willings
Press Guide

VOLUME 1: UNITED KINGDOM

Published by: Cision UK Ltd. Cision House, 16-22 Baltic Street West, London, EC1Y 0UL

Telephone: 0870 736 0010 E-mail: info.uk@cision.com Website: www.uk.cision.com

© Cision UK Ltd.

VAT registration number: 553 8580 17

Registered Office: Chess House, 34 Germain Street. Chesham Bucks HP5 1SJ

Volume 1 (UK) 2010	ISBN	978-1-906035-17-4
Volume 2 (Europe) 2010	ISBN	978-1-906035-18-1
Volume 3 (World) 2010	ISBN	978-1-906035-19-8
Volume 1 (UK) and 2 (Europe) 2010	ISBN	978-1-906035-20-4
Volume 1 (UK) and 3 (World) 2010	ISBN	978-1-906035-21-1
Volume 2 (Europe) and 3 (World) 2010	ISBN	978-1-906035-22-8
Volumes 1 (UK), 2 (Europe) and 3 (World) 2010	ISBN	978-1-906035-23-5

data publishers association

CISION UK LTD. IS A MEMBER OF THE DATA PUBLISHERS ASSOCIATION

SOFTWARE AND PAGE IMAGING BY DATA STANDARDS LTD, FROME.

PRINTING BY POLESTAR WHEATONS LTD, EXETER.

UNITED KINGDOM

Willings Press Guide

ABOUT WILLINGS

EDITORIAL POLICY

Willings Press Guide is published in three volumes. The editorial aim of Willings is to be a comprehensive, accurate and informative guide to the UK media industry (Volume 1) and to give details about the leading newspapers and periodicals in Europe (Volume 2), as well as other countries of the world (Volume 3).

For the purposes of Willings, ''media industry'' includes: newspapers, freesheets, magazines (business and consumer), journals, newsletters and any other publication appearing on a regular basis, including directories.

Willings has not set out to include manuals, maps, diaries, calendars, partworks or local periodicals with a very low circulation such as school magazines and local activity newsheets. Books not scheduled for publication at regular intervals are also excluded.

Each publication is listed free of charge with an extensive range of information about that title. ISSN numbers are included where available.

ENQUIRIES

FOR SUBSCRIPTION DETAILS

Contact the Willings Sales Team
Tel: (UK) 0870 736 0010 (Int) +44 (0)1494 797 225
Fax: (UK) 0870 736 0011 (Int) +44 (0)1494 797 224
Email: info.uk@cision.com

TO UPDATE ENTRY DETAILS

Contact the Research team
Tel: 0870 736 0010
Fax: 0870 736 0011
Email: changes.uk@cision.com

ABBREVIATIONS USED WITHIN THIS PUBLICATION

dps double page spread
ibc inside back cover
ifc inside front cover
lpc lines per cm
obc outside back cover
rop run of page
scc single column cm
UA Unitary Authority

iii

CONTENTS

CONTENTS

Welcome to the 2010 edition of the Willings Press Guide.

The Willings Press Guide has been a media staple for almost as long as there's been media, becoming affectionately known as the "Press Bible" early on in its history. Still as relevant today, it offers you easy and comprehensive access to media worldwide.

The 2010 edition brings you approximately 72,000 entries, and you will notice that there have been changes in the make up of two of our comprehensive three volumes. These are as a direct result of world changes - volume two contains the expanded Europe, including Cyprus and Turkey, while Europe has been excluded from volume three. We have continued our coverage of emerging markets, such as China, India and Brazil, and have also increased our coverage in established markets, such as the US and Canada.

As you are aware, local research and knowledge are the base on which our success has always been built, and the 2010 edition is no different. As always, our trusted directory has been compiled from local expertise at grassroots level worldwide, so you can be sure of its accuracy and relevance to your business, and our team of dedicated professional researchers are tireless in their determination to ensure that the entries submitted are accurate. In an uncertain world, at least you can still rely on Willings bringing you in depth, accurate and relevant coverage.

In addition, we make it easy for you to keep ahead of emerging trends and worldwide changes in the media with our online service www.willingspress.com, which is updated quarterly. You can also get lists and labels produced from the website, which further eases your job of keeping in touch with the media, and if you would like online access to this data, contact us about subscribing.

I know that you will find the 2010 edition an essential tool for your business, and would love to hear any feedback that you may have – please contact me at research.europe@cision.com. If you are looking for more information about our other products or services, please contact the Sales team on 0870 736 0010 (+44 1494 797 225 from outside the UK).

Falk Rehkopf
Head of European Research

CISION
Global Media Intelligence.

willings
Press Guide

TOP TITLES BY CIRCULATION

A guide to top circulation newspapers and periodicals in the UK. All figures quoted are the latest available to us at the time of going to press.

ABC denotes authenticated by the Audit Bureau of Circulations and VFD (used for Free Newspapers) indicates Verified Free Distribution, also authenticated by the ABC. BPA relates to figures supplied by the British Periodical Association.

NATIONAL DAILIES

	TITLE	PUBLISHER	CIRCULATION	AUDIT DATE
1	The Sun	News Group Newspapers Ltd	3,128,501	ABC 03/08/2009 to 30/08/2009
2	Daily Mail	Associated Newspapers Ltd	2,228,897	ABC 29/12/2008 to 25/01/2009
3	Daily Mirror	Trinity Mirror	1,324,883	ABC 03/08/2009 to 30/08/2009
4	Daily Star	Express Newspapers Ltd	886,814	ABC 03/08/2009 to 30/08/2009
5	The Daily Telegraph	Telegraph Media Group Ltd	814,087	ABC 03/08/2009 to 30/08/2009
6	Daily Express	Express Newspapers Ltd	730,234	ABC 03/08/2009 to 30/08/2009
7	The Times	Times Newspapers Ltd	576,185	ABC 03/08/2009 to 30/08/2009
8	Financial Times	Financial Times	395,845	ABC 03/08/2009 to 30/08/2009
9	The Guardian	Guardian Media Group plc	311,387	ABC 03/08/2009 to 30/08/2009
10	The Independent	Independent News and Media (UK) Ltd	187,837	ABC 03/08/2009 to 30/08/2009
11	Daily Sport	Sport Newspapers Ltd	72,592	Publisher's Statement

NATIONAL SUNDAYS

	TITLE	PUBLISHER	CIRCULATION	AUDIT DATE
1	News of the World	News Group Newspapers Ltd	3,120,991	ABC 03/08/2009 to 30/08/2009
2	The Mail on Sunday	Associated Newspapers Ltd	2,013,742	ABC 03/08/2009 to 30/08/2009
3	Sunday Mirror	Trinity Mirror	1,237,227	ABC 03/08/2009 to 30/08/2009
4	The Sunday Times	Times Newspapers Ltd	1,164,831	ABC 03/08/2009 to 30/08/2009
5	Sunday Express	Express Newspapers Ltd	646,861	ABC 03/08/2009 to 30/08/2009
6	The Sunday Telegraph	Telegraph Media Group Ltd	599,131	ABC 03/08/2009 to 30/08/2009
7	The People	Trinity Mirror	586,414	ABC 03/08/2009 to 30/08/2009
8	Daily Star Sunday	Express Newspapers Ltd	401,305	ABC 03/08/2009 to 30/08/2009
9	The Observer	Guardian Media Group plc	361,761	ABC 03/08/2009 to 30/08/2009
10	The Independent on Sunday	Independent News and Media (UK) Ltd	160,809	ABC 03/08/2009 to 30/08/2009
11	Sunday Sport	Sport Newspapers Ltd	70,796	Publisher's Statement

TOP TITLES BY CIRCULATION

REGIONAL MORNINGS, EVENINGS AND SUNDAYS - TOP 50

	TITLE	PUBLISHER	CIRCULATION	AUDIT DATE
1	Sunday Mail	Scottish Daily Record & Sunday Mail Ltd	428,613	ABC 03/08/2009 to 30/08/2009
2	The Sunday Post (Dundee)	D.C. Thomson & Co Ltd	354,870	ABC 03/08/2009 to 30/08/2009
3	Daily Record	Trinity Mirror	347,302	ABC 03/08/2009 to 30/08/2009
4	London Evening Standard	Evening Press Ltd	263,312	ABC 30/03/2009 to 26/04/2009
5	Express & Star	Midland News Association	140,001	Publisher's Statement
6	Liverpool Echo	Liverpool Daily Post & Echo Ltd	109,458	Publisher's Statement
7	Scottish Review of Books	Scottish Review of Books	100,000	Publisher's Statement
8	Manchester Evening News	Manchester Evening News Ltd	82,445	Publisher's Statement
9	The Press & Journal (Aberdeen)	Aberdeen Journals Ltd	81,956	ABC 01/01/2007 to 01/07/2007
10	Evening Times (Glasgow)	Newsquest Herald & Times Ltd	79,087	Publisher's Statement
11	Evening Chronicle (Newcastle)	NCJ Media Ltd	78,804	Publisher's Statement
12	Birmingham Mail	Trinity Mirror	78,178	ABC 02/01/2006 to 02/07/2006
13	Belfast Telegraph	Independent News and Media (UK) Ltd	75,602	ABC 02/07/2007 to 30/12/2007
14	Sunday Life (Belfast)	Independent News and Media (UK) Ltd	74,886	ABC 01/01/2007 to 01/07/2007
15	The Courier and Advertiser	D.C. Thomson & Co Ltd	73,485	ABC 02/07/2007 to 30/12/2007
16	Shropshire Star	Midland News Association	72,000	Publisher's Statement
17	Sunday World Northern Ireland Edition	Sunday Newspapers Ltd	71,000	Publisher's Statement
18	Leicester Mercury	Leicester Mercury Media Group Ltd	70,028	ABC 02/07/2007 to 30/12/2007
19	Sunday Herald Magazine	Newsquest Sunday Herald Ltd	70,000	Publisher's Statement
20	Sunday Sun	NCJ Media Ltd	68,033	ABC 02/07/2007 to 30/12/2007
21	The News (Portsmouth)	Portsmouth Publishing & Printing Ltd	65,000	Publisher's Statement
22	Scotland on Sunday	The Scotsman Publications Ltd	65,000	ABC 03/08/2009 to 30/08/2009
23	Eastern Daily Press (Norwich)	Archant Norfolk	64,700	ABC 02/07/2007 to 30/12/2007
24	The Sentinel Stoke-on-Trent	Staffordshire Sentinel News & Media Ltd	61,910	ABC 02/07/2007 to 30/12/2007
25	Hull Daily Mail	Mail News & Media Ltd	59,689	ABC 01/01/2007 to 01/07/2007
26	Sunday Mercury (Birmingham)	BPM Media (Midlands)	59,339	ABC 02/07/2007 to 30/12/2007
27	The Herald (Glasgow)	Newsquest Herald & Times Ltd	58,157	ABC 03/08/2009 to 30/08/2009
28	Nottingham Evening Post	Nottingham Post Media Group Ltd	57,699	ABC 02/07/2007 to 30/12/2007
29	Yorkshire Evening Post	Yorkshire Post Newspapers Ltd	56,647	Publisher's Statement
30	The Star Sheffield	Sheffield Newspapers Ltd	56,363	Publisher's Statement
31	Evening News (Edinburgh)	The Scotsman Publications Ltd	53,675	Publisher's Statement
32	Evening Express (Aberdeen)	Aberdeen Journals Ltd	53,384	ABC 02/07/2007 to 30/12/2007
33	South Wales Evening Post	South West Wales Media Ltd	51,329	ABC 02/07/2007 to 30/12/2007
34	Evening Post (Bristol)	Bristol News & Media Ltd	51,287	ABC 02/07/2007 to 30/12/2007
35	Evening Gazette (Middlesbrough)	Gazette Media Company Ltd	50,920	ABC 02/07/2007 to 30/12/2007
36	The Scotsman	The Scotsman Publications Ltd	50,750	ABC 03/08/2009 to 30/08/2009
37	The Northern Echo (Darlington)	Newsquest Yorkshire and North East (Darlington)	50,256	ABC 02/07/2007 to 30/12/2007
38	Yorkshire Post	Johnston Press plc	49,031	ABC 02/07/2007 to 30/12/2007
39	Coventry Telegraph	Midland Newspapers Ltd	48,025	Publisher's Statement
40	The Irish News	Irish News Ltd	47,790	ABC 02/07/2007 to 30/12/2007
41	South Wales Echo	Media Wales Ltd	46,127	ABC 02/07/2007 to 30/12/2007
42	Sunday Herald	Newsquest Sunday Herald Ltd	44,048	ABC 03/08/2009 to 30/08/2009
43	Sunderland Echo	Northeast Press Ltd	42,910	ABC 02/07/2007 to 30/12/2007
44	Derby Telegraph	Derby Daily Telegraph Ltd	42,726	ABC 02/07/2007 to 30/12/2007
45	Western Daily Press Bristol	Bristol News and Media	41,639	ABC 02/07/2007 to 30/12/2007
46	Wales on Sunday	Media Wales Ltd	41,199	ABC 02/07/2007 to 30/12/2007
47	Western Morning News	South West Media Group Ltd	41,154	ABC 02/07/2007 to 30/12/2007
48	The Herald (Plymouth)	South West Media Group Ltd	40,384	ABC 02/01/2006 to 02/07/2006
49	The Southern Daily Echo (Southampton)	Newsquest (Media Group) Ltd	39,174	ABC 02/07/2007 to 30/12/2007
50	Western Mail (Cardiff)	Media Wales Ltd	37,576	ABC 02/07/2007 to 30/12/2007

WEEKLY NEWSPAPERS - TOP 50

	TITLE	PUBLISHER	CIRCULATION	AUDIT DATE
1	West Notts & Derbyshire Recorder Series	Nottingham Post Media Group Ltd	260,441	VFD 02/07/2007 to 30/12/2007
2	Nottingham and Long Eaton Topper	Topper Newspapers Ltd	209,222	VFD 02/07/2007 to 30/12/2007
3	Birmingham Mail Extra	Trinity Mirror	177,201	VFD 02/07/2007 to 30/12/2007
4	Community Telegraph Series	Belfast Telegraph Newspapers Ltd	166,375	VFD 02/07/2007 to 30/12/2007
5	Bristol Observer Series	Bristol News & Media Ltd	165,769	VFD 02/07/2007 to 30/12/2007
6	Leicester Mail Series	Leicester Mercury Media Group Ltd	141,536	VFD 02/07/2007 to 30/12/2007
7	Journal Series Portsmouth	Portsmouth Publishing & Printing Ltd	136,795	VFD 02/07/2007 to 30/12/2007
8	Wirral Globe Series	Newsquest (Northwest) Ltd	133,193	VFD 02/07/2007 to 30/12/2007
9	Aldershot Mail and News Series	Aldershot News Ltd	131,660	VFD 02/07/2007 to 30/12/2007
10	Leeds Weekly News Series	Yorkshire Post Newspapers Ltd	124,534	VFD 02/07/2007 to 30/12/2007
11	Coventry Times	Midland Newspapers Ltd	121,430	VFD 02/07/2007 to 30/12/2007
12	Derby Express and Messenger Series	Derby Daily Telegraph Ltd	111,621	VFD 02/07/2007 to 30/12/2007
13	The Glaswegian Series	Scottish Daily Record & Sunday Mail Ltd	104,175	VFD 02/07/2007 to 30/12/2007
14	Advertiser Series (Ashton)	MEN Media	104,047	VFD 02/07/2007 to 30/12/2007
15	Sheffield Weekly Gazette	Sheffield Newspapers Ltd	103,897	VFD 02/07/2007 to 30/12/2007
16	Advertiser Series (Stoke-on-Trent)	Northcliffe Media Ltd	103,429	VFD 02/07/2007 to 30/12/2007
17	Croydon Guardian	Newsquest Media Group	99,753	VFD 02/07/2007 to 30/12/2007
18	Trafford Metro News	MEN Media	98,936	VFD 21/05/2007 to 01/07/2007
19	MK News	LSN Media	95,945	VFD 02/07/2007 to 30/12/2007
20	The Extra (Plymouth)	South West Media Group Ltd	93,894	VFD 02/07/2007 to 30/12/2007
21	Enfield Independent		92,538	VFD 01/01/2007 to 01/07/2007
22	Sutton Coldfield Observer Series	Central Independent News & Media Ltd	91,245	VFD 02/07/2007 to 30/12/2007
23	Chester Standard Series	NWN Media Ltd	90,394	VFD 02/07/2007 to 30/12/2007
24	The Oldham Advertiser	MEN Media	86,749	VFD 02/07/2007 to 30/12/2007
25	The Comet Series	Archant Herts & Cambs	85,226	VFD 02/07/2007 to 30/12/2007
26	Solihull News	BPM Media (Midlands)	79,221	VFD 30/07/2007 to 30/12/2007
27	East End Life	Tower Hamlets Council	78,914	VFD 02/07/2007 to 30/12/2007
28	St. Helens Star	Newsquest Media Group	78,827	VFD 02/07/2007 to 30/12/2007
29	St. Helens Reporter Series	Lancashire Publications Ltd	78,750	VFD 02/07/2007 to 30/12/2007
30	Bedfordshire Times & Citizen Series	Johnston Press plc	78,119	VFD 02/07/2007 to 30/12/2007
31	Aberdeen Citizen	Aberdeen Journals Ltd	76,408	VFD 02/07/2007 to 30/12/2007
32	Solihull, Shirley & Arden Observer Series	Bullivant Media Limited	73,823	VFD 02/07/2007 to 30/12/2007
33	Harrow Times	Newsquest Media Group	70,992	VFD 02/07/2007 to 30/12/2007
34	Wolverhampton Chronicle	Express & Star Ltd	68,351	VFD 02/07/2007 to 30/12/2007
35	Romford and Havering Weekly Post	Archant East London & Essex	68,181	VFD 02/07/2007 to 30/12/2007
36	Star Series (Selby & York)	Newsquest Yorkshire and North East (York)	67,353	VFD 02/07/2007 to 30/12/2007
37	Swansea Herald of Wales	South West Wales Media Ltd	67,297	VFD 02/07/2007 to 30/12/2007
38	Slough Express	Baylis & Co.	66,727	VFD 02/07/2007 to 30/12/2007
39	Walsall Advertiser	Central Independent News & Media Ltd	65,616	VFD 02/07/2007 to 30/12/2007
40	Walsall Chronicle	Express & Star Ltd	65,414	VFD 02/07/2007 to 30/12/2007
41	Preston Reporter Series	Lancashire Evening Post Ltd	64,110	VFD 02/07/2007 to 30/12/2007
42	Blackpool, Fylde and Wyre Reporter	Johnston Press plc	64,017	VFD 01/01/2007 to 01/07/2007
43	Sutton Coldfield News	Trinity Mirror Midlands	62,017	VFD 02/07/2007 to 30/12/2007
44	Leigh Reporter	Lancashire Publications Ltd	61,041	VFD 02/07/2007 to 30/12/2007
45	Telford Journal	Shropshire Newspapers Ltd	61,000	VFD 02/07/2007 to 30/12/2007
46	Oxford Star	Newsquest (Oxfordshire) Ltd	60,647	VFD 02/07/2007 to 30/12/2007
47	Bolton Journal	Newsquest Media Group	59,893	VFD 02/07/2007 to 30/12/2007
48	Blackburn Citizen	Newsquest Lancashire Limited	59,248	VFD 02/07/2007 to 30/12/2007
49	Mansfield and Ashfield Observer	Wilfred Edmunds	58,599	VFD 02/07/2007 to 30/12/2007
50	The Burton & South Derbyshire Advertiser	Staffordshire Newspapers Ltd	57,692	VFD 02/07/2007 to 30/12/2007

TOP TITLES BY CIRCULATION

FREE NEWSPAPERS - TOP 50

	TITLE	PUBLISHER	CIRCULATION	AUDIT DATE
1	Metro (London)	Associated Newspapers Ltd	742,291	ABC 26/11/2007 to 30/12/2007
2	London Lite	Associated Newspapers Ltd	400,547	ABC 2009
3	West Notts & Derbyshire Recorder Series	Nottingham Post Media Group Ltd	260,441	VFD 02/07/2007 to 30/12/2007
4	Nottingham and Long Eaton Topper	Topper Newspapers Ltd	209,222	VFD 02/07/2007 to 30/12/2007
5	Birmingham Mail Extra	Trinity Mirror	177,201	VFD 02/07/2007 to 30/12/2007
6	Community Telegraph Series	Belfast Telegraph Newspapers Ltd	166,375	VFD 02/07/2007 to 30/12/2007
7	Bristol Observer Series	Bristol News & Media Ltd	165,769	VFD 02/07/2007 to 30/12/2007
8	Leicester Mail Series	Leicester Mercury Media Group Ltd	141,536	VFD 02/07/2007 to 30/12/2007
9	Journal Series Portsmouth	Portsmouth Publishing & Printing Ltd	136,795	VFD 02/07/2007 to 30/12/2007
10	Wirral Globe Series	Newsquest (Northwest) Ltd	133,193	VFD 02/07/2007 to 30/12/2007
11	Leeds Weekly News Series	Yorkshire Post Newspapers Ltd	124,534	VFD 02/07/2007 to 30/12/2007
12	Coventry Times	Midland Newspapers Ltd	121,430	VFD 02/07/2007 to 30/12/2007
13	Derby Express and Messenger Series	Derby Daily Telegraph Ltd	111,621	VFD 02/07/2007 to 30/12/2007
14	The Glaswegian Series	Scottish Daily Record & Sunday Mail Ltd	104,175	VFD 02/07/2007 to 30/12/2007
15	Advertiser Series (Ashton)	MEN Media	104,047	VFD 02/07/2007 to 30/12/2007
16	Sheffield Weekly Gazette	Sheffield Newspapers Ltd	103,897	VFD 02/07/2007 to 30/12/2007
17	Advertiser Series (Stoke-on-Trent)	Northcliffe Media Ltd	103,429	VFD 02/07/2007 to 30/12/2007
18	Bedfordshire on Sunday	LSN Media	101,346	VFD 02/07/2007 to 30/12/2007
19	Croydon Guardian	Newsquest Media Group	99,753	VFD 02/07/2007 to 30/12/2007
20	Trafford Metro News	MEN Media	98,936	VFD 21/05/2007 to 01/07/2007
21	MK News	LSN Media	95,945	VFD 02/07/2007 to 30/12/2007
22	The Extra (Plymouth)	South West Media Group Ltd	93,894	VFD 02/07/2007 to 30/12/2007
23	Enfield Independent		92,538	VFD 01/01/2007 to 01/07/2007
24	Sutton Coldfield Observer Series	Central Independent News & Media Ltd	91,245	VFD 02/07/2007 to 30/12/2007
25	Chester Standard Series	NWN Media Ltd	90,394	VFD 02/07/2007 to 30/12/2007
26	The Oldham Advertiser	MEN Media	86,749	VFD 02/07/2007 to 30/12/2007
27	City A.M.	City AM	86,522	ABC 26/11/2007 to 30/12/2007
28	Solihull News	BPM Media (Midlands)	79,221	VFD 30/07/2007 to 30/12/2007
29	East End Life	Tower Hamlets Council	78,914	VFD 02/07/2007 to 30/12/2007
30	St. Helens Star	Newsquest Media Group	78,827	VFD 02/07/2007 to 30/12/2007
31	St. Helens Reporter Series	Lancashire Publications Ltd	78,750	VFD 02/07/2007 to 30/12/2007
32	Bedfordshire Times & Citizen Series	Johnston Press plc	78,119	VFD 02/07/2007 to 30/12/2007
33	Aberdeen Citizen	Aberdeen Journals Ltd	76,408	VFD 02/07/2007 to 30/12/2007
34	Solihull, Shirley & Arden Observer Series	Bullivant Media Limited	73,823	VFD 02/07/2007 to 30/12/2007
35	Harrow Times	Newsquest Media Group	70,992	VFD 02/07/2007 to 30/12/2007
36	Wolverhampton Chronicle	Express & Star Ltd	68,351	VFD 02/07/2007 to 30/12/2007
37	Romford and Havering Weekly Post	Archant East London & Essex	68,181	VFD 02/07/2007 to 30/12/2007
38	Star Series (Selby & York)	Newsquest Yorkshire and North East (York)	67,353	VFD 02/07/2007 to 30/12/2007
39	Swansea Herald of Wales	South West Wales Media Ltd	67,297	VFD 02/07/2007 to 30/12/2007
40	Slough Express	Baylis & Co.	66,727	VFD 02/07/2007 to 30/12/2007
41	Walsall Advertiser	Central Independent News & Media Ltd	65,616	VFD 02/07/2007 to 30/12/2007
42	Walsall Chronicle	Express & Star Ltd	65,414	VFD 02/07/2007 to 30/12/2007
43	Preston Reporter Series	Lancashire Evening Post Ltd	64,110	VFD 02/07/2007 to 30/12/2007
44	Blackpool, Fylde and Wyre Reporter	Johnston Press plc	64,017	VFD 01/01/2007 to 01/07/2007
45	Sutton Coldfield News	Trinity Mirror Midlands	62,017	VFD 02/07/2007 to 30/12/2007
46	Leigh Reporter	Lancashire Publications Ltd	61,041	VFD 02/07/2007 to 30/12/2007
47	Telford Journal	Shropshire Newspapers Ltd	61,000	VFD 02/07/2007 to 30/12/2007
48	Oxford Star	Newsquest (Oxfordshire) Ltd	60,647	VFD 02/07/2007 to 30/12/2007
49	Bolton Journal	Newsquest Media Group	59,893	VFD 02/07/2007 to 30/12/2007
50	Blackburn Citizen	Newsquest Lancashire Limited	59,248	VFD 02/07/2007 to 30/12/2007

Business Publications - Top 50

	TITLE	PUBLISHER	CIRCULATION	AUDIT DATE
1	National Geographic Magazine	National Geographic Society	340,264	ABC 01/01/2009 to 30/06/2009
2	First Voice of Business	NFSE (Sales Ltd)	202,111	ABC 01/07/2008 to 30/06/2009
3	Business Network	FSB Publications	201,476	ABC 01/07/2008 to 30/06/2009
4	New Scientist	Reed Business Information	160,633	ABC 01/01/2009 to 30/06/2009
5	Accountancy	Wolters Kluwer (UK) Ltd	153,169	ABC 01/07/2008 to 30/06/2009
6	Financial Management	Caspian Publishing	152,429	ABC 01/07/2007 to 30/06/2008
7	Computer Weekly	Reed Business Information	139,122	BPA W 01/06/2007 to 31/12/2007
8	People Management	Redactive Media Group	132,168	ABC 01/07/2008 to 30/06/2009
9	Accounting & Business	Certified Accountants Publications Limited	127,734	ABC 01/07/2007 to 30/06/2008
10	BMJ British Medical Journal	British Medical Association	122,239	ABC 01/07/2006 to 30/06/2007
11	Law Society Gazette	The Law Society	118,927	ABC 01/07/2007 to 30/06/2008
12	Professional Builder	Hamerville Magazines Ltd	108,502	ABC 02/07/2007 to 30/12/2007
13	Fortune	Time Inc.	105,967	ABC 01/07/2008 to 31/12/2008
14	Profile	Prospect	100,423	ABC 01/07/2007 to 30/06/2008
15	Management Today	Haymarket Brand Media	100,016	ABC 01/07/2008 to 30/06/2009
16	CNBC European Business	Ink Publishing	96,477	BPA W 2008
17	RICS Business	Atom Publishing Ltd	96,033	ABC 01/07/2008 to 30/06/2009
18	Computing	Incisive Media	93,362	BPA W 01/07/2008 to 31/12/2008
19	Professional Manager	The Chartered Management Institute	81,977	ABC 01/07/2008 to 30/06/2009
20	Professional Engineering	Professional Engineering Publishing Ltd	76,665	ABC 01/01/2008 to 31/12/2008
21	The Gas Installer	Corgi	74,913	ABC 01/01/2008 to 31/12/2008
22	Farmers Weekly	Reed Business Information	68,461	ABC 01/01/2008 to 31/12/2008
23	Nursing Standard	RCN Publishing Co Ltd	68,046	ABC 01/01/2008 to 31/12/2008
24	Professional Electrician and Installer	Hamerville Magazines Ltd	66,117	ABC 01/01/2007 to 01/07/2007
25	Professional Heating and Plumbing Installer	Hamerville Magazines Ltd	63,541	ABC 02/07/2007 to 30/12/2007
26	Professional Motor Mechanic	Hamerville Magazines Ltd	63,216	ABC 01/01/2007 to 01/07/2007
27	Genetic Engineering News	Mary Ann Liebert, Inc.	59,560	BPA W 01/01/2007 to 30/06/2007
28	The Pharmaceutical Journal	RPS Publishing	56,963	ABC 01/01/2008 to 31/12/2008
29	Accountancy Age	Incisive Media	56,794	ABC 01/07/2007 to 30/06/2008
30	Director	Director Publications Ltd	56,701	ABC 01/07/2008 to 30/06/2009
31	Auto Service & Repair	Ten Alps Publishing	55,230	ABC 01/07/2007 to 30/06/2008
32	New Civil Engineer	EMAP Insight	54,747	ABC 01/07/2008 to 30/06/2009
33	Industrial Engineering News Europe	Thomas Industrial Media bvba	53,061	BPA W 01/01/2007 to 30/06/2007
34	Farmers Guardian	UBM Information (Preston)	51,668	ABC 01/01/2008 to 31/12/2008
35	Medical Device & Diagnostics Industry	Canon Communications	50,540	BPA W 01/07/2006 to 31/12/2006
36	The Trader	Metropolis International (UK) Limited	50,469	VFD 01/01/2007 to 01/07/2007
37	Retail Express	Newtrade Publishing Ltd	50,301	ABC 01/01/2009 to 30/06/2009
38	Microwave Journal	Horizon House Publications Ltd	50,000	BPA W 01/01/2008 to 30/06/2008
39	British Farmer and Grower	Associa Ltd	49,200	ABC 01/01/2008 to 31/12/2008
40	Chemistry World	Royal Society of Chemistry	47,042	ABC 01/01/2008 to 31/12/2008
41	Personnel Today	Reed Business Information	43,633	ABC 01/07/2008 to 30/06/2009
42	Convenience Store	William Reed Business Media	42,518	ABC 01/07/2008 to 30/06/2009
43	Community Care	Reed Business Information	42,052	ABC 01/07/2008 to 30/06/2009
44	Flight International	Reed Business Information	42,016	BPA W 01/07/2007 to 31/12/2007
45	Money Week	Fleet Street Publications Ltd	41,282	ABC 01/01/2009 to 30/06/2009
46	Real Business	Caspian Publishing	40,982	ABC 01/07/2007 to 30/06/2008
47	Electronics Weekly	Reed Business Information	40,778	BPA W 01/01/2008 to 30/06/2008
48	Supply Management	Redactive Media Group	40,559	ABC 01/01/2008 to 31/12/2008
49	PASS	Wolters Kluwer (UK) Ltd	40,000	ABC 01/07/2007 to 30/06/2008
50	Independent Retail News	Metropolis International Group Ltd	39,709	ABC 01/07/2008 to 30/06/2009

TOP TITLES BY CIRCULATION

TOP TITLES BY CIRCULATION

CONSUMER PUBLICATIONS - TOP 50

	TITLE	PUBLISHER	CIRCULATION	AUDIT DATE
1	SKY Mag	BSKYB Publications Ltd	7,545,510	ABC 01/01/2009 to 30/06/2009
2	The National Trust Magazine	The National Trust	1,752,636	ABC 01/01/2008 to 31/12/2008
3	Sainsbury's Fresh Ideas	Seven Squared	1,499,499	ABC 01/01/2009 to 30/06/2009
4	TVChoice	H. Bauer Publishing	1,335,894	ABC 01/01/2009 to 30/06/2009
5	What's On TV	IPC TX	1,272,586	ABC 01/01/2009 to 30/06/2009
6	Morrisons	Result Customer Communications	1,100,000	ABC 01/01/2009 to 31/03/2009
7	The Somerfield Magazine	PSP Rare Publishing	1,003,795	ABC 01/01/2009 to 30/06/2009
8	Radio Times	BBC Worldwide Publishing	966,098	ABC 01/01/2009 to 30/06/2009
9	Take A Break	H. Bauer Publishing	920,060	ABC 01/01/2009 to 30/06/2009
10	Sky Kids Magazine	John Brown Group	755,141	ABC 01/01/2009 to 30/06/2009
11	Saga Magazine	Saga Publishing Ltd	653,930	ABC 01/01/2009 to 30/06/2009
12	hotcourses	Hotcourses	651,720	ABC/E 01/01/2009 to 31/01/2009
13	Birds - The Magazine of the RSPB	The Royal Society for the Protection of Birds	625,553	ABC 01/01/2009 to 30/06/2009
14	OK!	Northern & Shell plc	599,847	ABC 01/01/2009 to 30/06/2009
15	Reader's Digest	Reader's Digest Association Ltd	541,282	ABC 01/01/2009 to 30/06/2009
16	Closer	Bauer Media	530,371	ABC 01/01/2009 to 30/06/2009
17	Time Magazine	TIME Magazines Europe Limited	527,501	ABC 01/01/2009 to 30/06/2009
18	Glamour	Conde Nast Publications Ltd	526,145	ABC 01/01/2009 to 30/06/2009
19	Pet People	Sunday Publishing	524,476	ABC 01/01/2008 to 31/12/2008
20	Shortlist	Shortlist Media Ltd	510,720	ABC 01/01/2009 to 30/06/2009
21	Heat	Bauer Media	445,192	ABC 01/01/2009 to 30/06/2009
22	Cosmopolitan	National Magazine Company Ltd	441,663	ABC 01/01/2009 to 30/06/2009
23	Chat	IPC Connect Ltd	434,929	ABC 01/01/2009 to 30/06/2009
24	Good Housekeeping	National Magazine Company Ltd	410,011	ABC 01/01/2009 to 30/06/2009
25	Emma's Diary Pregnancy Guide	Lifecycle Marketing Limited	407,191	ABC 01/01/2009 to 30/06/2009
26	new!	Express Newspapers Ltd	400,189	ABC 01/01/2009 to 30/06/2009
27	HELLO!	HELLO! Ltd	397,634	ABC 01/01/2009 to 30/06/2009
28	V - The Vauxhall Magazine	Stream Publishing Ltd	396,294	ABC 01/01/2007 to 31/12/2007
29	That's Life	H. Bauer Publishing	386,875	ABC 01/01/2009 to 30/06/2009
30	Now	IPC Connect Ltd	384,356	ABC 01/01/2009 to 30/06/2009
31	The Caravan Club Magazine	The Caravan Club	374,390	ABC 01/01/2008 to 31/12/2008
32	Legion	Redactive Media Group	367,895	ABC 01/01/2008 to 31/12/2008
33	woman&home	IPC Media Ltd	350,212	ABC 01/01/2009 to 30/06/2009
34	The Garden	RHS Media	342,858	ABC 01/01/2009 to 30/06/2009
35	Woman's Weekly	IPC Media Ltd	335,118	ABC 01/01/2009 to 30/06/2009
36	Woman	IPC Connect Ltd	331,065	ABC 01/01/2009 to 30/06/2009
37	BBC Good Food	BBC Worldwide Publishing	323,171	ABC 01/01/2009 to 30/06/2009
38	Pick Me Up	IPC Connect Ltd	323,171	ABC 01/01/2009 to 30/06/2009
39	Waitrose Food Illustrated	John Brown Group	321,886	ABC 01/01/2009 to 30/06/2009
40	Star	Northern & Shell plc	317,940	ABC 01/01/2009 to 30/06/2009
41	Reveal	National Magazine Company Ltd	315,660	ABC 01/01/2009 to 30/06/2009
42	Look	IPC Connect Ltd	315,410	ABC 01/01/2009 to 30/06/2009
43	People's Friend	D.C. Thomson & Co Ltd	313,711	ABC 01/01/2009 to 30/06/2009
44	TV Times	IPC TX	311,307	ABC 01/01/2009 to 30/06/2009
45	Love It!	Hubert Burda Media UK	308,304	ABC 01/01/2009 to 30/06/2009
46	Woman's Own	IPC Media Ltd	307,407	ABC 01/01/2009 to 30/06/2009
47	Sainsbury's Magazine	Seven Publishing	301,842	ABC 01/01/2009 to 30/06/2009
48	Yours	Bauer Consumer Media Ltd (Media House)	301,089	ABC 01/01/2009 to 30/06/2009
49	Sainsbury's Fresh Ideas For Young Families	Seven Squared	299,625	ABC 01/07/2008 to 31/12/2008
50	Best	National Magazine Company Ltd	296,971	ABC 01/01/2009 to 30/06/2009

LAUNCHES

A launch is defined as a magazine or newspaper that was first published in 2009. Complete entries can be found in Section 4, UK media.

WILLINGS UK LAUNCHES

TITLE	PUBLISHER	SECTION
3D Artist	Imagine Publishing	Consumer
Bicester Community Times	Community Times UK Ltd	Consumer
Business North West Magazine	Mellor Media Ltd	Business
Chuggington	D.C. Thomson & Co Ltd	Consumer
CIBSE Journal	Chartered Institute of Building Services Engineers	Business
Cruise International	The Chelsea Magazine Company	Consumer
design footprint	LDI Media (UK)	Business
Eat In	H. Bauer Publishing	Consumer
Emigrant	GoodPoint Press LLP	Consumer
Environment Industry Magazine	Enviromedia Ltd	Business
Escapism Travel Magazine	Revolution Publishing	Consumer
Expert Investor Europe (EIE)	Last Word Media	Business
Fighting Fit	Newsquest Specialist Media Ltd	Consumer
filmstar	Blackfish Publishing Ltd	Consumer
Gas Technology News	Gas Technology News Ltd	Business
H&K	Lighthouse Publishing	Consumer
Horizons	Cedar Communications	Consumer
IP&E Industrial Plant & Equipment Ireland	Western Business Publishing	Business
The Knitter	Future Publishing Ltd	Consumer
Large Manchester	Large Publishing Ltd	Consumer
Large Students	Large Publishing Ltd	Consumer
London Property	LTP Publications	Consumer
LOVE magazine		Consumer
Luxury Meetings	Big Publishing	Business
The Montebury Magazine		Consumer
New Power	New Power Consulting	Business
Northern Ireland Medical Review/London Chemist Review	Medical Communications Ltd	Business
Offshore Technology	IMarEST	Business
Proceedings of ICE, Engineering History and Heritage	Thomas Telford Ltd	Business
Prom	Maze Media (2000) Ltd	Consumer
RECHARGE	NHST Media Group	Business
The Red Bulletin	Red Bulletin	Consumer

LAUNCHES CONTINUED

WILLINGS UK LAUNCHES (CONTINUED)

TITLE	PUBLISHER	SECTION
Registered Gas Engineer	The Team	Business
Risk Management Professional	Perspective Publishing Ltd	Business
SpareRoom	PPS	Consumer
Tradex News	Business and Industry Today Ltd	Business
Triathlon Plus	Future Publishing Ltd	Consumer
Waybuloo	BBC Children's Magazines	Consumer
Wired	Conde Nast Publications Ltd	Business
YourDeal		Newspaper
YourSandwich		Newspaper

Willings Volume 1
Section 1

Titles Index
Index to UK Titles

This index cross refers to all Newspapers, Magazines
and Periodicals within Section 4 (a) Newspapers,
4 (b) Business Magazines and other Periodicals and
4 (c) Consumer Magazines and other Periodicals.

Index to UK Titles

Index to UK Titles

Index to UK Titles

Index to UK Titles

Index to UK Titles

Index to UK Titles

Index to UK Titles

J

Index to UK Titles

Index to UK Titles

Index to UK Titles

Section 1 UK Titles Index

Index to UK Titles

Index to UK Titles

Index to UK Titles

T

Index to UK Titles

Index to UK Titles

Willings Volume 1
Section 2

Periodicals Index
Index to Periodicals by Classification

For quick access to a particular area of interest or a specialist subject, UK periodicals appear under 364 classifications in 84 groupings. This index cross-refers to all periodicals in Section 4. The section is preceded by two summaries of categories, one in A-Z order and one by grouping.

Categories A-Z

B = Business Publication   C = Consumer Publication

Business

Section 2 UK Periodicals by Classification

Agriculture & Farming

Agriculture & Farming

Agriculture & Farming - Regional

Agriculture & Farming Related

Agriculture - Machinery & Plant

Agriculture - Supplies & Services

Dairy Farming

Livestock

Milk

Poultry

Antiques

Applied Science & Laboratories

Architecture & Building

Architecture

Building

Building Related

Cleaning & Maintenance

Interior Design & Flooring

Planning & Housing

Surveying

Aviation & Aeronautics

Airlines

Airports

Aviation & Aeronautics

Section 2 UK Periodicals by Classification

Education Related

Education Teachers

Junior Education

Preparatory & Independent Schools

Special Needs Education

Teachers & Education Management

Clothing & Textiles

Clothing & Textiles

Knitwear

Lingerie, Hosiery/Swimwear

Co-Operatives

Commerce, Industry & Management

Commerce Related

Section 2 UK Periodicals by Classification

Business

Commerce, Industry & Management

Commercial Design

Company Secretaries

Industry & Factories

International Commerce

Purchasing

Quality Assurance

Small Business

Trade Unions

Training & Recruitment

Business

Work Study

Communications, Advertising & Marketing

Broadcasting

Communications Related

Communications, Advertising & Marketing

Conferences & Exhibitions

Press

Public Relations

Selling

Computers & Automation

Automation & Instrumentation

Computers Related

Data Processing

Section 2 UK Periodicals by Classification

Business

Data Transmission

Multimedia

Personal Computers

Professional Personal Computers

Construction

Construction Related

General (Construction)

Roads

Water Engineering

Cosmetics & Hairdressing

Cosmetics

Cosmetics & Hairdressing Related

Hairdressing

Decorating & Paint

Decorating & Paint

Paint - Technical Manufacture

Defence

JANE'S MILITARY COMMUNICATIONS *(Annual)* 514
JANE'S MILITARY VEHICLES & LOGISTICS *(Quarterly)* .. 514
JANE'S MINES & MINE CLEARANCE *(Quarterly)* 514
JANE'S MISSILES & ROCKETS *(Monthly)* 514
JANE'S NAVAL WEAPONS SYSTEMS *(Monthly)* 514
JANE'S NAVY INTERNATIONAL *(10 issues yearly)* 514
JANE'S NUCLEAR, BIOLOGICAL AND CHEMICAL DEFENCE *(Quarterly)* 514
JANE'S POLICE & HOMELAND SECURITY EQUIPMENT *(Quarterly)* 514
JANE'S RADAR AND ELECTRONIC WARFARE *(Quarterly)* 515
JANE'S UNDERWATER WARFARE SYSTEMS *(Annual)* .. 515
JANE'S UNMANNED AERIAL VEHICLES & TARGETS *(Monthly)* 515
JANE'S WORLD AIR FORCES *(Monthly)* 515
JANE'S WORLD ARMIES *(Monthly)* 515
JANE'S WORLD INSURGENCY & TERRORISM *(Monthly)* 515
JOURNAL OF THE ROYAL HIGHLAND FUSILIERS *(Annual)* 526
MILITARY LOGISTICS INTERNATIONAL *(6 issues yearly)* 560
MILITARY TRAINING & SIMULATION NEWS *(6 issues yearly)* 560
NAVY NEWS *(Monthly)* 573
THE OFFICER *(6 issues yearly)* 586
RAF NEWS *(25 issues yearly)* 636
RAIDER *(Monthly)* 636
THE ROYAL AIR FORCE YEARBOOK *(Annual)* 649
ROYAL ARMY DENTAL CORPS BULLETIN *(Annual)* 649
ROYAL MILITARY POLICE JOURNAL *(3 issues yearly)* ... 649
RUSI DEFENCE SYSTEMS *(3 issues yearly)* 650
RUSI JOURNAL *(6 issues yearly)* 650
THE SAPPER *(6 issues yearly)* 652
SOLDIER *(Monthly)* 666
THE THIN RED LINE *(Half-yearly)* 687
THE VOLUNTEER *(Quarterly)* 709
WARFARE *(Quarterly)* 709
WARSHIPS INTERNATIONAL FLEET REVIEW *(Monthly)* . 709

Drinks & Licensed Trade

Brewing

THE BREWER & DISTILLER INTERNATIONAL *(Monthly)* 318
BREWERS' GUARDIAN *(10 issues yearly)* 318

Drinks, Licensed Trade, Wines & Spirits

BAR MAGAZINE *(Monthly)* 308
BIIBUSINESS *(10 issues yearly)* 312
CLASS MAGAZINE *(10 issues yearly)* 353
DECANTER *(Monthly)* 382
DRAM - DRINKS RETAILING & MARKETING *(Monthly)* ... 390
THE DRINKS BUSINESS *(Monthly)* 390
DRINKS INTERNATIONAL *(Monthly)* 390
HOSPITALITY REVIEW NI *(11 issues yearly)* 475
IBD MEMBERS HANDBOOK *(Annual)* 479
IMBIBE *(6 issues yearly)* 482
LCN LICENSED & CATERING NEWS *(11 issues yearly)* ... 534
M&C REPORT *(Monthly)* 546
MORNING ADVERTISER *(Weekly)* 566
THE NATIONAL BARTENDER *(10 issues yearly)* 571
ON TRADE SCOTLAND *(Monthly)* 588
THE PUBLICAN *(42 issues yearly)* 632
SCOTTISH LICENSED TRADE NEWS *(24 issues yearly)* .. 656
THE SPIRITS BUSINESS *(7 issues yearly)* 671
THEME MAGAZINE *(Monthly)* 686
WORLD DRINKS REPORT *(25 issues yearly)* 717

Licensed Trade, Wines & Spirits

CIRCLE UPDATE *(5 issues yearly)* 351
HARPERS WINE AND SPIRIT *(26 issues yearly)* 465
THE IWSR DRINKS RECORD *(11 issues yearly)* 511

Off-Licence

OLN OFF LICENCE NEWS *(24 issues yearly)* 587

Electrical

CABLETALK *(Monthly)* 337
CONNECTIONS *(Quarterly)* 366
ECN ELECTRICAL CONTRACTING NEWS *(Monthly)* 393
ELECTRICAL & MECHANICAL CONTRACTOR *(10 issues yearly)* 397
ELECTRICAL ENGINEERING *(10 issues yearly)* 397
ELECTRICAL REVIEW *(11 issues yearly)* 398
ELECTRICAL TIMES *(11 issues yearly)* 398
ELECTRICAL WHOLESALER *(Monthly)* 398
ELECTROFACTS *(5 issues yearly)* 398
ENGINEERING AND TECHNOLOGY *(21 issues yearly)* ... 404
EPA *(Monthly)* 408
EUROPEAN DAILY ELECTRICITY MARKETS *(260 issues yearly)* 414
HIGHWAY ELECTRICAL NEWS *(6 issues yearly)* 471
THE IET STUDENT & YOUNG PROFESSIONAL MAGAZINE *(3 issues yearly)* 481
INTERNATIONAL JOURNAL OF ELECTRONICS *(Monthly)* 499
INTERNATIONAL RENTAL NEWS *(9 issues yearly)* 503
LEDS MAGAZINE *(6 issues yearly)* 535
LIGHTING *(Monthly)* 539
THE LIGHTING JOURNAL *(6 issues yearly)* 539
MONDO*ARC *(6 issues yearly)* 565
NCN NETWORK COMMUNICATIONS NEWS *(Monthly)* .. 573
NORTHERN IRELANDS ELECTRICAL MAGAZINE *(Quarterly)* 581
PANEL & SYSTEM BUILDING *(8 issues yearly)* 594
POWER ENGINEERING INTERNATIONAL *(11 issues yearly)* 613
PROFESSIONAL ELECTRICIAN AND INSTALLER *(11 issues yearly)* 623
SPARKS MAGAZINE *(Half-yearly)* 669
TOTAL LIGHTING *(Monthly)* 690
WIREIN *(6 issues yearly)* 714
WIRING MATTERS *(Quarterly)* 715

Electrical Retail Trade

General (Electrical Retail Trade)

CUE ENTERTAINMENT *(Monthly)* 378
CUSTOM INSTALLER *(Monthly)* 379
ERT *(26 issues yearly)* 409
ERT IRELAND *(6 issues yearly)* 409
GET CONNECTED MAGAZINE *(Monthly)* 454
THE INDEPENDENT ELECTRICAL RETAILER *(Monthly)* . 485

Radio & Hi-Fi

COMMONWEALTH BROADCASTER *(Quarterly)* 359
SVI MAGAZINE *(10 issues yearly)* 679

TV

TELEVISION *(10 issues yearly)* 685

Video

DVD & BEYOND *(Annual)* 392
HCD *(10 issues yearly)* 466
IOV FOCUS *(Monthly)* 507
IVCA UPDATE *(6 issues yearly)* 511
TELEVISUAL *(Monthly)* 685

Electronics

General (Electronics)

AUTOMOTIVE ELECTRONICS *(6 issues yearly)* 304
BROADBAND *(3 issues yearly)* 324
CEMA CONSUMER ELECTRONICS *(Monthly)* 344
CIE *(10 issues yearly)* 351
CIRCUIT WORLD *(Quarterly)* 351
COIL WINDING INTERNATIONAL AND ELECTRICAL INSULATION MAGAZINE *(6 issues yearly)* 357
CONNECTINGINDUSTRY.COM ELECTRONICS *(Monthly)* 365
EASTERN EUROPEAN WIRELESS COMMUNICATIONS *(6 issues yearly)* 393
EDN EUROPE *(Monthly)* 395
ELECTRO OPTICS *(6 issues yearly)* 398
ELECTRONIC DESIGN EUROPE *(26 issues yearly)* 398
ELECTRONIC PRODUCT DESIGN *(Monthly)* 398
ELECTRONIC PRODUCTION *(Quarterly)* 398
ELECTRONICS MANUFACTURE & TEST *(Monthly)* 399
ELECTRONICS SOURCING *(Monthly)* 399
ELECTRONICS WEEKLY *(47 issues yearly)* 399
ELECTRONICS WORLD *(Monthly)* 399
EMBEDDED SYSTEMS EUROPE *(10 issues yearly)* 400
EMBEDDED TECHNOLOGY JOURNAL *(Weekly)* 400
THE EMC JOURNAL *(6 issues yearly)* 400
EPN *(Monthly)* 408
EUROASIA SEMICONDUCTOR *(Monthly)* 412
EUROPEAN ELECTRONICS ENGINEER *(Half-yearly)* 415
EUROPEAN ELECTRONICS MARKETS FORECAST *(Monthly)* 415
GLOBAL SMT AND PACKAGING *(Monthly)* 457
IEICE TRANSACTIONS ON ELECTRONICS *(Monthly)* 481
IEICE TRANSACTIONS ON FUNDAMENTALS OF ELECTRONICS, COMMUNICATIONS & COMPUTER SCIENCE *(Monthly)* 481
IMAGING AND MACHINE VISION EUROPE *(6 issues yearly)* 482
INSTALLATION EUROPE *(Monthly)* 491
INTERNATIONAL JOURNAL OF CONTROL *(Monthly)* 498
MICROELECTRONICS INTERNATIONAL *(3 issues yearly)* 559
MICROWAVE JOURNAL *(Monthly)* 559
MICROWAVES AND RF MAGAZINE *(Monthly)* 559
NEW ELECTRONICS *(22 issues yearly)* 575
NORTHERN AFRICAN WIRELESS COMMUNICATIONS *(6 issues yearly)* 580
POWER ELECTRONICS EUROPE *(8 issues yearly)* 613
RESIDENTIAL SYSTEMS EUROPE *(6 issues yearly)* 643
SEMICONDUCTOR FABTECH *(Quarterly)* 659
SERVICE MANAGEMENT *(9 issues yearly)* 660
SOLDERING & SURFACE MOUNT TECHNOLOGY *(Quarterly)* 666
SOUTHERN AFRICAN WIRELESS COMMUNICATIONS *(6 issues yearly)* 668
TEST MAGAZINE *(Quarterly)* 685

Telecommunications

3G SOLUTIONS FOR OPERATORS *(Quarterly)* 280
3 G WIRELESS BROADBAND *(26 issues yearly)* 280
ASIACOM *(23 issues yearly)* 300
BT TODAY *(6 issues yearly)* 325
CALL CENTRE EUROPE *(6 issues yearly)* 337
CAPACITY *(11 issues yearly)* 339
CCF *(Monthly)* 344
COMMS BUSINESS *(Monthly)* 360
COMMS DEALER *(Monthly)* 360
COMMUNICATIONS AFRICA *(6 issues yearly)* 360
CONNECTED *(8 issues yearly)* 365
CONVERGENCE WORLD *(6 issues yearly)* 371
CTO WORLD *(Quarterly)* 378
EUROPEAN COMMUNICATIONS *(Quarterly)* 414
GLOBAL TELECOMS BUSINESS *(6 issues yearly)* 457
INFO *(6 issues yearly)* 487
INFORMATION WORLD REVIEW *(10 issues yearly)* 488
INTERNATIONAL COMMUNICATION GAZETTE *(6 issues yearly)* 495
JOURNAL OF TELECOMMUNICATIONS MANAGEMENT *(Quarterly)* 527
THE JOURNAL OF THE INSTITUTE OF TELECOMMUNICATIONS PROFESSIONALS *(Quarterly)* 527
LAND MOBILE *(11 issues yearly)* 532
MICROSOFT CONNECTIONS IN COMMUNICATIONS *(Quarterly)* 559
MOBILE *(Weekly)* 563
MOBILE BUSINESS *(Monthly)* 563
MOBILE CHOICE *(13 issues yearly)* 563
MOBILE CHOICE FOR BUSINESS *(Quarterly)* 563
MOBILE COMMUNICATIONS EUROPE *(23 issues yearly)* 563
MOBILE COMMUNICATIONS INTERNATIONAL *(10 issues yearly)* 563
MOBILE ENTERTAINMENT *(Monthly)* 564
MOBILE EUROPE *(10 issues yearly)* 564
MOBILE FRONTIERS *(Quarterly)* 564
MOBILE MEDIA *(23 issues yearly)* 564
MOBILE NEWS *(25 issues yearly)* 564
TELECOM MARKETS *(23 issues yearly)* 684
TELECOMS INSIGHT *(Monthly)* 684
TELEMEDIA MAGAZINE *(6 issues yearly)* 685
TOTAL TELECOM MAGAZINE *(11 issues yearly)* 690
VANILLAPLUS MAGAZINE *(6 issues yearly)* 705
VIA INMARSAT *(Quarterly)* 707
WIRELESS BUSINESS REVIEW *(Quarterly)* 714

Energy, Fuel & Nuclear

AFRICAN ENERGY *(24 issues yearly)* 287
BIOFUELS INTERNATIONAL *(10 issues yearly)* 313
BOILING POINT *(Half-yearly)* 316
COALTRANS INTERNATIONAL *(6 issues yearly)* 357
CONNECTINGINDUSTRY.COM ENERGY MANAGEMENT *(Quarterly)* 365
COSPP - COGENERATION AND ON-SITE POWER PRODUCTION *(6 issues yearly)* 373
DIESEL & GAS TURBINE WORLDWIDE *(10 issues yearly)* 387
EIBI ENERGY IN BUILDINGS & INDUSTRY *(10 issues yearly)* 397
ENERGY *(13 issues yearly)* 402
ENERGY ACTION *(3 issues yearly)* 402
ENERGY ECONOMIST *(Monthly)* 402
ENERGY ENGINEERING *(6 issues yearly)* 402
ENERGY IN EAST EUROPE *(24 issues yearly)* 402
ENERGY MANAGEMENT BRIEFING *(Monthly)* 402
ENERGY NOW *(6 issues yearly)* 403
ENERGY POLICY *(Monthly)* 403
ENERGY WORLD *(11 issues yearly)* 403
EU ENERGY *(26 issues yearly)* 411
EUROPEAN POWER DAILY *(300 issues yearly)* 418
GAS TURBINE WORLD *(6 issues yearly)* 452
GLOBAL SOLAR TECHNOLOGY *(6 issues yearly)* 457
INSIDE NRC *(26 issues yearly)* 490
INTERNATIONAL COAL REPORT *(Weekly)* 495
MCCLOSKEY'S COAL UK *(Monthly)* 554

Section 2 UK Periodicals by Classification

Business

Engineering & Machinery

CAD & CIM (Computer Integrated Manufacture)

Engineering & Machinery

Engineering - Design

Engineering Related

Finishing

Hydraulic Power

Machinery, Machine Tools & Metalworking

Pipelines

Production & Mechanical Engineering

Environment & Pollution

Finance & Economics

Accountancy

Section 2 **UK Periodicals by Classification**

Business

Health Education

Health Medical Related

Hospitals

Medical Engineering Technology

Medical Equipment

Mental Health

Nursing

Business

Section 2　UK Periodicals by Classification

Business

Local Government, Leisure & Recreation

Civil Service

Community Care & Social Services

Leisure, Recreation & Entertainment

Local Government

Local Government Finance

Local Government Related

Parks

Police

Public Health & Cleaning

Swimming Pools

Marine & Shipping

Boat Trade

Commercial Fishing

Marine & Shipping

Section 2 UK Periodicals by Classification

Section 2 UK Periodicals by Classification

Section 2 UK Periodicals by Classification

Toy Trade & Sports Goods

Sports Goods

Toy Trade

Toy Trade - Baby Goods

Transport

Bus & Coach Transport

Commercial Vehicles

Electric Vehicles

Freight

General (Transport)

Railways

Transport Related

Travel & Tourism

Adult & Gay Magazines

Adult Magazines

Gay & Lesbian Magazines

Men's Lifestyle Magazines

Consumer

Angling & Fishing

Animals & Pets

Animals & Pets

Animals & Pets Protection

Bees

Birds

Cats

Dogs

Fish

Horses & Ponies

Consumer Electronics

Consumer Electronics Related

Games

Hi-Fi & Recording

Home Computing

Video & DVD

Current Affairs & Politics

Education

Adult Education

Careers

Crafts

Education Related

General (Education)

Preparatory & Junior Education

Teachers

Ethnic

Gardening

Consumer

Holidays

Hotel Magazines

In-Flight Magazines

Travel

Motoring & Cycling

Club Cars

Cycling

Motor Sports

Section 2 UK Periodicals by Classification

Consumer

Motorcycling

Motoring

Motoring & Cycling Related

Veteran Cars

Music & Performing Arts

Cinema

Dance

Music

Opera

Pop Music

Consumer

Recreation & Leisure

Boating & Yachting

Camping & Caravanning

Children & Youth

Hostelling

Recreation & Leisure Related

Religious

Rural & Regional Interest

Regional Interest Channel Islands

Regional Interest English Counties

Section 2 UK Periodicals by Classification

Consumer

Section 2 UK Periodicals by Classification

Food & Cookery

Hair & Beauty

Home & Family

Home Purchase

Lifestyle

Personal Finance

Consumer

SHORTCUT CONFIDENTIAL (Monthly) 980
SKIPTON LIFE (Half-yearly) 983
SMART INVESTOR (3 issues yearly) 984
TRUST (Half-yearly) 1016
WHAT INVESTMENT (Monthly) 1033
WHAT INVESTMENT TRUST (Quarterly) 1033
WHICH? MONEY (Monthly) 1036
YOUR MONEY (3 issues yearly) 1048

Retirement

AT EASE (Half-yearly) 743
CHOICE (Monthly) 777
THE CIVIL SERVICE PENSIONER (Quarterly) 780
LET'S TALK! (Monthly) 888
LIFETIME (Monthly) 890
MATURE TIMES (Monthly) 901
OUR TIME (Quarterly) 931
PENNANT (Half-yearly) 937
PEVEREL LIFE AND STYLE (3 issues yearly) 940
PRIME OF LIFE (Monthly) 952
PROBUS MAGAZINE (Quarterly) 953
SAGA MAGAZINE (Monthly) 970
THERE'S MORE TO LIFE (Quarterly) 1005
TOUCHDOWN BRITISH AIRWAYS (Half-yearly) 1012
UNITE MAGAZINE (8 issues yearly) 1019
YOURS (26 issues yearly) 1049

Secretary & PA

BRISTOL SECRETARY (Monthly) 762
EXECUTARY NEWS (6 issues yearly) 823
EXECUTIVE PA (6 issues yearly) 823
LONDON P.A. (Quarterly) 895
OFFICE PROFESSIONAL (Quarterly) 927
OS MAGAZINE (6 issues yearly) 930
SMART PA (6 issues yearly) 984
THAMES VALLEY SECRETARY (Quarterly) 1004

Slimming & Health

THE ALTERNATIVE GUIDE (Quarterly) 733
BE (3 issues yearly) 750
BODY & SOUL (6 issues yearly) 759
BOOST YOUR WEIGHT LOSS! (3 issues yearly) 760
BOOTS HEALTH & BEAUTY (6 issues yearly) 760
CADUCEUS (Quarterly) 767
CELEBRITY DIET NOW (Half-yearly) 774
CROSSED GRAIN (3 issues yearly) 797
ELIXIR (Quarterly) 814
EMBODY (Quarterly) 814
FOODS MATTER (Monthly) 835
HARPERS 4 LIFE (Monthly) 854
HEALTH & FITNESS MAGAZINE (Monthly) 855
HEALTH & HOMEOPATHY (Quarterly) 855
THE HEALTH STORE MAGAZINE (6 issues yearly) 855
HEALTHY (8 issues yearly) 856
HEART HEALTH (6 issues yearly) 856
HORIZONS (Half-yearly) 863
ICON (INTEGRATED CANCER AND ONCOLOGY NEWS)
  (Quarterly) 866
INTHEPINK (Annual) 872
LIGHTER LIFE (9 issues yearly) 890
NATURAL HEALTH (Monthly) 917
NATURAL LIFESTYLE MAGAZINE (Monthly) 917
NUTRITION & HEALING (Monthly) 926
OPTIMUM NUTRITION (Quarterly) 929
PURPLE (Quarterly) 956

ROSEMARY CONLEY DIET & FITNESS MAGAZINE (9 issues
  yearly) 967
SHIATSU SOCIETY NEWS (Quarterly) 979
SLIM AT HOME (10 issues yearly) 984
SLIMMING WORLD (7 issues yearly) 984
SMILEGUIDE (Annual) 985
SPA SECRETS MAGAZINE (Quarterly) 989
SPA WELLBEING (Quarterly) 989
SPA WORLD (6 issues yearly) 989
SWEET MAGAZINE (7 issues yearly) 1000
TOP SANTE HEALTH & BEAUTY (Monthly) 1009
WEEKEND (Weekly) 1029
WEIGHT WATCHERS MAGAZINE (Monthly) 1029
WELLBEING MAGAZINE (6 issues yearly) 1030
WHAT DOCTORS DON'T TELL YOU (Monthly) 1032
WOMAN'S HEALTH (Annual) 1040
WOMEN'S FITNESS (13 issues yearly) 1040
YOGA AND HEALTH (Monthly) 1044
YOGA MAGAZINE (MIND BODY SPIRIT) (Monthly) 1044
YOU ME BABY (Monthly) 1046

Teenage

BIG CHEESE (Monthly) 754
BLISS (13 issues yearly) 757
CARIS (Quarterly) 772
EDUC8 MAGAZINE (6 issues yearly) 813
EXPOSURE (6 issues yearly) 824
FIRST NEWS (Weekly) 832
FLIPSIDE (8 issues yearly) 833
FRESH (10 issues yearly) 838
GO GIRL (17 issues yearly) 844
GVZ (Monthly) 852
I-D MAGAZINE (6 issues yearly) 866
INDIANA JONES THE OFFICIAL MAGAZINE (6 issues
  yearly) 869
MIZZ (26 issues yearly) 907
THE NEWSPAPER (6 issues yearly) 921
PROM (Annual) 954
SHOUT MAGAZINE (26 issues yearly) 981
STAR GIRL MAGAZINE (Monthly) 994
SUGAR (Monthly) 997
TORCHWOOD (13 issues yearly) 1010
X-PRESS (Annual) 1043
YOUNG SCOT PORTAL (Quarterly) 1046

Women's Interest

BELLA (Weekly) 752
BEST (Weekly) 753
BH THE MAGAZINE (Monthly) 754
BM (Quarterly) 758
THE CELEBRITY ANGELS SERIES (6 issues yearly) 774
CHAT (Weekly) 775
COAST (10 issues yearly) 785
COMPANY MAGAZINE (Monthly) 787
COSMOPOLITAN (Monthly) 791
DARE (7 issues yearly) 801
EASY LIVING (Monthly) 812
ECOIDEAS (Quarterly) 812
ELITE MAGAZINE (Quarterly) 814
ELLE (Monthly) 814
ESSENTIALS (Monthly) 820
FULL HOUSE (Weekly) 839
IN STYLE (Monthly) 868
LADIES FIRST (Quarterly) 884
THE LADY (Weekly) 885
LIFESCAPE (6 issues yearly) 889

LOOK (Weekly) 896
LOVE IT! (Weekly) 897
MARIE CLAIRE (Monthly) 900
MORE (Weekly) 910
MY WEEKLY (Weekly) 915
NO.1 (17 issues yearly) 922
NORTHERN WOMAN (10 issues yearly) 924
NOW (Weekly) 925
PEOPLE'S FRIEND (Weekly) 937
PICK ME UP (Weekly) 941
PINK RIBBON (Annual) 942
PRIDE MAGAZINE (Monthly) 949
PRIMA (Monthly) 949
PSYCHOLOGIES (Monthly) 955
REAL PEOPLE (Weekly) 961
RED (Monthly) 962
THE REGISTER - NWR NATIONAL MAGAZINE (Half-
  yearly) 964
REVEAL (Weekly) 965
SCARLET (Monthly) 972
SHE (Monthly) 979
SO ESTEEM (6 issues yearly) 985
TAKE A BREAK (Weekly) 1001
TAKE A BREAK SPECIALS (8 issues yearly) 1001
TESCO: THE MAGAZINE (6 issues yearly) 1004
TFT - THE FEMALE TOUCH (Quarterly) 1004
THAT'S LIFE (Weekly) 1004
TOWNSWOMAN (Quarterly) 1012
VANITY FAIR (Monthly) 1021
WI LIFE (8 issues yearly) 1037
WI NEWS (ESSEX) (Monthly) 1037
WI NEWS MAGAZINE (SUFFOLK EAST) (Monthly) 1037
WI NEWS MAGAZINE (SUFFOLK WEST) (Monthly) 1037
WI NEWS MAGAZINE (WEST KENT) (Monthly) 1037
WM (Quarterly) 1039
WOMAN (Weekly) 1039
WOMAN'S OWN (Weekly) 1040
WOMAN'S WEEKLY (Weekly) 1040
WOMAN'S WORLD (Annual) 1040
WOMEN'S NEWS (6 issues yearly) 1040
ZEST (Monthly) 1050

Women's Interest - Fashion

10 MAGAZINE (Quarterly) 723
ALEF (Quarterly) 732
ASOS (Monthly) 742
BURDA MODEMAGAZIN (Monthly) 766
GLAMOUR (Monthly) 843
GRAZIA (Weekly) 848
HARPER'S BAZAAR (Monthly) 854
HARVEY NICHOLS EDIT (Half-yearly) 855
LET THEM EAT CAKE (Quarterly) 888
LOVE MAGAZINE (Half-yearly) 897
MY BRENT CROSS (Half-yearly) 914
PLASTIQUE (Quarterly) 943
RANDOM MAGAZINE (Half-yearly) 961
RUBBISH (Annual) 969
ST FASHION (Half-yearly) 992
VOGUE (Monthly) 1024
W (Monthly) 1025

Women's Interest Related

AFF JOURNAL (Quarterly) 730
THE BARKER (3 issues yearly) 747
TIME FOR U (Quarterly) 1007
WRVS ACTION (Half-yearly) 1043

Willings Volume 1
Section 3

Newspapers Index

Index to UK Newspapers by frequency and area

National, regional dailies and weekly/local papers, with circulations. This index cross-refers to all newspapers in Section 4 (a) Newspapers. At the front of the section is a summary of counties and regional areas, with page numbers.

Towns & Counties/Unitary Authorities

National Daily Newspapers

Title	Average net circulation*	Page No.
DAILY EXPRESS (am)	730,234	124
DAILY MAIL (am)	2,228,897	124
DAILY MIRROR (am)	1,324,883	125
DAILY SPORT (am)	72,592	125
DAILY STAR (am)	886,814	125
THE DAILY TELEGRAPH (am)	814,087	125
FINANCIAL TIMES (am)	395,845	127
THE GUARDIAN (am)	311,387	128
THE INDEPENDENT (am)	187,837	129
THE SUN (am)	3,128,501	133
THE TIMES (am)	576,185	136

National Sunday Newspapers

Title	Average net circulation*	Page No.
DAILY STAR SUNDAY	401,305	125
THE INDEPENDENT ON SUNDAY	160,809	129
THE MAIL ON SUNDAY	2,013,742	130
NEWS OF THE WORLD	3,120,991	131
THE OBSERVER	361,761	131
THE PEOPLE	586,414	131
SUNDAY EXPRESS	646,861	133
SUNDAY MIRROR	1,237,227	134
SUNDAY SPORT	70,796	134
THE SUNDAY TELEGRAPH	599,131	134
THE SUNDAY TIMES	1,164,831	134

*Certified average net sales per issue. ABC August 3 2009 to August 30 2007

Regional Daily & Sunday Newspapers — Quick reference guide to regional daily and Sunday newspapers by area

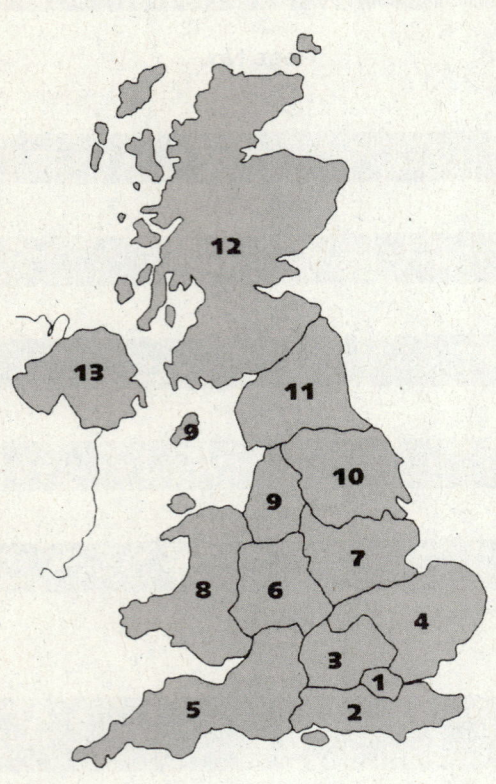

Most local newspapers are published weekly and many are published in 'Series', i.e. have the same editorial content. Free distribution newspapers are denoted by F

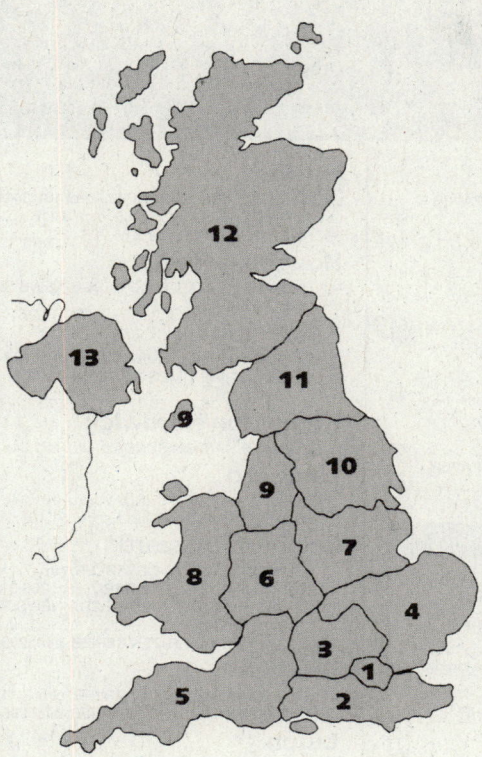

1 London

2 Southern

Kent, Hampshire, East Sussex, West Sussex

3 Home Counties

Bedfordshire, Berkshire, Buckinghamshire, Hertfordshire, Oxfordshire

4 East Anglia

Cambridgeshire, Essex, Norfolk, Northamptonshire, Suffolk

5 South West

Channel Islands, Cornwall, Devon, Dorset, Gloucestershire, Somerset, Wiltshire

6 West Midlands

Herefordshire, Shropshire, Warwickshire, West Midlands, Worcestershire

7 East Midlands

Derbyshire, Leicestershire, Lincolnshire, Rutland, Nottinghamshire

8 Wales

9 North West

Cheshire, Greater Manchester, Lancashire, Merseyside

10 North East

East Riding of Yorkshire, North Yorkshire, South Yorkshire, West Yorkshire

11 Northern

Cumbria, Co Durham, Northumberland, Tyne & Wear

12 Scotland

13 Northern Ireland

Non-Nationals - England

Title (Day/am/pm)	Circ.	Page No.	Title (Day/am/pm)	Circ.	Page No.	Title (Day/am/pm)	Circ.	Page No.

Non-Nationals

Local/Weekly Newspapers   Regional Daily Newspapers   Regional Sunday Newspapers

ENGLAND

- [D] ES MAGAZINE [F] 179
- [D] LONDON EVENING STANDARD, circ. 263,312 214
- [D] LONDON LITE, circ. 400,547 [F] 214
- [W] LONDON VOICE SERIES, circ. 220,000 [F] 214
- [D] METRO (LONDON), circ. 742,291 [F] 221
- [D] MIDLAND EDITION, circ. 5,000 [F] 222
- [W] SOUTHERN COUNTIES TELEGRAPH, circ. 45,000 [F] 252

Barking & Dagenham Borough

Barking
- [W] BARKING AND DAGENHAM POST, circ. 13,084 145
- [W] ESSEX ENQUIRER SERIES, circ. 57,859 [F] 180
- [W] ILFORD RECORDER SERIES, circ. 15,074 202
- [W] YELLOW ADVERTISER GROUP SERIES (ESSEX), circ. 434,612 [F] 278

Chadwell Heath
- [W] ILFORD RECORDER SERIES, circ. 15,074 202
- [W] ROMFORD RECORDER, circ. 28,302 241
- [W] YELLOW ADVERTISER GROUP SERIES (ESSEX), circ. 434,612 [F] 278

Dagenham
- [W] BARKING AND DAGENHAM POST, circ. 13,084 145
- [W] ESSEX ENQUIRER SERIES, circ. 57,859 [F] 180
- [W] ILFORD RECORDER SERIES, circ. 15,074 202
- [W] YELLOW ADVERTISER GROUP SERIES (ESSEX), circ. 434,612 [F] 278

Barnet Borough

Barnet
- [W] AVENUES SERIES, circ. 142,000 [F] 143
- [W] GAZETTE, ADVERTISER AND PRESS NEWSPAPER SERIES, circ. 270,519 188
- [W] HENDON TIMES SERIES, circ. 116,302 [F] 197

Church End
- [W] HENDON TIMES SERIES, circ. 116,302 [F] 197

Cockfosters
- [W] ENFIELD INDEPENDENT, circ. 92,538 [F] 179
- [W] GAZETTE, ADVERTISER AND PRESS NEWSPAPER SERIES, circ. 270,519 188
- [W] HENDON TIMES SERIES, circ. 116,302 [F] 197

Cricklewood
- [W] GAZETTE, ADVERTISER AND PRESS NEWSPAPER SERIES, circ. 270,519 188
- [W] HARROW OBSERVER & LEADER SERIES, circ. 116,846 195

Edgware
- [W] GAZETTE, ADVERTISER AND PRESS NEWSPAPER SERIES, circ. 270,519 188
- [W] HARROW OBSERVER & LEADER SERIES, circ. 116,846 195
- [W] HENDON TIMES SERIES, circ. 116,302 [F] 197

Finchley
- [W] AVENUES SERIES, circ. 142,000 [F] 143
- [W] GAZETTE, ADVERTISER AND PRESS NEWSPAPER SERIES, circ. 270,519 188
- [W] HENDON TIMES SERIES, circ. 116,302 [F] 197

Golders Green
- [W] GAZETTE, ADVERTISER AND PRESS NEWSPAPER SERIES, circ. 270,519 188
- [W] HAM & HIGH SERIES, circ. 9,619 194
- [W] HENDON TIMES SERIES, circ. 116,302 [F] 197

Hendon
- [W] AVENUES SERIES, circ. 142,000 [F] 143
- [W] GAZETTE, ADVERTISER AND PRESS NEWSPAPER SERIES, circ. 270,519 188
- [W] HENDON TIMES SERIES, circ. 116,302 [F] 197

Mill Hill
- [W] GAZETTE, ADVERTISER AND PRESS NEWSPAPER SERIES, circ. 270,519 188
- [W] HENDON TIMES SERIES, circ. 116,302 [F] 197

Monken Hadley
- [W] GAZETTE, ADVERTISER AND PRESS NEWSPAPER SERIES, circ. 270,519 188

New Barnet
- [W] HENDON TIMES SERIES, circ. 116,302 [F] 197

North End
- [W] HAM & HIGH SERIES, circ. 9,619 194
- [W] HENDON TIMES SERIES, circ. 116,302 [F] 197

Totteridge
- [W] AVENUES SERIES, circ. 142,000 [F] 143

Whetstone
- [W] AVENUES SERIES, circ. 142,000 [F] 143
- [W] GAZETTE, ADVERTISER AND PRESS NEWSPAPER SERIES, circ. 270,519 188

Bedfordshire

- [W] FOCUS SERIES, circ. 47,000 [F] 186

Ampthill
- [S] BEDFORDSHIRE ON SUNDAY, circ. 101,346 [F] 146
- [W] BEDFORDSHIRE TIMES & CITIZEN SERIES, circ. 78,119 [F] 147

Arlesey
- [S] BEDFORDSHIRE ON SUNDAY, circ. 101,346 [F] 146
- [W] BIGGLESWADE CHRONICLE, circ. 8,116 148
- [W] THE COMET SERIES, circ. 85,226 164

Barton-le-Clay
- [W] LUTON NEWS AND DUNSTABLE GAZETTE SERIES, circ. 14,316 216

Bedford
- [S] BEDFORDSHIRE ON SUNDAY, circ. 101,346 [F] 146
- [W] BEDFORDSHIRE TIMES & CITIZEN SERIES, circ. 78,119 [F] 147

Biggleswade
- [S] BEDFORDSHIRE ON SUNDAY, circ. 101,346 [F] 146
- [W] BIGGLESWADE CHRONICLE, circ. 8,116 148
- [W] THE COMET SERIES, circ. 85,226 164

Bromham
- [S] BEDFORDSHIRE ON SUNDAY, circ. 101,346 [F] 146
- [W] BEDFORDSHIRE TIMES & CITIZEN SERIES, circ. 78,119 [F] 147

Caddington
- [D] LONDON EVENING STANDARD, circ. 263,312 214
- [W] LUTON NEWS AND DUNSTABLE GAZETTE SERIES, circ. 14,316 216

Clapham
- [S] BEDFORDSHIRE ON SUNDAY, circ. 101,346 [F] 146
- [W] BEDFORDSHIRE TIMES & CITIZEN SERIES, circ. 78,119 [F] 147

Cranfield
- [W] MILTON KEYNES CITIZEN SERIES, circ. 205,772 [F] . 223

Dunstable
- [S] BEDFORDSHIRE ON SUNDAY, circ. 101,346 [F] 146
- [W] HERALD AND POST (LUTON & DUNSTABLE), circ. 90,526 [F] 197
- [D] LONDON EVENING STANDARD, circ. 263,312 214
- [W] LUTON & DUNSTABLE EXPRESS & NEWS SERIES, circ. 95,089 [F] 216

Eaton Bray
- [W] LEIGHTON BUZZARD OBSERVER, circ. 7,114 211
- [D] LONDON EVENING STANDARD, circ. 263,312 214
- [W] LUTON NEWS AND DUNSTABLE GAZETTE SERIES, circ. 14,316 216

Flitwick
- [S] BEDFORDSHIRE ON SUNDAY, circ. 101,346 [F] 146
- [W] BEDFORDSHIRE TIMES & CITIZEN SERIES, circ. 78,119 [F] 147

Harlington
- [W] LUTON & DUNSTABLE EXPRESS & NEWS SERIES, circ. 95,089 [F] 216

Henlow
- [S] BEDFORDSHIRE ON SUNDAY, circ. 101,346 [F] 146
- [W] BIGGLESWADE CHRONICLE, circ. 8,116 148
- [W] THE COMET SERIES, circ. 85,226 164

Houghton Regis
- [W] LUTON & DUNSTABLE EXPRESS & NEWS SERIES, circ. 95,089 [F] 216

Kempston
- [S] BEDFORDSHIRE ON SUNDAY, circ. 101,346 [F] 146
- [W] BEDFORDSHIRE TIMES & CITIZEN SERIES, circ. 78,119 [F] 147

Kempston Hardwick
- [S] BEDFORDSHIRE ON SUNDAY, circ. 101,346 [F] 146

Langford
- [S] BEDFORDSHIRE ON SUNDAY, circ. 101,346 [F] 146
- [W] BIGGLESWADE CHRONICLE, circ. 8,116 148

Leighton Buzzard
- [W] LEIGHTON BUZZARD OBSERVER, circ. 7,114 211
- [D] LONDON EVENING STANDARD, circ. 263,312 214
- [W] LUTON & DUNSTABLE EXPRESS & NEWS SERIES, circ. 95,089 [F] 216
- [W] MILTON KEYNES CITIZEN SERIES, circ. 205,772 [F] . 223

Linslade
- [W] LEIGHTON BUZZARD OBSERVER, circ. 7,114 211
- [W] MILTON KEYNES CITIZEN SERIES, circ. 205,772 [F] . 223

Luton
- [W] HERALD AND POST (LUTON & DUNSTABLE), circ. 90,526 [F] 197
- [D] LONDON EVENING STANDARD, circ. 263,312 214
- [W] LUTON & DUNSTABLE EXPRESS & NEWS SERIES, circ. 95,089 [F] 216
- [W] LUTON NEWS AND DUNSTABLE GAZETTE SERIES, circ. 14,316 216

Potton
- [S] BEDFORDSHIRE ON SUNDAY, circ. 101,346 [F] 146
- [W] BIGGLESWADE CHRONICLE, circ. 8,116 148

Sandy
- [S] BEDFORDSHIRE ON SUNDAY, circ. 101,346 [F] 146
- [W] BIGGLESWADE CHRONICLE, circ. 8,116 148
- [D] CAMBRIDGE NEWS, circ. 26,242 157
- [W] THE COMET SERIES, circ. 85,226 164

Shefford
- [W] BIGGLESWADE CHRONICLE, circ. 8,116 148
- [W] THE COMET SERIES, circ. 85,226 164

Stotfold
- [W] BIGGLESWADE CHRONICLE, circ. 8,116 148
- [W] THE COMET SERIES, circ. 85,226 164

Wootton
- [S] BEDFORDSHIRE ON SUNDAY, circ. 101,346 [F] 146
- [W] BEDFORDSHIRE TIMES & CITIZEN SERIES, circ. 78,119 [F] 147

Berkshire

- [W] GUARDIAN SERIES (WILTSHIRE, HAMPSHIRE AND SURREY), circ. 175,000 [F] 193
- [W] SOUTHERN COUNTIES TELEGRAPH, circ. 45,000 [F] 252

Arborfield
- [D] LONDON EVENING STANDARD, circ. 263,312 214
- [W] READING CHRONICLE SERIES, circ. 105,389 239
- [W] READING POST SERIES, circ. 84,500 239
- [W] WOKINGHAM AND BRACKNELL TIMES SERIES, circ. 6,430 277

Ascot
- [W] BRACKNELL FOREST & WOKINGHAM STANDARD SERIES, circ. 50,824 [F] 150
- [W] BRACKNELL NEWS SERIES, circ. 60,433 151
- [D] LONDON EVENING STANDARD, circ. 263,312 214
- [W] READING CHRONICLE SERIES, circ. 105,389 239
- [W] SLOUGH EXPRESS, circ. 66,727 [F] 249
- [W] SOUTH BUCKS AND BERKSHIRE NEWS SERIES, circ. 50,000 [F] 249
- [W] THE VILLAGER, circ. 8,000 [F] 267

[W] **Local/Weekly Newspapers**   [D] **Regional Daily Newspapers**   [S] **Regional Sunday Newspapers**   [F] **Free Newspapers**

Title (Day/am/pm)	Circ.	Page No.

W WOKINGHAM AND BRACKNELL TIMES SERIES, circ. 6,430 277

Bracknell
W BRACKNELL FOREST & WOKINGHAM STANDARD SERIES, circ. 50,824 F 150
W BRACKNELL NEWS SERIES, circ. 60,433 151
D LONDON EVENING STANDARD, circ. 263,312 214
W READING CHRONICLE SERIES, circ. 105,389 239
W SOUTH BUCKS AND BERKSHIRE NEWS SERIES, circ. 50,000 F 249
W WOKINGHAM AND BRACKNELL TIMES SERIES, circ. 6,430 277

Burghfield Common
D LONDON EVENING STANDARD, circ. 263,312 214
W READING CHRONICLE SERIES, circ. 105,389 239
W READING POST SERIES, circ. 84,500 239

Colnbrook
D LONDON EVENING STANDARD, circ. 263,312 214

Cookham
D LONDON EVENING STANDARD, circ. 263,312 214
W MAIDENHEAD ADVERTISER SERIES, circ. 75,397 217
W SLOUGH & WINDSOR OBSERVER SERIES, circ. 65,542 248

Crowthorne
W ALDERSHOT MAIL AND NEWS SERIES, circ. 131,660 140
W BRACKNELL FOREST & WOKINGHAM STANDARD SERIES, circ. 50,824 F 150
W BRACKNELL NEWS SERIES, circ. 60,433 151
D LONDON EVENING STANDARD, circ. 263,312 214
W READING CHRONICLE SERIES, circ. 105,389 239
W WOKINGHAM AND BRACKNELL TIMES SERIES, circ. 6,430 277

Datchet
D LONDON EVENING STANDARD, circ. 263,312 214
W SLOUGH & WINDSOR OBSERVER SERIES, circ. 65,542 248
W SLOUGH EXPRESS, circ. 66,727 F 249

Earley
W WOKINGHAM AND BRACKNELL TIMES SERIES, circ. 6,430 277

Eton
D LONDON EVENING STANDARD, circ. 263,312 214
W SLOUGH & WINDSOR OBSERVER SERIES, circ. 65,542 248

Hungerford
W GUARDIAN SERIES (WILTSHIRE, HAMPSHIRE AND SURREY), circ. 175,000 F 193
W NEWBURY WEEKLY NEWS SERIES, circ. 63,367 226

Lambourn
W NEWBURY WEEKLY NEWS SERIES, circ. 63,367 226

Langley
W SLOUGH & WINDSOR OBSERVER SERIES, circ. 65,542 248
W SLOUGH EXPRESS, circ. 66,727 F 249
W SOUTH BUCKS AND BERKSHIRE NEWS SERIES, circ. 50,000 F 249

Maidenhead
D LONDON EVENING STANDARD, circ. 263,312 214
W MAIDENHEAD ADVERTISER SERIES, circ. 75,397 217
W SLOUGH & WINDSOR OBSERVER SERIES, circ. 65,542 248
W SLOUGH EXPRESS, circ. 66,727 F 249
W SOUTH BUCKS AND BERKSHIRE NEWS SERIES, circ. 50,000 F 249

Mortimer
D LONDON EVENING STANDARD, circ. 263,312 214
W READING CHRONICLE SERIES, circ. 105,389 239
W READING POST SERIES, circ. 84,500 239

Newbury
W GUARDIAN SERIES (WILTSHIRE, HAMPSHIRE AND SURREY), circ. 175,000 F 193
W NEWBURY WEEKLY NEWS SERIES, circ. 63,367 226
W OXFORD JOURNAL, circ. 40,000 F 234
W READING CHRONICLE SERIES, circ. 105,389 239

Old Windsor
D LONDON EVENING STANDARD, circ. 263,312 214
W SLOUGH & WINDSOR OBSERVER SERIES, circ. 65,542 248
W SLOUGH EXPRESS, circ. 66,727 F 249

Pangbourne
D LONDON EVENING STANDARD, circ. 263,312 214

Reading
D LONDON EVENING STANDARD, circ. 263,312 214
W READING CHRONICLE SERIES, circ. 105,389 239
W READING POST SERIES, circ. 84,500 239

Sandhurst
W ALDERSHOT MAIL AND NEWS SERIES, circ. 131,660 140
W BRACKNELL FOREST & WOKINGHAM STANDARD SERIES, circ. 50,824 F 150
W BRACKNELL NEWS SERIES, circ. 60,433 151
D LONDON EVENING STANDARD, circ. 263,312 214
W WOKINGHAM AND BRACKNELL TIMES SERIES, circ. 6,430 277

Slough
W SLOUGH & WINDSOR OBSERVER SERIES, circ. 65,542 248
W SLOUGH EXPRESS, circ. 66,727 F 249
W SOUTH BUCKS AND BERKSHIRE NEWS SERIES, circ. 50,000 F 249

Sonning
W HENLEY STANDARD, circ. 12,049 197
W READING CHRONICLE SERIES, circ. 105,389 239
W READING POST SERIES, circ. 84,500 239
W WOKINGHAM AND BRACKNELL TIMES SERIES, circ. 6,430 277

Spencers Wood
D LONDON EVENING STANDARD, circ. 263,312 214
W READING CHRONICLE SERIES, circ. 105,389 239
W READING POST SERIES, circ. 84,500 239

Sunningdale
D LONDON EVENING STANDARD, circ. 263,312 214
W SLOUGH & WINDSOR OBSERVER SERIES, circ. 65,542 248
W THE VILLAGER, circ. 8,000 F 267

Thatcham
W NEWBURY WEEKLY NEWS SERIES, circ. 63,367 226
W OXFORD JOURNAL, circ. 40,000 F 234
W READING CHRONICLE SERIES, circ. 105,389 239

Theale
W NEWBURY WEEKLY NEWS SERIES, circ. 63,367 226

Twyford
W HENLEY STANDARD, circ. 12,049 197
D LONDON EVENING STANDARD, circ. 263,312 214
W MAIDENHEAD ADVERTISER SERIES, circ. 75,397 217
W READING CHRONICLE SERIES, circ. 105,389 239

Wargrave
W HENLEY STANDARD, circ. 12,049 197
D LONDON EVENING STANDARD, circ. 263,312 214
W MAIDENHEAD ADVERTISER SERIES, circ. 75,397 217
W READING CHRONICLE SERIES, circ. 105,389 239
W WOKINGHAM AND BRACKNELL TIMES SERIES, circ. 6,430 277

Windsor
D LONDON EVENING STANDARD, circ. 263,312 214
W SLOUGH & WINDSOR OBSERVER SERIES, circ. 65,542 248
W SLOUGH EXPRESS, circ. 66,727 F 249
W SOUTH BUCKS AND BERKSHIRE NEWS SERIES, circ. 50,000 F 249

Wokingham
W BRACKNELL FOREST & WOKINGHAM STANDARD SERIES, circ. 50,824 F 150
W BRACKNELL NEWS SERIES, circ. 60,433 151
D LONDON EVENING STANDARD, circ. 263,312 214
W READING CHRONICLE SERIES, circ. 105,389 239
W SOUTH BUCKS AND BERKSHIRE NEWS SERIES, circ. 50,000 F 249
W WOKINGHAM AND BRACKNELL TIMES SERIES, circ. 6,430 277

Woodley
W READING CHRONICLE SERIES, circ. 105,389 239
W WOKINGHAM AND BRACKNELL TIMES SERIES, circ. 6,430 277

Wraysbury
D LONDON EVENING STANDARD, circ. 263,312 214
W SLOUGH & WINDSOR OBSERVER SERIES, circ. 65,542 248
W SLOUGH EXPRESS, circ. 66,727 F 249

Bexley Borough
W BEXLEY CHRONICLE SERIES, circ. 40,000 F 148
W KENT ON SATURDAY, circ. 40,000 F 206
W TIMES AND REPORTER SERIES (KENT), circ. 154,146 263

Bexley
W THE MERCURY AND POST SERIES, circ. 166,029 F 219
W NEWS SHOPPER SERIES, circ. 308,920 F 228

Bexleyheath
W GATEWAY NEWS, circ. 22,000 F 188
W THE MERCURY AND POST SERIES, circ. 166,029 F 219
W NEWS SHOPPER SERIES, circ. 308,920 F 228

Erith
W GATEWAY NEWS, circ. 22,000 F 188
W NEWS SHOPPER SERIES, circ. 308,920 F 228

Sidcup
W NEWS SHOPPER SERIES, circ. 308,920 F 228

Thamesmead
W GATEWAY NEWS, circ. 22,000 F 188

Welling
W NEWS SHOPPER SERIES, circ. 308,920 F 228

Brent Borough
W HARROW TIMES, circ. 70,992 F 195

Brent
W HARROW OBSERVER & LEADER SERIES, circ. 116,846 195
W NORTH WEST LONDON NEWSPAPER SERIES, circ. 54,733 230

Kenton
W HARROW OBSERVER & LEADER SERIES, circ. 116,846 195

Kilburn
W HAM & HIGH SERIES, circ. 9,619 194

Neasden
W HARROW OBSERVER & LEADER SERIES, circ. 116,846 195
W LONDON NEWSPAPER GROUP SERIES, circ. 69,601 214

Wembley
W HARROW OBSERVER & LEADER SERIES, circ. 116,846 195
W SOUTH BUCKS AND BERKSHIRE NEWS SERIES, circ. 50,000 F 249

Willesden
W HARROW OBSERVER & LEADER SERIES, circ. 116,846 195

Bristol UA
W THE BATH CHRONICLE, circ. 20,000 146
W GUARDIAN SERIES (WILTSHIRE, HAMPSHIRE AND SURREY), circ. 175,000 F 193

Bristol
W BRISTOL OBSERVER SERIES, circ. 165,769 F 152
D EVENING POST (BRISTOL), circ. 51,287 181
D WESTERN DAILY PRESS BRISTOL, circ. 41,639 272

Kingswood
W BRISTOL OBSERVER SERIES, circ. 165,769 F 152

Bromley Borough
W KENT ON SATURDAY, circ. 40,000 F 206
W TIMES AND REPORTER SERIES (KENT), circ. 154,146 263

Beckenham
W NEWS SHOPPER SERIES, circ. 308,920 F 228

Biggin Hill
W BROMLEY AND BIGGIN HILL NEWS SERIES F 153
W NEWS SHOPPER SERIES, circ. 308,920 F 228
W SEVENOAKS CHRONICLE SERIES, circ. 105,776 246

Bromley
W BROMLEY AND BIGGIN HILL NEWS SERIES F 153
W EAST LONDON ADVERTISER, circ. 9,204 177
W NEWS SHOPPER SERIES, circ. 308,920 F 228

Chislehurst
W NEWS SHOPPER SERIES, circ. 308,920 F 228

Cudham
W BROMLEY AND BIGGIN HILL NEWS SERIES F 153

Downe
W BROMLEY AND BIGGIN HILL NEWS SERIES F 153

Farnborough
W BROMLEY AND BIGGIN HILL NEWS SERIES F 153

Non-Nationals - England

Hayes
W BROMLEY AND BIGGIN HILL NEWS SERIES F 153
W NEWS SHOPPER SERIES, circ. 308,920 F 228
W SOUTH BUCKS AND BERKSHIRE NEWS SERIES,
circ. 50,000 F 249

Keston
W BROMLEY AND BIGGIN HILL NEWS SERIES F 153
W NEWS SHOPPER SERIES, circ. 308,920 F 228

Orpington
W BROMLEY AND BIGGIN HILL NEWS SERIES F 153
W NEWS SHOPPER SERIES, circ. 308,920 F 228

Penge
W NEWS SHOPPER SERIES, circ. 308,920 F 228

West Wickham
W BROMLEY AND BIGGIN HILL NEWS SERIES F 153

Buckinghamshire
W FOCUS SERIES, circ. 47,000 F 186
D LONDON EVENING STANDARD, circ. 263,312 214
W SOUTHERN COUNTIES TELEGRAPH,
circ. 45,000 F 252

Amersham
W THE BUCKINGHAMSHIRE EXAMINER AND ADVERTISER
SERIES, circ. 13,568 153
W BUCKS FREE PRESS SERIES, circ. 85,396 154
W SOUTH BUCKS AND BERKSHIRE NEWS SERIES,
circ. 50,000 F 249

Aston Clinton
W BUCKS ADVERTISER & THAME GAZETTE SERIES,
circ. 41,849 F 153
W THE BUCKS HERALD SERIES, circ. 17,964 154

Aylesbury
W BUCKS ADVERTISER & THAME GAZETTE SERIES,
circ. 41,849 F 153
W THE BUCKS HERALD SERIES, circ. 17,964 154

Beaconsfield
W THE BUCKINGHAMSHIRE EXAMINER AND ADVERTISER
SERIES, circ. 13,568 153
W BUCKS FREE PRESS SERIES, circ. 85,396 154

Bletchley
W MILTON KEYNES CITIZEN SERIES, circ. 205,772 F . 223

Bourne End
W BUCKS FREE PRESS SERIES, circ. 85,396 154
W MAIDENHEAD ADVERTISER SERIES, circ. 75,397 217
W SOUTH BUCKS AND BERKSHIRE NEWS SERIES,
circ. 50,000 F 249

Buckingham
W BUCKINGHAM ADVERTISER SERIES, circ. 19,132 153
W MK NEWS, circ. 95,945 F 223

Burnham
W MAIDENHEAD ADVERTISER SERIES, circ. 75,397 217
W SLOUGH & WINDSOR OBSERVER SERIES,
circ. 65,542 248
W SLOUGH EXPRESS, circ. 66,727 F 249

Chalfont St. Giles
W THE BUCKINGHAMSHIRE EXAMINER AND ADVERTISER
SERIES, circ. 13,568 153
W BUCKS FREE PRESS SERIES, circ. 85,396 154

Chalfont St. Peter
W THE BUCKINGHAMSHIRE EXAMINER AND ADVERTISER
SERIES, circ. 13,568 153

Chesham
W THE BUCKINGHAMSHIRE EXAMINER AND ADVERTISER
SERIES, circ. 13,568 153
W BUCKS FREE PRESS SERIES, circ. 85,396 154
W SOUTH BUCKS AND BERKSHIRE NEWS SERIES,
circ. 50,000 F 249

Denham Green
W THE BUCKINGHAMSHIRE EXAMINER AND ADVERTISER
SERIES, circ. 13,568 153

Farnham Royal
W THE BUCKINGHAMSHIRE EXAMINER AND ADVERTISER
SERIES, circ. 13,568 153
W SLOUGH & WINDSOR OBSERVER SERIES,
circ. 65,542 248
W SLOUGH EXPRESS, circ. 66,727 F 249

Flackwell Heath
W BUCKS FREE PRESS SERIES, circ. 85,396 154

Gerrards Cross
W THE BUCKINGHAMSHIRE EXAMINER AND ADVERTISER
SERIES, circ. 13,568 153
W BUCKS FREE PRESS SERIES, circ. 85,396 154
W SOUTH BUCKS AND BERKSHIRE NEWS SERIES,
circ. 50,000 F 249

Great Kingshill
W BUCKS FREE PRESS SERIES, circ. 85,396 154

Great Missenden
W THE BUCKINGHAMSHIRE EXAMINER AND ADVERTISER
SERIES, circ. 13,568 153
W THE BUCKS HERALD SERIES, circ. 17,964 154

Haddenham
W BUCKS ADVERTISER & THAME GAZETTE SERIES,
circ. 41,849 F 153
W THE BUCKS HERALD SERIES, circ. 17,964 154

Hazlemere
W THE BUCKINGHAMSHIRE EXAMINER AND ADVERTISER
SERIES, circ. 13,568 153
W BUCKS FREE PRESS SERIES, circ. 85,396 154

High Wycombe
W BUCKS FREE PRESS SERIES, circ. 85,396 154
W SOUTH BUCKS AND BERKSHIRE NEWS SERIES,
circ. 50,000 F 249

Hughenden Valley
W BUCKS FREE PRESS SERIES, circ. 85,396 154

Iver
W THE BUCKINGHAMSHIRE EXAMINER AND ADVERTISER
SERIES, circ. 13,568 153
W SLOUGH & WINDSOR OBSERVER SERIES,
circ. 65,542 248
W SLOUGH EXPRESS, circ. 66,727 F 249

Iver Heath
W SLOUGH & WINDSOR OBSERVER SERIES,
circ. 65,542 248
W SLOUGH EXPRESS, circ. 66,727 F 249

Ivinghoe
W THE BUCKS HERALD SERIES, circ. 17,964 154
W LEIGHTON BUZZARD OBSERVER, circ. 7,114 211

Lane End
W BUCKS FREE PRESS SERIES, circ. 85,396 154

Marlow
W BUCKS FREE PRESS SERIES, circ. 85,396 154
W MAIDENHEAD ADVERTISER SERIES, circ. 75,397 217

Milton Keynes
W MILTON KEYNES CITIZEN SERIES, circ. 205,772 F . 223
W MK NEWS, circ. 95,945 F 223

Naphill
W BUCKS FREE PRESS SERIES, circ. 85,396 154

Newport Pagnell
W MILTON KEYNES CITIZEN SERIES, circ. 205,772 F . 223

Olney
W MILTON KEYNES CITIZEN SERIES, circ. 205,772 F . 223

Pitstone
W THE BUCKS HERALD SERIES, circ. 17,964 154
W LEIGHTON BUZZARD OBSERVER, circ. 7,114 211

Prestwood
W THE BUCKINGHAMSHIRE EXAMINER AND ADVERTISER
SERIES, circ. 13,568 153
W BUCKS FREE PRESS SERIES, circ. 85,396 154
W THE BUCKS HERALD SERIES, circ. 17,964 154

Princes Risborough
W BUCKS ADVERTISER & THAME GAZETTE SERIES,
circ. 41,849 F 153
W BUCKS FREE PRESS SERIES, circ. 85,396 154
W THE BUCKS HERALD SERIES, circ. 17,964 154

Seer Green
W THE BUCKINGHAMSHIRE EXAMINER AND ADVERTISER
SERIES, circ. 13,568 153
W BUCKS FREE PRESS SERIES, circ. 85,396 154

Stoke Poges
W THE BUCKINGHAMSHIRE EXAMINER AND ADVERTISER
SERIES, circ. 13,568 153
W SOUTH BUCKS AND BERKSHIRE NEWS SERIES,
circ. 50,000 F 249

Stony Stratford
W MILTON KEYNES CITIZEN SERIES, circ. 205,772 F . 223

Walter's Ash
W BUCKS FREE PRESS SERIES, circ. 85,396 154

Wendover
W BUCKS ADVERTISER & THAME GAZETTE SERIES,
circ. 41,849 F 153
W THE BUCKS HERALD SERIES, circ. 17,964 154

Winslow
W BUCKINGHAM ADVERTISER SERIES, circ. 19,132 153

Woburn Sands
W MILTON KEYNES CITIZEN SERIES, circ. 205,772 F . 223

Wolverton
W MILTON KEYNES CITIZEN SERIES, circ. 205,772 F . 223

Cambridgeshire

Abington
D CAMBRIDGE NEWS, circ. 26,242 157

Balsham
D CAMBRIDGE NEWS, circ. 26,242 157

Bassingbourn
D CAMBRIDGE NEWS, circ. 26,242 157

Brampton
D CAMBRIDGE NEWS, circ. 26,242 157
W CAMBRIDGE WEEKLY NEWS & CRIER SERIES,
circ. 208,805 F 157
W TOWN CRIER SERIES, circ. 43,550 F 265

Buckden
D CAMBRIDGE NEWS, circ. 26,242 157
W TOWN CRIER SERIES, circ. 43,550 F 265

Cambridge
D CAMBRIDGE NEWS, circ. 26,242 157
W CAMBRIDGE WEEKLY NEWS & CRIER SERIES,
circ. 208,805 F 157

Chatteris
D CAMBRIDGE NEWS, circ. 26,242 157
W CAMBS TIMES, circ. 22,000 F 157
W FENLAND CITIZEN SERIES, circ. 41,075 F 184

Cottenham
D CAMBRIDGE NEWS, circ. 26,242 157
W CAMBRIDGE WEEKLY NEWS & CRIER SERIES,
circ. 208,805 F 157

Earith
D CAMBRIDGE NEWS, circ. 26,242 157

Eaton Socon
D CAMBRIDGE NEWS, circ. 26,242 157
W CAMBRIDGE WEEKLY NEWS & CRIER SERIES,
circ. 208,805 F 157
W TOWN CRIER SERIES, circ. 43,550 F 265

Ely
D CAMBRIDGE NEWS, circ. 26,242 157
W CAMBRIDGE WEEKLY NEWS & CRIER SERIES,
circ. 208,805 F 157
W ELY STANDARD SERIES, circ. 21,797 F 179
W NEWMARKET JOURNAL SERIES, circ. 10,186 226

Fulbourn
D CAMBRIDGE NEWS, circ. 26,242 157
W CAMBRIDGE WEEKLY NEWS & CRIER SERIES,
circ. 208,805 F 157

Gamlingay
W BIGGLESWADE CHRONICLE, circ. 8,116 148
D CAMBRIDGE NEWS, circ. 26,242 157

Girton
D CAMBRIDGE NEWS, circ. 26,242 157
W CAMBRIDGE WEEKLY NEWS & CRIER SERIES,
circ. 208,805 F 157

Godmanchester
D CAMBRIDGE NEWS, circ. 26,242 157

Great Shelford
D CAMBRIDGE NEWS, circ. 26,242 157
W CAMBRIDGE WEEKLY NEWS & CRIER SERIES,
circ. 208,805 F 157

Harston
D CAMBRIDGE NEWS, circ. 26,242 157

Histon
D CAMBRIDGE NEWS, circ. 26,242 157

W Local/Weekly Newspapers   D Regional Daily Newspapers   S Regional Sunday Newspapers   F Free Newspapers

Title (Day/am/pm) | Circ. | Page No.

Huntingdon
[D] CAMBRIDGE NEWS, circ. 26,242 ... 157
[W] CAMBRIDGE WEEKLY NEWS & CRIER SERIES, circ. 208,805 [F] ... 157
[D] ET LIFE ... 180
[D] EVENING TELEGRAPH (PETERBOROUGH), circ. 18,542 ... 182
[W] THE HUNTS POST, circ. 48,786 ... 201
[W] TOWN CRIER SERIES, circ. 43,550 [F] ... 265

Linton
[D] CAMBRIDGE NEWS, circ. 26,242 ... 157
[W] CAMBRIDGE WEEKLY NEWS & CRIER SERIES, circ. 208,805 [F] ... 157
[W] THE REPORTER (SAFFRON WALDEN, STANSTED & SAWSTON), circ. 25,073 [F] ... 240

Little Paxton
[D] CAMBRIDGE NEWS, circ. 26,242 ... 157
[W] CAMBRIDGE WEEKLY NEWS & CRIER SERIES, circ. 208,805 [F] ... 157
[W] TOWN CRIER SERIES, circ. 43,550 [F] ... 265

Littleport
[D] EASTERN DAILY PRESS (NORWICH), circ. 64,700 ... 178
[W] ELY STANDARD SERIES, circ. 21,797 [F] ... 179

Longstanton
[D] CAMBRIDGE NEWS, circ. 26,242 ... 157
[W] CAMBRIDGE WEEKLY NEWS & CRIER SERIES, circ. 208,805 [F] ... 157

March
[W] CAMBS TIMES, circ. 22,000 [F] ... 157
[D] EASTERN DAILY PRESS (NORWICH), circ. 64,700 ... 178
[D] ET LIFE ... 180
[D] EVENING TELEGRAPH (PETERBOROUGH), circ. 18,542 ... 182
[W] FENLAND CITIZEN SERIES, circ. 41,075 [F] ... 184

Melbourn
[D] CAMBRIDGE NEWS, circ. 26,242 ... 157

Oakington
[D] CAMBRIDGE NEWS, circ. 26,242 ... 157

Peterborough
[D] ET LIFE ... 180
[D] EVENING TELEGRAPH (PETERBOROUGH), circ. 18,542 ... 182
[W] PETERBOROUGH CITIZEN, circ. 49,258 [F] ... 235

Ramsey
[D] ET LIFE ... 180
[D] EVENING TELEGRAPH (PETERBOROUGH), circ. 18,542 ... 182
[W] THE HUNTS POST, circ. 48,786 ... 201
[W] TOWN CRIER SERIES, circ. 43,550 [F] ... 265

Sawston
[D] CAMBRIDGE NEWS, circ. 26,242 ... 157
[W] CAMBRIDGE WEEKLY NEWS & CRIER SERIES, circ. 208,805 [F] ... 157
[W] HAVERHILL ECHO, circ. 4,927 ... 196
[W] THE REPORTER (SAFFRON WALDEN, STANSTED & SAWSTON), circ. 25,073 [F] ... 240

Sawtry
[D] CAMBRIDGE NEWS, circ. 26,242 ... 157
[W] CAMBRIDGE WEEKLY NEWS & CRIER SERIES, circ. 208,805 [F] ... 157
[W] TOWN CRIER SERIES, circ. 43,550 [F] ... 265

Soham
[D] CAMBRIDGE NEWS, circ. 26,242 ... 157
[W] ELY STANDARD SERIES, circ. 21,797 [F] ... 179
[W] NEWMARKET JOURNAL SERIES, circ. 10,186 ... 226

Somersham
[D] CAMBRIDGE NEWS, circ. 26,242 ... 157

St. Ives
[D] CAMBRIDGE NEWS, circ. 26,242 ... 157
[W] CAMBRIDGE WEEKLY NEWS & CRIER SERIES, circ. 208,805 [F] ... 157
[W] THE HUNTS POST, circ. 48,786 ... 201
[W] TOWN CRIER SERIES, circ. 43,550 [F] ... 265

St. Neots
[D] CAMBRIDGE NEWS, circ. 26,242 ... 157
[W] CAMBRIDGE WEEKLY NEWS & CRIER SERIES, circ. 208,805 [F] ... 157
[W] THE HUNTS POST, circ. 48,786 ... 201
[W] TOWN CRIER SERIES, circ. 43,550 [F] ... 265

Sutton
[D] CAMBRIDGE NEWS, circ. 26,242 ... 157
[W] CAMBRIDGE WEEKLY NEWS & CRIER SERIES, circ. 208,805 [F] ... 157
[W] ELY STANDARD SERIES, circ. 21,797 [F] ... 179

Warboys
[D] CAMBRIDGE NEWS, circ. 26,242 ... 157
[W] CAMBRIDGE WEEKLY NEWS & CRIER SERIES, circ. 208,805 [F] ... 157
[W] TOWN CRIER SERIES, circ. 43,550 [F] ... 265

Waterbeach
[D] CAMBRIDGE NEWS, circ. 26,242 ... 157
[W] CAMBRIDGE WEEKLY NEWS & CRIER SERIES, circ. 208,805 [F] ... 157

Whittlesey
[W] CAMBS TIMES, circ. 22,000 [F] ... 157

Willingham
[D] CAMBRIDGE NEWS, circ. 26,242 ... 157

Wisbech
[W] CAMBS TIMES, circ. 22,000 [F] ... 157
[D] EASTERN DAILY PRESS (NORWICH), circ. 64,700 ... 178
[D] ET LIFE ... 180
[D] EVENING TELEGRAPH (PETERBOROUGH), circ. 18,542 ... 182
[W] FENLAND CITIZEN SERIES, circ. 41,075 [F] ... 184
[W] WISBECH STANDARD, circ. 19,100 [F] ... 276

Wittering
[D] ET LIFE ... 180
[D] EVENING TELEGRAPH (PETERBOROUGH), circ. 18,542 ... 182

Yaxley
[D] ET LIFE ... 180
[D] EVENING TELEGRAPH (PETERBOROUGH), circ. 18,542 ... 182
[W] PETERBOROUGH CITIZEN, circ. 49,258 [F] ... 235

Camden Borough

Bloomsbury
[W] ISLINGTON GAZETTE & JOURNAL SERIES, circ. 52,062 ... 204

Camden
[W] AVENUES SERIES, circ. 142,000 [F] ... 143
[W] GREATER LONDON CHRONICLE, circ. 5,000 [F] ... 193
[W] HAM & HIGH SERIES, circ. 9,619 ... 194
[W] ISLINGTON GAZETTE & JOURNAL SERIES, circ. 52,062 ... 204
[W] JOURNAL SERIES, circ. 101,283 [F] ... 205
[W] NORTH WEST LONDON NEWSPAPER SERIES, circ. 54,733 ... 230

Hampstead
[W] AVENUES SERIES, circ. 142,000 [F] ... 143
[W] GREATER LONDON CHRONICLE, circ. 5,000 [F] ... 193
[W] HAM & HIGH SERIES, circ. 9,619 ... 194
[W] JOURNAL SERIES, circ. 101,283 [F] ... 205
[D] LONDON EVENING STANDARD, circ. 263,312 ... 214

Kentish Town
[W] AVENUES SERIES, circ. 142,000 [F] ... 143
[W] HAM & HIGH SERIES, circ. 9,619 ... 194
[W] ISLINGTON GAZETTE & JOURNAL SERIES, circ. 52,062 ... 204
[W] JOURNAL SERIES, circ. 101,283 [F] ... 205

Primrose Hill
[W] JOURNAL SERIES, circ. 101,283 [F] ... 205

St. Pancras
[W] ISLINGTON GAZETTE & JOURNAL SERIES, circ. 52,062 ... 204

Cheshire

Alderley Edge
[W] WILMSLOW EXPRESS, circ. 16,609 [F] ... 275

Alsager
[W] ADVERTISER SERIES (SOUTH CHESHIRE), circ. 25,694 [F] ... 140
[W] ADVERTISER SERIES (STOKE-ON-TRENT), circ. 103,429 [F] ... 140
[W] CHRONICLE SERIES (CREWE), circ. 42,988 ... 162
[W] CONGLETON CHRONICLE SERIES, circ. 16,900 ... 165
[D] THE SENTINEL STOKE-ON-TRENT, circ. 61,910 ... 245

Chester
[W] YR ANGOR (LIVERPOOL), circ. 3,000 ... 142
[W] CHESTER CHRONICLE SERIES, circ. 85,077 ... 160
[W] CHESTER STANDARD SERIES, circ. 90,394 [F] ... 160
[D] EVENING LEADER, circ. 21,180 ... 181
[D] LIVERPOOL DAILY POST, circ. 15,581 ... 213

Congleton
[W] ADVERTISER SERIES (SOUTH CHESHIRE), circ. 25,694 [F] ... 140
[W] CONGLETON CHRONICLE SERIES, circ. 16,900 ... 165
[D] MANCHESTER EVENING NEWS, circ. 82,445 ... 217
[W] MOORLANDS TRADER, circ. 15,689 [F] ... 224
[D] THE SENTINEL STOKE-ON-TRENT, circ. 61,910 ... 245

Crewe
[W] CHRONICLE SERIES (CREWE), circ. 42,988 ... 162
[W] CREWE GUARDIAN SERIES, circ. 39,786 [F] ... 168
[D] THE SENTINEL STOKE-ON-TRENT, circ. 61,910 ... 245

Cuddington
[W] THE CHRONICLE, circ. 15,000 [F] ... 161
[D] MANCHESTER EVENING NEWS, circ. 82,445 ... 217
[W] WARRINGTON GUARDIAN SERIES, circ. 111,077 ... 269

Culcheth
[W] LEIGH REPORTER, circ. 61,041 [F] ... 211

Deeside
[D] EVENING LEADER, circ. 21,180 ... 181
[W] FLINTSHIRE CHRONICLE ... 185

Disley
[D] MANCHESTER EVENING NEWS, circ. 82,445 ... 217

Ellesmere Port
[W] CHESTER CHRONICLE SERIES, circ. 85,077 ... 160
[W] CHESTER STANDARD SERIES, circ. 90,394 [F] ... 160
[W] ELLESMERE PORT PIONEER, circ. 5,203 ... 179
[D] LIVERPOOL ECHO, circ. 109,458 ... 213

Frodsham
[W] CHESTER CHRONICLE SERIES, circ. 85,077 ... 160
[W] RUNCORN & WIDNES NEWS & HERALD SERIES, circ. 42,205 ... 242
[W] RUNCORN & WIDNES WORLD, circ. 39,234 [F] ... 242

Great Sankey
[W] WARRINGTON GUARDIAN SERIES, circ. 111,077 ... 269

Helsby
[W] CHESTER CHRONICLE SERIES, circ. 85,077 ... 160
[W] RUNCORN & WIDNES NEWS & HERALD SERIES, circ. 42,205 ... 242
[W] RUNCORN & WIDNES WORLD, circ. 39,234 [F] ... 242

Holmes Chapel
[W] ADVERTISER SERIES (SOUTH CHESHIRE), circ. 25,694 [F] ... 140
[W] CHRONICLE SERIES (CREWE), circ. 42,988 ... 162
[W] CONGLETON CHRONICLE SERIES, circ. 16,900 ... 165
[D] MANCHESTER EVENING NEWS, circ. 82,445 ... 217
[D] THE SENTINEL STOKE-ON-TRENT, circ. 61,910 ... 245
[W] STOCKPORT EXPRESS AND TIMES SERIES, circ. 112,974 ... 256
[W] WARRINGTON GUARDIAN SERIES, circ. 111,077 ... 269

Knutsford
[D] MANCHESTER EVENING NEWS, circ. 82,445 ... 217
[W] WARRINGTON GUARDIAN SERIES, circ. 111,077 ... 269

Lymm
[W] SOUTH WARRINGTON NEWS, circ. 10,000 [F] ... 251
[W] WARRINGTON GUARDIAN SERIES, circ. 111,077 ... 269

Macclesfield
[W] MACCLESFIELD EXPRESS AND TIMES SERIES, circ. 45,030 ... 216
[D] MANCHESTER EVENING NEWS, circ. 82,445 ... 217
[W] MOORLANDS TRADER, circ. 15,689 [F] ... 224

Marple
[W] STOCKPORT EXPRESS AND TIMES SERIES, circ. 112,974 ... 256

Middlewich
[W] THE CHRONICLE, circ. 15,000 [F] ... 161
[W] CHRONICLE SERIES (CREWE), circ. 42,988 ... 162
[D] MANCHESTER EVENING NEWS, circ. 82,445 ... 217
[W] MID-CHESHIRE GUARDIAN SERIES, circ. 21,051 ... 222
[D] THE SENTINEL STOKE-ON-TRENT, circ. 61,910 ... 245
[W] WARRINGTON GUARDIAN SERIES, circ. 111,077 ... 269

Nantwich
[W] CHRONICLE SERIES (CREWE), circ. 42,988 ... 162
[W] CREWE GUARDIAN SERIES, circ. 39,786 [F] ... 168

Neston
[W] CHESTER CHRONICLE SERIES, circ. 85,077 ... 160
[W] CHESTER STANDARD SERIES, circ. 90,394 [F] ... 160
[W] ELLESMERE PORT PIONEER, circ. 5,203 ... 179
[W] WIRRAL GLOBE SERIES, circ. 133,193 [F] ... 275
[W] WIRRAL NEWS SERIES, circ. 132,829 [F] ... 276

Northwich
[W] THE CHRONICLE, circ. 15,000 [F] ... 161

[W] **Local/Weekly Newspapers** [D] **Regional Daily Newspapers** [S] **Regional Sunday Newspapers** [F] **Free Newspapers**

Non-Nationals - England

Title *(Day/am/pm)*	Circ.	Page No.

D MANCHESTER EVENING NEWS, circ. 82,445 217
W MID-CHESHIRE GUARDIAN SERIES, circ. 21,051 222
SOUTH WARRINGTON NEWS, circ. 10,000 251
W WARRINGTON GUARDIAN SERIES, circ. 111,077 ... 269

Penketh
W WARRINGTON GUARDIAN SERIES, circ. 111,077 ... 269

Poynton
W MACCLESFIELD EXPRESS AND TIMES SERIES, circ. 45,030 216
D MANCHESTER EVENING NEWS, circ. 82,445 217
STOCKPORT EXPRESS AND TIMES SERIES, circ. 112,974 256

Prestbury
W MACCLESFIELD EXPRESS AND TIMES SERIES, circ. 45,030 216

Runcorn
D LIVERPOOL DAILY POST, circ. 15,581 213
D LIVERPOOL ECHO, circ. 109,458 213
W RUNCORN & WIDNES NEWS & HERALD SERIES, circ. 42,205 242
W RUNCORN & WIDNES WORLD, circ. 39,234 F ... 242

Sandbach
W CHRONICLE SERIES (CREWE), circ. 42,988 162
W CONGLETON CHRONICLE SERIES, circ. 16,900 165
W CREWE GUARDIAN SERIES, circ. 39,786 F 168
D MANCHESTER EVENING NEWS, circ. 82,445 217
D THE SENTINEL STOKE-ON-TRENT, circ. 61,910 245

Saughall
W CHESTER CHRONICLE SERIES, circ. 85,077 160
D EVENING LEADER, circ. 21,180 181

Shavington
D THE SENTINEL STOKE-ON-TRENT, circ. 61,910 245

Stockton Heath
W SOUTH WARRINGTON NEWS, circ. 10,000 F 251
W WARRINGTON GUARDIAN SERIES, circ. 111,077 269

Thelwall
D MANCHESTER EVENING NEWS, circ. 82,445 217
W WARRINGTON GUARDIAN SERIES, circ. 111,077 269

Warrington
D LIVERPOOL DAILY POST, circ. 15,581 213
D LIVERPOOL ECHO, circ. 109,458 213
D MANCHESTER EVENING NEWS, circ. 82,445 217
W SOUTH WARRINGTON NEWS, circ. 10,000 F 251
W WARRINGTON GUARDIAN SERIES, circ. 111,077 269

Weaverham
D MANCHESTER EVENING NEWS, circ. 82,445 217
W WARRINGTON GUARDIAN SERIES, circ. 111,077 269

Widnes
D LIVERPOOL ECHO, circ. 109,458 213
D MANCHESTER EVENING NEWS, circ. 82,445 217
W RUNCORN & WIDNES NEWS & HERALD SERIES, circ. 42,205 242
W RUNCORN & WIDNES WORLD, circ. 39,234 F ... 242

Willaston
W CHESTER CHRONICLE SERIES, circ. 85,077 160
D LIVERPOOL DAILY POST, circ. 15,581 213
D LIVERPOOL ECHO, circ. 109,458 213
W WIRRAL GLOBE SERIES, circ. 133,193 F 275
W WIRRAL NEWS SERIES, circ. 132,829 F 276

Wilmslow
D MANCHESTER EVENING NEWS, circ. 82,445 217
W WILMSLOW EXPRESS, circ. 16,609 F 275

Winsford
W THE CHRONICLE, circ. 15,000 F 161
W MID-CHESHIRE GUARDIAN SERIES, circ. 21,051 222
W WARRINGTON GUARDIAN SERIES, circ. 111,077 269

City of London
D CITY A.M., circ. 86,522 F 162
W CITY OF LONDON & DOCKLAND TIMES, circ. 20,000 162
W NEWHAM RECORDER, circ. 13,531 226

Cornwall
S SUNDAY INDEPENDENT (PLYMOUTH), circ. 32,000 . 258

Bodmin
W CORNISH GUARDIAN SERIES, circ. 32,982 165
W NORTH CORNWALL ADVERTISER, circ. 37,000 F ... 229
W THE PACKET SERIES, circ. 90,472 234
D WESTERN MORNING NEWS, circ. 41,154 272

Bude
W CORNISH & DEVON POST SERIES, circ. 13,257 165
W CORNISH GUARDIAN SERIES, circ. 32,982 165
W NORTH CORNWALL ADVERTISER, circ. 37,000 F ... 229

Callington
W CORNISH & DEVON POST SERIES, circ. 13,257 165
W CORNISH TIMES & GAZETTE SERIES, circ. 51,000 ... 165
D THE HERALD (PLYMOUTH), circ. 40,384 198
W TAVISTOCK TIMES GAZETTE SERIES, circ. 13,000 ... 262

Camborne
W THE HUNTS POST, circ. 48,786 201
W THE PACKET SERIES, circ. 90,472 234
W THE WEST BRITON SERIES, circ. 39,343 270
D WESTERN MORNING NEWS, circ. 41,154 272

Camelford
W CORNISH & DEVON POST SERIES, circ. 13,257 165
W CORNISH GUARDIAN SERIES, circ. 32,982 165
W NORTH CORNWALL ADVERTISER, circ. 37,000 F ... 229
D WESTERN MORNING NEWS, circ. 41,154 272

Delabole
W NORTH CORNWALL ADVERTISER, circ. 37,000 F ... 229

Falmouth
W THE PACKET SERIES, circ. 90,472 234
W THE WEST BRITON SERIES, circ. 39,343 270
D WESTERN MORNING NEWS, circ. 41,154 272

Fowey
W CORNISH GUARDIAN (LOSTWITHIEL & FOWEY) 165
W CORNISH GUARDIAN SERIES, circ. 32,982 165
W CORNISH TIMES & GAZETTE SERIES, circ. 51,000 ... 165
W MID CORNWALL ADVERTISER, circ. 59,750 F 221
W ST. AUSTELL VOICE 253

Foxhole
W CORNISH GUARDIAN SERIES, circ. 32,982 165
W THE PACKET SERIES, circ. 90,472 234
D WESTERN MORNING NEWS, circ. 41,154 272

Gunnislake
D THE HERALD (PLYMOUTH), circ. 40,384 198
W TAVISTOCK TIMES GAZETTE SERIES, circ. 13,000 ... 262

Hayle
W THE CORNISHMAN, circ. 18,189 166
W THE PACKET SERIES, circ. 90,472 234
W ST. IVES TIMES & ECHO SERIES, circ. 3,930 254
W THE WEST BRITON SERIES, circ. 39,343 270
D WESTERN MORNING NEWS, circ. 41,154 272

Helston
W THE PACKET SERIES, circ. 90,472 234
W THE WEST BRITON SERIES, circ. 39,343 270
D WESTERN MORNING NEWS, circ. 41,154 272

Launceston
W CORNISH & DEVON POST SERIES, circ. 13,257 165
W CORNISH GUARDIAN SERIES, circ. 32,982 165
W CORNISH TIMES & GAZETTE SERIES, circ. 51,000 ... 165
W NORTH CORNWALL ADVERTISER, circ. 37,000 F ... 229
W TAVISTOCK TIMES GAZETTE SERIES, circ. 13,000 ... 262
D WESTERN MORNING NEWS, circ. 41,154 272

Liskeard
W CORNISH GUARDIAN SERIES, circ. 32,982 165
W CORNISH TIMES & GAZETTE SERIES, circ. 51,000 ... 165
D THE HERALD (PLYMOUTH), circ. 40,384 198
D WESTERN MORNING NEWS, circ. 41,154 272

Looe
W CORNISH GUARDIAN SERIES, circ. 32,982 165
W CORNISH TIMES & GAZETTE SERIES, circ. 51,000 ... 165
D WESTERN MORNING NEWS, circ. 41,154 272

Lostwithiel
W CORNISH GUARDIAN (LOSTWITHIEL & FOWEY) 165
W CORNISH GUARDIAN SERIES, circ. 32,982 165
W CORNISH TIMES & GAZETTE SERIES, circ. 51,000 ... 165
W MID CORNWALL ADVERTISER, circ. 59,750 F 221
W ST. AUSTELL VOICE 253

Millbrook
D THE HERALD (PLYMOUTH), circ. 40,384 198

Nanpean
W CORNISH GUARDIAN SERIES, circ. 32,982 165
W THE PACKET SERIES, circ. 90,472 234
D WESTERN MORNING NEWS, circ. 41,154 272

Newquay
W CORNISH GUARDIAN SERIES, circ. 32,982 165
W MID CORNWALL ADVERTISER, circ. 59,750 F 221
W THE NEWQUAY VOICE, circ. 5,000 226
D WESTERN MORNING NEWS, circ. 41,154 272

Par
W CORNISH GUARDIAN SERIES, circ. 32,982 165
W THE PACKET SERIES, circ. 90,472 234
W WESTERN MORNING NEWS, circ. 41,154 272

Penryn
W THE PACKET SERIES, circ. 90,472 234
W THE WEST BRITON SERIES, circ. 39,343 270
D WESTERN MORNING NEWS, circ. 41,154 272

Penzance
W THE CORNISHMAN, circ. 18,189 166
W THE PACKET SERIES, circ. 90,472 234
D WESTERN MORNING NEWS, circ. 41,154 272

Perranporth
W THE PACKET SERIES, circ. 90,472 234
W WESTERN MORNING NEWS, circ. 41,154 272

Polperro
W CORNISH TIMES & GAZETTE SERIES, circ. 51,000 ... 165

Redruth
W THE PACKET SERIES, circ. 90,472 234
W THE WEST BRITON SERIES, circ. 39,343 270
D WESTERN MORNING NEWS, circ. 41,154 272

Saltash
W CORNISH TIMES & GAZETTE SERIES, circ. 51,000 ... 165
W THE EXTRA (PLYMOUTH), circ. 93,894 F 184
D THE HERALD (PLYMOUTH), circ. 40,384 198
D WESTERN MORNING NEWS, circ. 41,154 272

St. Agnes
W MID CORNWALL ADVERTISER, circ. 59,750 F 221
W THE PACKET SERIES, circ. 90,472 234

St. Austell
W CORNISH GUARDIAN SERIES, circ. 32,982 165
W MID CORNWALL ADVERTISER, circ. 59,750 F 221
W THE PACKET SERIES, circ. 90,472 234
W ST. AUSTELL VOICE 253
D WESTERN MORNING NEWS, circ. 41,154 272

St. Blazey
W CORNISH GUARDIAN SERIES, circ. 32,982 165
W THE PACKET SERIES, circ. 90,472 234
W ST. AUSTELL VOICE 253
W WESTERN MORNING NEWS, circ. 41,154 272

St. Columb Major
W MID CORNWALL ADVERTISER, circ. 59,750 F 221

St. Columb Road
W CORNISH GUARDIAN SERIES, circ. 32,982 165
D THE HERALD (PLYMOUTH), circ. 40,384 198
W THE PACKET SERIES, circ. 90,472 234
D WESTERN MORNING NEWS, circ. 41,154 272

St. Ives
W THE CORNISHMAN, circ. 18,189 166
W THE PACKET SERIES, circ. 90,472 234
W ST. IVES TIMES & ECHO SERIES, circ. 3,930 254
D WESTERN MORNING NEWS, circ. 41,154 272

St. Just
W THE CORNISHMAN, circ. 18,189 166
D WESTERN MORNING NEWS, circ. 41,154 272

Stratton
W CORNISH & DEVON POST SERIES, circ. 13,257 165
W NORTH CORNWALL ADVERTISER, circ. 37,000 F ... 229

Torpoint
W CORNISH TIMES & GAZETTE SERIES, circ. 51,000 ... 165
W THE EXTRA (PLYMOUTH), circ. 93,894 F 184
D THE HERALD (PLYMOUTH), circ. 40,384 198

Truro
W CORNISH GUARDIAN SERIES, circ. 32,982 165
W MID CORNWALL ADVERTISER, circ. 59,750 F 221
W THE PACKET SERIES, circ. 90,472 234
W THE WEST BRITON SERIES, circ. 39,343 270
D WESTERN MORNING NEWS, circ. 41,154 272

Wadebridge
W CORNISH & DEVON POST SERIES, circ. 13,257 165
W CORNISH GUARDIAN SERIES, circ. 32,982 165
W NORTH CORNWALL ADVERTISER, circ. 37,000 F ... 229
D WESTERN MORNING NEWS, circ. 41,154 272

Croydon Borough
W KENT ON SATURDAY, circ. 40,000 F 206

Addington
W CROYDON ADVERTISER & POST SERIES, circ. 203,807 168

Title (Day/am/pm)	Circ.	Page No.	Title (Day/am/pm)	Circ.	Page No.	Title (Day/am/pm)	Circ.	Page No.

Coulsdon
W CROYDON ADVERTISER & POST SERIES, circ. 203,807 168

Croydon
W CROYDON ADVERTISER & POST SERIES, circ. 203,807 168
W CROYDON GUARDIAN, circ. 99,753 F 168
W GUARDIAN SERIES (WILTSHIRE, HAMPSHIRE AND SURREY), circ. 175,000 F 193
W SOUTH BUCKS AND BERKSHIRE NEWS SERIES, circ. 50,000 F 249

Purley
W CROYDON ADVERTISER & POST SERIES, circ. 203,807 168

Thornton Heath
W SURREY COMET, circ. 10,182 260

Cumbria
S THE SUNDAY POST (DUNDEE), circ. 354,870 258

Alston
W CUMBERLAND & WESTMORLAND HERALD SERIES, circ. 18,703 169
D EVENING CHRONICLE (NEWCASTLE), circ. 78,804 ... 180
W HEXHAM COURANT, circ. 18,379 199

Ambleside
W WESTMORLAND GAZETTE NEWSPAPER SERIES, circ. 56,020 273

Appleby
W CUMBERLAND & WESTMORLAND HERALD SERIES, circ. 18,703 169
W WESTMORLAND GAZETTE NEWSPAPER SERIES, circ. 56,020 273

Arnside
W LAKELAND ECHO, circ. 13,866 F 208
W WESTMORLAND GAZETTE NEWSPAPER SERIES, circ. 56,020 273

Aspatria
W THE CUMBERLAND NEWS & GAZETTE SERIES, circ. 98,340 169
D NEWS & STAR (CARLISLE) 227
W TIMES AND STAR SERIES, circ. 17,215 263

Barrow-in-Furness
W THE ADVERTISER BARROW AND WEST CUMBERLAND, circ. 39,535 F 138
W LAKELAND ECHO, circ. 13,866 F 208
D NORTH WEST EVENING MAIL (BARROW), circ. 18,520 230

Bowness on Windermere
W LAKELAND ECHO, circ. 13,866 F 208
W WESTMORLAND GAZETTE NEWSPAPER SERIES, circ. 56,020 273

Brampton
W THE CUMBERLAND NEWS & GAZETTE SERIES, circ. 98,340 169
D NEWS & STAR (CARLISLE) 227

Broughton-in-Furness
D NORTH WEST EVENING MAIL (BARROW), circ. 18,520 230

Carlisle
W THE CUMBERLAND NEWS & GAZETTE SERIES, circ. 98,340 169
D NEWS & STAR (CARLISLE) 227
S SUNDAY SUN, circ. 68,033 259

Cleator Moor
W WHITEHAVEN NEWS, circ. 17,330 274

Cockermouth
W THE CUMBERLAND NEWS & GAZETTE SERIES, circ. 98,340 169
W THE KESWICK REMINDER, circ. 4,500 207
D NEWS & STAR (CARLISLE) 227
W TIMES AND STAR SERIES, circ. 17,215 263

Coniston
D NORTH WEST EVENING MAIL (BARROW), circ. 18,520 230
W WESTMORLAND GAZETTE NEWSPAPER SERIES, circ. 56,020 273

Dalston
D NEWS & STAR (CARLISLE) 227

Dalton-in-Furness
D NORTH WEST EVENING MAIL (BARROW), circ. 18,520 230

Egremont
D NEWS & STAR (CARLISLE) 227
W WHITEHAVEN NEWS, circ. 17,330 274

Frizington
D NEWS & STAR (CARLISLE) 227
S SUNDAY SUN, circ. 68,033 259
W WHITEHAVEN NEWS, circ. 17,330 274

Grange-over-Sands
W LAKELAND ECHO, circ. 13,866 F 208
D NORTH WEST EVENING MAIL (BARROW), circ. 18,520 230
W WESTMORLAND GAZETTE NEWSPAPER SERIES, circ. 56,020 273

Grasmere
W WESTMORLAND GAZETTE NEWSPAPER SERIES, circ. 56,020 273

Harrington
D NEWS & STAR (CARLISLE) 227

Kendal
W LAKELAND ECHO, circ. 13,866 F 208
D LANCASHIRE EVENING POST, circ. 31,225 208
W WESTMORLAND GAZETTE NEWSPAPER SERIES, circ. 56,020 273

Keswick
W CUMBERLAND & WESTMORLAND HERALD SERIES, circ. 18,703 169
W THE CUMBERLAND NEWS & GAZETTE SERIES, circ. 98,340 169
W THE KESWICK REMINDER, circ. 4,500 207
D NEWS & STAR (CARLISLE) 227
W TIMES AND STAR SERIES, circ. 17,215 263

Kirkby Lonsdale
W LAKELAND ECHO, circ. 13,866 F 208
W WESTMORLAND GAZETTE NEWSPAPER SERIES, circ. 56,020 273

Kirkby Stephen
W CUMBERLAND & WESTMORLAND HERALD SERIES, circ. 18,703 169
W WESTMORLAND GAZETTE NEWSPAPER SERIES, circ. 56,020 273

Levens
W LAKELAND ECHO, circ. 13,866 F 208

Longtown
W THE CUMBERLAND NEWS & GAZETTE SERIES, circ. 98,340 169
W ESKDALE AND LIDDESDALE ADVERTISER, circ. 1,800 180
D NEWS & STAR (CARLISLE) 227

Maryport
W THE CUMBERLAND NEWS & GAZETTE SERIES, circ. 98,340 169
D NEWS & STAR (CARLISLE) 227
W TIMES AND STAR SERIES, circ. 17,215 263

Millom
W THE ADVERTISER BARROW AND WEST CUMBERLAND, circ. 39,535 F 138
D NORTH WEST EVENING MAIL (BARROW), circ. 18,520 230
W WHITEHAVEN NEWS, circ. 17,330 274

Milnthorpe
W LAKELAND ECHO, circ. 13,866 F 208
W WESTMORLAND GAZETTE NEWSPAPER SERIES, circ. 56,020 273

Penrith
W CUMBERLAND & WESTMORLAND HERALD SERIES, circ. 18,703 169
D NEWS & STAR (CARLISLE) 227

Seascale
W WHITEHAVEN NEWS, circ. 17,330 274

Seaton
D NEWS & STAR (CARLISLE) 227

Sedbergh
W WESTMORLAND GAZETTE NEWSPAPER SERIES, circ. 56,020 273

Silloth
W THE CUMBERLAND NEWS & GAZETTE SERIES, circ. 98,340 169

D NEWS & STAR (CARLISLE) 227

St. Bees
W WHITEHAVEN NEWS, circ. 17,330 274

Ulverston
W THE ADVERTISER BARROW AND WEST CUMBERLAND, circ. 39,535 F 138
W LAKELAND ECHO, circ. 13,866 F 208
D NORTH WEST EVENING MAIL (BARROW), circ. 18,520 230
W WESTMORLAND GAZETTE NEWSPAPER SERIES, circ. 56,020 273

Whitehaven
W THE CUMBERLAND NEWS & GAZETTE SERIES, circ. 98,340 169
D NEWS & STAR (CARLISLE) 227
W WHITEHAVEN NEWS, circ. 17,330 274

Wigton
W THE CUMBERLAND NEWS & GAZETTE SERIES, circ. 98,340 169
W THE KESWICK REMINDER, circ. 4,500 207
D NEWS & STAR (CARLISLE) 227

Windermere
W LAKELAND ECHO, circ. 13,866 F 208
D NORTH WEST EVENING MAIL (BARROW), circ. 18,520 230
W WESTMORLAND GAZETTE NEWSPAPER SERIES, circ. 56,020 273

Workington
W THE CUMBERLAND NEWS & GAZETTE SERIES, circ. 98,340 169
D NEWS & STAR (CARLISLE) 227
W TIMES AND STAR SERIES, circ. 17,215 263

Derbyshire

Alfreton
W CHAD SERIES MANSFIELD, circ. 61,097 158
D DERBYSHIRE TIMES SERIES, circ. 40,241 172
W JOURNAL & ADVERTISER SERIES, circ. 30,000 F ... 205
W RIPLEY & HEANOR NEWS, circ. 10,394 240
S SUNDAY MERCURY (BIRMINGHAM), circ. 59,339 ... 258
W WEST NOTTS & DERBYSHIRE RECORDER SERIES, circ. 260,441 F 271

Ambergate
W BELPER NEWS, circ. 3,632 147
D DERBY TELEGRAPH, circ. 42,726 172
D DERBYSHIRE TIMES SERIES, circ. 40,241 172
W RIPLEY & HEANOR NEWS, circ. 10,394 240

Ashbourne
W ASHBOURNE NEWS TELEGRAPH, circ. 7,000 143
D BURTON MAIL, circ. 14,658 155
W CHEADLE TIMES & ECHO SERIES, circ. 11,000 159
D DERBY TELEGRAPH, circ. 42,726 172
W MOORLANDS TRADER, circ. 15,689 F 224

Bakewell
W BUXTON ADVERTISER AND TIMES SERIES, circ. 39,607 156
D DERBYSHIRE TIMES SERIES, circ. 40,241 172
W MATLOCK MERCURY, circ. 8,192 218
S SUNDAY MERCURY (BIRMINGHAM), circ. 59,339 ... 258

Belper
W BELPER NEWS, circ. 3,632 147
W DERBY EXPRESS AND MESSENGER SERIES, circ. 111,621 F 172
D DERBY TELEGRAPH, circ. 42,726 172
W JOURNAL & ADVERTISER SERIES, circ. 30,000 F ... 205
W RIPLEY & HEANOR NEWS, circ. 10,394 240

Blackwell
D DERBYSHIRE TIMES SERIES, circ. 40,241 172

Bolsover
W CHAD SERIES MANSFIELD, circ. 61,097 158
W CHESTERFIELD & DRONFIELD ADVERTISER SERIES, circ. 74,963 F 160
W GUARDIAN SERIES (WORKSOP), circ. 95,428 193

Borrowash
D DERBY TELEGRAPH, circ. 42,726 172
W WEST NOTTS & DERBYSHIRE RECORDER SERIES, circ. 260,441 F 271

Breaston
D DERBY TELEGRAPH, circ. 42,726 172
W WEST NOTTS & DERBYSHIRE RECORDER SERIES, circ. 260,441 F 271

W **Local/Weekly Newspapers**   D **Regional Daily Newspapers**   S **Regional Sunday Newspapers**   F **Free Newspapers**

Non-Nationals - England

Title (Day/am/pm)	Circ.	Page No.

Buxton
W BUXTON ADVERTISER AND TIMES SERIES, circ. 39,607 156
D MANCHESTER EVENING NEWS, circ. 82,445 217
W MOORLANDS TRADER, circ. 15,689 F 224

Chesterfield
W CHESTERFIELD & DRONFIELD ADVERTISER SERIES, circ. 74,963 F 160
W CHESTERFIELD EXPRESS, circ. 34,842 F 160
W DERBYSHIRE TIMES SERIES, circ. 40,241 172
W GUARDIAN SERIES (WORKSOP), circ. 95,428 193
W THE MERCURY NEWSPAPER, circ. 40,000 F 219
D THE STAR SHEFFIELD, circ. 56,363 255

Clay Cross
W CHESTERFIELD & DRONFIELD ADVERTISER SERIES, circ. 74,963 F 160
W CHESTERFIELD EXPRESS, circ. 34,842 F 160

Creswell
W DERBYSHIRE TIMES SERIES, circ. 40,241 172
D THE STAR SHEFFIELD, circ. 56,363 255

Crich
W BELPER NEWS, circ. 3,632 147
D DERBY TELEGRAPH, circ. 42,726 172
W DERBYSHIRE TIMES SERIES, circ. 40,241 172
W RIPLEY & HEANOR NEWS, circ. 10,394 240

Derby
W BELPER NEWS, circ. 3,632 147
W DERBY EXPRESS AND MESSENGER SERIES, circ. 111,621 F 172
D DERBY TELEGRAPH, circ. 42,726 172
W MIDLANDS FOCUS, circ. 5,000 F 222

Dronfield
W CHESTERFIELD & DRONFIELD ADVERTISER SERIES, circ. 74,963 F 160
W DERBYSHIRE TIMES SERIES, circ. 40,241 172
W THE MERCURY NEWSPAPER, circ. 40,000 F 219
W SHEFFIELD WEEKLY GAZETTE, circ. 103,897 F 246

Duffield
W BELPER NEWS, circ. 3,632 147
W DERBY EXPRESS AND MESSENGER SERIES, circ. 111,621 F 172

Eckington
W CHESTERFIELD & DRONFIELD ADVERTISER SERIES, circ. 74,963 F 160
W SHEFFIELD WEEKLY GAZETTE, circ. 103,897 F 246

Egginton
D BURTON MAIL, circ. 14,658 155

Etwall
D DERBY TELEGRAPH, circ. 42,726 172
W MIDLANDS FOCUS, circ. 5,000 F 222

Glossop
W ADVERTISER SERIES (ASHTON), circ. 104,047 F 139
W ASHTON-UNDER-LYNE REPORTER SERIES, circ. 25,000 143
W BUXTON ADVERTISER AND TIMES SERIES, circ. 39,607 156
D MANCHESTER EVENING NEWS, circ. 82,445 217

Hatton
D BIRMINGHAM POST (CITY/LONDON OFFICE) 149
D BURTON MAIL, circ. 14,658 155
D DERBY TELEGRAPH, circ. 42,726 172
W MIDLANDS FOCUS, circ. 5,000 F 222
S SUNDAY MERCURY (BIRMINGHAM), circ. 59,339 258

Heage
W BELPER NEWS, circ. 3,632 147
D DERBY TELEGRAPH, circ. 42,726 172
W DERBYSHIRE TIMES SERIES, circ. 40,241 172
W RIPLEY & HEANOR NEWS, circ. 10,394 240

Heanor
W DERBY EXPRESS AND MESSENGER SERIES, circ. 111,621 F 172
D DERBY TELEGRAPH, circ. 42,726 172
W RIPLEY & HEANOR NEWS, circ. 10,394 240

Ilkeston
W DERBY EXPRESS AND MESSENGER SERIES, circ. 111,621 F 172
D DERBY TELEGRAPH, circ. 42,726 172
W ILKESTON ADVERTISER, circ. 8,488 202
W JOURNAL & ADVERTISER SERIES, circ. 30,000 F 205
D NOTTINGHAM EVENING POST, circ. 57,699 232
W RIPLEY & HEANOR NEWS, circ. 10,394 240
W WEST NOTTS & DERBYSHIRE RECORDER SERIES, circ. 260,441 F 271

Long Eaton
W JOURNAL & ADVERTISER SERIES, circ. 30,000 F 205
W LOUGHBOROUGH ECHO SERIES, circ. 72,916 215
W NOTTINGHAM AND LONG EATON TOPPER, circ. 209,222 F 232
D NOTTINGHAM EVENING POST, circ. 57,699 232
W WEST NOTTS & DERBYSHIRE RECORDER SERIES, circ. 260,441 F 271

Matlock
D DERBY TELEGRAPH, circ. 42,726 172
W DERBYSHIRE TIMES SERIES, circ. 40,241 172
W MATLOCK MERCURY, circ. 8,192 218

Melbourne
W BURTON MAIL, circ. 14,658 155
W DERBY EXPRESS AND MESSENGER SERIES, circ. 111,621 F 172

Mosborough
W SHEFFIELD TELEGRAPH, circ. 22,162 246
W SHEFFIELD WEEKLY GAZETTE, circ. 103,897 F 246
D THE STAR SHEFFIELD, circ. 56,363 255

New Mills
W ASHTON-UNDER-LYNE REPORTER SERIES, circ. 25,000 143
W STOCKPORT EXPRESS AND TIMES SERIES, circ. 112,974 256

Newton Solney
D BURTON MAIL, circ. 14,658 155

North Wingfield
W DERBYSHIRE TIMES SERIES, circ. 40,241 172
D THE STAR SHEFFIELD, circ. 56,363 255

Pilsley
D DERBY TELEGRAPH, circ. 42,726 172
W DERBYSHIRE TIMES SERIES, circ. 40,241 172

Pinxton
W WEST NOTTS & DERBYSHIRE RECORDER SERIES, circ. 260,441 F 271

Ripley
W DERBY EXPRESS AND MESSENGER SERIES, circ. 111,621 F 172
W DERBYSHIRE TIMES SERIES, circ. 40,241 172
W RIPLEY & HEANOR NEWS, circ. 10,394 240

Sandiacre
W ILKESTON ADVERTISER, circ. 8,488 202
W WEST NOTTS & DERBYSHIRE RECORDER SERIES, circ. 260,441 F 271

Shirland
D DERBY TELEGRAPH, circ. 42,726 172
W DERBYSHIRE TIMES SERIES, circ. 40,241 172

South Normanton
W CHAD SERIES MANSFIELD, circ. 61,097 158
W WEST NOTTS & DERBYSHIRE RECORDER SERIES, circ. 260,441 F 271

Swadlincote
W THE BURTON & SOUTH DERBYSHIRE ADVERTISER, circ. 57,692 F 155
D BURTON MAIL, circ. 14,658 155
S SUNDAY MERCURY (BIRMINGHAM), circ. 59,339 258
W TRIDENT MIDLAND NEWSPAPERS SERIES, circ. 46,151 265

Tibshelf
D DERBY TELEGRAPH, circ. 42,726 172
W DERBYSHIRE TIMES SERIES, circ. 40,241 172

West Hallam
D DERBY TELEGRAPH, circ. 42,726 172
W ILKESTON ADVERTISER, circ. 8,488 202
W WEST NOTTS & DERBYSHIRE RECORDER SERIES, circ. 260,441 F 271

Whaley Bridge
D MANCHESTER EVENING NEWS, circ. 82,445 217
W STOCKPORT EXPRESS AND TIMES SERIES, circ. 112,974 256

Wingerworth
W DERBYSHIRE TIMES SERIES, circ. 40,241 172
D THE STAR SHEFFIELD, circ. 56,363 255

Wirksworth
W MATLOCK MERCURY, circ. 8,192 218

Devon

S SUNDAY INDEPENDENT (PLYMOUTH), circ. 32,000 258

Ashburton
D HERALD EXPRESS, circ. 23,987 198
D THE HERALD (PLYMOUTH), circ. 40,384 198
W MID-DEVON ADVERTISER SERIES, circ. 60,000 222

Axminster
W BRIDPORT & LYME REGIS NEWS SERIES, circ. 10,576 152
D EXPRESS & ECHO (EXETER), circ. 20,767 183
W MIDWEEK HERALD, circ. 34,000 F 223
W PULMANS WEEKLY NEWS AND ADVERTISER SERIES, circ. 22,000 238

Barnstaple
W NORTH DEVON GAZETTE, circ. 51,438 F 229
W NORTH DEVON JOURNAL SERIES, circ. 30,759 229
D WESTERN MORNING NEWS, circ. 41,154 272

Bere Alston
D THE HERALD (PLYMOUTH), circ. 40,384 198

Bideford
W NORTH DEVON GAZETTE, circ. 51,438 F 229
W NORTH DEVON JOURNAL SERIES, circ. 30,759 229
D WESTERN MORNING NEWS, circ. 41,154 272

Bovey Tracey
D HERALD EXPRESS, circ. 23,987 198
W MID-DEVON ADVERTISER SERIES, circ. 60,000 222

Braunton
W NORTH DEVON JOURNAL SERIES, circ. 30,759 229

Bridestowe
W CORNISH & DEVON POST SERIES, circ. 13,257 165

Brixham
D HERALD EXPRESS, circ. 23,987 198
W SOUTH HAMS NEWSPAPERS GROUP, circ. 41,491 250
W TORBAY WEEKENDER SERIES, circ. 53,152 F 264

Buckfastleigh
D HERALD EXPRESS, circ. 23,987 198
D THE HERALD (PLYMOUTH), circ. 40,384 198
W MID-DEVON ADVERTISER SERIES, circ. 60,000 222

Budleigh Salterton
D EXPRESS & ECHO (EXETER), circ. 20,767 183
W THE JOURNAL SERIES (EXMOUTH), circ. 9,140 205

Chagford
W CORNISH & DEVON POST SERIES, circ. 13,257 165

Chudleigh
D HERALD EXPRESS, circ. 23,987 198
W MID-DEVON ADVERTISER SERIES, circ. 60,000 222

Chulmleigh
D CREDITON COUNTRY COURIER, circ. 4,500 168
D EXPRESS & ECHO (EXETER), circ. 20,767 183

Colyton
D EXPRESS & ECHO (EXETER), circ. 20,767 183
W MIDWEEK HERALD, circ. 34,000 F 223
W PULMANS WEEKLY NEWS AND ADVERTISER SERIES, circ. 22,000 238

Crediton
W CREDITON COUNTRY COURIER, circ. 4,500 168
D EXPRESS & ECHO (EXETER), circ. 20,767 183
W THE GAZETTE SERIES (MID DEVON), circ. 12,086 190
W STAR AND EXPRESS SERIES, circ. 95,047 F 255

Cullompton
D EXPRESS & ECHO (EXETER), circ. 20,767 183
W THE GAZETTE SERIES (MID DEVON), circ. 12,086 190
W STAR AND EXPRESS SERIES, circ. 95,047 F 255

Dartmouth
D HERALD EXPRESS, circ. 23,987 198
W SOUTH HAMS NEWSPAPERS GROUP, circ. 41,491 250
D WESTERN MORNING NEWS, circ. 41,154 272

Dawlish
W DAWLISH GAZETTE, circ. 13,251 171
D EXPRESS & ECHO (EXETER), circ. 20,767 183
D HERALD EXPRESS, circ. 23,987 198
W MID-DEVON ADVERTISER SERIES, circ. 60,000 222
D WESTERN MORNING NEWS, circ. 41,154 272

Exeter
W CREDITON COUNTRY COURIER, circ. 4,500 168
W THE EXETER TIMES, circ. 43,972 F 182
D EXPRESS & ECHO (EXETER), circ. 20,767 183
W WESTERN DAILY PRESS BRISTOL, circ. 41,639 272
D WESTERN MORNING NEWS, circ. 41,154 272

Exmouth
D EXPRESS & ECHO (EXETER), circ. 20,767 183

W Local/Weekly Newspapers   D Regional Daily Newspapers   S Regional Sunday Newspapers   F Free Newspapers

Title (Day/am/pm)	Circ.	Page No.

W THE JOURNAL SERIES (EXMOUTH), circ. 9,140 205
D WESTERN DAILY PRESS BRISTOL, circ. 41,639 272
W WESTERN MORNING NEWS, circ. 41,154 272

Fremington
W NORTH DEVON GAZETTE, circ. 51,438 F 229
D WESTERN MORNING NEWS, circ. 41,154 272

Great Torrington
W NORTH DEVON GAZETTE, circ. 51,438 F 229
W NORTH DEVON JOURNAL SERIES, circ. 30,759 229
D WESTERN MORNING NEWS, circ. 41,154 272

Holsworthy
W CORNISH & DEVON POST SERIES, circ. 13,257 165
W NORTH DEVON GAZETTE, circ. 51,438 F 229
W NORTH DEVON JOURNAL SERIES, circ. 30,759 229

Honiton
D EXPRESS & ECHO (EXETER), circ. 20,767 183
W MIDWEEK HERALD, circ. 34,000 F 223
W PULMANS WEEKLY NEWS AND ADVERTISER SERIES,
     circ. 22,000 238
W WESTERN MORNING NEWS, circ. 41,154 272

Horrabridge
D EXPRESS & ECHO (EXETER), circ. 20,767 183
D HERALD EXPRESS, circ. 23,987 198
D WESTERN MORNING NEWS, circ. 41,154 272

Ilfracombe
W NORTH DEVON GAZETTE, circ. 51,438 F 229
W NORTH DEVON JOURNAL SERIES, circ. 30,759 229

Ivybridge
W THE EXTRA (PLYMOUTH), circ. 93,894 F 184
D THE HERALD (PLYMOUTH), circ. 40,384 198
W SOUTH HAMS NEWSPAPERS GROUP, circ. 41,491 . 250
D WESTERN MORNING NEWS, circ. 41,154 272

Kingsbridge
D HERALD EXPRESS, circ. 23,987 198
D THE HERALD (PLYMOUTH), circ. 40,384 198
W SOUTH HAMS NEWSPAPERS GROUP, circ. 41,491 . 250
D WESTERN MORNING NEWS, circ. 41,154 272

Kingskerswell
D HERALD EXPRESS, circ. 23,987 198
W TORBAY WEEKENDER SERIES, circ. 53,152 F ... 264

Kingsteignton
D HERALD EXPRESS, circ. 23,987 198
W MID-DEVON ADVERTISER SERIES, circ. 60,000 222
W TORBAY WEEKENDER SERIES, circ. 53,152 F ... 264

Lifton
D THE HERALD (PLYMOUTH), circ. 40,384 198

Lydford
D THE HERALD (PLYMOUTH), circ. 40,384 198

Lynton
W NORTH DEVON JOURNAL SERIES, circ. 30,759 229

Modbury
D THE HERALD (PLYMOUTH), circ. 40,384 198

Moretonhampstead
D EXPRESS & ECHO (EXETER), circ. 20,767 183
D HERALD EXPRESS, circ. 23,987 198
W MID-DEVON ADVERTISER SERIES, circ. 60,000 222

Newton Abbot
D EXPRESS & ECHO (EXETER), circ. 20,767 183
D HERALD EXPRESS, circ. 23,987 198
D THE HERALD (PLYMOUTH), circ. 40,384 198
W MID-DEVON ADVERTISER SERIES, circ. 60,000 222
W TORBAY WEEKENDER SERIES, circ. 53,152 F ... 264
D WESTERN DAILY PRESS BRISTOL, circ. 41,639 272
D WESTERN MORNING NEWS, circ. 41,154 272

North Tawton
D EXPRESS & ECHO (EXETER), circ. 20,767 183

Northam
W NORTH DEVON GAZETTE, circ. 51,438 F 229
W WESTERN MORNING NEWS, circ. 41,154 272

Okehampton
W CORNISH & DEVON POST SERIES, circ. 13,257 165
W CREDITON COUNTRY COURIER, circ. 4,500 168
D EXPRESS & ECHO (EXETER), circ. 20,767 183
W TAVISTOCK TIMES GAZETTE SERIES, circ. 13,000 .. 262
D WESTERN MORNING NEWS, circ. 41,154 272

Ottery St. Mary
D EXPRESS & ECHO (EXETER), circ. 20,767 183
W PULMANS WEEKLY NEWS AND ADVERTISER SERIES,
     circ. 22,000 238
W SIDMOUTH HERALD SERIES, circ. 7,134 248

Paignton
D HERALD EXPRESS, circ. 23,987 198
W TORBAY WEEKENDER SERIES, circ. 53,152 F 264
W WESTERN MORNING NEWS, circ. 41,154 272

Plymouth
W THE EXTRA (PLYMOUTH), circ. 93,894 F 184
D THE HERALD (PLYMOUTH), circ. 40,384 198
W SOUTH HAMS NEWSPAPERS GROUP, circ. 41,491 . 250
D WESTERN MORNING NEWS, circ. 41,154 272

Plympton
W THE EXTRA (PLYMOUTH), circ. 93,894 F 184
D THE HERALD (PLYMOUTH), circ. 40,384 198
W SOUTH HAMS NEWSPAPERS GROUP, circ. 41,491 . 250
D WESTERN MORNING NEWS, circ. 41,154 272

Plymstock
W THE EXTRA (PLYMOUTH), circ. 93,894 F 184

Princetown
D THE HERALD (PLYMOUTH), circ. 40,384 198

Seaton
D EXPRESS & ECHO (EXETER), circ. 20,767 183
W MIDWEEK HERALD, circ. 34,000 F 223
W PULMANS WEEKLY NEWS AND ADVERTISER SERIES,
     circ. 22,000 238

Sidmouth
D EXPRESS & ECHO (EXETER), circ. 20,767 183
W SIDMOUTH HERALD SERIES, circ. 7,134 248

South Brent
D HERALD EXPRESS, circ. 23,987 198
D THE HERALD (PLYMOUTH), circ. 40,384 198

South Hams
W THE EXTRA (PLYMOUTH), circ. 93,894 F 184
W SOUTH HAMS NEWSPAPERS GROUP, circ. 41,491 . 250

South Molton
D EXPRESS & ECHO (EXETER), circ. 20,767 183
W THE GAZETTE SERIES (MID DEVON), circ. 12,086 190
W NORTH DEVON GAZETTE, circ. 51,438 F 229
W NORTH DEVON JOURNAL SERIES, circ. 30,759 229

South Zeal
D THE HERALD (PLYMOUTH), circ. 40,384 198

Tavistock
W CORNISH & DEVON POST SERIES, circ. 13,257 165
W THE EXTRA (PLYMOUTH), circ. 93,894 F 184
D THE HERALD (PLYMOUTH), circ. 40,384 198
W TAVISTOCK TIMES GAZETTE SERIES, circ. 13,000 ... 262
D WESTERN MORNING NEWS, circ. 41,154 272

Teignmouth
D EXPRESS & ECHO (EXETER), circ. 20,767 183
D HERALD EXPRESS, circ. 23,987 198
W MID-DEVON ADVERTISER SERIES, circ. 60,000 222
W TEIGNMOUTH NEWS, circ. 10,500 F 262

Thurlestone
D THE HERALD (PLYMOUTH), circ. 40,384 198

Tiverton
W CREDITON COUNTRY COURIER, circ. 4,500 168
D EXPRESS & ECHO (EXETER), circ. 20,767 183
W THE GAZETTE SERIES (MID DEVON), circ. 12,086 190
W STAR AND EXPRESS SERIES, circ. 95,047 F 255
D WESTERN DAILY PRESS BRISTOL, circ. 41,639 272
D WESTERN MORNING NEWS, circ. 41,154 272

Topsham
W THE JOURNAL SERIES (EXMOUTH), circ. 9,140 205

Torbay
D HERALD EXPRESS, circ. 23,987 198
W TORBAY WEEKENDER SERIES, circ. 53,152 F 264
D WESTERN MORNING NEWS, circ. 41,154 272

Torquay
D HERALD EXPRESS, circ. 23,987 198
W TORBAY WEEKENDER SERIES, circ. 53,152 F 264
W WESTERN MORNING NEWS, circ. 41,154 272

Torrington
W NORTH DEVON GAZETTE, circ. 51,438 F 229

Totnes
D HERALD EXPRESS, circ. 23,987 198
D THE HERALD (PLYMOUTH), circ. 40,384 198
W SOUTH HAMS NEWSPAPERS GROUP, circ. 41,491 . 250
D WESTERN MORNING NEWS, circ. 41,154 272

Woodbury
W THE JOURNAL SERIES (EXMOUTH), circ. 9,140 205

Yealmpton
D THE HERALD (PLYMOUTH), circ. 40,384 198

Yelverton
D THE HERALD (PLYMOUTH), circ. 40,384 198

Dorset

W LYME REGIS NEWS 216

Bere Regis
D DORSET ECHO, circ. 18,803 173

Blandford Forum
W ADVERTISER SERIES (POOLE & SWANAGE),
     circ. 163,340 F 140
D DAILY ECHO (BOURNEMOUTH), circ. 32,441 170
D DORSET ECHO, circ. 18,803 173
D WESTERN DAILY PRESS BRISTOL, circ. 41,639 272
W WESTERN GAZETTE AND YEOVIL TIMES SERIES,
     circ. 79,876 272

Bournemouth
W ADVERTISER SERIES (POOLE & SWANAGE),
     circ. 163,340 F 140
D DAILY ECHO (BOURNEMOUTH), circ. 32,441 170

Bovington Camp
D DORSET ECHO, circ. 18,803 173
D WESTERN DAILY PRESS BRISTOL, circ. 41,639 272
W WESTERN GAZETTE AND YEOVIL TIMES SERIES,
     circ. 79,876 272

Bridport
W BRIDPORT & LYME REGIS NEWS SERIES,
     circ. 10,576 152
D DORSET ECHO, circ. 18,803 173
D WESTERN DAILY PRESS BRISTOL, circ. 41,639 272
W WESTERN GAZETTE AND YEOVIL TIMES SERIES,
     circ. 79,876 272

Christchurch
W ADVERTISER & TIMES SERIES, circ. 21,421 138
W ADVERTISER SERIES (POOLE & SWANAGE),
     circ. 163,340 F 140
D DAILY ECHO (BOURNEMOUTH), circ. 32,441 170

Dorchester
D DORSET ADVERTISER, circ. 35,843 F 173
D DORSET ECHO, circ. 18,803 173
D WESTERN DAILY PRESS BRISTOL, circ. 41,639 272
W WESTERN GAZETTE AND YEOVIL TIMES SERIES,
     circ. 79,876 272

Easton
D DORSET ECHO, circ. 18,803 173
D WESTERN DAILY PRESS BRISTOL, circ. 41,639 . 272

Ferndown
D DAILY ECHO (BOURNEMOUTH), circ. 32,441 170

Fortuneswell
D DORSET ECHO, circ. 18,803 173

Gillingham
W WESTERN GAZETTE AND YEOVIL TIMES SERIES,
     circ. 79,876 272

Highcliffe
W ADVERTISER & TIMES SERIES, circ. 21,421 138
W NEW FOREST POST INCORPORATING FOREST &
     WATERSIDE OBSERVER, circ. 46,546 F 225

Lyme Regis
W BRIDPORT & LYME REGIS NEWS SERIES,
     circ. 10,576 152
D DORSET ECHO, circ. 18,803 173
W MIDWEEK HERALD, circ. 34,000 F 223
W PULMANS WEEKLY NEWS AND ADVERTISER SERIES,
     circ. 22,000 238
D WESTERN DAILY PRESS BRISTOL, circ. 41,639 272
W WESTERN GAZETTE AND YEOVIL TIMES SERIES,
     circ. 79,876 272

Overcombe
D DORSET ECHO, circ. 18,803 173
D WESTERN DAILY PRESS BRISTOL, circ. 41,639 272

Poole
W ADVERTISER SERIES (POOLE & SWANAGE),
     circ. 163,340 F 140
D DAILY ECHO (BOURNEMOUTH), circ. 32,441 170

Portland
W DORSET ADVERTISER, circ. 35,843 F 173

Shaftesbury
D DAILY ECHO (BOURNEMOUTH), circ. 32,441 170
D DORSET ECHO, circ. 18,803 173

W **Local/Weekly Newspapers**   D **Regional Daily Newspapers**   S **Regional Sunday Newspapers**   F **Free Newspapers**

Non-Nationals - England

Title (Day/am/pm)	Circ.	Page No.

W WESTERN GAZETTE AND YEOVIL TIMES SERIES, circ. 79,876 272

Sherborne
D DORSET ECHO, circ. 18,803 173
S STAR AND EXPRESS SERIES, circ. 95,047 F 255
D WESTERN DAILY PRESS BRISTOL, circ. 41,639 272
W WESTERN GAZETTE AND YEOVIL TIMES SERIES, circ. 79,876 272

Sturminster Newton
D DAILY ECHO (BOURNEMOUTH), circ. 32,441 170
D DORSET ECHO, circ. 18,803 173

Swanage
W ADVERTISER SERIES (POOLE & SWANAGE), circ. 163,340 F 140
D DAILY ECHO (BOURNEMOUTH), circ. 32,441 170
D DORSET ECHO, circ. 18,803 173

Wareham
W ADVERTISER SERIES (POOLE & SWANAGE), circ. 163,340 F 140
D DAILY ECHO (BOURNEMOUTH), circ. 32,441 170
D DORSET ECHO, circ. 18,803 173

Weston
D DORSET ECHO, circ. 18,803 173
D WESTERN DAILY PRESS BRISTOL, circ. 41,639 272

Weymouth
W DORSET ADVERTISER, circ. 35,843 F 173
D DORSET ECHO, circ. 18,803 173
W WESTERN GAZETTE AND YEOVIL TIMES SERIES, circ. 79,876 272

Wimborne
D DAILY ECHO (BOURNEMOUTH), circ. 32,441 170
W SALISBURY JOURNAL & AVON ADVERTISER SERIES, circ. 99,503 243

Durham County
W TEESDALE MERCURY, circ. 6,479 262

Aycliffe
W ADVERTISER SERIES (DURHAM), circ. 193,884 F ... 139

Barnard Castle
W DARLINGTON & STOCKTON TIMES SERIES, circ. 27,577 171
D THE NORTHERN ECHO (DARLINGTON), circ. 50,256 232
S SUNDAY SUN, circ. 68,033 259

Billingham
D EVENING GAZETTE (MIDDLESBROUGH), circ. 50,920 181
D HARTLEPOOL MAIL, circ. 18,223 195
W HERALD AND POST SERIES (TEESSIDE), circ. 232,382 F 197

Bishop Auckland
W ADVERTISER SERIES (DURHAM), circ. 193,884 F ... 139
W HERALD AND POST SERIES (TEESSIDE), circ. 232,382 F 197
D THE NORTHERN ECHO (DARLINGTON), circ. 50,256 232
S SUNDAY SUN, circ. 68,033 259
W WEAR VALLEY MERCURY, circ. 2,000 269
W WEARDALE GAZETTE, circ. 2,000 269

Blackhall Colliery
D EVENING CHRONICLE (NEWCASTLE), circ. 78,804 ... 180
D HARTLEPOOL MAIL, circ. 18,223 195
D THE JOURNAL (NEWCASTLE), circ. 35,476 205
D THE NORTHERN ECHO (DARLINGTON), circ. 50,256 232
W STAR SERIES, circ. 138,751 F 255
S SUNDAY SUN, circ. 68,033 259
D SUNDERLAND ECHO, circ. 42,910 259

Boldon
D THE SHIELDS GAZETTE, circ. 18,726 247
D SUNDERLAND ECHO, circ. 42,910 259

Bowburn
W ADVERTISER SERIES (DURHAM), circ. 193,884 F ... 139
D EVENING CHRONICLE (NEWCASTLE), circ. 78,804 ... 180
D THE JOURNAL (NEWCASTLE), circ. 35,476 205
D THE NORTHERN ECHO (DARLINGTON), circ. 50,256 232
S SUNDAY SUN, circ. 68,033 259
D SUNDERLAND ECHO, circ. 42,910 259

Brandon
S SUNDAY SUN, circ. 68,033 259

Burnopfield
D EVENING CHRONICLE (NEWCASTLE), circ. 78,804 ... 180
D THE JOURNAL (NEWCASTLE), circ. 35,476 205
D THE NORTHERN ECHO (DARLINGTON), circ. 50,256 232
S SUNDAY SUN, circ. 68,033 259

Castleside
W ADVERTISER SERIES (DURHAM), circ. 193,884 F ... 139
D EVENING CHRONICLE (NEWCASTLE), circ. 78,804 ... 180
D THE JOURNAL (NEWCASTLE), circ. 35,476 205
D THE NORTHERN ECHO (DARLINGTON), circ. 50,256 232
S SUNDAY SUN, circ. 68,033 259

Chester-le-Street
W ADVERTISER SERIES (DURHAM), circ. 193,884 F ... 139
S SUNDAY SUN, circ. 68,033 259

Chilton
W ADVERTISER SERIES (DURHAM), circ. 193,884 F ... 139
W COMMUNITY NEWSPAPER SERIES, circ. 28,500 F 164
D THE JOURNAL (NEWCASTLE), circ. 35,476 205
D THE NORTHERN ECHO (DARLINGTON), circ. 50,256 232
S SUNDAY SUN, circ. 68,033 259

Consett
W ADVERTISER SERIES (DURHAM), circ. 193,884 F ... 139
D EVENING CHRONICLE (NEWCASTLE), circ. 78,804 ... 180
D THE JOURNAL (NEWCASTLE), circ. 35,476 205

Cornforth
W ADVERTISER SERIES (DURHAM), circ. 193,884 F ... 139
D EVENING CHRONICLE (NEWCASTLE), circ. 78,804 ... 180
D THE JOURNAL (NEWCASTLE), circ. 35,476 205
D THE NORTHERN ECHO (DARLINGTON), circ. 50,256 232
S SUNDAY SUN, circ. 68,033 259
D SUNDERLAND ECHO, circ. 42,910 259

Coundon
W ADVERTISER SERIES (DURHAM), circ. 193,884 F ... 139
W DARLINGTON & STOCKTON TIMES SERIES, circ. 27,577 171

Crook
W ADVERTISER SERIES (DURHAM), circ. 193,884 F ... 139
D THE JOURNAL (NEWCASTLE), circ. 35,476 205
D THE NORTHERN ECHO (DARLINGTON), circ. 50,256 232
S SUNDAY SUN, circ. 68,033 259
W WEAR VALLEY MERCURY, circ. 2,000 269

Darlington
W ADVERTISER SERIES (DURHAM), circ. 193,884 F ... 139
W DARLINGTON & STOCKTON TIMES SERIES, circ. 27,577 171
W HERALD AND POST SERIES (TEESSIDE), circ. 232,382 F 197
D THE NORTHERN ECHO (DARLINGTON), circ. 50,256 232
S SUNDAY SUN, circ. 68,033 259

Durham City
W ADVERTISER SERIES (DURHAM), circ. 193,884 F ... 139
D DURHAM TIMES, circ. 6,000 176
D EVENING CHRONICLE (NEWCASTLE), circ. 78,804 ... 180
D THE JOURNAL (NEWCASTLE), circ. 35,476 205
D THE NORTHERN ECHO (DARLINGTON), circ. 50,256 232
S SUNDAY SUN, circ. 68,033 259
D SUNDERLAND ECHO, circ. 42,910 259
W WEAR VALLEY MERCURY, circ. 2,000 269

Eaglescliffe
W DARLINGTON & STOCKTON TIMES SERIES, circ. 27,577 171
D EVENING GAZETTE (MIDDLESBROUGH), circ. 50,920 181
D THE NORTHERN ECHO (DARLINGTON), circ. 50,256 232

Easington
W STAR SERIES, circ. 138,751 F 255
S SUNDAY SUN, circ. 68,033 259
D SUNDERLAND ECHO, circ. 42,910 259

Esh Winning
W ADVERTISER SERIES (DURHAM), circ. 193,884 F ... 139
D EVENING CHRONICLE (NEWCASTLE), circ. 78,804 ... 180
D THE JOURNAL (NEWCASTLE), circ. 35,476 205
D THE NORTHERN ECHO (DARLINGTON), circ. 50,256 232
S SUNDAY SUN, circ. 68,033 259
D SUNDERLAND ECHO, circ. 42,910 259

Evenwood
W DARLINGTON & STOCKTON TIMES SERIES, circ. 27,577 171
D THE JOURNAL (NEWCASTLE), circ. 35,476 205
D THE NORTHERN ECHO (DARLINGTON), circ. 50,256 232
S SUNDAY SUN, circ. 68,033 259

Ferryhill
W ADVERTISER SERIES (DURHAM), circ. 193,884 F ... 139
W COMMUNITY NEWSPAPER SERIES, circ. 28,500 F 164
W DARLINGTON & STOCKTON TIMES SERIES, circ. 27,577 171
D THE JOURNAL (NEWCASTLE), circ. 35,476 205
D THE NORTHERN ECHO (DARLINGTON), circ. 50,256 232
S SUNDAY SUN, circ. 68,033 259

Great Lumley
W ADVERTISER SERIES (DURHAM), circ. 193,884 F ... 139
D THE JOURNAL (NEWCASTLE), circ. 35,476 ....:. 205
D THE NORTHERN ECHO (DARLINGTON), circ. 50,256 232
S SUNDAY SUN, circ. 68,033 259
D SUNDERLAND ECHO, circ. 42,910 259

Hartlepool
D EVENING GAZETTE (MIDDLESBROUGH), circ. 50,920 181
D HARTLEPOOL MAIL, circ. 18,223 195
W STAR SERIES, circ. 138,751 F 255
S SUNDAY SUN, circ. 68,033 259

Hurworth-on-Tees
W ADVERTISER SERIES (DURHAM), circ. 193,884 F ... 139
W DARLINGTON & STOCKTON TIMES SERIES, circ. 27,577 171
D EVENING GAZETTE (MIDDLESBROUGH), circ. 50,920 181
D THE JOURNAL (NEWCASTLE), circ. 35,476 205
D THE NORTHERN ECHO (DARLINGTON), circ. 50,256 232
S SUNDAY SUN, circ. 68,033 259

Lanchester
W ADVERTISER SERIES (DURHAM), circ. 193,884 F ... 139

Langley Park
W ADVERTISER SERIES (DURHAM), circ. 193,884 F ... 139
D EVENING CHRONICLE (NEWCASTLE), circ. 78,804 ... 180
D THE JOURNAL (NEWCASTLE), circ. 35,476 205
D THE NORTHERN ECHO (DARLINGTON), circ. 50,256 232
S SUNDAY SUN, circ. 68,033 259
D SUNDERLAND ECHO, circ. 42,910 259

Leadgate
W ADVERTISER SERIES (DURHAM), circ. 193,884 F ... 139
D EVENING CHRONICLE (NEWCASTLE), circ. 78,804 ... 180
D THE JOURNAL (NEWCASTLE), circ. 35,476 205
D THE NORTHERN ECHO (DARLINGTON), circ. 50,256 232
S SUNDAY SUN, circ. 68,033 259

Murton
D EVENING CHRONICLE (NEWCASTLE), circ. 78,804 ... 180
D THE JOURNAL (NEWCASTLE), circ. 35,476 205
D THE NORTHERN ECHO (DARLINGTON), circ. 50,256 232
W STAR SERIES, circ. 138,751 F 255
S SUNDAY SUN, circ. 68,033 259
D SUNDERLAND ECHO, circ. 42,910 259

Newton Aycliffe
W HERALD AND POST SERIES (TEESSIDE), circ. 232,382 F 197
W NEWTON NEWS, circ. 15,000 F 228
D THE NORTHERN ECHO (DARLINGTON), circ. 50,256 232
S SUNDAY SUN, circ. 68,033 259

Norton
W HERALD AND POST SERIES (TEESSIDE), circ. 232,382 F 197

Ouston
W ADVERTISER SERIES (DURHAM), circ. 193,884 F ... 139
D THE NORTHERN ECHO (DARLINGTON), circ. 50,256 232
D SUNDERLAND ECHO, circ. 42,910 259

Pelton
W ADVERTISER SERIES (DURHAM), circ. 193,884 F ... 139
D THE JOURNAL (NEWCASTLE), circ. 35,476 205
D THE NORTHERN ECHO (DARLINGTON), circ. 50,256 232
S SUNDAY SUN, circ. 68,033 259
D SUNDERLAND ECHO, circ. 42,910 259

Peterlee
D HARTLEPOOL MAIL, circ. 18,223 195
D THE JOURNAL (NEWCASTLE), circ. 35,476 205
W STAR SERIES, circ. 138,751 F 255
S SUNDAY SUN, circ. 68,033 259
D SUNDERLAND ECHO, circ. 42,910 259

Sacriston
W ADVERTISER SERIES (DURHAM), circ. 193,884 F ... 139
D THE JOURNAL (NEWCASTLE), circ. 35,476 205
D THE NORTHERN ECHO (DARLINGTON), circ. 50,256 232
S SUNDAY SUN, circ. 68,033 259
D SUNDERLAND ECHO, circ. 42,910 259

Seaham
D EVENING CHRONICLE (NEWCASTLE), circ. 78,804 ... 180
D THE JOURNAL (NEWCASTLE), circ. 35,476 205
W STAR SERIES, circ. 138,751 F 255
D SUNDERLAND ECHO, circ. 42,910 259

Sedgefield
W ADVERTISER SERIES (DURHAM), circ. 193,884 F ... 139
W DARLINGTON & STOCKTON TIMES SERIES, circ. 27,577 171

W Local/Weekly Newspapers   D Regional Daily Newspapers   S Regional Sunday Newspapers   F Free Newspapers

Title (Day/am/pm)	Circ.	Page No.

W HERALD AND POST SERIES (TEESSIDE), circ. 232,382 F 197
S SUNDAY SUN, circ. 68,033 259

Shildon
W COMMUNITY NEWSPAPER SERIES, circ. 28,500 F 164
W HERALD AND POST SERIES (TEESSIDE), circ. 232,382 F 197
S SUNDAY SUN, circ. 68,033 259

Shotton Colliery
D EVENING CHRONICLE (NEWCASTLE), circ. 78,804 ... 180
D HARTLEPOOL MAIL, circ. 18,223 195
D THE JOURNAL (NEWCASTLE), circ. 35,476 205
D THE NORTHERN ECHO (DARLINGTON), circ. 50,256 232
W STAR SERIES, circ. 138,751 F 255
S SUNDAY SUN, circ. 68,033 259
D SUNDERLAND ECHO, circ. 42,910 259

South Hetton
D EVENING CHRONICLE (NEWCASTLE), circ. 78,804 ... 180
D THE JOURNAL (NEWCASTLE), circ. 35,476 205
D THE NORTHERN ECHO (DARLINGTON), circ. 50,256 232
W STAR SERIES, circ. 138,751 F 255
S SUNDAY SUN, circ. 68,033 259
D SUNDERLAND ECHO, circ. 42,910 259

Spennymoor
W ADVERTISER SERIES (DURHAM), circ. 193,884 F ... 139
W COMMUNITY NEWSPAPER SERIES, circ. 28,500 F 164
W HERALD AND POST SERIES (TEESSIDE), circ. 232,382 F 197
D THE JOURNAL (NEWCASTLE), circ. 35,476 205
D THE NORTHERN ECHO (DARLINGTON), circ. 50,256 232
S SUNDAY SUN, circ. 68,033 259

Stanley
W ADVERTISER SERIES (DURHAM), circ. 193,884 F ... 139

Stockton-on-Tees
W DARLINGTON & STOCKTON TIMES SERIES, circ. 27,577 171
D EVENING GAZETTE (MIDDLESBROUGH), circ. 50,920 181
W HERALD AND POST SERIES (TEESSIDE), circ. 232,382 F 197
D THE NORTHERN ECHO (DARLINGTON), circ. 50,256 232
S SUNDAY SUN, circ. 68,033 259

Ushaw Moor
W ADVERTISER SERIES (DURHAM), circ. 193,884 F ... 139
D EVENING CHRONICLE (NEWCASTLE), circ. 78,804 ... 180
D THE JOURNAL (NEWCASTLE), circ. 35,476 205
D THE NORTHERN ECHO (DARLINGTON), circ. 50,256 232
S SUNDAY SUN, circ. 68,033 259
D SUNDERLAND ECHO, circ. 42,910 259

Willington
S SUNDAY SUN, circ. 68,033 259
W WEAR VALLEY MERCURY, circ. 2,000 269

Wingate
D HARTLEPOOL MAIL, circ. 18,223 195
D THE JOURNAL (NEWCASTLE), circ. 35,476 205
D THE NORTHERN ECHO (DARLINGTON), circ. 50,256 232
W STAR SERIES, circ. 138,751 F 255
S SUNDAY SUN, circ. 68,033 259
D SUNDERLAND ECHO, circ. 42,910 259

Witton Gilbert
W ADVERTISER SERIES (DURHAM), circ. 193,884 F ... 139
D THE JOURNAL (NEWCASTLE), circ. 35,476 205
D THE NORTHERN ECHO (DARLINGTON), circ. 50,256 232
S SUNDAY SUN, circ. 68,033 259
D SUNDERLAND ECHO, circ. 42,910 259

Yarm
W DARLINGTON & STOCKTON TIMES SERIES, circ. 27,577 171
W HERALD AND POST SERIES (TEESSIDE), circ. 232,382 F 197

Ealing Borough

Acton
W THE GAZETTE AND LEADER SERIES, circ. 88,667 189
W GREATER LONDON CHRONICLE, circ. 5,000 F 193
D LONDON EVENING STANDARD, circ. 263,312 214
W TIMES SERIES (RICHMOND), circ. 152,627 264

Ealing
W THE GAZETTE AND LEADER SERIES, circ. 88,667 189
W GREATER LONDON CHRONICLE, circ. 5,000 F 193
W NORTH WEST LONDON NEWSPAPER SERIES, circ. 54,733 230
W SOUTH BUCKS AND BERKSHIRE NEWS SERIES, circ. 50,000 F 249

Greenford
W THE GAZETTE AND LEADER SERIES, circ. 88,667 189

Northolt
W THE GAZETTE AND LEADER SERIES, circ. 88,667 189

Southall
W THE GAZETTE AND LEADER SERIES, circ. 88,667 189
W SOUTH BUCKS AND BERKSHIRE NEWS SERIES, circ. 50,000 F 249

East Riding of Yorkshire
W BEVERLEY GUARDIAN, circ. 19,600 F 148
W BRIDLINGTON FREE PRESS SERIES, circ. 31,298 F ... 152
D DRIFFIELD TIMES, circ. 5,211 174
D LIFE AND STYLE 212
D YORKSHIRE POST, circ. 49,031 279
D YORKSHIRE POST (CITY/LONDON OFFICE) 279

Beverley
W BEVERLEY GUARDIAN, circ. 19,600 F 148
W DRIFFIELD TIMES SERIES, circ. 29,611 174
W HULL ADVERTISER SERIES, circ. 136,869 F 201
D HULL DAILY MAIL, circ. 59,689 201

Bridlington
W DRIFFIELD TIMES SERIES, circ. 29,611 174
D HULL DAILY MAIL, circ. 59,689 201
D THE PRESS (YORK), circ. 35,761 238
D SCARBOROUGH EVENING NEWS, circ. 17,239 244

Brough
W JOURNAL & ADVERTISER SERIES, circ. 30,000 F ... 205

Driffield
W DRIFFIELD TIMES, circ. 5,211 174
W DRIFFIELD TIMES SERIES, circ. 29,611 174

Great Driffield
W DRIFFIELD TIMES SERIES, circ. 29,611 174
D HULL DAILY MAIL, circ. 59,689 201
S SCARBOROUGH EVENING NEWS, circ. 17,239 244

Haltemprice
D HULL DAILY MAIL, circ. 59,689 201

Hedon
W HOLDERNESS GAZETTE SERIES, circ. 10,032 200
W HULL ADVERTISER SERIES, circ. 136,869 F 201
D HULL DAILY MAIL, circ. 59,689 201
W JOURNAL & ADVERTISER SERIES, circ. 30,000 F ... 205

Hessle
W HULL ADVERTISER SERIES, circ. 136,869 F 201

Hornsea
W HOLDERNESS GAZETTE SERIES, circ. 10,032 200
W HORNSEA & DISTRICT POST, circ. 28,000 F 200
W HULL ADVERTISER SERIES, circ. 136,869 F 201
D HULL DAILY MAIL, circ. 59,689 201

Howden
W GOOLE, HOWDEN COURIER, circ. 15,419 F 192
W GOOLE TIMES, circ. 10,149 192

Kingston-upon-Hull
W HULL ADVERTISER SERIES, circ. 136,869 F 201
D HULL DAILY MAIL, circ. 59,689 201
W JOURNAL & ADVERTISER SERIES, circ. 30,000 F ... 205

Market Weighton
W HULL ADVERTISER SERIES, circ. 136,869 F 201
D HULL DAILY MAIL, circ. 59,689 201
W POCKLINGTON POST, circ. 4,605 236
D THE PRESS (YORK), circ. 35,761 238
W STAR SERIES (SELBY & YORK), circ. 67,353 F 255

North Ferriby
W HULL ADVERTISER SERIES, circ. 136,869 F 201
D HULL DAILY MAIL, circ. 59,689 201

Patrington
W HOLDERNESS GAZETTE SERIES, circ. 10,032 200
W HULL ADVERTISER SERIES, circ. 136,869 F 201

Pocklington
W POCKLINGTON POST, circ. 4,605 236
D THE PRESS (YORK), circ. 35,761 238
D SCARBOROUGH EVENING NEWS, circ. 17,239 244
W STAR SERIES (SELBY & YORK), circ. 67,353 F 255

Stamford Bridge
W POCKLINGTON POST, circ. 4,605 236
D THE PRESS (YORK), circ. 35,761 238

Swanland
W HULL ADVERTISER SERIES, circ. 136,869 F 201
D HULL DAILY MAIL, circ. 59,689 201

Thorngumbald
W HULL ADVERTISER SERIES, circ. 136,869 F 201
D HULL DAILY MAIL, circ. 59,689 201

Withernsea
W HOLDERNESS GAZETTE SERIES, circ. 10,032 200
W HULL ADVERTISER SERIES, circ. 136,869 F 201
D HULL DAILY MAIL, circ. 59,689 201

East Sussex

Battle
W HASTINGS OBSERVER SERIES, circ. 36,478 196

Bexhill-on-Sea
W ADNEWS SERIES (BEXHILL & HASTINGS), circ. 51,080 F 138
W HASTINGS OBSERVER SERIES, circ. 36,478 196

Brighton
D THE ARGUS, circ. 32,788 142
W BRIGHTON AND HOVE LEADER SERIES, circ. 138,468 F 152
D LONDON EVENING STANDARD, circ. 263,312 214
D METRO (LONDON), circ. 742,291 F 221

Buxted
W SUSSEX EXPRESS SERIES, circ. 14,779 260

Crowborough
D KENT & SUSSEX COURIER SERIES, circ. 110,491 206
W SUSSEX EXPRESS SERIES, circ. 14,779 260

Eastbourne
D THE ARGUS, circ. 32,788 142
W EASTBOURNE AND DISTRICT ADVERTISER, circ. 48,729 F 178
W EASTBOURNE HERALD & GAZETTE SERIES, circ. 88,233 178

Forest Row
W EAST GRINSTEAD COURIER & OBSERVER, circ. 15,000 177

Hailsham
W EASTBOURNE AND DISTRICT ADVERTISER, circ. 48,729 F 178
W EASTBOURNE HERALD & GAZETTE SERIES, circ. 88,233 178
W SUSSEX EXPRESS SERIES, circ. 14,779 260

Hartfield
W EAST GRINSTEAD COURIER & OBSERVER, circ. 15,000 177

Hastings
W ADNEWS SERIES (BEXHILL & HASTINGS), circ. 51,080 F 138
D THE ARGUS, circ. 32,788 142
W HASTINGS OBSERVER SERIES, circ. 36,478 196

Heathfield
D KENT & SUSSEX COURIER SERIES, circ. 110,491 206
W SUSSEX EXPRESS SERIES, circ. 14,779 260

Hove
D THE ARGUS, circ. 32,788 142
W BRIGHTON AND HOVE LEADER SERIES, circ. 138,468 F 152
D LONDON EVENING STANDARD, circ. 263,312 214

Lewes
D THE ARGUS, circ. 32,788 142
W BRIGHTON AND HOVE LEADER SERIES, circ. 138,468 F 152
W SUSSEX EXPRESS SERIES, circ. 14,779 260

Newhaven
W BRIGHTON AND HOVE LEADER SERIES, circ. 138,468 F 152
W SUSSEX EXPRESS SERIES, circ. 14,779 260

Peacehaven
D THE ARGUS, circ. 32,788 142
W BRIGHTON AND HOVE LEADER SERIES, circ. 138,468 F 152
W SUSSEX EXPRESS SERIES, circ. 14,779 260

Pevensey
W EASTBOURNE AND DISTRICT ADVERTISER, circ. 48,729 F 178
W EASTBOURNE HERALD & GAZETTE SERIES, circ. 88,233 178
W SUSSEX EXPRESS SERIES, circ. 14,779 260

Polegate
W EASTBOURNE HERALD & GAZETTE SERIES, circ. 88,233 178

W **Local/Weekly Newspapers**   D **Regional Daily Newspapers**   S **Regional Sunday Newspapers**   F **Free Newspapers**

Non-Nationals - England

Title (Day/am/pm) Circ. Page No.

[W] SUSSEX EXPRESS SERIES, circ. 14,779 260

Portslade-by-Sea

[D] THE ARGUS, circ. 32,788 142
[W] BRIGHTON AND HOVE LEADER SERIES, circ. 138,468 [F] 152
[D] LONDON EVENING STANDARD, circ. 263,312 214

Ringmer

[D] THE ARGUS, circ. 32,788 142
[W] BRIGHTON AND HOVE LEADER SERIES, circ. 138,468 [F] 152
[W] SUSSEX EXPRESS SERIES, circ. 14,779 260

Robertsbridge

[W] HASTINGS OBSERVER SERIES, circ. 36,478 196

Rottingdean

[D] THE ARGUS, circ. 32,788 142

Rye

[W] HASTINGS OBSERVER SERIES, circ. 36,478 196

Saltdean

[D] THE ARGUS, circ. 32,788 142
[W] BRIGHTON AND HOVE LEADER SERIES, circ. 138,468 [F] 152

Seaford

[W] BRIGHTON AND HOVE LEADER SERIES, circ. 138,468 [F] 152
[W] EASTBOURNE AND DISTRICT ADVERTISER, circ. 48,729 [F] 178
[W] EASTBOURNE HERALD & GAZETTE SERIES, circ. 88,233 178
[W] SUSSEX EXPRESS SERIES, circ. 14,779 260

Selsey

[W] BOGNOR REGIS AND CHICHESTER GUARDIAN, circ. 41,368 [F] 149

St. Leonards

[W] HASTINGS OBSERVER SERIES, circ. 36,478 196

Uckfield

[W] BRIGHTON AND HOVE LEADER SERIES, circ. 138,468 [F] 152
[W] KENT & SUSSEX COURIER SERIES, circ. 110,491 206
[W] SUSSEX EXPRESS SERIES, circ. 14,779 260

Wadhurst

[W] KENT & SUSSEX COURIER SERIES, circ. 110,491 206

Enfield Borough

Edmonton

[W] ENFIELD INDEPENDENT, circ. 92,538 [F] 179
[W] GAZETTE, ADVERTISER AND PRESS NEWSPAPER SERIES, circ. 270,519 188
[W] HENDON TIMES SERIES, circ. 116,302 [F] 197
[W] ISLINGTON GAZETTE & JOURNAL SERIES, circ. 52,062 204

Enfield

[W] ENFIELD INDEPENDENT, circ. 92,538 [F] 179
[W] GAZETTE, ADVERTISER AND PRESS NEWSPAPER SERIES, circ. 270,519 188
[W] HENDON TIMES SERIES, circ. 116,302 [F] 197
[W] THE HERTS AND LEA VALLEY STAR, circ. 52,060 [F] 199

Palmers Green

[W] ENFIELD INDEPENDENT, circ. 92,538 [F] 179
[W] GAZETTE, ADVERTISER AND PRESS NEWSPAPER SERIES, circ. 270,519 188
[W] HENDON TIMES SERIES, circ. 116,302 [F] 197

Ponders End

[W] ENFIELD INDEPENDENT, circ. 92,538 [F] 179
[W] HENDON TIMES SERIES, circ. 116,302 [F] 197

Southgate

[W] ENFIELD INDEPENDENT, circ. 92,538 [F] 179
[W] GAZETTE, ADVERTISER AND PRESS NEWSPAPER SERIES, circ. 270,519 188
[W] HENDON TIMES SERIES, circ. 116,302 [F] 197

Winchmore Hill

[W] ENFIELD INDEPENDENT, circ. 92,538 [F] 179
[W] HENDON TIMES SERIES, circ. 116,302 [F] 197

Essex

[W] ESSEX ENQUIRER SERIES, circ. 57,859 [F] 180

Ardleigh

[W] ESSEX COUNTY STANDARD, circ. 20,316 180

Aveley

[W] ESSEX ENQUIRER SERIES, circ. 57,859 [F] 180
[D] LONDON EVENING STANDARD, circ. 263,312 214
[W] ROMFORD RECORDER, circ. 28,302 241
[W] THURROCK GAZETTE, circ. 57,080 [F] 263
[W] YELLOW ADVERTISER GROUP SERIES (ESSEX), circ. 434,612 [F] 278

Basildon

[D] ECHO (BASILDON), circ. 34,844 178
[W] ESSEX ENQUIRER SERIES, circ. 57,859 [F] 180
[D] LONDON EVENING STANDARD, circ. 263,312 214
[W] SOUTHEND STANDARD SERIES, circ. 204,783 [F] 252
[W] YELLOW ADVERTISER GROUP SERIES (ESSEX), circ. 434,612 [F] 278

Benfleet

[D] ECHO (BASILDON), circ. 34,844 178
[D] LONDON EVENING STANDARD, circ. 263,312 214
[W] SOUTHEND STANDARD SERIES, circ. 204,783 [F] 252

Bicknacre

[W] ESSEX CHRONICLE SERIES, circ. 35,461 180
[D] LONDON EVENING STANDARD, circ. 263,312 214
[W] WEEKLY NEWS SERIES (CHELMSFORD), circ. 59,949 [F] 269
[W] YELLOW ADVERTISER GROUP SERIES (ESSEX), circ. 434,612 [F] 278

Billericay

[W] BRENTWOOD GAZETTE SERIES, circ. 14,679 151
[D] ECHO (BASILDON), circ. 34,844 178
[W] ESSEX ENQUIRER SERIES, circ. 57,859 [F] 180
[D] LONDON EVENING STANDARD, circ. 263,312 214
[W] ROMFORD RECORDER, circ. 28,302 241
[W] SOUTHEND STANDARD SERIES, circ. 204,783 [F] 252
[W] YELLOW ADVERTISER GROUP SERIES (ESSEX), circ. 434,612 [F] 278

Boreham

[W] ESSEX CHRONICLE SERIES, circ. 35,461 180
[D] LONDON EVENING STANDARD, circ. 263,312 214
[W] YELLOW ADVERTISER GROUP SERIES (ESSEX), circ. 434,612 [F] 278

Braintree

[W] BRAINTREE & WITHAM TIMES & GAZETTE SERIES, circ. 39,857 151
[D] DAILY GAZETTE, circ. 22,131 170
[W] ESSEX CHRONICLE SERIES, circ. 35,461 180
[D] LONDON EVENING STANDARD, circ. 263,312 214
[W] THE TRIBUNE & COURIER SERIES, circ. 10,000 [F] 265
[W] YELLOW ADVERTISER GROUP SERIES (ESSEX), circ. 434,612 [F] 278

Brentwood

[W] BRENTWOOD GAZETTE SERIES, circ. 14,679 151
[W] ESSEX ENQUIRER SERIES, circ. 57,859 [F] 180
[D] LONDON EVENING STANDARD, circ. 263,312 214
[W] ROMFORD RECORDER, circ. 28,302 241
[W] SOUTHEND STANDARD SERIES, circ. 204,783 [F] 252
[W] YELLOW ADVERTISER GROUP SERIES (ESSEX), circ. 434,612 [F] 278

Brightlingsea

[D] DAILY GAZETTE, circ. 22,131 170
[W] ESSEX COUNTY STANDARD, circ. 20,316 180
[W] GAZETTE AND STANDARD SERIES (EAST ESSEX), circ. 22,625 189
[W] WEEKLY NEWS SERIES (COLCHESTER), circ. 59,962 [F] 270

Buckhurst Hill

[W] GUARDIAN AND INDEPENDENT SERIES, circ. 22,432 193

Burnham-on-Crouch

[W] ESSEX CHRONICLE SERIES, circ. 35,461 180
[D] LONDON EVENING STANDARD, circ. 263,312 214
[W] MALDON & BURNHAM STANDARD SERIES, circ. 9,687 217

Canvey Island

[D] ECHO (BASILDON), circ. 34,844 178
[W] LEIGH TIMES SERIES, circ. 67,000 211
[D] LONDON EVENING STANDARD, circ. 263,312 214
[W] SOUTHEND STANDARD SERIES, circ. 204,783 [F] 252

Chelmsford

[D] DAILY GAZETTE, circ. 22,131 170
[D] EA WEEK 176
[D] EAST ANGLIAN DAILY TIMES, circ. 34,392 176
[W] ESSEX CHRONICLE SERIES, circ. 35,461 180
[W] ESSEX ENQUIRER SERIES, circ. 57,859 [F] 180
[D] LONDON EVENING STANDARD, circ. 263,312 214
[W] WEEKLY NEWS SERIES (CHELMSFORD), circ. 59,949 [F] 269
[W] YELLOW ADVERTISER GROUP SERIES (ESSEX), circ. 434,612 [F] 278

Chigwell

[W] GUARDIAN AND INDEPENDENT SERIES, circ. 22,432 193
[W] ILFORD RECORDER SERIES, circ. 15,074 202
[D] LONDON EVENING STANDARD, circ. 263,312 214

Chipping Ongar

[W] ESSEX CHRONICLE SERIES, circ. 35,461 180
[D] LONDON EVENING STANDARD, circ. 263,312 214

Clacton

[D] DAILY GAZETTE, circ. 22,131 170
[D] EA WEEK 176
[D] EAST ANGLIAN DAILY TIMES, circ. 34,392 176
[W] GAZETTE AND STANDARD SERIES (EAST ESSEX), circ. 22,625 189
[W] WEEKLY NEWS SERIES (COLCHESTER), circ. 59,962 [F] 270

Coggeshall

[W] BRAINTREE & WITHAM TIMES & GAZETTE SERIES, circ. 39,857 151
[W] ESSEX COUNTY STANDARD, circ. 20,316 180

Colchester

[D] DAILY GAZETTE, circ. 22,131 170
[D] EA WEEK 176
[D] EAST ANGLIAN DAILY TIMES, circ. 34,392 176
[W] ESSEX COUNTY STANDARD, circ. 20,316 180
[W] THE TRIBUNE & COURIER SERIES, circ. 10,000 [F] 265
[W] WEEKLY NEWS SERIES (COLCHESTER), circ. 59,962 [F] 270
[W] YELLOW ADVERTISER GROUP SERIES (ESSEX), circ. 434,612 [F] 278

Danbury

[W] ESSEX CHRONICLE SERIES, circ. 35,461 180
[D] LONDON EVENING STANDARD, circ. 263,312 214
[W] MALDON & BURNHAM STANDARD SERIES, circ. 9,687 217
[W] WEEKLY NEWS SERIES (CHELMSFORD), circ. 59,949 [F] 269
[W] YELLOW ADVERTISER GROUP SERIES (ESSEX), circ. 434,612 [F] 278

Doddinghurst

[W] BRENTWOOD GAZETTE SERIES, circ. 14,679 151
[D] LONDON EVENING STANDARD, circ. 263,312 214
[W] ROMFORD RECORDER, circ. 28,302 241
[W] SOUTHEND STANDARD SERIES, circ. 204,783 [F] 252
[W] YELLOW ADVERTISER GROUP SERIES (ESSEX), circ. 434,612 [F] 278

Earls Colne

[D] DAILY GAZETTE, circ. 22,131 170
[D] EA WEEK 176
[D] EAST ANGLIAN DAILY TIMES, circ. 34,392 176
[W] SUFFOLK FREE PRESS, circ. 9,596 257

Epping

[W] GUARDIAN AND INDEPENDENT SERIES, circ. 22,432 193
[W] HARLOW STAR, circ. 38,743 195
[W] YELLOW ADVERTISER GROUP SERIES (ESSEX), circ. 434,612 [F] 278

Frinton

[D] DAILY GAZETTE, circ. 22,131 170
[W] GAZETTE AND STANDARD SERIES (EAST ESSEX), circ. 22,625 189
[W] WEEKLY NEWS SERIES (COLCHESTER), circ. 59,962 [F] 270

Grays

[D] ECHO (BASILDON), circ. 34,844 178
[W] ESSEX ENQUIRER SERIES, circ. 57,859 [F] 180
[D] LONDON EVENING STANDARD, circ. 263,312 214
[W] THURROCK GAZETTE, circ. 57,080 [F] 263

Great Dunmow

[W] BRAINTREE & WITHAM TIMES & GAZETTE SERIES, circ. 39,857 151
[W] DUNMOW BROADCAST AND RECORDER, circ. 11,945 [F] 176
[W] ESSEX CHRONICLE SERIES, circ. 35,461 180
[W] HERTS & ESSEX OBSERVER SERIES, circ. 30,375 199
[D] LONDON EVENING STANDARD, circ. 263,312 214

Great Wakering

[D] ECHO (BASILDON), circ. 34,844 178
[D] LONDON EVENING STANDARD, circ. 263,312 214

Great Waltham

[W] ESSEX CHRONICLE SERIES, circ. 35,461 180

Hadleigh

[W] ADVERTISER SERIES (IPSWICH), circ. 82,067 [F] 139
[D] EVENING STAR, circ. 19,707 181

[W] Local/Weekly Newspapers [D] Regional Daily Newspapers [S] Regional Sunday Newspapers [F] Free Newspapers

Title (Day/am/pm) Circ. Page No.

[W] SOUTHEND STANDARD SERIES, circ. 204,783 [F] 252
[W] SUFFOLK FREE PRESS, circ. 9,596 257

Halstead
[W] BRAINTREE & WITHAM TIMES & GAZETTE SERIES, circ. 39,857 151
[D] DAILY GAZETTE, circ. 22,131 170
[W] SUFFOLK FREE PRESS, circ. 9,596 257

Harlow
[W] HARLOW HERALD, circ. 48,648 [F] 195
[W] HARLOW STAR, circ. 38,743 195
[D] LONDON EVENING STANDARD, circ. 263,312 214

Harwich
[D] DAILY GAZETTE, circ. 22,131 170
[D] EA WEEK 176
[D] EAST ANGLIAN DAILY TIMES, circ. 34,392 176
[W] GAZETTE AND STANDARD SERIES (EAST ESSEX), circ. 22,625 189
[W] WEEKLY NEWS SERIES (COLCHESTER), circ. 59,962 [F] 270

Hatfield Peverel
[W] BRAINTREE & WITHAM TIMES & GAZETTE SERIES, circ. 39,857 151
[D] DAILY GAZETTE, circ. 22,131 170
[D] EA WEEK 176
[D] EAST ANGLIAN DAILY TIMES, circ. 34,392 176
[W] ESSEX CHRONICLE SERIES, circ. 35,461 180
[D] LONDON EVENING STANDARD, circ. 263,312 214
[W] YELLOW ADVERTISER GROUP SERIES (ESSEX), circ. 434,612 [F] 278

Hockley
[D] ECHO (BASILDON), circ. 34,844 178
[W] ESSEX ENQUIRER SERIES, circ. 57,859 [F] 180
[D] LONDON EVENING STANDARD, circ. 263,312 214
[W] SOUTHEND STANDARD SERIES, circ. 204,783 [F] 252

Hullbridge
[D] ECHO (BASILDON), circ. 34,844 178
[D] LONDON EVENING STANDARD, circ. 263,312 214
[W] SOUTHEND STANDARD SERIES, circ. 204,783 [F] 252
[W] YELLOW ADVERTISER GROUP SERIES (ESSEX), circ. 434,612 [F] 278

Ingatestone
[W] ESSEX CHRONICLE SERIES, circ. 35,461 180
[D] LONDON EVENING STANDARD, circ. 263,312 214
[W] SOUTHEND STANDARD SERIES, circ. 204,783 [F] 252

Jaywick
[D] DAILY GAZETTE, circ. 22,131 170
[D] EA WEEK 176
[D] EAST ANGLIAN DAILY TIMES, circ. 34,392 176
[W] GAZETTE AND STANDARD SERIES (EAST ESSEX), circ. 22,625 189

Kelvedon
[W] ESSEX CHRONICLE SERIES, circ. 35,461 180
[W] ESSEX COUNTY STANDARD, circ. 20,316 180
[D] LONDON EVENING STANDARD, circ. 263,312 214
[W] THE TRIBUNE & COURIER SERIES, circ. 10,000 [F] .. 265

Kelvedon Hatch
[W] BRENTWOOD GAZETTE SERIES, circ. 14,679 151
[D] LONDON EVENING STANDARD, circ. 263,312 214
[W] YELLOW ADVERTISER GROUP SERIES (ESSEX), circ. 434,612 [F] 278

Linford
[D] LONDON EVENING STANDARD, circ. 263,312 214
[W] THURROCK GAZETTE, circ. 57,080 [F] 263
[W] YELLOW ADVERTISER GROUP SERIES (ESSEX), circ. 434,612 [F] 278

Little Baddow
[D] EA WEEK 176
[D] EAST ANGLIAN DAILY TIMES, circ. 34,392 176
[W] ESSEX CHRONICLE SERIES, circ. 35,461 180
[D] LONDON EVENING STANDARD, circ. 263,312 214
[W] WEEKLY NEWS SERIES (CHELMSFORD), circ. 59,949 [F] 269
[W] YELLOW ADVERTISER GROUP SERIES (ESSEX), circ. 434,612 [F] 278

Little Clacton
[D] DAILY GAZETTE, circ. 22,131 170
[D] EA WEEK 176
[D] EAST ANGLIAN DAILY TIMES, circ. 34,392 176
[W] GAZETTE AND STANDARD SERIES (EAST ESSEX), circ. 22,625 189

Little Wakering
[D] ECHO (BASILDON), circ. 34,844 178
[D] LONDON EVENING STANDARD, circ. 263,312 214
[W] SOUTHEND STANDARD SERIES, circ. 204,783 [F] 252

Loughton
[W] GUARDIAN AND INDEPENDENT SERIES, circ. 22,432 193
[D] LONDON EVENING STANDARD, circ. 263,312 214
[W] YELLOW ADVERTISER GROUP SERIES (ESSEX), circ. 434,612 [F] 278

Maldon
[D] DAILY GAZETTE, circ. 22,131 170
[W] ESSEX CHRONICLE SERIES, circ. 35,461 180
[D] LONDON EVENING STANDARD, circ. 263,312 214
[W] MALDON & BURNHAM STANDARD SERIES, circ. 9,687 217
[W] YELLOW ADVERTISER GROUP SERIES (ESSEX), circ. 434,612 [F] 278

Manningtree
[D] DAILY GAZETTE, circ. 22,131 170
[W] ESSEX COUNTY STANDARD, circ. 20,316 180
[W] GAZETTE AND STANDARD SERIES (EAST ESSEX), circ. 22,625 189
[W] GREATER IPSWICH COMMUNITY NEWS SERIES, circ. 38,500 [F] 192

Marks Tey
[D] DAILY GAZETTE, circ. 22,131 170
[D] EA WEEK 176
[D] EAST ANGLIAN DAILY TIMES, circ. 34,392 176

Newport
[W] WALDEN LOCAL, circ. 14,000 [F] 267

North Weald Bassett
[W] BRENTWOOD GAZETTE SERIES, circ. 14,679 151
[W] GUARDIAN AND INDEPENDENT SERIES, circ. 22,432 193
[W] HARLOW STAR, circ. 38,743 195
[D] LONDON EVENING STANDARD, circ. 263,312 214

Ongar
[W] BRENTWOOD GAZETTE SERIES, circ. 14,679 151
[W] GUARDIAN AND INDEPENDENT SERIES, circ. 22,432 193

Purfleet
[W] THURROCK GAZETTE, circ. 57,080 [F] 263

Rayleigh
[D] ECHO (BASILDON), circ. 34,844 178
[W] ESSEX ENQUIRER SERIES, circ. 57,859 [F] 180
[W] LEIGH TIMES SERIES, circ. 67,000 211
[D] LONDON EVENING STANDARD, circ. 263,312 214
[W] SOUTHEND STANDARD SERIES, circ. 204,783 [F] 252

Rochford
[D] ECHO (BASILDON), circ. 34,844 178
[D] LONDON EVENING STANDARD, circ. 263,312 214
[W] SOUTHEND STANDARD SERIES, circ. 204,783 [F] 252

Saffron Walden
[D] CAMBRIDGE NEWS, circ. 26,242 157
[W] CAMBRIDGE WEEKLY NEWS & CRIER SERIES, circ. 208,805 [F] 157
[W] HERTS & ESSEX OBSERVER SERIES, circ. 30,375 199
[W] THE REPORTER (SAFFRON WALDEN, STANSTED & SAWSTON), circ. 25,073 [F] 240
[W] WALDEN LOCAL, circ. 14,000 [F] 267

Sible Hedingham
[D] DAILY GAZETTE, circ. 22,131 170
[D] EA WEEK 176
[D] EAST ANGLIAN DAILY TIMES, circ. 34,392 176
[W] SUFFOLK FREE PRESS, circ. 9,596 257

Silver End
[W] BRAINTREE & WITHAM TIMES & GAZETTE SERIES, circ. 39,857 151
[D] DAILY GAZETTE, circ. 22,131 170
[D] EA WEEK 176
[D] EAST ANGLIAN DAILY TIMES, circ. 34,392 176
[W] ESSEX CHRONICLE SERIES, circ. 35,461 180
[D] LONDON EVENING STANDARD, circ. 263,312 214

South Ockendon
[D] LONDON EVENING STANDARD, circ. 263,312 214
[W] THURROCK GAZETTE, circ. 57,080 [F] 263

South Woodham Ferrers
[D] ECHO (BASILDON), circ. 34,844 178
[W] ESSEX CHRONICLE SERIES, circ. 35,461 180
[D] LONDON EVENING STANDARD, circ. 263,312 214
[W] MALDON & BURNHAM STANDARD SERIES, circ. 9,687 217
[W] WEEKLY NEWS SERIES (CHELMSFORD), circ. 59,949 [F] 269

Southend
[D] ECHO (BASILDON), circ. 34,844 178
[W] LEIGH TIMES SERIES, circ. 67,000 211
[D] LONDON EVENING STANDARD, circ. 263,312 214
[W] SOUTHEND STANDARD SERIES, circ. 204,783 [F] 252
[W] YELLOW ADVERTISER GROUP SERIES (ESSEX), circ. 434,612 [F] 278

Southminster
[D] LONDON EVENING STANDARD, circ. 263,312 214
[W] MALDON & BURNHAM STANDARD SERIES, circ. 9,687 217

Stanford-le-Hope
[D] ECHO (BASILDON), circ. 34,844 178
[D] LONDON EVENING STANDARD, circ. 263,312 214
[W] THURROCK GAZETTE, circ. 57,080 [F] 263

Stansted
[D] CAMBRIDGE NEWS, circ. 26,242 157
[W] CAMBRIDGE WEEKLY NEWS & CRIER SERIES, circ. 208,805 [F] 157
[W] ESSEX CHRONICLE SERIES, circ. 35,461 180
[W] HERTS & ESSEX OBSERVER SERIES, circ. 30,375 199
[D] LONDON EVENING STANDARD, circ. 263,312 214
[W] THE REPORTER (SAFFRON WALDEN, STANSTED & SAWSTON), circ. 25,073 [F] 240

Thaxted
[W] BRAINTREE & WITHAM TIMES & GAZETTE SERIES, circ. 39,857 151
[W] THE REPORTER (SAFFRON WALDEN, STANSTED & SAWSTON), circ. 25,073 [F] 240
[W] WALDEN LOCAL, circ. 14,000 [F] 267

Theydon Bois
[W] GUARDIAN AND INDEPENDENT SERIES, circ. 22,432 193
[D] LONDON EVENING STANDARD, circ. 263,312 214
[W] YELLOW ADVERTISER GROUP SERIES (ESSEX), circ. 434,612 [F] 278

Thurrock
[W] ESSEX ENQUIRER SERIES, circ. 57,859 [F] 180
[W] ROMFORD RECORDER, circ. 28,302 241
[W] THURROCK GAZETTE, circ. 57,080 [F] 263
[W] YELLOW ADVERTISER GROUP SERIES (ESSEX), circ. 434,612 [F] 278

Tilbury
[D] ECHO (BASILDON), circ. 34,844 178
[D] LONDON EVENING STANDARD, circ. 263,312 214
[W] THURROCK GAZETTE, circ. 57,080 [F] 263

Tiptree
[D] DAILY GAZETTE, circ. 22,131 170
[W] ESSEX CHRONICLE SERIES, circ. 35,461 180
[W] ESSEX COUNTY STANDARD, circ. 20,316 180
[D] LONDON EVENING STANDARD, circ. 263,312 214
[W] MALDON & BURNHAM STANDARD SERIES, circ. 9,687 217
[W] THE TRIBUNE & COURIER SERIES, circ. 10,000 [F] .. 265
[W] WEEKLY NEWS SERIES (COLCHESTER), circ. 59,962 [F] 270

Tollesbury
[W] MALDON & BURNHAM STANDARD SERIES, circ. 9,687 217

Waltham Abbey
[W] GUARDIAN AND INDEPENDENT SERIES, circ. 22,432 193
[W] THE HERTS AND LEA VALLEY STAR, circ. 52,060 [F] 199
[D] LONDON EVENING STANDARD, circ. 263,312 214
[W] MERCURY SERIES (HODDESDON), circ. 10,921 220

Weeley
[D] DAILY GAZETTE, circ. 22,131 170
[D] EA WEEK 176
[D] EAST ANGLIAN DAILY TIMES, circ. 34,392 176
[W] GAZETTE AND STANDARD SERIES (EAST ESSEX), circ. 22,625 189

West Bergholt
[D] DAILY GAZETTE, circ. 22,131 170
[D] EA WEEK 176
[D] EAST ANGLIAN DAILY TIMES, circ. 34,392 176
[W] YELLOW ADVERTISER GROUP SERIES (ESSEX), circ. 434,612 [F] 278

West Mersea
[D] DAILY GAZETTE, circ. 22,131 170
[W] THE TRIBUNE & COURIER SERIES, circ. 10,000 [F] .. 265
[W] WEEKLY NEWS SERIES (COLCHESTER), circ. 59,962 [F] 270

Westcliff-on-Sea
[W] ESSEX ENQUIRER SERIES, circ. 57,859 [F] 180

Wickford
[W] BRENTWOOD GAZETTE SERIES, circ. 14,679 151

[W] **Local/Weekly Newspapers** [D] **Regional Daily Newspapers** [S] **Regional Sunday Newspapers** [F] **Free Newspapers**

Non-Nationals - England

Title (Day/am/pm)	Circ.	Page No.

[D] ECHO (BASILDON), circ. 34,844 178
[W] ESSEX CHRONICLE SERIES, circ. 35,461 180
[W] ESSEX ENQUIRER SERIES, circ. 57,859 [F] 180
[W] LEIGH TIMES SERIES, circ. 67,000 211
[D] LONDON EVENING STANDARD, circ. 263,312 214
[W] SOUTHEND STANDARD SERIES, circ. 204,783 [F] ... 252

Wickham Bishops
[W] BRAINTREE & WITHAM TIMES & GAZETTE SERIES, circ. 39,857 151
[D] DAILY GAZETTE, circ. 22,131 170
[D] EA WEEK 176
[D] EAST ANGLIAN DAILY TIMES, circ. 34,392 176
[W] ESSEX CHRONICLE SERIES, circ. 35,461 180
[D] LONDON EVENING STANDARD, circ. 263,312 214

Witham
[W] BRAINTREE & WITHAM TIMES & GAZETTE SERIES, circ. 39,857 151
[D] DAILY GAZETTE, circ. 22,131 170
[W] ESSEX CHRONICLE SERIES, circ. 35,461 180
[D] LONDON EVENING STANDARD, circ. 263,312 214
[W] YELLOW ADVERTISER GROUP SERIES (ESSEX), circ. 434,612 [F] 278

Wivenhoe
[W] ESSEX COUNTY STANDARD, circ. 20,316 180
[W] WEEKLY NEWS SERIES (COLCHESTER), circ. 59,962 [F] 270

Writtle
[D] EA WEEK 176
[D] EAST ANGLIAN DAILY TIMES, circ. 34,392 176
[W] ESSEX CHRONICLE SERIES, circ. 35,461 180
[D] LONDON EVENING STANDARD, circ. 263,312 214
[W] WEEKLY NEWS SERIES (CHELMSFORD), circ. 59,949 [F] 269
[W] YELLOW ADVERTISER GROUP SERIES (ESSEX), circ. 434,612 [F] 278

Gloucestershire
[D] THE CITIZEN (GLOUCESTER), circ. 26,259 162
[W] GUARDIAN SERIES (WILTSHIRE, HAMPSHIRE AND SURREY), circ. 175,000 [F] 193

Ashchurch
[W] EVESHAM OBSERVER SERIES, circ. 35,917 182
[W] GLOUCESTER AND CHELTENHAM NEWS SERIES, circ. 57,197 [F] 191
[D] GLOUCESTERSHIRE ECHO, circ. 21,074 191
[S] SUNDAY MERCURY (BIRMINGHAM), circ. 59,339 258
[D] WESTERN DAILY PRESS BRISTOL, circ. 41,639 272

Bishop's Cleeve
[W] GLOUCESTER AND CHELTENHAM NEWS SERIES, circ. 57,197 [F] 191

Bourton-on-the-Water
[W] EVESHAM OBSERVER SERIES, circ. 35,917 182
[D] GLOUCESTERSHIRE ECHO, circ. 21,074 191
[W] WILTS & GLOUCESTERSHIRE STANDARD SERIES, circ. 14,652 275

Chalford
[W] STROUD NEWS AND JOURNAL, circ. 17,227 257

Charlton Kings
[W] GLOUCESTER AND CHELTENHAM NEWS SERIES, circ. 57,197 [F] 191
[D] GLOUCESTERSHIRE ECHO, circ. 21,074 191
[W] INDEPENDENT SERIES (GLOUCESTERSHIRE), circ. 47,848 [F] 202
[S] SUNDAY MERCURY (BIRMINGHAM), circ. 59,339 258
[D] WESTERN DAILY PRESS BRISTOL, circ. 41,639 272

Cheltenham
[W] GLOUCESTER AND CHELTENHAM NEWS SERIES, circ. 57,197 [F] 191
[D] GLOUCESTERSHIRE ECHO, circ. 21,074 191
[W] INDEPENDENT SERIES (GLOUCESTERSHIRE), circ. 47,848 [F] 202
[S] SUNDAY MERCURY (BIRMINGHAM), circ. 59,339 258
[D] WESTERN DAILY PRESS BRISTOL, circ. 41,639 272

Chipping Campden
[W] EVESHAM JOURNAL SERIES, circ. 32,275 182
[W] EVESHAM OBSERVER SERIES, circ. 35,917 182
[D] GLOUCESTERSHIRE ECHO, circ. 21,074 191

Chipping Sodbury
[D] EVENING POST (BRISTOL), circ. 51,287 181
[W] GLOUCESTERSHIRE GAZETTE SERIES, circ. 15,614 191
[W] WESTERN DAILY PRESS BRISTOL, circ. 41,639 272

Churchdown
[W] GLOUCESTER AND CHELTENHAM NEWS SERIES, circ. 57,197 [F] 191
[D] GLOUCESTERSHIRE ECHO, circ. 21,074 191

[W] INDEPENDENT SERIES (GLOUCESTERSHIRE), circ. 47,848 [F] 202
[S] SUNDAY MERCURY (BIRMINGHAM), circ. 59,339 258
[D] WESTERN DAILY PRESS BRISTOL, circ. 41,639 272

Cinderford
[W] FOREST OF DEAN AND WYE VALLEY REVIEW, circ. 43,124 [F] 186
[W] THE FORESTER (FOREST OF DEAN), circ. 13,000 186

Cirencester
[D] GLOUCESTERSHIRE ECHO, circ. 21,074 191
[W] INDEPENDENT SERIES (GLOUCESTERSHIRE), circ. 47,848 [F] 202
[S] SUNDAY MERCURY (BIRMINGHAM), circ. 59,339 258
[S] SWINDON ADVERTISER, circ. 22,469 261
[W] WESTERN DAILY PRESS BRISTOL, circ. 41,639 272
[W] WILTS & GLOUCESTERSHIRE STANDARD SERIES, circ. 14,652 275

Coleford
[W] FOREST OF DEAN AND WYE VALLEY REVIEW, circ. 43,124 [F] 186
[W] THE FORESTER (FOREST OF DEAN), circ. 13,000 186
[S] SUNDAY MERCURY (BIRMINGHAM), circ. 59,339 258

Dursley
[W] INDEPENDENT SERIES (GLOUCESTERSHIRE), circ. 47,848 [F] 202
[W] STROUD LIFE 257
[S] SUNDAY MERCURY (BIRMINGHAM), circ. 59,339 258
[D] WESTERN DAILY PRESS BRISTOL, circ. 41,639 272

Fairford
[D] GLOUCESTERSHIRE ECHO, circ. 21,074 191
[S] SUNDAY MERCURY (BIRMINGHAM), circ. 59,339 258
[S] SWINDON ADVERTISER, circ. 22,469 261
[W] WILTS & GLOUCESTERSHIRE STANDARD SERIES, circ. 14,652 275

Frampton Cotterell
[D] EVENING POST (BRISTOL), circ. 51,287 181
[W] GLOUCESTERSHIRE GAZETTE SERIES, circ. 15,614 191
[D] WESTERN DAILY PRESS BRISTOL, circ. 41,639 272

Gloucester
[W] GLOUCESTER AND CHELTENHAM NEWS SERIES, circ. 57,197 [F] 191
[W] INDEPENDENT SERIES (GLOUCESTERSHIRE), circ. 47,848 [F] 202
[S] SUNDAY MERCURY (BIRMINGHAM), circ. 59,339 258
[D] WESTERN DAILY PRESS BRISTOL, circ. 41,639 272

Innsworth
[W] GLOUCESTER AND CHELTENHAM NEWS SERIES, circ. 57,197 [F] 191
[W] INDEPENDENT SERIES (GLOUCESTERSHIRE), circ. 47,848 [F] 202
[S] SUNDAY MERCURY (BIRMINGHAM), circ. 59,339 258
[D] WESTERN DAILY PRESS BRISTOL, circ. 41,639 272

Lechlade
[D] SWINDON ADVERTISER, circ. 22,469 261
[W] WESTERN DAILY PRESS BRISTOL, circ. 41,639 272
[W] WILTS & GLOUCESTERSHIRE STANDARD SERIES, circ. 14,652 275

Lydney
[W] FOREST OF DEAN AND WYE VALLEY REVIEW, circ. 43,124 [F] 186
[W] THE FORESTER (FOREST OF DEAN), circ. 13,000 186

Mangotsfield
[W] BRISTOL OBSERVER SERIES, circ. 165,769 [F] 152
[D] EVENING POST (BRISTOL), circ. 51,287 181
[D] WESTERN DAILY PRESS BRISTOL, circ. 41,639 272

Minchinhampton
[W] STROUD NEWS AND JOURNAL, circ. 17,227 257

Moreton-in-Marsh
[W] EVESHAM JOURNAL SERIES, circ. 32,275 182
[W] EVESHAM OBSERVER SERIES, circ. 35,917 182
[D] GLOUCESTERSHIRE ECHO, circ. 21,074 191
[W] WILTS & GLOUCESTERSHIRE STANDARD SERIES, circ. 14,652 275

Nailsworth
[D] EVENING POST (BRISTOL), circ. 51,287 181
[W] INDEPENDENT SERIES (GLOUCESTERSHIRE), circ. 47,848 [F] 202
[W] STROUD LIFE 257
[W] STROUD NEWS AND JOURNAL, circ. 17,227 257
[D] WESTERN DAILY PRESS BRISTOL, circ. 41,639 272

Newent
[W] THE FORESTER (FOREST OF DEAN), circ. 13,000 186
[W] MALVERN GAZETTE & LEDBURY REPORTER SERIES, circ. 17,001 217

Northleach
[D] GLOUCESTERSHIRE ECHO, circ. 21,074 191
[W] WESTERN DAILY PRESS BRISTOL, circ. 41,639 272
[W] WILTS & GLOUCESTERSHIRE STANDARD SERIES, circ. 14,652 275

Painswick
[W] STROUD NEWS AND JOURNAL, circ. 17,227 257

Pucklechurch
[D] EVENING POST (BRISTOL), circ. 51,287 181
[D] WESTERN DAILY PRESS BRISTOL, circ. 41,639 272

Purton
[D] SWINDON ADVERTISER, circ. 22,469 261
[D] WESTERN DAILY PRESS BRISTOL, circ. 41,639 272
[W] WILTS & GLOUCESTERSHIRE STANDARD SERIES, circ. 14,652 275

South Cerney
[W] INDEPENDENT SERIES (GLOUCESTERSHIRE), circ. 47,848 [F] 202

Stonehouse
[W] INDEPENDENT SERIES (GLOUCESTERSHIRE), circ. 47,848 [F] 202
[W] STROUD NEWS AND JOURNAL, circ. 17,227 257

Stow-on-the-Wold
[W] EVESHAM JOURNAL SERIES, circ. 32,275 182
[W] EVESHAM OBSERVER SERIES, circ. 35,917 182
[D] GLOUCESTERSHIRE ECHO, circ. 21,074 191
[W] WILTS & GLOUCESTERSHIRE STANDARD SERIES, circ. 14,652 275

Stroud
[D] EVENING POST (BRISTOL), circ. 51,287 181
[W] GLOUCESTER AND CHELTENHAM NEWS SERIES, circ. 57,197 [F] 191
[D] GLOUCESTERSHIRE ECHO, circ. 21,074 191
[W] INDEPENDENT SERIES (GLOUCESTERSHIRE), circ. 47,848 [F] 202
[W] STROUD LIFE 257
[W] STROUD NEWS AND JOURNAL, circ. 17,227 257
[S] SUNDAY MERCURY (BIRMINGHAM), circ. 59,339 258
[W] WESTERN DAILY PRESS BRISTOL, circ. 41,639 272

Tetbury
[W] INDEPENDENT SERIES (GLOUCESTERSHIRE), circ. 47,848 [F] 202
[W] STROUD NEWS AND JOURNAL, circ. 17,227 257
[D] WESTERN DAILY PRESS BRISTOL, circ. 41,639 272
[W] WILTS & GLOUCESTERSHIRE STANDARD SERIES, circ. 14,652 275

Tewkesbury
[W] EVESHAM OBSERVER SERIES, circ. 35,917 182
[W] GLOUCESTER AND CHELTENHAM NEWS SERIES, circ. 57,197 [F] 191
[D] GLOUCESTERSHIRE ECHO, circ. 21,074 191
[W] MALVERN GAZETTE & LEDBURY REPORTER SERIES, circ. 17,001 217
[S] SUNDAY MERCURY (BIRMINGHAM), circ. 59,339 258
[D] WESTERN DAILY PRESS BRISTOL, circ. 41,639 272

Thornbury
[W] BRISTOL OBSERVER SERIES, circ. 165,769 [F] 152
[W] GLOUCESTERSHIRE GAZETTE SERIES, circ. 15,614 191

Winchcombe
[D] GLOUCESTERSHIRE ECHO, circ. 21,074 191

Winterbourne
[W] GLOUCESTERSHIRE GAZETTE SERIES, circ. 15,614 191

Wotton-under-Edge
[W] GLOUCESTERSHIRE GAZETTE SERIES, circ. 15,614 191
[W] INDEPENDENT SERIES (GLOUCESTERSHIRE), circ. 47,848 [F] 202

Yate
[W] BRISTOL OBSERVER SERIES, circ. 165,769 [F] 152
[W] GLOUCESTERSHIRE GAZETTE SERIES, circ. 15,614 191

Greater Manchester
[W] JOURNAL & ADVERTISER SERIES, circ. 30,000 [F] ... 205
[D] MANCHESTER EVENING NEWS, circ. 82,445 217
[W] TRAFFORD METRO NEWS, circ. 98,936 [F] 265

Abram
[D] LANCASHIRE EVENING POST, circ. 31,225 208

Altrincham
[W] SALE & ALTRINCHAM MESSENGER SERIES, circ. 72,335 [F] 243

Ashton-in-Makerfield
[D] LANCASHIRE EVENING POST, circ. 31,225 208

[W] Local/Weekly Newspapers   [D] Regional Daily Newspapers   [S] Regional Sunday Newspapers   [F] Free Newspapers

Title (Day/am/pm)	Circ.	Page No.

W THE WIGAN OBSERVER, REPORTER AND NEWS SERIES, circ. 141,632 274

Ashton-under-Lyne
W ADVERTISER SERIES (ASHTON), circ. 104,047 F 139
W ASHTON-UNDER-LYNE REPORTER SERIES, circ. 25,000 143

Aspull
D LANCASHIRE EVENING POST, circ. 31,225 208
W THE WIGAN OBSERVER, REPORTER AND NEWS SERIES, circ. 141,632 274

Atherton
D THE BOLTON NEWS, circ. 29,552 150
W LEIGH REPORTER, circ. 61,041 F 211
W LEIGH, TYLDESLEY AND ATHERTON JOURNAL, circ. 61,475 F 211

Audenshaw
W ADVERTISER SERIES (ASHTON), circ. 104,047 F 139
W ASHTON-UNDER-LYNE REPORTER SERIES, circ. 25,000 143

Blackrod
W THE ADVERTISER (HORWICH, WESTHOUGHTON & DISTRICT), circ. 36,000 F 139
W BOLTON JOURNAL, circ. 59,893 F 149

Bolton
W THE ADVERTISER (HORWICH, WESTHOUGHTON & DISTRICT), circ. 36,000 F 139
W BOLTON JOURNAL, circ. 59,893 F 149
D THE BOLTON NEWS, circ. 29,552 150

Boothstown
W LEIGH REPORTER, circ. 61,041 F 211

Bowdon
W SALE & ALTRINCHAM MESSENGER SERIES, circ. 72,335 F 243

Bradshaw
W BOLTON JOURNAL, circ. 59,893 F 149
D THE BOLTON NEWS, circ. 29,552 150

Bramhall
W STOCKPORT EXPRESS AND TIMES SERIES, circ. 112,974 256

Bredbury
W STOCKPORT EXPRESS AND TIMES SERIES, circ. 112,974 256

Bromley Cross
W BOLTON JOURNAL, circ. 59,893 F 149
D THE BOLTON NEWS, circ. 29,552 150

Burnage
W SOUTH MANCHESTER REPORTER, circ. 49,449 F . 250
W STOCKPORT EXPRESS AND TIMES SERIES, circ. 112,974 256

Bury
D THE BOLTON NEWS, circ. 29,552 150
W BURY TIMES SERIES, circ. 69,393 155
D LANCASHIRE TELEGRAPH, circ. 32,716 209

Cadishead
W SALFORD ADVERTISER SERIES, circ. 123,190 F 243

Chadderton
W CHRONICLE WEEKEND OLDHAM, circ. 68,414 F 162
W MIDDLETON & NORTH MANCHESTER GUARDIAN & ADVERTISER SERIES, circ. 93,756 222
W THE OLDHAM ADVERTISER, circ. 86,749 F 233
D OLDHAM EVENING CHRONICLE, circ. 20,976 233

Cheadle
D MANCHESTER EVENING NEWS, circ. 82,445 217
W STOCKPORT EXPRESS AND TIMES SERIES, circ. 112,974 256

Cheetham Hill
W MIDDLETON & NORTH MANCHESTER GUARDIAN & ADVERTISER SERIES, circ. 93,756 222
W SALFORD ADVERTISER SERIES, circ. 123,190 F 243

Crumpsall
W MIDDLETON & NORTH MANCHESTER GUARDIAN & ADVERTISER SERIES, circ. 93,756 222
W SALFORD ADVERTISER SERIES, circ. 123,190 F 243

Delph
W THE OLDHAM ADVERTISER, circ. 86,749 F 233

Denton
W ADVERTISER SERIES (ASHTON), circ. 104,047 F 139
W ASHTON-UNDER-LYNE REPORTER SERIES, circ. 25,000 143

Didsbury
W SOUTH MANCHESTER REPORTER, circ. 49,449 F . 250
W STOCKPORT EXPRESS AND TIMES SERIES, circ. 112,974 256

Droylsden
W ADVERTISER SERIES (ASHTON), circ. 104,047 F 139
W ASHTON-UNDER-LYNE REPORTER SERIES, circ. 25,000 143

Dukinfield
W ADVERTISER SERIES (ASHTON), circ. 104,047 F 139
W ASHTON-UNDER-LYNE REPORTER SERIES, circ. 25,000 143

Eccles
W SALFORD ADVERTISER SERIES, circ. 123,190 F 243

Failsworth
W CHRONICLE WEEKEND OLDHAM, circ. 68,414 F 162
W THE OLDHAM ADVERTISER, circ. 86,749 233
D OLDHAM EVENING CHRONICLE, circ. 20,976 233

Fallowfield
W SOUTH MANCHESTER REPORTER, circ. 49,449 F . 250
W STOCKPORT EXPRESS AND TIMES SERIES, circ. 112,974 256

Farnworth
W BOLTON JOURNAL, circ. 59,893 F 149
D THE BOLTON NEWS, circ. 29,552 150

Golborne
W LEIGH REPORTER, circ. 61,041 F 211
W LEIGH, TYLDESLEY AND ATHERTON JOURNAL, circ. 61,475 F 211
W WARRINGTON GUARDIAN SERIES, circ. 111,077 269
W THE WIGAN OBSERVER, REPORTER AND NEWS SERIES, circ. 141,632 274

Gorton
W ASHTON-UNDER-LYNE REPORTER SERIES, circ. 25,000 143
W MIDDLETON & NORTH MANCHESTER GUARDIAN & ADVERTISER SERIES, circ. 93,756 222

Grasscroft
W THE OLDHAM ADVERTISER, circ. 86,749 F 233

Hale
W SALE & ALTRINCHAM MESSENGER SERIES, circ. 72,335 F 243

Hazel Grove
W STOCKPORT EXPRESS AND TIMES SERIES, circ. 112,974 256

Heywood
W HEYWOOD ADVERTISER, circ. 6,999 199
D MANCHESTER EVENING NEWS, circ. 82,445 217

Hindley
D THE BOLTON NEWS, circ. 29,552 150
D LANCASHIRE EVENING POST, circ. 31,225 208
W LEIGH, TYLDESLEY AND ATHERTON JOURNAL, circ. 61,475 F 211

Horwich
W THE ADVERTISER (HORWICH, WESTHOUGHTON & DISTRICT), circ. 36,000 F 139
W BOLTON JOURNAL, circ. 59,893 F 149
D THE BOLTON NEWS, circ. 29,552 150

Hyde
W ADVERTISER SERIES (ASHTON), circ. 104,047 F 139
W ASHTON-UNDER-LYNE REPORTER SERIES, circ. 25,000 143

Ince-in-Makerfield
D LANCASHIRE EVENING POST, circ. 31,225 208
W THE WIGAN OBSERVER, REPORTER AND NEWS SERIES, circ. 141,632 274

Irlam
W SALFORD ADVERTISER SERIES, circ. 123,190 F 243

Leigh
D THE BOLTON NEWS, circ. 29,552 150
D LANCASHIRE TELEGRAPH, circ. 32,716 209
W LEIGH REPORTER, circ. 61,041 F 211
W LEIGH, TYLDESLEY AND ATHERTON JOURNAL, circ. 61,475 F 211
D MANCHESTER EVENING NEWS, circ. 82,445 217

Levenshulme
W MIDDLETON & NORTH MANCHESTER GUARDIAN & ADVERTISER SERIES, circ. 93,756 222
W SOUTH MANCHESTER REPORTER, circ. 49,449 F . 250

Little Lever
W BOLTON JOURNAL, circ. 59,893 F 149
D THE BOLTON NEWS, circ. 29,552 150

Littleborough
W ROCHDALE OBSERVER SERIES, circ. 40,000 240

Longdendale
W ADVERTISER SERIES (ASHTON), circ. 104,047 F 139

Manchester
W ADVERTISER (NORTH EAST MANCHESTER), circ. 86,500 F 139

Middleton
W MIDDLETON & NORTH MANCHESTER GUARDIAN & ADVERTISER SERIES, circ. 93,756 222

Milnrow
W ROCHDALE OBSERVER SERIES, circ. 40,000 240

Mossley
W ADVERTISER SERIES (ASHTON), circ. 104,047 F 139
W ASHTON-UNDER-LYNE REPORTER SERIES, circ. 25,000 143
W CHRONICLE WEEKEND OLDHAM, circ. 68,414 F 162
D OLDHAM EVENING CHRONICLE, circ. 20,976 233

Moston
W MIDDLETON & NORTH MANCHESTER GUARDIAN & ADVERTISER SERIES, circ. 93,756 222

Oldham
W CHRONICLE WEEKEND OLDHAM, circ. 68,414 F 162
W THE OLDHAM ADVERTISER, circ. 86,749 F 233
D OLDHAM EVENING CHRONICLE, circ. 20,976 233

Partington
W SALE & ALTRINCHAM MESSENGER SERIES, circ. 72,335 F 243

Pendlebury
W SALFORD ADVERTISER SERIES, circ. 123,190 F 243

Prestwich
W BURY TIMES SERIES, circ. 69,393 155
W SALFORD ADVERTISER SERIES, circ. 123,190 F 243

Radcliffe
D THE BOLTON NEWS, circ. 29,552 150
W BURY TIMES SERIES, circ. 69,393 155
W SALFORD ADVERTISER SERIES, circ. 123,190 F 243

Ramsbottom
W BURY TIMES SERIES, circ. 69,393 155
W ROSSENDALE FREE PRESS, circ. 14,288 241

Rochdale
D MANCHESTER EVENING NEWS, circ. 82,445 217
W ROCHDALE OBSERVER SERIES, circ. 40,000 240

Romiley
W STOCKPORT EXPRESS AND TIMES SERIES, circ. 112,974 256

Royton
W CHRONICLE WEEKEND OLDHAM, circ. 68,414 F 162
W THE OLDHAM ADVERTISER, circ. 86,749 F 233
D OLDHAM EVENING CHRONICLE, circ. 20,976 233
W ROCHDALE OBSERVER SERIES, circ. 40,000 240

Saddleworth
W ADVERTISER SERIES (ASHTON), circ. 104,047 F 139
W ASHTON-UNDER-LYNE REPORTER SERIES, circ. 25,000 143
W CHRONICLE WEEKEND OLDHAM, circ. 68,414 F 162
W THE OLDHAM ADVERTISER, circ. 86,749 F 233
D OLDHAM EVENING CHRONICLE, circ. 20,976 233

Sale
D MANCHESTER EVENING NEWS, circ. 82,445 217
W SALE & ALTRINCHAM MESSENGER SERIES, circ. 72,335 F 243

Salford
W SALFORD ADVERTISER SERIES, circ. 123,190 F 243

Shaw
W CHRONICLE WEEKEND OLDHAM, circ. 68,414 F 162
W THE OLDHAM ADVERTISER, circ. 86,749 F 233
W ROCHDALE OBSERVER SERIES, circ. 40,000 240

Shevington
D LANCASHIRE EVENING POST, circ. 31,225 208
W THE WIGAN OBSERVER, REPORTER AND NEWS SERIES, circ. 141,632 274

Stalybridge
W ADVERTISER SERIES (ASHTON), circ. 104,047 F 139

Section 3 Index to UK Newspapers

Non-Nationals - England

Title (Day/am/pm)	Circ.	Page No.
W ASHTON-UNDER-LYNE REPORTER SERIES, circ. 25,000		143

Standish
D LANCASHIRE EVENING POST, circ. 31,225		208
W THE WIGAN OBSERVER, REPORTER AND NEWS SERIES, circ. 141,632		274

Stockport
D MANCHESTER EVENING NEWS, circ. 82,445		217
D STOCKPORT CITIZEN, circ. 60,000 F		256
W STOCKPORT EXPRESS AND TIMES SERIES, circ. 112,974		256

Stretford
W SALE & ALTRINCHAM MESSENGER SERIES, circ. 72,335 F		243

Swinton
W SALFORD ADVERTISER SERIES, circ. 123,190 F		243

Tyldesley
D THE BOLTON NEWS, circ. 29,552		150
W LEIGH REPORTER, circ. 61,041 F		211
W LEIGH, TYLDESLEY AND ATHERTON JOURNAL, circ. 61,475 F		211

Uppermill
W THE OLDHAM ADVERTISER, circ. 86,749 F		233

Urmston
W SALE & ALTRINCHAM MESSENGER SERIES, circ. 72,335 F		243

Walkden
D THE BOLTON NEWS, circ. 29,552		150
W SALFORD ADVERTISER SERIES, circ. 123,190 F		243

Westhoughton
W THE ADVERTISER (HORWICH, WESTHOUGHTON & DISTRICT), circ. 36,000 F		139
W BOLTON JOURNAL, circ. 59,893 F		149
D THE BOLTON NEWS, circ. 29,552		150
W LEIGH REPORTER, circ. 61,041 F		211

Whitefield
W BURY TIMES SERIES, circ. 69,393		155
W SALFORD ADVERTISER SERIES, circ. 123,190 F		243

Wigan
W THE ADVERTISER (HORWICH, WESTHOUGHTON & DISTRICT), circ. 36,000 F		139
D LANCASHIRE EVENING POST, circ. 31,225		208
W LEIGH, TYLDESLEY AND ATHERTON JOURNAL, circ. 61,475 F		211
W WIGAN EVENING POST, circ. 9,075		274
W THE WIGAN OBSERVER, REPORTER AND NEWS SERIES, circ. 141,632		274

Withington
W SOUTH MANCHESTER REPORTER, circ. 49,449 F		250
W STOCKPORT EXPRESS AND TIMES SERIES, circ. 112,974		256

Worsley
D THE BOLTON NEWS, circ. 29,552		150
W SALFORD ADVERTISER SERIES, circ. 123,190 F		243

Wythenshawe
W WYTHENSHAWE WORLD, circ. 29,000 F		278

Greenwich Borough

Eltham
W BEXLEY CHRONICLE SERIES, circ. 40,000 F		148
W NEWS SHOPPER SERIES, circ. 308,920 F		228
W TIMES AND REPORTER SERIES (KENT), circ. 154,146		263

Greenwich
W BEXLEY CHRONICLE SERIES, circ. 40,000 F		148
W THE DOCKLANDS AND PENINSULA SERIES, circ. 31,500 F		173
W THE MERCURY AND POST SERIES, circ. 166,029 F		219
W NEWS SHOPPER SERIES, circ. 308,920 F		228
W TIMES AND REPORTER SERIES (KENT), circ. 154,146		263

Woolwich
W NEWS SHOPPER SERIES, circ. 308,920 F		228

Hackney Borough

Hackney
W HACKNEY GAZETTE, circ. 10,331		194

Shoreditch
W EAST LONDON ADVERTISER, circ. 9,204		177

W HACKNEY GAZETTE, circ. 10,331		194

Stamford Hill
W HACKNEY GAZETTE, circ. 10,331		194

Stoke Newington
W GREATER LONDON CHRONICLE, circ. 5,000 F		193
W HACKNEY GAZETTE, circ. 10,331		194
W ISLINGTON GAZETTE & JOURNAL SERIES, circ. 52,062		204

Hammersmith Borough

Fulham
W THE GAZETTE AND LEADER SERIES, circ. 88,667		189
W LONDON NEWSPAPER GROUP SERIES, circ. 69,601		214
W NORTH WEST LONDON NEWSPAPER SERIES, circ. 54,733		230

Hammersmith
W THE GAZETTE AND LEADER SERIES, circ. 88,667		189
W GREATER LONDON CHRONICLE, circ. 5,000 F		193
W LONDON NEWSPAPER GROUP SERIES, circ. 69,601		214
W NORTH WEST LONDON NEWSPAPER SERIES, circ. 54,733		230
W TIMES SERIES (RICHMOND), circ. 152,627		264

Shepherds Bush
W THE GAZETTE AND LEADER SERIES, circ. 88,667		189

Hampshire
W GUARDIAN SERIES (WILTSHIRE, HAMPSHIRE AND SURREY), circ. 175,000 F		193
W THE MEON VALLEY NEWS, circ. 52,500 F		219
W SOUTHERN COUNTIES TELEGRAPH, circ. 45,000 F		252

Aldershot
W ALDERSHOT MAIL AND NEWS SERIES, circ. 131,660		140
W ALTON POST GAZETTE, TIMES & MAIL SERIES, circ. 30,000		141

Alresford
W ALTON POST GAZETTE, TIMES & MAIL SERIES, circ. 30,000		141
W FARNHAM HERALD SERIES, circ. 31,000		184
W HAMPSHIRE CHRONICLE SERIES, circ. 16,122		195

Alton
W ALTON POST GAZETTE, TIMES & MAIL SERIES, circ. 30,000		141
W FARNHAM HERALD SERIES, circ. 31,000		184
W HAMPSHIRE CHRONICLE SERIES, circ. 16,122		195

Andover
W ANDOVER ADVERTISER SERIES, circ. 39,707		141
W HAMPSHIRE CHRONICLE SERIES, circ. 16,122		195
W THE INDEPENDENT OBSERVER SERIES, circ. 14,000 F		202
W SALISBURY JOURNAL & AVON ADVERTISER SERIES, circ. 99,503		243

Ashurst
D THE SOUTHERN DAILY ECHO (SOUTHAMPTON), circ. 39,174		252

Barton-on-Sea
W ADVERTISER & TIMES SERIES, circ. 21,421		138
D DAILY ECHO (BOURNEMOUTH), circ. 32,441		170
W NEW FOREST POST INCORPORATING FOREST & WATERSIDE OBSERVER, circ. 46,546 F		225
D THE SOUTHERN DAILY ECHO (SOUTHAMPTON), circ. 39,174		252

Basingstoke
W BASINGSTOKE AND NORTH HANTS GAZETTE SERIES, circ. 77,769		146
W BASINGSTOKE OBSERVER, circ. 24,000 F		146
W THE INDEPENDENT OBSERVER SERIES, circ. 14,000 F		202

Beaulieu
W ADVERTISER & TIMES SERIES, circ. 21,421		138
W NEW FOREST POST INCORPORATING FOREST & WATERSIDE OBSERVER, circ. 46,546 F		225
D THE SOUTHERN DAILY ECHO (SOUTHAMPTON), circ. 39,174		252

Bishop's Waltham
W THE INDEPENDENT OBSERVER SERIES, circ. 14,000 F		202
W THE NEWS EXTRA AND ADVERTISER SERIES, circ. 143,103 F		227
D THE NEWS (PORTSMOUTH), circ. 65,000		228

D THE SOUTHERN DAILY ECHO (SOUTHAMPTON), circ. 39,174		252

Bordon
W ALTON POST GAZETTE, TIMES & MAIL SERIES, circ. 30,000		141
W FARNHAM HERALD SERIES, circ. 31,000		184
W THE MESSENGER, circ. 40,348 F		220
W PETERSFIELD POST SERIES, circ. 8,218		236

Bransgore
W NEW FOREST POST INCORPORATING FOREST & WATERSIDE OBSERVER, circ. 46,546 F		225

Brockenhurst
W ADVERTISER & TIMES SERIES, circ. 21,421		138
D DAILY ECHO (BOURNEMOUTH), circ. 32,441		170
W NEW FOREST POST INCORPORATING FOREST & WATERSIDE OBSERVER, circ. 46,546 F		225

Brook
W THE NEWS EXTRA AND ADVERTISER SERIES, circ. 143,103 F		227

Burley
W NEW FOREST POST INCORPORATING FOREST & WATERSIDE OBSERVER, circ. 46,546 F		225

Bursledon
W THE NEWS EXTRA AND ADVERTISER SERIES, circ. 143,103 F		227

Colden Common
W HAMPSHIRE CHRONICLE SERIES, circ. 16,122		195
D THE SOUTHERN DAILY ECHO (SOUTHAMPTON), circ. 39,174		252

Denmead
W JOURNAL SERIES PORTSMOUTH, circ. 136,795 F		205
D THE NEWS (PORTSMOUTH), circ. 65,000		228

Eastleigh
W HAMPSHIRE CHRONICLE SERIES, circ. 16,122		195
W THE NEWS EXTRA AND ADVERTISER SERIES, circ. 143,103 F		227
D THE NEWS (PORTSMOUTH), circ. 65,000		228
D THE SOUTHERN DAILY ECHO (SOUTHAMPTON), circ. 39,174		252

Emsworth
W EMS VALLEY GAZETTE, circ. 4,700 F		179
W JOURNAL SERIES PORTSMOUTH, circ. 136,795 F		205
D THE NEWS (PORTSMOUTH), circ. 65,000		228
W SOUTHDOWN OBSERVER SERIES, circ. 35,161		251

Fareham
W JOURNAL SERIES PORTSMOUTH, circ. 136,795 F		205
W THE NEWS EXTRA AND ADVERTISER SERIES, circ. 143,103 F		227
D THE NEWS (PORTSMOUTH), circ. 65,000		228
D THE SOUTHERN DAILY ECHO (SOUTHAMPTON), circ. 39,174		252

Farnborough
W ALDERSHOT MAIL AND NEWS SERIES, circ. 131,660		140

Fawley
W NEW FOREST POST INCORPORATING FOREST & WATERSIDE OBSERVER, circ. 46,546 F		225
D THE SOUTHERN DAILY ECHO (SOUTHAMPTON), circ. 39,174		252

Fleet
W ALDERSHOT MAIL AND NEWS SERIES, circ. 131,660		140

Fordingbridge
D DAILY ECHO (BOURNEMOUTH), circ. 32,441		170
W SALISBURY JOURNAL & AVON ADVERTISER SERIES, circ. 99,503		243

Four Marks
W ALTON POST GAZETTE, TIMES & MAIL SERIES, circ. 30,000		141
W FARNHAM HERALD SERIES, circ. 31,000		184
W HAMPSHIRE CHRONICLE SERIES, circ. 16,122		195
D THE SOUTHERN DAILY ECHO (SOUTHAMPTON), circ. 39,174		252

Frogmore
W ALDERSHOT MAIL AND NEWS SERIES, circ. 131,660		140

Gosport
W JOURNAL SERIES PORTSMOUTH, circ. 136,795 F		205
W THE NEWS EXTRA AND ADVERTISER SERIES, circ. 143,103 F		227
D THE NEWS (PORTSMOUTH), circ. 65,000		228

W Local/Weekly Newspapers   D Regional Daily Newspapers   S Regional Sunday Newspapers   F Free Newspapers

Title (Day/am/pm)	Circ.	Page No.	Title (Day/am/pm)	Circ.	Page No.	Title (Day/am/pm)	Circ.	Page No.

Hamble
[W] THE NEWS EXTRA AND ADVERTISER SERIES, circ. 143,103 [F] 227
[D] THE SOUTHERN DAILY ECHO (SOUTHAMPTON), circ. 39,174 252

Hartley Wintney
[W] BASINGSTOKE AND NORTH HANTS GAZETTE SERIES, circ. 77,769 146

Havant
[W] JOURNAL SERIES PORTSMOUTH, circ. 136,795 [F] . 205
[D] THE NEWS (PORTSMOUTH), circ. 65,000 228

Hayling Island
[W] HAYLING ISLANDER, circ. 11,350 [F] 196
[D] THE NEWS (PORTSMOUTH), circ. 65,000 228

Headley
[W] ALTON POST GAZETTE, TIMES & MAIL SERIES, circ. 30,000 141
[W] FARNHAM HERALD SERIES, circ. 31,000 [F] 184
[W] THE MESSENGER, circ. 40,348 [F] 220
[D] THE NEWS (PORTSMOUTH), circ. 65,000 228
[W] PETERSFIELD POST SERIES, circ. 8,218 236

Hedge End
[W] HAMPSHIRE CHRONICLE SERIES, circ. 16,122 195
[W] THE NEWS EXTRA AND ADVERTISER SERIES, circ. 143,103 [F] 227
[D] THE SOUTHERN DAILY ECHO (SOUTHAMPTON), circ. 39,174 252

Hook
[W] BASINGSTOKE AND NORTH HANTS GAZETTE SERIES, circ. 77,769 146
[W] SURREY COMET, circ. 10,182 260

Horndean
[W] JOURNAL SERIES PORTSMOUTH, circ. 136,795 [F] . 205
[W] PETERSFIELD POST SERIES, circ. 8,218 236

Hythe
[W] ADVERTISER & TIMES SERIES, circ. 21,421 138
[W] NEW FOREST POST INCORPORATING FOREST & WATERSIDE OBSERVER, circ. 46,546 [F] 225
[D] THE SOUTHERN DAILY ECHO (SOUTHAMPTON), circ. 39,174 252

King's Worthy
[W] HAMPSHIRE CHRONICLE SERIES, circ. 16,122 195
[D] THE SOUTHERN DAILY ECHO (SOUTHAMPTON), circ. 39,174 252

Kingsclere
[D] THE SOUTHERN DAILY ECHO (SOUTHAMPTON), circ. 39,174 252

Lee-on-the-Solent
[W] JOURNAL SERIES PORTSMOUTH, circ. 136,795 [F] . 205
[D] THE NEWS (PORTSMOUTH), circ. 65,000 228
[D] THE SOUTHERN DAILY ECHO (SOUTHAMPTON), circ. 39,174 252

Liphook
[W] ALTON POST GAZETTE, TIMES & MAIL SERIES, circ. 30,000 141
[W] FARNHAM HERALD SERIES, circ. 31,000 184
[W] PETERSFIELD POST SERIES, circ. 8,218 236

Liss
[W] FARNHAM HERALD SERIES, circ. 31,000 184
[W] PETERSFIELD POST SERIES, circ. 8,218 236

Locks Heath
[W] JOURNAL SERIES PORTSMOUTH, circ. 136,795 [F] . 205

Lymington
[W] ADVERTISER & TIMES SERIES, circ. 21,421 138
[D] DAILY ECHO (BOURNEMOUTH), circ. 32,441 170
[W] NEW FOREST POST INCORPORATING FOREST & WATERSIDE OBSERVER, circ. 46,546 [F] 225
[D] THE SOUTHERN DAILY ECHO (SOUTHAMPTON), circ. 39,174 252

Lyndhurst
[W] ADVERTISER & TIMES SERIES, circ. 21,421 138
[W] NEW FOREST POST INCORPORATING FOREST & WATERSIDE OBSERVER, circ. 46,546 [F] 225
[D] THE SOUTHERN DAILY ECHO (SOUTHAMPTON), circ. 39,174 252

Marchwood
[D] THE SOUTHERN DAILY ECHO (SOUTHAMPTON), circ. 39,174 252

Medstead
[W] ALTON POST GAZETTE, TIMES & MAIL SERIES, circ. 30,000 141

Milford-on-Sea
[W] ADVERTISER & TIMES SERIES, circ. 21,421 138
[D] DAILY ECHO (BOURNEMOUTH), circ. 32,441 170
[W] NEW FOREST POST INCORPORATING FOREST & WATERSIDE OBSERVER, circ. 46,546 [F] 225
[D] THE SOUTHERN DAILY ECHO (SOUTHAMPTON), circ. 39,174 252

Netley
[W] THE NEWS EXTRA AND ADVERTISER SERIES, circ. 143,103 [F] 227
[D] THE SOUTHERN DAILY ECHO (SOUTHAMPTON), circ. 39,174 252

Netley Marsh
[W] THE NEWS EXTRA AND ADVERTISER SERIES, circ. 143,103 [F] 227
[D] THE SOUTHERN DAILY ECHO (SOUTHAMPTON), circ. 39,174 252

New Milton
[W] ADVERTISER & TIMES SERIES, circ. 21,421 138
[D] DAILY ECHO (BOURNEMOUTH), circ. 32,441 170
[W] NEW FOREST POST INCORPORATING FOREST & WATERSIDE OBSERVER, circ. 46,546 [F] 225
[D] THE SOUTHERN DAILY ECHO (SOUTHAMPTON), circ. 39,174 252

North Baddesley
[W] THE NEWS EXTRA AND ADVERTISER SERIES, circ. 143,103 [F] 227

Odiham
[W] BASINGSTOKE AND NORTH HANTS GAZETTE SERIES, circ. 77,769 146

Old Basing
[W] BASINGSTOKE AND NORTH HANTS GAZETTE SERIES, circ. 77,769 146
[D] THE SOUTHERN DAILY ECHO (SOUTHAMPTON), circ. 39,174 252

Overton
[W] BASINGSTOKE AND NORTH HANTS GAZETTE SERIES, circ. 77,769 146

Petersfield
[W] ALTON POST GAZETTE, TIMES & MAIL SERIES, circ. 30,000 141
[W] FARNHAM HERALD SERIES, circ. 31,000 184
[W] THE MESSENGER, circ. 40,348 [F] 220
[D] THE NEWS (PORTSMOUTH), circ. 65,000 228
[W] PETERSFIELD POST SERIES, circ. 8,218 236

Portsmouth
[W] JOURNAL SERIES PORTSMOUTH, circ. 136,795 [F] . 205
[D] THE NEWS (PORTSMOUTH), circ. 65,000 228

Ringwood
[W] ADVERTISER & TIMES SERIES, circ. 21,421 138
[D] DAILY ECHO (BOURNEMOUTH), circ. 32,441 170
[W] SALISBURY JOURNAL & AVON ADVERTISER SERIES, circ. 99,503 243

Romsey
[W] HAMPSHIRE CHRONICLE SERIES, circ. 16,122 195
[W] THE INDEPENDENT OBSERVER SERIES, circ. 14,000 [F] 202
[D] THE SOUTHERN DAILY ECHO (SOUTHAMPTON), circ. 39,174 252

Southampton
[W] HAMPSHIRE CHRONICLE SERIES, circ. 16,122 195
[W] THE NEWS EXTRA AND ADVERTISER SERIES, circ. 143,103 [F] 227
[D] THE SOUTHERN DAILY ECHO (SOUTHAMPTON), circ. 39,174 252

Southbourne
[D] THE ARGUS, circ. 32,788 142
[D] THE NEWS (PORTSMOUTH), circ. 65,000 228
[W] SOUTHDOWN OBSERVER SERIES, circ. 35,161 251

Southsea
[W] JOURNAL SERIES PORTSMOUTH, circ. 136,795 [F] . 205

Stockbridge
[W] THE INDEPENDENT OBSERVER SERIES, circ. 14,000 [F] 202
[D] THE SOUTHERN DAILY ECHO (SOUTHAMPTON), circ. 39,174 252

Stubbington
[W] JOURNAL SERIES PORTSMOUTH, circ. 136,795 [F] . 205

(Hamble continued - right column top)
[W] THE NEWS EXTRA AND ADVERTISER SERIES, circ. 143,103 [F] 227
[D] THE NEWS (PORTSMOUTH), circ. 65,000 228
[D] THE SOUTHERN DAILY ECHO (SOUTHAMPTON), circ. 39,174 252

Sway
[W] NEW FOREST POST INCORPORATING FOREST & WATERSIDE OBSERVER, circ. 46,546 [F] 225

Tadley
[W] BASINGSTOKE AND NORTH HANTS GAZETTE SERIES, circ. 77,769 146
[W] NEWBURY WEEKLY NEWS SERIES, circ. 63,367 226
[W] READING CHRONICLE SERIES, circ. 105,389 239

Totton
[W] NEW FOREST POST INCORPORATING FOREST & WATERSIDE OBSERVER, circ. 46,546 [F] 225
[D] THE SOUTHERN DAILY ECHO (SOUTHAMPTON), circ. 39,174 252

Twyford
[D] THE SOUTHERN DAILY ECHO (SOUTHAMPTON), circ. 39,174 252

Waterlooville
[W] JOURNAL SERIES PORTSMOUTH, circ. 136,795 [F] . 205
[D] THE NEWS (PORTSMOUTH), circ. 65,000 228

West End
[W] HAMPSHIRE CHRONICLE SERIES, circ. 16,122 195
[W] THE NEWS EXTRA AND ADVERTISER SERIES, circ. 143,103 [F] 227
[D] THE SOUTHERN DAILY ECHO (SOUTHAMPTON), circ. 39,174 252

Whitchurch
[W] ANDOVER ADVERTISER SERIES, circ. 39,707 141
[W] BASINGSTOKE AND NORTH HANTS GAZETTE SERIES, circ. 77,769 146
[D] THE SOUTHERN DAILY ECHO (SOUTHAMPTON), circ. 39,174 252

Winchester
[W] ALTON POST GAZETTE, TIMES & MAIL SERIES, circ. 30,000 141
[W] HAMPSHIRE CHRONICLE SERIES, circ. 16,122 195
[W] THE INDEPENDENT OBSERVER SERIES, circ. 14,000 [F] 202
[D] THE NEWS (PORTSMOUTH), circ. 65,000 228
[D] THE SOUTHERN DAILY ECHO (SOUTHAMPTON), circ. 39,174 252

Yateley
[W] ALDERSHOT MAIL AND NEWS SERIES, circ. 131,660 140
[W] BRACKNELL FOREST & WOKINGHAM STANDARD SERIES, circ. 50,824 [F] 150

Haringey Borough

Crouch End
[W] AVENUES SERIES, circ. 142,000 [F] 143
[W] HENDON TIMES SERIES, circ. 116,302 [F] 197
[W] ISLINGTON GAZETTE & JOURNAL SERIES, circ. 52,062 204

Haringey
[W] ENFIELD INDEPENDENT, circ. 92,538 [F] 179
[W] GAZETTE, ADVERTISER AND PRESS NEWSPAPER SERIES, circ. 270,519 188
[W] HAM & HIGH SERIES, circ. 9,619 194
[W] HENDON TIMES SERIES, circ. 116,302 [F] 197
[W] ISLINGTON GAZETTE & JOURNAL SERIES, circ. 52,062 204

Highgate
[W] AVENUES SERIES, circ. 142,000 [F] 143
[W] HAM & HIGH SERIES, circ. 9,619 194
[W] ISLINGTON GAZETTE & JOURNAL SERIES, circ. 52,062 204

Hornsey
[W] ENFIELD INDEPENDENT, circ. 92,538 [F] 179
[W] HENDON TIMES SERIES, circ. 116,302 [F] 197
[W] ISLINGTON GAZETTE & JOURNAL SERIES, circ. 52,062 204

Muswell Hill
[W] AVENUES SERIES, circ. 142,000 [F] 143
[W] HENDON TIMES SERIES, circ. 116,302 [F] 197
[W] ISLINGTON GAZETTE & JOURNAL SERIES, circ. 52,062 204

Tottenham
[W] ENFIELD INDEPENDENT, circ. 92,538 [F] 179

[W] Local/Weekly Newspapers   [D] Regional Daily Newspapers   [S] Regional Sunday Newspapers   [F] Free Newspapers

Non-Nationals - England

Title (Day/am/pm)	Circ.	Page No.

W GAZETTE, ADVERTISER AND PRESS NEWSPAPER SERIES, circ. 270,519 188
W HENDON TIMES SERIES, circ. 116,302 [F] 197
W ISLINGTON GAZETTE & JOURNAL SERIES, circ. 52,062 204

Wood Green
W ENFIELD INDEPENDENT, circ. 92,538 [F] 179
W GAZETTE, ADVERTISER AND PRESS NEWSPAPER SERIES, circ. 270,519 188
W HENDON TIMES SERIES, circ. 116,302 [F] 197
W ISLINGTON GAZETTE & JOURNAL SERIES, circ. 52,062 204

Harrow Borough
W HARROW TIMES, circ. 70,992 [F] 195

Harrow
W HARROW OBSERVER & LEADER SERIES, circ. 116,846 195
W HENDON TIMES SERIES, circ. 116,302 [F] 197
W NORTH WEST LONDON NEWSPAPER SERIES, circ. 54,733 230
W SOUTH BUCKS AND BERKSHIRE NEWS SERIES, circ. 50,000 [F] 249

Harrow Weald
W HARROW OBSERVER & LEADER SERIES, circ. 116,846 195

Harrow on the Hill
W HARROW OBSERVER & LEADER SERIES, circ. 116,846 195

Pinner
W HARROW OBSERVER & LEADER SERIES, circ. 116,846 195

Stanmore
W HARROW OBSERVER & LEADER SERIES, circ. 116,846 195
W HENDON TIMES SERIES, circ. 116,302 [F] 197

Wealdstone
W HARROW OBSERVER & LEADER SERIES, circ. 116,846 195

Havering Borough
W ROMFORD AND HAVERING WEEKLY POST, circ. 68,181 [F] 241

Harold Hill
W BRENTWOOD GAZETTE SERIES, circ. 14,679 151
W ROMFORD RECORDER, circ. 28,302 241

Harold Wood
W BRENTWOOD GAZETTE SERIES, circ. 14,679 151
W ROMFORD RECORDER, circ. 28,302 241

Havering
W BRENTWOOD GAZETTE SERIES, circ. 14,679 151
W ESSEX ENQUIRER SERIES, circ. 57,859 [F] 180
W ROMFORD RECORDER, circ. 28,302 241

Havering atte Bower
W ROMFORD RECORDER, circ. 28,302 241

Hornchurch
W BRENTWOOD GAZETTE SERIES, circ. 14,679 151
W ESSEX ENQUIRER SERIES, circ. 57,859 [F] 180
W ROMFORD RECORDER, circ. 28,302 241
W YELLOW ADVERTISER GROUP SERIES (ESSEX), circ. 434,612 [F] 278

Rainham
W ESSEX ENQUIRER SERIES, circ. 57,859 [F] 180
W MEDWAY NEWS SERIES, circ. 135,720 219
W YELLOW ADVERTISER GROUP SERIES (ESSEX), circ. 434,612 [F] 278

Romford
W BRENTWOOD GAZETTE SERIES, circ. 14,679 151
W ESSEX ENQUIRER SERIES, circ. 57,859 [F] 180
W ROMFORD RECORDER, circ. 28,302 241
W YELLOW ADVERTISER GROUP SERIES (ESSEX), circ. 434,612 [F] 278

Upminster
W BRENTWOOD GAZETTE SERIES, circ. 14,679 151
W YELLOW ADVERTISER GROUP SERIES (ESSEX), circ. 434,612 [F] 278

Herefordshire
W ADMAG NEWSPAPERS SERIES, circ. 181,809 [F] 137
S SUNDAY MERCURY (BIRMINGHAM), circ. 59,339 258

Bromyard
W HEREFORD TIMES, circ. 39,876 198
W MALVERN GAZETTE & LEDBURY REPORTER SERIES, circ. 17,001 217
D WORCESTER NEWS, circ. 18,491 277

Hereford
W CHRONICLE & JOURNAL SERIES, circ. 87,901 161
W HEREFORD TIMES, circ. 39,876 198
D WESTERN DAILY PRESS BRISTOL, circ. 41,639 272
D WORCESTER NEWS, circ. 18,491 277

Ledbury
W HEREFORD TIMES, circ. 39,876 198
W MALVERN GAZETTE & LEDBURY REPORTER SERIES, circ. 17,001 217
D WESTERN DAILY PRESS BRISTOL, circ. 41,639 272
D WORCESTER NEWS, circ. 18,491 277

Leominster
W CHRONICLE & JOURNAL SERIES, circ. 87,901 161
W HEREFORD TIMES, circ. 39,876 198
W LUDLOW ADVERTISER SERIES, circ. 5,924 215
W WESTERN DAILY PRESS BRISTOL, circ. 41,639 272

Ross-on-Wye
W CHRONICLE & JOURNAL SERIES, circ. 87,901 161
W FOREST OF DEAN AND WYE VALLEY REVIEW, circ. 43,124 [F] 186
W THE FORESTER (FOREST OF DEAN), circ. 13,000 186
W HEREFORD TIMES, circ. 39,876 198
W THE ROSS GAZETTE, circ. 6,500 241
D WESTERN DAILY PRESS BRISTOL, circ. 41,639 272

Hertfordshire
W FOCUS SERIES, circ. 47,000 [F] 186
D LONDON EVENING STANDARD, circ. 263,312 214

Aldenham
W BOREHAMWOOD & ELSTREE TIMES, circ. 14,614 [F] 150

Baldock
D CAMBRIDGE NEWS, circ. 26,242 157
W THE COMET SERIES, circ. 85,226 164
W ROYSTON CROW, circ. 15,578 [F] 242

Barley
D CAMBRIDGE NEWS, circ. 26,242 157

Berkhamsted
W GAZETTE & HERALD EXPRESS SERIES (HEMEL HEMPSTEAD), circ. 62,882 188

Bishop's Stortford
W HARLOW HERALD, circ. 48,648 [F] 195
W HERTS & ESSEX OBSERVER SERIES, circ. 30,375 199

Borehamwood
W BOREHAMWOOD & ELSTREE TIMES, circ. 14,614 [F] 150
W HENDON TIMES SERIES, circ. 116,302 [F] 197

Bovingdon
W GAZETTE & HERALD EXPRESS SERIES (HEMEL HEMPSTEAD), circ. 62,882 188

Brookmans Park
W WELWYN & HATFIELD TIMES & HERALD SERIES, circ. 59,549 270

Broxbourne
W GAZETTE, ADVERTISER AND PRESS NEWSPAPER SERIES, circ. 270,519 188
W HERTFORDSHIRE MERCURY SERIES, circ. 26,720 .. 199
W THE HERTS AND LEA VALLEY STAR, circ. 52,060 [F] 199
W MERCURY SERIES (HODDESDON), circ. 10,921 220
W WELWYN & HATFIELD TIMES & HERALD SERIES, circ. 59,549 270

Buntingford
D CAMBRIDGE NEWS, circ. 26,242 157
W HERTFORDSHIRE MERCURY SERIES, circ. 26,720 .. 199
W ROYSTON CROW, circ. 15,578 [F] 242

Bushey
W AVENUES SERIES, circ. 142,000 [F] 143
W WATFORD OBSERVER SERIES, circ. 70,708 269

Cheshunt
W GAZETTE, ADVERTISER AND PRESS NEWSPAPER SERIES, circ. 270,519 188
W THE HERTS AND LEA VALLEY STAR, circ. 52,060 [F] 199
W MERCURY SERIES (HODDESDON), circ. 10,921 220
W WELWYN & HATFIELD TIMES & HERALD SERIES, circ. 59,549 270

Chorleywood
W AVENUES SERIES, circ. 142,000 [F] 143
W THE BUCKINGHAMSHIRE EXAMINER AND ADVERTISER SERIES, circ. 13,568 153
W REVIEW SERIES, circ. 67,666 [F] 240
W WATFORD OBSERVER SERIES, circ. 70,708 269

Codicote
W WELWYN & HATFIELD TIMES & HERALD SERIES, circ. 59,549 270

Cuffley
W GAZETTE, ADVERTISER AND PRESS NEWSPAPER SERIES, circ. 270,519 188
W MERCURY SERIES (HODDESDON), circ. 10,921 220
W WELWYN & HATFIELD TIMES & HERALD SERIES, circ. 59,549 [F] 270

Elstree
W BOREHAMWOOD & ELSTREE TIMES, circ. 14,614 [F] 150
W HENDON TIMES SERIES, circ. 116,302 [F] 197

Harmer Green
W REVIEW SERIES, circ. 67,666 [F] 240
W WELWYN & HATFIELD TIMES & HERALD SERIES, circ. 59,549 270

Harpenden
W FOCUS SERIES, circ. 47,000 [F] 186
W HERTS ADVERTISER, circ. 50,520 199
W REVIEW SERIES, circ. 67,666 [F] 240

Hatfield
W REVIEW SERIES, circ. 67,666 [F] 240
W WELWYN & HATFIELD TIMES & HERALD SERIES, circ. 59,549 270

Hemel Hempstead
W GAZETTE & HERALD EXPRESS SERIES (HEMEL HEMPSTEAD), circ. 62,882 188

Hertford
W HERTFORDSHIRE MERCURY SERIES, circ. 26,720 .. 199
W THE HERTS AND LEA VALLEY STAR, circ. 52,060 [F] 199
W WELWYN & HATFIELD TIMES & HERALD SERIES, circ. 59,549 270

Hitchin
W THE COMET SERIES, circ. 85,226 164

Hoddesdon
W HERTFORDSHIRE MERCURY SERIES, circ. 26,720 .. 199
W THE HERTS AND LEA VALLEY STAR, circ. 52,060 [F] 199
W MERCURY SERIES (HODDESDON), circ. 10,921 220

Kings Langley
W AVENUES SERIES, circ. 142,000 [F] 143
W GAZETTE & HERALD EXPRESS SERIES (HEMEL HEMPSTEAD), circ. 62,882 188
W WATFORD OBSERVER SERIES, circ. 70,708 269

Knebworth
W THE COMET SERIES, circ. 85,226 164
W WELWYN & HATFIELD TIMES & HERALD SERIES, circ. 59,549 270

Letchworth
W THE COMET SERIES, circ. 85,226 164

London Colney
W HERTS ADVERTISER, circ. 50,520 199

Markyate
W HERTS ADVERTISER, circ. 50,520 199
W REVIEW SERIES, circ. 67,666 [F] 240

Potters Bar
W GAZETTE, ADVERTISER AND PRESS NEWSPAPER SERIES, circ. 270,519 188
W HENDON TIMES SERIES, circ. 116,302 [F] 197
W WELWYN & HATFIELD TIMES & HERALD SERIES, circ. 59,549 270

Radlett
W BOREHAMWOOD & ELSTREE TIMES, circ. 14,614 [F] 150
W FOCUS SERIES, circ. 47,000 [F] 186
W HERTS ADVERTISER, circ. 50,520 199
W REVIEW SERIES, circ. 67,666 [F] 240

Redbourn
W HERTS ADVERTISER, circ. 50,520 199
W REVIEW SERIES, circ. 67,666 [F] 240

Rickmansworth
W AVENUES SERIES, circ. 142,000 [F] 143
W REVIEW SERIES, circ. 67,666 [F] 240

W Local/Weekly Newspapers   D Regional Daily Newspapers   S Regional Sunday Newspapers   [F] Free Newspapers

Title (Day/am/pm)	Circ.	Page No.

W SOUTH BUCKS AND BERKSHIRE NEWS SERIES, circ. 50,000 F 249
W WATFORD OBSERVER SERIES, circ. 70,708 269

Royston
D CAMBRIDGE NEWS, circ. 26,242 157
W CAMBRIDGE WEEKLY NEWS & CRIER SERIES, circ. 208,805 F 157
W HERTFORDSHIRE MERCURY SERIES, circ. 26,720 .. 199
W ROYSTON CROW, circ. 15,578 F 242

Sawbridgeworth
W HARLOW HERALD, circ. 48,648 F 195
W HARLOW STAR, circ. 38,743 195
W HERTS & ESSEX OBSERVER SERIES, circ. 30,375 199

Shenley
W BOREHAMWOOD & ELSTREE TIMES, circ. 14,614 F 150

South Oxhey
W WATFORD OBSERVER SERIES, circ. 70,708 269

St. Albans
W FOCUS SERIES, circ. 47,000 F 186
W HERTS ADVERTISER, circ. 50,520 199
W REVIEW SERIES, circ. 67,666 F 240

Stevenage
W THE COMET SERIES, circ. 85,226 164
W HERTFORDSHIRE MERCURY SERIES, circ. 26,720 .. 199

Tewin
W REVIEW SERIES, circ. 67,666 F 240
W WELWYN & HATFIELD TIMES & HERALD SERIES, circ. 59,549 270

Tring
W GAZETTE & HERALD EXPRESS SERIES (HEMEL HEMPSTEAD), circ. 62,882 188

Waltham Cross
W ENFIELD INDEPENDENT, circ. 92,538 F 179
W GAZETTE, ADVERTISER AND PRESS NEWSPAPER SERIES, circ. 270,519 188
W HENDON TIMES SERIES, circ. 116,302 F 197
W HERTFORDSHIRE MERCURY SERIES, circ. 26,720 .. 199
W THE HERTS AND LEA VALLEY STAR, circ. 52,060 F 199
W MERCURY SERIES (HODDESDON), circ. 10,921 220
W WELWYN & HATFIELD TIMES & HERALD SERIES, circ. 59,549 270

Ware
W HERTFORDSHIRE MERCURY SERIES, circ. 26,720 .. 199
W THE HERTS AND LEA VALLEY STAR, circ. 52,060 F 199
W WELWYN & HATFIELD TIMES & HERALD SERIES, circ. 59,549 270

Watford
W AVENUES SERIES, circ. 142,000 F 143
W REVIEW SERIES, circ. 67,666 F 240
W SOUTH BUCKS AND BERKSHIRE NEWS SERIES, circ. 50,000 F 249
W WATFORD OBSERVER SERIES, circ. 70,708 269

Welwyn
W WELWYN & HATFIELD TIMES & HERALD SERIES, circ. 59,549 270

Welwyn Garden City
W REVIEW SERIES, circ. 67,666 F 240
W WELWYN & HATFIELD TIMES & HERALD SERIES, circ. 59,549 270

Wheathampstead
W HERTS ADVERTISER, circ. 50,520 199
W REVIEW SERIES, circ. 67,666 F 240

Hillingdon Borough

Harefield
W UXBRIDGE GAZETTE SERIES, circ. 73,269 266

Harlington
W UXBRIDGE GAZETTE SERIES, circ. 73,269 266

Hayes
W UXBRIDGE GAZETTE SERIES, circ. 73,269 266

Heathrow
W SOUTH BUCKS AND BERKSHIRE NEWS SERIES, circ. 50,000 F 249

Hillingdon
W UXBRIDGE GAZETTE SERIES, circ. 73,269 266

Northwood
W UXBRIDGE GAZETTE SERIES, circ. 73,269 266

Ruislip
W SOUTH BUCKS AND BERKSHIRE NEWS SERIES, circ. 50,000 F 249
W UXBRIDGE GAZETTE SERIES, circ. 73,269 266

Uxbridge
W SOUTH BUCKS AND BERKSHIRE NEWS SERIES, circ. 50,000 F 249
W UXBRIDGE GAZETTE SERIES, circ. 73,269 266

West Drayton
W SOUTH BUCKS AND BERKSHIRE NEWS SERIES, circ. 50,000 F 249
W UXBRIDGE GAZETTE SERIES, circ. 73,269 266

Yiewsley
W SOUTH BUCKS AND BERKSHIRE NEWS SERIES, circ. 50,000 F 249

Hounslow Borough

Bedfont
W STAINES INFORMER SERIES, circ. 197,957 254
W TIMES SERIES (RICHMOND), circ. 152,627 264

Brentford
W HOUNSLOW CHRONICLE, circ. 60,000 201
W TIMES SERIES (RICHMOND), circ. 152,627 264

Chiswick
W HOUNSLOW CHRONICLE, circ. 60,000 201
W TIMES SERIES (RICHMOND), circ. 152,627 264

Cranford
W TIMES SERIES (RICHMOND), circ. 152,627 264

Feltham
W HOUNSLOW CHRONICLE, circ. 60,000 201
W STAINES INFORMER SERIES, circ. 197,957 254
W TIMES SERIES (RICHMOND), circ. 152,627 264

Hanworth
W INFORMER SERIES (KINGSTON), circ. 95,129 F 203
W STAINES INFORMER SERIES, circ. 197,957 254
W TIMES SERIES (RICHMOND), circ. 152,627 264

Heston
W TIMES SERIES (RICHMOND), circ. 152,627 264

Hounslow
W GUARDIAN & NEWS SERIES (SUTTON), circ. 315,438 193
W HOUNSLOW CHRONICLE, circ. 60,000 201
W SOUTH BUCKS AND BERKSHIRE NEWS SERIES, circ. 50,000 F 249
W TIMES SERIES (RICHMOND), circ. 152,627 264

Isleworth
W GREATER LONDON CHRONICLE, circ. 5,000 F 193
W TIMES SERIES (RICHMOND), circ. 152,627 264

Osterley
W TIMES SERIES (RICHMOND), circ. 152,627 264

Isle of Wight
W ISLE OF WIGHT COUNTY PRESS, circ. 38,492 204
W THE ISLE OF WIGHT GAZETTE F 204
D THE NEWS (PORTSMOUTH), circ. 65,000 228
D THE SOUTHERN DAILY ECHO (SOUTHAMPTON), circ. 39,174 252

Isles of Scilly

Hugh Town
D WESTERN MORNING NEWS, circ. 41,154 272

Islington Borough

Finsbury Park
W GREATER LONDON CHRONICLE, circ. 5,000 F 193
W ISLINGTON GAZETTE & JOURNAL SERIES, circ. 52,062 204

Highbury
W ISLINGTON GAZETTE & JOURNAL SERIES, circ. 52,062 204

Islington
W GREATER LONDON CHRONICLE, circ. 5,000 F 193
W HACKNEY GAZETTE, circ. 10,331 194
HAM HAM & HIGH SERIES, circ. 9,619 194
W ISLINGTON GAZETTE & JOURNAL SERIES, circ. 52,062 204

Tufnell Park
W AVENUES SERIES, circ. 142,000 F 143

Kensington & Chelsea Borough
W KENSINGTON AND CHELSEA TIMES, circ. 30,000 F 206

Chelsea
W NORTH WEST LONDON NEWSPAPER SERIES, circ. 54,733 230

Kensington
W LONDON NEWSPAPER GROUP SERIES, circ. 69,601 214
W NORTH WEST LONDON NEWSPAPER SERIES, circ. 54,733 230

Kent
W KENT ON SATURDAY, circ. 40,000 F 206
S KENT ON SUNDAY, circ. 2,370 F 207
D LONDON EVENING STANDARD, circ. 263,312 214
W SOUTHERN COUNTIES TELEGRAPH, circ. 45,000 F 252

Ashford
W ADSCENE, HERALD & EXPRESS SERIES (FOLKESTONE), circ. 108,975 138
W EXPRESS EXTRA SERIES KENT, circ. 79,557 183
W YOURKENT SERIES, circ. 120,000 F 279

Borough Green
W SEVENOAKS CHRONICLE SERIES, circ. 105,776 246

Broadstairs
W ISLE OF THANET GAZETTE SERIES, circ. 74,337 204

Canterbury
W ADSCENE (CANTERBURY), circ. 53,724 F 138
W CANTERBURY EXTRA SERIES, circ. 107,124 F 158
W KENTISH GAZETTE SERIES, circ. 25,591 207
W YOURKENT SERIES, circ. 120,000 F 279

Chatham
W KENT MESSENGER GROUP NEWSPAPERS, circ. 116,430 206
W MEDWAY MESSENGER AND EXTRA SERIES, circ. 120,252 218
W MEDWAY NEWS SERIES, circ. 135,720 219

Cliffe
W MEDWAY NEWS SERIES, circ. 135,720 219

Cliffe Woods
W MEDWAY NEWS SERIES, circ. 135,720 219

Cranbrook
W KENT & SUSSEX COURIER SERIES, circ. 110,491 206
W KENT MESSENGER GROUP NEWSPAPERS, circ. 116,430 206

Cuxton
W MEDWAY NEWS SERIES, circ. 135,720 219

Dartford
W DARTFORD MESSENGER, circ. 4,049 171
W GATEWAY NEWS, circ. 22,000 F 188
W GRAVESEND MESSENGER SERIES, circ. 40,890 192
W NEWS SHOPPER SERIES, circ. 308,920 F 228
W TIMES AND REPORTER SERIES (KENT), circ. 154,146 263

Deal
W ADSCENE, HERALD & EXPRESS SERIES (FOLKESTONE), circ. 108,975 138
W MERCURY SERIES (KENT), circ. 13,841 220

Dover
W ADSCENE, HERALD & EXPRESS SERIES (FOLKESTONE), circ. 108,975 138
W EXPRESS EXTRA SERIES KENT, circ. 79,557 183
W MERCURY SERIES (KENT), circ. 13,841 220
W YOURKENT SERIES, circ. 120,000 F 279

Dymchurch
W ADSCENE, HERALD & EXPRESS SERIES (FOLKESTONE), circ. 108,975 138
W EXPRESS EXTRA SERIES KENT, circ. 79,557 183

East Malling
W KENT MESSENGER GROUP NEWSPAPERS, circ. 116,430 206

Edenbridge
W CHRONICLE SERIES, circ. 17,100 F 162
W COUNTY BORDER NEWS SERIES, circ. 28,000 F ... 166
W KENT & SUSSEX COURIER SERIES, circ. 110,491 206

W **Local/Weekly Newspapers**   D **Regional Daily Newspapers**   S **Regional Sunday Newspapers**   F **Free Newspapers**

Non-Nationals - England

Title (Day/am/pm)	Circ.	Page No.

Eynsford
W TIMES AND REPORTER SERIES (KENT), circ. 154,146 263

Farningham
W TIMES AND REPORTER SERIES (KENT), circ. 154,146 263

Faversham
W ADSCENE (CANTERBURY), circ. 53,724 [F] 138
W CANTERBURY EXTRA SERIES, circ. 107,124 [F] 158
W EAST KENT GAZETTE SERIES, circ. 29,121 177
W KENTISH GAZETTE SERIES, circ. 25,591 207

Folkestone
W ADSCENE, HERALD & EXPRESS SERIES (FOLKESTONE), circ. 108,975 138
W EXPRESS EXTRA SERIES KENT, circ. 79,557 183

Gillingham
W KENT MESSENGER GROUP NEWSPAPERS, circ. 116,430 206
W MEDWAY MESSENGER AND EXTRA SERIES, circ. 120,252 218
W MEDWAY NEWS SERIES, circ. 135,720 219

Gravesend
W GRAVESEND MESSENGER SERIES, circ. 40,890 192
W TIMES AND REPORTER SERIES (KENT), circ. 154,146 263

Hadlow
W KENT & SUSSEX COURIER SERIES, circ. 110,491 206

Hawkhurst
W KENT & SUSSEX COURIER SERIES, circ. 110,491 206

Herne Bay
W ADSCENE (CANTERBURY), circ. 53,724 [F] 138
W CANTERBURY EXTRA SERIES, circ. 107,124 [F] 158
W KENTISH GAZETTE SERIES, circ. 25,591 207
W WHITSTABLE & HERNE BAY TIMES SERIES, circ. 5,564 274

Hextable
W NEWS SHOPPER SERIES, circ. 308,920 [F] 228
W TIMES AND REPORTER SERIES (KENT), circ. 154,146 263

Higham
W GRAVESEND MESSENGER SERIES, circ. 40,890 192
W MEDWAY NEWS SERIES, circ. 135,720 219

Hoo St. Werburgh
W MEDWAY NEWS SERIES, circ. 135,720 219

Hythe
W ADSCENE, HERALD & EXPRESS SERIES (FOLKESTONE), circ. 108,975 138
W EXPRESS EXTRA SERIES KENT, circ. 79,557 183

Isle of Sheppey
W EAST KENT GAZETTE SERIES, circ. 29,121 177
W SHEERNESS TIMES GUARDIAN, circ. 8,549 246

Isle of Thanet
W ISLE OF THANET GAZETTE SERIES, circ. 74,337 204
W YOURKENT SERIES, circ. 120,000 [F] 279

Istead Rise
W GRAVESEND MESSENGER SERIES, circ. 40,890 192
W TIMES AND REPORTER SERIES (KENT), circ. 154,146 263

Kemsing
W SEVENOAKS CHRONICLE SERIES, circ. 105,776 246

Longfield
W GRAVESEND MESSENGER SERIES, circ. 40,890 192
W TIMES AND REPORTER SERIES (KENT), circ. 154,146 263

Lydd
W EXPRESS EXTRA SERIES KENT, circ. 79,557 183

Maidstone
W DOWNS MAIL SERIES, circ. 62,000 [F] 174
W KENT MESSENGER GROUP NEWSPAPERS, circ. 116,430 206
W MEDWAY NEWS SERIES, circ. 135,720 219
W YOURKENT SERIES, circ. 120,000 [F] 279

Manston
W ISLE OF THANET GAZETTE SERIES, circ. 74,337 204

Margate
W ISLE OF THANET GAZETTE SERIES, circ. 74,337 204

Medway
W KENT MESSENGER GROUP NEWSPAPERS, circ. 116,430 206
W MEDWAY MESSENGER AND EXTRA SERIES, circ. 120,252 218
W MEDWAY NEWS SERIES, circ. 135,720 219
W YOURKENT SERIES, circ. 120,000 [F] 279

Meopham
W GRAVESEND MESSENGER SERIES, circ. 40,890 192
W MEDWAY NEWS SERIES, circ. 135,720 219

Minster
W EAST KENT GAZETTE SERIES, circ. 29,121 177
W ISLE OF THANET GAZETTE SERIES, circ. 74,337 204

New Ash Green
W GRAVESEND MESSENGER SERIES, circ. 40,890 192
W TIMES AND REPORTER SERIES (KENT), circ. 154,146 263

New Romney
W ADSCENE, HERALD & EXPRESS SERIES (FOLKESTONE), circ. 108,975 138
W EXPRESS EXTRA SERIES KENT, circ. 79,557 183

Newington
W MEDWAY NEWS SERIES, circ. 135,720 219

Northfleet
W GRAVESEND MESSENGER SERIES, circ. 40,890 192

Otford
W SEVENOAKS CHRONICLE SERIES, circ. 105,776 246

Paddock Wood
W KENT & SUSSEX COURIER SERIES, circ. 110,491 206
W KENT MESSENGER GROUP NEWSPAPERS, circ. 116,430 206

Pembury
W KENT & SUSSEX COURIER SERIES, circ. 110,491 206
W KENT MESSENGER GROUP NEWSPAPERS, circ. 116,430 206

Queensborough
W EAST KENT GAZETTE SERIES, circ. 29,121 177

Ramsgate
W ISLE OF THANET GAZETTE SERIES, circ. 74,337 204

Rochester
W MEDWAY MESSENGER AND EXTRA SERIES, circ. 120,252 218
W MEDWAY NEWS SERIES, circ. 135,720 219

Romney Marsh
W ADSCENE, HERALD & EXPRESS SERIES (FOLKESTONE), circ. 108,975 138
W EXPRESS EXTRA SERIES KENT, circ. 79,557 183

Sandwich
W MERCURY SERIES (KENT), circ. 13,841 220

Sevenoaks
W KM EXTRA SERIES (MAIDSTONE, TONBRIDGE AND TUNBRIDGE WELLS), circ. 60,000 [F] 208

Sheerness
W EAST KENT GAZETTE SERIES, circ. 29,121 177
W SHEERNESS TIMES GUARDIAN, circ. 8,549 246

Sittingbourne
W EAST KENT GAZETTE SERIES, circ. 29,121 177
W KENT MESSENGER GROUP NEWSPAPERS, circ. 116,430 206
W SHEERNESS TIMES GUARDIAN, circ. 8,549 246
W YOURKENT SERIES, circ. 120,000 [F] 279

Snodland
W MEDWAY NEWS SERIES, circ. 135,720 219

South Darenth
W TIMES AND REPORTER SERIES (KENT), circ. 154,146 263

Staplehurst
W KENT MESSENGER GROUP NEWSPAPERS, circ. 116,430 206

Strood
W MEDWAY MESSENGER AND EXTRA SERIES, circ. 120,252 218
W MEDWAY NEWS SERIES, circ. 135,720 219

Sutton at Hone
W NEWS SHOPPER SERIES, circ. 308,920 [F] 228
W TIMES AND REPORTER SERIES (KENT), circ. 154,146 263

Swanley
W BEXLEY CHRONICLE SERIES, circ. 40,000 [F] 148
W DARTFORD MESSENGER, circ. 4,049 171
W GRAVESEND MESSENGER SERIES, circ. 40,890 192
W NEWS SHOPPER SERIES, circ. 308,920 [F] 228
W TIMES AND REPORTER SERIES (KENT), circ. 154,146 263

Tenterden
W EXPRESS EXTRA SERIES KENT, circ. 79,557 183

Tonbridge
W KENT & SUSSEX COURIER SERIES, circ. 110,491 206
W KENT MESSENGER GROUP NEWSPAPERS, circ. 116,430 206
W KM EXTRA SERIES (MAIDSTONE, TONBRIDGE AND TUNBRIDGE WELLS), circ. 60,000 [F] 208

Tunbridge Wells
W KENT & SUSSEX COURIER SERIES, circ. 110,491 206
W KM EXTRA SERIES (MAIDSTONE, TONBRIDGE AND TUNBRIDGE WELLS), circ. 60,000 [F] 208

Weald
W KENT & SUSSEX COURIER SERIES, circ. 110,491 206
W KENT MESSENGER GROUP NEWSPAPERS, circ. 116,430 206
W SEVENOAKS CHRONICLE SERIES, circ. 105,776 246

West Kingsdown
W SEVENOAKS CHRONICLE SERIES, circ. 105,776 246

Westerham
W COUNTY BORDER NEWS SERIES, circ. 28,000 [F] 166
W SEVENOAKS CHRONICLE SERIES, circ. 105,776 246

Whitstable
W ADSCENE (CANTERBURY), circ. 53,724 [F] 138
W CANTERBURY EXTRA SERIES, circ. 107,124 [F] 158
W KENTISH GAZETTE SERIES, circ. 25,591 207
W WHITSTABLE & HERNE BAY TIMES SERIES, circ. 5,564 274

Kingston Borough

Chessington
W INFORMER SERIES (KINGSTON), circ. 95,129 [F] 203
W SURREY COMET, circ. 10,182 260
W TIMES SERIES (RICHMOND), circ. 152,627 264

Kingston upon Thames
W GUARDIAN & NEWS SERIES (SUTTON), circ. 315,438 193
W GUARDIAN SERIES (WILTSHIRE, HAMPSHIRE AND SURREY), circ. 175,000 [F] 193
W INFORMER SERIES (KINGSTON), circ. 95,129 [F] 203
W SURREY COMET, circ. 10,182 260
W TIMES SERIES (RICHMOND), circ. 152,627 264

New Malden
W INFORMER SERIES (KINGSTON), circ. 95,129 [F] 203
W SURREY COMET, circ. 10,182 260
W TIMES SERIES (RICHMOND), circ. 152,627 264

Surbiton
W INFORMER SERIES (KINGSTON), circ. 95,129 [F] 203
W SURREY COMET, circ. 10,182 260
W TIMES SERIES (RICHMOND), circ. 152,627 264

Tolworth
W INFORMER SERIES (KINGSTON), circ. 95,129 [F] 203

Lambeth Borough
W SOUTH LONDON PRESS SERIES, circ. 41,016 250

Clapham
W GUARDIAN & NEWS SERIES (SUTTON), circ. 315,438 193

Lambeth
W GUARDIAN & NEWS SERIES (SUTTON), circ. 315,438 193
W THE MERCURY AND POST SERIES, circ. 166,029 [F] 219

Streatham
W GREATER LONDON CHRONICLE, circ. 5,000 [F] 193
W GUARDIAN & NEWS SERIES (SUTTON), circ. 315,438 193
W THE MERCURY AND POST SERIES, circ. 166,029 [F] 219

Lancashire
W YR ANGOR (LIVERPOOL), circ. 3,000 142

Accrington
W ACCRINGTON OBSERVER, circ. 14,586 137
W BLACKBURN CITIZEN, circ. 59,248 [F] 149

W Local/Weekly Newspapers   D Regional Daily Newspapers   S Regional Sunday Newspapers   F Free Newspapers

Section 3 Index to UK Newspapers

Title (Day/am/pm)	Circ.	Page No.

Ⓓ LANCASHIRE TELEGRAPH, circ. 32,716 209

Adlington
Ⓦ THE ADVERTISER (HORWICH, WESTHOUGHTON & DISTRICT), circ. 36,000 Ⓕ 139
Ⓓ THE BOLTON NEWS, circ. 29,552 150
Ⓦ CHORLEY GUARDIAN SERIES, circ. 13,664 160
Ⓓ LANCASHIRE EVENING POST, circ. 31,225 208

Aintree
Ⓓ LIVERPOOL DAILY POST, circ. 15,581 213
Ⓓ LIVERPOOL ECHO, circ. 109,458 213
Ⓦ LIVERPOOL WEEKLY MERSEYMART & STAR SERIES, circ. 128,081 Ⓕ 213
Ⓦ SOUTHPORT, ORMSKIRK & FORMBY CHAMPION SERIES, circ. 94,383 Ⓕ 252

Appley Bridge
Ⓓ LANCASHIRE EVENING POST, circ. 31,225 208
Ⓓ LIVERPOOL DAILY POST, circ. 15,581 213
Ⓓ LIVERPOOL ECHO, circ. 109,458 213
Ⓦ ORMSKIRK ADVERTISER SERIES, circ. 30,165 233
Ⓦ THE WIGAN OBSERVER, REPORTER AND NEWS SERIES, circ. 141,632 274

Bacup
Ⓓ MANCHESTER EVENING NEWS, circ. 82,445 217
Ⓦ ROSSENDALE FREE PRESS, circ. 14,288 241

Banks
Ⓓ LANCASHIRE EVENING POST, circ. 31,225 208
Ⓓ LIVERPOOL DAILY POST, circ. 15,581 213
Ⓓ LIVERPOOL ECHO, circ. 109,458 213
Ⓦ SOUTHPORT, ORMSKIRK & FORMBY CHAMPION SERIES, circ. 94,383 Ⓕ 252
Ⓦ SOUTHPORT VISITER SERIES, circ. 73,905 252

Barnoldswick
Ⓦ THE BURNLEY AND PENDLE CITIZEN, circ. 55,649 Ⓕ 154
Ⓦ CRAVEN HERALD & PIONEER, circ. 17,661 167
Ⓦ LEADER TIMES SERIES, circ. 71,447 210

Barrowford
Ⓦ THE BURNLEY AND PENDLE CITIZEN, circ. 55,649 Ⓕ 154
Ⓓ LANCASHIRE TELEGRAPH, circ. 32,716 209
Ⓦ LEADER TIMES SERIES, circ. 71,447 210

Blackburn
Ⓦ BLACKBURN CITIZEN, circ. 59,248 Ⓕ 149
Ⓓ LANCASHIRE TELEGRAPH, circ. 32,716 209
Ⓓ MANCHESTER EVENING NEWS, circ. 82,445 217

Blackpool
Ⓦ BLACKPOOL, FYLDE AND WYRE REPORTER, circ. 64,017 Ⓕ 149
Ⓓ THE GAZETTE (BLACKPOOL), circ. 36,500 189
Ⓓ LANCASHIRE TELEGRAPH, circ. 32,716 209
Ⓓ MANCHESTER EVENING NEWS, circ. 82,445 217

Brierfield
Ⓓ LANCASHIRE TELEGRAPH, circ. 32,716 209
Ⓦ LEADER TIMES SERIES, circ. 71,447 210

Burnley
Ⓦ BLACKBURN CITIZEN, circ. 59,248 Ⓕ 149
Ⓦ THE BURNLEY AND PENDLE CITIZEN, circ. 55,649 Ⓕ 154
Ⓦ BURNLEY EXPRESS AND REPORTER SERIES, circ. 85,199 154
Ⓓ LANCASHIRE TELEGRAPH, circ. 32,716 209
Ⓦ LEADER TIMES SERIES, circ. 71,447 210
Ⓓ MANCHESTER EVENING NEWS, circ. 82,445 217

Burscough Bridge
Ⓓ LANCASHIRE EVENING POST, circ. 31,225 208
Ⓓ LIVERPOOL DAILY POST, circ. 15,581 213
Ⓓ LIVERPOOL ECHO, circ. 109,458 213
Ⓦ ORMSKIRK ADVERTISER SERIES, circ. 30,165 233
Ⓦ SOUTHPORT, ORMSKIRK & FORMBY CHAMPION SERIES, circ. 94,383 Ⓕ 252

Carnforth
Ⓦ LANCASTER GUARDIAN SERIES, circ. 16,306 209
Ⓦ VISITOR (MORECAMBE), circ. 13,030 267
Ⓦ WESTMORLAND GAZETTE NEWSPAPER SERIES, circ. 56,020 273

Chorley
Ⓦ THE ADVERTISER (HORWICH, WESTHOUGHTON & DISTRICT), circ. 36,000 Ⓕ 139
Ⓦ BLACKBURN CITIZEN, circ. 59,248 Ⓕ 149
Ⓓ THE BOLTON NEWS, circ. 29,552 150
Ⓦ CHORLEY CITIZEN, circ. 32,921 Ⓕ 160
Ⓦ CHORLEY GUARDIAN SERIES, circ. 13,664 160
Ⓓ LANCASHIRE EVENING POST, circ. 31,225 208
Ⓓ LANCASHIRE TELEGRAPH, circ. 32,716 209
Ⓓ MANCHESTER EVENING NEWS, circ. 82,445 217

Ⓦ THE WIGAN OBSERVER, REPORTER AND NEWS SERIES, circ. 141,632 274

Church
Ⓦ BLACKBURN CITIZEN, circ. 59,248 Ⓕ 149
Ⓓ LANCASHIRE EVENING POST, circ. 31,225 208
Ⓓ LANCASHIRE TELEGRAPH, circ. 32,716 209

Clayton le Moors
Ⓓ LANCASHIRE TELEGRAPH, circ. 32,716 209
Ⓦ MIDDLETON & NORTH MANCHESTER GUARDIAN & ADVERTISER SERIES, circ. 93,756 222

Cleveleys
Ⓦ BLACKPOOL, FYLDE AND WYRE REPORTER, circ. 64,017 Ⓕ 149
Ⓓ THE GAZETTE (BLACKPOOL), circ. 36,500 189

Clifton
Ⓦ LYTHAM ST ANNES EXPRESS SERIES, circ. 9,663 ... 216
Ⓦ SALFORD ADVERTISER SERIES, circ. 123,190 Ⓕ 243

Clitheroe
Ⓦ BURNLEY EXPRESS AND REPORTER SERIES, circ. 85,199 154
Ⓓ LANCASHIRE TELEGRAPH, circ. 32,716 209

Colne
Ⓦ BLACKBURN CITIZEN, circ. 59,248 Ⓕ 149
Ⓦ THE BURNLEY AND PENDLE CITIZEN, circ. 55,649 Ⓕ 154
Ⓓ LANCASHIRE TELEGRAPH, circ. 32,716 209
Ⓦ LEADER TIMES SERIES, circ. 71,447 210

Coppull
Ⓦ CHORLEY GUARDIAN SERIES, circ. 13,664 160
Ⓓ LANCASHIRE EVENING POST, circ. 31,225 208

Croston
Ⓦ CHORLEY GUARDIAN SERIES, circ. 13,664 160
Ⓓ LANCASHIRE EVENING POST, circ. 31,225 208
Ⓦ ORMSKIRK ADVERTISER SERIES, circ. 30,165 233

Darwen
Ⓦ BLACKBURN CITIZEN, circ. 59,248 Ⓕ 149
Ⓓ THE BOLTON NEWS, circ. 29,552 150
Ⓓ LANCASHIRE TELEGRAPH, circ. 32,716 209
Ⓓ MANCHESTER EVENING NEWS, circ. 82,445 217

Earby
Ⓦ THE BURNLEY AND PENDLE CITIZEN, circ. 55,649 Ⓕ 154
Ⓦ CRAVEN HERALD & PIONEER, circ. 17,661 167
Ⓦ LEADER TIMES SERIES, circ. 71,447 210

Eccleston
Ⓦ CHORLEY GUARDIAN SERIES, circ. 13,664 160
Ⓓ LANCASHIRE EVENING POST, circ. 31,225 208
Ⓦ ORMSKIRK ADVERTISER SERIES, circ. 30,165 233

Euxton
Ⓦ CHORLEY GUARDIAN SERIES, circ. 13,664 160
Ⓓ LANCASHIRE EVENING POST, circ. 31,225 208

Fleetwood
Ⓦ BLACKPOOL, FYLDE AND WYRE REPORTER, circ. 64,017 Ⓕ 149
Ⓦ FLEETWOOD WEEKLY NEWS, circ. 12,000 185
Ⓓ THE GAZETTE (BLACKPOOL), circ. 36,500 189

Freckleton
Ⓦ BLACKPOOL, FYLDE AND WYRE REPORTER, circ. 64,017 Ⓕ 149
Ⓓ THE GAZETTE (BLACKPOOL), circ. 36,500 189

Fylde
Ⓦ FLEETWOOD WEEKLY NEWS, circ. 12,000 185
Ⓦ LYTHAM ST ANNES EXPRESS SERIES, circ. 9,663 ... 216

Garstang
Ⓦ BLACKPOOL, FYLDE AND WYRE REPORTER, circ. 64,017 Ⓕ 149
Ⓦ THE GARSTANG & LONGRIDGE COURIER & NEWS SERIES, circ. 5,026 188
Ⓓ THE GAZETTE (BLACKPOOL), circ. 36,500 189
Ⓓ LANCASHIRE EVENING POST, circ. 31,225 208
Ⓦ LANCASTER GUARDIAN SERIES, circ. 16,306 209

Gosnargh
Ⓦ LONGRIDGE & RIBBLE VALLEY NEWS AND ADVERTISER, circ. 3,289 214

Great Harwood
Ⓓ LANCASHIRE TELEGRAPH, circ. 32,716 209

Grimsargh
Ⓦ LONGRIDGE & RIBBLE VALLEY NEWS AND ADVERTISER, circ. 3,289 214

Halsall
Ⓦ ORMSKIRK ADVERTISER SERIES, circ. 30,165 233
Ⓦ SOUTHPORT, ORMSKIRK & FORMBY CHAMPION SERIES, circ. 94,383 Ⓕ 252
Ⓦ SOUTHPORT VISITER SERIES, circ. 73,905 252

Haslingden
Ⓦ ROSSENDALE FREE PRESS, circ. 14,288 241

Hesketh Bank
Ⓦ ORMSKIRK ADVERTISER SERIES, circ. 30,165 233
Ⓦ SOUTHPORT, ORMSKIRK & FORMBY CHAMPION SERIES, circ. 94,383 Ⓕ 252
Ⓦ SOUTHPORT VISITER SERIES, circ. 73,905 252

Heysham
Ⓦ LANCASTER GUARDIAN SERIES, circ. 16,306 209

Higher Walton
Ⓓ LANCASHIRE EVENING POST, circ. 31,225 208

Hurst Green
Ⓦ LONGRIDGE & RIBBLE VALLEY NEWS AND ADVERTISER, circ. 3,289 214

Kearsley
Ⓓ THE BOLTON NEWS, circ. 29,552 150

Kirkham
Ⓦ BLACKPOOL, FYLDE AND WYRE REPORTER, circ. 64,017 Ⓕ 149
Ⓓ THE GAZETTE (BLACKPOOL), circ. 36,500 189
Ⓓ LANCASHIRE EVENING POST, circ. 31,225 208
Ⓦ LYTHAM ST ANNES EXPRESS SERIES, circ. 9,663 ... 216

Lancaster
Ⓓ LANCASHIRE EVENING POST, circ. 31,225 208
Ⓓ LANCASHIRE TELEGRAPH, circ. 32,716 209
Ⓦ LANCASTER AND MORECAMBE REPORTER, circ. 45,846 Ⓕ 209
Ⓦ LANCASTER GUARDIAN SERIES, circ. 16,306 209
Ⓦ VISITOR (MORECAMBE), circ. 13,030 267

Leyland
Ⓦ BLACKBURN CITIZEN, circ. 59,248 Ⓕ 149
Ⓦ CHORLEY GUARDIAN SERIES, circ. 13,664 160
Ⓓ LANCASHIRE EVENING POST, circ. 31,225 208
Ⓓ LANCASHIRE TELEGRAPH, circ. 32,716 209
Ⓓ MANCHESTER EVENING NEWS, circ. 82,445 217
Ⓦ PRESTON REPORTER SERIES, circ. 64,110 Ⓕ 238

Longridge
Ⓦ BLACKBURN CITIZEN, circ. 59,248 Ⓕ 149
Ⓦ THE GARSTANG & LONGRIDGE COURIER & NEWS SERIES, circ. 5,026 188
Ⓓ LANCASHIRE EVENING POST, circ. 31,225 208
Ⓦ LONGRIDGE & RIBBLE VALLEY NEWS AND ADVERTISER, circ. 3,289 214

Longton
Ⓓ LANCASHIRE EVENING POST, circ. 31,225 208

Lytham St. Annes
Ⓦ BLACKPOOL, FYLDE AND WYRE REPORTER, circ. 64,017 Ⓕ 149
Ⓓ THE GAZETTE (BLACKPOOL), circ. 36,500 189
Ⓓ LANCASHIRE TELEGRAPH, circ. 32,716 209
Ⓦ LYTHAM ST ANNES EXPRESS SERIES, circ. 9,663 ... 216

Morecambe
Ⓓ LANCASHIRE EVENING POST, circ. 31,225 208
Ⓦ LANCASTER AND MORECAMBE REPORTER, circ. 45,846 Ⓕ 209
Ⓦ LANCASTER GUARDIAN SERIES, circ. 16,306 209
Ⓓ MANCHESTER EVENING NEWS, circ. 82,445 217
Ⓦ VISITOR (MORECAMBE), circ. 13,030 267

Nelson
Ⓦ BLACKBURN CITIZEN, circ. 59,248 Ⓕ 149
Ⓦ THE BURNLEY AND PENDLE CITIZEN, circ. 55,649 Ⓕ 154
Ⓓ LANCASHIRE TELEGRAPH, circ. 32,716 209
Ⓦ LEADER TIMES SERIES, circ. 71,447 210

Ormskirk
Ⓓ LIVERPOOL ECHO, circ. 109,458 213
Ⓦ ORMSKIRK ADVERTISER SERIES, circ. 30,165 233
Ⓦ SOUTHPORT, ORMSKIRK & FORMBY CHAMPION SERIES, circ. 94,383 Ⓕ 252

Orrell
Ⓓ LANCASHIRE EVENING POST, circ. 31,225 208
Ⓦ THE WIGAN OBSERVER, REPORTER AND NEWS SERIES, circ. 141,632 274

Oswaldtwistle
Ⓓ LANCASHIRE TELEGRAPH, circ. 32,716 209

Ⓦ Local/Weekly Newspapers   Ⓓ Regional Daily Newspapers   Ⓢ Regional Sunday Newspapers   Ⓕ Free Newspapers

Non-Nationals - England

Title (Day/am/pm)	Circ.	Page No.

Padiham
W THE BURNLEY AND PENDLE CITIZEN, circ. 55,649 F 154
W BURNLEY EXPRESS AND REPORTER SERIES, circ. 85,199 154
D LANCASHIRE TELEGRAPH, circ. 32,716 ... 209

Parbold
D LANCASHIRE EVENING POST, circ. 31,225 ... 208
D LIVERPOOL DAILY POST, circ. 15,581 213
D LIVERPOOL ECHO, circ. 109,458 213
W ORMSKIRK ADVERTISER SERIES, circ. 30,165 ... 233
W SOUTHPORT, ORMSKIRK & FORMBY CHAMPION SERIES, circ. 94,383 F 252

Pendle
W THE BURNLEY AND PENDLE CITIZEN, circ. 55,649 F 154
W BURNLEY EXPRESS AND REPORTER SERIES, circ. 85,199 154
D LANCASHIRE TELEGRAPH, circ. 32,716 ... 209
W LEADER TIMES SERIES, circ. 71,447 210

Poulton le Fylde
W BLACKPOOL, FYLDE AND WYRE REPORTER, circ. 64,017 F 149
W FLEETWOOD WEEKLY NEWS, circ. 12,000 ... 185
D THE GAZETTE (BLACKPOOL), circ. 36,500 ... 189

Preston
W BLACKBURN CITIZEN, circ. 59,248 F 149
D LANCASHIRE EVENING POST, circ. 31,225 ... 208
W PRESTON REPORTER SERIES, circ. 64,110 F ... 238

Rainford
W ORMSKIRK ADVERTISER SERIES, circ. 30,165 ... 233
W ST. HELENS STAR, circ. 78,827 F 253

Rawtenstall
D LANCASHIRE TELEGRAPH, circ. 32,716 ... 209
W ROSSENDALE FREE PRESS, circ. 14,288 ... 241

Ribchester
W LONGRIDGE & RIBBLE VALLEY NEWS AND ADVERTISER, circ. 3,289 214

Rishton
D LANCASHIRE TELEGRAPH, circ. 32,716 ... 209

Rossendale
D LANCASHIRE TELEGRAPH, circ. 32,716 ... 209
D MANCHESTER EVENING NEWS, circ. 82,445 ... 217
W ROSSENDALE FREE PRESS, circ. 14,288 ... 241

Skelmersdale
W ORMSKIRK ADVERTISER SERIES, circ. 30,165 ... 233
W SOUTHPORT, ORMSKIRK & FORMBY CHAMPION SERIES, circ. 94,383 F 252

South Ribble
W CHORLEY GUARDIAN SERIES, circ. 13,664 ... 160
D LANCASHIRE EVENING POST, circ. 31,225 ... 208

Tarleton
W ORMSKIRK ADVERTISER SERIES, circ. 30,165 ... 233
W SOUTHPORT, ORMSKIRK & FORMBY CHAMPION SERIES, circ. 94,383 F 252
W SOUTHPORT VISITER SERIES, circ. 73,905 ... 252

Thornton Cleveleys
W BLACKPOOL, FYLDE AND WYRE REPORTER, circ. 64,017 F 149
W FLEETWOOD WEEKLY NEWS, circ. 12,000 ... 185

Tottington
W BURY TIMES SERIES, circ. 69,393 155

Warton
D LANCASHIRE EVENING POST, circ. 31,225 ... 208
W LYTHAM ST ANNES EXPRESS SERIES, circ. 9,663 ... 216

Whalley
W BURNLEY EXPRESS AND REPORTER SERIES, circ. 85,199 154
W SOUTH MANCHESTER REPORTER, circ. 49,449 F ... 250

Whitworth
D LANCASHIRE TELEGRAPH, circ. 32,716 ... 209
W ROCHDALE OBSERVER SERIES, circ. 40,000 ... 240
W ROSSENDALE FREE PRESS, circ. 14,288 ... 241

Leicestershire
W JOURNAL & ADVERTISER SERIES, circ. 30,000 F ... 205
D LEICESTER MERCURY, circ. 70,028 210

Anstey
W LEICESTER MAIL SERIES, circ. 141,536 F ... 210
D LEICESTER MERCURY, circ. 70,028 210

W THE MESSENGER SERIES (LEICESTERSHIRE & RUTLAND), circ. 50,000 F 221
S SUNDAY MERCURY (BIRMINGHAM), circ. 59,339 ... 258

Ashby-de-la-Zouch
W THE BURTON & SOUTH DERBYSHIRE ADVERTISER, circ. 57,692 F 155
D BURTON MAIL, circ. 14,658 155
W LEICESTER MAIL SERIES, circ. 141,536 F ... 210
D LEICESTER MERCURY, circ. 70,028 210
D LOUGHBOROUGH ECHO SERIES, circ. 72,916 ... 215
W THE MESSENGER SERIES (LEICESTERSHIRE & RUTLAND), circ. 50,000 F 221
W TRIDENT MIDLAND NEWSPAPERS SERIES, circ. 46,151 265

Barrow-upon-Soar
W LEICESTER MAIL SERIES, circ. 141,536 F ... 210
D LEICESTER MERCURY, circ. 70,028 210
S SUNDAY MERCURY (BIRMINGHAM), circ. 59,339 ... 258

Birstall
W THE BIRSTALL POST, circ. 5,200 F 149
W EXPRESS & CHRONICLE 183
D LEICESTER MERCURY, circ. 70,028 210

Blaby
W LEICESTER MAIL SERIES, circ. 141,536 F ... 210

Bottesford
W SCUNTHORPE TARGET, circ. 58,333 F 244

Broughton Astley
W THE HINCKLEY TIMES & HERALD SERIES, circ. 46,769 200
D LEICESTER MERCURY, circ. 70,028 210
S SUNDAY MERCURY (BIRMINGHAM), circ. 59,339 ... 258

Castle Donington
W DERBY EXPRESS AND MESSENGER SERIES, circ. 111,621 F 172
W LOUGHBOROUGH ECHO SERIES, circ. 72,916 ... 215

Coalville
W LEICESTER MAIL SERIES, circ. 141,536 F ... 210
D LEICESTER MERCURY, circ. 70,028 210
W LOUGHBOROUGH ECHO SERIES, circ. 72,916 ... 215
W TRIDENT MIDLAND NEWSPAPERS SERIES, circ. 46,151 265

Cosby
W THE HINCKLEY TIMES & HERALD SERIES, circ. 46,769 200
D LEICESTER MERCURY, circ. 70,028 210
S SUNDAY MERCURY (BIRMINGHAM), circ. 59,339 ... 258

Countesthorpe
W LEICESTER MAIL SERIES, circ. 141,536 F ... 210
D LEICESTER MERCURY, circ. 70,028 210
S SUNDAY MERCURY (BIRMINGHAM), circ. 59,339 ... 258

Desford
W THE HINCKLEY TIMES & HERALD SERIES, circ. 46,769 200
W LEICESTER MAIL SERIES, circ. 141,536 F ... 210
D LEICESTER MERCURY, circ. 70,028 210
S SUNDAY MERCURY (BIRMINGHAM), circ. 59,339 ... 258

Donisthorpe
D BURTON MAIL, circ. 14,658 155

Earl Shilton
W THE HINCKLEY TIMES & HERALD SERIES, circ. 46,769 200

East Goscote
W LEICESTER MAIL SERIES, circ. 141,536 F ... 210
D LEICESTER MERCURY, circ. 70,028 210
S SUNDAY MERCURY (BIRMINGHAM), circ. 59,339 ... 258

Fleckney
D LEICESTER MERCURY, circ. 70,028 210
S SUNDAY MERCURY (BIRMINGHAM), circ. 59,339 ... 258

Great Glen
W LEICESTER MAIL SERIES, circ. 141,536 F ... 210
D LEICESTER MERCURY, circ. 70,028 210
W THE MESSENGER SERIES (LEICESTERSHIRE & RUTLAND), circ. 50,000 F 221
S SUNDAY MERCURY (BIRMINGHAM), circ. 59,339 ... 258

Groby
W LEICESTER MAIL SERIES, circ. 141,536 F ... 210
D LEICESTER MERCURY, circ. 70,028 210
S SUNDAY MERCURY (BIRMINGHAM), circ. 59,339 ... 258

Hinckley
D COVENTRY TELEGRAPH, circ. 48,025 167

W THE HINCKLEY TIMES & HERALD SERIES, circ. 46,769 200
D LEICESTER MERCURY, circ. 70,028 210
D NUNEATON NEWS, circ. 15,000 232

Ibstock
W LEICESTER MAIL SERIES, circ. 141,536 F ... 210
D LEICESTER MERCURY, circ. 70,028 210
S SUNDAY MERCURY (BIRMINGHAM), circ. 59,339 ... 258
W TRIDENT MIDLAND NEWSPAPERS SERIES, circ. 46,151 265

Kibworth Harcourt
D LEICESTER MERCURY, circ. 70,028 210
S SUNDAY MERCURY (BIRMINGHAM), circ. 59,339 ... 258

Kirby Muxloe
W LEICESTER MAIL SERIES, circ. 141,536 F ... 210
D LEICESTER MERCURY, circ. 70,028 210
S SUNDAY MERCURY (BIRMINGHAM), circ. 59,339 ... 258

Leicester
W LEICESTER MAIL SERIES, circ. 141,536 F ... 210
D LEICESTER MERCURY, circ. 70,028 210

Loughborough
W LEICESTER MAIL SERIES, circ. 141,536 F ... 210
D LEICESTER MERCURY, circ. 70,028 210
W LOUGHBOROUGH ECHO SERIES, circ. 72,916 ... 215

Lutterworth
W THE MAIL SERIES, circ. 12,552 217
W THE MESSENGER SERIES (LEICESTERSHIRE & RUTLAND), circ. 50,000 F 221
W THE RUGBY OBSERVER SERIES, circ. 42,974 F ... 242

Market Harborough
D LEICESTER MERCURY, circ. 70,028 210
W THE MAIL SERIES, circ. 12,552 217
W NORTHANTS HERALD AND POST SERIES, circ. 128,956 F 231

Markfield
W LEICESTER MAIL SERIES, circ. 141,536 F ... 210
D LEICESTER MERCURY, circ. 70,028 210
S SUNDAY MERCURY (BIRMINGHAM), circ. 59,339 ... 258
W TRIDENT MIDLAND NEWSPAPERS SERIES, circ. 46,151 265

Measham
D BURTON MAIL, circ. 14,658 155

Melton Mowbray
D LEICESTER MERCURY, circ. 70,028 210
W RUTLAND TIMES, circ. 4,562 243
W TIMES SERIES (MELTON MOWBRAY), circ. 25,726 ... 264

Mountsorrel
W LEICESTER MAIL SERIES, circ. 141,536 F ... 210
D LEICESTER MERCURY, circ. 70,028 210
S SUNDAY MERCURY (BIRMINGHAM), circ. 59,339 ... 258

Narborough
W LEICESTER MAIL SERIES, circ. 141,536 F ... 210
D LEICESTER MERCURY, circ. 70,028 210
S SUNDAY MERCURY (BIRMINGHAM), circ. 59,339 ... 258

Newbold Verdon
W THE HINCKLEY TIMES & HERALD SERIES, circ. 46,769 200
D LEICESTER MERCURY, circ. 70,028 210
S SUNDAY MERCURY (BIRMINGHAM), circ. 59,339 ... 258

Oadby
W LEICESTER MAIL SERIES, circ. 141,536 F ... 210
D LEICESTER MERCURY, circ. 70,028 210

Quorndon
W LEICESTER MAIL SERIES, circ. 141,536 F ... 210
D LEICESTER MERCURY, circ. 70,028 210

Ratby
W LEICESTER MAIL SERIES, circ. 141,536 F ... 210
D LEICESTER MERCURY, circ. 70,028 210

Sapcote
W THE HINCKLEY TIMES & HERALD SERIES, circ. 46,769 200
D LEICESTER MERCURY, circ. 70,028 210
S SUNDAY MERCURY (BIRMINGHAM), circ. 59,339 ... 258

Shepshed
W LEICESTER MAIL SERIES, circ. 141,536 F ... 210
W LOUGHBOROUGH ECHO SERIES, circ. 72,916 ... 215

Sileby
W LEICESTER MAIL SERIES, circ. 141,536 F ... 210
D LEICESTER MERCURY, circ. 70,028 210
S SUNDAY MERCURY (BIRMINGHAM), circ. 59,339 ... 258

W Local/Weekly Newspapers   D Regional Daily Newspapers   S Regional Sunday Newspapers   F Free Newspapers

Title (Day/am/pm)	Circ.	Page No.

Stoney Stanton
W THE HINCKLEY TIMES & HERALD SERIES,
circ. 46,769 200
W LEICESTER MAIL SERIES, circ. 141,536 F 210
D LEICESTER MERCURY, circ. 70,028 210
S SUNDAY MERCURY (BIRMINGHAM), circ. 59,339 258

Whetstone
W LEICESTER MAIL SERIES, circ. 141,536 F 210
D LEICESTER MERCURY, circ. 70,028 210
S SUNDAY MERCURY (BIRMINGHAM), circ. 59,339 258

Wigston
W LEICESTER MAIL SERIES, circ. 141,536 F 210
D LEICESTER MERCURY, circ. 70,028 210

Lewisham Borough
W SOUTH LONDON PRESS SERIES, circ. 41,016 250

Catford
W THE MERCURY AND POST SERIES, circ. 166,029 F 219
W NEWS SHOPPER SERIES, circ. 308,920 F 228

Deptford
W THE MERCURY AND POST SERIES, circ. 166,029 F 219

Lewisham
W THE MERCURY AND POST SERIES, circ. 166,029 F 219
W NEWS SHOPPER SERIES, circ. 308,920 F 228

Lincolnshire
D LIFE AND STYLE 212
D YORKSHIRE POST (CITY/LONDON OFFICE) 279

Alford
D GRIMSBY TELEGRAPH, circ. 34,590 193
W LIFE, circ. 48,406 F 212
W LOUTH LEADER AND CITIZEN SERIES, circ. 101,326 215
W SKEGNESS STANDARD AND CITIZEN SERIES,
circ. 23,645 248
W TARGET SERIES, circ. 82,742 F 262

Appleby
W SCUNTHORPE TARGET, circ. 58,333 F 244

Barton-upon-Humber
D GRIMSBY TELEGRAPH, circ. 34,590 193
W LIFE, circ. 48,406 F 212
W SCUNTHORPE TARGET, circ. 58,333 F 244
D SCUNTHORPE TELEGRAPH, circ. 20,568 245

Boston
W BOSTON STANDARD AND CITIZEN SERIES,
circ. 53,935 150
D LINCOLNSHIRE ECHO, circ. 22,263 212
W TARGET SERIES, circ. 82,742 F 262

Bourne
D ET LIFE 180
D EVENING TELEGRAPH (PETERBOROUGH),
circ. 18,542 182
W LINCOLNSHIRE FREE PRESS SERIES, circ. 33,071 ..212
W THE LOCAL (BOURNE, THE DEEPINGS), circ. 3,600 . 213
W RUTLAND & STAMFORD MERCURY AND CITIZEN
SERIES, circ. 20,490 243

Bracebridge Heath
W LINCOLN TARGET SERIES, circ. 47,371 F 212
D LINCOLNSHIRE ECHO, circ. 22,263 212

Brigg
W LIFE, circ. 48,406 F 212
W MARKET RASEN MAIL, circ. 4,550 218
W SCUNTHORPE TARGET, circ. 58,333 F 244
D SCUNTHORPE TELEGRAPH, circ. 20,568 245

Broughton
W THE MESSENGER SERIES (LEICESTERSHIRE &
RUTLAND), circ. 50,000 F 221
W SCUNTHORPE TARGET, circ. 58,333 F 244

Burwell
D GRIMSBY TELEGRAPH, circ. 34,590 193
W LIFE, circ. 48,406 F 212

Caistor
D GRIMSBY TELEGRAPH, circ. 34,590 193
W LIFE, circ. 48,406 F 212
W MARKET RASEN MAIL, circ. 4,550 218

Cleethorpes
D GRIMSBY TELEGRAPH, circ. 34,590 193
W LIFE, circ. 48,406 F 212
D YORKSHIRE POST, circ. 49,031 279

Coningsby
W BOSTON STANDARD AND CITIZEN SERIES,
circ. 53,935 150
W HORNCASTLE NEWS, circ. 5,450 200
D LINCOLNSHIRE ECHO, circ. 22,263 212
W TARGET SERIES, circ. 82,742 F 262

Cranwell Airfield
D LINCOLNSHIRE ECHO, circ. 22,263 212
W SLEAFORD STANDARD AND CITIZEN SERIES,
circ. 4,771 248
W TARGET SERIES, circ. 82,742 F 262

Crowle
W THE EPWORTH BELLS & CROWLE ADVERTISER,
circ. 3,136 179
W GAINSBOROUGH NEWS AND STANDARD SERIES,
circ. 5,000 187
W SCUNTHORPE TARGET, circ. 58,333 F 244
D SCUNTHORPE TELEGRAPH, circ. 20,568 245

Deeping St. James
D ET LIFE 180
D EVENING TELEGRAPH (PETERBOROUGH),
circ. 18,542 182

Dunholme
W LINCOLN TARGET SERIES, circ. 47,371 F 212
D LINCOLNSHIRE ECHO, circ. 22,263 212

Epworth
W THE EPWORTH BELLS & CROWLE ADVERTISER,
circ. 3,136 179
W GAINSBOROUGH NEWS AND STANDARD SERIES,
circ. 5,000 187
W LIFE, circ. 48,406 F 212
W SCUNTHORPE TARGET, circ. 58,333 F 244
D SCUNTHORPE TELEGRAPH, circ. 20,568 245

Gainsborough
W GAINSBOROUGH NEWS AND STANDARD SERIES,
circ. 5,000 187
W LINCOLN TARGET SERIES, circ. 47,371 F 212
D LINCOLNSHIRE ECHO, circ. 22,263 212
W RETFORD GAINSBOROUGH AND WORKSOP TIMES,
circ. 10,913 240

Goole
W GOOLE, HOWDEN COURIER, circ. 15,419 F 192
D GOOLE TIMES, circ. 10,149 192
D HULL DAILY MAIL, circ. 59,689 201
W THE PRESS (YORK), circ. 35,761 238

Grantham
W GRANTHAM CITIZEN & JOURNAL SERIES,
circ. 36,579 192
D LINCOLNSHIRE ECHO, circ. 22,263 212

Grimsby
D GRIMSBY TELEGRAPH, circ. 34,590 193
W LIFE, circ. 48,406 F 212

Haxey
W DONCASTER FREE PRESS, circ. 34,029 173
W SCUNTHORPE TARGET, circ. 58,333 F 244
D THE STAR SHEFFIELD, circ. 56,363 255

Heighington
W LINCOLN TARGET SERIES, circ. 47,371 F 212
D LINCOLNSHIRE ECHO, circ. 22,263 212

Holbeach
W LINCOLNSHIRE FREE PRESS SERIES, circ. 33,071 ..212
W TARGET SERIES, circ. 82,742 F 262

Holton le Clay
D GRIMSBY TELEGRAPH, circ. 34,590 193
W LIFE, circ. 48,406 F 212

Horncastle
W HORNCASTLE NEWS, circ. 5,450 200
D LINCOLNSHIRE ECHO, circ. 22,263 212
W TARGET SERIES, circ. 82,742 F 262

Humberston
D GRIMSBY TELEGRAPH, circ. 34,590 193
W LIFE, circ. 48,406 F 212

Immingham
D GRIMSBY TELEGRAPH, circ. 34,590 193
W LIFE, circ. 48,406 F 212

Ingoldmells
W SKEGNESS STANDARD AND CITIZEN SERIES,
circ. 23,645 248
W TARGET SERIES, circ. 82,742 F 262

Kirton
W BOSTON STANDARD AND CITIZEN SERIES,
circ. 53,935 150
D LINCOLNSHIRE ECHO, circ. 22,263 212
W SCUNTHORPE TARGET, circ. 58,333 F 244
W TARGET SERIES, circ. 82,742 F 262

Laceby
D GRIMSBY TELEGRAPH, circ. 34,590 193
W LIFE, circ. 48,406 F 212

Legbourne
W TARGET SERIES, circ. 82,742 F 262

Lincoln
W LINCOLN TARGET SERIES, circ. 47,371 F 212
D LINCOLNSHIRE ECHO, circ. 22,263 212

Little Cawthorpe
W TARGET SERIES, circ. 82,742 F 262

Long Sutton
W FENLAND CITIZEN SERIES, circ. 41,075 F 184
W LINCOLNSHIRE FREE PRESS SERIES, circ. 33,071 ..212
W WISBECH STANDARD, circ. 19,100 F 276

Louth
D GRIMSBY TELEGRAPH, circ. 34,590 193
W LIFE, circ. 48,406 F 212
W LOUTH LEADER AND CITIZEN SERIES, circ. 101,326 215
W TARGET SERIES, circ. 82,742 F 262

Mablethorpe
D GRIMSBY TELEGRAPH, circ. 34,590 193
W LIFE, circ. 48,406 F 212
W LOUTH LEADER AND CITIZEN SERIES, circ. 101,326 215
W TARGET SERIES, circ. 82,742 F 262

Market Deeping
D ET LIFE 180
D EVENING TELEGRAPH (PETERBOROUGH),
circ. 18,542 182
W LINCOLNSHIRE FREE PRESS SERIES, circ. 33,071 ..212
W THE LOCAL (BOURNE, THE DEEPINGS), circ. 3,600 . 213
W RUTLAND & STAMFORD MERCURY AND CITIZEN
SERIES, circ. 20,490 243

Market Rasen
D GRIMSBY TELEGRAPH, circ. 34,590 193
W LIFE, circ. 48,406 F 212
D LINCOLNSHIRE ECHO, circ. 22,263 212
W MARKET RASEN MAIL, circ. 4,550 218
W TARGET SERIES, circ. 82,742 F 262

Messingham
W SCUNTHORPE TARGET, circ. 58,333 F 244
D SCUNTHORPE TELEGRAPH, circ. 20,568 245

Metheringham
W LINCOLN TARGET SERIES, circ. 47,371 F 212
D LINCOLNSHIRE ECHO, circ. 22,263 212

Nettleham
W LINCOLN TARGET SERIES, circ. 47,371 F 212
D LINCOLNSHIRE ECHO, circ. 22,263 212

New Waltham
D GRIMSBY TELEGRAPH, circ. 34,590 193
W LIFE, circ. 48,406 F 212

Pinchbeck
W LINCOLNSHIRE FREE PRESS SERIES, circ. 33,071 ..212

Ruskington
D LINCOLNSHIRE ECHO, circ. 22,263 212
W SLEAFORD STANDARD AND CITIZEN SERIES,
circ. 4,771 248
W TARGET SERIES, circ. 82,742 F 262

Saxilby
W LINCOLN TARGET SERIES, circ. 47,371 F 212
D LINCOLNSHIRE ECHO, circ. 22,263 212

Scawby
W SCUNTHORPE TARGET, circ. 58,333 F 244

Scunthorpe
W JOURNAL & ADVERTISER SERIES, circ. 30,000 F ... 205
W SCUNTHORPE TARGET, circ. 58,333 F 244
D SCUNTHORPE TELEGRAPH, circ. 20,568 245
D YORKSHIRE POST, circ. 49,031 279

Skegness
D GRIMSBY TELEGRAPH, circ. 34,590 193
W LIFE, circ. 48,406 F 212
D LINCOLNSHIRE ECHO, circ. 22,263 212
W SKEGNESS STANDARD AND CITIZEN SERIES,
circ. 23,645 248
W TARGET SERIES, circ. 82,742 F 262

W **Local/Weekly Newspapers**　　D **Regional Daily Newspapers**　　S **Regional Sunday Newspapers**　　F **Free Newspapers**

Non-Nationals - England

Title (Day/am/pm)	Circ.	Page No.

Skellingthorpe
W LINCOLN TARGET SERIES, circ. 47,371 F 212
D LINCOLNSHIRE ECHO, circ. 22,263 212

Sleaford
D LINCOLNSHIRE ECHO, circ. 22,263 212
W SLEAFORD STANDARD AND CITIZEN SERIES,
   circ. 4,771 248
W TARGET SERIES, circ. 82,742 F 262

Spalding
D ET LIFE 180
D EVENING TELEGRAPH (PETERBOROUGH),
   circ. 18,542 182
W LINCOLNSHIRE FREE PRESS SERIES, circ. 33,071 ..212
W TARGET SERIES, circ. 82,742 F 262

Spilsby
D LINCOLNSHIRE ECHO, circ. 22,263 212
W SKEGNESS STANDARD AND CITIZEN SERIES,
   circ. 23,645 248
W TARGET SERIES, circ. 82,742 F 262

Stamford
D ET LIFE 180
D EVENING TELEGRAPH (PETERBOROUGH),
   circ. 18,542 182
W RUTLAND & STAMFORD MERCURY AND CITIZEN
   SERIES, circ. 20,490 243
W RUTLAND TIMES, circ. 4,562 243

Sutton-on-Sea
W LOUTH LEADER AND CITIZEN SERIES, circ. 101,326 215

Syston
W LEICESTER MAIL SERIES, circ. 141,536 F 210
W TIMES SERIES (MELTON MOWBRAY), circ. 25,726 ... 264

Waddington
D EXPRESS & STAR (CITY/LONDON OFFICE) 183

Waltham
D GRIMSBY TELEGRAPH, circ. 34,590 193
W HERTFORDSHIRE MERCURY SERIES, circ. 26,720 ...199
W LIFE, circ. 48,406 F 212

Washingborough
W LINCOLN TARGET SERIES, circ. 47,371 F 212
D LINCOLNSHIRE ECHO, circ. 22,263 212

Welton
W LINCOLN TARGET SERIES, circ. 47,371 F 212
D LINCOLNSHIRE ECHO, circ. 22,263 212

Winterton
W SCUNTHORPE TARGET, circ. 58,333 F 244

Woodhall Spa
W HORNCASTLE NEWS, circ. 5,450 200
D LINCOLNSHIRE ECHO, circ. 22,263 212
W TARGET SERIES, circ. 82,742 F 262

London East
W ESSEX ENQUIRER SERIES, circ. 57,859 F 180

London South
W TIMES AND REPORTER SERIES (KENT),
   circ. 154,146 263

Merseyside

Bebington
D LIVERPOOL ECHO, circ. 109,458 213
W WIRRAL GLOBE SERIES, circ. 133,193 F 275
W WIRRAL NEWS SERIES, circ. 132,829 F 276

Billinge
W ST. HELENS STAR, circ. 78,827 F 253

Birkenhead
W YR ANGOR (LIVERPOOL), circ. 3,000 142
D LIVERPOOL DAILY POST, circ. 15,581 213
D LIVERPOOL ECHO, circ. 109,458 213
W WIRRAL GLOBE SERIES, circ. 133,193 F 275
W WIRRAL NEWS SERIES, circ. 132,829 F 276

Bootle
W CROSBY HERALD & BOOTLE TIMES SERIES,
   circ. 28,145 168
D LIVERPOOL DAILY POST, circ. 15,581 213

Crosby
W CROSBY HERALD & BOOTLE TIMES SERIES,
   circ. 28,145 168
D LIVERPOOL DAILY POST, circ. 15,581 213
D LIVERPOOL ECHO, circ. 109,458 213

Formby
W FORMBY TIMES, circ. 3,885 186
D LIVERPOOL ECHO, circ. 109,458 213
W SOUTHPORT, ORMSKIRK & FORMBY CHAMPION
   SERIES, circ. 94,383 F 252

Greasby
W CHESTER CHRONICLE SERIES, circ. 85,077 160
D LIVERPOOL DAILY POST, circ. 15,581 213
D LIVERPOOL ECHO, circ. 109,458 213
W WIRRAL GLOBE SERIES, circ. 133,193 F 275
W WIRRAL NEWS SERIES, circ. 132,829 F 276

Haydock
W ST. HELENS REPORTER SERIES, circ. 78,750 F 253
W ST. HELENS STAR, circ. 78,827 F 253
W THE WIGAN OBSERVER, REPORTER AND NEWS
   SERIES, circ. 141,632 274

Heswall
W CHESTER CHRONICLE SERIES, circ. 85,077 160
W WIRRAL GLOBE SERIES, circ. 133,193 F 275
W WIRRAL NEWS SERIES, circ. 132,829 F 276

Hoylake
W WIRRAL GLOBE SERIES, circ. 133,193 F 275
W WIRRAL NEWS SERIES, circ. 132,829 F 276

Huyton
W THE CHALLENGE, circ. 75,000 F 159
W LIVERPOOL WEEKLY MERSEYMART & STAR SERIES,
   circ. 128,081 F 213

Kirkby
W THE CHALLENGE, circ. 75,000 F 159

Knowsley
W THE CHALLENGE, circ. 75,000 F 159
W LIVERPOOL WEEKLY MERSEYMART & STAR SERIES,
   circ. 128,081 F 213
W ST. HELENS REPORTER SERIES, circ. 78,750 F ..253

Litherland
D LIVERPOOL DAILY POST, circ. 15,581 213
D LIVERPOOL ECHO, circ. 109,458 213

Liverpool
W YR ANGOR (LIVERPOOL), circ. 3,000 142
W THE CHALLENGE, circ. 75,000 F 159
D LIVERPOOL DAILY POST, circ. 15,581 213
D LIVERPOOL ECHO, circ. 109,458 213
W LIVERPOOL WEEKLY MERSEYMART & STAR SERIES,
   circ. 128,081 F 213

Lydiate
D LIVERPOOL DAILY POST, circ. 15,581 213
D LIVERPOOL ECHO, circ. 109,458 213
W LIVERPOOL WEEKLY MERSEYMART & STAR SERIES,
   circ. 128,081 F 213

Maghull
D LIVERPOOL DAILY POST, circ. 15,581 213
D LIVERPOOL ECHO, circ. 109,458 213
W LIVERPOOL WEEKLY MERSEYMART & STAR SERIES,
   circ. 128,081 F 213
W SOUTHPORT, ORMSKIRK & FORMBY CHAMPION
   SERIES, circ. 94,383 F 252

Moreton
D LIVERPOOL DAILY POST, circ. 15,581 213
D LIVERPOOL ECHO, circ. 109,458 213
W WIRRAL GLOBE SERIES, circ. 133,193 F 275
W WIRRAL NEWS SERIES, circ. 132,829 F 276

Newton-le-Willows
W ST. HELENS STAR, circ. 78,827 F 253

Prescot
W THE CHALLENGE, circ. 75,000 F 159
W ST. HELENS REPORTER SERIES, circ. 78,750 F ..253
W ST. HELENS STAR, circ. 78,827 F 253
W THE WIGAN OBSERVER, REPORTER AND NEWS
   SERIES, circ. 141,632 274

Rainhill
W ST. HELENS STAR, circ. 78,827 F 253

Sefton
W FORMBY TIMES, circ. 3,885 186
W LIVERPOOL WEEKLY MERSEYMART & STAR SERIES,
   circ. 128,081 F 213

Southport
D LANCASHIRE EVENING POST, circ. 31,225 208
D LIVERPOOL DAILY POST, circ. 15,581 213
D LIVERPOOL ECHO, circ. 109,458 213
W SOUTHPORT, ORMSKIRK & FORMBY CHAMPION
   SERIES, circ. 94,383 F 252
W SOUTHPORT VISITER SERIES, circ. 73,905 252

St. Helens
D LIVERPOOL DAILY POST, circ. 15,581 213
D LIVERPOOL ECHO, circ. 109,458 213
D MANCHESTER EVENING NEWS, circ. 82,445 217
W ST. HELENS REPORTER SERIES, circ. 78,750 F 253
W ST. HELENS STAR, circ. 78,827 F 253

Wallasey
D LIVERPOOL DAILY POST, circ. 15,581 213
D LIVERPOOL ECHO, circ. 109,458 213
W WIRRAL GLOBE SERIES, circ. 133,193 F 275
W WIRRAL NEWS SERIES, circ. 132,829 F 276

West Kirby
W WIRRAL GLOBE SERIES, circ. 133,193 F 275
W WIRRAL NEWS SERIES, circ. 132,829 F 276

Whiston
W THE CHALLENGE, circ. 75,000 F 159

Wirral
W WIRRAL GLOBE SERIES, circ. 133,193 F 275
W WIRRAL NEWS SERIES, circ. 132,829 F 276

Merton Borough

Merton
W GUARDIAN & NEWS SERIES (SUTTON),
   circ. 315,438 193

Mitcham
W GUARDIAN & NEWS SERIES (SUTTON),
   circ. 315,438 193
W SURREY COMET, circ. 10,182 260

Morden
W GUARDIAN & NEWS SERIES (SUTTON),
   circ. 315,438 193
W SURREY COMET, circ. 10,182 260

Wimbledon
W GUARDIAN & NEWS SERIES (SUTTON),
   circ. 315,438 193
W SURREY COMET, circ. 10,182 260

Newham Borough

W NEWHAM RECORDER, circ. 13,531 226
W STRATFORD & NEWHAM EXPRESS, circ. 49,981 F . 257

East Ham
W YELLOW ADVERTISER GROUP SERIES (ESSEX),
   circ. 434,612 F 278

Newham
W YELLOW ADVERTISER GROUP SERIES (ESSEX),
   circ. 434,612 F 278

Stratford
W WALTHAM FOREST GUARDIAN & INDEPENDENT
   SERIES, circ. 52,115 268
W YELLOW ADVERTISER GROUP SERIES (ESSEX),
   circ. 434,612 F 278

Norfolk

D EASTERN DAILY PRESS (NORWICH), circ. 64,700 178

Attleborough
W DISS EXPRESS, circ. 8,486 173
W NORFOLK COUNTY WEEKLIES SERIES, circ. 82,422 229

Aylsham
W ANGLIA ADVERTISER SERIES, circ. 94,387 F 142
W NORFOLK COUNTY WEEKLIES SERIES, circ. 82,422 229

Belton
W GREAT YARMOUTH ADVERTISER SERIES,
   circ. 84,667 F 192

Brundall
D NORWICH EVENING NEWS, circ. 22,914 232

Caister-on-Sea
W GREAT YARMOUTH MERCURY, circ. 18,367 192
D NORWICH EVENING NEWS, circ. 22,914 232

Cromer
W NORFOLK COUNTY WEEKLIES SERIES, circ. 82,422 229

Dereham
W NORFOLK COUNTY WEEKLIES SERIES, circ. 82,422 229

Dersingham
W THE CITIZEN (LYNN & DISTRICT), circ. 39,962 F ... 162
W LYNN NEWS SERIES, circ. 48,609 216

W **Local/Weekly Newspapers**   D **Regional Daily Newspapers**   S **Regional Sunday Newspapers**   F **Free Newspapers**

Title (Day/am/pm)	Circ.	Page No.

Diss
W DISS EXPRESS, circ. 8,486 173
D EA WEEK 176
D EAST ANGLIAN DAILY TIMES, circ. 34,392 176
W NORFOLK COUNTY WEEKLIES SERIES, circ. 82,422 229

Downham Market
W THE CITIZEN (LYNN & DISTRICT), circ. 39,962 F 162
W LYNN NEWS SERIES, circ. 48,609 216
W NORFOLK COUNTY WEEKLIES SERIES, circ. 82,422 229

East Dereham
W NORFOLK COUNTY WEEKLIES SERIES, circ. 82,422 229

Fakenham
W LYNN NEWS SERIES, circ. 48,609 216
W NORFOLK COUNTY WEEKLIES SERIES, circ. 82,422 229

Feltwell
W BURY FREE PRESS & CITIZEN SERIES, circ. 53,112 . 155
D EA WEEK 176
D EAST ANGLIAN DAILY TIMES, circ. 34,392 176

Gorleston
W GREAT YARMOUTH ADVERTISER SERIES,
    circ. 84,667 F 192
W GREAT YARMOUTH MERCURY, circ. 18,367 192

Great Yarmouth
W GREAT YARMOUTH ADVERTISER SERIES,
    circ. 84,667 F 192
W GREAT YARMOUTH MERCURY, circ. 18,367 192
D NORWICH EVENING NEWS, circ. 22,914 232

Harleston
W COMMUNITY NEWS SERIES, circ. 31,000 F 164
W DISS EXPRESS, circ. 8,486 173
W NORFOLK COUNTY WEEKLIES SERIES, circ. 82,422 229

Heacham
W THE CITIZEN (LYNN & DISTRICT), circ. 39,962 F 162
W LYNN NEWS SERIES, circ. 48,609 216

Hemsby
W GREAT YARMOUTH ADVERTISER SERIES,
    circ. 84,667 F 192
W GREAT YARMOUTH MERCURY, circ. 18,367 192
D NORWICH EVENING NEWS, circ. 22,914 232

Hethersett
W NORFOLK COUNTY WEEKLIES SERIES, circ. 82,422 229
D NORWICH EVENING NEWS, circ. 22,914 232

Holt
W NORFOLK COUNTY WEEKLIES SERIES, circ. 82,422 229

Hoveton
W NORFOLK COUNTY WEEKLIES SERIES, circ. 82,422 229
D NORWICH EVENING NEWS, circ. 22,914 232

Hunstanton
W THE CITIZEN (LYNN & DISTRICT), circ. 39,962 F .. 162
W LYNN NEWS SERIES, circ. 48,609 216

King's Lynn
W THE CITIZEN (LYNN & DISTRICT), circ. 39,962 F .. 162
W LYNN NEWS SERIES, circ. 48,609 216

Loddon
D NORWICH EVENING NEWS, circ. 22,914 232

North Walsham
W ANGLIA ADVERTISER SERIES, circ. 94,387 F 142
W NORFOLK COUNTY WEEKLIES SERIES, circ. 82,422 229

Norwich
W ANGLIA ADVERTISER SERIES, circ. 94,387 F 142
D NORWICH EVENING NEWS, circ. 22,914 232

Outwell
D ET LIFE 180
D EVENING TELEGRAPH (PETERBOROUGH),
    circ. 18,542 182
W FENLAND CITIZEN SERIES, circ. 41,075 F 184
W WISBECH STANDARD, circ. 19,100 F 276

Poringland
D NORWICH EVENING NEWS, circ. 22,914 232

Sheringham
W NORFOLK COUNTY WEEKLIES SERIES, circ. 82,422 229

Spixworth
D NORWICH EVENING NEWS, circ. 22,914 232

Stalham
W NORFOLK COUNTY WEEKLIES SERIES, circ. 82,422 229

Swaffham
D CAMBRIDGE NEWS, circ. 26,242 157
W LYNN NEWS SERIES, circ. 48,609 216
W NORFOLK COUNTY WEEKLIES SERIES, circ. 82,422 229

Taverham
W NORWICH EVENING NEWS, circ. 22,914 232

Terrington St. Clement
W THE CITIZEN (LYNN & DISTRICT), circ. 39,962 F .. 162
W LYNN NEWS SERIES, circ. 48,609 216
W WISBECH STANDARD, circ. 19,100 F 276

Thetford
W BURY FREE PRESS & CITIZEN SERIES, circ. 53,112 . 155
W MERCURY SERIES, circ. 45,543 F 220
W NORFOLK COUNTY WEEKLIES SERIES, circ. 82,422 229

Watton
W NORFOLK COUNTY WEEKLIES SERIES, circ. 82,422 229

Wells-next-the-Sea
W NORFOLK COUNTY WEEKLIES SERIES, circ. 82,422 229

Wroxham
W GREAT YARMOUTH MERCURY, circ. 18,367 192
W NORFOLK COUNTY WEEKLIES SERIES, circ. 82,422 229
D NORWICH EVENING NEWS, circ. 22,914 232

Wymondham
W DISS EXPRESS, circ. 8,486 173
W NORFOLK COUNTY WEEKLIES SERIES, circ. 82,422 229
D NORWICH EVENING NEWS, circ. 22,914 232

North Yorkshire
W JOURNAL & ADVERTISER SERIES, circ. 30,000 F ... 205
D LIFE AND STYLE 212
D YORKSHIRE POST, circ. 49,031 279
D YORKSHIRE POST (CITY/LONDON OFFICE) 279

Bedale
W ACKRILL NEWSPAPER SERIES, circ. 64,177 137
W ADVERTISER SERIES (DURHAM), circ. 193,884 F ... 139
W DARLINGTON & STOCKTON TIMES SERIES,
    circ. 27,577 171

Bishopthorpe
D THE NORTHERN ECHO (DARLINGTON), circ. 50,256 232
D THE PRESS (YORK), circ. 35,761 238

Boroughbridge
W ACKRILL NEWSPAPER SERIES, circ. 64,177 137

Boston Spa
W ACKRILL NEWSPAPER SERIES, circ. 64,177 137
D THE PRESS (YORK), circ. 35,761 238
D YORKSHIRE EVENING POST, circ. 56,647 279

Brotton
W ADVERTISER SERIES (DURHAM), circ. 193,884 F ... 139
D EVENING GAZETTE (MIDDLESBROUGH),
    circ. 50,920 181

Catterick
W ACKRILL NEWSPAPER SERIES, circ. 64,177 137
W ADVERTISER SERIES (DURHAM), circ. 193,884 F ... 139
W DARLINGTON & STOCKTON TIMES SERIES,
    circ. 27,577 171
D THE NORTHERN ECHO (DARLINGTON), circ. 50,256 232
S SUNDAY SUN, circ. 68,033 259

Catterick Garrison
W ACKRILL NEWSPAPER SERIES, circ. 64,177 137
W DARLINGTON & STOCKTON TIMES SERIES,
    circ. 27,577 171
D THE NORTHERN ECHO (DARLINGTON), circ. 50,256 232
S SUNDAY SUN, circ. 68,033 259

Copmanthorpe
D THE NORTHERN ECHO (DARLINGTON), circ. 50,256 232
D THE PRESS (YORK), circ. 35,761 238

Dunnington
D THE NORTHERN ECHO (DARLINGTON), circ. 50,256 232
D POCKLINGTON POST, circ. 4,605 236
D THE PRESS (YORK), circ. 35,761 238

Easingwold
W EASINGWOLD ADVERTISER & WEEKLY NEWS,
    circ. 3,500 176
W STAR SERIES (SELBY & YORK), circ. 67,353 F ... 255

Eastfield
W THE MERCURY SERIES (SCARBOROUGH),
    circ. 5,853 220
D THE NORTHERN ECHO (DARLINGTON), circ. 50,256 232
D THE PRESS (YORK), circ. 35,761 238
D SCARBOROUGH EVENING NEWS, circ. 17,239 244

(untitled, right column top)
S SUNDAY SUN, circ. 68,033 259
W TRADER SCARBOROUGH, FILEY AND HUNMANBY,
    circ. 35,900 F 265

Eston
D EVENING GAZETTE (MIDDLESBROUGH),
    circ. 50,920 181
D THE NORTHERN ECHO (DARLINGTON), circ. 50,256 232

Filey
W THE MERCURY SERIES (SCARBOROUGH),
    circ. 5,853 220
D SCARBOROUGH EVENING NEWS, circ. 17,239 244
W TRADER SCARBOROUGH, FILEY AND HUNMANBY,
    circ. 35,900 F 265

Glusburn
W CRAVEN HERALD & PIONEER, circ. 17,661 167
D TELEGRAPH & ARGUS, circ. 37,371 262

Great Ayton
W DARLINGTON & STOCKTON TIMES SERIES,
    circ. 27,577 171
W HERALD AND POST SERIES (TEESSIDE),
    circ. 232,382 F 197

Guisborough
W ADVERTISER SERIES (DURHAM), circ. 193,884 F ... 139
W DARLINGTON & STOCKTON TIMES SERIES,
    circ. 27,577 171
D EVENING GAZETTE (MIDDLESBROUGH),
    circ. 50,920 181
W HERALD AND POST SERIES (TEESSIDE),
    circ. 232,382 F 197
W WHITBY GAZETTE SERIES, circ. 12,017 274

Harrogate
W ACKRILL NEWSPAPER SERIES, circ. 64,177 137
W JOURNAL & ADVERTISER SERIES, circ. 30,000 F .. 205
D THE PRESS (YORK), circ. 35,761 238
D YORKSHIRE EVENING POST, circ. 56,647 279

Haxby
D THE NORTHERN ECHO (DARLINGTON), circ. 50,256 232
D THE PRESS (YORK), circ. 35,761 238

Helmsley
W GAZETTE & HERALD (RYEDALE & SCARBOROUGH),
    circ. 13,184 188
D THE PRESS (YORK), circ. 35,761 238

Hunmanby
W THE MERCURY SERIES (SCARBOROUGH),
    circ. 5,853 220
W TRADER SCARBOROUGH, FILEY AND HUNMANBY,
    circ. 35,900 F 265

Ingleton
W CRAVEN HERALD & PIONEER, circ. 17,661 167
W LANCASTER GUARDIAN SERIES, circ. 16,306 209
W WESTMORLAND GAZETTE NEWSPAPER SERIES,
    circ. 56,020 273

Kirkbymoorside
W GAZETTE & HERALD (RYEDALE & SCARBOROUGH),
    circ. 13,184 188
W THE MERCURY SERIES (SCARBOROUGH),
    circ. 5,853 220

Knaresborough
W ACKRILL NEWSPAPER SERIES, circ. 64,177 137
D THE PRESS (YORK), circ. 35,761 238
D YORKSHIRE EVENING POST, circ. 56,647 279

Leyburn
W DARLINGTON & STOCKTON TIMES SERIES,
    circ. 27,577 171

Loftus
W ADVERTISER SERIES (DURHAM), circ. 193,884 F ... 139
D EVENING GAZETTE (MIDDLESBROUGH),
    circ. 50,920 181
W WHITBY GAZETTE SERIES, circ. 12,017 274

Malton
W GAZETTE & HERALD (RYEDALE & SCARBOROUGH),
    circ. 13,184 188
W THE MERCURY SERIES (SCARBOROUGH),
    circ. 5,853 220
D THE PRESS (YORK), circ. 35,761 238
D SCARBOROUGH EVENING NEWS, circ. 17,239 244

Marske-by-the-Sea
W ADVERTISER SERIES (DURHAM), circ. 193,884 F ... 139
D EVENING GAZETTE (MIDDLESBROUGH),
    circ. 50,920 181
W HERALD AND POST SERIES (TEESSIDE),
    circ. 232,382 F 197
D THE NORTHERN ECHO (DARLINGTON), circ. 50,256 232

W Local/Weekly Newspapers   D Regional Daily Newspapers   S Regional Sunday Newspapers   F Free Newspapers

Non-Nationals - England

Title *(Day/am/pm)*	Circ.	Page No.	Title *(Day/am/pm)*	Circ.	Page No.	Title *(Day/am/pm)*	Circ.	Page No.

Middlesbrough
[D] EVENING GAZETTE (MIDDLESBROUGH), circ. 50,920 181
[W] HERALD AND POST SERIES (TEESSIDE), circ. 232,382 [F] 197
[D] THE NORTHERN ECHO (DARLINGTON), circ. 50,256 232
[S] SUNDAY SUN, circ. 68,033 259

New Marske
[W] ADVERTISER SERIES (DURHAM), circ. 193,884 [F] ... 139
[D] EVENING GAZETTE (MIDDLESBROUGH), circ. 50,920 181
[W] HERALD AND POST SERIES (TEESSIDE), circ. 232,382 [F] 197
[D] THE NORTHERN ECHO (DARLINGTON), circ. 50,256 232

Northallerton
[W] ACKRILL NEWSPAPER SERIES, circ. 64,177 137
[W] ADVERTISER SERIES (DURHAM), circ. 193,884 [F] ... 139
[W] DARLINGTON & STOCKTON TIMES SERIES, circ. 27,577 171
[D] EVENING GAZETTE (MIDDLESBROUGH), circ. 50,920 181
[W] HERALD AND POST SERIES (TEESSIDE), circ. 232,382 [F] 197
[D] THE NORTHERN ECHO (DARLINGTON), circ. 50,256 232
[D] THE PRESS (YORK), circ. 35,761 238

Norton
[W] COMMUNITY NEWSLETTER SERIES, circ. 42,000 [F] 164
[D] SCARBOROUGH EVENING NEWS, circ. 17,239 244

Pateley Bridge
[W] ACKRILL NEWSPAPER SERIES, circ. 64,177 137

Pickering
[W] GAZETTE & HERALD (RYEDALE & SCARBOROUGH), circ. 13,184 188
[W] THE MERCURY SERIES (SCARBOROUGH), circ. 5,853 220
[D] THE PRESS (YORK), circ. 35,761 238
[D] SCARBOROUGH EVENING NEWS, circ. 17,239 244

Redcar
[W] ADVERTISER SERIES (DURHAM), circ. 193,884 [F] ... 139
[D] EVENING GAZETTE (MIDDLESBROUGH), circ. 50,920 181
[W] HERALD AND POST SERIES (TEESSIDE), circ. 232,382 [F] 197
[W] WHITBY GAZETTE SERIES, circ. 12,017 274

Richmond
[W] ACKRILL NEWSPAPER SERIES, circ. 64,177 137
[W] ADVERTISER SERIES (DURHAM), circ. 193,884 [F] ... 139
[W] DARLINGTON & STOCKTON TIMES SERIES, circ. 27,577 171
[D] THE NORTHERN ECHO (DARLINGTON), circ. 50,256 232
[S] SUNDAY SUN, circ. 68,033 259

Ripon
[W] ACKRILL NEWSPAPER SERIES, circ. 64,177 137
[W] DARLINGTON & STOCKTON TIMES SERIES, circ. 27,577 171
[D] THE NORTHERN ECHO (DARLINGTON), circ. 50,256 232

Ryedale
[W] GAZETTE & HERALD (RYEDALE & SCARBOROUGH), circ. 13,184 188

Saltburn
[W] ADVERTISER SERIES (DURHAM), circ. 193,884 [F] ... 139
[W] DARLINGTON & STOCKTON TIMES SERIES, circ. 27,577 171
[D] EVENING GAZETTE (MIDDLESBROUGH), circ. 50,920 181
[W] HERALD AND POST SERIES (TEESSIDE), circ. 232,382 [F] 197
[W] WHITBY GAZETTE SERIES, circ. 12,017 274

Scalby
[W] THE MERCURY SERIES (SCARBOROUGH), circ. 5,853 220
[D] THE NORTHERN ECHO (DARLINGTON), circ. 50,256 232
[D] THE PRESS (YORK), circ. 35,761 238
[D] SCARBOROUGH EVENING NEWS, circ. 17,239 244
[S] SUNDAY SUN, circ. 68,033 259
[W] TRADER SCARBOROUGH, FILEY AND HUNMANBY, circ. 35,900 [F] 265

Scarborough
[W] GAZETTE & HERALD (RYEDALE & SCARBOROUGH), circ. 13,184 188
[W] THE MERCURY SERIES (SCARBOROUGH), circ. 5,853 220
[D] THE PRESS (YORK), circ. 35,761 238
[D] SCARBOROUGH EVENING NEWS, circ. 17,239 244
[S] SUNDAY SUN, circ. 68,033 259

Scotch Corner
[D] THE NORTHERN ECHO (DARLINGTON), circ. 50,256 232

Selby
[D] THE PRESS (YORK), circ. 35,761 238
[S] SELBY POST, circ. 5,000 245
[W] SELBY TIMES SERIES, circ. 22,001 245
[W] STAR SERIES (SELBY & YORK), circ. 67,353 [F] 255
[D] YORKSHIRE EVENING POST, circ. 56,647 279

Settle
[W] CRAVEN HERALD & PIONEER, circ. 17,661 167
[W] LANCASTER GUARDIAN SERIES, circ. 16,306 209

Sherburn
[W] THE MERCURY SERIES (SCARBOROUGH), circ. 5,853 220

Skelton
[W] ADVERTISER SERIES (DURHAM), circ. 193,884 [F] ... 139
[D] EVENING GAZETTE (MIDDLESBROUGH), circ. 50,920 181
[W] HERALD AND POST SERIES (TEESSIDE), circ. 232,382 [F] 197
[D] THE NORTHERN ECHO (DARLINGTON), circ. 50,256 232

Skipton
[W] BRADFORD TARGET SERIES, circ. 88,522 [F] 151
[W] CRAVEN HERALD & PIONEER, circ. 17,661 167
[D] TELEGRAPH & ARGUS, circ. 37,371 262

South Bank
[D] EVENING GAZETTE (MIDDLESBROUGH), circ. 50,920 181
[W] HERALD AND POST SERIES (TEESSIDE), circ. 232,382 [F] 197
[D] THE NORTHERN ECHO (DARLINGTON), circ. 50,256 232

Spofforth
[D] THE PRESS (YORK), circ. 35,761 238

Stokesley
[W] DARLINGTON & STOCKTON TIMES SERIES, circ. 27,577 171
[D] EVENING GAZETTE (MIDDLESBROUGH), circ. 50,920 181
[W] HERALD AND POST SERIES (TEESSIDE), circ. 232,382 [F] 197
[D] THE NORTHERN ECHO (DARLINGTON), circ. 50,256 232

Strensall
[D] THE NORTHERN ECHO (DARLINGTON), circ. 50,256 232
[D] THE PRESS (YORK), circ. 35,761 238

Tadcaster
[W] ACKRILL NEWSPAPER SERIES, circ. 64,177 137
[D] THE PRESS (YORK), circ. 35,761 238
[D] YORKSHIRE EVENING POST, circ. 56,647 279

Thirsk
[W] ACKRILL NEWSPAPER SERIES, circ. 64,177 137
[W] ADVERTISER SERIES (DURHAM), circ. 193,884 [F] ... 139
[W] DARLINGTON & STOCKTON TIMES SERIES, circ. 27,577 171
[D] THE NORTHERN ECHO (DARLINGTON), circ. 50,256 232
[D] THE PRESS (YORK), circ. 35,761 238

Thornaby-on-Tees
[D] EVENING GAZETTE (MIDDLESBROUGH), circ. 50,920 181
[W] HERALD AND POST SERIES (TEESSIDE), circ. 232,382 [F] 197

Whitby
[D] EVENING GAZETTE (MIDDLESBROUGH), circ. 50,920 181
[D] SCARBOROUGH EVENING NEWS, circ. 17,239 244
[S] SUNDAY SUN, circ. 68,033 259
[W] WHITBY GAZETTE SERIES, circ. 12,017 274

York
[D] THE PRESS (YORK), circ. 35,761 238
[W] STAR SERIES (SELBY & YORK), circ. 67,353 [F] 255
[D] YORKSHIRE EVENING POST, circ. 56,647 279

Northamptonshire
[S] NORTHANTS ON SUNDAY, circ. 50,000 [F] 231

Abington
[W] NORTHANTS HERALD AND POST SERIES, circ. 128,956 [F] 231

Brackley
[W] BANBURY GUARDIAN REVIEW SERIES, circ. 55,138 145
[W] BUCKINGHAM ADVERTISER SERIES, circ. 19,132 153
[W] NORTHANTS HERALD AND POST SERIES, circ. 128,956 [F] 231

Brixworth
[D] NORTHAMPTON CHRONICLE AND ECHO, circ. 20,070 231
[W] NORTHAMPTON MERCURY, circ. 48,615 [F] 231
[W] NORTHANTS HERALD AND POST SERIES, circ. 128,956 [F] 231

Bugbrooke
[D] NORTHAMPTON CHRONICLE AND ECHO, circ. 20,070 231
[W] NORTHAMPTON MERCURY, circ. 48,615 [F] 231
[W] NORTHANTS HERALD AND POST SERIES, circ. 128,956 [F] 231

Burton Latimer
[D] NORTHAMPTONSHIRE EVENING TELEGRAPH, circ. 22,915 231
[W] NORTHANTS HERALD AND POST SERIES, circ. 128,956 [F] 231
[W] NORTHANTS MERCURY & CITIZEN SERIES, circ. 49,503 [F] 231

Corby
[D] NORTHAMPTONSHIRE EVENING TELEGRAPH, circ. 22,915 231
[W] NORTHANTS HERALD AND POST SERIES, circ. 128,956 [F] 231
[W] NORTHANTS MERCURY & CITIZEN SERIES, circ. 49,503 [F] 231

Daventry
[D] COVENTRY TELEGRAPH, circ. 48,025 167
[D] DAVENTRY EXPRESS AND REVIEW SERIES, circ. 9,323 171
[D] NORTHAMPTON CHRONICLE AND ECHO, circ. 20,070 231
[W] THE RUGBY OBSERVER SERIES, circ. 42,974 [F] 242

Deanshanger
[W] MILTON KEYNES CITIZEN SERIES, circ. 205,772 [F] . 223
[D] NORTHAMPTON CHRONICLE AND ECHO, circ. 20,070 231

Desborough
[W] THE MAIL SERIES, circ. 12,552 217
[D] NORTHAMPTONSHIRE EVENING TELEGRAPH, circ. 22,915 231
[W] NORTHANTS HERALD AND POST SERIES, circ. 128,956 [F] 231
[W] NORTHANTS MERCURY & CITIZEN SERIES, circ. 49,503 [F] 231

Earls Barton
[D] NORTHAMPTON CHRONICLE AND ECHO, circ. 20,070 231
[D] NORTHAMPTONSHIRE EVENING TELEGRAPH, circ. 22,915 231
[W] NORTHANTS MERCURY & CITIZEN SERIES, circ. 49,503 [F] 231

Finedon
[D] NORTHAMPTONSHIRE EVENING TELEGRAPH, circ. 22,915 231
[W] NORTHANTS HERALD AND POST SERIES, circ. 128,956 [F] 231
[W] NORTHANTS MERCURY & CITIZEN SERIES, circ. 49,503 [F] 231

Hardingstone
[D] NORTHAMPTON CHRONICLE AND ECHO, circ. 20,070 231
[W] NORTHAMPTON MERCURY, circ. 48,615 [F] 231
[W] NORTHANTS HERALD AND POST SERIES, circ. 128,956 [F] 231

Higham Ferrers
[D] NORTHAMPTONSHIRE EVENING TELEGRAPH, circ. 22,915 231
[W] NORTHANTS HERALD AND POST SERIES, circ. 128,956 [F] 231
[W] NORTHANTS MERCURY & CITIZEN SERIES, circ. 49,503 [F] 231

Irchester
[D] NORTHAMPTONSHIRE EVENING TELEGRAPH, circ. 22,915 231
[W] NORTHANTS HERALD AND POST SERIES, circ. 128,956 [F] 231
[W] NORTHANTS MERCURY & CITIZEN SERIES, circ. 49,503 [F] 231

[W] **Local/Weekly Newspapers**   [D] **Regional Daily Newspapers**   [S] **Regional Sunday Newspapers**   [F] **Free Newspapers**

Title (Day/am/pm)	Circ.	Page No.

Irthlingborough
W NORTHANTS HERALD AND POST SERIES, circ. 128,956 F 231

D NORTHAMPTONSHIRE EVENING TELEGRAPH, circ. 22,915 231
W NORTHANTS HERALD AND POST SERIES, circ. 128,956 F 231
W NORTHANTS MERCURY & CITIZEN SERIES, circ. 49,503 F 231

Kettering
D NORTHAMPTONSHIRE EVENING TELEGRAPH, circ. 22,915 231
W NORTHANTS HERALD AND POST SERIES, circ. 128,956 F 231
W NORTHANTS MERCURY & CITIZEN SERIES, circ. 49,503 F 231

Long Buckby
W DAVENTRY EXPRESS AND REVIEW SERIES, circ. 9,323 171
D NORTHAMPTON CHRONICLE AND ECHO, circ. 20,070 231
W NORTHANTS HERALD AND POST SERIES, circ. 128,956 F 231

Middleton Cheney
W BANBURY GUARDIAN REVIEW SERIES, circ. 55,138 145
W OXFORD MAIL, circ. 25,426 234
S SUNDAY MERCURY (BIRMINGHAM), circ. 59,339 258

Northampton
D NORTHAMPTON CHRONICLE AND ECHO, circ. 20,070 231
W NORTHAMPTON MERCURY, circ. 48,615 F 231
W NORTHANTS HERALD AND POST SERIES, circ. 128,956 F 231

Oundle
D ET LIFE 180
D EVENING TELEGRAPH (PETERBOROUGH), circ. 18,542 182
D NORTHAMPTONSHIRE EVENING TELEGRAPH, circ. 22,915 231
W RUTLAND & STAMFORD MERCURY AND CITIZEN SERIES, circ. 20,490 243

Raunds
D NORTHAMPTONSHIRE EVENING TELEGRAPH, circ. 22,915 231
W NORTHANTS HERALD AND POST SERIES, circ. 128,956 F 231
W NORTHANTS MERCURY & CITIZEN SERIES, circ. 49,503 F 231

Rothwell
D NORTHAMPTONSHIRE EVENING TELEGRAPH, circ. 22,915 231
W NORTHANTS HERALD AND POST SERIES, circ. 128,956 F 231
W NORTHANTS MERCURY & CITIZEN SERIES, circ. 49,503 F 231

Rushden
D NORTHAMPTONSHIRE EVENING TELEGRAPH, circ. 22,915 231
W NORTHANTS HERALD AND POST SERIES, circ. 128,956 F 231
W NORTHANTS MERCURY & CITIZEN SERIES, circ. 49,503 F 231

Thrapston
D NORTHAMPTONSHIRE EVENING TELEGRAPH, circ. 22,915 231

Towcester
W BUCKINGHAM ADVERTISER SERIES, circ. 19,132 153
D NORTHAMPTON CHRONICLE AND ECHO, circ. 20,070 231
W NORTHANTS HERALD AND POST SERIES, circ. 128,956 F 231

Wellingborough
D NORTHAMPTONSHIRE EVENING TELEGRAPH, circ. 22,915 231
W NORTHANTS HERALD AND POST SERIES, circ. 128,956 F 231
W NORTHANTS MERCURY & CITIZEN SERIES, circ. 49,503 F 231

Wollaston
D NORTHAMPTONSHIRE EVENING TELEGRAPH, circ. 22,915 231
W NORTHANTS MERCURY & CITIZEN SERIES, circ. 49,503 F 231

Wootton
W LYNN NEWS SERIES, circ. 48,609 216
W NORTHAMPTON MERCURY, circ. 48,615 F 231

W NORTHANTS HERALD AND POST SERIES, circ. 128,956 F 231

Northumberland
S THE SUNDAY POST (DUNDEE), circ. 354,870 258

Alnmouth
D EVENING CHRONICLE (NEWCASTLE), circ. 78,804 ... 180

Alnwick
D EVENING CHRONICLE (NEWCASTLE), circ. 78,804 ... 180
D THE JOURNAL (NEWCASTLE), circ. 35,476 205
W NORTHUMBERLAND GAZETTE, circ. 10,815 232
S SUNDAY SUN, circ. 68,033 259

Amble
D EVENING CHRONICLE (NEWCASTLE), circ. 78,804 ... 180
W NORTHUMBERLAND GAZETTE, circ. 10,815 232
S SUNDAY SUN, circ. 68,033 259

Ashington
W CHRONICLE EXTRA SERIES (TYNE & WEAR), circ. 387,488 F 161
D EVENING CHRONICLE (NEWCASTLE), circ. 78,804 ... 180
D THE JOURNAL (NEWCASTLE), circ. 35,476 205
W NEWS GUARDIAN SERIES, circ. 131,934 F 227
S SUNDAY SUN, circ. 68,033 259

Bedlington
W CHRONICLE EXTRA SERIES (TYNE & WEAR), circ. 387,488 F 161
D EVENING CHRONICLE (NEWCASTLE), circ. 78,804 ... 180
D THE JOURNAL (NEWCASTLE), circ. 35,476 205
W NEWS GUARDIAN SERIES, circ. 131,934 F 227
S SUNDAY SUN, circ. 68,033 259

Bellingham
W HEXHAM COURANT, circ. 18,379 199
D THE JOURNAL (NEWCASTLE), circ. 35,476 205

Berwick-upon-Tweed
W BERWICK ADVERTISER AND GAZETTE SERIES, circ. 17,626 147

Blyth
W CHRONICLE EXTRA SERIES (TYNE & WEAR), circ. 387,488 F 161
D EVENING CHRONICLE (NEWCASTLE), circ. 78,804 ... 180
D THE JOURNAL (NEWCASTLE), circ. 35,476 205
W NEWS GUARDIAN SERIES, circ. 131,934 F 227
S SUNDAY SUN, circ. 68,033 259

Corbridge
W HEXHAM COURANT, circ. 18,379 199
D THE JOURNAL (NEWCASTLE), circ. 35,476 205
S SUNDAY SUN, circ. 68,033 259

Cramlington
W NEWS GUARDIAN SERIES, circ. 131,934 F 227

Guide Post
W CHRONICLE EXTRA SERIES (TYNE & WEAR), circ. 387,488 F 161
D EVENING CHRONICLE (NEWCASTLE), circ. 78,804 ... 180
D THE JOURNAL (NEWCASTLE), circ. 35,476 205
W NEWS GUARDIAN SERIES, circ. 131,934 F 227
S SUNDAY SUN, circ. 68,033 259

Haltwhistle
W THE CUMBERLAND NEWS & GAZETTE SERIES, circ. 98,340 169
W HEXHAM COURANT, circ. 18,379 199
D THE JOURNAL (NEWCASTLE), circ. 35,476 205
S SUNDAY SUN, circ. 68,033 259

Hexham
W HEXHAM COURANT, circ. 18,379 199
D THE JOURNAL (NEWCASTLE), circ. 35,476 205
S SUNDAY SUN, circ. 68,033 259

Morpeth
W CHRONICLE EXTRA SERIES (TYNE & WEAR), circ. 387,488 F 161
D EVENING CHRONICLE (NEWCASTLE), circ. 78,804 ... 180
D THE JOURNAL (NEWCASTLE), circ. 35,476 205
W MORPETH HERALD INC PONTELAND OBSERVER, circ. 2,947 224
W NEWS GUARDIAN SERIES, circ. 131,934 F 227
S SUNDAY SUN, circ. 68,033 259

Newbiggin-by-the-Sea
D EVENING CHRONICLE (NEWCASTLE), circ. 78,804 ... 180
D THE JOURNAL (NEWCASTLE), circ. 35,476 205
W NEWS GUARDIAN SERIES, circ. 131,934 F 227
S SUNDAY SUN, circ. 68,033 259

Otterburn
D EVENING CHRONICLE (NEWCASTLE), circ. 78,804 ... 180

Painshawfield
D THE JOURNAL (NEWCASTLE), circ. 35,476 205
S SUNDAY SUN, circ. 68,033 259

Pegswood
W CHRONICLE EXTRA SERIES (TYNE & WEAR), circ. 387,488 F 161
D EVENING CHRONICLE (NEWCASTLE), circ. 78,804 ... 180
D THE JOURNAL (NEWCASTLE), circ. 35,476 205
W MORPETH HERALD INC PONTELAND OBSERVER, circ. 2,947 224
W NEWS GUARDIAN SERIES, circ. 131,934 F 227
S SUNDAY SUN, circ. 68,033 259

Ponteland
W HEXHAM COURANT, circ. 18,379 199
W MORPETH HERALD INC PONTELAND OBSERVER, circ. 2,947 224

Prudhoe
W HEXHAM COURANT, circ. 18,379 199
S SUNDAY SUN, circ. 68,033 259

Seaton Delaval
W NEWS GUARDIAN SERIES, circ. 131,934 F 227
S SUNDAY SUN, circ. 68,033 259

Seaton Sluice
W CHRONICLE EXTRA SERIES (TYNE & WEAR), circ. 387,488 F 161
D EVENING CHRONICLE (NEWCASTLE), circ. 78,804 ... 180
D THE JOURNAL (NEWCASTLE), circ. 35,476 205
W NEWS GUARDIAN SERIES, circ. 131,934 F 227
S SUNDAY SUN, circ. 68,033 259

Tyne Valley
W HEXHAM COURANT, circ. 18,379 199

Wooler
W BERWICK ADVERTISER AND GAZETTE SERIES, circ. 17,626 147
D THE JOURNAL (NEWCASTLE), circ. 35,476 205
W NORTHUMBERLAND GAZETTE, circ. 10,815 232

Nottinghamshire
D NOTTINGHAM EVENING POST, circ. 57,699 232
W THE SHERWOOD VILLAGER, circ. 20,000 F 246

Arnold
W JOURNAL & ADVERTISER SERIES, circ. 30,000 F ... 205
W WEST NOTTS & DERBYSHIRE RECORDER SERIES, circ. 260,441 F 271

Awsworth
D DERBY TELEGRAPH, circ. 42,726 172
W EASTWOOD & KIMBERLEY ADVERTISER, circ. 4,189 178
W ILKESTON ADVERTISER, circ. 8,488 202
W WEST NOTTS & DERBYSHIRE RECORDER SERIES, circ. 260,441 F 271

Beeston
W JOURNAL & ADVERTISER SERIES, circ. 30,000 F ... 205
S SUNDAY MERCURY (BIRMINGHAM), circ. 59,339 258
W WEST NOTTS & DERBYSHIRE RECORDER SERIES, circ. 260,441 F 271

Bilsthorpe
W CHAD SERIES MANSFIELD, circ. 61,097 158
W WEST NOTTS & DERBYSHIRE RECORDER SERIES, circ. 260,441 F 271

Bingham
W JOURNAL & ADVERTISER SERIES, circ. 30,000 F ... 205
W NEWARK ADVERTISER SERIES, circ. 50,000 226

Bircotes
W GUARDIAN SERIES (WORKSOP), circ. 95,428 193
W RETFORD GAINSBOROUGH AND WORKSOP TIMES, circ. 10,913 240
D THE STAR SHEFFIELD, circ. 56,363 255

Blidworth
W CHAD SERIES MANSFIELD, circ. 61,097 158
W MANSFIELD AND ASHFIELD OBSERVER, circ. 58,599 F 218
W WEST NOTTS & DERBYSHIRE RECORDER SERIES, circ. 260,441 F 271

Boughton
W CHAD SERIES MANSFIELD, circ. 61,097 158
W MANSFIELD AND ASHFIELD OBSERVER, circ. 58,599 F 218
W WEST NOTTS & DERBYSHIRE RECORDER SERIES, circ. 260,441 F 271

Brinsley
D DERBY TELEGRAPH, circ. 42,726 172
W DERBYSHIRE TIMES SERIES, circ. 40,241 172

W **Local/Weekly Newspapers**   D **Regional Daily Newspapers**   S **Regional Sunday Newspapers**   F **Free Newspapers**

Section 3 Index to UK Newspapers

Non-Nationals - England

Title (Day/am/pm)	Circ.	Page No.

W EASTWOOD & KIMBERLEY ADVERTISER, circ. 4,189 178

Bulwell
W HUCKNALL & BULWELL DISPATCH, circ. 8,426 201

Burton Joyce
W JOURNAL & ADVERTISER SERIES, circ. 30,000 [F] ...205
W WEST NOTTS & DERBYSHIRE RECORDER SERIES, circ. 260,441 [F] 271

Calverton
W JOURNAL & ADVERTISER SERIES, circ. 30,000 [F] ...205
W WEST NOTTS & DERBYSHIRE RECORDER SERIES, circ. 260,441 [F] 271

Carlton
W JOURNAL & ADVERTISER SERIES, circ. 30,000 [F] ...205
W WEST NOTTS & DERBYSHIRE RECORDER SERIES, circ. 260,441 [F] 271

Carlton in Lindrick
W GUARDIAN SERIES (WORKSOP), circ. 95,428 193
W RETFORD GAINSBOROUGH AND WORKSOP TIMES, circ. 10,913 240
D THE STAR SHEFFIELD, circ. 56,363 255

Cotgrave
W JOURNAL & ADVERTISER SERIES, circ. 30,000 [F] ...205
W WEST NOTTS & DERBYSHIRE RECORDER SERIES, circ. 260,441 [F] 271

East Leake
W JOURNAL & ADVERTISER SERIES, circ. 30,000 [F] ...205
W WEST NOTTS & DERBYSHIRE RECORDER SERIES, circ. 260,441 [F] 271

East Retford
W GUARDIAN SERIES (WORKSOP), circ. 95,428 193
W RETFORD GAINSBOROUGH AND WORKSOP TIMES, circ. 10,913 240
D THE STAR SHEFFIELD, circ. 56,363 255

Eastwood
W EASTWOOD & KIMBERLEY ADVERTISER, circ. 4,189 178
W RIPLEY & HEANOR NEWS, circ. 10,394 240

Edwinstowe
W CHAD SERIES MANSFIELD, circ. 61,097 158
W MANSFIELD AND ASHFIELD OBSERVER, circ. 58,599 [F] 218
W WEST NOTTS & DERBYSHIRE RECORDER SERIES, circ. 260,441 [F] 271

Farnsfield
W CHAD SERIES MANSFIELD, circ. 61,097 158
W WEST NOTTS & DERBYSHIRE RECORDER SERIES, circ. 260,441 [F] 271

Harworth
W COMMUNITY NEWSLETTER SERIES, circ. 42,000 [F] 164
W GUARDIAN SERIES (WORKSOP), circ. 95,428 193
W RETFORD GAINSBOROUGH AND WORKSOP TIMES, circ. 10,913 240
D THE STAR SHEFFIELD, circ. 56,363 255

Hucknall
W HUCKNALL & BULWELL DISPATCH, circ. 8,426 201

Keyworth
W JOURNAL & ADVERTISER SERIES, circ. 30,000 [F] ...205
W WEST NOTTS & DERBYSHIRE RECORDER SERIES, circ. 260,441 [F] 271

Kimberley
W EASTWOOD & KIMBERLEY ADVERTISER, circ. 4,189 178

Kirkby in Ashfield
W CHAD SERIES MANSFIELD, circ. 61,097 158
W MANSFIELD AND ASHFIELD OBSERVER, circ. 58,599 [F] 218
W WEST NOTTS & DERBYSHIRE RECORDER SERIES, circ. 260,441 [F] 271

Langold
W GUARDIAN SERIES (WORKSOP), circ. 95,428 193
W RETFORD GAINSBOROUGH AND WORKSOP TIMES, circ. 10,913 240
D THE STAR SHEFFIELD, circ. 56,363 255

Mansfield
W CHAD SERIES MANSFIELD, circ. 61,097 158
W JOURNAL & ADVERTISER SERIES, circ. 30,000 [F] ...205
W MANSFIELD AND ASHFIELD OBSERVER, circ. 58,599 [F] 218
W THE MERCURY NEWSPAPER, circ. 40,000 [F] 219
W WEST NOTTS & DERBYSHIRE RECORDER SERIES, circ. 260,441 [F] 271

Mansfield Woodhouse
W CHAD SERIES MANSFIELD, circ. 61,097 158

W MANSFIELD AND ASHFIELD OBSERVER, circ. 58,599 [F] 218
W WEST NOTTS & DERBYSHIRE RECORDER SERIES, circ. 260,441 [F] 271

Newark-on-Trent
W JOURNAL & ADVERTISER SERIES, circ. 30,000 [F] ...205
W NEWARK ADVERTISER SERIES, circ. 50,000 226

Nottingham
W JOURNAL & ADVERTISER SERIES, circ. 30,000 [F] ...205
W NOTTINGHAM AND LONG EATON TOPPER, circ. 209,222 [F] 232
W WEST NOTTS & DERBYSHIRE RECORDER SERIES, circ. 260,441 [F] 271

Ollerton
W CHAD SERIES MANSFIELD, circ. 61,097 158
W NEWARK ADVERTISER SERIES, circ. 50,000 226
W RETFORD GAINSBOROUGH AND WORKSOP TIMES, circ. 10,913 240

Radcliffe-on-Trent
W JOURNAL & ADVERTISER SERIES, circ. 30,000 [F] ...205
W WEST NOTTS & DERBYSHIRE RECORDER SERIES, circ. 260,441 [F] 271

Rainworth
W CHAD SERIES MANSFIELD, circ. 61,097 158
W MANSFIELD AND ASHFIELD OBSERVER, circ. 58,599 [F] 218
W WEST NOTTS & DERBYSHIRE RECORDER SERIES, circ. 260,441 [F] 271

Ravenshead
W CHAD SERIES MANSFIELD, circ. 61,097 158

Retford
W GUARDIAN SERIES (WORKSOP), circ. 95,428 193
W RETFORD GAINSBOROUGH AND WORKSOP TIMES, circ. 10,913 240
D THE STAR SHEFFIELD, circ. 56,363 255

Ruddington
W JOURNAL & ADVERTISER SERIES, circ. 30,000 [F] ...205
W WEST NOTTS & DERBYSHIRE RECORDER SERIES, circ. 260,441 [F] 271

Selston
D DERBY TELEGRAPH, circ. 42,726 172
W DERBYSHIRE TIMES SERIES, circ. 40,241 172
W EASTWOOD & KIMBERLEY ADVERTISER, circ. 4,189 178
W RIPLEY & HEANOR NEWS, circ. 10,394 240

Southwell
W JOURNAL & ADVERTISER SERIES, circ. 30,000 [F] ...205
W NEWARK ADVERTISER SERIES, circ. 50,000 226

Stapleford
W ILKESTON ADVERTISER, circ. 8,488 202
W WEST NOTTS & DERBYSHIRE RECORDER SERIES, circ. 260,441 [F] 271

Sutton-in-Ashfield
W CHAD SERIES MANSFIELD, circ. 61,097 158
W MANSFIELD AND ASHFIELD OBSERVER, circ. 58,599 [F] 218
W WEST NOTTS & DERBYSHIRE RECORDER SERIES, circ. 260,441 [F] 271

Tuxford
W GUARDIAN SERIES (WORKSOP), circ. 95,428 193
W RETFORD GAINSBOROUGH AND WORKSOP TIMES, circ. 10,913 240
D THE STAR SHEFFIELD, circ. 56,363 255

Underwood
W CHAD SERIES MANSFIELD, circ. 61,097 158
W DERBYSHIRE TIMES SERIES, circ. 40,241 172
W EASTWOOD & KIMBERLEY ADVERTISER, circ. 4,189 178
W WEST NOTTS & DERBYSHIRE RECORDER SERIES, circ. 260,441 [F] 271

Warsop
W CHAD SERIES MANSFIELD, circ. 61,097 158
W MANSFIELD AND ASHFIELD OBSERVER, circ. 58,599 [F] 218
W WEST NOTTS & DERBYSHIRE RECORDER SERIES, circ. 260,441 [F] 271

West Bridgford
W JOURNAL & ADVERTISER SERIES, circ. 30,000 [F] ...205
W WEST NOTTS & DERBYSHIRE RECORDER SERIES, circ. 260,441 [F] 271

Worksop
W GUARDIAN SERIES (WORKSOP), circ. 95,428 193
W RETFORD GAINSBOROUGH AND WORKSOP TIMES, circ. 10,913 240

D THE STAR SHEFFIELD, circ. 56,363 255

Oxfordshire

W HERALD AND TIMES SERIES OXON, circ. 36,327 197
W OXFORD STAR, circ. 60,647 [F] 234

Abingdon
W OXFORD JOURNAL, circ. 40,000 [F] 234
D OXFORD MAIL, circ. 25,426 234

Banbury
W BANBURY GUARDIAN REVIEW SERIES, circ. 55,138 145
W OXFORD JOURNAL, circ. 40,000 [F] 234
D OXFORD MAIL, circ. 25,426 234

Benson
D OXFORD MAIL, circ. 25,426 234

Berinsfield
D OXFORD MAIL, circ. 25,426 234

Bicester
W BUCKINGHAM ADVERTISER SERIES, circ. 19,132 ... 153
W OXFORD JOURNAL, circ. 40,000 [F] 234
D OXFORD MAIL, circ. 25,426 234

Bloxham
W BANBURY GUARDIAN REVIEW SERIES, circ. 55,138 145
S SUNDAY MERCURY (BIRMINGHAM), circ. 59,339 258

Burford
S SUNDAY MERCURY (BIRMINGHAM), circ. 59,339 258

Carterton
D OXFORD MAIL, circ. 25,426 234
W WITNEY AND WEST OXFORDSHIRE GAZETTE, circ. 7,518 276

Chalgrove
D OXFORD MAIL, circ. 25,426 234

Charlbury
D OXFORD MAIL, circ. 25,426 234
W WILTS & GLOUCESTERSHIRE STANDARD SERIES, circ. 14,652 275

Chinnor
W BUCKS ADVERTISER & THAME GAZETTE SERIES, circ. 41,849 [F] 153
W BUCKS FREE PRESS SERIES, circ. 85,396 154

Chipping Norton
W BANBURY GUARDIAN REVIEW SERIES, circ. 55,138 145
W EVESHAM JOURNAL SERIES, circ. 32,275 182
W OXFORD JOURNAL, circ. 40,000 [F] 234
S SUNDAY MERCURY (BIRMINGHAM), circ. 59,339 258
W WITNEY AND WEST OXFORDSHIRE GAZETTE, circ. 7,518 276

Cholsey
D OXFORD MAIL, circ. 25,426 234
W READING CHRONICLE SERIES, circ. 105,389 239
W READING POST SERIES, circ. 84,500 239

Didcot
W OXFORD JOURNAL, circ. 40,000 [F] 234
D OXFORD MAIL, circ. 25,426 234

Faringdon
W FARINGDON FOLLY, circ. 2,500 184
W OXFORD JOURNAL, circ. 40,000 [F] 234

Goring
W HENLEY STANDARD, circ. 12,049 197
D OXFORD MAIL, circ. 25,426 234
W READING CHRONICLE SERIES, circ. 105,389 239

Grove
W OXFORD JOURNAL, circ. 40,000 [F] 234
D OXFORD MAIL, circ. 25,426 234

Henley-on-Thames
W HENLEY STANDARD, circ. 12,049 197
W READING CHRONICLE SERIES, circ. 105,389 239

Kennington
D OXFORD MAIL, circ. 25,426 234

Kidlington
W OXFORD JOURNAL, circ. 40,000 [F] 234

Oxford
W OXFORD JOURNAL, circ. 40,000 [F] 234
D OXFORD MAIL, circ. 25,426 234

Shipton-u-Wychwood
D OXFORD MAIL, circ. 25,426 234
W WILTS & GLOUCESTERSHIRE STANDARD SERIES, circ. 14,652 275

W **Local/Weekly Newspapers** D **Regional Daily Newspapers** S **Regional Sunday Newspapers** [F] **Free Newspapers**

Title *(Day/am/pm)*	Circ.	Page No.

Shrivenham
D OXFORD MAIL, circ. 25,426 234

Sonning Common
W READING POST SERIES, circ. 84,500 239

Streatley
W READING CHRONICLE SERIES, circ. 105,389 239

Thame
W BUCKS ADVERTISER & THAME GAZETTE SERIES, circ. 41,849 F 153
W BUCKS FREE PRESS SERIES, circ. 85,396 154
W THE BUCKS HERALD SERIES, circ. 17,964 154
D OXFORD MAIL, circ. 25,426 234

Wallingford
W OXFORD JOURNAL, circ. 40,000 F 234
D OXFORD MAIL, circ. 25,426 234

Wantage
W OXFORD JOURNAL, circ. 40,000 F 234
D OXFORD MAIL, circ. 25,426 234
W WANTAGE AND GROVE REVIEW F 268

Wheatley
D OXFORD MAIL, circ. 25,426 234

Witney
W OXFORD JOURNAL, circ. 40,000 F 234
D OXFORD MAIL, circ. 25,426 234
S SUNDAY MERCURY (BIRMINGHAM), circ. 59,339 ... 258
W WITNEY AND WEST OXFORDSHIRE GAZETTE, circ. 7,518 276

Woodstock
D OXFORD MAIL, circ. 25,426 234
W WITNEY AND WEST OXFORDSHIRE GAZETTE, circ. 7,518 276

Redbridge Borough

Hainault
W ILFORD RECORDER SERIES, circ. 15,074 202

Ilford
W ILFORD RECORDER SERIES, circ. 15,074 202

Redbridge
W ILFORD RECORDER SERIES, circ. 15,074 202
W WANSTEAD AND WOODFORD GUARDIAN, circ. 4,745 268
W YELLOW ADVERTISER GROUP SERIES (ESSEX), circ. 434,612 F 278

Wanstead
W GUARDIAN AND INDEPENDENT SERIES, circ. 22,432 193
W ILFORD RECORDER SERIES, circ. 15,074 202
W WANSTEAD AND WOODFORD GUARDIAN, circ. 4,745 268

Woodford
W GUARDIAN AND INDEPENDENT SERIES, circ. 22,432 193
W ILFORD RECORDER SERIES, circ. 15,074 202
W WANSTEAD AND WOODFORD GUARDIAN, circ. 4,745 268

Richmond upon Thames Borough

Barnes
W INFORMER SERIES (KINGSTON), circ. 95,129 F 203
W TIMES SERIES (RICHMOND), circ. 152,627 264

Hampton
W INFORMER SERIES (KINGSTON), circ. 95,129 F 203
W TIMES SERIES (RICHMOND), circ. 152,627 264

Kew
W INFORMER SERIES (KINGSTON), circ. 95,129 F 203

Mortlake
W TIMES SERIES (RICHMOND), circ. 152,627 264

Richmond upon Thames
W GUARDIAN & NEWS SERIES (SUTTON), circ. 315,438 193
W GUARDIAN SERIES (WILTSHIRE, HAMPSHIRE AND SURREY), circ. 175,000 F 193
W HOUNSLOW CHRONICLE, circ. 60,000 201
W INFORMER SERIES (KINGSTON), circ. 95,129 F 203
W SURREY COMET, circ. 10,182 260
W TIMES SERIES (RICHMOND), circ. 152,627 264

Teddington
W HOUNSLOW CHRONICLE, circ. 60,000 201

W INFORMER SERIES (KINGSTON), circ. 95,129 F 203
W TIMES SERIES (RICHMOND), circ. 152,627 264

Twickenham
W HOUNSLOW CHRONICLE, circ. 60,000 201
W INFORMER SERIES (KINGSTON), circ. 95,129 F 203
W SOUTH BUCKS AND BERKSHIRE NEWS SERIES, circ. 50,000 F 249
W TIMES SERIES (RICHMOND), circ. 152,627 264

Rutland UA

W YR ANGOR (LIVERPOOL), circ. 3,000 142
W JOURNAL & ADVERTISER SERIES, circ. 30,000 F ... 205
W LEICESTER MAIL SERIES, circ. 141,536 F 210
D LEICESTER MERCURY, circ. 70,028 210
W RUTLAND & STAMFORD MERCURY AND CITIZEN SERIES, circ. 20,490 243

Oakham
D LEICESTER MERCURY, circ. 70,028 210
W THE MESSENGER SERIES (LEICESTERSHIRE & RUTLAND), circ. 50,000 F 221
W RUTLAND TIMES, circ. 4,562 243

Uppingham
W THE MESSENGER SERIES (LEICESTERSHIRE & RUTLAND), circ. 50,000 F 221
W RUTLAND TIMES, circ. 4,562 243

Shropshire

W NEWPORT & MARKET DRAYTON ADVERTISER SERIES, circ. 9,112 226

Albrighton
D THE BIRMINGHAM POST, circ. 12,997 149
D BIRMINGHAM POST (CITY/LONDON OFFICE) 149
W BRIDGNORTH JOURNAL, circ. 9,126 152
D SHROPSHIRE STAR, circ. 72,000 247
D SHROPSHIRE STAR (CITY/LONDON OFFICE) 247
S SUNDAY MERCURY (BIRMINGHAM), circ. 59,339 ... 258
W TELFORD JOURNAL, circ. 61,000 F 262

Bayston Hill
D THE BIRMINGHAM POST, circ. 12,997 149
D BIRMINGHAM POST (CITY/LONDON OFFICE) 149
W CHRONICLE & JOURNAL SERIES, circ. 87,901 161
D SHROPSHIRE STAR, circ. 72,000 247
D SHROPSHIRE STAR (CITY/LONDON OFFICE) 247
S SUNDAY MERCURY (BIRMINGHAM), circ. 59,339 ... 258

Bridgnorth
D THE BIRMINGHAM POST, circ. 12,997 149
D BIRMINGHAM POST (CITY/LONDON OFFICE) 149
W BRIDGNORTH JOURNAL, circ. 9,126 152
D SHROPSHIRE STAR, circ. 72,000 247
D SHROPSHIRE STAR (CITY/LONDON OFFICE) 247

Broseley
D THE BIRMINGHAM POST, circ. 12,997 149
D BIRMINGHAM POST (CITY/LONDON OFFICE) 149
W BRIDGNORTH JOURNAL, circ. 9,126 152
D SHROPSHIRE STAR, circ. 72,000 247
D SHROPSHIRE STAR (CITY/LONDON OFFICE) 247
S SUNDAY MERCURY (BIRMINGHAM), circ. 59,339 ... 258
W TELFORD JOURNAL, circ. 61,000 F 262

Church Stretton
W CHRONICLE & JOURNAL SERIES, circ. 87,901 161
W LUDLOW ADVERTISER SERIES, circ. 5,924 215
D SHROPSHIRE STAR, circ. 72,000 247
D SHROPSHIRE STAR (CITY/LONDON OFFICE) 247

Donnington
D THE BIRMINGHAM POST, circ. 12,997 149
D BIRMINGHAM POST (CITY/LONDON OFFICE) 149
D SHROPSHIRE STAR, circ. 72,000 247
D SHROPSHIRE STAR (CITY/LONDON OFFICE) 247
S SUNDAY MERCURY (BIRMINGHAM), circ. 59,339 ... 258
W TELFORD JOURNAL, circ. 61,000 F 262

Ellesmere
W OSWESTRY AND BORDER COUNTIES ADVERTIZER, circ. 10,969 234
D SHROPSHIRE STAR, circ. 72,000 247
D SHROPSHIRE STAR (CITY/LONDON OFFICE) 247
W WHITCHURCH HERALD, circ. 4,586 274

Gobowen
D THE BIRMINGHAM POST, circ. 12,997 149
D BIRMINGHAM POST (CITY/LONDON OFFICE) 149
D EVENING LEADER, circ. 21,180 181
W OSWESTRY AND BORDER COUNTIES ADVERTIZER, circ. 10,969 234
D SHROPSHIRE STAR, circ. 72,000 247
D SHROPSHIRE STAR (CITY/LONDON OFFICE) 247

Hadley
D THE BIRMINGHAM POST, circ. 12,997 149
D BIRMINGHAM POST (CITY/LONDON OFFICE) 149
D SHROPSHIRE STAR, circ. 72,000 247
D SHROPSHIRE STAR (CITY/LONDON OFFICE) 247
S SUNDAY MERCURY (BIRMINGHAM), circ. 59,339 258
W TELFORD JOURNAL, circ. 61,000 F 262

Highley
W BRIDGNORTH JOURNAL, circ. 9,126 152

Ludlow
W CHRONICLE & JOURNAL SERIES, circ. 87,901 161
W HEREFORD TIMES, circ. 39,876 198
W LUDLOW ADVERTISER SERIES, circ. 5,924 215
D SHROPSHIRE STAR, circ. 72,000 247
D SHROPSHIRE STAR (CITY/LONDON OFFICE) 247

Madeley
D THE BIRMINGHAM POST, circ. 12,997 149
D BIRMINGHAM POST (CITY/LONDON OFFICE) 149
D SHROPSHIRE STAR, circ. 72,000 247
D SHROPSHIRE STAR (CITY/LONDON OFFICE) 247
S SUNDAY MERCURY (BIRMINGHAM), circ. 59,339 258
W TELFORD JOURNAL, circ. 61,000 F 262

Market Drayton
D THE SENTINEL STOKE-ON-TRENT, circ. 61,910 245
D SHROPSHIRE STAR, circ. 72,000 247
D SHROPSHIRE STAR (CITY/LONDON OFFICE) 247

Much Wenlock
W BRIDGNORTH JOURNAL, circ. 9,126 152

Oakengates
D THE BIRMINGHAM POST, circ. 12,997 149
D BIRMINGHAM POST (CITY/LONDON OFFICE) 149
D SHROPSHIRE STAR, circ. 72,000 247
D SHROPSHIRE STAR (CITY/LONDON OFFICE) 247
S SUNDAY MERCURY (BIRMINGHAM), circ. 59,339 258
W TELFORD JOURNAL, circ. 61,000 F 262

Oswestry
W OSWESTRY AND BORDER COUNTIES ADVERTIZER, circ. 10,969 234
D SHROPSHIRE STAR, circ. 72,000 247
D SHROPSHIRE STAR (CITY/LONDON OFFICE) 247

Shifnal
D THE BIRMINGHAM POST, circ. 12,997 149
D BIRMINGHAM POST (CITY/LONDON OFFICE) 149
W BRIDGNORTH JOURNAL, circ. 9,126 152
D SHROPSHIRE STAR, circ. 72,000 247
D SHROPSHIRE STAR (CITY/LONDON OFFICE) 247

Shrewsbury
W ADMAG NEWSPAPERS SERIES, circ. 181,809 F 137
W CHRONICLE & JOURNAL SERIES, circ. 87,901 161
D SHROPSHIRE STAR, circ. 72,000 247
D SHROPSHIRE STAR (CITY/LONDON OFFICE) 247

Telford
W ADMAG NEWSPAPERS SERIES, circ. 181,809 F 137
D THE BIRMINGHAM POST, circ. 12,997 149
D BIRMINGHAM POST (CITY/LONDON OFFICE) 149
D SHROPSHIRE STAR, circ. 72,000 247
D SHROPSHIRE STAR (CITY/LONDON OFFICE) 247
W TELFORD JOURNAL, circ. 61,000 F 262

Telford Dawley
D THE BIRMINGHAM POST, circ. 12,997 149
D BIRMINGHAM POST (CITY/LONDON OFFICE) 149
D SHROPSHIRE STAR, circ. 72,000 247
D SHROPSHIRE STAR (CITY/LONDON OFFICE) 247
S SUNDAY MERCURY (BIRMINGHAM), circ. 59,339 258
W TELFORD JOURNAL, circ. 61,000 F 262

Wellington
D THE BIRMINGHAM POST, circ. 12,997 149
D BIRMINGHAM POST (CITY/LONDON OFFICE) 149
D SHROPSHIRE STAR, circ. 72,000 247
D SHROPSHIRE STAR (CITY/LONDON OFFICE) 247
S SUNDAY MERCURY (BIRMINGHAM), circ. 59,339 258
W TELFORD JOURNAL, circ. 61,000 F 262

Wem
W CHRONICLE & JOURNAL SERIES, circ. 87,901 161
D SHROPSHIRE STAR, circ. 72,000 247
D SHROPSHIRE STAR (CITY/LONDON OFFICE) 247
W WHITCHURCH HERALD, circ. 4,586 274

Whitchurch
W CHRONICLE & JOURNAL SERIES, circ. 87,901 161
D SHROPSHIRE STAR, circ. 72,000 247
D SHROPSHIRE STAR (CITY/LONDON OFFICE) 247
W WHITCHURCH HERALD, circ. 4,586 274

W **Local/Weekly Newspapers**   D **Regional Daily Newspapers**   S **Regional Sunday Newspapers**   F **Free Newspapers**

Section 3 Index to UK Newspapers

Non-Nationals - England

Title *(Day/am/pm)*	Circ.	Page No.

Whittington
D THE BIRMINGHAM POST, circ. 12,997 149
D BIRMINGHAM POST (CITY/LONDON OFFICE) 149
W LICHFIELD MERCURY SERIES, circ. 81,365 F 211
W OSWESTRY AND BORDER COUNTIES ADVERTIZER, circ. 10,969 234
D SHROPSHIRE STAR, circ. 72,000 247
D SHROPSHIRE STAR (CITY/LONDON OFFICE) 247

Somerset
W STAR AND EXPRESS SERIES, circ. 95,047 F 255
S SUNDAY INDEPENDENT (PLYMOUTH), circ. 32,000 . 258
W WEST SOMERSET POST, circ. 9,000 F 271

Backwell
W CLEVEDON NEWSPAPERS SERIES, circ. 86,840 F . 163
W WESTON & SOMERSET MERCURY SERIES, circ. 18,600 273

Banwell
W ADMAG (WESTON-SUPER-MARE), circ. 41,589 F ... 138
W CLEVEDON NEWSPAPERS SERIES, circ. 86,840 F . 163
D EVENING POST (BRISTOL), circ. 51,287 181
D WESTERN DAILY PRESS BRISTOL, circ. 41,639 272
W WESTON & SOMERSET MERCURY SERIES, circ. 18,600 273

Bath
W GUARDIAN SERIES (WILTSHIRE, HAMPSHIRE AND SURREY), circ. 175,000 F 193

Bridgwater
W BRIDGWATER TIMES, circ. 25,677 F 152
W MERCURY AND WEEKLY NEWS SERIES, circ. 16,156 219

Burnham-on-Sea
W ADMAG (WESTON-SUPER-MARE), circ. 41,589 F ... 138
W CLEVEDON NEWSPAPERS SERIES, circ. 86,840 F . 163
W MERCURY AND WEEKLY NEWS SERIES, circ. 16,156 219
W WESTON & SOMERSET MERCURY SERIES, circ. 18,600 273

Chard
W CHARD & ILMINSTER NEWS, circ. 7,677 159
W PULMANS WEEKLY NEWS AND ADVERTISER SERIES, circ. 22,000 238
W WESTERN GAZETTE AND YEOVIL TIMES SERIES, circ. 79,876 272
D WESTERN MORNING NEWS, circ. 41,154 272

Cheddar
W MID SOMERSET NEWS & MEDIA, circ. 32,945 221
W WESTON & SOMERSET MERCURY SERIES, circ. 18,600 : 273

Chew Magna
W CHEW VALLEY GAZETTE, circ. 14,500 F 160

Chew Stoke
W CHEW VALLEY GAZETTE, circ. 14,500 F 160

Clevedon
W CLEVEDON NEWSPAPERS SERIES, circ. 86,840 F . 163
W WESTON & SOMERSET MERCURY SERIES, circ. 18,600 273

Congresbury
W CLEVEDON NEWSPAPERS SERIES, circ. 86,840 F . 163
W WESTON & SOMERSET MERCURY SERIES, circ. 18,600 273

Crewkerne
W CHARD & ILMINSTER NEWS, circ. 7,677 159
W PULMANS WEEKLY NEWS AND ADVERTISER SERIES, circ. 22,000 238
W WESTERN GAZETTE AND YEOVIL TIMES SERIES, circ. 79,876 272

Crowcombe
W WEST SOMERSET FREE PRESS SERIES, circ. 18,391 271

Dunster
W WEST SOMERSET FREE PRESS SERIES, circ. 18,391 271

Easton-in-Gordano
W CLEVEDON NEWSPAPERS SERIES, circ. 86,840 F . 163
D EVENING POST (BRISTOL), circ. 51,287 181
D WESTERN DAILY PRESS BRISTOL, circ. 41,639 272

Frome
W GUARDIAN SERIES (WILTSHIRE, HAMPSHIRE AND SURREY), circ. 175,000 F 193
W THE MELKSHAM INDEPENDENT NEWS SERIES, circ. 32,700 F 219

W SOMERSET STANDARD & GUARDIAN SERIES, circ. 16,198 249

Glastonbury
W MID SOMERSET NEWS & MEDIA, circ. 32,945 221
W WESTERN GAZETTE AND YEOVIL TIMES SERIES, circ. 79,876 272

Highbridge
W CLEVEDON NEWSPAPERS SERIES, circ. 86,840 F . 163
W MERCURY AND WEEKLY NEWS SERIES, circ. 16,156 219
W WESTON & SOMERSET MERCURY SERIES, circ. 18,600 273

Ilminster
W CHARD & ILMINSTER NEWS, circ. 7,677 159
W WESTERN GAZETTE AND YEOVIL TIMES SERIES, circ. 79,876 272

Keynsham
W BRISTOL OBSERVER SERIES, circ. 165,769 F 152

Langport
W WESTERN GAZETTE AND YEOVIL TIMES SERIES, circ. 79,876 272

Long Ashton
D EVENING POST (BRISTOL), circ. 51,287 181
D WESTERN DAILY PRESS BRISTOL, circ. 41,639 272
W WESTON & SOMERSET MERCURY SERIES, circ. 18,600 273

Martock
W WESTERN GAZETTE AND YEOVIL TIMES SERIES, circ. 79,876 272

Midsomer Norton
W MIDSOMER NORTON, RADSTOCK & DISTRICT JOURNAL, circ. 14,100 F 222
W SOMERSET STANDARD & GUARDIAN SERIES, circ. 16,198 249

Minehead
W SOMERSET COUNTY GAZETTE SERIES, circ. 29,688 249
W WEST SOMERSET FREE PRESS SERIES, circ. 18,391 271
D WESTERN DAILY PRESS BRISTOL, circ. 41,639 272

Nailsea
W CLEVEDON NEWSPAPERS SERIES, circ. 86,840 F . 163
W WESTON & SOMERSET MERCURY SERIES, circ. 18,600 273

Paulton
D EVENING POST (BRISTOL), circ. 51,287 181
W SOMERSET STANDARD & GUARDIAN SERIES, circ. 16,198 249
D WESTERN DAILY PRESS BRISTOL, circ. 41,639 272

Porlock
W WEST SOMERSET FREE PRESS SERIES, circ. 18,391 271

Portishead
W CLEVEDON NEWSPAPERS SERIES, circ. 86,840 F . 163
W WESTON & SOMERSET MERCURY SERIES, circ. 18,600 273

Radstock
W MIDSOMER NORTON, RADSTOCK & DISTRICT JOURNAL, circ. 14,100 F 222
W SOMERSET STANDARD & GUARDIAN SERIES, circ. 16,198 249

Shepton Mallet
W MID SOMERSET NEWS & MEDIA, circ. 32,945 221
W WESTERN GAZETTE AND YEOVIL TIMES SERIES, circ. 79,876 272

Somerton
W MID SOMERSET NEWS & MEDIA, circ. 32,945 221
W WESTERN GAZETTE AND YEOVIL TIMES SERIES, circ. 79,876 272

Street
W MID SOMERSET NEWS & MEDIA, circ. 32,945 221
W WESTERN GAZETTE AND YEOVIL TIMES SERIES, circ. 79,876 272

Taunton
W EXPRESS & ECHO (EXETER), circ. 20,767 183
W SOMERSET COUNTY GAZETTE SERIES, circ. 29,688 249
D WESTERN MORNING NEWS, circ. 41,154 272

Watchet
W SOMERSET COUNTY GAZETTE SERIES, circ. 29,688 249

W WEST SOMERSET FREE PRESS SERIES, circ. 18,391 271

Wellington
W SOMERSET COUNTY GAZETTE SERIES, circ. 29,688 249
W WELLINGTON WEEKLY NEWS, circ. 5,000 270
D WESTERN DAILY PRESS BRISTOL, circ. 41,639 272
D WESTERN MORNING NEWS, circ. 41,154 272

Wells
W MID SOMERSET NEWS & MEDIA, circ. 32,945 221
W WESTERN GAZETTE AND YEOVIL TIMES SERIES, circ. 79,876 272

Weston Super Mare
W ADMAG (WESTON-SUPER-MARE), circ. 41,589 F ... 138
W CLEVEDON NEWSPAPERS SERIES, circ. 86,840 F . 163
D EVENING POST (BRISTOL), circ. 51,287 181
W WESTON & SOMERSET MERCURY SERIES, circ. 18,600 273

Williton
W SOMERSET COUNTY GAZETTE SERIES, circ. 29,688 249
W WEST SOMERSET FREE PRESS SERIES, circ. 18,391 271

Wincanton
W WESTERN GAZETTE AND YEOVIL TIMES SERIES, circ. 79,876 272

Winscombe
W ADMAG (WESTON-SUPER-MARE), circ. 41,589 F ... 138
W CLEVEDON NEWSPAPERS SERIES, circ. 86,840 F . 163
D EVENING POST (BRISTOL), circ. 51,287 181
D WESTERN DAILY PRESS BRISTOL, circ. 41,639 272
W WESTON & SOMERSET MERCURY SERIES, circ. 18,600 273

Wiveliscombe
W SOMERSET COUNTY GAZETTE SERIES, circ. 29,688 249
W WELLINGTON WEEKLY NEWS, circ. 5,000 270

Yatton
W CLEVEDON NEWSPAPERS SERIES, circ. 86,840 F . 163
W WESTON & SOMERSET MERCURY SERIES, circ. 18,600 273

Yeovil
W WESTERN GAZETTE AND YEOVIL TIMES SERIES, circ. 79,876 272
D WESTERN MORNING NEWS, circ. 41,154 272

South Yorkshire
D LIFE AND STYLE 212
D YORKSHIRE POST, circ. 49,031 279
D YORKSHIRE POST (CITY/LONDON OFFICE) 279

Anston
W ROTHERHAM ADVERTISER AND RECORD SERIES, circ. 94,605 241
D THE STAR SHEFFIELD, circ. 56,363 255

Armthorpe
W COMMUNITY NEWSLETTER SERIES, circ. 42,000 F 164
W DONCASTER ADVERTISER, circ. 56,077 F 173
W DONCASTER FREE PRESS, circ. 34,029 173
D THE STAR SHEFFIELD, circ. 56,363 255

Askern
W COMMUNITY NEWSLETTER SERIES, circ. 42,000 F 164
W DONCASTER FREE PRESS, circ. 34,029 173
D THE STAR SHEFFIELD, circ. 56,363 255

Barnsley
W BARNSLEY CHRONICLE & INDEPENDENT SERIES, circ. 122,314 145
W ROTHERHAM GAZETTE SERIES, circ. 60,000 F 241
W SOUTH YORKSHIRE TIMES, circ. 5,862 251
D THE STAR SHEFFIELD, circ. 56,363 255

Bawtry
W COMMUNITY NEWSLETTER SERIES, circ. 42,000 F 164
W GUARDIAN SERIES (WORKSOP), circ. 95,428 193

Beighton
W THE MERCURY NEWSPAPER, circ. 40,000 F 219
W SHEFFIELD JOURNAL SERIES, circ. 56,889 F 246
W SHEFFIELD TELEGRAPH, circ. 22,162 246
W SHEFFIELD WEEKLY GAZETTE, circ. 103,897 F 246
D THE STAR SHEFFIELD, circ. 56,363 255

Bentley
W COMMUNITY NEWSLETTER SERIES, circ. 42,000 F 164

W **Local/Weekly Newspapers**   D **Regional Daily Newspapers**   S **Regional Sunday Newspapers**   F **Free Newspapers**

Title (Day/am/pm)	Circ.	Page No.	Title (Day/am/pm)	Circ.	Page No.	Title (Day/am/pm)	Circ.	Page No.

Bessacarr
W DONCASTER ADVERTISER, circ. 56,077 F 173
W DONCASTER FREE PRESS, circ. 34,029 173
D THE STAR SHEFFIELD, circ. 56,363 255

Birdwell
W BARNSLEY CHRONICLE & INDEPENDENT SERIES,
   circ. 122,314 145
D THE STAR SHEFFIELD, circ. 56,363 255

Brierley
W BARNSLEY CHRONICLE & INDEPENDENT SERIES,
   circ. 122,314 145
D THE STAR SHEFFIELD, circ. 56,363 255

Carcroft
W DONCASTER ADVERTISER, circ. 56,077 F 173
W DONCASTER FREE PRESS, circ. 34,029 173
D THE STAR SHEFFIELD, circ. 56,363 255

Chapeltown
W THE MERCURY NEWSPAPER, circ. 40,000 F 219
W SHEFFIELD JOURNAL SERIES, circ. 56,889 F 246
W SHEFFIELD TELEGRAPH, circ. 22,162 246
W SHEFFIELD WEEKLY GAZETTE, circ. 103,897 F 246
D THE STAR SHEFFIELD, circ. 56,363 255

Conisbrough
W COMMUNITY NEWSLETTER SERIES, circ. 42,000 F 164
W DEARNE VALLEY WEEKENDER, circ. 50,550 F 171
W SOUTH YORKSHIRE TIMES, circ. 5,862 251

Cudworth
W BARNSLEY CHRONICLE & INDEPENDENT SERIES,
   circ. 122,314 145

Darfield
W BARNSLEY CHRONICLE & INDEPENDENT SERIES,
   circ. 122,314 145

Darton
W BARNSLEY CHRONICLE & INDEPENDENT SERIES,
   circ. 122,314 145

Dearne
W BARNSLEY CHRONICLE & INDEPENDENT SERIES,
   circ. 122,314 145

Dinnington
W GUARDIAN SERIES (WORKSOP), circ. 95,428 193

Dodworth
W BARNSLEY CHRONICLE & INDEPENDENT SERIES,
   circ. 122,314 145
D THE STAR SHEFFIELD, circ. 56,363 255

Doncaster
W DEARNE VALLEY WEEKENDER, circ. 50,550 F 171
W DONCASTER ADVERTISER, circ. 56,077 F 173
W DONCASTER FREE PRESS, circ. 34,029 173
W JOURNAL & ADVERTISER SERIES, circ. 30,000 F 205
W ROTHERHAM GAZETTE SERIES, circ. 60,000 F 241
W SOUTH YORKSHIRE TIMES, circ. 5,862 251
D THE STAR SHEFFIELD, circ. 56,363 255

Finningley
W DONCASTER ADVERTISER, circ. 56,077 F 173

Grimethorpe
W BARNSLEY CHRONICLE & INDEPENDENT SERIES,
   circ. 122,314 145

Hatfield
W DONCASTER ADVERTISER, circ. 56,077 F 173
W DONCASTER FREE PRESS, circ. 34,029 173
W GOOLE TIMES, circ. 10,149 192
D THE STAR SHEFFIELD, circ. 56,363 255
W THORNE AND DISTRICT GAZETTE, circ. 19,000 F 263

Hoyland
W BARNSLEY CHRONICLE & INDEPENDENT SERIES,
   circ. 122,314 145
W SOUTH YORKSHIRE TIMES, circ. 5,862 251

Kirk Sandall
W DONCASTER ADVERTISER, circ. 56,077 F 173
W DONCASTER FREE PRESS, circ. 34,029 173
D THE STAR SHEFFIELD, circ. 56,363 255

Maltby
W GUARDIAN SERIES (WORKSOP), circ. 95,428 193
W ROTHERHAM ADVERTISER AND RECORD SERIES,
   circ. 94,605 241

Mexborough
W DEARNE VALLEY WEEKENDER, circ. 50,550 F 171
W DONCASTER FREE PRESS, circ. 34,029 173

W ROTHERHAM ADVERTISER AND RECORD SERIES,
   circ. 94,605 241
W SOUTH YORKSHIRE TIMES, circ. 5,862 251
D THE STAR SHEFFIELD, circ. 56,363 255

Moorends
W DONCASTER FREE PRESS, circ. 34,029 173
W GOOLE TIMES, circ. 10,149 192
D THE STAR SHEFFIELD, circ. 56,363 255

New Rossington
W DONCASTER FREE PRESS, circ. 34,029 173
D THE STAR SHEFFIELD, circ. 56,363 255

Oughtibridge
W SHEFFIELD TELEGRAPH, circ. 22,162 246
W SHEFFIELD WEEKLY GAZETTE, circ. 103,897 F 246
D THE STAR SHEFFIELD, circ. 56,363 255

Penistone
W BARNSLEY CHRONICLE & INDEPENDENT SERIES,
   circ. 122,314 145
D THE STAR SHEFFIELD, circ. 56,363 255

Rawmarsh
W THE MERCURY NEWSPAPER, circ. 40,000 F 219
W ROTHERHAM ADVERTISER AND RECORD SERIES,
   circ. 94,605 241
W SOUTH YORKSHIRE TIMES, circ. 5,862 251
D THE STAR SHEFFIELD, circ. 56,363 255

Rotherham
W GUARDIAN SERIES (WORKSOP), circ. 95,428 193
W THE MERCURY NEWSPAPER, circ. 40,000 F 219
W ROTHERHAM ADVERTISER AND RECORD SERIES,
   circ. 94,605 241
W ROTHERHAM GAZETTE SERIES, circ. 60,000 F 241
D THE STAR SHEFFIELD, circ. 56,363 255

Sheffield
W JOURNAL & ADVERTISER SERIES, circ. 30,000 F 205
W THE MERCURY NEWSPAPER, circ. 40,000 F 219
W SHEFFIELD JOURNAL SERIES, circ. 56,889 F 246
W SHEFFIELD TELEGRAPH, circ. 22,162 246
W SHEFFIELD WEEKLY GAZETTE, circ. 103,897 F 246
W SOUTH YORKSHIRE TIMES, circ. 5,862 251
D THE STAR SHEFFIELD, circ. 56,363 255

Stainforth
W THORNE AND DISTRICT GAZETTE, circ. 19,000 F 263

Stocksbridge
W THE MERCURY NEWSPAPER, circ. 40,000 F 219
W SHEFFIELD JOURNAL SERIES, circ. 56,889 F 246
W SHEFFIELD TELEGRAPH, circ. 22,162 246

Swinton
W DEARNE VALLEY WEEKENDER, circ. 50,550 F 171
D THE STAR SHEFFIELD, circ. 56,363 255

Thorne
W DONCASTER FREE PRESS, circ. 34,029 173
W GOOLE TIMES, circ. 10,149 192
W THORNE AND DISTRICT GAZETTE, circ. 19,000 F 263

Thurcroft
W ROTHERHAM ADVERTISER AND RECORD SERIES,
   circ. 94,605 241
D THE STAR SHEFFIELD, circ. 56,363 255

Thurnscoe
W BARNSLEY CHRONICLE & INDEPENDENT SERIES,
   circ. 122,314 145
W DEARNE VALLEY WEEKENDER, circ. 50,550 F 171
W DONCASTER FREE PRESS, circ. 34,029 173
W ROTHERHAM ADVERTISER AND RECORD SERIES,
   circ. 94,605 241
W SOUTH YORKSHIRE TIMES, circ. 5,862 251
D THE STAR SHEFFIELD, circ. 56,363 255

Wath upon Dearne
W BARNSLEY CHRONICLE & INDEPENDENT SERIES,
   circ. 122,314 145
W DEARNE VALLEY WEEKENDER, circ. 50,550 F 171
W DONCASTER FREE PRESS, circ. 34,029 173
W ROTHERHAM ADVERTISER AND RECORD SERIES,
   circ. 94,605 241
W SOUTH YORKSHIRE TIMES, circ. 5,862 251
D THE STAR SHEFFIELD, circ. 56,363 255

Wombwell
W BARNSLEY CHRONICLE & INDEPENDENT SERIES,
   circ. 122,314 145
W DEARNE VALLEY WEEKENDER, circ. 50,550 F 171
W THE MERCURY NEWSPAPER, circ. 40,000 F 219
W SOUTH YORKSHIRE TIMES, circ. 5,862 251

Worsbrough
W BARNSLEY CHRONICLE & INDEPENDENT SERIES,
   circ. 122,314 145
D THE STAR SHEFFIELD, circ. 56,363 255

Southwark Borough
W SOUTH LONDON PRESS SERIES, circ. 41,016 250

Dulwich
W GUARDIAN & NEWS SERIES (SUTTON),
   circ. 315,438 193

Rotherhithe
W THE DOCKLANDS AND PENINSULA SERIES,
   circ. 31,500 F 173

Southwark
W THE MERCURY AND POST SERIES, circ. 166,029 F 219
W SOUTHWARK NEWS SERIES, circ. 59,300 252

Sydenham
W THE MERCURY AND POST SERIES, circ. 166,029 F 219

West Norwood
W GUARDIAN & NEWS SERIES (SUTTON),
   circ. 315,438 193

Staffordshire
W EAST STAFFORDSHIRE JOURNAL INCORPORATING
   STAFFS BUSINESS TIMES, circ. 5,000 F 178
W YOUR LEEK PAPER, circ. 4,500 279

Alrewas
D BURTON MAIL, circ. 14,658 155
W LICHFIELD MERCURY SERIES, circ. 81,365 F 211

Armitage
D BIRMINGHAM MAIL, circ. 78,178 148
D THE BIRMINGHAM POST, circ. 12,997 149
D BIRMINGHAM POST (CITY/LONDON OFFICE) 149
W CHASE POST SERIES (LICHFIELD & RUGELEY),
   circ. 27,653 F 159
D EXPRESS & STAR, circ. 140,001 183
D EXPRESS & STAR (CITY/LONDON OFFICE) 183
W LICHFIELD MERCURY SERIES, circ. 81,365 F 211
W STAFFORDSHIRE NEWSLETTER SERIES,
   circ. 24,500 254
S SUNDAY MERCURY (BIRMINGHAM), circ. 59,339 258

Ashley
D THE SENTINEL STOKE-ON-TRENT, circ. 61,910 245

Barton-under-Needwood
D BURTON MAIL, circ. 14,658 155
W LICHFIELD MERCURY SERIES, circ. 81,365 F 211

Biddulph
W ADVERTISER SERIES (SOUTH CHESHIRE),
   circ. 25,694 F 140
W ADVERTISER SERIES (STOKE-ON-TRENT),
   circ. 103,429 F 140
W CONGLETON CHRONICLE SERIES, circ. 16,900 165
W MOORLANDS TRADER, circ. 15,689 F 224
W POST & TIMES SERIES, circ. 16,304 237
D THE SENTINEL STOKE-ON-TRENT, circ. 61,910 245

Blythe Bridge
W CHEADLE TIMES & ECHO SERIES, circ. 11,000 159

Branston
D BURTON MAIL, circ. 14,658 155

Burntwood
W THE CANNOCK & LICHFIELD CHRONICLE SERIES,
   circ. 65,761 F 157
W CHASE POST SERIES BURNTWOOD & CANNOCK,
   circ. 49,453 F 159
W CHASE POST SERIES (LICHFIELD & RUGELEY),
   circ. 27,653 F 159
W LICHFIELD MERCURY SERIES, circ. 81,365 F 211

Burslem
W ADVERTISER SERIES (STOKE-ON-TRENT),
   circ. 103,429 F 140

Burton upon Trent
W THE BURTON & SOUTH DERBYSHIRE ADVERTISER,
   circ. 57,692 F 155
D BURTON MAIL, circ. 14,658 155
D DERBY TELEGRAPH, circ. 42,726 172

Cannock
D BIRMINGHAM MAIL, circ. 78,178 148
D THE BIRMINGHAM POST, circ. 12,997 149
D BIRMINGHAM POST (CITY/LONDON OFFICE) 149
W THE CANNOCK & LICHFIELD CHRONICLE SERIES,
   circ. 65,761 F 157

W **Local/Weekly Newspapers**   D **Regional Daily Newspapers**   S **Regional Sunday Newspapers**   F **Free Newspapers**

Non-Nationals - England

Title *(Day/am/pm)* Circ. Page No.

[W] CHASE POST SERIES BURNTWOOD & CANNOCK, circ. 49,453 [F] ... 159
[D] EXPRESS & STAR, circ. 140,001 ... 183
[D] EXPRESS & STAR (CITY/LONDON OFFICE) ... 183
[W] LICHFIELD MERCURY SERIES, circ. 81,365 [F] ... 211
[D] SHROPSHIRE STAR (CITY/LONDON OFFICE) ... 247
[W] WOLVERHAMPTON CHRONICLE, circ. 68,351 [F] ... 277

Cheadle
[W] ADVERTISER SERIES (STOKE-ON-TRENT), circ. 103,429 [F] ... 140
[W] CHEADLE TIMES & ECHO SERIES, circ. 11,000 ... 159
[W] MOORLANDS TRADER, circ. 15,689 [F] ... 224
[W] POST & TIMES SERIES, circ. 16,304 ... 237
[D] THE SENTINEL STOKE-ON-TRENT, circ. 61,910 ... 245

Cheddleton
[W] ADVERTISER SERIES (STOKE-ON-TRENT), circ. 103,429 [F] ... 140
[W] MOORLANDS TRADER, circ. 15,689 [F] ... 224

Eccleshall
[D] THE SENTINEL STOKE-ON-TRENT, circ. 61,910 ... 245
[W] STAFFORD POST SERIES, circ. 36,712 [F] ... 254

Fazeley
[D] BIRMINGHAM MAIL, circ. 78,178 ... 148
[D] THE BIRMINGHAM POST, circ. 12,997 ... 149
[D] BIRMINGHAM POST (CITY/LONDON OFFICE) ... 149
[D] EXPRESS & STAR, circ. 140,001 ... 183
[D] EXPRESS & STAR (CITY/LONDON OFFICE) ... 183
[S] SUNDAY MERCURY (BIRMINGHAM), circ. 59,339 ... 258
[W] TAMWORTH HERALD SERIES, circ. 58,633 ... 262

Fenton
[W] ADVERTISER SERIES (STOKE-ON-TRENT), circ. 103,429 [F] ... 140

Forsbrook
[W] CHEADLE TIMES & ECHO SERIES, circ. 11,000 ... 159

Gnosall
[D] THE BIRMINGHAM POST, circ. 12,997 ... 149
[D] BIRMINGHAM POST (CITY/LONDON OFFICE) ... 149
[D] EXPRESS & STAR, circ. 140,001 ... 183
[D] EXPRESS & STAR (CITY/LONDON OFFICE) ... 183
[D] THE SENTINEL STOKE-ON-TRENT, circ. 61,910 ... 245
[W] STAFFORD POST SERIES, circ. 36,712 [F] ... 254
[W] STAFFORDSHIRE NEWSLETTER SERIES, circ. 24,500 ... 254
[S] SUNDAY MERCURY (BIRMINGHAM), circ. 59,339 ... 258

Great Wyrley
[D] BIRMINGHAM MAIL, circ. 78,178 ... 148
[D] THE BIRMINGHAM POST, circ. 12,997 ... 149
[D] BIRMINGHAM POST (CITY/LONDON OFFICE) ... 149
[D] EXPRESS & STAR, circ. 140,001 ... 183
[D] EXPRESS & STAR (CITY/LONDON OFFICE) ... 183
[W] LICHFIELD MERCURY SERIES, circ. 81,365 [F] ... 211
[S] SUNDAY MERCURY (BIRMINGHAM), circ. 59,339 ... 258

Hanley
[W] ADVERTISER SERIES (STOKE-ON-TRENT), circ. 103,429 [F] ... 140

Hednesford
[W] THE CANNOCK & LICHFIELD CHRONICLE SERIES, circ. 65,761 [F] ... 157
[W] LICHFIELD MERCURY SERIES, circ. 81,365 [F] ... 211

Kinver
[D] BIRMINGHAM MAIL, circ. 78,178 ... 148
[D] THE BIRMINGHAM POST, circ. 12,997 ... 149
[D] BIRMINGHAM POST (CITY/LONDON OFFICE) ... 149
[D] EXPRESS & STAR, circ. 140,001 ... 183
[D] EXPRESS & STAR (CITY/LONDON OFFICE) ... 183
[W] STOURBRIDGE NEWS, circ. 51,747 [F] ... 256
[S] SUNDAY MERCURY (BIRMINGHAM), circ. 59,339 ... 258

Leek
[W] ADVERTISER SERIES (STOKE-ON-TRENT), circ. 103,429 [F] ... 140
[W] CHEADLE TIMES & ECHO SERIES, circ. 11,000 ... 159
[W] MOORLANDS TRADER, circ. 15,689 [F] ... 224
[W] POST & TIMES SERIES, circ. 16,304 ... 237
[D] THE SENTINEL STOKE-ON-TRENT, circ. 61,910 ... 245
[W] YOUR LEEK PAPER, circ. 4,500 ... 279

Lichfield
[D] BIRMINGHAM MAIL, circ. 78,178 ... 148
[D] THE BIRMINGHAM POST, circ. 12,997 ... 149
[D] BIRMINGHAM POST (CITY/LONDON OFFICE) ... 149
[W] THE CANNOCK & LICHFIELD CHRONICLE SERIES, circ. 65,761 [F] ... 157
[W] CHASE POST SERIES BURNTWOOD & CANNOCK, circ. 49,453 [F] ... 159
[W] CHASE POST SERIES (LICHFIELD & RUGELEY), circ. 27,653 [F] ... 159
[D] EXPRESS & STAR, circ. 140,001 ... 183
[D] EXPRESS & STAR (CITY/LONDON OFFICE) ... 183
[W] LICHFIELD MERCURY SERIES, circ. 81,365 [F] ... 211
[D] SHROPSHIRE STAR (CITY/LONDON OFFICE) ... 247
[S] SUNDAY MERCURY (BIRMINGHAM), circ. 59,339 ... 258
[W] WOLVERHAMPTON CHRONICLE, circ. 68,351 [F] ... 277

Madeley
[D] THE BIRMINGHAM POST, circ. 12,997 ... 149
[D] THE SENTINEL STOKE-ON-TRENT, circ. 61,910 ... 245

Meir
[W] CHEADLE TIMES & ECHO SERIES, circ. 11,000 ... 159

Newcastle-under-Lyme
[W] ADVERTISER SERIES (STOKE-ON-TRENT), circ. 103,429 [F] ... 140
[D] THE SENTINEL STOKE-ON-TRENT, circ. 61,910 ... 245

Norton Canes
[W] LICHFIELD MERCURY SERIES, circ. 81,365 [F] ... 211

Rangemore
[D] BURTON MAIL, circ. 14,658 ... 155

Rolleston
[D] THE BIRMINGHAM POST, circ. 12,997 ... 149
[D] BIRMINGHAM POST (CITY/LONDON OFFICE) ... 149
[D] BURTON MAIL, circ. 14,658 ... 155
[D] DERBY TELEGRAPH, circ. 42,726 ... 172
[W] MIDLANDS FOCUS, circ. 5,000 [F] ... 222
[S] SUNDAY MERCURY (BIRMINGHAM), circ. 59,339 ... 258

Rugeley
[D] BIRMINGHAM MAIL, circ. 78,178 ... 148
[D] THE BIRMINGHAM POST, circ. 12,997 ... 149
[D] BIRMINGHAM POST (CITY/LONDON OFFICE) ... 149
[W] THE CANNOCK & LICHFIELD CHRONICLE SERIES, circ. 65,761 [F] ... 157
[W] CHASE POST SERIES BURNTWOOD & CANNOCK, circ. 49,453 [F] ... 159
[W] CHASE POST SERIES (LICHFIELD & RUGELEY), circ. 27,653 [F] ... 159
[D] EXPRESS & STAR, circ. 140,001 ... 183
[D] EXPRESS & STAR (CITY/LONDON OFFICE) ... 183
[W] LICHFIELD MERCURY SERIES, circ. 81,365 [F] ... 211
[W] STAFFORDSHIRE NEWSLETTER SERIES, circ. 24,500 ... 254
[W] WOLVERHAMPTON CHRONICLE, circ. 68,351 [F] ... 277

Sedgley
[W] DUDLEY NEWS & COUNTY EXPRESS, circ. 38,894 [F] ... 175

Stafford
[D] EXPRESS & STAR, circ. 140,001 ... 183
[D] EXPRESS & STAR (CITY/LONDON OFFICE) ... 183
[D] THE SENTINEL STOKE-ON-TRENT, circ. 61,910 ... 245
[D] SHROPSHIRE STAR (CITY/LONDON OFFICE) ... 247
[W] THE STAFFORD & STONE CHRONICLE, circ. 37,057 [F] ... 254
[W] STAFFORD POST SERIES, circ. 36,712 [F] ... 254
[W] STAFFORDSHIRE NEWSLETTER SERIES, circ. 24,500 ... 254
[S] SUNDAY MERCURY (BIRMINGHAM), circ. 59,339 ... 258

Stoke-on-Trent
[W] ADVERTISER SERIES (STOKE-ON-TRENT), circ. 103,429 [F] ... 140
[D] THE SENTINEL STOKE-ON-TRENT, circ. 61,910 ... 245

Stone
[D] EXPRESS & STAR, circ. 140,001 ... 183
[D] EXPRESS & STAR (CITY/LONDON OFFICE) ... 183
[D] THE SENTINEL STOKE-ON-TRENT, circ. 61,910 ... 245
[W] THE STAFFORD & STONE CHRONICLE, circ. 37,057 [F] ... 254
[W] STAFFORD POST SERIES, circ. 36,712 [F] ... 254
[W] STAFFORDSHIRE NEWSLETTER SERIES, circ. 24,500 ... 254
[W] WOLVERHAMPTON CHRONICLE, circ. 68,351 [F] ... 277

Tamworth
[D] BIRMINGHAM MAIL, circ. 78,178 ... 148
[D] THE BIRMINGHAM POST, circ. 12,997 ... 149
[D] BIRMINGHAM POST (CITY/LONDON OFFICE) ... 149
[W] TAMWORTH HERALD SERIES, circ. 58,633 ... 262

Tean
[W] CHEADLE TIMES & ECHO SERIES, circ. 11,000 ... 159

Tunstall
[W] ADVERTISER SERIES (STOKE-ON-TRENT), circ. 103,429 [F] ... 140

Tutbury
[D] BURTON MAIL, circ. 14,658 ... 155

Uttoxeter
[D] BURTON MAIL, circ. 14,658 ... 155
[W] CHEADLE TIMES & ECHO SERIES, circ. 11,000 ... 159
[D] DERBY TELEGRAPH, circ. 42,726 ... 172
[W] POST & TIMES SERIES, circ. 16,304 ... 237
[D] THE SENTINEL STOKE-ON-TRENT, circ. 61,910 ... 245
[W] STAFFORDSHIRE NEWSLETTER SERIES, circ. 24,500 ... 254
[W] UTTOXETER ADVERTISER, circ. 4,200 ... 266

Weston Coyney
[W] CHEADLE TIMES & ECHO SERIES, circ. 11,000 ... 159

Wombourne
[D] THE BIRMINGHAM POST, circ. 12,997 ... 149
[D] BIRMINGHAM POST (CITY/LONDON OFFICE) ... 149
[D] EXPRESS & STAR, circ. 140,001 ... 183
[D] EXPRESS & STAR (CITY/LONDON OFFICE) ... 183
[W] THE NEWS & OBSERVER SERIES, circ. 131,457 ... 227
[S] SUNDAY MERCURY (BIRMINGHAM), circ. 59,339 ... 258

Yoxall
[D] BURTON MAIL, circ. 14,658 ... 155
[W] LICHFIELD MERCURY SERIES, circ. 81,365 [F] ... 211

Suffolk

Aldeburgh
[W] ADVERTISER SERIES (IPSWICH), circ. 82,067 [F] ... 139
[W] COMMUNITY NEWS SERIES, circ. 31,000 [F] ... 164

Beccles
[W] COMMUNITY NEWS SERIES, circ. 31,000 [F] ... 164
[D] EASTERN DAILY PRESS (NORWICH), circ. 64,700 ... 178
[W] NORFOLK COUNTY WEEKLIES SERIES, circ. 82,422 229

Brandon
[D] EASTERN DAILY PRESS (NORWICH), circ. 64,700 ... 178
[W] NORFOLK COUNTY WEEKLIES SERIES, circ. 82,422 229

Bungay
[W] COMMUNITY NEWS SERIES, circ. 31,000 [F] ... 164
[D] EASTERN DAILY PRESS (NORWICH), circ. 64,700 ... 178
[W] NORFOLK COUNTY WEEKLIES SERIES, circ. 82,422 229

Bury St. Edmunds
[W] BURY FREE PRESS & CITIZEN SERIES, circ. 53,112 . 155
[W] CAMBRIDGE WEEKLY NEWS & CRIER SERIES, circ. 208,805 [F] ... 157
[D] EA WEEK ... 176
[D] EAST ANGLIAN DAILY TIMES, circ. 34,392 ... 176
[W] MERCURY SERIES, circ. 45,543 [F] ... 220

Capel St. Mary
[D] EA WEEK ... 176
[D] EAST ANGLIAN DAILY TIMES, circ. 34,392 ... 176
[D] EVENING STAR, circ. 19,707 ... 181
[W] GREATER IPSWICH COMMUNITY NEWS SERIES, circ. 38,500 [F] ... 192

Clare
[W] HAVERHILL ECHO, circ. 4,927 ... 196
[W] SUFFOLK FREE PRESS, circ. 9,596 ... 257

Claydon
[W] GREATER IPSWICH COMMUNITY NEWS SERIES, circ. 38,500 [F] ... 192

Eye
[W] DISS EXPRESS, circ. 8,486 ... 173

Felixstowe
[W] ADVERTISER SERIES (IPSWICH), circ. 82,067 [F] ... 139
[D] EA WEEK ... 176
[D] EAST ANGLIAN DAILY TIMES, circ. 34,392 ... 176
[D] EVENING STAR, circ. 19,707 ... 181

Framlingham
[W] ADVERTISER SERIES (IPSWICH), circ. 82,067 [F] ... 139
[W] COMMUNITY NEWS SERIES, circ. 31,000 [F] ... 164
[W] DISS EXPRESS, circ. 8,486 ... 173

Halesworth
[W] COMMUNITY NEWS SERIES, circ. 31,000 [F] ... 164
[D] EA WEEK ... 176
[D] EAST ANGLIAN DAILY TIMES, circ. 34,392 ... 176
[D] EASTERN DAILY PRESS (NORWICH), circ. 64,700 ... 178
[W] NORFOLK COUNTY WEEKLIES SERIES, circ. 82,422 229

Haverhill
[D] CAMBRIDGE NEWS, circ. 26,242 ... 157
[W] CAMBRIDGE WEEKLY NEWS & CRIER SERIES, circ. 208,805 [F] ... 157
[D] EA WEEK ... 176
[D] EAST ANGLIAN DAILY TIMES, circ. 34,392 ... 176
[W] HAVERHILL ECHO, circ. 4,927 ... 196

Ipswich
[W] ADVERTISER SERIES (IPSWICH), circ. 82,067 [F] ... 139
[D] EA WEEK ... 176

[W] **Local/Weekly Newspapers** [D] **Regional Daily Newspapers** [S] **Regional Sunday Newspapers** [F] **Free Newspapers**

Title (Day/am/pm) Circ. Page No.

[D] EAST ANGLIAN DAILY TIMES, circ. 34,392 ... 176
[D] EVENING STAR, circ. 19,707 ... 181
[W] GREATER IPSWICH COMMUNITY NEWS SERIES, circ. 38,500 [F] ... 192

Kessingland
[D] EA WEEK ... 176
[D] EAST ANGLIAN DAILY TIMES, circ. 34,392 ... 176
[D] EASTERN DAILY PRESS (NORWICH), circ. 64,700 ... 178
[W] LOWESTOFT JOURNAL, circ. 18,333 ... 215

Lakenheath
[W] BURY FREE PRESS & CITIZEN SERIES, circ. 53,112 . 155
[D] EA WEEK ... 176
[D] EAST ANGLIAN DAILY TIMES, circ. 34,392 ... 176
[D] EASTERN DAILY PRESS (NORWICH), circ. 64,700 ... 178

Lavenham
[W] SUFFOLK FREE PRESS, circ. 9,596 ... 257

Leiston
[W] COMMUNITY NEWS SERIES, circ. 31,000 [F] ... 164

Long Melford
[W] SUFFOLK FREE PRESS, circ. 9,596 ... 257

Lowestoft
[D] EA WEEK ... 176
[D] EAST ANGLIAN DAILY TIMES, circ. 34,392 ... 176
[D] EASTERN DAILY PRESS (NORWICH), circ. 64,700 ... 178
[W] LOWESTOFT JOURNAL, circ. 18,333 ... 215

Mildenhall
[W] BURY FREE PRESS & CITIZEN SERIES, circ. 53,112 . 155
[W] CAMBRIDGE WEEKLY NEWS & CRIER SERIES, circ. 208,805 [F] ... 157
[W] NEWMARKET JOURNAL SERIES, circ. 10,186 ... 226

Needham Market
[W] BURY FREE PRESS & CITIZEN SERIES, circ. 53,112 . 155

Newmarket
[D] CAMBRIDGE NEWS, circ. 26,242 ... 157
[W] CAMBRIDGE WEEKLY NEWS & CRIER SERIES, circ. 208,805 [F] ... 157
[D] EA WEEK ... 176
[D] EAST ANGLIAN DAILY TIMES, circ. 34,392 ... 176
[W] MERCURY SERIES, circ. 45,543 [F] ... 220
[W] NEWMARKET JOURNAL SERIES, circ. 10,186 ... 226

Saxmundham
[W] ADVERTISER SERIES (IPSWICH), circ. 82,067 [F] ... 139
[W] COMMUNITY NEWS SERIES, circ. 31,000 [F] ... 164
[D] EA WEEK ... 176
[D] EAST ANGLIAN DAILY TIMES, circ. 34,392 ... 176

Southwold
[W] COMMUNITY NEWS SERIES, circ. 31,000 [F] ... 164
[D] EA WEEK ... 176
[D] EASTERN DAILY PRESS (NORWICH), circ. 64,700 ... 178
[W] LOWESTOFT JOURNAL, circ. 18,333 ... 215

Stowmarket
[W] ADVERTISER SERIES (IPSWICH), circ. 82,067 [F] ... 139
[W] BURY FREE PRESS & CITIZEN SERIES, circ. 53,112 . 155
[D] EA WEEK ... 176
[D] EAST ANGLIAN DAILY TIMES, circ. 34,392 ... 176
[D] EVENING STAR, circ. 19,707 ... 181
[W] GREATER IPSWICH COMMUNITY NEWS SERIES, circ. 38,500 [F] ... 192

Sudbury
[W] MERCURY SERIES, circ. 45,543 [F] ... 220
[W] SUFFOLK FREE PRESS, circ. 9,596 ... 257

Woodbridge
[W] ADVERTISER SERIES (IPSWICH), circ. 82,067 [F] ... 139
[W] COMMUNITY NEWS SERIES, circ. 31,000 [F] ... 164
[D] EA WEEK ... 176
[D] EAST ANGLIAN DAILY TIMES, circ. 34,392 ... 176
[D] EVENING STAR, circ. 19,707 ... 181
[W] GREATER IPSWICH COMMUNITY NEWS SERIES, circ. 38,500 [F] ... 192

Surrey
[D] LONDON EVENING STANDARD, circ. 263,312 ... 214
[W] SOUTH BUCKS AND BERKSHIRE NEWS SERIES, circ. 50,000 [F] ... 249
[W] SOUTHERN COUNTIES TELEGRAPH, circ. 45,000 [F] ... 252

Addlestone
[W] STAINES INFORMER SERIES, circ. 197,957 ... 254
[W] WOKING NEWS & MAIL SERIES, circ. 9,002 ... 276
[W] WOKING REVIEW SERIES, circ. 41,114 [F] ... 276

Ash
[W] ALDERSHOT MAIL AND NEWS SERIES, circ. 131,660 ... 140

Ashford
[W] STAINES INFORMER SERIES, circ. 197,957 ... 254

Ashtead
[W] ADVERTISER SERIES (SURREY), circ. 11,382 ... 140
[W] GUARDIAN & NEWS SERIES (SUTTON), circ. 315,438 ... 193
[W] SURREY COMET, circ. 10,182 ... 260

Banstead
[W] CROYDON ADVERTISER & POST SERIES, circ. 203,807 ... 168
[W] GUARDIAN & NEWS SERIES (SUTTON), circ. 315,438 ... 193
[W] SURREY MIRROR SERIES, circ. 40,632 ... 260

Beare Green
[W] ADVERTISER SERIES (SURREY), circ. 11,382 ... 140

Betchworth
[W] ADVERTISER SERIES (SURREY), circ. 11,382 ... 140

Bletchingley
[W] COUNTY BORDER NEWS SERIES, circ. 28,000 [F] ... 166
[W] SURREY MIRROR SERIES, circ. 40,632 ... 260

Byfleet
[W] STAINES INFORMER SERIES, circ. 197,957 ... 254
[W] WOKING NEWS & MAIL SERIES, circ. 9,002 ... 276
[W] WOKING REVIEW SERIES, circ. 41,114 [F] ... 276

Camberley
[W] ALDERSHOT MAIL AND NEWS SERIES, circ. 131,660 ... 140
[W] GUARDIAN SERIES (WILTSHIRE, HAMPSHIRE AND SURREY), circ. 175,000 [F] ... 193
[W] SOUTH BUCKS AND BERKSHIRE NEWS SERIES, circ. 50,000 [F] ... 249

Capel
[W] ADVERTISER SERIES (SURREY), circ. 11,382 ... 140

Caterham
[W] CHRONICLE SERIES, circ. 17,100 [F] ... 162
[W] COUNTY BORDER NEWS SERIES, circ. 28,000 [F] ... 166
[W] CROYDON ADVERTISER & POST SERIES, circ. 203,807 ... 168
[W] SURREY MIRROR SERIES, circ. 40,632 ... 260

Chertsey
[W] STAINES INFORMER SERIES, circ. 197,957 ... 254

Chobham
[W] SURREY COMET, circ. 10,182 ... 260
[W] WOKING NEWS & MAIL SERIES, circ. 9,002 ... 276

Claygate
[W] GUARDIAN & NEWS SERIES (SUTTON), circ. 315,438 ... 193
[W] SURREY COMET, circ. 10,182 ... 260

Cobham
[W] ADVERTISER SERIES (SURREY), circ. 11,382 ... 140
[W] GRAVESEND MESSENGER SERIES, circ. 40,890 ... 192
[W] GUARDIAN & NEWS SERIES (SUTTON), circ. 315,438 ... 193
[W] STAINES INFORMER SERIES, circ. 197,957 ... 254
[W] SURREY TIMES & ADVERTISER SERIES, circ. 63,655 ... 260

Cranleigh
[W] SURREY TIMES & ADVERTISER SERIES, circ. 63,655 ... 260
[W] WEST SUSSEX COUNTY TIMES SERIES, circ. 54,814 ... 271

Dorking
[W] ADVERTISER SERIES (SURREY), circ. 11,382 ... 140
[W] GUARDIAN & NEWS SERIES (SUTTON), circ. 315,438 ... 193
[W] GUARDIAN SERIES (WILTSHIRE, HAMPSHIRE AND SURREY), circ. 175,000 [F] ... 193
[W] SURREY TIMES & ADVERTISER SERIES, circ. 63,655 ... 260

East Horsley
[W] ADVERTISER SERIES (SURREY), circ. 11,382 ... 140

Egham
[W] SOUTH BUCKS AND BERKSHIRE NEWS SERIES, circ. 50,000 [F] ... 249
[W] STAINES INFORMER SERIES, circ. 197,957 ... 254

Epsom
[W] CROYDON ADVERTISER & POST SERIES, circ. 203,807 ... 168
[W] GUARDIAN & NEWS SERIES (SUTTON), circ. 315,438 ... 193
[W] SURREY COMET, circ. 10,182 ... 260

Esher
[W] GUARDIAN & NEWS SERIES (SUTTON), circ. 315,438 ... 193
[W] STAINES INFORMER SERIES, circ. 197,957 ... 254
[W] SURREY COMET, circ. 10,182 ... 260
[W] SURREY TIMES & ADVERTISER SERIES, circ. 63,655 ... 260

Ewell
[W] GUARDIAN & NEWS SERIES (SUTTON), circ. 315,438 ... 193
[W] SURREY COMET, circ. 10,182 ... 260

Farnham
[W] ALDERSHOT MAIL AND NEWS SERIES, circ. 131,660 ... 140
[W] ALTON POST GAZETTE, TIMES & MAIL SERIES, circ. 30,000 ... 141
[W] FARNHAM HERALD SERIES, circ. 31,000 ... 184

Godalming
[W] THE MESSENGER, circ. 40,348 [F] ... 220
[W] SURREY TIMES & ADVERTISER SERIES, circ. 63,655 ... 260

Godstone
[W] COUNTY BORDER NEWS SERIES, circ. 28,000 [F] ... 166

Guildford
[W] ALDERSHOT MAIL AND NEWS SERIES, circ. 131,660 ... 140
[W] GUARDIAN SERIES (WILTSHIRE, HAMPSHIRE AND SURREY), circ. 175,000 [F] ... 193
[W] SOUTH BUCKS AND BERKSHIRE NEWS SERIES, circ. 50,000 [F] ... 249
[W] SURREY TIMES & ADVERTISER SERIES, circ. 63,655 ... 260

Haslemere
[W] ALTON POST GAZETTE, TIMES & MAIL SERIES, circ. 30,000 ... 141
[W] FARNHAM HERALD SERIES, circ. 31,000 ... 184
[W] THE MESSENGER, circ. 40,348 [F] ... 220

Hersham
[W] STAINES INFORMER SERIES, circ. 197,957 ... 254
[W] SURREY COMET, circ. 10,182 ... 260
[W] SURREY TIMES & ADVERTISER SERIES, circ. 63,655 ... 260

Hindhead
[W] ALTON POST GAZETTE, TIMES & MAIL SERIES, circ. 30,000 ... 141
[W] FARNHAM HERALD SERIES, circ. 31,000 ... 184

Holmwood
[W] ADVERTISER SERIES (SURREY), circ. 11,382 ... 140

Horley
[W] CRAWLEY OBSERVER, TIMES AND HERALD SERIES, circ. 45,052 ... 167
[W] REDHILL REIGATE HORLEY LIFE, circ. 33,771 [F] ... 239
[W] SOUTH BUCKS AND BERKSHIRE NEWS SERIES, circ. 50,000 [F] ... 249
[W] SURREY MIRROR SERIES, circ. 40,632 ... 260

Kenley
[W] CROYDON ADVERTISER & POST SERIES, circ. 203,807 ... 168

Leatherhead
[W] ADVERTISER SERIES (SURREY), circ. 11,382 ... 140
[W] GUARDIAN & NEWS SERIES (SUTTON), circ. 315,438 ... 193
[W] SOUTH BUCKS AND BERKSHIRE NEWS SERIES, circ. 50,000 [F] ... 249
[W] SURREY TIMES & ADVERTISER SERIES, circ. 63,655 ... 260

Leigh
[W] ADVERTISER SERIES (SURREY), circ. 11,382 ... 140

Limpsfield
[W] CHRONICLE SERIES, circ. 17,100 [F] ... 162
[W] COUNTY BORDER NEWS SERIES, circ. 28,000 [F] ... 166

Lingfield
[W] CHRONICLE SERIES, circ. 17,100 [F] ... 162
[W] COUNTY BORDER NEWS SERIES, circ. 28,000 [F] ... 166
[W] EAST GRINSTEAD COURIER & OBSERVER, circ. 15,000 ... 177
[W] SURREY MIRROR SERIES, circ. 40,632 ... 260

[W] **Local/Weekly Newspapers** [D] **Regional Daily Newspapers** [S] **Regional Sunday Newspapers** [F] **Free Newspapers**

Non-Nationals - England

Title (Day/am/pm)	Circ.	Page No.

Molesey
W GUARDIAN & NEWS SERIES (SUTTON), circ. 315,438 193
W STAINES INFORMER SERIES, circ. 197,957 254
W SURREY TIMES & ADVERTISER SERIES, circ. 63,655 260

Newdigate
W ADVERTISER SERIES (SURREY), circ. 11,382 140

Ockley
W ADVERTISER SERIES (SURREY), circ. 11,382 140

Ottershaw
W STAINES INFORMER SERIES, circ. 197,957 254

Oxshott
W ADVERTISER SERIES (SURREY), circ. 11,382 140

Oxted
W CHRONICLE SERIES, circ. 17,100 F 162
W COUNTY BORDER NEWS SERIES, circ. 28,000 F ... 166
W SURREY MIRROR SERIES, circ. 40,632 260

Redhill
W GUARDIAN SERIES (WILTSHIRE, HAMPSHIRE AND SURREY), circ. 175,000 F 193
W REDHILL REIGATE HORLEY LIFE, circ. 33,771 F 239
W SOUTH BUCKS AND BERKSHIRE NEWS SERIES, circ. 50,000 F 249
W SURREY MIRROR SERIES, circ. 40,632 260

Reigate
W GUARDIAN SERIES (WILTSHIRE, HAMPSHIRE AND SURREY), circ. 175,000 F 193
W REDHILL REIGATE HORLEY LIFE, circ. 33,771 F 239
W SURREY MIRROR SERIES, circ. 40,632 260

Salfords
W SURREY MIRROR SERIES, circ. 40,632 260

Send
W WOKING REVIEW SERIES, circ. 41,114 F 276

Shepperton
W STAINES INFORMER SERIES, circ. 197,957 254

Staines
W STAINES INFORMER SERIES, circ. 197,957 254

Sunbury
W STAINES INFORMER SERIES, circ. 197,957 254

Virginia Water
W STAINES INFORMER SERIES, circ. 197,957 254
W THE VILLAGER, circ. 8,000 F 267

Walton-on-Thames
W GUARDIAN & NEWS SERIES (SUTTON), circ. 315,438 193
W GUARDIAN SERIES (WILTSHIRE, HAMPSHIRE AND SURREY), circ. 175,000 F 193
W STAINES INFORMER SERIES, circ. 197,957 254
W SURREY COMET, circ. 10,182 260
W SURREY TIMES & ADVERTISER SERIES, circ. 63,655 260

West Byfleet
W WOKING NEWS & MAIL SERIES, circ. 9,002 276

Weybridge
W GUARDIAN & NEWS SERIES (SUTTON), circ. 315,438 193
W STAINES INFORMER SERIES, circ. 197,957 254
W SURREY COMET, circ. 10,182 260
W SURREY TIMES & ADVERTISER SERIES, circ. 63,655 260

Whyteleafe
W COUNTY BORDER NEWS SERIES, circ. 28,000 F ... 166
W CROYDON ADVERTISER & POST SERIES, circ. 203,807 168

Woking
W GUARDIAN SERIES (WILTSHIRE, HAMPSHIRE AND SURREY), circ. 175,000 F 193
W STAINES INFORMER SERIES, circ. 197,957 254
W SURREY TIMES & ADVERTISER SERIES, circ. 63,655 260
W WOKING NEWS & MAIL SERIES, circ. 9,002 276
W WOKING REVIEW SERIES, circ. 41,114 F 276

Sutton Borough

Carshalton
W CROYDON ADVERTISER & POST SERIES, circ. 203,807 168

Sutton
W CROYDON ADVERTISER & POST SERIES, circ. 203,807 168
W GUARDIAN & NEWS SERIES (SUTTON), circ. 315,438 193
W GUARDIAN SERIES (WILTSHIRE, HAMPSHIRE AND SURREY), circ. 175,000 F 193
W SURREY COMET, circ. 10,182 260

Wallington
W CROYDON ADVERTISER & POST SERIES, circ. 203,807 168

Worcester Park
W GUARDIAN & NEWS SERIES (SUTTON), circ. 315,438 193
W SURREY COMET, circ. 10,182 260

Tower Hamlets Borough

W EAST LONDON ADVERTISER, circ. 9,204 177
W NEWHAM RECORDER, circ. 13,531 226

Docklands
W CITY OF LONDON & DOCKLAND TIMES, circ. 20,000 162
W THE DOCKLANDS AND PENINSULA SERIES, circ. 31,500 F 173
W THE WHARF, 33,442 F 273

Limehouse
W THE DOCKLANDS AND PENINSULA SERIES, circ. 31,500 F 173

Spitalfields
W EAST LONDON ADVERTISER, circ. 9,204 177

Tower Hamlets
W EAST END LIFE, circ. 78,914 F 177

Wapping
W THE DOCKLANDS AND PENINSULA SERIES, circ. 31,500 F 173

Whitechapel
W EAST LONDON ADVERTISER, circ. 9,204 177

Tyne & Wear

Blaydon
D EVENING CHRONICLE (NEWCASTLE), circ. 78,804 ... 180
D THE JOURNAL (NEWCASTLE), circ. 35,476 205
D THE NORTHERN ECHO (DARLINGTON), circ. 50,256 232
S SUNDAY SUN, circ. 68,033 259

Chopwell
D EVENING CHRONICLE (NEWCASTLE), circ. 78,804 ... 180
D THE JOURNAL (NEWCASTLE), circ. 35,476 205
S SUNDAY SUN, circ. 68,033 259

Cleadon
W CHRONICLE EXTRA SERIES (TYNE & WEAR), circ. 387,488 F 161
D EVENING CHRONICLE (NEWCASTLE), circ. 78,804 ... 180
D THE JOURNAL (NEWCASTLE), circ. 35,476 205
D THE SHIELDS GAZETTE, circ. 18,726 247
S SUNDAY SUN, circ. 68,033 259
D SUNDERLAND ECHO, circ. 42,910 259

Dudley
W NEWS GUARDIAN SERIES, circ. 131,934 F 227

Felling
W CHRONICLE EXTRA SERIES (TYNE & WEAR), circ. 387,488 F 161
D EVENING CHRONICLE (NEWCASTLE), circ. 78,804 ... 180
D THE JOURNAL (NEWCASTLE), circ. 35,476 205
D THE NORTHERN ECHO (DARLINGTON), circ. 50,256 232
S SUNDAY SUN, circ. 68,033 259

Gateshead
W CHRONICLE EXTRA SERIES (TYNE & WEAR), circ. 387,488 F 161
D EVENING CHRONICLE (NEWCASTLE), circ. 78,804 ... 180
D THE JOURNAL (NEWCASTLE), circ. 35,476 205
S SUNDAY SUN, circ. 68,033 259

Gosforth
W CHRONICLE EXTRA SERIES (TYNE & WEAR), circ. 387,488 F 161
D EVENING CHRONICLE (NEWCASTLE), circ. 78,804 ... 180
D THE JOURNAL (NEWCASTLE), circ. 35,476 205
S SUNDAY SUN, circ. 68,033 259

Hebburn
D THE SHIELDS GAZETTE, circ. 18,726 247
W STAR SERIES, circ. 138,751 F 255

Hetton-le-Hole
W STAR SERIES, circ. 138,751 F 255
D SUNDERLAND ECHO, circ. 42,910 259

Houghton-le-Spring
W STAR SERIES, circ. 138,751 F 255
D SUNDERLAND ECHO, circ. 42,910 259

Jarrow
D THE SHIELDS GAZETTE, circ. 18,726 247
W STAR SERIES, circ. 138,751 F 255

Killingworth
W CHRONICLE EXTRA SERIES (TYNE & WEAR), circ. 387,488 161
D EVENING CHRONICLE (NEWCASTLE), circ. 78,804 ... 180
D THE JOURNAL (NEWCASTLE), circ. 35,476 205
S SUNDAY SUN, circ. 68,033 259

Long Benton
D EVENING CHRONICLE (NEWCASTLE), circ. 78,804 ... 180
D THE JOURNAL (NEWCASTLE), circ. 35,476 205
S SUNDAY SUN, circ. 68,033 259

Newburn
W CHRONICLE EXTRA SERIES (TYNE & WEAR), circ. 387,488 F 161
D EVENING CHRONICLE (NEWCASTLE), circ. 78,804 ... 180
D THE JOURNAL (NEWCASTLE), circ. 35,476 205
D THE NORTHERN ECHO (DARLINGTON), circ. 50,256 232
S SUNDAY SUN, circ. 68,033 259

Newcastle upon Tyne
W CHRONICLE EXTRA SERIES (TYNE & WEAR), circ. 387,488 F 161
D EVENING CHRONICLE (NEWCASTLE), circ. 78,804 ... 180
D THE JOURNAL (NEWCASTLE), circ. 35,476 205
S SUNDAY SUN, circ. 68,033 259
D SUNDERLAND ECHO, circ. 42,910 259

North Shields
W CHRONICLE EXTRA SERIES (TYNE & WEAR), circ. 387,488 F 161
W NEWS GUARDIAN SERIES, circ. 131,934 F 227

Rowlands Gill
D EVENING CHRONICLE (NEWCASTLE), circ. 78,804 ... 180
D THE JOURNAL (NEWCASTLE), circ. 35,476 205
D THE NORTHERN ECHO (DARLINGTON), circ. 50,256 232
S SUNDAY SUN, circ. 68,033 259

Ryton
D EVENING CHRONICLE (NEWCASTLE), circ. 78,804 ... 180
D THE JOURNAL (NEWCASTLE), circ. 35,476 205
D THE NORTHERN ECHO (DARLINGTON), circ. 50,256 232
S SUNDAY SUN, circ. 68,033 259

Shiremoor
W CHRONICLE EXTRA SERIES (TYNE & WEAR), circ. 387,488 F 161
D EVENING CHRONICLE (NEWCASTLE), circ. 78,804 ... 180
D THE JOURNAL (NEWCASTLE), circ. 35,476 205
W NEWS GUARDIAN SERIES, circ. 131,934 F 227
S SUNDAY SUN, circ. 68,033 259

South Shields
W CHRONICLE EXTRA SERIES (TYNE & WEAR), circ. 387,488 F 161
D EVENING CHRONICLE (NEWCASTLE), circ. 78,804 ... 180
D THE JOURNAL (NEWCASTLE), circ. 35,476 205
D THE SHIELDS GAZETTE, circ. 18,726 247
W STAR SERIES, circ. 138,751 F 255
S SUNDAY SUN, circ. 68,033 259
D SUNDERLAND ECHO, circ. 42,910 259

Sunderland
D EVENING CHRONICLE (NEWCASTLE), circ. 78,804 ... 180
D THE JOURNAL (NEWCASTLE), circ. 35,476 205
W STAR SERIES, circ. 138,751 F 255
S SUNDAY SUN, circ. 68,033 259
D SUNDERLAND ECHO, circ. 42,910 259

Sunniside
W CHRONICLE EXTRA SERIES (TYNE & WEAR), circ. 387,488 F 161
D EVENING CHRONICLE (NEWCASTLE), circ. 78,804 ... 180
D THE JOURNAL (NEWCASTLE), circ. 35,476 205
D THE NORTHERN ECHO (DARLINGTON), circ. 50,256 232
S SUNDAY SUN, circ. 68,033 259

Tynemouth
W NEWS GUARDIAN SERIES, circ. 131,934 F 227

Wallsend
W CHRONICLE EXTRA SERIES (TYNE & WEAR), circ. 387,488 F 161

W **Local/Weekly Newspapers**   D **Regional Daily Newspapers**   S **Regional Sunday Newspapers**   F **Free Newspapers**

Title (Day/am/pm)	Circ.	Page No.

Ⓦ NEWS GUARDIAN SERIES, circ. 131,934 Ⓕ 227

Washington
Ⓦ STAR SERIES, circ. 138,751 Ⓕ 255
Ⓓ SUNDERLAND ECHO, circ. 42,910 259

Whickham
Ⓦ CHRONICLE EXTRA SERIES (TYNE & WEAR), circ. 387,488 Ⓕ 161
Ⓓ THE JOURNAL (NEWCASTLE), circ. 35,476 205
Ⓓ THE NORTHERN ECHO (DARLINGTON), circ. 50,256 232
Ⓢ SUNDAY SUN, circ. 68,033 259

Whitburn
Ⓓ THE SHIELDS GAZETTE, circ. 18,726 247
Ⓓ SUNDERLAND ECHO, circ. 42,910 259

Whitley Bay
Ⓦ CHRONICLE EXTRA SERIES (TYNE & WEAR), circ. 387,488 Ⓕ 161
Ⓦ NEWS GUARDIAN SERIES, circ. 131,934 Ⓕ 227

Wide Open
Ⓦ CHRONICLE EXTRA SERIES (TYNE & WEAR), circ. 387,488 Ⓕ 161
Ⓓ EVENING CHRONICLE (NEWCASTLE), circ. 78,804 .. 180
Ⓓ THE JOURNAL (NEWCASTLE), circ. 35,476 205
Ⓢ SUNDAY SUN, circ. 68,033 259

Waltham Forest Borough

Chingford
Ⓦ GUARDIAN AND INDEPENDENT SERIES, circ. 22,432 193
Ⓦ WALTHAM FOREST GUARDIAN & INDEPENDENT SERIES, circ. 52,115 268
Ⓦ YELLOW ADVERTISER GROUP SERIES (ESSEX), circ. 434,612 Ⓕ 278

Leyton
Ⓦ GUARDIAN AND INDEPENDENT SERIES, circ. 22,432 193
Ⓦ WALTHAM FOREST GUARDIAN & INDEPENDENT SERIES, circ. 52,115 268
Ⓦ YELLOW ADVERTISER GROUP SERIES (ESSEX), circ. 434,612 Ⓕ 278

Leytonstone
Ⓦ GUARDIAN AND INDEPENDENT SERIES, circ. 22,432 193
Ⓦ WALTHAM FOREST GUARDIAN & INDEPENDENT SERIES, circ. 52,115 268
Ⓦ YELLOW ADVERTISER GROUP SERIES (ESSEX), circ. 434,612 Ⓕ 278

Waltham Forest
Ⓦ WALTHAM FOREST GUARDIAN & INDEPENDENT SERIES, circ. 52,115 268
Ⓦ YELLOW ADVERTISER GROUP SERIES (ESSEX), circ. 434,612 Ⓕ 278

Walthamstow
Ⓦ GUARDIAN AND INDEPENDENT SERIES, circ. 22,432 193
Ⓦ WALTHAM FOREST GUARDIAN & INDEPENDENT SERIES, circ. 52,115 268
Ⓦ YELLOW ADVERTISER GROUP SERIES (ESSEX), circ. 434,612 Ⓕ 278

Wandsworth Borough

Ⓦ SOUTH LONDON PRESS SERIES, circ. 41,016 250

Balham
Ⓦ GUARDIAN & NEWS SERIES (SUTTON), circ. 315,438 193

Battersea
Ⓦ GUARDIAN & NEWS SERIES (SUTTON), circ. 315,438 193

Putney
Ⓦ GUARDIAN & NEWS SERIES (SUTTON), circ. 315,438 193
Ⓦ LONDON NEWSPAPER GROUP SERIES, circ. 69,601 214
Ⓦ SURREY COMET, circ. 10,182 260

Tooting
Ⓦ GUARDIAN & NEWS SERIES (SUTTON), circ. 315,438 193
Ⓦ THE MERCURY AND POST SERIES, circ. 166,029 Ⓕ 219

Wandsworth
Ⓦ GUARDIAN & NEWS SERIES (SUTTON), circ. 315,438 193
Ⓦ THE MERCURY AND POST SERIES, circ. 166,029 Ⓕ 219
Ⓦ SURREY COMET, circ. 10,182 260

Warwickshire

Ⓓ COVENTRY TELEGRAPH, circ. 48,025 167

Alcester
Ⓓ BIRMINGHAM MAIL, circ. 78,178 148
Ⓦ LEAMINGTON & STRATFORD OBSERVER SERIES, circ. 90,456 Ⓕ 210
Ⓦ REDDITCH ADVERTISER AND CHRONICLE SERIES, circ. 46,343 Ⓕ 239
Ⓦ REDDITCH AND BROMSGROVE STANDARD SERIES, circ. 89,270 Ⓕ 239
Ⓦ STRATFORD-UPON-AVON HERALD SERIES, circ. 70,303 257

Atherstone
Ⓓ BIRMINGHAM MAIL, circ. 78,178 148
Ⓦ NUNEATON NEWS, circ. 15,000 232
Ⓦ NUNEATON TRIBUNE, circ. 54,756 Ⓕ 233
Ⓦ TAMWORTH HERALD SERIES, circ. 58,633 262

Baddesley Ensor
Ⓓ BIRMINGHAM MAIL, circ. 78,178 148
Ⓓ THE BIRMINGHAM POST, circ. 12,997 149
Ⓓ BIRMINGHAM POST (CITY/LONDON OFFICE) 149
Ⓢ SUNDAY MERCURY (BIRMINGHAM), circ. 59,339 ... 258
Ⓦ TAMWORTH HERALD SERIES, circ. 58,633 262

Bedworth
Ⓓ THE BIRMINGHAM POST, circ. 12,997 149
Ⓓ BIRMINGHAM POST (CITY/LONDON OFFICE) 149
Ⓦ NUNEATON NEWS, circ. 15,000 232
Ⓦ NUNEATON TRIBUNE, circ. 54,756 Ⓕ 233

Bidford-on-Avon
Ⓓ BIRMINGHAM MAIL, circ. 78,178 148
Ⓦ LEAMINGTON & STRATFORD OBSERVER SERIES, circ. 90,456 Ⓕ 210
Ⓦ REDDITCH ADVERTISER AND CHRONICLE SERIES, circ. 46,343 Ⓕ 239

Bulkington
Ⓦ NUNEATON TRIBUNE, circ. 54,756 Ⓕ 233

Coleshill
Ⓓ BIRMINGHAM MAIL, circ. 78,178 148
Ⓓ THE BIRMINGHAM POST, circ. 12,997 149
Ⓓ BIRMINGHAM POST (CITY/LONDON OFFICE) 149
Ⓦ TAMWORTH HERALD SERIES, circ. 58,633 262

Dordon
Ⓓ BIRMINGHAM MAIL, circ. 78,178 148
Ⓓ THE BIRMINGHAM POST, circ. 12,997 149
Ⓓ BIRMINGHAM POST (CITY/LONDON OFFICE) 149
Ⓢ SUNDAY MERCURY (BIRMINGHAM), circ. 59,339 ... 258
Ⓦ TAMWORTH HERALD SERIES, circ. 58,633 262

Hartshill
Ⓓ THE BIRMINGHAM POST, circ. 12,997 149
Ⓓ BIRMINGHAM POST (CITY/LONDON OFFICE) 149
Ⓓ LEICESTER MERCURY, circ. 70,028 210
Ⓦ NUNEATON NEWS, circ. 15,000 232
Ⓦ NUNEATON TRIBUNE, circ. 54,756 Ⓕ 233
Ⓢ SUNDAY MERCURY (BIRMINGHAM), circ. 59,339 ... 258

Henley-in-Arden
Ⓓ BIRMINGHAM MAIL, circ. 78,178 148
Ⓦ SOLIHULL NEWS, circ. 79,221 Ⓕ 249
Ⓦ SOLIHULL, SHIRLEY & ARDEN OBSERVER SERIES, circ. 73,823 Ⓕ 249
Ⓦ STRATFORD-UPON-AVON HERALD SERIES, circ. 70,303 257

Kenilworth
Ⓓ BIRMINGHAM MAIL, circ. 78,178 148
Ⓓ THE BIRMINGHAM POST, circ. 12,997 149
Ⓓ BIRMINGHAM POST (CITY/LONDON OFFICE) 149
Ⓦ LEAMINGTON & STRATFORD OBSERVER SERIES, circ. 90,456 Ⓕ 210
Ⓦ LEAMINGTON SPA COURIER SERIES, circ. 56,996 ... 210
Ⓦ TIMES SERIES (COVENTRY, LEAMINGTON, WARWICK & KENILWORTH), circ. 50,913 Ⓕ 264

Kineton
Ⓓ THE BIRMINGHAM POST, circ. 12,997 149
Ⓓ BIRMINGHAM POST (CITY/LONDON OFFICE) 149

Kingsbury
Ⓓ BIRMINGHAM MAIL, circ. 78,178 148
Ⓓ THE BIRMINGHAM POST, circ. 12,997 149
Ⓓ BIRMINGHAM POST (CITY/LONDON OFFICE) 149
Ⓓ EXPRESS & STAR, circ. 140,001 183
Ⓓ EXPRESS & STAR (CITY/LONDON OFFICE) 183
Ⓢ SUNDAY MERCURY (BIRMINGHAM), circ. 59,339 ... 258

Leamington Spa
Ⓓ BIRMINGHAM MAIL, circ. 78,178 148
Ⓓ THE BIRMINGHAM POST, circ. 12,997 149
Ⓓ BIRMINGHAM POST (CITY/LONDON OFFICE) 149

Ⓦ LEAMINGTON & STRATFORD OBSERVER SERIES, circ. 90,456 Ⓕ 210
Ⓦ LEAMINGTON SPA COURIER SERIES, circ. 56,996 ... 210
Ⓦ SOLIHULL NEWS, circ. 79,221 Ⓕ 249
Ⓦ TIMES SERIES (COVENTRY, LEAMINGTON, WARWICK & KENILWORTH), circ. 50,913 Ⓕ 264

Nuneaton
Ⓓ LEICESTER MERCURY, circ. 70,028 210
Ⓦ NUNEATON NEWS, circ. 15,000 232
Ⓦ NUNEATON TRIBUNE, circ. 54,756 Ⓕ 233

Polesworth
Ⓓ BIRMINGHAM MAIL, circ. 78,178 148
Ⓓ THE BIRMINGHAM POST, circ. 12,997 149
Ⓓ BIRMINGHAM POST (CITY/LONDON OFFICE) 149
Ⓢ SUNDAY MERCURY (BIRMINGHAM), circ. 59,339 ... 258
Ⓦ TAMWORTH HERALD SERIES, circ. 58,633 262

Rugby
Ⓦ RUGBY ADVERTISER AND REVIEW SERIES, circ. 56,936 242
Ⓦ THE RUGBY OBSERVER SERIES, circ. 42,974 Ⓕ 242
Ⓦ THE RUGBY TIMES, circ. 33,944 Ⓕ 242

Shipston-on-Stour
Ⓓ BIRMINGHAM MAIL, circ. 78,178 148
Ⓦ STRATFORD-UPON-AVON HERALD SERIES, circ. 70,303 257

Southam
Ⓓ BIRMINGHAM MAIL, circ. 78,178 148
Ⓓ THE BIRMINGHAM POST, circ. 12,997 149
Ⓓ BIRMINGHAM POST (CITY/LONDON OFFICE) 149
Ⓦ LEAMINGTON & STRATFORD OBSERVER SERIES, circ. 90,456 Ⓕ 210
Ⓦ LEAMINGTON SPA COURIER SERIES, circ. 56,996 ... 210
Ⓢ SUNDAY MERCURY (BIRMINGHAM), circ. 59,339 ... 258

Stratford-upon-Avon
Ⓓ BIRMINGHAM MAIL, circ. 78,178 148
Ⓓ THE BIRMINGHAM POST, circ. 12,997 149
Ⓓ BIRMINGHAM POST (CITY/LONDON OFFICE) 149
Ⓦ LEAMINGTON & STRATFORD OBSERVER SERIES, circ. 90,456 Ⓕ 210
Ⓦ STRATFORD-UPON-AVON HERALD SERIES, circ. 70,303 257

Studley
Ⓓ BIRMINGHAM MAIL, circ. 78,178 148

Warwick
Ⓓ THE BIRMINGHAM POST, circ. 12,997 149
Ⓓ BIRMINGHAM POST (CITY/LONDON OFFICE) 149
Ⓦ LEAMINGTON & STRATFORD OBSERVER SERIES, circ. 90,456 Ⓕ 210
Ⓦ LEAMINGTON SPA COURIER SERIES, circ. 56,996 ... 210
Ⓦ SOLIHULL NEWS, circ. 79,221 Ⓕ 249
Ⓦ TIMES SERIES (COVENTRY, LEAMINGTON, WARWICK & KENILWORTH), circ. 50,913 Ⓕ 264

Water Orton
Ⓓ BIRMINGHAM MAIL, circ. 78,178 148
Ⓓ THE BIRMINGHAM POST, circ. 12,997 149
Ⓓ BIRMINGHAM POST (CITY/LONDON OFFICE) 149
Ⓓ EXPRESS & STAR, circ. 140,001 183
Ⓓ EXPRESS & STAR (CITY/LONDON OFFICE) 183
Ⓦ SOLIHULL NEWS, circ. 79,221 Ⓕ 249
Ⓢ SUNDAY MERCURY (BIRMINGHAM), circ. 59,339 ... 258
Ⓦ SUTTON COLDFIELD OBSERVER SERIES, circ. 91,245 Ⓕ 261

Wellesbourne
Ⓓ BIRMINGHAM MAIL, circ. 78,178 148
Ⓓ THE BIRMINGHAM POST, circ. 12,997 149
Ⓓ BIRMINGHAM POST (CITY/LONDON OFFICE) 149
Ⓦ EVESHAM JOURNAL SERIES, circ. 32,275 182
Ⓦ STRATFORD-UPON-AVON HERALD SERIES, circ. 70,303 257
Ⓢ SUNDAY MERCURY (BIRMINGHAM), circ. 59,339 ... 258

West Midlands

Ⓢ SUNDAY MERCURY (BIRMINGHAM), circ. 59,339 ... 258

Acocks Green
Ⓦ SOLIHULL NEWS, circ. 79,221 Ⓕ 249

Aldridge
Ⓓ BIRMINGHAM MAIL, circ. 78,178 148
Ⓓ THE BIRMINGHAM POST, circ. 12,997 149
Ⓓ BIRMINGHAM POST (CITY/LONDON OFFICE) 149
Ⓓ EXPRESS & STAR, circ. 140,001 183
Ⓓ EXPRESS & STAR (CITY/LONDON OFFICE) 183
Ⓦ THE NEWS & OBSERVER SERIES, circ. 131,457 227
Ⓦ WALSALL ADVERTISER, circ. 65,616 Ⓕ 268

Balsall
Ⓓ BIRMINGHAM MAIL, circ. 78,178 148

Ⓦ **Local/Weekly Newspapers**   Ⓓ **Regional Daily Newspapers**   Ⓢ **Regional Sunday Newspapers**   Ⓕ **Free Newspapers**

Non-Nationals - England

Title (Day/am/pm)	Circ.	Page No.

D THE BIRMINGHAM POST, circ. 12,997 149
D BIRMINGHAM POST (CITY/LONDON OFFICE) 149

Balsall Common
W LEAMINGTON SPA COURIER SERIES, circ. 56,996 ... 210
W SOLIHULL NEWS, circ. 79,221 F 249
W SOLIHULL, SHIRLEY & ARDEN OBSERVER SERIES, circ. 73,823 249

Birmingham
D BIRMINGHAM MAIL, circ. 78,178 148
D BIRMINGHAM MAIL EXTRA, circ. 177,201 F 148
D THE BIRMINGHAM POST, circ. 12,997 149
D BIRMINGHAM POST (CITY/LONDON OFFICE) 149
D EXPRESS & STAR, circ. 140,001 183
D EXPRESS & STAR (CITY/LONDON OFFICE) 183
D SHROPSHIRE STAR (CITY/LONDON OFFICE) 247

Bloxwich
D BIRMINGHAM MAIL, circ. 78,178 148
D THE BIRMINGHAM POST, circ. 12,997 149
D BIRMINGHAM POST (CITY/LONDON OFFICE) 149
D EXPRESS & STAR, circ. 140,001 183
D EXPRESS & STAR (CITY/LONDON OFFICE) 183
W THE NEWS & OBSERVER SERIES, circ. 131,457 227
W WALSALL ADVERTISER, circ. 65,616 F 268

Brierley Hill
W DUDLEY NEWS & COUNTY EXPRESS, circ. 38,894 F 175

Brownhills
D BIRMINGHAM MAIL, circ. 78,178 148
D THE BIRMINGHAM POST, circ. 12,997 149
D BIRMINGHAM POST (CITY/LONDON OFFICE) 149
W CHASE POST SERIES BURNTWOOD & CANNOCK, circ. 49,453 F 159
D EXPRESS & STAR, circ. 140,001 183
D EXPRESS & STAR (CITY/LONDON OFFICE) 183
W THE NEWS & OBSERVER SERIES, circ. 131,457 227
W WALSALL ADVERTISER, circ. 65,616 F 268

Castle Bromwich
D THE BIRMINGHAM POST, circ. 12,997 149
D BIRMINGHAM POST (CITY/LONDON OFFICE) 149

Chelmsley Wood
D BIRMINGHAM MAIL, circ. 78,178 148
D THE BIRMINGHAM POST, circ. 12,997 149
D BIRMINGHAM POST (CITY/LONDON OFFICE) 149

Cheswick Green
D BIRMINGHAM MAIL, circ. 78,178 148
D THE BIRMINGHAM POST, circ. 12,997 149
W SOLIHULL NEWS, circ. 79,221 F 249
W SOLIHULL, SHIRLEY & ARDEN OBSERVER SERIES, circ. 73,823 249

Coventry
D THE BIRMINGHAM POST, circ. 12,997 149
D BIRMINGHAM POST (CITY/LONDON OFFICE) 149
W COVENTRY OBSERVER, circ. 122,552 F 167
D COVENTRY TELEGRAPH, circ. 48,025 167
W COVENTRY TIMES, circ. 121,430 F 167
W TIMES SERIES (COVENTRY, LEAMINGTON, WARWICK & KENILWORTH), circ. 50,913 F 264

Cradley Heath
W HALESOWEN NEWS, circ. 41,019 F 194

Darlaston
W THE NEWS & OBSERVER SERIES, circ. 131,457 227

Dudley
D BIRMINGHAM MAIL, circ. 78,178 148
D THE BIRMINGHAM POST, circ. 12,997 149
D BIRMINGHAM POST (CITY/LONDON OFFICE) 149
D DUDLEY CHRONICLE SERIES, circ. 168,985 F 174
W DUDLEY NEWS & COUNTY EXPRESS, circ. 38,894 F 175
D EXPRESS & STAR, circ. 140,001 183
D EXPRESS & STAR (CITY/LONDON OFFICE) 183
D SHROPSHIRE STAR (CITY/LONDON OFFICE) 247
W WOLVERHAMPTON CHRONICLE, circ. 68,351 F 277

Erdington
D BIRMINGHAM MAIL, circ. 78,178 148
D THE BIRMINGHAM POST, circ. 12,997 149
W SUTTON COLDFIELD NEWS, circ. 62,017 F 261
W SUTTON COLDFIELD OBSERVER SERIES, circ. 91,245 F 261
W WOLVERHAMPTON CHRONICLE, circ. 68,351 F 277

Great Barr
D BIRMINGHAM MAIL EXTRA, circ. 177,201 F 148
W SANDWELL AND GREAT BARR CHRONICLE SERIES, circ. 94,540 F 244
D SHROPSHIRE STAR (CITY/LONDON OFFICE) 247

W SUTTON COLDFIELD OBSERVER SERIES, circ. 91,245 F 261
W WOLVERHAMPTON CHRONICLE, circ. 68,351 F 277

Halesowen
D BIRMINGHAM MAIL, circ. 78,178 148
D THE BIRMINGHAM POST, circ. 12,997 149
D BIRMINGHAM POST (CITY/LONDON OFFICE) 149
W DUDLEY CHRONICLE SERIES, circ. 168,985 F 174
D EXPRESS & STAR, circ. 140,001 183
D EXPRESS & STAR (CITY/LONDON OFFICE) 183
W HALESOWEN NEWS, circ. 41,019 F 194
W WOLVERHAMPTON CHRONICLE, circ. 68,351 F 277

Hall Green
W SOLIHULL NEWS, circ. 79,221 F 249
W SOLIHULL, SHIRLEY & ARDEN OBSERVER SERIES, circ. 73,823 249

Hampton-in-Arden
D BIRMINGHAM MAIL, circ. 78,178 148
D THE BIRMINGHAM POST, circ. 12,997 149
D BIRMINGHAM POST (CITY/LONDON OFFICE) 149

Handsworth Wood
W SUTTON COLDFIELD OBSERVER SERIES, circ. 91,245 F 261

Kingswinford
W STOURBRIDGE NEWS, circ. 51,747 F 256

Knowle
D BIRMINGHAM MAIL, circ. 78,178 148
D THE BIRMINGHAM POST, circ. 12,997 149
D BIRMINGHAM POST (CITY/LONDON OFFICE) 149
W SOLIHULL NEWS, circ. 79,221 F 249
W SOLIHULL, SHIRLEY & ARDEN OBSERVER SERIES, circ. 73,823 F 249

Meriden
D BIRMINGHAM MAIL, circ. 78,178 148
D THE BIRMINGHAM POST, circ. 12,997 149
D BIRMINGHAM POST (CITY/LONDON OFFICE) 149
D COVENTRY TELEGRAPH, circ. 48,025 167

Oldbury
W HALESOWEN NEWS, circ. 41,019 F 194
W THE NEWS & OBSERVER SERIES, circ. 131,457 227
W SANDWELL AND GREAT BARR CHRONICLE SERIES, circ. 94,540 F 244
D SHROPSHIRE STAR (CITY/LONDON OFFICE) 247

Pelsall
D BIRMINGHAM MAIL, circ. 78,178 148
D THE BIRMINGHAM POST, circ. 12,997 149
D BIRMINGHAM POST (CITY/LONDON OFFICE) 149
D EXPRESS & STAR, circ. 140,001 183
D EXPRESS & STAR (CITY/LONDON OFFICE) 183
W WALSALL ADVERTISER, circ. 65,616 F 268

Rowley Regis
W HALESOWEN NEWS, circ. 41,019 F 194
W SANDWELL AND GREAT BARR CHRONICLE SERIES, circ. 94,540 F 244

Rushall
D BIRMINGHAM MAIL, circ. 78,178 148
D THE BIRMINGHAM POST, circ. 12,997 149
D BIRMINGHAM POST (CITY/LONDON OFFICE) 149
D EXPRESS & STAR, circ. 140,001 183
D EXPRESS & STAR (CITY/LONDON OFFICE) 183
W WALSALL ADVERTISER, circ. 65,616 F 268

Sandwell
D EXPRESS & STAR, circ. 140,001 183
D EXPRESS & STAR (CITY/LONDON OFFICE) 183
W WOLVERHAMPTON CHRONICLE, circ. 68,351 F 277

Shelfield
D BIRMINGHAM MAIL, circ. 78,178 148
D THE BIRMINGHAM POST, circ. 12,997 149
D BIRMINGHAM POST (CITY/LONDON OFFICE) 149
D EXPRESS & STAR, circ. 140,001 183
D EXPRESS & STAR (CITY/LONDON OFFICE) 183
W WALSALL ADVERTISER, circ. 65,616 F 268

Smethwick
W SANDWELL AND GREAT BARR CHRONICLE SERIES, circ. 94,540 F 244
D SHROPSHIRE STAR (CITY/LONDON OFFICE) 247

Solihull
D BIRMINGHAM MAIL, circ. 78,178 148
D THE BIRMINGHAM POST, circ. 12,997 149
D BIRMINGHAM POST (CITY/LONDON OFFICE) 149
D COVENTRY TELEGRAPH, circ. 48,025 167
W SOLIHULL NEWS, circ. 79,221 F 249
W SOLIHULL, SHIRLEY & ARDEN OBSERVER SERIES, circ. 73,823 249

Stourbridge
D BIRMINGHAM MAIL, circ. 78,178 148
D THE BIRMINGHAM POST, circ. 12,997 149
D BIRMINGHAM POST (CITY/LONDON OFFICE) 149
W DUDLEY CHRONICLE SERIES, circ. 168,985 F 174
D EXPRESS & STAR, circ. 140,001 183
W STOURBRIDGE NEWS, circ. 51,747 F 256
W WOLVERHAMPTON CHRONICLE, circ. 68,351 F 277

Sutton Coldfield
D BIRMINGHAM MAIL, circ. 78,178 148
D THE BIRMINGHAM POST, circ. 12,997 149
D BIRMINGHAM POST (CITY/LONDON OFFICE) 149
W SUTTON COLDFIELD NEWS, circ. 62,017 F 261
W SUTTON COLDFIELD OBSERVER SERIES, circ. 91,245 F 261

Tipton
W THE NEWS & OBSERVER SERIES, circ. 131,457 227
W SANDWELL AND GREAT BARR CHRONICLE SERIES, circ. 94,540 F 244

Walsall
D BIRMINGHAM MAIL, circ. 78,178 148
D THE BIRMINGHAM POST, circ. 12,997 149
D BIRMINGHAM POST (CITY/LONDON OFFICE) 149
D EXPRESS & STAR, circ. 140,001 183
D EXPRESS & STAR (CITY/LONDON OFFICE) 183
W THE NEWS & OBSERVER SERIES, circ. 131,457 227
D SHROPSHIRE STAR (CITY/LONDON OFFICE) 247
W WALSALL ADVERTISER, circ. 65,616 F 268
W WALSALL CHRONICLE, circ. 65,414 F 268
W WOLVERHAMPTON CHRONICLE, circ. 68,351 F 277

Warley
D BIRMINGHAM MAIL, circ. 78,178 148
D THE BIRMINGHAM POST, circ. 12,997 149
D BIRMINGHAM POST (CITY/LONDON OFFICE) 149
D EXPRESS & STAR, circ. 140,001 183
D EXPRESS & STAR (CITY/LONDON OFFICE) 183

Wednesbury
W THE NEWS & OBSERVER SERIES, circ. 131,457 227
W SANDWELL AND GREAT BARR CHRONICLE SERIES, circ. 94,540 F 244
D SHROPSHIRE STAR (CITY/LONDON OFFICE) 247

West Bromwich
D BIRMINGHAM MAIL, circ. 78,178 148
D THE BIRMINGHAM POST, circ. 12,997 149
D BIRMINGHAM POST (CITY/LONDON OFFICE) 149
D EXPRESS & STAR, circ. 140,001 183
D EXPRESS & STAR (CITY/LONDON OFFICE) 183
W THE NEWS & OBSERVER SERIES, circ. 131,457 227
W SANDWELL AND GREAT BARR CHRONICLE SERIES, circ. 94,540 F 244
D SHROPSHIRE STAR (CITY/LONDON OFFICE) 247
W SUTTON COLDFIELD OBSERVER SERIES, circ. 91,245 F 261

Willenhall
W THE NEWS & OBSERVER SERIES, circ. 131,457 227
W WALSALL ADVERTISER, circ. 65,616 F 268
W WOLVERHAMPTON CHRONICLE, circ. 68,351 F 277

Wolverhampton
D THE BIRMINGHAM POST, circ. 12,997 149
D BIRMINGHAM POST (CITY/LONDON OFFICE) 149
D EXPRESS & STAR, circ. 140,001 183
D EXPRESS & STAR (CITY/LONDON OFFICE) 183
D SHROPSHIRE STAR (CITY/LONDON OFFICE) 247
W WOLVERHAMPTON CHRONICLE, circ. 68,351 F 277

Yardley
W SOLIHULL NEWS, circ. 79,221 F 249

West Sussex
W SOUTH BUCKS AND BERKSHIRE NEWS SERIES, circ. 50,000 F 249

Angmering-on-Sea
W LITTLEHAMPTON GAZETTE, circ. 9,839 213
W WORTHING ADVERTISER AND HERALD SERIES, circ. 90,862 277
W WORTHING GUARDIAN, circ. 35,000 F 277

Arundel
W LITTLEHAMPTON GAZETTE, circ. 9,839 213
W THE NEWS (PORTSMOUTH), circ. 65,000 228
W WEST SUSSEX GAZETTE, circ. 8,683 271
W WORTHING ADVERTISER AND HERALD SERIES, circ. 90,862 277

Ashington
W WEST SUSSEX COUNTY TIMES SERIES, circ. 54,814 271
W WEST SUSSEX GAZETTE, circ. 8,683 271

W Local/Weekly Newspapers   D Regional Daily Newspapers   S Regional Sunday Newspapers   F Free Newspapers

Section 3 Index to UK Newspapers

Title (Day/am/pm)	Circ.	Page No.

Barnham

W THE ARGUS, circ. 32,788 142
W BOGNOR REGIS AND CHICHESTER GUARDIAN,
  circ. 41,368 F 149
W SOUTHDOWN OBSERVER SERIES, circ. 35,161 251
W WEST SUSSEX GAZETTE, circ. 8,683 271

Billingshurst

W WEST SUSSEX COUNTY TIMES SERIES,
  circ. 54,814 271
W WEST SUSSEX GAZETTE, circ. 8,683 271

Bognor Regis

D THE ARGUS, circ. 32,788 142
W BOGNOR REGIS AND CHICHESTER GUARDIAN,
  circ. 41,368 F 149
D THE NEWS (PORTSMOUTH), circ. 65,000 228
W SOUTHDOWN OBSERVER SERIES, circ. 35,161 251
W WEST SUSSEX GAZETTE, circ. 8,683 271

Bosham

W SOUTHDOWN OBSERVER SERIES, circ. 35,161 251
W WEST SUSSEX GAZETTE, circ. 8,683 271

Burgess Hill

D THE ARGUS, circ. 32,788 142
W BRIGHTON AND HOVE LEADER SERIES,
  circ. 138,468 F 152
W MID SUSSEX TIMES AND CITIZEN SERIES,
  circ. 42,701 221

Chanctonbury

W WEST SUSSEX COUNTY TIMES SERIES,
  circ. 54,814 271
W WORTHING ADVERTISER AND HERALD SERIES,
  circ. 90,862 277

Chichester

D THE ARGUS, circ. 32,788 142
W BOGNOR REGIS AND CHICHESTER GUARDIAN,
  circ. 41,368 F 149
D THE NEWS (PORTSMOUTH), circ. 65,000 228
W SOUTH BUCKS AND BERKSHIRE NEWS SERIES,
  circ. 50,000 F 249
W SOUTHDOWN OBSERVER SERIES, circ. 35,161 251
W WEST SUSSEX GAZETTE, circ. 8,683 271

Copthorne

W CRAWLEY OBSERVER, TIMES AND HERALD SERIES,
  circ. 45,052 167
W EAST GRINSTEAD COURIER & OBSERVER,
  circ. 15,000 177

Crawley

D THE ARGUS, circ. 32,788 142
W CRAWLEY NEWS, circ. 33,782 F 167
W CRAWLEY OBSERVER, TIMES AND HERALD SERIES,
  circ. 45,052 167
D LONDON EVENING STANDARD, circ. 263,312 214
W SOUTH BUCKS AND BERKSHIRE NEWS SERIES,
  circ. 50,000 F 249
W WEST SUSSEX GAZETTE, circ. 8,683 271

Crawley Down

D THE ARGUS, circ. 32,788 142
W CRAWLEY NEWS, circ. 33,782 F 167
W CRAWLEY OBSERVER, TIMES AND HERALD SERIES,
  circ. 45,052 167
W EAST GRINSTEAD COURIER & OBSERVER,
  circ. 15,000 177

East Grinstead

W EAST GRINSTEAD COURIER & OBSERVER,
  circ. 15,000 177
D LONDON EVENING STANDARD, circ. 263,312 214
W WEST SUSSEX GAZETTE, circ. 8,683 271

East Wittering

D THE ARGUS, circ. 32,788 142
W BOGNOR REGIS AND CHICHESTER GUARDIAN,
  circ. 41,368 F 149
W SOUTHDOWN OBSERVER SERIES, circ. 35,161 251

Gatwick

W CRAWLEY NEWS, circ. 33,782 F 167
W CRAWLEY OBSERVER, TIMES AND HERALD SERIES,
  circ. 45,052 167
W REDHILL REIGATE HORLEY LIFE, circ. 33,771 F 239
W SURREY MIRROR SERIES, circ. 40,632 260

Haywards Heath

W BRIGHTON AND HOVE LEADER SERIES,
  circ. 138,468 F 152
W MID SUSSEX TIMES AND CITIZEN SERIES,
  circ. 42,701 221

Henfield

W WEST SUSSEX COUNTY TIMES SERIES,
  circ. 54,814 271
W WEST SUSSEX GAZETTE, circ. 8,683 271

Horsham

D THE ARGUS, circ. 32,788 142
W WEST SUSSEX COUNTY TIMES SERIES,
  circ. 54,814 271
W WEST SUSSEX GAZETTE, circ. 8,683 271

Hurstpierpoint

D THE ARGUS, circ. 32,788 142
W MID SUSSEX TIMES AND CITIZEN SERIES,
  circ. 42,701 221

Keymer

D THE ARGUS, circ. 32,788 142
W MID SUSSEX TIMES AND CITIZEN SERIES,
  circ. 42,701 221

Lancing

W SHOREHAM & STEYNING HERALD SERIES,
  circ. 4,215 247
W WEST SUSSEX GAZETTE, circ. 8,683 271
W WORTHING ADVERTISER AND HERALD SERIES,
  circ. 90,862 277
W WORTHING GUARDIAN, circ. 35,000 F 277

Littlehampton

W LITTLEHAMPTON GAZETTE, circ. 9,839 213
W WEST SUSSEX GAZETTE, circ. 8,683 271
W WORTHING ADVERTISER AND HERALD SERIES,
  circ. 90,862 277

Middleton-on-Sea

W SOUTHDOWN OBSERVER SERIES, circ. 35,161 251

Midhurst

W THE MESSENGER, circ. 40,348 F 220
W SOUTHDOWN OBSERVER SERIES, circ. 35,161 251
W WEST SUSSEX GAZETTE, circ. 8,683 271

Petworth

W THE MESSENGER, circ. 40,348 F 220
W SOUTHDOWN OBSERVER SERIES, circ. 35,161 251
W WEST SUSSEX GAZETTE, circ. 8,683 271

Pulborough

W SOUTHDOWN OBSERVER SERIES, circ. 35,161 251
W WEST SUSSEX COUNTY TIMES SERIES,
  circ. 54,814 271
W WEST SUSSEX GAZETTE, circ. 8,683 271
W WORTHING ADVERTISER AND HERALD SERIES,
  circ. 90,862 277

Rustington

W LITTLEHAMPTON GAZETTE, circ. 9,839 213
W WORTHING ADVERTISER AND HERALD SERIES,
  circ. 90,862 277
W WORTHING GUARDIAN, circ. 35,000 F 277

Shoreham-by-Sea

W SHOREHAM & STEYNING HERALD SERIES,
  circ. 4,215 247
W SOUTH BUCKS AND BERKSHIRE NEWS SERIES,
  circ. 50,000 F 249
W WEST SUSSEX GAZETTE, circ. 8,683 271
W WORTHING ADVERTISER AND HERALD SERIES,
  circ. 90,862 277

Sompting

D THE ARGUS, circ. 32,788 142
W SHOREHAM & STEYNING HERALD SERIES,
  circ. 4,215 247
W WEST SUSSEX GAZETTE, circ. 8,683 271
W WORTHING ADVERTISER AND HERALD SERIES,
  circ. 90,862 277
W WORTHING GUARDIAN, circ. 35,000 F 277

Southwater

D THE ARGUS, circ. 32,788 142
W WEST SUSSEX COUNTY TIMES SERIES,
  circ. 54,814 271
W WEST SUSSEX GAZETTE, circ. 8,683 271

Southwick

W BRIGHTON AND HOVE LEADER SERIES,
  circ. 138,468 F 152

Steyning

W SHOREHAM & STEYNING HERALD SERIES,
  circ. 4,215 247
W WEST SUSSEX COUNTY TIMES SERIES,
  circ. 54,814 271
W WEST SUSSEX GAZETTE, circ. 8,683 271
W WORTHING GUARDIAN, circ. 35,000 F 277

Storrington

W WEST SUSSEX COUNTY TIMES SERIES,
  circ. 54,814 271
W WEST SUSSEX GAZETTE, circ. 8,683 271
W WORTHING ADVERTISER AND HERALD SERIES,
  circ. 90,862 277

West Chiltington

D THE ARGUS, circ. 32,788 142
W SOUTHDOWN OBSERVER SERIES, circ. 35,161 251

Westergate

D THE ARGUS, circ. 32,788 142
W BOGNOR REGIS AND CHICHESTER GUARDIAN,
  circ. 41,368 F 149
W SOUTHDOWN OBSERVER SERIES, circ. 35,161 251
W WEST SUSSEX GAZETTE, circ. 8,683 271

Worthing

D THE ARGUS, circ. 32,788 142
W SOUTH BUCKS AND BERKSHIRE NEWS SERIES,
  circ. 50,000 F 249
W WEST SUSSEX GAZETTE, circ. 8,683 271
W WORTHING ADVERTISER AND HERALD SERIES,
  circ. 90,862 277
W WORTHING GUARDIAN, circ. 35,000 F 277

Yapton

D THE ARGUS, circ. 32,788 142
W BOGNOR REGIS AND CHICHESTER GUARDIAN,
  circ. 41,368 F 149
W LITTLEHAMPTON GAZETTE, circ. 9,839 213
W WEST SUSSEX GAZETTE, circ. 8,683 271

West Yorkshire

W JOURNAL & ADVERTISER SERIES, circ. 30,000 F ... 205
W LIFE AND STYLE 212
D YORKSHIRE POST, circ. 49,031 279
D YORKSHIRE POST (CITY/LONDON OFFICE) 279

Ackworth Moor Top

D THE STAR SHEFFIELD, circ. 56,363 255
D YORKSHIRE EVENING POST, circ. 56,647 279

Addingham

W ACKRILL NEWSPAPER SERIES, circ. 64,177 137
W BRADFORD TARGET SERIES, circ. 88,522 F 151
W ILKLEY GAZETTE, circ. 5,860 202
D TELEGRAPH & ARGUS, circ. 37,371 262
D YORKSHIRE EVENING POST, circ. 56,647 279

Baildon

D TELEGRAPH & ARGUS, circ. 37,371 262
D YORKSHIRE EVENING POST, circ. 56,647 279

Bardsey

W ACKRILL NEWSPAPER SERIES, circ. 64,177 137
D THE PRESS (YORK), circ. 35,761 238
D YORKSHIRE EVENING POST, circ. 56,647 279

Batley

W BATLEY NEWS SERIES, circ. 8,551 146
W EXPRESS & CHRONICLE 183
D HUDDERSFIELD DAILY EXAMINER, circ. 25,898 201
W THE PRESS (DEWSBURY) 238
D TELEGRAPH & ARGUS, circ. 37,371 262
D YORKSHIRE EVENING POST, circ. 56,647 279

Bingley

W BRADFORD TARGET SERIES, circ. 88,522 F 151
W KEIGHLEY NEWS SERIES, circ. 39,727 206
D TELEGRAPH & ARGUS, circ. 37,371 262
D YORKSHIRE EVENING POST, circ. 56,647 279

Birstall

W BATLEY NEWS SERIES, circ. 8,551 146
D HUDDERSFIELD DAILY EXAMINER, circ. 25,898 201
W MORLEY OBSERVER & ADVERTISER, circ. 5,000 224
W THE PRESS (DEWSBURY) 238
W SPENBOROUGH GUARDIAN, circ. 7,743 253

Blackley

W MIDDLETON & NORTH MANCHESTER GUARDIAN &
  ADVERTISER SERIES, circ. 93,756 222

Bradford

W BRADFORD TARGET SERIES, circ. 88,522 F 151
W BRIGHOUSE ECHO, circ. 6,629 152
W SPENBOROUGH GUARDIAN, circ. 7,743 253
D TELEGRAPH & ARGUS, circ. 37,371 262
D YORKSHIRE EVENING POST, circ. 56,647 279

Bramhope

W WHARFE VALLEY TIMES SERIES, circ. 63,868 F 273
W WHARFEDALE & AIREDALE OBSERVER, circ. 5,181 . 273
D YORKSHIRE EVENING POST, circ. 56,647 279

W Local/Weekly Newspapers D Regional Daily Newspapers S Regional Sunday Newspapers F Free Newspapers

Non-Nationals - England

Title (Day/am/pm)	Circ.	Page No.

Brighouse
W BRIGHOUSE ECHO, circ. 6,629 152
W CALDERDALE NEWS, circ. 36,000 F 156
D EVENING COURIER (HALIFAX), circ. 19,956 181
W EXPRESS & CHRONICLE 183
D HUDDERSFIELD DAILY EXAMINER, circ. 25,898 201

Burley in Wharfedale
W ILKLEY GAZETTE, circ. 5,860 202
W WHARFE VALLEY TIMES SERIES, circ. 63,868 F 273
D YORKSHIRE EVENING POST, circ. 56,647 279

Castleford
W PONTEFRACT & CASTLEFORD EXPRESS & EXTRA SERIES, circ. 57,152 236
D YORKSHIRE EVENING POST, circ. 56,647 279

Clayton West
W EXAMINER WEEKLY, circ. 55,322 F 182
W EXPRESS & CHRONICLE 183
D HUDDERSFIELD DAILY EXAMINER, circ. 25,898 201
W MIDDLETON & NORTH MANCHESTER GUARDIAN & ADVERTISER SERIES, circ. 93,756 222

Cleckheaton
W THE PRESS (DEWSBURY) 238
W SPENBOROUGH GUARDIAN, circ. 7,743 253
D TELEGRAPH & ARGUS, circ. 37,371 262

Colne Valley
W EXAMINER WEEKLY, circ. 55,322 F 182
W EXPRESS & CHRONICLE 183

Crofton
D YORKSHIRE EVENING POST, circ. 56,647 279

Denby Dale
W EXPRESS & CHRONICLE 183
D HUDDERSFIELD DAILY EXAMINER, circ. 25,898 201
W RIPLEY & HEANOR NEWS, circ. 10,394 240
W WAKEFIELD EXPRESS SERIES, circ. 83,674 267

Dewsbury
W DEWSBURY REPORTER AND ADVERTISER SERIES, circ. 11,468 173
W THE PRESS (DEWSBURY) 238
D TELEGRAPH & ARGUS, circ. 37,371 262
D YORKSHIRE EVENING POST, circ. 56,647 279

East Keswick
W ACKRILL NEWSPAPER SERIES, circ. 64,177 137
W THE PRESS (YORK), circ. 35,761 238
D YORKSHIRE EVENING POST, circ. 56,647 279

Elland
W CALDERDALE NEWS, circ. 36,000 F 156
D EVENING COURIER (HALIFAX), circ. 19,956 181

Featherstone
W PONTEFRACT & CASTLEFORD EXPRESS & EXTRA SERIES, circ. 57,152 236
D YORKSHIRE EVENING POST, circ. 56,647 279

Fitzwilliam
W HEMSWORTH AND SOUTH ELMSALL EXPRESS, circ. 6,453 197
D THE STAR SHEFFIELD, circ. 56,363 255
D YORKSHIRE EVENING POST, circ. 56,647 279

Garforth
W LEEDS WEEKLY NEWS SERIES, circ. 124,534 F 210
D YORKSHIRE EVENING POST, circ. 56,647 279

Gildersome
W LEEDS WEEKLY NEWS SERIES, circ. 124,534 F 210
W MORLEY OBSERVER & ADVERTISER, circ. 5,000 224

Great Preston
D YORKSHIRE EVENING POST, circ. 56,647 279

Guiseley
W BRADFORD TARGET SERIES, circ. 88,522 F 151
D TELEGRAPH & ARGUS, circ. 37,371 262
W WHARFE VALLEY TIMES SERIES, circ. 63,868 F 273
W WHARFEDALE & AIREDALE OBSERVER, circ. 5,181 . 273
D YORKSHIRE EVENING POST, circ. 56,647 279

Halifax
W BRIGHOUSE ECHO, circ. 6,629 152
W CALDERDALE NEWS, circ. 36,000 F 156
D EVENING COURIER (HALIFAX), circ. 19,956 181
W JOURNAL & ADVERTISER SERIES, circ. 30,000 F .. 205
D YORKSHIRE EVENING POST, circ. 56,647 279

Haworth
W KEIGHLEY NEWS SERIES, circ. 39,727 206
D TELEGRAPH & ARGUS, circ. 37,371 262
D YORKSHIRE EVENING POST, circ. 56,647 279

Hebden Bridge
D EVENING COURIER (HALIFAX), circ. 19,956 181
W HEBDEN BRIDGE TIMES, circ. 3,349 196

Heckmondwike
W EXPRESS & CHRONICLE 183
D HUDDERSFIELD DAILY EXAMINER, circ. 25,898 201
W THE PRESS (DEWSBURY) 238
W SPENBOROUGH GUARDIAN, circ. 7,743 253
D TELEGRAPH & ARGUS, circ. 37,371 262

Hemsworth
W HEMSWORTH AND SOUTH ELMSALL EXPRESS, circ. 6,453 197

Holme Valley
W EXAMINER WEEKLY, circ. 55,322 F 182

Holmfirth
W EXPRESS & CHRONICLE 183
D HUDDERSFIELD DAILY EXAMINER, circ. 25,898 201

Holywell Green
W EXAMINER WEEKLY, circ. 55,322 F 182
W EXPRESS & CHRONICLE 183
D HUDDERSFIELD DAILY EXAMINER, circ. 25,898 201

Honley
W EXAMINER WEEKLY, circ. 55,322 F 182
W EXPRESS & CHRONICLE 183
D HUDDERSFIELD DAILY EXAMINER, circ. 25,898 201

Horbury
W WAKEFIELD EXPRESS SERIES, circ. 83,674 267

Horsforth
W WHARFE VALLEY TIMES SERIES, circ. 63,868 F 273
W WHARFEDALE & AIREDALE OBSERVER, circ. 5,181 . 273
D YORKSHIRE EVENING POST, circ. 56,647 279

Huddersfield
W BRIGHOUSE ECHO, circ. 6,629 152
W EXAMINER WEEKLY, circ. 55,322 F 182
W EXPRESS & CHRONICLE 183
D HUDDERSFIELD DAILY EXAMINER, circ. 25,898 201
W JOURNAL & ADVERTISER SERIES, circ. 30,000 F ... 205

Ilkley
W BRADFORD TARGET SERIES, circ. 88,522 F 151
W ILKLEY GAZETTE, circ. 5,860 202
D TELEGRAPH & ARGUS, circ. 37,371 262
W WHARFE VALLEY TIMES SERIES, circ. 63,868 F 273
D YORKSHIRE EVENING POST, circ. 56,647 279

Keighley
W BRADFORD TARGET SERIES, circ. 88,522 F 151
W KEIGHLEY NEWS SERIES, circ. 39,727 206
D TELEGRAPH & ARGUS, circ. 37,371 262
D YORKSHIRE EVENING POST, circ. 56,647 279

Kippax
W LEEDS WEEKLY NEWS SERIES, circ. 124,534 F 210
D YORKSHIRE EVENING POST, circ. 56,647 279

Knottingley
W PONTEFRACT & CASTLEFORD EXPRESS & EXTRA SERIES, circ. 57,152 236
D YORKSHIRE EVENING POST, circ. 56,647 279

Leeds
W JOURNAL & ADVERTISER SERIES, circ. 30,000 F ... 205
W LEEDS WEEKLY NEWS SERIES, circ. 124,534 F 210
W MORLEY OBSERVER & ADVERTISER, circ. 5,000 224
D YORKSHIRE EVENING POST, circ. 56,647 279

Liversedge
W SPENBOROUGH GUARDIAN, circ. 7,743 253
D YORKSHIRE EVENING POST, circ. 56,647 279

Lofthouse
W WAKEFIELD EXPRESS SERIES, circ. 83,674 267
D YORKSHIRE EVENING POST, circ. 56,647 279

Marsden
W EXPRESS & CHRONICLE 183
D HUDDERSFIELD DAILY EXAMINER, circ. 25,898 201

Meltham
W EXPRESS & CHRONICLE 183

Menston
W ACKRILL NEWSPAPER SERIES, circ. 64,177 137
W ILKLEY GAZETTE, circ. 5,860 202
W WHARFE VALLEY TIMES SERIES, circ. 63,868 F 273
W WHARFEDALE & AIREDALE OBSERVER, circ. 5,181 . 273
D YORKSHIRE EVENING POST, circ. 56,647 279

Mirfield
W DEWSBURY REPORTER AND ADVERTISER SERIES, circ. 11,468 173
W EXPRESS & CHRONICLE 183
D HUDDERSFIELD DAILY EXAMINER, circ. 25,898 201
W THE PRESS (DEWSBURY) 238

Morley
W LEEDS WEEKLY NEWS SERIES, circ. 124,534 F 210
W MORLEY OBSERVER & ADVERTISER, circ. 5,000 224
D YORKSHIRE EVENING POST, circ. 56,647 279

Mytholmroyd
D EVENING COURIER (HALIFAX), circ. 19,956 181
W HEBDEN BRIDGE TIMES, circ. 3,349 196

Normanton
W WAKEFIELD EXPRESS SERIES, circ. 83,674 267
D YORKSHIRE EVENING POST, circ. 56,647 279

Ossett
W WAKEFIELD EXPRESS SERIES, circ. 83,674 267
D YORKSHIRE EVENING POST, circ. 56,647 279

Otley
D TELEGRAPH & ARGUS, circ. 37,371 262
W WHARFE VALLEY TIMES SERIES, circ. 63,868 F . 273
W WHARFEDALE & AIREDALE OBSERVER, circ. 5,181 . 273
D YORKSHIRE EVENING POST, circ. 56,647 279

Pontefract
W PONTEFRACT & CASTLEFORD EXPRESS & EXTRA SERIES, circ. 57,152 236
D YORKSHIRE EVENING POST, circ. 56,647 279

Pudsey
D TELEGRAPH & ARGUS, circ. 37,371 262
W WHARFE VALLEY TIMES SERIES, circ. 63,868 F . 273
D YORKSHIRE EVENING POST, circ. 56,647 279

Queensbury
D EVENING COURIER (HALIFAX), circ. 19,956 181
D TELEGRAPH & ARGUS, circ. 37,371 262
D YORKSHIRE EVENING POST, circ. 56,647 279

Ripponden
D EVENING COURIER (HALIFAX), circ. 19,956 181

Rishworth
D EVENING COURIER (HALIFAX), circ. 19,956 181

Rothwell
W WAKEFIELD EXPRESS SERIES, circ. 83,674 267
D YORKSHIRE EVENING POST, circ. 56,647 279

Ryhill
W WAKEFIELD EXPRESS SERIES, circ. 83,674 267
D YORKSHIRE EVENING POST, circ. 56,647 279

Shelf
D YORKSHIRE EVENING POST, circ. 56,647 279

Shelley
W EXAMINER WEEKLY, circ. 55,322 F 182
W EXPRESS & CHRONICLE 183
D HUDDERSFIELD DAILY EXAMINER, circ. 25,898 201

Shipley
W BRADFORD TARGET SERIES, circ. 88,522 F 151
D TELEGRAPH & ARGUS, circ. 37,371 262
D YORKSHIRE EVENING POST, circ. 56,647 279

Silsden
W KEIGHLEY NEWS SERIES, circ. 39,727 206
D YORKSHIRE EVENING POST, circ. 56,647 279

Skelmanthorpe
W EXAMINER WEEKLY, circ. 55,322 F 182
W EXPRESS & CHRONICLE 183
D HUDDERSFIELD DAILY EXAMINER, circ. 25,898 201

Slaithwaite
W EXPRESS & CHRONICLE 183
D HUDDERSFIELD DAILY EXAMINER, circ. 25,898 201

South Elmsall
W HEMSWORTH AND SOUTH ELMSALL EXPRESS, circ. 6,453 197
W SOUTH YORKSHIRE TIMES, circ. 5,862 251

South Kirkby
W HEMSWORTH AND SOUTH ELMSALL EXPRESS, circ. 6,453 197

Sowerby Bridge
W CALDERDALE NEWS, circ. 36,000 F 156
D EVENING COURIER (HALIFAX), circ. 19,956 181

W **Local/Weekly Newspapers**   D **Regional Daily Newspapers**   S **Regional Sunday Newspapers**   F **Free Newspapers**

Title (Day/am/pm)	Circ.	Page No.

Stainland
D EVENING COURIER (HALIFAX), circ. 19,956 181

Steeton
W KEIGHLEY NEWS SERIES, circ. 39,727 206
D TELEGRAPH & ARGUS, circ. 37,371 262
D YORKSHIRE EVENING POST, circ. 56,647 279

Swillington
W LEEDS WEEKLY NEWS SERIES, circ. 124,534 F ... 210
D YORKSHIRE EVENING POST, circ. 56,647 279

Todmorden
D EVENING COURIER (HALIFAX), circ. 19,956 181
D MANCHESTER EVENING NEWS, circ. 82,445 217
D TODMORDEN NEWS, circ. 4,049 264

Wakefield
W JOURNAL & ADVERTISER SERIES, circ. 30,000 F ... 205
W WAKEFIELD EXPRESS SERIES, circ. 83,674 267
D YORKSHIRE EVENING POST, circ. 56,647 279

Wetherby
W ACKRILL NEWSPAPER SERIES, circ. 64,177 137
W JOURNAL & ADVERTISER SERIES, circ. 30,000 F ... 205
D THE PRESS (YORK), circ. 35,761 238
D YORKSHIRE EVENING POST, circ. 56,647 279

Wilsden
W BRADFORD TARGET SERIES, circ. 88,522 F 151
D TELEGRAPH & ARGUS, circ. 37,371 262
D YORKSHIRE EVENING POST, circ. 56,647 279

Woodkirk
W MORLEY OBSERVER & ADVERTISER, circ. 5,000 224

Yeadon
D TELEGRAPH & ARGUS, circ. 37,371 262
W WHARFE VALLEY TIMES SERIES, circ. 63,868 F ... 273
W WHARFEDALE & AIREDALE OBSERVER, circ. 5,181 . 273
D YORKSHIRE EVENING POST, circ. 56,647 279

Westminster Borough
W THE WESTMINSTER NEWS, circ. 10,000 F 273

Maida Vale
W HAM & HIGH SERIES, circ. 9,619 194

Marylebone
W HAM & HIGH SERIES, circ. 9,619 194
W LONDON NEWSPAPER GROUP SERIES,
circ. 69,601 214

Paddington
W GREATER LONDON CHRONICLE, circ. 5,000 F ... 193
W LONDON NEWSPAPER GROUP SERIES,
circ. 69,601 214
W NORTH WEST LONDON NEWSPAPER SERIES,
circ. 54,733 230

Pimlico
W LONDON NEWSPAPER GROUP SERIES,
circ. 69,601 214

St. John's Wood
W HAM & HIGH SERIES, circ. 9,619 194

Westminster
W LONDON NEWSPAPER GROUP SERIES,
circ. 69,601 214
W NORTH WEST LONDON NEWSPAPER SERIES,
circ. 54,733 230

Wiltshire
W THE BATH CHRONICLE, circ. 20,000 146
W GUARDIAN SERIES (WILTSHIRE, HAMPSHIRE AND
SURREY), circ. 175,000 F 193
W SOUTHERN COUNTIES TELEGRAPH,
circ. 45,000 F 252

Amesbury
W SALISBURY JOURNAL & AVON ADVERTISER SERIES,
circ. 99,503 243

Bradford-on-Avon
D WESTERN DAILY PRESS BRISTOL, circ. 41,639 272
W WILTSHIRE TIMES & NEWS SERIES, circ. 67,360 275

Calne
D WESTERN DAILY PRESS BRISTOL, circ. 41,639 272
W WILTSHIRE GAZETTE AND HERALD SERIES,
circ. 50,397 275
W WILTSHIRE TIMES & NEWS SERIES, circ. 67,360 275

Chippenham
D WESTERN DAILY PRESS BRISTOL, circ. 41,639 272

W WILTSHIRE GAZETTE AND HERALD SERIES,
circ. 50,397 275
W WILTSHIRE TIMES & NEWS SERIES, circ. 67,360 275

Corsham
W WILTSHIRE GAZETTE AND HERALD SERIES,
circ. 50,397 275
W WILTSHIRE TIMES & NEWS SERIES, circ. 67,360 275

Cricklade
D WESTERN DAILY PRESS BRISTOL, circ. 41,639 272
W WILTS & GLOUCESTERSHIRE STANDARD SERIES,
circ. 14,652 275

Devizes
D WESTERN DAILY PRESS BRISTOL, circ. 41,639 272
W WILTSHIRE GAZETTE AND HERALD SERIES,
circ. 50,397 275

Highworth
D SWINDON ADVERTISER, circ. 22,469 261
D WESTERN DAILY PRESS BRISTOL, circ. 41,639 272
W WILTS & GLOUCESTERSHIRE STANDARD SERIES,
circ. 14,652 275

Ludgershall
W ANDOVER ADVERTISER SERIES, circ. 39,707 141
W SALISBURY JOURNAL & AVON ADVERTISER SERIES,
circ. 99,503 243
D THE SOUTHERN DAILY ECHO (SOUTHAMPTON),
circ. 39,174 252

Lyneham
D SWINDON ADVERTISER, circ. 22,469 261
D WESTERN DAILY PRESS BRISTOL, circ. 41,639 272
W WILTSHIRE GAZETTE AND HERALD SERIES,
circ. 50,397 275

Malmesbury
W INDEPENDENT SERIES (GLOUCESTERSHIRE),
circ. 47,848 F 202
D WESTERN DAILY PRESS BRISTOL, circ. 41,639 272
W WILTS & GLOUCESTERSHIRE STANDARD SERIES,
circ. 14,652 275
W WILTSHIRE GAZETTE AND HERALD SERIES,
circ. 50,397 275

Marlborough
D SWINDON ADVERTISER, circ. 22,469 261
D WESTERN DAILY PRESS BRISTOL, circ. 41,639 272
W WILTSHIRE GAZETTE AND HERALD SERIES,
circ. 50,397 275

Melksham
W THE MELKSHAM INDEPENDENT NEWS SERIES,
circ. 32,700 F 219
D WESTERN DAILY PRESS BRISTOL, circ. 41,639 272
W WILTSHIRE TIMES & NEWS SERIES, circ. 67,360 275

Pewsey
W WILTSHIRE GAZETTE AND HERALD SERIES,
circ. 50,397 275

Salisbury
W SALISBURY JOURNAL & AVON ADVERTISER SERIES,
circ. 99,503 243
D THE SOUTHERN DAILY ECHO (SOUTHAMPTON),
circ. 39,174 252

Swindon
W GUARDIAN SERIES (WILTSHIRE, HAMPSHIRE AND
SURREY), circ. 175,000 F 193
D SWINDON ADVERTISER, circ. 22,469 261
D SWINDON STAR, circ. 48,248 F 261
D WESTERN DAILY PRESS BRISTOL, circ. 41,639 272
W WILTSHIRE GAZETTE AND HERALD SERIES,
circ. 50,397 275

Tidworth
W ANDOVER ADVERTISER SERIES, circ. 39,707 141
W SALISBURY JOURNAL & AVON ADVERTISER SERIES,
circ. 99,503 243

Trowbridge
D WESTERN DAILY PRESS BRISTOL, circ. 41,639 272
W WILTSHIRE TIMES & NEWS SERIES, circ. 67,360 275

Warminster
W THE MELKSHAM INDEPENDENT NEWS SERIES,
circ. 32,700 F 219
W SOMERSET STANDARD & GUARDIAN SERIES,
circ. 16,198 249
W WARMINSTER JOURNAL, circ. 5,000 269
D WESTERN DAILY PRESS BRISTOL, circ. 41,639 272
W WILTSHIRE TIMES & NEWS SERIES, circ. 67,360 275

Westbury
W THE MELKSHAM INDEPENDENT NEWS SERIES,
circ. 32,700 F 219

W SOMERSET STANDARD & GUARDIAN SERIES,
circ. 16,198 249
W WARMINSTER JOURNAL, circ. 5,000 269
W WILTSHIRE TIMES & NEWS SERIES, circ. 67,360 275

Wilton
W SALISBURY JOURNAL & AVON ADVERTISER SERIES,
circ. 99,503 243

Wootton Bassett
D WESTERN DAILY PRESS BRISTOL, circ. 41,639 272
W WILTSHIRE GAZETTE AND HERALD SERIES,
circ. 50,397 275

Wroughton
D SWINDON ADVERTISER, circ. 22,469 261
D WESTERN DAILY PRESS BRISTOL, circ. 41,639 272
W WILTSHIRE GAZETTE AND HERALD SERIES,
circ. 50,397 275

Worcestershire
W BROMSGROVE ADVERTISER SERIES, circ. 37,530 ... 153
S SUNDAY MERCURY (BIRMINGHAM), circ. 59,339 258

Alvechurch
W BROMSGROVE ADVERTISER SERIES, circ. 37,530 ... 153
W REDDITCH ADVERTISER AND CHRONICLE SERIES,
circ. 46,343 F 239

Astwood Bank
D BIRMINGHAM MAIL, circ. 78,178 148
D THE BIRMINGHAM POST, circ. 12,997 149
D BIRMINGHAM POST (CITY/LONDON OFFICE) 149
W REDDITCH ADVERTISER AND CHRONICLE SERIES,
circ. 46,343 F 239

Barnt Green
D BIRMINGHAM MAIL, circ. 78,178 148
D THE BIRMINGHAM POST, circ. 12,997 149
D BIRMINGHAM POST (CITY/LONDON OFFICE) 149
W BROMSGROVE ADVERTISER SERIES, circ. 37,530 ... 153
D EXPRESS & STAR, circ. 140,001 183
D EXPRESS & STAR (CITY/LONDON OFFICE) 183

Bewdley
D BIRMINGHAM MAIL, circ. 78,178 148
D THE BIRMINGHAM POST, circ. 12,997 149
D BIRMINGHAM POST (CITY/LONDON OFFICE) 149
D EXPRESS & STAR, circ. 140,001 183
D EXPRESS & STAR (CITY/LONDON OFFICE) 183
W THE SHUTTLE INCORPORATING KIDDERMINSTER
TIMES AND STOURPORT NEWS, circ. 40,450 248

Broadway
D THE BIRMINGHAM POST, circ. 12,997 149
D BIRMINGHAM POST (CITY/LONDON OFFICE) 149
W EVESHAM OBSERVER SERIES, circ. 35,917 182
D GLOUCESTERSHIRE ECHO, circ. 21,074 191

Bromsgrove
D BIRMINGHAM MAIL, circ. 78,178 148
D THE BIRMINGHAM POST, circ. 12,997 149
D BIRMINGHAM POST (CITY/LONDON OFFICE) 149
W BROMSGROVE ADVERTISER SERIES, circ. 37,530 ... 153
W REDDITCH AND BROMSGROVE STANDARD SERIES,
circ. 89,270 F 239
D WORCESTER NEWS, circ. 18,491 277

Catshill
D BIRMINGHAM MAIL, circ. 78,178 148
D THE BIRMINGHAM POST, circ. 12,997 149
D BIRMINGHAM POST (CITY/LONDON OFFICE) 149
D EXPRESS & STAR, circ. 140,001 183
D EXPRESS & STAR (CITY/LONDON OFFICE) 183

Droitwich
W BERROWS WORCESTER JOURNAL, circ. 48,097 ... 147
D BIRMINGHAM MAIL, circ. 78,178 148
W BROMSGROVE ADVERTISER SERIES, circ. 37,530 ... 153
W REDDITCH AND BROMSGROVE STANDARD SERIES,
circ. 89,270 F 239
D WORCESTER NEWS, circ. 18,491 277

Evesham
D BIRMINGHAM MAIL, circ. 78,178 148
W EVESHAM JOURNAL SERIES, circ. 32,275 182
W EVESHAM OBSERVER SERIES, circ. 35,917 182
D GLOUCESTERSHIRE ECHO, circ. 21,074 191
D WORCESTER NEWS, circ. 18,491 277

Fernhill Heath
W BERROWS WORCESTER JOURNAL, circ. 48,097 ... 147
D THE BIRMINGHAM POST, circ. 12,997 149
D BIRMINGHAM POST (CITY/LONDON OFFICE) 149
D WORCESTER NEWS, circ. 18,491 277
W THE WORCESTER STANDARD, circ. 52,412 F 277

W **Local/Weekly Newspapers**   D **Regional Daily Newspapers**   S **Regional Sunday Newspapers**   F **Free Newspapers**

Non-Nationals - Channel Islands

Title (Day/am/pm)	Circ.	Page No.

Great Malvern
D THE BIRMINGHAM POST, circ. 12,997 149
D BIRMINGHAM POST (CITY/LONDON OFFICE) 149
W MALVERN GAZETTE & LEDBURY REPORTER SERIES, circ. 17,001 217

Hagley
D BIRMINGHAM MAIL, circ. 78,178 148
D THE BIRMINGHAM POST, circ. 12,997 149
D BIRMINGHAM POST (CITY/LONDON OFFICE) 149
D EXPRESS & STAR, circ. 140,001 183
D EXPRESS & STAR (CITY/LONDON OFFICE) 183
W STOURBRIDGE NEWS, circ. 51,747 F 256

Kempsey
D WORCESTER NEWS, circ. 18,491 277

Kidderminster
D BIRMINGHAM MAIL, circ. 78,178 148
D THE BIRMINGHAM POST, circ. 12,997 149
D BIRMINGHAM POST (CITY/LONDON OFFICE) 149
D EXPRESS & STAR, circ. 140,001 183
D EXPRESS & STAR (CITY/LONDON OFFICE) 183
D SHROPSHIRE STAR (CITY/LONDON OFFICE) 247
W THE SHUTTLE INCORPORATING KIDDERMINSTER TIMES AND STOURPORT NEWS, circ. 40,450 248
W WOLVERHAMPTON CHRONICLE, circ. 68,351 F 277
D WORCESTER NEWS, circ. 18,491 277

Malvern
W MALVERN GAZETTE & LEDBURY REPORTER SERIES, circ. 17,001 217
D WORCESTER NEWS, circ. 18,491 277

Pershore
W BERROWS WORCESTER JOURNAL, circ. 48,097 147
W EVESHAM JOURNAL SERIES, circ. 32,275 182
W EVESHAM OBSERVER SERIES, circ. 35,917 182
W WORCESTER NEWS, circ. 18,491 277

Powick
D WORCESTER NEWS, circ. 18,491 277
W THE WORCESTER STANDARD, circ. 52,412 F 277

Redditch
D BIRMINGHAM MAIL, circ. 78,178 148
D THE BIRMINGHAM POST, circ. 12,997 149
D BIRMINGHAM POST (CITY/LONDON OFFICE) 149
W REDDITCH ADVERTISER AND CHRONICLE SERIES, circ. 46,343 F 239
W REDDITCH AND BROMSGROVE STANDARD SERIES, circ. 89,270 F 239

Stourport-on-Severn
D BIRMINGHAM MAIL, circ. 78,178 148
D THE BIRMINGHAM POST, circ. 12,997 149
D BIRMINGHAM POST (CITY/LONDON OFFICE) 149
D EXPRESS & STAR, circ. 140,001 183
D EXPRESS & STAR (CITY/LONDON OFFICE) 183
W THE SHUTTLE INCORPORATING KIDDERMINSTER TIMES AND STOURPORT NEWS, circ. 40,450 248

Tenbury Wells
D THE BIRMINGHAM POST, circ. 12,997 149
D BIRMINGHAM POST (CITY/LONDON OFFICE) 149
W CHRONICLE & JOURNAL SERIES, circ. 87,901 161
W HEREFORD TIMES, circ. 39,876 198
W LUDLOW ADVERTISER SERIES, circ. 5,924 215

Upton-upon-Severn
W BERROWS WORCESTER JOURNAL, circ. 48,097 147
W MALVERN GAZETTE & LEDBURY REPORTER SERIES, circ. 17,001 217
D WORCESTER NEWS, circ. 18,491 277
W THE WORCESTER STANDARD, circ. 52,412 F 277

Worcester
W BERROWS WORCESTER JOURNAL, circ. 48,097 147
D EXPRESS & STAR, circ. 140,001 183
D EXPRESS & STAR (CITY/LONDON OFFICE) 183
D WORCESTER NEWS, circ. 18,491 277
W THE WORCESTER STANDARD, circ. 52,412 F 277

CHANNEL ISLANDS

Channel Islands
D GUERNSEY PRESS AND STAR, circ. 16,196 193

Alderney
W GUERNSEY WEEKLY PRESS AND STAR, circ. 700,000 194
W THE VISITOR (GUERNSEY), circ. 16,000 F 267

Guernsey
W GUERNSEY GLOBE, circ. 20,000 F 193

D GUERNSEY PRESS AND STAR, circ. 16,196 193
W GUERNSEY WEEKLY PRESS AND STAR, circ. 700,000 194
W THE VISITOR (GUERNSEY), circ. 16,000 F 267

Herm
W GUERNSEY WEEKLY PRESS AND STAR, circ. 700,000 194
W THE VISITOR (GUERNSEY), circ. 16,000 F 267

Jersey
D JERSEY EVENING POST, circ. 21,100 204

Sark
W GUERNSEY WEEKLY PRESS AND STAR, circ. 700,000 194
W THE VISITOR (GUERNSEY), circ. 16,000 F 267

St. Peter Port
D GUERNSEY PRESS AND STAR, circ. 16,196 193

ISLE OF MAN

Isle of Man
W ISLE OF MAN NEWSPAPERS, circ. 61,849 204

Douglas
W ISLE OF MAN NEWSPAPERS, circ. 61,849 204

NORTHERN IRELAND
D BELFAST TELEGRAPH, circ. 75,602 147
D THE IRISH NEWS, circ. 47,790 203
D NEWS LETTER, circ. 26,477 228
S SUNDAY LIFE (BELFAST), circ. 74,886 258
S SUNDAY WORLD NORTHERN IRELAND EDITION, circ. 71,000 259

Co. Antrim
S THE SUNDAY POST (DUNDEE), circ. 354,870 258

Ahoghill
W BALLYMENA TIMES SERIES, circ. 4,428 144
W DUNGANNON OBSERVER SERIES 175

Andersonstown
W ANDERSONSTOWN NEWS SERIES, circ. 14,598 141

Antrim
W ANTRIM GUARDIAN SERIES, circ. 14,794 142
W BALLYMENA TIMES SERIES, circ. 4,428 144
W NORTH BELFAST NEWS, circ. 5,374 229

Ballycastle
W BALLYMONEY AND MOYLE TIMES, circ. 8,000 144
W THE CHRONICLE AND LEADER SERIES (COLERAINE), circ. 43,841 161
W DUNGANNON OBSERVER SERIES 175

Ballyclare
W ANTRIM GUARDIAN SERIES, circ. 14,794 142
W EAST ANTRIM GAZETTE SERIES, circ. 3,607 176
W THE TIMES SERIES, circ. 47,517 264

Ballymena
W BALLYMENA TIMES SERIES, circ. 4,428 144
W DUNGANNON OBSERVER SERIES 175

Ballymoney
W BALLYMENA TIMES SERIES, circ. 4,428 144
W BALLYMONEY AND MOYLE TIMES, circ. 8,000 144
W THE CHRONICLE AND LEADER SERIES (COLERAINE), circ. 43,841 161
W NORTHERN CONSTITUTION SERIES, circ. 5,500 231

Broughshane
W BALLYMENA TIMES SERIES, circ. 4,428 144
W DUNGANNON OBSERVER SERIES 175

Bushmills
W BALLYMONEY AND MOYLE TIMES, circ. 8,000 144
W THE CHRONICLE AND LEADER SERIES (COLERAINE), circ. 43,841 161

Carnlough
W THE TIMES SERIES, circ. 47,517 264

Carrickfergus
W EAST ANTRIM GAZETTE SERIES, circ. 3,607 176
W THE TIMES SERIES, circ. 47,517 264

Crumlin
W ANTRIM GUARDIAN SERIES, circ. 14,794 142

W LISBURN ECHO, circ. 23,101 F 212
W ULSTER STAR, circ. 9,767 266

Cullybackey
W BALLYMENA TIMES SERIES, circ. 4,428 144
W DUNGANNON OBSERVER SERIES 175

Dunloy
W THE CHRONICLE AND LEADER SERIES (COLERAINE), circ. 43,841 161
W DUNGANNON OBSERVER SERIES 175
W NORTHERN CONSTITUTION SERIES, circ. 5,500 231

Dunmurry
W DOWN RECORDER, circ. 11,711 174
W LEADER (COUNTY DOWN SERIES), circ. 3,778 209
W LISBURN ECHO, circ. 23,101 F 212
W ULSTER STAR, circ. 9,767 266

Greenisland
W EAST ANTRIM GAZETTE SERIES, circ. 3,607 176
W THE TIMES SERIES, circ. 47,517 264

Larne
W THE TIMES SERIES, circ. 47,517 264

Mossley
W COMMUNITY TELEGRAPH SERIES, circ. 166,375 F 164
W THE TIMES SERIES, circ. 47,517 264

Newtownabbey
W COMMUNITY TELEGRAPH SERIES, circ. 166,375 F 164
W THE TIMES SERIES, circ. 47,517 264

Portrush
W THE CHRONICLE AND LEADER SERIES (COLERAINE), circ. 43,841 161
W COLERAINE TIMES, circ. 7,387 163
W DUNGANNON OBSERVER SERIES 175
W NORTHERN CONSTITUTION SERIES, circ. 5,500 231

Randalstown
W ANTRIM GUARDIAN SERIES, circ. 14,794 142
W BALLYMENA TIMES SERIES, circ. 4,428 144
W DUNGANNON OBSERVER SERIES 175

Whitehead
W EAST ANTRIM GAZETTE SERIES, circ. 3,607 176
W THE TIMES SERIES, circ. 47,517 264

Co. Armagh
S THE SUNDAY POST (DUNDEE), circ. 354,870 258

Armagh
W DUNGANNON NEWS & TYRONE COURIER, circ. 15,083 175
W NEWRY DEMOCRAT, circ. 8,371 227
W PORTADOWN TIMES INC. CRAIGAVON NEWS, circ. 10,401 237
W ULSTER GAZETTE, circ. 10,025 266

Bessbrook
W NEWRY DEMOCRAT, circ. 8,371 227
W ULSTER GAZETTE, circ. 10,025 266

Crossmaglen
W DUNGANNON OBSERVER SERIES 175
W THE EXAMINER, circ. 9,000 182
W NEWRY REPORTER, circ. 14,474 227
W ULSTER GAZETTE, circ. 10,025 266

Keady
W DUNGANNON OBSERVER SERIES 175
W ULSTER GAZETTE, circ. 10,025 266

Markethill
W DUNGANNON OBSERVER SERIES 175
W PORTADOWN TIMES INC. CRAIGAVON NEWS, circ. 10,401 237
W ULSTER GAZETTE, circ. 10,025 266

Newry
W THE COUNTY DOWN OUTLOOK, circ. 3,972 166
W DUNGANNON OBSERVER SERIES 175
W THE EXAMINER, circ. 9,000 182
W MOURNE OBSERVER SERIES, circ. 11,639 225
W NEWRY DEMOCRAT, circ. 8,371 227
W NEWRY REPORTER, circ. 14,474 227

Richill
W DUNGANNON NEWS & TYRONE COURIER, circ. 15,083 175
W DUNGANNON OBSERVER SERIES 175
W PORTADOWN TIMES INC. CRAIGAVON NEWS, circ. 10,401 237
W ULSTER GAZETTE, circ. 10,025 266

W Local/Weekly Newspapers   D Regional Daily Newspapers   S Regional Sunday Newspapers   F Free Newspapers

Title (Day/am/pm)	Circ.	Page No.	Title (Day/am/pm)	Circ.	Page No.	Title (Day/am/pm)	Circ.	Page No.

W **Local/Weekly Newspapers**   D **Regional Daily Newspapers**   S **Regional Sunday Newspapers**   F **Free Newspapers**

Section 3 Index to UK Newspapers

Non-Nationals - Scotland

Title (Day/am/pm)	Circ.	Page No.

Portaferry
W COUNTY DOWN SPECTATOR AND ULSTER STANDARD SERIES, circ. 11,994 ... 166
W DOWN DEMOCRAT, circ. 3,389 ... 174
W DOWN RECORDER, circ. 11,711 ... 174
W NEWTOWNARDS CHRONICLE, circ. 9,956 ... 229

Portavogie
W COUNTY DOWN SPECTATOR AND ULSTER STANDARD SERIES, circ. 11,994 ... 166
W DOWN DEMOCRAT, circ. 3,389 ... 174
W DOWN RECORDER, circ. 11,711 ... 174
W NEWTOWNARDS CHRONICLE, circ. 9,956 ... 229

Rathfriland
W BANBRIDGE CHRONICLE, circ. 5,957 ... 144
W THE COUNTY DOWN OUTLOOK, circ. 3,972 ... 166
W NEWRY DEMOCRAT, circ. 8,371 ... 227

Rostrevor
W THE COUNTY DOWN OUTLOOK, circ. 3,972 ... 166
W DOWN RECORDER, circ. 11,711 ... 174
W DUNGANNON OBSERVER SERIES ... 175
W NEWRY DEMOCRAT, circ. 8,371 ... 227
W NEWRY REPORTER, circ. 14,474 ... 227

Saintfield
W DOWN DEMOCRAT, circ. 3,389 ... 174
W DOWN RECORDER, circ. 11,711 ... 174
W LEADER (COUNTY DOWN SERIES), circ. 3,778 ... 209
W MOURNE OBSERVER SERIES, circ. 11,639 ... 225
W NEWTOWNARDS CHRONICLE, circ. 9,956 ... 229

Waringstown
W DUNGANNON OBSERVER SERIES ... 175

Fermanagh
W DUNGANNON OBSERVER SERIES ... 175
W FERMANAGH HERALD, circ. 13,593 ... 185
S THE SUNDAY POST (DUNDEE), circ. 354,870 ... 258

Enniskillen
W DUNGANNON OBSERVER SERIES ... 175
W IMPARTIAL REPORTER, circ. 14,444 ... 202

Irvinestown
W DUNGANNON OBSERVER SERIES ... 175
W IMPARTIAL REPORTER, circ. 14,444 ... 202

Lisnaskea
W DUNGANNON OBSERVER SERIES ... 175
W IMPARTIAL REPORTER, circ. 14,444 ... 202

Tyrone

Castlederg
W DUNGANNON OBSERVER SERIES ... 175
W TYRONE CONSTITUTION AND STRABANE WEEKLY NEWS SERIES, circ. 12,516 ... 266

Coalisland
W DUNGANNON NEWS & TYRONE COURIER, circ. 15,083 ... 175
W MID ULSTER MAIL SERIES, circ. 19,763 ... 221
W TYRONE TIMES AND DUNGANNON GAZETTE, circ. 5,000 ... 266

Cookstown
W DUNGANNON NEWS & TYRONE COURIER, circ. 15,083 ... 175
W DUNGANNON OBSERVER SERIES ... 175
W MID ULSTER MAIL SERIES, circ. 19,763 ... 221
W TYRONE TIMES AND DUNGANNON GAZETTE, circ. 5,000 ... 266

Dungannon
W DUNGANNON NEWS & TYRONE COURIER, circ. 15,083 ... 175
W DUNGANNON OBSERVER SERIES ... 175
W MID ULSTER MAIL SERIES, circ. 19,763 ... 221
W PORTADOWN TIMES INC. CRAIGAVON NEWS, circ. 10,401 ... 237
W TYRONE TIMES AND DUNGANNON GAZETTE, circ. 5,000 ... 266

Fintona
W DUNGANNON OBSERVER SERIES ... 175
W TYRONE CONSTITUTION AND STRABANE WEEKLY NEWS SERIES, circ. 12,516 ... 266

Moy
W DUNGANNON NEWS & TYRONE COURIER, circ. 15,083 ... 175
W PORTADOWN TIMES INC. CRAIGAVON NEWS, circ. 10,401 ... 237

W TYRONE TIMES AND DUNGANNON GAZETTE, circ. 5,000 ... 266
W ULSTER GAZETTE, circ. 10,025 ... 266

Moygashel
W DUNGANNON NEWS & TYRONE COURIER, circ. 15,083 ... 175
W DUNGANNON OBSERVER SERIES ... 175

Newtownstewart
W DUNGANNON OBSERVER SERIES ... 175
W TYRONE CONSTITUTION AND STRABANE WEEKLY NEWS SERIES, circ. 12,516 ... 266

Omagh
W DUNGANNON NEWS & TYRONE COURIER, circ. 15,083 ... 175
W DUNGANNON OBSERVER SERIES ... 175
W TYRONE CONSTITUTION AND STRABANE WEEKLY NEWS SERIES, circ. 12,516 ... 266

Sion Mills
W DUNGANNON OBSERVER SERIES ... 175
W THE SENTINEL SERIES, circ. 42,840 ... 245
W TYRONE CONSTITUTION AND STRABANE WEEKLY NEWS SERIES, circ. 12,516 ... 266

Strabane
W DERRY JOURNAL SERIES, circ. 72,956 ... 172
W TYRONE CONSTITUTION AND STRABANE WEEKLY NEWS SERIES, circ. 12,516 ... 266

SCOTLAND
D DAILY RECORD, circ. 347,302 ... 170
D DAILY RECORD (EDINBURGH OFFICE) ... 170
D THE HERALD (GLASGOW), circ. 58,157 ... 198
D THE HERALD (GLASGOW) (CITY/LONDON OFFICE) . 198
D THE HERALD (GLASGOW) (EDINBURGH OFFICE) ... 198
D THE HERALD MAGAZINE ... 198
D SATURDAY PLUS F ... 244
S SCOTLAND ON SUNDAY, circ. 65,000 ... 244
S SCOTLAND ON SUNDAY (CITY/LONDON OFFICE) ... 244
D THE SCOTSMAN, circ. 50,750 ... 244
D THE SCOTSMAN (CITY/LONDON OFFICE) ... 244
D THE SCOTSMAN (GLASGOW OFFICE) ... 244
D THE SCOTSMAN MAGAZINE ... 244
D SCOTTISH REVIEW OF BOOKS, circ. 100,000 ... 244
D SEVEN DAYS ... 246
D SPECTRUM MAGAZINE SCOTLAND ON SUNDAY ... 253
S SUNDAY HERALD, circ. 44,048 ... 258
D SUNDAY HERALD (EDINBURGH) ... 258
D SUNDAY HERALD MAGAZINE, circ. 70,000 ... 258
S SUNDAY MAIL, circ. 428,613 ... 258
S THE SUNDAY POST (DUNDEE), circ. 354,870 ... 258
D THE SUNDAY POST (GLASGOW OFFICE) ... 259
D THE SUNDAY POST (LONDON OFFICE) ... 259

Aberdeenshire UA
D THE PRESS & JOURNAL (ABERDEEN), circ. 81,956 .. 237

Aboyne
W DEESIDE PIPER AND HERALD SERIES, circ. 8,595 ... 171
D EVENING EXPRESS (ABERDEEN), circ. 53,384 ... 181

Alford
W DEESIDE PIPER AND HERALD SERIES, circ. 8,595 ... 171

Badenoch
W STRATHSPEY & BADENOCH HERALD, circ. 4,844 ... 257

Ballater
W DEESIDE PIPER AND HERALD SERIES, circ. 8,595 ... 171
D EVENING EXPRESS (ABERDEEN), circ. 53,384 ... 181

Banchory
W DEESIDE PIPER AND HERALD SERIES, circ. 8,595 ... 171
D EVENING EXPRESS (ABERDEEN), circ. 53,384 ... 181

Banff
W THE BANFFSHIRE JOURNAL, circ. 4,994 ... 145
D EVENING EXPRESS (ABERDEEN), circ. 53,384 ... 181

Braemar
W DEESIDE PIPER AND HERALD SERIES, circ. 8,595 ... 171
D EVENING EXPRESS (ABERDEEN), circ. 53,384 ... 181

Cornhill
W THE BANFFSHIRE JOURNAL, circ. 4,994 ... 145

Ellon
W ADVERTISER SERIES IN ABERDEENSHIRE, circ. 15,000 ... 139
W THE ELLON TIMES AND EAST GORDON ADVERTISER, circ. 2,416 ... 179
D EVENING EXPRESS (ABERDEEN), circ. 53,384 ... 181

W NORTH EAST WEEKLY, circ. 10,000 F ... 229

Fraserburgh
D EVENING EXPRESS (ABERDEEN), circ. 53,384 ... 181
W THE FRASERBURGH HERALD, circ. 5,878 ... 187
W NORTH EAST WEEKLY, circ. 10,000 F ... 229

Huntly
D EVENING EXPRESS (ABERDEEN), circ. 53,384 ... 181
W HUNTLY EXPRESS, circ. 3,300 ... 201

Inverurie
W ADVERTISER SERIES IN ABERDEENSHIRE, circ. 15,000 ... 139
D EVENING EXPRESS (ABERDEEN), circ. 53,384 ... 181
W INVERURIE HERALD, circ. 9,000 ... 203

Kemnay
W INVERURIE HERALD, circ. 9,000 ... 203

Macduff
W THE BANFFSHIRE JOURNAL, circ. 4,994 ... 145

Mintlaw
W BUCHAN OBSERVER, circ. 7,786 ... 153
D EVENING EXPRESS (ABERDEEN), circ. 53,384 ... 181

Peterhead
W BUCHAN OBSERVER, circ. 7,786 ... 153
D EVENING EXPRESS (ABERDEEN), circ. 53,384 ... 181
W NORTH EAST WEEKLY, circ. 10,000 F ... 229

Portlethen
D EVENING EXPRESS (ABERDEEN), circ. 53,384 ... 181

Portsoy
W BANFFSHIRE ADVERTISER, circ. 4,500 ... 145
W THE BANFFSHIRE JOURNAL, circ. 4,994 ... 145

Stonehaven
D THE COURIER AND ADVERTISER, circ. 73,485 ... 166
D EVENING EXPRESS (ABERDEEN), circ. 53,384 ... 181
W MEARNS LEADER, circ. 4,450 ... 218
W MONTROSE REVIEW SERIES, circ. 6,217 ... 224

Tarland
W DEESIDE PIPER AND HERALD SERIES, circ. 8,595 ... 171

Turriff
W ADVERTISER SERIES IN ABERDEENSHIRE, circ. 15,000 ... 139
W THE BANFFSHIRE JOURNAL, circ. 4,994 ... 145
D EVENING EXPRESS (ABERDEEN), circ. 53,384 ... 181

Angus UA
D EVENING TELEGRAPH & POST (DUNDEE), circ. 24,349 ... 181
D THE PRESS & JOURNAL (ABERDEEN), circ. 81,956 .. 237

Arbroath
W ARBROATH HERALD & GAZETTE SERIES, circ. 10,156 ... 142
D THE COURIER AND ADVERTISER, circ. 73,485 ... 166

Brechin
W BRECHIN ADVERTISER, circ. 2,931 ... 151
D THE COURIER AND ADVERTISER, circ. 73,485 ... 166

Carnoustie
W ARBROATH HERALD & GAZETTE SERIES, circ. 10,156 ... 142
D THE COURIER AND ADVERTISER, circ. 73,485 ... 166

Edzell
W BRECHIN ADVERTISER, circ. 2,931 ... 151

Forfar
D THE COURIER AND ADVERTISER, circ. 73,485 ... 166
W FORFAR DISPATCH SERIES, circ. 5,653 ... 186

Kirriemuir
W FORFAR DISPATCH SERIES, circ. 5,653 ... 186

Montrose
D THE COURIER AND ADVERTISER, circ. 73,485 ... 166
D EVENING EXPRESS (ABERDEEN), circ. 53,384 ... 181
W MONTROSE REVIEW SERIES, circ. 6,217 ... 224

Argyll & Bute UA
W DUNOON OBSERVER & ARGYLLSHIRE STANDARD, circ. 6,500 ... 176
W ILEACH, circ. 2,500 ... 202

Arden
W HELENSBURGH ADVERTISER, circ. 6,730 ... 196

Argyll
W ARGYLLSHIRE ADVERTISER ... 142

W Local/Weekly Newspapers   D Regional Daily Newspapers   S Regional Sunday Newspapers   F Free Newspapers

Title (Day/am/pm)	Circ.	Page No.

W OBAN TIMES & WEST HIGHLAND TIMES, circ. 17,421 233

Arrochar
W HELENSBURGH ADVERTISER, circ. 6,730 196

Bowmore
W OBAN TIMES & WEST HIGHLAND TIMES, circ. 17,421 233

Campbeltown
W CAMPBELTOWN COURIER, circ. 7,347 157
W OBAN TIMES & WEST HIGHLAND TIMES, circ. 17,421 233

Cardross
W DUMBARTON AND VALE OF LEVEN REPORTER, circ. 4,332 175
W HELENSBURGH ADVERTISER, circ. 6,730 196

Clynder
W HELENSBURGH ADVERTISER, circ. 6,730 196

Dunoon
W DUNOON OBSERVER & ARGYLLSHIRE STANDARD, circ. 6,500 176

Garelochhead
W HELENSBURGH ADVERTISER, circ. 6,730 196

Helensburgh
W CLYDE WEEKLY NEWS, circ. 5,339 F 163
W HELENSBURGH ADVERTISER, circ. 6,730 196
W LENNOX SERIES, circ. 12,307 211

Inveraray
W ARGYLLSHIRE ADVERTISER 142
W CAMPBELTOWN COURIER, circ. 7,347 157

Kilcreggan
W HELENSBURGH ADVERTISER, circ. 6,730 196

Lochgilphead
W ARGYLLSHIRE ADVERTISER 142
W CAMPBELTOWN COURIER, circ. 7,347 157
W OBAN TIMES & WEST HIGHLAND TIMES, circ. 17,421 233

Luss
W DUMBARTON AND VALE OF LEVEN REPORTER, circ. 4,332 175
W HELENSBURGH ADVERTISER, circ. 6,730 196

Millport
W LARGS & MILLPORT WEEKLY NEWS, circ. 5,958 209

Oban
W OBAN TIMES & WEST HIGHLAND TIMES, circ. 17,421 233

Port Ellen
W OBAN TIMES & WEST HIGHLAND TIMES, circ. 17,421 233

Rhu
W HELENSBURGH ADVERTISER, circ. 6,730 196

Rosneath
W HELENSBURGH ADVERTISER, circ. 6,730 196

Rothesay
W THE BUTEMAN, circ. 4,000 155

Strachur
W ARGYLLSHIRE ADVERTISER 142

Tarbert
W ARGYLLSHIRE ADVERTISER 142
W CAMPBELTOWN COURIER, circ. 7,347 157

Taynuilt
W OBAN TIMES & WEST HIGHLAND TIMES, circ. 17,421 233

City of Aberdeen UA
D THE PRESS & JOURNAL (ABERDEEN), circ. 81,956 ..237

Aberdeen
W ABERDEEN CITIZEN, circ. 76,408 F 137
D EVENING EXPRESS (ABERDEEN), circ. 53,384 181
W NORTH EAST WEEKLY, circ. 10,000 F 229

Cove Bay
W ABERDEEN CITIZEN, circ. 76,408 F 137
D EVENING EXPRESS (ABERDEEN), circ. 53,384 181
W MONTROSE REVIEW SERIES, circ. 6,217 224

Dyce
W ABERDEEN CITIZEN, circ. 76,408 F 137

Peterculter
W DEESIDE PIPER AND HERALD SERIES, circ. 8,595 ... 171

Westhill
W ABERDEEN CITIZEN, circ. 76,408 F 137
D EVENING EXPRESS (ABERDEEN), circ. 53,384 181

City of Dundee UA
D EVENING TELEGRAPH & POST (DUNDEE), circ. 24,349 181

Broughty Ferry
W ARBROATH HERALD & GAZETTE SERIES, circ. 10,156 142

Dundee
D THE COURIER AND ADVERTISER, circ. 73,485 166

City of Edinburgh UA
D EVENING NEWS (EDINBURGH), circ. 53,675 181
W THE GAZETTE SERIES (EDINBURGH), circ. 12,000 F 189

Danderhall
W DALKEITH ADVERTISER SERIES, circ. 60,690 170
D EVENING NEWS (EDINBURGH), circ. 53,675 181

Edinburgh
D EVENING NEWS (EDINBURGH), circ. 53,675 181
W HERALD AND POST SERIES (EDINBURGH), circ. 166,378 F 197
W NORTH EDINBURGH NEWS (NEN), circ. 14,500 F ... 230

Kirkliston
D EVENING NEWS (EDINBURGH), circ. 53,675 181

South Queensferry
D EVENING NEWS (EDINBURGH), circ. 53,675 181
F FIFE AND KINROSS EXTRA, circ. 52,464 F 185
W LINLITHGOWSHIRE JOURNAL AND GAZETTE SERIES, circ. 8,632 212

Winchburgh
D EVENING NEWS (EDINBURGH), circ. 53,675 181
W WEST LOTHIAN COURIER, circ. 17,229 271

Clackmannanshire UA
F FIFE AND KINROSS EXTRA, circ. 52,464 F 185

Alloa
W ALLOA AND HILLFOOTS ADVERTISER, circ. 9,119 141
W ALLOA AND HILLFOOTS WEE COUNTY NEWS, circ. 6,587 141
F FIFE AND KINROSS EXTRA, circ. 52,464 F 185
W STIRLING SHOPPER SERIES, circ. 7,049 F 256

Alva
W ALLOA AND HILLFOOTS ADVERTISER, circ. 9,119 141
W ALLOA AND HILLFOOTS WEE COUNTY NEWS, circ. 6,587 141
W STIRLING OBSERVER SERIES, circ. 16,849 255
W STIRLING SHOPPER SERIES, circ. 7,049 F 256

Clackmannan
W ALLOA AND HILLFOOTS ADVERTISER, circ. 9,119 141
W ALLOA AND HILLFOOTS WEE COUNTY NEWS, circ. 6,587 141
W STIRLING OBSERVER SERIES, circ. 16,849 255
W STIRLING SHOPPER SERIES, circ. 7,049 F 256

Dollar
W ALLOA AND HILLFOOTS ADVERTISER, circ. 9,119 141
W ALLOA AND HILLFOOTS WEE COUNTY NEWS, circ. 6,587 141
F FIFE AND KINROSS EXTRA, circ. 52,464 F 185

Hillfoots
W ALLOA AND HILLFOOTS ADVERTISER, circ. 9,119 141
W STIRLING OBSERVER SERIES, circ. 16,849 255
W STIRLING SHOPPER SERIES, circ. 7,049 F 256

Menstrie
W ALLOA AND HILLFOOTS ADVERTISER, circ. 9,119 141
W ALLOA AND HILLFOOTS WEE COUNTY NEWS, circ. 6,587 141
W STIRLING OBSERVER SERIES, circ. 16,849 255
W STIRLING SHOPPER SERIES, circ. 7,049 F 256

Tillicoultry
W ALLOA AND HILLFOOTS ADVERTISER, circ. 9,119 141
W ALLOA AND HILLFOOTS WEE COUNTY NEWS, circ. 6,587 141

Dumfries & Galloway UA
D NEWS & STAR (CARLISLE) 227

W NITHSDALE NEWS, circ. 2,100 229

Annan
W ANNANDALE OBSERVER SERIES, circ. 36,203 142
W DUMFRIES & GALLOWAY STANDARD, circ. 27,257 ..175
D NEWS & STAR (CARLISLE) 227

Annandale
W DUMFRIES AND GALLOWAY NEWS SERIES, circ. 16,631 175
W ESKDALE AND LIDDESDALE ADVERTISER, circ. 1,800 180

Castle Douglas
W ANNANDALE OBSERVER SERIES, circ. 36,203 142
W DUMFRIES AND GALLOWAY NEWS SERIES, circ. 16,631 175
W GALLOWAY GAZETTE, circ. 6,296 187

Dalbeattie
W ANNANDALE OBSERVER SERIES, circ. 36,203 142
W DUMFRIES AND GALLOWAY NEWS SERIES, circ. 16,631 175
W GALLOWAY GAZETTE, circ. 6,296 187

Dalton
W WESTMORLAND GAZETTE NEWSPAPER SERIES, circ. 56,020 273

Dumfries
W ANNANDALE OBSERVER SERIES, circ. 36,203 142
W DUMFRIES & GALLOWAY STANDARD, circ. 27,257 ..175

Eskdale
W ESKDALE AND LIDDESDALE ADVERTISER, circ. 1,800 180

Galloway
W GALLOWAY GAZETTE, circ. 6,296 187

Gretna
D NEWS & STAR (CARLISLE) 227

Kirkconnel
W ANNANDALE OBSERVER SERIES, circ. 36,203 142
W CUMNOCK CHRONICLE, circ. 7,680 169

Kirkcudbright
W ANNANDALE OBSERVER SERIES, circ. 36,203 142
W DUMFRIES AND GALLOWAY NEWS SERIES, circ. 16,631 175
W GALLOWAY GAZETTE, circ. 6,296 187

Langholm
W ANNANDALE OBSERVER SERIES, circ. 36,203 142
W ESKDALE AND LIDDESDALE ADVERTISER, circ. 1,800 180
W HAWICK NEWS, circ. 5,462 196
D NEWS & STAR (CARLISLE) 227
W SOUTHERN REPORTER, circ. 18,310 252

Locharbriggs
W ANNANDALE OBSERVER SERIES, circ. 36,203 142

Lockerbie
W ANNANDALE OBSERVER SERIES, circ. 36,203 142
W DUMFRIES & GALLOWAY STANDARD, circ. 27,257 ..175
W ESKDALE AND LIDDESDALE ADVERTISER, circ. 1,800 180

Moffat
W ANNANDALE OBSERVER SERIES, circ. 36,203 142
W DUMFRIES & GALLOWAY STANDARD, circ. 27,257 ..175

New Galloway
W DUMFRIES AND GALLOWAY NEWS SERIES, circ. 16,631 175

Newton
W MIDDLETON & NORTH MANCHESTER GUARDIAN & ADVERTISER SERIES, circ. 93,756 222

Newton Stewart
W GALLOWAY GAZETTE, circ. 6,296 187
W STRANRAER & WIGTOWNSHIRE FREE PRESS, circ. 7,733 257

Sanquhar
W CUMNOCK CHRONICLE, circ. 7,680 169
W DUMFRIES & GALLOWAY STANDARD, circ. 27,257 ..175

Stranraer
W DUMFRIES AND GALLOWAY NEWS SERIES, circ. 16,631 175
W GALLOWAY GAZETTE, circ. 6,296 187
W STRANRAER & WIGTOWNSHIRE FREE PRESS, circ. 7,733 257

Non-Nationals - Scotland

Title (Day/am/pm)	Circ.	Page No.

Wigtown
W DUMFRIES AND GALLOWAY NEWS SERIES, circ. 16,631 175
W GALLOWAY GAZETTE, circ. 6,296 187
W STRANRAER & WIGTOWNSHIRE FREE PRESS, circ. 7,733 257

East Ayrshire UA

Auchinleck
W AYRSHIRE POST, circ. 26,863 144
W CUMNOCK CHRONICLE, circ. 7,680 169

Bellsbank
W CUMNOCK CHRONICLE, circ. 7,680 169

Catrine
W AYRSHIRE POST, circ. 26,863 144
W CUMNOCK CHRONICLE, circ. 7,680 169

Crosshouse
W IRVINE TIMES, circ. 3,599 203
W KILMARNOCK STANDARD, circ. 17,311 207

Cumnock
W AYRSHIRE POST, circ. 26,863 144
W CUMNOCK CHRONICLE, circ. 7,680 169

Darvel
W KILMARNOCK STANDARD, circ. 17,311 207

Drongan
W AYRSHIRE POST, circ. 26,863 144
W CUMNOCK CHRONICLE, circ. 7,680 169

Galston
W KILMARNOCK STANDARD, circ. 17,311 207

Kilmarnock
W AYRSHIRE WORLD SERIES, circ. 16,827 F 144
W KILMARNOCK STANDARD, circ. 17,311 207

Kilmaurs
W KILMARNOCK STANDARD, circ. 17,311 207

Mauchline
W AYRSHIRE POST, circ. 26,863 144
W CUMNOCK CHRONICLE, circ. 7,680 169

Muirkirk
W AYRSHIRE POST, circ. 26,863 144
W CUMNOCK CHRONICLE, circ. 7,680 169

New Cumnock
W CUMNOCK CHRONICLE, circ. 7,680 169

Newmilns
W KILMARNOCK STANDARD, circ. 17,311 207

Patna
W AYRSHIRE POST, circ. 26,863 144
W CUMNOCK CHRONICLE, circ. 7,680 169

Stewarton
W IRVINE TIMES, circ. 3,599 203
W KILMARNOCK STANDARD, circ. 17,311 207

East Dunbartonshire UA

Bearsden
W THE GLASGOW EXTRA SERIES, circ. 100,810 F 190
W THE GLASWEGIAN SERIES, circ. 104,175 F 190
W MILNGAVIE & BEARSDEN HERALD, circ. 6,622 223

Bishopbriggs
W KIRKINTILLOCH & BISHOPBRIGGS HERALD SERIES, circ. 34,797 208

Chryston
W AIRDRIE & COATBRIDGE ADVERTISER, circ. 16,621 140
D EVENING TIMES (GLASGOW), circ. 79,087 182

Glenboig
W AIRDRIE & COATBRIDGE ADVERTISER, circ. 16,621 140
D EVENING TIMES (GLASGOW), circ. 79,087 182
W LANARKSHIRE WORLD, circ. 35,172 F 208

Kirkintilloch
W THE GLASWEGIAN SERIES, circ. 104,175 F 190
W KIRKINTILLOCH & BISHOPBRIGGS HERALD SERIES, circ. 34,797 208

Lennoxtown
D EVENING TIMES (GLASGOW), circ. 79,087 182
W KIRKINTILLOCH & BISHOPBRIGGS HERALD SERIES, circ. 34,797 208

Lenzie
W THE GLASWEGIAN SERIES, circ. 104,175 F 190
W KIRKINTILLOCH & BISHOPBRIGGS HERALD SERIES, circ. 34,797 208

Milngavie
W THE GLASGOW EXTRA SERIES, circ. 100,810 F 190
W THE GLASWEGIAN SERIES, circ. 104,175 F 190
W MILNGAVIE & BEARSDEN HERALD, circ. 6,622 223

Milton of Campsie
D EVENING TIMES (GLASGOW), circ. 79,087 182
W KIRKINTILLOCH & BISHOPBRIGGS HERALD SERIES, circ. 34,797 208

Stepps
D EVENING TIMES (GLASGOW), circ. 79,087 182
W KIRKINTILLOCH & BISHOPBRIGGS HERALD SERIES, circ. 34,797 208

Strathblane
W MILNGAVIE & BEARSDEN HERALD, circ. 6,622 223

Torrance
D EVENING TIMES (GLASGOW), circ. 79,087 182
W KIRKINTILLOCH & BISHOPBRIGGS HERALD SERIES, circ. 34,797 208

East Lothian UA
W BERWICKSHIRE NEWS AND EAST LOTHIAN HERALD, circ. 5,957 147
W DALKEITH ADVERTISER SERIES, circ. 60,690 170
D EVENING NEWS (EDINBURGH), circ. 53,675 181
W THE LOTHIAN TIMES (EAST LOTHIAN EDITION), circ. 48,838 F 215

Cockenzie
W DALKEITH ADVERTISER SERIES, circ. 60,690 170

Dunbar
W DALKEITH ADVERTISER SERIES, circ. 60,690 170
W EAST LOTHIAN COURIER, circ. 14,074 177
D EVENING NEWS (EDINBURGH), circ. 53,675 181

Haddington
W DALKEITH ADVERTISER SERIES, circ. 60,690 170
W EAST LOTHIAN COURIER, circ. 14,074 177
D EVENING NEWS (EDINBURGH), circ. 53,675 181

Musselburgh
W DALKEITH ADVERTISER SERIES, circ. 60,690 170
W EAST LOTHIAN COURIER, circ. 14,074 177

North Berwick
W EAST LOTHIAN COURIER, circ. 14,074 177

Ormiston
W DALKEITH ADVERTISER SERIES, circ. 60,690 170

Prestonpans
W DALKEITH ADVERTISER SERIES, circ. 60,690 170
W EAST LOTHIAN COURIER, circ. 14,074 177

East Renfrewshire UA

Barrhead
W THE PAISLEY AND RENFREWSHIRE GAZETTE SERIES, circ. 19,577 234
D PAISLEY DAILY EXPRESS, circ. 9,528 235
W RENFREWSHIRE WORLD, circ. 15,670 F 239

Eaglesham
W EAST KILBRIDE NEWS, circ. 12,712 177
D EVENING TIMES (GLASGOW), circ. 79,087 182

Newton Mearns
D EVENING TIMES (GLASGOW), circ. 79,087 182
W THE GLASGOW EXTRA SERIES, circ. 100,810 F 190
W THE GLASWEGIAN SERIES, circ. 104,175 F 190
W THE PAISLEY AND RENFREWSHIRE GAZETTE SERIES, circ. 19,577 234

Falkirk UA

Bo'ness
W FALKIRK & GRANGEMOUTH ADVERTISER SERIES, circ. 51,805 F 184
W LINLITHGOWSHIRE JOURNAL AND GAZETTE SERIES, circ. 8,632 212

Denny
W FALKIRK & GRANGEMOUTH ADVERTISER SERIES, circ. 51,805 F 184
W THE FALKIRK HERALD, circ. 28,779 184
W STIRLING OBSERVER SERIES, circ. 16,849 255
W STIRLING SHOPPER SERIES, circ. 7,049 F 256

Falkirk
D EVENING TIMES (GLASGOW), circ. 79,087 182
W FALKIRK & GRANGEMOUTH ADVERTISER SERIES, circ. 51,805 F 184
W THE FALKIRK HERALD, circ. 28,779 184

Grangemouth
D EVENING TIMES (GLASGOW), circ. 79,087 182
W FALKIRK & GRANGEMOUTH ADVERTISER SERIES, circ. 51,805 F 184
W THE FALKIRK HERALD, circ. 28,779 184

Stenhousemuir
W FALKIRK & GRANGEMOUTH ADVERTISER SERIES, circ. 51,805 F 184
W THE FALKIRK HERALD, circ. 28,779 184

Fife UA

Anstruther
W EAST FIFE MAIL, circ. 10,982 177

Ballingry
W CENTRAL FIFE TIMES AND ADVERTISER, circ. 7,013 158
D THE COURIER AND ADVERTISER, circ. 73,485 166

Buckhaven
D THE COURIER AND ADVERTISER, circ. 73,485 166
W EAST FIFE MAIL, circ. 10,982 177

Burntisland
D THE COURIER AND ADVERTISER, circ. 73,485 166
D EVENING TELEGRAPH & POST (DUNDEE), circ. 24,349 181
W FIFE AND KINROSS EXTRA, circ. 52,464 F 185
W FIFE LEADER AND FREE PRESS SERIES, circ. 135,799 185

Cardenden
W CENTRAL FIFE TIMES AND ADVERTISER, circ. 7,013 158
D THE COURIER AND ADVERTISER, circ. 73,485 166
W FIFE AND KINROSS EXTRA, circ. 52,464 F 185
W FIFE LEADER AND FREE PRESS SERIES, circ. 135,799 185

Cowdenbeath
W CENTRAL FIFE TIMES AND ADVERTISER, circ. 7,013 158
W FIFE AND KINROSS EXTRA, circ. 52,464 F 185

Crossford
D THE COURIER AND ADVERTISER, circ. 73,485 166
W DUNFERMLINE PRESS AND WEST OF FIFE ADVERTISER, circ. 21,005 175

Cupar
D THE COURIER AND ADVERTISER, circ. 73,485 166
D EVENING TELEGRAPH & POST (DUNDEE), circ. 24,349 181
W FIFE HERALD INC. FIFE NEWS AND KINROSSHIRE ADVERTISER, circ. 13,116 185

Dalgety Bay
D THE COURIER AND ADVERTISER, circ. 73,485 166
W DUNFERMLINE PRESS AND WEST OF FIFE ADVERTISER, circ. 21,005 175
W FIFE AND KINROSS EXTRA, circ. 52,464 F 185

Dunfermline
D THE COURIER AND ADVERTISER, circ. 73,485 166
W DUNFERMLINE PRESS AND WEST OF FIFE ADVERTISER, circ. 21,005 175
D EVENING TELEGRAPH & POST (DUNDEE), circ. 24,349 181
W FIFE AND KINROSS EXTRA, circ. 52,464 F 185

Falkland
W FIFE HERALD INC. FIFE NEWS AND KINROSSHIRE ADVERTISER, circ. 13,116 185
W GLENROTHES GAZETTE LESLIE AND MARKINCH NEWS, circ. 6,133 191

Glenrothes
D THE COURIER AND ADVERTISER, circ. 73,485 166
D EVENING TELEGRAPH & POST (DUNDEE), circ. 24,349 181
W FIFE LEADER AND FREE PRESS SERIES, circ. 135,799 185
W GLENROTHES GAZETTE LESLIE AND MARKINCH NEWS, circ. 6,133 191

High Valleyfield
D THE COURIER AND ADVERTISER, circ. 73,485 166
W DUNFERMLINE PRESS AND WEST OF FIFE ADVERTISER, circ. 21,005 175

Inverkeithing
D THE COURIER AND ADVERTISER, circ. 73,485 166

Title (Day/am/pm)	Circ.	Page No.

W DUNFERMLINE PRESS AND WEST OF FIFE ADVERTISER, circ. 21,005 175
W FIFE AND KINROSS EXTRA, circ. 52,464 F 185

Kelty
W CENTRAL FIFE TIMES AND ADVERTISER, circ. 7,013 158
D THE COURIER AND ADVERTISER, circ. 73,485 166
W DUNFERMLINE PRESS AND WEST OF FIFE ADVERTISER, circ. 21,005 175

Kincardine
W ALLOA AND HILLFOOTS ADVERTISER, circ. 9,119 ... 141
W ALLOA AND HILLFOOTS WEE COUNTY NEWS, circ. 6,587 141
W DUNFERMLINE PRESS AND WEST OF FIFE ADVERTISER, circ. 21,005 175
W FIFE AND KINROSS EXTRA, circ. 52,464 F 185

Kinghorn
D THE COURIER AND ADVERTISER, circ. 73,485 166
D EVENING TELEGRAPH & POST (DUNDEE), circ. 24,349 181
W FIFE LEADER AND FREE PRESS SERIES, circ. 135,799 185

Kirkcaldy
D THE COURIER AND ADVERTISER, circ. 73,485 166
D EVENING TELEGRAPH & POST (DUNDEE), circ. 24,349 181
W FIFE LEADER AND FREE PRESS SERIES, circ. 135,799 185

Ladybank
W FIFE HERALD INC. FIFE NEWS AND KINROSSHIRE ADVERTISER, circ. 13,116 185

Leslie
W GLENROTHES GAZETTE LESLIE AND MARKINCH NEWS, circ. 6,133 191

Leuchars
D THE COURIER AND ADVERTISER, circ. 73,485 166
D EVENING TELEGRAPH & POST (DUNDEE), circ. 24,349 181

Leven
D THE COURIER AND ADVERTISER, circ. 73,485 166
W EAST FIFE MAIL, circ. 10,982 177

Lochgelly
W CENTRAL FIFE TIMES AND ADVERTISER, circ. 7,013 158
W FIFE AND KINROSS EXTRA, circ. 52,464 F 185

Markinch
W GLENROTHES GAZETTE LESLIE AND MARKINCH NEWS, circ. 6,133 191

Newburgh
W FIFE HERALD INC. FIFE NEWS AND KINROSSHIRE ADVERTISER, circ. 13,116 185

Newport-on-Tay
W FIFE HERALD INC. FIFE NEWS AND KINROSSHIRE ADVERTISER, circ. 13,116 185

Oakley
D THE COURIER AND ADVERTISER, circ. 73,485 166
W DUNFERMLINE PRESS AND WEST OF FIFE ADVERTISER, circ. 21,005 175

Rosyth
W DUNFERMLINE PRESS AND WEST OF FIFE ADVERTISER, circ. 21,005 175
W FIFE AND KINROSS EXTRA, circ. 52,464 F 185

St. Andrews
D THE COURIER AND ADVERTISER, circ. 73,485 166
W ST. ANDREWS CITIZEN 253

Tayport
W FIFE HERALD INC. FIFE NEWS AND KINROSSHIRE ADVERTISER, circ. 13,116 185

Glasgow UA

Baillieston
W AIRDRIE & COATBRIDGE ADVERTISER, circ. 16,621 140
W THE GLASWEGIAN SERIES, circ. 104,175 F 190

Bridgeton
W THE GLASWEGIAN SERIES, circ. 104,175 F 190

Cambuslang
W RUTHERGLEN REFORMER, circ. 4,277 243

Castlemilk
W RUTHERGLEN REFORMER, circ. 4,277 243

East Kilbride
W EAST KILBRIDE MAIL, circ. 26,000 F 177
W EAST KILBRIDE NEWS, circ. 12,712 177
W EVENING TIMES (GLASGOW), circ. 79,087 182
W LANARKSHIRE WORLD, circ. 35,172 F 208

Eastwood
W THE GLASGOW EXTRA SERIES, circ. 100,810 F 190
W THE GLASWEGIAN SERIES, circ. 104,175 F 190

Giffnock
D EVENING TIMES (GLASGOW), circ. 79,087 182
W THE GLASGOW EXTRA SERIES, circ. 100,810 F 190
W THE GLASWEGIAN SERIES, circ. 104,175 F 190
W THE PAISLEY AND RENFREWSHIRE GAZETTE SERIES, circ. 19,577 234

Glasgow
D EVENING TIMES (GLASGOW), circ. 79,087 182
W THE GLASGOW EXTRA SERIES, circ. 100,810 F 190
W THE GLASWEGIAN SERIES, circ. 104,175 F 190
W LOCAL NEWS (GLASGOW) SERIES, circ. 40,000 F .. 213

Partick
W THE GLASGOW EXTRA SERIES, circ. 100,810 F 190

Rutherglen
W RUTHERGLEN REFORMER, circ. 4,277 243

Uddingston
W LANARKSHIRE EXTRA SERIES, circ. 46,000 F 208
W LANARKSHIRE WORLD, circ. 35,172 F 208
W MOTHERWELL TIMES SERIES, circ. 13,718 224

Highland UA

W GAZETA Z HIGHLAND, circ. 20,000 F 188
D THE PRESS & JOURNAL (ABERDEEN), circ. 81,956 .. 237

Alness
W HIGHLAND NEWS SERIES, circ. 26,799 199
W NORTH STAR, circ. 5,365 230
W ROSS-SHIRE JOURNAL AND HERALD SERIES, circ. 21,182 241

Arisaig
W OBAN TIMES & WEST HIGHLAND TIMES, circ. 17,421 233

Aviemore
D EVENING EXPRESS (ABERDEEN), circ. 53,384 181
W HIGHLAND NEWS SERIES, circ. 26,799 199
W STRATHSPEY & BADENOCH HERALD, circ. 4,844 ... 257

Ballachulish
W OBAN TIMES & WEST HIGHLAND TIMES, circ. 17,421 233

Caithness
W JOHN O'GROAT JOURNAL SERIES, circ. 15,717 204

Carrbridge
W STRATHSPEY & BADENOCH HERALD, circ. 4,844 ... 257

Cromarty
W NORTH STAR, circ. 5,365 230
W ROSS-SHIRE JOURNAL AND HERALD SERIES, circ. 21,182 241

Dingwall
W HIGHLAND NEWS SERIES, circ. 26,799 199
W INVERNESS COURIER SERIES, circ. 30,383 203
W NORTH STAR, circ. 5,365 230
W ROSS-SHIRE JOURNAL AND HERALD SERIES, circ. 21,182 241

Fort William
W HIGHLAND NEWS SERIES, circ. 26,799 199
W OBAN TIMES & WEST HIGHLAND TIMES, circ. 17,421 233

Grantown-on-Spey
D EVENING EXPRESS (ABERDEEN), circ. 53,384 181
W STRATHSPEY & BADENOCH HERALD, circ. 4,844 ... 257

Invergordon
W HIGHLAND NEWS SERIES, circ. 26,799 199
W NORTH STAR, circ. 5,365 230
W ROSS-SHIRE JOURNAL AND HERALD SERIES, circ. 21,182 241

Inverness
W HIGHLAND NEWS SERIES, circ. 26,799 199
W INVERNESS COURIER SERIES, circ. 30,383 203
W NAIRNSHIRE TELEGRAPH 225

Isle of Skye
W OBAN TIMES & WEST HIGHLAND TIMES, circ. 17,421 233

W ROSS-SHIRE JOURNAL AND HERALD SERIES, circ. 21,182 241
W WEST HIGHLAND FREE PRESS, circ. 8,712 271

Kingussie
W STRATHSPEY & BADENOCH HERALD, circ. 4,844 257

Kyle of Lochalsh
W NORTH STAR, circ. 5,365 230
W OBAN TIMES & WEST HIGHLAND TIMES, circ. 17,421 233
W WEST HIGHLAND FREE PRESS, circ. 8,712 271

Mallaig
W HIGHLAND NEWS SERIES, circ. 26,799 199
W OBAN TIMES & WEST HIGHLAND TIMES, circ. 17,421 233

Nairn
W HIGHLAND NEWS SERIES, circ. 26,799 199
W INVERNESS COURIER SERIES, circ. 30,383 203
W NAIRNSHIRE TELEGRAPH 225

Newtonmore
W STRATHSPEY & BADENOCH HERALD, circ. 4,844 257

Onich
W OBAN TIMES & WEST HIGHLAND TIMES, circ. 17,421 233

Portree
W HIGHLAND NEWS SERIES, circ. 26,799 199
W OBAN TIMES & WEST HIGHLAND TIMES, circ. 17,421 233

Spean Bridge
W HIGHLAND NEWS SERIES, circ. 26,799 199

Strathspey
W STRATHSPEY & BADENOCH HERALD, circ. 4,844 257

Strontian
W OBAN TIMES & WEST HIGHLAND TIMES, circ. 17,421 233

Tain
W HIGHLAND NEWS SERIES, circ. 26,799 199
W NORTH STAR, circ. 5,365 230
W ROSS-SHIRE JOURNAL AND HERALD SERIES, circ. 21,182 241

Ullapool
W HIGHLAND NEWS SERIES, circ. 26,799 199
W NORTH STAR, circ. 5,365 230
W ROSS-SHIRE JOURNAL AND HERALD SERIES, circ. 21,182 241

Inverclyde UA

W LARGS & MILLPORT WEEKLY NEWS, circ. 5,958 209

Gourock
D GREENOCK TELEGRAPH, circ. 17,667 193
W INVERCLYDE EXTRA, circ. 18,979 F 203

Greenock
D EVENING TIMES (GLASGOW), circ. 79,087 182
D GREENOCK TELEGRAPH, circ. 17,667 193
W INVERCLYDE EXTRA, circ. 18,979 F 203

Inverkip
D GREENOCK TELEGRAPH, circ. 17,667 193
W INVERCLYDE EXTRA, circ. 18,979 F 203

Kilmacolm
D GREENOCK TELEGRAPH, circ. 17,667 193
W THE PAISLEY AND RENFREWSHIRE GAZETTE SERIES, circ. 19,577 234

Port Glasgow
D GREENOCK TELEGRAPH, circ. 17,667 193
W INVERCLYDE EXTRA, circ. 18,979 F 203

Skelmorlie
D GREENOCK TELEGRAPH, circ. 17,667 193
W INVERCLYDE EXTRA, circ. 18,979 F 203

Wemyss Bay
D GREENOCK TELEGRAPH, circ. 17,667 193
W INVERCLYDE EXTRA, circ. 18,979 F 203

Midlothian UA

W THE ADVERTISER (MIDLOTHIAN), circ. 7,126 139
W EVENING NEWS (EDINBURGH), circ. 53,675 181
W THE LOTHIAN TIMES (EAST LOTHIAN EDITION), circ. 48,838 F 215
W LOTHIAN TIMES (MIDLOTHIAN) F 215

W **Local/Weekly Newspapers**   D **Regional Daily Newspapers**   S **Regional Sunday Newspapers**   F **Free Newspapers**

Non-Nationals - Scotland

Title (*Day/am/pm*) Circ. Page No.

Bonnyrigg
[W] DALKEITH ADVERTISER SERIES, circ. 60,690 170

Dalkeith
[W] DALKEITH ADVERTISER SERIES, circ. 60,690 170
[D] EVENING NEWS (EDINBURGH), circ. 53,675 181

Gorebridge
[W] DALKEITH ADVERTISER SERIES, circ. 60,690 170

Loanhead
[W] DALKEITH ADVERTISER SERIES, circ. 60,690 170
[D] EVENING NEWS (EDINBURGH), circ. 53,675 181

Mayfield
[W] DALKEITH ADVERTISER SERIES, circ. 60,690 170
[D] EVENING NEWS (EDINBURGH), circ. 53,675 181

Penicuik
[W] DALKEITH ADVERTISER SERIES, circ. 60,690 170
[W] PEEBLESSHIRE NEWS, circ. 5,013 235

Moray UA

[W] GAZETA Z HIGHLAND, circ. 20,000 [F] 188
[D] THE PRESS & JOURNAL (ABERDEEN), circ. 81,956 .. 237

Buckie
[W] BANFFSHIRE ADVERTISER, circ. 4,500 145
[W] THE BANFFSHIRE JOURNAL, circ. 4,994 145
[W] NORTHERN SCOT AND MORAY & NAIRN EXPRESS, circ. 18,203 232

Cullen
[W] BANFFSHIRE ADVERTISER, circ. 4,500 145
[W] THE BANFFSHIRE JOURNAL, circ. 4,994 145
[D] EVENING EXPRESS (ABERDEEN), circ. 53,384 181
[W] NORTHERN SCOT AND MORAY & NAIRN EXPRESS, circ. 18,203 232

Elgin
[D] EVENING EXPRESS (ABERDEEN), circ. 53,384 181
[W] NORTHERN SCOT AND MORAY & NAIRN EXPRESS, circ. 18,203 232

Fochabers
[W] BANFFSHIRE ADVERTISER, circ. 4,500 145
[W] NORTHERN SCOT AND MORAY & NAIRN EXPRESS, circ. 18,203 232

Forres
[D] EVENING EXPRESS (ABERDEEN), circ. 53,384 181
[W] FORRES GAZETTE, circ. 3,630 186
[W] HIGHLAND NEWS SERIES, circ. 26,799 199
[W] NAIRNSHIRE TELEGRAPH 225
[W] NORTHERN SCOT AND MORAY & NAIRN EXPRESS, circ. 18,203 232

Keith
[W] BANFFSHIRE HERALD, circ. 3,000 145
[W] NORTHERN SCOT AND MORAY & NAIRN EXPRESS, circ. 18,203 232

Kinloss
[W] FORRES GAZETTE, circ. 3,630 186

Lossiemouth
[W] NORTHERN SCOT AND MORAY & NAIRN EXPRESS, circ. 18,203 232

North Ayrshire UA

Ardrossan
[W] ARDROSSAN & SALTCOATS HERALD, circ. 14,615 .. 142
[W] AYRSHIRE WORLD SERIES, circ. 16,827 [F] 144

Arran
[W] THE ARRAN BANNER, circ. 3,458 143

Beith
[W] ARDROSSAN & SALTCOATS HERALD, circ. 14,615 .. 142

Dalry
[W] ARDROSSAN & SALTCOATS HERALD, circ. 14,615 .. 142

Dreghorn
[W] AYRSHIRE WORLD SERIES, circ. 16,827 [F] 144
[W] THE IRVINE HERALD AND KILWINNING CHRONICLE, circ. 10,490 203
[W] IRVINE TIMES, circ. 3,599 203

Dundonald
[W] AYRSHIRE WORLD SERIES, circ. 16,827 [F] 144
[W] KILMARNOCK STANDARD, circ. 17,311 207

Irvine
[W] AYRSHIRE WORLD SERIES, circ. 16,827 [F] 144
[W] THE IRVINE HERALD AND KILWINNING CHRONICLE, circ. 10,490 203
[W] IRVINE TIMES, circ. 3,599 203

Kilbirnie
[W] ARDROSSAN & SALTCOATS HERALD, circ. 14,615 .. 142

Kilwinning
[W] AYRSHIRE WORLD SERIES, circ. 16,827 [F] 144
[W] THE IRVINE HERALD AND KILWINNING CHRONICLE, circ. 10,490 203
[W] IRVINE TIMES, circ. 3,599 203

Largs
[W] AYRSHIRE WORLD SERIES, circ. 16,827 [F] 144
[D] GREENOCK TELEGRAPH, circ. 17,667 193
[W] LARGS & MILLPORT WEEKLY NEWS, circ. 5,958 209

Saltcoats
[W] ARDROSSAN & SALTCOATS HERALD, circ. 14,615 .. 142
[W] AYRSHIRE WORLD SERIES, circ. 16,827 [F] 144

Stevenston
[W] ARDROSSAN & SALTCOATS HERALD, circ. 14,615 .. 142
[W] AYRSHIRE WORLD SERIES, circ. 16,827 [F] 144
[W] THE IRVINE HERALD AND KILWINNING CHRONICLE, circ. 10,490 203

West Kilbride
[W] ARDROSSAN & SALTCOATS HERALD, circ. 14,615 .. 142

North Lanarkshire UA

[W] CARLUKE GAZETTE 158
[W] HAMILTON ADVERTISER, circ. 23,013 194
[W] KIRKINTILLOCH & BISHOPBRIGGS HERALD SERIES, circ. 34,797 208
[W] LANARK GAZETTE 208

Airdrie
[W] AIRDRIE & COATBRIDGE ADVERTISER, circ. 16,621 140
[D] EVENING TIMES (GLASGOW), circ. 79,087 182
[W] LANARKSHIRE WORLD, circ. 35,172 [F] 208

Bellshill
[W] HAMILTON ADVERTISER, circ. 23,013 194
[W] LANARKSHIRE EXTRA SERIES, circ. 46,000 [F] 208
[W] MOTHERWELL TIMES SERIES, circ. 13,718 224

Bothwell
[W] LANARKSHIRE EXTRA SERIES, circ. 46,000 [F] 208
[W] LANARKSHIRE WORLD, circ. 35,172 [F] 208
[W] MOTHERWELL TIMES SERIES, circ. 13,718 224

Caldercruix
[W] AIRDRIE & COATBRIDGE ADVERTISER, circ. 16,621 140
[D] EVENING TIMES (GLASGOW), circ. 79,087 182
[W] LANARKSHIRE WORLD, circ. 35,172 [F] 208

Chapelhall
[W] AIRDRIE & COATBRIDGE ADVERTISER, circ. 16,621 140
[D] EVENING TIMES (GLASGOW), circ. 79,087 182
[W] LANARKSHIRE WORLD, circ. 35,172 [F] 208

Cleland
[W] MOTHERWELL TIMES SERIES, circ. 13,718 224
[W] WISHAW PRESS, circ. 9,997 276

Coatbridge
[W] AIRDRIE & COATBRIDGE ADVERTISER, circ. 16,621 140
[D] EVENING TIMES (GLASGOW), circ. 79,087 182
[W] LANARKSHIRE WORLD, circ. 35,172 [F] 208

Cumbernauld
[W] CUMBERNAULD NEWS AND KILSYTH CHRONICLE SERIES, circ. 11,853 169

Harthill
[D] EVENING NEWS (EDINBURGH), circ. 53,675 181
[W] WEST LOTHIAN COURIER, circ. 17,229 271

Kilsyth
[W] CUMBERNAULD NEWS AND KILSYTH CHRONICLE SERIES, circ. 11,853 169

Law
[W] CARLUKE AND LANARK GAZETTE SERIES, circ. 12,363 158
[W] LANARK & CARLUKE ADVERTISER 208

Motherwell
[D] EVENING TIMES (GLASGOW), circ. 79,087 182
[W] HAMILTON ADVERTISER, circ. 23,013 194
[W] LANARKSHIRE EXTRA SERIES, circ. 46,000 [F] 208
[W] LANARKSHIRE WORLD, circ. 35,172 [F] 208
[W] MOTHERWELL TIMES SERIES, circ. 13,718 224
[W] WISHAW PRESS, circ. 9,997 276

Newarthill
[W] MOTHERWELL TIMES SERIES, circ. 13,718 224

Overtown
[W] HAMILTON ADVERTISER, circ. 23,013 194
[W] LANARKSHIRE WORLD, circ. 35,172 [F] 208
[W] WISHAW PRESS, circ. 9,997 276

Shotts
[W] HAMILTON ADVERTISER, circ. 23,013 194
[W] LANARKSHIRE WORLD, circ. 35,172 [F] 208
[W] WISHAW PRESS, circ. 9,997 276

Viewpark
[W] LANARKSHIRE WORLD, circ. 35,172 [F] 208
[W] MOTHERWELL TIMES SERIES, circ. 13,718 224

Wishaw
[W] HAMILTON ADVERTISER, circ. 23,013 194
[W] LANARKSHIRE EXTRA SERIES, circ. 46,000 [F] 208
[W] LANARKSHIRE WORLD, circ. 35,172 [F] 208
[W] WISHAW PRESS, circ. 9,997 276

Orkney Islands UA

[W] THE ORCADIAN, circ. 10,183 233
[W] ORKNEY TODAY, circ. 5,993 233
[D] THE PRESS & JOURNAL (ABERDEEN), circ. 81,956 .. 237

Perth & Kinross UA

[D] EVENING TELEGRAPH & POST (DUNDEE), circ. 24,349 181
[D] THE PRESS & JOURNAL (ABERDEEN), circ. 81,956 .. 237

Alyth
[D] THE COURIER AND ADVERTISER, circ. 73,485 166

Auchterarder
[D] THE COURIER AND ADVERTISER, circ. 73,485 166
[W] STRATHEARN HERALD, circ. 3,047 257

Blairgowrie
[D] THE COURIER AND ADVERTISER, circ. 73,485 166
[W] PERTHSHIRE ADVERTISER SERIES, circ. 36,056 235

Coupar Angus
[D] THE COURIER AND ADVERTISER, circ. 73,485 166

Crieff
[D] THE COURIER AND ADVERTISER, circ. 73,485 166
[W] STRATHEARN HERALD, circ. 3,047 257

Kinross
[W] FIFE AND KINROSS EXTRA, circ. 52,464 [F] 185
[W] FIFE HERALD INC. FIFE NEWS AND KINROSSHIRE ADVERTISER, circ. 13,116 185
[W] PERTHSHIRE ADVERTISER SERIES, circ. 36,056 235

New Scone
[D] THE COURIER AND ADVERTISER, circ. 73,485 166

Perth
[D] THE COURIER AND ADVERTISER, circ. 73,485 166
[W] PERTHSHIRE ADVERTISER SERIES, circ. 36,056 235

Pitlochry
[D] THE COURIER AND ADVERTISER, circ. 73,485 166

Strathearn
[W] STRATHEARN HERALD, circ. 3,047 257

Renfrewshire UA

Bishopton
[D] EVENING TIMES (GLASGOW), circ. 79,087 182
[W] THE GLASGOW EXTRA SERIES, circ. 100,810 [F] 190
[W] THE PAISLEY AND RENFREWSHIRE GAZETTE SERIES, circ. 19,577 234
[W] RENFREWSHIRE WORLD, circ. 15,670 [F] 239

Bridge of Weir
[W] THE GLASGOW EXTRA SERIES, circ. 100,810 [F] 190
[W] THE PAISLEY AND RENFREWSHIRE GAZETTE SERIES, circ. 19,577 234
[D] PAISLEY DAILY EXPRESS, circ. 9,528 235

Elderslie
[D] PAISLEY DAILY EXPRESS, circ. 9,528 235

Houston
[D] EVENING TIMES (GLASGOW), circ. 79,087 182
[W] THE GLASGOW EXTRA SERIES, circ. 100,810 [F] 190
[W] THE PAISLEY AND RENFREWSHIRE GAZETTE SERIES, circ. 19,577 234
[D] PAISLEY DAILY EXPRESS, circ. 9,528 235
[W] RENFREWSHIRE WORLD, circ. 15,670 [F] 239

Johnstone
[W] THE GLASGOW EXTRA SERIES, circ. 100,810 [F] 190

[W] Local/Weekly Newspapers [D] Regional Daily Newspapers [S] Regional Sunday Newspapers [F] Free Newspapers

W **Local/Weekly Newspapers**   D **Regional Daily Newspapers**   S **Regional Sunday Newspapers**   F **Free Newspapers**

Non-Nationals - Wales

Title (Day/am/pm)	Circ.	Page No.

W STIRLING SHOPPER SERIES, circ. 7,049 F 256

West Dunbartonshire UA

Alexandria
W CLYDE WEEKLY NEWS, circ. 5,339 F 163
W DUMBARTON AND VALE OF LEVEN REPORTER,
circ. 4,332 175

Balloch
W DUMBARTON AND VALE OF LEVEN REPORTER,
circ. 4,332 175

Clydebank
W CLYDE WEEKLY NEWS, circ. 5,339 F 163
W CLYDEBANK POST, circ. 12,981 163
D EVENING TIMES (GLASGOW), circ. 79,087 182

Dumbarton
W CLYDE WEEKLY NEWS, circ. 5,339 F 163
W DUMBARTON AND VALE OF LEVEN REPORTER,
circ. 4,332 175
D EVENING TIMES (GLASGOW), circ. 79,087 182
W LENNOX SERIES, circ. 12,307 211

Erskine
W THE GLASGOW EXTRA SERIES, circ. 100,810 F 190
W THE PAISLEY AND RENFREWSHIRE GAZETTE SERIES,
circ. 19,577 234
W RENFREWSHIRE WORLD, circ. 15,670 F 239

Inchinnan
D EVENING TIMES (GLASGOW), circ. 79,087 182
W THE GLASGOW EXTRA SERIES, circ. 100,810 F 190
W THE PAISLEY AND RENFREWSHIRE GAZETTE SERIES,
circ. 19,577 234

Renfrew
W THE GLASGOW EXTRA SERIES, circ. 100,810 F 190
W THE PAISLEY AND RENFREWSHIRE GAZETTE SERIES,
circ. 19,577 234
D PAISLEY DAILY EXPRESS, circ. 9,528 235
W RENFREWSHIRE WORLD, circ. 15,670 F 239

West Lothian UA

D EVENING NEWS (EDINBURGH), circ. 53,675 181
W HERALD AND POST SERIES (EDINBURGH),
circ. 166,378 F 197
W WEST LOTHIAN COURIER, circ. 17,229 271

Armadale
W WEST LOTHIAN COURIER, circ. 17,229 271

Bathgate
D EVENING NEWS (EDINBURGH), circ. 53,675 181
W WEST LOTHIAN COURIER, circ. 17,229 271

Blackburn
W WEST LOTHIAN COURIER, circ. 17,229 271

Broxburn
W WEST LOTHIAN COURIER, circ. 17,229 271

East Calder
D EVENING NEWS (EDINBURGH), circ. 53,675 181
W WEST LOTHIAN COURIER, circ. 17,229 271

Fauldhouse
W WEST LOTHIAN COURIER, circ. 17,229 271

Linlithgow
D EVENING NEWS (EDINBURGH), circ. 53,675 181
W FALKIRK & GRANGEMOUTH ADVERTISER SERIES,
circ. 51,805 F 184
W LINLITHGOWSHIRE JOURNAL AND GAZETTE SERIES,
circ. 8,632 212
W WEST LOTHIAN COURIER, circ. 17,229 271

Livingston
W WEST LOTHIAN COURIER, circ. 17,229 271

Polbeth
D EVENING NEWS (EDINBURGH), circ. 53,675 181
W WEST LOTHIAN COURIER, circ. 17,229 271

Stoneyburn
D EVENING NEWS (EDINBURGH), circ. 53,675 181
W WEST LOTHIAN COURIER, circ. 17,229 271

Whitburn
W WEST LOTHIAN COURIER, circ. 17,229 271

Western Isles UA

D THE PRESS & JOURNAL (ABERDEEN), circ. 81,956 .. 237
W STORNOWAY GAZETTE AND WEST COAST
ADVERTISER, circ. 13,006 256
W WEST HIGHLAND FREE PRESS, circ. 8,712 271

Stornoway
W HIGHLAND NEWS SERIES, circ. 26,799 199
W STORNOWAY GAZETTE AND WEST COAST
ADVERTISER, circ. 13,006 256

WALES

W Y CYMRO, circ. 6,000 169
D WESTERN MAIL (CARDIFF), circ. 37,576 272

Blaenau Gwent UA

W THE CARDIFF & SOUTH WALES ADVERTISER,
circ. 30,000 F 158

Abertillery
W GWENT GAZETTE, circ. 11,495 194
S WALES ON SUNDAY, circ. 41,199 267

Brynmawr
W ABERGAVENNY CHRONICLE SERIES, circ. 15,000 ... 137
W GWENT GAZETTE, circ. 11,495 194

Cwm
W GWENT GAZETTE, circ. 11,495 194
D SOUTH WALES ARGUS, circ. 28,879 250
D SOUTH WALES ECHO, circ. 46,127 251
S WALES ON SUNDAY, circ. 41,199 267

Ebbw Vale
W GWENT GAZETTE, circ. 11,495 194

Gilwern
W ABERGAVENNY CHRONICLE SERIES, circ. 15,000 ... 137
D SOUTH WALES ARGUS, circ. 28,879 250
S WALES ON SUNDAY, circ. 41,199 267

Tredegar
W GWENT GAZETTE, circ. 11,495 194
D SOUTH WALES ARGUS, circ. 28,879 250
S WALES ON SUNDAY, circ. 41,199 267

Bridgend UA

W THE CARDIFF & SOUTH WALES ADVERTISER,
circ. 30,000 F 158

Aberkenfig
W GLAMORGAN GAZETTE SERIES, circ. 21,504 190
D SOUTH WALES ECHO, circ. 46,127 251
S WALES ON SUNDAY, circ. 41,199 267

Bridgend
W CARDIFF POST SERIES, circ. 103,812 F 158
W GEM SERIES, circ. 36,196 F 190
W GLAMORGAN GAZETTE SERIES, circ. 21,504 190
D SOUTH WALES ECHO, circ. 46,127 251
S WALES ON SUNDAY, circ. 41,199 267

Bryncoch
W GLAMORGAN GAZETTE SERIES, circ. 21,504 190
D SOUTH WALES ECHO, circ. 46,127 251
S WALES ON SUNDAY, circ. 41,199 267

Croeserw
W PONTYPRIDD AND LLANTRISANT OBSERVER,
circ. 11,429 236
D SOUTH WALES ECHO, circ. 46,127 251
S WALES ON SUNDAY, circ. 41,199 267

Maesteg
W CARDIFF POST SERIES, circ. 103,812 F 158
W GLAMORGAN GAZETTE SERIES, circ. 21,504 190

Pencoed
W GLAMORGAN GAZETTE SERIES, circ. 21,504 190
D SOUTH WALES ECHO, circ. 46,127 251
S WALES ON SUNDAY, circ. 41,199 267

Pontycymer
W GLAMORGAN GAZETTE SERIES, circ. 21,504 190
D SOUTH WALES ECHO, circ. 46,127 251
S WALES ON SUNDAY, circ. 41,199 267

Porthcawl
W CARDIFF POST SERIES, circ. 103,812 F 158
W GEM SERIES, circ. 36,196 F 190
W GLAMORGAN GAZETTE SERIES, circ. 21,504 190
D SOUTH WALES ECHO, circ. 46,127 251
S WALES ON SUNDAY, circ. 41,199 267

Pyle
W GLAMORGAN GAZETTE SERIES, circ. 21,504 190
D SOUTH WALES ECHO, circ. 46,127 251
S WALES ON SUNDAY, circ. 41,199 267

Caerphilly UA

W THE CARDIFF & SOUTH WALES ADVERTISER,
circ. 30,000 F 158

Abercarn
W CAERPHILLY CAMPAIGN SERIES, circ. 70,860 F 156
D SOUTH WALES ARGUS, circ. 28,879 250
D SOUTH WALES ECHO, circ. 46,127 251
S WALES ON SUNDAY, circ. 41,199 267

Bargoed
W CAERPHILLY CAMPAIGN SERIES, circ. 70,860 F 156
D SOUTH WALES ECHO, circ. 46,127 251
S WALES ON SUNDAY, circ. 41,199 267

Bedwas
W CAERPHILLY CAMPAIGN SERIES, circ. 70,860 F 156
D SOUTH WALES ARGUS, circ. 28,879 250
D SOUTH WALES ECHO, circ. 46,127 251
S WALES ON SUNDAY, circ. 41,199 267

Blackwood
W CAERPHILLY CAMPAIGN SERIES, circ. 70,860 F 156
D SOUTH WALES ARGUS, circ. 28,879 250
S WALES ON SUNDAY, circ. 41,199 267

Caerphilly
W CAERPHILLY CAMPAIGN SERIES, circ. 70,860 F 156
D SOUTH WALES ECHO, circ. 46,127 251
S WALES ON SUNDAY, circ. 41,199 267

Gelligaer
W CAERPHILLY CAMPAIGN SERIES, circ. 70,860 F 156
D SOUTH WALES ECHO, circ. 46,127 251
S WALES ON SUNDAY, circ. 41,199 267

Gilfach Goch
S WALES ON SUNDAY, circ. 41,199 267

Llanbradach
W CAERPHILLY CAMPAIGN SERIES, circ. 70,860 F 156
D SOUTH WALES ECHO, circ. 46,127 251
S WALES ON SUNDAY, circ. 41,199 267

Nelson
D SOUTH WALES ECHO, circ. 46,127 251
S WALES ON SUNDAY, circ. 41,199 267

New Tredegar
W CAERPHILLY CAMPAIGN SERIES, circ. 70,860 F 156
D SOUTH WALES ECHO, circ. 46,127 251
S WALES ON SUNDAY, circ. 41,199 267

Newbridge
W CAERPHILLY CAMPAIGN SERIES, circ. 70,860 F 156
D SOUTH WALES ARGUS, circ. 28,879 250
D SOUTH WALES ECHO, circ. 46,127 251
S WALES ON SUNDAY, circ. 41,199 267

Oakdale
W CAERPHILLY CAMPAIGN SERIES, circ. 70,860 F 156
D SOUTH WALES ARGUS, circ. 28,879 250
S WALES ON SUNDAY, circ. 41,199 267

Pontllanfraith
W CAERPHILLY CAMPAIGN SERIES, circ. 70,860 F 156
D SOUTH WALES ARGUS, circ. 28,879 250
S WALES ON SUNDAY, circ. 41,199 267

Rhymney
D SOUTH WALES ECHO, circ. 46,127 251
S WALES ON SUNDAY, circ. 41,199 267

Rhymney Valley
W CAERPHILLY CAMPAIGN SERIES, circ. 70,860 F 156

Risca
W THE FREE PRESS NEWSPAPER SERIES,
circ. 11,281 187
W NEWPORT & CWMBRAN WEEKLY ARGUS,
circ. 34,670 F 226
D SOUTH WALES ARGUS, circ. 28,879 250
S WALES ON SUNDAY, circ. 41,199 267

Cardiff UA

W THE CARDIFF & SOUTH WALES ADVERTISER,
circ. 30,000 F 158

Cardiff
W YR ANGOR (LIVERPOOL), circ. 3,000 142
W CARDIFF POST SERIES, circ. 103,812 F 158
D SOUTH WALES ECHO, circ. 46,127 251
S WALES ON SUNDAY, circ. 41,199 267

Radyr
W CARDIFF POST SERIES, circ. 103,812 F 158
D SOUTH WALES ECHO, circ. 46,127 251

W **Local/Weekly Newspapers**   D **Regional Daily Newspapers**   S **Regional Sunday Newspapers**   F **Free Newspapers**

Title (Day/am/pm)	Circ.	Page No.

S WALES ON SUNDAY, circ. 41,199 267

Taff's Well
W PONTYPRIDD AND LLANTRISANT OBSERVER, circ. 11,429 236
D SOUTH WALES ECHO, circ. 46,127 251
S TAFOD ELAÍ, circ. 800 261
S WALES ON SUNDAY, circ. 41,199 267

Carmarthenshire UA
W THE CARDIFF & SOUTH WALES ADVERTISER, circ. 30,000 F 158

Ammanford
W GLO MÂN, circ. 600 191
W JOURNAL SERIES (CARMARTHEN), circ. 20,800 205
W LLANELLI STAR SERIES, circ. 15,699 213
D SOUTH WALES EVENING POST, circ. 51,329 251
W SOUTH WALES GUARDIAN SERIES, circ. 8,533 251
S WALES ON SUNDAY, circ. 41,199 267

Brynamman
W SOUTH WALES GUARDIAN SERIES, circ. 8,533 251

Burry Port
W LLANELLI STAR SERIES, circ. 15,699 213

Carmarthen
W JOURNAL SERIES (CARMARTHEN), circ. 20,800 205
W LLANELLI STAR SERIES, circ. 15,699 213
D SOUTH WALES EVENING POST, circ. 51,329 251
W SOUTH WALES GUARDIAN SERIES, circ. 8,533 251
W WESTERN TELEGRAPH SERIES, circ. 25,627 273

Cross Hands
W LLANELLI STAR SERIES, circ. 15,699 213
W PAPUR Y CWM, circ. 1,200 235
W SOUTH WALES GUARDIAN SERIES, circ. 8,533 251

Cwmllynfell
W LLAIS, circ. 990 213
D SOUTH WALES EVENING POST, circ. 51,329 251
W SOUTH WALES GUARDIAN SERIES, circ. 8,533 251
S WALES ON SUNDAY, circ. 41,199 267

Glanaman
W JOURNAL SERIES (CARMARTHEN), circ. 20,800 205
D SOUTH WALES EVENING POST, circ. 51,329 251
W SOUTH WALES GUARDIAN SERIES, circ. 8,533 251
S WALES ON SUNDAY, circ. 41,199 267

Kidwelly
W LLANELLI STAR SERIES, circ. 15,699 213

Llandovery
W BRECON AND RADNOR EXPRESS, circ. 27,326 151
W JOURNAL SERIES (CARMARTHEN), circ. 20,800 205
W SOUTH WALES GUARDIAN SERIES, circ. 8,533 251

Llandybie
W SOUTH WALES GUARDIAN SERIES, circ. 8,533 251

Llanelli
W LLANELLI STAR SERIES, circ. 15,699 213
W PAPUR Y CWM, circ. 1,200 235
D SOUTH WALES EVENING POST, circ. 51,329 251
S WALES ON SUNDAY, circ. 41,199 267

Pembrey
W LLANELLI STAR SERIES, circ. 15,699 213

Pontyberem
W LLANELLI STAR SERIES, circ. 15,699 213
W PAPUR Y CWM, circ. 1,200 235
D SOUTH WALES EVENING POST, circ. 51,329 251
W SOUTH WALES GUARDIAN SERIES, circ. 8,533 251
S WALES ON SUNDAY, circ. 41,199 267

Trimsaran
W LLANELLI STAR SERIES, circ. 15,699 213
W PAPUR Y CWM, circ. 1,200 235
D SOUTH WALES EVENING POST, circ. 51,329 251
S WALES ON SUNDAY, circ. 41,199 267

Whitland
W JOURNAL SERIES (CARMARTHEN), circ. 20,800 205
W TENBY, NARBERTH & WHITLAND OBSERVER SERIES, circ. 7,431 263
W WESTERN TELEGRAPH SERIES, circ. 25,627 273

Ceredigion UA
D Y DAILY POST CYMRAEG 170
D DAILY POST (WALES), circ. 36,432 170

Aberaeron
W THE CAMBRIAN NEWS SERIES, circ. 24,400 156
W Y GAMBO, circ. 1,300 188

W TIVY-SIDE ADVERTISER, circ. 8,720 264

Aberystwyth
W YR ANGOR (ABERYSTWYTH), circ. 700 142
W YR ANGOR (LIVERPOOL), circ. 3,000 142
W BLEWYN GLAS, circ. 1,200 149
W THE CAMBRIAN NEWS SERIES, circ. 24,400 156
W Y TINCER, circ. 1,200 264
S WALES ON SUNDAY, circ. 41,199 267

Cardigan
W THE CAMBRIAN NEWS SERIES, circ. 24,400 156
W COUNTY ECHO AND ST. DAVIDS CITY CHRONICLE, circ. 3,500 166
W Y GAMBO, circ. 1,300 188
W Y GARTHEN, circ. 700 188
W JOURNAL SERIES (CARMARTHEN), circ. 20,800 205
W TIVY-SIDE ADVERTISER, circ. 8,720 264
W WALES ON SUNDAY, circ. 41,199 267
W WESTERN TELEGRAPH SERIES, circ. 25,627 273

Lampeter
W THE CAMBRIAN NEWS SERIES, circ. 24,400 156
W Y GARTHEN, circ. 700 188
S WALES ON SUNDAY, circ. 41,199 267

New Quay
W TIVY-SIDE ADVERTISER, circ. 8,720 264

Newcastle Emlyn
W THE CAMBRIAN NEWS SERIES, circ. 24,400 156
W Y GAMBO, circ. 1,300 188
W Y GARTHEN, circ. 700 188
W JOURNAL SERIES (CARMARTHEN), circ. 20,800 205
W TIVY-SIDE ADVERTISER, circ. 8,720 264

Conwy UA
D Y DAILY POST CYMRAEG 170
D DAILY POST (WALES), circ. 36,432 170

Abergele
W THE JOURNAL RHYL, PRESTATYN AND ABERGELE, circ. 30,287 F 205
W VISITOR SERIES, circ. 27,702 267

Betws-y-Coed
W NORTH WALES WEEKLY NEWS SERIES, circ. 17,314 230

Colwyn Bay
W NORTH WALES WEEKLY NEWS SERIES, circ. 17,314 230
W THE PIONEER (NORTH WALES), circ. 30,672 236

Conwy
W NORTH WALES WEEKLY NEWS SERIES, circ. 17,314 230
W THE PIONEER (NORTH WALES), circ. 30,672 236

Deganwy
W NORTH WALES WEEKLY NEWS SERIES, circ. 17,314 230
W THE PIONEER (NORTH WALES), circ. 30,672 236
S WALES ON SUNDAY, circ. 41,199 267

Llandudno
W NORTH WALES WEEKLY NEWS SERIES, circ. 17,314 230
W THE PIONEER (NORTH WALES), circ. 30,672 236

Llandudno Junction
W NORTH WALES WEEKLY NEWS SERIES, circ. 17,314 230
W THE PIONEER (NORTH WALES), circ. 30,672 236
S WALES ON SUNDAY, circ. 41,199 267

Llanrwst
W NORTH WALES WEEKLY NEWS SERIES, circ. 17,314 230

Penmaenmawr
W NORTH WALES WEEKLY NEWS SERIES, circ. 17,314 230

Penrhyn Bay
W NORTH WALES WEEKLY NEWS SERIES, circ. 17,314 230
W THE PIONEER (NORTH WALES), circ. 30,672 236
S WALES ON SUNDAY, circ. 41,199 267

Rhos-on-Sea
W THE PIONEER (NORTH WALES), circ. 30,672 236

Denbighshire UA
D Y DAILY POST CYMRAEG 170
D DAILY POST (WALES), circ. 36,432 170

Cefn-Mawr
D EVENING LEADER, circ. 21,180 181
D SHROPSHIRE STAR, circ. 72,000 247
D SHROPSHIRE STAR (CITY/LONDON OFFICE) 247
S WALES ON SUNDAY, circ. 41,199 267
W WREXHAM LEADER, circ. 42,138 F 278

Corwen
W DENBIGHSHIRE FREE PRESS SERIES, circ. 7,148 172
W NORTH WALES SERIES 230
W YOUR VALE, circ. 7,992 F 279

Denbigh
W DENBIGHSHIRE FREE PRESS SERIES, circ. 7,148 172
W Y GADLAS, circ. 1,600 187
W YOUR VALE, circ. 7,992 F 279

Dyserth
W THE JOURNAL RHYL, PRESTATYN AND ABERGELE, circ. 30,287 F 205
W VISITOR SERIES, circ. 27,702 267
S WALES ON SUNDAY, circ. 41,199 267

Llangollen
D EVENING LEADER, circ. 21,180 181
D SHROPSHIRE STAR, circ. 72,000 247
D SHROPSHIRE STAR (CITY/LONDON OFFICE) 247
W WREXHAM CHRONICLE, circ. 38,278 F 278

Prestatyn
D EVENING LEADER, circ. 21,180 181
W Y GLANNAU, circ. 1,000 190
W THE JOURNAL RHYL, PRESTATYN AND ABERGELE, circ. 30,287 F 205
W VISITOR SERIES, circ. 27,702 267

Rhuddlan
W Y GLANNAU, circ. 1,000 190
W THE JOURNAL RHYL, PRESTATYN AND ABERGELE, circ. 30,287 F 205
W VISITOR SERIES, circ. 27,702 267

Rhyl
W YR ANGOR (LIVERPOOL), circ. 3,000 142
D EVENING LEADER, circ. 21,180 181
W Y GLANNAU, circ. 1,000 190
W THE JOURNAL RHYL, PRESTATYN AND ABERGELE, circ. 30,287 F 205
W VISITOR SERIES, circ. 27,702 267

Ruthin
W Y BEDOL, circ. 2,500 147
W DENBIGHSHIRE FREE PRESS SERIES, circ. 7,148 172
W YOUR VALE, circ. 7,992 F 279

St. Asaph
W DENBIGHSHIRE FREE PRESS SERIES, circ. 7,148 172
W Y GLANNAU, circ. 1,000 190
W THE JOURNAL RHYL, PRESTATYN AND ABERGELE, circ. 30,287 F 205
W VISITOR SERIES, circ. 27,702 267

Flintshire UA
D Y DAILY POST CYMRAEG 170
W FLINTSHIRE STANDARD, circ. 31,482 F 186

Bagillt
D EVENING LEADER, circ. 21,180 181
S WALES ON SUNDAY, circ. 41,199 267

Buckley
W FLINTSHIRE CHRONICLE 185

Flint
W FLINTSHIRE CHRONICLE 185

Hawarden
D EVENING LEADER, circ. 21,180 181
S WALES ON SUNDAY, circ. 41,199 267

Holywell
W FLINTSHIRE CHRONICLE 185
W Y GLANNAU, circ. 1,000 190

Hope
D EVENING LEADER, circ. 21,180 181
D SHROPSHIRE STAR, circ. 72,000 247
D SHROPSHIRE STAR (CITY/LONDON OFFICE) 247
S WALES ON SUNDAY, circ. 41,199 267
W WREXHAM LEADER, circ. 42,138 F 278

Llay
D EVENING LEADER, circ. 21,180 181
D NENE, circ. 850 225
D SHROPSHIRE STAR, circ. 72,000 247
D SHROPSHIRE STAR (CITY/LONDON OFFICE) 247
S WALES ON SUNDAY, circ. 41,199 267
W WREXHAM LEADER, circ. 42,138 F 278

W **Local/Weekly Newspapers**   D **Regional Daily Newspapers**   S **Regional Sunday Newspapers**   F **Free Newspapers**

Non-Nationals - Wales

Title (Day/am/pm)	Circ.	Page No.

Mold
W YR ANGOR (LIVERPOOL), circ. 3,000 142
W FLINTSHIRE CHRONICLE 185

Penyffordd
D EVENING LEADER, circ. 21,180 181
S WALES ON SUNDAY, circ. 41,199 267

Shotton
D EVENING LEADER, circ. 21,180 181
S WALES ON SUNDAY, circ. 41,199 267

Gwynedd UA
D Y DAILY POST CYMRAEG 170
D DAILY POST (WALES), circ. 36,432 170

Bala
W THE CAMBRIAN NEWS SERIES, circ. 24,400 156
D DENBIGHSHIRE FREE PRESS SERIES, circ. 7,148 172
W PETHE PENLLYN, circ. 600 236

Bangor
W THE CAERNARFON HERALD SERIES, circ. 35,574 ... 156
W NORTH WALES CHRONICLE, circ. 33,870 F 230
S WALES ON SUNDAY, circ. 41,199 267

Barmouth
W THE CAMBRIAN NEWS SERIES, circ. 24,400 156
W NORTH WALES SERIES 230
S WALES ON SUNDAY, circ. 41,199 267

Bethesda
W NORTH WALES CHRONICLE, circ. 33,870 F 230

Blaenau Ffestiniog
W THE CAMBRIAN NEWS SERIES, circ. 24,400 156

Caernarfon
W YR ANGOR (LIVERPOOL), circ. 3,000 142
W THE CAERNARFON HERALD SERIES, circ. 35,574 ... 156
W NORTH WALES CHRONICLE, circ. 33,870 F 230

Dolgellau
W THE CAMBRIAN NEWS SERIES, circ. 24,400 156
W Y DYDD, circ. 1,000 176

Llanfairfechan
W NORTH WALES WEEKLY NEWS SERIES,
circ. 17,314 230

Porthmadog
W THE CAERNARFON HERALD SERIES, circ. 35,574 ... 156
W THE CAMBRIAN NEWS SERIES, circ. 24,400 156

Pwllheli
W THE CAERNARFON HERALD SERIES, circ. 35,574 ... 156
W THE CAMBRIAN NEWS SERIES, circ. 24,400 156
W LLANW LLYN, circ. 2,250 213

Tywyn
W THE CAMBRIAN NEWS SERIES, circ. 24,400 156
W DAIL DYSYNNI, circ. 1,000 169

Isle of Anglesey UA
W THE CAERNARFON HERALD SERIES, circ. 35,574 ... 156
D Y DAILY POST CYMRAEG 170
D DAILY POST (WALES), circ. 36,432 170
W Y RHWYD, circ. 1,350 240

Amlwch
W YR ARWYDD, circ. 1,400 143
W NORTH WALES CHRONICLE, circ. 33,870 F 230

Holyhead
W THE CAERNARFON HERALD SERIES, circ. 35,574 ... 156
W NORTH WALES CHRONICLE, circ. 33,870 F 230
S WALES ON SUNDAY, circ. 41,199 267

Llanfairpwllgwyngyll
W NORTH WALES CHRONICLE, circ. 33,870 F 230
S WALES ON SUNDAY, circ. 41,199 267

Llangefni
W YR ANGOR (LIVERPOOL), circ. 3,000 142
W Y GLORIAN, circ. 1,700 191
W NORTH WALES CHRONICLE, circ. 33,870 F 230

Menai Bridge
W NORTH WALES CHRONICLE, circ. 33,870 F 230
S WALES ON SUNDAY, circ. 41,199 267

Valley
W NORTH WALES CHRONICLE, circ. 33,870 F 230
S WALES ON SUNDAY, circ. 41,199 267

Merthyr Tydfil UA
W THE CARDIFF & SOUTH WALES ADVERTISER,
circ. 30,000 F 158

Abercarnaid
W MERTHYR EXPRESS 220
W MERTHYR EXPRESS SERIES, circ. 17,138 220
D SOUTH WALES ECHO, circ. 46,127 251
S WALES ON SUNDAY, circ. 41,199 267

Merthyr Tydfil
W MERTHYR EXPRESS 220
W MERTHYR EXPRESS SERIES, circ. 17,138 220
D SOUTH WALES ECHO, circ. 46,127 251
S WALES ON SUNDAY, circ. 41,199 267

Merthyr Vale
W MERTHYR EXPRESS 220
W MERTHYR EXPRESS SERIES, circ. 17,138 220
D SOUTH WALES ECHO, circ. 46,127 251
S WALES ON SUNDAY, circ. 41,199 267

Treharris
D SOUTH WALES ECHO, circ. 46,127 251
S WALES ON SUNDAY, circ. 41,199 267

Troedyrhiw
W MERTHYR EXPRESS 220
W MERTHYR EXPRESS SERIES, circ. 17,138 220
D SOUTH WALES ECHO, circ. 46,127 251
S WALES ON SUNDAY, circ. 41,199 267

Monmouthshire UA
W THE CARDIFF & SOUTH WALES ADVERTISER,
circ. 30,000 F 158

Abergavenny
W ABERGAVENNY CHRONICLE SERIES, circ. 15,000 ... 137
W THE FREE PRESS NEWSPAPER SERIES,
circ. 11,281 187
W GWENT GAZETTE, circ. 11,495 194
W HEREFORD TIMES, circ. 39,876 198
D SOUTH WALES ARGUS, circ. 28,879 250
S WALES ON SUNDAY, circ. 41,199 267

Caldicot
W FOREST OF DEAN AND WYE VALLEY REVIEW,
circ. 43,124 F 186
W THE FREE PRESS NEWSPAPER SERIES,
circ. 11,281 187

Chepstow
W FOREST OF DEAN AND WYE VALLEY REVIEW,
circ. 43,124 F 186
W THE FORESTER (FOREST OF DEAN), circ. 13,000 186
W THE FREE PRESS NEWSPAPER SERIES,
circ. 11,281 187
D SOUTH WALES ARGUS, circ. 28,879 250
D WESTERN DAILY PRESS BRISTOL, circ. 41,639 272

Monmouth
W ABERGAVENNY CHRONICLE SERIES, circ. 15,000 ... 137
W FOREST OF DEAN AND WYE VALLEY REVIEW,
circ. 43,124 F 186
W THE FORESTER (FOREST OF DEAN), circ. 13,000 186
W THE FREE PRESS NEWSPAPER SERIES,
circ. 11,281 187
W HEREFORD TIMES, circ. 39,876 198
W MONMOUTHSHIRE BEACON AND MERLIN SERIES,
circ. 10,800 224
D SOUTH WALES ARGUS, circ. 28,879 250
D WESTERN DAILY PRESS BRISTOL, circ. 41,639 272

Sedbury
W THE FREE PRESS NEWSPAPER SERIES,
circ. 11,281 187
D SOUTH WALES ARGUS, circ. 28,879 250
S WALES ON SUNDAY, circ. 41,199 267
D WESTERN DAILY PRESS BRISTOL, circ. 41,639 272

Tutshill
W THE FREE PRESS NEWSPAPER SERIES,
circ. 11,281 187
D SOUTH WALES ARGUS, circ. 28,879 250
S WALES ON SUNDAY, circ. 41,199 267
D WESTERN DAILY PRESS BRISTOL, circ. 41,639 272

Neath & Port Talbot UA
W THE CARDIFF & SOUTH WALES ADVERTISER,
circ. 30,000 F 158

Glyn Neath
W NEATH GUARDIAN SERIES, circ. 4,402 225

Neath
W THE COURIER SERIES (NEATH & PORT TALBOT),
circ. 16,695 167
W NEATH AND PORT TALBOT TRIBUNE,
circ. 46,000 F 225
W NEATH GUARDIAN SERIES, circ. 4,402 225
D SOUTH WALES EVENING POST, circ. 51,329 251
S WALES ON SUNDAY, circ. 41,199 267

Port Talbot
W THE COURIER SERIES (NEATH & PORT TALBOT),
circ. 16,695 167
W NEATH AND PORT TALBOT TRIBUNE,
circ. 46,000 F 225
W NEATH GUARDIAN SERIES, circ. 4,402 225
D SOUTH WALES EVENING POST, circ. 51,329 251
S WALES ON SUNDAY, circ. 41,199 267

Resolven
W NEATH GUARDIAN SERIES, circ. 4,402 225
D SOUTH WALES EVENING POST, circ. 51,329 251
S WALES ON SUNDAY, circ. 41,199 267

Seven Sisters
W NEATH GUARDIAN SERIES, circ. 4,402 225
D SOUTH WALES EVENING POST, circ. 51,329 251
S WALES ON SUNDAY, circ. 41,199 267

Newport UA
W THE CARDIFF & SOUTH WALES ADVERTISER,
circ. 30,000 F 158

Caerleon
W THE FREE PRESS NEWSPAPER SERIES,
circ. 11,281 187
D SOUTH WALES ARGUS, circ. 28,879 250
S WALES ON SUNDAY, circ. 41,199 267

Newport
W THE FREE PRESS NEWSPAPER SERIES,
circ. 11,281 187
W NEWPORT & CWMBRAN WEEKLY ARGUS,
circ. 34,670 F 226
D SOUTH WALES ARGUS, circ. 28,879 250
D SOUTH WALES ECHO, circ. 46,127 251
S WALES ON SUNDAY, circ. 41,199 267

Pembrokeshire UA

Fishguard
W COUNTY ECHO AND ST. DAVIDS CITY CHRONICLE,
circ. 3,500 166
W TIVY-SIDE ADVERTISER, circ. 8,720 264
W WESTERN TELEGRAPH SERIES, circ. 25,627 273

Haverfordwest
W COUNTY ECHO AND ST. DAVIDS CITY CHRONICLE,
circ. 3,500 166
W MILFORD & WEST WALES MERCURY, circ. 5,565 223
S WALES ON SUNDAY, circ. 41,199 267
W WESTERN TELEGRAPH SERIES, circ. 25,627 273

Milford Haven
W MILFORD & WEST WALES MERCURY, circ. 5,565 223
W WESTERN TELEGRAPH SERIES, circ. 25,627 273

Narberth
W TENBY, NARBERTH & WHITLAND OBSERVER SERIES,
circ. 7,431 263
W WESTERN TELEGRAPH SERIES, circ. 25,627 273

Newport
W TIVY-SIDE ADVERTISER, circ. 8,720 264

Neyland
W MILFORD & WEST WALES MERCURY, circ. 5,565 223
W WESTERN TELEGRAPH SERIES, circ. 25,627 273

Pembroke
W MILFORD & WEST WALES MERCURY, circ. 5,565 223
W TENBY, NARBERTH & WHITLAND OBSERVER SERIES,
circ. 7,431 263
S WALES ON SUNDAY, circ. 41,199 267
W WESTERN TELEGRAPH SERIES, circ. 25,627 273

Pembroke Dock
W MILFORD & WEST WALES MERCURY, circ. 5,565 223
W TENBY, NARBERTH & WHITLAND OBSERVER SERIES,
circ. 7,431 263
S WALES ON SUNDAY, circ. 41,199 267
W WESTERN TELEGRAPH SERIES, circ. 25,627 273

Saundersfoot
W TENBY, NARBERTH & WHITLAND OBSERVER SERIES,
circ. 7,431 263

W **Local/Weekly Newspapers**   D **Regional Daily Newspapers**   S **Regional Sunday Newspapers**   F **Free Newspapers**

Title (Day/am/pm)	Circ.	Page No.	Title (Day/am/pm)	Circ.	Page No.	Title (Day/am/pm)	Circ.	Page No.

St. David's

W COUNTY ECHO AND ST. DAVIDS CITY CHRONICLE, circ. 3,500 166
W WESTERN TELEGRAPH SERIES, circ. 25,627 273

Tenby

W TENBY, NARBERTH & WHITLAND OBSERVER SERIES, circ. 7,431 263
W WESTERN TELEGRAPH SERIES, circ. 25,627 273

Powys UA

D Y DAILY POST CYMRAEG 170
D DAILY POST (WALES), circ. 36,432 170

Abertridwr

W CAERPHILLY CAMPAIGN SERIES, circ. 70,860 F 156
D SOUTH WALES ECHO, circ. 46,127 251
S WALES ON SUNDAY, circ. 41,199 267

Brecon

W BRECON AND RADNOR EXPRESS, circ. 27,326 151
W HEREFORD TIMES, circ. 39,876 198
S WALES ON SUNDAY, circ. 41,199 267

Builth Wells

W BRECON AND RADNOR EXPRESS, circ. 27,326 151
W POWYS COUNTY TIMES, EXPRESS & GAZETTE, circ. 17,628 237

Crickhowell

W ABERGAVENNY CHRONICLE SERIES, circ. 15,000 ... 137
W BRECON AND RADNOR EXPRESS, circ. 27,326 151
D SOUTH WALES ARGUS, circ. 28,879 250
S WALES ON SUNDAY, circ. 41,199 267

Hay-on-Wye

W BRECON AND RADNOR EXPRESS, circ. 27,326 151
W HEREFORD TIMES, circ. 39,876 198

Knighton

W BRECON AND RADNOR EXPRESS, circ. 27,326 151
W HEREFORD TIMES, circ. 39,876 198
W POWYS COUNTY TIMES, EXPRESS & GAZETTE, circ. 17,628 237
D SHROPSHIRE STAR, circ. 72,000 247
D SHROPSHIRE STAR (CITY/LONDON OFFICE) 247

Llandrindod Wells

W BRECON AND RADNOR EXPRESS, circ. 27,326 151
W CHRONICLE & JOURNAL SERIES, circ. 87,901 161
W POWYS COUNTY TIMES, EXPRESS & GAZETTE, circ. 17,628 237

Llanfyllin

W OSWESTRY AND BORDER COUNTIES ADVERTIZER, circ. 10,969 234
W PLU'R GWEUNYDD, circ. 750 236
W POWYS COUNTY TIMES, EXPRESS & GAZETTE, circ. 17,628 237
D SHROPSHIRE STAR, circ. 72,000 247
D SHROPSHIRE STAR (CITY/LONDON OFFICE) 247

Llanidloes

W THE CAMBRIAN NEWS SERIES, circ. 24,400 156
W POWYS COUNTY TIMES, EXPRESS & GAZETTE, circ. 17,628 237
D SHROPSHIRE STAR, circ. 72,000 247
D SHROPSHIRE STAR (CITY/LONDON OFFICE) 247

Machynlleth

W BLEWYN GLAS, circ. 1,200 149
W THE CAMBRIAN NEWS SERIES, circ. 24,400 156
W POWYS COUNTY TIMES, EXPRESS & GAZETTE, circ. 17,628 237
D SHROPSHIRE STAR, circ. 72,000 247
D SHROPSHIRE STAR (CITY/LONDON OFFICE) 247

Montgomery

W ADMAG NEWSPAPERS SERIES, circ. 181,809 F ... 137
W POWYS COUNTY TIMES, EXPRESS & GAZETTE, circ. 17,628 237
D SHROPSHIRE STAR, circ. 72,000 247
D SHROPSHIRE STAR (CITY/LONDON OFFICE) 247

Newtown

W BLEWYN GLAS, circ. 1,200 149
W POWYS COUNTY TIMES, EXPRESS & GAZETTE, circ. 17,628 237
W SEREN HAFREN, circ. 500 245
D SHROPSHIRE STAR, circ. 72,000 247
D SHROPSHIRE STAR (CITY/LONDON OFFICE) 247

Presteigne

W BRECON AND RADNOR EXPRESS, circ. 27,326 151
W HEREFORD TIMES, circ. 39,876 198
W POWYS COUNTY TIMES, EXPRESS & GAZETTE, circ. 17,628 237

D SHROPSHIRE STAR, circ. 72,000 247
D SHROPSHIRE STAR (CITY/LONDON OFFICE) 247

Rhayader

W BRECON AND RADNOR EXPRESS, circ. 27,326 151
W THE CAMBRIAN NEWS SERIES, circ. 24,400 156
W POWYS COUNTY TIMES, EXPRESS & GAZETTE, circ. 17,628 237
D SHROPSHIRE STAR, circ. 72,000 247
D SHROPSHIRE STAR (CITY/LONDON OFFICE) 247

Senghenydd

W CAERPHILLY CAMPAIGN SERIES, circ. 70,860 F ... 156
D SOUTH WALES ECHO, circ. 46,127 251
S WALES ON SUNDAY, circ. 41,199 267

Welshpool

W PLU'R GWEUNYDD, circ. 750 236
W POWYS COUNTY TIMES, EXPRESS & GAZETTE, circ. 17,628 237
D SHROPSHIRE STAR, circ. 72,000 247
D SHROPSHIRE STAR (CITY/LONDON OFFICE) 247

Ystalyfera

W LLAIS, circ. 990 213
D SOUTH WALES EVENING POST, circ. 51,329 251
D SOUTH WALES GUARDIAN SERIES, circ. 8,533 251
S WALES ON SUNDAY, circ. 41,199 267

Ystradgynlais

W BRECON AND RADNOR EXPRESS, circ. 27,326 151
D SOUTH WALES EVENING POST, circ. 51,329 251
D SOUTH WALES GUARDIAN SERIES, circ. 8,533 251
S WALES ON SUNDAY, circ. 41,199 267

Rhondda Cynon Taff UA

W THE CARDIFF & SOUTH WALES ADVERTISER, circ. 30,000 F 158

Abercynon

W CYNON VALLEY LEADER, circ. 10,137 169
D SOUTH WALES ECHO, circ. 46,127 251
S WALES ON SUNDAY, circ. 41,199 267

Aberdare

W CLOCHDAR, circ. 550 163
W CYNON VALLEY LEADER, circ. 10,137 169
D SOUTH WALES ECHO, circ. 46,127 251
S WALES ON SUNDAY, circ. 41,199 267

Beddau

W PONTYPRIDD AND LLANTRISANT OBSERVER, circ. 11,429 236
D SOUTH WALES ECHO, circ. 46,127 251
S WALES ON SUNDAY, circ. 41,199 267

Church Village

W PONTYPRIDD AND LLANTRISANT OBSERVER, circ. 11,429 236
D SOUTH WALES ECHO, circ. 46,127 251
S WALES ON SUNDAY, circ. 41,199 267

Cwmbach

W CYNON VALLEY LEADER, circ. 10,137 169
D SOUTH WALES ECHO, circ. 46,127 251
S WALES ON SUNDAY, circ. 41,199 267

Ferndale

W CAERPHILLY CAMPAIGN SERIES, circ. 70,860 F ... 156
D SOUTH WALES ECHO, circ. 46,127 251
S WALES ON SUNDAY, circ. 41,199 267

Glyncoch

W PONTYPRIDD AND LLANTRISANT OBSERVER, circ. 11,429 236
D SOUTH WALES ECHO, circ. 46,127 251
S WALES ON SUNDAY, circ. 41,199 267

Llanharan

W GLAMORGAN GAZETTE SERIES, circ. 21,504 190
W PONTYPRIDD AND LLANTRISANT OBSERVER, circ. 11,429 236
D SOUTH WALES ECHO, circ. 46,127 251
S WALES ON SUNDAY, circ. 41,199 267

Llanharry

W GLAMORGAN GAZETTE SERIES, circ. 21,504 190
D SOUTH WALES ECHO, circ. 46,127 251
S WALES ON SUNDAY, circ. 41,199 267

Llantrisant

W CAERPHILLY CAMPAIGN SERIES, circ. 70,860 F 156
W CARDIFF POST SERIES, circ. 103,812 F 158
W PONTYPRIDD AND LLANTRISANT OBSERVER, circ. 11,429 236
D SOUTH WALES ECHO, circ. 46,127 251
W TAFOD ELAÍ, circ. 800 261
S WALES ON SUNDAY, circ. 41,199 267

Maerdy

D SOUTH WALES ECHO, circ. 46,127 251
S WALES ON SUNDAY, circ. 41,199 267

Mountain Ash

W CAERPHILLY CAMPAIGN SERIES, circ. 70,860 F ... 156
W CYNON VALLEY LEADER, circ. 10,137 169
D SOUTH WALES ECHO, circ. 46,127 251
S WALES ON SUNDAY, circ. 41,199 267

Pentyrch

D SOUTH WALES ECHO, circ. 46,127 251
W TAFOD ELAÍ, circ. 800 261
S WALES ON SUNDAY, circ. 41,199 267

Pontyclun

W PONTYPRIDD AND LLANTRISANT OBSERVER, circ. 11,429 236
D SOUTH WALES ECHO, circ. 46,127 251
S WALES ON SUNDAY, circ. 41,199 267

Pontypridd

W CAERPHILLY CAMPAIGN SERIES, circ. 70,860 F 156
W PONTYPRIDD AND LLANTRISANT OBSERVER, circ. 11,429 236
D SOUTH WALES ECHO, circ. 46,127 251
W TAFOD ELAÍ, circ. 800 261
S WALES ON SUNDAY, circ. 41,199 267

Rhondda

W CAERPHILLY CAMPAIGN SERIES, circ. 70,860 F ... 156
W RHONDDA LEADER, circ. 12,500 240
D SOUTH WALES ECHO, circ. 46,127 251
S WALES ON SUNDAY, circ. 41,199 267

Tonyrefail

W PONTYPRIDD AND LLANTRISANT OBSERVER, circ. 11,429 236
D SOUTH WALES ECHO, circ. 46,127 251
W TAFOD ELAÍ, circ. 800 261
S WALES ON SUNDAY, circ. 41,199 267

Swansea UA

W THE CARDIFF & SOUTH WALES ADVERTISER, circ. 30,000 F 158

Bishopston

D SOUTH WALES EVENING POST, circ. 51,329 251
W SWANSEA HERALD OF WALES, circ. 67,297 F 261
S WALES ON SUNDAY, circ. 41,199 267

Clydach

W LLAIS, circ. 990 213
D SOUTH WALES EVENING POST, circ. 51,329 251
W SOUTH WALES GUARDIAN SERIES, circ. 8,533 251
W SWANSEA HERALD OF WALES, circ. 67,297 F 261
S WALES ON SUNDAY, circ. 41,199 267

Gorseinon

W LLANELLI STAR SERIES, circ. 15,699 213
W SWANSEA HERALD OF WALES, circ. 67,297 F 261

Gowerton

W LLANELLI STAR SERIES, circ. 15,699 213

Loughor

W LLANELLI STAR SERIES, circ. 15,699 213

Pen-clawdd

D SOUTH WALES EVENING POST, circ. 51,329 251
W SWANSEA HERALD OF WALES, circ. 67,297 F 261
S WALES ON SUNDAY, circ. 41,199 267

Pontardawe

W THE COURIER SERIES (NEATH & PORT TALBOT), circ. 16,695 167
W LLAIS, circ. 990 213
W SOUTH WALES GUARDIAN SERIES, circ. 8,533 251

Pontardulais

W LLANELLI STAR SERIES, circ. 15,699 213
W SOUTH WALES GUARDIAN SERIES, circ. 8,533 251

Southgate

D SOUTH WALES EVENING POST, circ. 51,329 251
W SWANSEA HERALD OF WALES, circ. 67,297 F 261
S WALES ON SUNDAY, circ. 41,199 267

Swansea

W YR ANGOR (LIVERPOOL), circ. 3,000 142
W THE COURIER SERIES (NEATH & PORT TALBOT), circ. 16,695 167
W LLAIS, circ. 990 213
D SOUTH WALES EVENING POST, circ. 51,329 251
W SOUTH WALES GUARDIAN SERIES, circ. 8,533 251
W SWANSEA HERALD OF WALES, circ. 67,297 F 261
S WALES ON SUNDAY, circ. 41,199 267

W Local/Weekly Newspapers   D Regional Daily Newspapers   S Regional Sunday Newspapers   F Free Newspapers

Non-Nationals - Wales

Title (Day/am/pm)	Circ.	Page No.

Torfaen UA

Blaenavon
W ABERGAVENNY CHRONICLE SERIES, circ. 15,000 ... 137
W THE FREE PRESS NEWSPAPER SERIES,
circ. 11,281 187

Cwmavon
W THE FREE PRESS NEWSPAPER SERIES,
circ. 11,281 187
S WALES ON SUNDAY, circ. 41,199 267

Cwmbran
W THE FREE PRESS NEWSPAPER SERIES,
circ. 11,281 187
W NEWPORT & CWMBRAN WEEKLY ARGUS,
circ. 34,670 F 226
D SOUTH WALES ARGUS, circ. 28,879 250
D SOUTH WALES ECHO, circ. 46,127 251
S WALES ON SUNDAY, circ. 41,199 267

Pontypool
W THE FREE PRESS NEWSPAPER SERIES,
circ. 11,281 187
D SOUTH WALES ARGUS, circ. 28,879 250
S WALES ON SUNDAY, circ. 41,199 267

Vale of Glamorgan UA

W THE CARDIFF & SOUTH WALES ADVERTISER,
circ. 30,000 F 158

Barry
W BARRY & DISTRICT NEWS SERIES, circ. 12,864 145
W CARDIFF POST SERIES, circ. 103,812 F 158
W GEM SERIES, circ. 36,196 F 190
D SOUTH WALES ECHO, circ. 46,127 251
S WALES ON SUNDAY, circ. 41,199 267

Cowbridge
W CARDIFF POST SERIES, circ. 103,812 F 158
W GEM SERIES, circ. 36,196 F 190
D SOUTH WALES ECHO, circ. 46,127 251

Dinas Powis
W BARRY & DISTRICT NEWS SERIES, circ. 12,864 145
W CARDIFF POST SERIES, circ. 103,812 F 158
W PENARTH TIMES, circ. 6,183 235
D SOUTH WALES ECHO, circ. 46,127 251

S WALES ON SUNDAY, circ. 41,199 267

Llantwit Major
W BARRY & DISTRICT NEWS SERIES, circ. 12,864 145
W CARDIFF POST SERIES, circ. 103,812 F 158
W GEM SERIES, circ. 36,196 190
D SOUTH WALES ECHO, circ. 46,127 251

Penarth
W BARRY & DISTRICT NEWS SERIES, circ. 12,864 145
W CARDIFF POST SERIES, circ. 103,812 F 158
W PENARTH TIMES, circ. 6,183 235
D SOUTH WALES ECHO, circ. 46,127 251
S WALES ON SUNDAY, circ. 41,199 267

Rhoose
W BARRY & DISTRICT NEWS SERIES, circ. 12,864 145
W CARDIFF POST SERIES, circ. 103,812 F 158
W GEM SERIES, circ. 36,196 F 190

St. Athan
W BARRY & DISTRICT NEWS SERIES, circ. 12,864 145
W CARDIFF POST SERIES, circ. 103,812 F 158
W GEM SERIES, circ. 36,196 F 190
D SOUTH WALES ECHO, circ. 46,127 251
S WALES ON SUNDAY, circ. 41,199 267

Wrexham UA

D Y DAILY POST CYMRAEG 170
D DAILY POST (WALES), circ. 36,432 170

Brymbo
D EVENING LEADER, circ. 21,180 181
D SHROPSHIRE STAR, circ. 72,000 247
D SHROPSHIRE STAR (CITY/LONDON OFFICE) 247
S WALES ON SUNDAY, circ. 41,199 267
W WREXHAM LEADER, circ. 42,138 F 278

Chirk
D EVENING LEADER, circ. 21,180 181
O OSWESTRY AND BORDER COUNTIES ADVERTIZER,
circ. 10,969 234
D SHROPSHIRE STAR, circ. 72,000 247
D SHROPSHIRE STAR (CITY/LONDON OFFICE) 247
S WALES ON SUNDAY, circ. 41,199 267
W WREXHAM LEADER, circ. 42,138 F 278

Coedpoeth
D SHROPSHIRE STAR, circ. 72,000 247

D SHROPSHIRE STAR (CITY/LONDON OFFICE) 247
S WALES ON SUNDAY, circ. 41,199 267
W WREXHAM LEADER, circ. 42,138 F 278

Gresford
D EVENING LEADER, circ. 21,180 181
W NENE, circ. 850 225
D SHROPSHIRE STAR, circ. 72,000 247
D SHROPSHIRE STAR (CITY/LONDON OFFICE) 247
S WALES ON SUNDAY, circ. 41,199 267
W WREXHAM LEADER, circ. 42,138 F 278

Gwersyllt
D EVENING LEADER, circ. 21,180 181
D SHROPSHIRE STAR, circ. 72,000 247
D SHROPSHIRE STAR (CITY/LONDON OFFICE) 247
S WALES ON SUNDAY, circ. 41,199 267
W WREXHAM LEADER, circ. 42,138 F 278

Rhosllanerchrugog
D EVENING LEADER, circ. 21,180 181
W NENE, circ. 850 225
D SHROPSHIRE STAR, circ. 72,000 247
D SHROPSHIRE STAR (CITY/LONDON OFFICE) 247
S WALES ON SUNDAY, circ. 41,199 267
W WREXHAM LEADER, circ. 42,138 F 278

Rossett
D EVENING LEADER, circ. 21,180 181
D SHROPSHIRE STAR, circ. 72,000 247
D SHROPSHIRE STAR (CITY/LONDON OFFICE) 247
S WALES ON SUNDAY, circ. 41,199 267
W WREXHAM LEADER, circ. 42,138 F 278

Ruabon
D EVENING LEADER, circ. 21,180 181
W NENE, circ. 850 225
D SHROPSHIRE STAR, circ. 72,000 247
D SHROPSHIRE STAR (CITY/LONDON OFFICE) 247
S WALES ON SUNDAY, circ. 41,199 267
W WREXHAM LEADER, circ. 42,138 F 278

Wrexham
W YR ANGOR (LIVERPOOL), circ. 3,000 142
D EVENING LEADER, circ. 21,180 181
W NENE, circ. 850 225
D SHROPSHIRE STAR, circ. 72,000 247
D SHROPSHIRE STAR (CITY/LONDON OFFICE) 247
W WREXHAM CHRONICLE, circ. 38,278 F 278
W WREXHAM LEADER, circ. 42,138 F 278

Willings Volume 1
Section 4

UK Media

Section 4 comprises 3 sub-sections called 4 (a) Newspapers,
4 (b) Business Magazines and Periodicals and
4 (c) Consumer Magazines and Periodicals. You will find
the National Newspapers listed at the beginning of Section 4 (a),
followed by the Non-Nationals.
Information on publications outside the UK can be found
in Volume 2 (Western Europe) and Volume 3 (World).

National Newspapers

ARTS
634472U65A-93_782

Tel: 020 7005 2000 **Fax:** 020 7005 2466
Email: arts@independent.co.uk
Frequency: Mornings - Published Monday to Friday within The Independent
Editor: David Lister
Summary of Content: Section covering features, profiles, reviews and previews of events in the cinema, theatre, architecture, visual arts, radio and music.
Section of: The Independent
NATIONAL DAILY & SUNDAY NEWSPAPERS: National Daily Newspapers

BIZARRE
41728U65A-120_720

Tel: 020 7782 4000 **Fax:** 020 7782 4350
Email: biz@the-sun.co.uk
Frequency: Mornings - Published within The Sun
Editor: Gordon Smart
Summary of Content: Show business gossip and interviews.
Section of: The Sun
NATIONAL DAILY & SUNDAY NEWSPAPERS: National Daily Newspapers

BOOKS ON FRIDAY
628702U65A-20_710

Tel: 020 7938 6701 **Fax:** 020 7937 0332
Email: sandra.parsons@dailymail.co.uk
Frequency: Weekly - Published on Friday within the Daily Mail
Editor: Sandra Parsons
Summary of Content: Section including book reviews and literary news.
ADVERTISING: Rates on application
Section of: Daily Mail
NATIONAL DAILY & SUNDAY NEWSPAPERS: National Daily Newspapers

BRICKS AND MORTAR
767252U65A-130_863

Tel: 020 7782 5000 **Fax:** 020 7782 7550
Email: property@thetimes.co.uk
Frequency: Weekly - Published on Friday within The Times
Editor: Anne Ashworth
Summary of Content: Section covering all aspects of property, from the economics of interest rates to the homes of the rich and famous.
ADVERTISING RATES:
SCC £67.00
Section of: The Times
NATIONAL DAILY & SUNDAY NEWSPAPERS: National Daily Newspapers

BUSINESS
41677U65A-90_740

Formerly: Finance Guardian
Tel: 020 3353 2000
Frequency: Mornings - Published within The Guardian
Editor: Deborah Hargreaves
Summary of Content: Section covering finance and investment, including share prices.
ADVERTISING: Rates on application
Section of: The Guardian
NATIONAL DAILY & SUNDAY NEWSPAPERS: National Daily Newspapers

BUSINESS
41693U65A-93_720

Tel: 020 7005 2636 **Fax:** 020 7005 2098
Email: businessnews@independent.co.uk
Frequency: Mornings - Published within The Independent
Editor: Jeremy Warner
Summary of Content: Reports on business and City news.
Section of: The Independent
NATIONAL DAILY & SUNDAY NEWSPAPERS: National Daily Newspapers

CAREER
633849U65A-130_710

Formerly: Times Appointments First Executive
Tel: 020 7782 5618 **Fax:** 020 7782 5751
Email: career@thetimes.co.uk
Publisher: Times Newspapers Ltd
Frequency: Weekly - Published on Thursday within The Times

Editor: Carol Lewis
Summary of Content: Section listing jobs, opportunities and features for graduates up to middle management.
ADVERTISING RATES:
SCC £67.00
Section of: The Times
NATIONAL DAILY & SUNDAY NEWSPAPERS: National Daily Newspapers

CAREER MAIL
41604U65A-20_720

Tel: 020 7938 6137 **Fax:** 020 7937 8161
Frequency: Weekly - Published on Thursdays within the Daily Mail
Editor: Charlotte Beugge
Summary of Content: Section carrying features on career development and work, plus appointments listings.
ADVERTISING: Rates on application
Section of: Daily Mail
NATIONAL DAILY & SUNDAY NEWSPAPERS: National Daily Newspapers

CASHPOINT
707138U65A-40_712

Tel: 01621 817818 **Fax:** 020 8612 7401
Email: rcxsd@waitrose.com
Frequency: 26 issues yearly - Published every other Tuesday within the Daily Star
Editor: Michelle Carter
Summary of Content: Section covering personal finance issues.
Section of: Daily Star
NATIONAL DAILY & SUNDAY NEWSPAPERS: National Daily Newspapers

CELEBS ON SUNDAY
41871U65H-50

Formerly: M Celebs
Editorial Address: 22nd Floor, 1 Canada Square, Canary Wharf, LONDON, E14 5AP **Tel:** 020 7293 3000
Fax: 020 7293 2655
Email: celebs@sundaymirror.co.uk
Advertising Address: As above. **Fax:** 020 7293 3280
Web site: http://www.sundaymirror.co.uk
Publisher: Trinity Mirror
Date Established: 2002
Frequency: Weekly - See main record for circulation figure
Editor: Dan Lloyd; **Features Editor:** Lara Kilner
Summary of Content: Magazine covering celebrity news, health, fitness, beauty, fashion and food. Includes television listings.
ADVERTISING RATES:
Full Page Colour £26600.00
Copy instructions: Copy Date: 3 weeks prior to publication date
Supplement to: Sunday Mirror
NATIONAL DAILY & SUNDAY NEWSPAPERS: National Colour Supplements

CITY & BUSINESS
41658U65A-10_720

Tel: 020 8612 7000 **Fax:** 0871 520 7766
Frequency: Mornings - Published within the Daily Express
Editor: Stephen Kahn
Summary of Content: Section covering companies news and share prices.
ADVERTISING: Rates on application
Section of: Daily Express
NATIONAL DAILY & SUNDAY NEWSPAPERS: National Daily Newspapers

CITY & FINANCE
41605U65A-20_730

Tel: 020 7938 6990 **Fax:** 020 7937 7374
Email: city@dailymail.co.uk
Frequency: Mornings - Published within the Daily Mail from Monday to Saturday
Editor: Alex Brummer
Summary of Content: Section covering business and finance.
ADVERTISING: Rates on application
Section of: Daily Mail
NATIONAL DAILY & SUNDAY NEWSPAPERS: National Daily Newspapers

DAILY EXPRESS
41655U65A-10

Formerly: The Express
Editorial Address: The Northern & Shell Building, 10 Lower Thames Street, LONDON, EC3R 6EN **Tel:** 020 8612 7000
Fax: 0871 520 7702
Email: news.desk@express.co.uk
Advertising Address: As above. **Tel:** 0871 434 1010
Email: melanie.danks@express.co.uk
Web site: http://www.express.co.uk
Publisher: Express Newspapers Ltd
Frequency: Mornings - Not published on Sunday

Cover Price: £0.40
Circulation: 730,234 (ABC 03/08/2009 to 30/08/2009)
Editor: Peter Hill; **News Editor:** Geoff Maynard; **Features Editor:** Fergus Kelly; **Advertising Manager:** Melanie Danks
Summary of Content: Tabloid-sized newspaper covering national and international news with features on business and finance, education, appointments, lifestyle, entertainment and sport.
Twitter: http://twitter.com/daily_express.
ADVERTISING RATES:
Full Page Mono £23765.00
Full Page Colour £31500.00
SCC £97.00
Agency Commission: 15%
Mechanical Data: Type Area: 345 x 245mm, No. of Columns (Display): 7, Col Widths (Display): 37mm, Col Length: 345mm, Page Width: 245mm
Copy instructions: Copy Date: Mono 7 days Colour 10 days prior to publication date
Sections:
City & Business
Daily Express Careers
Daily Express Sport
Express Woman
Goal Express
Money
Motoring
Start Your Own Business
Travel
TV Express
The Weekend Starts Here
Supplement(s): Daily Express Saturday - 52xY
NATIONAL DAILY & SUNDAY NEWSPAPERS: National Daily Newspapers

DAILY EXPRESS CAREERS
41663U65A-10_722

Formerly: Careers Express
Tel: 020 8612 7000 **Fax:** 0871 520 7766
Frequency: Weekly - Published on Thursdays within the Daily Express
Editor: Ben West
Summary of Content: Section covering careers, education and appointments.
ADVERTISING: Rates on application
Section of: Daily Express
NATIONAL DAILY & SUNDAY NEWSPAPERS: National Daily Newspapers

DAILY EXPRESS SATURDAY
41864U65H-8

Formerly: The Express Saturday
Editorial Address: The Northern & Shell Building, 10 Lower Thames Street, LONDON, EC3R 6EN **Tel:** 020 8612 7000
Fax: 0871 434 7305
Email: saturdayexpress@express.co.uk
Advertising Address: As above. **Tel:** 0871 434 1010
Fax: 0871 520 7766
Email: tarun.naipaul@express.co.uk
Web site: http://www.express.co.uk
Publisher: Express Newspapers Ltd
Frequency: Weekly - See main record for circulation figure
Cover Price: £0.70
Editor: Carly Smith; **Features Editor:** Justine Holman; **Advertising Manager:** Tarun Naipaul
Summary of Content: Magazine containing television and radio listings, celebrity features, fashion, beauty, interiors, food, property and gardening.
ADVERTISING RATES:
Full Page Colour £30000.00
Agency Commission: 15%
Mechanical Data: Type Area: 265 x 195mm, Bleed Size: 306 x 232mm, Trim Size: 300 x 226mm, No. of Columns (Display): 7, Col Length: 265mm, Page Width: 195mm, Film: Digital
Copy instructions: Copy Date: 9 working days prior to publication date
Average advertising content per issue: 40%
Supplement to: Daily Express
NATIONAL DAILY & SUNDAY NEWSPAPERS: National Colour Supplements

DAILY EXPRESS SPORT
41660U65A-10_725

Formerly: The Express Sport
Tel: 020 8612 7000 **Fax:** 020 7922 7896
Frequency: Mornings - Published within the Daily Express
Editor: Bill Bradshaw
Summary of Content: Section covering sports news and fixtures.
ADVERTISING: Rates on application
Section of: Daily Express
NATIONAL DAILY & SUNDAY NEWSPAPERS: National Daily Newspapers

DAILY MAIL
41602U65A-20

Editorial Address: Northcliffe House, 2 Derry Street, LONDON, W8 5TT **Tel:** 020 7938 6000 **Fax:** 020 7937 4463

Email: news@dailymail.co.uk
Advertising Address: As above.
Email: john.teal@dailymail.co.uk
Web site: http://www.dailymail.co.uk
Publisher: Associated Newspapers Ltd
Date Established: 1896
Frequency: Mornings - Published Monday - Saturday
Cover Price: £0.50
Circulation: 2,228,897 (ABC 29/12/2008 to 25/01/2009)
Editor: Keith Poole; **News Editor:** Keith Poole; **Features Editor:** Jim Gillespie; **Editor-in-Chief:** Paul Dacre;
Advertising Director: John Teal
Summary of Content: Tabloid sized newspaper covering national and international news with features on travel, finance, sport, women's interest, entertainment and health.
Twitter: http://twitter.com/mailonline
ADVERTISING RATES:
Full Page Mono £32508.00
Full Page Colour £45612.00
SCC £129.00
Agency Commission: 15%
Mechanical Data: Col Length: 360mm, No. of Columns (Display): 7, Col Widths (Display): 35mm, Film: Digital, Page Width: 268mm, Type Area: 360 x 268mm
Sections:
Books on Friday
Career Mail
City & Finance
Femail Magazine
Good Health
It's Friday
Lifestyle
Money Mail
Property Mail
Sportsmail
TravelMail
Supplement(s): Daily Mail Weekend - 52xY
NATIONAL DAILY & SUNDAY NEWSPAPERS: National Daily Newspapers

DAILY MAIL (CITY OFFICE)   324854U65E-20

Editorial Address: Northcliffe House, 2 Derry Street, LONDON, W8 5TT **Tel:** 020 7938 6990 **Fax:** 020 7937 7374
Email: city@dailymail.co.uk
Publisher: Associated Newspapers Ltd
Editor: Alex Brummer
Summary of Content: Accepts news on banking, business, economics and Unit Trusts.
ADVERTISING: No Advertising taken
NATIONAL DAILY & SUNDAY NEWSPAPERS: National Daily City Office

DAILY MAIL (MANCHESTER OFFICE)   707694U65C-122

Editorial Address: Acresfield, 8-10 Exchange Street, St. Anns Square, MANCHESTER, M2 7HA **Tel:** 0161 836 5050 **Fax:** 0161 836 5068
Email: manchester@dailymail.co.uk
Publisher: Associated Newspapers Ltd
Editor: James Tozer
ADVERTISING: No Advertising taken
NATIONAL DAILY & SUNDAY NEWSPAPERS: National Daily Regional Offices

DAILY MAIL WEEKEND   41862U65H-10

Editorial Address: Northcliffe House, 2 Derry Street, LONDON, W8 5TT **Tel:** 020 7938 6000 **Fax:** 020 7938 6117
Advertising Address: As above.
Email: catryn.brogan@dailymail.co.uk
Web site: http://www.dailymail.co.uk
Publisher: Associated Newspapers Ltd
Date Established: 1993
Frequency: Weekly - Published on Saturday. See main record for circulation figure
Editor: Amber Bayliss; **Features Editor:** Nicole Mowbray
Summary of Content: Magazine featuring TV and radio listings, celebrity interviews, travel and lifestyle.
ADVERTISING RATES:
Full Page Colour £41970.00
Agency Commission: 15%
Mechanical Data: Bleed Size: 367 x 298mm, Trim Size: 359 x 290mm, Type Area: 330 x 262mm, Col Length: 330mm, Film: Digital, Page Width: 262mm, No. of Columns (Display): 7
Average advertising content per issue: 18%
Supplement to Daily Mail
NATIONAL DAILY & SUNDAY NEWSPAPERS: National Colour Supplements

DAILY MIRROR   41706U65A-100

Formerly: The Mirror
Editorial Address: 1 Canada Square, Canary Wharf, LONDON, E14 5AP **Tel:** 020 7293 3000
Email: mirrornews@mirror.co.uk

Advertising Address: As above. **Fax:** 020 7293 3285
Email: andy.whelan@mgn.co.uk
Web site: http://www.mirror.co.uk
Publisher: Trinity Mirror
Frequency: Mornings - Not published on Sunday
Cover Price: £0.45
Circulation: 1,324,883 (ABC 03/08/2009 to 30/08/2009)
Editor: Anthony Harwood; **News Editor:** Barry Rabbetts;
Managing Editor: Eugene Duffy
Summary of Content: Tabloid-sized newspaper covering national and international news stories, with articles on finance, entertainment, television, show-biz and sport.
Twitter: http://twitter.com/DailyMirror.
ADVERTISING RATES:
Full Page Mono £29000.00
Full Page Colour £36800.00
SCC £112.00
Mechanical Data: Type Area: 340 x 265mm, No. of Columns (Display): 7, Print Process: Web-fed offset litho, Col Widths (Display): 35mm, Col Length: 340mm, Page Width: 265mm
Sections:
Mirror FC
Mirror Mania
Mirror Money
Mirror Racing
Mirror Sport
The Mirror Works
Racing Post Extra
The Review
Editions:
Daily Mirror (Northern Ireland Edition)
Supplement(s): The Ticket - 52xY, We Love Telly! - 52xY, Your Life - 104xY
NATIONAL DAILY & SUNDAY NEWSPAPERS: National Daily Newspapers

DAILY MIRROR (BELFAST)   41842U65C-350

Formerly: The Mirror (Belfast)
Editorial Address: 415 Holywood Road, BELFAST, BT4 2GU **Tel:** 028 9056 8000 **Fax:** 028 9056 8005
Email: irish@mgn.co.uk
Publisher: Trinity Mirror
Frequency: Daily
Editor: News Desk; **News Editor:** Joe Gorrod
ADVERTISING: No Advertising taken
NATIONAL DAILY & SUNDAY NEWSPAPERS: National Daily Regional Offices

DAILY MIRROR (BIRMINGHAM OFFICE)   41819U65C-45

Formerly: The Mirror (Birmingham Office)
Editorial Address: Weaman Street, Queensway, BIRMINGHAM, B4 6AT **Tel:** 0121 234 5000
Publisher: Trinity Mirror
Editor: Rod Chaytor
ADVERTISING: No Advertising taken
NATIONAL DAILY & SUNDAY NEWSPAPERS: National Daily Regional Offices

DAILY MIRROR (OLDHAM OFFICE)   41833U65C-203

Formerly: The Mirror (Oldham Office)
Editorial Address: Hollinwood Avenue, Chadderton, OLDHAM, OL9 8EP **Tel:** 0161 683 6074 **Fax:** 0161 683 6065
Email: s.white@mirror.co.uk
Web site: http://www.mirror.co.uk
Publisher: Trinity Mirror
Frequency: Daily
Editor: Stephen White
ADVERTISING: No Advertising taken
NATIONAL DAILY & SUNDAY NEWSPAPERS: National Daily Regional Offices

DAILY SPORT   41614U65A-30

Editorial Address: 19 Great Ancoats Street, MANCHESTER, M60 4BT **Tel:** 0161 236 4466 **Fax:** 0161 236 4535
Email: neil.goodwin@sportnewspapers.co.uk
Advertising Address: As above. **Tel:** 0161 237 4600 **Fax:** 0161 237 4612
Email: advertising@sportnewspapers.co.uk
Web site: http://www.dailysport.com
Publisher: Sport Newspapers Ltd
Frequency: Mornings - Published Monday to Saturday
Cover Price: £0.50
Circulation: 72,592 (Publisher's Statement)
Editor: Neil Goodwin; **News Editor:** Neil Goodwin;
Publisher: David Sullivan
Summary of Content: Tabloid sized newspaper with general interest features, show-biz news and sport.
Twitter: http://twitter.com/daily_sport.
ADVERTISING RATES:
Full Page Mono £2000.00

Full Page Colour £2400.00
SCC £25.00
Agency Commission: 10%
Mechanical Data: Col Length: 350mm, Film: Digital, Type Area: 350 x 262mm, Col Widths (Display): 34mm, No. of Columns (Display): 7, Page Width: 262mm
Copy instructions: Copy Date: 12 noon 2 days prior to publication date
Average advertising content per issue: 70%
NATIONAL DAILY & SUNDAY NEWSPAPERS: National Daily Newspapers

DAILY STAR   41615U65A-40

Editorial Address: The Northern & Shell Building, 10 Lower Thames Street, LONDON, EC3R 6EN **Tel:** 0871 434 1010
Fax: 020 8612 7401
Email: news@dailystar.co.uk
Advertising Address: As above. **Fax:** 0871 434 2753
Email: jason.campbell@express.co.uk
Web site: http://www.dailystar.co.uk
Publisher: Express Newspapers Ltd
Date Established: 1978
Frequency: Mornings - Published Monday to Saturday
Cover Price: £0.20
Circulation: 886,814 (ABC 03/08/2009 to 30/08/2009)
Editor: Ian Trueman; **News Editor:** Jon Lockett
Summary of Content: Tabloid sized newspaper covering general interest stories, show-biz news and sport.
Twitter: http://twitter.com/daily_star.
ADVERTISING RATES:
SCC £97.00
Agency Commission: 15%
Mechanical Data: Type Area: 345 x 275mm, Col Widths (Display): 37mm, No. of Columns (Display): 7, Film: Digital, Col Length: 345mm, Page Width: 275mm
Sections:
Cashpoint
Go For It
Starform
Supplement(s): HotTV - 52xY
NATIONAL DAILY & SUNDAY NEWSPAPERS: National Daily Newspapers

DAILY STAR (GLASGOW OFFICE)   41836U65C-271

Editorial Address: Citypoint 2, 25 Tyndrum Street, GLASGOW, G4 0JY **Tel:** 0141 352 2544 **Fax:** 0141 352 2555
Email: scot.news@express.co.uk
Publisher: Express Newspapers Ltd
Editor: Nick Gates
ADVERTISING: No Advertising taken
NATIONAL DAILY & SUNDAY NEWSPAPERS: National Daily Regional Offices

DAILY STAR SUNDAY   761885U65B-72

Editorial Address: The Northern & Shell Building, 10 Lower Thames Street, LONDON, EC3R 6EN **Tel:** 0871 520 7424
Fax: 0871 434 7967
Email: michael.booker@dailystar.co.uk
Advertising Address: As above. **Tel:** 0871 520 2766
Email: michelle.payne@express.co.uk
Web site: http://www.dailystarsunday.co.uk
Publisher: Express Newspapers Ltd
Date Established: 2002
Frequency: Sunday
Cover Price: £0.85
Circulation: 401,305 (ABC 03/08/2009 to 30/08/2009)
Editor: Michael Booker; **News Editor:** Michael Booker;
Advertising Manager: Jason Campbell
Summary of Content: Tabloid-sized newspaper covering general interest stories, show-biz news and sport.
Twitter: http://twitter.com/daily_star.
ADVERTISING RATES:
Full Page Mono £21070.00
Full Page Colour £28420.00
SCC £86.00
Agency Commission: 15%
Mechanical Data: Type Area: 350 x 275mm, Col Length: 350mm, Page Width: 275mm, No. of Columns (Display): 7, Col Widths (Display): 37mm, Film: Digital
Copy instructions: Copy Date: 2 days prior to publication date
Average advertising content per issue: 35%
Editions:
Daily Star Sunday Scotland
Supplement(s): Take 5 - 52xY
NATIONAL DAILY & SUNDAY NEWSPAPERS: National Sunday Newspapers

THE DAILY TELEGRAPH   41623U65A-50

Editorial Address: 111 Buckingham Palace Road, LONDON, SW1W 0DT **Tel:** 020 7931 2000
Fax: 020 7931 2938
Email: dtnews@telegraph.co.uk
Advertising Address: As above.

Email: ken.breen@telegraph.co.uk
Web site: http://www.telegraph.co.uk
Publisher: Telegraph Media Group Ltd
Frequency: Mornings - Not published on Sunday
Cover Price: £0.80
Circulation: 814,087 (ABC 03/08/2009 to 30/08/2009)
Editor: William Lewis; **News Editor:** Chris Evans; **Features Editor:** Genevieve Fox; **Editor-in-Chief:** William Lewis
Summary of Content: Broadsheet-sized, quality newspaper providing in-depth national and international news with political coverage, business and financial news, appointments, property, arts, travel and sport.
Twitter: http://twitter.com/dailytelegraph.
ADVERTISING RATES:
Full Page Mono £46000.00
Full Page Colour £59000.00
SCC £106.00
Agency Commission: 15%
Mechanical Data: No. of Columns (Display): 8, Col Length: 540mm, Col Widths (Display): 39mm, Film: Digital, Page Width: 340mm, Type Area: 540 x 340mm
Copy instructions: Copy Date: 7 days prior to publication date
Sections:
The Daily Telegraph Business
The Daily Telegraph Business2 + Jobs
The Daily Telegraph Gardening
The Daily Telegraph Motoring
The Daily Telegraph Property
The Daily Telegraph Review
The Daily Telegraph Sport
The Daily Telegraph Travel
The Daily Telegraph Weekend
The Daily Telegraph Your Business
The Daily Telegraph Your Money
Media News
Supplement(s): The Daily Telegraph Television & Radio Seven-Day Guide - 52xY, London Property - 52xY, Telegraph Magazine - 52xY, Ultratravel - 4xY
NATIONAL DAILY & SUNDAY NEWSPAPERS: National Daily Newspapers

THE DAILY TELEGRAPH BUSINESS
41631U65A-50_720
Formerly: The Daily Telegraph Business News
Tel: 020 7931 2000 **Fax:** 020 7538 7177
Email: city@telegraph.co.uk
Frequency: Mornings - Published within The Daily Telegraph
Editor: Damian Reece
Summary of Content: Covers business and companies news and share prices.
ADVERTISING: Rates on application
Section of: The Daily Telegraph
NATIONAL DAILY & SUNDAY NEWSPAPERS: National Daily Newspapers

THE DAILY TELEGRAPH BUSINESS2 + JOBS
41628U65A-50_713
Formerly: The Daily Telegraph Appointments Business File
Tel: 020 7931 2000 **Fax:** 020 7538 7177
Web site: http://www.businessfile.co.uk
Frequency: Weekly - Published on Thursday within The Daily Telegraph, is also duplicated in The Sunday Telegraph
Editor: Richard Tyler
Summary of Content: Section containing business news and features plus executive level appointments.
ADVERTISING: Rates on application
Section of: The Daily Telegraph
NATIONAL DAILY & SUNDAY NEWSPAPERS: National Daily Newspapers

THE DAILY TELEGRAPH (CITY OFFICE)
41855U65E-50
Editorial Address: 111 Buckingham Palace Road, LONDON, SW1W 0DT **Tel:** 020 7931 2710
Fax: 020 7931 2760
Email: city@telegraph.co.uk
Publisher: Telegraph Media Group Ltd
Editor: City News Desk; **Executive Editor:** Richard Fletcher
ADVERTISING: No Advertising taken
NATIONAL DAILY & SUNDAY NEWSPAPERS: National Daily City Office

THE DAILY TELEGRAPH (EDINBURGH OFFICE)
41834U65C-240
Editorial Address: Barclay House, Holyrood Road, EDINBURGH, EH8 8AS **Tel:** 0131 620 4214
Email: auslan.cramb@telegraph.co.uk
Publisher: Telegraph Media Group Ltd
Editor: Auslan Cramb
ADVERTISING: No Advertising taken
NATIONAL DAILY & SUNDAY NEWSPAPERS: National Daily Regional Offices

THE DAILY TELEGRAPH GARDENING
707025U65A-50_730
Tel: 020 7931 2000 **Fax:** 020 7538 7244
Email: gardening@telegraph.co.uk
Frequency: Weekly - Published on Saturday within The Daily Telegraph
Editor: Kylie O'Brien
Summary of Content: Section covering all types of gardening from urban to rural.
ADVERTISING: Rates on application
Section of: The Daily Telegraph
NATIONAL DAILY & SUNDAY NEWSPAPERS: National Daily Newspapers

THE DAILY TELEGRAPH (MANCHESTER OFFICE)
41824U65C-130
Editorial Address: Longbridge Road, Trafford Park, MANCHESTER, M17 1SL **Tel:** 0161 868 1090
Fax: 0161 868 1095
Email: nigel.bunyan@telegraph.co.uk
Publisher: Telegraph Media Group Ltd
Editor: Nigel Bunyan
ADVERTISING: No Advertising taken
NATIONAL DAILY & SUNDAY NEWSPAPERS: National Daily Regional Offices

THE DAILY TELEGRAPH (MIDLANDS OFFICE)
41817U65C-70
Formerly: The Daily Telegraph (Birmingham Office)
Editorial Address: 111 Buckingham Palace Road, LONDON, SW1W 0DT **Tel:** 01332 738100
Fax: 01332 738138
Email: nick.britten@telegraph.co.uk
Web site: http://www.telegraph.co.uk
Publisher: Telegraph Media Group Ltd
Editor: Nick Britten
ADVERTISING: No Advertising taken
NATIONAL DAILY & SUNDAY NEWSPAPERS: National Daily Regional Offices

THE DAILY TELEGRAPH MOTORING
41633U65A-50_780
Tel: 020 7931 2000 **Fax:** 020 7538 6139
Frequency: Weekly - Published on Saturday within The Daily Telegraph
Editor: Peter Hall
Summary of Content: Review of new car models, features on motoring safety and style, and new car technology.
ADVERTISING: Rates on application
Section of: The Daily Telegraph
NATIONAL DAILY & SUNDAY NEWSPAPERS: National Daily Newspapers

THE DAILY TELEGRAPH PROPERTY
41635U65A-50_785
Tel: 020 7931 2000 **Fax:** 020 7538 7247
Email: property@telegraph.co.uk
Frequency: Weekly - Published on Saturday within The Daily Telegraph
Editor: Kylie O'Brien
Summary of Content: Section covering the property market.
ADVERTISING: Rates on application
Section of: The Daily Telegraph
NATIONAL DAILY & SUNDAY NEWSPAPERS: National Daily Newspapers

THE DAILY TELEGRAPH REVIEW
41629U65A-50_714
Formerly: The Daily Telegraph Arts + Books
Tel: 020 7931 2000 **Fax:** 020 7538 7650
Frequency: Weekly - Published on Saturday within The Daily Telegraph
Editor: Tom Horan
Summary of Content: Book, theatre, dance, opera, music and gallery reviews.
ADVERTISING: Rates on application
Section of: The Daily Telegraph
NATIONAL DAILY & SUNDAY NEWSPAPERS: National Daily Newspapers

THE DAILY TELEGRAPH SPORT
41636U65A-50_787
Tel: 020 7931 2000 **Fax:** 020 7513 2507
Email: sport@telegraph.co.uk
Frequency: Mornings - Published within The Daily Telegraph
Editor: Keith Perry
Summary of Content: Carries news and features on sporting events, personalities and results.

ADVERTISING: Rates on application
Section of: The Daily Telegraph
NATIONAL DAILY & SUNDAY NEWSPAPERS: National Daily Newspapers

THE DAILY TELEGRAPH TRAVEL
41637U65A-50_790
Tel: 020 7931 2000 **Fax:** 020 7538 6802
Email: traveldesk@telegraph.co.uk
Frequency: Weekly - Published on Saturday within The Daily Telegraph
Editor: Graham Boynton
Summary of Content: Section featuring travel and holidays.
ADVERTISING: Rates on application
Section of: The Daily Telegraph
NATIONAL DAILY & SUNDAY NEWSPAPERS: National Daily Newspapers

THE DAILY TELEGRAPH WEEKEND
41638U65A-50_800
Tel: 020 7931 2000 **Fax:** 020 7538 7244
Email: weekend@telegraph.co.uk
Frequency: Weekly - Published on Saturday within The Daily Telegraph
Editor: Jon Stock
Summary of Content: Features on home, gardening, fashion, travel, food and drink.
ADVERTISING: Rates on application
Section of: The Daily Telegraph
NATIONAL DAILY & SUNDAY NEWSPAPERS: National Daily Newspapers

THE DAILY TELEGRAPH YOUR BUSINESS
41630U65A-50_810
Formerly: Business Monitor
Tel: 020 7931 2000 **Fax:** 020 7538 7177
Frequency: Weekly - Published on Mondays within The Daily Telegraph
Editor: Richard Tyler
Summary of Content: Section featuring a weekly focus on growing businesses.
ADVERTISING: Rates on application
Section of: The Daily Telegraph
NATIONAL DAILY & SUNDAY NEWSPAPERS: National Daily Newspapers

THE DAILY TELEGRAPH YOUR MONEY
41634U65A-50_820
Tel: 020 7931 2000 **Fax:** 020 7628 0290
Frequency: Weekly - Published on Saturday within The Daily Telegraph
Editor: Ian Cowie
Summary of Content: Section about personal finance.
ADVERTISING: Rates on application
Section of: The Daily Telegraph
NATIONAL DAILY & SUNDAY NEWSPAPERS: National Daily Newspapers

ECOSSE
26163U65D-6
Editorial Address: 6th Floor, Guildhall, 57 Queen Street, GLASGOW, G1 3EN **Tel:** 0141 420 5100
Email: joan.mcalpine@sunday-times.co.uk
Advertising Address: As above. **Fax:** 0141 420 5341
Email: andrew.hylden@newsint.co.uk
Web site: http://www.sunday-times.co.uk
Publisher: News International (Scotland) Ltd
Frequency: Weekly
Editor: Joan McAlpine; **Advertising Manager:** Andrew Hylden
Summary of Content: Scottish features and listings supplement of The Sunday Times Scotland includes coverage of arts and culture, lifestyle, travel, food and restaurants with news analysis and profiles.
ADVERTISING RATES:
Full Page Mono £8856.00
Full Page Colour £11513.00
SCC £20.50
Agency Commission: 15%
Mechanical Data: Type Area: 540 x 343mm, Col Length: 540mm, Page Width: 343mm, Col Widths (Display): 46mm, No. of Columns (Display): 8, Film: Digital
Copy instructions: Copy Date: Thursday prior to publication date
Average advertising content per issue: 30%
Supplement to: The Sunday Times Scotland
NATIONAL DAILY & SUNDAY NEWSPAPERS: National Sunday Regional Offices

EXPRESS WOMAN
41661U65A-10_790

Formerly: Life
Tel: 020 8612 7000 **Fax:** 0871 520 7766
Frequency: Mornings - Published daily within the Daily Express
Editor: Tina Moran
Summary of Content: Section covering lifestyles, relationships, children, work, fashion, beauty, health, fitness and women's interest.
ADVERTISING: Rates on application
Section of: Daily Express
NATIONAL DAILY & SUNDAY NEWSPAPERS: National Daily Newspapers

FABULOUS
41874U65H-60

Formerly: Sunday
Editorial Address: 1 Virginia Street, LONDON, E98 1SU
Tel: 020 7782 7000 **Fax:** 020 7782 7474
Email: farzana.parkar@fabulousmag.co.uk
Advertising Address: As above.
Email: jane.west@newsint.co.uk
Web site: http://www.fabulousmag.co.uk
Publisher: News Group Newspapers Ltd
Date Established: 1981
Frequency: Weekly - See main record for circulation figure
Editor: Laura Bond; **Executive Editor:** Rachel Richardson;
Features Editor: Sinead McIntyre
Summary of Content: Magazine covering celebrities, fashion, beauty and real-life, with its own dedicated website www.fabulousmag.co.uk.
ADVERTISING RATES:
Full Page Colour £31500.00
Agency Commission: 15%
Mechanical Data: Type Area: 259 x 204mm, Bleed Size: 291 x 233mm, Trim Size: 283 x 225mm, Film: Digital, Col Length: 259mm, Page Width: 204mm
Copy instructions: Copy Date: 20 working days prior to publication date
Average advertising content per issue: 20%
Supplement to: News of the World
NATIONAL DAILY & SUNDAY NEWSPAPERS: National Colour Supplements

FAVOURITE
41733U65A-120_890

Formerly: They're Off
Tel: 020 7782 4000 **Fax:** 020 7782 4655
Email: trevor.clements@the-sun.co.uk
Frequency: Weekly - Published on Saturday within The Sun
Editor: Trevor Clements
Summary of Content: Section concerned with horse racing and football, containing news, form guides and tips.
Section of: The Sun
NATIONAL DAILY & SUNDAY NEWSPAPERS: National Daily Newspapers

FEMAIL MAGAZINE
41607U65A-20_750

Tel: 020 7938 6736 **Fax:** 020 7938 4076
Email: femail@dailymail.co.uk
Web site: http://www.femail.co.uk
Frequency: Weekly - Published on Thursdays within the Daily Mail
Editor: Nicola Dawson
Summary of Content: Section covering fashion, beauty and women's interest features.
ADVERTISING: Rates on application
Section of: Daily Mail
NATIONAL DAILY & SUNDAY NEWSPAPERS: National Daily Newspapers

FILM AND MUSIC
41678U65A-90_745

Formerly: Friday Review
Tel: 020 3353 2000
Frequency: Weekly - Published on Fridays within The Guardian
Editor: Michael Hann
Summary of Content: Section covering the arts, film, television and music.
ADVERTISING: Rates on application
Section of: The Guardian
NATIONAL DAILY & SUNDAY NEWSPAPERS: National Daily Newspapers

FINANCIAL SUNDAY EXPRESS
41781U65B-30_710

Formerly: Serious Money
Tel: 020 8612 7162 **Fax:** 0871 434 7643
Email: tracey.boles@express.co.uk
Frequency: Sunday - Published within the Sunday Express
Editor: Tracey Boles
Summary of Content: Section covering business and financial news, e-commerce and computing.

ADVERTISING RATES:
SCC £166.00
Section of: Sunday Express
NATIONAL DAILY & SUNDAY NEWSPAPERS: National Sunday Newspapers

FINANCIAL TIMES
41666U65A-80

Editorial Address: 1 Southwark Bridge, LONDON, SE1 9HL
Tel: 020 7873 3000
Email: news.desk@ft.com
Advertising Address: As above.
Email: ukads@ft.com
Web site: http://www.ft.com
ISSN: 0307-1766
Publisher: Financial Times
Date Established: 1888
Frequency: Mornings - Not published on Sunday
Cover Price: £1.80
Circulation: 395,845 (ABC 03/08/2009 to 30/08/2009)
Editor: Lionel Barber; **News Editor:** Robert Shrimsley;
Executive Editor: Hugh Carnegy; **Advertising Manager:** Robert Jolliffe
Summary of Content: Broadsheet-sized quality newspaper providing in-depth business and financial news, analysis and coverage of world markets and industries. Also includes features on IT and personal finance with national and international news, sport and entertainment.
Twitter: http://twitter.com/FinancialTImes.
ADVERTISING RATES:
Full Page Mono £40400.00
Full Page Colour £56300.00
SCC £95.00
Sections:
Financial Times Appointments
Financial Times Companies & Markets
FT Digital Business
FT Life and Arts
FT Money Guide
Editions:
Financial Times (Irish Office)
FTpm
Supplement(s): Financial Times Weekend Magazine - 52xY, FT Global Traveller - 7xY, FT Money - 52xY, FT Wealth Magazine, FTfm - 50xY, House and Home - 52xY, How To Spend It - 26xY
NATIONAL DAILY & SUNDAY NEWSPAPERS: National Daily Newspapers

FINANCIAL TIMES APPOINTMENTS
763141U65A-80_801

Tel: 020 7873 3000
Frequency: Weekly - Published on Thursday within the Financial Times
Summary of Content: Section covering interesting and original angles on the world of employment and management with an international slant.
ADVERTISING: Rates on application
Section of: Financial Times
NATIONAL DAILY & SUNDAY NEWSPAPERS: National Daily Newspapers

FINANCIAL TIMES (BIRMINGHAM OFFICE)
41818U65C-40

Editorial Address: Suite 310, Somerville House, 20-22 Harborne Road, BIRMINGHAM, B15 3AA
Tel: 0121 454 0922
Web site: http://www.ft.vom/guthrie
Publisher: Financial Times
Editor: Jonathan Guthrie
ADVERTISING: No Advertising taken
NATIONAL DAILY & SUNDAY NEWSPAPERS: National Daily Regional Offices

FINANCIAL TIMES COMPANIES & MARKETS
41673U65A-80_800

Tel: 020 7873 3000 **Fax:** 020 7873 3074
Email: patrick.jenkins@ft.com
Frequency: Mornings - Published Monday to Friday within the Financial Times
Editor: Patrick Jenkins
Summary of Content: Section covering UK and international companies news, share prices and currencies information.
ADVERTISING: Rates on application
Section of: Financial Times
NATIONAL DAILY & SUNDAY NEWSPAPERS: National Daily Newspapers

FINANCIAL TIMES (EDINBURGH OFFICE)
41835U65C-250

Editorial Address: PR by email only **Tel:** 0131 220 1420
Fax: 0131 220 1578
Email: andrew.bolger@ft.com

Publisher: Financial Times
Editor: Andrew Bolger
ADVERTISING: No Advertising taken
NATIONAL DAILY & SUNDAY NEWSPAPERS: National Daily Regional Offices

FINANCIAL TIMES (MANCHESTER OFFICE)
41826U65C-140

Editorial Address: Alexandra Buildings, Queen Street, MANCHESTER, M2 5LF **Tel:** 0161 834 9381
Fax: 0161 832 9248
Email: leanne.badham@ft.com
Web site: http://www.ft.com
Publisher: Financial Times
Editor: News Desk
ADVERTISING: No Advertising taken
NATIONAL DAILY & SUNDAY NEWSPAPERS: National Daily Regional Offices

FINANCIAL TIMES WEEKEND MAGAZINE
1616181U65H-102

Editorial Address: 1 Southwark Bridge, LONDON, SE1 9HL
Tel: 020 7873 3000 **Fax:** 020 7873 4952
Email: eaw@ft.com
Advertising Address: As above. **Fax:** 020 7873 4336
Email: andrea.frias-andrade@ft.com
Web site: http://www.ft.com
Publisher: Financial Times
Date Established: 2003
Frequency: Weekly - Published on Saturday. See main record for circulation figure
Editor: Natalie Coley; **Advertising Manager:** Andrea Frias-Andrade
Summary of Content: Magazine containing in-depth current affairs articles also includes books and arts reviews.
Readership/Target Audience: Read by readers of the Financial Times.
ADVERTISING RATES:
Full Page Colour £8500.00
Agency Commission: 15%
Copy instructions: Copy Date: 1 week prior to publication date
Supplement to: Financial Times
NATIONAL DAILY & SUNDAY NEWSPAPERS: National Colour Supplements

FT DIGITAL BUSINESS
41670U65A-80_750

Formerly: FT Information Technology
Tel: 020 7873 3000 **Fax:** 020 7873 4343
Email: digitalbusiness@ft.com
Web site: http://www.ft.com/ftit
Editor: Peter Whitehead
Summary of Content: Section providing coverage of all areas of the technology and telecommunications industry, from enterprise software to computer games, online business to 3G.
ADVERTISING: Rates on application
Section of: Financial Times
NATIONAL DAILY & SUNDAY NEWSPAPERS: National Daily Newspapers

FT LIFE AND ARTS
41672U65A-80_780

Formerly: FT Weekend
Tel: 020 7873 3000 **Fax:** 020 7873 3929
Email: ftweekend@ft.com
Frequency: Weekly - Published on Saturdays within the Financial Times
Editor: Lucy Tuck
Summary of Content: Features on the arts, motoring, sports, gardening, travel, food, property, fashion and book reviews.
ADVERTISING: Rates on application
Section of: Financial Times
NATIONAL DAILY & SUNDAY NEWSPAPERS: National Daily Newspapers

FT MONEY GUIDE
1625940U65A-80_802

Tel: 020 7873 3000 **Fax:** 020 7873 3197
Email: ftreports@ft.com
Frequency: Monthly - Published on the last Saturday of the month within the Financial Times
Editor: Kevin Brown
Summary of Content: Section taking an in-depth look at personal investment.
ADVERTISING: Rates on application
Section of: Financial Times
NATIONAL DAILY & SUNDAY NEWSPAPERS: National Daily Newspapers

G2
41679U65A-90_750

Tel: 020 3353 2000
Email: g2@guardian.co.uk
Frequency: Mornings - Published within The Guardian Monday to Friday
Editor: Emily Wilson
Summary of Content: Section covering the arts, style, fashion, architecture, education, news features, work, TV and radio guide and TV Review.
ADVERTISING: Rates on application
Section of: The Guardian
NATIONAL DAILY & SUNDAY NEWSPAPERS: National Daily Newspapers

THE GAME
766868U65A-130_861

Tel: 020 7782 5000 **Fax:** 020 7782 5211
Email: sport@thetimes.co.uk
Web site: http://www.timesonline.co.uk/thegame
Frequency: Weekly - Published on Monday within the Times
Editor: Craig Tregurtha
Summary of Content: Section covering football news, results, reactions, previews and features.
ADVERTISING RATES:
SCC £67.00
Section of: The Times
NATIONAL DAILY & SUNDAY NEWSPAPERS: National Daily Newspapers

GO FOR IT
41621U65A-40_760

Formerly: Pack Yer Bags
Tel: 0871 434 1010
Frequency: Weekly - Published on Saturdays within the Daily Star
Editor: Vicky Lissaman
Summary of Content: Section concerned with travel and holidays.
Section of: Daily Star
NATIONAL DAILY & SUNDAY NEWSPAPERS: National Daily Newspapers

GOAL EXPRESS
707088U65A-10_750

Tel: 020 8612 7000 **Fax:** 0871 520 7766
Email: exsport@express.co.uk
Frequency: Weekly - Published on Monday within the Daily Express
Editor: Tony Banks
Summary of Content: Section focusing on news and views of weekend football.
ADVERTISING: No Advertising taken
Section of: Daily Express
NATIONAL DAILY & SUNDAY NEWSPAPERS: National Daily Newspapers

GOOD HEALTH
41608U65A-20_760

Tel: 020 7938 6000 **Fax:** 020 7938 4076
Frequency: Weekly - Published on Tuesdays within the Daily Mail
Summary of Content: Section about personal and family health.
ADVERTISING: Rates on application
Section of: Daily Mail
NATIONAL DAILY & SUNDAY NEWSPAPERS: National Daily Newspapers

GRADUATE
41684U65A-90_791

Formerly: Guardian Rise
Tel: 020 3353 2000
Frequency: Weekly - Published on Saturdays within The Guardian
Editor: Ian Wylie
Summary of Content: Section containing careers advice and information for university students and graduates. Includes appointments listings.
ADVERTISING: Rates on application
Section of: The Guardian
NATIONAL DAILY & SUNDAY NEWSPAPERS: National Daily Newspapers

THE GUARDIAN
41674U65A-90

Editorial Address: Kings Place, 90 York Way, LONDON, N1 9GU **Tel:** 020 3353 2000 **Fax:** 020 7837 2114
Email: national@guardian.co.uk
Advertising Address: 119 Farringdon Road, LONDON, EC1R 3ER **Tel:** 020 7278 2332 **Fax:** 020 7728 1449
Email: chris.pelekanou@guardian.co.uk
Web site: http://www.guardian.co.uk
Publisher: Guardian Media Group plc
Date Established: 1821
Frequency: Mornings - Not published on Sunday
Cover Price: £0.90
Circulation: 311,387 (ABC 03/08/2009 to 30/08/2009)

Editor: News Desk; **Executive Editor:** Sheila Fitzsimons; **Managing Editor:** Chris Elliott
Summary of Content: Berliner-sized quality newspaper containing in-depth national and international news with political and financial coverage, social issues, media, education, IT, jobs, travel, sport, arts and entertainment. A digital edition is also available.
Twitter: http://twitter.com/guardian
ADVERTISING RATES:
Full Page Mono £11400.00
Full Page Colour £18000.00
Agency Commission: 15%
Mechanical Data: Col Length: 440mm, No. of Columns (Display): 10, Col Widths (Display): 44mm, Type Area: 440 x 285mm, Page Width: 285mm, Film: Digital
Copy instructions: Copy Date: 5 days prior to publication date
Sections:
Business
Film and Music
G
Graduate
The Guardian Consumer
The Guardian Education
The Guardian Office Hours
The Guardian Review
The Guardian Society
The Guardian Sport
The Guardian Travel
The Guardian Weekend Sport
Media Guardian
Money
Technology
Supplement(s): Family - 52xY, The Guardian Weekend - 52xY, The Guide (Guardian) - 52xY, Work - 52xY, Your Baby - 1xY
NATIONAL DAILY & SUNDAY NEWSPAPERS: National Daily Newspapers

THE GUARDIAN CONSUMER
41680U65A-90_760

Tel: 020 3353 2000
Frequency: Weekly - Published once a month on Wednesdays within The Guardian
Editor: Amy Fleming
Summary of Content: Section concerned with consumer affairs.
ADVERTISING: Rates on application
Section of: The Guardian
NATIONAL DAILY & SUNDAY NEWSPAPERS: National Daily Newspapers

THE GUARDIAN EDUCATION
41681U65A-90_770

Tel: 020 3353 2000
Email: alice.woolley@guardian.co.uk
Frequency: Weekly - Published on Tuesdays within The Guardian
Editor: Claire Phipps
Summary of Content: News and features on education and educational policies.
ADVERTISING: Rates on application
Section of: The Guardian
NATIONAL DAILY & SUNDAY NEWSPAPERS: National Daily Newspapers

THE GUARDIAN (LEEDS OFFICE)
41822U65C-85

Editorial Address: Cragg Mount, Woodlands Drive, Rawdon, LEEDS, LS19 6JZ **Tel:** 0113 250 9422
Email: martin.wainwright@guardian.co.uk
Web site: http://www.guardian.co.uk
Publisher: Guardian Media Group plc
Editor: Martin Wainwright
ADVERTISING: No Advertising taken
NATIONAL DAILY & SUNDAY NEWSPAPERS: National Daily Regional Offices

THE GUARDIAN (MANCHESTER OFFICE)
41827U65C-150

Editorial Address: 1 Scott Place, MANCHESTER, M3 3GG
Tel: 0161 908 3898
Web site: http://www.guardian.co.uk
Publisher: Guardian Media Group plc
Editor: Martin Wainwright
ADVERTISING: No Advertising taken
NATIONAL DAILY & SUNDAY NEWSPAPERS: National Daily Regional Offices

THE GUARDIAN OFFICE HOURS
622779U65A-90_787

Tel: 020 3353 2000
Email: office.hours@guardian.co.uk
Frequency: Weekly - Published on Monday within The Guardian

Editor: Vicky Frost
Summary of Content: Section covering career issues relevant to secretaries, office administrators and PAs.
ADVERTISING: Rates on application
Section of: The Guardian
NATIONAL DAILY & SUNDAY NEWSPAPERS: National Daily Newspapers

THE GUARDIAN REVIEW
41685U65A-90_792

Formerly: The Guardian Saturday Review
Tel: 020 3353 2000
Email: lisa.allardice@guardian.co.uk
Frequency: Weekly - Published on Saturdays within The Guardian
Editor: Lisa Allardice
Summary of Content: Section covering the arts and books, including profiles of famous people.
ADVERTISING: Rates on application
Section of: The Guardian
NATIONAL DAILY & SUNDAY NEWSPAPERS: National Daily Newspapers

THE GUARDIAN SOCIETY
41686U65A-90_795

Tel: 020 3353 2000
Frequency: Weekly - Published on Wednesdays within The Guardian
Editor: Alison Benjamin
Summary of Content: Section reporting on social and environmental issues.
ADVERTISING: Rates on application
Section of: The Guardian
NATIONAL DAILY & SUNDAY NEWSPAPERS: National Daily Newspapers

THE GUARDIAN SPORT
41687U65A-90_800

Tel: 020 3353 2000
Web site: http://www.football.guardian.co.uk
Frequency: Mornings - Published Monday to Friday within The Guardian
Editor: Ben Clissitt
Summary of Content: Section covering sports news and fixtures.
ADVERTISING: Rates on application
Section of: The Guardian
NATIONAL DAILY & SUNDAY NEWSPAPERS: National Daily Newspapers

THE GUARDIAN TRAVEL
41688U65A-90_805

Tel: 020 7278 2332 **Fax:** 020 7239 9935
Frequency: Weekly - Published on Saturdays within The Guardian
Editor: Isabel Choat
Summary of Content: Section covering all aspects of travel.
ADVERTISING: Rates on application
Section of: The Guardian
NATIONAL DAILY & SUNDAY NEWSPAPERS: National Daily Newspapers

THE GUARDIAN WEEKEND
41865U65H-30

Editorial Address: Kings Place, 90 York Way, LONDON, N1 9GU **Tel:** 020 3353 2000
Email: weekend@guardian.co.uk
Advertising Address: As above. **Tel:** 020 7239 9917
Email: nicola.warren@guardian.co.uk
Web site: http://www.guardian.co.uk
Publisher: Guardian Media Group plc
Frequency: Weekly - Published on Saturday. See main record for circulation figure
Editor: Sue Matthias
Summary of Content: Investigative features and coverage of fashion, food and drink, homes, interiors and gardening.
ADVERTISING RATES:
Full Page Colour £11000.00
Agency Commission: 15%
Mechanical Data: Type Area: 260 x 213mm, Trim Size: 292 x 246mm, Bleed Size: 298 x 249mm, Col Length: 260mm, Page Width: 213mm, Film: Digital
Copy instructions: Copy Date: 10 working days prior to publication date
Supplement to: The Guardian
NATIONAL DAILY & SUNDAY NEWSPAPERS: National Colour Supplements

THE GUARDIAN WEEKEND SPORT
41689U65A-90_820

Tel: 020 7239 9519 **Fax:** 020 7713 4107
Frequency: Weekly - Published on Saturdays within The Guardian
Editor: Adam Sills
Summary of Content: Section covering all aspects of sport.
ADVERTISING: Rates on application

Section of: The Guardian
NATIONAL DAILY & SUNDAY NEWSPAPERS: National Daily Newspapers

HEALTH
707912U65A-120_805

Formerly: Health +
Tel: 020 7782 4000 **Fax:** 020 7772 4070
Email: health@the-sun.co.uk
Frequency: Weekly - Published on Thursday within The Sun
Summary of Content: Section covering features and articles on medical and health issues.
Section of: The Sun
NATIONAL DAILY & SUNDAY NEWSPAPERS: National Daily Newspapers

HOMES AND HOLIDAYS
1642163U65B-40_782

Tel: 020 7293 3272 **Fax:** 020 7293 3073
Email: features@sundaymirror.co.uk
Frequency: Weekly
Editor: Jill Main; **Features Editor:** Jill Main
Summary of Content: Section covering holiday destinations and information also, tips and advice on improving your house, with expert advice on how to make money from your home.
Mechanical Data: Type Area: 328 x 250mm, Col Length: 328mm, Page Width: 250mm, Trim Size: 344 x 268mm, Bleed Size: 356 x 274mm, No. of Columns (Display): 7, Col Widths (Display): 37.5mm, Film: Digital
Section of: Sunday Mirror
NATIONAL DAILY & SUNDAY NEWSPAPERS: National Sunday Newspapers

IN GEAR
632116U65B-70_775

Formerly: Driving
Tel: 020 7782 5000 **Fax:** 020 7782 5100
Email: ingear@sunday-times.co.uk
Frequency: Sunday - Published within The Sunday Times
Editor: Emma Smith
Summary of Content: Section covering motoring issues, road safety and car profiles.
ADVERTISING RATES:
SCC £105.00
Section of: The Sunday Times
NATIONAL DAILY & SUNDAY NEWSPAPERS: National Sunday Newspapers

THE INDEPENDENT
41692U65A-93

Editorial Address: Northcliffe House, 2 Derry Street, LONDON, W8 5TT **Tel:** 020 7005 2000 **Fax:** 020 7005 2999
Email: newseditor@independent.co.uk
Advertising Address: As above. **Fax:** 020 7005 2581
Email: k.pearman@independent.co.uk
Web site: http://www.independent.co.uk
Publisher: Independent News and Media (UK) Ltd
Frequency: Mornings - Not published on Sunday
Cover Price: £0.80
Circulation: 187,837 (ABC 03/08/2009 to 30/08/2009)
Editor: News Desk; **News Editor:** Oliver Wright; **Executive Editor:** Ben Preston; **Features Editor:** Rebecca Armstrong; **Editor-in-Chief:** Simon Kelner; **Managing Director:** Simon Kelner; **Managing Editor:** Imogen Haddon
Summary of Content: Compact-sized quality newspaper, containing in-depth national and international news with coverage of politics, finance, media, IT, education, jobs, sport, travel, arts and entertainment.
Twitter: http://twitter.com/TheIndyNews.
ADVERTISING RATES:
Full Page Mono £9380.00
Full Page Colour £14484.00
SCC £44.00
Agency Commission: 15%
Mechanical Data: Col Widths (Display): 34mm, No. of Columns (Display): 7, Col Length: 340mm, Type Area: 340 x 262mm, Print Process: Web-fed offset litho, Film: Digital, Page Width: 262mm
Copy instructions: Copy Date: mono 2 working days colour 7 working days prior to publication date
Sections:
Arts
Business
The Independent Education
The Independent Property
The Independent Review
The Independent Sport
The Information Daily
Media Weekly
Network
Traveller
Supplement(s): FE - 4xY, The Independent Arts & Books Review - 52xY, The Independent Magazine - 52xY, The Information - 52xY, Life - 365xY, Save and Spend - 52xY
NATIONAL DAILY & SUNDAY NEWSPAPERS: National Daily Newspapers

THE INDEPENDENT ARTS & BOOKS REVIEW
1665009U65A-93_838

Editorial Address: For all contact details see main record, The Independent **Tel:** 020 7005 2000 **Fax:** 020 7005 2466
Email: d.lister@independent.co.uk
Frequency: Weekly - Published on Friday within The Independent
Editor: David Lister
Summary of Content: Cultural supplement embracing diverse areas of the arts including a lengthy cover story on a topical cultural issue, or interview with a leading arts figure, has features and reviews on film, pop and rock, jazz and world music, a books interview and reviews.
Supplement to: The Independent
NATIONAL DAILY & SUNDAY NEWSPAPERS: National Daily Newspapers

THE INDEPENDENT EDUCATION
41695U65A-93_740

Tel: 020 7005 2000 **Fax:** 020 7005 2143
Frequency: Weekly - Published on Thursdays within The Independent
Editor: Lucy Hodges
Summary of Content: Covers education and appointments.
Section of: The Independent
NATIONAL DAILY & SUNDAY NEWSPAPERS: National Daily Newspapers

THE INDEPENDENT MAGAZINE
41866U65H-34

Editorial Address: Northcliffe House, 2 Derry Street, LONDON, W8 5TT **Tel:** 020 7005 2000 **Fax:** 020 7005 2799
Email: magazine@independent.co.uk
Advertising Address: As above. **Fax:** 020 7005 2581
Email: c.evans@independent.co.uk
Web site: http://www.independent.co.uk
Publisher: Independent News and Media (UK) Ltd
Frequency: Weekly - Published on Saturday. See main record for circulation figure
Editor: Charlotte Philby
Summary of Content: Magazine containing general features including fashion, style, interiors, food and drink.
ADVERTISING RATES:
Full Page Colour £10000.00
Agency Commission: 15%
Mechanical Data: No. of Columns (Display): 6, Film: Digital
Copy instructions: Copy Date: 12 days prior to publication date
Average advertising content per issue: 20%
Supplement to: The Independent
NATIONAL DAILY & SUNDAY NEWSPAPERS: National Colour Supplements

THE INDEPENDENT ON SUNDAY
41750U65B-3

Editorial Address: Northcliffe House, 2 Derry Street, LONDON, W8 5TT **Tel:** 020 7005 2000 **Fax:** 020 7005 2047
Email: sundaynews@independent.co.uk
Advertising Address: As above. **Fax:** 020 7005 2581
Email: s.wheeleri@independent.co.uk
Web site: http://www.independent.co.uk
Publisher: Independent News and Media (UK) Ltd
Frequency: Sunday
Cover Price: £1.80
Circulation: 160,809 (ABC 03/08/2009 to 30/08/2009)
Editor: Peter Victor; **Executive Editor:** Lisa Markwell; **Editor-in-Chief:** Simon Kelner; **Managing Editor:** Imogen Haddon
Summary of Content: Compact-sized quality Sunday newspaper containing in-depth national and international news with coverage of politics, finance, IT, education, careers, jobs, sport, travel, arts, culture and entertainment.
Twitter: http://twitter.com/TheIndyNews.
ADVERTISING RATES:
Full Page Mono £8570.00
Full Page Colour £13050.00
SCC £42.00
Mechanical Data: Type Area: 340 x 262mm, Col Length: 340mm, Page Width: 262mm, Col Widths (Display): 34mm, No. of Columns (Display): 7, Print Process: Web offset, Film: Digital
Copy instructions: Copy Date: 3 days prior to publication date
Sections:
The Independent on Sunday Business
The Independent on Sunday Money
Sportsweek
Travel Section
Supplement(s): The New Review - 52xY
NATIONAL DAILY & SUNDAY NEWSPAPERS: National Sunday Newspapers

THE INDEPENDENT ON SUNDAY BUSINESS
41752U65B-3_720

Tel: 020 7005 2000 **Fax:** 020 7005 2096
Email: m.pagano@independent.co.uk

Frequency: Sunday - Published within The Independent on Sunday
Editor: Margareta Pagano
Summary of Content: Section containing business news, property, telecoms, media, technology and market information reports.
ADVERTISING RATES:
Full Page Mono £8570.00
Full Page Colour £13050.00
SCC £42.00
Section of: The Independent on Sunday
NATIONAL DAILY & SUNDAY NEWSPAPERS: National Sunday Newspapers

THE INDEPENDENT ON SUNDAY MONEY
41754U65B-3_760

Tel: 020 7005 2000 **Fax:** 020 7005 2098
Frequency: Sunday - Published within The Independent on Sunday
Editor: Julian Knight
Summary of Content: Section concerned with all aspects of personal finance.
ADVERTISING: Rates on application
Section of: The Independent on Sunday
NATIONAL DAILY & SUNDAY NEWSPAPERS: National Sunday Newspapers

THE INDEPENDENT PROPERTY
768645U65A-93_836

Tel: 020 7005 2000 **Fax:** 020 7005 2824
Email: b.davison@independent.co.uk
Frequency: Weekly - Published on Wednesday within The Independent
Editor: Christian Broughton
Summary of Content: Section looking at the property market including trends and lifestyle features.
Section of: The Independent
NATIONAL DAILY & SUNDAY NEWSPAPERS: National Daily Newspapers

THE INDEPENDENT REVIEW
41702U65A-93_825

Formerly: The Review
Tel: 020 7005 2000 **Fax:** 020 7005 2182
Frequency: Mornings - Published Monday to Friday within The Independent
Summary of Content: Daily section with features, comment, arts, listings, television, lifestyle and travel.
Section of: The Independent
NATIONAL DAILY & SUNDAY NEWSPAPERS: National Daily Newspapers

THE INDEPENDENT SPORT
41704U65A-93_760

Tel: 020 7005 2000 **Fax:** 020 7005 2894
Email: m.tench@independent.co.uk
Frequency: Mornings - Published within The Independent
Editor: Chris Broughton
Summary of Content: Section containing fixtures, news, reports and features on sport.
Section of: The Independent
NATIONAL DAILY & SUNDAY NEWSPAPERS: National Daily Newspapers

THE INFORMATION DAILY
41699U65A-93_788

Tel: 020 7005 2000 **Fax:** 020 7005 2182
Email: information@independent.co.uk
Frequency: Mornings - Published Monday to Friday within the Independent
Editor: Stuart Price
Summary of Content: Section containing television and radio listings plus cinema and arts listings.
Section of: The Independent
NATIONAL DAILY & SUNDAY NEWSPAPERS: National Daily Newspapers

IT'S FRIDAY
41610U65A-20_770

Tel: 020 7938 6585 **Fax:** 020 7938 7671
Frequency: Weekly - Published on Fridays within the Daily Mail
Editor: Win Blackmore
Summary of Content: Section carrying news and gossip from the world of entertainment. Includes film, music, theatre, dance, book reviews and a shopping page.
ADVERTISING: Rates on application
Section of: Daily Mail
NATIONAL DAILY & SUNDAY NEWSPAPERS: National Daily Newspapers

LIFE
1746360U65H-116

Formerly: Extra
Editorial Address: Northcliffe House, 2 Derry Street, LONDON, W8 5TT **Tel:** 020 7005 2719 **Fax:** 020 7005 2939
Email: features@independent.co.uk
Advertising Address: As above. **Tel:** 020 7005 2000
Fax: 020 7005 2581
Email: k.pearman@independent.co.uk
Web site: http://www.independent.co.uk
Publisher: Independent News and Media (UK) Ltd
Frequency: Daily - For circulation see main record
Editor: Jamie Merrill, **Executive Editor:** Adam Leigh;
Features Editor: Susie Rushton; **Advertising Manager:** Darren Evans
Summary of Content: Features supplement with articles covering lifestyle, art and culture, beauty, health and environmental issues.
ADVERTISING RATES:
Full Page Mono £10472.00
Full Page Colour £16660.00
SCC £44.00
Agency Commission: 15%
Copy instructions: Copy Date: Mono 2 working days prior to publication date Colour 7 working days prior to publication date
Supplement to: The Independent
NATIONAL DAILY & SUNDAY NEWSPAPERS: National Colour Supplements

LIVE
41869U65H-42

Formerly: Live Night & Day
Editorial Address: Northcliffe House, 2 Derry Street, LONDON, W8 5TT **Tel:** 020 7938 6000
Advertising Address: As above. **Tel:** 020 7938 7312
Fax: 020 7937 5320
Email: advertising@mailonsunday.co.uk
Publisher: Associated Newspapers Ltd
Frequency: Weekly - See main record for circulation figure
Editor: Andrew Davies; **Advertising Manager:** Joanne Shorrock
Summary of Content: Magazine containing interviews and entertainment coverage with features on: going-out, clubbing, male trends, gadgets and technology. Includes Choice, a television listings section.
ADVERTISING RATES:
Full Page Mono £43567.00
Full Page Colour £43567.00
Mechanical Data: Bleed Size: 358 x 274mm, Trim Size: 350 x 270mm, Print Process: Offset litho, Col Length: 320mm, Page Width: 242mm, Type Area: 320 x 242mm, Film: Digital
Copy instructions: Copy Date: 10 working days prior to publication date
Supplement to: The Mail on Sunday
NATIONAL DAILY & SUNDAY NEWSPAPERS: National Colour Supplements

THE MAIL ON SUNDAY
41759U65B-5

Editorial Address: Northcliffe House, 2 Derry Street, LONDON, W8 5TT **Tel:** 020 7938 6000 **Fax:** 020 7937 3829
Email: news@mailonsunday.co.uk
Advertising Address: As above. **Fax:** 020 7937 5320
Email: steve.maddren@mailonsunday.co.uk
Web site: http://www.mailonsunday.co.uk
Publisher: Associated Newspapers Ltd
Date Established: 1982
Frequency: Sunday
Cover Price: £1.50
Circulation: 2,013,742 (ABC 03/08/2009 to 30/08/2009)
Editor: Peter Wright; **News Editor:** David Dillon **Features Editor:** Sian James; **Editor-in-Chief:** Paul Dacre;
Advertising Manager: Steve Maddren **Advertising Director:** Simon Davies
Summary of Content: Tabloid-sized Sunday newspaper covering national and international news with features on travel, finance, sport, women's interest, entertainment and health.
Twitter: http://twitter.com/mailonline.
ADVERTISING RATES:
Full Page Mono £39300.00
Full Page Colour £55800.00
Agency Commission: 15%
Mechanical Data: Col Length: 358mm, No. of Columns (Display): 7, Page Width: 268mm, Type Area: 358 x 268mm, Film: Digital
Copy instructions: Copy Date: Mono Thursday 10.30am prior to publication date Colour Wednesday 3.30pm prior to publication date
Sections:
The Mail on Sunday
Supplement(s): Live - 52xY, You Magazine The Mail on Sunday - 52xY
NATIONAL DAILY & SUNDAY NEWSPAPERS: National Sunday Newspapers

THE MAIL ON SUNDAY 2
1831421U65B-5_882

Email: news@mailonsunday.co.uk
Frequency: Weekly - Published on Sunday
Editor: Peter Wright
Summary of Content: Section featuring reviews, health, property, travel, critics and puzzles.
Section of: The Mail on Sunday
NATIONAL DAILY & SUNDAY NEWSPAPERS: National Sunday Newspapers

MEDIA GUARDIAN
41691U65A-90_860

Tel: 020 3353 2000
Email: jane.martinson@guardian.co.uk
Frequency: Weekly - Published on Mondays within The Guardian
Editor: Jane Martinson
Summary of Content: Section focusing on the media industry with news, features, profiles and appointments.
ADVERTISING: Rates on application
Section of: The Guardian
NATIONAL DAILY & SUNDAY NEWSPAPERS: National Daily Newspapers

MEDIA NEWS
41639U65A-50_883

Tel: 020 7931 2000 **Fax:** 020 7538 7878
Frequency: Weekly - Published on Thursday within The Daily Telegraph
Editor: Tom Leonard
Summary of Content: Section covering media news.
ADVERTISING: Rates on application
Section of: The Daily Telegraph
NATIONAL DAILY & SUNDAY NEWSPAPERS: National Daily Newspapers

MEDIA WEEKLY
41700U65A-93_790

Formerly: Media
Tel: 020 7005 2000 **Fax:** 020 7005 2307
Frequency: Weekly - Published on Mondays within The Independent
Editor: Ian Burrell
Summary of Content: Provides detailed analysis across all sections of the media and includes interviews with high profile figures.
Section of: The Independent
NATIONAL DAILY & SUNDAY NEWSPAPERS: National Daily Newspapers

MIRROR FC
1647184U65A-100_901

Tel: 020 7293 2432 **Fax:** 020 7293 3739
Email: fc@mirror.co.uk
Frequency: Weekly - Published on Saturday during the football season, within the Daily Mirror
Editor: Steve Anglesea
Summary of Content: Section providing a guide to the weekend's professional football, focusing mainly on the Premiership, it has features, statistics, previews and interviews.
ADVERTISING: Rates on application
Section of: Daily Mirror
NATIONAL DAILY & SUNDAY NEWSPAPERS: National Daily Newspapers

MIRROR MANIA
41714U65A-100_760

Tel: 020 7293 3386 **Fax:** 020 7293 3739
Email: dean.morse@mirror.co.uk
Frequency: Weekly - Published on Monday within the Daily Mirror
Editor: Dean Morse
Summary of Content: Section focusing on football with news and results.
ADVERTISING: Rates on application
Section of: Daily Mirror
NATIONAL DAILY & SUNDAY NEWSPAPERS: National Daily Newspapers

MIRROR MONEY
41715U65A-100_770

Tel: 020 7293 3650 **Fax:** 020 7293 3801
Email: money@mirror.co.uk
Frequency: Weekly - Published on Wednesday within the Daily Mirror
Editor: Tricia Phillips
Summary of Content: Personal finance guide.
ADVERTISING: Rates on application
Section of: Daily Mirror
NATIONAL DAILY & SUNDAY NEWSPAPERS: National Daily Newspapers

MIRROR RACING
41716U65A-100_800

Tel: 020 7293 3284 **Fax:** 020 7293 3739
Email: david.mitchell@mirror.co.uk
Frequency: Mornings - Published Monday to Friday within the Daily Mirror
Editor: Dave Mitchell
Summary of Content: Section covering racing features and fixtures.
ADVERTISING: Rates on application
Section of: Daily Mirror
NATIONAL DAILY & SUNDAY NEWSPAPERS: National Daily Newspapers

MIRROR SPORT
41717U65A-100_850

Tel: 020 7293 3386 **Fax:** 020 7293 3739
Email: dean.morse@mirror.co.uk
Frequency: Mornings - Published within the Daily Mirror
Editor: Dean Morse
Summary of Content: Sports news, features and fixtures.
ADVERTISING: Rates on application
Section of: Daily Mirror
NATIONAL DAILY & SUNDAY NEWSPAPERS: National Daily Newspapers

THE MIRROR WORKS
41719U65A-100_890

Tel: 020 7293 3000 **Fax:** 020 7293 3544
Email: t.phillips@mirror.co.uk
Frequency: Weekly - Published on Thursday within the Daily Mirror
Editor: Tricia Phillips
Summary of Content: Features on employment plus job adverts.
ADVERTISING: Rates on application
Section of: Daily Mirror
NATIONAL DAILY & SUNDAY NEWSPAPERS: National Daily Newspapers

MONEY
41662U65A-10_820

Tel: 020 8612 7000 **Fax:** 0871 520 7766
Frequency: Weekly - Published on Wednesdays within the Daily Express
Editor: Chris Torney
Summary of Content: Section containing personal finance.
ADVERTISING: Rates on application
Section of: Daily Express
NATIONAL DAILY & SUNDAY NEWSPAPERS: National Daily Newspapers

MONEY
41682U65A-90_785

Formerly: Guardian Jobs & Money
Tel: 020 3353 2000
Email: money@guardian.co.uk
Frequency: Weekly - Published on Saturdays within The Guardian
Editor: Patrick Collinson
Summary of Content: Section with reports on the job market and money features.
ADVERTISING: Rates on application
Section of: The Guardian
NATIONAL DAILY & SUNDAY NEWSPAPERS: National Daily Newspapers

MONEY MAIL
41611U65A-20_790

Tel: 020 7938 6137 **Fax:** 020 7937 8161
Email: money.press@dailymail.co.uk
Frequency: Weekly - Published on Wednesdays within the Daily Mail
Editor: Tony Hazell
Summary of Content: Section reporting on personal finance issues such as pensions, savings and investments.
ADVERTISING: Rates on application
Section of: Daily Mail
NATIONAL DAILY & SUNDAY NEWSPAPERS: National Daily Newspapers

MOTORING
755514U65A-10_822

Tel: 020 8612 7000 **Fax:** 0871 520 7766
Email: nat.barnes@express.co.uk
Frequency: Weekly - Published on Saturday within the Daily Express
Summary of Content: Section covering cars and motoring, includes new car and motorcycle launches.
ADVERTISING: Rates on application
Section of: Daily Express
NATIONAL DAILY & SUNDAY NEWSPAPERS: National Daily Newspapers

NETWORK
41701U65A-93_810

Tel: 020 7005 2000 **Fax:** 020 7005 2939
Frequency: Weekly - Published on Mondays within The Independent
Editor: Simon O'Hagan
Summary of Content: Section with news and features on the IT industry, including new products.
Section of: The Independent
NATIONAL DAILY & SUNDAY NEWSPAPERS: National Daily Newspapers

THE NEW REVIEW
41875U65H-70

Formerly: The Sunday Review
Editorial Address: Northcliffe House, 2 Derry Street, LONDON, W8 5TT **Tel:** 020 7005 2000 **Fax:** 020 7005 2627
Email: newreview@independent.co.uk
Advertising Address: As above.
Email: p.ellwood@independent.co.uk
Web site: http://www.independent.co.uk
Publisher: Independent News and Media (UK) Ltd
Date Established: 1989
Frequency: Weekly - See main record for circulation figure
Editor: Lisa Markwell
Summary of Content: Contains features on arts, music, books, culture, fashion, cookery, food and drink, architecture and women's interest.
ADVERTISING RATES:
Full Page Mono £10000.00
Full Page Colour £10000.00
Agency Commission: 15%
Mechanical Data: Type Area: 310 x 232mm, Bleed Size: 348 x 276mm, Col Length: 310mm, Page Width: 232mm, Trim Size: 340 x 270mm, Film: Digital
Copy instructions: Copy Date: 14 working days prior to publication date
Supplement to: The Independent on Sunday
NATIONAL DAILY & SUNDAY NEWSPAPERS: National Colour Supplements

NEWS OF THE WORLD
41768U65B-10

Editorial Address: 1 Virginia Street, LONDON, E98 1NW
Tel: 020 7782 4000 **Fax:** 020 7583 9504
Email: newsdesk@notw.co.uk
Advertising Address: As above. **Fax:** 020 7782 7191
Email: jane.west@newsint.co.uk
Web site: http://www.newsoftheworld.co.uk
Publisher: News Group Newspapers Ltd
Date Established: 1843
Frequency: Sunday
Cover Price: £0.85
Circulation: 3,120,991 (ABC 03/08/2009 to 30/08/2009)
Editor: Neil McLeod; **News Editor:** James Mellor; **Executive Editor:** Neil Wallis; **Features Editor:** Matthew Nixson; **Managing Editor:** Stuart Kuttner
Summary of Content: Newspaper covering national and international news stories, with articles on lifestyle, health, fashion, entertainment, television, show-biz and sport.
ADVERTISING RATES:
Full Page Mono £41816.00
Full Page Colour £56180.00
SCC £183.00
Mechanical Data: Page Width: 264mm, Col Length: 338mm, Col Widths (Display): 34mm, No. of Columns (Display): 7, Type Area: 338 x 264mm, Film: Digital
Copy instructions: Copy Date: Mono 2pm 1 working day prior Colour 3 working days prior to publication date
Sections:
Score
Supplement(s): Fabulous - 52xY
NATIONAL DAILY & SUNDAY NEWSPAPERS: National Sunday Newspapers

NEWS OF THE WORLD (GLASGOW OFFICE)
41849U65D-100

Editorial Address: 5th Floor, Guildhall, 57 Queen Street, GLASGOW, G1 3EN **Tel:** 0141 420 5254 **Fax:** 0141 420 5255
Email: scottish.news@notw.co.uk
Publisher: News Group Newspapers Ltd
Editor: Craig Jackson; **News Editor:** Craig Jackson
ADVERTISING: No Advertising taken
NATIONAL DAILY & SUNDAY NEWSPAPERS: National Sunday Regional Offices

NEWS OF THE WORLD (MANCHESTER OFFICE)
41845U65D-20

Editorial Address: 16th Floor, 111 Piccadilly, MANCHESTER, M1 2HY **Tel:** 0161 935 5290
Fax: 0161 228 2927
Publisher: News Group Newspapers Ltd
Editor: Keith Gladdis
ADVERTISING: No Advertising taken
NATIONAL DAILY & SUNDAY NEWSPAPERS: National Sunday Regional Offices

THE OBSERVER
41770U65B-20

Editorial Address: Kings Place, 90 York Way, LONDON, N1 9GU **Tel:** 020 3353 2000
Email: news@observer.co.uk
Advertising Address: 119 Farringdon Road, LONDON, EC1R 3ER **Tel:** 020 7239 9735
Email: alexandra.turner@guardian.co.uk
Web site: http://www.observer.co.uk
Publisher: Guardian Media Group plc
Date Established: 1791
Frequency: Sunday
Cover Price: £1.90
Circulation: 361,761 (ABC 03/08/2009 to 30/08/2009)
Editor: John Mulholland; **News Editor:** Chris Boffey; **Managing Editor:** Jan Thompson
Summary of Content: Berliner-sized quality Sunday newspaper containing in-depth national and international news with political and financial coverage, social issues, media, education, IT, jobs, travel, sport, arts and entertainment. A digital edition is also available.
ADVERTISING RATES:
Full Page Mono £13933.00
Full Page Colour £22000.00
Agency Commission: 15%
Mechanical Data: Film: Digital, Col Length: 440mm, No. of Columns (Display): 10
Copy instructions: Copy Date: Mono Friday 3pm prior to publication date Colour Wednesday 12pm prior to publication date
Sections:
The Observer Business & Media
The Observer Cash
The Observer Escape
The Observer Review
The Observer Sport
Editions:
Observer (North)
Observer Scotland
Supplement(s): Observer Film Quarterly - 4xY, The Observer Food Monthly - 12xY, Observer Music Monthly - 12xY, The Observer Sport Monthly - 12xY, Observer Woman - 12xY, OM The Observer Magazine - 52xY
NATIONAL DAILY & SUNDAY NEWSPAPERS: National Sunday Newspapers

THE OBSERVER BUSINESS & MEDIA
41771U65B-20_721

Tel: 020 3353 2000
Email: business@observer.co.uk
Frequency: Weekly - Published within The Observer
Editor: Ruth Sunderland
Summary of Content: Section containing business news and features. Also covers careers and media news.
ADVERTISING: Rates on application
Section of: The Observer
NATIONAL DAILY & SUNDAY NEWSPAPERS: National Sunday Newspapers

THE OBSERVER CASH
41772U65B-20_725

Email: cash@observer.co.uk
Frequency: Weekly - Published within The Observer
Editor: Lisa Bachelor
Summary of Content: Section covering personal finance and property.
ADVERTISING: Rates on application
Copy instructions: Copy Date: Mono Friday 3pm prior to publication date Colour Wednesday 3pm prior to publication date
Section of: The Observer
NATIONAL DAILY & SUNDAY NEWSPAPERS: National Sunday Newspapers

THE OBSERVER ESCAPE
41773U65B-20_737

Tel: 020 3353 2000
Email: escape@observer.co.uk
Frequency: Weekly - Published within The Observer
Editor: Joanne O'Connor
Summary of Content: Section covering travel.
ADVERTISING: Rates on application
Copy instructions: Copy Date: Mono Thursday 3pm prior to publication date Colour Wednesday 3pm prior to publication date
Section of: The Observer
NATIONAL DAILY & SUNDAY NEWSPAPERS: National Sunday Newspapers

THE OBSERVER REVIEW
41774U65B-20_781

Tel: 020 3353 2000
Email: review@observer.co.uk
Frequency: Weekly - Published within The Observer
Editor: Jane Ferguson
Summary of Content: Contains features, music, film, television, arts and book reviews.
ADVERTISING: Rates on application

Copy instructions: Copy Date: Mono Thursday 3pm prior to publication date Colour Wednesday 12pm prior to publication date
Section of: The Observer
NATIONAL DAILY & SUNDAY NEWSPAPERS: National Sunday Newspapers

THE OBSERVER SPORT
41776U65B-20_841

Tel: 020 3353 2000
Email: sport@observer.co.uk
Frequency: Weekly - Published within The Observer
Editor: Brian Oliver
Summary of Content: Section containing sports news, features and fixtures.
ADVERTISING: Rates on application
Section of: The Observer
NATIONAL DAILY & SUNDAY NEWSPAPERS: National Sunday Newspapers

OBSERVER WOMAN
1705324U65H-113

Editorial Address: Kings Place, 90 York Way, LONDON, N1 9GU **Tel:** 020 3353 2000
Email: observer.woman@observer.co.uk
Advertising Address: 119 Farringdon Road, LONDON, EC1R 3ER **Tel:** 020 7278 2332 **Fax:** 020 7278 1448
Email: joe.doherty@guardian.co.uk
Web site: http://www.observer.co.uk/woman
Publisher: Guardian Media Group plc
Date Established: 2006
Frequency: Monthly - See main record for circulation figure
Editor: Eva Wiseman; **Advertising Manager:** Joe Doherty
Summary of Content: Lifestyle supplement with items of interest to men and women. Includes a section covering fashion, shopping, gadgets and beauty, with features on relationships and lifestyles as well as interviews with high profile celebrities.
ADVERTISING RATES:
Full Page Colour £11000.00
Mechanical Data: Type Area: 260 x 198mm, Bleed Size: 301 x 232mm, Trim Size: 291 x 222mm, Col Length: 260mm, Page Width: 198mm, Film: Digital
Copy instructions: Copy Date: 10 days prior to publication date
Supplement to: The Observer
NATIONAL DAILY & SUNDAY NEWSPAPERS: National Colour Supplements

OM THE OBSERVER MAGAZINE
41867U65H-36

Formerly: Observer Magazine
Editorial Address: Kings Place, 90 York Way, LONDON, N1 9GU **Tel:** 020 3353 2000
Email: magazine@observer.co.uk
Advertising Address: 119 Farringdon Road, LONDON, EC1R 3ER **Tel:** 020 7239 9917
Email: michael.craigg@guardian.co.uk
Publisher: Guardian Media Group plc
Frequency: Weekly - See main record for circulation figure
Editor: Allan Jenkins; **Features Editor:** Ian Tucker; **Advertising Manager:** Michael Craigg
Summary of Content: Magazine containing features and interviews plus coverage of fashion, food and drink, health, motoring, gardening and interiors.
ADVERTISING RATES:
Full Page Colour £10000.00
Mechanical Data: Type Area: 250 x 187mm, Bleed Size: 281 x 216mm, Trim Size: 271 x 206mm, Col Length: 250mm, Page Width: 187mm, Film: Digital
Copy instructions: Copy Date: 14 working days prior to publication date
Supplement to: The Observer
NATIONAL DAILY & SUNDAY NEWSPAPERS: National Colour Supplements

THE PEOPLE
41790U65B-45

Formerly: Sunday People
Editorial Address: 1 Canada Square, Canary Wharf, LONDON, E14 5AP **Tel:** 020 7293 3000 **Fax:** 020 7293 3517
Email: peoplenews@mgn.co.uk
Advertising Address: As above. **Fax:** 020 7293 3405
Email: caroline.kildare-morgan@mgn.co.uk
Web site: http://www.people.co.uk
Publisher: Trinity Mirror
Frequency: Sunday
Cover Price: £0.90
Circulation: 586,414 (ABC 03/08/2009 to 30/08/2009)
Editor: Lloyd Embley; **News Editor:** Lee Harpin; **Features Editor:** Caroline Waterston; **Advertising Manager:** Caroline Kildare-Morgan
Summary of Content: Tabloid-sized Sunday newspaper covering general interest stories, show-biz and sport.
ADVERTISING RATES:
Full Page Mono £23100.00
Full Page Colour £29500.00
SCC £89.00

National Newspapers

Mechanical Data: Film: Digital, Col Length: 341mm, No. of Columns (Display): 7, Col Widths (Display): 34mm, Type Area: 341 x 265mm, Page Width: 265mm
Copy instructions: Copy Date: Mono 5 days Colour 7 days prior to publication date
Sections:
The SP
Editions:
People Scotland
Supplement(s): Take it Easy - 52xY
NATIONAL DAILY & SUNDAY NEWSPAPERS: National Sunday Newspapers

PROPERTY MAIL
764358U65A-20_815
Tel: 020 7938 6000 **Fax:** 020 7938 6755
Email: property@dailymail.co.uk
Frequency: Weekly - Published on Friday within the Daily Mail
Editor: Jenny Coad
Summary of Content: Section looking at residential property including celebrity driven articles, the housing market and new developments.
ADVERTISING: Rates on application
Section of: Daily Mail
NATIONAL DAILY & SUNDAY NEWSPAPERS: National Daily Newspapers

PUBLIC SECTOR
1620650U65A-130_864
Formerly: Public Agenda
Tel: 020 7782 5651 **Fax:** 020 7782 5125
Email: agenda@thetimes.co.uk
Frequency: Weekly - Published on Friday within The Times
Summary of Content: Digest of the professional public sector media.
ADVERTISING: No Advertising taken
Section of: The Times
NATIONAL DAILY & SUNDAY NEWSPAPERS: National Daily Newspapers

RACING POST EXTRA
762987U65A-100_900
Formerly: The Winner
Tel: 020 7293 3284 **Fax:** 020 7293 3739
Email: david.mitchell@mirror.co.uk
Frequency: Weekly - Published on Saturday within the Daily Mirror
Editor: Dave Mitchell
Summary of Content: Section covering racing news, results, fixtures and articles on betting and tips.
ADVERTISING: Rates on application
Section of: Daily Mirror
NATIONAL DAILY & SUNDAY NEWSPAPERS: National Daily Newspapers

THE REVIEW
41711U65A-100_750
Formerly: Mega Mirror
Tel: 020 7293 3000 **Fax:** 020 7293 3834
Email: alun.palmer@mirror.co.uk
Frequency: Weekly - Published on Saturday within the Daily Mirror
Editor: Alun Palmer
Summary of Content: Section covering homes, travel, music, DVDs, gadgets, books, gardening and food and drink.
ADVERTISING: Rates on application
Section of: Daily Mirror
NATIONAL DAILY & SUNDAY NEWSPAPERS: National Daily Newspapers

S THE SUNDAY EXPRESS
41873U65H-58
Formerly: The Sunday Express Magazine
Editorial Address: The Northern & Shell Building, 10 Lower Thames Street, LONDON, EC3R 6EN **Tel:** 020 8612 7000
Fax: 0871 434 7305
Email: benita.adesuyan@express.co.uk
Advertising Address: As above. **Tel:** 0871 434 1010
Fax: 0871 521 2753
Email: tarun.naipaul@express.co.uk
Publisher: Express Newspapers Ltd
Frequency: Weekly - See main record for circulation figure Free to qualifying individuals
Editor: Benita Adesuyan; **Advertising Manager:** Tarun Naipaul
Summary of Content: Magazine containing features and interviews plus shopping, home entertainment, health, interiors, food and gardening.
ADVERTISING RATES:
Full Page Mono £27500.00
Full Page Colour £27500.00
Mechanical Data: Type Area: 240 x 206mm, Bleed Size: 281 x 234mm, Trim Size: 275 x 228mm, Col Length: 240mm, Page Width: 206mm
Copy instructions: Copy Date: 10 days prior to publication date

Supplement to: Sunday Express
NATIONAL DAILY & SUNDAY NEWSPAPERS: National Colour Supplements

SAVE AND SPEND
41698U65A-93_780
Formerly: The Independent Your Money
Editorial Address: For all contact details see main record, The Independent **Tel:** 020 7005 2062 **Fax:** 020 7005 2098
Email: cash@independent.co.uk
Frequency: Weekly - Published on Saturdays within The Independent
Editor: David Prosser
Summary of Content: Section covering personal finance.
Supplement to: The Independent
NATIONAL DAILY & SUNDAY NEWSPAPERS: National Daily Newspapers

SCORE
706686U65B-10_750
Tel: 020 7782 4372 **Fax:** 020 7782 4393
Email: mike.dunn@news-of-the-world.co.uk
Frequency: Weekly
Editor: Mike Dunn
Summary of Content: Section covering football news, results and statistics.
Section of: News of the World
NATIONAL DAILY & SUNDAY NEWSPAPERS: National Sunday Newspapers

SCOTTISH DAILY EXPRESS (GLASGOW)
41838U65C-275
Formerly: Scottish Express (Glasgow)
Editorial Address: Citypoint 2, 25 Tyndrum Street, GLASGOW, G4 0JY **Tel:** 0141 352 2521 **Fax:** 0141 352 2555
Email: scot.news@express.co.uk
Web site: http://www.scottishdailyexpress.co.uk
Publisher: Express Newspapers Ltd
Date Established: 1928
Frequency: Daily
Cover Price: £0.35
Circulation: 80,000 (Publisher's Statement)
Editor: Tom Martin; **News Editor:** Tom Fullerton; **Executive Editor:** David Hamilton
ADVERTISING: No Advertising taken
NATIONAL DAILY & SUNDAY NEWSPAPERS: National Daily Regional Offices

SCOTTISH DAILY MAIL
41837U65C-277
Editorial Address: 20 Waterloo Street, GLASGOW, G2 6DB
Tel: 0141 331 4700 **Fax:** 0141 331 4707
Email: scotland@dailymail.co.uk
Advertising Address: Media Link, Pavilion 1, Castlecraig Business Park, Players Road, STIRLING, FK7 7SH
Tel: 01786 433100 **Fax:** 01786 433101
Email: gill.dolan@media-link.co.uk
Publisher: Associated Newspapers Ltd
Circulation: 128,604 (ABC 29/01/2007 to 25/02/2007)
Editor: Tim Knowles; **News Editor:** Tim Knowles
ADVERTISING RATES:
Full Page Mono £5040.00
Full Page Colour £6300.00
Agency Commission: 10%
Mechanical Data: Type Area: 360 x 268mm, Col Length: 360mm, Page Width: 268mm, Film: Digital, Col Widths (Display): 35mm, No. of Columns (Display): 7
Copy instructions: Copy Date: 4 days prior to publication date
Average advertising content per issue: 50%
NATIONAL DAILY & SUNDAY NEWSPAPERS: National Daily Regional Offices

SCOTTISH DAILY MIRROR (GLASGOW OFFICE)
41839U65C-278
Formerly: Scottish Mirror Glasgow Office
Editorial Address: One Central Quay, GLASGOW, G3 8DA
Tel: 0141 221 2121 **Fax:** 0141 309 3351
Email: reporters@mirror.co.uk
Web site: http://www.mirror.co.uk
Publisher: Trinity Mirror
Editor: Maggie Barry; **Circulation Manager:** Mark Wright
ADVERTISING: No Advertising taken
NATIONAL DAILY & SUNDAY NEWSPAPERS: National Daily Regional Offices

SCOTTISH MAIL ON SUNDAY
41848U65D-99
Formerly: Mail on Sunday in Scotland
Editorial Address: Clydesdale Bank Exchange, 20 Waterloo Street, GLASGOW, G2 6DB **Tel:** 0141 331 4700
Fax: 0141 331 4752
Email: scotland@mailonsunday.co.uk
Publisher: Associated Newspapers Ltd

Frequency: Weekly
Cover Price: £1.50
Circulation: 111,553 (Publisher's Statement)
Editor: Jamie Macaskill
ADVERTISING: No Advertising taken
NATIONAL DAILY & SUNDAY NEWSPAPERS: National Sunday Regional Offices

THE SCOTTISH SUN (GLASGOW OFFICE)
41840U65C-280
Formerly: The Scottish Sun
Editorial Address: Guildhall, 57 Queen Street, GLASGOW, G1 3EN **Tel:** 0141 420 5200 **Fax:** 0141 420 5248
Email: scoop@thesun.co.uk
Web site: http://www.thescottishsun.co.uk/scotsol/homepage
Publisher: News Group Newspapers Ltd
Editor: Alan Muir; **News Editor:** Alan Muir; **Executive Editor:** Mike Kiernan; **Features Editor:** Gill Smith; **Managing Director:** Steven Walker
Summary of Content: Newspaper covering political, business, sports etc. news of Scotland.
Readership/Target Audience: Aimed at Scottish people.
ADVERTISING: No Advertising taken
NATIONAL DAILY & SUNDAY NEWSPAPERS: National Daily Regional Offices

SCOTTISH SUNDAY EXPRESS
41850U65D-130
Editorial Address: Citypoint 2, 25 Tyndrum Street, GLASGOW, G4 0JY **Tel:** 0141 352 2519 **Fax:** 0141 352 2599
Email: scotsunday@express.co.uk
Advertising Address: The Northern & Shell Building, 10 Lower Thames Street, LONDON, EC3R 6EN
Tel: 0871 520 2758 **Fax:** 0871 434 2753
Email: iain.mcmaster@express.co.uk
Web site: http://www.express.co.uk
Publisher: Express Newspapers Ltd
Frequency: Weekly
Cover Price: £1.30
Circulation: 65,000 (Publisher's Statement)
Editor: Derek Lambie; **Advertising Manager:** Iain McMaster
ADVERTISING RATES:
Full Page Mono £4655.00
Full Page Colour £7105.00
SCC £19.00
Agency Commission: 10%
Mechanical Data: Type Area: 345 x 275mm, Col Length: 345mm, Page Width: 275mm, Film: Digital
Copy instructions: Copy Date: 2 days prior to publication date
Average advertising content per issue: 45%
NATIONAL DAILY & SUNDAY NEWSPAPERS: National Sunday Regional Offices

SCREEN
1647183U65A-130_865
Tel: 020 7782 7434 **Fax:** 020 7782 5203
Email: alex.oconnell@thetimes.co.uk
Frequency: Weekly - Published on Thursday within The Times
Editor: Alex O'Connell
Summary of Content: Section covering film reviews with features on current and future releases, retrospectives and interviews.
ADVERTISING RATES:
SCC £67.00
Section of: The Times
NATIONAL DAILY & SUNDAY NEWSPAPERS: National Daily Newspapers

SEVEN
1703691U65H-111
Editorial Address: 111 Buckingham Palace Road, LONDON, SW1W 0DT **Tel:** 020 7931 2000
Advertising Address: As above.
Email: david.wilcox@telegraph.co.uk
Publisher: Telegraph Media Group Ltd
Frequency: Sunday - See main record for circulation figure
Editor: Ross Jones
Summary of Content: Magazine containing arts and culture features and reviews with entertainment coverage and TV and radio listings.
ADVERTISING RATES:
Full Page Colour £17767.00
Agency Commission: 10%
Mechanical Data: Type Area: 277 x 236mm, Bleed Size: 321 x 280mm, Trim Size: 311 x 270mm, Col Length: 277mm, Col Widths (Display): 36mm, No. of Columns (Display): 6, Page Width: 236mm, Film: Digital
Copy instructions: Copy Date: 10 days prior to publication date
Average advertising content per issue: 30%
Supplement to: The Sunday Telegraph
NATIONAL DAILY & SUNDAY NEWSPAPERS: National Colour Supplements

THE SP
766858U65B-45_700

Tel: 020 7293 3503 **Fax:** 020 7293 2403
Email: sport@people.co.uk
Frequency: Sunday - Published within The People
Editor: James Brown
Summary of Content: Section containing the latest sports news, results and features.
ADVERTISING: Rates on application
Section of: The People
NATIONAL DAILY & SUNDAY NEWSPAPERS: National Sunday Newspapers

SPORTSMAIL
41613U65A-20_840

Tel: 020 7938 6202 **Fax:** 020 7938 4053
Frequency: Mornings
Editor: Lee Clayton
Summary of Content: Section carrying sports news and features. Published within the Daily Mail.
ADVERTISING: Rates on application
Section of: Daily Mail
NATIONAL DAILY & SUNDAY NEWSPAPERS: National Daily Newspapers

SPORTSWEEK
41757U65B-3_920

Formerly: The Independent on Sunday Sport
Tel: 020 7005 2847 **Fax:** 020 7005 2894
Frequency: Sunday - Published within The Independent on Sunday
Editor: Marc Padgett
Summary of Content: Section containing sports reports and fixtures.
ADVERTISING RATES:
Full Page Mono £8570.00
Full Page Colour £13050.00
SCC £42.00
Section of: The Independent on Sunday
NATIONAL DAILY & SUNDAY NEWSPAPERS: National Sunday Newspapers

STARFORM
41622U65A-40_810

Tel: 020 7922 7400 **Fax:** 020 7922 7961
Frequency: Mornings - Published on Saturday within the Daily Star
Editor: Tony Lewis
Summary of Content: Section concerned with horse racing, containing news, form guides and tips.
Readership/Target Audience: Aimed at those interested in horse racing.
Section of: Daily Star
NATIONAL DAILY & SUNDAY NEWSPAPERS: National Daily Newspapers

START YOUR OWN BUSINESS
41659U65A-10_730

Formerly: EX Enterprise Express
Tel: 020 8612 7000 **Fax:** 0871 520 7766
Frequency: Mornings - Published within the Daily Express on Mondays
Editor: Chris Torney
Summary of Content: Section containing news and features aimed at people running and setting up small businesses.
ADVERTISING: Rates on application
Section of: Daily Express
NATIONAL DAILY & SUNDAY NEWSPAPERS: National Daily Newspapers

STELLA
41876U65H-78

Formerly: Sunday Telegraph Magazine
Editorial Address: 111 Buckingham Palace Road, LONDON, SW1W 0DT **Tel:** 020 7931 3490
Fax: 020 7931 3426
Email: stella@telegraph.co.uk
Advertising Address: As above. **Tel:** 020 7931 2000
Email: vanessa.gartell@telegraph.co.uk
Web site: http://www.telegraph.co.uk/stellamagazine
Publisher: Telegraph Media Group Ltd
Date Established: 2005
Frequency: Weekly - See main record for circulation figure
Editor: Nisha Diu; **Features Editor:** Kate Salter; **Advertising Manager:** Carley Ayres
Summary of Content: Magazine containing interviews, profiles, investigative stories and features on fashion, beauty, interiors, restaurants, food and drink.
ADVERTISING RATES:
Full Page Colour £17767.00
Mechanical Data: Type Area: 240 X 170mm, Bleed Size: 285 x 215mm, Trim Size: 275 x 205mm, Col Length: 240mm, Page Width: 170mm, Film: Digital
Copy instructions: Copy Date: 21 days prior to publication date

---

Supplement to: The Sunday Telegraph
NATIONAL DAILY & SUNDAY NEWSPAPERS: National Colour Supplements

THE SUN
41722U65A-120

Editorial Address: 1 Virginia Street, LONDON, E98 1SN
Tel: 020 7782 4000 **Fax:** 020 7782 4095
Email: news@the-sun.co.uk
Advertising Address: As above. **Fax:** 020 7782 7262
Email: jane.west@newsint.co.uk
Web site: http://www.the-sun.co.uk
ISSN: 0307-2681
Publisher: News Group Newspapers Ltd
Frequency: Mornings - Not published on Sunday
Cover Price: £0.30
Circulation: 3,128,501 (ABC 03/08/2009 to 30/08/2009)
Editor: News Desk; **Features Editor:** Gavin Glicksman
Summary of Content: Tabloid-sized newspaper covering national and international news stories, with articles on finance, entertainment, television, show-biz and sport. Twitter: http://twitter.com/thesun_news.
ADVERTISING RATES:
Full Page Mono £43540.00
Full Page Colour £55502.00
SCC £182.00
Mechanical Data: Type Area: 338 x 264mm, Col Length: 338mm, No. of Columns (Display): 7, Col Widths (Display): 34mm, Print Process: Offset-litho, Film: Digital, Page Width: 264mm
Sections:
Bizarre
Favourite
Health
Sun City
Sun Fashion
Sun Fit Squad
Sun Motors
Sun Sport
Sun Super Goals
Sun Woman
Sun World
Supplement(s): Cashflow - 26xY, The TV Mag - 52xY
NATIONAL DAILY & SUNDAY NEWSPAPERS: National Daily Newspapers

THE SUN (BIRMINGHAM OFFICE)
41820U65C-50

Editorial Address: 6th Floor, Albany House, Hurst Street, BIRMINGHAM, B5 4BD **Tel:** 0121 622 7307
Publisher: News Group Newspapers Ltd
Editor: Andrew Parker
NATIONAL DAILY & SUNDAY NEWSPAPERS: National Daily Regional Offices

SUN CITY
41729U65A-120_800

Formerly: Sun Money
Tel: 020 7782 4000 **Fax:** 020 7782 5605
Email: ian.king@the-sun.co.uk
Frequency: Mornings - Published within The Sun
Editor: Steve Hawkes
Summary of Content: Personal finance guide.
Section of: The Sun
NATIONAL DAILY & SUNDAY NEWSPAPERS: National Daily Newspapers

SUN FASHION
1882009U65A-120_892

Frequency: 104 issues yearly - Published Friday and Saturday within the Sun
Section of: The Sun
NATIONAL DAILY & SUNDAY NEWSPAPERS: National Daily Newspapers

SUN FIT SQUAD
1882008U65A-120_891

Frequency: Weekly - Published on Monday within the Sun
Section of: The Sun
NATIONAL DAILY & SUNDAY NEWSPAPERS: National Daily Newspapers

SUN MOTORS
754847U65A-120_770

Tel: 020 7782 4000 **Fax:** 020 7782 4063
Frequency: Weekly - Published on Friday within The Sun
Editor: Ken Gibson
Summary of Content: Section focusing on motoring news.
Section of: The Sun
NATIONAL DAILY & SUNDAY NEWSPAPERS: National Daily Newspapers

---

SUN SPORT
41730U65A-120_810

Tel: 020 7782 4000 **Fax:** 020 7782 4074
Email: sport@the-sun.co.uk
Frequency: Mornings - Published within The Sun
Editor: Steve Waring
Summary of Content: Section covering all sports issues, news and results.
Section of: The Sun
NATIONAL DAILY & SUNDAY NEWSPAPERS: National Daily Newspapers

SUN SUPER GOALS
41731U65A-120_820

Tel: 020 7782 4200 **Fax:** 020 7782 4074
Frequency: 104 issues yearly - Published on Monday and Saturday within The Sun
Editor: Steve Waring
Summary of Content: Section covering football news and features.
Section of: The Sun
NATIONAL DAILY & SUNDAY NEWSPAPERS: National Daily Newspapers

SUN WOMAN
41732U65A-120_880

Tel: 020 7782 4000 **Fax:** 020 7782 4063
Email: sharon.hendry@the-sun.co.uk
Frequency: 104 issues yearly - Published on Tuesday and Wednesday within The Sun
Editor: Sally Brook
Summary of Content: Features and interviews of interest to women.
Section of: The Sun
NATIONAL DAILY & SUNDAY NEWSPAPERS: National Daily Newspapers

SUN WORLD
634483U65A-120_885

Tel: 020 7782 4284 **Fax:** 020 7782 4063
Email: lisa.minot@the-sun.co.uk
Frequency: Weekly - Published on Saturday within The Sun
Editor: Lisa Minot
Summary of Content: Travel section with destination profiles and features, interviews and a consumer page.
Section of: The Sun
NATIONAL DAILY & SUNDAY NEWSPAPERS: National Daily Newspapers

SUNDAY EXPRESS
41778U65B-30

Editorial Address: The Northern & Shell Building, 10 Lower Thames Street, LONDON, EC3R 6EN **Tel:** 020 8612 7000
Fax: 0871 434 7300
Email: news.desk@express.co.uk
Advertising Address: As above. **Tel:** 0871 434 1010
Fax: 0871 434 2753
Email: jane.putley@express.co.uk
Web site: http://www.express.co.uk/Sunday
Publisher: Express Newspapers Ltd
Frequency: Sunday
Cover Price: £1.30
Circulation: 646,861 (ABC 03/08/2009 to 30/08/2009)
Editor: Martin Townsend; **News Editor:** Stephen Rigley; **Features Editor:** Amy Packer; **Advertising Manager:** Stephanie Wilkes
Summary of Content: Tabloid-sized Sunday newspaper covering national and international news with features on business and finance, education, appointments, lifestyle, travel, entertainment and sport.
Twitter: http://twitter.com/daily_express.
ADVERTISING RATES:
Full Page Mono £28420.00
Full Page Colour £40670.00
SCC £166.00
Agency Commission: 15%
Mechanical Data: Type Area: 345 x 275mm, Col Widths (Display): 37mm, No. of Columns (Display): 7, Film: Digital, Col Length: 345mm, Page Width: 275mm
Copy instructions: Copy Date: Mono Friday prior to publication date Colour Thursday prior to publication date
Average advertising content per issue: 35%
Sections:
Financial Sunday Express
Sunday Express Property
Sunday Express Review
Sunday Express Sport
Sunday Express Travel
Your Money
Supplement(s): S The Sunday Express - 52xY
NATIONAL DAILY & SUNDAY NEWSPAPERS: National Sunday Newspapers

SUNDAY EXPRESS PROPERTY
754882U65B-30_810

Tel: 020 8612 7440
Email: jane.slade@express.co.uk
Frequency: Sunday - Published within the Sunday Express

National Newspapers

Section 4 (a) Newspapers

Editor: Jane Slade
Summary of Content: Section covering all aspects of property maintenance, buying and selling.
ADVERTISING: Rates on application
Section of: Sunday Express
NATIONAL DAILY & SUNDAY NEWSPAPERS: National Sunday Newspapers

SUNDAY EXPRESS REVIEW 634224U65B-30_824
Formerly: Enjoy
Tel: 020 7922 7124 **Fax:** 020 7922 7300
Email: giulia.rhodes@express.co.uk
Publisher: Express Newspapers Ltd
Frequency: Sunday - Published within the Sunday Express
Editor: Amy Packer
Summary of Content: Entertainment and free time section covering music, film, books, theatre, fashion, style and TV, with profiles, reviews, lifestyles, features, and celebrity interviews.
ADVERTISING: Rates on application
Section of: Sunday Express
NATIONAL DAILY & SUNDAY NEWSPAPERS: National Sunday Newspapers

SUNDAY EXPRESS SPORT 41783U65B-30_825
Tel: 01772 833116 **Fax:** 020 7922 7896
Frequency: Sunday - Published within the Sunday Express
Editor: Scott Wilson
Summary of Content: Section covering all sports news.
ADVERTISING: Rates on application
Section of: Sunday Express
NATIONAL DAILY & SUNDAY NEWSPAPERS: National Sunday Newspapers

SUNDAY EXPRESS TRAVEL 754880U65B-30_840
Tel: 020 8612 7678 **Fax:** 0871 520 7678
Email: travel@express.co.uk
Frequency: Sunday - Published within the Sunday Express
Editor: Jane Memmler
Summary of Content: Section covering international travel and holidays.
ADVERTISING: Rates on application
Section of: Sunday Express
NATIONAL DAILY & SUNDAY NEWSPAPERS: National Sunday Newspapers

SUNDAY MIRROR 41786U65B-40
Editorial Address: 1 Canada Square, Canary Wharf, LONDON, E14 5AP **Tel:** 020 7293 3000 **Fax:** 020 7293 3587
Email: news@sundaymirror.co.uk
Advertising Address: As above. **Fax:** 020 7293 3280
Email: catherine.allen@mgn.co.uk
Web site: http://www.sundaymirror.co.uk
Publisher: Trinity Mirror
Frequency: Sunday
Cover Price: £0.95
Circulation: 1,237,227 (ABC 03/08/2009 to 30/08/2009)
Editor: Tina Weaver; **News Editor:** James Saville; **Features Editor:** Jill Main; **Advertising Manager:** Catherine Allen
Summary of Content: Tabloid-sized Sunday newspaper covering national and international news stories, with articles on finance, entertainment, television, show-biz and sport.
Twitter: http://twitter.com/DailyMirror.
ADVERTISING RATES:
Full Page Mono £30300.00
Full Page Colour £38600.00
SCC £128.00
Agency Commission: 15%
Mechanical Data: Type Area: 341 x 265mm, No. of Columns (Display): 7, Col Length: 341mm, Page Width: 265mm, Film: Digital
Sections:
Homes and Holidays
Sunday Mirror Sport
Supplement(s): Celebs on Sunday - 52xY
NATIONAL DAILY & SUNDAY NEWSPAPERS: National Sunday Newspapers

SUNDAY MIRROR (BELFAST) 41852U65D-270
Editorial Address: 415 Holywood Road, BELFAST, BT4 2GU **Tel:** 028 9056 8000 **Fax:** 028 9056 8059
Email: victoria.mcmahon@mgn.co.uk
Publisher: Trinity Mirror
Editor: Victoria McMahon
ADVERTISING: No Advertising taken
NATIONAL DAILY & SUNDAY NEWSPAPERS: National Sunday Regional Offices

SUNDAY MIRROR (GLASGOW OFFICE)
1644041U65D-282
Editorial Address: One Central Quay, GLASGOW, G3 8DA
Tel: 0141 309 3271 **Fax:** 0141 309 3527
Email: s.martin@sundaymirror.co.uk
Publisher: Trinity Mirror
Editor: Stephen Martin
ADVERTISING: No Advertising taken
NATIONAL DAILY & SUNDAY NEWSPAPERS: National Sunday Regional Offices

SUNDAY MIRROR SPORT 41789U65B-40_781
Tel: 020 7293 3492 **Fax:** 020 7293 3644
Frequency: Sunday - Published within the Sunday Mirror
Editor: David Walker
Summary of Content: Section covering sports news, features, fixtures and reports. Includes 'The Prem' which covers match reports from the premiership.
Section of: Sunday Mirror
NATIONAL DAILY & SUNDAY NEWSPAPERS: National Sunday Newspapers

SUNDAY SPORT 41795U65B-55
Editorial Address: 19 Great Ancoats Street, MANCHESTER, M60 4BT **Tel:** 0161 236 4466 **Fax:** 0161 236 4535
Email: james.crisp@sportnewspapers.co.uk
Advertising Address: As above. **Tel:** 0161 237 4600
Fax: 0161 237 4612
Email: tracey.lawson@sportnewspapers.co.uk
Web site: http://www.sundaysport.com
Publisher: Sport Newspapers Ltd
Date Established: 1986
Frequency: Sunday
Cover Price: £0.80
Circulation: 70,796 (Publisher's Statement)
Editor: James Crisp; **News Editor:** Neil Goodwin
Summary of Content: Tabloid-sized Sunday newspaper with general interest features, show-biz news and sport.
Twitter: http://twitter.com/daily_sport.
ADVERTISING RATES:
Full Page Mono £2000.00
Full Page Colour £2400.00
SCC £25.00
Mechanical Data: Page Width: 262mm, Col Length: 350mm, No. of Columns (Display): 7, Film: Digital, Col Widths (Display): 34mm, Type Area: 350 x 262mm
Copy instructions: Copy Date: Thursday 12 noon prior to publication date
Supplement(s): Bare & Naked - 26xY
NATIONAL DAILY & SUNDAY NEWSPAPERS: National Sunday Newspapers

THE SUNDAY TELEGRAPH 41796U65B-60
Editorial Address: 111 Buckingham Palace Road, LONDON, SW1W 0DT **Tel:** 020 7931 2000
Email: stnews@telegraph.co.uk
Advertising Address: As above.
Email: mathew.watkins@telegraph.co.uk
Web site: http://www.telegraph.co.uk
Publisher: Telegraph Media Group Ltd
Date Established: 1961
Frequency: Sunday
Cover Price: £1.90
Circulation: 599,131 (ABC 03/08/2009 to 30/08/2009)
Editor: News Desk; **News Editor:** James Hall; **Editor-in-Chief:** William Lewis; **Advertising Manager:** Alex Blaikley
Summary of Content: Broadsheet-sized quality Sunday newspaper providing in-depth national and international news with political coverage, business, city and finance news, appointments, property, arts, travel and sports coverage.
Twitter: http://twitter.com/dailytelegraph.
ADVERTISING RATES:
Full Page Mono £34000.00
Full Page Colour £42000.00
SCC £80.00
Agency Commission: 15%
Mechanical Data: Col Length: 540mm, Col Widths (Display): 39mm, No. of Columns (Display): 8, Film: Digital, Type Area: 540 x 340mm, Page Width: 340mm
Copy instructions: Copy Date: Friday 4pm prior to publication date
Sections:
The Sunday Telegraph Business
The Sunday Telegraph Home and Living
The Sunday Telegraph Money & Jobs
The Sunday Telegraph Sport
The Sunday Telegraph Travel
Supplement(s): Seven - 52xY, ST Children's Style - 2xY, ST Fashion - 2xY, ST Men - 2xY, Stella - 52xY
NATIONAL DAILY & SUNDAY NEWSPAPERS: National Sunday Newspapers

THE SUNDAY TELEGRAPH BUSINESS
41800U65B-60_781
Tel: 020 7931 2000
Email: cityeditor@telegraph.co.uk
Frequency: Sunday - Published within The Sunday Telegraph
Editor: Dan Roberts
Summary of Content: Section covering news and features on business.
ADVERTISING RATES:
SCC £80.00
Section of: The Sunday Telegraph
NATIONAL DAILY & SUNDAY NEWSPAPERS: National Sunday Newspapers

THE SUNDAY TELEGRAPH (CITY OFFICE) 41858U65F-90
Editorial Address: 111 Buckingham Palace Road, LONDON, SW1W 0DT **Tel:** 020 7931 2000
Fax: 020 7931 2760
Email: city@telegraph.co.uk
Publisher: Telegraph Media Group Ltd
Executive Editor: Richard Fletcher
ADVERTISING: No Advertising taken
NATIONAL DAILY & SUNDAY NEWSPAPERS: National Sunday City Office

THE SUNDAY TELEGRAPH HOME AND LIVING 1641323U65B-60_823
Formerly: The Sunday Telegraph House and Living
Tel: 020 7931 2000
Email: homeandliving@telegraph.co.uk
Frequency: Sunday - Published within The Sunday Telegraph
Editor: Bernice Davison
Summary of Content: Section covering buying and selling in the housing market including DIY and gardening.
ADVERTISING RATES:
SCC £62.00
Section of: The Sunday Telegraph
NATIONAL DAILY & SUNDAY NEWSPAPERS: National Sunday Newspapers

THE SUNDAY TELEGRAPH MONEY & JOBS 41801U65B-60_810
Formerly: The Sunday Telegraph Money
Tel: 020 7931 2000
Frequency: Sunday - Published within The Sunday Telegraph
Editor: Paul Farrow
Summary of Content: Section covering all aspects of personal finance.
ADVERTISING RATES:
SCC £85.00
Section of: The Sunday Telegraph
NATIONAL DAILY & SUNDAY NEWSPAPERS: National Sunday Newspapers

THE SUNDAY TELEGRAPH SPORT
41803U65B-60_821
Tel: 020 7931 2000
Frequency: Sunday - Published within The Sunday Telegraph
Summary of Content: Section containing news and features on sport.
ADVERTISING RATES:
SCC £80.00
Section of: The Sunday Telegraph
NATIONAL DAILY & SUNDAY NEWSPAPERS: National Sunday Newspapers

THE SUNDAY TELEGRAPH TRAVEL
622828U65B-60_822
Tel: 020 7931 2000
Email: traveldesk@telegraph.co.uk
Frequency: Sunday - Published within The Sunday Telegraph
Editor: Graham Boynton
Summary of Content: Section covering travel and holidays.
ADVERTISING RATES:
SCC £78.00
Section of: The Sunday Telegraph
NATIONAL DAILY & SUNDAY NEWSPAPERS: National Sunday Newspapers

THE SUNDAY TIMES 41804U65B-70
Editorial Address: 1 Pennington Street, LONDON, E98 1ST
Tel: 020 7782 5000 **Fax:** 020 7782 5731
Email: newsdesk@sunday-times.co.uk

Advertising Address: 1 Virginia Street, LONDON, E98 1PL
Tel: 020 7782 7000
Email: jane.west@newsint.co.uk
Web site: http://www.sunday-times.co.uk
Publisher: Times Newspapers Ltd
Frequency: Sunday
Cover Price: £2.00
Circulation: 1,164,831 (ABC 03/08/2009 to 30/08/2009)
Editor: John Witherow; **News Editor:** Nicholas Hellen;
Executive Editor: Tristan Davies; **Managing Editor:** Richard Caseby
Summary of Content: Broadsheet-sized quality Sunday newspaper containing in-depth national and international news with coverage of politics, finance, media, IT, education, law, property, jobs, sport, travel, arts and entertainment.
Twitter: http://twitter.com/TimesOnline.
ADVERTISING RATES:
Full Page Mono £60690.00
Full Page Colour £90065.00
SCC £144.00
Mechanical Data: Col Length: 540mm, No. of Columns (Display): 8, Col Widths (Display): 39mm, Type Area: 540 x 343mm, Page Width: 343mm
Copy instructions: Copy Date: Mono 2 working days Colour 3 working days prior to publication date
Sections:
In Gear
The Sunday Times Appointments
The Sunday Times Business
The Sunday Times Home
The Sunday Times Money
The Sunday Times News Review
The Sunday Times Sport
The Sunday Times Travel
Supplement(s): The Sunday Times Culture - 52xY, The Sunday Times Magazine - 52xY, The Sunday Times Style - 52xY
NATIONAL DAILY & SUNDAY NEWSPAPERS: National Sunday Newspapers

THE SUNDAY TIMES APPOINTMENTS

41808U65B-70_715

Tel: 020 7782 5000
Frequency: Sunday - Published within The Sunday Times
Editor: Sian Griffiths
Summary of Content: Section containing news and features on careers, work and education, plus appointments listings.
ADVERTISING: Rates on application
Section of: The Sunday Times
NATIONAL DAILY & SUNDAY NEWSPAPERS: National Sunday Newspapers

THE SUNDAY TIMES BUSINESS

41810U65B-70_730

Tel: 020 7782 5000 **Fax:** 020 7782 5765
Email: john.waples@sunday-times.co.uk
Frequency: Sunday - Published within The Sunday Times
Editor: John Waples
Summary of Content: Section carrying business and city news.
ADVERTISING RATES:
Full Page Mono £60675.00
Full Page Colour £90090.00
SCC £144.00
Section of: The Sunday Times
NATIONAL DAILY & SUNDAY NEWSPAPERS: National Sunday Newspapers

THE SUNDAY TIMES CULTURE 41877U65H-79

Editorial Address: 1 Pennington Street, LONDON, E98 1ST
Tel: 020 7782 5000 **Fax:** 020 7782 5776
Email: culture@sunday-times.co.uk
Advertising Address: 1 Virginia Street, LONDON, E98 1PL
Tel: 020 7782 7608
Email: sarah.walker@newsint.co.uk
Publisher: Times Newspapers Ltd
Frequency: Weekly - See main record for circulation figure
Editor: Helen Hawkins
Summary of Content: Magazine covering art, film, theatre, music, dance and books, includes television and radio listings and a consumer guide to the Internet and domestic digital technology. No business or e-commerce.
ADVERTISING RATES:
Full Page Colour £31660.00
SCC £204.00
Mechanical Data: Col Length: 281.5mm, No. of Columns (Display): 5, Type Area: 281.5 x 250mm, Col Widths (Display): 46mm, Page Width: 250mm
Copy instructions: Copy Date: 2 Tuesdays prior to publication date
Supplement to: The Sunday Times
NATIONAL DAILY & SUNDAY NEWSPAPERS: National Colour Supplements

THE SUNDAY TIMES HOME 41813U65B-70_750

Formerly: The Sunday Times Property
Tel: 020 7782 5000 **Fax:** 020 7782 5706
Email: property@sunday-times.co.uk
Frequency: Sunday - Published within The Sunday Times
Editor: Peter Conradi
Summary of Content: Section with features on the property market and property listings.
ADVERTISING RATES:
SCC £105.00
Section of: The Sunday Times
NATIONAL DAILY & SUNDAY NEWSPAPERS: National Sunday Newspapers

THE SUNDAY TIMES MAGAZINE

41878U65H-82

Editorial Address: 1 Pennington Street, LONDON, E98 1SD
Tel: 020 7782 5000 **Fax:** 020 7867 0410
Email: amy.turner@sunday-times.co.uk
Advertising Address: 1 Virginia Street, LONDON, E98 1PL
Tel: 020 7782 4000
Email: jane.west@newsint.co.uk
Publisher: Times Newspapers Ltd
Frequency: Weekly - See main record for circulation figure
Editor: Amy Turner
Summary of Content: Magazine containing features and interviews.
ADVERTISING RATES:
Full Page Colour £19000.00
Mechanical Data: Film: Digital, Type Area: 274 x 212mm, Col Length: 274mm, Bleed Size: 303 x 238mm, Trim Size: 297 x 232mm, Page Width: 212mm
Copy instructions: Copy Date: 24 working days prior to publication date
Supplement to: The Sunday Times
NATIONAL DAILY & SUNDAY NEWSPAPERS: National Colour Supplements

THE SUNDAY TIMES MONEY 41811U65B-70_770

Tel: 020 7782 5757 **Fax:** 020 7782 5689
Frequency: Sunday - Published within The Sunday Times
Editor: Kathryn Cooper
Summary of Content: Reports and investigations on personal finance issues.
ADVERTISING RATES:
Full Page Mono £56230.00
Full Page Colour £78355.00
SCC £135.00
Section of: The Sunday Times
NATIONAL DAILY & SUNDAY NEWSPAPERS: National Sunday Newspapers

THE SUNDAY TIMES NEWS REVIEW

41812U65B-70_780

Tel: 020 7782 5000 **Fax:** 020 7782 5479
Frequency: Sunday - Published within The Sunday Times
Editor: Susannah Herbert
Summary of Content: Section containing reviews, analysis and comment on the week's news stories, plus profiles and interviews.
ADVERTISING RATES:
Full Page Mono £52500.00
Full Page Colour £78300.00
SCC £131.00
Section of: The Sunday Times
NATIONAL DAILY & SUNDAY NEWSPAPERS: National Sunday Newspapers

THE SUNDAY TIMES SCOTLAND

41851U65D-150

Editorial Address: 6th Floor, Guildhall, 57 Queen Street, GLASGOW, G1 3EN **Tel:** 0141 420 5100 **Fax:** 0141 420 5262
Email: brenda.diver@sunday-times.co.uk
Advertising Address: As above.
Email: lynne.robertson@newsint.co.uk
Web site: http://www.timesonline.co.uk
Publisher: News International (Scotland) Ltd
Frequency: Weekly
Cover Price: £1.90
Circulation: 89,000 (Publisher's Statement)
Editor: News Desk; **Features Editor:** Joan McAlpine
Summary of Content: Newspaper covering news and events in Scotland.
Readership/Target Audience: Aimed at Scottish people.
ADVERTISING RATES:
SCC £22.50
Agency Commission: 10%
Mechanical Data: Type Area: 540 x 343mm, Col Length: 540mm, Page Width: 343mm, Col Widths (Display): 39mm, No. of Columns (Display): 8, Film: Digital
Copy instructions: Copy Date: Thursday 4pm prior to publication date

Supplement(s): Ecosse - 52xY
NATIONAL DAILY & SUNDAY NEWSPAPERS: National Sunday Regional Offices

THE SUNDAY TIMES SPORT 41814U65B-70_800

Tel: 020 7782 5718 **Fax:** 020 7782 5720
Frequency: Sunday - Published within The Sunday Times
Editor: Alex Butler
Summary of Content: Section covering sports news and fixtures plus motoring.
ADVERTISING RATES:
Full Page Mono £57330.00
Full Page Colour £83060.00
SCC £137.00
Section of: The Sunday Times
NATIONAL DAILY & SUNDAY NEWSPAPERS: National Sunday Newspapers

THE SUNDAY TIMES STYLE 41879U65H-85

Editorial Address: 1 Pennington Street, LONDON, E98 1ST
Tel: 020 7782 5000 **Fax:** 020 7782 5120
Email: ststyle@sunday-times.co.uk
Advertising Address: 1 Virginia Street, LONDON, E98 1PL
Tel: 020 7782 4000
Email: jane.west@newsint.co.uk
Publisher: Times Newspapers Ltd
Frequency: Weekly - See main record for circulation figure
Usual Pagination: 68
Editor: Gemma Soames; **Features Editor:** Jessica Brinton
Summary of Content: Magazine containing features on fashion, lifestyle, food and drink, health and interiors.
ADVERTISING RATES:
Full Page Colour £38500.00
Agency Commission: 15%
Mechanical Data: Type Area: 271 x 188mm, Col Length: 271mm, Bleed Size: 303 x 220mm, Trim Size: 297 x 210mm, Page Width: 188mm
Copy instructions: Copy Date: 15 working days prior to publication date
Supplement to: The Sunday Times
NATIONAL DAILY & SUNDAY NEWSPAPERS: National Colour Supplements

THE SUNDAY TIMES TRAVEL 41815U65B-70_840

Tel: 020 7782 5000 **Fax:** 020 7782 5540
Email: travel@sunday-times.co.uk
Frequency: Sunday - Published within The Sunday Times
Editor: Christine Walker
Summary of Content: Reports on travel destinations worldwide.
ADVERTISING RATES:
Full Page Mono £29140.00
Full Page Colour £42655.00
SCC £131.00
Section of: The Sunday Times
NATIONAL DAILY & SUNDAY NEWSPAPERS: National Sunday Newspapers

TAKE 5 1666008U65H-104

Editorial Address: The Northern & Shell Building, 10 Lower Thames Street, LONDON, EC3R 6EN **Tel:** 0871 520 1000
Email: victoria.lissaman@dailystar.co.uk
Advertising Address: As above. **Fax:** 0871 434 2753
Email: steve.molloy@express.co.uk
Publisher: Express Newspapers Ltd
Date Established: 2005
Frequency: Weekly - See main record for circulation figure
Cover Price: Free
Usual Pagination: 48
Editor: Vicky Lissaman; **Advertising Manager:** Steve Molloy
Summary of Content: Magazine covering listings, celebrity and real life stories.
ADVERTISING RATES:
Full Page Colour £12000.00
Copy instructions: Copy Date: Tuesday 12pm 2 weeks prior to publication date
Supplement to: Daily Star Sunday
NATIONAL DAILY & SUNDAY NEWSPAPERS: National Colour Supplements

TAKE IT EASY 41870U65H-48

Formerly: The People Magazine
Editorial Address: 1 Canada Square, Canary Wharf, LONDON, E14 5AP **Tel:** 020 7293 3039 **Fax:** 020 7293 3517
Email: magazine@people.co.uk
Advertising Address: As above. **Tel:** 020 7293 3000
Fax: 020 7293 3285
Email: vanessa.burke@mgn.co.uk
Publisher: Trinity Mirror
Frequency: Weekly - See main record for circulation figure. Published on Sunday
Usual Pagination: 40
Editor: Hanna Tavner

Summary of Content: Women's weekly magazine containing real life stories, health, beauty, fashion, cookery and celebrity interviews. Also includes TV listings.
ADVERTISING RATES:
Full Page Colour £21300.00
Agency Commission: 15%
Mechanical Data: Type Area: 257 x 195mm, Bleed Size: 283 x 221mm, Trim Size: 275 x 213mm, Col Length: 257mm, Page Width: 195mm, Film: Digital
Copy instructions: Copy Date: 3 weeks prior to publication date
Average advertising content per issue: 25%
Supplement to: The People
NATIONAL DAILY & SUNDAY NEWSPAPERS: National Colour Supplements

TECHNOLOGY
41683U65A-90_790
Tel: 020 3353 2000
Email: tech@guardian.co.uk
Frequency: Weekly - Published on Thursdays within The Guardian
Editor: Charles Arthur
Summary of Content: Section covering consumer and business technology including hardware, software, Internet and gadgets.
ADVERTISING: Rates on application
Section of: The Guardian
NATIONAL DAILY & SUNDAY NEWSPAPERS: National Daily Newspapers

TELEGRAPH MAGAZINE
41880U65H-90
Editorial Address: 111 Buckingham Palace Road, LONDON, SW1W 0DT **Tel:** 020 7931 2000
Fax: 020 7931 3418
Email: satmag@telegraph.co.uk
Advertising Address: As above.
Email: carley.ayres@telegraph.co.uk
Publisher: Telegraph Media Group Ltd
Frequency: Weekly - Published on Saturdays. See main record for circulation figure
Editor: Michele Lavery; **Features Editor:** Jessamy Calkin
Summary of Content: Magazine covering fashion, beauty, home and lifestyle.
ADVERTISING: Rates on application
Agency Commission: 15%
Copy instructions: Copy Date: 21 days prior to publication date
Supplement to: The Daily Telegraph
NATIONAL DAILY & SUNDAY NEWSPAPERS: National Colour Supplements

THE TIMES
41734U65A-130
Editorial Address: 1 Pennington Street, LONDON, E98 1TT
Tel: 020 7782 5000 **Fax:** 020 7782 5988
Email: home.news@thetimes.co.uk
Advertising Address: 1 Virginia Street, LONDON, E98 1PL
Tel: 020 7782 5000 **Fax:** 020 7782 7123
Email: jane.west@newsint.co.uk
Web site: http://www.thetimes.co.uk
Publisher: Times Newspapers Ltd
Date Established: 1785
Frequency: Mornings - Published Monday - Saturday
Cover Price: £0.90
Circulation: 576,185 (ABC 03/08/2009 to 30/08/2009)
Editor: Newsdesk; **Executive Editor:** Alex O'Connell; **Managing Editor:** David Chappell
Summary of Content: Compact-sized quality newspaper, containing in-depth national and international news with coverage of politics, finance, media, IT, education, law, jobs, sport, travel, arts and entertainment.
Twitter: http://twitter.com/TimesOnline.
ADVERTISING RATES:
Full Page Mono £16645.00
Full Page Colour £27195.00
SCC £75.00
Mechanical Data: Col Length: 340mm, No. of Columns (Display): 7, Film: Digital, Col Widths (Display): 34mm, Type Area: 340 x 264mm, Page Width: 264mm
Copy instructions: Copy Date: Mono 2 working days Colour 3 working days prior to publication date
Sections:
Bricks and Mortar
Career
The Game
Public Sector
Screen
Times
The Times Business
The Times Crème
The Times Law
The Times Money
The Times Sport
The Times Travel
Supplement(s): LUXX - 6xY, Playlist - 52xY, The Times Books - 52xY, The Times Magazine - 52xY, Weekend - 52xY
NATIONAL DAILY & SUNDAY NEWSPAPERS: National Daily Newspapers

TIMES 2
41743U65A-130_800
Formerly: T2
Tel: 020 7782 5330 **Fax:** 020 7782 5203
Frequency: Mornings - Published Monday - Friday within The Times
Editor: Emma Tucker
Summary of Content: Section covering the arts, style, features, education, parenting, health, travel, television and radio.
ADVERTISING RATES:
SCC £67.00
Mechanical Data: Type Area: 325 x 265mm, Col Length: 325mm, No. of Columns (Display): 6, Col Widths (Display): 41mm
Section of: The Times
NATIONAL DAILY & SUNDAY NEWSPAPERS: National Daily Newspapers

THE TIMES BUSINESS
41739U65A-130_720
Formerly: Business
Tel: 020 7782 5113 **Fax:** 020 7782 5112
Email: david.wighton@thetimes.co.uk
Frequency: Mornings - Published everyday within The Times
Editor: David Wighton
Summary of Content: News and features about companies including share price lists.
ADVERTISING RATES:
SCC £67.00
Section of: The Times
NATIONAL DAILY & SUNDAY NEWSPAPERS: National Daily Newspapers

THE TIMES CRÈME
41744U65A-130_810
Formerly: The Times Crème de la Crème
Tel: 020 7782 5920 **Fax:** 020 7782 5124
Email: creme@thetimes.co.uk
Frequency: Weekly - Published on Wednesday within The Times
Editor: Julie Daniels
Summary of Content: Section dealing with secretarial careers and appointments.
ADVERTISING RATES:
SCC £67.00
Section of: The Times
NATIONAL DAILY & SUNDAY NEWSPAPERS: National Daily Newspapers

THE TIMES (EDINBURGH OFFICE)
624223U65C-260
Editorial Address: Scot House, 10 South St. Andrew Street, EDINBURGH, EH2 2AZ **Tel:** 0131 624 8353
Email: david.lister@thetimes.co.uk
Web site: http://www.thetimes.co.uk
Publisher: Times Newspapers Ltd
Editor: David Lister
ADVERTISING: No Advertising taken
NATIONAL DAILY & SUNDAY NEWSPAPERS: National Daily Regional Offices

THE TIMES (GLASGOW OFFICE)
41841U65C-551
Editorial Address: 57 Queen Street, GLASGOW, G1 3EN
Tel: 0141 420 5296
Publisher: Times Newspapers Ltd
Editor: Melanie Reid
ADVERTISING: No Advertising taken
NATIONAL DAILY & SUNDAY NEWSPAPERS: National Daily Regional Offices

THE TIMES LAW
623335U65A-130_840
Formerly: The Legal Section
Tel: 020 7782 5000 **Fax:** 020 7782 5002
Frequency: Weekly - Published on Tuesday within The Times
Editor: Frances Gibb
Summary of Content: Section covering legal issues, including news, analysis and appointments.
ADVERTISING RATES:
SCC £67.00
Section of: The Times
NATIONAL DAILY & SUNDAY NEWSPAPERS: National Daily Newspapers

THE TIMES MAGAZINE
41881U65H-95
Editorial Address: 1 Pennington Street, LONDON, E98 1TD
Tel: 020 7782 5954 **Fax:** 020 7782 5075
Email: magazine@thetimes.co.uk
Advertising Address: 1 Virginia Street, LONDON, E98 1PL
Tel: 020 7782 7000

Email: jane.west@newsint.co.uk
Publisher: Times Newspapers Ltd
Frequency: Weekly - Published on Saturday. See main record for circulation figure
Editor: Alexia Skinitis
Summary of Content: Magazine covering fashion, food, beauty, interiors and general features.
ADVERTISING RATES:
Full Page Colour £16540.00
Mechanical Data: Bleed Size: 276 x 236mm, Trim Size: 270 x 230mm
Supplement to: The Times
NATIONAL DAILY & SUNDAY NEWSPAPERS: National Colour Supplements

THE TIMES (MANCHESTER OFFICE)
41829U65C-163.
Editorial Address: 111 Piccadilly, MANCHESTER, M1 2HY
Tel: 0161 935 5350
Email: russell.jenkins@thetimes.co.uk
Publisher: Times Newspapers Ltd
Editor: Russell Jenkins
ADVERTISING: No Advertising taken
NATIONAL DAILY & SUNDAY NEWSPAPERS: National Daily Regional Offices

THE TIMES MONEY
41747U65A-130_850
Tel: 020 7782 5080 **Fax:** 020 7782 5082
Email: anne.ashworth@thetimes.co.uk
Frequency: Weekly - Published on Saturday within The Times
Editor: Andrew Ellson
Summary of Content: Features on personal finance.
ADVERTISING RATES:
SCC £75.00
Section of: The Times
NATIONAL DAILY & SUNDAY NEWSPAPERS: National Daily Newspapers

THE TIMES SPORT
41742U65A-130_780
Formerly: The Times Sports Daily
Tel: 020 7782 5945 **Fax:** 020 7782 5211
Email: sport@thetimes.co.uk
Frequency: Mornings - Published Monday to Saturday within The Times
Editor: Tim Hallissey
Summary of Content: Sports news and reports.
ADVERTISING RATES:
SCC £63.00
Section of: The Times
NATIONAL DAILY & SUNDAY NEWSPAPERS: National Daily Newspapers

THE TIMES TRAVEL
629225U65A-130_855
Tel: 020 7782 5173 **Fax:** 020 7782 5927
Email: travel@thetimes.co.uk
Frequency: Weekly - Published on Saturday within The Times
Editor: Kathleen Wyatt
Summary of Content: Articles and features on travel, holidays and places to visit.
ADVERTISING RATES:
SCC £75.00
Section of: The Times
NATIONAL DAILY & SUNDAY NEWSPAPERS: National Daily Newspapers

TRAVEL
755639U65A-10_832
Tel: 020 8612 7000 **Fax:** 0871 520 7766
Email: travel@express.co.uk
Frequency: Weekly - Published on Saturday within the Daily Express
Editor: Jane Memmler
Summary of Content: Section covering travel and holidays.
ADVERTISING: Rates on application
Section of: Daily Express
NATIONAL DAILY & SUNDAY NEWSPAPERS: National Daily Newspapers

TRAVEL SECTION
766960U65B-3_922
Formerly: The Compact Traveller
Tel: 020 7005 2798 **Fax:** 020 7005 2428
Email: k.simon@independent.co.uk
Frequency: Sunday - Published within The Independent on Sunday
Editor: Kate Simon
Summary of Content: Travel section looking at different types of holiday destinations.
ADVERTISING RATES:
Full Page Mono £8570.00
Full Page Colour £13050.00

SCC £42.00
Section of: The Independent on Sunday
NATIONAL DAILY & SUNDAY NEWSPAPERS: National
Sunday Newspapers

TRAVELLER
41705U65A-93_835

Tel: 020 7005 2000 **Fax:** 020 7005 2428
Frequency: Weekly - Published on Saturday within The
Independent
Editor: Simon Calder
Summary of Content: Section covering travel and holidays.
Section of: The Independent
NATIONAL DAILY & SUNDAY NEWSPAPERS: National
Daily Newspapers

TRAVELMAIL
41606U65A-20_860

Formerly: Travel
Tel: 020 7938 6000 **Fax:** 020 7938 6755
Frequency: Weekly - Published on Wednesdays and
Saturdays within the Daily Mail
Editor: Mark Palmer
Summary of Content: Section with features on travel
destinations in the UK and abroad.
ADVERTISING: Rates on application
Section of: Daily Mail
NATIONAL DAILY & SUNDAY NEWSPAPERS: National
Daily Newspapers

TV EXPRESS
633854U65A-10_835

Formerly: Antenna
Tel: 020 8612 7000 **Fax:** 0871 520 7766
Frequency: Mornings - Published in the Daily Express
Monday to Friday
Summary of Content: Section containing TV and Radio
listings with interviews and reviews.
ADVERTISING: Rates on application
Section of: Daily Express
NATIONAL DAILY & SUNDAY NEWSPAPERS: National
Daily Newspapers

THE WEEKEND STARTS HERE
41664U65A-10_845

Formerly: Simply the Best
Tel: 020 8612 7000 **Fax:** 0871 520 7766
Frequency: Weekly - Published on Fridays within the Daily
Express
Editor: Tinu Majekodunmi
Summary of Content: Guide to film, music, theatre,
comedy, art and television. Contains listings and features.
ADVERTISING: Rates on application
Section of: Daily Express
NATIONAL DAILY & SUNDAY NEWSPAPERS: National
Daily Newspapers

YOU MAGAZINE THE MAIL ON SUNDAY
41882U65H-100

Formerly: You The Mail on Sunday
Editorial Address: Northcliffe House, 2 Derry Street,
LONDON, W8 5TT **Tel:** 020 7938 6000 **Fax:** 020 7938 4609
Advertising Address: As above. **Fax:** 020 7937 5320
Email: simon.davies@mailonsunday.co.uk
Publisher: Associated Newspapers Ltd
Frequency: Weekly - See main record for circulation figure
Editor: Sue Peart; **Advertisement Director:** Simon Davies
Summary of Content: Magazine covering general features
including fashion, food, beauty and health.
ADVERTISING RATES:
Full Page Colour ....:......... £28500.00
Mechanical Data: Type Area: 262 x 209mm, Bleed Size:
292 x 235mm, Trim Size: 286 x 232mm, Col Length: 262mm,
Film: Digital
Copy instructions: Copy Date: 10 days prior to publication
date
Supplement to: The Mail on Sunday
NATIONAL DAILY & SUNDAY NEWSPAPERS: National
Colour Supplements

YOUR MONEY
1606523U65B-30_841

Tel: 020 7922 2994 **Fax:** 020 7922 7643
Email: david.prosser@express.co.uk
Frequency: Sunday - Published within the Sunday Express
Editor: Chris Torney
Summary of Content: Section covering all areas of personal
finance.
ADVERTISING: Rates on application
Section of: Sunday Express
NATIONAL DAILY & SUNDAY NEWSPAPERS: National
Sunday Newspapers

Non-National Newspapers

ABERAERON & NEW QUAY CAMBRIAN NEWS
763773U72C-30_180

Formerly: Teifi Valley & Cambrian News
Frequency: Weekly
Cover Price: £0.65
ADVERTISING: Rates on application
Part of Series, see entry for: The Cambrian News Series
LOCAL NEWSPAPERS: Local Newspapers Wales

ABERDEEN CITIZEN
44859U72D-9

Formerly: Aberdeen Herald & Post
Editorial Address: PO Box 43, Lang Stracht, Mastrick,
ABERDEEN, AB15 6DF **Tel:** 01224 690222
Fax: 01224 699575
Email: ee.news@ajl.co.uk
Advertising Address: As above. **Tel:** 01224 343305
Fax: 01224 344108
Email: l.smyth@ajl.co.uk
Web site: http://www.thisisaberdeen.co.uk
Publisher: Aberdeen Journals Ltd
Date Established: 1980
Frequency: Weekly
Cover Price: Free
Circulation: 76,408 (VFD 02/07/2007 to 30/12/2007)
Editor: News Desk; **Features Editor:** Marie-Claire Jones;
Advertising Manager: Liam Smyth
ADVERTISING: Rates on application
Agency Commission: 10%
Copy instructions: Copy Date: 2 days prior to publication
date
Average advertising content per issue: 75%
LOCAL NEWSPAPERS: Local Newspapers Scotland

ABERGAVENNY CHRONICLE
44749U72C-15_120

Frequency: Weekly
Cover Price: £0.32
ADVERTISING: Rates on application
Part of Series, see entry for: Abergavenny Chronicle Series
LOCAL NEWSPAPERS: Local Newspapers Wales

ABERGAVENNY CHRONICLE SERIES
44748U72C-15

Editorial Address: Tindle House, 13 Nevill Street,
ABERGAVENNY, NP7 5AA **Tel:** 01873 852187
Fax: 01873 857677
Advertising Address: As above.
Email: advertising@tindlenews.co.uk
Publisher: Abergavenny Chronicle Ltd
Frequency: Weekly - Published every Thursday
Cover Price: £0.40
Circulation: 15,000 (Publisher's Statement)
Editor: Liz Davis; **Advertising Manager:** Mary Purcell
Language(s): English; Welsh
ADVERTISING: Rates on application
Mechanical Data: Col Length: 550mm, Col Widths (Display):
36mm, No. of Columns (Display): 10, Type Area: 550 x
396mm, Print Process: Web-fed offset litho, Film: Digital,
Page Width: 396mm
**Series owner and contact point for the following titles,
see individual entries:**
Abergavenny Chronicle
Crickhowell and Abergavenny Chronicle
LOCAL NEWSPAPERS: Local Newspapers Wales

ABERGELE & ST ASAPH VISITOR
44847U72C-357_220

Frequency: Weekly
Cover Price: £0.60
Circulation: 3,503 (ABC 02/07/2007 to 30/12/2007)
Part of Series, see entry for: Visitor Series
LOCAL NEWSPAPERS: Local Newspapers Wales

ABERYSTWYTH CAMBRIAN NEWS
763769U72C-30_110

Formerly: The Aberystwyth & Cambrian News
Frequency: Weekly
Cover Price: £0.65
ADVERTISING: Rates on application
Part of Series, see entry for: The Cambrian News Series
LOCAL NEWSPAPERS: Local Newspapers Wales

ACCRINGTON OBSERVER
43943U72B-1910

Editorial Address: 1 Scott Place, MANCHESTER, M3 3RN
Tel: 01254 871444 **Fax:** 01254 872259
Email: accringtonobserver@menmedia.co.uk
Advertising Address: As above. **Tel:** 0161 829 3300
Email: mark.stansfield@menmediasales.co.uk
Web site: http://www.accringtonobserver.co.uk
Publisher: MEN Media
Frequency: Weekly - Published on Friday
Cover Price: £0.52
Circulation: 14,586 (ABC 02/07/2007 to 30/12/2007)
Editor: Stuart Robertson; **News Editor:** Lisa Kenyon
ADVERTISING RATES:
SCC £4.65
Agency Commission: 10%
Mechanical Data: Page Width: 267mm, Print Process: Web-
fed litho, Film: Digital, Type Area: 340 x 267mm, Col Length:
340mm, Col Widths (Display): 27mm, No. of Columns
(Display): 9
Copy instructions: Copy Date: Wednesday 4pm prior to
publication date
LOCAL NEWSPAPERS: Local Newspapers English
Counties

ACKRILL NEWSPAPER SERIES
44646U72B-3588

Formerly: Ackrill Newspapers
Editorial Address: 1 Cardale Park, Beckwith Head Road,
HARROGATE, HG3 1RZ **Tel:** 01423 564321
Fax: 01423 707440
Email: ackrill.news@ypn.co.uk
Advertising Address: As above. **Fax:** 01423 531431
Email: ackrill.sales@ypn.co.uk
Web site: http://www.harrogateadvertiser.net
Publisher: Ackrill Group Ltd
Frequency: Weekly - Published on Tuesday, Wednesday &
Friday
Circulation: 64,177 (Combined Circulation)
Editor: Tom Hay; **News Editor:** Tom Hay; **Editor-in-Chief:**
Jean MacQuarrie
ADVERTISING RATES:
Full Page Mono £7034.72
Full Page Colour £9145.14
SCC £11.42
Agency Commission: 10%
Mechanical Data: Type Area: 560 x 324.25mm, Col Length:
560mm, Page Width: 324.25mm, No. of Columns (Display):
11
**Series owner and contact point for the following titles,
see individual entries:**
Harrogate Advertiser
Knaresborough Post
North Yorkshire News
Pateley Bridge & Nidderdale Herald
Ripon Gazette & Boroughbridge Herald
Wetherby, Boston Spa & Tadcaster News
Supplement(s): Business Pink - 6xY, Motors - 52xY,
Property - 52xY, The Society - 12xY, Weekend - 52xY,
Yorkshire's Finest - 12xY
LOCAL NEWSPAPERS: Local Newspapers English
Counties

ADDLESTONE & BYFLEET REVIEW
44421U72B-3170_120

Frequency: Weekly
Cover Price: Free
Part of Series, see entry for: Woking Review Series
LOCAL NEWSPAPERS: Local Newspapers English
Counties

ADMAG NEWSPAPERS SERIES
1655834U72B-3955

Formerly: Hereford Admag
Editorial Address: Red Barn Drive, HEREFORD, HR4 9QL
Tel: 01432 376121 **Fax:** 01432 353231
Email: newsdesk@admagnewspapers.co.uk
Advertising Address: 3-4 Shoplatch, SHREWSBURY, SY1
1HF **Tel:** 01743 239150
Email: jan.edwards@admagnewspapers.co.uk
Publisher: Central Independent News & Media Ltd
Frequency: Weekly - Published on Wednesday
Cover Price: Free
Circulation: 181,809 (Combined Circulation)
Editor: Richard Green; **Advertising Manager:** Jan Edwards
Summary of Content: Not looking for hard news related
press releases.
ADVERTISING: Rates on application
**Series owner and contact point for the following titles,
see individual entries:**
Hereford Admag
Montgomeryshire Advertiser
Shrewsbury Admag
Telford and Wrekin Admag
LOCAL NEWSPAPERS: Local Newspapers English
Counties

Non-National Newspapers

ADMAG (WESTON-SUPER-MARE)

1647247U72B-3952

Editorial Address: 32 Waterloo Street, WESTON-SUPER-MARE, BS23 1LW **Tel:** 01934 422622 **Fax:** 01934 422633
Advertising Address: As above. **Tel:** 01934 422555
Email: sally.cook@archant.co.uk
Publisher: Archant South West
Frequency: Weekly
Cover Price: Free
Circulation: 41,589 (VFD 02/07/2007 to 30/12/2007)
ADVERTISING: Rates on application
LOCAL NEWSPAPERS: Local Newspapers English Counties

ADNEWS BEXHILL

44424U72B-3200_110

Frequency: Weekly
Cover Price: Free
Circulation: 18,309 (Publisher's Statement)
Part of Series, see entry for: Adnews Series (Bexhill & Hastings)
LOCAL NEWSPAPERS: Local Newspapers English Counties

ADNEWS HASTINGS

44425U72B-3200_120

Frequency: Weekly
Cover Price: Free
Circulation: 32,771 (Publisher's Statement)
Part of Series, see entry for: Adnews Series (Bexhill & Hastings)
LOCAL NEWSPAPERS: Local Newspapers English Counties

ADNEWS SERIES (BEXHILL & HASTINGS)

44423U72B-3200

Formerly: Bexhill-on-Sea Observer & News Series
Editorial Address: 18 Sackville Road, BEXHILL-ON-SEA, TN39 3JL **Tel:** 01424 730555 **Fax:** 01424 730832
Email: bexobs@trbeckett.co.uk
Advertising Address: Woods House, Telford Road, ST. LEONARDS-ON-SEA, TN38 9LZ **Tel:** 01424 854242
Fax: 01424 852850
Email: hayley.scott@jpress.co.uk
Web site: http://www.bexhilltoday.co.uk
Publisher: T.R. Beckett Ltd
Frequency: Weekly - Published on Wednesday
Cover Price: Free
Circulation: 51,080 (Publisher's Statement)
Editor: Lynda Turner; **Advertising Manager:** Hayley Scott
ADVERTISING RATES:
Full Page Mono £3066.12
Full Page Colour £3985.95
Mechanical Data: Type Area: 340 x 277mm, Col Length: 340mm, No. of Columns (Display): 9, Col Widths (Display): 29mm, Film: Digital, Page Width: 277mm
Copy instructions: Copy Date: Monday 4pm prior to publication date
Average advertising content per issue: 65%
Series owner and contact point for the following titles, see individual entries:
Adnews Bexhill
Adnews Hastings
LOCAL NEWSPAPERS: Local Newspapers English Counties

ADSCENE (ASHFORD)

43873U72B-1750_110

Frequency: Weekly
Cover Price: Free
Circulation: 18,957 (Publisher's Statement)
ADVERTISING: Rates on application
Part of Series, see entry for: Adscene, Herald & Express Series (Folkestone)
LOCAL NEWSPAPERS: Local Newspapers English Counties

ADSCENE (CANTERBURY)

43845U72B-1745

Formerly: Canterbury Times Series
Editorial Address: Newspaper House, Simmonds Road, Wincheap, CANTERBURY, CT1 3YR **Tel:** 01227 767321
Fax: 01227 456344
Email: newsdesk.canterbury@krnmedia.co.uk
Advertising Address: As above. **Tel:** 01227 473313
Fax: 01227 456444
Email: sales.canterbury@kentregionalnewspapers.co.uk
Publisher: Kent Regional News and Media
Date Established: 1973
Frequency: Weekly - Published on Friday
Cover Price: Free
Circulation: 53,724 (VFD 02/07/2007 to 30/12/2007)
News Editor: Roger Kasper; **Advertising Manager:** Tracy Newton

ADVERTISING RATES:
Full Page Mono £680.00
Full Page Colour £924.80
SCC £7.00
Mechanical Data: Page Width: 262mm, Film: Digital, Col Length: 340mm, Type Area: 340 x 262mm, No. of Columns (Display): 8
Copy instructions: Copy Date: Monday prior to publication date
Supplement(s): Relax - 52xY
LOCAL NEWSPAPERS: Local Newspapers English Counties

ADSCENE (DEAL, DOVER & FOLKESTONE)

43874U72B-1750_120

Formerly: Adscene (Shepway).
Frequency: Weekly
Cover Price: Free
Circulation: 55,148 (VFD 02/07/2007 to 30/12/2007)
ADVERTISING: Rates on application
Part of Series, see entry for: Adscene, Herald & Express Series (Folkestone)
LOCAL NEWSPAPERS: Local Newspapers English Counties

ADSCENE, HERALD & EXPRESS SERIES (FOLKESTONE)

43872U72B-1750

Editorial Address: Westcliff House, Westcliff Gardens, FOLKESTONE, CT20 1FH **Tel:** 01303 850999
Fax: 01303 850618
Email: newsdesk.folkestone@krnmedia.co.uk
Advertising Address: As above.
Email: danielle.johnson@krnmedia.co.uk
Web site: http://www.ickent.co.uk
Publisher: Northcliffe Media Ltd
Date Established: 1891
Frequency: Weekly - Published every Thursday
Circulation: 108,975 (Combined Circulation)
Editor: Simon Finlay; **Advertising Manager:** Danielle Johnson
ADVERTISING: Rates on application
Series owner and contact point for the following titles, see individual entries:
Adscene (Ashford)
Adscene (Deal, Dover & Folkestone)
Dover Express
Folkestone Herald
Hythe Herald
Romney Marsh Herald
Supplement(s): Driving Forces - 52xY, Kentish Property Times - 52xY
LOCAL NEWSPAPERS: Local Newspapers English Counties

ADSCENE (SITTINGBOURNE & SHEPPEY)

27411U72B-1790_130

Frequency: Weekly
Cover Price: Free
Circulation: 15,200 (Publisher's Statement)
Usual Pagination: 28
ADVERTISING: Rates on application
Part of Series, see entry for: East Kent Gazette Series
LOCAL NEWSPAPERS: Local Newspapers English Counties

ADSCENE (THANET)

43882U72B-1830_130

Formerly: Adscene (Thanet & District)
Frequency: Weekly - Published on Thursday
Cover Price: Free
Circulation: 52,075 (VFD 02/07/2007 to 30/12/2007)
ADVERTISING: Rates on application
Part of Series, see entry for: Isle of Thanet Gazette Series
LOCAL NEWSPAPERS: Local Newspapers English Counties

THE ADVERTISER

44478U72B-3330_180

Formerly: Worthing Advertiser
Web site: http://www.worthingherald.co.uk
Frequency: Weekly - Published on Friday
Cover Price: Free
Circulation: 73,250 (Publisher's Statement)
Part of Series, see entry for: Worthing Advertiser and Herald Series
LOCAL NEWSPAPERS: Local Newspapers English Counties

ADVERTISER & TIMES SERIES

43727U72B-1337

Editorial Address: 62 Old Milton Road, NEW MILTON, BH25 6EH **Tel:** 01425 615501 **Fax:** 01425 638635
Email: news@advertiserandtimes.co.uk

Advertising Address: As above. **Tel:** 01425 613384
Fax: 01425 610257
Email: advertising@advertiserandtimes.co.uk
Web site: http://www.advertiserandtimes.co.uk
Publisher: Advertiser & Times (Hants)
Date Established: 1929
Frequency: Weekly
Cover Price: £0.30
Circulation: 21,421 (Publisher's Statement)
Editor: Andy Sherwood; **News Editor:** Andy Sherwood; **Advertising Manager:** Jackie Lebburn
ADVERTISING RATES:
Full Page Mono £1052.80
Agency Commission: 10%
Mechanical Data: Page Width: 403mm, No. of Columns (Display): 8, Type Area: 560 x 403mm, Col Length: 560mm, Col Widths (Display): 48mm
Copy instructions: Copy Date: 8 days prior to publication date
Average advertising content per issue: 60%
Series owner and contact point for the following titles, see individual entries:
Lymington Times
New Milton Advertiser
LOCAL NEWSPAPERS: Local Newspapers English Counties

THE ADVERTISER BARROW AND WEST CUMBERLAND

43444U72B-605

Editorial Address: Newspaper House, Abbey Road, BARROW-IN-FURNESS, LA14 5QS **Tel:** 01229 840150
Fax: 01229 840164
Email: news@nwemail.co.uk
Advertising Address: As above. **Tel:** 01229 840127
Fax: 01229 832141
Email: sharon.granville@cngroup.co.uk
Web site: http://www.nwemail.co.uk
Publisher: Cumbrian Newspapers Ltd
Frequency: Weekly
Cover Price: Free
Circulation: 39,535 (VFD 02/07/2007 to 30/12/2007)
Editor: Phil Pearson; **Advertising Manager:** Sharon Granville
ADVERTISING RATES:
Full Page Colour £2371.60
SCC £9.68
Agency Commission: 10%
Mechanical Data: Type Area: 350 x 266mm, Page Width: 266mm, Col Length: 350mm, No. of Columns (Display): 7, Film: Digital
Copy instructions: Copy Date: Tuesday 2.30pm prior to publication date
Average advertising content per issue: 60%
LOCAL NEWSPAPERS: Local Newspapers English Counties

THE ADVERTISER (CHESTER-LE-STREET)

43570U72B-915_140

Formerly: Chester-le-Street Advertiser
Frequency: Weekly
Cover Price: Free
Circulation: 16,733 (VFD 02/07/2007 to 30/12/2007)
ADVERTISING RATES:
Full Page Mono £3421.08
Full Page Colour £4276.35
SCC £11.18
Part of Series, see entry for: Advertiser Series (Durham)
LOCAL NEWSPAPERS: Local Newspapers English Counties

THE ADVERTISER (CONSETT & STANLEY)

43571U72B-915_150

Formerly: Consett & Stanley Advertiser
Frequency: Weekly
Cover Price: Free
Circulation: 30,418 (VFD 02/07/2007 to 30/12/2007)
ADVERTISING RATES:
Full Page Mono £3421.08
Full Page Colour £4276.35
SCC £11.18
Part of Series, see entry for: Advertiser Series (Durham)
LOCAL NEWSPAPERS: Local Newspapers English Counties

THE ADVERTISER (DARLINGTON, AYCLIFFE & SEDGEFIELD)

43572U72B-915_160

Formerly: Darlington, Aycliffe & Sedgefield Advertiser
Frequency: Weekly
Cover Price: Free
Circulation: 63,349 (VFD 02/07/2007 to 30/12/2007)
ADVERTISING RATES:
Full Page Mono £4152.42
Full Page Colour £5190.52

SCC £13.57
Part of Series, see entry for: Advertiser Series (Durham)
LOCAL NEWSPAPERS: Local Newspapers English Counties

THE ADVERTISER (DURHAM)

43573U72B-915_180

Formerly: Durham Advertiser
Frequency: Weekly
Cover Price: Free
Circulation: 27,102 (VFD 02/07/2007 to 30/12/2007)
ADVERTISING RATES:
Full Page Mono £3421.08
Full Page Colour £4276.35
SCC £11.18
Part of Series, see entry for: Advertiser Series (Durham)
LOCAL NEWSPAPERS: Local Newspapers English Counties

THE ADVERTISER ENFIELD 42995U72A-120_110

Frequency: Weekly
Cover Price: Free
Circulation: 86,839 (Publisher's Statement)
ADVERTISING RATES:
SCC £9.35
Part of Series, see entry for: Gazette, Advertiser and Press Newspaper Series
LOCAL NEWSPAPERS: Local Newspapers Greater London

THE ADVERTISER GREAT YARMOUTH AND GORLESTON

44144U72B-2447_110

Formerly: Great Yarmouth and Gorleston Advertiser
Frequency: Weekly
Cover Price: Free
Circulation: 40,469 (VFD 02/07/2007 to 30/12/2007)
ADVERTISING RATES:
Full Page Mono £1658.88
Part of Series, see entry for: Great Yarmouth Advertiser Series
LOCAL NEWSPAPERS: Local Newspapers English Counties

THE ADVERTISER (HORWICH, WESTHOUGHTON & DISTRICT)

43675U72B-1152

Editorial Address: Bentham House, 147-149 Chorley New Road, Horwich, BOLTON, BL6 5QE **Tel:** 01204 696916
Fax: 01204 691139
Email: advertiser@news4u.co.uk
Advertising Address: As above.
Email: advertiser@news4u.co.uk
Publisher: Advertiser Newspapers
Date Established: 1980
Frequency: 14 issues yearly - Published 2nd Tuesday of each month
Cover Price: Free
Circulation: 36,000 (Publisher's Statement)
Editor: Steve Crawshaw; **Features Editor:** Carol Thomson;
Advertising Manager: Steve Crawshaw
ADVERTISING RATES:
Full Page Colour £931.00
SCC £3.50
Agency Commission: 10%
Mechanical Data: Col Widths (Display): 37mm, Type Area: 380 x 270mm, No. of Columns (Display): 7, Col Length: 380mm, Page Width: 270mm, Print Process: Web-fed offset litho
Copy instructions: Copy Date: 1 week prior to publication date
Average advertising content per issue: 60%
LOCAL NEWSPAPERS: Local Newspapers English Counties

THE ADVERTISER (MIDLOTHIAN)

44900U72D-270_130

Frequency: Weekly
Cover Price: £0.42
Circulation: 7,126 (ABC 02/07/2007 to 30/12/2007)
Part of Series, see entry for: Dalkeith Advertiser Series
LOCAL NEWSPAPERS: Local Newspapers Scotland

THE ADVERTISER (NEWBURY)

43267U72B-170_150

Frequency: Weekly
Cover Price: Free
Circulation: 39,587 (Publisher's Statement)
ADVERTISING: Rates on application

Part of Series, see entry for: Newbury Weekly News Series
LOCAL NEWSPAPERS: Local Newspapers English Counties

ADVERTISER (NORTH EAST MANCHESTER)

43695U72B-1203_100

Formerly: Express Moston, Middleton, Blackley & Crumpsall
Frequency: Weekly
Cover Price: Free
Circulation: 86,500 (Publisher's Statement)
ADVERTISING RATES:
SCC £6.55
Part of Series, see entry for: Middleton & North Manchester Guardian & Advertiser Series
LOCAL NEWSPAPERS: Local Newspapers English Counties

THE ADVERTISER NORTH NORFOLK

706946U72B-3954_101

Formerly: North Norfolk Advertiser
Frequency: Weekly
Cover Price: Free
Circulation: 13,377 (Publisher's Statement)
ADVERTISING: Rates on application
Part of Series, see entry for: Anglia Advertiser Series
LOCAL NEWSPAPERS: Local Newspapers English Counties

THE ADVERTISER (NORTH YORKSHIRE)

43574U72B-915_230

Formerly: North Yorkshire Advertiser
Frequency: Weekly
Cover Price: Free
Circulation: 27,219 (VFD 02/07/2007 to 30/12/2007)
ADVERTISING RATES:
Full Page Mono £642.60
Full Page Colour 803.25
SCC £2.10
Part of Series, see entry for: Advertiser Series (Durham)
LOCAL NEWSPAPERS: Local Newspapers English Counties

THE ADVERTISER NORWICH

44145U72B-3954_100

Formerly: Norwich Advertiser
Frequency: Weekly
Cover Price: Free
Circulation: 80,133 (VFD 02/07/2007 to 30/12/2007)
ADVERTISING: Rates on application
Part of Series, see entry for: Anglia Advertiser Series
LOCAL NEWSPAPERS: Local Newspapers English Counties

THE ADVERTISER PRESTWICH, WHITEFIELD & RADCLIFFE 43716U72B-1290_120

Frequency: Weekly
Cover Price: Free
Circulation: 34,576 (VFD 02/07/2007 to 30/12/2007)
Part of Series, see entry for: Salford Advertiser Series
LOCAL NEWSPAPERS: Local Newspapers English Counties

ADVERTISER SERIES (ASHTON)

43676U72B-1153

Editorial Address: 35-37 Booth Street, ASHTON-UNDER-LYNE, OL6 7LB **Tel:** 0161 339 7611 **Fax:** 0161 343 2997
Email: tamesideadvertiser@menwn.co.uk
Advertising Address: Wood Street, Hollywood, STOCKPORT, SK3 0AB **Tel:** 0161 480 4491
Fax: 0161 480 4837
Email: mark.stansfield@menmediasales.co.uk
Web site: http://www.tamesideadvertiser.co.uk
Publisher: MEN Media
Date Established: 1979
Frequency: Weekly - Published on Thursday
Cover Price: Free
Circulation: 104,047 (VFD 02/07/2007 to 30/12/2007)
Advertising Manager: Mark Stansfield
ADVERTISING: Rates on application
Agency Commission: 10%
Mechanical Data: Page Width: 267mm, Film: Digital, Type Area: 340 x 267mm, Col Length: 340mm, Col Widths (Display): 27mm, No. of Columns (Display): 9
Copy instructions: Copy Date: Tuesday 3.30pm prior to publication date
Series owner and contact point for the following titles, see individual entries:
The Glossop Advertiser

Tameside Advertiser
LOCAL NEWSPAPERS: Local Newspapers English Counties

ADVERTISER SERIES (DURHAM)

43569U72B-915

Editorial Address: PO Box 14, Priestgate, DARLINGTON, DL1 1NF **Tel:** 01325 381313 **Fax:** 01325 505268
Email: advertiser.editorial@nne.co.uk
Advertising Address: As above. **Fax:** 01325 384311
Email: trish.booth@nne.co.uk
Web site: http://www.thisisthenortheast.co.uk/advertiser
Publisher: Newsquest Yorkshire and North East (Darlington)
Frequency: Weekly
Cover Price: Free
Circulation: 193,884 (Combined Circulation)
Editor: Nigel Burton; **Managing Director:** David Coates
ADVERTISING: Rates on application
Copy instructions: Copy Date: 6 days prior to publication date
Average advertising content per issue: 70%
Series owner and contact point for the following titles, see individual entries:
The Advertiser (Chester-le-Street)
The Advertiser (Consett & Stanley)
The Advertiser (Darlington, Aycliffe & Sedgefield)
The Advertiser (Durham)
The Advertiser (North Yorkshire)
The Advertiser (Wear Valley)
LOCAL NEWSPAPERS: Local Newspapers English Counties

ADVERTISER SERIES IN ABERDEENSHIRE

44860U72D-10

Editorial Address: 16 High Street, TURRIFF, AB53 4DT
Tel: 01888 563589 **Fax:** 01888 563936
Email: newsdesk@wpeters.co.uk
Advertising Address: As above.
Email: adverts@wpeters.co.uk
Publisher: W. Peters and Son Ltd
Date Established: 1930
Frequency: Weekly
Circulation: 15,000 (Publisher's Statement)
Editor: Jan Mackie; **Managing Director:** David George;
Advertising Manager: Neil Bremner
ADVERTISING RATES:
Full Page Mono £725.00
SCC £3.25
Agency Commission: 10%
Mechanical Data: Col Length: 390mm, Col Widths (Display): 42mm, No. of Columns (Display): 6, Type Area: 390 x 275mm, Print Process: Litho, Trim Size: 312 x 430mm, Page Width: 275mm, Film: Digital
Copy instructions: Copy Date: Tuesday 11am prior to publication date
Series owner and contact point for the following titles, see individual entries:
Ellon & District Advertiser
Inverurie Advertiser
Turriff & District Advertiser
LOCAL NEWSPAPERS: Local Newspapers Scotland

ADVERTISER SERIES (IPSWICH)

44341U72B-3078

Formerly: Ipswich Advertiser
Editorial Address: Press House, 30 Lower Brook Street, IPSWICH, IP4 1AN **Tel:** 01473 324696
Email: mercury@archant.co.uk
Advertising Address: As above. **Tel:** 01473 230023
Fax: 01473 324830
Email: james.east@archant.co.uk
Web site: http://www.ipswichadvertiser.co.uk
Publisher: Archant Suffolk
Frequency: Weekly - Published on Thursday
Cover Price: Free
Circulation: 82,067 (Combined Circulation)
Editor: Charlotte Smith-Jarvis; **Managing Director:** Stuart McCreery; **Advertising Manager:** James East
ADVERTISING RATES:
Full Page Mono £3098.88
Full Page Colour £4028.54
SCC £10.76
Agency Commission: 10%
Mechanical Data: Film: Digital, Type Area: 360 x 270mm, Col Length: 360mm, Page Width: 270mm, Col Widths (Display): 32mm, No. of Columns (Display): 8
Copy instructions: Copy Date: Tuesday 5pm prior to publication date
Average advertising content per issue: 65%
Series owner and contact point for the following titles, see individual entries:
The Coastal Advertiser
Felixstowe Advertiser
The Hadleigh Advertiser
Ipswich Advertiser

Non-National Newspapers

Stowmarket Advertiser
LOCAL NEWSPAPERS: Local Newspapers English Counties

ADVERTISER SERIES (POOLE & SWANAGE)
43552U72B-902
Editorial Address: Richmond Hill, BOURNEMOUTH, BH2 6HH **Tel:** 01202 554601 **Fax:** 01202 292115
Email: newsdesk@bournemouthecho.co.uk
Advertising Address: As above. **Tel:** 01202 411422 **Fax:** 01202 294289
Email: debi.thorne@bournemouthecho.co.uk
Web site: http://www.bournemouthecho.co.uk
Publisher: Newsquest (Media Group) Ltd
Date Established: 1980
Frequency: Weekly
Cover Price: Free
Circulation: 163,340 (Combined Circulation)
Editor: Andy Martin; **News Editor:** Andy Martin; **Editor-in-Chief:** Neal Butterworth; **Managing Director:** Mike Wright
ADVERTISING: Rates on application
Agency Commission: 10%
Average advertising content per issue: 70%
Series owner and contact point for the following titles, see individual entries:
Bournemouth Advertiser
Christchurch Advertiser
Poole & Dorset Advertiser
Swanage & Wareham Advertiser
The Vale Advertiser
LOCAL NEWSPAPERS: Local Newspapers English Counties

ADVERTISER SERIES (SOUTH CHESHIRE)
43346U72B-423
Formerly: Advertiser Series (Biddulph & Congleton)
Editorial Address: 26 High Street, CREWE, CW2 7BN
Tel: 01782 602764 **Fax:** 01270 258469
Email: emma.king@thesentinel.co.uk
Advertising Address: 21-24 Smithfield Centre, Haywood Street, LEEK, ST13 5JL **Tel:** 01260 281012
Fax: 01538 392249
Email: jane.barlow@thepostandtimes.co.uk
Web site: http://www.thisissentinel.co.uk
Publisher: Northcliffe Media Ltd
Date Established: 1986
Frequency: Weekly - Published Thursday
Cover Price: Free
Circulation: 25,694 (VFD 20/08/2007 to 30/12/2007)
Editor: Emma King; **Advertising Manager:** Jane Barlow
ADVERTISING RATES:
SCC £3.45
Agency Commission: 10%
Mechanical Data: No. of Columns (Display): 8, Type Area: 360 x 265mm, Col Length: 360mm, Page Width: 265mm, Col Widths (Display): 30mm; Film: Digital
Copy instructions: Copy Date: Tuesday 12pm prior to publication date
Average advertising content per issue: 48%
Series owner and contact point for the following titles, see individual entries:
Alsager Advertiser
The Congleton Advertiser
South Cheshire Advertiser
LOCAL NEWSPAPERS: Local Newspapers English Counties

ADVERTISER SERIES (STOKE-ON-TRENT)
44286U72B-2956
Editorial Address: Sentinel House, Forge Lane, Etruria, STOKE-ON-TRENT, ST1 5SS **Tel:** 01782 602525
Fax: 01782 280781
Email: newsdesk@thesentinel.co.uk
Advertising Address: As above. **Fax:** 01782 262617
Email: advertiser@thesentinel.co.uk
Web site: http://www.thisisthesentinel.co.uk
Publisher: Northcliffe Media Ltd
Date Established: 1975
Frequency: Weekly
Cover Price: Free
Circulation: 103,429 (VFD 02/07/2007 to 30/12/2007)
Editor: Charlotte Littlejones; **Editor-in-Chief:** Mike Sassi; **Advertising Manager:** Lyn Rowe
ADVERTISING: Rates on application
Series owner and contact point for the following titles, see individual entries:
The Moorlands Advertiser
Newcastle Advertiser
The Potteries Advertiser
Supplement(s): Business Weekly - 52xY, The Sentinel - 52xY
LOCAL NEWSPAPERS: Local Newspapers English Counties

ADVERTISER SERIES (SURREY)
44351U72B-3095
Editorial Address: 80 South Street, DORKING, RH4 2HE
Tel: 01306 886661 **Fax:** 01306 886939
Email: editor@dorkingadvertiser.co.uk
Advertising Address: Trinity House, 51 London Road, REIGATE, RH2 9PR **Tel:** 01737 732000 **Fax:** 01737 732098
Email: matthew.bingham@essnmedia.co.uk
Web site: http://www.icsurreyonline.co.uk
Publisher: East Surrey & Sussex Newspapers plc
Frequency: Weekly - Published on Thursday
Cover Price: £0.60
Circulation: 11,382 (Combined Circulation)
Editor: Ursula Hudson; **Advertising Manager:** Matthew Bingham
ADVERTISING RATES:
SCC £12.30
Mechanical Data: Type Area: 360 x 270mm, Col Widths (Display): 32mm, Col Length: 360mm, Page Width: 270mm, No. of Columns (Display): 8
Copy instructions: Copy Date: Tuesday 12.00 noon prior to publication date
Series owner and contact point for the following titles, see individual entries:
Dorking Advertiser
Leatherhead Advertiser
Supplement(s): The Guide - 52xY
LOCAL NEWSPAPERS: Local Newspapers English Counties

THE ADVERTISER (STRATHKELVIN)
44984U72D-630_200
Formerly: Strathkelvin Advertiser
Frequency: Weekly
Cover Price: Free
Circulation: 23,022 (ABC 04/07/2005 to 01/01/2006)
Part of Series, see entry for: Kirkintilloch & Bishopbriggs Herald Series
LOCAL NEWSPAPERS: Local Newspapers Scotland

THE ADVERTISER WAVENEY
44147U72B-2447_190
Formerly: Waveney Advertiser
Frequency: Weekly
Cover Price: Free
Circulation: 43,113 (VFD 02/07/2007 to 30/12/2007)
ADVERTISING RATES:
Full Page Mono £1658.88
Part of Series, see entry for: Great Yarmouth Advertiser Series
LOCAL NEWSPAPERS: Local Newspapers English Counties

THE ADVERTISER (WEAR VALLEY)
43575U72B-915_250
Formerly: Wear Valley Advertiser
Frequency: Weekly
Cover Price: Free
Circulation: 29,063 (VFD 02/07/2007 to 30/12/2007)
ADVERTISING RATES:
Full Page Mono £4152.42
Full Page Colour £5190.52
SCC £13.57
Part of Series, see entry for: Advertiser Series (Durham)
LOCAL NEWSPAPERS: Local Newspapers English Counties

AINTREE & MAGHULL CHAMPION
44105U72B-2388_140
Formerly: Maghull Champion
Frequency: Weekly
Cover Price: Free
ADVERTISING RATES:
Full Page Mono £476.00
SCC £1.75
Part of Series, see entry for: Southport, Ormskirk & Formby Champion Series
LOCAL NEWSPAPERS: Local Newspapers English Counties

AIRDRIE & COATBRIDGE ADVERTISER
44864U72D-20
Editorial Address: 5/15 Bank Street, AIRDRIE, ML6 6AF
Tel: 01236 748048 **Fax:** 01236 748098
Email: acadvertiser@s-un.co.uk
Advertising Address: Press Buildings, Campbell Street, Hamilton, AIRDRIE, ML3 6AX **Tel:** 01698 282222
Fax: 01698 425706
Email: kclark@s-un.co.uk
Web site: http://www.iclanarkshire.co.uk
Publisher: Scottish & Universal Newspapers Ltd

Frequency: Weekly - Published on Wednesday
Cover Price: £0.73
Circulation: 16,621 (ABC 02/07/2007 to 30/12/2007)
Editor: Wendy Scott
ADVERTISING: Rates on application
LOCAL NEWSPAPERS: Local Newspapers Scotland

AIRE, WHARFE AND WORTH VALLEYS TARGET
1772447U72B-3747_141
Formerly: Bingley Target
Frequency: Weekly
Cover Price: Free
Part of Series, see entry for: Bradford Target Series
LOCAL NEWSPAPERS: Local Newspapers English Counties

ALCESTER CHRONICLE
44625U72B-3568_110
Frequency: Weekly
Cover Price: Free
Part of Series, see entry for: Redditch Advertiser and Chronicle Series
LOCAL NEWSPAPERS: Local Newspapers English Counties

ALDERSHOT AND FARNBOROUGH COURIER
44360U72B-1382_140
Formerly: Farnborough Courier
Frequency: Weekly - Circulation figure is for Courier Series including Farnborough Courier, Fleet & District Courier, Hart District Courier, Yateley & District Courier and Camberley Courier
Cover Price: Free
Circulation: 71,686 (ABC 01/01/2007 to 01/07/2007)
ADVERTISING: Rates on application
Part of Series, see entry for: Aldershot Mail and News Series
LOCAL NEWSPAPERS: Local Newspapers English Counties

ALDERSHOT MAIL AND NEWS SERIES
43757U72B-1382
Formerly: News Group
Editorial Address: 35-39 High Street, ALDERSHOT, GU11 1BH **Tel:** 01252 339760 **Fax:** 01252 339770
Email: newsdesk@aldershot.co.uk
Advertising Address: 192 Victoria Road, ALDERSHOT, GU11 1JZ **Tel:** 01252 316311 **Fax:** 01252 343042
Email: advertising@starnewspaper.co.uk
Web site: http://www.aldershot.co.uk
Publisher: Aldershot News Ltd
Date Established: 1894
Frequency: Weekly - Circulation figures for the Aldershot Courier and Aldershot News & Mail are the total figures for their respective series
Circulation: 131,660 (VFD 02/07/2007 to 30/12/2007)
Editor: Claire Youngs; **News Editor:** Claire Youings
ADVERTISING: Rates on application
Series owner and contact point for the following titles, see individual entries:
Aldershot and Farnborough Courier
Aldershot News & Mail
Ash & Farnham Mail & News
Camberley News & Mail
Farnborough News & Mail
Fleet & Hart Courier
Fleet News & Mail
Sandhurst & Crowthorne News & Mail
Yateley News & Mail
Supplement(s): What's On - 52xY
LOCAL NEWSPAPERS: Local Newspapers English Counties

ALDERSHOT NEWS & MAIL
43759U72B-1382_110
Formerly: Aldershot News
Frequency: Weekly
Cover Price: £0.37
Circulation: 22,200 (Publisher's Statement)
ADVERTISING: Rates on application
Part of Series, see entry for: Aldershot Mail and News Series
LOCAL NEWSPAPERS: Local Newspapers English Counties

ALFRETON CHAD
44173U72B-2580_110
Publisher: Wilfred Edmunds
Frequency: Weekly - Published on Friday
Cover Price: Free
Circulation: 16,104 (VFD 02/07/2007 to 30/12/2007)
ADVERTISING RATES:
SCC £4.87

Part of Series, see entry for: Chad Series Mansfield
LOCAL NEWSPAPERS: Local Newspapers English Counties

ALLANWATER NEWS
1753417U72D-1022
Formerly: Allan Water News
Editorial Address: 10 Mar Street, ALLOA, FK10 1HR
Tel: 01259 724724 **Fax:** 01259 723250
Email: editor@forthindependentnewspapers.co.uk
Advertising Address: As above.
Email: admanager@wee-county-news.co.uk
Publisher: Forth Independent Newspapers
Date Established: 2006
Frequency: Weekly
Cover Price: Free
Circulation: 8,000 (Publisher's Statement)
Editor: Ronnie Paterson; **Advertising Manager:** Laura Evans
Summary of Content: Website covering newspaper Allan Water News.
Readership/Target Audience: Aimed at people interested in news, living in Scotland.
ADVERTISING: Rates on application
LOCAL NEWSPAPERS: Local Newspapers Scotland

ALLOA AND HILLFOOTS ADVERTISER
44865U72D-30
Editorial Address: 39 Drysdale Street, ALLOA, FK10 1JA
Tel: 01259 214416 **Fax:** 01259 722375
Email: editorial@alloaadvertiser.co.uk
Advertising Address: As above.
Email: advertising@alloaadvertiser.co.uk
Web site: http://www.alloaadvertiser.com
Publisher: Clyde & Forth Press Group
Date Established: 1841
Frequency: Weekly
Cover Price: £0.45
Circulation: 9,119 (ABC 02/07/2007 to 30/12/2007)
Editor: Kevin McRoberts; **News Editor:** Hamish Hutchinson; **Advertising Manager:** Roberta Bell
ADVERTISING RATES:
Full Page Mono £2076.00
Full Page Colour £4152.00
SCC £7.46
Agency Commission: 10%
Mechanical Data: Type Area: 330 x 265.5mm, Col Length: 330mm, Col Widths (Display): 31mm, No. of Columns (Display): 8, Film: Negative, wrong reading, emulsion side up, Print Process: Web-fed offset litho, Page Width: 265.5mm
Copy instructions: Copy Date: Monday 4pm prior to publication date
Average advertising content per issue: 50%
LOCAL NEWSPAPERS: Local Newspapers Scotland

ALLOA & HILLFOOTS SHOPPER
45034U72D-930_120
Frequency: Weekly - See Stirling Shopper for circulation figure
Cover Price: Free
ADVERTISING: Rates on application
Part of Series, see entry for: Stirling Shopper Series
LOCAL NEWSPAPERS: Local Newspapers Scotland

ALLOA AND HILLFOOTS WEE COUNTY NEWS
44866U72D-40
Editorial Address: 10 Mar Street, ALLOA, FK10 1HR
Tel: 01259 724724 **Fax:** 01259 724725
Email: editor@wee-county-news.co.uk
Advertising Address: As above. **Fax:** 01259 723250
Email: admanager@wee-county-news.co.uk
Web site: http://www.wee-county-news.co.uk
Publisher: Forth Independent Newspapers
Date Established: 1995
Frequency: Weekly - Published on Tuesday
Cover Price: £0.41
Circulation: 6,587 (ABC 02/07/2007 to 30/12/2007)
Editor: News Desk; **Advertising Manager:** Laura Evans
ADVERTISING: Rates on application
Agency Commission: 10%
Copy instructions: Copy Date: Monday prior to publication date
Average advertising content per issue: 45%
LOCAL NEWSPAPERS: Local Newspapers Scotland

ALRESFORD ADVERTISER
43731U72B-1339_150
Frequency: Weekly
Cover Price: Free

Part of Series, see entry for: Alton Post Gazette, Times & Mail Series
LOCAL NEWSPAPERS: Local Newspapers English Counties

ALSAGER ADVERTISER
1664311U72B-423_132
Frequency: Weekly
Cover Price: Free
Part of Series, see entry for: Advertiser Series (South Cheshire)
LOCAL NEWSPAPERS: Local Newspapers English Counties

ALTON HERALD
44370U72B-3120_110
Email: alton.herald@internet-today.co.uk
Web site: http://www.tindlenews.co.uk
Frequency: Weekly - Published on Thursday
Cover Price: £0.50
Part of Series, see entry for: Farnham Herald Series
LOCAL NEWSPAPERS: Local Newspapers English Counties

ALTON POST GAZETTE
43732U72B-1339_170
Formerly: Alton Gazette
Frequency: Weekly
Cover Price: £0.20
Part of Series, see entry for: Alton Post Gazette, Times & Mail Series
LOCAL NEWSPAPERS: Local Newspapers English Counties

ALTON POST GAZETTE, TIMES & MAIL SERIES
43730U72B-1339
Formerly: Alton Post Gazette and Alresford Advertiser Series
Editorial Address: 24 High Street, ALTON, GU34 1BN
Tel: 01420 84446 **Fax:** 01420 542547
Email: postgazette.news@tindlenews.co.uk
Advertising Address: As above.
Email: postgazette.admin@tindlenews.co.uk
Publisher: Tindle Newspapers Ltd
Date Established: 1886
Frequency: Weekly - Published on Wednesday
Cover Price: £0.20
Free to qualifying individuals
Circulation: 30,000 (Publisher's Statement)
Editor: Amanda Barnes; **Advertising Manager:** Alan Wooler
ADVERTISING RATES:
SCC £3.85
Agency Commission: 10%
Mechanical Data: Col Length: 390mm, Col Widths (Display): 30mm, Type Area: 390 x 270mm, Page Width: 270mm, No. of Columns (Display): 8, Film: Digital
Copy instructions: Copy Date: Thursday 4pm prior to publication date
Average advertising content per issue: 60%
Series owner and contact point for the following titles, see individual entries:
Alresford Advertiser
Alton Post Gazette
Alton Times & Mail
Bordon Times & Mail
Haslemere Times & Mail
Liphook Times & Mail
Petersfield Times & Mail
Surrey & Hants News
LOCAL NEWSPAPERS: Local Newspapers English Counties

ALTON TIMES & MAIL
44386U72B-1339_180
Frequency: Weekly - Circulation figure includes the Bordon Times & Mail, the Haslemere Times & Mail, the Liphook Times & Mail and the Petersfield Times & Mail
Cover Price: Free
Circulation: 25,440 (VFD 02/07/2007 to 30/12/2007)
Part of Series, see entry for: Alton Post Gazette, Times & Mail Series
LOCAL NEWSPAPERS: Local Newspapers English Counties

AMERSHAM EXAMINER
43296U72B-240_110
Formerly: Amersham Advertiser
Cover Price: £0.55
Part of Series, see entry for: The Buckinghamshire Examiner and Advertiser Series
LOCAL NEWSPAPERS: Local Newspapers English Counties

ANDERSONSTOWN NEWS (MONDAY)
623758U72E-3_110
Frequency: Weekly
Cover Price: £0.65
Circulation: 8,538 (ABC 01/01/2007 to 30/12/2007)
ADVERTISING RATES:
Full Page Mono £930.24
Full Page Colour £1209.30
Part of Series, see entry for: Andersonstown News Series
LOCAL NEWSPAPERS: Local Newspapers Northern Ireland

ANDERSONSTOWN NEWS SERIES
45051U72E-3
Formerly: Andersonstown News
Editorial Address: Teach Basil, 2 Hannahstown Hill, BELFAST, BT17 0LT **Tel:** 028 9061 9000
Fax: 028 9062 0602
Email: r.livingstone@belfastmediagroup.com
Advertising Address: As above. **Tel:** 028 9060 9000
Fax: 028 9060 5533
Email: j.odonnell@belfastmediagroup.com
Web site: http://www.belfastmedia.com
Publisher: Belfast Media Group
Frequency: 104 issues yearly
Circulation: 14,598 (ABC 01/01/2007 to 30/12/2007)
Editor: Ciara McGuigan; **News Editor:** Robin Livingstone; **Features Editor:** Ciara McGuigan; **Advertising Manager:** Jacqueline O'Donnell
ADVERTISING: Rates on application
Mechanical Data: Type Area: 340 x 260mm, Col Length: 340mm, Page Width: 260mm, Film: Digital, No. of Columns (Display): 6
Copy instructions: Copy Date: 2 working days prior to publication date
Series owner and contact point for the following titles, see individual entries:
Andersonstown News (Monday)
Andersonstown News (Thursday)
Supplement(s): Business & Recruitment - 52xY, Homes - 36xY, Motoring - 52xY
LOCAL NEWSPAPERS: Local Newspapers Northern Ireland

ANDERSONSTOWN NEWS (THURSDAY)
623765U72E-3_120
Frequency: Weekly
Cover Price: £0.65
Circulation: 14,100 (ABC 02/01/2006 to 31/12/2006)
ADVERTISING RATES:
Full Page Mono £1191.36
Full Page Colour £1548.45
Part of Series, see entry for: Andersonstown News Series
LOCAL NEWSPAPERS: Local Newspapers Northern Ireland

ANDOVER ADVERTISER
43734U72B-1340_110
Frequency: Weekly
Cover Price: £0.60
Circulation: 15,776 (ABC 01/01/2007 to 30/12/2007)
ADVERTISING RATES:
Full Page Colour £1890.00
Part of Series, see entry for: Andover Advertiser Series
LOCAL NEWSPAPERS: Local Newspapers English Counties

ANDOVER ADVERTISER SERIES
43733U72B-1340
Editorial Address: Advertiser House, 24-32 London Street, ANDOVER, SP10 2PE **Tel:** 01264 321205
Fax: 01264 338723
Email: newsdesk@andoveradvertiser.co.uk
Advertising Address: As above. **Tel:** 01264 323456
Fax: 01264 332174
Email: sales@andoveradvertiser.co.uk
Web site: http://www.andoveradvertiser.co.uk
Publisher: Newsquest (Media Group) Ltd
Date Established: 1858
Frequency: Weekly
Circulation: 39,707 (Combined Circulation)
Editor: Dick Bellringer; **News Editor:** Dick Bellringer; **Managing Director:** John Banks
ADVERTISING: Rates on application
Agency Commission: 10%
Copy instructions: Copy Date: 3 days prior to publication date
Average advertising content per issue: 40%
Series owner and contact point for the following titles, see individual entries:
Andover Advertiser
Midweek Advertiser
LOCAL NEWSPAPERS: Local Newspapers English Counties

Non-National Newspapers

ANGLIA ADVERTISER SERIES
1655656U72B-3954

Editorial Address: Prospect House, Rouen Road, NORWICH, NR1 1RE **Tel:** 01603 772487 **Fax:** 01603 666781
Email: sarah.wade@archant.co.uk
Advertising Address: As above.
Email: janice.mark@archant.co.uk
Web site: http://www.advertiser24.co.uk
Publisher: Archant Norfolk
Frequency: Weekly
Cover Price: Free
Circulation: 94,387 (Combined Circulation)
Editor: Sarah Wade; **Advertising Manager:** Janice Mark
ADVERTISING: Rates on application
Copy instructions: Copy Date: Tuesday 5pm prior to publication date
Average advertising content per issue: 65%
Series owner and contact point for the following titles, see individual entries:
The Advertiser North Norfolk
The Advertiser Norwich
LOCAL NEWSPAPERS: Local Newspapers English Counties

YR ANGOR (ABERYSTWYTH)
761713U72J-12

Editorial Address: 4 Ty Mawr, Padarn Terrace, Llanbadarn Fawr, ABERYSTWYTH, SY23 3RG **Tel:** 01970 623396
Advertising Address: 37 Cefn Esgair, Llanbadarn Fawr, ABERYSTWYTH, SY23 3JG **Tel:** 01970 617019
Email: kathleenberwyn@hotmail.com
Publisher: Lolfa Tal-y-bont (Aberystwyth)
Frequency: 10 issues yearly - Not published in August or September
Cover Price: £0.40
Circulation: 700 (Publisher's Statement)
Editor: David Greaney; **Advertising Manager:** Kathleen Evans
Summary of Content: Welsh language community newspaper including articles on churches and chapels, sports, schools and societies.
Language(s): Welsh
Readership/Target Audience: Aimed at Welsh speaking readers with an interest in the local area.
ADVERTISING: Rates on application
Copy instructions: Copy Date: 14 days prior to publication date
Average advertising content per issue: 25%
LOCAL NEWSPAPERS: Community Newsletters

YR ANGOR (LIVERPOOL)
761764U72J-15

Editorial Address: 32 Garth Drive, LIVERPOOL, L18 6HW
Tel: 0151 724 1989 **Fax:** 0151 724 5691
Email: ben@garthdrive.fsnet.co.uk
Advertising Address: As above.
Email: ben@garthdrive.fsnet.co.uk
Web site: http://www.liverpool-welsh.co.uk
Publisher: Modern Welsh Publications Ltd
Date Established: 1979
Frequency: 10 issues yearly - Not published in January or August
Cover Price: £0.40
Annual Sub.: £7.00
Circulation: 3,000 (Publisher's Statement)
Usual Pagination: 12
Editor: Ben Rees; **Advertising Manager:** Ben Rees
Summary of Content: Welsh language community newspaper featuring local news, articles, poetry and ecological issues.
Language(s): Welsh
Readership/Target Audience: Aimed at Welsh speaking readers in Lancashire.
ADVERTISING RATES:
Full Page Mono £100.00
LOCAL NEWSPAPERS: Community Newsletters

ANNANDALE HERALD
44914U72D-325_110

Frequency: Weekly - Published on Thursday
Cover Price: £0.45
Circulation: 3,172 (ABC 02/07/2007 to 30/12/2007)
ADVERTISING: Rates on application
Part of Series, see entry for: Annandale Observer Series
LOCAL NEWSPAPERS: Local Newspapers Scotland

ANNANDALE OBSERVER
44915U72D-325_120

Frequency: Weekly - Published on Friday
Cover Price: £0.48
Circulation: 6,737 (ABC 02/07/2007 to 30/12/2007)
ADVERTISING: Rates on application
Part of Series, see entry for: Annandale Observer Series
LOCAL NEWSPAPERS: Local Newspapers Scotland

ANNANDALE OBSERVER SERIES
44913U72D-325

Formerly: Dumfriesshire Newspapers
Editorial Address: 96 High Street, ANNAN, DG12 6EJ
Tel: 01461 202417 **Fax:** 01461 205472
Email: newsdesk@dngonline.co.uk
Advertising Address: As above. **Fax:** 01461 205659
Email: advertising@dngonline.co.uk
Web site: http://www.annandaleobserver.co.uk
Publisher: DNG Media
Frequency: Weekly
Circulation: 36,203 (Combined Circulation)
Editor: Fiona Reid; **Managing Director:** William Laidlaw;
Advertising Director: Graeme McGregor
ADVERTISING: Rates on application
Agency Commission: 10%
Series owner and contact point for the following titles, see individual entries:
Annandale Herald
Annandale Observer
Dumfries Courier
Moffat News
Supplement(s): Flair - 12xY
LOCAL NEWSPAPERS: Local Newspapers Scotland

ANTRIM GUARDIAN
45053U72E-20_120

Frequency: Weekly
Cover Price: £0.95
Part of Series, see entry for: Antrim Guardian Series
LOCAL NEWSPAPERS: Local Newspapers Northern Ireland

ANTRIM GUARDIAN SERIES
45052U72E-20

Formerly: Ballymena Guardian Series
Editorial Address: 5 Railway Street, ANTRIM, BT41 4AE
Tel: 028 9446 2624 **Fax:** 028 9446 5551
Email: editor@antrimguardian.co.uk
Advertising Address: As above.
Email: advertising@antrimguardian.co.uk
Web site: http://www.ulsternet-ni.co.uk
Publisher: Alpha Newspaper Group
Date Established: 1970
Frequency: Weekly - Published on Tuesday
Circulation: 14,794 (ABC 02/07/2007 to 30/12/2007)
Editor: Liam Heffron
ADVERTISING RATES:
Full Page Mono £2557.00
Full Page Colour £4346.90
SCC £4.65
Agency Commission: 10%
Mechanical Data: No. of Columns (Display): 10, Film: Digital
Copy instructions: Copy Date: 2 days prior to publication date
Series owner and contact point for the following titles, see individual entries:
Antrim Guardian
Ballymena Guardian
LOCAL NEWSPAPERS: Local Newspapers Northern Ireland

ANTRIM TIMES
45057U72E-30_120

Frequency: Weekly
Cover Price: £0.90
Part of Series, see entry for: Ballymena Times Series
LOCAL NEWSPAPERS: Local Newspapers Northern Ireland

ARBROATH HERALD
1833068U72D-60_100

Editorial Address: For all contact details see main edition, Arbroath Herald
Frequency: Weekly
Cover Price: £0.48
Part of Series, see entry for: Arbroath Herald & Gazette Series
LOCAL NEWSPAPERS: Local Newspapers Scotland

ARBROATH HERALD & GAZETTE SERIES
44867U72D-60

Formerly: Arbroath Herald
Editorial Address: 21 Market Place, ARBROATH, DD11 1HR **Tel:** 01241 872274 **Fax:** 01241 878789
Email: arbroath.herald@jnscotland.co.uk
Advertising Address: As above. **Fax:** 01241 431435
Email: arbroath.ads@jnscotland.co.uk
Web site: http://www.arbroathherald.co.uk
Publisher: Angus County Press Ltd
Date Established: 1885
Frequency: Weekly
Circulation: 10,156 (ABC 01/01/2007 to 01/07/2007)
Editor: Brian Stormont; **News Editor:** Brian Forsyth;
Advertising Manager: Jason Black
ADVERTISING RATES:
Full Page Mono £1742.00
Full Page Colour £2612.93

SCC £7.64
Agency Commission: 10%
Mechanical Data: Type Area: 340 x 272mm, Col Length: 340mm, No. of Columns (Display): 7, Col Widths (Display): 36mm, Film: Digital, Page Width: 272mm
Copy instructions: Copy Date: Tuesday 5pm prior to publication date
Average advertising content per issue: 35%
Series owner and contact point for the following titles, see individual entries:
Arbroath Herald
Guide & Gazette (Broughty Ferry)
LOCAL NEWSPAPERS: Local Newspapers Scotland

ARDEN OBSERVER
1665529U72B-3961_103

Frequency: Weekly - Published on Thursday
Cover Price: Free
Circulation: 46,655 (Publisher's Statement)
Part of Series, see entry for: Solihull, Shirley & Arden Observer Series
LOCAL NEWSPAPERS: Local Newspapers English Counties

ARDROSSAN & SALTCOATS HERALD
44868U72D-70

Editorial Address: Dock Road, ARDROSSAN, KA22 8DA
Tel: 01294 464321 **Fax:** 01294 466590
Email: editorial.ah@cfpress.co.uk
Advertising Address: As above.
Email: advertising.ah@cfpress.co.uk
Web site: http://www.ardrossanherald.com
Publisher: Clyde & Forth Press Group
Frequency: Weekly - Published on Wednesday
Cover Price: £0.55
Circulation: 14,615 (ABC 01/01/2007 to 30/12/2007)
Editor: Lauren Campbell; **News Editor:** Lauren Campbell;
Advertising Manager: Fiona Aitken
ADVERTISING RATES:
SCC £11.41
Agency Commission: 10%
Mechanical Data: Type Area: 330 x 266mm, No. of Columns (Display): 8, Col Widths (Display): 30mm, Col Length: 330mm, Page Width: 266mm, Film: Digital
Copy instructions: Copy Date: Monday 5pm prior to publication date
Average advertising content per issue: 50%
LOCAL NEWSPAPERS: Local Newspapers Scotland

ARFON-DWYFOR CAMBRIAN NEWS
1659703U72C-30_182

Formerly: Arfon-Dwyfor and Cambrian News
Frequency: Weekly
Cover Price: £0.65
ADVERTISING: Rates on application
Part of Series, see entry for: The Cambrian News Series
LOCAL NEWSPAPERS: Local Newspapers Wales

THE ARGUS
42003U67B-100

Formerly: The Argus (Brighton)
Editorial Address: Argus House, Crowhurst Road, Hollingbury, BRIGHTON, BN1 8AR **Tel:** 01273 544544
Fax: 01273 505703
Email: news@theargus.co.uk
Advertising Address: As above. **Fax:** 01273 889500
Email: nikki.sitwell@theargus.co.uk
Web site: http://www.theargus.co.uk
Publisher: Newsquest (Sussex) Ltd
Date Established: 1880
Frequency: Daily - Not published on Sunday
Cover Price: £0.38
Circulation: 32,788 (Publisher's Statement)
Editor: Lee Gibbs; **News Editor:** Lee Gibbs; **Features Editor:** Kim Protheroe; **Group Editor:** Michael Beard
ADVERTISING RATES:
Full Page Mono £1103.00
Full Page Colour £1324.00
SCC £7.98
Agency Commission: 10%
Mechanical Data: No. of Columns (Display): 9, Type Area: 340 x 259mm, Film: Digital, Col Length: 340mm, Page Width: 259mm
Copy instructions: Copy Date: 2 days prior to publication date
Supplement(s): Body & Soul - 52xY, Business (The Argus) - 52xY, The Guide - 52xY, Motoring - 52xY, Property - 52xY, Rant - 52xY, Weekend - 52xY, Woman - 52xY
REGIONAL DAILY & SUNDAY NEWSPAPERS: Regional Daily Newspapers

ARGYLLSHIRE ADVERTISER
44869U72D-75

Editorial Address: 44 Argyll Street, LOCHGILPHEAD, PA31 8NB **Tel:** 01546 602345 **Fax:** 01546 602661

Email: editor@argyllshireadvertiser.co.uk
Advertising Address: As above. **Tel:** 01586 602345
Email: adverts@campbeltowncourier.co.uk
Web site: http://www.argyllshireadvertiser.co.uk
Publisher: Wyvex Media Group
Date Established: 1861
Frequency: Weekly - Published on Friday. Circulation figure is incorporated into Campbeltown Courier
Cover Price: £0.62
Editor: Jenny Sutherland; **Managing Director:** Howard Bennett; **Advertising Manager:** Anne Martin
ADVERTISING RATES:
SCC £4.75
Agency Commission: 10%
Mechanical Data: Type Area: 340 x 249mm, Page Width: 249mm, Film: Digital, Col Length: 340mm, No. of Columns (Display): 7
Copy instructions: Copy Date: Tuesday prior to publication date
Supplement(s): Holiday West Highland - 4xY
LOCAL NEWSPAPERS: Local Newspapers Scotland

ARMAGH OBSERVER
45090U72E-120_120
Frequency: Weekly
Cover Price: £0.70
Part of Series, see entry for: Dungannon Observer Series
LOCAL NEWSPAPERS: Local Newspapers Northern Ireland

ARMTHORPE COMMUNITY NEWSLETTER
1647020U72B-3950_100
Frequency: Monthly
Cover Price: Free
Circulation: 6,000 (Publisher's Statement)
ADVERTISING: Rates on application
Part of Series, see entry for: Community Newsletter Series
LOCAL NEWSPAPERS: Local Newspapers English Counties

THE ARRAN BANNER
44870U72D-83
Editorial Address: BRODICK, Isle of Arran, KA27 8AJ
Tel: 01770 302142 **Fax:** 01770 302021
Email: editorial@arranbanner.co.uk
Advertising Address: As above.
Email: adverts@arranbanner.co.uk
Web site: http://www.arranbanner.co.uk
Publisher: Wyvex Media Group
Date Established: 1974
Frequency: Weekly - Published on Saturday
Cover Price: £0.50
Circulation: 3,458 (ABC 01/01/2007 to 30/12/2007)
Editor: Howard Driver; **Advertising Manager:** Fiona Simpson; **Group Editor:** Stewart MacKenzie
ADVERTISING RATES:
Full Page Mono £632.00
Full Page Colour £821.60
Agency Commission: 10%
Mechanical Data: Film: Digital, Type Area: 345 x 272mm, Col Length: 345mm, Page Width: 272mm
Copy instructions: Copy Date: Tuesday 4pm prior to publication date
Supplement(s): Holiday Arran - 1xY
LOCAL NEWSPAPERS: Local Newspapers Scotland

ARTS, BOOKS & CINEMA
1813572U67H-432
Editorial Address: For all contact details see main record, The Herald (Glasgow)
Frequency: Weekly
ADVERTISING: Rates on application
Supplement to: The Herald (Glasgow)
REGIONAL DAILY & SUNDAY NEWSPAPERS: Regional Colour Supplements

YR ARWYDD
1644469U72J-325
Editorial Address: Sir Thomas Jones School, Amlwch, ANGLESEY, LL68 9TH **Tel:** 01407 830287
Fax: 01407 830967
Frequency: 10 issues yearly - Not published in January and August
Cover Price: £0.30
Circulation: 1,400 (Publisher's Statement)
Editor: Ann Jones
Summary of Content: Welsh language community newspaper covering local news and community related items with features covering local events, cookery, poetry, religion and places of historical interest.
Language(s): Welsh
Readership/Target Audience: Aimed at Welsh speakers and the local community.
ADVERTISING: No Advertising taken
LOCAL NEWSPAPERS: Community Newsletters

ASCOT NEWS
43250U72B-150_110
Frequency: Weekly - Circulation incorporated into Bracknell News Series
Cover Price: £0.27
Part of Series, see entry for: Bracknell News Series
LOCAL NEWSPAPERS: Local Newspapers English Counties

ASH & FARNHAM MAIL & NEWS
43760U72B-1382_120
Formerly: Ash & Farnham Mail
Frequency: Weekly - Circulation figure is incorporated into the Aldershot Mail & News
Cover Price: £0.22
ADVERTISING: Rates on application
Part of Series, see entry for: Aldershot Mail and News Series
LOCAL NEWSPAPERS: Local Newspapers English Counties

ASHBOURNE NEWS TELEGRAPH
43464U72B-670
Editorial Address: 6 Market Place, ASHBOURNE, DE6 1ES
Tel: 01335 342847 **Fax:** 01335 300124
Email: editorial@ashbournenewstelegraph.co.uk
Advertising Address: As above. **Tel:** 01335 300200
Email: judy.smith@staffordshirenewspapers.co.uk
Web site: http://www.ashbournenewstelegraph.co.uk
Publisher: Staffordshire Newspapers Ltd
Frequency: Weekly - Published on Wednesday
Cover Price: £0.40
Circulation: 7,000 (Publisher's Statement)
Editor: News Desk; **Advertising Manager:** Judith Smith
ADVERTISING RATES:
Full Page Mono £1086.75
Full Page Colour £1467.11
SCC £3.45
Agency Commission: 10%
Mechanical Data: Col Widths (Display): 28mm, Col Length: 350mm, Page Width: 268mm, Film: Digital, Type Area: 350 x 268mm, No. of Columns (Display): 9
Copy instructions: Copy Date: Friday 4pm prior to publication date
Average advertising content per issue: 50%
LOCAL NEWSPAPERS: Local Newspapers English Counties

ASHBURTON, BUCKFASTLEIGH & MID-DEVON ADVERTISER
43512U72B-827_140
Frequency: Weekly
Cover Price: £0.35
Part of Series, see entry for: Mid-Devon Advertiser Series
LOCAL NEWSPAPERS: Local Newspapers English Counties

ASHBY ECHO
44007U72B-2150_282
Frequency: Weekly - Circulation figure is incorporated into the Coalville Echo
Cover Price: Free
ADVERTISING RATES:
SCC £5.25
Part of Series, see entry for: Loughborough Echo Series
LOCAL NEWSPAPERS: Local Newspapers English Counties

ASHBY TIMES
44033U72B-2193_110
Frequency: Weekly - Circulation figure is incorporated into the Coalville Times
Cover Price: £0.39
ADVERTISING: Rates on application
Part of Series, see entry for: Trident Midland Newspapers Series
LOCAL NEWSPAPERS: Local Newspapers English Counties

ASHFIELD CHAD
44174U72B-2580_120
Frequency: Weekly - Circulation figure is incorporated into the Mansfield Chad
Cover Price: £0.58
ADVERTISING RATES:
SCC £6.80
Part of Series, see entry for: Chad Series Mansfield
LOCAL NEWSPAPERS: Local Newspapers English Counties

ASHTON-UNDER-LYNE REPORTER SERIES
43681U72B-1160
Editorial Address: Park House, 5 Acres Lane, STALYBRIDGE, SK15 2JR **Tel:** 0161 303 1910
Fax: 0161 303 1922
Email: editorial@tameside-reporter.co.uk
Advertising Address: As above. **Tel:** 0161 304 7691
Fax: 0161 304 8484
Email: janebates@tameside-reporter.co.uk
Web site: http://www.tamesidereporter.co.uk
Publisher: Ashton Weekly Newspapers Ltd
Date Established: 1850
Frequency: Weekly
Cover Price: £0.38
Circulation: 25,000 (Combined Circulation)
Editor: Nigel Skinner; **News Editor:** Clare Wallace; **Managing Director:** Chris Wright
ADVERTISING: Rates on application
Agency Commission: 10%
Mechanical Data: Type Area: 390 x 286.5mm, Col Length: 390mm, Page Width: 286.5mm, Film: Digital
Copy instructions: Copy Date: 2 days prior to publication date
Average advertising content per issue: 50%
Series owner and contact point for the following titles, see individual entries:
Glossop Chronicle incorporating High Peak Reporter
Tameside Reporter
LOCAL NEWSPAPERS: Local Newspapers English Counties

ASKERN, CAMPSALL & NORTON COMMUNITY NEWSLETTER
1647019U72B-3950_101
Frequency: Monthly
Cover Price: Free
Circulation: 6,000 (Publisher's Statement)
ADVERTISING: Rates on application
Part of Series, see entry for: Community Newsletter Series
LOCAL NEWSPAPERS: Local Newspapers English Counties

ATHERSTONE HERALD
44323U72B-3040_110
Frequency: Weekly - Circulation figure also includes Tamworth Herald and the Coleshill Herald
Cover Price: £0.55
Circulation: 25,380 (ABC 02/07/2007 to 30/12/2007)
ADVERTISING: Rates on application
Part of Series, see entry for: Tamworth Herald Series
LOCAL NEWSPAPERS: Local Newspapers English Counties

AVENUES (NORTH WEST EDITION)
1665302U72A-1311_102
Editorial Address: For all contact details see main edition, Avenues
Frequency: Weekly
Cover Price: Free
Circulation: 50,000 (Publisher's Statement)
ADVERTISING: Rates on application
Part of Series, see entry for: Avenues Series
LOCAL NEWSPAPERS: Local Newspapers Greater London

AVENUES SERIES
1665240U72A-1311
Formerly: Avenues
Editorial Address: Arden House, Arden Grove, HARPENDEN, AL5 4SJ **Tel:** 01582 984940
Fax: 0870 8632589
Email: editorial@avenuesonline.co.uk
Advertising Address: As above.
Email: production@avenuesonline.co.uk
Web site: http://www.avenuespublishing.co.uk
ISSN: 1477-3112
Publisher: Avenues Publishing
Date Established: 2001
Frequency: Weekly
Cover Price: Free
Circulation: 142,000 (Combined Circulation)
Editor: News Desk; **Advertising Manager:** Angela Stevenson
ADVERTISING: Rates on application
Series owner and contact point for the following titles, see individual entries:
Avenues (North West Edition)
Avenues (South West Herts Edition)
LOCAL NEWSPAPERS: Local Newspapers Greater London

AVENUES (SOUTH WEST HERTS EDITION)
1805234U72A-1311_104
Frequency: Weekly
Cover Price: Free

Non-National Newspapers

Circulation: 60,000 (Publisher's Statement)
ADVERTISING: Rates on application
Part of Series, see entry for: Avenues Series
LOCAL NEWSPAPERS: Local Newspapers Greater London

AVON ADVERTISER HANTS & DORSET EDITION
44566U72B-3520_191
Frequency: Weekly
Cover Price: Free
Circulation: 37,838 (VFD 04/07/2005 to 01/01/2006)
ADVERTISING RATES:
SCC £2.65
Part of Series, see entry for: Salisbury Journal & Avon Advertiser Series
LOCAL NEWSPAPERS: Local Newspapers English Counties

AVON ADVERTISER SALISBURY EDITION
44567U72B-3520_192
Formerly: Avon Advertiser Salisbury and Andover Edition
Frequency: Weekly
Cover Price: Free
Circulation: 34,670 (VFD 01/01/2007 to 01/07/2007)
ADVERTISING RATES:
SCC £5.30
Part of Series, see entry for: Salisbury Journal & Avon Advertiser Series
LOCAL NEWSPAPERS: Local Newspapers English Counties

AYR ADVERTISER
44872U72D-90_110
Frequency: Weekly
Cover Price: £0.55
Part of Series, see entry for: Ayr Advertiser Series
LOCAL NEWSPAPERS: Local Newspapers Scotland

AYR ADVERTISER SERIES
44871U72D-90
Editorial Address: The Herald Building, Dock Road, ARDROSSAN, KA22 8DA Tel: 01292 267631
Fax: 01292 265535
Email: editorial.aa@cfpress.co.uk
Advertising Address: PO Box 8663, ARDROSSAN, KA22 8BX Tel: 01294 464321 Fax: 01294 466590
Email: advertising.aa@cfpress.co.uk
Web site: http://www.ayradvertiser.com
Publisher: Clyde & Forth Press Group
Date Established: 1803
Frequency: Weekly - Published on Tuesday
Circulation: 6,069 (ABC 01/01/2007 to 30/12/2007)
Editor: Frank Cassidy; News Editor: Frank Cassidy;
Advertising Manager: Fiona Aitken
ADVERTISING RATES:
Full Page Mono £1443.52
Full Page Colour £2150.28
SCC £5.43
Agency Commission: 10%
Mechanical Data: Type Area: 330 x 266mm, No. of Columns (Display): 8, Col Length: 330mm, Col Widths (Display): 33mm, Film: Digital
Copy instructions: Copy Date: Monday 12pm prior to publication date
Average advertising content per issue: 25%
Series owner and contact point for the following titles, see individual entries:
Ayr Advertiser
Carrick Herald
Troon & Prestwick Times
LOCAL NEWSPAPERS: Local Newspapers Scotland

AYRSHIRE POST
44879U72D-100
Editorial Address: Nile Court, 154 High Street, AYR, KA7 1PX Tel: 01292 262200 Fax: 01292 611930
Email: ayrshirepost@s-un.co.uk
Advertising Address: 34 Mackintosh Place, South Newmoor Industrial Estate, IRVINE, KA11 4JY
Tel: 01294 202054 Fax: 01294 213982
Email: emacdonald@s-un.co.uk
Publisher: Scottish & Universal Newspapers Ltd
Date Established: 1888
Frequency: Weekly - Published on Friday
Cover Price: £0.80
Circulation: 26,863 (ABC 02/07/2007 to 30/12/2007)
Editor: News Desk; Features Editor: Yonnie McInnes;
Managing Director: Alex Cargill; Advertising Manager: Eleanor MacDonald; Group Editor: Alan Woodison
ADVERTISING RATES:
SCC £11.40
Agency Commission: 10%
Mechanical Data: Col Length: 390mm, Col Widths (Display): 30mm, No. of Columns (Display): 8, Type Area: 390 x 268mm, Page Width: 268mm, Film: Digital

Copy instructions: Copy Date: Monday 5pm prior to publication date
LOCAL NEWSPAPERS: Local Newspapers Scotland

AYRSHIRE WORLD
1601098U72C-103_100
Frequency: Weekly
Cover Price: Free
Circulation: 11,294 (Publisher's Statement)
ADVERTISING RATES:
SCC £8.90
Part of Series, see entry for: Ayrshire World Series
LOCAL NEWSPAPERS: Local Newspapers Scotland

AYRSHIRE WORLD SERIES
44880U72D-103
Formerly: Ayrshire World
Editorial Address: 19 Bank Street, IRVINE, KA12 0AJ
Tel: 01294 272233 Fax: 01294 202072
Email: irvineherald@s-un.co.uk
Advertising Address: 34 Mackintosh Place, South Newmoor Industrial Estate, IRVINE, KA11 4JY
Tel: 01294 222288 Fax: 01294 213982
Email: ppaterson@s-un.co.uk
Web site: http://www.icayrshire.co.uk
Publisher: Scottish & Universal Newspapers Ltd
Frequency: Weekly - Published on Thursday
Cover Price: Free
Circulation: 16,827 (Combined Circulation)
Editor: Eric McGowan
ADVERTISING: Rates on application
Agency Commission: 10%
Mechanical Data: Type Area: 390 x 268mm, Page Width: 268mm, Film: Digital, Col Length: 390mm, No. of Columns (Display): 8
Copy instructions: Copy Date: Monday prior to publication date
Series owner and contact point for the following titles, see individual entries:
Ayrshire World
North Ayrshire World
LOCAL NEWSPAPERS: Local Newspapers Scotland

BALHAM & TOOTING GUARDIAN
1695653U72A-128_247
Frequency: Weekly - See Putney & Wandsworth Guardian for circulation figure
Cover Price: Free
Part of Series, see entry for: Guardian & News Series (Sutton)
LOCAL NEWSPAPERS: Local Newspapers Greater London

BALLYCLARE GAZETTE AND EAST ANTRIM GAZETTE
45064U72E-55_140
Formerly: Ballyclare Gazette
Frequency: Weekly
Cover Price: £0.85
(Publisher's Statement)
Part of Series, see entry for: East Antrim Gazette Series
LOCAL NEWSPAPERS: Local Newspapers Northern Ireland

BALLYMENA CHRONICLE & ANTRIM OBSERVER
45091U72E-120_130
Frequency: Weekly
Cover Price: £0.40
Part of Series, see entry for: Dungannon Observer Series
LOCAL NEWSPAPERS: Local Newspapers Northern Ireland

BALLYMENA GUARDIAN
45055U72E-20_180
Formerly: East Antrim Guardian
Frequency: Weekly
Cover Price: £0.95
(Publisher's Statement)
Part of Series, see entry for: Antrim Guardian Series
LOCAL NEWSPAPERS: Local Newspapers Northern Ireland

BALLYMENA TIMES
45058U72E-30_130
Frequency: Weekly
Cover Price: £0.90
Part of Series, see entry for: Ballymena Times Series
LOCAL NEWSPAPERS: Local Newspapers Northern Ireland

BALLYMENA TIMES SERIES
45056U72E-30
Editorial Address: 22-24 Ballymoney Street, BALLYMENA, BT43 6AL Tel: 028 2565 3300 Fax: 028 2564 1517
Email: dessie.blackadder@jpress.co.uk
Advertising Address: As above.
Email: stephanie.manson@jpress.co.uk

Web site: http://www.ballymenatimes.com
Publisher: Johnston Press plc
Frequency: Weekly - Published on Tuesday
Circulation: 4,428 (ABC 02/07/2007 to 30/12/2007)
Editor: Dessie Blackadder; Features Editor: Karen Fullerton; Advertising Manager: Stephanie Manson
ADVERTISING RATES:
Full Page Mono £1667.70
Full Page Colour £2417.75
Mechanical Data: Trim Size: 420 x 297mm, Film: Digital, No. of Columns (Display): 9
Copy instructions: Copy Date: Friday 2.00pm prior to publication date
Series owner and contact point for the following titles, see individual entries:
Antrim Times
Ballymena Times
LOCAL NEWSPAPERS: Local Newspapers Northern Ireland

BALLYMONEY AND MOYLE TIMES
45059U72E-35
Formerly: Ballymoney Times
Editorial Address: 6 Church Street, BALLYMONEY, BT53 6DL Tel: 028 2766 6216 Fax: 028 2766 7066
Email: lyle.mcmullan@jpress.co.uk
Advertising Address: As above. Tel: 028 7035 5260
Email: carmel.taylor@jpress.co.uk
Web site: http://www.ballymoneytoday.co.uk
Publisher: Morton Newspapers Ltd
Date Established: 1988
Frequency: Weekly
Cover Price: £0.95
Circulation: 8,000 (Publisher's Statement)
Editor: Lyle McMullan; Advertising Manager: Carmel Taylor
ADVERTISING RATES:
Full Page Mono £1667.00
Full Page Colour £2418.17
SCC £5.45
Agency Commission: 10%
Mechanical Data: Col Length: 340mm, Page Width: 265mm, Film: Digital, Type Area: 340 x 265mm, No. of Columns (Display): 9, Col Widths (Display): 28mm
Copy instructions: Copy Date: Monday 1pm prior to publication date
Average advertising content per issue: 50%
LOCAL NEWSPAPERS: Local Newspapers Northern Ireland

BANBRIDGE CHRONICLE
45060U72E-40
Editorial Address: 14 Bridge Street, BANBRIDGE, BT32 3JS Tel: 028 4066 2322 Fax: 028 4062 4397
Email: news@banbridgechronicle.com
Advertising Address: As above.
Email: advertising@banbridgechronicle.com
Web site: http://www.banbridgechronicle.com
Publisher: Banbridge Chronicle Press Ltd
Date Established: 1874
Frequency: Weekly
Cover Price: £0.90
Circulation: 5,957 (ABC 02/07/2007 to 30/12/2007)
Editor: Bryan Hooks; Advertising Director: David Hodgett
ADVERTISING RATES:
Full Page Mono £1465.20
Full Page Colour £1978.00
SCC £5.50
Agency Commission: 15%
Mechanical Data: Page Width: 265mm, Type Area: 333 x 265mm, Col Length: 333mm, No. of Columns (Display): 8, Col Widths (Display): 35.5mm, Film: Digital
Copy instructions: Copy Date: Tuesday 12.00 prior to publication date
Average advertising content per issue: 50%
LOCAL NEWSPAPERS: Local Newspapers Northern Ireland

BANBRIDGE LEADER
45102U72E-156_120
Frequency: Weekly
Cover Price: £0.95
Part of Series, see entry for: Leader (County Down Series)
LOCAL NEWSPAPERS: Local Newspapers Northern Ireland

THE BANBURY & DISTRICT REVIEW
44213U72B-2690_120
Formerly: The Banbury & District Citizen
Frequency: Weekly - Published on Friday
Cover Price: Free
Circulation: 33,003 (VFD 02/07/2007 to 30/12/2007)
Part of Series, see entry for: Banbury Guardian Review Series
LOCAL NEWSPAPERS: Local Newspapers English Counties

BANBURY GUARDIAN
272B-2690_140

Frequency: Weekly - Published on Thursday
Cover Price: £0.45
Circulation: 17,135 (ABC 02/07/2007 to 30/12/2007)
Part of Series, see entry for: Banbury Guardian Review Series
LOCAL NEWSPAPERS: Local Newspapers English Counties

BANBURY GUARDIAN REVIEW SERIES
44212U72B-2690

Formerly: Banbury Guardian Citizen Series
Editorial Address: 7 North Bar, BANBURY, OX16 0TQ
Tel: 01295 227799 **Fax:** 01295 270734
Email: editorial@banburyguardian.co.uk
Advertising Address: As above. **Tel:** 01295 227777
Fax: 01295 257689
Email: pauline.nicklin@banburyguardian.co.uk
Web site: http://www.banburyguardian.co.uk
Publisher: Central Counties Newspapers South Ltd
Frequency: Weekly
Circulation: 55,138 (Combined Circulation)
Editor: Jason Gibbins; **Advertising Manager:** Pauline Nicklin
ADVERTISING RATES:
SCC £8.00
Agency Commission: 10%
Mechanical Data: Col Widths (Display): 28mm, No. of Columns (Display): 11, Film: Digital
Copy instructions: Copy Date: Monday 5pm prior to publication date
Average advertising content per issue: 65%
Series owner and contact point for the following titles, see individual entries:
The Banbury & District Review
Banbury Guardian
The Commuter
LOCAL NEWSPAPERS: Local Newspapers English Counties

BANFFSHIRE ADVERTISER
44881U72D-110

Editorial Address: 13-15 West Church Street, BUCKIE, AB56 1BN **Tel:** 01542 832265 **Fax:** 01542 834316
Email: mail@banffshireadvertiser.co.uk
Advertising Address: As above.
Email: adverts@banffshireadvertiser.co.uk
Publisher: J & M Publishing
Date Established: 1881
Frequency: Weekly - Published on Tuesday
Cover Price: £0.45
Circulation: 4,500 (Publisher's Statement)
Editor: Alan Beresford
ADVERTISING RATES:
Full Page Mono £500.00
Full Page Colour £600.00
Agency Commission: 10%
Mechanical Data: Page Width: 263mm, Col Widths (Display): 33mm, No. of Columns (Display): 7, Film: Digital, Type Area: 370 x 263mm, Col Length: 370mm
Copy instructions: Copy Date: Friday 5.00pm prior to publication date
Average advertising content per issue: 40%
LOCAL NEWSPAPERS: Local Newspapers Scotland

BANFFSHIRE HERALD
44882U72D-120

Editorial Address: 181 Mid Street, KEITH, AB55 5BL
Tel: 01542 886262 **Fax:** 01542 886059
Email: mail@banffshireherald.co.uk
Advertising Address: As above.
Email: mail@banffshireherald.co.uk
Publisher: J & M Publishing
Frequency: Weekly - Published on Friday
Cover Price: £0.45
Circulation: 3,000 (Publisher's Statement)
Editor: Lorna Campbell
ADVERTISING RATES:
Full Page Mono £500.00
Full Page Colour £600.00
SCC £3.30
Agency Commission: 10%
Mechanical Data: Page Width: 263mm, Col Widths (Display): 33mm, No. of Columns (Display): 7, Film: Digital, Type Area: 370 x 263mm, Col Length: 370mm
Copy instructions: Copy Date: Wednesday 12.30pm prior to publication date
Average advertising content per issue: 40%
LOCAL NEWSPAPERS: Local Newspapers Scotland

THE BANFFSHIRE JOURNAL
44883U72D-130

Editorial Address: 22 Old Market Place, BANFF, AB45 1GE
Tel: 01261 812551 **Fax:** 01261 815611
Email: editor@banffshire-journal.co.uk
Advertising Address: As above.

Email: advertising@banffshire-journal.co.uk
Web site: http://www.banffshire-journal.co.uk
Publisher: Moray & Nairn Newspaper Co Ltd
Date Established: 1845
Frequency: Weekly - Published on Tuesday
Cover Price: £0.55
Circulation: 4,994 (ABC 01/01/2007 to 30/12/2007)
Editor: George Boardman
ADVERTISING: Rates on application
Agency Commission: 10%
Copy instructions: Copy Date: Friday 12 noon prior to publication date
Average advertising content per issue: 45%
LOCAL NEWSPAPERS: Local Newspapers Scotland

BANGOR & ANGLESEY MAIL
44758U72C-70_105

Frequency: Weekly
Cover Price: Free
Circulation: 10,687 (VFD 02/07/2007 to 30/12/2007)
ADVERTISING RATES:
Full Page Mono £1224.00
Full Page Colour £1657.20
SCC £4.25
Part of Series, see entry for: The Caernarfon Herald Series
LOCAL NEWSPAPERS: Local Newspapers Wales

BARKING AND DAGENHAM POST
43056U72A-101

Formerly: Post Newspapers
Editorial Address: Media House, 539 High Road, ILFORD, IG1 1UD **Tel:** 020 8477 3778 **Fax:** 020 8709 0047
Email: postnewsdesk@archant.co.uk
Advertising Address: As above. **Tel:** 020 8478 4444
Email: steve.sabine@archant.co.uk
Web site: http://www.bdpost.co.uk
Publisher: Archant London
Date Established: 1923
Frequency: Weekly
Cover Price: £0.55
Circulation: 13,084 (ABC 02/07/2007 to 30/12/2007)
Editor: News Desk; **Advertising Manager:** Steve Sabine
ADVERTISING RATES:
Full Page Mono £2835.00
Full Page Colour £3035.00
SCC £9.00
Agency Commission: 10%
Mechanical Data: Type Area: 350 x 267mm, Col Length: 350mm, Page Width: 267mm, No. of Columns (Display): 9, Col Widths (Display): 27mm, Film: Digital
Copy instructions: Copy Date: 2 days prior to publication date
Average advertising content per issue: 40%
LOCAL NEWSPAPERS: Local Newspapers Greater London

BARKING & DAGENHAM RECORDER
43064U72A-230_140

Frequency: Weekly
Cover Price: £0.50
Part of Series, see entry for: Ilford Recorder Series
LOCAL NEWSPAPERS: Local Newspapers Greater London

BARNET & POTTERS BAR TIMES
43043U72A-200_110

Frequency: Weekly
Cover Price: Free
Circulation: 37,623 (VFD 02/07/2007 to 30/12/2007)
ADVERTISING RATES:
SCC £3.30
Part of Series, see entry for: Hendon Times Series
LOCAL NEWSPAPERS: Local Newspapers Greater London

BARNOLDSWICK & EARBY TIMES
43989U72B-2040_120

Frequency: Weekly - Published on Friday. See Nelson Leader for circulation figure
Cover Price: £0.70
ADVERTISING RATES:
Full Page Mono £1306.62
Full Page Colour £1698.60
SCC £4.27
Part of Series, see entry for: Leader Times Series
LOCAL NEWSPAPERS: Local Newspapers English Counties

BARNSLEY CHRONICLE
44672U72B-3670_120

Frequency: Weekly - Published on Friday
Cover Price: £0.55
Circulation: 43,365 (ABC 02/07/2007 to 30/12/2007)
ADVERTISING RATES:
Full Page Mono £3150.00

Full Page Colour £3520.00
SCC £6.23
Part of Series, see entry for: Barnsley Chronicle & Independent Series
Supplement(s): Motoring - 52xY, Property - 52xY
LOCAL NEWSPAPERS: Local Newspapers English Counties

BARNSLEY CHRONICLE & INDEPENDENT SERIES
44671U72B-3670

Editorial Address: 47 Church Street, BARNSLEY, S70 2AS
Tel: 01226 734734 **Fax:** 01226 734455
Email: editorial@barnsley-chronicle.co.uk
Advertising Address: As above. **Tel:** 01226 734666
Fax: 01226 734343
Email: mikes@barnsley-chronicle.co.uk
Web site: http://www.barnsley-chronicle.co.uk
Publisher: Barnsley Chronicle Ltd
Date Established: 1858
Frequency: Weekly
Circulation: 122,314 (Combined Circulation)
Editor: Steph Daley; **News Editor:** Steph Daley; **Managing Director:** Nicholas Hewitt; **Advertising Manager:** Mike Shenton
Summary of Content: Features news specific to Barnsley, no regional content.
ADVERTISING RATES:
Full Page Mono £3150.00
Full Page Colour £3520.00
SCC £6.23
Agency Commission: 10%
Mechanical Data: Col Widths (Display): 35mm, No. of Columns (Display): 10, Film: Digital
Copy instructions: Copy Date: 2 days prior to publication date
Average advertising content per issue: 54%
Series owner and contact point for the following titles, see individual entries:
Barnsley Chronicle
Independent Barnsley
Supplement(s): Business - 12xY, First Class - 3xY, Moving Up - 1xY
LOCAL NEWSPAPERS: Local Newspapers English Counties

BARNSLEY GAZETTE
1698043U72B-3982_100

Frequency: 26 issues yearly
Cover Price: Free
Part of Series, see entry for: Rotherham Gazette Series
LOCAL NEWSPAPERS: Local Newspapers English Counties

BARRHEAD NEWS
45012U72D-820_120

Frequency: Weekly - Circulation figure includes the Gazette (Renfrewshire). Published on Wednesday
Cover Price: £0.45
Circulation: 10,258 (ABC 01/01/2007 to 30/12/2007)
ADVERTISING RATES:
SCC £8.75
Part of Series, see entry for: The Paisley and Renfrewshire Gazette Series
LOCAL NEWSPAPERS: Local Newspapers Scotland

BARRY & DISTRICT NEWS
706968U72C-50_105

Frequency: Weekly
Circulation: 6,755 (ABC 02/07/2007 to 30/12/2007)
Part of Series, see entry for: Barry & District News Series
LOCAL NEWSPAPERS: Local Newspapers Wales

BARRY & DISTRICT NEWS SERIES
44751U72C-50

Formerly: Barry and District News
Editorial Address: 156 Holton Road, BARRY, CF63 4TY
Tel: 01446 733456 **Fax:** 01446 732719
Email: barrynews@gwent-wales.co.uk
Advertising Address: As above.
Email: andrea.hall@gwent-wales.co.uk
Web site: http://www.barryanddistrictnews.co.uk
Publisher: Newsquest (Media Group) Ltd
Frequency: Weekly - Published on Thursday
Cover Price: £0.40
Circulation: 12,864 (Combined Circulation)
Editor: Shira Valek; **Advertising Manager:** Andrea Hall
ADVERTISING RATES:
Full Page Mono £1355.58
Full Page Colour £1694.48
SCC £4.43
Agency Commission: 10%
Mechanical Data: Type Area: 340 x 259mm, No. of Columns (Display): 9, Col Length: 340mm, Page Width: 259mm

Non-National Newspapers

Copy instructions: Copy Date: Friday 4pm prior to publication date
Average advertising content per issue: 45%
Series owner and contact point for the following titles, see individual entries:
Barry & District News
Penarth Times
Supplement(s): This is the Vale - 2xY
LOCAL NEWSPAPERS: Local Newspapers Wales

BARRY POST
44772U72C-95_105

Frequency: Weekly
Cover Price: Free
Circulation: 22,155 (VFD 01/01/2007 to 01/07/2007)
ADVERTISING RATES:
SCC £4.11
Copy instructions: Copy Date: Friday 5.30pm prior to publication date
Part of Series, see entry for: Cardiff Post Series
LOCAL NEWSPAPERS: Local Newspapers Wales

BASILDON, BILLERICAY AND WICKFORD RECORDER
43643U72B-1080_130

Formerly: Basildon Recorder
Frequency: Weekly
Cover Price: Free
Circulation: 53,820 (VFD 02/07/2007 to 30/12/2007)
ADVERTISING: Rates on application
Part of Series, see entry for: Southend Standard Series
LOCAL NEWSPAPERS: Local Newspapers English Counties

BASINGSTOKE AND NORTH HANTS GAZETTE SERIES
43738U72B-1345

Editorial Address: Gazette House, Pelton Road, BASINGSTOKE, RG21 6YD **Tel:** 01256 337444
Fax: 01256 337425
Email: newsdesk@basingstokegazette.co.uk
Advertising Address: As above. **Tel:** 01256 337489
Fax: 01256 840369
Email: advertising@basingstokegazette.co.uk
Web site: http://www.basingstokegazette.co.uk
Publisher: Newsquest
Frequency: Weekly
Circulation: 77,769 (Combined Circulation)
Editor: Hugh Cadman; **News Editor:** Hugh Cadman
ADVERTISING RATES:
Full Page Mono £2126.70
Full Page Colour £2126.70
SCC £7.16
Agency Commission: 10%
Mechanical Data: Col Length: 340mm, No. of Columns (Display): 9, Type Area: 340 x 264mm, Bleed Size: 5mm, Trim Size: 290 x 275mm, Page Width: 264mm, Print Process: Web-fed offset litho
Series owner and contact point for the following titles, see individual entries:
The Extra for Basingstoke and North Hampshire
The Gazette (Basingstoke and North Hants (Mon))
The Gazette (Basingstoke and North Hants (Thurs))
LOCAL NEWSPAPERS: Local Newspapers English Counties

BASINGSTOKE OBSERVER
623231U72B-1346

Editorial Address: 2nd Floor, Paddington House, Festival Place, BASINGSTOKE, RG21 7LJ **Tel:** 01256 694120
Fax: 01256 694133
Email: s.davies@basingstokeobserver.co.uk
Advertising Address: As above.
Email: j.ryan@basingstokeobserver.co.uk
Web site: http://www.basingstokeobserver.co.uk
Publisher: Tri-Media Publishing
Date Established: 2000
Frequency: Weekly - Published on Thursday
Cover Price: Free
Circulation: 24,000 (Publisher's Statement)
Editor: Steve Davies; **Advertising Manager:** John Ryan
ADVERTISING RATES:
Full Page Mono £1579.00
Full Page Colour £1829.50
SCC £4.50
Agency Commission: 10%
Mechanical Data: Col Widths (Display): 27.5mm, Type Area: 340 x 264mm, Col Length: 340mm, No. of Columns (Display): 9, Page Width: 264mm, Film: Digital
Copy instructions: Copy Date: Monday 5pm prior to publication date
Average advertising content per issue: 60%
Supplement(s): Basingstoke & Northamptonshire Living - 12xY
LOCAL NEWSPAPERS: Local Newspapers English Counties

THE BATH CHRONICLE
41983U72B-4058

Editorial Address: Westpoint, James Street West, BATH, BA1 2DA **Tel:** 01225 322322 **Fax:** 01225 322291
Email: news@bathchron.co.uk
Advertising Address: As above.
Email: j.bates@bathchron.co.uk
Web site: http://www.thisisbath.co.uk
Publisher: Bath News & Media
Date Established: 1760
Frequency: Weekly - Published on Thursday
Cover Price: £0.60
Circulation: 20,000 (Publisher's Statement)
Editor: Paul Wiltshire; **News Editor:** Paul Wiltshire;
Features Editor: Jackie Chappell; **Managing Director:** Sarah Irvine; **Advertising Manager:** Jayne Bates
ADVERTISING RATES:
Full Page Mono £1676.16
Full Page Colour £2093.50
Mechanical Data: Film: Digital
Copy instructions: Copy Date: 6 days prior to publication date
Average advertising content per issue: 30%
Supplement(s): The Business - 12xY, Drive - 52xY, Final Score - 52xY, The Guide - 52xY, Life and Soul - 52xY, Property Weekly - 52xY, Recruitment - 52xY
LOCAL NEWSPAPERS: Local Newspapers English Counties

BATLEY NEWS
44689U72B-3740_120

Frequency: Weekly
Cover Price: £0.45
Part of Series, see entry for: Batley News Series
LOCAL NEWSPAPERS: Local Newspapers English Counties

BATLEY NEWS SERIES
44688U72B-3740

Editorial Address: 11 Commercial Street, BATLEY, WF17 5HL **Tel:** 01924 472121 **Fax:** 01924 473678
Email: batleyeditorial@ywng.co.uk
Advertising Address: 17 Wellington Road, DEWSBURY, WF13 1HQ **Tel:** 01924 468282 **Fax:** 01924 457652
Email: davina.turton@ywng.co.uk
Web site: http://www.batleynews.co.uk
Publisher: The Reporter Ltd
Frequency: Weekly - Published on Friday
Circulation: 8,551 (ABC 02/07/2007 to 30/12/2007)
Editor: Vicky Dacre; **News Editor:** Vicky Dacre
ADVERTISING RATES:
Full Page Mono £957.78
Full Page Colour £1245.12
Agency Commission: 10%
Mechanical Data: Type Area: 340mm x 274mm, Col Length: 340mm, No. of Columns (Display): 9, Page Width: 274mm, Film: Digital
Average advertising content per issue: 30%
Series owner and contact point for the following titles, see individual entries:
Batley News
Birstall News
LOCAL NEWSPAPERS: Local Newspapers English Counties

BATTERSEA & CLAPHAM GUARDIAN
1695654U72A-128_246

Frequency: Weekly - See Putney & Wandsworth Guardian for circulation figure
Cover Price: Free
Part of Series, see entry for: Guardian & News Series (Sutton)
LOCAL NEWSPAPERS: Local Newspapers Greater London

BATTLE OBSERVER
1835418U72B-3225_201

Frequency: Weekly - Published on Friday. Circulation is included in Rye Observer
Cover Price: £0.40
ADVERTISING: Rates on application
Part of Series, see entry for: Hastings Observer Series
LOCAL NEWSPAPERS: Local Newspapers English Counties

BEACONSFIELD ADVERTISER
43297U72B-240_130

Cover Price: £0.55
Part of Series, see entry for: The Buckinghamshire Examiner and Advertiser Series
LOCAL NEWSPAPERS: Local Newspapers English Counties

BEARWOOD NEWS
1818525U72B-3467_21

Frequency: Weekly - Published on Thursday
Cover Price: Free
ADVERTISING RATES:
SCC £4.46
Part of Series, see entry for: The News & Observer Series
LOCAL NEWSPAPERS: Local Newspapers English Counties

BECCLES AND BUNGAY JOURNAL
44134U72B-2437_120

ISSN: 0958-2908
Frequency: Weekly
Cover Price: £0.55
Circulation: 7,322 (ABC 02/07/2007 to 30/12/2007)
ADVERTISING: Rates on application
Part of Series, see entry for: Norfolk County Weeklies Series
LOCAL NEWSPAPERS: Local Newspapers English Counties

BECCLES AND BUNGAY JOURNAL (BUNGAY EDITION)
1656995U72B-2437_241

Frequency: Weekly - See the Beccles and Bungay Journal for circulation figure
Cover Price: £0.55
ADVERTISING: Rates on application
Part of Series, see entry for: Norfolk County Weeklies Series
LOCAL NEWSPAPERS: Local Newspapers English Counties

BECCLES AND BUNGAY JOURNAL (HALESWORTH EDITION)
1656994U72B-2437_242

Frequency: Weekly - See the Beccles and Bungay Journal for circulation figure
Cover Price: £0.55
ADVERTISING: Rates on application
Part of Series, see entry for: Norfolk County Weeklies Series
LOCAL NEWSPAPERS: Local Newspapers English Counties

BECCLES INDEPENDENT
44334U72B-3072_12

Frequency: Monthly
Cover Price: Free
Circulation: 7,000 (Publisher's Statement)
Part of Series, see entry for: Community News Series
LOCAL NEWSPAPERS: Local Newspapers English Counties

BEDFORDSHIRE ON SUNDAY
43229U67C-

Editorial Address: 22 Mill Street, BEDFORD, MK40 3HD
Tel: 01234 300888 **Fax:** 01234 369592
Email: editor@lsnmedia.co.uk
Advertising Address: As above. **Tel:** 01234 369582
Fax: 01234 306604
Email: gemma.dunne@bedsonsunday.com
Web site: http://www.bedsonsunday.com
Publisher: LSN Media
Date Established: 1977
Frequency: Sunday
Cover Price: Free
Circulation: 101,346 (VFD 02/07/2007 to 30/12/2007)
Editor: Chris Gill; **Managing Director:** Mike Richardson
ADVERTISING RATES:
Full Page Mono £2756.25
Full Page Colour £3445.31
SCC £8.75
Mechanical Data: Col Length: 350mm, No. of Columns (Display): 9, Film: Digital, Page Width: 268mm, Type Area: 350 x 268mm
Copy instructions: Copy Date: Thursday 5.30pm prior to publication date
Editions:
Bedfordshire on Sunday Borough Edition
Bedfordshire on Sunday Mid Edition
REGIONAL DAILY & SUNDAY NEWSPAPERS: Regional Sunday Newspapers

BEDFORDSHIRE ON SUNDAY BOROUGH EDITION
43231U67C-3_52

Frequency: Sunday
Cover Price: Free
Circulation: 60,896 (VFD 02/07/2007 to 30/12/2007)
Edition of: Bedfordshire on Sunday
REGIONAL DAILY & SUNDAY NEWSPAPERS: Regional Sunday Newspapers

BEDFORDSHIRE ON SUNDAY MID EDITION

43230U67C-3_560

Frequency: Sunday
Cover Price: Free
Circulation: 40,450 (VFD 02/07/2007 to 30/12/2007)
Edition of: Bedfordshire on Sunday
REGIONAL DAILY & SUNDAY NEWSPAPERS: Regional Sunday Newspapers

BEDFORDSHIRE TIMES & CITIZEN SERIES

43232U72B-84

Editorial Address: 11-13 Mill Street, BEDFORD, MK40 3EU
Tel: 01234 409100 **Fax:** 01234 409199
Email: editorial@timesandcitizen.co.uk
Advertising Address: As above. **Tel:** 01234 405060
Tel: 01234 409140
Email: advertising@timesandcitizen.co.uk
Web site: http://www.bedfordtoday.co.uk
Publisher: Johnston Press plc
Date Established: 1880
Frequency: Weekly - Published on Thursday
Cover Price: Free
Circulation: 78,119 (VFD 02/07/2007 to 30/12/2007)
Editor: News Desk; **News Editor:** Ben Raza
ADVERTISING: Rates on application
Series owner and contact point for the following titles, see individual entries:
Times & Citizen Bedford Borough Edition
Times & Citizen Mid Bedfordshire Edition
LOCAL NEWSPAPERS: Local Newspapers English Counties

Y BEDOL

761699U72J-18

Editorial Address: Elfair, Clwyd Street, RUTHIN, LL15 1HW
Tel: 01824 702179 **Fax:** 01824 704741
Email: papurbro@ybedol.fsnet.co.uk
Frequency: 11 issues yearly - Not published in August
Cover Price: £0.40
Circulation: 2,500 (Publisher's Statement)
Editor: Hafina Clwyd
Summary of Content: Welsh language community newspaper.
Language(s): Welsh
Readership/Target Audience: Aimed at Welsh speaking readers in the local area.
ADVERTISING: No Advertising taken
LOCAL NEWSPAPERS: Community Newsletters

BELFAST NEWS

45061U72E-50

Editorial Address: 2 Esky Drive, Carn Industrial Area, Portadown, CRAIGAVON, BT63 5YY **Tel:** 028 3839 5599
Fax: 028 3839 3941
Email: rankin.armstrong@newsletter.co.uk
Advertising Address: Metro Building, 6-9 Donegall Square South, BELFAST, BT1 5JA **Tel:** 028 9089 7700
Fax: 028 9089 7744
Email: conor.o'kane@jpress.co.uk
Publisher: Johnston Press
Date Established: 1998
Frequency: Weekly - Published on Thursday
Cover Price: Free
Circulation: 46,094 (VFD 02/07/2007 to 30/12/2007)
Editor: Rankin Armstrong; **Advertising Manager:** Conor O'Kane
ADVERTISING RATES:
Full Page Mono £1943.00
Full Page Colour £2720.00
SCC £6.35
Agency Commission: 15%
Mechanical Data: Type Area: 340 x 265mm, No. of Columns (Display): 9, Col Length: 340mm, Page Width: 265mm, Film: Digital
Copy instructions: Copy Date: Tuesday 4pm prior to publication date
LOCAL NEWSPAPERS: Local Newspapers Northern Ireland

BELFAST TELEGRAPH

42266U67B-2370

Formerly: Belfast Telegraph (City Edition)
Editorial Address: 124-144 Royal Avenue, BELFAST, BT1 1EB **Tel:** 028 9026 4000 **Fax:** 028 9055 4506
Email: newseditor@belfasttelegraph.co.uk
Advertising Address: Mediaforce, 1 Gunpowder Square, Fleet Street, LONDON, EC4A 3EP **Tel:** 020 7583 2100
Fax: 020 7353 2111
Email: sgill@mediaforce.co.uk
Web site: http://www.belfasttelegraph.co.uk
Publisher: Independent News and Media (UK) Ltd
Date Established: 1870
Frequency: Evenings - Not published on Sunday
Cover Price: £0.60
Circulation: 75,602 (ABC 02/07/2007 to 30/12/2007)

Editor: Ronan Henry; **News Editor:** Ronan Henry; **Features Editor:** Gail Walker; **Advertising Manager:** Scott Gill;
Publisher: Sam McIlveen
ADVERTISING RATES:
SCC £19.30
Agency Commission: 15%
Mechanical Data: Page Width: 342mm, Type Area: 560 x 342mm, Col Widths (Display): 32mm, No. of Columns (Display): 10, Col Length: 560mm, Film: Digital
Copy instructions: Copy Date: 3 days prior to publication date
Average advertising content per issue: 40%
Editions:
Belfast Telegraph (County)
Belfast Telegraph (Final Edition)
Belfast Telegraph (Morning Edition)
Belfast Telegraph (Northwest)
Supplement(s): 24/7 - 52xY, Business Telegraph - 52xY, Homefinder - 52xY, Jobfinder - 104xY
REGIONAL DAILY & SUNDAY NEWSPAPERS: Regional Daily Newspapers

BELFAST TELEGRAPH (COUNTY)

42269U67B-2370_530

Edition of: Belfast Telegraph
REGIONAL DAILY & SUNDAY NEWSPAPERS: Regional Daily Newspapers

BELFAST TELEGRAPH (FINAL EDITION)

1665758U67B-2370_592

Frequency: Evenings
Cover Price: £0.60
Edition of: Belfast Telegraph
REGIONAL DAILY & SUNDAY NEWSPAPERS: Regional Daily Newspapers

BELFAST TELEGRAPH (MORNING EDITION)

1667632U67B-2370_591

Frequency: Mornings
Cover Price: £0.60
Edition of: Belfast Telegraph
REGIONAL DAILY & SUNDAY NEWSPAPERS: Regional Daily Newspapers

BELFAST TELEGRAPH (NORTHWEST)

42271U67B-2370_590

Formerly: Belfast Telegraph (Londonderry)
Edition of: Belfast Telegraph
REGIONAL DAILY & SUNDAY NEWSPAPERS: Regional Daily Newspapers

BELLSHILL SPEAKER

44998U72D-740_120

Frequency: Weekly
Cover Price: £0.36
Part of Series, see entry for: Motherwell Times Series
LOCAL NEWSPAPERS: Local Newspapers Scotland

BELPER EXPRESS

43477U72B-695_120

Frequency: Weekly
Cover Price: Free
Part of Series, see entry for: Derby Express and Messenger Series
LOCAL NEWSPAPERS: Local Newspapers English Counties

BELPER NEWS

43465U72B-680

Editorial Address: 8 The Courtyard, Market Place, BELPER, DE56 1FZ **Tel:** 01773 881100 **Fax:** 01773 822428
Email: editor@belpernews.co.uk
Advertising Address: As above.
Email: deborah.beeley@derbyshiretimes.co.uk
Web site: http://www.belpernews.co.uk
Publisher: Wilfred Edmunds Ltd
Date Established: 1896
Frequency: Weekly
Cover Price: £0.35
Circulation: 3,632 (ABC 02/07/2007 to 30/12/2007)
Editor: Laura Hammond
ADVERTISING RATES:
Full Page Mono £865.98
Full Page Colour £1125.77
SCC £2.83
Agency Commission: 10%
Mechanical Data: Col Length: 340mm, Page Width: 271mm, Film: Digital, Type Area: 340 x 271mm, No. of Columns (Display): 9

Copy instructions: Copy Date: Monday noon prior to publication date
LOCAL NEWSPAPERS: Local Newspapers English Counties

BENTLEY AND ARKSEY COMMUNITY NEWSLETTER

1692787U72B-3950_106

Frequency: Monthly
Cover Price: Free
Circulation: 6,000 (Publisher's Statement)
ADVERTISING: Rates on application
Part of Series, see entry for: Community Newsletter Series
LOCAL NEWSPAPERS: Local Newspapers English Counties

BERROWS WORCESTER JOURNAL

44605U72B-3556

Editorial Address: Hylton Road, WORCESTER, WR2 5JX
Tel: 01905 748200 **Fax:** 01905 742277
Email: wenedit@worcesternews.co.uk
Advertising Address: As above. **Fax:** 01905 742375
Email: julia.lancett@midlands.newsquest.co.uk
Web site: http://www.berrowsjournal.co.uk
Publisher: Newsquest Media Group
Frequency: Weekly - Published every Friday
Free to qualifying individuals
Circulation: 48,097 (VFD 02/07/2007 to 30/12/2007)
Editor: Stephanie Preece; **News Editor:** Stephanie Preece
ADVERTISING: Rates on application
LOCAL NEWSPAPERS: Local Newspapers English Counties

BERWICK ADVERTISER

761953U72B-2520_130

Frequency: Weekly
Cover Price: £0.62
Circulation: 7,931 (ABC 02/07/2007 to 30/12/2007)
ADVERTISING RATES:
SCC £8.30
Mechanical Data: Type Area: 550 x 333mm, Col Length: 550mm, Page Width: 333mm, No. of Columns (Display): 11
Part of Series, see entry for: Berwick Advertiser and Gazette Series
LOCAL NEWSPAPERS: Local Newspapers English Counties

BERWICK ADVERTISER AND GAZETTE SERIES

44165U72B-2520

Editorial Address: 90 Marygate, BERWICK-UPON-TWEED, TD15 1BW **Tel:** 01289 306677 **Fax:** 01289 307377
Email: iansmith@tweeddalepress.co.uk
Advertising Address: As above. **Fax:** 01289 334454
Email: jobell@tweeddalepress.co.uk
Web site: http://www.berwickadvertiser.co.uk
Publisher: Tweeddale Press Group
Date Established: 1806
Frequency: Weekly
Circulation: 17,626 (Combined Circulation)
Editor: Stuart Laundy; **Advertising Manager:** Jo Bell
ADVERTISING: Rates on application
Mechanical Data: Type Area: 550 x 333mm, Col Length: 550mm, Col Widths (Display): 28mm, Page Width: 333mm, No. of Columns (Display): 11
Series owner and contact point for the following titles, see individual entries:
Berwick Advertiser
Berwick Gazette
LOCAL NEWSPAPERS: Local Newspapers English Counties

BERWICK GAZETTE

44166U72B-2520_140

Frequency: Weekly
Cover Price: Free
Circulation: 10,106 (Publisher's Statement)
ADVERTISING RATES:
SCC £3.64
Mechanical Data: Type Area: 340 x 272mm, Col Length: 340mm, Page Width: 272mm, No. of Columns (Display): 9
Part of Series, see entry for: Berwick Advertiser and Gazette Series
LOCAL NEWSPAPERS: Local Newspapers English Counties

BERWICKSHIRE NEWS AND EAST LOTHIAN HERALD

44167U72B-2525

Editorial Address: 90 Marygate, BERWICK-UPON-TWEED, TD15 1BW **Tel:** 01289 306677 **Fax:** 01289 307377
Email: sandybrydon@tweeddalepress.co.uk
Advertising Address: As above. **Fax:** 01289 334454
Email: jobell@tweeddalepress.co.uk
Web site: http://www.berwickshirenews.co.uk

Non-National Newspapers

Publisher: Tweeddale Press Group
Date Established: 1869
Frequency: Weekly
Cover Price: £0.62
Circulation: 5,957 (ABC 02/07/2007 to 30/12/2007)
Editor: Sandy Brydon; **Advertising Manager:** Jo Bell
ADVERTISING RATES:
SCC £8.30
Agency Commission: 10%
Mechanical Data: Col Length: 550mm, Col Widths (Display): 28mm, No. of Columns (Display): 11, Print Process: Litho, Type Area: 550 x 333mm, Film: Digital, Page Width: 333mm
Average advertising content per issue: 40%
LOCAL NEWSPAPERS: Local Newspapers English Counties

BEVERLEY ADVERTISER
44639U72B-3582_120

Formerly: Beverley & East Yorkshire Advertiser
Frequency: Weekly - Published on Thursday
Cover Price: Free
Circulation: 19,962 (VFD 02/07/2007 to 30/12/2007)
ADVERTISING RATES:
SCC £3.40
Part of Series, see entry for: Hull Advertiser Series
LOCAL NEWSPAPERS: Local Newspapers English Counties

BEVERLEY GUARDIAN
44631U72B-3576_120

Frequency: Weekly
Cover Price: Free
Circulation: 19,600 (Publisher's Statement)
Summary of Content: News, sport and entertainment.
Copy instructions: Copy Date: Wednesday 5pm prior to publication date
Part of Series, see entry for: Driffield Times Series
LOCAL NEWSPAPERS: Local Newspapers English Counties

BEXHILL-ON-SEA OBSERVER
44426U72B-3225_140

Frequency: Weekly
Cover Price: £0.42
Circulation: 9,623 (ABC 02/07/2007 to 30/12/2007)
ADVERTISING: Rates on application
Part of Series, see entry for: Hastings Observer Series
LOCAL NEWSPAPERS: Local Newspapers English Counties

BEXLEY CHRONICLE SERIES
1623615U72A-1303

Editorial Address: Andrew House, Granville Road, SIDCUP, DA14 4BN **Tel:** 020 8302 6150 **Fax:** 020 8300 2315
Email: newsdesk@bexleychronicle.com
Advertising Address: As above.
Email: newsdesk@bexleychronicle.com
Web site: http://www.bexleychronicle.com
Publisher: Stone Leisure Ltd
Frequency: Monthly
Cover Price: Free
Circulation: 40,000 (Publisher's Statement)
Editor: Bob Griffiths
ADVERTISING RATES:
Full Page Mono £937.00
Full Page Colour £1041.11
SCC £5.00
Agency Commission: 10%
Mechanical Data: Type Area: 360 x 268mm, Col Length: 360mm, Page Width: 268mm, Print Process: Web-fed, No. of Columns (Display): 8, Col Widths (Display): 30mm, Film: Digital
Copy instructions: Copy Date: 1 week prior to publication date
Average advertising content per issue: 50%
Series owner and contact point for the following titles, see individual entries:
Bexleyheath Chronicle
Blackfen and Eltham Chronicle
Sidcup Chronicle
Swanley Chronicle
Thamesmead Chronicle
LOCAL NEWSPAPERS: Local Newspapers Greater London

BEXLEY TIMES
43908U72B-1875_150

Formerly: Bexley Times (Erith & Crayford Edition)
Frequency: Weekly
Cover Price: £0.35
Circulation: 65,923 (VFD 02/07/2007 to 30/12/2007)
ADVERTISING RATES:
SCC £3.00

Part of Series, see entry for: Times and Reporter Series (Kent)
LOCAL NEWSPAPERS: Local Newspapers English Counties

BEXLEYHEATH CHRONICLE
1626387U72A-1303_100

Frequency: Monthly
Cover Price: Free
Part of Series, see entry for: Bexley Chronicle Series
LOCAL NEWSPAPERS: Local Newspapers Greater London

BICESTER REVIEW
43292U72B-230_120

Frequency: Weekly
Cover Price: Free
Circulation: 9,402 (VFD 02/07/2007 to 30/12/2007)
Part of Series, see entry for: Buckingham Advertiser Series
LOCAL NEWSPAPERS: Local Newspapers English Counties

BIDDULPH CHRONICLE
43360U72B-445_110

Frequency: Weekly
Cover Price: £0.40
Part of Series, see entry for: Congleton Chronicle Series
LOCAL NEWSPAPERS: Local Newspapers English Counties

BIGGIN HILL NEWS
43837U72A-400_120

Date Established: 1966
Frequency: Weekly - Published on Thursday
Cover Price: Free
Part of Series, see entry for: Bromley and Biggin Hill News Series
LOCAL NEWSPAPERS: Local Newspapers Greater London

BIGGLESWADE CHRONICLE
43235U72B-90

Editorial Address: 7 High Street, BIGGLESWADE, SG18 0JB **Tel:** 01767 222555 **Fax:** 01767 224466
Email: editorial@biggleswadechronicle.co.uk
Advertising Address: As above. **Tel:** 01767 222333
Email: sue.bower@bedsnews.com
Web site: http://www.biggleswadetoday.co.uk
Publisher: Johnston Press plc
Date Established: 1891
Frequency: Weekly - Published on Friday
Cover Price: £0.43
Circulation: 8,116 (Publisher's Statement)
Editor: James Stewart; **Advertising Manager:** Sue Bower
ADVERTISING RATES:
Full Page Mono £1331.10
Full Page Colour £1663.87
SCC £5.10
Agency Commission: 10%
Mechanical Data: Col Length: 340mm, No. of Columns (Display): 9, Page Width: 268mm, Type Area: 340 x 268mm, Film: Digital, Col Widths (Display): 26.8mm
Copy instructions: Copy Date: Wednesday 5.00pm prior to publication date
Average advertising content per issue: 40%
LOCAL NEWSPAPERS: Local Newspapers English Counties

BILLERICAY AND WICKFORD GAZETTE
43592U72B-965_103

Frequency: Weekly - See main series record for circulation figure
Cover Price: £0.65
Part of Series, see entry for: Brentwood Gazette Series
LOCAL NEWSPAPERS: Local Newspapers English Counties

BINGHAM ADVERTISER AND SOUTH NOTTS ADVERTISER
44190U72B-2620_200

Formerly: South Notts Advertiser
Frequency: Weekly
Cover Price: £0.50
Part of Series, see entry for: Newark Advertiser Series
LOCAL NEWSPAPERS: Local Newspapers English Counties

BIRMINGHAM MAIL
41987U67B-30

Formerly: Birmingham Evening Mail
Editorial Address: 6th Floor, Fort Dunlop, Fort Parkway, BIRMINGHAM, B24 9FF **Tel:** 0121 236 3366
Fax: 0121 233 0271
Email: newsdesk@birminghammail.net
Advertising Address: As above. **Fax:** 0121 234 5752

Email: john_allen@mrn.co.uk
Web site: http://www.birminghammail.net
Publisher: Trinity Mirror
Date Established: 1870
Frequency: Evenings
Cover Price: £0.40
Circulation: 78,178 (ABC 02/01/2006 to 02/07/2006)
Editor: Andy Richards; **Features Editor:** Paul Fulford;
Advertising Manager: John Allen
ADVERTISING RATES:
SCC £33.90
Mechanical Data: Print Process: Web-fed offset litho, Page Width: 264mm, Type Area: 340 x 264mm, Col Length: 340mm, No. of Columns (Display): 9, Film: Digital
Copy instructions: Copy Date: 2 days prior to publication date
Editions:
Birmingham Mail (Black Country)
Birmingham Mail (Central City Final)
Birmingham Mail (City Final)
Birmingham Mail (Weekend Edition)
Supplement(s): City Mail - 12xY
REGIONAL DAILY & SUNDAY NEWSPAPERS: Regional Daily Newspapers

---

BIRMINGHAM MAIL (BLACK COUNTRY)
41990U67B-30_520

Formerly: Black Country Mail
Frequency: Daily
ADVERTISING RATES:
SCC £33.90
Edition of: Birmingham Mail
REGIONAL DAILY & SUNDAY NEWSPAPERS: Regional Daily Newspapers

---

BIRMINGHAM MAIL (CENTRAL CITY FINAL)
1655225U67B-30_521

Formerly: Birmingham Evening Mail (City Final)
Frequency: Daily
ADVERTISING RATES:
SCC £33.90
Edition of: Birmingham Mail
REGIONAL DAILY & SUNDAY NEWSPAPERS: Regional Daily Newspapers

---

BIRMINGHAM MAIL (CITY FINAL)
1698974U67B-30_526

Formerly: Birmingham Mail (North City Final)
Frequency: Daily
Cover Price: £0.40
ADVERTISING RATES:
SCC £33.90
Edition of: Birmingham Mail
REGIONAL DAILY & SUNDAY NEWSPAPERS: Regional Daily Newspapers

---

BIRMINGHAM MAIL EXTRA
44539U72B-3428

Formerly: Birmingham News Series
Editorial Address: BPM Media, Floor 6, Fort Dunlop, Fort Parkway, BIRMINGHAM, B24 9FF **Tel:** 0121 236 3366
Fax: 0121 233 0271
Email: newsdesk@birminghammail.net
Advertising Address: PO Box 18, Weaman Street, BIRMINGHAM, B4 6AX **Tel:** 0121 236 3366
Fax: 0121 234 5190
Web site: http://www.birminghammail.net
Publisher: Trinity Mirror
Frequency: Weekly - Published on Thursday
Cover Price: Free
Circulation: 177,201 (VFD 02/07/2007 to 30/12/2007)
Usual Pagination: 50
Editor: Andy Richards; **Features Editor:** Paul Fulford
ADVERTISING RATES:
Full Page Mono £6003.72
Full Page Colour £8105.02
SCC £17.32
Mechanical Data: Type Area: 340 x 264mm, No. of Columns (Display): 9, Col Length: 340mm, Page Width: 264mm, Film: Digital
Copy instructions: Copy Date: 1 day prior to publication date
Supplement(s): The Property News - 52xY
LOCAL NEWSPAPERS: Local Newspapers English Counties

BIRMINGHAM MAIL (WEEKEND EDITION)
1702950U67B-30_528

Frequency: Weekly
Cover Price: £0.40
ADVERTISING RATES:
SCC £33.90

Edition of: Birmingham Mail
REGIONAL DAILY & SUNDAY NEWSPAPERS: Regional Daily Newspapers

THE BIRMINGHAM POST
41992U67B-40
Editorial Address: 6th Floor, Fort Dunlop, Fort Parkway, BIRMINGHAM, B4 9FF **Tel:** 0121 236 3366
Fax: 0121 234 5667
Email: postnewsdesk@birminghampost.net
Advertising Address: As above. **Fax:** 0121 234 5757
Email: john_allen@mrn.co.uk
Web site: http://www.birminghampost.net
Publisher: BPM Media (Midlands)
Frequency: Mornings
Cover Price: £0.70
Circulation: 12,997 (Publisher's Statement)
Editor: Sarah Probert; **News Editor:** Sarah Probert;
Executive Editor: Mike Hughes; **Advertising Manager:** John Allen
ADVERTISING RATES:
Full Page Mono £6884.06
Full Page Colour £9293.48
SCC £11.59
Agency Commission: 10%
Mechanical Data: Col Widths (Display): 28mm, Type Area: 540 x 323mm, Col Length: 540mm, Film: Digital, No. of Columns (Display): 11, Page Width: 323mm
Copy instructions: Copy Date: 2 days prior to publication date
Average advertising content per issue: 40%
Editions:
Birmingham Post (City Edition)
Birmingham Post (First Edition)
Supplement(s): Business & Property Review - 52xY, Post People - 52xY, Post Property - 52xY
REGIONAL DAILY & SUNDAY NEWSPAPERS: Regional Daily Newspapers

BIRMINGHAM POST (CITY EDITION)
41993U67B-40_530
Edition of: The Birmingham Post
REGIONAL DAILY & SUNDAY NEWSPAPERS: Regional Daily Newspapers

BIRMINGHAM POST (CITY/LONDON OFFICE)
42300U67D-60
Editorial Address: 1 Canada Square, Canary Wharf, LONDON, E14 5AP **Tel:** 020 7293 3459 **Fax:** 020 7293 3400
Email: jon_walker@mrn.co.uk
Publisher: Trinity Mirror
Cover Price: £0.60
Editor: Jonathan Walker
REGIONAL DAILY & SUNDAY NEWSPAPERS: Regional Daily Sunday London City Office

BIRMINGHAM POST (FIRST EDITION)
41994U67B-40_560
Formerly: Birmingham Post(County Edition)
Edition of: The Birmingham Post
REGIONAL DAILY & SUNDAY NEWSPAPERS: Regional Daily Newspapers

BIRSTALL NEWS
44690U72B-3740_130
Frequency: Weekly
Cover Price: £0.45
Part of Series, see entry for: Batley News Series
LOCAL NEWSPAPERS: Local Newspapers English Counties

THE BIRSTALL POST
44743U72B-2100
Editorial Address: Longslade College, Wanlip Lane, Birstall, LEICESTER, LE4 4GH **Tel:** 0116 267 4213
Fax: 0116 267 4213
Email: editor@birstallpost.co.uk
Advertising Address: As above.
Email: editor@birstallpost.co.uk
Web site: http://www.birstallpost.co.uk
Publisher: The Birstall Post Society
Date Established: 1983
Frequency: Monthly
Cover Price: Free
Circulation: 5,200 (Publisher's Statement)
Editor: Jerry Jackson; **Advertising Manager:** Jerry Jackson
ADVERTISING RATES:
Full Page Mono £350.00
Mechanical Data: Trim Size: 420 x 297mm, Film: Digital, Type Area: 390 x 279mm, Col Length: 390mm, Page Width: 279mm
LOCAL NEWSPAPERS: Local Newspapers English Counties

BISHOPBRIGGS HERALD
44980U72D-630_130
Frequency: Weekly - Circulation figure is incorporated into the Kirkintilloch Herald
Cover Price: £0.29
Part of Series, see entry for: Kirkintilloch & Bishopbriggs Herald Series
LOCAL NEWSPAPERS: Local Newspapers Scotland

BISHOP'S STORTFORD OBSERVER
43803U72B-1545_170
Formerly: Herts & Essex Observer
Frequency: Weekly - Circulation figure includes Dunmow and Waldon Observer and Stansted Observer
Cover Price: £0.52
Circulation: 15,552 (ABC 02/07/2007 to 30/12/2007)
Part of Series, see entry for: Herts & Essex Observer Series
LOCAL NEWSPAPERS: Local Newspapers English Counties

BLACKBURN CITIZEN
43946U72B-1917
Formerly: Blackburn Citizen Series
Editorial Address: Newspaper House, High Street, BLACKBURN, BB1 1HT **Tel:** 01254 298205
Fax: 01254 680429
Email: lt_editorial@lancashire.newsquest.co.uk
Advertising Address: As above. **Tel:** 01254 678678
Email: sarah.wheildon@nqnw.co.uk
Web site: http://www.lancashiretelegraph.co.uk
Publisher: Newsquest Lancashire Limited
Frequency: Weekly
Cover Price: Free
Circulation: 59,248 (VFD 02/07/2007 to 30/12/2007)
Editor: Ian Singleton; **News Editor:** Ian Singleton
ADVERTISING RATES:
Full Page Mono £1008.00
Full Page Colour £1260.00
SCC £3.20
Agency Commission: 10%
Mechanical Data: Page Width: 273mm, Film: Digital, Print Process: Web-fed offset litho, Type Area: 350 x 273mm, Col Length: 350mm, Col Widths (Display): 27mm, No. of Columns (Display): 9
Copy instructions: Copy Date: Monday 4.30pm prior to publication date
Average advertising content per issue: 60%
LOCAL NEWSPAPERS: Local Newspapers English Counties

BLACKFEN AND ELTHAM CHRONICLE
1681784U72A-1303_104
Frequency: Monthly
Cover Price: Free
Part of Series, see entry for: Bexley Chronicle Series
LOCAL NEWSPAPERS: Local Newspapers Greater London

BLACKPOOL, FYLDE AND WYRE REPORTER
765061U72B-3921
Formerly: Blackpool Reporter Series
Editorial Address: Avroe House, Avroe Crescent, Blackpool Business Park, BLACKPOOL, FY4 2DP **Tel:** 01253 400888
Fax: 01253 361870
Email: jon.rhodes@blackpoolgazette.co.uk
Advertising Address: As above. **Fax:** 01253 361898
Email: joanne.lee@blackpoolgazette.co.uk
Web site: http://www.blackpoolgazette.co.uk
Publisher: Johnston Press plc
Date Established: 1999
Frequency: Weekly
Cover Price: Free
Circulation: 64,017 (VFD 01/01/2007 to 01/07/2007)
Editor: Jon Rhodes; **News Editor:** Jon Rhodes; **Advertising Manager:** Joanne Lee
ADVERTISING: Rates on application
LOCAL NEWSPAPERS: Local Newspapers English Counties

BLACKWOOD CAMPAIGN
44765U72C-78_115
Frequency: Weekly
Cover Price: Free
Circulation: 13,258 (VFD 02/07/2007 to 30/12/2007)
Part of Series, see entry for: Caerphilly Campaign Series
LOCAL NEWSPAPERS: Local Newspapers Wales

BLAIRGOWRIE ADVERTISER
45018U72D-830_120
Frequency: Weekly - Published on Thursday
Cover Price: £0.42
Circulation: 3,231 (ABC 02/07/2007 to 30/12/2007)
Part of Series, see entry for: Perthshire Advertiser Series
LOCAL NEWSPAPERS: Local Newspapers Scotland

BLEWYN GLAS
761708U72J-25
Editorial Address: 85 Tregarth, MACHYNLLETH, SY20 8HY **Tel:** 01654 702881
Advertising Address: Cefnrhosan, Aberhosan, MACHYNLLETH, SY20 8RA **Tel:** 01654 702459
Frequency: 11 issues yearly - Not published in August
Cover Price: £0.30
Circulation: 1,200 (Publisher's Statement)
Editor: Eirian Jones; **Advertising Manager:** Dwynwen Humphries
Summary of Content: Welsh language community newspaper featuring village news, a diary of events, poetry and a letters page.
Language(s): Welsh
Readership/Target Audience: Aimed at Welsh speaking readers in the Machynlleth area.
ADVERTISING RATES:
Full Page Mono £60.00
Mechanical Data: Film: Digital, Type Area: 350 x 110mm, Col Length: 350mm, Page Width: 110mm
Copy instructions: Copy Date: 2nd Tuesday of the month prior to publication date
Average advertising content per issue: 25%
LOCAL NEWSPAPERS: Community Newsletters

BLYTHE & FORSBROOK TIMES
44298U72B-2970_110
Frequency: Weekly - Published on Wednesday
Cover Price: £0.40
Part of Series, see entry for: Cheadle Times & Echo Series
LOCAL NEWSPAPERS: Local Newspapers English Counties

BOGNOR REGIS AND CHICHESTER GUARDIAN
44451U72B-3275
Formerly: Bognor Regis and Chichester Journal & Guardian Series
Editorial Address: Unicorn House, 8 Eastgate Square, CHICHESTER, PO19 1JN **Tel:** 01243 539389
Fax: 01243 539386
Email: janet.philip@chiobserver.co.uk
Advertising Address: As above. **Tel:** 01243 532532
Fax: 01243 776854
Email: kate.newton@chiobserver.co.uk
Web site: http://www.chichester.co.uk
Publisher: Sussex Newspapers Ltd
Frequency: Weekly
Cover Price: Free
Circulation: 41,368 (Publisher's Statement)
Editor: Janet Philip
ADVERTISING RATES:
Full Page Mono £5242.16
Agency Commission: 10%
Mechanical Data: Col Length: 340mm, No. of Columns (Display): 9, Type Area: 340 x 272mm, Page Width: 272mm, Film: Digital
Copy instructions: Copy Date: Friday 5pm prior to publication date
LOCAL NEWSPAPERS: Local Newspapers English Counties

BOGNOR REGIS OBSERVER
44469U72B-3326_130
Frequency: Weekly
Part of Series, see entry for: Southdown Observer Series
LOCAL NEWSPAPERS: Local Newspapers English Counties

BOLSOVER ADVERTISER
43471U72B-691_105
Frequency: 26 issues yearly
Cover Price: Free
Circulation: 11,412 (VFD 02/07/2007 to 30/12/2007)
ADVERTISING: Rates on application
Part of Series, see entry for: Chesterfield & Dronfield Advertiser Series
LOCAL NEWSPAPERS: Local Newspapers English Counties

BOLTON JOURNAL
43684U72B-1166
Formerly: Bolton Journal Series
Editorial Address: Newspaper House, Churchgate, BOLTON, BL1 1DE **Tel:** 01204 522345 **Fax:** 01204 528304
Email: newsdesk@theboltonnews.co.uk
Advertising Address: As above. **Tel:** 01204 537235
Fax: 01204 537432
Web site: http://www.theboltonnews.co.uk
Publisher: Newsquest Media Group

Non-National Newspapers

Frequency: Weekly - Published on Thursday
Cover Price: Free
Circulation: 59,893 (VFD 02/07/2007 to 30/12/2007)
Editor: James Higgins; **Advertising Manager:** Beverley Shepherd
ADVERTISING: Rates on application
LOCAL NEWSPAPERS: Local Newspapers English Counties

THE BOLTON NEWS
41997U67B-70
Formerly: Bolton Evening News
Editorial Address: Newspaper House, Churchgate, BOLTON, BL1 1DE **Tel:** 01204 522345 **Fax:** 01204 537427
Email: newsdesk@theboltonnews.co.uk
Advertising Address: As above. **Fax:** 01204 537432
Email: twaddington@lancashire.newsquest.co.uk
Web site: http://www.thisisbolton.co.uk
Publisher: Newsquest (Lancs)
Date Established: 1867
Frequency: Mornings - Not published on Sunday
Cover Price: £0.40
Circulation: 29,552 (ABC 02/07/2007 to 30/12/2007)
Editor: James Higgins; **Features Editor:** Andrew Mosley;
Managing Director: Jan Lever; **Advertising Manager:** Trish Waddington
ADVERTISING RATES:
SCC £6.00
Agency Commission: 10%
Mechanical Data: Type Area: 350 x 273mm, Print Process: Web-fed offset litho, Col Length: 350mm, No. of Columns (Display): 9, Film: Digital, Page Width: 273mm
Copy instructions: Copy Date: 2 days prior to publication date
Average advertising content per issue: 35%
Supplement(s): Motors - 52xY, Property For Sale - 52xY, Property Plus - 52xY
REGIONAL DAILY & SUNDAY NEWSPAPERS: Regional Daily Newspapers

BO'NESS JOURNAL
717877U72D-690_110
Frequency: Weekly
Cover Price: £0.40
Part of Series, see entry for: Linlithgowshire Journal and Gazette Series
LOCAL NEWSPAPERS: Local Newspapers Scotland

BOOTLE TIMES
44090U72B-2319_130
Frequency: Weekly - Published Thursdays
Cover Price: Free
Circulation: 16,824 (VFD 02/07/2007 to 30/12/2007)
ADVERTISING RATES:
SCC £3.56
Part of Series, see entry for: Crosby Herald & Bootle Times Series
LOCAL NEWSPAPERS: Local Newspapers English Counties

BORDER TELEGRAPH
44884U72D-160
Editorial Address: 113 Channel Street, GALASHIELS, TD1 1BN **Tel:** 01896 758395 **Fax:** 01896 759395
Email: editorial@bordertelegraph.com
Advertising Address: 113 High Street, GALASHIELS, TD1 1SB **Tel:** 01896 758395 **Fax:** 01896 759395
Email: ghill@bordertelegraph.com
Web site: http://www.bordertelegraph.com
Publisher: Border Weeklies Ltd
Date Established: 1896
Frequency: Weekly - Published on Wednesday
Cover Price: £0.40
Circulation: 4,362 (ABC 02/07/2007 to 30/12/2007)
Editor: Atholl Innes; **Advertising Manager:** Gillian Hill
ADVERTISING RATES:
Full Page Mono £999.60
Full Page Colour £1649.20
SCC £3.57
Agency Commission: 10%
Mechanical Data: Col Widths (Display): 31mm, Film: Digital, Page Width: 265.5mm, No. of Columns (Display): 8, Col Length: 350mm, Type Area: 350 x 265.5mm
Copy instructions: Copy Date: Thursday 5pm prior to publication date
Average advertising content per issue: 40%
LOCAL NEWSPAPERS: Local Newspapers Scotland

BORDON HERALD
44371U72B-3120_120
Frequency: Weekly
Cover Price: £0.50
Part of Series, see entry for: Farnham Herald Series
LOCAL NEWSPAPERS: Local Newspapers English Counties

BORDON POST
43773U72B-1383_130
Frequency: Weekly
Cover Price: £0.35
Part of Series, see entry for: Petersfield Post Series
LOCAL NEWSPAPERS: Local Newspapers English Counties

BORDON TIMES & MAIL
44387U72B-1339_190
Frequency: Weekly - Circulation figure is incorporated into the Alton Times & Mail
Cover Price: Free
Part of Series, see entry for: Alton Post Gazette, Times & Mail Series
LOCAL NEWSPAPERS: Local Newspapers English Counties

BOREHAMWOOD & ELSTREE TIMES
43784U72B-1494
Editorial Address: 71 Church Road, LONDON, NW4 4DN
Tel: 020 8953 3391 **Fax:** 020 8207 3713
Email: bwnews@london.newsquest.co.uk
Advertising Address: As above. **Tel:** 020 8359 5959
Fax: 020 8203 5141
Email: ngleeson@london.newsquest.co.uk
Web site: http://www.borehamwoodtimes.co.uk
Publisher: Newsquest (North London)
Date Established: 1936
Frequency: Weekly - Published on Friday
Cover Price: Free
Circulation: 14,614 (VFD 02/07/2007 to 30/12/2007)
Usual Pagination: 136
Editor: News Desk
ADVERTISING RATES:
Full Page Mono £470.00
Full Page Colour £470.00
SCC £2.70
Agency Commission: 10%
Mechanical Data: Col Widths (Display): 27.5mm, Film: Digital, Col Length: 350mm, Page Width: 265mm, Type Area: 350 x 265mm, No. of Columns (Display): 9
Copy instructions: Copy Date: Tuesday 4pm
LOCAL NEWSPAPERS: Local Newspapers English Counties

BOSTON CITIZEN
1656217U72B-2196_101
Frequency: Weekly - Circulation figure includes Louth Citizen and Skegness Citizen and Sleaford Citizen
Cover Price: Free
Circulation: 41,886 (ABC 02/07/2007 to 30/12/2007)
ADVERTISING RATES:
Full Page Mono £1652.40
Full Page Colour £2148.12
Part of Series, see entry for: Boston Standard and Citizen Series
LOCAL NEWSPAPERS: Local Newspapers English Counties

BOSTON STANDARD
1656218U72B-2196_100
Date Established: 1912
Frequency: Weekly
Cover Price: £0.40
Circulation: 12,049 (ABC 02/07/2007 to 30/12/2007)
ADVERTISING RATES:
Full Page Mono £973.80
Full Page Colour £1265.94
Part of Series, see entry for: Boston Standard and Citizen Series
LOCAL NEWSPAPERS: Local Newspapers English Counties

BOSTON STANDARD AND CITIZEN SERIES
44037U72B-2196
Formerly: Boston Standard
Editorial Address: 5-6 Church Lane, BOSTON, PE21 6ND
Tel: 01205 311433 **Fax:** 01205 352913
Email: warren.moody@jpress.co.uk
Advertising Address: As above.
Email: lisa.mitchell@jpress.co.uk
Web site: http://www.bostonstandard.co.uk
Publisher: Lincolnshire Newspapers Ltd
Date Established: 1912
Frequency: Weekly - Published every Wednesday
Circulation: 53,935 (Combined Circulation)
News Editor: Stephen Stray; **Managing Director:** Paul Robins; **Advertising Manager:** Lisa Mitchell
ADVERTISING: Rates on application
Agency Commission: 10%
Mechanical Data: Page Width: 270mm, Film: Digital, Type Area: 340 x 270mm, Col Length: 340mm, Col Widths (Display): 28mm, No. of Columns (Display): 9
Copy instructions: Copy Date: Monday 5pm prior to publication date

Average advertising content per issue: 60%
Series owner and contact point for the following titles, see individual entries:
Boston Citizen
Boston Standard
Supplement(s): Property Today - 52xY
LOCAL NEWSPAPERS: Local Newspapers English Counties

BOSTON TARGET
44084U72B-2287_120
Frequency: Weekly
Cover Price: Free
Circulation: 27,340 (VFD 02/07/2007 to 30/12/2007)
Part of Series, see entry for: Target Series
LOCAL NEWSPAPERS: Local Newspapers English Counties

BOURNEMOUTH ADVERTISER
43553U72B-902_110
Frequency: Weekly
Cover Price: Free
Circulation: 59,921 (VFD 02/07/2007 to 30/12/2007)
ADVERTISING: Rates on application
Part of Series, see entry for: Advertiser Series (Poole & Swanage)
LOCAL NEWSPAPERS: Local Newspapers English Counties

BOVEY TRACEY, CHUDLEIGH & MID-DEVON ADVERTISER
43513U72B-827_145
Frequency: Weekly
Cover Price: £0.35
Part of Series, see entry for: Mid-Devon Advertiser Series
LOCAL NEWSPAPERS: Local Newspapers English Counties

BRACKLEY & TOWCESTER ADVERTISER
43293U72B-230_125
Frequency: Weekly - Circulation figure is incorporated into the Buckingham & Winslow Advertiser
Cover Price: £0.47
Part of Series, see entry for: Buckingham Advertiser Series
LOCAL NEWSPAPERS: Local Newspapers English Counties

BRACKLEY & TOWCESTER POST
44163U72B-2500_200
Frequency: Weekly
Cover Price: Free
Circulation: 11,877 (VFD 02/07/2007 to 30/12/2007)
ADVERTISING RATES:
SCC £2.94
Part of Series, see entry for: Northants Herald and Post Series
LOCAL NEWSPAPERS: Local Newspapers English Counties

BRACKNELL & ASCOT TIMES
43286U72B-210_120
Frequency: Weekly - Circulation figure is incorporated into the Wokingham Times
Cover Price: £0.35
Part of Series, see entry for: Wokingham and Bracknell Times Series
LOCAL NEWSPAPERS: Local Newspapers English Counties

BRACKNELL FOREST & WOKINGHAM STANDARD SERIES
43287U72B-3941
Formerly: Bracknell & Wokingham Standard Series
Editorial Address: Unit 5, Anvil Court, 44 Denmark Street, WOKINGHAM, RG40 2BB **Tel:** 0118 936 6180
Fax: 0118 936 6190
Email: editorial@bracknellstandard.co.uk
Advertising Address: As above.
Email: reception@wokingham-times.co.uk
Web site: http://www.getbracknell.co.uk
Publisher: Surrey & Berkshire Media Group
Frequency: Weekly - Published on Thursday
Cover Price: Free
Circulation: 50,824 (VFD 02/07/2007 to 30/12/2007)
Editor: Alison Hepworth; **Publisher:** Kim Chapman
ADVERTISING RATES:
SCC £4.85
Mechanical Data: Col Widths (Display): 30mm, Page Width: 277mm, Type Area: 350 x 277mm, Col Length: 350mm, No. of Columns (Display): 9, Film: Digital

Series owner and contact point for the following titles, see individual entries:
Bracknell Forest Standard
Wokingham Standard
LOCAL NEWSPAPERS: Local Newspapers English Counties

BRACKNELL FOREST STANDARD

1732606U72B-3941_100

Formerly: Bracknell Standard
Frequency: Weekly
Cover Price: Free
Part of Series, see entry for: Bracknell Forest & Wokingham Standard Series
LOCAL NEWSPAPERS: Local Newspapers English Counties

BRACKNELL MIDWEEK

43251U72B-150_115

Formerly: Midweek News
Frequency: Weekly - Published on Wednesday. Circulation figure includes the Wokingham Midweek
Cover Price: Free
Circulation: 50,485 (VFD 30/07/2007 to 30/12/2007)
Part of Series, see entry for: Bracknell News Series
LOCAL NEWSPAPERS: Local Newspapers English Counties

BRACKNELL NEWS

43252U72B-150_120

Frequency: Weekly - Published on Thursday. Circulation figure is for Bracknell News Series which includes Ascot News, Wokingham News and Crowthorne, Owlsmoor & Sandhurst Newsweek
Cover Price: £0.27
Circulation: 5,588 (ABC 02/07/2007 to 30/12/2007)
Part of Series, see entry for: Bracknell News Series
LOCAL NEWSPAPERS: Local Newspapers English Counties

BRACKNELL NEWS SERIES

43249U72B-150

Editorial Address: South Hill, Ringmead, BRACKNELL, RG12 7PA **Tel:** 01344 456611 **Fax:** 01344 426840
Email: news@bracknellnews.co.uk
Advertising Address: 50-56 Portman Road, READING, RG30 1BA **Tel:** 0118 950 3050 **Fax:** 0118 939 1619
Email: dtonna@berksmedia.co.uk
Web site: http://www.bracknellnews.co.uk
Publisher: Berkshire Media Group Ltd
Frequency: Weekly - Published on Wednesday and Thursday
Cover Price: £0.55
Circulation: 60,433 (Combined Circulation)
Editor: Richard Crowe; **News Editor:** Richard Crowe; **Editor-in-Chief:** Sally Stevens; **Advertising Manager:** Dene Tonna
ADVERTISING RATES:
Full Page Mono £3687.36
Full Page Colour £3687.36
Agency Commission: 10%
Mechanical Data: No. of Columns (Display): 8, Type Area: 340 x 262mm, Col Length: 340mm, Page Width: 262mm, Film: Digital, Col Widths (Display): 31mm
Copy instructions: Copy Date: Monday 10.00 am prior to publication date
Average advertising content per issue: 60%
Series owner and contact point for the following titles, see individual entries:
Ascot News
Bracknell Midweek
Bracknell News
Wokingham Midweek
Wokingham News and Crowthorne and Sandhurst Newsweek
Supplement(s): Business - 12xY
LOCAL NEWSPAPERS: Local Newspapers English Counties

BRADFORD TARGET

44693U72B-3747_120

Formerly: Bradford Star
Frequency: Weekly
Cover Price: Free
Circulation: 48,411 (VFD 02/07/2007 to 30/12/2007)
Part of Series, see entry for: Bradford Target Series
LOCAL NEWSPAPERS: Local Newspapers English Counties

BRADFORD TARGET SERIES

44691U72B-3747

Formerly: Bradford Star and Target Series
Editorial Address: Hall Ings, BRADFORD, BD1 1JR
Tel: 01274 729511 **Fax:** 01274 723634
Email: newsdesk@bradford.newsquest.co.uk
Advertising Address: As above. **Fax:** 01274 724907

Email: adsales@bradford.newsquest.co.uk
Web site: http://www.thetelegraphandargus.co.uk
Publisher: Newsquest Yorkshire and North East (Bradford)
Frequency: Weekly
Cover Price: Free
Circulation: 88,522 (Combined Circulation)
Editor: Perry Austin-Clarke
ADVERTISING RATES:
SCC £4.60
Agency Commission: 10%
Mechanical Data: Type Area: 350 x 261mm, Page Width: 261mm, Film: Negative, wrong reading, emulsion side up. Positive, right reading, emulsion side down. Digital, Col Length: 350mm, No. of Columns (Display): 8, Print Process: Web-fed offset litho, Col Widths (Display): 30mm
Copy instructions: Copy Date: Monday 12pm prior to publication date
Series owner and contact point for the following titles, see individual entries:
Aire, Wharfe and Worth Valleys Target
Bradford Target
LOCAL NEWSPAPERS: Local Newspapers English Counties

BRAINTREE & WITHAM TIMES & GAZETTE SERIES

43586U72B-950

Editorial Address: 76 High Street, BRAINTREE, CM7 1JP
Tel: 01376 343344 **Fax:** 01376 552811
Email: bwtnews@nqe.com
Advertising Address: Wickham House, 1 Northgate Street, COLCHESTER, CO1 1HA **Tel:** 01206 506000
Fax: 01206 508298
Email: braintreeads@nqe.com
Web site: http://www.braintreeandwithamtimes.co.uk
Publisher: Newsquest (Essex) Ltd
Date Established: 1929
Frequency: Weekly - Published on Wednesday and Friday
Circulation: 39,857 (Combined Circulation)
Editor: News Desk; **Advertising Manager:** Louise Woodman
ADVERTISING: Rates on application
Agency Commission: 10%
Mechanical Data: Page Width: 267mm, Col Widths (Display): 27mm, Film: Digital, Col Length: 340mm, No. of Columns (Display): 9, Type Area: 340 x 267mm, Print Process: Web offset
Copy Date: Tuesday 10am prior to publicaton date
Average advertising content per issue: 70%
Series owner and contact point for the following titles, see individual entries:
Braintree & Witham Times incorporating the Dunmow, Thated and Felsted Times
Braintree and Witham Weekly News
Halstead Gazette
Witham & Braintree Times
LOCAL NEWSPAPERS: Local Newspapers English Counties

BRAINTREE & WITHAM TIMES INCORPORATING THE DUNMOW, THATED AND FELSTED TIMES

43587U72B-950_120

Formerly: Braintree & Witham Times
Frequency: Weekly - Published on Wednesday. Circulation figure also includes the Dunmow, Thaxted and Felsted Times and the Witham & Braintree Times
Cover Price: £0.55
Circulation: 13,618 (ABC 02/07/2007 to 30/12/2007)
ADVERTISING RATES:
SCC £5.55
Part of Series, see entry for: Braintree & Witham Times & Gazette Series
LOCAL NEWSPAPERS: Local Newspapers English Counties

BRAINTREE AND WITHAM WEEKLY NEWS

43599U72B-950_201

Formerly: Essex Weekly News Braintree, Witham
Frequency: Weekly
Cover Price: Free
Circulation: 20,988 (VFD 02/07/2007 to 30/12/2007)
ADVERTISING RATES:
SCC £5.55
Part of Series, see entry for: Braintree & Witham Times & Gazette Series
LOCAL NEWSPAPERS: Local Newspapers English Counties

BRECHIN ADVERTISER

44885U72D-170

Editorial Address: 13 Swan Street, BRECHIN, DD9 6EE
Tel: 01356 622767 **Fax:** 01307 466923
Email: advertisernews@brechinadvertiser.com

Advertising Address: As above. **Fax:** 01356 625507
Email: advertiseradverts@brechinadvertiser.com
Web site: http://www.brechinadvertiser.com
Publisher: Angus County Press Ltd
Date Established: 1848
Frequency: Weekly
Cover Price: £0.50
Circulation: 2,931 (ABC 02/07/2007 to 30/12/2007)
Editor: Alan Ducat; **Advertising Manager:** Linda Ruxton
ADVERTISING RATES:
Full Page Mono £647.36
Full Page Colour £970.86
SCC £2.72
Agency Commission: 10%
Mechanical Data: Col Length: 340mm, Col Widths (Display): 28mm, Page Width: 700mm, No. of Columns (Display): 9, Type Area: 340mm x 700mm, Print Process: Web-fed offset litho, Film: Digital
Copy instructions: Copy Date: Monday 5pm prior to publication date
LOCAL NEWSPAPERS: Local Newspapers Scotland

BRECON AND RADNOR EXPRESS

44752U72C-60

Formerly: Brecon and Radnor Express Series
Editorial Address: 11 The Bulwark, BRECON, LD3 7AE
Tel: 01874 610111 **Fax:** 01874 624097
Email: theeditor@brecon-radnor.co.uk
Advertising Address: As above. **Fax:** 01874 624359
Email: advertising@brecon-radnor.co.uk
Web site: http://www.brecon-radnor-today.co.uk/tn/index.cfm
Publisher: Brecon and Radnor Express Ltd
Date Established: 1882
Frequency: Weekly
Cover Price: £0.50
Circulation: 27,326 (Publisher's Statement)
Editor: Julie Chappell; **News Editor:** Twm Owen; **Advertising Manager:** Sandie Wickens
Summary of Content: Weekly broadsheet newspaper providing local news and sports.
ADVERTISING RATES:
Full Page Mono £2880.90
Full Page Colour £3457.08
SCC £4.85
Agency Commission: 10%
Mechanical Data: No. of Columns (Display): 11, Col Widths (Display): 29mm, Film: Digital
Copy instructions: Copy Date: Monday 5pm prior to publication date
Average advertising content per issue: 40%
LOCAL NEWSPAPERS: Local Newspapers Wales

BRENTWOOD GAZETTE

43593U72B-965_105

Formerly: Brentwood Gazette & Mid Essex Recorder
Frequency: Weekly - See main series record for circulation figure
Cover Price: £0.65
Part of Series, see entry for: Brentwood Gazette Series
LOCAL NEWSPAPERS: Local Newspapers English Counties

BRENTWOOD GAZETTE SERIES

43591U72B-965

Editorial Address: Westway, CHELMSFORD, CM1 3BE
Tel: 01245 600700 **Fax:** 01277 219172
Email: editorial@gazettenews.co.uk
Advertising Address: As above. **Fax:** 01245 603424
Email: sarah.woodley-dyne@essexchronicle.co.uk
Web site: http://www.thisistotalessex.co.uk
Publisher: Essex Chronicle Media Group Ltd
Date Established: 1919
Frequency: Weekly - The circulation figure is the total figure for all series members
Circulation: 14,679 (ABC 02/07/2007 to 30/12/2007)
Editor: Deanne Blaylock; **Managing Director:** Richard Karn; **Advertising Manager:** Sarah Woodley-Dyne
ADVERTISING RATES:
Full Page Mono £2016.00
SCC £7.00
Mechanical Data: Film: Digital, Page Width: 270mm, Type Area: 360 x 270mm, Col Length: 360mm, Col Widths (Display): 31mm, No. of Columns (Display): 8
Copy instructions: Copy Date: 1 week prior to publication date
Series owner and contact point for the following titles, see individual entries:
Billericay and Wickford Gazette
Brentwood Gazette
Ongar & North Weald Gazette
Supplement(s): Business - 52xY, Go - 52xY, Property - 52xY
LOCAL NEWSPAPERS: Local Newspapers English Counties

BRENTWOOD WEEKLY NEWS

43597U72B-1080_221

Email: community@nqe.com
Web site: http://www.brentwoodweeklynews.co.uk
Frequency: Weekly
Cover Price: Free
Circulation: 36,263 (VFD 02/07/2007 to 30/12/2007)
ADVERTISING: Rates on application
Part of Series, see entry for: Southend Standard Series
LOCAL NEWSPAPERS: Local Newspapers English Counties

BRIDGNORTH JOURNAL

44230U72B-2810

Editorial Address: 50A High Street, BRIDGNORTH, WV16 4DX **Tel:** 01746 761411 **Fax:** 01746 763733
Email: news@bridgnorthjournal.co.uk
Advertising Address: As above.
Email: jrichardson@shropshirestar.co.uk
Web site: http://www.bridgnorthjournal.com
Publisher: Shropshire Newspapers Ltd
Date Established: 1859
Frequency: Weekly - Published on Friday
Cover Price: £0.40
Circulation: 9,126 (ABC 02/07/2007 to 30/12/2007)
Editor: John Griffiths; **Managing Director:** Steve Brown; **Advertising Manager:** Jonathan Richardson
ADVERTISING RATES:
Full Page Mono £1082.00
Full Page Colour £1407.00
Agency Commission: 10%
Mechanical Data: Type Area: 410 x 305mm, Col Length: 410mm, Col Widths (Display): 35mm, Film: Digital, No. of Columns (Display): 8, Page Width: 305mm
Copy instructions: Copy Date: Tuesday 12pm prior to publication date
Average advertising content per issue: 60%
Supplement(s): Bridgnorth Life - 4xY, Home Improvements - 4xY, Shropshire Life - 12xY
LOCAL NEWSPAPERS: Local Newspapers English Counties

BRIDGWATER MERCURY

44260U72B-2875_101

Frequency: Weekly - Circulation figure includes the Burnham & Highbridge Mercury
Cover Price: £0.50
Circulation: 13,109 (ABC 01/01/2007 to 30/12/2007)
ADVERTISING RATES:
SCC £4.00
Part of Series, see entry for: Mercury and Weekly News Series
LOCAL NEWSPAPERS: Local Newspapers English Counties

BRIDGWATER TIMES

761667U72B-2910

Formerly: Bridgwater Times Series
Editorial Address: Southover, WELLS, BA5 1UH
Tel: 01749 832300 **Fax:** 01749 832347
Email: times@midsomnews.co.uk
Advertising Address: Midsomer News and Media, Southover, WELLS, BA5 1UH **Tel:** 01749 832300
Fax: 01749 832346
Email: admin@midsomnews.co.uk
Web site: http://www.thisisbridgwater.co.uk
Publisher: Northcliffe Media Ltd
Frequency: Weekly - Published on Thursday
Cover Price: Free
Circulation: 25,677 (VFD 02/07/2007 to 30/12/2007)
Editor: Tim Lethaby; **News Editor:** Tim Lethaby
ADVERTISING RATES:
Full Page Mono £964.80
Full Page Colour £1206.00
Agency Commission: 10%
Mechanical Data: Page Width: 270mm, Film: Digital, Type Area: 360 x 270mm, No. of Columns (Display): 8, Col Length: 360mm, Col Widths (Display): 31mm
Copy instructions: Copy Date: Monday 12 noon prior to publication date
LOCAL NEWSPAPERS: Local Newspapers English Counties

BRIDLINGTON FREE PRESS

44628U72B-3574_120

Frequency: Weekly
Cover Price: £0.48
Circulation: 15,458 (ABC 02/07/2007 to 30/12/2007)
ADVERTISING RATES:
Full Page Mono £2061.00
Full Page Colour £2732.00
SCC £6.87
Part of Series, see entry for: Bridlington Free Press Series
LOCAL NEWSPAPERS: Local Newspapers English Counties

BRIDLINGTON FREE PRESS SERIES

44627U72B-3574

Editorial Address: 3 Prospect Street, BRIDLINGTON, YO15 2AQ **Tel:** 01262 677338 **Fax:** 01262 607525
Email: newsdesk@bridlingtonfreepress.co.uk
Advertising Address: As above. **Tel:** 01262 606606
Fax: 01262 604556
Email: joanna.machin@yrnltd.co.uk
Web site: http://www.bridlingtontoday.co.uk
Publisher: Yorkshire Regional Newspapers Ltd
Date Established: 1859
Frequency: Weekly - Published on Thursday
Circulation: 31,298 (Combined Circulation)
Editor: John Edwards; **Managing Director:** Jason Rusedavis; **Advertising Manager:** Joanna Machin
ADVERTISING: Rates on application
Agency Commission: 10%
Mechanical Data: Type Area: 340 x 274mm, Col Length: 340mm, No. of Columns (Display): 9, Page Width: 274mm, Film: Digital
Copy instructions: Copy Date: Monday 5.00pm prior to publication date
Average advertising content per issue: 60%
Series owner and contact point for the following titles, see individual entries:
Bridlington Free Press
Bridlington Gazette & Herald incorporating The Leader
LOCAL NEWSPAPERS: Local Newspapers English Counties

BRIDLINGTON GAZETTE & HERALD INCORPORATING THE LEADER

44629U72B-3574_140

Frequency: Weekly
Cover Price: Free
Circulation: 15,840 (Publisher's Statement)
ADVERTISING RATES:
Full Page Mono £955.00
Full Page Colour £1064.00
SCC £4.46
Part of Series, see entry for: Bridlington Free Press Series
LOCAL NEWSPAPERS: Local Newspapers English Counties

BRIDPORT & LYME REGIS NEWS SERIES

43562U72B-905

Editorial Address: 67 East Street, BRIDPORT, DT6 3LB
Tel: 01308 425884 **Fax:** 01308 425031
Email: news@bridportnews.co.uk
Advertising Address: As above. **Tel:** 01308 422388
Fax: 01308 458080
Email: ads@bridportnews.co.uk
Web site: http://www.bridportnews.co.uk
Publisher: Newsquest Media Group
Date Established: 1855
Frequency: Weekly
Circulation: 10,576 (ABC 01/01/2007 to 30/12/2007)
Usual Pagination: 48
Editor: Chris Carson
ADVERTISING RATES:
Full Page Mono £1020.60
Full Page Colour £1134.00
SCC £3.60
Agency Commission: 10%
Mechanical Data: Page Width: 264mm, No. of Columns (Display): 9, Film: Digital, Col Length: 350mm, Type Area: 350 x 264mm, Col Widths (Display): 28mm
Copy instructions: Copy Date: Tuesday 12pm prior to publication date
Average advertising content per issue: 50%
Series owner and contact point for the following titles, see individual entries:
Bridport News
Lyme Regis News
LOCAL NEWSPAPERS: Local Newspapers English Counties

BRIDPORT NEWS

43563U72B-905_120

Frequency: Weekly
Cover Price: £0.40
Part of Series, see entry for: Bridport & Lyme Regis News Series
LOCAL NEWSPAPERS: Local Newspapers English Counties

BRIGHOUSE ECHO

44694U72B-3750

Editorial Address: West Park Street, BRIGHOUSE, HD6 1JW **Tel:** 01484 714617 **Fax:** 01484 400087
Email: stephen.firth@brighouseecho.co.uk
Advertising Address: As above. **Tel:** 01484 721911
Email: advertising.brighouse@halifaxcourier.co.uk
Web site: http://www.brighouseecho.co.uk
Publisher: Johnston Press plc

Date Established: 1887
Frequency: Weekly
Cover Price: £0.45
Circulation: 6,629 (ABC 02/07/2007 to 30/12/2007)
Usual Pagination: 18
Editor: Stephen Firth; **Advertising Manager:** Rachael Hamer
ADVERTISING RATES:
SCC £3.89
Agency Commission: 10%
Mechanical Data: Page Width: 324mm, Film: Digital, Print Process: Web-fed offset litho, Type Area: 560mm x 324mm, No. of Columns (Display): 11, Col Length: 560mm
Copy instructions: Copy Date: Tuesday 5pm prior to publication date
Supplement(s): Choices - 4xY, Lifestyle - 52xY, Motors Today - 52xY
LOCAL NEWSPAPERS: Local Newspapers English Counties

BRIGHTON & HOVE LEADER

44428U72B-3210_120

Frequency: Weekly
Cover Price: Free
Circulation: 68,040 (Publisher's Statement)
Part of Series, see entry for: Brighton and Hove Leader Series
LOCAL NEWSPAPERS: Local Newspapers English Counties

BRIGHTON AND HOVE LEADER SERIES

44427U72B-3210

Editorial Address: Argus House, Crowhurst Road, Hollingbury, BRIGHTON, BN1 8AR **Tel:** 01273 544544
Fax: 01273 544723
Email: leader@leaderseries.co.uk
Advertising Address: As above. **Fax:** 01273 889500
Email: david.maguire@theargus.co.uk
Web site: http://www.theargus.co.uk
Publisher: Newsquest (Sussex) Ltd
Frequency: Weekly
Cover Price: Free
Circulation: 138,468 (Combined Circulation)
Usual Pagination: 44
Editor: Chris Chandler; **Advertising Manager:** David Maguire; **Group Editor:** Chris Chandler
ADVERTISING RATES:
Full Page Mono £2356.00
Full Page Colour £2664.00
SCC £19.40
Agency Commission: 10%
Mechanical Data: Col Length: 340mm, No. of Columns (Display): 9, Type Area: 340 x 259mm, Film: Digital, Page Width: 259mm, Col Widths (Display): 27mm
Copy instructions: Copy Date: Monday prior to publication date
Average advertising content per issue: 70%
Series owner and contact point for the following titles, see individual entries:
Brighton & Hove Leader
Mid Sussex Leader
South Coast Leader
Uckfield Leader
LOCAL NEWSPAPERS: Local Newspapers English Counties

BRISTOL OBSERVER SERIES

43203U72B-20

Editorial Address: Temple Way, BRISTOL, BS99 7HD
Tel: 0117 934 3000 **Fax:** 0117 934 3575
Email: epnews@bepp.co.uk
Advertising Address: As above. **Fax:** 0117 934 3577
Email: observer@bepp.co.uk
Publisher: Bristol News & Media Ltd
Frequency: Weekly
Cover Price: Free
Circulation: 165,769 (VFD 02/07/2007 to 30/12/2007)
Editor: News Desk
ADVERTISING RATES:
Full Page Mono £3902.40
Full Page Colour £4878.00
Agency Commission: 10%
Copy instructions: Copy Date: 1 week prior to publication date
Series owner and contact point for the following titles, see individual entries:
Observer (East, Kingswood & Keynsham)
Observer (South Gloucestershire)
Observer (South West)
LOCAL NEWSPAPERS: Local Newspapers English Counties

BRIXHAM NEWS

43535U72B-854_211

Frequency: Weekly
Cover Price: Free

Part of Series, see entry for: South Hams Newspapers Group
LOCAL NEWSPAPERS: Local Newspapers English Counties

BROMLEY AND BIGGIN HILL NEWS SERIES
43838U72A-400

Editorial Address: Winterton House, High Street, WESTERHAM, TN16 1AT **Tel:** 01959 564766
Fax: 01959 562760
Email: bheditor@googlemail.com
Advertising Address: As above.
Email: adinfo@internet-today.co.uk
Web site: http://www.tindlenews.co.uk
Publisher: Biggin Hill News Ltd
Frequency: Weekly - Published on Thursday
Cover Price: Free
Editor: Luke King
ADVERTISING RATES:
SCC £5.90
Agency Commission: 10%
Mechanical Data: Page Width: 265mm, Col Widths (Display): 29.6mm, Film: Digital, Type Area: 340 x 265mm, Col Length: 340mm, No. of Columns (Display): 8
Copy instructions: Copy Date: Tuesday 5pm prior to publication date
Series owner and contact point for the following titles, see individual entries:
Biggin Hill News
Bromley News
Supplement(s): Biggin Hill Air Fair - 1xY, Bridal Elegance - 1xY, Education - 2xY, Essentially West Wycombe and Hayes - 4xY, Glovebox - 4xY
LOCAL NEWSPAPERS: Local Newspapers Greater London

BROMLEY NEWS
761959U72A-400_130

Date Established: 1981
Cover Price: Free
Part of Series, see entry for: Bromley and Biggin Hill News Series
LOCAL NEWSPAPERS: Local Newspapers Greater London

BROMLEY TIMES
43909U72B-1875_160

Formerly: Kentish Times Bromley & Beckenham Edition
Frequency: Weekly
Cover Price: Free
Circulation: 80,500 (Publisher's Statement)
ADVERTISING RATES:
SCC £3.50
Part of Series, see entry for: Times and Reporter Series (Kent)
LOCAL NEWSPAPERS: Local Newspapers English Counties

BROMSGROVE ADVERTISER
44607U72B-3558_130

Frequency: Weekly
Cover Price: £0.55
Free to qualifying individuals
Part of Series, see entry for: Bromsgrove Advertiser Series
LOCAL NEWSPAPERS: Local Newspapers English Counties

BROMSGROVE ADVERTISER SERIES
44606U72B-3558

Formerly: Bromsgrove Advertiser & Messenger Series
Editorial Address: 5 High Street, BROMSGROVE, B61 8AJ
Tel: 01527 837000 **Fax:** 01527 889055
Email: advertiser@midlands.newsquest.co.uk
Advertising Address: As above. **Tel:** 01527 879211
Fax: 01527 877456
Email: bob.price@midlands.newsquest.co.uk
Web site: http://www.bromsgroveadvertiser.co.uk
Publisher: Newsquest Media Group
Frequency: Weekly - Published on Wednesday
Circulation: 37,530 (VFD 02/07/2007 to 30/12/2007)
Editor: Alan Wallcroft; **Managing Director:** Michael Donovan
ADVERTISING RATES:
Full Page Colour £1130.06
Agency Commission: 10%
Mechanical Data: Type Area: 350 x 268mm, Page Width: 268mm, Film: Negative, right reading, emulsion side down. Digital, Col Widths (Display): 28mm, Col Length: 350mm, No. of Columns (Display): 9
Copy instructions: Copy Date: 1 week prior to publication date
Average advertising content per issue: 78%
Series owner and contact point for the following titles, see individual entries:
Bromsgrove Advertiser

Droitwich Spa Advertiser
LOCAL NEWSPAPERS: Local Newspapers English Counties

BROMSGROVE STANDARD
44621U72B-3566_130

Frequency: Weekly - Circulation figure includes the Droitwich Spa Standard
Cover Price: Free
Circulation: 40,349 (VFD 02/07/2007 to 30/12/2007)
ADVERTISING RATES:
SCC £5.66
Part of Series, see entry for: Redditch and Bromsgrove Standard Series
LOCAL NEWSPAPERS: Local Newspapers English Counties

BUCHAN OBSERVER
44886U72D-190

Editorial Address: 28-30 Seagate, PETERHEAD, AB42 1JP
Tel: 01779 472184 **Fax:** 01779 871321
Email: ken.duncan@jpress.co.uk
Advertising Address: 17 Chapel Street, PETERHEAD, AB42 1TH **Tel:** 01779 871330 **Fax:** 01779 871371
Email: phyllis.mundie@buchanobserver.co.uk
Web site: http://www.buchanobserver.com
Publisher: Johnston Press plc
Frequency: Weekly - Published on Tuesday
Cover Price: £0.45
Circulation: 7,786 (ABC 02/07/2007 to 30/12/2007)
Editor: Ken Duncan; **Features Editor:** Ken Duncan
ADVERTISING RATES:
Full Page Mono £820.00
Full Page Colour £1066.00
SCC £3.35
Agency Commission: 10%
Mechanical Data: Col Widths (Display): 28mm, Col Length: 340mm, Film: Digital, No. of Columns (Display): 9, Type Area: 340 x 272mm, Print Process: Web-fed offset litho, Page Width: 272mm
Copy instructions: Copy Date: 3 days prior to publication date
Average advertising content per issue: 40%
Supplement(s): Drive - 52xY
LOCAL NEWSPAPERS: Local Newspapers Scotland

BUCKINGHAM ADVERTISER SERIES
43291U72B-230

Editorial Address: Riverside, 61-62 Well Street, BUCKINGHAM, MK18 1EN **Tel:** 01280 827940
Fax: 01280 823729
Email: editorial@buckinghamadvertiser.co.uk
Advertising Address: As above.
Email: vicky.key@ccnltd.com
Web site: http://www.buckinghamonline.co.uk
Publisher: Central Counties Newspapers South Ltd
Date Established: 1853
Frequency: Weekly
Circulation: 19,132 (Combined Circulation)
Editor: Rob Gibbard; **Advertising Manager:** Victoria Key
ADVERTISING RATES:
SCC £5.42
Mechanical Data: Type Area: 340 x 265mm, Col Length: 340mm, Page Width: 265mm
Copy instructions: Copy Date: Tuesday 5.00pm prior to publication date
Average advertising content per issue: 60%
Series owner and contact point for the following titles, see individual entries:
Bicester Review
Brackley & Towcester Advertiser
Buckingham & Winslow Advertiser
LOCAL NEWSPAPERS: Local Newspapers English Counties

BUCKINGHAM & WINSLOW ADVERTISER
43294U72B-230_130

Frequency: Weekly - Circulation figure includes the Brackley & Towcester Advertiser
Cover Price: £0.47
Circulation: 9,730 (ABC 02/07/2007 to 30/12/2007)
Part of Series, see entry for: Buckingham Advertiser Series
LOCAL NEWSPAPERS: Local Newspapers English Counties

BUCKINGHAMSHIRE ADVERTISER
43298U72B-240_150

Cover Price: £0.55
Part of Series, see entry for: The Buckinghamshire Examiner and Advertiser Series
LOCAL NEWSPAPERS: Local Newspapers English Counties

BUCKINGHAMSHIRE EXAMINER
43302U72B-240_170

Formerly: The Bucks Examiner
Date Established: 1889
Cover Price: £0.55
Part of Series, see entry for: The Buckinghamshire Examiner and Advertiser Series
LOCAL NEWSPAPERS: Local Newspapers English Counties

THE BUCKINGHAMSHIRE EXAMINER AND ADVERTISER SERIES
43295U72B-240

Formerly: Bucks Examiner and Advertiser Series
Editorial Address: West London & Bucks Newspaper, 2nd floor, Belmont Chambers, 28 Bakers Road, UXBRIDGE, UB8 1RG **Tel:** 01895 451000
Email: bucksnews@trinitysouth.co.uk
Advertising Address: As above.
Email: advertisingchesham@trinitysouth.co.uk
Web site: http://www.buckinghamshireexaminer.co.uk
Publisher: Trinity Mirror Southern
Frequency: Weekly - Published on Thursday
Circulation: 13,568 (ABC 02/07/2007 to 30/12/2007)
Usual Pagination: 64
Editor: News Desk
ADVERTISING RATES:
Full Page Mono £3536.00
Full Page Colour £3889.00
SCC £12.35
Mechanical Data: Page Width: 262mm, Type Area: 340 x 262mm, Col Length: 340mm, No. of Columns (Display): 8, Col Widths (Display): 31mm, Film: Digital
Copy instructions: Copy Date: Tuesday 4pm prior to publication date
Series owner and contact point for the following titles, see individual entries:
Amersham Examiner
Beaconsfield Advertiser
Buckinghamshire Advertiser
Buckinghamshire Examiner
LOCAL NEWSPAPERS: Local Newspapers English Counties

BUCKS ADVERTISER
43300U72B-250_130

Frequency: Weekly
Cover Price: Free
ADVERTISING RATES:
SCC £4.65
Part of Series, see entry for: Bucks Advertiser & Thame Gazette Series
LOCAL NEWSPAPERS: Local Newspapers English Counties

BUCKS ADVERTISER & THAME GAZETTE SERIES
43299U72B-250

Editorial Address: The Gatehouse, Gatehouse Road, AYLESBURY, HP19 8ED **Tel:** 01296 619700
Email: editorial@bucksherald.co.uk
Advertising Address: As above.
Email: jo.measey@ccnltd.com
Web site: http://www.aylesburytoday.co.uk
Publisher: Central Counties Newspapers South Ltd
Frequency: Weekly - Published every Friday
Cover Price: Free
Circulation: 41,849 (ABC 01/01/2007 to 01/07/2007)
Usual Pagination: 80
Editor: Tim Green; **Advertising Director:** Jo Measey
ADVERTISING RATES:
SCC £8.96
Agency Commission: 10%
Mechanical Data: Type Area: 340 x 268mm, Page Width: 268mm, Col Length: 340mm, No. of Columns (Display): 9, Film: Digital, Col Widths (Display): 28mm
Copy instructions: Copy Date: Wednesday 5pm prior to publication date
Series owner and contact point for the following titles, see individual entries:
Bucks Advertiser
Thame Gazette
LOCAL NEWSPAPERS: Local Newspapers English Counties

BUCKS FREE PRESS
43304U72B-280_120

Frequency: Weekly - Circulation figure also includes the Amersham & Chesham Free Press and the Marlow Free Press
Cover Price: £0.50
Circulation: 23,716 (ABC 02/07/2007 to 30/12/2007)
Part of Series, see entry for: Bucks Free Press Series
LOCAL NEWSPAPERS: Local Newspapers English Counties

BUCKS FREE PRESS SERIES
43303U72B-280

Editorial Address: Loudwater Mill, Station Road, Loudwater, HIGH WYCOMBE, HP10 9TY **Tel:** 01494 755000
Fax: 01494 534015
Email: bfpnews@london.newsquest.co.uk
Advertising Address: As above. **Fax:** 01494 441977
Email: bfpads@london.newsquest.co.uk
Web site: http://www.bucksfreepress.co.uk
Publisher: Newsquest Media Group
Date Established: 1856
Frequency: Weekly
Circulation: 85,396 (Combined Circulation)
Editor: Steve Cohen; **Features Editor:** Lindi Bilgorri;
Publisher: Vic Catanach
ADVERTISING RATES:
Full Page Colour £1000.00
Agency Commission: 10%
Mechanical Data: Col Widths (Display): 27.5mm, No. of Columns (Display): 9
Copy instructions: Copy Date: Wednesday 1pm prior to publication date
Series owner and contact point for the following titles, see individual entries:
Bucks Free Press
Marlow Free Press
Midweek
South Bucks Star
LOCAL NEWSPAPERS: Local Newspapers English Counties

THE BUCKS HERALD
1763622U72B-290_100

Frequency: Weekly
Cover Price: £0.45
Usual Pagination: 68
ADVERTISING RATES:
Full Page Mono £2895.20
Full Page Colour £3763.76
SCC £4.70
Part of Series, see entry for: The Bucks Herald Series
LOCAL NEWSPAPERS: Local Newspapers English Counties

THE BUCKS HERALD SERIES
43307U72B-290

Formerly: The Bucks Herald
Editorial Address: The Gatehouse, Gatehouse Way, AYLESBURY, HP19 8DB **Tel:** 01296 619777
Fax: 01296 393096
Email: editorial@bucksherald.co.uk
Advertising Address: As above. **Tel:** 01296 619700
Fax: 01296 393451
Email: jo@ccnltd.com
Web site: http://www.aylesburytoday.co.uk
Publisher: Central Counties Newspapers South Ltd
Frequency: Weekly
Circulation: 17,964 (ABC 02/07/2007 to 30/12/2007)
Editor: Ellen Campbell; **Advertising Director:** Jo Measey
Agency Commission: 10%
Mechanical Data: Type Area: 540 x 328mm, Page Width: 328mm, Film: Digital, Col Length: 540mm, No. of Columns (Display): 11, Col Widths (Display): 28mm
Copy instructions: Copy Date: Monday 5pm prior to publication date
Series owner and contact point for the following titles, see individual entries:
The Bucks Herald
The Commuter Herald
Supplement(s): BH The Magazine - 12xY
LOCAL NEWSPAPERS: Local Newspapers English Counties

BUDE & STRATTON POST
43413U72B-520_110

Frequency: Weekly
Cover Price: £0.65
ADVERTISING RATES:
Full Page Mono £3360.00
Full Page Colour £3710.00
SCC £6.00
Mechanical Data: Type Area: 560 x 366mm, Col Length: 560mm, Col Widths (Display): 34mm, No. of Columns (Display): 10, Page Width: 366mm, Film: Digital
Part of Series, see entry for: Cornish & Devon Post Series
LOCAL NEWSPAPERS: Local Newspapers English Counties

THE BUDLEIGH JOURNAL
43506U72B-810_160

Formerly: Journal Budleigh Salterton
Frequency: Weekly - Circulation figure incorporated in The Exmouth Journal
Cover Price: £0.50
ADVERTISING RATES:
SCC £3.80
Part of Series, see entry for: The Journal Series (Exmouth)
LOCAL NEWSPAPERS: Local Newspapers English Counties

BUNGAY AND HARLESTON COMMUNITY NEWS
44335U72B-3072_130

Frequency: Monthly
Cover Price: Free
Circulation: 5,700 (Publisher's Statement)
Part of Series, see entry for: Community News Series
LOCAL NEWSPAPERS: Local Newspapers English Counties

BUNTINGFORD & ROYSTON MERCURY
43797U72B-1520_140

Formerly: Royston & Buntingford Mercury
Frequency: Weekly
Cover Price: £0.60
ADVERTISING: Rates on application
Part of Series, see entry for: Hertfordshire Mercury Series
LOCAL NEWSPAPERS: Local Newspapers English Counties

BURNHAM & HIGHBRIDGE MERCURY
44261U72B-2875_102

Frequency: Weekly - Circulation figure is incorporated into the Bridgwater Mercury
Cover Price: £0.50
ADVERTISING RATES:
SCC £4.00
Part of Series, see entry for: Mercury and Weekly News Series
LOCAL NEWSPAPERS: Local Newspapers English Counties

BURNHAM & HIGHBRIDGE TIMES
43221U72B-40_181

Frequency: Weekly
Cover Price: Free
Circulation: 12,969 (VFD 02/07/2007 to 30/12/2007)
ADVERTISING RATES:
Full Page Mono £1368.00
Full Page Colour £1710.00
Part of Series, see entry for: Clevedon Newspapers Series
LOCAL NEWSPAPERS: Local Newspapers English Counties

BURNHAM AND HIGHBRIDGE WEEKLY NEWS
768733U72B-2875_100

Frequency: Weekly
Cover Price: £0.40
Circulation: 3,047 (ABC 01/01/2007 to 30/12/2007)
ADVERTISING RATES:
SCC £1.65
Part of Series, see entry for: Mercury and Weekly News Series
LOCAL NEWSPAPERS: Local Newspapers English Counties

BURNHAM STANDARD
43631U72B-1070_140

Formerly: Maldon & Burnham Standard
Frequency: Weekly
Cover Price: £0.48
Part of Series, see entry for: Maldon & Burnham Standard Series
LOCAL NEWSPAPERS: Local Newspapers English Counties

THE BURNLEY AND PENDLE CITIZEN
43954U72B-1930

Formerly: Burnley Citizen Series
Editorial Address: Newspaper House, High Street, BLACKBURN, BB1 1HT **Tel:** 01254 678678
Fax: 01254 680429
Email: lt_editorial@lancashire.newsquest.co.uk
Advertising Address: As above. **Fax:** 01254 696020
Email: sarah.wheildon@nqnw.co.uk
Web site: http://www.thisislancashire.co.uk
Publisher: Newsquest Media Group
Frequency: Weekly - Published on Thursday
Cover Price: Free
Circulation: 55,649 (VFD 02/07/2007 to 30/12/2007)
Usual Pagination: 40
Editor: Ian Singleton; **News Editor:** Ian Singleton;
Advertising Manager: Sarah Wheildon
ADVERTISING RATES:
Full Page Mono £1008.00
Full Page Colour £1260.00
SCC £3.20
Agency Commission: 10%
Mechanical Data: Page Width: 273mm, Film: Digital, Type Area: 350 x 273mm, Col Length: 350mm, No. of Columns (Display): 9, Col Widths (Display): 27.5mm

Copy instructions: Copy Date: Tuesday 4pm prior to publication date
Average advertising content per issue: 75%
LOCAL NEWSPAPERS: Local Newspapers English Counties

BURNLEY & PENDLE REPORTER
1693349U72B-1940_223

Frequency: Weekly - Circulation figure is a combined figure and includes the Clitheroe & Whalley Reporter and the Pendle & Burnley Reporter
Cover Price: Free
Circulation: 55,941 (ABC 01/01/2007 to 01/07/2007)
ADVERTISING RATES:
Full Page Mono £4332.96
Full Page Colour £5632.84
SCC £14.16
Part of Series, see entry for: Burnley Express and Reporter Series
LOCAL NEWSPAPERS: Local Newspapers English Counties

BURNLEY EXPRESS AND REPORTER SERIES
43957U72B-1940

Formerly: Burnley Express Series
Editorial Address: Bull Street, BURNLEY, BB11 1DP **Tel:** 01282 478155 **Fax:** 01282 439863
Email: margaret.parsons@eastlancsnews.co.uk
Advertising Address: As above. **Tel:** 01282 426161
Fax: 01282 435332
Email: helen.foulds@eastlancsnews.co.uk
Web site: http://www.burnleyexpress.net
Publisher: East Lancashire Newspapers Ltd
Date Established: 1877
Circulation: 85,199 (Combined Circulation)
Editor: Margaret Parsons; **News Editor:** Margaret Parsons;
Advertising Manager: Helen Foulds
ADVERTISING RATES:
Full Page Mono £4332.96
Full Page Colour £5632.84
SCC £14.16
Agency Commission: 10%
Mechanical Data: Film: Digital, Type Area: 340 x 274mm, Col Length: 340mm, Page Width: 274mm, No. of Columns (Display): 9
Series owner and contact point for the following titles, see individual entries:
Burnley & Pendle Reporter
Burnley Express (Friday)
Burnley Express (Tuesday)
Clitheroe & Whalley Reporter
Padiham and District Express (Fri)
Padiham and District Express (Tue)
Pendle & Burnley Reporter
Pendle Express (Tuesday)
Supplement(s): Motors Today, Property Today
LOCAL NEWSPAPERS: Local Newspapers English Counties

BURNLEY EXPRESS (FRIDAY)
43959U72B-1940_130

Frequency: Weekly - Circulation figure includes Padiham and District Express (Fri)
Cover Price: £0.65
Circulation: 17,647 (ABC 02/07/2007 to 30/12/2007)
ADVERTISING RATES:
Full Page Mono £4332.96
Full Page Colour £5632.84
SCC £14.16
Copy instructions: Copy Date: Wednesday, 4pm, prior to publication date
Part of Series, see entry for: Burnley Express and Reporter Series
LOCAL NEWSPAPERS: Local Newspapers English Counties

BURNLEY EXPRESS (TUESDAY)
43958U72B-1940_120

Frequency: Weekly - Circulation figure includes Padiham and District Express (Tuesday) and the Pendle Express (Tuesday)
Cover Price: £0.50
Circulation: 11,611 (ABC 02/07/2007 to 30/12/2007)
ADVERTISING RATES:
Full Page Mono £4332.96
Full Page Colour £5632.84
SCC £14.16
Copy instructions: Copy Date: Friday, 5pm, prior to publication date
Part of Series, see entry for: Burnley Express and Reporter Series
LOCAL NEWSPAPERS: Local Newspapers English Counties

BURNTWOOD MERCURY
44306U72B-2990_110

Frequency: Weekly - Circulation figure is incorporated into the Lichfield Mercury
Cover Price: Free
ADVERTISING RATES:
SCC £5.25
Part of Series, see entry for: Lichfield Mercury Series
LOCAL NEWSPAPERS: Local Newspapers English Counties

THE BURNTWOOD POST
44296U72B-2965_130

Formerly: Burntwood Chase Post
Frequency: Weekly
Cover Price: Free
Part of Series, see entry for: Chase Post Series Burntwood & Cannock
LOCAL NEWSPAPERS: Local Newspapers English Counties

THE BURTON & SOUTH DERBYSHIRE ADVERTISER
44287U72B-2957

Editorial Address: 65-68 High Street, BURTON-ON-TRENT, DE14 1LE **Tel:** 01283 512345 **Fax:** 01283 515351
Email: editorial@burtonmail.co.uk
Advertising Address: As above. **Fax:** 01283 510075
Email: advertising@burtonmail.co.uk
Web site: http://www.burtonmail.co.uk
Publisher: Staffordshire Newspapers Ltd
Frequency: Weekly - Published on Wednesday
Cover Price: Free
Circulation: 57,692 (VFD 02/07/2007 to 30/12/2007)
Usual Pagination: 32
Editor: Andrew Parker; **Editor-in-Chief:** Andrew Parker; **Managing Director:** Mike Richardson; **Advertising Manager:** Guy Helliker
ADVERTISING RATES:
SCC £6.75
Agency Commission: 10%
Mechanical Data: Type Area: 350 x 276mm, Col Length: 350mm, Col Widths (Display): 31mm, No. of Columns (Display): 8, Print Process: Web-fed offset litho, Film: Digital, Page Width: 276mm
Copy instructions: Copy Date: Friday 12 noon prior to publication date
LOCAL NEWSPAPERS: Local Newspapers English Counties

BURTON MAIL
42016U67B-135

Editorial Address: 65-68 High Street, BURTON-ON-TRENT, DE14 1LE **Tel:** 01283 512345 **Fax:** 01283 515351
Email: editorial@burtonmail.co.uk
Advertising Address: As above. **Fax:** 01283 510075
Email: keyaccount@burtonmail.co.uk
Web site: http://www.burtonmail.co.uk
Publisher: Staffordshire Newspapers Ltd
Date Established: 1898
Frequency: Mornings - Not published on Sunday
Cover Price: £0.38
Circulation: 14,658 (ABC 02/07/2007 to 30/12/2007)
Editor: Andrew Parker; **Managing Director:** Mike Richardson
ADVERTISING RATES:
SCC £5.70
Agency Commission: 10%
Mechanical Data: Col Length: 360mm, Col Widths (Display): 28mm, Film: Digital, No. of Columns (Display): 9, Type Area: 350 x 268mm, Page Width: 276mm
Copy instructions: Copy Date: 9.30am 1 day prior to publication date
Average advertising content per issue: 25%
REGIONAL DAILY & SUNDAY NEWSPAPERS: Regional Daily Newspapers

BURY FREE PRESS & CITIZEN SERIES
44327U72B-3071

Editorial Address: Kings Road, BURY ST. EDMUNDS, IP33 3ET **Tel:** 01284 768911 **Fax:** 01284 755619
Email: news@buryfreepress.co.uk
Advertising Address: As above.
Email: yvonne.harbutt@buryfreepress.co.uk
Web site: http://www.buryfreepress.co.uk
Publisher: Johnston Press plc
Date Established: 1784
Frequency: Weekly - Published on Wednesday and Friday
Cover Price: £0.60
Free to qualifying individuals
Circulation: 53,112 (Combined Circulation)
Usual Pagination: 104
Editor: Lesley Anslow; **News Editor:** Lesley Anslow; **Managing Director:** Richard Parkinson; **Advertising Manager:** Yvonne Harbutt
ADVERTISING RATES:
Full Page Mono £2837.00

Full Page Colour £3688.00
Agency Commission: 10%
Mechanical Data: Print Process: Web-fed offset litho, Col Widths (Display): 26mm, Col Length: 340mm, Type Area: 340 x 270mm, No. of Columns (Display): 9, Page Width: 270mm, Film: Digital
Copy instructions: Copy Date: Wednesday 1pm prior to publication date
Average advertising content per issue: 60%
Series owner and contact point for the following titles, see individual entries:
Bury Free Press Mildenhall
Bury Free Press Stowmarket News
Bury Free Press Thetford & Brandon News
Bury Free Press Town and Villages Edition
The Citizen (Bury St. Edmunds & Thetford)
Supplement(s): Exclusive - 12xY, Lifestyle - 52xY
LOCAL NEWSPAPERS: Local Newspapers English Counties

BURY FREE PRESS MILDENHALL
44331U72B-3071_170

Frequency: Weekly - Circulation figure also includes the Bury Free Press Stowmarket News, the Bury Free Press Thetford & Brandon News and the Bury Free Press Town & Villages Edition
Cover Price: £0.60
Circulation: 27,159 (ABC 02/07/2007 to 30/12/2007)
Part of Series, see entry for: Bury Free Press & Citizen Series
LOCAL NEWSPAPERS: Local Newspapers English Counties

BURY FREE PRESS STOWMARKET NEWS
44330U72B-3071_160

Frequency: Weekly - Circulation figure is incorporated into the Bury Free Press Mildenhall
Cover Price: £0.60
Part of Series, see entry for: Bury Free Press & Citizen Series
LOCAL NEWSPAPERS: Local Newspapers English Counties

BURY FREE PRESS THETFORD & BRANDON NEWS
44332U72B-3071_250

Frequency: Weekly - Circulation figure is incorporated into the Bury Free Press Mildenhall
Cover Price: £0.60
Part of Series, see entry for: Bury Free Press & Citizen Series
LOCAL NEWSPAPERS: Local Newspapers English Counties

BURY FREE PRESS TOWN AND VILLAGES EDITION
44328U72B-3071_150

Frequency: Weekly - Circulation figure is incorporated into the Bury Free Press Mildenhall
Cover Price: £0.60
Part of Series, see entry for: Bury Free Press & Citizen Series
LOCAL NEWSPAPERS: Local Newspapers English Counties

BURY JOURNAL
43691U72B-1170_190

Frequency: Weekly
Cover Price: Free
Circulation: 39,562 (VFD 02/07/2007 to 30/12/2007)
ADVERTISING: Rates on application
Part of Series, see entry for: Bury Times Series
LOCAL NEWSPAPERS: Local Newspapers English Counties

BURY ST EDMUNDS MERCURY
44349U72B-3088_130

Formerly: Bury Mercury
Frequency: Weekly
Cover Price: Free
Circulation: 27,290 (VFD 02/07/2007 to 30/12/2007)
Part of Series, see entry for: Mercury Series
LOCAL NEWSPAPERS: Local Newspapers English Counties

BURY TIMES
43689U72B-1170_120

Formerly: Bury Times (Friday)
Frequency: Weekly - Published on Thursday. Circulation figure includes Bury Times (Ramsbottom & Tottington Edition)
Cover Price: £0.50
Circulation: 23,047 (ABC 02/07/2007 to 30/12/2007)

ADVERTISING: Rates on application
Part of Series, see entry for: Bury Times Series
LOCAL NEWSPAPERS: Local Newspapers English Counties

BURY TIMES (RAMSBOTTOM & TOTTINGTON EDITION)
1693456U72B-1170_211

Frequency: Weekly - See Bury Times for circulation figure
Cover Price: £0.50
ADVERTISING: Rates on application
Part of Series, see entry for: Bury Times Series
LOCAL NEWSPAPERS: Local Newspapers English Counties

BURY TIMES SERIES
43688U72B-1170

Editorial Address: Market Street, BURY, BL9 0PF
Tel: 0161 764 9421 **Fax:** 0161 797 4056
Email: steve.orrell@lancashire.newsquest.co.uk
Advertising Address: Newspaper House, Churchgate, BOLTON, BL1 1DE **Tel:** 01204 522333 **Fax:** 01204 537432
Email: classified@lancashire.newsquest.co.uk
Web site: http://www.thisisbury.co.uk
Publisher: Newsquest Media Group
Frequency: Weekly
Circulation: 69,393 (Combined Circulation)
Usual Pagination: 120
Editor: Steve Orrell; **News Editor:** Steve Orrell; **Managing Director:** Jan Lever
ADVERTISING: Rates on application
Agency Commission: 10%
Copy instructions: Copy Date: 3 days prior to publication date
Series owner and contact point for the following titles, see individual entries:
Bury Journal
Bury Times
Bury Times (Ramsbottom & Tottington Edition)
Prestwich & Whitefield Guide
Radcliffe Times
LOCAL NEWSPAPERS: Local Newspapers English Counties

BUSINESS
41647U67B-9009_701

Formerly: Business Day
Tel: 020 7938 6902 **Fax:** 020 7938 6916
Email: citydesk@standard.co.uk
Frequency: Evenings - Published daily within the London Evening Standard
Editor: Chris Blackhurst
Summary of Content: Section covering City news.
ADVERTISING: Rates on application
Part of Series, see entry for: London Evening Standard
REGIONAL DAILY & SUNDAY NEWSPAPERS: Regional Daily Newspapers

BUSINESS7
1881720U72A-650_100

Frequency: Weekly
Cover Price: Free
Summary of Content: Section focusing on local business stories and issues affecting the world of commerce.
Part of Series, see entry for: The Wharf
LOCAL NEWSPAPERS: Local Newspapers Greater London

THE BUTEMAN
44887U72D-200

Editorial Address: 5 Victoria Street, Rothesay, ISLE OF BUTE, PA20 0AJ **Tel:** 01700 502503 **Fax:** 01700 505159
Email: bute.newsdesk@buteman.com
Advertising Address: As above. **Tel:** 01700 502931
Email: bute.advertising@buteman.com
Publisher: Angus County Press Ltd
Date Established: 1854
Frequency: Weekly - Published on Friday
Cover Price: £0.44
Circulation: 4,000 (Publisher's Statement)
Editor: Craig Borland
ADVERTISING RATES:
Full Page Mono ....,........ £1140.00
Full Page Colour £1710.00
SCC £4.67
Agency Commission: 10%
Mechanical Data: Col Widths (Display): 28mm, No. of Columns (Display): 9, Page Width: 272mm, Col Length: 340mm, Type Area: 340 x 272mm, Film: Digital
Copy instructions: Copy Date: Tuesday 4pm prior to publication date
Average advertising content per issue: 25%
LOCAL NEWSPAPERS: Local Newspapers Scotland

BUXTON ADVERTISER
43467U72B-690_130

Frequency: Weekly
Cover Price: £0.45

Non-National Newspapers

Circulation: 13,022 (ABC 02/07/2007 to 30/12/2007)
ADVERTISING: Rates on application
Part of Series, see entry for: Buxton Advertiser and Times Series
LOCAL NEWSPAPERS: Local Newspapers English Counties

BUXTON ADVERTISER AND TIMES SERIES
43466U72B-690

Editorial Address: 10 Scarsdale Place, BUXTON, SK17 6EG
Tel: 01298 767080 Fax: 01298 70411
Email: news@buxtonadvertiser.co.uk
Advertising Address: As above. Tel: 01298 767070
Email: advertising@buxtonadvertiser.co.uk
Web site: http://www.buxtonadvertiser.co.uk
Publisher: Derbyshire Times Newspaper Group
Frequency: Weekly - Published on Thursday
Circulation: 39,607 (Combined Circulation)
Usual Pagination: 44
Editor: John Phillips; News Editor: Emma Downes;
Advertising Manager: Lorraine Gerrard
ADVERTISING: Rates on application
Agency Commission: 10%
Copy instructions: Copy Date: Monday 5.00pm prior to publication date
Average advertising content per issue: 60%
Series owner and contact point for the following titles, see individual entries:
Buxton Advertiser
Buxton Advertiser (Town)
Buxton Times
Glossop Courier
High Peak Courier
LOCAL NEWSPAPERS: Local Newspapers English Counties

BUXTON ADVERTISER (TOWN)
1792964U72B-690_191

Frequency: Weekly - See Buxton Advertiser for circulation figure
Cover Price: £0.45
ADVERTISING: Rates on application
Part of Series, see entry for: Buxton Advertiser and Times Series
LOCAL NEWSPAPERS: Local Newspapers English Counties

BUXTON TIMES
43468U72B-690_180

Frequency: Weekly
Cover Price: Free
Circulation: 5,532 (VFD 02/07/2007 to 30/12/2007)
ADVERTISING: Rates on application
Part of Series, see entry for: Buxton Advertiser and Times Series
LOCAL NEWSPAPERS: Local Newspapers English Counties

BYFLEET NEWS & MAIL, INCORPORATING WEST BYFLEET, PYRFORD & NEW HAW
44417U72B-3169_120

Formerly: Byfleet, West Byfleet & Pyrford News & Mail
Frequency: Weekly
Cover Price: £0.32
Part of Series, see entry for: Woking News & Mail Series
LOCAL NEWSPAPERS: Local Newspapers English Counties

CAERNARFON & DENBIGH HERALD (ARFON EDITION)
44759U72C-70_110

Frequency: Weekly - Circulation figure includes Caernarfon & Denbigh Herald (South Edition)
Cover Price: £0.65
Circulation: 14,085 (ABC 02/07/2007 to 30/12/2007)
ADVERTISING RATES:
Full Page Mono £1138.00
Full Page Colour £1536.30
SCC £3.95
Part of Series, see entry for: The Caernarfon Herald Series
LOCAL NEWSPAPERS: Local Newspapers Wales

CAERNARFON & DENBIGH HERALD (SOUTH EDITION)
44760U72C-70_120

Frequency: Weekly - For circulation see Caernarfon & Denbigh Herald (Arfon Edition)
Cover Price: £0.65
ADVERTISING RATES:
Full Page Mono £1138.00
Full Page Colour £1536.30
SCC £3.95

Part of Series, see entry for: The Caernarfon Herald Series
LOCAL NEWSPAPERS: Local Newspapers Wales

THE CAERNARFON HERALD SERIES
44757U72C-70

Editorial Address: 14 Eastgate Street, CAERNARFON, LL55 1AG Tel: 01286 671111 Fax: 01286 676937
Email: caernarfon.herald@northwalesnews.co.uk
Advertising Address: Vale Road, Llandudno Junction, CONWAY, LL31 9SL Tel: 01492 579455 Fax: 01492 580126
Email: simon.davis@northwalesnews.co.uk
Web site: http://www.icnorthwales.co.uk
Publisher: North Wales Independent Publications
Frequency: Weekly
Cover Price: £0.65
Circulation: 35,574 (Combined Circulation)
Editor: Helen Harper; Advertising Manager: Simon Davis; Group Editor: Jeff Eames
ADVERTISING RATES:
Full Page Mono £2318.00
Full Page Colour £3129.30
SCC 8.05
Agency Commission: 10%
Mechanical Data: Film: Digital
Copy instructions: Copy Date: 4 days prior to publication date
Series owner and contact point for the following titles, see individual entries:
Bangor & Anglesey Mail
Caernarfon & Denbigh Herald (Arfon Edition)
Caernarfon & Denbigh Herald (South Edition)
Holyhead Anglesey Mail
LOCAL NEWSPAPERS: Local Newspapers Wales

CAERPHILLY CAMPAIGN
44766U72C-78_120

Frequency: Weekly
Cover Price: Free
Circulation: 27,895 (VFD 02/07/2007 to 30/12/2007)
Part of Series, see entry for: Caerphilly Campaign Series
LOCAL NEWSPAPERS: Local Newspapers Wales

CAERPHILLY CAMPAIGN SERIES
44763U72C-78

Editorial Address: 4A Market Street, CAERPHILLY, CF83 1NX Tel: 029 2085 1100 Fax: 029 2088 7065
Email: charles.booth@gwent-wales.co.uk
Advertising Address: As above.
Email: andrea.hall@gwent-wales.co.uk
Web site: http://www.campaignseries.co.uk
Publisher: Newsquest (Media Group) Ltd
Frequency: Weekly - Published on Wednesday
Cover Price: Free
Circulation: 70,860 (Combined Circulation)
Editor: Charles Booth; Advertising Manager: Andrea Hall
ADVERTISING RATES:
SCC £7.75
Agency Commission: 10%
Mechanical Data: Type Area: 340 x 250mm, Col Length: 340mm, Col Widths (Display): 27mm, No. of Columns (Display): 9, Page Width: 250mm, Film: Digital
Copy instructions: Copy Date: Thursday 4pm prior to publication date
Average advertising content per issue: 75%
Series owner and contact point for the following titles, see individual entries:
Blackwood Campaign
Caerphilly Campaign
LOCAL NEWSPAPERS: Local Newspapers Wales

CAITHNESS COURIER
44976U72D-580_140

Frequency: Weekly - Published on Wednesday
Cover Price: £0.60
Circulation: 6,956 (ABC 01/01/2007 to 30/12/2007)
ADVERTISING RATES:
Full Page Mono £2200.00
Full Page Colour £2860.00
SCC £4.00
Part of Series, see entry for: John O'Groat Journal Series
LOCAL NEWSPAPERS: Local Newspapers Scotland

CALDERDALE NEWS
44695U72B-3755

Editorial Address: PO Box 19, King Cross Street, HALIFAX, HX1 2SF Tel: 01422 260214 Fax: 01422 330021
Email: tim.worsnop@halifaxcourier.co.uk
Advertising Address: As above. Tel: 01422 260200
Fax: 01422 260282
Email: sarah.lister@halifaxcourier.co.uk
Web site: http://www.halifaxtoday.co.uk
Publisher: Halifax Courier Ltd
Frequency: Weekly - Published on Thursday
Cover Price: Free
Circulation: 36,000 (Publisher's Statement)

Usual Pagination: 20
Editor: Tim Worsnop; News Editor: Sophie McCandlish;
Features Editor: Tim Worsnop; Managing Director: Darron McLoughlin; Advertising Manager: Sarah Lister
ADVERTISING RATES:
SCC £12.45
Agency Commission: 10%
Mechanical Data: Col Length: 340mm, No. of Columns (Display): 9, Print Process: Web-fed offset litho, Type Area: 340 x 274mm, Page Width: 274mm
Copy instructions: Copy Date: Monday 5pm prior to publication date
Average advertising content per issue: 64%
LOCAL NEWSPAPERS: Local Newspapers English Counties

CAMBERLEY NEWS & MAIL 43762U72B-1382_128

Formerly: Camberley News
Frequency: Weekly - Circulation figure is incorporated into the Aldershot News
Cover Price: £0.37
ADVERTISING: Rates on application
Part of Series, see entry for: Aldershot Mail and News Series
LOCAL NEWSPAPERS: Local Newspapers English Counties

CAMBORNE REDRUTH PACKET
43427U72B-553_110

Frequency: Weekly - Circulation figure also includes the Falmouth Packet and the Helston Packet
Circulation: 19,673 (VFD 02/07/2007 to 30/12/2007)
ADVERTISING RATES:
Full Page Mono £1165.50
Full Page Colour £1573.43
SCC £3.70
Part of Series, see entry for: The Packet Series
LOCAL NEWSPAPERS: Local Newspapers English Counties

CAMBORNE REDRUTH TINNER
43433U72B-560_110

Frequency: Weekly
Cover Price: Free
Circulation: 16,314 (Publisher's Statement)
ADVERTISING: Rates on application
Part of Series, see entry for: The Packet Series
LOCAL NEWSPAPERS: Local Newspapers English Counties

CAMBOURNE WEEKLY NEWS
1749965U72B-350_203

Frequency: Weekly
Cover Price: Free
Circulation: 1,500 (Publisher's Statement)
ADVERTISING RATES:
SCC £3.45
Part of Series, see entry for: Cambridge Weekly News & Crier Series
LOCAL NEWSPAPERS: Local Newspapers English Counties

THE CAMBRIAN NEWS SERIES 44770U72C-30

Formerly: Cambrian News
Editorial Address: PO Box 4, ABERYSTWYTH, SY23 3WB Tel: 01970 615000 Fax: 01970 624699
Email: edit@cambrian-news.co.uk
Advertising Address: Unit 7, Aberystwyth Science Park, Ceredigion, ABERYSTWYTH, SY23 3AH Tel: 01970 611611 Fax: 01970 611925
Email: doug@regionaladvertising.co.uk
Web site: http://www.aberystwyth-today.co.uk
Publisher: Cambrian News (Aberystwyth) Ltd
Date Established: 1860
Frequency: Weekly - Published on Thursday
Cover Price: £0.65
Circulation: 24,400 (Publisher's Statement)
Editor: Simon Middlehurst; News Editor: Simon Middlehurst; Advertising Manager: Doug Price
Language(s): English; Welsh
ADVERTISING RATES:
Full Page Mono £2246.40
SCC £7.80
Agency Commission: 10%
Mechanical Data: Type Area: 360 x 270mm, Page Width: 270mm, Film: Digital, Col Length: 360mm, No. of Columns (Display): 8, Col Widths (Display): 31mm
Copy instructions: Copy Date: Friday 4pm prior to publication date
Average advertising content per issue: 40%

Section 4 (a) Newspapers

Series owner and contact point for the following titles, see individual entries:
Aberaeron & New Quay Cambrian News
Aberystwyth Cambrian News
Arfon-Dwyfor Cambrian News
Dysynni Cambrian News
Lampeter & Tregaron Cambrian News
Machynlleth Cambrian News
Meirionnydd Cambrian News
LOCAL NEWSPAPERS: Local Newspapers Wales

CAMBRIDGE EVENING NEWS (CITY FINAL)
1753002U67B-140_500
Frequency: Daily
Cover Price: £0.40
ADVERTISING: Rates on application
Edition of: Cambridge News
REGIONAL DAILY & SUNDAY NEWSPAPERS: Regional Daily Newspapers

CAMBRIDGE NEWS
42017U67B-140
Formerly: Cambridge Evening News
Editorial Address: Winship Road, Milton, CAMBRIDGE, CB24 6PP **Tel:** 01223 434434 **Fax:** 01223 434415
Email: newsdesk@cambridge-news.co.uk
Advertising Address: As above. **Tel:** 01223 434343
Fax: 01223 434222
Email: advertising@cambridge-news.co.uk
Web site: http://www.cambridge-news.co.uk
Publisher: Cambridge Newspapers Ltd
Frequency: Daily - Published four times a day
Cover Price: £0.45
Circulation: 26,242 (Publisher's Statement)
Editor: John Deex; **News Editor:** Paul Holland; **Features Editor:** Paul Kirkley; **Managing Director:** Graham Ayers;
Advertising Manager: Louise Shephard
ADVERTISING: Rates on application
Agency Commission: 10%
Copy instructions: Copy Date: 2 days prior to publication date
Average advertising content per issue: 35%
Editions:
Cambridge Evening News (City Final)
Cambridge News (Cambridge)
Cambridge News (Newmarket/Ely)
Cambridge News (Sunrise Edition)
Supplement(s): The Magazine - 50xY, Property News - 52xY, Style Magazine - 12xY
REGIONAL DAILY & SUNDAY NEWSPAPERS: Regional Daily Newspapers

CAMBRIDGE NEWS & CRIER
43315U72B-350_201
Formerly: Cambridge Crier
Frequency: Weekly
Cover Price: Free
Circulation: 42,077 (VFD 01/01/2007 to 01/07/2007)
Usual Pagination: 40
ADVERTISING RATES:
SCC £7.10
Part of Series, see entry for: Cambridge Weekly News & Crier Series
LOCAL NEWSPAPERS: Local Newspapers English Counties

CAMBRIDGE NEWS (CAMBRIDGE)
1814059U67B-140_502
Frequency: Mornings
Cover Price: £0.40
ADVERTISING: Rates on application
Edition of: Cambridge News
REGIONAL DAILY & SUNDAY NEWSPAPERS: Regional Daily Newspapers

CAMBRIDGE NEWS (NEWMARKET/ELY)
1814057U67B-140_501
Frequency: Mornings
Cover Price: £0.40
ADVERTISING: Rates on application
Edition of: Cambridge News
REGIONAL DAILY & SUNDAY NEWSPAPERS: Regional Daily Newspapers

CAMBRIDGE NEWS (SUNRISE EDITION)
1826652U67B-140_503
Frequency: Mornings
Cover Price: £0.40
ADVERTISING: Rates on application
Edition of: Cambridge News
REGIONAL DAILY & SUNDAY NEWSPAPERS: Regional Daily Newspapers

CAMBRIDGE WEEKLY NEWS & CRIER SERIES
43316U72B-350
Editorial Address: Winship Road, Milton, CAMBRIDGE, CB24 6PP **Tel:** 01223 434434 **Fax:** 01223 434415
Email: newsdesk@cambridge-news.co.uk
Advertising Address: As above.
Email: advertising@cambridge-news.co.uk
Web site: http://www.cambridge-news.co.uk
Publisher: Cambridge Newspapers Ltd
Frequency: Weekly
Cover Price: Free
Circulation: 208,805 (Combined Circulation)
Usual Pagination: 48
Editor: Nigel Brookes; **Managing Director:** Graham Ayers;
Advertising Manager: Chris Brown; **Group Editor:** Paul Brackley
ADVERTISING RATES:
Full Page Mono £2945.25
Full Page Colour £3828.56
Mechanical Data: Type Area: 350 x 268mm, Col Length: 350mm, Page Width: 268mm, Film: Digital, No. of Columns (Display): 9, Col Widths (Display): 28mm
Copy instructions: Copy Date: Monday 5pm prior to publication date
Series owner and contact point for the following titles, see individual entries:
Cambourne Weekly News
Cambridge News & Crier
Ely Weekly News
Haverhill Weekly News
Histon and Impington Crier
Huntingdon Weekly News
Newmarket Weekly News
Royston Weekly News
Saffron Walden Weekly News
Sawston Crier
St. Ives Weekly News
St. Neots Weekly News
LOCAL NEWSPAPERS: Local Newspapers English Counties

CAMBS TIMES
43326U72B-360
Formerly: Cambridgeshire Times Series
Editorial Address: 51 High Street, MARCH, PE15 9JJ
Tel: 01354 652621 **Fax:** 01354 657676
Email: editor@cambs-times.co.uk
Advertising Address: As above. **Fax:** 01354 652751
Email: sales@cambs-times.co.uk
Web site: http://www.cambstimes24.co.uk
Publisher: Archant Herts & Cambs
Date Established: 1872
Frequency: Weekly - Published every Friday
Cover Price: Free
Circulation: 22,000 (Publisher's Statement)
Usual Pagination: 72
Editor: John Elworthy; **Advertising Manager:** Nick Boister
ADVERTISING RATES:
Full Page Mono £1340.28
Full Page Colour £1742.36
SCC £4.38
Agency Commission: 10%
Mechanical Data: No. of Columns (Display): 9, Col Widths (Display): 26.3mm, Film: Digital
Copy instructions: Copy Date: Wednesday 2pm prior to publication date
Average advertising content per issue: 60%
LOCAL NEWSPAPERS: Local Newspapers English Counties

CAMDEN GAZETTE
1683494U72A-240_201
Frequency: Weekly
Cover Price: Free
Circulation: 15,327 (Publisher's Statement)
ADVERTISING RATES:
SCC £10.00
Part of Series, see entry for: Islington Gazette & Journal Series
LOCAL NEWSPAPERS: Local Newspapers Greater London

CAMDEN NEW JOURNAL
43077U72A-242_140
Frequency: Weekly
Cover Price: Free
Circulation: 53,943 (Publisher's Statement)
ADVERTISING RATES:
Full Page Mono £1862.00
Full Page Colour £2234.40
SCC £7.00
Part of Series, see entry for: Journal Series
LOCAL NEWSPAPERS: Local Newspapers Greater London

CAMELFORD & DELABOLE POST
43414U72B-520_130
Frequency: Weekly
Cover Price: £0.65

ADVERTISING RATES:
Full Page Mono £3360.00
Full Page Colour £3710.00
SCC £6.00
Mechanical Data: Type Area: 560 x 366mm, Col Length: 560mm, Col Widths (Display): 34mm, Page Width: 366mm, Film: Digital, No. of Columns (Display): 10
Part of Series, see entry for: Cornish & Devon Post Series
LOCAL NEWSPAPERS: Local Newspapers English Counties

CAMELFORD, DELABOLE, BOSCASTLE & TINTAGEL JOURNAL GAZETTE
43417U72B-520_160
Frequency: Monthly
Cover Price: Free
ADVERTISING: Rates on application
Mechanical Data: Type Area: 360 x 255mm, Col Length: 360mm, Col Widths (Display): 34mm, No. of Columns (Display): 7, Page Width: 255mm, Film: Digital
Part of Series, see entry for: Cornish & Devon Post Series
LOCAL NEWSPAPERS: Local Newspapers English Counties

CAMPBELTOWN COURIER
44888U72D-220
Editorial Address: Main and Longrow South, CAMPBELTOWN, PA28 6AE **Tel:** 01586 554646
Fax: 01586 553006
Email: editor@campbeltowncourier.co.uk
Advertising Address: As above.
Email: adverts@campbeltowncourier.co.uk
Web site: http://www.campbeltowncourier.co.uk
Publisher: Wyvex Media Group
Frequency: Weekly - Published on Friday
Cover Price: £0.62
Circulation: 7,347 (ABC 01/01/2007 to 30/12/2007)
Editor: Joanne Simms; **Features Editor:** Joanne Simms;
Managing Director: Howard Bennett; **Advertising Manager:** Anne Martin; **Publisher:** Joan Bennett
ADVERTISING RATES:
Full Page Mono £1108.00
Full Page Colour £1300.00
SCC £4.25
Agency Commission: 10%
Mechanical Data: Col Length: 330mm, Col Widths (Display): 35mm, No. of Columns (Display): 7, Print Process: Web-fed offset litho, Film: Digital, Type Area: 330 x 263mm, Page Width: 263mm
Copy instructions: Copy Date: Tuesday prior to publication date
Average advertising content per issue: 60%
LOCAL NEWSPAPERS: Local Newspapers Scotland

THE CANNOCK & RUGELEY CHRONICLE
1682058U72B-2960_100
Frequency: Weekly
Cover Price: Free
Part of Series, see entry for: The Cannock & Lichfield Chronicle Series
LOCAL NEWSPAPERS: Local Newspapers English Counties

THE CANNOCK & LICHFIELD CHRONICLE SERIES
44289U72B-2960
Formerly: The Cannock & Rugeley Chronicle
Editorial Address: 51-53 Queen Street, WOLVERHAMPTON, WV1 1ES **Tel:** 01543 465304
Fax: 01902 319467
Email: cannockchron@expressandstar.co.uk
Advertising Address: Queens Square, CANNOCK, WS11 1EA **Tel:** 01543 506311 **Fax:** 01543 465308
Email: a.roberts@expressandstar.co.uk
Web site: http://www.yourchronicle.com
Publisher: Express & Star Ltd
Frequency: Weekly
Cover Price: Free
Circulation: 65,761 (Publisher's Statement)
Usual Pagination: 50
Editor: Mark Shipp; **Advertising Manager:** Alison Roberts
ADVERTISING RATES:
Full Page Mono £1476.00
Full Page Colour £1918.00
SCC £4.50
Mechanical Data: Type Area: 410 x 305mm, No. of Columns (Display): 9, Col Length: 410mm, Page Width: 305mm, Col Widths (Display): 32mm, Film: Digital
Copy instructions: Copy Date: Tuesday 1pm prior to publication date
Average advertising content per issue: 75%
Series owner and contact point for the following titles, see individual entries:
The Cannock & Rugeley Chronicle

The Lichfield & Burntwood Chronicle
LOCAL NEWSPAPERS: Local Newspapers English Counties

CANTERBURY EXTRA
43840U72B-1763_130
Frequency: Weekly
Cover Price: Free
Circulation: 56,865 (VFD 02/07/2007 to 30/12/2007)
ADVERTISING: Rates on application
Part of Series, see entry for: Canterbury Extra Series
LOCAL NEWSPAPERS: Local Newspapers English Counties

CANTERBURY EXTRA SERIES
43839U72B-1763
Editorial Address: Gazette House, 5-8 Estuary View Business Park, Boorman Way, WHITSTABLE, CT5 3SE
Tel: 01227 768181 **Fax:** 01227 762415
Email: kentishgazette@thekmgroup.co.uk
Advertising Address: As above. **Fax:** 01227 762327
Email: kbarry@thekmgroup.co.uk
Web site: http://www.kentonline.co.uk
Publisher: Kent Messenger Group
Frequency: Weekly
Cover Price: Free
Circulation: 107,124 (Combined Circulation)
Editor: Kathryn Tye; **News Editor:** Kathryn Tye
ADVERTISING: Rates on application
Agency Commission: 10%
Copy instructions: Copy Date: Friday 5pm prior to publication date
Average advertising content per issue: 74%
Series owner and contact point for the following titles, see individual entries:
Canterbury Extra
Herne Bay Extra
Thanet Extra
Whitstable Extra
LOCAL NEWSPAPERS: Local Newspapers English Counties

THE CARDIFF & SOUTH WALES ADVERTISER
1657766U72C-502
Editorial Address: 254 Cowbridge Road East, CARDIFF, CF5 1GZ **Tel:** 029 2040 2743 **Fax:** 029 2040 2744
Email: cardiff.advertiser@virgin.net
Advertising Address: As above. **Tel:** 029 2030 3900
Email: cardiff.advertiser@virgin.net
Publisher: Hot Press Publications
Frequency: Weekly - Published on Friday
Cover Price: Free
Circulation: 30,000 (Publisher's Statement)
Editor: David Hynes; **Advertising Manager:** Cheryl Willis
ADVERTISING RATES:
SCC £6.00
Agency Commission: 10%
Mechanical Data: Type Area: 350 x 285mm, Bleed Size: 365 x 300mm, Col Length: 350mm, Page Width: 285mm, No. of Columns (Display): 8, Film: Digital, Col Widths (Display): 33mm
Copy instructions: Copy Date: 1 week prior to publication date
Average advertising content per issue: 75%
LOCAL NEWSPAPERS: Local Newspapers Wales

CARDIFF POST SERIES
44771U72C-95
Editorial Address: 6 Park Street, CARDIFF, CF10 1XR
Tel: 029 2024 3600
Email: cardiff.post@mediawales.co.uk
Advertising Address: As above. **Tel:** 029 2022 3333
Email: denise.rich@mediawales.co.uk
Web site: http://www.icwales.co.uk
Publisher: Media Wales Ltd
Frequency: Weekly
Cover Price: Free
Circulation: 103,812 (Combined Circulation)
Editor: News Desk; **Advertisement Director:** Gerald Griffiths
ADVERTISING: Rates on application
Agency Commission: 10%
Mechanical Data: Film: Positive, right reading, emulsion side down, Type Area: 340 x 266mm, No. of Columns (Display): 8, Col Widths (Display): 32mm, Col Length: 340mm, Print Process: Web-fed offset litho, Page Width: 266mm
Copy instructions: Copy Date: Tuesday 5.30pm prior to publication date
Average advertising content per issue: 70%
Series owner and contact point for the following titles, see individual entries:
Barry Post
The Post Cardiff
LOCAL NEWSPAPERS: Local Newspapers Wales

CARDIGAN JOURNAL
706894U72C-220_120
Frequency: Weekly
Part of Series, see entry for: Journal Series (Carmarthen)
LOCAL NEWSPAPERS: Local Newspapers Wales

CARLUKE AND LANARK GAZETTE SERIES
44889U72D-230
Editorial Address: 3 High Street, CARLUKE, ML8 4AL
Tel: 01555 772226 **Fax:** 01555 771633
Email: clgazette@jnscotland.co.uk
Advertising Address: Redbrae Road, Camelon, FALKIRK, FK1 4AZ **Tel:** 01324 624959 **Fax:** 01324 629079
Email: clgazette@jnscotland.co.uk
Web site: http://www.carluketoday.co.uk
Publisher: Johnston Press plc
Date Established: 1906
Frequency: Weekly
Circulation: 12,363 (ABC 02/07/2007 to 30/12/2007)
Editor: Julie Currie; **Advertising Manager:** Anne Frew
ADVERTISING RATES:
Full Page Mono £2294.00
Full Page Colour £3441.00
SCC £3.80
Agency Commission: 10%
Mechanical Data: Film: Digital, Page Width: 333mm, Type Area: 550 x 333mm, Col Length: 550mm, No. of Columns (Display): 11, Col Widths (Display): 28mm
Copy instructions: Copy Date: Monday 12pm prior to publication date
Average advertising content per issue: 35%
Series owner and contact point for the following titles, see individual entries:
Carluke Gazette
Lanark Gazette
LOCAL NEWSPAPERS: Local Newspapers Scotland

CARLUKE GAZETTE
44890U72D-230_110
Frequency: Weekly
Cover Price: £0.42
Part of Series, see entry for: Carluke and Lanark Gazette Series
LOCAL NEWSPAPERS: Local Newspapers Scotland

CARMARTHEN JOURNAL
706993U72C-220_110
Frequency: Weekly
Part of Series, see entry for: Journal Series (Carmarthen)
LOCAL NEWSPAPERS: Local Newspapers Wales

CARRICK GAZETTE
44892U72D-236
Editorial Address: 32 Dalrymple Street, GIRVAN, KA26 9AE
Tel: 01465 712688 **Fax:** 01465 713775
Email: editorial@carrickgazette.com
Advertising Address: As above. **Tel:** 01465 714717
Email: vicky.bone@carrickgazette.com
Web site: http://www.carrickgazette.co.uk
Publisher: Johnston Press plc
Frequency: Weekly - Published on Thursday
Cover Price: £0.48
Circulation: 2,893 (ABC 02/07/2007 to 30/12/2007)
Editor: Alan Cameron; **Group Editor:** Archie Plunkett
ADVERTISING RATES:
Full Page Mono £1389.24
Full Page Colour £2086.92
SCC £4.54
Agency Commission: 10%
Mechanical Data: Type Area: 340 x 272mm, Col Length: 340mm, Col Widths (Display): 28mm, No. of Columns (Display): 9, Print Process: Web-fed offset litho, Film: Digital, Page Width: 272mm
Copy instructions: Copy Date: Monday 5pm prior to publication date
Average advertising content per issue: 50%
LOCAL NEWSPAPERS: Local Newspapers Scotland

CARRICK HERALD
44873U72D-90_140
Frequency: Weekly
Cover Price: £0.50
Part of Series, see entry for: Ayr Advertiser Series
LOCAL NEWSPAPERS: Local Newspapers Scotland

CARRICK TIMES AND EAST ANTRIM TIMES
45124U72E-226_120
Frequency: Weekly - Published on Thursday. Circulation figure is incorporated into the Larne Times & East Antrim Times
Cover Price: £0.90
Part of Series, see entry for: The Times Series
LOCAL NEWSPAPERS: Local Newspapers Northern Ireland

CARRICKFERGUS ADVERTISER AND EAST ANTRIM GAZETTE
768636U72E-55_141
Formerly: Carrickfergus Advertiser
Frequency: Weekly - see Ballyclare Gazette for circulation figure
Cover Price: £0.85
Part of Series, see entry for: East Antrim Gazette Series
LOCAL NEWSPAPERS: Local Newspapers Northern Ireland

CASTLE POINT ECHO INCLUDING RAYLEIGH & ROCHFORD
41982U67B-13_630
Formerly: Castle Point Evening Echo including Rayleigh & Rochford
Publisher: Newsquest (Essex) Ltd
Frequency: Mornings
Cover Price: £0.38
Edition of: Echo (Basildon)
REGIONAL DAILY & SUNDAY NEWSPAPERS: Regional Daily Newspapers

CATERHAM AND DISTRICT ADVERTISER
42970U72A-50_110
Frequency: Weekly - For circulation see Croydon Advertiser
Cover Price: £0.55
ADVERTISING RATES:
SCC £14.50
Part of Series, see entry for: Croydon Advertiser & Post Series
LOCAL NEWSPAPERS: Local Newspapers Greater London

CATERHAM MIRROR
44401U72B-3160_120
Frequency: Weekly - Circulation figure includes Horley and Gatwick Mirror Charlwood Smallfield Gatwick, Surrey Mirror Redhill, Reigate and Banstead and Surrey Mirror (Tandridge District Edition)
Cover Price: £0.40
Circulation: 11,826 (ABC 02/07/2007 to 30/12/2007)
Part of Series, see entry for: Surrey Mirror Series
LOCAL NEWSPAPERS: Local Newspapers English Counties

CENTRAL FIFE TIMES AND ADVERTISER
44893U72D-250
Editorial Address: 17 Bank Street, LOCHGELLY, KY5 9QQ
Tel: 01592 780342 **Fax:** 01592 784993
Email: timeseditor@dunfermlinepress.co.uk
Advertising Address: Dunfermline Press, Pitreavie Business Park, Queensferry Road, DUNFERMLINE, KY11 8QS
Tel: 01383 728201 **Fax:** 01383 737040
Email: advertising@dunfermlinepress.co.uk
Publisher: A. Romanes & Son Ltd
Date Established: 1892
Frequency: Weekly - Published every Thursday
Cover Price: £0.35
Circulation: 7,013 (ABC 02/07/2007 to 30/12/2007)
Editor: James Stark; **Advertising Manager:** Lynn Hubber
ADVERTISING RATES:
Full Page Mono £916.00
Full Page Colour £1832.00
SCC £3.47
Agency Commission: 10%
Mechanical Data: Type Area: 330 x 265.5mm, No. of Columns (Display): 8, Col Length: 330mm, Col Widths (Display): 31mm, Page Width: 265.5mm, Film: Digital
Copy instructions: Copy Date: Monday 4pm prior to publication date
LOCAL NEWSPAPERS: Local Newspapers Scotland

CENTRAL SOMERSET GAZETTE
44252U72B-2900_130
Frequency: Weekly - Circulation figure incorporated into the Cheddar Valley Gazette
Cover Price: £0.60
ADVERTISING RATES:
SCC £2.30
Part of Series, see entry for: Mid Somerset News & Media
LOCAL NEWSPAPERS: Local Newspapers English Counties

CHAD SERIES MANSFIELD
44172U72B-2580
Editorial Address: 121 Newgate Lane, MANSFIELD, NG18 2PA **Tel:** 01623 456789 **Fax:** 01623 464647
Email: newsdesk@chad.co.uk
Advertising Address: As above. **Tel:** 01623 464748
Fax: 01623 464749
Email: classified@chad.co.uk
Web site: http://www.chad.co.uk
Publisher: North Notts Newspapers Ltd
Date Established: 1952

Frequency: Weekly - Published on Wednesday
Circulation: 61,097 (Combined Circulation)
Editor: Ashley Booker; **News Editor:** Ashley Booker;
Managing Director: Dawn Sweeney; **Advertising Manager:** Samantha Bailey
ADVERTISING: Rates on application
Mechanical Data: Film: Digital, Type Area: 340 x 265mm, Page Width: 265mm, Col Length: 340mm, No. of Columns (Display): 9, Col Widths (Display): 27mm
Series owner and contact point for the following titles, see individual entries:
Alfreton Chad
Ashfield Chad
Mansfield Chad
Mansfield Woodhouse Chad
Rainworth Chad
Sherwood Chad
Shirebrook & Bolsover Chad
Warsop Chad
LOCAL NEWSPAPERS: Local Newspapers English Counties

THE CHALLENGE
44093U72B-2365
Formerly: Knowsley Challenge
Editorial Address: 36 Henry Street, LIVERPOOL, L1 5BS
Tel: 0151 706 7411 **Fax:** 0151 707 1678
Email: alan@merseymirror.com
Advertising Address: As above. **Tel:** 0151 709 7567
Email: andy@merseymirror.com
Web site: http://www.thechallenge.co.uk
Publisher: Mersey Mirror
Date Established: 1986
Frequency: Monthly - Published on the 2nd Monday in the month
Cover Price: Free
Circulation: 75,000 (Publisher's Statement)
Editor: Alan Birkett
ADVERTISING RATES:
Full Page Mono £910.00
Full Page Colour £1137.50
SCC £8.00
Agency Commission: 10%
Mechanical Data: Type Area: 335 x 262mm, Col Length: 335mm, Page Width: 262mm, No. of Columns (Display): 8, Col Widths (Display): 30mm, Film: Digital
Copy instructions: Copy Date: 1 week prior to publication date
Average advertising content per issue: 40%
LOCAL NEWSPAPERS: Local Newspapers English Counties

THE CHAPELTOWN AND DISTRICT JOURNAL
764747U72B-3712_120
Frequency: Weekly
Cover Price: Free
ADVERTISING RATES:
Full Page Mono £1138.32
Full Page Colour £1479.82
SCC £3.72
Part of Series, see entry for: Sheffield Journal Series
LOCAL NEWSPAPERS: Local Newspapers English Counties

CHARD ADVERTISER
1606278U72B-842_104
Formerly: Chard Advertiser & Clarion
Frequency: Weekly
Cover Price: Free
Circulation: 3,000 (Publisher's Statement)
Part of Series, see entry for: Pulmans Weekly News and Advertiser Series
LOCAL NEWSPAPERS: Local Newspapers English Counties

CHARD & ILMINSTER NEWS
44262U72B-3927
Editorial Address: 3A Fore Street, CHARD, TA20 1PH
Tel: 01460 238180 **Fax:** 01460 238188
Email: newsdesk@chardandilminsternews.co.uk
Advertising Address: As above. **Tel:** 01460 238170
Email: annie.corrick@chardandilminsternews.co.uk
Web site: http://www.chardandilminsternews.co.uk
ISSN: 0962-5089
Publisher: Newsquest (Media Group) Ltd
Date Established: 1874
Frequency: Weekly - Published on Wednesday
Cover Price: £0.40
Circulation: 7,677 (ABC 01/01/2007 to 30/12/2007)
Editor: Steve Sowder; **Editor-in-Chief:** Ken Bird
ADVERTISING RATES:
Full Page Mono £642.60
Full Page Colour £803.25
SCC £2.95
Agency Commission: 10%
Mechanical Data: Type Area: 315 x 264mm, Col Length: 315mm, Col Widths (Display): 28mm, No. of Columns

(Display): 9, Print Process: Web-fed offset litho, Film: Digital, Page Width: 264mm
Copy instructions: Copy Date: Friday 12pm prior to publication date
Average advertising content per issue: 40%
Supplement(s): On The Move - 52xY
LOCAL NEWSPAPERS: Local Newspapers English Counties

CHASE POST CANNOCK
44297U72B-2965_150
Frequency: Weekly
Cover Price: Free
Part of Series, see entry for: Chase Post Series Burntwood & Cannock
LOCAL NEWSPAPERS: Local Newspapers English Counties

CHASE POST SERIES BURNTWOOD & CANNOCK
44295U72B-2965
Editorial Address: 103-106 High Green Court, Newhall Street, CANNOCK, WS11 1AB **Tel:** 01543 501700
Fax: 01543 501759
Email: chase_post@mrn.co.uk
Advertising Address: As above.
Email: shaun_ricks@mrn.co.uk
Web site: http://www.iccannock.co.uk
Publisher: Trinity Mirror Midlands
Frequency: Weekly - Published on Thursday
Cover Price: Free
Circulation: 49,453 (VFD 13/08/2007 to 30/12/2007)
Usual Pagination: 104
Editor: Mike Lockley; **Advertising Manager:** Eve Corbett
ADVERTISING RATES:
Full Page Mono £2692.80
Full Page Colour £3635.28
SCC £8.80
Agency Commission: 10%
Mechanical Data: Type Area: 340 x 272mm, Col Length: 340mm, Col Widths (Display): 28mm, Page Width: 272mm, No. of Columns (Display): 9, Film: Digital
Copy instructions: Copy Date: Tuesday 5pm prior to publication date
Average advertising content per issue: 70%
Series owner and contact point for the following titles, see individual entries:
The Burntwood Post
Chase Post Cannock
LOCAL NEWSPAPERS: Local Newspapers English Counties

CHASE POST SERIES (LICHFIELD & RUGELEY)
44292U72B-2963
Editorial Address: 33 Bore Street, LICHFIELD, WS13 6LZ
Tel: 01543 258523 **Fax:** 01543 418251
Email: chase_post@mrn.co.uk
Advertising Address: 103-106 High Green Court, Newhall Street, CANNOCK, WS11 1GR **Tel:** 01543 501700
Fax: 01543 501759
Email: eve_corbett@mrn.co.uk
Web site: http://www.iclichfield.co.uk
Publisher: Midland Weekly Media
Frequency: Weekly - Published on Thursday
Cover Price: Free
Circulation: 27,653 (VFD 02/07/2007 to 30/12/2007)
Usual Pagination: 48
Editor: Theresa Bradley; **Advertising Manager:** Eve Corbett
ADVERTISING RATES:
SCC £4.10
Agency Commission: 10%
Mechanical Data: Type Area: 340 x 264mm, Col Length: 340mm, Col Widths (Display): 28mm, No. of Columns (Display): 9, Page Width: 264mm, Film: Digital
Copy instructions: Copy Date: Tuesday 5pm prior to publication date
Average advertising content per issue: 65%
Series owner and contact point for the following titles, see individual entries:
Lichfield Post
Rugeley Post
LOCAL NEWSPAPERS: Local Newspapers English Counties

CHEADLE & TEAN TIMES
44300U72B-2970_120
Frequency: Weekly - Published on Wednesday
Cover Price: £0.40
Part of Series, see entry for: Cheadle Times & Echo Series
LOCAL NEWSPAPERS: Local Newspapers English Counties

CHEADLE POST & TIMES
44311U72B-3005_120
Frequency: Weekly
Cover Price: £0.45
Circulation: 1,774 (ABC 02/07/2007 to 30/12/2007)

ADVERTISING RATES:
Full Page Mono £633.60
Full Page Colour £792.00
Part of Series, see entry for: Post & Times Series
LOCAL NEWSPAPERS: Local Newspapers English Counties

CHEADLE TIMES & ECHO SERIES
44298U72B-2970
Editorial Address: 18 Tape Street, Cheadle, STOKE-ON-TRENT, ST10 1BD **Tel:** 01538 752214 **Fax:** 01538 754465
Email: news@timesandecho.co.uk
Advertising Address: As above.
Email: adv@timesandecho.co.uk
Publisher: Times & Echo Newspapers
Frequency: Weekly - Published on Wednesday
Cover Price: £0.40
Circulation: 11,000 (Publisher's Statement)
Editor: Julie Bull; **Advertising Manager:** Lynn Smith
ADVERTISING RATES:
Full Page Mono £712.80
Full Page Colour £855.36
SCC £3.30
Agency Commission: 10%
Mechanical Data: Col Length: 360mm, Col Widths (Display): 41mm, No. of Columns (Display): 6, Page Width: 266mm, Film: Digital, Type Area: 360 x 266mm
Copy instructions: Copy Date: Tuesday 12pm prior to publication date
Average advertising content per issue: 60%
Series owner and contact point for the following titles, see individual entries:
Blythe & Forsbrook Times
Cheadle & Tean Times
Uttoxeter Echo
LOCAL NEWSPAPERS: Local Newspapers English Counties

CHEDDAR VALLEY GAZETTE
44253U72B-2900_140
Frequency: Weekly - Circulation figure includes the Central Somerset Gazette
Cover Price: £0.60
Circulation: 9,473 (ABC 02/07/2007 to 30/12/2007)
ADVERTISING RATES:
SCC £2.30
Part of Series, see entry for: Mid Somerset News & Media
LOCAL NEWSPAPERS: Local Newspapers English Counties

CHELMSFORD WEEKLY NEWS
43598U72B-990_120
Formerly: Chelmsford & South Woodham Weekly News
Frequency: Weekly
Cover Price: Free
Circulation: 47,517 (VFD 02/07/2007 to 30/12/2007)
ADVERTISING RATES:
Full Page Mono £700.00
Full Page Colour £795.00
SCC £4.30
Part of Series, see entry for: Weekly News Series (Chelmsford)
LOCAL NEWSPAPERS: Local Newspapers English Counties

CHELTENHAM NEWS
43659U72B-1125_100
Date Established: 1874
Frequency: Weekly - Circulation figure includes the Tewkesbury News
Cover Price: Free
Circulation: 24,772 (VFD 02/07/2007 to 30/12/2007)
Mechanical Data: Col Length: 360mm, No. of Columns (Display): 8
Part of Series, see entry for: Gloucester and Cheltenham News Series
LOCAL NEWSPAPERS: Local Newspapers English Counties

CHERTSEY, ADDLESTONE & BYFLEET HERALD
719139U72B-3137_110
Formerly: Chertsey Herald
Frequency: Weekly - Circulation figure also includes the Staines & Ashford News, the Staines & Egham News, the Sunbury & Shepperton Herald, the Walton & Weybridge Herald and the Woking Herald. Published on Wednesday
Cover Price: £0.35
Circulation: 13,916 (ABC 02/07/2007 to 30/12/2007)
Part of Series, see entry for: Staines Informer Series
LOCAL NEWSPAPERS: Local Newspapers English Counties

Non-National Newspapers

CHESHUNT AND WALTHAM MERCURY
43808U72B-1560_110
Frequency: Weekly
Cover Price: £0.60
Circulation: 5,779 (Publisher's Statement)
Part of Series, see entry for: Mercury Series (Hoddesdon)
LOCAL NEWSPAPERS: Local Newspapers English Counties

CHESTER AND DISTRICT STANDARD
1638970U72B-425_100
Frequency: Weekly
Cover Price: Free
Circulation: 57,191 (VFD 02/07/2007 to 30/12/2007)
ADVERTISING: Rates on application
Part of Series, see entry for: Chester Standard Series
LOCAL NEWSPAPERS: Local Newspapers English Counties

THE CHESTER CHRONICLE CITY EDITION
43351U72B-430_120
Formerly: Chronicle Chester City Edition
Frequency: Weekly - Published on Thursday. Circulation figure includes the Chronicle Chester County Edition, the Chronicle Fordsham and Helsby
Cover Price: £0.70
Circulation: 25,943 (ABC 02/07/2007 to 30/12/2007)
ADVERTISING RATES:
SCC £10.61
Part of Series, see entry for: Chester Chronicle Series
LOCAL NEWSPAPERS: Local Newspapers English Counties

THE CHESTER CHRONICLE COUNTRY EDITION
43352U72B-430_122
Formerly: Chronicle Chester Country Edition
Frequency: Weekly - Published on Thursday. Circulation figure is incorporated into the Chronicle Chester City Edition
Cover Price: £0.70
ADVERTISING RATES:
SCC £10.61
Part of Series, see entry for: Chester Chronicle Series
LOCAL NEWSPAPERS: Local Newspapers English Counties

CHESTER CHRONICLE SERIES
43350U72B-430
Formerly: Chronicle Series Chester
Editorial Address: Chronicle House, Commonhall Street, CHESTER, CH1 2AA **Tel:** 01244 340151 **Fax:** 01244 606498
Email: newsroom@cheshirenews.co.uk
Advertising Address: As above. **Fax:** 01244 606398
Email: chris.connolly@cheshirenews.co.uk
Web site: http://www.iccheshireonline.co.uk
Publisher: Trinity Mirror Cheshire
Date Established: 1775
Frequency: Weekly - Published on Tuesday and Thursday
Circulation: 85,077 (Combined Circulation)
Editor: Michael Green; **News Editor:** Barry Ellams; **Editor-in-Chief:** Eric Langton; **Managing Director:** Warren Butcher; **Advertising Manager:** Louise Barlow
ADVERTISING: Rates on application
Mechanical Data: No. of Columns (Display): 8, Type Area: 380 x 276mm, Col Length: 380mm, Page Width: 276mm, Film: Digital
Series owner and contact point for the following titles, see individual entries:
The Chester Chronicle City Edition
The Chester Chronicle Country Edition
Chronicle Extra
The Frodsham & Helsby Chronicle
Supplement(s): Classified - 52xY, The Guide - 52xY, Motoring - 52xY, Property - 52xY, Your Home - 52xY
LOCAL NEWSPAPERS: Local Newspapers English Counties

CHESTER EVENING LEADER
42230U67B-2080_530
Frequency: Evenings - Published Monday to Friday, Friday edition is published in the morning
ADVERTISING RATES:
SCC £8.50
Edition of: Evening Leader
REGIONAL DAILY & SUNDAY NEWSPAPERS: Regional Daily Newspapers

CHESTER STANDARD SERIES
43347U72B-425
Formerly: Chester and District Standard
Editorial Address: Linenhall House, Stanley Street, CHESTER, CH1 2LR **Tel:** 01244 304500 **Fax:** 01244 400022

Email: news@chesterstandard.co.uk
Advertising Address: As above. **Fax:** 01244 351536
Email: linda.johns@chesterstandard.co.uk
Web site: http://www.chesterstandard.co.uk
Publisher: NWN Media Ltd
Frequency: Weekly - Published on Thursday
Cover Price: Free
Circulation: 90,394 (VFD 02/07/2007 to 30/12/2007)
Editor: Paul Chamberlain; **Advertising Manager:** Linda Johns
ADVERTISING: Rates on application
Agency Commission: 10%
Copy instructions: Copy Date: Monday 5pm prior to publication date
Average advertising content per issue: 60%
Series owner and contact point for the following titles, see individual entries:
Chester and District Standard
Ellesmere Port and Neston Standard
Supplement(s): Lifestyle - 4xY, Property - 52xY
LOCAL NEWSPAPERS: Local Newspapers English Counties

CHESTERFIELD ADVERTISER
43472U72B-691_110
Frequency: Weekly
Cover Price: Free
Circulation: 53,265 (VFD 02/07/2007 to 30/12/2007)
ADVERTISING: Rates on application
Part of Series, see entry for: Chesterfield & Dronfield Advertiser Series
LOCAL NEWSPAPERS: Local Newspapers English Counties

CHESTERFIELD & DRONFIELD ADVERTISER SERIES
43470U72B-691
Editorial Address: 37 Station Road, CHESTERFIELD, S41 7XD **Tel:** 01246 504523 **Fax:** 01246 504579
Email: don.collins@derbyshiretimes.co.uk
Advertising Address: As above. **Tel:** 01246 504504
Fax: 01246 504557
Email: advertising@derbyshiretimes.co.uk
Publisher: Derbyshire Times Newspaper Group
Frequency: Weekly - Published on Wednesday and Friday
Cover Price: Free
Circulation: 74,963 (Combined Circulation)
Usual Pagination: 24
Editor: Don Collins
ADVERTISING: Rates on application
Agency Commission: 10%
Copy instructions: Copy Date: 1 week prior to publication date
Average advertising content per issue: 40%
Series owner and contact point for the following titles, see individual entries:
Bolsover Advertiser
Chesterfield Advertiser
Dronfield Advertiser
LOCAL NEWSPAPERS: Local Newspapers English Counties

CHESTERFIELD EXPRESS
43474U72B-692
Editorial Address: 37 Station Road, CHESTERFIELD, S41 7XD **Tel:** 01246 504675 **Fax:** 01246 504579
Email: chesterfield.express@derbyshiretimes.co.uk
Advertising Address: As above. **Tel:** 01246 504500
Fax: 01246 504557
Email: emma.wild@derbyshiretimes.co.uk
Web site: http://www.chesterfieldtoday.co.uk
Publisher: Derbyshire Times Newspaper Group
Frequency: Weekly - Published on Wednesday
Cover Price: Free
Circulation: 34,842 (VFD 02/07/2007 to 30/12/2007)
Editor: Allison Glossop
ADVERTISING RATES:
SCC £4.94
Mechanical Data: Film: Digital, Type Area: 340 x 271mm, No. of Columns (Display): 9, Col Length: 340mm, Page Width: 271mm
Copy instructions: Copy Date: Monday 11.00am prior to publication date
LOCAL NEWSPAPERS: Local Newspapers English Counties

CHEW VALLEY GAZETTE
43210U72B-21
Editorial Address: 5 South Parade, Chew Magna, BRISTOL, BS40 8SH **Tel:** 01275 332266 **Fax:** 01275 333067
Email: editorial@chewvalleygazette.co.uk
Advertising Address: As above.
Email: a.colston@chewvalleygazette.co.uk
Web site: http://www.chewvalleygazette.co.uk
Publisher: Chew Valley Gazette Ltd
Date Established: 1984

Frequency: Monthly
Cover Price: Free
Circulation: 14,500 (Publisher's Statement)
Usual Pagination: 48
Editor: Rowland Janes; **Advertising Manager:** Alison Colston
ADVERTISING RATES:
Full Page Mono £625.85
Full Page Colour £782.31
SCC £4.00
Agency Commission: 10%
Mechanical Data: Page Width: 270mm, Col Length: 360mm, No. of Columns (Display): 8, Col Widths (Display): 30mm, Type Area: 360 x 270mm
Average advertising content per issue: 50%
LOCAL NEWSPAPERS: Local Newspapers English Counties

CHICHESTER OBSERVER
44470U72B-3326_140
Frequency: Weekly
Part of Series, see entry for: Southdown Observer Series
LOCAL NEWSPAPERS: Local Newspapers English Counties

THE CHISWICK
1817454U72A-510_142
Frequency: Weekly
Cover Price: Free
Circulation: 18,831 (Publisher's Statement)
Part of Series, see entry for: Times Series (Richmond)
LOCAL NEWSPAPERS: Local Newspapers Greater London

CHOBHAM NEWS & MAIL INCORPORATING WINDLESHAM, BISLEY & WEST END
44418U72B-3169_150
Formerly: Chobham & Windlesham News & Mail
Frequency: Weekly
Cover Price: £0.32
Part of Series, see entry for: Woking News & Mail Series
LOCAL NEWSPAPERS: Local Newspapers English Counties

CHORLEY CITIZEN
1840315U72B-4156
Editorial Address: Nwespaper House, High Street, BLACKBURN, BB1 1HT **Tel:** 01254 298252
Fax: 01254 680429
Email: cgee@lancashirenewsquest.co.uk
Web site: http://www.thisislancashire.co.uk
Publisher: Newsquest Lancashire Limited
Frequency: Weekly - Published on Wednesday
Cover Price: Free
Circulation: 32,921 (VFD 02/07/2007 to 30/12/2007)
Editor: Chris Gee
ADVERTISING: Rates on application
LOCAL NEWSPAPERS: Local Newspapers English Counties

CHORLEY GUARDIAN
43965U72B-1950_130
Frequency: Weekly
Cover Price: £0.55
Part of Series, see entry for: Chorley Guardian Series
LOCAL NEWSPAPERS: Local Newspapers English Counties

CHORLEY GUARDIAN SERIES
43964U72B-1950
Editorial Address: 32A Market Street, CHORLEY, PR7 2RY **Tel:** 01257 264911 **Fax:** 01257 241358
Email: guardiannews@lep.co.uk
Advertising Address: Olivers Place, Fulwood, PRESTON, PR2 9ZA **Tel:** 01772 838050 **Fax:** 01772 204941
Email: katie.meiler@lep.co.uk
Web site: http://www.chorley-guardian.co.uk
Publisher: Lancashire Evening Post Ltd
Date Established: 1871
Frequency: Weekly - Published every Wednesday
Circulation: 13,664 (ABC 02/07/2007 to 30/12/2007)
Editor: Chris Maguire
ADVERTISING RATES:
Full Page Mono £1453.50
Full Page Colour £1891.08
SCC £4.75
Agency Commission: 10%
Mechanical Data: Type Area: 340 x 274mm, Page Width: 274mm, Film: Digital, Col Length: 340mm, No. of Columns (Display): 9
Copy instructions: Copy Date: Monday 5pm prior to publication date
Average advertising content per issue: 64%
Series owner and contact point for the following titles, see individual entries:
Chorley Guardian

Leyland Guardian
Supplement(s): First Class - 1xY, Guardian Angels - 1xY
LOCAL NEWSPAPERS: Local Newspapers English Counties

CHRISTCHURCH ADVERTISER

43554U72B-902_120

Frequency: Weekly
Cover Price: Free
Circulation: 22,120 (VFD 02/07/2007 to 30/12/2007)
ADVERTISING: Rates on application
Part of Series, see entry for: Advertiser Series (Poole & Swanage)
LOCAL NEWSPAPERS: Local Newspapers English Counties

THE CHRONICLE

43389U72B-482

Formerly: Northwich Chronicle & Mail Series
Editorial Address: Chronicle House, Commonhall Street, CHESTER, CH1 2AA **Tel:** 01244 606415
Email: midcheshire.news@cheshirenews.co.uk
Advertising Address: As above.
Email: trade.ads@buysell.co.uk
Web site: http://www.midcheshirechronicle.co.uk
Publisher: Trinity Mirror Cheshire
Frequency: Weekly - Published on Wednesday
Cover Price: Free
Circulation: 15,000 (Publisher's Statement)
Usual Pagination: 50
Editor: Andrew Bowan; **Managing Director:** Warren Butcher; **Advertising Manager:** Lena Edmondson
ADVERTISING: Rates on application
LOCAL NEWSPAPERS: Local Newspapers English Counties

CHRONICLE & JOURNAL SERIES

44231U72B-2812

Editorial Address: Chronicle House, Castle Foregate, SHREWSBURY, SY1 2DN **Tel:** 01743 248248
Fax: 01743 365242
Email: jbutterworth@shropshirestar.co.uk
Advertising Address: Ketley, TELFORD, TF1 5HU
Tel: 01952 242424 **Fax:** 01952 222451
Email: adverts@shropshirestar.co.uk
Web site: http://www.shrewsburychronicle.com
Publisher: Shropshire Newspapers Ltd
Frequency: Weekly
Circulation: 87,901 (Combined Circulation)
Editor: John Butterworth; **Managing Director:** Steve Brown; **Managing Editor:** John Butterworth
ADVERTISING: Rates on application
Agency Commission: 10%
Mechanical Data: Type Area: 410 x 305mm, Col Length: 410mm, Print Process: Web-fed offset litho, Film: Digital, Page Width: 305mm, Col Widths (Display): 35mm, No. of Columns (Display): 8
Copy instructions: Copy Date: 3 days prior to publication date
Average advertising content per issue: 60%
Series owner and contact point for the following titles, see individual entries:
Hereford & Leominster Journal
Ludlow Journal
Mid Wales Journal
North Shropshire Chronicle
Shrewsbury Chronicle
South Shropshire Journal
LOCAL NEWSPAPERS: Local Newspapers English Counties

THE CHRONICLE AND LEADER SERIES (COLERAINE)

45065U72E-60

Formerly: The Chronicle (Coleraine)
Editorial Address: 20 Railway Road, COLERAINE, BT52 1PD **Tel:** 028 7034 3344 **Fax:** 028 7034 3606
Email: editor@thechronicle.uk.com
Advertising Address: As above. **Fax:** 028 7032 9889
Email: advertising@northernnewspapers.co.uk
Web site: http://www.ulsternet-ni.co.uk
Publisher: Northern Alpha Newspaper Group
Frequency: Weekly
Circulation: 43,841 (Combined Circulation)
Editor: John Fillis; **News Editor:** John Fillis; **Managing Director:** Mary Taylor; **Publisher:** Mary Taylor
ADVERTISING RATES:
Full Page Mono £2557.00
Full Page Colour £4346.90
SCC £4.65
Agency Commission: 10%
Mechanical Data: Page Width: 336mm, Col Length: 550mm, Col Widths (Display): 31mm, Film: Digital, No. of Columns (Display): 10, Type Area: 550 x 336mm, Print Process: Web-fed offset litho

Copy instructions: Copy Date: Monday 4pm prior to publication date
Average advertising content per issue: 40%
Series owner and contact point for the following titles, see individual entries:
The Chronicle (Ballycastle)
The Chronicle (Ballymoney)
The Chronicle (Coleraine)
The Chronicle (Limavady)
The Leader (Coleraine)
LOCAL NEWSPAPERS: Local Newspapers Northern Ireland

THE CHRONICLE (BALLYCASTLE)

1668508U72E-60_103

Frequency: Weekly - See The Chronicle (Coleraine) for circulation figure
Cover Price: £0.85
Part of Series, see entry for: The Chronicle and Leader Series (Coleraine)
LOCAL NEWSPAPERS: Local Newspapers Northern Ireland

THE CHRONICLE (BALLYMONEY)

1668507U72E-60_102

Frequency: Weekly - See The Chronicle (Coleraine) for circulation figure
Cover Price: £0.85
Part of Series, see entry for: The Chronicle and Leader Series (Coleraine)
LOCAL NEWSPAPERS: Local Newspapers Northern Ireland

THE CHRONICLE (COLERAINE)

1655118U72E-60_101

Frequency: Weekly - Circulation figure includes The Chronicle (Ballycastle), The Chronicle (Limavady) and The Chronicle (Ballymoney)
Cover Price: £0.85
Circulation: 14,841 (ABC 02/07/2007 to 30/12/2007)
Part of Series, see entry for: The Chronicle and Leader Series (Coleraine)
LOCAL NEWSPAPERS: Local Newspapers Northern Ireland

CHRONICLE EXTRA

1750470U72B-430_132

Formerly: Midweek Chronicle
Frequency: Weekly - Published on Monday
Cover Price: Free
Circulation: 59,134 (VFD 02/07/2007 to 30/12/2007)
ADVERTISING RATES:
SCC £10.61
Part of Series, see entry for: Chester Chronicle Series
LOCAL NEWSPAPERS: Local Newspapers English Counties

CHRONICLE EXTRA DERWENTSIDE

1809851U72B-3362_251

Frequency: Weekly
Cover Price: Free
Circulation: 29,229 (Publisher's Statement)
ADVERTISING RATES:
SCC £4.10
Part of Series, see entry for: Chronicle Extra Series (Tyne & Wear)
LOCAL NEWSPAPERS: Local Newspapers English Counties

CHRONICLE EXTRA GATESHEAD

44485U72B-3362_150

Formerly: Herald & Post Gateshead
Frequency: Weekly
Cover Price: Free
Circulation: 56,659 (VFD 03/07/2006 to 31/12/2006)
ADVERTISING RATES:
SCC £8.05
Part of Series, see entry for: Chronicle Extra Series (Tyne & Wear)
LOCAL NEWSPAPERS: Local Newspapers English Counties

CHRONICLE EXTRA NEWCASTLE

44487U72B-3362_180

Formerly: Herald & Post Newcastle
Frequency: Weekly
Cover Price: Free
Circulation: 84,431 (VFD 03/07/2006 to 31/12/2006)
ADVERTISING RATES:
SCC £13.85

Part of Series, see entry for: Chronicle Extra Series (Tyne & Wear)
LOCAL NEWSPAPERS: Local Newspapers English Counties

CHRONICLE EXTRA NORTH TYNESIDE

44488U72B-3362_190

Formerly: Herald & Post North Tyneside
Frequency: Weekly
Cover Price: Free
Circulation: 66,255 (VFD 03/07/2006 to 31/12/2006)
ADVERTISING RATES:
SCC £7.95
Part of Series, see entry for: Chronicle Extra Series (Tyne & Wear)
LOCAL NEWSPAPERS: Local Newspapers English Counties

CHRONICLE EXTRA SERIES (TYNE & WEAR)

44484U72B-3362

Formerly: Herald & Post Series (Tyne & Wear)
Editorial Address: Groat Market, NEWCASTLE UPON TYNE, NE1 1ED **Tel:** 0191 232 7500 **Fax:** 0191 232236
Email: extra.newsdesk@ncjmedia.co.uk
Advertising Address: As above. **Fax:** 0191 230 0241
Email: sue.mcewan@ncjmedia.co.uk
Web site: http://www.icnewcastle.co.uk
Publisher: Trinity Mirror
Frequency: Weekly - Published on Wednesday
Cover Price: Free
Circulation: 387,488 (Combined Circulation)
Usual Pagination: 40
Editor: Zoe Burn; **News Editor:** Zoe Burn; **Advertising Manager:** Sue McEwan
ADVERTISING: Rates on application
Mechanical Data: Type Area: 350 x 278mm, Col Length: 350mm, No. of Columns (Display): 8, Print Process: Web offset, Film: Digital, Page Width: 278mm
Series owner and contact point for the following titles, see individual entries:
Chronicle Extra Derwentside
Chronicle Extra Gateshead
Chronicle Extra Newcastle
Chronicle Extra North Tyneside
Chronicle Extra South Tyneside
The Chronicle Extra Tyne West
Journal Extra
LOCAL NEWSPAPERS: Local Newspapers English Counties

CHRONICLE EXTRA SOUTH TYNESIDE

44490U72B-3362_250

Formerly: South Tyneside Herald & Post
Frequency: Weekly
Cover Price: Free
Circulation: 51,141 (VFD 06/11/2006 to 31/12/2006)
ADVERTISING RATES:
SCC £7.95
Part of Series, see entry for: Chronicle Extra Series (Tyne & Wear)
LOCAL NEWSPAPERS: Local Newspapers English Counties

THE CHRONICLE EXTRA TYNE WEST

1835744U72B-3362_252

Editorial Address: For all contact details see main record, Chronicle Extra Series (Tyne & Wear)
Frequency: Weekly
Cover Price: Free
Circulation: 29,000 (Publisher's Statement)
ADVERTISING RATES:
SCC £5.00
Part of Series, see entry for: Chronicle Extra Series (Tyne & Wear)
LOCAL NEWSPAPERS: Local Newspapers English Counties

THE CHRONICLE (GREAT BARR)

44524U72B-3418_160

Formerly: The Chronicle (Great Barr & Erdington)
Frequency: Weekly
Cover Price: Free
Circulation: 38,339 (VFD 03/07/2006 to 31/12/2006)
ADVERTISING RATES:
SCC £3.50
Part of Series, see entry for: Sandwell and Great Barr Chronicle Series
LOCAL NEWSPAPERS: Local Newspapers English Counties

Non-National Newspapers

THE CHRONICLE (LIMAVADY)
1668509U72E-60_104

Frequency: Weekly - See The Chronicle (Coleraine) for circulation figure
Cover Price: £0.85
Part of Series, see entry for: The Chronicle and Leader Series (Coleraine)
LOCAL NEWSPAPERS: Local Newspapers Northern Ireland

THE CHRONICLE (SANDBACH & MIDDLEWICH EDITION)
43356U72B-435_130

Formerly: Chronicle (Sandbach)
Frequency: Weekly - Circulation figure is incorporated into the Crewe Chronicle
Cover Price: £0.50
Part of Series, see entry for: Chronicle Series (Crewe)
LOCAL NEWSPAPERS: Local Newspapers English Counties

THE CHRONICLE (SANDWELL)
44525U72B-3418_200

Frequency: Weekly
Cover Price: Free
Circulation: 56,201 (VFD 03/07/2006 to 31/12/2006)
ADVERTISING RATES:
SCC £4.50
Part of Series, see entry for: Sandwell and Great Barr Chronicle Series
LOCAL NEWSPAPERS: Local Newspapers English Counties

CHRONICLE SERIES
43852U72B-1773

Formerly: Chronicle Series Kent
Editorial Address: Winterton House, High Street, WESTERHAM, TN16 1AT **Tel:** 01959 564766
Email: editorial.chronicle@internet-today.co.uk
Advertising Address: As above. **Fax:** 01959 562760
Email: paul.k@internet-today.co.uk
Publisher: Biggin Hill News Ltd
Date Established: 1994
Frequency: Monthly
Cover Price: Free
Circulation: 17,100 (Combined Circulation)
Usual Pagination: 20
Editor: Sigrid Sherrell
ADVERTISING RATES:
Full Page Mono £1496.00
Full Page Colour £1645.00
SCC £5.50
Agency Commission: 10%
Mechanical Data: Page Width: 265mm, Film: Digital, Type Area: 340 x 265mm, Col Length: 340mm, No. of Columns (Display): 8, Col Widths (Display): 29mm
Average advertising content per issue: 30%
Series owner and contact point for the following titles, see individual entries:
Edenbridge Chronicle
Tandridge Chronicle
LOCAL NEWSPAPERS: Local Newspapers English Counties

CHRONICLE SERIES (CREWE)
43355U72B-435

Editorial Address: 32-34 Victoria Street, CREWE, CW1 2JE **Tel:** 01270 255733 **Fax:** 01270 502439
Email: crewe.news@cheshirenews.co.uk
Advertising Address: As above. **Tel:** 01270 502400
Fax: 01270 502418
Email: crewe.advertising@cheshirenews.co.uk
Web site: http://www.cheshirenews.co.uk
Publisher: Trinity Mirror Cheshire
Frequency: Weekly - Published on Wednesday
Circulation: 42,988 (Combined Circulation)
Usual Pagination: 100
Editor: David Fox; **News Editor:** Antonia Merola
ADVERTISING RATES:
SCC £9.07
Agency Commission: 10%
Mechanical Data: Type Area: 350 x 272mm, Col Length: 350mm, Page Width: 272mm, Film: Digital
Series owner and contact point for the following titles, see individual entries:
The Chronicle (Sandbach & Middlewich Edition)
Crewe Chronicle
Crewe Mail
Nantwich Chronicle
LOCAL NEWSPAPERS: Local Newspapers English Counties

CHRONICLE WEEKEND OLDHAM
43693U72B-1185

Editorial Address: PO Box 47, 172 Union Street, OLDHAM, OL1 1EQ **Tel:** 0161 633 2121 **Fax:** 0161 652 2111
Email: editorial@oldham-chronicle.co.uk
Advertising Address: As above. **Fax:** 0161 627 0905
Email: jcwhitt@oldham-chronicle.co.uk
Web site: http://www.oldham-chronicle.co.uk
Publisher: Hirst Kidd & Rennie Ltd
Frequency: Weekly
Cover Price: Free
Circulation: 68,414 (Publisher's Statement)
Editor: Jim Williams; **News Editor:** Mike Attenborough; **Features Editor:** Paul Genty; **Managing Director:** Philip Hirst; **Advertising Manager:** Jim Whittingham
ADVERTISING RATES:
Full Page Mono £1007.76
Full Page Colour £1360.48
SCC £4.94
Agency Commission: 10%
Mechanical Data: Page Width: 265mm, Film: Digital, Type Area: 340 x 265mm, Col Length: 340mm, Col Widths (Display): 41mm, No. of Columns (Display): 6, Print Process: Offset litho
Copy instructions: Copy Date: Monday prior to publication date
Average advertising content per issue: 65%
LOCAL NEWSPAPERS: Local Newspapers English Counties

THE CITIZEN (BURY ST. EDMUNDS & THETFORD)
44329U72B-3071_154

Frequency: Weekly
Cover Price: Free
Circulation: 24,600 (Publisher's Statement)
Part of Series, see entry for: Bury Free Press & Citizen Series
LOCAL NEWSPAPERS: Local Newspapers English Counties

CITIZEN FIRST
43312U72B-310_190

Formerly: Tuesday Citizen
Frequency: Weekly
Cover Price: Free
Circulation: 86,518 (VFD 02/07/2007 to 30/12/2007)
ADVERTISING: Rates on application
Part of Series, see entry for: Milton Keynes Citizen Series
LOCAL NEWSPAPERS: Local Newspapers English Counties

THE CITIZEN (GLOUCESTER)
42063U67B-240

Editorial Address: 1 Clarence Parade, Cheltenham, GLOUCESTER, GL50 3NY **Tel:** 01452 420621
Fax: 01452 420664
Email: citizen.news@glosmedia.co.uk
Advertising Address: As above. **Tel:** 01452 424442
Email: kerry.stoddart@glosmedia.co.uk
Web site: http://www.thisisgloucestershire.co.uk
Publisher: Gloucestershire Media
Date Established: 1876
Frequency: Mornings
Cover Price: £0.37
Circulation: 26,259 (ABC 02/07/2007 to 30/12/2007)
Editor: Sally Munro; **Advertising Director:** Kerry Stoddart
ADVERTISING RATES:
Full Page Mono £2016.00
Full Page Colour £2520.00
SCC £7.00
Agency Commission: 10%
Mechanical Data: Col Length: 360mm, Type Area:'360 x 275mm, Film: Digital, No. of Columns (Display): 8, Page Width: 275mm
Copy instructions: Copy Date: 3 days prior to publication date
Editions:
Weekend Citizen
Supplement(s): Business (The Citizen (Gloucester)) - 52xY, Eating Out - 52xY, Going Out - 52xY, Jobs - 52xY, Motoring - 52xY, Property - 52xY, Sport Monday - 52xY, Weekend Magazine - 52xY, Young Sport - 104xY
REGIONAL DAILY & SUNDAY NEWSPAPERS: Regional Daily Newspapers

THE CITIZEN (LYNN & DISTRICT)
44126U72B-2429

Formerly: Citizen Series (Lynn & District)
Editorial Address: 57 Priestgate, PETERBOROUGH, PE1 1JW **Tel:** 01553 761188 **Fax:** 01553 817380
Email: newsdesk@lynnnews.co.uk
Advertising Address: Limes House, Purfleet Street, KING'S LYNN, PE30 1HL **Tel:** 01553 761188 **Fax:** 01553 817381
Email: angie.hastings@lynnnews.co.uk
Web site: http://www.lynnnews.co.uk

Publisher: East Midlands Newspapers Ltd
Date Established: 1986
Frequency: Weekly - Published on Wednesday
Cover Price: Free
Circulation: 39,962 (Publisher's Statement)
Usual Pagination: 28
Editor: Jo Garner; **Publisher:** David Dixon
ADVERTISING RATES:
Full Page Mono £1511.64
Full Page Colour £1965.12
SCC £4.94
Agency Commission: 10%
Mechanical Data: Type Area: 340 x 270mm, No. of Columns (Display): 9, Film: Digital, Col Length: 340mm, Page Width: 270mm, Col Widths (Display): 27mm
Average advertising content per issue: 75%
LOCAL NEWSPAPERS: Local Newspapers English Counties

CITY A.M.
1693586U67B-9018

Editorial Address: 12-14 Dowgate Hill, LONDON, EC4R 2SU **Tel:** 020 3167 4946 **Fax:** 020 7248 1729
Email: city@cityam.com
Advertising Address: As above.
Email: jeremy.slattery@cityam.com
Web site: http://www.cityam.com
Publisher: City AM
Frequency: Daily - Published Monday to Friday
Cover Price: Free
Circulation: 86,522 (ABC 26/11/2007 to 30/12/2007)
Editor: Kate Bartlett; **News Editor:** Ben Griffiths; **Features Editor:** Jeremy Hazlehurst
ADVERTISING RATES:
Full Page Mono £8000.00
Full Page Colour £8000.00
Agency Commission: 15%
Mechanical Data: Type Area: 350 x 259mm, Col Length: 350mm, Page Width: 259mm, No. of Columns (Display): 7, Film: Digital
Copy instructions: Copy Date: Friday 5pm prior to publication date
Average advertising content per issue: 33%
Supplement(s): Property - 26xY
REGIONAL DAILY & SUNDAY NEWSPAPERS: Regional Daily Newspapers

CITY LITE
1797207U67B-340_661

Frequency: Weekly
Cover Price: Free
Circulation: 7,000 (Print Run)
ADVERTISING: Rates on application
Edition of: Yorkshire Evening Post
REGIONAL DAILY & SUNDAY NEWSPAPERS: Regional Daily Newspapers

CITY LITE
1809956U67B-600_501

Frequency: Weekly
Cover Price: Free
Circulation: 10,000 (Print Run)
Edition of: Evening Telegraph (Peterborough)
REGIONAL DAILY & SUNDAY NEWSPAPERS: Regional Daily Newspapers

CITY OF LONDON & DOCKLAND TIMES
42967U72A-30

Editorial Address: 10 College East, Gunthorpe Street, LONDON, E1 7RL **Tel:** 020 7247 2524
Email: cldt@btinternet.com
Advertising Address: As above. **Fax:** 020 7247 8151
Email: cldt@btinternet.com
Publisher: City of London & Dockland Times
Date Established: 1984
Frequency: Weekly
Cover Price: £0.40
Circulation: 20,000 (Publisher's Statement)
Editor: Dennis Delderfield; **Advertising Manager:** Dennis Delderfield
ADVERTISING RATES:
Full Page Mono £912.00
SCC £4.00
Agency Commission: 15%
Mechanical Data: Page Width: 230mm, No. of Columns (Display): 4, Film: Digital, Type Area: 329 x 230mm, Col Length: 329mm, Col Widths (Display): 53mm
Copy instructions: Copy Date: 5 days prior to publication date
Average advertising content per issue: 25%
LOCAL NEWSPAPERS: Local Newspapers Greater London

CLACTON GAZETTE
43617U72B-1044_120

Frequency: Weekly - Circulation figure incorporates the Frinton & Walton Gazette
Cover Price: £0.55
Circulation: 16,296 (ABC 02/07/2007 to 30/12/2007)
ADVERTISING RATES:
Full Page Colour £772.00
SCC £4.65
Copy instructions: Copy Date: Tuesday 1pm prior to publication date
Part of Series, see entry for: Gazette and Standard Series (East Essex)
LOCAL NEWSPAPERS: Local Newspapers English Counties

CLACTON WEEKLY NEWS
43614U72B-1030_120

Formerly: Tendring Weekly News
Frequency: Weekly
Cover Price: Free
Circulation: 23,065 (Publisher's Statement)
ADVERTISING RATES:
Full Page Mono £310.00
Full Page Colour £405.00
SCC £2.40
Part of Series, see entry for: Weekly News Series (Colchester)
LOCAL NEWSPAPERS: Local Newspapers English Counties

CLEVEDON NEWSPAPERS SERIES
43220U72B-40

Formerly: South Avon Mercury Series
Editorial Address: Elton House, Albert Road, CLEVEDON, BS21 7SW **Tel:** 01179 343000 **Fax:** 01275 335147
Email: editor@clevedon.co.uk
Advertising Address: As above. **Tel:** 01275 335142
Fax: 01275 335146
Email: ads@clevedon.co.uk
Web site: http://www.thisisclevedon.co.uk
Publisher: North Somerset and Media LTD
Frequency: Weekly
Cover Price: Free
Circulation: 86,840 (Combined Circulation)
Editor: Carol Deacon; **Advertising Manager:** Ann Johnston
ADVERTISING RATES:
Full Page Mono £2030.04
Full Page Colour £2530.00
Agency Commission: 10%
Mechanical Data: Type Area: 360 x 272mm, Col Length: 360mm, Page Width: 272mm, Col Widths (Display): 31mm, No. of Columns (Display): 8, Film: Digital
Copy instructions: Copy Date: Monday 5pm prior to publication date
Average advertising content per issue: 70%
Series owner and contact point for the following titles, see individual entries:
Burnham & Highbridge Times
Mercury (Clevedon, Nailsea, Portishead & Yatton)
Supplement(s): What's On Where - 12xY
LOCAL NEWSPAPERS: Local Newspapers English Counties

CLITHEROE ADVERTISER AND TIMES
43967U72B-1960

Formerly: Clitheroe Advertiser and Times Series
Editorial Address: 3 King Street, CLITHEROE, BB7 2EW
Tel: 01200 422324 **Fax:** 01200 443467
Email: duncan.smith@eastlancsnews.co.uk
Advertising Address: As above. **Tel:** 01200 422323
Email: zoe.reynolds@eastlancsnews.co.uk
Web site: http://www.clitheroetoday.co.uk
Publisher: Johnston Press plc
Date Established: 1868
Frequency: Weekly - Published on Thursday
Cover Price: £0.70
Circulation: 9,170 (ABC 02/07/2007 to 30/12/2007)
Editor: Duncan Smith; **News Editor:** Duncan Smith; **Managing Director:** Sally O'Neill; **Advertising Manager:** Zoe Reynolds
Summary of Content: Weekly local newspaper with monthly free lifestyle magazine.
ADVERTISING: Rates on application
Agency Commission: 10%
Mechanical Data: Film: Digital, Type Area: 340 x 265mm, No. of Columns (Display): 9, Col Length: 340mm, Page Width: 265mm, Col Widths (Display): 28mm
Copy instructions: Copy Date: Tuesday 12 noon prior to publication date
LOCAL NEWSPAPERS: Local Newspapers English Counties

CLITHEROE & WHALLEY REPORTER
1693351U72B-1940_222

Frequency: Weekly - For circulation figure see the Burnley & Pendle Reporter
Cover Price: Free
ADVERTISING RATES:
Full Page Mono £4332.96
Full Page Colour £5632.84
SCC £14.16
Part of Series, see entry for: Burnley Express and Reporter Series
LOCAL NEWSPAPERS: Local Newspapers English Counties

CLOCHDAR
761565U72J-46

Editorial Address: 14 Clifton Street, ABERDARE, CF44 7PB
Tel: 01685 873440 **Fax:** 01685 873440
Email: eric.clochdar@gmail.com
Advertising Address: As above.
Email: eric.clochdar@gmail.com
Date Established: 1988
Frequency: 10 issues yearly - Not published in January and August
Cover Price: £0.25
Circulation: 550 (Publisher's Statement)
Editor: Eric Jones; **Advertising Manager:** Eric Jones
Summary of Content: Welsh language community newspaper including local news items, school news, gardening and cultural events.
Language(s): Welsh
Readership/Target Audience: Aimed at Welsh speaking readers in the Cynon Valley.
ADVERTISING RATES:
Full Page Mono £80.00
Mechanical Data: Film: Digital
Copy instructions: Copy Date: 2 weeks prior to publication date
Average advertising content per issue: 15%
LOCAL NEWSPAPERS: Community Newsletters

CLYDE WEEKLY NEWS
44896U72D-255

Editorial Address: 53 High Street, DUMBARTON, G82 1LS
Tel: 01389 742299 **Fax:** 01389 742488
Email: thelennox@s-un.co.uk
Advertising Address: As above. **Fax:** 01389 744538
Email: pdeads@s-un.co.uk
Publisher: Scottish & Universal Newspapers Ltd
Frequency: Weekly - Published on Thursday
Cover Price: Free
Circulation: 5,339 (Publisher's Statement)
Editor: Mark McLean
ADVERTISING RATES:
Full Page Mono £1575.00
Full Page Colour £2047.50
SCC £5.05
Agency Commission: 10%
Mechanical Data: Col Length: 390mm, No. of Columns (Display): 8, Type Area: 390 x 260mm, Page Width: 260mm
Copy instructions: Copy Date: Tuesday 11am prior to publication date
LOCAL NEWSPAPERS: Local Newspapers Scotland

CLYDEBANK POST
44894U72D-252

Editorial Address: 88 Dumbarton Road, CLYDEBANK, G81 1UG **Tel:** 0141 952 0565 **Fax:** 0141 952 7267
Email: editorial.cb@cfpress.co.uk
Advertising Address: As above. **Tel:** 0141 952 1345
Email: mhull@cfpress.co.uk
Publisher: Clyde & Forth Press Group
Frequency: Weekly - Published on Wednesday
Cover Price: £0.55
Circulation: 12,981 (ABC 01/01/2007 to 30/12/2007)
Editor: James Walsh; **News Editor:** Lynda Collins; **Advertising Manager:** Margaret Hull
ADVERTISING RATES:
Full Page Mono £1993.00
Full Page Colour £2989.00
SCC £7.55
Mechanical Data: Film: Digital, Page Width: 266mm, No. of Columns (Display): 8, Type Area: 330 x 266mm, Col Length: 330mm
Copy instructions: Copy Date: Monday 4pm prior to publication date
LOCAL NEWSPAPERS: Local Newspapers Scotland

COALVILLE ECHO
44008U72B-2150_281

Frequency: Weekly - Circulation figure also includes the Ashby Echo
Cover Price: Free
Circulation: 14,308 (Publisher's Statement)
ADVERTISING RATES:
SCC £5.25

Part of Series, see entry for: Loughborough Echo Series
LOCAL NEWSPAPERS: Local Newspapers English Counties

COALVILLE TIMES
44034U72B-2193_130

Frequency: Weekly - Circulation figure includes the Ashby Times and the Swadlincote Times
Cover Price: £0.39
Circulation: 9,151 (ABC 02/07/2007 to 30/12/2007)
ADVERTISING: Rates on application
Part of Series, see entry for: Trident Midland Newspapers Series
LOCAL NEWSPAPERS: Local Newspapers English Counties

COAST GAZETTE
42035U67B-170_550

Formerly: Evening Gazette (Clacton & Harwich)
Frequency: Daily
ADVERTISING: Rates on application
Edition of: Daily Gazette
REGIONAL DAILY & SUNDAY NEWSPAPERS: Regional Daily Newspapers

THE COASTAL ADVERTISER
44146U72B-3078_101

Formerly: The Suffolk Advertiser
Cover Price: Free
Circulation: 10,862 (VFD 05/11/2007 to 30/12/2007)
Editor: Mark Crossley
Summary of Content: Newspaper covering news, homes, jobs and cars for Framlingham, Leiston, Saxmundham, Wickham Market and Woodbridge, Suffolk.
Readership/Target Audience: Aimed at people living in this area.
Part of Series, see entry for: Advertiser Series (Ipswich)
LOCAL NEWSPAPERS: Local Newspapers English Counties

COASTAL JOURNAL
768519U72B-545_144

Frequency: Weekly - For circulation see Liskeard and Callington Gazette
Cover Price: Free
ADVERTISING RATES:
Full Page Mono £1065.60
Full Page Colour £1324.80
Part of Series, see entry for: Cornish Times & Gazette Series
LOCAL NEWSPAPERS: Local Newspapers English Counties

COLCHESTER GAZETTE (CHELMSFORD, WITHAM, BRAINTREE & MALDON)
42034U67B-170_530

Formerly: Evening Gazette (Chelmsford, Witham, Braintree & Maldon)
Frequency: Daily
ADVERTISING: Rates on application
Edition of: Daily Gazette
REGIONAL DAILY & SUNDAY NEWSPAPERS: Regional Daily Newspapers

COLCHESTER WEEKLY NEWS
43615U72B-1030_130

Formerly: Colchester and Mersea Weekly News
Frequency: Weekly
Cover Price: Free
Circulation: 36,897 (VFD 02/07/2007 to 30/12/2007)
ADVERTISING RATES:
Full Page Mono £440.00
Full Page Colour £535.00
SCC £3.60
Part of Series, see entry for: Weekly News Series (Colchester)
LOCAL NEWSPAPERS: Local Newspapers English Counties

COLERAINE TIMES
45066U72E-65

Editorial Address: 5 Stone Row, COLERAINE, BT52 1EP
Tel: 028 7035 5260 **Fax:** 028 7035 6186
Email: david.rankin@jpress.co.uk
Advertising Address: As above.
Email: adcr@mortonnewspapers.com
Web site: http://www.colerainetimes.co.uk
Publisher: Morton Newspapers Ltd
Date Established: 1990
Frequency: Weekly - Published on Tuesday
Cover Price: £0.95
Circulation: 7,387 (ABC 02/07/2007 to 30/12/2007)

Section 4 (a) Newspapers

Editor: David Rankin; **Advertising Manager:** Carmel Taylor
ADVERTISING RATES:
Full Page Mono £1667.00
Full Page Colour £2418.17
SCC £5.45
Agency Commission: 10%
Mechanical Data: Type Area: 340 x 265mm, No. of
Columns (Display): 9, Col Length: 340mm, Col Widths
(Display): 28mm, Page Width: 265mm, Film: Digital
Copy instructions: Copy Date: Monday prior to publication
date
Average advertising content per issue: 60%
LOCAL NEWSPAPERS: Local Newspapers Northern Ireland

COLESHILL HERALD (INCORPORATING THE COLESHILL CHRONICLE)

44324U72B-3040_120

Frequency: Weekly - Circulation figure is incorporated into
the Atherstone Herald
Cover Price: £0.55
ADVERTISING: Rates on application
Part of Series, see entry for: Tamworth Herald Series
LOCAL NEWSPAPERS: Local Newspapers English
Counties

COLNE TIMES

43990U72B-2040_130

Frequency: Weekly - Published on Friday. See Nelson
Leader for circulation figure
Cover Price: £0.70
ADVERTISING RATES:
Full Page Mono £1306.62
Full Page Colour £1698.60
SCC £4.27
Part of Series, see entry for: Leader Times Series
LOCAL NEWSPAPERS: Local Newspapers English
Counties

THE COMET HITCHIN EDITION

43811U72B-1580_130

Frequency: Weekly
Free to qualifying individuals
Circulation: 19,279 (VFD 02/07/2007 to 30/12/2007)
Part of Series, see entry for: The Comet Series
LOCAL NEWSPAPERS: Local Newspapers English
Counties

THE COMET LETCHWORTH & BALDOCK EDITION

43812U72B-1580_140

Frequency: Weekly
Free to qualifying individuals
Circulation: 22,098 (VFD 03/01/2005 to 03/07/2005)
Part of Series, see entry for: The Comet Series
LOCAL NEWSPAPERS: Local Newspapers English
Counties

THE COMET SERIES

43810U72B-1580

Formerly: North Herts Comet Series
Editorial Address: Bank House, Primett Road,
STEVENAGE, SG1 3EE **Tel:** 01438 866200
Fax: 01438 866215
Email: editorial@thecomet.net
Advertising Address: As above. **Tel:** 01438 866000
Fax: 01438 866060
Email: jackie.bevan@archant.co.uk
Web site: http://www.thecomet24.co.uk
Publisher: Archant Herts & Cambs
Date Established: 1971
Frequency: Weekly - Published every Thursday
Circulation: 85,226 (VFD 02/07/2007 to 30/12/2007)
Editor: John Adams; **News Editor:** John Adams; **Managing
Director:** Stuart McCreery; **Advertising Manager:** Jackie
Bevan
ADVERTISING RATES:
SCC £9.27
Agency Commission: 10%
Mechanical Data: Page Width: 263mm, Col Length:
360mm, Film: Digital, No. of Columns (Display): 9, Type
Area: 360 x 263mm, Col Widths (Display): 27mm
Copy instructions: Copy Date: Tuesday 12.00 pm prior to
publication date
**Series owner and contact point for the following titles,
see individual entries:**
The Comet Hitchin Edition
The Comet Letchworth & Baldock Edition
The Comet Stevenage Edition
LOCAL NEWSPAPERS: Local Newspapers English
Counties

THE COMET STEVENAGE EDITION

43813U72B-1580_150

Frequency: Weekly
Free to qualifying individuals
Circulation: 35,911 (VFD 31/10/2005 to 01/01/2006)
Part of Series, see entry for: The Comet Series
LOCAL NEWSPAPERS: Local Newspapers English
Counties

COMMUNITY NEWS SERIES

44333U72B-3072

Editorial Address: 27 Norwich Road, HALESWORTH, IP19
8BX **Tel:** 01986 834231 **Fax:** 01986 834270
Email: communitynews@micropress.co.uk
Advertising Address: As above.
Email: communitynews@micropress.co.uk
Publisher: Micropress
Date Established: 1975
Frequency: Monthly
Cover Price: Free
Circulation: 31,000 (Publisher's Statement)
Editor: Dennis Perkins; **News Editor:** Kate Hill; **Advertising
Manager:** Karen Taylor
ADVERTISING RATES:
Full Page Mono £310.00
Agency Commission: 10%
Mechanical Data: Page Width: 267mm, Film: Digital, Type
Area: 400 x 267mm, Col Length: 400mm, Col Widths
(Display): 35mm, No. of Columns (Display): 7
Copy instructions: Copy Date: 10 days prior to publication
date
Average advertising content per issue: 70%
**Series owner and contact point for the following titles,
see individual entries:**
Beccles Independent
Bungay and Harleston Community News
Framlingham Wickham Market and Debenham Community
News
Leiston Saxmundham Aldeburgh and District Community
News
Woodbridge Melton and District Community News
LOCAL NEWSPAPERS: Local Newspapers English
Counties

COMMUNITY NEWSLETTER SERIES

1645948U72B-3950

Editorial Address: Sunny Bar, DONCASTER, DN1 1NB
Tel: 01302 819111 **Fax:** 01302 348516
Email: newsletters@doncastertoday.co.uk
Advertising Address: As above. **Fax:** 01302 348525
Email: claire.ferguson@doncastertoday.co.uk
Web site: http://www.doncasterfreepress.co.uk
Publisher: South Yorkshire Newspapers Ltd
Date Established: 2002
Frequency: Monthly
Cover Price: Free
Circulation: 42,000 (Publisher's Statement)
Editor: Jim Oldfield
ADVERTISING: Rates on application
**Series owner and contact point for the following titles,
see individual entries:**
Armthorpe Community Newsletter
Askern, Campsall & Norton Community Newsletter
Bentley and Arksey Community Newsletter
Conisbrough and Denaby Community Newsletter
Rossington Community Newsletter
Sprotbrough, Scawsby & Cusworth Community Newsletter
Tickhill & Bawtry (plus Harworth) Community Newsletter
LOCAL NEWSPAPERS: Local Newspapers English
Counties

COMMUNITY NEWSPAPER SERIES

1657614U72B-3957

Editorial Address: 1st Floor Offices, Shildon Town Council,
Civic Hall Square, SHILDON, DL4 1AH **Tel:** 01388 775896
Fax: 01388 775896
Email: crier@talk21.com
Advertising Address: As above.
Email: crier@talk21.com
Publisher: Community Newspaper Support Association
Date Established: 1991
Frequency: Weekly
Cover Price: Free
Circulation: 28,500 (Combined Circulation)
Editor: Stephanie Ellis; **Advertising Manager:** Jeffrey Ridley
ADVERTISING: Rates on application
Agency Commission: 10%
Mechanical Data: Trim Size: 280 x 185mm, Film: Digital
Average advertising content per issue: 60%
**Series owner and contact point for the following titles,
see individual entries:**
Ferryhill and Chilton Chapter
Shildon and District Town Crier
The Spennynews
LOCAL NEWSPAPERS: Local Newspapers English
Counties

COMMUNITY TELEGRAPH EAST BELFAST

45074U72E-67_170

Formerly: Community Telegraph Stormont and Areas
Frequency: Weekly
Cover Price: Free
Circulation: 43,103 (VFD 26/11/2007 to 30/12/2007)
ADVERTISING RATES:
SCC £5.51
Copy instructions: Copy Date: Tuesday 11am prior to
publication date
Part of Series, see entry for: Community Telegraph Series
LOCAL NEWSPAPERS: Local Newspapers Northern Ireland

COMMUNITY TELEGRAPH NORTH BELFAST

45072U72E-67_160

Formerly: Community Telegraph North Belfast and Areas
Frequency: Weekly
Cover Price: Free
Circulation: 28,656 (VFD 02/07/2007 to 30/12/2007)
ADVERTISING RATES:
SCC £4.58
Copy instructions: Copy Date: Monday 11am prior to
publication date
Part of Series, see entry for: Community Telegraph Series
LOCAL NEWSPAPERS: Local Newspapers Northern Ireland

COMMUNITY TELEGRAPH NORTH DOWN AND ARDS

45069U72E-67_130

Formerly: Community Telegraph Bangor and Areas
Frequency: Weekly
Cover Price: Free
Circulation: 35,614 (VFD 26/11/2007 to 30/12/2007)
ADVERTISING RATES:
SCC £3.86
Copy instructions: Copy Date: Monday 11am prior to
publication date
Part of Series, see entry for: Community Telegraph Series
LOCAL NEWSPAPERS: Local Newspapers Northern Ireland

COMMUNITY TELEGRAPH SERIES

45067U72E-67

Editorial Address: 124-144 Royal Avenue, BELFAST, BT1
1EB **Tel:** 028 9026 4331 **Fax:** 028 9055 4504
Email: cteditorial@thect.co.uk
Advertising Address: 5th Floor, 124-144 Royal Avenue,
BELFAST, BT1 1EB **Tel:** 028 9026 4074 **Fax:** 028 9055 4504
Email: mark.reilly@thect.co.uk
Web site: http://www.thect.co.uk
Publisher: Belfast Telegraph Newspapers Ltd
Date Established: 1985
Frequency: Weekly
Cover Price: Free
Circulation: 166,375 (VFD 02/07/2007 to 30/12/2007)
Editor: Victoria Sloss; **Advertising Manager:** Mark Reilly
ADVERTISING RATES:
Full Page Mono £4896.00
Full Page Colour £6120.00
SCC £18.00
Agency Commission: 15%
Mechanical Data: Page Width: 272mm, Col Widths
(Display): 34mm, Type Area: 340 x 272mm, Col Length:
340mm, No. of Columns (Display): 8, Film: Digital
Average advertising content per issue: 60%
**Series owner and contact point for the following titles,
see individual entries:**
Community Telegraph East Belfast
Community Telegraph North Belfast
Community Telegraph North Down and Ards
Community Telegraph South Belfast
Community Telegraph West Belfast
LOCAL NEWSPAPERS: Local Newspapers Northern Ireland

COMMUNITY TELEGRAPH SOUTH BELFAST

45073U72E-67_165

Formerly: Community Telegraph Shaftesbury and Areas
Frequency: Weekly
Cover Price: Free
Circulation: 35,190 (VFD 26/11/2007 to 30/12/2007)
ADVERTISING RATES:
SCC £4.58
Copy instructions: Copy Date: Tuesday 11am prior to
publication date
Part of Series, see entry for: Community Telegraph Series
LOCAL NEWSPAPERS: Local Newspapers Northern Ireland

COMMUNITY TELEGRAPH WEST BELFAST

1813092U72E-67_171

Frequency: Weekly
Cover Price: Free
Circulation: 23,812 (Publisher's Statement)

ADVERTISING RATES:
SCC £3.30
Copy instructions: Copy Date: Monday 11am prior to publication date
Part of Series, see entry for: Community Telegraph Series
LOCAL NEWSPAPERS: Local Newspapers Northern Ireland

THE COMMUTER
1814056U72B-2690_141
Frequency: Weekly
Cover Price: Free
Circulation: 5,000 (Print Run)
Part of Series, see entry for: Banbury Guardian Review Series
LOCAL NEWSPAPERS: Local Newspapers English Counties

THE COMMUTER HERALD
1763677U72B-290_101
Frequency: Weekly
Cover Price: Free
ADVERTISING RATES:
SCC £2.50
Part of Series, see entry for: The Bucks Herald Series
LOCAL NEWSPAPERS: Local Newspapers English Counties

THE CONGLETON ADVERTISER
762062U72B-423_130
Formerly: Adnews (Congleton)
Frequency: Weekly
Cover Price: Free
Part of Series, see entry for: Advertiser Series (South Cheshire)
LOCAL NEWSPAPERS: Local Newspapers English Counties

CONGLETON CHRONICLE
43361U72B-445_120
Frequency: Weekly
Cover Price: £0.40
Part of Series, see entry for: Congleton Chronicle Series
LOCAL NEWSPAPERS: Local Newspapers English Counties

CONGLETON CHRONICLE SERIES
43359U72B-445
Editorial Address: 11 High Street, CONGLETON, CW12 1BW **Tel:** 01260 273737 **Fax:** 01260 280687
Email: chronicleseries@aol.com
Advertising Address: As above.
Email: chronads@aol.com
Web site: http://www.chronicleseries.co.uk
Publisher: Congleton Chronicle Ltd
Date Established: 1893
Frequency: Weekly - Published on Thursday
Circulation: 16,900 (Publisher's Statement)
Editor: Jeremy Condliffe; **Managing Director:** Jeremy Condliffe; **Advertising Manager:** Pam Austen
ADVERTISING RATES:
Full Page Mono £650.00
Full Page Colour £800.00
SCC £3.12
Agency Commission: 10%
Mechanical Data: Type Area: 360 x 266mm, Col Length: 360mm, Page Width: 266mm, Col Widths (Display): 41mm, No. of Columns (Display): 6, Film: Digital
Copy instructions: Copy Date: Monday 12noon prior to publication date
Average advertising content per issue: 60%
Series owner and contact point for the following titles, see individual entries:
Biddulph Chronicle
Congleton Chronicle
Sandbach Chronicle
LOCAL NEWSPAPERS: Local Newspapers English Counties

CONISBROUGH AND DENABY COMMUNITY NEWSLETTER
1692786U72B-3950_105
Frequency: Monthly
Cover Price: Free
Circulation: 6,000 (Publisher's Statement)
ADVERTISING: Rates on application
Part of Series, see entry for: Community Newsletter Series
LOCAL NEWSPAPERS: Local Newspapers English Counties

CORBY MERCURY & CITIZEN
44155U72B-2490_130
Formerly: Corby Citizen
Frequency: Weekly
Cover Price: Free
Circulation: 8,731 (VFD 03/07/2006 to 31/12/2006)
ADVERTISING: Rates on application
Part of Series, see entry for: Northants Mercury & Citizen Series
LOCAL NEWSPAPERS: Local Newspapers English Counties

CORNISH & DEVON POST SERIES
43412U72B-520
Editorial Address: Tindle House, Westgate Street, LAUNCESTON, PL15 7AL **Tel:** 01566 772424
Fax: 01566 778243
Email: k.whitford@thepost.uk.com
Advertising Address: As above. **Tel:** 01566 775500
Fax: 01566 778245
Email: j.ward@thepost.uk.com
Publisher: Cornish & Devon Post
Date Established: 1856
Frequency: Weekly
Circulation: 13,257 (Publisher's Statement)
Editor: Suzanne Cleave; **News Editor:** Suzanne Cleave;
Advertising Manager: Judy Ward
ADVERTISING: Rates on application
Agency Commission: 10%
Mechanical Data: Col Length: 560mm, Page Width: 366mm, Type Area: 560 x 366mm, Col Widths (Display): 34mm, No. of Columns (Display): 10, Film: Digital
Copy instructions: Copy Date: Monday 5pm prior to publication date
Average advertising content per issue: 50%
Series owner and contact point for the following titles, see individual entries:
Bude & Stratton Post
Camelford & Delabole Post
Camelford, Delabole, Boscastle & Tintagel Journal Gazette
The Holsworthy Post
Launceston & Cornish & Devon Post
Launceston, Holsworthy Bude & Stratton Journal Gazette
LOCAL NEWSPAPERS: Local Newspapers English Counties

CORNISH GUARDIAN (BODMIN)
765126U72B-530_120
Frequency: Weekly - See Cornish Guardian Series for combined circulation figure
Cover Price: £0.85
Part of Series, see entry for: Cornish Guardian Series
LOCAL NEWSPAPERS: Local Newspapers English Counties

CORNISH GUARDIAN (LOSTWITHIEL & FOWEY)
765130U72B-530_160
Frequency: Weekly - See Cornish Guardian Series for combined circulation figure
Cover Price: £0.85
Part of Series, see entry for: Cornish Guardian Series
LOCAL NEWSPAPERS: Local Newspapers English Counties

CORNISH GUARDIAN (NORTH CORNWALL)
765127U72B-530_130
Formerly: Cornish Guardian (Camelford & District)
Frequency: Weekly - See Cornish Guardian Series for combined circulation figure
Cover Price: £0.85
Part of Series, see entry for: Cornish Guardian Series
LOCAL NEWSPAPERS: Local Newspapers English Counties

CORNISH GUARDIAN SERIES
43419U72B-530
Editorial Address: 1 Town Arms Passage, BODMIN, PL31 2JQ **Tel:** 01726 76815 **Fax:** 01726 69694
Email: cgedit@c-dm.co.uk
Advertising Address: 30 Fore Street, BODMIN, PL31 2HQ
Tel: 0845 606 0311 **Fax:** 01872 247433
Email: trade.classifieds@c-dm.co.uk
Web site: http://www.thisiscornwall.co.uk
Publisher: Cornwall & Devon Media Limited
Date Established: 1901
Frequency: Weekly - Published on Wednesday
Cover Price: £0.85
Circulation: 32,982 (ABC 02/07/2007 to 30/12/2007)
Editor: Oscar Morse; **Editor-in-Chief:** Andy Cooper
ADVERTISING RATES:
Full Page Mono £1857.60
Full Page Colour £2322.00

SCC £6.45
Mechanical Data: Type Area: 360 x 268mm, No. of Columns (Display): 8, Col Length: 360mm, Page Width: 268mm, Col Widths (Display): 31.5mm, Film: Digital
Copy instructions: Copy Date: Monday 5pm prior to publication date
Series owner and contact point for the following titles, see individual entries:
Cornish Guardian (Bodmin)
Cornish Guardian (Lostwithiel & Fowey)
Cornish Guardian (North Cornwall)
Cornish Guardian (South East Cornwall)
Cornish Guardian (St. Austell)
Cornish Guardian (Wadebridge & Padstow)
Newquay Guardian
LOCAL NEWSPAPERS: Local Newspapers English Counties

CORNISH GUARDIAN (SOUTH EAST CORNWALL)
765129U72B-530_155
Formerly: Cornish Guardian (Liskeard & Looe)
Frequency: Weekly - See Cornish Guardian Series for combined circulation figure
Cover Price: £0.85
Part of Series, see entry for: Cornish Guardian Series
LOCAL NEWSPAPERS: Local Newspapers English Counties

CORNISH GUARDIAN (ST. AUSTELL)
765133U72B-530_185
Frequency: Weekly - See Cornish Guardian Series for combined circulation figure
Cover Price: £0.85
Part of Series, see entry for: Cornish Guardian Series
LOCAL NEWSPAPERS: Local Newspapers English Counties

CORNISH GUARDIAN (WADEBRIDGE & PADSTOW)
765134U72B-530_195
Frequency: Weekly - See Cornish Guardian Series for combined circulation figure
Cover Price: £0.85
Part of Series, see entry for: Cornish Guardian Series
LOCAL NEWSPAPERS: Local Newspapers English Counties

CORNISH TIMES
762191U72B-545_110
Frequency: Weekly
Cover Price: £0.60
Circulation: 15,000 (Publisher's Statement)
ADVERTISING RATES:
Full Page Mono £1209.60
Full Page Colour £1497.60
SCC £4.20
Mechanical Data: Col Length: 360mm, No. of Columns (Display): 8
Part of Series, see entry for: Cornish Times & Gazette Series
LOCAL NEWSPAPERS: Local Newspapers English Counties

CORNISH TIMES & GAZETTE SERIES
43424U72B-545
Formerly: Liskeard Times & Gazette
Editorial Address: Tindle Suite, Webbs House, The Parade, LISKEARD, PL14 6AH **Tel:** 01579 342174
Fax: 01579 341851
Email: editorial@cornish-times.co.uk
Advertising Address: As above. **Fax:** 01579 341852
Email: ct.advertising@internet-today.co.uk
Web site: http://www.liskeard-today.co.uk
Publisher: Putnam Newspapers Ltd
Frequency: Weekly - Published on Friday
Circulation: 51,000 (Combined Circulation)
Editor: John Noble; **Advertising Manager:** Hazel Bradley
ADVERTISING: Rates on application
Agency Commission: 10%
Mechanical Data: Type Area: 360 x 272mm, Page Width: 272mm, Col Widths (Display): 32mm, Film: Digital, No. of Columns (Display): 8, Col Length: 360mm
Copy instructions: Copy Date: Tuesday prior to publication date
Average advertising content per issue: 50%
Series owner and contact point for the following titles, see individual entries:
Coastal Journal
Cornish Times
Liskeard and Callington Gazette
Looe and Polperro Gazette
Saltash Journal
Torpoint Journal

Non-National Newspapers

Supplement(s): Countryside Today - 12xY, Prime of Life - 12xY
LOCAL NEWSPAPERS: Local Newspapers English Counties

THE CORNISHMAN
43420U72B-541

Editorial Address: Buriton House, Alverton Street, PENZANCE, TR18 2QP **Tel:** 01736 351146
Fax: 01736 350436
Email: cmnews@c-dm.co.uk
Advertising Address: As above. **Tel:** 01736 362247
Email: nmarriott@c-dm.co.uk
Web site: http://www.thisiscornwall.co.uk
Publisher: Cornwall & Devon Media Limited
Frequency: Weekly - Published on Thursday
Cover Price: £0.80
Circulation: 18,189 (ABC 01/01/2007 to 01/07/2007)
Editor: John Williams; **Editor-in-Chief:** Andy Cooper;
Advertising Manager: Nikki Marriot
ADVERTISING RATES:
Full Page Mono £1123.20
Full Page Colour £1516.32
SCC £3.90
Mechanical Data: Type Area: 360 x 268mm, No. of Columns (Display): 8, Col Widths (Display): 31.5mm, Col Length: 360mm, Page Width: 268mm, Film: Digital
Copy instructions: Copy Date: Monday 5pm prior to publication date
LOCAL NEWSPAPERS: Local Newspapers English Counties

CORWEN TIMES
44826U72C-275_130

Frequency: Weekly
Cover Price: £0.40
Part of Series, see entry for: North Wales Series
LOCAL NEWSPAPERS: Local Newspapers Wales

COTSWOLD JOURNAL
44611U72B-3560_120

Frequency: Weekly
ADVERTISING: Rates on application
Part of Series, see entry for: Evesham Journal Series
LOCAL NEWSPAPERS: Local Newspapers English Counties

COTSWOLDS OBSERVER
1808392U72B-4052_101

Frequency: Weekly - Published on Wednesday
Cover Price: £0.35
Free to qualifying individuals
Part of Series, see entry for: Evesham Observer Series
LOCAL NEWSPAPERS: Local Newspapers English Counties

COULSDON & PURLEY ADVERTISER
42973U72A-50_130

Frequency: Weekly - For circulation see Croydon Advertiser
Cover Price: £0.55
ADVERTISING RATES:
SCC £14.50
Part of Series, see entry for: Croydon Advertiser & Post Series
LOCAL NEWSPAPERS: Local Newspapers Greater London

COUNTY BORDER NEWS SERIES
43855U72B-1774

Editorial Address: 3 Ash Close, LINGFIELD, RH7 6HQ
Tel: 0 7814 458802 **Fax:** 01737 501052
Email: kevinwilliamblack@gmail.com
Advertising Address: Winterton House, High Street, WESTERHAM, TN16 1AT **Tel:** 01959 564766
Email: paul.k@internet-today.co.uk
Web site: http://www.countybordernews.com
Publisher: Biggin Hill News Ltd
Date Established: 1976
Frequency: Weekly
Cover Price: Free
Circulation: 28,000 (Publisher's Statement)
Editor: Kevin Black
ADVERTISING RATES:
Full Page Mono £1428.00
Full Page Colour £1836.00
SCC £5.25
Agency Commission: 10%
Mechanical Data: Page Width: 265mm, Film: Digital, Type Area: 340 x 265mm, Col Length: 340mm, No. of Columns (Display): 8, Col Widths (Display): 29.6mm
Series owner and contact point for the following titles, see individual entries:
Edenbridge County Border News
Godstone County Border News
Lingfield County Border News
Oxted County Border News
Tandridge County Border News
Westerham County Border News
LOCAL NEWSPAPERS: Local Newspapers English Counties

THE COUNTY DOWN OUTLOOK
45117U72E-69

Formerly: Outlook (Rathfriland)
Editorial Address: 8 Main Street, Rathfriland, NEWRY, BT34 5PS **Tel:** 028 4063 0202 **Fax:** 028 4063 1022
Email: news@outlooknews.co.uk
Advertising Address: As above.
Email: advertising@outlooknews.co.uk
Web site: http://www.ulsternet-ni.co.uk
Publisher: Alpha Newspaper Group
Date Established: 1940
Frequency: Weekly - Published every Tuesday evening
Cover Price: £0.85
Circulation: 3,972 (Publisher's Statement)
Editor: Alan McVeigh; **Advertising Manager:** Evelyn McCracken
ADVERTISING RATES:
Full Page Colour £1297.55
SCC £4.52
Agency Commission: 10%
Mechanical Data: Trim Size: 420 x 297mm, Col Widths (Display): 35mm, No. of Columns (Display): 7, Type Area: 410 x 272mm, Col Length: 410mm, Page Width: 272mm, Film: Digital
Copy instructions: Copy Date: Monday 5pm prior to publication date
LOCAL NEWSPAPERS: Local Newspapers Northern Ireland

COUNTY DOWN SPECTATOR AND ULSTER STANDARD
45076U72E-70_140

Frequency: Weekly
Cover Price: £0.70
Circulation: 10,916 (ABC 01/01/2007 to 30/12/2007)
ADVERTISING RATES:
SCC £3.80
Part of Series, see entry for: County Down Spectator and Ulster Standard Series
LOCAL NEWSPAPERS: Local Newspapers Northern Ireland

COUNTY DOWN SPECTATOR AND ULSTER STANDARD SERIES
45075U72E-70

Editorial Address: 91 Main Street, BANGOR, BT20 4AF
Tel: 028 9127 0270 **Fax:** 028 9127 1544
Email: editor@spectatornewspapers.co.uk
Advertising Address: As above.
Email: advertising@spectatornewspapers.co.uk
Web site: http://www.spectatornewspapers.co.uk
Publisher: D.E. Alexander & Sons Ltd.
Date Established: 1904
Frequency: Weekly
Circulation: 11,994 (Combined Circulation)
Editor: Paul Flowers; **Features Editor:** Paul Flowers
ADVERTISING RATES:
SCC £6.65
Agency Commission: 10%
Mechanical Data: Type Area: 560 x 366mm, Col Length: 560mm, Page Width: 366mm, Col Widths (Display): 33mm, No. of Columns (Display): 10, Film: Digital
Copy instructions: Copy Date: Wednesday 12pm prior to publication date
Series owner and contact point for the following titles, see individual entries:
County Down Spectator and Ulster Standard
Newtownards Spectator
LOCAL NEWSPAPERS: Local Newspapers Northern Ireland

COUNTY ECHO AND ST. DAVIDS CITY CHRONICLE
44780U72C-155

Formerly: County Echo (Fishguard)
Editorial Address: Parc Y Shwt, FISHGUARD, SA65 9AP
Tel: 01348 874445 **Fax:** 01348 873651
Email: countyecho@btconnect.com
Advertising Address: As above.
Email: countyecho@btconnect.com
Publisher: County Echo Newspapers Ltd
Date Established: 1893
Frequency: Weekly - Published on Friday
Cover Price: £0.38
Circulation: 3,500 (Publisher's Statement)
Editor: Dyllan Davis
Language(s): English; Welsh
ADVERTISING RATES:
Full Page Mono £882.00
Full Page Colour £1008.00
SCC £3.50
Mechanical Data: Type Area: 360 x 270mm, Col Length: 360mm, Page Width: 270mm, No. of Columns (Display): 8, Col Widths (Display): 31mm, Film: Digital

Copy instructions: Copy Date: Tuesday 4pm prior to publication date
Average advertising content per issue: 40%
LOCAL NEWSPAPERS: Local Newspapers Wales

COUNTY TIMES AND GAZETTE
44784U72C-160_130

Formerly: Powys County Times and Gazette
Frequency: Weekly
Cover Price: £0.65
Part of Series, see entry for: Powys County Times, Express & Gazette
LOCAL NEWSPAPERS: Local Newspapers Wales

THE COURIER
764074U72B-3705_130

Frequency: 26 issues yearly
Cover Price: Free
Circulation: 3,600 (Publisher's Statement)
ADVERTISING RATES:
Full Page Mono £240.00
Part of Series, see entry for: The Tribune & Courier Series
LOCAL NEWSPAPERS: Local Newspapers English Counties

THE COURIER AND ADVERTISER
42255U67B-2190

Formerly: The Courier and Advertiser (Dundee)
Editorial Address: 80 Kingsway East, DUNDEE, DD4 8SL
Tel: 01382 223131 **Fax:** 01382 454590
Email: courier@dcthomson.co.uk
Advertising Address: As above. **Tel:** 01382 455666
Fax: 01382 454599
Email: awatt@dcthomson.co.uk
Web site: http://www.thecourier.co.uk
Publisher: D.C. Thomson & Co Ltd
Date Established: 1801
Frequency: Mornings
Cover Price: £0.42
Circulation: 73,485 (ABC 02/07/2007 to 30/12/2007)
Editor: Mike Alexander; **News Editor:** Mike Alexander;
Features Editor: Catriona MacInnes
ADVERTISING RATES:
Full Page Mono £8030.00
Full Page Colour £10439.00
SCC £17.70
Agency Commission: 10%
Mechanical Data: Type Area: 540 x 340mm, No. of Columns (Display): 9, Print Process: Web-fed litho, Film: Positive, right reading, emulsion side up. Digital, Col Length: 540mm, Col Widths (Display): 35mm, Page Width: 340mm
Copy instructions: Copy Date: 5 days prior to publication date
Editions:
The Courier and Advertiser (Angus)
The Courier and Advertiser (Dundee)
The Courier and Advertiser (Fife)
The Courier and Advertiser (North East Fife)
The Courier and Advertiser (Perth)
REGIONAL DAILY & SUNDAY NEWSPAPERS: Regional Daily Newspapers

THE COURIER AND ADVERTISER (ANGUS)
1660264U67B-2190_500

Frequency: Mornings
Cover Price: £0.42
Edition of: The Courier and Advertiser
REGIONAL DAILY & SUNDAY NEWSPAPERS: Regional Daily Newspapers

THE COURIER AND ADVERTISER (DUNDEE)
1660268U67B-2190_504

Frequency: Mornings
Cover Price: £0.42
Edition of: The Courier and Advertiser
REGIONAL DAILY & SUNDAY NEWSPAPERS: Regional Daily Newspapers

THE COURIER AND ADVERTISER (FIFE)
1660267U67B-2190_503

Frequency: Mornings
Cover Price: £0.42
Edition of: The Courier and Advertiser
REGIONAL DAILY & SUNDAY NEWSPAPERS: Regional Daily Newspapers

THE COURIER AND ADVERTISER (NORTH EAST FIFE)
1660266U67B-2190_502
Frequency: Mornings
Cover Price: £0.42
Edition of: The Courier and Advertiser
REGIONAL DAILY & SUNDAY NEWSPAPERS: Regional Daily Newspapers

THE COURIER AND ADVERTISER (PERTH)
1660265U67B-2190_501
Frequency: Mornings
Cover Price: £0.42
Edition of: The Courier and Advertiser
REGIONAL DAILY & SUNDAY NEWSPAPERS: Regional Daily Newspapers

COURIER (EAST SUSSEX)
44432U72B-1835_201
Frequency: Weekly
Circulation: 4,137 (Publisher's Statement)
Part of Series, see entry for: Kent & Sussex Courier Series
LOCAL NEWSPAPERS: Local Newspapers English Counties

COURIER (EDENBRIDGE)
43897U72B-1835_110
Frequency: Weekly - Circulation figure also includes the Courier (Paddock Wood), Courier (Tonbridge), Courier (Tunbridge Wells) and Courier (Weald)
Circulation: 32,549 (ABC 02/07/2007 to 30/12/2007)
Part of Series, see entry for: Kent & Sussex Courier Series
LOCAL NEWSPAPERS: Local Newspapers English Counties

THE COURIER MIDWEEK
44513U72B-3386_150
Formerly: The Leamington and Mid-Warwickshire Review
Frequency: Weekly - Published on Thursday
Cover Price: Free
Circulation: 39,856 (VFD 02/01/2006 to 02/07/2006)
Part of Series, see entry for: Leamington Spa Courier Series
LOCAL NEWSPAPERS: Local Newspapers English Counties

COURIER (PADDOCK WOOD)
43896U72B-1835_120
Frequency: Weekly - Circulation figure is incorporated into the Courier (Edenbridge)
Part of Series, see entry for: Kent & Sussex Courier Series
LOCAL NEWSPAPERS: Local Newspapers English Counties

THE COURIER SERIES (NEATH & PORT TALBOT)
713790U72C-162
Editorial Address: PO Box 14, Adelaide Street, SWANSEA, SA1 1QT **Tel:** 01792 510000 **Fax:** 01792 469665
Email: chris.davies@swwmedia.co.uk
Advertising Address: As above. **Tel:** 01792 514545
Fax: 01792 514598
Web site: http://www.thisisswansea.co.uk
Publisher: South West Wales Media Ltd
Date Established: 1999
Frequency: Weekly - Published every Tuesday
Free to qualifying individuals
Circulation: 16,695 (Publisher's Statement)
Editor: Chris Davies; **News Editor:** Chris Davies
Language(s): English; Welsh
ADVERTISING RATES:
Full Page Mono £921.60
Full Page Colour £1152.00
SCC £3.20
Mechanical Data: Page Width: 270mm, Type Area: 360 x 270mm, Col Length: 360mm, Col Widths (Display): 32mm, No. of Columns (Display): 8, Film: Digital, Print Process: Web offset
Copy instructions: Copy Date: Friday 10am prior to publication date
Series owner and contact point for the following titles, see individual entries:
Neath Courier
Port Talbot Courier
Supplement(s): Negesydd - 6xY
LOCAL NEWSPAPERS: Local Newspapers Wales

COURIER (TONBRIDGE)
43898U72B-1835_130
Frequency: Weekly - Circulation figure is incorporated into the Courier (Edenbridge)
Part of Series, see entry for: Kent & Sussex Courier Series
LOCAL NEWSPAPERS: Local Newspapers English Counties

COURIER (TUNBRIDGE WELLS)
43899U72B-1835_150
Frequency: Weekly - Circulation figure is incorporated into the Courier (Edenbridge)
Part of Series, see entry for: Kent & Sussex Courier Series
LOCAL NEWSPAPERS: Local Newspapers English Counties

COURIER (WEALD)
43900U72B-1835_170
Frequency: Weekly - Circulation figure is incorporated into the Courier (Edenbridge)
Part of Series, see entry for: Kent & Sussex Courier Series
LOCAL NEWSPAPERS: Local Newspapers English Counties

COVENTRY OBSERVER
768243U72B-3928
Editorial Address: Unit B, Kings Chambers, Queens Road, COVENTRY, CV1 3EH **Tel:** 024 7649 5969
Fax: 024 7649 5998
Email: editor@coventryobserver.co.uk
Advertising Address: 1 The Courtyard, 707 Warwick Road, SOLIHULL, B91 3DA **Tel:** 024 7649 5969
Fax: 024 7649 5949
Email: kim.cooper@observerstandard.com
Web site: http://www.coventryobserver.co.uk
Publisher: Bullivant Media Limited
Date Established: 2002
Frequency: Weekly - Published on Thursday
Cover Price: Free
Circulation: 122,552 (Publisher's Statement)
Editor: Mike Green
ADVERTISING RATES:
Full Page Mono £3780.00
Full Page Colour £4725.00
Agency Commission: 10%
Mechanical Data: Page Width: 265mm, Film: Digital, Type Area: 350 x 265mm, Col Length: 350mm, Col Widths (Display): 27mm, No. of Columns (Display): 9
Copy instructions: Copy Date: Tuesday 5pm prior to publication date
Average advertising content per issue: 70%
LOCAL NEWSPAPERS: Local Newspapers English Counties

COVENTRY TELEGRAPH
42037U67B-180
Formerly: Coventry Evening Telegraph
Editorial Address: Corporation Street, COVENTRY, CV1 1FP **Tel:** 024 7663 3633 **Fax:** 024 7655 0869
Email: news@coventrytelegraph.net
Advertising Address: As above. **Fax:** 024 7622 4470
Email: sue_johnson@mrn.co.uk
Web site: http://iccoventry.icnetwork.co.uk
Publisher: Midland Newspapers Ltd
Frequency: Mornings
Cover Price: £0.40
Circulation: 48,025 (Publisher's Statement)
Usual Pagination: 52
Editor: Steve Williams; **Executive Editor:** Charles Barker;
Managing Director: Debbie Davies
ADVERTISING RATES:
SCC £15.70
Agency Commission: 10%
Mechanical Data: Film: Digital, Type Area: 340 x 264mm, Col Length: 340mm, Col Widths (Display): 28mm, No. of Columns (Display): 9, Page Width: 264mm
Copy instructions: Copy Date: 2 days prior to publication date
Average advertising content per issue: 75%
Editions:
Nuneaton Telegraph
Warwickshire Telegraph
Supplement(s): Game On - 52xY, Jobs - 52xY, Junior Sport - 52xY, Motors - 52xY, Property Guide - 52xY, Weekend - 52xY, What's On - 52xY, Your Life - 52xY
REGIONAL DAILY & SUNDAY NEWSPAPERS: Regional Daily Newspapers

COVENTRY TIMES
44527U72B-3447
Formerly: Coventry Citizen
Editorial Address: Corporation Street, COVENTRY, CV1 1FP **Tel:** 024 7650 0500 **Fax:** 024 7650 0232
Email: darren_parkin@mrn.co.uk
Advertising Address: As above. **Tel:** 024 7663 3633
Fax: 024 7650 0585
Email: craig_cooksley@mrn.co.uk
Web site: http://www.timeslive.com
Publisher: Midland Newspapers Ltd
Frequency: Weekly - Published on Thursday
Cover Price: Free
Circulation: 121,430 (VFD 02/07/2007 to 30/12/2007)
Editor: Darren Parkin; **News Editor:** Alan Harris;
Advertising Manager: Craig Cooksley

ADVERTISING RATES:
SCC £9.90
Mechanical Data: No. of Columns (Display): 9
LOCAL NEWSPAPERS: Local Newspapers English Counties

CRAIGAVON ECHO
45078U72E-80
Editorial Address: 14 Church Street, PORTADOWN, BT62 3LQ **Tel:** 028 3833 6111 **Fax:** 028 3835 0203
Email: alistair.bushe@jpress.co.uk
Advertising Address: As above.
Email: caroline.henderson@jpress.co.uk
Publisher: Morton Newspapers Ltd
Frequency: Weekly - Published every Friday
Circulation: 20,687 (VFD 02/07/2007 to 30/12/2007)
Editor: Alistair Bushe
ADVERTISING RATES:
Full Page Mono £1435.00
Full Page Colour £1937.00
SCC £4.70
Agency Commission: 10%
Mechanical Data: Type Area: 450 x 268mm, Col Length: 450mm, Col Widths (Display): 32mm, No. of Columns (Display): 9, Film: Digital, Page Width: 268mm
Copy instructions: Copy Date: Thursday 3pm prior to publication date
Average advertising content per issue: 70%
LOCAL NEWSPAPERS: Local Newspapers Northern Ireland

CRAVEN HERALD & PIONEER
44656U72B-3590
Formerly: Craven Herald & Pioneer Series
Editorial Address: 38 High Street, SKIPTON, BD23 1JU
Tel: 01756 792577 **Fax:** 01756 700310
Email: news@cravenherald.co.uk
Advertising Address: As above.
Email: gemma.aldersley@skipton.newsquest.co.uk
Web site: http://www.cravenherald.co.uk
Publisher: Newsquest Media Group
Date Established: 1853
Frequency: Weekly
Cover Price: £0.75
Circulation: 17,661 (ABC 02/07/2007 to 30/12/2007)
Editor: Lindsey Moore; **News Editor:** Lindsey Moore;
Features Editor: Lindsey Moore; **Advertising Manager:** Gemma Aldersley
ADVERTISING: Rates on application
Agency Commission: 10%
Mechanical Data: Print Process: Web-fed offset litho, Film: Digital
LOCAL NEWSPAPERS: Local Newspapers English Counties

CRAWLEY NEWS
44454U72B-3285
Editorial Address: 31-33 High Street, CRAWLEY, RH10 1BQ **Tel:** 01342 322659
Email: editor@crawleynews.co.uk
Advertising Address: 51 London Road, REIGATE, RH2 9PR
Tel: 01737 732000 **Fax:** 01737 732098
Email: matthew.bingham@essnmedia.co.uk
Web site: http://www.thisissussex.co.uk/crawley
Publisher: Northcliffe Media Ltd
Frequency: Weekly - Published on Wednesday
Cover Price: Free
Circulation: 33,782 (VFD 02/07/2007 to 30/12/2007)
Editor: Glenn Ebrey
ADVERTISING RATES:
SCC £5.68
Mechanical Data: Film: Digital, Type Area: 340 x 266mm, No. of Columns (Display): 8, Col Length: 340mm, Page Width: 266mm
Copy instructions: Copy Date: Monday 10am prior to publication date
LOCAL NEWSPAPERS: Local Newspapers English Counties

CRAWLEY OBSERVER
1814272U72B-3290_100
Frequency: Weekly - Published on Wednesday
Cover Price: £0.20
Circulation: 8,973 (ABC 01/01/2007 to 01/07/2007)
ADVERTISING RATES:
SCC £4.69
Part of Series, see entry for: Crawley Observer, Times and Herald Series
LOCAL NEWSPAPERS: Local Newspapers English Counties

CRAWLEY OBSERVER, TIMES AND HERALD SERIES
44455U72B-3290
Formerly: Crawley Observer and Herald Series
Editorial Address: 12 The Boulevard, CRAWLEY, RH10 1XY
Tel: 01293 562929 **Fax:** 01293 615589

Email: kirk.ward@sussexnewspapers.co.uk
Advertising Address: As above.
Email: richard.harmer@sussexnewspapers.co.uk
Web site: http://www.crawleyobserver.co.uk
Publisher: Sussex Newspapers Ltd
Frequency: Weekly
Circulation: 45,052 (Combined Circulation)
Editor: Kirk Ward; **Managing Director:** Carl Dimmock
ADVERTISING: Rates on application
Agency Commission: 10%
Mechanical Data: Col Length: 340mm, Page Width: 277mm, Col Widths (Display): 29mm, Film: Digital, Type Area: 340 x 277mm, No. of Columns (Display): 9
Copy instructions: Copy Date: 2 days prior to publication date
Average advertising content per issue: 60%
Series owner and contact point for the following titles, see individual entries:
Crawley Observer
Crawley Times
Weekend Herald
LOCAL NEWSPAPERS: Local Newspapers English Counties

CRAWLEY TIMES
1866688U72B-3290_102

Frequency: Weekly - Published on Friday
Cover Price: £0.50
Circulation: 1,500 (Publisher's Statement)
Part of Series, see entry for: Crawley Observer, Times and Herald Series
LOCAL NEWSPAPERS: Local Newspapers English Counties

CREDITON COUNTRY COURIER
43497U72B-785

Editorial Address: 102 High Street, CREDITON, EX17 3LF
Tel: 01363 774263 **Fax:** 01363 773545
Email: editor@creditoncouriernewspaper.co.uk
Advertising Address: As above.
Email: sales@creditoncouriernewspaper.co.uk
Web site: http://www.creditoncouriernewspaper.co.uk
Publisher: Crediton Country Courier
Date Established: 1974
Frequency: 26 issues yearly - Published on alternate Fridays
Cover Price: £0.50
Circulation: 4,500 (Publisher's Statement)
Editor: Alan Quick; **News Editor:** Arthur Sharp; **Advertising Manager:** Sarah Dickinson
ADVERTISING RATES:
Full Page Mono £428.40
SCC £1.70
Agency Commission: 10%
Mechanical Data: Type Area: 360 x 267.2mm, Col Length: 360mm, No. of Columns (Display): 7, Print Process: Web-fed offset litho, Film: Digital, Page Width: 267.2mm
Copy instructions: Copy Date: Monday prior to publication date
LOCAL NEWSPAPERS: Local Newspapers English Counties

THE CREDITON GAZETTE
43517U72B-805_140

Frequency: Weekly
Cover Price: £0.55
Part of Series, see entry for: The Gazette Series (Mid Devon)
LOCAL NEWSPAPERS: Local Newspapers English Counties

CREWE & NANTWICH GUARDIAN
43370U72B-464_140

Formerly: Crewe Guardian
Frequency: Weekly
Cover Price: Free
ADVERTISING: Rates on application
Part of Series, see entry for: Crewe Guardian Series
LOCAL NEWSPAPERS: Local Newspapers English Counties

CREWE CHRONICLE
43357U72B-435_190

Frequency: Weekly - Circulation figure includes the Nantwich Chronicle and the Sandbach Chronicle editions
Cover Price: £0.45
Circulation: 18,071 (ABC 02/07/2007 to 30/12/2007)
Part of Series, see entry for: Chronicle Series (Crewe)
LOCAL NEWSPAPERS: Local Newspapers English Counties

CREWE GUARDIAN SERIES
43369U72B-464

Editorial Address: Theatre Court, London Road, NORTHWICH, CW9 5HB **Tel:** 01606 813616

Email: crewe@guardiangrp.co.uk
Advertising Address: As above.
Email: carl.day@guardiangrp.co.uk
Web site: http://www.creweandnantwichguardian.co.uk
Publisher: Newsquest (Northwest) Ltd
Frequency: Weekly - Published on Thursday
Cover Price: Free
Circulation: 39,786 (VFD 02/07/2007 to 30/12/2007)
Editor: Mark Hilditch; **Managing Director:** Eleanor Underhill
ADVERTISING: Rates on application
Agency Commission: 10%
Average advertising content per issue: 60%
Series owner and contact point for the following titles, see individual entries:
Crewe & Nantwich Guardian
Nantwich Guardian
LOCAL NEWSPAPERS: Local Newspapers English Counties

CREWE MAIL
43379U72B-435_252

Formerly: The South Cheshire Mail
Frequency: Weekly
Cover Price: Free
Circulation: 24,917 (Publisher's Statement)
ADVERTISING RATES:
SCC £5.25
Part of Series, see entry for: Chronicle Series (Crewe)
LOCAL NEWSPAPERS: Local Newspapers English Counties

CREWKERNE ADVERTISER
44249U72B-842_105

Formerly: Crewkerne and District Advertiser
Frequency: Weekly
Cover Price: Free
Circulation: 4,000 (Publisher's Statement)
Part of Series, see entry for: Pulmans Weekly News and Advertiser Series
LOCAL NEWSPAPERS: Local Newspapers English Counties

CRICKHOWELL AND ABERGAVENNY CHRONICLE
44750U72C-15_140

Frequency: Weekly
ADVERTISING: Rates on application
Part of Series, see entry for: Abergavenny Chronicle Series
LOCAL NEWSPAPERS: Local Newspapers Wales

CROSBY HERALD
44091U72B-2319_140

Formerly: Crosby Herald incorporating Merseymart
Frequency: Weekly
Cover Price: £0.60
Circulation: 11,321 (ABC 02/07/2007 to 30/12/2007)
ADVERTISING RATES:
SCC £3.08
Part of Series, see entry for: Crosby Herald & Bootle Times Series
LOCAL NEWSPAPERS: Local Newspapers English Counties

CROSBY HERALD & BOOTLE TIMES SERIES
762043U72B-2319

Formerly: Crosby Herald & Times Series
Editorial Address: 26-32 Tulketh Street, SOUTHPORT, PR8 1BT **Tel:** 01704 536655
Email: newsdesk@crosbyherald.co.uk
Advertising Address: As above. **Fax:** 01704 532041
Email: glenn.lewin@liverpool.com
Web site: http://www.crosbyherald.co.uk
Publisher: Liverpool Daily Post & Echo Ltd
Date Established: 1894
Frequency: Weekly - Published on Thursday
Circulation: 28,145 (Combined Circulation)
Editor: Jamie Mcloughlin
ADVERTISING RATES:
SCC £5.54
Agency Commission: 10%
Mechanical Data: Type Area: 360 x 272mm, Col Length: 360mm, No. of Columns (Display): 8, Page Width: 272mm, Film: Digital
Copy instructions: Copy Date: Tuesday 1pm prior to publication date
Average advertising content per issue: 60%
Series owner and contact point for the following titles, see individual entries:
Bootle Times
Crosby Herald
LOCAL NEWSPAPERS: Local Newspapers English Counties

CROWTHORNE & SANDHURST TIMES
43288U72B-210_130

Frequency: Weekly - Circulation figure is incorporated into the Wokingham Times
Cover Price: £0.35
Part of Series, see entry for: Wokingham and Bracknell Times Series
LOCAL NEWSPAPERS: Local Newspapers English Counties

CROYDON ADVERTISER
42971U72A-50_120

Frequency: Weekly - Circulation figure is for Croydon Advertiser Series, including Caterham & District Advertiser, Coulsdon & Purley Advertiser, New Addington Advertiser and Sutton Advertiser
Cover Price: £0.55
Circulation: 19,386 (ABC 02/07/2007 to 30/12/2007)
ADVERTISING RATES:
SCC £14.50
Part of Series, see entry for: Croydon Advertiser & Post Series
LOCAL NEWSPAPERS: Local Newspapers Greater London

CROYDON ADVERTISER & POST SERIES
42969U72A-50

Formerly: Croydon Advertiser Series
Editorial Address: Jessop House, 100 Tamworth Road, CROYDON, CR0 1XX **Tel:** 020 8760 7600
Email: newsdesk@croydonadvertiser.co.uk
Advertising Address: As above.
Email: jakki.crotty@essnmedia.co.uk
Web site: http://www.thisiscroydontoday.co.uk
Publisher: Northcliffe Media Ltd
Date Established: 1869
Frequency: Weekly - Published on Wednesday and Friday
Circulation: 203,807 (Combined Circulation)
Editor: Andy Worden; **News Editor:** Jo Wadsworth
ADVERTISING: Rates on application
Agency Commission: 10%
Copy instructions: Copy Date: Tuesday 5pm prior to publication
Series owner and contact point for the following titles, see individual entries:
Caterham and District Advertiser
Coulsdon & Purley Advertiser
Croydon Advertiser
New Addington Advertiser
The Post
The Post Croydon Borough
The Post Sutton Borough
Sutton and Epsom Advertiser
LOCAL NEWSPAPERS: Local Newspapers Greater London

CROYDON GUARDIAN
42999U72A-60

Editorial Address: Unecol House, 819 London Road, SUTTON, SM3 9BN **Tel:** 020 8329 9244 **Fax:** 020 8329 9201
Email: newsdesk@croydonguardian.co.uk
Advertising Address: As above.
Email: croydonguardian@london.newsquest.co.uk
Web site: http://www.croydonguardian.co.uk
Publisher: Newsquest Media Group
Frequency: Weekly - Published on Wednesday
Cover Price: Free
Circulation: 99,753 (VFD 02/07/2007 to 30/12/2007)
Editor: Matthew Knowles; **Advertising Manager:** Leah Gauthier; **Managing Editor:** Andrew Parkes
ADVERTISING RATES:
Full Page Mono £950.95
Full Page Colour £1235.00
SCC £6.20
Agency Commission: 10%
Mechanical Data: Col Length: 315mm, Page Width: 267mm, Col Widths (Display): 27mm, Film: Digital, Type Area: 315 x 267mm, No. of Columns (Display): 9
Copy instructions: Copy Date: Friday 5.30pm prior to publication date
Average advertising content per issue: 30%
LOCAL NEWSPAPERS: Local Newspapers Greater London

THE CULM VALLEY GAZETTE
704448U72B-805_150

Formerly: The Gazette (Culm Valley)
Frequency: Weekly
Cover Price: £0.55
Part of Series, see entry for: The Gazette Series (Mid Devon)
LOCAL NEWSPAPERS: Local Newspapers English Counties

CUMBERLAND & WESTMORLAND HERALD
762174U72B-607_130

Frequency: Weekly
Cover Price: £0.55
Circulation: 18,703 (ABC 02/07/2007 to 30/12/2007)
Part of Series, see entry for: Cumberland & Westmorland Herald Series
LOCAL NEWSPAPERS: Local Newspapers English Counties

CUMBERLAND & WESTMORLAND HERALD SERIES
43445U72B-607

Editorial Address: 14 King Street, PENRITH, CA11 7AH
Tel: 01768 862313 **Fax:** 01768 890363
Email: lizs@cwherald.com
Advertising Address: As above. **Tel:** 01768 866755
Email: adverts@cwherald.com
Web site: http://www.cwherald.com
Publisher: Cumberland & Westmorland Herald
Date Established: 1870
Frequency: Weekly
Circulation: 18,703 (Combined Circulation)
Editor: Colin Maughan; **News Editor:** Liz Stannard;
Managing Director: Simon Veich; **Advertising Manager:** Vicki Richardson
ADVERTISING RATES:
Full Page Mono £3474.90
Full Page Colour £4256.75
SCC £7.15
Agency Commission: 10%
Mechanical Data: Col Length: 539mm, No. of Columns (Display): 9, Col Widths (Display): 39mm, Type Area: 539 x 388mm, Page Width: 388mm, Film: Digital
Copy instructions: Copy Date: Wednesday 12pm prior to publication date
Average advertising content per issue: 40%
Series owner and contact point for the following titles, see individual entries:
Cumberland & Westmorland Herald
Lake District Herald
LOCAL NEWSPAPERS: Local Newspapers English Counties

THE CUMBERLAND NEWS & GAZETTE SERIES
43446U72B-610

Formerly: The Cumberland News Series
Editorial Address: PO Box 7, Newspaper House, Dalston Road, CARLISLE, CA2 5UA **Tel:** 01228 612600
Fax: 01228 612640
Email: news@cumbrian-newspapers.co.uk
Advertising Address: As above.
Email: nicola.meredith@cumbrian-newspapers.co.uk
Web site: http://www.cumberland-news.co.uk
Publisher: Cumbrian Newspapers Ltd
Frequency: Weekly
Cover Price: £0.80
Circulation: 98,340 (Combined Circulation)
Editor: Sue Crawford; **News Editor:** Sue Crawford;
Features Editor: Mark Campbell; **Managing Director:** Terry Hall; **Advertising Director:** Terry Hall
ADVERTISING: Rates on application
Series owner and contact point for the following titles, see individual entries:
The Cumberland News (Brampton, Longtown & Haltwhistle)
The Cumberland News (City Edition)
The Cumberland News (County Edition)
The Cumberland News (Late Final Friday Edition)
The Cumberland News (Wigton, Aspatria, Silloth & Solway)
East Cumbrian Gazette
West Cumbrian Gazette
Supplement(s): Glamour - 12xY, Junior - 12xY, Learning - 12xY, Weddings - 12xY
LOCAL NEWSPAPERS: Local Newspapers English Counties

THE CUMBERLAND NEWS (BRAMPTON, LONGTOWN & HALTWHISTLE)
43447U72B-610_110

Frequency: Weekly
ADVERTISING: Rates on application
Part of Series, see entry for: The Cumberland News & Gazette Series
LOCAL NEWSPAPERS: Local Newspapers English Counties

THE CUMBERLAND NEWS (CITY EDITION)
43449U72B-610_130

Frequency: Weekly
Circulation: 34,509 (ABC 02/07/2007 to 30/12/2007)
ADVERTISING: Rates on application

Part of Series, see entry for: The Cumberland News & Gazette Series
LOCAL NEWSPAPERS: Local Newspapers English Counties

THE CUMBERLAND NEWS (COUNTY EDITION)
43450U72B-610_140

Frequency: Weekly
ADVERTISING: Rates on application
Part of Series, see entry for: The Cumberland News & Gazette Series
LOCAL NEWSPAPERS: Local Newspapers English Counties

THE CUMBERLAND NEWS (LATE FINAL FRIDAY EDITION)
43451U72B-610_170

Frequency: Weekly
ADVERTISING: Rates on application
Part of Series, see entry for: The Cumberland News & Gazette Series
LOCAL NEWSPAPERS: Local Newspapers English Counties

THE CUMBERLAND NEWS (WIGTON, ASPATRIA, SILLOTH & SOLWAY)
43448U72B-610_120

Frequency: Weekly
ADVERTISING: Rates on application
Part of Series, see entry for: The Cumberland News & Gazette Series
LOCAL NEWSPAPERS: Local Newspapers English Counties

CUMBERNAULD AND KILSYTH ADVERTISER
1656872U72D-258_102

Frequency: Weekly - Published on Friday
Cover Price: Free
Circulation: 17,716 (VFD 02/07/2007 to 30/12/2007)
Part of Series, see entry for: Cumbernauld News and Kilsyth Chronicle Series
LOCAL NEWSPAPERS: Local Newspapers Scotland

CUMBERNAULD NEWS
1638839U72D-258_100

Frequency: Weekly - Published on Wednesday. Circulation figure includes the Kilsyth Chronicle
Cover Price: £0.42
Circulation: 11,853 (ABC 02/07/2007 to 30/12/2007)
Part of Series, see entry for: Cumbernauld News and Kilsyth Chronicle Series
LOCAL NEWSPAPERS: Local Newspapers Scotland

CUMBERNAULD NEWS AND KILSYTH CHRONICLE SERIES
44897U72D-258

Formerly: Cumbernauld News and Kilsyth Chronicle
Editorial Address: 10-12 Tay Walk, Town Centre, Cumbernauld, GLASGOW, G67 1BU **Tel:** 01236 725578
Fax: 01236 729931
Email: editorial.cumbernauldnews@jnscotland.co.uk
Advertising Address: As above.
Email: cumbernauld.advertising@jnscotland.co.uk
Web site: http://www.cumbernauld-news.co.uk
Publisher: Johnston (Falkirk) Ltd
Date Established: 1961
Frequency: Weekly - Published every Wednesday and Friday
Circulation: 11,853 (ABC 02/07/2007 to 30/12/2007)
Editor: Alister Blyth
ADVERTISING RATES:
Full Page Mono £2215.71
Full Page Colour £3323.56
SCC £7.26
Agency Commission: 10%
Mechanical Data: Col Widths (Display): 28mm, Page Width: 272mm, Film: Digital, Col Length: 340mm, Type Area: 340 x 272mm, No. of Columns (Display): 9
Copy instructions: Copy Date: Monday 5pm prior to publication date
Average advertising content per issue: 50%
Series owner and contact point for the following titles, see individual entries:
Cumbernauld and Kilsyth Advertiser
Cumbernauld News
Kilsyth Chronicle
LOCAL NEWSPAPERS: Local Newspapers Scotland

CUMNOCK CHRONICLE
44898U72D-260

Editorial Address: 49 Ayr Road, CUMNOCK, KA18 1ED
Tel: 01290 421633 **Fax:** 01290 420832

Email: editorial.cc@cfpress.co.uk
Advertising Address: As above.
Email: advertising.cc@cfpress.co.uk
Web site: http://www.cumnockchronicle.com
Publisher: Clyde & Forth Press Group
Date Established: 1901
Frequency: Weekly - Published on Wednesday
Cover Price: £0.50
Circulation: 7,680 (ABC 01/01/2007 to 30/12/2007)
Editor: Douglas Skelton; **News Editor:** Roddie McVake
ADVERTISING RATES:
Full Page Mono £1723.92
Full Page Colour £2585.88
SCC £6.53
Mechanical Data: No. of Columns (Display): 8, Type Area: 330 x 266mm, Col Length: 330mm, Page Width: 266mm
Copy instructions: Copy Date: Tuesday 12pm prior to publication date
Average advertising content per issue: 40%
LOCAL NEWSPAPERS: Local Newspapers Scotland

Y CYFNOD
44828U72C-275_190

Frequency: Weekly
Cover Price: £0.40
Part of Series, see entry for: North Wales Series
LOCAL NEWSPAPERS: Local Newspapers Wales

Y CYMRO
44856U72C-500

Editorial Address: Cambrian News, 9 Bank Place, PORTHMADOG, LL49 9AA **Tel:** 01766 515514
Email: y-cymro@cambrian-news.co.uk
Advertising Address: Unit 7, Aberystwyth Science Park, ABERYSTWYTH, SY23 3AH **Tel:** 01970 612505
Fax: 01970 624699
Email: wendy@cambrian-news.co.uk
Publisher: Cambrian News (Aberystwyth) Ltd
Date Established: 1932
Frequency: Weekly
Cover Price: £0.50
Circulation: 6,000 (Publisher's Statement)
Editor: William Owen
Language(s): Welsh
ADVERTISING RATES:
Full Page Mono £1497.60
Full Page Colour £1972.80
SCC £5.20
Agency Commission: 10%
Mechanical Data: Film: Digital, No. of Columns (Display): 8, Type Area: 340 x 259mm, Col Length: 340mm, Page Width: 259mm, Col Widths (Display): 31mm
Copy instructions: Copy Date: Friday 10am prior to publication date
Average advertising content per issue: 25%
LOCAL NEWSPAPERS: Local Newspapers Wales

CYNON VALLEY LEADER
44785U72C-164

Editorial Address: 52-53 Glebeland Street, MERTHYR TYDFIL, CF47 8AT **Tel:** 01685 873136 **Fax:** 01685 884312
Email: cynon.valley.leader@mediawales.co.uk
Advertising Address: As above. **Tel:** 01685 856558
Fax: 01685 856556
Email: cynon.valley.leader@mediawales.co.uk
Web site: http://www.icwales.com
Publisher: Media Wales Ltd
Frequency: Weekly - Published on Wednesday
Cover Price: £0.63
Circulation: 10,137 (ABC 02/07/2007 to 30/12/2007)
Editor: Gary Marsh; **Features Editor:** Gary Marsh;
Advertising Manager: Robert Gray
ADVERTISING RATES:
SCC £4.54
Agency Commission: 10%
Mechanical Data: Type Area: 340 x 266mm, No. of Columns (Display): 8, Film: Digital, Col Widths (Display): 31.5mm, Col Length: 340mm, Page Width: 266mm
Copy instructions: Copy Date: 2 days prior to publication date
Average advertising content per issue: 30%
LOCAL NEWSPAPERS: Local Newspapers Wales

DAIL DYSYNNI
761662U72J-53

Editorial Address: 31 Ar Y Don, TYWYN, LL36 0DS
Tel: 01654 710428
Advertising Address: Fferm Penllyn, Neptune Road, TYWYN, LL36 0DP **Tel:** 01654 710094
Email: alun.win@btopenworld.com
Frequency: 11 issues yearly - Not published in September
Cover Price: £0.40
Circulation: 1,000 (Publisher's Statement)
Editor: Maldwyn Davies; **Advertising Manager:** Alun Evans
Summary of Content: Welsh language community newspaper covering local news, schooling, sports and includes a children's page.
Language(s): Welsh

Non-National Newspapers

Readership/Target Audience: Aimed at Welsh speaking readers with an interest in local affairs.
ADVERTISING RATES:
Full Page Mono £100.00
Full Page Colour £100.00
Mechanical Data: No. of Columns (Display): 3, Film: Digital
Copy instructions: Copy Date: 2 weeks prior to publication date
Average advertising content per issue: 10%
LOCAL NEWSPAPERS: Community Newsletters

DAILY ECHO (BOURNEMOUTH) 41998U67B-80

Editorial Address: Richmond Hill, BOURNEMOUTH, BH2 6HH **Tel:** 01202 554601 **Fax:** 01202 292115
Email: newsdesk@bournemouthecho.co.uk
Advertising Address: As above. **Tel:** 01202 295555
Fax: 01202 293676
Email: colette.crompton@bournemouthecho.co.uk
Web site: http://www.bournemouthecho.co.uk
Publisher: Newsquest Media Group
Date Established: 1900
Frequency: Daily
Cover Price: £0.38
Circulation: 32,441 (ABC 02/07/2007 to 30/12/2007)
Editor: Neal Butterworth; **News Editor:** Andy Martin;
Features Editor: Kevin Nash; **Managing Director:** Michael Wright
ADVERTISING: Rates on application
Copy instructions: Copy Date: 2 days prior to publication date
Supplement(s): Business South - 52xY, Homes and Property - 52xY, Jobs Today - 52xY, Lifetime - 52xY, Recruitment - 52xY, Society - 52xY, Sport on Monday - 52xY, Weekend Magazine - 52xY, What's On Guide - 52xY, Wheels - 52xY
REGIONAL DAILY & SUNDAY NEWSPAPERS: Regional Daily Newspapers

DAILY GAZETTE 42033U67B-170

Formerly: Colchester Gazette
Editorial Address: Oriel House, 43-44 North Hill, COLCHESTER, CO1 1TZ **Tel:** 01206 506000
Fax: 01206 508274
Email: gazette.newsdesk@nqe.com
Advertising Address: As above. **Fax:** 01206 508195
Email: s.morgan@nqe.com
Web site: http://www.gazette-news.co.uk
Publisher: Newsquest (Essex) Ltd
Date Established: 1970
Frequency: Daily - Published Monday to Friday
Cover Price: £0.38
Circulation: 22,131 (ABC 02/07/2007 to 30/12/2007)
Editor: Tom Parkes; **News Editor:** Dominic Bowers; **Editor-in-Chief:** Martin McNeil; **Managing Director:** Wayne Hutton
Agency Commission: 10%
Copy instructions: Copy Date: 1 day prior to publication date
Average advertising content per issue: 40%
Editions:
Coast Gazette
Colchester Gazette (Chelmsford, Witham, Braintree & Maldon)
Supplement(s): Ahead - 52xY, Business Gazette - 52xY, Gazette Family - 52xY, Motors - 52xY
REGIONAL DAILY & SUNDAY NEWSPAPERS: Regional Daily Newspapers

Y DAILY POST CYMRAEG 1666431U67H-353

Formerly: Yr Herald Cymraeg
Editorial Address: PO Box 202, Vale Road, LLANDUDNO JUNCTION, LL31 9ZD **Tel:** 01492 574455
Fax: 01492 574433
Email: yrheraldcymraeg@dailypost.co.uk
Advertising Address: 14 Eastgate Street, CAERNARFON, LL55 1AG **Tel:** 01286 681111 **Fax:** 01286 685440
Email: martin.r.williams@northwalesnews.co.uk
Web site: http://www.dailypostcymraeg.co.uk
Publisher: Liverpool Daily Post & Echo Ltd
Date Established: 1855
Frequency: Weekly - See main record for circulation figure
Editor: Tudur Huws Jones; **Advertising Manager:** Martin Williams
Summary of Content: Supplement published in Welsh covering news, current affairs and Welsh issues with interviews, entertainment coverage, arts and heritage features and events of interest to Welsh speakers.
Language(s): Welsh
ADVERTISING RATES:
SCC £11.00
Mechanical Data: Trim Size: 360 x 272mm, Col Widths (Display): 31mm, No. of Columns (Display): 8, Film: Digital
Supplement to: Daily Post (Wales)
REGIONAL DAILY & SUNDAY NEWSPAPERS: Regional Colour Supplements

DAILY POST (WALES) 42118U67B-9002

Formerly: Daily Post (Welsh Edition)
Editorial Address: PO Box 202, Vale Road, LLANDUDNO JUNCTION, LL31 9ZD **Tel:** 01492 574455
Fax: 01492 574433
Email: welshnews@dailypost.co.uk
Advertising Address: As above. **Tel:** 01492 574466
Fax: 01492 574422
Email: sharondoleman@dailypost.co.uk
Web site: http://www.dailypost.co.uk
Publisher: Trinity Mirror
Frequency: Mornings - Publishes Monday to Saturday
Cover Price: £0.42
Circulation: 36,432 (ABC 02/07/2007 to 30/12/2007)
Editor: Debbie James; **News Editor:** Debbie James
ADVERTISING RATES:
Full Page Mono £3038.40
Full Page Colour £4101.84
SCC £10.55
Agency Commission: 10%
Mechanical Data: Type Area: 360 x 272mm, Col Length: 360mm, No. of Columns (Display): 8, Col Widths (Display): 31mm, Film: Digital, Page Width: 272mm
Copy instructions: Copy Date: 2 days prior to publication date
Supplement(s): Y Daily Post Cymraeg - 52xY, Farm and Country - 52xY, Flashback - 52xY, Viva - 52xY, The Weekend Post - 52xY
REGIONAL DAILY & SUNDAY NEWSPAPERS: Regional Daily Newspapers

DAILY RECORD 42261U67B-2270

Formerly: Daily Record (Glasgow)
Editorial Address: 1 Central Quay, GLASGOW, G3 8DA
Tel: 0141 309 3000 **Fax:** 0141 309 3340
Email: reporters@dailyrecord.co.uk
Advertising Address: As above. **Fax:** 0141 309 3545
Email: advertisinginfo@dailyrecord.co.uk
Web site: http://www.dailyrecord.co.uk
Publisher: Trinity Mirror
Date Established: 1895
Frequency: Mornings
Cover Price: £0.35
Circulation: 347,302 (ABC 03/08/2009 to 30/08/2009)
Editor: News Desk; **News Editor:** Andy Lines; **Features Editor:** Melanie Harvey; **Managing Director:** Mark Hollinshead; **Managing Editor:** Derek Stuart-Brown; **Advertisement Director:** Denise West
ADVERTISING RATES:
Full Page Mono £9980.00
Full Page Colour £12974.00
SCC £42.80
Agency Commission: 15%
Mechanical Data: Type Area: 340 x 265mm, Col Widths (Display): 35mm, No. of Columns (Display): 7, Film: Digital, Col Length: 340mm, Page Width: 265mm
Copy instructions: Copy Date: 2 days prior to publication date
Average advertising content per issue: 60%
Editions:
Daily Record Aberdeen PM
Daily Record Dundee PM
Daily Record Edinburgh PM
Daily Record Glasgow PM
Supplement(s): Home Record - 52xY, Record Money - 52xY, Record Recruitment - 52xY, Road Record - 52xY, Saturday Plus - 52xY, Scotland Means Business - 4xY, Travel Select - 12xY, TV Magazine - 52xY, Vital & Living - 52xY, The Winner - 52xY, Young Scot Portal - 4xY
REGIONAL DAILY & SUNDAY NEWSPAPERS: Regional Daily Newspapers

DAILY RECORD ABERDEEN PM

1799990U67B-2270_502

Frequency: Evenings
Cover Price: Free
Edition of: Daily Record
REGIONAL DAILY & SUNDAY NEWSPAPERS: Regional Daily Newspapers

DAILY RECORD DUNDEE PM

1799991U67B-2270_503

Frequency: Evenings
Cover Price: Free
Edition of: Daily Record
REGIONAL DAILY & SUNDAY NEWSPAPERS: Regional Daily Newspapers

DAILY RECORD (EDINBURGH OFFICE)

624188U67E-200

Formerly: Daily Record (Glasgow) (Edinburgh Office)
Editorial Address: One Sixty, 160 Dundee Street, EDINBURGH, EH11 1DG **Tel:** 0131 225 4275
Fax: 0131 220 6478

Email: i.hope@dailyrecord.co.uk
Web site: http://www.dailyrecord.co.uk
Publisher: Trinity Mirror
Cover Price: £0.35
Usual Pagination: 50
Editor: Christopher Mooney
REGIONAL DAILY & SUNDAY NEWSPAPERS: Regional Offices

DAILY RECORD EDINBURGH PM

1779799U67B-2270_500

Frequency: Evenings
Cover Price: Free
Edition of: Daily Record
REGIONAL DAILY & SUNDAY NEWSPAPERS: Regional Daily Newspapers

DAILY RECORD GLASGOW PM

1779802U67B-2270_501

Frequency: Evenings
Cover Price: Free
Edition of: Daily Record
REGIONAL DAILY & SUNDAY NEWSPAPERS: Regional Daily Newspapers

DALKEITH ADVERTISER SERIES

44899U72D-270

Editorial Address: 12 High Street, DALKEITH, EH22 1HR
Tel: 0131 561 6615 **Fax:** 0131 561 6625
Email: alex.hogg@jnlothian.co.uk
Advertising Address: As above. **Tel:** 0131 561 6600
Email: advertising@jnlothian.co.uk
Web site: http://www.midlothianadvertiser.co.uk
Publisher: Johnston Press plc
Date Established: 1854
Frequency: Weekly - Published on Wednesday
Circulation: 60,690 (Combined Circulation)
Editor: Jo Robinson; **Advertising Manager:** Yvette Moore
ADVERTISING: Rates on application
Agency Commission: 10%
Mechanical Data: Film: Digital, Page Width: 272mm, Type Area: 340mm x 272mm, No. of Columns (Display): 9, Col Length: 340mm
Series owner and contact point for the following titles, see individual entries:
The Advertiser (Midlothian)
East Lothian News
The Lothian Times (East Lothian edition)
Lothian Times (Midlothian)
Musselburgh News
Peebles Times
Supplement(s): East Lothian Visitors' Guide - 1xY
LOCAL NEWSPAPERS: Local Newspapers Scotland

DARLINGTON & STOCKTON TIMES CLEVELAND

43578U72B-920_101

Frequency: Weekly
Part of Series, see entry for: Darlington & Stockton Times Series
LOCAL NEWSPAPERS: Local Newspapers English Counties

DARLINGTON & STOCKTON TIMES COUNTY DURHAM

43577U72B-920_100

Frequency: Weekly
Cover Price: £0.50
Part of Series, see entry for: Darlington & Stockton Times Series
LOCAL NEWSPAPERS: Local Newspapers English Counties

DARLINGTON AND STOCKTON TIMES, HAMBLETON

1895036U72B-920_103

Frequency: Weekly - Published on Friday
Cover Price: £0.50
Part of Series, see entry for: Darlington & Stockton Times Series
LOCAL NEWSPAPERS: Local Newspapers English Counties

DARLINGTON & STOCKTON TIMES, RICHMOND AND DALES

43579U72B-920_102

Formerly: Darlington & Stockton Times North Yorkshire
Frequency: Weekly
Part of Series, see entry for: Darlington & Stockton Times Series
LOCAL NEWSPAPERS: Local Newspapers English Counties

DARLINGTON & STOCKTON TIMES SERIES
43576U72B-920

Formerly: Darlington & Stockton Times
Editorial Address: PO Box 14, Priestgate, DARLINGTON, DL1 1NF **Tel:** 01325 381313 **Fax:** 01325 464637
Email: dst@nne.co.uk
Advertising Address: As above. **Fax:** 01325 384311
Email: displayadvertising@nne.co.uk
Web site: http://www.dst.co.uk
Publisher: Newsquest Yorkshire and North East (Darlington)
Date Established: 1847
Frequency: Weekly - Published on Friday
Circulation: 27,577 (ABC 02/07/2007 to 30/12/2007)
Editor: Newsdesk; **News Editor:** Mike Bridgen; **Managing Director:** David Coates; **Advertising Manager:** Trish Booth
ADVERTISING RATES:
Full Page Mono £6028.22
Full Page Colour £7535.27
SCC £10.34
Agency Commission: 10%
Mechanical Data: Type Area: 530 x 347mm, Col Length: 530mm, Page Width: 347mm, No. of Columns (Display): 11, Col Widths (Display): 29mm, Film: Digital
Copy instructions: Copy Date: Tuesday 3pm prior to publication date
Series owner and contact point for the following titles, see individual entries:
Darlington & Stockton Times Cleveland
Darlington & Stockton Times County Durham
Darlington and Stockton Times, Hambleton
Darlington & Stockton Times, Richmond and Dales
Supplement(s): Welcome to North Yorkshire - 1xY
LOCAL NEWSPAPERS: Local Newspapers English Counties

DARLINGTON HERALD & POST
43582U72B-3360_201

Formerly: Darlington & North Yorkshire Herald & Post
Frequency: Weekly - Published on Thursday
Cover Price: Free
Circulation: 36,898 (Publisher's Statement)
ADVERTISING RATES:
Full Page Mono £1725.00
Full Page Colour £2328.75
SCC £6.35
Part of Series, see entry for: Herald and Post Series (Teesside)
LOCAL NEWSPAPERS: Local Newspapers English Counties

DARTFORD AND SWANLEY TIMES
43911U72B-1875_200

Formerly: Swanley Times
Frequency: Weekly
Cover Price: £0.40
Circulation: 2,031 (ABC 01/01/2007 to 01/07/2007)
ADVERTISING RATES:
SCC £1.45
Part of Series, see entry for: Times and Reporter Series (Kent)
LOCAL NEWSPAPERS: Local Newspapers English Counties

DARTFORD MESSENGER
623108U72B-1782

Formerly: Dartford and Swanley Messenger
Editorial Address: 7 High Street, GRAVESEND, DA11 0BQ
Tel: 01474 564327 **Fax:** 01474 564304
Email: dartfordmessenger@thekmgroup.co.uk
Advertising Address: Medway House, Sir Thomas Longley Road, Medway City Estate, ROCHESTER, ME2 4DU
Tel: 020 8308 7406 **Fax:** 020 8300 0550
Email: jjarvis@thekmgroup.co.uk
Web site: http://www.kentonline.co.uk
Publisher: Kent Messenger Group
Date Established: 2000
Frequency: Weekly - Published on Thursday
Cover Price: £0.40
Circulation: 4,049 (Publisher's Statement)
Editor: Lauren Abbott; **News Editor:** Lauren Abbott; **Advertising Manager:** Jo-Anne Jarvis
ADVERTISING: Rates on application
Agency Commission: 10%
Copy instructions: Copy Date: Tuesday 5pm prior to publication date
LOCAL NEWSPAPERS: Local Newspapers English Counties

DARTMOUTH CHRONICLE
43542U72B-854_190

Formerly: South Hams Gazette & Dartmouth Chronicle
Frequency: Weekly
Cover Price: £0.35

Part of Series, see entry for: South Hams Newspapers Group
LOCAL NEWSPAPERS: Local Newspapers English Counties

DAVENTRY & WEST NORTHAMPTONSHIRE REVIEW
1657370U72B-2480_101

Frequency: Weekly - For circulation figure see the Rugby Review
Cover Price: Free
Part of Series, see entry for: Daventry Express and Review Series
LOCAL NEWSPAPERS: Local Newspapers English Counties

DAVENTRY EXPRESS
1657371U72B-2480_100

Frequency: Weekly
Cover Price: £0.42
Part of Series, see entry for: Daventry Express and Review Series
LOCAL NEWSPAPERS: Local Newspapers English Counties

DAVENTRY EXPRESS AND REVIEW SERIES
44152U72B-2480

Formerly: Daventry Express
Editorial Address: 63 High Street, DAVENTRY, NN11 4BQ
Tel: 01327 703383 **Fax:** 01327 300416
Email: editorial@daventryexpress.co.uk
Advertising Address: As above.
Email: advertising@daventryexpress.co.uk
Web site: http://www.daventrytoday.co.uk
Publisher: Central Counties Newspapers South Ltd
Frequency: Weekly - Published every Thursday
Circulation: 9,323 (ABC 02/07/2007 to 30/12/2007)
Editor: Alice Dyer
ADVERTISING RATES:
Full Page Mono £1156.00
Full Page Colour £1459.00
Agency Commission: 10%
Mechanical Data: Page Width: 265mm, Col Widths (Display): 28mm, Col Length: 340mm, Type Area: 340 x 265mm, Film: Digital, No. of Columns (Display): 9
Copy instructions: Copy Date: Tuesday 2pm prior to publication date
Average advertising content per issue: 63%
Series owner and contact point for the following titles, see individual entries:
Daventry & West Northamptonshire Review
Daventry Express
Supplement(s): Business Focus - 12xY
LOCAL NEWSPAPERS: Local Newspapers English Counties

DAWLISH GAZETTE
43498U72B-790

Formerly: Dawlish Gazette Series
Editorial Address: Gazette Office, 6 Park Road, DAWLISH, EX7 9LQ **Tel:** 01626 864161 **Fax:** 01626 888518
Email: mda.edit@internet-today.co.uk
Advertising Address: 39 Teign Street, TEIGNMOUTH, TQ14 8EA **Tel:** 01626 779494 **Fax:** 01626 777155
Email: teign.sales@internet-today.co.uk
Web site: http://www.dawlish-today.co.uk
Publisher: Dawlish Newspapers Ltd
Frequency: Weekly
Cover Price: £0.30
Circulation: 13,251 (Publisher's Statement)
Editor: Ruth Davey; **Advertising Manager:** Keith Hawkins
ADVERTISING RATES:
Full Page Mono £1368.00
Full Page Colour £1642.00
Agency Commission: 10%
Mechanical Data: Col Length: 360mm, No. of Columns (Display): 8, Film: Digital, Type Area: 360 x 262mm, Page Width: 262mm, Col Widths (Display): 30mm
Copy instructions: Copy Date: Monday 12pm prior to publication date
Average advertising content per issue: 55%
LOCAL NEWSPAPERS: Local Newspapers English Counties

DAWLISH POST
43511U72B-827_120

Frequency: Weekly
Cover Price: Free
Circulation: 4,850 (Publisher's Statement)
Part of Series, see entry for: Mid-Devon Advertiser Series
LOCAL NEWSPAPERS: Local Newspapers English Counties

DEARNE VALLEY WEEKENDER
44674U72B-3676

Formerly: Rotherham Advertiser
Editorial Address: Brookfields Way, Manvers, Wath Upon Dearne, ROTHERHAM, S63 5DL **Tel:** 01709 768014
Fax: 01709 768014
Email: howard.poucher@garnett-dickinson.co.uk
Advertising Address: 84 High Street, MEXBOROUGH, S64 9AU **Tel:** 01709 768000
Email: carol.colley@garnett-dickinson.co.uk
Web site: http://www.rotherhamadvertiser.co.uk
Publisher: Garnett Dickinson Group Ltd
Frequency: Weekly - Published every Friday
Cover Price: Free
Circulation: 50,550 (VFD 02/07/2007 to 30/12/2007)
Editor: Howard Poucher; **Advertising Manager:** Carol Colley
Summary of Content: Newspaper covering news and events in Rotherham.
Readership/Target Audience: Aimed at people living in this area.
ADVERTISING RATES:
SCC £4.65
Agency Commission: 10%
Mechanical Data: Type Area: 340 x 269mm, Col Length: 340mm, Page Width: 269mm, Film: Digital, Col Widths (Display): 31mm, No. of Columns (Display): 8
Copy instructions: Copy Date: Wednesday 4.30pm prior to publication date
Average advertising content per issue: 80%
LOCAL NEWSPAPERS: Local Newspapers English Counties

THE DEESIDE PIPER & HERALD
44907U72D-280_130

Frequency: Weekly - Circulation figure is incorporated into the Deeside Piper and Herald Series
Cover Price: £0.54
Part of Series, see entry for: Deeside Piper and Herald Series
LOCAL NEWSPAPERS: Local Newspapers Scotland

DEESIDE PIPER AND HERALD SERIES
44906U72D-280

Editorial Address: 1 Scott Skinner Square, BANCHORY, AB31 5SE **Tel:** 01330 824955 **Fax:** 01330 825236
Email: pipereditorial@deesidepiper.com
Advertising Address: As above.
Email: piperadverts@deesidepiper.com
Web site: http://www.deesidepiper.co.uk
Publisher: Angus County Press Ltd
Frequency: Weekly - Published on Thursday. Circulation figure includes the Deeside Piper, Donside Piper and Inverurie Herald
Cover Price: £0.55
Circulation: 8,595 (ABC 02/07/2007 to 30/12/2007)
Editor: Kim Walton
ADVERTISING RATES:
SCC £4.75
Agency Commission: 10%
Mechanical Data: Page Width: 272mm, Type Area: 340 x 272mm, Col Length: 340mm, No. of Columns (Display): 7, Col Widths (Display): 34mm, Print Process: Web-fed offset litho, Film: Digital
Copy instructions: Copy Date: Monday 3pm prior to publication date
Series owner and contact point for the following titles, see individual entries:
The Deeside Piper & Herald
The Donside Piper & Herald
LOCAL NEWSPAPERS: Local Newspapers Scotland

DEMOCRAT (DUNGANNON)
45096U72E-120_200

Frequency: Weekly
Cover Price: £0.40
Part of Series, see entry for: Dungannon Observer Series
LOCAL NEWSPAPERS: Local Newspapers Northern Ireland

DENBIGHSHIRE EVENING LEADER
1866631U67B-2080_681

Frequency: Evenings
ADVERTISING RATES:
SCC £8.50
Edition of: Evening Leader
REGIONAL DAILY & SUNDAY NEWSPAPERS: Regional Daily Newspapers

Non-National Newspapers

DENBIGHSHIRE FREE PRESS (CORWEN & BALA)
44787U72C-173_120

Frequency: Weekly
Part of Series, see entry for: Denbighshire Free Press Series
LOCAL NEWSPAPERS: Local Newspapers Wales

DENBIGHSHIRE FREE PRESS (DENBIGH & RUTHIN)
44788U72C-173_150

Frequency: Weekly
Part of Series, see entry for: Denbighshire Free Press Series
LOCAL NEWSPAPERS: Local Newspapers Wales

DENBIGHSHIRE FREE PRESS SERIES
44786U72C-173

Editorial Address: Mold Business Park, Wrexham Road, MOLD, CH7 1XY **Tel:** 01745 357500
Email: editor@denbighshirefreepress.co.uk
Advertising Address: 23 Kinmel Street, RHYL, LL18 1AH
Tel: 01745 357500 **Fax:** 01745 343510
Email: rebecca.marlow@nwn.co.uk
Web site: http://www.denbighshirefreepress.co.uk
Publisher: NWN Media Ltd
Date Established: 1881
Frequency: Weekly - Published on Thursday
Cover Price: £0.50
Circulation: 7,148 (ABC 02/07/2007 to 30/12/2007)
Editor: Nic Outterside; **Managing Director:** David Faulkaer; **Advertising Manager:** Rebecca Marlow
Language(s): English; Welsh
ADVERTISING RATES:
SCC £4.80
Mechanical Data: Page Width: 259mm, Type Area: 370 x 259mm, Col Length: 370mm, Col Widths (Display): 27mm, No. of Columns (Display): 9, Film: Digital
Copy instructions: Copy Date: Tuesday 5.30pm prior to publication date
Series owner and contact point for the following titles, see individual entries:
Denbighshire Free Press (Corwen & Bala)
Denbighshire Free Press (Denbigh & Ruthin)
LOCAL NEWSPAPERS: Local Newspapers Wales

DERBY EXPRESS
43478U72B-695_140

Frequency: Weekly
Cover Price: Free
Part of Series, see entry for: Derby Express and Messenger Series
LOCAL NEWSPAPERS: Local Newspapers English Counties

DERBY EXPRESS AND MESSENGER SERIES
43476U72B-695

Formerly: Derby Express Series
Editorial Address: Northcliffe House, Meadow Road, DERBY, DE1 2BH **Tel:** 01332 291111 **Fax:** 01332 253027
Email: hburton@derbytelegraph.co.uk
Advertising Address: As above. **Fax:** 01332 253011
Email: lhatton@derbytelegraph.co.uk
Web site: http://www.thisisderbyshire.co.uk
Publisher: Derby Daily Telegraph Ltd
Frequency: Weekly
Cover Price: Free
Circulation: 111,621 (VFD 02/07/2007 to 30/12/2007)
Editor: Hilary Burton; **Advertising Manager:** Lorraine Hatton
ADVERTISING RATES:
Full Page Colour £1200.00
Mechanical Data: Type Area: 360 x 269mm, Col Length: 360mm, Page Width: 269mm, No. of Columns (Display): 8, Col Widths (Display): 31mm, Film: Digital
Copy instructions: Copy Date: Mono 5pm Friday Colour 12pm Thursday prior to publication date
Average advertising content per issue: 80%
Series owner and contact point for the following titles, see individual entries:
Belper Express
Derby Express
Derby Messenger
Ilkeston Express
LOCAL NEWSPAPERS: Local Newspapers English Counties

DERBY MESSENGER
1866236U72B-695_171

Frequency: Weekly
Cover Price: Free
Part of Series, see entry for: Derby Express and Messenger Series
LOCAL NEWSPAPERS: Local Newspapers English Counties

DERBY TELEGRAPH
42048U67B-210

Formerly: Evening Telegraph (Derby)
Editorial Address: Northcliffe House, Meadow Road, DERBY, DE1 2BH **Tel:** 01332 291111
Email: newsdesk@derbytelegraph.co.uk
Advertising Address: As above. **Fax:** 01332 253011
Email: mlomas@derbytelegraph.co.uk
Web site: http://www.thisisderbyshire.co.uk
Publisher: Derby Daily Telegraph Ltd
Frequency: Mornings
Cover Price: £0.35
Circulation: 42,726 (ABC 02/07/2007 to 30/12/2007)
Editor: Newsdesk; **Features Editor:** Jill Gallone; **Managing Director:** Joanne Glynn; **Advertising Manager:** Michele Lomas
ADVERTISING RATES:
Full Page Mono £3330.00
Full Page Colour £4162.50
SCC £11.25
Mechanical Data: Type Area: 360 x 269mm, No. of Columns (Display): 8, Col Widths (Display): 31mm, Col Length: 360mm, Page Width: 269mm, Film: Digital, Print Process: Web-fed offset litho
Copy instructions: Copy Date: Mono 12pm 2 days prior to publication date Colour 2 days prior to publication date
REGIONAL DAILY & SUNDAY NEWSPAPERS: Regional Daily Newspapers

DERBYSHIRE TIMES ALFRETON
43488U72B-710_180

Frequency: Weekly
ADVERTISING: Rates on application
Part of Series, see entry for: Derbyshire Times Series
LOCAL NEWSPAPERS: Local Newspapers English Counties

DERBYSHIRE TIMES CHESTERFIELD/ CLAY CROSS
43486U72B-710_150

Frequency: Weekly
Cover Price: £0.35
ADVERTISING: Rates on application
Part of Series, see entry for: Derbyshire Times Series
LOCAL NEWSPAPERS: Local Newspapers English Counties

DERBYSHIRE TIMES MATLOCK/PEAK
43489U72B-710_190

Frequency: Weekly
ADVERTISING: Rates on application
Part of Series, see entry for: Derbyshire Times Series
LOCAL NEWSPAPERS: Local Newspapers English Counties

DERBYSHIRE TIMES SERIES
43484U72B-710

Formerly: Derbyshire Times and Chesterfield Gazette Series
Editorial Address: 37 Station Road, CHESTERFIELD, S41 7XD **Tel:** 01246 504500 **Fax:** 01246 504579
Email: editorial@derbyshiretimes.co.uk
Advertising Address: As above. **Fax:** 01246 504557
Email: carol.silcock@derbyshiretimes.co.uk
Web site: http://www.derbyshiretimes.co.uk
Publisher: Wilfred Edmunds Ltd
Frequency: Weekly - Published on Thursday
Cover Price: £0.55
Circulation: 40,241 (ABC 02/07/2007 to 30/12/2007)
Editor: Clare Morris
ADVERTISING: Rates on application
Series owner and contact point for the following titles, see individual entries:
Derbyshire Times Alfreton
Derbyshire Times Chesterfield/ Clay Cross
Derbyshire Times Matlock/Peak
LOCAL NEWSPAPERS: Local Newspapers English Counties

DEREHAM & FAKENHAM TIMES
44135U72B-2437_130

Frequency: Weekly
Cover Price: £0.55
Circulation: 8,141 (ABC 02/07/2007 to 30/12/2007)
ADVERTISING: Rates on application
Part of Series, see entry for: Norfolk County Weeklies Series
LOCAL NEWSPAPERS: Local Newspapers English Counties

DERRY JOURNAL (FRIDAY)
45080U72E-100_120

Frequency: Weekly
Cover Price: £0.90

Circulation: 20,898 (ABC 02/07/2007 to 30/12/2007)
ADVERTISING RATES:
Full Page Mono £3630.00
Full Page Colour £5082.00
SCC £6.00
Mechanical Data: Type Area: 560 x 328mm, Col Length: 560mm, Page Width: 328mm
Part of Series, see entry for: Derry Journal Series
LOCAL NEWSPAPERS: Local Newspapers Northern Ireland

DERRY JOURNAL SERIES
45079U72E-100

Editorial Address: 22 Buncrana Road, LONDONDERRY, BT48 8AA **Tel:** 028 7127 2200 **Fax:** 028 7127 2218
Email: erin.hutcheon@derryjournal.com
Advertising Address: As above. **Fax:** 028 7127 2225
Email: caroline.morris@derryjournal.com
Web site: http://www.derryjournal.com
Publisher: Derry Journal Ltd
Date Established: 1772
Frequency: Weekly
Circulation: 72,956 (Combined Circulation)
Editor: Erin Hutcheon; **News Editor:** Sean McLaughlin; **Advertising Manager:** Caroline Morris
ADVERTISING RATES:
Full Page Mono £6413.00
Full Page Colour £8978.00
SCC £10.60
Agency Commission: 10%
Mechanical Data: Type Area: 341 x 268mm, Col Length: 341mm, Page Width: 268mm, Col Widths (Display): 28mm, No. of Columns (Display): 9, Film: Digital
Copy instructions: Copy Date: 1pm 2 working days prior to publication date
Series owner and contact point for the following titles, see individual entries:
Derry Journal (Friday)
Derry Journal (Tuesday)
Foyle News
LOCAL NEWSPAPERS: Local Newspapers Northern Ireland

DERRY JOURNAL (TUESDAY)
45081U72E-100_130

Frequency: Weekly
Cover Price: £0.90
Circulation: 19,054 (ABC 02/07/2007 to 30/12/2007)
ADVERTISING RATES:
Full Page Mono £1805.40
Full Page Colour £2527.56
SCC £5.90
Part of Series, see entry for: Derry Journal Series
LOCAL NEWSPAPERS: Local Newspapers Northern Ireland

DERRY NEWS (MONDAY)
1687633U72E-101_100

Frequency: Weekly
Cover Price: £0.80
Circulation: 6,684 (ABC 02/07/2007 to 30/12/2007)
ADVERTISING: Rates on application
Copy instructions: Copy Date: Friday 12pm prior to publication date
Part of Series, see entry for: Derry News Series
LOCAL NEWSPAPERS: Local Newspapers Northern Ireland

DERRY NEWS SERIES
708160U72E-101

Formerly: Derry News
Editorial Address: 26 Balliniska Road, Springtown Industrial Estate, LONDONDERRY, BT48 0LY **Tel:** 028 7129 6600 **Fax:** 028 7129 6611
Email: eamonn@derrynews.net
Advertising Address: As above. **Fax:** 028 7129 6605
Email: admin@derrynews.net
Publisher: River Media
Date Established: 2001
Frequency: 104 issues yearly - Published Monday and Thursday
Circulation: 14,166 (ABC 02/07/2007 to 30/12/2007)
Editor: Ciaran O'Neill; **Advertising Manager:** Carol O Hagan; **Group Editor:** Ciaran O'Neill
ADVERTISING: Rates on application
Agency Commission: 10%
Copy instructions: Copy Date: 2 days prior to publication date
Average advertising content per issue: 40%
Series owner and contact point for the following titles, see individual entries:
Derry News (Monday)
Derry News (Thursday)
LOCAL NEWSPAPERS: Local Newspapers Northern Ireland

DERRY NEWS (THURSDAY)
1687634U72E-101_101

Frequency: Weekly
Cover Price: £0.80
Circulation: 7,482 (ABC 02/07/2007 to 30/12/2007)

ADVERTISING: Rates on application
Copy instructions: Copy Date: Tuesday 12pm prior to publication date
Part of Series, see entry for: Derry News Series
LOCAL NEWSPAPERS: Local Newspapers Northern Ireland

THE DEWSBURY REPORTER

44697U72B-3760_130

Formerly: The Reporter Dewsbury
Frequency: Weekly - Circulation figure includes The Mirfield Reporter
Cover Price: £0.42
Circulation: 11,468 (ABC 02/07/2007 to 30/12/2007)
ADVERTISING RATES:
Full Page Mono £1168.00
Full Page Colour £1519.00
SCC £3.82
Part of Series, see entry for: Dewsbury Reporter and Advertiser Series
LOCAL NEWSPAPERS: Local Newspapers English Counties

DEWSBURY REPORTER AND ADVERTISER SERIES

44696U72B-3760

Formerly: Dewsbury Reporter Series
Editorial Address: 17 Wellington Road, DEWSBURY, WF13 1HQ **Tel:** 01924 468282 **Fax:** 01924 487124
Email: dewsburyeditorial@ywng.co.uk
Advertising Address: As above. **Fax:** 01924 457652
Web site: http://www.dewsburyreporter.co.uk
Publisher: The Reporter Ltd
Date Established: 1858
Frequency: Weekly
Circulation: 11,468 (ABC 02/07/2007 to 30/12/2007)
Editor: Hannah Ridgeway; **News Editor:** Julie Bartram; **Features Editor:** Margaret Watson
ADVERTISING RATES:
Full Page Mono 2836.00
Full Page Colour 3687.00
SCC £9.27
Agency Commission: 10%
Mechanical Data: Type Area: 340mm x 274mm, Col Length: 340mm, No. of Columns (Display): 9, Page Width: 274mm, Col Widths (Display): 30mm, Film: Digital
Copy instructions: Copy Date: 2 days prior to publication date
Average advertising content per issue: 30%
Series owner and contact point for the following titles, see individual entries:
The Dewsbury Reporter
The Mirfield Reporter
Reporter Extra
Supplement(s): The Guide - 52xY
LOCAL NEWSPAPERS: Local Newspapers English Counties

DIDCOT HERALD

44224U72B-2720_130

Frequency: Weekly - Circulation can be found with the Abingdon Herald
Cover Price: £0.35
ADVERTISING RATES:
SCC £4.75
Part of Series, see entry for: Herald and Times Series Oxon
LOCAL NEWSPAPERS: Local Newspapers English Counties

DINNINGTON & MALTBY GUARDIAN

44202U72B-2670_120

Frequency: Weekly
Cover Price: £0.55
Circulation: 3,700 (Publisher's Statement)
ADVERTISING RATES:
SCC £5.14
Part of Series, see entry for: Guardian Series (Worksop)
LOCAL NEWSPAPERS: Local Newspapers English Counties

DINNINGTON & MALTBY TRADER NEWS

44208U72B-2670_181

Frequency: Weekly
Cover Price: Free
Circulation: 21,142 (VFD 02/07/2007 to 30/12/2007)
ADVERTISING RATES:
SCC £4.29
Part of Series, see entry for: Guardian Series (Worksop)
LOCAL NEWSPAPERS: Local Newspapers English Counties

DISS EXPRESS

44140U72B-2440

Formerly: Diss Express Series
Editorial Address: Norfolk & Suffolk House, Mere Street, DISS, IP22 4AE **Tel:** 01379 642264 **Fax:** 01379 650110
Email: editorial@dissexpress.co.uk
Advertising Address: As above.
Email: advertising@dissexpress.co.uk
Web site: http://www.disstoday.co.uk
Publisher: Johnston Press plc
Date Established: 1864
Frequency: Weekly - Published on Friday
Cover Price: £0.48
Circulation: 8,486 (ABC 02/07/2007 to 30/12/2007)
Editor: Catherine Morris; **Advertising Manager:** Ron Westrup
ADVERTISING RATES:
Full Page Mono £1753.38
Full Page Colour 2279.39
SCC £5.73
Agency Commission: 10%
Mechanical Data: Print Process: Web-fed offset litho, Col Widths (Display): 28mm, Col Length: 341mm, Type Area: 341 x 265mm, Page Width: 265mm, No. of Columns (Display): 9
Copy instructions: Copy Date: Wednesday 1pm prior to publication date
Average advertising content per issue: 45%
LOCAL NEWSPAPERS: Local Newspapers English Counties

DISS MERCURY

44136U72B-2437_140

Frequency: Weekly
Cover Price: Free
Circulation: 15,299 (VFD 02/07/2007 to 30/12/2007)
ADVERTISING: Rates on application
Part of Series, see entry for: Norfolk County Weeklies Series
LOCAL NEWSPAPERS: Local Newspapers English Counties

THE DOCKLANDS

1831093U72A-1322_100

Frequency: Weekly
Cover Price: Free
Part of Series, see entry for: The Docklands and Peninsula Series
LOCAL NEWSPAPERS: Local Newspapers Greater London

THE DOCKLANDS AND PENINSULA SERIES

1732845U72A-1322

Formerly: The Docklands
Editorial Address: 138 Cambridge Heath Road, Bethnal Green, LONDON, E1 5QJ **Tel:** 020 7791 7791
Email: docknews@archant.co.uk
Advertising Address: As above. **Fax:** 020 7791 7701
Email: lynn.grieveson@archant.co.uk
Web site: http://www.docklands24.co.uk
Publisher: Archant London
Date Established: 2006
Frequency: Weekly
Cover Price: Free
Circulation: 31,500 (Combined Circulation)
Editor: John Hyde
ADVERTISING RATES:
SCC £7.50
Copy instructions: Copy Date: Monday 11.00 am prior to publication date
Series owner and contact point for the following titles, see individual entries:
The Docklands
The Peninsula
LOCAL NEWSPAPERS: Local Newspapers Greater London

DONCASTER ADVERTISER

44675U72B-3677

Formerly: Doncaster Advertiser (East)
Editorial Address: Sunny Bar, DONCASTER, DN1 1NB
Tel: 01302 347299 **Fax:** 01302 348521
Email: advertiser@doncastertoday.co.uk
Advertising Address: As above. **Tel:** 01302 347232
Fax: 01302 348525
Email: eve.hanson@doncastertoday.co.uk
Publisher: South Yorkshire Newspapers Ltd
Date Established: 1974
Frequency: Weekly
Cover Price: Free
Circulation: 56,077 (VFD 02/07/2007 to 30/12/2007)
Editor: Martin Edmunds; **Managing Director:** Paul Bentham
ADVERTISING RATES:
Full Page Mono £749.70
Full Page Colour £974.61
SCC £3.50
Agency Commission: 10%

Mechanical Data: Type Area: 340 x 265mm, No. of Columns (Display): 9, Col Widths (Display): 28mm, Film: Digital, Type Area: 340mm, Page Width: 265mm
Copy instructions: Copy Date: Tuesday 6.00pm prior to publication date
Average advertising content per issue: 80%
LOCAL NEWSPAPERS: Local Newspapers English Counties

DONCASTER FREE PRESS

44677U72B-3680

Editorial Address: Sunny Bar, DONCASTER, DN1 1NB
Tel: 01302 347264 **Fax:** 01302 348523
Email: editorial@doncastertoday.co.uk
Advertising Address: As above. **Tel:** 01302 347241
Fax: 01302 348519
Email: advertising@doncastertoday.co.uk
Web site: http://www.doncasterfreepress.co.uk
Publisher: South Yorkshire Newspapers Ltd
Date Established: 1925
Frequency: Weekly - Published on Thursday
Cover Price: £0.60
Circulation: 34,029 (ABC 02/07/2007 to 30/12/2007)
Editor: Kath Finlay; **News Editor:** Kath Finlay; **Features Editor:** Darren Burke; **Editor-in-Chief:** Graeme Huston; **Managing Director:** Paul Bentham
ADVERTISING RATES:
Full Page Mono £1165.25
Full Page Colour £1516.54
Agency Commission: 10%
Mechanical Data: Type Area: 340 x 272mm, No. of Columns (Display): 9, Film: Digital, Col Length: 340mm, Page Width: 272mm, Col Widths (Display): 28mm
Copy instructions: Copy Date: Monday 6pm prior to publication date
Average advertising content per issue: 70%
Supplement(s): Profile - 6xY, Property Guide - 52xY, South Yorkshire Motor Guide - 52xY
LOCAL NEWSPAPERS: Local Newspapers English Counties

DONCASTER GAZETTE

1698045U72B-3982_101

Frequency: 26 issues yearly
Cover Price: Free
Part of Series, see entry for: Rotherham Gazette Series
LOCAL NEWSPAPERS: Local Newspapers English Counties

THE DONSIDE PIPER & HERALD

44908U72D-280_140

Frequency: Weekly - Circulation figure is incorporated into the Deeside Piper and Herald Series
Cover Price: £0.54
Part of Series, see entry for: Deeside Piper and Herald Series
LOCAL NEWSPAPERS: Local Newspapers Scotland

DORKING ADVERTISER

44352U72B-3095_140

Frequency: Weekly - Circulation figure also includes the Leatherhead Advertiser
Cover Price: £0.60
Circulation: 11,114 (ABC 02/07/2007 to 30/12/2007)
Part of Series, see entry for: Advertiser Series (Surrey)
LOCAL NEWSPAPERS: Local Newspapers English Counties

DORSET ADVERTISER

43556U72B-903

Formerly: Advertiser Series (Weymouth)
Editorial Address: Fleet House, Hampshire Road, Granby Industrial Estate, WEYMOUTH, DT4 9XD **Tel:** 01305 830930
Fax: 01305 830956
Email: newsdesk@dorsetecho.co.uk
Web site: http://www.dorsetecho.co.uk
Publisher: Newsquest (Media Group) Ltd
Frequency: Weekly - Published on Friday
Cover Price: Free
Circulation: 35,843 (Publisher's Statement)
Editor: James Tougout; **News Editor:** James Tougout; **Features Editor:** Ruth Meech
ADVERTISING: No Advertising taken
LOCAL NEWSPAPERS: Local Newspapers English Counties

DORSET ECHO

42197U67B-1140

Formerly: Dorset Evening Echo
Editorial Address: Fleet House, Hampshire Road, Granby Industrial Estate, WEYMOUTH, DT4 9XD **Tel:** 01305 830930
Fax: 01305 830956
Email: newsdesk@dorsetecho.co.uk
Advertising Address: As above. **Fax:** 01305 830869
Email: tracey.hajden@dorsetecho.co.uk
Web site: http://www.dorsetecho.co.uk

Publisher: Newsquest (Media Group) Ltd
Frequency: Evenings
Cover Price: £0.32
Circulation: 18,803 (ABC 02/07/2007 to 30/12/2007)
Editor: James Tourgout; **News Editor:** James Tourgout;
Features Editor: Diarmuid MacDonagh
ADVERTISING RATES:
SCC £5.97
Agency Commission: 10%
Mechanical Data: Col Length: 350mm, No. of Columns
(Display): 8, Type Area: 350 x 261mm, Page Width: 261mm,
Col Widths (Display): 30mm, Film: Digital
Copy instructions: Copy Date: 5pm 2 days prior to
publication date
Supplement(s): Dorset Echo Weekend Magazine - 52xY
REGIONAL DAILY & SUNDAY NEWSPAPERS: Regional
Daily Newspapers

DOVER AND DEAL EXTRA   43866U72B-1795_120
Frequency: Weekly - Circulation figure is incorporated into
the Extra (Folkestone and Hythe)
Cover Price: Free
Part of Series, see entry for: Express Extra Series Kent
LOCAL NEWSPAPERS: Local Newspapers English
Counties

DOVER EXPRESS   43875U72B-1750_125
Frequency: Weekly
Cover Price: £0.55
Circulation: 9,470 (ABC 02/07/2007 to 30/12/2007)
ADVERTISING: Rates on application
Part of Series, see entry for: Adscene, Herald & Express
Series (Folkestone)
LOCAL NEWSPAPERS: Local Newspapers English
Counties

DOVER MERCURY   43929U72B-1882_140
Frequency: Weekly - Circulation figure is incorporated into
the East Kent Mercury
Cover Price: £0.50
Part of Series, see entry for: Mercury Series (Kent)
LOCAL NEWSPAPERS: Local Newspapers English
Counties

DOWN DEMOCRAT   45084U72E-103
Editorial Address: 74 Market Street, DOWNPATRICK, BT30
6LZ **Tel:** 028 4461 4400 **Fax:** 028 4461 2221
Email: editor@downdemocrat.com
Advertising Address: As above.
Email: veronica.barr@downdemocrat.com
Web site: http://www.downdemocrat.com
Publisher: Irish Examiner
Date Established: 1992
Frequency: Weekly - Published on Tuesday
Cover Price: £0.85
Circulation: 3,389 (Publisher's Statement)
Editor: Colm Donnelly; **Advertising Manager:** Veronica Barr
ADVERTISING RATES:
SCC £3.50
Mechanical Data: Col Length: 330mm, Type Area: 330 x
265mm, Page Width: 265mm, Film: Digital, No. of Columns
(Display): 8, Col Widths (Display): 29mm
Copy instructions: Copy Date: Friday 12pm prior to
publication date
Supplement(s): Community Times - 52xY, Sport - 52xY
LOCAL NEWSPAPERS: Local Newspapers Northern Ireland

DOWN RECORDER   45085U72E-105
Editorial Address: 2-4 Church Street, DOWNPATRICK,
BT30 6EJ **Tel:** 028 4461 3711 **Fax:** 028 4461 4624
Email: editor@thedownrecorder.co.uk
Advertising Address: As above.
Email: advertising@thedownrecorder.co.uk
Web site: http://www.thedownrecorder.com
Publisher: W.Y. Crichton & Co Ltd
Date Established: 1836
Frequency: Weekly - Published on Wednesday
Cover Price: £0.65
Circulation: 11,711 (ABC 02/07/2007 to 30/12/2007)
Editor: Paul Symington; **Features Editor:** Marcus Crichton;
Advertising Manager: Caroline Rogan
ADVERTISING RATES:
Full Page Mono £1453.25
SCC £5.25
Mechanical Data: Type Area: 410 x 270mm, No. of
Columns (Display): 7, Col Length: 410mm, Page Width:
270mm
LOCAL NEWSPAPERS: Local Newspapers Northern Ireland

DOWNHAM NEWS   1702946U72B-2435_152
Frequency: Monthly
Cover Price: Free
Circulation: 6,500 (Publisher's Statement)
ADVERTISING RATES:
Full Page Mono £306.00
Full Page Colour £397.80
Part of Series, see entry for: Lynn News Series
LOCAL NEWSPAPERS: Local Newspapers English
Counties

DOWNS MAIL (EAST MAIDSTONE)
768239U72B-3660_100
Frequency: Monthly
Cover Price: Free
Circulation: 17,000 (Publisher's Statement)
Part of Series, see entry for: Downs Mail Series
LOCAL NEWSPAPERS: Local Newspapers English
Counties

DOWNS MAIL (MAIDSTONE TOWN)
768241U72B-3660_101
Frequency: Monthly
Cover Price: Free
Circulation: 30,000 (Publisher's Statement)
Part of Series, see entry for: Downs Mail Series
LOCAL NEWSPAPERS: Local Newspapers English
Counties

DOWNS MAIL SERIES   46926U72B-3660
Formerly: Downs Mail
Editorial Address: 2 Forge House, Bearsted Green
Business Park, Bearsted, MAIDSTONE, ME14 4DT
Tel: 01622 734735 **Fax:** 01622 631131
Email: dfowle2011@aol.com
Advertising Address: As above. **Tel:** 01622 630330
Email: info@downsmail.co.uk
Web site: http://www.downsmail.co.uk
Publisher: Mail Publications Ltd
Date Established: 1997
Frequency: Monthly
Cover Price: Free
Circulation: 62,000 (Combined Circulation)
Usual Pagination: 56
Editor: Murray Evans; **News Editor:** Stephen Eighteen
Readership/Target Audience: Read by residents and local
business people in Maidstone and the surrounding area.
ADVERTISING RATES:
Full Page Mono £1500.00
Full Page Colour £1585.00
Agency Commission: 10%
Mechanical Data: Col Length: 271mm, Col Widths (Display):
41.5mm, No. of Columns (Display): 4, Type Area: 271 x
181mm, Bleed Size: 298 x 205mm, Page Width: 181mm,
Film: Digital
Copy instructions: Copy Date: 10 days prior to publication
date
Average advertising content per issue: 60%
**Series owner and contact point for the following titles,
see individual entries:**
Downs Mail (East Maidstone)
Downs Mail (Maidstone Town)
Downs Mail (South & Weald)
Supplement(s): Mid-Kent Living - 12xY
LOCAL NEWSPAPERS: Local Newspapers English
Counties

DOWNS MAIL (SOUTH & WEALD)
768242U72B-3660_102
Frequency: Monthly
Cover Price: Free
Circulation: 15,000 (Publisher's Statement)
Part of Series, see entry for: Downs Mail Series
LOCAL NEWSPAPERS: Local Newspapers English
Counties

DRIFFIELD POST   44632U72B-3576_130
Frequency: Weekly
Cover Price: £0.40
Circulation: 4,800 (Publisher's Statement)
Summary of Content: News, sport and entertainment.
Copy instructions: Copy Date: Wednesday 12am prior to
publication date
Part of Series, see entry for: Driffield Times Series
LOCAL NEWSPAPERS: Local Newspapers English
Counties

DRIFFIELD TIMES   44633U72B-3576_140
Frequency: Weekly
Cover Price: £0.42

Circulation: 5,211 (ABC 02/07/2007 to 30/12/2007)
Summary of Content: Local news, sport and entertainment.
Copy instructions: Copy Date: Monday 5pm prior to
publication date
Part of Series, see entry for: Driffield Times Series
LOCAL NEWSPAPERS: Local Newspapers English
Counties

DRIFFIELD TIMES SERIES   44630U72B-3576
Editorial Address: Times House, Mill Street, DRIFFIELD,
YO25 6TN **Tel:** 01377 241414 **Fax:** 01377 241507
Email: editorial@driffieldtoday.co.uk
Advertising Address: As above. **Tel:** 01377 241122
Fax: 01377 241396
Email: jenny.harrison@ypn.co.uk
Web site: http://www.driffieldtoday.co.uk
Publisher: Yorkshire Regional Newspapers Ltd
Date Established: 1860
Frequency: Weekly
Circulation: 29,611 (Combined Circulation)
Editor: Dennis Sissons; **News Editor:** Steve Petch;
Advertising Manager: Shirley Ruston
ADVERTISING RATES:
SCC £11.40
Agency Commission: 10%
Mechanical Data: Type Area: 340 x 274mm, Col Length:
340mm, Page Width: 274mm, No. of Columns (Display): 9,
Col Widths (Display): 27mm, Film: Digital
Copy instructions: Copy Date: Monday 4pm prior to
publication date
**Series owner and contact point for the following titles,
see individual entries:**
Beverley Guardian
Driffield Post
Driffield Times
Supplement(s): Motoring Today - 52xY, Property Today -
52xY
LOCAL NEWSPAPERS: Local Newspapers English
Counties

DROITWICH SPA ADVERTISER
44609U72B-3558_160
Frequency: Weekly
Cover Price: Free
Part of Series, see entry for: Bromsgrove Advertiser Series
LOCAL NEWSPAPERS: Local Newspapers English
Counties

DROITWICH SPA STANDARD
44622U72B-3566_185
Frequency: Weekly - Circulation figure is included into the
Bromsgrove Standard
Cover Price: Free
ADVERTISING RATES:
SCC £5.66
Part of Series, see entry for: Redditch and Bromsgrove
Standard Series
LOCAL NEWSPAPERS: Local Newspapers English
Counties

DRONFIELD ADVERTISER   43473U72B-691_130
Frequency: Weekly
Cover Price: Free
Circulation: 10,286 (VFD 02/07/2007 to 30/12/2007)
ADVERTISING: Rates on application
Part of Series, see entry for: Chesterfield & Dronfield
Advertiser Series
LOCAL NEWSPAPERS: Local Newspapers English
Counties

DUDLEY CHRONICLE   44534U72B-3450_120
Frequency: Weekly
Cover Price: Free
Circulation: 46,972 (VFD 02/07/2007 to 30/12/2007)
ADVERTISING: Rates on application
Part of Series, see entry for: Dudley Chronicle Series
LOCAL NEWSPAPERS: Local Newspapers English
Counties

DUDLEY CHRONICLE SERIES   44533U72B-3450
Editorial Address: 51-53 Queen Street,
WOLVERHAMPTON, WV1 1ES **Tel:** 01384 353217
Fax: 01384 353221
Email: dudleychrons@expressandstar.co.uk
Advertising Address: Express & Star Regional Centre,
Hurst Business Park, Narrowboat Way, BRIERLEY HILL,
DY5 1ES **Tel:** 01384 355355 **Fax:** 01384 353222
Email: b.wain@expressandstar.co.uk
Web site: http://www.expressandstar.co.uk
Publisher: Express & Star Ltd
Frequency: Weekly - Published on Thursday

Cover Price: Free
Circulation: 168,985 (Combined Circulation)
Editor: John Nash; **Advertising Manager:** Brian Wain
ADVERTISING: Rates on application
Agency Commission: 10%
Copy instructions: Copy Date: Tuesday 1pm prior to publication date
Average advertising content per issue: 75%
Series owner and contact point for the following titles, see individual entries:
Dudley Chronicle
Halesowen Chronicle
Kidderminster Chronicle
Stourbridge Chronicle
LOCAL NEWSPAPERS: Local Newspapers English Counties

DUDLEY NEWS & COUNTY EXPRESS

44537U72B-3453

Editorial Address: St. John's House, St. John's Road, STOURBRIDGE, DY8 1EH **Tel:** 01384 358085
Fax: 01384 358252
Email: newsgrouped@midlands.newsquest.co.uk
Advertising Address: As above. **Tel:** 01384 358200
Fax: 01384 358253
Email: caroline.smith@midlands.newsquest.co.uk
Web site: http://www.dudleynews.co.uk
Publisher: Newsquest Midlands (South) Ltd
Frequency: Weekly - Published on Thursday
Cover Price: Free
Circulation: 38,894 (VFD 02/07/2007 to 30/12/2007)
Editor: News Desk; **Advertising Manager:** Caroline Smith; **Publisher:** Peter John
ADVERTISING RATES:
SCC £3.30
Mechanical Data: Type Area: 350 x 268mm, Col Length: 350mm, Page Width: 268mm, No. of Columns (Display): 9, Col Widths (Display): 28mm, Film: Digital
Copy instructions: Copy Date: Tuesday 12am prior to publication date
LOCAL NEWSPAPERS: Local Newspapers English Counties

DUMBARTON AND VALE OF LEVEN REPORTER

44909U72D-290

Editorial Address: 88 Dumbarton Road, CLYDEBANK, G81 1UG **Tel:** 01389 763335 **Fax:** 0141 952 7267
Email: editorial@dumbartonreporter.co.uk
Advertising Address: As above. **Tel:** 0141 952 1345
Email: advertising@cfpress.co.uk
Web site: http://www.dumbartonreporter.co.uk
Publisher: Clyde & Forth Press Group
Frequency: Weekly - Published on Tuesday
Cover Price: £0.50
Circulation: 4,332 (ABC 01/01/2007 to 30/12/2007)
Editor: Lorna Caitens; **Advertising Manager:** Lorna Scobie
ADVERTISING RATES:
Full Page Mono £792.00
Full Page Colour £1188.00
Agency Commission: 10%
Mechanical Data: No. of Columns (Display): 8, Type Area: 330mm x 266mm, Col Length: 330mm, Page Width: 266mm, Film: Digital
Copy instructions: Copy Date: Monday 10am prior to publication date
Average advertising content per issue: 40%
LOCAL NEWSPAPERS: Local Newspapers Scotland

DUMFRIES AND GALLOWAY NEWS SERIES

44947U72D-440

Formerly: Galloway News
Editorial Address: Unit 3A, Station Yard Industrial Estate, Oakwell Road, CASTLE DOUGLAS, DG7 1LA
Tel: 01556 504141 **Fax:** 01556 504159
Email: gallowaynews@s-un.co.uk
Advertising Address: As above. **Tel:** 01387 253123
Email: gallowaynews@s-un.co.uk
Web site: http://www.icdumfries.co.uk
Publisher: Scottish & Universal Newspapers Ltd
Frequency: Weekly - Published on Thursday and Friday
Circulation: 16,631 (Combined Circulation)
Usual Pagination: 48
Editor: Lee Kerr; **Advertising Manager:** Jane Milven
ADVERTISING: Rates on application
Series owner and contact point for the following titles, see individual entries:
Dumfries and Galloway Today
Galloway News
Supplement(s): Farming Review - 8xY
LOCAL NEWSPAPERS: Local Newspapers Scotland

DUMFRIES & GALLOWAY STANDARD

44910U72D-310

Editorial Address: Maxwell Town Industrial Estate, Glasgow Road, DUMFRIES, DG2 0NA **Tel:** 01387 255252
Fax: 01387 256613
Email: dgnews@s-un.co.uk
Advertising Address: As above. **Tel:** 01387 253123
Fax: 01387 268800
Email: dumfries_adv@s-un.co.uk
Web site: http://www.icdumfries.co.uk
Publisher: Scottish & Universal Newspapers Ltd
Frequency: 104 issues yearly - Published on Wednesday and Friday
Circulation: 27,257 (Publisher's Statement)
Editor: Iain Pollock; **Advertising Manager:** Jane Milven
ADVERTISING RATES:
Full Page Mono £2937.00
Full Page Colour £3962.50
Agency Commission: 10%
Mechanical Data: Film: Digital, Type Area: 340 x 265mm, Col Length: 340mm, Page Width: 265mm
Copy instructions: Copy Date: Monday 5pm prior to publication date
Average advertising content per issue: 45%
Series owner and contact point for the following titles, see individual entries:
Dumfries & Galloway Standard (Friday)
Dumfries & Galloway Standard (Wednesday)
LOCAL NEWSPAPERS: Local Newspapers Scotland

DUMFRIES & GALLOWAY STANDARD (FRIDAY)

44912U72D-310_140

Frequency: Weekly
Cover Price: £0.42
Circulation: 16,683 (ABC 02/07/2007 to 30/12/2007)
ADVERTISING: Rates on application
Part of Series, see entry for: Dumfries & Galloway Standard
LOCAL NEWSPAPERS: Local Newspapers Scotland

DUMFRIES & GALLOWAY STANDARD (WEDNESDAY)

44911U72D-310_130

Frequency: Weekly
Circulation: 10,574 (ABC 02/07/2007 to 30/12/2007)
ADVERTISING: Rates on application
Part of Series, see entry for: Dumfries & Galloway Standard
LOCAL NEWSPAPERS: Local Newspapers Scotland

DUMFRIES AND GALLOWAY TODAY

1605577U72D-440_100

Frequency: Weekly - Published on Friday
Cover Price: Free
Circulation: 6,831 (Publisher's Statement)
ADVERTISING: Rates on application
Part of Series, see entry for: Dumfries and Galloway News Series
LOCAL NEWSPAPERS: Local Newspapers Scotland

DUMFRIES COURIER

44916U72D-325_130

Frequency: Weekly - Published on Friday
Cover Price: Free
Circulation: 25,092 (VFD 02/07/2007 to 30/12/2007)
ADVERTISING: Rates on application
Part of Series, see entry for: Annandale Observer Series
LOCAL NEWSPAPERS: Local Newspapers Scotland

DUNDALK ADVERTISER

45086U72E-120_135

Email: editor@observernewspapersni.com
Frequency: Monthly
Cover Price: Free
Part of Series, see entry for: Dungannon Observer Series
LOCAL NEWSPAPERS: Local Newspapers Northern Ireland

DUNFERMLINE PRESS AND WEST OF FIFE ADVERTISER

44919U72D-328

Editorial Address: Pitreavie Business Park, Queensferry Road, DUNFERMLINE, KY11 8QS **Tel:** 01383 728201
Fax: 01383 737040
Email: newseditor@dunfermlinepress.co.uk
Advertising Address: As above.
Email: advertising@dunfermlinepress.co.uk
Web site: http://www.dunfermlinepress.co.uk
Publisher: The Dunfermline Press Group
Date Established: 1859
Frequency: Weekly
Cover Price: £0.60
Circulation: 21,005 (ABC 02/07/2007 to 30/12/2007)

Editor: Alastair McRoberts; **News Editor:** Alastair McRoberts; **Advertising Manager:** Lynn Hubber
ADVERTISING RATES:
Full Page Mono £4290.00
Full Page Colour £8580.00
SCC £7.80
Agency Commission: 10%
Mechanical Data: Type Area: 550 x 332.5mm, Col Length: 550mm, Col Widths (Display): 31mm, No. of Columns (Display): 10, Film: Digital, Page Width: 332.5mm
Copy instructions: Copy Date: Tuesday 4pm prior to publication date
Average advertising content per issue: 60%
LOCAL NEWSPAPERS: Local Newspapers Scotland

DUNGANNON NEWS & TYRONE COURIER

45087U72E-110

Editorial Address: 58 Scotch Street, DUNGANNON, BT70 1BD **Tel:** 028 8772 2271 **Fax:** 028 8772 6171
Email: newsdesk@tyronecourier.uk.com
Advertising Address: As above.
Email: advertising@tyronecourier.uk.com
Web site: http://www.ulsternet-ni.co.uk
Publisher: Tyrone Printing Co Ltd
Frequency: Weekly - Published on Wednesday
Cover Price: £0.95
Circulation: 15,083 (Publisher's Statement)
Editor: Ian Greer; **Features Editor:** Beulah-Anne Wallace
ADVERTISING RATES:
Full Page Mono £1047.55
Full Page Colour £1587.55
SCC £3.65
Agency Commission: 10%
Mechanical Data: Film: Digital, Page Width: 272mm, Col Length: 410mm, Type Area: 410 x 272mm, Col Widths (Display): 35mm, No. of Columns (Display): 7, Print Process: Web offset
Copy instructions: Copy Date: Mono Monday 5pm prior to puiblication date Colour Thursday 5pm prior to publication date
Average advertising content per issue: 40%
LOCAL NEWSPAPERS: Local Newspapers Northern Ireland

DUNGANNON OBSERVER

45092U72E-120_140

Frequency: Weekly
Cover Price: £0.40
Part of Series, see entry for: Dungannon Observer Series
LOCAL NEWSPAPERS: Local Newspapers Northern Ireland

DUNGANNON OBSERVER SERIES

45088U72E-120

Editorial Address: Ann Street, DUNGANNON, BT70 1ET
Tel: 028 8772 2557 **Fax:** 028 8772 7334
Email: editor@observernewspapersni.com
Advertising Address: As above.
Publisher: Observer Newspapers Northern Ireland Ltd
Frequency: Weekly
Editor: Desmond Mallon; **Features Editor:** Eithne Mallon; **Managing Director:** Desmond Mallon; **Advertising Manager:** Desmond Mallon
ADVERTISING RATES:
SCC £12.50
Mechanical Data: Type Area: 550 x 368mm, Col Length: 550mm, Film: Digital, No. of Columns (Display): 9, Page Width: 368mm
Series owner and contact point for the following titles, see individual entries:
Armagh Observer
Ballymena Chronicle & Antrim Observer
Democrat (Dungannon)
Dundalk Advertiser
Dungannon Observer
Fermanagh News
Lurgan & Portadown Examiner
Mid Ulster Observer
The Newry Advertiser
LOCAL NEWSPAPERS: Local Newspapers Northern Ireland

DUNMOW & STANSTED OBSERVER

43802U72B-1545_130

Formerly: Dunmow and Waldon Observer
Frequency: Weekly - See the Herts & Essex Observer for circulation figure
Cover Price: £0.55
Part of Series, see entry for: Herts & Essex Observer Series
LOCAL NEWSPAPERS: Local Newspapers English Counties

DUNMOW BROADCAST AND RECORDER
43603U72B-995

Editorial Address: 54 High Street, SAFFRON WALDEN, CB10 1EE **Tel:** 01371 874537 **Fax:** 01371 874538
Email: editor@dunmow-broadcast.co.uk
Advertising Address: 2 Angel Lane, GREAT DUNMOW, CM6 1AQ **Tel:** 01799 512880
Email: sales@dunmow-broadcast.co.uk
Web site: http://www.dunmow-broadcast.co.uk
Publisher: Archant Herts & Cambs
Frequency: Weekly - Published on Thursday
Cover Price: Free
Circulation: 11,945 (VFD 02/07/2007 to 30/12/2007)
Editor: Nick Thompson; **Advertising Manager:** Donna Neville
ADVERTISING: Rates on application
Agency Commission: 10%
Copy instructions: Copy Date: Tuesday 4pm prior to publication date
Average advertising content per issue: 40%
LOCAL NEWSPAPERS: Local Newspapers English Counties

DUNOON OBSERVER & ARGYLLSHIRE STANDARD
44920U72D-330

Editorial Address: 219 Argyll Street, DUNOON, PA23 7QT
Tel: 01369 703218 **Fax:** 01369 707850
Email: editorial@dunoon-observer.co.uk
Advertising Address: As above. **Tel:** 01369 706854
Fax: 01369 702462
Email: advertising@dunoon-observer.co.uk
Web site: http://www.dunoon-observer.co.uk
Publisher: E. & R. Inglis
Date Established: 1871
Frequency: Weekly
Cover Price: £0.60
Circulation: 6,500 (Publisher's Statement)
Editor: Colin Cameron; **Advertising Manager:** Susan Irwin
ADVERTISING RATES:
Full Page Mono £924.00
Full Page Colour £1152.80
SCC £3.85
Agency Commission: 10%
Mechanical Data: Page Width: 272mm, No. of Columns (Display): 6, Col Length: 400mm, Type Area: 400 x 272mm, Col Widths (Display): 42mm, Film: Digital
Copy instructions: Copy Date: Tuesday 12pm prior to publication date
Average advertising content per issue: 45%
LOCAL NEWSPAPERS: Local Newspapers Scotland

DUNSTABLE GAZETTE
43242U72B-137_110

Frequency: Weekly - Published on Thursday
Cover Price: £0.38
Circulation: 4,442 (ABC 02/07/2007 to 30/12/2007)
ADVERTISING: Rates on application
Part of Series, see entry for: Luton News and Dunstable Gazette Series
LOCAL NEWSPAPERS: Local Newspapers English Counties

DURHAM TIMES
1810536U72B-4055

Editorial Address: Ribble House, Unit 10, Mandale Park, Belmont Industrial Estate, DURHAM, DH1 1TH
Tel: 0191 384 4600
Email: durhamtimes@nne.co.uk
Advertising Address: Suite 2, Blackmoor Court, DURHAM, DH1 5ER **Tel:** 0191 374 0298 **Fax:** 0191 384 8817
Email: chris.miller@nne.co.uk
Web site: http://www.durhamtimes.co.uk
Publisher: Newsquest Yorkshire and North East (Darlington)
Date Established: 2007
Frequency: Weekly
Cover Price: £0.30
Free to qualifying individuals
Circulation: 6,000 (Publisher's Statement)
Editor: Tony Kearney
ADVERTISING: Rates on application
LOCAL NEWSPAPERS: Local Newspapers English Counties

Y DYDD
1644405U72C-501

Editorial Address: 9 Bank Place, PORTHMADOG, LL49 9AA **Tel:** 01766 515514 **Fax:** 01766 514738
Email: ydydd@cambrian-news.co.uk
Advertising Address: As above. **Tel:** 01766 513815
Fax: 01766 512817
Email: carolyn@cambrian-news.co.uk
ISSN: 1742-402X
Publisher: Cambrian News (Aberystwyth) Ltd
Frequency: Weekly - Published on Saturday
Cover Price: £0.30
Circulation: 1,000 (Publisher's Statement)

Editor: Iwan Jones; **Advertising Manager:** Carolyn Ballantyne
Language(s): English; Welsh
ADVERTISING RATES:
SCC £5.00
Agency Commission: 10%
Mechanical Data: Trim Size: 330 x 270mm, Film: Digital, No. of Columns (Display): 8, Page Width: 269mm
Copy instructions: Copy Date: Thursday 10am prior to publication date
LOCAL NEWSPAPERS: Local Newspapers Wales

DYSYNNI CAMBRIAN NEWS
1659702U72C-30_181

Formerly: Dysynni and Cambrian News
Frequency: Weekly
Cover Price: £0.65
ADVERTISING: Rates on application
Part of Series, see entry for: The Cambrian News Series
LOCAL NEWSPAPERS: Local Newspapers Wales

EA WEEK
633802U67H-75

Formerly: East Anglian Magazine
Editorial Address: Press House, 30 Lower Brook Street, IPSWICH, IP4 1AN **Tel:** 01473 324716
Email: dominic.castle@eadt.co.uk
Advertising Address: As above. **Tel:** 01473 324599
Fax: 01473 324626
Email: mark.gallant@archant.co.uk
Web site: http://www.eadt.co.uk
Publisher: Archant Suffolk
Date Established: 1990
Frequency: Weekly - Published on Saturday
Usual Pagination: 64
Editor: Dominic Castle; **Advertising Manager:** Mark Gallant
Summary of Content: Lifestyle magazine containing features on fashion, interiors, beauty, travel and gardening.
Readership/Target Audience: Aimed mainly at women between 25 and 85 years of age, living in East Anglia.
ADVERTISING RATES:
Full Page Colour £1535.00
Agency Commission: 10%
Mechanical Data: Type Area: 340 x 270mm, Col Widths (Display): 32mm, No. of Columns (Display): 8, Col Length: 340mm, Page Width: 270mm
Copy instructions: Copy Date: 2 weeks prior to publication date
Supplement to: East Anglian Daily Times
REGIONAL DAILY & SUNDAY NEWSPAPERS: Regional Colour Supplements

EALING LEADER
42988U72A-110_110

Frequency: Weekly
Cover Price: Free
Circulation: 75,102 (VFD 02/07/2007 to 30/12/2007)
ADVERTISING RATES:
SCC £11.00
Part of Series, see entry for: The Gazette and Leader Series
LOCAL NEWSPAPERS: Local Newspapers Greater London

EASINGWOLD ADVERTISER & WEEKLY NEWS
44657U72B-3600

Editorial Address: Advertiser Office, The Market Place, Easingwold, YORK, YO61 3AB **Tel:** 01347 821329
Fax: 01347 822576
Email: news@easingwoldadvertiser.com
Advertising Address: As above.
Email: tiser@ghsmith.com
Web site: http://www.easingwoldadvertiser.com
ISSN: 1749-5962
Publisher: G.H. Smith & Son
Date Established: 1892
Frequency: Weekly
Cover Price: £0.10
Circulation: 3,500 (Publisher's Statement)
Editor: Rupert Smith; **Advertising Manager:** Alex Smith
ADVERTISING RATES:
Full Page Mono £369.00
Full Page Colour £462.00
Mechanical Data: Col Length: 350mm, No. of Columns (Display): 6, Type Area: 350 x 280mm, Page Width: 280mm, Print Process: Litho, Col Widths (Display): 43mm
Copy instructions: Copy Date: Wednesday 12pm prior to publication date
LOCAL NEWSPAPERS: Local Newspapers English Counties

EAST ANGLIAN DAILY TIMES
42078U67B-300

Editorial Address: Press House, 30 Lower Brook Street, IPSWICH, IP4 1AN **Tel:** 01473 230023 **Fax:** 01473 324871
Email: news@eadt.co.uk
Advertising Address: As above. **Fax:** 01473 232529
Email: julian.evans@archant.co.uk

Web site: http://www.eadt.co.uk
Publisher: Archant Suffolk
Frequency: Mornings
Cover Price: £0.50
Circulation: 34,392 (ABC 02/07/2007 to 30/12/2007)
Editor: Brad Jones; **News Editor:** Brad Jones; **Features Editor:** Julian Ford; **Managing Director:** Stuart McCreery; **Advertising Manager:** Julian Evans
ADVERTISING RATES:
Full Page Mono £2522.88
Full Page Colour £3532.03
SCC £8.76
Agency Commission: 10%
Mechanical Data: Type Area: 360 x 270mm, Col Length: 360mm, No. of Columns (Display): 8, Film: Digital, Page Width: 270mm, Col Widths (Display): 32mm
Copy instructions: Copy Date: 2 days prior to publication date
Average advertising content per issue: 35%
Editions:
East Anglian Daily Times (East Edition)
East Anglian Daily Times (Essex)
East Anglian Daily Times (West Edition)
Supplement(s): Business East - 52xY, EA Week - 52xY
REGIONAL DAILY & SUNDAY NEWSPAPERS: Regional Daily Newspapers

EAST ANGLIAN DAILY TIMES (EAST EDITION)
42079U67B-300_540

Edition of: East Anglian Daily Times
REGIONAL DAILY & SUNDAY NEWSPAPERS: Regional Daily Newspapers

EAST ANGLIAN DAILY TIMES (ESSEX)
42080U67B-300_560

Edition of: East Anglian Daily Times
REGIONAL DAILY & SUNDAY NEWSPAPERS: Regional Daily Newspapers

EAST ANGLIAN DAILY TIMES (WEST EDITION)
42081U67B-300_660

Edition of: East Anglian Daily Times
REGIONAL DAILY & SUNDAY NEWSPAPERS: Regional Daily Newspapers

EAST ANTRIM ADVERTISER
45125U72E-226_130

Frequency: Weekly
Cover Price: Free
Circulation: 19,006 (Publisher's Statement)
Part of Series, see entry for: The Times Series
LOCAL NEWSPAPERS: Local Newspapers Northern Ireland

EAST ANTRIM GAZETTE SERIES
45062U72E-55

Formerly: Carrickfergus Advertiser and Ballyclare Gazette Series
Editorial Address: 6 Market Place, CARRICKFERGUS, BT38 7AW **Tel:** 028 9335 2967 **Fax:** 028 9335 2449
Email: news@carrickadvertiser.co.uk
Advertising Address: As above. **Tel:** 028 9336 3651
Fax: 028 9336 3092
Email: advertisingmanager@carrickadvertiser.co.uk
Web site: http://www.ulsternet-ni.co.uk
Publisher: Cerdac
Frequency: Weekly - Published on Tuesday
Circulation: 3,607 (ABC 02/07/2007 to 30/12/2007)
Editor: David Hall; **Advertising Manager:** Michelle Brennan
ADVERTISING RATES:
Full Page Mono £1047.85
Full Page Colour 1587.55
SCC £3.65
Agency Commission: 10%
Mechanical Data: Page Width: 272mm, Film: Digital, Type Area: 410 x 272mm, Col Length: 410mm, No. of Columns (Display): 7, Col Widths (Display): 35mm
Series owner and contact point for the following titles, see individual entries:
Ballyclare Gazette and East Antrim Gazette
Carrickfergus Advertiser and East Antrim Gazette
Larne Gazette and East Antrim Gazette
LOCAL NEWSPAPERS: Local Newspapers Northern Ireland

EAST CLEVELAND HERALD & POST
43409U72B-3360_140

Formerly: East Cleveland Herald & Post incorporating Teesside Times
Frequency: Weekly - Published on Wednesday
Cover Price: Free
Circulation: 47,122 (VFD 02/07/2007 to 30/12/2007)

ADVERTISING RATES:
Full Page Mono £2115.00
Full Page Colour £2855.25
SCC £7.80
Part of Series, see entry for: Herald and Post Series (Teesside)
LOCAL NEWSPAPERS: Local Newspapers English Counties

EAST CORNWALL TIMES
43545U72B-857_140

Frequency: Weekly
Cover Price: £0.55
Circulation: 750 (Publisher's Statement)
Part of Series, see entry for: Tavistock Times Gazette Series
LOCAL NEWSPAPERS: Local Newspapers English Counties

EAST CUMBRIAN GAZETTE
43453U72B-610_190

Frequency: Weekly
Cover Price: Free
Circulation: 36,160 (VFD 02/07/2007 to 30/12/2007)
ADVERTISING: Rates on application
Part of Series, see entry for: The Cumberland News & Gazette Series
LOCAL NEWSPAPERS: Local Newspapers English Counties

EAST END LIFE
42977U72A-80

Editorial Address: Mulberry Place, 5 Clove Crescent, LONDON, E14 2BG **Tel:** 020 7364 3179 **Fax:** 020 7364 4917
Email: eastendlife.news@towerhamlets.gov.uk
Advertising Address: As above. **Tel:** 020 7364 3059
Fax: 020 7364 4384
Email: chris.payne@towerhamlets.gov.uk
Web site: http://www.towerhamlets.gov.uk
Publisher: Tower Hamlets Council
Date Established: 1993
Frequency: Weekly
Cover Price: Free
Circulation: 78,914 (VFD 02/07/2007 to 30/12/2007)
Editor: Laraine Clay; **Advertising Manager:** Kim Chaplin
Language(s): Bengali; English; Somali
ADVERTISING RATES:
Full Page Mono £1300.00
Full Page Colour £1300.00
SCC £7.50
Agency Commission: 10%
Mechanical Data: No. of Columns (Display): 6, Type Area: 340 x 265mm, Col Length: 340mm, Col Widths (Display): 41mm, Film: Digital, Page Width: 265mm
Copy instructions: Copy Date: Wednesday 12pm prior to publication date
Average advertising content per issue: 50%
Supplement(s): Get a Life! - 12xY
LOCAL NEWSPAPERS: Local Newspapers Greater London

EAST FIFE MAIL
44922U72D-204

Editorial Address: 7 Mitchell Street, LEVEN, KY8 4HJ
Tel: 01333 423201 **Fax:** 01333 421915
Email: efmeditor@fifetoday.co.uk
Advertising Address: As above.
Email: mailads@fifetoday.co.uk
Web site: http://www.fifetoday.co.uk
Publisher: Strachan & Livingston Ltd
Date Established: 1911
Frequency: Weekly - Published on Wednesday
Cover Price: £0.40
Circulation: 10,982 (ABC 01/01/2007 to 01/07/2007)
Editor: Jerzy Morkis; **Advertising Manager:** Bill Morgan
ADVERTISING RATES:
SCC £4.81
Agency Commission: 10%
Mechanical Data: Col Length: 340mm, Type Area: 340 x 272mm, Page Width: 272mm, Col Widths (Display): 28mm, No. of Columns (Display): 9, Film: Digital
Copy instructions: Copy Date: Monday 1pm prior to publication date
Average advertising content per issue: 45%
LOCAL NEWSPAPERS: Local Newspapers Scotland

EAST GRINSTEAD COURIER & OBSERVER
44456U72B-3300

Formerly: East Grinstead Courier
Editorial Address: 37 High Street, EAST GRINSTEAD, RH19 3AF **Tel:** 01892 681000 **Fax:** 01892 510400
Email: editor.eastgrinstead@essnmedia.co.uk
Advertising Address: As above. **Fax:** 01342 410736
Email: geoff.ashton@courier.co.uk
Web site: http://www.thisiscourier.co.uk
Publisher: Northcliffe Media Ltd
Frequency: Weekly - Published on Thursday

Cover Price: £0.40
Free to qualifying individuals
Circulation: 15,000 (Publisher's Statement)
Editor: Emily Bridges; **Editor-in-Chief:** Ian Carter
ADVERTISING RATES:
Full Page Mono £1094.40
Full Page Colour £1258.56
SCC £3.80
Mechanical Data: Film: Digital, Page Width: 270mm, Type Area: 360 x 270mm, Col Length: 360mm, No. of Columns (Display): 8
LOCAL NEWSPAPERS: Local Newspapers English Counties

EAST HERTS HERALD
43791U72B-1600_282

Formerly: East Herts & Broxbourne Herald
Frequency: Weekly
Cover Price: Free
Circulation: 43,063 (VFD 02/07/2007 to 30/12/2007)
ADVERTISING RATES:
Full Page Mono £1953.72
SCC £6.03
Mechanical Data: Page Width: 263mm, Print Process: Web-fed offset litho, Col Length: 350mm, Col Widths (Display): 9, Type Area: 350 x 263mm, Col Widths (Display): 27mm, Film: Digital
Part of Series, see entry for: Welwyn & Hatfield Times & Herald Series
LOCAL NEWSPAPERS: Local Newspapers English Counties

EAST KENT GAZETTE
43861U72B-1790_140

Frequency: Weekly - Circulation figure also includes Sheppey Gazette
Cover Price: £0.50
Circulation: 11,515 (ABC 02/07/2007 to 30/12/2007)
Part of Series, see entry for: East Kent Gazette Series
LOCAL NEWSPAPERS: Local Newspapers English Counties

EAST KENT GAZETTE SERIES
43860U72B-1790

Editorial Address: North Kent Media Centre, 4 Ambley Green, Gillingham Business Park, GILLINGHAM, ME8 0NJ
Tel: 01634 236320 **Fax:** 01634 236331
Email: newsdesk.gazette@krnmedia.co.uk
Advertising Address: Press Centre, 19 High Street, SITTINGBOURNE, ME10 4AY **Tel:** 01795 475411
Fax: 01795 425596
Email: sales.ekg@kentregionalnewspapers.co.uk
Web site: http://www.thisiskent.co.uk
Publisher: Northcliffe Media Ltd
Date Established: 1855
Frequency: Weekly - Published on Wednesday
Circulation: 29,121 (Combined Circulation)
Editor: News Desk
ADVERTISING RATES:
Full Page Mono £682.50
Full Page Colour £761.25
SCC £4.99
Agency Commission: 10%
Mechanical Data: Film: Digital, Col Widths (Display): 31mm, No. of Columns (Display): 8
Copy instructions: Copy Date: 3 days prior to publication date
Average advertising content per issue: 40%
Series owner and contact point for the following titles, see individual entries:
Adscene (Sittingbourne & Sheppey)
East Kent Gazette
Faversham Times
Sheppey Gazette
LOCAL NEWSPAPERS: Local Newspapers English Counties

EAST KENT MERCURY
43930U72B-1882_160

Frequency: Weekly - Circulation figure includes the Dover Mercury
Cover Price: £0.50
Circulation: 13,841 (ABC 02/07/2007 to 30/12/2007)
Part of Series, see entry for: Mercury Series (Kent)
LOCAL NEWSPAPERS: Local Newspapers English Counties

EAST KILBRIDE MAIL
1641627U72D-1006

Editorial Address: 228 Eaglesham Road, East Kilbride, GLASGOW, G75 8RH **Tel:** 01355 270515
Fax: 01355 590748
Email: editorial@eastkilbridemail.com
Advertising Address: As above. **Tel:** 01355 271888
Email: sales@eastkilbridemail.com
Publisher: Forth Independent Newspapers
Date Established: 2004
Frequency: Weekly - Published on Wednesday

Cover Price: Free
Circulation: 26,000 (Publisher's Statement)
Editor: Willie Mack; **Advertising Manager:** Steve McDonald
ADVERTISING RATES:
Full Page Colour £1229.00
SCC £4.52
Agency Commission: 10%
Mechanical Data: Film: Digital, Type Area: 347 x 266mm, Col Length: 347mm, Page Width: 266mm
Copy instructions: Copy Date: Monday 5pm prior to publication date
Average advertising content per issue: 60%
LOCAL NEWSPAPERS: Local Newspapers Scotland

EAST KILBRIDE NEWS
44923U72D-340

Editorial Address: 2 Olympia Arcade, Town Centre, EAST KILBRIDE, G74 1LX **Tel:** 01355 265000 **Fax:** 01355 264488
Email: eknews@s-un.co.uk
Advertising Address: Scottish & Universal Newspapers Ltd, PO Box 2, Press Buildings, 9 Campbell Street, HAMILTON, ML3 6AX **Tel:** 01698 282222 **Fax:** 01698 425706
Email: cparker@s-un.co.uk
Web site: http://www.eknews.co.uk
Publisher: SUN Group Lanarkshire Region
Date Established: 1952
Frequency: Weekly - Published on Wednesday
Cover Price: £0.78
Circulation: 12,712 (ABC 02/07/2007 to 30/12/2007)
Editor: Louise Reilly; **Advertising Manager:** Caroline Parker
ADVERTISING RATES:
Full Page Mono £2464.80
Full Page Colour £3327.48
SCC £7.90
Mechanical Data: Type Area: 390 x 270mm, No. of Columns (Display): 8, Col Length: 390mm, Page Width: 270mm
Copy instructions: Copy Date: Tuesday 12 noon prior to publication date
LOCAL NEWSPAPERS: Local Newspapers Scotland

EAST LEEDS WEEKLY NEWS
44712U72B-3812_120

Frequency: Weekly
Cover Price: Free
Circulation: 34,725 (VFD 02/07/2007 to 30/12/2007)
ADVERTISING RATES:
SCC £4.75
Part of Series, see entry for: Leeds Weekly News Series
LOCAL NEWSPAPERS: Local Newspapers English Counties

EAST LONDON ADVERTISER
43151U72A-1301

Editorial Address: 138 Cambridge Heath Road, LONDON, E1 5QJ **Tel:** 020 7791 7799 **Fax:** 020 7790 0646
Email: ela.editorial@archant.co.uk
Advertising Address: As above. **Tel:** 020 7791 7791
Fax: 020 7791 7700
Email: darren.jackson@archant.co.uk
Web site: http://www.eastlondonadvertiser.co.uk
Publisher: Archant Regional
Date Established: 1866
Frequency: Weekly - Published on Thursday
Cover Price: £0.50
Circulation: 9,204 (ABC 02/07/2007 to 30/12/2007)
Editor: Mike Brooke; **News Editor:** Mike Brooke
ADVERTISING RATES:
Full Page Mono £2677.50
Full Page Colour £2827.50
SCC £8.00
Agency Commission: 10%
Mechanical Data: Film: Digital, Type Area: 350 x 265mm, No. of Columns (Display): 9, Col Widths (Display): 27.5mm, Page Width: 265mm, Col Length: 350mm
Copy instructions: Copy Date: Friday 4pm prior to publication date
Average advertising content per issue: 50%
LOCAL NEWSPAPERS: Local Newspapers Greater London

EAST LONDON ENQUIRER
623317U72B-1025_130

Formerly: East London Courier
Frequency: Weekly
Cover Price: Free
Part of Series, see entry for: Essex Enquirer Series
LOCAL NEWSPAPERS: Local Newspapers English Counties

EAST LOTHIAN COURIER
44924U72D-350

Editorial Address: 56 Court Street, HADDINGTON, EH41 3AF **Tel:** 01620 822451 **Fax:** 01620 826143
Email: editorial@eastlothiancourier.com
Advertising Address: As above.
Email: display@eastlothiancourier.com

Non-National Newspapers

Web site: http://www.eastlothiancourier.com
Publisher: The Dunfermline Press Group
Date Established: 1859
Frequency: Weekly - Published on Friday
Cover Price: £0.50
Circulation: 14,074 (ABC 02/07/2007 to 30/12/2007)
Editor: Robert Scott; **Advertising Manager:** Tammie McFarlane
ADVERTISING RATES:
Full Page Mono £1259.28
Full Page Colour £2102.34
SCC £4.77
Agency Commission: 10%
Mechanical Data: Col Length: 330mm, Col Widths (Display): 33mm, No. of Columns (Display): 8, Film: Digital, Type Area: 330mm x 265mm, Page Width: 265mm
Copy instructions: Copy Date: Tuesday 3pm prior to publication date
Average advertising content per issue: 40%
LOCAL NEWSPAPERS: Local Newspapers Scotland

EAST LOTHIAN NEWS
44901U72D-270_140

Frequency: Weekly - Circulation figure includes Musselburgh News
Cover Price: £0.42
Circulation: 4,726 (ABC 02/07/2007 to 30/12/2007)
Part of Series, see entry for: Dalkeith Advertiser Series
LOCAL NEWSPAPERS: Local Newspapers Scotland

EAST RIDING ADVERTISER
44640U72B-3582_140

Formerly: Haltemprice Advertiser
Frequency: Weekly - Published on Wednesday
Cover Price: Free
Circulation: 27,639 (VFD 02/07/2007 to 30/12/2007)
ADVERTISING RATES:
SCC £3.40
Part of Series, see entry for: Hull Advertiser Series
LOCAL NEWSPAPERS: Local Newspapers English Counties

EAST RIDING MAIL
42076U67B-290_520

Formerly: Hull Daily Mail Beverley and East Riding Edition
Frequency: Evenings
Circulation: 20,874 (Publisher's Statement)
ADVERTISING: Rates on application
Edition of: Hull Daily Mail
REGIONAL DAILY & SUNDAY NEWSPAPERS: Regional Daily Newspapers

EAST STAFFORDSHIRE JOURNAL INCORPORATING STAFFS BUSINESS TIMES
43483U72B-4057

Editorial Address: Journal House, 18 Curzon Street, DERBY, DE1 1LL **Tel:** 01332 294660 **Fax:** 01332 202393
Email: staffsjournal@hotmail.com
Advertising Address: As above. **Tel:** 01332 292228
Email: staffsjournal@hotmail.com
Publisher: JPC Ltd
Frequency: Weekly - Published on Thursday
Cover Price: Free
Circulation: 5,000 (Publisher's Statement)
Editor: Rebecca Goodwin; **News Editor:** Katie Fulard;
Advertising Manager: Rebecca Goodwin
ADVERTISING: Rates on application
LOCAL NEWSPAPERS: Local Newspapers English Counties

EASTBOURNE AND DISTRICT ADVERTISER
44438U72B-3240_130

Frequency: Weekly
Cover Price: Free
Circulation: 48,729 (Publisher's Statement)
Part of Series, see entry for: Eastbourne Herald & Gazette Series
LOCAL NEWSPAPERS: Local Newspapers English Counties

EASTBOURNE GAZETTE
44440U72B-3240_140

Frequency: Weekly
Cover Price: £0.35
Circulation: 10,975 (ABC 02/07/2007 to 30/12/2007)
Part of Series, see entry for: Eastbourne Herald & Gazette Series
LOCAL NEWSPAPERS: Local Newspapers English Counties

EASTBOURNE HERALD
44441U72B-3240_150

Frequency: Weekly
Cover Price: £0.48
Circulation: 24,528 (ABC 02/07/2007 to 30/12/2007)
Part of Series, see entry for: Eastbourne Herald & Gazette Series
Supplement(s): Access - 12xY, Baby of the Year - 12xY, Christmas Local - 12xY, Eastbourne Tennis - 12xY, Eastbourne's Finest - 12xY, Learn For Life - 12xY, Motoring Files - 12xY, New Horizons - 12xY, Perfect Day - 12xY, Primetime - 2xY, Property - 12xY, Red Arrows - 12xY, Student Guide - 12xY, Top Resort - 12xY, When You Lose A Loved One - 12xY
LOCAL NEWSPAPERS: Local Newspapers English Counties

EASTBOURNE HERALD & GAZETTE SERIES
44439U72B-3240

Formerly: Eastbourne Gazette & Herald Series
Editorial Address: Beckett House, 1 Commercial Road, EASTBOURNE, BN21 3XQ **Tel:** 01323 722091
Fax: 01323 431387
Email: eastbourne.herald@trbeckett.co.uk
Advertising Address: As above. **Fax:** 01323 411758
Email: denise.greaves@jpress.co.uk
Web site: http://www.eastbourneherald.co.uk
Publisher: T.R. Beckett Ltd
Frequency: Weekly - Published on Wednesday and Friday
Circulation: 88,233 (Combined Circulation)
Editor: Laura Sonier; **News Editor:** Laura Sonier
ADVERTISING RATES:
Full Page Mono £4183.00
Full Page Colour £5437.90
Agency Commission: 10%
Mechanical Data: Page Width: 277mm, Type Area: 340 x 277mm, Col Length: 340mm, No. of Columns (Display): 9, Col Widths (Display): 29mm, Film: Digital
Copy instructions: Copy Date: Friday 5pm prior to publication date
Average advertising content per issue: 70%
Series owner and contact point for the following titles, see individual entries:
Eastbourne and District Advertiser
Eastbourne Gazette
Eastbourne Herald
Hailsham Gazette
Seaford Gazette
Supplement(s): Etc - 4xY, Success Stories - 12xY
LOCAL NEWSPAPERS: Local Newspapers English Counties

EASTERN DAILY PRESS (GREATER NORWICH)
42136U67B-450_530

Formerly: Eastern Daily Press (Yarmouth & Greater Norwich)
Edition of: Eastern Daily Press (Norwich)
REGIONAL DAILY & SUNDAY NEWSPAPERS: Regional Daily Newspapers

EASTERN DAILY PRESS (NORTH & SOUTH)
749505U67B-450_580

Formerly: Eastern Daily Press (North)
Edition of: Eastern Daily Press (Norwich)
REGIONAL DAILY & SUNDAY NEWSPAPERS: Regional Daily Newspapers

EASTERN DAILY PRESS (NORWICH)
42134U67B-450

Editorial Address: Prospect House, Rouen Road, NORWICH, NR1 1RE **Tel:** 01603 628311 **Fax:** 01603 623871
Email: edpnewsdesk@archant.co.uk
Advertising Address: As above. **Fax:** 01603 615903
Email: jane.egle@archant.co.uk
Web site: http://www.edp24.co.uk
Publisher: Archant Norfolk
Date Established: 1870
Frequency: Mornings - Not published on Sunday
Cover Price: £0.48
Circulation: 64,700 (ABC 02/07/2007 to 30/12/2007)
Managing Director: Stephan Phillips
ADVERTISING RATES:
SCC £12.87
Agency Commission: 10%
Mechanical Data: Type Area: 340 x 270mm, Col Length: 340mm, Print Process: Offset litho, No. of Columns (Display): 8, Film: Digital, Col Widths (Display): 32mm, Page Width: 270mm
Copy instructions: Copy Date: 4 days prior to publication date
Average advertising content per issue: 35%
Editions:
Eastern Daily Press (Greater Norwich)
Eastern Daily Press (North & South)
Eastern Daily Press (Waveney)

Eastern Daily Press (West Norfolk & Fens)
Supplement(s): Event - 52xY, Jobsearch - 52xY, Motoring - 52xY, The Pink 'Un (Norwich), Sunday - 52xY, What's On - Daily Property - 52xY
REGIONAL DAILY & SUNDAY NEWSPAPERS: Regional Daily Newspapers

EASTERN DAILY PRESS (WAVENEY)
42137U67B-450_540

Formerly: Eastern Daily Press (Coastal)
Edition of: Eastern Daily Press (Norwich)
REGIONAL DAILY & SUNDAY NEWSPAPERS: Regional Daily Newspapers

EASTERN DAILY PRESS (WEST NORFOLK & FENS)
42138U67B-450_640

Edition of: Eastern Daily Press (Norwich)
REGIONAL DAILY & SUNDAY NEWSPAPERS: Regional Daily Newspapers

EASTWOOD & KIMBERLEY ADVERTISER
44181U72B-2590

Editorial Address: 8 Heanor Road, ILKESTON, DE7 8ER
Tel: 0115 944 6160 **Fax:** 0115 944 4990
Email: news@eastwoodadvertiser.co.uk
Advertising Address: As above.
Email: advertising@eastwoodadvertiser.co.uk
Web site: http://www.eastwoodadvertiser.co.uk
Publisher: Derbyshire Times Newspaper Group
Date Established: 1896
Frequency: Weekly - Published on Friday
Cover Price: £0.32
Circulation: 4,189 (ABC 02/07/2007 to 30/12/2007)
Editor: Laura Rands; **Advertising Manager:** Deborah Beeley; **Group Editor:** Amanda Hatfield
ADVERTISING RATES:
Full Page Mono £835.38
Full Page Colour £1085.99
SCC £2.73
Agency Commission: 10%
Mechanical Data: Type Area: 306 x 271mm, Col Length: 306mm, Col Widths (Display): 28mm, No. of Columns (Display): 9, Page Width: 271mm, Film: Digital
Copy instructions: Copy Date: Wednesday 12 noon prior to publication date
Average advertising content per issue: 50%
LOCAL NEWSPAPERS: Local Newspapers English Counties

ECHO (BASILDON)
41979U67B-13

Formerly: Evening Echo (Basildon)
Editorial Address: Newspaper House, Chester Hall Lane, BASILDON, SS14 3BL **Tel:** 01268 522792
Email: echonews@nqe.com
Advertising Address: As above. **Fax:** 01268 532060
Email: louise.woodman@nqe.com
Web site: http://www.echo-news.co.uk
Publisher: Newsquest (Essex) Ltd
Date Established: 1969
Frequency: Mornings
Cover Price: £0.38
Circulation: 34,844 (ABC 02/07/2007 to 30/12/2007)
Editor: Chris Hatton; **Features Editor:** Claire Borley;
Managing Director: Wayne Hutton; **Advertising Manager:** Louise Woodman
ADVERTISING RATES:
Full Page Mono £1680.00
Full Page Colour £1810.00
SCC £7.57
Agency Commission: 10%
Mechanical Data: Col Length: 340mm, Col Widths (Display): 29mm, Film: Digital, No. of Columns (Display): 9, Type Area: 340 x 274mm, Print Process: Web offset, Trim Size: 420 x 297mm, Page Width: 274mm
Copy instructions: Copy Date: 2 days prior to publication date
Editions:
Castle Point Echo including Rayleigh & Rochford
Southend Echo
Supplement(s): Business - 12xY, Echo Property - 52xY, Echo Woman - 52xY, Motoring Echo - 52xY
REGIONAL DAILY & SUNDAY NEWSPAPERS: Regional Daily Newspapers

EDENBRIDGE CHRONICLE
43853U72B-1773_110

Frequency: Monthly
Cover Price: Free
Circulation: 4,100 (Publisher's Statement)
Part of Series, see entry for: Chronicle Series
LOCAL NEWSPAPERS: Local Newspapers English Counties

EDENBRIDGE COUNTY BORDER NEWS

43856U72B-1774_120

Frequency: Weekly - Circulation figure incorporates Westerham County Border News
Cover Price: Free
Circulation: 6,500 (Publisher's Statement)
Part of Series, see entry for: County Border News Series
LOCAL NEWSPAPERS: Local Newspapers English Counties

EDGWARE & MILL HILL TIMES

43044U72A-200_120

Frequency: Weekly
Cover Price: Free
Circulation: 19,223 (VFD 02/07/2007 to 30/12/2007)
ADVERTISING RATES:
SCC £2.65
Part of Series, see entry for: Hendon Times Series
LOCAL NEWSPAPERS: Local Newspapers Greater London

ELLESMERE PORT AND NESTON STANDARD

43373U72B-425_101

Formerly: Ellesmere Port Standard
Email: news@chesterstandard.co.uk
Frequency: Weekly
Cover Price: Free
Circulation: 33,158 (VFD 02/01/2006 to 02/07/2006)
ADVERTISING: Rates on application
Part of Series, see entry for: Chester Standard Series
LOCAL NEWSPAPERS: Local Newspapers English Counties

ELLESMERE PORT PIONEER

43372U72B-470

Formerly: Ellesmere Port Pioneer & News Series
Editorial Address: Chronicle House, Commonhall Street, CHESTER, CH1 2AA **Tel:** 0151 356 2345
Fax: 0151 356 2131
Email: pioneer@cheshirenews.co.uk
Advertising Address: As above. **Tel:** 0151 227 2000
Email: ros.mcguire@liverpool.com
Web site: http://www.icccheshireonline.co.uk
Publisher: Trinity Mirror Cheshire
Date Established: 1920
Frequency: Weekly - Published on Wednesday
Cover Price: £0.55
Circulation: 5,203 (ABC 02/07/2007 to 30/12/2007)
Editor: Chris Smith; **News Editor:** Chris Smith
ADVERTISING RATES:
SCC £10.04
Mechanical Data: Type Area: 350 x 272mm, No. of Columns (Display): 8, Col Length: 350mm, Page Width: 272mm
Copy instructions: Copy Date: Tuesday 9.30am prior to publication date
LOCAL NEWSPAPERS: Local Newspapers English Counties

ELLON & DISTRICT ADVERTISER

44861U72D-10_140

Frequency: Weekly
Cover Price: £0.49
ADVERTISING RATES:
Full Page Mono £490.00
SCC £2.25
Part of Series, see entry for: Advertiser Series in Aberdeenshire
LOCAL NEWSPAPERS: Local Newspapers Scotland

THE ELLON TIMES AND EAST GORDON ADVERTISER

44930U72D-358

Editorial Address: 8 Bridge Street, ELLON, AB41 9AA
Tel: 01358 724488 **Fax:** 01358 726660
Email: ken.duncan@ellontimes.co.uk
Advertising Address: 17 Chapel Street, PETERHEAD, AB42 1TH **Tel:** 01779 871330 **Fax:** 01779 871331
Email: phyllis.mundie@jpress.co.uk
Publisher: Angus County Press Ltd
Date Established: 1990
Frequency: Weekly - Published on Thursday
Cover Price: £0.47
Circulation: 2,416 (ABC 02/07/2007 to 30/12/2007)
Editor: David Duncan
ADVERTISING RATES:
Full Page Mono £525.00
Full Page Colour £680.00
Agency Commission: 10%
Mechanical Data: Type Area: 340 x 268mm, Col Length: 340mm, Page Width: 268mm, No. of Columns (Display): 8, Film: Digital, Col Widths (Display): 30, Print Process: Web-fed offset litho

Copy instructions: Copy Date: 2 days prior to publication date
Average advertising content per issue: 40%
Supplement(s): Drive - 52xY
LOCAL NEWSPAPERS: Local Newspapers Scotland

ELY STANDARD

1864053U72B-370_100

Frequency: Weekly - Published on Thursday
Cover Price: Free
Circulation: 21,797 (Publisher's Statement)
ADVERTISING: Rates on application
Part of Series, see entry for: Ely Standard Series
LOCAL NEWSPAPERS: Local Newspapers English Counties

ELY STANDARD SERIES

43329U72B-370

Formerly: Ely Standard
Editorial Address: 38 Market Street, ELY, CB7 4LS
Tel: 01353 667831 **Fax:** 01353 667198
Email: editor@ely-standard.co.uk
Advertising Address: As above. **Fax:** 01353 666645
Email: nick.boister@archant.co.uk
Web site: http://www.elystandard24.co.uk
Publisher: Archant Herts & Cambs
Frequency: Weekly - Published on Thursday
Cover Price: Free
Circulation: 21,797 (Publisher's Statement)
Editor: Debbie Davies; **Advertising Manager:** Nick Boister
ADVERTISING RATES:
Full Page Mono £1250.64
Full Page Colour £1625.82
SCC £3.86
Agency Commission: 10%
Mechanical Data: No. of Columns (Display): 9, Col Widths (Display): 30mm, Film: Digital
Copy instructions: Copy Date: 2 days prior to publication date
Average advertising content per issue: 45%
Series owner and contact point for the following titles, see individual entries:
Ely Standard
Ely Standard (Soham Edition)
LOCAL NEWSPAPERS: Local Newspapers English Counties

ELY STANDARD (SOHAM EDITION)

1864054U72B-370_101

Frequency: Weekly - Published on Thursday. Circulation is combined with Ely Standard
Cover Price: Free
ADVERTISING: Rates on application
Part of Series, see entry for: Ely Standard Series
LOCAL NEWSPAPERS: Local Newspapers English Counties

ELY WEEKLY NEWS

43318U72B-350_160

Formerly: Ely Weekly News & Town Crier
Frequency: Weekly
Cover Price: Free
Circulation: 17,922 (VFD 02/07/2007 to 30/12/2007)
ADVERTISING RATES:
SCC £3.45
Part of Series, see entry for: Cambridge Weekly News & Crier Series
LOCAL NEWSPAPERS: Local Newspapers English Counties

EMS VALLEY GAZETTE

1647087U72B-3951

Editorial Address: Unicorn House, 8 Eastgate Square, CHICHESTER, PO19 1JN **Tel:** 01243 534133
Fax: 01243 539386
Email: colin.channon@chiobserver.co.uk
Advertising Address: As above. **Fax:** 01243 538032
Email: lesley.clunie@chiobserver.co.uk
Web site: http://www.chicester.co.uk
Publisher: Sussex Newspapers (Horsham) Ltd
Frequency: Monthly
Cover Price: Free
Circulation: 4,700 (Publisher's Statement)
Editor: Colin Channon; **Advertising Manager:** Lesley Clunie; **Group Editor:** Colin Channon
Summary of Content: Local News, features, sport relevant to the Emsworth residents.
ADVERTISING RATES:
Full Page Mono £492.32
Full Page Colour £640.02
Agency Commission: 10%
Mechanical Data: Type Area: 340 x 264mm, Col Length: 340mm, Page Width: 264mm, Film: Digital

Copy instructions: Copy Date: 1 week prior to publication date
LOCAL NEWSPAPERS: Local Newspapers English Counties

ENFIELD INDEPENDENT

42978U72A-200_142

Formerly: Enfield Independent Series
Frequency: Weekly - Published on Wednesday
Cover Price: Free
Circulation: 92,538 (VFD 01/01/2007 to 01/07/2007)
Editor: Charlie Stong
ADVERTISING: Rates on application
Part of Series, see entry for: Hendon Times Series
LOCAL NEWSPAPERS: Local Newspapers Greater London

EPPING FOREST GUARDIAN

43013U72A-132_160

Formerly: Epping Forest Guardian (Epping, Ongar & Villages)
Frequency: Weekly
Cover Price: £0.45
Circulation: 9,204 (ABC 02/07/2007 to 30/12/2007)
ADVERTISING: Rates on application
Part of Series, see entry for: Guardian and Independent Series
LOCAL NEWSPAPERS: Local Newspapers Greater London

EPPING FOREST INDEPENDENT

42982U72A-132_181

Formerly: Epping Forest Independent Series
Frequency: Weekly - Published on Friday
Cover Price: Free
Circulation: 13,228 (VFD 02/07/2007 to 30/12/2007)
ADVERTISING: Rates on application
Part of Series, see entry for: Guardian and Independent Series
LOCAL NEWSPAPERS: Local Newspapers Greater London

EPSOM GUARDIAN

43001U72A-128_130

Formerly: Epsom and Banstead Guardian
Frequency: Weekly - See Sutton Guardian for circulation figure
Cover Price: Free
Part of Series, see entry for: Guardian & News Series (Sutton)
LOCAL NEWSPAPERS: Local Newspapers Greater London

THE EPWORTH BELLS & CROWLE ADVERTISER

44678U72B-3690

Editorial Address: 13 Market Place, Epworth, DONCASTER, DN9 1EU **Tel:** 01427 875228
Fax: 01427 873900
Email: editorial@gooletoday.co.uk
Advertising Address: As above. **Tel:** 01427 872202
Email: ahuby@epworthtoday.co.uk
Web site: http://www.epworthbells.co.uk
Publisher: South Yorkshire Newspapers Ltd
Date Established: 1872
Frequency: Weekly - Published on Thursday
Cover Price: £0.42
Circulation: 3,136 (ABC 02/07/2007 to 30/12/2007)
Editor: Janet Harrison; **Advertising Manager:** Amanda Huby
ADVERTISING RATES:
Full Page Mono £197.92
Full Page Colour £257.90
SCC £1.72
Mechanical Data: No. of Columns (Display): 9, Type Area: 340 x 272mm, Col Length: 340mm, Page Width: 272mm, Film: Digital
LOCAL NEWSPAPERS: Local Newspapers English Counties

ES MAGAZINE

41863U67H-357

Editorial Address: Northcliffe House, 2 Derry Street, Kensington, LONDON, W8 5EE **Tel:** 020 7938 6000
Fax: 020 7937 9302
Email: andy.barker@standard.co.uk
Advertising Address: As above. **Fax:** 020 7937 0305
Email: adrian.milner@standard.co.uk
Publisher: Evening Standard Co Ltd
Frequency: Weekly - Published on Friday. See main record for circulation figure
Cover Price: Free
Editor: Andy Barker; **Features Editor:** Emilie McMeekan
Summary of Content: Magazine covering celebrity interviews, fashion, shopping and eateries. Includes a section featuring reviews of restaurants, bars, clubs and shops in London.
ADVERTISING RATES:
Full Page Mono £16800.00

Full Page Colour £16800.00
SCC £100.00
Mechanical Data: Page Width: 212mm, No. of Columns
(Display): 4, Type Area: 266 x 212mm, Col Length: 266mm,
Trim Size: 286 x 232mm, Bleed Size: 294 x 240mm, Film:
Digital
Copy instructions: Copy Date: 2 weeks prior to publication
date
Supplement to: London Evening Standard
REGIONAL DAILY & SUNDAY NEWSPAPERS: Regional
Colour Supplements

ESHER AND COBHAM GUARDIAN

43000U72A-128_125

Formerly: Elmbridge Guardian
Frequency: Weekly - Circulation figure was originally for the
Elmbridge Guardian
Cover Price: Free
Circulation: 41,685 (VFD 02/07/2007 to 30/12/2007)
Part of Series, see entry for: Guardian & News Series
(Sutton)
LOCAL NEWSPAPERS: Local Newspapers Greater London

ESKDALE AND LIDDESDALE
ADVERTISER

44931U72D-360

Editorial Address: Commercial House, High Street,
LANGHOLM, DG13 0JH **Tel:** 01387 380012
Fax: 01387 380979
Email: eskdale.news@cumbrian-newspapers.co.uk
Advertising Address: As above.
Email: eskdale.news@cumbrian-newspapers.co.uk
Web site: http://eladvertiser.co.uk
Publisher: Eskdale & Liddesdale Newspapers
Date Established: 1848
Frequency: Weekly - Published on Thursday
Cover Price: £0.45
Circulation: 1,800 (Publisher's Statement)
Editor: Rachel Norris; **News Editor:** Rachel Norris;
Advertising Manager: Sharon Turner
ADVERTISING RATES:
Full Page Mono £796.32
Full Page Colour £995.40
SCC £3.16
Agency Commission: 10%
Mechanical Data: Col Length: 360mm, Col Widths (Display):
33mm, No. of Columns (Display): 7, Print Process: Offset
litho, Type Area: 360 x 256mm, Page Width: 256mm, Film:
Digital
Copy instructions: Copy Date: Monday 3pm prior to
publication date
Average advertising content per issue: 45%
Supplement(s): Langholm Common Riding - 1xY
LOCAL NEWSPAPERS: Local Newspapers Scotland

ESSEX CHRONICLE

43605U72B-1015_110

Frequency: Weekly - Circulation figure incorporated in
Essex Chronicle Series
ADVERTISING: Rates on application
Part of Series, see entry for: Essex Chronicle Series
LOCAL NEWSPAPERS: Local Newspapers English
Counties

ESSEX CHRONICLE BRAINTREE

43606U72B-1015_120

Frequency: Weekly - Circulation figure incorporated in
Essex Chronicle Series
ADVERTISING: Rates on application
Part of Series, see entry for: Essex Chronicle Series
LOCAL NEWSPAPERS: Local Newspapers English
Counties

ESSEX CHRONICLE MALDON AND
BURNHAM

43608U72B-1015_160

Frequency: Weekly - Circulation figure incorporated in
Essex Chronicle Series
ADVERTISING: Rates on application
Part of Series, see entry for: Essex Chronicle Series
LOCAL NEWSPAPERS: Local Newspapers English
Counties

ESSEX CHRONICLE SERIES

43604U72B-1015

Editorial Address: Westway, CHELMSFORD, CM1 3BE
Tel: 01245 603360
Email: newsdesk@essexchronicle.co.uk
Advertising Address: As above. **Tel:** 01245 600700
Fax: 01245 603424
Email: sarah.woodley-dyne@essexchronicle.co.uk
Web site: http://www.totalessex.co.uk
Publisher: Essex Chronicle Media Group Ltd
Date Established: 1764

Frequency: Weekly - Circulation figure incorporates the
Essex Chronicle, the Essex Chronicle Braintree, the Essex
Chronicle Dunmow & Stansted, the Essex Chronicle Maldon
& Burnham, the Essex Chronicle Witham and the Essex
Chronicle Woodham. Published on Wednesday and
Thursday
Cover Price: £0.70
Circulation: 35,461 (ABC 02/07/2007 to 30/12/2007)
Editor: Paul Dent-Jones; **News Editor:** Paul Dent-Jones;
Managing Director: Richard Karn; **Advertising Manager:**
Sarah Woodley-Dyne
ADVERTISING: Rates on application
Mechanical Data: Page Width: 270mm, Type Area: 360 x
270mm, Col Length: 360mm, Col Widths (Display): 31mm,
No. of Columns (Display): 8
**Series owner and contact point for the following titles,
see individual entries:**
Essex Chronicle
Essex Chronicle Braintree
Essex Chronicle Maldon And Burnham
Supplement(s): Go! - 52xY
LOCAL NEWSPAPERS: Local Newspapers English
Counties

ESSEX COMMUNITY NEWS

634489U72B-3074_100

Frequency: Monthly
Cover Price: Free
Circulation: 3,650 (Publisher's Statement)
ADVERTISING: Rates on application
Part of Series, see entry for: Greater Ipswich Community
News Series
LOCAL NEWSPAPERS: Local Newspapers English
Counties

ESSEX COUNTY STANDARD

43611U72B-1020

Editorial Address: Oriel House, 43-44 North Hill,
COLCHESTER, CO1 1TZ **Tel:** 01206 508308
Fax: 01206 508274
Email: ecs.news@nqe.com
Advertising Address: Echo Newspapers, Newspaper
House, Chester Hall Lane, BASILDON, SS14 3BL
Tel: 01206 506000 **Fax:** 01206 508440
Email: basildon.adverts@nqe.com
Web site: http://www.essexcountystandard.co.uk
Publisher: Essex County Newspapers
Date Established: 1831
Frequency: Weekly - Published on Friday
Cover Price: £0.55
Circulation: 20,316 (ABC 02/07/2007 to 30/12/2007)
Editor: News Desk; **News Editor:** Wendy Brading;
Advertising Manager: Samantha Bruce
ADVERTISING RATES:
Full Page Mono £1035.00
Full Page Colour £1130.00
SCC £6.20
Agency Commission: 10%
Mechanical Data: Col Length: 340mm, Col Widths (Display):
27mm, Film: Digital, No. of Columns (Display): 9, Type Area:
340 x 267mm, Print Process: Web offset, Page Width:
267mm
Copy instructions: Copy Date: Tuesday 5pm prior to
publication date
Average advertising content per issue: 60%
Supplement(s): Property - 52xY
LOCAL NEWSPAPERS: Local Newspapers English
Counties

ESSEX ENQUIRER

623318U72B-1025_140

Formerly: Essex Courier
Frequency: Weekly
Cover Price: Free
Part of Series, see entry for: Essex Enquirer Series
LOCAL NEWSPAPERS: Local Newspapers English
Counties

ESSEX ENQUIRER SERIES

43612U72B-1025

Formerly: Essex Courier Series
Editorial Address: Independent House, Radford Business
Centre, Radford Way, BILLERICAY, CM12 0AA
Tel: 01277 627300 **Fax:** 01277 655925
Email: newsdesk@theenquirer.co.uk
Advertising Address: As above. **Tel:** 01277 627400
Fax: 01277 624749
Email: alex@theenquirer.co.uk
Web site: http://www.theenquirer.co.uk
Publisher: Typestyle Ltd
Date Established: 2002
Frequency: Weekly - Published on Thursday
Cover Price: Free
Circulation: 57,859 (Publisher's Statement)
Editor: Neil Speight; **Features Editor:** Nicola Moyne;
Managing Director: Andrew Diggory

ADVERTISING RATES:
Full Page Colour £3672.00
SCC £12.00
Agency Commission: 10%
Mechanical Data: Type Area: 340 x 267mm, Col Length:
340mm, No. of Columns (Display): 9, Film: Digital, Page
Width: 267mm, Col Widths (Display): 27mm
Copy instructions: Copy Date: 1 week prior to publication
date
**Series owner and contact point for the following titles,
see individual entries:**
East London Enquirer
Essex Enquirer
Supplement(s): VeggieTimes - 12xY
LOCAL NEWSPAPERS: Local Newspapers English
Counties

ET LIFE

1695525U67H-360

Editorial Address: New Priestgate House, 57 Priestgate,
PETERBOROUGH, PE1 1JW **Tel:** 01733 555111
Fax: 01733 313147
Email: julia.ogden@peterboroughtoday.co.uk
Advertising Address: As above. **Fax:** 01733 555188
Email: sasha.dean@peterboroughtoday.co.uk
Web site: http://www.peterboroughtoday.co.uk
Publisher: Johnston Press plc
Frequency: Evenings
Editor: Julia Ogden; **Features Editor:** Julia Ogden
Summary of Content: Supplement covering lifestyle and
women's interest features with items on fashion, health,
beauty, home interiors, food and TV listings.
Readership/Target Audience: Aimed at readers of the
Evening Telegraph (Peterborough).
ADVERTISING: Rates on application
Supplement to: Evening Telegraph (Peterborough)
REGIONAL DAILY & SUNDAY NEWSPAPERS: Regional
Colour Supplements

EVENING CHRONICLE (NEWCASTLE)

42126U67B-420

Editorial Address: Groat Market, NEWCASTLE UPON
TYNE, NE1 1ED **Tel:** 0191 232 7500 **Fax:** 0191 232 2256
Email: ec.news@ncjmedia.co.uk
Advertising Address: As above. **Fax:** 0191 230 4144
Email: julie.emmerson@ncjmedia.co.uk
Web site: http://www.chroniclelive.co.uk
Publisher: NCJ Media Ltd
Date Established: 1869
Frequency: Evenings
Cover Price: £0.42
Circulation: 78,804 (Publisher's Statement)
Editor: News Desk; **News Editor:** James Marley;
Managing Director: Steve Brown
ADVERTISING RATES:
Full Page Mono £6143.00
Full Page Colour £8293.05
Mechanical Data: Print Process: Web-fed offset litho, Type
Area: 350 x 277mm, Col Length: 350mm, Film: Positive, right
reading, emulsion side down. Digital, No. of Columns
(Display): 8, Page Width: 277mm
Copy instructions: Copy Date: Mono 2 days prior to
publication date Colour 5 days prior to publication date
Editions:
Evening Chronicle (Newcastle and Gateshead Edition)
Evening Chronicle (Northumberland and Coast Edition)
Evening Chronicle (Regionwide Edition)
Supplement(s): Community Chronicle - 52xY, Your Health -
52xY
REGIONAL DAILY & SUNDAY NEWSPAPERS: Regional
Daily Newspapers

EVENING CHRONICLE (NEWCASTLE
AND GATESHEAD EDITION)

761117U67B-420_530

Formerly: Evening Chronicle (Gateshead Edition)
Frequency: Evenings
Cover Price: £0.40
ADVERTISING RATES:
Full Page Mono £5964.00
Full Page Colour £7991.60
Edition of: Evening Chronicle (Newcastle)
REGIONAL DAILY & SUNDAY NEWSPAPERS: Regional
Daily Newspapers

EVENING CHRONICLE
(NORTHUMBERLAND AND COAST
EDITION)

761116U67B-420_520

Formerly: Evening Chronicle (Coast Edition)
Frequency: Evenings
Cover Price: £0.40
ADVERTISING RATES:
Full Page Mono £5964.00
Full Page Colour £7991.00

Edition of: Evening Chronicle (Newcastle)
REGIONAL DAILY & SUNDAY NEWSPAPERS: Regional Daily Newspapers

EVENING CHRONICLE (REGIONWIDE EDITION)
761115U67B-420_550

Formerly: Evening Chronicle (North Edition)
Frequency: Evenings
Cover Price: £0.40
ADVERTISING RATES:
Full Page Mono £5964.00
Full Page Colour £7991.00
Edition of: Evening Chronicle (Newcastle)
REGIONAL DAILY & SUNDAY NEWSPAPERS: Regional Daily Newspapers

EVENING COURIER (HALIFAX)
42069U67B-260

Editorial Address: PO Box 19, King Cross Street, HALIFAX, HX1 2SF **Tel:** 01422 260200 **Fax:** 01422 330021
Email: newsdesk@halifaxcourier.co.uk
Advertising Address: As above.
Email: admanager@halifaxcourier.co.uk
Web site: http://www.halifaxtoday.co.uk
Publisher: Halifax Courier Ltd
Date Established: 1832
Frequency: Evenings - Not published on Sunday
Cover Price: £0.40
Circulation: 19,956 (ABC 02/07/2007 to 30/12/2007)
Editor: Sophie McCandlish; **News Editor:** Sophie McCandlish; **Features Editor:** Tim Worsnop; **Advertising Manager:** Jason Shrimpton
ADVERTISING RATES:
SCC £13.71
Agency Commission: 10%
Mechanical Data: Type Area: 340 x 265mm, Page Width: 265mm, Print Process: Web-fed offset litho, Col Widths (Display): 28.5mm, Col Length: 340mm, No. of Columns (Display): 9, Film: Digital
Copy instructions: Copy Date: 2 days prior to publication date
Average advertising content per issue: 40%
Supplement(s): Local Life - 52xY
REGIONAL DAILY & SUNDAY NEWSPAPERS: Regional Daily Newspapers

EVENING EXPRESS (ABERDEEN)
42243U67B-2150

Editorial Address: PO Box 43, Lang Stracht, Mastrick, ABERDEEN, AB15 6DF **Tel:** 01224 690222
Fax: 01224 699575
Email: ee.news@ajl.co.uk
Advertising Address: As above.
Email: jim.bruce@ajl.co.uk
Web site: http://www.eveningexpress.co.uk
Publisher: Aberdeen Journals Ltd
Frequency: Evenings - Not published on Sunday
Cover Price: £0.36
Circulation: 53,384 (ABC 02/07/2007 to 30/12/2007)
Editor: Damian Bates; **News Editor:** Craig Walker;
Managing Director: Alan Scott
ADVERTISING RATES:
Full Page Mono £3948.00
Full Page Colour £5330.00
SCC £18.80
Agency Commission: 10%
Mechanical Data: Col Widths (Display): 41mm, Col Length: 350mm, No. of Columns (Display): 6, Film: Positive, right reading, emulsion side down. Digital
Copy instructions: Copy Date: 2 days prior to publication date
Average advertising content per issue: 35%
Editions:
Evening Express Extra
Evening Express Final Edition
Evening Express Late Final Edition
Supplement(s): Jobs & Employment - 52xY, Living - 52xY, Property - 52xY, What's On - 52xY
REGIONAL DAILY & SUNDAY NEWSPAPERS: Regional Daily Newspapers

EVENING EXPRESS EXTRA
42244U67B-2150_581

Formerly: Evening Express Banff & Buchan
Edition of: Evening Express (Aberdeen)
REGIONAL DAILY & SUNDAY NEWSPAPERS: Regional Daily Newspapers

EVENING EXPRESS FINAL EDITION
42245U67B-2150_540

Formerly: Evening Express City Edition (Aberdeen)
Edition of: Evening Express (Aberdeen)
REGIONAL DAILY & SUNDAY NEWSPAPERS: Regional Daily Newspapers

EVENING EXPRESS LATE FINAL EDITION
1620666U67B-2150_582

Edition of: Evening Express (Aberdeen)
REGIONAL DAILY & SUNDAY NEWSPAPERS: Regional Daily Newspapers

EVENING GAZETTE (MIDDLESBROUGH)
42125U67B-410

Editorial Address: Gazette Buildings, 105-111 Borough Road, MIDDLESBROUGH, TS1 3AZ **Tel:** 01642 245401
Fax: 01642 234228
Email: news@eveninggazette.co.uk
Advertising Address: As above. **Tel:** 01642 252525
Fax: 01642 234619
Email: fieldsales@gazettemedia.co.uk
Web site: http://www.gazettelive.co.uk
Publisher: Gazette Media Company Ltd
Date Established: 1869
Frequency: Evenings
Cover Price: £0.40
Circulation: 50,920 (ABC 02/07/2007 to 30/12/2007)
Editor: News Desk; **Executive Editor:** Sue Calvert;
Managing Director: Robert Cuffe; **Advertising Manager:** Coral Appleby
ADVERTISING RATES:
Full Page Mono £4050.00
Full Page Colour £5490.00
Mechanical Data: Type Area: 520 x 349mm, Film: Positive, right reading, emulsion side down. Digital, Col Length: 520mm, Page Width: 349mm, No. of Columns (Display): 8
Copy instructions: Copy Date: Mono 5pm 2 days prior to publication date Colour 7 days prior to publication date
Supplement(s): Evening Gazette Sports (Middlesbrough) - 260xY, Greenbits - 4xY, Health Gazette - 4xY, North East Vision - 4xY
REGIONAL DAILY & SUNDAY NEWSPAPERS: Regional Daily Newspapers

EVENING LEADER
42229U67B-2080

Editorial Address: Mold Business Park, Wrexham Road, MOLD, CH7 1XY **Tel:** 01352 707707 **Fax:** 01352 752180
Email: news@eveningleader.co.uk
Advertising Address: As above. **Fax:** 01352 700048
Email: advertising@eveningleader.co.uk
Web site: http://www.eveningleader.co.uk
Publisher: NWN Media Ltd
Frequency: Evenings - Published Monday to Friday, Friday edition is published in the morning
Circulation: 21,180 (ABC 02/07/2007 to 30/12/2007)
Editor: Jonathan Barnett; **Advertising Manager:** Miriam Reed
Readership/Target Audience: Circulated in Chester, Deeside, Denbighshire, Flintshire and Wrexham.
ADVERTISING RATES:
SCC £10.50
Mechanical Data: Col Length: 350mm, No. of Columns (Display): 9, Film: Digital, Type Area: 350 x 259mm, Page Width: 259mm
Copy instructions: Copy Date: 11.30am 2 days prior to publication date
Editions:
Chester Evening Leader
Denbighshire Evening Leader
Flintshire Evening Leader
Wrexham Evening Leader
Supplement(s): Bygones - 52xY, Gig Guide - 52xY, Junior Sports - 52xY, Living - 52xY, Weekend - 52xY
REGIONAL DAILY & SUNDAY NEWSPAPERS: Regional Daily Newspapers

EVENING NEWS (CITY FINAL EDITION) (EDINBURGH)
42258U67B-2230_510

Edition of: Evening News (Edinburgh)
REGIONAL DAILY & SUNDAY NEWSPAPERS: Regional Daily Newspapers

EVENING NEWS (EDINBURGH)
42257U67B-2230

Editorial Address: 108 Holyrood Road, EDINBURGH, EH8 8AS **Tel:** 0131 620 8620 **Fax:** 0131 620 8696
Email: news_en@scotsman.com
Advertising Address: As above. **Fax:** 0131 523 0322
Email: freeves@scotsman.com
Web site: http://www.edinburghnews.com
Publisher: The Scotsman Publications Ltd
Date Established: 1873
Frequency: Evenings
Cover Price: £0.35
Circulation: 53,675 (Publisher's Statement)
News Editor: Alan Young; **Features Editor:** Eaun McGrory;
Managing Director: Michael Johnston
ADVERTISING RATES:
Full Page Mono £4634.88

EVENING POST (BRISTOL)
42006U67B-110

Editorial Address: Temple Way, BRISTOL, BS99 7HD
Tel: 0117 934 3000 **Fax:** 0117 934 3575
Email: epnews@bepp.co.uk
Advertising Address: As above. **Fax:** 0117 934 3548
Email: s.spargo@bepp.co.uk
Web site: http://www.thisisbristol.co.uk
Publisher: Bristol News & Media Ltd
Date Established: 1932
Frequency: Evenings
Cover Price: £0.35
Circulation: 51,287 (ABC 02/07/2007 to 30/12/2007)
Editor: Rob Perkins; **News Editor:** Rob Perkins; **Features Editor:** Tim Davey; **Editor-in-Chief:** Mike Norton
ADVERTISING RATES:
Full Page Mono £4032.00
Full Page Colour £5040.00
SCC £14.00
Agency Commission: 10%
Mechanical Data: Type Area: 360 x 270mm, Col Widths (Display): 31mm, No. of Columns (Display): 8, Film: Positive, right reading, emulsion side down. Digital, Print Process: Web-fed offset litho, Col Length: 360mm, Page Width: 270mm
Copy instructions: Copy Date: 12.00pm 2 days prior to publication date
Editions:
Evening Post (Late Edition)
Supplement(s): Motorcycle - 12xY
REGIONAL DAILY & SUNDAY NEWSPAPERS: Regional Daily Newspapers

EVENING POST (LATE EDITION)
623437U67B-110_535

Formerly: Evening Post (Bristol Final)
Edition of: Evening Post (Bristol)
REGIONAL DAILY & SUNDAY NEWSPAPERS: Regional Daily Newspapers

EVENING POST NOTTINGHAM (FINAL)
1668005U67B-470_500

Frequency: Evenings
Cover Price: £0.33
Edition of: Nottingham Evening Post
REGIONAL DAILY & SUNDAY NEWSPAPERS: Regional Daily Newspapers

EVENING STAR
42082U67B-310

Formerly: Evening Star (Ipswich)
Editorial Address: Press House, 30 Lower Brook Street, IPSWICH, IP4 1AN **Tel:** 01473 230023 **Fax:** 01473 324850
Email: starnews@eveningstar.co.uk
Advertising Address: As above. **Tel:** 01473 320023
Fax: 01473 324625
Email: julian.evans@archant.co.uk
Web site: http://www.eveningstar.co.uk
Publisher: Archant Suffolk
Date Established: 1885
Frequency: Evenings
Cover Price: £0.45
Circulation: 19,707 (ABC 02/07/2007 to 30/12/2007)
Editor: Jess Gallagher; **News Editor:** Jess Gallagher;
Features Editor: James Marston; **Managing Director:** Stuart McCreery; **Advertising Manager:** Mark Gallant
ADVERTISING RATES:
Full Page Mono £2168.64
Full Page Colour £3036.10
Agency Commission: 10%
Mechanical Data: Film: Digital, Col Widths (Display): 32mm, Screen: 40 lpc, Type Area: 360 x 270mm, Col Length: 360mm, No. of Columns (Display): 8, Page Width: 270mm
Copy instructions: Copy Date: Mono 2 days Colour 5 days prior to publication date
Supplement(s): Grass Roots - 52xY, Star Weekly - 52xY
REGIONAL DAILY & SUNDAY NEWSPAPERS: Regional Daily Newspapers

EVENING TELEGRAPH & POST (DUNDEE)
42256U67B-2210

Editorial Address: 80 Kingsway East, DUNDEE, DD4 8SL
Tel: 01382 223131 **Fax:** 01382 454590

Full Page Colour £5793.60
Mechanical Data: Type Area: 340 x 277mm, Col Length: 340mm, Page Width: 277mm, Col Widths (Display): 32mm, No. of Columns (Display): 8, Film: Digital
Copy instructions: Copy Date: Wednesday 5pm prior to publication date
Editions:
Evening News (City Final Edition) (Edinburgh)
Supplement(s): The Guide - 52xY, Life & Style - 52xY
REGIONAL DAILY & SUNDAY NEWSPAPERS: Regional Daily Newspapers

Section 4 (a) Newspapers

Email: newsdesk@eveningtelegraph.co.uk
Advertising Address: As above. **Fax:** 01382 454599
Email: advertising-kingsway@dcthomson.co.uk
Web site: http://www.eveningtelegraph.co.uk
Publisher: D.C. Thomson & Co Ltd
Date Established: 1900
Frequency: Evenings - Published Monday to Friday
Cover Price: £0.32
Circulation: 24,349 (ABC 02/07/2007 to 30/12/2007)
Editor: Elaine Harrison; **News Editor:** Elaine Harrison;
Features Editor: Philip Smith; **Advertising Manager:** Craig McGeoghie
ADVERTISING RATES:
Full Page Mono £1400.00
SCC £6.60
Agency Commission: 10%
Mechanical Data: Type Area: 350 x 264mm, Screen: Digital, Col Length: 350mm, Col Widths (Display): 35mm, No. of Columns (Display): 7, Page Width: 264mm, Print Process: Web-fed offset litho
Copy instructions: Copy Date: 5pm 2 days prior to publication date
REGIONAL DAILY & SUNDAY NEWSPAPERS: Regional Daily Newspapers

EVENING TELEGRAPH (PETERBOROUGH)
42147U67B-600

Editorial Address: New Priestgate House, 57 Priestgate, PETERBOROUGH, PE1 1JW **Tel:** 01733 555111
Fax: 01733 313147
Email: news@peterboroughtoday.co.uk
Advertising Address: As above. **Fax:** 01733 555188
Email: richard.duxbury@peterboroughtoday.co.uk
Web site: http://www.peterboroughtoday.co.uk
Publisher: Johnston Press plc
Frequency: Evenings
Cover Price: £0.35
Circulation: 18,542 (Publisher's Statement)
Editor: Paul Grinnell; **News Editor:** Paul Grinnell; **Features Editor:** Julia Ogden; **Managing Director:** Amanda Davison-Young; **Advertising Manager:** Richard Duxbury
ADVERTISING RATES:
Full Page Mono £4605.00
Full Page Colour £7291.98
Agency Commission: 10%
Mechanical Data: Col Length: 340mm, No. of Columns (Display): 9, Type Area: 340 x 265mm, Print Process: Web-fed offset litho, Film: Digital, Page Width: 265mm
Copy instructions: Copy Date: 4.00 pm 2 days prior to publication date
Average advertising content per issue: 35%
Editions:
City Lite
Evening Telegraph (Peterborough) (City Final Edition)
Supplement(s): ET Business - 52xY, ET Life - Daily, The Guide - 52xY
REGIONAL DAILY & SUNDAY NEWSPAPERS: Regional Daily Newspapers

EVENING TELEGRAPH (PETERBOROUGH) (CITY FINAL EDITION)
1744356U67B-600_500

Frequency: Evenings
Cover Price: £0.35
Edition of: Evening Telegraph (Peterborough)
REGIONAL DAILY & SUNDAY NEWSPAPERS: Regional Daily Newspapers

EVENING TIMES (GLASGOW)
42262U67B-2290

Editorial Address: 200 Renfield Street, GLASGOW, G2 3QB
Tel: 0141 302 7000 **Fax:** 0141 302 6600
Email: news@eveningtimes.co.uk
Advertising Address: As above. **Tel:** 0141 302 6000
Fax: 0141 302 6203
Email: businesssales@gmgw.newsquest.co.uk
Web site: http://www.eveningtimes.co.uk
Publisher: Newsquest Herald & Times Ltd
Frequency: Evenings - Not published on Sunday
Cover Price: £0.40
Circulation: 79,087 (Publisher's Statement)
Editor: Yvonne Flynn; **News Editor:** Hugh Boag; **Editor-in-Chief:** Donald Martin; **Advertisement Director:** Ian Clarke
ADVERTISING RATES:
SCC £29.50
Mechanical Data: Film: Digital, Type Area: 360 x 255mm, Col Length: 360mm, No. of Columns (Display): 7, Col Widths (Display): 33mm, Page Width: 255mm
Copy instructions: Copy Date: Mono 10am 1 day prior Colour 4pm 2 days prior to publication date
Editions:
Evening Times (Glasgow) (Late News Extra)
Evening Times (Glasgow) (Late News Final)
Supplement(s): et - 52xY, TimesOut - 52xY
REGIONAL DAILY & SUNDAY NEWSPAPERS: Regional Daily Newspapers

EVENING TIMES (GLASGOW) (LATE NEWS EXTRA)
1660075U67B-2290_500

Frequency: Evenings
Cover Price: £0.40
Edition of: Evening Times (Glasgow)
REGIONAL DAILY & SUNDAY NEWSPAPERS: Regional Daily Newspapers

EVENING TIMES (GLASGOW) (LATE NEWS FINAL)
1660076U67B-2290_501

Formerly: Evening Times (Glasgow) (Late Night Special)
Frequency: Evenings
Cover Price: £0.40
Edition of: Evening Times (Glasgow)
REGIONAL DAILY & SUNDAY NEWSPAPERS: Regional Daily Newspapers

EVESHAM JOURNAL
44612U72B-3560_140

Frequency: Weekly
ADVERTISING: Rates on application
Part of Series, see entry for: Evesham Journal Series
LOCAL NEWSPAPERS: Local Newspapers English Counties

EVESHAM JOURNAL SERIES
44610U72B-3560

Editorial Address: Sapphire House, Crab Apple Way, Vale Park, EVESHAM, WR11 1GP **Tel:** 01386 444050
Fax: 01386 444078
Email: journal@midlands.newsquest.co.uk
Advertising Address: As above. **Tel:** 01386 442555
Fax: 01386 444077
Email: brian.strange@midlandsnewsquest.co.uk
Web site: http://www.eveshamjournal.co.uk
Publisher: Newsquest Media Group
Date Established: 1860
Frequency: Weekly - Published on Thursday
Cover Price: £0.55
Circulation: 32,275 (VFD 01/01/2007 to 01/07/2007)
Editor: News Desk
ADVERTISING: Rates on application
Agency Commission: 10%
Copy instructions: Copy Date: Tuesday 12pm prior to publication date
Average advertising content per issue: 65%
Series owner and contact point for the following titles, see individual entries:
Cotswold Journal
Evesham Journal
LOCAL NEWSPAPERS: Local Newspapers English Counties

EVESHAM OBSERVER
1808393U72B-4052_100

Frequency: Weekly - Published on Wednesday
Cover Price: £0.35
Free to qualifying individuals
(Publisher's Statement)
Part of Series, see entry for: Evesham Observer Series
LOCAL NEWSPAPERS: Local Newspapers English Counties

EVESHAM OBSERVER SERIES
1808476U72B-4052

Editorial Address: 8 King Charles Court, Vine Street, EVESHAM, WR11 4RF **Tel:** 01386 443699
Fax: 01386 443610
Email: editor@eveshamobserver.co.uk
Advertising Address: As above. **Tel:** 01386 48000
Fax: 01386 48050
Email: jo.williams@eveshamobserver.co.uk
Publisher: Bullivant Media Limited
Frequency: Weekly - Published on Wednesday
Free to qualifying individuals
Circulation: 35,917 (VFD 10/09/2007 to 30/12/2007)
Editor: Ian Dipple
ADVERTISING RATES:
Full Page Mono £1701.00
Full Page Colour £1701.00
SCC £5.40
Agency Commission: 10%
Mechanical Data: Type Area: 350 x 265mm, Col Length: 350mm, Page Width: 265mm, Film: Digital, Col Widths (Display): 35mm, No. of Columns (Display): 9
Copy instructions: Copy Date: Friday prior to publication date
Series owner and contact point for the following titles, see individual entries:
Cotswolds Observer
Evesham Observer
Tewkesbury Observer
LOCAL NEWSPAPERS: Local Newspapers English Counties

THE EXAMINER
1668511U72E-284

Editorial Address: Rathkeeland House, 1 Blaney Road, Crossmaglen, NEWRY, BT35 9JJ **Tel:** 028 3086 8500
Fax: 028 3086 8580
Email: theexaminer@btconnect.com
Advertising Address: As above.
Email: theexaminer@btconnect.com
ISSN: 1755-0734
Publisher: The Examiner
Date Established: 1992
Frequency: Weekly - Published on Monday
Cover Price: £0.60
Circulation: 9,000 (Publisher's Statement)
Editor: Gerry Murray; **Advertising Manager:** Tina Murray
ADVERTISING RATES:
Full Page Mono £400.00
Full Page Colour £500.00
SCC £2.10
Agency Commission: 15%
Mechanical Data: Type Area: 360 x 260mm, Col Length: 360mm, Page Width: 260mm, Film: Digital, Col Widths (Display): 40mm, No. of Columns (Display): 6
Copy instructions: Copy Date: Friday prior to publication date
Average advertising content per issue: 35%
LOCAL NEWSPAPERS: Local Newspapers Northern Ireland

EXAMINER WEEKLY
44705U72B-3780

Formerly: The Huddersfield Weekly News
Editorial Address: Queen Street South, HUDDERSFIELD, HD1 3DU **Tel:** 01484 430000 **Fax:** 01484 437789
Advertising Address: PO Box A26, Queen Street South, HUDDERSFIELD, HD1 3DU **Tel:** 01484 430000
Fax: 01484 437730
Email: anne.barrett@examiner.co.uk
Web site: http://www.ichuddersfield.co.uk
Publisher: Trinity Mirror
Frequency: Weekly - Published on Tuesday
Cover Price: Free
Circulation: 55,322 (VFD 02/07/2007 to 30/12/2007)
Editor: Chris Burgess
ADVERTISING RATES:
SCC £5.76
Agency Commission: 10%
Mechanical Data: Film: Digital, Type Area: 342 x 272mm, Col Length: 342mm, Page Width: 272mm, Col Widths (Display): 30mm, No. of Columns (Display): 8
Copy instructions: Copy Date: Thursday 12pm prior to publication date
LOCAL NEWSPAPERS: Local Newspapers English Counties

THE EXETER TIMES
43509U72B-825

Formerly: The Leader Exeter
Editorial Address: 17 Brest Road, Derriford, PLYMOUTH, PL6 5AA **Tel:** 01392 442211 **Fax:** 01392 442287
Email: eoldfield@expressandecho.co.uk
Advertising Address: As above. **Fax:** 01392 442294
Email: cedwards@expressandecho.co.uk
Web site: http://www.thisisexeter.co.uk
Publisher: South West Media Group Ltd
Frequency: Weekly
Cover Price: Free
Circulation: 43,972 (VFD 02/07/2007 to 30/12/2007)
Editor: Edward Oldfield
ADVERTISING RATES:
Full Page Mono £1497.60
Full Page Colour £1872.00
SCC £5.20
Agency Commission: 10%
Mechanical Data: Page Width: 268mm, Type Area: 360 x 268mm, Col Length: 360mm, Col Widths (Display): 31mm, No. of Columns (Display): 8, Print Process: Web-fed litho, Film: Digital, Screen: 34 lpc
Copy instructions: Copy Date: 12 noon 2 days prior to publication date
Average advertising content per issue: 70%
LOCAL NEWSPAPERS: Local Newspapers English Counties

EXMOUTH HERALD
43508U72B-810_200

Frequency: Weekly - Published on Friday
Cover Price: Free
Circulation: 16,856 (VFD 02/07/2007 to 30/12/2007)
ADVERTISING RATES:
SCC £4.00
Part of Series, see entry for: The Journal Series (Exmouth)
LOCAL NEWSPAPERS: Local Newspapers English Counties

THE EXMOUTH JOURNAL
43505U72B-810_140

Frequency: Weekly - Published on Thursday. Circulation figure incorporates The Journal (Budleigh Salterton)
Cover Price: £0.50

Circulation: 8,608 (ABC 02/07/2007 to 30/12/2007)
ADVERTISING RATES:
SCC £3.80
Part of Series, see entry for: The Journal Series (Exmouth)
LOCAL NEWSPAPERS: Local Newspapers English Counties

EXPRESS & CHRONICLE
44699U72B-4151
Formerly: Express & Chronicle Series (Huddersfield)
Editorial Address: Queen Street South, HUDDERSFIELD, HD1 3DU **Tel:** 01484 437713 **Fax:** 01484 437718
Email: editor@expressandchronicle.co.uk
Advertising Address: As above. **Tel:** 01484 430000
Fax: 01484 437730
Email: maureen.clark@examiner.co.uk
Publisher: Trinity Mirror Huddersfield Ltd
Frequency: Weekly - Published on Saturday
Editor: Chris Burgess
ADVERTISING RATES:
Full Page Mono £1748.32
Full Page Colour £2483.45
SCC £6.56
Agency Commission: 10%
Mechanical Data: Page Width: 261mm, No. of Columns (Display): 8, Type Area: 346 x 261mm, Col Length: 346mm
Supplement to: Huddersfield Daily Examiner
LOCAL NEWSPAPERS: Local Newspapers English Counties

EXPRESS & ECHO (EXETER)
42056U67B-230
Editorial Address: Heron Road, Sowton Industrial Estate, EXETER, EX2 7NF **Tel:** 01392 442211 **Fax:** 01392 442287
Email: echonews@expressandecho.co.uk
Advertising Address: As above. **Fax:** 01392 442422
Email: rwoodward@swmg.co.uk
Web site: http://www.thisisexeter.co.uk
Publisher: South West Media Group Ltd
Frequency: Mornings - Not published on Sunday
Cover Price: £0.35
Circulation: 20,767 (ABC 02/07/2007 to 30/12/2007)
Editor: News Desk; **News Editor:** Rob Sims; **Features Editor:** Becky Moran; **Advertising Director:** Ivor Bull
ADVERTISING RATES:
Full Page Mono £2016.00
Full Page Colour £2520.00
SCC £7.00
Agency Commission: 10%
Mechanical Data: Col Widths (Display): 31mm, Film: Digital, No. of Columns (Display): 8
Copy instructions: Copy Date: 2 days prior to publication date
Supplement(s): Drive - 52xY, Jobs - 52xY, Property Scene - 52xY
REGIONAL DAILY & SUNDAY NEWSPAPERS: Regional Daily Newspapers

---

EXPRESS & STAR
42199U67B-1150
Editorial Address: 51-53 Queen Street, WOLVERHAMPTON, WV1 1ES **Tel:** 01902 313131
Fax: 01902 319721
Email: newsdesk@expressandstar.co.uk
Advertising Address: As above. **Fax:** 01902 710106
Email: display@expressandstar.co.uk
Web site: http://www.expressandstar.com
Publisher: Midland News Association
Date Established: 1874
Frequency: Evenings - Circulation figure is only Monday to Friday
Circulation: 140,001 (Publisher's Statement)
Editor: Adrian Faber; **News Editor:** Bob Kane; **Features Editor:** Emma Farmer; **Managing Director:** Alan Harris; **Advertising Manager:** Paul Carter
Readership/Target Audience: Aimed at those within the West Midlands, Staffordshire, Shropshire and Worcestershire area.
ADVERTISING RATES:
SCC £24.50
Copy instructions: Copy Date: 3 days prior to publication date
Average advertising content per issue: 40%
Editions:
Express & Star (Cannock & Lichfield)
Express & Star (City)
Express & Star (Kidderminster)
Express & Star (Late Final)
Express & Star (Sandwell)
Express & Star (Stafford)
Express & Star (Walsall)
Express & Star (Wolverhampton)
Supplement(s): Venture - 4xY
REGIONAL DAILY & SUNDAY NEWSPAPERS: Regional Daily Newspapers

---

EXPRESS & STAR (CANNOCK & LICHFIELD)
42204U67B-1150_570
Formerly: Express & Star (Lichfield & Burntwood)
Edition of: Express & Star
REGIONAL DAILY & SUNDAY NEWSPAPERS: Regional Daily Newspapers

---

EXPRESS & STAR (CITY)
42200U67B-1150_520
Edition of: Express & Star
REGIONAL DAILY & SUNDAY NEWSPAPERS: Regional Daily Newspapers

---

EXPRESS & STAR (CITY/LONDON OFFICE)
42301U67D-75
Formerly: Express & Star (West Midlands) (City/London Office)
Editorial Address: Press Gallery, House of Commons, Westminster, LONDON, SW1A 0AA **Tel:** 020 7219 3381
Email: j.hipwood@expressandstar.co.uk
Web site: http://www.shropshirestar.co.uk
Publisher: Midland News Association
Editor: John Hipwood
ADVERTISING: No Advertising taken
REGIONAL DAILY & SUNDAY NEWSPAPERS: Regional Daily Sunday London City Office

---

EXPRESS & STAR (KIDDERMINSTER)
42203U67B-1150_560
Edition of: Express & Star
REGIONAL DAILY & SUNDAY NEWSPAPERS: Regional Daily Newspapers

---

EXPRESS & STAR (LATE FINAL)
42202U67B-1150_540
Formerly: Express & Star (Dudley)
Edition of: Express & Star
REGIONAL DAILY & SUNDAY NEWSPAPERS: Regional Daily Newspapers

---

EXPRESS & STAR (SANDWELL)
42205U67B-1150_610
Circulation: 19,290 (Publisher's Statement)
Edition of: Express & Star
REGIONAL DAILY & SUNDAY NEWSPAPERS: Regional Daily Newspapers

---

EXPRESS & STAR (STAFFORD)
42206U67B-1150_620
Edition of: Express & Star
REGIONAL DAILY & SUNDAY NEWSPAPERS: Regional Daily Newspapers

---

EXPRESS & STAR (WALSALL)
42208U67B-1150_640
Circulation: 22,180 (Publisher's Statement)
Edition of: Express & Star
REGIONAL DAILY & SUNDAY NEWSPAPERS: Regional Daily Newspapers

---

EXPRESS & STAR (WOLVERHAMPTON)
42209U67B-1150_670
Circulation: 46,843 (Publisher's Statement)
Edition of: Express & Star
REGIONAL DAILY & SUNDAY NEWSPAPERS: Regional Daily Newspapers

---

EXPRESS EXTRA SERIES KENT
43864U72B-1795
Editorial Address: Express House, 34-36 North Street, ASHFORD, TN24 8JR **Tel:** 01233 623232
Fax: 01233 626545
Email: kentishexpress@thekmgroup.co.uk
Advertising Address: As above.
Email: sodriscoll@thekmgroup.co.uk
Web site: http://www.kentonline.co.uk
Publisher: Kent Messenger Group
Frequency: Weekly - Published on Thursday
Circulation: 79,557 (Combined Circulation)
Editor: Robert Barman; **News Editor:** Alastair Irvine
ADVERTISING RATES:
Full Page Mono £1958.00
Agency Commission: 10%

Mechanical Data: Col Length: 340mm, No. of Columns (Display): 8, Type Area: 340 x 276mm, Col Widths (Display): 31mm, Page Width: 276mm, Film: Digital
Copy instructions: Copy Date: Friday prior to publication date
Average advertising content per issue: 80%
Series owner and contact point for the following titles, see individual entries:
Dover and Deal Extra
Extra (Ashford and Tenterden)
Extra (Folkestone and Hythe)
Kentish Express Ashford and District
Kentish Express Folkestone
Kentish Express Hythe and Romney Marsh
Kentish Express Tenterden
Supplement(s): Focus - 6xY
LOCAL NEWSPAPERS: Local Newspapers English Counties

EXPRESS ROCHDALE
43696U72B-1280_181
Frequency: Weekly
Cover Price: Free
Circulation: 50,345 (VFD 02/07/2007 to 30/12/2007)
ADVERTISING RATES:
SCC £6.15
Part of Series, see entry for: Rochdale Observer Series
LOCAL NEWSPAPERS: Local Newspapers English Counties

EXTRA (ASHFORD AND TENTERDEN)
43865U72B-1795_125
Formerly: Extra (Ashford and Villages)
Frequency: Weekly
Cover Price: Free
Part of Series, see entry for: Express Extra Series Kent
LOCAL NEWSPAPERS: Local Newspapers English Counties

THE EXTRA BEARSDEN, MILNGAVIE & WESTEND
44950U72D-450_120
Formerly: The Extra Bearsden, Milngavie & West End
Frequency: Weekly
Cover Price: Free
Circulation: 25,171 (VFD 06/08/2007 to 30/12/2007)
Part of Series, see entry for: The Glasgow Extra Series
LOCAL NEWSPAPERS: Local Newspapers Scotland

EXTRA (FOLKESTONE AND HYTHE)
43867U72B-1795_130
Frequency: Weekly - Circulation figure incorporates the Dover and Deal Extra
Cover Price: Free
Circulation: 56,824 (VFD 02/07/2007 to 30/12/2007)
Part of Series, see entry for: Express Extra Series Kent
LOCAL NEWSPAPERS: Local Newspapers English Counties

THE EXTRA FOR BASINGSTOKE AND NORTH HAMPSHIRE
43739U72B-1345_130
Formerly: Basingstoke Gazette Extra
Frequency: Weekly - Published on Wednesday
Cover Price: Free
Circulation: 42,857 (VFD 02/07/2007 to 30/12/2007)
ADVERTISING RATES:
Full Page Mono £1989.00
Full Page Colour £1989.00
SCC £6.70
Part of Series, see entry for: Basingstoke and North Hants Gazette Series
LOCAL NEWSPAPERS: Local Newspapers English Counties

THE EXTRA GLASGOW SOUTH & EASTWOOD
44951U72D-450_160
Frequency: Weekly
Cover Price: Free
Circulation: 36,350 (VFD 02/07/2007 to 30/12/2007)
Part of Series, see entry for: The Glasgow Extra Series
LOCAL NEWSPAPERS: Local Newspapers Scotland

EXTRA (MAIDSTONE, MID-KENT)
43891U72B-1840_200
Frequency: Weekly
Cover Price: Free
Circulation: 49,234 (VFD 02/07/2007 to 30/12/2007)

Part of Series, see entry for: Kent Messenger Group Newspapers
LOCAL NEWSPAPERS: Local Newspapers English Counties

THE EXTRA PAISLEY & RENFREWSHIRE

44952U72D-450_200
Formerly: The Extra Paisley, Renfrewshire & Gryffe
Frequency: Weekly
Cover Price: Free
Circulation: 34,335 (VFD 02/07/2007 to 30/12/2007)
Part of Series, see entry for: The Glasgow Extra Series
LOCAL NEWSPAPERS: Local Newspapers Scotland

THE EXTRA (PLYMOUTH)   43526U72B-838
Formerly: Extra Series (Plymouth)
Editorial Address: 17 Brest Road, Derriford Business Park, PLYMOUTH, PL6 5AA **Tel:** 01752 765500
Fax: 01752 765527
Email: news@theplymouthherald.co.uk
Advertising Address: As above. **Fax:** 01752 765515'
Email: rwoodward@swmg.co.uk
Web site: http://www.thisisplymouth.co.uk
Publisher: South West Media Group Ltd
Date Established: 1980
Frequency: Weekly - Published on Thursday
Cover Price: Free
Circulation: 93,894 (VFD 02/07/2007 to 30/12/2007)
Editor: Mike Bramhall; **Managing Director:** Duncan Currall;
Advertising Director: Paul Newman
ADVERTISING RATES:
Full Page Mono £3551.68
Full Page Colour £3189.60
SCC £8.86
Agency Commission: 10%
Mechanical Data: Type Area: 360 x 268mm, Film: Digital, Col Length: 360mm, Page Width: 268mm, No. of Columns (Display): 8
Copy instructions: Copy Date: 12pm Friday 1 week prior to publication date
Average advertising content per issue: 70%
LOCAL NEWSPAPERS: Local Newspapers English Counties

FALKIRK ADVERTISER   44933U72D-365_110
Frequency: Weekly
Cover Price: Free
Part of Series, see entry for: Falkirk & Grangemouth Advertiser Series
LOCAL NEWSPAPERS: Local Newspapers Scotland

FALKIRK & GRANGEMOUTH
ADVERTISER SERIES   44932U72D-365
Editorial Address: Redbrae Road, Camelon, FALKIRK, FK1 4ZA **Tel:** 01324 638314 **Fax:** 01324 473100
Email: editorial@falkirkherald.co.uk
Advertising Address: As above. **Tel:** 01324 624959
Fax: 01324 629079
Email: morag.munro@jnscotland.co.uk
Web site: http://www.falkirkherald.co.uk
Publisher: Johnston Press plc
Date Established: 1900
Frequency: Weekly - Published on Thursday
Cover Price: Free
Circulation: 51,805 (VFD 02/07/2007 to 30/12/2007)
Editor: News Desk; **Managing Director:** Richard Bell;
Advertising Manager: Kieran Koszary
ADVERTISING RATES:
Full Page Mono £2353.14
Full Page Colour £3529.71
SCC £7.69
Agency Commission: 10%
Mechanical Data: Page Width: 272mm, Film: Digital, Type Area: 340 x 272mm, Col Length: 340mm, No. of Columns (Display): 9, Col Widths (Display): 28mm
Copy instructions: Copy Date: Friday 5pm prior to publication date
Average advertising content per issue: 70%
Series owner and contact point for the following titles, see individual entries:
Falkirk Advertiser
Grangemouth Advertiser
Linlithgow Advertiser
LOCAL NEWSPAPERS: Local Newspapers Scotland

THE FALKIRK HERALD   44936U72D-380
Formerly: Falkirk Herald and Scottish Midlands Journal
Editorial Address: Redbrae Road, Camelon, FALKIRK, FK1 4ZA **Tel:** 01324 690243 **Fax:** 01324 629792
Email: editorial@falkirkherald.co.uk
Advertising Address: As above. **Tel:** 01324 624959
Fax: 01324 629079

Email: kieran.koszary@jnscotland.co.uk
Web site: http://www.falkirkherald.co.uk
Publisher: Johnston (Falkirk) Ltd
Date Established: 1845
Frequency: Weekly - Published on Thursday
Cover Price: £0.47
Circulation: 28,779 (ABC 02/07/2007 to 30/12/2007)
Editor: News Desk; **Group Editor:** Colin Hume
ADVERTISING RATES:
Full Page Mono £5705.15
Full Page Colour £8557.72
SCC £9.43
Agency Commission: 10%
Mechanical Data: Print Process: Web-fed offset litho, Type Area: 550 x 333mm, Col Length: 550mm, Col Widths (Display): 28mm, No. of Columns (Display): 11, Page Width: 333mm, Film: Digital
Copy instructions: Copy Date: Wednesday 2.00pm prior to publication date
Average advertising content per issue: 50%
LOCAL NEWSPAPERS: Local Newspapers Scotland

FALMOUTH PACKET   43428U72B-553_120
Frequency: Weekly
ADVERTISING RATES:
Full Page Mono £1165.50
Full Page Colour £1573.43
SCC £3.70
Part of Series, see entry for: The Packet Series
LOCAL NEWSPAPERS: Local Newspapers English Counties

FAREHAM & GOSPORT JOURNAL
43752U72B-1378_150
Frequency: Weekly
Cover Price: Free
Circulation: 48,950 (VFD 02/07/2007 to 30/12/2007)
Part of Series, see entry for: Journal Series Portsmouth
LOCAL NEWSPAPERS: Local Newspapers English Counties

FARINGDON FOLLY   1695529U72B-3973
Editorial Address: 9 Market Place, FARINGDON, SN7 7HL
Tel: 01367 243898 **Fax:** 01367 242372
Email: news@faringdonfolly.com
Advertising Address: As above.
Email: j.stayt@internet-today.co.uk
Publisher: Tindle Newspapers Ltd
Frequency: Monthly
Cover Price: £0.60
Circulation: 2,500 (Publisher's Statement)
Editor: Al Cane; **Advertising Manager:** Jackie Stayt
ADVERTISING RATES:
Full Page Mono £622.00
Full Page Colour £622.00
Agency Commission: 10%
Mechanical Data: Trim Size: 390 x 268mm, Film: Digital
Copy instructions: Copy Date: 16th of the month prior to publication date
LOCAL NEWSPAPERS: Local Newspapers English Counties

FARNBOROUGH NEWS & MAIL
43764U72B-1382_150
Formerly: Farnborough News
Frequency: Weekly - Circulation figure is incorporated into the Aldershot News & Mail
Cover Price: £0.37
ADVERTISING RATES:
SCC £11.64
Part of Series, see entry for: Aldershot Mail and News Series
LOCAL NEWSPAPERS: Local Newspapers English Counties

FARNHAM HERALD   44372U72B-3120_140
Frequency: Weekly
Cover Price: £0.50
Part of Series, see entry for: Farnham Herald Series
LOCAL NEWSPAPERS: Local Newspapers English Counties

FARNHAM HERALD SERIES   44369U72B-3120
Editorial Address: 114-115 West Street, FARNHAM, GU9 7HL **Tel:** 01252 725224 **Fax:** 01252 899267
Email: farnham-herald@internet-today.co.uk
Advertising Address: As above. **Fax:** 01252 899257
Email: bryan.buck@internet-today.co.uk
Web site: http://www.farnham-herald-today.co.uk
Publisher: Farnham Castle Newspapers Ltd

Date Established: 1895
Frequency: Weekly - Published on Thursday
Circulation: 31,000 (Publisher's Statement)
Editor: Tony Short; **Managing Director:** Brian Doel
ADVERTISING RATES:
SCC £10.21
Agency Commission: 10%
Mechanical Data: Type Area: 560 x 365mm, Col Length: 560mm, Page Width: 365mm, Col Widths (Display): 36mm, No. of Columns (Display): 10, Film: Positive, right reading, emulsion side down. Digital, Print Process: Offset litho
Copy instructions: Copy Date: Monday 12pm prior to publication date
Average advertising content per issue: 60%
Series owner and contact point for the following titles, see individual entries:
Alton Herald
Bordon Herald
Farnham Herald
Haslemere Herald
Liphook Herald
Petersfield Herald
Supplement(s): Herald Homes - 12xY
LOCAL NEWSPAPERS: Local Newspapers English Counties

FASHION & STYLE   1899300U67B-9087
Tel: 020 7938 7597
Email: fashion@standard.co.uk
Frequency: Weekly - Published on Tuesdays within the London Evening Standard
Editor: Laura Craik
Summary of Content: Section focusing on fashion, cosmetics and style.
ADVERTISING: Rates on application
Part of Series, see entry for: London Evening Standard
REGIONAL DAILY & SUNDAY NEWSPAPERS: Regional Daily Newspapers

FAVERSHAM NEWS   43903U72B-1870_135
Frequency: Weekly
Cover Price: £0.60
Circulation: 3,432 (ABC 02/07/2007 to 30/12/2007)
Part of Series, see entry for: Kentish Gazette Series
LOCAL NEWSPAPERS: Local Newspapers English Counties

FAVERSHAM TIMES   43862U72B-1790_150
Frequency: Weekly
Cover Price: £0.45
Circulation: 2,406 (ABC 02/07/2007 to 30/12/2007)
Part of Series, see entry for: East Kent Gazette Series
LOCAL NEWSPAPERS: Local Newspapers English Counties

FELIXSTOWE ADVERTISER
1656824U72B-3078_104
Frequency: Weekly - This is an edition of the Ipswich Advertiser
Cover Price: Free
Part of Series, see entry for: Advertiser Series (Ipswich)
LOCAL NEWSPAPERS: Local Newspapers English Counties

FENLAND CITIZEN, MARCH &
CHATTERIS   1831099U72B-380_100
Frequency: Weekly - Published on Wednesday
Cover Price: Free
Part of Series, see entry for: Fenland Citizen Series
LOCAL NEWSPAPERS: Local Newspapers English Counties

FENLAND CITIZEN SERIES   43330U72B-380
Editorial Address: 11 Union Street, WISBECH, PE13 1DN
Tel: 01945 586100 **Fax:** 01945 586139
Email: sarah.cliss@fenlandcitizen.co.uk
Advertising Address: As above. **Fax:** 01945 465912
Email: rop@fenlandcitizen.co.uk
Web site: http://www.fenlandcitizen.co.uk
Publisher: Johnston Press plc
Date Established: 1845
Frequency: Weekly - Published every Wednesday
Cover Price: Free
Circulation: 41,075 (VFD 02/07/2007 to 30/12/2007)
Editor: Sarah Cliss; **Managing Director:** Amanda Davison-Young; **Advertising Manager:** Jamie Paul; **Group Editor:** Jon Buss
ADVERTISING RATES:
Full Page Colour £1401.48
SCC £4.58
Agency Commission: 10%

Mechanical Data: Type Area: 340 x 270mm, No. of Columns (Display): 9, Col Widths (Display): 27mm, Film: Digital, Col Length: 340mm, Page Width: 270mm
Copy instructions: Copy Date: Monday 3pm prior to publication date
Average advertising content per issue: 66%
Series owner and contact point for the following titles, see individual entries:
Fenland Citizen, March & Chatteris
Fenland Citizen, Wisbech
LOCAL NEWSPAPERS: Local Newspapers English Counties

FENLAND CITIZEN, WISBECH

1831100U72B-380_101

Frequency: Weekly - Published on Wednesday
Cover Price: Free
Part of Series, see entry for: Fenland Citizen Series
LOCAL NEWSPAPERS: Local Newspapers English Counties

FERMANAGH HERALD

45097U72E-130

Editorial Address: 30 Belmore Street, ENNISKILLEN, BT74 6AA **Tel:** 028 6632 2066 **Fax:** 028 6632 5521
Email: editor@fermanaghherald.com
Advertising Address: As above.
Email: advertising@fermanaghherald.com
Web site: http://www.fermanaghherald.com
Publisher: North-West of Ireland Ptg. & Pub. Co. Ltd
Date Established: 1901
Frequency: Weekly
Cover Price: £0.95
Circulation: 13,593 (ABC 02/07/2007 to 30/12/2007)
Editor: Pauline Leary; **Advertising Manager:** Anne Mooney
ADVERTISING RATES:
SCC £4.10
Agency Commission: 10%
Mechanical Data: Page Width: 262mm, Type Area: 363 x 262mm, Col Length: 363mm, Col Widths (Display): 34mm, No. of Columns (Display): 7, Film: Digital
Copy instructions: Copy Date: Monday 3pm prior to publication date
Average advertising content per issue: 40%
LOCAL NEWSPAPERS: Local Newspapers Northern Ireland

FERMANAGH NEWS

45093U72E-120_150

Frequency: Weekly
Cover Price: £0.40
Part of Series, see entry for: Dungannon Observer Series
LOCAL NEWSPAPERS: Local Newspapers Northern Ireland

FERRYHILL AND CHILTON CHAPTER

1657568U72B-3957_102

Email: thechapter@talk21.com
Web site: http://www.thechapter.org
Frequency: Weekly
Cover Price: Free
Circulation: 9,000 (Publisher's Statement)
ADVERTISING RATES:
Full Page Mono £250.00
Part of Series, see entry for: Community Newspaper Series
LOCAL NEWSPAPERS: Local Newspapers English Counties

FIFE AND KINROSS EXTRA

44937U72D-385

Editorial Address: Pitreavie Business Park, Queensferry Road, DUNFERMLINE, KY11 8QS **Tel:** 01383 728201
Fax: 01383 737040
Email: extra@dunfermlinepress.co.uk
Advertising Address: As above.
Email: advertising@dunfermlinepress.co.uk
Publisher: The Dunfermline Press Group
Frequency: Weekly
Cover Price: Free
Circulation: 52,464 (VFD 02/07/2007 to 30/12/2007)
Editor: Andrew Cowie; **Advertising Manager:** Lynn Hubber
ADVERTISING RATES:
Full Page Mono £2041.00
Full Page Colour £4082.00
SCC £7.29
Agency Commission: 10%
Mechanical Data: Type Area: 350 x 265.5mm, Col Length: 350mm, Col Widths (Display): 31mm, No. of Columns (Display): 8, Film: Digital, Page Width: 265.5mm
Copy instructions: Copy Date: Tuesday 4pm prior to publication date
Average advertising content per issue: 70%
LOCAL NEWSPAPERS: Local Newspapers Scotland

FIFE FREE PRESS

44941U72D-395_130

Frequency: Weekly - Published on Thursday
Cover Price: £0.42
Circulation: 17,739 (ABC 02/07/2007 to 30/12/2007)
ADVERTISING: Rates on application
Part of Series, see entry for: Fife Leader and Free Press Series
LOCAL NEWSPAPERS: Local Newspapers Scotland

FIFE HERALD INC. FIFE NEWS AND KINROSSHIRE ADVERTISER

44938U72D-390

Editorial Address: George Inn Pend, Crossgate, CUPAR, KY15 5AB **Tel:** 01334 652206 **Fax:** 01334 655400
Email: edherald@fifetoday.co.uk
Advertising Address: As above.
Email: bill.williamson@fifetoday.co.uk
Web site: http://www.fifetoday.co.uk
Publisher: Strachan & Livingston Ltd
Date Established: 1822
Frequency: Weekly - Circulation figure is a combined figure for Fife Herald and St. Andrews Citizen
Cover Price: £0.44
Circulation: 13,116 (ABC 02/07/2007 to 30/12/2007)
Editor: Graeme Scott
ADVERTISING RATES:
SCC £4.94
Agency Commission: 10%
Mechanical Data: Col Length: 340mm, No. of Columns (Display): 9, Print Process: Web-fed offset litho, Type Area: 340 x 272mm, Page Width: 272mm, Film: Digital
Copy instructions: Copy Date: Wednesday 4.00pm prior to publication date
Average advertising content per issue: 50%
LOCAL NEWSPAPERS: Local Newspapers Scotland

FIFE LEADER AND FREE PRESS SERIES

44939U72D-395

Formerly: Fife Leader and Advertiser Series
Editorial Address: 23 Kirk Wynd, KIRKCALDY, KY1 1EP **Tel:** 01592 261451 **Fax:** 01592 204180
Email: ffpnews@fifetoday.co.uk
Advertising Address: As above. **Fax:** 01592 598834
Email: ffpadvertising@fifetoday.co.uk
Web site: http://www.fifetoday.co.uk
Publisher: Strachan & Livingston Ltd
Date Established: 1871
Frequency: Weekly - Published on Tuesday, Thursday and Friday
Circulation: 135,799 (Combined Circulation)
Editor: Allan Crow; **Advertising Manager:** John Mackay
ADVERTISING: Rates on application
Agency Commission: 10%
Copy instructions: Copy Date: 2 days prior to publication date
Average advertising content per issue: 60%
Series owner and contact point for the following titles, see individual entries:
Fife Free Press
Fife Leader North
Fife Leader South
Herald and Post Fife
LOCAL NEWSPAPERS: Local Newspapers Scotland

FIFE LEADER NORTH

44940U72D-395_140

Formerly: Fife Advertiser
Frequency: Weekly - Published on Monday
Cover Price: Free
Circulation: 24,043 (VFD 02/07/2007 to 30/12/2007)
ADVERTISING: Rates on application
Part of Series, see entry for: Fife Leader and Free Press Series
LOCAL NEWSPAPERS: Local Newspapers Scotland

FIFE LEADER SOUTH

44942U72D-395_180

Formerly: Fife Leader
Frequency: Weekly - Published on Monday
Cover Price: Free
Circulation: 49,140 (VFD 02/07/2007 to 30/12/2007)
Advertising Manager: Bill Morgan
ADVERTISING: Rates on application
Part of Series, see entry for: Fife Leader and Free Press Series
LOCAL NEWSPAPERS: Local Newspapers Scotland

FILEY & HUNMANBY MERCURY

44660U72B-3623_120

Frequency: Weekly - Published on Friday
Cover Price: £0.42
Circulation: 2,969 (ABC 02/07/2007 to 30/12/2007)

Part of Series, see entry for: The Mercury Series (Scarborough)
LOCAL NEWSPAPERS: Local Newspapers English Counties

FILM AND ARTS

762998U67B-9009_700

Formerly: Arts
Tel: 020 7938 6000 **Fax:** 020 7937 2648
Email: fiona.hughes@standard.co.uk
Frequency: Evenings - Published within the London Evening Standard
Editor: Fiona Hughes
Summary of Content: Section covering the arts including literature, music, dance, art, cinema and the theatre.
ADVERTISING: Rates on application
Part of Series, see entry for: London Evening Standard
REGIONAL DAILY & SUNDAY NEWSPAPERS: Regional Daily Newspapers

FLEET & HART COURIER

44361U72B-1382_170

Formerly: Fleet & District Courier
Frequency: Weekly - For circulation figure see Aldershot and Farnborough Courier
Cover Price: Free
ADVERTISING: Rates on application
Part of Series, see entry for: Aldershot Mail and News Series
LOCAL NEWSPAPERS: Local Newspapers English Counties

FLEET NEWS & MAIL

43766U72B-1382_175

Formerly: Fleet Mail
Frequency: Weekly - Circulation figure is incorporated into the Aldershot Mail & News
Cover Price: £0.22
ADVERTISING: Rates on application
Part of Series, see entry for: Aldershot Mail and News Series
LOCAL NEWSPAPERS: Local Newspapers English Counties

FLEETWOOD WEEKLY NEWS

43968U72B-1979

Formerly: Fleetwood Weekly News Series
Editorial Address: 168 Lord Street, FLEETWOOD, FY7 6SR **Tel:** 01253 772950 **Fax:** 01253 776058
Email: fwn@fleetwoodweekly.co.uk
Advertising Address: As above. **Tel:** 01253 772966
Fax: 01253 770518
Email: fwn@fleetwoodweekly.co.uk
Web site: http://www.fleetwoodtoday.co.uk
Publisher: Johnston Press plc
Frequency: Weekly - Published on Wednesday
Cover Price: £0.40
Circulation: 12,000 (Publisher's Statement)
Editor: Garry Millar; **Advertising Manager:** Jane Nicholson
ADVERTISING RATES:
Full Page Mono £1490.80
Full Page Colour £1938.03
Agency Commission: 10%
Mechanical Data: Type Area: 340 x 277mm, Col Length: 340mm, Page Width: 277mm, No. of Columns (Display): 9, Col Widths (Display): 29mm, Film: Digital
Copy instructions: Copy Date: Monday 5pm prior to publication date
Average advertising content per issue: 60%
LOCAL NEWSPAPERS: Local Newspapers English Counties

FLINTSHIRE CHRONICLE

44777U72C-135

Formerly: Chronicle Series (Flintshire)
Editorial Address: Office 2, Daniel Owen Precinct, MOLD, CH7 1AP **Tel:** 01244 821911 **Fax:** 01244 830786
Email: flintshire.news@cheshirenews.co.uk
Advertising Address: Chronicle House, Commonhall Street, CHESTER, CH1 2AA **Tel:** 01244 340151
Email: louise.barlow@cheshirenews.co.uk
Web site: http://www.flintshirechronicle.co.uk
Publisher: Trinity Mirror
Frequency: Weekly - Published on Friday
Cover Price: £0.70
Editor: Kevin Hughes; **News Editor:** Lois York; **Advertising Manager:** Louise Barlow
ADVERTISING: Rates on application
Supplement(s): Your Future - 52xY, Your Home - 52xY, Your Time - 52xY
LOCAL NEWSPAPERS: Local Newspapers Wales

Non-National Newspapers

Section 4 (a) Newspapers

FLINTSHIRE EVENING LEADER

42231U67B-2080_550

Frequency: Evenings - Published Monday to Friday, Friday edition is published in the morning
ADVERTISING RATES:
SCC £6.80
Edition of: Evening Leader
REGIONAL DAILY & SUNDAY NEWSPAPERS: Regional Daily Newspapers

FLINTSHIRE STANDARD

44789U72C-180

Formerly: Flintshire Leader & Standard
Editorial Address: Mold Business Park, Wrexham Road, MOLD, CH7 1XY **Tel:** 01352 707769 **Fax:** 01352 752180
Email: news@flintshireeveningleader.co.uk
Advertising Address: As above. **Tel:** 01352 707707
Fax: 01352 700048
Email: admanager@flintshireeveningleader.co.uk
Web site: http://www.flintshirestandard.co.uk
Publisher: NWN Media Ltd
Frequency: Weekly - Published every Thursday
Cover Price: Free
Circulation: 31,482 (VFD 02/07/2007 to 30/12/2007)
Editor: Steven Graves; **News Editor:** Steven Graves
ADVERTISING RATES:
Full Page Mono £1307.00
Full Page Colour £1699.10
Agency Commission: 10%
Mechanical Data: Film: Digital, Type Area: 350 x 259mm, Col Length: 350mm, No. of Columns (Display): 9, Col Widths (Display): 27mm, Page Width: 259mm
Copy instructions: Copy Date: Monday 5pm prior to publication date
LOCAL NEWSPAPERS: Local Newspapers Wales

FOCUS (COLOUR SUPPLEMENT)

44519U72B-3410_140

Frequency: Monthly
Cover Price: Free
ADVERTISING RATES:
Full Page Colour £1213.00
Mechanical Data: Type Area: 270 x 185mm, Col Length: 270mm, Page Width: 185mm, Film: Digital
Part of Series, see entry for: Stratford-upon-Avon Herald Series
LOCAL NEWSPAPERS: Local Newspapers English Counties

FOCUS SERIES

754845U72B-1496

Formerly: City Focus
Editorial Address: PO Box 238, ST. ALBANS, AL1 1WE
Tel: 01582 414876 **Fax:** 01582 654327
Email: editorial@focusnewspapers.co.uk
Advertising Address: As above.
Email: ads@focusnewspapers.co.uk
Web site: http://www.focusnewspapers.co.uk
Publisher: Focus Newspapers Ltd
Date Established: 2001
Frequency: Monthly
Cover Price: Free
Circulation: 47,000 (Publisher's Statement)
Editor: Stefanie Hayes; **Advertising Manager:** Stefanie Hayes
ADVERTISING: Rates on application
Agency Commission: 15%
Copy instructions: Copy Date: 3 days prior to publication date
Average advertising content per issue: 60%
Series owner and contact point for the following titles, see individual entries:
St. Albans Focus
Supplement(s): Business - 4xY, Education - 2xY, Health & Beauty - 4xY, Homes & Gardens - 4xY, Women - 4xY
LOCAL NEWSPAPERS: Local Newspapers English Counties

FOCUS (WEST KENT, EAST SUSSEX)

43901U72B-1835_200

Formerly: News in Focus
Frequency: Weekly
Cover Price: Free
Circulation: 67,950 (Publisher's Statement)
ADVERTISING RATES:
SCC £6.80
Part of Series, see entry for: Kent & Sussex Courier Series
LOCAL NEWSPAPERS: Local Newspapers English Counties

FOLKESTONE HERALD

43876U72B-1750_130

Frequency: Weekly - Circulation figure is for the Folkestone Herald Series which includes the Hythe Herald and the Romney Marsh Herald
Cover Price: £0.55
Circulation: 22,755 (ABC 02/07/2007 to 30/12/2007)
ADVERTISING: Rates on application
Part of Series, see entry for: Adscene, Herald & Express Series (Folkestone)
LOCAL NEWSPAPERS: Local Newspapers English Counties

THE FOREST JOURNAL

44574U72B-3520_140

Frequency: Weekly - See Salisbury Journal for circulation figure
Cover Price: £0.65
ADVERTISING RATES:
SCC £1.50
Part of Series, see entry for: Salisbury Journal & Avon Advertiser Series
LOCAL NEWSPAPERS: Local Newspapers English Counties

FOREST OF DEAN AND WYE VALLEY REVIEW

43661U72B-1115

Editorial Address: The Tindle Suite, Kings Buildings, Hill Street, LYDNEY, GL15 5HE **Tel:** 01594 841113
Fax: 01594 842386
Email: review-editor@internet-today.co.uk
Advertising Address: As above.
Email: review-adverts@internet-today.co.uk
Web site: http://www.forest-and-wye-today.co.uk
Publisher: Forest of Dean & Wye Valley Review Ltd
Date Established: 1982
Frequency: Weekly - Published on Wednesday
Cover Price: Free
Circulation: 43,124 (Publisher's Statement)
Editor: Ted Lamb; **Advertising Manager:** Nicki Read
ADVERTISING RATES:
Full Page Mono £1080.00
Full Page Colour £1350.00
Agency Commission: 10%
Mechanical Data: Trim Size: 360 x 276mm, Print Process: Web-fed offset litho, Film: Digital
Copy instructions: Copy Date: Tuesday 12pm prior to publication date
Average advertising content per issue: 65%
LOCAL NEWSPAPERS: Local Newspapers English Counties

THE FORESTER (FOREST OF DEAN)

43660U72B-1110

Editorial Address: 43-47 High Street, CINDERFORD, GL14 2SL **Tel:** 01594 820600 **Fax:** 01594 820610
Email: editor@theforester.co.uk
Advertising Address: As above.
Email: janet.miles@glosmedia.co.uk
Web site: http://www.www.thisisgloucestershire.co.uk
Publisher: Gloucestershire Media
Frequency: Weekly - Published on Thursday
Cover Price: £0.55
Circulation: 13,000 (Publisher's Statement)
Editor: Vivienne Hargreaves; **Advertising Manager:** Janet Miles
ADVERTISING RATES:
Full Page Mono £918.72
Full Page Colour £1127.52
SCC £2.90
Agency Commission: 15%
Mechanical Data: Type Area: 360 x 270mm, Page Width: 270mm, Film: Digital, Col Length: 360mm, Col Widths (Display): 27mm, No. of Columns (Display): 8
Copy instructions: Copy Date: Monday 1pm prior to publication date
Average advertising content per issue: 45%
Supplement(s): Homes & Gardens - 12xY, Leisure - 52xY, Motors - 52xY, Property - 52xY
LOCAL NEWSPAPERS: Local Newspapers English Counties

FORFAR DISPATCH

707397U72D-400_120

Frequency: Weekly
Cover Price: £0.56
Part of Series, see entry for: Forfar Dispatch Series
LOCAL NEWSPAPERS: Local Newspapers Scotland

FORFAR DISPATCH SERIES

44943U72D-400

Editorial Address: 117-119 Castle Street, FORFAR, DD8 3AH **Tel:** 01307 464899 **Fax:** 01307 466923
Email: dispatchnews@forfardispatch.com
Advertising Address: Craig O'Loch Road, FORFAR, DD8 1BT **Tel:** 01307 464899 **Fax:** 01307 466923

Email: zara.higgins@anguscountypress.com
Web site: http://www.forfardispatch.com
Publisher: Angus County Press Ltd
Date Established: 1884
Frequency: Weekly
Cover Price: £0.56
Circulation: 5,653 (ABC 02/07/2007 to 30/12/2007)
Editor: Alan Ducat; **Advertising Manager:** Zara Higgins
ADVERTISING RATES:
Full Page Mono £937.00
Full Page Colour £1201.00
SCC £3.72
Agency Commission: 10%
Mechanical Data: Col Length: 360mm, Page Width: 272mm, Film: Digital, No. of Columns (Display): 9, Print Process: Web-fed offset litho, Type Area: 360 x 272mm
Copy instructions: Copy Date: Monday 5pm prior to publication date
Average advertising content per issue: 40%
Series owner and contact point for the following titles, see individual entries:
Forfar Dispatch
Kirriemuir Herald
LOCAL NEWSPAPERS: Local Newspapers Scotland

FORMBY CHAMPION

44104U72B-2388_120

Frequency: Weekly
Cover Price: Free
ADVERTISING RATES:
Full Page Mono £952.00
SCC £3.50
Part of Series, see entry for: Southport, Ormskirk & Formby Champion Series
LOCAL NEWSPAPERS: Local Newspapers English Counties

FORMBY TIMES

44092U72B-2340

Editorial Address: 26-32 Tulketh Street, SOUTHPORT, PR8 1BT **Tel:** 01704 872237 **Fax:** 01704 875729
Email: newsdesk@formbytimes.co.uk
Advertising Address: As above. **Tel:** 01704 536655
Fax: 01704 532041
Email: rebecca.liggett@liverpool.com
Web site: http://www.formbytimes.co.uk
Publisher: Liverpool Daily Post & Echo Ltd
Date Established: 1894
Frequency: Weekly
Cover Price: £0.60
Circulation: 3,885 (Publisher's Statement)
Editor: Hazel Shaw; **Executive Editor:** Jamie Mcloughlin; **Managing Director:** Sara Wilde
ADVERTISING RATES:
SCC £2.17
Mechanical Data: Type Area: 360 x 272mm, No. of Columns (Display): 8, Col Length: 360mm, Page Width: 272mm, Film: Digital
LOCAL NEWSPAPERS: Local Newspapers English Counties

FORRES GAZETTE

44944U72D-406

Editorial Address: 133 High Street, FORRES, IV36 1DX
Tel: 01309 672615 **Fax:** 01309 674755
Email: editor@forres-gazette.co.uk
Advertising Address: As above. **Tel:** 01343 551100
Fax: 01343 541629
Email: advertising@northern-scot.co.uk
Web site: http://www.forres-gazette.co.uk
Publisher: Moray & Nairn Newspaper Co Ltd
Date Established: 1837
Frequency: Weekly
Cover Price: £0.63
Circulation: 3,630 (ABC 01/01/2007 to 30/12/2007)
Editor: Ken Smith
ADVERTISING RATES:
Full Page Mono £725.20
Full Page Colour £1048.95
SCC £2.80
Agency Commission: 10%
Mechanical Data: Film: Digital, Page Width: 263mm, Type Area: 370mm x 263mm, Col Length: 370mm, No. of Columns (Display): 7, Col Widths (Display): 37mm
Copy instructions: Copy Date: Friday 5pm prior to publication
Average advertising content per issue: 50%
LOCAL NEWSPAPERS: Local Newspapers Scotland

FOYLE NEWS

717676U72E-100_150

Frequency: Weekly
Cover Price: £0.50
Circulation: 2,621 (Publisher's Statement)
ADVERTISING RATES:
Full Page Mono £1040.40
Full Page Colour £1456.56
SCC £3.40

Part of Series, see entry for: Derry Journal Series
LOCAL NEWSPAPERS: Local Newspapers Northern Ireland

FRAMLINGHAM WICKHAM MARKET AND DEBENHAM COMMUNITY NEWS
44336U72B-3072_140

Frequency: Monthly
Cover Price: Free
Circulation: 4,600 (Publisher's Statement)
Part of Series, see entry for: Community News Series
LOCAL NEWSPAPERS: Local Newspapers English Counties

THE FRASERBURGH HERALD 44945U72D-420
Editorial Address: 60 High Street, FRASERBURGH, AB43 9HP **Tel:** 01346 513900 **Fax:** 01346 517378
Email: mark.jackson@jpress.co.uk
Advertising Address: 17 Chapel Street, PETERHEAD, AB42 1TH **Tel:** 01779 472017 **Fax:** 01779 871331
Email: phyllis.mundie@jpress.co.uk
Publisher: Johnston Press plc
Date Established: 1884
Frequency: Weekly
Cover Price: £0.45
Circulation: 5,878 (ABC 02/07/2007 to 30/12/2007)
Editor: Mark Jackson
ADVERTISING RATES:
Full Page Mono £795.00
Full Page Colour £1030.00
SCC £3.25
Agency Commission: 10%
Mechanical Data: Col Length: 340mm, Film: Digital, No. of Columns (Display): 8, Type Area: 340 x 268mm, Page Width: 268mm, Print Process: Web-fed offset litho
Copy instructions: Copy Date: 2 days prior to publication date
Average advertising content per issue: 40%
LOCAL NEWSPAPERS: Local Newspapers Scotland

THE FREE PRESS ABERGAVENNY, USK
707006U72C-182_110
Frequency: Weekly
Circulation: 1,420 (Publisher's Statement)
Part of Series, see entry for: The Free Press Newspaper Series
LOCAL NEWSPAPERS: Local Newspapers Wales

THE FREE PRESS CHEPSTOW, CALDICOT, MAGOR, WYE VALLEY
44791U72C-182_120
Frequency: Weekly
Circulation: 4,707 (Publisher's Statement)
Part of Series, see entry for: The Free Press Newspaper Series
LOCAL NEWSPAPERS: Local Newspapers Wales

THE FREE PRESS MONMOUTH, RAGLAN
707008U72C-182_130
Frequency: Weekly
Circulation: 1,383 (Publisher's Statement)
Part of Series, see entry for: The Free Press Newspaper Series
LOCAL NEWSPAPERS: Local Newspapers Wales

THE FREE PRESS NEWSPAPER SERIES
44790U72C-182
Editorial Address: 3 Portland Buildings, Commercial Street, PONTYPOOL, NP4 6JS **Tel:** 01495 751133
Fax: 01495 751911
Email: pontypoolnews@gwent-wales.co.uk
Advertising Address: Cardiff Road, Maesglas, NEWPORT, NP20 3QN **Tel:** 01633 810000 **Fax:** 01633 777160
Email: sales@gwent-wales.co.uk
Web site: http://www.freepressseries.co.uk
Publisher: Newsquest (Media Group) Ltd
Frequency: Weekly
Cover Price: £0.35
Circulation: 11,281 (Combined Circulation)
Editor: Leanne Fender; **Managing Editor:** Nicole Garnon
ADVERTISING RATES:
SCC £4.10
Agency Commission: 10%
Mechanical Data: Page Width: 259mm, Col Widths (Display): 27mm, Film: Digital, Type Area: 340 x 259mm, Col Length: 340mm, No. of Columns (Display): 9
Copy instructions: Copy Date: Friday prior to publication date
Average advertising content per issue: 40%

Series owner and contact point for the following titles, see individual entries:
The Free Press Abergavenny, Usk
The Free Press Chepstow, Caldicot, Magor, Wye Valley
The Free Press Monmouth, Raglan
The Free Press Pontypool, Cwmbran, Blaenavon
LOCAL NEWSPAPERS: Local Newspapers Wales

THE FREE PRESS PONTYPOOL, CWMBRAN, BLAENAVON
707009U72C-182_140
Frequency: Weekly
Circulation: 3,771 (ABC 02/07/2007 to 30/12/2007)
Part of Series, see entry for: The Free Press Newspaper Series
LOCAL NEWSPAPERS: Local Newspapers Wales

FRINTON AND WALTON GAZETTE
43618U72B-1044_140
Frequency: Weekly - Circulation figure incorporated into the Clacton Gazette
Cover Price: £0.55
ADVERTISING RATES:
Full Page Colour £772.00
SCC £4.65
Copy instructions: Copy Date: Tuesday 1pm prior to publication date
Part of Series, see entry for: Gazette and Standard Series (East Essex)
LOCAL NEWSPAPERS: Local Newspapers English Counties

THE FRODSHAM & HELSBY CHRONICLE
43354U72B-430_130
Formerly: Chronicle Frodsham & Helsby
Frequency: Weekly - Published on Thursday. Circulation figure is incorporated into the Chronicle Chester City Edition
Cover Price: £0.70
ADVERTISING RATES:
SCC £10.61
Part of Series, see entry for: Chester Chronicle Series
LOCAL NEWSPAPERS: Local Newspapers English Counties

FROME TIMES 44569U72B-3517_140
Frequency: 26 issues yearly
Cover Price: Free
Circulation: 12,000 (Publisher's Statement)
ADVERTISING RATES:
Full Page Colour £468.00
Part of Series, see entry for: The Melksham Independent News Series
LOCAL NEWSPAPERS: Local Newspapers English Counties

FULHAM & HAMMERSMITH CHRONICLE
43087U72A-300_147
Frequency: Weekly - Published on Thursday. Circulation figure includes Kensington & Chelsea News, Marylebone & Paddington Mercury and Westminster & Pimlico News
Cover Price: £0.45
Circulation: 3,256 (ABC 02/07/2007 to 30/12/2007)
ADVERTISING RATES:
SCC £13.93
Copy instructions: Copy Date: Tuesday 4pm prior to publication date
Part of Series, see entry for: London Newspaper Group Series
LOCAL NEWSPAPERS: Local Newspapers Greater London

Y GADLAS 761744U72J-77
Editorial Address: Swyddfa'r Gadlas, Canolfan Tan y Fron, Bylchau, DENBIGH, LL16 5LY **Tel:** 01745 870357
Fax: 01745 870357
Email: ygadlas1@btinternet.com
Advertising Address: As above.
Email: ygadlas1@btinternet.com
Date Established: 1976
Frequency: Monthly
Cover Price: £0.50
Circulation: 1,600 (Publisher's Statement)
Usual Pagination: 32
Editor: M. I. Davies; **Advertising Manager:** M. I. Davies
Summary of Content: Welsh language community newspaper covering local interest news and events.
Language(s): Welsh
Readership/Target Audience: Aimed at Welsh speaking readers with an interest in local affairs.
ADVERTISING RATES:
Full Page Mono £110.00
Mechanical Data: Film: Digital

Copy instructions: Copy Date: 3 weeks prior to publication date
Average advertising content per issue: 10%
LOCAL NEWSPAPERS: Community Newsletters

GAINSBOROUGH NEWS 44059U72B-2255_150
Formerly: Gainsborough Trader News
Frequency: Weekly
Cover Price: Free
Circulation: 17,000 (Publisher's Statement)
ADVERTISING RATES:
SCC £1.32
Part of Series, see entry for: Gainsborough News and Standard Series
LOCAL NEWSPAPERS: Local Newspapers English Counties

GAINSBOROUGH NEWS AND STANDARD SERIES
761979U72B-2255
Editorial Address: 5-7 Market Place, GAINSBOROUGH, DN21 2BP **Tel:** 01427 615323 **Fax:** 01427 613492
Email: editorial@gainsboroughtoday.co.uk
Advertising Address: As above.
Email: graham.hobbs@jpress.co.uk
Web site: http://www.gainsboroughstandard.co.uk
Publisher: South Yorkshire Newspapers Ltd
Date Established: 1855
Frequency: Weekly - Published on Thursday and Friday
Circulation: 5,000 (Combined Circulation)
Editor: Jackie Laver; **News Editor:** Jackie Laver
ADVERTISING: Rates on application
Series owner and contact point for the following titles, see individual entries:
Gainsborough News
Gainsborough Standard
LOCAL NEWSPAPERS: Local Newspapers English Counties

GAINSBOROUGH STANDARD
44058U72B-2255_170
Frequency: Weekly
Cover Price: £0.42
Circulation: 4,209 (ABC 02/07/2007 to 30/12/2007)
ADVERTISING RATES:
SCC £1.53
Part of Series, see entry for: Gainsborough News and Standard Series
LOCAL NEWSPAPERS: Local Newspapers English Counties

GAINSBOROUGH TARGET 44040U72B-2240_140
Frequency: Weekly
Cover Price: Free
Circulation: 13,775 (VFD 02/07/2007 to 30/12/2007)
ADVERTISING RATES:
SCC £3.60
Part of Series, see entry for: Lincoln Target Series
LOCAL NEWSPAPERS: Local Newspapers English Counties

GALLOWAY GAZETTE 44946U72D-430
Formerly: Galloway Gazette & Stranraer News
Editorial Address: 71 Victoria Street, NEWTON STEWART, DG8 6NL **Tel:** 01671 402503 **Fax:** 01671 403391
Email: editorial@gallowaygazette.com
Advertising Address: As above.
Email: advertising@gallowaygazette.com
Web site: http://www.gallowaygazette.com
Publisher: Johnston Press plc
Date Established: 1870
Frequency: Weekly - Published on Friday
Cover Price: £0.55
Annual Sub.: £46.12
Circulation: 6,296 (ABC 02/07/2007 to 30/12/2007)
Editor: Archie Plunkett; **Managing Director:** Keith McIntyre; **Advertising Manager:** Julie Hamilton; **Group Editor:** Archie Plunkett
ADVERTISING RATES:
Full Page Mono £1525.58
Full Page Colour £2289.56
SCC £6.60
Agency Commission: 10%
Mechanical Data: Col Length: 540mm, Type Area: 540 x 406mm, No. of Columns (Display): 7, Print Process: Web offset, Col Widths (Display): 34mm, Page Width: 406mm, Film: Digital
Copy instructions: Copy Date: Wednesday 3pm prior to publication date
Average advertising content per issue: 40%
LOCAL NEWSPAPERS: Local Newspapers Scotland

Non-National Newspapers

GALLOWAY NEWS
1605578U72D-440_101

Frequency: Weekly - Published on Thursday
Cover Price: £0.78
Circulation: 9,800 (Publisher's Statement)
ADVERTISING Rates on application
Part of Series, see entry for: Dumfries and Galloway News Series
LOCAL NEWSPAPERS: Local Newspapers Scotland

Y GAMBO
761761U72J-80

Editorial Address: Y Graig, Aberporth, CARDIGAN, SA43 2DU **Tel:** 01239 810555
Advertising Address: Derwen Deg, Penrhiwllan, LLANDYSUL, SA44 5NU **Tel:** 01559 371392
Email: johnygraig@tesco.net
Frequency: 10 issues yearly - Not published in August and September
Cover Price: £0.50
Circulation: 1,300 (Publisher's Statement)
Editor: John Davies; **Advertising Manager:** John Davies
Summary of Content: Welsh language newspaper, covering almost exclusively local news.
Language(s): Welsh
Readership/Target Audience: Aimed at Welsh speaking readers in South West Ceredigion.
ADVERTISING RATES:
Full Page Mono £80.00
Mechanical Data: Film: Digital
Copy instructions: Copy Date: 3 weeks prior to publication date
LOCAL NEWSPAPERS: Community Newsletters

THE GARSTANG & LONGRIDGE COURIER & NEWS SERIES
43971U72B-1985

Formerly: Garstang & Longridge Courier Series
Editorial Address: 7 Pringle Court, Parkhill Road, Garstang, PRESTON, PR3 1LN **Tel:** 01995 602494 **Fax:** 01995 601623
Email: garstang.courier@lep.co.uk
Advertising Address: Olivers Place, Eastway, Fulwood, PRESTON, PR2 9ZA **Tel:** 01772 254841 **Fax:** 01772 838199
Email: martin.woodhead@lep.co.uk
Web site: http://www.garstangcourier.co.uk
Publisher: Lancashire Evening Post Ltd
Date Established: 1963
Frequency: Weekly - Published on Wednesday
Circulation: 5,026 (ABC 02/07/2007 to 30/12/2007)
Editor: Richard Machin
ADVERTISING: Rates on application
Agency Commission: 10%
Copy instructions: Copy Date: Monday 5pm prior to publication date
Average advertising content per issue: 50%
Series owner and contact point for the following titles, see individual entries:
The Garstang Courier
The Longridge News
Supplement(s): Property - 52xY, Rural Life - 12xY
LOCAL NEWSPAPERS: Local Newspapers English Counties

THE GARSTANG COURIER
1832652U72B-1985_100

Frequency: Weekly - Published on Wednesday
Cover Price: £0.55
ADVERTISING: Rates on application
Part of Series, see entry for: The Garstang & Longridge Courier & News Series
LOCAL NEWSPAPERS: Local Newspapers English Counties

Y GARTHEN
761762U72J-83

Editorial Address: Heddfryn, New Inn, PENCADER, SA39 9AY **Tel:** 01559 384252
Email: ygarthen@papurbro.org
Advertising Address: As above.
Date Established: 1981
Frequency: 10 issues yearly - Not published in January and August
Cover Price: £0.45
Circulation: 700 (Publisher's Statement)
Usual Pagination: 28
Editor: Marina Davies; **Advertising Manager:** Marina Davies
Summary of Content: Newsletter covering community news and local stories with sport coverage, young farmers club and youth activity pages.
Language(s): Welsh
Readership/Target Audience: Aimed at Welsh speaking readers in the Teifi Valley.
ADVERTISING: Rates on application
Copy instructions: Copy Date: 20th of the month prior to publication date
LOCAL NEWSPAPERS: Community Newsletters

GATEWAY NEWS
1665697U72A-1312

Editorial Address: 2 Bertrand Way, Thamesmead, LONDON, SE28 8LL **Tel:** 0844 357 5356 **Fax:** 020 8320 7844
Email: editor@gatewaynews.co.uk
Advertising Address: As above. **Tel:** 020 8320 7844
Email: adverts@gatewaynews.co.uk
Web site: http://www.gatewaynews.co.uk
Date Established: 2005
Frequency: Monthly
Cover Price: Free
Circulation: 22,000 (Publisher's Statement)
Editor: Dwain Leaver; **Advertising Manager:** Dwain Leaver
ADVERTISING RATES:
Full Page Colour £872.00
Mechanical Data: Type Area: 366 x 266mm, Col Length: 366mm, Page Width: 266mm, No. of Columns (Display): 8, Film: Digital
Average advertising content per issue: 40%
LOCAL NEWSPAPERS: Local Newspapers Greater London

GAZETA Z HIGHLAND
1804613U72D-1024

Editorial Address: New Century House, Stadium Road, INVERNESS, IV1 1FG **Tel:** 01463 233059 **Fax:** 01463 732220
Email: h.macrae@spp-group.com
Advertising Address: As above. **Fax:** 01463 732289
Email: sales@ncpg.co.uk
Web site: http://www.gazeta-z-highland.co.uk
Publisher: Scottish Provincial Press
Date Established: 2007
Frequency: Monthly
Cover Price: Free
Circulation: 20,000 (Print Run)
Editor: Helen Macrae; **Advertising Manager:** Steve Barron
Summary of Content: Newspaper covering local community news and issues.
Language(s): English; Polish
Readership/Target Audience: Aimed at both the Scottish and Polish communities.
ADVERTISING RATES:
SCC £3.75
Agency Commission: 10%
Mechanical Data: Type Area: 370 x 261mm, Col Length: 370mm, Page Width: 261mm, Col Widths (Display): 31mm, No. of Columns (Display): 8, Film: Digital
Copy instructions: Copy Date: 1 week prior to publication date
Average advertising content per issue: 25%
LOCAL NEWSPAPERS: Local Newspapers Scotland

GAZETTE, ADVERTISER AND PRESS NEWSPAPER SERIES
42994U72A-120

Formerly: Gazette and Advertiser Newspaper Series
Editorial Address: 4th Floor, Refuge House, 9-10 River Front, ENFIELD, EN1 3SZ **Tel:** 020 8367 2345
Fax: 020 8366 9376
Email: news.enfield@nlhnews.co.uk
Advertising Address: As above. **Fax:** 020 8366 4013
Email: advertisingenfield@trinitysouth.co.uk
Web site: http://www.northlondon-today.co.uk
Publisher: Tindle Newspapers Ltd
Frequency: Weekly
Circulation: 270,519 (Combined Circulation)
Editor: Henry Ellis; **News Editor:** Henry Ellis; **Publisher:** Alison Cruse
ADVERTISING: Rates on application
Agency Commission: 10%
Mechanical Data: Page Width: 262mm, Type Area: 340 x 262mm, Col Length: 340mm, No. of Columns (Display): 8, Col Widths (Display): 31mm
Copy instructions: Copy Date: 2 days prior to publication date
Average advertising content per issue: 60%
Series owner and contact point for the following titles, see individual entries:
The Advertiser Enfield
The Gazette (Enfield)
The Haringey Advertiser
The Press Barnet, Whetstone & Potters Bar
The Press Hendon, Finchley, Edgware & Mill Hill
LOCAL NEWSPAPERS: Local Newspapers Greater London

GAZETTE & HERALD (BOX, CALNE, CHIPPENHAM, CORSHAM & LYNEHAM)
44585U72B-3540_155

Formerly: Calne Gazette & Herald
Frequency: Weekly - Circulation figure includes the Gazette & Herald (Devizes), the Gazette & Herald (Marlborough & Pewsey) and the Gazette & Herald (Malmesbury, Wootton Bassett, Wroughton, Highworth, Cricklade, Purton and Lechlade)
Cover Price: £0.65
Circulation: 26,508 (ABC 02/07/2007 to 30/12/2007)

Part of Series, see entry for: Wiltshire Gazette and Herald Series
LOCAL NEWSPAPERS: Local Newspapers English Counties

GAZETTE & HERALD (DEVIZES)
44586U72B-3540_150

Frequency: Weekly
Cover Price: £0.65
Part of Series, see entry for: Wiltshire Gazette and Herald Series
LOCAL NEWSPAPERS: Local Newspapers English Counties

GAZETTE & HERALD EXPRESS SERIES (HEMEL HEMPSTEAD)
43786U72B-1500

Editorial Address: 39 Marlowes, HEMEL HEMPSTEAD, HP1 1LH **Tel:** 01442 262311 **Fax:** 01442 261887
Email: editorial@hemelgazette.co.uk
Advertising Address: As above. **Fax:** 01442 241824
Email: advertising@hemelgazette.co.uk
Web site: http://www.hemeltoday.co.uk
Publisher: Central Counties Newspapers South Ltd
Frequency: Weekly
Circulation: 62,882 (Combined Circulation)
Editor: Ann Traynor; **News Editor:** Ann Traynor; **Advertising Manager:** Jill Manning
ADVERTISING: Rates on application
Agency Commission: 10%
Copy instructions: Copy Date: 1 week prior to publication date
Average advertising content per issue: 70%
Series owner and contact point for the following titles, see individual entries:
Gazette (Berkhamsted, Tring & the Langleys)
Gazette (Hemel Hempstead)
Herald Express Hemel Hempstead, Berkhamsted & Tring
LOCAL NEWSPAPERS: Local Newspapers English Counties

GAZETTE & HERALD (MARLBOROUGH & PEWSEY)
44587U72B-3540_160

Frequency: Weekly
Cover Price: £0.65
Part of Series, see entry for: Wiltshire Gazette and Herald Series
LOCAL NEWSPAPERS: Local Newspapers English Counties

GAZETTE & HERALD (RYEDALE & SCARBOROUGH)
44658U72B-3610

Editorial Address: PO Box 29, 76-86 Walmgate, YORK, YO1 9YN **Tel:** 01904 653051 **Fax:** 01904 567178
Email: gazette@gazetteherald.co.uk
Advertising Address: 22 Yorkersgate, MALTON, YO17 7AB **Tel:** 01653 699699 **Fax:** 01653 692294
Email: maltonsales@ycp.co.uk
Web site: http://www.gazetteherald.co.uk
Publisher: York & County Press
Date Established: 1790
Frequency: Weekly - Published on Wednesday
Cover Price: £0.70
Circulation: 13,184 (ABC 02/07/2007 to 30/12/2007)
Editor: Jamila Farooqi; **News Editor:** Jamila Farooqi; **Advertising Manager:** Charlotte Baker
ADVERTISING RATES:
Full Page Mono £2145.00
Full Page Colour £2681.00
SCC £3.25
Agency Commission: 10%
Mechanical Data: Film: Digital, Col Widths (Display): 27mm, Type Area: 550 x 351.5mm, No. of Columns (Display): 12, Col Length: 550mm
Copy instructions: Copy Date: Monday 12 noon prior to publication date
Average advertising content per issue: 50%
LOCAL NEWSPAPERS: Local Newspapers English Counties

GAZETTE & HERALD (SWINDON)
1605516U72B-3540_161

Frequency: Weekly
Cover Price: £0.50
Part of Series, see entry for: Wiltshire Gazette and Herald Series
LOCAL NEWSPAPERS: Local Newspapers English Counties

THE GAZETTE AND LEADER SERIES

42986U72A-110

Editorial Address: 93 Staines Road, HOUNSLOW, TW3 3JB
Tel: 020 8572 1816 **Fax:** 020 8840 0107
Email: edit@ealinggazette.co.uk
Advertising Address: 134-136 Broadway, LONDON, W13 0TL **Tel:** 020 8579 3131 **Fax:** 020 8840 0107
Email: ropeating@trinitysouth.co.uk
Web site: http://www.ealinggazette.co.uk
Publisher: Trinity Mirror Southern
Frequency: Weekly
Circulation: 88,667 (Combined Circulation)
Editor: News Desk; **Advertising Manager:** Amarjit Ram
ADVERTISING: Rates on application
Mechanical Data: Type Area: 340 x 262mm, Col Length: 340mm, Page Width: 262mm, Film: Digital, Col Widths (Display): 31mm, No. of Columns (Display): 8
Copy instructions: Copy Date: Wednesday 4pm prior to publication date
Series owner and contact point for the following titles, see individual entries:
Ealing Leader
Gazette (Ealing & Acton)
Gazette (Fulham)
Gazette (Greenford & Northolt)
Gazette (Hammersmith & Shepherds Bush)
Gazette (Southall)
LOCAL NEWSPAPERS: Local Newspapers Greater London

GAZETTE AND STANDARD SERIES (EAST ESSEX)

43616U72B-1044

Editorial Address: 28 Jackson Road, CLACTON-ON-SEA, CO15 1QL **Tel:** 01255 221221 **Fax:** 01255 432824
Email: cf.gazette@nqe.com
Advertising Address: Wickham House, 1 Northgate Street, COLCHESTER, CO1 1HA **Tel:** 01206 506000
Email: samantha.bruce@nqe.com
Web site: http://www.clactonandfrintongazette.co.uk
Publisher: Essex County Newspapers
Date Established: 1877
Frequency: Weekly
Circulation: 22,625 (Combined Circulation)
Editor: Dominic Bowers
ADVERTISING: Rates on application
Mechanical Data: No. of Columns (Display): 9, Col Widths (Display): 27mm, Print Process: Web-fed offset litho, Type Area: 340 x 267mm, Col Length: 340mm, Film: Digital, Page Width: 267mm
Series owner and contact point for the following titles, see individual entries:
Clacton Gazette
Frinton and Walton Gazette
Harwich and Manningtree Standard
Manningtree and Harwich Standard
LOCAL NEWSPAPERS: Local Newspapers English Counties

THE GAZETTE (BASINGSTOKE AND NORTH HANTS (MON))

43741U72B-1345_155

Frequency: Weekly
Cover Price: £0.55
Circulation: 10,085 (Publisher's Statement)
ADVERTISING RATES:
Full Page Mono £1377.00
Full Page Colour £1377.00
SCC £4.50
Copy instructions: Copy Date: Thursday 12 noon prior to publication date
Part of Series, see entry for: Basingstoke and North Hants Gazette Series
LOCAL NEWSPAPERS: Local Newspapers English Counties

THE GAZETTE (BASINGSTOKE AND NORTH HANTS (THURS))

43742U72B-1345_160

Formerly: The Gazette (Basingstoke and North Hants (Fri))
Frequency: Weekly
Cover Price: £0.55
Circulation: 24,827 (Publisher's Statement)
ADVERTISING RATES:
Full Page Mono £2126.70
Full Page Colour £2126.70
SCC £6.95
Copy instructions: Copy Date: Tuesday 12pm prior to publication date
Part of Series, see entry for: Basingstoke and North Hants Gazette Series
LOCAL NEWSPAPERS: Local Newspapers English Counties

GAZETTE (BERKHAMSTED, TRING & THE LANGLEYS)

1809545U72B-1500_141

Frequency: Weekly - See Gazette (Hemel Hempstead) for circulation figure
Cover Price: £0.45
ADVERTISING: Rates on application
Part of Series, see entry for: Gazette & Herald Express Series (Hemel Hempstead)
LOCAL NEWSPAPERS: Local Newspapers English Counties

THE GAZETTE (BLACKPOOL)

41996U67B-60

Editorial Address: Avroe House, Avroe Crescent, Blackpool Business Park, Squires Gate Lane, BLACKPOOL, FY4 2DP
Tel: 01253 400888 **Fax:** 01253 361870
Email: jon.rhodes@blackpoolgazette.co.uk
Advertising Address: As above. **Fax:** 01253 361898
Email: ava.makepeace@blackpoolgazette.co.uk
Web site: http://www.blackpoolgazette.co.uk
Publisher: Johnston Press plc
Date Established: 1873
Frequency: Evenings
Cover Price: £0.40
Circulation: 36,500 (Publisher's Statement)
Editor: Jon Rhodes; **News Editor:** Jon Rhodes; **Managing Director:** Darren Russell; **Advertising Manager:** Ava Makepeace
ADVERTISING: Rates on application
Copy instructions: Copy Date: 2 days prior to publication date
Editions:
The Gazette (Blackpool) (Fleetwood)
The Gazette (Blackpool) (Late Final)
Supplement(s): Life! - 52xY, Property Today - 52xY, The Weekend - 52xY, Wheels - 52xY
REGIONAL DAILY & SUNDAY NEWSPAPERS: Regional Daily Newspapers

THE GAZETTE (BLACKPOOL) (FLEETWOOD)

1660042U67B-60_500

Frequency: Evenings
Cover Price: £0.40
ADVERTISING: Rates on application
Edition of: The Gazette (Blackpool)
REGIONAL DAILY & SUNDAY NEWSPAPERS: Regional Daily Newspapers

THE GAZETTE (BLACKPOOL) (LATE FINAL)

1660043U67B-60_501

Frequency: Evenings
Cover Price: £0.40
ADVERTISING: Rates on application
Edition of: The Gazette (Blackpool)
REGIONAL DAILY & SUNDAY NEWSPAPERS: Regional Daily Newspapers

GAZETTE (EALING & ACTON)

42989U72A-110_140

Frequency: Weekly - Circulation figure includes the Gazette (Fulham), the Gazette (Greenford & Northolt), the Gazette Hammersmith & Shepherds Bush and the Gazette (Southall)
Cover Price: £0.55
Circulation: 12,007 (ABC 02/07/2007 to 30/12/2007)
ADVERTISING RATES:
SCC £12.00
Part of Series, see entry for: The Gazette and Leader Series
LOCAL NEWSPAPERS: Local Newspapers Greater London

THE GAZETTE (ENFIELD)

42997U72A-120_150

Formerly: Enfield Gazette
Frequency: Weekly
Cover Price: £0.40
Circulation: 30,000 (Publisher's Statement)
ADVERTISING RATES:
SCC £9.35
Part of Series, see entry for: Gazette, Advertiser and Press Newspaper Series
LOCAL NEWSPAPERS: Local Newspapers Greater London

GAZETTE (FULHAM)

42990U72A-110_150

Frequency: Weekly - Circulation figure is incorporated into the Gazette (Ealing & Acton)
Cover Price: £0.55
ADVERTISING RATES:
SCC £12.00
Part of Series, see entry for: The Gazette and Leader Series
LOCAL NEWSPAPERS: Local Newspapers Greater London

GAZETTE (GREENFORD & NORTHOLT)

42991U72A-110_160

Frequency: Weekly - Circulation figure is incorporated into the Gazette (Ealing & Acton)
Cover Price: £0.55
ADVERTISING RATES:
SCC £12.00
Part of Series, see entry for: The Gazette and Leader Series
LOCAL NEWSPAPERS: Local Newspapers Greater London

GAZETTE (HAMMERSMITH & SHEPHERDS BUSH)

42992U72A-110_180

Frequency: Weekly - Circulation figure is incorporated into the Gazette (Ealing & Acton)
Cover Price: £0.55
ADVERTISING RATES:
SCC £12.00
Part of Series, see entry for: The Gazette and Leader Series
LOCAL NEWSPAPERS: Local Newspapers Greater London

GAZETTE (HAREFIELD)

43159U72A-525_105

Frequency: Weekly - For circulation see Gazette (Uxbridge & West Drayton)
Cover Price: £0.40
ADVERTISING: Rates on application
Part of Series, see entry for: Uxbridge Gazette Series
LOCAL NEWSPAPERS: Local Newspapers Greater London

GAZETTE (HAYES & HARLINGTON)

43160U72A-525_110

Frequency: Weekly - For circulation see Gazette (Uxbridge & West Drayton)
Cover Price: £0.40
ADVERTISING: Rates on application
Part of Series, see entry for: Uxbridge Gazette Series
LOCAL NEWSPAPERS: Local Newspapers Greater London

GAZETTE (HEMEL HEMPSTEAD)

43788U72B-1500_140

Formerly: Gazette (Hemel Hempstead/Berkhamsted/Tring & the Langleys)
Frequency: Weekly - Circulation figure includes Gazette (Berkhamsted, Tring & the Langleys) Published on Wednesday
Cover Price: £0.45
Circulation: 13,455 (ABC 02/07/2007 to 30/12/2007)
ADVERTISING: Rates on application
Part of Series, see entry for: Gazette & Herald Express Series (Hemel Hempstead)
LOCAL NEWSPAPERS: Local Newspapers English Counties

GAZETTE (JARROW & HEBBURN)

42174U67B-1040_560

Cover Price: £0.38
Edition of: The Shields Gazette
REGIONAL DAILY & SUNDAY NEWSPAPERS: Regional Daily Newspapers

THE GAZETTE (RENFREWSHIRE)

45013U72D-820_180

Formerly: Johnstone & Linwood Gazette
Frequency: Weekly - Circulation figure is incorporated into the Barrhead News. Published on Wednesdays
Cover Price: £0.55
ADVERTISING RATES:
SCC £8.75
Part of Series, see entry for: The Paisley and Renfrewshire Gazette Series
LOCAL NEWSPAPERS: Local Newspapers Scotland

GAZETTE (RUISLIP & NORTHWOOD)

43161U72A-525_150

Frequency: Weekly - For circulation see Gazette (Uxbridge & West Drayton)
Cover Price: £0.40
ADVERTISING: Rates on application
Part of Series, see entry for: Uxbridge Gazette Series
LOCAL NEWSPAPERS: Local Newspapers Greater London

THE GAZETTE SERIES (EDINBURGH)

1800274U72D-1023

Editorial Address: 108 Holyrood Road, EDINBURGH, EH8 8AS **Tel:** 0131 620 8707

Section 4 (a) Newspapers

Email: gmilne@scotsman.com
Advertising Address: As above. **Tel:** 0131 620 8620
Email: louisa.lawson@scotsman.com
Publisher: The Scotsman Publications Ltd
Frequency: Monthly
Cover Price: Free
Circulation: 12,000 (Combined Circulation)
Editor: Gail Milne
ADVERTISING RATES:
Full Page Colour £918.00
SCC £3.00
Mechanical Data: Type Area: 340 x 277mm, Col Length:
340mm, Page Width: 277mm, Col Widths (Display): 32mm,
No. of Columns (Display): 9, Film: Digital
Copy instructions: Copy Date: Wednesday 5pm prior to
publication date
**Series owner and contact point for the following titles,
see individual entries:**
Leith Gazette
Morningside and Bruntsfield Gazette
Stockbridge and New Town Gazette
LOCAL NEWSPAPERS: Local Newspapers Scotland

THE GAZETTE SERIES (MID DEVON)
43516U72B-805

Formerly: The Mid Devon Gazette Series
Editorial Address: 29 Bampton Street, TIVERTON, EX16
6AG **Tel:** 01884 252725 **Fax:** 01884 243102
Email: news@middevongazette.co.uk
Advertising Address: As above. **Fax:** 01884 258527
Email: sales@middevongazette.co.uk
Web site: http://www.thisismiddevon.co.uk
Publisher: South West Media Group Ltd
Date Established: 1858
Frequency: Weekly - Published on Tuesday
Circulation: 12,086 (ABC 02/07/2007 to 30/12/2007)
Editor: Tim Hall; **Advertising Manager:** Veronica Tatnall
ADVERTISING RATES:
Full Page Mono £1051.20
SCC £3.65
Agency Commission: 10%
Mechanical Data: Page Width: 268mm, Type Area: 360 x
268mm, Col Length: 360mm, Col Widths (Display): 31mm,
No. of Columns (Display): 8, Film: Digital
Copy instructions: Copy Date: Thursday 5pm prior to
publication date
Average advertising content per issue: 70%
**Series owner and contact point for the following titles,
see individual entries:**
The Crediton Gazette
The Culm Valley Gazette
The Tiverton Gazette
LOCAL NEWSPAPERS: Local Newspapers English
Counties

GAZETTE (SOUTHALL)
42993U72A-110_220
Frequency: Weekly - Circulation figure is incorporated into
the Gazette (Ealing & Acton)
Cover Price: £0.55
ADVERTISING RATES:
SCC £12.00
Part of Series, see entry for: The Gazette and Leader
Series
LOCAL NEWSPAPERS: Local Newspapers Greater London

GAZETTE (UXBRIDGE AND WEST DRAYTON)
43162U72A-525_170
Frequency: Weekly - Circulation is for Uxbridge & West
Drayton Gazette Series including Gazette (Hayes &
Harlington), Gazette (Ruislip & Northwood) and Gazette
(Harefield)
Cover Price: £0.40
Circulation: 14,620 (ABC 02/07/2007 to 30/12/2007)
ADVERTISING: Rates on application
Part of Series, see entry for: Uxbridge Gazette Series
LOCAL NEWSPAPERS: Local Newspapers Greater London

GEM (BARRY)
44794U72C-185_120
Frequency: Weekly - Circulation is for Glamorgan Gem
Series including Gem (Cowbridge) and Gem (Llantwit Major)
Cover Price: Free
Circulation: 30,196 (Publisher's Statement)
Part of Series, see entry for: Gem Series
LOCAL NEWSPAPERS: Local Newspapers Wales

GEM (COWBRIDGE)
44795U72C-185_130
Frequency: Weekly - For circulation see Gem (Barry)
Cover Price: Free
Part of Series, see entry for: Gem Series
LOCAL NEWSPAPERS: Local Newspapers Wales

GEM (LLANTWIT MAJOR)
44796U72C-185_150
Frequency: Weekly - For circulation see Gem (Barry)
Cover Price: Free
Part of Series, see entry for: Gem Series
LOCAL NEWSPAPERS: Local Newspapers Wales

GEM (PORTHCAWL & BRIDGEND)
44756U72C-185_100
Formerly: Bridgend & Valleys Recorder
Frequency: Weekly
Cover Price: Free
Circulation: 6,000 (Publisher's Statement)
Part of Series, see entry for: Gem Series
LOCAL NEWSPAPERS: Local Newspapers Wales

GEM SERIES
44793U72C-185
Editorial Address: Graig House, 53 Eastgate, COWBRIDGE,
CF71 7EL **Tel:** 01446 774484
Email: ggem@internet-today.co.uk
Advertising Address: As above. **Fax:** 01446 774108
Email: ggem@internet-today.co.uk
Web site: http://www.cowbridge-today.co.uk
Publisher: Tindle Newspapers Ltd
Frequency: Weekly - Published on Thursday
Cover Price: Free
Circulation: 36,196 (Combined Circulation)
Editor: Caroline Attya; **Advertising Manager:** Garreth
Jamieson
ADVERTISING RATES:
Full Page Mono £2448.00
Full Page Colour £3182.40
SCC £8.50
Agency Commission: 10%
Mechanical Data: Type Area: 360 x 270mm, Col Length:
360mm, Col Widths (Display): 32mm, No. of Columns
(Display): 8, Page Width: 270mm, Film: Digital
Copy instructions: Copy Date: Monday 5pm prior to
publication date
Average advertising content per issue: 60%
**Series owner and contact point for the following titles,
see individual entries:**
Gem (Barry)
Gem (Cowbridge)
Gem (Llantwit Major)
Gem (Porthcawl & Bridgend)
LOCAL NEWSPAPERS: Local Newspapers Wales

GETREADING
1902261U72B-4163_101
Frequency: Weekly - Published on Friday
Cover Price: Free
Circulation: 71,000 (Publisher's Statement)
Part of Series, see entry for: Reading Post Series
LOCAL NEWSPAPERS: Local Newspapers English
Counties

GLAMORGAN GAZETTE
1659710U72C-190_100
Frequency: Weekly
Cover Price: £0.68
Part of Series, see entry for: Glamorgan Gazette Series
LOCAL NEWSPAPERS: Local Newspapers Wales

GLAMORGAN GAZETTE SERIES
44797U72C-190
Editorial Address: 2 Brackla Street Centre, BRIDGEND,
CF31 1DD **Tel:** 01656 304920 **Fax:** 01656 304904
Email: glamorgan.gazette@mediawales.co.uk
Advertising Address: Thomson House, Havelock Street,
CARDIFF, CF10 1XR **Tel:** 029 2058 3583
Fax: 029 2058 3553
Email: robert.gray@mediawales.co.uk
Web site: http://www.icwales.co.uk
Publisher: Celtic Newspapers Ltd
Frequency: Weekly - Published on Thursday
Circulation: 21,504 (ABC 02/07/2007 to 30/12/2007)
Editor: Deborah Rees
ADVERTISING RATES:
Full Page Mono £1816.00
Full Page Colour £2452.89
SCC £6.68
Agency Commission: 10%
Mechanical Data: Col Length: 340mm, Page Width:
266mm, Type Area: 340 x 266mm, No. of Columns (Display):
8
Copy instructions: Copy Date: Monday 1pm prior to
publication date
**Series owner and contact point for the following titles,
see individual entries:**
Glamorgan Gazette
Glamorgan Gazette (Valleys Edition)
Supplement(s): Entertainment - 52xY, Motors - 52xY
LOCAL NEWSPAPERS: Local Newspapers Wales

GLAMORGAN GAZETTE (VALLEYS EDITION)
1659709U72C-190_101
Frequency: Weekly
Cover Price: £0.68
Part of Series, see entry for: Glamorgan Gazette Series
LOCAL NEWSPAPERS: Local Newspapers Wales

Y GLANNAU
761751U72J-85
Editorial Address: Drws-y-Coed, Ffordd-y-Cwm,
DYSERTH, LL18 6HR **Tel:** 01745 570302
Email: gruffudd.roberts@btinternet.com
Advertising Address: 7 Kentigern Court, Elwy Park, ST.
ASAPH, LL17 0AX **Tel:** 01745 583971
Frequency: 10 issues yearly
Cover Price: £0.50
Circulation: 1,000 (Publisher's Statement)
Editor: Gruffudd Roberts; **Advertising Manager:** Myra
Hughes
Summary of Content: Welsh language local community
newsletter containing articles of local interest including
environmental, sport and leisure items.
Language(s): Welsh
Readership/Target Audience: Aimed at Welsh speakers
interested in the North Wales area.
ADVERTISING RATES:
Full Page Mono £80.00
Mechanical Data: Page Width: 210mm, Type Area: 290 x
210mm, Col Length: 290mm, Col Widths (Display): 70mm,
No. of Columns (Display): 3, Trim Size: 350 x 230mm
Copy instructions: Copy Date: 3 weeks prior to publication
date
LOCAL NEWSPAPERS: Community Newsletters

THE GLASGOW EXTRA SERIES
44949U72D-450
Formerly: Glasgow Extra & Courier Series
Editorial Address: Park House, Academy Park, Gower
Street, Pollokshields, GLASGOW, G51 1PT
Tel: 0141 427 7878 **Fax:** 0141 427 9780
Email: colin.macdonald@jnscotland.co.uk
Advertising Address: As above. **Fax:** 0141 427 0519
Email: sandra.weatherston@jpress.co.uk
Publisher: Johnston Press (Falkirk)
Date Established: 1982
Frequency: Weekly - Published on Thursday
Cover Price: Free
Circulation: 100,810 (Combined Circulation)
Usual Pagination: 44
Editor: Colin MacDonald; **News Editor:** Colin MacDonald
ADVERTISING RATES:
SCC £11.28
Agency Commission: 10%
Mechanical Data: Type Area: 345 x 272mm, Col Widths
(Display): 28mm, Col Length: 345mm, No. of Columns
(Display): 9, Page Width: 272mm, Film: Digital
Copy instructions: Copy Date: Tuesday 12pm prior to
publication date
Average advertising content per issue: 70%
**Series owner and contact point for the following titles,
see individual entries:**
The Extra Bearsden, Milngavie & Westend
The Extra Glasgow South & Eastwood
The Extra Paisley & Renfrewshire
LOCAL NEWSPAPERS: Local Newspapers Scotland

THE GLASWEGIAN NORTH
600888U72D-455_140
Frequency: Weekly
Cover Price: Free
Part of Series, see entry for: The Glaswegian Series
LOCAL NEWSPAPERS: Local Newspapers Scotland

THE GLASWEGIAN SERIES
44953U72D-455
Editorial Address: 1 Central Quay, GLASGOW, G3 8DA
Tel: 0141 309 3111 **Fax:** 0141 309 3351
Email: glaswegian@dailyrecord.co.uk
Advertising Address: As above. **Tel:** 0141 309 4970
Fax: 0141 309 3545
Email: advertising@dailyrecord.co.uk
Publisher: Scottish Daily Record & Sunday Mail Ltd
Frequency: Weekly - Published on Thursday
Cover Price: Free
Circulation: 104,175 (VFD 02/07/2007 to 30/12/2007)
Usual Pagination: 56
Editor: Peter Carroll
ADVERTISING RATES:
Full Page Mono £5497.00
Full Page Colour £6871.00
SCC £20.21
Agency Commission: 15%
Mechanical Data: Type Area: 341 x 265mm, Col Length:
341mm, Col Widths (Display): 30mm, No. of Columns
(Display): 8, Film: Digital, Page Width: 265mm
**Series owner and contact point for the following titles,
see individual entries:**
The Glaswegian North

The Glaswegian South
LOCAL NEWSPAPERS: Local Newspapers Scotland

THE GLASWEGIAN SOUTH
600889U72D-455_150

Frequency: Weekly
Cover Price: Free
Part of Series, see entry for: The Glaswegian Series
LOCAL NEWSPAPERS: Local Newspapers Scotland

GLENROTHES GAZETTE LESLIE AND MARKINCH NEWS
44954U72D-460

Editorial Address: 14 North Street, GLENROTHES, KY7 5NA **Tel:** 01592 753205 **Fax:** 01592 754261
Email: edgazette@fifetoday.co.uk
Advertising Address: As above. **Tel:** 01592 261451
Email: bill.morgan@fifetoday.co.uk
Web site: http://www.fifetoday.co.uk
Publisher: Strachan & Livingston Ltd
Date Established: 1962
Frequency: Weekly - Published on Wednesday
Cover Price: £0.35
Circulation: 6,133 (ABC 02/07/2007 to 30/12/2007)
Usual Pagination: 32
Editor: Gail Milne; **Advertising Manager:** Bill Morgan
ADVERTISING RATES:
SCC £3.79
Agency Commission: 10%
Mechanical Data: Col Widths (Display): 28mm, No. of Columns (Display): 9, Film: Digital
Copy instructions: Copy Date: Monday 4pm prior to publication date
Average advertising content per issue: 46%
LOCAL NEWSPAPERS: Local Newspapers Scotland

GLO MÂN
761615U72J-90

Editorial Address: 37 Waterloo Road, CAPEL HENDRE, SA18 3SF **Tel:** 01269 592142
Advertising Address: 37 College Street, AMMANFORD, SA18 2BU **Tel:** 01269 592142
Date Established: 1978
Frequency: 10 issues yearly - Not published in August and September
Cover Price: £0.50
Circulation: 600 (Publisher's Statement)
Editor: Edwyn Williams; **Advertising Manager:** Edwyn Collins
Summary of Content: Welsh language community magazine with a particular focus on local events containing articles on sports and youth interest.
Language(s): Welsh
Readership/Target Audience: Aimed at Welsh speaking readers with an interest in the local area.
ADVERTISING: Rates on application
Average advertising content per issue: 5%
LOCAL NEWSPAPERS: Community Newsletters

Y GLORIAN
1644465U72J-322

Editorial Address: Pros Kairon, Dwyran, LLANFAIRPWLLGWYNGYLL, LL61 6YU **Tel:** 01248 430507
Advertising Address: Gwel Eryri, Llangwyllog, Ynys Môn, LLANGEFNI, LL77 7PX **Tel:** 01248 723707
Email: nesta.pritchard@tiscali.co.uk
Frequency: 10 issues yearly - Not published in January and August
Cover Price: £0.40
Circulation: 1,700 (Publisher's Statement)
Editor: Gwen Lloyd Jones; **Advertising Manager:** Nesta Pritchard
Summary of Content: Welsh language community newspaper covering local news and community events including features on sport, schools, local history and heritage.
Language(s): Welsh
Readership/Target Audience: Aimed at the local community.
ADVERTISING RATES:
Full Page Mono £45.00
LOCAL NEWSPAPERS: Community Newsletters

THE GLOSSOP ADVERTISER
43678U72B-1153_120

Frequency: Weekly
Cover Price: Free
Circulation: 12,896 (VFD 02/07/2007 to 30/12/2007)
ADVERTISING RATES:
SCC £8.75
Part of Series, see entry for: Advertiser Series (Ashton)
LOCAL NEWSPAPERS: Local Newspapers English Counties

GLOSSOP CHRONICLE INCORPORATING HIGH PEAK REPORTER
43683U72B-1160_160

Frequency: Weekly
Cover Price: £0.38
Circulation: 10,000 (Publisher's Statement)
ADVERTISING: Rates on application
Part of Series, see entry for: Ashton-Under-Lyne Reporter Series
LOCAL NEWSPAPERS: Local Newspapers English Counties

GLOSSOP COURIER
706766U72B-690_185

Frequency: Weekly - Circulation figure is incorporated into the High Peak Courier
Cover Price: Free
ADVERTISING: Rates on application
Part of Series, see entry for: Buxton Advertiser and Times Series
LOCAL NEWSPAPERS: Local Newspapers English Counties

GLOUCESTER AND CHELTENHAM NEWS SERIES
43662U72B-1125

Formerly: Gloucester News
Editorial Address: 1 Clarence Parade, CHELTENHAM, GL50 3NY **Tel:** 01452 424442 **Fax:** 01452 420664
Email: editor@glosnews.co.uk
Advertising Address: As above.
Email: louise.baker@glosmedia.co.uk
Web site: http://www.thisisgloucestershire.co.uk
Publisher: Gloucestershire Media
Frequency: Weekly - Published on Thursday
Cover Price: Free
Circulation: 57,197 (Combined Circulation)
Editor: News Desk; **Advertising Director:** Kerry Stoddart
ADVERTISING RATES:
SCC £6.60
Mechanical Data: Film: Digital, Page Width: 275mm, Type Area: 360 x 275mm, No. of Columns (Display): 8, Col Length: 360mm, Col Widths (Display): 31mm
Copy instructions: Copy Date: 4 days prior to publication date
Series owner and contact point for the following titles, see individual entries:
Cheltenham News
Gloucester News
Tewkesbury News
LOCAL NEWSPAPERS: Local Newspapers English Counties

GLOUCESTER NEWS
1616531U72B-1125_101

Frequency: Weekly
Cover Price: Free
Circulation: 32,425 (VFD 02/07/2007 to 30/12/2007)
Part of Series, see entry for: Gloucester and Cheltenham News Series
LOCAL NEWSPAPERS: Local Newspapers English Counties

GLOUCESTERSHIRE ECHO
42029U67B-160

Editorial Address: 1 Clarence Parade, CHELTENHAM, GL50 3NY **Tel:** 01242 271900 **Fax:** 01242 271821
Email: echo.news@glosmedia.co.uk
Advertising Address: As above. **Fax:** 01242 271759
Email: kerry.stoddart@glosmedia.co.uk
Web site: http://www.thisisgloucestershire.co.uk
Publisher: Cheltenham Newspaper Company Ltd
Date Established: 1874
Frequency: Evenings
Cover Price: £0.35
Circulation: 21,074 (ABC 02/07/2007 to 30/12/2007)
Editor: Adrian Jones; **News Editor:** Adrian Jones; **Features Editor:** Tanya Gledhill; **Advertising Director:** Kerry Stoddart
ADVERTISING RATES:
Full Page Mono £2016.00
Full Page Colour £2520.00
SCC £7.00
Agency Commission: 10%
Mechanical Data: Col Length: 360mm, Col Widths (Display): 31mm, No. of Columns (Display): 8, Film: Digital, Type Area: 360 x 275mm, Page Width: 275mm
Copy instructions: Copy Date: 2 days prior to publication date
Average advertising content per issue: 48%
Supplement(s): Business (Gloucestershire Echo) - 52xY, Sport Monday - 52xY, Weekend - 52xY
REGIONAL DAILY & SUNDAY NEWSPAPERS: Regional Daily Newspapers

THE GLOUCESTERSHIRE GAZETTE
43212U72B-23_140

Formerly: The Gazette (Dursley, Wotton, Cam & the Vale of Berkeley)
Frequency: Weekly
Cover Price: £0.55
Part of Series, see entry for: Gloucestershire Gazette Series
LOCAL NEWSPAPERS: Local Newspapers English Counties

GLOUCESTERSHIRE GAZETTE SERIES
43211U72B-23

Formerly: Gazette Series (South Glos)
Editorial Address: Reliance House, Long Street, DURSLEY, GL11 4LS **Tel:** 01453 544000 **Fax:** 01453 540208
Email: gazette.news@dursleygazette.co.uk
Advertising Address: As above. **Tel:** 01453 540222
Fax: 01453 540212
Web site: http://www.thisisthesouthcotswolds.co.uk
Publisher: Newsquest (Media Group) Ltd
Date Established: 1879
Frequency: Weekly - Published on Thursday
Circulation: 15,614 (ABC 02/07/2007 to 30/12/2007)
Editor: Skip Walker; **News Editor:** Jeff Bolitho; **Managing Director:** Gavin Stacey; **Publisher:** Trevor Sallis
ADVERTISING RATES:
Full Page Mono £1891.08
Full Page Colour £2363.85
SCC 6.18
Agency Commission: 10%
Mechanical Data: Page Width: 259mm, Film: Digital, Type Area: 306 x 259mm, Col Length: 306mm, No. of Columns (Display): 9, Col Widths (Display): 27mm
Copy instructions: Copy Date: Tuesdays 4pm prior to publication date
Average advertising content per issue: 40%
Series owner and contact point for the following titles, see individual entries:
The Gloucestershire Gazette
Thornbury Gazette
Yate & Sodbury Gazette
LOCAL NEWSPAPERS: Local Newspapers English Counties

GLOUCESTERSHIRE INDEPENDENT CHELTENHAM EDITION
43664U72B-1144_150

Formerly: Cheltenham Independent
Frequency: Weekly - See main record for circulation
Cover Price: Free
Part of Series, see entry for: Independent Series (Gloucestershire)
LOCAL NEWSPAPERS: Local Newspapers English Counties

GLOUCESTERSHIRE INDEPENDENT GLOUCESTER EDITION
43665U72B-1144_170

Formerly: Gloucestershire Independent City Edition
Frequency: Weekly - See main record for circulation
Cover Price: Free
Part of Series, see entry for: Independent Series (Gloucestershire)
LOCAL NEWSPAPERS: Local Newspapers English Counties

GLOUCESTERSHIRE INDEPENDENT SOUTH OF GLOUCESTERSHIRE EDITION
43666U72B-1144_190

Formerly: Gloucestershire Independent County Edition
Frequency: Weekly - See main record for circulation
Cover Price: Free
Part of Series, see entry for: Independent Series (Gloucestershire)
LOCAL NEWSPAPERS: Local Newspapers English Counties

GO
1828027U72B-4136

Editorial Address: For all contact details see main record, Brentwood Gazette Series
Frequency: Weekly
ADVERTISING: Rates on application
Supplement to: Brentwood Gazette Series
LOCAL NEWSPAPERS: Local Newspapers English Counties

GODSTONE COUNTY BORDER NEWS

1665851U72B-1774_201

Frequency: Weekly - Circulation is incorporated into Oxted County Border News
Cover Price: Free
Part of Series, see entry for: County Border News Series
LOCAL NEWSPAPERS: Local Newspapers English Counties

GOOLE, HOWDEN COURIER

44041U72B-2199

Formerly: Goole, Howden, Thorne Courier
Editorial Address: 8 Pasture Road, GOOLE, DN14 6EZ
Tel: 01405 782410 **Fax:** 01405 762686
Email: editorial@gooletoday.co.uk
Advertising Address: As above.
Email: advertising@gooletoday.co.uk
Web site: http://www.goolecourier.co.uk
Publisher: South Yorkshire Newspapers Ltd
Date Established: 1985
Frequency: Weekly - Published on Thursday
Cover Price: Free
Cover Price: £0.32
Circulation: 15,419 (VFD 02/07/2007 to 30/12/2007)
Editor: Janet Harrison; **Advertising Manager:** Melanie Roberts
ADVERTISING RATES:
Full Page Mono £295.00
Full Page Colour £424.11
Agency Commission: 10%
Mechanical Data: Trim Size: 350 x 272mm, Film: Digital, No. of Columns (Display): 9
Copy instructions: Copy Date: Tuesday prior to publication date
Supplement(s): Motor Guide - 52xY
LOCAL NEWSPAPERS: Local Newspapers English Counties

GOOLE TIMES

44042U72B-2201

Editorial Address: 102 Boothferry Road, GOOLE, DN14 6AE **Tel:** 01405 720110 **Fax:** 01405 720003
Email: editorial@gooletimes.co.uk
Advertising Address: As above.
Email: advertising@gooletimes.co.uk
Web site: http://www.gooletimes.co.uk
Publisher: Chronicle Publications Ltd
Frequency: Weekly - Published on Thursday
Cover Price: £0.45
Circulation: 10,149 (ABC 01/01/2007 to 30/12/2007)
Usual Pagination: 56
Editor: Peter Butler; **Advertising Manager:** Natalie Stuart
ADVERTISING RATES:
Full Page Mono £1406.00
Full Page Colour £1556.00
SCC £3.80
Agency Commission: 10%
Mechanical Data: Col Length: 370mm, Type Area: 370 x 265mm, Page Width: 265mm, No. of Columns (Display): 10, Trim Size: 370 x 277mm, Bleed Size: 376 x 283mm, Film: Digital, Print Process: Web-fed offset
Copy instructions: Copy Date: Tuesday 4pm prior to publication date
Average advertising content per issue: 65%
LOCAL NEWSPAPERS: Local Newspapers English Counties

GRANGEMOUTH ADVERTISER

44934U72D-365_120

Frequency: Weekly
Cover Price: Free
Part of Series, see entry for: Falkirk & Grangemouth Advertiser Series
LOCAL NEWSPAPERS: Local Newspapers Scotland

GRANTHAM CITIZEN

44044U72B-2203_140

Frequency: Weekly - Published on Tuesday
Cover Price: Free
Circulation: 16,000 (Publisher's Statement)
ADVERTISING RATES:
Full Page Mono £902.70
Full Page Colour £1173.51
SCC 2.95
Part of Series, see entry for: Grantham Citizen & Journal Series
LOCAL NEWSPAPERS: Local Newspapers English Counties

GRANTHAM CITIZEN & JOURNAL SERIES

44043U72B-2203

Editorial Address: 46 High Street, GRANTHAM, NG31 6NE
Tel: 01476 562291 **Fax:** 01476 560564
Email: comment@granthamjournal.co.uk
Advertising Address: As above. **Fax:** 01476 541420

Email: lisa.williams@granthamjournal.co.uk
Web site: http://www.granthamjournal.co.uk
Publisher: Johnston Press plc
Date Established: 1854
Frequency: Weekly - Published on Tuesday & Friday
Circulation: 36,579 (Combined Circulation)
Editor: Bob Hart; **Editor-in-Chief:** Tim Robinson; **Managing Director:** Amanda Davison-Young
ADVERTISING RATES:
Full Page Mono £1615.68
Full Page Colour £2100.38
Agency Commission: 10%
Mechanical Data: No. of Columns (Display): 9, Col Widths (Display): 27mm, Type Area: 340 x 270mm, Col Length: 340mm, Page Width: 270mm, Film: Digital
Copy instructions: Copy Date: Tuesday 5pm prior to publication date
Average advertising content per issue: 62%
Series owner and contact point for the following titles, see individual entries:
Grantham Citizen
Grantham Journal
LOCAL NEWSPAPERS: Local Newspapers English Counties

GRANTHAM JOURNAL

44045U72B-2203_160

Frequency: Weekly - Published on Friday
Cover Price: £0.47
Circulation: 20,579 (ABC 02/07/2007 to 30/12/2007)
ADVERTISING RATES:
SCC £5.02
Part of Series, see entry for: Grantham Citizen & Journal Series
LOCAL NEWSPAPERS: Local Newspapers English Counties

GRAVESEND MESSENGER

1616056U72B-1820_131

Frequency: Weekly
Cover Price: £0.50
Circulation: 8,197 (ABC 02/07/2007 to 30/12/2007)
ADVERTISING RATES:
SCC £3.95
Part of Series, see entry for: Gravesend Messenger Series
LOCAL NEWSPAPERS: Local Newspapers English Counties

GRAVESEND MESSENGER SERIES

43879U72B-1820

Formerly: Gravesend Messenger and Extra Series
Editorial Address: 7 High Street, GRAVESEND, DA11 0BQ
Tel: 01474 564327 **Fax:** 01474 564304
Email: gravesendmessenger@thekmgroup.co.uk
Advertising Address: Medway House, Ginsburg Close, Sir Thomas Longley Road, Medway City Estate, ROCHESTER, ME2 4DU **Tel:** 01634 227980 **Fax:** 01634 718408
Email: jjarvis@thekmgroup.co.uk
Web site: http://www.gravesendmessenger.co.uk
Publisher: Kent Messenger Group
Date Established: 1998
Frequency: Weekly
Circulation: 40,890 (Combined Circulation)
Editor: Denise Eaton; **News Editor:** Lauren Abbott; **Advertising Manager:** Joanne Jarvis
ADVERTISING: Rates on application
Mechanical Data: Page Width: 276mm, Film: Digital, Type Area: 340 x 276mm, Col Length: 340mm, Col Widths (Display): 31mm, No. of Columns (Display): 8
Copy instructions: Copy Date: Friday 5pm prior to publication date
Series owner and contact point for the following titles, see individual entries:
Gravesend Messenger
Messenger Extra
LOCAL NEWSPAPERS: Local Newspapers English Counties

GRAVESEND REPORTER

43914U72B-1875_135

Frequency: Weekly
Cover Price: £0.40
Circulation: 5,692 (ABC 02/07/2007 to 30/12/2007)
ADVERTISING RATES:
SCC £1.45
Part of Series, see entry for: Times and Reporter Series (Kent)
LOCAL NEWSPAPERS: Local Newspapers English Counties

GREAT BARR OBSERVER

44550U72B-3027_130

Frequency: Weekly
Cover Price: Free
Circulation: 32,361 (VFD 02/07/2007 to 30/12/2007)

ADVERTISING RATES:
SCC £4.20
Part of Series, see entry for: Sutton Coldfield Observer Series
LOCAL NEWSPAPERS: Local Newspapers English Counties

GREAT YARMOUTH ADVERTISER SERIES

44143U72B-2447

Formerly: Suffolk Advertiser Series
Editorial Address: 169 King Street, GREAT YARMOUTH, NR30 2PA **Tel:** 01493 847961 **Fax:** 01493 847979
Advertising Address: 36 North Quay, GREAT YARMOUTH, NR30 1JE **Tel:** 01493 335000 **Fax:** 01493 652082
Email: adservice@archant.co.uk
Web site: http://www.advertiser-online.co.uk
Publisher: Archant Norfolk
Frequency: Weekly - Published on Thursday
Cover Price: Free
Circulation: 84,667 (Combined Circulation)
Usual Pagination: 40
Editor: Laura Bagshaw; **Advertising Manager:** Colin Huggins
ADVERTISING: Rates on application
Agency Commission: 10%
Mechanical Data: Col Length: 360mm, Col Widths (Display): 32mm, No. of Columns (Display): 8, Print Process: Web-fed offset litho, Type Area: 360 x 260mm, Film: Digital, Page Width: 260mm
Copy instructions: Copy Date: Tuesday 5pm prior to publication date
Series owner and contact point for the following titles, see individual entries:
The Advertiser Great Yarmouth and Gorleston
The Advertiser Waveney
Supplement(s): Chic - 4xY, Holidaymaker - 1xY, Homes and Gardens - 4xY
LOCAL NEWSPAPERS: Local Newspapers English Counties

GREAT YARMOUTH MERCURY

44129U72B-2433

Editorial Address: 169 King Street, GREAT YARMOUTH, NR30 2PA **Tel:** 01493 847940 **Fax:** 01493 847979
Email: anne.edwards@archant.co.uk
Advertising Address: 36 North Quay, GREAT YARMOUTH, NR30 1JE **Tel:** 01493 335000 **Fax:** 01493 652082
Email: adservice@archant.co.uk
Web site: http://www.yarmouthmercury24.co.uk
Publisher: Archant Norfolk
Date Established: 1880
Frequency: Weekly - Published on Friday
Cover Price: £0.55
Circulation: 18,367 (ABC 02/07/2007 to 30/12/2007)
Editor: Anne Edwards; **Advertising Manager:** Colin Huggins
ADVERTISING RATES:
Full Page Mono £1396.80
Full Page Colour £1815.84
SCC £4.85
Agency Commission: 10%
Mechanical Data: Type Area: 360 x 260mm, No. of Columns (Display): 8, Col Length: 360mm, Page Width: 260mm, Col Widths (Display): 32mm, Film: Digital
Copy instructions: Copy Date: Tuesday 5pm prior to publication date
LOCAL NEWSPAPERS: Local Newspapers English Counties

GREATER IPSWICH COMMUNITY NEWS

634488U72B-3074_200

Formerly: Ipswich Community News
Frequency: Monthly
Cover Price: Free
Circulation: 34,850 (Publisher's Statement)
ADVERTISING: Rates on application
Part of Series, see entry for: Greater Ipswich Community News Series
LOCAL NEWSPAPERS: Local Newspapers English Counties

GREATER IPSWICH COMMUNITY NEWS SERIES

634370U72B-3074

Formerly: Community News Series (Ipswich)
Editorial Address: 20 Wharfedale Road, IPSWICH, IP1 4JP
Tel: 01473 400632 **Fax:** 01473 400633
Email: mike@communitynews.demon.co.uk
Advertising Address: As above.
Email: dawn@communitynews.demon.co.uk
Publisher: Wharfedale (Publishing) Ltd
Date Established: 1964
Frequency: Monthly
Cover Price: Free

Circulation: 38,500 (Combined Circulation)
Editor: Mike Harrison; **Advertising Manager:** Dawn Harrison
ADVERTISING: Rates on application
Agency Commission: 10%
Copy instructions: Copy Date: 20th of the month prior to publication date
Average advertising content per issue: 50%
Series owner and contact point for the following titles, see individual entries:
Essex Community News
Greater Ipswich Community News
LOCAL NEWSPAPERS: Local Newspapers English Counties

GREATER LONDON CHRONICLE

625813U72A-35

Formerly: London Chronicle
Editorial Address: 3rd Floor, 53 Corporation Street, COVENTRY, CV1 1GX **Tel:** 024 7663 0558
Fax: 024 7622 0745
Email: editorial@greaterlondonchronicle.co.uk
Email: info@greaterlondonchronicle.co.uk
Advertising Address: As above.
Web site: http://www.greaterlondonchronicle.co.uk
Publisher: JPC Ltd
Frequency: Weekly - Published on Thursday
Cover Price: Free
Circulation: 5,000 (Publisher's Statement)
Editor: Michael Masih
ADVERTISING RATES:
SCC 9.00
Mechanical Data: Type Area: 360 x 264mm, Col Length: 360mm, Col Widths (Display): 3.3mm, No. of Columns (Display): 8, Page Width: 264mm, Film: Digital
Copy instructions: Copy Date: Mono 4.30pm Monday Colour 5.00pm Friday prior to publication
Average advertising content per issue: 80%
LOCAL NEWSPAPERS: Local Newspapers Greater London

GREENOCK TELEGRAPH

42264U67B-2330

Editorial Address: 2 Crawfurd Street, GREENOCK, PA15 1LH **Tel:** 01475 726511 **Fax:** 01475 783734
Email: editorial@greenocktelegraph.co.uk
Advertising Address: As above.
Email: advertising@greenocktelegraph.co.uk
Web site: http://www.greenocktelegraph.co.uk
Publisher: Clyde & Forth Press Group
Date Established: 1857
Frequency: Evenings - Not published on Sunday
Cover Price: £0.35
Circulation: 17,667 (Publisher's Statement)
Editor: News Desk; **News Editor:** Paul Ford; **Features Editor:** Elaine Bowers; **Managing Editor:** Tom McConigley
ADVERTISING RATES:
Full Page Mono £1734.00
Full Page Colour £2601.00
Agency Commission: 10%
Mechanical Data: Col Length: 330mm, No. of Columns (Display): 8, Col Widths (Display): 30mm, Type Area: 330 x 266mm, Print Process: Web offset, Page Width: 266mm, Film: Digital
Copy instructions: Copy Date: 2 days prior to publication date
Average advertising content per issue: 40%
REGIONAL DAILY & SUNDAY NEWSPAPERS: Regional Daily Newspapers

GRIMSBY TELEGRAPH

42068U67B-250

Formerly: Grimsby Evening Telegraph
Editorial Address: 80 Cleethorpe Road, GRIMSBY, DN31 3EH **Tel:** 01472 360360 **Fax:** 01472 372257
Email: newsdesk@grimsbytelegraph.co.uk
Advertising Address: As above. **Fax:** 01472 372235
Email: caroline.whelpton@gsmg.co.uk
Web site: http://www.thisisgrimsby.co.uk
Publisher: Grimsby & Scunthorpe Media Group
Date Established: 1897
Frequency: Daily
Cover Price: £0.36
Circulation: 34,590 (ABC 02/07/2007 to 30/12/2007)
Editor: Lucy Wood; **News Editor:** Lucy Wood
ADVERTISING: Rates on application
Supplement(s): Business Telegraph - 52xY, Homes Telegraph - 52xY, Life - 6xY, Motors - 52xY
REGIONAL DAILY & SUNDAY NEWSPAPERS: Regional Daily Newspapers

GUARDIAN AND INDEPENDENT SERIES

43012U72A-132

Formerly: Guardian Series (West Essex)
Editorial Address: 480 Larkshall Road, LONDON, E4 9GD
Tel: 01992 572285 **Fax:** 01992 574039

Email: dyeatman@london.newsquest.co.uk
Advertising Address: Guardian House, 480-500 Larkshall Road, Highams Park, LONDON, E4 9GD **Tel:** 020 8498 3400
Fax: 020 8531 2924
Email: tlittle@london.newsquest.co.uk
Web site: http://www.guardian-series.co.uk
Publisher: Newsquest (North London)
Frequency: Weekly - Published on Thursday and Friday
Circulation: 22,432 (Combined Circulation)
Usual Pagination: 80
Editor: Dominic Yeatman; **Features Editor:** Lindi Bilgorri
ADVERTISING: Rates on application
Series owner and contact point for the following titles, see individual entries:
Epping Forest Guardian
Epping Forest Independent
LOCAL NEWSPAPERS: Local Newspapers Greater London

GUARDIAN & NEWS SERIES (SUTTON)

42998U72A-128

Formerly: Guardian Series (Sutton)
Editorial Address: Unecol House, 819 London Road, SUTTON, SM3 9BN **Tel:** 020 8329 9244 **Fax:** 020 8330 9918
Email: sduggan@london.newsquest.co.uk
Advertising Address: As above. **Fax:** 020 8329 9201
Email: j.cheedle@london.newsquest.co.uk
Web site: http://www.yourlocalguardian.co.uk
Publisher: Newsquest Media Group
Date Established: 1980
Frequency: Weekly
Circulation: 315,438 (Combined Circulation)
Usual Pagination: 50
Editor: Sean Duggan; **Managing Director:** Howard Scott; **Advertising Manager:** John Cheedle; **Group Editor:** Sean Duggan
ADVERTISING: Rates on application
Agency Commission: 10%
Mechanical Data: Col Length: 350mm, No. of Columns (Display): 9, Type Area: 350 x 267mm, Page Width: 267mm, Film: Digital
Average advertising content per issue: 60%
Series owner and contact point for the following titles, see individual entries:
Balham & Tooting Guardian
Battersea & Clapham Guardian
Epsom Guardian
Esher and Cobham Guardian
Kingston Borough Guardian
Mitcham & Morden Guardian
Streatham, West Norwood & Crystal Palace Guardian
Sutton Guardian
Walton and Weybridge Guardian
Wandsworth & Putney Guardian
Wimbledon Guardian
LOCAL NEWSPAPERS: Local Newspapers Greater London

GUARDIAN (MIDDLETON & NORTH MANCHESTER)

768244U72B-1203_101

Frequency: Weekly
Cover Price: £0.50
Circulation: 7,256 (ABC 02/07/2007 to 30/12/2007)
ADVERTISING RATES:
SCC £3.80
Part of Series, see entry for: Middleton & North Manchester Guardian & Advertiser Series
LOCAL NEWSPAPERS: Local Newspapers English Counties

GUARDIAN SERIES (WILTSHIRE, HAMPSHIRE AND SURREY)

601275U72B-3455

Formerly: Guardian Series (Wiltshire & Hampshire)
Editorial Address: 53 Corporation Street, COVENTRY, CV1 1GX **Tel:** 024 7622 0742 **Fax:** 024 7622 5476
Email: wiltshireguardian@yahoo.com
Advertising Address: As above. **Tel:** 024 7663 0550
Email: advertising@wiltshireguardian.co.uk
Publisher: Guardian Series
Frequency: Weekly
Cover Price: Free
Circulation: 175,000 (Combined Circulation)
Editor: Jag Basra; **Managing Director:** Jag Basra
ADVERTISING RATES:
SCC £13.00
Agency Commission: 10%
Mechanical Data: Trim Size: 420 x 297mm, Film: Digital, Col Length: 360mm, No. of Columns (Display): 8, Col Widths (Display): 33mm
Copy instructions: Copy Date: Monday 12pm prior to publication date
Average advertising content per issue: 75%
Series owner and contact point for the following titles, see individual entries:
Hampshire Guardian
Surrey Guardian

Wiltshire Guardian
LOCAL NEWSPAPERS: Local Newspapers English Counties

GUARDIAN SERIES (WORKSOP)

44201U72B-2670

Editorial Address: 21-27 Ryton Street, WORKSOP, S80 2AY **Tel:** 01909 500500 **Fax:** 01909 474849
Email: newsroom@worksop-guardian.co.uk
Advertising Address: As above.
Email: louise.mchugh@worksop-guardian.co.uk
Web site: http://www.worksopguardian.co.uk
Publisher: South Yorkshire Newspapers Ltd
Date Established: 1896
Frequency: Weekly - Published on Wednesday, Thursday and Friday
Circulation: 95,428 (Combined Circulation)
Editor: Newsdesk; **News Editor:** Jackie Laver; **Managing Director:** Paul Bentham; **Advertising Manager:** Louise McHugh
ADVERTISING RATES:
SCC £20.35
Agency Commission: 10%
Mechanical Data: Type Area: 340 x 272mm, Col Length: 340mm, Page Width: 272mm, Film: Digital, No. of Columns (Display): 9
Series owner and contact point for the following titles, see individual entries:
Dinnington & Maltby Guardian
Dinnington & Maltby Trader News
Retford Trader Guardian
Worksop Guardian
Worksop Trader
LOCAL NEWSPAPERS: Local Newspapers English Counties

GUERNSEY GLOBE

45139U72F-5

Editorial Address: PO Box 57, Braye Road, Vale, GUERNSEY, GY1 3BW **Tel:** 01481 240240
Fax: 01481 240235
Email: newsroom@guernsey-press.com
Advertising Address: As above. **Fax:** 01481 240275
Email: abrun@guernsey-press.com
Publisher: Guernsey Press Co Ltd
Date Established: 1992
Frequency: Weekly
Cover Price: Free
Circulation: 20,000 (Publisher's Statement)
Editor: Emily Burden; **Advertising Manager:** Antony Brun
ADVERTISING RATES:
Full Page Mono £1020.00
Full Page Colour £2077.60
SCC £3.85
Agency Commission: 10%
Mechanical Data: Type Area: 400 x 262mm, Page Width: 262mm, No. of Columns (Display): 7, Col Length: 400mm, Col Widths (Display): 34mm, Film: Digital
Copy instructions: Copy Date: 3 days prior to publication date
Average advertising content per issue: 50%
LOCAL NEWSPAPERS: Local Newspapers Channel Islands

GUERNSEY PRESS AND STAR

42277U67B-2430

Formerly: Guernsey Evening Press & Star
Editorial Address: PO Box 57, Braye Road, Vale, GUERNSEY, GY1 3BW **Tel:** 01481 240240
Fax: 01481 240235
Email: newseditor@guernsey-press.com
Advertising Address: As above. **Fax:** 01481 240275
Email: gpads@guernsey-press.com
Web site: http://www.thisisguernsey.com/
Publisher: Guernsey Press Co Ltd
Date Established: 1897
Frequency: Daily
Cover Price: £0.45
Circulation: 16,196 (ABC 02/07/2007 to 30/12/2007)
Editor: Gemma Long; **News Editor:** Gemma Long; **Features Editor:** Di Digard; **Advertisement Director:** Antony Brun
Summary of Content: Gemma Hockey is the News Editor to whom press releases should be addressed.
ADVERTISING RATES:
Full Page Mono £2677.00
Full Page Colour £3847.20
SCC £10.07
Agency Commission: 10%
Mechanical Data: Col Length: 400mm, Col Widths (Display): 34mm, No. of Columns (Display): 7, Type Area: 400 x 262mm, Print Process: Web-fed offset litho, Film: Digital, Page Width: 262mm
Copy instructions: Copy Date: 3 days prior to publication date
Average advertising content per issue: 35%

Supplement(s): Careers - 4xY, Finance - 6xY, House and Home - 12xY, The Look - 2xY, The Week - 52xY
REGIONAL DAILY & SUNDAY NEWSPAPERS: Regional Daily Newspapers

GUERNSEY WEEKLY PRESS AND STAR
45140U72F-7

Formerly: Guernsey Weekly Press
Editorial Address: PO Box 57, Braye Road, Vale, GUERNSEY, GY1 3BW **Tel:** 01481 240240
Fax: 01481 240235
Email: newsroom@guernsey-press.com
Advertising Address: As above. **Tel:** 01481 240299
Fax: 01481 240275
Email: abrun@guernsey-press.com
Web site: http://www.thisisguernsey.com
Publisher: Guernsey Press Co Ltd
Frequency: Weekly
Cover Price: £0.45
Circulation: 700,000 (Publisher's Statement)
Editor: Richard Digard; **News Editor:** Gemma Long;
Features Editor: Di Digard; **Advertisement Director:** Antony Brun
ADVERTISING RATES:
Full Page Mono £1246.00
Full Page Colour £1800.00
Agency Commission: 10%
Mechanical Data: Col Length: 400mm, Col Widths (Display): 34mm, No. of Columns (Display): 7, Screen: 40 lpc, Type Area: 400 x 262mm, Page Width: 262mm
Copy instructions: Copy Date: 10am 3 days prior to publication date
Average advertising content per issue: 57%
LOCAL NEWSPAPERS: Local Newspapers Channel Islands

THE GUIDE
1850418U72B-4153

Editorial Address: 51 London Road, REIGATE, RH2 9PR
Tel: 01737 732000 **Fax:** 01737 732267
Email: theguide@essnmedia.co.uk
Web site: http://www.thisissurreytoday.co.uk
Publisher: Northcliffe Media Ltd
Frequency: Weekly - Published on Thursday
Editor: Deborah Tucknott
Summary of Content: What's on and leisure guide covering theatre, music and features.
ADVERTISING: Rates on application
Supplement to: Surrey Mirror Series
LOCAL NEWSPAPERS: Local Newspapers English Counties

THE GUIDE
1896224U72B-4160

Editorial Address: For all contact details see main record, Dewsbury Reporter and Advertiser Series
Frequency: Weekly
ADVERTISING: Rates on application
Supplement to: Dewsbury Reporter and Advertiser Series
LOCAL NEWSPAPERS: Local Newspapers English Counties

GUIDE & GAZETTE (BROUGHTY FERRY)
44956U72D-60_101

Frequency: Weekly
Cover Price: £0.42
Mechanical Data: Col Widths (Display): 36mm, Page Width: 272mm, Type Area: 340 x 272mm, Col Length: 340mm, No. of Columns (Display): 7, Film: Digital
Part of Series, see entry for: Arbroath Herald & Gazette Series
LOCAL NEWSPAPERS: Local Newspapers Scotland

GWENDRAETH JOURNAL
706895U72C-220_125

Frequency: Weekly
Part of Series, see entry for: Journal Series (Carmarthen)
LOCAL NEWSPAPERS: Local Newspapers Wales

GWENT GAZETTE
44800U72C-200

Editorial Address: 52-53 Glebeland Street, MERTHYR TYDFIL, CF47 8AT **Tel:** 01495 304589 **Fax:** 01495 306194
Email: gwent.gazette@mediawales.co.uk
Advertising Address: As above. **Tel:** 01685 856564
Fax: 01685 856556
Email: carol.jenkins@mediawales.co.uk
Web site: http://www.icwales.co.uk
Publisher: Trinity Mirror
Frequency: Weekly - Published on Wednesday
Cover Price: £0.63
Circulation: 11,495 (ABC 02/07/2007 to 30/12/2007)
Editor: Gordon Caldecott
ADVERTISING: Rates on application

HACKNEY GAZETTE
43021U72A-150

Formerly: Hackney Gazette & Express Series
Editorial Address: 138 Cambridge Heath Road, LONDON, E1 5QJ **Tel:** 020 7791 7788 **Fax:** 020 7791 7702
Email: hg.editorial@archant.co.uk
Advertising Address: As above. **Fax:** 020 7791 7700
Email: darren.jackson@archant.co.uk
Web site: http://www.hackneygazette.co.uk
Publisher: Archant London
Date Established: 1864
Frequency: Weekly - Published on Thursday
Cover Price: £0.50
Circulation: 10,331 (ABC 02/07/2007 to 30/12/2007)
Editor: News Desk; **News Editor:** Russ Lawrence;
Advertising Manager: Darren Jackson
ADVERTISING RATES:
Full Page Mono £2520.00
Full Page Colour £3235.00
SCC £8.00
Agency Commission: 10%
Mechanical Data: Col Widths (Display): 27mm, Film: Digital, No. of Columns (Display): 9
Copy instructions: Copy Date: Thursday prior to publication date
LOCAL NEWSPAPERS: Local Newspapers Greater London

THE HADLEIGH ADVERTISER
1826722U72B-3078_106

Frequency: Weekly
Cover Price: Free
Part of Series, see entry for: Advertiser Series (Ipswich)
LOCAL NEWSPAPERS: Local Newspapers English Counties

HAILSHAM GAZETTE
44442U72B-3240_160

Frequency: Weekly
Cover Price: £0.35
Circulation: 2,025 (Publisher's Statement)
Part of Series, see entry for: Eastbourne Herald & Gazette Series
LOCAL NEWSPAPERS: Local Newspapers English Counties

HALESOWEN CHRONICLE
44535U72B-3450_140

Frequency: Weekly
Cover Price: Free
Circulation: 38,925 (VFD 02/07/2007 to 30/12/2007)
ADVERTISING: Rates on application
Part of Series, see entry for: Dudley Chronicle Series
LOCAL NEWSPAPERS: Local Newspapers English Counties

HALESOWEN NEWS
44538U72B-3457

Formerly: Halesowen News and County Express
Editorial Address: St. John's House, St. John's Road, STOURBRIDGE, DY8 1EH **Tel:** 01384 358085
Fax: 01384 358252
Email: newsgrouped@midlands.newsquest.co.uk
Advertising Address: As above. **Tel:** 01384 358200
Fax: 01384 358253
Email: caroline.smith@midlands.newsquest.co.uk
Web site: http://www.halesowennews.co.uk
Publisher: Newsquest Midlands (South) Ltd
Frequency: Weekly - Published on Thursday
Cover Price: Free
Circulation: 41,019 (VFD 02/07/2007 to 30/12/2007)
Usual Pagination: 56
Editor: News Desk; **Managing Director:** Peter John
ADVERTISING RATES:
SCC £3.60
Agency Commission: 10%
Mechanical Data: Type Area: 350 x 270mm, Col Length: 350mm, Page Width: 270mm, No. of Columns (Display): 9, Col Widths (Display): 28mm, Film: Digital
Copy instructions: Copy Date: 2 days prior to publication date
Average advertising content per issue: 65%
LOCAL NEWSPAPERS: Local Newspapers English Counties

HALSTEAD GAZETTE
43590U72B-950_200

Frequency: Weekly - Published on Friday
Cover Price: £0.55
Circulation: 5,251 (ABC 02/07/2007 to 30/12/2007)

Copy instructions: Copy Date: Friday 5.00pm prior to publication date
Average advertising content per issue: 33%
LOCAL NEWSPAPERS: Local Newspapers Wales

ADVERTISING RATES:
SCC £3.30
Part of Series, see entry for: Braintree & Witham Times & Gazette Series
LOCAL NEWSPAPERS: Local Newspapers English Counties

HAM & HIGH BROADWAY
43025U72A-160_120

Formerly: Broadway Ham & High
Frequency: Weekly
Cover Price: £0.55
Part of Series, see entry for: Ham & High Series
LOCAL NEWSPAPERS: Local Newspapers Greater London

HAM & HIGH HAMPSTEAD & HIGHGATE EXPRESS
43026U72A-160_160

Frequency: Weekly
Cover Price: £0.55
Part of Series, see entry for: Ham & High Series
LOCAL NEWSPAPERS: Local Newspapers Greater London

HAM & HIGH SERIES
43024U72A-160

Editorial Address: 100A Avenue Road, Hampstead, LONDON, NW3 3HF **Tel:** 020 7433 0000 **Fax:** 020 7433 6229
Email: editorial@hamhigh.co.uk
Advertising Address: As above. **Fax:** 020 7433 6259
Email: elaine.allen2@archant.co.uk
Web site: http://www.hamhigh.co.uk
Publisher: Archant London
Frequency: Weekly - Published on Thursday and Friday
Circulation: 9,619 (ABC 02/07/2007 to 30/12/2007)
Editor: Ed Thomas; **News Editor:** Ed Thomas; **Features Editor:** Bridget Galton; **Managing Director:** Enzo Testa;
Publisher: Enzo Testa
ADVERTISING RATES:
Full Page Colour £4803.75
SCC £15.25
Agency Commission: 10%
Mechanical Data: Page Width: 265mm, Col Widths (Display): 27mm, Type Area: 360 x 265mm, No. of Columns (Display): 9, Col Length: 360mm, Film: Digital
Copy instructions: Copy Date: Monday 4.30pm prior to publication date
Average advertising content per issue: 60%
Series owner and contact point for the following titles, see individual entries:
Ham & High Broadway
Ham & High Hampstead & Highgate Express
Marylebone Express
The Wood & Vale Express
Supplement(s): Education - 4xY, Property - 52xY
LOCAL NEWSPAPERS: Local Newspapers Greater London

HAMILTON ADVERTISER
44957U72D-500

Formerly: Hamilton Advertiser Series
Editorial Address: Press Buildings, Campbell Street, HAMILTON, ML3 6AX **Tel:** 01698 283200
Fax: 01698 421168
Email: hamiltonadvertiser@s-un.co.uk
Advertising Address: As above.
Email: mscott@s-un.co.uk
Web site: http://www.icscotland.co.uk
Publisher: Scottish & Universal Newspapers Ltd
Frequency: Weekly - Published on Thursday. Circulation includes Lanark & Carluke Advertiser
Cover Price: £0.75
Circulation: 23,013 (ABC 02/07/2007 to 30/12/2007)
Usual Pagination: 96
Editor: John Rowbotham; **News Editor:** John Rowbotham;
Advertising Manager: Margaret Scott
ADVERTISING RATES:
SCC £12.55
LOCAL NEWSPAPERS: Local Newspapers Scotland

HAMMERSMITH & KENSINGTON TIMES
1804886U72A-385_142

Frequency: Weekly
Cover Price: £0.45
Part of Series, see entry for: North West London Newspaper Series
LOCAL NEWSPAPERS: Local Newspapers Greater London

HAMPSHIRE CHRONICLE
43748U72B-1370_120

Frequency: Weekly - Circulation figure includes the Hampshire Chronicle New Forest Edition and the Hampshire Chronicle South Hants Edition
Cover Price: £0.65
Circulation: 16,463 (Publisher's Statement)
ADVERTISING RATES:
SCC £5.10

Part of Series, see entry for: Hampshire Chronicle Series
LOCAL NEWSPAPERS: Local Newspapers English Counties

HAMPSHIRE CHRONICLE SERIES
43746U72B-1370

Editorial Address: Upper Brook Street, WINCHESTER, SO23 8AL **Tel:** 01962 860836 **Fax:** 01962 877507
Email: news@hampshirechronicle.co.uk
Advertising Address: Staple House, Staple Gardens, WINCHESTER, SO23 8SR **Tel:** 01962 841772
Fax: 01962 849362
Email: sue.meheux@hampshirechronicle.co.uk
Web site: http://www.hampshirechronicle.co.uk
Publisher: Newsquest (Media Group) Ltd
Date Established: 1772
Frequency: Weekly
Circulation: 16,122 (ABC 01/01/2007 to 30/12/2007)
Editor: Andrew Napier; **News Editor:** Andrew Napier;
Managing Director: Stewart Dunn; **Advertising Manager:** Sue Meheux; **Publisher:** Sue Meheux
ADVERTISING: Rates on application
Agency Commission: 10%
Mechanical Data: Page Width: 352.5mm, Film: Digital, Type Area: 540 x 352.5mm, Col Length: 540mm, Col Widths (Display): 28mm, No. of Columns (Display): 12
Copy instructions: Copy Date: Monday 5 pm prior to publication date
Average advertising content per issue: 45%
Series owner and contact point for the following titles, see individual entries:
Hampshire Chronicle
Hampshire Chronicle South Hants Edition
NewsExtra
Romsey Advertiser
LOCAL NEWSPAPERS: Local Newspapers English Counties

HAMPSHIRE CHRONICLE SOUTH HANTS EDITION
624005U72B-1370_140

Frequency: Weekly - Circulation figure is incorporated into the Hampshire Chronicle
Cover Price: £0.65
ADVERTISING RATES:
SCC £5.10
Part of Series, see entry for: Hampshire Chronicle Series
LOCAL NEWSPAPERS: Local Newspapers English Counties

HAMPSHIRE GUARDIAN
25940U72B-3455_120

Frequency: Weekly
Cover Price: Free
Circulation: 65,000 (Publisher's Statement)
Part of Series, see entry for: Guardian Series (Wiltshire, Hampshire and Surrey)
LOCAL NEWSPAPERS: Local Newspapers English Counties

HARBOROUGH HERALD & POST
44160U72B-2500_130

Frequency: Weekly
Cover Price: Free
Circulation: 6,117 (VFD 16/10/2006 to 31/12/2006)
ADVERTISING RATES:
SCC £2.94
Part of Series, see entry for: Northants Herald and Post Series
LOCAL NEWSPAPERS: Local Newspapers English Counties

THE HARBOROUGH MAIL
44026U72B-2168_110

Frequency: Weekly - Circulation figure includes the Lutterworth Mail
Cover Price: £0.47
Circulation: 12,552 (ABC 02/07/2007 to 30/12/2007)
Part of Series, see entry for: The Mail Series
LOCAL NEWSPAPERS: Local Newspapers English Counties

THE HARINGEY ADVERTISER
42996U72A-120_120

Formerly: Advertiser Crouch End & Hornsey
Frequency: Weekly - Published on Wednesday
Cover Price: Free
Circulation: 35,265 (Publisher's Statement)
ADVERTISING RATES:
SCC £7.40
Part of Series, see entry for: Gazette, Advertiser and Press Newspaper Series
LOCAL NEWSPAPERS: Local Newspapers Greater London

HARINGEY INDEPENDENT
1666200U72A-200_141

Formerly: Muswell Hill and Crouch End Times
Frequency: Weekly
Cover Price: Free
Circulation: 20,447 (VFD 01/01/2007 to 01/07/2007)
ADVERTISING: Rates on application
Part of Series, see entry for: Hendon Times Series
LOCAL NEWSPAPERS: Local Newspapers Greater London

HARLOW HERALD
43789U72B-1510

Formerly: Harlow Herald Series
Editorial Address: Unit G6, Peartree Business Park, South Road, Templefields, HARLOW, CM20 2BD
Tel: 01279 624331 **Fax:** 01279 624375
Email: heraldnews@archant.co.uk
Advertising Address: As above.
Email: malcolm.seeby@archant.co.uk
Web site: http://www.harlowherald24.co.uk
Publisher: Archant Regional
Frequency: Weekly
Cover Price: Free
Circulation: 48,648 (VFD 01/01/2007 to 01/07/2007)
Editor: Barry Hunt
ADVERTISING RATES:
SCC £6.03
Agency Commission: 10%
Mechanical Data: Col Length: 340mm, Page Width: 263mm, Type Area: 340 x 263mm, Film: Digital, Col Widths (Display): 26.3mm, No. of Columns (Display): 9
Copy instructions: Copy Date: Tuesday 4pm prior to publication date
Average advertising content per issue: 70%
LOCAL NEWSPAPERS: Local Newspapers English Counties

HARLOW STAR
43622U72B-1048

Formerly: Harlow Star Series
Editorial Address: 6 West Gate, HARLOW, CM20 1JW
Tel: 01279 451545 **Fax:** 01279 400570
Email: star@hertsessexnews.co.uk
Advertising Address: The Media Centre, 40 Ware Road, HERTFORD, SG13 7HU **Tel:** 01992 526600
Fax: 01992 526654
Email: advertising@hertsessexnews.co.uk
Web site: http://www.hertsessexnews.co.uk
Publisher: Herts & Essex Newspapers Ltd
Date Established: 1980
Frequency: Weekly - Published on Thursday
Cover Price: £0.50
Free to qualifying individuals
Circulation: 38,743 (VFD 02/07/2007 to 30/12/2007)
Usual Pagination: 90
Editor: Louise Sassoon; **News Editor:** Louise Sassoon;
Advertisement Director: Ricky Allan
ADVERTISING RATES:
Full Page Mono £1858.00
Full Page Colour £2043.00
SCC £5.90
Agency Commission: 10%
Mechanical Data: Film: Digital, Type Area: 350 x 268mm, Col Length: 350mm, Col Widths (Display): 28mm, No. of Columns (Display): 9, Print Process: Web-fed offset litho, Page Width: 268mm
Copy instructions: Copy Date: Tuesday 12.00pm prior to publication date
LOCAL NEWSPAPERS: Local Newspapers English Counties

HARROGATE ADVERTISER
44647U72B-3588_150

Frequency: Weekly
Cover Price: £0.60
Circulation: 16,046 (ABC 02/07/2007 to 30/12/2007)
ADVERTISING RATES:
SCC £10.14
Part of Series, see entry for: Ackrill Newspaper Series
LOCAL NEWSPAPERS: Local Newspapers English Counties

HARROW LEADER
633806U72A-170_110

Formerly: Harrow & Stanmore Leader
Frequency: Weekly - Published on Thursday
Cover Price: Free
Circulation: 70,466 (VFD 02/07/2007 to 30/12/2007)
ADVERTISING RATES:
SCC £11.10
Part of Series, see entry for: Harrow Observer & Leader Series
LOCAL NEWSPAPERS: Local Newspapers Greater London

HARROW OBSERVER
43034U72A-170_130

Frequency: Weekly - Published on Thursday. Circulation figure is for Harrow Observer Series, including Pinner Observer, Wembley Observer, Stanmore Observer and Willesden Observer
Cover Price: £0.35
Circulation: 7,703 (ABC 02/07/2007 to 30/12/2007)
ADVERTISING RATES:
SCC £11.70
Part of Series, see entry for: Harrow Observer & Leader Series
LOCAL NEWSPAPERS: Local Newspapers Greater London

HARROW OBSERVER & LEADER SERIES
43028U72A-170

Formerly: Harrow Observer, Leader & Independent Series
Editorial Address: Gazette House, 28 Bakers Road, UXBRIDGE, UB8 1RG **Tel:** 01895 451000
Fax: 020 8863 1727
Email: newsharrow@trinitysouth.co.uk
Advertising Address: As above. **Tel:** 020 8427 4404
Fax: 020 8803 1727
Email: stevebaker@trinitysouth.co.uk
Publisher: Trinity Mirror Southern
Date Established: 1895
Frequency: Weekly
Circulation: 116,846 (Combined Circulation)
Advertising Manager: Steve Baker
ADVERTISING: Rates on application
Agency Commission: 10%
Copy instructions: Copy Date: Tuesday 4pm prior to publication date
Average advertising content per issue: 50%
Series owner and contact point for the following titles, see individual entries:
Harrow Leader
Harrow Observer
Pinner Observer
Stanmore Observer
Wembley Leader
Wembley Observer
Willesden Leader
Willesden Observer
Supplement(s): Motoring - 52xY, Property - 52xY
LOCAL NEWSPAPERS: Local Newspapers Greater London

HARROW TIMES
43045U72A-172

Formerly: West London Times Series
Editorial Address: 71 Church Road, HENDON, NW4 4DN
Tel: 01923 216 304
Email: rsharp@london.newsquest.co.uk
Advertising Address: As above. **Tel:** 01923 216200
Email: harrowrop@london.newsquest.co.uk
Web site: http://www.harrowtimes.co.uk
Publisher: Newsquest Media Group
Date Established: 1997
Frequency: Weekly - Published on Thursday
Cover Price: Free
Circulation: 70,992 (VFD 02/07/2007 to 30/12/2007)
Editor: Rachel Sharp; **Advertising Manager:** Vina Dhaliwal
ADVERTISING: Rates on application
Agency Commission: 10%
Mechanical Data: Type Area: 350 x 265mm, Col Length: 350mm, Page Width: 265mm, No. of Columns (Display): 9, Col Widths (Display): 27mm, Film: Digital
Copy instructions: Copy Date: Tuesday 5pm prior to publication date
LOCAL NEWSPAPERS: Local Newspapers Greater London

HARTLEPOOL MAIL
42070U67B-265

Formerly: Hartlepool Mail (Final Edition)
Editorial Address: New Clarence House, Wesley Square, HARTLEPOOL, TS24 8BX **Tel:** 01429 239333
Fax: 01429 869024
Email: mail.news@northeast-press.co.uk
Advertising Address: As above. **Fax:** 01429 265818
Email: sheila.argument@northeast-press.co.uk
Web site: http://www.hartlepooltoday.co.uk
Publisher: Northeast Press Ltd
Date Established: 1877
Frequency: Evenings
Cover Price: £0.40
Circulation: 18,223 (ABC 02/07/2007 to 30/12/2007)
Editor: Ian Willis; **News Editor:** Ian Willis; **Managing Director:** Linda Burnside; **Advertising Manager:** Sheila Argument
ADVERTISING RATES:
Full Page Mono £3862.50
Full Page Colour £5021.25
Agency Commission: 10%
Mechanical Data: Type Area: 340 x 276mm, Col Length: 340mm, Col Widths (Display): 34mm, No. of Columns (Display): 9, Print Process: Web-fed offset litho, Film: Digital, Page Width: 276mm

Non-National Newspapers

Section 4 (a) Newspapers

Copy instructions: Copy Date: 12 noon 2 days prior to publication date
Average advertising content per issue: 30%
Editions:
Hartlepool Mail (First & County Edition)
Supplement(s): Aspiration Mail - 4xY, Business and Industrial Review - 2xY, Business Mail - 12xY, Out and About Guides - 1xY
REGIONAL DAILY & SUNDAY NEWSPAPERS: Regional Daily Newspapers

HARTLEPOOL MAIL (FIRST & COUNTY EDITION)
42071U67B-265_530
Formerly: Hartlepool Mail (County Edition)
Frequency: Evenings
Cover Price: £0.40
Edition of: Hartlepool Mail
REGIONAL DAILY & SUNDAY NEWSPAPERS: Regional Daily Newspapers

HARTLEPOOL STAR
44492U72B-3371_120
Frequency: Weekly
Cover Price: Free
Circulation: 25,585 (VFD 02/07/2007 to 30/12/2007)
ADVERTISING RATES:
SCC £6.80
Part of Series, see entry for: Star Series
LOCAL NEWSPAPERS: Local Newspapers English Counties

HARWICH AND MANNINGTREE STANDARD
43619U72B-1044_180
Frequency: Weekly - Circulation figure also includes the Manningtree & Harwich Standard
Cover Price: £0.48
Circulation: 6,329 (ABC 02/07/2007 to 30/12/2007)
ADVERTISING RATES:
Full Page Colour £405.00
SCC £2.60
Copy instructions: Copy Date: Tuesday 1pm prior to publication date
Part of Series, see entry for: Gazette and Standard Series (East Essex)
LOCAL NEWSPAPERS: Local Newspapers English Counties

HASLEMERE HERALD
44373U72B-3120_150
Frequency: Weekly
Cover Price: £0.50
Part of Series, see entry for: Farnham Herald Series
LOCAL NEWSPAPERS: Local Newspapers English Counties

HASLEMERE TIMES & MAIL
44388U72B-1339_200
Frequency: Weekly - Circulation figure is incorporated into the Alton Times & Mail
Cover Price: Free
Part of Series, see entry for: Alton Post Gazette, Times & Mail Series
LOCAL NEWSPAPERS: Local Newspapers English Counties

HASTINGS & ST LEONARDS OBSERVER
44436U72B-3225_170
Frequency: Weekly
Cover Price: £0.45
Circulation: 20,436 (ABC 02/07/2007 to 30/12/2007)
ADVERTISING: Rates on application
Part of Series, see entry for: Hastings Observer Series
LOCAL NEWSPAPERS: Local Newspapers English Counties

HASTINGS OBSERVER SERIES
44434U72B-3225
Formerly: East Sussex Observer Series
Editorial Address: Woods House, Telford Road, ST. LEONARDS-ON-SEA, TN38 9LZ **Tel:** 01424 854242
Fax: 01424 854284
Email: observer@trbeckett.co.uk
Advertising Address: As above. **Fax:** 01424 852850
Email: observerads.beckett@jpress.co.uk
Web site: http://www.hastingsobserver.co.uk
Publisher: T.R. Beckett Ltd
Date Established: 1859
Frequency: Weekly - Published on Friday
Circulation: 36,478 (Combined Circulation)

Editor: Angela Gallen; **News Editor:** Angela Gallen;
Advertising Manager: Hayley Scott; **Group Editor:** Peter Lindsey
ADVERTISING: Rates on application
Mechanical Data: Film: Digital
Copy instructions: Copy Date: Monday 4pm prior to publication date
Series owner and contact point for the following titles, see individual entries:
Battle Observer
Bexhill-on-Sea Observer
Hastings & St Leonards Observer
Rye Observer
LOCAL NEWSPAPERS: Local Newspapers English Counties

HAVANT & WATERLOOVILLE JOURNAL
43754U72B-1378_170
Frequency: Weekly
Cover Price: Free
Circulation: 28,894 (VFD 10/09/2007 to 30/12/2007)
Part of Series, see entry for: Journal Series Portsmouth
LOCAL NEWSPAPERS: Local Newspapers English Counties

HAVERHILL ECHO
44340U72B-3077
Editorial Address: 7 Queen's Square, HAVERHILL, CB9 9EG **Tel:** 01440 703456 **Fax:** 01440 764013
Email: news@haverhillecho.com
Advertising Address: As above. **Fax:** 01440 712684
Email: tracey.hills@jpress.co.uk
Web site: http://www.haverhilltoday.co.uk
ISSN: 0962-242X
Publisher: Johnston Press plc
Date Established: 1888
Frequency: Weekly - Published on Thursday
Cover Price: £0.42
Circulation: 4,927 (ABC 02/07/2007 to 30/12/2007)
Editor: Karen Steel; **Managing Director:** Richard Parkinson
ADVERTISING: Rates on application
LOCAL NEWSPAPERS: Local Newspapers English Counties

HAVERHILL WEEKLY NEWS
43319U72B-350_170
Frequency: Weekly
Cover Price: Free
Circulation: 13,149 (VFD 02/07/2007 to 30/12/2007)
ADVERTISING RATES:
SCC £3.45
Part of Series, see entry for: Cambridge Weekly News & Crier Series
LOCAL NEWSPAPERS: Local Newspapers English Counties

HAWICK NEWS
44960U72D-520
Formerly: Hawick News & Scottish Border Chronicle
Editorial Address: 3 Tower Knowe, HAWICK, TD9 9DQ
Tel: 01450 379690 **Fax:** 01450 376705
Email: hnnews@tweeddalepress.co.uk
Advertising Address: As above.
Email: janiscornwall@tweeddalepress.co.uk
Web site: http://www.hawick-news.co.uk
Publisher: Tweeddale Press Group
Date Established: 1881
Frequency: Weekly - Published on Friday
Cover Price: £0.50
Circulation: 5,462 (ABC 02/07/2007 to 30/12/2007)
Usual Pagination: 24
Editor: Jason Marshall; **Advertising Manager:** Janis Cornwall
ADVERTISING RATES:
Full Page Mono £1144.44
Full Page Colour £1716.66
Agency Commission: 10%
Mechanical Data: Type Area: 340 x 272mm, No. of Columns (Display): 9, Page Width: 272mm, Col Length: 340mm, Film: Digital, Col Widths (Display): 28mm
Copy instructions: Copy Date: Tuesday 5.00 pm prior to publication date
LOCAL NEWSPAPERS: Local Newspapers Scotland

HAYLE TIMES
43437U72B-580_130
Frequency: Weekly
Cover Price: £0.58
Circulation: 180 (Publisher's Statement)
Part of Series, see entry for: St. Ives Times & Echo Series
LOCAL NEWSPAPERS: Local Newspapers English Counties

HAYLING ISLANDER
43750U72B-1373
Editorial Address: 78 Elm Grove, HAYLING ISLAND, PO11 9EH **Tel:** 023 9246 3473 **Fax:** 023 9246 1685
Email: contactus@haylingislandtoday.co.uk
Advertising Address: As above.
Email: suzy.walker@jpress.co.uk
Web site: http://www.haylingtoday.co.uk
Publisher: Portsmouth Publishing & Printing Ltd
Date Established: 1973
Frequency: Monthly - Published on the 1st Tuesday of every month
Cover Price: Free
Circulation: 11,350 (Publisher's Statement)
Editor: Andrew Griffin; **Advertising Manager:** Suzy Walker
ADVERTISING RATES:
Full Page Mono £671.30
Full Page Colour £872.69
Agency Commission: 10%
Mechanical Data: Col Widths (Display): 29mm, Col Length: 340mm, No. of Columns (Display): 9, Print Process: Web-fed offset litho
Copy instructions: Copy Date: Friday prior to publication date
Average advertising content per issue: 50%
Supplement(s): Hayling Directory - 1xY, The Visitor's Guide - 1xY
LOCAL NEWSPAPERS: Local Newspapers English Counties

HEADINGLEY, ARMLEY & MEANWOOD WEEKLY NEWS
44715U72B-3812_180
Formerly: West Leeds Weekly News
Frequency: Weekly
Cover Price: Free
Circulation: 32,807 (Publisher's Statement)
ADVERTISING RATES:
SCC £4.30
Part of Series, see entry for: Leeds Weekly News Series
LOCAL NEWSPAPERS: Local Newspapers English Counties

HEALTH
763137U67B-9009_705
Formerly: Health & Fitness
Tel: 020 7938 6000 **Fax:** 020 7937 2648
Frequency: Weekly - Published on Tuesdays in the London Evening Standard
Editor: Sophie Goodchild
Summary of Content: Section looking at issues of health and fitness with tips, advice and features.
ADVERTISING: Rates on application
Part of Series, see entry for: London Evening Standard
REGIONAL DAILY & SUNDAY NEWSPAPERS: Regional Daily Newspapers

HEBDEN BRIDGE TIMES
44703U72B-3770
Editorial Address: 19A Crown Street, HEBDEN BRIDGE, HX7 8EH **Tel:** 01422 842106 **Fax:** 01422 842628
Email: norman.masters@halifaxcourier.co.uk
Advertising Address: As above. **Tel:** 01422 843073
Email: gemma.kipping@halifaxcourier.co.uk
Web site: http://www.hebdenbridgetimes.co.uk
Publisher: Johnston Press plc
Date Established: 1881
Frequency: Weekly - Published on Thursday
Cover Price: £0.44
Circulation: 3,349 (ABC 02/07/2007 to 30/12/2007)
Usual Pagination: 16
Editor: Norman Masters; **Managing Director:** Darron McLoughlin
ADVERTISING RATES:
SCC £13.71
Mechanical Data: Page Width: 335.5mm, Film: Digital, Col Widths (Display): 27.7mm, No. of Columns (Display): 11, Type Area: 560 x 335.5mm, Col Length: 560mm
Copy instructions: Copy Date: Tuesday 5pm prior to publication date
LOCAL NEWSPAPERS: Local Newspapers English Counties

HELENSBURGH ADVERTISER
44961U72D-530
Editorial Address: Clyde Weekly Press, 15 Colquhoun Square, HELENSBURGH, G84 8SE **Tel:** 01436 673434
Fax: 01436 671241
Email: editorial@helensburghadvertiser.co.uk
Advertising Address: As above. **Fax:** 0141 952 7267
Email: advertising.ha@cfpress.co.uk
Web site: http://www.helensburghadvertiser.co.uk
ISSN: 1356-8663
Publisher: Clyde & Forth Press Group
Frequency: Weekly - Published on Thursday
Cover Price: £0.50
Circulation: 6,730 (ABC 01/01/2007 to 30/12/2007)
Usual Pagination: 40

Editor: Tracy-Ann Carmichael; **Advertising Manager:** Margaret Hull
ADVERTISING RATES:
Full Page Mono £1544.40
Full Page Colour £2316.60
SCC £5.85
Agency Commission: 10%
Mechanical Data: Col Length: 330mm, Page Width: 266mm, Film: Digital, Col Widths (Display): 30.5mm, No. of Columns (Display): 8, Type Area: 330 x 266mm
Copy instructions: Copy Date: 2 days prior to publication date
Average advertising content per issue: 40%
LOCAL NEWSPAPERS: Local Newspapers Scotland

HELENSBURGH LENNOX   762424U72D-673_140
Formerly: Helensburgh Herald
Frequency: Weekly
Cover Price: £0.70
Part of Series, see entry for: Lennox Series
LOCAL NEWSPAPERS: Local Newspapers Scotland

HELSTON GAZETTE   43434U72B-560_120
Frequency: Weekly
Cover Price: Free
Circulation: 15,477 (Publisher's Statement)
ADVERTISING RATES:
Full Page Mono £352.50
Full Page Colour £475.88
SCC £2.35
Part of Series, see entry for: The Packet Series
LOCAL NEWSPAPERS: Local Newspapers English Counties

HELSTON PACKET   43429U72B-553_130
Frequency: Weekly - Circulation figure is incorporated into the Camborne Redruth Packet
ADVERTISING RATES:
Full Page Mono £456.75
Full Page Colour £616.61
SCC £1.45
Part of Series, see entry for: The Packet Series
LOCAL NEWSPAPERS: Local Newspapers English Counties

HEMSWORTH AND SOUTH ELMSALL EXPRESS   44704U72B-3775
Editorial Address: 23 Barnsley Road, South Elmsall, PONTEFRACT, WF9 2RN **Tel:** 01977 642214
Fax: 01977 642004
Email: rebeccawhittington@ywng.co.uk
Advertising Address: As above. **Tel:** 01977 604107
Email: johnsmith@pandcexpress.co.uk
Web site: http://www.hemsworthandsouthelmsallexpress.co.uk
Publisher: Yorkshire Weekly Newspaper Group Ltd
Frequency: Weekly
Cover Price: £0.40
Circulation: 6,453 (ABC 02/07/2007 to 30/12/2007)
Usual Pagination: 48
Editor: Rebecca Whittington; **News Editor:** Rebecca Whittington
ADVERTISING RATES:
SCC £4.14
Agency Commission: 10%
Mechanical Data: Col Widths (Display): 28mm, Col Length: 340mm, Page Width: 265mm, Film: Digital, Type Area: 340 x 265mm, No. of Columns (Display): 9
Copy instructions: Copy Date: Tuesday 11am prior to publication date
LOCAL NEWSPAPERS: Local Newspapers English Counties

HENDON & FINCHLEY TIMES   43046U72A-200_140
Frequency: Weekly
Cover Price: Free
Circulation: 39,009 (VFD 02/07/2007 to 30/12/2007)
ADVERTISING RATES:
SCC £3.45
Part of Series, see entry for: Hendon Times Series
LOCAL NEWSPAPERS: Local Newspapers Greater London

HENDON TIMES SERIES   43042U72A-200
Editorial Address: 71 Church Road, Hendon, LONDON, NW4 4DN **Tel:** 020 8359 5959 **Fax:** 020 8203 9106
Email: timesnews@london.newsquest.co.uk
Advertising Address: As above. **Fax:** 020 8203 5141
Email: isteel@london.newsquest.co.uk
Web site: http://www.times-series.co.uk
Publisher: Newsquest (North London)

Date Established: 1875
Frequency: Weekly - Published on Thursday & Friday
Cover Price: Free
Circulation: 116,302 (Combined Circulation)
Editor: Charlie Stong; **Features Editor:** Lindi Bilgorri; **Advertising Manager:** Ian Steel
ADVERTISING RATES:
SCC £12.05
Agency Commission: 10%
Mechanical Data: Col Length: 350mm, Type Area: 350 x 265mm, No. of Columns (Display): 9, Film: Digital, Page Width: 265mm
Copy instructions: Copy Date: Monday 5.00pm prior to publication date
Series owner and contact point for the following titles, see individual entries:
Barnet & Potters Bar Times
Edgware & Mill Hill Times
Enfield Independent
Haringey Independent
Hendon & Finchley Times
LOCAL NEWSPAPERS: Local Newspapers Greater London

HENLEY STANDARD   44221U72B-2710
Editorial Address: Caxton House, 1 Station Road, HENLEY-ON-THAMES, RG9 1AD **Tel:** 01491 419444
Fax: 01491 419401
Email: news@henleystandard.co.uk
Advertising Address: As above. **Fax:** 01491 419402
Email: adverts@higgsgroup.co.uk
Web site: http://www.henley-on-thames.com
Publisher: Higgs Group
Date Established: 1885
Frequency: Weekly
Cover Price: £0.50
Circulation: 12,049 (ABC 01/01/2007 to 30/12/2007)
Editor: Simon Bradshaw; **News Editor:** Richard Reed
ADVERTISING RATES:
Full Page Mono £1433.25
Full Page Colour £1863.23
Agency Commission: 10%
Mechanical Data: Col Length: 390mm, No. of Columns (Display): 7, Type Area: 390 x 283mm, Page Width: 283mm, Film: Digital, Print Process: Web-fed offset litho, Trim Size: 445 x 320mm, Col Widths (Display): 37mm
Copy instructions: Copy Date: Tuesday 12pm prior to publication date
Average advertising content per issue: 60%
LOCAL NEWSPAPERS: Local Newspapers English Counties

HERALD AND POST EDINBURGH   44926U72D-1009_100
Formerly: Edinburgh Herald & Post
Frequency: Weekly
Cover Price: Free
Circulation: 124,293 (VFD 13/08/2007 to 30/12/2007)
ADVERTISING: Rates on application
Part of Series, see entry for: Herald and Post Series (Edinburgh)
LOCAL NEWSPAPERS: Local Newspapers Scotland

HERALD AND POST FIFE   44918U72D-1009_102
Publisher: Strachan & Livingston Ltd
Frequency: Weekly
Cover Price: Free
Circulation: 44,877 (VFD 02/07/2007 to 30/12/2007)
ADVERTISING: Rates on application
Part of Series, see entry for: Fife Leader and Free Press Series
LOCAL NEWSPAPERS: Local Newspapers Scotland

HERALD AND POST (LUTON & DUNSTABLE)   43236U72B-132
Formerly: Herald and Post Series (Luton)
Editorial Address: Media House, 39 Upper George Street, LUTON, LU1 2RD **Tel:** 01582 700666 **Fax:** 01582 700660
Email: editorial@heraldpost.co.uk
Advertising Address: As above. **Tel:** 01582 700600
Fax: 01582 700610
Email: advertising@bedsnews.com
Web site: http://www.lutontoday.co.uk
Publisher: Johnston Press plc
Frequency: Weekly - Published on Thursday
Cover Price: Free
Circulation: 90,526 (Publisher's Statement)
Usual Pagination: 80
Editor: John Francis
ADVERTISING RATES:
Full Page Mono £2806.02
Full Page Colour £3647.83
SCC £9.17
Agency Commission: 10%

Mechanical Data: Type Area: 340 x 268mm, Col Length: 340mm, Col Widths (Display): 28mm, No. of Columns (Display): 9, Page Width: 268mm, Film: Digital
Copy instructions: Copy Date: Monday prior to publication date
Average advertising content per issue: 80%
LOCAL NEWSPAPERS: Local Newspapers English Counties

HERALD AND POST (RUNCORN)   43378U72B-484_181
Formerly: Runcorn Herald and Post
Frequency: Weekly - Published on Friday
Cover Price: Free
Circulation: 28,486 (VFD 02/07/2007 to 30/12/2007)
ADVERTISING: Rates on application
Part of Series, see entry for: Runcorn & Widnes News & Herald Series
LOCAL NEWSPAPERS: Local Newspapers English Counties

HERALD AND POST SERIES (EDINBURGH)   1657191U72D-1009
Editorial Address: 108 Holyrood Road, EDINBURGH, EH8 8AS **Tel:** 0131 620 8620
Email: edinhp@scotsman.com
Advertising Address: As above. **Tel:** 0131 620 8342
Fax: 0131 523 0298
Email: mince@scotsman.com
Publisher: The Scotsman Publications Ltd
Frequency: Weekly
Cover Price: Free
Circulation: 166,378 (Combined Circulation)
Editor: Hugh Jarvis; **Advertising Manager:** Mhairi Ince
ADVERTISING: Rates on application
Copy instructions: Copy Date: Tuesday 10am prior to publication date
Series owner and contact point for the following titles, see individual entries:
Herald and Post Edinburgh
Herald and Post West Lothian
LOCAL NEWSPAPERS: Local Newspapers Scotland

HERALD AND POST SERIES (TEESSIDE)   43408U72B-3360
Editorial Address: Gazette Buildings, 105-111 Borough Road, MIDDLESBROUGH, TS1 3AZ **Tel:** 01642 234355
Fax: 01642 232014
Email: sue.giles@gazettemedia.co.uk
Advertising Address: As above. **Tel:** 01642 252525
Fax: 01642 254764
Email: fieldsales@gazettemedia.co.uk
Web site: http://www.gazettelive.co.uk/heraldandpost
Publisher: Trinity Mirror
Frequency: Weekly - Published on Thursay and Friday
Cover Price: Free
Circulation: 232,382 (Combined Circulation)
Usual Pagination: 44
Editor: Sue Giles
ADVERTISING: Rates on application
Mechanical Data: Film: Digital, Type Area: 340 x 266mm, Page Width: 266mm, Col Widths (Display): 31.5mm, Col Length: 340mm, No. of Columns (Display): 8
Copy instructions: Copy Date: Monday 12pm prior to publication date
Series owner and contact point for the following titles, see individual entries:
Darlington Herald & Post
East Cleveland Herald & Post
Middlesbrough Herald & Post
North Yorkshire Herald & Post
South Durham Herald & Post
Stockton & Billingham Herald & Post
LOCAL NEWSPAPERS: Local Newspapers English Counties

HERALD AND POST WEST LOTHIAN   45042U72D-1009_101
Formerly: West Lothian Herald & Post
Frequency: Weekly
Cover Price: Free
Circulation: 42,085 (VFD 03/09/2007 to 30/12/2007)
ADVERTISING: Rates on application
Part of Series, see entry for: Herald and Post Series (Edinburgh)
LOCAL NEWSPAPERS: Local Newspapers Scotland

HERALD AND TIMES SERIES OXON   44222U72B-2720
Editorial Address: Newspaper House, Osney Mead, OXFORD, OX2 0EJ **Tel:** 01865 425262 **Fax:** 01865 425554

Non-National Newspapers

Email: news@nqo.com
Advertising Address: As above. **Tel:** 01865 425275
Fax: 01865 425557
Email: retail.admin@nqo.com
Web site: http://www.oxfordmail.co.uk
Publisher: Newsquest (Oxfordshire) Ltd
Frequency: Weekly
Circulation: 36,327 (Combined Circulation)
Usual Pagination: 72
Editor: Jason Collie; **News Editor:** Jason Collie; **Managing Director:** Shamus Donald; **Advertising Manager:** Julian Richings
ADVERTISING: Rates on application
Agency Commission: 10%
Copy instructions: Copy Date: Monday 9.30am prior to publication date
Series owner and contact point for the following titles, see individual entries:
The Abingdon Herald
Didcot Herald
The Oxford Times
Wallingford Herald
Wantage & Grove Herald
Supplement(s): Banbury Lifestyle - 12xY, Bride & Groom - 2xY, In Business - 12xY, Intuition - 4xY, Oxfordshire Limited Edition - 12xY
LOCAL NEWSPAPERS: Local Newspapers English Counties

HERALD EXPRESS
42196U67B-1090

Formerly: Herald Express (Torquay)
Editorial Address: Harmsworth House, Barton Hill Road, TORQUAY, TQ2 8JN **Tel:** 01803 676000 **Fax:** 01803 676228
Email: newsdesk@heraldexpress.co.uk
Advertising Address: As above. **Fax:** 01803 676799
Email: pnewman@swmg.co.uk
Web site: http://www.thisissouthdevon.co.uk
Publisher: South West Media Group Ltd
Date Established: 1925
Frequency: Daily
Cover Price: £0.37
Circulation: 23,987 (ABC 02/07/2007 to 30/12/2007)
Editor: Ellen Grindley; **News Editor:** Ellen Grindley;
Managing Director: Chris Coward; **Advertising Manager:** Paul Newman
ADVERTISING RATES:
SCC £6.20
Agency Commission: 10%
Mechanical Data: Col Length: 360mm, No. of Columns (Display): 8, Col Widths (Display): 31.5mm, Film: Digital
Copy instructions: Copy Date: 2 days prior to publication date
Editions:
Herald Express (Bay and County)
Herald Express (Brixham and Southhams)
Herald Express (Newton and Teign)
Supplement(s): Business (Herald Express) - 52xY, Bygones - 52xY, Class of 2007 - 52xY, Drive - 52xY, On the Town What's on Now - 52xY, Property - 52xY
REGIONAL DAILY & SUNDAY NEWSPAPERS: Regional Daily Newspapers

HERALD EXPRESS (BAY AND COUNTY)
763357U67B-1090_550

Frequency: Evenings
Cover Price: £0.37
Edition of: Herald Express
REGIONAL DAILY & SUNDAY NEWSPAPERS: Regional Daily Newspapers

HERALD EXPRESS HEMEL HEMPSTEAD, BERKHAMSTED & TRING
43787U72B-1500_120

Frequency: Weekly - Published on Thursday
Cover Price: Free
Circulation: 49,427 (VFD 02/07/2007 to 30/12/2007)
ADVERTISING: Rates on application
Part of Series, see entry for: Gazette & Herald Express Series (Hemel Hempstead)
LOCAL NEWSPAPERS: Local Newspapers English Counties

HERALD EXPRESS (NEWTON AND TEIGN)
763361U67B-1090_580

Frequency: Evenings
Cover Price: £0.75
Edition of: Herald Express
REGIONAL DAILY & SUNDAY NEWSPAPERS: Regional Daily Newspapers

THE HERALD (GLASGOW)
42263U67B-2310

Editorial Address: 200 Renfield Street, GLASGOW, G2 3QB
Tel: 0141 302 7000 **Fax:** 0141 302 7007
Email: news@theherald.co.uk
Advertising Address: As above. **Fax:** 0141 302 6363
Email: daniel.mccomiskey@glasgow.newsquest
Web site: http://www.theherald.co.uk
Publisher: Newsquest Herald & Times Ltd
Frequency: Mornings
Cover Price: £0.70
Circulation: 58,157 (ABC 03/08/2009 to 30/08/2009)
Editor: Calum MacDonald; **News Editor:** Calum MacDonald; **Features Editor:** Mark Smith; **Editor-in-Chief:** Donald Martin
ADVERTISING RATES:
Full Page Mono £11500.00
Full Page Colour £14950.00
SCC £26.50
Mechanical Data: Page Width: 349mm, Type Area: 540 x 349mm, Col Length: 540mm, No. of Columns (Display): 8, Film: Digital, Col Widths (Display): 41mm
Copy instructions: Copy Date: 2 days prior to publication date
Average advertising content per issue: 50%
Supplement(s): Arts, Books & Cinema - 52xY, The Herald Business Magazine - 10xY, The Herald Magazine - 52xY, The Herald Society - 52xY
REGIONAL DAILY & SUNDAY NEWSPAPERS: Regional Daily Newspapers

THE HERALD (GLASGOW) (CITY/LONDON OFFICE)
42305U67D-250

Editorial Address: 30 Cannon Street, LONDON, EC4M 6YJ
Tel: 020 7618 3443 **Fax:** 020 7618 3455
Email: business@theherald.co.uk
Web site: http://www.theherald.co.uk
Publisher: Newsquest Herald & Times Ltd
Date Established: 1783
Cover Price: £0.55
ADVERTISING: Rates on application
REGIONAL DAILY & SUNDAY NEWSPAPERS: Regional Daily Sunday London City Office

THE HERALD (GLASGOW) (EDINBURGH OFFICE)
42310U67E-300

Editorial Address: Bearford House, 39 Hanover Street, EDINBURGH, EH2 2PJ **Tel:** 0131 240 0270
Email: edinburgh@theherald.co.uk
Web site: http://www.theherald.co.uk
Publisher: Newsquest Herald & Times Ltd
Cover Price: £0.65
Usual Pagination: 50
Editor: Brian Donnelly
ADVERTISING: No Advertising taken
REGIONAL DAILY & SUNDAY NEWSPAPERS: Regional Offices

HERALD LEADER
44302U72B-3040_181

Formerly: Tamworth Herald Extra
Email: tamworth.editorial@cintamworth.co.uk
Frequency: Weekly
Cover Price: Free
Circulation: 33,253 (VFD 02/07/2007 to 30/12/2007)
Usual Pagination: 28
ADVERTISING: Rates on application
Part of Series, see entry for: Tamworth Herald Series
LOCAL NEWSPAPERS: Local Newspapers English Counties

THE HERALD MAGAZINE
1664996U67H-352

Editorial Address: 200 Renfield Street, GLASGOW, G2 3QB
Tel: 0141 302 7003 **Fax:** 0141 302 7177
Email: magazine@theherald.co.uk
Advertising Address: As above. **Tel:** 0141 302 6000
Fax: 0141 302 6363
Email: christine.sermanni@glasgow.newsquest.co.uk
Web site: http://www.theherald.co.uk
Publisher: Newsquest Herald & Times Ltd
Frequency: Weekly - Published on Saturday within The Herald
Editor: Kathleen Morgan
Summary of Content: Lifestyle magazine containing interviews and reportage, with features on travel, fashion, film, music and celebrities. Also includes radio and TV listings and previews with restaurant reviews.
ADVERTISING RATES:
Full Page Colour £6500.00
Mechanical Data: Type Area: 344 x 260mm, Col Length: 344mm, Page Width: 260mm, No. of Columns (Display): 7, Col Widths (Display): 34mm, Film: Digital
Supplement to: The Herald (Glasgow)
REGIONAL DAILY & SUNDAY NEWSPAPERS: Regional Colour Supplements

THE HERALD (PLYMOUTH)
42148U67B-650

Formerly: Evening Herald (Plymouth)
Editorial Address: 17 Brest Road, Derriford Business Park, PLYMOUTH, PL6 5AA **Tel:** 01752 765500 .
Fax: 01752 765527
Email: news@theplymouthherald.co.uk
Advertising Address: As above. **Fax:** 01752 765515
Email: rwoodward@swmg.co.uk
Web site: http://www.thisisplymouth.co.uk
Publisher: South West Media Group Ltd
Frequency: Mornings - Not published on Sunday
Cover Price: £0.36
Circulation: 40,384 (ABC 02/01/2006 to 02/07/2006)
Editor: James Garnett; **News Editor:** James Garnett;
Advertising Manager: Roger Woodward; **Advertisement Director:** Paul Newman
ADVERTISING RATES:
Full Page Mono £2609.28
Full Page Colour £3261.60
SCC £9.06
Agency Commission: 10%
Mechanical Data: Film: Digital, Type Area: 360 x 268mm, Col Length: 360mm, No. of Columns (Display): 8, Col Widths (Display): 31mm, Page Width: 268mm
Copy instructions: Copy Date: 2 days prior to publication date
Supplement(s): Home Seeker - 52xY, Motors - 52xY, Sport - 52xY
REGIONAL DAILY & SUNDAY NEWSPAPERS: Regional Daily Newspapers

HEREFORD ADMAG
1656461U72B-3955_100

Frequency: Weekly
Cover Price: Free
Circulation: 59,445 (VFD 02/07/2007 to 30/12/2007)
ADVERTISING RATES:
SCC £3.70
Part of Series, see entry for: Admag Newspapers Series
LOCAL NEWSPAPERS: Local Newspapers English Counties

HEREFORD & LEOMINSTER JOURNAL
44232U72B-2812_130

Frequency: Weekly
Cover Price: Free
Circulation: 49,593 (VFD 02/07/2007 to 30/12/2007)
ADVERTISING: Rates on application
Part of Series, see entry for: Chronicle & Journal Series
LOCAL NEWSPAPERS: Local Newspapers English Counties

HEREFORD TIMES
43780U72B-143

Formerly: Hereford Times Series
Editorial Address: Holmer Road, HEREFORD, HR4 9UJ
Tel: 01432 274413 **Fax:** 01432 845897
Email: htnewsdesk@midlands.newsquest.co.uk
Advertising Address: As above. **Fax:** 01432 845898
Email: hereford.fieldsales@midlands.newsquest.co.uk
Web site: http://www.herefordtimes.com
Publisher: Newsquest Media Group
Date Established: 1832
Frequency: Weekly
Cover Price: £0.65
Circulation: 39,876 (ABC 02/07/2007 to 30/12/2007)
Usual Pagination: 120
Editor: Newsdesk; **News Editor:** Ian Morris; **Advertising Manager:** Tina Hurley
ADVERTISING RATES:
SCC £4.9
Agency Commission: 10%
Mechanical Data: Type Area: 350 x 268mm, Page Width: 268mm, Film: Digital, Col Length: 350mm, No. of Columns (Display): 9, Col Widths (Display): 28mm
Copy instructions: Copy Date: 3 days prior to publication date
LOCAL NEWSPAPERS: Local Newspapers English Counties

HERNE BAY EXTRA
43842U72B-1763_17

Frequency: Weekly
Cover Price: Free
ADVERTISING: Rates on application
Part of Series, see entry for: Canterbury Extra Series
LOCAL NEWSPAPERS: Local Newspapers English Counties

HERNE BAY GAZETTE
43904U72B-1870_14

Frequency: Weekly
Cover Price: £0.60
Circulation: 4,392 (ABC 02/07/2007 to 30/12/2007)

Part of Series, see entry for: Kentish Gazette Series
LOCAL NEWSPAPERS: Local Newspapers English Counties

HERNE BAY TIMES
43941U72B-1902_120

Frequency: Weekly
Cover Price: £0.35
Part of Series, see entry for: Whitstable & Herne Bay Times Series
LOCAL NEWSPAPERS: Local Newspapers English Counties

HERTFORDSHIRE MERCURY
43796U72B-1520_120

Frequency: Weekly
Cover Price: £0.60
ADVERTISING: Rates on application
Part of Series, see entry for: Hertfordshire Mercury Series
LOCAL NEWSPAPERS: Local Newspapers English Counties

HERTFORDSHIRE MERCURY SERIES
43795U72B-1520

Editorial Address: The Media Centre, 40 Ware Road, HERTFORD, SG13 7HU **Tel:** 01992 526625
Fax: 01992 526645
Email: mercury@hertsessexnews.co.uk
Advertising Address: As above. **Tel:** 01992 526600
Fax: 01992 526654
Email: advertising@hertsessexnews.co.uk
Web site: http://www.hertfordshiremercury.co.uk
Publisher: Herts & Essex Newspapers Ltd
Frequency: Weekly - Published on Friday
Circulation: 26,720 (ABC 02/07/2007 to 30/12/2007)
Usual Pagination: 140
Editor: Abigayle Barber; **News Editor:** Abigayle Barber;
Advertisement Director: Ricky Allan
ADVERTISING RATES:
Full Page Mono £2220.75
Full Page Colour £2385.75
SCC £7.05
Agency Commission: 10%
Mechanical Data: Page Width: 268mm, Col Widths (Display): 28mm, Type Area: 350 x 268mm, Col Length: 350mm, No. of Columns (Display): 9, Film: Digital
Copy instructions: Copy Date: Tuesday 4pm prior to publication date
Average advertising content per issue: 70%
Series owner and contact point for the following titles, see individual entries:
Buntingford & Royston Mercury
Hertfordshire Mercury
LOCAL NEWSPAPERS: Local Newspapers English Counties

HERTS ADVERTISER
43800U72B-1530

Formerly: Herts Advertiser St. Albans & Harpenden
Editorial Address: Unit 1, Sandridge Park, Porters Wood, ST. ALBANS, AL3 6PH **Tel:** 01727 865165
Fax: 01727 736527
Email: herts.advertiser@archant.co.uk
Advertising Address: As above. **Tel:** 01727 736400
Fax: 01727 736455
Email: esther.roscoe@archant.co.uk
Web site: http://www.hertsad.co.uk
Publisher: Archant Herts & Cambs
Date Established: 1855
Frequency: Weekly - Published on Thursday
Free to qualifying individuals
Circulation: 50,520 (VFD 03/09/2007 to 30/12/2007)
Editor: Madeleine Burton; **News Editor:** Madeleine Burton;
Managing Director: Stuart McCreery; **Advertising Manager:** Esther Roscoe
ADVERTISING RATES:
Full Page Colour £2750.00
SCC £8.50
Agency Commission: 10%
Mechanical Data: Page Width: 263mm, Print Process: Web-offset litho, Type Area: 360 x 263mm, Col Length: 360mm, No. of Columns (Display): 9, Col Widths (Display): 27mm, Film: Digital
Copy instructions: Copy Date: Monday 5.30pm prior to publication date
Average advertising content per issue: 85%
Supplement(s): Motoring, Property
LOCAL NEWSPAPERS: Local Newspapers English Counties

HERTS AND ESSEX ADVERTISER
1682046U72B-159_198

Formerly: Berkshire and Middlesex Advertiser
Frequency: Weekly - Published on Mondays

Cover Price: Free
ADVERTISING RATES:
Full Page Mono £699.00
Full Page Colour £900.00
Part of Series, see entry for: South Bucks and Berkshire News Series
LOCAL NEWSPAPERS: Local Newspapers English Counties

HERTS & ESSEX OBSERVER SERIES
43801U72B-1545

Editorial Address: 12 North Street, BISHOP'S STORTFORD, CM23 2LQ **Tel:** 01279 866355
Fax: 01279 507780
Email: observer@hertsessexnews.co.uk
Advertising Address: The Media Centre, 40 Ware Road, HERTFORD, SG13 7HU **Tel:** 01992 526666
Fax: 01992 526687
Email: advertising@hertsessexnews.co.uk
Web site: http://www.hertsandessexobserver.co.uk
Publisher: Herts & Essex Observer Newspapers
Date Established: 1861
Frequency: Weekly - Published on Thursday
Circulation: 30,375 (Combined Circulation)
Editor: Sandra Perry; **News Editor:** Sandra Perry;
Managing Director: Paul Thompson; **Advertising Director:** Richard Byham
ADVERTISING RATES:
Full Page Mono £1622.25
Full Page Colour £1622.25
Agency Commission: 10%
Mechanical Data: Page Width: 268mm, Film: Digital, Type Area: 350 x 268mm, Col Length: 350mm, No. of Columns (Display): 9
Copy instructions: Copy Date: Thursday 4pm prior to publication date
Average advertising content per issue: 63%
Series owner and contact point for the following titles, see individual entries:
Bishop's Stortford Observer
Dunmow & Stansted Observer
Herts and Essex Star Classified
Supplement(s): Driving - 52xY, Homeworks - 4xY, Property - 52xY
LOCAL NEWSPAPERS: Local Newspapers English Counties

HERTS AND ESSEX STAR CLASSIFIED
718255U72B-1545_180

Frequency: Weekly - Published on Tuesday
Cover Price: Free
Circulation: 14,823 (VFD 03/07/2006 to 31/12/2006)
Editor: Sarosh Daruvala
Part of Series, see entry for: Herts & Essex Observer Series
LOCAL NEWSPAPERS: Local Newspapers English Counties

THE HERTS AND LEA VALLEY STAR
43799U72B-1525

Formerly: Hertfordshire Star
Editorial Address: The Media Centre, 40 Ware Road, HERTFORD, SG13 7HU **Tel:** 01992 526600
Fax: 01992 526645
Email: hertsstar@hertsessexnews.co.uk
Advertising Address: As above. **Fax:** 01992 526687
Email: advertising@hertsessexnews.co.uk
Web site: http://www.hertfordshiremercury.co.uk
Publisher: Herts & Essex Newspapers Ltd
Frequency: Weekly
Cover Price: Free
Circulation: 52,060 (ABC 14/05/2007 to 01/07/2007)
Usual Pagination: 64
Editor: Abigayle Barber; **News Editor:** Abigayle Barber;
Managing Director: Graham Ayres; **Advertising Manager:** Claire Estherby; **Publisher:** Ricky Allan
ADVERTISING RATES:
Full Page Mono £1858.50
Full Page Colour £2044.35
SCC £5.90
Agency Commission: 10%
Mechanical Data: Page Width: 268mm, Film: Digital, Type Area: 350 x 268mm, Col Length: 350mm, Col Widths (Display): 28mm, No. of Columns (Display): 9
Copy instructions: Copy Date: Tuesday noon prior to publication date
Average advertising content per issue: 75%
LOCAL NEWSPAPERS: Local Newspapers English Counties

HEXHAM COURANT
44168U72B-2530

Editorial Address: Beaumont Street, HEXHAM, NE46 3NA
Tel: 01434 602351 **Fax:** 01434 607872
Email: news@hexham-courant.co.uk

Advertising Address: As above.
Email: sandy.rutherford@hexham-courant.co.uk
Web site: http://www.hexham-courant.co.uk
Publisher: J. Catherall & Co (Printers) Ltd
Date Established: 1864
Frequency: Weekly - Published on Friday
Cover Price: £0.65
Circulation: 18,379 (ABC 02/07/2007 to 30/12/2007)
Editor: Brian Tilley; **Advertising Manager:** Sandy Rutherford
ADVERTISING RATES:
SCC £7.50
Agency Commission: 10%
Mechanical Data: Col Length: 540mm, Col Widths (Display): 37mm, No. of Columns (Display): 9, Film: Digital, Type Area: 540 x 366mm, Page Width: 366mm
Copy instructions: Copy Date: Tuesday 5.00pm prior to publication date
Average advertising content per issue: 50%
Supplement(s): Community Guide - 1xY, Environment - 1xY, Farm & Country - 2xY, Tynedale Visitor - 1xY, Tynedale Weddings - 2xY
LOCAL NEWSPAPERS: Local Newspapers English Counties

HEYWOOD ADVERTISER
43698U72B-1205

Editorial Address: Drake Street, ROCHDALE, OL16 1PH
Tel: 01706 360626 **Fax:** 01706 366711
Email: heywoodadvertiser@menwn.co.uk
Advertising Address: Wood Street, Hollywood, STOCKPORT, SK3 0AB **Tel:** 0161 480 4491
Fax: 0161 480 4837
Email: laura.norfolk@menmediasales.co.uk
Web site: http://www.heywoodadvertiser.co.uk
Publisher: MEN Media
Date Established: 1855
Frequency: Weekly - Published on Thursday
Cover Price: £0.49
Circulation: 6,999 (ABC 02/07/2007 to 30/12/2007)
Editor: Paul Harrison; **News Editor:** Emma Ferguson
ADVERTISING RATES:
Full Page Mono £948.60
Full Page Colour £1328.04
SCC £3.10
Agency Commission: 10%
Mechanical Data: Page Width: 267mm, Film: Digital, Type Area: 340 x 267mm, Col Length: 340mm, Col Widths (Display): 27mm, No. of Columns (Display): 9
Copy instructions: Copy Date: Tuesday 3.30pm prior to publication date
Average advertising content per issue: 60%
LOCAL NEWSPAPERS: Local Newspapers English Counties

HIGH PEAK COURIER
43469U72B-690_190

Frequency: Weekly - Circulation figure includes the Glossop Courier
Cover Price: Free
Circulation: 21,053 (VFD 02/07/2007 to 30/12/2007)
ADVERTISING: Rates on application
Part of Series, see entry for: Buxton Advertiser and Times Series
LOCAL NEWSPAPERS: Local Newspapers English Counties

HIGHLAND NEWS
44963U72D-540_150

Frequency: Weekly - Published on Thursday
Cover Price: £0.55
Circulation: 8,548 (ABC 01/01/2007 to 30/12/2007)
Part of Series, see entry for: Highland News Series
LOCAL NEWSPAPERS: Local Newspapers Scotland

HIGHLAND NEWS SERIES
44962U72D-540

Editorial Address: New Century House, Stadium Road, INVERNESS, IV1 1FG **Tel:** 01463 732222 **Fax:** 01463 732220
Email: newsdesk@highland-news.co.uk
Advertising Address: As above. **Fax:** 01463 732273
Email: ads@highland-news.co.uk
Web site: http://www.highland-news.co.uk
Publisher: Scottish Provincial Press
Date Established: 1883
Frequency: Weekly - Published on Thursday
Circulation: 26,799 (Combined Circulation)
Editor: Newsdesk; **Managing Director:** Roy Fox; **Group Editor:** Paul Breen
ADVERTISING RATES:
Full Page Mono £3966.40
Full Page Colour £5949.60
Agency Commission: 10%
Mechanical Data: Film: Digital, Col Length: 370mm, No. of Columns (Display): 8, Type Area: 370 x 276mm, Page Width: 276mm
Copy instructions: Copy Date: Tuesday 12.00pm prior to publication date

Section 4 (a) Newspapers

Series owner and contact point for the following titles, see individual entries:
Highland News
Inverness Herald
LOCAL NEWSPAPERS: Local Newspapers Scotland

THE HILLSBOROUGH AND DISTRICT JOURNAL
764746U72B-3712_135
Frequency: Weekly
Cover Price: Free
ADVERTISING RATES:
Full Page Mono £844.56
Full Page Colour £1097.93
SCC £2.76
Part of Series, see entry for: Sheffield Journal Series
LOCAL NEWSPAPERS: Local Newspapers English Counties

HINCKLEY HERALD & CLASSIFIED JOURNAL
44009U72B-2120_130
Formerly: Hinckley & South Leicestershire Herald & Journal
Email: hinckleytimes@mrn.co.uk
Web site: http://www.hinckley-times.co.uk
Frequency: Weekly - Published on Tuesday
Cover Price: Free
Circulation: 30,901 (VFD 02/07/2007 to 30/12/2007)
ADVERTISING: Rates on application
Part of Series, see entry for: The Hinckley Times & Herald Series
LOCAL NEWSPAPERS: Local Newspapers English Counties

THE HINCKLEY TIMES
762192U72B-2120_150
Frequency: Weekly - Published on Thursday
Cover Price: £0.52
Circulation: 15,868 (ABC 02/07/2007 to 30/12/2007)
ADVERTISING: Rates on application
Part of Series, see entry for: The Hinckley Times & Herald Series
LOCAL NEWSPAPERS: Local Newspapers English Counties

THE HINCKLEY TIMES & HERALD SERIES
44010U72B-2120
Formerly: The Hinckley Times
Editorial Address: Brunel Road, HINCKLEY, LE10 0AB
Tel: 01455 891965 **Fax:** 01455 891968
Email: hinckleytimes@mrn.co.uk
Advertising Address: As above. **Tel:** 01455 891678
Fax: 01455 632774
Email: retail_hinckley@mrn.co.uk
Web site: http://www.hinckley-times.co.uk
Publisher: Trinity Mirror
Frequency: Weekly - Published on Thursday
Circulation: 46,769 (Combined Circulation)
Editor: Ian Gallagher; **Advertising Manager:** Karen Goodall
ADVERTISING: Rates on application
Agency Commission: 10%
Copy instructions: Copy Date: 2 days prior to publication date
Average advertising content per issue: 40%
Series owner and contact point for the following titles, see individual entries:
Hinckley Herald & Classified Journal
The Hinckley Times
Supplement(s): The Guide - 52xY, Times Homes - 52xY
LOCAL NEWSPAPERS: Local Newspapers English Counties

HISTON AND IMPINGTON CRIER
761153U72B-350_173
Frequency: Monthly
Cover Price: Free
Circulation: 3,000 (Publisher's Statement)
ADVERTISING RATES:
SCC £7.10
Part of Series, see entry for: Cambridge Weekly News & Crier Series
LOCAL NEWSPAPERS: Local Newspapers English Counties

HODDESDON AND BROXBOURNE MERCURY
43809U72B-1560_120
Frequency: Weekly
Cover Price: £0.60
Circulation: 5,142 (Publisher's Statement)
Part of Series, see entry for: Mercury Series (Hoddesdon)
LOCAL NEWSPAPERS: Local Newspapers English Counties

HOLDERNESS ADVERTISER
44641U72B-3582_145
Frequency: Weekly - Published on Wednesday
Cover Price: Free
Circulation: 14,810 (VFD 02/07/2007 to 30/12/2007)
ADVERTISING RATES:
SCC £3.40
Part of Series, see entry for: Hull Advertiser Series
LOCAL NEWSPAPERS: Local Newspapers English Counties

HOLDERNESS GAZETTE
44635U72B-3578_140
Frequency: Weekly
Cover Price: £0.38
Circulation: 4,749 (ABC 03/07/2006 to 31/12/2006)
Part of Series, see entry for: Holderness Gazette Series
LOCAL NEWSPAPERS: Local Newspapers English Counties

HOLDERNESS GAZETTE SERIES
44634U72B-3578
Editorial Address: 1 Seaside Road, WITHERNSEA, HU19 2DL **Tel:** 01964 611587 **Fax:** 01964 615303
Email: news@holderness-gazette.co.uk
Advertising Address: As above. **Tel:** 01964 612777
Email: advertising@holderness-gazette.co.uk
Web site: http://www.holderness-gazette.co.uk
Publisher: Holderness Newspapers Ltd
Date Established: 1910
Frequency: Weekly - Published on Thursday
Circulation: 10,032 (Combined Circulation)
Usual Pagination: 48
Editor: Chris Leak; **Advertising Manager:** Cheryl Jones
ADVERTISING RATES:
Full Page Mono £660.00
Full Page Colour £826.00
SCC £2.36
Agency Commission: 10%
Mechanical Data: Type Area: 350 x 265mm, Col Length: 350mm, Page Width: 265mm, Col Widths (Display): 31mm, No. of Columns (Display): 8, Film: Digital
Copy instructions: Copy Date: Tuesday 5pm prior to publication date
Average advertising content per issue: 60%
Series owner and contact point for the following titles, see individual entries:
Holderness Gazette
Hornsea Gazette
Supplement(s): Holiday - 1xY
LOCAL NEWSPAPERS: Local Newspapers English Counties

THE HOLSWORTHY POST
43416U72B-520_150
Frequency: Weekly
Cover Price: £0.65
ADVERTISING RATES:
Full Page Mono £3360.00
Full Page Colour £3710.00
SCC £6.00
Mechanical Data: Type Area: 560 x 366mm, Col Length: 560mm, Col Widths (Display): 34mm, No. of Columns (Display): 10, Page Width: 366mm, Film: Digital
Part of Series, see entry for: Cornish & Devon Post Series
LOCAL NEWSPAPERS: Local Newspapers English Counties

HOLYHEAD ANGLESEY MAIL
44761U72C-70_170
Frequency: Weekly
Cover Price: £0.65
Circulation: 10,802 (ABC 02/07/2007 to 30/12/2007)
ADVERTISING RATES:
Full Page Mono £1224.00
Full Page Colour £1657.20
SCC £4.25
Part of Series, see entry for: The Caernarfon Herald Series
LOCAL NEWSPAPERS: Local Newspapers Wales

HOLYWOOD ADVERTISER
1668510U72E-286
Editorial Address: 99 Princess Gardens, HOLYWOOD, BT18 0PW **Tel:** 028 9042 7115
Email: b.johnston@spectatornewspapers.co.uk
Advertising Address: As above.
Email: b.johnston@spectatornewspapers.co.uk
Publisher: Holywood Advertiser
Date Established: 1983
Frequency: Monthly
Cover Price: Free
Circulation: 5,000 (Publisher's Statement)
Editor: Bernard Johnston; **Advertising Manager:** Bernard Johnston
ADVERTISING RATES:
Full Page Mono £500.00

Full Page Colour £600.00
SCC £3.00
Agency Commission: 15%
Mechanical Data: Type Area: 360 x 255mm, Col Length: 360mm, Page Width: 255mm, No. of Columns (Display): 7
Copy instructions: Copy Date: Middle of each month
Average advertising content per issue: 70%
LOCAL NEWSPAPERS: Local Newspapers Northern Ireland

HONITON ADVERTISER
1606274U72B-842_102
Frequency: Weekly - Circulation figure includes the Ottery Advertiser and Colyton Advertiser
Cover Price: £0.40
Circulation: 5,000 (Publisher's Statement)
Part of Series, see entry for: Pulmans Weekly News and Advertiser Series
LOCAL NEWSPAPERS: Local Newspapers English Counties

HORLEY & GATWICK MIRROR
44402U72B-3160_140
Formerly: Horley and Gatwick Mirror Charlwood Smallfield Gatwick
Frequency: Weekly
Cover Price: £0.40
Part of Series, see entry for: Surrey Mirror Series
LOCAL NEWSPAPERS: Local Newspapers English Counties

HORNCASTLE NEWS
44049U72B-2210
Editorial Address: Church Lane, HORNCASTLE, LN9 5HW
Tel: 01507 526868 **Fax:** 01507 522025
Email: sean.topham@jpress.co.uk
Advertising Address: As above. **Fax:** 01507 353201
Email: karen.griggs@jpress.co.uk
Web site: http://www.horncastlenews.co.uk
Publisher: Johnston Publishing Ltd
Date Established: 1885
Frequency: Weekly - Published on Wednesday
Cover Price: £0.42
Circulation: 5,450 (Publisher's Statement)
Usual Pagination: 32
Editor: Sean Topham; **Features Editor:** Alison Sandilands; **Advertising Manager:** Karen Griggs; **Managing Editor:** Tim Robinson
ADVERTISING RATES:
Full Page Mono £869.04
Full Page Colour £1129.70
Agency Commission: 10%
Mechanical Data: Type Area: 340 x 265mm, Col Length: 340mm, No. of Columns (Display): 9, Page Width: 265mm, Film: Digital
Copy instructions: Copy Date: Monday 12pm prior to publication date
Average advertising content per issue: 65%
LOCAL NEWSPAPERS: Local Newspapers English Counties

HORNCASTLE TARGET
44085U72B-2287_125
Formerly: Coningsby and Horncastle Target
Frequency: Weekly - Circulation figure includes the Skegness and Spilsby Target
Cover Price: Free
Circulation: 24,358 (VFD 02/07/2007 to 30/12/2007)
Part of Series, see entry for: Target Series
LOCAL NEWSPAPERS: Local Newspapers English Counties

HORNSEA & DISTRICT POST
44637U72B-3580
Editorial Address: Blundell's Corner, Beverley Road, HULL, HU3 1XS **Tel:** 01482 315183 **Fax:** 01482 217686
Email: advertiser@mailnewsmedia.co.uk
Advertising Address: 5A North Bar Within, BEVERLEY, HU17 8AP **Tel:** 01482 870777 **Fax:** 01482 872170
Email: p.jessop@mailnewsmedia.co.uk
Web site: http://www.thisishull.co.uk
Publisher: Mail News & Media Ltd
Date Established: 1987
Frequency: Monthly
Cover Price: Free
Circulation: 28,000 (Publisher's Statement)
Usual Pagination: 12
Editor: News Desk; **Advertising Manager:** Paula Jessop
ADVERTISING: Rates on application
LOCAL NEWSPAPERS: Local Newspapers English Counties

HORNSEA GAZETTE
44636U72B-3578_150
Frequency: Weekly
Cover Price: £0.38

Circulation: 5,283 (Publisher's Statement)
Part of Series, see entry for: Holderness Gazette Series
LOCAL NEWSPAPERS: Local Newspapers English Counties

HORNSEY & CROUCH END JOURNAL
43071U72A-240_140

Frequency: Weekly - Circulation figure includes Muswell Hill Journal
Cover Price: £0.40
Circulation: 5,877 (ABC 02/07/2007 to 30/12/2007)
ADVERTISING RATES:
SCC £10.00
Part of Series, see entry for: Islington Gazette & Journal Series
LOCAL NEWSPAPERS: Local Newspapers Greater London

HORSHAM ADVERTISER
44472U72B-3328_160

Formerly: Horsham & Storrington Advertiser
Frequency: Weekly
Cover Price: Free
Circulation: 33,200 (Publisher's Statement)
Mechanical Data: Type Area: 340 x 277mm, Col Length: 340mm, Page Width: 277mm, Col Widths (Display): 29mm, No. of Columns (Display): 9, Screen: 40 lpc, Film: Digital
Copy instructions: Copy Date: Friday prior to publication date
Part of Series, see entry for: West Sussex County Times Series
LOCAL NEWSPAPERS: Local Newspapers English Counties

HOUGHTON STAR
44493U72B-3371_125

Frequency: Weekly
Cover Price: Free
Circulation: 10,944 (VFD 02/07/2007 to 30/12/2007)
ADVERTISING RATES:
SCC £4.48
Part of Series, see entry for: Star Series
LOCAL NEWSPAPERS: Local Newspapers English Counties

HOUNSLOW & BRENTFORD TIMES
43127U72A-510_120

Formerly: Brentford, Chiswick & Isleworth Times including Hounslow, Feltham & Hanworth
Frequency: Weekly - See Richmond & Twickenham Times for circulation figure
Cover Price: £0.45
Usual Pagination: 80
Part of Series, see entry for: Times Series (Richmond)
LOCAL NEWSPAPERS: Local Newspapers Greater London

HOUNSLOW CHRONICLE
43097U72A-320

Formerly: Hounslow Chronicle Series
Editorial Address: 93 Staines Road, HOUNSLOW, TW3 3JB
Tel: 020 8572 1816 **Fax:** 020 8741 1973
Email: newshounslow@trinitysouth.co.uk
Advertising Address: 2 High Street, TEDDINGTON, TW11
NEW **Tel:** 020 8943 5171 **Fax:** 020 8977 7741
Email: nslsales@trinitysouth.co.uk
Web site: http://www.hounslowchronicle.co.uk
Publisher: North Surrey and London Newspapers
Frequency: Weekly - Published on Friday
Cover Price: £0.50
Circulation: 60,000 (Publisher's Statement)
Usual Pagination: 52
Editor: Adrian Seal; **Advertising Manager:** Jenny Dash
ADVERTISING: Rates on application
Agency Commission: 10%
LOCAL NEWSPAPERS: Local Newspapers Greater London

HUCKNALL & BULWELL DISPATCH
44182U72B-2600

Editorial Address: Yorke Street, HUCKNALL, NG15 7BT
Tel: 0115 953 6552 **Fax:** 0115 953 6551
Email: newsdesk@hucknall-dispatch.co.uk
Advertising Address: As above. **Tel:** 01623 450229
Fax: 0115 953 6550
Email: haroldine.lockwood@chad.co.uk
Web site: http://www.hucknalldispatch.co.uk
Publisher: Wilfred Edmunds
Date Established: 1903
Frequency: Weekly - Published on Friday
Cover Price: £0.40
Circulation: 8,426 (ABC 02/07/2007 to 30/12/2007)
Editor: Richard Silverwood; **News Editor:** Richard Silverwood; **Features Editor:** Richard Silverwood;
Advertising Manager: Haroldine Lockwood

ADVERTISING RATES:
Full Page Mono £1358.64
Agency Commission: 10%
Mechanical Data: Col Widths (Display): 27mm, Page Width: 268mm, Col Length: 350mm, No. of Columns (Display): 9, Type Area: 350 x 268mm
Copy instructions: Copy Date: Wednesday 12pm prior to publication date
Average advertising content per issue: 60%
LOCAL NEWSPAPERS: Local Newspapers English Counties

HUDDERSFIELD DAILY EXAMINER
42073U67B-280

Editorial Address: PO Box A26, Queen Street South, HUDDERSFIELD, HD1 2TD **Tel:** 01484 430000
Fax: 01484 437789
Email: editorial@examiner.co.uk
Advertising Address: As above. **Fax:** 01484 437730
Email: anne.barrett@examiner.co.uk
Web site: http://www.examiner.co.uk
Publisher: Trinity Mirror
Frequency: Evenings - Not published on Sunday
Cover Price: £0.46
Circulation: 25,898 (Publisher's Statement)
Editor: News Desk; **News Editor:** Neil Atkinson; **Executive Editor:** Michael O'Connell; **Advertising Manager:** Anne Barrett
ADVERTISING RATES:
SCC £6.56
Agency Commission: 10%
Mechanical Data: Film: Digital, Type Area: 342 x 272mm, Col Length: 342mm, No. of Columns (Display): 8, Page Width: 272mm
Copy instructions: Copy Date: 5pm 2 days prior to publication date
Supplement(s): Express & Chronicle - 52xY, Fresh - 52xY, Motors - 52xY, Property - 52xY
REGIONAL DAILY & SUNDAY NEWSPAPERS: Regional Daily Newspapers

THE HULL ADVERTISER (EAST)
44642U72B-3582_150

Frequency: Weekly - Published on Thursday
Cover Price: Free
Circulation: 39,622 (VFD 02/07/2007 to 30/12/2007)
ADVERTISING RATES:
SCC £6.30
Part of Series, see entry for: Hull Advertiser Series
LOCAL NEWSPAPERS: Local Newspapers English Counties

HULL ADVERTISER SERIES
44638U72B-3582

Editorial Address: Blundell's Corner, Beverley Road, HULL, HU3 1XS **Tel:** 01482 315184
Email: advertiser@mailnewsmedia.co.uk
Advertising Address: As above. **Tel:** 01482 327111
Fax: 01482 315485
Email: s.howes@mailnewsmedia.co.uk
Web site: http://www.thisishullandeastriding.co.uk
Publisher: Mail News & Media Ltd
Frequency: Weekly - Published on Wednesday and Thursday
Cover Price: Free
Circulation: 136,869 (Combined Circulation)
Editor: John Meehan; **Managing Director:** Phil Inman; **Advertising Manager:** Sarah Howes
ADVERTISING RATES:
Full Page Mono £4435.20
Full Page Colour £5543.70
Agency Commission: 10%
Mechanical Data: Col Length: 360mm, Page Width: 268mm, Type Area: 360 x 268mm, No. of Columns (Display): 8, Film: Digital, Col Widths (Display): 28mm, Print Process: Web-fed offset litho
Copy instructions: Copy Date: Friday 4pm prior to publication date
Average advertising content per issue: 70%
Series owner and contact point for the following titles, see individual entries:
Beverley Advertiser
East Riding Advertiser
Holderness Advertiser
The Hull Advertiser (East)
The Hull Advertiser (West)
LOCAL NEWSPAPERS: Local Newspapers English Counties

THE HULL ADVERTISER (WEST)
44643U72B-3582_160

Frequency: Weekly - Published on Thursday
Cover Price: Free
Circulation: 34,836 (VFD 02/07/2007 to 30/12/2007)

ADVERTISING RATES:
SCC £6.30
Part of Series, see entry for: Hull Advertiser Series
LOCAL NEWSPAPERS: Local Newspapers English Counties

HULL DAILY MAIL
42074U67B-290

Editorial Address: Blundell's Corner, Beverley Road, HULL, HU3 1XS **Tel:** 01482 327111 **Fax:** 01482 315353
Email: news@mailnewsmedia.co.uk
Advertising Address: As above. **Tel:** 01482 315388
Email: a.malton@mailnewsmedia.co.uk
Web site: http://www.thisishullandeastriding.co.uk
Publisher: Mail News & Media Ltd
Frequency: Daily
Cover Price: £0.38
Circulation: 59,689 (ABC 01/01/2007 to 01/07/2007)
Editor: Rick Lyon; **News Editor:** Rick Lyon; **Features Editor:** Bryan Marshall; **Managing Director:** Phil Inman; **Advertising Manager:** Amanda Malton
ADVERTISING RATES:
Full Page Mono £4204.80
Full Page Colour £5256.00
Agency Commission: 10%
Mechanical Data: Type Area: 360 x 268mm, Col Length: 360mm, Col Widths (Display): 31mm, No. of Columns (Display): 8, Film: Digital, Page Width: 268mm
Copy instructions: Copy Date: Mono 5pm 2 days prior Colour 5pm 3 days prior to publication date
Average advertising content per issue: 60%
Editions:
East Riding Mail
Hull Daily Mail (Final)
Supplement(s): The Business - 52xY, Drive - 52xY, Femail - 52xY, The Guide - 52xY, Home - 52xY, Hot Shots - 52xY
REGIONAL DAILY & SUNDAY NEWSPAPERS: Regional Daily Newspapers

HULL DAILY MAIL (FINAL)
42075U67B-290_521

Frequency: Evenings
Edition of: Hull Daily Mail
REGIONAL DAILY & SUNDAY NEWSPAPERS: Regional Daily Newspapers

HUNTINGDON WEEKLY NEWS
43320U72B-350_175

Frequency: Weekly
Cover Price: Free
Circulation: 14,681 (Publisher's Statement)
ADVERTISING RATES:
SCC £3.45
Part of Series, see entry for: Cambridge Weekly News & Crier Series
LOCAL NEWSPAPERS: Local Newspapers English Counties

HUNTLY EXPRESS
44967U72D-550

Editorial Address: 9 Gordon Street, HUNTLY, AB54 8AJ
Tel: 01466 793622 **Fax:** 01466 794994
Email: mail@huntlyexpress.co.uk
Advertising Address: As above.
Email: mail@huntlyexpress.co.uk
Publisher: J & M Publishing
Date Established: 1863
Frequency: Weekly
Cover Price: £0.45
Circulation: 3,300 (Publisher's Statement)
Usual Pagination: 16
Editor: Pat Scott; **News Editor:** Pat Scott
ADVERTISING RATES:
Full Page Mono £500.00
Full Page Colour £600.00
Agency Commission: 10%
Mechanical Data: Page Width: 263mm, Col Widths (Display): 33mm, No. of Columns (Display): 7, Film: Digital, Type Area: 370 x 263mm, Col Length: 370mm
Copy instructions: Copy Date: Wednesday 12.30pm prior to publication date
Average advertising content per issue: 40%
LOCAL NEWSPAPERS: Local Newspapers Scotland

THE HUNTS POST
43331U72B-390

Formerly: The Hunts Post Series
Editorial Address: 30 High Street, HUNTINGDON, PE29 3TB **Tel:** 01480 411481 **Fax:** 01480 443446
Email: editor@huntspost.co.uk
Advertising Address: As above. **Fax:** 01480 433316
Email: lesley.godfrey@archant.co.uk
Web site: http://www.huntspost24.co.uk
Publisher: Archant Herts & Cambs
Date Established: 1870
Frequency: Weekly
Cover Price: £0.75

Non-National Newspapers

Free to qualifying individuals
Circulation: 48,786 (VFD 02/07/2007 to 30/12/2007)
Editor: Andy Veale; **Managing Director:** Stuart McCreery;
Advertising Manager: Lesley Godfrey
ADVERTISING RATES:
Full Page Mono £2037.96
Full Page Colour £2650.32
Agency Commission: 10%
Mechanical Data: Trim Size: 360 x 263mm
Copy instructions: Copy Date: Monday 5pm prior to publication date
LOCAL NEWSPAPERS: Local Newspapers English Counties

HYTHE HERALD
43877U72B-1750_150
Frequency: Weekly
Cover Price: £0.55
ADVERTISING: Rates on application
Part of Series, see entry for: Adscene, Herald & Express Series (Folkestone)
LOCAL NEWSPAPERS: Local Newspapers English Counties

ILEACH
754745U72D-553
Editorial Address: Main Street, BOWMORE, PA43 7JH
Tel: 01496 810355 **Fax:** 01496 810647
Email: editor@ileach.co.uk
Advertising Address: As above.
Email: ileach@ileach.co.uk
Web site: http://www.ileach.co.uk
Publisher: Ileach
Date Established: 1973
Frequency: 26 issues yearly
Cover Price: £0.85
Circulation: 2,500 (Publisher's Statement)
Editor: Carl Reavey; **Advertising Manager:** Alison MacTaggart
Language(s): English; Gaelic
ADVERTISING RATES:
Full Page Mono £239.00
Mechanical Data: Trim Size: 420 x 297mm, Film: Digital
Copy instructions: Copy Date: Tuesday noon prior to publication date
LOCAL NEWSPAPERS: Local Newspapers Scotland

ILFORD RECORDER
43066U72A-230_170
Formerly: Ilford Recorder (Wanstead/Woodford)
Frequency: Weekly
Cover Price: £0.50
Part of Series, see entry for: Ilford Recorder Series
LOCAL NEWSPAPERS: Local Newspapers Greater London

ILFORD RECORDER SERIES
43063U72A-230
Editorial Address: Media House, 539 High Road, ILFORD, IG1 1UD **Tel:** 020 8477 3800 **Fax:** 020 8477 3801
Email: newsdesk@ilfordrecorder.co.uk
Advertising Address: As above. **Tel:** 020 8478 4444
Fax: 020 8477 3710
Email: graham.willis@archant.co.uk
Web site: http://www.ilfordrecorder.co.uk
Publisher: Archant East London & Essex
Date Established: 1898
Frequency: Weekly - Published on Thursday
Circulation: 15,074 (ABC 02/07/2007 to 30/12/2007)
Usual Pagination: 106
Editor: Sally Lowe; **News Editor:** Sally Lowe; **Advertising Manager:** Graham Willis
ADVERTISING RATES:
Full Page Mono £2835.00
Full Page Colour £3035.00
SCC £9.00
Agency Commission: 10%
Mechanical Data: Type Area: 350 x 267mm, Col Length: 350mm, Col Widths (Display): 27mm, No. of Columns (Display): 9, Film: Digital, Page Width: 267mm
Copy instructions: Copy Date: Tuesday noon prior to publication date
Average advertising content per issue: 60%
Series owner and contact point for the following titles, see individual entries:
Barking & Dagenham Recorder
Ilford Recorder
LOCAL NEWSPAPERS: Local Newspapers Greater London

ILKESTON ADVERTISER
43494U72B-730
Formerly: Ilkeston Advertiser and Erewash Valley Weekly News
Editorial Address: 8 Heanor Road, ILKESTON, DE7 8ER
Tel: 0115 944 6160 **Fax:** 0115 944 4990
Email: news@ilkestonadvertiser.co.uk
Advertising Address: As above.
Email: deborah.beeley@derbyshiretimes.co.uk
Web site: http://www.ilkestonadvertiser.co.uk

Publisher: Johnston Press plc
Date Established: 1800
Frequency: Weekly
Cover Price: £0.40
Circulation: 8,488 (ABC 02/07/2007 to 30/12/2007)
Editor: News Desk; **Advertising Manager:** Deborah Beeley
ADVERTISING RATES:
Full Page Mono £918.00
Full Page Colour £1193.40
SCC £3.00
Agency Commission: 10%
Mechanical Data: Type Area: 306 x 271mm, No. of Columns (Display): 9, Col Length: 306mm, Page Width: 271mm, Col Widths (Display): 28mm, Film: Digital
Copy instructions: Copy Date: Tuesday 12pm prior to publication date
Average advertising content per issue: 40%
LOCAL NEWSPAPERS: Local Newspapers English Counties

ILKESTON EXPRESS
43479U72B-695_170
Frequency: Weekly
Cover Price: Free
Part of Series, see entry for: Derby Express and Messenger Series
LOCAL NEWSPAPERS: Local Newspapers English Counties

ILKLEY GAZETTE
44706U72B-3795
Editorial Address: 8 Wells Road, ILKLEY, LS29 9JD
Tel: 01943 603483 **Fax:** 01943 604583
Email: paul.l@wharfedalenewspapers.co.uk
Advertising Address: As above. **Fax:** 01943 816224
Email: gemma.aldersley@wharfedale.newsquest.co.uk
Web site: http://www.ilkleygazette.co.uk
Publisher: Newsquest Yorkshire and North East (Bradford)
Date Established: 1861
Frequency: Weekly - Published on Thursday
Cover Price: £0.75
Circulation: 5,860 (ABC 02/07/2007 to 30/12/2007)
Editor: Paul Langan; **Managing Director:** Charles Birrell
ADVERTISING RATES:
Full Page Mono £2257.80
Full Page Colour £2826.72
SCC £3.87
Agency Commission: 10%
Mechanical Data: Type Area: 530 x 346mm, Col Length: 530mm, No. of Columns (Display): 12, Page Width: 346mm, Col Widths (Display): 27mm, Film: Digital
Copy instructions: Copy Date: Tuesday 12pm prior to publication date
Average advertising content per issue: 40%
LOCAL NEWSPAPERS: Local Newspapers English Counties

IMPARTIAL REPORTER
45098U72E-140
Formerly: Impartial Reporter & Farmers' Journal (Enniskillen)
Editorial Address: 8-10 East Bridge Street, ENNISKILLEN, BT74 7BT **Tel:** 028 6632 4422 **Fax:** 028 6632 5047
Email: dmcdaniel@impartialreporter.com
Advertising Address: As above. **Tel:** 028 6632 4425
Fax: 028 6632 5969
Email: jclarke@impartialreporter.com
Web site: http://www.impartialreporter.com
Publisher: William Trimble Ltd
Date Established: 1825
Frequency: Weekly - Published on Thursday
Cover Price: £0.85
Circulation: 14,444 (ABC 02/07/2007 to 30/12/2007)
Editor: Denzil McDaniel; **Advertising Manager:** June Clarke; **Managing Editor:** Denzil McDaniel
ADVERTISING RATES:
Full Page Mono £1944.00
Full Page Colour £2444.00
SCC £4.00
Agency Commission: 10%
Mechanical Data: Col Length: 540mm, Page Width: 345mm, Film: Digital, No. of Columns (Display): 9, Col Widths (Display): 35mm, Type Area: 540 x 345mm
Copy instructions: Copy Date: Monday 5.30pm prior to publication date
Average advertising content per issue: 40%
LOCAL NEWSPAPERS: Local Newspapers Northern Ireland

INDEPENDENT BARNSLEY
44673U72B-3670_160
Frequency: Weekly - Published on Tuesday
Cover Price: Free
Circulation: 78,949 (VFD 09/07/2007 to 30/12/2007)
ADVERTISING RATES:
SCC £4.50
Part of Series, see entry for: Barnsley Chronicle & Independent Series
LOCAL NEWSPAPERS: Local Newspapers English Counties

THE INDEPENDENT BASINGSTOKE
1749199U72B-1400_102
Frequency: Weekly
Cover Price: Free
Circulation: 14,000 (Publisher's Statement)
ADVERTISING RATES:
SCC £5.50
Part of Series, see entry for: The Independent Observer Series
LOCAL NEWSPAPERS: Local Newspapers English Counties

THE INDEPENDENT OBSERVER SERIES
754778U72B-1400
Formerly: The Observer Independent Series
Editorial Address: 20 Moorside Road, WINCHESTER, SO23 7RX **Tel:** 01962 859559 **Fax:** 01962 870957
Email: winchobs@aol.com
Advertising Address: Suite 20, Cavendish Centre, WINCHESTER, SO23 0LB **Tel:** 01962 859559
Fax: 01962 870957
Email: rich@observerrecruitment.co.uk
Web site: http://www.hantsdirect.com
Publisher: Hampshire Media Ltd
Frequency: Weekly - Published on Thursday
Cover Price: Free
Circulation: 14,000 (Combined Circulation)
Editor: Mark O'Connor
ADVERTISING RATES:
SCC £9.00
Agency Commission: 10%
Mechanical Data: Film: Digital, Page Width: 262mm, Col Length: 340mm, Col Widths (Display): 31mm, No. of Columns (Display): 8, Type Area: 340 x 262mm
Copy instructions: Copy Date: Tuesday 1pm prior to publication date
Series owner and contact point for the following titles, see individual entries:
The Independent Basingstoke
The Mid Hampshire Observer
The West Hampshire Observer
LOCAL NEWSPAPERS: Local Newspapers English Counties

INDEPENDENT SERIES (GLOUCESTERSHIRE)
43663U72B-1144
Editorial Address: Reliance House, Long Street, DURSLEY, GL11 4LS **Tel:** 01453 544000 **Fax:** 01453 540208
Email: gazette.news@dursleygazette.co.uk
Advertising Address: As above. **Fax:** 01453 540212
Web site: http://www.gazetteseries.co.uk
Publisher: Newsquest (Media Group) Ltd
Date Established: 1985
Frequency: Weekly
Cover Price: Free
Circulation: 47,848 (VFD 01/01/2007 to 01/07/2007)
Usual Pagination: 64
Editor: Skip Walker; **Managing Director:** Gavin Stacey; **Publisher:** Trevor Sallis
ADVERTISING RATES:
SCC £5.50
Mechanical Data: Film: Digital, Col Length: 340mm, Col Widths (Display): 27mm, Page Width: 259mm, No. of Columns (Display): 9, Type Area: 340 x 259mm
Copy instructions: Copy Date: Monday 4pm prior to publication date
Series owner and contact point for the following titles, see individual entries:
Gloucestershire Independent Cheltenham Edition
Gloucestershire Independent Gloucester Edition
Gloucestershire Independent South of Gloucestershire Edition
LOCAL NEWSPAPERS: Local Newspapers English Counties

INFORMER (KINGSTON)
43067U72A-232_120
Frequency: Weekly
Cover Price: Free
Circulation: 51,007 (VFD 02/07/2007 to 30/12/2007)
Part of Series, see entry for: Informer Series (Kingston)
LOCAL NEWSPAPERS: Local Newspapers Greater London

INFORMER (RICHMOND & TWICKENHAM)
629714U72A-232_150
Publisher: South News plc
Frequency: Weekly
Cover Price: Free
Circulation: 46,236 (VFD 02/07/2007 to 30/12/2007)
Part of Series, see entry for: Informer Series (Kingston)
LOCAL NEWSPAPERS: Local Newspapers Greater London

INFORMER SERIES (KINGSTON)

43068U72A-232

Editorial Address: 93 Staines Road, HOUNSLOW, TW3 3JB
Tel: 020 8572 1816 **Fax:** 020 8741 1973
Email: newskingston@trinitysouth.co.uk
Advertising Address: Informer House, 2 High Street, TEDDINGTON, TW11 8EW **Tel:** 020 8943 5171
Fax: 020 8977 7741
Email: nslsales@trinitysouth.co.uk
Publisher: Trinity Mirror Southern
Frequency: Weekly - Published on Friday
Cover Price: Free
Circulation: 95,129 (Combined Circulation)
Editor: Daniel Lyons; **News Editor:** Daniel Lyons;
Advertising Manager: Niki Hornsby
ADVERTISING RATES:
Full Page Mono £3147.04
Full Page Colour £3933.80
SCC £11.57
Agency Commission: 10%
Mechanical Data: Col Length: 340mm, Col Widths (Display): 31mm, No. of Columns (Display): 8, Print Process: Web offset, Type Area: 340 x 262mm, Page Width: 262mm, Film: Digital
Copy instructions: Copy Date: Tuesday 4.00pm prior to publication date
Average advertising content per issue: 52%
Series owner and contact point for the following titles, see individual entries:
Informer (Kingston)
Informer (Richmond & Twickenham)
LOCAL NEWSPAPERS: Local Newspapers Greater London

INTERNATIONAL HERALD TRIBUNE

41859U65G-150

Editorial Address: 1 New Oxford Street, LONDON, WC1A 1NU **Tel:** 020 7061 3500 **Fax:** 020 7061 3529
Email: iht@iht.com
Advertising Address: As above.
Email: sadams@iht.com
Web site: http://www.iht.com
ISSN: 0294-8052
Publisher: International Herald Tribune
Frequency: Mornings - Published Monday to Saturday
Cover Price: £1.30
Circulation: 242,182 (Publisher's Statement)
Executive Editor: Alison Smale; **Managing Editor:** Tom Redburn
Summary of Content: News content: General news, business and financial, arts, leisure, entertainment, fashion, new technology and the internet.
Readership/Target Audience: International business readers and decision makers.
ADVERTISING RATES:
Full Page Mono $78985.00
Full Page Colour $96985.00
Agency Commission: 15%
Mechanical Data: No. of Columns (Display): 6, Col Widths (Display): 53mm, Type Area: 530 x 337mm, Film: Digital, Col Length: 530mm, Page Width: 337mm
Copy instructions: Copy Date: Mono 5 days prior to publication date Colour 5 days prior to publication date
NATIONAL DAILY & SUNDAY NEWSPAPERS: International Daily Newspapers

INVERCLYDE EXTRA

44895U72D-253

Formerly: Clyde Post
Editorial Address: 2 Crawfurd Street, GREENOCK, PA15 1LH **Tel:** 01475 726511 **Fax:** 01475 783734
Email: editorial@greenocktelegraph.co.uk
Advertising Address: As above.
Email: advertising@greenocktelegraph.co.uk
Publisher: Clyde & Forth Press Group
Frequency: Weekly - Published every Wednesday
Cover Price: Free
Circulation: 18,979 (VFD 09/07/2007 to 30/12/2007)
Editor: Wendy Metcalfe
ADVERTISING RATES:
Full Page Mono £1734.00
Full Page Colour £2601.00
SCC £7.30
Agency Commission: 10%
Mechanical Data: Film: Positive, right reading, emulsion side down, Col Widths (Display): 30mm, Print Process: Web-fed offset litho, Screen: 40 lpc, Col Length: 330mm, No. of Columns (Display): 8, Type Area: 330 x 266mm, Page Width: 266mm
Copy instructions: Copy Date: Thursday 4pm prior to publication date
Average advertising content per issue: 66%
LOCAL NEWSPAPERS: Local Newspapers Scotland

INVERNESS COURIER (FRIDAY)

44970U72D-560_140

Frequency: Weekly
Cover Price: £0.70
Circulation: 17,609 (ABC 01/01/2007 to 30/12/2007)
ADVERTISING RATES:
Full Page Mono £6517.50
Full Page Colour £9776.00
SCC £11.85
Copy instructions: Copy Date: Tuesday 12.00 noon prior to publication dates
Part of Series, see entry for: Inverness Courier Series
LOCAL NEWSPAPERS: Local Newspapers Scotland

INVERNESS COURIER SERIES

44968U72D-560

Editorial Address: New Century House, Stadium Road, INVERNESS, IV1 1FG **Tel:** 01463 233059 **Fax:** 01463 243439
Email: editorial@inverness-courier.co.uk
Advertising Address: As above. **Fax:** 01463 238223
Email: sales@inverness-courier.co.uk
Web site: http://www.inverness-courier.co.uk
Publisher: Scottish Provincial Press
Frequency: 104 issues yearly - Published bi-weekly
Circulation: 30,383 (ABC 01/01/2007 to 30/12/2007)
Usual Pagination: 36
Editor: Helen Patterson; **News Editor:** Helen Patterson;
Features Editor: Callum Macloud; **Advertising Manager:** Trish Gunn
ADVERTISING RATES:
Full Page Mono £9150.00
Full Page Colour £13725
SCC £16.55
Agency Commission: 10%
Mechanical Data: Col Widths (Display): 35mm, No. of Columns (Display): 10
Average advertising content per issue: 70%
Series owner and contact point for the following titles, see individual entries:
Inverness Courier (Friday)
Inverness Courier (Tuesday)
LOCAL NEWSPAPERS: Local Newspapers Scotland

INVERNESS COURIER (TUESDAY)

44969U72D-560_120

Frequency: Weekly
Cover Price: £0.55
Circulation: 12,774 (ABC 01/01/2007 to 30/12/2007)
ADVERTISING RATES:
Full Page Mono £6517.50
Full Page Colour £9776.00
SCC £11.85
Copy instructions: Copy Date: Thursday 12.00 noon prior to publication date
Part of Series, see entry for: Inverness Courier Series
LOCAL NEWSPAPERS: Local Newspapers Scotland

INVERNESS HERALD

44964U72D-540_155

Formerly: Inverness & Nairn Herald
Frequency: Weekly - Published on Friday
Cover Price: Free
Circulation: 18,132 (VFD 01/01/2007 to 01/07/2007)
Part of Series, see entry for: Highland News Series
LOCAL NEWSPAPERS: Local Newspapers Scotland

INVERURIE ADVERTISER

44862U72D-10_160

Frequency: Weekly
Cover Price: £0.49
ADVERTISING RATES:
Full Page Mono £490.00
SCC £2.25
Part of Series, see entry for: Advertiser Series in Aberdeenshire
LOCAL NEWSPAPERS: Local Newspapers Scotland

INVERURIE HERALD

44971U72D-568

Editorial Address: 15B High Street, INVERURIE, AB51 3QA
Tel: 01467 625150 **Fax:** 01467 622251
Email: heraldnews@inverurieherald.com
Advertising Address: As above.
Email: heraldadverts@inverurieherald.com
Web site: http://www.inverurieherald.com
Publisher: Angus County Press Ltd
Date Established: 1989
Frequency: Weekly - Circulation figure is incorporated into the Deeside Piper and Herald Series
Cover Price: £0.40
Circulation: 9,000 (Publisher's Statement)
Usual Pagination: 40
Editor: David Duncan
ADVERTISING RATES:
SCC £4.80

Mechanical Data: No. of Columns (Display): 7, Col Widths (Display): 36mm, Film: Digital
Copy instructions: Copy Date: Monday 3pm prior to publication date
Average advertising content per issue: 50%
LOCAL NEWSPAPERS: Local Newspapers Scotland

IPSWICH ADVERTISER

1655664U72B-3078_100

Frequency: Weekly
Cover Price: Free
Circulation: 66,826 (VFD 02/07/2007 to 30/12/2007)
Part of Series, see entry for: Advertiser Series (Ipswich)
LOCAL NEWSPAPERS: Local Newspapers English Counties

THE IRISH NEWS

42272U67B-2390

Editorial Address: 113-117 Donegall Street, BELFAST, BT1 2GE **Tel:** 028 9032 2226 **Fax:** 028 9033 7505
Email: newsdesk@irishnews.com
Advertising Address: As above. **Fax:** 028 9033 7508
Email: s.higgins@irishnews.com
Web site: http://www.irishnews.com
Publisher: Irish News Ltd
Date Established: 1891
Frequency: Mornings
Cover Price: £0.70
Circulation: 47,790 (ABC 02/07/2007 to 30/12/2007)
Editor: Noel Doran; **News Editor:** Billy Foley; **Features Editor:** William Scholes; **Managing Director:** Dominic Fitzpatrick
ADVERTISING RATES:
SCC £11.50
Agency Commission: 15%
Mechanical Data: Film: Digital, Col Length: 340mm, Type Area: 340 x 265mm, No. of Columns (Display): 8, Col Widths (Display): 30.5mm, Page Width: 265mm
Copy instructions: Copy Date: 2 days prior to publication date
Average advertising content per issue: 40%
REGIONAL DAILY & SUNDAY NEWSPAPERS: Regional Daily Newspapers

THE IRVINE HERALD AND KILWINNING CHRONICLE

44972U72D-570

Editorial Address: 19 Bank Street, IRVINE, KA12 0AJ
Tel: 01294 272233 **Fax:** 01294 202072
Email: irvineherald@s-un.co.uk
Advertising Address: 34 Mackintosh Place, South Newmoor Industrial Estate, IRVINE, KA11 4JY
Tel: 01294 222288 **Fax:** 01294 213982
Email: pre-press@s-un.co.uk
Web site: http://www.icayrshire.co.uk
Publisher: Scottish and Universal Newspapers Hamilton
Date Established: 1872
Frequency: Weekly
Cover Price: £0.70
Circulation: 10,490 (ABC 02/07/2007 to 30/12/2007)
Usual Pagination: 130
Editor: Lex Brown; **News Editor:** Lex Brown; **Advertising Manager:** Sheena Thomson
ADVERTISING RATES:
Full Page Mono £1346.40
Full Page Colour £1817.64
SCC £5.94
Agency Commission: 10%
Mechanical Data: Type Area: 340 x 265mm, Col Length: 340mm, Page Width: 265mm, Col Widths (Display): 27mm, No. of Columns (Display): 9
Copy instructions: Copy Date: Monday 5pm prior to publication date
Average advertising content per issue: 50%
LOCAL NEWSPAPERS: Local Newspapers Scotland

IRVINE TIMES

44973U72D-575

Editorial Address: 43 Bank Street, IRVINE, KA12 0LL
Tel: 01294 273421 **Fax:** 01294 277719
Email: editorial.it@cfpress.co.uk
Advertising Address: As above.
Email: advertising.it@cfpress.co.uk
Web site: http://www.irvinetimes.com
Publisher: Clyde & Forth Press Group
Frequency: Weekly - Published on Wednesday
Cover Price: £0.50
Circulation: 3,599 (ABC 01/01/2007 to 30/12/2007)
Usual Pagination: 48
Editor: Billy Bain
ADVERTISING RATES:
Full Page Mono £902.88
Full Page Colour £1354.32
SCC £3.42
Agency Commission: 10%
Mechanical Data: Col Length: 330mm, No. of Columns (Display): 8, Type Area: 330 x 266mm, Page Width: 266mm, Col Widths (Display): 30mm, Film: Digital

Non-National Newspapers

Section 4 (a) Newspapers

Copy instructions: Copy Date: Monday 12pm prior to publication date
Average advertising content per issue: 50%
LOCAL NEWSPAPERS: Local Newspapers Scotland

THE ISLAND TIMES
43638U72B-1079_130

Frequency: Monthly
Cover Price: Free
Circulation: 15,000 (Publisher's Statement)
ADVERTISING RATES:
Full Page Mono £275.00
Full Page Colour £400.00
SCC £5.00
Part of Series, see entry for: Leigh Times Series
LOCAL NEWSPAPERS: Local Newspapers English Counties

ISLE OF MAN COURIER
45143U72G-10_120

Frequency: Weekly - Published on Thursday
Cover Price: Free
Circulation: 36,318 (VFD 02/07/2007 to 30/12/2007)
Mechanical Data: Col Length: 340mm, No. of Columns (Display): 9, Col Widths (Display): 28mm, Type Area: 340 x 268mm, Page Width: 268mm, Film: Digital
Part of Series, see entry for: Isle of Man Newspapers
LOCAL NEWSPAPERS: Local Newspapers Isle of Man

ISLE OF MAN EXAMINER
45144U72G-10_140

Frequency: Weekly - Published on Tuesday
Cover Price: £0.50
Circulation: 13,276 (ABC 02/07/2007 to 30/12/2007)
Mechanical Data: Col Length: 540mm, Page Width: 328mm, No. of Columns (Display): 11, Type Area: 540 x 328mm, Film: Digital, Col Widths (Display): 28mm
Part of Series, see entry for: Isle of Man Newspapers
LOCAL NEWSPAPERS: Local Newspapers Isle of Man

ISLE OF MAN NEWSPAPERS
45142U72G-10

Formerly: Isle of Man Courier Series
Editorial Address: Publishing House, Peel Road, DOUGLAS, IM1 5PZ **Tel:** 01624 695695 **Fax:** 01624 611149
Email: newsdesk@newsiom.co.im
Advertising Address: As above. **Tel:** 01624 695608
Fax: 01624 661041
Email: ads@newsiom.co.im
Web site: http://www.iomtoday.co.im
Publisher: Johnston Press plc
Frequency: Weekly
Circulation: 61,849 (Combined Circulation)
Editor: Paul Speller; **News Editor:** Paul Speller; **Advertising Manager:** Gen Hicks
ADVERTISING RATES:
SCC £10.02
Agency Commission: 10%
Average advertising content per issue: 70%
Series owner and contact point for the following titles, see individual entries:
Isle of Man Courier
Isle of Man Examiner
Manx Independent
Supplement(s): Outlook Magazine - 12xY
LOCAL NEWSPAPERS: Local Newspapers Isle of Man

ISLE OF THANET GAZETTE MARGATE, RAMSGATE, BROADSTAIRS
43883U72B-1830_150

Frequency: Weekly - Published on Friday
Cover Price: £0.40
Circulation: 14,077 (ABC 02/07/2007 to 30/12/2007)
ADVERTISING: Rates on application
Part of Series, see entry for: Isle of Thanet Gazette Series
LOCAL NEWSPAPERS: Local Newspapers English Counties

ISLE OF THANET GAZETTE SERIES
43880U72B-1830

Editorial Address: Suite 1, 3rd Floor, Mill Lane House, Mill Lane, MARGATE, CT9 1JU **Tel:** 01843 578150
Fax: 01843 578170
Email: newsdesk.thanet@krnmedia.co.uk
Advertising Address: As above.
Email: sales.thanet@kentregionalnewspapers.co.uk
Web site: http://www.thisiskent.co.uk
Publisher: Kent Regional News and Media
Date Established: 1869
Frequency: Weekly
Circulation: 74,337 (Combined Circulation)
Editor: Rebecca Smith; **Advertising Manager:** Erika Osborne
ADVERTISING: Rates on application

Mechanical Data: Film: Digital, Page Width: 262mm, Type Area: 340 x 262mm, Col Length: 340mm, No. of Columns (Display): 8, Col Widths (Display): 34mm
Series owner and contact point for the following titles, see individual entries:
Adscene (Thanet)
Isle of Thanet Gazette Margate, Ramsgate, Broadstairs
Thanet Times
Supplement(s): Daytripper - 1xY, Exclusively Yours - 4xY, Motors - 52xY, Property - 52xY, Wedding - 2xY
LOCAL NEWSPAPERS: Local Newspapers English Counties

ISLE OF WIGHT COUNTY PRESS
43836U72B-1710

Editorial Address: Brannon House, 123 Pyle Street, NEWPORT, PO30 1ST **Tel:** 01983 522210
Fax: 01983 528920
Email: editor@iwcp2.demon.co.uk
Advertising Address: As above. **Tel:** 01983 521333
Fax: 01983 527204
Email: adman@iwcpress.demon.co.uk
Web site: http://www.iwcp.co.uk
Publisher: Isle of Wight County Press Ltd
Date Established: 1884
Frequency: Weekly - Published on Friday
Cover Price: £0.65
Circulation: 38,492 (ABC 02/07/2007 to 30/12/2007)
Usual Pagination: 60
Editor: Suzanne Pert; **News Editor:** Suzanne Pert; **Features Editor:** Mary McBride; **Managing Director:** Robin Freeman
ADVERTISING RATES:
Full Page Mono £1780.00
Full Page Colour £2136.00
SCC £3.94
Agency Commission: 10%
Mechanical Data: Col Length: 580mm, Col Widths (Display): 37mm, Film: Digital, No. of Columns (Display): 9, Type Area: 580 x 365mm, Page Width: 365mm
Copy instructions: Copy Date: Monday prior to publication date
Average advertising content per issue: 60%
LOCAL NEWSPAPERS: Local Newspapers English Counties

THE ISLE OF WIGHT GAZETTE
1923841U72B-4164

Editorial Address: Unit 18, Spithead Business Centre, Newport Road, Sandown, ISLE OF WIGHT, PO36 9PH
Tel: 01983 402599 **Fax:** 01983 404819
Email: newsdesk@iwgazette.co.uk
Frequency: Weekly
Cover Price: Free
Editor: Jason Kay; **Features Editor:** Jo Macaulay
Summary of Content: Newspaper covering news and features from the Isle of Wight. The newspaper raises money for a local charity called The Mount Batten Hospice.
Readership/Target Audience: Aimed at people of all ages across the Isle of Man.
LOCAL NEWSPAPERS: Local Newspapers English Counties

ISLINGTON GAZETTE
43073U72A-240_180

Formerly: Islington Gazette & Stoke Newington Observer
Frequency: Weekly - Circulation figure includes Islington Gazette EC1
Cover Price: £0.40
Circulation: 10,992 (ABC 02/07/2007 to 30/12/2007)
ADVERTISING RATES:
SCC £15.00
Part of Series, see entry for: Islington Gazette & Journal Series
LOCAL NEWSPAPERS: Local Newspapers Greater London

ISLINGTON GAZETTE & JOURNAL SERIES
43069U72A-240

Editorial Address: 161 Tottenham Lane, LONDON, N8 9BU
Tel: 020 8342 5777 **Fax:** 020 8342 5730
Email: nlnews@archant.co.uk
Advertising Address: As above. **Tel:** 020 8342 5700
Fax: 020 8342 5720
Email: melanie.balban@archant.co.uk
Web site: http://www.islingtongazette.co.uk
Publisher: Archant London
Date Established: 1856
Frequency: Weekly
Circulation: 52,062 (Combined Circulation)
Editor: Tony Allcock; **Advertising Manager:** Melanie Balban; **Group Editor:** Tony Allcock
ADVERTISING: Rates on application
Mechanical Data: Col Widths (Display): 26.5 mm, No. of Columns (Display): 9, Type Area: 265 x 247.5mm, Col Length: 265mm, Page Width: 247.5mm, Film: Digital

Copy instructions: Copy Date: Tuesday 12 noon prior to publication date
Series owner and contact point for the following titles, see individual entries:
Camden Gazette
Hornsey & Crouch End Journal
Islington Gazette
Islington Gazette EC
Muswell Hill Journal
Tottenham, Wood Green & Edmonton Journal
Supplement(s): Trends - 4xY
LOCAL NEWSPAPERS: Local Newspapers Greater London

ISLINGTON GAZETTE EC1
719347U72A-240_183

Frequency: Weekly - Circulation figure is incorporated into the Islington Gazette
Cover Price: £0.40
ADVERTISING RATES:
SCC £15.00
Part of Series, see entry for: Islington Gazette & Journal Series
LOCAL NEWSPAPERS: Local Newspapers Greater London

ISLINGTON TRIBUNE
1638698U72A-242_181

Frequency: Weekly
Cover Price: Free
Circulation: 17,340 (ABC 02/01/2006 to 02/07/2006)
Summary of Content: Newspaper covering news and events in Islington.
Readership/Target Audience: Aimed at people interested in everyday's life and living in this area.
ADVERTISING: Rates on application
Part of Series, see entry for: Journal Series
LOCAL NEWSPAPERS: Local Newspapers Greater London

IVYBRIDGE & SOUTH BRENT GAZETTE
43539U72B-854_130

Formerly: Ivybridge, South Brent & South Hams Gazette
Frequency: Weekly
Cover Price: £0.35
Part of Series, see entry for: South Hams Newspapers Group
LOCAL NEWSPAPERS: Local Newspapers English Counties

JERSEY EVENING POST
42278U67B-2450

Editorial Address: PO Box 582, Five Oaks, St. Saviour, JERSEY, JE4 8XQ **Tel:** 01534 611611 **Fax:** 01534 611622
Email: editorial@jerseyeveningpost.com
Advertising Address: As above. **Tel:** 01534 611699
Email: advertising@jerseyeveningpost.com
Web site: http://www.thisisjersey.com
Publisher: Jersey Evening Post Ltd
Date Established: 1890
Frequency: Evenings - Not published on Sunday
Cover Price: £0.45
Circulation: 21,100 (ABC 02/07/2007 to 30/12/2007)
Editor: Chris Bright; **News Editor:** Carl Walker; **Features Editor:** Anna Plunkett-Cole; **Managing Director:** Jerry Ramsden
ADVERTISING RATES:
SCC £11.97
Mechanical Data: Page Width: 262mm, Type Area: 400 x 262mm, Col Length: 400mm, No. of Columns (Display): 7, Film: Digital
Supplement(s): The Week - 52xY
REGIONAL DAILY & SUNDAY NEWSPAPERS: Regional Daily Newspapers

JOHN O'GROAT JOURNAL
44977U72D-580_180

Formerly: John O'Groat Journal and Weekly Advertiser
Frequency: Weekly - Published on Friday
Cover Price: £0.68
Circulation: 8,761 (ABC 01/01/2007 to 30/12/2007)
ADVERTISING RATES:
Full Page Mono £2200.00
Full Page Colour £2860.00
SCC £4.00
Part of Series, see entry for: John O'Groat Journal Series
LOCAL NEWSPAPERS: Local Newspapers Scotland

JOHN O'GROAT JOURNAL SERIES
44975U72D-580

Editorial Address: 42 Union Street, WICK, KW1 5ED
Tel: 01955 602424 **Fax:** 01955 604822
Email: editor@nosn.co.uk
Advertising Address: As above.
Email: advertising@nosn.co.uk
Web site: http://www.johnogroat-journal.co.uk
Publisher: North of Scotland Newspapers
Frequency: Weekly - Published on Wednesday and Friday

Circulation: 15,717 (Combined Circulation)
Editor: Karen Steven; **Advertising Manager:** Sheona Campbell
ADVERTISING RATES:
Full Page Mono £3300.00
Full Page Colour £4290.00
SCC £7.80
Agency Commission: 10%
Mechanical Data: Type Area: 550 x 377mm, Col Length: 550mm, Col Widths (Display): 35mm, No. of Columns (Display): 10, Page Width: 377mm, Film: Digital
Copy instructions: Copy Date: Monday 10am prior to publication date
Series owner and contact point for the following titles, see individual entries:
Caithness Courier
John O'Groat Journal
Supplement(s): Caithness Property Journal - 12xY, Home Improvements - 2xY
LOCAL NEWSPAPERS: Local Newspapers Scotland

JOURNAL & ADVERTISER SERIES

44195U72B-2659

Formerly: Times Today Series
Editorial Address: Unit 3, Grove House, Bridgford Road, West Bridgford, NOTTINGHAM, NG2 6AP
Tel: 0115 981 4043 **Fax:** 0115 945 5893
Email: editorial@nottinghamjournal.com
Advertising Address: As above. **Tel:** 0115 981 5020
Email: melanie.lupton@nottinghamjournal.com
Publisher: JPC Group
Frequency: Weekly - Published on Thursday and Friday
Cover Price: Free
Circulation: 30,000 (Combined Circulation)
Usual Pagination: 12
Editor: Ed Palmer; **Features Editor:** Rob Macpherson; **Managing Director:** Philip Cound
ADVERTISING RATES:
Full Page Mono £2288.00
Agency Commission: 10%
Mechanical Data: Type Area: 360 x 262mm, Col Length: 360mm, No. of Columns (Display): 8, Page Width: 262mm, Film: Digital, Col Widths (Display): 30mm
Copy instructions: Copy Date: Monday prior to publication date
Average advertising content per issue: 50%
Series owner and contact point for the following titles, see individual entries:
The Lancashire Advertiser
Nottingham & Trent Valley Journal
LOCAL NEWSPAPERS: Local Newspapers English Counties

THE JOURNAL (CITY EDITION) (NEWCASTLE)

42128U67B-430_505

Frequency: Mornings
Edition of: The Journal (Newcastle)
REGIONAL DAILY & SUNDAY NEWSPAPERS: Regional Daily Newspapers

THE JOURNAL (CUMBRIA, TEESIDE AND THE BORDERS)

42129U67B-430_510

Formerly: The Journal (Cumbria, Borders, Teeside and Co. Durham)
Frequency: Mornings
Edition of: The Journal (Newcastle)
REGIONAL DAILY & SUNDAY NEWSPAPERS: Regional Daily Newspapers

THE JOURNAL (DURHAM)

758398U67B-430_520

Frequency: Mornings
Edition of: The Journal (Newcastle)
REGIONAL DAILY & SUNDAY NEWSPAPERS: Regional Daily Newspapers

JOURNAL EXTRA

44489U72B-3362_200

Formerly: Chronicle Extra Northumberland
Frequency: Weekly
Cover Price: Free
Circulation: 70,773 (VFD 03/07/2006 to 31/12/2006)
ADVERTISING RATES:
SCC £7.95
Part of Series, see entry for: Chronicle Extra Series (Tyne & Wear)
LOCAL NEWSPAPERS: Local Newspapers English Counties

THE JOURNAL (HAMBLE VALLEY)

43753U72B-1378_160

Formerly: Hamble Valley Journal
Frequency: Weekly
Cover Price: Free
Circulation: 11,688 (VFD 01/11/2004 to 02/01/2005)
Part of Series, see entry for: Journal Series Portsmouth
LOCAL NEWSPAPERS: Local Newspapers English Counties

THE JOURNAL (NEWCASTLE)

42127U67B-430

Editorial Address: Groat Market, NEWCASTLE UPON TYNE, NE1 1ED **Tel:** 0191 232 7500 **Fax:** 0191 201 6044
Email: jnl.newsdesk@ncjmedia.co.uk
Advertising Address: As above. **Fax:** 0191 230 4144
Email: callcentre@ncjmedia.co.uk
Web site: http://www.journallive.com
Publisher: NCJ Media Ltd
Frequency: Mornings
Cover Price: £0.50
Circulation: 35,476 (ABC 02/07/2007 to 30/12/2007)
Editor: Jon Tunney; **News Editor:** Jon Tunney; **Managing Director:** Steve Brown; **Advertising Manager:** Jack Ford
ADVERTISING RATES:
Full Page Mono £4018.00
Full Page Colour £7118.55
Mechanical Data: Type Area: 350 x 278mm, Col Length: 350mm, Page Width: 278mm, Film: Digital, No. of Columns (Display): 8
Editions:
The Journal (City Edition) (Newcastle)
The Journal (Cumbria, Teeside and the Borders)
The Journal (Durham)
The Journal (Northumberland)
The Journal (Tyneside)
The Journal (Wearside)
Supplement(s): Culture - 12xY, Executive Motoring - 52xY, Homemaker - 52xY, Northern Business - 52xY, Racing Plus - 52xY, Weekend - 52xY
REGIONAL DAILY & SUNDAY NEWSPAPERS: Regional Daily Newspapers

THE JOURNAL (NORTHUMBERLAND)

42130U67B-430_560

Frequency: Mornings
Edition of: The Journal (Newcastle)
REGIONAL DAILY & SUNDAY NEWSPAPERS: Regional Daily Newspapers

THE JOURNAL RHYL, PRESTATYN AND ABERGELE

44801U72C-215

Editorial Address: 23 Kinmel Street, RHYL, LL18 1AH
Tel: 01745 357500 **Fax:** 01745 343510
Email: editor@rhyljournal.co.uk
Advertising Address: As above.
Email: admanager@rhyljournal.co.uk
Web site: http://www.rhyljournal.co.uk
Publisher: NWN Media Ltd
Frequency: Weekly - Published on Wednesday
Cover Price: Free
Circulation: 30,287 (VFD 02/07/2007 to 30/12/2007)
Editor: Terry Canty; **Advertising Manager:** Mandy Ellis
ADVERTISING RATES:
SCC £5.35
Agency Commission: 10%
Mechanical Data: Page Width: 259mm, Type Area: 370 x 259mm, Col Length: 370mm, Col Widths (Display): 27mm, No. of Columns (Display): 9, Film: Digital
Copy instructions: Copy Date: Monday 1pm prior to publication date
Average advertising content per issue: 70%
LOCAL NEWSPAPERS: Local Newspapers Wales

JOURNAL SERIES

43076U72A-242

Editorial Address: 40 Camden Road, LONDON, NW1 9DR
Tel: 020 7419 9000 **Fax:** 020 7482 7317
Email: editorial@camdennewjournal.co.uk
Advertising Address: As above. **Fax:** 020 7209 1322
Email: aharding@camdennewjournal.co.uk
Web site: http://www.thecnj.com
Publisher: New Journal Enterprises Ltd
Date Established: 1982
Frequency: Weekly - Published on Thursday and Friday
Cover Price: Free
Circulation: 101,283 (Combined Circulation)
Usual Pagination: 48
Editor: Richard Osley; **News Editor:** Richard Osley; **Advertising Manager:** Alan Harding
ADVERTISING: Rates on application
Agency Commission: 10%
Mechanical Data: Type Area: 340 x 259mm, Col Length: 340mm, Page Width: 259mm, Film: Digital, No. of Columns (Display): 7, Col Widths (Display): 34mm

Copy instructions: Copy Date: Monday 5pm prior to publication date
Series owner and contact point for the following titles, see individual entries:
Camden New Journal
Islington Tribune
West End Extra
Supplement(s): The Review - 52xY
LOCAL NEWSPAPERS: Local Newspapers Greater London

JOURNAL SERIES (CARMARTHEN)

44776U72C-220

Formerly: Carmarthen Journal incorporating The Welshman
Editorial Address: 18 King Street, CARMARTHEN, SA31 1BN **Tel:** 01267 227222 **Fax:** 01267 227229
Email: journal.star@swwmedia.co.uk
Advertising Address: As above. **Fax:** 01267 227256
Email: eirlys.peck@swwmedia.co.uk
Web site: http://www.thisiscarmarthenshire.co.uk
Publisher: South West Wales Media Ltd
Date Established: 1810
Frequency: Weekly - Published on Wednesday
Cover Price: £0.55
Circulation: 20,800 (ABC 02/07/2007 to 30/12/2007)
Editor: Cathryn Ings; **Managing Director:** Blanche Sainsbury
Language(s): English; Welsh
ADVERTISING RATES:
Full Page Mono £1711.00
SCC £5.40
Agency Commission: 15%
Mechanical Data: Col Length: 360mm, Col Widths (Display): 32mm, No. of Columns (Display): 8, Type Area: 360 x 270mm, Film: Digital, Page Width: 270mm
Copy instructions: Copy Date: Monday 12 noon prior to publication date
Series owner and contact point for the following titles, see individual entries:
Cardigan Journal
Carmarthen Journal
Gwendraeth Journal
Llandovery Journal
Llandysul Journal
St. Clears & Whitland Journal
LOCAL NEWSPAPERS: Local Newspapers Wales

THE JOURNAL SERIES (EXMOUTH)

43504U72B-810

Editorial Address: Fair Oak Close, Exeter Airport Business Park, Clyst Honiton, EXETER, EX5 2UL **Tel:** 01392 888505
Fax: 01392 888499
Email: exmouth.editorial@archant.co.uk
Advertising Address: As above. **Tel:** 01392 888444
Fax: 01392 888470
Email: stacey.hughes2@archant.co.uk
Web site: http://www.exmouthjournal.co.uk
Publisher: Archant South West
Frequency: Weekly
Circulation: 9,140 (Combined Circulation)
Editor: Phil Griffin; **Advertising Manager:** Stacey Hughes
ADVERTISING: Rates on application
Agency Commission: 10%
Mechanical Data: Col Length: 365mm, Type Area: 365 x 270mm, Col Widths (Display): 27mm, Page Width: 270mm, No. of Columns (Display): 9
Copy instructions: Copy Date: Tuesday 3pm prior to publication date
Average advertising content per issue: 40%
Series owner and contact point for the following titles, see individual entries:
The Budleigh Journal
Exmouth Herald
The Exmouth Journal
LOCAL NEWSPAPERS: Local Newspapers English Counties

JOURNAL SERIES PORTSMOUTH

43751U72B-1378

Editorial Address: The News Centre, Hilsea, PORTSMOUTH, PO2 9SX **Tel:** 023 9266 4488
Fax: 023 9267 3363
Email: newsdesk@thenews.co.uk
Advertising Address: As above. **Fax:** 023 9269 0544
Email: rob.thomas@thenews.co.uk
Web site: http://www.portsmouth.co.uk
Publisher: Portsmouth Publishing & Printing Ltd
Frequency: Weekly - Published on Thursday
Cover Price: Free
Circulation: 136,795 (VFD 02/07/2007 to 30/12/2007)
Editor: Graeme Patfield; **News Editor:** Graeme Patfield; **Features Editor:** Simon Toft; **Managing Director:** Gary Fearon
ADVERTISING RATES:
Full Page Mono £4097.34
Full Page Colour £5326.54
Agency Commission: 10%

Section 4 (a) Newspapers

Mechanical Data: Col Widths (Display): 29mm, Col Length: 340mm, No. of Columns (Display): 9, Page Width: 277mm, Type Area: 340 x 277mm, Film: Digital
Copy instructions: Copy Date: 3 days prior to publication date
Average advertising content per issue: 65%
Series owner and contact point for the following titles, see individual entries:
Fareham & Gosport Journal
Havant & Waterlooville Journal
The Journal (Hamble Valley)
Portsmouth & Southsea Journal
LOCAL NEWSPAPERS: Local Newspapers English Counties

THE JOURNAL (TYNESIDE) 42131U67B-430_610
Frequency: Mornings
Edition of: The Journal (Newcastle)
REGIONAL DAILY & SUNDAY NEWSPAPERS: Regional Daily Newspapers

---

THE JOURNAL (WEARSIDE) 42132U67B-430_630
Frequency: Mornings
Edition of: The Journal (Newcastle)
REGIONAL DAILY & SUNDAY NEWSPAPERS: Regional Daily Newspapers

---

KEIGHLEY NEWS 44708U72B-3810_140
Tel: 01535 606611
Frequency: Weekly - Published on Friday
Cover Price: £0.65
Circulation: 14,894 (ABC 02/07/2007 to 30/12/2007)
ADVERTISING: Rates on application
Part of Series, see entry for: Keighley News Series
LOCAL NEWSPAPERS: Local Newspapers English Counties

KEIGHLEY NEWS SERIES 44707U72B-3810
Editorial Address: 80-86 North Street, KEIGHLEY, BD21 3AG **Tel:** 01535 606611 **Fax:** 01535 210444
Email: alistair.shand@keighleynews.co.uk
Advertising Address: As above.
Email: kym.hall@bradford.newsquest.co.uk
Web site: http://www.keighleynews.co.uk
Publisher: Newsquest Yorkshire and North East (Bradford)
Date Established: 1864
Frequency: Weekly - Published on Wednesday and Thursday
Circulation: 39,727 (Combined Circulation)
Editor: Alistair Shand; **News Editor:** Alistair Shand;
Advertising Manager: Kym Hall
ADVERTISING: Rates on application
Agency Commission: 10%
Copy instructions: Copy Date: Tuesday 5pm prior to publication date
Series owner and contact point for the following titles, see individual entries:
Keighley News
Keighley Target
LOCAL NEWSPAPERS: Local Newspapers English Counties

KEIGHLEY TARGET 44709U72B-3810_160
Formerly: Keighley News Midweek
Frequency: Weekly - Published on Friday. Circulation figure includes the Craven Target
Cover Price: Free
Circulation: 24,833 (VFD 02/07/2007 to 30/12/2007)
ADVERTISING: Rates on application
Part of Series, see entry for: Keighley News Series
LOCAL NEWSPAPERS: Local Newspapers English Counties

KENILWORTH OBSERVER 44507U72B-3382_130
Frequency: Weekly
Cover Price: Free
ADVERTISING: Rates on application
Part of Series, see entry for: Leamington & Stratford Observer Series
LOCAL NEWSPAPERS: Local Newspapers English Counties

KENILWORTH TIMES 1698077U72B-3964_100
Formerly: Kenilworth Citizen
Frequency: Weekly - Published on Thursday
Cover Price: Free
Circulation: 50,913 (VFD 02/07/2007 to 30/12/2007)

Part of Series, see entry for: Times Series (Coventry, Leamington, Warwick & Kenilworth)
LOCAL NEWSPAPERS: Local Newspapers English Counties

KENILWORTH WEEKLY NEWS 44505U72B-3386_201
Web site: http://www.kenilworthonline.co.uk
Frequency: Weekly - Published on Friday
Cover Price: £0.42
Circulation: 3,727 (ABC 02/07/2007 to 30/12/2007)
Part of Series, see entry for: Leamington Spa Courier Series
LOCAL NEWSPAPERS: Local Newspapers English Counties

THE KENNETT & NORTH WILTSHIRE STAR 43735U72B-3540_130
Formerly: Devizes, Melksham, Vale of Pewsey & Marlborough News
Frequency: Weekly - Published on Wednesday
Cover Price: Free
Circulation: 23,889 (VFD 02/07/2007 to 30/12/2007)
Part of Series, see entry for: Wiltshire Gazette and Herald Series
LOCAL NEWSPAPERS: Local Newspapers English Counties

KENSINGTON & CHELSEA NEWS 43089U72A-300_170
Frequency: Weekly - Published on Thursday. For circulation see Fulham & Hammersmith Chronicle
Cover Price: £0.45
ADVERTISING RATES:
SCC £13.93
Copy instructions: Copy Date: Tuesday 4pm prior to publication date
Part of Series, see entry for: London Newspaper Group Series
LOCAL NEWSPAPERS: Local Newspapers Greater London

KENSINGTON AND CHELSEA TIMES 1641186U72A-1314
Editorial Address: 112 Barnfield Avenue, KINGSTON ON THAMES, KL2 5RT **Tel:** 020 8549 7811 **Fax:** 020 8541 0077
Email: kensingtonnews@btconnect.com
Advertising Address: As above.
Email: kensingtonnews@btconnect.com
Publisher: Westminster Times Ltd
Frequency: Monthly
Cover Price: Free
Circulation: 30,000 (Publisher's Statement)
Usual Pagination: 24
Editor: Catherine Farrell; **Features Editor:** Katya Kan;
Advertising Manager: Oscar Conrad; **Publisher:** Oscar Conrad
ADVERTISING RATES:
Full Page Colour £800.00
Agency Commission: 15%
Mechanical Data: Page Width: 260mm, Type Area: 350 x 260mm, Col Length: 350mm, Trim Size: 380 x 289mm
Copy instructions: Copy Date: 3 days prior to publication date
Average advertising content per issue: 50%
LOCAL NEWSPAPERS: Local Newspapers Greater London

KENT & SUSSEX COURIER SERIES 43895U72B-1835
Editorial Address: Longfield Road, TUNBRIDGE WELLS, TN2 3HL **Tel:** 01892 681000 **Fax:** 01892 510400
Email: editor@courier.co.uk
Advertising Address: As above. **Fax:** 01892 543181
Email: lucy.farrant@courier.co.uk
Web site: http://www.thisiscourier.co.uk
Publisher: Courier Media Group Ltd
Frequency: Weekly
Circulation: 110,491 (Combined Circulation)
Editor: John McCready; **Editor-in-Chief:** John McCready;
Managing Director: Richard Karn
ADVERTISING RATES:
SCC £9.40
Agency Commission: 10%
Mechanical Data: Type Area: 360 x 270mm, Col Length: 360mm, Film: Digital, No. of Columns (Display): 8, Print Process: Web-fed offset litho, Page Width: 270mm
Average advertising content per issue: 60%
Series owner and contact point for the following titles, see individual entries:
Courier (East Sussex)
Courier (Edenbridge)
Courier (Paddock Wood)

Courier (Tonbridge)
Courier (Tunbridge Wells)
Courier (Weald)
Focus (West Kent, East Sussex)
LOCAL NEWSPAPERS: Local Newspapers English Counties

KENT MESSENGER GROUP NEWSPAPERS 43885U72B-1840
Formerly: Kent Messenger Extra Series
Editorial Address: 6-7 Middle Row, MAIDSTONE, ME14 1TG **Tel:** 01622 695666 **Fax:** 01622 7664988
Email: messengernews@thekmgroup.co.uk
Advertising Address: Messenger House, New Hythe Lane, Larkfield, AYLESFORD, ME20 6SG **Tel:** 01622 717880
Fax: 01622 719637
Email: rdadson@thekmgroup.co.uk
Web site: http://www.kentmessenger.co.uk
Publisher: Kent Messenger Group
Frequency: Weekly - Published on Friday
Circulation: 116,430 (Combined Circulation)
Editor: News Desk
ADVERTISING: Rates on application
Agency Commission: 10%
Mechanical Data: Page Width: 276mm, Type Area: 340 x 276mm, Col Length: 340mm, No. of Columns (Display): 8, Col Widths (Display): 31mm, Film: Digital
Copy instructions: Copy Date: Wednesday 5pm prior to publication date
Average advertising content per issue: 50%
Series owner and contact point for the following titles, see individual entries:
Extra (Maidstone, Mid-Kent)
Kent Messenger (Maidstone)
Kent Messenger (Malling & District)
Kent Messenger (Weald)
Sittingbourne Extra
LOCAL NEWSPAPERS: Local Newspapers English Counties

KENT MESSENGER (MAIDSTONE) 43887U72B-1840_160
Frequency: Weekly - Circulation figure includes the Kent Messenger (Malling & District), Kent Messenger (Medway Towns) and Kent Messenger (Weald)
Cover Price: £0.70
Circulation: 51,810 (ABC 02/07/2007 to 30/12/2007)
ADVERTISING RATES:
Full Page Mono £3685.60
Full Page Colour £4607.00
Part of Series, see entry for: Kent Messenger Group Newspapers
LOCAL NEWSPAPERS: Local Newspapers English Counties

KENT MESSENGER (MALLING & DISTRICT) 43888U72B-1840_170
Frequency: Weekly
Cover Price: £0.70
ADVERTISING RATES:
Full Page Mono £3685.60
Full Page Colour £4607.00
Part of Series, see entry for: Kent Messenger Group Newspapers
LOCAL NEWSPAPERS: Local Newspapers English Counties

KENT MESSENGER (WEALD) 43889U72B-1840_180
Formerly: Kent Messenger (Weald & Tunbridge Wells)
Frequency: Weekly
Cover Price: £0.60
ADVERTISING RATES:
Full Page Mono £3685.50
Full Page Colour £4607.00
Part of Series, see entry for: Kent Messenger Group Newspapers
LOCAL NEWSPAPERS: Local Newspapers English Counties

KENT ON SATURDAY 1666933U72B-3963
Formerly: Kentish Saturday Observer
Editorial Address: KoS Media Ltd, Apple Barn, Hythe Road, Smeeth, ASHFORD, TN25 6SR **Tel:** 01303 817000
Fax: 01303 817002
Email: editorial@kosmedia.co.uk
Advertising Address: As above. **Fax:** 01303 817001
Email: advertising@kosmedia.co.uk
Web site: http://www.kentnews.co.uk
ISSN: 1745-9451
Publisher: Kos Media Ltd
Date Established: 2005

Frequency: Weekly
Cover Price: Free
Circulation: 40,000 (Publisher's Statement)
Editor: News Desk; **Advertising Manager:** Ynez Coton
ADVERTISING RATES:
SCC £16.48
Agency Commission: 10%
Mechanical Data: Type Area: 360 x 268mm, Col Length: 360mm, Page Width: 268mm, Col Widths (Display): 30mm, No. of Columns (Display): 8, Film: Digital
Average advertising content per issue: 50%
LOCAL NEWSPAPERS: Local Newspapers English Counties

KENT ON SUNDAY
767054U67C-101

Editorial Address: Apple Barn, Smeeth, ASHFORD, TN25 6SR **Tel:** 01303 817000 **Fax:** 01303 817002
Email: editorial@kosmedia.co.uk
Advertising Address: As above. **Fax:** 01303 817001
Email: advertising@kosmedia.co.uk
Web site: http://www.kentnews.co.uk
Publisher: Kos Media Ltd
Frequency: Sunday
Cover Price: Free
Circulation: 2,370 (Publisher's Statement)
Editor: Ian Patel; **Managing Director:** Paul Stannard; **Advertising Manager:** Mary Hopper
ADVERTISING RATES:
SCC £9.20
Agency Commission: 10%
Mechanical Data: Page Width: 268mm, Col Length: 360mm, No. of Columns (Display): 8, Type Area: 360 x 268mm, Film: Digital, Col Widths (Display): 30mm
Copy instructions: Copy Date: Wednesday 5pm prior to publication date
Average advertising content per issue: 50%
Supplement(s): Creative Appointments - 52xY, Exclusive and New Homes - 52xY, Review on Sunday - 52xY, Sunday Motoring - 52xY
REGIONAL DAILY & SUNDAY NEWSPAPERS: Regional Sunday Newspapers

KENTISH EXPRESS ASHFORD AND DISTRICT
43868U72B-1795_150

Frequency: Weekly - Circulation figure is incorporated into the Kentish Express Folkestone
Cover Price: £0.45
Part of Series, see entry for: Express Extra Series Kent
LOCAL NEWSPAPERS: Local Newspapers English Counties

KENTISH EXPRESS FOLKESTONE
43869U72B-1795_170

Formerly: Folkestone Express
Frequency: Weekly - Circulation figure includes Kentish Express Ashford and District; Kentish Express (Hythe and Romney Marsh); Kentish Express (Tenterden)
Cover Price: £0.45
Circulation: 22,733 (ABC 02/07/2007 to 30/12/2007)
Part of Series, see entry for: Express Extra Series Kent
LOCAL NEWSPAPERS: Local Newspapers English Counties

KENTISH EXPRESS HYTHE AND ROMNEY MARSH
43870U72B-1795_175

Frequency: Weekly - Circulation figure is incorporated into the Kentish Express Folkestone
Cover Price: £0.45
Part of Series, see entry for: Express Extra Series Kent
LOCAL NEWSPAPERS: Local Newspapers English Counties

KENTISH EXPRESS TENTERDEN
43871U72B-1795_180

Frequency: Weekly - Circulation figure is incorporated into the Kentish Express Folkestone
Cover Price: £0.45
Part of Series, see entry for: Express Extra Series Kent
LOCAL NEWSPAPERS: Local Newspapers English Counties

KENTISH GAZETTE CANTERBURY AND DISTRICT
43905U72B-1870_150

Frequency: Weekly - Circulation figure includes the Whitstable Gazette
Cover Price: £0.45
Circulation: 17,767 (ABC 02/07/2007 to 30/12/2007)
Part of Series, see entry for: Kentish Gazette Series
LOCAL NEWSPAPERS: Local Newspapers English Counties

KENTISH GAZETTE SERIES
43902U72B-1870

Editorial Address: Gazette House, 5-8 Boorman Way, Estuary View Business Park, WHITSTABLE, CT5 3SE
Tel: 01227 768181 **Fax:** 01227 762415
Email: kentishgazette@thekmgroup.co.uk
Advertising Address: As above. **Fax:** 01227 762327
Email: cwatson@thekmgroup.co.uk
Web site: http://www.kentishgazette.co.uk
Publisher: Kent Messenger Group
Date Established: 1717
Frequency: Weekly
Circulation: 25,591 (ABC 02/07/2007 to 30/12/2007)
Editor: News Desk; **Advertising Manager:** Caroline Watson
ADVERTISING RATES:
SCC £7.45
Agency Commission: 10%
Mechanical Data: Page Width: 276mm, Film: Digital, Col Length: 340mm, Col Widths (Display): 31mm, No. of Columns (Display): 8, Type Area: 340 x 276mm
Copy instructions: Copy Date: Tuesday 5pm prior to publication date
Average advertising content per issue: 60%
Series owner and contact point for the following titles, see individual entries:
Faversham News
Herne Bay Gazette
Kentish Gazette Canterbury and District
Whitstable Gazette
Supplement(s): Homes - 52xY, Motoring - 52xY, What's On - 52xY
LOCAL NEWSPAPERS: Local Newspapers English Counties

THE KESWICK REMINDER
43455U72B-630

Editorial Address: 32-34 Station Street, KESWICK, CA12 5HF **Tel:** 01768 772140 **Fax:** 01768 771203
Email: news@keswickreminder.co.uk
Advertising Address: As above.
Email: advertising@keswickreminder.co.uk
Publisher: G.W. McKane & Son
Date Established: 1896
Frequency: Weekly - Published on Friday
Cover Price: £0.20
Circulation: 4,500 (Publisher's Statement)
Editor: Jane Grave; **Advertising Manager:** Wendy Stephenson
ADVERTISING RATES:
Full Page Mono £643.00
SCC £2.55
Agency Commission: 10%
Mechanical Data: Print Process: Sheet-fed offset litho, Col Length: 480mm, Col Widths (Display): 42mm, Type Area: 480 x 322mm, Page Width: 322mm, Film: Digital, No. of Columns (Display): 7
Copy instructions: Copy Date: Wednesday 12pm prior to publication date
Average advertising content per issue: 60%
LOCAL NEWSPAPERS: Local Newspapers English Counties

KETTERING MERCURY & CITIZEN
44156U72B-2490_170

Formerly: Kettering Citizen
Frequency: Weekly
Cover Price: Free
Circulation: 18,350 (VFD 03/07/2006 to 31/12/2006)
ADVERTISING: Rates on application
Part of Series, see entry for: Northants Mercury & Citizen Series
LOCAL NEWSPAPERS: Local Newspapers English Counties

KIDDERMINSTER CHRONICLE
44563U72B-3510_150

Frequency: Weekly
Cover Price: Free
Circulation: 37,234 (VFD 02/07/2007 to 30/12/2007)
ADVERTISING: Rates on application
Part of Series, see entry for: Dudley Chronicle Series
LOCAL NEWSPAPERS: Local Newspapers English Counties

KILBURN TIMES
43121U72A-385_110

Frequency: Weekly - Circulation figure includes the Willesden & Brent Times
Cover Price: £0.45
Circulation: 21,648 (Publisher's Statement)
Part of Series, see entry for: North West London Newspaper Series
LOCAL NEWSPAPERS: Local Newspapers Greater London

KILMARNOCK STANDARD
44978U72D-610

Formerly: Kilmarnock Standard Ayrshire Weekly News and Irvine Valley News
Editorial Address: 25 Portland Gate, Portland Street, KILMARNOCK, KA1 1JN **Tel:** 01563 525115
Fax: 01563 571527
Email: kilmarnockstandard@s-un.co.uk
Advertising Address: 34 Mackintosh Place, South Newmoor Industrial Estate, IRVINE, KA11 4JY
Tel: 01294 222288 **Fax:** 01294 213982
Email: klamont@s-un.co.uk
Web site: http://www.icayrshire.co.uk
Publisher: Scottish & Universal Newspapers Ltd
Date Established: 1863
Frequency: Weekly - Published on Wednesday
Cover Price: £0.80
Circulation: 17,311 (ABC 02/07/2007 to 30/12/2007)
Usual Pagination: 128
Editor: Stef Lach; **Advertising Manager:** Karen Lamont
ADVERTISING RATES:
Full Page Mono £3447.60
Full Page Colour £4654.26
Agency Commission: 10%
Mechanical Data: Col Length: 340mm, Col Widths (Display): 27mm, No. of Columns (Display): 9, Page Width: 265mm, Type Area: 340 x 265mm, Film: Digital
Copy instructions: Copy Date: 5pm Monday prior to publication date
Average advertising content per issue: 50%
LOCAL NEWSPAPERS: Local Newspapers Scotland

KILSYTH CHRONICLE
1638840U72D-258_101

Frequency: Weekly - Published on Wednesday. See the Cumbernauld News for combined circulation figure
Cover Price: £0.42
Part of Series, see entry for: Cumbernauld News and Kilsyth Chronicle Series
LOCAL NEWSPAPERS: Local Newspapers Scotland

KINCARDINESHIRE OBSERVER
44994U72D-730_150

Frequency: Weekly - Published on Friday
Cover Price: £0.38
Circulation: 1,112 (ABC 02/07/2007 to 30/12/2007)
ADVERTISING RATES:
Full Page Mono £845.00
Full Page Colour £1267.00
SCC £3.43
Copy instructions: Copy Date: Tuesday 5pm prior to publication date
Part of Series, see entry for: Montrose Review Series
LOCAL NEWSPAPERS: Local Newspapers Scotland

KINGSBRIDGE & SALCOMBE GAZETTE
43540U72B-854_140

Formerly: Kingsbridge, Salcombe & South Hams Gazette
Frequency: Weekly
Cover Price: £0.35
Part of Series, see entry for: South Hams Newspapers Group
LOCAL NEWSPAPERS: Local Newspapers English Counties

KINGSTEIGNTON & MID-DEVON ADVERTISER
1706664U72B-827_181

Frequency: Weekly
Cover Price: £0.40
Part of Series, see entry for: Mid-Devon Advertiser Series
LOCAL NEWSPAPERS: Local Newspapers English Counties

KINGSTON BOROUGH GUARDIAN
43002U72A-128_140

Frequency: Weekly
Cover Price: Free
Circulation: 49,430 (VFD 02/07/2007 to 30/12/2007)
Part of Series, see entry for: Guardian & News Series (Sutton)
LOCAL NEWSPAPERS: Local Newspapers Greater London

KIRKHAM AND FYLDE EXPRESS
43986U72B-2005_140

Frequency: Weekly - Circulation figure is incorporated into the Lytham St. Annes Express
Part of Series, see entry for: Lytham St Annes Express Series
LOCAL NEWSPAPERS: Local Newspapers English Counties

Non-National Newspapers

KIRKINTILLOCH & BISHOPBRIGGS HERALD SERIES
44979U72D-630

Editorial Address: 11 Dalrymple Court, Townhead, KIRKINTILLOCH, G66 3AA **Tel:** 0141 775 0040
Fax: 0141 776 2218
Email: kirkyherald@jnscotland.co.uk
Advertising Address: As above.
Email: kirkintilloch.ads@jnscotland.co.uk
Web site: http://www.kirkintilloch-herald.co.uk
Publisher: Johnston Press plc
Frequency: Weekly - Published on Wednesday
Circulation: 34,797 (Combined Circulation)
Usual Pagination: 40
Editor: Alan Muir; **Advertising Manager:** Elaine Livingstone
ADVERTISING RATES:
Full Page Mono £2754.47
Full Page Colour £6017.49
Agency Commission: 10%
Mechanical Data: Page Width: 272mm, Film: Digital, Type Area: 340 x 272mm, Col Length: 340mm, No. of Columns (Display): 9, Col Widths (Display): 28mm
Copy instructions: Copy Date: Monday 10am prior to publication date
Average advertising content per issue: 40%
Series owner and contact point for the following titles, see individual entries:
The Advertiser (Strathkelvin)
Bishopbriggs Herald
Kirkintilloch Herald
Kirkintilloch Herald North Lanarkshire Edition
Springburn Herald
LOCAL NEWSPAPERS: Local Newspapers Scotland

KIRKINTILLOCH HERALD
44981U72D-630_160

Frequency: Weekly - Circulation figure includes the Bishopsbrigg Herald, the Springburn Herald and the Kirkintilloch Herald North Lanarkshire Edition
Cover Price: £0.29
Circulation: 11,775 (ABC 02/07/2007 to 30/12/2007)
Part of Series, see entry for: Kirkintilloch & Bishopbriggs Herald Series
LOCAL NEWSPAPERS: Local Newspapers Scotland

KIRKINTILLOCH HERALD NORTH LANARKSHIRE EDITION
44982U72D-630_170

Frequency: Weekly - Circulation figure is incorporated into the Kirkintilloch Herald
Cover Price: £0.29
Part of Series, see entry for: Kirkintilloch & Bishopbriggs Herald Series
LOCAL NEWSPAPERS: Local Newspapers Scotland

KIRRIEMUIR HERALD
707392U72D-400_130

Frequency: Weekly
Cover Price: £0.56
Part of Series, see entry for: Forfar Dispatch Series
LOCAL NEWSPAPERS: Local Newspapers Scotland

KM EXTRA (MAIDSTONE)
1644552U72B-3947

Formerly: KM Extra (Sevenoaks)
Frequency: Weekly
Cover Price: Free
Part of Series, see entry for: KM Extra Series (Maidstone, Tonbridge and Tunbridge Wells)
LOCAL NEWSPAPERS: Local Newspapers English Counties

KM EXTRA SERIES (MAIDSTONE, TONBRIDGE AND TUNBRIDGE WELLS)
1616118U72B-3933

Formerly: KM Extra Series (Sevenoaks, Tonbridge and Tunbridge Wells)
Editorial Address: 6-7 Middle Row, MAIDSTONE, ME14 1TG **Tel:** 01892 525111
Email: twellsextra@thekmgroup.co.uk
Advertising Address: As above. **Tel:** 01892 544747
Fax: 01892 545445
Email: chollis@thekmgroup.co.uk
Web site: http://www.kentmessenger.co.uk
Publisher: Kent Messenger Group
Frequency: Weekly - Published on Thursday
Cover Price: Free
Circulation: 60,000 (Publisher's Statement)
Editor: News Desk; **Advertising Manager:** Clive Hollis
ADVERTISING RATES:
Full Page Mono £1196.80
Full Page Colour £1496.00
SCC £4.40
Agency Commission: 10%

Mechanical Data: Type Area: 340 x 276mm, Col Length: 340mm, Col Widths (Display): 31mm, No. of Columns (Display): 8, Page Width: 276mm, Film: Digital
Copy instructions: Copy Date: Monday prior to publication date
Average advertising content per issue: 70%
Series owner and contact point for the following titles, see individual entries:
KM Extra (Maidstone)
KM Extra (Tonbridge)
KM Extra (Tunbridge Wells)
LOCAL NEWSPAPERS: Local Newspapers English Counties

KM EXTRA (TONBRIDGE)
43893U72B-3933_101

Formerly: Extra (Tonbridge)
Frequency: Weekly
Cover Price: Free
Part of Series, see entry for: KM Extra Series (Maidstone, Tonbridge and Tunbridge Wells)
LOCAL NEWSPAPERS: Local Newspapers English Counties

KM EXTRA (TUNBRIDGE WELLS)
43894U72B-3933_100

Formerly: Extra (Tunbridge Wells)
Frequency: Weekly
Cover Price: Free
Part of Series, see entry for: KM Extra Series (Maidstone, Tonbridge and Tunbridge Wells)
LOCAL NEWSPAPERS: Local Newspapers English Counties

KNARESBOROUGH POST
44649U72B-3588_180

Frequency: Weekly
Cover Price: £0.60
Circulation: 3,528 (ABC 02/07/2007 to 30/12/2007)
ADVERTISING RATES:
SCC £10.14
Part of Series, see entry for: Ackrill Newspaper Series
LOCAL NEWSPAPERS: Local Newspapers English Counties

KNUTSFORD GUARDIAN
43396U72B-500_140

Frequency: Weekly
Cover Price: £0.50
Circulation: 6,583 (ABC 02/07/2007 to 30/12/2007)
ADVERTISING: Rates on application
Part of Series, see entry for: Warrington Guardian Series
LOCAL NEWSPAPERS: Local Newspapers English Counties

LAKE DISTRICT HERALD
762175U72B-607_160

Frequency: Weekly - Circulation included in Cumberland & Westmorland Herald
Cover Price: £0.55
Part of Series, see entry for: Cumberland & Westmorland Herald Series
LOCAL NEWSPAPERS: Local Newspapers English Counties

LAKELAND ECHO
43456U72B-1987

Editorial Address: 12 Victoria Street, MORECAMBE, LA4 4AG **Tel:** 01524 833111 **Fax:** 01524 834024
Email: lakeland.echo@lmnews.co.uk
Advertising Address: As above. **Fax:** 01524 420939
Email: advertising@lmnews.co.uk
Web site: http://www.lakelandtoday.co.uk
Publisher: Lancaster and Morecambe Newspapers
Frequency: Weekly
Cover Price: Free
Circulation: 13,866 (Publisher's Statement)
Editor: Lauren Holden; **Advertising Director:** Debs Stuchbury
ADVERTISING: Rates on application
Agency Commission: 10%
Copy instructions: Copy Date: Monday 12.30am prior to publication date
Average advertising content per issue: 70%
LOCAL NEWSPAPERS: Local Newspapers English Counties

LAMPETER & TREGARON CAMBRIAN NEWS
763770U72C-30_150

Formerly: Lampeter, Coast & Cambrian News
Frequency: Weekly
Cover Price: £0.65
ADVERTISING: Rates on application

Part of Series, see entry for: The Cambrian News Series
LOCAL NEWSPAPERS: Local Newspapers Wales

LANARK & CARLUKE ADVERTISER
44959U72D-1033

Editorial Address: Press Buildings, Campbell Street, HAMILTON, ML3 6AX **Tel:** 01698 205202
Email: gtopp@lcadvertiser.co.uk
Web site: http://www.icscotland.co.uk
Publisher: Scottish & Universal Newspapers Ltd
Frequency: Weekly - Circulation is included in Hamilton Advertiser
Cover Price: £0.70
Editor: George Topp; **News Editor:** George Topp
ADVERTISING: Rates on application
LOCAL NEWSPAPERS: Local Newspapers Scotland

LANARK GAZETTE
44891U72D-230_170

Frequency: Weekly
Cover Price: £0.42
Part of Series, see entry for: Carluke and Lanark Gazette Series
LOCAL NEWSPAPERS: Local Newspapers Scotland

LANARKSHIRE EXTRA SERIES
44985U72D-664

Formerly: Lanarkshire People Series
Editorial Address: 29 Hope Street, MOTHERWELL, ML1 1BT **Tel:** 01698 242553 **Fax:** 01698 269399
Email: lanedit@jpress.co.uk
Advertising Address: As above. **Tel:** 01698 261321
Fax: 01698 275177
Email: suzanne.ohare@jpress.co.uk
Web site: http://www.motherwelltimes.co.uk
Publisher: Johnston Press plc
Date Established: 1981
Frequency: Weekly - Published on Thursday
Cover Price: Free
Circulation: 46,000 (Publisher's Statement)
Usual Pagination: 36
Editor: Martin Clark
ADVERTISING RATES:
SCC £12.75
Agency Commission: 10%
Copy instructions: Copy Date: Monday 5pm prior to publication date
Average advertising content per issue: 55%
Series owner and contact point for the following titles, see individual entries:
North Lanarkshire Extra
South Lanarkshire Extra
Strathaven Extra
LOCAL NEWSPAPERS: Local Newspapers Scotland

LANARKSHIRE WORLD
45045U72D-1000

Formerly: World Series
Editorial Address: Press Buildings, Campbell Street, HAMILTON, ML3 6AX **Tel:** 01698 283200
Fax: 01698 421168
Email: hamiltonadvertiser@s-un.co.uk
Advertising Address: As above. **Fax:** 01698 425706
Email: tele-ad@s-un.co.uk
Web site: http://www.inside-scotland.co.uk
Publisher: Scottish & Universal Newspapers Ltd
Frequency: Weekly - Published on Friday
Cover Price: Free
Circulation: 35,172 (VFD 02/07/2007 to 30/12/2007)
Editor: Joseph Kelly
ADVERTISING: Rates on application
LOCAL NEWSPAPERS: Local Newspapers Scotland

THE LANCASHIRE ADVERTISER
1805688U72B-2659_175

Frequency: Weekly
Cover Price: Free
Part of Series, see entry for: Journal & Advertiser Series
LOCAL NEWSPAPERS: Local Newspapers English Counties

LANCASHIRE EVENING POST
42160U67B-900

Editorial Address: Olivers Place, Eastway, Fulwood, PRESTON, PR2 9ZA **Tel:** 01772 254841 **Fax:** 01772 880173
Email: lep.newsdesk@lep.co.uk
Advertising Address: As above. **Fax:** 01772 556683
Email: lep.advertising@jpress.co.uk
Web site: http://www.lep.co.uk
Publisher: Lancashire Evening Post Ltd
Frequency: Evenings
Cover Price: £0.32

Circulation: 31,225 (Publisher's Statement)
Editor: News Desk; Features Editor: Peter Richardson;
Managing Director: Margaret Hilton
ADVERTISING RATES:
SCC £14.09
Mechanical Data: Film: Digital, Page Width: 278mm, Col
Length: 340mm, No. of Columns (Display): 9, Col Widths
(Display): 29mm, Type Area: 340 x 278mm
Copy instructions: Copy Date: 12pm 1 day prior to
publication date
Editions:
Lancashire Evening Post (Chorley Edition)
Lancashire Evening Post (County Edition)
Supplement(s): Business and Education - 52xY, Property
and Motors - 52xY, Week Ahead - 52xY, What Women Want
- 52xY
REGIONAL DAILY & SUNDAY NEWSPAPERS: Regional
Daily Newspapers

LANCASHIRE EVENING POST (CHORLEY EDITION)
42161U67B-900_530
ADVERTISING RATES:
SCC £8.59
Edition of: Lancashire Evening Post
REGIONAL DAILY & SUNDAY NEWSPAPERS: Regional
Daily Newspapers

LANCASHIRE EVENING POST (COUNTY EDITION)
42162U67B-900_550
ADVERTISING RATES:
SCC £8.59
Edition of: Lancashire Evening Post
REGIONAL DAILY & SUNDAY NEWSPAPERS: Regional
Daily Newspapers

LANCASHIRE EVENING TELEGRAPH (BURNLEY, PENDLE AND ROSSENDALE)
1660034U67B-50_500
Frequency: Evenings
Cover Price: £0.38
Edition of: Lancashire Telegraph
REGIONAL DAILY & SUNDAY NEWSPAPERS: Regional
Daily Newspapers

LANCASHIRE TELEGRAPH
41995U67B-50
Formerly: Lancashire Evening Telegraph
Editorial Address: Newspaper House, High Street,
BLACKBURN, BB1 1HT Tel: 01254 678678
Fax: 01254 680429
Email: lt_editorial@lancashire.newsquest.co.uk
Advertising Address: As above. Fax: 01254 298181
Email: sarah.wheildon@nqnw.co.uk
Web site: http://www.lancashiretelegraph.co.uk
Publisher: Newsquest (Let/Citizen) Ltd
Frequency: Mornings - Not published on Sunday
Cover Price: £0.38
Circulation: 32,716 (ABC 03/07/2006 to 31/12/2006)
Editor: Ian Singleton; News Editor: Ian Singleton; Features
Editor: John Anson; Advertising Manager: Sharon How
ADVERTISING RATES:
SCC £6.80
Mechanical Data: Col Length: 350mm, No. of Columns
(Display): 9, Film: Digital, Col Widths (Display): 27mm, Type
Area: 350 x 273mm, Print Process: Web-fed offset litho,
Page Width: 273mm
Copy instructions: Copy Date: 2 days prior to publication
date
Editions:
Lancashire Evening Telegraph (Burnley, Pendle and
Rossendale)
REGIONAL DAILY & SUNDAY NEWSPAPERS: Regional
Daily Newspapers

LANCASTER AND MORECAMBE REPORTER
1695423U72B-3983
Editorial Address: 12 Victoria Street, MORECAMBE, LA4
4AG Tel: 01524 833111 Fax: 01524 834024
Email: lauren.holden@lmnews.co.uk
Advertising Address: As above. Fax: 01524 420939
Email: advertising@lmnews.co.uk
Publisher: Lancaster and Morecambe Newspapers
Frequency: Weekly
Cover Price: Free
Circulation: 45,846 (VFD 02/07/2007 to 30/12/2007)
Editor: Lauren Holden; Advertisement Director: Debs
Stuchbury
ADVERTISING: Rates on application
Agency Commission: 10%
Copy instructions: Copy Date: 2 days prior to publication
date

Average advertising content per issue: 70%
LOCAL NEWSPAPERS: Local Newspapers English
Counties

LANCASTER GUARDIAN BENTHAM EDITION
43976U72B-1990_110
Frequency: Weekly - Circulation figure incorporated in
Lancaster Guardian Series
ADVERTISING: Rates on application
Part of Series, see entry for: Lancaster Guardian Series
LOCAL NEWSPAPERS: Local Newspapers English
Counties

LANCASTER GUARDIAN CITY EDITION
43979U72B-1990_170
Frequency: Weekly - Circulation figure incorporated in
Lancaster Guardian Series
ADVERTISING: Rates on application
Part of Series, see entry for: Lancaster Guardian Series
LOCAL NEWSPAPERS: Local Newspapers English
Counties

LANCASTER GUARDIAN SERIES
43975U72B-1990
Editorial Address: 29 Common Garden Street,
LANCASTER, LA1 1XD Tel: 01524 32525
Fax: 01524 842157
Email: guardian@lmnews.co.uk
Advertising Address: 12 Victoria Street, MORECAMBE,
LA4 4AG Tel: 01524 833111 Fax: 01524 420939
Email: advertising@lmnews.co.uk
Web site: http://www.lancasterguardian.co.uk
Publisher: Lancaster and Morecambe Newspapers
Date Established: 1837
Frequency: Weekly - Published on Friday
Cover Price: £0.70
Circulation: 16,306 (ABC 02/07/2007 to 30/12/2007)
Editor: Louise Bryning; News Editor: Louise Bryning;
Managing Director: Michael Harper; Advertisement
Director: Debs Stuchbury
ADVERTISING: Rates on application
Agency Commission: 10%
Copy instructions: Copy Date: Tuesday 2.30pm prior to
publication date
Average advertising content per issue: 55%
Series owner and contact point for the following titles,
see individual entries:
Lancaster Guardian Bentham Edition
Lancaster Guardian City Edition
Morecambe Guardian
LOCAL NEWSPAPERS: Local Newspapers English
Counties

LANCING HERALD
44465U72B-3323_110
Frequency: Weekly - Circulation figure is incorporated into
the Worthing Herald
Cover Price: £0.32
ADVERTISING: Rates on application
Part of Series, see entry for: Shoreham & Steyning Herald
Series
LOCAL NEWSPAPERS: Local Newspapers English
Counties

LARGS & MILLPORT WEEKLY NEWS
44988U72D-669
Editorial Address: 22 Dock Road, ARDROSSAN, KA22 8DA
Tel: 01475 689009
Email: editorial@largsnews.co.uk
Advertising Address: 3 Lade Street, LARGS, KA30 8BA
Tel: 01475 689009 Fax: 01475 676468
Email: advertising.ln@cfpress.co.uk
Web site: http://www.largsandmillportnews.com
Publisher: Clyde & Forth Press Group
Date Established: 1877
Frequency: Weekly - Published on Wednesday
Cover Price: £0.55
Circulation: 5,958 (ABC 01/01/2007 to 30/12/2007)
Usual Pagination: 28
Editor: Drew Cochrane
ADVERTISING RATES:
SCC £6.20
Agency Commission: 10%
Mechanical Data: No. of Columns (Display): 8, Type Area:
330 x 266mm, Col Length: 330mm, Page Width: 266mm, Col
Widths (Display): 30mm, Film: Digital
Copy instructions: Copy Date: Monday 5pm prior to
publication date
Average advertising content per issue: 50%
LOCAL NEWSPAPERS: Local Newspapers Scotland

LARNE GAZETTE AND EAST ANTRIM GAZETTE
45063U72E-55_120
Formerly: Larne Gazette
Frequency: Weekly
Part of Series, see entry for: East Antrim Gazette Series
LOCAL NEWSPAPERS: Local Newspapers Northern Ireland

LARNE TIMES AND EAST ANTRIM TIMES
45126U72E-226_140
Frequency: Weekly - Published on Thursday. Circulation
figure includes the Carrick Times & East Antrim Times and
the Newtonabbey Times & East Antrim Times
Cover Price: £0.90
Circulation: 9,943 (ABC 02/07/2007 to 30/12/2007)
Part of Series, see entry for: The Times Series
LOCAL NEWSPAPERS: Local Newspapers Northern Ireland

LAUNCESTON & CORNISH & DEVON POST
43415U72B-520_140
Frequency: Weekly
Cover Price: £0.65
ADVERTISING RATES:
Full Page Mono £3360.00
Full Page Colour £3710.00
SCC £6.00
Mechanical Data: Type Area: 560 x 366mm, Col Length:
560mm, Col Widths (Display): 34mm, No. of Columns
(Display): 10, Page Width: 366mm, Film: Digital
Part of Series, see entry for: Cornish & Devon Post Series
LOCAL NEWSPAPERS: Local Newspapers English
Counties

LAUNCESTON, HOLSWORTHY BUDE & STRATTON JOURNAL GAZETTE
43418U72B-520_180
Frequency: Weekly
Cover Price: Free
ADVERTISING RATES:
Full Page Mono £1146.60
Full Page Colour £1496.60
Mechanical Data: Type Area: 360 x 255mm, Col Length:
360mm, Col Widths (Display): 34mm, No. of Columns
(Display): 7, Page Width: 255mm, Film: Digital
Part of Series, see entry for: Cornish & Devon Post Series
LOCAL NEWSPAPERS: Local Newspapers English
Counties

THE LEADER (COLERAINE)
45100U72E-60_100
Frequency: 45 issues yearly
Cover Price: Free
Circulation: 29,000 (Publisher's Statement)
Advertising Manager: Richard Stratton
ADVERTISING RATES:
Full Page Mono £910.90
Full Page Colour £1547.00
SCC £3.45
Copy instructions: Copy Date: Friday 10am prior to
publication date
Part of Series, see entry for: The Chronicle and Leader
Series (Coleraine)
LOCAL NEWSPAPERS: Local Newspapers Northern Ireland

LEADER (COUNTY DOWN SERIES)
45101U72E-156
Editorial Address: 25 Bridge Street, BANBRIDGE, BT32
3JL Tel: 028 4066 2745 Fax: 028 4062 6378
Email: mark.weir@banbridgeleader.co.uk
Advertising Address: As above.
Email: anita.murray@jpress.co.uk
Web site: http://www.banbridgeleader.co.uk
Publisher: Morton Newspapers Ltd
Frequency: Weekly - Published on Tuesday
Circulation: 3,778 (ABC 02/07/2007 to 30/12/2007)
Editor: Mark Weir; Advertising Manager: Anita Murray
ADVERTISING RATES:
Full Page Mono £1481.05
Full Page Colour £2147.70
SCC £4.85
Mechanical Data: Col Length: 340mm, Col Widths (Display):
28mm, No. of Columns (Display): 9, Type Area: 340 x
268mm, Page Width: 268mm, Film: Digital
Copy instructions: Copy Date: Friday 4pm prior to
publication date
Series owner and contact point for the following titles,
see individual entries:
Banbridge Leader
The Leader (Dromore)
LOCAL NEWSPAPERS: Local Newspapers Northern Ireland

THE LEADER (DROMORE)
45103U72E-156_160

Frequency: Weekly
Cover Price: £0.95
Part of Series, see entry for: Leader (County Down Series)
LOCAL NEWSPAPERS: Local Newspapers Northern Ireland

THE LEADER MABLETHORPE AND SUTTON-ON-SEA
44063U72B-2263_120

Formerly: The Leader Mablethorpe, Sutton & Alford
Frequency: Weekly - Circulation figure includes the Louth Leader
Cover Price: £0.45
Circulation: 10,326 (ABC 02/07/2007 to 30/12/2007)
ADVERTISING: Rates on application
Part of Series, see entry for: Louth Leader and Citizen Series
LOCAL NEWSPAPERS: Local Newspapers English Counties

LEADER (NORTH WEST LEICESTERSHIRE & SOUTH DERBYSHIRE)
44035U72B-2193_150

Frequency: Weekly
Cover Price: Free
Circulation: 37,000 (Publisher's Statement)
ADVERTISING: Rates on application
Part of Series, see entry for: Trident Midland Newspapers Series
LOCAL NEWSPAPERS: Local Newspapers English Counties

LEADER TIMES SERIES
43988U72B-2040

Formerly: Nelson Leader and Colne Times Series
Editorial Address: 37 Scotland Road, NELSON, BB9 7UT
Tel: 01282 612561 **Fax:** 01282 618626
Email: peter.dewhurst@eastlancsnews.co.uk
Advertising Address: Bull Street, BURNLEY, BB11 1DP
Tel: 01282 426161 **Fax:** 01282 435332
Email: donna.wiggan@eastlancsnews.co.uk
Web site: http://www.pendletoday.co.uk
Publisher: East Lancashire Newspapers Ltd
Date Established: 1874
Frequency: Weekly - Published every Friday
Circulation: 71,447 (Combined Circulation)
Usual Pagination: 40
Editor: Andrew Spencer; **News Editor:** Peter Dewhurst
ADVERTISING RATES:
Full Page Mono £1306.62
Full Page Colour £1698.60
SCC £4.27
Agency Commission: 10%
Mechanical Data: Type Area: 340 x 274mm, Col Length: 340mm, Page Width: 274mm, Film: Digital, No. of Columns (Display): 9
Copy instructions: Copy Date: Wednesday 12.00pm prior to publication date
Average advertising content per issue: 45%
Series owner and contact point for the following titles, see individual entries:
Barnoldswick & Earby Times
Colne Times
Nelson Leader
Pendle and Burnley Reporter
LOCAL NEWSPAPERS: Local Newspapers English Counties

LEAMINGTON & STRATFORD OBSERVER SERIES
44506U72B-3382

Editorial Address: 45 The Parade, LEAMINGTON SPA, CV32 4BL **Tel:** 01926 451900 **Fax:** 01926 429012
Email: editor@leamingtonobserver.co.uk
Advertising Address: As above. **Fax:** 01926 451754
Email: adverts@leamingtonobserver.co.uk
Web site: http://www.leamingtonobserver.com
Publisher: Bullivant Media Limited
Date Established: 1989
Frequency: Weekly - Published on Thursday
Cover Price: Free
Circulation: 90,456 (Combined Circulation)
Editor: Ian Hughes; **Managing Director:** Chris Bullivant
ADVERTISING: Rates on application
Copy instructions: Copy Date: Tuesday 5.00pm prior to publication date
Series owner and contact point for the following titles, see individual entries:
Kenilworth Observer
Royal Leamington Spa Observer
Southam Observer
Stratford Upon-Avon & Arden Observer
Warwick Observer
LOCAL NEWSPAPERS: Local Newspapers English Counties

LEAMINGTON SPA COURIER
44514U72B-3386_180

Frequency: Weekly - Published on Friday. Circulation figure includes the Warwick Courier
Cover Price: £0.42
Circulation: 13,413 (ABC 02/07/2007 to 30/12/2007)
Part of Series, see entry for: Leamington Spa Courier Series
LOCAL NEWSPAPERS: Local Newspapers English Counties

LEAMINGTON SPA COURIER SERIES
44512U72B-3386

Editorial Address: 32 Hamilton Terrace, LEAMINGTON SPA, CV32 4LY **Tel:** 01926 457755 **Fax:** 01926 339960
Email: editorial@leamingtoncourier.co.uk
Advertising Address: As above. **Tel:** 01926 457777
Fax: 01926 451690
Email: karen.davies@ccnltd.com
Web site: http://www.leamingtontoday.co.uk
Publisher: Central Counties Newspapers South Ltd
Date Established: 1828
Frequency: Weekly
Circulation: 56,996 (Combined Circulation)
Editor: Simon Steele; **Advertising Manager:** Karen Davies; **Group Editor:** Martin Lawson
ADVERTISING RATES:
Full Page Mono £2004.30
SCC £6.55
Mechanical Data: No. of Columns (Display): 9, Col Widths (Display): 28mm, Film: Digital, Type Area: 340 x 268mm, Col Length: 340mm, Page Width: 268mm
Copy instructions: Copy Date: Wednesday 12pm prior to publication date
Average advertising content per issue: 65%
Series owner and contact point for the following titles, see individual entries:
The Courier Midweek
Kenilworth Weekly News
Leamington Spa Courier
Warwick Courier
Supplement(s): Business Focus - 12xY, Warwickshire Choice - 12xY
LOCAL NEWSPAPERS: Local Newspapers English Counties

LEATHERHEAD ADVERTISER
44353U72B-3095_160

Frequency: Weekly - Circulation figure is incorporated into the Dorking Advertiser
Cover Price: £0.60
Part of Series, see entry for: Advertiser Series (Surrey)
LOCAL NEWSPAPERS: Local Newspapers English Counties

LEDBURY REPORTER
27414U72B-3564_100

Frequency: Weekly
Cover Price: £0.55
ADVERTISING: Rates on application
Part of Series, see entry for: Malvern Gazette & Ledbury Reporter Series
LOCAL NEWSPAPERS: Local Newspapers English Counties

LEEDS WEEKLY NEWS SERIES
44711U72B-3812

Editorial Address: PO Box 49, Wellington Street, LEEDS, LS1 1LW **Tel:** 0113 238 8773
Email: lwneditorial@ypn.co.uk
Advertising Address: PO Box 168, Wellington Street, LEEDS, LS1 1RF **Tel:** 0113 238 8767 **Fax:** 0113 238 8484
Email: tony.sharma@ypn.co.uk
Publisher: Yorkshire Post Newspapers Ltd
Date Established: 1980
Frequency: Weekly
Cover Price: Free
Circulation: 124,534 (VFD 02/07/2007 to 30/12/2007)
Editor: Laura Bowyer; **Advertising Manager:** Tony Sharma
ADVERTISING RATES:
SCC £14.85
Agency Commission: 10%
Mechanical Data: Type Area: 340 x 274mm, No. of Columns (Display): 9, Col Widths (Display): 26.5mm, Col Length: 340mm, Page Width: 274mm, Film: Digital
Copy instructions: Copy Date: Mono Tuesday noon Colour Monday 5pm prior to publication date
Average advertising content per issue: 68%
Series owner and contact point for the following titles, see individual entries:
East Leeds Weekly News
Headingley, Armley & Meanwood Weekly News
Morley, Beeston & Hunslet Weekly News

North Leeds Weekly News
LOCAL NEWSPAPERS: Local Newspapers English Counties

LEEK POST & TIMES
44312U72B-3005_130

Frequency: Weekly
Cover Price: £0.40
Circulation: 10,987 (ABC 02/07/2007 to 30/12/2007)
ADVERTISING RATES:
Full Page Mono £979.20
Full Page Colour £1224.00
Part of Series, see entry for: Post & Times Series
LOCAL NEWSPAPERS: Local Newspapers English Counties

LEICESTER MAIL
44016U72B-2135_150

Frequency: Weekly - Circulation incorporates the figure for Oadby and Wigston Mail
Cover Price: Free
Circulation: 89,525 (VFD 02/07/2007 to 30/12/2007)
ADVERTISING RATES:
SCC £13.80
Part of Series, see entry for: Leicester Mail Series
LOCAL NEWSPAPERS: Local Newspapers English Counties

LEICESTER MAIL SERIES
44011U72B-2135

Editorial Address: St. George Street, LEICESTER, LE1 9FJ
Tel: 0116 222 4627 **Fax:** 0116 222 4669
Email: gemmacollins@leicestermercury.co.uk
Advertising Address: As above. **Tel:** 0116 222 4128
Fax: 0116 262 4687
Email: retail@leicestermercury.co.uk
Web site: http://www.thisisleicestershire.co.uk
Publisher: Leicester Mercury Media Group Ltd
Date Established: 1975
Frequency: Weekly
Cover Price: Free
Circulation: 141,536 (VFD 02/07/2007 to 30/12/2007)
Editor: Gemma Collins; **Advertising Manager:** Lee Smith
ADVERTISING RATES:
SCC £20.00
Agency Commission: 10%
Mechanical Data: Type Area: 360 x 277mm, Col Length: 360mm, No. of Columns (Display): 8, Col Widths (Display): 32mm, Film: Digital, Page Width: 277mm
Copy instructions: Copy Date: Thursday 12pm prior to publication date
Average advertising content per issue: 70%
Series owner and contact point for the following titles, see individual entries:
Leicester Mail
Loughborough Mail
Mail (Coalville & District)
Oadby and Wigston Mail
LOCAL NEWSPAPERS: Local Newspapers English Counties

LEICESTER MERCURY
42104U67B-360

Editorial Address: St. George Street, LEICESTER, LE1 9FQ
Tel: 0116 251 2512 **Fax:** 0116 253 0645
Email: newsdesk@leicestermercury.co.uk
Advertising Address: As above. **Fax:** 0116 262 4608
Email: enquiries@leicestermercury.co.uk
Web site: http://www.thisisleicestershire.co.uk
Publisher: Leicester Mercury Media Group Ltd
Frequency: Daily - Not published on Sunday
Cover Price: £0.35
Circulation: 70,028 (ABC 02/07/2007 to 30/12/2007)
Editor: Keith Perch; **News Editor:** Mark Charlton; **Features Editor:** Alex Dawson
ADVERTISING RATES:
SCC £20.25
Agency Commission: 10%
Mechanical Data: Type Area: 360 x 277mm, Col Length: 360mm, Page Width: 277mm, Film: Digital
Editions:
Leicester Mercury (City Edition)
Leicester Mercury (County Edition)
REGIONAL DAILY & SUNDAY NEWSPAPERS: Regional Daily Newspapers

LEICESTER MERCURY (CITY EDITION)
42105U67B-360_530

Edition of: Leicester Mercury
REGIONAL DAILY & SUNDAY NEWSPAPERS: Regional Daily Newspapers

LEICESTER MERCURY (COUNTY EDITION)
42107U67B-360_570

Formerly: Leicester Mercury (Loughborough Edition)
Edition of: Leicester Mercury
REGIONAL DAILY & SUNDAY NEWSPAPERS: Regional Daily Newspapers

LEIGH & WESTCLIFF TIMES
43639U72B-1079_150

Frequency: 26 issues yearly
Cover Price: Free
Circulation: 28,000 (Publisher's Statement)
ADVERTISING RATES:
Full Page Mono £275.00
Full Page Colour £400.00
SCC £5.00
Part of Series, see entry for: Leigh Times Series
LOCAL NEWSPAPERS: Local Newspapers English Counties

LEIGH REPORTER
43700U72B-1227

Editorial Address: Magnum House, 33 Lord Street, LEIGH, WN7 1BY **Tel:** 01942 603334 **Fax:** 01942 674124
Email: wendy.moss@lancspublications.co.uk
Advertising Address: As above. **Fax:** 01942 262209
Email: tammy.mckenna@lancspublications.co.uk
Web site: http://www.leighreporter.co.uk
Publisher: Lancashire Publications Ltd
Frequency: Weekly - Published on Thursday
Cover Price: Free
Circulation: 61,041 (VFD 02/07/2007 to 30/12/2007)
Editor: Wendy Moss; **News Editor:** Wendy Moss; **Features Editor:** Wendy Moss; **Advertising Manager:** Tammy McKenna; **Group Editor:** Gillian Gray
ADVERTISING RATES:
Full Page Colour £2752.78
SCC £6.92
Agency Commission: 10%
Mechanical Data: Type Area: 340 x 270mm, No. of Columns (Display): 9, Col Length: 340mm, Page Width: 270mm, Col Widths (Display): 29mm, Film: Digital
Copy instructions: Copy Date: Tuesday 12pm prior to publication date
Average advertising content per issue: 70%
LOCAL NEWSPAPERS: Local Newspapers English Counties

LEIGH TIMES SERIES
43637U72B-1079

Formerly: Southend Times Series
Editorial Address: 106 The Broadway, LEIGH-ON-SEA, SS9 1AB **Tel:** 01702 477666 **Fax:** 01702 478710
Email: editor@leightimes.co.uk
Advertising Address: As above.
Email: mike@leightimes.co.uk
Publisher: Leigh Times Ltd
Date Established: 1982
Circulation: 67,000 (Combined Circulation)
Editor: Michael Guy; **Managing Director:** Michael Guy; **Advertising Manager:** Lisa Miller; **Publisher:** Michael Guy
ADVERTISING: Rates on application
Agency Commission: 10%
Mechanical Data: No. of Columns (Display): 8, Col Widths (Display): 31mm, Trim Size: 360 x 265mm
Copy instructions: Copy Date: Wednesday 12pm prior to publication date
Average advertising content per issue: 70%
Series owner and contact point for the following titles, see individual entries:
The Island Times
Leigh & Westcliff Times
Rayleigh & Eastwood Times
LOCAL NEWSPAPERS: Local Newspapers English Counties

LEIGH, TYLDESLEY AND ATHERTON JOURNAL
43699U72B-1225

Formerly: The Journal (Leigh, Tyldesley and Atherton)
Editorial Address: 44-46 Railway Road, LEIGH, WN7 4AT
Tel: 01942 670669 **Fax:** 01942 670479
Email: bgomm@lancashire.newsquest.co.uk
Advertising Address: As above. **Tel:** 01942 672241
Email: ads@leighjournal.co.uk
Web site: http://www.leighjournal.co.uk
Publisher: Newsquest Media Group
Date Established: 1874
Frequency: Weekly - Published on Thursday
Cover Price: Free
Circulation: 61,475 (Publisher's Statement)
Editor: Brian Gomm; **News Editor:** Brian Gomm; **Advertising Manager:** Julie Collinson
ADVERTISING RATES:
SCC £2.25
Agency Commission: 10%

Mechanical Data: No. of Columns (Display): 9, Col Widths (Display): 27.5mm, Film: Digital
Copy instructions: Copy Date: Tuesday 3pm prior to publication date
Average advertising content per issue: 60%
LOCAL NEWSPAPERS: Local Newspapers English Counties

LEIGHTON BUZZARD NEWS
43247U72B-4158_100

Formerly: Leighton Buzzard on Sunday
Frequency: Weekly - Published on Wednesday
Cover Price: Free
Circulation: 16,566 (VFD 02/07/2007 to 30/12/2007)
Part of Series, see entry for: Luton & Dunstable Express & News Series
LOCAL NEWSPAPERS: Local Newspapers English Counties

LEIGHTON BUZZARD OBSERVER
43240U72B-135

Editorial Address: 17 Bridge Street, LEIGHTON BUZZARD, LU7 1AH **Tel:** 01525 372051 **Fax:** 01525 850043
Email: news@lbobserver.co.uk
Advertising Address: As above. **Tel:** 01525 858400
Fax: 01525 853949
Email: sales@lbobserver.co.uk
Web site: http://www.leightonbuzzardtoday.co.uk
Publisher: Johnston Press plc
Date Established: 1861
Frequency: Weekly
Cover Price: £0.42
Circulation: 7,114 (ABC 02/07/2007 to 30/12/2007)
Editor: News Desk; **Editor-in-Chief:** John Francis
ADVERTISING RATES:
Full Page Mono £1422.90
SCC £4.65
Agency Commission: 10%
Mechanical Data: Page Width: 268mm, Film: Digital, Type Area: 340 x 268mm, Col Length: 340mm, Col Widths (Display): 28mm, No. of Columns (Display): 9, Print Process: Web-fed offset litho
Copy instructions: Copy Date: Friday prior to publication date
LOCAL NEWSPAPERS: Local Newspapers English Counties

LEIGHTON - LINSLADE CITIZEN
43310U72B-310_170

Formerly: Leighton-Buzzard and Linslade Citizen
Frequency: Weekly
Cover Price: Free
Circulation: 16,177 (VFD 02/07/2007 to 30/12/2007)
ADVERTISING: Rates on application
Part of Series, see entry for: Milton Keynes Citizen Series
LOCAL NEWSPAPERS: Local Newspapers English Counties

LEISTON SAXMUNDHAM ALDEBURGH AND DISTRICT COMMUNITY NEWS
44337U72B-3072_150

Frequency: Monthly
Cover Price: Free
Circulation: 7,600 (Publisher's Statement)
Part of Series, see entry for: Community News Series
LOCAL NEWSPAPERS: Local Newspapers English Counties

LEITH GAZETTE
1800034U72D-1023_100

Formerly: Leith and Portobellow Gazette
Frequency: Monthly
Cover Price: Free
Circulation: 4,000 (Publisher's Statement)
Part of Series, see entry for: The Gazette Series (Edinburgh)
LOCAL NEWSPAPERS: Local Newspapers Scotland

THE LENNOX
762423U72D-673_150

Formerly: Lennox Herald
Frequency: Weekly
Cover Price: £0.70
Part of Series, see entry for: Lennox Series
LOCAL NEWSPAPERS: Local Newspapers Scotland

LENNOX SERIES
44989U72D-673

Formerly: Lennox Herald Series
Editorial Address: 53 High Street, DUMBARTON, G82 1LS
Tel: 01389 742299 **Fax:** 01389 742488
Email: thelennox@s-un.co.uk
Advertising Address: As above. **Tel:** 0141 887 7911
Email: tgraham@s-un.co.uk
Web site: http://www.lennoxherald.co.uk
Publisher: Scottish & Universal Newspapers Ltd
Frequency: Weekly - Published on Wednesday
Circulation: 12,307 (ABC 02/07/2007 to 30/12/2007)
Usual Pagination: 48
Editor: Marc McLean; **Advertising Manager:** Trisha Graham
ADVERTISING RATES:
Full Page Mono £1630.00
Full Page Colour £2119.00
Mechanical Data: Type Area: 390 x 260mm, No. of Columns (Display): 9, Col Length: 390mm, Page Width: 260mm, Film: Digital
Series owner and contact point for the following titles, see individual entries:
Helensburgh Lennox
The Lennox
LOCAL NEWSPAPERS: Local Newspapers Scotland

LEYLAND GUARDIAN
43966U72B-1950_150

Frequency: Weekly
Cover Price: £0.55
Part of Series, see entry for: Chorley Guardian Series
LOCAL NEWSPAPERS: Local Newspapers English Counties

LEYLAND REPORTER
43997U72B-2052_150

Frequency: Weekly
Cover Price: Free
Part of Series, see entry for: Preston Reporter Series
LOCAL NEWSPAPERS: Local Newspapers English Counties

THE LICHFIELD & BURNTWOOD CHRONICLE
1682044U72B-2960_101

Frequency: Weekly
Cover Price: Free
Part of Series, see entry for: The Cannock & Lichfield Chronicle Series
LOCAL NEWSPAPERS: Local Newspapers English Counties

LICHFIELD MERCURY
44308U72B-2990_150

Frequency: Weekly - Circulation figure includes the Burntwood Mercury
Cover Price: Free
Circulation: 36,781 (VFD 02/07/2007 to 30/12/2007)
ADVERTISING RATES:
SCC £5.25
Part of Series, see entry for: Lichfield Mercury Series
LOCAL NEWSPAPERS: Local Newspapers English Counties

LICHFIELD MERCURY SERIES
44305U72B-2990

Formerly: Lichfield & Rugeley Mercury Series
Editorial Address: Ventura Park Road, Bitterscote, TAMWORTH, B78 3LZ **Tel:** 01827 848586
Fax: 01827 848640
Email: mercury.editorial@cintamworth.co.uk
Advertising Address: As above. **Fax:** 01827 848488
Email: hayley.pearce@cintamworth.co.uk
Web site: http://www.thisislichfield.co.uk
Publisher: Central Independent News & Media Ltd
Date Established: 1815
Frequency: Weekly - Published on Thursday
Cover Price: Free
Circulation: 81,365 (Combined Circulation)
Editor: Andy Kerr; **Group Editor:** Gary Phelps
Summary of Content: Local News, Sports and Features.
ADVERTISING: Rates on application
Agency Commission: 10%
Mechanical Data: No. of Columns (Display): 9, Col Widths (Display): 28mm, Film: Digital
Copy instructions: Copy Date: Tuesday 3pm prior to publication date
Average advertising content per issue: 70%
Series owner and contact point for the following titles, see individual entries:
Burntwood Mercury
Lichfield Mercury
Rugeley Mercury
LOCAL NEWSPAPERS: Local Newspapers English Counties

LICHFIELD POST
44293U72B-2963_130

Frequency: Weekly - Published on Thursday
Cover Price: Free
ADVERTISING RATES:
SCC £4.10
Part of Series, see entry for: Chase Post Series (Lichfield & Rugeley)
LOCAL NEWSPAPERS: Local Newspapers English Counties

LIFE
44066U72B-2206

Formerly: Grimsby Target
Editorial Address: 80 Cleethorpe Road, GRIMSBY, DN31 3EH **Tel:** 01472 360360 **Fax:** 01472 372257
Email: newsdesk@grimsbytelegraph.co.uk
Advertising Address: As above. **Fax:** 01472 372235
Email: matthew.stinson@gsmg.co.uk
Web site: http://www.thisisgrimsby.co.uk
Publisher: Grimsby & Scunthorpe Media Group
Frequency: Weekly - Published on Thursdays
Cover Price: Free
Circulation: 48,406 (VFD 03/07/2006 to 31/12/2006)
Editor: Lucy Wood; **News Editor:** Lucy Wood; **Features Editor:** James Harrington; **Advertising Director:** Claire Arthur
ADVERTISING: Rates on application
Agency Commission: 10%
Mechanical Data: Film: Digital, No. of Columns (Display): 8, Col Widths (Display): 31mm, Print Process: Web-fed offset litho
Copy instructions: Copy Date: Friday 3.30pm prior to publication date
Average advertising content per issue: 60%
LOCAL NEWSPAPERS: Local Newspapers English Counties

LIFE AND STYLE
1774727U67H-430

Editorial Address: PO Box 168, Wellington Street, LEEDS, LS1 1RF **Tel:** 0113 243 2701 **Fax:** 0113 238 8521
Email: catherine.scott@ypn.co.uk
Advertising Address: As above. **Fax:** 0113 383 1389
Email: joanna.wade@ypn.co.uk
Publisher: Johnston Press plc
Date Established: 2006
Frequency: Weekly - Published on Wednesday. See main record for circulation figure
Cover Price: £0.42
Editor: Catherine Scott
Summary of Content: Lifestyle supplement covering fashion, beauty, health, shopping and home with interviews and human interest stories.
Readership/Target Audience: Aimed at readers of the Yorkshire Post.
ADVERTISING RATES:
Full Page Mono £5064.00
Full Page Colour £6583.59
Agency Commission: 10%
Mechanical Data: Type Area: 340 x 274mm, Col Length: 340mm, Col Widths (Display): 30mm, No. of Columns (Display): 9, Film: Digital, Page Width: 274mm
Copy instructions: Copy Date: 1 week prior to publication date
Average advertising content per issue: 20%
Supplement to: Yorkshire Post
REGIONAL DAILY & SUNDAY NEWSPAPERS: Regional Colour Supplements

LINCOLN TARGET
762128U72B-2240_160

Frequency: Weekly
Cover Price: Free
Circulation: 33,596 (VFD 02/07/2007 to 30/12/2007)
ADVERTISING RATES:
SCC £5.40
Part of Series, see entry for: Lincoln Target Series
LOCAL NEWSPAPERS: Local Newspapers English Counties

LINCOLN TARGET SERIES
44053U72B-2240

Formerly: Lincoln Target
Editorial Address: Brayford Wharf East, LINCOLN, LN5 7AT
Tel: 01522 820000 **Fax:** 01522 804493
Email: news@lincolnshireecho.co.uk
Advertising Address: As above. **Fax:** 01522 804491
Email: adverts@lincolnshireecho.co.uk
Web site: http://www.thisislincolnshire.co.uk
Publisher: Lincolnshire Media Ltd
Frequency: Weekly - Published on Thursday
Cover Price: Free
Circulation: 47,371 (Combined Circulation)
Editor: Dan Sharp; **News Editor:** Dan Sharp; **Managing Director:** Mark Price; **Managing Editor:** Nick Purkiss
ADVERTISING RATES:
SCC £5.40

Mechanical Data: Film: Digital, Page Width: 269mm, Col Length: 365mm, No. of Columns (Display): 8, Type Area: 365 x 269mm, Print Process: Web-fed offset litho
Series owner and contact point for the following titles, see individual entries:
Gainsborough Target
Lincoln Target
LOCAL NEWSPAPERS: Local Newspapers English Counties

LINCOLNSHIRE ECHO
42111U67B-365

Editorial Address: Brayford Wharf East, LINCOLN, LN5 7AT
Tel: 01522 820000 **Fax:** 01522 804493
Email: news@lincolnshireecho.co.uk
Advertising Address: As above. **Tel:** 01522 804480
Fax: 01522 804491
Email: adverts@lincolnshireecho.co.uk
Web site: http://www.thisislincolnshire.co.uk
Publisher: Lincolnshire Media Ltd
Date Established: 1893
Frequency: Daily - Not published on Sunday
Cover Price: £0.36
Circulation: 22,263 (ABC 02/07/2007 to 30/12/2007)
Editor: Dan Sharp; **News Editor:** Dan Sharp; **Features Editor:** Sarah Overton; **Managing Director:** Mark Price;
Advertising Manager: Lucy Alcorn
ADVERTISING RATES:
Full Page Mono £1900.80
Full Page Colour £2376.00
SCC £6.60
Agency Commission: 10%
Mechanical Data: Col Length: 365mm, No. of Columns (Display): 8, Print Process: Web-fed offset litho, Type Area: 365 x 269mm, Film: Digital, Page Width: 269mm
Copy instructions: Copy Date: 2 days prior to publication date
Average advertising content per issue: 40%
Supplement(s): Home and Garden - 12xY, Property Echo - 52xY, This Is Motors - 52xY, This is The Business - 12xY
REGIONAL DAILY & SUNDAY NEWSPAPERS: Regional Daily Newspapers

LINCOLNSHIRE FREE PRESS
44055U72B-2250_150

Frequency: Weekly - Published on Tuesday
Cover Price: £0.37
Circulation: 18,222 (ABC 02/07/2007 to 30/12/2007)
ADVERTISING RATES:
SCC £4.69
Part of Series, see entry for: Lincolnshire Free Press Series
LOCAL NEWSPAPERS: Local Newspapers English Counties

LINCOLNSHIRE FREE PRESS SERIES
44054U72B-2250

Editorial Address: Priory House, The Crescent, SPALDING, PE11 1AB **Tel:** 01775 725021 **Fax:** 01775 714744
Email: david.crossley@jpress.co.uk
Advertising Address: As above. **Fax:** 01775 765444
Email: gill.wheldon@jpress.co.uk
Web site: http://www.spaldingtoday.co.uk
Publisher: Johnston Press plc
Date Established: 1847
Frequency: Weekly
Circulation: 33,071 (Combined Circulation)
Editor: David Crossley; **News Editor:** David Crossley;
Group Editor: Jon Buss
ADVERTISING: Rates on application
Agency Commission: 10%
Mechanical Data: Col Widths (Display): 27mm, No. of Columns (Display): 9, Film: Digital
Average advertising content per issue: 57%
Series owner and contact point for the following titles, see individual entries:
Lincolnshire Free Press
Spalding Guardian
LOCAL NEWSPAPERS: Local Newspapers English Counties

LINGFIELD COUNTY BORDER NEWS
1665850U72B-1774_202

Frequency: Weekly - Circulation is incorporated into Oxted County Border News
Cover Price: Free
Part of Series, see entry for: County Border News Series
LOCAL NEWSPAPERS: Local Newspapers English Counties

LINLITHGOW ADVERTISER
44935U72D-365_130

Frequency: Weekly
Cover Price: Free

Part of Series, see entry for: Falkirk & Grangemouth Advertiser Series
LOCAL NEWSPAPERS: Local Newspapers Scotland

LINLITHGOW GAZETTE
44990U72D-690_130

Email: journal.gazette@jnscotland.co.uk
Frequency: Weekly
Cover Price: £0.40
Part of Series, see entry for: Linlithgowshire Journal and Gazette Series
LOCAL NEWSPAPERS: Local Newspapers Scotland

LINLITHGOWSHIRE JOURNAL AND GAZETTE SERIES
717859U72D-690

Editorial Address: 114 High Street, LINLITHGOW, EH49 7AQ **Tel:** 01506 844592 **Fax:** 01506 670281
Email: editorial@journalandgazette.co.uk
Advertising Address: As above.
Email: kieran.koszary@jnscotland.co.uk
Web site: http://www.linlithgowtodaygazette.co.uk
Publisher: Johnston (Falkirk) Ltd
Date Established: 1891
Frequency: Weekly
Circulation: 8,632 (ABC 02/07/2007 to 30/12/2007)
Editor: Jackie Mitchell; **Advertising Manager:** Kieran Koszary
ADVERTISING RATES:
Full Page Mono £1055.70
Full Page Colour £1583.55
SCC £3.45
Mechanical Data: Film: Digital, Page Width: 272mm, Col Widths (Display): 28mm, Type Area: 340 x 272mm, Col Length: 340mm, No. of Columns (Display): 9
Series owner and contact point for the following titles, see individual entries:
Bo'ness Journal
Linlithgow Gazette
Queensferry Gazette
LOCAL NEWSPAPERS: Local Newspapers Scotland

LIPHOOK HERALD
1640803U72B-3120_181

Frequency: Weekly
Cover Price: £0.50
Part of Series, see entry for: Farnham Herald Series
LOCAL NEWSPAPERS: Local Newspapers English Counties

LIPHOOK TIMES & MAIL
44389U72B-1339_210

Frequency: Weekly - Circulation figure is incorporated into the Alton Times & Mail
Cover Price: Free
Part of Series, see entry for: Alton Post Gazette, Times & Mail Series
LOCAL NEWSPAPERS: Local Newspapers English Counties

LISBURN ECHO
45104U72E-157

Editorial Address: 12A Bow Street, LISBURN, BT28 1BN
Tel: 028 9267 9111 **Fax:** 028 9260 2904
Email: news@ulsterstar.co.uk
Advertising Address: As above.
Web site: http://www.lisburntoday.co.uk
Publisher: Morton Newspapers Ltd
Frequency: Weekly
Cover Price: Free
Circulation: 23,101 (VFD 02/07/2007 to 30/12/2007)
Editor: David Fletcher; **Advertising Manager:** Liz Milburne
ADVERTISING RATES:
Full Page Mono £1435.15
Full Page Colour £2080.00
SCC £4.70
Mechanical Data: Col Length: 340mm, Page Width: 268mm, Type Area: 340 x 268mm, No. of Columns (Display): 9
Copy instructions: Copy Date: Thursday midday prior to publication date
LOCAL NEWSPAPERS: Local Newspapers Northern Ireland

LISKEARD AND CALLINGTON GAZETTE
43425U72B-545_140

Formerly: Liskeard, Looe, Saltash and Callington Gazette
Frequency: Weekly - Circulation figure is for Liskeard and Callington Gazette, Looe and Polperro Gazette, Coastal Journal, Saltash Journal and Torpoint Journal
Cover Price: Free
Circulation: 36,000 (Publisher's Statement)
ADVERTISING RATES:
Full Page Mono £1065.60
Full Page Colour £1324.80
SCC £3.70

Part of Series, see entry for: Cornish Times & Gazette Series
LOCAL NEWSPAPERS: Local Newspapers English Counties

LITTLEHAMPTON GAZETTE
44459U72B-3319

Editorial Address: 34 Beach Road, LITTLEHAMPTON, BN17 5HT **Tel:** 01903 714135 **Fax:** 01903 739060
Email: roger.green@littlehamptongazette.co.uk
Advertising Address: Cannon House, Chatsworth Road, WORTHING, BN11 1NA **Tel:** 01903 282387
Fax: 01903 216087
Web site: http://www.littlehamptongazette.co.uk
Publisher: Portsmouth Publishing & Printing Ltd
Date Established: 1893
Frequency: Weekly - Published on Thursday
Cover Price: £0.42
Circulation: 9,839 (ABC 02/07/2007 to 30/12/2007)
Editor: Roger Green; **Advertising Manager:** Jane Bell
ADVERTISING RATES:
SCC £3.76
Mechanical Data: Type Area: 340 x 277mm, No. of Columns (Display): 9, Col Length: 340mm, Page Width: 277mm, Film: Digital
LOCAL NEWSPAPERS: Local Newspapers English Counties

LIVERPOOL DAILY POST
42115U67B-370

Formerly: Daily Post (Liverpool)
Editorial Address: PO Box 48, Old Hall Street, LIVERPOOL, L69 3EB **Tel:** 0151 227 2000 **Fax:** 0151 472 2506
Email: andykelly@dailypost.co.uk
Advertising Address: As above. **Fax:** 0151 473 0105
Email: frank.notton@liverpool.com
Web site: http://www.liverpooldailypost.co.uk
ISSN: 0962-7553
Publisher: Liverpool Daily Post & Echo Ltd
Frequency: Mornings - Published Monday to Friday
Cover Price: £0.55
Circulation: 15,581 (ABC 02/07/2007 to 30/12/2007)
Editor: Mark Thomas; **Features Editor:** Emma Johnson
ADVERTISING RATES:
Full Page Mono £2902.00
Full Page Colour £3917.70
SCC £10.08
Agency Commission: 10%
Mechanical Data: Type Area: 360 x 272mm, Col Length: 360mm, Col Widths (Display): 31mm, No. of Columns (Display): 8, Film: Digital, Page Width: 272mm
Copy instructions: Copy Date: 2 days prior to publication date
Average advertising content per issue: 40%
Supplement(s): Box Office - 52xY, Daysix (Leisure and Lifestyle) - 52xY, Elegant Homes - 52xY, Golf Northwest - 52xY, LDP Business - 12xY, Post Match - 52xY, Style City - 52xY
REGIONAL DAILY & SUNDAY NEWSPAPERS: Regional Daily Newspapers

LIVERPOOL ECHO
42119U67B-380

Editorial Address: PO Box 48, Old Hall Street, LIVERPOOL, L69 3EB **Tel:** 0151 227 2000 **Fax:** 0151 472 2474
Advertising Address: As above. **Fax:** 0151 330 5024
Email: chris.forsyth@liverpool.com
Web site: http://www.liverpoolecho.co.uk
Publisher: Liverpool Daily Post & Echo Ltd
Frequency: Evenings
Cover Price: £0.45
Circulation: 109,458 (Publisher's Statement)
Editor: Maria Breslin; **News Editor:** Maria Breslin; **Features Editor:** Jane Haase; **Managing Director:** Sara Wilde
ADVERTISING RATES:
SCC £27.64
Agency Commission: 10%
Mechanical Data: Col Length: 360mm, Col Widths (Display): 31mm, No. of Columns (Display): 8, Film: Digital, Type Area: 360 x 272mm, Page Width: 272mm
Copy instructions: Copy Date: 2 working days prior to publication date
Editions:
Liverpool Echo (Main Extra)
Supplement(s): Football Echo (Liverpool) - 52xY
REGIONAL DAILY & SUNDAY NEWSPAPERS: Regional Daily Newspapers

LIVERPOOL ECHO (MAIN EXTRA)
1660030U67B-380_501

Formerly: Liverpool Echo (Extra)
Frequency: Daily
Cover Price: £0.45
Edition of: Liverpool Echo
REGIONAL DAILY & SUNDAY NEWSPAPERS: Regional Daily Newspapers

LIVERPOOL WEEKLY MERSEYMART & STAR SERIES
44094U72B-2383

Formerly: Liverpool Weekly Star Series
Editorial Address: Liverpool Echo and Daily Post Building, Old Hall Street, LIVERPOOL, L69 3EB **Tel:** 0151 227 2000
Fax: 0151 285 8403
Email: lwng.newsdesk@liverpool.com
Advertising Address: 6 Allerton Road, Mossley Hill, LIVERPOOL, L18 1LN **Tel:** 0151 227 2000
Email: karen.williams@cheshirenews.co.uk
Web site: http://www.icliverpool.co.uk
Publisher: Trinity Mirror
Frequency: Weekly
Cover Price: Free
Circulation: 128,081 (Combined Circulation)
Editor: Jane Clare; **Advertising Manager:** Debbie McGraw
ADVERTISING: Rates on application
Agency Commission: 10%
Copy instructions: Copy Date: 3 working days prior to publication date
Series owner and contact point for the following titles, see individual entries:
Maghull & Aintree Star
Merseymart and Star Huyton and Roby
Merseymart West Derby & Tuebrook
South Liverpool Merseymart
Star and Merseymart Anfield & Walton
LOCAL NEWSPAPERS: Local Newspapers English Counties

LLAIS
761562U72J-140

Editorial Address: Afallon, 23 Kingrosia Parc, Clydach, SWANSEA, SA6 5PN **Tel:** 01792 842853
Advertising Address: As above.
Frequency: 10 issues yearly - Not published in August and September
Cover Price: £0.40
Circulation: 990 (Publisher's Statement)
Editor: John Evans; **Advertising Manager:** John Evans
Summary of Content: Welsh language community newspaper featuring arts, book reviews, letters, local news and an editorial column.
Language(s): Welsh
Readership/Target Audience: Aimed at Welsh speaking readers with an interest in local affairs.
ADVERTISING: Rates on application
LOCAL NEWSPAPERS: Community Newsletters

LLANDOVERY JOURNAL
706896U72C-220_130

Frequency: Weekly
Part of Series, see entry for: Journal Series (Carmarthen)
LOCAL NEWSPAPERS: Local Newspapers Wales

LLANDYSUL JOURNAL
706897U72C-220_140

Frequency: Weekly
Part of Series, see entry for: Journal Series (Carmarthen)
LOCAL NEWSPAPERS: Local Newspapers Wales

LLANELLI STAR
44806U72C-230_150

Frequency: Weekly
Cover Price: £0.55
Part of Series, see entry for: Llanelli Star Series
LOCAL NEWSPAPERS: Local Newspapers Wales

LLANELLI STAR SERIES
44803U72C-230

Editorial Address: 11 Cowell Street, LLANELLI, SA15 1UU
Tel: 01554 745334 **Fax:** 01554 745335
Email: journal.star@swwmedia.co.uk
Advertising Address: 18 King Street, CAMARTHAN, SA31 1BN **Tel:** 01267 227222 **Fax:** 01267 227256
Email: eirlys.peck@swwmedia.co.uk
Web site: http://www.thisisllanellistar.co.uk
Publisher: South West Wales Media Ltd
Date Established: 1907
Frequency: Weekly - Published on Wednesday
Circulation: 15,699 (ABC 02/07/2007 to 30/12/2007)
Editor: Bede MacGowan; **Managing Director:** Blanche Sainsbury; **Advertising Manager:** Eirlys Peck
Language(s): English; Welsh
ADVERTISING RATES:
Full Page Mono £1647.00
Full Page Colour £2058.00
Agency Commission: 15%
Mechanical Data: Col Length: 360mm, Col Widths (Display): 32mm, No. of Columns (Display): 8, Film: Digital, Type Area: 360 x 270mm, Page Width: 270mm
Copy instructions: Copy Date: Monday 12pm prior to publication date
Average advertising content per issue: 50%
Series owner and contact point for the following titles, see individual entries:
Llanelli Star

West Wales Tribune
Supplement(s): Business Plus - 12xY, Joio - 52xY, Your Home - 52xY
LOCAL NEWSPAPERS: Local Newspapers Wales

LLANW LLYN
1644421U72J-323

Editorial Address: Flat 2, Avondale, Abersoch, PWLLHELI, LL53 7DT **Tel:** 01758 712580
Email: twrog@jones692.orangehome.co.uk
Frequency: 11 issues yearly - Not published in August
Cover Price: £0.40
Circulation: 2,250 (Publisher's Statement)
Editor: Twrog Jones
Summary of Content: Welsh language community newspaper covering local news and events including coverage of shows and festivals and items on local history.
Language(s): Welsh
Readership/Target Audience: Aimed at the local community.
ADVERTISING: No Advertising taken
LOCAL NEWSPAPERS: Community Newsletters

THE LOCAL (BOURNE, THE DEEPINGS)
44060U72B-2258

Formerly: Bourne Local Series
Editorial Address: 28A West Street, BOURNE, PE10 9NE
Tel: 01778 425876 **Fax:** 01778 394087
Email: news@bournelocal.co.uk
Advertising Address: As above.
Email: lucy.greenwood@jpress.co.uk
Web site: http://www.bournelocal.co.uk
ISSN: 1350-8997
Publisher: East Midlands Newspapers Ltd
Date Established: 1989
Frequency: Weekly - Published on Friday
Cover Price: £0.40
Circulation: 3,600 (Publisher's Statement)
Editor: Paul Clark; **Managing Director:** Amanda Davison-Young; **Advertising Manager:** Lucy Greenwood
ADVERTISING: Rates on application
LOCAL NEWSPAPERS: Local Newspapers English Counties

LOCAL NEWS FOR SOUTHSIDERS
1819048U72D-698_100

Frequency: Monthly
Cover Price: Free
Circulation: 20,000 (Publisher's Statement)
Part of Series, see entry for: Local News (Glasgow) Series
LOCAL NEWSPAPERS: Local Newspapers Scotland

LOCAL NEWS FOR WESTENDERS
1819049U72D-698_101

Frequency: Monthly
Cover Price: Free
Circulation: 20,000 (Publisher's Statement)
Part of Series, see entry for: Local News (Glasgow) Series
LOCAL NEWSPAPERS: Local Newspapers Scotland

LOCAL NEWS (GLASGOW) SERIES
45001U72D-698

Formerly: Local News for Southsiders
Editorial Address: Suite 9, 2nd Floor, 73 Robertson Street, GLASGOW, G2 8QD **Tel:** 0141 226 4898
Fax: 0141 226 4708
Email: localnews@btconnect.com
Advertising Address: As above.
Email: localnews@btconnect.com
Web site: http://www.localnewsglasgow.co.uk
Publisher: Yam Publications Ltd
Date Established: 1997
Frequency: Monthly
Cover Price: Free
Circulation: 40,000 (Combined Circulation)
Editor: Grace Franklin
Language(s): Arabic; Chinese; English; Urdu
Readership/Target Audience: Circulates in: south of the River Clyde and most of the communities north of the River Clyde particularly around the west end of the city.
ADVERTISING RATES:
SCC £6.00
Mechanical Data: Col Length: 365mm, Col Widths (Display): 34mm, No. of Columns (Display): 7, Type Area: 365 x 270mm, Page Width: 270mm
Copy instructions: Copy Date: 24th of the month prior to publication date
Average advertising content per issue: 50%
Series owner and contact point for the following titles, see individual entries:
Local News for Southsiders

Section 4 (a) Newspapers

Local News for Westenders
LOCAL NEWSPAPERS: Local Newspapers Scotland

LONDON EVENING STANDARD

41641U67B-9009

Formerly: Evening Standard
Editorial Address: Northcliffe House, 2 Derry Street, LONDON, W8 5TT **Tel:** 020 7938 6000
Email: news@standard.co.uk
Advertising Address: As above. **Fax:** 020 7937 7929
Email: mark.service@standard.co.uk
Web site: http://www.standard.co.uk
Publisher: Evening Press Ltd
Frequency: Evenings - Published Monday to Friday
Cover Price: Free
Circulation: 263,312 (ABC 30/03/2009 to 26/04/2009)
Editor: Newsdesk; **News Editor:** Hugh Dougherty;
Features Editor: Charlotte Ross; **Managing Director:** Andrew Mullins; **Advertising Manager:** Mark Service;
Managing Editor: Doug Wills
Summary of Content: Tabloid-sized newspaper covering national, international and regional news for London and the South-East. Includes coverage of city news, sport, lifestyle, travel, entertainment and guides to London.
ADVERTISING RATES:
Full Page Mono £20160.00
Full Page Colour £30240.00
SCC £80.00
Series owner and contact point for the following titles, see individual entries:
Business
Fashion & Style
Film and Arts
Health
London Evening Standard Homes & Property
London Jobs
London Life
Media
Sport
Travel
Trends
Editions:
London Evening Standard (Late Night Final)
London Evening Standard (News Extra)
London Evening Standard (West End Final)
Supplement(s): ES Magazine - 52xY
REGIONAL DAILY & SUNDAY NEWSPAPERS: Regional Daily Newspapers

LONDON EVENING STANDARD HOMES & PROPERTY

41648U67B-9009_702

Formerly: Evening Standard Homes & Property
Tel: 020 7938 6000 **Fax:** 020 7938 7249
Frequency: Weekly - Published on Wednesday within the London Evening Standard
Circulation: 389,837 (Publisher's Statement)
Editor: Janice Morley
Summary of Content: Section covering all aspects of buying and selling property with features on interiors, property maintenance, garden design and personal finance.
ADVERTISING: Rates on application
Part of Series, see entry for: London Evening Standard
REGIONAL DAILY & SUNDAY NEWSPAPERS: Regional Daily Newspapers

LONDON EVENING STANDARD (LATE NIGHT FINAL)

41644U67B-9009_709

Formerly: Evening Standard (Late Night Final)
ADVERTISING: Rates on application
Edition of: London Evening Standard
REGIONAL DAILY & SUNDAY NEWSPAPERS: Regional Daily Newspapers

LONDON EVENING STANDARD (NEWS EXTRA)

41645U67B-9009_600

Formerly: Evening Standard (News Extra)
Frequency: 250 issues yearly
ADVERTISING: Rates on application
Edition of: London Evening Standard
REGIONAL DAILY & SUNDAY NEWSPAPERS: Regional Daily Newspapers

LONDON EVENING STANDARD (WEST END FINAL)

41646U67B-9009_500

Formerly: Evening Standard (West End Final)
Editorial Address: For all contact details see main edition, Evening Standard
Frequency: Evenings
Cover Price: £0.40
ADVERTISING: Rates on application

Edition of: London Evening Standard
REGIONAL DAILY & SUNDAY NEWSPAPERS: Regional Daily Newspapers

LONDON INFORMER

43081U72A-300_167

Formerly: Kensington & Chelsea Informer
Frequency: Weekly - Published on Friday. Circulation figure includes Marylebone & Paddington Informer, Hammersmith & Fulham Informer and Westminster & Pimlico Informer
Cover Price: Free
Circulation: 66,345 (Publisher's Statement)
ADVERTISING RATES:
SCC £14.51
Copy instructions: Copy Date: Wednesday 4pm prior to publication date
Part of Series, see entry for: London Newspaper Group Series
LOCAL NEWSPAPERS: Local Newspapers Greater London

LONDON JOBS

41649U67B-9009_703

Formerly: Evening Standard Just the Job
Tel: 020 7938 6000
Email: londonjobs@standard.co.uk
Web site: http://www.londonjobs.co.uk
Frequency: Weekly - Published on Monday within the London Evening Standard
Summary of Content: Section featuring information on careers and appointments.
ADVERTISING: Rates on application
Part of Series, see entry for: London Evening Standard
REGIONAL DAILY & SUNDAY NEWSPAPERS: Regional Daily Newspapers

LONDON LIFE

1899299U67B-9086

Tel: 020 7938 7586
Email: features@standard.co.uk
Frequency: Weekly - Published on Thursday within The London Evening Standard
Editor: Charlotte Ross
Summary of Content: Section focusing on issues affecting Londoners.
ADVERTISING: Rates on application
Part of Series, see entry for: London Evening Standard
REGIONAL DAILY & SUNDAY NEWSPAPERS: Regional Daily Newspapers

LONDON LITE

1777373U67B-9031

Editorial Address: Northcliffe House, 2 Derry Street, LONDON, W8 5TT **Tel:** 020 7938 6000
Advertising Address: As above.
Email: karen.glanville@standard.co.uk
Web site: http://www.thelondonlite.co.uk
Publisher: Associated Newspapers Ltd
Date Established: 2006
Frequency: Evenings
Cover Price: Free
Circulation: 400,547 (ABC 2009)
Editor: Bo Wilson; **News Editor:** Bo Wilson; **Features Editor:** Tracey Blake; **Advertising Manager:** Karen Glanville
Summary of Content: Free evening publication focussing on news, celebrities and entertainment.
ADVERTISING RATES:
Full Page Mono £17640.00
Full Page Colour £17640.00
SCC £70.00
Mechanical Data: Type Area: 360 x 268mm, Col Length: 360mm, Page Width: 268mm, Col Widths (Display): 35mm, No. of Columns (Display): 7, Film: Digital
Copy instructions: Copy Date: 2 working days prior to publication date
REGIONAL DAILY & SUNDAY NEWSPAPERS: Regional Daily Newspapers

LONDON NEWSPAPER GROUP SERIES

43086U72A-300

Formerly: London Newspaper Group
Editorial Address: 93 Staines Road, HOUNSLOW, TW3 3JB
Tel: 020 8572 1816 **Fax:** 020 8741 1973
Email: newshammersmith@trinitysouth.co.uk
Advertising Address: Informer House, 2 High Street, TEDDINGTON, TW11 8EW **Tel:** 020 8943 5171
Fax: 020 8977 7741
Email: nslsales@trinitysouth.co.uk
Publisher: Trinity Mirror Southern
Frequency: Weekly
Circulation: 69,601 (Combined Circulation)
Editor: News Desk; **Advertising Manager:** Niki Hornsby
ADVERTISING: Rates on application
Agency Commission: 10%
Mechanical Data: Type Area: 340 x 262mm, Col Length: 340mm, Page Width: 262mm, Col Widths (Display): 31mm, No. of Columns (Display): 8, Film: Digital

Average advertising content per issue: 50%
Series owner and contact point for the following titles, see individual entries:
Fulham & Hammersmith Chronicle
Kensington & Chelsea News
London Informer
Marylebone, Paddington and Pimlico Mercury
LOCAL NEWSPAPERS: Local Newspapers Greater London

LONDON VOICE

1626333U72A-1302_100

Frequency: 26 issues yearly
Cover Price: Free
ADVERTISING: Rates on application
Part of Series, see entry for: London Voice Series
LOCAL NEWSPAPERS: Local Newspapers Greater London

LONDON VOICE BEXLEY & GREENWICH

1626334U72A-1302_101

Frequency: 26 issues yearly
Cover Price: Free
ADVERTISING: Rates on application
Part of Series, see entry for: London Voice Series
LOCAL NEWSPAPERS: Local Newspapers Greater London

LONDON VOICE SERIES

1613566U72A-1302

Formerly: London Voice
Editorial Address: 11 Heather Close, LONDON, SW8 3BS
Tel: 020 7720 4150 **Fax:** 020 7720 4150
Email: raymondross11540@aol.com
Advertising Address: As above.
Email: dvhrt@aol.com
Publisher: London Voice Publishing
Date Established: 2002
Frequency: 26 issues yearly
Cover Price: Free
Circulation: 220,000 (Publisher's Statement)
Editor: Raymond Ross; **News Editor:** Raymond Ross;
Features Editor: Charles Anderson; **Advertising Manager:** David Hart; **Managing Editor:** David Hart
ADVERTISING: Rates on application
Series owner and contact point for the following titles, see individual entries:
London Voice
London Voice Bexley & Greenwich
LOCAL NEWSPAPERS: Local Newspapers Greater London

LONDONDERRY SENTINEL

45122U72E-220_140

Formerly: The Sentinel (Londonderry)
Frequency: Weekly - Published on Wednesday
Cover Price: £0.85
Circulation: 4,785 (ABC 02/07/2007 to 30/12/2007)
Part of Series, see entry for: The Sentinel Series
LOCAL NEWSPAPERS: Local Newspapers Northern Ireland

LONG EATON RECORDER

768338U72B-2666_211

Frequency: Weekly
Cover Price: Free
Circulation: 46,386 (VFD 02/07/2007 to 30/12/2007)
ADVERTISING: Rates on application
Part of Series, see entry for: West Notts & Derbyshire Recorder Series
LOCAL NEWSPAPERS: Local Newspapers English Counties

LONGRIDGE & RIBBLE VALLEY NEWS AND ADVERTISER

43984U72B-1999

Editorial Address: 7 Pringle Court, Parkhill Road, Garstang, PRESTON, PR3 1LN **Tel:** 01995 605910 **Fax:** 01995 601623
Email: longridge.news@lep.co.uk
Advertising Address: Olivers Place, Eastway, Fulwood, PRESTON, PR2 9ZA **Tel:** 01772 838146 **Fax:** 01772 204941
Email: andy.skelding@lep.co.uk
Web site: http://www.longridgenews.co.uk
Publisher: Lancashire Evening Post Ltd
Frequency: Weekly - Published on Wednesday
Cover Price: £0.55
Circulation: 3,289 (ABC 02/07/2007 to 30/12/2007)
Editor: Richard Machin; **Advertising Manager:** Andy Skelding
ADVERTISING RATES:
SCC £2.89
Agency Commission: 10%
Mechanical Data: Page Width: 274mm, Col Length: 340mm, Col Widths (Display): 30mm, No. of Columns (Display): 9, Type Area: 340 x 274mm, Film: Digital
Copy instructions: Copy Date: Monday 5pm prior to publication date
Average advertising content per issue: 50%
LOCAL NEWSPAPERS: Local Newspapers English Counties

THE LONGRIDGE NEWS
1832653U72B-1985_101
Formerly: The Longridge Courier
Frequency: Weekly - Published on Wednesday
Cover Price: £0.55
ADVERTISING: Rates on application
Part of Series, see entry for: The Garstang & Longridge Courier & News Series
LOCAL NEWSPAPERS: Local Newspapers English Counties

LOOE AND POLPERRO GAZETTE
767524U72B-545_141
Frequency: Weekly - For circulation, see Liskeard and Callington Gazette
Cover Price: Free
ADVERTISING RATES:
Full Page Mono £1065.60
Full Page Colour £1324.80
SCC £3.70
Part of Series, see entry for: Cornish Times & Gazette Series
LOCAL NEWSPAPERS: Local Newspapers English Counties

THE LOTHIAN TIMES (EAST LOTHIAN EDITION)
44902U72D-270_170
Frequency: Weekly - Circulation figure is a combined figure comprising The Lothian Times (East Lothian edition), Midlothian Times and Peebles Times
Cover Price: Free
Circulation: 48,838 (VFD 02/07/2007 to 30/12/2007)
Part of Series, see entry for: Dalkeith Advertiser Series
LOCAL NEWSPAPERS: Local Newspapers Scotland

LOTHIAN TIMES (MIDLOTHIAN)
44903U72D-270_175
Formerly: Midlothian Times
Frequency: Weekly - Please see The Lothian Times (East Lothian edition) for circulation figures
Cover Price: Free
Part of Series, see entry for: Dalkeith Advertiser Series
LOCAL NEWSPAPERS: Local Newspapers Scotland

LOUGHBOROUGH ECHO
44022U72B-2150_170
Frequency: Weekly - Circulation figure also includes the Shepshed Echo
Cover Price: £0.50
Circulation: 21,438 (ABC 02/07/2007 to 30/12/2007)
ADVERTISING RATES:
SCC £5.25
Part of Series, see entry for: Loughborough Echo Series
LOCAL NEWSPAPERS: Local Newspapers English Counties

LOUGHBOROUGH ECHO SERIES
44020U72B-2150
Editorial Address: Royal Way, Off Belton Road West Extension, LOUGHBOROUGH, LE11 5XR **Tel:** 01509 232632
Fax: 01509 240016
Email: matt_jarram@mrn.co.uk
Advertising Address: As above. **Fax:** 01509 238363
Email: echoadvertising@mrn.co.uk
Web site: http://www.icloughborough.co.uk
Publisher: Trinity Mirror
Frequency: Weekly
Circulation: 72,916 (Combined Circulation)
Editor: Matt Jarram
ADVERTISING RATES:
SCC £5.25
Agency Commission: 10%
Mechanical Data: Film: Digital, Col Length: 340mm, Page Width: 264mm, Type Area: 340 x 264mm, No. of Columns (Display): 9
Average advertising content per issue: 60%
Series owner and contact point for the following titles, see individual entries:
Ashby Echo
Coalville Echo
Loughborough Echo
Loughborough Echo Trader Xtra
Shepshed Echo
LOCAL NEWSPAPERS: Local Newspapers English Counties

LOUGHBOROUGH ECHO TRADER XTRA
44021U72B-2150_140
Frequency: Weekly
Cover Price: Free
Circulation: 35,351 (Publisher's Statement)

ADVERTISING RATES:
SCC £5.25
Part of Series, see entry for: Loughborough Echo Series
LOCAL NEWSPAPERS: Local Newspapers English Counties

LOUGHBOROUGH MAIL
44017U72B-2135_160
Frequency: Weekly
Cover Price: Free
Circulation: 31,438 (VFD 02/07/2007 to 30/12/2007)
ADVERTISING RATES:
SCC £5.35
Part of Series, see entry for: Leicester Mail Series
LOCAL NEWSPAPERS: Local Newspapers English Counties

LOUTH CITIZEN
1655841U72B-2263_161
Frequency: Weekly - For circulation figure see Boston Citizen
Cover Price: Free
ADVERTISING: Rates on application
Part of Series, see entry for: Louth Leader and Citizen Series
LOCAL NEWSPAPERS: Local Newspapers English Counties

LOUTH LEADER
44061U72B-2263_160
Formerly: Louth Standard
Frequency: Weekly - Circulation figure is incorporated into The Leader Mablethorpe, Sutton & Alford
Cover Price: £0.45
ADVERTISING: Rates on application
Part of Series, see entry for: Louth Leader and Citizen Series
LOCAL NEWSPAPERS: Local Newspapers English Counties

LOUTH LEADER AND CITIZEN SERIES
44062U72B-2263
Formerly: Louth Leader Series
Editorial Address: 44 Eastgate, LOUTH, LN11 9NJ
Tel: 01507 353200 **Fax:** 01507 617401
Email: charles.ladbrook@jpress.co.uk
Advertising Address: As above. **Fax:** 01507 353201
Email: lisa.mitchell@jpress.co.uk
Web site: http://www.louthtoday.co.uk
Publisher: Johnston Press plc
Frequency: Weekly - Published on Wednesday
Circulation: 101,326 (Combined Circulation)
Editor: Charles Ladbrook; **Advertising Manager:** Lisa Mitchell
ADVERTISING: Rates on application
Agency Commission: 10%
Copy instructions: Copy Date: Friday prior to publication date
Average advertising content per issue: 50%
Series owner and contact point for the following titles, see individual entries:
The Leader Mablethorpe and Sutton-on-Sea
Louth Citizen
Louth Leader
LOCAL NEWSPAPERS: Local Newspapers English Counties

LOUTH TARGET
44065U72B-2287_132
Formerly: Louth Target Series
Frequency: Weekly - Circulation figure includes the Mablethorpe and Alford Target and the Market Rasen Target
Cover Price: Free
Circulation: 13,776 (VFD 02/07/2007 to 30/12/2007)
Part of Series, see entry for: Target Series
LOCAL NEWSPAPERS: Local Newspapers English Counties

LOWESTOFT JOURNAL
44342U72B-3080
Editorial Address: 147 London Road North, LOWESTOFT, NR32 1NB **Tel:** 01502 525820 **Fax:** 01502 525848
Email: lowestoft.journal@archant.co.uk
Advertising Address: High Street, Gorleston, GREAT YARMOUTH, NR31 6RL **Tel:** 01493 335000
Email: bonnie.rayner@archant.co.uk
Web site: http://www.lowestoftjournal24.co.uk
Publisher: Archant Norfolk
Date Established: 1873
Frequency: Weekly - Published on Friday
Cover Price: £0.55
Circulation: 18,333 (ABC 02/07/2007 to 30/12/2007)
Editor: Russell Cook; **Managing Director:** Stephan Phillips
ADVERTISING RATES:
SCC £5.74

Agency Commission: 10%
Mechanical Data: Page Width: 270mm, Type Area: 360 x 270mm, Col Length: 360mm, No. of Columns (Display): 8, Col Widths (Display): 32mm, Film: Digital
Copy instructions: Copy Date: Wednesday 5pm prior to publication date
Average advertising content per issue: 40%
LOCAL NEWSPAPERS: Local Newspapers English Counties

LUDLOW ADVERTISER
44240U72B-2820_150
Frequency: Weekly
Cover Price: £0.40
Part of Series, see entry for: Ludlow Advertiser Series
LOCAL NEWSPAPERS: Local Newspapers English Counties

LUDLOW ADVERTISER SERIES
44239U72B-2820
Editorial Address: Holmer Road, HEREFORD, HR4 9UJ
Tel: 01584 873796 **Fax:** 01584 878442
Email: lanews@midlands.newsquest.co.uk
Advertising Address: Old Post Office, 7 Corve Street, LUDLOW, SY8 1QE **Tel:** 01584 872183 **Fax:** 01584 878442
Email: laadvertising@midlands.newsquest.co.uk
Web site: http://www.ludlowadvertiser.co.uk
Publisher: Newsquest Media Group
Frequency: Weekly - Published on Thursday
Circulation: 5,924 (ABC 02/07/2007 to 30/12/2007)
Editor: Adrian Kibbler; **News Editor:** Adrian Kibbler
ADVERTISING RATES:
Full Page Mono £607.95
Full Page Colour £740.25
Agency Commission: 10%
Mechanical Data: No. of Columns (Display): 9, Col Widths (Display): 28mm, Film: Digital
Copy instructions: Copy Date: Tuesday 12 noon prior to publication date
Average advertising content per issue: 65%
Series owner and contact point for the following titles, see individual entries:
Ludlow Advertiser
Tenbury Wells Advertiser
LOCAL NEWSPAPERS: Local Newspapers English Counties

LUDLOW JOURNAL
44234U72B-2812_175
Frequency: Weekly
Cover Price: Free
Circulation: 9,130 (VFD 02/07/2007 to 30/12/2007)
ADVERTISING: Rates on application
Part of Series, see entry for: Chronicle & Journal Series
LOCAL NEWSPAPERS: Local Newspapers English Counties

LURGAN & PORTADOWN EXAMINER
45094U72E-120_160
Frequency: Weekly
Cover Price: £0.40
Part of Series, see entry for: Dungannon Observer Series
LOCAL NEWSPAPERS: Local Newspapers Northern Ireland

LURGAN MAIL
45105U72E-170
Formerly: Lurgan Mail incorporating The Craigavon Times
Editorial Address: 4A High Street, LURGAN, BT66 8AW
Tel: 028 3832 7777 **Fax:** 028 3832 5271
Email: clint.aiken@jpress.co.uk
Advertising Address: As above.
Email: robert.abraham@jpress.co.uk
Web site: http://www.lurgantoday.co.uk
Publisher: Morton Newspapers Ltd
Frequency: Weekly - Published on Wednesday
Cover Price: £0.95
Circulation: 8,632 (ABC 02/07/2007 to 30/12/2007)
Editor: Clint Aiken; **Advertising Manager:** Robert Abraham
ADVERTISING RATES:
Full Page Mono £1530.00
Full Page Colour £1912.50
SCC £5.00
Agency Commission: 10%
Mechanical Data: Type Area: 340 x 268mm, Col Length: 340mm, Print Process: Web-fed offset litho, Film: Digital, No. of Columns (Display): 9, Col Widths (Display): 32mm, Page Width: 268mm
Copy instructions: Copy Date: Tuesday 5pm prior to publication date
LOCAL NEWSPAPERS: Local Newspapers Northern Ireland

Non-National Newspapers

LUTON & DUNSTABLE EXPRESS
43248U72B-4158_101

Formerly: Luton & Dunstable on Sunday
Frequency: Weekly - Published on Wednesday
Cover Price: Free
Circulation: 67,106 (VFD 02/07/2007 to 30/12/2007)
Part of Series, see entry for: Luton & Dunstable Express & News Series
LOCAL NEWSPAPERS: Local Newspapers English Counties

LUTON & DUNSTABLE EXPRESS & NEWS SERIES
43245U72B-4158

Formerly: Luton & Dunstable on Sunday
Editorial Address: 28 King Street, LUTON, LU1 2DP
Tel: 01582 707707 **Fax:** 01582 707708
Email: editor@ldexpress.co.uk
Advertising Address: As above. **Tel:** 01582 700800
Fax: 01582 700801
Email: advertising@ldexpress.co.uk
Web site: http://www.ldexpress.co.uk
Publisher: LSN Media
Frequency: Weekly - Published on Wednesday
Cover Price: Free
Circulation: 95,089 (Publisher's Statement)
Editor: Craig Lewis; **News Editor:** Craig Lewis
ADVERTISING RATES:
SCC £7.20
Agency Commission: 10%
Mechanical Data: Type Area: 350 x 268mm, Col Length: 350mm, Film: Digital, No. of Columns (Display): 9, Page Width: 268mm
Copy instructions: Copy Date: Friday 5.30pm prior to publication date
Average advertising content per issue: 65%
Series owner and contact point for the following titles, see individual entries:
Leighton Buzzard News
Luton & Dunstable Express
Supplement(s): Bedfordshire Property - 52xY
LOCAL NEWSPAPERS: Local Newspapers English Counties

LUTON NEWS
43244U72B-137_150

Frequency: Weekly - Published on Wednesday
Cover Price: £0.38
Circulation: 9,874 (ABC 02/07/2007 to 30/12/2007)
ADVERTISING: Rates on application
Part of Series, see entry for: Luton News and Dunstable Gazette Series
LOCAL NEWSPAPERS: Local Newspapers English Counties

LUTON NEWS AND DUNSTABLE GAZETTE SERIES
43241U72B-137

Formerly: Luton News and Leader Series
Editorial Address: Media House, 39 Upper George Street, LUTON, LU1 2RD **Tel:** 01582 700600 **Fax:** 01582 526012
Email: editorial@lutonnews.co.uk
Advertising Address: As above. **Tel:** 01582 700601
Fax: 01582 700610
Web site: http://www.lutontoday.co.uk
Publisher: Johnston Press plc
Frequency: Weekly - Published on a Wednesday
Circulation: 14,316 (ABC 02/07/2007 to 30/12/2007)
Editor: Geoff Cox; **Advertising Manager:** Debbie Robinson
ADVERTISING: Rates on application
Agency Commission: 10%
Copy instructions: Copy Date: Monday 5pm prior to publication date
Series owner and contact point for the following titles, see individual entries:
Dunstable Gazette
Luton News
Supplement(s): Business Monthly - 12xY
LOCAL NEWSPAPERS: Local Newspapers English Counties

THE LUTTERWORTH MAIL
44027U72B-2168_150

Frequency: Weekly - Circulation figure is incorporated into the Harborough Mail
Cover Price: £0.47
Part of Series, see entry for: The Mail Series
LOCAL NEWSPAPERS: Local Newspapers English Counties

THE LUTTERWORTH OBSERVER
1817456U72B-3392_101

Frequency: Weekly - Published on Thursdays
Cover Price: Free
Circulation: 10,469 (VFD 02/07/2007 to 30/12/2007)

ADVERTISING RATES:
Full Page Mono £945.00
Part of Series, see entry for: The Rugby Observer Series
LOCAL NEWSPAPERS: Local Newspapers English Counties

LYME REGIS NEWS
43564U72B-905_140

Frequency: Weekly
Cover Price: £0.40
Part of Series, see entry for: Bridport & Lyme Regis News Series
LOCAL NEWSPAPERS: Local Newspapers English Counties

LYMINGTON TIMES
43728U72B-1337_150

Frequency: Weekly
Cover Price: £0.20
Part of Series, see entry for: Advertiser & Times Series
LOCAL NEWSPAPERS: Local Newspapers English Counties

LYNN NEWS (FRIDAY)
44132U72B-2435_150

Frequency: Weekly
Cover Price: £0.52
Circulation: 28,839 (ABC 02/07/2007 to 30/12/2007)
ADVERTISING RATES:
Full Page Mono £2221.56
Full Page Colour £2888.03
Part of Series, see entry for: Lynn News Series
LOCAL NEWSPAPERS: Local Newspapers English Counties

LYNN NEWS SERIES
44130U72B-2435

Editorial Address: Limes House, Purfleet Street, KING'S LYNN, PE30 1HL **Tel:** 01773 555111 **Fax:** 01553 767627
Email: newsdesk@lynnnews.co.uk
Advertising Address: As above. **Tel:** 01553 762001
Fax: 01553 817381
Email: vicky.smith@lynnnews.co.uk
Web site: http://www.lynnnews.co.uk
Publisher: East Midlands Newspapers Ltd
Date Established: 1841
Frequency: 104 issues yearly
Circulation: 48,609 (ABC 02/07/2007 to 30/12/2007)
News Editor: Donna Semmens; **Advertising Manager:** Vicky Smith; **Group Editor:** Jon Buss
ADVERTISING RATES:
Full Page Mono £4253.40
Full Page Colour £5529.42
Agency Commission: 10%
Mechanical Data: Col Length: 340mm, Film: Digital, No. of Columns (Display): 9, Type Area: 340 x 265mm, Page Width: 265mm
Copy instructions: Copy Date: 3 working days prior to publication date
Average advertising content per issue: 63%
Series owner and contact point for the following titles, see individual entries:
Downham News
Lynn News (Friday)
Lynn News (Tuesday)
LOCAL NEWSPAPERS: Local Newspapers English Counties

LYNN NEWS (TUESDAY)
44131U72B-2435_140

Frequency: Weekly
Cover Price: £0.52
Circulation: 19,770 (ABC 02/07/2007 to 30/12/2007)
ADVERTISING RATES:
Full Page Mono £1713.06
Full Page Colour £2227.08
Part of Series, see entry for: Lynn News Series
LOCAL NEWSPAPERS: Local Newspapers English Counties

LYTHAM ST. ANNES EXPRESS
43987U72B-2005_150

Frequency: Weekly
Part of Series, see entry for: Lytham St Annes Express Series
LOCAL NEWSPAPERS: Local Newspapers English Counties

LYTHAM ST ANNES EXPRESS SERIES
43985U72B-2005

Editorial Address: 12 St. Annes Road West, LYTHAM ST. ANNES, FY8 1RF **Tel:** 01253 724236 **Fax:** 01253 714924
Email: news@lsaexpress.co.uk

Advertising Address: Blackpool Gazette, Avroe House, Avroe Crescent, Blackpool Business Park, LANCS, FY4 4DD
Tel: 01253 400888 **Fax:** 01253 406600
Email: display@blackpoolgazette.co.uk
Web site: http://www.lythamstannesexpress.co.uk
Publisher: Johnston Press plc
Frequency: Weekly - Published on Thursday
Cover Price: £0.47
Circulation: 9,663 (ABC 02/07/2007 to 30/12/2007)
Editor: Gordon McCully; **Advertising Manager:** Joanne Lee
ADVERTISING RATES:
Full Page Mono £1556.00
Full Page Colour £2290.00
SCC £6.00
Agency Commission: 10%
Mechanical Data: Type Area: 340 x 274mm, Col Length: 340mm, Page Width: 274mm, No. of Columns (Display): 9, Col Widths (Display): 30mm, Film: Digital
Copy instructions: Copy Date: Tuesday 12 noon prior to publication date
Average advertising content per issue: 60%
Series owner and contact point for the following titles, see individual entries:
Kirkham and Fylde Express
Lytham St. Annes Express
Supplement(s): Fashion Elite - 2xY, Fylde By Air - 2xY, Leisure Express - 52xY, Property Today - 52xY, Rural Life - 2xY, School Report - 12xY, Society - 12xY
LOCAL NEWSPAPERS: Local Newspapers English Counties

MABLETHORPE AND ALFORD TARGET
1646146U72B-2287_172

Frequency: Weekly
Cover Price: Free
Part of Series, see entry for: Target Series
LOCAL NEWSPAPERS: Local Newspapers English Counties

MACCLESFIELD EXPRESS
43383U72B-479_120

Frequency: Weekly - Published on Wednesday
Cover Price: £0.50
Circulation: 16,307 (ABC 02/07/2007 to 30/12/2007)
ADVERTISING RATES:
SCC £7.75
Agency Commission: 10%
Part of Series, see entry for: Macclesfield Express and Times Series
LOCAL NEWSPAPERS: Local Newspapers English Counties

MACCLESFIELD EXPRESS AND TIMES SERIES
43382U72B-479

Editorial Address: 37 Chestergate, MACCLESFIELD, SK11 6AL **Tel:** 01625 424445 **Fax:** 01625 618853
Email: macclesfieldexpress@menwn.co.uk
Advertising Address: Wood Street, Hollywood, STOCKPORT, SK3 0AB **Tel:** 0161 480 4491
Fax: 0161 480 4837
Email: mark.wroe@menmediasales.co.uk
Web site: http://www.macclesfield-express.co.uk
Publisher: MEN Media
Frequency: Weekly
Circulation: 45,030 (Combined Circulation)
Editor: Charlotte Cox; **News Editor:** Charlotte Cox
ADVERTISING: Rates on application
Agency Commission: 10%
Mechanical Data: Type Area: 340 x 267mm, Col Length: 340mm, Page Width: 267mm, No. of Columns (Display): 9, Col Widths (Display): 27mm, Film: Digital
Copy instructions: Copy Date: Tuesday 3.00pm prior to publication date
Series owner and contact point for the following titles, see individual entries:
Macclesfield Express
Macclesfield Times
Poynton Times
LOCAL NEWSPAPERS: Local Newspapers English Counties

MACCLESFIELD TIMES
43384U72B-479_140

Frequency: Weekly - Published on Thursday
Cover Price: Free
Circulation: 23,353 (VFD 02/07/2007 to 30/12/2007)
ADVERTISING RATES:
SCC £4.75
Agency Commission: 10%
Part of Series, see entry for: Macclesfield Express and Times Series
LOCAL NEWSPAPERS: Local Newspapers English Counties

MACHYNLLETH CAMBRIAN NEWS

763771U72C-30_160

Formerly: Montgomery & Radnor Cambrian News
Frequency: Weekly
Cover Price: £0.65
ADVERTISING: Rates on application
Part of Series, see entry for: The Cambrian News Series
LOCAL NEWSPAPERS: Local Newspapers Wales

MAGHULL & AINTREE STAR

44095U72B-2383_110

Formerly: Star and Merseymart Maghull and Aintree
Frequency: Weekly
Cover Price: Free
Circulation: 13,492 (VFD 02/07/2007 to 30/12/2007)
ADVERTISING: Rates on application
Part of Series, see entry for: Liverpool Weekly Merseymart & Star Series
LOCAL NEWSPAPERS: Local Newspapers English Counties

MAIDENHEAD ADVERTISER

761643U72B-160_160

Frequency: Weekly - Circulation figure incorporates the Twyford Advertiser
Cover Price: £0.40
Circulation: 23,450 (ABC 02/07/2007 to 30/12/2007)
ADVERTISING: Rates on application
Part of Series, see entry for: Maidenhead Advertiser Series
LOCAL NEWSPAPERS: Local Newspapers English Counties

MAIDENHEAD ADVERTISER SERIES

43265U72B-160

Formerly: Maidenhead Advertiser
Editorial Address: 48 Bell Street, MAIDENHEAD, SL6 1HX
Tel: 01628 417834 **Fax:** 01628 678245
Email: news@baylismedia.co.uk
Advertising Address: As above. **Tel:** 01628 680680
Fax: 01628 683700
Email: adverts@maidenads.co.uk
Web site: http://www.maidenhead-advertiser.co.uk
Publisher: Baylis & Co.
Date Established: 1869
Frequency: Weekly
Circulation: 75,397 (Combined Circulation)
Editor: Glenn Mitchell; **Advertisement Director:** Edward Pearce
ADVERTISING: Rates on application
Series owner and contact point for the following titles, see individual entries:
Maidenhead Advertiser
Slough and South Bucks Express
Twyford Advertiser
Windsor, Eton and Ascot Express
Supplement(s): Berkshire Living - 4xY, Business Monthly - 12xY, Leisure & Lifestyle - 52xY, Weddings etc - 2xY
LOCAL NEWSPAPERS: Local Newspapers English Counties

MAIDSTONE ADSCENE

43848U72B-1881_110

Formerly: Maidstone Adscene (Malling & District)
Frequency: Weekly
Cover Price: Free
Circulation: 44,773 (Publisher's Statement)
ADVERTISING: Rates on application
Part of Series, see entry for: Medway News Series
LOCAL NEWSPAPERS: Local Newspapers English Counties

MAIL (COALVILLE & DISTRICT)

44014U72B-2135_135

Formerly: Mail Coalville & Whitwick
Frequency: Weekly
Cover Price: Free
Circulation: 20,573 (VFD 20/08/2007 to 30/12/2007)
ADVERTISING RATES:
SCC £3.20
Part of Series, see entry for: Leicester Mail Series
LOCAL NEWSPAPERS: Local Newspapers English Counties

THE MAIL SERIES

44025U72B-2168

Editorial Address: 9 Northampton Road, MARKET HARBOROUGH, LE16 9HB **Tel:** 01858 436060
Fax: 01858 410097
Email: alex.blackwell@harboroughmail.co.uk
Advertising Address: As above.
Email: andy.cox@harboroughmail.co.uk

Web site: http://www.harboroughmail.co.uk
Publisher: Johnston Press plc
Date Established: 1854
Frequency: Weekly - Published on Thursday
Cover Price: £0.47
Circulation: 12,552 (Combined Circulation)
Editor: Alex Blackwell; **News Editor:** Alex Blackwell;
Managing Director: Simon Kennedy
ADVERTISING RATES:
Full Page Mono £1187.28
Full Page Colour £1543.46
SCC £3.88
Agency Commission: 10%
Mechanical Data: Col Length: 340mm, No. of Columns (Display): 9, Type Area: 340 x 265mm, Page Width: 265mm, Col Widths (Display): 27mm, Film: Digital
Copy instructions: Copy Date: Tuesday 12am prior to publication date
Average advertising content per issue: 60%
Series owner and contact point for the following titles, see individual entries:
The Harborough Mail
The Lutterworth Mail
LOCAL NEWSPAPERS: Local Newspapers English Counties

MALDON & BURNHAM STANDARD SERIES

43629U72B-1070

Editorial Address: Oriel House, 43-44 North Hill, COLCHESTER, CO1 1TZ **Tel:** 01206 508249
Fax: 01206 508274
Email: mbsdistrict@nqe.com
Advertising Address: Newspaper House, Chester Hall Lane, BASILDON, SS14 3BL **Tel:** 01245 393444
Fax: 01245 344211
Email: debbie.walker@nqe.com
Web site: http://www.maldonandburnhamstandard.co.uk
Publisher: Newsquest (Essex) Ltd
Frequency: Weekly - Published on Wednesday
Circulation: 9,687 (ABC 02/07/2007 to 30/12/2007)
Editor: Ainsley Davidson; **Advertising Manager:** Debbie Walker
ADVERTISING RATES:
Full Page Mono £595.00
Full Page Colour £690.00
SCC £3.90
Agency Commission: 10%
Mechanical Data: Col Length: 340mm, Film: Negative, right reading, emulsion side down, No. of Columns (Display): 9, Type Area: 340 x 267mm, Page Width: 267mm
Copy instructions: Copy Date: Monday 1pm prior to publication date
Series owner and contact point for the following titles, see individual entries:
Burnham Standard
Maldon Standard
LOCAL NEWSPAPERS: Local Newspapers English Counties

MALDON STANDARD

43630U72B-1070_120

Formerly: Burnham & Maldon Standard
Frequency: Weekly
Cover Price: £0.48
Part of Series, see entry for: Maldon & Burnham Standard Series
LOCAL NEWSPAPERS: Local Newspapers English Counties

MALLING CHRONICLE

43932U72B-1885_160

Formerly: Sevenoaks Chronicle (Malling Edition)
Frequency: Weekly - Circulation figure is incorporated into the Sevenoaks Chronicle Town edition
Cover Price: £0.60
ADVERTISING RATES:
SCC £5.70
Part of Series, see entry for: Sevenoaks Chronicle Series
LOCAL NEWSPAPERS: Local Newspapers English Counties

MALTON & PICKERING MERCURY

44661U72B-3623_145

Formerly: Ryedale Mercury
Frequency: Weekly - Published on Thursday
Cover Price: £0.44
Circulation: 2,884 (ABC 02/07/2007 to 30/12/2007)
Part of Series, see entry for: The Mercury Series (Scarborough)
LOCAL NEWSPAPERS: Local Newspapers English Counties

MALVERN GAZETTE

1616093U72B-3564_101

Frequency: Weekly
Cover Price: £0.55
ADVERTISING: Rates on application
Part of Series, see entry for: Malvern Gazette & Ledbury Reporter Series
LOCAL NEWSPAPERS: Local Newspapers English Counties

MALVERN GAZETTE & LEDBURY REPORTER SERIES

44618U72B-3564

Formerly: Malvern Gazette & Ledbury Reporter
Editorial Address: Broads Bank, MALVERN, WR14 2HP
Tel: 01684 892200 **Fax:** 01684 568313
Email: mgnewsdesk@midlands.newsquest.co.uk
Advertising Address: As above.
Email: jenny.burgess@midlands.newsquest.co.uk
Web site: http://www.malverngazette.co.uk
Publisher: Newsquest Media Group
Date Established: 1898
Frequency: Weekly - Published on Friday
Circulation: 17,001 (ABC 02/07/2007 to 30/12/2007)
Editor: John Murphy; **News Editor:** Suzanne Black;
Advertising Manager: Jenny Burgess
ADVERTISING: Rates on application
Agency Commission: 10%
Copy instructions: Copy Date: Tuesday prior to publication date
Average advertising content per issue: 65%
Series owner and contact point for the following titles, see individual entries:
Ledbury Reporter
Malvern Gazette
Supplement(s): Weekender - 52xY
LOCAL NEWSPAPERS: Local Newspapers English Counties

MANCHESTER EVENING NEWS 42121U67B-400

Editorial Address: 1 Scott Place, Hardman Street, MANCHESTER, M3 3RN **Tel:** 0161 832 7200
Fax: 0161 211 2034
Email: newsdesk@men-news.co.uk
Advertising Address: As above. **Fax:** 0161 829 3310
Email: ads@menmediasales.co.uk
Web site: http://www.manchestereveningnews.co.uk
Publisher: Manchester Evening News Ltd
Frequency: Evenings - Not published on Sunday
Cover Price: £0.38
Free to qualifying individuals
Circulation: 82,445 (Publisher's Statement)
Editor: News Desk; **News Editor:** Sarah Lester; **Features Editor:** Deanna Delamotta
ADVERTISING RATES:
SCC £38.65
Agency Commission: 10%
Mechanical Data: Type Area: 340 x 267mm, Print Process: Web-fed offset litho, Page Width: 267mm, Film: Digital, Col Length: 340mm, No. of Columns (Display): 9, Col Widths (Display): 30m
Copy instructions: Copy Date: 2 days prior to publication date
Average advertising content per issue: 70%
Editions:
Manchester Evening News (Home)
Manchester Evening News (Main)
Supplement(s): Home - 52xY
REGIONAL DAILY & SUNDAY NEWSPAPERS: Regional Daily Newspapers

MANCHESTER EVENING NEWS (HOME)

42122U67B-400_120

Formerly: Manchester Evening News (3rd Edition)
Frequency: Mornings
Cover Price: £0.35
Edition of: Manchester Evening News
REGIONAL DAILY & SUNDAY NEWSPAPERS: Regional Daily Newspapers

MANCHESTER EVENING NEWS (MAIN)

42123U67B-400_130

Formerly: Manchester Evening News (2nd Edition)
Frequency: Evenings
Cover Price: £0.35
Edition of: Manchester Evening News
REGIONAL DAILY & SUNDAY NEWSPAPERS: Regional Daily Newspapers

MANNINGTREE AND HARWICH STANDARD

43620U72B-1044_200

Frequency: Weekly - Circulation figure is incorporated into the Harwich & Manningtree Standard
Cover Price: £0.48

Non-National Newspapers

Section 4 (a) Newspapers

ADVERTISING RATES:
Full Page Colour £405.00
SCC £2.60
Part of Series, see entry for: Gazette and Standard Series (East Essex)
LOCAL NEWSPAPERS: Local Newspapers English Counties

MANSFIELD AND ASHFIELD OBSERVER
44186U72B-2610
Editorial Address: 121 Newgate Lane, MANSFIELD, NG18 2PA **Tel:** 01623 450298 **Fax:** 01623 464647
Email: tony.spittles@chad.co.uk
Advertising Address: As above. **Tel:** 01623 456789 **Fax:** 01623 465556
Email: classified@chad.co.uk
Web site: http://www.chad.co.uk
Publisher: Wilfred Edmunds
Date Established: 1969
Frequency: Weekly - Published on Thursday
Cover Price: Free
Circulation: 58,599 (VFD 02/07/2007 to 30/12/2007)
Editor: Tony Spittles; **News Editor:** Tony Spittles; **Features Editor:** Tony Spittles; **Managing Director:** Dawn Sweeney; **Advertising Manager:** Samantha Bailey; **Publisher:** Tony Spittles
ADVERTISING RATES:
Full Page Mono £2261.34
Full Page Colour £2939.74
SCC £7.39
Mechanical Data: Film: Digital, Type Area: 370 x 270mm, No. of Columns (Display): 9, Page Width: 270mm, Col Length: 370mm
Copy instructions: Copy Date: Monday 5pm prior to publication date
LOCAL NEWSPAPERS: Local Newspapers English Counties

MANSFIELD & ASHFIELD RECORDER
44200U72B-2666_210
Frequency: Weekly
Cover Price: Free
Circulation: 62,151 (VFD 02/07/2007 to 30/12/2007)
ADVERTISING: Rates on application
Part of Series, see entry for: West Notts & Derbyshire Recorder Series
LOCAL NEWSPAPERS: Local Newspapers English Counties

MANSFIELD CHAD
44175U72B-2580_130
Frequency: Weekly - Published on Wednesday. Circulation figure incorporates the Mansfield Woodhouse Chad, the Rainworth Chad, the Ashfield Chad, the Sherwood Chad, the Shirebrook & Bolsover Chad and the Warsop Chad
Cover Price: £0.58
Circulation: 44,993 (ABC 02/07/2007 to 30/12/2007)
ADVERTISING RATES:
SCC £9.12
Part of Series, see entry for: Chad Series Mansfield
LOCAL NEWSPAPERS: Local Newspapers English Counties

MANSFIELD WOODHOUSE CHAD
44179U72B-2580_140
Frequency: Weekly - Circulation figure is included into the Mansfield Chad
Cover Price: £0.47
ADVERTISING: Rates on application
Part of Series, see entry for: Chad Series Mansfield
LOCAL NEWSPAPERS: Local Newspapers English Counties

MANX INDEPENDENT
45145U72G-10_200
Frequency: Weekly - Published on Friday
Cover Price: £0.44
Circulation: 12,255 (ABC 02/07/2007 to 30/12/2007)
ADVERTISING: Rates on application
Mechanical Data: No. of Columns (Display): 9, Film: Digital, Type Area: 340 x 268mm, Col Length: 340mm, Page Width: 268mm, Col Widths (Display): 28mm
Part of Series, see entry for: Isle of Man Newspapers
LOCAL NEWSPAPERS: Local Newspapers Isle of Man

MARKET DRAYTON ADVERTISER
44244U72B-2830_140
Frequency: Weekly - Circulation figure is incorporated into the Newport Advertiser
Cover Price: £0.40
ADVERTISING: Rates on application

Part of Series, see entry for: Newport & Market Drayton Advertiser Series
LOCAL NEWSPAPERS: Local Newspapers English Counties

MARKET RASEN MAIL
44068U72B-2269
Editorial Address: Waverley Court, Queen Street, MARKET RASEN, LN8 3EH **Tel:** 01673 844644 **Fax:** 01673 842879
Email: jason.hippisley@jpress.co.uk
Advertising Address: 44 Eastgate, LOUTH, LN11 9NJ
Tel: 01507 353200 **Fax:** 01507 35301
Email: fiona.leak@jpress.co.uk
Web site: http://www.marketrasenmail.co.uk
Publisher: Lincolnshire Newspapers Ltd
Date Established: 1856
Frequency: Weekly - Published on Wednesday
Cover Price: £0.45
Circulation: 4,550 (ABC 02/07/2007 to 30/12/2007)
Editor: Jason Hippisley
ADVERTISING: Rates on application
LOCAL NEWSPAPERS: Local Newspapers English Counties

MARLOW FREE PRESS
43305U72B-280_140
Frequency: Weekly - Circulation figure is incorporated into the Bucks Free Press
Cover Price: £0.50
Part of Series, see entry for: Bucks Free Press Series
LOCAL NEWSPAPERS: Local Newspapers English Counties

MARYLEBONE EXPRESS
1665335U72A-160_182
Frequency: Weekly
Cover Price: £0.55
Part of Series, see entry for: Ham & High Series
LOCAL NEWSPAPERS: Local Newspapers Greater London

MARYLEBONE, PADDINGTON AND PIMLICO MERCURY
43090U72A-300_190
Formerly: Marylebone & Paddington Mercury
Frequency: Weekly - Published on Thursday. For circulation see Fulham & Hammersmith Chronicle
Cover Price: £0.45
ADVERTISING RATES:
SCC £13.93
Copy instructions: Copy Date: Tuesday 4pm prior to publication date
Part of Series, see entry for: London Newspaper Group Series
LOCAL NEWSPAPERS: Local Newspapers Greater London

MATLOCK MERCURY
43495U72B-750
Editorial Address: 4 Firs Parade, MATLOCK, DE4 3AS
Tel: 01629 762130 **Fax:** 01629 584270
Email: news@matlockmercury.co.uk
Advertising Address: As above. **Tel:** 01629 762120
Email: gary.blurton@derbyshiretimes.co.uk
Web site: http://www.matlockmercury.co.uk
Publisher: Wilfred Edmunds Ltd
Frequency: Weekly - Published on Thursday
Cover Price: £0.40
Circulation: 8,192 (ABC 02/07/2007 to 30/12/2007)
Editor: Newsdesk; **Advertising Manager:** Gary Blurton
ADVERTISING RATES:
SCC £3.00
Agency Commission: 10%
Mechanical Data: Col Length: 340mm, Page Width: 271mm, Type Area: 340 x 271mm, No. of Columns (Display): 9, Film: Digital
Copy instructions: Copy Date: Monday 5pm prior to publication date
LOCAL NEWSPAPERS: Local Newspapers English Counties

MEARNS LEADER
44995U72D-710
Formerly: The Leader inc. Mearns Leader & Kincardineshire Mail
Editorial Address: 12 Ann Street, STONEHAVEN, AB39 2ER
Tel: 01569 762139 **Fax:** 01569 766940
Email: leadernews@mearnsleader.com
Advertising Address: As above.
Email: leaderadverts@mearnsleader.com
Web site: http://www.mearnstoday.co.uk
Publisher: Johnston Press plc
Frequency: Weekly - Published on Friday
Cover Price: £0.54
Circulation: 4,450 (ABC 02/07/2007 to 30/12/2007)
Editor: John McIntosh; **Advertising Manager:** Elaine Dalglish

ADVERTISING RATES:
Full Page Mono £750.00
Full Page Colour £849.66
SCC £3.68
Agency Commission: 10%
Mechanical Data: Page Width: 272mm, Type Area: 340 x 272mm, Film: Digital, Col Length: 340mm, Col Widths (Display): 36mm, No. of Columns (Display): 9, Print Process: Web-fed offset litho
Copy instructions: Copy Date: Tuesday 5pm prior to publication date
Average advertising content per issue: 60%
LOCAL NEWSPAPERS: Local Newspapers Scotland

MEDIA
41651U67B-9009_704
Tel: 020 7938 6000 **Fax:** 020 7937 2648
Frequency: Weekly - Published on Wednesday within the London Evening Standard
Editor: Andrew Neather
Summary of Content: Section covering media news.
ADVERTISING: Rates on application
Part of Series, see entry for: London Evening Standard
REGIONAL DAILY & SUNDAY NEWSPAPERS: Regional Daily Newspapers

MEDWAY ADSCENE (GILLINGHAM, CHATHAM, ROCHESTER, STROOD, RAINHAM)
43847U72B-1881_125
Formerly: Adscene (Medway & District)
Frequency: Weekly
Cover Price: Free
Circulation: 77,309 (Publisher's Statement)
ADVERTISING: Rates on application
Part of Series, see entry for: Medway News Series
LOCAL NEWSPAPERS: Local Newspapers English Counties

MEDWAY EXTRA
43937U72B-1898_150
Frequency: Weekly
Cover Price: Free
Circulation: 78,652 (Publisher's Statement)
ADVERTISING RATES:
Full Page Mono £1713.60
Full Page Colour £2142.00
SCC £6.30
Copy instructions: Copy Date: 5 days prior to publication date
Part of Series, see entry for: Medway Messenger and Extra Series
LOCAL NEWSPAPERS: Local Newspapers English Counties

MEDWAY MESSENGER
1616055U72B-1898_171
Frequency: 104 issues yearly
Cover Price: £0.35
Circulation: 41,600 (Publisher's Statement)
ADVERTISING RATES:
Full Page Mono £1632.00
Full Page Colour £2040.00
SCC £6.00
Copy instructions: Copy Date: 5 days prior to publication date
Part of Series, see entry for: Medway Messenger and Extra Series
LOCAL NEWSPAPERS: Local Newspapers English Counties

MEDWAY MESSENGER AND EXTRA SERIES
43935U72B-1898
Formerly: West Kent Extra Series
Editorial Address: Medway House, Ginsbury Close, Sir Thomas Longley Road, Medway City Estate, ROCHESTER, ME2 4DU **Tel:** 01634 227834 **Fax:** 01634 715256
Email: medwaymessenger@thekmgroup.co.uk
Advertising Address: As above. **Tel:** 01634 2277971
Fax: 01634 718408
Email: jcallis@kmfm.co.uk
Web site: http://www.kentonline.co.uk
Publisher: Kent Messenger Group
Frequency: 104 issues yearly
Circulation: 120,252 (Combined Circulation)
Editor: Newsdesk; **News Editor:** Sarah Clarke
ADVERTISING RATES:
Full Page Mono £1664.64
Full Page Colour £1958.40
Agency Commission: 10%
Mechanical Data: Film: Digital, Col Widths (Display): 31mm, No. of Columns (Display): 8
Copy instructions: Copy Date: 5 days prior to publication date
Average advertising content per issue: 40%

Series owner and contact point for the following titles, see individual entries:
Medway Extra
Medway Messenger
LOCAL NEWSPAPERS: Local Newspapers English Counties

MEDWAY NEWS SERIES
43846U72B-1881

Formerly: Chatham & Medway News Series
Editorial Address: North Kent Media Centre, 4 Ambley Green, Gillingham Business Park, GILLINGHAM, ME8 0NJ
Tel: 01634 236320
Email: newsdesk.medway@krnmedia.co.uk
Advertising Address: As above.
Email: sales.medway@krnmedia.co.uk
Publisher: Kent Regional News and Media
Frequency: Weekly - Published on Tuesday and Friday
Circulation: 135,720 (Combined Circulation)
Editor: Nicola Jordan; **Advertising Manager:** Erika Osborne
ADVERTISING: Rates on application
Agency Commission: 10%
Mechanical Data: Page Width: 262mm, Film: Digital, Type Area: 340 x 262mm, Col Length: 340mm, No. of Columns (Display): 8, Col Widths (Display): 34mm
Average advertising content per issue: 40%
Series owner and contact point for the following titles, see individual entries:
Maidstone Adscene
Medway Adscene (Gillingham, Chatham, Rochester, Strood, Rainham)
News
LOCAL NEWSPAPERS: Local Newspapers English Counties

MEIRIONNYDD CAMBRIAN NEWS
1659704U72C-30_183

Formerly: Meirionnydd and Cambrian News
Frequency: Weekly
Cover Price: £0.65
ADVERTISING: Rates on application
Part of Series, see entry for: The Cambrian News Series
LOCAL NEWSPAPERS: Local Newspapers Wales

MELKSHAM INDEPENDENT NEWS
44570U72B-3517_180

Frequency: 26 issues yearly
Cover Price: Free
Circulation: 12,100 (Publisher's Statement)
ADVERTISING RATES:
Full Page Colour £468.00
Part of Series, see entry for: The Melksham Independent News Series
LOCAL NEWSPAPERS: Local Newspapers English Counties

THE MELKSHAM INDEPENDENT NEWS SERIES
44568U72B-3517

Editorial Address: 31 Market Place, MELKSHAM, SN12 6ES **Tel:** 01225 704761 **Fax:** 01225 708081
Email: newsdesk2@btconnect.com
Advertising Address: As above.
Email: newsdesk2@btconnect.com
Publisher: Wiltshire Publications Ltd
Frequency: 26 issues yearly
Cover Price: Free
Circulation: 32,700 (Combined Circulation)
Editor: Ian Drew; **Advertising Manager:** Ian Drew
ADVERTISING: Rates on application
Copy instructions: Copy Date: Friday prior to publication date
Average advertising content per issue: 50%
Series owner and contact point for the following titles, see individual entries:
Frome Times
Melksham Independent News
White Horse News
LOCAL NEWSPAPERS: Local Newspapers English Counties

MELTON CITIZEN
44030U72B-2192_110

Frequency: Weekly - Published on Tuesday
Cover Price: Free
Circulation: 12,800 (Publisher's Statement)
ADVERTISING RATES:
Full Page Mono £908.82
Full Page Colour £1179.14
SCC £2.97
Copy instructions: Copy Date: Friday 5.00pm prior to publication date

Part of Series, see entry for: Times Series (Melton Mowbray)
LOCAL NEWSPAPERS: Local Newspapers English Counties

MELTON TIMES
44031U72B-2192_120

Frequency: Weekly - Published on Thursday
Cover Price: £0.47
Circulation: 12,926 (ABC 02/07/2007 to 30/12/2007)
ADVERTISING RATES:
Full Page Mono £1545.30
Full Page Colour £2008.89
SCC £5.05
Copy instructions: Copy Date: Tuesday 2.30pm prior to publication date
Part of Series, see entry for: Times Series (Melton Mowbray)
LOCAL NEWSPAPERS: Local Newspapers English Counties

MENDIP MESSENGER
44258U72B-2900_160

Formerly: Mid Somerset Times
Frequency: Weekly
Cover Price: Free
Circulation: 14,217 (Publisher's Statement)
ADVERTISING RATES:
SCC £2.30
Mechanical Data: Trim Size: 250 x 180mm
Part of Series, see entry for: Mid Somerset News & Media
LOCAL NEWSPAPERS: Local Newspapers English Counties

THE MEON VALLEY NEWS
763200U72B-3525

Editorial Address: Woodlands, Old Mill Lane, Broad Halfpenny Down, Hambleton, WATERLOOVILLE, PO8 0SE
Tel: 023 9263 2767 **Fax:** 023 9263 2929
Email: editorial@mvn.org.uk
Advertising Address: As above.
Web site: http://www.mvn.org.uk
Publisher: Harmsworth Printing (Staverton) Ltd
Date Established: 1985
Frequency: Monthly
Cover Price: Free
Circulation: 52,500 (Publisher's Statement)
Editor: Angela Ennis; **Advertising Manager:** Christine Miller
ADVERTISING RATES:
SCC £7.00
Agency Commission: 10%
Mechanical Data: Type Area: 360 x 265mm, Col Length: 360mm, No. of Columns (Display): 8, Col Widths (Display): 30mm, Print Process: Web-offset litho, Film: Digital, Page Width: 265mm
Copy instructions: Copy Date: 10 days prior to publication
LOCAL NEWSPAPERS: Local Newspapers English Counties

THE MERCURY AND POST SERIES
43140U72A-460

Formerly: South London Press & Mercury Series
Editorial Address: 2-4 Leigham Court Road, LONDON, SW16 2PD **Tel:** 020 8769 4444 **Fax:** 020 8769 1742
Email: mercury@slp.co.uk
Advertising Address: As above. **Fax:** 020 8664 7247
Email: markbrown@slp.co.uk
Web site: http://www.icsouthlondon.co.uk
Publisher: Tindle Newspapers Ltd
Date Established: 1865
Frequency: Weekly - Published on Wednesday and Thursday
Cover Price: Free
Circulation: 166,029 (Combined Circulation)
Editor: Keely Sherbird
ADVERTISING: Rates on application
Copy instructions: Copy Date: Monday 1pm before publication
Series owner and contact point for the following titles, see individual entries:
The Mercury Bexley Borough
The Mercury Greenwich Borough
The Mercury Lewisham Borough
The Post Mitcham, Morden & Wimbledon
The Post, Streatham, Clapham & Crystal Palace
LOCAL NEWSPAPERS: Local Newspapers Greater London

MERCURY AND WEEKLY NEWS SERIES
44248U72B-2875

Editorial Address: Royal Clarence House, York Buildings, BRIDGWATER, TA6 3AT **Tel:** 01278 727950
Fax: 01278 452184
Email: newsdesk@bridgwatermercury.co.uk
Advertising Address: As above.
Email: sales@bridgwatermercury.co.uk

Web site: http://www.bridgwatermercury.co.uk
Publisher: Newsquest (Media Group) Ltd
Date Established: 1857
Frequency: Weekly - Published on Tuesday and Wednesday
Circulation: 16,156 (Combined Circulation)
Editor: Matthew Colledge; **News Editor:** Matthew Colledge;
Advertising Manager: Nick Grabham
ADVERTISING: Rates on application
Agency Commission: 10%
Copy instructions: Copy Date: Thursday 4pm prior to publication date
Series owner and contact point for the following titles, see individual entries:
Bridgwater Mercury
Burnham & Highbridge Mercury
Burnham and Highbridge Weekly News
LOCAL NEWSPAPERS: Local Newspapers English Counties

THE MERCURY BEXLEY BOROUGH
43137U72A-460_251

Frequency: Weekly
Cover Price: Free
Circulation: 12,999 (Publisher's Statement)
ADVERTISING: Rates on application
Part of Series, see entry for: The Mercury and Post Series
LOCAL NEWSPAPERS: Local Newspapers Greater London

MERCURY (CLEVEDON, NAILSEA, PORTISHEAD & YATTON)
43222U72B-40_140

Frequency: Weekly
Cover Price: Free
Circulation: 35,808 (VFD 02/07/2007 to 30/12/2007)
ADVERTISING RATES:
Full Page Mono £1368.00
Full Page Colour £1710.00
Part of Series, see entry for: Clevedon Newspapers Series
LOCAL NEWSPAPERS: Local Newspapers English Counties

THE MERCURY GREENWICH BOROUGH
43138U72A-460_252

Frequency: Weekly
Cover Price: Free
Circulation: 51,396 (VFD 02/04/2007 to 01/07/2007)
ADVERTISING: Rates on application
Part of Series, see entry for: The Mercury and Post Series
LOCAL NEWSPAPERS: Local Newspapers Greater London

THE MERCURY LEWISHAM BOROUGH
43141U72A-460_110

Frequency: Weekly
Cover Price: Free
Circulation: 32,560 (Publisher's Statement)
ADVERTISING: Rates on application
Part of Series, see entry for: The Mercury and Post Series
LOCAL NEWSPAPERS: Local Newspapers Greater London

THE MERCURY NEWSPAPER
44679U72B-3700

Formerly: The Mercury Newspaper South Yorks, N. East Derbyshire & North Notts
Editorial Address: PO Box 3689, SHEFFIELD, S2 7WS
Tel: 0114 276 3633 **Fax:** 0114 276 3644
Email: david@mercurynewspaper.co.uk
Advertising Address: 4B Queens Road, SHEFFIELD, S2 4DG **Tel:** 0114 276 3633 **Fax:** 0114 276 3644
Email: sales@mercurynewspaper.co.uk
Web site: http://www.mercurynewspaper.co.uk
Publisher: Sheffield Mercury Ltd
Frequency: Weekly
Cover Price: Free
Circulation: 40,000 (Publisher's Statement)
Editor: David Hayes; **Managing Director:** David Hayes;
Advertising Manager: David Hayes
ADVERTISING RATES:
Full Page Mono £576.00
Full Page Colour £700.00
SCC £3.00
Agency Commission: 15%
Mechanical Data: Col Length: 360mm, Page Width: 255mm, Type Area: 360 x 255mm, Col Widths (Display): 30mm, No. of Columns (Display): 8, Film: Digital
Copy instructions: Copy Date: Tuesday 3pm prior to publication date
Average advertising content per issue: 50%
LOCAL NEWSPAPERS: Local Newspapers English Counties

Non-National Newspapers

Section 4 (a) Newspapers

MERCURY SERIES
44348U72B-3088

Formerly: West Suffolk Mercury Series
Editorial Address: Press House, 30 Lower Brook Street, IPSWICH, IP4 1AN **Tel:** 01473 324696 **Fax:** 01473 324934
Email: mercury@archant.co.uk
Advertising Address: As above. **Tel:** 01284 230023
Fax: 01284 702970
Email: peter.mayhew@archant.co.uk
Publisher: Archant Suffolk
Frequency: Weekly
Cover Price: Free
Circulation: 45,543 (VFD 02/07/2007 to 30/12/2007)
Editor: Mark Crossley; **Managing Director:** Stuart McCreery
ADVERTISING RATES:
Full Page Mono £1543.68
Full Page Colour £2006.78
SCC £5.36
Agency Commission: 10%
Mechanical Data: Page Width: 270mm, Type Area: 360 x 270mm, Col Length: 360mm, Col Widths (Display): 33mm, No. of Columns (Display): 8, Film: Digital
Copy instructions: Copy Date: Monday 12 noon prior to publication date
Average advertising content per issue: 65%
Series owner and contact point for the following titles, see individual entries:
Bury St Edmunds Mercury
Sudbury Mercury
LOCAL NEWSPAPERS: Local Newspapers English Counties

MERCURY SERIES (HODDESDON)
43807U72B-1560

Editorial Address: The Media Centre, 40 Ware Road, HERTFORD, SG13 7HU **Tel:** 01992 526600
Fax: 01992 526645
Email: mercury@hertsessexnews.co.uk
Advertising Address: As above. **Tel:** 01992 526666
Fax: 01992 526686
Email: advertising@hertsessexnews.co.uk
Web site: http://www.hertfordshiremercury.co.uk
Publisher: Herts & Essex Newspapers Ltd
Frequency: Weekly - Published every Friday
Circulation: 10,921 (Combined Circulation)
Usual Pagination: 130
Editor: Abigayle Barber; **News Editor:** Abigayle Barber;
Advertising Manager: Karen Church
ADVERTISING RATES:
Full Page Mono £2281.00
Full Page Colour £2446.00
Agency Commission: 10%
Mechanical Data: Page Width: 270mm, Col Widths (Display): 31mm, No. of Columns (Display): 8, Type Area: 350 x 270mm, Col Length: 350mm, Film: Digital, Print Process: Web-fed offset litho
Copy instructions: Copy Date: Friday prior to publication date
Average advertising content per issue: 70%
Series owner and contact point for the following titles, see individual entries:
Cheshunt and Waltham Mercury
Hoddesdon and Broxbourne Mercury
LOCAL NEWSPAPERS: Local Newspapers English Counties

MERCURY SERIES (KENT)
43928U72B-1882

Editorial Address: 13 Queen Street, DEAL, CT14 6EX
Tel: 01304 365526 **Fax:** 01304 374770
Email: mercurynews@thekmgroup.co.uk
Advertising Address: 25 High Street, DOVER, CT16 1EB
Tel: 01304 240380 **Fax:** 01304 208108
Email: sswan@thekmgroup.co.uk
Web site: http://www.kentonline.co.uk
Publisher: Kent Messenger Group
Date Established: 1865
Frequency: Weekly - Published on Thursday
Circulation: 13,841 (Combined Circulation)
Usual Pagination: 70
Editor: Graham Smith; **Advertising Manager:** Sharon Swann
ADVERTISING RATES:
Full Page Mono £1115.20
Full Page Colour £1394.00
SCC £4.10
Agency Commission: 10%
Copy instructions: Copy Date: Tuesday 12pm prior to publication date
Series owner and contact point for the following titles, see individual entries:
Dover Mercury
East Kent Mercury
LOCAL NEWSPAPERS: Local Newspapers English Counties

THE MERCURY SERIES (SCARBOROUGH)
44659U72B-3623

Editorial Address: 17-23 Aberdeen Walk, SCARBOROUGH, YO11 1BB **Tel:** 01723 363636 **Fax:** 01723 379033
Email: stephanie.pride@yrnltd.co.uk
Advertising Address: As above. **Tel:** 01723 383838
Fax: 01723 383825
Email: advertising@scarborougheveningnews.co.uk
Web site: http://www.scarboroughevingnews.co.uk
Publisher: Yorkshire Regional Newspapers Ltd
Frequency: Weekly - Published on Wednesday and Saturday
Circulation: 5,853 (Combined Circulation)
Usual Pagination: 36
Editor: Ed Asquith; **Managing Director:** Jason Rewsw-Davies; **Advertising Manager:** Nicola Fisher
ADVERTISING: Rates on application
Agency Commission: 10%
Series owner and contact point for the following titles, see individual entries:
Filey & Hunmanby Mercury
Malton & Pickering Mercury
LOCAL NEWSPAPERS: Local Newspapers English Counties

MERIONETH EXPRESS
44827U72C-275_160

Frequency: Weekly
Cover Price: £0.40
Part of Series, see entry for: North Wales Series
LOCAL NEWSPAPERS: Local Newspapers Wales

MERSEYMART AND STAR HUYTON AND ROBY
44096U72B-2383_120

Frequency: Weekly
Cover Price: Free
Circulation: 7,563 (Publisher's Statement)
ADVERTISING: Rates on application
Part of Series, see entry for: Liverpool Weekly Merseymart & Star Series
LOCAL NEWSPAPERS: Local Newspapers English Counties

MERSEYMART WEST DERBY & TUEBROOK
44099U72B-2383_190

Formerly: Merseymart and Star West Derby & Tuebrook
Frequency: Weekly
Cover Price: Free
Circulation: 24,558 (VFD 02/07/2007 to 30/12/2007)
ADVERTISING: Rates on application
Part of Series, see entry for: Liverpool Weekly Merseymart & Star Series
LOCAL NEWSPAPERS: Local Newspapers English Counties

MERTHYR EXPRESS
625579U72C-240_110

Frequency: Weekly
Cover Price: £0.60
ADVERTISING RATES:
Full Page Mono £1436.00
Full Page Colour £1868.00
Part of Series, see entry for: Merthyr Express Series
LOCAL NEWSPAPERS: Local Newspapers Wales

MERTHYR EXPRESS SERIES
44808U72C-240

Editorial Address: 52-53 Glebeland Street, MERTHYR TYDFIL, CF47 8AT **Tel:** 01685 856500 **Fax:** 01685 856520
Email: merthyr.express@mediawales.co.uk
Advertising Address: Thomson House, Havelock Street, CARDIFF, CF1 1XR **Tel:** 01685 856558 **Fax:** 01685 856556
Email: robert.gray@mediawales.co.uk
Web site: http://www.icwales.co.uk
Publisher: Celtic Newspapers Ltd
Frequency: Weekly - Published on Thursday
Circulation: 17,138 (ABC 02/07/2007 to 30/12/2007)
Editor: Gordon Caldecott
ADVERTISING RATES:
Full Page Mono £1669.63
Full Page Colour £2251.58
Agency Commission: 10%
Mechanical Data: Film: Digital, No. of Columns (Display): 8, Col Widths (Display): 31.5mm
Copy instructions: Copy Date: Friday 5pm prior to publication date
Average advertising content per issue: 20%
Series owner and contact point for the following titles, see individual entries:
Merthyr Express
Rhymney Valley Express
LOCAL NEWSPAPERS: Local Newspapers Wales

THE MESSENGER
44376U72B-3130

Editorial Address: Tindle House, High Street, BORDON, GU35 0AY **Tel:** 01420 485183 **Fax:** 01420 541018
Email: messenger.editorial@tindlenews.co.uk
Advertising Address: 2 Kings Road, HASLEMERE, GU27 2QA **Tel:** 01428 653999 **Fax:** 01428 661658
Email: advertising@messenger-online.co.uk
Web site: http://www.messenger-online.co.uk
Publisher: Tindle Newspapers Ltd
Date Established: 1981
Frequency: Weekly - Published on Monday
Cover Price: Free
Circulation: 40,348 (Publisher's Statement)
Editor: Joyce Sharland-Brown
ADVERTISING RATES:
Full Page Mono £1133.00
Full Page Colour £1416.50
SCC £3.85
Agency Commission: 10%
Mechanical Data: Col Length: 390mm, Col Widths (Display): 33mm, No. of Columns (Display): 8, Type Area: 390 x 270mm, Trim Size: 420 x 300mm, Page Width: 270mm
Copy instructions: Copy Date: Friday 12pm prior to publication date
Average advertising content per issue: 60%
LOCAL NEWSPAPERS: Local Newspapers English Counties

THE MESSENGER (BRADGATE PARK, SOUTH LEICESTERSHIRE)
1805239U72B-4051_100

Formerly: The Advertiser (Bradgate Park, South Leicestershire)
Frequency: Weekly
Cover Price: Free
Circulation: 8,000 (Publisher's Statement)
ADVERTISING RATES:
SCC £1.00
Part of Series, see entry for: The Messenger Series (Leicestershire & Rutland)
LOCAL NEWSPAPERS: Local Newspapers English Counties

MESSENGER EXTRA
43936U72B-1820_132

Formerly: Gravesend Extra
Frequency: Weekly
Cover Price: Free
Circulation: 32,693 (VFD 02/07/2007 to 30/12/2007)
ADVERTISING RATES:
SCC £4.55
Part of Series, see entry for: Gravesend Messenger Series
LOCAL NEWSPAPERS: Local Newspapers English Counties

THE MESSENGER (GREAT GLEN, SOUTH LEICESTERSHIRE)
1835204U72B-4051_102

Formerly: The Advertiser (Great Glen, South Leicestershire)
Frequency: Weekly
Cover Price: Free
ADVERTISING RATES:
SCC £1.00
Part of Series, see entry for: The Messenger Series (Leicestershire & Rutland)
LOCAL NEWSPAPERS: Local Newspapers English Counties

THE MESSENGER (LUTTERWORTH & BROUGHTON)
1805240U72B-4051_101

Formerly: The Advertiser (Lutterworth & Broughton)
Frequency: Weekly
Cover Price: Free
Circulation: 10,000 (Publisher's Statement)
ADVERTISING RATES:
SCC £1.00
Part of Series, see entry for: The Messenger Series (Leicestershire & Rutland)
LOCAL NEWSPAPERS: Local Newspapers English Counties

THE MESSENGER (MARKET BOSWORTH, RUTLAND)
1835205U72B-4051_103

Formerly: The Advertiser (Market Bosworth, Rutland)
Frequency: Weekly
Cover Price: Free

ADVERTISING RATES:
SCC £1.00
Part of Series, see entry for: The Messenger Series
(Leicestershire & Rutland)
LOCAL NEWSPAPERS: Local Newspapers English
Counties

THE MESSENGER SERIES (LEICESTERSHIRE & RUTLAND)

1805237U72B-4051

Formerly: The Advertiser Series (Leicestershire & Rutland)
Editorial Address: St. George Street, LEICESTER, LE1 9FQ
Tel: 0116 251 2512 **Fax:** 0116 222 4669
Email: gemmacollins@leicestermercury.co.uk
Advertising Address: As above.
Email: sonia.bradford@leicestermercury.co.uk
Publisher: Leicester Mercury Media Group Ltd
Date Established: 2007
Frequency: Weekly
Cover Price: Free
Circulation: 50,000 (Publisher's Statement)
Editor: Gemma Collins
ADVERTISING: Rates on application
Mechanical Data: No. of Columns (Display): 8, Trim Size:
360 x 277mm
Copy instructions: Copy Date: Thursday 5pm prior to
publication
**Series owner and contact point for the following titles,
see individual entries:**
The Messenger (Bradgate Park, South Leicestershire)
The Messenger (Great Glen, South Leicestershire)
The Messenger (Lutterworth & Broughton)
The Messenger (Market Bosworth, Rutland)
LOCAL NEWSPAPERS: Local Newspapers English
Counties

METRO (LONDON)

42120U67B-387

Editorial Address: Northcliffe House, 2 Derry Street,
LONDON, W8 5TT **Tel:** 020 7651 5200 **Fax:** 020 7651-5202
Email: news.london@ukmetro.co.uk
Advertising Address: As above. **Fax:** 020 7651 5342
Email: james.hooper@ukmetro.co.uk
Web site: http://www.metro.co.uk
Publisher: Associated Newspapers Ltd
Date Established: 1999
Frequency: Mornings
Cover Price: Free
Circulation: 742,291 (ABC 26/11/2007 to 30/12/2007)
Editor: Kenny Campbell; **News Editor:** Sarah Getty;
Features Editor: Kieran Meeke; **Managing Director:** Steve
Auckland; **Managing Editor:** Graeme Fort; **Group Editor:**
Kenny Campbell
Readership/Target Audience: Read by professional men
and women aged between 18 and 44 years old living and
working in London.
ADVERTISING RATES:
SCC £121.00
Agency Commission: 15%
Mechanical Data: Type Area: 350 x 268mm, Col Length:
350mm, Page Width: 268mm, No. of Columns (Display): 7,
Col Widths (Display): 35mm, Film: Digital
Average advertising content per issue: 45%
REGIONAL DAILY & SUNDAY NEWSPAPERS: Regional
Daily Newspapers

METRO (SCOTLAND)

633930U67B-325

Editorial Address: Clydesdale Bank Exchange, 20 Waterloo
Street, GLASGOW G2 6DB **Tel:** 0141 225 3336
Fax: 0141 225 3316
Email: news.scotland@ukmetro.co.uk
Web site: http://www.metro.co.uk
Publisher: Associated Newspapers Ltd
Date Established: 2001
Frequency: Mornings - Publishes Monday to Friday
Cover Price: Free
Circulation: 128,318 (ABC 26/11/2007 to 30/12/2007)
Editor: Steve Deal
ADVERTISING RATES:
SCC £25.00
Agency Commission: 10%
Mechanical Data: Col Length: 340mm, Col Widths (Display):
34mm, No. of Columns (Display): 7, Film: Digital, Type Area:
340 x 268mm, Page Width: 268mm
Copy instructions: Copy Date: 2 days prior to publication
date
Average advertising content per issue: 40%
REGIONAL DAILY & SUNDAY NEWSPAPERS: Regional
Daily Newspapers

MID CORNWALL ADVERTISER

43422U72B-3939

Editorial Address: Tindle House, 2 Trevanson Street,
WADEBRIDGE, PL27 7AW **Tel:** 01208 815096
Fax: 01208 815935
Email: fi.nca@internet-today.co.uk
Advertising Address: As above.
Email: editorial.nca@internet-today.co.uk
Web site: http://www.cornwalladvertisers.co.uk
Publisher: North Cornwall Advertiser Ltd
Date Established: 1994
Frequency: Monthly
Cover Price: Free
Circulation: 59,750 (Publisher's Statement)
Editor: Fiona Jolley; **Advertising Manager:** Linden Jones
ADVERTISING RATES:
Full Page Mono £720.00
Full Page Colour £795.00
SCC £5.40
Agency Commission: 15%
Mechanical Data: Film: Digital, No. of Columns (Display): 8
Copy instructions: Copy Date: 1 week prior to publication
date
Average advertising content per issue: 50%
LOCAL NEWSPAPERS: Local Newspapers English
Counties

THE MID HAMPSHIRE OBSERVER

1640805U72B-1400_101

Frequency: Weekly
Cover Price: Free
ADVERTISING RATES:
SCC £5.50
Part of Series, see entry for: The Independent Observer
Series
LOCAL NEWSPAPERS: Local Newspapers English
Counties

MID SOMERSET NEWS & MEDIA

44251U72B-2900

Formerly: Mid Somerset Newspapers
Editorial Address: Southover, WELLS, BA5 1UH
Tel: 01749 832300 **Fax:** 01749 832347
Email: editor@midsomnews.co.uk
Advertising Address: As above. **Fax:** 01749 832332
Email: vicki.stoodley@midsomnews.co.uk
Web site: http://www.thisissomerset.co.uk
Publisher: Bath News & Media
Date Established: 1851
Frequency: Weekly
Circulation: 32,945 (Combined Circulation)
Editor: Philip Welch; **News Editor:** Laura Thorpe;
Advertisement Director: Vicki Stoodley
ADVERTISING RATES:
Full Page Mono £1526.40
Full Page Colour £1908.00
SCC £5.30
Mechanical Data: Page Width: 270mm, Film: Digital, Type
Area: 360 x 270mm, Col Length: 360mm, No. of Columns
(Display): 8, Col Widths (Display): 33mm
**Series owner and contact point for the following titles,
see individual entries:**
Central Somerset Gazette
Cheddar Valley Gazette
Mendip Messenger
Shepton Mallet Journal
Wells Journal
LOCAL NEWSPAPERS: Local Newspapers English
Counties

MID SUSSEX CITIZEN

44462U72B-3322_130

Frequency: Weekly
Cover Price: Free
Circulation: 29,750 (Publisher's Statement)
Copy instructions: Copy Date: Monday, 5pm prior to
publication date
Part of Series, see entry for: Mid Sussex Times and Citizen
Series
LOCAL NEWSPAPERS: Local Newspapers English
Counties

MID SUSSEX LEADER

628701U72B-3210_130

Frequency: Weekly
Cover Price: Free
Circulation: 37,292 (Publisher's Statement)

Part of Series, see entry for: Brighton and Hove Leader
Series
LOCAL NEWSPAPERS: Local Newspapers English
Counties

MID SUSSEX TIMES

44463U72B-3322_150

Frequency: Weekly
Cover Price: £0.38
Circulation: 12,539 (ABC 02/07/2007 to 30/12/2007)
Copy instructions: Copy Date: Tuesday, 5pm prior to
publication date
Part of Series, see entry for: Mid Sussex Times and Citizen
Series
LOCAL NEWSPAPERS: Local Newspapers English
Counties

MID SUSSEX TIMES AND CITIZEN SERIES

44461U72B-3322

Editorial Address: 7-9 South Road, HAYWARDS HEATH,
RH16 4LE **Tel:** 01444 452201 **Fax:** 01444 416611
Email: middy.news@sussexnewspapers.co.uk
Advertising Address: As above. **Fax:** 01444 416241
Email: vanessa.lover@sussexnewspapers.co.uk
Web site: http://www.midsussextoday.co.uk
Publisher: Sussex (Southern) Newspapers Ltd
Date Established: 1881
Frequency: Weekly
Circulation: 42,701 (Combined Circulation)
Usual Pagination: 92
Editor: Diane Jones; **Advertising Manager:** Vanessa Lover
ADVERTISING RATES:
Full Page Mono £2160.00
Full Page Colour £2808.00
Agency Commission: 10%
Mechanical Data: Film: Digital, Type Area: 340 x 265mm,
Col Length: 340mm, Page Width: 265mm, No. of Columns
(Display): 9
Copy instructions: Copy Date: Individual advertising copy
deadlines available for series members
**Series owner and contact point for the following titles,
see individual entries:**
Mid Sussex Citizen
Mid Sussex Times
LOCAL NEWSPAPERS: Local Newspapers English
Counties

MID-ULSTER ECHO

45107U72E-180_110

Frequency: Weekly
Cover Price: Free
Circulation: 9,587 (Publisher's Statement)
Part of Series, see entry for: Mid Ulster Mail Series
LOCAL NEWSPAPERS: Local Newspapers Northern
Ireland

MID ULSTER MAIL SERIES

45106U72E-180

Editorial Address: 52 Oldtown Street, COOKSTOWN, BT80
8BB **Tel:** 028 8676 2288 **Fax:** 028 8676 4295
Email: mark.bain@midulstermail.co.uk
Advertising Address: As above.
Email: claire.speers@jpress.co.uk
Web site: http://www.midulstermail.co.uk
Publisher: Morton Newspapers Ltd
Date Established: 1890
Frequency: Weekly - Published on Thursday
Circulation: 19,763 (Combined Circulation)
Editor: Gillian McDade; **Managing Director:** Jean Long;
Advertising Manager: Claire Speers
ADVERTISING RATES:
SCC £5.00
Agency Commission: 10%
Mechanical Data: Col Length: 340mm, No. of Columns
(Display): 9, Type Area: 340 x 268mm, Page Width: 268mm,
Film: Digital, Col Widths (Display): 30mm
Copy instructions: Copy Date: Tuesday 4pm prior to
publication date
Average advertising content per issue: 40%
**Series owner and contact point for the following titles,
see individual entries:**
Mid-Ulster Echo
Mid-Ulster Mail (South Derry)
Mid-Ulster Mail (Tyrone)
LOCAL NEWSPAPERS: Local Newspapers Northern
Ireland

MID-ULSTER MAIL (SOUTH DERRY)

45108U72E-180_120

Frequency: Weekly - Circulation figure includes Mid-Ulster Mail (Tyrone)
Cover Price: £0.85
Circulation: 10,176 (ABC 02/07/2007 to 30/12/2007)
Part of Series, see entry for: Mid Ulster Mail Series
LOCAL NEWSPAPERS: Local Newspapers Northern Ireland

MID-ULSTER MAIL (TYRONE)

45109U72E-180_140

Frequency: Weekly - Circulation figure is incorporated into the Mid-Ulster Mail (South Derry)
Cover Price: £0.85
Part of Series, see entry for: Mid Ulster Mail Series
LOCAL NEWSPAPERS: Local Newspapers Northern Ireland

MID ULSTER OBSERVER

45095U72E-120_170

Frequency: Weekly
Cover Price: £0.70
Part of Series, see entry for: Dungannon Observer Series
LOCAL NEWSPAPERS: Local Newspapers Northern Ireland

MID WALES JOURNAL

44235U72B-2812_180

Frequency: Weekly
Cover Price: £0.50
Circulation: 4,500 (Publisher's Statement)
ADVERTISING: Rates on application
Part of Series, see entry for: Chronicle & Journal Series
LOCAL NEWSPAPERS: Local Newspapers English Counties

MID-CHESHIRE GUARDIAN SERIES

1804093U72B-4050

Editorial Address: 3 Theatre Court, London Road, NORTHWICH, CW9 5HB **Tel:** 01606 813617
Fax: 01606 331893
Email: northwich@guardiangrp.co.uk
Advertising Address: 15 Market Street, NORTHWICH, CW9 5DT **Tel:** 01606 813600 **Fax:** 01606 330216
Email: fwright@guardiangrp.co.uk
Web site: http://www.northwichguardian.co.uk
Publisher: Newsquest (Northwest) Ltd
Frequency: Weekly
Circulation: 21,051 (Combined Circulation)
Editor: Gina Bebbington
ADVERTISING RATES:
Full Page Mono £846.56
Full Page Colour £1058.20
SCC £4.30
Agency Commission: 10%
Mechanical Data: Type Area: 350 x 268mm, Col Length: 350mm, Page Width: 268mm, Col Widths (Display): 27.7mm, No. of Columns (Display): 9, Film: Digital
Average advertising content per issue: 40%
Series owner and contact point for the following titles, see individual entries:
Middlewich Guardian
Northwich Guardian
Winsford Guardian
LOCAL NEWSPAPERS: Local Newspapers English Counties

MID-DEVON ADVERTISER SERIES

43510U72B-827

Editorial Address: Old Manor House, 63 Wolborough Street, NEWTON ABBOT, TQ12 1NE **Tel:** 01626 353555
Fax: 01626 333589
Email: mda.news@tindlenews.co.uk
Advertising Address: As above. **Tel:** 01626 355566
Email: mda.sales@internet-today.co.uk
Web site: http://www.middevonadvertiser.co.uk
Publisher: Devon & Cornwall Newspapers Ltd
Frequency: Weekly - Published on Friday
Circulation: 60,000 (Publisher's Statement)
Editor: Ruth Davey; **News Editor:** John Balment;
Advertising Manager: Vanessa Ewers
ADVERTISING RATES:
SCC £6.10
Agency Commission: 10%
Mechanical Data: Type Area: 360 x 262mm, Col Length: 360mm, Page Width: 262mm, No. of Columns (Display): 8, Col Widths (Display): 30mm, Film: Digital

Copy instructions: Copy Date: 3 days prior to publication date
Average advertising content per issue: 40%
Series owner and contact point for the following titles, see individual entries:
Ashburton, Buckfastleigh & Mid-Devon Advertiser
Bovey Tracey, Chudleigh & Mid-Devon Advertiser
Dawlish Post
Kingsteignton & Mid-Devon Advertiser
Newton Abbot & Mid-Devon Advertiser
Teignmouth Post & Gazette
LOCAL NEWSPAPERS: Local Newspapers English Counties

MIDDLESBROUGH HERALD & POST

43410U72B-3360_170

Formerly: Middlesbrough Herald & Post inc Teesside Times
Frequency: Weekly - Published on Wednesday
Cover Price: Free
Circulation: 43,761 (VFD 02/07/2007 to 30/12/2007)
ADVERTISING RATES:
Full Page Mono £2660.00
Full Page Colour £3591.00
SCC £9.80
Part of Series, see entry for: Herald and Post Series (Teesside)
LOCAL NEWSPAPERS: Local Newspapers English Counties

MIDDLETON & NORTH MANCHESTER GUARDIAN & ADVERTISER SERIES

43697U72B-1203

Formerly: Guardian & Advertiser Series
Editorial Address: 1 Scott Place, MANCHESTER, M3 3RN
Tel: 0161 643 3615
Email: middletonguardian@menmedia.co.uk
Advertising Address: Wood Street, Hollywood, STOCKPORT, SK3 0AB **Tel:** 0161 480 4491
Email: mark.stansfield@menmediasales.co.uk
Web site: http://www.middletonguardian.co.uk
Publisher: MEN Media
Date Established: 1877
Frequency: Weekly
Circulation: 93,756 (Combined Circulation)
Editor: Gerry Sammon; **News Editor:** Dan Thompson;
Advertising Manager: Mark Stansfield
ADVERTISING: Rates on application
Agency Commission: 10%
Mechanical Data: Page Width: 267mm, Film: Digital, Type Area: 340 x 267mm, Col Length: 340mm, Col Widths (Display): 27mm, No. of Columns (Display): 9
Average advertising content per issue: 60%
Series owner and contact point for the following titles, see individual entries:
Advertiser (North East Manchester)
Guardian (Middleton & North Manchester)
LOCAL NEWSPAPERS: Local Newspapers English Counties

MIDDLEWICH GUARDIAN

1804122U72B-4050_100

Frequency: Weekly - See Winsford Guardian for circulation figure
Cover Price: £0.50
Part of Series, see entry for: Mid-Cheshire Guardian Series
LOCAL NEWSPAPERS: Local Newspapers English Counties

MIDHURST & PETWORTH OBSERVER

44460U72B-3326_141

Frequency: Weekly
Usual Pagination: 48
Part of Series, see entry for: Southdown Observer Series
LOCAL NEWSPAPERS: Local Newspapers English Counties

MIDLAND EDITION

755526U72B-3464

Editorial Address: Suite 5A, 5th Floor, Medusa House, St. Johns Road, STOURBRIDGE, DY8 1YS **Tel:** 01384 379523
Fax: 01384 379551
Email: steve.baker@twenty4medialimited.co.uk
Advertising Address: As above.
Web site: http://www.twenty4medialimited.co.uk
Publisher: Twenty 4 Media Ltd
Date Established: 2002
Frequency: 26 issues yearly
Cover Price: Free
Circulation: 5,000 (Publisher's Statement)

Editor: Steve Baker; **Features Editor:** Andrew Davies;
Advertising Manager: Steve Baker
ADVERTISING RATES:
Full Page Mono £975.00
Full Page Colour £1170.00
Mechanical Data: Type Area: 340 x 261mm, Col Length: 340mm, Page Width: 261mm, Film: Digital
LOCAL NEWSPAPERS: Local Newspapers English Counties

MIDLANDS FOCUS

43480U72B-705

Formerly: Midlands Review
Editorial Address: Journal House, 18 Curzon Street, DERBY, DE1 1LL **Tel:** 01332 242044 **Fax:** 01332 202671
Email: editorial@live.co.uk
Advertising Address: As above.
Email: editorial@live.co.uk
Publisher: JPC Ltd
Frequency: Weekly - Published on Thursday
Cover Price: Free
Circulation: 5,000 (Publisher's Statement)
Editor: Rebecca Goodwin; **News Editor:** Julie Scott;
Features Editor: Julie Scott; **Advertising Manager:** Julie Scott
ADVERTISING RATES:
SCC £14.00
Agency Commission: 10%
Mechanical Data: Type Area: 360 x 262mm, Col Length: 360mm, Col Widths (Display): 31mm, No. of Columns (Display): 8, Page Width: 262mm, Film: Digital
Copy instructions: Copy Date: Wednesday 4pm prior to publication date
Average advertising content per issue: 75%
LOCAL NEWSPAPERS: Local Newspapers English Counties

MIDSOMER NORTON, RADSTOCK & DISTRICT JOURNAL

1638706U72B-3940

Formerly: Midsomer Norton & Radstock Journal
Editorial Address: 7 Frome Road, RADSTOCK, BA3 3PT
Tel: 01761 432309 **Fax:** 01761 437810
Email: mnrjournal@btconnect.com
Advertising Address: As above.
Email: mnrjournal@btconnect.com
Publisher: Midsomer Norton, Radstock & District Journal
Date Established: 1980
Frequency: Weekly
Cover Price: Free
Circulation: 14,100 (Publisher's Statement)
Editor: George Donkin; **Managing Director:** George Donkin;
Advertising Manager: George Donkin
ADVERTISING RATES:
Full Page Mono £310.00
Agency Commission: 10%
Mechanical Data: Type Area: 300 x 205mm, Col Length: 300mm, Page Width: 205mm, No. of Columns (Display): 5, Film: Digital
Copy instructions: Copy Date: Monday 5pm prior to publication date
LOCAL NEWSPAPERS: Local Newspapers English Counties

MIDWEEK

43306U72B-280_200

Formerly: Bucks Free Press Midweek
Frequency: Weekly
Cover Price: £0.25
Circulation: 5,466 (ABC 02/07/2007 to 30/12/2007)
ADVERTISING RATES:
Full Page Colour £500.00
Part of Series, see entry for: Bucks Free Press Series
LOCAL NEWSPAPERS: Local Newspapers English Counties

MIDWEEK ADVERTISER

43737U72B-1340_150

Formerly: Avon Midweek Advertiser
Frequency: Weekly
Cover Price: Free
Circulation: 23,931 (ABC 01/01/2007 to 01/07/2007)
ADVERTISING RATES:
Full Page Colour £1323.00
Part of Series, see entry for: Andover Advertiser Series
LOCAL NEWSPAPERS: Local Newspapers English Counties

MIDWEEK GUARDIAN (WARRINGTON)

43400U72B-500_230

Frequency: Weekly
Cover Price: Free
Circulation: 67,976 (VFD 02/07/2007 to 30/12/2007)
ADVERTISING: Rates on application
Part of Series, see entry for: Warrington Guardian Series
LOCAL NEWSPAPERS: Local Newspapers English Counties

MIDWEEK HERALD

43532U72B-829

Formerly: Midweek Herald (Sidmouth)
Editorial Address: Fair Oak Close, Exeter Airport Business Park, Clyst Honiton, EXETER, EX5 2UL **Tel:** 01392 888488
Fax: 01395 888551
Email: midweek@archant.co.uk
Advertising Address: As above. **Tel:** 01392 888444
Fax: 01392 888470
Email: stacey.hughes@archant.co.uk
Web site: http://www.midweekherald.co.uk
Publisher: Archant South West
Frequency: Weekly - Published on Wednesday
Cover Price: Free
Circulation: 34,000 (Publisher's Statement)
Editor: Belinda Bennett; **Advertising Manager:** Stacey Hughes
ADVERTISING RATES:
Full Page Mono £1717.20
Full Page Colour £1867.20
SCC £5.30
Agency Commission: 10%
Mechanical Data: Type Area: 365 x 270mm, No. of Columns (Display): 9, Col Widths (Display): 27mm, Col Length: 365mm, Page Width: 270mm, Film: Digital
Copy instructions: Copy Date: Friday 3pm prior to publication date
Average advertising content per issue: 70%
LOCAL NEWSPAPERS: Local Newspapers English Counties

MIDWEEK OBSERVER

1657143U72B-190_254

Formerly: Royal Borough Midweek
Frequency: Weekly
Cover Price: Free
Circulation: 50,000 (Publisher's Statement)
Part of Series, see entry for: Slough & Windsor Observer Series
LOCAL NEWSPAPERS: Local Newspapers English Counties

MIDWEEK STRATFORD-UPON-AVON

44520U72B-3410_160

Frequency: Weekly
Cover Price: Free
Circulation: 53,025 (Publisher's Statement)
ADVERTISING RATES:
Full Page Colour £2268.00
Mechanical Data: Page Width: 256mm, Film: Digital, Col Length: 350mm, No. of Columns (Display): 7, Type Area: 350 x 256mm, Col Widths (Display): 34mm
Part of Series, see entry for: Stratford-upon-Avon Herald Series
LOCAL NEWSPAPERS: Local Newspapers English Counties

MIDWEEK VISITER (FORMBY EDITION)

1744953U72B-2400_191

Frequency: Weekly - See Midweek Visiter (Southport) for circulation figure
Cover Price: Free
ADVERTISING: Rates on application
Part of Series, see entry for: Southport Visiter Series
LOCAL NEWSPAPERS: Local Newspapers English Counties

MIDWEEK VISITER (SOUTHPORT)

44111U72B-2400_190

Frequency: Weekly - Circulation figure includes Midweek Visiter (Formby Edition)
Cover Price: Free
Circulation: 57,979 (ABC 17/07/2006 to 31/12/2006)
ADVERTISING: Rates on application
Part of Series, see entry for: Southport Visiter Series
LOCAL NEWSPAPERS: Local Newspapers English Counties

MILDENHALL JOURNAL

44344U72B-3081_150

Frequency: Weekly
Cover Price: £0.42

Part of Series, see entry for: Newmarket Journal Series
LOCAL NEWSPAPERS: Local Newspapers English Counties

MILFORD & WEST WALES MERCURY

44809U72C-241

Formerly: Milford Mercury Series
Editorial Address: 92 Charles Street, MILFORD HAVEN, SA73 2HE **Tel:** 01646 698971 **Fax:** 01646 693941
Email: fraser.watson@gwent-wales.co.uk
Advertising Address: Old Hakin Road, HAVERFORDWEST, SA61 1XF **Tel:** 01437 765000
Web site: http://www.milfordmercury.co.uk
Publisher: Newsquest Wales & Gloucestershire
Frequency: Weekly - Published on Thursday
Cover Price: £0.45
Circulation: 5,565 (ABC 02/07/2007 to 30/12/2007)
Editor: Fraser Watson; **Advertising Manager:** Andrew Plant; **Group Editor:** Fiona Phillips
ADVERTISING RATES:
SCC £3.10
Mechanical Data: Film: Digital
Copy instructions: Copy Date: Tuesday 4.00pm prior to publication date
LOCAL NEWSPAPERS: Local Newspapers Wales

MILLOM & WEST CUMBRIA EVENING MAIL

41976U67B-10_560

Frequency: Evenings
Edition of: North West Evening Mail (Barrow)
REGIONAL DAILY & SUNDAY NEWSPAPERS: Regional Daily Newspapers

MILNGAVIE & BEARSDEN HERALD

44992U72D-720

Editorial Address: 27 Stewart Street, Milngavie, GLASGOW, G62 6BW **Tel:** 0141 956 3533
Fax: 0141 956 7096
Email: mbherald@jnscotland.co.uk
Advertising Address: As above.
Email: linda.bruce@jpress.co.uk
Web site: http://milngavietoday.co.uk
Publisher: Johnston (Falkirk) Ltd
Date Established: 1901
Frequency: Weekly - Published on Friday
Cover Price: £0.32
Circulation: 6,622 (ABC 02/07/2007 to 30/12/2007)
Editor: Newsdesk; **Managing Director:** Richard Bell
ADVERTISING RATES:
SCC £5.17
Agency Commission: 10%
Mechanical Data: Col Widths (Display): 28mm, Page Width: 272mm, Film: Digital, Col Length: 340mm, Type Area: 340 x 272mm, No. of Columns (Display): 9
Copy instructions: Copy Date: Tuesday 5pm prior to publication date
Average advertising content per issue: 35%
LOCAL NEWSPAPERS: Local Newspapers Scotland

MILTON KEYNES CITIZEN

43311U72B-310_180

Frequency: Weekly
Cover Price: Free
Circulation: 103,077 (VFD 02/07/2007 to 30/12/2007)
ADVERTISING: Rates on application
Part of Series, see entry for: Milton Keynes Citizen Series
LOCAL NEWSPAPERS: Local Newspapers English Counties

MILTON KEYNES CITIZEN SERIES

43309U72B-310

Editorial Address: Napier House, Auckland Park, Bond Avenue, Mount Farm, Bletchley, MILTON KEYNES, MK1 1BU **Tel:** 01908 372279 **Fax:** 01908 632214
Email: editorial@mkcitizen.co.uk
Advertising Address: As above. **Tel:** 01908 371133
Fax: 01908 371112
Email: advertising@mkcitizen.co.uk
Web site: http://www.miltonkeynes.co.uk
Publisher: Johnston Press plc
Frequency: Weekly
Cover Price: Free
Circulation: 205,772 (Combined Circulation)
Editor: Steve Larner; **News Editor:** Steve Larner; **Features Editor:** Sam Gilprow; **Advertising Manager:** Claire Duffy
ADVERTISING: Rates on application
Average advertising content per issue: 82%
Series owner and contact point for the following titles, see individual entries:
Citizen First
Leighton - Linslade Citizen
Milton Keynes Citizen

Supplement(s): Citisport - 52xY, Milton Keynes Business Citizen - 11xY
LOCAL NEWSPAPERS: Local Newspapers English Counties

THE MIRFIELD REPORTER

44698U72B-3760_160

Frequency: Weekly - See The Dewsbury Reporter for circulation figure
Cover Price: £0.42
ADVERTISING RATES:
Full Page Mono £1168.00
Full Page Colour £1519.00
SCC £3.82
Part of Series, see entry for: Dewsbury Reporter and Advertiser Series
LOCAL NEWSPAPERS: Local Newspapers English Counties

MITCHAM & MORDEN GUARDIAN

1695652U72A-128_248

Frequency: Weekly
Cover Price: Free
Part of Series, see entry for: Guardian & News Series (Sutton)
LOCAL NEWSPAPERS: Local Newspapers Greater London

MK NEWS

43313U72B-3929

Formerly: Buckinghamshire on Sunday and MK News Series
Editorial Address: 1 Diamond Court, Opal Drive, Fox Milne, MILTON KEYNES, MK15 0DU **Tel:** 01908 689595
Fax: 01908 689550
Email: editor@mk-news.co.uk
Advertising Address: As above.
Email: advertising@mk-news.co.uk
Web site: http://www.mk-news.co.uk
Publisher: LSN Media
Date Established: 1997
Frequency: Weekly - Published Wednesdays
Cover Price: Free
Circulation: 95,945 (VFD 02/07/2007 to 30/12/2007)
Editor: David Gale; **Advertising Manager:** Samantha Thompson
ADVERTISING RATES:
Full Page Colour £955.00
Agency Commission: 10%
Mechanical Data: Type Area: 360 x 263mm, No. of Columns (Display): 9, Film: Digital, Col Length: 360mm, Page Width: 263mm
Average advertising content per issue: 70%
LOCAL NEWSPAPERS: Local Newspapers English Counties

MOFFAT NEWS

44917U72D-325_170

Frequency: Weekly - Published on Thursday
Cover Price: £0.45
Circulation: 1,202 (ABC 02/07/2007 to 30/12/2007)
ADVERTISING: Rates on application
Part of Series, see entry for: Annandale Observer Series
LOCAL NEWSPAPERS: Local Newspapers Scotland

MONDAY SPORT

45733U67B-9079

Formerly: Yorkshire Sports
Date Established: 1900
Frequency: Weekly - Published on Monday. See main record for circulation figure
Free to qualifying individuals
Summary of Content: Section covering local sports.
ADVERTISING: Rates on application
Part of Series, see entry for: Telegraph & Argus
REGIONAL DAILY & SUNDAY NEWSPAPERS: Regional Daily Newspapers

MONMOUTH MERLIN

1695532U72C-244_101

Frequency: Monthly
Cover Price: Free
Circulation: 4,000 (Publisher's Statement)
ADVERTISING RATES:
Full Page Mono £576.00
Full Page Colour £633.60
SCC £2.00
Part of Series, see entry for: Monmouthshire Beacon and Merlin Series
LOCAL NEWSPAPERS: Local Newspapers Wales

Non-National Newspapers

MONMOUTHSHIRE BEACON
1695531U72C-244_100
Frequency: Weekly - Published on Thursday
Cover Price: £0.35
Circulation: 6,300 (Publisher's Statement)
Part of Series, see entry for: Monmouthshire Beacon and Merlin Series
LOCAL NEWSPAPERS: Local Newspapers Wales

MONMOUTHSHIRE BEACON AND MERLIN SERIES
44813U72C-244
Formerly: Monmouthshire Beacon
Editorial Address: 56 Monnow Street, MONMOUTH, NP25 3XJ **Tel:** 01600 712142 **Fax:** 01600 715531
Email: robert.williams@tindlenews.co.uk
Advertising Address: As above.
Email: beacon.ads@internet-today.co.uk
Web site: http://www.monmouth-today.co.uk
ISSN: 0964-2119
Publisher: Tindle Newspapers Ltd
Circulation: 10,800 (Combined Circulation)
Editor: Robert Williams; **Advertising Manager:** Lee Whiteland
ADVERTISING RATES:
Full Page Mono £1036.80
Full Page Colour £1140.48
SCC £3.60
Agency Commission: 10%
Mechanical Data: Col Length: 360mm, Page Width: 270mm, Film: Digital, Type Area: 360 x 270mm, No. of Columns (Display): 8
Copy instructions: Copy Date: 4pm on Friday prior to publication date
Series owner and contact point for the following titles, see individual entries:
Monmouth Merlin
Monmouthshire Beacon
Wye Valley Merlin
LOCAL NEWSPAPERS: Local Newspapers Wales

MONTGOMERYSHIRE ADVERTISER
1656435U72B-3955_102
Frequency: Monthly
Cover Price: Free
Circulation: 20,000 (Publisher's Statement)
ADVERTISING RATES:
SCC £1.90
Part of Series, see entry for: Admag Newspapers Series
LOCAL NEWSPAPERS: Local Newspapers English Counties

MONTROSE REVIEW
44996U72D-730_180
Frequency: Weekly - Published on Thursday
Cover Price: £0.50
Circulation: 5,105 (ABC 02/07/2007 to 30/12/2007)
ADVERTISING RATES:
Full Page Mono £934.00
Full Page Colour £1215.00
SCC £3.68
Part of Series, see entry for: Montrose Review Series
LOCAL NEWSPAPERS: Local Newspapers Scotland

MONTROSE REVIEW SERIES
44993U72D-730
Editorial Address: 59 John Street, MONTROSE, DD10 8QU
Tel: 01674 672605 **Fax:** 01674 676232
Email: reviewnews@montrosereview.com
Advertising Address: As above.
Email: reviewadverts@montrosereview.com
Web site: http://www.montrosetoday.co.uk
Publisher: Johnston Press plc
Date Established: 1811
Frequency: Weekly
Circulation: 6,217 (Combined Circulation)
Usual Pagination: 40
Editor: Charles Wallace; **Managing Director:** Angus Morrison
ADVERTISING: Rates on application
Agency Commission: 10%
Copy instructions: Copy Date: Monday 5pm prior to publication date
Average advertising content per issue: 60%
Series owner and contact point for the following titles, see individual entries:
Kincardineshire Observer
Montrose Review
LOCAL NEWSPAPERS: Local Newspapers Scotland

THE MOORLANDS ADVERTISER
762063U72B-423_120
Formerly: The Biddulph Advertiser
Frequency: Weekly

Cover Price: Free
Circulation: 22,046 (VFD 02/07/2007 to 30/12/2007)
ADVERTISING: Rates on application
Part of Series, see entry for: Advertiser Series (Stoke-on-Trent)
LOCAL NEWSPAPERS: Local Newspapers English Counties

MOORLANDS TRADER
1660451U72B-3958
Editorial Address: 11 High Street, CONGLETON, CW12 1BW **Tel:** 01260 291638 **Fax:** 01538 382204
Email: moorlandstraderuk@yahoo.co.uk
Advertising Address: As above. **Fax:** 01260 280687
Email: moorlandstraderuk@yahoo.co.uk
Publisher: Congleton Chronicle Ltd
Date Established: 2000
Frequency: 26 issues yearly - Published on Friday
Cover Price: Free
Circulation: 15,689 (Publisher's Statement)
Editor: Jeremy Condliffe; **Advertising Manager:** James Bell
ADVERTISING RATES:
Full Page Mono £450.00
Full Page Colour £500.00
SCC £3.20
Agency Commission: 10%
Mechanical Data: Type Area: 365 x 266mm, Col Length: 365mm, Col Widths (Display): 41mm, No. of Columns (Display): 6, Page Width: 266mm, Print Process: Web-fed offset litho, Film: Digital
Average advertising content per issue: 70%
LOCAL NEWSPAPERS: Local Newspapers English Counties

MORECAMBE GUARDIAN
43980U72B-1990_180
Frequency: Weekly - Circulation figure incorporated in Lancaster Guardian Series
ADVERTISING: Rates on application
Part of Series, see entry for: Lancaster Guardian Series
LOCAL NEWSPAPERS: Local Newspapers English Counties

MORLEY, BEESTON & HUNSLET WEEKLY NEWS
44714U72B-3812_170
Formerly: South Leeds Weekly News
Frequency: Weekly
Cover Price: Free
Circulation: 29,938 (Publisher's Statement)
ADVERTISING RATES:
SCC £4.50
Part of Series, see entry for: Leeds Weekly News Series
LOCAL NEWSPAPERS: Local Newspapers English Counties

MORLEY OBSERVER & ADVERTISER
44717U72B-3823
Formerly: Morley Observer Series
Editorial Address: 40 Queen Street, Morley, LEEDS, LS27 9BR **Tel:** 0113 252 3456 **Fax:** 0113 252 9432
Email: editorial@morleytoday.co.uk
Advertising Address: Express House, Southgate, WAKEFIELD, WF1 1TE **Tel:** 01924 375111
Fax: 01924 290451
Email: bobbie.robinson@wakefieldexpress.co.uk
Web site: http://www.morleyobserver.co.uk
Publisher: Yorkshire Weekly Newspaper Group Ltd
Date Established: 1871
Frequency: Weekly - Published on Wednesday
Cover Price: £0.40
Circulation: 5,000 (Publisher's Statement)
Editor: Sarah Hall; **Group Editor:** Mark Bradley
ADVERTISING RATES:
Full Page Mono £1919.56
Full Page Colour £2490.23
Agency Commission: 10%
Mechanical Data: Page Width: 274mm, Col Widths (Display): 27mm, Film: Digital, Type Area: 340 x 274mm, Col Length: 340mm, No. of Columns (Display): 9
Copy instructions: Copy Date: Friday 5pm prior to publication date
Supplement(s): Leisure Guide - 52xY, Motors Today - 52xY, Property Today - 52xY
LOCAL NEWSPAPERS: Local Newspapers English Counties

MORNINGSIDE AND BRUNTSFIELD GAZETTE
1800032U72D-1023_101
Frequency: Monthly
Cover Price: Free
Circulation: 4,000 (Publisher's Statement)

Part of Series, see entry for: The Gazette Series (Edinburgh)
LOCAL NEWSPAPERS: Local Newspapers Scotland

MORPETH HERALD INC PONTELAND OBSERVER
44169U72B-2550
Editorial Address: 17 Newgate Street, MORPETH, NE61 1AW **Tel:** 01670 517171 **Fax:** 01670 503805
Email: morpeth.herald@northeast-press.co.uk
Advertising Address: As above. **Tel:** 01670 516066
Fax: 01670 512516
Email: dawn.owens@northeast-press.co.uk
Web site: http://www.morpethherald.co.uk
Publisher: Northeast Press Ltd
Date Established: 1854
Frequency: Weekly - Published on Thursday
Cover Price: £0.45
Circulation: 2,947 (ABC 02/07/2007 to 30/12/2007)
Usual Pagination: 20
Editor: Terry Hackett; **Advertising Manager:** Dawn Owens
ADVERTISING RATES:
Full Page Mono £2790.00
Full Page Colour £3627.00
Agency Commission: 10%
Mechanical Data: Type Area: 560 x 338mm, Col Length: 560mm, No. of Columns (Display): 11, Page Width: 338mm, Film: Digital
Copy instructions: Copy Date: Monday 5.00pm prior to publication date
Average advertising content per issue: 60%
Supplement(s): Motors Today - 12xY
LOCAL NEWSPAPERS: Local Newspapers English Counties

MOTHERWELL TIMES
44999U72D-740_150
Frequency: Weekly
Cover Price: £0.36
Part of Series, see entry for: Motherwell Times Series
LOCAL NEWSPAPERS: Local Newspapers Scotland

MOTHERWELL TIMES SERIES
44997U72D-740
Editorial Address: 29 Hope Street, MOTHERWELL, ML1 1BT **Tel:** 01698 264611 **Fax:** 01698 275177
Email: motherwell.times@jnscotland.co.uk
Advertising Address: As above.
Email: suzanne.o'hare@jnscotland.co.uk
Web site: http://www.motherwelltoday.co.uk
Publisher: Johnston (Falkirk) Ltd
Date Established: 1883
Frequency: Weekly - Published on Wednesday
Circulation: 13,718 (ABC 02/07/2007 to 30/12/2007)
Usual Pagination: 28
Editor: Martin Clark
ADVERTISING RATES:
SCC £8.31
Agency Commission: 10%
Mechanical Data: Page Width: 272mm, Film: Digital, Type Area: 340 x 272mm, Col Length: 340mm, No. of Columns (Display): 9, Col Widths (Display): 28mm
Copy instructions: Copy Date: Monday 5pm prior to publication date
Average advertising content per issue: 38%
Series owner and contact point for the following titles, see individual entries:
Bellshill Speaker
Motherwell Times
LOCAL NEWSPAPERS: Local Newspapers Scotland

MOTORS
1828030U72C-519
Editorial Address: For all contact details see main record, Glamorgan Gazette Series
Frequency: Weekly
ADVERTISING: Rates on application
Supplement to: Glamorgan Gazette Series
LOCAL NEWSPAPERS: Local Newspapers Wales

MOURNE OBSERVER (DOWN EDITION)
45111U72E-190_140
Frequency: Weekly
Cover Price: £0.90
Part of Series, see entry for: Mourne Observer Series
LOCAL NEWSPAPERS: Local Newspapers Northern Ireland

MOURNE OBSERVER SERIES
45110U72E-190

Editorial Address: Castlewellan Road, NEWCASTLE, BT33 0JX **Tel:** 028 4372 2666 **Fax:** 028 4372 4566
Email: editor@mourneobserver.com
Advertising Address: As above.
Email: mourneobserver@btconnect.com
Web site: http://www.mourneobserver.com
Publisher: Mourne Observer Ltd.
Date Established: 1949
Frequency: Weekly - Published on Wednesday
Circulation: 11,639 (ABC 02/07/2007 to 30/12/2007)
Editor: Terence Bowman; **News Editor:** Terence Bowman;
Features Editor: Terence Bowman; **Managing Director:**
David Hawthorne; **Advertising Manager:** Alice Bleue
ADVERTISING RATES:
Full Page Colour £1200.00
SCC £4.00
Agency Commission: 15%
Mechanical Data: Type Area: 340 x 265mm, Col Length:
340mm, Col Widths (Display): 30.5mm, No. of Columns
(Display): 8; Page Width: 265mm; Film: Digital
Copy instructions: Copy Date: 2 days prior to publication
date
Average advertising content per issue: 60%
**Series owner and contact point for the following titles,
see individual entries:**
Mourne Observer (Down Edition)
Mourne Observer (South Down Edition)
LOCAL NEWSPAPERS: Local Newspapers Northern Ireland

MOURNE OBSERVER (SOUTH DOWN EDITION)
45112U72E-190_160

Frequency: Weekly
Cover Price: £0.90
Part of Series, see entry for: Mourne Observer Series
LOCAL NEWSPAPERS: Local Newspapers Northern Ireland

MUSSELBURGH NEWS
44904U72D-270_180

Frequency: Weekly - Circulation figure is incorporated into
East Lothian News
Cover Price: £0.42
Part of Series, see entry for: Dalkeith Advertiser Series
LOCAL NEWSPAPERS: Local Newspapers Scotland

MUSWELL HILL JOURNAL
43074U72A-240_190

Frequency: Weekly - Circulation figure is incorporated into
the Hornsey & Crouch End Journal
Cover Price: £0.40
ADVERTISING RATES:
SCC £10.00
Part of Series, see entry for: Islington Gazette & Journal
Series
LOCAL NEWSPAPERS: Local Newspapers Greater London

NAIRNSHIRE TELEGRAPH
45000U72D-760

Editorial Address: 10 Leopold Street, NAIRN, IV12 4BG
Tel: 01667 453258 **Fax:** 01667 452379
Email: ed@nairnshiretelegraph.com
Advertising Address: As above.
Email: nairnshire.telegraph@btinternet.com
Publisher: Nairnshire Telegraph
Date Established: 1853
Frequency: Weekly
Cover Price: £0.40
Usual Pagination: 12
Editor: Iain Bain; **Advertising Manager:** Iain Bain
ADVERTISING RATES:
Full Page Mono £492.10
SCC £1.90
Agency Commission: 10%
Mechanical Data: Col Length: 370mm, Col Widths (Display):
35mm, No. of Columns (Display): 7, Type Area: 370 x
262mm, Page Width: 262mm, Film: Digital
Copy instructions: Copy Date: Wednesday 12pm prior to
publication date
LOCAL NEWSPAPERS: Local Newspapers Scotland

NANTWICH CHRONICLE
43358U72B-435_250

Frequency: Weekly - Circulation figure is incorporated into
the Crewe Chronicle
Cover Price: £0.45
Part of Series, see entry for: Chronicle Series (Crewe)
LOCAL NEWSPAPERS: Local Newspapers English
Counties

NANTWICH GUARDIAN
43371U72B-464_190

Frequency: Weekly
Cover Price: Free
ADVERTISING: Rates on application

Part of Series, see entry for: Crewe Guardian Series
LOCAL NEWSPAPERS: Local Newspapers English
Counties

NARBERTH & WHITLAND OBSERVER
713634U72C-352_130

Frequency: Weekly
Circulation: 1,088 (Publisher's Statement)
Part of Series, see entry for: Tenby, Narberth & Whitland
Observer Series
LOCAL NEWSPAPERS: Local Newspapers Wales

NEATH AND PORT TALBOT TRIBUNE
44833U72C-310

Formerly: Port Talbot Tribune Series
Editorial Address: PO Box 14, Adelaide Street, SWANSEA,
SA1 1QT **Tel:** 01792 510000 **Fax:** 01792 469665
Email: tribune@swwmedia.co.uk
Advertising Address: As above. **Fax:** 01792 514598
Email: michelle.baxter@swwmedia.co.uk
Web site: http://www.thisisswansea.co.uk
Publisher: South West Wales Media Ltd
Date Established: 1990
Frequency: Monthly
Cover Price: Free
Circulation: 46,000 (Publisher's Statement)
Editor: Chris Davies; **News Editor:** Chris Davies;
Advertising Manager: Steve Williams
Language(s): English; Welsh
ADVERTISING RATES:
SCC £6.40
Agency Commission: 10%
Mechanical Data: Type Area: 360 x 270mm, Col Length:
360mm, No. of Columns (Display): 8, Col Widths (Display):
32mm, Page Width: 270mm, Film: Digital
Copy instructions: Copy Date: 1 week prior to publication
date
Average advertising content per issue: 60%
LOCAL NEWSPAPERS: Local Newspapers Wales

NEATH COURIER
713794U72C-162_150

Frequency: Weekly
Cover Price: £0.20
Part of Series, see entry for: The Courier Series (Neath &
Port Talbot)
LOCAL NEWSPAPERS: Local Newspapers Wales

NEATH GUARDIAN
44815U72C-250_150

Frequency: Weekly
Part of Series, see entry for: Neath Guardian Series
LOCAL NEWSPAPERS: Local Newspapers Wales

NEATH GUARDIAN SERIES
44814U72C-250

Editorial Address: 2 Brackla Street Centre, BRIDGEND,
CF31 1DD **Tel:** 01656 304927
Email: guardian@mediawales.co.uk
Advertising Address: 17 Queen Street, NEATH, SA11 1DN
Tel: 01639 795792 **Fax:** 01639 778884
Email: gary.bacon@mediawales.co.uk
Web site: http://www.mediawales.co.uk
Publisher: Media Wales Ltd
Frequency: Weekly - Published on Wednesday
Cover Price: £0.53
Circulation: 4,402 (ABC 02/07/2007 to 30/12/2007)
Editor: Deborah Reef; **Advertising Manager:** Gary Bacon
ADVERTISING RATES:
Full Page Mono £1667.36
Full Page Colour £2249.44
SCC £6.13
Agency Commission: 10%
Mechanical Data: Col Length: 340mm, Col Widths (Display):
31.5mm, No. of Columns (Display): 8, Type Area: 340 x
266mm, Page Width: 266mm, Film: Digital
Copy instructions: Copy Date: Friday 4pm prior to
publication date
Average advertising content per issue: 40%
**Series owner and contact point for the following titles,
see individual entries:**
Neath Guardian
Port Talbot Guardian
LOCAL NEWSPAPERS: Local Newspapers Wales

NELSON LEADER
43991U72B-2040_160

Frequency: Weekly - Published on Friday. Circulation figure
includes the Colne Times and Barnoldswick and Earby
Times
Cover Price: £0.70
Circulation: 15,329 (ABC 02/07/2007 to 30/12/2007)
ADVERTISING RATES:
Full Page Mono £1306.62

Full Page Colour £1698.60
SCC £4.27
Part of Series, see entry for: Leader Times Series
LOCAL NEWSPAPERS: Local Newspapers English
Counties

NENE
761725U72J-175

Editorial Address: 76 Stryd Osborne, Rhosllanerchgrugog,
WREXHAM, LL14 2HT **Tel:** 01978 842075
Email: papurbronene@btinternet.com
Advertising Address: Cil Haul, Erwgerrig,
Rhosllanerchgrugog, WREXHAM, LL14 2BS
Tel: 01978 840646
Frequency: 11 issues yearly - Not published in August
Cover Price: £0.40
Circulation: 850 (Publisher's Statement)
Usual Pagination: 20
Editor: Gareth Hughes; **Advertising Manager:** Towyn
Rogers
Summary of Content: Local community newspaper
featuring items of local interest including music, drama,
politics and the environment.
Language(s): Welsh
Readership/Target Audience: Aimed at Welsh speaking
readers in Wrexham and the surrounding area.
ADVERTISING RATES:
Full Page Mono £100.00
Mechanical Data: No. of Columns (Display): 4
Copy instructions: Copy Date: Last Tuesday of the month
prior to publication date
Average advertising content per issue: 15%
LOCAL NEWSPAPERS: Community Newsletters

NEW ADDINGTON ADVERTISER
42974U72A-50_170

Frequency: Weekly - For circulation see Croydon Advertiser
Cover Price: £0.55
ADVERTISING RATES:
SCC £14.50
Part of Series, see entry for: Croydon Advertiser & Post
Series
LOCAL NEWSPAPERS: Local Newspapers Greater London

NEW FOREST POST INCORPORATING FOREST & WATERSIDE OBSERVER
43756U72B-1379

Formerly: New Forest Post
Editorial Address: Canterbury House, 41 Gosport Street,
LYMINGTON, SO41 9BB **Tel:** 01590 613804
Fax: 01590 689073
Email: chris.yandell@dailyecho.co.uk
Advertising Address: As above. **Tel:** 01590 613888
Fax: 01590 678727
Email: joanne.london@newforestpost.co.uk
Web site: http://www.thisishampshire.net
Publisher: Newsquest (Media Group) Ltd
Frequency: Weekly - Published on Thursday
Cover Price: Free
Circulation: 46,546 (VFD 02/07/2007 to 30/12/2007)
Usual Pagination: 40
Editor: Chris Yandell; **Advertising Manager:** Joanne
London
ADVERTISING RATES:
Full Page Mono £1544.40
Full Page Colour £1716.00
SCC £5.45
Agency Commission: 10%
Mechanical Data: Page Width: 261mm, Film: Digital, Col
Length: 350mm, Col Widths (Display): 28mm, No. of
Columns (Display): 9, Type Area: 350 x 261mm
Copy instructions: Copy Date: Monday 5pm prior to
publication date
Average advertising content per issue: 65%
LOCAL NEWSPAPERS: Local Newspapers English
Counties

NEW MILTON ADVERTISER
43729U72B-1337_170

Frequency: Weekly
Cover Price: £0.20
ADVERTISING RATES:
Full Page Mono £985.60
SCC £2.20
Part of Series, see entry for: Advertiser & Times Series
LOCAL NEWSPAPERS: Local Newspapers English
Counties

NEWARK ADVERTISER
44189U72B-2620_180

Frequency: Weekly
Cover Price: £0.50
Part of Series, see entry for: Newark Advertiser Series
LOCAL NEWSPAPERS: Local Newspapers English
Counties

Non-National Newspapers

NEWARK ADVERTISER SERIES

44187U72B-2620

Editorial Address: Appleton Gate, NEWARK, NG24 1JX
Tel: 01636 681234 **Fax:** 01636 681122
Email: news@newarkadvertiser.co.uk
Advertising Address: As above. **Tel:** 01636 681111
Email: ads@newarkadvertiser.co.uk
Web site: http://www.newarkadvertiser.co.uk
Publisher: Newark Advertiser Ltd
Date Established: 1854
Frequency: Weekly
Cover Price: £0.50
Circulation: 50,000 (Publisher's Statement)
Usual Pagination: 64
Editor: Lucy Millard; **Editor-in-Chief:** Roger Parlby
ADVERTISING RATES:
SCC £7.06
Mechanical Data: Film: Digital, Col Widths (Display): 26mm,
No. of Columns (Display): 9
**Series owner and contact point for the following titles,
see individual entries:**
Bingham Advertiser and South Notts Advertiser
Newark Advertiser
Ollerton Advertiser
Southwell Advertiser
Trader Pictorial (Newark)
LOCAL NEWSPAPERS: Local Newspapers English
Counties

NEWBURY AND THATCHAM CHRONICLE

43271U72B-180_180

Frequency: Weekly
Cover Price: Free
Circulation: 13,594 (VFD 02/07/2007 to 30/12/2007)
ADVERTISING RATES:
Full Page Mono £1245.76
Full Page Colour £1557.20
SCC £4.58
Part of Series, see entry for: Reading Chronicle Series
LOCAL NEWSPAPERS: Local Newspapers English
Counties

NEWBURY PROPERTY NEWS

623303U72B-170_155

Frequency: Weekly
Cover Price: Free
ADVERTISING: Rates on application
Part of Series, see entry for: Newbury Weekly News Series
LOCAL NEWSPAPERS: Local Newspapers English
Counties

NEWBURY WEEKLY NEWS

43268U72B-170_160

Frequency: Weekly
Cover Price: £0.60
Circulation: 23,095 (ABC 02/07/2007 to 30/12/2007)
ADVERTISING: Rates on application
Part of Series, see entry for: Newbury Weekly News Series
LOCAL NEWSPAPERS: Local Newspapers English
Counties

NEWBURY WEEKLY NEWS SERIES

43266U72B-170

Editorial Address: Newspaper House, Faraday Road,
NEWBURY, RG14 2DW **Tel:** 01635 564539
Fax: 01635 522922
Email: editor@newburynews.co.uk
Advertising Address: As above. **Tel:** 01635 550444
Fax: 01635 46052
Email: advert@newburynews.co.uk
Web site: http://www.newburynews.co.uk
Publisher: Newbury Weekly News (Printers) Ltd
Date Established: 1867
Frequency: Weekly
Cover Price: £0.60
Circulation: 63,367 (Combined Circulation)
Editor: Martin Robertshaw; **Managing Director:** Adrian
Martin
ADVERTISING: Rates on application
Agency Commission: 10%
Mechanical Data: No. of Columns (Display): 8, Col Widths
(Display):
Average advertising content per issue: 50%
**Series owner and contact point for the following titles,
see individual entries:**
The Advertiser (Newbury)
Newbury Property News
Newbury Weekly News
Supplement(s): Newbury Business Today - 12xY, Out &
About - 12xY
LOCAL NEWSPAPERS: Local Newspapers English
Counties

NEWCASTLE ADVERTISER

624348U72B-2956_130

Frequency: Weekly
Cover Price: Free
ADVERTISING: Rates on application
Part of Series, see entry for: Advertiser Series (Stoke-on-
Trent)
LOCAL NEWSPAPERS: Local Newspapers English
Counties

NEWHAM RECORDER

43103U72A-350

Formerly: Newham Recorder Series
Editorial Address: Media House, 539 High Road, ILFORD,
IG1 1UD **Tel:** 020 8472 1421 **Fax:** 020 8471 7908
Email: colin.grainger@newhamrecorder.co.uk
Advertising Address: 182-184 High Street North, East Ham,
LONDON, E6 2JD **Tel:** 020 8472 1421 **Fax:** 020 8471 7908
Email: maggie.duggan@archant.co.uk
Web site: http://www.newhamrecorder.co.uk
Publisher: Archant East London & Essex
Date Established: 1969
Frequency: Weekly - Published on Wednesday
Cover Price: £0.50
Circulation: 13,531 (ABC 02/07/2007 to 30/12/2007)
Editor: Colin Grainger; **News Editor:** Pat Coughtrey
ADVERTISING RATES:
Full Page Mono £2835.00
Full Page Colour £3135.00
SCC £9.00
Agency Commission: 10%
Mechanical Data: Col Length: 350mm, No. of Columns
(Display): 9, Type Area: 350 x 267mm, Page Width: 267mm,
Film: Digital, Col Widths (Display): 27mm
Copy instructions: Copy Date: Mono Monday Colour Friday
Average advertising content per issue: 60%
LOCAL NEWSPAPERS: Local Newspapers Greater London

NEWMARKET JOURNAL

44345U72B-3081_160

Frequency: Weekly
Cover Price: £0.42
Part of Series, see entry for: Newmarket Journal Series
LOCAL NEWSPAPERS: Local Newspapers English
Counties

NEWMARKET JOURNAL SERIES

44343U72B-3081

Editorial Address: Rookery House, The guineas,
NEWMARKET, CB8 8SY **Tel:** 01638 668441
Fax: 01638 665547
Email: alison.hayes@newmarketjournal.co.uk
Advertising Address: As above. **Fax:** 01638 561502
Email: paul.taylor@newmarketjournal.co.uk
Web site: http://www.newmarketjournal.co.uk
Publisher: Johnston Press plc
Date Established: 1872
Frequency: Weekly - Published on Thursday
Circulation: 10,186 (ABC 02/07/2007 to 30/12/2007)
Usual Pagination: 56
Editor: Alison Hayes
ADVERTISING RATES:
Full Page Mono £2071.00
Full Page Colour £2588.75
SCC £6.77
Agency Commission: 10%
Mechanical Data: Col Widths (Display): 26.8mm, Col
Length: 340mm, Type Area: 340 x 270mm, Print Process:
Web-fed offset litho, Page Width: 270mm, Film: Digital, No.
of Columns (Display): 9
Copy instructions: Copy Date: Monday 5pm prior to
publication date
Average advertising content per issue: 38%
**Series owner and contact point for the following titles,
see individual entries:**
Mildenhall Journal
Newmarket Journal
Soham & Ely Journal
Supplement(s): Lifestyle - 52xY
LOCAL NEWSPAPERS: Local Newspapers English
Counties

NEWMARKET WEEKLY NEWS

43321U72B-350_180

Frequency: Weekly
Cover Price: Free
Circulation: 16,267 (VFD 02/07/2007 to 30/12/2007)
ADVERTISING RATES:
SCC £3.45
Part of Series, see entry for: Cambridge Weekly News &
Crier Series
LOCAL NEWSPAPERS: Local Newspapers English
Counties

NEWPORT ADVERTISER

44243U72B-2830_120

Frequency: Weekly - Circulation figure includes the Market
Drayton Advertiser
Cover Price: £0.40
Circulation: 9,112 (ABC 02/07/2007 to 30/12/2007)
ADVERTISING: Rates on application
Part of Series, see entry for: Newport & Market Drayton
Advertiser Series
LOCAL NEWSPAPERS: Local Newspapers English
Counties

NEWPORT & CWMBRAN WEEKLY ARGUS

44818U72C-260

Editorial Address: Cardiff Road, Maesglas, NEWPORT,
NP20 3QN **Tel:** 01633 810000 **Fax:** 01633 777023
Email: nicole.garnon@gwent-wales.co.uk
Advertising Address: As above. **Tel:** 01633 777215
Fax: 01633 777160
Email: sharon.hutchinson@gwent-wales.co.uk
Web site: http://www.southwalesargus.co.uk
Publisher: Newsquest Media Group
Date Established: 1859
Frequency: Weekly - Published every Wednesday
Cover Price: Free
Circulation: 34,670 (VFD 20/08/2007 to 30/12/2007)
Editor: Nicole Garnon; **Advertising Manager:** Sharon
Hutchinson; **Managing Editor:** Nicole Garnon
Language(s): English; Welsh
ADVERTISING RATES:
Full Page Mono £1236.24
Full Page Colour £2798.00
SCC £6.40
Agency Commission: 10%
Mechanical Data: No. of Columns (Display): 9, Type Area:
340 x 259mm, Col Length: 340mm, Page Width: 259mm,
Film: Digital
Copy instructions: Copy Date: 2 days 4pm prior to
publication date
Average advertising content per issue: 85%
LOCAL NEWSPAPERS: Local Newspapers Wales

NEWPORT & MARKET DRAYTON ADVERTISER SERIES

44242U72B-2830

Editorial Address: 32 St. Mary Street, NEWPORT, TF10 7AL
Tel: 01952 811500 **Fax:** 01952 820013
Email: staylor@shropshirestar.co.uk
Advertising Address: As above.
Email: newportads@shropshirestar.co.uk
Web site: http://www.newportadvertiser.co.uk
Publisher: Midland News Association
Frequency: Weekly - Published on Friday
Circulation: 9,112 (Combined Circulation)
Editor: Samantha Taylor; **Advertising Manager:** Andrea
Lumb
ADVERTISING: Rates on application
Agency Commission: 10%
Copy instructions: Copy Date: Wednesday 12am prior to
publication date
**Series owner and contact point for the following titles,
see individual entries:**
Market Drayton Advertiser
Newport Advertiser
LOCAL NEWSPAPERS: Local Newspapers English
Counties

NEWQUAY GUARDIAN

765131U72B-530_170

Formerly: Cornish Guardian (Newquay District)
Frequency: Weekly - See Cornish Guardian Series for
combined circulation figure
Cover Price: £0.65
Part of Series, see entry for: Cornish Guardian Series
LOCAL NEWSPAPERS: Local Newspapers English
Counties

THE NEWQUAY VOICE

768536U72B-3926

Editorial Address: 4 Beachfield Avenue, NEWQUAY, TR7
1DR **Tel:** 01637 878298 **Fax:** 01637 859080
Email: editorial@newquayvoice.co.uk
Advertising Address: As above. **Tel:** 01637 876260
Email: sales@newquayvoice.co.uk
Web site: http://www.newquayvoice.co.uk
Publisher: AD Sales
Date Established: 2001
Frequency: Weekly - Published on Wednesday
Cover Price: £0.40
Circulation: 5,000 (Publisher's Statement)
Editor: Matt Bond
ADVERTISING RATES:
Full Page Colour £988.00
SCC £2.50
Agency Commission: 10%

Mechanical Data: Type Area: 393 x 284mm, Col Length: 393mm, Page Width: 284mm, No. of Columns (Display): 8, Col Widths (Display): 33.75mm, Film: Digital
Copy instructions: Copy Date: Friday prior to publication date
Average advertising content per issue: 35%
LOCAL NEWSPAPERS: Local Newspapers English Counties

THE NEWRY ADVERTISER   45050U72E-120_180
Formerly: Advertiser (Newry)
Email: editor@observernewspapersni.com
Frequency: Monthly
Cover Price: Free
Part of Series, see entry for: Dungannon Observer Series
LOCAL NEWSPAPERS: Local Newspapers Northern Ireland

NEWRY DEMOCRAT   45113U72E-195
Editorial Address: 45 Hill Street, NEWRY, BT34 1AF
Tel: 028 3025 1250 Fax: 028 3025 1017
Email: jackie.mckeown@newrydemocrat.com
Advertising Address: As above. Tel: 028 3025 1017
Email: louis.ohare@newrydemocrat.com
Web site: http://www.newrydemocrat.com
Publisher: Thomas Crosbie Holdings Ltd
Frequency: Weekly - Published on Monday
Cover Price: £0.95
Circulation: 8,371 (ABC 02/07/2007 to 30/12/2007)
Editor: Jackie McKeown
Language(s): English; Polish
ADVERTISING RATES:
Full Page Mono £792.00
Full Page Colour £1056.00
SCC £3.00
Agency Commission: 10%
Mechanical Data: Col Length: 330mm, Col Widths (Display): 36mm, No. of Columns (Display): 8, Type Area: 330 x 265mm, Film: Digital, Page Width: 265mm
Copy instructions: Copy Date: Friday 3pm prior to publication date
Average advertising content per issue: 40%
LOCAL NEWSPAPERS: Local Newspapers Northern Ireland

NEWRY REPORTER   45114U72E-197
Editorial Address: 4 Margaret Street, NEWRY, BT34 1DF
Tel: 028 3026 7633 Fax: 028 3026 3157
Email: editor@newryreporter.com
Advertising Address: As above.
Email: advertising@newryreporter.com
Web site: http://www.newryreporter.com
Publisher: Edward Hodgett Ltd
Date Established: 1867
Frequency: Weekly - Published on Wednesday
Cover Price: £0.90
Circulation: 14,474 (ABC 02/07/2007 to 30/12/2007)
Editor: Austin Smyth; Advertising Manager: Edward Hodgett
ADVERTISING RATES:
Full Page Mono £1386.00
Full Page Colour £1871.40
SCC £4.95
Agency Commission: 10%
Mechanical Data: Type Area: 400 x 270mm, No. of Columns (Display): 7, Col Length: 400mm, Page Width: 270mm, Col Widths (Display): 34mm, Film: Digital
Copy instructions: Copy Date: Tuesday 1pm prior to publication date
Average advertising content per issue: 70%
LOCAL NEWSPAPERS: Local Newspapers Northern Ireland

NEWS   43851U72B-1881_140
Formerly: Medway Standard
Frequency: Weekly
Cover Price: £0.35
Circulation: 3,496 (Publisher's Statement)
ADVERTISING: Rates on application
Part of Series, see entry for: Medway News Series
LOCAL NEWSPAPERS: Local Newspapers English Counties

THE NEWS & OBSERVER SERIES
    44540U72B-3467
Formerly: The News Series
Editorial Address: 103-106 High Green Court, Newhall Street, CANNOCK, WS11 1AB Tel: 01922 636666
Fax: 01922 616905
Email: walsall_observer@mrn.co.uk
Advertising Address: MWM North Ltd, High Green Court, Newhall Street, CANNOCK, WS11 1GR Tel: 01543 501700
Fax: 01543 501793
Email: walsall_display@mrn.co.uk
Web site: http://www.icwalsall.co.uk

Publisher: Trinity Mirror Midlands
Frequency: Weekly
Circulation: 131,457 (Combined Circulation)
Editor: Mike Lockley; Advertising Manager: Jon Cottrell
ADVERTISING: Rates on application
Agency Commission: 10%
Copy instructions: Copy Date: Wednesday 4pm prior to publication date
Average advertising content per issue: 70%
Series owner and contact point for the following titles, see individual entries:
Bearwood News
Oldbury News
Tipton News
Wednesbury News
West Bromwich News
LOCAL NEWSPAPERS: Local Newspapers English Counties

NEWS & STAR (CARLISLE)   42023U67B-150
Editorial Address: PO Box 7, Newspaper House, Dalston Road, CARLISLE, CA2 5UA Tel: 01228 612600
Fax: 01228 612640
Email: news@cumbrian-newspapers.co.uk
Advertising Address: As above. Fax: 01228 612613
Email: nicola.meredith@cumbrian-newspapers.co.uk
Web site: http://www.newsandstar.co.uk
Publisher: Cumbrian Newspapers Ltd
Frequency: Evenings
Cover Price: £0.45
Editor: Sue Crawford; News Editor: Sue Crawford; Features Editor: Mark Campbell
ADVERTISING RATES:
SCC £11.53
Mechanical Data: Col Length: 350mm, No. of Columns (Display): 7, Film: Digital, Type Area: 350 x 249mm, Page Width: 249mm
Copy instructions: Copy Date: 2 days prior to publication date
Editions:
News & Star (Final)
News & Star (Late Final)
News & Star (West Cumbrian)
REGIONAL DAILY & SUNDAY NEWSPAPERS: Regional Daily Newspapers

NEWS & STAR (FINAL)   1657509U67B-150_681
Cover Price: £0.42
Edition of: News & Star (Carlisle)
REGIONAL DAILY & SUNDAY NEWSPAPERS: Regional Daily Newspapers

NEWS & STAR (LATE FINAL)   42024U67B-150_540
Formerly: News & Star (Late Final) (Cumbria)
Cover Price: £0.42
Edition of: News & Star (Carlisle)
REGIONAL DAILY & SUNDAY NEWSPAPERS: Regional Daily Newspapers

NEWS & STAR (WEST CUMBRIAN)
    42025U67B-150_680
Formerly: West Cumbrian News & Star
Cover Price: £0.42
Edition of: News & Star (Carlisle)
REGIONAL DAILY & SUNDAY NEWSPAPERS: Regional Daily Newspapers

THE NEWS (ASHTON)   752690U72B-1310_190
Frequency: Monthly
Cover Price: Free
Circulation: 26,389 (Publisher's Statement)
ADVERTISING: Rates on application
Mechanical Data: Col Length: 350mm, No. of Columns (Display): 9
Part of Series, see entry for: The Wigan Observer, Reporter and News Series
LOCAL NEWSPAPERS: Local Newspapers English Counties

THE NEWS EXTRA AND ADVERTISER SERIES   43775U72B-1338
Formerly: The Advertiser Series (Southampton)
Editorial Address: Newspaper House, Test Lane, Redbridge, SOUTHAMPTON, SO16 9JX Tel: 023 8042 4520
Fax: 023 8042 4525
Email: newsdesk@dailyecho.co.uk
Advertising Address: As above. Tel: 023 8042 4777
Fax: 023 8042 4928
Email: tracey.richards@dailyecho.co.uk
Web site: http://www.thisishampshire.net
Publisher: Newsquest (Media Group) Ltd

Frequency: Weekly
Cover Price: Free
Circulation: 143,103 (Publisher's Statement)
Editor: Gordon Sutter; News Editor: Gordon Sutter
ADVERTISING RATES:
Full Page Mono £3331.12
Full Page Colour £3701.25
SCC £11.75
Agency Commission: 10%
Mechanical Data: Type Area: 370 x 264mm, No. of Columns (Display): 9, Col Length: 370mm, Page Width: 264mm
Series owner and contact point for the following titles, see individual entries:
The News Extra and Advertiser (West Edition)
The News Extra Southampton Edition (East and West)
LOCAL NEWSPAPERS: Local Newspapers English Counties

THE NEWS EXTRA AND ADVERTISER (WEST EDITION)   43776U72B-1338_160
Formerly: The News Extra and Advertiser (East Edition)
Frequency: Weekly
Cover Price: Free
Part of Series, see entry for: The News Extra and Advertiser Series
LOCAL NEWSPAPERS: Local Newspapers English Counties

THE NEWS EXTRA SOUTHAMPTON EDITION (EAST AND WEST)
    600867U72B-1338_170
Formerly: The News Extra and Advertiser (West Edition)
Frequency: Weekly
Cover Price: Free
Part of Series, see entry for: The News Extra and Advertiser Series
LOCAL NEWSPAPERS: Local Newspapers English Counties

THE NEWS (FAREHAM & GOSPORT)
    42157U67B-800_550
Cover Price: £0.40
Edition of: The News (Portsmouth)
REGIONAL DAILY & SUNDAY NEWSPAPERS: Regional Daily Newspapers

NEWS GUARDIAN   44503U72B-3372_220
Formerly: Whitley Bay News Guardian
Frequency: Weekly
Cover Price: Free
Circulation: 59,976 (VFD 02/07/2007 to 30/12/2007)
Part of Series, see entry for: News Guardian Series
LOCAL NEWSPAPERS: Local Newspapers English Counties

NEWS GUARDIAN SERIES   44499U72B-3372
Formerly: Whitley Bay News Guardian Series
Editorial Address: Guardian House, 33-35 Park View, WHITLEY BAY, NE26 2TP Tel: 0191 251 8484
Fax: 0191 251 8566
Email: ross.weeks@northeast-press.co.uk
Advertising Address: 17 Newgate Street, MORPETH, NE61 1AW Tel: 01670 516066 Fax: 01670 503805
Email: helen.lockyer@northeast-press.co.uk
Web site: http://www.newsguardian.co.uk
Publisher: Johnston Press plc
Frequency: Weekly - Published on Thursday
Cover Price: Free
Circulation: 131,934 (Combined Circulation)
Editor: Ross Weeks
ADVERTISING RATES:
Full Page Mono £5665.00
SCC £18.64
Agency Commission: 10%
Copy instructions: Copy Date: Monday 12.00pm prior to publication date
Average advertising content per issue: 75%
Series owner and contact point for the following titles, see individual entries:
News Guardian
News Post Leader (Blyth Valley)
News Post Leader (Wansbeck)
LOCAL NEWSPAPERS: Local Newspapers English Counties

THE NEWS (HAVANT & WATERLOOVILLE)   42158U67B-800_570
Cover Price: £0.40

Edition of: The News (Portsmouth)
REGIONAL DAILY & SUNDAY NEWSPAPERS: Regional Daily Newspapers

NEWS LETTER
42276U67B-2410

Editorial Address: 2 Esky Drive, Carn Industrial Estate, Portadown, CRAIGAVON, BT63 5YY **Tel:** 028 3839 5577
Fax: 028 3839 5599
Email: newsdesk@newsletter.co.uk
Advertising Address: The Metro Building, 6-9 Donegall Square South, BELFAST, BT1 5JA **Tel:** 028 9089 7702
Fax: 028 9089 7744
Email: pamela.arnold@jpress.co.uk
Web site: http://www.newsletter.co.uk
Publisher: Johnston Press
Date Established: 1737
Frequency: Mornings
Cover Price: £0.62
Circulation: 26,477 (ABC 02/07/2007 to 30/12/2007)
Editor: Rankin Armstrong; **News Editor:** Karen Grimason;
Advertising Manager: Pamela Arnold
ADVERTISING RATES:
Full Page Mono £3274.00
Full Page Colour £4584.00
Agency Commission: 10%
Mechanical Data: Type Area: 340 x 268mm, Col Length: 340mm, No. of Columns (Display): 9, Print Process: Web-fed offset, Page Width: 268mm
Copy instructions: Copy Date: 2 days prior to publication date
Average advertising content per issue: 15%
Editions:
News Letter (Belfast Edition)
Supplement(s): Business (News Letter) - 52xY, Farming Life - 104xY, Lifestyle - 52xY, PM - 52xY, Property Today - 52xY, Sports Ulster - 52xY
REGIONAL DAILY & SUNDAY NEWSPAPERS: Regional Daily Newspapers

NEWS LETTER (BELFAST EDITION)
1665554U67B-2410_500

Frequency: Daily
Cover Price: £0.60
ADVERTISING: Rates on application
Edition of: News Letter
REGIONAL DAILY & SUNDAY NEWSPAPERS: Regional Daily Newspapers

THE NEWS (PORTSMOUTH)
42155U67B-800

Editorial Address: The News Centre, Hilsea, PORTSMOUTH, PO2 9SX **Tel:** 023 9266 4488
Fax: 023 9267 3363
Email: newsdesk@thenews.co.uk
Advertising Address: As above. **Fax:** 023 9269 0544
Email: rob.thomas@thenews.co.uk
Web site: http://www.portsmouth.co.uk
Publisher: Portsmouth Publishing & Printing Ltd
Date Established: 1877
Frequency: Evenings
Cover Price: £0.40
Annual Sub.: £112.32
Circulation: 65,000 (Publisher's Statement)
Editor: Simon Toft; **News Editor:** Graeme Patfield;
Features Editor: Simon Toft; **Managing Director:** Gary Fearon
ADVERTISING RATES:
Full Page Mono £4675.00
Full Page Colour £6077.50
SCC £15.28
Agency Commission: 10%
Mechanical Data: Col Widths (Display): 28mm, Col Length: 340mm, No. of Columns (Display): 9, Film: Digital, Type Area: 340 x 265mm, Page Width: 265mm
Copy instructions: Copy Date: 2 days prior to publication date
Average advertising content per issue: 37%
Editions:
The News (Fareham & Gosport)
The News (Havant & Waterlooville)
Supplement(s): Free Ads - 52xY, Lifestyle - 52xY, Motoring Guide - 52xY, The Portsmouth and South-East Hampshire Property Guide - 52xY, Recruitment - 52xY, Sports Mail (Portsmouth) - 52xY, Weekend - 52xY
REGIONAL DAILY & SUNDAY NEWSPAPERS: Regional Daily Newspapers

NEWS POST LEADER (BLYTH VALLEY)
44500U72B-3372_160

Formerly: News Post Leader
Frequency: Weekly - Circulation figure includes News Post Leader (Wansbeck)
Cover Price: Free
Circulation: 71,821 (Publisher's Statement)

Part of Series, see entry for: News Guardian Series
LOCAL NEWSPAPERS: Local Newspapers English Counties

NEWS POST LEADER (WANSBECK)
1698331U72B-3372_221

Frequency: Weekly - See News Post Leader (Blyth Valley) for circulation figure
Cover Price: Free
Part of Series, see entry for: News Guardian Series
LOCAL NEWSPAPERS: Local Newspapers English Counties

NEWS SHOPPER (BEXLEY)
43109U72A-360_140

Formerly: News Shopper (Bexleyheath & Welling)
Frequency: Weekly
Cover Price: Free
Circulation: 69,561 (VFD 02/07/2007 to 30/12/2007)
ADVERTISING: Rates on application
Part of Series, see entry for: News Shopper Series
LOCAL NEWSPAPERS: Local Newspapers Greater London

NEWS SHOPPER (BROMLEY)
43110U72A-360_150

Formerly: News Shopper (Bromley & Hayes)
Frequency: Weekly
Cover Price: Free
Circulation: 96,447 (VFD 02/07/2007 to 30/12/2007)
ADVERTISING: Rates on application
Part of Series, see entry for: News Shopper Series
LOCAL NEWSPAPERS: Local Newspapers Greater London

NEWS SHOPPER (DARTFORD & SWANLEY)
43111U72A-360_155

Frequency: Weekly
Cover Price: Free
Circulation: 53,179 (VFD 01/01/2007 to 01/07/2007)
ADVERTISING: Rates on application
Part of Series, see entry for: News Shopper Series
LOCAL NEWSPAPERS: Local Newspapers Greater London

NEWS SHOPPER (GRAVESHAM)
43113U72A-360_163

Formerly: News Shopper (Gravesham Borough)
Frequency: Weekly
Cover Price: Free
ADVERTISING: Rates on application
Part of Series, see entry for: News Shopper Series
LOCAL NEWSPAPERS: Local Newspapers Greater London

NEWS SHOPPER (GREENWICH & CHARLTON)
43114U72A-360_165

Frequency: Weekly
Cover Price: Free
ADVERTISING: Rates on application
Part of Series, see entry for: News Shopper Series
LOCAL NEWSPAPERS: Local Newspapers Greater London

NEWS SHOPPER (LEWISHAM & CATFORD)
43115U72A-360_170

Frequency: Weekly
Cover Price: Free
Circulation: 80,998 (VFD 02/07/2007 to 30/12/2007)
ADVERTISING: Rates on application
Part of Series, see entry for: News Shopper Series
LOCAL NEWSPAPERS: Local Newspapers Greater London

NEWS SHOPPER SERIES
43107U72A-360

Editorial Address: Mega House, Crest View Drive, Petts Wood, ORPINGTON, BR5 1BT **Tel:** 01689 836211
Fax: 01689 875367
Email: newsroom@london.newsquest.co.uk
Advertising Address: As above. **Fax:** 01689 890253
Email: lwright@london.newsquest.co.uk
Web site: http://www.newsshopper.co.uk
Publisher: Newsquest Media Group
Date Established: 1965
Frequency: Weekly - Published on Wednesday
Cover Price: Free
Circulation: 308,920 (Combined Circulation)
Editor: Glyn Garlick; **News Editor:** Glyn Garlick;
Advertising Manager: Louisa Wright
ADVERTISING: Rates on application
Agency Commission: 10%

Copy instructions: Copy Date: Friday 5pm prior to publication date
Average advertising content per issue: 65%
Series owner and contact point for the following titles, see individual entries:
News Shopper (Bexley)
News Shopper (Bromley)
News Shopper (Dartford & Swanley)
News Shopper (Gravesham)
News Shopper (Greenwich & Charlton)
News Shopper (Lewisham & Catford)
LOCAL NEWSPAPERS: Local Newspapers Greater London

THE NEWS (STANDISH)
752691U72B-1310_200

Frequency: Monthly
Cover Price: Free
Circulation: 10,000 (Publisher's Statement)
ADVERTISING: Rates on application
Mechanical Data: Col Length: 350mm, No. of Columns (Display): 9
Part of Series, see entry for: The Wigan Observer, Reporter and News Series
LOCAL NEWSPAPERS: Local Newspapers English Counties

NEWSEXTRA
624433U72B-1370_110

Formerly: Eastleigh News Extra
Frequency: Weekly - Circulation figure also includes the Winchester News Extra
Cover Price: Free
Circulation: 58,412 (Publisher's Statement)
ADVERTISING RATES:
SCC £3.75
Part of Series, see entry for: Hampshire Chronicle Series
LOCAL NEWSPAPERS: Local Newspapers English Counties

NEWTON ABBOT & DISTRICT WEEKENDER
43550U72B-885_140

Formerly: Newton Weekender
Frequency: Weekly
Cover Price: Free
Circulation: 13,062 (VFD 02/07/2007 to 30/12/2007)
Part of Series, see entry for: Torbay Weekender Series
LOCAL NEWSPAPERS: Local Newspapers English Counties

NEWTON ABBOT & MID-DEVON ADVERTISER
43514U72B-827_150

Frequency: Weekly
Cover Price: £0.35
Circulation: 13,266 (Publisher's Statement)
Part of Series, see entry for: Mid-Devon Advertiser Series
LOCAL NEWSPAPERS: Local Newspapers English Counties

NEWTON NEWS
43584U72B-934

Editorial Address: St. Cuthberts Way, Aycliffe Business Park, NEWTON AYCLIFFE, DL5 6DX **Tel:** 01325 300212
Fax: 01325 312893
Email: syd@gonp.co.uk
Advertising Address: As above.
Email: paul@gonp.co.uk
Web site: http://www.newtonnews.co.uk
Publisher: Newton Press
Date Established: 1959
Frequency: Weekly
Cover Price: Free
Circulation: 15,000 (Publisher's Statement)
Usual Pagination: 8
Editor: Syd Howarth; **Advertising Manager:** Paul Howarth
ADVERTISING RATES:
Full Page Mono £800.00
Full Page Colour £1200.00
SCC £3.00
Agency Commission: 15%
Mechanical Data: Col Length: 400mm, Col Widths (Display): 33mm, Type Area: 400 x 293mm, Print Process: Web-fed litho, Page Width: 293mm, No. of Columns (Display): 8, Film: Digital
Copy instructions: Copy Date: Wednesday 5pm prior to publication date
Average advertising content per issue: 45%
LOCAL NEWSPAPERS: Local Newspapers English Counties

NEWTOWNABBEY TIMES AND EAST ANTRIM TIMES
45127U72E-226_160

Frequency: Weekly - Published on Thursday. Circulation figure is incorporated into the Larne Times & East Antrim Times
Cover Price: £0.90
Part of Series, see entry for: The Times Series
LOCAL NEWSPAPERS: Local Newspapers Northern Ireland

NEWTOWNARDS CHRONICLE
45115U72E-200

Editorial Address: 25 Frances Street, NEWTOWNARDS, BT23 7DT **Tel:** 028 9181 3333 **Fax:** 028 9182 0087
Email: news@ardschronicle.co.uk
Advertising Address: As above.
Email: advertising@ardschronicle.co.uk
Publisher: Newtownards Chronicle Ltd
Date Established: 1873
Frequency: Weekly - Published on Thursday
Cover Price: £0.70
Circulation: 9,956 (ABC 01/01/2007 to 30/12/2007)
Editor: John Savage; **Managing Director:** I. Alexander;
Advertising Manager: Brian Sloan
ADVERTISING RATES:
Full Page Mono £2240.00
Agency Commission: 10%
Mechanical Data: Type Area: 560mm x 336mm, Col Length: 560mm, Page Width: 336mm, Film: Digital, No. of Columns (Display): 10, Col Width (Display): 33mm
Copy instructions: Copy Date: Tuesday 5pm prior to publication date
Average advertising content per issue: 50%
LOCAL NEWSPAPERS: Local Newspapers Northern Ireland

NEWTOWNARDS SPECTATOR
45077U72E-70_160

Frequency: Weekly
Cover Price: £0.70
Circulation: 1,078 (ABC 01/01/2007 to 30/12/2007)
ADVERTISING RATES:
SCC ....:............................ £3.80
Part of Series, see entry for: County Down Spectator and Ulster Standard Series
LOCAL NEWSPAPERS: Local Newspapers Northern Ireland

NITHSDALE NEWS
1605550U72D-1002

Formerly: Upper Nithsdale News
Editorial Address: Whitehill Farmhouse, Crawick, SANQUHAR, DG4 6JW **Tel:** 01659 50942
Fax: 0870 123 1659
Email: contact@weepaper.com
Advertising Address: As above.
Email: ads@weepaper.com
Web site: http://www.weepaper.com
Publisher: Daisybakers
Date Established: 1993
Frequency: 26 issues yearly
Cover Price: £0.50
Circulation: 2,100 (Publisher's Statement)
Editor: Alison Daniels; **Advertising Manager:** Carol Baker
ADVERTISING RATES:
Full Page Mono £220.00
Mechanical Data: Film: Digital
LOCAL NEWSPAPERS: Local Newspapers Scotland

NORFOLK COUNTY WEEKLIES SERIES
44133U72B-2437

Editorial Address: Prospect House, Rouen Road, NORWICH, NR1 1RE **Tel:** 01603 772402 **Fax:** 01603 666781
Email: terry.redhead@archant.co.uk
Advertising Address: Archant North, 36 North Quay, GREAT YARMOUTH, NR30 1JE **Tel:** 01493 335000
Fax: 01493 652082
Email: colin.huggins@archant.co.uk
Publisher: Archant Norfolk
Frequency: Weekly
Circulation: 82,422 (Combined Circulation)
Editor: Terry Redhead; **Managing Director:** Stephan Phillips; **Advertising Manager:** Colin Huggins; **Group Editor:** Terry Redhead
ADVERTISING: Rates on application
Series owner and contact point for the following titles, see individual entries:
Beccles and Bungay Journal
Beccles and Bungay Journal (Bungay Edition)
Beccles and Bungay Journal (Halesworth Edition)
Dereham & Fakenham Times
Diss Mercury
North Norfolk News
Swaffham and Watton Times
Thetford and Brandon Times
Wymondham & Attleborough Mercury
LOCAL NEWSPAPERS: Local Newspapers English Counties

NORTH AYRSHIRE WORLD
27491U72D-103_101

Frequency: Weekly
Cover Price: Free
Circulation: 2,083 (Publisher's Statement)
ADVERTISING RATES:
SCC £6.20
Part of Series, see entry for: Ayrshire World Series
LOCAL NEWSPAPERS: Local Newspapers Scotland

NORTH BELFAST NEWS
1643543U72E-283

Editorial Address: 253-255 Antrim Road, BELFAST, BT15 2GY **Tel:** 028 9058 4444 **Fax:** 028 9058 4450
Email: m.mccourt@belfastmediagroup.com
Advertising Address: Teach Basil, 2 Hannahstown Hill, BELFAST, BT17 0LT **Tel:** 028 90 61 9000
Email: j.odonnell@belfastmediagroup.com
Web site: http://www.belfastmedia.com
ISSN: 1462-107X
Publisher: Belfast Media Group
Date Established: 1998
Frequency: Weekly - Published on Thursday
Cover Price: £0.70
Circulation: 5,374 (ABC 01/01/2007 to 30/12/2007)
Editor: Maria McCourt
ADVERTISING RATES:
Full Page Mono £930.24
Full Page Colour £1209.31
Agency Commission: 10%
Mechanical Data: Film: Digital
Supplement(s): Business - 52xY, Car and Homes - 52xY
LOCAL NEWSPAPERS: Local Newspapers Northern Ireland

NORTH CORNWALL ADVERTISER
43421U72B-543

Formerly: Cornwall Advertiser Series
Editorial Address: Tindle House, 2 Trevanson Street, WADEBRIDGE, PL27 7AW **Tel:** 01208 815096
Fax: 01208 815935
Email: editorial.nca@internet-today.co.uk
Advertising Address: As above.
Email: editorial.nca@internet-today.co.uk
Web site: http://www.cornwalladvertisers.co.uk
Publisher: North Cornwall Advertiser Ltd
Date Established: 1986
Frequency: Monthly
Cover Price: Free
Circulation: 37,000 (Publisher's Statement)
Editor: Linden Jones; **Advertising Manager:** Linden Jones
ADVERTISING RATES:
Full Page Mono £720.00
Full Page Colour £795.00
SCC £4.95
Agency Commission: 15%
Mechanical Data: Col Length: 360mm, Col Widths (Display): 31mm, No. of Columns (Display): 8, Type Area: 360 x 269mm, Print Process: Web-fed offset litho, Page Width: 269mm, Film: Digital
Copy instructions: Copy Date: 7 days prior to publication date
Average advertising content per issue: 50%
LOCAL NEWSPAPERS: Local Newspapers English Counties

NORTH DEVON GAZETTE
43519U72B-832

Formerly: North Devon Gazette & Advertiser
Editorial Address: Unit 3, Old Station Road, BARNSTAPLE, EX32 8PB **Tel:** 01271 345056 **Fax:** 01271 341667
Email: dave.tanner@archant.co.uk
Advertising Address: As above. **Tel:** 01271 344303
Fax: 01271 328896
Email: lyn.brodie@archant.co.uk
Web site: http://www.northdevongazette.co.uk
Publisher: Archant South West
Date Established: 1856
Frequency: Weekly - Published on Wednesday
Cover Price: Free
Circulation: 51,438 (VFD 02/07/2007 to 30/12/2007)
Editor: David Tanner; **Advertising Manager:** Lyn Brodie
ADVERTISING RATES:
Full Page Mono £1591.20
Full Page Colour £1969.88
SCC £5.20
Agency Commission: 10%
Mechanical Data: Col Widths (Display): 25mm, No. of Columns (Display): 9, Film: Digital, Page Width: 261mm, Type Area: 340 x 261mm, Col Length: 340mm
Copy instructions: Copy Date: Monday 5pm prior to publication date
Average advertising content per issue: 66%
LOCAL NEWSPAPERS: Local Newspapers English Counties

NORTH DEVON JOURNAL (BARNSTAPLE EDITION)
43524U72B-833_120

Formerly: North Devon Journal
Frequency: Weekly
Part of Series, see entry for: North Devon Journal Series
LOCAL NEWSPAPERS: Local Newspapers English Counties

NORTH DEVON JOURNAL (BIDEFORD EDITION)
43525U72B-833_140

Formerly: North Devon Journal (Torridge Edition)
Frequency: Weekly
Part of Series, see entry for: North Devon Journal Series
LOCAL NEWSPAPERS: Local Newspapers English Counties

NORTH DEVON JOURNAL (HOLSWORTHY EDITION)
1746715U72B-833_141

Frequency: Weekly
Part of Series, see entry for: North Devon Journal Series
LOCAL NEWSPAPERS: Local Newspapers English Counties

NORTH DEVON JOURNAL (ILFRACOMBE EDITION)
623973U72B-833_130

Frequency: Weekly
Part of Series, see entry for: North Devon Journal Series
LOCAL NEWSPAPERS: Local Newspapers English Counties

NORTH DEVON JOURNAL SERIES
43523U72B-833

Editorial Address: Avery House, Liberty Road, Roundswell Business Park, BARNSTAPLE, EX31 3TL **Tel:** 01271 343064
Fax: 01271 347457
Email: editorial@northdevonjournal.co.uk
Advertising Address: As above. **Fax:** 01271 347420
Email: dsawyer@c-dm.co.uk
Web site: http://www.thisisnorthdevon.co.uk
Publisher: Cornwall & Devon Media Limited
Date Established: 1824
Frequency: Weekly - Published on Thursday
Cover Price: £0.80
Circulation: 30,759 (ABC 02/07/2007 to 30/12/2007)
Usual Pagination: 72
Editor: Owen Jones; **Editor-in-Chief:** Andy Cooper; **Managing Director:** Tony Hazell; **Advertising Manager:** Dale Sawyer
ADVERTISING RATES:
Full Page Mono £1756.80
Full Page Colour £2195.50
SCC £6.10
Mechanical Data: Type Area: 360 x 268.1mm, Col Widths (Display): 31.5mm, No. of Columns (Display): 8, Col Length: 360mm, Page Width: 268.1mm, Film: Digital
Copy instructions: Copy Date: Monday 12 noon 3 days prior to publication date
Series owner and contact point for the following titles, see individual entries:
North Devon Journal (Barnstaple Edition)
North Devon Journal (Bideford Edition)
North Devon Journal (Holsworthy Edition)
North Devon Journal (Ilfracombe Edition)
LOCAL NEWSPAPERS: Local Newspapers English Counties

NORTH EAST WEEKLY
1697237U72D-1017

Editorial Address: 10 Rose Street, PETERHEAD, AB42 1DB **Tel:** 01779 480851 **Fax:** 01779 480851
Email: sales@buchanadvertiser.co.uk
Advertising Address: As above.
Email: sales@buchanadvertiser.co.uk
Web site: http://www.buchanadvertiser.co.uk
Publisher: Buchan Associates
Frequency: Weekly - Published on Thursday
Cover Price: Free
Circulation: 10,000 (Publisher's Statement)
Editor: Alan Buchan; **Advertising Manager:** Alan Buchan
ADVERTISING RATES:
Full Page Mono £70.00
Mechanical Data: Type Area: 277 x 190mm, Col Length: 277mm, Page Width: 190mm, Film: Digital
Copy instructions: Copy Date: Monday 5pm prior to publication date
LOCAL NEWSPAPERS: Local Newspapers Scotland

Non-National Newspapers

NORTH EDINBURGH NEWS (NEN)
45002U72D-767

Formerly: North Edinburgh News NEN
Editorial Address: 222 Crewe Road North, EDINBURGH, EH5 2NS **Tel:** 0131 467 3972 **Fax:** 0131 467 3973
Email: mary@northedinburghnews.co.uk
Advertising Address: As above.
Email: mary@northedinburghnews.co.uk
Web site: http://www.northedinburghnews.co.uk
Publisher: North Edinburgh News
Date Established: 1980
Frequency: Monthly
Cover Price: Free
Circulation: 14,500 (Publisher's Statement)
Editor: Mary Burnside; **Advertising Manager:** Mary Burnside
Readership/Target Audience: Circulates in: North Edinburgh.
ADVERTISING RATES:
Full Page Mono £577.50
Full Page Colour £663.00
SCC £5.75
Agency Commission: 10%
Mechanical Data: Col Widths (Display): 52mm, No. of Columns (Display): 5, Type Area: 340x 280mm, Page Width: 280mm, Col Length: 340mm, Film: Digital
Average advertising content per issue: 25%
LOCAL NEWSPAPERS: Local Newspapers Scotland

NORTH LANARKSHIRE EXTRA
44987U72D-664_160

Formerly: Motherwell Extra
Frequency: Weekly
Cover Price: Free
ADVERTISING RATES:
SCC £8.35
Part of Series, see entry for: Lanarkshire Extra Series
LOCAL NEWSPAPERS: Local Newspapers Scotland

NORTH LEEDS WEEKLY NEWS
44713U72B-3812_160

Frequency: Weekly
Cover Price: Free
Circulation: 30,882 (VFD 02/07/2007 to 30/12/2007)
ADVERTISING RATES:
SCC £4.25
Part of Series, see entry for: Leeds Weekly News Series
LOCAL NEWSPAPERS: Local Newspapers English Counties

NORTH NORFOLK NEWS
44137U72B-2437_180

Frequency: Weekly
Cover Price: £0.55
Circulation: 8,797 (Publisher's Statement)
ADVERTISING: Rates on application
Part of Series, see entry for: Norfolk County Weeklies Series
LOCAL NEWSPAPERS: Local Newspapers English Counties

NORTH SHROPSHIRE CHRONICLE
44236U72B-2812_185

Frequency: Weekly - Circulation figure incorporated into Shrewsbury Chronicle
Cover Price: £0.50
ADVERTISING: Rates on application
Part of Series, see entry for: Chronicle & Journal Series
LOCAL NEWSPAPERS: Local Newspapers English Counties

NORTH SOMERSET TIMES
31111U72B-60_180

Frequency: Weekly
Cover Price: Free
Circulation: 30,992 (VFD 02/07/2007 to 30/12/2007)
ADVERTISING: Rates on application
Part of Series, see entry for: Weston & Somerset Mercury Series
Supplement(s): Property Times - 52xY
LOCAL NEWSPAPERS: Local Newspapers English Counties

NORTH STAR
45003U72D-770

Formerly: North Star (Dingwall)
Editorial Address: Dochcarty Road, DINGWALL, IV15 9UG
Tel: 01349 863248 **Fax:** 01349 863456
Email: northstar@spp-group.com
Advertising Address: New Century House, Stadium Road, INVERNESS, IV1 1FG **Tel:** 01463 732222 **Fax:** 01463 732273
Email: b.mccoll@highland-news.co.uk

Web site: http://www.highland-news.co.uk
Publisher: Scottish Provincial Press
Date Established: 1893
Frequency: Weekly - Published on Thursday
Cover Price: £0.68
Circulation: 5,365 (ABC 01/01/2007 to 30/12/2007)
Usual Pagination: 56
Editor: Jackie MacKenzie; **Group Editor:** Paul Breen
ADVERTISING RATES:
Full Page Mono £3966.40
Full Page Colour £5949.60
SCC £13.40
Agency Commission: 10%
Mechanical Data: Page Width: 276mm, Type Area: 370 x 276mm, Film: Digital, No. of Columns (Display): 8, Col Length: 370mm
Copy instructions: Copy Date: Tuesday 12pm prior to publication date
LOCAL NEWSPAPERS: Local Newspapers Scotland

NORTH WALES CHRONICLE
44821U72C-270

Formerly: North Wales Chronicle Series
Editorial Address: 302 High Street, BANGOR, LL57 1UL
Tel: 01248 387400 **Fax:** 01248 354793
Email: news@northwaleschronicle.co.uk
Advertising Address: As above.
Email: julie.foster@nwn.co.uk
Web site: http://www.northwaleschronicle.co.uk
Publisher: NWN Media Ltd
Date Established: 1808
Frequency: Weekly - Published on Thursday
Cover Price: Free
Circulation: 33,870 (VFD 02/07/2007 to 30/12/2007)
Editor: Alex Ballard; **Advertising Manager:** Julie Foster
ADVERTISING RATES:
Full Page Mono £1718.28
Full Page Colour £2233.76
SCC £5.16
Agency Commission: 10%
Mechanical Data: Type Area: 370 x 259mm, Col Length: 370mm, Col Widths (Display): 27mm, No. of Columns (Display): 9, Film: Digital, Page Width: 259mm
Copy instructions: Copy Date: Tuesday 2.00pm prior to publication date
Average advertising content per issue: 60%
LOCAL NEWSPAPERS: Local Newspapers Wales

NORTH WALES SERIES
44825U72C-275

Editorial Address: County Press Buildings, Station Road, BALA, LL23 7PG **Tel:** 01678 520262
Email: cyfnod@tiscali.co.uk
Advertising Address: As above. **Fax:** 01678 521251
Email: cyfnod@tiscali.co.uk
Publisher: Gwasg Y Sir
Frequency: Weekly - Published on Wednesday
Editor: Gwyn Evans; **Advertising Manager:** Gareth Evans;
Publisher: Gwyn Evans
ADVERTISING RATES:
Full Page Mono £500.00
SCC £6.00
Agency Commission: 10%
Mechanical Data: Type Area: 400 x 280mm, Col Length: 400mm, Col Widths (Display): 45mm, No. of Columns (Display): 6, Page Width: 280mm, Film: Digital
Copy instructions: Copy Date: 1 week prior to publication date
Series owner and contact point for the following titles, see individual entries:
Corwen Times
Y Cyfnod
Merioneth Express
LOCAL NEWSPAPERS: Local Newspapers Wales

NORTH WALES WEEKLY NEWS (COLWYN BAY EDITION)
27476U72C-280_130

Frequency: Weekly
Cover Price: £0.70
ADVERTISING: Rates on application
Part of Series, see entry for: North Wales Weekly News Series
LOCAL NEWSPAPERS: Local Newspapers Wales

NORTH WALES WEEKLY NEWS (CONWY VALLEY EDITION)
27478U72C-280_150

Frequency: Weekly
Cover Price: £0.70
ADVERTISING: Rates on application
Part of Series, see entry for: North Wales Weekly News Series
LOCAL NEWSPAPERS: Local Newspapers Wales

NORTH WALES WEEKLY NEWS (GENERAL EDITION)
27477U72C-280_180

Frequency: Weekly
Cover Price: £0.70
ADVERTISING: Rates on application
Part of Series, see entry for: North Wales Weekly News Series
LOCAL NEWSPAPERS: Local Newspapers Wales

NORTH WALES WEEKLY NEWS SERIES
44829U72C-280

Formerly: North Wales Weekly News
Editorial Address: Vale Road, LLANDUDNO JUNCTION, LL31 9SL **Tel:** 01492 584321 **Fax:** 01492 596498
Email: news.desk@northwalesnews.co.uk
Advertising Address: As above. **Fax:** 01492 574422
Email: sharon.doleman@dailypost.co.uk
Web site: http://www.northwalesweeklynews.co.uk
Publisher: Trinity Mirror
Frequency: Weekly - Published on Thursday
Circulation: 17,314 (ABC 02/07/2007 to 30/12/2007)
Editor: Dan Owen; **Advertising Manager:** Sharon Doleman
ADVERTISING: Rates on application
Series owner and contact point for the following titles, see individual entries:
North Wales Weekly News (Colwyn Bay Edition)
North Wales Weekly News (Conwy Valley Edition)
North Wales Weekly News (General Edition)
Supplement(s): Your Property - 51xY
LOCAL NEWSPAPERS: Local Newspapers Wales

NORTH WEST EVENING MAIL (BARROW)
41975U67B-10

Formerly: North West Evening Mail (Cumbria)
Editorial Address: Newspaper House, Abbey Road, BARROW-IN-FURNESS, LA14 5QS **Tel:** 01229 821835
Fax: 01229 840164
Email: news@nwemail.co.uk
Advertising Address: As above. **Fax:** 01229 832141
Email: maria.woods@cngroup.co.uk
Web site: http://www.nwemail.co.uk
Publisher: Furness Newspapers Ltd
Date Established: 1898
Frequency: Evenings - Not published on Sunday
Cover Price: £0.39
Circulation: 18,520 (ABC 02/07/2007 to 30/12/2007)
Editor: Jonathan Lee; **News Editor:** Robert Johnson
ADVERTISING RATES:
Full Page Mono £2371.60
Full Page Colour £2371.60
SCC £9.68
Agency Commission: 10%
Mechanical Data: Page Width: 266mm, Col Length: 350mm, No. of Columns (Display): 7, Film: Digital, Type Area: 350 x 266mm
Copy instructions: Copy Date: 11.30am 1 day prior to publication date
Average advertising content per issue: 50%
Editions:
Millom & West Cumbria Evening Mail
Ulverston & South Lakes Evening Mail
Supplement(s): Motors - 52xY, Property - 52xY
REGIONAL DAILY & SUNDAY NEWSPAPERS: Regional Daily Newspapers

NORTH WEST LONDON NEWSPAPER SERIES
43119U72A-385

Editorial Address: 100A Avenue Road, LONDON, NW3 3HF
Tel: 020 7433 6000 **Fax:** 020 8962 6159
Email: tim.cole@archant.co.uk
Advertising Address: As above. **Tel:** 020 7433 0000
Fax: 020 7453 6259
Email: elaine.allen2@archant.co.uk
Web site: http://www.wbtimes.co.uk
Publisher: Archant London
Frequency: Weekly - Published on Thursday
Circulation: 54,733 (Combined Circulation)
Editor: Andy McCorkell; **News Editor:** Andy McCorkell
ADVERTISING RATES:
Full Page Colour £4803.75
SCC £15.25
Agency Commission: 10%
Mechanical Data: Col Length: 360mm, Type Area: 360 x 265mm, Page Width: 265mm, No. of Columns (Display): 9, Film: Digital, Col Widths (Display): 27mm
Copy instructions: Copy Date: Monday 4.30pm prior to publication date
Series owner and contact point for the following titles, see individual entries:
Hammersmith & Kensington Times
Kilburn Times
Paddington & Westminster Times
Wembley & Kingsbury Times

Willesden & Brent Times
LOCAL NEWSPAPERS: Local Newspapers Greater London

NORTH YORKSHIRE HERALD & POST

622898U72B-3360_203

Frequency: Weekly - Published on Thursday
Cover Price: Free
Circulation: 14,039 (Publisher's Statement)
ADVERTISING RATES:
Full Page Mono £1145.00
Full Page Colour £1545.75
SCC £4.25
Part of Series, see entry for: Herald and Post Series
(Teesside)
LOCAL NEWSPAPERS: Local Newspapers English
Counties

NORTH YORKSHIRE NEWS 44651U72B-3588_195

Formerly: North Yorkshire News (Richmond)
Frequency: Weekly
Cover Price: Free
Circulation: 31,574 (VFD 02/07/2007 to 30/12/2007)
ADVERTISING RATES:
SCC £5.51
Part of Series, see entry for: Ackrill Newspaper Series
LOCAL NEWSPAPERS: Local Newspapers English
Counties

NORTHAMPTON CHRONICLE AND ECHO

42133U67B-440

Formerly: Chronicle and Echo (Northampton)
Editorial Address: Upper Mounts, NORTHAMPTON, NN1
3HR, **Tel:** 01604 467000 **Fax:** 01604 467200
Email: editor@northantsnews.co.uk
Advertising Address: As above. **Fax:** 01604 467240
Email: michael.loveridge@northantsnews.co.uk
Web site: http://www.northamptonchron.co.uk
Publisher: Northamptonshire Newspapers Ltd
Frequency: Evenings
Cover Price: £0.40
Circulation: 20,070 (ABC 02/07/2007 to 30/12/2007)
Editor: Richard Edmondson; **News Editor:** Richard
Edmondson; **Features Editor:** Lily Canter; **Managing
Director:** Nick Mills; **Advertising Manager:** Michael
Loveridge
ADVERTISING RATES:
Full Page Mono £2701.98
Full Page Colour £3512.57
SCC £8.83
Mechanical Data: Type Area: 340 x 265mm, Col Length:
340mm, No. of Columns (Display): 9, Film: Digital, Page
Width: 265mm
Copy instructions: Copy Date: 2 days prior to publication
date
Supplement(s): Business - 52xY, Jobs - 52xY, Motors -
52xY, Property - 52xY, Sport - 52xY, TV Week - 52xY
REGIONAL DAILY & SUNDAY NEWSPAPERS: Regional
Daily Newspapers

NORTHAMPTON HERALD & POST

44162U72B-2500_150

Frequency: Weekly
Cover Price: Free
Circulation: 48,954 (VFD 02/07/2007 to 30/12/2007)
ADVERTISING RATES:
Full Page Mono £2172.60
Full Page Colour £2933.01
SCC £7.10
Part of Series, see entry for: Northants Herald and Post
Series
LOCAL NEWSPAPERS: Local Newspapers English
Counties

NORTHAMPTON MERCURY 44153U72B-2484

Editorial Address: Upper Mounts, NORTHAMPTON, NN1
3HR **Tel:** 01604 467000 **Fax:** 01604 467190
Email: editor@northantsnews.co.uk
Advertising Address: As above. **Fax:** 01604 467240
Email: stacey.mcfaul@northantsnews.co.uk
Web site: http://www.northantsnews.com
Publisher: Northamptonshire Newspapers Ltd
Date Established: 1720
Frequency: Weekly - Published on Thursday
Cover Price: Free
Circulation: 48,615 (VFD 03/07/2006 to 31/12/2006)
Usual Pagination: 60
Editor: Steve Scoles; **Managing Director:** Nick Mills;
Advertising Manager: Stacey McFaul
ADVERTISING RATES:
SCC £9.12
Agency Commission: 10%

Mechanical Data: Type Area: 340 x 268mm, No. of
Columns (Display): 9, Col Widths (Display): 28mm, Film:
Digital, Col Length: 340mm, Page Width: 268mm
Copy instructions: Copy Date: 2 days prior to publication
date
Average advertising content per issue: 30%
Supplement(s): Motors - 52xY, Property Today - 52xY
LOCAL NEWSPAPERS: Local Newspapers English
Counties

NORTHAMPTONSHIRE EVENING
TELEGRAPH 42085U67B-315

Formerly: Evening Telegraph (Kettering)
Editorial Address: Newspaper House, Ise Park, Rothwell
Road, KETTERING, NN16 8GA **Tel:** 01536 506100
Fax: 01536 506195
Email: et.newsdesk@northantsnews.co.uk
Advertising Address: As above. **Fax:** 01536 506196
Email: amanda.hamilton@northantsnews.co.uk
Web site: http://www.northantset.co.uk
Publisher: Johnston Press plc
Date Established: 1897
Frequency: Evenings
Cover Price: £0.38
Circulation: 22,915 (Publisher's Statement)
Usual Pagination: 40
Editor: David Brennan; **News Editor:** David Brennan;
Features Editor: Joni Ager; **Advertising Manager:** Amanda
Hamilton
ADVERTISING RATES:
SCC £8.59
Agency Commission: 10%
Mechanical Data: Col Length: 340mm, No. of Columns
(Display): 9, Film: Positive, right reading, emulsion side
down. Digital, Type Area: 340 x 268mm, Page Width:
268mm
Copy instructions: Copy Date: 2 days prior to publication
date
Average advertising content per issue: 60%
Supplement(s): Gardening - 12xY, Home and New Cars -
12xY, Jobs Today - 52xY, Property - 52xY
REGIONAL DAILY & SUNDAY NEWSPAPERS: Regional
Daily Newspapers

NORTHANTS HERALD AND POST
SERIES 44158U72B-2500

Editorial Address: Newspaper House, 9 Derngate,
NORTHAMPTON, NN1 1NN **Tel:** 01604 614600
Fax: 01604 614649
Email: chris.gill@hpnorthants.co.uk
Advertising Address: As above. **Fax:** 01604 614724
Email: hpretailsales@mrn.co.uk
Web site: http://www.icnorthants.co.uk
Publisher: LSN Media
Frequency: Weekly - Published Thursday and Friday
Cover Price: Free
Circulation: 128,956 (Combined Circulation)
Usual Pagination: 40
Editor: Chris Gill; **Advertising Manager:** Candy Thompson
ADVERTISING: Rates on application
Mechanical Data: Page Width: 264mm, Type Area: 340 x
264mm, Col Length: 340mm, Col Widths (Display): 28mm,
No. of Columns (Display): 9
**Series owner and contact point for the following titles,
see individual entries:**
Brackley & Towcester Post
Harborough Herald & Post
Northampton Herald & Post
Wellingborough & Rushden Herald & Post
Supplement(s): Property Direct - 52xY
LOCAL NEWSPAPERS: Local Newspapers English
Counties

NORTHANTS MERCURY & CITIZEN
SERIES 44154U72B-2490

Formerly: Northants Citizen Series
Editorial Address: Newspaper House, Ise Park, Rothwell
Road, KETTERING, NN16 8GA **Tel:** 01536 506100
Fax: 01536 506195
Email: et.newsdesk@northantsnews.co.uk
Advertising Address: As above. **Tel:** 01536 506506
Fax: 01536 506196
Web site: http://www.northantset.co.uk
Publisher: Northamptonshire Newspapers Ltd
Frequency: Weekly - Published on Thursday
Cover Price: Free
Circulation: 49,503 (Publisher's Statement)
Editor: David Brennan; **News Editor:** David Brennan
ADVERTISING: Rates on application
Agency Commission: 10%
Mechanical Data: Type Area: 340 x 268mm, Col Length:
340mm, No. of Columns (Display): 9, Film: Digital, Page
Width: 268mm
Copy instructions: Copy Date: 2 days prior to publication
date

**Series owner and contact point for the following titles,
see individual entries:**
Corby Mercury & Citizen
Kettering Mercury & Citizen
Wellingborough and Rushden Mercury & Citizen
LOCAL NEWSPAPERS: Local Newspapers English
Counties

NORTHANTS ON SUNDAY 713830U67C-24

Editorial Address: Upper Mounts, NORTHAMPTON, NN1
3HR **Tel:** 01604 467000 **Fax:** 01604 467190
Email: editor@northantsnews.co.uk
Advertising Address: As above.
Web site: http://www.northantsnews.com
Publisher: Johnston Press plc
Date Established: 2001
Frequency: Sunday
Cover Price: Free
Circulation: 50,000 (Publisher's Statement)
Editor: Steve Scoles; **News Editor:** Steve Scoles; **Features
Editor:** Steve Scoles; **Group Editor:** Jeremy Clifford
ADVERTISING: Rates on application
Mechanical Data: Type Area: 350 x 268mm, Col Length:
350mm, No. of Columns (Display): 8
Editions:
Northants on Sunday (North)
REGIONAL DAILY & SUNDAY NEWSPAPERS: Regional
Sunday Newspapers

NORTHANTS ON SUNDAY (NORTH)

1668035U67C-24_500

Frequency: Sunday
Cover Price: Free
Edition of: Northants on Sunday
REGIONAL DAILY & SUNDAY NEWSPAPERS: Regional
Sunday Newspapers

NORTHERN CONSTITUTION
(COLERAINE EDITION) 1639075U72E-205_102

Frequency: Weekly
Cover Price: £0.85
Part of Series, see entry for: Northern Constitution Series
LOCAL NEWSPAPERS: Local Newspapers Northern Ireland

NORTHERN CONSTITUTION (LIMAVADY
EDITION) 1639073U72E-205_100

Frequency: Weekly
Cover Price: £0.85
Part of Series, see entry for: Northern Constitution Series
LOCAL NEWSPAPERS: Local Newspapers Northern Ireland

NORTHERN CONSTITUTION
(MAGHERAFELT) 1639074U72E-205_101

Formerly: Northern Constitution (South Londonderry Edition)
Frequency: Weekly
Part of Series, see entry for: Northern Constitution Series
LOCAL NEWSPAPERS: Local Newspapers Northern Ireland

NORTHERN CONSTITUTION SERIES

45116U72E-205

Formerly: Northern Constitution
Editorial Address: 23 Main Street, Limavady, CO.
LONDONDERRY, BT49 OEP **Tel:** 028 7776 2130
Fax: 028 7776 3986
Email: limavady.news@northernconstitution.co.uk
Advertising Address: 20 Railway Road, COLERAINE, BT52
1PD **Tel:** 028 7034 3344 **Fax:** 028 7032 9889
Email: advertising@northernnewspapers.co.uk
Web site: http://www.ulsternet-ni.co.uk
Publisher: Northern Alpha Newspaper Group
Frequency: Weekly - Published on Wednesday
Circulation: 5,500 (Publisher's Statement)
Editor: Jennifer Church
ADVERTISING RATES:
Full Page Mono £1488.00
Full Page Colour £2529.00
SCC £4.65
Agency Commission: 10%
Mechanical Data: Col Length: 400mm, Col Widths (Display):
31mm, Film: Negative, wrong reading, emulsion side up, No.
of Columns (Display): 10, Type Area: 340 x 268mm, Print
Process: Web offset, Screen: 40 lpc, Page Width: 268mm
Copy instructions: Copy Date: Tuesday 5pm prior to
publication date
Average advertising content per issue: 40%
**Series owner and contact point for the following titles,
see individual entries:**
Northern Constitution (Coleraine Edition)
Northern Constitution (Limavady Edition)

Section 4 (a) Newspapers

Northern Constitution (Magherafelt)
LOCAL NEWSPAPERS: Local Newspapers Northern Ireland

THE NORTHERN ECHO (COUNTY DURHAM EDITION)
42044U67B-200_540
Formerly: Northern Echo (South West Durham Edition)
Edition of: The Northern Echo (Darlington)
REGIONAL DAILY & SUNDAY NEWSPAPERS: Regional Daily Newspapers

THE NORTHERN ECHO (DARLINGTON)
42043U67B-200
Editorial Address: PO Box 14, Priestgate, DARLINGTON, DL1 1NF **Tel:** 01325 381313 **Fax:** 01325 380539
Email: newsdesk@nne.co.uk
Advertising Address: As above. **Fax:** 01325 384311
Email: lynda.winfield@nne.co.uk
Web site: http://www.northernecho.co.uk
Publisher: Newsquest Yorkshire and North East (Darlington)
Date Established: 1870
Frequency: Mornings
Cover Price: £0.40
Circulation: 50,256 (ABC 02/07/2007 to 30/12/2007)
Editor: Nigel Burton; **News Editor:** Nigel Burton; **Managing Director:** David Coates
ADVERTISING RATES:
Full Page Mono £10002.00
Full Page Colour £12502.50
SCC £18.21
Mechanical Data: Col Length: 340mm, No. of Columns (Display): 9, Type Area: 340 x 283mm, Page Width: 283mm, Col Widths (Display): 29mm, Film: Digital
Editions:
The Northern Echo (County Durham Edition)
The Northern Echo (Darlington, Tees Valley & North Yorkshire Edition)
Supplement(s): 7 Days - 52xY, Football - 48xY, Homes & Property - 52xY, Living - 12xY, Local Heroes - 52xY, Motoring - 52xY, NE Magazine - 12xY, Racing North - 2xY, Sport - 52xY
REGIONAL DAILY & SUNDAY NEWSPAPERS: Regional Daily Newspapers

THE NORTHERN ECHO (DARLINGTON, TEES VALLEY & NORTH YORKSHIRE EDITION)
42047U67B-200_670
Formerly: Northern Echo (Tees Valley Edition)
Edition of: The Northern Echo (Darlington)
REGIONAL DAILY & SUNDAY NEWSPAPERS: Regional Daily Newspapers

NORTHERN SCOT AND MORAY & NAIRN EXPRESS
45004U72D-780
Editorial Address: 74-76 South Street, ELGIN, IV30 1JG
Tel: 01343 548777 **Fax:** 01343 545629
Email: admin@northern-scot.co.uk
Advertising Address: As above. **Fax:** 01343 541629
Email: advertising@northern-scot.co.uk
Web site: http://www.northern-scot.co.uk
Publisher: Moray & Nairn Newspaper Co Ltd
Date Established: 1880
Frequency: Weekly
Cover Price: £0.68
Circulation: 18,203 (ABC 01/01/2007 to 30/12/2007)
Usual Pagination: 36
Editor: Mike Collins; **Advertising Manager:** Sue Pilkington
ADVERTISING RATES:
Full Page Mono £6239.00
Full Page Colour £9355.00
SCC £11.34
Agency Commission: 10%
Mechanical Data: Col Widths (Display): 35mm, Page Width: 377mm, Film: Digital, Type Area: 550mm x 377mm, Col Length: 550mm, No. of Columns (Display): 10
Copy instructions: Copy Date: Tuesday 4.30pm prior to publication date
Average advertising content per issue: 50%
Supplement(s): Midweek Extra - 52xY
LOCAL NEWSPAPERS: Local Newspapers Scotland

NORTHUMBERLAND GAZETTE
44170U72B-2560
Editorial Address: 32 Bondgate Without, ALNWICK, NE66 1PN **Tel:** 01665 602234 **Fax:** 01665 602472
Email: northumberland.gazette@northeast-press.co.uk
Advertising Address: As above. **Tel:** 01665 604944
Email: dawn@northeast-press.co.uk
Web site: http://www.northumberlandgazette.co.uk
Publisher: Northeast Press Ltd
Date Established: 1854
Frequency: Weekly - Published on Thursday

Cover Price: £0.60
Circulation: 10,815 (ABC 02/07/2007 to 30/12/2007)
Editor: Janet Hall; **Managing Director:** Stuart Birkett; **Advertising Manager:** Dawn Owens
ADVERTISING RATES:
Full Page Mono £3776.00
Full Page Colour £4908.00
Agency Commission: 10%
Mechanical Data: Col Widths (Display): 30.7mm, Page Width: 345mm, Type Area: 560 x 345mm, Col Length: 560mm, No. of Columns (Display): 11
Copy instructions: Copy Date: Monday 5pm prior to publication date
Supplement(s): Diary of Events - 1xY, Farming Surveys - 3xY, First Class - 1xY, Holiday Guide - 1xY, Motors Today - 12xY, Northumberland Now - 12xY
LOCAL NEWSPAPERS: Local Newspapers English Counties

NORTH-WEST ECHO
45120U72E-220_110
Frequency: Weekly - Published on Tuesday
Cover Price: Free
Circulation: 31,726 (Publisher's Statement)
ADVERTISING RATES:
Full Page Mono £1392.00
Full Page Colour £1908.60
SCC £4.55
Part of Series, see entry for: The Sentinel Series
LOCAL NEWSPAPERS: Local Newspapers Northern Ireland

NORTHWICH GUARDIAN
43398U72B-4050_102
Frequency: Weekly
Cover Price: £0.50
Circulation: 14,750 (ABC 02/07/2007 to 30/12/2007)
Part of Series, see entry for: Mid-Cheshire Guardian Series
LOCAL NEWSPAPERS: Local Newspapers English Counties

NORWICH EVENING NEWS
42139U67B-460
Formerly: Evening News Norwich
Editorial Address: Prospect House, Rouen Road, NORWICH, NR1 1RE **Tel:** 01603 628311 **Fax:** 01603 219060
Email: eveningnews@archant.co.uk
Advertising Address: As above. **Fax:** 01603 615343
Email: julie.brown@archant.co.uk
Web site: http://www.eveningnews24.co.uk
Publisher: Archant Norfolk
Date Established: 1882
Frequency: Evenings - Not published on Sunday
Cover Price: £0.40
Circulation: 22,914 (ABC 02/07/2007 to 30/12/2007)
Editor: Tim Williams; **Features Editor:** Derek James; **Managing Director:** Stephan Phillips; **Advertising Manager:** Julie Brown
ADVERTISING RATES:
Full Page Mono £2217.60
Full Page Colour £2882.88
Agency Commission: 10%
Mechanical Data: Page Width: 270mm, Type Area: 360 x 270mm, No. of Columns (Display): 8, Col Widths (Display): 32mm, Film: Digital, Col Length: 360mm
Copy instructions: Copy Date: 2 working days prior to publication date
Supplement(s): Going Out, Life Matters, Staying In
REGIONAL DAILY & SUNDAY NEWSPAPERS: Regional Daily Newspapers

NOTTINGHAM AND LONG EATON TOPPER
44192U72B-2623
Editorial Address: Maychalk House, 8 Musters Road, West Bridgford, NOTTINGHAM, NG2 7PL **Tel:** 0115 969 6000
Fax: 0115 982 1874
Email: john.topper@btconnect.com
Advertising Address: As above. **Fax:** 0115 982 6565
Web site: http://www.toppernewspapers.co.uk
Publisher: Topper Newspapers Ltd
Date Established: 1994
Frequency: Weekly - Published on Wednesday
Cover Price: Free
Circulation: 209,222 (VFD 02/07/2007 to 30/12/2007)
Usual Pagination: 64
Editor: John Howorth; **News Editor:** Simon Holmes; **Advertising Manager:** Alice Hall
ADVERTISING RATES:
Full Page Mono £2562.00
Full Page Colour £3330.00
SCC £9.15
Agency Commission: 10%
Mechanical Data: Trim Size: 350 x 260mm, Film: Digital, No. of Columns (Display): 8
Copy instructions: Copy Date: Friday prior to publication date

---

Average advertising content per issue: 20%
LOCAL NEWSPAPERS: Local Newspapers English Counties

NOTTINGHAM & TRENT VALLEY JOURNAL
44193U72B-2659_172
Frequency: Weekly
Cover Price: Free
Circulation: 15,000 (Publisher's Statement)
Usual Pagination: 12
Part of Series, see entry for: Journal & Advertiser Series
LOCAL NEWSPAPERS: Local Newspapers English Counties

NOTTINGHAM EVENING POST
42140U67B-470
Formerly: Evening Post Nottingham
Editorial Address: Castle Wharf House, NOTTINGHAM, NG1 7EU **Tel:** 0115 948 2000
Email: newsdesk@nottinghameveningpost.co.uk
Advertising Address: As above. **Fax:** 0115 964 4097
Email: advertising@nottinghameveningpost.co.uk
Web site: http://www.thisisnottingham.co.uk
Publisher: Nottingham Post Media Group Ltd
Date Established: 1878
Frequency: 313 issues yearly
Cover Price: £0.33
Circulation: 57,699 (ABC 02/07/2007 to 30/12/2007)
Editor: Steven Fletcher; **News Editor:** Steven Fletcher; **Features Editor:** Jeremy Lewis; **Advertising Manager:** James Crudgington
ADVERTISING RATES:
SCC £16.90
Mechanical Data: Col Length: 360mm, No. of Columns (Display): 8, Print Process: Web-fed offset litho, Film: Negative, right reading, emulsion side down. Digital, Type Area: 360 x 277mm, Page Width: 277mm
Copy instructions: Copy Date: 2 days prior to publication date
Editions:
Evening Post Nottingham (Final)
Supplement(s): Business (Evening Post Nottingham) - 52xY, Bygones - 12xY, Commercial Property - 52xY, Homes to Buy - 52xY, Homes to Rent - 52xY, Jobs Extra - 52xY, Motoring Post - 52xY, Post People - 52xY, Seven Days - 52xY
REGIONAL DAILY & SUNDAY NEWSPAPERS: Regional Daily Newspapers

NOTTINGHAM RECORDER
44199U72B-2666_170
Frequency: Weekly
Cover Price: Free
Circulation: 151,904 (VFD 02/07/2007 to 30/12/2007)
ADVERTISING: Rates on application
Part of Series, see entry for: West Notts & Derbyshire Recorder Series
LOCAL NEWSPAPERS: Local Newspapers English Counties

NUNEATON NEWS
42144U67B-478
Formerly: Heartland Evening News (Nuneaton Area)
Editorial Address: Newspaper House, 11-15 Newtown Road, NUNEATON, CV11 4HP **Tel:** 024 7635 3534
Fax: 024 7635 3481
Email: editorial@hen-news.co.uk
Advertising Address: As above.
Email: annette.shillito@staffordshirenewspapers.co.uk
Web site: http://www.nuneaton-news.co.uk
Publisher: Staffordshire Newspapers Ltd
Frequency: Evenings - Not published on Sunday. Circulation of Wednesday edition is 45000
Cover Price: £0.30
Circulation: 15,000 (Publisher's Statement)
Editor: Claire Harrison; **Managing Director:** Gary Matthews
ADVERTISING RATES:
Full Page Mono £1202.24
Agency Commission: 10%
Mechanical Data: Type Area: 350 x 268mm, Col Length: 350mm, No. of Columns (Display): 9, Film: Digital, Page Width: 268mm
Copy instructions: Copy Date: 12 noon 1 day prior to publication date
Supplement(s): Property - 52xY
REGIONAL DAILY & SUNDAY NEWSPAPERS: Regional Daily Newspapers

NUNEATON TELEGRAPH
42041U67B-180_610
Formerly: Nuneaton Evening Telegraph
Cover Price: £0.40
Edition of: Coventry Telegraph
REGIONAL DAILY & SUNDAY NEWSPAPERS: Regional Daily Newspapers

NUNEATON TRIBUNE
44522U72B-3413

Formerly: Nuneaton Weekly Tribune
Editorial Address: Brunel Road, HINCKLEY, LE10 0AB
Tel: 01455 891965 **Fax:** 01455 891968
Email: nuneatontribune@mrn.co.uk
Advertising Address: Corporation Street, COVENTRY, CV1
1FP **Tel:** 024 7663 3633
Email: business@coventry-telegraph.co.uk
Web site: http://www.nuneatontribune.net
Publisher: Trinity Mirror
Frequency: Weekly - Published on Thursday
Cover Price: Free
Circulation: 54,756 (VFD 02/07/2007 to 30/12/2007)
Editor: Emma Ray; **News Editor:** Emma Ray
ADVERTISING RATES:
Full Page Mono £1836.00
Full Page Colour £2478.00
SCC £6.00
Mechanical Data: Film: Digital, Type Area: 340 x 264mm,
No. of Columns (Display): 9, Col Length: 340mm, Page
Width: 264mm
LOCAL NEWSPAPERS: Local Newspapers English
Counties

OADBY AND WIGSTON MAIL
44018U72B-2135_170

Frequency: Weekly - Circulation figure incorporated in the
Leicester Mail
Cover Price: Free
ADVERTISING RATES:
SCC £13.80
Part of Series, see entry for: Leicester Mail Series
LOCAL NEWSPAPERS: Local Newspapers English
Counties

OBAN TIMES & WEST HIGHLAND TIMES
45006U72D-800

Formerly: Oban Times Series
Editorial Address: PO Box 1, Crannog Lane, OBAN, PA34
4HB **Tel:** 01631 568000 **Fax:** 01631 568001
Email: editor@obantimes.co.uk
Advertising Address: As above.
Email: editor@obantimes.co.uk
Web site: http://www.obantimes.co.uk
Publisher: Wyvex Media Group
Date Established: 1861
Frequency: Weekly
Cover Price: £0.70
Circulation: 17,421 (ABC 01/01/2007 to 30/12/2007)
Usual Pagination: 24
Editor: Stewart MacKenzie; **Advertising Manager:** Anne
Martin
ADVERTISING RATES:
SCC £8.65
Mechanical Data: No. of Columns (Display): 10, Col Widths
(Display): 35mm, Type Area: 550 x 357mm, Col Length:
550mm, Page Width: 357mm, Film: Digital
Copy instructions: Copy Date: Tuesday 10.00am prior to
publication date
LOCAL NEWSPAPERS: Local Newspapers Scotland

OBSERVER (EAST, KINGSWOOD & KEYNSHAM)
43204U72B-20_105

Formerly: Bristol Observer (East, Kingswood & Keynsham)
Frequency: Weekly - Published on Friday
Cover Price: Free
Circulation: 62,890 (VFD 02/07/2007 to 30/12/2007)
ADVERTISING RATES:
SCC £5.60
Part of Series, see entry for: Bristol Observer Series
LOCAL NEWSPAPERS: Local Newspapers English
Counties

OBSERVER (SOUTH GLOUCESTERSHIRE)
43207U72B-20_140

Formerly: Bristol Observer (South Glo'shire)
Frequency: Weekly - Published on Wednesday
Cover Price: Free
Circulation: 33,491 (VFD 02/07/2007 to 30/12/2007)
ADVERTISING RATES:
SCC £3.40
Part of Series, see entry for: Bristol Observer Series
LOCAL NEWSPAPERS: Local Newspapers English
Counties

OBSERVER (SOUTH WEST)
43209U72B-20_150

Formerly: Observer (South Bristol)
Frequency: Weekly - Published on Friday
Cover Price: Free
Circulation: 34,492 (VFD 02/07/2007 to 30/12/2007)

ADVERTISING RATES:
SCC £4.35
Part of Series, see entry for: Bristol Observer Series
LOCAL NEWSPAPERS: Local Newspapers English
Counties

OKEHAMPTON TIMES
43546U72B-857_160

Frequency: Weekly
Cover Price: £0.55
Circulation: 4,000 (Publisher's Statement)
Part of Series, see entry for: Tavistock Times Gazette
Series
LOCAL NEWSPAPERS: Local Newspapers English
Counties

• OLDBURY NEWS
1818523U72B-3467_212

Frequency: Weekly - Published on Thursday
Cover Price: Free
ADVERTISING RATES:
SCC £4.46
Part of Series, see entry for: The News & Observer Series
LOCAL NEWSPAPERS: Local Newspapers English
Counties

THE OLDHAM ADVERTISER
43679U72B-1245

Formerly: Advertiser (Oldham)
Editorial Address: 70 Yorkshire Street, OLDHAM, OL1 1SR
Tel: 0161 626 3663 **Fax:** 0161 626 3449
Email: oldhamadvertiser@menwn.co.uk
Advertising Address: 82-86 Drake Street, ROCHDALE,
OL11 5JL **Tel:** 01706 354321 **Fax:** 01706 750227
Email: mark.stansfield@menmediasales.co.uk
Web site: http://www.oldhamadvertiser.co.uk
Publisher: MEN Media
Date Established: 1982
Frequency: Weekly - Published on Thursday
Cover Price: Free
Circulation: 86,749 (VFD 02/07/2007 to 30/12/2007)
Usual Pagination: 88
Editor: Carl Marsden; **News Editor:** Carl Marsden
ADVERTISING RATES:
SCC £5.55
Agency Commission: 10%
Mechanical Data: Page Width: 267mm, Film: Digital, Type
Area: 340 x 267mm, Col Length: 340mm, Col Widths
(Display): 27mm, No. of Columns (Display): 9
Copy instructions: Copy Date: Tuesday 3.30pm prior to
publication date
Average advertising content per issue: 60%
LOCAL NEWSPAPERS: Local Newspapers English
Counties

OLDHAM EVENING CHRONICLE
42145U67B-490

Formerly: Evening Chronicle (Oldham)
Editorial Address: PO Box 47, 172 Union Street, OLDHAM,
OL1 1EQ **Tel:** 0161 633 2121 **Fax:** 0161 652 2111
Email: editorial@oldham-chronicle.co.uk
Advertising Address: As above. **Fax:** 0161 627 0905
Email: advertising@oldham-chronicle.co.uk
Web site: http://www.oldham-chronicle.co.uk
Publisher: Hirst Kidd & Rennie Ltd
Frequency: Evenings
Cover Price: £0.45
Circulation: 20,976 (ABC 02/07/2007 to 30/12/2007)
Editor: Jim Williams; **Managing Director:** Philip Hirst;
Advertising Manager: Jim Whittingham
ADVERTISING RATES:
Full Page Mono £1350.48
Full Page Colour £1823.15
SCC £6.62
Agency Commission: 10%
Mechanical Data: Col Length: 340mm, Type Area: 340 x
265mm, Page Width: 265mm, Film: Digital, No. of Columns
(Display): 6, Col Widths (Display): 41mm
Copy instructions: Copy Date: 12 noon 2 days prior to
publication date
Average advertising content per issue: 40%
REGIONAL DAILY & SUNDAY NEWSPAPERS: Regional
Daily Newspapers

OLLERTON ADVERTISER
44188U72B-2620_130

Formerly: Dukeries Advertiser
Frequency: Weekly
Cover Price: £0.50
Part of Series, see entry for: Newark Advertiser Series
LOCAL NEWSPAPERS: Local Newspapers English
Counties

ONGAR & NORTH WEALD GAZETTE
43595U72B-965_120

Formerly: Ongar Gazette
Frequency: Weekly - See main series record for circulation
figure
Cover Price: £0.65
Part of Series, see entry for: Brentwood Gazette Series
LOCAL NEWSPAPERS: Local Newspapers English
Counties

THE ORCADIAN
45010U72D-810

Editorial Address: 50 Albert Street, KIRKWALL, KW15 1HQ
Tel: 01856 878000 **Fax:** 01856 878001
Email: newsroom@orcadian.co.uk
Advertising Address: Hells Half Acre, Hatston Industrial
Estate, KIRKWALL, KW15 1DW **Tel:** 01856 879000
Fax: 01856 879001
Email: adverts@orcadian.co.uk
Web site: http://www.orcadian.co.uk
Publisher: The Orcadian Ltd
Date Established: 1854
Frequency: Weekly - Published on Thursday
Cover Price: £0.70
Circulation: 10,183 (ABC 02/07/2007 to 30/12/2007)
Editor: Sigurd Towrie; **Advertising Manager:** Julie Hellewel
ADVERTISING RATES:
Full Page Mono £1080.00
Full Page Colour £1440.00
Agency Commission: 10%
Mechanical Data: Col Length: 400mm, Col Widths (Display):
41mm, Film: Digital, Type Area: 400 x 261mm, Page Width:
261mm, No. of Columns (Display): 6
Copy instructions: Copy Date: Monday 5pm prior to
publication date
Average advertising content per issue: 35%
Supplement(s): Orcadian Farmer - 2xY
LOCAL NEWSPAPERS: Local Newspapers Scotland

ORKNEY TODAY
1626956U72D-1003

Editorial Address: Unit 1, Kiln Corner, Ayre Road,
KIRKWALL, KW15 1QX **Tel:** 01856 888810
Fax: 01856 888811
Email: editorial@orkneytoday.co.uk
Advertising Address: As above. **Tel:** 01856 888817
Email: adverts@orkneytoday.co.uk
Web site: http://www.orkneytoday.co.uk
Publisher: Orkney Today Ltd
Date Established: 2003
Frequency: Weekly - Published on Thursday
Cover Price: £0.75
Circulation: 5,993 (ABC 02/07/2007 to 30/12/2007)
Editor: News Desk
ADVERTISING RATES:
Full Page Mono £702.00
Full Page Colour £936.00
Agency Commission: 10%
Mechanical Data: Type Area: 360 x 276mm, No. of
Columns (Display): 6, Col Length: 360mm, Page Width:
276mm, Film: Digital, Col Widths (Display): 42mm
Copy instructions: Copy Date: Tuesday 1pm prior to
publication date
Supplement(s): Motoring - 12xY
LOCAL NEWSPAPERS: Local Newspapers Scotland

ORMSKIRK ADVERTISER
43994U72B-2050_120

Formerly: Advertiser Ormskirk
Frequency: Weekly - Circulation figure includes the
Skelmersdale Advertiser
Cover Price: £0.60
Circulation: 11,482 (ABC 02/07/2007 to 30/12/2007)
Part of Series, see entry for: Ormskirk Advertiser Series
LOCAL NEWSPAPERS: Local Newspapers English
Counties

ORMSKIRK ADVERTISER SERIES
43992U72B-2050

Editorial Address: 26-32 Tulketh Street, SOUTHPORT, PR8
1BT **Tel:** 01695 572501 **Fax:** 01695 570129
Email: newsdesk@ormskirkadvertiser.co.uk
Advertising Address: As above. **Tel:** 01704 536655
Fax: 01704 532041
Email: glenn.lewin@liverpool.com
Web site: http://www.ormskirkadvertiser.co.uk
Publisher: Liverpool Daily Post & Echo Ltd
Date Established: 1853
Frequency: Weekly - Published on Thursday
Circulation: 30,165 (Combined Circulation)
Editor: Gary Stewart; **News Editor:** Gary Stewart;
Advertising Manager: Glenn Lewin
ADVERTISING RATES:
SCC £5.93
Agency Commission: 10%

Non-National Newspapers

Mechanical Data: Film: Digital, **Col Length:** 360mm, **No. of Columns (Display):** 8, **Type Area:** 360 x 272mm, **Page Width:** 272mm
Copy instructions: Copy Date: Tuesday 5pm prior to publication date
Average advertising content per issue: 60%
Series owner and contact point for the following titles, see individual entries:
Ormskirk Advertiser
Skelmersdale Advertiser
LOCAL NEWSPAPERS: Local Newspapers English Counties

ORMSKIRK & WEST LANCS CHAMPION
44106U72B-2388_160

Frequency: Weekly
Cover Price: Free
ADVERTISING RATES:
Full Page Mono £680.00
SCC £2.50
Part of Series, see entry for: Southport, Ormskirk & Formby Champion Series
LOCAL NEWSPAPERS: Local Newspapers English Counties

OSSETT & HORBURY OBSERVER
44730U72B-3910_160

Frequency: Weekly
Cover Price: Free
Circulation: 11,367 (VFD 02/07/2007 to 30/12/2007)
ADVERTISING RATES:
Full Page Mono £945.54
Full Page Colour £1229.20
SCC £3.09
Part of Series, see entry for: Wakefield Express Series
LOCAL NEWSPAPERS: Local Newspapers English Counties

OSWESTRY AND BORDER COUNTIES ADVERTIZER
44245U72B-2835

Editorial Address: 16-18 Oswald Road, OSWESTRY, SY11 1RE **Tel:** 01691 655321 **Fax:** 01691 652530
Email: news@bordercountiesadvertizer.co.uk
Advertising Address: As above.
Email: admanager@bordercountiesadvertizer.co.uk
Web site: http://www.bordercountiesadvertizer.co.uk
Publisher: NWN Media Ltd
Date Established: 1849
Frequency: Weekly - Published on Tuesday
Cover Price: £0.55
Circulation: 10,969 (ABC 02/07/2007 to 30/12/2007)
Editor: Susan Perry; **Advertising Manager:** Ginny Rogers
ADVERTISING RATES:
Full Page Mono £1823.85
Full Page Colour £2371.01
SCC £5.79
Agency Commission: 10%
Mechanical Data: Col Widths (Display): 27mm, **No. of Columns (Display):** 9, **Page Width:** 259mm, **Type Area:** 350 x 259mm, **Col Length:** 350mm, **Film:** Digital
Copy instructions: Copy Date: Friday morning prior to publication date
Average advertising content per issue: 40%
Supplement(s): Property - 48xY
LOCAL NEWSPAPERS: Local Newspapers English Counties

OTTERY ADVERTISER
767282U72B-842_100

Formerly: Ottery St Mary Advertiser
Frequency: Weekly - Circulation figure is incorporated into the Honiton Advertiser
Cover Price: Free
Part of Series, see entry for: Pulmans Weekly News and Advertiser Series
LOCAL NEWSPAPERS: Local Newspapers English Counties

OTTERY HERALD
1732514U72B-850_100

Frequency: Weekly
Cover Price: £0.36
ADVERTISING RATES:
SCC £3.60
Part of Series, see entry for: Sidmouth Herald Series
LOCAL NEWSPAPERS: Local Newspapers English Counties

OXFORD JOURNAL
44216U72B-2705

Formerly: Courier Series
Editorial Address: 7-11 Cholswell Court, Cholswell Road, Shippon, ABINGDON, OX13 6HX **Tel:** 01235 553444
Fax: 01235 547819

Email: ric.sumner@youroxfordshire.co.uk
Advertising Address: 9-11 Cholswell Court, Cholswell Road, Shippon, ABINGDON, OX13 6HX **Tel:** 01235 547809
Fax: 01235 554465
Email: fatimam@courier.co.uk
Web site: http://www.youroxfordshire.co.uk
Publisher: Tri Media Group
Date Established: 1982
Frequency: Weekly - Published on Thursday
Cover Price: Free
Circulation: 40,000 (Publisher's Statement)
News Editor: Ric Sumner; **Advertising Manager:** Fatima Mansoor; **Group Editor:** Hartley Milner
ADVERTISING RATES:
Full Page Mono £3888.00
Full Page Colour £5184.00
SCC £12.00
Mechanical Data: Type Area: 340 x 264mm, **Col Length:** 340mm, **Page Width:** 264mm, **No. of Columns (Display):** 9, **Film:** Digital
Copy instructions: Copy Date: Tuesday 5.30pm prior to publication date
Supplement(s): Auto Weekly - 52xY
LOCAL NEWSPAPERS: Local Newspapers English Counties

OXFORD MAIL
42146U67B-500

Editorial Address: Newspaper House, Osney Mead, OXFORD, OX2 0EJ **Tel:** 01865 425262 **Fax:** 01865 425554
Email: news@nqo.com
Advertising Address: As above. **Fax:** 01865 425557
Email: retail.admin@nqo.com
Web site: http://www.oxfordmail.co.uk
Publisher: Newsquest (Oxfordshire) Ltd
Frequency: Mornings
Cover Price: £0.35
Circulation: 25,426 (Publisher's Statement)
Editor: Simon O'Neill; **News Editor:** Jason Collie; **Managing Director:** Shamus Donald
ADVERTISING RATES:
SCC £8.10
Agency Commission: 10%
Mechanical Data: Type Area: 340 x 258.2mm, **Col Length:** 340mm, **No. of Columns (Display):** 9, **Film:** Digital, **Page Width:** 258.2mm
Copy instructions: Copy Date: 2 days prior to publication date
Supplement(s): Sports Extra - 52xY
REGIONAL DAILY & SUNDAY NEWSPAPERS: Regional Daily Newspapers

---

OXFORD STAR
44228U72B-2740

Editorial Address: Newspaper House, Osney Mead, OXFORD, OX2 0EJ **Tel:** 01865 425262 **Fax:** 01865 425554
Email: news@nqo.com
Advertising Address: As above. **Tel:** 01865 420420
Fax: 01865 425557
Email: advertising@nqo.com
Web site: http://www.oxfordmail.co.uk
Publisher: Newsquest (Oxfordshire) Ltd
Frequency: Weekly - Published on Thursday
Cover Price: Free
Circulation: 60,647 (VFD 02/07/2007 to 30/12/2007)
Editor: Jason Collie; **News Editor:** Jason Collie; **Managing Director:** Shamus Donald; **Advertising Manager:** Julian Richings
ADVERTISING RATES:
SCC £5.15
Agency Commission: 10%
Mechanical Data: No. of Columns (Display): 9, **Film:** Digital, **Type Area:** 340 x 258.2mm, **Col Length:** 340mm, **Page Width:** 258.2mm
LOCAL NEWSPAPERS: Local Newspapers English Counties

THE OXFORD TIMES
44225U72B-2720_170

Frequency: Weekly
Cover Price: £0.60
Circulation: 22,793 (ABC 02/07/2007 to 30/12/2007)
ADVERTISING RATES:
SCC £8.45
Mechanical Data: Col Length: 540mm, **No. of Columns (Display):** 12, **Film:** Digital, **Type Area:** 540 x 345mm, **Page Width:** 345mm
Part of Series, see entry for: Herald and Times Series Oxon
Supplement(s): In Business The Oxford Times - 12xY, Oxfordshire Homes - 4xY
LOCAL NEWSPAPERS: Local Newspapers English Counties

OXTED COUNTY BORDER NEWS
1665852U72B-1774_203

Frequency: Weekly - Cirulation figure incorporates Godstone, Lingfield and Tanbridge
Cover Price: Free
Circulation: 21,500 (Publisher's Statement)
Part of Series, see entry for: County Border News Series
LOCAL NEWSPAPERS: Local Newspapers English Counties

THE PACKET SERIES
43426U72B-553

Editorial Address: 3 Falmouth Business Park, Bickland Water Road, FALMOUTH, TR11 4SZ **Tel:** 01326 213333
Fax: 01326 318749
Email: editorial@packetseries.co.uk
Advertising Address: As above. **Fax:** 01326 212084
Email: advertising@packetseries.co.uk
Web site: http://www.thepacket.co.uk
Publisher: Newsquest Media Group
Frequency: Weekly - Published on Wednesday
Circulation: 90,472 (Combined Circulation)
Editor: Stephen Ivall
ADVERTISING: Rates on application
Agency Commission: 10%
Mechanical Data: Type Area: 350 x 264mm, **Col Length:** 350mm, **No. of Columns (Display):** 9, **Col Widths (Display):** 28mm, **Film:** Digital, **Page Width:** 264mm
Average advertising content per issue: 50%
Series owner and contact point for the following titles, see individual entries:
Camborne Redruth Packet
Camborne Redruth Tinner
Falmouth Packet
Helston Gazette
Helston Packet
Penwith Pirate
Truro Packet
Supplement(s): Royal Cornwall Show - 1xY
LOCAL NEWSPAPERS: Local Newspapers English Counties

PADDINGTON & WESTMINSTER TIMES
1804887U72A-385_141

Frequency: Weekly
Cover Price: £0.40
Part of Series, see entry for: North West London Newspaper Series
LOCAL NEWSPAPERS: Local Newspapers Greater London

PADIHAM AND DISTRICT EXPRESS (FRI)
43961U72B-1940_200

Frequency: Weekly - Circulation figure is incorporated into the Burnley Express (Friday)
Cover Price: £0.52
ADVERTISING RATES:
Full Page Mono £4332.96
Full Page Colour £5632.84
SCC £14.16
Part of Series, see entry for: Burnley Express and Reporter Series
LOCAL NEWSPAPERS: Local Newspapers English Counties

PADIHAM AND DISTRICT EXPRESS (TUE)
43960U72B-1940_180

Frequency: Weekly - Circulation figure is incorporated into the Burnley Express (Tuesday)
Cover Price: £0.38
ADVERTISING RATES:
Full Page Mono £4332.96
Full Page Colour £5632.84
SCC £14.16
Part of Series, see entry for: Burnley Express and Reporter Series
LOCAL NEWSPAPERS: Local Newspapers English Counties

THE PAISLEY AND RENFREWSHIRE GAZETTE SERIES
45011U72D-820

Formerly: The Gazette Series (Paisley)
Editorial Address: 6 Glasgow Road, PAISLEY, PA1 3XB **Tel:** 0141 889 0511 **Fax:** 0141 889 9836
Email: editorial.gaz@cfpress.co.uk
Advertising Address: As above. **Tel:** 0141 887 9300
Email: advertising.gaz@cfpress.co.uk
Web site: http://www.paisleygazette.co.uk
Publisher: Clyde & Forth Press Group
Frequency: Weekly
Circulation: 19,577 (Combined Circulation)
Usual Pagination: 40
Editor: News Desk

ADVERTISING RATES:
Full Page Mono £3424.08
SCC £12.97
Mechanical Data: Type Area: 330 x 266mm, Col Length:
330mm, Col Widths (Display): 30mm, No. of Columns
(Display): 8, Page Width: 266mm, Film: Digital
**Series owner and contact point for the following titles,
see individual entries:**
Barrhead News
The Gazette (Renfrewshire)
Paisley People
LOCAL NEWSPAPERS: Local Newspapers Scotland

PAISLEY DAILY EXPRESS
42265U67B-2350
Editorial Address: 14 New Street, PAISLEY, PA1 1YA
Tel: 0141 887 7911 **Fax:** 0141 887 6254
Email: pde@s-un.co.uk
Advertising Address: As above. **Tel:** 0141 887 7744
Fax: 0141 889 7148
Email: pgraham@s-un.co.uk
Web site: http://www.paisleydailyexpress.co.uk
Publisher: Scottish & Universal Newspapers Ltd
Frequency: Mornings - Not published on Sunday
Cover Price: £0.42
Circulation: 9,528 (ABC 02/07/2007 to 30/12/2007)
Editor: Anne Dalrymple; **News Editor:** Gavin Pennie;
Features Editor: Anne Dalrymple; **Advertising Manager:**
Patricia Graham
ADVERTISING RATES:
Full Page Mono £2100.35
Full Page Colour £2730.44
SCC £7.95
Agency Commission: 10%
Mechanical Data: Col Length: 340mm, No. of Columns
(Display): 9, Film: Digital
Copy instructions: Copy Date: 3 days prior to publication
date
REGIONAL DAILY & SUNDAY NEWSPAPERS: Regional
Daily Newspapers

PAISLEY PEOPLE
45015U72D-820_220
Formerly: Paisley and District People
Frequency: Weekly - Published on Friday
Cover Price: Free
Circulation: 9,319 (VFD 23/07/2007 to 30/12/2007)
ADVERTISING RATES:
SCC £8.55
Part of Series, see entry for: The Paisley and Renfrewshire
Gazette Series
LOCAL NEWSPAPERS: Local Newspapers Scotland

PAPUR Y CWM
761619U72J-205
Editorial Address: Brynteg, Heol Maes-y-Bont, Castell-y-
Rhingyll, LLANELLI, SA14 7NA **Tel:** 01269 842151
Fax: 01269 832170
Email: dafyddtomos@btopenworld.com
Advertising Address: As above.
Email: dafyddguard-papurycwm@yahoo.co.uk
Date Established: 1982
Frequency: 10 issues yearly - Not published in August and
September
Cover Price: £0.45
Circulation: 1,200 (Publisher's Statement)
Editor: Dafydd Thomas; **Advertising Manager:** Dafydd
Thomas
Summary of Content: Welsh language community
newspaper covering sports, schooling, village news, arts,
local history, cookery, travel and a children's corner.
Language(s): Welsh
Readership/Target Audience: Aimed at Welsh speaking
readers in the Gwendraeth Valleys.
ADVERTISING RATES:
SCC £3.00
Agency Commission: 10%
Mechanical Data: Film: Digital, No. of Columns (Display): 4
Copy instructions: Copy Date: 12th of the month prior to
publication date
Average advertising content per issue: 30%
LOCAL NEWSPAPERS: Community Newsletters

PATELEY BRIDGE & NIDDERDALE HERALD
44653U72B-3588_200
Frequency: Weekly
Cover Price: £0.60
Circulation: 1,782 (ABC 02/07/2007 to 30/12/2007)
ADVERTISING RATES:
SCC £10.14
Part of Series, see entry for: Ackrill Newspaper Series
LOCAL NEWSPAPERS: Local Newspapers English
Counties

PEEBLES TIMES
44905U72D-270_190
Frequency: Weekly - Please see The Lothian Times (East
Lothian edition) for circulation figures
Cover Price: Free
Part of Series, see entry for: Dalkeith Advertiser Series
LOCAL NEWSPAPERS: Local Newspapers Scotland

PEEBLESSHIRE NEWS
45016U72D-823
Editorial Address: 40 Northgate, PEEBLES, EH45 8BZ
Tel: 01721 720884 **Fax:** 01721 721492
Email: editorial@peeblesshirenews.com
Advertising Address: 113 High Street, GALASHIELS, TD1
1SB **Tel:** 01896 758395 **Fax:** 01896 759395
Email: display@bordertelegraph.com
Web site: http://www.peeblesshirenews.com
Publisher: Border Weeklies Ltd
Frequency: Weekly - Published on Friday
Cover Price: £0.40
Circulation: 5,013 (ABC 02/07/2007 to 30/12/2007)
Usual Pagination: 28
Editor: Atholl Innes; **Advertising Manager:** Gillian Hell
ADVERTISING RATES:
Full Page Mono £357.00
Full Page Colour £589.00
Agency Commission: 10%
Mechanical Data: Page Width: 265.5mm, Col Widths
(Display): 31mm, Film: Digital, Col Length: 360mm, Type
Area: 360mm x 265.5mm, No. of Columns (Display): 8
Copy instructions: Copy Date: Tuesday 5pm prior to
publication date
Average advertising content per issue: 40%
LOCAL NEWSPAPERS: Local Newspapers Scotland

PENARTH TIMES
44830U72C-50_110
Frequency: Weekly
Circulation: 6,183 (ABC 02/07/2007 to 30/12/2007)
Part of Series, see entry for: Barry & District News Series
LOCAL NEWSPAPERS: Local Newspapers Wales

PENDLE & BURNLEY REPORTER
1693348U72B-1940_221
Frequency: Weekly - For circulation figure see the Burnley &
Pendle Reporter
Cover Price: Free
ADVERTISING RATES:
Full Page Mono £4332.96
Full Page Colour £5632.84
SCC £14.16
Part of Series, see entry for: Burnley Express and Reporter
Series
LOCAL NEWSPAPERS: Local Newspapers English
Counties

PENDLE AND BURNLEY REPORTER
1656957U72B-2040_161
Frequency: Weekly - Published on Thursday
Cover Price: Free
Circulation: 56,118 (VFD 02/07/2007 to 30/12/2007)
ADVERTISING RATES:
Full Page Mono £1306.62
Full Page Colour £1698.60
SCC £4.27
Part of Series, see entry for: Leader Times Series
LOCAL NEWSPAPERS: Local Newspapers English
Counties

PENDLE EXPRESS (TUESDAY)
43962U72B-1940_220
Frequency: Weekly - Circulation figure is incorporated into
the Burnley Express (Tuesday)
Cover Price: £0.38
ADVERTISING RATES:
Full Page Mono £4332.96
Full Page Colour £5632.84
SCC £14.16
Copy instructions: Copy Date: Wednesday, 4pm, prior to
publication date
Part of Series, see entry for: Burnley Express and Reporter
Series
LOCAL NEWSPAPERS: Local Newspapers English
Counties

THE PENINSULA
1831095U72A-1322_101
Frequency: Weekly
Cover Price: Free
Part of Series, see entry for: The Docklands and Peninsula
Series
LOCAL NEWSPAPERS: Local Newspapers Greater London

PENWITH PIRATE
43435U72B-560_160
Frequency: Weekly
Cover Price: Free
Circulation: 25,234 (Publisher's Statement)
ADVERTISING RATES:
Full Page Mono £787.50
Full Page Colour £1063.13
SCC £2.50
Part of Series, see entry for: The Packet Series
LOCAL NEWSPAPERS: Local Newspapers English
Counties

PERTH SHOPPER
45021U72D-830_160
Frequency: Weekly - Published on Friday
Cover Price: Free
Circulation: 7,413 (Publisher's Statement)
Copy instructions: Copy Date: Wednesday noon prior to
publication date
Part of Series, see entry for: Perthshire Advertiser Series
LOCAL NEWSPAPERS: Local Newspapers Scotland

PERTHSHIRE ADVERTISER FRIDAY
45020U72D-830_140
Frequency: Weekly
Cover Price: £0.56
Circulation: 16,520 (ABC 02/07/2007 to 30/12/2007)
Copy instructions: Copy Date: Wednesday 1pm prior to
publication date
Part of Series, see entry for: Perthshire Advertiser Series
LOCAL NEWSPAPERS: Local Newspapers Scotland

PERTHSHIRE ADVERTISER SERIES
45017U72D-830
Editorial Address: 58 Watergate, PERTH, PH1 5TF
Tel: 01738 626211 **Fax:** 01738 493277
Email: pa@s-un.co.uk
Advertising Address: As above. **Fax:** 01738 493299
Email: lgardiner@s-un.co.uk
Web site: http://www.icperthshire.co.uk
Publisher: Scottish & Universal Newspapers Ltd
Frequency: 100 issues yearly
Circulation: 36,056 (Combined Circulation)
Usual Pagination: 52
Editor: Alison Lowson
ADVERTISING RATES:
SCC £23.50
Agency Commission: 10%
Mechanical Data: Page Width: 270mm, Type Area: 390 x
270mm, Col Length: 390mm, No. of Columns (Display): 8,
Col Widths (Display): 31mm, Film: Digital
Average advertising content per issue: 60%
**Series owner and contact point for the following titles,
see individual entries:**
Blairgowrie Advertiser
Perth Shopper
Perthshire Advertiser Friday
Perthshire Advertiser Tuesday
LOCAL NEWSPAPERS: Local Newspapers Scotland

PERTHSHIRE ADVERTISER TUESDAY
45019U72D-830_130
Frequency: Weekly
Cover Price: £0.56
Circulation: 8,892 (ABC 02/07/2007 to 30/12/2007)
Copy instructions: Copy Date: Friday 1pm prior to
publication date
Part of Series, see entry for: Perthshire Advertiser Series
LOCAL NEWSPAPERS: Local Newspapers Scotland

PETERBOROUGH CITIZEN
43334U72B-400
Editorial Address: New Priestgate House, 57 Priestgate,
PETERBOROUGH, PE1 1JW **Tel:** 01733 555111
Fax: 01733 313147
Email: news@peterboroughtoday.co.uk
Advertising Address: As above. **Fax:** 01733 555188
Email: richard.duxbury@peterboroughtoday.co.uk
Web site: http://www.peterboroughtoday.co.uk
Publisher: Johnston Press plc
Frequency: Weekly - Published on Thursday
Cover Price: Free
Circulation: 49,258 (VFD 02/07/2007 to 30/12/2007)
Editor: Paul Grinnell; **News Editor:** Paul Grinnell;
Advertising Manager: Richard Duxbury
ADVERTISING RATES:
Full Page Mono £2622.42
Full Page Colour £3185.46
Agency Commission: 10%
Mechanical Data: Type Area: 340 x 270mm, No. of
Columns (Display): 9, Col Length: 340mm, Col Widths
(Display): 27mm, Page Width: 270mm, Print Process: Digital

Copy instructions: Copy Date: Tuesday 2.00 pm prior to publication date
Average advertising content per issue: 60%
LOCAL NEWSPAPERS: Local Newspapers English Counties

PETERLEE STAR
44494U72B-3371_130
Frequency: Weekly
Cover Price: Free
Circulation: 17,371 (VFD 02/07/2007 to 30/12/2007)
ADVERTISING RATES:
SCC £4.46
Part of Series, see entry for: Star Series
LOCAL NEWSPAPERS: Local Newspapers English Counties

PETERSFIELD HERALD
44374U72B-3120_180
Frequency: Weekly
Cover Price: £0.50
Part of Series, see entry for: Farnham Herald Series
LOCAL NEWSPAPERS: Local Newspapers English Counties

PETERSFIELD POST
43774U72B-1383_180
Frequency: Weekly
Cover Price: £0.35
Part of Series, see entry for: Petersfield Post Series
LOCAL NEWSPAPERS: Local Newspapers English Counties

PETERSFIELD POST SERIES
43772U72B-1383
Editorial Address: 33 High Street, PETERSFIELD, GU32 3JR **Tel:** 01730 268021 **Fax:** 01730 266721
Email: david.jones@thepost.co.uk
Advertising Address: As above. **Tel:** 01730 266331
Email: jo.barlow@thepost.co.uk
Web site: http://www.petersfield.co.uk
Publisher: Portsmouth Publishing & Printing Ltd
Frequency: Weekly - Published on Wednesday
Circulation: 8,218 (ABC 02/07/2007 to 30/12/2007)
Editor: David Jones; **Advertising Manager:** Jo Barlow
ADVERTISING RATES:
SCC £4.47
Agency Commission: 10%
Mechanical Data: Page Width: 277mm, Film: Digital, Type Area: 345 x 277mm, Col Length: 345mm, No. of Columns (Display): 9
Copy instructions: Copy Date: Friday 12pm prior to publication date
Series owner and contact point for the following titles, see individual entries:
Bordon Post
Petersfield Post
LOCAL NEWSPAPERS: Local Newspapers English Counties

PETERSFIELD TIMES & MAIL
44390U72B-1339_220
Formerly: Petersfield Mail
Frequency: Weekly - Circulation figure is incorporated into the Alton Times & Mail
Cover Price: Free
Part of Series, see entry for: Alton Post Gazette, Times & Mail Series
LOCAL NEWSPAPERS: Local Newspapers English Counties

PETHE PENLLYN
761763U72J-208
Editorial Address: Nant-y-Llyn, Llanuwchllyn, BALA, LL23 7DF **Tel:** 01678 540384
Email: beryl@nantyllyn.fsnet.co.uk
Advertising Address: Ffynnon Wen, CORWEN, LL21 OST **Tel:** 01490 440350
Email: ffynnonwen@btinternet.com
Frequency: 10 issues yearly - Not published in September or January
Cover Price: £0.30
Circulation: 600 (Publisher's Statement per month)
Editor: Beryl Griffiths; **Advertising Manager:** Elsbeth Jones
Summary of Content: Welsh language newspaper covering local news, schooling, agriculture and featuring poetry and competitions.
Language(s): Welsh
Readership/Target Audience: Aimed at Welsh speaking readers in Bala and the surrounding area.
ADVERTISING: Rates on application
Copy instructions: Copy Date: 10th of the month prior to publication date
LOCAL NEWSPAPERS: Community Newsletters

PINNER OBSERVER
43035U72A-170_160
Frequency: Weekly - Published on Thursday. For circulation, see Harrow Observer
Cover Price: £0.35
ADVERTISING RATES:
SCC £11.70
Part of Series, see entry for: Harrow Observer & Leader Series
LOCAL NEWSPAPERS: Local Newspapers Greater London

THE PIONEER (NORTH WALES)
44831U72C-305
Editorial Address: 22 Penrhyn Road, COLWYN BAY, LL29 8HY **Tel:** 01492 531188 **Fax:** 01492 533564
Email: news@northwalespioneer.co.uk
Advertising Address: As above.
Email: admanager@northwalespioneer.co.uk
Web site: http://www.northwalespioneer.co.uk
Publisher: NWN Media Ltd
Frequency: Weekly - Published on Wednesday
Cover Price: £0.50
Free to qualifying individuals
Circulation: 30,672 (VFD 02/07/2007 to 30/12/2007)
Editor: Terry Canty; **Advertising Manager:** Claire Bryce; **Group Editor:** Steve Rogers
Language(s): English; Welsh
ADVERTISING RATES:
Full Page Mono £2129.40
Full Page Colour £2768.22
Agency Commission: 10%
Mechanical Data: Page Width: 259mm, Type Area: 350 x 259mm, Col Length: 350mm, Col Widths (Display): 27mm, No. of Columns (Display): 9, Film: Digital
Copy instructions: Copy Date: Monday morning prior to publication date
LOCAL NEWSPAPERS: Local Newspapers Wales

PLU'R GWEUNYDD
761706U72J-210
Editorial Address: Eirianfa, New Road, Llanfair Caereinion, WELSHPOOL, SY21 0SB **Tel:** 01938 810048
Fax: 01938 810785
Email: clicied@btconnect.com
Frequency: 11 issues yearly - Not published in August
Cover Price: £0.40
Circulation: 750 (Publisher's Statement)
Editor: Mary Steele
Summary of Content: Welsh language community newspaper covering local news with a section for learners of Welsh and a children's corner.
Language(s): Welsh
Readership/Target Audience: Aimed at Welsh speaking readers in Llanfair Caereinion and the surrounding area.
ADVERTISING: No Advertising taken
LOCAL NEWSPAPERS: Community Newsletters

PLYMPTON, PLYMSTOCK & IVYBRIDGE NEWS
43541U72B-854_160
Frequency: Weekly
Cover Price: Free
Part of Series, see entry for: South Hams Newspapers Group
LOCAL NEWSPAPERS: Local Newspapers English Counties

POCKLINGTON POST
44645U72B-3625
Formerly: Pocklington, Market Weighton & District Post
Editorial Address: 2 Railway Street, Pocklington, YORK, YO42 2QZ **Tel:** 01759 301003 **Fax:** 01759 305890
Email: news@pocklingtontoday.co.uk
Advertising Address: As above. **Tel:** 01759 303772
Email: advertising@pocklingtontoday.co.uk
Web site: http://www.pocklingtontoday.co.uk
Publisher: Yorkshire Regional Newspapers Ltd
Frequency: Weekly - Published on Thursday
Cover Price: £0.60
Circulation: 4,605 (ABC 02/07/2007 to 30/12/2007)
Editor: Nick Frame; **Advertising Manager:** Charlotte Jackson
ADVERTISING RATES:
Full Page Mono £1435.14
Full Page Colour £1865.68
SCC £4.98
Agency Commission: 10%
Mechanical Data: Col Length: 320mm, Page Width: 274mm, Film: Digital, Type Area: 320 x 274mm, No. of Columns (Display): 9
Copy instructions: Copy Date: Tuesday 12 noon prior to publication date
Average advertising content per issue: 55%
LOCAL NEWSPAPERS: Local Newspapers English Counties

PONTEFRACT & CASTLEFORD EXPRESS
44721U72B-3835_150
Frequency: Weekly - Published on Thursday
Cover Price: £0.55
Circulation: 24,117 (ABC 02/07/2007 to 30/12/2007)
ADVERTISING RATES:
Full Page Mono £1683.00
Full Page Colour £2187.90
SCC £5.50
Part of Series, see entry for: Pontefract & Castleford Express & Extra Series
LOCAL NEWSPAPERS: Local Newspapers English Counties

PONTEFRACT & CASTLEFORD EXPRESS & EXTRA SERIES
44720U72B-3835
Editorial Address: 12 Bank Street, CASTLEFORD, WF10 1HZ **Tel:** 01977 737200 **Fax:** 01977 737201
Email: editorial@pandctoday.co.uk
Advertising Address: 1 Front Street, PONTEFRACT, WS8 1BL **Tel:** 01977 702151 **Fax:** 01977 799043
Email: advertising@pandcexpress.co.uk
Web site: http://www.pontefractandcastlefordtoday.co.uk
Publisher: Yorkshire Weekly Newspaper Group Ltd
Date Established: 1880
Frequency: Weekly
Circulation: 57,152 (Combined Circulation)
Editor: Newsdesk; **News Editor:** Julie Sambrook
Agency Commission: 10%
Mechanical Data: Type Area: 340 x 274mm, Col Length: 340mm, Page Width: 274mm, Col Widths (Display): 27.78mm, No. of Columns (Display): 9
Copy instructions: Copy Date: Tuesday 2pm prior to publication date
Series owner and contact point for the following titles, see individual entries:
Pontefract & Castleford Express
Pontefract & Castleford Extra
Supplement(s): Leisure Guide - 52xY, Motors - 52xY, Property Guide - 52xY
LOCAL NEWSPAPERS: Local Newspapers English Counties

PONTEFRACT & CASTLEFORD EXTRA
44722U72B-3835_160
Frequency: Weekly - Published on Friday
Cover Price: Free
Circulation: 33,035 (VFD 04/07/2005 to 01/01/2006)
ADVERTISING RATES:
Full Page Mono £1477.98
Full Page Colour £1921.37
SCC £4.83
Part of Series, see entry for: Pontefract & Castleford Express & Extra Series
LOCAL NEWSPAPERS: Local Newspapers English Counties

PONTYPRIDD AND LLANTRISANT OBSERVER
44832U72C-306
Editorial Address: 10 Market Street, PONTYPRIDD, CF37 2ST **Tel:** 01443 665161 **Fax:** 01443 665181
Email: pontypridd.observer@mediawales.co.uk
Advertising Address: 52-53 Glebeland Street, MERTHYR TYDFIL, CF47 8AT **Tel:** 01685 856558 **Fax:** 01685 856556
Email: cydna.thomas@mediawales.co.uk
Web site: http://www.walesonline.co.uk
Publisher: Trinity Mirror
Frequency: Weekly - Published on Wednesday
Cover Price: £0.68
Circulation: 11,429 (ABC 02/07/2007 to 30/12/2007)
Editor: Mari Ropstad
ADVERTISING: Rates on application
LOCAL NEWSPAPERS: Local Newspapers Wales

POOLE & DORSET ADVERTISER
43555U72B-902_170
Frequency: Weekly
Cover Price: Free
Circulation: 58,227 (VFD 02/07/2007 to 30/12/2007)
ADVERTISING: Rates on application
Part of Series, see entry for: Advertiser Series (Poole & Swanage)
LOCAL NEWSPAPERS: Local Newspapers English Counties

PORT TALBOT COURIER
713795U72C-162_170
Frequency: Weekly
Cover Price: £0.20
Part of Series, see entry for: The Courier Series (Neath & Port Talbot)
LOCAL NEWSPAPERS: Local Newspapers Wales

PORT TALBOT GUARDIAN
44816U72C-250_170

Publisher: Wilfred Edmunds
Frequency: Weekly
Part of Series, see entry for: Neath Guardian Series
LOCAL NEWSPAPERS: Local Newspapers Wales

PORTADOWN TIMES INC. CRAIGAVON NEWS
45118U72E-215

Editorial Address: 14 Church Street, Portadown, CRAIGAVON, BT62 3LQ **Tel:** 028 3833 6111
Fax: 028 3835 0203
Email: editor@portadowntimes.co.uk
Advertising Address: As above.
Email: victor.kelly@jpress.co.uk
Web site: http://www.portadowntimes.co.uk
Publisher: Morton Newspapers Ltd
Date Established: 1924
Frequency: Weekly - Published on Friday
Cover Price: £0.95
Circulation: 10,401 (ABC 02/07/2007 to 30/12/2007)
Editor: Alister Bushe; **Managing Director:** Jean Long;
Advertising Manager: Victor Kelly
ADVERTISING RATES:
Full Page Mono £1591.00
Full Page Colour £2148.80
Agency Commission: 10%
Mechanical Data: Col Length: 340mm, Col Widths (Display): 28mm, No. of Columns (Display): 9, Print Process: Web-fed offset litho, Type Area: 340 x 268mm, Page Width: 268mm, Film: Digital
Copy instructions: Copy Date: Wednesday 12pm prior to publication date
Average advertising content per issue: 60%
LOCAL NEWSPAPERS: Local Newspapers Northern Ireland

PORTSMOUTH & SOUTHSEA JOURNAL
43755U72B-1378_190

Frequency: Weekly
Cover Price: Free
Circulation: 58,951 (VFD 24/09/2007 to 30/12/2007)
Part of Series, see entry for: Journal Series Portsmouth
LOCAL NEWSPAPERS: Local Newspapers English Counties

THE POST
43052U72A-50_190

Formerly: Epsom & Banstead Post
Frequency: Weekly
Cover Price: Free
Circulation: 28,066 (ABC 01/01/2007 to 01/07/2007)
ADVERTISING RATES:
SCC £9.70
Part of Series, see entry for: Croydon Advertiser & Post Series
LOCAL NEWSPAPERS: Local Newspapers Greater London

POST & TIMES SERIES
44310U72B-3005

Editorial Address: 21-24 The Smithfield Centre, LEEK, ST13 5JW **Tel:** 01538 399599 **Fax:** 01538 392249
Advertising Address: As above.
Email: rachel.bailey@thepostandtimes.co.uk
Web site: http://www.thepostandtimes.co.uk
Publisher: Northcliffe Media Ltd
Date Established: 1870
Frequency: Weekly
Circulation: 16,304 (ABC 02/07/2007 to 30/12/2007)
Editor: Rob Cotterill
ADVERTISING: Rates on application
Agency Commission: 10%
Mechanical Data: No. of Columns (Display): 8, Type Area: 360 x 265mm, Page Width: 265mm, Col Length: 360mm, Film: Digital
Copy instructions: Copy Date: Monday 1.30pm prior to publication date
Average advertising content per issue: 60%
Series owner and contact point for the following titles, see individual entries:
Cheadle Post & Times
Leek Post & Times
Uttoxeter Post & Times
LOCAL NEWSPAPERS: Local Newspapers English Counties

THE POST CARDIFF
44774U72C-95_130

Frequency: Weekly
Cover Price: Free
Circulation: 71,627 (Publisher's Statement)
ADVERTISING RATES:
SCC £12.01
Copy instructions: Copy Date: Tuesday 5.30pm prior to publication date

Part of Series, see entry for: Cardiff Post Series
LOCAL NEWSPAPERS: Local Newspapers Wales

THE POST CROYDON BOROUGH
42972U72A-50_185

Frequency: Weekly
Cover Price: Free
Circulation: 98,175 (Publisher's Statement)
ADVERTISING RATES:
SCC £9.70
Part of Series, see entry for: Croydon Advertiser & Post Series
LOCAL NEWSPAPERS: Local Newspapers Greater London

THE POST MITCHAM, MORDEN & WIMBLEDON
43186U72A-50_250

Formerly: The Post Wimbledon, Morden & Mitcham
Email: edit@croydonadvertiser.co.uk
Frequency: Weekly
Cover Price: Free
Circulation: 37,485 (Publisher's Statement)
ADVERTISING: Rates on application
Part of Series, see entry for: The Mercury and Post Series
LOCAL NEWSPAPERS: Local Newspapers Greater London

POST PLUS
42315U67H-350

Formerly: The Sunday Post Magazine
Editorial Address: The Sunday Post, 2 Albert Square, DUNDEE, DD1 9QJ **Tel:** 01382 223131 **Fax:** 01382 201064
Email: magazine@sundaypost.com
Advertising Address: As above. **Tel:** 01382 575149
Fax: 01382 454599
Email: teleads@dcthomson.co.uk
Web site: http://www.sundaypost.com
Publisher: D.C. Thomson & Co Ltd
Date Established: 1988
Frequency: Monthly
Cover Price: Free
Circulation: 378,639 (Publisher's Statement)
Editor: Jan Gooderham; **Advertising Manager:** Bob Walker
Summary of Content: Family interest magazine covering fashion, cookery, celebrity interviews and features.
Readership/Target Audience: Aimed at families.
ADVERTISING RATES:
Full Page Mono £9960.00
Full Page Colour £12375.00
Agency Commission: 15%
Mechanical Data: Type Area: 256 x 196mm, Col Widths (Display): 45mm, No. of Columns (Display): 4, Bleed Size: 283 x 216mm, Trim Size: 277 x 210mm, Col Length: 256mm, Film: Digital, Page Width: 196mm
Copy instructions: Copy Date: 3 weeks prior to publication date
Supplement to: The Sunday Post (Dundee)
REGIONAL DAILY & SUNDAY NEWSPAPERS: Regional Colour Supplements

THE POST, STREATHAM, CLAPHAM & CRYSTAL PALACE
43142U72A-460_120

Formerly: The Post, Streatham, Clapham & West Norwood
Frequency: Weekly
Cover Price: Free
Circulation: 30,158 (VFD 02/07/2007 to 30/12/2007)
ADVERTISING: Rates on application
Part of Series, see entry for: The Mercury and Post Series
LOCAL NEWSPAPERS: Local Newspapers Greater London

THE POST SUTTON BOROUGH
42976U72A-50_200

Formerly: Sutton Borough Independent
Frequency: Weekly
Cover Price: Free
Circulation: 54,211 (Publisher's Statement)
ADVERTISING RATES:
SCC £9.70
Part of Series, see entry for: Croydon Advertiser & Post Series
LOCAL NEWSPAPERS: Local Newspapers Greater London

THE POTTERIES ADVERTISER
624346U72B-2956_110

Frequency: Weekly
Cover Price: Free
ADVERTISING: Rates on application
Part of Series, see entry for: Advertiser Series (Stoke-on-Trent)
LOCAL NEWSPAPERS: Local Newspapers English Counties

POWYS COUNTY TIMES AND EXPRESS MONTGOMERYSHIRE
44783U72C-160_120

Formerly: Powys County Times and Express Machynlleth Edition
Frequency: Weekly
Cover Price: £0.65
Part of Series, see entry for: Powys County Times, Express & Gazette
LOCAL NEWSPAPERS: Local Newspapers Wales

POWYS COUNTY TIMES, EXPRESS & GAZETTE
44781U72C-160

Formerly: Powys County Times & Express
Editorial Address: 11C Broad Street, WELSHPOOL, SY21 7LE **Tel:** 01938 553354 **Fax:** 01938 554667
Email: news@countytimes.co.uk
Advertising Address: As above.
Email: dave.gregory@nwn.co.uk
Web site: http://www.countytimes.co.uk
Publisher: NWN Media Ltd
Frequency: Weekly
Circulation: 17,628 (ABC 02/07/2007 to 30/12/2007)
Editor: Nick Knight
Language(s): English; Welsh
ADVERTISING RATES:
Full Page Mono £1921.50
Full Page Colour £2497.95
SCC £6.10
Agency Commission: 10%
Mechanical Data: Col Length: 350mm, Col Widths (Display): 27mm, Page Width: 259mm, No. of Columns (Display): 9, Print Process: Web-fed offset litho, Type Area: 350 x 259mm
Copy instructions: Copy Date: Tuesday 10am prior to publication date
Average advertising content per issue: 40%
Series owner and contact point for the following titles, see individual entries:
County Times and Gazette
Powys County Times and Express Montgomeryshire
LOCAL NEWSPAPERS: Local Newspapers Wales

POYNTON TIMES
43385U72B-479_160

Frequency: Weekly - Published on Thursday
Cover Price: Free
Circulation: 5,370 (VFD 02/07/2007 to 30/12/2007)
ADVERTISING RATES:
SCC £4.75
Agency Commission: 10%
Part of Series, see entry for: Macclesfield Express and Times Series
LOCAL NEWSPAPERS: Local Newspapers English Counties

PRESCOT & KNOWSLEY REPORTER (INCORPORATING ST. HELENS)
44101U72B-2386_160

Formerly: Prescot Reporter incorporating St. Helens Reporter
Frequency: Weekly
Cover Price: Free
Part of Series, see entry for: St. Helens Reporter Series
LOCAL NEWSPAPERS: Local Newspapers English Counties

PRESCOT NEWS
1799440U72B-1310_271

Frequency: Monthly
Cover Price: Free
Circulation: 10,000 (Print Run)
ADVERTISING: Rates on application
Part of Series, see entry for: The Wigan Observer, Reporter and News Series
LOCAL NEWSPAPERS: Local Newspapers English Counties

THE PRESS & JOURNAL (ABERDEEN)
42247U67B-2170

Editorial Address: PO Box 43, Lang Stracht, Mastrick, ABERDEEN, AB15 6DF **Tel:** 01224 690222
Fax: 01224 663575
Email: pj.newsdesk@ajl.co.uk
Advertising Address: As above. **Fax:** 01224 341212
Email: jim.bruce@ajl.co.uk
Web site: http://www.pressandjournal.co.uk
Publisher: Aberdeen Journals Ltd
Date Established: 1747
Frequency: Mornings
Cover Price: £0.44
Circulation: 81,956 (ABC 01/01/2007 to 01/07/2007)
Editor: Derek Tucker; **News Editor:** Andrew Kellock;
Features Editor: Sonja Cox; **Managing Director:** Alan Scott

Non-National Newspapers

ADVERTISING RATES:
Full Page Mono £11550.00
Full Page Colour £15500.00
SCC £26.25
Agency Commission: 10%
Mechanical Data: Type Area: 550 x 356mm, Col Length: 550mm, Page Width: 356mm, No. of Columns (Display): 8, Film: Digital
Copy instructions: Copy Date: 2 days prior to publication date
Average advertising content per issue: 40%
Editions:
The Press & Journal (Aberdeen)
The Press & Journal (Aberdeenshire)
The Press & Journal (Highland Edition)
The Press & Journal (Inverness)
The Press & Journal (Latest)
The Press & Journal (Moray)
The Press & Journal (North East)
Supplement(s): Energy - 13xY
REGIONAL DAILY & SUNDAY NEWSPAPERS: Regional Daily Newspapers

THE PRESS & JOURNAL (ABERDEEN)
42248U67B-2170_520
Formerly: Press & Journal (Aberdeen Edition)
Frequency: Mornings
Edition of: The Press & Journal (Aberdeen)
REGIONAL DAILY & SUNDAY NEWSPAPERS: Regional Daily Newspapers

THE PRESS & JOURNAL (ABERDEENSHIRE)
42252U67B-2170_570
Edition of: The Press & Journal (Aberdeen)
REGIONAL DAILY & SUNDAY NEWSPAPERS: Regional Daily Newspapers

THE PRESS & JOURNAL (HIGHLAND EDITION)
42251U67B-2170_560
Edition of: The Press & Journal (Aberdeen)
REGIONAL DAILY & SUNDAY NEWSPAPERS: Regional Daily Newspapers

THE PRESS & JOURNAL (INVERNESS)
1840760U67B-2170_606
Edition of: The Press & Journal (Aberdeen)
REGIONAL DAILY & SUNDAY NEWSPAPERS: Regional Daily Newspapers

THE PRESS & JOURNAL (LATEST)
42249U67B-2170_530
Formerly: The Press & Journal (South)
Edition of: The Press & Journal (Aberdeen)
REGIONAL DAILY & SUNDAY NEWSPAPERS: Regional Daily Newspapers

THE PRESS & JOURNAL (MORAY)
42253U67B-2170_600
Edition of: The Press & Journal (Aberdeen)
REGIONAL DAILY & SUNDAY NEWSPAPERS: Regional Daily Newspapers

THE PRESS & JOURNAL (NORTH EAST)
624919U67B-2170_605
Edition of: The Press & Journal (Aberdeen)
REGIONAL DAILY & SUNDAY NEWSPAPERS: Regional Daily Newspapers

THE PRESS BARNET, WHETSTONE & POTTERS BAR
42962U72A-120_152
Formerly: Press Barnet & Whetstone
Frequency: Weekly
Cover Price: Free
Circulation: 43,775 (Publisher's Statement)
ADVERTISING RATES:
SCC £7.40
Part of Series, see entry for: Gazette, Advertiser and Press Newspaper Series
LOCAL NEWSPAPERS: Local Newspapers Greater London

THE PRESS (DEWSBURY)
761477U72B-3757
Editorial Address: Edward Latham House, 1 Oates Street, DEWSBURY, WF13 1BB **Tel:** 01924 439498
Fax: 01924 457994
Email: news@thepressnews.co.uk

Advertising Address: As above.
Email: advertising@thepressnews.co.uk
Web site: http://www.thepressnews.co.uk
Publisher: Newspost Ltd
Date Established: 2002
Frequency: Weekly
Cover Price: £0.40
Free to qualifying individuals
Editor: Martin Shaw; **Advertising Manager:** David Baird
ADVERTISING RATES:
SCC £6.50
Agency Commission: 10%
Mechanical Data: Page Width: 254mm, Film: Digital, Type Area: 360 x 254mm, Col Length: 360mm, No. of Columns (Display): 8
Copy instructions: Copy Date: Wednesday 5pm prior to publication date
LOCAL NEWSPAPERS: Local Newspapers English Counties

THE PRESS HENDON, FINCHLEY, EDGWARE & MILL HILL
42964U72A-120_154
Formerly: Press Hendon and Finchley Edition
Frequency: Weekly
Cover Price: Free
Circulation: 74,640 (Publisher's Statement)
ADVERTISING RATES:
SCC £7.40
Part of Series, see entry for: Gazette, Advertiser and Press Newspaper Series
LOCAL NEWSPAPERS: Local Newspapers Greater London

THE PRESS (YORK)
42213U67B-1180
Formerly: Evening Press (York)
Editorial Address: PO Box 29, 76-86 Walmgate, YORK, YO1 9YN **Tel:** 01904 653051 **Fax:** 01904 612853
Email: newsdesk@thepress.co.uk
Advertising Address: As above. **Fax:** 01904 611488
Email: advertising@ycp.co.uk
Web site: http://www.yorkpress.co.uk
Publisher: Newsquest Yorkshire and North East (York)
Frequency: Daily
Cover Price: £0.40
Circulation: 35,761 (ABC 04/07/2005 to 01/01/2006)
Editor: Scott Armstrong
ADVERTISING RATES:
Full Page Mono £2754.00
Full Page Colour 3442.50
SCC £9.00
Agency Commission: 10%
Mechanical Data: Page Width: 351mm, Film: Digital, No. of Columns (Display): 9, Type Area: 550 x 351mm, Col Length: 550mm
Copy instructions: Copy Date: 3 working days prior to publication date
Average advertising content per issue: 70%
Supplement(s): Home & Garden - 3xY, Life & Times - 52xY, York twenty4seven - 52xY
REGIONAL DAILY & SUNDAY NEWSPAPERS: Regional Daily Newspapers

PRESTON REPORTER
43998U72B-2052_180
Frequency: Weekly
Cover Price: Free
Part of Series, see entry for: Preston Reporter Series
LOCAL NEWSPAPERS: Local Newspapers English Counties

PRESTON REPORTER SERIES
43996U72B-2052
Editorial Address: Olivers Place, Eastway, Fulwood, PRESTON, PR2 9ZA **Tel:** 01772 254841 **Fax:** 01772 880173
Email: lep.newsdesk@lep.co.uk
Advertising Address: As above. **Fax:** 01772 838199
Email: mark.fry@lep.co.uk
Web site: http://www.lep.co.uk/thereporter
Publisher: Lancashire Evening Post Ltd
Frequency: Weekly
Cover Price: Free
Circulation: 64,110 (VFD 02/07/2007 to 30/12/2007)
Editor: Nicola Adam; **Features Editor:** Peter Richardson; **Managing Director:** Margaret Hilton
ADVERTISING RATES:
Full Page Colour £4186.08
SCC £6.17
Agency Commission: 10%
Mechanical Data: Type Area: 340 x 274mm, Page Width: 274mm, Film: Digital, Col Length: 340mm, Col Widths (Display): 30mm, No. of Columns (Display): 9
Copy instructions: Copy Date: Tuesday 12pm prior to publication date
Average advertising content per issue: 70%
Series owner and contact point for the following titles, see individual entries:
Leyland Reporter

Preston Reporter
LOCAL NEWSPAPERS: Local Newspapers English Counties

PRESTWICH & WHITEFIELD GUIDE
43692U72B-1170_200
Frequency: Weekly
Cover Price: £0.30
Circulation: 4,063 (ABC 02/07/2007 to 30/12/2007)
Advertising Manager: Philip Wheelhouse
ADVERTISING: Rates on application
Part of Series, see entry for: Bury Times Series
LOCAL NEWSPAPERS: Local Newspapers English Counties

PRINCETOWN GAZETTE
43547U72B-857_170
Frequency: Weekly
Cover Price: £0.55
Circulation: 500 (Publisher's Statement)
Part of Series, see entry for: Tavistock Times Gazette Series
LOCAL NEWSPAPERS: Local Newspapers English Counties

PROPERTY CHRONICLE
43276U72B-180_290
Frequency: Weekly
Cover Price: Free
ADVERTISING RATES:
Full Page Mono £2880.48
Full Page Colour £3600.60
SCC £10.59
Part of Series, see entry for: Reading Chronicle Series
LOCAL NEWSPAPERS: Local Newspapers English Counties

PUDSEY TIMES
44723U72B-3919_171
Frequency: Weekly
Cover Price: Free
Circulation: 21,905 (VFD 02/07/2007 to 30/12/2007)
ADVERTISING: Rates on application
Copy instructions: Copy Date: Monday 4pm prior to publication date
Part of Series, see entry for: Wharfe Valley Times Series
LOCAL NEWSPAPERS: Local Newspapers English Counties

PULMANS WEEKLY NEWS AND ADVERTISER SERIES
43530U72B-842
Formerly: Pulmans Weekly News Series
Editorial Address: Tindle House, South Street, AXMINSTER, EX13 5AD **Tel:** 01297 631120
Fax: 01297 35417
Email: pulmans@tindlenews.co.uk
Advertising Address: As above. **Tel:** 01297 32443
Fax: 01297 35160
Email: pulmans@internet-today.co.uk
Publisher: Tindle Newspapers Ltd
Frequency: Weekly - Published on Wednesday
Circulation: 22,000 (Combined Circulation)
Editor: Kate Erin-Mews; **Advertising Manager:** Harriet Parkin
ADVERTISING RATES:
Full Page Mono £832.00
SCC £3.60
Mechanical Data: Type Area: 390 x 270mm, Page Width: 270mm, Col Length: 390mm, No. of Columns (Display): 8, Film: Digital
Copy instructions: Copy Date: Monday 5pm prior to publication date
Series owner and contact point for the following titles, see individual entries:
Chard Advertiser
Crewkerne Advertiser
Honiton Advertiser
Ottery Advertiser
Pulmans Weekly News Devon & Somerset
LOCAL NEWSPAPERS: Local Newspapers English Counties

PULMANS WEEKLY NEWS DEVON & SOMERSET
767369U72B-842_101
Frequency: Weekly
Cover Price: £0.40
Circulation: 10,000 (Publisher's Statement)
Part of Series, see entry for: Pulmans Weekly News and Advertiser Series
LOCAL NEWSPAPERS: Local Newspapers English Counties

QUEENSFERRY GAZETTE
717869U72D-690_150

Frequency: Weekly
Cover Price: £0.40
Part of Series, see entry for: Linlithgowshire Journal and Gazette Series
LOCAL NEWSPAPERS: Local Newspapers Scotland

RADCLIFFE TIMES
43705U72B-1170_210

Frequency: Weekly
Cover Price: £0.50
Circulation: 2,721 (Publisher's Statement)
Advertising Manager: Janet Campbell
ADVERTISING: Rates on application
Part of Series, see entry for: Bury Times Series
LOCAL NEWSPAPERS: Local Newspapers English Counties

RAINWORTH CHAD
44177U72B-2580_150

Frequency: Weekly - Circulation figure is incorporated into the Mansfield Chad
Part of Series, see entry for: Chad Series Mansfield
LOCAL NEWSPAPERS: Local Newspapers English Counties

RAYLEIGH & EASTWOOD TIMES
43640U72B-1079_160

Frequency: Monthly
Cover Price: Free
Circulation: 15,000 (Publisher's Statement)
ADVERTISING RATES:
Full Page Mono £275.00
Full Page Colour £400.00
SCC £5.00
Part of Series, see entry for: Leigh Times Series
LOCAL NEWSPAPERS: Local Newspapers English Counties

RAYLEIGH, ROCHFORD & CASTLE POINT STANDARD
1626345U72B-1080_222

Frequency: Weekly
Cover Price: Free
Circulation: 53,688 (VFD 02/07/2007 to 30/12/2007)
ADVERTISING: Rates on application
Mechanical Data: Type Area: 340 x 267mm, Col Length: 340mm, Page Width: 267mm, No. of Columns (Display): 9, Col Widths (Display): 27mm, Film: Positive, right reading, emulsion side down, Print Process: Web-fed offset litho
Part of Series, see entry for: Southend Standard Series
LOCAL NEWSPAPERS: Local Newspapers English Counties

READING CHRONICLE
43272U72B-180_200

Frequency: Weekly - Circulation figure includes the Woodley Chronicle
Cover Price: £0.55
Circulation: 11,056 (ABC 02/07/2007 to 30/12/2007)
ADVERTISING RATES:
Full Page Mono £3255.84
Full Page Colour £4069.80
SCC £11.97
Part of Series, see entry for: Reading Chronicle Series
LOCAL NEWSPAPERS: Local Newspapers English Counties

READING CHRONICLE SERIES
43270U72B-180

Editorial Address: 50-56 Portman Road, READING, RG30 1BA **Tel:** 0118 950 3030 **Fax:** 0118 963 3171
Email: news@readingchronicle.co.uk
Advertising Address: As above.
Web site: http://www.readingchronicle.co.uk
Publisher: Berkshire Media Group Ltd
Date Established: 1825
Frequency: Weekly - Published on Wednesday & Thursday
Circulation: 105,389 (Combined Circulation)
Editor: Maurice O'Brien; **News Editor:** Maurice O'Brien;
Editor-in-Chief: Sally Stevens
ADVERTISING: Rates on application
Agency Commission: 10%
Mechanical Data: Type Area: 340 x 260.2mm, Col Length: 328mm, No. of Columns (Display): 8
Average advertising content per issue: 33%
Series owner and contact point for the following titles, see individual entries:
Kronika Reading
Newbury and Thatcham Chronicle
Property Chronicle
Reading Chronicle
The Reading Midweek
Woodley and Earley Chronicle

Supplement(s): The Guide - 52xY
LOCAL NEWSPAPERS: Local Newspapers English Counties

THE READING MIDWEEK
43273U72B-180_205

Formerly: The Chronicle Extra
Frequency: Weekly - Published on Wednesday
Cover Price: Free
Circulation: 75,739 (VFD 01/01/2007 to 01/07/2007)
ADVERTISING RATES:
Full Page Mono £3092.64
Full Page Colour £3865.80
SCC £11.37
Part of Series, see entry for: Reading Chronicle Series
LOCAL NEWSPAPERS: Local Newspapers English Counties

READING POST
1902258U72B-4163_100

Frequency: Weekly - Published on Wednesday
Cover Price: £0.40
Circulation: 13,500 (Publisher's Statement)
Part of Series, see entry for: Reading Post Series
LOCAL NEWSPAPERS: Local Newspapers English Counties

READING POST SERIES
42165U72B-4163

Formerly: Reading Evening Post
Editorial Address: 8 Tessa Road, READING, RG1 8NS
Tel: 0118 918 3000 **Fax:** 0118 959 9363
Email: editorial@reading-epost.co.uk
Advertising Address: As above. **Tel:** 0118 921 7700
Fax: 0118 958 8229
Email: display@reading-epost.co.uk
Web site: http://www.getreading.co.uk
Publisher: Surrey & Berkshire Media Group
Frequency: Evenings - Published on Wednesday and Friday
Circulation: 84,500 (Combined Circulation)
Editor: Andy Murrill; **News Editor:** Sarah Dave; **Features Editor:** Phil Creighton; **Managing Director:** Paul O'Halloran
ADVERTISING RATES:
Full Page Mono £2841.30
Full Page Colour £3694.95
SCC £11.73
Agency Commission: 10%
Mechanical Data: Type Area: 346 x 277mm, Col Length: 346mm, Film: Digital, No. of Columns (Display): 9, Col Widths (Display): 29mm, Page Width: 277mm
Copy instructions: Copy Date: 3 days prior to publication date
Average advertising content per issue: 40%
Series owner and contact point for the following titles, see individual entries:
getreading
Reading Post
LOCAL NEWSPAPERS: Local Newspapers English Counties

REDDITCH ADVERTISER
44626U72B-3568_170

Formerly: Redditch Advertiser inc The Redditch Indicator
Frequency: Weekly
Cover Price: Free
Part of Series, see entry for: Redditch Advertiser and Chronicle Series
LOCAL NEWSPAPERS: Local Newspapers English Counties

REDDITCH ADVERTISER AND CHRONICLE SERIES
44624U72B-3568

Formerly: Redditch Advertiser/ Indicator Series
Editorial Address: Grosvenor House, Prospect Hill, REDDITCH, B97 4DL **Tel:** 01527 453535 **Fax:** 01527 453534
Email: redditcheditorial@midlands.newsquest.co.uk
Advertising Address: As above. **Tel:** 01527 453500
Fax: 01527 453805
Email: gill.cook@midlands.newsquest.co.uk
Web site: http://www.redditchadvertiser.co.uk
Publisher: Newsquest Media Group
Date Established: 1859
Frequency: Weekly - Published on Wednesday
Cover Price: Free
Circulation: 46,343 (VFD 02/07/2007 to 30/12/2007)
Editor: Helen Clarke; **Managing Director:** Mike Donovan
ADVERTISING RATES:
Full Page Mono £1354.50
Full Page Colour £1694.70
SCC £4.30
Agency Commission: 10%
Mechanical Data: Page Width: 268mm, Screen: Mono 34 lpc Colour 40 lpc, Col Length: 350mm, Col Widths (Display): 28mm, No. of Columns (Display): 9, Film: Negative, right reading, emulsion side down. Digital, Type Area: 350 x 268mm

Copy instructions: Copy Date: Tuesday 12pm prior to publication date
Average advertising content per issue: 65%
Series owner and contact point for the following titles, see individual entries:
Alcester Chronicle
Redditch Advertiser
LOCAL NEWSPAPERS: Local Newspapers English Counties

REDDITCH & ALCESTER STANDARD
44623U72B-3566_210

Formerly: Redditch Standard
Frequency: Weekly
Cover Price: Free
Circulation: 48,921 (VFD 02/07/2007 to 30/12/2007)
ADVERTISING RATES:
SCC £5.66
Part of Series, see entry for: Redditch and Bromsgrove Standard Series
LOCAL NEWSPAPERS: Local Newspapers English Counties

REDDITCH AND BROMSGROVE STANDARD SERIES
44619U72B-3566

Editorial Address: Webb House, 20A Church Green East, REDDITCH, B98 8BP **Tel:** 01527 588688 **Fax:** 01527 584371
Email: editor@redditchstandard.co.uk
Advertising Address: As above.
Email: dawn.goodyer@observerstandard.com
Web site: http://www.redditchstandard.co.uk
Publisher: Bullivant Media Limited
Date Established: 1996
Frequency: Weekly - Published on Friday
Cover Price: Free
Circulation: 89,270 (Combined Circulation)
Editor: Andrew Powell; **News Editor:** Andrew Powell;
Features Editor: Andrew Powell
ADVERTISING: Rates on application
Agency Commission: 10%
Mechanical Data: Col Widths (Display): 27mm, No. of Columns (Display): 9, Film: Digital, Type Area: 350 x 265mm, Col Length: 350mm, Page Width; 265mm
Copy instructions: Copy Date: Wednesday 5pm prior to publication date
Series owner and contact point for the following titles, see individual entries:
Bromsgrove Standard
Droitwich Spa Standard
Redditch & Alcester Standard
LOCAL NEWSPAPERS: Local Newspapers English Counties

REDHILL REIGATE HORLEY LIFE
44375U72B-3123

Formerly: Horley Life Series
Editorial Address: Argus House, Crowhurst Road, Hollingbury, BRIGHTON, BN1 8AR **Tel:** 01273 544544
Fax: 01403 544723
Email: editorial@lifenewspapers.co.uk
Advertising Address: As above. **Fax:** 01273 889500
Email: iain.houston@theargus.co.uk
Web site: http://www.redhillandreigatelife.co.uk
Publisher: Newsquest (Sussex) Ltd
Frequency: Weekly - Published on Wednesday
Cover Price: Free
Circulation: 33,771 (Publisher's Statement)
Usual Pagination: 40
Editor: Chris Chandler; **Advertising Manager:** Iain Houston
ADVERTISING RATES:
Full Page Mono £1071.00
Full Page Colour £1286.00
Agency Commission: 10%
Mechanical Data: Col Length: 360mm, No. of Columns (Display): 9, Type Area: 360 x 276mm, Page Width: 276mm, Col Widths (Display): 28mm, Film: Digital
Copy instructions: Copy Date: 1 week prior to publication date
Average advertising content per issue: 30%
LOCAL NEWSPAPERS: Local Newspapers English Counties

RENFREWSHIRE WORLD
45022U72D-835

Editorial Address: 14 New Street, PAISLEY, PA1 1YA
Tel: 0141 887 7911 **Fax:** 0141 887 6254
Email: pde@s-un.co.uk
Advertising Address: As above. **Tel:** 0141 887 7744
Fax: 0141 889 7148
Email: pdeads@s-un.co.uk
Web site: http://www.icrenfrewshire.co.uk
Publisher: Scottish & Universal Newspapers Ltd
Frequency: Weekly - Published on Thursday
Cover Price: Free
Circulation: 15,670 (Publisher's Statement)

Non-National Newspapers

Editor: Anne Dalrymple; **News Editor:** Gavin Penny;
Advertising Manager: Patricia Graham
ADVERTISING: Rates on application
Mechanical Data: Type Area: 340 x 267mm, Page Width:
267mm, Col Length: 340mm, No. of Columns (Display): 8,
Film: Digital
Copy instructions: Copy Date: 2 days prior to publication
date
LOCAL NEWSPAPERS: Local Newspapers Scotland

REPORTER EXTRA
1664312U72B-3760_161

Formerly: The Weekly Advertiser (Dewsbury)
Frequency: Weekly
Cover Price: Free
Circulation: 44,583 (VFD 17/09/2007 to 30/12/2007)
ADVERTISING RATES:
Full Page Mono £1526.00
Full Page Colour £1985.00
SCC £4.99
Part of Series, see entry for: Dewsbury Reporter and
Advertiser Series
LOCAL NEWSPAPERS: Local Newspapers English
Counties

THE REPORTER (SAFFRON WALDEN, STANSTED & SAWSTON)
43632U72B-1077

Formerly: Saffron Walden & Stansted Reporter Series
Editorial Address: 54 High Street, SAFFRON WALDEN,
CB10 1EE **Tel:** 01799 512880 **Fax:** 01799 527310
Email: editor@saffronwalden-reporter.co.uk
Advertising Address: As above. **Tel:** 01799 525100
Fax: 01799 513382
Email: carla.thomas@archant.co.uk
Web site: http://www.saffronwalden-reporter.co.uk
ISSN: 1468-7327
Publisher: Archant Herts & Cambs
Frequency: Weekly - Published on Thursday
Cover Price: Free
Circulation: 25,073 (VFD 02/07/2007 to 30/12/2007)
Editor: Barry Hunt
ADVERTISING RATES:
Full Page Mono £1458.00
Agency Commission: 10%·
Mechanical Data: Type Area: 360 x 263mm, No. of
Columns (Display): 9, Col Length: 360mm, Col Widths
(Display): 27mm, Page Width: 263mm, Film: Digital
Copy instructions: Copy Date: Tuesday 4pm prior to
publication date
Average advertising content per issue: 30%
LOCAL NEWSPAPERS: Local Newspapers English
Counties

RETFORD GAINSBOROUGH AND WORKSOP TIMES
44194U72B-2650

Formerly: Retford Times Gainsborough & Worksop
Editorial Address: Chancery Court, 32 West Street,
RETFORD, DN22 6ES **Tel:** 01777 704444
Fax: 01777 708791
Email: news@retfordtimes.co.uk
Advertising Address: As above. **Tel:** 01777 702275
Email: adverts@retfordtimes.co.uk
Web site: http://www.thisisretford.co.uk
Publisher: Lincolnshire Media Ltd
Date Established: 1869
Frequency: Weekly
Cover Price: £0.40
Circulation: 10,913 (ABC 02/07/2007 to 30/12/2007)
Editor: Nick Purkiss; **News Editor:** Steve Cawthorne;
Managing Director: Mark Price; **Managing Editor:** Nick
Purkiss
ADVERTISING RATES:
Full Page Mono £1209.00
Full Page Colour £1512.00
SCC £4.20
Agency Commission: 10%
Mechanical Data: Col Widths (Display): 30mm, Film: Digital,
Page Width: 269mm, Type Area: 360 x 269mm, Col Length:
360mm, No. of Columns (Display): 8
Copy instructions: Copy Date: 2 days prior to publication
date
Average advertising content per issue: 40%
LOCAL NEWSPAPERS: Local Newspapers English
Counties

RETFORD TRADER GUARDIAN
44204U72B-2670_170

Formerly: Guardian (Retford)
Publisher: South Yorkshire Newspapers Ltd
Frequency: Weekly
Cover Price: Free
Circulation: 23,287 (VFD 02/07/2007 to 30/12/2007)
ADVERTISING RATES:
SCC £7.37

Part of Series, see entry for: Guardian Series (Worksop)
LOCAL NEWSPAPERS: Local Newspapers English
Counties

REVIEW SERIES
43816U72B-1586

Formerly: Observer & Review Series
Editorial Address: Observer House, Caxton Court, Caxton
Way, Watford Business Park, WATFORD, WD18 8RJ
Tel: 01923 216296 **Fax:** 01923 243738
Email: stalbansnews@london.newsquest.co.uk
Advertising Address: As above. **Tel:** 01923 216216
Fax: 01923 222737
Email: ljayson@london.newsquest.co.uk
Web site: http://www.stalbansreview.co.uk
Publisher: Newsquest (North London)
Date Established: 1972
Frequency: Weekly - Published Wednesday and Thursday
Cover Price: Free
Circulation: 67,666 (Combined Circulation)
Editor: Alex Lewis; **Features Editor:** Lindi Bilgorri; **Group
Editor:** Peter Wilson-Leary
ADVERTISING RATES:
SCC £5.50
Agency Commission: 10%
Mechanical Data: Type Area: 350 x 265mm, No. of
Columns (Display): 9, Col Length: 350mm, Col Widths
(Display): 27mm, Page Width: 265mm, Film: Digital
Copy instructions: Copy Date: 2 days prior to publication
date
Average advertising content per issue: 40%
**Series owner and contact point for the following titles,
see individual entries:**
Review Welwyn Hatfield Edition
St. Albans & Harpenden Review
LOCAL NEWSPAPERS: Local Newspapers English
Counties

REVIEW WELWYN HATFIELD EDITION
43819U72B-1586_180

Frequency: Weekly
Cover Price: Free
Circulation: 19,096 (VFD 02/07/2007 to 30/12/2007)
Part of Series, see entry for: Review Series
LOCAL NEWSPAPERS: Local Newspapers English
Counties

RHONDDA LEADER
44836U72C-325

Editorial Address: 10 Market Street, PONTYPRIDD, CF37
2ST **Tel:** 01443 665151 **Fax:** 01443 665181
Email: rhondda.leader@mediawales.co.uk
Advertising Address: 52-53 Glebeland Street, MERTHYR
TYDFIL, CF47 8AT **Tel:** 01685 856569 **Fax:** 01685 856556
Email: rob.gray@mediawales.co.uk
Web site: http://www.icwales.co.uk
Publisher: Media Wales Ltd
Frequency: Weekly - Published on Thursday
Cover Price: £0.68
Circulation: 12,500 (ABC 02/07/2007 to 30/12/2007)
Editor: Wayne Nowaczwk; **Advertising Manager:** Robert
Gray
ADVERTISING RATES:
SCC £3.74
Agency Commission: 10%
Mechanical Data: Col Length: 340mm, Col Widths (Display):
31.5mm, Film: Digital, No. of Columns (Display): 8, Type
Area: 340 x 277mm, Page Width: 277mm
Copy instructions: Copy Date: Monday 1pm prior to
publication date
LOCAL NEWSPAPERS: Local Newspapers Wales

Y RHWYD
761669U72J-230

Editorial Address: Afallon, Caergeiliog, HOLYHEAD, LL65
3YG **Tel:** 01407 742040
Advertising Address: Crud Yr Awel, 6 Llain Fain, Llain
Goch, HOLYHEAD, LL65 1NF **Tel:** 01407 762090
Frequency: 10 issues yearly - Not published in January or
September
Cover Price: £0.40
Circulation: 1,350 (Publisher's Statement)
Editor: Arthur Roberts; **Advertising Manager:** Gladys
Pritchard
Summary of Content: Welsh language community
newspaper covering local news. Includes articles on sport,
nature, children's columns and crosswords.
Language(s): Welsh
Readership/Target Audience: Aimed at Welsh speaking
people with an interest in local affairs, living in North-West
Anglesey.
ADVERTISING RATES:
Full Page Mono £55.00
Mechanical Data: Film: Digital
Copy instructions: Copy Date: 10 days prior to publication
date
LOCAL NEWSPAPERS: Community Newsletters

RHYL & PRESTATYN VISITOR
44846U72C-357_150

Frequency: Weekly
Cover Price: Free
Circulation: 24,199 (Publisher's Statement)
Part of Series, see entry for: Visitor Series
LOCAL NEWSPAPERS: Local Newspapers Wales

RHYMNEY VALLEY EXPRESS
625580U72C-240_120

Formerly: Rhymney Valley
Frequency: Weekly
Cover Price: £0.60
Part of Series, see entry for: Merthyr Express Series
LOCAL NEWSPAPERS: Local Newspapers Wales

RICHMOND & TWICKENHAM TIMES
43129U72A-510_130

Frequency: Weekly - Circulation figure includes Hounslow &
Brentford Times
Cover Price: £0.50
Circulation: 10,256 (ABC 02/07/2007 to 30/12/2007)
Usual Pagination: 80
Part of Series, see entry for: Times Series (Richmond)
LOCAL NEWSPAPERS: Local Newspapers Greater London

RIPLEY & HEANOR NEWS
43496U72B-760

Editorial Address: 27 Grosvenor Road, RIPLEY, DE5 3JE
Tel: 01773 514170 **Fax:** 01773 570109
Email: news@rhnews.co.uk
Advertising Address: As above. **Tel:** 01773 514151
Email: rachel.nicholson@rhnews.co.uk
Web site: http://www.ripleyandheanornews.co.uk
Publisher: Derbyshire Times Newspaper Group
Date Established: 1889
Frequency: Weekly - Published on Thursday
Cover Price: £0.40
Circulation: 10,394 (ABC 02/07/2007 to 30/12/2007)
Editor: Richard Woolley; **Managing Director:** Dawn
Sweeney; **Group Editor:** Amanda Hatfield
ADVERTISING RATES:
SCC £3.40
Agency Commission: 10%
Mechanical Data: Col Widths (Display): 28mm, No. of
Columns (Display): 9, Film: Digital
Copy instructions: Copy Date: Tuesday 2.00pm prior to
publication date
Average advertising content per issue: 40%
Supplement(s): Female Focus - 4xY, Home is Where the
Heart Is - 4xY, Motoring Guide - 52xY, Property Guide -
52xY
LOCAL NEWSPAPERS: Local Newspapers English
Counties

RIPON GAZETTE & BOROUGHBRIDGE HERALD
44654U72B-3588_210

Frequency: Weekly
Cover Price: £0.60
Circulation: 6,088 (ABC 02/07/2007 to 30/12/2007)
ADVERTISING RATES:
SCC £6.31
Part of Series, see entry for: Ackrill Newspaper Series
LOCAL NEWSPAPERS: Local Newspapers English
Counties

ROCHDALE OBSERVER (SATURDAY)
43711U72B-1280_180

Frequency: Weekly
Cover Price: £0.55
Circulation: 22,664 (ABC 02/07/2007 to 30/12/2007)
ADVERTISING RATES:
SCC £8.00
Part of Series, see entry for: Rochdale Observer Series
LOCAL NEWSPAPERS: Local Newspapers English
Counties

ROCHDALE OBSERVER SERIES
43709U72B-1280

Editorial Address: Observer Buildings, 82-86 Drake Street,
ROCHDALE, OL16 1PH **Tel:** 01706 354321
Fax: 01706 526314
Email: rochdaleobserver@menmedia.co.uk
Advertising Address: As above. **Fax:** 01706 750227
Email: geoff.jepson@gmwn.co.uk
Web site: http://www.rochdaleobserver.co.uk
Publisher: MEN Media
Date Established: 1856
Frequency: 104 issues yearly - Published Wednesday and
Saturday

Circulation: 40,000 (Combined Circulation)
Editor: Stephanie Nelson; News Editor: Stephanie Nelson;
Advertising Manager: Geoff Jepson
ADVERTISING: Rates on application
Agency Commission: 10%
Average advertising content per issue: 60%
Series owner and contact point for the following titles,
see individual entries:
Express Rochdale
Rochdale Observer (Saturday)
Rochdale Observer (Wednesday)
LOCAL NEWSPAPERS: Local Newspapers English
Counties

ROCHDALE OBSERVER (WEDNESDAY)

43710U72B-1280_140

Frequency: Weekly
Cover Price: £0.42
Circulation: 15,951 (ABC 02/07/2007 to 30/12/2007)
ADVERTISING RATES:
SCC £6.50
Part of Series, see entry for: Rochdale Observer Series
LOCAL NEWSPAPERS: Local Newspapers English
Counties

ROE VALLEY SENTINEL

45121U72E-220_120

Frequency: Weekly - Published on Wednesday
Cover Price: £0.85
Circulation: 6,329 (Publisher's Statement)
Part of Series, see entry for: The Sentinel Series
LOCAL NEWSPAPERS: Local Newspapers Northern Ireland

ROMFORD AND HAVERING WEEKLY POST

43061U72A-101_180

Formerly: Romford and Havering Free Post
Editorial Address: Media House, 539 High Road, ILFORD,
IG1 1UD Tel: 01708 771500 Fax: 01708 771520
Email: news.desk@romfordrecorder.co.uk
Advertising Address: As above.
Email: janette.clark@archant.co.uk
Publisher: Archant East London & Essex
Frequency: Weekly
Cover Price: Free
Circulation: 68,181 (VFD 02/07/2007 to 30/12/2007)
Editor: Sheena McKenzie; Advertising Manager: Janette
Clark
ADVERTISING RATES:
Full Page Mono £2520.00
Full Page Colour £3150.00
Agency Commission: 10%
Mechanical Data: Type Area: 350 x 267mm, Col Length:
350mm, Page Width: 267mm, Col Widths (Display): 27.5mm,
No. of Columns (Display): 9, Film: Digital
Copy instructions: Copy Date: Monday 4pm prior to
publication date
Average advertising content per issue: 60%
LOCAL NEWSPAPERS: Local Newspapers Greater London

ROMFORD RECORDER

43131U72A-430

Formerly: Romford Recorder Series
Editorial Address: Media House, 539 High Road, ILFORD,
IG1 1UD Tel: 01708 771500 Fax: 01708 771520
Email: news.desk@romfordrecorder.co.uk
Advertising Address: As above. Fax: 01708 771521
Email: janette.clark@archant.co.uk
Web site: http://www.romfordrecorder.co.uk
Publisher: Archant East London & Essex
Frequency: Weekly - Published on Friday
Cover Price: £0.55
Circulation: 28,302 (ABC 02/07/2007 to 30/12/2007)
Editor: Sheena McKenzie
ADVERTISING RATES:
SCC £9.00
Mechanical Data: Type Area: 350 x 267mm, Col Length:
350mm, No. of Columns (Display): 9, Page Width: 267mm,
Film: Digital
Copy instructions: Copy Date: Tuesday 5.30pm prior to
publication date
LOCAL NEWSPAPERS: Local Newspapers Greater London

ROMNEY MARSH HERALD

43878U72B-1750_180

Frequency: Weekly
Cover Price: £0.55
ADVERTISING: Rates on application
Part of Series, see entry for: Adscene, Herald & Express
Series (Folkestone)
LOCAL NEWSPAPERS: Local Newspapers English
Counties

ROMSEY ADVERTISER

43749U72B-1370_145

Frequency: Weekly
Cover Price: £0.45
Circulation: 7,084 (ABC 01/01/2007 to 30/12/2007)
ADVERTISING RATES:
SCC £2.80
Part of Series, see entry for: Hampshire Chronicle Series
LOCAL NEWSPAPERS: Local Newspapers English
Counties

THE ROSS GAZETTE

43783U72B-1480

Editorial Address: 54A Broad Street, ROSS-ON-WYE, HR9
7DY Tel: 01989 562007 Fax: 01989 768023
Email: ross.gazette@tindlenews.co.uk
Advertising Address: As above.
Email: ross.advertising@internet-today.co.uk
ISSN: 1368-8057
Publisher: The Ross Gazette Ltd
Date Established: 1867
Frequency: Weekly - Published on Wednesday
Cover Price: £0.32
Circulation: 6,500 (Publisher's Statement)
Editor: Chris Robertson; Advertising Manager: Lee
Whiteland
ADVERTISING RATES:
SCC £3.60
Agency Commission: 10%
Mechanical Data: Col Length: 390mm, Col Widths (Display):
30.25mm, No. of Columns (Display): 8, Print Process: Web-
fed offset litho, Type Area: 390 x 270mm, Page Width:
270mm, Film: Digital
Copy instructions: Copy Date: Monday 12 noon prior to
publication date
Average advertising content per issue: 33%
Supplement(s): The Ross Recorder - 12xY
LOCAL NEWSPAPERS: Local Newspapers English
Counties

ROSSENDALE FREE PRESS

43999U72B-2053

Formerly: Rossendale Series
Editorial Address: 1 Scott Place, MANCHESTER, M3 3RN
Tel: 0161 211 2955 Fax: 0161 211 2911
Email: freepressnews@menmedia.co.uk
Advertising Address: As above. Tel: 0161 480 4491
Email: mark.stansfield@menmediasales.co.uk
Web site: http://www.therossendalefreepress.co.uk
ISSN: 0963-7575
Publisher: MEN Media
Date Established: 1883
Frequency: Weekly - Published on Friday
Cover Price: £0.55
Circulation: 14,288 (ABC 02/07/2007 to 30/12/2007)
Editor: Lisa Kenyon; News Editor: Lisa Kenyon
ADVERTISING RATES:
SCC £4.90
Agency Commission: 10%
Mechanical Data: Page Width: 267mm, Film: Digital, Type
Area: 340 x 267mm, Col Length: 340mm, Col Widths
(Display): 27mm, No. of Columns (Display): 9
Copy instructions: Copy Date: Wednesday 4pm prior to
publication date
Average advertising content per issue: 60%
LOCAL NEWSPAPERS: Local Newspapers English
Counties

ROSSINGTON COMMUNITY NEWSLETTER

1647021U72B-3950_102

Frequency: Monthly
Cover Price: Free
Circulation: 6,000 (Publisher's Statement)
ADVERTISING: Rates on application
Part of Series, see entry for: Community Newsletter Series
LOCAL NEWSPAPERS: Local Newspapers English
Counties

ROSS-SHIRE HERALD

1697361U72D-840_100

Frequency: Weekly
Cover Price: Free
Circulation: 10,298 (ABC 01/01/2007 to 30/12/2007)
Part of Series, see entry for: Ross-shire Journal and Herald
Series
LOCAL NEWSPAPERS: Local Newspapers Scotland

ROSS-SHIRE JOURNAL

1697426U72D-840_101

Frequency: Weekly
Cover Price: £0.68
Circulation: 10,884 (ABC 02/01/2006 to 31/12/2006)
Part of Series, see entry for: Ross-shire Journal and Herald
Series
LOCAL NEWSPAPERS: Local Newspapers Scotland

ROSS-SHIRE JOURNAL AND HERALD SERIES

45024U72D-840

Formerly: Ross-shire Journal
Editorial Address: Dochcarty Road, DINGWALL, IV15 9UG
Tel: 01349 863436 Fax: 01349 866741
Email: editor@rsjournal.co.uk
Advertising Address: As above. Fax: 01349 863456
Email: sales@rsjournal.co.uk
Web site: http://www.ross-shirejournal.co.uk
Publisher: Scottish Provincial Press
Date Established: 1875
Frequency: Weekly - Published on Friday
Circulation: 21,182 (Combined Circulation)
Editor: Hector MacKenzie; Advertising Manager: Gail
Henderson-Gray
Language(s): English; Gaelic
ADVERTISING RATES:
Full Page Mono £3382.50
Full Page Colour £5073.75
Mechanical Data: Type Area: 550 x 277mm, No. of
Columns (Display): 10, Col Widths (Display): 35mm, Col
Length: 550mm, Page Width: 277mm, Film: Digital
Copy instructions: Copy Date: Tuesday 12 noon prior to
publication date
Series owner and contact point for the following titles,
see individual entries:
Ross-shire Herald
Ross-shire Journal
LOCAL NEWSPAPERS: Local Newspapers Scotland

ROTHERHAM ADVERTISER AND RECORD SERIES

762262U72B-3925

Editorial Address: Brookfields Way, Manvers, Wath Upon
Dearne, ROTHERHAM, S63 5DL Tel: 01709 768146
Email: howard.poucher@garnett-dickinson.co.uk
Advertising Address: 67 Wellgate, ROTHERHAM, S60 2LT
Tel: 01709 768000 Fax: 01709 360236
Email: peter.chubb@garnett-dickinson.co.uk
Web site: http://www.rotherhamadvertiser.com
Publisher: Garnett Dickinson Group Ltd
Frequency: Weekly
Circulation: 94,605 (Combined Circulation)
Editor: Howard Poucher; Advertising Manager: Peter
Chubb
ADVERTISING: Rates on application
Agency Commission: 10%
Mechanical Data: Page Width: 265mm, Type Area: 340 x
265mm, Col Length: 340mm, Col Widths (Display): 30mm,
No. of Columns (Display): 8, Film: Digital
Average advertising content per issue: 55%
Supplement(s): Chase - 4xY
LOCAL NEWSPAPERS: Local Newspapers English
Counties

ROTHERHAM GAZETTE

1698042U72B-3982_102

Frequency: 26 issues yearly
Cover Price: Free
Part of Series, see entry for: Rotherham Gazette Series
LOCAL NEWSPAPERS: Local Newspapers English
Counties

ROTHERHAM GAZETTE SERIES

1698041U72B-3982

Editorial Address: Mexborough Business Centre, College
Road, MEXBOROUGH, S64 9JP Tel: 01709 581400
Fax: 01709 581339
Email: info@gazettenewspapers.org.uk
Advertising Address: The Brampton Centre, Brampton
Road, Wath-upon-Dearne, ROTHERHAM, S63 6BB
Tel: 01709 581400 Fax: 01709 581339
Email: info@gazettenewspapers.org.uk
Publisher: Denby Print Ltd
Frequency: 26 issues yearly
Cover Price: Free
Circulation: 60,000 (Publisher's Statement)
Advertising Manager: Carol Lunn
ADVERTISING RATES:
Full Page Mono £1088.00
SCC £4.50
Agency Commission: 10%
Mechanical Data: Type Area: 340 x 261mm, Col Length:
340mm, Page Width: 261mm, Film: Digital, No. of Columns
(Display): 8
Copy instructions: Copy Date: Monday prior to publication
date
Series owner and contact point for the following titles,
see individual entries:
Barnsley Gazette
Doncaster Gazette
Rotherham Gazette
LOCAL NEWSPAPERS: Local Newspapers English
Counties

Non-National Newspapers

ROTHWELL & OULTON EXTRA
1663896U72B-3910_231

Frequency: Weekly - See Wakefield Extra for circulation figure
Cover Price: Free
ADVERTISING RATES:
Full Page Mono £1655.46
Full Page Colour £2152.10
SCC £5.41
Part of Series, see entry for: Wakefield Express Series
LOCAL NEWSPAPERS: Local Newspapers English Counties

ROYAL BOROUGH OBSERVER
43283U72B-190_253

Formerly: Windsor, Ascot & Maidenhead Observer
Frequency: Weekly - Circulation figure includes the Slough & South Bucks Observer
Circulation: 12,500 (Publisher's Statement)
Part of Series, see entry for: Slough & Windsor Observer Series
LOCAL NEWSPAPERS: Local Newspapers English Counties

ROYAL LEAMINGTON SPA OBSERVER
44508U72B-3382_150

Frequency: Weekly
Cover Price: Free
Circulation: 47,456 (VFD 02/07/2007 to 30/12/2007)
ADVERTISING: Rates on application
Part of Series, see entry for: Leamington & Stratford Observer Series
LOCAL NEWSPAPERS: Local Newspapers English Counties

ROYAL LEAMINGTON SPA TIMES
1698081U72B-3964_102

Frequency: Weekly - Published on Wednesday
Cover Price: Free
Part of Series, see entry for: Times Series (Coventry, Leamington, Warwick & Kenilworth)
LOCAL NEWSPAPERS: Local Newspapers English Counties

ROYSTON CROW
43820U72B-1588

Formerly: Royston & Baldock Crow Series
Editorial Address: Heath House, Princes Mews, ROYSTON, SG8 9RT **Tel:** 01763 245241 **Fax:** 01763 242231
Email: news@royston-crow.co.uk
Advertising Address: Bank House, Primett Road, Stevenage, HERTFORDSHIRE, SG1 3EE **Tel:** 01438 866000
Fax: 01438 866060
Email: sales@royston-crow.co.uk
Web site: http://www.roystoncrow.co.uk
Publisher: Archant Herts & Cambs
Frequency: Weekly - Published on Thursday
Cover Price: Free
Circulation: 15,578 (VFD 02/07/2007 to 30/12/2007)
Editor: Darren Isted; **Advertising Manager:** Jackie Bevan
ADVERTISING RATES:
Full Page Mono £1506.60
Full Page Colour £1807.92
SCC £4.65
Agency Commission: 10%
Mechanical Data: Type Area: 360 x 270mm, Col Widths (Display): 27mm, Page Width: 270mm, Col Length: 360mm, No. of Columns (Display): 9
Copy instructions: Copy Date: Tuesday 5pm prior to publication date
Average advertising content per issue: 47.87%
LOCAL NEWSPAPERS: Local Newspapers English Counties

ROYSTON WEEKLY NEWS
43322U72B-350_185

Frequency: Weekly
Cover Price: Free
Circulation: 13,717 (VFD 02/07/2007 to 30/12/2007)
ADVERTISING RATES:
SCC £3.45
Part of Series, see entry for: Cambridge Weekly News & Crier Series
LOCAL NEWSPAPERS: Local Newspapers English Counties

RUGBY ADVERTISER
1646140U72B-3400_100

Frequency: Weekly
Cover Price: £0.35
Circulation: 10,891 (ABC 02/07/2007 to 30/12/2007)

ADVERTISING RATES:
Full Page Mono £1545.30
Full Page Colour £2008.89
SCC £5.05
Part of Series, see entry for: Rugby Advertiser and Review Series
LOCAL NEWSPAPERS: Local Newspapers English Counties

RUGBY ADVERTISER AND REVIEW SERIES
44516U72B-3400

Formerly: Rugby Advertiser
Editorial Address: 2 Albert Street, RUGBY, CV21 2RS
Tel: 01788 539977 **Fax:** 01788 539960
Email: editorial@rugbyadvertiser.co.uk
Advertising Address: As above. **Tel:** 01788 539999
Fax: 01788 541274
Email: ginny.hunter@hoenews.com
Web site: http://www.rugbyadvertiser.co.uk
Publisher: Johnston Press plc
Date Established: 1846
Frequency: Weekly
Cover Price: £0.35
Circulation: 56,936 (Combined Circulation)
Editor: Philip Hibble; **News Editor:** Philip Hibble
ADVERTISING RATES:
Full Page Mono £2270.52
Full Page Colour £2951.67
SCC £7.42
Agency Commission: 10%
Mechanical Data: Type Area: 340 x 268mm, Col Length: 340mm, Col Widths (Display): 25mm, Page Width: 268mm, No. of Columns (Display): 9, Film: Digital
Copy instructions: Copy Date: Tuesday 1pm prior to publication date
Average advertising content per issue: 60%
Series owner and contact point for the following titles, see individual entries:
Rugby Advertiser
Rugby Review
LOCAL NEWSPAPERS: Local Newspapers English Counties

THE RUGBY OBSERVER
1817455U72B-3392_100

Frequency: Weekly - Published on Thursdays
Cover Price: Free
Circulation: 41,260 (VFD 03/07/2006 to 31/12/2006)
Usual Pagination: 80
ADVERTISING RATES:
Full Page Mono £1795.00
Part of Series, see entry for: The Rugby Observer Series
LOCAL NEWSPAPERS: Local Newspapers English Counties

THE RUGBY OBSERVER SERIES
44517U72B-3392

Formerly: The Rugby Observer
Editorial Address: 28 Regent Street, RUGBY, CV21 2PS
Tel: 01788 535147 **Fax:** 01788 577114
Email: editor@observerstandard.com
Advertising Address: 45 The Parade, LEAMINGTON SPA, CV32 4BL **Tel:** 01926 451900 **Fax:** 01926 451754
Email: dawn.jones@observerstandard.com
Web site: http://www.therugbyobserver.co.uk
Publisher: Bullivant Media Limited
Date Established: 1991
Frequency: Weekly - Published on Thursday
Cover Price: Free
Circulation: 42,974 (Publisher's Statement)
Editor: Chris Smith
ADVERTISING: Rates on application
Agency Commission: 10%
Copy instructions: Copy Date: Tuesday 5pm prior to publication date
Average advertising content per issue: 70%
Series owner and contact point for the following titles, see individual entries:
The Lutterworth Observer
The Rugby Observer
LOCAL NEWSPAPERS: Local Newspapers English Counties

RUGBY REVIEW
1646141U72B-3400_101

ISSN: 0962-3035
Frequency: Weekly
Cover Price: Free
Circulation: 46,045 (Publisher's Statement)
ADVERTISING RATES:
Full Page Mono £1193.40
Full Page Colour £1551.42
SCC £3.90

Part of Series, see entry for: Rugby Advertiser and Review Series
LOCAL NEWSPAPERS: Local Newspapers English Counties

THE RUGBY TIMES
1750250U72B-4046

Editorial Address: Coventry Newspapers Ltd, Corporation Street, COVENTRY, CV1 1FP **Tel:** 024 7663 3633
Fax: 024 7650 0232
Email: darren_parkin@mrn.co.uk
Advertising Address: As above. **Fax:** 024 7650 0583
Email: retail_fieldsales@mrn.co.uk
Web site: http://www.timeslive.com
Publisher: Trinity Mirror
Date Established: 2006
Frequency: Weekly
Cover Price: Free
Circulation: 33,944 (Publisher's Statement)
Editor: Darren Parkin; **Advertising Manager:** Alex Blasdale
ADVERTISING RATES:
SCC £5.85
Agency Commission: 10%
Copy instructions: Copy Date: Friday 5pm prior to publication date
LOCAL NEWSPAPERS: Local Newspapers English Counties

RUGELEY MERCURY
44309U72B-2990_16

Formerly: Rugeley and Cannock Mercury
Web site: http://www.thisisrugeley.co.uk
Frequency: Weekly
Cover Price: Free
Circulation: 9,445 (VFD 02/07/2007 to 30/12/2007)
ADVERTISING RATES:
SCC £5.1
Part of Series, see entry for: Lichfield Mercury Series
LOCAL NEWSPAPERS: Local Newspapers English Counties

RUGELEY POST
44294U72B-2963_19

Frequency: Weekly
Cover Price: Free
ADVERTISING RATES:
SCC £4.1
Part of Series, see entry for: Chase Post Series (Lichfield & Rugeley)
LOCAL NEWSPAPERS: Local Newspapers English Counties

RUNCORN & WIDNES NEWS & HERALD SERIES
43390U72B-48

Formerly: Runcorn & Widnes Weekly News Series
Editorial Address: 2 Robert Street, WIDNES, WA8 6LY
Tel: 0151 422 3560 **Fax:** 0151 423 1336
Email: runcorn.news@cheshirenews.co.uk
Advertising Address: 123 Main Street, FRODSHAM, WA6 7AF **Tel:** 01928 736220 **Fax:** 01928 736208
Email: trade.ads@buysell.co.uk
Web site: http://www.iccheshireonline.co.uk
Publisher: Trinity Mirror Cheshire
Date Established: 1874
Frequency: Weekly - Published on Thursday and Friday
Circulation: 42,205 (Combined Circulation)
Editor: Rob Hopkins; **News Editor:** Adrian Short; **Advertising Manager:** Vivienne Morgan
ADVERTISING: Rates on application
Copy instructions: Copy Date: Tuesday 12.30pm prior to publication date
Series owner and contact point for the following titles, see individual entries:
Herald and Post (Runcorn)
Runcorn Weekly News
Widnes Weekly News
LOCAL NEWSPAPERS: Local Newspapers English Counties

RUNCORN & WIDNES WORLD
43391U72B-48

Formerly: Runcorn World Series
Editorial Address: The Academy, Bridge Street, WARRINGTON, WA1 2RU **Tel:** 01925 434116
Fax: 01925 434115
Email: newsroom@worldgroup.co.uk
Advertising Address: As above. **Tel:** 01925 434000
Fax: 01925 434059
Email: djohnson@guardiangrp.co.uk
Web site: http://www.runcornandwidnesworld.co.uk
Publisher: Newsquest Media Group
Frequency: Weekly - Published on Wednesday
Cover Price: Free
Circulation: 39,234 (Publisher's Statement)
Editor: Barbara Jordan; **Advertising Manager:** David Johnson

ADVERTISING: Rates on application
Agency Commission: 10%
Copy instructions: Copy Date: Monday 5pm prior to publication date
Average advertising content per issue: 70%
LOCAL NEWSPAPERS: Local Newspapers English Counties

RUNCORN WEEKLY NEWS
765064U72B-484_160

Frequency: Weekly - Circulation includes Widnes Weekly News. Published on Thursday
Cover Price: £0.60
Circulation: 12,802 (ABC 02/07/2007 to 30/12/2007)
ADVERTISING: Rates on application
Part of Series, see entry for: Runcorn & Widnes News & Herald Series
LOCAL NEWSPAPERS: Local Newspapers English Counties

RUTHERGLEN REFORMER
45023U72D-838

Formerly: Reformer (Rutherglen)
Editorial Address: 89 Main Street, Rutherglen, GLASGOW, G73 2JQ **Tel:** 0141 647 2271 **Fax:** 0141 613 1298
Email: rutherglenreformer@s-un.co.uk
Advertising Address: Press Buildings, Campbell Street, HAMILTON, ML3 6AX **Tel:** 01698 283200
Fax: 01698 425706
Web site: http://www.iclanarkshire.co.uk
Publisher: Scottish and Universal Newspapers Hamilton
Date Established: 1875
Frequency: Weekly - Published on Wednesday
Cover Price: £0.70
Circulation: 4,277 (ABC 02/07/2007 to 30/12/2007)
Editor: Kenny Smith; **Advertising Manager:** Caroline Parker
ADVERTISING RATES:
Full Page Mono £1731.60
Full Page Colour £2337.66
SCC £5.55
Mechanical Data: Type Area: 390 x 270mm, No. of Columns (Display): 8, Col Length: 390mm, Page Width: 270mm
LOCAL NEWSPAPERS: Local Newspapers Scotland

RUTLAND & STAMFORD MERCURY AND CITIZEN SERIES
44069U72B-2274

Editorial Address: Mercury House, 7 Sheep Market, STAMFORD, PE9 2QZ **Tel:** 01780 762255
Fax: 01780 751371
Email: smeditor@stamfordmercury.co.uk
Advertising Address: As above.
Email: emma.thornton@stamfordmercury.co.uk
Web site: http://www.stamfordmercury.co.uk
Publisher: Johnston Press plc
Date Established: 1695
Frequency: Weekly - Published on Tuesday and Friday
Circulation: 20,490 (ABC 02/07/2007 to 30/12/2007)
Editor: Lisa Bruen; **News Editor:** Lisa Bruen
ADVERTISING RATES:
SCC £6.89
Agency Commission: 10%
Mechanical Data: Type Area: 340 x 270mm, Col Length: 340mm, Col Widths (Display): 27mm, No. of Columns (Display): 9, Page Width: 270mm, Film: Digital
Copy instructions: Copy Date: Monday 5.00pm prior to publication date
Average advertising content per issue: 65%
Series owner and contact point for the following titles, see individual entries:
Rutland Mercury
The Stamford, Bourne and The Deepings Citizen
Stamford Mercury (Bourne Edition)
Stamford Mercury (Stamford and Deepings Edition)
Supplement(s): Mercury Property Today - 52xY
LOCAL NEWSPAPERS: Local Newspapers English Counties

RUTLAND MERCURY
44070U72B-2274_150

Frequency: Weekly - Circulation figure includes Stamford Mercury (Bourne Edition) and Stamford Mercury (Stamford and Deepings Edition)
Cover Price: £0.50
Circulation: 20,490 (ABC 02/07/2007 to 30/12/2007)
Part of Series, see entry for: Rutland & Stamford Mercury and Citizen Series
LOCAL NEWSPAPERS: Local Newspapers English Counties

RUTLAND TIMES
44028U72B-2191

Editorial Address: Times House, 43 South Street, OAKHAM, LE15 6BG **Tel:** 01572 758888 **Fax:** 01572 755599
Email: rutland.editorial@jpress.co.uk
Advertising Address: As above. **Fax:** 01572 758109
Email: robbie.stinson@jpress.co.uk

Web site: http://www.rutland-times.co.uk
Publisher: Johnston Press plc
Frequency: Weekly - Published on Thursday
Cover Price: £0.45
Circulation: 4,562 (ABC 02/07/2007 to 30/12/2007)
Editor: Richard Yetman; **News Editor:** Andrea Scholes; **Managing Director:** Amanda Davison-Young; **Advertising Manager:** Robbie Stinson
ADVERTISING RATES:
Full Page Mono £1377.00
Full Page Colour £1790.10
SCC £4.50
Agency Commission: 10%
Mechanical Data: Page Width: 270mm, Col Length: 340mm, Film: Digital, No. of Columns (Display): 9, Type Area: 340 x 270mm, Col Widths (Display): 30mm, Bleed Size: 344 x 274mm
Copy instructions: Copy Date: Tuesday 4pm prior to publication date
Average advertising content per issue: 40%
Supplement(s): Embrace - 12xY
LOCAL NEWSPAPERS: Local Newspapers English Counties

RYE OBSERVER
44437U72B-3225_200

Formerly: Rye & Battle Observer
Frequency: Weekly - Circulation figure is for the Rye & Battle Observer Series, including Battle Observer
Cover Price: £0.40
Circulation: 6,419 (ABC 02/07/2007 to 30/12/2007)
ADVERTISING: Rates on application
Part of Series, see entry for: Hastings Observer Series
LOCAL NEWSPAPERS: Local Newspapers English Counties

SAFFRON WALDEN WEEKLY NEWS
43323U72B-350_190

Frequency: Weekly
Cover Price: Free
Circulation: 19,531 (VFD 02/07/2007 to 30/12/2007)
ADVERTISING RATES:
SCC £3.45
Part of Series, see entry for: Cambridge Weekly News & Crier Series
LOCAL NEWSPAPERS: Local Newspapers English Counties

SALE & ALTRINCHAM MESSENGER
43713U72B-1287_150

Frequency: Weekly
Cover Price: Free
Circulation: 47,625 (VFD 02/07/2007 to 30/12/2007)
ADVERTISING: Rates on application
Part of Series, see entry for: Sale & Altrincham Messenger Series
LOCAL NEWSPAPERS: Local Newspapers English Counties

SALE & ALTRINCHAM MESSENGER SERIES
43712U72B-1287

Editorial Address: 7 Crossford Court, Dane Road, SALE, M33 7BZ **Tel:** 0161 908 3380 **Fax:** 0161 908 3403
Email: sam.editorial@messengergrp.co.uk
Advertising Address: As above. **Fax:** 0161 908 3402
Email: nick.fellows@messengergrp.co.uk
Web site: http://www.messengernewspapers.co.uk
ISSN: 1466-3066
Publisher: Newsquest Media Group
Date Established: 1974
Frequency: Weekly - Published on Thursday
Cover Price: Free
Circulation: 72,335 (Combined Circulation)
Editor: Carla Flynn; **Features Editor:** Christine Klabacher; **Advertising Manager:** Nick Fellows; **Publisher:** Nuala O'Rourke
ADVERTISING: Rates on application
Mechanical Data: No. of Columns (Display): 9, Col Length: 340mm, Film: Digital
Series owner and contact point for the following titles, see individual entries:
Sale & Altrincham Messenger
Stretford & Urmston Messenger
LOCAL NEWSPAPERS: Local Newspapers English Counties

SALFORD ADVERTISER
43717U72B-1290_140

Formerly: Advertiser & Salford City Reporter
Frequency: Weekly
Cover Price: Free
Circulation: 88,614 (VFD 02/07/2007 to 30/12/2007)

Part of Series, see entry for: Salford Advertiser Series
LOCAL NEWSPAPERS: Local Newspapers English Counties

SALFORD ADVERTISER SERIES
43715U72B-1290

Formerly: Salford City Reporter & Advertiser Series
Editorial Address: 30 Church Street, Eccles, MANCHESTER, M30 0DF **Tel:** 0161 789 5015
Fax: 0161 787 8081
Email: salfordadvertiser@menmedia.co.uk
Advertising Address: Drake Street, ROCHDALE, OL16 1PH **Tel:** 01706 354321 **Fax:** 01706 750227
Email: mark.stansfield@menmediasales.co.uk
Web site: http://www.salfordadvertiser.co.uk
Publisher: MEN Media
Frequency: Weekly - Published every Thursday
Cover Price: Free
Circulation: 123,190 (Combined Circulation)
Editor: Vince Hale; **Advertising Manager:** Mark Stansfield
ADVERTISING RATES:
SCC £8.25
Agency Commission: 10%
Mechanical Data: Page Width: 267mm, Film: Digital, Type Area: 340 x 267mm, Col Length: 340mm, Col Widths (Display): 27mm, No. of Columns (Display): 9
Copy instructions: Copy Date: Tuesday 3.30pm prior to publication date
Average advertising content per issue: 60%
Series owner and contact point for the following titles, see individual entries:
The Advertiser Prestwich, Whitefield & Radcliffe
Salford Advertiser
LOCAL NEWSPAPERS: Local Newspapers English Counties

SALISBURY JOURNAL
44575U72B-3520_190

Frequency: Weekly - Circulation figure includes Amesbury Journal and The Forest Journal
Cover Price: £0.65
Circulation: 26,995 (ABC 01/01/2007 to 30/12/2007)
ADVERTISING RATES:
SCC £6.00
Part of Series, see entry for: Salisbury Journal & Avon Advertiser Series
LOCAL NEWSPAPERS: Local Newspapers English Counties

SALISBURY JOURNAL & AVON ADVERTISER SERIES
44572U72B-3520

Formerly: Salisbury Newspapers Series
Editorial Address: Rollestone House, 8-12 Rollestone Street, SALISBURY, SP1 1DY **Tel:** 01722 426511
Fax: 01722 321854
Email: newsdesk@salisburyjournal.co.uk
Advertising Address: As above. **Tel:** 01722 426500
Fax: 01722 426591
Email: sales@salisburyjournal.co.uk
Web site: http://www.thisissalisbury.co.uk
Publisher: Salisbury Newspapers Ltd
Date Established: 1729
Frequency: Weekly - Published on Wednesday and Thursday
Circulation: 99,503 (Combined Circulation)
Editor: Morwenna Blake; **News Editor:** Morwenna Blake; **Advertising Manager:** Debbie Potter; **Publisher:** Bill Browne
ADVERTISING: Rates on application
Agency Commission: 10%
Copy instructions: Copy Date: Monday 5pm prior to publication date
Series owner and contact point for the following titles, see individual entries:
Avon Advertiser Hants & Dorset Edition
Avon Advertiser Salisbury Edition
The Forest Journal
Salisbury Journal
LOCAL NEWSPAPERS: Local Newspapers English Counties

SALTASH JOURNAL
764864U72B-545_142

Frequency: Weekly - For circulation, see Liskeard and Callington Gazette
Cover Price: Free
ADVERTISING RATES:
Full Page Mono £1065.60
Full Page Colour £1324.80
SCC £3.70
Part of Series, see entry for: Cornish Times & Gazette Series
LOCAL NEWSPAPERS: Local Newspapers English Counties

Non-National Newspapers

SANDBACH CHRONICLE
43362U72B-445_150

Frequency: Weekly
Cover Price: £0.40
Part of Series, see entry for: Congleton Chronicle Series
LOCAL NEWSPAPERS: Local Newspapers English Counties

SANDHURST & CROWTHORNE NEWS & MAIL
43769U72B-1382_210

Formerly: Sandhurst & Crowthorne News
Frequency: Weekly - Circulation figure is incorporated into the Aldershot News & Mail
Cover Price: £0.37
ADVERTISING: Rates on application
Part of Series, see entry for: Aldershot Mail and News Series
LOCAL NEWSPAPERS: Local Newspapers English Counties

SANDWELL AND GREAT BARR CHRONICLE SERIES
44523U72B-3418

Formerly: Birmingham Chronicle Series
Editorial Address: 51-53 Queen Street, WOLVERHAMPTON, WV1 1ES **Tel:** 01902 313131
Fax: 01902 319467
Email: sandwellchronicle@expressandstar.co.uk
Advertising Address: Black Lake, WEST BROMWICH, B70 0QB **Tel:** 0121 553 7171 **Fax:** 0121 553 4668
Email: b.wain@expressandstar.co.uk
Web site: http://www.yourchronicle.com
Publisher: Express & Star Ltd
Frequency: Weekly - Published on Thursday
Cover Price: Free
Circulation: 94,540 (Combined Circulation)
Editor: Leon Burakowski; **Advertising Manager:** Brian Wain
ADVERTISING: Rates on application
Copy instructions: Copy Date: Tuesday 12 noon prior to publication date
Series owner and contact point for the following titles, see individual entries:
The Chronicle (Great Barr)
The Chronicle (Sandwell)
Supplement(s): Out and About - 2xY
LOCAL NEWSPAPERS: Local Newspapers English Counties

SATURDAY PLUS
46106U67H-431

Formerly: Saturday
Editorial Address: 1 Central Quay, GLASGOW, G3 8DA
Tel: 0141 309 3344 **Fax:** 0141 309 3850
Email: l.cowan@sundaymail.co.uk
Advertising Address: As above. **Tel:** 0141 248 2727
Fax: 0141 309 3545
Email: advertising@dailyrecord.co.uk
Web site: http://www.dailyrecord.co.uk
Publisher: Trinity Mirror
Frequency: Weekly - See main record for circulation figure
Cover Price: Free
Usual Pagination: 24
Editor: Liz Cowan; **Editor-in-Chief:** Bruce Waddell; **Managing Director:** Mark Hollinshead; **Advertising Manager:** Shelly Dee Vallance
Summary of Content: Lifestyle magazine with features on celebrities, gardening, interiors, health & parenting, restaurants, days out, travel and shopping.
Readership/Target Audience: Read primarily by women aged 20 years old and over.
ADVERTISING RATES:
Full Page Colour £12000.00
Agency Commission: 15%
Mechanical Data: Film: Digital
Copy instructions: Copy Date: 8 days prior to publication date
Average advertising content per issue: 30%
Supplement to: Daily Record
REGIONAL DAILY & SUNDAY NEWSPAPERS: Regional Colour Supplements

SAWSTON CRIER
1655746U72B-350_202

Frequency: Monthly
Cover Price: Free
Circulation: 3,000 (Publisher's Statement)
ADVERTISING RATES:
SCC £7.10
Part of Series, see entry for: Cambridge Weekly News & Crier Series
LOCAL NEWSPAPERS: Local Newspapers English Counties

SCARBOROUGH EVENING NEWS
42166U67B-1010

Editorial Address: 17-23 Aberdeen Walk, SCARBOROUGH, YO11 1BB **Tel:** 01723 363636 **Fax:** 01723 379033
Email: editorial@ynlltd.co.uk
Advertising Address: As above. **Fax:** 01723 383825
Email: jenny.harrison@ypn.co.uk
Web site: http://www.scarboroughevingnews.co.uk/
Publisher: Yorkshire Regional Newspapers Ltd
Date Established: 1882
Frequency: Evenings - Not published on Sunday
Cover Price: £0.37
Circulation: 17,239 (Publisher's Statement)
Editor: John Ritchie; **News Editor:** John Ritchie; **Managing Director:** Jason Rewse-Davis
ADVERTISING RATES:
Full Page Mono £1989.00
Full Page Colour £2585.70
SCC £6.50
Agency Commission: 10%
Mechanical Data: Col Length: 340mm, No. of Columns (Display): 9, Film: Digital, Col Widths (Display): 28mm, Page Width: 274mm, Type Area: 340 x 274mm
Copy instructions: Copy Date: 2 days prior to publication date
Average advertising content per issue: 30%
Supplement(s): Local Life - 4xY
REGIONAL DAILY & SUNDAY NEWSPAPERS: Regional Daily Newspapers

SCOTLAND ON SUNDAY
42295U67C-36

Editorial Address: 108 Holyrood Road, EDINBURGH, EH8 8AS **Tel:** 0131 620 8620 **Fax:** 0131 620 8491
Email: jwatson@scotlandonsunday.com
Advertising Address: As above. **Tel:** 0131 620 8963
Fax: 0131 523 0373
Email: avipond@scotsman.com
Web site: http://www.scotlandonsunday.com
Publisher: The Scotsman Publications Ltd
Date Established: 1988
Frequency: Sunday
Cover Price: £1.40
Circulation: 65,000 (ABC 03/08/2009 to 30/08/2009)
Editor: News Desk; **News Editor:** Jeremy Watson; **Managing Director:** Michael Johnston
ADVERTISING RATES:
Full Page Mono £11668.80
Full Page Colour £14586.00
SCC £26.52
Agency Commission: 15%
Mechanical Data: No. of Columns (Display): 8, Col Widths (Display): 410mm, Col Length: 550mm, Type Area: 550 x 356mm
Copy instructions: Copy Date: Friday 12 noon prior to publication date
Average advertising content per issue: 30%
Supplement(s): Appointments - 52xY, At Home - 52xY, Business (Scotland on Sunday) - 52xY, Review - 52xY, Spectrum Magazine Scotland on Sunday - 52xY, Sport - 52xY
REGIONAL DAILY & SUNDAY NEWSPAPERS: Regional Sunday Newspapers

SCOTLAND ON SUNDAY (CITY/LONDON OFFICE)
42306U67D-280

Formerly: Scotland on Sunday Edinburgh City/London Office
Editorial Address: Dolphyn Court, 10-11 Great Turnstile, LONDON, WC1V 7JU **Tel:** 020 7025 3637
Email: tmurden@scotlandonsunday.com
Web site: http://www.scotlandonsunday.com
Publisher: The Scotsman Publications Ltd
Date Established: 1988
Frequency: Sunday
Cover Price: £1.40
Editor: Martin Flanagan
ADVERTISING: No Advertising taken
REGIONAL DAILY & SUNDAY NEWSPAPERS: Regional Daily Sunday London City Office

THE SCOTSMAN
42260U67B-2250

Editorial Address: 108 Holyrood Road, EDINBURGH, EH8 8AS **Tel:** 0131 620 8620 **Fax:** 0131 620 8616
Email: newsdesk_ts@scotsman.com
Advertising Address: As above. **Tel:** 0131 620 8978
Fax: 0131 523 0322
Web site: http://www.scotsman.com
Publisher: The Scotsman Publications Ltd
Frequency: Mornings - Not published on Sunday
Cover Price: £0.70
Circulation: 50,750 (ABC 03/08/2009 to 30/08/2009)
Editor: Frank O'Donnell; **Executive Editor:** Bill Jamieson; **Managing Director:** Michael Johnston
ADVERTISING RATES:
Full Page Mono £5100.00

Full Page Colour £6120.00
SCC £25.00
Supplement(s): Critique - 52xY, Education - 52xY, Friday Review - 52xY, IT and IP - 52xY, The Scotsman Magazine - 52xY, SW - 52xY
REGIONAL DAILY & SUNDAY NEWSPAPERS: Regional Daily Newspapers

THE SCOTSMAN (CITY/LONDON OFFICE)
42307U67D-320

Formerly: The Scotsman (Edinburgh) (City/London Office)
Editorial Address: Dolphyn Court, 10-11 Great Turnstile, LONDON, WC1V 7JU **Tel:** 020 7025 3635
Email: mflanagan@scotsman.com
Web site: http://www.scotsman.com
Publisher: The Scotsman Publications Ltd
Cover Price: £0.70
Editor: Martin Flanagan; **Circulation Manager:** Ken Reed
ADVERTISING: No Advertising taken
REGIONAL DAILY & SUNDAY NEWSPAPERS: Regional Daily Sunday London City Office

THE SCOTSMAN (GLASGOW OFFICE)
42311U67E-500

Editorial Address: 80 St. Vincent Street, GLASGOW, G2 5UB **Tel:** 0141 236 6400 **Fax:** 0141 236 6417
Email: newsdesk_ts@scotsman.com
Web site: http://www.scotsman.com
Publisher: The Scotsman Publications Ltd
Date Established: 1816
Editor: Craig Brown
REGIONAL DAILY & SUNDAY NEWSPAPERS: Regional Offices

THE SCOTSMAN MAGAZINE
624240U67H-376

Editorial Address: 108 Holyrood Road, EDINBURGH, EH8 8AS **Tel:** 0131 620 8620 **Fax:** 0131 620 8617
Advertising Address: As above. **Fax:** 0131 523 0373
Web site: http://www.scotsman.com
Publisher: The Scotsman Publications Ltd
Frequency: Weekly - See main record for circulation figure
Editor: Alison Gray
Summary of Content: Lifestyle magazine covering fashion, beauty and style with celebrity interviews.
ADVERTISING RATES:
Full Page Colour £5469.75
Mechanical Data: Type Area: 332 x 254mm, Bleed Size: 368 x 286mm, Trim Size: 356 x 282mm, Col Length: 332mm, Page Width: 254mm, Film: Digital
Copy instructions: Copy Date: 1 week prior to publication date
Supplement to: The Scotsman
REGIONAL DAILY & SUNDAY NEWSPAPERS: Regional Colour Supplements

SCOTTISH REVIEW OF BOOKS
1667077U67H-355

Editorial Address: 42 New Street, MUSSELBURGH, EH21 6JN **Tel:** 0131 665 7885 **Fax:** 0131 665 7885
Email: aftaylor2000@aol.com
Advertising Address: 200 Renfield Street, GLASGOW, G2 3QB **Tel:** 0141 302 6021 **Fax:** 0141 302 6363
Email: pauline.cairns@glasgow.newsquest.co.uk
Publisher: Scottish Review of Books
Frequency: Quarterly
Annual Sub.: £12.00
Circulation: 100,000 (Publisher's Statement)
Editor: Alan Taylor; **Advertising Manager:** Pauline Cairns
Summary of Content: Publication with book reviews, essays and interviews covering Scottish books and writers.
ADVERTISING RATES:
SCC £15.00
Mechanical Data: Type Area: 335 x 248mm, Bleed Size: 373 x 278mm, Trim Size: 357 x 270mm, Col Length: 335mm, Page Width: 248mm
Supplement to: Sunday Herald
REGIONAL DAILY & SUNDAY NEWSPAPERS: Regional Colour Supplements

SCUNTHORPE TARGET
44073U72B-227

Formerly: Scunthorpe Target Series
Editorial Address: 4-5 Park Square, SCUNTHORPE, DN15 6JH **Tel:** 01724 273273 **Fax:** 01724 273101
Email: newsdesk@scunthorpetarget.co.uk
Advertising Address: As above. **Tel:** 01724 273113
Email: claire.arthur@gsmg.co.uk
Web site: http://www.thisisscunthorpe.co.uk
Publisher: Grimsby & Scunthorpe Media Group
Frequency: Weekly
Cover Price: Free
Circulation: 58,333 (Publisher's Statement)

Editor: Mike Underwood; **News Editor:** Vicky Cottam; **Advertisement Director:** Claire Arthur
ADVERTISING RATES:
SCC £6.40
Mechanical Data: Col Length: 360mm, No. of Columns (Display): 8, Type Area: 360 x 268mm, Page Width: 268mm, Col Widths (Display): 31mm, Print Process: Web-fed offset litho, Film: Digital
Copy instructions: Copy Date: Friday 5pm prior to publication date
LOCAL NEWSPAPERS: Local Newspapers English Counties

SCUNTHORPE TELEGRAPH
42167U67B-1015
Formerly: Scunthorpe Evening Telegraph
Editorial Address: 4-5 Park Square, Laneham Street, SCUNTHORPE, DN15 6JH **Tel:** 01724 273273
Fax: 01724 273101
Email: newsdesk@scunthorpetelegraph.co.uk
Advertising Address: As above.
Email: adverts@gsmg.co.uk
Web site: http://www.thisisscunthorpe.co.uk
Publisher: Grimsby & Scunthorpe Media Group
Frequency: Mornings - Not published on Sunday
Cover Price: £0.36
Circulation: 20,568 (ABC 02/07/2007 to 30/12/2007)
News Editor: Vicky Cottam
ADVERTISING RATES:
Full Page Mono 1932.48
Full Page Colour 2415.60
Copy instructions: Copy Date: 3.30pm 2 days prior to publication date
Supplement(s): 24/7 - 52xY, Matchday - 52xY, Motors - 52xY, Nostalgia - 12xY, Property - 52xY, Sport Extra - 52xY, Trains - 4xY
REGIONAL DAILY & SUNDAY NEWSPAPERS: Regional Daily Newspapers

SEAFORD GAZETTE
44443U72B-3240_170
Frequency: Weekly
Cover Price: £0.35
Circulation: 1,712 (Publisher's Statement)
Part of Series, see entry for: Eastbourne Herald & Gazette Series
LOCAL NEWSPAPERS: Local Newspapers English Counties

SEAHAM STAR
44495U72B-3371_136
Frequency: Weekly
Cover Price: Free
Circulation: 8,906 (VFD 02/07/2007 to 30/12/2007)
ADVERTISING RATES:
SCC £4.48
Part of Series, see entry for: Star Series
LOCAL NEWSPAPERS: Local Newspapers English Counties

SELBY POST
706728U72B-3640
Editorial Address: 11 The Crescent, SELBY, YO8 4PD
Tel: 01757 291087 **Fax:** 01757 707787
Email: editorial@selbypost.co.uk
Advertising Address: 102 Boothferry Road, GOOLE, DN14 5AE **Tel:** 01405 720110 **Fax:** 01405 720003
Email: advertising@gooletimes.co.uk
Web site: http://www.selbypost.co.uk
Publisher: Chronicle Publications Ltd
Date Established: 2000
Frequency: Weekly - Published on Thursday
Cover Price: £0.10
Circulation: 5,000 (Publisher's Statement)
Usual Pagination: 56
Editor: Dan Murphy; **News Editor:** Dan Murphy;
Advertising Manager: Natalie Stuart
ADVERTISING RATES:
Full Page Mono £1406.00
Full Page Colour £1556.00
SCC £3.80
Agency Commission: 10%
Mechanical Data: No. of Columns (Display): 10, Trim Size: 370 x 265mm, Bleed Size: 376 x 283mm, Film: Digital, Print Process: Web-fed offset
Copy instructions: Copy Date: Tuesday, 4pm prior to publication date
Average advertising content per issue: 65%
LOCAL NEWSPAPERS: Local Newspapers English Counties

SELBY STAR
44666U72B-3645_190
Frequency: Weekly
Cover Price: Free
Circulation: 15,454 (VFD 02/07/2007 to 30/12/2007)
ADVERTISING RATES:
Full Page Mono £428.40

Full Page Colour £535.00
SCC £1.40
Part of Series, see entry for: Star Series (Selby & York)
LOCAL NEWSPAPERS: Local Newspapers English Counties

SELBY TIMES
44664U72B-3643_170
Frequency: Weekly
Cover Price: £0.40
Circulation: 8,926 (ABC 02/07/2007 to 30/12/2007)
ADVERTISING RATES:
SCC £2.70
Copy instructions: Copy Date: Tuesday 11am prior to publication date
Part of Series, see entry for: Selby Times Series
LOCAL NEWSPAPERS: Local Newspapers English Counties

SELBY TIMES COURIER
44663U72B-3643_160
Formerly: Selby Times Extra
Frequency: Weekly
Cover Price: Free
Circulation: 13,075 (VFD 02/01/2006 to 02/07/2006)
ADVERTISING RATES:
SCC £2.56
Copy instructions: Copy Date: Wednesday 12pm prior to publication date
Part of Series, see entry for: Selby Times Series
LOCAL NEWSPAPERS: Local Newspapers English Counties

SELBY TIMES SERIES
44662U72B-3643
Editorial Address: 74-76 Gowthorpe, SELBY, YO8 4ET
Tel: 01757 702198 **Fax:** 01757 705468
Email: editorial@selbytimes.co.uk
Advertising Address: As above. **Tel:** 01757 702802
Email: lorainelaybourn@selbytimes.co.uk
Web site: http://www.selbytimes.co.uk
Publisher: South Yorkshire Newspapers Ltd
Frequency: Weekly - Published on Thursday
Circulation: 22,001 (Combined Circulation)
Editor: Richard Parker
ADVERTISING RATES:
SCC £3.61
Agency Commission: 10%
Mechanical Data: Type Area: 340 x 274mm, Col Length: 340mm, Page Width: 274mm, No. of Columns (Display): 9, Col Widths (Display): 27.78mm, Film: Digital
Copy instructions: Copy Date: Tuesday 11am prior to publication date
Series owner and contact point for the following titles, see individual entries:
Selby Times
Selby Times Courier
LOCAL NEWSPAPERS: Local Newspapers English Counties

SELKIRK WEEKEND ADVERTISER
45025U72D-870
Editorial Address: The Hermitage, High Street, SELKIRK, TD7 4DA **Tel:** 01750 721581 **Fax:** 01750 721239
Email: theweepaper@tweeddalepress.co.uk
Advertising Address: As above.
Email: southernsales@tweeddalepress.co.uk
Web site: http://www.selkirktoday.co.uk
Publisher: Tweeddale Press Group
Frequency: Weekly
Cover Price: £0.30
Circulation: 3,500 (Publisher's Statement)
Editor: Bob Burgess
ADVERTISING RATES:
Full Page Mono £657.90
Full Page Colour £980.90
SCC £2.21
Agency Commission: 10%
Mechanical Data: Type Area: 340 x 272mm, No. of Columns (Display): 9, Col Length: 340mm, Page Width: 272mm, Film: Digital
Copy instructions: Copy Date: Monday 10am prior to publication date
LOCAL NEWSPAPERS: Local Newspapers Scotland

THE SENTINEL (CHESHIRE)
1657250U67B-1060_612
Frequency: Daily
Cover Price: £0.32
ADVERTISING: Rates on application
Edition of: The Sentinel Stoke-on-Trent
REGIONAL DAILY & SUNDAY NEWSPAPERS: Regional Daily Newspapers

THE SENTINEL (CITY FINAL)
42182U67B-1060_610
Cover Price: £0.32
ADVERTISING: Rates on application
Edition of: The Sentinel Stoke-on-Trent
REGIONAL DAILY & SUNDAY NEWSPAPERS: Regional Daily Newspapers

THE SENTINEL (FIRST)
1657248U67B-1060_611
Frequency: Daily
Cover Price: £0.32
ADVERTISING: Rates on application
Edition of: The Sentinel Stoke-on-Trent
REGIONAL DAILY & SUNDAY NEWSPAPERS: Regional Daily Newspapers

THE SENTINEL (MOORLANDS)
42180U67B-1060_580
Cover Price: £0.32
ADVERTISING: Rates on application
Edition of: The Sentinel Stoke-on-Trent
REGIONAL DAILY & SUNDAY NEWSPAPERS: Regional Daily Newspapers

THE SENTINEL SERIES
45119U72E-220
Editorial Address: Suite 3, Spencer House, 33 Spencer Road, LONDONDERRY, BT47 6AA **Tel:** 028 7134 8889
Fax: 028 7134 4763
Email: eamon.sweeney@jpress.co.uk
Advertising Address: As above.
Email: garth.mellon@jpress.co.uk
Web site: http://www.londonderrysentinel.co.uk
Publisher: Johnston Press plc
Date Established: 1829
Frequency: Weekly
Circulation: 42,840 (Combined Circulation)
Editor: Eamon Sweeney
ADVERTISING RATES:
Full Page Mono £1484.10
Full Page Colour £2151.96
Agency Commission: 10%
Mechanical Data: Type Area: 340 x 268mm, Col Length: 340mm, Col Widths (Display): 28mm, No. of Columns (Display): 9, Page Width: 268mm, Film: Digital
Series owner and contact point for the following titles, see individual entries:
Londonderry Sentinel
North-West Echo
Roe Valley Sentinel
LOCAL NEWSPAPERS: Local Newspapers Northern Ireland

THE SENTINEL STOKE-ON-TRENT
42177U67B-1060
Editorial Address: Sentinel House, Etruria, STOKE-ON-TRENT, ST1 5SS **Tel:** 01782 602525 **Fax:** 01782 201167
Email: newsdesk@thesentinel.co.uk
Advertising Address: As above. **Fax:** 01782 262617
Email: wendy.wilson@thesentinel.co.uk
Web site: http://www.thisisthesentinel.co.uk
Publisher: Staffordshire Sentinel News & Media Ltd
Date Established: 1854
Frequency: Daily
Cover Price: £0.33
Circulation: 61,910 (ABC 02/07/2007 to 30/12/2007)
Editor: Robert Andrews; **News Editor:** Robert Andrews; **Features Editor:** Richard Bramwell; **Editor-in-Chief:** Mike Sassi; **Managing Director:** Tim Saunders; **Advertising Manager:** Wendy Wilson
ADVERTISING RATES:
Full Page Mono £3398.40
Full Page Colour £4248.00
Agency Commission: 10%
Mechanical Data: Col Widths (Display): 30mm, Col Length: 360mm, No. of Columns (Display): 8, Film: Digital, Page Width: 265mm, Type Area: 360 x 265mm
Copy instructions: Copy Date: 2 days prior to publication date
Editions:
The Sentinel (Cheshire)
The Sentinel (City Final)
The Sentinel (First)
The Sentinel (Moorlands)
Supplement(s): Going Out - 52xY, Staying In - 52xY
REGIONAL DAILY & SUNDAY NEWSPAPERS: Regional Daily Newspapers

SEREN HAFREN
761703U72J-250
Editorial Address: Bacheldre, 11 Hillside Avenue, NEWTOWN, SY16 2PS **Tel:** 01686 626202
Email: meirion.nansi@tiscali.co.uk
Advertising Address: Rhoslwyn, 21 Oaktree Avenue, Barnfields, NEWTOWN, SY16 2LF **Tel:** 01686 625711

Email: anne.rees@drenewydd.freeserve.co.uk
Frequency: 11 issues yearly - Not published in August
Cover Price: £0.40
Circulation: 500 (Publisher's Statement)
Editor: Nansi Lloyd Ellis; **Advertising Manager:** Anne Rees
Summary of Content: Welsh language newspaper covering news from the local villages, including a Welsh learners column and sections on farming, schooling and a children's page.
Language(s): Welsh
Readership/Target Audience: Aimed at Welsh speaking readers in the Severn Valley.
ADVERTISING RATES:
Full Page Mono £80.00
SCC £5.00
Mechanical Data: Col Widths (Display): 70mm, No. of Columns (Display): 3, Film: Digital
Copy instructions: Copy Date: 7 days prior to publication date
Average advertising content per issue: 12%
LOCAL NEWSPAPERS: Community Newsletters

SEVEN DAYS
42316U67H-279
Formerly: XS
Editorial Address: Sunday Mail, One Central Quay, GLASGOW, G3 8DA **Tel:** 0141 309 3871 **Fax:** 0141 309 3587
Email: l.cowan@sundaymail.co.uk
Advertising Address: As above. **Tel:** 0141 248 2727
Fax: 0141 309 3545
Email: p.genasi@dailyrecord.co.uk
Web site: http://www.sundaymail.co.uk
Publisher: Trinity Mirror
Frequency: Weekly - Published on Sunday. See main record for circulation figure
Editor: Liz Cowan; **Advertising Manager:** Paul Genasi
Summary of Content: Magazine containing celebrity and show-biz features, articles on films, music, travel, entertainment and medical issues and an events and listings guide.
ADVERTISING: Rates on application
Supplement to: Sunday Mail
REGIONAL DAILY & SUNDAY NEWSPAPERS: Regional Colour Supplements

SEVENOAKS CHRONICLE SERIES
43931U72B-1885
Formerly: Sevenoaks Chronicle & Focus Series
Editorial Address: 54 High Street, SEVENOAKS, TN13 1JG
Tel: 01732 228000 **Fax:** 01732 456286
Email: reporters@sevenoaks-chronicle.co.uk
Advertising Address: Longfield Road, TUNBRIDGE WELLS, TN2 3HL **Tel:** 01892 681000 **Fax:** 01892 543181
Email: advertising@courier.co.uk
Web site: http://www.thisiskent.co.uk
Publisher: Courier Media Group Ltd
Date Established: 1881
Frequency: Weekly - Published every Thursday
Circulation: 105,776 (Combined Circulation)
Editor-in-Chief: John McCready; **Advertising Director:** David Hobden
ADVERTISING RATES:
Full Page Mono £7286.40
Full Page Colour £8379.36
SCC £25.30
Agency Commission: 10%
Mechanical Data: Type Area: 360 x 270mm, Page Width: 270mm, Col Widths (Display): 32mm, No. of Columns (Display): 8, Col Length: 360mm, Film: Digital
Copy instructions: Copy Date: Monday Tuesday and Thursday 5pm prior to publication date
Average advertising content per issue: 60%
Series owner and contact point for the following titles, see individual entries:
Malling Chronicle
Sevenoaks Chronicle (Sevenoaks Town Edition)
Sevenoaks Chronicle (Westerham Edition)
Supplement(s): Days Out - 1xY, Dining Out - 2xY
LOCAL NEWSPAPERS: Local Newspapers English Counties

SEVENOAKS CHRONICLE (SEVENOAKS TOWN EDITION)
717985U72B-1885_165
Frequency: Weekly - Circulation figure includes the Sevenoaks Chronicle Westerham & Edenbridge edition and the Malling Chronicle
Cover Price: £0.60
Circulation: 12,212 (ABC 02/07/2007 to 30/12/2007)
ADVERTISING RATES:
SCC £5.70
Part of Series, see entry for: Sevenoaks Chronicle Series
LOCAL NEWSPAPERS: Local Newspapers English Counties

SEVENOAKS CHRONICLE (WESTERHAM EDITION)
717983U72B-1885_170
Formerly: Sevenoaks Chronicle (Westerham & Edenbridge Edition)
Frequency: Weekly - Circulation figure is incorporated into the Sevenoaks Chronicle Town edition
Cover Price: £0.60
ADVERTISING RATES:
SCC £5.70
Part of Series, see entry for: Sevenoaks Chronicle Series
LOCAL NEWSPAPERS: Local Newspapers English Counties

SHANKILL MIRROR
1668593U72E-285
Editorial Address: 2 Forthriver Crescent, BELFAST, BT13 3SS **Tel:** 028 9072 9000 **Fax:** 028 9072 9002
Email: news@shankillmirror.com
Advertising Address: As above.
Email: sales@shankillmirror.com
Web site: http://www.shankillmirror.com
Publisher: Shankill Community Media Ltd
Frequency: 19 issues yearly
Cover Price: Free
Circulation: 38,000 (Publisher's Statement)
Editor: John MacVicar
ADVERTISING RATES:
Full Page Mono £932.40
Full Page Colour £1398.60
SCC £5.00
Agency Commission: 15%
Mechanical Data: Type Area: 364 x 262mm, Col Length: 364m, Page Width: 262mm, No. of Columns (Display): 6, Film: Digital
LOCAL NEWSPAPERS: Local Newspapers Northern Ireland

SHEERNESS TIMES GUARDIAN
43934U72B-1890
Formerly: Sheerness Times Guardian and Extra Series
Editorial Address: 44 High Street, SHEERNESS, ME12 1NL
Tel: 01795 580300 **Fax:** 01795 660515
Email: timesguardian@thekmgroup.co.uk
Advertising Address: As above.
Email: timesguardian@thekmgroup.co.uk
Web site: http://www.timesguardian.co.uk
Publisher: Kent Messenger Group
Date Established: 1858
Frequency: Weekly - Published on Thursday
Cover Price: £0.50
Circulation: 8,549 (ABC 02/07/2007 to 30/12/2007)
Editor: Nathan Rao; **Advertising Manager:** Sharon Patrick
ADVERTISING: Rates on application
Agency Commission: 10%
Copy instructions: Copy Date: Friday 5pm prior to publication date
Average advertising content per issue: 70%
Supplement(s): Kent Business - 12xY, What's On - 52xY
LOCAL NEWSPAPERS: Local Newspapers English Counties

SHEFFIELD JOURNAL SERIES
44682U72B-3712
Formerly: Sheffield Journal
Editorial Address: York Street, SHEFFIELD, S1 1PU
Tel: 0114 276 7676 **Fax:** 0114 272 5978
Advertising Address: As above. **Fax:** 0114 242 1282
Email: katie.mitchell@sheffieldnewspapers.co.uk
Web site: http://www.star.co.uk
Publisher: Sheffield Newspapers Ltd
Frequency: Weekly
Cover Price: Free
Circulation: 56,889 (VFD 02/07/2007 to 30/12/2007)
Editor: Charles Smith; **News Editor:** Charles Smith
ADVERTISING: Rates on application
Agency Commission: 10%
Mechanical Data: Film: Digital, Col Length: 340mm, Page Width: 272mm, Type Area: 340 x 272mm, No. of Columns (Display): 9
Copy instructions: Copy Date: Monday 5pm prior to publication date
Average advertising content per issue: 60%
Series owner and contact point for the following titles, see individual entries:
The Chapeltown and District Journal
The Hillsborough and District Journal
The Stocksbridge and District Journal
LOCAL NEWSPAPERS: Local Newspapers English Counties

SHEFFIELD TELEGRAPH
44683U72B-3714
Editorial Address: York Street, SHEFFIELD, S1 1PU
Tel: 0114 276 7676 **Fax:** 0114 272 5978
Email: sheffieldtelegraph@sheffieldnewspapers.co.uk
Advertising Address: As above. **Fax:** 0114 252 1227
Email: carolyn.rawlings@sheffieldnewspapers.co.uk

Web site: http://www.sheffieldtelegraph.co.uk
Publisher: Sheffield Newspapers Ltd
Date Established: 1989
Frequency: Weekly
Cover Price: £0.80
Circulation: 22,162 (ABC 02/07/2007 to 30/12/2007)
Editor: Peter Kay; **News Editor:** Peter Kay; **Features Editor:** Peter Kay; **Managing Director:** Mark Rodgers; **Advertising Manager:** Carolyn Rawlings
ADVERTISING RATES:
Full Page Mono £2931.48
Full Page Colour £3812.76
Mechanical Data: Type Area: 340 x 265mm, Page Width: 265mm, No. of Columns (Display): 9, Col Length: 340mm
Copy instructions: Copy Date: 12 noon 2 days prior to publication
LOCAL NEWSPAPERS: Local Newspapers English Counties

SHEFFIELD WEEKLY GAZETTE
44684U72B-3715
Editorial Address: York Street, SHEFFIELD, S1 1PU
Tel: 0114 276 7676 **Fax:** 0114 252 1266
Advertising Address: As above. **Fax:** 0114 252 1227
Email: melinda.gore@sheffieldnewspapers.co.uk
Web site: http://www.thestar.co.uk
Publisher: Sheffield Newspapers Ltd
Frequency: Weekly
Cover Price: Free
Circulation: 103,897 (VFD 02/07/2007 to 30/12/2007)
Editor: Newsdesk
ADVERTISING RATES:
Full Page Colour £4936.00
SCC £12.41
Agency Commission: 10%
Mechanical Data: Film: Digital, Type Area: 340 x 272mm, No. of Columns (Display): 9, Col Length: 340mm, Page Width: 272mm
Copy instructions: Copy Date: Tuesday 12.30pm prior to publication date
Supplement(s): Sheffield Gazette Motor Guide - 52xY
LOCAL NEWSPAPERS: Local Newspapers English Counties

SHEPPEY GAZETTE
43863U72B-1790_190
Frequency: Weekly - Circulation figure is incorporated into the East Kent Gazette
Cover Price: £0.42
Part of Series, see entry for: East Kent Gazette Series
LOCAL NEWSPAPERS: Local Newspapers English Counties

SHEPSHED ECHO
44023U72B-2150_220
Frequency: Weekly - Circulation figure is incorporated into the Loughborough Echo
Cover Price: £0.48
ADVERTISING RATES:
SCC £5.25
Part of Series, see entry for: Loughborough Echo Series
LOCAL NEWSPAPERS: Local Newspapers English Counties

SHEPTON MALLET JOURNAL
44254U72B-2900_180
Frequency: Weekly - Circulation figure includes the Wells Journal
Cover Price: £0.60
Circulation: 9,255 (ABC 02/07/2007 to 30/12/2007)
ADVERTISING RATES:
SCC £2.30
Part of Series, see entry for: Mid Somerset News & Media
LOCAL NEWSPAPERS: Local Newspapers English Counties

SHERWOOD CHAD
44176U72B-2580_160
Frequency: Weekly - Circulation figure is incorporated into the Mansfield Chad
ADVERTISING: Rates on application
Part of Series, see entry for: Chad Series Mansfield
LOCAL NEWSPAPERS: Local Newspapers English Counties

THE SHERWOOD VILLAGER
624736U72B-2655
Editorial Address: PO Box 8455, NEWARK, NG23 5WX
Tel: 01636 525607
Email: johnclawson@xln.co.uk
Advertising Address: As above. **Fax:** 01636 525503
Email: johnclawson@xln.co.uk
Publisher: Bellcourt Limited
Date Established: 1990

Frequency: Monthly
Cover Price: Free
Circulation: 20,000 (Publisher's Statement)
Usual Pagination: 16
Editor: John Clawson; **Managing Director:** John Clawson;
Advertising Manager: John Clawson
ADVERTISING RATES:
Full Page Mono £458.13
SCC £3.75
Agency Commission: 10%
Mechanical Data: Film: Digital, Col Length: 365mm, Col Widths (Display): 36mm, No. of Columns (Display): 7
Average advertising content per issue: 40%
LOCAL NEWSPAPERS: Local Newspapers English Counties

THE SHETLAND TIMES
45026U72D-890

Editorial Address: Gremista Industrial Estate, Gremista, Lerwick, SHETLAND, ZE1 0PX **Tel:** 01595 693622
Fax: 01595 694637
Email: editorial@shetland-times.co.uk
Advertising Address: As above.
Email: adverts@shetland-times.co.uk
Web site: http://www.shetlandtoday.co.uk
Publisher: The Shetland Times Ltd
Frequency: Weekly - Published on Friday
Cover Price: £0.75
Annual Sub.: £70.72
Circulation: 11,438 (ABC 02/07/2007 to 30/12/2007)
Editor: Jim Tait; **News Editor:** Jim Tait; **Advertising Manager:** Vivienne Henderson
ADVERTISING RATES:
SCC £2.75
Agency Commission: 10%
Mechanical Data: Type Area: 400 x 255mm, Col Length: 400mm, Col Widths (Display): 40mm, No. of Columns (Display): 6, Print Process: Web-fed offset litho, Page Width: 255mm, Film: Digital
Copy instructions: Copy Date: Tuesday 5pm prior to publication date
LOCAL NEWSPAPERS: Local Newspapers Scotland

THE SHIELDS GAZETTE
42173U67B-1040

Formerly: Gazette South Shields
Editorial Address: Chapter Row, SOUTH SHIELDS, NE33 1BL **Tel:** 0191 427 4800 **Fax:** 0191 456 8270
Email: gazette.news@northeast-press.co.uk
Advertising Address: As above. **Fax:** 0191 427 0864
Email: kathleen.grieves@northeast-press.co.uk
Web site: http://www.shieldsgazette.com
Publisher: Northeast Press Ltd
Date Established: 1849
Frequency: Evenings
Cover Price: £0.42
Circulation: 18,726 (ABC 02/07/2007 to 30/12/2007)
Editor: John Szymanski; **News Editor:** Helen Charlton; **Managing Director:** Stuart Birkett; **Advertising Manager:** Kathleen Grieves
ADVERTISING RATES:
Full Page Mono £1979.82
Full Page Colour £2572.94
Mechanical Data: Col Length: 340mm, No. of Columns (Display): 9, Film: Digital, Type Area: 340 x 276mm, Page Width: 276mm
Copy instructions: Copy Date: 2 days prior to publication date
Editions:
Gazette (Jarrow & Hebburn)
The Shields Gazette (Final Edition)
REGIONAL DAILY & SUNDAY NEWSPAPERS: Regional Daily Newspapers

THE SHIELDS GAZETTE (FINAL EDITION)
1695155U67B-1040_561

Frequency: Weekly
Cover Price: £0.38
Edition of: The Shields Gazette
REGIONAL DAILY & SUNDAY NEWSPAPERS: Regional Daily Newspapers

SHILDON AND DISTRICT TOWN CRIER
1657611U72B-3957_101

Web site: http://www.shildontowncrier.com
Frequency: Weekly
Cover Price: Free
Circulation: 8,000 (Publisher's Statement)
ADVERTISING RATES:
Full Page Mono £250.00
Part of Series, see entry for: Community Newspaper Series
LOCAL NEWSPAPERS: Local Newspapers English Counties

SHIREBROOK & BOLSOVER CHAD
44178U72B-2580_170

Frequency: Weekly - Circulation figure is incorporated into the Mansfield Chad
ADVERTISING: Rates on application
Part of Series, see entry for: Chad Series Mansfield
LOCAL NEWSPAPERS: Local Newspapers English Counties

SHIRLEY OBSERVER
1775005U72B-3961_102

Frequency: Weekly
Cover Price: Free
Part of Series, see entry for: Solihull, Shirley & Arden Observer Series
LOCAL NEWSPAPERS: Local Newspapers English Counties

SHOREHAM & STEYNING HERALD SERIES
44464U72B-3323

Editorial Address: Cannon House, Chatsworth Road, WORTHING, BN11 1NA **Tel:** 01903 282390
Fax: 01903 520000
Email: shorehamherald@btopenworld.com
Advertising Address: As above. **Tel:** 01903 230051
Fax: 01903 216087
Email: dsmith@worthingtoday.co.uk
Web site: http://www.shorehamherald.co.uk
Publisher: Sussex Newspapers Ltd
Frequency: Weekly - Published on Thursday
Circulation: 4,215.(Combined Circulation)
Editor: Michelle Nevell; **Managing Director:** Karl Dimmock;
Advertising Manager: David Smith
ADVERTISING: Rates on application
Agency Commission: 10%
Copy instructions: Copy Date: Monday 12pm prior to publication date
Average advertising content per issue: 50%
Series owner and contact point for the following titles, see individual entries:
Lancing Herald
Shoreham Herald
Steyning Herald
LOCAL NEWSPAPERS: Local Newspapers English Counties

SHOREHAM HERALD
44466U72B-3323_150

Frequency: Weekly - Circulation figure includes the Steyning Herald
Cover Price: £0.30
Circulation: 4,296 (ABC 02/07/2007 to 30/12/2007)
ADVERTISING: Rates on application
Part of Series, see entry for: Shoreham & Steyning Herald Series
LOCAL NEWSPAPERS: Local Newspapers English Counties

SHREWSBURY ADMAG
1656434U72B-3955_103

Frequency: Weekly
Cover Price: Free
Circulation: 54,012 (VFD 02/07/2007 to 30/12/2007)
ADVERTISING RATES:
SCC £3.70
Part of Series, see entry for: Admag Newspapers Series
LOCAL NEWSPAPERS: Local Newspapers English Counties

SHREWSBURY CHRONICLE
44237U72B-2812_210

Frequency: Weekly - Circulation figure includes North Shropshire Chronicle
Cover Price: £0.50
Circulation: 15,629 (ABC 02/07/2007 to 30/12/2007)
ADVERTISING: Rates on application
Part of Series, see entry for: Chronicle & Journal Series
LOCAL NEWSPAPERS: Local Newspapers English Counties

SHROPSHIRE STAR
42188U67B-1083

Editorial Address: Ketley, TELFORD, TF1 5HU
Tel: 01952 242424 **Fax:** 01952 254605
Email: newsroom@shropshirestar.co.uk
Advertising Address: As above. **Fax:** 01952 222451
Email: advertising@shropshirestar.co.uk
Web site: http://www.shropshirestar.com
Publisher: Midland News Association
Date Established: 1964
Frequency: Evenings
Cover Price: £0.38
Circulation: 72,000 (Publisher's Statement)

Editor: Sarah-Jane Smith; **News Editor:** Jon Simcock;
Managing Director: Steve Brown; **Advertising Manager:** Gareth Cadwallader
ADVERTISING RATES:
SCC £9.00
Agency Commission: 15%
Mechanical Data: Type Area: 410 x 305mm, Col Length: 410mm, Page Width: 305mm, Film: Digital
Copy instructions: Copy Date: 12 noon 1 day prior to publication date
Average advertising content per issue: 40%
Editions:
Shropshire Star (Bridgnorth)
Shropshire Star (Mid-Wales)
Shropshire Star (North)
Shropshire Star (Oswestry Edition)
Shropshire Star (Shrewsbury)
Shropshire Star (South)
Shropshire Star (Telford)
Supplement(s): Shropshire Magazine - 12xY
REGIONAL DAILY & SUNDAY NEWSPAPERS: Regional Daily Newspapers

SHROPSHIRE STAR (BRIDGNORTH)
42190U67B-1083_520

ADVERTISING: Rates on application
Edition of: Shropshire Star
REGIONAL DAILY & SUNDAY NEWSPAPERS: Regional Daily Newspapers

SHROPSHIRE STAR (CITY/LONDON OFFICE)
42302U67D-117

Editorial Address: Press Gallery, House of Commons, Westminster, LONDON, SW1A 1AA **Tel:** 020 7219 3381
Email: j.hipwood@expressandstar.co.uk
Web site: http://www.shropshirestar.com
Publisher: Midland News Association
Editor: John Hipwood
ADVERTISING: No Advertising taken
REGIONAL DAILY & SUNDAY NEWSPAPERS: Regional Daily Sunday London City Office

SHROPSHIRE STAR (MID-WALES)
42191U67B-1083_580

ADVERTISING: Rates on application
Edition of: Shropshire Star
REGIONAL DAILY & SUNDAY NEWSPAPERS: Regional Daily Newspapers

SHROPSHIRE STAR (NORTH)
42192U67B-1083_590

Circulation: 9,112 (Publisher's Statement)
ADVERTISING: Rates on application
Edition of: Shropshire Star
REGIONAL DAILY & SUNDAY NEWSPAPERS: Regional Daily Newspapers

SHROPSHIRE STAR (OSWESTRY EDITION)
42189U67B-1083_600

Formerly: Shropshire Star (Border)
Circulation: 6,740 (Publisher's Statement)
ADVERTISING: Rates on application
Edition of: Shropshire Star
REGIONAL DAILY & SUNDAY NEWSPAPERS: Regional Daily Newspapers

SHROPSHIRE STAR (SHREWSBURY)
42193U67B-1083_620

ADVERTISING: Rates on application
Edition of: Shropshire Star
REGIONAL DAILY & SUNDAY NEWSPAPERS: Regional Daily Newspapers

SHROPSHIRE STAR (SOUTH)
42194U67B-1083_630

ADVERTISING: Rates on application
Edition of: Shropshire Star
REGIONAL DAILY & SUNDAY NEWSPAPERS: Regional Daily Newspapers

SHROPSHIRE STAR (TELFORD)
42195U67B-1083_660

ADVERTISING: Rates on application

Edition of: Shropshire Star
REGIONAL DAILY & SUNDAY NEWSPAPERS: Regional Daily Newspapers

THE SHUTTLE INCORPORATING KIDDERMINSTER TIMES AND STOURPORT NEWS
44614U72B-3562

Formerly: Kidderminster Shuttle Series
Editorial Address: 6 Towers Buildings, Blackwell Street, KIDDERMINSTER, DY10 2DY **Tel:** 01562 633330
Fax: 01562 633332
Email: peter.mcmillian@midlands.newsquest.co.uk
Advertising Address: As above. **Tel:** 01562 633300
Email: ross.walmsley@midlands.newsquest.co.uk
Web site: http://www.kiddermintershuttle.co.uk
Publisher: Newsquest Media Group
Date Established: 1870
Frequency: Weekly - Published on Thursday
Free to qualifying individuals
Circulation: 40,450 (VFD 02/07/2007 to 30/12/2007)
Editor: Peter McMillan; **Managing Director:** Peter John; **Advertising Manager:** Ross Walmsley
Summary of Content: There may be a charge for colour separation.
ADVERTISING: Rates on application
Agency Commission: 10%
Average advertising content per issue: 65%
LOCAL NEWSPAPERS: Local Newspapers English Counties

SIDCUP CHRONICLE
1626388U72A-1303_101

Frequency: Monthly
Cover Price: Free
Part of Series, see entry for: Bexley Chronicle Series
LOCAL NEWSPAPERS: Local Newspapers Greater London

SIDMOUTH HERALD
1732521U72B-850_101

Frequency: Weekly
Cover Price: £0.36
ADVERTISING RATES:
SCC £3.60
Part of Series, see entry for: Sidmouth Herald Series
LOCAL NEWSPAPERS: Local Newspapers English Counties

SIDMOUTH HERALD SERIES
43531U72B-850

Formerly: Sidmouth Herald
Editorial Address: Fair Oak Close, Exeter Airport, Clyst Honiton, Clyst Honiton, EXETER, EX5 2UL
Tel: 01395 515191 **Fax:** 01395 579159
Email: emma.silverthorne@archant.co.uk
Advertising Address: As above. **Tel:** 01392 888400
Fax: 01392 888470
Email: traudi.coates@archant.co.uk
Web site: http://www.sidmouthherald.co.uk
Publisher: Archant South West
Date Established: 1849
Frequency: Weekly - Published on Friday
Circulation: 7,134 (ABC 02/07/2007 to 30/12/2007)
Editor: News Desk; **Managing Director:** Bernard Driscoll; **Advertising Manager:** Traudi Coates
ADVERTISING: Rates on application
Agency Commission: 10%
Mechanical Data: Col Length: 360mm, Type Area: 360 x 270mm, Col Widths (Display): 27mm, No. of Columns (Display): 9, Page Width: 270mm, Film: Digital
Copy instructions: Copy Date: Tuesday 2pm prior to publication date
Average advertising content per issue: 68%
Series owner and contact point for the following titles, see individual entries:
Ottery Herald
Sidmouth Herald
Supplement(s): Views - 4xY
LOCAL NEWSPAPERS: Local Newspapers English Counties

SITTINGBOURNE EXTRA
43938U72B-1840_100

Frequency: Weekly
Cover Price: Free
Circulation: 15,386 (VFD 02/07/2007 to 30/12/2007)
ADVERTISING: Rates on application
Part of Series, see entry for: Kent Messenger Group Newspapers
LOCAL NEWSPAPERS: Local Newspapers English Counties

SKEGNESS AND SPILSBY TARGET
44088U72B-2287_160

Formerly: Skegness Target
Frequency: Weekly - See Coningsby and Horncastle Target for circulation figure
Cover Price: Free
Part of Series, see entry for: Target Series
LOCAL NEWSPAPERS: Local Newspapers English Counties

SKEGNESS CITIZEN
1656198U72B-2280_121

Frequency: Weekly
Cover Price: Free
Circulation: 12,500 (Publisher's Statement)
Part of Series, see entry for: Skegness Standard and Citizen Series
LOCAL NEWSPAPERS: Local Newspapers English Counties

SKEGNESS STANDARD
44078U72B-2280_115

Formerly: Skegness Standard incorporating Skegness News
Frequency: Weekly - Circulation figure includes the Alford Standard and Spilsby Standard
Cover Price: £0.47
Circulation: 11,145 (ABC 02/07/2007 to 30/12/2007)
Part of Series, see entry for: Skegness Standard and Citizen Series
LOCAL NEWSPAPERS: Local Newspapers English Counties

SKEGNESS STANDARD AND CITIZEN SERIES
44075U72B-2280

Editorial Address: Unit 22, The Hildreds, SKEGNESS, PE25 3NU **Tel:** 01754 897120 **Fax:** 01754 610987
Email: rebekah.gunn@jpress.co.uk
Advertising Address: As above. **Fax:** 01754 610366
Email: lisa.mitchell@jpress.co.uk
Web site: http://www.www.skegnessstandard.co.uk
Publisher: Johnston Press plc
Date Established: 1922
Frequency: Weekly - Published on Wednesday
Cover Price: £0.47
Circulation: 23,645 (Combined Circulation)
Editor: Rebekah Gunn
ADVERTISING RATES:
Full Page Mono £979.20
Full Page Colour £1272.96
Agency Commission: 10%
Mechanical Data: Type Area: 340 x 270mm, Col Length: 340mm, Col Widths (Display): 28mm, No. of Columns (Display): 9, Print Process: Web-fed offset litho, Page Width: 270mm, Film: Digital
Copy instructions: Copy Date: Monday 4pm prior to publication date
Average advertising content per issue: 60%
Series owner and contact point for the following titles, see individual entries:
Skegness Citizen
Skegness Standard
Spilsby Standard
LOCAL NEWSPAPERS: Local Newspapers English Counties

SKELMERSDALE ADVERTISER
43995U72B-2050_130

Formerly: Advertiser Skelmersdale
Frequency: Weekly - Circulation figure is incorporated into the Ormskirk Advertiser
Cover Price: £0.60
Part of Series, see entry for: Ormskirk Advertiser Series
LOCAL NEWSPAPERS: Local Newspapers English Counties

THE SKELMERSDALE CHAMPION
44108U72B-2388_200

Frequency: Weekly
Cover Price: Free
Circulation: 17,897 (VFD 02/07/2007 to 30/12/2007)
ADVERTISING RATES:
Full Page Mono £1346.40
SCC £4.95
Part of Series, see entry for: Southport, Ormskirk & Formby Champion Series
LOCAL NEWSPAPERS: Local Newspapers English Counties

SLEAFORD CITIZEN
1656199U72B-2283_101

Frequency: Weekly
Cover Price: Free

Circulation: 613 (Publisher's Statement)
ADVERTISING RATES:
Full Page Mono £1377.00
Full Page Colour £1790.10
SCC £4.50
Part of Series, see entry for: Sleaford Standard and Citizen Series
LOCAL NEWSPAPERS: Local Newspapers English Counties

SLEAFORD STANDARD
1656203U72B-2283_100

Date Established: 1924
Frequency: Weekly
Cover Price: £0.40
Circulation: 4,158 (ABC 02/07/2007 to 30/12/2007)
ADVERTISING RATES:
Full Page Mono £765.00
Full Page Colour £994.50
SCC £2.50
Part of Series, see entry for: Sleaford Standard and Citizen Series
LOCAL NEWSPAPERS: Local Newspapers English Counties

SLEAFORD STANDARD AND CITIZEN SERIES
44081U72B-2283

Formerly: Sleaford Standard
Editorial Address: 28 Handley Street, SLEAFORD, NG34 7TQ **Tel:** 01529 416340 **Fax:** 01529 413239
Email: john.lavery@jpress.co.uk
Advertising Address: 11 Union Street, WISBECH, PE13 1DN **Tel:** 01945 586126 **Fax:** 01945 465912
Email: james.paul@jpress.co.uk
Web site: http://www.sleafordstandard.co.uk
Publisher: Johnston Press plc
Frequency: Weekly
Circulation: 4,771 (Combined Circulation)
Editor: John Lavery; **News Editor:** Andy Hubbert; **Advertising Manager:** Jamie Paul; **Managing Editor:** Tim Robinson
ADVERTISING: Rates on application
Agency Commission: 10%
Mechanical Data: Film: Digital, Col Length: 340mm, Col Widths (Display): 28mm, No. of Columns (Display): 9, Type Area: 340 x 270mm, Print Process: Web-fed offset lino, Page Width: 270mm
Copy instructions: Copy Date: Monday, 4pm prior to publication date
Average advertising content per issue: 60%
Series owner and contact point for the following titles, see individual entries:
Sleaford Citizen
Sleaford Standard
LOCAL NEWSPAPERS: Local Newspapers English Counties

SLEAFORD TARGET
44087U72B-2287_140

Frequency: Weekly
Cover Price: Free
Circulation: 17,268 (VFD 02/07/2007 to 30/12/2007)
Part of Series, see entry for: Target Series
LOCAL NEWSPAPERS: Local Newspapers English Counties

SLOUGH AND SOUTH BUCKS EXPRESS
43257U72B-160_192

Formerly: Slough Express
Frequency: Weekly
Cover Price: Free
Circulation: 51,947 (VFD 20/08/2007 to 30/12/2007)
Part of Series, see entry for: Maidenhead Advertiser Series
LOCAL NEWSPAPERS: Local Newspapers English Counties

SLOUGH & SOUTH BUCKS OBSERVER
43281U72B-190_177

Formerly: Slough & Langley Observer
Frequency: Weekly - Circulation figure is incorporated into the Royal Borough Observer
Cover Price: £0.45
Part of Series, see entry for: Slough & Windsor Observer Series
LOCAL NEWSPAPERS: Local Newspapers English Counties

SLOUGH & WINDSOR OBSERVER SERIES
43278U72B-190

Formerly: Slough, Eton & Windsor Series
Editorial Address: Upton Court, Datchet Road, SLOUGH, SL3 7NR **Tel:** 01753 523355 **Fax:** 01753 627211

Email: newsroom@sloughobserver.co.uk
Advertising Address: As above. **Fax:** 01753 627210
Email: advertising@sloughobserver.co.uk
Web site: http://www.sloughobserver.co.uk
Publisher: Berkshire Media Group Ltd
Frequency: Weekly
Circulation: 65,542 (Combined Circulation)
Editor: Roger Hawes; **Advertising Manager:** Alan Rogers
ADVERTISING RATES:
Full Page Mono £2150.00
SCC £7.20
Agency Commission: 10%
Mechanical Data: Type Area: 330 x 264.5mm, Col Length:
330mm, Col Widths (Display): 33mm, No. of Columns
(Display): 8, Page Width: 264.5mm, Film: Digital
Copy instructions: Copy Date: Wednesday 3pm prior to
publication date
Average advertising content per issue: 55%
**Series owner and contact point for the following titles,
see individual entries:**
Midweek Observer
Royal Borough Observer
Slough & South Bucks Observer
LOCAL NEWSPAPERS: Local Newspapers English
Counties

SLOUGH EXPRESS
43255U72B-158
Formerly: Slough Express Series
Editorial Address: 487 Ipswich Road, SLOUGH, SL1 4EP
Tel: 01753 825111 **Fax:** 01753 849545
Email: expressnews@baylismedia.co.uk
Advertising Address: As above. **Fax:** 01753 692254
Email: advertising@sloughexpress.co.uk
Web site: http://www.windsorexpress.co.uk
Publisher: Baylis & Co.
Frequency: Weekly - Published on Friday
Cover Price: Free
Circulation: 66,727 (VFD 02/07/2007 to 30/12/2007)
ADVERTISING RATES:
SCC £13.27
Mechanical Data: Type Area: 340 x 265mm, Col Length:
340mm, Page Width: 265mm, Col Widths (Display): 31mm,
No. of Columns (Display): 8, Film: Digital
Copy instructions: Copy Date: Tuesday 5pm prior to
publication date
LOCAL NEWSPAPERS: Local Newspapers English
Counties

SOHAM & ELY JOURNAL
44346U72B-3081_170
Frequency: Weekly
Cover Price: £0.42
Part of Series, see entry for: Newmarket Journal Series
LOCAL NEWSPAPERS: Local Newspapers English
Counties

SOLIHULL NEWS
44544U72B-3470
Formerly: Solihull News and Guardian Series
Editorial Address: 6th Floor, Fort Dunlop, BIRMINGHAM,
B4 9FF **Tel:** 0121 236 3366
Email: solihull_news@mrn.co.uk
Advertising Address: As above. **Tel:** 0121 711 3993
Fax: 0121 704 3338
Email: solihull_timesdisplay@mrn.co.uk
Web site: http://www.icsolihull.co.uk
Publisher: BPM Media (Midlands)
Date Established: 1931
Frequency: Weekly - Published on Friday
Cover Price: Free
Circulation: 79,221 (VFD 30/07/2007 to 30/12/2007)
Editor: Sheila Grandfield; **News Editor:** Sheila Grandfield;
Managing Director: Tony Lennox
ADVERTISING: Rates on application
Agency Commission: 10%
Average advertising content per issue: 70%
LOCAL NEWSPAPERS: Local Newspapers English
Counties

SOLIHULL OBSERVER
1667974U72B-3961_101
Frequency: Weekly - Published on Thursday
Cover Price: Free
Circulation: 73,823 (Publisher's Statement)
Part of Series, see entry for: Solihull, Shirley & Arden
Observer Series
LOCAL NEWSPAPERS: Local Newspapers English
Counties

SOLIHULL, SHIRLEY & ARDEN OBSERVER SERIES
1665513U72B-3961
Formerly: Solihull and Shirley Observer Series
Editorial Address: 45 The Parade, LEAMINGTON SPA,
CV32 4BZ **Tel:** 01926 451900 **Fax:** 01926 451754
Email: chris.willmott@bullivantmedia.com

Advertising Address: As above.
Email: wayne.lovelock@bullivantmedia.com
Web site: http://www.solihullobserver.co.uk
Publisher: Bullivant Media Limited
Date Established: 2005
Frequency: Weekly - Published on Thursday
Cover Price: Free
Circulation: 73,823 (VFD 02/07/2007 to 30/12/2007)
Editor: Chris Willmott; **News Editor:** Steve Hayes
ADVERTISING RATES:
Full Page Mono £2315.00
Full Page Colour £2894.06
Mechanical Data: Type Area: 350 x 265mm, Col Length:
350mm, Page Width: 265mm, No. of Columns (Display): 9,
Film: Digital, Col Widths (Display): 27mm
Copy instructions: Copy Date: Tuesday 5.30pm prior to
publication date
**Series owner and contact point for the following titles,
see individual entries:**
Arden Observer
Shirley Observer
Solihull Observer
LOCAL NEWSPAPERS: Local Newspapers English
Counties

SOMERSET COUNTY GAZETTE SERIES
44259U72B-2930
Editorial Address: 44 St. James Street, TAUNTON, TA1
1JR **Tel:** 01823 365100 **Fax:** 01823 365200
Email: newsdesk@countygazette.co.uk
Advertising Address: As above. **Tel:** 01823 365000
Fax: 01823 365240
Email: leon.lee@countygazette.co.uk
Web site: http://www.somersetcountygazette.co.uk
Publisher: Newsquest (Media Group) Ltd
Date Established: 1836
Frequency: Weekly
Cover Price: £0.70
Circulation: 29,688 (ABC 01/01/2007 to 30/12/2007)
Editor: Alex Cameron; **News Editor:** Alex Cameron; **Editor-
in-Chief:** Ken Bird; **Managing Director:** Vincent Boni
ADVERTISING RATES:
Full Page Mono £1675.80
Full Page Colour £2094.75
SCC £7.00
Agency Commission: 10%
Mechanical Data: Type Area: 350 x 264mm, Col Widths
(Display): 28mm, Page Width: 264mm, Film: Digital, Col
Length: 350mm, No. of Columns (Display): 9
Copy instructions: Copy Date: Tuesday 11am prior to
publication date
Average advertising content per issue: 50%
**Series owner and contact point for the following titles,
see individual entries:**
Somerset County Gazette (Taunton Edition)
West Somerset County Gazette
LOCAL NEWSPAPERS: Local Newspapers English
Counties

SOMERSET COUNTY GAZETTE (TAUNTON EDITION)
44263U72B-2930_190
Formerly: Somerset County Gazette
Frequency: Weekly
Cover Price: £0.70
Part of Series, see entry for: Somerset County Gazette
Series
LOCAL NEWSPAPERS: Local Newspapers English
Counties

SOMERSET GUARDIAN
43218U72B-2933_150
Frequency: Weekly
Cover Price: £0.50
Circulation: 8,617 (ABC 02/07/2007 to 30/12/2007)
Part of Series, see entry for: Somerset Standard &
Guardian Series
LOCAL NEWSPAPERS: Local Newspapers English
Counties

SOMERSET MERCURY
1703587U72B-60_181
Frequency: Weekly - See Weston & Somerset Mercury for
circulation figure
Cover Price: £0.50
ADVERTISING: Rates on application
Part of Series, see entry for: Weston & Somerset Mercury
Series
LOCAL NEWSPAPERS: Local Newspapers English
Counties

SOMERSET STANDARD
43219U72B-2933_160
Formerly: Frome and Somerset Standard
Frequency: Weekly
Cover Price: £0.50

Circulation: 7,581 (ABC 03/07/2006 to 31/12/2006)
Part of Series, see entry for: Somerset Standard &
Guardian Series
LOCAL NEWSPAPERS: Local Newspapers English
Counties

SOMERSET STANDARD & GUARDIAN SERIES
43217U72B-2933
Editorial Address: Westpoint, James Street West, BATH,
BA1 2DA **Tel:** 01225 322322 **Fax:** 01225 322292
Email: editor@somersetguardian.co.uk
Advertising Address: 78B High Street, Midsomer Norton,
RADSTOCK, BA3 2DE **Tel:** 01761 417778
Fax: 01761 419128
Email: r.taylor@westnews.co.uk
Web site: http://www.thisissomerset.co.uk
Publisher: Bath News & Media
Frequency: Weekly
Cover Price: £0.50
Circulation: 16,198 (Combined Circulation)
Editor: Emma Dance; **News Editor:** Emma Dance; **Editor-
in-Chief:** Sam Holliday; **Advertising Manager:** Jane Bates
ADVERTISING RATES:
SCC £5.65
Agency Commission: 10%
Mechanical Data: Type Area: 360 x 270mm, Col Length:
360mm, Page Width: 270mm, Film: Digital
Copy instructions: Copy Date: Friday prior to publication
date
**Series owner and contact point for the following titles,
see individual entries:**
Somerset Guardian
Somerset Standard
LOCAL NEWSPAPERS: Local Newspapers English
Counties

SOUTH BELFAST NEWS
1687353U72E-287
Editorial Address: Teach Basil, 2 Hannahstown Hill,
BELFAST, BT17 0LT **Tel:** 028 9060 8807
Fax: 028 9060 5501
Email: m.mccourt@belfastmediagroup.com
Advertising Address: As above. **Tel:** 028 9061 9000
Fax: 028 9060 5533
Email: j.odonnell@belfastmediagroup.com
Web site: http://www.irelandclick.com
ISSN: 1473-1452
Publisher: Belfast Media Group
Frequency: Weekly - Published on Wednesday
Cover Price: £0.65
Free to qualifying individuals
Circulation: 2,091 (Publisher's Statement)
Editor: Maria McCourt
ADVERTISING RATES:
Full Page Mono £930.24
Full Page Colour £1209.30
Agency Commission: 15%
Mechanical Data: Type Area: 340 x 260mm, Col Length:
340mm, Page Width: 260mm, No. of Columns (Display): 6,
Film: Digital, Col Widths (Display): 42mm
Copy instructions: Copy Date: 1 day prior to publication
date
Average advertising content per issue: 20%
LOCAL NEWSPAPERS: Local Newspapers Northern Ireland

SOUTH BUCKS AND BERKSHIRE NEWS
43262U72B-159_140
Formerly: Greater London Review
Frequency: Weekly - Published on Thursday
Cover Price: Free
ADVERTISING RATES:
Full Page Mono £699.00
Full Page Colour £900.00
Part of Series, see entry for: South Bucks and Berkshire
News Series
LOCAL NEWSPAPERS: Local Newspapers English
Counties

SOUTH BUCKS AND BERKSHIRE NEWS SERIES
43261U72B-159
Formerly: Herald & Post Series (Slough)
Editorial Address: 70A High Street, SLOUGH, SL1 1EL
Tel: 01753 535535 **Fax:** 01753 531852
Email: southbucks.berksnews@live.co.uk
Advertising Address: As above.
Email: sales@advertsales.orangehome.co.uk
Web site: http://www.southbucksberksnews.co.uk
Publisher: Harmsworth Printing Ltd
Frequency: Weekly - Published on a Friday
Cover Price: Free
Circulation: 50,000 (Publisher's Statement)
Editor: Joanne Spicer; **Advertising Manager:** Joanne
Spicer
ADVERTISING: Rates on application

Non-National Newspapers

Agency Commission: 10%
Mechanical Data: Col Length: 360mm, No. of Columns (Display): 8, Film: Digital, Col Widths (Display): 32mm, Page Width: 268mm, Type Area: 360 x 268mm
Copy instructions: Copy Date: Wednesday prior to publication date
Series owner and contact point for the following titles, see individual entries:
Herts and Essex Advertiser
South Bucks and Berkshire News
Surrey and Sussex Telegraph
LOCAL NEWSPAPERS: Local Newspapers English Counties

SOUTH BUCKS STAR
43314U72B-280_201
Frequency: Weekly
Cover Price: Free
Circulation: 50,622 (VFD 02/07/2007 to 30/12/2007)
ADVERTISING RATES:
Full Page Colour £800.00
Part of Series, see entry for: Bucks Free Press Series
LOCAL NEWSPAPERS: Local Newspapers English Counties

SOUTH CHESHIRE ADVERTISER
768457U72B-2956_131
Frequency: Weekly
Cover Price: Free
Part of Series, see entry for: Advertiser Series (South Cheshire)
LOCAL NEWSPAPERS: Local Newspapers English Counties

SOUTH COAST LEADER
44429U72B-3210_140
Frequency: Weekly
Cover Price: Free
Circulation: 23,136 (Publisher's Statement)
Part of Series, see entry for: Brighton and Hove Leader Series
LOCAL NEWSPAPERS: Local Newspapers English Counties

SOUTH DEVON AND PLYMOUTH TIMES
43536U72B-854_212
Frequency: Weekly
Cover Price: £0.30
Part of Series, see entry for: South Hams Newspapers Group
LOCAL NEWSPAPERS: Local Newspapers English Counties

SOUTH DURHAM HERALD & POST
43583U72B-3360_202
Frequency: Weekly - Published on Thursday
Cover Price: Free
Circulation: 28,278 (Publisher's Statement)
ADVERTISING RATES:
Full Page Mono £1665.00
Full Page Colour £2244.75
SCC £6.15
Part of Series, see entry for: Herald and Post Series (Teesside)
LOCAL NEWSPAPERS: Local Newspapers English Counties

SOUTH HAMS NEWSPAPERS GROUP
43538U72B-854
Editorial Address: 101-103 Fore Street, KINGSBRIDGE, TQ7 1AF **Tel:** 01548 856353 **Fax:** 01548 853836
Email: shn@internet-today.co.uk
Advertising Address: As above. **Tel:** 01548 853334
Fax: 01548 856499
Email: sh.ads@internet-today.co.uk
Web site: http://www.tindlenews.co.uk
Publisher: Tindle Newspapers Ltd
Frequency: Weekly
Circulation: 41,491 (Publisher's Statement)
Editor: Steve Harvey; **Advertising Manager:** Jane Wood
ADVERTISING RATES:
Full Page Mono £1523.52
Full Page Colour £1981.44
SCC £5.29
Agency Commission: 10%
Mechanical Data: Col Length: 360mm, Type Area: 360 x 262mm, Page Width: 262mm, Film: Digital, Col Widths (Display): 30mm, No. of Columns (Display): 8
Copy instructions: Copy Date: Tuesday 12pm prior to publication date
Average advertising content per issue: 60%

Series owner and contact point for the following titles, see individual entries:
Brixham News
Dartmouth Chronicle
Ivybridge & South Brent Gazette
Kingsbridge & Salcombe Gazette
Plympton, Plymstock & Ivybridge News
South Devon and Plymouth Times
Totnes News
Totnes Times
LOCAL NEWSPAPERS: Local Newspapers English Counties

THE SOUTH LAKES CITIZEN (INCORPORATING THE LAKES LEADER)
43459U72B-3931_101
Frequency: Weekly
Cover Price: Free
Circulation: 21,184 (VFD 02/07/2007 to 30/12/2007)
Part of Series, see entry for: Westmorland Gazette Newspaper Series
LOCAL NEWSPAPERS: Local Newspapers English Counties

SOUTH LANARKSHIRE EXTRA
44986U72D-664_140
Formerly: Hamilton Extra
Frequency: Weekly
Cover Price: Free
ADVERTISING RATES:
SCC £8.35
Part of Series, see entry for: Lanarkshire Extra Series
LOCAL NEWSPAPERS: Local Newspapers Scotland

SOUTH LIVERPOOL MERSEYMART
44098U72B-2383_180
Formerly: Merseymart South Liverpool
Frequency: Weekly
Cover Price: Free
Circulation: 51,566 (VFD 02/07/2007 to 30/12/2007)
ADVERTISING: Rates on application
Part of Series, see entry for: Liverpool Weekly Merseymart & Star Series
LOCAL NEWSPAPERS: Local Newspapers English Counties

SOUTH LONDON PRESS (FRIDAY EDITION)
43144U72A-1310_101
Frequency: Weekly
Cover Price: £0.40
Circulation: 21,939 (Publisher's Statement)
Part of Series, see entry for: South London Press Series
LOCAL NEWSPAPERS: Local Newspapers Greater London

SOUTH LONDON PRESS SERIES
1656873U72A-1310
Editorial Address: 2-4 Leigham Court Road, LONDON, SW16 2PD **Tel:** 020 8710 6430 **Fax:** 020 8769 1742
Email: newsdesk@slp.co.uk
Advertising Address: As above. **Tel:** 020 8769 4444
Fax: 020 8710 6547
Email: customerservices@slp.co.uk
Web site: http://www.southlondonpress.co.uk
Publisher: Tindle Newspapers Ltd
Frequency: Weekly - Published on Tuesday and Friday
Cover Price: £0.50
Circulation: 41,016 (Combined Circulation)
Editor: News Desk; **News Editor:** Lawrence Conway
ADVERTISING RATES:
SCC £36.50
Agency Commission: 10%
Mechanical Data: Type Area: 340 x 262mm, Col Length: 340mm, Page Width: 262mm, Col Widths (Display): 31mm, No. of Columns (Display): 8, Film: Digital
Copy instructions: Copy Date: 7 days prior to publication date
Average advertising content per issue: 30%
Series owner and contact point for the following titles, see individual entries:
South London Press (Friday Edition)
South London Press (Tuesday Edition)
LOCAL NEWSPAPERS: Local Newspapers Greater London

SOUTH LONDON PRESS (TUESDAY EDITION)
43143U72A-1310_100
Formerly: South London Press
Frequency: Weekly
Cover Price: £0.40
Circulation: 19,077 (ABC 01/01/2007 to 01/07/2007)

Part of Series, see entry for: South London Press Series
LOCAL NEWSPAPERS: Local Newspapers Greater London

SOUTH MANCHESTER REPORTER
43706U72B-1295
Formerly: Reporter Series (South Manchester)
Editorial Address: 24 School Lane, Didsbury, MANCHESTER, M20 6RG **Tel:** 0161 446 2213
Fax: 0161 434 9921
Email: southmanchesterreporter@menwn.co.uk
Advertising Address: Wood Street, Hollywood, STOCKPORT, SK3 0AB **Tel:** 0161 475 4818
Fax: 0161 475 4894
Email: andy.harrison@gmwn.co.uk
Web site: http://www.southmanchesterreporter.co.uk
Publisher: MEN Media
Frequency: Weekly - Published on Thursday
Cover Price: Free
Circulation: 49,449 (VFD 06/08/2007 to 30/12/2007)
Editor: Gareth Tidman; **Advertising Manager:** Andy Harrison
ADVERTISING RATES:
SCC £5.90
Agency Commission: 10%
Mechanical Data: Page Width: 267mm, Film: Digital, Type Area: 340 x 267mm, Col Length: 340mm, Col Widths (Display): 27mm, No. of Columns (Display): 9
Copy instructions: Copy Date: Wednesday 12 noon prior to publication date
Average advertising content per issue: 60%
LOCAL NEWSPAPERS: Local Newspapers English Counties

SOUTH SHROPSHIRE JOURNAL
44238U72B-2812_220
Frequency: Weekly
Cover Price: £0.50
Circulation: 8,689 (ABC 02/07/2007 to 30/12/2007)
ADVERTISING: Rates on application
Part of Series, see entry for: Chronicle & Journal Series
LOCAL NEWSPAPERS: Local Newspapers English Counties

SOUTH TYNE STAR
44496U72B-3371_138
Frequency: Weekly
Cover Price: Free
Circulation: 26,486 (VFD 02/07/2007 to 30/12/2007)
ADVERTISING RATES:
SCC £6.90
Part of Series, see entry for: Star Series
LOCAL NEWSPAPERS: Local Newspapers English Counties

SOUTH WALES ARGUS
42234U67B-2090
Editorial Address: Cardiff Road, Maesglas, NEWPORT, NP20 3QN **Tel:** 01633 777229 **Fax:** 01633 777202
Email: newsdesk@southwalesargus.co.uk
Advertising Address: As above. **Tel:** 01633 810000
Fax: 01633 777160
Email: sales@gwent-wales.co.uk
Web site: http://www.southwalesargus.co.uk
Publisher: South Wales Argus Ltd
Frequency: Evenings
Cover Price: £0.38
Circulation: 28,879 (Publisher's Statement)
Editor: Maria Williams; **News Editor:** Maria Williams;
Managing Director: Gavin Stacey; **Publisher:** Trevor Sallis
Readership/Target Audience: Circulates in: Newport, Gwent and surrounding areas.
ADVERTISING RATES:
SCC £10.90
Agency Commission: 10%
Mechanical Data: No. of Columns (Display): 9, Film: Digital, Col Widths (Display): 27mm
Copy instructions: Copy Date: 2 days prior to publication date
Average advertising content per issue: 30%
Editions:
South Wales Argus (Monmouthshire)
South Wales Argus (Newport)
South Wales Argus (Torfaen)
South Wales Argus (Valleys)
Supplement(s): Business Update - 24xY, Escape - 12xY, Motors - 52xY, Primetime - 12xY, Property Argus - 52xY, Venue - 52xY
REGIONAL DAILY & SUNDAY NEWSPAPERS: Regional Daily Newspapers

Part of Series, see entry for: South London Press Series
LOCAL NEWSPAPERS: Local Newspapers Greater London

SOUTH WALES ARGUS (MONMOUTHSHIRE)

42235U67B-2090_590

Edition of: South Wales Argus
REGIONAL DAILY & SUNDAY NEWSPAPERS: Regional Daily Newspapers

SOUTH WALES ARGUS (NEWPORT)

42236U67B-2090_610

Edition of: South Wales Argus
REGIONAL DAILY & SUNDAY NEWSPAPERS: Regional Daily Newspapers

SOUTH WALES ARGUS (TORFAEN)

42237U67B-2090_680

Edition of: South Wales Argus
REGIONAL DAILY & SUNDAY NEWSPAPERS: Regional Daily Newspapers

SOUTH WALES ARGUS (VALLEYS)

42238U67B-2090_690

Edition of: South Wales Argus
REGIONAL DAILY & SUNDAY NEWSPAPERS: Regional Daily Newspapers

SOUTH WALES ECHO

42216U67B-2050

Editorial Address: 6 Park Street, CARDIFF, CF10 1XR
Tel: 029 2022 3333
Email: echo.newsdesk@mediawales.co.uk
Advertising Address: As above.
Email: sarah.champ@@mediawales.co.uk
Web site: http://www.icwales.com
Publisher: Media Wales Ltd
Frequency: Evenings
Cover Price: £0.43
Circulation: 46,127 (ABC 02/07/2007 to 30/12/2007)
Editor: Nick Machin; **Advertising Manager:** Gerald Griffiths
ADVERTISING RATES:
SCC £19.24
Agency Commission: 10%
Mechanical Data: No. of Columns (Display): 8, Film: Digital, Col Length: 340mm, Page Width: 266mm, Type Area: 340 x 266mm
Copy instructions: Copy Date: 2 days prior to publication date
Editions:
South Wales Echo (Bridgend & Valleys Edition)
South Wales Echo (City Final)
Supplement(s): Business (South Wales Echo) - 4xY, Entertainment - 52xY, Holidays - 12xY, Junior Sport - 12xY, Motors - 52xY, Sport - 52xY, Time to Remember - 12xY, Weekender - 52xY
REGIONAL DAILY & SUNDAY NEWSPAPERS: Regional Daily Newspapers

SOUTH WALES ECHO (BRIDGEND & VALLEYS EDITION)

42222U67B-2050_690

Formerly: South Wales Echo Valleys
Edition of: South Wales Echo
REGIONAL DAILY & SUNDAY NEWSPAPERS: Regional Daily Newspapers

SOUTH WALES ECHO (CITY FINAL)

42220U67B-2050_530

Formerly: South Wales Echo City
Edition of: South Wales Echo
REGIONAL DAILY & SUNDAY NEWSPAPERS: Regional Daily Newspapers

SOUTH WALES EVENING POST

42239U67B-2110

Editorial Address: PO Box 14, Adelaide Street, SWANSEA, SA1 1QT **Tel:** 01792 510000 **Fax:** 01792 514697
Email: peter.slee@swwmedia.co.uk
Advertising Address: As above. **Fax:** 01792 514599
Email: steve.williams@swwmedia.co.uk
Web site: http://www.thisisswansea.co.uk
Publisher: South West Wales Media Ltd
Date Established: 1897
Frequency: Evenings
Cover Price: £0.36
Circulation: 51,329 (ABC 02/07/2007 to 30/12/2007)
Editor: Spencer Feeney; **News Editor:** Chris Davies;
Features Editor: Peter Slee; **Managing Director:** Blanche Sainsbury; **Advertising Manager:** Steve Williams;
Circulation Manager: Paul Jenkins
Summary of Content: Covers national and regional Welsh news.

ADVERTISING RATES:
Full Page Mono £2960.00
Full Page Colour £3456.00
SCC £9.60
Agency Commission: 10%
Mechanical Data: Col Length: 360mm, No. of Columns (Display): 8, Film: Digital, Type Area: 360 x 270mm, Print Process: Web offset, Page Width: 270mm
Copy instructions: Copy Date: Mono 2 days Colour 3 days prior to publication date
Editions:
South Wales Evening Post (Llanelli & Carmarthen)
South Wales Evening Post (Neath and Port Talbot)
South Wales Evening Post (Swansea)
Supplement(s): Business Plus - 12xY
REGIONAL DAILY & SUNDAY NEWSPAPERS: Regional Daily Newspapers

SOUTH WALES EVENING POST (LLANELLI & CARMARTHEN)

42240U67B-2110_580

Edition of: South Wales Evening Post
REGIONAL DAILY & SUNDAY NEWSPAPERS: Regional Daily Newspapers

SOUTH WALES EVENING POST (NEATH AND PORT TALBOT)

42241U67B-2110_600

Edition of: South Wales Evening Post
REGIONAL DAILY & SUNDAY NEWSPAPERS: Regional Daily Newspapers

SOUTH WALES EVENING POST (SWANSEA)

42242U67B-2110_650

Editor: Spencer Feeney
Edition of: South Wales Evening Post
REGIONAL DAILY & SUNDAY NEWSPAPERS: Regional Daily Newspapers

SOUTH WALES GUARDIAN

44838U72C-340_130

Formerly: Swansea Valley Guardian
Frequency: Weekly
Cover Price: £0.45
Part of Series, see entry for: South Wales Guardian Series
LOCAL NEWSPAPERS: Local Newspapers Wales

SOUTH WALES GUARDIAN SERIES

44837U72C-340

Editorial Address: 37 Quay Street, AMMANFORD, SA18 3BS **Tel:** 01269 592074 **Fax:** 01269 591020
Email: mike.lewis@southwalesguardian.co.uk
Advertising Address: As above. **Fax:** 01269 596314
Email: michelle.lewis@gwent-wales.co.uk
Web site: http://www.southwalesguardian.co.uk
Publisher: Newsquest (Media Group) Ltd
Date Established: 1955
Frequency: Weekly - Published on Wednesday
Circulation: 8,533 (ABC 02/07/2007 to 30/12/2007)
Editor: Mike Lewis; **Features Editor:** Clare Salter;
Advertising Manager: Michelle Lewis
Language(s): English; Welsh
ADVERTISING RATES:
Full Page Mono £1162.80
Full Page Colour £1395.36
SCC £3.80
Agency Commission: 10%
Mechanical Data: Col Widths (Display): 27mm, Col Length: 340mm, Type Area: 340 x 259mm, No. of Columns (Display): 9, Page Width: 259mm
Copy instructions: Copy Date: Monday 4pm prior to publication date
Average advertising content per issue: 35%
Series owner and contact point for the following titles, see individual entries:
South Wales Guardian
Towy Valley Guardian
Supplement(s): Wheels - 12xY
LOCAL NEWSPAPERS: Local Newspapers Wales

SOUTH WARRINGTON NEWS

626089U72B-490

Editorial Address: 52 Walton Road, Stockton Heath, WARRINGTON, WA4 6NL **Tel:** 01925 600601
Fax: 01925 264102
Email: editor@southwarringtonnews.co.uk
Advertising Address: As above.
Email: sales@southwarrington.co.uk
Web site: http://www.southwarrington.com
Publisher: North West News Ltd
Date Established: 1993
Frequency: Monthly
Cover Price: Free

Circulation: 10,000 (Publisher's Statement)
Editor: B. Hardman; **Features Editor:** Claire Brook;
Advertising Manager: B. Hardman
ADVERTISING RATES:
Full Page Mono £1701.63
Full Page Colour £2051.28
SCC £6.16
Agency Commission: 10%
Mechanical Data: Col Length: 370mm, Col Widths (Display): 27mm, No. of Columns (Display): 9, Type Area: 370 x 259mm, Print Process: Web-fed offset litho, Page Width: 259mm
Copy instructions: Copy Date: 2 days prior to publication date
Average advertising content per issue: 70%
LOCAL NEWSPAPERS: Local Newspapers English Counties

SOUTH WOODHAM WEEKLY NEWS

759801U72B-990_180

Formerly: South Woodham and Maldon Weekly News
Frequency: Weekly
Cover Price: Free
Circulation: 12,432 (VFD 03/07/2006 to 31/12/2006)
ADVERTISING RATES:
Full Page Mono £205.00
Full Page Colour £300.00
SCC £1.90
Part of Series, see entry for: Weekly News Series (Chelmsford)
LOCAL NEWSPAPERS: Local Newspapers English Counties

SOUTH YORKSHIRE TIMES

44685U72B-3720

Formerly: South Yorkshire Times Series
Editorial Address: 27-29 High Street, MEXBOROUGH, S64 9AF **Tel:** 01709 303055 **Fax:** 01709 303098
Email: editorial@dearnetoday.co.uk
Advertising Address: 29 High Street, MEXBOROUGH, S64 9AF **Tel:** 01709 303030
Email: spotts@doncastertoday.co.uk
Web site: http://www.southyorkshiretimes.co.uk
Publisher: South Yorkshire Newspapers Ltd
Date Established: 1877
Frequency: Weekly - Published on Thursday
Cover Price: £0.33
Circulation: 5,862 (ABC 02/07/2007 to 30/12/2007)
Editor: News Desk; **Advertising Manager:** Gail Beeson
ADVERTISING: Rates on application
Supplement(s): South Yorkshire Motor Guide - 52xY, South Yorkshire Property Guide - 52xY
LOCAL NEWSPAPERS: Local Newspapers English Counties

SOUTHAM OBSERVER

44509U72B-3382_170

Frequency: Weekly
Cover Price: Free
ADVERTISING: Rates on application
Part of Series, see entry for: Leamington & Stratford Observer Series
LOCAL NEWSPAPERS: Local Newspapers English Counties

SOUTHDOWN OBSERVER SERIES

44468U72B-3326

Editorial Address: Unicorn House, 8 Eastgate Square, CHICHESTER, PO19 1JN **Tel:** 01243 534132
Fax: 01243 539386
Email: news@chiobserver.co.uk
Advertising Address: As above. **Tel:** 01243 532532
Fax: 01243 776854
Email: margaret.race@chiobserver.co.uk
Web site: http://www.www.chichester.co.uk
Publisher: Johnston Press plc
Frequency: Weekly
Cover Price: £0.50
Circulation: 35,161 (ABC 02/07/2007 to 30/12/2007)
Editor: Kelly Frank; **News Editor:** Kelly Frank
ADVERTISING RATES:
Full Page Mono £5148.00
Full Page Colour £6693.00
SCC £8.51
Agency Commission: 10%
Mechanical Data: Trim Size: 560 x 339mm, Col Widths (Display): 29mm, No. of Columns (Display): 11, Film: Digital
Copy instructions: Copy Date: Monday 5pm prior to publication date
Average advertising content per issue: 60%
Series owner and contact point for the following titles, see individual entries:
Bognor Regis Observer
Chichester Observer

Non-National Newspapers

Midhurst & Petworth Observer
LOCAL NEWSPAPERS: Local Newspapers English Counties

SOUTHEND ECHO
41981U67B-13_600

Formerly: Southend Evening Echo
Frequency: Mornings
Cover Price: £0.38
Edition of: Echo (Basildon)
REGIONAL DAILY & SUNDAY NEWSPAPERS: Regional Daily Newspapers

SOUTHEND STANDARD
43646U72B-1080_200

Formerly: Southend Standard Southend Borough
Frequency: Weekly - Published on Wednesday
Cover Price: Free
Circulation: 61,012 (VFD 02/07/2007 to 30/12/2007)
ADVERTISING: Rates on application
Part of Series, see entry for: Southend Standard Series
LOCAL NEWSPAPERS: Local Newspapers English Counties

SOUTHEND STANDARD SERIES
43642U72B-1080

Formerly: Standard Recorder Series
Editorial Address: 18 Clarence Road, SOUTHEND-ON-SEA, SS1 1AN **Tel:** 01702 321150 **Fax:** 01702 321159
Email: echonews@nqe.com
Advertising Address: Newspaper House, Chester Hall Lane, BASILDON, SS14 3BL **Tel:** 01268 522792
Fax: 01268 532060
Email: stephen.golding@nqe.com
Web site: http://www.southendstandard.co.uk
Publisher: Echo Newspapers
Frequency: Weekly
Cover Price: Free
Circulation: 204,783 (Combined Circulation)
Editor: David Giles; **News Editor:** David Giles; **Features Editor:** Claire Borley; **Advertising Manager:** Stephen Golding
ADVERTISING: Rates on application
Agency Commission: 10%
Average advertising content per issue: 75%
Series owner and contact point for the following titles, see individual entries:
Basildon, Billericay and Wickford Recorder
Brentwood Weekly News
Rayleigh, Rochford & Castle Point Standard
Southend Standard
LOCAL NEWSPAPERS: Local Newspapers English Counties

SOUTHERN COUNTIES TELEGRAPH
1639897U72B-3944

Editorial Address: 2nd Floor, 53 Corporation Street, COVENTRY, CV1 1GX **Tel:** 024 7663 0894
Fax: 024 7625 2110
Email: warren@southerncountiesonline.co.uk
Advertising Address: As above.
Email: sales@southerncountiesonline.co.uk
Web site: http://www.southerncountiesonline.co.uk
Publisher: JPC
Date Established: 2001
Frequency: Weekly - Published on Monday
Cover Price: Free
Circulation: 45,000 (Publisher's Statement)
Editor: Keira Byrne; **News Editor:** Warren Gibbons
ADVERTISING RATES:
SCC £10.70
Agency Commission: 10%
Mechanical Data: Film: Digital
Copy instructions: Copy Date: 2 days prior to publication date
Average advertising content per issue: 75%
LOCAL NEWSPAPERS: Local Newspapers English Counties

THE SOUTHERN DAILY ECHO (SOUTHAMPTON)
42176U67B-1050

Editorial Address: Newspaper House, Test Lane, Redbridge, SOUTHAMPTON, SO16 9JX **Tel:** 023 8042 4777
Fax: 023 8042 4545
Email: newsdesk@dailyecho.co.uk
Advertising Address: As above. **Fax:** 023 8042 4770
Email: tracey.richards@dailyecho.co.uk
Web site: http://www.dailyecho.co.uk
Publisher: Newsquest (Media Group) Ltd
Frequency: Evenings - Not published on Sunday
Cover Price: £0.38
Circulation: 39,174 (ABC 02/07/2007 to 30/12/2007)

Editor: Gordon Sutter; **News Editor:** Gordon Sutter;
Features Editor: Andy Bissell; **Managing Director:** Stewart Dunn
ADVERTISING: Rates on application
Agency Commission: 10%
Copy instructions: Copy Date: 2 days prior to publication date
Average advertising content per issue: 35%
Editions:
The Southern Daily Echo (Town and County)
Supplement(s): Business (The Southern Daily Echo (Southampton)) - 52xY, Homes and Property - 52xY, Life - 52xY, The Pink Southampton - 52xY, Recruitment - 52xY, Weekender - 52xY, Wheels - 52xY
REGIONAL DAILY & SUNDAY NEWSPAPERS: Regional Daily Newspapers

THE SOUTHERN DAILY ECHO (TOWN AND COUNTY)
1691331U67B-1050_500

Frequency: Daily
Cover Price: £0.35
ADVERTISING: Rates on application
Edition of: The Southern Daily Echo (Southampton)
REGIONAL DAILY & SUNDAY NEWSPAPERS: Regional Daily Newspapers

SOUTHERN REPORTER
45027U72D-910

Editorial Address: The Hermitage, High Street, SELKIRK, TD7 4DA **Tel:** 01750 21581 **Fax:** 01750 21239
Email: susanwindram@tweeddalepress.co.uk
Advertising Address: As above.
Email: edithscott@tweeddalepress.co.uk
Web site: http://www.thesouthernreporter.co.uk
Publisher: Tweeddale Press Group
Date Established: 1855
Frequency: Weekly
Cover Price: £0.70
Circulation: 18,310 (ABC 02/07/2007 to 30/12/2007)
Editor: Mark Entwistle; **Group Editor:** Susan Windram
ADVERTISING RATES:
SCC £9.90
Agency Commission: 10%
Mechanical Data: Type Area: 550 x 333mm, Col Length: 550mm, Col Widths (Display): 28mm, No. of Columns (Display): 11, Page Width: 333mm, Film: Digital
Copy instructions: Copy Date: Friday prior to publication date
LOCAL NEWSPAPERS: Local Newspapers Scotland

THE SOUTHPORT CHAMPION
44107U72B-2388_180

Frequency: Weekly - Circulation figure is for Champion Series including Formby Champion, Ormskirk & West Lancs Champion and Aintree & Maghull Champion
Cover Price: Free
Circulation: 76,486 (VFD 02/07/2007 to 30/12/2007)
ADVERTISING RATES:
Full Page Mono £1700.00
SCC £6.25
Part of Series, see entry for: Southport, Ormskirk & Formby Champion Series
LOCAL NEWSPAPERS: Local Newspapers English Counties

SOUTHPORT, ORMSKIRK & FORMBY CHAMPION SERIES
44103U72B-2388

Formerly: Champion Series
Editorial Address: Clare House, 166 Lord Street, SOUTHPORT, PR9 0QA **Tel:** 01704 392400
Fax: 01704 501678
Email: editorial@champnews.com
Advertising Address: As above. **Tel:** 01704 392392
Fax: 01704 531327
Email: phil.lilley@champnews.com
Web site: http://www.champnews.com
Publisher: Champion Media Group
Frequency: Weekly - Published on Wednesday
Cover Price: Free
Circulation: 94,383 (Combined Circulation)
Editor: News Desk; **Managing Director:** Betty Drummond;
Advertising Director: Phil Lilley
ADVERTISING RATES:
Full Page Mono £2257.60
SCC £8.30
Agency Commission: 10%
Mechanical Data: Type Area: 340 x 265mm, No. of Columns (Display): 8, Col Length: 340mm, Print Process: Web-fed offset litho, Page Width: 265mm, Trim Size: 400 x 300mm, Col Widths (Display): 30mm, Film: Digital
Copy instructions: Copy Date: Monday 2pm prior to publication date
Average advertising content per issue: 67%

Series owner and contact point for the following titles, see individual entries:
Aintree & Maghull Champion
Formby Champion
Ormskirk & West Lancs Champion
The Skelmersdale Champion
The Southport Champion
LOCAL NEWSPAPERS: Local Newspapers English Counties

SOUTHPORT REPORTER
1629338U72B-3937_101

Frequency: Weekly
Cover Price: Free
ADVERTISING: Rates on application
Part of Series, see entry for: Mersey and Southport Reporter Series
LOCAL NEWSPAPERS: Local Newspapers English Counties

SOUTHPORT VISITER
44110U72B-2400_180

Frequency: Weekly
Cover Price: £0.50
Circulation: 15,926 (ABC 02/07/2007 to 30/12/2007)
ADVERTISING: Rates on application
Part of Series, see entry for: Southport Visiter Series
LOCAL NEWSPAPERS: Local Newspapers English Counties

SOUTHPORT VISITER SERIES
44109U72B-2400

Editorial Address: 26-32 Tulketh Street, SOUTHPORT, PR8 1BT **Tel:** 01704 536655 **Fax:** 01704 398297
Email: visiternews@southportvisiter.co.uk
Advertising Address: As above. **Tel:** 01704 530600
Fax: 01704 532041
Email: sue.watkinson@southportvisiter.co.uk
Web site: http://www.southportvisiter.co.uk
Publisher: Liverpool Daily Post & Echo Ltd
Date Established: 1844
Frequency: Weekly
Cover Price: £0.65
Circulation: 73,905 (Combined Circulation)
Editor: Andrew Brown; **News Editor:** Jamie Mcloughlin
ADVERTISING: Rates on application
Series owner and contact point for the following titles, see individual entries:
Midweek Visiter (Formby Edition)
Midweek Visiter (Southport)
Southport Visiter
Supplement(s): The Guide - 12xY
LOCAL NEWSPAPERS: Local Newspapers English Counties

SOUTHWARK NEWS
1665981U72A-470_100

Frequency: Weekly - Published on Thursday
Cover Price: £0.30
Usual Pagination: 20
Part of Series, see entry for: Southwark News Series
LOCAL NEWSPAPERS: Local Newspapers Greater London

SOUTHWARK NEWS SERIES
43147U72A-470

Formerly: Southwark News
Editorial Address: Unit A302, Tower Bridge Business Complex, Clements Road, LONDON, SE16 4DG
Tel: 020 7231 5258 **Fax:** 020 7237 1578
Email: news@southwarknews.org
Advertising Address: As above. **Tel:** 020 7232 1639
Email: ads@southwarknews.org
Web site: http://www.southwarknews.co.uk
Publisher: Southward Newspaper Ltd.
Date Established: 1987
Circulation: 59,300 (Publisher's Statement)
Editor: Anthony Phillips; **Group Editor:** Kevin Quinn
ADVERTISING RATES:
Full Page Colour £1400.00
SCC £5.00
Agency Commission: 10%
Mechanical Data: Col Length: 360mm, Type Area: 360 x 270mm, No. of Columns (Display): 8, Col Widths (Display): 27mm, Film: Digital, Page Width: 270mm
Copy instructions: Copy Date: Monday prior to publication date
Average advertising content per issue: 30%
Series owner and contact point for the following titles, see individual entries:
Southwark News
Southwark Weekender
Supplement(s): Education Guide - 1xY, Taste - 1xY
LOCAL NEWSPAPERS: Local Newspapers Greater London

SOUTHWARK WEEKENDER
1665975U72A-470_101
Web site: http://www.southwarkweekender.co.uk
Frequency: Monthly
Cover Price: Free
Part of Series, see entry for: Southwark News Series
LOCAL NEWSPAPERS: Local Newspapers Greater London

SOUTHWELL ADVERTISER
1615614U72B-2620_251
Frequency: Weekly
Part of Series, see entry for: Newark Advertiser Series
LOCAL NEWSPAPERS: Local Newspapers English Counties

SPALDING GUARDIAN
44056U72B-2250_190
Frequency: Weekly - Published on Thursday
Cover Price: £0.37
Circulation: 14,849 (ABC 02/07/2007 to 30/12/2007)
ADVERTISING RATES:
SCC £3.91
Part of Series, see entry for: Lincolnshire Free Press Series
LOCAL NEWSPAPERS: Local Newspapers English Counties

SPECTRUM MAGAZINE SCOTLAND ON SUNDAY
42314U67H-300
Editorial Address: 108 Holyrood Road, EDINBURGH, EH8 8AS **Tel:** 0131 620 8620 **Fax:** 0131 523 0316
Email: spectrumsos@scotsman.com
Advertising Address: As above. **Fax:** 0131 523 0348
Email: adverts@scotsman.com
Web site: http://www.scotsman.com
Publisher: The Scotsman Publications Ltd
Date Established: 1997
Frequency: Weekly - See main record for circulation figure
Cover Price: £1.40
Editor: Clare Trodden; **Advertising Manager:** Carol Gibson
Summary of Content: Magazine covering celebrity interviews, topical features and articles on films, books, food, fashion, art, gardening, travel, lifestyle and property. Also contains a what's on guide and TV and radio listings.
ADVERTISING: Rates on application
Supplement to: Scotland on Sunday
REGIONAL DAILY & SUNDAY NEWSPAPERS: Regional Colour Supplements

SPENBOROUGH GUARDIAN
44724U72B-3880
Formerly: Spenborough Guardian Series
Editorial Address: 1 Market Street, CLECKHEATON, BD19 3RT **Tel:** 01274 874635 **Fax:** 01274 851304
Email: margaret.heward@ywng.co.uk
Advertising Address: 17 Wellington Road, DEWSBURY, WF13 1HQ **Tel:** 01924 468282 **Fax:** 01924 457652
Email: joanne.gilbert@ywng.co.uk
Web site: http://www.spenboroughguardian.co.uk
Publisher: Dewsbury Reporter Group
Date Established: 1867
Frequency: Weekly
Cover Price: £0.45
Circulation: 7,743 (ABC 02/07/2007 to 30/12/2007)
Editor: Margaret Heward; **News Editor:** Margaret Heward; **Features Editor:** Margaret Heward; **Managing Director:** Helen Oldham
ADVERTISING RATES:
SCC £5.09
Agency Commission: 10%
Mechanical Data: Col Widths (Display): 28mm, Film: Digital, Type Area: 340mm x 265mm, Col Length: 340mm, No. of Columns (Display): 9, Page Width: 265mm
Copy instructions: Copy Date: 3 days prior to publication date
LOCAL NEWSPAPERS: Local Newspapers English Counties

THE SPENNYNEWS
1657613U72B-3957_100
Email: spennynews@talk21.com
Web site: http://www.spennynews.com
Frequency: 26 issues yearly
Cover Price: Free
Circulation: 11,500 (Publisher's Statement)
ADVERTISING RATES:
Full Page Mono £250.00
Part of Series, see entry for: Community Newspaper Series
LOCAL NEWSPAPERS: Local Newspapers English Counties

SPILSBY STANDARD
44079U72B-2280_120
Frequency: Weekly - For circulation see Skegness Standard incorporating Skegness News
Cover Price: £0.47
Part of Series, see entry for: Skegness Standard and Citizen Series
LOCAL NEWSPAPERS: Local Newspapers English Counties

SPORT
41652U67B-9009_706
Formerly: Standard Sport
Tel: 020 7938 6000 **Fax:** 020 7937 3304
Frequency: Mornings - Published within the London Evening Standard
Editor: Steve McKenlay
Summary of Content: Section covering sports news, features and fixtures.
ADVERTISING: Rates on application
Part of Series, see entry for: London Evening Standard
REGIONAL DAILY & SUNDAY NEWSPAPERS: Regional Daily Newspapers

SPRINGBURN HERALD
44983U72D-630_190
Frequency: Weekly - Circulation figure is incorporated into the Kirkintilloch Herald
Cover Price: £0.29
Part of Series, see entry for: Kirkintilloch & Bishopbriggs Herald Series
LOCAL NEWSPAPERS: Local Newspapers Scotland

SPROTBROUGH, SCAWSBY & CUSWORTH COMMUNITY NEWSLETTER
1647022U72B-3950_103
Frequency: Monthly
Cover Price: Free
Circulation: 6,000 (Publisher's Statement)
ADVERTISING: Rates on application
Part of Series, see entry for: Community Newsletter Series
LOCAL NEWSPAPERS: Local Newspapers English Counties

ST. ALBANS & HARPENDEN REVIEW
625410U72B-1586_160
Formerly: Review Harpenden Edition
Frequency: Weekly
Cover Price: Free
Circulation: 48,570 (VFD 03/07/2006 to 31/12/2006)
Part of Series, see entry for: Review Series
LOCAL NEWSPAPERS: Local Newspapers English Counties

ST. ALBANS FOCUS
1640577U72B-1496_100
Frequency: Monthly
Cover Price: Free
ADVERTISING: Rates on application
Part of Series, see entry for: Focus Series
LOCAL NEWSPAPERS: Local Newspapers English Counties

ST. ANDREWS CITIZEN
45028U72D-913
Editorial Address: 5A Greyfriars Garden, ST. ANDREWS, KY16 9HG **Tel:** 01334 473464 **Fax:** 01334 479014
Email: edcitizen@fifetoday.co.uk
Advertising Address: As above. **Tel:** 01334 475855
Email: margaret.mackie@fifetoday.co.uk
Web site: http://www.fifetoday.co.uk
Publisher: Strachan & Livingston Ltd
Date Established: 1871
Frequency: Weekly - Published on Friday
Cover Price: £0.42
Editor: Mike Rankin
ADVERTISING RATES:
Full Page Mono £9858.28
Full Page Colour £14787.42
SCC £32.22
Agency Commission: 10%
Mechanical Data: Col Length: 340mm, Col Widths (Display): 30mm, No. of Columns (Display): 9, Print Process: Web offset, Type Area: 340 x 272mm, Page Width: 272mm
Copy instructions: Copy Date: Wednesday 11am prior to publication date
Average advertising content per issue: 50%
LOCAL NEWSPAPERS: Local Newspapers Scotland

ST. AUSTELL VOICE
1749165U72B-4045
Editorial Address: 16 Truro Road, ST. AUSTELL, PL25 5JB
Tel: 01726 67722 **Fax:** 01726 67300
Email: editorial@staustellvoice.co.uk

Advertising Address: As above.
Email: sales@staustellvoice.co.uk
Publisher: AD Sales
Frequency: Weekly
Cover Price: £0.45
Editor: Phillip Lamphee
ADVERTISING RATES:
Full Page Colour £988.00
Agency Commission: 10%
Mechanical Data: Type Area: 380 x 284mm, Col Length: 380mm, Page Width: 284mm, Col Widths (Display): 34mm, No. of Columns (Display): 8, Film: Digital
Copy instructions: Copy Date: 1 week prior to publication date
LOCAL NEWSPAPERS: Local Newspapers English Counties

ST. CLEARS & WHITLAND JOURNAL
706898U72C-220_150
Frequency: Weekly
Part of Series, see entry for: Journal Series (Carmarthen)
LOCAL NEWSPAPERS: Local Newspapers Wales

ST. HELENS REPORTER
44102U72B-2386_180
Formerly: St. Helens Reporter incorporating The Prescot Reporter
Frequency: Weekly
Cover Price: Free
Part of Series, see entry for: St. Helens Reporter Series
LOCAL NEWSPAPERS: Local Newspapers English Counties

ST. HELENS REPORTER SERIES
44100U72B-2386
Editorial Address: Bank House, Claughton Street, ST. HELENS, WA10 1RL **Tel:** 01744 22285 **Fax:** 01744 451389
Email: sthelens.reporter@lancspublications.co.uk
Advertising Address: As above.
Email: jackie.kennedy@lancspublications.co.uk
Web site: http://www.sthelenstoday.net
Publisher: Lancashire Publications Ltd
Date Established: 1865
Frequency: Weekly - Published on Wednesday
Cover Price: Free
Circulation: 78,750 (VFD 02/07/2007 to 30/12/2007)
Editor: Andrew Moffatt; **News Editor:** Andrew Moffatt
ADVERTISING RATES:
SCC £10.56
Agency Commission: 10%
Mechanical Data: Type Area: 340 x 276mm, Col Length: 340mm, Page Width: 276mm, No. of Columns (Display): 9
Copy instructions: Copy Date: Tuesday 11.30am prior to publication date
Average advertising content per issue: 70%
Series owner and contact point for the following titles, see individual entries:
Prescot & Knowsley Reporter (incorporating St. Helens)
St. Helens Reporter
LOCAL NEWSPAPERS: Local Newspapers English Counties

ST. HELENS STAR
44112U72B-2410
Editorial Address: 23A Hardshaw Street, ST. HELENS, WA10 1RT **Tel:** 01744 762766 **Fax:** 01744 762767
Email: steve.leary@sthelensstar.co.uk
Advertising Address: As above. **Tel:** 01744 751441
Fax: 01744 762741
Email: sthelens-advertise@newsquest.co.uk
Web site: http://www.sthelensstar.co.uk
Publisher: Newsquest Media Group
Date Established: 1973
Frequency: Weekly
Cover Price: Free
Circulation: 78,827 (VFD 02/07/2007 to 30/12/2007)
Usual Pagination: 104
Editor: Steve Leary
ADVERTISING RATES:
Full Page Mono £1055.25
Full Page Colour £1319.06
SCC £4.00
Agency Commission: 10%
Mechanical Data: Type Area: 350 x 268mm, Col Length: 350mm, Col Widths (Display): 27mm, No. of Columns (Display): 9, Print Process: Web-fed offset litho, Page Width: 268mm, Film: Digital, Bleed Size: +3mm
Copy instructions: Copy Date: Tuesday 4pm prior to publication date
Average advertising content per issue: 70%
Supplement(s): Lifestyle - 4xY
LOCAL NEWSPAPERS: Local Newspapers English Counties

Non-National Newspapers

ST. IVES TIMES & ECHO
43438U72B-580_150

Frequency: Weekly
Cover Price: £0.58
Circulation: 3,750 (Publisher's Statement)
Part of Series, see entry for: St. Ives Times & Echo Series
LOCAL NEWSPAPERS: Local Newspapers English Counties

ST. IVES TIMES & ECHO SERIES
43436U72B-580

Editorial Address: High Street, ST. IVES, TR26 1RS
Tel: 01736 795813 **Fax:** 01736 793536
Email: news@stivesnews.co.uk
Advertising Address: As above.
Email: tim@stivesnews.co.uk
Web site: http://www.stivesnews.co.uk
Publisher: St. Ives Printing and Publishing Company
Frequency: Weekly - Published on Friday
Cover Price: £0.63
Circulation: 3,930 (Combined Circulation)
Editor: Toni Carver; **Features Editor:** Toni Carver
ADVERTISING RATES:
Full Page Mono £838.00
SCC £2.85
Agency Commission: 10%
Mechanical Data: Type Area: 420 x 295mm, Col Length: 420mm, Col Widths (Display): 40mm, No. of Columns (Display): 7, Film: Digital, Page Width: 295mm
Copy instructions: Copy Date: 5 days prior to publication date
Average advertising content per issue: 30%
Series owner and contact point for the following titles, see individual entries:
Hayle Times
St. Ives Times & Echo
LOCAL NEWSPAPERS: Local Newspapers English Counties

ST. IVES WEEKLY NEWS
43324U72B-350_195

Frequency: Weekly
Cover Price: Free
Circulation: 13,421 (Publisher's Statement)
ADVERTISING RATES:
SCC £3.45
Part of Series, see entry for: Cambridge Weekly News & Crier Series
LOCAL NEWSPAPERS: Local Newspapers English Counties

ST. NEOTS WEEKLY NEWS
43325U72B-350_200

Frequency: Weekly
Cover Price: Free
Circulation: 13,674 (Publisher's Statement)
ADVERTISING RATES:
SCC £3.45
Part of Series, see entry for: Cambridge Weekly News & Crier Series
LOCAL NEWSPAPERS: Local Newspapers English Counties

THE STAFFORD & STONE CHRONICLE
44314U72B-3476

Formerly: Stafford Chronicle
Editorial Address: 51-53 Queen Street, WOLVERHAMPTON, WV1 1ES **Tel:** 01902 313131
Fax: 01785 245207
Email: staffordchronicle@expressandstar.co.uk
Advertising Address: As above. **Tel:** 01785 273900
Fax: 01785 273985
Email: staffordchronadv@expressandstar.co.uk
Web site: http://www.yourchronicle.com
Publisher: Express & Star Ltd
Frequency: Weekly
Cover Price: Free
Circulation: 37,057 (Publisher's Statement)
Usual Pagination: 48
Editor: Sarah Taylor; **Advertising Manager:** Nicola Flood
ADVERTISING RATES:
Full Page Mono £1312.00
Full Page Colour £1705.00
SCC £4.00
Agency Commission: 10%
Mechanical Data: Type Area: 410 x 307mm, No. of Columns (Display): 9, Col Length: 410mm, Page Width: 307mm, Film: Digital
Copy instructions: Copy Date: Tuesday 12pm prior to publication date
Average advertising content per issue: 70%
LOCAL NEWSPAPERS: Local Newspapers English Counties

STAFFORD POST
1849424U72B-3025_100

Frequency: Weekly
Cover Price: Free
ADVERTISING: Rates on application
Part of Series, see entry for: Stafford Post Series
LOCAL NEWSPAPERS: Local Newspapers English Counties

STAFFORD POST SERIES
44546U72B-3025

Formerly: Stafford Post
Editorial Address: 35 Eastgate Street, STAFFORD, ST16 2LZ **Tel:** 01785 212364 **Fax:** 01785 225458
Email: stafford_post@mrn.co.uk
Advertising Address: As above.
Email: nicki_warrillow@mrn.co.uk
Web site: http://www.icstafford.co.uk
Publisher: Trinity Mirror Midlands
Date Established: 1980
Frequency: Weekly - Published on Wednesday
Cover Price: Free
Circulation: 36,712 (VFD 02/07/2007 to 30/12/2007)
Editor: Mike Lockley; **Advertising Manager:** Nicola Warrillow
ADVERTISING RATES:
Full Page Mono £1667.70
Full Page Colour £2168.01
SCC £5.45
Agency Commission: 10%
Mechanical Data: Col Length: 340mm, Type Area: 340 x 264mm, Page Width: 264mm, No. of Columns (Display): 9, Film: Digital, Col Widths (Display): 28mm
Copy instructions: Copy Date: Monday noon prior to publication date
Average advertising content per issue: 70%
Series owner and contact point for the following titles, see individual entries:
Stafford Post
Stone Post
LOCAL NEWSPAPERS: Local Newspapers English Counties

STAFFORDSHIRE NEWSLETTER, AT THE HEART OF STAFFORDSHIRE & RUGELEY
44318U72B-3020_157

Formerly: Staffordshire Newsletter Stafford Edition
Frequency: Weekly
Circulation: 21,500 (Publisher's Statement)
Part of Series, see entry for: Staffordshire Newsletter Series
LOCAL NEWSPAPERS: Local Newspapers English Counties

STAFFORDSHIRE NEWSLETTER SERIES
44315U72B-3020

Editorial Address: The Publishing Centre, Derby Street, STAFFORD, ST16 2DT **Tel:** 01785 257700
Fax: 01785 253287
Email: editor@staffordshirenewsletter.co.uk
Advertising Address: As above.
Email: leanne.scoins@staffordshirenewspapers.co.uk
Web site: http://www.staffordshirenewsletter.co.uk
Publisher: Staffordshire Newspapers Ltd
Date Established: 1906
Frequency: Weekly - Published on Thursday
Cover Price: £0.60
Circulation: 24,500 (Publisher's Statement)
Editor: Diana Nevin
Summary of Content: Local news items, reports, community news and entertainments.
Readership/Target Audience: Local residents.
ADVERTISING RATES:
SCC £8.15
Agency Commission: 10%
Mechanical Data: Type Area: 350 x 268mm, Page Width: 268mm, Col Widths (Display): 28mm, Film: Digital, Col Length: 350mm, No. of Columns (Display): 9
Copy instructions: Copy Date: 2 days prior to publication date
Series owner and contact point for the following titles, see individual entries:
Staffordshire Newsletter, at the Heart of Staffordshire & Rugeley
Staffordshire Newsletter Stone Edition
Supplement(s): Staffordshire Guide - 1xY
LOCAL NEWSPAPERS: Local Newspapers English Counties

STAFFORDSHIRE NEWSLETTER STONE EDITION
44319U72B-3020_160

Frequency: Weekly
Circulation: 3,000 (Publisher's Statement)

Part of Series, see entry for: Staffordshire Newsletter Series
LOCAL NEWSPAPERS: Local Newspapers English Counties

STAINES & ASHFORD NEWS
44380U72B-3137_155

Frequency: Weekly - Circulation figure is incorporated into the Chertsey, Addlestone & Byfleet Herald
Cover Price: £0.35
Part of Series, see entry for: Staines Informer Series
LOCAL NEWSPAPERS: Local Newspapers English Counties

STAINES & EGHAM NEWS
44382U72B-3137_180

Frequency: Weekly - Circulation figure is incorporated into the Chertsey, Addlestone & Byfleet Herald
Cover Price: £0.35
Part of Series, see entry for: Staines Informer Series
LOCAL NEWSPAPERS: Local Newspapers English Counties

STAINES INFORMER
44378U72B-3137_140

Frequency: Weekly - Published on Thursday
Cover Price: Free
Circulation: 49,462 (VFD 02/07/2007 to 30/12/2007)
Part of Series, see entry for: Staines Informer Series
LOCAL NEWSPAPERS: Local Newspapers English Counties

STAINES INFORMER SERIES
44377U72B-3137

Editorial Address: 89 Eastworth Road, CHERTSEY, KT16 8DX **Tel:** 01932 561111 **Fax:** 01932 568235
Email: surreynewspapers@trinitysouth.co.uk
Advertising Address: As above. **Tel:** 01932 561122
Fax: 01932 566804
Email: fieldsaleschertsey@trinitysouth.co.uk
Web site: http://www.surreyherald.co.uk
Publisher: Trinity Mirror Southern
Frequency: Weekly
Circulation: 197,957 (Combined Circulation)
Editor: News Desk; **Advertising Manager:** Rachel Atherbury
ADVERTISING RATES:
Full Page Mono £3054.56
Full Page Colour £3970.93
Agency Commission: 10%
Mechanical Data: Film: Digital, Type Area: 340 x 262mm, Col Length: 340mm, Page Width: 262mm, Col Widths (Display): 31mm, No. of Columns (Display): 8
Average advertising content per issue: 80%
Series owner and contact point for the following titles, see individual entries:
Chertsey, Addlestone & Byfleet Herald
Staines & Ashford News
Staines & Egham News
Staines Informer
Sunbury & Shepperton Herald
Walton and Weybridge Herald
Walton & Weybridge Informer
Woking Informer
LOCAL NEWSPAPERS: Local Newspapers English Counties

THE STAMFORD, BOURNE AND THE DEEPINGS CITIZEN
1655835U72B-2274_171

Frequency: Weekly
Cover Price: Free
Circulation: 10,113 (VFD 02/07/2007 to 30/12/2007)
Part of Series, see entry for: Rutland & Stamford Mercury and Citizen Series
LOCAL NEWSPAPERS: Local Newspapers English Counties

STAMFORD MERCURY (BOURNE EDITION)
44071U72B-2274_160

Frequency: Weekly - Circulation figure is incorporated into the Rutland Mercury
Cover Price: £0.50
Part of Series, see entry for: Rutland & Stamford Mercury and Citizen Series
LOCAL NEWSPAPERS: Local Newspapers English Counties

STAMFORD MERCURY (STAMFORD AND DEEPINGS EDITION)
44072U72B-2274_170

Frequency: Weekly - Circulation figure is incorporated into the Rutland Mercury
Cover Price: £0.50

Part of Series, see entry for: Rutland & Stamford Mercury and Citizen Series
LOCAL NEWSPAPERS: Local Newspapers English Counties

STANMORE OBSERVER   1641183U72A-170_191
Frequency: Weekly - Published on Thursday. For circulation, see Harrow Observer
Cover Price: £0.35
ADVERTISING RATES:
SCC £11.70
Part of Series, see entry for: Harrow Observer & Leader Series
LOCAL NEWSPAPERS: Local Newspapers Greater London

STAR AND EXPRESS SERIES   44264U72B-2934
Formerly: Somerset Star and Express Series
Editorial Address: 44 St. James Street, TAUNTON, TA1 1JR **Tel:** 01823 365100 **Fax:** 01823 365200
Email: newsdesk@countygazette.co.uk
Advertising Address: As above. **Tel:** 01823 365000
Fax: 01823 365240
Email: sales@countygazette.co.uk
Web site: http://www.somersetcountygazette.co.uk
Publisher: Newsquest (Media Group) Ltd
Date Established: 1985
Frequency: Weekly
Cover Price: Free
Circulation: 95,047 (Combined Circulation)
Editor: News Desk; **Editor-in-Chief:** Ken Bird; **Managing Director:** Vincent Boni; **Advertising Manager:** Karen Bosley
ADVERTISING RATES:
Full Page Mono £3030.30
Full Page Colour £3787.88
SCC £15.05
Agency Commission: 10%
Mechanical Data: Type Area: 350 x 264mm, Col Length: 350mm, No. of Columns (Display): 9, Col Widths (Display): 28mm, Film: Digital, Print Process: Web-fed offset litho, Page Width: 264mm
Copy instructions: Copy Date: Monday prior to publication date
Average advertising content per issue: 70%
Series owner and contact point for the following titles, see individual entries:
The Star (Bridgewater)
The Star (Mid Devon)
The Star (Taunton & Wellington)
Yeovil Express
LOCAL NEWSPAPERS: Local Newspapers English Counties

STAR AND MERSEYMART ANFIELD & WALTON   44097U72B-2383_160
Frequency: Weekly
Cover Price: Free
Circulation: 30,902 (VFD 02/07/2007 to 30/12/2007)
ADVERTISING: Rates on application
Part of Series, see entry for: Liverpool Weekly Merseymart & Star Series
LOCAL NEWSPAPERS: Local Newspapers English Counties

THE STAR (BRIDGEWATER)   44265U72B-2934_110
Formerly: The Star (Sedgemoor)
Frequency: Weekly
Cover Price: Free
Circulation: 19,463 (VFD 01/01/2007 to 01/07/2007)
ADVERTISING RATES:
Full Page Mono £976.50
Full Page Colour £1220.63
SCC £3.30
Part of Series, see entry for: Star and Express Series
LOCAL NEWSPAPERS: Local Newspapers English Counties

THE STAR DONCASTER   42170U67B-1030_560
Formerly: Doncaster Star
Cover Price: £0.40
Edition of: The Star Sheffield
REGIONAL DAILY & SUNDAY NEWSPAPERS: Regional Daily Newspapers

STAR LITE   1800040U67B-1030_642
Frequency: Weekly
Cover Price: Free
Circulation: 5,000 (Print Run)
Edition of: The Star Sheffield
REGIONAL DAILY & SUNDAY NEWSPAPERS: Regional Daily Newspapers

THE STAR (MID DEVON)   44266U72B-2934_130
Frequency: Weekly
Cover Price: Free
Circulation: 18,354 (VFD 02/07/2007 to 30/12/2007)
ADVERTISING RATES:
Full Page Mono £573.30
Full Page Colour £716.63
SCC £3.30
Part of Series, see entry for: Star and Express Series
LOCAL NEWSPAPERS: Local Newspapers English Counties

STAR SERIES   44491U72B-3371
Editorial Address: Echo House, Pennywell, SUNDERLAND, SR4 9ER **Tel:** 0191 501 7208 **Fax:** 0191 534 5975
Email: echo.news@northeast-press.co.uk
Advertising Address: As above. **Tel:** 0191 501 5800
Fax: 0191 534 7497
Email: lynn.wild@northeast-press.co.uk
Web site: http://www.northeast-press.co.uk
Publisher: Northeast Press Ltd
Date Established: 1988
Frequency: Weekly
Cover Price: Free
Circulation: 138,751 (Combined Circulation)
Editor: Peter Jeffrey; **Managing Director:** Stuart Birkett
ADVERTISING RATES:
SCC £19.25
Agency Commission: 10%
Mechanical Data: Col Length: 340mm, Page Width: 276mm, Type Area: 340 x 276mm, Col Widths (Display): 28mm, No. of Columns (Display): 9
Copy instructions: Copy Date: 7 days prior to publication date
Average advertising content per issue: 65%
Series owner and contact point for the following titles, see individual entries:
Hartlepool Star
Houghton Star
Peterlee Star
Seaham Star
South Tyne Star
Sunderland Star
Washington Star
LOCAL NEWSPAPERS: Local Newspapers English Counties

STAR SERIES (SELBY & YORK)   44665U72B-3645
Formerly: Star & Gazette Series
Editorial Address: PO Box 29, 76-86 Walmgate, YORK, YO1 9YN **Tel:** 01904 653051 **Fax:** 01904 612853
Email: lynne.martin@thepress.co.uk
Advertising Address: As above. **Fax:** 01904 611488
Email: alyson.liversedge@ycp.co.uk
Web site: http://www.yorkpress.co.uk
Publisher: Newsquest Yorkshire and North East (York)
Frequency: Weekly - Published every Thursday
Cover Price: Free
Circulation: 67,353 (VFD 02/07/2007 to 30/12/2007)
Editor: Lynne Martin
ADVERTISING: Rates on application
Agency Commission: 10%
Mechanical Data: Col Widths (Display): 32mm, No. of Columns (Display): 9, Film: Digital
Copy instructions: Copy Date: Thursday 12pm prior to publication date
Average advertising content per issue: 80%
Series owner and contact point for the following titles, see individual entries:
Selby Star
York Star
LOCAL NEWSPAPERS: Local Newspapers English Counties

THE STAR SHEFFIELD   42168U67B-1030
Editorial Address: York Street, SHEFFIELD, S1 1PU
Tel: 0114 276 7676 **Fax:** 0114 272 5978
Email: starnews@sheffieldnewspapers.co.uk
Advertising Address: As above. **Fax:** 0114 252 1377
Email: marcus.schofield@sheffieldnewspapers.co.uk
Web site: http://www.thestar.co.uk
Publisher: Sheffield Newspapers Ltd
Date Established: 1870
Frequency: Evenings - Not published on Sunday
Cover Price: £0.40
Circulation: 56,363 (Publisher's Statement)
Editor: Newsdesk; **News Editor:** Charles Smith; **Features Editor:** Martin Smith; **Managing Director:** Mark Rodgers
ADVERTISING RATES:
SCC £21.74
Agency Commission: 10%
Mechanical Data: Col Length: 340mm, No. of Columns (Display): 9, Film: Digital, Type Area: 340 x 268mm, Page Width: 268mm
Copy instructions: Copy Date: Mono 2 days Colour 4 days prior to publication date

Editions:
The Star Doncaster
Star Lite
The Star Sheffield (City Edition)
REGIONAL DAILY & SUNDAY NEWSPAPERS: Regional Daily Newspapers

THE STAR SHEFFIELD (CITY EDITION)   1667575U67B-1030_641
Formerly: Star Sheffield (District Edition)
Frequency: Evenings
Cover Price: £0.40
Edition of: The Star Sheffield
REGIONAL DAILY & SUNDAY NEWSPAPERS: Regional Daily Newspapers

THE STAR (TAUNTON & WELLINGTON)   44267U72B-2934_150
Frequency: Weekly
Cover Price: Free
Circulation: 28,794 (VFD 02/07/2007 to 30/12/2007)
ADVERTISING RATES:
Full Page Mono £715.05
Full Page Colour £893.82
SCC £4.15
Part of Series, see entry for: Star and Express Series
LOCAL NEWSPAPERS: Local Newspapers English Counties

STEYNING HERALD   44467U72B-3323_170
Frequency: Weekly - Circulation figure is incorporated into the Shoreham Herald
Cover Price: £0.30
ADVERTISING: Rates on application
Part of Series, see entry for: Shoreham & Steyning Herald Series
LOCAL NEWSPAPERS: Local Newspapers English Counties

STIRLING NEWS INCORPORATING ALLOA AND HILLFOOT WEEKENDER   45029U72D-915
Formerly: Stirling News incorporating Alloa and Hillfoot News Extra
Editorial Address: 39 Drysdale Street, ALLOA, FK10 1JA
Tel: 01259 214416 **Fax:** 01259 722375
Email: stirling@dunfermlinepress.co.uk
Advertising Address: As above.
Email: advertising@alloaadvertiser.co.uk
Publisher: The Dunfermline Press Group
Frequency: Weekly
Cover Price: Free
Circulation: 27,192 (VFD 02/07/2007 to 30/12/2007)
Editor: Nicola Findlay; **Advertising Manager:** Roberta Bell
ADVERTISING RATES:
Full Page Mono £2052.00
Full Page Colour £4104.00
SCC £7.46
Agency Commission: 10%
Mechanical Data: Film: Digital, Col Widths (Display): 31mm, Type Area: 330 x 265.5mm, No. of Columns (Display): 8, Col Length: 330mm, Page Width: 265.5mm
Copy instructions: Copy Date: 2 days prior to publication date
Average advertising content per issue: 50%
LOCAL NEWSPAPERS: Local Newspapers Scotland

STIRLING OBSERVER COUNTY EDITION   45031U72D-920_110
Frequency: Weekly - Published on Friday
Cover Price: £0.80
ADVERTISING RATES:
Full Page Mono £2580.00
Full Page Colour £3483.00
SCC £8.20
Part of Series, see entry for: Stirling Observer Series
LOCAL NEWSPAPERS: Local Newspapers Scotland

STIRLING OBSERVER SERIES   45030U72D-920
Editorial Address: 34 Upper Craigs, STIRLING, FK8 2DW
Tel: 01786 451110 **Fax:** 01786 459429
Email: observer@s-un.co.uk
Advertising Address: As above. **Tel:** 01786 451111
Fax: 01786 449463
Email: adv-observer@s-un.co.uk
Web site: http://www.stirlingobserver.co.uk
Publisher: Scottish & Universal Newspapers Ltd
Date Established: 1836
Frequency: 104 issues yearly
Cover Price: £0.85

Non-National Newspapers

Circulation: 16,849 (Publisher's Statement)
Editor: Donald Morton; **Advertising Manager:** Alison Millar
ADVERTISING RATES:
Full Page Mono £6098.00
Full Page Colour £8232.00
SCC £19.40
Agency Commission: 10%
Mechanical Data: Film: Digital, Type Area: 340 x 265mm,
Col Length: 340mm, Page Width: 265mm, No. of Columns
(Display): 9
Average advertising content per issue: 40%
**Series owner and contact point for the following titles,
see individual entries:**
Stirling Observer County Edition
Stirling Observer Town Edition
LOCAL NEWSPAPERS: Local Newspapers Scotland

STIRLING OBSERVER TOWN EDITION
45032U72D-920_130
Frequency: Weekly - Published on Wednesday
Cover Price: £0.80
ADVERTISING RATES:
Full Page Mono £2580.00
Full Page Colour £3483.00
SCC £8.20
Part of Series, see entry for: Stirling Observer Series
LOCAL NEWSPAPERS: Local Newspapers Scotland

STIRLING SHOPPER
45035U72D-930_180
Frequency: Weekly - Circulation includes Alloa Shopper
Cover Price: Free
Circulation: 7,049 (Publisher's Statement)
Part of Series, see entry for: Stirling Shopper Series
LOCAL NEWSPAPERS: Local Newspapers Scotland

STIRLING SHOPPER SERIES
45033U72D-930
Editorial Address: 34 Upper Craigs, STIRLING, FK8 2DW
Tel: 01786 451110 **Fax:** 01786 459429
Email: observer@s-un.co.uk
Advertising Address: As above. **Tel:** 01786 451111
Fax: 01786 449463
Email: adv-observer@s-un.co.uk
Web site: http://www.stirlingobserver.co.uk
Publisher: Scottish & Universal Newspapers Ltd
Date Established: 1836
Frequency: Weekly - Published on Thursday
Cover Price: Free
Circulation: 7,049 (Combined Circulation)
Editor: Alan Rennie; **Advertising Manager:** Alison Millar
ADVERTISING RATES:
Full Page Mono £2194.00
Full Page Colour £2961.90
SCC £7.05
Agency Commission: 10%
Mechanical Data: No. of Columns (Display): 9, Col Widths
(Display): 27mm, Film: Digital, Type Area: 340 x 265mm, Col
Length: 340mm, Page Width: 265mm
Copy instructions: Copy Date: 1 week prior to publication
date
Average advertising content per issue: 40%
**Series owner and contact point for the following titles,
see individual entries:**
Alloa & Hillfoots Shopper
Stirling Shopper
LOCAL NEWSPAPERS: Local Newspapers Scotland

STOCKBRIDGE AND NEW TOWN GAZETTE
1800035U72D-1023_102
Frequency: Monthly
Cover Price: Free
Circulation: 4,000 (Publisher's Statement)
Part of Series, see entry for: The Gazette Series
(Edinburgh)
LOCAL NEWSPAPERS: Local Newspapers Scotland

STOCKPORT CITIZEN
1640889U72B-3945
Formerly: The Citizen (Stockport)
Editorial Address: 62 Argyll Road, CHEADLE, SK8 2LH
Tel: 0161 491 4073
Email: citizenmatters@aol.com
Advertising Address: 4A Ravenoak Road, CHEADLE
HULME, SK8 7BL **Tel:** 0161 486 1100
Email: citizenpapers@aol.com
Web site: http://www.stockportcitizen.co.uk
Publisher: Citizen Newspapers Ltd
Date Established: 2001
Frequency: 26 issues yearly
Cover Price: Free
Circulation: 60,000 (Publisher's Statement)
Editor: Mike Sheils; **Advertising Manager:** Mike Sheils

ADVERTISING: Rates on application
LOCAL NEWSPAPERS: Local Newspapers English
Counties

STOCKPORT EXPRESS
43720U72B-1300_110
Frequency: Weekly - Published every Wednesday
Cover Price: £0.44
Circulation: 14,516 (ABC 02/07/2007 to 30/12/2007)
ADVERTISING RATES:
SCC £7.10
Part of Series, see entry for: Stockport Express and Times
Series
LOCAL NEWSPAPERS: Local Newspapers English
Counties

STOCKPORT EXPRESS AND TIMES SERIES
43719U72B-1300
Editorial Address: Wood Street, Hollywood, STOCKPORT,
SK3 0AB **Tel:** 0161 475 4834 **Fax:** 0161 475 4868
Email: stockportexpress@menwn.co.uk
Advertising Address: As above. **Tel:** 0161 480 4491
Fax: 0161 480 4837
Email: mark.wroe@menmediasales.co.uk
Web site: http://www.stockportexpress.co.uk
Publisher: MEN Media
Frequency: Weekly
Circulation: 112,974 (Combined Circulation)
Editor: Paul Maher; **News Editor:** Paul Maher; **Features
Editor:** Lisa Cooper
ADVERTISING: Rates on application
Agency Commission: 10%
Mechanical Data: Page Width: 267mm, Film: Digital, Type
Area: 340 x 267mm, Col Length: 340mm, Col Widths
(Display): 27mm, No. of Columns (Display): 9
Copy instructions: Copy Date: Tuesday 1.00pm prior to
publication date
**Series owner and contact point for the following titles,
see individual entries:**
Stockport Express
Stockport Times East
Stockport Times West
LOCAL NEWSPAPERS: Local Newspapers English
Counties

STOCKPORT TIMES EAST
43721U72B-1300_120
Frequency: Weekly - Published every Thursday
Cover Price: Free
Circulation: 51,409 (VFD 02/07/2007 to 30/12/2007)
ADVERTISING RATES:
SCC £6.85
Agency Commission: 10%
Part of Series, see entry for: Stockport Express and Times
Series
LOCAL NEWSPAPERS: Local Newspapers English
Counties

STOCKPORT TIMES WEST
43722U72B-1300_140
Frequency: Weekly - Published every Thursday
Cover Price: Free
Circulation: 47,049 (VFD 02/07/2007 to 30/12/2007)
ADVERTISING RATES:
SCC £6.85
Agency Commission: 10%
Part of Series, see entry for: Stockport Express and Times
Series
LOCAL NEWSPAPERS: Local Newspapers English
Counties

THE STOCKSBRIDGE AND DISTRICT JOURNAL
764748U72B-3712_180
Frequency: Weekly
Cover Price: Free
ADVERTISING RATES:
Full Page Mono £746.64
Full Page Colour £970.63
SCC £2.44
Part of Series, see entry for: Sheffield Journal Series
LOCAL NEWSPAPERS: Local Newspapers English
Counties

STOCKTON & BILLINGHAM HERALD & POST
43411U72B-3360_200
Formerly: Stockton and District Herald & Post
Frequency: Weekly - Published on Wednesday
Cover Price: Free
Circulation: 63,647 (VFD 02/07/2007 to 30/12/2007)
ADVERTISING RATES:
Full Page Mono £2775.00
Full Page Colour £3746.25
SCC £10.20

Part of Series, see entry for: Herald and Post Series
(Teesside)
LOCAL NEWSPAPERS: Local Newspapers English
Counties

STONE POST
1849425U72B-3025_101
Frequency: Weekly - Published on Wednesday
Cover Price: Free
ADVERTISING: Rates on application
Part of Series, see entry for: Stafford Post Series
LOCAL NEWSPAPERS: Local Newspapers English
Counties

STORNOWAY GAZETTE AND WEST COAST ADVERTISER
45036U72D-950
Editorial Address: 10 Francis Street, STORNOWAY, HS1
2XE **Tel:** 01851 702687 **Fax:** 01851 705019
Email: newsdesk@stornowaygazette.co.uk
Advertising Address: As above. **Fax:** 01851 706424
Email: advertising@stornowaygazette.co.uk
Web site: http://www.stornowaygazette.co.uk
Publisher: Johnston Press plc
Frequency: Weekly - Published on Thursday
Cover Price: £0.65
Circulation: 13,006 (ABC 02/07/2007 to 30/12/2007)
Editor: Melinda Gillen; **Managing Director:** Angus Morrison;
Advertising Manager: Michelle Macaulay
Language(s): English; Gaelic
ADVERTISING: Rates on application
LOCAL NEWSPAPERS: Local Newspapers Scotland

STOURBRIDGE CHRONICLE
44536U72B-3450_180
Frequency: Weekly
Cover Price: Free
Circulation: 45,854 (VFD 02/07/2007 to 30/12/2007)
ADVERTISING: Rates on application
Part of Series, see entry for: Dudley Chronicle Series
LOCAL NEWSPAPERS: Local Newspapers English
Counties

STOURBRIDGE NEWS
44547U72B-3477
Formerly: Stourbridge News & County Express
Editorial Address: St. John's House, St. John's Road,
STOURBRIDGE, DY8 1EH **Tel:** 01384 358225
Fax: 01384 358252
Email: newsgrouped@midlands.newsquest.co.uk
Advertising Address: As above. **Tel:** 01384 358200
Fax: 01384 358253
Email: caroline.smith@midlands.newsquest.co.uk
Web site: http://www.stourbridgenews.co.uk
Publisher: Newsquest Media Group
Frequency: Weekly - Published on Thursdays
Cover Price: Free
Circulation: 51,747 (VFD 02/07/2007 to 30/12/2007)
Usual Pagination: 136
Editor: News Desk; **Advertising Manager:** Caroline Smith;
Publisher: Peter John
ADVERTISING: Rates on application
LOCAL NEWSPAPERS: Local Newspapers English
Counties

STOWMARKET ADVERTISER
1656822U72B-3078_105
Frequency: Weekly - This is an edition of the Ipswich
Advertiser
Cover Price: Free
Part of Series, see entry for: Advertiser Series (Ipswich)
LOCAL NEWSPAPERS: Local Newspapers English
Counties

STRABANE CHRONICLE
45134U72E-270_190
Frequency: Weekly - Published on Thursday
Circulation: 5,307 (ABC 02/07/2007 to 30/12/2007)
Part of Series, see entry for: Ulster Herald Series
LOCAL NEWSPAPERS: Local Newspapers Northern Ireland

STRABANE WEEKLY NEWS
45129U72E-230_160
Frequency: Weekly
Cover Price: £0.70
Circulation: 2,996 (Publisher's Statement)
ADVERTISING: Rates on application
Part of Series, see entry for: Tyrone Constitution and
Strabane Weekly News Series
LOCAL NEWSPAPERS: Local Newspapers Northern Ireland

STRANRAER & WIGTOWNSHIRE FREE PRESS

45037U72D-955

Formerly: Wigtown Free Press and Stranraer Advertiser
Editorial Address: St. Andrew Street, STRANRAER, DG9 7EB **Tel:** 01776 702551 **Fax:** 01776 706695
Email: alan.hall@stranraer-freepress.co.uk
Advertising Address: As above.
Email: sales@stranraer-freepress.co.uk
Web site: http://www.stranraer-freepress.co.uk
ISSN: 1468-6384
Publisher: Stranraer & Wigtownshire Free Press
Date Established: 1842
Frequency: Weekly - Published on Thursday
Cover Price: £0.65
Circulation: 7,733 (ABC 01/01/2007 to 30/12/2007)
Editor: Alan Hall
ADVERTISING RATES:
Full Page Mono £1440.00
Full Page Colour £2280.00
SCC £6.00
Mechanical Data: No. of Columns (Display): 6, Type Area: 394 x 284mm, Col Length: 394mm, Col Widths (Display): 44mm, Film: Digital, Page Width: 284mm
Copy instructions: Copy Date: Tuesday 12 noon prior to publication date
LOCAL NEWSPAPERS: Local Newspapers Scotland

STRATFORD & NEWHAM EXPRESS

43148U72A-480

Formerly: Stratford & Newham Express Series
Editorial Address: 539 High Road, ILFORD, IG1 1UD
Tel: 020 8472 1421 **Fax:** 020 8471 7908
Email: pat.coughtrey@newhamrecorder.co.uk
Advertising Address: As above.
Email: kevin.poulter@archant.co.uk
Web site: http://www.stratfordandnewhamexpress.co.uk
Publisher: Archant Regional
Date Established: 1850
Frequency: Weekly
Cover Price: Free
Circulation: 49,981 (VFD 03/07/2006 to 31/12/2006)
Editor: Colin Grainger; **News Editor:** Pat Coughtrey
ADVERTISING RATES:
Full Page Mono £1775.50
Full Page Colour £2221.88
SCC £7.90
Mechanical Data: No. of Columns (Display): 9, Col Widths (Display): 27.5mm, Film: Digital
Copy instructions: Copy Date: Monday 5.30pm prior to publication date
Average advertising content per issue: 60%
LOCAL NEWSPAPERS: Local Newspapers Greater London

STRATFORD-UPON-AVON HERALD

44521U72B-3410_200

Frequency: Weekly
Cover Price: £0.35
Circulation: 17,278 (Publisher's Statement)
ADVERTISING RATES:
Full Page Colour £4499.00
Mechanical Data: Page Width: 330mm, Film: Digital, Type Area: 540 x 330mm, Col Length: 540mm, No. of Columns (Display): 9, Col Widths (Display): 34mm
Part of Series, see entry for: Stratford-upon-Avon Herald Series
LOCAL NEWSPAPERS: Local Newspapers English Counties

STRATFORD UPON-AVON & ARDEN OBSERVER

44510U72B-3382_200

Formerly: Stratford Upon-Avon-Observer
Frequency: Weekly
Cover Price: Free
Circulation: 43,000 (Publisher's Statement)
ADVERTISING: Rates on application
Part of Series, see entry for: Leamington & Stratford Observer Series
LOCAL NEWSPAPERS: Local Newspapers English Counties

STRATFORD-UPON-AVON HERALD SERIES

44518U72B-3410

Editorial Address: York House, 17 Rother Street, STRATFORD-UPON-AVON, CV37 6NB **Tel:** 01789 266261
Fax: 01789 269519
Email: news@stratford-herald.com
Advertising Address: As above.
Email: publishing@stratford-herald.com
Web site: http://www.stratford-herald.com
Publisher: George Boyden & Son
Date Established: 1860
Frequency: Weekly

Circulation: 70,303 (Combined Circulation)
Usual Pagination: 40
Editor: Philippa Prankard; **News Editor:** Philippa Prankard;
Advertising Manager: Tracy Thompson
ADVERTISING: Rates on application
Agency Commission: 10%
Average advertising content per issue: 60%
Series owner and contact point for the following titles, see individual entries:
Focus (Colour Supplement)
Midweek Stratford-upon-Avon
Stratford-upon-Avon Herald
LOCAL NEWSPAPERS: Local Newspapers English Counties

STRATHAVEN EXTRA

1647094U72D-664_161

Frequency: Weekly
Cover Price: Free
ADVERTISING RATES:
SCC £6.00
Part of Series, see entry for: Lanarkshire Extra Series
LOCAL NEWSPAPERS: Local Newspapers Scotland

STRATHEARN HERALD

45038U72D-960

Editorial Address: 7 East High Street, CRIEFF, PH7 3AF
Tel: 01764 656501 **Fax:** 01764 656502
Email: herald@s-un.co.uk
Advertising Address: 58 Watergate, PERTH, PH1 5TF
Tel: 01738 626211 **Fax:** 01738 493299
Email: lgardiner@s-un.co.uk
Web site: http://www.strathearnherald.co.uk
Publisher: Scottish & Universal Newspapers Ltd
Date Established: 1856
Frequency: Weekly - Published on Thursday
Cover Price: £0.72
Circulation: 3,047 (ABC 02/07/2007 to 30/12/2007)
Editor: Caroline Boxer
ADVERTISING RATES:
SCC £5.70
Mechanical Data: Page Width: 270mm, Type Area: 390 x 270mm, Col Length: 390mm, Col Widths (Display): 31mm, No. of Columns (Display): 8, Film: Digital
LOCAL NEWSPAPERS: Local Newspapers Scotland

STRATHSPEY & BADENOCH HERALD

45039U72D-964

Editorial Address: 44 High Street, GRANTOWN-ON-SPEY, PH26 3EH **Tel:** 01479 872102 **Fax:** 01479 873435
Email: editorial@sbherald.co.uk
Advertising Address: As above.
Email: advertising@northern-scot.co.uk
Web site: http://www.sbherald.co.uk
Publisher: Moray & Nairn Newspaper Co Ltd
Frequency: Weekly - Published on Wednesday
Cover Price: £0.55
Circulation: 4,844 (ABC 01/01/2007 to 30/12/2007)
Editor: Gavin Musgrove; **Advertising Manager:** Jacqui O'Rourke
ADVERTISING RATES:
SCC £3.40
Agency Commission: 10%
Mechanical Data: Col Widths (Display): 35mm, Page Width: 377mm, Film: Digital, Type Area: 550 x 377mm, Col Length: 550mm, No. of Columns (Display): 10
Copy instructions: Copy Date: Monday 3.45pm prior to publication date
Average advertising content per issue: 45%
LOCAL NEWSPAPERS: Local Newspapers Scotland

STREATHAM, WEST NORWOOD & CRYSTAL PALACE GUARDIAN

43004U72A-128_200

Formerly: Streatham, Clapham & Dulwich Guardian
Frequency: Weekly
Cover Price: Free
Circulation: 22,992 (Publisher's Statement)
Part of Series, see entry for: Guardian & News Series (Sutton)
LOCAL NEWSPAPERS: Local Newspapers Greater London

STRETFORD & URMSTON MESSENGER

43714U72B-1287_190

Frequency: Weekly
Cover Price: Free
Circulation: 24,710 (VFD 02/07/2007 to 30/12/2007)
ADVERTISING: Rates on application
Part of Series, see entry for: Sale & Altrincham Messenger Series
LOCAL NEWSPAPERS: Local Newspapers English Counties

STROUD LIFE

1837012U72B-4152

Editorial Address: 1 Clarence Parade, CHELTENHAM, GL50 3NY **Tel:** 01452 424442
Email: stroudlife@glosmedia.co.uk
Advertising Address: 14 Union Street, STROUD, GL5 2HE
Tel: 01453 759799 **Fax:** 01453 757711
Email: sadie.malin@glosmedia.co.uk
Web site: http://www.thisisgloucestershire.co.uk/stroud
Publisher: Gloucestershire Media
Date Established: 2008
Frequency: Weekly
Cover Price: £0.20
Editor: Ian Mean
ADVERTISING: Rates on application
LOCAL NEWSPAPERS: Local Newspapers English Counties

STROUD NEWS AND JOURNAL

43667U72B-1145

Editorial Address: 6 Lansdown, STROUD, GL5 1BE
Tel: 01453 762412 **Fax:** 01453 764165
Email: snjnews@stroudnewsandjournal.co.uk
Advertising Address: As above. **Tel:** 01453 751567
Fax: 01453 752979
Email: dean.amos@gwent-wales.co.uk
Web site: http://www.stroudnewsandjournal.co.uk
Publisher: Newsquest Wales & Gloucestershire
Date Established: 1854
Frequency: Weekly - Published on Wednesday
Cover Price: £0.55
Circulation: 17,227 (ABC 02/07/2007 to 30/12/2007)
Usual Pagination: 64
Editor: Sue Smith; **News Editor:** Tamash Lal; **Managing Director:** Gavin Stacey; **Advertising Manager:** Dean Amos;
Publisher: Trevor Sallis
ADVERTISING RATES:
Full Page Mono £1759.50
SCC £5.75
Agency Commission: 10%
Mechanical Data: Film: Digital, Col Length: 340mm, No. of Columns (Display): 9, Type Area: 340 x 259mm, Page Width: 259mm
Copy instructions: Copy Date: Monday 5pm prior to publication date
Average advertising content per issue: 65%
Supplement(s): Christmas Gift Guide - 1xY, Eating Out - 2xY, Education - 4xY, Homes & Gardens - 2xY, SNJ Direct - 52xY, Weddings - 2xY
LOCAL NEWSPAPERS: Local Newspapers English Counties

SUDBURY MERCURY

44350U72B-3088_190

Formerly: West Suffolk Mercury - Sudbury Edition
Frequency: Weekly
Cover Price: Free
Circulation: 18,253 (VFD 02/07/2007 to 30/12/2007)
Part of Series, see entry for: Mercury Series
LOCAL NEWSPAPERS: Local Newspapers English Counties

SUFFOLK FREE PRESS

44347U72B-3083

Editorial Address: Borehamgate, SUDBURY, CO10 2EE
Tel: 01787 375271 **Fax:** 01787 880301
Email: jonathan.schofield@sudburytoday.co.uk
Advertising Address: As above. **Fax:** 01787 311174
Email: paul.taylor@suffolkfreepress.co.uk
Web site: http://www.suffolkfreepress.co.uk
Publisher: Johnston Press plc
Date Established: 1855
Frequency: Weekly - Published on Thursday
Cover Price: £0.47
Circulation: 9,596 (ABC 02/07/2007 to 30/12/2007)
Usual Pagination: 44
Editor: Jonathan Schofield; **Managing Director:** Richard Parkinson
ADVERTISING RATES:
Full Page Mono £2028.00
Full Page Colour £2406.30
SCC £6.63
Agency Commission: 10%
Mechanical Data: Col Widths (Display): 26mm, Col Length: 340mm, Type Area: 340 x 266mm, Page Width: 266mm, Film: Digital, No. of Columns (Display): 9
Copy instructions: Copy Date: Monday 5.00pm prior to publication date
Average advertising content per issue: 38%
Supplement(s): LifeStyle - 52xY
LOCAL NEWSPAPERS: Local Newspapers English Counties

Non-National Newspapers

SUNBURY & SHEPPERTON HERALD

44384U72B-3137_250

Formerly: Surrey Herald (Sunbury & Shepperton)
Frequency: Weekly - Circulation figure is incorporated into the Chertsey, Addlestone & Byfleet Herald
Cover Price: £0.35
Part of Series, see entry for: Staines Informer Series
LOCAL NEWSPAPERS: Local Newspapers English Counties

SUNDAY HERALD

42296U67C-38

Editorial Address: 200 Renfield Street, GLASGOW, G2 3QB
Tel: 0141 302 7800 **Fax:** 0141 302 7863
Email: news@sundayherald.com
Advertising Address: As above. **Tel:** 0141 302 7000
Fax: 0141 302 6010
Email: announcements@glasgow.newsquest.co.uk
Web site: http://www.sundayherald.com
Publisher: Newsquest Sunday Herald Ltd
Date Established: 1999
Frequency: Sunday
Cover Price: £1.40
Circulation: 44,048 (ABC 03/08/2009 to 30/08/2009)
Editor: News Desk; **Editor-in-Chief:** Donald Martin
ADVERTISING RATES:
Full Page Mono £6562.50
Full Page Colour £8531.25
SCC £15.00
Mechanical Data: Type Area: 344 x 260mm, Col Length: 344mm, No. of Columns (Display): 7, Col Widths (Display): 34mm, Page Width: 260mm, Film: Digital
Copy instructions: Copy Date: Thursday 5pm prior to publication date
Average advertising content per issue: 20%
Supplement(s): Fresh - 10xY, Scottish Review of Books - 4xY, Sunday Herald Magazine - 52xY
REGIONAL DAILY & SUNDAY NEWSPAPERS: Regional Sunday Newspapers

SUNDAY HERALD (EDINBURGH)

1639143U67E-551

Editorial Address: Bearford House, 39 Hanover Street, EDINBURGH, EH2 2PJ **Tel:** 0141 302 7000
Fax: 0141 302 7007
Email: edinburgh@theherald.co.uk
Web site: http://www.sundayherald.com
Publisher: Newsquest Sunday Herald Ltd
Date Established: 1999
Cover Price: £1.00
Editor: News Desk
ADVERTISING: No Advertising taken
REGIONAL DAILY & SUNDAY NEWSPAPERS: Regional Offices

SUNDAY HERALD MAGAZINE

31257U67H-325

Editorial Address: 200 Renfield Street, GLASGOW, G2 3QB
Tel: 0141 302 7800 **Fax:** 0141 302 7863
Email: magazine@sundayherald.com
Advertising Address: As above. **Tel:** 0141 302 7000
Fax: 0141 302 6363
Email: announcements@glasgow.newsquest.co.uk
Web site: http://www.sundayherald.com
Publisher: Newsquest Sunday Herald Ltd
Date Established: 1999
Frequency: Weekly
Cover Price: £1.60
Circulation: 70,000 (Publisher's Statement)
Editor: Susan Flockhart
Summary of Content: Magazine covering arts, entertainment, political and cultural events in Scotland with books and arts reviews, interviews, political features and TV listings. Also contains celebrity interviews, topical and general interest features.
ADVERTISING RATES:
Full Page Colour £3000.00
Mechanical Data: Type Area: 270 x 205mm, Bleed Size: 303 x 233mm, Trim Size: 297 x 230mm, Col Length: 270mm, Film: Digital, Col Widths (Display): 48mm, No. of Columns (Display): 4, Page Width: 205mm
Copy instructions: Copy Date: Thursday 1 week prior to publication date
Average advertising content per issue: 20%
Supplement to: Sunday Herald
REGIONAL DAILY & SUNDAY NEWSPAPERS: Regional Colour Supplements

SUNDAY INDEPENDENT (BRISTOL, SOMERSET & YEOVIL)

1643942U67C-30_500

Formerly: Sunday Independent (Bristol & Somerset)
Frequency: Sunday
Cover Price: £0.70

Edition of: Sunday Independent (Plymouth)
REGIONAL DAILY & SUNDAY NEWSPAPERS: Regional Sunday Newspapers

SUNDAY INDEPENDENT (CORNWALL)

1643940U67C-30_501

Frequency: Sunday
Cover Price: £0.70
Edition of: Sunday Independent (Plymouth)
REGIONAL DAILY & SUNDAY NEWSPAPERS: Regional Sunday Newspapers

SUNDAY INDEPENDENT (PLYMOUTH)

42282U67C-30

Editorial Address: The Tindle Suite, Webbs House, The Parade, LISKEARD, PL14 6AH **Tel:** 01579 342174
Fax: 01579 341851
Email: ct.edit@internet-today.co.uk
Advertising Address: As above. **Fax:** 01579 341852
Email: sales@sundayindependent.co.uk
Publisher: Tindle Newspapers Ltd
Date Established: 1808
Frequency: Sunday
Cover Price: £0.70
Circulation: 32,000 (Publisher's Statement)
Usual Pagination: 80
Editor: John Noble
ADVERTISING RATES:
Full Page Mono £1625.40
Full Page Colour £1869.21
Agency Commission: 10%
Mechanical Data: No. of Columns (Display): 8, Film: Digital
Copy instructions: Copy Date: Thursday 5pm prior to publication date
Average advertising content per issue: 35%
Editions:
Sunday Independent (Bristol, Somerset & Yeovil)
Sunday Independent (Cornwall)
REGIONAL DAILY & SUNDAY NEWSPAPERS: Regional Sunday Newspapers

SUNDAY JOURNAL

1647506U67C-102

Editorial Address: 22 Buncrana Road, LONDONDERRY, BT48 8AA **Tel:** 028 7127 2200 **Fax:** 028 7127 2204
Email: ellen.doherty@derryjournal.com
Advertising Address: As above. **Fax:** 028 7127 2225
Email: caroline.morris@derryjournal.com
Web site: http://www.sundayjournal.ie
Publisher: Derry Journal Ltd
Frequency: Sunday
Cover Price: £0.80
Circulation: 7,096 (ABC 02/07/2007 to 30/12/2007)
Editor: Martin McGinley; **Advertising Manager:** Caroline Morris
Summary of Content: Local news and features focusing on family and specialist features.
ADVERTISING RATES:
Full Page Mono £1239.30
Full Page Colour £1735.02
Agency Commission: 10%
Mechanical Data: Type Area: 340 x 268mm, Col Length: 340mm, Page Width: 268mm, Col Widths (Display): 28mm, No. of Columns (Display): 9, Film: Digital
Copy instructions: Copy Date: Thursday 4.00pm prior to publication date
Average advertising content per issue: 40%
REGIONAL DAILY & SUNDAY NEWSPAPERS: Regional Sunday Newspapers

SUNDAY LIFE (BELFAST)

42298U67C-58

Editorial Address: 124-144 Royal Avenue, BELFAST, BT1 1EB **Tel:** 028 9026 4000 **Fax:** 028 9055 4507
Email: mhill@belfasttelegraph.co.uk
Advertising Address: As above.
Email: p.beatty@belfasttelegraph.co.uk
Web site: http://www.sundaylife.co.uk
Publisher: Independent News and Media (UK) Ltd
Frequency: Sunday
Cover Price: £1.10
Circulation: 74,886 (ABC 01/01/2007 to 01/07/2007)
Editor: Martin Breen; **Features Editor:** Jane Hardy;
Managing Director: Michael Brophy
ADVERTISING RATES:
SCC £19.88
Agency Commission: 10%
Mechanical Data: Type Area: 342 x 272mm, Col Length: 342mm, Film: Digital, No. of Columns (Display): 10, Col Widths (Display): 32mm, Page Width: 272mm
Copy instructions: Copy Date: 1 week prior to publication date
Average advertising content per issue: 60%
REGIONAL DAILY & SUNDAY NEWSPAPERS: Regional Sunday Newspapers

SUNDAY MAIL

42297U67C-40

Formerly: Sunday Mail (Glasgow)
Editorial Address: 1 Central Quay, GLASGOW, G3 8DA
Tel: 0141 309 3000 **Fax:** 0141 309 3587
Email: mailbox@sundaymail.co.uk
Advertising Address: As above. **Fax:** 0141 309 3545
Email: advertising@dailyrecord.co.uk
Web site: http://www.sundaymail.co.uk
Publisher: Scottish Daily Record & Sunday Mail Ltd
Frequency: Sunday
Cover Price: £1.30
Circulation: 428,613 (ABC 03/08/2009 to 30/08/2009)
Usual Pagination: 80
Editor: Brendan McGinty; **News Editor:** Brendan McGinty;
Managing Director: Mark Hollinshead; **Advertising Manager:** Ian MacGillivray
Readership/Target Audience: Circulates throughout Scotland.
ADVERTISING RATES:
Full Page Mono £13890.00
Full Page Colour £18057.00
Agency Commission: 15%
Mechanical Data: Type Area: 340 x 265mm, Col Widths (Display): 35mm, No. of Columns (Display): 7, Film: Digital, Col Length: 340mm, Page Width: 265mm
Copy instructions: Copy Date: 2 days prior to publication date
Average advertising content per issue: 40%
Supplement(s): Mail Motors - 52xY, Right at Home - 52xY, Seven Days - 52xY
REGIONAL DAILY & SUNDAY NEWSPAPERS: Regional Sunday Newspapers

SUNDAY MERCURY (BIRMINGHAM)

42280U67C-10

Editorial Address: 6th Floor, Fort Dunlop, Fort Parkway, BIRMINGHAM, B24 9FF **Tel:** 0121 236 3366
Fax: 0121 234 5877
Email: sundaymercury@sundaymercury.net
Advertising Address: PO Box 18, Weaman Street, BIRMINGHAM, B4 6AX **Tel:** 0121 236 3366
Fax: 0121 234 5865
Email: andrea_watkeys@mrn.co.uk
Web site: http://www.sundaymercury.net
Publisher: BPM Media (Midlands)
Frequency: Sunday
Cover Price: £0.90
Circulation: 59,339 (ABC 02/07/2007 to 30/12/2007)
Editor: Steve Dyson; **News Editor:** Tony Larner; **Executive Editor:** Paul Cole; **Features Editor:** Lorne Jackson
ADVERTISING RATES:
Full Page Mono £5266.26
Full Page Colour £7109.45
SCC £17.21
Mechanical Data: Col Length: 340mm, Film: Digital, No. of Columns (Display): 9, Type Area: 340 x 264mm, Col Widths (Display): 28mm, Page Width: 264mm
Copy instructions: Copy Date: 4 days prior to publication date
Average advertising content per issue: 40%
REGIONAL DAILY & SUNDAY NEWSPAPERS: Regional Sunday Newspapers

SUNDAY POST ABERDEEN AND SHETLAND

42285U67C-35_510

Frequency: Sunday
Cover Price: £0.95
Edition of: The Sunday Post (Dundee)
REGIONAL DAILY & SUNDAY NEWSPAPERS: Regional Sunday Newspapers

SUNDAY POST CENTRAL SCOTLAND

42286U67C-35_530

Frequency: Sunday
Cover Price: £0.95
Edition of: The Sunday Post (Dundee)
REGIONAL DAILY & SUNDAY NEWSPAPERS: Regional Sunday Newspapers

THE SUNDAY POST (DUNDEE)

42284U67C-35

Editorial Address: 2 Albert Square, DUNDEE, DD1 9QJ
Tel: 01382 223131 **Fax:** 01382 201064
Email: mail@sundaypost.com
Advertising Address: As above. **Tel:** 01382 575149
Fax: 01382 454599
Email: advertising-meadowside@dcthomson.co.uk
Web site: http://www.sundaypost.com
Publisher: D.C. Thomson & Co Ltd
Date Established: 1919
Frequency: Sunday
Cover Price: £0.95
Circulation: 354,870 (ABC 03/08/2009 to 30/08/2009)

Editor: David Pollington; **News Editor:** Tom McKay; **Features Editor:** Bruce Allan; **Advertising Manager:** Bob Walker
ADVERTISING RATES:
Full Page Mono £10670.00
Full Page Colour £12804.00
SCC £48.50
Agency Commission: 10%
Mechanical Data: Print Process: Web-fed offset litho, Type Area: 350 x 264mm, Col Widths (Display): 26mm, Col Length: 350mm, No. of Columns (Display): 7, Page Width: 264mm
Copy instructions: Copy Date: Mono 4 days prior to publication date Colour 6 days prior to publication date
Editions:
Sunday Post Aberdeen and Shetland
Sunday Post Central Scotland
Sunday Post Dundee Edition
Sunday Post Edinburgh and Lothian
Sunday Post England and Ireland
Sunday Post Fife
Sunday Post Glasgow City
Sunday Post Inverness
Sunday Post Lanarkshire and Argyll
Sunday Post Scottish Borders
Supplement(s): Post Plus - 12xY
REGIONAL DAILY & SUNDAY NEWSPAPERS: Regional Sunday Newspapers

SUNDAY POST DUNDEE EDITION
42287U67C-35_540
Frequency: Sunday
Cover Price: £0.95
Edition of: The Sunday Post (Dundee)
REGIONAL DAILY & SUNDAY NEWSPAPERS: Regional Sunday Newspapers

SUNDAY POST EDINBURGH AND LOTHIAN
42288U67C-35_550
Frequency: Sunday
Cover Price: £0.95
Edition of: The Sunday Post (Dundee)
REGIONAL DAILY & SUNDAY NEWSPAPERS: Regional Sunday Newspapers

SUNDAY POST ENGLAND AND IRELAND
42289U67C-35_560
Frequency: Sunday
Cover Price: £0.95
Edition of: The Sunday Post (Dundee)
REGIONAL DAILY & SUNDAY NEWSPAPERS: Regional Sunday Newspapers

SUNDAY POST FIFE
42290U67C-35_570
Frequency: Sunday
Cover Price: £0.95
Edition of: The Sunday Post (Dundee)
REGIONAL DAILY & SUNDAY NEWSPAPERS: Regional Sunday Newspapers

SUNDAY POST GLASGOW CITY
42291U67C-35_580
Frequency: Sunday
Cover Price: £0.95
Edition of: The Sunday Post (Dundee)
REGIONAL DAILY & SUNDAY NEWSPAPERS: Regional Sunday Newspapers

THE SUNDAY POST (GLASGOW OFFICE)
42312U67E-550
Editorial Address: 144 Port Dundas Road, GLASGOW, G4 0HZ **Tel:** 0141 332 9933 **Fax:** 0141 331 1595
Email: newsdesk@sundaypost.com
Web site: http://www.sundaypost.com
Publisher: D.C. Thomson & Co Ltd
Cover Price: £0.95
Editor: Colin Grant; **News Editor:** Colin Grant
REGIONAL DAILY & SUNDAY NEWSPAPERS: Regional Offices

SUNDAY POST INVERNESS
42292U67C-35_590
Frequency: Sunday
Cover Price: £0.95
Edition of: The Sunday Post (Dundee)
REGIONAL DAILY & SUNDAY NEWSPAPERS: Regional Sunday Newspapers

SUNDAY POST LANARKSHIRE AND ARGYLL
42293U67C-35_600
Frequency: Sunday
Cover Price: £0.95
Edition of: The Sunday Post (Dundee)
REGIONAL DAILY & SUNDAY NEWSPAPERS: Regional Sunday Newspapers

THE SUNDAY POST (LONDON OFFICE)
42308U67D-400
Formerly: The Sunday Post (Scotland) (London Office)
Editorial Address: 185 Fleet Street, LONDON, EC4A 2HS
Tel: 020 7400 1030 **Fax:** 020 7400 1089
Email: gsherriff@sundaypost.com
Web site: http://www.sundaypost.com
Publisher: D.C. Thomson & Co Ltd
Frequency: Weekly
Cover Price: £1.00
Editor: Gavin Sherriff
REGIONAL DAILY & SUNDAY NEWSPAPERS: Regional Daily Sunday London City Office

SUNDAY POST SCOTTISH BORDERS
42294U67C-35_650
Frequency: Sunday
Cover Price: £0.95
Edition of: The Sunday Post (Dundee)
REGIONAL DAILY & SUNDAY NEWSPAPERS: Regional Sunday Newspapers

SUNDAY SUN
42281U67C-20
Formerly: Sunday Sun (Newcastle)
Editorial Address: Groat Market, NEWCASTLE UPON TYNE, NE1 1ED **Tel:** 0191 201 6201 **Fax:** 0191 201 6180
Email: scoop.sundaysun@ncjmedia.co.uk
Advertising Address: As above. **Tel:** 0191 232 7500
Fax: 0191 230 4144
Email: jane.holmes@ncjmedia.co.uk
Web site: http://www.sundaysun.co.uk
Publisher: NCJ Media Ltd
Date Established: 1919
Frequency: Sunday
Cover Price: £0.85
Circulation: 68,033 (ABC 02/07/2007 to 30/12/2007)
Editor: News Desk; **News Editor:** Mike Kelly; **Managing Director:** Steve Brown; **Advertising Manager:** Jane Holmes
ADVERTISING RATES:
Full Page Mono £4648.00
Full Page Colour £6274.00
SCC £16.60
Agency Commission: 10%
Mechanical Data: Type Area: 350 x 277mm, Print Process: Web offset, Col Length: 350mm, Page Width: 277mm, No. of Columns (Display): 8, Film: Digital
Average advertising content per issue: 60%
Editions:
Sunday Sun (City)
Sunday Sun (Coast)
Supplement(s): Choice - 52xY
REGIONAL DAILY & SUNDAY NEWSPAPERS: Regional Sunday Newspapers

SUNDAY SUN (CITY)
1668047U67C-20_501
Frequency: Sunday
Cover Price: £0.80
Edition of: Sunday Sun
REGIONAL DAILY & SUNDAY NEWSPAPERS: Regional Sunday Newspapers

SUNDAY SUN (COAST)
1668044U67C-20_500
Frequency: Sunday
Cover Price: £0.80
Edition of: Sunday Sun
REGIONAL DAILY & SUNDAY NEWSPAPERS: Regional Sunday Newspapers

SUNDAY WORLD NORTHERN IRELAND EDITION
42299U67C-100
Editorial Address: 3-5 Commercial Court, Off Hill Street, BELFAST, BT1 2NB **Tel:** 028 9023 8118 **Fax:** 028 9023 8120
Email: richard.sullivan@nth.sundayworld.com
Advertising Address: As above. **Tel:** 028 9040 8731
Fax: 028 9023 6155
Email: graeme.smith@sundayworld.com
Publisher: Sunday Newspapers Ltd
Frequency: Sunday
Cover Price: £1.00
Circulation: 71,000 (Publisher's Statement)

Editor: Richard Sullivan; **News Editor:** Richard Sullivan; **Features Editor:** Roisin Gorman; **Advertising Manager:** Graeme Smith
ADVERTISING RATES:
Full Page Mono £2580.00
Full Page Colour £4450.00
SCC £18.00
Agency Commission: 15%
Mechanical Data: Col Length: 336mm, No. of Columns (Display): 7, Film: Digital, Col Widths (Display): 35mm, Page Width: 269mm, Type Area: 336 x 269mm
Copy instructions: Copy Date: Friday am prior to publication date
Average advertising content per issue: 5%
REGIONAL DAILY & SUNDAY NEWSPAPERS: Regional Sunday Newspapers

SUNDERLAND ECHO
42184U67B-1070
Editorial Address: Echo House, Pennywell, SUNDERLAND, SR4 9ER **Tel:** 0191 501 5800 **Fax:** 0191 534 5975
Email: echo.news@northeast-press.co.uk
Advertising Address: As above. **Fax:** 0191 534 3807
Email: sharon.ewart@northeast-press.co.uk
Web site: http://www.sunderlandecho.com
Publisher: Northeast Press Ltd
Date Established: 1873
Frequency: Evenings
Cover Price: £0.42
Circulation: 42,910 (ABC 02/07/2007 to 30/12/2007)
Editor: Peter Jeffrey; **News Editor:** Peter Jeffrey; **Features Editor:** Steve Sharpe; **Managing Director:** Stuart Birkett
ADVERTISING RATES:
Full Page Mono £3090.00
Full Page Colour £4017.00
SCC £11.74
Agency Commission: 10%
Mechanical Data: Type Area: 340 x 276mm, Col Widths (Display): 28mm, Page Width: 276mm, Bleed Size: +3mm, Col Length: 340mm, No. of Columns (Display): 9, Film: Digital
Copy instructions: Copy Date: 2 working days prior to publication date
Average advertising content per issue: 32%
Supplement(s): Portfolio - 12xY
REGIONAL DAILY & SUNDAY NEWSPAPERS: Regional Daily Newspapers

SUNDERLAND STAR
44497U72B-3371_140
Frequency: Weekly
Cover Price: Free
Circulation: 32,229 (VFD 02/07/2007 to 30/12/2007)
ADVERTISING RATES:
SCC £6.80
Part of Series, see entry for: Star Series
LOCAL NEWSPAPERS: Local Newspapers English Counties

SURREY ADVERTISER (CRANLEIGH & VILLAGES)
44411U72B-3165_190
Frequency: Weekly - Circulation figure is incorporated into the Surrey Advertiser (Guildford Town)
Cover Price: £0.55
ADVERTISING: Rates on application
Part of Series, see entry for: Surrey Times & Advertiser Series
LOCAL NEWSPAPERS: Local Newspapers English Counties

SURREY ADVERTISER (DORKING & DISTRICT)
44412U72B-3165_200
Frequency: Weekly - Circulation figure is incorporated into the Surrey Advertiser (Guildford Town)
Cover Price: £0.55
ADVERTISING: Rates on application
Part of Series, see entry for: Surrey Times & Advertiser Series
LOCAL NEWSPAPERS: Local Newspapers English Counties

SURREY ADVERTISER (ELMBRIDGE)
1665472U72B-3165_233
Formerly: Surrey Advertiser (Esher and Cobham)
Frequency: Weekly - Circulation figure is incorporated into the Surrey Advertiser (Guildford Town)
Cover Price: £0.52
ADVERTISING: Rates on application
Part of Series, see entry for: Surrey Times & Advertiser Series
LOCAL NEWSPAPERS: Local Newspapers English Counties

Non-National Newspapers

SURREY ADVERTISER (GODALMING & VILLAGES)
44413U72B-3165_210
Frequency: Weekly - Circulation figure is incorporated into the Surrey Advertiser (Guildford Town)
Cover Price: £0.55
ADVERTISING: Rates on application
Part of Series, see entry for: Surrey Times & Advertiser Series
LOCAL NEWSPAPERS: Local Newspapers English Counties

SURREY ADVERTISER (GUILDFORD EAST)
1665471U72B-3165_232
Frequency: Weekly - Circulation figure is incorporated into the Surrey Advertiser (Guildford Town)
Cover Price: £0.55
ADVERTISING: Rates on application
Part of Series, see entry for: Surrey Times & Advertiser Series
LOCAL NEWSPAPERS: Local Newspapers English Counties

SURREY ADVERTISER (GUILDFORD TOWN)
44410U72B-3165_170
Frequency: Weekly - Published on Friday. Circulation figure includes the Surrey Advertiser (Cranleigh & Villages), the Surrey Advertiser (Dorking & District), the Surrey Advertiser (Godalming & Villages) Surrey Advertiser (Leatherhead & District), Surrey Advertiser (Woking), Surrey Advertiser (Elmbridge), Surrey Advertiser (Guildford West) and the Surrey Advertiser (Guildford East)
Cover Price: £0.55
Circulation: 30,163 (ABC 02/07/2007 to 30/12/2007)
ADVERTISING: Rates on application
Part of Series, see entry for: Surrey Times & Advertiser Series
LOCAL NEWSPAPERS: Local Newspapers English Counties

SURREY ADVERTISER (GUILDFORD WEST)
1665470U72B-3165_231
Frequency: Weekly - Circulation figure is incorporated into the Surrey Advertiser (Guildford Town)
Cover Price: £0.55
ADVERTISING: Rates on application
Part of Series, see entry for: Surrey Times & Advertiser Series
LOCAL NEWSPAPERS: Local Newspapers English Counties

SURREY ADVERTISER (LEATHERHEAD & DISTRICT)
44414U72B-3165_230
Frequency: Weekly - Circulation figure is incorporated into the Surrey Advertiser (Guildford Town)
Cover Price: £0.55
ADVERTISING: Rates on application
Part of Series, see entry for: Surrey Times & Advertiser Series
LOCAL NEWSPAPERS: Local Newspapers English Counties

SURREY ADVERTISER (WOKING)
1665475U72B-3165_234
Frequency: Weekly - Circulation figure is incorporated into the Surrey Advertiser (Guildford Town)
Cover Price: £0.55
ADVERTISING: Rates on application
Part of Series, see entry for: Surrey Times & Advertiser Series
LOCAL NEWSPAPERS: Local Newspapers English Counties

SURREY & HANTS NEWS
44391U72B-1339_230
Frequency: Weekly
Cover Price: Free
Circulation: 13,554 (Publisher's Statement)
Part of Series, see entry for: Alton Post Gazette, Times & Mail Series
LOCAL NEWSPAPERS: Local Newspapers English Counties

SURREY AND SUSSEX TELEGRAPH
768375U72B-159_197
Formerly: Surrey Telegraph
Frequency: Weekly - Published on Friday
Cover Price: Free
ADVERTISING RATES:
Full Page Mono £699.00

Full Page Colour £900.00
Part of Series, see entry for: South Bucks and Berkshire News Series
LOCAL NEWSPAPERS: Local Newspapers English Counties

SURREY COMET
43152U72A-500
Formerly: Surrey Comet Series
Editorial Address: Unecol House, 819 London Road, NORTH CHEAM, SM3 9BN **Tel:** 020 8329 9244
Fax: 020 8329 9201
Email: newsdesk@surreycomet.co.uk
Advertising Address: As above. **Tel:** 020 8329 9420
Email: mburgess@london.newsquest.co.uk
Web site: http://www.surreycomet.co.uk
Publisher: Newsquest Media Group
Date Established: 1864
Frequency: Weekly - Published on Wednesday. This circulation figure is a combined figure including the Surrey Comet and Wandsworth Borough News
Cover Price: £0.40
Circulation: 10,182 (ABC 02/07/2007 to 30/12/2007)
Editor: David Rankin; **Features Editor:** June Sampson; **Managing Editor:** Andrew Parkes; **Group Editor:** Sean Duggan
ADVERTISING RATES:
Full Page Mono £550.00
Full Page Colour £612.00
Agency Commission: 10%
Mechanical Data: Type Area: 350 x 267mm, Col Length: 350mm, Page Width: 267mm, Film: Digital
Copy instructions: Copy Date: 3 days prior to publication date
Average advertising content per issue: 25%
LOCAL NEWSPAPERS: Local Newspapers Greater London

SURREY GUARDIAN
1623222U72B-3455_141
Frequency: Weekly
Cover Price: Free
Circulation: 45,000 (Publisher's Statement)
Part of Series, see entry for: Guardian Series (Wiltshire, Hampshire and Surrey)
LOCAL NEWSPAPERS: Local Newspapers English Counties

SURREY MIRROR REDHILL, REIGATE AND BANSTEAD
44404U72B-3160_190
Frequency: Weekly
Cover Price: £0.40
Part of Series, see entry for: Surrey Mirror Series
LOCAL NEWSPAPERS: Local Newspapers English Counties

SURREY MIRROR SERIES
44400U72B-3160
Editorial Address: 51 London Road, REIGATE, RH2 9PR
Tel: 01737 732000 **Fax:** 01737 732267
Email: editor@surreymirror.co.uk
Advertising Address: As above.
Email: classified@essnmedia.co.uk
Web site: http://www.icsurreyonline.co.uk
Publisher: Northcliffe Media Ltd
Frequency: Weekly - Published every Wednesday and Thursday
Circulation: 40,632 (Combined Circulation)
Usual Pagination: 22
Editor: Jazzmin Jiwa; **Features Editor:** Christine Malthouse; **Editor-in-Chief:** Ian Carter
ADVERTISING RATES:
SCC £12.08
Agency Commission: 10%
Series owner and contact point for the following titles, see individual entries:
Caterham Mirror
Horley & Gatwick Mirror
Surrey Mirror Redhill, Reigate and Banstead
Surrey Mirror (Tandridge District Edition)
Supplement(s): The Guide - 52xY
LOCAL NEWSPAPERS: Local Newspapers English Counties

SURREY MIRROR (TANDRIDGE DISTRICT EDITION)
44405U72B-3160_210
Frequency: Weekly
Cover Price: £0.40
Part of Series, see entry for: Surrey Mirror Series
LOCAL NEWSPAPERS: Local Newspapers English Counties

SURREY TIMES
44409U72B-3165_150
Formerly: Guildford Times
Frequency: Weekly
Cover Price: Free
Circulation: 33,492 (VFD 01/01/2007 to 01/07/2007)
ADVERTISING: Rates on application
Part of Series, see entry for: Surrey Times & Advertiser Series
LOCAL NEWSPAPERS: Local Newspapers English Counties

SURREY TIMES & ADVERTISER SERIES
44406U72B-3165
Formerly: Surrey Times/Advertiser Series
Editorial Address: Stoke Mill, Woking Road, GUILDFORD, GU1 1QA **Tel:** 01483 508900 **Fax:** 01483 508930
Email: editorial@surreyad.co.uk
Advertising Address: As above. **Tel:** 01483 508700
Fax: 01483 508851
Email: salessupport@surreyad.co.uk
Web site: http://www.surreyad.co.uk
Publisher: Surrey & Berkshire Media Group
Frequency: Weekly
Circulation: 63,655 (Combined Circulation)
Usual Pagination: 76
Editor: Tony Green; **News Editor:** Tony Green; **Features Editor:** Lauren Margrave; **Advertising Manager:** Natalie Gold
ADVERTISING: Rates on application
Agency Commission: 10%
Copy instructions: Copy Date: 3 days prior to publication date
Average advertising content per issue: 65%
Series owner and contact point for the following titles, see individual entries:
Surrey Advertiser (Cranleigh & Villages)
Surrey Advertiser (Dorking & District)
Surrey Advertiser (Elmbridge)
Surrey Advertiser (Godalming & Villages)
Surrey Advertiser (Guildford East)
Surrey Advertiser (Guildford Town)
Surrey Advertiser (Guildford West)
Surrey Advertiser (Leatherhead & District)
Surrey Advertiser (Woking)
Surrey Times
Supplement(s): Business Extra - 4xY, House & Garden - 4xY, What's On - 52xY
LOCAL NEWSPAPERS: Local Newspapers English Counties

SUSSEX EXPRESS HAILSHAM, POLEGATE & HERSTMONCEUX
44446U72B-3270_130
Frequency: Weekly
Cover Price: £0.32
Part of Series, see entry for: Sussex Express Series
LOCAL NEWSPAPERS: Local Newspapers English Counties

SUSSEX EXPRESS LEWES, RINGMER, CHAILEY & NEWICK
44447U72B-3270_140
Frequency: Weekly
Cover Price: £0.32
Part of Series, see entry for: Sussex Express Series
LOCAL NEWSPAPERS: Local Newspapers English Counties

SUSSEX EXPRESS NEWHAVEN AND SEAFORD
44450U72B-3270_200
Formerly: Sussex Express Newhaven, Peacehaven, Telscombe, E. Saltdean
Frequency: Weekly
Cover Price: £0.32
Part of Series, see entry for: Sussex Express Series
LOCAL NEWSPAPERS: Local Newspapers English Counties

SUSSEX EXPRESS SERIES
44444U72B-3270
Editorial Address: Temple House, 25-26 High Street, LEWES, BN7 2LU **Tel:** 01273 480601 **Fax:** 01273 486997
Email: sussex.express@sussexnewspapers.co.uk
Advertising Address: As above. **Fax:** 01273 476524
Email: sussex.express@sussexnewspapers.co.uk
Web site: http://www.sussexexpress.co.uk
Publisher: Johnston Press plc
Date Established: 1837
Frequency: Weekly - Published on Friday
Cover Price: £0.38
Circulation: 14,779 (ABC 02/07/2007 to 30/12/2007)
Usual Pagination: 70

Editor: Mike Mackenzie; **Advertising Manager:** Geoff Hough
ADVERTISING RATES:
SCC £9.67
Agency Commission: 10%
Mechanical Data: Type Area: 340 x 277mm, Col Length: 340mm, Page Width: 277mm, Col Widths (Display): 29mm, No. of Columns (Display): 9, Film: Digital
Copy instructions: Copy Date: Tuesday 4pm prior to publication date
Series owner and contact point for the following titles, see individual entries:
Sussex Express Hailsham, Polegate & Herstmonceux
Sussex Express Lewes, Ringmer, Chailey & Newick
Sussex Express Newhaven and Seaford
Sussex Express Uckfield, Heathfield & Crowborough
Supplement(s): Sussex Motoring - 3xY
LOCAL NEWSPAPERS: Local Newspapers English Counties

SUSSEX EXPRESS UCKFIELD, HEATHFIELD & CROWBOROUGH

44448U72B-3270_160

Frequency: Weekly
Cover Price: £0.32
Part of Series, see entry for: Sussex Express Series
LOCAL NEWSPAPERS: Local Newspapers English Counties

SUTTON AND EPSOM ADVERTISER

42975U72A-50_175

Formerly: Sutton Advertiser
Frequency: Weekly - For circulation see Croydon Advertiser
Cover Price: £0.55
ADVERTISING RATES:
SCC £14.50
Part of Series, see entry for: Croydon Advertiser & Post Series
LOCAL NEWSPAPERS: Local Newspapers Greater London

SUTTON COLDFIELD NEWS

44548U72B-3480

Editorial Address: BPM Media, Floor 6, BIRMINGHAM, B24 9FF **Tel:** 0121 355 7070 **Fax:** 0121 321 3092
Email: sutton_news@mrn.co.uk
Advertising Address: 35 Birmingham Road, SUTTON COLDFIELD, B72 1QE **Tel:** 01827 308000
Fax: 0121 321 3092
Email: sutton_sales@mrn.co.uk
Web site: http://www.icsuttoncoldfield.co.uk
Publisher: Trinity Mirror Midlands
Date Established: 1870
Frequency: Weekly - Published on Friday
Cover Price: Free
Circulation: 62,017 (VFD 02/07/2007 to 30/12/2007)
Usual Pagination: 62
Editor: News Desk
ADVERTISING RATES:
Full Page Mono £2019.60
Full Page Colour £2726.46
SCC £6.78
Agency Commission: 10%
Mechanical Data: Type Area: 340 x 272mm, No. of Columns (Display): 9, Col Length: 340mm, Col Widths (Display): 28mm, Page Width: 272mm, Film: Digital
Copy instructions: Copy Date: Wednesday prior to publication date
Average advertising content per issue: 70%
LOCAL NEWSPAPERS: Local Newspapers English Counties

SUTTON COLDFIELD OBSERVER

44553U72B-3027_190

Frequency: Weekly
Cover Price: Free
Circulation: 58,884 (VFD 02/07/2007 to 30/12/2007)
ADVERTISING RATES:
SCC £6.10
Part of Series, see entry for: Sutton Coldfield Observer Series
LOCAL NEWSPAPERS: Local Newspapers English Counties

SUTTON COLDFIELD OBSERVER SERIES

44549U72B-3027

Editorial Address: Ventura Park Road, Bitterscote, TAMWORTH, B78 3LZ **Tel:** 0121 355 6061
Fax: 01827 848640
Email: suttonobserver@cintamworth.co.uk
Advertising Address: As above. **Tel:** 01827 848586
Fax: 0845 600 8392
Email: richard.clay@cintamworth.co.uk
Web site: http://www.thisissuttoncoldfield.co.uk

Publisher: Central Independent News & Media Ltd
Date Established: 1985
Frequency: Weekly - Published every Friday
Cover Price: Free
Circulation: 91,245 (VFD 02/07/2007 to 30/12/2007)
Usual Pagination: 160
Editor: Laura Vickers; **News Editor:** Laura Vickers;
Advertising Manager: Richard Clay; **Group Editor:** Gary Phelps
ADVERTISING: Rates on application
Agency Commission: 10%
Mechanical Data: Page Width: 276mm, Col Widths (Display): 29mm, Type Area: 360 x 276mm, Col Length: 360mm, No. of Columns (Display): 9, Film: Digital
Copy instructions: Copy Date: Wednesday 12pm prior to publication date
Series owner and contact point for the following titles, see individual entries:
Great Barr Observer
Sutton Coldfield Observer
LOCAL NEWSPAPERS: Local Newspapers English Counties

SUTTON GUARDIAN

43006U72A-128_220

Frequency: Weekly - Circulation figure includes Epsom Guardian
Cover Price: Free
Circulation: 103,463 (VFD 02/07/2007 to 30/12/2007)
Part of Series, see entry for: Guardian & News Series (Sutton)
LOCAL NEWSPAPERS: Local Newspapers Greater London

SWADLINCOTE TIMES

44036U72B-2193_200

Frequency: Weekly - Circulation figure is incorporated into the Coalville Times
Cover Price: £0.39
ADVERTISING: Rates on application
Part of Series, see entry for: Trident Midland Newspapers Series
LOCAL NEWSPAPERS: Local Newspapers English Counties

SWAFFHAM AND WATTON TIMES

1656993U72B-2437_243

Frequency: Weekly - See the Thetford and Brandon Times for circulation
Cover Price: Free
ADVERTISING: Rates on application
Part of Series, see entry for: Norfolk County Weeklies Series
LOCAL NEWSPAPERS: Local Newspapers English Counties

SWANAGE & WAREHAM ADVERTISER

43560U72B-902_171

Formerly: Swanage & District Advertiser
Frequency: Weekly
Cover Price: Free
Circulation: 13,072 (VFD 02/01/2006 to 02/07/2006)
ADVERTISING: Rates on application
Part of Series, see entry for: Advertiser Series (Poole & Swanage)
LOCAL NEWSPAPERS: Local Newspapers English Counties

SWANLEY CHRONICLE

1656815U72A-1303_103

Frequency: Monthly
Cover Price: Free
Part of Series, see entry for: Bexley Chronicle Series
LOCAL NEWSPAPERS: Local Newspapers Greater London

SWANSEA HERALD OF WALES

44841U72C-350

Formerly: Herald of Wales
Editorial Address: PO Box 14, Adelaide St, SWANSEA, SA1 1QT **Tel:** 01792 514606 **Fax:** 01792 469665
Email: postnews@swwmedia.co.uk
Advertising Address: As above. **Tel:** 01792 514571
Fax: 01792 514598
Email: steve.williams@swwmedia.co.uk
Web site: http://www.thisisswansea.co.uk
Publisher: South West Wales Media Ltd
Frequency: Weekly - Published on Wednesday
Cover Price: Free
Circulation: 67,297 (VFD 02/07/2007 to 30/12/2007)
Editor: Chris Davies; **News Editor:** Chris Davies; **Features Editor:** Peter Slee; **Advertising Manager:** Steve Williams
ADVERTISING RATES:
Full Page Mono £1180.80
Full Page Colour £1476.00
SCC £4.10

Agency Commission: 10%
Mechanical Data: Page Width: 270mm, Type Area: 360 x 270mm, Col Length: 360mm, Col Widths (Display): 32mm, No. of Columns (Display): 8, Film: Digital, Print Process: Web-fed offset litho
Copy instructions: Copy Date: Friday 5pm prior to publication date
Average advertising content per issue: 70%
LOCAL NEWSPAPERS: Local Newspapers Wales

SWINDON ADVERTISER

42187U67B-1080

Formerly: Evening Advertiser (Swindon)
Editorial Address: 100 Victoria Road, SWINDON, SN1 3BE
Tel: 01793 528144 **Fax:** 01793 501888
Email: newsdesk@swindonadvertiser.co.uk
Advertising Address: As above. **Fax:** 01793 501700
Web site: http://www.swindonadvertiser.co.uk
Publisher: Newsquest (Wiltshire) Ltd
Date Established: 1854
Frequency: Evenings
Cover Price: £0.35
Circulation: 22,469 (Publisher's Statement)
Editor: Dave King; **News Editor:** Kevin Burchall; **Features Editor:** Jaine Blackman; **Managing Director:** Mark Suddaby
ADVERTISING RATES:
SCC £7.25
Mechanical Data: No. of Columns (Display): 9
Copy instructions: Copy Date: 1 working day prior to publication date
Supplement(s): Wiltshire Business - 11xY
REGIONAL DAILY & SUNDAY NEWSPAPERS: Regional Daily Newspapers

SWINDON STAR

44594U72B-3942

Editorial Address: 100 Victoria Road, SWINDON, SN1 3BE
Tel: 01793 528144 **Fax:** 01793 501888
Email: editor@swindonadvertiser.co.uk
Advertising Address: As above. **Fax:** 01793 501771
Email: ahollands@newswilts.co.uk
Web site: http://www.swindonadvertiser.co.uk
Publisher: Newsquest (Wiltshire) Ltd
Frequency: Weekly
Cover Price: Free
Circulation: 48,248 (VFD 02/07/2007 to 30/12/2007)
Editor: Kevin Burchall; **News Editor:** Kevin Burchall; **Features Editor:** Jaine Blackman
ADVERTISING RATES:
SCC £9.00
Mechanical Data: Film: Digital, Col Length: 340mm, Page Width: 269mm, Type Area: 340 x 269mm, No. of Columns (Display): 9
Copy instructions: Copy Date: 12 noon 2 days prior to publication date
LOCAL NEWSPAPERS: Local Newspapers English Counties

TAFOD ELAÍ

761566U72J-260

Editorial Address: Hendre, 4 Pantbach, Pentyrch, CARDIFF, CF15 9TG **Tel:** 029 2089 0040
Email: pentyrch@tesco.net
Advertising Address: As above.
Email: pentyrch@tesco.net
Web site: http://www.tafelai.com
Date Established: 1985
Frequency: 10 issues yearly - Not published in January and August
Cover Price: £0.60
Circulation: 800 (Publisher's Statement)
Editor: Penri Williams; **Advertising Manager:** Penri Williams
Summary of Content: Welsh language community newspaper containing news from the local villages including schooling, sports and a list of upcoming Welsh activities.
Language(s): Welsh
Readership/Target Audience: Aimed at Welsh speaking readers with an interest in local affairs.
ADVERTISING RATES:
Full Page Mono £120.00
Mechanical Data: Film: Digital
Copy instructions: Copy Date: 20th of the month prior to publication date
Average advertising content per issue: 15%
LOCAL NEWSPAPERS: Community Newsletters

TAMESIDE ADVERTISER

43677U72B-1153_110

Formerly: Advertiser Aston, Audenshaw & District
Frequency: Weekly
Cover Price: Free
Circulation: 91,151 (VFD 02/07/2007 to 30/12/2007)
ADVERTISING RATES:
SCC £8.75
Part of Series, see entry for: Advertiser Series (Ashton)
LOCAL NEWSPAPERS: Local Newspapers English Counties

Non-National Newspapers

Section 4 (a) Newspapers

TAMESIDE REPORTER
43682U72B-1160_110

Formerly: Tameside Reporter Audenshaw, Stalybridge, Dukinfield & District
Frequency: Weekly
Cover Price: £0.38
Circulation: 15,000 (Publisher's Statement)
ADVERTISING: Rates on application
Part of Series, see entry for: Ashton-Under-Lyne Reporter Series
LOCAL NEWSPAPERS: Local Newspapers English Counties

TAMWORTH HERALD
44325U72B-3040_180

Frequency: Weekly - Circulation figure is incorporated into the Atherstone Herald
Cover Price: £0.55
ADVERTISING: Rates on application
Part of Series, see entry for: Tamworth Herald Series
LOCAL NEWSPAPERS: Local Newspapers English Counties

TAMWORTH HERALD SERIES
44322U72B-3040

Editorial Address: Ventura Park Road, Bitterscote, TAMWORTH, B78 3LZ **Tel:** 01827 848600
Fax: 01827 848640
Email: tamworth.editorial@cintamworth.co.uk
Advertising Address: As above. **Fax:** 0845 600 8392
Email: tina.mcfadden@cintamworth.co.uk
Web site: http://www.thisistamworth.co.uk
Publisher: Northcliffe Media Ltd
Date Established: 1868
Frequency: Weekly
Circulation: 58,633 (Combined Circulation)
Editor: Lindsey Smith; **Advertisement Director:** Tina McFadden
ADVERTISING: Rates on application
Series owner and contact point for the following titles, see individual entries:
Atherstone Herald
Coleshill Herald (incorporating The Coleshill Chronicle)
Herald Leader
Tamworth Herald
Supplement(s): GCSE and A level Results - 1xY
LOCAL NEWSPAPERS: Local Newspapers English Counties

TANDRIDGE CHRONICLE
43854U72B-1773_150

Date Established: 1997
Frequency: Monthly
Cover Price: Free
Circulation: 13,000 (Publisher's Statement)
Part of Series, see entry for: Chronicle Series
LOCAL NEWSPAPERS: Local Newspapers English Counties

TANDRIDGE COUNTY BORDER NEWS
43857U72B-1774_180

Frequency: Weekly - Circulation is incorporated into Oxted County Border News
Cover Price: Free
Part of Series, see entry for: County Border News Series
LOCAL NEWSPAPERS: Local Newspapers English Counties

TARGET SERIES
44083U72B-2287

Editorial Address: 16 Wide Bargate, BOSTON, PE21 6SR
Tel: 01205 315000 **Fax:** 01205 315045
Email: news@targetseries.co.uk
Advertising Address: As above. **Fax:** 01205 315025
Email: adverts@targetseries.co.uk
Web site: http://www.thisisboston.co.uk
Publisher: Lincolnshire Media Ltd
Frequency: Weekly - Published on Wednesday
Cover Price: Free
Circulation: 82,742 (Combined Circulation)
Usual Pagination: 84
Editor: Graeme Holmes; **News Editor:** Graeme Holmes;
Advertising Manager: James Barnes; **Managing Editor:** Nick Purkiss
ADVERTISING RATES:
Full Page Mono £1872.00
Full Page Colour £2340.00
Agency Commission: 10%
Mechanical Data: Col Widths (Display): 30mm, No. of Columns (Display): 8, Film: Digital
Copy instructions: Copy Date: Monday 5pm prior to publication date
Average advertising content per issue: 50%
Series owner and contact point for the following titles, see individual entries:
Boston Target
Horncastle Target

Louth Target
Mablethorpe and Alford Target
Skegness and Spilsby Target
Sleaford Target
LOCAL NEWSPAPERS: Local Newspapers English Counties

TAVISTOCK TIMES GAZETTE
43548U72B-857_200

Frequency: Weekly
Cover Price: £0.55
Circulation: 7,800 (Publisher's Statement)
Part of Series, see entry for: Tavistock Times Gazette Series
LOCAL NEWSPAPERS: Local Newspapers English Counties

TAVISTOCK TIMES GAZETTE SERIES
43544U72B-857

Editorial Address: Tindle House, 14 Brook Street, TAVISTOCK, PL19 0HD **Tel:** 01822 613666
Fax: 01822 617352
Email: tavistock@internet-today.co.uk
Advertising Address: As above. **Fax:** 01822 618222
Email: tavy@internet-today.co.uk
Web site: http://www.tavistock-today.co.uk
Publisher: Tavistock Newspapers Ltd
Date Established: 1857
Frequency: Weekly
Circulation: 13,000 (Combined Circulation)
Editor: Colin Brent; **Managing Director:** Brian Doel;
Advertising Manager: Lyn Roberts
ADVERTISING RATES:
Full Page Mono £1050.00
Full Page Colour £1300.00
SCC £4.20
Agency Commission: 10%
Mechanical Data: Page Width: 262mm, Type Area: 360 x 262mm, Col Length: 360mm, Film: Digital, No. of Columns (Display): 8, Col Widths (Display): 30mm
Copy instructions: Copy Date: Tuesday 11am prior to publication date
Average advertising content per issue: 60%
Series owner and contact point for the following titles, see individual entries:
East Cornwall Times
Okehampton Times
Princetown Gazette
Tavistock Times Gazette
LOCAL NEWSPAPERS: Local Newspapers English Counties

TEESDALE MERCURY
43585U72B-940

Editorial Address: 24 Market Place, BARNARD CASTLE, DL12 8NB **Tel:** 01833 637140 **Fax:** 01833 638633
Email: editor@teesdalemercury.co.uk
Advertising Address: As above. **Tel:** 01833 633612
Email: kateware@teesdalemercury.co.uk
Web site: http://www.teesdalemercury.co.uk
Publisher: Teesdale Mercury Ltd
Date Established: 1854
Frequency: Weekly - Published on Wednesday
Cover Price: £0.40
Circulation: 6,479 (ABC 02/07/2007 to 30/12/2007)
Editor: Adrian Braddy; **Advertising Manager:** Kate Ware
ADVERTISING RATES:
Full Page Mono £810.00
Full Page Colour £1300.00
SCC £3.10
Agency Commission: 10%
Mechanical Data: Col Widths (Display): 45mm, No. of Columns (Display): 7, Film: Digital, Col Length: 450mm, Page Width: 338mm, Print Process: Offset sheet fed litho, Type Area: 450 x 338mm
Copy instructions: Copy Date: Friday prior to publication date
Average advertising content per issue: 50%
Supplement(s): Dale Life - 4xY
LOCAL NEWSPAPERS: Local Newspapers English Counties

TEIGNMOUTH NEWS
43500U72B-870

Editorial Address: 39 Teign Street, TEIGNMOUTH, TQ14 8EA **Tel:** 01626 778029 **Fax:** 01626 777155
Email: teignmouth@internet-today.co.uk
Advertising Address: As above. **Tel:** 01626 779494
Email: teign.sales@internet-today.co.uk
Publisher: Dawlish Newspapers Ltd
Date Established: 1983
Frequency: Weekly
Cover Price: Free
Circulation: 10,500 (Publisher's Statement)
Editor: Ruth Davey; **Advertising Manager:** Keith Hawkins

ADVERTISING RATES:
Full Page Mono £1368.00
Full Page Colour £1641.60
SCC £4.75
Agency Commission: 10%
Mechanical Data: Page Width: 262mm, Col Length: 360mm, No. of Columns (Display): 8, Type Area: 360 x 262mm
Copy instructions: Copy Date: Monday 12 noon prior to publication date
Average advertising content per issue: 55%
LOCAL NEWSPAPERS: Local Newspapers English Counties

TEIGNMOUTH POST & GAZETTE
43515U72B-827_180

Frequency: Weekly
Cover Price: £0.35
Part of Series, see entry for: Mid-Devon Advertiser Series
LOCAL NEWSPAPERS: Local Newspapers English Counties

TELEGRAPH & ARGUS
41999U67B-90

Formerly: Telegraph & Argus (Bradford)
Editorial Address: Hall Ings, BRADFORD, BD1 1JR
Tel: 01274 729511 **Fax:** 01274 723634
Email: newsdesk@telegraphandargus.co.uk
Advertising Address: As above. **Fax:** 01274 724907
Email: adsales@bradford.newsquest.co.uk
Web site: http://www.thetelegraphandargus.co.uk
Publisher: Newsquest Yorkshire and North East (Bradford)
Frequency: Evenings - Not published on Sunday
Cover Price: £0.40
Circulation: 37,371 (Publisher's Statement)
Editor: Perry Austin-Clarke; **Advertising Manager:** Janet Dutton; **Managing Editor:** Peter Orme
ADVERTISING RATES:
SCC £7.50
Agency Commission: 10%
Mechanical Data: Print Process: Web-fed offset litho, Page Width: 259mm, No. of Columns (Display): 9, Col Length: 340mm, Film: Digital, Type Area: 340 x 259mm, Col Widths (Display): 27mm
Copy instructions: Copy Date: 4pm 2 days prior to publication date
Series owner and contact point for the following titles, see individual entries:
Monday Sport
Supplement(s): Saturday Space - 52xY, Thursday Play - 52xY, Tuesday People - 52xY
REGIONAL DAILY & SUNDAY NEWSPAPERS: Regional Daily Newspapers

TELFORD AND WREKIN ADMAG
1656433U72B-3955_101

Frequency: Weekly
Cover Price: Free
Circulation: 48,302 (VFD 02/07/2007 to 30/12/2007)
ADVERTISING RATES:
SCC £2.90
Part of Series, see entry for: Admag Newspapers Series
LOCAL NEWSPAPERS: Local Newspapers English Counties

TELFORD JOURNAL
44246U72B-2860

Editorial Address: Waterloo Road, Ketley, TELFORD, TF1 5HU **Tel:** 01952 242424 **Fax:** 01952 254605
Email: staylor@shropshirestar.co.uk
Advertising Address: As above. **Fax:** 01952 222451
Email: pguy@shropshirestar.co.uk
Web site: http://www.telfordjournal.com
Publisher: Shropshire Newspapers Ltd
Frequency: Weekly - Published on Thursday
Cover Price: Free
Circulation: 61,000 (VFD 02/07/2007 to 30/12/2007)
Usual Pagination: 56
Editor: David Sharp; **Managing Director:** Steve Brown
Summary of Content: Newspaper covering all the latest news from the Telford region.
Readership/Target Audience: Aimed at people living in this area.
ADVERTISING RATES:
Full Page Mono £1886.00
Full Page Colour £2451.00
SCC £5.75
Agency Commission: 10%
Mechanical Data: Page Width: 305mm, Type Area: 410 x 305mm, Col Length: 410mm, Film: Digital, Print Process: Web-fed offset litho
Copy instructions: Copy Date: Tuesday 12 noon prior to publication date
LOCAL NEWSPAPERS: Local Newspapers English Counties

TENBURY WELLS ADVERTISER

44241U72B-2820_180

Frequency: Weekly
Cover Price: £0.40
Part of Series, see entry for: Ludlow Advertiser Series
LOCAL NEWSPAPERS: Local Newspapers English Counties

TENBY, NARBERTH & WHITLAND OBSERVER SERIES

44842U72C-352

Editorial Address: Tindle House, Warren Street, TENBY, SA70 7JY **Tel:** 01834 843262 **Fax:** 01834 844774
Email: editor@thetenbyobserver.co.uk
Advertising Address: As above.
Email: advertising@thetenbyobserver.co.uk
Web site: http://www.tenby-today.co.uk
Publisher: Tenby Observer Ltd
Date Established: 1853
Frequency: Weekly
Cover Price: £0.44
Circulation: 7,431 (Publisher's Statement)
Editor: Neil Dickinson; **Advertising Manager:** Clare Townend
ADVERTISING RATES:
Full Page Mono £826.56
SCC £3.28
Agency Commission: 10%
Mechanical Data: Type Area: 360 x 272mm, Col Length: 360mm, Col Widths (Display): 35mm, No. of Columns (Display): 7, Page Width: 272mm
Copy instructions: Copy Date: Tuesday 4pm prior to publication date
Average advertising content per issue: 40%
Series owner and contact point for the following titles, see individual entries:
Narberth & Whitland Observer
Tenby Observer
LOCAL NEWSPAPERS: Local Newspapers Wales

TENBY OBSERVER

713629U72C-352_160

Frequency: Weekly
Circulation: 6,343 (Publisher's Statement)
Part of Series, see entry for: Tenby, Narberth & Whitland Observer Series
LOCAL NEWSPAPERS: Local Newspapers Wales

TEWKESBURY NEWS

1663904U72B-1125_102

Frequency: Weekly - For circulation figure see Cheltenham News
Cover Price: Free
Part of Series, see entry for: Gloucester and Cheltenham News Series
LOCAL NEWSPAPERS: Local Newspapers English Counties

TEWKESBURY OBSERVER

1840352U72B-4052_102

Frequency: Weekly - Published on Wednesday
Cover Price: £0.35
(Publisher's Statement)
Part of Series, see entry for: Evesham Observer Series
LOCAL NEWSPAPERS: Local Newspapers English Counties

THAME GAZETTE

43301U72B-250_180

Frequency: Weekly
Cover Price: Free
ADVERTISING RATES:
SCC £4.65
Part of Series, see entry for: Bucks Advertiser & Thame Gazette Series
LOCAL NEWSPAPERS: Local Newspapers English Counties

THAMESMEAD CHRONICLE

1656814U72A-1303_102

Frequency: Monthly
Cover Price: Free
Part of Series, see entry for: Bexley Chronicle Series
LOCAL NEWSPAPERS: Local Newspapers Greater London

THANET EXTRA

43843U72B-1763_190

Frequency: Weekly
Cover Price: Free
Circulation: 50,211 (VFD 02/07/2007 to 30/12/2007)
ADVERTISING: Rates on application

Part of Series, see entry for: Canterbury Extra Series
LOCAL NEWSPAPERS: Local Newspapers English Counties

THANET TIMES

43884U72B-1830_200

Frequency: Weekly - Published on Tuesday
Cover Price: £0.35
Circulation: 8,185 (ABC 02/07/2007 to 30/12/2007)
ADVERTISING: Rates on application
Part of Series, see entry for: Isle of Thanet Gazette Series
LOCAL NEWSPAPERS: Local Newspapers English Counties

THETFORD AND BRANDON TIMES

44138U72B-2437_230

Formerly: The Thetford and Watton Times
Frequency: Weekly - Circulation figure is a combined figure including the Swaffham and Watton Times
Cover Price: Free
Circulation: 25,178 (VFD 02/07/2007 to 30/12/2007)
ADVERTISING: Rates on application
Part of Series, see entry for: Norfolk County Weeklies Series
LOCAL NEWSPAPERS: Local Newspapers English Counties

THORNBURY GAZETTE

43215U72B-23_230

Frequency: Weekly
Cover Price: £0.55
Part of Series, see entry for: Gloucestershire Gazette Series
LOCAL NEWSPAPERS: Local Newspapers English Counties

THORNE AND DISTRICT GAZETTE

1685826U72B-3975

Editorial Address: Sunny Bar, DONCASTER, DN1 1NB
Tel: 01302 347264 **Fax:** 01302 348523
Email: editorial@thornetoday.co.uk
Advertising Address: Gazette House, King Street, Thorne, DONCASTER, DN8 5BA **Tel:** 01302 347241
Fax: 01302 348519
Email: eve@doncastertoday.co.uk
Web site: http://www.thornetoday.co.uk
Publisher: South Yorkshire Newspapers Ltd
Frequency: Weekly - Published on Thursday
Cover Price: Free
Circulation: 19,000 (Publisher's Statement)
Editor: Janet Harrison; **News Editor:** Janet Harrison;
Advertising Manager: Eve Hanson
ADVERTISING RATES:
Full Page Mono £385.56
Full Page Colour £502.29
Agency Commission: 10%
Mechanical Data: Type Area: 340 x 280mm, Col Length: 340mm, Page Width: 280mm, Col Widths (Display): 28mm, No. of Columns (Display): 9, Film: Digital
Copy instructions: Copy Date: Tuesday 12 noon prior to publication date
Average advertising content per issue: 60%
LOCAL NEWSPAPERS: Local Newspapers English Counties

THURROCK GAZETTE

43648U72B-1090

Editorial Address: 91 Orsett Road, GRAYS, RM17 5EX
Tel: 01375 411502 **Fax:** 01375 411508
Email: alex.ellis@nqe.com
Advertising Address: As above. **Tel:** 01375 411510
Fax: 01375 411509
Email: debbie.walker@nqe.com
Web site: http://www.thurrockgazette.co.uk
Publisher: Newsquest (Essex) Ltd
Date Established: 1884
Frequency: Weekly - Published on Friday
Cover Price: Free
Circulation: 57,080 (VFD 02/07/2007 to 30/12/2007)
Usual Pagination: 140
Advertising Manager: Debbie Walker
ADVERTISING RATES:
SCC £4.50
Agency Commission: 10%
Mechanical Data: Page Width: 274mm, Type Area: 340 x 274mm, Col Length: 340mm, No. of Columns (Display): 9, Col Widths (Display): 29mm, Film: Digital
Copy instructions: Copy Date: Tuesday 10am prior to publication date
Average advertising content per issue: 80%
LOCAL NEWSPAPERS: Local Newspapers English Counties

TICKHILL & BAWTRY (PLUS HARWORTH) COMMUNITY NEWSLETTER

1647023U72B-3950_104

Frequency: Monthly
Cover Price: Free
Circulation: 6,000 (Publisher's Statement)
ADVERTISING: Rates on application
Part of Series, see entry for: Community Newsletter Series
LOCAL NEWSPAPERS: Local Newspapers English Counties

TIMES & CITIZEN BEDFORD BOROUGH EDITION

43233U72B-84_120

Frequency: Weekly
Cover Price: Free
Circulation: 60,690 (VFD 02/07/2007 to 30/12/2007)
ADVERTISING: Rates on application
Part of Series, see entry for: Bedfordshire Times & Citizen Series
LOCAL NEWSPAPERS: Local Newspapers English Counties

TIMES & CITIZEN MID BEDFORDSHIRE EDITION

43234U72B-84_140

Frequency: Weekly
Cover Price: Free
Circulation: 17,429 (VFD 30/07/2007 to 30/12/2007)
ADVERTISING: Rates on application
Part of Series, see entry for: Bedfordshire Times & Citizen Series
LOCAL NEWSPAPERS: Local Newspapers English Counties

TIMES AND REPORTER SERIES (KENT)

43907U72B-1875

Formerly: Times and Express Series (Kent)
Editorial Address: Roxby House, 20-22 Station Road, SIDCUP, DA15 7EJ **Tel:** 020 8269 7000 **Fax:** 020 8269 7070
Advertising Address: As above. **Fax:** 020 8269 7060
Email: john.haynes@archant.co.uk
Publisher: Archant London
Frequency: Weekly - Published on Thursdays
Circulation: 154,146 (Combined Circulation)
Editor: Kate Bryson; **News Editor:** Michael Adkins;
Advertising Manager: John Haynes
ADVERTISING: Rates on application
Agency Commission: 10%
Mechanical Data: Type Area: 350 x 265mm, Col Length: 350mm, Col Widths (Display): 27.5mm, No. of Columns (Display): 9, Page Width: 265mm, Film: Digital
Copy instructions: Copy Date: Tuesday 12.00 prior to publication date
Series owner and contact point for the following titles, see individual entries:
Bexley Times
Bromley Times
Dartford and Swanley Times
Gravesend Reporter
Supplement(s): Kentish Times Magazine - 52xY
LOCAL NEWSPAPERS: Local Newspapers English Counties

TIMES AND STAR (COCKERMOUTH)

1647349U72B-640_101

Frequency: Weekly
Cover Price: £0.60
Part of Series, see entry for: Times and Star Series
LOCAL NEWSPAPERS: Local Newspapers English Counties

TIMES AND STAR (MARYPORT)

1647350U72B-640_102

Frequency: Weekly
Cover Price: £0.60
Part of Series, see entry for: Times and Star Series
LOCAL NEWSPAPERS: Local Newspapers English Counties

TIMES AND STAR SERIES

43457U72B-640

Formerly: West Cumberland Times & Star
Editorial Address: 23 Oxford Street, WORKINGTON, CA14 2AN **Tel:** 01900 607610 **Fax:** 01900 607645
Email: news@times-and-star.co.uk
Advertising Address: As above. **Tel:** 01900 607662
Email: jackie.clemence@cumbrian-newspapers.co.uk
Web site: http://www.timesandstar.co.uk
Publisher: Cumbrian Newspapers Ltd
Date Established: 1964

Non-National Newspapers

Frequency: Weekly - Published on Friday
Circulation: 17,215 (ABC 02/07/2007 to 30/12/2007)
Editor: Nicole Regan; **Managing Director:** Terry Hall
ADVERTISING RATES:
Full Page Mono £4752.00
Full Page Colour £4752.00
SCC £8.80
Mechanical Data: Col Length: 540mm, Page Width:
357mm, Film: Digital, Type Area: 540 x 357mm, No. of
Columns (Display): 10
**Series owner and contact point for the following titles,
see individual entries:**
Times and Star (Cockermouth)
Times and Star (Maryport)
Times and Star (Workington)
Supplement(s): Cumbria Weddings - 6xY, Futures - 12xY,
Glamour - 4xY, Go West - 1xY, Homestyle - 4xY
LOCAL NEWSPAPERS: Local Newspapers English
Counties

TIMES AND STAR (WORKINGTON)
1647351U72B-640_100

Formerly: Times and Star (West Cumberland)
Frequency: Weekly
Cover Price: £0.60
Part of Series, see entry for: Times and Star Series
LOCAL NEWSPAPERS: Local Newspapers English
Counties

THE TIMES SERIES
45123U72E-226

Editorial Address: 8 Dunluce Street, LARNE, BT40 1JG
Tel: 028 2827 2303 **Fax:** 028 2826 0255
Email: news@larnetimes.co.uk
Advertising Address: 14 Portland Avenue,
GLENGORMLEY, BT36 5EY **Tel:** 028 9084 3621
Email: roy.sharpe@jpresstimes.co.uk
Web site: http://www.mortonnewspapers.com
Publisher: Johnston Press
Frequency: Weekly
Circulation: 47,517 (VFD 02/07/2007 to 30/12/2007)
Editor: Hugh Vance; **Features Editor:** Valerie Martin;
Managing Director: Jean Long; **Advertising Manager:** Lee-
Ann Gregson
ADVERTISING RATES:
SCC £5.60
**Series owner and contact point for the following titles,
see individual entries:**
Carrick Times and East Antrim Times
East Antrim Advertiser
Larne Times and East Antrim Times
Newtownabbey Times and East Antrim Times
LOCAL NEWSPAPERS: Local Newspapers Northern Ireland

TIMES SERIES (COVENTRY, LEAMINGTON, WARWICK & KENILWORTH)
1666040U72B-3964

Formerly: Times Series (Coventry)
Editorial Address: Corporation Street, COVENTRY, CV1
1FP **Tel:** 024 7650 0500 **Fax:** 024 7655 3820
Email: darren_parkin@mrn.co.uk
Advertising Address: As above. **Tel:** 024 7663 3633
Email: retail_fieldsales@mrn.co.uk
Web site: http://www.timeslive.com
Publisher: Trinity Mirror
Frequency: Weekly
Cover Price: Free
Circulation: 50,913 (Combined Circulation)
Editor: Darren Parkin; **Advertising Manager:** Hazel Pilling
ADVERTISING RATES:
Full Page Mono £1912.00
Full Page Colour £2581.87
Agency Commission: 10%
Mechanical Data: Col Widths (Display): 28mm, No. of
Columns (Display): 9, Page Width: 264mm
Copy instructions: Copy Date: Monday 5pm prior to
publication date
**Series owner and contact point for the following titles,
see individual entries:**
Kenilworth Times
Royal Leamington Spa Times
Warwick Times
LOCAL NEWSPAPERS: Local Newspapers English
Counties

TIMES SERIES (MELTON MOWBRAY)
44029U72B-2192

Editorial Address: 49 Nottingham Street, MELTON
MOWBRAY, LE13 1NT **Tel:** 01664 410041
Fax: 01664 412515
Email: tara.rippin@meltontoday.co.uk
Advertising Address: As above. **Fax:** 01664 410042
Email: graham.kirk@meltontimes.co.uk
Web site: http://www.meltontoday.co.uk

Publisher: Johnston Press plc
Date Established: 1859
Frequency: Weekly
Circulation: 25,726 (Combined Circulation)
Editor: Michael Cooke; **Managing Director:** Paul Robins;
Advertising Manager: Graham Kirk
ADVERTISING RATES:
Full Page Mono £1982.88
Full Page Colour £2577.72
SCC £6.48
Agency Commission: 10%
Mechanical Data: Col Widths (Display): 27mm, No. of
Columns (Display): 9, Film: Digital, Type Area: 340 x 270mm,
Col Length: 340mm, Page Width: 270mm
Average advertising content per issue: 64%
**Series owner and contact point for the following titles,
see individual entries:**
Melton Citizen
Melton Times
LOCAL NEWSPAPERS: Local Newspapers English
Counties

TIMES SERIES (RICHMOND)
43125U72A-510

Formerly: Times & Guardian Series (Richmond)
Editorial Address: 29-39 London Road, TWICKENHAM,
TW1 3SZ **Tel:** 020 8744 4200 **Fax:** 020 8744 4299
Email: rtt@london.newsquest.co.uk
Advertising Address: As above.
Email: mburgess@london.newsquest.co.uk
Web site: http://www.rttimes.co.uk
Publisher: Newsquest Media Group
Date Established: 1873
Frequency: Weekly - Published on Friday
Circulation: 152,627 (Combined Circulation)
Editor: Daniel Menhinnitt; **News Editor:** Gerry Holt;
Advertising Manager: Melanie Burgess
ADVERTISING RATES:
Full Page Mono £1200.00
SCC £4.50
Agency Commission: 10%
Mechanical Data: Col Length: 560mm, No. of Columns
(Display): 12, Type Area: 560 x 357mm, Page Width: 357mm,
Film: Digital
**Series owner and contact point for the following titles,
see individual entries:**
The Chiswick
Hounslow & Brentford Times
Richmond & Twickenham Times
LOCAL NEWSPAPERS: Local Newspapers Greater London

Y TINCER
761756U72J-262

Editorial Address: Rhos Helyg, 23 Maes Yr Efail, Penrhyn-
coch, ABERYSTWYTH, SY23 3HE **Tel:** 01970 828017
Email: rhoshelyg@btinternet.com
Advertising Address: As above.
Email: rhoshelyg@btinternet.com
ISSN: 0963-925X
Publisher: Y Tincer Committee
Date Established: 1977
Frequency: 10 issues yearly - Published on 3rd Thursday of
the month but not published in July and August
Cover Price: £0.40
Annual Sub.: £9.00
Circulation: 1,200 (Publisher's Statement)
Editor: Ceris Gruffudd; **Advertising Manager:** Ceris
Gruffudd
Summary of Content: Welsh language community
newspaper featuring local news, an events calendar and
children's corner.
Language(s): Welsh
Readership/Target Audience: Aimed at Welsh speaking
readers living in North Ceredigion.
ADVERTISING: Rates on application
LOCAL NEWSPAPERS: Community Newsletters

TIPTON NEWS
1818522U72B-3467_213

Frequency: Weekly - Published on Thursday
Cover Price: Free
ADVERTISING RATES:
SCC £4.46
Part of Series, see entry for: The News & Observer Series
LOCAL NEWSPAPERS: Local Newspapers English
Counties

THE TIVERTON GAZETTE
43518U72B-805_160

Formerly: The Gazette (Tiverton)
Frequency: Weekly
Cover Price: £0.55
Part of Series, see entry for: The Gazette Series (Mid
Devon)
LOCAL NEWSPAPERS: Local Newspapers English
Counties

TIVY-SIDE ADVERTISER
44843U72C-355

Editorial Address: 39 St. Mary Street, CARDIGAN, SA43
1EU **Tel:** 01239 614343 **Fax:** 01239 615386
Email: tivyside@gwent-wales.co.uk
Advertising Address: Press Building, Merlins Bridge,
HAVERFORDWEST, SA61 1XF **Tel:** 01437 765000
Fax: 01437 760482
Email: mark.sainsbury@gwent-wales.co.uk
Web site: http://www.tivyside.co.uk
Publisher: Newsquest Wales & Gloucestershire
Date Established: 1866
Frequency: Weekly - Published on Tuesday
Cover Price: £0.50
Circulation: 8,720 (Publisher's Statement)
Editor: Sue Lewis; **Advertising Manager:** Mark Sainsbury
ADVERTISING RATES:
Full Page Mono £1285.00
Full Page Colour £1606.00
SCC £4.00
Agency Commission: 10%
Mechanical Data: Type Area: 340 x 259mm, No. of
Columns (Display): 9, Col Length: 340mm, Col Widths
(Display): 27mm, Page Width: 259mm, Film: Digital
Copy instructions: Copy Date: Friday 4.30pm prior to
publication date
LOCAL NEWSPAPERS: Local Newspapers Wales

TODMORDEN NEWS
44727U72B-3900

Editorial Address: Fielden Square, Rochdale Road,
TODMORDEN, OL14 7LD **Tel:** 01706 815731
Fax: 01706 816071
Email: john.greenwood@halifaxcourier.co.uk
Advertising Address: As above. **Tel:** 01706 815231
Web site: http://www.todmordennews.co.uk
Publisher: Johnston Press plc
Date Established: 1853
Frequency: Weekly
Cover Price: £0.44
Circulation: 4,049 (ABC 02/07/2007 to 30/12/2007)
Editor: Stephen Firth; **Features Editor:** Stephen Firth;
Managing Director: Darron McLoughlin
ADVERTISING: Rates on application
Mechanical Data: Col Widths (Display): 27.78mm, Film:
Digital, No. of Columns (Display): 11
Copy instructions: Copy Date: Tuesday 5pm prior to
publication date
Supplement(s): Motoring - 52xY
LOCAL NEWSPAPERS: Local Newspapers English
Counties

TORBAY WEEKENDER
43551U72B-885_155

Frequency: Weekly
Cover Price: Free
Circulation: 40,090 (VFD 02/07/2007 to 30/12/2007)
Part of Series, see entry for: Torbay Weekender Series
LOCAL NEWSPAPERS: Local Newspapers English
Counties

TORBAY WEEKENDER SERIES
43549U72B-885

Editorial Address: Harmsworth House, Barton Hill Road,
TORQUAY, TQ2 8JN **Tel:** 01803 676284 **Fax:** 01803 676499
Email: weekender@heraldexpress.co.uk
Advertising Address: As above. **Tel:** 01803 676000
Email: dpearce@swmg.co.uk
Web site: http://www.thisissouthdevon.co.uk
Publisher: South West Media Group Ltd
Frequency: Weekly - Published on Thursday
Cover Price: Free
Circulation: 53,152 (Combined Circulation)
Usual Pagination: 32
Editor: Tracey Gwynne; **Advertising Manager:** David
Pearce
ADVERTISING RATES:
Full Page Mono £1958.40
Full Page Colour £2448.00
SCC £6.80
Agency Commission: 10%
Mechanical Data: Col Length: 360mm, Film: Digital, No. of
Columns (Display): 8, Type Area: 360 x 288mm, Print
Process: Web-fed offset litho, Page Width: 288mm, Col
Widths (Display): 36mm
Copy instructions: Copy Date: Friday 5pm prior to
publication date
**Series owner and contact point for the following titles,
see individual entries:**
Newton Abbot & District Weekender
Torbay Weekender
LOCAL NEWSPAPERS: Local Newspapers English
Counties

TORPOINT JOURNAL
767528U72B-545_143

Frequency: Weekly - For circulation, see Liskeard and
Callington Gazette
Cover Price: Free

ADVERTISING RATES:
Full Page Mono £1065.60
Full Page Colour £1324.80
SCC £3.70
Part of Series, see entry for: Cornish Times & Gazette Series
LOCAL NEWSPAPERS: Local Newspapers English Counties

TOTNES NEWS
43543U72B-854_210

Frequency: Weekly
Cover Price: Free
Part of Series, see entry for: South Hams Newspapers Group
LOCAL NEWSPAPERS: Local Newspapers English Counties

TOTNES TIMES
43537U72B-854_213

Frequency: Weekly
Cover Price: £0.30
Part of Series, see entry for: South Hams Newspapers Group
LOCAL NEWSPAPERS: Local Newspapers English Counties

TOTTENHAM, WOOD GREEN & EDMONTON JOURNAL
43075U72A-240_200

Formerly: Tottenham & Wood Green Journal
Frequency: Weekly
Cover Price: £0.40
Circulation: 19,866 (Publisher's Statement)
ADVERTISING RATES:
SCC £10.00
Part of Series, see entry for: Islington Gazette & Journal Series
LOCAL NEWSPAPERS: Local Newspapers Greater London

TOWN CENTRE NEWS (WIGAN)
1799439U72B-1310_272

Frequency: Monthly
Cover Price: Free
Circulation: 10,000 (Print Run)
ADVERTISING: Rates on application
Part of Series, see entry for: The Wigan Observer, Reporter and News Series
LOCAL NEWSPAPERS: Local Newspapers English Counties

TOWN CRIER HUNTINGDON
43344U72B-415_160

Frequency: Weekly
Cover Price: Free
ADVERTISING RATES:
Full Page Mono £765.00
Full Page Colour £994.50
SCC £7.36
Part of Series, see entry for: Town Crier Series
LOCAL NEWSPAPERS: Local Newspapers English Counties

TOWN CRIER SERIES
43341U72B-415

Formerly: Citizen Series
Editorial Address: Priory House, Priory Lane, ST. NEOTS, PE19 2BH **Tel:** 01480 402100 **Fax:** 01480 402132
Email: tceditorial@towncrierseries.co.uk
Advertising Address: As above. **Fax:** 01480 215246
Email: sally.huckle@towncrierseries.co.uk
Publisher: Johnston Press plc
Frequency: Weekly
Cover Price: Free
Circulation: 43,550 (VFD 02/07/2007 to 30/12/2007)
Usual Pagination: 106
Editor: Matt Cornish; **Advertising Manager:** Sally Huckle
ADVERTISING RATES:
Full Page Mono £2034.90
Full Page Colour £2645.37
Agency Commission: 10%
Mechanical Data: Col Widths (Display): 26.8mm, Page Width: 270mm, Film: Digital, Type Area: 340 x 270mm, Col Length: 340mm, No. of Columns (Display): 9
Copy instructions: Copy Date: Monday 5.30pm prior to publication date
Average advertising content per issue: 65%
Series owner and contact point for the following titles, see individual entries:
Town Crier Huntingdon
Town Crier St. Neots
LOCAL NEWSPAPERS: Local Newspapers English Counties

TOWN CRIER ST. NEOTS
43342U72B-415_140

Frequency: Weekly
Cover Price: Free
ADVERTISING RATES:
Full Page Mono £765.00
Full Page Colour £994.50
SCC £7.36
Part of Series; see entry for: Town Crier Series
LOCAL NEWSPAPERS: Local Newspapers English Counties

TOWY VALLEY GUARDIAN
44840U72C-340_170

Frequency: Weekly
Cover Price: £0.45
Part of Series, see entry for: South Wales Guardian Series
LOCAL NEWSPAPERS: Local Newspapers Wales

TRADER PICTORIAL (NEWARK)
44046U72B-2620_250

Formerly: Grantham Trader Series
Frequency: Weekly
Cover Price: Free
Circulation: 38,766 (Publisher's Statement)
Part of Series, see entry for: Newark Advertiser Series
LOCAL NEWSPAPERS: Local Newspapers English Counties

TRADER SCARBOROUGH, FILEY AND HUNMANBY
44668U72B-3647

Editorial Address: 17-23 Aberdeen Walk, SCARBOROUGH, YO11 1BB **Tel:** 01723 363636 **Fax:** 01723 379580
Email: john.ritchie@yrnltd.co.uk
Advertising Address: As above. **Tel:** 01723 352269
Email: amanda.cashmore@jpress.co.uk
Web site: http://www.scarboroughtoday.co.uk
Publisher: Yorkshire Regional Newspapers Ltd
Frequency: Daily - Not published on Sunday
Cover Price: Free
Circulation: 35,900 (Publisher's Statement)
Usual Pagination: 24
Editor: John Ritchie; **Advertising Manager:** Amanda Cashmore
ADVERTISING RATES:
SCC £4.55
Agency Commission: 10%
Mechanical Data: No. of Columns (Display): 9, Col Widths (Display): 27.78mm, Film: Digital
Copy instructions: Copy Date: Tuesday 4pm prior to publication date
Average advertising content per issue: 70%
LOCAL NEWSPAPERS: Local Newspapers English Counties

TRAFFORD METRO NEWS
43701U72B-1230

Formerly: Manchester Metro News (Trafford Edition)
Editorial Address: 1 Scott Place, MANCHESTER, SK3 0AB
Tel: 0161 211 2537 **Fax:** 0161 475 4868
Email: news@metro-news.co.uk
Advertising Address: As above. **Tel:** 0161 832 7200
Fax: 0161 480 4837
Email: karen.smith@menmediasales.co.uk
Web site: http://www.metronews.co.uk
Publisher: MEN Media
Date Established: 1987
Frequency: Weekly - Published on Friday
Cover Price: Free
Circulation: 98,936 (VFD 21/05/2007 to 01/07/2007)
Editor: Bethan Dorsett
ADVERTISING RATES:
Full Page Mono £2524.50
Full Page Colour £3534.30
Mechanical Data: Type Area: 340 x 267mm, Col Length: 340mm, Page Width: 267mm, Film: Digital, No. of Columns (Display): 9
LOCAL NEWSPAPERS: Local Newspapers English Counties

TRAVEL
1606536U67B-9009_708

Tel: 020 7938 7584 **Fax:** 020 7938 3637
Email: traveldesk@standard.co.uk
Web site: http://www.thisistravel.co.uk
Frequency: 156 issues yearly - Published Monday, Wednesday and Friday within The London Evening Standard
Editor: Simon Davis
Summary of Content: Section featuring leisure holidays and travel both in the UK and abroad.
ADVERTISING: Rates on application
Part of Series, see entry for: London Evening Standard
REGIONAL DAILY & SUNDAY NEWSPAPERS: Regional Daily Newspapers

TRENDS
1899298U67B-9085

Tel: 020 3367 7000
Frequency: Weekly - Published on Mondays within the London Evening Standard
Editor: Sarah Sands
Summary of Content: Section featuring lifestyle trends.
Part of Series, see entry for: London Evening Standard
REGIONAL DAILY & SUNDAY NEWSPAPERS: Regional Daily Newspapers

THE TRIBUNE
764150U72B-3705_160

Frequency: 26 issues yearly
Cover Price: Free
Circulation: 6,000 (Publisher's Statement)
ADVERTISING RATES:
Full Page Mono £270.00
Part of Series, see entry for: The Tribune & Courier Series
LOCAL NEWSPAPERS: Local Newspapers English Counties

THE TRIBUNE & COURIER SERIES
764073U72B-3705

Editorial Address: 46 High Street, West Mersea, COLCHESTER, CO5 8QA **Tel:** 01206 382935
Fax: 01206 384190
Email: editorialmic@btconnect.com
Advertising Address: As above. **Tel:** 01206 381555
Email: infomic@btconnect.com
Publisher: Mersea Island Communications
Date Established: 1993
Frequency: 26 issues yearly
Cover Price: Free
Circulation: 10,000 (Publisher's Statement)
Editor: Paula Shaw; **Publisher:** Glynis Softley
ADVERTISING: Rates on application
Mechanical Data: Film: Digital, No. of Columns (Display): 4, Type Area: 277 x 185mm, Col Length: 277mm, Page Width: 185mm
Copy instructions: Copy Date: 11 days prior to publication date
Average advertising content per issue: 50%
Series owner and contact point for the following titles, see individual entries:
The Courier
The Tribune
LOCAL NEWSPAPERS: Local Newspapers English Counties

TRIDENT MIDLAND NEWSPAPERS SERIES
44032U72B-2193

Editorial Address: Bridge Road, COALVILLE, LE67 3QP
Tel: 01530 813101 **Fax:** 01530 811361
Email: editor@timesandleader.co.uk
Advertising Address: As above.
Email: advertising@timesandleader.co.uk
Publisher: Trident Midland Newspapers
Date Established: 1895
Frequency: Weekly
Circulation: 46,151 (Combined Circulation)
Usual Pagination: 40
Editor: Ian Sleigh; **Advertising Manager:** Judith Leake
ADVERTISING: Rates on application
Series owner and contact point for the following titles, see individual entries:
Ashby Times
Coalville Times
Leader (North West Leicestershire & South Derbyshire)
Swadlincote Times
LOCAL NEWSPAPERS: Local Newspapers English Counties

TROON & PRESTWICK TIMES
44874U72D-90_180

Frequency: Weekly
Cover Price: £0.50
Part of Series, see entry for: Ayr Advertiser Series
LOCAL NEWSPAPERS: Local Newspapers Scotland

TRURO PACKET
43431U72B-553_210

Formerly: Truro & Newquay Packet
Frequency: Weekly
Circulation: 13,774 (VFD 02/07/2007 to 30/12/2007)
ADVERTISING RATES:
Full Page Mono £992.25
Full Page Colour £1339.53
SCC £2.50
Part of Series, see entry for: The Packet Series
LOCAL NEWSPAPERS: Local Newspapers English Counties

Non-National Newspapers

Section 4 (a) Newspapers

TURRIFF & DISTRICT ADVERTISER
44863U72D-10_180

Frequency: Weekly
ADVERTISING RATES:
Full Page Mono £490.00
SCC £2.25
Part of Series, see entry for: Advertiser Series in Aberdeenshire
LOCAL NEWSPAPERS: Local Newspapers Scotland

TWYFORD ADVERTISER
761645U72B-160_190

Frequency: Weekly - Circulation is incorporated into the Maidenhead Advertiser
Cover Price: £0.40
ADVERTISING: Rates on application
Part of Series, see entry for: Maidenhead Advertiser Series
LOCAL NEWSPAPERS: Local Newspapers English Counties

TYRONE CONSTITUTION
45130U72E-230_180

Frequency: Weekly
Cover Price: £0.85
Circulation: 9,520 (Publisher's Statement)
ADVERTISING: Rates on application
Part of Series, see entry for: Tyrone Constitution and Strabane Weekly News Series
LOCAL NEWSPAPERS: Local Newspapers Northern Ireland

TYRONE CONSTITUTION AND STRABANE WEEKLY NEWS SERIES
45128U72E-230

Editorial Address: 25-27 High Street, OMAGH, BT78 1BD
Tel: 028 8224 2721 **Fax:** 028 8224 3549
Email: news@tyronecon.co.uk
Advertising Address: As above.
Email: ulster@ulsternet-ni.co.uk
Web site: http://www.ulsternet-ni.co.uk
Publisher: Alpha Newspaper Group
Frequency: Weekly - Published on Thursday
Circulation: 12,516 (Combined Circulation)
Editor: Wesley Atchison; **Advertising Manager:** Amanda Rice
ADVERTISING RATES:
Full Page Mono £540.00
Full Page Colour £1047.55
Agency Commission: 10%
Mechanical Data: Page Width: 272mm, Film: Digital, Col Length: 410mm, Col Widths (Display): 35mm, Type Area: 410 x 272mm, No. of Columns (Display): 7
Copy instructions: Copy Date: Mono Tuesday 4pm prior to publication date Colour 7 days prior to publication date
Average advertising content per issue: 35%
Series owner and contact point for the following titles, see individual entries:
Strabane Weekly News
Tyrone Constitution
Supplement(s): Omagh Christmas - 1xY, Out & About at Easter - 1xY, Weddings - 1xY
LOCAL NEWSPAPERS: Local Newspapers Northern Ireland

TYRONE HERALD
1659804U72E-270_201

Frequency: Weekly - Published on Monday
Cover Price: £0.50
Circulation: 6,591 (ABC 02/07/2007 to 30/12/2007)
Part of Series, see entry for: Ulster Herald Series
LOCAL NEWSPAPERS: Local Newspapers Northern Ireland

TYRONE TIMES AND DUNGANNON GAZETTE
45131U72E-250

Editorial Address: Unit B, Buttermarket Centre, Thomas Street, DUNGANNON, BT70 1HN **Tel:** 028 8775 2801
Fax: 028 8775 2819
Email: peter.bayne@jpress.co.uk
Advertising Address: As above.
Email: claire.speers@jpress.co.uk
Web site: http://www.tyronetoday.com
Publisher: Morton Newspapers Ltd
Frequency: Weekly - Published on Tuesday
Cover Price: £0.80
Circulation: 5,000 (Publisher's Statement)
Editor: Peter Bayne; **Advertising Manager:** Claire Speers
ADVERTISING RATES:
Full Page Mono £1584.00
Full Page Colour £1980.00
SCC £4.70
Mechanical Data: Type Area: 340 x 268mm, No. of Columns (Display): 8, Col Length: 340mm, Page Width: 268mm, Film: Digital
Copy instructions: Copy Date: Friday 1pm prior to publication date
LOCAL NEWSPAPERS: Local Newspapers Northern Ireland

UCKFIELD LEADER
1655349U72B-3210_141

Frequency: Weekly
Cover Price: Free
Circulation: 10,000 (Publisher's Statement)
Part of Series, see entry for: Brighton and Hove Leader Series
LOCAL NEWSPAPERS: Local Newspapers English Counties

ULSTER GAZETTE
45132U72E-260

Formerly: Ulster Gazette & Armagh Standard
Editorial Address: 56 Scotch Street, ARMAGH, BT61 7DQ
Tel: 028 3752 2639 **Fax:** 028 3752 7029
Email: newsdesk@ulstergazette.co.uk
Advertising Address: As above.
Email: advertising@ulstergazette.co.uk
Web site: http://www.ulster-ni.co.uk
Publisher: Ulster Gazette (Armagh) Ltd.
Frequency: Weekly - Published on Wednesday
Cover Price: £0.95
Circulation: 10,025 (Publisher's Statement)
Editor: Richard Burden; **Advertising Manager:** Paddy Scott
ADVERTISING RATES:
SCC £3.65
Agency Commission: 10%
Mechanical Data: Type Area: 410 x 272mm, No. of Columns (Display): 7, Col Length: 410mm, Page Width: 272mm, Film: Digital, Col Widths (Display): 35mm
Copy instructions: Copy Date: 3 days prior to publication date
Average advertising content per issue: 40%
LOCAL NEWSPAPERS: Local Newspapers Northern Ireland

ULSTER HERALD
45135U72E-270_200

Formerly: Ulster Herald and Provincial Advertiser
Frequency: Weekly - Published on Thursday
Cover Price: £0.75
Circulation: 12,679 (ABC 02/07/2007 to 30/12/2007)
Part of Series, see entry for: Ulster Herald Series
LOCAL NEWSPAPERS: Local Newspapers Northern Ireland

ULSTER HERALD SERIES
45133U72E-270

Editorial Address: 14 John Street, OMAGH, BT78 1DT
Tel: 028 8224 3444 **Fax:** 028 8224 2206
Email: editor@ulsterherald.com
Advertising Address: As above. **Fax:** 028 8225 5953
Email: advertising@ulsterherald.com
Web site: http://www.ulsterherald.com
Publisher: North-West of Ireland Ptg. & Pub. Co. Ltd
Date Established: 1901
Frequency: Weekly - Published on Monday and Thursday
Circulation: 21,967 (Combined Circulation)
Editor: Dominic McClements; **Advertising Manager:** Roisin Kerrigan
Language(s): English; Gaelic
ADVERTISING RATES:
Full Page Mono £1083.60
Full Page Colour £1517.04
SCC £4.30
Agency Commission: 10%
Mechanical Data: Type Area: 363 x 262mm, Col Length: 363mm, No. of Columns (Display): 7, Page Width: 262mm, Film: Digital
Copy instructions: Copy Date: Tuesday 1pm prior to publication date
Average advertising content per issue: 40%
Series owner and contact point for the following titles, see individual entries:
Strabane Chronicle
Tyrone Herald
Ulster Herald
Supplement(s): Property - 52xY, The Scene - 52xY, Sportsweek - 52xY
LOCAL NEWSPAPERS: Local Newspapers Northern Ireland

ULSTER STAR
45136U72E-280

Formerly: Ulster Star Series
Editorial Address: 12A Bow Street, LISBURN, BT28 1BN
Tel: 028 9267 9111 **Fax:** 028 9260 2904
Email: news@ulsterstar.co.uk
Advertising Address: As above.
Email: andrinaoprey@jpress.co.uk
Web site: http://www.lisburntoday.co.uk
Publisher: Morton Newspapers Ltd
Date Established: 1957
Frequency: Weekly - Published on Thursday
Cover Price: £0.98
Circulation: 9,767 (ABC 02/07/2007 to 30/12/2007)
Editor: David Fletcher; **Advertising Manager:** Andrina O'Prey
ADVERTISING RATES:
Full Page Mono £1638.00
Full Page Colour £2374.00

Agency Commission: 10%
Mechanical Data: Col Length: 340mm, Type Area: 340 x 268mm, No. of Columns (Display): 9, Page Width: 268mm, Col Widths (Display): 28mm, Print Process: Web-fed offset litho
Copy instructions: Copy Date: Wednesday 12 noon prior to publication date
LOCAL NEWSPAPERS: Local Newspapers Northern Ireland

ULVERSTON & SOUTH LAKES EVENING MAIL
41978U67B-10_650

Frequency: Evenings
Edition of: North West Evening Mail (Barrow)
REGIONAL DAILY & SUNDAY NEWSPAPERS: Regional Daily Newspapers

UTTOXETER ADVERTISER
44326U72B-3050

Editorial Address: Lion Buildings, 8 Market Place, UTTOXETER, ST14 8HP **Tel:** 01889 565048
Fax: 01889 563061
Email: reporters@uttoxeteradvertiser.co.uk
Advertising Address: As above. **Tel:** 01889 562050
Email: gill.conroy@staffordshirenewspapers.co.uk
Web site: http://www.uttoxeteradvertiser.co.uk
Publisher: Staffordshire Newspapers Ltd
Frequency: Weekly - Published on Wednesday
Cover Price: £0.45
Circulation: 4,200 (Publisher's Statement)
Usual Pagination: 16
Editor: James Brindle
ADVERTISING RATES:
Full Page Mono £740.25
Full Page Colour £999.34
SCC £2.35
Agency Commission: 10%
Mechanical Data: Type Area: 350 x 268mm, Col Length: 350mm, No. of Columns (Display): 9, Page Width: 268mm, Film: Digital
Copy instructions: Copy Date: Friday 5.00pm prior to publication date
Average advertising content per issue: 40%
LOCAL NEWSPAPERS: Local Newspapers English Counties

UTTOXETER ECHO
44301U72B-2970_200

Frequency: Weekly - Published on Wednesday
Cover Price: £0.40
Part of Series, see entry for: Cheadle Times & Echo Series
LOCAL NEWSPAPERS: Local Newspapers English Counties

UTTOXETER POST & TIMES
44313U72B-3005_150

Frequency: Weekly
Cover Price: £0.40
Circulation: 3,543 (ABC 02/07/2007 to 30/12/2007)
ADVERTISING RATES:
Full Page Mono £705.60
Full Page Colour £882.00
Part of Series, see entry for: Post & Times Series
LOCAL NEWSPAPERS: Local Newspapers English Counties

UXBRIDGE & HAYES LEADER SOUTH EDITION
43165U72A-525_200

Frequency: Weekly - For circulation see Uxbridge & Ruislip Leader North Edition
Cover Price: Free
ADVERTISING: Rates on application
Part of Series, see entry for: Uxbridge Gazette Series
LOCAL NEWSPAPERS: Local Newspapers Greater London

UXBRIDGE & RUISLIP LEADER NORTH EDITION
43166U72A-525_210

Formerly: Uxbridge Leader North Edition
Frequency: Weekly - Circulation is for Uxbridge Leader Series including Uxbridge & Hayes Leader South Edition
Cover Price: Free
Circulation: 58,649 (VFD 02/07/2007 to 30/12/2007)
ADVERTISING: Rates on application
Part of Series, see entry for: Uxbridge Gazette Series
LOCAL NEWSPAPERS: Local Newspapers Greater London

UXBRIDGE GAZETTE SERIES
43158U72A-525

Editorial Address: Gazette House, 28 Bakers Road, UXBRIDGE, UB8 1RG **Tel:** 01895 451021
Fax: 01895 451050
Email: editoraluxbridge@trinitysouth.co.uk
Advertising Address: As above. **Tel:** 01895 451000
Fax: 01895 451090

Email: advertisinguxbridge@trinitysouth.co.uk
Web site: http://www.icuxbridge.co.uk
Publisher: Trinity Mirror
Frequency: Weekly
Circulation: 73,269 (Combined Circulation)
Editor: Shujaul Azam; **Features Editor:** Siba Matti; **Editor-in-Chief:** Adrian Seal; **Managing Director:** Simon Edgley;
Advertising Manager: Vanessa Hillman
ADVERTISING: Rates on application
Agency Commission: 10%
Copy instructions: Copy Date: Monday 4pm prior to publication date
Average advertising content per issue: 40%
Series owner and contact point for the following titles, see individual entries:
Gazette (Harefield)
Gazette (Hayes & Harlington)
Gazette (Ruislip & Northwood)
Gazette (Uxbridge and West Drayton)
Uxbridge & Hayes Leader South Edition
Uxbridge & Ruislip Leader North Edition
LOCAL NEWSPAPERS: Local Newspapers Greater London

THE VALE ADVERTISER   1655117U72B-902_173
Frequency: Weekly
Cover Price: Free
Circulation: 10,000 (Publisher's Statement)
ADVERTISING: Rates on application
Part of Series, see entry for: Advertiser Series (Poole & Swanage)
LOCAL NEWSPAPERS: Local Newspapers English Counties

THE VILLAGER   44415U72B-3167
Formerly: Virginia Water Villager Series
Editorial Address: Ocean House, The Ring, BRACKNELL, RG12 1AX **Tel:** 01344 456611
Email: villagernews@berksmedia.co.uk
Advertising Address: Upton Court, Datchet Road, SLOUGH, SL3 7NR **Tel:** 01753 523355 **Fax:** 01753 627210
Email: sales@thevillager.co.uk
Web site: http://www.thevillager.co.uk
Publisher: Berkshire Media Group Ltd
Date Established: 1997
Frequency: 25 issues yearly - Published on Wednesday
Cover Price: Free
Circulation: 8,000 (Publisher's Statement)
Usual Pagination: 40
Editor: Lauren Everitt; **Advertising Manager:** Alan Rogers
ADVERTISING RATES:
Full Page Mono £620.40
Full Page Colour £655.40
SCC £2.35
Agency Commission: 10%
Mechanical Data: Col Length: 340mm, Col Widths (Display): 30mm, No. of Columns (Display): 8, Type Area: 340 x 264mm, Print Process: Web-fed offset litho, Film: Digital, Page Width: 264mm
Copy instructions: Copy Date: Thursday 4pm prior to publication date
Average advertising content per issue: 70%
LOCAL NEWSPAPERS: Local Newspapers English Counties

THE VISITOR (GUERNSEY)   1664933U72F-9
Editorial Address: PO Box 57, Braye Road, Vale, GUERNSEY, GY1 3BW **Tel:** 01481 240240
Fax: 01481 240275
Email: jtodd@guernsey-press.com
Advertising Address: As above.
Email: rguilbert@guernsey-press.com
Web site: http://www.thisisguernsey.com
Publisher: Guernsey Press Co Ltd
Date Established: 1987
Frequency: Monthly
Cover Price: Free
Circulation: 16,000 (Publisher's Statement)
Editor: Julie Todd; **Advertising Manager:** Becky Guilbert
ADVERTISING RATES:
Full Page Colour £1800.00
Mechanical Data: Film: Digital, Trim Size: 245 x 170mm
LOCAL NEWSPAPERS: Local Newspapers Channel Islands

VISITOR (MORECAMBE)   44005U72B-2090
Editorial Address: 12 Victoria Street, MORECAMBE, LA4 4AG **Tel:** 01524 833111 **Fax:** 01524 834024
Email: visitor@lmnews.co.uk
Advertising Address: As above. **Fax:** 01524 420939
Email: ads.lmn@lmnews.co.uk
Web site: http://www.thevisitor.co.uk
Publisher: Lancaster and Morecambe Newspapers
Frequency: Weekly - Published on Wednesday
Cover Price: £0.60
Circulation: 13,030 (ABC 02/07/2007 to 30/12/2007)

Usual Pagination: 56
Editor: Glen Cooper; **News Editor:** Ingrid Kent; **Features Editor:** Ingrid Kent
ADVERTISING: Rates on application
Agency Commission: 10%
Mechanical Data: Col Length: 340mm, Page Width: 274mm, Type Area: 340 x 274mm, No. of Columns (Display): 9, Col Widths (Display): 29mm, Film: Digital
Copy instructions: Copy Date: Monday prior to publication date
Supplement(s): Motor Guide - 52xY, Property Guide - 52xY
LOCAL NEWSPAPERS: Local Newspapers English Counties

VISITOR SERIES   44845U72C-357
Editorial Address: 84 High Street, RHYL, LL18 1UB
Tel: 01745 334144 **Fax:** 01745 337862
Email: martin.williams@northwalesnews.co.uk
Advertising Address: PO Box 202, Vale Road, LLANDUDNO JUNCTION, LL31 9ZD **Tel:** 01492 584321
Fax: 01492 574422
Email: sharon.doleman@dailypost.co.uk
Web site: http://www.icnorthwales.co.uk
Publisher: Trinity Mirror
Frequency: Weekly - Published on Wednesday
Circulation: 27,702 (Combined Circulation)
Editor: Martin Williams; **News Editor:** Martin Williams;
Executive Editor: Dan Owen; **Editor-in-Chief:** Alan Davies;
Advertising Manager: Sharon Doleman
ADVERTISING RATES:
Full Page Mono £1195.00
SCC £4.15
Mechanical Data: Page Width: 272mm, Type Area: 360 x 272mm, No. of Columns (Display): 8, Col Length: 360mm
Series owner and contact point for the following titles, see individual entries:
Abergele & St Asaph Visitor
Rhyl & Prestatyn Visitor
LOCAL NEWSPAPERS: Local Newspapers Wales

WAKEFIELD EXPRESS (CITY EDITION)
44731U72B-3910_180
Frequency: Weekly - Circulation figure includes the Wakefield Express (Horbury), the Wakefield Express (Osset), the Wakefield Express (Rothwell) and the Normanton and Wakefield Express
Cover Price: £0.45
Circulation: 32,642 (ABC 02/07/2007 to 30/12/2007)
ADVERTISING RATES:
Full Page Mono £1973.70
Full Page Colour £2565.81
SCC £6.45
Part of Series, see entry for: Wakefield Express Series
LOCAL NEWSPAPERS: Local Newspapers English Counties

WAKEFIELD EXPRESS (HORBURY)
44732U72B-3910_190
Frequency: Weekly - Circulation figure is incorporated into the Wakefield Express (City Edition)
Cover Price: £0.45
ADVERTISING RATES:
Full Page Mono £1973.70
Full Page Colour £2565.81
SCC £6.45
Part of Series, see entry for: Wakefield Express Series
LOCAL NEWSPAPERS: Local Newspapers English Counties

WAKEFIELD EXPRESS (NORMANTON)
44733U72B-3910_200
Formerly: Normanton & Wakefield Express
Frequency: Weekly - Circulation figure is incorporated into the Wakefield Express (City Edition)
Cover Price: £0.45
ADVERTISING RATES:
Full Page Mono £1973.70
Full Page Colour £2565.81
SCC £6.45
Part of Series, see entry for: Wakefield Express Series
LOCAL NEWSPAPERS: Local Newspapers English Counties

WAKEFIELD EXPRESS (OSSETT)
44734U72B-3910_210
Frequency: Weekly - Circulation figure is incorporated into the Wakefield Express (City Edition)
Cover Price: £0.45
ADVERTISING RATES:
Full Page Mono £1973.70
Full Page Colour £2565.81
SCC £6.45

Part of Series, see entry for: Wakefield Express Series
LOCAL NEWSPAPERS: Local Newspapers English Counties

WAKEFIELD EXPRESS SERIES
44728U72B-3910
Editorial Address: Express House, Southgate, WAKEFIELD, WF1 1TE **Tel:** 01924 375111 **Fax:** 01924 433040
Email: editorial@wakefieldexpress.co.uk
Advertising Address: As above. **Fax:** 01924 290451
Email: advertising@wakefieldexpress.co.uk
Web site: http://www.wakefieldexpress.co.uk
Publisher: Yorkshire Weekly Newspaper Group Ltd
Date Established: 1854
Frequency: Weekly - Published every Friday
Circulation: 83,674 (Combined Circulation)
Usual Pagination: 30
Editor: Lisa Rookes; **Managing Director:** Helen Oldham;
Advertising Manager: Karen Curren
ADVERTISING: Rates on application
Agency Commission: 10%
Average advertising content per issue: 60%
Series owner and contact point for the following titles, see individual entries:
Ossett & Horbury Observer
Rothwell & Oulton Extra
Wakefield Express (City Edition)
Wakefield Express (Horbury)
Wakefield Express (Normanton)
Wakefield Express (Ossett)
Wakefield Extra
Supplement(s): Leisure - 52xY, Motoring - 52xY, Property - 52xY, Sport - 52xY
LOCAL NEWSPAPERS: Local Newspapers English Counties

WAKEFIELD EXTRA   44729U72B-3910_150
Frequency: Weekly - Circulation figure includes the Rothwell & Oulton Extra
Cover Price: Free
Circulation: 39,665 (VFD 10/09/2007 to 30/12/2007)
ADVERTISING RATES:
Full Page Mono £1655.46
Full Page Colour £2152.10
SCC £5.41
Part of Series, see entry for: Wakefield Express Series
LOCAL NEWSPAPERS: Local Newspapers English Counties

WALDEN LOCAL   43649U72B-1091
Editorial Address: 10 Emson Close, SAFFRON WALDEN, CB10 1HL **Tel:** 01799 516161 **Fax:** 01799 520561
Email: editor@waldenlocal.co.uk
Advertising Address: As above.
Email: sales@waldenlocal.co.uk
Web site: http://www.waldenlocal.com
Publisher: Local Publications (Saffron Walden) Ltd
Frequency: Weekly - Published on Wednesday
Cover Price: Free
Circulation: 14,000 (Publisher's Statement)
Usual Pagination: 20
Editor: John Brooker; **Managing Director:** Louise Cordall;
Advertising Manager: Karen Bouch
ADVERTISING RATES:
Full Page Mono £380.00
Full Page Colour £400.00
SCC £2.50
Agency Commission: 10%
Mechanical Data: Page Width: 265mm, Film: Digital, Col Length: 365mm, No. of Columns (Display): 8, Col Widths (Display): 30mm, Type Area: 365 x 265mm, Print Process: Web-fed offset litho
Copy instructions: Copy Date: 2 days prior to publication date
Average advertising content per issue: 75%
LOCAL NEWSPAPERS: Local Newspapers English Counties

WALES ON SUNDAY   42283U67C-34
Editorial Address: 6 Park Street, CARDIFF, CF10 1XR
Tel: 029 2024 3600
Email: wosmail@mediawales.co.uk
Advertising Address: As above. **Tel:** 029 2022 3333
Email: denise.rich@mediawales.co.uk
Web site: http://www.icwales.co.uk
Publisher: Media Wales Ltd
Frequency: Sunday
Cover Price: £0.85
Circulation: 41,199 (ABC 02/07/2007 to 30/12/2007)
Editor: Tim Gordon; **Executive Editor:** Wayne Davies;
Features Editor: Margaret O'Reilly; **Advertising Manager:** Gerald Griffiths
ADVERTISING RATES:
SCC £10.74

Agency Commission: 10%
Mechanical Data: Film: Positive, right reading, emulsion side down, No. of Columns (Display): 8, Col Widths (Display): 32mm, Col Length: 340mm, Print Process: Web-fed offset litho, Type Area: 340 x 266mm, Page Width: 266mm
Copy instructions: Copy Date: Thursday prior to publication date
Average advertising content per issue: 40%
Editions:
Wales on Sunday (Gwent Edition)
Wales on Sunday (North Wales Edition)
Wales on Sunday (South Wales Edition)
Wales on Sunday (West Wales Edition)
Supplement(s): Life on Sunday - 52xY, Sport on Sunday - 52xY
REGIONAL DAILY & SUNDAY NEWSPAPERS: Regional Sunday Newspapers

WALES ON SUNDAY (GWENT EDITION)
1665160U67C-34_500
Frequency: Sunday
Cover Price: £0.85
Edition of: Wales on Sunday
REGIONAL DAILY & SUNDAY NEWSPAPERS: Regional Sunday Newspapers

WALES ON SUNDAY (NORTH WALES EDITION)
1665164U67C-34_502
Frequency: Sunday
Cover Price: £0.85
Edition of: Wales on Sunday
REGIONAL DAILY & SUNDAY NEWSPAPERS: Regional Sunday Newspapers

WALES ON SUNDAY (SOUTH WALES EDITION)
1665162U67C-34_504
Frequency: Sunday
Cover Price: £0.85
Edition of: Wales on Sunday
REGIONAL DAILY & SUNDAY NEWSPAPERS: Regional Sunday Newspapers

WALES ON SUNDAY (WEST WALES EDITION)
1665161U67C-34_503
Frequency: Sunday
Cover Price: £0.85
Edition of: Wales on Sunday
REGIONAL DAILY & SUNDAY NEWSPAPERS: Regional Sunday Newspapers

THE WALL STREET JOURNAL EUROPE
41860U65G-350
Editorial Address: 10 Fleet Place, Limeburner Lane, LONDON, EC4M 7QN Tel: 020 7842 9200
Fax: 020 7842 9201
Email: london.news@wsj.com
Advertising Address: 90 Long Acre, LONDON, WC2E 9PR
Tel: 020 7842 9600 Fax: 020 7842 9650
Email: tracey.lehane@dowjones.com
Web site: http://www.wsje.com
Publisher: Dow Jones & Co Inc.
Frequency: Mornings - Published Monday to Friday
Cover Price: £1.20
Circulation: 79,579 (ABC 01/07/2008 to 31/12/2008)
Usual Pagination: 32
Editor: Neil McIntosh; Managing Editor: Jesse Lewis
Summary of Content: News content: Mainly business and financial.
ADVERTISING RATES:
Full Page Mono $44312.00
Full Page Colour $54112.00
Agency Commission: 15%
Mechanical Data: Col Length: 355mm, No. of Columns (Display): 5, Page Width: 254mm, Col Widths (Display): 35mm, Print Process: Offset litho, Type Area: 355 x 254mm
Copy instructions: Copy Date: 2 weeks prior to publication date
NATIONAL DAILY & SUNDAY NEWSPAPERS: International Daily Newspapers

WALLINGFORD HERALD
44226U72B-2720_190
Frequency: Weekly - Circulation figure can be found with the Abingdon Herald
Cover Price: £0.35
ADVERTISING RATES:
SCC £4.75
Part of Series, see entry for: Herald and Times Series Oxon
LOCAL NEWSPAPERS: Local Newspapers English Counties

WALSALL ADVERTISER
44556U72B-3060
Formerly: Walsall Advertiser & Midweek Series
Editorial Address: Ventura Park Road, Bitterscote, TAMWORTH, B78 3LZ Tel: 01827 848435
Fax: 01827 848640
Email: walsall.editorial@cintamworth.co.uk
Advertising Address: As above. Tel: 01827 848586
Fax: 0845 600 8391
Email: cin.retail@cintamworth.co.uk
Web site: http://www.thisiswalsallonline.co.uk
Publisher: Central Independent News & Media Ltd
Frequency: Weekly
Cover Price: Free
Circulation: 65,616 (VFD 02/07/2007 to 30/12/2007)
Editor: Laura Vickers; News Editor: Laura Vickers;
Managing Director: Tim Saunders; Advertising Manager: Jackie Keeling; Group Editor: Gary Phelps
ADVERTISING: Rates on application
Agency Commission: 10%
Copy instructions: Copy Date: Tuesday 12pm prior to publication date
LOCAL NEWSPAPERS: Local Newspapers English Counties

WALSALL CHRONICLE
44526U72B-3489
Editorial Address: 51-53 Queen Street, WOLVERHAMPTON, WV1 1ES Tel: 01902 313131
Fax: 01902 319467
Email: walsallchronicle@expressandstar.co.uk
Advertising Address: Hatherton Street, WALSALL, WS1 1ES Tel: 01922 444444 Fax: 01922 444300
Email: walsallchronicle@expressandstar.co.uk
Publisher: Express & Star Ltd
Frequency: Weekly - Published on Thursday
Cover Price: Free
Circulation: 65,414 (VFD 02/07/2007 to 30/12/2007)
Editor: Danny Farragher; Advertising Manager: Stuart Perkins
ADVERTISING RATES:
SCC £3.75
Agency Commission: 10%
Mechanical Data: Type Area: 410 x 305mm, No. of Columns (Display): 8, Col Length: 410mm, Page Width: 305mm, Film: Digital
Copy instructions: Copy Date: Monday 12pm prior to publication date
Average advertising content per issue: 75%
LOCAL NEWSPAPERS: Local Newspapers English Counties

WALTHAM FOREST GUARDIAN
43168U72A-534_120
Formerly: Guardian (Chingford)
Frequency: Weekly
Cover Price: £0.45
Circulation: 13,845 (ABC 03/07/2006 to 31/12/2006)
ADVERTISING RATES:
Full Page Mono £545.00
Full Page Colour £545.00
SCC £4.05
Part of Series, see entry for: Waltham Forest Guardian & Independent Series
LOCAL NEWSPAPERS: Local Newspapers Greater London

WALTHAM FOREST GUARDIAN & INDEPENDENT SERIES
43167U72A-534
Formerly: Waltham Forest Guardian Series
Editorial Address: 480-500 Larkshall Road, Highams Park, LONDON, E4 9GD Tel: 020 8498 3400 Fax: 020 8531 2017
Email: jmoyes@london.newsquest.co.uk
Advertising Address: As above. Fax: 020 8531 2924
Email: tfrost@london.newsquest.co.uk
Web site: http://www.guardian-series.co.uk
Publisher: Newsquest Media Group
Frequency: Weekly - Published on Thursday
Circulation: 52,115 (Combined Circulation)
Editor: Jonathan Bunn; Features Editor: Lindi Bilgorri;
Advertising Manager: Tracey Frost
ADVERTISING: Rates on application
Agency Commission: 10%
Average advertising content per issue: 30%
Series owner and contact point for the following titles, see individual entries:
Waltham Forest Guardian
Waltham Forest Independent
LOCAL NEWSPAPERS: Local Newspapers Greater London

WALTHAM FOREST INDEPENDENT
42984U72A-534_190
Frequency: Weekly
Cover Price: Free
Circulation: 38,270 (VFD 02/07/2007 to 30/12/2007)

ADVERTISING RATES:
Full Page Mono £305.00
Full Page Colour £305.00
SCC £2.30
Part of Series, see entry for: Waltham Forest Guardian & Independent Series
LOCAL NEWSPAPERS: Local Newspapers Greater London

WALTON AND WEYBRIDGE GUARDIAN
1702944U72A-128_249
Frequency: Weekly - See Esher and Cobham Guardian for circulation figure
Cover Price: Free
Part of Series, see entry for: Guardian & News Series (Sutton)
LOCAL NEWSPAPERS: Local Newspapers Greater London

WALTON AND WEYBRIDGE HERALD
719140U72B-3137_300
Frequency: Weekly - Circulation figure is incorporated into the Chertsey, Addlestone & Byfleet Herald
Cover Price: £0.35
Part of Series, see entry for: Staines Informer Series
LOCAL NEWSPAPERS: Local Newspapers English Counties

WALTON & WEYBRIDGE INFORMER
762369U72B-3137_280
Frequency: Weekly - Published on Thursday
Cover Price: Free
Circulation: 46,812 (VFD 02/07/2007 to 30/12/2007)
Part of Series, see entry for: Staines Informer Series
LOCAL NEWSPAPERS: Local Newspapers English Counties

WANDSWORTH & PUTNEY GUARDIAN
43020U72A-128_230
Formerly: Putney & Wandsworth Guardian
Frequency: Weekly
Cover Price: Free
Circulation: 97,868 (VFD 27/08/2007 to 30/12/2007)
Part of Series, see entry for: Guardian & News Series (Sutton)
LOCAL NEWSPAPERS: Local Newspapers Greater London

WANSTEAD AND WOODFORD GUARDIAN
43177U72A-550
Formerly: Independent and Guardian Series
Editorial Address: Guardian House, 480-500 Larkshall Road, Highams Park, LONDON, E4 9GD Tel: 020 8498 3460
Fax: 020 8531 2017
Email: dyeatman@london.newsquest.co.uk
Advertising Address: As above. Tel: 020 8498 3400
Fax: 020 8531 2924
Email: pcarr@london.newsquest.co.uk
Web site: http://www.guardian-series.co.uk
Publisher: Newsquest Media Group
Frequency: Weekly - Published on Thursday
Cover Price: £0.45
Circulation: 4,745 (ABC 02/07/2007 to 30/12/2007)
Editor: Sam Adams; Managing Editor: Anthony Longdon
ADVERTISING RATES:
SCC £1.75
Agency Commission: 10%
Mechanical Data: Type Area: 350 x 265mm, Page Width: 265mm, Col Length: 350mm, Col Widths (Display): 27.5mm, No. of Columns (Display): 9, Film: Digital
Copy instructions: Copy Date: 3 days prior to publication date
Average advertising content per issue: 40%
LOCAL NEWSPAPERS: Local Newspapers Greater London

WANTAGE & GROVE HERALD
44227U72B-2720_200
Frequency: Weekly - Circulation figure is incorporated into the Abingdon Herald
Cover Price: £0.35
ADVERTISING RATES:
SCC £4.75
Part of Series, see entry for: Herald and Times Series Oxon
LOCAL NEWSPAPERS: Local Newspapers English Counties

WANTAGE AND GROVE REVIEW
43269U72B-4049
Editorial Address: PO Box 6098, NEWBURY, RG14 9BN
Tel: 01635 297000 Fax: 01635 297000
Email: wantageandgrove@btconnect.com

Advertising Address: As above.
Email: wantageandgrove@btconnect.com
Publisher: At Review Publishing
Frequency: 26 issues yearly
Cover Price: Free
Editor: Tanya Blanchard; **Advertising Manager:** Tanya Blanchard
ADVERTISING: Rates on application
LOCAL NEWSPAPERS: Local Newspapers English Counties

WARMINSTER JOURNAL   44578U72B-3530
Editorial Address: 36 Market Place, WARMINSTER, BA12 9AN **Tel:** 01985 213030 **Fax:** 01985 217680
Email: news@warminsterjournal.co.uk
Advertising Address: As above.
Email: adverts@warminsterjournal.co.uk
Web site: http://www.warminsterjournal.co.uk
ISSN: 1470-3238
Publisher: Coates & Parker Ltd
Date Established: 1881
Frequency: Weekly
Cover Price: £0.35
Circulation: 5,000 (Publisher's Statement)
Editor: Diana Watkins; **Advertising Manager:** Diana Watkins
ADVERTISING RATES:
Full Page Mono £342.00
Full Page Colour £393.30
SCC £1.80
Agency Commission: 10%
Mechanical Data: Page Width: 258mm, Type Area: 380 x 258mm, Col Length: 380mm, No. of Columns (Display): 5, Col Widths (Display): 50mm
Copy instructions: Copy Date: Tuesday 10am prior to publication date
Average advertising content per issue: 45%
LOCAL NEWSPAPERS: Local Newspapers English Counties

WARRINGTON GUARDIAN   43399U72B-500_220
Frequency: Weekly
Cover Price: £0.50
Circulation: 35,522 (ABC 02/07/2007 to 30/12/2007)
ADVERTISING: Rates on application
Part of Series, see entry for: Warrington Guardian Series
LOCAL NEWSPAPERS: Local Newspapers English Counties

WARRINGTON GUARDIAN SERIES
43395U72B-500
Editorial Address: The Academy, 138 Bridge Street, WARRINGTON, WA1 2RU **Tel:** 01925 434000
Fax: 01925 434115
Email: newsdesk@guardiangrp.co.uk
Advertising Address: As above. **Fax:** 01925 434050
Email: djohnson@guardiangrp.co.uk
Web site: http://www.warringtonguardian.co.uk
Publisher: Newsquest (Northwest) Ltd
Date Established: 1853
Frequency: Weekly
Circulation: 111,077 (Combined Circulation)
Editor: Gareth Dunning; **News Editor:** Gareth Dunning; **Features Editor:** Andrew Moores; **Managing Director:** Eleanor Underhill; **Advertising Manager:** Dave Johnson
ADVERTISING: Rates on application
Series owner and contact point for the following titles, see individual entries:
Knutsford Guardian
Midweek Guardian (Warrington)
Warrington Guardian
LOCAL NEWSPAPERS: Local Newspapers English Counties

WARSOP CHAD   44180U72B-2580_180
Frequency: Weekly - Circulation figure is included into the Mansfield Chad
ADVERTISING: Rates on application
Part of Series, see entry for: Chad Series Mansfield
LOCAL NEWSPAPERS: Local Newspapers English Counties

WARWICK COURIER   44515U72B-3386_200
Frequency: Weekly - Published on Friday. Circulation figure is incorporated into the Leamington Spa Courier
Cover Price: £0.42
Part of Series, see entry for: Leamington Spa Courier Series
LOCAL NEWSPAPERS: Local Newspapers English Counties

WARWICK OBSERVER   44511U72B-3382_250
Frequency: Weekly
Cover Price: Free
ADVERTISING: Rates on application
Part of Series, see entry for: Leamington & Stratford Observer Series
LOCAL NEWSPAPERS: Local Newspapers English Counties

WARWICK TIMES   1698078U72B-3964_101
Frequency: Weekly - Published on Wednesday
Cover Price: Free
Part of Series, see entry for: Times Series (Coventry, Leamington, Warwick & Kenilworth)
LOCAL NEWSPAPERS: Local Newspapers English Counties

WARWICKSHIRE TELEGRAPH   42040U67B-180_590
Formerly: Warwickshire Evening Telegraph
Cover Price: £0.40
Edition of: Coventry Telegraph
REGIONAL DAILY & SUNDAY NEWSPAPERS: Regional Daily Newspapers

WASHINGTON STAR   44498U72B-3371_150
Frequency: Weekly
Cover Price: Free
Circulation: 17,230 (VFD 02/07/2007 to 30/12/2007)
ADVERTISING RATES:
SCC £4.95
Part of Series, see entry for: Star Series
LOCAL NEWSPAPERS: Local Newspapers English Counties

WATFORD FREE   43830U72B-1599_130
Formerly: Watford Free Observer
Frequency: Weekly - Published on Wednesday
Cover Price: Free
Circulation: 50,425 (VFD 02/07/2007 to 30/12/2007)
ADVERTISING RATES:
SCC £6.20
Part of Series, see entry for: Watford Observer Series
LOCAL NEWSPAPERS: Local Newspapers English Counties

THE WATFORD OBSERVER   43831U72B-1599_150
Frequency: Weekly - Published on Friday
Cover Price: £0.45
Circulation: 20,283 (ABC 02/07/2007 to 30/12/2007)
ADVERTISING RATES:
SCC £6.00
Part of Series, see entry for: Watford Observer Series
LOCAL NEWSPAPERS: Local Newspapers English Counties

WATFORD OBSERVER SERIES   43828U72B-1599
Editorial Address: Observer House, Caxton Court, Caxton Way, Watford Business Park, WATFORD, WD18 8RJ
Tel: 01923 216216 **Fax:** 01923 243738
Email: editor@watfordobserver.co.uk
Advertising Address: As above. **Fax:** 01923 235201
Email: observerads@london.newsquest.co.uk
Web site: http://www.watfordobserver.co.uk
Publisher: Newsquest (North London)
Date Established: 1863
Frequency: Weekly
Circulation: 70,708 (Combined Circulation)
Editor: Martin Buhagiar; **Features Editor:** Lindi Bilgorri; **Group Editor:** Martin Buhagiar
ADVERTISING: Rates on application
Agency Commission: 10%
Copy instructions: Copy Date: 2 days prior to publication date
Average advertising content per issue: 40%
Series owner and contact point for the following titles, see individual entries:
Watford Free
The Watford Observer
Supplement(s): Newsquest Hertfordshire, Buckinghamshire & Middlesex - 1xY
LOCAL NEWSPAPERS: Local Newspapers English Counties

WEAR VALLEY MERCURY   1772526U72B-4047
Editorial Address: 43 Hope Street, CROOK, DL15 9HU
Tel: 01388 768758 **Fax:** 01388 767529
Email: editorial@wearvalleymercury.co.uk
Advertising Address: As above.

Email: geraldhirst@wearvalleymercury.co.uk
Web site: http://www.wearvalleymercury.co.uk
Publisher: Teesdale Mercury Ltd
Date Established: 2006
Frequency: Weekly
Cover Price: £0.32
Circulation: 2,000 (Publisher's Statement)
Editor: Duncan Leatherdale
ADVERTISING RATES:
Full Page Mono £580.00
Mechanical Data: Type Area: 450 x 338mm, Col Length: 450mm, Page Width: 338mm, Col Widths (Display): 45mm, No. of Columns (Display): 7, Film: Digital
Copy instructions: Copy Date: Wednesday 9am prior to publication date
Average advertising content per issue: 25%
LOCAL NEWSPAPERS: Local Newspapers English Counties

WEARDALE GAZETTE   1616239U72B-3934
Editorial Address: 6 Market Place, Stanhope, BISHOP AUCKLAND, DL13 2UJ **Tel:** 01388 527700
Fax: 01388 527706
Email: anitaatkinson128@btinternet.com
Advertising Address: As above.
Email: wp@weardalegazette.co.uk
Web site: http://www.weardalegazette.co.uk
Publisher: Weardale Gazette & Publishing Co Ltd
Frequency: 24 issues yearly
Cover Price: £0.60
Circulation: 2,000 (Publisher's Statement)
Editor: Anita Atkinson
ADVERTISING RATES:
Full Page Mono £429.00
Mechanical Data: Film: Digital, Type Area: 393 x 275mm, Col Length: 393mm, Page Width: 275mm
Copy instructions: Copy Date: 1 week prior to publication date
LOCAL NEWSPAPERS: Local Newspapers English Counties

WEDNESBURY NEWS   1818526U72B-3467_215
Frequency: Weekly
Cover Price: Free
ADVERTISING RATES:
SCC £4.46
Part of Series, see entry for: The News & Observer Series
LOCAL NEWSPAPERS: Local Newspapers English Counties

WEEKEND CITIZEN   1615525U67B-240_671
Frequency: Weekly - Published on Saturday
Cover Price: £0.40
ADVERTISING: Rates on application
Edition of: The Citizen (Gloucester)
REGIONAL DAILY & SUNDAY NEWSPAPERS: Regional Daily Newspapers

WEEKEND HERALD   1814271U72B-3290_101
Frequency: Weekly
Cover Price: Free
Circulation: 36,079 (ABC 03/07/2006 to 31/12/2006)
ADVERTISING RATES:
SCC £5.55
Part of Series, see entry for: Crawley Observer, Times and Herald Series
LOCAL NEWSPAPERS: Local Newspapers English Counties

WEEKLY NEWS SERIES (CHELMSFORD)
43596U72B-990
Editorial Address: Newspaper House, Chester Hall Lane, BASILDON, SS14 3BL **Tel:** 01268 522792
Email: cwnnews@nqe.com
Advertising Address: As above. **Tel:** 01245 469432
Email: tom.walters@nqe.com
Web site: http://www.chelmsfordweeklynews.co.uk
Publisher: Newsquest (Essex) Ltd
Date Established: 1862
Frequency: Weekly
Cover Price: Free
Circulation: 59,949 (Combined Circulation)
Editor: Denise Rigby; **Advertising Manager:** Tom Walters
ADVERTISING RATES:
Full Page Mono £965.00
Full Page Colour £1060.00
SCC £7.75
Mechanical Data: Col Length: 340mm, Col Widths (Display): 27mm, Film: Digital, No. of Columns (Display): 9, Type Area: 340 x 267mm, Print Process: Web-fed offset litho, Page Width: 267mm

Non-National Newspapers

Copy instructions: Copy Date: Tuesday 1pm prior to publication date
Series owner and contact point for the following titles, see individual entries:
Chelmsford Weekly News
South Woodham Weekly News
LOCAL NEWSPAPERS: Local Newspapers English Counties

WEEKLY NEWS SERIES (COLCHESTER)
43613U72B-1030

Formerly: Express Series
Editorial Address: Oriel House, 43-44 North Hill, COLCHESTER, CO1 1TZ **Tel:** 01206 508280
Fax: 01206 508274
Email: gazette.newsdesk@nqe.com
Advertising Address: Wickham House, 1 Northgate Street, COLCHESTER, CO1 1HA **Tel:** 01206 506000
Fax: 01206 508195
Email: samantha.bruce@nqe.com
Web site: http://www.gazette_news.co.uk
Publisher: Essex County Newspapers
Frequency: Weekly - Published on Thursday
Cover Price: Free
Circulation: 59,962 (Combined Circulation)
Editor: News Desk
ADVERTISING RATES:
Full Page Mono £575.00
Full Page Colour £670.00
SCC £4.65
Mechanical Data: Type Area: 340 x 267mm, Col Length: 340mm, No. of Columns (Display): 9, Film: Digital, Col Widths (Display): 27mm, Page Width: 267mm
Copy instructions: Copy Date: Friday 5pm prior to publication date
Average advertising content per issue: 87%
Series owner and contact point for the following titles, see individual entries:
Clacton Weekly News
Colchester Weekly News
LOCAL NEWSPAPERS: Local Newspapers English Counties

WELLINGBOROUGH & RUSHDEN HERALD & POST
44164U72B-2500_220

Frequency: Weekly
Cover Price: Free
Circulation: 25,518 (VFD 02/07/2007 to 30/12/2007)
ADVERTISING RATES:
SCC £7.10
Part of Series, see entry for: Northants Herald and Post Series
LOCAL NEWSPAPERS: Local Newspapers English Counties

WELLINGBOROUGH AND RUSHDEN MERCURY & CITIZEN
44157U72B-2490_200

Formerly: Wellingborough and Rushden Citizen
Frequency: Weekly
Cover Price: Free
Circulation: 21,581 (VFD 03/07/2006 to 31/12/2006)
ADVERTISING: Rates on application
Part of Series, see entry for: Northants Mercury & Citizen Series
LOCAL NEWSPAPERS: Local Newspapers English Counties

WELLINGTON WEEKLY NEWS
44270U72B-2937

Editorial Address: 26 High Street, WELLINGTON, TA21 8RA **Tel:** 01823 662439 **Fax:** 01823 665793
Email: wellyedit@tindlenews.co.uk
Advertising Address: As above. **Tel:** 01823 664633
Email: wwnadvertising@internet-today.co.uk
Web site: http://www.wellington-today.co.uk
Publisher: Tindle Newspapers Ltd
Date Established: 1860
Frequency: Weekly - Published on Wednesday
Cover Price: £0.45
Circulation: 5,000 (Publisher's Statement)
Editor: Chris Alder
ADVERTISING RATES:
Full Page Mono £849.60
Full Page Colour £1062.00
SCC £2.95
Agency Commission: 10%
Mechanical Data: Film: Digital, Page Width: 270mm, Col Length: 360mm, Col Widths (Display): 31mm, No. of Columns (Display): 8, Type Area: 360 x 270mm
Copy instructions: Copy Date: Friday 2pm prior to publication date
Average advertising content per issue: 30%
LOCAL NEWSPAPERS: Local Newspapers English Counties

WELLS JOURNAL
44255U72B-2900_200

Frequency: Weekly - Circulation figure is incorporated into the Shepton Mallet Journal
Cover Price: £0.60
ADVERTISING RATES:
SCC £2.30
Part of Series, see entry for: Mid Somerset News & Media
LOCAL NEWSPAPERS: Local Newspapers English Counties

WELWYN & HATFIELD TIMES
43834U72B-1600_200

Frequency: Weekly - Circulation figure includes Welwyn & Hatfield Times Potters Bar Edition
Cover Price: £0.50
Circulation: 16,486 (ABC 02/07/2007 to 30/12/2007)
ADVERTISING RATES:
Full Page Mono £2349.00
Full Page Colour £2449.00
SCC £7.25
Part of Series, see entry for: Welwyn & Hatfield Times & Herald Series
LOCAL NEWSPAPERS: Local Newspapers English Counties

WELWYN & HATFIELD TIMES & HERALD SERIES
43832U72B-1600

Formerly: Welwyn & Hatfield Times Series
Editorial Address: 31A Howardsgate, WELWYN GARDEN CITY, AL8 6AP **Tel:** 01707 327551 **Fax:** 01707 384195
Email: whtimes@archant.co.uk
Advertising Address: Bank House, Primett Road, STEVENAGE, SG1 3EE **Tel:** 01438 866000
Email: esther.roscoe@archant.co.uk
Web site: http://www.whtimes.co.uk
Publisher: Archant Herts & Cambs
Date Established: 1928
Frequency: Weekly
Circulation: 59,549 (Combined Circulation)
Editor: Chris Lennon; **News Editor:** Chris Lennon;
Managing Director: Stuart McCreery; **Advertising Manager:** Esther Roscoe
ADVERTISING: Rates on application
Agency Commission: 10%
Mechanical Data: Page Width: 263mm, Type Area: 360 x 263mm, Col Length: 360mm, No. of Columns (Display): 9, Col Widths (Display): 27mm, Film: Digital
Copy instructions: Copy Date: Monday 3pm prior to publication date
Average advertising content per issue: 85%
Series owner and contact point for the following titles, see individual entries:
East Herts Herald
Welwyn & Hatfield Times
Welwyn & Hatfield Times Potters Bar Edition
LOCAL NEWSPAPERS: Local Newspapers English Counties

WELWYN & HATFIELD TIMES POTTERS BAR EDITION
43835U72B-1600_280

Frequency: Weekly - For circulation see Welwyn & Hatfield Times
Cover Price: £0.50
ADVERTISING RATES:
Full Page Mono £2349.00
Full Page Colour £2449.00
SCC £7.25
Part of Series, see entry for: Welwyn & Hatfield Times & Herald Series
LOCAL NEWSPAPERS: Local Newspapers English Counties

WEMBLEY & KINGSBURY TIMES
43096U72A-385_135

Formerly: Wembley & Kingsbury Chronicle
Frequency: Weekly
Cover Price: Free
Circulation: 33,085 (VFD 02/07/2007 to 30/12/2007)
Part of Series, see entry for: North West London Newspaper Series
LOCAL NEWSPAPERS: Local Newspapers Greater London

WEMBLEY LEADER
43032U72A-170_180

Frequency: Weekly - Published on Wednesday. Circulation figure for Wembley Leader Series, including Willisden Leader
Cover Price: Free
Circulation: 38,677 (VFD 02/07/2007 to 30/12/2007)
ADVERTISING RATES:
SCC £11.10

Part of Series, see entry for: Harrow Observer & Leader Series
LOCAL NEWSPAPERS: Local Newspapers Greater London

WEMBLEY OBSERVER
43037U72A-170_190

Frequency: Weekly - Published on Thursday. For circulation, see Harrow Observer
Cover Price: £0.35
ADVERTISING RATES:
SCC £11.70
Part of Series, see entry for: Harrow Observer & Leader Series
LOCAL NEWSPAPERS: Local Newspapers Greater London

THE WEST BRITON FALMOUTH & PENRYN EDITION
43441U72B-590_120

Frequency: Weekly
Cover Price: £0.85
Part of Series, see entry for: The West Briton Series
LOCAL NEWSPAPERS: Local Newspapers English Counties

THE WEST BRITON HELSTON & THE LIZARD EDITION
43442U72B-590_130

Frequency: Weekly
Cover Price: £0.85
Part of Series, see entry for: The West Briton Series
LOCAL NEWSPAPERS: Local Newspapers English Counties

THE WEST BRITON REDRUTH, CAMBORNE & HAYLE EDITION
43440U72B-590_110

Frequency: Weekly
Cover Price: £0.85
Part of Series, see entry for: The West Briton Series
LOCAL NEWSPAPERS: Local Newspapers English Counties

THE WEST BRITON SERIES
43439U72B-590

Editorial Address: Harmsworth House, City Wharf, Malpas Road, TRURO, TR1 1QH **Tel:** 01872 271451
Fax: 01872 247435
Email: jreines@c-dm.co.uk
Advertising Address: As above. **Tel:** 0845 606 0311
Fax: 01872 247436
Email: ccarter@c-dm.co.uk
Web site: http://www.thisiscornwall.co.uk
Publisher: Cornwall & Devon Media Limited
Date Established: 1810
Frequency: Weekly - Published on Thursday
Circulation: 39,343 (ABC 02/07/2007 to 30/12/2007)
Editor: Carolyn Thomas; **Features Editor:** Colin Gregory;
Editor-in-Chief: Andy Cooper
ADVERTISING RATES:
Full Page Mono £2088.40
Full Page Colour £2610.50
SCC £7.25
Agency Commission: 15%
Mechanical Data: Col Length: 360mm, Col Widths (Display): 31.5mm, Type Area: 360 x 268mm, Page Width: 268mm, No. of Columns (Display): 8, Film: Digital
Copy instructions: Copy Date: Friday, 5pm prior to publication date
Average advertising content per issue: 40%
Series owner and contact point for the following titles, see individual entries:
The West Briton Falmouth & Penryn Edition
The West Briton Helston & The Lizard Edition
The West Briton Redruth, Camborne & Hayle Edition
The West Briton Truro & Mid Cornwall Edition
LOCAL NEWSPAPERS: Local Newspapers English Counties

THE WEST BRITON TRURO & MID CORNWALL EDITION
43443U72B-590_140

Frequency: Weekly
Cover Price: £0.85
Part of Series, see entry for: The West Briton Series
LOCAL NEWSPAPERS: Local Newspapers English Counties

WEST BROMWICH NEWS
1818524U72B-3467_214

Frequency: Weekly - Published on Thursday
Cover Price: Free
ADVERTISING RATES:
SCC £4.46

Part of Series, see entry for: The News & Observer Series
LOCAL NEWSPAPERS: Local Newspapers English Counties

WEST CUMBRIAN GAZETTE 43454U72B-610_210
Frequency: Weekly
Cover Price: Free
Circulation: 27,671 (VFD 02/07/2007 to 30/12/2007)
ADVERTISING: Rates on application
Part of Series, see entry for: The Cumberland News & Gazette Series
LOCAL NEWSPAPERS: Local Newspapers English Counties

WEST END EXTRA 43078U72A-242_180
Cover Price: Free
Summary of Content: Newspaper covering news and events of West End of London.
Readership/Target Audience: Aimed at people interested in this part of the city and/or living here.
ADVERTISING: Rates on application
Part of Series, see entry for: Journal Series
LOCAL NEWSPAPERS: Local Newspapers Greater London

THE WEST HAMPSHIRE OBSERVER
1640806U72B-1400_100
Frequency: Weekly
Cover Price: Free
ADVERTISING RATES:
SCC £5.00
Part of Series, see entry for: The Independent Observer Series
LOCAL NEWSPAPERS: Local Newspapers English Counties

WEST HIGHLAND FREE PRESS 45040U72D-970
Editorial Address: Industrial Estate, Isle of Skye, BROADFORD, IV49 9AP **Tel:** 01471 822464
Fax: 01471 822694
Email: newsdesk@whfp.co.uk
Advertising Address: As above.
Email: advertising@whfp.co.uk
Web site: http://www.whfp.com
Publisher: West Highland Publishing Co. Ltd
Frequency: Weekly - Published on Thursday
Cover Price: £0.65
Circulation: 8,712 (ABC 02/07/2007 to 30/12/2007)
Editor: Ian McCormack; **Advertising Manager:** Anne O'Lone
ADVERTISING RATES:
Full Page Mono ....:...... £800.00
Full Page Colour £1040.00
Agency Commission: 10%
Mechanical Data: Col Length: 370mm, Page Width: 266mm, Col Widths (Display): 41mm, Type Area: 370 x 266mm, No. of Columns (Display): 6, Film: Digital
Copy instructions: Copy Date: Tuesday 11am prior to publication date
Average advertising content per issue: 30%
Supplement(s): An Gaidheal Ur - 52xY
LOCAL NEWSPAPERS: Local Newspapers Scotland

WEST LOTHIAN COURIER 45041U72D-972
Editorial Address: 20-22 King Street, BATHGATE, EH48 1AX **Tel:** 01506 633544 **Fax:** 01506 650578
Email: wlothiancourier@s-un.co.uk
Advertising Address: As above. **Fax:** 01506 653526
Email: sswan@s-un.co.uk
Web site: http://www.wlcourier.co.uk
Publisher: S.U.N Ltd
Date Established: 1872
Frequency: Weekly - Published on Thursday
Cover Price: £0.78
Circulation: 17,229 (ABC 02/07/2007 to 30/12/2007)
Editor: News Desk; **Managing Director:** Belle Steven;
Advertising Manager: Sharon Swan
ADVERTISING RATES:
Full Page Mono £3121.20
Full Page Colour £4123.62
SCC £10.20
Agency Commission: 10%
Mechanical Data: Col Length: 340mm, No. of Columns (Display): 9, Film: Digital, Type Area: 340 x 265mm, Page Width: 265mm
Copy instructions: Copy Date: Tuesday 4pm prior to publication date
LOCAL NEWSPAPERS: Local Newspapers Scotland

WEST NOTTS & DERBYSHIRE RECORDER SERIES 44198U72B-2666
Editorial Address: Castle Wharf House, NOTTINGHAM, NG1 7EU **Tel:** 0115 948 2000 **Fax:** 0115 964 4032
Email: newsdesk@nottinghameveningpost.co.uk
Advertising Address: Unit 7, Brunts Business Centre, Samuel Brunts Way, MANSFIELD, NG18 2AH
Tel: 01623 420000 **Fax:** 01623 420900
Email: karen.millward@nottinghameveningpost.co.uk
Web site: http://www.thisisnottingham.co.uk
Publisher: Nottingham Post Media Group Ltd
Frequency: Weekly - Published on Thursday
Cover Price: Free
Circulation: 260,441 (VFD 02/07/2007 to 30/12/2007)
Editor: Steven Fletcher; **News Editor:** Steven Fletcher;
Advertising Manager: Karen Millward
ADVERTISING: Rates on application
Mechanical Data: No. of Columns (Display): 8, Print Process: Web-fed offset litho, Film: Negative, right reading, emulsion side down
Series owner and contact point for the following titles, see individual entries:
Long Eaton Recorder
Mansfield & Ashfield Recorder
Nottingham Recorder
LOCAL NEWSPAPERS: Local Newspapers English Counties

WEST SOMERSET COUNTY GAZETTE
768734U72B-2930_191
Formerly: Somerset County Gazette (Minehead Edition)
Frequency: Weekly
Cover Price: £0.70
Part of Series, see entry for: Somerset County Gazette Series
LOCAL NEWSPAPERS: Local Newspapers English Counties

WEST SOMERSET DIARY 1644046U72B-2940_141
Frequency: Monthly
Cover Price: Free
Circulation: 8,000 (Publisher's Statement)
ADVERTISING: Rates on application
Part of Series, see entry for: West Somerset Free Press Series
LOCAL NEWSPAPERS: Local Newspapers English Counties

WEST SOMERSET FREE PRESS
44272U72B-2940_120
Frequency: Weekly - Published on Friday. Circulation figure also includes the West Somerset News Trader
Cover Price: £0.45
Circulation: 10,391 (ABC 01/01/2007 to 30/12/2007)
ADVERTISING: Rates on application
Part of Series, see entry for: West Somerset Free Press Series
LOCAL NEWSPAPERS: Local Newspapers English Counties

WEST SOMERSET FREE PRESS SERIES
44271U72B-2940
Editorial Address: 5 Long Street, WILLITON, TA4 4QN
Tel: 01984 632731 **Fax:** 01984 633099
Email: wsfp.news@internet-today.co.uk
Advertising Address: As above.
Email: freepress@internet-today.co.uk
Web site: http://www.west-somerset-today.co.uk
Publisher: Tindle Newspapers Ltd
Date Established: 1860
Frequency: Published on Wednesday and Friday
Circulation: 18,391 (Combined Circulation)
Editor: Gareth Purcell; **Advertising Manager:** David Tucker
ADVERTISING: Rates on application
Agency Commission: 10%
Copy instructions: Copy Date: Tuesday 2pm prior to publication date
Average advertising content per issue: 60%
Series owner and contact point for the following titles, see individual entries:
West Somerset Diary
West Somerset Free Press
West Somerset News Trader
Supplement(s): Equine - 1xY, Motoring - 1xY, Railway - 1xY, Wedding - 2xY
LOCAL NEWSPAPERS: Local Newspapers English Counties

WEST SOMERSET NEWS TRADER
44273U72B-2940_140
Formerly: Minehead News Trader
Frequency: Weekly - Published on Wednesday. Circulation figure is incorporated into the West Somerset Free Press
Cover Price: Free
ADVERTISING: Rates on application
Part of Series, see entry for: West Somerset Free Press Series
LOCAL NEWSPAPERS: Local Newspapers English Counties

WEST SOMERSET POST 1743221U72B-4041
Formerly: The Crier
Editorial Address: 1 Twyford Place, WELLINGTON, TA21 8BZ **Tel:** 01823 663146 **Fax:** 01823 663146
Email: news@westsomersetpost.com
Advertising Address: Central House, Summerland Place, MINEHEAD, TA24 5BT **Tel:** 01643 888215
Fax: 01643 709677
Email: sales@westsomersetpost.com
Web site: http://www.wspostnews.blogspot.com
Publisher: Post News Group Ltd
Date Established: 1994
Frequency: Weekly - Published on Thursday
Cover Price: Free
Circulation: 9,000 (Publisher's Statement)
Usual Pagination: 32
Editor: John Thorne; **Advertising Manager:** John Thorne
ADVERTISING RATES:
Full Page Mono £355.00
Full Page Colour £355.00
Agency Commission: 25%
Mechanical Data: Film: Digital, Type Area: 355 x 261mm, Trim Size: 365 x 281mm, Col Length: 343mm, Col Widths (Display): 40.2mm, No. of Columns (Display): 6, Page Width: 261mm
Copy instructions: Copy Date: 3 days prior to publication date
Average advertising content per issue: 67%
LOCAL NEWSPAPERS: Local Newspapers English Counties

WEST SUSSEX COUNTY TIMES
44473U72B-3328_190
Frequency: Weekly
Cover Price: £0.45
Circulation: 21,614 (ABC 02/07/2007 to 30/12/2007)
Mechanical Data: Type Area: 560 x 339mm, Col Length: 560mm, Page Width: 339mm, No. of Columns (Display): 11, Col Widths (Display): 29mm, Screen: 40 lpc, Film: Digital
Copy instructions: Copy Date: Tuesday prior to publication date
Part of Series, see entry for: West Sussex County Times Series
LOCAL NEWSPAPERS: Local Newspapers English Counties

WEST SUSSEX COUNTY TIMES SERIES
44471U72B-3328
Editorial Address: 14-16 Market Square, HORSHAM, RH12 1HD **Tel:** 01403 751200 **Fax:** 01403 751248
Email: tim.raw@sussexnewspapers.co.uk
Advertising Address: As above. **Fax:** 01403 751260
Email: lisa.jones@sussexnewspapers.co.uk
Web site: http://www.horshamtoday.co.uk
Publisher: Sussex Newspapers (Horsham) Ltd
Date Established: 1869
Frequency: Weekly
Cover Price: £0.48
Circulation: 54,814 (Combined Circulation)
Editor: Tim Raw; **Managing Director:** Karl Dimmock
ADVERTISING RATES:
SCC £10.88
Agency Commission: 10%
Mechanical Data: No. of Columns (Display): 11, Col Widths (Display): 30mm, Film: Digital, Type Area: 560 x 340mm, Col Length: 560mm, Page Width: 340mm
Copy instructions: Copy Date: Friday prior to publication date
Series owner and contact point for the following titles, see individual entries:
Horsham Advertiser
West Sussex County Times
LOCAL NEWSPAPERS: Local Newspapers English Counties

WEST SUSSEX GAZETTE 44474U72B-3329
Editorial Address: 14-16 Market Square, HORSHAM, RH12 1HD **Tel:** 01403 751218
Email: jeannie.knight@westsussextoday.co.uk

Section 4 (a) Newspapers

Advertising Address: Unicorn House, Eastgate Square, CHICHESTER, PO19 1JN **Tel:** 01243 532532
Fax: 01243 776854
Email: margaret.race@chiobserver.co.uk
Web site: http://www.westsussextoday.co.uk
Publisher: Johnston Press plc
Date Established: 1853
Frequency: Weekly
Cover Price: £0.35
Circulation: 8,683 (ABC 02/07/2007 to 30/12/2007)
Editor: Jeannie Knight; **News Editor:** Jeannie Knight
ADVERTISING RATES:
SCC £5.66
Agency Commission: 10%
Mechanical Data: Col Length: 560mm, Col Widths (Display): 29mm, Film: Digital, No. of Columns (Display): 11, Type Area: 560 x 339mm, Page Width: 339mm
Copy instructions: Copy Date: Monday 5pm prior to publication date
Average advertising content per issue: 50%
LOCAL NEWSPAPERS: Local Newspapers English Counties

WEST WALES TRIBUNE
1813457U72C-230_161
Frequency: Monthly
Cover Price: Free
Part of Series, see entry for: Llanelli Star Series
LOCAL NEWSPAPERS: Local Newspapers Wales

WESTERHAM COUNTY BORDER NEWS
43858U72B-1774_200
Frequency: Weekly - See Edenbridge County Border News for circulation
Cover Price: Free
Part of Series, see entry for: County Border News Series
LOCAL NEWSPAPERS: Local Newspapers English Counties

WESTERN DAILY PRESS (BATH & WILTSHIRE)
42015U67B-120_680
Formerly: Western Daily Press Wiltshire
ADVERTISING RATES:
SCC £3.35
Edition of: Western Daily Press Bristol
REGIONAL DAILY & SUNDAY NEWSPAPERS: Regional Daily Newspapers

WESTERN DAILY PRESS BRISTOL
42010U67B-120
Editorial Address: Temple Way, BRISTOL, BS99 7HD
Tel: 0117 934 3000 **Fax:** 0117 934 3574
Email: wdnews@bepp.co.uk
Advertising Address: As above. **Fax:** 0117 934 3571
Email: s.spargo@bepp.co.uk
Web site: http://www.westerndailypress.co.uk
Publisher: Bristol News and Media
Date Established: 1858
Frequency: Mornings
Cover Price: £0.45
Circulation: 41,639 (ABC 02/07/2007 to 30/12/2007)
Editor: Cathy Ellis; **News Editor:** Cathy Ellis, **Features Editor:** Tim Davey
ADVERTISING RATES:
Full Page Mono £2692.80
Full Page Colour £3366.00
SCC £9.35
Agency Commission: 10%
Mechanical Data: Col Length: 360mm, Type Area: 360 x 270mm, No. of Columns (Display): 8, Page Width: 270mm, Film: Digital
Copy instructions: Copy Date: 48 working hours prior to publication date
Editions:
Western Daily Press (Bath & Wiltshire)
Western Daily Press Severnside
Western Daily Press (Somerset & Late City)
Supplement(s): Riders - 52xY, West Country Life - 52xY
REGIONAL DAILY & SUNDAY NEWSPAPERS: Regional Daily Newspapers

WESTERN DAILY PRESS SEVERNSIDE
42013U67B-120_650
ADVERTISING RATES:
SCC £2.40
Edition of: Western Daily Press Bristol
REGIONAL DAILY & SUNDAY NEWSPAPERS: Regional Daily Newspapers

WESTERN DAILY PRESS (SOMERSET & LATE CITY)
42014U67B-120_660
Formerly: Western Daily Press Somerset
Frequency: Mornings
ADVERTISING RATES:
SCC £4.55
Edition of: Western Daily Press Bristol
REGIONAL DAILY & SUNDAY NEWSPAPERS: Regional Daily Newspapers

WESTERN GAZETTE AND YEOVIL TIMES SERIES
44274U72B-2950
Editorial Address: Sherborne Road, YEOVIL, BA21 4YA
Tel: 01935 700500 **Fax:** 01935 426963
Email: newsdesk@westgaz.co.uk
Advertising Address: As above. **Fax:** 01935 432266
Email: ads@westgaz.co.uk
Web site: http://www.westgaz.co.uk
Publisher: The Western Gazette Co. Ltd
Date Established: 1737
Frequency: Weekly
Circulation: 79,876 (Combined Circulation)
Editor: Zena O'Rourke; **Features Editor:** Tori Birch;
Managing Director: Jackie Dean; **Advertising Director:** Nikki Leggett
ADVERTISING RATES:
Full Page Mono £2822.40
Full Page Colour £3528.00
SCC £9.80
Agency Commission: 10%
Mechanical Data: Col Length: 360mm, Col Widths (Display): 31mm, Page Width: 270mm, Type Area: 360 x 270mm, No. of Columns (Display): 8
Copy instructions: Copy Date: Tuesday 11am prior to publication date
Series owner and contact point for the following titles, see individual entries:
Western Gazette (Crewkerne & Chard Edition)
Western Gazette (North Dorset Edition)
Western Gazette (Sherborne Edition)
Western Gazette (South Somerset Edition)
Western Gazette (West Dorset Edition)
Western Gazette (Yeovil & District Edition)
Yeovil Times
LOCAL NEWSPAPERS: Local Newspapers English Counties

WESTERN GAZETTE (CREWKERNE & CHARD EDITION)
44278U72B-2950_170
Formerly: Western Gazette (Crewkerne)
Frequency: Weekly - Circulation figure is incorporated into the Western Gazette (Mendips edition)
Cover Price: £0.60
Part of Series, see entry for: Western Gazette and Yeovil Times Series
LOCAL NEWSPAPERS: Local Newspapers English Counties

WESTERN GAZETTE (NORTH DORSET EDITION)
44281U72B-2950_200
Formerly: Western Gazette (Shaftesbury, Gillingham)
Frequency: Weekly - Circulation figure is incorporated into the Western Gazette (Mendips edition)
Cover Price: £0.60
Part of Series, see entry for: Western Gazette and Yeovil Times Series
LOCAL NEWSPAPERS: Local Newspapers English Counties

WESTERN GAZETTE (SHERBORNE EDITION)
44282U72B-2950_210
Frequency: Weekly - Circulation figure is incorporated into the Western Gazette (Mendips edition)
Cover Price: £0.60
Part of Series, see entry for: Western Gazette and Yeovil Times Series
LOCAL NEWSPAPERS: Local Newspapers English Counties

WESTERN GAZETTE (SOUTH SOMERSET EDITION)
44280U72B-2950_190
Formerly: Western Gazette (Mendips Edition)
Frequency: Weekly - Circulation figure includes the Western Gazette (North Dorset edition), the Western Gazette (Crewkerne & Chard edition), the Western Gazette (South Somerset edition), Western Gazette (West Dorset edition), the Western Gazette (Sherborne edition) and the Western Gazette (Yeovil & District edition)
Cover Price: £0.60
Circulation: 35,174 (ABC 02/07/2007 to 30/12/2007)

Part of Series, see entry for: Western Gazette and Yeovil Times Series
LOCAL NEWSPAPERS: Local Newspapers English Counties

WESTERN GAZETTE (WEST DORSET EDITION)
44284U72B-2950_230
Formerly: Western Gazette (Dorchester & Weymouth Edition)
Frequency: Weekly - Circulation figure is incorporated into the Western Gazette (Mendips edition)
Cover Price: £0.60
Part of Series, see entry for: Western Gazette and Yeovil Times Series
LOCAL NEWSPAPERS: Local Newspapers English Counties

WESTERN GAZETTE (YEOVIL & DISTRICT EDITION)
44285U72B-2950_240
Frequency: Weekly - Circulation figure is incorporated into the Western Gazette (Mendips edition)
Cover Price: £0.60
Part of Series, see entry for: Western Gazette and Yeovil Times Series
LOCAL NEWSPAPERS: Local Newspapers English Counties

WESTERN MAIL (CARDIFF)
42223U67B-2070
Editorial Address: 6 Park Street, CARDIFF, CF10 1XR
Tel: 029 2022 3333 **Fax:** 029 2058 3652
Email: newsdesk@walesonline.co.uk
Advertising Address: As above.
Email: denise.rich@mediawales.co.uk
Web site: http://www.walesonline.co.uk
Publisher: Media Wales Ltd
Date Established: 1869
Frequency: Mornings - Not published on Sunday
Cover Price: £0.35
Circulation: 37,576 (ABC 02/07/2007 to 30/12/2007)
Editor: News Desk; **Features Editor:** Peter Morrell
Language(s): English; Welsh
ADVERTISING RATES:
SCC £21.14
Agency Commission: 10%
Mechanical Data: Film: Digital, Type Area: 340 x 266mm, Col Length: 340mm, Page Width: 266mm, Col Widths (Display): 32mm, No. of Columns (Display): 8
Editions:
Western Mail (First Edition)
Supplement(s): Box Office - 52xY, Business (Western Mail (Cardiff)) - 52xY, Education - 52xY, Jobs - 52xY, The Magazine - 52xY, Motoring - 52xY, Sport - 52xY, Welsh Homes & Magazine - 52xY, WM - 4xY, WM - 52xY
REGIONAL DAILY & SUNDAY NEWSPAPERS: Regional Daily Newspapers

WESTERN MAIL (FIRST EDITION)
1829836U67B-2070_500
Frequency: Mornings - Not published on Sunday
Cover Price: £0.35
Language(s): English; Welsh
ADVERTISING: Rates on application
Edition of: Western Mail (Cardiff)
REGIONAL DAILY & SUNDAY NEWSPAPERS: Regional Daily Newspapers

WESTERN MORNING NEWS
42152U67B-700
Formerly: Western Morning News (Plymouth)
Editorial Address: 17 Brest Road, Derriford Business Park, PLYMOUTH, PL6 5AA **Tel:** 01752 765538
Fax: 01752 765535
Email: wmnnewsdesk@westernmorningnews.co.uk
Advertising Address: As above. **Tel:** 01752 765500
Fax: 01752 765655
Web site: http://www.thisiswesternmorningnews.co.uk
Publisher: South West Media Group Ltd
Frequency: Mornings
Cover Price: £0.45
Circulation: 41,154 (ABC 02/07/2007 to 30/12/2007)
Editor: Steve Grant; **News Editor:** Steve Grant; **Features Editor:** Su Carroll; **Managing Director:** Duncan Currall; **Advertisement Director:** Lesa Brown
ADVERTISING RATES:
Full Page Mono £2534.40
Full Page Colour £3168.00
SCC £8.80
Agency Commission: 10%
Mechanical Data: Film: Negative, right reading, emulsion side down. Digital
Copy instructions: Copy Date: 12 noon 2 days prior to publication date

Editions:
Western Morning News (Cornwall Edition)
Western Morning News (Devon Edition)
REGIONAL DAILY & SUNDAY NEWSPAPERS: Regional
Daily Newspapers

WESTERN MORNING NEWS (CORNWALL EDITION)
42153U67B-700_530
Edition of: Western Morning News
REGIONAL DAILY & SUNDAY NEWSPAPERS: Regional
Daily Newspapers

WESTERN MORNING NEWS (DEVON EDITION)
42154U67B-700_550
Edition of: Western Morning News
REGIONAL DAILY & SUNDAY NEWSPAPERS: Regional
Daily Newspapers

WESTERN TELEGRAPH (EAST)
1813183U72C-400_101
Frequency: Weekly
Cover Price: £0.60
Part of Series, see entry for: Western Telegraph Series
LOCAL NEWSPAPERS: Local Newspapers Wales

WESTERN TELEGRAPH (FIRST)
1813184U72C-400_100
Frequency: Weekly
Cover Price: £0.60
Part of Series, see entry for: Western Telegraph Series
LOCAL NEWSPAPERS: Local Newspapers Wales

WESTERN TELEGRAPH (NORTH)
1813185U72C-400_102
Frequency: Weekly
Cover Price: £0.60
Part of Series, see entry for: Western Telegraph Series
LOCAL NEWSPAPERS: Local Newspapers Wales

WESTERN TELEGRAPH SERIES
44848U72C-400
Formerly: Western Telegraph Pembrokeshire
Editorial Address: Press Buildings, Old Hakin Road, Merlins
Bridge, HAVERFORDWEST, SA61 1XF **Tel:** 01437 763133
Fax: 01437 761793
Email: lee.day@gwent-wales.co.uk
Advertising Address: As above. **Tel:** 01437 765000
Fax: 01437 760482
Email: peter.blacker@gwent-wales.co.uk
Web site: http://www.westerntelegraph.co.uk
Publisher: Newsquest (Media Group) Ltd
Date Established: 1854
Frequency: Weekly
Circulation: 25,627 (ABC 02/07/2007 to 30/12/2007)
Editor: Lee Day; **News Editor:** Lee Day; **Publisher:** Peter
John
ADVERTISING RATES:
Full Page Mono £2295.00
Full Page Colour £2417.56
Agency Commission: 10%
Mechanical Data: Type Area: 340 x 259mm, Col Length:
340mm, Col Widths (Display): 27mm, No. of Columns
(Display): 9, Page Width: 259mm, Film: Digital
Copy instructions: Copy Date: Friday 4.30pm prior to
publication date
Average advertising content per issue: 60%
**Series owner and contact point for the following titles,
see individual entries:**
Western Telegraph (East)
Western Telegraph (First)
Western Telegraph (North)
Supplement(s): Buzz - 3xY, Local Business - 12xY, Motors
and Property - 52xY, New Cars - 9xY, Property - 12xY,
Spring Guide - 1xY, Summer Guide - 2xY
LOCAL NEWSPAPERS: Local Newspapers Wales

THE WESTMINSTER NEWS
1793867U72A-1323
Editorial Address: Davina House, Suite 205, 137-149
Goswell Road, LONDON, EC1V 7ET **Tel:** 07709 301763
Email: editor@sketchnews.co.uk
Advertising Address: As above. **Tel:** 020 7328 7251
Email: editor@sketchnews.co.uk
Web site: http://www.thewestminsternews.co.uk
Publisher: Sketch News
Date Established: 2006
Frequency: Monthly
Cover Price: Free
Circulation: 10,000 (Print Run)

Editor: David Noakes; **Features Editor:** Sophie Sweatman;
Publisher: David Hetherington
ADVERTISING RATES:
Full Page Mono £700.00
Full Page Colour £900.00
Agency Commission: 10%
Mechanical Data: Type Area: 350 x 260mm, Col Length:
350mm, Page Width: 260mm, Film: Digital, Trim Size: 380 x
290mm
Average advertising content per issue: 50%
LOCAL NEWSPAPERS: Local Newspapers Greater London

WESTMORLAND GAZETTE
43460U72B-3931_100
Frequency: Weekly
Cover Price: £0.75
Circulation: 30,787 (ABC 02/07/2007 to 30/12/2007)
Part of Series, see entry for: Westmorland Gazette
Newspaper Series
LOCAL NEWSPAPERS: Local Newspapers English
Counties

WESTMORLAND GAZETTE NEWSPAPER SERIES
43458U72B-3931
Formerly: Westmorland Gazette Series
Editorial Address: 1 Wainwright's Yard, KENDAL, LA9 4DP
Tel: 01539 710100 **Fax:** 01539 720990
Email: newsdesk@kendal.newsquest.co.uk
Advertising Address: 1 Wainwrights Yard, KENDAL, LA9
4DP **Tel:** 01539 720555 **Fax:** 01539 723618
Email: martin.leonard@kendal.newsquest.co.uk
Web site: http://www.thewestmorlandgazette.co.uk
Publisher: Westmorland Gazette Newspapers
Frequency: Weekly
Circulation: 56,020 (Combined Circulation)
Editor: Mike Addison; **News Editor:** Mike Addison;
Advertising Manager: Martin Leonard; **Group Editor:** Kevin
Young
ADVERTISING RATES:
SCC £7.78
Agency Commission: 10%
Mechanical Data: Col Length: 530mm, No. of Columns
(Display): 12, Type Area: 530 x 351mm, Print Process: Web-
fed offset litho, Page Width: 351mm
Copy instructions: Copy Date: 3 days prior to publication
date
Average advertising content per issue: 60%
**Series owner and contact point for the following titles,
see individual entries:**
The South Lakes Citizen (incorporating The Lakes Leader)
Westmorland Gazette
LOCAL NEWSPAPERS: Local Newspapers English
Counties

WESTON & SOMERSET MERCURY
43227U72B-60_140
Formerly: Weston Mercury
Frequency: Weekly - Circulation figure is for the Weston &
Somerset Mercury and Somerset Mercury
Cover Price: £0.50
Circulation: 16,280 (ABC 02/07/2007 to 30/12/2007)
ADVERTISING: Rates on application
Part of Series, see entry for: Weston & Somerset Mercury
Series
LOCAL NEWSPAPERS: Local Newspapers English
Counties

WESTON & SOMERSET MERCURY SERIES
43224U72B-60
Editorial Address: 32 Waterloo Street, WESTON-SUPER-
MARE, BS23 1LW **Tel:** 01934 422522 **Fax:** 01934 422600
Email: newsdesk@thewestonmercury.co.uk
Advertising Address: As above. **Tel:** 01934 422555
Fax: 01934 422633
Email: sally.cook@archant.co.uk
Web site: http://www.westonmercury.co.uk
Publisher: Archant South West
Date Established: 1843
Frequency: Weekly
Free to qualifying individuals
Circulation: 18,600 (Publisher's Statement)
Editor: Simon Angear; **News Editor:** Simon Angear;
Features Editor: Sarah Whitchurch; **Managing Director:**
Bernard Driscoll; **Advertising Manager:** Sally Cook;
Managing Editor: Judi Kisiel
ADVERTISING: Rates on application
**Series owner and contact point for the following titles,
see individual entries:**
North Somerset Times
Somerset Mercury
Weston & Somerset Mercury
LOCAL NEWSPAPERS: Local Newspapers English
Counties

WETHERBY, BOSTON SPA & TADCASTER NEWS
44655U72B-3588_230
Frequency: Weekly
Cover Price: £0.60
Circulation: 5,159 (ABC 02/07/2007 to 30/12/2007)
ADVERTISING RATES:
SCC £5.62
Part of Series, see entry for: Ackrill Newspaper Series
LOCAL NEWSPAPERS: Local Newspapers English
Counties

THE WHARF
43185U72A-650
Editorial Address: 1 Canada Square, Canary Wharf,
LONDON, E14 5AP **Tel:** 020 7510 6306 **Fax:** 020 7293 2264
Email: newsdesk@wharf.co.uk
Advertising Address: As above. **Tel:** 020 7510 6055
Email: simon.copcutt@wharf.co.uk
Web site: http://www.wharf.co.uk
Publisher: Trinity Mirror
Frequency: Weekly - Published on Thursday
Cover Price: Free
Circulation: 33,442 (Publisher's Statement)
Usual Pagination: 56
Editor: Giles Broadbent; **Advertising Manager:** Simon
Copcutt
ADVERTISING RATES:
Full Page Mono £2312.00
Full Page Colour £3005.00
SCC £8.50
Agency Commission: 10%
Mechanical Data: Page Width: 265.5mm, Type Area: 340 x
265.5mm, Col Length: 340mm, Col Widths (Display): 31mm,
No. of Columns (Display): 8, Film: Digital
Copy instructions: Copy Date: Mono Monday 5pm Colour
Friday 3pm prior to publication date
Average advertising content per issue: 30%
**Series owner and contact point for the following titles,
see individual entries:**
Business
LOCAL NEWSPAPERS: Local Newspapers Greater London

WHARFE VALLEY TIMES
44737U72B-3919_150
Formerly: Wharfe Valley Times Otley & Aireborough Edition
Frequency: Weekly
Cover Price: Free
Circulation: 41,963 (VFD 02/07/2007 to 30/12/2007)
ADVERTISING: Rates on application
Copy instructions: Copy Date: Tuesday 12pm prior to
publication date
Part of Series, see entry for: Wharfe Valley Times Series
LOCAL NEWSPAPERS: Local Newspapers English
Counties

WHARFE VALLEY TIMES SERIES
44736U72B-3919
Editorial Address: Yorkshire Post News, PO Box 49,
Wellington Street, LEEDS, LS1 1RF **Tel:** 0113 238 8773
Email: wvt.news@ypn.co.uk
Advertising Address: As above. **Tel:** 0113 238 8704
Fax: 0113 238 8484
Email: leedsfree.display@ypn.co.uk
Publisher: Johnston Press plc
Frequency: Weekly
Cover Price: Free
Circulation: 63,868 (Combined Circulation)
Editor: Sheila Holmes; **Advertising Manager:** Tony Shama
ADVERTISING: Rates on application
Agency Commission: 10%
Mechanical Data: Film: Digital, Col Widths (Display): 27mm,
Page Width: 274mm, No. of Columns (Display): 9, Col
Length: 340mm, Type Area: 340 x 274mm
Average advertising content per issue: 68%
**Series owner and contact point for the following titles,
see individual entries:**
Pudsey Times
Wharfe Valley Times
LOCAL NEWSPAPERS: Local Newspapers English
Counties

WHARFEDALE & AIREDALE OBSERVER
44740U72B-3920
Formerly: Wharfedale Observer & Express Series
Editorial Address: 8 Wells Road, ILKLEY, LS29 9JD
Tel: 01943 607022 **Fax:** 01943 604583
Email: paul.l@ilkley.newsquest.co.uk
Advertising Address: As above. **Tel:** 01943 603483
Fax: 01943 816224
Email: gemma.aldersley@wharfedale.newsquest.co.uk
Web site: http://www.thisisbradford.co.uk
Publisher: Newsquest Yorkshire and North East (Bradford)
Frequency: Weekly - Published on Thursday
Cover Price: £0.75
Circulation: 5,181 (ABC 02/07/2007 to 30/12/2007)

Non-National Newspapers

Editor: Paul Langan; **Advertising Manager:** Gemma Aldersley
ADVERTISING RATES:
Full Page Mono £2069.00
Full Page Colour £2587.00
Agency Commission: 10%
Mechanical Data: Page Width: 346mm, Film: Digital, Type Area: 530 x 346mm, Col Length: 530mm, No. of Columns (Display): 12
Copy instructions: Copy Date: Tuesday 12pm prior to publication date
Average advertising content per issue: 50%
LOCAL NEWSPAPERS: Local Newspapers English Counties

WHITBY GAZETTE (FRIDAY)
624934U72B-3650_110
Frequency: Weekly
Cover Price: £0.40
Circulation: 12,017 (ABC 02/07/2007 to 30/12/2007)
Part of Series, see entry for: Whitby Gazette Series
LOCAL NEWSPAPERS: Local Newspapers English Counties

WHITBY GAZETTE SERIES
44669U72B-3650
Editorial Address: 17-18 Bridge Street, WHITBY, YO22 4BG **Tel:** 01947 602836 **Fax:** 01947 820535
Email: editorial@whitbygazette.co.uk
Advertising Address: As above. **Fax:** 01947 829916
Email: andy.longhurst@yrnltd.co.uk
Web site: http://www.whitbygazette.co.uk
ISSN: 0963-4657
Publisher: Yorkshire Regional Newspapers Ltd
Frequency: 104 issues yearly
Circulation: 12,017 (ABC 02/07/2007 to 30/12/2007)
Editor: Damian Holmes; **Advertising Manager:** Andy Longhurst
ADVERTISING RATES:
Full Page Mono £1866.60
Full Page Colour £2426.58
SCC £6.10
Agency Commission: 10%
Mechanical Data: Type Area: 340 x 274mm, Col Length: 340mm, Page Width: 274mm, No. of Columns (Display): 9, Film: Digital
Average advertising content per issue: 58%
Series owner and contact point for the following titles, see individual entries:
Whitby Gazette (Friday)
Whitby Gazette (Tuesday)
LOCAL NEWSPAPERS: Local Newspapers English Counties

WHITBY GAZETTE (TUESDAY)
624927U72B-3650_120
Frequency: Weekly
Cover Price: £0.30
Circulation: 6,285 (ABC 02/07/2007 to 30/12/2007)
Part of Series, see entry for: Whitby Gazette Series
LOCAL NEWSPAPERS: Local Newspapers English Counties

WHITCHURCH HERALD
44247U72B-2870
Editorial Address: Chronicle House, Commonhall Street, CHESTER, CH1 2AA **Tel:** 01244 606409 **Fax:** 01244 606496
Email: whitchurch.news@cheshirenews.co.uk
Advertising Address: As above. **Tel:** 01948 665768
Fax: 01948 667174
Email: judith.large@cheshirenews.co.uk
Web site: http://www.icccheshireonline.co.uk
Publisher: Trinity Mirror Cheshire
Date Established: 1869
Frequency: Weekly
Cover Price: £0.50
Circulation: 4,586 (ABC 02/07/2007 to 30/12/2007)
Editor: Andrew Bowan; **Editor-in-Chief:** Eric Langton; **Advertising Manager:** Judith Large
ADVERTISING RATES:
Full Page Mono £1133.92
Full Page Colour £1530.79
SCC £3.73
Agency Commission: 10%
Mechanical Data: No. of Columns (Display): 8, Type Area: 380 x 276mm, Col Length: 380mm, Page Width: 276mm, Film: Digital
Copy instructions: Copy Date: Tuesday 1pm prior to publication date
Average advertising content per issue: 50%
LOCAL NEWSPAPERS: Local Newspapers English Counties

WHITE HORSE NEWS
44571U72B-3517_210
Frequency: 26 issues yearly
Cover Price: Free
Circulation: 8,600 (Publisher's Statement)
ADVERTISING RATES:
Full Page Colour £468.00
Part of Series, see entry for: The Melksham Independent News Series
LOCAL NEWSPAPERS: Local Newspapers English Counties

WHITEHAVEN NEWS
43462U72B-660
Editorial Address: 148 Queen Street, WHITEHAVEN, CA28 7AZ **Tel:** 01946 595100 **Fax:** 01946 595102
Email: news@whitehaven-news.co.uk
Advertising Address: 23 Oxford Street, WORKINGTON, CA14 2AN **Tel:** 01900 607600 **Fax:** 01900 607601
Email: jackie.clemence@cn-group.co.uk
Web site: http://www.whitehaven-news.co.uk
Publisher: Cumbrian Newspapers Ltd
Frequency: Weekly - Published on Thursday
Cover Price: £0.52
Circulation: 17,330 (ABC 02/07/2007 to 30/12/2007)
Editor: Alan Cleaver; **News Editor:** Alan Cleaver; **Managing Director:** Kerry Hall; **Advertising Manager:** Jackie Clemence
ADVERTISING RATES:
Full Page Mono £3960.09
Full Page Colour £4401.00
SCC £8.15
Copy instructions: Copy Date: Tuesday 5pm prior to publication date
LOCAL NEWSPAPERS: Local Newspapers English Counties

WHITSTABLE & HERNE BAY TIMES SERIES
43939U72B-1902
Editorial Address: Newspaper House, Simmonds Road, Wincheap, CANTERBURY, CT1 3YR **Tel:** 01227 771515
Fax: 01227 770768
Email: newsdesk.times@krnmedia.co.uk
Advertising Address: 136 Cromwell Road, WHITSTABLE, CT5 1NG **Tel:** 01227 771515 **Fax:** 01227 456444
Email: sales.canterbury@kentregionalnewspapers.co.uk
Publisher: Kent Regional News and Media
Date Established: 1863
Frequency: Weekly - Published on Thursday
Cover Price: £0.40
Circulation: 5,564 (ABC 02/07/2007 to 30/12/2007)
Editor: John Nurden; **News Editor:** Roger Kasper; **Advertising Manager:** Karen Shelby
ADVERTISING RATES:
SCC £2.40
Agency Commission: 10%
Mechanical Data: No. of Columns (Display): 8, Col Widths (Display): 31mm, Film: Digital
Copy instructions: Copy Date: 2 days prior to publication date
Average advertising content per issue: 60%
Series owner and contact point for the following titles, see individual entries:
Herne Bay Times
Whitstable Times
LOCAL NEWSPAPERS: Local Newspapers English Counties

WHITSTABLE EXTRA
43844U72B-1763_200
Frequency: Weekly
Cover Price: Free
ADVERTISING: Rates on application
Part of Series, see entry for: Canterbury Extra Series
LOCAL NEWSPAPERS: Local Newspapers English Counties

WHITSTABLE GAZETTE
43906U72B-1870_200
Frequency: Weekly - Circulation figure is incorporated into the Kentish Gazette Canterbury & District
Cover Price: £0.45
Part of Series, see entry for: Kentish Gazette Series
LOCAL NEWSPAPERS: Local Newspapers English Counties

WHITSTABLE TIMES
43942U72B-1902_150
Frequency: Weekly
Cover Price: £0.35
Part of Series, see entry for: Whitstable & Herne Bay Times Series
LOCAL NEWSPAPERS: Local Newspapers English Counties

WIDNES WEEKLY NEWS
43403U72B-484_180
Frequency: Weekly - See Runcorn Weekly News for circulation figure
Cover Price: £0.60
ADVERTISING: Rates on application
Part of Series, see entry for: Runcorn & Widnes News & Herald Series
LOCAL NEWSPAPERS: Local Newspapers English Counties

WIGAN EVENING POST
42198U67B-1141
Editorial Address: Martland Mill, Martland Mill Lane, WIGAN, WN5 0LX **Tel:** 01942 506221 **Fax:** 01942 221223
Email: jean.fisher@lancspublications.co.uk
Advertising Address: As above. **Tel:** 01942 228000
Fax: 01942 226110
Email: wep.advertising@lancspublications.co.uk
Web site: http://www.wigantoday.net
Publisher: Lancashire Publications Ltd (Wigan)
Frequency: Evenings
Cover Price: £0.40
Circulation: 9,075 (Publisher's Statement)
Editor: Charles Graham; **Features Editor:** Peter Richardson; **Advertising Manager:** Louise Dugdill
ADVERTISING RATES:
Full Page Mono £1040.40
Full Page Colour £1392.30
Agency Commission: 10%
Mechanical Data: Type Area: 340 x 278mm, Col Widths (Display): 30mm, Digital: 30mm, Col Length: 340mm, No. of Columns (Display): 9, Page Width: 278mm
Copy instructions: Copy Date: 2 days prior to publication date
Supplement(s): Freetime - 52xY
REGIONAL DAILY & SUNDAY NEWSPAPERS: Regional Daily Newspapers

WIGAN OBSERVER
719150U72B-1310_250
Frequency: Weekly
Cover Price: £0.65
Circulation: 17,181 (ABC 02/07/2007 to 30/12/2007)
ADVERTISING: Rates on application
Mechanical Data: Col Length: 350mm, No. of Columns (Display): 9
Part of Series, see entry for: The Wigan Observer, Reporter and News Series
LOCAL NEWSPAPERS: Local Newspapers English Counties

THE WIGAN OBSERVER, REPORTER AND NEWS SERIES
43724U72B-1310
Editorial Address: Martland Mill, Martland Mill Lane, WIGAN, WN5 0LX **Tel:** 01942 228000 **Fax:** 01942 221223
Email: gillian.gray@lancspublications.co.uk
Advertising Address: As above. **Fax:** 01942 226110
Email: allen.crawford@lancspublications.co.uk
Web site: http://www.wigantoday.net
Publisher: Johnston Press plc
Frequency: Weekly - Published on Tuesday and Thursday
Circulation: 141,632 (Combined Circulation)
Editor: Charles Graham; **Advertising Director:** Allen Crawford
ADVERTISING: Rates on application
Agency Commission: 10%
Mechanical Data: No. of Columns (Display): 9, Type Area: 340 x 274mm, Col Length: 340mm, Col Widths (Display): 29mm, Page Width: 274mm, Film: Digital
Copy instructions: Copy Date: Monday 5pm prior to publication date
Series owner and contact point for the following titles, see individual entries:
The News (Ashton)
The News (Standish)
Prescot News
Town Centre News (Wigan)
Wigan Observer
Wigan Reporter
LOCAL NEWSPAPERS: Local Newspapers English Counties

WIGAN REPORTER
43725U72B-1310_270
Formerly: Wigan Reporter incorporating Ashton Reporter
Frequency: Weekly
Cover Price: Free
Circulation: 68,062 (Publisher's Statement)
ADVERTISING: Rates on application
Mechanical Data: Col Length: 350mm, No. of Columns (Display): 9
Part of Series, see entry for: The Wigan Observer, Reporter and News Series
LOCAL NEWSPAPERS: Local Newspapers English Counties

WILLESDEN & BRENT TIMES

43124U72A-385_140

Formerly: Willesden & Brent Chronicle
Frequency: Weekly - Circulation figure is incorporated into Kilburn Times
Cover Price: £0.45
Part of Series, see entry for: North West London Newspaper Series
LOCAL NEWSPAPERS: Local Newspapers Greater London

WILLESDEN LEADER

43033U72A-170_100

Formerly: Brent Leader
Frequency: Weekly - Published on Wednesday. For circulation, see Wembley Leader
Cover Price: Free
ADVERTISING RATES:
SCC £11.10
Part of Series, see entry for: Harrow Observer & Leader Series
LOCAL NEWSPAPERS: Local Newspapers Greater London

WILLESDEN OBSERVER

43039U72A-170_120

Formerly: Harrow Independent
Frequency: Weekly - Published on Thursday. For circulation, see Harrow Observer
Cover Price: £0.35
ADVERTISING RATES:
SCC £11.70
Part of Series, see entry for: Harrow Observer & Leader Series
LOCAL NEWSPAPERS: Local Newspapers Greater London

WILMSLOW EXPRESS

43404U72B-512

Formerly: Wilmslow Express Series
Editorial Address: 15 Water Lane, WILMSLOW, SK9 5AE
Tel: 01625 529333 **Fax:** 01625 549660
Email: wilmslowexpress@menwn.co.uk
Advertising Address: Wood Street, Hollywood, STOCKPORT, SK3 0AB **Tel:** 0161 475 4818
Fax: 0161 475 4894
Email: mark.stansfield@menmediasales.co.uk
Web site: http://www.thewilmslowexpress.co.uk
Publisher: MEN Media
Date Established: 1850
Frequency: Weekly - Published on Thursday
Cover Price: Free
Circulation: 16,609 (VFD 02/07/2007 to 30/12/2007)
Editor: Betty Anderson; **News Editor:** Betty Anderson
ADVERTISING RATES:
SCC £6.70
Agency Commission: 10%
Mechanical Data: Page Width: 267mm, Film: Digital, Type Area: 340 x 267mm, Col Length: 340mm, No. of Columns (Display): 9, Col Widths (Display): 27mm
Copy instructions: Copy Date: Tuesday 3pm prior to publication date
Average advertising content per issue: 60%
LOCAL NEWSPAPERS: Local Newspapers English Counties

WILTS & GLOUCESTERSHIRE STANDARD (COTSWOLD EDITION)

43672U72B-1150_200

Formerly: Wilts & Gloucestershire Standard
Frequency: Weekly
Part of Series, see entry for: Wilts & Gloucestershire Standard Series
LOCAL NEWSPAPERS: Local Newspapers English Counties

WILTS & GLOUCESTERSHIRE STANDARD (NORTH WILTSHIRE EDITION)

43670U72B-1150_130

Formerly: Malmesbury Standard
Frequency: Weekly - Circulation figure is incorporated into the Wilts & Gloucestershire Standard (Cotswold Edition)
Cover Price: £0.45
Part of Series, see entry for: Wilts & Gloucestershire Standard Series
LOCAL NEWSPAPERS: Local Newspapers English Counties

WILTS & GLOUCESTERSHIRE STANDARD SERIES

43669U72B-1150

Editorial Address: 74 Dyer Street, CIRENCESTER, GL7 2PW **Tel:** 01285 642642 **Fax:** 01285 654460
Email: simon.davies@gwent-wales.co.uk
Advertising Address: As above. **Fax:** 01285 885606
Email: richard.evans@gwent-wales.co.uk

Web site: http://www.wiltsglosstandard.co.uk
Publisher: Newsquest (Media Group) Ltd
Date Established: 1837
Frequency: Weekly
Cover Price: £0.55
Circulation: 14,652 (ABC 02/07/2007 to 30/12/2007)
Editor: Simon Davies; **News Editor:** Simon Davies;
Advertising Manager: Richard Evans
ADVERTISING RATES:
SCC £6.00
Agency Commission: 10%
Mechanical Data: Col Length: 340mm, Col Widths (Display): 27mm, No. of Columns (Display): 9, Page Width: 259mm, Type Area: 340 x 259mm, Film: Digital
Copy instructions: Copy Date: Monday 5.00pm prior to publication date
Average advertising content per issue: 65%
Series owner and contact point for the following titles, see individual entries:
Wilts & Gloucestershire Standard (Cotswold Edition)
Wilts & Gloucestershire Standard (North Wiltshire Edition)
Supplement(s): Cotswold Essence - 4xY
LOCAL NEWSPAPERS: Local Newspapers English Counties

WILTSHIRE GAZETTE AND HERALD SERIES

44584U72B-3540

Editorial Address: 14 Market Place, DEVIZES, SN10 1HT
Tel: 01380 723501 **Fax:** 01380 729042
Email: glawrence@newswilts.co.uk
Advertising Address: As above. **Fax:** 01380 720559
Email: pnorris@newswilts.co.uk
Web site: http://www.gazetteandherald.co.uk
Publisher: Newsquest (Wiltshire) Ltd
Frequency: Weekly
Circulation: 50,397 (Combined Circulation)
Editor: Jo Moore; **Advertising Manager:** Pam Norris
ADVERTISING RATES:
Full Page Mono £2080.80
Full Page Colour £2601.00
SCC £6.80
Agency Commission: 10%
Mechanical Data: Page Width: 269mm, Col Widths (Display): 27mm, Type Area: 340 x 269mm, Film: Digital, Col Length: 340mm, No. of Columns (Display): 9
Copy instructions: Copy Date: Monday prior to publication date
Series owner and contact point for the following titles, see individual entries:
Gazette & Herald (Box, Calne, Chippenham, Corsham & Lyneham)
Gazette & Herald (Devizes)
Gazette & Herald (Marlborough & Pewsey)
Gazette & Herald (Swindon)
The Kennett & North Wiltshire Star
Supplement(s): Confetti - 1xY, Homeworks - 2xY, Lifestyle - 6xY, Town Guide - 1xY
LOCAL NEWSPAPERS: Local Newspapers English Counties

WILTSHIRE GUARDIAN

44583U72B-3455_140

Frequency: Weekly
Cover Price: Free
Circulation: 65,000 (Publisher's Statement)
Part of Series, see entry for: Guardian Series (Wiltshire, Hampshire and Surrey)
LOCAL NEWSPAPERS: Local Newspapers English Counties

WILTSHIRE STAR

44577U72B-3550_130

Formerly: West and North Wiltshire Star
Frequency: Weekly
Cover Price: Free
Circulation: 48,038 (VFD 02/07/2007 to 30/12/2007)
ADVERTISING: Rates on application
Part of Series, see entry for: Wiltshire Times & News Series
LOCAL NEWSPAPERS: Local Newspapers English Counties

THE WILTSHIRE TIMES AND CHIPPENHAM NEWS

44601U72B-3550_210

Formerly: The Wiltshire Times
Frequency: Weekly - Circulation figure includes the Chippenham News
Cover Price: £0.60
Circulation: 19,177 (ABC 02/07/2007 to 30/12/2007)
ADVERTISING: Rates on application
Part of Series, see entry for: Wiltshire Times & News Series
LOCAL NEWSPAPERS: Local Newspapers English Counties

WILTSHIRE TIMES & NEWS SERIES

44595U72B-3550

Editorial Address: 15 Duke Street, TROWBRIDGE, BA14 8EF **Tel:** 01225 773600 **Fax:** 01225 773690
Email: wtimes@newswilts.co.uk
Advertising Address: As above. **Tel:** 01225 777292
Fax: 01225 773691
Email: lwrintnore@newswilts.co.uk
Web site: http://www.wiltshiretimes.co.uk
Publisher: Newsquest (Wiltshire) Ltd
Date Established: 1854
Frequency: Weekly - Published Thursday and Friday
Circulation: 67,360 (Combined Circulation)
Editor: Craig Evry; **News Editor:** Craig Evry; **Advertising Manager:** Lisa Wrintnore
ADVERTISING: Rates on application
Agency Commission: 10%
Copy instructions: Copy Date: Monday prior to publication date
Average advertising content per issue: 55%
Series owner and contact point for the following titles, see individual entries:
Wiltshire Star
The Wiltshire Times and Chippenham News
Supplement(s): Driving Times - 52xY, Moving Times - 52xY, Wessex in Business - 12xY
LOCAL NEWSPAPERS: Local Newspapers English Counties

WIMBLEDON GUARDIAN

43017U72A-128_240

Formerly: Wimbledon, Mitcham & Morden Guardian
Frequency: Weekly
Cover Price: Free
Part of Series, see entry for: Guardian & News Series (Sutton)
LOCAL NEWSPAPERS: Local Newspapers Greater London

WINDSOR, ETON AND ASCOT EXPRESS

43259U72B-160_193

Formerly: Windsor and Eton Express
Frequency: Weekly
Cover Price: Free
Part of Series, see entry for: Maidenhead Advertiser Series
LOCAL NEWSPAPERS: Local Newspapers English Counties

WINSFORD GUARDIAN

43401U72B-4050_101

Formerly: Winsford & Middlewich Guardian
Frequency: Weekly
Cover Price: £0.50
Circulation: 6,343 (ABC 02/07/2007 to 30/12/2007)
Part of Series, see entry for: Mid-Cheshire Guardian Series
LOCAL NEWSPAPERS: Local Newspapers English Counties

WIRRAL GLOBE BEBINGTON & BROMBOROUGH EDITION

44114U72B-2423_110

Frequency: Weekly
Cover Price: Free
ADVERTISING RATES:
SCC £1.90
Part of Series, see entry for: Wirral Globe Series
LOCAL NEWSPAPERS: Local Newspapers English Counties

WIRRAL GLOBE BIRKENHEAD EDITION

44115U72B-2423_130

Frequency: Weekly
Cover Price: Free
ADVERTISING RATES:
SCC £2.10
Part of Series, see entry for: Wirral Globe Series
LOCAL NEWSPAPERS: Local Newspapers English Counties

WIRRAL GLOBE SERIES

44113U72B-2423

Formerly: Wirral Globe
Editorial Address: Haymarket Court, Hinson Street, BIRKENHEAD, CH41 5BX **Tel:** 0151 906 3050
Fax: 0151 906 3049
Email: globe.editorial@wirral-globe.co.uk
Advertising Address: As above. **Tel:** 0151 906 3000
Email: tmcbride@wirral-globe.co.uk
Web site: http://www.wirralglobe.co.uk
Publisher: Newsquest (Northwest) Ltd
Date Established: 1973
Frequency: Weekly - Published on Wednesday
Cover Price: Free
Circulation: 133,193 (VFD 02/07/2007 to 30/12/2007)

Non-National Newspapers

Editor: Leigh Marles; **News Editor:** Justin Dunn; **Features Editor:** Catherine Lawlor; **Advertising Manager:** Julie McKee
ADVERTISING: Rates on application
Agency Commission: 10%
Mechanical Data: Type Area: 350 x 268mm, Col Length: 350mm, No. of Columns (Display): 9, Col Widths (Display): 27.5mm, Film: Digital, Page Width: 268mm
Copy instructions: Copy Date: Monday 4pm prior to publication date
Average advertising content per issue: 70%
Series owner and contact point for the following titles, see individual entries:
Wirral Globe Bebington & Bromborough Edition
Wirral Globe Birkenhead Edition
Wirral Globe Wallasey and Moreton Edition
Wirral Globe West Wirral Edition
Supplement(s): Property Select - 52xY
LOCAL NEWSPAPERS: Local Newspapers English Counties

WIRRAL GLOBE WALLASEY AND MORETON EDITION
44118U72B-2423_190
Frequency: Weekly
Cover Price: Free
ADVERTISING RATES:
SCC £2.10
Part of Series, see entry for: Wirral Globe Series
LOCAL NEWSPAPERS: Local Newspapers English Counties

WIRRAL GLOBE WEST WIRRAL EDITION
44117U72B-2423_170
Formerly: Wirral Globe Hoylake & West Kirby Edition
Frequency: Weekly
Cover Price: Free
ADVERTISING RATES:
SCC £2.10
Part of Series, see entry for: Wirral Globe Series
LOCAL NEWSPAPERS: Local Newspapers English Counties

WIRRAL NEWS, BIRKENHEAD
44121U72B-2426_130
Formerly: Birkenhead News
Frequency: Weekly
Cover Price: Free
Circulation: 39,729 (VFD 02/07/2007 to 30/12/2007)
Part of Series, see entry for: Wirral News Series
LOCAL NEWSPAPERS: Local Newspapers English Counties

WIRRAL NEWS, BROMBOROUGH AND BEBINGTON
44120U72B-2426_120
Formerly: Bromborough and Bebington News
Frequency: Weekly
Cover Price: Free
Circulation: 23,169 (VFD 02/07/2007 to 30/12/2007)
Part of Series, see entry for: Wirral News Series
LOCAL NEWSPAPERS: Local Newspapers English Counties

WIRRAL NEWS, HESWALL, HOYLAKE, WEST KIRBY AND NESTON
44122U72B-2426_150
Formerly: Heswall News
Frequency: Weekly
Cover Price: Free
Circulation: 22,795 (VFD 02/07/2007 to 30/12/2007)
Part of Series, see entry for: Wirral News Series
LOCAL NEWSPAPERS: Local Newspapers English Counties

WIRRAL NEWS SERIES
44119U72B-2426
Editorial Address: 76 Hamilton Street, BIRKENHEAD, CH41 5AN **Tel:** 0151 288 7653 **Fax:** 0151 647 6933
Email: newsdesk@wirralnews.co.uk
Advertising Address: As above. **Tel:** 0151 647 7111
Email: ros.mcguire@liverpool.com
Web site: http://www.wirralnews.co.uk
Publisher: Trinity Mirror
Date Established: 1856
Frequency: Weekly - Published on Wednesday
Cover Price: Free
Circulation: 132,829 (Combined Circulation)
Editor: News Desk; **Managing Director:** Sara Wilde; **Advertising Manager:** Ros McGuire
ADVERTISING RATES:
Full Page Mono £4042.00
Full Page Colour £5456.70

SCC £14.04
Agency Commission: 10%
Mechanical Data: Film: Digital, Page Width: 272mm, Col Length: 360mm, Type Area: 360 x 272mm, Col Widths (Display): 31mm, No. of Columns (Display): 8
Copy instructions: Copy Date: Friday 5pm prior to publication date
Average advertising content per issue: 66%
Series owner and contact point for the following titles, see individual entries:
Wirral News, Birkenhead
Wirral News, Bromborough and Bebington
Wirral News, Heswall, Hoylake, West Kirby and Neston
Wirral News, Wallasey
LOCAL NEWSPAPERS: Local Newspapers English Counties

WIRRAL NEWS, WALLASEY
44125U72B-2426_190
Formerly: Wallasey News
Frequency: Weekly
Cover Price: Free
Circulation: 35,017 (VFD 02/07/2007 to 30/12/2007)
Part of Series, see entry for: Wirral News Series
LOCAL NEWSPAPERS: Local Newspapers English Counties

WISBECH STANDARD
43345U72B-420
Editorial Address: 34 Market Place, WISBECH, PE13 1DP
Tel: 01945 584447 **Fax:** 01945 475887
Email: editor@wisbech-standard.co.uk
Advertising Address: As above. **Tel:** 01354 652621
Fax: 01354 652751
Email: nick.boister@archant.co.uk
Web site: http://www.wisbech-standard.co.uk
Publisher: Archant Herts & Cambs
Date Established: 1888
Frequency: Weekly - Published on Friday
Cover Price: Free
Circulation: 19,100 (Publisher's Statement)
Editor: John Elworthy; **Advertising Manager:** Nick Boister
ADVERTISING RATES:
Full Page Mono £1360.80
Full Page Colour £1769.00
Agency Commission: 10%
Mechanical Data: Type Area: 360 x 263mm, No. of Columns (Display): 9, Col Length: 360mm, Col Widths (Display): 27mm, Page Width: 263mm, Film: Digital
Copy instructions: Copy Date: Wednesday 2pm prior to publication date
Average advertising content per issue: 60%
LOCAL NEWSPAPERS: Local Newspapers English Counties

WISHAW PRESS
45044U72D-990
Editorial Address: 354 Main Street, WISHAW, ML2 7NG
Tel: 01698 373111 **Fax:** 01698 375679
Email: wishawpress@s-un.co.uk
Advertising Address: The Hamilton Advertiser, Press Buildings, Campbell Street, HAMILTON, ML3 6AX
Tel: 01698 283200 **Fax:** 01698 425706
Email: cparker@s-un.co.uk
Web site: http://www.iclanarkshire.co.uk
Publisher: Scottish & Universal Newspapers Ltd
Date Established: 1869
Frequency: Weekly - Published on Wednesday
Cover Price: £0.73
Circulation: 9,997 (ABC 02/07/2007 to 30/12/2007)
Advertising Manager: Caroline Parker
ADVERTISING RATES:
SCC £6.70
Mechanical Data: Type Area: 390 x 270mm, No. of Columns (Display): 8, Col Length: 390mm, Page Width: 270mm, Film: Digital
LOCAL NEWSPAPERS: Local Newspapers Scotland

WITHAM & BRAINTREE TIMES
43589U72B-950_160
Frequency: Weekly - Published on Wednesday. Circulation figure is incorporated into the Braintree & Witham Times
Cover Price: £0.55
ADVERTISING RATES:
SCC £5.55
Part of Series, see entry for: Braintree & Witham Times & Gazette Series
LOCAL NEWSPAPERS: Local Newspapers English Counties

WITNEY AND WEST OXFORDSHIRE GAZETTE
44229U72B-2750
Editorial Address: 47 Market Square, WITNEY, OX28 6AG
Tel: 01993 773133 **Fax:** 01993 706797
Email: witney@nqo.com

Advertising Address: Newspaper House, Osney Mead, OXFORD, OX2 0EJ **Tel:** 01865 425275 **Fax:** 01865 425557
Email: retail.admin@nqo.com
Web site: http://www.witneygazette.net
Publisher: Newsquest (Oxfordshire) Ltd
Date Established: 1882
Frequency: Weekly
Cover Price: £0.35
Circulation: 7,518 (ABC 02/07/2007 to 30/12/2007)
Editor: David Horne; **Advertising Manager:** Julian Richings
ADVERTISING RATES:
SCC £4.10
Agency Commission: 10%
Mechanical Data: Type Area: 340 x 258.2mm, Col Length: 340mm, No. of Columns (Display): 9, Page Width: 258.2mm, Film: Digital
LOCAL NEWSPAPERS: Local Newspapers English Counties

WOKING INFORMER
762370U72B-3137_290
Frequency: Weekly - Published on Thursday
Cover Price: Free
Circulation: 36,765 (VFD 02/07/2007 to 30/12/2007)
Part of Series, see entry for: Staines Informer Series
LOCAL NEWSPAPERS: Local Newspapers English Counties

WOKING NEWS & MAIL
44419U72B-3169_180
Frequency: Weekly
Cover Price: £0.32
Part of Series, see entry for: Woking News & Mail Series
LOCAL NEWSPAPERS: Local Newspapers English Counties

WOKING NEWS & MAIL SERIES
44416U72B-3169
Editorial Address: Stoke Mill, Woking Road, GUILDFORD, GU1 1QA **Tel:** 01483 755755 **Fax:** 01483 776945
Email: newsandmail@woking.co.uk
Advertising Address: As above. **Tel:** 01483 508700
Fax: 01483 508851
Email: displayadvertising@surreyad.co.uk
Web site: http://www.woking.co.uk
Publisher: Surrey & Berkshire Media Group
Date Established: 1894
Frequency: Weekly - Published on Thursday
Circulation: 9,002 (ABC 02/07/2007 to 30/12/2007)
Editor: Nicola Rider; **News Editor:** Nicola Rider
ADVERTISING RATES:
SCC £5.85
Mechanical Data: Trim Size: 560 x 347, No. of Columns (Display): 10, Film: Digital
Series owner and contact point for the following titles, see individual entries:
Byfleet News & Mail, incorporating West Byfleet, Pyrford & New Haw
Chobham News & Mail incorporating Windlesham, Bisley & West End
Woking News & Mail
Supplement(s): What's On - 52xY
LOCAL NEWSPAPERS: Local Newspapers English Counties

WOKING REVIEW
44422U72B-3170_190
Frequency: Weekly
Cover Price: Free
Part of Series, see entry for: Woking Review Series
LOCAL NEWSPAPERS: Local Newspapers English Counties

WOKING REVIEW SERIES
44420U72B-3170
Editorial Address: Stoke Mill, Woking Road, GUILDFORD, GU1 1QA **Tel:** 01483 755755 **Fax:** 01483 776945
Email: review@woking.co.uk
Advertising Address: As above. **Tel:** 01483 508700
Email: salessupport@surreyad.co.uk
Web site: http://www.woking.co.uk
Publisher: Surrey & Berkshire Media Group
Frequency: Weekly - Published on Thursday
Cover Price: Free
Circulation: 41,114 (VFD 02/07/2007 to 30/12/2007)
Editor: Nicola Rider; **News Editor:** Nicola Rider;
Advertising Manager: Kerry Wright
ADVERTISING RATES:
Full Page Mono £1960.00
Agency Commission: 10%
Mechanical Data: Page Width: 277mm, Type Area: 350 x 277mm, Col Length: 350mm, Col Widths (Display): 32mm, No. of Columns (Display): 8, Print Process: Web-fed offset litho, Film: Digital
Copy instructions: Copy Date: 4 days prior to publication date

Average advertising content per issue: 40%
Series owner and contact point for the following titles,
see individual entries:
Addlestone & Byfleet Review
Woking Review
Supplement(s): Property Weekly - 52xY
LOCAL NEWSPAPERS: Local Newspapers English
Counties

WOKINGHAM AND BRACKNELL TIMES SERIES

43285U72B-210

Editorial Address: Unit 5, Anvil Court, 44 Denmark Street,
WOKINGHAM, RG40 2BB **Tel:** 0118 936 6188
Fax: 0118 936 6190
Email: editorial@wokingham-times.co.uk
Advertising Address: 8 Tessa Road, READING, RG1 8NS
Tel: 0118 918 3000 **Fax:** 0118 958 8229
Email: advertising@reading-epost.co.uk
Web site: http://www.getwokingham.co.uk
Publisher: Surrey & Berkshire Media Group
Frequency: Weekly - Published Wednesday
Circulation: 6,430 (Combined Circulation)
Editor: Vicky Corbett; **News Editor:** Vicky Corbett
ADVERTISING RATES:
Full Page Mono £3073.84
Full Page Colour £3995.99
Mechanical Data: Type Area: 560 x 339mm, Col Length:
560mm, No. of Columns (Display): 11, Film: Digital, Page
Width: 339mm
Copy instructions: Copy Date: Monday 12 noon prior to
publication date
Series owner and contact point for the following titles,
see individual entries:
Bracknell & Ascot Times
Crowthorne & Sandhurst Times
Wokingham Times
Supplement(s): The Property Paper - 52xY
LOCAL NEWSPAPERS: Local Newspapers English
Counties

WOKINGHAM MIDWEEK

1655352U72B-150_191

Frequency: Weekly - See Midweek News for circulation
figure
Cover Price: Free
Part of Series, see entry for: Bracknell News Series
LOCAL NEWSPAPERS: Local Newspapers English
Counties

WOKINGHAM NEWS AND CROWTHORNE AND SANDHURST NEWSWEEK

43254U72B-150_190

Formerly: Wokingham News
Frequency: Weekly
Cover Price: £0.60
Part of Series, see entry for: Bracknell News Series
LOCAL NEWSPAPERS: Local Newspapers English
Counties

WOKINGHAM STANDARD

1732607U72B-3941_101

Frequency: Weekly
Cover Price: Free
Part of Series, see entry for: Bracknell Forest &
Wokingham Standard Series
LOCAL NEWSPAPERS: Local Newspapers English
Counties

WOKINGHAM TIMES

43290U72B-210_160

Frequency: Weekly - Circulation figure includes the
Bracknell & Ascot Times and the Crowthorne & Sandhurst
Times
Cover Price: £0.35
Circulation: 6,430 (ABC 02/07/2007 to 30/12/2007)
Part of Series, see entry for: Wokingham and Bracknell
Times Series
LOCAL NEWSPAPERS: Local Newspapers English
Counties

WOLVERHAMPTON CHRONICLE

44562U72B-3510

Formerly: Wolverhampton Chronicle Series
Editorial Address: 51-53 Queen Street,
WOLVERHAMPTON, WV1 1ES **Tel:** 01902 319496
Fax: 01902 319467
Email: wolchron@expressandstar.co.uk
Advertising Address: As above. **Tel:** 01902 313131
Email: display@expressandstar.co.uk
Web site: http://www.yourchronicle.com
Publisher: Express & Star Ltd
Frequency: Weekly - Published on Thursdays
Cover Price: Free

Circulation: 68,351 (VFD 02/07/2007 to 30/12/2007)
Editor: Sol Buckner; **Managing Director:** Alan Harris;
Advertising Manager: Glyn Law; **Group Editor:** Sue
Attwater
ADVERTISING RATES:
SCC £6.15
Mechanical Data: Type Area: 410 x 305mm, Col Length:
410mm, Page Width: 305mm
Copy instructions: Copy Date: Tuesday 12pm prior to
publication date
Average advertising content per issue: 75%
LOCAL NEWSPAPERS: Local Newspapers English
Counties

THE WOOD & VALE EXPRESS

1609426U72A-160_181

Frequency: Weekly
Cover Price: £0.55
Part of Series, see entry for: Ham & High Series
LOCAL NEWSPAPERS: Local Newspapers Greater London

WOODBRIDGE MELTON AND DISTRICT COMMUNITY NEWS

44338U72B-3072_160

Frequency: Monthly
Cover Price: Free
Circulation: 6,100 (Publisher's Statement)
Part of Series, see entry for: Community News Series
LOCAL NEWSPAPERS: Local Newspapers English
Counties

WOODLEY AND EARLEY CHRONICLE

43275U72B-180_280

Formerly: Woodley Chronicle
Frequency: Weekly - Circulation figure is incorporated into
the Reading Chronicle
Cover Price: £0.55
ADVERTISING RATES:
Full Page Mono £3255.84
Full Page Colour £4069.80
SCC £11.97
Part of Series, see entry for: Reading Chronicle Series
LOCAL NEWSPAPERS: Local Newspapers English
Counties

WORCESTER NEWS

42210U67B-1160

Formerly: Evening News (Worcester)
Editorial Address: Berrows House, Hylton Road,
WORCESTER, WR2 5JX **Tel:** 01905 748200
Fax: 01905 742277
Email: wenedit@worcesternews.co.uk
Advertising Address: As above.
Email: sales@newsquestmidlands.co.uk
Web site: http://www.worcesternews.co.uk
Publisher: Newsquest Media Group
Date Established: 1937
Frequency: Daily
Cover Price: £0.35
Circulation: 18,491 (ABC 01/01/2007 to 01/07/2007)
Editor: Stephanie Preece; **News Editor:** Stephanie Preece;
Features Editor: David Chapman
ADVERTISING: Rates on application
Supplement(s): Motoring News - 52xY, Weekend News and
Entertainment - 52xY
REGIONAL DAILY & SUNDAY NEWSPAPERS: Regional
Daily Newspapers

THE WORCESTER STANDARD

628840U72B-3570

Formerly: Worcester Gazette and Standard Series
Editorial Address: 51A Upper Tything, WORCESTER, WR1
1JY **Tel:** 01905 726200 **Fax:** 01905 613915
Email: editor@worcesterstandard.co.uk
Advertising Address: As above.
Email: gill.drinkwater@observerstandard.com
Web site: http://www.worcesterstandard.co.uk
ISSN: 1472-152X
Publisher: Bullivant Media Limited
Date Established: 2000
Frequency: Weekly
Cover Price: Free
Circulation: 52,412 (Publisher's Statement)
Editor: Kara Bradley; **Advertising Manager:** Gill Drinkwater
ADVERTISING RATES:
Full Page Mono £1701.00
Full Page Colour £2126.25
SCC £5.40
Agency Commission: 10%
Mechanical Data: Col Length: 350mm, Page Width:
265mm, Film: Digital, Type Area: 350 x 265mm, No. of
Columns (Display): 9

Copy instructions: Copy Date: Wednesday 5pm prior to
publication date
Average advertising content per issue: 65%
LOCAL NEWSPAPERS: Local Newspapers English
Counties

WORKSOP GUARDIAN

44205U72B-2670_175

Frequency: Weekly
Cover Price: £0.55
Circulation: 17,788 (ABC 02/07/2007 to 30/12/2007)
ADVERTISING RATES:
SCC £6.42
Part of Series, see entry for: Guardian Series (Worksop)
LOCAL NEWSPAPERS: Local Newspapers English
Counties

WORKSOP TRADER

44210U72B-2670_183

Publisher: South Yorkshire Newspapers Ltd
Frequency: Weekly
Cover Price: Free
Circulation: 29,511 (VFD 02/07/2007 to 30/12/2007)
ADVERTISING RATES:
SCC £4.99
Part of Series, see entry for: Guardian Series (Worksop)
LOCAL NEWSPAPERS: Local Newspapers English
Counties

WORTHING ADVERTISER AND HERALD SERIES

44475U72B-3330

Editorial Address: Cannon House, Chatsworth Road,
WORTHING, BN11 1NA **Tel:** 01903 230051
Fax: 01903 520000
Email: letters@worthingherald.co.uk
Advertising Address: As above. **Fax:** 01903 216087
Email: michelle.vallis@worthingtoday.co.uk
Web site: http://www.worthingherald.co.uk
Publisher: Portsmouth Publishing & Printing Ltd
Frequency: Weekly - Published on Wednesday and
Thursday
Circulation: 90,862 (Combined Circulation)
Editor: Nicola McLarnon; **News Editor:** Nicola McLarnon;
Managing Director: Karl Dimmock; **Advertising Manager:**
Michelle Vallis
ADVERTISING RATES:
SCC £15.64
Agency Commission: 10%
Mechanical Data: Type Area: 360 x 265mm, Film: Digital,
Col Length: 360mm, Page Width: 265mm
Copy instructions: Copy Date: 3 days prior to publication
date
Series owner and contact point for the following titles,
see individual entries:
The Advertiser
Worthing Herald
Supplement(s): Simply Sussex - 4xY
LOCAL NEWSPAPERS: Local Newspapers English
Counties

WORTHING GUARDIAN

44480U72B-3335

Formerly: Worthing Guardian Series
Editorial Address: Cannon House, Chatsworth Road,
WORTHING, BN11 1NA **Tel:** 01903 230051
Fax: 01903 520000
Email: letters@worthingtoday.co.uk
Advertising Address: As above. **Fax:** 01903 216087
Email: suzie.yates@jpress.co.uk
Publisher: Johnston Press plc
Frequency: Weekly
Cover Price: Free
Circulation: 35,000 (Publisher's Statement)
Editor: Sam Woodman; **Advertising Manager:** Suzie Yates
ADVERTISING RATES:
SCC £7.76
Agency Commission: 10%
Mechanical Data: Film: Digital
Copy instructions: Copy Date: Tuesday 4pm prior to
publication date
LOCAL NEWSPAPERS: Local Newspapers English
Counties

WORTHING HERALD

44479U72B-3330_190

Advertising Address: Cannon House, Chatsworth Road,
WORTHING, BN11 1NA
Frequency: Weekly - Published on Thursday. Circulation
figure includes the Lancing Herald
Cover Price: £0.32
Circulation: 17,612 (ABC 02/07/2007 to 30/12/2007)
Summary of Content: Local newspaper with news, sport,
jobs, property, cars and entertainment from Worthing and
the surrounding areas.

Non-National Newspapers

Part of Series, see entry for: Worthing Advertiser and Herald Series
LOCAL NEWSPAPERS: Local Newspapers English Counties

WREXHAM CHRONICLE
44855U72C-450
Formerly: Wrexham Mail
Editorial Address: Office 2, Daniel Owen Precinct, MOLD, CH7 1AP **Tel:** 01978 351515 **Fax:** 01244 830786
Email: wrexham.news@cheshirenews.co.uk
Advertising Address: 31 Henblas Street, WREXHAM, LL13 8AD **Tel:** 01244 606339 **Fax:** 01244 606398
Email: ros.mcguire@liverpool.com
Web site: http://www.icnorthwales.co.uk
Publisher: Trinity Mirror Cheshire
Frequency: Weekly - Published on Thursday
Cover Price: Free
Circulation: 38,278 (Publisher's Statement)
Editor: Kevin Hughes; **Advertising Manager:** Louise Barlow; **Group Editor:** Kevin Hughes
ADVERTISING RATES:
Full Page Mono £1666.00
Full Page Colour £2249.00
SCC £5.95
Agency Commission: 10%
Mechanical Data: Type Area: 350 x 272mm, No. of Columns (Display): 8, Film: Digital, Page Width: 272mm, Col Length: 350mm, Col Widths (Display): 31mm
Copy instructions: Copy Date: Tuesday 12.30pm prior to publication date
Average advertising content per issue: 50%
LOCAL NEWSPAPERS: Local Newspapers Wales

WREXHAM EVENING LEADER
42233U67B-2080_680
Frequency: Evenings - Published Monday to Friday, Friday edition is published in the morning
ADVERTISING RATES:
SCC £4.60
Edition of: Evening Leader
REGIONAL DAILY & SUNDAY NEWSPAPERS: Regional Daily Newspapers

WREXHAM LEADER
44854U72C-410
Editorial Address: 45 King Street, WREXHAM, LL11 1HR
Tel: 01978 355151 **Fax:** 01978 311421
Email: news@wrexhamleader.co.uk
Advertising Address: Mold Business Park, Wrexham Road, MOLD, CH7 1XY **Tel:** 01352 707707 **Fax:** 01352 700048
Email: melanie.egan@nwn.co.uk
Web site: http://www.wrexhamleader.co.uk
Publisher: NWN Media Ltd
Date Established: 1920
Frequency: Weekly - Published every Friday
Cover Price: Free
Circulation: 42,138 (VFD 03/12/2007 to 30/12/2007)
Editor: Barrie Jones; **Editor-in-Chief:** Barrie Jones
ADVERTISING RATES:
Full Page Mono £3502.80
Full Page Colour £4594.59
SCC £5.35
Agency Commission: 10%
Mechanical Data: Type Area: 550 x 415mm, Col Length: 550mm, Page Width: 415mm, Col Widths (Display): 34.6mm, No. of Columns (Display): 12, Film: Digital
Copy instructions: Copy Date: Monday 5pm prior to publication date
Supplement(s): Property Guide - 52xY
LOCAL NEWSPAPERS: Local Newspapers Wales

WYE VALLEY MERLIN
1695534U72C-244_102
Frequency: Monthly
Cover Price: Free
Circulation: 500 (Publisher's Statement)
Part of Series, see entry for: Monmouthshire Beacon and Merlin Series
LOCAL NEWSPAPERS: Local Newspapers Wales

WYMONDHAM & ATTLEBOROUGH MERCURY
44139U72B-2437_240
Frequency: Weekly
Cover Price: Free
Circulation: 17,685 (VFD 02/07/2007 to 30/12/2007)
ADVERTISING: Rates on application
Part of Series, see entry for: Norfolk County Weeklies Series
LOCAL NEWSPAPERS: Local Newspapers English Counties

WYTHENSHAWE WORLD
43726U72B-1317
Editorial Address: 495 Altrincham Road, Baguley, MANCHESTER, M23 1AR **Tel:** 0161 998 4786
Fax: 0161 998 2486
Email: newsdesk@wythenshaweworld.com
Advertising Address: As above.
Email: wytworld@ntlworld.com
Web site: http://wythenshaweworld.com
Publisher: Wythenshawe World Ltd
Frequency: 26 issues yearly
Cover Price: Free
Circulation: 29,000 (Publisher's Statement)
Editor: John Oatway
ADVERTISING RATES:
Full Page Mono £525.00
Full Page Colour £675.00
SCC £4.00
Agency Commission: 10%
Mechanical Data: Film: Digital, Page Width: 262mm, Type Area: 390 x 262mm, Col Length: 390mm, Col Widths (Display): 30mm, No. of Columns (Display): 8
Copy instructions: Copy Date: Tuesday 4pm prior to publication date
LOCAL NEWSPAPERS: Local Newspapers English Counties

YATE & SODBURY GAZETTE
43214U72B-23_200
Formerly: Chipping Sodbury & Yate Gazette
Frequency: Weekly
Cover Price: £0.55
Part of Series, see entry for: Gloucestershire Gazette Series
LOCAL NEWSPAPERS: Local Newspapers English Counties

YATELEY NEWS & MAIL
43771U72B-1382_260
Formerly: Yateley News
Frequency: Weekly - Circulation figure is incorporated into the Aldershot News & Mail
Cover Price: £0.37
ADVERTISING: Rates on application
Part of Series, see entry for: Aldershot Mail and News Series
LOCAL NEWSPAPERS: Local Newspapers English Counties

YELLOW ADVERTISER (BARKING & DAGENHAM)
43188U72B-1094_110
Formerly: Yellow Advertiser (Barking/Dagenham/ Beckton/ East Ham)
Frequency: Weekly
Cover Price: Free
Circulation: 17,862 (Publisher's Statement)
ADVERTISING: Rates on application
Part of Series, see entry for: Yellow Advertiser Group Series (Essex)
LOCAL NEWSPAPERS: Local Newspapers English Counties

YELLOW ADVERTISER (BASILDON)
43651U72B-1094_120
Frequency: Weekly
Cover Price: Free
Circulation: 55,445 (Publisher's Statement)
ADVERTISING: Rates on application
Part of Series, see entry for: Yellow Advertiser Group Series (Essex)
LOCAL NEWSPAPERS: Local Newspapers English Counties

YELLOW ADVERTISER (BRENTWOOD & SHENFIELD)
43653U72B-1094_130
Formerly: Yellow Advertiser (Brentwood)
Frequency: Weekly
Cover Price: Free
Circulation: 15,038 (Publisher's Statement)
ADVERTISING: Rates on application
Part of Series, see entry for: Yellow Advertiser Group Series (Essex)
LOCAL NEWSPAPERS: Local Newspapers English Counties

YELLOW ADVERTISER (CASTLE POINT & ROCHFORD)
43654U72B-1094_140
Frequency: Weekly
Cover Price: Free
Circulation: 47,285 (Publisher's Statement)
ADVERTISING: Rates on application

Part of Series, see entry for: Yellow Advertiser Group Series (Essex)
LOCAL NEWSPAPERS: Local Newspapers English Counties

YELLOW ADVERTISER (CHELMSFORD & MALDON)
43655U72B-1094_150
Frequency: Weekly
Cover Price: Free
Circulation: 34,610 (Publisher's Statement)
ADVERTISING: Rates on application
Part of Series, see entry for: Yellow Advertiser Group Series (Essex)
LOCAL NEWSPAPERS: Local Newspapers English Counties

YELLOW ADVERTISER GROUP SERIES (ESSEX)
43650U72B-1094
Formerly: Yellow Advertiser Group (Essex)
Editorial Address: Acorn House, Great Oaks, BASILDON, SS14 1AH **Tel:** 01268 503400 **Fax:** 01268 503480
Email: newsdesk@yellowad.co.uk
Advertising Address: As above. **Fax:** 01268 503418
Email: kentodd@yellowad.co.uk
Web site: http://www.icessex.co.uk
Publisher: Tindle Newspapers Ltd
Frequency: Weekly - Published on Thursday and Friday
Cover Price: Free
Circulation: 434,612 (Combined Circulation)
Editor: Greg Fidgeon; **News Editor:** Steve Neale; **Features Editor:** Liz Wade
ADVERTISING: Rates on application
Agency Commission: 10%
Copy instructions: Copy Date: 2 days prior to publication date
Average advertising content per issue: 75%
Series owner and contact point for the following titles, see individual entries:
Yellow Advertiser (Barking & Dagenham)
Yellow Advertiser (Basildon)
Yellow Advertiser (Brentwood & Shenfield)
Yellow Advertiser (Castle Point & Rochford)
Yellow Advertiser (Chelmsford & Maldon)
Yellow Advertiser (Havering)
Yellow Advertiser (Redbridge)
Yellow Advertiser (Southend)
Yellow Advertiser (Stratford & Newham)
Yellow Advertiser (Thurrock)
Yellow Advertiser (Waltham Forest)
LOCAL NEWSPAPERS: Local Newspapers English Counties

YELLOW ADVERTISER (HAVERING)
43191U72B-1094_180
Formerly: Yellow Advertiser (Hornchurch & Romford)
Frequency: Weekly
Cover Price: Free
Circulation: 68,234 (Publisher's Statement)
ADVERTISING: Rates on application
Part of Series, see entry for: Yellow Advertiser Group Series (Essex)
LOCAL NEWSPAPERS: Local Newspapers English Counties

YELLOW ADVERTISER (REDBRIDGE)
43189U72B-1094_220
Frequency: Weekly
Cover Price: Free
Circulation: 49,983 (Publisher's Statement)
ADVERTISING: Rates on application
Part of Series, see entry for: Yellow Advertiser Group Series (Essex)
LOCAL NEWSPAPERS: Local Newspapers English Counties

YELLOW ADVERTISER (SOUTHEND)
43657U72B-1094_240
Frequency: Weekly
Cover Price: Free
Circulation: 62,842 (Publisher's Statement)
ADVERTISING: Rates on application
Part of Series, see entry for: Yellow Advertiser Group Series (Essex)
LOCAL NEWSPAPERS: Local Newspapers English Counties

YELLOW ADVERTISER (STRATFORD & NEWHAM)
1818403U72B-1094_301
Frequency: Weekly
Cover Price: Free

Circulation: 8,000 (Publisher's Statement)
ADVERTISING: Rates on application
Part of Series, see entry for: Yellow Advertiser Group
Series (Essex)
LOCAL NEWSPAPERS: Local Newspapers English
Counties

YELLOW ADVERTISER (THURROCK)
43658U72B-1094_250
Formerly: Yellow Advertiser (Thurrock & Lakeside)
Frequency: Weekly
Cover Price: Free
Circulation: 39,865 (Publisher's Statement)
ADVERTISING: Rates on application
Part of Series, see entry for: Yellow Advertiser Group
Series (Essex)
LOCAL NEWSPAPERS: Local Newspapers English
Counties

YELLOW ADVERTISER (WALTHAM FOREST)
43192U72B-1094_300
Frequency: Weekly
Cover Price: Free
Circulation: 35,448 (Publisher's Statement)
ADVERTISING: Rates on application
Part of Series, see entry for: Yellow Advertiser Group
Series (Essex)
LOCAL NEWSPAPERS: Local Newspapers English
Counties

YEOVIL EXPRESS
44268U72B-2934_170
Frequency: Weekly
Cover Price: Free
Circulation: 28,436 (VFD 02/07/2007 to 30/12/2007)
ADVERTISING RATES:
Full Page Mono £765.45
Full Page Colour £956.82
SCC £4.30
Part of Series, see entry for: Star and Express Series
LOCAL NEWSPAPERS: Local Newspapers English
Counties

YEOVIL TIMES
44275U72B-2950_160
Frequency: Weekly
Cover Price: Free
Circulation: 44,702 (VFD 01/01/2007 to 01/07/2007)
Part of Series, see entry for: Western Gazette and Yeovil
Times Series
LOCAL NEWSPAPERS: Local Newspapers English
Counties

YORK STAR
44667U72B-3645_230
Frequency: Weekly
Cover Price: Free
Circulation: 51,899 (VFD 02/07/2007 to 30/12/2007)
ADVERTISING RATES:
Full Page Mono £1667.70
Full Page Colour £2084.63
SCC £5.45
Mechanical Data: Screen: 33 lpc, Film: Negative, right
reading, emulsion side down
Part of Series, see entry for: Star Series (Selby & York)
LOCAL NEWSPAPERS: Local Newspapers English
Counties

YORKSHIRE EVENING POST
42089U67B-340
Editorial Address: PO Box 168, Wellington Street, LEEDS,
LS1 1RF **Tel:** 0113 243 2701 **Fax:** 0113 238 8536
Email: eped@ypn.co.uk
Advertising Address: As above. **Fax:** 0113 238 8535
Email: nicola.atkinson@ypn.co.uk
Web site: http://www.yorkshireeveningpost.com
Publisher: Yorkshire Post Newspapers Ltd
Date Established: 1890
Frequency: Evenings
Cover Price: £0.37
Circulation: 56,647 (Publisher's Statement)
Editor: News Desk; **News Editor:** Gillian Haworth;
Features Editor: Jayne Dawson; **Managing Director:** Chris
Green; **Advertising Manager:** Nicola Atkinson
ADVERTISING: Rates on application
Agency Commission: 10%
Copy instructions: Copy Date: 2 days prior to publication
date
Average advertising content per issue: 30%
Editions:
City Lite
Yorkshire Evening Post (Main Edition)
Yorkshire Evening Post (Wakefield)

Supplement(s): 24SEVEN - 52xY, Drive It - 52xY, Homes -
52xY, Jobs - 52xY, Motors - 52xY, Scene - 52xY, Women's
Post - 52xY
REGIONAL DAILY & SUNDAY NEWSPAPERS: Regional
Daily Newspapers

YORKSHIRE EVENING POST (MAIN EDITION)
42094U67B-340_580
Formerly: Yorkshire Evening Post (Leeds Final)
Cover Price: £0.30
ADVERTISING: Rates on application
Edition of: Yorkshire Evening Post
REGIONAL DAILY & SUNDAY NEWSPAPERS: Regional
Daily Newspapers

YORKSHIRE EVENING POST (WAKEFIELD)
42096U67B-340_660
ADVERTISING: Rates on application
Edition of: Yorkshire Evening Post
REGIONAL DAILY & SUNDAY NEWSPAPERS: Regional
Daily Newspapers

YORKSHIRE POST
42098U67B-355
Editorial Address: PO Box 168, Wellington Street, LEEDS,
LS1 1RF **Tel:** 0113 243 2701 **Fax:** 0113 238 8521
Email: yp.newsdesk@ypn.co.uk
Advertising Address: As above. **Fax:** 0113 383 1524
Email: john.bottomley@ypn.co.uk
Web site: http://www.yorkshirepost.co.uk
Publisher: Johnston Press plc
Frequency: Mornings
Cover Price: £0.48
Circulation: 49,031 (ABC 02/07/2007 to 30/12/2007)
Editor: Hannah Start; **News Editor:** Hannah Start; **Features
Editor:** Sarah Freeman; **Advertising Manager:** John
Bottomley
ADVERTISING RATES:
Full Page Mono £10194.00
Full Page Colour £13253.00
Agency Commission: 10%
Mechanical Data: Col Length: 560mm, No. of Columns
(Display): 11, Film: Digital, Col Widths (Display): 27mm
Copy instructions: Copy Date: 2 days prior to publication
date
Editions:
Yorkshire Post (Hull & East Riding Edition)
Yorkshire Post (North Yorkshire Edition)
Yorkshire Post (South Yorkshire Edition)
Yorkshire Post (West Riding Edition)
Supplement(s): Business Week - 52xY, Country Week -
52xY, Life and Style - 52xY, Yorkshire Post Magazine - 52xY
REGIONAL DAILY & SUNDAY NEWSPAPERS: Regional
Daily Newspapers

YORKSHIRE POST (CITY/LONDON OFFICE)
42304U67D-170
Editorial Address: Dolphyn Court, 10-11 Great Turnstile,
LONDON, WC1V 7JU **Tel:** 020 7025 3640
Email: ros.snowdon@ypn.co.uk
Web site: http://www.thisisleeds.co.uk
Publisher: Johnston Press plc
Frequency: 313 issues yearly - Monday to Saturday
Cover Price: £0.45
Editor: Ros Snowdon
REGIONAL DAILY & SUNDAY NEWSPAPERS: Regional
Daily Sunday London City Office

YORKSHIRE POST (HULL & EAST RIDING EDITION)
42100U67B-355_560
Edition of: Yorkshire Post
REGIONAL DAILY & SUNDAY NEWSPAPERS: Regional
Daily Newspapers

YORKSHIRE POST (NORTH YORKSHIRE EDITION)
42101U67B-355_600
Edition of: Yorkshire Post
REGIONAL DAILY & SUNDAY NEWSPAPERS: Regional
Daily Newspapers

YORKSHIRE POST (SOUTH YORKSHIRE EDITION)
42102U67B-355_640
Edition of: Yorkshire Post
REGIONAL DAILY & SUNDAY NEWSPAPERS: Regional
Daily Newspapers

YORKSHIRE POST (WEST RIDING EDITION)
42103U67B-355_680
Edition of: Yorkshire Post
REGIONAL DAILY & SUNDAY NEWSPAPERS: Regional
Daily Newspapers

YOUR LEEK PAPER
1623326U72B-3935
Editorial Address: 19 Getliffes Yard, Derby Street, LEEK,
ST13 6HU **Tel:** 01538 371800 **Fax:** 01538 371810
Email: info@yourleekpaper.co.uk
Advertising Address: As above.
Email: info@yourleekpaper.co.uk
Web site: http://www.yourleekpaper.co.uk
Publisher: Staffordshire Newspapers Ltd
Date Established: 2003
Frequency: Weekly - Published on Wednesday
Cover Price: £0.25
Circulation: 4,500 (Publisher's Statement)
Editor: Philip Jenkins; **News Editor:** James Benstead;
Advertising Manager: Angela Wynne
ADVERTISING RATES:
SCC £2.80
Agency Commission: 10%
Mechanical Data: Col Length: 360mm, Col Widths (Display):
34mm, No. of Columns (Display): 9, Type Area: 360 x
265mm, Page Width: 265mm, Film: Digital
Copy instructions: Copy Date: Friday 4.30pm prior to
publication date
Average advertising content per issue: 30%
LOCAL NEWSPAPERS: Local Newspapers English
Counties

YOUR VALE
44844U72C-356
Formerly: The Vale Advertiser
Editorial Address: 84 High Street, RHYL, LL18 1UB
Tel: 01745 345895 **Fax:** 01745 337862
Email: david.simister@northwalesnews.co.uk
Advertising Address: As above. **Tel:** 01745 345880
Fax: 01745 355516
Email: sharon.dolman@dailypost.co.uk
Web site: http://www.yourvale.co.uk
Publisher: Trinity Mirror
Frequency: Weekly - Published on Wednesday
Cover Price: Free
Circulation: 7,992 (Publisher's Statement)
Editor: David Simister; **News Editor:** Martin Williams;
Advertising Manager: Sharon Dolman
ADVERTISING RATES:
Full Page Mono £1138.00
Agency Commission: 10%
Mechanical Data: Page Width: 272mm, Film: Digital, Type
Area: 360 x 272mm, Col Length: 360mm, No. of Columns
(Display): 8
Copy instructions: Copy Date: Wednesday 10.30am prior
to publication date
LOCAL NEWSPAPERS: Local Newspapers Wales

YOURDEAL
1895882U72B-4101_108
Web site: http://www.yourdeal-sandwich.co.uk
Date Established: 2009
Frequency: Weekly - Published on Wednesday
Cover Price: Free
Circulation: 9,500 (Print Run)
ADVERTISING RATES:
SCC £4.95
Part of Series, see entry for: YourKent Series
LOCAL NEWSPAPERS: Local Newspapers English
Counties

YOURKENT SERIES
1827086U72B-4101
Editorial Address: Apple Barn, Smeeth, ASHFORD, TN25
6SR **Tel:** 01303 817000 **Fax:** 01303 817002
Email: editorial@kosmedia.co.uk
Advertising Address: As above. **Tel:** 01303 817150
Fax: 01303 817001
Email: sales@kosmedia.co.uk
Web site: http://www.yourkenttv.co.uk
Publisher: Kos Media Ltd
Date Established: 2007
Frequency: Weekly - Published on Wednesday
Cover Price: Free
Circulation: 120,000 (Combined Circulation)
Editor: Gary Wright; **News Editor:** Jon Coates; **Group
Editor:** Gary Wright
ADVERTISING: Rates on application
Mechanical Data: Type Area: 360 x 268mm, Col Length:
360mm, Page Width: 268mm, Col Widths (Display): 30mm,
No. of Columns (Display): 8, Film: Digital
**Series owner and contact point for the following titles,
see individual entries:**
Your Canterbury
Your Medway
Your Swale
YourAshford

Business Magazines

YourDeal
YourDover
YourMaidstone
YourSandwich
YourShepway
YourThanet
LOCAL NEWSPAPERS: Local Newspapers English Counties

YOURSANDWICH
1895883U72B-4101_109

Web site: http://www.yoursandwich.co.uk
Date Established: 2009
Frequency: Weekly - Published on Wednesday
Circulation: 9,500 (Print Run)
ADVERTISING RATES:
SCC £4.95
Part of Series, see entry for: YourKent Series
LOCAL NEWSPAPERS: Local Newspapers English Counties

YOURTHANET
1827095U72B-4101_107

Web site: http://www.yourthanet.co.uk
Frequency: Weekly - Published on Wednesday
Cover Price: Free
Circulation: 15,000 (Publisher's Statement)
ADVERTISING RATES:
SCC £4.95
Part of Series, see entry for: YourKent Series
LOCAL NEWSPAPERS: Local Newspapers English Counties

Business Magazines

'T' MAG
37082U14F-76

Formerly: 't' Magazine (training, education, employment)
Editorial Address: Alex Wood Hall, Norfolk Street, CAMBRIDGE, CB1 2LD **Tel:** 01223 358700
Fax: 01223 358766
Email: hugh@tmag.co.uk
Advertising Address: As above.
Email: info@tmag.co.uk
Web site: http://www.tmag.co.uk
ISSN: 1359-2319
Publisher: T magazine Ltd
Frequency: 10 issues yearly
Annual Sub.: £99.95
Circulation: 500 (Publisher's Statement)
Usual Pagination: 36
Editor: Hugh Lloyd Jones; **Advertising Manager:** Simon Shaw; **Publisher:** Simon Shaw
Summary of Content: Magazine covering learning and development, training, education and the future of employment.
Readership/Target Audience: Read by senior and middle managers at further and higher education providers, private training providers, policy-making bodies, skills councils, research organisations, local councils and training managers in companies and public organisations.
ADVERTISING RATES:
Full Page Colour £900.00
Agency Commission: 10%
Mechanical Data: Trim Size: 297 x 210mm, Bleed Size: 303 x 216mm, Film: Positive, right reading, emulsion side down. Digital
Copy instructions: Copy Date: 15th of the month prior to publication date
BUSINESS: COMMERCE, INDUSTRY & MANAGEMENT: Training & Recruitment

20/20 EUROPE
40402U56E-20

Editorial Address: PR by email only **Tel:** 01580 852445
Email: c.norton@fabianogroup.com
Advertising Address: Fabiano Editore, Regione San Giovanni, 40, 14053 CANELLI (AT) **Tel:** 0141 82 78 01
Fax: 0141 82 78 300
Email: c.borello@fabianogroup.com
Web site: http://www.2020europe.eu
Publisher: Fabiano Srl
Date Established: 1989
Frequency: 5 issues yearly
Annual Sub.: EUR100.00
Circulation: 26,900 (Publisher's Statement)
Editor: Clodagh Norton; **Advertising Manager:** Chiara Borello

Summary of Content: Magazine covering international fashion, new products, retailing and business news.
Language(s): English; French; German; Italian; Spanish
Readership/Target Audience: Read by optical retailers throughout Europe.
ADVERTISING RATES:
Full Page Colour EUR7900.00
Mechanical Data: Bleed Size: 306 x 236mm, Trim Size: 300 x 230mm, Film: Digital
BUSINESS: HEALTH & MEDICAL: Optics

24HOUSING
1864052U32G-182

Editorial Address: Fortis et Fides, Whitestone Business Park, Whitestone, HEREFORD, HR1 3SE **Tel:** 01432 852522
Email: michelle.pacey@24dash.com
Web site: http://www.24dash.com/magazine
Publisher: allpay.net Ltd
Frequency: Monthly
Cover Price: £3.95
Annual Sub.: £47.50
Editor: Jane Gething-Lewis
Summary of Content: Magazine focusing on social housing including in-depth reports, interviews and news about the sector.
Readership/Target Audience: Aimed at housing professionals.
BUSINESS: LOCAL GOVERNMENT, LEISURE & RECREATION: Community Care & Social Services

3G SOLUTIONS FOR OPERATORS
624119U18B-60

Formerly: 3G Strategies for Operators
Editorial Address: PO Box 23, DURSLEY, GL11 5WA
Tel: 01453 861390 **Fax:** 01453 860483
Email: info@kavamedia.com
Advertising Address: As above.
Email: richard@kavamedia.com
Web site: http://www.kavamedia.com/3gsolutions
ISSN: 1470-6474
Publisher: Kava Media
Date Established: 2000
Frequency: Quarterly
Cover Price: Free
Circulation: 26,500 (Publisher's Statement)
Usual Pagination: 36
Editor: Richard Kennedy; **Advertising Manager:** Richard Kennedy
Summary of Content: Magazine examining the evolution of 3G business models, development of revenue streams and UMTS roll out and how companies achieve differentiation in the marketplace.
Readership/Target Audience: Aimed at global network operators.
ADVERTISING: Rates on application
BUSINESS: ELECTRONICS: Telecommunications

3 G WIRELESS BROADBAND
1601521U18B-1940

Formerly: Wireless Broadband Analyst
Editorial Address: Mortimer House, 37-41 Mortimer Street, LONDON, W1T 3JH **Tel:** 020 7017 5000 **Fax:** 020 7017 5418
Email: julian.bright@informa.com
Web site: http://www.baskervilletelecoms.com/planetwireless
ISSN: 1474-5666
Publisher: T&F Informa Group PLC
Date Established: 2001
Frequency: 26 issues yearly
Annual Sub.: £1495.00
Usual Pagination: 24
Editor: Julian Bright; **Publisher:** Mark Newman
Summary of Content: Newsletter covering Bluetooth, WLAN and the Wireless Enterprise with wireless strategies and solutions and the latest platforms, applications and technologies.
Readership/Target Audience: Aimed at high level IT and wireless executives.
ADVERTISING: No Advertising taken
BUSINESS: ELECTRONICS: Telecommunications

5 TO 7 EDUCATOR
704848U62C-170

Formerly: Five to Eleven
Editorial Address: St. Judes Church, Dulwich Road, LONDON, SE24 0PB **Tel:** 020 7738 5454
Fax: 020 7733 2325
Email: sonali@markallengroup.com
Advertising Address: As above. **Fax:** 020 7326 4835
Email: matt@markallengroup.com
Web site: http://www.fivetoseven.co.uk
ISSN: 1473-4044
Publisher: MA Education Ltd
Date Established: 2001
Frequency: Monthly - Published on 2nd Tuesday of the month prior cover date
Cover Price: £3.99

Free to qualifying individuals
Annual Sub.: £54.00
Circulation: 16,000 (Publisher's Statement)
Usual Pagination: 68
Editor: Sonali Hindmarch
Summary of Content: Publication covering all aspects of the National Curriculum including practical and helpful information on training, special needs and child health. Also contains book reviews.
Readership/Target Audience: Aimed at professionals working in key stage 1 education.
ADVERTISING RATES:
Full Page Mono £995.00
Full Page Colour £995.00
Agency Commission: 10%
Mechanical Data: Type Area: 262 x 195mm, Bleed Size: 303 x 236mm, Trim Size: 297 x 230mm, Col Length: 262mm, Page Width: 195mm, Film: Digital, Print Process: Litho
Copy instructions: Copy Date: 2 weeks prior to publication date
Average advertising content per issue: 20%
BUSINESS: CHURCH & SCHOOL EQUIPMENT & EDUCATION: Junior Education

8020 EUROPA
1799612U5R-688

Editorial Address: 3rd Floor, Armstrong House, 38 Market Square, UXBRIDGE, UB8 1TG **Tel:** 01895 454595
Email: john.garratt@8020europa.com
Advertising Address: As above. **Fax:** 01895 454598
Email: john.chapman@iteuropa.com
Web site: http://www.8020europa.com
Publisher: BPL Business Media Ltd
Date Established: 2006
Frequency: 10 issues yearly - Published the 1st week of the cover month
Cover Price: Free
Circulation: 20,000 (Publisher's Statement)
Usual Pagination: 64
Editor: John Garratt; **Advertising Manager:** John Chapman
Summary of Content: Magazine focusing on the key issues affecting the European IT market and the primary channels that serve it. Features industry and marketing news and tracks key developments in marketing, regulations, legislation, finance, recruitment and training.
Language(s): English; French; German; Italian; Spanish
Readership/Target Audience: Aimed at directors in ICT channel organisations, vendors, resellers and developers.
ADVERTISING RATES:
Full Page Colour EUR5625.00
Agency Commission: 10%
Mechanical Data: Type Area: 265 x 185mm, Bleed Size: 303 x 216mm, Trim Size: 297 x 210mm, Col Length: 265mm, Page Width: 185mm, Film: Digital
Copy instructions: Copy Date: 2 weeks prior to publication date
Average advertising content per issue: 25%
BUSINESS: COMPUTERS & AUTOMATION: Computers Related

AA FILES
35809U4A-10

Editorial Address: 36 Bedford Square, LONDON, WC1B 3ES **Tel:** 020 7887 4000 **Fax:** 020 7414 0783
Email: weaver_to@aaschool.ac.uk
Web site: http://www.aaschool.ac.uk
ISSN: 0261-6823
Publisher: Architectural Association
Date Established: 1982
Frequency: Half-yearly
Annual Sub.: £32.00
Circulation: 3,500 (Publisher's Statement)
Usual Pagination: 88
Editor: Thomas Weaver; **Circulation Manager:** Kirsten Morphet
Summary of Content: Journal containing the history and theory of architecture, art and design, contemporary projects, exhibition reviews and book reviews.
Readership/Target Audience: Aimed at architects, teachers and students of architecture and design.
ADVERTISING: No Advertising taken
BUSINESS: ARCHITECTURE & BUILDING: Architecture

ABC AND D ARCHITECT BUILDER CONTRACTOR & DEVELOPER
35880U4E-20

Editorial Address: 2 Sugar Brook Court, Aston Road, BROMSGROVE, B60 3EX **Tel:** 01527 834451
Fax: 01527 574388
Email: claire.mackle@centaur.co.uk
Advertising Address: As above. **Fax:** 01527 834482
Email: angela.joel@centaur.co.uk
Web site: http://www.abc-d.co.uk
Publisher: Centaur Business Intelligence
Date Established: 1988
Frequency: Monthly - Published in the 1st week of the cover month
Cover Price: Free
Circulation: 21,000 (ABC 01/07/2008 to 30/06/2009)

Usual Pagination: 84
Editor: Claire Mackle
Summary of Content: Magazine covering news, features and product reviews for building industry professionals.
Readership/Target Audience: Read primarily by architectural practices, larger building contractors and professionals who specify in building products.
ADVERTISING RATES:
Full Page Mono £1400.00
Full Page Colour £1900.00
Mechanical Data: Type Area: 267 x 190mm, Bleed Size: 303 x 216mm, Trim Size: 297 x 210mm, Film: Digital, Col Length: 267mm, Page Width: 190mm
Copy instructions: Copy Date: 5 weeks prior to publication date
Supplement(s): Heating, Ventilation and Energy Efficiency - 1xY, Housebuilder - 1xY
BUSINESS: ARCHITECTURE & BUILDING: Building

ABERDEEN AND GRAMPIAN CHAMBER OF COMMERCE BUSINESS BULLETIN
41433U63D-12

Formerly: Aberdeen Chamber of Commerce Business Bulletin
Editorial Address: Greenhole Place, Bridge of Don Industrial Estate, ABERDEEN, AB23 8EU **Tel:** 01224 343900
Fax: 01224 343943
Email: business.bulletin@agcc.co.uk
Advertising Address: As above.
Email: gary.boyd@agcc.co.uk
Web site: http://www.agcc.co.uk
Publisher: Aberdeen and Grampian Chamber of Commerce
Frequency: 10 issues yearly
Annual Sub.: £30.00
Circulation: 7,000 (Publisher's Statement)
Usual Pagination: 44
Editor: Kate Yuill
Summary of Content: Chamber of Commerce update including information and advice on business issues, members' news and training and international trade news.
Readership/Target Audience: Read by Aberdeen and Grampian Chamber of Commerce members and the local business community.
ADVERTISING RATES:
Full Page Colour £750.00
Agency Commission: 10%
Mechanical Data: Bleed Size: 301 x 214mm, Trim Size: 297 x 210mm, Film: Digital
Average advertising content per issue: 25%
BUSINESS: REGIONAL BUSINESS: Regional Business Scotland

ABERDEEN PETROLEUM REPORT
38568U33-1_5

Editorial Address: Unit 12, Wellheads Crescent Industrial Estate, Wellheads Crescent, ABERDEEN, AB21 7GA
Tel: 0870 438 0001 **Fax:** 0870 438 0002
Email: info@aproil.co.uk
ISSN: 0263-5054
Publisher: Aberdeen Petroleum Publishing Ltd
Date Established: 1981
Frequency: Weekly
Annual Sub.: £600.00
Usual Pagination: 12
Editor: Kevin Daley
Summary of Content: Newsletter covering North Sea, Atlantic margin and North West European upstream oil and gas.
Readership/Target Audience: Aimed at people working within the oil and gas industry.
ADVERTISING: No Advertising taken
Supplement(s): Features List - 3xY
BUSINESS: OIL & PETROLEUM

ABERDEEN-ANGUS REVIEW
37852U21D-50

Editorial Address: Pedigree House, 6 King's Place, PERTH, PH2 8AD **Tel:** 01738 622477 **Fax:** 01738 636436
Email: info@aberdeen-angus.co.uk
Advertising Address: 11 Sunnyside Gardens, DRUMOAK, AB31 5EZ **Tel:** 01330 811616 **Fax:** 01330 811616
Email: info@aberdeen-angus.co.uk
Publisher: Aberdeen-Angus Cattle Society
Date Established: 1923
Frequency: Annual - Published in January
Cover Price: £6.00
Circulation: 4,000 (Publisher's Statement)
Usual Pagination: 120
Editor: Eddie Gillanders
Summary of Content: Journal containing news, features and technical articles on the breeding of Aberdeen-Angus cattle.
Readership/Target Audience: Aimed at all members and breeders within the UK and some abroad.
ADVERTISING RATES:
Full Page Mono £325.00
Full Page Colour £375.00

Agency Commission: 10%
Mechanical Data: Type Area: 265 x 185mm, Print Process: Litho, Col Length: 265mm, Page Width: 185mm, Bleed Size: +3mm, Trim Size: 297 x 210mm, Film: Digital
Copy instructions: Copy Date: November 1st
Average advertising content per issue: 50%
BUSINESS: AGRICULTURE & FARMING: Livestock

ABSOLUTE RETURN
1776139U1F-629

Editorial Address: Nestor House, Playhouse Yard, LONDON, EC4V 5EX **Tel:** 020 7779 7330
Fax: 020 7779 7331
Email: info@hedgefundintelligence.com
Advertising Address: As above.
Email: jwillis@hedgefundintelligence.com
Web site: http://www.hedgefundintelligence.com
Publisher: Hedge Fund Intelligence
Date Established: 2003
Frequency: 10 issues yearly - July/August and December/January are joint issues
Annual Sub.: £950.00
Usual Pagination: 52
Editor: Neil Wilson; **Advertising Manager:** John Willis
Summary of Content: Magazine containing news and analysis on new US fund launches, interviews with industry leaders, analysis of trends, US performance data and strategy analysis.
Readership/Target Audience: Aimed at qualified investors and industry professionals.
ADVERTISING RATES:
Full Page Mono $10000.00
Mechanical Data: Type Area: 236 x 175mm, Bleed Size: 278 x 211mm, Trim Size: 272 x 205mm, Col Length: 236mm, Page Width: 175mm, Film: Digital
Copy instructions: Copy Date: 17th of the month prior to publication date
BUSINESS: FINANCE & ECONOMICS: Investment

ABTA GOLF
759569U50-4_50

Editorial Address: 197-199 City Road, LONDON, EC1V 1JN
Tel: 020 7253 9906 **Fax:** 020 7253 9907
Email: editorial@abtamagazine.co.uk
Advertising Address: As above. **Fax:** 020 7253 9909
Email: tania@abtamagazine.co.uk
Web site: http://www.absolutepublishing.com
Publisher: Absolute Publishing Ltd
Date Established: 1997
Frequency: Annual - Published in December
Free to qualifying individuals
Circulation: 250 (Publisher's Statement)
Editor: Glen Mutel; **Managing Director:** Matthew Jackson;
Advertising Manager: Tania Kreindler
Summary of Content: Publication promoting golf clubs, resorts, destinations and hotels, which cater for golfers and their families to the travel trade.
Readership/Target Audience: Read by ABTA travel agents and tour operators as well as those attending the International Golf Travel Market.
ADVERTISING RATES:
Full Page Colour £8750.00
Agency Commission: 10%
Mechanical Data: Type Area: 261 x 177mm, Col Length: 261mm, Trim Size: 297 x 210mm, Bleed Size: 307 x 220mm, Page Width: 177mm, Film: Digital
Copy instructions: Copy Date: September 4th
Average advertising content per issue: 40%
BUSINESS: TRAVEL & TOURISM

ABTA MAGAZINE
39712U50-5

Editorial Address: 197-199 City Road, LONDON, EC1V 1JN
Tel: 020 7253 9906 **Fax:** 020 77253 9907
Email: editorial@absolutepublishing.com
Advertising Address: As above. **Fax:** 020 7253 9907
Email: sales@abtamagazine.co.uk
Web site: http://www.absolutepublishing.com/travel/abtamagazine/tabid/62/Default.aspx
Publisher: Absolute Publishing Ltd
Date Established: 1997
Frequency: Monthly - Published on the 1st Monday of the cover month
Free to qualifying individuals
Annual Sub.: £26.00
Circulation: 12,413 (ABC 01/07/2008 to 30/06/2009)
Usual Pagination: 146
Editor: Pat Riddell; **Managing Director:** Matthew Jackson;
Publisher: Peter Levinger
Summary of Content: Travel trade magazine featuring membership news and travel features.
Readership/Target Audience: Aimed at members of ABTA, travel agents, tour operators and corporate travel planners.
ADVERTISING RATES:
Full Page Colour £5150.00
Agency Commission: 10%
Mechanical Data: Film: Digital, Type Area: 261 x 177mm, Col Length: 261mm, Page Width: 177mm, Bleed Size: 307 x 220mm, Trim Size: 297 x 210mm

---

Copy instructions: Copy Date: 10th of month prior to publication date
Average advertising content per issue: 35%
Supplement(s): Croatia - 1xY, Gay & Lesbian - 1xY, Iceland - 1xY, India - 1xY, Indian Ocean - 1xY, Jordan - 1xY, Lithuania - 1xY, Malta - 1xY, Middle East - 1xY, Oman - 1xY
BUSINESS: TRAVEL & TOURISM

ACB NEWS
39941U55-3

Editorial Address: Dept. Clinical Biochemistry, City Hospital, Dudley Road, BIRMINGHAM, B18 7QH
Tel: 0121 507 5353 **Fax:** 0121 765 4224
Email: editor.acbnews@acb.org.uk
Advertising Address: PRC Associates Ltd, The Annexe, Fitznells Manor, Chessington Road, EWELL, KT17 1TF
Tel: 020 8786 7376 **Fax:** 020 8786 7262
Email: mail@prcassoc.co.uk
Web site: http://www.acb.org.uk
ISSN: 0141-8912
Publisher: PRC Associates Ltd
Date Established: 1950
Frequency: Monthly
Annual Sub.: £24.00
Circulation: 2,750 (Publisher's Statement)
Usual Pagination: 32
Editor: Jonathan Berg
Summary of Content: Magazine containing technical information as well as Association news and coming events.
Readership/Target Audience: Read by qualified clinical biochemists, NHS scientists and medical consultants in the UK and overseas hospital laboratories.
ADVERTISING RATES:
Full Page Mono £590.00
Full Page Colour £1210.00
Agency Commission: 10%
Mechanical Data: Film: Digital, Type Area: 210 x 153mm, Bleed Size: 246 x 181mm, Trim Size: 240 x 175mm, Col Length: 210mm, Page Width: 153mm
Copy instructions: Copy Date: 10th of the month prior to publication date
Average advertising content per issue: 30%
BUSINESS: APPLIED SCIENCE & LABORATORIES

ACCESS ALL AREAS
35628U2C-10

Editorial Address: 1 Canada Square, 19th Floor, Canary Wharf, LONDON, E14 5AP **Tel:** 020 7772 8300
Fax: 020 7772 8596
Email: nic.howden@oceanmedia.co.uk
Advertising Address: Bank House, 23 Warwick Road, COVENTRY, CV1 2EW **Tel:** 024 7657 1171
Fax: 024 7657 1172
Email: michelle.tayton@oceanmedia.co.uk
Web site: http://www.access-aa.co.uk
Publisher: Ocean Media Group Ltd
Date Established: 1993
Frequency: 10 issues yearly - Published on the 18th of the month prior to cover month
Free to qualifying individuals
Annual Sub.: £45.00
Circulation: 7,500 (Publisher's Statement)
Usual Pagination: 40
Editor: Nic Howden; **Managing Director:** Trevor Barratt
Summary of Content: Magazine covering events, industry news and legislative issues.
Readership/Target Audience: Read by events organisers, council entertainment officers, personnel and marketing managers.
ADVERTISING RATES:
Full Page Colour £2200.00
Agency Commission: 10%
Mechanical Data: Film: Digital; Type Area: 395 x 272mm, Bleed Size: 426 x 303mm, Col Length: 395mm, Page Width: 272mm
Copy instructions: Copy Date: 1st of the month prior to publication date
Average advertising content per issue: 40%
BUSINESS: COMMUNICATIONS, ADVERTISING & MARKETING: Conferences & Exhibitions

---

ACCESS INTERNATIONAL
39082U42R-20

Editorial Address: Southfields, Southview Road, WADHURST, TN5 6TP **Tel:** 01892 784088
Fax: 01892 786257
Email: murray.pollok@khl.com
Advertising Address: As above. **Fax:** 01892 784086
Email: wil.holloway@khl.com
Web site: http://www.khl.com
ISSN: 1352-7517
Publisher: KHL Group
Date Established: 1994
Frequency: 8 issues yearly - Published in the 2nd week of the cover month
Cover Price: £8.00
Free to qualifying individuals
Annual Sub.: £85.00
Circulation: 8,024 (Publisher's Statement)
Usual Pagination: 52

Business Magazines

Editor: Maria Hadlow; **Managing Editor:** Murray Pollok; **Publisher:** James King
Summary of Content: Magazine covering the worldwide aerial work platform industry, focusing on the use of powered aerial work platforms and non-powered access equipment including scaffolding. Also the official magazine of the International Powered Access Federation (IPAF).
Readership/Target Audience: Read by buyers and users of all types of access equipment, including powered aerial platforms and scaffolding.
ADVERTISING RATES:
Full Page Colour £3400.00
Agency Commission: 10%
Mechanical Data: Page Width: 184mm, Type Area: 268 x 184mm, Col Length: 268mm, Trim Size: 297 x 210mm, Bleed Size: 303 x 216mm, Film: Digital
Copy instructions: Copy Date: 3 weeks prior to publication date
Average advertising content per issue: 60%
Supplement(s): Access Yearbook - 1xY
BUSINESS: CONSTRUCTION: Construction Related

ACCESS JOURNAL　　　　1646091U4R-617
Editorial Address: 105 Judd Street, LONDON, WC1H 9NE
Tel: 020 7391 2002 **Fax:** 020 7387 7109
Email: henry.french@rnib.org.uk
Web site: http://www.rnib.org.uk
Publisher: Royal National Institute of the Blind
Date Established: 2000
Frequency: Quarterly
Annual Sub.: £20.00
Circulation: 450 (Publisher's Statement)
Usual Pagination: 32
Editor: Henry French
Summary of Content: Journal focusing on accessible environments. Includes up-to-date news on policy, legislation, research and environmental developments in the field of buildings, streets and transport.
Readership/Target Audience: Aimed at access groups, architects, surveyors, building managers and owners of small businesses.
ADVERTISING: No Advertising taken
BUSINESS: ARCHITECTURE & BUILDING: Building Related

ACCESS YEARBOOK　　　　600989U42R-30
Editorial Address: For all contact details see main record, Access International
Frequency: Annual - Published in December
Language(s): Chinese; English; French; German; Italian; Spanish
Mechanical Data: Type Area: 268 x 184mm, Col Length: 268mm, Film: Digital, Bleed Size: 303 x 216mm, Trim Size: 297 x 210mm, Page Width: 184mm
Copy instructions: Copy Date: 3 weeks prior to publication date
Supplement to: Access International
BUSINESS: CONSTRUCTION: Construction Related

ACCOMMODATION MANAGEMENT
　　　　36584U11A-123
Formerly: Housekeeping Today
Editorial Address: 2 Cheltenham Mount, HARROGATE, HG1 1DL **Tel:** 01423 569676 **Fax:** 01423 569677
Email: kate@pelgrp.com
Advertising Address: As above.
Email: debbie@pelgrp.com
Web site: http://www.amuk.info
Publisher: Pelican Magazines Ltd
Date Established: 1991
Frequency: Quarterly - Published in the middle of the 2nd cover month
Free to qualifying individuals
Annual Sub.: £26.00
Circulation: 5,000 (Publisher's Statement)
Usual Pagination: 36
Editor: Kate Jackson; **Group Editor:** Leslie Charneca
Summary of Content: Journal of the UK Housekeepers Association (UKHA), covering senior executive housekeepers in hotels, private hospitals and residential educational establishments.
Readership/Target Audience: Aimed at those within the housekeeping profession and accommodation management.
ADVERTISING RATES:
Full Page Colour £895.00
Agency Commission: 10%
Mechanical Data: Trim Size: 297 x 210mm, Bleed Size: 303 x 213mm, Film: Digital
Average advertising content per issue: 40%
BUSINESS: CATERING: Catering, Hotels & Restaurants

ACCOUNTANCY　　　　35026U1B-10
Editorial Address: 145 London Road, KINGSTON UPON THAMES, KT2 6SR **Tel:** 020 8247 1389 **Fax:** 020 8247 1424
Email: accountancynews@cch.co.uk

Advertising Address: As above. **Tel:** 020 8247 1350
Fax: 020 8247 1388
Email: mark.cleeve@cch.co.uk
Web site: http://www.accountancymagazine.com
ISSN: 0001-4664
Publisher: Wolters Kluwer (UK) Ltd
Date Established: 1889
Frequency: Monthly
Annual Sub.: £77.20
Circulation: 153,169 (ABC 01/07/2008 to 30/06/2009)
Usual Pagination: 128
Editor: Sally Percy; **Features Editor:** Penny Sukhraj
Summary of Content: Journal covering articles on accounting developments, auditing, finance, profit improvement, taxation, financial law, technology business and management.
Readership/Target Audience: Aimed at chartered accountants and finance professionals.
ADVERTISING RATES:
Full Page Colour £10145.00
Agency Commission: 10%
Mechanical Data: Type Area: 270 x 200mm, Col Length: 270mm, Film: Positive, right reading, emulsion side down. Digital, No. of Columns (Display): 4, Bleed Size: 303 x 216mm, Trim Size: 297 x 210mm, Page Width: 200mm, Print Process: Web-fed offset litho
Copy instructions: Copy Date: 4 weeks prior to publication date
Average advertising content per issue: 50%
Supplement(s): Finance Directors - 4xY, Practice Matters - 2xY
BUSINESS: FINANCE & ECONOMICS: Accountancy

ACCOUNTANCY AGE　　　　35027U1B-15
Editorial Address: 32-34 Broadwick Street, LONDON, W1A 2HG **Tel:** 020 7316 9000 **Fax:** 020 7316 9250
Email: news@accountancyage.com
Advertising Address: As above. **Fax:** 020 7316 9350
Email: kevin.sinclair@incisivemedia.com
Web site: http://www.accountancyage.com
ISSN: 0001-4672
Publisher: Incisive Media
Date Established: 1969
Frequency: Weekly
Free to qualifying individuals
Annual Sub.: £100.00
Circulation: 56,794 (ABC 01/07/2007 to 30/06/2008)
Usual Pagination: 40
Editor: Rachael Singh; **Features Editor:** Kevin Reed
Summary of Content: Journal containing news of developments in accountancy, finance, business, taxation and computer programs. Includes features on business recovery, consultancy, corporate finance, human resources, audit and networking.
Twitter: http://twitter.com/accountancyage.
Readership/Target Audience: Aimed at fully qualified accountants working in the UK.
ADVERTISING RATES:
Full Page Colour £5640.00
SCC £47.00
Agency Commission: 10%
Mechanical Data: Film: Digital
Copy instructions: Copy Date: 1 week prior to publication date
Supplement(s): Best Practice - 11xY, Management Briefings - 12xY, Young Professional - 11xY
BUSINESS: FINANCE & ECONOMICS: Accountancy

THE ACCOUNTANT　　　　601014U1B-21
Editorial Address: The Colonnades, 34 Porchester Road, LONDON, W2 6ES **Tel:** 020 7563 5631 **Fax:** 020 7563 5601
Email: arvind.hickman@vrlknowledgebank.com
Web site: http://www.worldaccountingintelligence.com
Publisher: VRL Knowledge Bank Ltd
Frequency: Monthly
Annual Sub.: £777.00
Usual Pagination: 20
Editor: Carolyn Canham
Summary of Content: Newsletter covering a mixture of news, analysis and interviews. Includes country surveys and reports on the development of accounting standards and practices worldwide.
Readership/Target Audience: Aimed at accountants.
ADVERTISING: No Advertising taken
BUSINESS: FINANCE & ECONOMICS: Accountancy

ACCOUNTING & BUSINESS　　　　35029U1B-25
Editorial Address: 29 Lincoln's Inn Fields, LONDON, WC2A 3EE **Tel:** 020 7059 5966 **Fax:** 020 7059 5771
Email: chris.quick@accaglobal.com
Advertising Address: Educate Ltd, 91-93 Southwark Street, LONDON, SE1 0HX **Tel:** 020 7902 1200
Email: lisa.peake@accaglobal.com
Web site: http://www.accaglobal.com
ISSN: 1460-406X
Publisher: Certified Accountants Publications Limited
Date Established: 1998

Frequency: 10 issues yearly - Combined issues published July/August and November/December
Free to qualifying individuals
Annual Sub.: £85.00
Circulation: 127,734 (ABC 01/07/2007 to 30/06/2008)
Usual Pagination: 88
Editor: Chris Quick; **Advertising Manager:** Lisa Peake
Summary of Content: Magazine with articles that cover business and professional developments worldwide.
Twitter: http://twitter.com/ACCANews.
Readership/Target Audience: Aimed at members of ACCA, corporations, executive agencies, professional partnerships and international bodies, accountants and finance professionals.
ADVERTISING RATES:
Full Page Colour £7950.00
Agency Commission: 10%
Mechanical Data: Type Area: 237 x 190mm, Bleed Size: 280 x 220mm, Trim Size: 275 x 215mm, Col Length: 237mm, Film: Digital, Page Width: 190mm
Copy instructions: Copy Date: 18th of the month prior to publication date
Average advertising content per issue: 30%
BUSINESS: FINANCE & ECONOMICS: Accountancy

ACCOUNTING & BUSINESS RESEARCH
　　　　35049U1B-26
Editorial Address: University of Edinburgh Business School, William Robertson Building, 50 George Square, EDINBURGH, EH8 9JY **Tel:** 0131 651 5245
Fax: 0131 650 8337
Email: abr-editor@ed.ac.uk
Web site: http://www.abr-journal.com
ISSN: 0001-4788
Publisher: Wolters Kluwer (UK) Ltd
Date Established: 1970
Frequency: Quarterly - A specials issue is published once a year
Annual Sub.: £50.00
Usual Pagination: 90
Editor: Pauline Weetman
Summary of Content: Publication containing research studies concerned with accountancy and related disciplines.
Readership/Target Audience: Aimed primarily at teachers of accounting in universities and libraries.
ADVERTISING: No Advertising taken
BUSINESS: FINANCE & ECONOMICS: Accountancy

ACCOUNTING, AUDITING & ACCOUNTABILITY JOURNAL　　　　20152U1B-33
Editorial Address: Howard House, Wagon Lane, BINGLEY, BD16 1WA **Tel:** 01274 777700 **Fax:** 01274 785200
Email: slinacre@emeraldinsight.com
Web site: http://www.emeraldinsight.com
ISSN: 0951-3574
Publisher: Emerald Group Publishing Ltd
Date Established: 1988
Frequency: 6 issues yearly
Usual Pagination: 120
Editor: Simon Linacre; **Publisher:** Simon Linacre
Summary of Content: Journal exploring the philosophies and traditions that underpin the accounting profession.
Readership/Target Audience: Read by accounting and management researchers, undergraduate and postgraduate students, accounting and auditing policy makers.
ADVERTISING: No Advertising taken
BUSINESS: FINANCE & ECONOMICS: Accountancy

ACCOUNTING TECHNICIAN　　　　35031U1B-43
Editorial Address: The Pall Mall Deposit, 124-128 Barlby Road, LONDON, W10 6BL **Tel:** 020 8962 3020
Fax: 020 8962 8689
Email: aat@thinkpublishing.co.uk
Web site: http://www.accountingtechnician.co.uk
ISSN: 1358-6297
Publisher: Think Publishing Ltd
Date Established: 1999
Frequency: 11 issues yearly - Combined issues December/January
Cover Price: £2.95
Free to qualifying individuals
Circulation: 113,000 (Publisher's Statement)
Usual Pagination: 56
Editor: Sarah Notton; **News Editor:** Matt Packer
Summary of Content: Magazine covering business, accounting and training issues affecting accounting professionals.
Readership/Target Audience: Read by members and students of the Association of Accounting Technicians.
ADVERTISING: No Advertising taken
BUSINESS: FINANCE & ECONOMICS: Accountancy

ACE DIRECTORY
37565U19A-20

Editorial Address: Alliance House, 12 Caxton Street, LONDON, SW1H 0QL **Tel:** 020 7222 6557
Fax: 020 7222 0750
Email: awalker@acenet.co.uk
Advertising Address: Hardy Publishing Ltd, New Loom House, 101 Back Church Lane, LONDON, E1 1LU
Tel: 020 7709 0303 **Fax:** 020 7709 1227
Email: jennifer@thehardygroup.co.uk
Web site: http://www.acenet.co.uk
ISSN: 1351-3672
Publisher: Association for consultancy and engineering
Date Established: 1993
Frequency: Annual
Annual Sub.: £35.00
Circulation: 5,000 (Publisher's Statement)
Usual Pagination: 300
Editor: Andy Walker; **Advertising Manager:** Danny Henderson; **Advertising Director:** Jennifer Allen
Summary of Content: Directory containing details of ACE firms that lists by area, name and engineering discipline.
Readership/Target Audience: Aimed at people wishing to use the services of a consulting engineer.
ADVERTISING RATES:
Full Page Colour £1100.00
Agency Commission: 10%
Mechanical Data: Type Area: 250 x 176mm, Bleed Size: +3mm, Trim Size: 297 x 210mm, Page Width: 176mm, Film: Digital, Col Length: 250mm
Copy instructions: Copy Date: January 1st
Average advertising content per issue: 95%
BUSINESS: ENGINEERING & MACHINERY

ACOUSTICS BULLETIN
39942U55-5

Editorial Address: 39 Garners Lane, STOCKPORT, SK3 8SD **Tel:** 0161 487 2225 **Fax:** 0871 994 1778
Email: ian@acia-acoustics.co.uk
Advertising Address: 77A St. Peters Street, ST. ALBANS, AL1 3BN **Tel:** 01727 848195 **Fax:** 01727 850553
Email: ioa@ioa.org.uk
Web site: http://www.ioa.org.uk
Publisher: Institute of Acoustics
Date Established: 1976
Frequency: 6 issues yearly
Cover Price: £25.00
Annual Sub.: £120.00
Circulation: 2,600 (Publisher's Statement)
Editor: Ian Bennett; **Advertising Manager:** Dennis Baylis
Summary of Content: Journal of the Institute of Acoustics. Covering all aspects of acoustics and the wide range of applications which it embraces.
Readership/Target Audience: Aimed at Institute members.
ADVERTISING RATES:
Full Page Mono £800.00
Full Page Colour £800.00
Agency Commission: 10%
Mechanical Data: Print Process: Litho, Type Area: 254 x 184mm, Film: Digital, Col Length: 254mm, Trim Size: 297 x 210mm, Page Width: 184mm
Copy instructions: Copy Date: 4 weeks prior to publication date
Average advertising content per issue: 25%
BUSINESS: APPLIED SCIENCE & LABORATORIES

THE ACQUIRER
34904U1A-15

Editorial Address: 198 Kings Road, LONDON, SW3 5XP
Tel: 020 7368 7199
Email: sr1@caspianpublishing.co.uk
Advertising Address: As above.
Web site: http://www.caspianpublishing.co.uk
ISSN: 0966-7784
Publisher: Caspian Publishing
Frequency: 3 issues yearly
Free to qualifying individuals
Circulation: 30,000 (Publisher's Statement)
Usual Pagination: 20
Editor: Stuart Rock; **Publisher:** Mike Bokaie
Summary of Content: Corporate finance magazine from Livingstone Guarantee, covering acquisitions and mergers.
Readership/Target Audience: Aimed at small to medium businesses.
ADVERTISING: No Advertising taken
BUSINESS: FINANCE & ECONOMICS

ACQUISITION FINANCE
1663651U1A-306

Editorial Address: 28 Sandford Street, LICHFIELD, WS13 6QA **Tel:** 0870 242 7021 **Fax:** 0870 242 7023
Email: editorial@amgl.co.uk
Advertising Address: As above.
Email: jason.wynn@amgl.co.uk
Web site: http://www.amgl.co.uk
Publisher: Assertive Media Group Limited
Date Established: 2003
Frequency: Monthly
Annual Sub.: £59.00
Circulation: 7,114 (Publisher's Statement)

Usual Pagination: 60
Editor: Charlotte Abbott
Summary of Content: Magazine covering corporate finance matters, transactions and current affairs.
Readership/Target Audience: Aimed at dealmakers and advisers.
ADVERTISING RATES:
Full Page Mono .,...................................... £1980.00
Full Page Colour £1980.00
Agency Commission: 10%
Mechanical Data: Film: Digital
Average advertising content per issue: 40%
BUSINESS: FINANCE & ECONOMICS

ACQUISITIONS MONTHLY
34905U1A-20

Editorial Address: Aldgate House, 33 Aldgate High Street, LONDON, EC3N 1DL **Tel:** 020 7369 7000
Fax: 020 7369 7585
Email: henry.gibbon@thomsonreuters.com
Advertising Address: As above. **Fax:** 020 7369 7766
Email: stephen.howard@thomsonreuters.com
Web site: http://www.aqm-e.com
ISSN: 0952-3618
Publisher: Thomson Reuters
Frequency: Monthly - Published around the 1st of the cover month
Annual Sub.: £489.00
Circulation: 21,000 (Publisher's Statement)
Editor: Henry Gibbon; **Editor-in-Chief:** Henry Gibbon;
Managing Director: Elly Hardwick; **Advertising Director:** Stephen Howard
Summary of Content: Guide to international mergers, acquisitions and management buyouts, with in-depth analysis and profiles.
Readership/Target Audience: Read by business financial executives, company directors, merchant bankers, lawyers, accountants and advisers.
ADVERTISING RATES:
Full Page Mono £5200.00
Full Page Colour £5200.00
Agency Commission: 10%
Mechanical Data: Film: Digital, Type Area: 260 x 175mm, Col Length: 260mm, Page Width: 175mm, Trim Size: 297 x 210mm, Bleed Size: 303 x 216mm
Copy instructions: Copy Date: 1 week prior to publication date
Average advertising content per issue: 13%
Supplement(s): MBO - 1xY
BUSINESS: FINANCE & ECONOMICS

ACR NEWS
35763U3C-7

Formerly: AC & R News
Editorial Address: Faversham House, 232A Addington Road, SOUTH CROYDON, CR2 8LE **Tel:** 020 8651 7100
Fax: 020 8651 7117
Email: neil.everitt@fav-house.com
Advertising Address: As above.
Email: jan.thorpe@fav-house.com
Web site: http://www.acr-news.com
ISSN: 0266-6871
Publisher: Faversham House Group Ltd
Date Established: 1984
Frequency: Monthly
Free to qualifying individuals
Annual Sub.: £49.00
Circulation: 9,480 (ABC 01/01/2008 to 31/12/2008)
Usual Pagination: 60
Editor: Neil Everitt; **Advertising Manager:** Jan Thorpe;
Publisher: Jan Thorpe
Summary of Content: Journal covering all aspects of the air conditioning and refrigeration industry.
Readership/Target Audience: Read by air conditioning and refrigeration operatives and experts.
ADVERTISING RATES:
Full Page Mono £1400.00
Full Page Colour £1800.00
Agency Commission: 10%
Mechanical Data: Col Length: 270mm, Type Area: 270 x 180mm, Page Width: 180mm, Trim Size: 297 x 210mm, Bleed Size: 303 x 216mm, Film: Digital
Copy instructions: Copy Date: 2 weeks prior to publication date
Average advertising content per issue: 60%
BUSINESS: HEATING & VENTILATION: Refrigeration & Ventilation

ACR TODAY
35764U3C-10

Editorial Address: The Maltings, West Street, BOURNE, PE10 9PH **Tel:** 01778 391000 **Fax:** 01778 394748
Email: philc@warnersgroup.co.uk
Advertising Address: As above. **Fax:** 01778 392079
Email: julietg@warnersgroup.co.uk
Web site: http://www.acrtoday.co.uk
ISSN: 0957-7726
Publisher: Warners Group Publications plc
Date Established: 1989

Frequency: Monthly - Published in the 1st week of the cover month
Cover Price: Free
Circulation: 10,765 (ABC 01/01/2008 to 31/12/2008)
Usual Pagination: 52
Editor: Phil Creaney; **Publisher:** Juliet Goss
Summary of Content: Magazine containing news and information on a wide range of refrigeration and air conditioning topics.
Readership/Target Audience: Aimed at air conditioning and refrigeration engineers, consultants, specifiers and end users.
ADVERTISING RATES:
Full Page Mono £1515.00
Full Page Colour £1515.00
Agency Commission: 10%
Mechanical Data: Type Area: 275 x 190mm, Bleed Size: 303 x 216mm, Trim Size: 297 x 210mm, Col Length: 275mm, Film: Digital, Page Width: 190mm
Copy instructions: Copy Date: 4 weeks prior to publication date
Average advertising content per issue: 50%
BUSINESS: HEATING & VENTILATION: Refrigeration & Ventilation

ACTION NETWORK
41427U14A-505

Editorial Address: 2 Alexandra Gate, Ffordd Pengam, CARDIFF, CF24 2SA **Tel:** 029 2089 4888
Fax: 029 2089 4889
Email: actionadcopy@aol.com
Advertising Address: As above.
Email: actionadsales@aol.com
Web site: http://www.actionmag.org
Publisher: Hog Fever Ltd
Date Established: 1996
Frequency: 9 issues yearly
Cover Price: Free
Circulation: 15,000 (Publisher's Statement)
Usual Pagination: 52
Editor: Malcolm Lee; **Advertising Manager:** Penny Lee
Summary of Content: National business magazine covering management strategy, business schools, general news, overseas travel, conservation, celebrities, sport and music.
Readership/Target Audience: Aimed at managers, executives and professionals.
ADVERTISING RATES:
Full Page Colour £2365.00
Agency Commission: 10%
Mechanical Data: Type Area: 276 x 196mm, Col Length: 276mm, Page Width: 196mm, Bleed Size: +5mm, Film: Digital
Copy instructions: Copy Date: 1 week prior to publication date
Average advertising content per issue: 40%
BUSINESS: COMMERCE, INDUSTRY & MANAGEMENT

THE ACTUARY
35100U1A-22

Editorial Address: 32-34 Broadwick Street, LONDON, W1A 2HG **Tel:** 020 7316 9000 **Fax:** 020 7316 9313
Email: philip.harding@incisivemedia.com
Advertising Address: As above.
Email: philip.harding@incisivemedia.com
Web site: http://www.the-actuary.org.uk
ISSN: 0960-457X
Publisher: Incisive Media
Date Established: 1990
Frequency: 11 issues yearly - Published on the last Thursday of the month prior to cover date
Cover Price: £5.00
Free to qualifying individuals
Circulation: 19,964 (ABC 01/07/2008 to 30/06/2009)
Usual Pagination: 68
Editor: Marjorie Ngwenya; **News Editor:** Louisa Lobo;
Features Editor: Tracey Brown; **Advertising Manager:** Philip Harding; **Managing Editor:** Sharon Maguire;
Publisher: Philip Harding
Summary of Content: Magazine representing the actuarial profession within the UK. Includes commercial, financial, and technical advice underpinning the operation of insurance companies, pension funds and other institutions.
Readership/Target Audience: Read by members of the Faculty and Institute of Actuaries and those involved in the Staple Inn Actuarial Society.
ADVERTISING RATES:
Full Page Colour £2520.00
Agency Commission: 10%
Mechanical Data: Film: Digital, Page Width: 180mm, Type Area: 267 x 180mm, Bleed Size: 303 x 216mm, Trim Size: 297 x 210mm, Col Length: 267mm
Copy instructions: Copy Date: 2 weeks prior to publication date
BUSINESS: FINANCE & ECONOMICS

ACW AIR CARGO WEEK
39625U49C-1_20

Formerly: ACW
Editorial Address: Darby House, Bletchingley Road, Merstham, REDHILL, RH1 3TT **Tel:** 01737 645777
Fax: 01737 645888
Email: imj@aircargoweek.com
Advertising Address: As above.
Email: sales@a-zgroup.com
Web site: http://www.azfreight.com
Publisher: A-Z Group Ltd
Date Established: 1998
Frequency: Weekly - Published every Monday
Free to qualifying individuals
Annual Sub.: £100.00
Circulation: 12,032 (ABC 01/01/2008 to 31/12/2008)
Usual Pagination: 16
Editor: Ian Martin Jones
Summary of Content: Newspaper containing global news, analysis of the air cargo industry and a wide range of regional features.
Readership/Target Audience: Aimed at air cargo professionals and those using air cargo services.
ADVERTISING RATES:
Full Page Colour £5200.00
Agency Commission: 10%
Mechanical Data: Type Area: 370 x 270mm, Col Length: 370mm, Page Width: 270mm, Bleed Size: 396 x 296mm, Trim Size: 390 x 290mm
Copy instructions: Copy Date: 1 week prior to publication date
BUSINESS: TRANSPORT: Freight

ADDICTION
24908U56L-2

Editorial Address: National Addiction Centre PO48, 4 Windsor Walk, LONDON, SE5 8AF **Tel:** 020 7848 0452
Fax: 020 7848 5966
Email: gill@addictionjournal.org
Advertising Address: 9600 Garsington Road, Cowley, OXFORD, OX4 2DQ **Tel:** 01865 476271 **Fax:** 01865 471271
Email: joanna.baker@wiley.com
Web site: http://www.addictionjournal.org
ISSN: 0965-2140
Publisher: Wiley-Blackwell Publishing
Date Established: 1884
Frequency: Monthly
Free to qualifying individuals
Annual Sub.: £335.00
Circulation: 1,600 (Publisher's Statement)
Usual Pagination: 180
Editor: Molly Jarvis
Summary of Content: Journal covering all aspects of addiction.
Readership/Target Audience: Read by scientists, practitioners and policy-makers.
ADVERTISING RATES:
Full Page Mono £540.00
Full Page Colour £1300.00
Agency Commission: 10%
Mechanical Data: Trim Size: 276 x 210mm, Type Area: 230 x 170mm, Col Length: 230mm, Page Width: 170mm, Film: Digital, Bleed Size: +6mm
Copy instructions: Copy Date: 6 weeks prior to publication date
BUSINESS: HEALTH & MEDICAL: Disability & Rehabilitation

ADDICTION TODAY
40449U56L-4

Editorial Address: 193 Victoria Street, LONDON, SW1E 5NE **Tel:** 020 7233 5333 **Fax:** 020 7233 8123
Email: editor@addictiontoday.org
Advertising Address: As above. **Tel:** 0845 345 5251
Fax: 0870 836 2388
Email: david@addictiontoday.org
Web site: http://www.addictiontoday.org
ISSN: 1471-5511
Publisher: Addiction Recovery Foundation
Date Established: 1989
Frequency: 6 issues yearly
Free to qualifying individuals
Annual Sub.: £45.00
Circulation: 5,000 (Publisher's Statement)
Usual Pagination: 36
Editor: Deirdre Boyd; **Advertising Manager:** David Leonard
Summary of Content: Magazine containing articles on practical education for all professionals involved in addiction recovery.
Readership/Target Audience: Aimed at treatment providers, purchasers and policy makers throughout the UK.
ADVERTISING RATES:
Full Page Mono £910.00
Full Page Colour £1115.00
Agency Commission: 10%
Mechanical Data: Type Area: 277 x 190mm, Col Length: 277mm, Page Width: 190mm
Copy instructions: Copy Date: 7th of the month prior to publication date
Average advertising content per issue: 20%
BUSINESS: HEALTH & MEDICAL: Disability & Rehabilitation

ADDITIVES FOR POLYMERS
38812U39-1_50

Editorial Address: The Boulevard, Langford Lane, KIDLINGTON, OX5 1GB **Tel:** 01865 843000
Fax: 01865 843971
Email: carolineedser@hotmail.com
Web site: http://www.additivesforpolymer.com
ISSN: 0306-3747
Publisher: Elsevier Ltd
Frequency: Monthly
Usual Pagination: 12
Editor: Caroline Edser
Summary of Content: Newsletter containing details of relevant polymer additives materials and products, new applications, new research and technical developments, company news, market trends, legislation, environment, health and safety issues, new publications and related conferences.
Readership/Target Audience: Read by plastics technologists, senior technical management, personnel in companies manufacturing polymers, polymer equipment, and composites, or supplying the processed raw materials.
ADVERTISING: No Advertising taken
BUSINESS: PLASTICS & RUBBER

ADINEWS
38363U31D-2

Formerly: adiNEWS & Motorcycle Trainer
Editorial Address: The Lansdowne Building, Crowhurst Road, Hollingbury, BRIGHTON, BN1 8AF **Tel:** 01273 566058
Fax: 01273 566059
Email: editorial@adinews.co.uk
Advertising Address: As above. **Tel:** 01273 554102
Email: advertising@adinews.co.uk
Web site: http://www.adinews.co.uk
ISSN: 1471-8685
Publisher: DSN Publishing
Date Established: 2000
Frequency: Monthly
Cover Price: £3.00
Annual Sub.: £30.00
Circulation: 14,000 (Publisher's Statement)
Usual Pagination: 68
Editor: Paul Caddick; **Advertising Manager:** Christie Rigg; **Managing Editor:** Paul Caddick
Summary of Content: Magazine covering all aspects of driving instructor training and road safety, car news, motoring news and industry related news, plus helpful articles on the realities of working as an instructor and trainer.
Readership/Target Audience: Aimed at driving instructors of all levels, driving training professionals and road safety professionals.
ADVERTISING RATES:
Full Page Colour £1980.00
Agency Commission: 10%
Mechanical Data: Bleed Size: 303 x 216mm, Page Width: 190mm, No. of Columns (Display): 4, Type Area: 277 x 190mm, Col Length: 277mm, Trim Size: 297 x 210mm, Film: Digital
Copy instructions: Copy Date: 10 working days prior to publication date
Average advertising content per issue: 32%
BUSINESS: MOTOR TRADE: Driving Schools

ADMAP
35466U2A-20

Editorial Address: Ivory Square, Plantation Wharf, LONDON, SW11 3UE **Tel:** 020 7326 8611
Email: colin.grimshaw@warc.com
Advertising Address: Crown House, 72 Hammersmith Road, LONDON, W14 8TH **Tel:** 020 7470 2442
Fax: 020 7470 2441
Email: clare.beveridge@warc.com
Web site: http://www.admapmagazine.com
ISSN: 0001-8295
Publisher: WARC Ltd
Date Established: 1964
Frequency: 11 issues yearly - Published on the 1st of the month
Annual Sub.: £280.00
Circulation: 12,000 (Publisher's Statement)
Usual Pagination: 60
Editor: Colin Grimshaw; **Publisher:** Matthew Coombs
Summary of Content: Magazine containing marketing and advertising papers with a research and media bias, publishing original articles.
Readership/Target Audience: Aimed at decision makers and managers in market research, advertising and marketing communications, and advertiser companies.
ADVERTISING RATES:
Full Page Mono £1452.00
Full Page Colour £2328.00
Agency Commission: 10%
Mechanical Data: Page Width: 180mm, Col Length: 280mm, Print Process: Offset litho, Type Area: 280 x 180mm, Bleed Size: 303 x 216mm, Trim Size: 297 x 210mm, Film: Digital

Copy instructions: Copy Date: 2 weeks prior to publication date
BUSINESS: COMMUNICATIONS, ADVERTISING & MARKETING

ADOPTION & FOSTERING
38449U32G-10

Editorial Address: Saffron House, 6-10 Kirby Street, LONDON, EC1N 8TS **Tel:** 020 7421 2600
Fax: 020 7421 2601
Email: miranda.davies@baaf.org.uk
Advertising Address: As above. **Fax:** 020 7593 2601
Email: miranda.davies@baaf.org.uk
Web site: http://www.baaf.org.uk
ISSN: 0308-5759
Publisher: British Association for Adoption and Fostering
Date Established: 1953
Frequency: Quarterly
Cover Price: £12.00
Annual Sub.: £60.00
Circulation: 4,800 (Publisher's Statement)
Usual Pagination: 96
Editor: Roger Bullock; **Advertising Manager:** Miranda Davies
Summary of Content: International journal containing features written by scholars and practitioners in the child care field. Also includes articles on legislation, medical research and book reviews.
Readership/Target Audience: Aimed at local authority and voluntary adoption agencies, medical and child care professionals and university social work departments.
ADVERTISING RATES:
Full Page Mono £440.00
Mechanical Data: Page Width: 152mm, Type Area: 210 x 152mm, Col Length: 210mm
Average advertising content per issue: 5%
BUSINESS: LOCAL GOVERNMENT, LEISURE & RECREATION: Community Care & Social Services

ADULTS LEARNING
41107U62F-20

Editorial Address: 21 De Montfort Street, LEICESTER, LE1 7GE **Tel:** 0116 204 4200 **Fax:** 0116 204 4262
Email: paul.stanistreet@niace.org.uk
Advertising Address: As above. **Fax:** 0116 285 4514
Web site: http://www.niace.org.uk
ISSN: 0955-2308
Publisher: National Institute of Adult Continuing Education
Date Established: 1995
Frequency: 10 issues yearly - Published monthly except July and August
Annual Sub.: £34.00
Circulation: 2,500 (Publisher's Statement)
Usual Pagination: 32
Editor: Paul Stanistreet; **Advertising Manager:** Paul Stanistreet
Summary of Content: Journal containing information and news of developments, research and good practice in adult education and training at all levels.
Readership/Target Audience: Read by adult education and training professionals.
ADVERTISING RATES:
Full Page Mono £411.25
Full Page Colour £528.75
Mechanical Data: Type Area: 269 x 190mm, Col Length: 269mm, Page Width: 190mm, Bleed Size: 303 x 216mm, Trim Size: 279 x 190mm, Film: Digital
Copy instructions: Copy Date: 5th of cover month
BUSINESS: CHURCH & SCHOOL EQUIPMENT & EDUCATION: Adult Education

ADVANCE LIST
1810849U64K-656

Editorial Address: Zenith House, 155 Curtain Road, LONDON, EC2A 3QY **Tel:** 020 7613 2299
Fax: 020 7613 3822
Email: newsbreaks@londonatlarge.com
Web site: http://www.londonatlarge.com
Publisher: London At Large Ltd
Frequency: Weekly
Annual Sub.: £1500.00
Circulation: 3,000 (Publisher's Statement)
Editor: Kerri Darn; **Managing Director:** Chris Parkinson
Summary of Content: Publication featuring a celebrity and event diary, releases, key dates of interest, gigs, exhibitions, TV production information, film news and breaking news from all categories.
Readership/Target Audience: Aimed at media professionals.
ADVERTISING: No Advertising taken
BUSINESS: OTHER CLASSIFICATIONS: Cinema Entertainment

ADVANCE PRODUCTION NEWS
26082U64K-80

Editorial Address: Meridian House, Royal Hill, LONDON, SE10 8RD **Tel:** 020 8305 6905
Email: alan@crimsonuk.com
Web site: http://www.crimsonuk.com

Publisher: Crimson Communications
Date Established: 1999
Frequency: Monthly
Annual Sub.: £350.00
Usual Pagination: 100
Editor: Alan Williams; **Managing Director:** Alan Williams
Summary of Content: Magazine giving advance information on television programmes and films about to be made in the UK. Also includes media diary and reviews.
Readership/Target Audience: Aimed at PR companies, casting agents, magazine editors, camera crews and all those with an interest in pre-production news.
ADVERTISING: No Advertising taken
BUSINESS: OTHER CLASSIFICATIONS: Cinema Entertainment

ADVANCED CERAMICS REPORT 36608U12A-5
Editorial Address: 9A Victoria Square, DROITWICH, WR9 8DE **Tel:** 0870 165 7211 **Fax:** 0870 165 7212
Email: acr@intnews.com
Web site: http://www.performance-materials.net
ISSN: 0268-9847
Publisher: International Newsletters
Date Established: 1986
Frequency: Monthly
Annual Sub.: £467.00
Usual Pagination: 12
Editor: Sobie Akram; **Publisher:** Nick Butler
Summary of Content: Newsletter for senior management involved in high technology ceramics and ceramic composites.
Readership/Target Audience: Read by senior managers in research, design, production and engineering in companies manufacturing or using ceramics.
ADVERTISING: No Advertising taken
BUSINESS: CERAMICS, POTTERY & GLASS: Ceramics & Pottery

ADVANCED COMPOSITES BULLETIN
38813U39-2
Editorial Address: 9A Victoria Square, DROITWICH, WR9 8DE **Tel:** 0870 165 7211 **Fax:** 0870 165 7212
Email: acb@intnews.com
Web site: http://www.performance-materials.net
ISSN: 0951-953X
Publisher: International Newsletters
Date Established: 1987
Frequency: Monthly
Annual Sub.: £490.00
Usual Pagination: 12
Editor: Nick Butler; **Circulation Manager:** Guy Kitteringham
Summary of Content: Publication containing worldwide coverage of new composite materials, processing, testing and applications.
Readership/Target Audience: Aimed at suppliers and end-users in the aerospace, automotive, electronics, construction and defence industries and general engineering industries.
ADVERTISING: No Advertising taken
BUSINESS: PLASTICS & RUBBER

ADVANCES IN ENGINEERING SOFTWARE 37681U19J-20
Editorial Address: Wessex Institute of Technology, Ashurst Lodge, Ashurst, SOUTHAMPTON, SO40 7AA
Tel: 023 8029 3223 **Fax:** 023 8029 2853
Web site: http://www.elsevier.com/locate/advengsoft
ISSN: 0965-9978
Publisher: Elsevier Ltd
Date Established: 1969
Frequency: Monthly
Annual Sub.: EUR1768.00
Usual Pagination: 86
Editor: Robert Adey
Summary of Content: Journal reporting on recent and projected computer-based engineering techniques including aerospace, civil and environmental engineering with an emphasis on research development leading to problem solving.
Readership/Target Audience: Aimed at researchers in universities and industry.
ADVERTISING: No Advertising taken
BUSINESS: ENGINEERING & MACHINERY: CAD & CIM (Computer Integrated Manufacture)

ADVANCES IN TEXTILES TECHNOLOGY
39495U47A-1
Formerly: High Performance Textiles
Editorial Address: 9A Victoria Square, DROITWICH, WR9 8DE **Tel:** 0870 165 7211 **Fax:** 0870 165 7212
Email: editorial@intnews.com
Web site: http://www.technical-textiles.net
ISSN: 0144-5871
Publisher: International Newsletters

Date Established: 1980
Frequency: 8 issues yearly
Annual Sub.: £417.00
Usual Pagination: 12
Editor: Nick Butler; **Advertising Manager:** David Kay
Summary of Content: Newsletter focusing on high performance textiles, including product development and research.
Readership/Target Audience: Read mainly by management in the textile industry.
BUSINESS: CLOTHING & TEXTILES

ADVERTISING EXPENDITURE FORECASTS
601494U2A-35
Editorial Address: 24 Percy Street, LONDON, W1T 2BS
Tel: 020 7961 1192 **Fax:** 020 7291 1199
Email: publications@zenithoptimedia.com
Advertising Address: As above.
Web site: http://www.zenithoptimedia.com
ISSN: 0968-2163
Publisher: Zenith Optimedia Group
Date Established: 1988
Frequency: Quarterly
Annual Sub.: £1155.00
Usual Pagination: 230
Editor: Jonathan Barnard
Summary of Content: Report covering expenditure by medium in fifty-seven countries featuring commentary and forecasts compiled with local market intelligence and rapid cross-referencing and trend analysis.
Readership/Target Audience: Aimed at those in the banking, consultancy and advertising industries.
ADVERTISING: No Advertising taken
BUSINESS: COMMUNICATIONS, ADVERTISING & MARKETING

THE ADVISER 38450U32G-15
Editorial Address: The Development Centre, Wolverhampton Science Park, WOLVERHAMPTON, WV10 9RT **Tel:** 01902 310568 **Fax:** 01902 710068
Email: alan.markey@citizensadvice.org.uk
Advertising Address: As above.
Email: sharanjit.kaur@citizensadvice.org.uk
Web site: http://www.advisermagazine.org.uk
ISSN: 0950-5458
Publisher: National Association of Citizens Advice Bureaux
Date Established: 1986
Frequency: 6 issues yearly - Published end of month prior to cover date
Cover Price: £7.00
Annual Sub.: £45.00
Circulation: 3,000 (Publisher's Statement)
Usual Pagination: 52
Editor: Alan Markey; **Advertising Manager:** Sharanjit Kaur
Summary of Content: Publication containing a guide to housing, social security, employment, consumer and money advice. Also has Abstracts section which contains summaries of cases including the most important decisions of the Social Security and Child Support Commissions.
Readership/Target Audience: Aimed at advisors, practitioners and others working in the field of social welfare.
ADVERTISING RATES:
Full Page Mono £650.00
Mechanical Data: Type Area: 265 x 180mm, Col Length: 265mm, Trim Size: 297 x 210mm, Page Width: 180mm, Film: Digital
Average advertising content per issue: 10%
BUSINESS: LOCAL GOVERNMENT, LEISURE & RECREATION: Community Care & Social Services

THE ADVOCATE 40040U55-56
Formerly: The Herald
Editorial Address: Best View, Upton Lane, Dundry, BRISTOL, BS41 8NS **Tel:** 0117 964 4088
Email: wadeseducation@sky.com
Web site: http://www.wadeseducation.btik.com
Publisher: Western Alcohol & Drugs Education Society
Date Established: 1830
Frequency: 3 issues yearly - Published in March, July and November
Cover Price: Free
Circulation: 200 (Publisher's Statement)
Usual Pagination: 24
Editor: Angela Bebbington
Summary of Content: Facts, figures and articles concerning alcohol and drugs. Advertising our educational material.
Readership/Target Audience: Aimed at members of the Western Alcohol & Drugs Education Society, the general public, schools and community networks.
ADVERTISING: No Advertising taken
BUSINESS: APPLIED SCIENCE & LABORATORIES

AEC MAGAZINE 37688U19J-21
Formerly: CADDESK AEC
Editorial Address: 93A Rivington Street, LONDON, EC2A 3AY **Tel:** 020 3355 7310 **Fax:** 020 3355 7319
Email: greg@x3dmedia.com
Advertising Address: As above.
Email: tony@x3dmedia.com
Web site: http://www.aecmag.com
Publisher: X3D Media
Frequency: 6 issues yearly - Published in the 2nd week of the 1st cover month
Free to qualifying individuals
Circulation: 10,000 (Publisher's Statement)
Usual Pagination: 40
Editor: Greg Corke; **Managing Editor:** Greg Corke
Summary of Content: Independent magazine giving news, product reviews, user comments, case studies and buyers guides relating to IT and CAD in architecture, engineering and construction.
Readership/Target Audience: Read by architects, engineers and construction managers.
ADVERTISING RATES:
Full Page Mono £2032.00
Full Page Colour £2562.00
Agency Commission: 10%
Mechanical Data: Page Width: 190mm, Type Area: 280 x 190mm, Col Length: 280mm, Trim Size: 297 x 210mm, Bleed Size: 303 x 216mm, Film: Digital
Copy instructions: Copy Date: 2nd week of the month prior to publication date
Average advertising content per issue: 40%
BUSINESS: ENGINEERING & MACHINERY: CAD & CIM (Computer Integrated Manufacture)

AEP APPOINTMENTS BROADSHEET
41137U62H-10
Editorial Address: 26 The Avenue, DURHAM, DH1 4ED
Tel: 0191 384 9512 **Fax:** 0191 386 5287
Email: lynn@aep.org.uk
Advertising Address: As above.
Email: lynn@aep.org.uk
Publisher: Association of Educational Psychologists
Frequency: Weekly
Circulation: 3,080 (Publisher's Statement)
Editor: Lynn Flowers; **Advertising Manager:** Lynn Flowers
Summary of Content: Publication containing advertisements for educational psychologists.
Readership/Target Audience: Aimed at educational psychologists.
ADVERTISING: Rates on application
BUSINESS: CHURCH & SCHOOL EQUIPMENT & EDUCATION: Careers

THE AERONAUTICAL JOURNAL 36318U6A-13
Editorial Address: 4 Hamilton Place, LONDON, W1J 7BQ
Tel: 020 7670 4300 **Fax:** 020 7670 4359
Email: publications@aerosociety.com
Web site: http://www.aerosociety.com
ISSN: 0001-9240
Publisher: Royal Aeronautical Society
Date Established: 1897
Frequency: Monthly
Cover Price: £36.00
Annual Sub.: £375.00
Circulation: 1,500 (Publisher's Statement)
Usual Pagination: 56
Editor: Chris Male; **Editor-in-Chief:** Peter Bearman; **Managing Editor:** Chris Male; **Publisher:** Keith Mans
Summary of Content: Journal of the Royal Aeronautical Society. Publishes refereed technical and engineering papers on all aerospace sciences.
Readership/Target Audience: Read by professionals in the aeronautical industry, research organisations and academia.
ADVERTISING: No Advertising taken
BUSINESS: AVIATION & AERONAUTICS

AEROSPACE ENGINEERING 36398U6D-10
Editorial Address: 5 Church Avenue, FARNBOROUGH, GU14 7AY **Tel:** 01252 515562 **Fax:** 724 776 9765
Email: richardgardner@btinternet.com
Advertising Address: University House, 11-13 Lower Grosvenor Place, LONDON, SW1W 0EX **Tel:** 020 7834 7676 **Fax:** 020 7973 0076
Email: media@alaincharles.com
Web site: http://www.sae.org
Publisher: Society of Automotive Engineers Inc.
Frequency: 10 issues yearly - Published in the 1st week of the cover month
Annual Sub.: £135.00
Circulation: 30,000 (Publisher's Statement)
Usual Pagination: 20
Editor: Richard Gardner; **Advertising Manager:** Richard Rozelaar
Summary of Content: Journal covering international developments in aerospace technology and design.

Readership/Target Audience: Aimed at managing directors, manufacturers and designers interested in Aerospace Technology.
ADVERTISING RATES:
Full Page Mono $6140.00
Full Page Colour $8040.00
Agency Commission: 15%
Mechanical Data: Bleed Size: 282 x 212mm, Page Width: 177mm, Trim Size: 276 x 206mm, Type Area: 254 x 177mm, Col Length: 254mm, Film: Digital
Copy instructions: Copy Date: 3 weeks prior to publication date
Average advertising content per issue: 40%
BUSINESS: AVIATION & AERONAUTICS: Aviation Engineering Equipment

AEROSPACE INTERNATIONAL   36320U6A-18

Editorial Address: 4 Hamilton Place, LONDON, W1J 7BQ
Tel: 020 7670 4300 **Fax:** 020 7670 4359
Email: publications@aerosociety.com
Web site: http://www.aerosociety.com
ISSN: 0305-0831
Publisher: Royal Aeronautical Society
Date Established: 1973
Frequency: Monthly - Published on the 25th of the month prior to cover date
Free to qualifying individuals
Annual Sub.: £120.00
Circulation: 17,299 (Publisher's Statement)
Usual Pagination: 36
Editor: Richard Gardner; **Features Editor:** Bill Read
Summary of Content: Magazine of the Royal Aeronautical Society containing current industry news plus specialist features on air transport, defence, airports, engineering, MRO, ATC, training, safety, commercial and space articles.
Readership/Target Audience: Read by qualified aeronautical engineers, pilots, maintenance engineers, air traffic controllers, academics, politicians and those interested in aviation.
ADVERTISING: No Advertising taken
BUSINESS: AVIATION & AERONAUTICS

AEROSPACE MANUFACTURING   1775551U6A-206

Editorial Address: Featherstone House, 375 High Street, ROCHESTER, ME1 1DA **Tel:** 01634 830566
Fax: 01634 408488
Email: newsdesk@aero-mag.com
Advertising Address: As above.
Email: mdeadman@aero-mag.com
Web site: http://www.aero-mag.com
Publisher: MIT Publishing
Date Established: 2006
Frequency: 10 issues yearly - Published in the 1st week of the month prior to cover month
Cover Price: EUR20.00
Free to qualifying individuals
Circulation: 9,927 (ABC 01/07/2006 to 30/06/2007)
Usual Pagination: 76
Editor: Mike Richardson
Summary of Content: Publication covering the design, production and supply chain of the European civil and defence aerospace industries.
Readership/Target Audience: Aimed at decision makers involved in design, production and procurement within the civil and defence aerospace industry.
ADVERTISING RATES:
Full Page Colour £3900.00
Agency Commission: 10%
Mechanical Data: Type Area: 267 x 180mm, Bleed Size: 303 x 216mm, Trim Size: 297 x 210mm, Col Length: 267mm, Page Width: 180mm, Film: Digital
Copy instructions: Copy Date: 4 weeks prior to publication date
Average advertising content per issue: 40%
BUSINESS: AVIATION & AERONAUTICS

THE AEROSPACE PROFESSIONAL   1655939U6A-202

Editorial Address: 4 Hamilton Place, LONDON, W1J 7BQ
Tel: 020 7670 4300
Web site: http://www.aerosociety.com
Publisher: Royal Aeronautical Society
Date Established: 1999
Frequency: Monthly
Free to qualifying individuals
Circulation: 19,000 (Publisher's Statement)
Usual Pagination: 20
Editor: Chris Male
Summary of Content: Magazine of the Royal Aeronautical Society covering news of the society and its branches and divisions.
Readership/Target Audience: Aimed at qualified aeronautical engineers and pilots.
ADVERTISING: No Advertising taken
BUSINESS: AVIATION & AERONAUTICS

AEROSPACE TESTING INTERNATIONAL
1616089U6D-501

Editorial Address: Abinger House, Church Street, DORKING, RH4 1DF **Tel:** 01306 743744 **Fax:** 01306 887546
Email: c.hounsfield@ukintpress.com
Advertising Address: As above. **Fax:** 01306 742525
Email: c.flanagan@ukintpress.com
Web site: http://www.ukipme.com
Publisher: UKIP Media & Events Ltd
Date Established: 2001
Frequency: Quarterly
Cover Price: Free
Circulation: 10,462 (ABC 01/01/2008 to 31/12/2008)
Usual Pagination: 160
Editor: Christopher Hounsfield; **Managing Director:** Graham Johnson; **Advertising Manager:** Cheryl Flanagan
Summary of Content: Publication featuring news, features and technical articles covering every aspect of aerospace testing and test engineering.
Readership/Target Audience: Aimed at aeronautical engineers and other aerospace professionals.
ADVERTISING RATES:
Full Page Colour £4150.00
Agency Commission: 15%
Mechanical Data: Type Area: 276 x 200mm, Bleed Size: 306 x 236mm, Trim Size: 300 x 230mm, Col Length: 276mm, Page Width: 200mm, Film: Digital
BUSINESS: AVIATION & AERONAUTICS: Aviation Engineering Equipment

AFASIC NEWS   754184U62G-30

Editorial Address: 20 Bowling Green Lane, LONDON, EC1R 0BD **Tel:** 020 7490 9410 **Fax:** 020 7251 2834
Email: carol.lingwood@btopenworld.com
Web site: http://www.afasic.org.uk
ISSN: 1354-2499
Publisher: Afasic
Date Established: 1968
Frequency: 3 issues yearly - Published in January, May and September
Cover Price: Free
Circulation: 2,000 (Publisher's Statement)
Usual Pagination: 16
Editor: Carol Lingwood
Summary of Content: Magazine about children with speech and language impairments and disabilities, covering special education needs, speech and language therapy, courses, training and research, and books relating to developmental speech and language impairments.
Readership/Target Audience: Read by young people with speech and language impairments, their parents and carers and the professionals who look after them.
ADVERTISING: No Advertising taken
BUSINESS: CHURCH & SCHOOL EQUIPMENT & EDUCATION: Special Needs Education

AFRICA AND MIDDLE EAST TEXTILES
39479U47A-5

Formerly: African and Middle East Textiles
Editorial Address: University House, 11-13 Lower Grosvenor Place, LONDON, SW1W 0EX **Tel:** 020 7834 7676
Fax: 020 7973 0076
Email: zsa.tebbit@alaincharles.com
Advertising Address: As above.
Email: post@alaincharles.com
Web site: http://www.alaincharles.com
ISSN: 0144-7521
Publisher: Alain Charles Publishing Ltd
Date Established: 1980
Frequency: Quarterly
Free to qualifying individuals
Annual Sub.: $60.00
Circulation: 10,559 (Publisher's Statement)
Usual Pagination: 48
Editor: Zsa Tebbit; **Publisher:** Derek Fordham
Summary of Content: Journal covering textile and apparel manufacturing, research, production and marketing in Africa and the Middle East.
Language(s): English; French
Readership/Target Audience: Read by executives in the apparel and textile industries.
ADVERTISING RATES:
Full Page Mono $3270.00
Full Page Colour $4810.00
Agency Commission: 15%
Mechanical Data: Type Area: 292 x 208mm, Bleed Size: 298 x 214mm, Film: Digital, Type Area: 266 x 180mm, Col Length: 266mm, Page Width: 180mm
Copy instructions: Copy Date: 1 week prior to publication date
Average advertising content per issue: 30%
BUSINESS: CLOTHING & TEXTILES

AFRICA ASIA CONFIDENTIAL   1835396U14C-371

Editorial Address: 73 Farringdon Road, LONDON, EC1M 3JQ **Tel:** 020 7831 3511 **Fax:** 020 7831 6778

Email: info@africa-confidential.com
Publisher: Asempa Limited
Frequency: Monthly
Annual Sub.: £300.00
Editor: Patrick Smith; **Managing Editor:** Clare Tauben
Summary of Content: Newsletter providing reports, comment and analysis covering the entire African and Asian continents. Also reports on international issues affecting the social, political and economic future.
Readership/Target Audience: Read by politicians, officials, military personnel and academics.
ADVERTISING: No Advertising taken
BUSINESS: COMMERCE, INDUSTRY & MANAGEMENT: International Commerce

AFRICA CONFIDENTIAL   36914U14C-2_3

Editorial Address: 73 Farringdon Road, LONDON, EC1M 3JQ **Tel:** 020 7831 3511 **Fax:** 020 7831 6778
Email: info@africa-confidential.com
Web site: http://www.africa-confidential.com
ISSN: 0044-6483
Publisher: Asempa Limited
Date Established: 1960
Frequency: 25 issues yearly
Annual Sub.: £695.00
Circulation: 3,000 (Publisher's Statement)
Usual Pagination: 12
Editor: Patrick Smith; **Managing Editor:** Clare Tauben
Summary of Content: Newsletter providing reports, comment and analysis covering the entire African continent. Also reports on international issues affecting the social, political and economic future of Africa.
Readership/Target Audience: Read by politicians, business people, military personnel and academics.
ADVERTISING: No Advertising taken
BUSINESS: COMMERCE, INDUSTRY & MANAGEMENT: International Commerce

AFRICA HEALTH   629369U56A-169

Formerly: Mera (Medical Education Resource Africa)
Editorial Address: Vine House, Fair Green, Reach, CAMBRIDGE, CB25 0JD **Tel:** 01638 743633
Fax: 01638 743998
Email: info@fsg.co.uk
Advertising Address: As above.
Email: jo@fsg.co.uk
Web site: http://www.fsg.co.uk
ISSN: 1478-2642
Publisher: FSG Communications Ltd
Date Established: 2002
Frequency: 6 issues yearly
Free to qualifying individuals
Annual Sub.: £65.00
Circulation: 12,500 (Publisher's Statement)
Usual Pagination: 112
Editor: Penny Lang; **Publisher:** Bryan Pearson
Summary of Content: Magazine covering clinical and other information relevant to the developing world including epidemiological information, news on management issues and updates on clinical practice.
Readership/Target Audience: Aimed at doctors and other senior health professionals and policymakers in Africa.
ADVERTISING RATES:
Full Page Mono £1569.00
Full Page Colour £2088.00
Agency Commission: 10%
Mechanical Data: Type Area: 254 x 178mm, Bleed Size: 285 x 205mm, Trim Size: 280 x 200mm, Film: Digital, Col Length: 254mm, Page Width: 178mm
Copy instructions: Copy Date: 1 week prior to publication date
Average advertising content per issue: 40%
BUSINESS: HEALTH & MEDICAL

AFRICA MONITOR   36981U14C-207

Editorial Address: Mermaid House, 2 Puddle Dock, LONDON, EC4V 3DS **Tel:** 020 7248 0468
Fax: 020 7248 0467
Email: emartins@businessmonitor.com
Web site: http://www.businessmonitor.com
ISSN: 1362-4423
Publisher: Business Monitor International Ltd
Date Established: 1996
Frequency: Monthly
Circulation: 555 (Publisher's Statement)
Usual Pagination: 8
Editor: Elizabeth Martins; **Publisher:** Richard Londesborough
Summary of Content: Publication covering economic and political developments in Africa including government, economy, finance and the business environment.
Readership/Target Audience: Aimed at investors who have invested or who are looking to invest in Africa.
ADVERTISING: No Advertising taken
BUSINESS: COMMERCE, INDUSTRY & MANAGEMENT: International Commerce

AFRICA OIL AND GAS

601344U33-1_7

Formerly: Hart Africa Oil and Gas
Editorial Address: PO Box 503, WINCHESTER, SO23 3DG
Tel: 01962 711756 **Fax:** 01276 713126
Email: mdixon@africaoilandgas.com
Advertising Address: As above.
Web site: http://www.africaoilandgas.com
Publisher: Fraser Publications Ltd
Frequency: 25 issues yearly
Annual Sub.: £645.00
Usual Pagination: 8
Editor: Mark Dixon; **Circulation Manager:** Sam Williams
Summary of Content: Newsletter covering oil and gas developments and political and economic risks in Africa.
Readership/Target Audience: Aimed at business development executives in the oil and gas industry.
ADVERTISING: No Advertising taken
BUSINESS: OIL & PETROLEUM

AFRICA TODAY

601252U14A-3_50

Editorial Address: Suite 2, 2nd Floor, AMC House, 12 Cumberland Avenue, LONDON, NW10 7QL
Tel: 020 8838 5900 **Fax:** 020 8838 3700
Email: carol.ibb@btinternet.com
Advertising Address: Africa Media International, Laurel Cottage, CUMBRIA, LA20 6HU **Tel:** 01229 715000
Email: carol.ibb@btinternet.com
Web site: http://www.africatoday.com
Publisher: Afro Media (UK) Ltd
Frequency: Monthly - Published in the 3rd week of every month
Annual Sub.: £30.00
Circulation: 57,000 (Publisher's Statement)
Editor: Kayode Soyinka; **Editor-in-Chief:** Kayode Soyinka; **Advertising Director:** Carol Filby; **Publisher:** Kayode Soyinka
Summary of Content: Magazine concerned with news and business features.
Readership/Target Audience: Aimed at professionals, decision makers, industrialists, government officials including ministers, civil servants and diplomats, travelling foreign investors in African markets, managers and CEOs.
ADVERTISING RATES:
Full Page Mono £4700.00
Full Page Colour £6290.00
Agency Commission: 15%
Mechanical Data: Trim Size: 280 x 213mm, Type Area: 260 x 195mm, Bleed Size: 286 x 219mm, Film: Digital, Col Length: 260mm, Page Width: 195mm
Copy instructions: Copy Date: 1st of month prior to publication
BUSINESS: COMMERCE, INDUSTRY & MANAGEMENT

AFRICAHEDGE

1776089U1F-627

Formerly: South AfricaHedge
Editorial Address: Nestor House, Playhouse Yard, LONDON, EC4V 5EX **Tel:** 020 7779 7330
Fax: 020 7779 7331
Email: info@hedgefundintelligence.com
Advertising Address: As above.
Email: jwillis@hedgefundintelligence.com
Web site: http://www.hedgefundintelligence.com
Publisher: Hedge Fund Intelligence
Frequency: 10 issues yearly - July/August and December/January are joint issues
Annual Sub.: £700.00
Usual Pagination: 20
Editor: Gwyneth Roberts; **Advertising Manager:** John Willis
Summary of Content: Newsletter containing new fund launches, latest developments amongst listed funds, news and interviews with the people behind some of the best hedge fund returns in the world, comprehensive performance data on South Africa funds and inside information on investment opportunities in the rest of Africa.
Readership/Target Audience: Aimed at investors, hedge fund managers, service providers and others wishing to be kept up to date with the latest developments in the hedge fund industry.
ADVERTISING RATES:
Full Page Mono £2000.00
Mechanical Data: Type Area: 244 x 185mm, Bleed Size: 278 x 211mm, Trim Size: 272 x 205mm, Col Length: 244mm, Page Width: 185mm, Film: Digital
Copy instructions: Copy Date: 1st of the publication month
BUSINESS: FINANCE & ECONOMICS: Investment

AFRICAN BUSINESS

36916U14C-3

Editorial Address: 7 Coldbath Square, LONDON, EC1R 4LQ **Tel:** 020 7841 3210 **Fax:** 020 7841 3211
Email: editorial@africasia.com
Advertising Address: As above. **Tel:** 020 7713 7711
Fax: 020 7713 7898
Email: advertising@africasia.com
Web site: http://www.africasia.com
ISSN: 0141-3929
Publisher: IC Publications Ltd

Date Established: 1966
Frequency: 11 issues yearly - Published around the last Wednesday of the month prior to cover month
Cover Price: £2.70
Annual Sub.: £36.00
Circulation: 26,314 (ABC 01/01/2008 to 31/12/2008)
Usual Pagination: 68
Editor: Anver Versi; **Advertising Manager:** Omar Ben Yedder; **Publisher:** Omar Ben-Yedder
Summary of Content: Journal specialising in African economic, financial business and development issues.
Readership/Target Audience: Read by Pan-African decision-makers and business people.
ADVERTISING RATES:
Full Page Colour £5800.00
Agency Commission: 15%
Mechanical Data: Type Area: 242 x 186mm, Bleed Size: 276 x 216mm, Trim Size: 270 x 210mm, Col Length: 242mm, Film: Digital, Page Width: 186mm
Copy instructions: Copy Date: 2 weeks prior to publication date
Average advertising content per issue: 10%
BUSINESS: COMMERCE, INDUSTRY & MANAGEMENT: International Commerce

AFRICAN ENERGY

718040U58-4

Editorial Address: 19 Wellington Square, HASTINGS, TN34 1PB **Tel:** 01424 721667 **Fax:** 01424 721721
Email: thalia@africa-energy.com
Web site: http://www.africa-energy.com
Publisher: Cross-Border Information
Date Established: 1998
Frequency: 24 issues yearly
Annual Sub.: £875.00
Usual Pagination: 22
Editor: Thalia Griffiths; **News Editor:** Thalia Griffiths
Summary of Content: Newsletter containing the latest information and evaluation on important inter-governmental deals, financing facilities and new projects for the African power, oil and gas industry.
Readership/Target Audience: Aimed at those interested in African Energy.
ADVERTISING: Rates on application
BUSINESS: ENERGY, FUEL & NUCLEAR

AFRICAN FARMING AND FOOD PROCESSING

37745U21A-50

Editorial Address: University House, 11-13 Lower Grosvenor Place, LONDON, SW1W 0EX **Tel:** 020 7834 7676
Fax: 020 7973 0076
Email: jonquil.phelan@alaincharles.com
Advertising Address: As above.
Email: irene.greve@alaincharles.com
Web site: http://www.alaincharles.com
ISSN: 0266-8017
Publisher: Alain Charles Publishing Ltd
Date Established: 1980
Frequency: 6 issues yearly - Published around the 1st of the 2nd cover month
Free to qualifying individuals
Annual Sub.: £54.00
Circulation: 10,365 (Publisher's Statement)
Usual Pagination: 36
Editor: Jonquil Phelan; **Managing Editor:** Jonquil Phelan; **Publisher:** Nick Fordham
Summary of Content: Magazine covering agricultural developments, new technology and farm management in Africa.
Readership/Target Audience: Read by farmers, plantation owners, politicians, members of co-operatives and aid agency workers in Africa.
ADVERTISING RATES:
Full Page Colour £2650.00
Agency Commission: 15%
Mechanical Data: Type Area: 266 x 180mm, Col Length: 266mm, Bleed Size: 298 x 214mm, Trim Size: 292 x 208mm, Page Width: 180mm, Film: Digital
Copy instructions: Copy Date: 2 weeks prior to publication date
Average advertising content per issue: 35%
BUSINESS: AGRICULTURE & FARMING

AFRICAN JOURNAL OF ECOLOGY

25121U57-1_90

Editorial Address: Environment Department, University of York, Heslington, YORK, YO10 5DD **Tel:** 01904 434059
Email: sa29@york.ac.uk
Web site: http://www.blackwellpublishing.com/journal.asp?ref=0141-6707
Publisher: Wiley-Blackwell Publishing
Date Established: 1963
Frequency: Quarterly
Annual Sub.: £545.00
Circulation: 3,719 (Publisher's Statement)
Usual Pagination: 120
Editor: Shona Attridge

Summary of Content: Journal publishing original scientific research into the animals and plants of Africa.
Language(s): English; French
Readership/Target Audience: Read by academics and professionals working in the field.
ADVERTISING: No Advertising taken
BUSINESS: ENVIRONMENT & POLLUTION

AFRICAN REVIEW OF BUSINESS AND TECHNOLOGY

36918U14C-3_5

Editorial Address: University House, 11-13 Lower Grosvenor Place, LONDON, SW1W 0EX **Tel:** 020 7834 7676
Fax: 020 7973 0076
Email: jonquil.phelan@alaincharles.com
Advertising Address: As above.
Email: pallavi.pandey@alaincharles.com
Web site: http://www.alaincharles.com
ISSN: 0954-6782
Publisher: Alain Charles Publishing Ltd
Date Established: 1964
Frequency: 11 issues yearly - Published in the last week of the month prior to the cover month
Cover Price: £6.00
Free to qualifying individuals
Annual Sub.: £60.00
Circulation: 13,440 (ABC 01/07/2008 to 30/06/2009)
Usual Pagination: 60
Editor: Jonquil Phelan; **Managing Editor:** Jonquil Phelan; **Publisher:** Nick Fordham
Summary of Content: Magazine covering management, technology, finance, construction, transport and infrastructure.
Readership/Target Audience: Aimed at senior executives in African businesses or government departments.
ADVERTISING RATES:
Full Page Mono EUR4490.00
Full Page Colour EUR6610.00
Agency Commission: 15%
Mechanical Data: Type Area: 266 x 180mm, Bleed Size: 298 x 214mm, Trim Size: 292 x 208mm, Col Length: 266mm, Page Width: 180mm, Film: Digital
Average advertising content per issue: 40%
BUSINESS: COMMERCE, INDUSTRY & MANAGEMENT: International Commerce

AFTERMARKET

38280U31A-2

Editorial Address: Crystal House, 14 London Road, RAINHAM, ME8 6YX **Tel:** 01634 261262 **Fax:** 01634 360514
Email: tom@aftermarket.co.uk
Advertising Address: As above.
Email: sales@aftermarket.co.uk
Web site: http://www.aftermarketnetwork.com
Publisher: Crystal Communications
Date Established: 1992
Frequency: 10 issues yearly - Published in the last week of the month prior to the cover date
Free to qualifying individuals
Annual Sub.: £60.00
Circulation: 30,151 (ABC 01/07/2008 to 30/06/2009)
Usual Pagination: 60
Advertising Manager: Paul Dearing; **Publisher:** Jim Dunn
Summary of Content: Magazine containing regular technical and training updates, a new product and equipment guide and a free reader enquiry service.
Readership/Target Audience: Aimed at wholesalers, franchised dealers, independent garages, fast-fits, body shops and MOT stations primarily for passenger cars and light commercial vehicles.
ADVERTISING RATES:
Full Page Colour £3517.00
Agency Commission: 10%
Mechanical Data: Film: Digital, No. of Columns (Display): 4, Type Area: 270 x 190mm, Print Process: Web-fed offset, Bleed Size: 303 x 216mm, Trim Size: 297 x 210mm, Col Length: 270mm, Page Width: 190mm
Copy instructions: Copy Date: 4 weeks prior to publication date
Average advertising content per issue: 40%
BUSINESS: MOTOR TRADE: Motor Trade Accessories

AGBIOTECH NEWS AND INFORMATION

37926U21R-40

Editorial Address: Nosworthy Way, WALLINGFORD, OX10 8DE **Tel:** 01491 832111 **Fax:** 01491 833508
Email: d.hemming@cabi.org
Web site: http://www.agbiotechnet.com
ISSN: 0954-9897
Publisher: CABI
Frequency: Monthly
Annual Sub.: £95.00
Editor: David Hemming
Summary of Content: Journal covering molecular techniques, genetic engineering, cloning and gene sequencing, cell tissue and embryo manipulation, waste and organic by-product processing, economics and social and legal aspects.

Business Magazines

Section 4 (b) Business Magazines

Readership/Target Audience: Aimed at scientists, policy makers, commercial companies, members of government and investors involved in agricultural biotechnology.
ADVERTISING: No Advertising taken
BUSINESS: AGRICULTURE & FARMING: Agriculture & Farming Related

---

AGBIOTECH REPORTER
601485U21A-54_10

Formerly: AgraFood Biotech
Editorial Address: 80 Calverley Road, TUNBRIDGE WELLS, TN1 2UN **Tel:** 020 7017 7500 **Fax:** 020 7017 7599
Email: marketing@agra-net.com
Web site: http://www.agra-net.com
ISSN: 1757-2029
Publisher: Agra Informa Ltd
Date Established: 1999
Frequency: 24 issues yearly
Annual Sub.: £796.00
Usual Pagination: 26
Summary of Content: Newsletter reporting on biotechnology in food production, processing and product manufacturing.
Readership/Target Audience: Aimed at members of the European and International food industry.
ADVERTISING: No Advertising taken
BUSINESS: AGRICULTURE & FARMING

AGE AGENDA BULLETIN
1865036U56B-305

Editorial Address: Astral House, 1268 London Road, LONDON, SW16 4ER **Tel:** 020 8765 7200
Fax: 020 8764 6594
Email: diana.fawcett@ace.org.uk
Web site: http://www.ageconcern.org.uk
Publisher: Age Concern England
Date Established: 2007
Frequency: Monthly
Annual Sub.: £34.00
Circulation: 1,280 (Publisher's Statement)
Editor: Diana Fawcett
Summary of Content: Bulletin covering issues concerning older people, offering information for those looking after older people and coverage of policy, legislation news and new reports.
Readership/Target Audience: Aimed at those working with and for older people.
ADVERTISING: Rates on application
BUSINESS: HEALTH & MEDICAL: Nursing

AGE AND AGEING
24472U56A-1_50

Editorial Address: 72 Prince Street, BRISTOL, BS1 4QD
Tel: 0117 370 0988 **Fax:** 0117 903 0505
Email: office@ageingmedicine.com
Advertising Address: Great Clarendon Street, OXFORD, OX2 6DP **Tel:** 01865 354637
Email: elisabetta.sheffield@oxfordjournals.org
Web site: http://www.oup.co.uk/jnls
ISSN: 0002-0729
Publisher: OUP
Date Established: 1972
Frequency: 6 issues yearly
Annual Sub.: £180.00
Editor: Katy Ladbrook
Summary of Content: Journal focusing on referred articles on geriatric medicine and gerontology, reporting observations, advances and developments in the clinical, psychological and epidemiological aspects of later life.
Readership/Target Audience: Read by geriatricians, psycho geriatricians and GPs with a special interest in the elderly.
ADVERTISING RATES:
Full Page Mono £742.00
Full Page Colour £1236.00
Agency Commission: 10%
Mechanical Data: Print Process: Litho, Type Area: 255 x 178mm, Trim Size: 279 x 216mm, Bleed Size: 285 x 222mm, Col Length: 255mm, Film: Digital, Page Width: 178mm
BUSINESS: HEALTH & MEDICAL

AGEING AND SOCIETY
40293U56B-7

Editorial Address: The Edinburgh Building, Shaftesbury Road, CAMBRIDGE, CB2 2RU **Tel:** 01223 312393
Fax: 01223 315052
Email: a.warnes@sheffield.ac.uk
Advertising Address: As above. **Tel:** 01223 325757
Email: ad_sales@cambridge.org
Web site: http://journals.cambridge.org/jid_aso
ISSN: 0144-686X
Publisher: Cambridge University Press
Date Established: 1981
Frequency: 6 issues yearly
Annual Sub.: £55.00
Editor: Tony Warnes
Summary of Content: International interdisciplinary journal devoted to publishing papers which further the understanding of human ageing, book reviews, review

---

symposia, extracts of relevant articles in other journals, and progress reports on research areas.
Readership/Target Audience: Read by lecturers, researchers, academics in social sciences and cultural studies, social gerontologists, social service health professionals and governmental departments.
ADVERTISING RATES:
Full Page Mono £460.00
Mechanical Data: Film: Digital, Type Area: 190 x 115mm, Col Length: 190mm, Page Width: 115mm
Copy instructions: Copy Date: 8 weeks prior to publication date
BUSINESS: HEALTH & MEDICAL: Nursing

AGENDANI
1790171U32A-264

Editorial Address: Davidson House, Glenavy Road Business Park, Moira, CRAIGAVON, BT67 0LT
Tel: 028 9261 9933 **Fax:** 028 9261 9951
Email: info@agendani.com
Advertising Address: As above.
Email: dan.mcquade@agendani.com
Web site: http://www.agendani.com
ISSN: 1752-4466
Publisher: bmf Publishing
Date Established: 2006
Frequency: 10 issues yearly - Published in the 1st week of the 1st cover month
Cover Price: £2.95
Annual Sub.: £29.50
Circulation: 6,458 (ABC 01/07/2008 to 30/06/2009)
Usual Pagination: 120
Editor: Owen McQuade; **Managing Editor:** Owen McQuade
Summary of Content: Public affairs magazine covering public policy from health and education to the economy.
Readership/Target Audience: Aimed at senior managers in the public, private and voluntary sectors.
ADVERTISING RATES:
Full Page Colour £1495.00
Agency Commission: 15%
Mechanical Data: Type Area: 235 x 170mm, Bleed Size: 303 x 216mm, Trim Size: 297 x 210mm, Col Length: 235mm, Page Width: 170mm, Film: Digital
Copy instructions: Copy Date: 1 week prior to publication date
BUSINESS: LOCAL GOVERNMENT, LEISURE & RECREATION: Local Government

---

AGRA EUROPE
37746U21A-53

Editorial Address: 80 Calverley Road, TUNBRIDGE WELLS, TN1 2UN **Tel:** 020 7017 7500 **Fax:** 020 7017 7599
Email: marketing@agra-net.com
Web site: http://www.agra-net.com
ISSN: 0002-1024
Publisher: Agra Informa Ltd
Date Established: 1963
Frequency: Weekly
Annual Sub.: £3170.00
Usual Pagination: 40
Circulation Manager: Barbara Mason
Summary of Content: Newsletter providing news, analysis and comment on European and international agricultural policy and trade.
Readership/Target Audience: Read by food companies, agribusiness and governments.
ADVERTISING: No Advertising taken
BUSINESS: AGRICULTURE & FARMING

AGRAFOOD EAST EUROPE
37748U21A-54_15

Formerly: East Europe Agriculture and Food Monthly
Editorial Address: 80 Calverley Road, TUNBRIDGE WELLS, TN1 2UN **Tel:** 020 7017 7500 **Fax:** 020 7017 7599
Email: marketing@agra-net.com
Web site: http://www.agra-net.com
ISSN: 1466-500X
Publisher: Agra Informa Ltd
Date Established: 1982
Frequency: Weekly
Annual Sub.: £1132.00
Usual Pagination: 36
Summary of Content: Newsletter covering analysis and comment on production, policy, prices, trade, joint ventures and company news in Central and Eastern Europe. Includes EU enlargement, agricultural policy, exports and imports, supply and demand balances, trade policy and rural and agri-environmental policy.
Readership/Target Audience: Read by those involved in industry, trade and government.
ADVERTISING: No Advertising taken
BUSINESS: AGRICULTURE & FARMING

AGRAFOOD EUROPE
37749U21A-54_30

Editorial Address: 80 Calverley Road, TUNBRIDGE WELLS, TN1 2UN **Tel:** 020 7017 7500 **Fax:** 020 7017 7599
Email: marketing@agra-net.com
Web site: http://www.agra-net.com

ISSN: 1361-9810
Publisher: Agra Informa Ltd
Frequency: Monthly
Annual Sub.: £732.00
Usual Pagination: 40
Circulation Manager: Sue Crouch
Summary of Content: Report on agricultural markets, policy and trade in the European Union.
Readership/Target Audience: Read by European agribusiness, food companies and institutions.
ADVERTISING: No Advertising taken
BUSINESS: AGRICULTURE & FARMING

AGREEMENT
1902858U1E-408

Editorial Address: Talbot Hays Farm, WINCHESTER, RG27 8BZ **Tel:** 01252 843566 **Fax:** 01252 843566
Email: rosalind.renshaw@googlemail.com
Publisher: The National Association of Estate Agents
Frequency: 6 issues yearly
Cover Price: Free
Editor: Rosalind Renshaw
Summary of Content: Journal of the Association of Residential Letting Agents.
Readership/Target Audience: Aimed at those with an interest in the private rented sector.
BUSINESS: FINANCE & ECONOMICS: Property

AGROW WORLD CROP PROTECTION NEWS
36643U13-10

Editorial Address: Telephone House, 69-77 Paul Street, LONDON, EC2A 4LQ **Tel:** 020 7017 6843
Fax: 020 7017 6838
Email: agrow@informa.com
Advertising Address: As above. **Tel:** 020 7017 5000
Fax: 020 7017 6787
Email: robin.baker@informa.com
Web site: http://www.agrow.co.uk
ISSN: 0268-313X
Publisher: Informa UK Limited
Frequency: 24 issues yearly
Annual Sub.: £950.00
Circulation: 1,500 (Publisher's Statement)
Usual Pagination: 24
Editor: Sanjiv Rana; **Advertising Manager:** Robin Baker
Summary of Content: Newsletter covering company news, new products, market information, regulatory affairs and political reports.
Readership/Target Audience: Aimed at executives in the crop protection industry, agrochemical manufacturers, distributors and biotechnology company personnel.
ADVERTISING RATES:
Full Page Mono £1180.00
Full Page Colour £1575.00
Agency Commission: 10%
Mechanical Data: Film: Digital, Type Area: 260 x 185mm, Col Length: 260mm, Trim Size: 295 x 208mm, Bleed Size: 303 x 216mm, Page Width: 185mm
Copy instructions: Copy Date: Mono 10 days Colour 14 days prior to publication date
Average advertising content per issue: 25%
BUSINESS: CHEMICALS

AID AUTOMOTIVE INDUSTRY DATA NEWSLETTER
38277U31A-3

Editorial Address: Fairview, 31 Cape Road, WARWICK, CV34 4JP **Tel:** 01926 410040 **Fax:** 01926 776252
Email: peter.schmidt@eagleaid.com
Web site: http://www.eagleaid.com
ISSN: 0951-158X
Publisher: AID Ltd
Date Established: 1983
Frequency: 24 issues yearly
Annual Sub.: £479.00
Circulation: 14,000 (Publisher's Statement)
Usual Pagination: 20
Editor: Peter Schmidt; **Editor-in-Chief:** Peter Schmidt; **Publisher:** Peter Schmidt
Summary of Content: Newsletter about the automotive industry worldwide. Main emphasis on Europe plus quarterly market coverage of USA, Japan, China, Russia and Korea.
Readership/Target Audience: Aimed at Senior Decision makers at automotive and component manufacturers. International shipping and steel companies as well as auto industry analysts and investment banks.
ADVERTISING: No Advertising taken
BUSINESS: MOTOR TRADE: Motor Trade Accessories

AIDS
24435U56A-2_50

Editorial Address: 250 Waterloo Road, LONDON, SE1 8RD
Tel: 020 7981 0676 **Fax:** 020 7981 0556
Email: phil.daly@wolterskluwer.com
Advertising Address: The Point of Difference, 4 Chase Side Avenue, LONDON, SW20 8LU **Tel:** 020 8542 3200
Fax: 020 8543 3810

Email: pointofdiff@btinternet.com
Web site: http://www.aidsonline.com
ISSN: 0269-9370
Publisher: Lippincott Williams & Wilkins
Date Established: 1987
Frequency: 18 issues yearly
Annual Sub.: $525.00
Circulation: 1,297 (Publisher's Statement)
Usual Pagination: 192
Editor: Jenna Williams; **Advertising Manager:** Bill D'Sa
Summary of Content: Journal focusing on HIV/AIDS prevention strategy, drugs, clinical advances, epidemiological and social impact.
Readership/Target Audience: Aimed at AIDS/HIV clinicians, academics and health workers.
ADVERTISING RATES:
Full Page Mono $1900.00
Full Page Colour $3875.00
Agency Commission: 15%
Mechanical Data: Type Area: 254 x 178mm, Trim Size: 276 x 207mm, Bleed Size: 282 x 213mm, Film: Digital, Col Length: 254mm, Page Width: 178mm
Average advertising content per issue: 15%
BUSINESS: HEALTH & MEDICAL

AIDS CARE
40130U56A-3
Editorial Address: 4 Park Square, Milton Park, ABINGDON, OX14 4RN **Tel:** 020 7017 6000 **Fax:** 020 7017 6336
Email: ellie.gilroy@tandf.co.uk
Advertising Address: As above. **Fax:** 020 7017 6713
Email: jenna.johnston@tandf.co.uk
Web site: http://www.informaworld.com/caic
ISSN: 0954-0121
Publisher: Routledge, Taylor & Francis
Date Established: 1988
Frequency: 10 issues yearly
Annual Sub.: £368.00
Circulation: 600 (Publisher's Statement)
Usual Pagination: 136
Editor: Ellie Gilroy; **Advertising Manager:** Jenna Johnston
Summary of Content: Journal providing a forum for publishing in one authoritative source research and reports from the many complementary disciplines involved in the AIDS/HIV field. These include psychology, sociology, epidemiology, social work and anthropology, social aspects of medicine, nursing, education, health education, law, administration, counselling including various approaches such as behavioural therapy, psychotherapy and family therapy.
Readership/Target Audience: Aimed at psychologists, sociologists, epidemiologists, social workers, anthropologists, medical practitioners, psychiatrists, nurses, health education teachers, public health specialists and counsellors.
ADVERTISING RATES:
Full Page Mono £300.00
Agency Commission: 10%
Mechanical Data: Type Area: 210 x 130mm, Trim Size: 240 x 165mm, Col Length: 210mm, Page Width: 130mm, Film: Digital
BUSINESS: HEALTH & MEDICAL

THE AIM & PLUS DEAL MONITOR
758636U1F-4
Formerly: The AIM & OFEX Deal Monitor
Editorial Address: 3rd Floor, Henry Thomas House, 5-11 Worship Street, LONDON, EC2A 2BH **Tel:** 020 7562 3370
Email: dealmonitor@t1ps.com
Advertising Address: As above. **Fax:** 020 7628 3815
Email: robert.tyson@t1ps.com
Web site: http://www.dealmonitor.co.uk
Publisher: T1ps.com Limited
Date Established: 2001
Frequency: 6 issues yearly
Annual Sub.: £465.00
Usual Pagination: 48
Editor: Richard Gill; **Advertising Manager:** Robert Tyson; **Managing Editor:** Richard Gill
Summary of Content: Newsletter covering information and analysis relating to the Alternative Investment Market and PLUS trading faculty. Includes market news, investment trends, acquisitions and listings of deal activities. Covers articles on fees and commissions and broker and adviser changes.
Readership/Target Audience: Aimed at corporate finance advisers, accountants, lawyers, finance directors and chief executives of companies on or considering joining AIM or OFEX.
ADVERTISING: Rates on application
BUSINESS: FINANCE & ECONOMICS: Investment

THE AIM AND PLUS NEWSLETTER
21802U1F-577
Formerly: The AIM and OFEX Newsletter
Editorial Address: 3rd Floor, Henry Thomas House, 5-11 Worship Street, LONDON, EC2A 2BH **Tel:** 020 7562 3370
Fax: 020 7628 3815
Email: richard.gill@t1ps.com
Advertising Address: As above.
Email: robert.tyson@t1ps.com
ISSN: 1464-2522
Publisher: T1ps.com Limited
Date Established: 1995
Frequency: Monthly
Annual Sub.: £295.00
Usual Pagination: 24
Editor: Richard Gill; **Advertising Manager:** Robert Tyson
Summary of Content: Investment newsletter covering shares quoted on the Alternative Investment Market and the PLUS market.
Readership/Target Audience: Aimed at private and professional investors.
ADVERTISING: Rates on application
Agency Commission: 10%
Average advertising content per issue: 20%
BUSINESS: FINANCE & ECONOMICS: Investment

AIM BULLETIN
1805025U1F-636
Editorial Address: 4th Floor, Bankside House, 107 Leadenhall Street, LONDON, EC3A 4AF **Tel:** 020 7743 0050
Fax: 020 7504 3627
Email: info@sharecast.com
Advertising Address: As above.
Email: advertising@digitallook.com
Web site: http://www.aimbulletin.com
Publisher: Digital Look Ltd
Frequency: Quarterly - Published at the end of the cover month
Free to qualifying individuals
Circulation: 5,000 (Publisher's Statement)
Editor: Philip Whiterow
Summary of Content: Magazine containing news, features and other items of interest to the alternative investment market.
Readership/Target Audience: Aimed at AIM members and advisors.
ADVERTISING RATES:
Full Page Colour £2000.00
Agency Commission: 10%
Mechanical Data: Type Area: 267 x 180mm, Bleed Size: 303 x 216mm, Trim Size: 297 x 210mm, Col Length: 267mm, Page Width: 180mm, Film: Digital
Copy instructions: Copy Date: 25th of the month prior to publication date
Average advertising content per issue: 40%
BUSINESS: FINANCE & ECONOMICS: Investment

AIMA JOURNAL
1810338U1F-643
Editorial Address: 167 Fleet Street, LONDON, EC4A 2EA **Tel:** 020 7822 8380 **Fax:** 020 7822 8381
Email: editor@aima.org
Web site: http://www.aima.org
ISSN: 1479-0971
Publisher: Alternative Investment Management Association
Date Established: 1997
Frequency: Quarterly
Free to qualifying individuals
Annual Sub.: £100.00
Circulation: 6,500 (Publisher's Statement)
Usual Pagination: 52
Editor: Emma Mugridge; **Managing Editor:** Emma Mugridge
Summary of Content: Journal of the Alternative Investment Management Association.
Readership/Target Audience: Aimed at global membership, government bodies, policy makers and their advisors, regulatory and tax authorities institutional investors and the media.
ADVERTISING: No Advertising taken
BUSINESS: FINANCE & ECONOMICS: Investment

AIR & BUSINESS TRAVEL NEWS
1865039U50-244
Editorial Address: Cardinal House, 39-40 Albemarle Street, LONDON, W1S 4TE **Tel:** 020 7647 6330 **Fax:** 020 7647 6331
Email: editorial@panaceapublishing.co.uk
Web site: http://www.abtn.co.uk
Publisher: Panacea Publishing
Frequency: Daily
Cover Price: Free
Circulation: 37,000 (Publisher's Statement per month)
Editor: Tom Otley
Summary of Content: Newsletter covering the weeks news in the air travel business and managed business travel as well as associated travel interests including airlines, hotels, rail, car hire and ground transport.

Readership/Target Audience: Aimed at the business travel buyers, the suppliers, the travel management companies and the travel buyers.
ADVERTISING: Rates on application
BUSINESS: TRAVEL & TOURISM

AIR CADET
38851U40-7
Editorial Address: Headquarters Air Cadets, RAF Cranwell, SLEAFORD, NG34 8HB **Tel:** 01400 267630
Fax: 01400 261517
Email: editoraircadet@hotmail.com
Advertising Address: Mongoose Media, 2 Lonsdale Road, LONDON, NW6 6RD **Tel:** 020 7306 0300
Fax: 020 7306 0301
Email: aircadet@mongoosemedia.com
Web site: http://www.aircadets.org
Publisher: Warners Group Publications plc
Date Established: 1941
Frequency: 6 issues yearly
Free to qualifying individuals
Annual Sub.: £5.00
Circulation: 47,000 (Publisher's Statement)
Usual Pagination: 32
Editor: Carol McCombe
Summary of Content: Magazine containing news and features of general and specialist interest.
Readership/Target Audience: Aimed at air cadets in the 13 to 20 age group and adult volunteers.
ADVERTISING RATES:
Full Page Colour £810.00
Agency Commission: 10%
Mechanical Data: Bleed Size: 303 x 216mm, Page Width: 180mm, Film: Digital, Type Area: 265 x 180mm, Col Length: 265mm
Copy instructions: Copy Date: 3rd of the month prior to publication date
BUSINESS: DEFENCE

AIR CARGO NEWS
39627U49C-5
Editorial Address: Headline House, Chaucer Road, ASHFORD, TW15 2QT **Tel:** 01784 255000
Fax: 01784 246189
Email: w.masters@aircargonews.net
Advertising Address: As above.
Email: o.king@aircargonews.net
Web site: http://www.aircargonews.net
Publisher: Air Cargo Media Ltd
Date Established: 1983
Frequency: 25 issues yearly
Annual Sub.: £95.00
Circulation: 14,499 (ABC 01/01/2008 to 31/12/2008)
Usual Pagination: 24
Editor: Wendy Masters; **Advertising Manager:** Oliver King
Summary of Content: Journal containing international news and features on the specialist air cargo market.
Readership/Target Audience: Read by exporters, importers, forwarding agents and airline personnel.
ADVERTISING RATES:
Full Page Mono £5803.00
Full Page Colour £7570.00
Agency Commission: 10%
Mechanical Data: Type Area: 370 x 262mm, Bleed Size: 395 x 295mm, Trim Size: 390 x 290mm, Film: Digital, Col Length: 370mm, Page Width: 262mm
Copy instructions: Copy Date: 2 weeks prior to publication date
Average advertising content per issue: 50%
BUSINESS: TRANSPORT: Freight

AIR CARGO YEARBOOK
629434U49C-7
Editorial Address: 16 Hampden Gurney Street, LONDON, W1H 5AL **Tel:** 020 7724 3456 **Fax:** 020 7724 2632
Email: info@airtransportpubs.com
Advertising Address: As above.
Email: rosa@airtransportpubs.com
Web site: http://www.airtransportpubs.com
ISSN: 1476-2684
Publisher: Air Transport Publications Ltd
Date Established: 2002
Frequency: Annual - Published in April
Free to qualifying individuals
Annual Sub.: £110.00
Circulation: 3,500 (Publisher's Statement)
Editor: John White; **Managing Director:** Gulia Selby; **Advertising Manager:** Rosa Bellanca; **Managing Editor:** John White
Summary of Content: Publication containing articles which focus on international air cargo trends, developments and statistics. Also includes directories covering airlines, airports, cargo handling agents, GSAs, and manufacturers and suppliers of airport and airline cargo handling equipment, systems and services.
Readership/Target Audience: Aimed at senior air cargo executives and those within the air transport industry.
ADVERTISING RATES:
Full Page Colour £3100.00
Agency Commission: 10%

Business Magazines

Mechanical Data: Trim Size: 280 x 203mm, Bleed Size: 288 x 211mm, Film: Digital
Copy instructions: Copy Date: 31st March
Average advertising content per issue: 30%
BUSINESS: TRANSPORT: Freight

AIR INTERNATIONAL
36324U6A-25

Editorial Address: PO Box 100, STAMFORD, PE9 1XQ
Tel: 01780 755131 **Fax:** 01780 757261
Email: mark.ayton@keypublishing.com
Advertising Address: As above. **Fax:** 01780 751323
Email: geoff.butler@keypublishing.com
Web site: http://www.airinternational.com
ISSN: 0306-5634
Publisher: Key Publishing Ltd
Frequency: Monthly - Published on the last Thursday of the month prior to cover date
Cover Price: £3.50
Annual Sub.: £31.50
Circulation: 11,344 (ABC 01/01/2008 to 31/12/2008)
Usual Pagination: 84
Editor: Mark Ayton; **News Editor:** Dave Willis; **Managing Director:** Adrian Cox
Summary of Content: Magazine covering news and features on civil and military aviation.
Readership/Target Audience: Read by senior defence and aerospace executives.
ADVERTISING RATES:
Full Page Colour £3445.00
SCC £20.00
Agency Commission: 10%
Mechanical Data: Type Area: 267 x 180mm, Bleed Size: 307 x 215mm, Trim Size: 297 x 210mm, Col Length: 267mm, Film: Digital, Page Width: 180mm
Copy instructions: Copy Date: 3 weeks prior to publication date
Average advertising content per issue: 20%
BUSINESS: AVIATION & AERONAUTICS

THE AIR LETTER
36325U6A-28

Editorial Address: 42 Markham Court, CAMBERLEY, GU15 3HJ **Tel:** 01276 502571 **Fax:** 01276 501654
Email: newsroom@airletter.com
Web site: http://www.airletter.com
Publisher: The Air Letter
Date Established: 1932
Frequency: 250 issues yearly
Annual Sub.: £785.00
Usual Pagination: 8
Editor: Andrew Campbell; **Publisher:** Tim O'Shea
Summary of Content: Newsletter reporting on international news, politics, technology and economics in the aerospace industry.
Readership/Target Audience: Read by executives, organisations and government agencies.
ADVERTISING: No Advertising taken
BUSINESS: AVIATION & AERONAUTICS

AIR MAIL
38852U40-10

Editorial Address: Unit 3, 5 Sybron Way, Millbrook Industrial Estate, CROWBOROUGH, TN6 3DZ
Tel: 01892 600192 **Fax:** 01892 665375
Email: colin.pullen@rafatrad.co.uk
Advertising Address: As above.
Email: adverts@rafatrad.co.uk
Web site: http://www.rafatrad.co.uk
ISSN: 0002-2446
Publisher: RAFATRAD Ltd
Date Established: 1940
Frequency: Quarterly
Free to qualifying individuals
Circulation: 64,406 (Publisher's Statement)
Usual Pagination: 64
Editor: Colin Pullen; **Advertising Manager:** Colin Pullen
Summary of Content: Journal of the Royal Air Force Association, containing articles about the RAF past and present.
Readership/Target Audience: Read by serving and ex-RAF members.
ADVERTISING RATES:
Full Page Mono £1082.00
Full Page Colour £1483.00
Agency Commission: 10%
Mechanical Data: Film: Digital, Type Area: 263 x 182mm, Bleed Size: 303 x 216mm, Trim Size: 297 x 210mm, Col Length: 263mm, Page Width: 182mm, No. of Columns (Display): 2, Print Process: Web offset
Copy instructions: Copy Date: Beginning of the month prior to publication date
Average advertising content per issue: 25%
BUSINESS: DEFENCE

AIR QUALITY MANAGEMENT
40620U57-2

Editorial Address: 100 Avenue Road, Swiss Cottage, LONDON, NW3 3PF **Tel:** 020 7393 7000 **Fax:** 020 7393 7010

Email: bell.freelance@gmail.com
Web site: http://www.air-quality-management.co.uk
Publisher: GEE Publishing Ltd
Date Established: 1995
Frequency: Monthly
Annual Sub.: £309.00
Usual Pagination: 12
Editor: Robert Bell
Summary of Content: Newsletter providing news and features on all aspects of local air quality management, including policy, technology and research into health effects.
Readership/Target Audience: Aimed at people working in the environmental and public health sectors and in industry.
ADVERTISING: No Advertising taken
BUSINESS: ENVIRONMENT & POLLUTION

AIR TRAFFIC TECHNOLOGY INTERNATIONAL
1616087U6D-502

Editorial Address: Abinger House, Church Street, DORKING, RH4 1DF **Tel:** 01306 743744 **Fax:** 01306 887546
Email: a.pickering@ukintpress.com
Advertising Address: As above. **Fax:** 01306 742525
Email: c.scott@ukintpress.com
Web site: http://www.ukintpress.com
Publisher: UKIP Media & Events Ltd
Frequency: Annual - Published in October
Editor: Andrew Pickering
Summary of Content: Magazine focusing on the latest air traffic technology, products, services, simulation and training.
Readership/Target Audience: Aimed at air traffic professionals, aviation authority managers and other aviation professionals.
ADVERTISING RATES:
Full Page Colour £5175.00
Agency Commission: 15%
Mechanical Data: Bleed Size: 303 x 216mm, Trim Size: 297 x 210mm, Film: Digital
Average advertising content per issue: 25%
BUSINESS: AVIATION & AERONAUTICS: Aviation Engineering Equipment

AIR TRANSPORT WORLD
36328U6A-35

Editorial Address: 34A West Street, MARLOW, SL7 2NB
Tel: 01628 477775 **Fax:** 01628 481111
Email: cathybuyck@aol.com
Advertising Address: As above.
Email: ann.haigh@penton.com
Web site: http://www.atwonline.com
ISSN: 0002-2543
Publisher: Penton Media
Date Established: 1964
Frequency: Monthly - Published around the end of the cover month
Free to qualifying individuals
Annual Sub.: $105.00
Circulation: 38,054 (BPA Worldwide 01/01/2008 to 30/06/2008)
Usual Pagination: 84
Editor: Perry Flint; **News Editor:** Brian Straus; **Editor-in-Chief:** Perry Flint; **Managing Director:** Ann Haigh; **Advertising Manager:** Ann Haigh; **Managing Editor:** Kathryn Young
Summary of Content: Journal covering all aspects of airlines management.
Readership/Target Audience: Read by senior executives in the commercial airline industry.
ADVERTISING RATES:
Full Page Mono $11096.00
Full Page Colour $13765.00
Agency Commission: 15%
Mechanical Data: Type Area: 254 x 178mm, Bleed Size: 279 x 203mm, Trim Size: 273 x 197mm, Col Length: 254mm, Page Width: 178mm, Film: Digital
Copy instructions: Copy Date: 6th of the month prior to publication date
BUSINESS: AVIATION & AERONAUTICS

AIRCRAFT COMMERCE
708204U6A-20

Editorial Address: Suite 2B, Bishops Wheel House, Albion Way, HORSHAM, RH12 1AH **Tel:** 01403 230302
Fax: 01403 230525
Email: charles@aircraft-commerce.com
Advertising Address: As above.
Email: sales@aircraft-commerce.com
Web site: http://www.aircraft-commerce.com
ISSN: 1463-1873
Publisher: Nimrod Publications
Date Established: 1998
Frequency: 6 issues yearly
Free to qualifying individuals
Annual Sub.: £197.00
Circulation: 9,024 (BPA Worldwide 01/01/2007 to 01/07/2007)
Usual Pagination: 52

Editor: Charles Williams; **Advertising Manager:** Charles Williams; **Publisher:** Charles Williams
Summary of Content: Magazine covering all aspects of the economics and management of air transport.
Readership/Target Audience: Aimed at decision makers and executives within the aircraft industry.
ADVERTISING RATES:
Full Page Colour $7500.00
Agency Commission: 15%
Mechanical Data: Page Width: 183mm, Film: Digital, Trim Size: 297 x 215mm, Type Area: 273 x 183mm, Col Length: 273mm
Copy instructions: Copy Date: 1 week prior to publication date
Average advertising content per issue: 35%
BUSINESS: AVIATION & AERONAUTICS

AIRCRAFT ENGINEERING AND AEROSPACE TECHNOLOGY: AN INTERNATIONAL JOURNAL
36399U6D-40

Formerly: Aircraft Engineering and Aerospace Technology
Editorial Address: 15 Haslemere Road, Crouch End, LONDON, N8 9QP **Tel:** 020 8340 9265 **Fax:** 020 8340 9265
Email: tersv@aol.com
Web site: http://www.emeraldinsight.com/aeat.htm
ISSN: 0002-2667
Publisher: Emerald Group Publishing Ltd
Date Established: 1928
Frequency: 6 issues yearly
Usual Pagination: 106
Editor: Terry Savage; **Advertising Manager:** Andrea Marsden; **Publisher:** Harry Colson
Summary of Content: Publication containing peer-reviewed academic papers on research and development in the aerospace industry.
Readership/Target Audience: Read by chief engineers, aircraft design engineers and maintenance departments of the major airlines, military, aerospace companies, and university research departments.
ADVERTISING: No Advertising taken
BUSINESS: AVIATION & AERONAUTICS: Aviation Engineering Equipment

AIRCRAFT ILLUSTRATED
36329U6A-21

Editorial Address: Riverdene Business Park, Molesey Road, HERSHAM, KT12 4RG **Tel:** 01932 266600
Fax: 01932 266601
Email: amy.bridges@ianallanpublishing.co.uk
Advertising Address: Foundry Road, STAMFORD, PE9 2PP
Tel: 01780 484634 **Fax:** 01780 763388
Email: kirsty.flatt@ianallanpublishing.co.uk
Web site: http://www.aircraftillustrated.com
ISSN: 0002-2675
Publisher: Ian Allan Publishing Ltd
Date Established: 1967
Frequency: Monthly
Cover Price: £3.80
Annual Sub.: £45.60
Circulation: 35,000 (Publisher's Statement)
Usual Pagination: 100
Publisher: Paul Appleton
Summary of Content: Publication covering both military and civil aviation news and features.
Readership/Target Audience: Read by military and civil aviation industry personnel, serving RAF officers and cadets, aircraft preservationists, modellers, air travellers and enthusiasts.
ADVERTISING RATES:
Full Page Colour £800.00
SCC £10.00
Agency Commission: 10%
Mechanical Data: Bleed Size: 303 x 216mm, Film: Digital, Trim Size: 297 x 210mm, Type Area: 265 x 185mm, Col Length: 265mm, Page Width: 185mm
Copy instructions: Copy Date: 1 month prior to publication date
Average advertising content per issue: 20%
BUSINESS: AVIATION & AERONAUTICS

AIRCRAFT INTERIORS INTERNATIONAL
36417U6F-40

Editorial Address: Abinger House, Church Street, DORKING, RH4 1DF **Tel:** 01306 743744 **Fax:** 01306 887546
Email: aircraftinteriors@ukintpress.com
Advertising Address: As above. **Fax:** 01306 742525
Email: aircraftinteriors@ukintpress.com
Web site: http://www.ukipme.com
ISSN: 1463-8932
Publisher: UKIP Media & Events Ltd
Date Established: 1998
Frequency: 5 issues yearly - Published around the middle of the cover date
Free to qualifying individuals
Annual Sub.: £28.00
Circulation: 14,490 (BPA Worldwide 01/07/2007 to 31/12/2007)

Usual Pagination: 112
Editor: Anthony James; **Managing Director:** Graham Johnson; **Advertising Manager:** Simon Hughes
Summary of Content: Magazine containing world news, new product reviews, interviews, case studies on aircraft interior industry developments, systems appraisals and technology profiles.
Readership/Target Audience: Aimed at designers, engineers, brand managers and department managers engaged in all aspects of aircraft interior design and completion, including airlines, interior design consultants, aircraft manufacturers and completion centres.
ADVERTISING RATES:
Full Page Colour £3925.00
Mechanical Data: Film: Digital, Trim Size: 300 x 230mm, Type Area: 276 x 200mm, Col Length: 276mm, Page Width: 200mm
BUSINESS: AVIATION & AERONAUTICS: Airlines

AIRCRAFT MAINTENANCE & ENGINEERING DIRECTORY
629437U6D-90

Editorial Address: 16 Hampden Gurney Street, LONDON, W1H 5AL **Tel:** 020 7724 3456 **Fax:** 020 7724 2632
Email: info@airtransportpubs.com
Advertising Address: As above.
Email: advertising@airtransportpubs.com
Web site: http://www.airtransportpubs.com
ISSN: 1369-1031
Publisher: Air Transport Publications Ltd
Date Established: 1997
Frequency: Annual - Published in May
Cover Price: £90.00
Free to qualifying individuals
Circulation: 3,500 (Publisher's Statement)
Usual Pagination: 376
Editor: Sarah Murray; **Advertising Manager:** Jina Lawrence
Summary of Content: Directory focusing on industry articles and statistics, and airline and world fleet data. Includes directories of airlines, third party services and manufacturers and suppliers of support equipment, systems and services.
Readership/Target Audience: Aimed at senior management within the airline and aircraft MRO industry worldwide.
ADVERTISING RATES:
Full Page Colour £3400.00
Agency Commission: 10%
Mechanical Data: Bleed Size: 288 x 211mm, Trim Size: 280 x 203mm, Film: Digital
Copy instructions: Copy Date: 4 weeks prior to publication date
Average advertising content per issue: 40%
BUSINESS: AVIATION & AERONAUTICS: Aviation Engineering Equipment

---

AIRCRAFT TECHNOLOGY ENGINEERING & MAINTENANCE
36401U6D-150

Editorial Address: Ludgate House, 245 Blackfriars Road, LONDON, SE1 9UY **Tel:** 020 7579 4840 **Fax:** 020 7579 4848
Email: daniellah@aviation-industry.com
Advertising Address: As above.
Email: simonb@aviation-industry.com
Web site: http://www.aviationindustrygroup.com
ISSN: 0967-439X
Publisher: UBM Aviation
Date Established: 1992
Frequency: 7 issues yearly - Published on the 10th of the cover month
Cover Price: £25.00
Free to qualifying individuals
Annual Sub.: £150.00
Circulation: 10,387 (BPA Worldwide 01/01/2008 to 30/06/2008)
Usual Pagination: 88
Editor: Daniella Horwitz
Summary of Content: International aviation magazine covering civil aircraft design, manufacturing and maintenance (MRO) sectors.
Readership/Target Audience: Read by the management staff of aircraft and component manufacturers, airline manufacturers, airline management executives and MRO professionals working within the commercial aviation industry.
ADVERTISING RATES:
Full Page Mono £3451.00
Full Page Colour £5310.00
Agency Commission: 15%
Mechanical Data: Type Area: 258 x 186mm, Film: Digital, Print Process: Offset-litho, Bleed Size: 284 x 216mm, Trim Size: 278 x 210mm, Col Length: 258mm, Page Width: 186mm, No. of Columns (Display): 3
Copy instructions: Copy Date: 20th of the month prior to the first cover month
Average advertising content per issue: 40%
Supplement(s): The Engine Yearbook - 1xY
BUSINESS: AVIATION & AERONAUTICS: Aviation Engineering Equipment

---

AIRCRAFT VALUE JOURNAL
36330U6A-22

Editorial Address: 23 Cherry Lane, Bearley, STRATFORD-UPON-AVON, CV37 0SX **Tel:** 01789 730283
Fax: 01789 730309
Email: info@aircraftvalues.net
Web site: http://www.aircraftvalues.net
ISSN: 0966-0348
Publisher: Aircraft Value Analysis Co
Frequency: 6 issues yearly
Annual Sub.: £100.00
Usual Pagination: 24
Editor: Paul Leighton
Summary of Content: Publication covering analytical assessment of aircraft values, the various factors that affect them and of the users of such equipment.
Readership/Target Audience: Aimed at the aviation community, banks, financial institutions, lessors and airlines.
ADVERTISING: No Advertising taken
BUSINESS: AVIATION & AERONAUTICS

AIRFINANCE ANNUAL
36371U6A-55

Editorial Address: 1 North Hill, COLCHESTER, CO1 1DZ
Tel: 01206 579591 **Fax:** 01206 765309
Email: lisa@euromoney-yearbooks.co.uk
Advertising Address: As above.
Email: lisa@euromoney-yearbooks.co.uk
Web site: http://www.euromoney-yearbooks.co.uk
ISSN: 0266-2132
Publisher: Euromoney Institutional Investor plc
Date Established: 1984
Frequency: Annual - Published in September
Cover Price: £195.00
Circulation: 10,000 (Publisher's Statement)
Usual Pagination: 300
Editor: Lisa Paul
Summary of Content: Journal providing country by country profiles illustrating the composition of the domestic aviation market, focusing on operators, manufacturers and financiers, the regulatory, legal and taxation framework, export credit facilities and documentation.
Readership/Target Audience: Aimed at senior executives in all major carriers, financiers, and sundry service suppliers to the international commercial aviation finance market.
ADVERTISING: Rates on application
Agency Commission: 15%
Average advertising content per issue: 20%
BUSINESS: AVIATION & AERONAUTICS

AIRFINANCE JOURNAL
36418U6F-50

Editorial Address: Nestor House, Playhouse Yard, LONDON, EC4V 5EX **Tel:** 020 7779 8888
Fax: 020 7779 8525
Email: awhyte@euromoneyplc.com
Advertising Address: As above. **Fax:** 020 7779 8353
Email: aleggatt@euromoneyplc.com
Web site: http://www.airfinancejournal.com
ISSN: 0143-2257
Publisher: Euromoney Institutional Investor plc
Date Established: 1980
Frequency: 10 issues yearly - Published on the 1st of the cover month
Cover Price: £65.00
Annual Sub.: £550.00
Circulation: 2,803 (ABC 01/07/2008 to 30/06/2009)
Usual Pagination: 44
Editor: Sophie Segal; **Advertising Manager:** Andrew Leggatt; **Group Editor:** Alasdair Whyte
Summary of Content: Magazine covering corporate and asset financing within the commercial aerospace industry.
Readership/Target Audience: Read by financiers, airline personnel, lawyers, manufacturers and insurers.
ADVERTISING RATES:
Full Page Colour £7704.00
Agency Commission: 10%
Mechanical Data: Film: Digital, Trim Size: 286 x 210mm, Bleed Size: 292 x 216mm
Copy instructions: Copy Date: 1 week prior to publication date
Average advertising content per issue: 28%
BUSINESS: AVIATION & AERONAUTICS: Airlines

AIRFORCES MONTHLY
38853U40-8

Editorial Address: PO Box 100, STAMFORD, PE9 1XQ
Tel: 01780 755131 **Fax:** 01780 751323
Email: edafm@keypublishing.com
Advertising Address: As above.
Email: geoff.butler@keypublishing.com
Web site: http://www.airforcesmonthly.com
Publisher: Key Publishing Ltd
Frequency: Monthly
Cover Price: £3.70
Circulation: 20,750 (ABC 01/01/2008 to 31/12/2008)
Usual Pagination: 84
Editor: Alan Warnes; **News Editor:** Dave Allport; **Managing Director:** Adrian Cox

---

Summary of Content: Magazine containing news about modern military aircraft.
Readership/Target Audience: Aimed at the military, airspace personnel, industry and military enthusiasts.
ADVERTISING RATES:
Full Page Colour £1449.00
SCC £20.00
Agency Commission: 10%
Mechanical Data: Film: Digital, Bleed Size: 307 x 220mm, Trim Size: 297 x 210mm, Type Area: 287 x 200mm, Col Length: 287mm, Page Width: 200mm
Copy instructions: Copy Date: 2 weeks prior to publication date
BUSINESS: DEFENCE

AIRLINE BUSINESS
36419U6F-70

Editorial Address: Quadrant House, The Quadrant, SUTTON, SM2 5AS **Tel:** 020 8652 3500 **Fax:** 020 8652 3842
Email: airline.business@flightglobal.com
Advertising Address: As above. **Fax:** 020 8652 8923
Email: shaun.barton@rbi.co.uk
Web site: http://www.airlinebusiness.com
ISSN: 0268-7615
Publisher: Reed Business Information
Date Established: 1985
Frequency: Monthly - Published on the last Wednesday of the month
Free to qualifying individuals
Annual Sub.: £87.00
Circulation: 24,986 (BPA Worldwide 01/07/2007 to 31/12/2007)
Usual Pagination: 78
Editor: Mark Pilling; **Features Editor:** Kerry Ezard
Summary of Content: Publication covering the financial and commercial aspects of airline management.
Readership/Target Audience: Read by senior management of the civil airline industry, plus associated finance, leasing, manufacturing and legal companies.
ADVERTISING RATES:
Full Page Mono £5245.00
Full Page Colour £6850.00
Agency Commission: 10%
Mechanical Data: Page Width: 181mm, Type Area: 246 x 181mm, Col Length: 246mm, Film: Digital, Bleed Size: 273 x 200mm, Trim Size: 267 x 197mm
Copy instructions: Copy Date: 1 week prior to publication date
Supplement(s): Airline Industry Guide - 1xY, Bridging the GAAP - 1xY, IT Trends Survey - 1xY
BUSINESS: AVIATION & AERONAUTICS: Airlines

AIRLINE CARGO MANAGEMENT
1655351U49C-503

Editorial Address: 16 Hampden Gurney Street, LONDON, W1H 5AL **Tel:** 020 7724 3456
Email: editor@airlinecargomanagement.com
Advertising Address: As above. **Fax:** 020 7724 2632
Email: rosa@airtransportpubs.com
Web site: http://www.airlinecargomanagement.com
ISSN: 1478-5358
Publisher: Air Transport Publications Ltd
Date Established: 2002
Frequency: Quarterly
Free to qualifying individuals
Circulation: 6,009 (BPA Worldwide 01/07/2007 to 31/12/2007)
Usual Pagination: 64
Editor: Alexandra Lennane; **Advertising Manager:** Rosa Bellanca
Summary of Content: Magazine focusing on international air cargo management issues.
Readership/Target Audience: Aimed at senior airline and airport cargo managers and ground handling executives.
ADVERTISING RATES:
Full Page Colour £2950.00
Agency Commission: 10%
Mechanical Data: Bleed Size: 288 x 211mm, Trim Size: 280 x 203mm, Film: Digital
Copy instructions: Copy Date: 4 weeks prior to publication date
Average advertising content per issue: 40%
BUSINESS: TRANSPORT: Freight

AIRLINE FLEET MANAGEMENT
36420U6F-72

Formerly: Airline Fleet and Network Management
Editorial Address: Ludgate House, 245 Blackfriars Road, LONDON, SE1 9UY **Tel:** 020 7579 4840 **Fax:** 020 7579 4848
Email: philipt@aviation-industry.com
Advertising Address: As above.
Email: philipt@aviation-industry.com
Web site: http://www.aviationindustrygroup.com
ISSN: 1466-3767
Publisher: UBM Aviation
Date Established: 1998
Frequency: 8 issues yearly
Annual Sub.: £115.00

Business Magazines

Circulation: 16,000 (Publisher's Statement)
Usual Pagination: 70
Editor: Philip Tozer-Pennington; **Managing Director:** Philip Tozer-Pennington; **Advertising Manager:** Philip Tozer-Pennington
Summary of Content: Magazine covering the selection, acquisition, finance and trading of commercial aircraft.
Readership/Target Audience: Aimed at professionals working within airline fleet planning, purchasing, finance and trading departments.
ADVERTISING RATES:
Full Page Mono £2736.00
Full Page Colour £4208.00
Agency Commission: 15%
Mechanical Data: Col Widths (Display): 58mm, No. of Columns (Display): 3, Bleed Size: 284 x 216mm, Film: Digital, Trim Size: 278 x 210mm
Average advertising content per issue: 25%
BUSINESS: AVIATION & AERONAUTICS: Airlines

AIRPORT EQUIPMENT & SERVICES BUYERS' GUIDE
629436U6B-57

Formerly: Airport Yearbook
Editorial Address: 16 Hampden Gurney Street, LONDON, W1H 5AL **Tel:** 020 7724 3456 **Fax:** 020 7724 2632
Email: info@airtransportpubs.com
Advertising Address: As above.
Email: besem@airtransportpubs.com
Web site: http://www.airtransportpubs.com
ISSN: 1750-693X
Publisher: Air Transport Publications Ltd
Date Established: 2006
Frequency: Annual - Published in July
Cover Price: £110.00
Free to qualifying individuals
Circulation: 3,500 (Publisher's Statement)
Usual Pagination: 350
Editor: Sarah Murray; **Managing Director:** Gulia Selby; **Advertising Manager:** Bessem Bikhazi
Summary of Content: Yearbook including directories of airports, airport authorities, and manufacturers and suppliers of airport equipment, systems and services.
Readership/Target Audience: Aimed at senior executives within airports worldwide.
ADVERTISING RATES:
Full Page Colour £3250.00
Agency Commission: 10%
Mechanical Data: Film: Digital, Trim Size: 280 x 203mm, Bleed Size: 288 x 211mm
Average advertising content per issue: 40%
BUSINESS: AVIATION & AERONAUTICS: Airports

THE AIRPORT OPERATOR
1641121U6B-354

Editorial Address: 3A Gatwick Metro Centre, Balcombe Road, HORLEY, RH6 9GA **Tel:** 01293 783851
Fax: 01293 782959
Email: james@pps-publications.com
Advertising Address: As above.
Email: james@pps-publications.com
Web site: http://www.aoa.org.uk
Publisher: PPS Publications Ltd
Frequency: Quarterly
Free to qualifying individuals
Circulation: 4,000 (Publisher's Statement)
Usual Pagination: 52
Editor: Ross Falconer; **Advertising Manager:** James Nixon
Summary of Content: Magazine covering the UK airport and aviation industry.
Readership/Target Audience: Aimed at airport executives, legislators and relevant regulators.
ADVERTISING: Rates on application
Agency Commission: 10%
Mechanical Data: Type Area: 270 x 190mm, Trim Size: 297 x 210mm, Bleed Size: 303 x 216mm, Col Length: 270mm, Film: Digital, Page Width: 190mm
Copy instructions: Copy Date: 2 weeks prior to publication date
Average advertising content per issue: 40%
BUSINESS: AVIATION & AERONAUTICS: Airports

AIRPORT WORLD
36376U6B-55

Editorial Address: 26-30 London Road, TWICKENHAM, TW1 3RW **Tel:** 020 8831 7507 **Fax:** 020 8891 0123
Email: joe@insightgrp.co.uk
Advertising Address: As above. **Tel:** 020 8831 7500
Email: jonathan@insightgrp.co.uk
Web site: http://www.airport-world.com
Publisher: Insight Media Ltd
Date Established: 1996
Frequency: 6 issues yearly
Free to qualifying individuals
Annual Sub.: £80.00
Circulation: 7,000 (Publisher's Statement)
Usual Pagination: 68
Editor: Joe Bates

Summary of Content: Magazine dealing with airport development and business strategies.
Language(s): Chinese; English
Readership/Target Audience: Aimed at airport senior and middle management. Primary circulation supplied by Airports Council International.
ADVERTISING RATES:
Full Page Colour £4000.00
Agency Commission: 15%
Mechanical Data: Film: Digital, Type Area: 265 x 185mm, Col Length: 265mm, Bleed Size: 303 x 216mm, Trim Size: 297 x 210mm, Page Width: 185mm
Average advertising content per issue: 40%
BUSINESS: AVIATION & AERONAUTICS: Airports

AIRPORTS INTERNATIONAL
36377U6B-60

Editorial Address: PO Box 100, STAMFORD, PE9 1XQ
Tel: 01780 755131 **Fax:** 01780 757261
Email: tom.allett@keypublishing.com
Advertising Address: As above.
Email: brodie.baxter@keypublishing.com
Web site: http://www.airportsint.com
Publisher: Key Publishing Ltd
Date Established: 1968
Frequency: 9 issues yearly
Free to qualifying individuals
Annual Sub.: £95.00
Circulation: 12,100 (ABC 01/01/2008 to 31/12/2008)
Usual Pagination: 48
Editor: Tom Allett
Summary of Content: Magazine covering all aspects of ground based civil aviation operations. Features include buyers guides to equipment, airport safety and airport development.
Readership/Target Audience: Aimed at airport directors and managers, operations directors, ground handling and ATC and ATM industry personnel worldwide.
ADVERTISING RATES:
Full Page Colour £3939.00
Agency Commission: 10%
Mechanical Data: Type Area: 269 x 186mm, Bleed Size: 303 x 216mm, Trim Size: 297 x 210mm, Film: Digital, Col Length: 269mm, Page Width: 186mm
Copy instructions: Copy Date: 3 weeks prior to publication date
Average advertising content per issue: 30%
BUSINESS: AVIATION & AERONAUTICS: Airports

AIRPORTS OF THE WORLD
1820185U6B-357

Editorial Address: PO Box 100, STAMFORD, PE9 1XQ
Tel: 01780 755131 **Fax:** 01780 757261
Email: mark.nicholls@keypublishing.com
Advertising Address: As above. **Fax:** 01780 751323
Email: andrew.mason@keypublishing.com
Web site: http://www.airportsworld.com
Publisher: Key Publishing Ltd
Date Established: 2005
Frequency: 6 issues yearly
Cover Price: £3.80
Circulation: 35,000 (Print Run)
Usual Pagination: 84
Editor: Mark Nicholls
Summary of Content: Magazine covering articles on airports around the world including features on jobs at airports, behind the scenes at airports, technical articles and developments.
Readership/Target Audience: Aimed at aviation enthusiasts, airport employees and those working in the industry.
ADVERTISING RATES:
Full Page Colour £1315.00
Agency Commission: 10%
Mechanical Data: Type Area: 287 x 200mm, Bleed Size: 307 x 220mm, Trim Size: 297 x 210mm, Col Length: 287mm, Page Width: 200mm, Film: Digital
Copy instructions: Copy Date: 3 weeks prior to publication date
Average advertising content per issue: 10%
BUSINESS: AVIATION & AERONAUTICS: Airports

AJ SPECIFICATION
35780U4A-11

Formerly: AJ Focus
Editorial Address: Greater London House, Hampstead Road, LONDON, NW1 7EJ **Tel:** 020 7728 5000
Email: architecturepr@emap.com
Advertising Address: As above.
Email: tom.peardon@emap.com
Web site: http://www.architectsjournal.co.uk
Publisher: EMAP Insight
Date Established: 1986
Frequency: Monthly - Published on the 3rd Thursday of the cover month
Free to qualifying individuals
Annual Sub.: £40.00
Usual Pagination: 68
Editor: Tally Wade

Summary of Content: Journal covering the design, development, manufacture and use of products for the building industry. Features include new products, products in practice, factory focus and the showcase section.
Readership/Target Audience: Read by architects, technicians, engineers and surveyors.
ADVERTISING RATES:
Full Page Colour £2943.00
Mechanical Data: Film: Digital, Type Area: 231 x 186 mm, Col Length: 231mm, Trim Size: 265 x 210mm, Bleed Size: 271 x 216mm, Page Width: 186mm
Copy instructions: Copy Date: 3 weeks prior to publication date
Supplement to: The Architects' Journal
BUSINESS: ARCHITECTURE & BUILDING: Architecture

ALA BULLETIN
39127U44-169

Formerly: The Bulletin of the Agricultural Law Association
Editorial Address: Kimblewick Cottage, Prince Albert Road, West Mersea, COLCHESTER, CO5 8AZ **Tel:** 01206 383521
Email: geoff@geoffwhittaker.com
Web site: http://www.ala.org.uk
Publisher: Agricultural Law Association
Date Established: 1985
Frequency: Quarterly
Annual Sub.: £70.00
Circulation: 1,200 (Publisher's Statement)
Usual Pagination: 20
Editor: Geoff Whittaker
Summary of Content: Technical and political commentary and updates of rural professional interest.
Readership/Target Audience: Aimed at members and prospective members of the Agricultural Law Association.
ADVERTISING: No Advertising taken
BUSINESS: LEGAL

ALCOHOL & ALCOHOLISM
40517U56R-5

Editorial Address: 35 Morningside Park, EDINBURGH, EH10 5HD **Tel:** 0131 537 6557 **Fax:** 0131 537 6866
Email: jonathan.chick@gmail.com
Advertising Address: Great Clarendon Street, OXFORD, OX2 6DP **Tel:** 01865 353907
Email: jnlsadvertising@oxfordjournals.org
Web site: http://www.oup.co.uk/jnls
Publisher: OUP
Date Established: 1966
Frequency: 6 issues yearly
Annual Sub.: £400.00
Circulation: 900 (Publisher's Statement)
Usual Pagination: 120
Editor: Jonathan Chick
Summary of Content: Journal containing papers on clinical, biomedical, psychological and sociological aspects of alcoholism and alcohol research.
Readership/Target Audience: Read by scientists and treatment practitioners in the private and public sectors.
ADVERTISING RATES:
Full Page Mono £646.00
Full Page Colour £1076.00
Agency Commission: 10%
Mechanical Data: Type Area: 255 x 178mm, Print Process: Litho, Trim Size: 279 x 216mm, Film: Digital, Col Length: 285 x 222mm, Page Width: 180mm
BUSINESS: HEALTH & MEDICAL: Health Medical Related

ALERT MAGAZINE
1623510U53-679

Editorial Address: Retra House, St. John's Terrace, 1 Ampthill Street, BEDFORD, MK42 9EY **Tel:** 01234 269110
Fax: 01234 269609
Email: alert@retra.co.uk
Advertising Address: As above.
Email: alert@retra.co.uk
Web site: http://www.retra.co.uk
Publisher: RETRA
Frequency: 6 issues yearly
Cover Price: Free
Circulation: 2,000 (Publisher's Statement)
Usual Pagination: 28
Editor: Louise Lloyd-Jones; **Advertising Manager:** Louise Lloyd-Jones
Summary of Content: Magazine covering the independent electrical retailing trade.
Readership/Target Audience: Read by members of retra (Radio, Electrical and Television Retailers' Association).
ADVERTISING RATES:
Full Page Colour £850.00
Mechanical Data: Film: Digital, Type Area: 275 x 185mm, Bleed Size: 303 x 216mm, Trim Size: 297 x 210mm, Col Length: 275mm, Page Width: 185mm
Copy instructions: Copy Date: 15 days prior to publication date
Average advertising content per issue: 20%
BUSINESS: RETAILING & WHOLESALING

ALIMENTOS Y BEBIDAS, LATINOAMÉRICA
1750356U22R-763

Editorial Address: Lodge House, Lodge Lane, Langham, COLCHESTER, CO4 5NE **Tel:** 01206 233156
Fax: 01206 233157
Email: c.rowan@foodandbeverageinternational.com
Advertising Address: As above.
Email: m.byrne@foodandbeverageinternational.com
Web site: http://www.foodandbeverageinternational.com
ISSN: 1752-0681
Publisher: Zenith International Publishing
Date Established: 2006
Frequency: 6 issues yearly
Free to qualifying individuals
Circulation: 13,200 (Publisher's Statement)
Usual Pagination: 52
Editor: Claire Rowan; **Executive Editor:** Maureen Byrne;
Advertising Manager: Maureen Byrne; **Managing Editor:** Claire Rowan; **Publisher:** Maureen Byrne
Summary of Content: Magazine covering the latest food and beverage manufacturing news and technology, food and drink product formulation and launches and the latest technical developments in processing, packaging, ingredients and food safety. Published in both Spanish and Portuguese.
Language(s): Portuguese; Spanish
Readership/Target Audience: Aimed at food and drink manufacturers throughout Latin America.
ADVERTISING RATES:
Full Page Colour $3750.00
BUSINESS: FOOD: Food Related

ALLERGY NEWSLETTER
40450U56L-5

Editorial Address: PO Box 278, TWICKENHAM, TW1 4QQ
Tel: 020 8892 4949 **Fax:** 020 8892 4950
Email: aaallergy@btconnect.com
Advertising Address: As above.
Email: aaallergy@btconnect.com
Web site: http://www.actionagainstallergy.co.uk
Publisher: Action Against Allergy
Date Established: 1978
Frequency: 3 issues yearly - Published in March, July and November
Cover Price: £5.00
Free to qualifying individuals
Annual Sub.: £15.00
Circulation: 1,500 (Publisher's Statement)
Usual Pagination: 48
Editor: Patricia Schooling
Summary of Content: Newsletter containing news, views and tips for AAA members, plus conference reports and articles by allergists. Covers the whole spectrum of medical research, diagnostic practice and treatment of allergies and allergy-related illness. Regular feature on products and services to help the allergy sufferer.
Readership/Target Audience: Aimed at allergy sufferers and health professionals dealing with allergic illness.
ADVERTISING RATES:
Full Page Colour £350.00
Agency Commission: 10%
Mechanical Data: Trim Size: 210 x 148mm, Bleed Size: +3mm, Film: Digital, Type Area: 190 x 125mm, Col Length: 190mm, Page Width: 125mm
Copy instructions: Copy Date: 3 weeks prior to publication
Average advertising content per issue: 35%
BUSINESS: HEALTH & MEDICAL: Disability & Rehabilitation

ALLIANCE MAGAZINE
1732559U1P-282

Formerly: Alliance
Editorial Address: 1st Floor, Corsham Street, LONDON, N1 6DR **Tel:** 020 7608 1862 **Fax:** 020 7608 1862
Email: alliance@alliancemagazine.org
Advertising Address: As above.
Email: alliance@alliancemagazine.org
Web site: http://www.alliancemagazine.org
ISSN: 1359-4621
Publisher: Alliance Publishing Trust
Date Established: 1998
Frequency: Quarterly - Published at the beginning of the cover month March, June, September and December
Free to qualifying individuals
Annual Sub.: £89.00
Circulation: 16,000 (Publisher's Statement)
Usual Pagination: 64
Editor: Caroline Hartnell; **Advertising Manager:** Radwan Siddiq; **Publisher:** David Drewery
Summary of Content: Magazine covering in-depth coverage and different perspectives on issues relating to philanthropy and social investment.
Language(s): English; Spanish
Readership/Target Audience: Aimed at corporate backers and those working in the giving sector.
ADVERTISING RATES:
Full Page Colour £1750.00
Mechanical Data: Type Area: 226 x 182mm, Col Length: 226mm, Page Width: 182mm, Film: Digital
Copy instructions: Copy Date: 2 weeks prior to publication date

Average advertising content per issue: 5%
BUSINESS: FINANCE & ECONOMICS: Fundraising

ALTERNATIVE INSURANCE CAPITAL
35102U1D-12

Editorial Address: Informa House, 30-32 Mortimer Street, LONDON, W1W 7RE **Tel:** 020 7017 4020
Fax: 020 7436 8414
Email: graham.village@informa.com
Web site: http://www.evandale.co.uk
ISSN: 1369-9628
Publisher: Informa PLC
Date Established: 1991
Frequency: Monthly
Annual Sub.: £1284.00
Usual Pagination: 16
Editor: Graham Village
Summary of Content: Newsletter providing news and comment on financial reinsurance, insurance futures, risk securitization and capital market products.
Readership/Target Audience: Aimed at members of the insurance industry.
ADVERTISING: No Advertising taken
BUSINESS: FINANCE & ECONOMICS: Insurance

ALUMINIUM INTERNATIONAL TODAY
38142U27-2

Formerly: Aluminium Today
Editorial Address: Westgate House, 120-130 Station Road, REDHILL, RH1 1ET **Tel:** 01737 768611 **Fax:** 01737 855474
Email: aluminium@uk.dmgworldmedia.com
Advertising Address: As above. **Tel:** 01737 855000
Email: kenclark@dmgworldmedia.com
Web site: http://www.aluminiumtoday.com
ISSN: 1475-455X
Publisher: DMG Business Media
Date Established: 1980
Frequency: 6 issues yearly
Cover Price: £35.00
Free to qualifying individuals
Annual Sub.: £193.00
Circulation: 7,000 (Publisher's Statement)
Usual Pagination: 48
Editor: Tim Smith
Summary of Content: Journal of aluminium production and processing. Includes industry news, technical features, products and services and diary of events.
Language(s): Chinese; English; Russian
Readership/Target Audience: Aimed at production directors, metallurgists, works managers and quality control managers.
ADVERTISING RATES:
Full Page Colour £3320.00
Agency Commission: 10%
Mechanical Data: Film: Digital, Type Area: 265 x 185mm, Bleed Size: 305 x 213mm, Trim Size: 297 x 210mm, Col Length: 265mm, Page Width: 185mm
Average advertising content per issue: 45%
Editions:
Annual Buyers Guide
BUSINESS: METAL, IRON & STEEL

ALUMINIUM TIMES
629539U27-3

Editorial Address: Gresham House, 54 High Street, SHOREHAM-BY-SEA, BN43 5DB **Tel:** 01273 453033
Fax: 01273 453085
Email: johnclarke@mmcpublications.co.uk
Advertising Address: As above.
Email: johnclarke@mmcpublications.co.uk
Web site: http://www.mmcpublications.co.uk
ISSN: 1465-8240
Publisher: Modern Media Communications Ltd
Date Established: 1998
Frequency: 5 issues yearly
Cover Price: £15.00
Free to qualifying individuals
Annual Sub.: £72.00
Circulation: 5,000 (Publisher's Statement)
Usual Pagination: 72
Editor: John Clarke; **Advertising Manager:** John Clarke;
Publisher: John Clarke
Summary of Content: Magazine covering news, product information, technical articles and profiles of companies and leading figures in the aluminium and light metals industry.
Readership/Target Audience: Aimed at managers of companies in primary and secondary sectors, rolling mills and extruding aluminium works who are involved with the decision of purchasing consumables and equipment.
ADVERTISING RATES:
Full Page Colour £1710.00
Agency Commission: 10%
Mechanical Data: Type Area: 265 x 185mm, Col Length: 265mm, No. of Columns (Display): 2, Bleed Size: 303 x 213mm, Trim Size: 297 x 210mm, Page Width: 185mm, Film: Digital

Copy instructions: Copy Date: 3 weeks prior to publication date
Average advertising content per issue: 40%
Supplement(s): Industry Maps - 2xY
BUSINESS: METAL, IRON & STEEL

ALUMINIUM WORLD
1640860U27-203

Editorial Address: 32 Woodstock Grove, LONDON, W12 8LE **Tel:** 020 7616 0800 **Fax:** 020 7616 0810
Email: charris@sovereign-publications.com
Advertising Address: As above.
Email: chris.harris@sovereign-publications.com
Web site: http://www.aluminiumworld.com
Publisher: Sovereign Publications Ltd
Frequency: Half-yearly - Published in spring and autumn
Free to qualifying individuals
Circulation: 9,000 (Publisher's Statement)
Editor: Chris Harris; **Advertising Manager:** Christopher Harris
Summary of Content: Magazine covering new process and product technology for the international aluminium industry.
Readership/Target Audience: Aimed at decision makers within the aluminium industry.
ADVERTISING RATES:
Full Page Colour £4950.00
Mechanical Data: Film: Digital
Copy instructions: Copy Date: 6 weeks prior to publication date
BUSINESS: METAL, IRON & STEEL

AM
38288U31A-17

Editorial Address: Media House, Lynchwood, Peterborough Business Park, PETERBOROUGH, PE2 6EA
Tel: 01733 468261 **Fax:** 01733 468632
Email: tim.rose@bauermedia.co.uk
Advertising Address: As above. **Tel:** 01733 468000
Fax: 01733 468350
Email: stuart.pask@emap.com
Web site: http://www.am-online.com
Publisher: Bauer Media Ltd (Orton)
Date Established: 1990
Frequency: 26 issues yearly
Cover Price: £4.20
Free to qualifying individuals
Annual Sub.: £99.00
Circulation: 17,383 (ABC 01/01/2008 to 31/12/2008)
Usual Pagination: 48
Editor: Tim Rose
Summary of Content: Journal covering business information for the UK automotive industry.
Readership/Target Audience: Read by senior personnel of franchised dealers, vehicle manufacturers, independent car dealers, independent service and repair garages and motor parts distributors.
ADVERTISING RATES:
Full Page Colour £5120.00
Agency Commission: 10%
Mechanical Data: Trim Size: 380 x 280mm, Type Area: 352 x 250mm, Bleed Size: 386 x 286mm, Col Length: 352mm, Page Width: 250mm, Film: Digital
Copy instructions: Copy Date: 1 week prior to publication date
Average advertising content per issue: 40%
BUSINESS: MOTOR TRADE: Motor Trade Accessories

AMBITIONS
1664229U50-213

Editorial Address: Ocean Point One, 94 Ocean Drive, EDINBURGH, EH6 6JH **Tel:** 0131 472 2222
Email: ambitions@visitscotland.com
Advertising Address: 2 Marshall Street, LONDON, W1T 2HS **Tel:** 020 7692 9292 **Fax:** 020 7692 9393
Email: amf@lps.co.uk
Web site: http://www.visitscotland.org
Publisher: Engage Group Ltd
Date Established: 2004
Frequency: 3 issues yearly
Cover Price: Free
Circulation: 11,000 (Publisher's Statement)
Editor: Clare Damodaran
Summary of Content: Magazine covering news, comment and features on the Scottish tourism industry.
Readership/Target Audience: Aimed at those involved in the Scottish tourism industry.
ADVERTISING RATES:
Full Page Colour £895.00
Mechanical Data: Type Area: 260 x 205mm, Bleed Size: 295 x 225mm, Col Length: 260mm, Page Width: 205mm, Film: Digital
Average advertising content per issue: 30%
BUSINESS: TRAVEL & TOURISM

AMBULANCE TODAY
1637737U56P-101

Editorial Address: 41 Canning Street, LIVERPOOL, L8 7NN
Tel: 0151 708 8864
Email: heneghandeclan@yahoo.co.uk

Business Magazines

Advertising Address: As above. **Fax:** 0151 708 8864
Publisher: Wordplay Publishing Ltd
Date Established: 2001
Frequency: Quarterly
Free to qualifying individuals
Annual Sub: £19.80
Circulation: 10,000 (Publisher's Statement)
Editor: Declan Heneghan; **Advertising Manager:** Declan Heneghan; **Publisher:** Declan Heneghan
Summary of Content: Magazine covering all aspects of ambulance affairs, including good practice, health and safety, clinical governance, supplies and support. Also includes news and human interests stories.
Readership/Target Audience: Aimed at ambulance staff and those working in the NHS, Red Cross and St John Ambulance.
ADVERTISING RATES:
Full Page Colour £1500.00
Agency Commission: 15%
Mechanical Data: Bleed Size: 303 x 216mm, Trim Size: 297 x 210mm, Film: Digital
Copy instructions: Copy Date: 20th of the month prior to publication date
Average advertising content per issue: 50%
Supplement(s): Ambulance Tomorrow - 1xY
BUSINESS: HEALTH & MEDICAL: Casualty & Emergency

AMBULANCE UK
40508U56P-7
Editorial Address: Media House, 48 High Street, SWANLEY, BR8 8BQ **Tel:** 01322 660434 **Fax:** 01322 666539
Email: mediajournals@aol.com
Advertising Address: As above.
Email: mediajournals@aol.com
Web site: http://www.mediapublishingcompany.com
Publisher: Media Publishing
Date Established: 1984
Frequency: 6 issues yearly - Published on the 20th of the cover month
Annual Sub: £24.00
Circulation: 5,500 (Publisher's Statement)
Usual Pagination: 64
Editor: Barry Johns; **Managing Director:** Terry Gardner; **Advertising Manager:** Terry Gardner; **Publisher:** Terry Gardner
Summary of Content: Journal for the public and private sector ambulance services with articles on communications, training, vehicles, clothing and safety.
Readership/Target Audience: Read by chief ambulance officers, chief executives, chairmen and other senior personnel of ambulance authorities and private ambulance stations.
ADVERTISING RATES:
Full Page Mono £750.00
Full Page Colour £1200.00
Agency Commission: 10%
Mechanical Data: Type Area: 270 x 185mm, Trim Size: 297 x 210mm, Bleed Size: 303 x 216mm, Film: Digital, Col Length: 270mm, Page Width: 185mm
Copy instructions: Copy Date: 2 weeks prior to publication date
BUSINESS: HEALTH & MEDICAL: Casualty & Emergency

AMED NEWS
37025U14F-2
Editorial Address: 7-8 Roman Way, Small Business Park, London Road, Godmanchester, HUNTINGDON, PE29 2LN **Tel:** 01480 459575 **Fax:** 01480 450721
Email: amedoffice@amed.org.uk
Advertising Address: As above.
Email: amedoffice@amed.org.uk
Web site: http://www.amed.org.uk
Publisher: The Association for Management Education & Development
Date Established: 1981
Frequency: Quarterly
Annual Sub: £100.00
Circulation: 700 (Publisher's Statement)
Usual Pagination: 20
Editor: Terry Gibson; **Advertising Manager:** Concepta Wayment; **Managing Editor:** Terry Gibson
Summary of Content: Newsletter of the Association for Management Education and Development, containing the latest practices and issues around organisational development, events listings and national, international and regional news.
Readership/Target Audience: Read by development and training executives, human resources managers and development consultants.
ADVERTISING RATES:
Full Page Colour £650.00
Mechanical Data: Film: Digital, Type Area: 255 x 130mm, Col Length: 255mm, Page Width: 130mm
Average advertising content per issue: 15%
BUSINESS: COMMERCE, INDUSTRY & MANAGEMENT: Training & Recruitment

AMENITY MACHINERY & EQUIPMENT
38417U32D-20
Editorial Address: Offices 2 & 3, Brixfield Farm, Sunrising Hill, Kineton, WARWICK, CV35 0ED **Tel:** 01926 691212
Fax: 01926 642060
Email: journals@acp-publishers.co.uk
Advertising Address: As above.
Email: journals@acp-publishers.co.uk
ISSN: 1464-9586
Publisher: ACP Publishers Ltd
Date Established: 1998
Frequency: 10 issues yearly - Published on the 15th of the cover month
Free to qualifying individuals
Annual Sub: £25.00
Circulation: 8,230 (ABC 01/07/2008 to 30/06/2009)
Usual Pagination: 48
Editor: Malcolm Benjamin; **Publisher:** Malcolm Benjamin
Summary of Content: Magazine covering machinery news, use, technical features and management, with sections on vintage equipment, green space management and environmental requirements.
Readership/Target Audience: Aimed at landscape contractors, equipment dealers, local authorities, as well as owners of country houses, caravan parks and golf courses.
ADVERTISING RATES:
Full Page Colour £1250.00
SCC £10.00
Agency Commission: 10%
Mechanical Data: Page Width: 190mm, Film: Digital, Type Area: 270 x 190mm, Col Length: 270mm, Trim Size: 297 x 210mm, Bleed Size: 305 x 216mm
Copy instructions: Copy Date: 28th of the month prior to publication date
Average advertising content per issue: 40%
BUSINESS: LOCAL GOVERNMENT, LEISURE & RECREATION: Parks

AMERICAFRUIT MAGAZINE
624899U26C-2
Editorial Address: 1 Nine Elms Lane, LONDON, SW8 5NQ **Tel:** 020 7501 3700 **Fax:** 020 7498 6472
Email: maura@fruitnet.com
Advertising Address: As above.
Email: rodrigo@fruitnet.com
Web site: http://www.americafruit.com
Publisher: Market Intelligence Ltd
Date Established: 2000
Frequency: 6 issues yearly - Published in the last week of the month prior to cover month
Annual Sub: $85.00
Circulation: 3,000 (Publisher's Statement)
Usual Pagination: 60
Editor: Maura Maxwell; **Advertising Manager:** Rodrigo Magdaleno
Summary of Content: Magazine covering news and features relevant to the fresh produce industry of the Americas.
Readership/Target Audience: Aimed at buyers, suppliers and senior managers of large fruit and vegetable companies.
ADVERTISING RATES:
Full Page Mono $1430.00
Full Page Colour $2250.00
Agency Commission: 10%
Mechanical Data: Col Length: 260mm, Page Width: 170mm, Film: Digital, Type Area: 260 x 170mm, Bleed Size: 303 x 216mm, Trim Size: 297 x 210mm
Copy instructions: Copy Date: 2 weeks prior to publication date
Average advertising content per issue: 40%
BUSINESS: GARDEN TRADE

AMERICAN MOTORCYCLE DEALER
38352U31B-15
Editorial Address: Kenwood House, 1 Upper Grosvenor Road, TUNBRIDGE WELLS, TN1 2DU **Tel:** 01892 511516
Fax: 01892 511517
Email: amd@dealer-world.com
Advertising Address: As above.
Email: amd@dealer-world.com
Web site: http://www.dealer-world.com
ISSN: 1465-7627
Publisher: Dealer-World.com
Frequency: Monthly
Free to qualifying individuals
Circulation: 12,500 (Publisher's Statement)
Usual Pagination: 40
Editor: Alan Franck; **Advertising Manager:** Steve Rix; **Group Editor:** Alan Franck; **Publisher:** Robin Bradley
Summary of Content: Industry and product news magazine covering parts and accessories for the American made motorcycle market.
Readership/Target Audience: Aimed at international Harley-Davidson dealers and specialist distributors.
ADVERTISING RATES:
Full Page Colour £1895.00
SCC £30.00

Mechanical Data: Trim Size: 297 x 210mm, Bleed Size: 303 x 216mm
Copy instructions: Copy Date: 30 days prior to publication date
Average advertising content per issue: 50%
BUSINESS: MOTOR TRADE: Motorcycle Trade

AMICUS CURIAE
23770U44-135
Editorial Address: Charles Clore House, 17 Russell Square, LONDON, WC1B 5DR **Tel:** 020 7862 5800
Fax: 020 7862 5855
Email: julian.harris@sas.ac.uk
Web site: http://www.ials.sas.ac.uk
ISSN: 1461-2097
Publisher: IALS
Frequency: 6 issues yearly
Free to qualifying individuals
Editor: Julian Harris
Summary of Content: Journal containing articles on a wide variety of subjects, including commercial law and International and European topics presented in a direct and readable style, written by both academic and practitioner lawyers.
Readership/Target Audience: Aimed at the legal profession.
ADVERTISING: No Advertising taken
BUSINESS: LEGAL

AMMO
1644516U2A-656
Editorial Address: 45 Fouberts Place, LONDON, W1F 7QH
Tel: 020 7575 1935
Email: matthew@ammo.xtremeinformation.com
Web site: http://www.ammo.co.uk
Publisher: Xtreme Information
Date Established: 1994
Frequency: Weekly
Annual Sub: £1975.00
Circulation: 300 (Publisher's Statement)
Usual Pagination: 50
Editor: Matthew Carlton
Summary of Content: Bulletin covering future events and business information.
Readership/Target Audience: Aimed at advertising agencies, PR agencies and media and communications agencies.
ADVERTISING: No Advertising taken
BUSINESS: COMMUNICATIONS, ADVERTISING & MARKETING

AMSPAR MAGAZINE
40136U56A-14
Editorial Address: Tavistock House North, Tavistock Square, LONDON, WC1H 9LN **Tel:** 020 7387 6005
Fax: 020 7388 2648
Email: info@amspar.co.uk
Advertising Address: As above.
Email: info@amspar.co.uk
Web site: http://www.amspar.com
Publisher: AMSPAR
Date Established: 1972
Frequency: Quarterly
Cover Price: £3.00
Circulation: 4,000 (Publisher's Statement)
Usual Pagination: 18
Editor: Tom Brownlie; **Advertising Manager:** Christine Denmark
Summary of Content: Magazine containing Association news and articles about primary and secondary care and qualifications in the sector.
Readership/Target Audience: Read by members of the Association of Medical Secretaries, practice managers, administrators, receptionists and Amspar students.
ADVERTISING RATES:
Full Page Mono £675.00
Mechanical Data: Type Area: 275 x 190mm, Trim Size: 297 x 210mm, Bleed Size: 303 x 216mm, Col Length: 275mm, Film: Digital, Page Width: 190mm
Copy instructions: Copy Date: 3 weeks prior to publication date
Average advertising content per issue: 5%
BUSINESS: HEALTH & MEDICAL

ANAESTHESIA
40138U56A-20
Editorial Address: 9600 Garsington Road, Cowley, OXFORD, OX4 2DQ **Tel:** 01865 776868 **Fax:** 01865 471423
Email: anaesthesia@nottingham.ac.uk
Advertising Address: As above.
Email: nchesher@wiley.com
Web site: http://www.blackwell-synergy.com/loi/ana
ISSN: 0003-2409
Publisher: Wiley-Blackwell Publishing
Date Established: 1997
Frequency: Monthly
Annual Sub: £146.00
Circulation: 11,224 (Publisher's Statement)
Usual Pagination: 104

Editor: Sue Jarvis
Summary of Content: Journal of the Association of Anaesthetists of Great Britain and Ireland.
Readership/Target Audience: Read by anaesthetists, pharmacologists and associated clinicians worldwide.
ADVERTISING RATES:
Full Page Mono £582.00
Full Page Colour £1367.00
Agency Commission: 10%
Mechanical Data: Page Width: 180mm, Type Area: 245 x 180mm, Col Length: 245mm, Trim Size: 276 x 210mm, Bleed Size: 282 x 216mm, Film: Digital
Copy instructions: Copy Date: 3 weeks prior to publication date
BUSINESS: HEALTH & MEDICAL

ANAESTHESIA POINTS WEST
40139U56A-25
Editorial Address: Department of Anaesthesia, Royal Devon and Exeter Hospital, Barrack Road, EXETER
Tel: 01392 411611
Email: james.pittman@rdeft.nhs.uk
Advertising Address: As above.
Email: james.pittman@rdeft.nhs.uk
Publisher: Society of Anaesthetists of the SW Region
Date Established: 1968
Frequency: Half-yearly - Published in May and October
Circulation: 750 (Publisher's Statement)
Usual Pagination: 50
Editor: James Pittman; **Advertising Manager:** James Pittman
Summary of Content: Journal of The Society of Anaesthetists of the South Western Region. Contains original articles and items of general interest.
Readership/Target Audience: Read by members of The Society of Anaesthetists.
ADVERTISING: Rates on application
BUSINESS: HEALTH & MEDICAL

ANALYST
39944U55-20
Editorial Address: Thomas Graham House, Science Park, Milton Road, CAMBRIDGE, CB4 0WF **Tel:** 01223 420066
Fax: 01223 420247
Email: analyst@rsc.org
Advertising Address: As above. **Tel:** 01223 432246
Fax: 01223 426017
Email: advertising@rsc.org
Web site: http://www.rsc.org/analyst
ISSN: 0003-2654
Publisher: Royal Society of Chemistry
Date Established: 1876
Frequency: Monthly
Annual Sub.: £1302.00
Usual Pagination: 200
Editor: Niamh O'Connor; **Managing Editor:** Niamh O'Connor
Summary of Content: Journal containing primary papers and reviews on any aspect of analytical and bioanalytical science.
Readership/Target Audience: Aimed at analytical and bioanalytical chemists.
ADVERTISING RATES:
Full Page Colour £890.00
SCC £26.00
Agency Commission: 10%
Mechanical Data: Type Area: 252 x 188mm, Bleed Size: 281 x 216mm, Col Length: 252mm, Trim Size: 275 x 210mm, Film: Digital, Page Width: 188mm
BUSINESS: APPLIED SCIENCE & LABORATORIES

ANALYTICAL ABSTRACTS
36693U37-1_20
Editorial Address: Thomas Graham House, Science Park, Milton Road, CAMBRIDGE, CB4 0WF **Tel:** 01223 420066
Fax: 01223 420247
Email: analyticalabstracts@rsc.org
Advertising Address: As above. **Tel:** 01223 432246
Fax: 01223 426017
Email: advertising@rsc.org
Web site: http://www.rsc.org/aa
ISSN: 0003-2689
Publisher: Royal Society of Chemistry
Date Established: 1954
Frequency: Monthly
Annual Sub.: £1455.00
Circulation: 1,250 (Publisher's Statement)
Advertising Manager: Ian Swain
Summary of Content: Journal providing abstracts of papers, books and application notes of importance and interest to analytical chemists. Also covers biochemistry, pharmaceutical chemistry, food and agro-chemistry, environmental chemistry, apparatus and techniques, general analytical chemistry and inorganic chemistry.
Readership/Target Audience: Aimed at working analytical chemists.
ADVERTISING RATES:
Full Page Mono £890.00

Mechanical Data: Type Area: 252 x 188mm, Bleed Size: 281 x 216mm, Col Length: 252mm, Page Width: 188mm, Trim Size: 275 x 210mm
BUSINESS: PHARMACEUTICAL & CHEMISTS

ANATOLIA
1804694U50-237
Editorial Address: Bournemouth University, Talbot Campus, Fern Barrow, POOLE, BH12 5BB
Tel: 01202 961524 **Fax:** 01202 965228
Email: afyall@bournemouth.ac.uk
Web site: http://www.anatoliajournal.com
Publisher: Anatolia
Date Established: 1997
Frequency: Half-yearly - Published in summer and winter
Summary of Content: Journal focusing on tourism and hospitality research. Contains articles relating to the understanding, practice and education of tourism and hospitality.
Readership/Target Audience: Aimed at academics.
ADVERTISING: No Advertising taken
BUSINESS: TRAVEL & TOURISM

ANGLIA BUSINESS
41279U63B-437
Formerly: Anglia Industry and Business
Editorial Address: The Publishing House, 119 Newland Street, WITHAM, CM8 1WF **Tel:** 01376 521900
Fax: 01376 521901
Email: steed@acguk.com
Advertising Address: As above.
Email: mail@acguk.com
Web site: http://www.acguk.com
Publisher: ACG Publications
Date Established: 1982
Frequency: 6 issues yearly - Published on the last Friday of the cover month
Cover Price: Free
Circulation: 15,500 (Publisher's Statement)
Usual Pagination: 60
Editor: Steed Webzell; **Advertising Manager:** Steed Webzell
Summary of Content: Business to business publication providing information on different aspects of the services and manufacturing industries.
Readership/Target Audience: Aimed at managers and owners within the East of England business environment.
ADVERTISING RATES:
Full Page Colour £1865.00
Agency Commission: 10%
Mechanical Data: Type Area: 268 x 190mm, Col Length: 268mm, Bleed Size: 307 x 220mm, Trim Size: 297 x 210mm, Page Width: 190mm, Film: Digital
Copy instructions: Copy Date: 2 weeks prior to publication date
Average advertising content per issue: 40%
BUSINESS: REGIONAL BUSINESS: Regional Business English Counties

ANGLIA FARMER
37883U21J-8
Formerly: Anglia Farmer and Contractor
Editorial Address: National Rural Enterprise Centre, Stoneleigh Park, KENILWORTH, CV8 2RR
Tel: 024 7685 3056
Email: editor@ruralcity.co.uk
Advertising Address: 27 Norwich Road, HALESWORTH, IP19 8BX **Tel:** 01986 834250 **Fax:** 01986 834255
Email: chloe@micropress.co.uk
Publisher: BC Publications
Date Established: 1981
Frequency: Monthly - Published the 1st week of the month Free to qualifying individuals
Annual Sub.: £18.00
Circulation: 7,000 (Publisher's Statement)
Usual Pagination: 32
Editor: Johann Tasker; **Managing Director:** Simon Tooth
Summary of Content: Journal covering items of agricultural relevance to East Anglia.
Readership/Target Audience: Read by farmers and growers in the Eastern Counties, as well as allied trades and supply organisations.
ADVERTISING RATES:
Full Page Colour £800.00
SCC £7.20
Agency Commission: 10%
Mechanical Data: Col Length: 270mm, Type Area: 270 x 188mm, Page Width: 188mm, No. of Columns (Display): 4, Col Widths (Display): 35mm, Trim Size: 290 x 210mm, Bleed Size: 305 x 214mm, Film: Digital
Copy instructions: Copy Date: 2 weeks prior to publication date
Average advertising content per issue: 40%
BUSINESS: AGRICULTURE & FARMING: Agriculture & Farming - Regional

ANIMAL PHARM - WORLD ANIMAL HEALTH AND NUTRITION NEWS
41524U64H-130
Editorial Address: Telephone House, 69-77 Paul Street, LONDON, EC2A 4LQ **Tel:** 020 7017 5000
Fax: 020 7017 6838
Email: jamie.day@informa.com
Advertising Address: As above. **Fax:** 020 7017 6787
Email: natasha.bailey@informa.com
Web site: http://www.animalpharmnews.com
Publisher: Informa Pharma
Date Established: 1982
Frequency: 24 issues yearly
Annual Sub.: £480.00
Circulation: 1,500 (Publisher's Statement)
Usual Pagination: 24
Editor: Jamie Day; **Publisher:** Phil Solomon
Summary of Content: Newsletter reporting on developments in the world of animal health-care and nutrition markets.
Readership/Target Audience: Aimed at the producers of animal medicines and health treatments, regulatory authorities, animal feed producers, research bodies, vets and universities.
ADVERTISING RATES:
Full Page Colour £1805.00
Agency Commission: 10%
Mechanical Data: Type Area: 277 x 190mm, Bleed Size: 303 x 216mm, Trim Size: 295 x 208mm, Print Process: Offset litho, Col Length: 277mm, Page Width: 190mm, Film: Digital
Copy instructions: Copy Date: 7 days prior to publication date
Supplement(s): Animal Farm Insight - 3xY
BUSINESS: OTHER CLASSIFICATIONS: Veterinary

ANIMAL WELFARE
41541U64H-135
Editorial Address: The Old School, Brewhouse Hill, Wheathampstead, ST. ALBANS, AL4 8AN
Tel: 01582 831818 **Fax:** 01582 831414
Email: ufaw@ufaw.org.uk
Web site: http://www.ufaw.org.uk
ISSN: 0962-7286
Publisher: Universities Federation for Animal Welfare
Date Established: 1992
Frequency: Quarterly
Annual Sub.: £75.00
Circulation: 700 (Publisher's Statement)
Usual Pagination: 150
Editor: James Kirkwood; **Editor-in-Chief:** James Kirkwood
Summary of Content: The Journal publishes the results of scientific research and technical studies relating to the welfare of animals kept on farms, in laboratories, zoos and as companions or managed in the wild. Also includes reviews of recent animal welfare publications.
Readership/Target Audience: Aimed at all those involved with animal welfare science and those concerned with and responsible for the care and welfare of animals.
ADVERTISING: No Advertising taken
BUSINESS: OTHER CLASSIFICATIONS: Veterinary

ANNUAL BIBLIOGRAPHY OF ENGLISH LANGUAGE & LITERATURE
40920U60B-11_5
Editorial Address: c/o Cambridge University Library, West Road, CAMBRIDGE, CB3 9DR **Tel:** 01223 333058
Email: abell@bibl.org
Web site: http://www.mhra.org.uk
ISSN: 0066-3786
Publisher: Modern Humanities Research Association
Date Established: 1921
Frequency: Annual - Usually October
Annual Sub.: £183.00
Circulation: 600 (Publisher's Statement)
Usual Pagination: 1428
Editor: Jennifer Fellows
Summary of Content: Publication containing listings of all scholarly articles, books and reviews concerning English language and literature and related topics published anywhere in the world, and in any language. (Education and pedagogical subjects, and the medical application of linguistics are excluded).
Readership/Target Audience: Aimed at researchers, librarians and students.
ADVERTISING: No Advertising taken
BUSINESS: PUBLISHING: Libraries

ANTI-CANCER DRUGS
38724U56A-27
Editorial Address: 250 Waterloo Road, LONDON, SE1 8RD
Tel: 020 7981 0676 **Fax:** 020 7981 0556
Email: phil.daly@wolterskluwer.com
Advertising Address: The Point of Difference, 4 Chase Side Avenue, LONDON, SW20 8LU **Tel:** 020 8542 3200
Fax: 020 8543 3810
Email: pointofdiff@btinternet.com
Web site: http://www.anti-cancerdrugs.com

Business Magazines

ISSN: 0959-4973
Publisher: Lippincott Williams & Wilkins
Date Established: 1990
Frequency: 10 issues yearly
Annual Sub.: $507.00
Circulation: 80 (Publisher's Statement)
Usual Pagination: 128
Editor: Phil Daly; **Advertising Manager:** Bill D'Sa;
Publisher: Phil Daly
Summary of Content: Journal covering innovations in therapeutic agents against cancer, clinical trials and pre-clinical development of anti-cancer drugs.
Readership/Target Audience: Aimed at oncologists and haematologists.
ADVERTISING RATES:
Full Page Mono $765.00
Full Page Colour $1645.00
Agency Commission: 15%
Mechanical Data: Col Length: 254mm, Trim Size: 276 x 207mm, Type Area: 254 x 178mm, Bleed Size: 286 x 213mm, Film: Positive right reading, emulsion side down. Digital, Page Width: 178mm
Copy instructions: Copy Date: 6 weeks prior to publication date
BUSINESS: HEALTH & MEDICAL

ANTI-CORROSION METHODS & MATERIALS
37621U19C-10
Editorial Address: Howard House, Wagon Lane, BINGLEY, BD16 1WA **Tel:** 01274 777700 **Fax:** 01274 785200
Email: t.liskiewicz@leeds.ac.uk
Web site: http://www.emeraldinsight.com
ISSN: 0003-5599
Publisher: Emerald Group Publishing Ltd
Date Established: 1953
Frequency: 6 issues yearly
Annual Sub.: £1139.00
Usual Pagination: 92
Editor: Tomasz Liskiewicz; **Publisher:** Harry Colson
Summary of Content: Journal covering all aspects of corrosion management, prevention and control.
Readership/Target Audience: Read by production managers, works managers and researchers interested in, or having a responsibility for corrosion control and prevention.
ADVERTISING: No Advertising taken
BUSINESS: ENGINEERING & MACHINERY: Finishing

ANTI-INFECTIVE DRUG NEWS
1799490U37-425
Editorial Address: Lincoln House, City Fields Business Park, City Fields Way, Tangmere, CHICHESTER, PO20 2FS
Tel: 01243 756038 **Fax:** 01243 533418
Email: healthcare@espicom.com
Web site: http://www.espicom.com
ISSN: 1471-8294
Publisher: Espicom Ltd
Date Established: 2000
Frequency: 22 issues yearly
Annual Sub.: £560.00
Circulation: 600 (Publisher's Statement)
Usual Pagination: 16
Editor: Mike O'Harrow
Summary of Content: Newsletter focusing on commercial and scientific developments in anti-infective drugs.
Readership/Target Audience: Aimed at senior executives in pharmaceutical companies.
ADVERTISING: No Advertising taken
BUSINESS: PHARMACEUTICAL & CHEMISTS

ANTIQUARIAN HOROLOGY
36439U7-10
Editorial Address: New House, High Street, Ticehurst, WADHURST, TN5 7AL **Tel:** 01580 200155
Fax: 01580 201323
Email: secretary@ahsoc.demon.co.uk
Advertising Address: 10 Strathmore Close, CATERHAM, CR3 5EQ **Tel:** 01883 348082 **Fax:** 01833 344772
Email: anthonyjlaw@hotmail.com
Web site: http://www.ahsoc.demon.co.uk
ISSN: 0003-5785
Publisher: The Antiquarian Horological Society
Date Established: 1953
Frequency: Quarterly
Annual Sub.: £40.00
Circulation: 2,500 (Publisher's Statement)
Usual Pagination: 108
Editor: Peter de Clercq; **Advertising Manager:** Pamela Law
Summary of Content: Journal containing information concerning antique clocks, watches and other time telling instruments, plus the proceedings of the Antiquarian Horological Society.
Readership/Target Audience: Read by those who collect, restore and study antique clocks, watches and sun-dials.
ADVERTISING RATES:
Full Page Mono £156.00
Full Page Colour £385.00
Mechanical Data: Type Area: 215 x 146mm, Col Length: 215mm, Page Width: 146mm, Print Process: Litho, Bleed

Size: 253 x 184mm, Trim Size: 248 x 178mm, Col Widths (Display): 70mm, No. of Columns (Display): 2
Copy instructions: Copy Date: 6 weeks prior to publication date
Average advertising content per issue: 20%
BUSINESS: ANTIQUES

THE ANTIQUE TRADE CALENDAR
36451U7-82
Editorial Address: 32 Fredericks Place, LONDON, N12 8QE
Tel: 020 8446 3604 **Fax:** 020 8922 8257
Advertising Address: As above.
Publisher: GP London
Date Established: 1992
Frequency: Quarterly
Cover Price: £1.50
Annual Sub.: £9.00
Circulation: 9,000 (Publisher's Statement)
Usual Pagination: 160
Editor: Stephen Browning
Summary of Content: Great Britain's guide to antique fairs, markets and centres.
Readership/Target Audience: Aimed at the antiques trade and serious collectors.
ADVERTISING RATES:
Full Page Mono £110.00
Agency Commission: 10%
Average advertising content per issue: 50%
BUSINESS: ANTIQUES

ANTIQUES DIARY
36442U7-97
Editorial Address: PO Box 6271, CHRISTCHURCH, BH23 9BF **Tel:** 01425 280340
Email: jack.fowler3@ntlworld.com
Advertising Address: As above. **Fax:** 01425 270279
Email: antiquesdiary@btconnect.com
Web site: http://www.antiquesdiaryonline.co.uk
Publisher: Antiques Diary
Date Established: 1986
Frequency: 6 issues yearly
Cover Price: £1.50
Annual Sub.: £13.00
Circulation: 5,000 (Publisher's Statement)
Usual Pagination: 140
Editor: Jack Fowler; **Features Editor:** Jack Fowler;
Advertising Manager: Peter Allwright; **Managing Editor:** Peter Allwright; **Publisher:** Peter Allwright
Summary of Content: Regional guide to antique fairs, markets and auctions.
Readership/Target Audience: Aimed at collectors, organisers and participants in fairs, markets and auctions in the UK.
ADVERTISING RATES:
Full Page Mono £170.00
Full Page Colour £212.50
Agency Commission: 10%
Mechanical Data: Type Area: 195 x 133mm, Col Length: 195mm, Trim Size: 210 x 148mm, Page Width: 133mm, Film: Digital
Copy instructions: Copy Date: 2 months prior to publication date
Average advertising content per issue: 30%
BUSINESS: ANTIQUES

THE ANTIQUES FAIRS & CENTRES GUIDE
36443U7-99
Editorial Address: Castle Ash, Birmingham Road, Blakedown, KIDDERMINSTER, DY10 3JE **Tel:** 01562 701490
Fax: 01562 700001
Email: editorial@antiquesmagazine.com
Advertising Address: As above.
Email: sales@antiquesmagazine.com
Web site: http://www.antiquesfairs.com
Publisher: H.P. Publishing
Date Established: 1986
Frequency: Half-yearly - Published in December and June
Cover Price: £2.75
Free to qualifying individuals
Circulation: 20,000 (Publisher's Statement)
Usual Pagination: 68
Editor: John Hubbard; **Advertising Manager:** Louise Ford
Summary of Content: Guide containing information regarding buying and selling of antiques, news of forthcoming auctions and antiques fairs.
Readership/Target Audience: Aimed at people interested in buying and selling antiques.
ADVERTISING RATES:
Full Page Colour £1375.00
Agency Commission: 15%
Mechanical Data: Type Area: 264 x 182mm, Bleed Size: 303 x 216mm, Trim Size: 297 x 210mm, Col Length: 264mm, Page Width: 182mm
Copy instructions: Copy Date: 6 weeks prior to publication date
Average advertising content per issue: 65%

Supplement to: Antiques Magazine
BUSINESS: ANTIQUES

ANTIQUES TRADE GAZETTE
36445U7-100
Editorial Address: 115 Shaftesbury Avenue, LONDON, WC2H 8AD **Tel:** 020 7420 6600 **Fax:** 020 7420 6633
Email: editorial@antiquestradegazette.com
Advertising Address: As above. **Tel:** 020 7420 6644
Fax: 020 7420 6655
Email: sales@antiquestradegazette.com
Web site: http://www.antiquestradegazette.com
ISSN: 0306-1051
Publisher: Metropress Ltd.
Date Established: 1971
Frequency: Weekly
Cover Price: £2.00
Annual Sub.: £79.00
Usual Pagination: 80
Editor: Ivan Macquisten; **Editor-in-Chief:** Mark Bridge;
Advertising Manager: Mark Holdaway
Summary of Content: Journal covering news, features and market analysis on fine art and antiques both in the UK and overseas.
Readership/Target Audience: Read by antique dealers, auctioneers and serious collectors.
ADVERTISING RATES:
Full Page Mono £1450.00
Full Page Colour £1740.00
Agency Commission: 15%
Mechanical Data: Page Width: 216mm, Type Area: 308 x 216mm, Col Length: 308mm, Film: Positive, right reading, emulsion side down. Digital, No. of Columns (Display): 6, Print Process: Web-fed offset litho
Copy instructions: Copy Date: Tuesday 12 noon prior to publication date
Average advertising content per issue: 65%
BUSINESS: ANTIQUES

APCJ ASIA PACIFIC COATINGS JOURNAL
37279U16B-2
Formerly: Paint & Ink International
Editorial Address: Westgate House, 120-130 Station Road, REDHILL, RH1 1ET **Tel:** 01737 855000 **Fax:** 01737 855034
Email: gregmorris@dmgworldmedia.com
Advertising Address: As above. **Tel:** 01737 855328
Email: jeffmontgomery@uk.dmgworldmedia.com
Web site: http://www.coatingsgroup.com
ISSN: 1648-1412
Publisher: DMG World Media
Date Established: 1879
Frequency: 6 issues yearly
Cover Price: £28.00
Free to qualifying individuals
Annual Sub.: £107.00
Circulation: 5,900 (Publisher's Statement)
Usual Pagination: 36
Editor: Elit Kane
Summary of Content: Journal covering all aspects of coatings manufacture, commercial and legislative news worldwide and other articles on the industry.
Readership/Target Audience: Read by paint and printing ink manufacturers and suppliers of raw materials throughout the Asia Pacific region.
ADVERTISING RATES:
Full Page Mono £2769.00
Full Page Colour £4714.00
Agency Commission: 10%
Mechanical Data: Film: Digital, Page Width: 185mm, Type Area: 265 x 185mm, Col Length: 265mm, Trim Size: 297 x 210mm, Bleed Size: 303 x 216mm
BUSINESS: DECORATING & PAINT: Paint - Technical Manufacture

APF ASIA PACIFIC FIRE
765512U54A-226
Editorial Address: The Abbey Manor Business Centre, The Abbey, Preston Road, YEOVIL, BA20 2EN
Tel: 01935 426428 **Fax:** 01935 426926
Email: mark.seton@apfmag.com
Advertising Address: As above.
Email: mark.seton@apfmag.com
Web site: http://www.mdmpublishing.com
ISSN: 1476-1386
Publisher: MDM Publishing Ltd
Date Established: 2002
Frequency: Quarterly - Published on the 1st Monday of the cover month
Free to qualifying individuals
Annual Sub.: £35.00
Circulation: 7,000 (Publisher's Statement)
Usual Pagination: 72
Editor: Mark Seton; **Advertising Manager:** Mark Seton;
Publisher: Mark Seton
Summary of Content: Magazine covering top quality articles and the latest industry news from the world of Fire Protection and Fire-fighting in the Asia Pacific countries.

Readership/Target Audience: Aimed at those involved within the Asia Pacific Fire Protection and Fire Service Industry.
ADVERTISING RATES:
Full Page Mono £1265.00
Full Page Colour £1750.00
Agency Commission: 10%
Mechanical Data: Bleed Size: 303 x 216mm, Trim Size: 297 x 210mm, Page Width: 185mm, Type Area: 275 x 185mm, Col Length: 275mm, Film: Digital
Copy instructions: Copy Date: 7th of the month prior to publication date
Average advertising content per issue: 40%
BUSINESS: SAFETY & SECURITY: Fire Fighting

APPLIED CLINICAL TRIALS   38725U37-1_70
Editorial Address: PO Box 114, Hawarden, DEESIDE, CH5 3ZA **Tel:** 01244 538583
Email: philipward1@btconnect.com
Advertising Address: Advanstar House, Park West, Sealand Road, CHESTER, CH1 4RN **Tel:** 01925 732797
Fax: 01925 732798
Email: wblow@advanstar.com
Web site: http://www.actmagazine.com
Publisher: Advanstar Communications (U.K.) Ltd
Frequency: Monthly - Published on the 1st Wednesday of the cover month
Free to qualifying individuals
Circulation: 20,150 (BPA Worldwide)
Editor: Philip Ward; **Advertising Manager:** Wayne Blow
Summary of Content: Magazine covering all aspects of the clinical trials and drug development sectors.
Readership/Target Audience: Read by project managers, clinical research associates and regulatory managers in pharmaceutical companies.
ADVERTISING: Rates on application
Agency Commission: 15%
Copy instructions: Copy Date: 4 weeks prior to publication date
Average advertising content per issue: 50%
BUSINESS: PHARMACEUTICAL & CHEMISTS

APPLIED COGNITIVE PSYCHOLOGY
40605U56R-7
Editorial Address: The Atrium, Southern Gate, CHICHESTER, PO19 8SQ **Tel:** 01243 779777
Fax: 01243 775878
Advertising Address: As above.
Email: adsales@wiley.co.uk
Web site: http://www.interscience.wiley.com
ISSN: 0888-4080
Publisher: John Wiley & Sons Ltd
Frequency: 9 issues yearly
Annual Sub.: $1120.00
Usual Pagination: 104
Editor: Graham Davies; **Advertising Manager:** Faith Pidduck
Summary of Content: Journal containing papers dealing with psychological analyses of memory, learning, thinking, problem solving, language and consciousness as they occur in the real world.
Readership/Target Audience: Aimed at academics and practitioners in psychology and related professions interested in ergonomic, legal, educational, industrial rehabilitation and psycho-medical problems.
ADVERTISING RATES:
Full Page Mono £1175.00
Full Page Colour £2575.00
Agency Commission: 10%
Mechanical Data: Print Process: Sheet-fed litho, Film: Mono: Negative, right reading, emulsion side up Colour: Positive, right reading, emulsion side down. Digital, Type Area: 230 x 150mm, Trim Size: 250 x 165mm, Bleed Size: 256 x 171mm, Col Length: 250mm, Page Width: 165mm
BUSINESS: HEALTH & MEDICAL: Health Medical Related

APPLIED LINGUISTICS   30078U62A-504
Editorial Address: Great Clarendon Street, OXFORD, OX2 6DP **Tel:** 01865 353907 **Fax:** 01865 353485
Email: applied-linguistics@open.ac.uk
Advertising Address: 60 Upper Broadmoor Road, CROWTHORNE, RG45 7DE **Tel:** 01344 779945
Fax: 01344 779945
Email: lhann@lhms.fsnet.co.uk
Web site: http://www3.oup.co.uk/applij
ISSN: 0142-6001
Publisher: OUP
Date Established: 1980
Frequency: Quarterly
Cover Price: £17.00
Annual Sub.: £54.00
Usual Pagination: 144
Editor: Ken Hyland
Summary of Content: Journal containing studies on the relationship between theoretical and practical aspects of language education.

Readership/Target Audience: Read by language testers, linguists, psycholinguists, social psychologists, sociolinguists, speech pathologists, speech therapists and translators.
ADVERTISING RATES:
Full Page Mono £340.00
Agency Commission: 10%
Mechanical Data: Type Area: 200 x 130mm, Col Length: 200mm, Page Width: 130mm, Film: Digital
Copy instructions: Copy Date: 12th of the month prior to publication date
BUSINESS: CHURCH & SCHOOL EQUIPMENT & EDUCATION: Education

THE APPOINTMENT   39793U53-9
Editorial Address: The Old Bank, 349 Archway Road, Highgate, LONDON, N6 5AA **Tel:** 020 8340 3366
Fax: 020 8340 8866
Email: editorial@theappointment.co.uk
Advertising Address: As above.
Email: advertising@theappointment.co.uk
Web site: http://www.theappointment.co.uk
ISSN: 1366-6932
Publisher: The Appointment Ltd
Date Established: 1997
Frequency: 23 issues yearly - Published on the first and the middle Saturday of the month
Cover Price: £1.50
Annual Sub.: £30.00
Circulation: 30,000 (Publisher's Statement)
Usual Pagination: 32
Editor: Calum MacLeod; **Advertising Manager:** Adam Tomkinson; **Publisher:** Adam Tomkinson
Summary of Content: Magazine focusing on news and developments within the retail, fashion and hospitality industries. Features include profiles of leading retailers, practical career guidance, industry trends, retail industry salary surveys, business comment and e-commerce.
Readership/Target Audience: Read by retail, fashion and hospitality professionals at management level across all business functions.
ADVERTISING RATES:
Full Page Mono £6200.00
Full Page Colour £6500.00
Agency Commission: 15%
Mechanical Data: Film: Digital, Bleed Size: 303 x 213mm, Type Area: 267 x 185mm, Page Width: 185mm, Col Length: 267mm, Trim Size: 297 x 210mm
Copy instructions: Copy Date: 5 days prior to publication date
Average advertising content per issue: 60%
BUSINESS: RETAILING & WHOLESALING

APPROPRIATE TECHNOLOGY   40621U21R-1506
Editorial Address: Grenville Court, Britwell Road, Burnham, SLOUGH, SL1 8DF **Tel:** 01628 600499 **Fax:** 01628 600488
Email: info@researchinformation.co.uk
Advertising Address: As above.
Email: info@researchinformation.co.uk
Web site: http://www.researchinformation.co.uk
ISSN: 0305-0920
Publisher: Research Information Ltd
Date Established: 1973
Frequency: Quarterly - Published the middle of the cover month
Annual Sub.: £150.00
Circulation: 3,000 (Publisher's Statement)
Usual Pagination: 72
Editor: David Dixon; **Advertising Manager:** Ras Patel; **Publisher:** Kumar Patel
Summary of Content: International magazine communicating new practical technologies, policies and ideas addressing the elimination of poverty and hunger.
Readership/Target Audience: Read by fieldworkers, educators and policy makers.
ADVERTISING RATES:
Full Page Mono £750.00
Full Page Colour £995.00
Agency Commission: 10%
Mechanical Data: Type Area: 254 x 178mm, Col Length: 254mm, Page Width: 178mm, Film: Digital
Copy instructions: Copy Date: 15th of the month prior to publication date
BUSINESS: AGRICULTURE & FARMING: Agriculture & Farming Related

AQUACULTURE NUTRITION   39392U45B-7
Editorial Address: 9600 Garsington Road, Cowley, OXFORD, OX4 2DQ **Tel:** 01865 476517 **Fax:** 01865 714591
Email: anu@oxon.blackwellpublishing.com
Web site: http://www.blackwellpublishing.com/anu
ISSN: 1353-5773
Publisher: Wiley-Blackwell Publishing
Date Established: 1996
Frequency: 6 issues yearly
Circulation: 300 (Publisher's Statement)
Usual Pagination: 112

Editor: Martin Tilly
Summary of Content: Journal featuring papers on practical and theoretical topics relevant to freshwater and marine aquaculture; also covers conservation of freshwater and marine fish and the creation, development and management of commercial and recreational freshwater and marine fisheries.
Readership/Target Audience: Aimed at those involved in fish nutrition and processing, as well as the aqua-feed industry.
ADVERTISING: No Advertising taken
BUSINESS: MARINE & SHIPPING: Commercial Fishing

AQUACULTURE RESEARCH   39379U45B-10
Editorial Address: 9600 Garsington Road, Cowley, OXFORD, OX4 2DQ **Tel:** 01865 776868 **Fax:** 01865 714591
Email: mtilly@wiley.com
Advertising Address: As above. **Fax:** 01865 471267
Email: craig.pickett@oxon.blackwellpublishing.com
Web site: http://www.blackwellpublishing.com/are
ISSN: 1355-557X
Publisher: Wiley-Blackwell Publishing
Frequency: 16 issues yearly
Annual Sub.: £1498.00
Circulation: 550 (Publisher's Statement)
Usual Pagination: 96
Editor: Martin Tilly
Summary of Content: Journal featuring papers on applied and scientific research relevant to freshwater, brackish and marine aquaculture.
Readership/Target Audience: Read by academics, scientists and students in the field of aquaculture.
ADVERTISING RATES:
Full Page Mono £450.00
Full Page Colour £850.00
Agency Commission: 10%
Mechanical Data: Type Area: 230 x 170mm, Trim Size: 276 x 210mm, Col Length: 230mm, Page Width: 170mm, Bleed Size: +3mm, Film: Digital
Copy instructions: Copy Date: 6 weeks prior to publication date
BUSINESS: MARINE & SHIPPING: Commercial Fishing

THE AQUANAUT   38569U33-1_10
Editorial Address: Bon Accord House, Riverside Drive, ABERDEEN, AB11 7SL **Tel:** 01224 597800
Fax: 01224 580320
Email: sheywood@ods-petrodata.com
Web site: http://www.petrodata.co.uk
Publisher: ODS-Petrodata UK Ltd
Date Established: 1985
Frequency: Monthly
Annual Sub.: $1000.00
Circulation: 120 (Publisher's Statement)
Usual Pagination: 12
Editor: Shaun Heywood
Summary of Content: Newsletter on the underwater engineering industry.
Readership/Target Audience: Aimed at oil contractors.
ADVERTISING: No Advertising taken
BUSINESS: OIL & PETROLEUM

ARAB BANKER   1657701U1C-352
Editorial Address: PO Box 13666, LONDON, SW14 8WF **Tel:** 020 8392 1122 **Fax:** 020 8392 1422
Email: sajidrizvi@eapgroup.com
Advertising Address: As above.
Email: sales@eapgroup.com
Web site: http://www.arab-banker.com
ISSN: 0261-2925
Publisher: EAP Group Business Media
Date Established: 1981
Frequency: Quarterly
Free to qualifying individuals
Circulation: 11,000 (Print Run)
Usual Pagination: 52
Editor: Sajid Rizvi; **Advertising Manager:** Sajid Rizvi; **Publisher:** Sajid Rizvi
Summary of Content: Magazine focusing on banking and finance in the Middle East.
Readership/Target Audience: Aimed at senior banking personnel and government officials.
ADVERTISING RATES:
Full Page Mono £3950.00
Full Page Colour £4475.00
Agency Commission: 10%
Mechanical Data: Type Area: 250 x 180mm, Bleed Size: 303 x 216mm, Trim Size: 297 x 210mm, Col Length: 250mm, Page Width: 180mm, Print Process: Sheet-fed litho, Film: Digital, Col Widths (Display): 180mm
Average advertising content per issue: 30%
BUSINESS: FINANCE & ECONOMICS: Banking

Business Magazines

ARAB-BRITISH BUSINESS
1666999U14C-358

Editorial Address: 43 Upper Grosvenor Street, LONDON, W1K 2NJ **Tel:** 020 7235 4363 **Fax:** 020 7245 6688
Email: d.morgan@abcc.org.uk
Advertising Address: As above.
Email: el-idrissi@abcc.org.uk
Web site: http://www.abcc.org.uk
Publisher: Arab-British Chamber of Commerce
Frequency: 22 issues yearly
Cover Price: Free
Circulation: 2,000 (Publisher's Statement)
Editor: David Morgan; **Advertising Manager:** Abdeslam El-Idrissi
Summary of Content: Bulletin covering all aspects of British trade with the Arab world. Includes articles on conferences, events, law, trade and regulations.
Readership/Target Audience: Aimed at members of the Arab-British Chamber of Commerce.
ADVERTISING: Rates on application
BUSINESS: COMMERCE, INDUSTRY & MANAGEMENT: International Commerce

ARC
35418U1M-5

Formerly: USRO Update
Editorial Address: 8 Leake Street, LONDON, SE1 7NN
Tel: 020 7401 5555 **Fax:** 020 7401 5550
Email: arc@fda.org.uk
Web site: http://www.fda.org.uk
Publisher: Association of Revenue and Customs
Frequency: 10 issues yearly
Circulation: 2,800 (Publisher's Statement)
Usual Pagination: 16
Editor: Liz Bullivant
Summary of Content: Journal featuring news and developments within the Inland Revenue and HM Customs and Excise.
Readership/Target Audience: Aimed at senior tax inspectors and senior revenue officials.
ADVERTISING: No Advertising taken
BUSINESS: FINANCE & ECONOMICS: Taxation

ARC MAGAZINE
40879U60B-150

Formerly: Society of Archivists Newsletter
Editorial Address: Unit 25, The Coach House, 2 Upper York Street, BRISTOL, BS2 8QN **Tel:** 0117 923 2951
Email: arceditor@]societymediasales.co.uk
Advertising Address: As above. **Tel:** 0117 904 1283
Email: jed.wells@dpmedia.co.uk
Web site: http://www.archives.org.uk
ISSN: 0142-2278
Publisher: DP Media
Frequency: Monthly
Free to qualifying individuals
Circulation: 2,150 (Publisher's Statement)
Usual Pagination: 40
Summary of Content: Journal containing news, information and ideas relevant to the profession including archive conservation and records management.
Readership/Target Audience: Read by members of the Society of Archivists and those concerned with the archive and records management industry.
ADVERTISING RATES:
Full Page Colour £705.00
Mechanical Data: Col Length: 270mm, Trim Size: 291 x 204mm, Type Area: 270 x 190mm, Page Width: 190mm, Bleed Size: 297 x 210mm, Film: Digital
Supplement(s): ARC Recruitment - 11xY, ARC Recruitment Plus - 12xY
BUSINESS: PUBLISHING: Libraries

ARCA NEWS
1647083U57-128

Editorial Address: 18 Generator Hall, Electric Wharf, COVENTRY, CV1 4JL **Tel:** 0870 199 4044
Fax: 0870 777 4360
Email: info@simplymarcomms.co.uk
Advertising Address: As above.
Email: info@simplymarcomms.co.uk
Web site: http://www.arca.org.uk
Publisher: Simply Marcomms
Date Established: 1990
Frequency: Quarterly
Free to qualifying individuals
Circulation: 3,000 (Publisher's Statement)
Usual Pagination: 32
Editor: Kirstie Colledge; **Advertising Manager:** Nicky Lewis
Summary of Content: Journal covering all aspects of asbestos management, asbestos surveying and asbestos removal.
Readership/Target Audience: Aimed at asbestos removal contractors and anyone involved in the management of asbestos in buildings.
ADVERTISING: Rates on application
BUSINESS: ENVIRONMENT & POLLUTION

ARCHITECTS CHOICE
35822U4A-304

Editorial Address: 4th Floor, Geneva House, Park Road, PETERBOROUGH, PE1 2UX **Tel:** 01733 756555
Fax: 01733 760505
Email: ac@onecoms.co.uk
Advertising Address: As above.
Email: mark.hickey@onecoms.co.uk
Web site: http://www.onecoms.co.uk
Publisher: Media One Communications Ltd.
Date Established: 1997
Frequency: Monthly
Cover Price: £3.75
Free to qualifying individuals
Circulation: 8,500 (Publisher's Statement)
Usual Pagination: 36
Editor: Jade Tilley
Summary of Content: Magazine covering products, news, applications and features on architectural projects.
Readership/Target Audience: Read by designers and architects.
ADVERTISING RATES:
Full Page Colour £565.00
Agency Commission: 10%
Mechanical Data: Trim Size: 297 x 210mm, Film: Digital
Average advertising content per issue: 20%
BUSINESS: ARCHITECTURE & BUILDING: Architecture

ARCHITECTS DATAFILE
35785U4A-25

Editorial Address: Cointronic House, Station Road, HEATHFIELD, TN21 8DF **Tel:** 01435 865797
Fax: 01435 867635
Email: editorial@netmagmedia.eu
Advertising Address: As above. **Tel:** 01435 863500
Fax: 01435 863897
Web site: http://www.adfonline.eu
Publisher: Parker Ellis Publishing Ltd
Date Established: 1993
Frequency: Monthly - Published around the middle of the cover month
Cover Price: Free
Circulation: 17,997 (ABC 01/07/2008 to 30/06/2009)
Usual Pagination: 56
Editor: Patricia Percival
Summary of Content: Magazine covering projects, new products and technical information.
Readership/Target Audience: Aimed at working architects.
ADVERTISING RATES:
Full Page Mono £1425.00
Full Page Colour £1425.00
Agency Commission: 10%
Mechanical Data: Trim Size: 297 x 210mm, Film: Digital, Bleed Size: 303 x 216mm
Copy instructions: Copy Date: 4 weeks prior to publication date
Average advertising content per issue: 33%
BUSINESS: ARCHITECTURE & BUILDING: Architecture

THE ARCHITECTS' JOURNAL
35786U4A-30

Editorial Address: Greater London House, Hampstead Road, LONDON, NW1 7EJ **Tel:** 020 7728 5000
Fax: 020 7728 4666
Email: kieran.long@emap.com
Advertising Address: As above. **Fax:** 020 7505 7650
Email: tom.peardon@emap.com
Web site: http://www.architectsjournal.co.uk
ISSN: 0003-8466
Publisher: EMAP Insight
Frequency: Weekly
Cover Price: £4.00
Annual Sub.: £150.00
Circulation: 9,088 (ABC 01/07/2008 to 30/06/2009)
Usual Pagination: 68
Editor: Rory Olcayto; **News Editor:** Richard Waite;
Features Editor: Rory Olcayto; **Managing Director:** Natasha Christie-Miller
Summary of Content: Magazine containing industry news on architecture and building techniques and practices.
Twitter: http://twitter.com/architectsjrnal
Readership/Target Audience: Read by building industry professionals.
ADVERTISING RATES:
Full Page Mono £3237.00
Full Page Colour £3237.00
Agency Commission: 10%
Mechanical Data: Bleed Size: 271 x 216mm, Trim Size: 265 x 210mm, Film: Digital, Type Area: 231 x 186mm, Col Length: 231mm, Page Width: 186mm
Copy instructions: Copy Date: 2 weeks prior to publication date
Supplement(s): AJ Specification - 12xY
BUSINESS: ARCHITECTURE & BUILDING: Architecture

ARCHITECTURAL DESIGN
1773013U4A-320

Editorial Address: Third Floor, International House, 7 High Street, LONDON, W5 5DB **Tel:** 020 8326 3800
Fax: 020 8326 3801

Web site: http://www.wiley.com
ISSN: 0003-8504
Publisher: John Wiley & Sons Ltd
Date Established: 1930
Frequency: 6 issues yearly
Cover Price: £22.99
Annual Sub.: £110.00
Circulation: 5,000 (Publisher's Statement)
Usual Pagination: 128
Editor: Helen Castle
Summary of Content: Magazine covering architecture and design.
Readership/Target Audience: Aimed at architects and architectural students.
BUSINESS: ARCHITECTURE & BUILDING: Architecture

ARCHITECTURAL HERITAGE
35813U4A-55

Editorial Address: The Glasite Meeting House, 33 Barony Street, EDINBURGH, EH3 6NX **Tel:** 0131 557 0019
Fax: 0131 557 0049
Email: director@ahss.org.uk
Advertising Address: 22 George Square, EDINBURGH, EH8 9LF **Tel:** 0131 650 4220 **Fax:** 0131 662 0053
Email: journals@eup.ed.ac.uk
Web site: http://www.ahss.org.uk
ISSN: 1350-7524
Publisher: Edinburgh University Press Ltd
Frequency: Annual - Published in September
Usual Pagination: 128
Editor: Neil Gregory; **Advertising Manager:** Wendy Gardiner
Summary of Content: Journal presenting Scottish-related architectural and art historical research as well as insights into the development of the profession and its social background.
Readership/Target Audience: Aimed at architects, art historians and interested enthusiasts.
ADVERTISING RATES:
Full Page Mono £250.00
Mechanical Data: Trim Size: 247 x 177mm, Film: Digital
Copy instructions: Copy Date: 8 weeks prior to publication date
Average advertising content per issue: 5%
BUSINESS: ARCHITECTURE & BUILDING: Architecture

ARCHITECTURAL IRONMONGERY JOURNAL
35952U4R-50

Editorial Address: 8 Stepney Green, LONDON, E1 3JU
Tel: 020 7790 3431 **Fax:** 020 7790 8517
Email: info@gai.org.uk
Advertising Address: As above.
Email: info@gai.org.uk
Web site: http://www.gai.org.uk
ISSN: 0959-986X
Publisher: The Guild of Architectural Ironmongers
Date Established: 1990
Frequency: Quarterly
Cover Price: Free
Circulation: 6,000 (Publisher's Statement)
Usual Pagination: 36
Editor: Helen Curry; **Advertisement Director:** Helen Curry;
Publisher: Gary Amer
Summary of Content: Magazine of the Guild of Architectural Ironmongers. Covers news, information and features.
Readership/Target Audience: Read by manufacturers, distributors and specifiers of architectural hardware.
ADVERTISING RATES:
Full Page Mono £1175.00
Full Page Colour £1450.00
Agency Commission: 10%
Mechanical Data: Type Area: 270 x 181mm, Bleed Size: 304 x 213mm, Film: Digital, Col Length: 270mm, Page Width: 181mm
Copy instructions: Copy Date: 1 month prior to publication date
Average advertising content per issue: 40%
BUSINESS: ARCHITECTURE & BUILDING: Building Related

THE ARCHITECTURAL REVIEW
35788U4A-60

Editorial Address: Greater London House, Hampstead Road, LONDON, NW1 7EJ **Tel:** 020 7728 4589
Email: paul.finch@emap.com
Advertising Address: As above. **Tel:** 020 7728 5000
Email: francine.libessart@emap.com
Web site: http://www.arplus.com
ISSN: 0003-861X
Publisher: EMAP Insight
Date Established: 1896
Frequency: Monthly - Published on the 1st of the cover month
Cover Price: £8.00
Annual Sub.: £89.00
Circulation: 14,869 (ABC 01/07/2008 to 30/06/2009)
Usual Pagination: 100

Editor: Paul Finch; **Editor-in-Chief:** Kieran Long; **Managing Editor:** Catherine Slessor
Summary of Content: International journal focusing on architecture, interior design, landscape and process. Twitter: http://twitter.com/AR_at_large.
Readership/Target Audience: Aimed at architects, interior designers and landscape architects.
ADVERTISING RATES:
Full Page Colour £3000.00
Agency Commission: 10%
Mechanical Data: Col Length: 266mm, Type Area: 266 x 192mm, Bleed Size: 303 x 236mm, Trim Size: 297 x 230mm, Film: Digital, Page Width: 192mm
Copy instructions: Copy Date: 2 weeks prior to publication date
Average advertising content per issue: 30%
BUSINESS: ARCHITECTURE & BUILDING: Architecture

ARCHITECTURAL TECHNOLOGY
35789U4A-63
Formerly: Chartered Institute of Architectural Technologists
Editorial Address: 397 City Road, LONDON, EC1V 1NH
Tel: 020 7278 2206 **Fax:** 020 7837 3194
Email: info@ciat.org.uk
Advertising Address: As above.
Email: adam@ciat.org.uk
Web site: http://www.ciat.org.uk
ISSN: 1361-326X
Publisher: Chartered Institute of Architectural Technologists
Date Established: 1983
Frequency: 6 issues yearly
Free to qualifying individuals
Annual Sub.: £15.00
Circulation: 10,500 (Publisher's Statement)
Usual Pagination: 32
Editor: Hugh Morrison; **Advertising Manager:** Adam Endacott
Summary of Content: Publication of the Chartered Institute of Architectural Technologists featuring news within the construction industry and architectural technology.
Readership/Target Audience: Aimed at Architectural Technologists and associated professionals.
ADVERTISING RATES:
Full Page Mono £930.00
Full Page Colour £930.00
Agency Commission: 10%
Mechanical Data: Type Area: 267 x 188mm, Bleed Size: 305 x 216mm, Trim Size: 297 x 210mm, Film: Positive, right reading, emulsion side down. Digital, Col Length: 267mm, Page Width: 188mm
Copy instructions: Copy Date: 2 weeks prior to publication date
Average advertising content per issue: 30%
BUSINESS: ARCHITECTURE & BUILDING: Architecture

ARCHITECTURE TODAY
35790U4A-65
Editorial Address: 161 Rosebery Avenue, LONDON, EC1R 4QX **Tel:** 020 7837 0143 **Fax:** 020 7837 0155
Email: editorial@architecturetoday.co.uk
Advertising Address: As above.
Email: alan.i@architecturetoday.co.uk
Web site: http://www.architecturetoday.co.uk
ISSN: 0958-6407
Publisher: Architecture Today plc
Date Established: 1989
Frequency: 10 issues yearly
Cover Price: £4.50
Free to qualifying individuals
Annual Sub.: £45.00
Circulation: 21,193 (ABC 01/07/2008 to 30/06/2009)
Usual Pagination: 100
Editor: Ian Latham; **Advertising Manager:** Alan Irvine; **Managing Editor:** Susan Warlow
Summary of Content: Magazine containing building features, European news, practice articles and special features.
Readership/Target Audience: Aimed at registered architects practising in the UK.
ADVERTISING RATES:
Full Page Mono £2140.00
Full Page Colour £3110.00
Agency Commission: 10%
Mechanical Data: Type Area: 254 x 178mm, Bleed Size: 305 x 213mm, Trim Size: 297 x 210mm, Film: Digital, Col Length: 254mm, Page Width: 178mm
Average advertising content per issue: 50%
Supplement(s): AT Handbook - 4xY, Ecotech - 2xY
BUSINESS: ARCHITECTURE & BUILDING: Architecture

ARCHITEXT
1644301U4A-316
Editorial Address: Unit 8, Chorley West Business Park, Ackhurst Road, CHORLEY, PR7 1NL **Tel:** 0870 444 8955
Email: editorial@euromedia-al.com
Advertising Address: As above. **Fax:** 0870 447 8956
Email: sales@euromedia-al.co.uk
Publisher: Euromedia Associates Ltd

Date Established: 2005
Frequency: 5 issues yearly
Free to qualifying individuals
Circulation: 10,000 (Publisher's Statement)
Editor: Richard Cheesbrough; **Advertising Manager:** Gemma Winstanley
Summary of Content: Magazine covering all aspects of construction services with a large focus on building regulations.
Readership/Target Audience: Aimed at architects, property developers, housing associations and local authorities.
ADVERTISING RATES:
Full Page Colour £18000.00
Mechanical Data: Trim Size: 297 x 210mm, Bleed Size: 303 x 216mm
BUSINESS: ARCHITECTURE & BUILDING: Architecture

ARENA
37174U14L-85
Editorial Address: 188 Wilmslow Road, MANCHESTER, M14 6LJ **Tel:** 0161 224 2804 **Fax:** 0161 249 2490
Email: arena@usdaw.org.uk
Advertising Address: Century One Publishing, Arquen House, 4-6 Spicer Street, ST. ALBANS, AL3 4PQ
Tel: 01727 893894 **Fax:** 01727 893895
Email: enquiries@centuryonepublishing.ltd.uk
Web site: http://www.usdaw.org.uk
Publisher: USDAW
Date Established: 1998
Frequency: Quarterly
Free to qualifying individuals
Annual Sub.: £20.00
Circulation: 370,000 (Publisher's Statement)
Usual Pagination: 24
Editor: Peter Rees-Farrell; **Advertising Manager:** Nick Simpson
Summary of Content: Magazine of the Union of Shop, Distributive and Allied Workers.
Readership/Target Audience: Read by union members, Members of Parliament and company managers.
ADVERTISING RATES:
Full Page Colour £6950.00
Agency Commission: 10%
Mechanical Data: Type Area: 284 x 190mm, Bleed Size: 303 x 216mm, Trim Size: 297 x 210mm, Col Length: 284mm, Film: Digital, Page Width: 190mm
BUSINESS: COMMERCE, INDUSTRY & MANAGEMENT: Trade Unions

ARGUS FSU ENERGY
38570U33-1_13
Editorial Address: 175 St. John Street, LONDON, EC1V 4LW **Tel:** 020 7780 4200 **Fax:** 020 7780 4201
Email: fsuenergy@argusmediagroup.com
Web site: http://www.argusonline.com
ISSN: 1368-7425
Publisher: Argus Media Ltd
Date Established: 1996
Frequency: Weekly
Usual Pagination: 16
Editor: John Gawthrop; **Executive Editor:** Euan Craik; **Publisher:** Adrian Binks
Summary of Content: Newsletter covering oil and gas intelligence in Eastern Europe and the former Soviet Union.
Readership/Target Audience: Aimed at executives within the oil industry and those with a financial interest.
ADVERTISING: No Advertising taken
BUSINESS: OIL & PETROLEUM

ARGUS FUNDAMENTALS
38621U33-43
Formerly: Petroleum Argus Fundamentals
Editorial Address: 175 St. John Street, LONDON, EC1V 4LW **Tel:** 020 7780 4200 **Fax:** 020 7780 4201
Email: agm@argusmediagroup.com
Web site: http://www.argusmediagroup.com
Publisher: Argus Media Ltd
Date Established: 1990
Frequency: Monthly
Usual Pagination: 28
Editor: Richard Child; **Editor-in-Chief:** Ian Bourne; **Publisher:** Adrian Binks
Summary of Content: Publication containing statistical analysis of the energy markets.
Readership/Target Audience: Aimed at oil market analysts.
ADVERTISING: No Advertising taken
BUSINESS: OIL & PETROLEUM

ARIEL
1667382U2D-144
Editorial Address: Room 2425, White City, 201 Wood Lane, LONDON, W12 7TS **Tel:** 020 8008 4224
Email: ariel.team@bbc.co.uk
Publisher: BBC
Frequency: Weekly
Free to qualifying individuals
Annual Sub.: £50.00

Circulation: 23,000 (Publisher's Statement)
Usual Pagination: 16
Editor: Clare Bolt; **Features Editor:** Clare Bolt
Summary of Content: Magazine covering news, features and comment about the BBC and the media industry.
Readership/Target Audience: Aimed at BBC employees and stakeholders.
ADVERTISING: No Advertising taken
BUSINESS: COMMUNICATIONS, ADVERTISING & MARKETING: Broadcasting

THE ARK
37832U21D-60
Editorial Address: Ewell House, Graveney Road, Goodstone, FAVERSHAM, ME13 8UP **Tel:** 01795 535468
Fax: 01795 535469
Email: editorial@thearkmagazine.co.uk
Advertising Address: As above.
Email: ads@dthearkmagazine.co.uk
Web site: http://www.rbst.org.uk
ISSN: 0306-8870
Publisher: GTC
Date Established: 1974
Frequency: Quarterly
Annual Sub.: £20.00
Circulation: 8,000 (Publisher's Statement)
Usual Pagination: 44
Editor: Rachel Kelly; **Advertising Manager:** Melanie Richards
Summary of Content: Magazine of the Rare Breeds Survival Trust. Covers news, events and articles on rare breeds of farm animals.
Readership/Target Audience: Read by members.
ADVERTISING RATES:
Full Page Colour £575.00
Agency Commission: 10%
Mechanical Data: Type Area: 260 x 180mm, Print Process: Offset litho, Col Length: 260mm, No. of Columns (Display): 4, Trim Size: 297 x 210mm, Bleed Size: 303 x 210mm, Page Width: 180mm
Copy instructions: Copy Date: 10th of the month prior to publication date
Average advertising content per issue: 15%
BUSINESS: AGRICULTURE & FARMING: Livestock

ARLIS/UK & IRELAND ANNUAL DIRECTORY
40883U60B-11
Editorial Address: Victoria and Albert Museum, Cromwell Road, South Kensington, LONDON, SW7 2RL
Tel: 020 7942 2317
Email: arlis@vam.ac.uk
Advertising Address: As above.
Email: arlis@vam.ac.uk
Web site: http://www.arlis.org.uk
ISSN: 0954-0679
Publisher: ARLIS/UK & Ireland
Frequency: Annual - Published in March
Free to qualifying individuals
Annual Sub.: £45.00
Circulation: 500 (Publisher's Statement)
Usual Pagination: 64
Editor: Business Manager; **Advertising Manager:** Natasha Held
Summary of Content: Publication containing a directory of members and subscribers.
Readership/Target Audience: Aimed at members of the society, art publishers and other relevant organisations.
ADVERTISING RATES:
Full Page Mono £165.00
Mechanical Data: Type Area: 242 x 170mm, Col Length: 242mm, Page Width: 170mm, Bleed Size: 303 x 216mm, Trim Size: 297 x 210mm
BUSINESS: PUBLISHING: Libraries

AROUND ARENA
1804691U11A-223
Editorial Address: 70 Copthorne Avenue, BROMLEY, BR2 8NN **Tel:** 020 3087 2378
Email: lorraine@arena.org.uk
Web site: http://www.arena.org.uk
Publisher: Arena
Frequency: Quarterly
Cover Price: Free
Circulation: 3,000 (Publisher's Statement)
Usual Pagination: 6
Editor: Lorraine Wood
Summary of Content: Newsletter containing industry and business news for the hospitality sector.
Readership/Target Audience: Aimed at members of Arena, including operators, wholesalers, distributors, manufacturers and service providers.
ADVERTISING: No Advertising taken
BUSINESS: CATERING: Catering, Hotels & Restaurants

ART BUSINESS TODAY
41597U64Q-20

Editorial Address: 16-18 Empress Place, LONDON, SW6 1TT **Tel:** 020 7381 6616 **Fax:** 020 7381 2596
Email: abt@fineart.co.uk
Advertising Address: As above.
Email: sales@fineart.co.uk
Web site: http://www.abtonline.co.uk
Publisher: The Fine Art Trade Guild
Date Established: 1906
Frequency: 5 issues yearly
Annual Sub.: £26.00
Circulation: 5,000 (Publisher's Statement)
Usual Pagination: 80
Editor: Annabelle Ruston; **Managing Director:** Rosie Sumner; **Managing Editor:** Annabelle Ruston; **Publisher:** Rosie Sumner
Summary of Content: Publication containing features relevant to the art trade, such as gallery design, picture selling and framing methods.
Readership/Target Audience: Read by gallery owners, framers, artists, publishers, fine art printers, frame manufacturers, designers and trade suppliers.
ADVERTISING RATES:
Full Page Colour £1820.00
Agency Commission: 10%
Mechanical Data: Film: Digital, Page Width: 190mm, Type Area: 277 x 190mm, Col Length: 277mm, Bleed Size: 303 x 216mm, Trim Size: 297 x 210mm
Copy instructions: Copy Date: 4 weeks prior to publication date
BUSINESS: OTHER CLASSIFICATIONS: Framing

ART BUYER
1696588U53-692

Editorial Address: 1 Churchgates, The Wilderness, BERKHAMSTED, HP4 2UB **Tel:** 01442 289930
Fax: 01442 289950
Advertising Address: As above.
Email: christine@lemapublishing.co.uk
Publisher: Lema Publishing
Date Established: 2008
Frequency: Annual - Published in May
Cover Price: Free
Circulation: 5,000 (Publisher's Statement)
Usual Pagination: 72
Editor: Jacqui Parr
Summary of Content: Magazine devoted to art, design and image licensing. Includes company profiles and information from licensors and agents involved in marketing all types of art-based properties around the world.
Readership/Target Audience: Aimed at decision makers in the art licensing industry.
ADVERTISING RATES:
Full Page Colour £1300.00
BUSINESS: RETAILING & WHOLESALING

ART DESIGN & COMMUNICATION IN HIGHER EDUCATION
1696242U62R-489

Editorial Address: Chelsea College of Art and Design, 16 John Islip Street, LONDON, SW1P 4JU **Tel:** 020 7514 7818
Email: l.drew@chelsea.arts.ac.uk
Web site: http://www.intellectbooks.co.uk
ISSN: 1474-273X
Publisher: Intellect Ltd
Date Established: 2002
Frequency: 3 issues yearly
Annual Sub.: £30.00
Usual Pagination: 80
Editor: Laura Lanceley
Summary of Content: Refereed journal that aims to inform, stimulate and promote the development of research with a learning and teaching focus for art, design and communication within higher education.
Readership/Target Audience: Aimed at academics.
ADVERTISING: Rates on application
BUSINESS: CHURCH & SCHOOL EQUIPMENT & EDUCATION: Education Related

ART LIBRARIES JOURNAL
25298U60B-11_7

Editorial Address: 10 Prevetts Way, ALDEBURGH, IP15 5LT **Tel:** 01728 451948
Email: g.varley@arlis2.demon.co.uk
Advertising Address: Victoria and Albert Museum, Cromwell Road, South Kensington, LONDON, SW7 2RL
Tel: 020 7942 2317
Email: arlis@vam.ac.uk
Web site: http://www.arlis.org.uk
ISSN: 0307-4722
Publisher: ARLIS/UK & Ireland
Date Established: 1976
Frequency: Quarterly
Cover Price: £50.00
Circulation: 750 (Publisher's Statement)
Usual Pagination: 48
Editor: Gillian Varley; **Advertising Manager:** Natasha Held

Summary of Content: Journal concentrating on the librarianship and documentation of art, architecture and design.
Language(s): English; French; German; Spanish
Readership/Target Audience: Aimed at art librarians in academic, public and special libraries, museums, booksellers, publishers, students and other interested readers throughout the world.
ADVERTISING RATES:
Full Page Mono £115.00
Mechanical Data: Type Area: 242 x 170mm, Col Length: 242mm, Page Width: 170mm, Film: Digital, Trim Size: 297 x 210mm, Bleed Size: +3mm
Copy instructions: Copy Date: 4 weeks prior to publication date
BUSINESS: PUBLISHING: Libraries

ARTS RESEARCH DIGEST
625419U32H-10

Editorial Address: Corbridge Business Centre, Tinklers Yard, CORBRIDGE, NE45 5SB **Tel:** 01434 636089
Email: enquiries@arts-research-digest.com
Advertising Address: As above.
Email: enquiries@arts-research-digest.com
Web site: http://www.arts-research-digest.com
ISSN: 1353-0305
Publisher: Arts Research Limited
Date Established: 1994
Frequency: 3 issues yearly - Published in March, July and November
Annual Sub.: £72.00
Circulation: 600 (Publisher's Statement)
Usual Pagination: 48
Editor: Annie Livesey; **Advertising Manager:** Carol Marshall
Summary of Content: Journal providing an overview of recent and current research in the arts and cultural sectors.
Readership/Target Audience: Aimed at local authorities, academics, researchers, policy makers, consultants, practitioners, funding agencies, universities, colleges and arts organisations.
ADVERTISING RATES:
Full Page Mono £100.00
Full Page Colour £250.00
Copy instructions: Copy Date: 6 weeks prior to publication date
BUSINESS: LOCAL GOVERNMENT, LEISURE & RECREATION: Leisure, Recreation & Entertainment

ARTSPROFESSIONAL
711965U64P-25

Editorial Address: PO Box 1010, Histon, CAMBRIDGE, CB24 9WH **Tel:** 01223 200200 **Fax:** 01223 200201
Email: editors@artsprofessional.co.uk
Advertising Address: As above.
Email: ads@artsprofessional.co.uk
Web site: http://www.artsprofessional.co.uk
ISSN: 1474-385X
Publisher: Arts Intelligence Ltd
Date Established: 2001
Frequency: 24 issues yearly - No issue mid-August or late December
Cover Price: £3.75
Annual Sub.: £84.00
Circulation: 7,500 (Publisher's Statement)
Usual Pagination: 16
Editor: Catherine Rose; **Publisher:** Brian Whitehead
Summary of Content: Magazine containing news and features relating to the management, administration, funding and development of the arts sector across all art forms and types of organisation.
Readership/Target Audience: Read by managers, administrators and officers at all levels in arts and related organisations.
ADVERTISING RATES:
Full Page Mono £1290.00
Full Page Colour £1350.00
Agency Commission: 10%
Mechanical Data: Page Width: 188mm, Type Area: 269 x 188mm, Col Length: 269mm, Trim Size: 297 x 210mm, Film: Digital
Copy instructions: Copy Date: Tuesday prior to publication date
Average advertising content per issue: 30%
BUSINESS: OTHER CLASSIFICATIONS: Museums

ASIA AND MIDDLE EAST FOOD TRADE
37938U22A-20

Editorial Address: PO Box 125, STOWMARKET, IP14 1PB
Tel: 01449 771200
Email: editor@ameft.com
Advertising Address: As above.
Email: transnational@mwmedia.uk.com
Web site: http://www.ameft.com
ISSN: 0265-6469
Publisher: J Latke Publishing
Frequency: Quarterly
Annual Sub.: EUR40.00
Circulation: 19,506 (Publisher's Statement)
Usual Pagination: 76

Editor: Sarah Zimmer
Summary of Content: Publication focusing on new products, trends in food and catering equipment technology and consumption patterns in Asian and Middle Eastern markets.
Readership/Target Audience: Aimed at food and beverage importers, commercial caterers, large retailers, equipment buyers and distributors.
ADVERTISING RATES:
Full Page Mono EUR2940.00
Full Page Colour EUR3960.00
Agency Commission: 15%
Mechanical Data: Page Width: 178mm, Type Area: 256 x 178mm, Bleed Size: 283 x 213mm, Trim Size: 280 x 210mm, Col Length: 256mm, Film: Digital
BUSINESS: FOOD

ASIA MONITOR
36980U14C-200

Formerly: Indian Subcontinent Monitor
Editorial Address: Mermaid House, 2 Puddle Dock, LONDON, EC4V 4DU **Tel:** 020 7248 0468
Fax: 020 7248 0467
Email: ysano@businessmonitor.com
Web site: http://www.businessmonitor.com
ISSN: 0265-2601
Publisher: Business Monitor International Ltd
Date Established: 1989
Frequency: Monthly
Circulation: 1,000 (Publisher's Statement)
Usual Pagination: 16
Editor: Yoel Sano; **Publisher:** Richard Londesborough
Summary of Content: Briefing covering political, economic, financial and business environments and developments.
Readership/Target Audience: Aimed at company executives, directors and financial consultants.
ADVERTISING: No Advertising taken
Editions:
China and North East Asia Monitor
South Asia Monitor
South East Asia Monitor Volume 1
South East Asia Monitor Volume 2
BUSINESS: COMMERCE, INDUSTRY & MANAGEMENT: International Commerce

ASIA PACIFIC PERSONAL CARE
1640365U15A-19

Editorial Address: Step House, North Farm Road, TUNBRIDGE WELLS, TN2 3DR **Tel:** 01892 518877
Fax: 01892 616177
Email: nicholasmarshall@stepcomms.com
Advertising Address: As above.
Email: joshtaylor@stepex.com
Web site: http://www.personalcaremagazine.com
ISSN: 1470-8213
Publisher: Step Communications Ltd
Frequency: 9 issues yearly - Published in the 1st week of the month
Cover Price: Free
Circulation: 10,091 (Publisher's Statement)
Usual Pagination: 76
Editor: Nicholas Marshall; **Advertising Manager:** Josh Taylor; **Managing Editor:** Nicholas Marshall
Summary of Content: Magazine covering the application of new materials and ingredients for personal care products.
Language(s): Chinese; English; Japanese; Korean
Readership/Target Audience: Aimed at cosmetic scientists, formulating chemists, dermatologists, microbiologists, marketing personnel, production staff and company owners.
ADVERTISING RATES:
Full Page Mono £1725.0
Full Page Colour £1875.0
Agency Commission: 10%
Mechanical Data: Type Area: 258 x 180mm, Bleed Size: 303 x 216mm, Trim Size: 297 x 210mm, Film: Digital, Col Length: 258mm, Page Width: 180mm
Copy instructions: Copy Date: 3 weeks prior to publication date
Average advertising content per issue: 30%
BUSINESS: COSMETICS & HAIRDRESSING: Cosmetics

ASIACOM
37414U18B-3

Editorial Address: Mortimer House, 37-41 Mortimer Street, LONDON, W1P 3JH **Tel:** 020 7017 4800 **Fax:** 020 7017 428
Email: nicole.mccormick@informa.com
Web site: http://www.telecom.com
ISSN: 1084-0710
Publisher: Informa Telecoms and Media Group
Frequency: 23 issues yearly
Annual Sub.: £750.00
Usual Pagination: 12
Editor: Nicole McCormick; **Managing Editor:** Nicole McCormick
Summary of Content: Magazine covering news of interest to the TV, cable, and telecommunications industry throughout the Asia-Pacific region.

Readership/Target Audience: Aimed at those within the TV, cable, and telecommunications industry.
ADVERTISING: No Advertising taken
BUSINESS: ELECTRONICS: Telecommunications

ASIAFRUIT MAGAZINE
38113U26C-5
Editorial Address: 1 Nine Elms Lane, LONDON, SW8 5NQ
Tel: 020 7501 3700 **Fax:** 020 7498 6472
Email: john@fruitnet.com
Advertising Address: As above.
Email: linda@fruitnet.com
Web site: http://www.fruitnet.com
Publisher: Market Intelligence Ltd
Date Established: 1995
Frequency: 6 issues yearly - Published on the last Friday of the month prior to cover date
Annual Sub.: £65.00
Circulation: 5,000 (Publisher's Statement)
Usual Pagination: 120
Editor: Steven Maxwell; **News Editor:** Steven Maxwell;
Managing Director: Chris White; **Advertising Manager:** Linda Bloomfield; **Publisher:** Chris White
Summary of Content: Magazine covering the marketing and distribution of fresh fruit and vegetables in Asia.
Language(s): Chinese; English
Readership/Target Audience: Aimed at those involved in the fresh produce business.
ADVERTISING RATES:
Full Page Colour $2250.00
Agency Commission: 10%
Mechanical Data: Type Area: 260 x 170mm, Col Length: 260mm, Trim Size: 297 x 210mm, Bleed Size: 303 x 216mm, Page Width: 170mm, Film: Digital
Copy instructions: Copy Date: 2 weeks prior to publication date
Average advertising content per issue: 35%
BUSINESS: GARDEN TRADE

ASIAHEDGE
1645514U1F-630
Editorial Address: Nestor House, Playhouse Yard, LONDON, EC4V 5EX **Tel:** 020 7779 7330
Fax: 020 7779 7331
Email: info@hedgefundintelligence.com
Advertising Address: As above.
Email: jwillis@hedgefundintelligence.com
Web site: http://www.hedgefundintelligence.com
Publisher: Hedge Fund Intelligence
Frequency: 10 issues yearly - July/August and November/December are combined issues
Annual Sub.: £850.00
Editor: Paul Storey; **Advertising Manager:** John Willis
Summary of Content: Newsletter providing investors and asset allocators with names and strategies of promising new Asian funds, monitoring the performance of established managers, alerting service providers to potential business opportunities and providing comprehensive league tables on Asian funds.
Readership/Target Audience: Aimed at investors, asset allocators, hedge fund managers, service providers and anyone else wishing to be kept up to date with the latest developments in the industry.
ADVERTISING RATES:
Full Page Mono £5950.00
Mechanical Data: Type Area: 244 x 185mm, Bleed Size: 278 x 211mm, Trim Size: 272 x 205mm, Col Length: 244mm, Page Width: 185mm, Film: Digital
Copy instructions: Copy Date: 10th of the publication month
BUSINESS: FINANCE & ECONOMICS: Investment

ASIAN ENTERPRISE
1849805U14C-376
Editorial Address: Waterfront Studios, 1 Dock Road, LONDON, E16 1AG **Tel:** 020 7476 9400 **Fax:** 020 7476 9450
Email: info@generalweb.biz
Advertising Address: As above.
Email: info@generalweb.biz
Web site: http://www.asianenterprise.biz
Publisher: General Communications International Ltd
Date Established: 2007
Frequency: Quarterly
Cover Price: £3.95
Free to qualifying individuals
Circulation: 15,000 (Controlled Circulation)
Usual Pagination: 68
Publisher: Karim Ullah
Summary of Content: Magazine showcasing achievements of Asian businessmen and women both in the UK and abroad. Contains profiles and interviews with leading personalities, analysis, business trends and features.
Readership/Target Audience: Aimed at businessmen and women of sub-continental background.
ADVERTISING RATES:
Full Page Colour EUR6715.00
BUSINESS: COMMERCE, INDUSTRY & MANAGEMENT: International Commerce

ASIAN ENVIRONMENTAL TECHNOLOGY
40622U57-4
Editorial Address: Oak Court Business Centre, Sandridge Park, Porters Wood, ST. ALBANS, AL3 6PH
Tel: 01727 858840 **Fax:** 01727 840310
Email: info@envirotechpubs.com
Advertising Address: As above.
Email: info@envirotechpubs.com
Web site: http://www.envirotech-online.com
ISSN: 1363-7134
Publisher: Environmental Technology Publications Ltd
Date Established: 1996
Frequency: Quarterly
Cover Price: Free
Circulation: 23,334 (Publisher's Statement)
Usual Pagination: 60
Editor: Marcus Pattison; **Managing Director:** Marcus Pattison; **Advertising Manager:** Marcus Pattison;
Publisher: Marcus Pattison
Summary of Content: Magazine containing product news and articles on the latest developments in pollution monitoring, water and waste management and treatment, air analysis and clean up.
Readership/Target Audience: Aimed at environmental scientists and decision makers throughout Asia and Australasia.
ADVERTISING RATES:
Full Page Mono £4250.00
Full Page Colour £5045.00
Agency Commission: 15%
Mechanical Data: Type Area: 370 x 250mm, Bleed Size: 406 x 286mm, Trim Size: 400 x 280mm, Col Length: 370mm, Page Width: 250mm, Film: Digital
Copy instructions: Copy Date: 5th of the month prior to publication date
Average advertising content per issue: 50%
BUSINESS: ENVIRONMENT & POLLUTION

ASIAN INFRASTRUCTURE
39566U49A-20
Formerly: Asian Infrastructure Monthly
Editorial Address: Raggett House, Bowdens, LANGPORT, TA10 0DD **Tel:** 01458 259683 **Fax:** 01458 259684
Email: lalsop@asiaint.com
ISSN: 1472-9943
Publisher: Intelligence Research Ltd
Date Established: 1995
Frequency: Monthly
Annual Sub.: £695.00
Usual Pagination: 60
Editor: Louise Alsop
Summary of Content: Newsletter containing news, analysis and comment on ports, roads, railways, airports, mass transit systems, urban development, water supply and sanitation in Asia.
Readership/Target Audience: Read by engineering companies and designers, bankers, lawyers, project financiers, accountants, management consultants, construction companies and transport operators.
ADVERTISING: No Advertising taken
BUSINESS: TRANSPORT

ASIAN OIL & GAS
38571U33-1_15
Editorial Address: The Arena, Stockley Park, UXBRIDGE, UB11 1AA **Tel:** 020 8899 1765 **Fax:** 020 8534 5396
Email: dmorgan@offshore-engineer.com
Advertising Address: 168 St. Johns Hill, SEVENOAKS, TN13 3PF **Tel:** 01732 459683
Email: neil@aladltd.co.uk
Web site: http://www.oilonline.com
Publisher: Atlantic Communications
Frequency: 6 issues yearly - Published at the beginning of the 2nd cover month
Free to qualifying individuals
Circulation: 6,530 (Publisher's Statement)
Usual Pagination: 52
Editor: David Morgan; **Editor-in-Chief:** David Morgan
Summary of Content: Publication covering the oil and gas industry in Asia including current and future technology involved in on and off shore exploration, production and processing.
Readership/Target Audience: Aimed at operations managers in oil and gas organisations.
ADVERTISING RATES:
Full Page Mono $3925.00
Full Page Colour $4700.00
Mechanical Data: Page Width: 190mm, Film: Digital, Type Area: 254 x 190mm, Col Length: 254mm, Trim Size: 286 x 210mm, Bleed Size: 293 x 215mm
Copy instructions: Copy Date: 4 weeks prior to publication date
BUSINESS: OIL & PETROLEUM

ASIAN TRADER
37939U22A-50
Editorial Address: Garavi Gujarat House, 1 Silex Street, LONDON, SE1 0DW **Tel:** 020 7654 7740 **Fax:** 020 7261 0055
Email: tanuja@gujarat.co.uk

Advertising Address: As above.
Email: paul.gray@amg.biz
Web site: http://asiantrader.biz
ISSN: 0961-7132
Publisher: Asian Trade Publications Ltd
Date Established: 1985
Frequency: 25 issues yearly
Cover Price: £3.00
Free to qualifying individuals
Circulation: 35,238 (ABC 01/07/2007 to 30/06/2008)
Usual Pagination: 42
Editor: Tanuja Parekh; **Executive Editor:** Shailesh Solanki;
Advertising Manager: Paul Gray; **Managing Editor:** Kalpesh Solanki
Summary of Content: Journal containing news on the independent retail sector, features on product categories, news on the cash and carry wholesale sector and newspaper/magazine sector.
Language(s): English; Gujarati; Urdu
Readership/Target Audience: Aimed at off-licences, grocers and newsagents.
ADVERTISING RATES:
Full Page Colour £3301.00
Agency Commission: 10%
Mechanical Data: Film: Digital, Trim Size: 297 x 210mm
Copy instructions: Copy Date: 2 weeks prior to publication date
Average advertising content per issue: 40%
BUSINESS: FOOD

ASIA-PACIFIC BAKER
36454U8A-20
Editorial Address: 1st Floor Offices, 1-3 Station Road East, OXTED, RH8 0BD **Tel:** 01883 734582 **Fax:** 01883 713640
Email: evie@crier.co.uk
Advertising Address: As above.
Email: nthorp@crier.co.uk
Web site: http://www.worldbakers.com
ISSN: 1461-3050
Publisher: Crier Media Group
Date Established: 1997
Frequency: Quarterly - Published on the 20th of the cover month
Free to qualifying individuals
Annual Sub.: £46.00
Circulation: 8,347 (Publisher's Statement)
Usual Pagination: 48
Editor: Evie Serventi; **Managing Director:** John Whitbread;
Publisher: John Whitbread
Summary of Content: Magazine covering news, market trends, bakery processing and ingredients.
Readership/Target Audience: Aimed at bakers throughout the Asia-Pacific rim.
ADVERTISING RATES:
Full Page Colour £2450.00
Mechanical Data: Page Width: 186mm, Type Area: 270 x 186mm, Col Length: 270mm, Trim Size: 297 x 210mm, Film: Digital
Copy instructions: Copy Date: 4 weeks prior to publication date
Average advertising content per issue: 25%
BUSINESS: BAKING & CONFECTIONERY: Baking

ASIA-PACIFIC ENGINEER
713567U19F-99
Formerly: Asia-Pacific Process Engineer
Editorial Address: Europa House, 13-17 Ironmonger Row, LONDON, EC1V 3QG **Tel:** 020 7253 2545
Fax: 020 7608 1600
Email: editorial@setform.com
Web site: http://www.engineerlive.com
Publisher: Setform Ltd
Date Established: 2000
Frequency: Half-yearly - Published in June and December
Cover Price: Free
Circulation: 10,000 (Publisher's Statement)
Usual Pagination: 88
Editor: Paul Boughton; **Managing Director:** Mike Bishop
Summary of Content: Magazine covering all aspects of process engineering throughout Asia.
Readership/Target Audience: Aimed at senior engineers and design engineers within the processing industries.
ADVERTISING: No Advertising taken
BUSINESS: ENGINEERING & MACHINERY: Production & Mechanical Engineering

ASKFIRA NEWS
38057U23A-20
Formerly: FIRA Promotional Newsletter
Editorial Address: Maxwell Road, STEVENAGE, SG1 2EW
Tel: 01438 777700 **Fax:** 01438 777800
Email: info@fira.co.uk
Web site: http://www.fira.co.uk
Publisher: FIRA International Ltd
Date Established: 2001
Frequency: Quarterly
Cover Price: Free
Circulation: 7,000 (Publisher's Statement)
Usual Pagination: 16

Editor: Geoff Covey
Summary of Content: Newsletter covering all aspects of furniture production. Includes articles on design, health and safety, environment, sustainability quality, ergonomics, materials, complaint resolution and training.
Readership/Target Audience: Aimed at members and prospective members of the Furniture Industry Research Association.
ADVERTISING: No Advertising taken
BUSINESS: FURNISHINGS & FURNITURE

ASLEF LOCOMOTIVE JOURNAL
37193U14L-420

Formerly: Locomotive Journal
Editorial Address: 9 Arkwright Road, Hampstead, LONDON, NW3 6AB **Tel:** 020 7317 8600 **Fax:** 020 7794 6406
Email: journal@aslef.org.uk
Web site: http://www.aslef.org.uk
Publisher: ASLEF
Date Established: 1880
Frequency: Monthly
Cover Price: £1.00
Free to qualifying individuals
Circulation: 18,500 (Publisher's Statement)
Usual Pagination: 24
Editor: Chris Proctor
Summary of Content: Journal of the Associated Society of Locomotive Engineers and Firemen.
Readership/Target Audience: Aimed at ASLEF members.
ADVERTISING: No Advertising taken
BUSINESS: COMMERCE, INDUSTRY & MANAGEMENT: Trade Unions

ASPHALT NOW
708185U42B-5

Editorial Address: 14A Eccleston Street, LONDON, SW1W 9LT **Tel:** 020 7730 1100 **Fax:** 020 7730 2213
Email: info@asphaltuk.org
Web site: http://www.asphaltuk.org
ISSN: 1460-8383
Publisher: HMPR
Date Established: 1997
Frequency: Half-yearly - Published in May and November
Cover Price: Free
Circulation: 14,000 (Publisher's Statement)
Usual Pagination: 8
Editor: Helen Melhuish
Summary of Content: Magazine of the Asphalt Industry Alliance featuring news and information on the asphalt industry.
Readership/Target Audience: Aimed at those with an interest in the asphalt industry and maintenance of roads.
ADVERTISING: No Advertising taken
BUSINESS: CONSTRUCTION: Roads

ASPIRE
1668614U11A-201

Editorial Address: Progressive House, 2 Maidstone Road, Sidcup, PULBOROUGH, DA14 5HZ **Tel:** 0845 000 2500
Email: davidf@dewberryredpoint.co.uk
Advertising Address: As above.
Email: danielh@dewberryredpoint.co.uk
Web site: http://www.dewberryredpoint.co.uk
Publisher: Dewberry Redpoint Ltd
Date Established: 2004
Frequency: Quarterly
Free to qualifying individuals
Circulation: 6,000 (Publisher's Statement)
Usual Pagination: 82
Editor: David Hurst
Summary of Content: Magazine covering property, products and people involved in the hospitality industry.
Readership/Target Audience: Aimed at senior management within the hospitality sector.
ADVERTISING RATES:
Full Page Colour £2500.00
BUSINESS: CATERING: Catering, Hotels & Restaurants

ASSEMBLY AUTOMATION
35980U5A-5

Editorial Address: 17 Old Lane, Low Mill Village, Addingham, ILKLEY, LS29 0SA **Tel:** 01943 830399
Fax: 01943 831876
Email: news@engineeringfirst.com
Web site: http://www.emeraldinsight.com/aa.htm
ISSN: 0144-5154
Publisher: Emerald Group Publishing Ltd
Frequency: Quarterly
Annual Sub.: £2699.00
Circulation: 4,000 (Publisher's Statement)
Usual Pagination: 90
Editor: Clive Loughlin
Summary of Content: Journal covering international developments in dedicated and programme assembly on the latest trends towards flexible manufacture.

Readership/Target Audience: Read by engineers and managers who develop and apply assembly automation systems.
ADVERTISING: No Advertising taken
BUSINESS: COMPUTERS & AUTOMATION: Automation & Instrumentation

---

THE ASSESSOR
1640324U31A-392

Editorial Address: Ewell House, Graveney Road, FAVERSHAM, ME13 8UP **Tel:** 01795 542436
Fax: 01795 535469
Email: editorial@iaea.uk.com
Advertising Address: As above. **Tel:** 01795 535468
Email: ads@iaea.uk.com
Web site: http://www.iaea.uk.com
Publisher: GTC
Frequency: 6 issues yearly
Free to qualifying individuals
Usual Pagination: 28
Editor: Eleanor Sheath; **Advertising Manager:** Steven Riley
Summary of Content: Publication covering all matters of relevance to automobile assessors including news, new products, latest models, road and car safety issues and car manufacture.
Readership/Target Audience: Aimed at automobile assessors and sent to all members of the IAEA.
ADVERTISING RATES:
Full Page Colour £750.00
SCC £12.50
Agency Commission: 10%
Mechanical Data: Type Area: 275 x 188mm, Bleed Size: 303 x 216mm, Trim Size: 297 x 210mm, Col Length: 275mm, Page Width: 188mm, Print Process: Litho, Col Widths (Display): 42mm, No. of Columns (Display): 4, Film: Digital
Copy instructions: Copy Date: 23rd of the month prior to publication date
Average advertising content per issue: 20%
BUSINESS: MOTOR TRADE: Motor Trade Accessories

ASSISTIVE TECHNOLOGIES
40463U56L-18

Formerly: Motion Technology Today
Editorial Address: 47 Church Street, BARNSLEY, S70 2AS
Tel: 01226 734407 **Fax:** 01226 734477
Email: dm@whpl.net
Advertising Address: As above. **Tel:** 01226 734333
Email: advertising@assistivetechnologies.co.uk
Web site: http://www.assistivetechnologies.co.uk
Publisher: Wharncliffe Publishing Ltd
Date Established: 1998
Frequency: 6 issues yearly
Free to qualifying individuals
Annual Sub.: £45.00
Circulation: 6,000 (Publisher's Statement)
Usual Pagination: 32
Editor: Nicola Hyde; **News Editor:** Nicola Hyde; **Group Editor:** Andrew Harrod; **Circulation Manager:** Kelly Tarff
Summary of Content: Magazine covering news and issues relating to the orthotics, prosthetics, rehabilitation and mobility market including company profiles, interviews and exhibitions coverage.
Readership/Target Audience: Aimed at workers in the health and medical industry and engineers in rehabilitation and mobility, along with mobility end users.
ADVERTISING RATES:
Full Page Colour £1300.00
Agency Commission: 10%
Mechanical Data: Type Area: 320 x 220mm, Bleed Size: 346 x 246mm, Col Length: 320mm, Page Width: 220mm, Film: Digital, Trim Size: 340 x 240mm
Average advertising content per issue: 40%
BUSINESS: HEALTH & MEDICAL: Disability & Rehabilitation

ASSOCIATION MANAGEMENT QUARTERLY
1656463U14A-532

Formerly: Association Management
Editorial Address: The Old Pottery, Fulneck, PUDSEY, LS28 8NT **Tel:** 0113 255 6896
Email: louise@louisewrites.co.uk
Advertising Address: Red Spot Media Solutions Ltd, Southfield House, Southfields Business Park, Falcon Way, BOURNE, PE10 0FF **Tel:** 01778 392580 **Fax:** 01778 426411
Email: sue@redspotmediasolutions.co.uk
Publisher: Mypec
Date Established: 1989
Frequency: Quarterly
Free to qualifying individuals
Annual Sub.: £46.00
Circulation: 3,500 (Publisher's Statement)
Usual Pagination: 28
Editor: Louise Clarke
Summary of Content: Magazine covering all aspects of the association sector. Includes articles on legal, finance, health and safety and conference and venue information.
Readership/Target Audience: Aimed at chief executives and association secretaries in societies, institutes and trade unions.

ADVERTISING RATES:
Full Page Colour £1190.00
SCC £15.00
Agency Commission: 10%
Mechanical Data: Film: Digital, Type Area: 261 x 174mm, Col Length: 261mm, Page Width: 174mm, Print Process: Web-fed offset litho, Col Widths (Display): 42mm, No. of Columns (Display): 4
Copy instructions: Copy Date: 3 weeks prior to publication date
Average advertising content per issue: 20%
BUSINESS: COMMERCE, INDUSTRY & MANAGEMENT

ASSOCIATION MEETINGS INTERNATIONAL
35629U2C-17

Editorial Address: Woodley House, Oak Road, RIVENHALL END, CM8 3HE **Tel:** 01376 512700 **Fax:** 01376 502691
Email: robspalding@btinternet.com
Advertising Address: Kings House, Cantelupe Road, EAST GRINSTEAD, RH19 3BE **Tel:** 01342 306700
Fax: 01342 302554
Email: npresident@cat-publications.com
Web site: http://www.meetpie.com
Publisher: Conference & Travel Publications Ltd
Frequency: 6 issues yearly - Published on the 1st Monday of the cover month
Cover Price: Free
Circulation: 10,000 (Publisher's Statement)
Usual Pagination: 56
Editor: Rob Spalding; **Managing Director:** Martin Lewis
Summary of Content: Magazine for those involved in planning and organising conferences and meetings for members of associations around the world.
Readership/Target Audience: Aimed at organisers and association executives responsible for the planning and organisation of association conventions, congresses and meetings, both national and international.
ADVERTISING RATES:
Full Page Colour £3195.00
Agency Commission: 10%
Mechanical Data: Bleed Size: 303 x 216mm, Trim Size: 297 x 210mm, Film: Digital
Copy instructions: Copy Date: 13th of the month prior to publication date
Average advertising content per issue: 50%
BUSINESS: COMMUNICATIONS, ADVERTISING & MARKETING: Conferences & Exhibitions

---

ASSOCIATION OF INDEPENDENT MUSEUMS (AIM) BULLETIN
41587U64P-27

Formerly: Association of Independent Museums Bulletin
Editorial Address: Lindford Cottage, Church Lane, Cocking, MIDHURST, GU29 0HW **Tel:** 01730 812419
Fax: 01730 812419
Email: heavyhorse@mistral.co.uk
Advertising Address: As above.
Email: heavyhorse@mistral.co.uk
Web site: http://www.aim-museums.co.uk
ISSN: 0142-887X
Publisher: Association of Independent Museums
Date Established: 1977
Frequency: 6 issues yearly - Published on the 1st of the month
Annual Sub.: £70.00
Circulation: 1,300 (Publisher's Statement)
Usual Pagination: 16
Editor: Diana Zeuner; **Advertising Manager:** Diana Zeuner
Summary of Content: Bulletin of The Association of Independent Museums. Contains information on independent museums and heritage organisations.
Readership/Target Audience: Aimed at individual museum professionals, conservation press, media, designers, consultants, freelancers and commercial suppliers.
ADVERTISING RATES:
Full Page Colour £355.00
Agency Commission: 10%
Mechanical Data: Trim Size: 273 x 190mm, Film: Digital
Copy instructions: Copy Date: 26th of the month prior to publication date
Average advertising content per issue: 25%
BUSINESS: OTHER CLASSIFICATIONS: Museums

ASTHMA MAGAZINE
624436U56A-28_50

Formerly: Asthma News
Editorial Address: Summit House, 70 Wilson Street, LONDON, EC2A 2DB **Tel:** 0845 603 8143
Fax: 020 7256 6075
Email: editor@asthma.org.uk
Advertising Address: As above. **Tel:** 020 7786 4900
Email: chodder@asthma.org.uk
Web site: http://www.asthma.org.uk
ISSN: 1356-3440
Publisher: Asthma Enterprises Limited
Date Established: 1993
Frequency: Quarterly
Annual Sub.: £12.00

Circulation: 11,000 (Publisher's Statement)
Usual Pagination: 36
Editor: Elizabeth McGrath; **News Editor:** Hannah Devman;
Advertising Manager: Clare Hodder
Summary of Content: Magazine with the latest news on asthma care and developments in research. Also includes handy hints on coping and living with asthma and news on the charity's campaigning and other activities.
Readership/Target Audience: Aimed at members of Asthma UK and people with an interest in asthma.
ADVERTISING RATES:
Full Page Colour £1250.00
Mechanical Data: Bleed Size: +3mm, Trim Size: 300 x 230mm
BUSINESS: HEALTH & MEDICAL

ASTRONOMY & GEOPHYSICS   39946U55-33
Editorial Address: Department of Physics & Astronomy, Leeds University, LEEDS, LS2 9JT **Tel:** 0113 343 6672
Fax: 0113 343 3900
Email: s.bowler@leeds.ac.uk
Advertising Address: 9600 Garsington Road, Cowley, OXFORD, OX4 2DQ **Tel:** 01865 776868 **Fax:** 01865 714591
Email: craig.pickett@oxon.blackwellpublishing.com
Web site: http://www.blackwellpublishing.com/journals
ISSN: 1366-8781
Publisher: Wiley-Blackwell Publishing
Date Established: 1997
Frequency: 6 issues yearly
Annual Sub.: £78.00
Circulation: 3,500 (Publisher's Statement)
Usual Pagination: 40
Editor: Sue Bowler; **Publisher:** Miriam Maus
Summary of Content: Journal of the Royal Astronomical Society, covering research reviews, news and conference reports.
Readership/Target Audience: Read by professional astronomers, geophysicists and members.
ADVERTISING RATES:
Full Page Mono £600.00
Full Page Colour £1300.00
Agency Commission: 10%
Mechanical Data: Page Width: 177mm, Type Area: 253 x 177mm, Col Length: 253mm, Trim Size: 297 x 210mm, Film: Digital, Bleed Size: 303 x 216mm
Copy instructions: Copy Date: 4 weeks prior to publication date
BUSINESS: APPLIED SCIENCE & LABORATORIES

AT HANDBOOK   35791U4A-72
Formerly: AT Detail
Editorial Address: 161 Rosebery Avenue, LONDON, EC1R 4QX **Tel:** 020 7837 0143 **Fax:** 020 7837 0155
Email: products@architecturetoday.co.uk
Advertising Address: As above.
Email: alan.i@architecturetoday.co.uk
Web site: http://www.architecturetoday.co.uk
Publisher: Architecture Today plc
Date Established: 2001
Frequency: Quarterly
Cover Price: Free
Circulation: 21,178 (Publisher's Statement 01/07/2007 to 30/06/2008)
Usual Pagination: 52
Editor: Susan Warlow; **Advertising Manager:** Alan Irvine
Summary of Content: Magazine covering all aspects of new projects and developments, including product information, services and current trade exhibitions.
Readership/Target Audience: Aimed at specifiers in the construction industry.
ADVERTISING RATES:
Full Page Mono £2140.00
Full Page Colour £3110.00
Agency Commission: 10%
Mechanical Data: Col Length: 254mm, Page Width: 178mm, Type Area: 254 x 178mm, Bleed Size: 305 x 213mm, Trim Size: 297 x 210mm, Film: Digital
Copy instructions: Copy Date: 28 days prior to publication date
Supplement to: Architecture Today
BUSINESS: ARCHITECTURE & BUILDING: Architecture

ATTIRE ACCESSORIES   1819917U47A-589
Editorial Address: Broseley House, Newlands Drive, WITHAM, CM8 2UL **Tel:** 01376 514000 **Fax:** 01376 514555
Email: jenniferk@klinedavis.com
Advertising Address: As above.
Email: stephenl@attireaccessories.com
Web site: http://www.attireaccessories.com
ISSN: 1758-0919
Publisher: Kline Davis Ltd
Date Established: 2007
Frequency: 6 issues yearly
Free to qualifying individuals
Circulation: 6,300 (Publisher's Statement)

Editor: Jennifer Kettle; **Advertising Manager:** Stephen Lampshire
Summary of Content: Magazine providing product and market analysis and the latest trends with information on trade shows, financial and legal matters and reviews on new and innovative products.
Readership/Target Audience: Aimed at buyers in independent fashion shops, jewellers, boutiques, shoe shops, bag shops, accessory shops and buyers in national fashion chains and department stores.
ADVERTISING RATES:
Full Page Colour £1475.00
Agency Commission: 10%
Mechanical Data: Bleed Size: 325 x 237mm, Trim Size: 319 x 231mm, Film: Digital
Average advertising content per issue: 40%
BUSINESS: CLOTHING & TEXTILES

ATTIRE BRIDAL   1852532U47A-593
Editorial Address: Broseley House, Newland Drive, WITHAM, CM8 2UL **Tel:** 01376 535609 **Fax:** 01376 514555
Email: editor@attirebridal.com
Advertising Address: As above. **Tel:** 01376 565612
Email: frankiej@attirebridal.com
Web site: http://www.attirebridal.com
ISSN: 1758-0072
Publisher: Kline Davis Ltd
Date Established: 2007
Frequency: 6 issues yearly
Free to qualifying individuals
Circulation: 2,721 (ABC 01/07/2008 to 30/06/2009)
Usual Pagination: 100
Editor: Rebecca Winward
Summary of Content: Magazine covering fashion, visual merchandising, trader show previews and industry news.
Readership/Target Audience: Aimed at bridal retailers.
ADVERTISING: Rates on application
BUSINESS: CLOTHING & TEXTILES

ATTRACTIONS MANAGEMENT   41472U64A-36
Editorial Address: Portmill House, Portmill Lane, HITCHIN, SG5 1DJ **Tel:** 01462 431385 **Fax:** 01462 433909
Email: attractions@leisuremedia.com
Advertising Address: As above.
Email: juliebadrick@leisuremedia.com
Web site: http://www.attractionsmanagement.co.uk
Publisher: The Leisure Media Company Ltd
Date Established: 1995
Frequency: Quarterly - Published at the beginning of the 1st week of the cover month
Cover Price: £3.00
Circulation: 6,000 (Publisher's Statement)
Usual Pagination: 100
Editor: Kathleen Whyman; **Advertising Manager:** Julie Badrick; **Managing Editor:** Kathleen Whyman; **Publisher:** Julie Badrick
Summary of Content: Publication covering business issues in the theme parks, science centres, zoos and aquariums, visitor attractions, museums and heritage, galleries and waterpark markets.
Readership/Target Audience: Aimed at owners, operators, investors, designers and consultants in the theme parks, science centres, zoos and aquariums, visitor attractions, museums and heritage, galleries and water park markets.
ADVERTISING RATES:
Full Page Colour £1790.00
Agency Commission: 10%
Mechanical Data: Type Area: 260 x 172mm, Bleed Size: 303 x 213mm, Trim Size: 297 x 210mm, Col Length: 260mm, Print Process: Web-fed offset litho, Film: Digital, Page Width: 172mm
Copy instructions: Copy Date: 2 weeks prior to publication date
Average advertising content per issue: 25%
BUSINESS: OTHER CLASSIFICATIONS: Amusement Trade

AUDIENCE   714100U61-4
Editorial Address: 26 Dorset Street, LONDON, W1U 8AP
Tel: 020 7486 7007 **Fax:** 020 7486 2002
Email: steve@audience.uk.com
Advertising Address: As above.
Email: phil@audience.uk.com
Web site: http://www.audience.uk.com
Publisher: Audience Media Ltd
Date Established: 1999
Frequency: Monthly
Cover Price: £5.85
Annual Sub.: £70.00
Circulation: 5,000 (Publisher's Statement)
Usual Pagination: 40
Editor: Stephen Parker; **News Editor:** James Drury; **Managing Editor:** Stephen Parker
Summary of Content: Magazine focusing on the international contemporary live music industry.
Readership/Target Audience: Aimed at concert promoters, venues, booking agents, record and publishing company

executives, equipment and transport companies, festivals, lawyers and accountants.
ADVERTISING: Rates on application
BUSINESS: MUSIC TRADE

AUDIO MEDIA   40933U61-6
Editorial Address: 1st Floor, 1 Cabot House, Compass Point Business Park, Stocks Bridge Way, ST. IVES, PE27 5JL **Tel:** 01480 461555 **Fax:** 01480 461550
Email: pr@audiomedia.com
Advertising Address: As above.
Email: n.humbert@audiomedia.com
Web site: http://www.audiomedia.com
ISSN: 0960-7471
Publisher: IMAS Publishing (UK) Ltd
Date Established: 1990
Frequency: Monthly - Published on the 1st Monday of the cover month
Cover Price: £3.80
Free to qualifying individuals
Circulation: 10,297 (Publisher's Statement)
Usual Pagination: 88
Editor: Paul Mac; **News Editor:** Paul Holmes; **Managing Director:** Angela Brown; **Advertising Manager:** Nick Humbert; **Publisher:** Nick Humbert
Summary of Content: Magazine about sound recording, post-production, broadcast, live sound, video and film sound.
Language(s): English; French; German; Japanese
Readership/Target Audience: Aimed at audio professionals.
ADVERTISING RATES:
Full Page Colour £1950.00
Agency Commission: 10%
Mechanical Data: Col Length: 262mm, Film: Digital, Type Area: 262 x 186mm, Bleed Size: 304 x 217mm, Trim Size: 297 x 210mm, Page Width: 186mm
Copy instructions: Copy Date: 3 weeks prior to publication date
Average advertising content per issue: 54%
BUSINESS: MUSIC TRADE

AUDIO PRO INTERNATIONAL   1827718U2D-153
Editorial Address: Saxon House, 6A St Andrew Street, HERTFORD, SG14 1JA **Tel:** 01992 535646
Fax: 01992 535648
Email: andy.low@intentmedia.co.uk
Advertising Address: As above.
Email: darrell.carter@intentmedia.co.uk
Web site: http://www.audioprointernational.com
Publisher: Intent Media
Frequency: 11 issues yearly
Cover Price: Free
Circulation: 5,500 (Publisher's Statement)
Editor: Andrew Low; **Advertising Manager:** Darrell Carter; **Managing Editor:** Andy Barrett
Summary of Content: Magazine covering the audio industry. Featuring live sound, commercial audio, install, recording, post production and broadcast.
Readership/Target Audience: Aimed at present and future audio professionals.
ADVERTISING RATES:
Full Page Colour £1220.00
Agency Commission: 10%
Mechanical Data: Type Area: 290 x 206mm, Bleed Size: 321 x 236mm, Trim Size: 315 x 230mm, Col Length: 290mm, Page Width: 206mm, Film: Digital
Copy instructions: Copy Date: 2 weeks prior to publication date
Average advertising content per issue: 50%
BUSINESS: COMMUNICATIONS, ADVERTISING & MARKETING: Broadcasting

AUDITORIA   762936U32H-450
Editorial Address: Abinger House, Church Street, DORKING, RH4 1DF **Tel:** 01306 743744 **Fax:** 01306 742525
Email: a.james@ukintpress.com
Advertising Address: As above.
Email: damien@ukpress.com
Web site: http://www.ukintpress.com
Publisher: UKIP Media & Events Ltd
Date Established: 2002
Frequency: Annual - Published in September
Free to qualifying individuals
Annual Sub.: £105.00
Circulation: 11,500 (Publisher's Statement)
Usual Pagination: 104
Editor: Anthony James; **Advertising Manager:** Damien de Roche
Summary of Content: Magazine covering entertainment venue design, technology and operations. Includes views, surveys, interviews and market studies.
Readership/Target Audience: Aimed at owners and operators of convention centres, concert halls, arenas, concert halls and performing arts facilities.
ADVERTISING RATES:
Full Page Colour £3950.00

Business Magazines

Agency Commission: 10%
Mechanical Data: Type Area: 255 x 195mm, Bleed Size: 281 x 221mm, Trim Size: 275 x 215mm, Col Length: 255mm, Page Width: 195mm, Film: Digital
BUSINESS: LOCAL GOVERNMENT, LEISURE & RECREATION: Leisure, Recreation & Entertainment

AUTHENTICATION NEWS
1702773U54C-324
Editorial Address: 2A High Street, SHEPPERTON, TW17 9AW Tel: 01932 269917 Fax: 01932 269918
Email: info@authenticationnews.info
Web site: http://www.authenticationnews.info
ISSN: 1368-857X
Publisher: Reconnaissance International Ltd
Date Established: 1995
Frequency: Monthly
Annual Sub.: £497.00
Usual Pagination: 12
Editor: Astrid Mitchell; Managing Editor: Astrid Mitchell
Summary of Content: Newsletter covering brand protection, document security and personal identification.
Readership/Target Audience: Aimed at brand owners, document issuers, packaging and labelling converters, security printers and suppliers and vendors of authentication technologies.
ADVERTISING: No Advertising taken
BUSINESS: SAFETY & SECURITY: Security

AUTISM
40504U56N-1
Editorial Address: 1 Oliver's Yard, 55 City Road, LONDON, EC1Y 1SP Tel: 020 7324 8500 Fax: 020 7324 8600
Email: autism@nas.org.uk
Advertising Address: As above.
Email: advertising@sagepub.co.uk
ISSN: 1362-3613
Publisher: Sage Publications
Date Established: 1997
Frequency: 6 issues yearly
Cover Price: £13.00
Annual Sub.: £58.00
Circulation: 1,000 (Publisher's Statement)
Usual Pagination: 112
Editor: Dermot Bowler; Advertising Manager: Sheena Karim
Summary of Content: Journal covering the subject of autism and autism related disorders.
Readership/Target Audience: Aimed at academics and professionals within the psychology and neurology fields.
ADVERTISING RATES:
Full Page Mono £500.00
Agency Commission: 5%
Mechanical Data: Page Width: 140mm, Type Area: 210 x 140mm, Col Length: 210mm, Film: Digital
Copy instructions: Copy Date: 12 weeks prior to publication date
BUSINESS: HEALTH & MEDICAL: Mental Health

AUTO
38278U31A-11
Editorial Address: Meridien House, 42 Upper Berkeley Street, LONDON, W1H 5QJ Tel: 01256 477548
Fax: 01256 477548
Email: kenrogers.press@gmail.com
Advertising Address: As above. Tel: 020 7616 0800
Fax: 020 7616 0810
Email: lgarrett@sovereign-publications.com
Web site: http://www.sovereign-publications.com
Publisher: Sovereign Publications Ltd
Date Established: 1998
Frequency: Half-yearly - Published in January and June
Cover Price: Free
Circulation: 10,000 (Publisher's Statement)
Usual Pagination: 160
Editor: Ken Rogers
Summary of Content: Magazine providing a review of new developments and technologies relating to materials used in automotive design, component technology, manufacturing and production, as well as examining policies and issues facing the automotive industry.
Readership/Target Audience: Aimed at top executives, engineers and technicians in the motor industry.
ADVERTISING RATES:
Full Page Mono £6950.00
Full Page Colour £7950.00
Agency Commission: 10%
Mechanical Data: Type Area: 255 x 180mm, Col Length: 255mm, Page Width: 180mm, Bleed Size: 303 x 216mm, Trim Size: 297 x 210mm, Film: Digital
Copy instructions: Copy Date: End of November
Average advertising content per issue: 40%
BUSINESS: MOTOR TRADE: Motor Trade Accessories

AUTO ID EUROPE
1658969U5A-234
Editorial Address: Oak House Mews, 43 The Parade, Claygate, ESHER, KT10 0PD Tel: 01392 202591
Email: kevin@via-medialtd.com

Advertising Address: As above. Fax: 01372 472862
Email: robert@via-medialtd.com
Web site: http://www.autoideurope.com
ISSN: 1748-0396
Publisher: Via Media Ltd
Frequency: Quarterly
Free to qualifying individuals
Circulation: 10,000 (Publisher's Statement)
Usual Pagination: 44
Editor: Kevin Robinson; Advertising Manager: Robert Fulwell
Summary of Content: Magazine covering all aspects of data capture technology and applications.
Readership/Target Audience: Aimed at those working within the supply chain industry.
ADVERTISING RATES:
Full Page Colour £2800.00
Agency Commission: 15%
Mechanical Data: Film: Digital, Type Area: 250 x 180mm, Bleed Size: 286 x 216mm, Trim Size: 280 x 210mm, Col Length: 250mm, Page Width: 180mm
Copy instructions: Copy Date: 3weeks prior to publication date
Average advertising content per issue: 30%
BUSINESS: COMPUTERS & AUTOMATION: Automation & Instrumentation

AUTO RETAIL BULLETIN
1645361U31A-377
Editorial Address: 44 Station Road, Woodford Halse, DAVENTRY, NN11 3RB Tel: 01327 264188
Fax: 01327 264189
Email: rupert@auto-retail.com
Web site: http://www.auto-retail.com
ISSN: 1755-4292
Publisher: Automotive Retail Ltd
Date Established: 2004
Frequency: Monthly
Annual Sub.: £295.00
Circulation: 1,000 (Publisher's Statement)
Usual Pagination: 28
Editor: Rupert Saunders
Summary of Content: Publication covering all aspects of the automotive retail industry including the latest news and analysis.
Readership/Target Audience: Aimed at senior directors within the automotive retail industry.
ADVERTISING: No Advertising taken
BUSINESS: MOTOR TRADE: Motor Trade Accessories

AUTO SERVICE & REPAIR
1800318U31A-394
Editorial Address: 9 Savoy Street, LONDON, WC2E 7HR
Tel: 020 8808 5116
Email: neil@featurebank.co.uk
Web site: http://www.tenalpspublishing.com
Publisher: Ten Alps Publishing
Date Established: 2006
Frequency: 6 issues yearly - Published around the 1st week of the cover month
Cover Price: £3.95
Free to qualifying individuals
Circulation: 55,230 (ABC 01/01/2007 to 30/06/2007)
Usual Pagination: 60
Editor: Neil Kennett
Summary of Content: Magazine containing practical business and technical information.
Readership/Target Audience: Aimed at owners of independent automotive workshops and technicians.
ADVERTISING: No Advertising taken
BUSINESS: MOTOR TRADE: Motor Trade Accessories

AUTO VENDING
36603U11B-30
Editorial Address: Rephoto House, Plough Road, Smallfield, HORLEY, RH6 9EZ Tel: 01342 844444
Fax: 01342 844488
Email: amanda-roberts@btconnect.com
Advertising Address: As above.
Email: gavin.rimmer@rephotopublishing.co.uk
Web site: http://www.auto-vending.co.uk
Publisher: Rephoto Publishing Ltd
Date Established: 1991
Frequency: Monthly - Published at the end of the 1st week of the cover month
Annual Sub.: £60.00
Circulation: 7,500 (Publisher's Statement)
Usual Pagination: 44
Editor: Amanda Roberts
Summary of Content: Magazine containing news, products, developments, people and events relevant to the automatic vending industry. Also includes articles on specifiers of automatic vending equipment and services.
Readership/Target Audience: Aimed at people working within the industry, end-users, specifiers and all other interested bodies.
ADVERTISING RATES:
Full Page Colour £1995.00
Agency Commission: 10%

Mechanical Data: Type Area: 270 x 190mm, Bleed Size: 303 x 216mm, Trim Size: 297 x 210mm, Col Length: 270mm, Page Width: 190mm, Film: Digital
Copy instructions: Copy Date: 20th of the month prior to publication date
Average advertising content per issue: 40%
Supplement(s): Water, Water, Water - 5xY
BUSINESS: CATERING: Vending Machines

AUTOIMMUNE DRUG FOCUS
1799442U37-423
Editorial Address: Lincoln House, City Fields Business Park, City Fields Way, Tangmere, CHICHESTER, PO20 2FS
Tel: 01243 756016 Fax: 01243 533418
Email: healthcare@espicom.com
Web site: http://www.espicom.com
Publisher: Espicom Ltd
Frequency: Monthly
Annual Sub.: £560.00
Usual Pagination: 20
Editor: Johanna Shiu
Summary of Content: Newsletter covering developments in autoimmune drugs. Provides company and drug indexes as well as information on future conferences. Includes articles on diabetes, inflammatory bowel diseases, multiple sclerosis, musculoskeletal disorders, psoriasis and general developments.
Readership/Target Audience: Aimed at senior executives in pharmaceutical companies.
ADVERTISING: No Advertising taken
BUSINESS: PHARMACEUTICAL & CHEMISTS

AUTOMOTIVATION
1656553U31R-60
Editorial Address: 2 New Street, WARWICK, CV34 4RX
Tel: 01926 493330 Fax: 01926 492203
Email: richybarnett@hotmail.com
Advertising Address: As above.
Email: sales@panaceamarketing.co.uk
Web site: http://www.automotivation.info
Publisher: Panacea Marketing Ltd
Date Established: 2003
Frequency: Quarterly
Cover Price: Free
Circulation: 25,000 (Publisher's Statement)
Editor: Richard Barnett; Advertising Manager: Keeley Marvin
Summary of Content: Magazine covering industry news, legislation and advice on the automotive trade.
Readership/Target Audience: Aimed at garage mechanics.
ADVERTISING RATES:
Full Page Colour £2200.00
Agency Commission: 10%
Mechanical Data: Trim Size: 297 x 210mm, Bleed Size: 303 x 216mm, Film: Digital
Copy instructions: Copy Date: 3 weeks prior to publication date
Average advertising content per issue: 35%
BUSINESS: MOTOR TRADE: Motor Trade Related

AUTOMOTIVE DESIGN ASIA
1638916U31A-376
Editorial Address: Hawley Mill, Hawley Road, DARTFORD, DA2 7TJ Tel: 01322 221144 Fax: 01322 221188
Email: etranter@findlay.co.uk
Advertising Address: As above.
Email: bstyles@findlay.co.uk
Web site: http://www.automotivedesignasia.com
ISSN: 1741-721X
Publisher: Findlay Media Ltd
Date Established: 2003
Frequency: 6 issues yearly
Free to qualifying individuals
Annual Sub.: £110.00
Circulation: 20,000 (BPA Worldwide 01/01/2007 to 30/06/2007)
Usual Pagination: 52
Editor: Ed Tranter; Advertising Manager: Beau Styles; Publisher: Beau Styles
Summary of Content: Magazine containing reports on technological developments in components systems and materials specified by senior research and development, design engineers and purchasing managers, who work with Asian vehicle manufacturers and their tier one and two suppliers.
Readership/Target Audience: Aimed at engineers in vehicle engineering design and R&D centres throughout Asia and Pacific regions.
ADVERTISING: Rates on application
Mechanical Data: Type Area: 266 x 184mm, Bleed Size: 303 x 216mm, Trim Size: 297 x 210mm, Col Length: 266mm, Page Width: 184mm
BUSINESS: MOTOR TRADE: Motor Trade Accessories

AUTOMOTIVE ELECTRONICS
1660744U18A-9018
Editorial Address: Prudence Place, Proctor Way, LUTON, LU2 9PE Tel: 01582 722460

Email: steve.rogerson@journalist.co.uk
Advertising Address: As above.
Email: david@automotive-electronics.co.uk
Web site: http://www.automotive-electronics.co.uk
Publisher: MT Publications Ltd
Date Established: 2005
Frequency: 6 issues yearly
Cover Price: Free
Circulation: 4,000 (Publisher's Statement)
Usual Pagination: 36
Editor: Steve Rogerson; **Advertising Manager:** David
Williams; **Publisher:** David Williams
Summary of Content: Magazine focusing on all internal and
external vehicle electronic systems.
Readership/Target Audience: Aimed at design engineers
and technical management working in vehicle
manufacturing, OEM and research and development sites.
ADVERTISING RATES:
Full Page Colour £1418.00
Agency Commission: 10%
Mechanical Data: Bleed Size: 306 x 216mm, Trim Size: 297
x 210mm, Film: Digital
Copy instructions: Copy Date: 4 weeks prior to publication
date
Average advertising content per issue: 40%
BUSINESS: ELECTRONICS

AUTOMOTIVE ENGINEER　　　37651U19F-101

Editorial Address: 1 Birdcage Walk, LONDON, SW1H 9JJ
Tel: 020 7304 6809
Email: ae@pepublishing.com
Advertising Address: As above. **Tel:** 020 7222 3337
Fax: 020 7799 2479
Email: christianlf@pepublishing.com
Web site: http://www.ae-plus.com
ISSN: 0307-6490
Publisher: Professional Engineering Publishing Ltd
Frequency: 11 issues yearly - Published in the 1st week of
the cover month
Annual Sub.: £313.00
Circulation: 33,000 (Publisher's Statement)
Usual Pagination: 56
Editor: Tristan Honeywill; **Publisher:** Paul Williams
Summary of Content: Magazine covering development of
cars, commercial vehicles, motor sport, fuel cell cars,
hybrids, automotive technology, powertrain, drivetrain,
brakes, steering, components, design, electronics, lighting,
interiors, materials, manufacturing, rapid prototyping, safety,
research and development, software, testing and telematics.
Readership/Target Audience: Read by engineers,
executives, managers and consultants working for OEMs
and suppliers. It also goes to academia, government
organisations and other automotive engineering societies.
ADVERTISING RATES:
Full Page Mono £5400.00
Full Page Colour £6400.00
Agency Commission: 15%
Mechanical Data: Type Area: 255 x 180mm, Bleed Size:
303 x 216mm, Trim Size: 297 x 210mm, Col Length: 255mm,
Page Width: 180mm, Film: Digital
Copy instructions: Copy Date: 1 week prior to publication
date
Average advertising content per issue: 30%
BUSINESS: ENGINEERING & MACHINERY: Production &
Mechanical Engineering

AUTOMOTIVE ENGINEERING INTERNATIONAL　　38285U31A-16_13

Editorial Address: Lee Farm, Fyfield, ESSEX, CM5 0RN
Tel: 724 776 4841
Email: stuart.birch@btopenworld.com
Advertising Address: University House, 11-13 Lower
Grosvenor Place, LONDON, SW1W 0EX **Tel:** 020 7834 7676
Fax: 020 7973 0076
Email: media@alaincharles.com
Web site: http://www.sae.org
ISSN: 0098-2571
Publisher: Society of Automotive Engineers Inc.
Date Established: 1917
Frequency: Monthly - Published in the 1st week of the cover
month
Circulation: 124,082 (Publisher's Statement)
Editor: Stuart Birch; **Advertising Manager:** Richard
Rozelaar
Summary of Content: Magazine providing information,
news and features on new vehicles, advances in technology,
manufacturing and improved vehicle systems.
Readership/Target Audience: Aimed at manufacturers of
vehicles and parts worldwide.
ADVERTISING RATES:
Full Page Mono $9910.00
Full Page Colour $12110.00
Agency Commission: 15%
Mechanical Data: Print Process: Offset litho, Bleed Size:
282 x 212mm, Type Area: 254 x 177mm, Page Width:
177mm, Col Length: 254mm, Trim Size: 276 x 206mm, Film:
Digital

Copy instructions: Copy Date: 2nd week of the month prior
to publication date
Average advertising content per issue: 50%
BUSINESS: MOTOR TRADE: Motor Trade Accessories

AUTOMOTIVE INDUSTRIES　　1698264U31R-61

Editorial Address: 3rd Floor, Roman House, 296 Golders
Green Road, LONDON, NW11 9PY **Tel:** 020 8764 9696
Email: nickpalmen@autoindustry.us
Advertising Address: As above. **Fax:** 020 8458 7130
Email: advertising@autoindustry.us
Web site: http://www.ai-online.com
ISSN: 1099-4130
Publisher: Worldwide Purchasing
Date Established: 1895
Frequency: Monthly - Published around the 1st Monday of
the cover month
Free to qualifying individuals
Annual Sub.: $88.00
Circulation: 69,989 (Publisher's Statement)
Editor: Nick Palmen; **Advertising Director:** Robert White
Summary of Content: Magazine focusing on the automotive
industry including design, production, opinion and analysis.
Readership/Target Audience: Aimed at key decision
makers in the automotive manufacturing industry.
ADVERTISING RATES:
Full Page Mono $9000.00
Full Page Colour $9000.00
Agency Commission: 15%
Mechanical Data: Type Area: 247 x 183mm, Bleed Size:
273 x 209mm, Trim Size: 267 x 203mm, Col Length: 247mm,
Page Width: 183mm, Film: Digital
Copy instructions: Copy Date: 4 weeks prior to publication
date
Average advertising content per issue: 30%
BUSINESS: MOTOR TRADE: Motor Trade Related

AUTOMOTIVE INSIGHT　　1796255U31A-393

Editorial Address: 201 Great Portland Street, LONDON,
W1W 5AB **Tel:** 020 7307 3424 **Fax:** 020 7580 6376
Email: alexwells@rmif.co.uk
Advertising Address: PW Media & Publishing Ltd, 2nd
Floor, 2-4 St. Nicholas Street, WORCESTER, WR1 1UW
Tel: 01905 723008 **Fax:** 01905 612039
Email: alexwells@rmif.co.uk
Web site: http://www.rmif.co.uk
Publisher: PW Media & Publishing Ltd
Date Established: 2007
Frequency: 10 issues yearly - Double issues published in
January/February and August/September
Free to qualifying individuals
Circulation: 9,000 (Publisher's Statement)
Usual Pagination: 44
Editor: Vaughan Freeman; **Advertising Manager:** Alex
Wells
Summary of Content: Magazine covering all aspects of the
retail motor industry, including vehicle retail and repair,
MOTs, motor cycle rider training, customer reception to
back end business processes. Delivers information and
analysis on market forces and trends.
Readership/Target Audience: Aimed at decision makers
within the Retail Motor Industry.
ADVERTISING RATES:
Full Page Colour £1200.00
Mechanical Data: Type Area: 277 x 190mm, Trim Size: 297
x 210mm, Bleed Size: 303 x 216mm, Col Length: 277mm,
Page Width: 190mm, Film: Digital
Copy instructions: Copy Date: 3 weeks prior to publication
date
BUSINESS: MOTOR TRADE: Motor Trade Accessories

AUTOMOTIVE LOGISTICS　　758606U31R-16

Editorial Address: Lamb House, Church Street, LONDON,
W4 2PD **Tel:** 020 8987 0968
Email: christopher.ludwig@ultimamedia.com
Advertising Address: As above. **Tel:** 020 8987 0900
Fax: 020 8987 0948
Email: louis.yiakoumi@ultimamedia.com
Web site: http://www.automotivelogisticsmagazine.com
ISSN: 1471-6003
Publisher: Ultima Media Ltd
Date Established: 1998
Frequency: Quarterly
Free to qualifying individuals
Annual Sub.: £48.00
Circulation: 9,000 (BPA Worldwide 01/01/2007 to
30/06/2007)
Usual Pagination: 68
Editor: Christopher Ludwig; **News Editor:** Marcus Williams;
Advertising Manager: Louis Yiakoumi; **Publisher:** Louis
Yiakoumi
Summary of Content: Magazine covering all aspects of
logistics in the automotive industry. Contains interviews,
company profiles, news roundup, major suppliers and
regional focus.

Readership/Target Audience: Read by senior management
of logistics companies, vehicle makers, automotive industry
suppliers and logistic service providers.
ADVERTISING RATES:
Full Page Colour £5250.00
Agency Commission: 10%
Mechanical Data: Trim Size: 297 x 210mm, Film: Digital
Copy instructions: Copy Date: 3 weeks prior to publication
date
BUSINESS: MOTOR TRADE: Motor Trade Related

AUTOMOTIVE MANUFACTURER　　1655829U31A-380

Editorial Address: 15-19 Great Chapel Street, LONDON,
W1F 8FN **Tel:** 020 7758 3047 **Fax:** 020 7758 3001
Email: markbursa@aol.com
Advertising Address: As above. **Tel:** 020 7758 3000
Email: s.wright@cavendishgroup.co.uk
Web site: http://www.cavendishgroup.co.uk
Publisher: Cavendish Group
Date Established: 2004
Frequency: Quarterly - Published at the end of the cover
month
Free to qualifying individuals
Circulation: 10,000 (Publisher's Statement)
Editor: Mark Bursa; **Advertising Manager:** Simon Wright
Summary of Content: Magazine covering information on
European car manufacturing technologies.
Readership/Target Audience: Aimed at chief engineers,
manufacturing directors and car designers.
ADVERTISING RATES:
Full Page Colour £5650.00
Agency Commission: 15%
Mechanical Data: Type Area: 258 x 186mm, Bleed Size:
292 x 218mm, Trim Size: 286 x 212mm, Col Length: 258mm,
Page Width: 186mm, Film: Digital
Copy instructions: Copy Date: 6 weeks prior to publication
date
Average advertising content per issue: 30%
BUSINESS: MOTOR TRADE: Motor Trade Accessories

AUTOMOTIVE MANUFACTURING SOLUTIONS　　623167U31A-17_7

Editorial Address: Lamb House, Church Street, LONDON,
W4 2PD **Tel:** 020 8987 0900 **Fax:** 020 8987 0948
Email: julian.buckley@ultimamedia.com
Advertising Address: As above. **Tel:** 020 8987 0931
Email: andrew.fallon@ultimamedia.com
Web site: http://www.automotivemanufacturingsolutions.
com
ISSN: 1354-4306
Publisher: Ultima Media Ltd
Date Established: 2000
Frequency: 6 issues yearly - Published around the 1st of the
1st cover month
Cover Price: Free
Circulation: 9,000 (BPA Worldwide 01/01/2007 to
30/06/2007)
Usual Pagination: 84
Editor: Julian Buckley; **Advertising Manager:** Andrew
Fallon; **Publisher:** Andrew Fallon
Summary of Content: Magazine offering an insight into the
latest manufacturing technologies being employed by
leading auto manufacturers and suppliers. Contains a highly
focused manufacturing news section and several news
analysis features. Interviews from heads of manufacturing,
supplier profiles and strategies, regional reports, case
studies and factory visits.
Readership/Target Audience: Aimed at specifiers and
purchasers of machinery and equipment at automaker and
supplier plants.
ADVERTISING RATES:
Full Page Colour £6950.00
Mechanical Data: Type Area: 277 x 190mm, Bleed Size:
303 x 216mm, Trim Size: 297 x 210mm, Col Length: 277mm,
Page Width: 190mm, Film: Digital
Copy instructions: Copy Date: 1st week of the month prior
to 1st cover month
Average advertising content per issue: 25%
Supplement(s): Automotive Manufacturing Solutions
Directory - 1xY, Automotive Paintshop Solutions - 1xY
BUSINESS: MOTOR TRADE: Motor Trade Accessories

AUTOMOTIVE QUARTERLY REVIEW　　38303U31A-17_20

Editorial Address: Chase Farm Barn, Southburgh,
THETFORD, IP25 7SU **Tel:** 01362 820130
Fax: 01362 821578
Email: jontystorey@aol.com
Web site: http://www.automotiveworld.com
Publisher: Young Communications Media Ltd
Date Established: 1998
Frequency: Quarterly
Annual Sub.: £595.00
Usual Pagination: 300
Editor: Jonathan Storey

Summary of Content: Publication providing up-to-date analysis of the performance of major passenger vehicle manufacturing groups. Also contains the latest financial results and news of the world's principal car makers, including a detailed source of new registration and production data.
Readership/Target Audience: Aimed at the global automotive industry.
ADVERTISING: No Advertising taken
BUSINESS: MOTOR TRADE: Motor Trade Accessories

AUTOMOTIVE TESTING TECHNOLOGY INTERNATIONAL
38321U31A-152

Formerly: Testing Technology International
Editorial Address: Abinger House, Church Street, DORKING, RH4 1DF **Tel:** 01306 743744 **Fax:** 01306 887546
Email: testing@ukintpress.com
Advertising Address: As above. **Fax:** 01306 742525
Email: jason.sullivan@ukintpress.com
Web site: http://www.ukintpress.com
ISSN: 1461-8966
Publisher: UKIP Media & Events Ltd
Frequency: Quarterly
Free to qualifying individuals
Annual Sub.: £125.00
Circulation: 20,000 (Publisher's Statement)
Usual Pagination: 100
Editor: Adam Gavine; **Editor-in-Chief:** Adam Gavine;
Advertising Manager: Jason Sullivan
Summary of Content: Magazine covering the development of cars including durability and crash testing.
Readership/Target Audience: Aimed at engineers worldwide.
ADVERTISING RATES:
Full Page Colour £3650.00
Agency Commission: 15%
Mechanical Data: Type Area: 270 x 180mm, Bleed Size: 303 x 216mm, Col Length: 270mm, Page Width: 180mm, Film: Digital, Trim Size: 297 x 210mm
Copy instructions: Copy Date: 3 weeks prior to publication date
Average advertising content per issue: 33%
Supplement(s): Crashtest Technology International - 2xY
BUSINESS: MOTOR TRADE: Motor Trade Accessories

AUTOTIMES
764906U31A-373

Editorial Address: 85 Elwyn Road, MARCH, PE15 9DB
Tel: 01354 656555 **Fax:** 01354 660999
Email: andyh.stonecross@btconnect.com
Advertising Address: As above.
Email: steph.stonecross@btconnect.com
Web site: http://www.autotimes.co.uk
ISSN: 1477-562X
Publisher: Stone Cross Publishing Ltd
Date Established: 2002
Frequency: Monthly
Free to qualifying individuals
Annual Sub.: £60.00
Circulation: 20,000 (Publisher's Statement)
Usual Pagination: 48
Editor: Andy Hurst; **Features Editor:** Vaughan Freeman;
Editor-in-Chief: Andy Hurst
Summary of Content: Magazine covering parts and equipment purchasing, industry issues including legal and financial and all subjects relating to the motor industry aftermarket.
Readership/Target Audience: Aimed at owners and directors of independent and franchised garages, bodyshops, retail accessory shops, MOT centres and vehicle manufacturers.
ADVERTISING RATES:
Full Page Mono £2485.00
Full Page Colour £2635.00
Agency Commission: 10%
Mechanical Data: Film: Digital, Col Length: 270mm, Page Width: 190mm, Type Area: 270 x 190mm, Bleed Size: 303 x 216mm, Trim Size: 297 x 210mm
Average advertising content per issue: 40%
BUSINESS: MOTOR TRADE: Motor Trade Accessories

AV MAGAZINE
35661U2D-7

Editorial Address: 174 Hammersmith Road, LONDON, W6 7JP **Tel:** 020 8267 8005 **Fax:** 020 8267 8008
Email: avnewsdesk@haymarket.com
Advertising Address: As above. **Tel:** 020 8267 5000
Fax: 020 8267 4287
Email: katherine.gordon@haymarket.com
Web site: http://www.avinteractive.co.uk
ISSN: 1361-3685
Publisher: Haymarket Specialist Publications
Date Established: 1972
Frequency: Monthly - Published on the 1st of the cover month
Cover Price: £4.95
Free to qualifying individuals
Annual Sub.: £53.00

Circulation: 15,019 (ABC 01/07/2006 to 30/06/2007)
Usual Pagination: 80
Editor: Bhavna Mistry
Summary of Content: Magazine focusing on audio-visual applications in business and education.
Readership/Target Audience: Read by managers within the audio-visual communications industry and regular end-user companies.
ADVERTISING RATES:
Full Page Colour £3240.00
Agency Commission: 10%
Mechanical Data: Col Length: 265mm, Film: Digital, Type Area: 265 x 195mm, Print Process: Web-fed offset litho, Bleed Size: 305 x 235mm, Trim Size: 295 x 225mm, Page Width: 195mm
Copy instructions: Copy Date: 10th of the month prior to cover month
BUSINESS: COMMUNICATIONS, ADVERTISING & MARKETING: Broadcasting

---

AV NEWS
752730U2D-10

Editorial Address: Tormore House, 150 High Street, DEAL, CT14 6BG **Tel:** 01304 239988
Email: editorial@avnews.co.uk
Advertising Address: As above.
Email: sales@avnews.co.uk
Web site: http://www.avnews.co.uk
Publisher: Blue and Green Ltd
Date Established: 2001
Frequency: Monthly
Free to qualifying individuals
Circulation: 7,802 (Publisher's Statement)
Editor: Lindsey Reynolds; **Advertising Manager:** Bryan Denyer
Summary of Content: Trade magazine for dealers, resellers and retailers of audio-visual equipment and services in business-to-business and consumer markets.
Readership/Target Audience: Read by resellers, dealers and retailers specialist, independent and multiples in AV, IT, office equipment, home cinema and specified vertical markets as well as manufacturers and distributors.
ADVERTISING RATES:
Full Page Colour £2680.00
Agency Commission: 10%
Mechanical Data: Type Area: 366 x 266mm, Trim Size: 390 x 290mm, Film: Digital, Col Length: 366mm, Page Width: 266mm, Bleed Size: 396 x 296mm
Copy instructions: Copy Date: 12th of the month prior to publication date
Average advertising content per issue: 50%
BUSINESS: COMMUNICATIONS, ADVERTISING & MARKETING: Broadcasting

---

AVIATION NEWS
36326U6A-31

Formerly: Air Pictorial
Editorial Address: Drury Lane, ST. LEONARDS-ON-SEA, TN38 9BJ **Tel:** 01424 205536 **Fax:** 01424 443693
Email: editor@aviation-news.co.uk
Advertising Address: As above. **Tel:** 01424 720477
Email: advertising@aviation-news.co.uk
Web site: http://www.aviation-news.co.uk
ISSN: 0965-1891
Publisher: HPC Publishing
Date Established: 1939
Frequency: Monthly
Cover Price: £3.80
Free to qualifying individuals
Annual Sub.: £45.00
Circulation: 20,000 (Publisher's Statement)
Usual Pagination: 86
Advertising Manager: Rosemary Beckwith; **Publisher:** Derek Knoll
Summary of Content: Magazine covering all aspects of the aircraft industry. Includes in-depth reports on airlines, staff and airports.
Readership/Target Audience: Read by RAF servicemen, aviators, enthusiasts and industry.
ADVERTISING RATES:
Full Page Mono £324.00
Full Page Colour £404.00
Agency Commission: 10%
Mechanical Data: Page Width: 185mm, Film: Digital, Type Area: 275 x 185mm, Bleed Size: 306 x 216mm, Trim Size: 297 x 210mm, Col Length: 275mm
Copy instructions: Copy Date: 6 weeks prior to publication date
Supplement(s): Air Events - 1xY
BUSINESS: AVIATION & AERONAUTICS

AVIATION SECURITY INTERNATIONAL
36424U6F-78

Editorial Address: 375 Upper Richmond Road West, East Sheen, LONDON, SW14 7NX **Tel:** 91 804 2577
Email: editor@avsec.com
Advertising Address: 64 Castle Road, ST. ALBANS, AL1 5DG **Tel:** 01727 843915 **Fax:** 01727 830204
Email: kathryn@asi-mag.com

Web site: http://www.asi-mag.com
ISSN: 1352-0148
Publisher: ASI Publications Ltd
Date Established: 1992
Frequency: 6 issues yearly
Annual Sub.: EUR196.00
Circulation: 8,000 (Publisher's Statement)
Usual Pagination: 48
Editor: Philip Baum; **Advertising Manager:** Kathryn McGowan; **Publisher:** Adrian Broadbent
Summary of Content: Magazine covering news, features and products on the security of the world's airlines and airports.
Readership/Target Audience: Read by airline security managers, cabin crew trainers and director generals of civil aviation authorities.
ADVERTISING RATES:
Full Page Colour £1500.00
Agency Commission: 10%
Mechanical Data: Film: Digital, Type Area: 240 x 180mm, Print Process: Offset litho, Bleed Size: 290 x 220mm, Trim Size: 280 x 210mm, Col Length: 240mm, Page Width: 180mm
Copy instructions: Copy Date: Last week of the month prior to 1st cover month
BUSINESS: AVIATION & AERONAUTICS: Airlines

AVIATION STRATEGY
36332U6A-63

Editorial Address: James House, 1st Floor, 22-24 Corsham Street, LONDON, N1 6DR **Tel:** 020 7490 5215
Fax: 020 7490 5218
Email: info@aviationeconomics.com
Web site: http://www.aviationeconomics.com
ISSN: 1463-9254
Publisher: Aviation Economics
Date Established: 1997
Frequency: 10 issues yearly - Jan/Feb and July/August issues combined
Annual Sub.: £420.00
Circulation: 500 (Publisher's Statement)
Usual Pagination: 24
Editor: Julian Longin; **Publisher:** Keith McMullan
Summary of Content: Journal covering detailed analysis and briefings on contemporary aviation issues, companies and markets. Also includes reports on aviation developments.
Readership/Target Audience: Read by aviation executives, financiers and aerospace manufacturers.
ADVERTISING: No Advertising taken
BUSINESS: AVIATION & AERONAUTICS

AVIATION WEEK & SPACE TECHNOLOGY
36391U6C-100

Editorial Address: 43 Raleigh Park Road, OXFORD, OX2 9AZ **Tel:** 01865 726128
Email: barrie@aviationweek.com
Advertising Address: Five Oaks, Cansey Lane, Bradfield, MANNINGTREE, CO11 2XE **Tel:** 01255 871070
Fax: 01255 871071
Email: mike.elmes@aerospacemedia.co.uk
Web site: http://www.aviationnow.com/awst
ISSN: 0005-2175
Publisher: The McGraw-Hill Companies
Frequency: Weekly
Cover Price: $6.00
Circulation: 105,000 (Publisher's Statement)
Usual Pagination: 74
Editor: Douglas Barrie
Summary of Content: Journal covering news and events in the fields of aviation and space technology.
Readership/Target Audience: Read by personnel within the aerospace industry, airline and government officials.
ADVERTISING RATES:
Full Page Mono $17705.00
Full Page Colour $20645.00
Agency Commission: 15%
Mechanical Data: Type Area: 248 x 178mm, Bleed Size: 273 x 200mm, Trim Size: 267 x 197mm, Col Length: 248mm, Page Width: 178mm, Film: Digital
Copy instructions: Copy Date: 2 weeks prior to publication date
Average advertising content per issue: 35%
Supplement(s): Aviation Week Sourcebook - 1xY
BUSINESS: AVIATION & AERONAUTICS: Space Research

AWD WELDING BUSINESS BULLETIN
1799437U19A-562

Formerly: Business Bulletin
Editorial Address: Securehold Business Centre, Studley Road, REDDITCH, B98 7LG **Tel:** 01952 290036
Fax: 01952 290037
Email: info@awd.org.uk
Advertising Address: Clark Associates, 24 Moorhouse Close, Wellington, TELFORD, TF1 2BF **Tel:** 01952 250311
Fax: 01952 250312
Email: info@awd.com

Web site: http://www.awd.org.uk
Publisher: Association of Welding Distributors
Frequency: 3 issues yearly - Published in spring, summer and winter
Free to qualifying individuals
Circulation: 2,000 (Publisher's Statement)
Usual Pagination: 36
Editor: Martin Clark; **Advertising Director:** Martin Clark
Summary of Content: Magazine focusing on welding products. Contains market information, company profiles, product reviews, interviews, safety and legal updates.
Readership/Target Audience: Aimed at members of the Association of Welding Distributors, manufacturers, distributors, wholesalers and consultants working in the welding supply industry.
ADVERTISING RATES:
Full Page Colour £1210.00
Agency Commission: 10%
Mechanical Data: Trim Size: 300 x 213mm, Bleed Size: 303 x 216mm, Col Widths (Display): 57mm, No. of Columns (Display): 3, Print Process: Litho, Type Area: 274 x 182mm, Col Length: 274mm, Page Width: 182mm, Film: Digital
Copy instructions: Copy Date: 4 weeks prior to publication date
BUSINESS: ENGINEERING & MACHINERY

AWE INTERNATIONAL
1685679U57-136
Editorial Address: 1st Floor, Suite One, St. Albans Chambers, 15-16 St. Alban Street, WEYMOUTH, DT4 8PY
Tel: 01305 785199 **Fax:** 01305 772722
Email: nigel@bay-publishing.com
Advertising Address: As above.
Email: nick@bay-publishing.com
Web site: http://www.aweimagazine.com
ISSN: 1745-3623
Publisher: Bay Publishing Ltd
Date Established: 2005
Frequency: Quarterly - Published around the 1st of the cover month
Cover Price: Free
Annual Sub.: £65.00
Circulation: 9,600 (Publisher's Statement)
Usual Pagination: 72
Editor: Nigel Fellows; **Advertising Manager:** Nick Limm; **Publisher:** Nigel Fellows
Summary of Content: Magazine focusing on environmental monitoring and analysis and process emissions control. Topics covered include regulations, news, law and product reviews.
Readership/Target Audience: Aimed at environmental consultants, analysts, chemists, bio chemists, purchasing managers and facilities managers.
ADVERTISING RATES:
Full Page Colour £2700.00
Agency Commission: 10%
Mechanical Data: Type Area: 270 x 180mm, Bleed Size: 303 x 216mm, Trim Size: 297 x 210mm, Col Length: 270mm, Page Width: 180mm, Film: Digital
Average advertising content per issue: 40%
BUSINESS: ENVIRONMENT & POLLUTION

THE AYRSHIRE JOURNAL
37833U21D-75
Editorial Address: 17 Barns Street, AYR, KA7 1XB
Tel: 01292 267123 **Fax:** 01292 611973
Email: society@ayrshirescs.org
Advertising Address: As above.
Email: society@ayrshirescs.org
Web site: http://www.ayrshires.org
Publisher: Ayrshire Cattle Society
Frequency: 3 issues yearly - Varies
Annual Sub.: £12.00
Circulation: 1,200 (Publisher's Statement)
Usual Pagination: 48
Editor: Irene Kirkpatrick
Summary of Content: Journal covering all aspects of Ayrshire cattle.
Readership/Target Audience: Read by dairy farmers and technical advisors in colleges and universities.
ADVERTISING: Rates on application
BUSINESS: AGRICULTURE & FARMING: Livestock

A-Z AIR FREIGHTERS GUIDE
39626U49C-2
Editorial Address: Darby House, Bletchingley Road, Merstham, REDHILL, RH1 3TT **Tel:** 01737 645777
Fax: 01737 645888
Email: ij@a-zgroup.com
Advertising Address: As above.
Email: rb@a-zgroup.com
Web site: http://www.azfreight.com
Publisher: A-Z Group Ltd
Date Established: 1998
Frequency: Annual - Published in June
Annual Sub.: £195.00
Circulation: 4,500 (Publisher's Statement)
Usual Pagination: 300

Editor: Ian Martin Jones; **Managing Director:** Norman Bamford; **Managing Editor:** Ian Martin Jones
Summary of Content: Directory containing details of all cargo aircraft dimensions, airlines and airfreight.
Readership/Target Audience: Aimed at air cargo industry professionals, senior executives of cargo airlines, charter brokers and freight forwarders.
ADVERTISING RATES:
Full Page Colour £3250.00
Agency Commission: 10%
Mechanical Data: Type Area: 257 x 182mm, Col Length: 257mm, Page Width: 182mm, Film: Digital, Bleed Size: +3mm, Trim Size: 297 x 210mm
Copy instructions: Copy Date: 6 weeks prior to publication date
Average advertising content per issue: 10%
BUSINESS: TRANSPORT: Freight

A-Z WORLD AIRPORTS GUIDE
36372U6B-3
Formerly: A-Z World Airports Directory
Editorial Address: Darby House, Bletchingley Road, Merstham, REDHILL, RH1 3TT **Tel:** 01737 645777
Fax: 01737 645888
Email: info@a-zgroup.com
Advertising Address: As above.
Email: info@a-zgroup.com
Web site: http://www.azworldairports.com
Publisher: A-Z Group Ltd
Date Established: 1998
Frequency: Annual - Published in September
Annual Sub.: £65.00
Usual Pagination: 264
Editor: Ian Jones; **Managing Director:** Norman Bamford; **Advertising Manager:** Norman Bamford; **Managing Editor:** Ian Jones
Summary of Content: Publication providing comprehensive details of over one thousand of the world's major airports.
Readership/Target Audience: Aimed at airport operators, airlines, general sales agents, courier companies, shippers, tour operators and cargo consolidators.
ADVERTISING: Rates on application
Agency Commission: 10%
BUSINESS: AVIATION & AERONAUTICS: Airports

A-Z WORLDWIDE AIRFREIGHT DIRECTORY
39650U49C-3
Editorial Address: Darby House, Bletchingley Road, Merstham, REDHILL, RH1 3TT **Tel:** 01737 645777
Fax: 01737 645888
Email: imj@aircargoweek.com
Advertising Address: As above.
Email: sales@a-zfreight.com
Web site: http://www.azfreight.com
Publisher: A-Z Group Ltd
Date Established: 1987
Frequency: Half-yearly - Published in January and July
Annual Sub.: £130.00
Circulation: 9,700 (Publisher's Statement)
Usual Pagination: 740
Editor: Ian Martin Jones; **Managing Director:** Norman Bamford; **Managing Editor:** Ian Martin Jones
Summary of Content: Directory featuring cargo agents, world time zones, maps, airport and city codes, airlines, airfreight and chartered brokers.
Readership/Target Audience: Aimed at those working within the air cargo services including; general sales agents, freight forwarders, courier handling agents, express operators and courier service suppliers.
ADVERTISING RATES:
Full Page Mono £3250.00
Full Page Colour £4000.00
Agency Commission: 10%
Mechanical Data: Trim Size: 277 x 210mm, Bleed Size: 283 x 216mm, Type Area: 257 x 190mm, Col Length: 257mm, Page Width: 190mm, Film: Digital
Copy instructions: Copy Date: 6 weeks prior to publication date
BUSINESS: TRANSPORT: Freight

B2B MARKETING
1645448U2A-659
Editorial Address: 1st Floor, Colonial Buildings, 59-61 Hatton Garden, LONDON, EC1N 8LS **Tel:** 020 3077 0068
Fax: 020 7438 1377
Email: info@b2bm.biz
Advertising Address: As above.
Email: david.lewis@b2bm.biz
Web site: http://www.b2bm.biz
ISSN: 1477-4895
Publisher: Silver Bullet Publishing
Date Established: 2004
Frequency: 10 issues yearly - Published in the 2nd week of the cover month
Annual Sub.: £99.00
Circulation: 6,000 (ABC 01/07/2006 to 30/06/2007)
Usual Pagination: 64
Editor: Joel Harrison; **Advertising Manager:** David Lewis

Summary of Content: Magazine covering all aspects of marketing to a business audience, with an emphasis on practical hands-on content aimed at helping practitioners improve their effectiveness.
Readership/Target Audience: Aimed at senior marketing professionals and those working in the marketing services sector.
ADVERTISING RATES:
Full Page Colour £3000.00
Agency Commission: 10%
Mechanical Data: Type Area: 260 x 175mm, Bleed Size: 303 x 216mm, Trim Size: 297 x 210mm, Col Length: 260mm, Page Width: 175mm, Film: Digital
Copy instructions: Copy Date: 3 weeks prior to publication date
Average advertising content per issue: 33%
BUSINESS: COMMUNICATIONS, ADVERTISING & MARKETING

BACK TO SCHOOL BOOKSELLER
40806U60A-9
Editorial Address: 5th Floor, Endeavour House, 189 Shaftesbury Avenue, LONDON, WC2H 8TJ
Tel: 020 7420 6104 **Fax:** 020 7420 6103
Email: hannah.davies@bookseller.co.uk
Advertising Address: As above. **Tel:** 020 7420 6108
Email: david.wright@bookseller.co.uk
Web site: http://www.thebookseller.com
ISSN: 0006-7539
Publisher: Bookseller Publications
Date Established: 1999
Frequency: Annual - Published in June
Cover Price: £4.40
Circulation: 12,700 (Publisher's Statement)
Usual Pagination: 52
Editor: Hannah Davies; **Editor-in-Chief:** Neill Denny; **Managing Director:** Nigel Roby; **Advertising Director:** David Wright
Summary of Content: Magazine covering all aspects of the book trade. Contains news, features and book reviews.
Readership/Target Audience: Read by publishers, booksellers and librarians.
ADVERTISING RATES:
Full Page Colour £2328.00
Agency Commission: 10%
Mechanical Data: Bleed Size: 303 x 230mm, Film: Digital, Type Area: 297 x 224mm, Col Length: 297mm, Page Width: 224mm
Copy instructions: Copy Date: 2 weeks prior to publication date
Average advertising content per issue: 40%
Supplement to: The Bookseller
BUSINESS: PUBLISHING: Publishing & Book Trade

BAGMA BULLETIN
762664U21E-871
Editorial Address: 1st Floor, Entrance B, Salamander Quay West, Park Lane, HAREFIELD, UB9 6NZ **Tel:** 0870 205 2924
Fax: 0870 205 2934
Email: michaelweedon@indices.co.uk
Advertising Address: As above.
Email: simongreen@indices.co.uk
Web site: http://www.bagma.com
Publisher: Indices Publications Ltd
Frequency: 6 issues yearly
Cover Price: Free
Circulation: 3,500 (Publisher's Statement)
Usual Pagination: 16
Editor: Michael Weedon; **Publisher:** Michael Weedon
Summary of Content: Official journal of the British Agriculture and Garden Machinery Association containing news and features on all aspects of agricultural, garden and forestry machinery.
Readership/Target Audience: Read by those involved in agriculture, gardening and forestry.
ADVERTISING RATES:
Full Page Colour £1000.00
Mechanical Data: Page Width: 190mm, Col Length: 264mm, Film: Digital, Type Area: 264 x 190mm, Bleed Size: 303 x 213mm, Trim Size: 297 x 210mm
BUSINESS: AGRICULTURE & FARMING: Agriculture - Machinery & Plant

---

BALANCE
40518U56R-10
Editorial Address: 10 Parkway, Camden, LONDON, NW1 7AA **Tel:** 020 7424 1000 **Fax:** 020 7424 1001
Email: balance@diabetes.org.uk
Web site: http://www.diabetes.org.uk
ISSN: 0005-4216
Publisher: Diabetes UK
Date Established: 1935
Frequency: 6 issues yearly
Cover Price: £3.50
Free to qualifying individuals
Circulation: 175,000 (Publisher's Statement)
Usual Pagination: 80
Editor: Martin Cullen

Business Magazines

Summary of Content: Health and lifestyle magazine published by Diabetes UK. Contains medical articles, healthy eating diets and junior balance as well as competitions.
Readership/Target Audience: Aimed at members of Diabetes UK, clinics and those suffering from diabetes.
ADVERTISING: No Advertising taken
BUSINESS: HEALTH & MEDICAL: Health Medical Related

THE BALTIC
39321U45A-20
Editorial Address: The Diary House, Rickett Street, LONDON, SW6 1RU **Tel:** 020 7386 6120
Email: lucy.budd@mar-media.com
Advertising Address: As above. **Tel:** 020 7386 6100
Fax: 020 7381 8890
Email: alex.corboude@mar-media.com
Web site: http://www.thebaltic.com
ISSN: 0967-0394
Publisher: Maritime Media Ltd
Frequency: Quarterly - Published around the 20th of the month prior to cover date
Annual Sub.: £110.00
Circulation: 4,000 (Publisher's Statement)
Usual Pagination: 80
Editor: Lucy Budd; **Advertising Manager:** Alex Corboude
Summary of Content: Magazine of the Baltic Exchange, covering maritime trading matters.
Readership/Target Audience: Read by members of the exchange, consultants and surveyors, ship owners and operators, freight forwarders, ship management companies, maritime lawyers and arbitrators, charterers and brokers, liner companies and shipping agents.
ADVERTISING RATES:
Full Page Colour £5950.00
Agency Commission: 10%
Mechanical Data: Type Area: 254 x 178mm, Page Width: 178mm, Col Length: 254mm, Bleed Size: 303 x 216mm, Trim Size: 297 x 210mm, Film: Digital
Copy instructions: Copy Date: 3 weeks prior to publication date
Average advertising content per issue: 30%
BUSINESS: MARINE & SHIPPING

THE BANKER
35064U1C-50
Editorial Address: 1 Southwark Bridge, LONDON, SE1 9HL
Tel: 020 7873 3000
Email: brian.caplen@ft.com
Advertising Address: As above.
Email: adrian.northey@ft.com
Web site: http://www.thebanker.com
ISSN: 0005-5395
Publisher: FT Group
Date Established: 1926
Frequency: Monthly
Annual Sub.: £245.00
Circulation: 28,022 (ABC 01/07/2008 to 30/06/2009)
Usual Pagination: 150
Editor: Brian Caplen; **Editor-in-Chief:** Stephen Timewell;
Managing Director: Caspar De Bono
Summary of Content: Journal featuring articles on international banking, finance, economics, banking technology and capital markets.
Readership/Target Audience: Aimed at senior bankers, corporate treasurers and financial directors of companies.
ADVERTISING RATES:
Full Page Colour £11500.00
Agency Commission: 10%
Mechanical Data: Bleed Size: 303 x 216mm, Trim Size: 297 x 210mm, Film: Digital, Type Area: 266 x 182mm, Col Length: 266mm, Page Width: 182mm
Copy instructions: Copy Date: 20th of the month prior to publication date
BUSINESS: FINANCE & ECONOMICS: Banking

BANKING AUTOMATION BULLETIN
35062U1C-20
Formerly: BABE Banking Automation Bulletin for Europe
Editorial Address: 304 Sandycombe Road, Kew Gardens, RICHMOND, TW9 3NG **Tel:** 020 8940 1398
Fax: 020 8940 1527
Email: bulletin@rbrlondon.com
Web site: http://www.rbrlondon.com
ISSN: 1351-5543
Publisher: Retail Banking Research Ltd
Date Established: 1979
Frequency: Monthly
Annual Sub.: £490.00
Circulation: 2,000 (Publisher's Statement)
Usual Pagination: 10
Editor: Dominic Hirsch
Summary of Content: Magazine focusing on developments in automated banking and payment systems in Europe and worldwide.
Language(s): Arabic; English; French; German; Greek; Italian; Spanish; Turkish

Readership/Target Audience: Aimed at senior bankers and executives.
ADVERTISING: No Advertising taken
BUSINESS: FINANCE & ECONOMICS: Banking

BANKING TECHNOLOGY
35067U1C-60
Editorial Address: Telephone House, 69-77 Paul Street, LONDON, EC2A 4LQ **Tel:** 020 7017 4019
Fax: 020 7017 4085
Email: news@bankingtech.com
Advertising Address: As above. **Tel:** 020 7017 4600
Email: hamish.mcarthur@informa.com
Web site: http://www.bankingtech.com
ISSN: 0266-0865
Publisher: Informa PLC
Date Established: 1984
Frequency: 10 issues yearly - Published in the 1st week of the cover month
Free to qualifying individuals
Annual Sub.: £425.00
Circulation: 8,060 (ABC 01/07/2008 to 30/06/2009)
Usual Pagination: 68
Editor: David Bannister
Summary of Content: Magazine covering financial technology, systems, services and the latest developments.
Readership/Target Audience: Aimed at senior executives in management in the financial services industry. Also marketing and data processing divisions of banks, savings banks and brokers.
ADVERTISING RATES:
Full Page Colour £5059.00
Agency Commission: 10%
Mechanical Data: Trim Size: 297 x 210mm, Bleed Size: 303 x 216mm, Type Area: 264 x 169mm, Col Length: 264mm, Page Width: 169mm, Film: Digital
Copy instructions: Copy Date: 2 weeks prior to publication date
Average advertising content per issue: 25%
BUSINESS: FINANCE & ECONOMICS: Banking

THE BAPCO JOURNAL
36206U5E-30
Editorial Address: 32 Vauxhall Bridge Road, LONDON, SW1V 2SS **Tel:** 020 7973 6400
Email: jm.sanchez@hgluk.com
Advertising Address: As above. **Fax:** 020 7233 5052
Email: a.mitchell@hgluk.com
Web site: http://www.bapcojournal.com
ISSN: 1475-861X
Publisher: Hemming Group Ltd
Date Established: 1995
Frequency: 6 issues yearly - Published the 3rd week of the month
Free to qualifying individuals
Annual Sub.: £35.00
Circulation: 5,000 (Publisher's Statement)
Usual Pagination: 52
Editor: Jose Sanchez; **Advertising Manager:** Andy Mitchell
Summary of Content: Official publication of The British Association of Public Safety Communications Officers. Covers news, information technology and communications, features, developments and articles on all aspects of communications within the public safety arena.
Readership/Target Audience: Aimed at emergency services, local authorities central government, rescue services, public utilities, public transport and other agencies involved in public safety and homeland security.
ADVERTISING RATES:
Full Page Colour £1900.00
SCC £25.00
Agency Commission: 10%
Mechanical Data: Type Area: 284 x 210mm, Col Length: 284mm, Trim Size: 306 x 229mm, Bleed Size: 312 x 235mm, Film: Digital, Page Width: 210mm
Copy instructions: Copy Date: 2 weeks prior to publication date
Average advertising content per issue: 40%
BUSINESS: COMPUTERS & AUTOMATION: Data Transmission

THE BAR DIRECTORY
39281U44-150
Editorial Address: 100 Avenue Road, Swiss Cottage, LONDON, NW3 3PF **Tel:** 020 7393 7000 **Fax:** 020 7393 7010
Advertising Address: 2nd Floor, 100 Avenue Road, LONDON, NW3 3PF **Tel:** 020 7393 7000 **Fax:** 020 7393 7790
Email: tom.clark@mail.thomson.com
Web site: http://www.legalhub.co.uk
Publisher: Sweet & Maxwell Ltd
Frequency: Annual - Published in October
Annual Sub.: £140.00
Circulation: 2,000 (Publisher's Statement)
Usual Pagination: 1980
Editor: Anne Kemsley
Summary of Content: Published in association with the General Council of the Bar. Contains information on chambers and individual barristers along with commentary on the work of the Bar.
Readership/Target Audience: Aimed at solicitors.

ADVERTISING RATES:
Full Page Mono £881.25
Mechanical Data: Film: Digital, Type Area: 210 x 130mm, Page Width: 130mm, Col Length: 210mm
Copy instructions: Copy Date: June 1st
BUSINESS: LEGAL

BAR MAGAZINE
1654815U9A-254
Formerly: The Venue
Editorial Address: 61 St. Luke's Avenue, LONDON, SW4 7LG **Tel:** 020 7627 4506
Email: mark@cimltd.co.uk
Advertising Address: Barham Court, Teston, MAIDSTONE, ME18 5BZ **Tel:** 01622 618799 **Fax:** 01622 618793
Email: katie@cimltd.co.uk
Web site: http://www.barmagazine.co.uk
Publisher: CIM LLP
Date Established: 1999
Frequency: Monthly - Published at the end of the month prior to cover month
Free to qualifying individuals
Annual Sub.: £32.00
Circulation: 9,800 (Publisher's Statement)
Usual Pagination: 56
Editor: Mark Ludmon; **Advertising Manager:** Katie Johnson
Summary of Content: Magazine covering news and information for the bar industry, including drinks and design.
Readership/Target Audience: Aimed at decision-makers and people with purchase power throughout the licensed trade and related industries.
ADVERTISING RATES:
Full Page Colour £2002.00
Agency Commission: 10%
Mechanical Data: Type Area: 300 x 230mm, Col Length: 300mm, Page Width: 230mm
Copy instructions: Copy Date: 1st week of the month prior to publication date
Average advertising content per issue: 50%
BUSINESS: DRINKS & LICENSED TRADE: Drinks, Licensed Trade, Wines & Spirits

BARNARDO'S TODAY
35452U1P-20
Editorial Address: Tanners Lane, Barkingside, ILFORD, IG6 1QG **Tel:** 020 8550 8822 **Fax:** 020 8550 0429
Email: suzanne.westbury@barnardos.org.uk
Web site: http://www.barnardos.org.uk
ISSN: 1460-9681
Publisher: Barnardo's
Date Established: 1975
Frequency: Half-yearly - Published in March and October
Cover Price: Free
Circulation: 65,000 (Publisher's Statement)
Usual Pagination: 20
Editor: Suzanne Westbury
Summary of Content: Journal containing news and features on the charity's work with children in the community.
Readership/Target Audience: Aimed at supporters and prospective supporters.
ADVERTISING: No Advertising taken
BUSINESS: FINANCE & ECONOMICS: Fundraising

THE BARRISTER
1805772U44-3047
Editorial Address: 21A-23A Dudden Hill Lane, LONDON, NW10 2ET **Tel:** 0870 766 2715
Email: admin@barristermagazine.com
Advertising Address: As above.
Email: admin@barristermagazine.com
Web site: http://www.barristermagazine.com
Publisher: Media Management Corporation Ltd
Date Established: 1999
Frequency: Quarterly
Annual Sub.: £20.00
Circulation: 7,500 (Publisher's Statement)
Editor: Nigel Simmonds; **Advertising Manager:** Mark Turnbull
Summary of Content: Magazine providing a topical review of legal and political issues. Includes articles on expert witnesses, legal and financial services, information technology, charitable trusts and education.
Readership/Target Audience: Aimed at practising barristers in chambers.
ADVERTISING RATES:
Full Page Colour £2350.00
Mechanical Data: Trim Size: 297 x 210mm, Type Area: 255 x 180mm, Col Length: 255mm, Page Width: 180mm, Film: Digital, Col Widths (Display): 55mm, Bleed Size: 307 x 220mm
Copy instructions: Copy Date: 4 weeks prior to publication date
BUSINESS: LEGAL

BARTS AND THE LONDON CHRONICLE

40343U56C-42

Formerly: Barts Journal
Editorial Address: Queen Mary University of London,
Alumni Relations Office, Mile End Road, LONDON, E1 4NS
Tel: 020 7882 3732 **Fax:** 020 7882 3706
Email: batlaa@qmul.ac.uk
Web site: http://www.batlaa.org
ISSN: 1470-2282
Publisher: Barts and The London Alumni Association
Date Established: 1999
Frequency: Half-yearly - Published in April and October
Cover Price: Free
Circulation: 13,000 (Publisher's Statement)
Usual Pagination: 50
Editor: Jo Stiles
Summary of Content: Journal containing articles on topical
subjects related to the medical professions, news of the
College, its former staff and students, current medical
research, news of student clubs and societies.
Readership/Target Audience: Circulated to members of
the Barts and The London Alumni Association, staff and
students of Barts and The London, Queen Mary's School of
Medicine.
ADVERTISING: No Advertising taken
BUSINESS: HEALTH & MEDICAL: Hospitals

BASE METALS MONTHLY

1687346U27-205

Editorial Address: Nestor House, Playhouse Yard,
LONDON, EC4V 5EX **Tel:** 020 7827 9977
Fax: 020 7827 6430
Email: acole@metalbulletinresearch.com
Web site: http://www.metalbulletinresearch.com
Publisher: Metal Bulletin plc
Frequency: Monthly
Circulation: 100 (Publisher's Statement)
Editor: Andy Cole
Summary of Content: Report focusing on long-term
forecasts, detailed supply-demand balances and in-depth
analytical research.
Readership/Target Audience: Aimed at metal producers,
consumers and traders.
ADVERTISING: No Advertising taken
BUSINESS: METAL, IRON & STEEL

BASELINE MAGAZINE

1791209U4E-441

Editorial Address: Unit 6, Crown Yard, Bedgebury Estate,
Bedgebury Road, Goudhurst, CRANBROOK, TN17 2QZ
Tel: 01580 213500 **Fax:** 01580 213600
Email: baseline@octoberbuildingmedia.co.uk
Advertising Address: As above.
Email: baselinemagazine@octoberbuildingmedia.co.uk
Web site: http://www.octoberbuildingmedia.co.uk
Publisher: October Building Media Ltd
Date Established: 2006
Frequency: 10 issues yearly - Published the 1st Monday in
the 1st week of cover month
Cover Price: Free
Circulation: 30,000 (Publisher's Statement)
Usual Pagination: 52
Editor: Brett Pearson; **Advertising Manager:** Brett Pearson;
Publisher: Brett Pearson
Summary of Content: Magazine covering new products,
building regulations and business advice.
Readership/Target Audience: Aimed at builders and
general tradesmen using the Buildbase chain of builders'
merchants.
ADVERTISING RATES:
Full Page Colour £1750.00
Agency Commission: 10%
Mechanical Data: Type Area: 277 x 190mm, Bleed Size:
303 x 216mm, Trim Size: 297 x 210mm, Col Length: 277mm,
Film: Digital, Page Width: 190mm
Copy instructions: Copy Date: 4 weeks prior to publication
date
Average advertising content per issue: 40%
BUSINESS: ARCHITECTURE & BUILDING: Building

BATHROOM JOURNAL

38073U23C-6

Editorial Address: Napier House, 11 Surrey Street,
LOWESTOFT, NR32 1LJ **Tel:** 01502 517115
Fax: 01502 517117
Email: editor@bathroomjournal.co.uk
Advertising Address: As above.
Email: jenny@bathroomjournal.co.uk
Web site: http://www.craftsmanpublishing.co.uk
ISSN: 1366-946X
Publisher: CPC Ltd
Date Established: 1997
Frequency: 6 issues yearly
Free to qualifying individuals
Annual Sub.: £15.00
Circulation: 7,800 (Publisher's Statement)
Usual Pagination: 32

Editor: Jan Orchard; **Managing Director:** Melvyn Earle
Advertising Manager: Jenny Lawrence
Summary of Content: Journal covering all aspects of the
professional bathroom and tile industries.
Readership/Target Audience: Aimed at bathroom and tile
retailers and specialists.
ADVERTISING RATES:
Full Page Colour £1095.00
Agency Commission: 10%
Mechanical Data: Type Area: 271 x 187mm, Bleed Size:
303 x 213mm, Trim Size: 297 x 210mm, Film: Digital, Col
Length: 271mm, Page Width: 187mm
Average advertising content per issue: 42%
BUSINESS: FURNISHINGS & FURNITURE: Furnishings &
Furniture - Kitchens & Bathrooms

THE BATOD MAGAZINE

41146U62J-40

Editorial Address: PR by email only **Tel:** 0845 643 5181
Fax: 0845 643 5181
Email: magazine@batod.org.uk
Advertising Address: 41 The Orchard, Leven, BEVERLEY,
HU17 5QA **Tel:** 01964 544243 **Fax:** 01964 544243
Email: advertising@batod.org.uk
Web site: http://www.batod.org.uk
ISSN: 1366-0799
Publisher: British Association of Teachers of the Deaf
Frequency: 5 issues yearly - Published on the 20th of the
cover month
Free to qualifying individuals
Circulation: 1,800 (Publisher's Statement)
Usual Pagination: 56
Editor: Paul Simpson; **Advertising Manager:** Arnold
Underwood
Summary of Content: Magazine dealing with general issues
relevant to teachers of the deaf including government
legislation, professional developments and dissemination of
good practice.
Readership/Target Audience: Aimed at Teachers of the
Deaf and associated professionals.
ADVERTISING RATES:
Full Page Mono £260.00
Full Page Colour £440.00
Mechanical Data: Film: Digital, Trim Size: 270 x 170mm
Copy instructions: Copy Date: 6 weeks prior to publication
date
Average advertising content per issue: 20%
BUSINESS: CHURCH & SCHOOL EQUIPMENT &
EDUCATION: Teachers & Education Management

BATTERIES AND ENERGY STORAGE
TECHNOLOGY

1616371U49F-101

Editorial Address: 70 Goring Road, GORING-BY-SEA,
BN12 4AB **Tel:** 0845 194 7338 **Fax:** 0845 194 7739
Email: gerry@bestmag.co.uk
Advertising Address: As above.
Email: advertising@bestmag.co.uk
Web site: http://www.bestmag.co.uk
ISSN: 1741-8666
Publisher: Energy Storage Publishing Ltd
Date Established: 2003
Frequency: Quarterly
Free to qualifying individuals
Annual Sub.: £90.00
Circulation: 6,000 (Publisher's Statement)
Usual Pagination: 148
Editor: Gerry Woolf; **Advertising Manager:** Karen Hampton;
Publisher: Gerry Woolf
Summary of Content: Magazine containing information on
electrochemical and energy storage systems - batteries and
battery making, supercaps, stationary fuel cells and all their
applications. Includes features and technical articles based
on first hand reports from conferences and plant and
laboratory visits as well as the latest news and product
reviews.
Readership/Target Audience: Read by battery
manufacturing company managers, telecom and automotive
manufacturers.
ADVERTISING RATES:
Full Page Mono £1190.00
Full Page Colour £1700.00
Agency Commission: 10%
Mechanical Data: Type Area: 272 x 184mm, Col Length:
272mm, Page Width: 184mm, Bleed Size: 303 x 216mm,
Trim Size: 297 x 210mm, Film: Digital
Copy instructions: Copy Date: 30 days prior to publication
date
Average advertising content per issue: 60%
BUSINESS: TRANSPORT: Electric Vehicles

BATTERIES INTERNATIONAL

39695U49F-50

Editorial Address: The Cricketers, Station Road, Amberley,
ARUNDEL, BN18 9LT **Tel:** 01798 839338
Fax: 0700 600 4918
Email: editor@batteriesinternational.com
Advertising Address: As above. **Fax:** 01580 712323
Email: advertising@batteriesinternational.com
Web site: http://www.batteriesinternational.com

ISSN: 0957-9249
Publisher: Mustard Seeds Publishing
Date Established: 1989
Frequency: Quarterly
Free to qualifying individuals
Annual Sub.: £105.00
Circulation: 5,000 (Controlled Circulation)
Usual Pagination: 48
Editor: Mike Halls; **Advertising Manager:** Don Cleary;
Publisher: Don Cleary
Summary of Content: Magazine covering all types of
battery manufacturing, battery chemistry, energy storage
and battery applications, including electric vehicles.
Readership/Target Audience: Read by battery
manufacturing companies worldwide, clients, distributors
and equipment suppliers.
ADVERTISING RATES:
Full Page Mono EUR2250.00
Full Page Colour EUR2250.00
Agency Commission: 10%
Mechanical Data: Type Area: 272 x 184mm, Trim Size: 297
x 210mm, Film: Positive, right reading, emulsion side down,
Print Process: Sheet-fed offset litho, Col Length: 272mm,
Bleed Size: 300 x 213mm, Page Width: 184mm
Copy instructions: Copy Date: 1 week prior to publication
date
Average advertising content per issue: 30%
BUSINESS: TRANSPORT: Electric Vehicles

BATTLESPACE NEWS

1616022U40-419

Editorial Address: 2nd Floor Flat, 8 Sinclair Gardens,
LONDON, W14 0AT **Tel:** 020 7610 5520 **Fax:** 020 7610 5520
Email: j.nettlefold@battle-technology.com
Advertising Address: As above.
Email: j.nettlefold@battle-technology.com
Web site: http://www.battle-technology.com
Publisher: Battlespace Publications
Date Established: 1998
Frequency: 6 issues yearly - Published in the middle of the
cover month
Free to qualifying individuals
Annual Sub.: £333.00
Circulation: 7,149 (Publisher's Statement)
Usual Pagination: 60
Editor: Julian Nettlefold; **Advertising Manager:** Julian
Nettlefold
Summary of Content: International newspaper focusing on
news and information about new defence systems and
defence electronics.
Readership/Target Audience: Read by defence industry
professionals, military personnel and government officials.
ADVERTISING RATES:
Full Page Mono £2155.00
Full Page Colour £2940.00
Mechanical Data: Film: Digital, Trim Size: 297 x 210mm,
Bleed Size: 303 x 216mm
BUSINESS: DEFENCE

BDA NEWS

40374U56D-15

Editorial Address: 64 Wimpole Street, LONDON, W1G 8YS
Tel: 020 7935 0875 **Fax:** 020 7563 4581
Email: g.jackson@bda.org
Advertising Address: BDA, 4 Crinan Street, LONDON, N1
9XW **Tel:** 020 7843 4785 **Fax:** 020 7843 4725
Email: s.kydas@nature.com
Web site: http://www.bda.org
ISSN: 0961-9755
Publisher: British Dental Association
Date Established: 1980
Frequency: Monthly
Free to qualifying individuals
Circulation: 20,004 (ABC 01/01/2008 to 31/12/2008)
Usual Pagination: 40
Editor: Graeme Jackson
Summary of Content: The British Dental Association news
magazine. Contains articles affecting both the business and
professional interests of dentists.
Readership/Target Audience: Aimed at members of the
BDA.
ADVERTISING RATES:
Full Page Mono £2801.00
Full Page Colour £2801.00
Agency Commission: 10%
Mechanical Data: Bleed Size: +3mm, Trim Size: 297 x
210mm, Film: Digital
Copy instructions: Copy Date: 10 days prior to publication
date
Average advertising content per issue: 40%
BUSINESS: HEALTH & MEDICAL: Dental

BDJ BRITISH DENTAL JOURNAL

40375U56D-25

Editorial Address: The Macmillan Building, 4 Crinan Street,
LONDON, N1 9XW **Tel:** 020 7843 3680 **Fax:** 020 7843 4725
Email: bdjeditorial@nature.com
Advertising Address: As above. **Tel:** 020 7833 4000

Business Magazines

Email: a.mason@nature.com
Web site: http://www.bdj.co.uk
ISSN: 0007-0610
Publisher: Nature Publishing Group
Date Established: 1880
Frequency: 24 issues yearly
Annual Sub.: EUR380.00
Circulation: 20,562 (ABC 01/01/2008 to 31/12/2008)
Usual Pagination: 80
Editor: Arveen Bajaj; **News Editor:** Arveen Bajaj; **Editor-in-Chief:** Stephen Hancocks; **Publisher:** Kim Black-Totham
Summary of Content: Journal of the British Dental Association. Contains scientific articles, reviews of current dental topics, news and views from the world of dentistry.
Readership/Target Audience: Read by BDA members, dental practitioners, researchers, academic dentists, dental teachers and dental students.
ADVERTISING RATES:
Full Page Colour £2801.00
Agency Commission: 10%
Mechanical Data: Type Area: 266 x 181mm, Col Length: 266mm, Trim Size: 297 x 210mm, Film: Digital, Page Width: 181mm, Bleed Size: +3mm
Copy instructions: Copy Date: 10 days prior to publication date
Average advertising content per issue: 30%
BUSINESS: HEALTH & MEDICAL: Dental

BEAUTY MAGAZINE 37243U15A-10_50
Editorial Address: 207 Linen Hall, 162-168 Regent Street, LONDON, W1B 5TB **Tel:** 020 7434 1530 **Fax:** 020 7437 0915
Email: info@beauty-magazine.co.uk
Advertising Address: As above.
Email: carrie.culbertson@1530.com
Web site: http://www.beauty-magazine.co.uk
Publisher: Communications International Group
Frequency: Monthly - Published in the 1st week of the cover month
Cover Price: £3.20
Free to qualifying individuals
Annual Sub.: £70.00
Circulation: 13,139 (ABC 01/01/2006 to 31/12/2006)
Usual Pagination: 36
Editor: Cara Whitehouse; **Advertising Manager:** Carrie Culbertson
Summary of Content: Magazine covering UK product features and the latest news from the cosmetics industry, focusing on new services and techniques.
Readership/Target Audience: Aimed at beauty counter, pharmacy assistants, managers and buyers. Also chemists, wholesalers and marketing staff within the UK cosmetics industry.
ADVERTISING RATES:
Full Page Colour £3230.00
Agency Commission: 10%
Mechanical Data: Bleed Size: 309 x 228mm, Trim Size: 303 x 222mm, Type Area: 264 x 198mm, Col Length: 264mm, Page Width: 198mm, Film: Digital
Copy instructions: Copy Date: 4 weeks prior to publication date
Average advertising content per issue: 30%
BUSINESS: COSMETICS & HAIRDRESSING: Cosmetics

BED & BREAKFAST NEWS 711921U50-12_30
Formerly: Bed & Breakfast News and Views
Editorial Address: PO Box 533, NORTHWICH, CW9 9DZ
Tel: 01606 784524
Email: bedandbreakfastnews@yahoo.co.uk
Advertising Address: As above. **Tel:** 01565 755033
Fax: 01565 755607
Email: bedandbreakfastnews@yahoo.co.uk
Web site: http://www.bandbnews.co.uk
Publisher: Christine Stalker
Date Established: 2001
Frequency: Monthly - Published on the 1st of the cover month
Annual Sub.: £35.00
Circulation: 17,000 (Publisher's Statement)
Usual Pagination: 20
Editor: Christine Stalker; **Advertising Manager:** Christine Stalker
Summary of Content: Magazine containing industry specific tourist industry news and products, small business information and company profiles.
Readership/Target Audience: Aimed at bed and breakfast proprietors, guest house and small hotels with up to twelve bedrooms.
ADVERTISING RATES:
Full Page Colour £600.00
Agency Commission: 10%
Mechanical Data: Trim Size: 297 x 210mm, Film: Digital
Copy instructions: Copy Date: 7th of the month prior to publication date
Average advertising content per issue: 35%
BUSINESS: TRAVEL & TOURISM

BEEF FARMER 37834U21D-150
Editorial Address: The Sheep Centre, MALVERN, WR13 6PH **Tel:** 01684 565533 **Fax:** 01684 565577
Email: info@shepherdpublishing.co.uk
Advertising Address: As above.
Email: info@shepherdpublishing.co.uk
ISSN: 1471-8413
Publisher: Shepherd Publishing Ltd
Date Established: 1997
Frequency: Quarterly
Annual Sub.: £50.00
Circulation: 5,000 (Publisher's Statement)
Usual Pagination: 32
Editor: Sheila Spence; **Advertising Manager:** Howard Venters; **Publisher:** Howard Venters
Summary of Content: Journal of the National Beef Association. Covers articles on breeding, veterinary advice, feeding and new products.
Readership/Target Audience: Read by association members, beef producers and related industry members.
ADVERTISING RATES:
Full Page Colour £1470.00
SCC £10.95
Agency Commission: 10%
Mechanical Data: Trim Size: 297 x 210mm, Film: Digital, Bleed Size: 301 x 214mm, Col Widths (Display): 90mm, No. of Columns (Display): 2
Copy instructions: Copy Date: 1 month prior to publication date
Average advertising content per issue: 40%
Official Journal of: National Beef Association
BUSINESS: AGRICULTURE & FARMING: Livestock

BEHAVIORAL ECOLOGY 601476U55-9016
Editorial Address: Institute of Zoology, Zoological Society of London, Regents Park, LONDON, NW1 4RY
Tel: 01865 353907 **Fax:** 01865 353485
Email: beedit@ioz.ac.uk
Advertising Address: Great Clarendon Street, OXFORD, OX2 6DP **Tel:** 01865 354767
Email: jnlsadvertising@oxfordjournals.org
Web site: http://www.oup.co.uk/jnls
ISSN: 1045-2249
Publisher: OUP
Date Established: 1989
Frequency: 6 issues yearly
Cover Price: £11.00
Annual Sub.: £52.00
Usual Pagination: 132
Editor: Will Cresswell; **Advertising Manager:** Elisabetta Palanghi Sheffield
Summary of Content: The official journal of the International Society for Behavioral Ecology, which includes studies on the whole range of behaving organisms, including plants, invertebrates, vertebrates and humans.
Readership/Target Audience: Aimed at all members of the International Society for Behavioral Ecology.
ADVERTISING RATES:
Full Page Mono £1409.00
Full Page Colour £2348.00
Agency Commission: 10%
Mechanical Data: Trim Size: 276 x 210mm, Bleed Size: 282 x 216mm, Type Area: 2454 x 178mm, Col Length: 254mm, Print Process: Litho, Page Width: 178mm, Film: Digital
BUSINESS: APPLIED SCIENCE & LABORATORIES

BELFAST GAZETTE 39283U44-152
Editorial Address: 16 Arthur Street, BELFAST, BT1 4GD
Tel: 028 9089 5135 **Fax:** 028 9023 5401
Email: belfast.gazette@tso.co.uk
Web site: http://www.belfast-gazette.co.uk
ISSN: 0951-0370
Publisher: TSO
Date Established: 1921
Frequency: Weekly
Cover Price: £0.75
Annual Sub.: £68.00
Editor: Shirley McMaster
Summary of Content: Publication containing official, statutory, legal, bankruptcy and liquidation notices relating to Northern Ireland.
Readership/Target Audience: Aimed at Government departments, libraries, solicitors and large credit information firms.
ADVERTISING: No Advertising taken
BUSINESS: LEGAL

BELUX 37724U20-165
Formerly: The Journal (Belgian-Luxembourg Chamber of Commerce)
Editorial Address: 105 Ferriby Road, HESSLE, HU13 0HX
Tel: 0870 246 1610 **Fax:** 0870 429 2148
Email: info@blcc.co.uk
Advertising Address: As above.
Email: info@blcc.co.uk
Web site: http://www.blcc.co.uk

ISSN: 1357-6879
Publisher: Belgian-Luxembourg Chamber of Commerce
Frequency: Quarterly - Published in the middle of the month
Free to qualifying individuals
Circulation: 4,500 (Publisher's Statement)
Usual Pagination: 20
Editor: Michel van Hoonacker; **Advertising Manager:** Michel van Hoonacker
Summary of Content: Magazine covering events, news concerning Chamber of Commerce members and financial and legal matters.
Readership/Target Audience: Read by those aiming to do business in Belgium, Luxembourg and UK.
ADVERTISING: Rates on application
BUSINESS: IMPORT & EXPORT

BENCHMARK 37684U19J-23
Editorial Address: Prospect House, Stanley Boulevard, Hamilton Intnl Technology Park, Blantyre, GLASGOW, G72 0BN **Tel:** 01355 225688 **Fax:** 01698 823311
Email: info@nafems.org
Advertising Address: As above.
Email: paul.steward@nafems.org
Web site: http://www.nafems.org
ISSN: 0951-6859
Publisher: NAFEMS
Date Established: 1984
Frequency: Quarterly
Free to qualifying individuals
Annual Sub.: £40.00
Circulation: 6,000 (Publisher's Statement)
Usual Pagination: 40
Editor: David Quinn; **Advertising Manager:** Paul Steward
Summary of Content: Journal featuring engineering design and analysis, finite element analysis, computational fluid dynamics, CAD, CAM and CAE.
Readership/Target Audience: Read by engineers, analysts, designers, engineering managers and training officers.
ADVERTISING RATES:
Full Page Colour £1500.00
Mechanical Data: Bleed Size: +6mm, Film: Digital, Trim Size: 297 x 210mm
Copy instructions: Copy Date: 6 weeks prior to publication date
Average advertising content per issue: 15%
BUSINESS: ENGINEERING & MACHINERY: CAD & CIM (Computer Integrated Manufacture)

BENCHMARK 1776547U54C-328
Editorial Address: PO Box 332, DARTFORD, DA1 9FF
Tel: 01342 837897
Email: editorial@proactivpubs.co.uk
Advertising Address: As above. **Tel:** 020 8295 1414
Fax: 020 8295 1401
Email: david.lewis@proactivpubs.co.uk
Web site: http://www.benchmarkmagazine.co.uk
ISSN: 1750-1040
Publisher: Pro-Activ Publications Ltd
Date Established: 2006
Frequency: 6 issues yearly - Published around the last week of the 1st cover month
Cover Price: £8.00
Annual Sub.: £24.00
Circulation: 10,000 (Publisher's Statement)
Usual Pagination: 72
Editor: Pete Conway; **Advertisement Director:** David Lewis
Summary of Content: Magazine covering independent performance related testing of electronic security systems.
Readership/Target Audience: Aimed at installers and integrators of electronic security systems, specifiers, consultants and users of electronic security solutions.
ADVERTISING RATES:
Full Page Colour £2100.00
Mechanical Data: Type Area: 275 x 185mm, Bleed Size: 303 x 216mm, Trim Size: 297 x 210mm, Col Length: 275mm, Page Width: 185mm, Film: Digital
Copy instructions: Copy Date: 1 week prior to publication date
BUSINESS: SAFETY & SECURITY: Security

BENEFITS 20396U32R-494
Editorial Address: 4th Floor, Beacon House, Queens Road, BRISTOL, BS8 1QU **Tel:** 0117 331 4054 **Fax:** 0117 331 4093
Email: fran.bennett@socres.ox.ac.uk
Advertising Address: As above.
Email: jessica.hughes@bristol.ac.uk
Web site: http://www.policypress.org.uk
ISSN: 0962-7898
Publisher: The Policy Press
Date Established: 1991
Frequency: 3 issues yearly - Published in February, June and October
Annual Sub.: £50.00
Usual Pagination: 48
Editor: Kathryn King; **Advertising Manager:** Jessica Hughes

Summary of Content: Journal covering social security research, policy and practice.
Readership/Target Audience: Aimed at academics and people working in local government and the voluntary sector.
ADVERTISING RATES:
Full Page Mono £200.00
Mechanical Data: Type Area: 203 x 120mm, Bleed Size: 258 x 178mm, Col Length: 203mm, Page Width: 120mm, Film: Digital
Copy instructions: Copy Date: 8 weeks prior to publication date
BUSINESS: LOCAL GOVERNMENT, LEISURE & RECREATION: Local Government Related

---

BENEFITS & COMPENSATION INTERNATIONAL
35351U1H-10

Editorial Address: East Wing, Fourth Floor, Hope House, 45 Great Peter Street, LONDON, SW1P 3LT **Tel:** 020 7222 0288
Fax: 020 7799 2163
Email: editorial@benecompintl.com
Advertising Address: As above.
Email: advertising@benecompintl.com
Web site: http://www.benecompintl.com
ISSN: 0268-764X
Publisher: Pension Publications Ltd
Date Established: 1971
Frequency: 10 issues yearly
Annual Sub.: £380.00
Circulation: 901 (Publisher's Statement)
Usual Pagination: 38
Editor: Alexandra Hain-Cole
Summary of Content: Magazine covering employee benefits around the world. Follows salary and bonus trends and stock options.
Readership/Target Audience: Read by directors and employees of multinational companies and their advisers.
ADVERTISING RATES:
Full Page Mono £2995.00
Full Page Colour £3680.00
Agency Commission: 15%
Mechanical Data: Film: Digital, Type Area: 255 x 183mm, Bleed Size: 310 x 220mm, Trim Size: 297 x 210mm, Col Length: 255mm, Page Width: 183mm, Print Process: Offset litho
Copy instructions: Copy Date: 6 weeks prior to publication date
BUSINESS: FINANCE & ECONOMICS: Pensions

BENELUX UNQUOTE
1750385U1F-620

Editorial Address: 4th Floor, Haymarket House, 28-29 Haymarket, LONDON, SW1Y 4RX **Tel:** 020 7004 7471
Fax: 020 7004 7548
Email: kimberly.romaine@incisivemedia.com
Advertising Address: Haymarket House, 28-29 Haymarket, LONDON, SW1Y 4RX **Tel:** 020 7484 9700
Fax: 020 7004 7548
Email: stephen.osullivan@incisivemedia.com
Web site: http://www.unquote.com
Publisher: Incisive Media Investments
Frequency: 10 issues yearly
Annual Sub.: £795.00
Circulation: 45 (Publisher's Statement)
Usual Pagination: 30
Editor: Kimberly Romaine; **Advertising Manager:** Stephen O'Sullivan
Summary of Content: Newsletter covering private equity transactions in the Benelux region.
Readership/Target Audience: Aimed at people in the private equity industry.
ADVERTISING RATES:
Full Page Mono £1650.00
Full Page Colour £3300.00
Agency Commission: 10%
Mechanical Data: Bleed Size: 286 x 222mm, Trim Size: 280 x 216mm, Film: Digital
BUSINESS: FINANCE & ECONOMICS: Investment

BERMUDA REINSURANCE
1791186U1D-422

Editorial Address: 15-17 Newton Way, Woolsthorpe By Colsterworth, GRANTHAM, NG33 5NR **Tel:** 020 8290 4943
Fax: 020 7681 1248
Email: nlipinski@newtonmedia.co.uk
Advertising Address: As above. **Tel:** 020 8313 3967
Email: nlipinski@newtonmedia.co.uk
Web site: http://www.bermudareinsurancemagazine.com
ISSN: 1749-4508
Publisher: Newton Media Ltd
Date Established: 2005
Frequency: 5 issues yearly
Annual Sub.: £175.00
Editor: Nicholas Lipinski; **Advertising Manager:** Nicholas Lipinski; **Publisher:** Nicholas Lipinski
Summary of Content: Magazine covering news and opinion from the Bermuda reinsurance market.

Readership/Target Audience: Aimed at senior management in insurance and reinsurance companies, reinsurance brokers and their service providers.
ADVERTISING RATES:
Full Page Mono £4650.00
Full Page Colour £4650.00
Agency Commission: 10%
Mechanical Data: Type Area: 270 x 185mm, Bleed Size: 303 x 216mm, Trim Size: 297 x 210mm, Col Length: 270mm, Page Width: 185mm, Film: Digital
Copy instructions: Copy Date: 10th of the month prior to publication date
Average advertising content per issue: 25%
BUSINESS: FINANCE & ECONOMICS: Insurance

BERNOULLI
1740123U31A-391

Editorial Address: 841 High Road, Finchley, LONDON, N12 8PT **Tel:** 020 8446 2100 **Fax:** 020 8446 2191
Email: william.kimberley@racetechmag.com
Advertising Address: As above.
Email: info@racetechmag.com
Web site: http://www.racetechmag.com
ISSN: 1751-2670
Publisher: Racecar Graphic Ltd
Date Established: 2006
Frequency: Quarterly
Cover Price: £10.00
Circulation: 10,000 (Publisher's Statement)
Usual Pagination: 100
Editor: William Kimberley; **Advertising Manager:** Soheila Kimberley
Summary of Content: Magazine covering the theory and practice of road and race car aerodynamics.
Readership/Target Audience: Aimed at those involved in optimising the performance of road and race cars, from design right through to the actual competitive events.
ADVERTISING RATES:
Full Page Mono £2500.00
Full Page Colour £3000.00
Mechanical Data: Trim Size: 297 x 210mm, Bleed Size: 303 x 216mm, Type Area: 277 x 190mm, Col Length: 277mm, Page Width: 190mm
BUSINESS: MOTOR TRADE: Motor Trade Accessories

BEST PRACTICE
763758U63B-2481

Editorial Address: 33 Middle Meadow Avenue, BIRMINGHAM, B32 1NU **Tel:** 0121 687 1054
Fax: 0121 687 1051
Email: bestpracticeuk@live.com
Advertising Address: As above.
Email: bestpracticeuk@aol.com
Web site: http://www.bestpracticeuk.co.uk
Publisher: Fresh Media UK Ltd
Date Established: 1998
Frequency: 26 issues yearly
Cover Price: £2.00
Free to qualifying individuals
Circulation: 5,000 (Publisher's Statement)
Editor: Andre Laurent; **Advertising Manager:** Andre Laurent
Summary of Content: Magazine containing an informative mix of business trends, latest products and updates for industry and commerce, recognising best practice and commitment to excellence.
Readership/Target Audience: Aimed at named decision makers within industry and commerce. Covers new products, company developments and case studies.
ADVERTISING: Rates on application
BUSINESS: REGIONAL BUSINESS: Regional Business English Counties

---

BEST PRACTICE & RESEARCH CLINICAL ENDOCRINOLOGY & METABOLISM
40576U56R-9_50

Formerly: Bailliere's Clinical Endocrinology & Metabolism
Editorial Address: The Boulevard, Langford Lane, KIDLINGTON, OX5 1GB **Tel:** 01865 843823
Fax: 01865 843997
Email: andrew.miller@elsevier.com
Web site: http://www.intl.elsevierhealth.com/journals/beem
ISSN: 1521-690X
Publisher: Elsevier Ltd
Date Established: 1986
Frequency: 6 issues yearly
Annual Sub.: EUR234.00
Circulation: 600 (Publisher's Statement)
Usual Pagination: 200
Editor: Andrew Miller
Summary of Content: Journal about current research and best practice in endocrinology and metabolism with each issue themed around a single topic.
Readership/Target Audience: Aimed at doctors, consultants and specialists.
ADVERTISING: No Advertising taken
BUSINESS: HEALTH & MEDICAL: Health Medical Related

BETTER BUSINESS
37118U14H-13_5

Editorial Address: 1st Floor, Northumbria House, 5 Delta Bank Road, Metro Riverside Park, GATESHEAD, NE11 9DJ
Tel: 0191 461 8000 **Fax:** 0191 461 8001
Email: news@better-business.co.uk
Advertising Address: As above.
Email: j.stockdale@cobwebinfo.com
Web site: http://www.better-business.co.uk
ISSN: 1369-5053
Publisher: Cobweb Information Ltd
Date Established: 1992
Frequency: 10 issues yearly
Annual Sub.: £48.00
Circulation: 1,000 (Controlled Circulation)
Usual Pagination: 28
Editor: Richard Reed
Summary of Content: Publication containing practical business information and advice.
Readership/Target Audience: Aimed at small business owners and managers, freelancers and self-employed people.
ADVERTISING RATES:
Full Page Colour £1500.00
Agency Commission: 10%
Mechanical Data: Type Area: 303 x 206mm, Film: Digital, Col Length: 303mm, Bleed Size: +3mm, Page Width: 206mm
Copy instructions: Copy Date: 1st of the month prior to publication date
Average advertising content per issue: 10%
BUSINESS: COMMERCE, INDUSTRY & MANAGEMENT: Small Business

BETTING BUSINESS
1655552U64A-175

Editorial Address: 50 Upper North Street, BRIGHTON, BN1 3FH **Tel:** 020 8563 8425 **Fax:** 01273 204827
Email: am@sjc.co.uk
Advertising Address: Bolton Technology Exchange, 33 Queensbrook, BOLTON, BL1 4AY **Tel:** 01204 396397
Fax: 01204 392748
Email: njudson@gbmedia.eu
Web site: http://www.betting-business.co.uk
Publisher: Gaming Business Media
Date Established: 2004
Frequency: Monthly
Cover Price: £5.20
Circulation: 2,600 (Publisher's Statement)
Usual Pagination: 40
Editor: Andrew McCarron; **Managing Editor:** Ken Scott
Summary of Content: Magazine covering the latest business developments within the betting industry.
Readership/Target Audience: Aimed at betting office managers and online betting operators.
ADVERTISING RATES:
Full Page Mono £960.00
Full Page Colour £1200.00
Agency Commission: 10%
Mechanical Data: Film: Digital, Type Area: 312 x 219mm, Col Length: 312mm, Page Width: 219mm, Bleed Size: 346 x 246mm, Trim Size: 340 x 240mm
Copy instructions: Copy Date: 10 days prior to publication date
BUSINESS: OTHER CLASSIFICATIONS: Amusement Trade

BEVERAGE INNOVATION
627328U22R-360

Formerly: softdrinksworld
Editorial Address: 7 Kingsmead Square, BATH, BA1 2AB
Tel: 01225 327890 **Fax:** 01225 327891
Email: info@zipublishing.com
Advertising Address: As above.
Email: mcj@zipublishing.com
Web site: http://www.foodbev.com
Publisher: Zenith International
Date Established: 2000
Frequency: 10 issues yearly - Double issues in July and December
Free to qualifying individuals
Annual Sub.: £110.00
Circulation: 17,598 (Publisher's Statement)
Usual Pagination: 70
Editor: Claire Phoenix
Summary of Content: Magazine covering all aspects of news relating to the global non alcoholic drinks industry including interviews, new technology and product reviews and analysis.
Language(s): English; French; German; Italian; Spanish
Readership/Target Audience: Aimed at those working in the non-alcoholic drinks, water and dairy industries including suppliers, retailers, manufacturers, financial analysts, marketing and public relations brand managers.
ADVERTISING RATES:
Full Page Colour £2435.00
Agency Commission: 10%
Mechanical Data: Trim Size: 297 x 210mm, Col Widths (Display): 43mm, No. of Columns (Display): 4, Film: Digital, Print Process: Offset litho, Bleed Size: 303 x 213mm
Average advertising content per issue: 35%
BUSINESS: FOOD: Food Related

Business Magazines

BFM - BUSINESS AND FINANCE MIDLANDS
711707U63B-1780

Formerly: Business and Finance Midlands
Editorial Address: 65 Church Street, BIRMINGHAM, B3 2DP **Tel:** 0121 262 3727
Email: mark_bfm@yahoo.co.uk
Advertising Address: As above.
Email: mark_bfm@yahoo.co.uk
Publisher: Midlands Business Media Ltd
Date Established: 1999
Frequency: 8 issues yearly - Published on the 2nd Tuesday of the month
Annual Sub.: £49.00
Circulation: 7,500 (Publisher's Statement)
Usual Pagination: 68
Editor: Fred Bromwich; **Advertising Manager:** Mark Dorey;
Publisher: Mark Dorey
Summary of Content: Magazine covering corporate finance for the professional sector in the Midlands.
Readership/Target Audience: Aimed at corporate executives and directors of all Midlands based business with a turnover of £3 million.
ADVERTISING: Rates on application
Mechanical Data: Bleed Size: 303 x 216mm, Trim Size: 297 x 210mm, Type Area: 267 x 180mm, Film: Digital, Col Length: 267mm, Page Width: 180mm
Copy instructions: Copy Date: 3 weeks prior to publication date
Supplement(s): Legal 500 - 1xY
BUSINESS: REGIONAL BUSINESS: Regional Business English Counties

BIALL BRITISH & IRISH ASSOCIATION OF LAW LIBRARIANS NEWSLETTER
40855U44-152_50

Editorial Address: 7 Thornhaugh Street, Russell Square, LONDON, WC1H 0XG **Tel:** 020 7898 4155
Fax: 020 7898 4159
Email: ss104@soas.ac.uk
Web site: http://www.biall.org.uk
Publisher: BIALL
Frequency: 6 issues yearly
Cover Price: Free
Circulation: 850 (Publisher's Statement)
Usual Pagination: 20
Editor: Jon Beaumont
Summary of Content: Newsletter of BIALL, covering news about law libraries, legal publications, legal databases, software products and conferences.
Readership/Target Audience: Read by members of BIALL.
ADVERTISING: No Advertising taken
BUSINESS: LEGAL

BICYCLE TRADE AND INDUSTRY
38356U31C-20

Editorial Address: 97 Front Street, Whickham, NEWCASTLE UPON TYNE, NE16 4JL **Tel:** 0191 488 1947
Email: kate@tradeandindustry.net
Advertising Address: As above.
Email: kate@tradeandindustry.net
Web site: http://www.tradeandindustry.net
Publisher: KSA Partnership
Date Established: 1980
Frequency: Monthly
Cover Price: Free
Circulation: 3,500 (Publisher's Statement)
Usual Pagination: 8
Editor: Peter Lumley; **Advertisement Director:** Kate Spencer; **Publisher:** Peter Lumley
Summary of Content: Magazine containing news and current affairs of interest to anyone dealing with the British bicycle trade.
Readership/Target Audience: Aimed at retailers, distributors and manufacturers.
ADVERTISING RATES:
Full Page Colour £1148.00
Agency Commission: 10%
Mechanical Data: Type Area: 260 x 183mm, Col Length: 260mm, Page Width: 183mm, Film: Digital
Copy instructions: Copy Date: Last week of the month prior to publication date
Average advertising content per issue: 40%
BUSINESS: MOTOR TRADE: Bicycle Trade

BIFALINK
39629U49C-15

Editorial Address: Redfern House, Browells Lane, FELTHAM, TW13 7EP **Tel:** 020 8844 2266
Fax: 020 8890 5546
Email: bifa@bifa.org
Advertising Address: 2 Park Lane, Earls Colne, COLCHESTER, CO6 2RJ **Tel:** 01787 222434
Fax: 01787 220465
Email: pedwards.parklane@virgin.net
Web site: http://www.bifa.org
Publisher: Park Lane Publishing

Date Established: 1989
Frequency: Monthly
Cover Price: £3.00
Free to qualifying individuals
Annual Sub.: £36.00
Circulation: 6,500 (Publisher's Statement)
Usual Pagination: 20
Editor: Sharon Hammond; **Advertising Manager:** Peter Edwards
Summary of Content: News from the British International Freight Association.
Readership/Target Audience: Aimed at BIFA members.
ADVERTISING RATES:
Full Page Colour £2195.00
Mechanical Data: Type Area: 277 x 190mm, Col Length: 277mm, Page Width: 190mm, Trim Size: 297 x 210mm, Bleed Size: 303 x 216mm, Film: Digital
BUSINESS: TRANSPORT: Freight

BIIBUSINESS
36491U9A-20

Editorial Address: The Annexe, Sycamore Design, Hanover Close, 85 Mount Ephraim, TUNBRIDGE WELLS, TN4 8BU **Tel:** 01892 544340 **Fax:** 01892 545138
Email: biibiz@ak3000.com
Advertising Address: Wessex House, 80 Park Street, CAMBERLEY, GU15 3PT **Tel:** 01795 535468
Fax: 01276 23045
Email: ads@bii-business.co.uk
Web site: http://www.bii.org
Publisher: BII
Date Established: 1983
Frequency: 10 issues yearly
Free to qualifying individuals
Annual Sub.: £50.00
Circulation: 16,107 (ABC 01/07/2006 to 30/06/2007)
Usual Pagination: 36
Editor: Andrew Palmer
Summary of Content: Official journal of The BII, the professional body for the licensed retail sector, providing information for licensees and their staff.
Readership/Target Audience: Read by members of the BII and those within the industry.
ADVERTISING RATES:
Full Page Mono £2150.00
Full Page Colour £2150.00
Agency Commission: 10%
Mechanical Data: Film: Digital, Bleed Size: 296 x 236mm, Trim Size: 290 x 230mm
Copy instructions: Copy Date: 20 days prior to publication date
Average advertising content per issue: 40%
BUSINESS: DRINKS & LICENSED TRADE: Drinks, Licensed Trade, Wines & Spirits

BIKE BIZ
624267U31C-10

Formerly: BicycleBusiness
Editorial Address: Benton Bridge Cottage, Jesmond Dene, NEWCASTLE UPON TYNE, NE7 7DA **Tel:** 0191 265 2062
Email: carlton.reid@intentmedia.co.uk
Advertising Address: Saxon House, 6A St. Andrew Street, HERTFORD, SG14 1JA **Tel:** 01992 535647
Fax: 01992 535648
Email: carly.bailey@intentmedia.co.uk
Web site: http://www.bikebiz.co.uk
ISSN: 1476-1505
Publisher: Intent Media
Date Established: 1999
Frequency: Monthly
Cover Price: Free
Circulation: 2,500 (Publisher's Statement)
Usual Pagination: 44
Editor: Carlton Reid
Summary of Content: Magazine containing news and articles on new products and developments within the bicycle industry. Also contains reports on international cycling events.
Readership/Target Audience: Aimed at suppliers and independent bicycle dealers.
ADVERTISING RATES:
Full Page Colour £775.00
Agency Commission: 10%
Mechanical Data: Type Area: 290 x 206mm, Col Length: 290mm, Page Width: 206mm, Bleed Size: 321 x 236mm, Film: Digital, Trim Size: 315 x 230mm
BUSINESS: MOTOR TRADE: Bicycle Trade

THE BILL OF MIDDLESEX
1851527U44-3056

Editorial Address: 4th Floor, Orleans House, Edmund Street, LIVERPOOL, L3 9NG **Tel:** 0151 236 4141
Fax: 0141 236 0440
Email: phillightfoot@benhampublishing.com
Web site: http://www.benhampublishing.com/magazines.htm
Publisher: Benham Publishing Limited
Frequency: Quarterly
Cover Price: Free

Circulation: 1,500 (Publisher's Statement)
Usual Pagination: 36
Editor: Phil Lightfoot
Summary of Content: Official magazine of the Middlesex Law Society. Features society news, members events and awards and the law supply chain.
Readership/Target Audience: Aimed at members of the Middlesex Law Society.
BUSINESS: LEGAL

BINGO LINK
765111U64A-171

Editorial Address: Lexham House, 75 High Street, DUNSTABLE, LU6 1JF **Tel:** 01582 860900
Fax: 01582 860901
Email: bingolink@bingo-association.co.uk
Advertising Address: Associa, North Gate, Uppingham, OAKHAM, LE15 9PL **Tel:** 01572 824263
Web site: http://www.bingo-association.co.uk
Publisher: The Bingo Association
Date Established: 1983
Frequency: Quarterly
Cover Price: £4.00
Free to qualifying individuals
Annual Sub.: £15.00
Circulation: 1,200 (Publisher's Statement)
Usual Pagination: 20
Editor: Steven Baldwin; **Advertising Manager:** Wendy Rose; **Publisher:** Steven Baldwin
Summary of Content: Magazine covering all aspects of the bingo industry including news, developments and products.
Readership/Target Audience: Aimed at bingo club owners, operators and managers.
ADVERTISING RATES:
Full Page Colour £1700.00
Agency Commission: 10%
Mechanical Data: Type Area: 250 x 195mm, Col Length: 250mm, Trim Size: 278 x 210mm, Bleed Size: 284 x 216mm, Page Width: 195mm, No. of Columns (Display): 2
Average advertising content per issue: 30%
BUSINESS: OTHER CLASSIFICATIONS: Amusement Trade

BINSTED'S BOTTLING DIRECTORY
38700U35-5

Editorial Address: Attwood House, Mansfield Park, Four Marks, ALTON, GU34 5PZ **Tel:** 01420 568900
Fax: 01420 565995
Email: editorial@binstedgroup.com
Advertising Address: As above. **Fax:** 01420 565994
Email: andrew.flew@binstedgroup.com
Web site: http://www.binstedgroup.com
Publisher: The Binsted Group plc
Date Established: 1976
Frequency: Annual - Published in August
Cover Price: £100.00
Usual Pagination: 240
Editor: Julie Foskett
Summary of Content: Directory focusing on beverage producers, packers and manufacturers, trade associations, contract bottlers and packers, machinery and service suppliers guide.
Readership/Target Audience: Aimed at brewing, bottling and canning plant managers and sales suppliers to the industry.
ADVERTISING RATES:
Full Page Mono £995.00
Full Page Colour £1535.00
Mechanical Data: Type Area: 229 x 178mm, Bleed Size: 286 x 216mm, Trim Size: 280 x 210mm, Film: Digital, Col Length: 229mm, Page Width: 178mm
BUSINESS: PACKAGING & BOTTLING

BINSTED'S DIRECTORY OF FOOD TRADE MARKS & BRAND NAMES
37992U22A-53

Editorial Address: Station House, Hortons Way, WESTERHAM, TN16 1BZ **Tel:** 01959 563944
Fax: 01959 561285
Email: info@foodtradereview.com
Advertising Address: As above.
Email: info@foodtradereview.com
Web site: http://www.foodtradereview.com
ISSN: 0067-8651
Publisher: Food Trade Press Ltd
Date Established: 1959
Frequency: Annual - Published in October
Annual Sub.: £85.00
Circulation: 1,600 (Publisher's Statement)
Usual Pagination: 548
Editor: Colette Binsted; **Advertising Manager:** Adrian Binsted
Summary of Content: Directory containing the latest listings of all brand names used in food, with full company addresses.
Readership/Target Audience: Aimed at large food companies in the UK and Overseas.

ADVERTISING RATES:
Full Page Mono £240.00
Agency Commission: 10%
Mechanical Data: Type Area: 180 x 125mm, Print Process: Offset litho, Bleed Size: 224 x 146mm, Trim Size: 218 x 148mm, No. of Columns (Display): 1, Col Length: 180mm, Page Width: 125mm, Film: Digital
Average advertising content per issue: 2%
BUSINESS: FOOD

THE BIOCHEMIST
39949U55-37

Editorial Address: 3rd Floor, Eagle House, 16 Procter Street, LONDON, WC1V 6NX **Tel:** 020 7280 4100
Fax: 020 7280 4169
Email: editorial@biochemistry.org
Advertising Address: As above.
Email: editorial@biochemistry.org
Web site: http://www.biochemist.com
ISSN: 0954-982X
Publisher: The Biochemical Society
Date Established: 1978
Frequency: 6 issues yearly
Free to qualifying individuals
Annual Sub.: £49.00
Circulation: 6,236 (Publisher's Statement)
Usual Pagination: 64
Editor: Mark Burgess; **Executive Editor:** Mark Burgess; **Managing Director:** Rhonda Oliver; **Advertising Manager:** Mark Burgess
Summary of Content: Journal of the Biochemical Society containing interviews, features, application stories, book reviews, comment, education and policy.
Readership/Target Audience: Read by biochemists, molecular life scientists, students, research directors and senior personnel in commercial and academic life-science ventures.
ADVERTISING RATES:
Full Page Mono £950.00
Full Page Colour £1200.00
Agency Commission: 10%
Mechanical Data: Type Area: 255 x 185mm, Col Length: 255mm, Bleed Size: 281 x 216mm, Film: Digital, Page Width: 185mm
Average advertising content per issue: 10%
BUSINESS: APPLIED SCIENCE & LABORATORIES

BIOFUELS INTERNATIONAL
1804491U58-185

Editorial Address: Marshall House, 124 Middleton Road, MORDEN, SM4 6RW **Tel:** 020 8687 4126
Fax: 020 8687 4130
Email: margaret@biofuels-news.com
Advertising Address: As above. **Tel:** 020 8648 7092
Email: andrew@biofuels-news.com
Web site: http://www.biofuels-news.com
ISSN: 1754-2170
Publisher: Horseshoe Media Ltd
Date Established: 2007
Frequency: 10 issues yearly
Annual Sub.: £195.00
Circulation: 3,000 (Publisher's Statement)
Usual Pagination: 76
Editor: Margaret Garn; **Managing Director:** Peter Patterson; **Advertising Manager:** Pierre-Gomis Diallo
Summary of Content: Magazine focusing on biofuels including biodiesel, bioethanol and biomass. Contains news and updates, country focus reports, interviews, technology and details of exhibitions and conferences.
Readership/Target Audience: Aimed at managers in production and process plants, suppliers and distributors, financial institutions, government departments, NGOs, traders, consultants and trade associations.
ADVERTISING: Rates on application
Agency Commission: 15%
Copy instructions: Copy Date: 3 weeks prior to publication date
Average advertising content per issue: 30%
BUSINESS: ENERGY, FUEL & NUCLEAR

BIOINFORMATICS
25795U64F-9

Editorial Address: Great Clarendon Street, OXFORD, OX2 6DP **Tel:** 01865 353907 **Fax:** 01865 353985
Email: bioinformatics@editorialoffice.co.uk
Advertising Address: As above. **Fax:** 01865 353774
Email: steve.simmonds@oxfordjournals.org
Web site: http://www.oup.co.uk/jnls
ISSN: 1367-4803
Publisher: OUP
Date Established: 1985
Frequency: 24 issues yearly
Annual Sub.: £373.00
Circulation: 1,000 (Publisher's Statement)
Usual Pagination: 88
Editor: A. Bateman; **Executive Editor:** A. Bateman
Summary of Content: Contains papers on new algorithms, programs, software, reports, reviews, surveys covering aspects of computer applications in life sciences.
Readership/Target Audience: Aimed at biologists.

ADVERTISING RATES:
Full Page Mono £742.00
Full Page Colour £1236.00
Agency Commission: 10%
Mechanical Data: Type Area: 255 x 178mm, Trim Size: 279 x 216mm, Bleed Size: 285 x 222mm, Film: Digital, Print Process: Litho, Col Length: 255mm, Page Width: 178mm
BUSINESS: OTHER CLASSIFICATIONS: Biology

BIOLOGIST
41491U64F-10

Editorial Address: 9 Red Lion Court, LONDON, EC4A 3EF
Tel: 020 7936 5900 **Fax:** 020 7936 5901
Email: biologist@iob.org
Advertising Address: Impact Media, The Mere, Mere Road, Bitteswell, LUTTERWORTH, LE17 4LH **Tel:** 01455 554148
Fax: 01455 559620
Email: greavesval@yahoo.co.uk
Web site: http://www.iob.org
ISSN: 0006-3347
Publisher: Institute of Biology
Date Established: 1953
Frequency: Quarterly
Free to qualifying individuals
Annual Sub.: £110.00
Circulation: 15,000 (Publisher's Statement)
Usual Pagination: 60
Editor: Simon Napper; **Advertising Manager:** Valerie Greaves
Summary of Content: Journal covering the diversity within biological research today including authoritative review articles on science policy and new developments or controversial issues.
Readership/Target Audience: Aimed at professional biologists, educators and students at all levels, as well as the interested amateur.
ADVERTISING RATES:
Full Page Mono £700.00
Full Page Colour £850.00
SCC £15.53
Agency Commission: 10%
Mechanical Data: Col Length: 272mm, Film: Digital, Type Area: 272 x 180mm, Print Process: Sheet-fed offset litho, Bleed Size: 303 x 216mm, Trim Size: 297 x 210mm, Page Width: 180mm
Copy instructions: Copy Date: 1st of month prior to publication date
Average advertising content per issue: 5%
BUSINESS: OTHER CLASSIFICATIONS: Biology

BIOMEDICAL MATERIALS
40519U56R-20

Editorial Address: 9A Victoria Square, DROITWICH, WR9 8DE **Tel:** 0870 165 7211 **Fax:** 0870 165 7212
Email: editorial@intnews.com
Web site: http://www.performance-materials.com
ISSN: 0955-7717
Publisher: International Newsletters
Frequency: Monthly
Annual Sub.: £427.00
Usual Pagination: 12
Editor: Paula Read; **Circulation Manager:** Guy Kitteringham
Summary of Content: Newsletter about the latest developments in biomedical materials.
Readership/Target Audience: Read by design and production managers, technologists, R&D personnel, researchers and academics.
ADVERTISING: No Advertising taken
BUSINESS: HEALTH & MEDICAL: Health Medical Related

THE BIOMEDICAL SCIENTIST
39950U55-38

Editorial Address: Foxgloves, Sutton St. Nicholas, HEREFORD, HR1 3AY **Tel:** 01432 882077
Email: brnation@ukonline.co.uk
Advertising Address: Step House, North Farm Road, TUNBRIDGE WELLS, TN2 3DR **Tel:** 01892 518877
Fax: 01892 616177
Email: trevorsoutherden@stepex.com
ISSN: 1352-7673
Publisher: Step Publishing Ltd
Date Established: 1934
Frequency: Monthly
Free to qualifying individuals
Annual Sub.: £110.00
Circulation: 18,000 (Publisher's Statement)
Usual Pagination: 100
Editor: Brian Nation; **Publisher:** Trevor Moon
Summary of Content: Journal containing news on scientific and management subjects, including symposia reports.
Readership/Target Audience: Read by biomedical scientists and clinical scientists.
ADVERTISING RATES:
Full Page Colour £1545.00
Agency Commission: 10%
Mechanical Data: Type Area: 258 x 180mm, Bleed Size: 303 x 216mm, Trim Size: 297 x 210mm, Print Process: Web-fed offset litho, Film: Digital, Col Length: 258mm, Page Width: 180mm

Supplement(s): Pathology in Practice ~ 4xY
BUSINESS: APPLIED SCIENCE & LABORATORIES

BIOMETRIC TECHNOLOGY TODAY
35982U5A-40

Editorial Address: The Boulevard, Langford Lane, KIDLINGTON, OX5 1GB **Tel:** 029 2056 0458
Email: m.lockie@btopenworld.com
Web site: http://www.compseconline.com
ISSN: 0969-4765
Publisher: Elsevier Ltd
Date Established: 1993
Frequency: 10 issues yearly
Annual Sub.: EUR748.00
Usual Pagination: 12
Editor: Mark Lockie; **Publisher:** Steve Barrett
Summary of Content: Journal covering automatic personal identification and verification technologies.
Readership/Target Audience: Aimed at governments, retailers and those involved in the transport industry and financial sector. Also healthcare providers, computer manufacturers and systems integrators.
ADVERTISING: No Advertising taken
BUSINESS: COMPUTERS & AUTOMATION: Automation & Instrumentation

BIOMETRIKA
40038U55-38_20

Editorial Address: Great Clarendon Street, OXFORD, OX2 6DP **Tel:** 01865 353907 **Fax:** 01865 353485
Email: biometrika@epfl.ch
Web site: http://biomet.oupjournals.org
ISSN: 0006-3444
Publisher: OUP
Date Established: 1901
Frequency: Quarterly
Cover Price: £10.00
Annual Sub.: £33.00
Usual Pagination: 250
Editor: A. Davison
Summary of Content: Journal containing statistical theory and applications.
Readership/Target Audience: Aimed at academics and researchers concerned with applied mathematics, statistics and probability.
ADVERTISING: No Advertising taken
BUSINESS: APPLIED SCIENCE & LABORATORIES

BIOSCIENCE LAW REVIEW
623246U44-153

Editorial Address: Office G18, Spinners Court, 55 West End, WITNEY, OX28 1NH **Tel:** 01993 706183
Fax: 01993 709410
Email: bio@lawtext.com
Web site: http://www.lawtext.com
ISSN: 1365-8867
Publisher: Lawtext Publishing Ltd
Date Established: 1997
Frequency: 6 issues yearly
Annual Sub.: £290.00
Usual Pagination: 50
Editor: Nick Gingell; **Managing Editor:** Nick Gingell; **Publisher:** Nick Gingell
Summary of Content: Magazine containing legal analysis and news on legal developments in the field of bio-science.
Readership/Target Audience: Aimed at patent agents, patent attorneys and lawyers in private practice and in-house who advise bio-science industries.
ADVERTISING: No Advertising taken
BUSINESS: LEGAL

BIOSTATISTICS
601422U55-38_40

Editorial Address: Department of Mathematics and Statistics, Lancaster University, Bailrigg, LANCASTER, LA1 4YB **Tel:** 01524 593747 **Fax:** 01524 592681
Email: p.diggle@lancaster.ac.uk
Web site: http://biostatistics.oxfordjournals.org
ISSN: 1465-4644
Publisher: OUP
Date Established: 2000
Frequency: Quarterly
Cover Price: £38.00
Annual Sub.: £131.00
Usual Pagination: 164
Editor: Peter Diggle
Summary of Content: Journal publishing papers that develop and apply innovative statistical methods to problems of human health and disease including basic biomedical sciences. The focus is on methods and applications.
Readership/Target Audience: Aimed at academics and researchers in biostatistics.
ADVERTISING: No Advertising taken
BUSINESS: APPLIED SCIENCE & LABORATORIES

BIOTECH INTERNATIONAL

39952U55-38_50

Editorial Address: 2 Claridge Court, Lower Kings Road, BERKHAMSTED, HP4 2AF **Tel:** 01442 877777
Fax: 01442 870617
Email: bobw@lansdowne-media.co.uk
Advertising Address: As above.
Email: bobw@lansdowne-media.co.uk
Web site: http://www.labint-online.com
Frequency: 6 issues yearly
Cover Price: Free
Circulation: 24,000 (Publisher's Statement)
Usual Pagination: 36
Editor: Bob Warren; **Advertising Manager:** Bob Warren; **Publisher:** Bernard Leger
Summary of Content: Publication covering all aspects of technology from life science research to industrial biology and in particular bioprocessing equipment.
Readership/Target Audience: Aimed at the entrepreneurial life science and academic research sectors.
ADVERTISING RATES:
Full Page Mono EUR5500.00
Full Page Colour EUR7500.00
Agency Commission: 15%
Mechanical Data: Type Area: 254 x 182mm, Col Length: 254mm, Page Width: 182mm, Bleed Size: 288 x 222mm, Film: Digital
Average advertising content per issue: 60%
BUSINESS: APPLIED SCIENCE & LABORATORIES

BIOTECHNOLOGY AND APPLIED BIOCHEMISTRY

40123U55-39

Editorial Address: Third Floor, Eagle House, 16 Procter Street, LONDON, WC1V 6NX **Tel:** 020 7828 4110
Fax: 020 7280 4169
Email: editorial@portlandpress.com
Web site: http://www.babonline.org
ISSN: 0885-4513
Publisher: Portland Press Ltd
Frequency: Monthly
Free to qualifying individuals
Annual Sub.: £279.00
Usual Pagination: 72
Editor: Stuart Hobday; **Executive Editor:** Stuart Hobday
Summary of Content: Journal of new technologies for the processing of natural and recombinant biological molecules, novel expression systems, new cell-culture and fermentation methods, healthcare contributions related to the commercialisation of novel medicines, process engineering aspects of new therapeutic proteins, antibodies and genes, tissue engineering, stem-cell and cell therapeutics and nanotechnology.
Readership/Target Audience: Aimed at biotechnologists.
ADVERTISING: No Advertising taken
BUSINESS: APPLIED SCIENCE & LABORATORIES

BIOTECHNOLOGY & GENETIC ENGINEERING REVIEWS

41499U64F-12

Editorial Address: Manor Farm, Church Lane, Thrumpton, NOTTINGHAM, NG11 0AX **Tel:** 0115 951 6149
Fax: 0115 951 6142
Email: steve.harding@hottingham.ac.uk
Web site: http://www.nottingham.ac.uk/ncmh
ISSN: 0264-8725
Publisher: Nottingham University Press
Date Established: 1984
Frequency: Annual
Annual Sub.: £75.00
Circulation: 300 (Publisher's Statement)
Usual Pagination: 400
Editor: S. Harding
Summary of Content: Contains important developments in industrial, agricultural and medical applications of biotechnology, with particular emphasis on the genetic manipulation of the organisms concerned.
Readership/Target Audience: Aimed at postgraduate students and researchers.
ADVERTISING: No Advertising taken
BUSINESS: OTHER CLASSIFICATIONS: Biology

BIRMINGHAM LAW SOCIETY BULLETIN

39124U44-155

Editorial Address: 8 Temple Street, BIRMINGHAM, B2 5BT
Tel: 0121 643 9116 **Fax:** 0121 633 3507
Email: becky@birminghamlawsociety.co.uk
Advertising Address: 2nd Floor, Richardson House, 21-24 New Street, WORCESTER, WR1 2DP **Tel:** 01905 723011
Email: ali@pw-media.co.uk
Web site: http://www.birminghamlawsociety.co.uk
Publisher: PW Media & Publishing Ltd
Date Established: 1980
Frequency: 10 issues yearly
Free to qualifying individuals
Annual Sub.: £200.00
Circulation: 3,500 (Publisher's Statement)
Usual Pagination: 28

Editor: Veronica Dean; **Advertising Manager:** Alison Jones; **Publisher:** Dawn Pardoe
Summary of Content: Journal of the Birmingham Law Society containing news and features relating to the legal profession and the law.
Readership/Target Audience: Aimed at law professionals.
ADVERTISING RATES:
Full Page Colour £1300.00
Agency Commission: 10%
Mechanical Data: Type Area: 277 x 190mm, Film: Digital, Bleed Size: 303 x 216mm, Trim Size: 297 x 210mm, Col Length: 277mm, Page Width: 190mm
Copy instructions: Copy Date: 2 weeks prior to publication date
Average advertising content per issue: 40%
BUSINESS: LEGAL

BISCUIT WORLD

36462U8B-20

Editorial Address: 1st Floor Offices, 1-3 Station Road East, OXTED, RH8 0BD **Tel:** 01883 734582 **Fax:** 01883 713640
Email: joyce@crier.co.uk
Advertising Address: As above.
Email: nthorp@crier.co.uk
Web site: http://www.biscuitonline.com
ISSN: 1462-7302
Publisher: Crier Media Group
Date Established: 1998
Frequency: Quarterly - Published on the 1st of the cover months
Annual Sub.: £55.00
Circulation: 4,317 (Publisher's Statement)
Usual Pagination: 52
Editor: Evie Serventi; **Publisher:** John Whitbread
Summary of Content: Magazine covering world news and market trends in biscuit manufacturing. Features include technical and scientific reports, product reviews and ingredients.
Readership/Target Audience: Aimed at biscuit producers, producers of ingredients and those involved in the process of biscuit manufacturing.
ADVERTISING RATES:
Full Page Colour EUR3000.00
Mechanical Data: Type Area: 270 x 186mm, Col Length: 270mm, Page Width: 186mm, Film: Digital, Trim Size: 297 x 210mm, Bleed Size: 306 x 216mm
Copy instructions: Copy Date: 4 weeks prior to publication date
Average advertising content per issue: 25%
BUSINESS: BAKING & CONFECTIONERY: Confectionery Manufacturing

BJA: BRITISH JOURNAL OF ANAESTHESIA

601423U56A-29

Editorial Address: Academic Anaesthesia Unit, Floor K, Royal Hallamshire Hospital, Glossop Road, SHEFFIELD, S10 2JF **Tel:** 0114 226 1087 **Fax:** 0114 226 1462
Email: bja@sheffield.ac.uk
Advertising Address: Oxford University Press, Great Clarendon Street, OXFORD, OX2 6DP **Tel:** 01865 354637
Fax: 01865 353774
Email: steve.simmonds@oxfordjournals.org
Web site: http://www.oup.co.uk/jnls
ISSN: 0007-0912
Publisher: OUP
Date Established: 1923
Frequency: Monthly
Annual Sub.: £230.00
Usual Pagination: 150
Editor: Charles Reilly
Summary of Content: Journal of the College of Anaesthetists.
Readership/Target Audience: Aimed at 8000 members and fellows of the College of Anaesthetists, plus non-member subscribers.
ADVERTISING RATES:
Full Page Mono £742.00
Full Page Colour £1236.00
Agency Commission: 10%
Mechanical Data: Page Width: 178mm, Type Area: 255 x 178mm, Col Length: 255mm, Trim Size: 280 x 216mm, Bleed Size: 286 x 222mm, Print Process: Litho, Screen: 54 lpc, Film: Positive, right reading, emulsion side down. Digital
Copy instructions: Copy Date: 5 weeks prior to publication date
BUSINESS: HEALTH & MEDICAL

BKU MAGAZINE

22850U23C-7

Formerly: Bathroom & Kitchen Update
Editorial Address: 15A London Road, MAIDSTONE, ME16 8LY **Tel:** 01622 687031 **Fax:** 01622 757646
Email: bathroom@datateam.co.uk
Advertising Address: As above.
Email: bathroom@datateam.co.uk
Web site: http://www.bathroomandkitchenupdate.com
ISSN: 1475-6919
Publisher: Datateam Publishing Ltd
Date Established: 1997

Frequency: Monthly - Published in the 1st week of the cover month
Cover Price: Free
Circulation: 4,554 (ABC 01/01/2008 to 31/12/2008)
Usual Pagination: 52
Editor: Jacqui Hunter; **Advertising Manager:** Roz Rustell
Summary of Content: Magazine covering information and articles on different products within the kitchen and bathroom.
Readership/Target Audience: Aimed at independent and multiple retailers, property developers and merchants.
ADVERTISING RATES:
Full Page Mono £1122.00
Full Page Colour £1782.00
SCC £15.00
Agency Commission: 10%
Mechanical Data: Type Area: 275 x 195mm, Print Process: Sheet-fed offset litho, Bleed Size: 312 x 235mm, Trim Size: 306 x 229mm, Film: Digital, Col Length: 275mm, Page Width: 195mm
Copy instructions: Copy Date: 15th of the month prior to publication date
Average advertising content per issue: 40%
BUSINESS: FURNISHINGS & FURNITURE: Furnishings & Furniture - Kitchens & Bathrooms

BLINDS & SHUTTERS

35953U4R-300

Editorial Address: 173 High Street, RICKMANSWORTH, WD3 1AY **Tel:** 01923 692671 **Fax:** 01923 692679
Email: m.downs@turretgroup.com
Advertising Address: As above. **Tel:** 01923 692660
Email: j.sardakis@turretgroup.com
Web site: http://www.blindsmagazine.co.uk
ISSN: 0305-733X
Publisher: Turret Group Ltd.
Date Established: 1957
Frequency: Quarterly - Published on the 10th of the cover month
Free to qualifying individuals
Annual Sub.: £49.00
Circulation: 5,624 (ABC 01/07/2008 to 30/06/2009)
Usual Pagination: 100
Editor: Matthew Downs; **Advertising Manager:** Julie Saridakis; **Publisher:** Sarah Williams
Summary of Content: Magazine containing news and views on the latest blinds, awnings and shutters and their many applications.
Readership/Target Audience: Aimed at architects, specifiers, construction companies, facilities managers, designers, retailers, fitters, contractors and manufacturers.
ADVERTISING RATES:
Full Page Colour £930.00
Agency Commission: 10%
Mechanical Data: Type Area: 254 x 178mm, Trim Size: 297 x 210mm, Bleed Size: 303 x 216mm, Col Length: 254mm, Page Width: 178mm, Film: Digital
Copy instructions: Copy Date: 2 weeks prior to publication date
Average advertising content per issue: 60%
BUSINESS: ARCHITECTURE & BUILDING: Building Related

BLOOD PRESSURE MONITORING

40239U56A-51_30

Editorial Address: 250 Waterloo Road, LONDON, SE1 8RD
Tel: 020 7981 0676 **Fax:** 020 7981 0556
Email: magda.lewandowska@wolterskluwer.com
Advertising Address: The Point of Difference, 4 Chase Side Avenue, LONDON, SW20 8LU **Tel:** 020 8542 3200
Fax: 020 8543 3810
Email: pointofdiff@btinternet.com
Web site: http://www.bpmonitoring.com
ISSN: 1359-5237
Publisher: Lippincott Williams & Wilkins
Frequency: 6 issues yearly
Annual Sub.: £342.00
Circulation: 94 (Publisher's Statement)
Usual Pagination: 64
Editor: William White; **Editor-in-Chief:** William White; **Advertising Manager:** Dick Bower
Summary of Content: Journal containing material covering all aspects of manual, automated and ambulatory monitoring of blood pressure and its variability including device technology and assessment, blood pressure variability, clinical pharmacology and therapeutics, clinical practice and epidemiology.
Readership/Target Audience: Specialists involved in all aspects of blood pressure measurement and variability.
ADVERTISING RATES:
Full Page Mono $765.00
Full Page Colour $1645.00
Agency Commission: 15%
Mechanical Data: Trim Size: 276 x 207mm, Type Area: 254 x 178mm, Bleed Size: 282 x 213mm, Film: Positve, right reading, emulsion side down. Digital, Col Length: 254mm, Page Width: 178mm
Copy instructions: Copy Date: 6 weeks prior to publication date

Average advertising content per issue: 5%
BUSINESS: HEALTH & MEDICAL

BLOW
1685479U47A-579

Formerly: Super Blow
Editorial Address: 29-35 Rathbone Street, LONDON, W1T
1NJ **Tel:** 020 7436 9449 **Fax:** 020 7436 7027
Email: info@blow.co.uk
Advertising Address: As above.
Email: michael@blow.co.uk
Web site: http://www.blow.co.uk
Publisher: Blow
Date Established: 1993
Frequency: Half-yearly - Published in February and October
Cover Price: Free
Circulation: 7,500 (Publisher's Statement)
Editor: Michael Oliveira-Salac
Summary of Content: Magazine covering profiles of new
designers and their collections. Also covers exhibitions,
fashion shows and parties.
Readership/Target Audience: Aimed at fashion industry
buyers.
ADVERTISING: Rates on application
BUSINESS: CLOTHING & TEXTILES

BLUEPRINT
37145U4A-322

Editorial Address: Boundary House, 91-93 Charterhouse
Street, LONDON, EC1M 6HR **Tel:** 020 7336 5200
Email: pkelly@blueprintmagazine.co.uk
Advertising Address: As above. **Fax:** 020 7336 5201
Email: jmaughan@wilmington.co.uk
Web site: http://www.blueprintmagazine.co.uk
ISSN: 0268-4926
Publisher: Progressive Media Publications
Date Established: 1983
Frequency: Monthly
Cover Price: £4.75
Circulation: 6,233 (ABC 01/07/2008 to 30/06/2009)
Usual Pagination: 116
Editor: Peter Kelly
Summary of Content: Magazine for leading architects and
designers.
Readership/Target Audience: Read by architects, interior
designers and those with a strong interest in design.
ADVERTISING RATES:
Full Page Colour £2453.00
Agency Commission: 10%
Mechanical Data: Type Area: 302 x 220mm, Bleed Size:
334 x 254mm, Trim Size: 328 x 248mm, Col Length: 302mm,
Page Width: 220mm, Film: Digital
Average advertising content per issue: 40%
BUSINESS: ARCHITECTURE & BUILDING: Architecture

BLUEPRINT
1700488U54R-334

Editorial Address: 4th Floor, Orleans House, Edmund
Street, LIVERPOOL, L3 9NG **Tel:** 0151 236 4141
Fax: 0151 236 0440
Email: blueprint@benhampublishing.com
Advertising Address: As above.
Email: blueprint@benhampublishing.com
Web site: http://www.benhampublishing.com/magazines.
htm
Publisher: Benham Publishing Limited
Date Established: 2003
Frequency: Quarterly
Free to qualifying individuals
Circulation: 2,500 (Publisher's Statement)
Usual Pagination: 60
Editor: Ian Fletcher; **Managing Director:** Ian Fletcher;
Advertising Manager: Ian Fletcher
Summary of Content: Magazine covering emergency
planning, crisis management and disaster response.
Readership/Target Audience: Aimed at local government,
national government, heavy industry, utilities, emergency
services, volunteers organisations, disaster response
charities, educational establishments, the legal profession
and independent consultants.
ADVERTISING RATES:
Full Page Mono £1300.00
Full Page Colour £1500.00
BUSINESS: SAFETY & SECURITY: Safety Related

BMA NEWS
40142U56A-30_120

Editorial Address: BMA House, Tavistock Square,
LONDON, WC1H 9JP **Tel:** 020 7383 6122
Fax: 020 7383 6566
Email: bmanews@bma.org.uk
Advertising Address: As above. **Tel:** 020 7383 6181
Fax: 020 7383 6556
Email: bmanews@bma.org.uk
Web site: http://www.bma.org.uk
Publisher: British Medical Association
Date Established: 2001
Frequency: Weekly

Free to qualifying individuals
Annual Sub.: £82.00
Circulation: 100,000 (Publisher's Statement)
Usual Pagination: 16
Editor: Lisa Pritchard; **News Editor:** Lisa Pritchard
Summary of Content: Magazine containing news about the
British Medical Association, NHS news, medical politics,
features and analysis.
Readership/Target Audience: Read by members of the
British Medical Association.
ADVERTISING RATES:
Full Page Mono £3045.00
Full Page Colour £4860.00
Mechanical Data: Bleed Size: 393 x 286mm, Print Process:
Web-fed offset litho, Film: Digital, Trim Size: 387 x 280mm
Copy instructions: Copy Date: 10 days prior to publication
date
Supplement to: BMJ British Medical Journal
BUSINESS: HEALTH & MEDICAL

BMJ BRITISH MEDICAL JOURNAL
40143U56A-50

Editorial Address: BMA House, Tavistock Square,
LONDON, WC1H 9JR **Tel:** 020 7387 4499
Fax: 020 7383 6418
Email: editor@bmj.com
Advertising Address: As above. **Fax:** 020 7383 6556
Email: displaysales@bmj.com
Web site: http://www.bmj.com
Publisher: British Medical Association
Date Established: 1840
Frequency: Weekly
Annual Sub.: £167.00
Circulation: 122,239 (ABC 01/07/2006 to 30/06/2007)
Usual Pagination: 88
Editor: Annabel Ferriman; **News Editor:** Annabel Ferriman
Summary of Content: Journal of the British Medical
Association.
Twitter: http://twitter.com/bmj_latest.
Readership/Target Audience: Read by general
practitioners and hospital doctors.
ADVERTISING: Rates on application
Copy instructions: Copy Date: 12 days prior to publication
date
Editions:
BMJ Clinical Research
BMJ Compact
BMJ General Practice
BMJ International
Supplement(s): BMA News - 51xY, BMJ Careers - 51xY
BUSINESS: HEALTH & MEDICAL

BMJ BUILDERS MERCHANTS JOURNAL
35882U4E-40

Editorial Address: Faversham House, 232A Addington
Road, SOUTH CROYDON, CR2 8LE **Tel:** 020 8651 7100
Fax: 020 8651 7117
Email: fiona.russellhorne@fav-house.com
Advertising Address: As above. **Tel:** 020 8651 7152
Email: george.gash@fav-house.com
Web site: http://www.buildersmerchantsjournal.net
ISSN: 0268-1423
Publisher: Faversham House Group Ltd
Date Established: 1920
Frequency: Monthly - Published in the 2nd week of the
cover month
Free to qualifying individuals
Annual Sub.: £85.00
Circulation: 7,455 (ABC 01/07/2008 to 30/06/2009)
Usual Pagination: 60
Editor: Fiona Russell Horne; **Advertising Manager:** George
Gash; **Publisher:** Colin Petty
Summary of Content: Magazine containing news and
features on new products in the building materials supply
industry.
Readership/Target Audience: Read by senior management
working within the building materials supply industry.
ADVERTISING RATES:
Full Page Colour £2150.00
SCC £39.00
Agency Commission: 10%
Mechanical Data: Type Area: 254 x 178mm, Col Length:
254mm, Page Width: 178mm, Trim Size: 297 x 210mm,
Bleed Size: 303 x 213mm, Print Process: Sheet-fed offset
litho, Film: Digital, Col Widths (Display): 42mm, No. of
Columns (Display): 4
Copy instructions: Copy Date: 15th of the month prior to
publication date
Average advertising content per issue: 55%
Supplement(s): Official Guide to the Industry Conference -
1xY, Official Report to the Industry Conference - 1xY,
Trailblazers - 1xY
BUSINESS: ARCHITECTURE & BUILDING: Building

BOARD CONVERTING NEWS INTERNATIONAL
38706U36-1_50

Editorial Address: 1 Salisbury Office Park, London Road,
SALISBURY, SP1 3HP **Tel:** 01722 337038
Email: publications@brunton.co.uk
Advertising Address: As above.
Email: publications@brunton.co.uk
Web site: http://www.brunton.co.uk
Publisher: Brunton Business Publications Ltd
Frequency: 26 issues yearly
Annual Sub.: £60.00
Circulation: 7,250 (Publisher's Statement)
Usual Pagination: 20
Editor: Dan Brunton; **Managing Director:** Michael Brunton;
Advertising Manager: Michael Brunton; **Publisher:** Michael
Brunton
Summary of Content: News sheet for the corrugated and
carton industry.
Readership/Target Audience: Read by plant managers and
production managers.
ADVERTISING RATES:
Full Page Colour £795.00
Agency Commission: 10%
Mechanical Data: Type Area: 247 x 183mm, Col Length:
247mm, Page Width: 183mm, Bleed Size: 281 x 202mm,
Trim Size: 275 x 197mm, Film: Digital
Copy instructions: Copy Date: 10 days prior to publication
date
BUSINESS: PAPER

BOARD MARKET DIGEST
38707U36-1_75

Editorial Address: PO Box 2002, WATFORD, WD25 9ZT
Tel: 01923 894777 **Fax:** 01923 894888
Email: enquiries@pplresearch.co.uk
ISSN: 1358-0671
Publisher: PPL Research Ltd
Date Established: 1986
Frequency: Monthly
Annual Sub.: £330.00
Circulation: 400 (Publisher's Statement)
Usual Pagination: 12
Editor: Lawrence Turk; **Managing Director:** Lawrence Turk;
Publisher: Lawrence Turk; **Circulation Manager:** Anne
Lovelock
Summary of Content: Market data and analyses on the
packaging paper and board market.
Readership/Target Audience: Aimed at professional
buyers and suppliers of packaging papers and boards.
ADVERTISING: No Advertising taken
BUSINESS: PAPER

BOARDING SCHOOL
41099U62E-50

Editorial Address: Grosvenor Gardens House, 35-37
Grosvenor Gardens, LONDON, SW1W 0BS
Tel: 020 7798 1580 **Fax:** 020 7798 1581
Email: bsa@boarding.org.uk
Advertising Address: 12 Deben Mill Business Centre,
Melton, WOODBRIDGE, IP12 1BL **Tel:** 01394 389850
Fax: 01394 386893
Email: enquiries@johncatt.co.uk
Web site: http://www.boarding.org.uk
Publisher: John Catt Educational Ltd
Date Established: 1986
Frequency: Half-yearly - Published in May and November
Cover Price: £2.00
Free to qualifying individuals
Circulation: 3,000 (Publisher's Statement)
Usual Pagination: 48
Editor: Richard Davison
Summary of Content: Magazine publishing articles on
boarding and education and reports on developments in
boarding schools.
Readership/Target Audience: Read by head teachers,
bursars, teachers, pastoral staff and politicians. Sent to
members and associate members as one of the services
provided by the association.
ADVERTISING RATES:
Full Page Colour £1820.00
Agency Commission: 10%
Mechanical Data: Trim Size: 297 x 210mm, Film: Digital
Copy instructions: Copy Date: 4 weeks prior to publication
date
Average advertising content per issue: 25%
BUSINESS: CHURCH & SCHOOL EQUIPMENT &
EDUCATION: Preparatory & Independent Schools

BOARDROOM EDGE
1827783U14R-511

Editorial Address: PR by email only
Email: thollydavis@gmail.com
Advertising Address: The Coach House, Knowle Hill,
EVESHAM, WR11 7EN **Tel:** 07776 206077
Email: rich@boardroomedge.com
Web site: http://www.boardroomedge.com
Publisher: Boardroom Edge LLP
Date Established: 2007
Frequency: 6 issues yearly

Business Magazines

Cover Price: Free
Circulation: 8,000 (Print Run)
Editor: Tricia Holly Davis; Advertising Manager: Richard Roe
Summary of Content: Magazine covering the boardroom issues of working with a new energy, environment and ethics agenda whilst sustaining and growing profitability.
Readership/Target Audience: Aimed at boardroom executives in UK companies and organisations.
ADVERTISING RATES:
Full Page Colour £5250.00
Agency Commission: 10%
Mechanical Data: Bleed Size: 303 x 216mm, Trim Size: 297 x 210mm, Film: Digital
Copy instructions: Copy Date: 3 weeks prior to publication date
Average advertising content per issue: 20%
BUSINESS: COMMERCE, INDUSTRY & MANAGEMENT: Commerce Related

BOATING BUSINESS
39420U45E-30
Editorial Address: The Old Mill, Lower Quay, FAREHAM, PO16 0RA Tel: 01892 545696 Fax: 01329 825330
Email: pnash@boatingbusiness.com
Advertising Address: As above. Tel: 01329 820477
Email: lcurtis@boatingbusiness.com
Web site: http://www.boatingbusiness.com
Publisher: Mercator Media Ltd
Date Established: 1983
Frequency: Monthly - Published on the 1st Wednesday of the cover month
Free to qualifying individuals
Annual Sub.: £63.00
Circulation: 6,000 (Publisher's Statement)
Usual Pagination: 28
Editor: Peter Nash; Advertising Manager: Lorraine Curtis
Summary of Content: Magazine covering news, features, new products, personnel movements and developments within the British leisure marine industry.
Readership/Target Audience: Read by the boating and yachting trade.
ADVERTISING RATES:
Full Page Mono £1775.00
Full Page Colour £2345.00
Agency Commission: 10%
Mechanical Data: Col Length: 268mm, Col Widths (Display): 37mm, Film: Digital, No. of Columns (Display): 5, Type Area: 268 x 205mm, Print Process: Offset litho, Page Width: 205mm, Bleed Size: 298 x 231mm, Trim Size: 292 x 225mm
Copy instructions: Copy Date: 2 weeks prior to publication date
Average advertising content per issue: 20%
BUSINESS: MARINE & SHIPPING: Boat Trade

BODY & SOCIETY
48760U62R-471
Editorial Address: The Theory, Culture & Society Centre, Faculty of Humanities, The Nottingham Trent University, Clifton Lane, NOTTINGHAM, NG11 8NS Tel: 0115 848 6330
Fax: 0115 848 6331
Email: tcs@ntu.ac.uk
Advertising Address: 1 Oliver's Yard, 55 City Road, LONDON, EC1Y 1SP Tel: 020 7324 8500
Fax: 020 7324 8600
Email: advertising@sagepub.co.uk
Web site: http://www.sagepub.co.uk
ISSN: 1357-034X
Publisher: Sage Publications
Date Established: 1995
Frequency: Quarterly
Annual Sub.: £41.00
Circulation: 425 (Publisher's Statement)
Usual Pagination: 144
Editor: Mike Featherstone; Advertising Manager: Sheena Karim; Managing Editor: Tomoko Tamari
Summary of Content: Magazine containing information on the social and cultural analysis of the human body.
Readership/Target Audience: Aimed at those with an interest or working in the field of humanities.
ADVERTISING RATES:
Full Page Mono £500.00
Agency Commission: 5%
Mechanical Data: Film: Digital, Col Length: 205mm, Page Width: 130mm, Type Area: 205 X 130mm
Copy instructions: Copy Date: 12 weeks prior to publication date
BUSINESS: CHURCH & SCHOOL EQUIPMENT & EDUCATION: Education Related

BODY LANGUAGE
45411U56R-511
Formerly: Body Language Plastics & Cosmetic Surgery
Editorial Address: 69 Grand Parade, BRIGHTON, BN2 9TS
Tel: 01273 606799
Email: editorial@bodylanguage.net
Advertising Address: As above. Tel: 020 7514 5976
Email: ra@nmp-eu.com
Web site: http://www.bodylanguage.net
Publisher: Wigmore Medical Limited

Date Established: 1998
Frequency: 6 issues yearly
Cover Price: £7.00
Annual Sub.: £42.00
Circulation: 6,500 (Publisher's Statement)
Usual Pagination: 88
Editor: David Williams; Publisher: Bedo Eghiayan
Summary of Content: Magazine providing independent information on treatments and procedures within the cosmetic surgery sector.
Readership/Target Audience: Aimed at practitioners.
ADVERTISING RATES:
Full Page Colour £1995.00
Agency Commission: 10%
Mechanical Data: Film: Digital, Type Area: 260 x 184mm, Bleed Size: 303 x 216mm, Trim Size: 297 x 210mm, Col Length: 260mm, Page Width: 184mm
Copy instructions: Copy Date: 2 weeks prior to publication date
Average advertising content per issue: 40%
BUSINESS: HEALTH & MEDICAL: Health Medical Related

BODY MAGAZINE
38367U31R-20
Editorial Address: Belmont House, 102 Finkle Lane, Gildersome, LEEDS, LS27 7TW Tel: 0113 253 8333
Fax: 0113 238 1892
Email: body@vbra.co.uk
Advertising Address: As above.
Email: bev@vbra.co.uk
Web site: http://www.vbra.co.uk
ISSN: 0006-5501
Publisher: Vehicle Builders & Repairers Association
Date Established: 1919
Frequency: 10 issues yearly
Annual Sub.: £40.00
Circulation: 6,000 (Publisher's Statement)
Usual Pagination: 44
Editor: Judi Barton
Summary of Content: Journal of the Vehicle Builders and Repairers Association Ltd covering the automotive body repair industry and commercial vehicle body building industry. Features on new products and equipment, legislation, health and safety, environment, management and training.
Readership/Target Audience: Aimed at bodyshops, cv bodybuilders, training centres, insurance engineers, insurance companies and manufacturers, distributors and importers of vehicles and relevant equipment, products and services.
ADVERTISING RATES:
Full Page Mono £720.00
Full Page Colour £1300.00
SCC £18.00
Agency Commission: 10%
Mechanical Data: Trim Size: 297 x 210mm, Page Width: 190mm, Col Length: 273mm, Film: Digital, Bleed Size: 303 x 216mm, Type Area: 273 x 190mm
Average advertising content per issue: 35%
BUSINESS: MOTOR TRADE: Motor Trade Related

BODYSHOP BUYERS GUIDE
38338U31A-22
Editorial Address: The Firs, High Street, Whitchurch, AYLESBURY, HP22 4JU Tel: 01296 642800
Fax: 01296 640044
Advertising Address: As above.
Email: info@bodyshopmag.com
Web site: http://www.bodyshopmag.com
Publisher: Plenham Ltd
Date Established: 1990
Frequency: Annual - Published in December
Cover Price: Free
Circulation: 7,500 (Publisher's Statement)
Usual Pagination: 100
Editor: Amy Manson; Publisher: Christopher Mann
Summary of Content: Guide containing a directory of manufacturers, suppliers and distributors to the automotive refinish industry.
Readership/Target Audience: Aimed at key personnel of auto and commercial vehicle refinish industry establishments.
ADVERTISING RATES:
Full Page Mono £1425.00
Full Page Colour £2175.00
Agency Commission: 10%
Mechanical Data: Film: Positive, right reading, emulsion side down, Screen: Mono 60 lpc Colour 70 lpc, Print Process: Litho, Trim Size: 297 x 210mm, Bleed Size: 303 x 216mm, Col Length: 270mm, Col Widths (Display): 48mm, No. of Columns (Display): 4, Type Area: 270 x 190mm, Page Width: 190mm
Copy instructions: Copy Date: Late September prior to publication date
Average advertising content per issue: 70%
BUSINESS: MOTOR TRADE: Motor Trade Accessories

BODYSHOP MAGAZINE
38295U31A-30
Editorial Address: The Firs, High Street, Whitchurch, AYLESBURY, HP22 4JU Tel: 01296 642800
Fax: 01296 640044
Email: kelly@bodyshopmag.com
Advertising Address: As above.
Email: julie@bodyshopmag.com
Web site: http://www.bodyshopmag.com
ISSN: 1465-9514
Publisher: Plenham Ltd
Frequency: Monthly
Cover Price: £5.00
Free to qualifying individuals
Annual Sub.: £55.00
Circulation: 9,392 (ABC 01/07/2008 to 30/06/2009)
Usual Pagination: 68
Editor: Kelly Dalwood; Managing Director: David Young; Publisher: Christopher Mann
Summary of Content: Magazine covering both the car and commercial vehicle refinishing and crash repair market.
Readership/Target Audience: Read by proprietors, key personnel of body shops, factors and distributors, specialist bodybuilders, coachbuilders, product manufacturers, vehicle manufacturers and insurance companies.
ADVERTISING RATES:
Full Page Mono £1525.00
Full Page Colour £2275.00
Agency Commission: 10%
Mechanical Data: Type Area: 275 x 190mm, Col Length: 275mm, Col Widths (Display): 44mm, Film: Digital, No. of Columns (Display): 4, Bleed Size: 303 x 216mm, Trim Size: 297 x 210mm, Print Process: Litho, Page Width: 190mm
Average advertising content per issue: 50%
BUSINESS: MOTOR TRADE: Motor Trade Accessories

BOILING POINT
40791U58-211
Editorial Address: PO Box 900, BROMLEY, BR1 9FF
Tel: 020 7193 3699 Fax: 0870 137 2360
Email: boilingpoint@hedon.info
Web site: http://www.hedon.info
ISSN: 0263-3167
Publisher: Eco Ltd
Date Established: 1982
Frequency: Half-yearly
Cover Price: Free
Circulation: 2,000 (Publisher's Statement)
Usual Pagination: 40
Editor: Grant Ballard-Tremeer
Summary of Content: International journal dealing with all aspects of household energy in the developing world.
Language(s): English; French
Readership/Target Audience: Aimed at development practitioners.
ADVERTISING: No Advertising taken
BUSINESS: ENERGY, FUEL & NUCLEAR

THE BONDHOLDER
35225U1F-65
Editorial Address: Fitzroy House, 13-17 Epworth Street, LONDON, EC2A 4DL Tel: 020 7825 8100
Fax: 020 7608 2032
Email: enquiries@interactivedata.com
Advertising Address: As above.
Email: david.gilbert@interactivedata.com
ISSN: 0961-8171
Publisher: Interactive Data (Europe) Limited
Date Established: 1872
Frequency: Weekly
Annual Sub.: £3035.00
Editor: David Gilbert
Summary of Content: Magazine specialising in bonds, equities and securities.
Readership/Target Audience: Aimed at investment bankers.
ADVERTISING: Rates on application
Agency Commission: 10%
Copy instructions: Copy Date: Friday of the week prior to publication date
Average advertising content per issue: 10%
BUSINESS: FINANCE & ECONOMICS: Investment

BONE MARROW TRANSPLANTATION
24505U56A-51_35
Editorial Address: Haematology Department, Hammersmith Hospital, LONDON, W12 0NN Tel: 020 8383 3233
Fax: 020 8740 9679
Email: bmtran@imperial.ac.uk
Web site: http://www.naturesj.com/bmt
ISSN: 0268-3369
Publisher: Nature Publishing Group
Date Established: 1986
Frequency: 24 issues yearly
Annual Sub.: £421.00
Circulation: 2,000 (Publisher's Statement)
Usual Pagination: 90
Editor: Linda Casey; Editor-in-Chief: J.M. Goldman

Summary of Content: Journal focusing on aspects of clinical and basic haemopoietic stem cell transplantation.
Readership/Target Audience: Aimed at the medical profession.
ADVERTISING: No Advertising taken
BUSINESS: HEALTH & MEDICAL

THE BOOK COLLECTOR
40835U60A-12

Editorial Address: PO Box 12426, LONDON, W11 3GW
Tel: 020 7727 4340 **Fax:** 020 7792 3492
Email: editor@thebookcollector.co.uk
Advertising Address: 32 Swift Way, Thurlby, BOURNE, PE10 0QA **Tel:** 01778 338095 **Fax:** 01778 338096
Email: info@thebookcollector.co.uk
Web site: http://www.thebookcollector.co.uk
ISSN: 0006-7237
Publisher: The Collector Ltd
Date Established: 1952
Frequency: Quarterly
Annual Sub.: £42.00
Circulation: 1,400 (Publisher's Statement)
Editor: Nicolas Barker; **Advertising Manager:** Patricia Cooper
Summary of Content: Journal containing articles of interest to book collectors, booksellers and librarians, including sales, catalogues, exhibitions, publications, book reviews and current events.
Readership/Target Audience: Aimed at book collectors, bibliographers and university and public libraries in the UK and USA.
ADVERTISING RATES:
Full Page Mono £220.00
Agency Commission: 10%
Mechanical Data: Type Area: 164 x 101mm, Col Length: 164mm, Page Width: 101mm
Average advertising content per issue: 25%
BUSINESS: PUBLISHING: Publishing & Book Trade

BOOK PEOPLE
1898696U60A-66

Editorial Address: Queen Anne House, LUCTON, HR6 9PN
Tel: 0845 658 0068 **Fax:** 0845 658 0069
Email: paul@book-people.net
Web site: http://www.book-people.net
Publisher: Rigden Thorne
Frequency: Monthly
Annual Sub.: £18.00
Editor: Paul Thorne
Summary of Content: Magazine covering the world of publishing.
Readership/Target Audience: Aimed at the book and journal publishing community.
BUSINESS: PUBLISHING: Publishing & Book Trade

BOOK WORLD
40807U60A-26_50

Editorial Address: 2 Caversham Street, LONDON, SW3 4AH **Tel:** 020 7351 4995 **Fax:** 020 7351 4995
Email: leonard.holdsworth@btopenworld.com
Advertising Address: As above.
Email: leonard.holdsworth@btinternet.com
Publisher: Christchurch Publishers Ltd
Date Established: 1971
Frequency: Monthly
Cover Price: £2.50
Annual Sub.: £30.00
Circulation: 6,000 (Publisher's Statement)
Usual Pagination: 96
Editor: Leonard Holdsworth; **Advertising Manager:** Leonard Holdsworth; **Managing Editor:** Leonard Holdsworth
Summary of Content: Magazine containing book features and book reviews.
Readership/Target Audience: Read by serious book collectors, publishers, librarians and booksellers.
ADVERTISING RATES:
Full Page Mono £600.00
Full Page Colour £950.00
Agency Commission: 15%
Mechanical Data: Print Process: Web-fed offset litho, Film: Digital
Copy instructions: Copy Date: 4 weeks prior to publication date
Average advertising content per issue: 25%
BUSINESS: PUBLISHING: Publishing & Book Trade

THE BOOKPLATE JOURNAL
40837U60A-15_50

Editorial Address: 22 Broomy Hill, HEREFORD, HR4 0LH
Tel: 01432 352536
Email: editor@bookplatesociety.org
ISSN: 0264-3693
Publisher: The Bookplate Society
Date Established: 1983
Frequency: Half-yearly - Published in March and September
Annual Sub.: £30.00
Circulation: 300 (Publisher's Statement)
Usual Pagination: 72

Editor: Peter Youatt
Summary of Content: Journal about collectors, artists and designers of book plates; contains articles and reviews.
Readership/Target Audience: Aimed at bibliographers, librarians and collectors, artists and designers of book plates.
ADVERTISING: No Advertising taken
BUSINESS: PUBLISHING: Publishing & Book Trade

THE BOOKSELLER
40811U60A-25

Editorial Address: 5th Floor, Endeavour House, 189 Shaftesbury Avenue, LONDON, WC2H 8TJ
Tel: 020 7420 6006 **Fax:** 020 7420 6103
Email: philip.jones@bookseller.co.uk
Advertising Address: As above. **Tel:** 020 7420 6000
Fax: 020 7420 6102
Email: nicola.chin@bookseller.co.uk
Web site: http://www.thebookseller.com
ISSN: 0006-7539
Publisher: Nielsen Business Media
Date Established: 1858
Frequency: Weekly - Published on Friday
Cover Price: £4.40
Annual Sub.: £170.00
Circulation: 9,698 (Publisher's Statement)
Editor: Philip Jones; **News Editor:** Katie Coyne; **Features Editor:** Tom Tivnan; **Editor-in-Chief:** Neill Denny; **Managing Director:** Nigel Roby; **Managing Editor:** Philip Jones
Summary of Content: Magazine covering news and information on the book publishing trade.
Readership/Target Audience: Aimed at booksellers, librarians and publishers, reviewers, literary agents, authors and the media.
ADVERTISING RATES:
Full Page Colour £2382.00
Agency Commission: 10%
Mechanical Data: Trim Size: 297 x 224mm, Bleed Size: 303 x 230mm, Film: Digital
Copy instructions: Copy Date: 1 week prior to publication date
Average advertising content per issue: 50%
Supplement(s): Back to School Bookseller - 1xY, Buyers Guide - 2xY, Children's Bookseller - 2xY, Frankfurt Book Fair Preview - 1xY, Graphic Novels and Manga Supplement - 1xY, Independent Publishers Catalogue - 1xY, London Book Fair Preview - 1xY, Paperback Preview - 2xY, Travel Bookseller - 2xY
BUSINESS: PUBLISHING: Publishing & Book Trade

BOOKSELLING ESSENTIALS
40812U60A-26

Formerly: Bookselling
Editorial Address: 272 Vauxhall Bridge Road, LONDON, SW1V 1BA **Tel:** 020 7802 0802 **Fax:** 020 7802 0803
Email: meryl.halls@booksellers.org.uk
Web site: http://www.booksellers.org.uk
Publisher: The Booksellers Association of the UK & Ireland Ltd
Frequency: Quarterly
Free to qualifying individuals
Circulation: 3,800 (Publisher's Statement)
Usual Pagination: 4
Editor: Meryl Halls
Summary of Content: Official journal of the Booksellers Association. Gives news of the Association's services and activities and includes information about events and general developments in the book trade.
Readership/Target Audience: Aimed at those within the industry.
ADVERTISING: No Advertising taken
BUSINESS: PUBLISHING: Publishing & Book Trade

BPI
38785U38-5

Formerly: British Photographic Industry News
Editorial Address: PO Box 107, PETERBOROUGH, PE6 6AJ **Tel:** 01778 380835 **Fax:** 01778 380835
Email: lynne@bpinews.orangehome.co.uk
Advertising Address: The Mill, Bearwalden Business Park, Wendens Ambo, SAFFRON WALDEN, CB11 4GB
Tel: 01799 544200 **Fax:** 01799 544202
Email: sam.scott@archant.co.uk
Web site: http://www.archant.co.uk
Publisher: Archant Specialist Ltd (Saffron Walden)
Date Established: 1975
Frequency: Monthly - Published in the 1st week of the cover month
Cover Price: £2.50
Free to qualifying individuals
Annual Sub.: £30.00
Circulation: 4,233 (Publisher's Statement)
Usual Pagination: 24
Editor: Peter Corbett; **Advertising Director:** Sam Scott-Smith
Summary of Content: Magazine containing news, views and advice on the activities and products of the photographic trade.

Readership/Target Audience: Aimed at retailers, distributors and manufacturers of photographic products.
ADVERTISING RATES:
Full Page Mono £1420.00
Full Page Colour £1420.00
Agency Commission: 10%
Mechanical Data: Col Length: 277mm, Page Width: 190mm, Trim Size: 297 x 210mm, Bleed Size: 303 x 216mm, Type Area: 277 x 190mm, Film: Digital
Copy instructions: Copy Date: 2 weeks prior to publication date
Average advertising content per issue: 45%
BUSINESS: PHOTOGRAPHIC TRADE

BPW NEWS
36723U14A-15

Editorial Address: 74 Fairfield Rise, BILLERICAY, CM12 9NU **Tel:** 01225 837251
Email: hq@bpwuk.co.uk
Advertising Address: As above.
Web site: http://www.bpwuk.co.uk
Publisher: Business and Professional Women UK Ltd
Frequency: Quarterly
Annual Sub.: £20.00
Circulation: 1,000 (Publisher's Statement)
Usual Pagination: 8
Editor: Nikki Bennett Willetts
Summary of Content: Official magazine of Business and Professional Women UK Ltd. Contains information, news and features of interest to working women.
Readership/Target Audience: Aimed at business and professional women.
ADVERTISING: No Advertising taken
BUSINESS: COMMERCE, INDUSTRY & MANAGEMENT

BQ MAGAZINE
1896993U63-2

Editorial Address: Unit 10, Baird Close, Stephenson Industrial Estate, Washington, TYNE AND WEAR, NE37 3HL
Tel: 0191 419 3221
Email: editor@bq-magazine.co.uk
Web site: http://www.bq-magazine.co.uk
Publisher: Room 501 Publishing
Frequency: Quarterly
Cover Price: £2.95
Circulation: 10,000 (Publisher's Statement)
Editor: Brian Nicholls
Summary of Content: Magazine covering business and lifestyle in the North East.
Readership/Target Audience: Aimed at people living in the North East of England.
BUSINESS: REGIONAL BUSINESS

BRAIN
40116U55-40_60

Editorial Address: Level 5, Addenbrooke's Hospital, Hills Road, CAMBRIDGE, CB2 2QQ **Tel:** 01223 331141
Fax: 01223 767382
Email: brain@medschl.cam.ac.uk
Advertising Address: Oxford University Press, Great Clarendon Street, OXFORD, OX2 6DP **Tel:** 01865 353907
Fax: 01865 353485
Email: steve.simmonds@oxfordjournals.org
Web site: http://brain.oupjournals.org
ISSN: 0006-8950
Publisher: OUP
Date Established: 1877
Frequency: Monthly
Cover Price: £22.00
Annual Sub.: £215.00
Usual Pagination: 238
Editor: Alastair Compston; **Managing Editor:** Eleanor Riches
Summary of Content: Journal covering clinical neurology and related disciplines in the basic neurological sciences where relevant to clinical problems.
Readership/Target Audience: Aimed at academics and practitioners in their neurosciences.
ADVERTISING RATES:
Full Page Mono £742.00
Full Page Colour £1236.00
Agency Commission: 10%
Mechanical Data: Type Area: 255 x 178mm, Col Length: 255mm, Trim Size: 279 x 216mm, Bleed Size: 285 x 222mm, Film: Digital, Print Process: Litho, Page Width: 178mm
BUSINESS: APPLIED SCIENCE & LABORATORIES

BRAIN INJURY
40474U56L-6_20

Editorial Address: Telephone House, 69-77 Paul Street, LONDON, EC2A 4LQ **Tel:** 020 7017 5000
Fax: 020 7017 6955
Advertising Address: As above. **Tel:** 01235 828600
Fax: 01235 829000
Web site: http://www.informaworld.com/braininjury
ISSN: 0269-9052
Publisher: Informa Healthcare
Date Established: 1986
Frequency: 14 issues yearly

Business Magazines

Annual Sub.: £1390.00
Usual Pagination: 96
Editor: Sally Howells; **Advertising Manager:** Di Owen;
Managing Editor: Sally Howells
Summary of Content: Journal covering all aspects of brain injury from basic science, neurological techniques and outcomes to vocational aspects, with studies of rehabilitation and outcome of both patients and their families.
Readership/Target Audience: Aimed at basic scientists, neurosurgeons or rehabilitation specialists.
BUSINESS: HEALTH & MEDICAL: Disability & Rehabilitation

BRAND LABEL UK
1864572U53-710

Editorial Address: 7 Bay Hall, Willow Land, Birkby, HUDDERSFIELD, HD1 5EN **Tel:** 01484 321000
Fax: 01484 321001
Email: j.muff@brandlabeluk.co.uk
Advertising Address: As above.
Email: j.muff@brandlabeluk.co.uk
Web site: http://www.planet-group.net
Publisher: The Planet Group (UK) Ltd
Frequency: 6 issues yearly
Cover Price: £12.00
Annual Sub.: £48.00
Circulation: 5,000 (Publisher's Statement)
Editor: Jane Muff
Summary of Content: Magazine focusing on the brand label sector providing a comprehensive source of information for the industry.
Readership/Target Audience: Aimed at manufacturers, buyers, marketeers, technologists and category managers.
ADVERTISING RATES:
Full Page Colour £3995.00
BUSINESS: RETAILING & WHOLESALING

BRAND - THE JOURNAL OF BRAND PROTECTION
38711U36-2

Formerly: PPA - business intelligence for packagers
Editorial Address: Cleeve Road, LEATHERHEAD, KT22 7RU **Tel:** 01372 802000 **Fax:** 01372 802079
Email: publications@pira-international.com
Web site: http://www.intertechpira.com
ISSN: 1475-0929
Publisher: PIRA International
Date Established: 2001
Frequency: 10 issues yearly
Annual Sub.: £575.00
Usual Pagination: 48
Editor: Sara Ver-Bruggen; **Managing Director:** Dave Simmons; **Publisher:** Rav Lally
Summary of Content: Publication covering news and analysis of brand protection technologies and brand packaging technologies.
Readership/Target Audience: Aimed at senior and technical managers within the paper and packaging supply chain.
ADVERTISING: No Advertising taken
BUSINESS: PAPER

BRAZIL BUSINESS BRIEF
36924U14C-19

Editorial Address: 32 Green Street, LONDON, W1K 7AT
Tel: 020 7399 9281 **Fax:** 020 7499 0186
Email: brazilianchamber@brazilianchamber.org.uk
Advertising Address: As above. **Tel:** 020 7221 7179
Email: comersio@brazilianchamber.org.uk
Publisher: Brazilian Chamber of Commerce in Great Britain
Frequency: 5 issues yearly
Free to qualifying individuals
Circulation: 1,000 (Publisher's Statement)
Usual Pagination: 48
Editor: Patricia Bourne; **Advertising Manager:** Valentina Ravagni
Summary of Content: Magazine containing news from the Brazilian Chamber of Commerce in Great Britain, covering politics, business and investment issues.
Readership/Target Audience: Aimed at businessmen and investors. Distributed to members of the Brazilian Chamber of Commerce in Great Britain.
ADVERTISING: Rates on application
Average advertising content per issue: 20%
BUSINESS: COMMERCE, INDUSTRY & MANAGEMENT: International Commerce

BREAKTIME MAGAZINE
1642079U62A-513

Editorial Address: Breaktime House, 2 Glencoe Road, POOLE, BH12 2DW **Tel:** 01202 722458 **Fax:** 0871 218 0096
Email: breaktime@breaktimemagazine.co.uk
Web site: http://www.breaktimemagazine.co.uk
Publisher: Breaktime Magazines Ltd
Date Established: 2004
Frequency: 3 issues yearly - Published in January, late April/early May and September
Cover Price: £2.50

Free to qualifying individuals
Annual Sub.: £6.00
Circulation: 30,000 (Publisher's Statement)
Usual Pagination: 100
Editor: Lucy Richmond
Summary of Content: Magazine covering features and articles of interest to teaching professionals including educational resources, government initiatives, student careers, outdoor education, venues and attractions suitable for school visits and competitions for the class and teacher.
Readership/Target Audience: Aimed at teaching professionals, schools and LEAs in the UK.
BUSINESS: CHURCH & SCHOOL EQUIPMENT & EDUCATION: Education

THE BREWER & DISTILLER INTERNATIONAL
36505U9B-30

Formerly: The Brewer & Distiller
Editorial Address: 33 Clarges Street, LONDON, W1J 7EE
Tel: 020 7499 8144 **Fax:** 020 7499 1156
Email: editor@ibd.org.uk
Advertising Address: The Clockhouse Studio, Clock House Lane, Bramley, GUILDFORD, GU5 0AP **Tel:** 01483 893100
Fax: 01483 894500
Email: sally.carter@carlingpartnership.co.uk
Web site: http://www.ibd.org.uk
ISSN: 1753-2086
Publisher: The Institute of Brewing & Distilling
Date Established: 2000
Frequency: Monthly - Published around the 7th of the cover month
Free to qualifying individuals
Annual Sub.: £72.00
Circulation: 4,500 (Publisher's Statement)
Usual Pagination: 48
Editor: Roger Putman
Summary of Content: Journal containing scientific and technical articles about all aspects of the brewery, distilling and allied industries. Also contains a news section for industry announcements and new products.
Readership/Target Audience: Aimed at technical brewers, brewery production directors, plant managers, maltsters, chemists, engineers and beer service managers.
ADVERTISING RATES:
Full Page Mono £1100.00
Full Page Colour £1100.00
Agency Commission: 10%
Mechanical Data: Bleed Size: 303 x 216mm, Print Process: Offset litho, Film: Positive right reading emulsion side down. Digital, Trim Size: 297 x 210mm
BUSINESS: DRINKS & LICENSED TRADE: Brewing

BREWERS' GUARDIAN
36506U9B-32

Editorial Address: 3rd Floor, Alma House, Alma Road, REIGATE, RH2 0AX **Tel:** 01737 735018 **Fax:** 01737 735195
Email: larry@advantagepublishing.co.uk
Advertising Address: As above.
Email: kamini@advantagepublishing.co.uk
Web site: http://www.brewersguardian.com
ISSN: 0006-9728
Publisher: Advantage Publishing Ltd
Date Established: 1871
Frequency: 10 issues yearly - Published at the beginning of the cover month
Annual Sub.: £75.00
Circulation: 3,100 (Publisher's Statement)
Usual Pagination: 48
Editor: Larry Nelson; **Advertising Manager:** Kamini Dickie
Summary of Content: International journal featuring technological developments and market trends, giving an overview of the brewing industry. Each issue contains news and opinion pieces together with in-depth features for an objective overview of the industry today.
Readership/Target Audience: Read by brewery industry executives worldwide.
ADVERTISING RATES:
Full Page Mono £750.00
Full Page Colour £1200.00
Agency Commission: 10%
Mechanical Data: Type Area: 260 x 185mm, Bleed Size: 303 x 226mm, Trim Size: 297 x 210mm, No. of Columns (Display): 1, Col Length: 260mm, Page Width: 185mm, Film: Digital
Copy instructions: Copy Date: 2 weeks prior to publication date
Average advertising content per issue: 40%
BUSINESS: DRINKS & LICENSED TRADE: Brewing

BRIDAL BUYER
39480U47A-14

Editorial Address: 114 Cholmley Gardens, LONDON, NW6 1UP **Tel:** 020 7431 2259 **Fax:** 020 7431 7411
Email: bridalbuyer@rogolgoodkind.co.uk
Advertising Address: 1 Canada Square, 19th Floor, Canary Wharf, LONDON, E14 5AP **Tel:** 020 7772 8300
Fax: 020 7772 8332
Email: nardene.smith@oceanmedia.co.uk

Web site: http://www.bridalbuyer.com
Publisher: Ocean Media Group Ltd
Date Established: 1989
Frequency: 6 issues yearly
Free to qualifying individuals
Annual Sub.: £58.00
Circulation: 2,512 (Publisher's Statement)
Usual Pagination: 88
Editor: Susi Rogol; **Advertising Manager:** Nardene Smith
Summary of Content: Magazine focused on the UK bridalwear market including wedding dresses and groomswear, bridesmaids, mother of the bride, accessories and lingerie. Also contains merchandise information and solid business advice to retailers, including legal, financial and marketing.
Readership/Target Audience: Aimed at bridal retailers, suppliers and manufacturers.
ADVERTISING RATES:
Full Page Colour £2240.00
Agency Commission: 10%
Mechanical Data: Type Area: 336 x 243mm, Bleed Size: +6mm, Col Length: 336mm, Page Width: 243mm, Film: Digital
Copy instructions: Copy Date: 3 weeks prior to publication date
BUSINESS: CLOTHING & TEXTILES

BRIDGE DESIGN & ENGINEERING
38961U42A-6,_50

Editorial Address: 32 Vauxhall Bridge Road, LONDON, SW1V 2SS **Tel:** 020 7973 4697 **Fax:** 020 7973 4797
Email: h.russell@hgluk.com
Advertising Address: As above. **Tel:** 020 7973 4698
Email: l.bentley@hgluk.com
Web site: http://www.bridgeweb.com
ISSN: 1359-7493
Publisher: Hemming Group Ltd
Date Established: 1995
Frequency: Quarterly - Published at the end of the cover month
Cover Price: £27.00
Annual Sub.: £105.00
Circulation: 5,000 (Publisher's Statement)
Editor: Helena Russell; **Managing Director:** Graham Bond; **Publisher:** Graham Bond
Summary of Content: Magazine containing international coverage of the design, construction, maintenance and management of bridges, with technical articles from industry experts and site reports.
Readership/Target Audience: Aimed at designers, builders, architects and specialist manufacturers.
ADVERTISING RATES:
Full Page Colour £2480.00
Agency Commission: 10%
Mechanical Data: Bleed Size: 307 x 240mm, Trim Size: 297 x 230mm, Type Area: 262 x 202mm, Film: Positive, right reading, emulsion side down, Col Length: 262mm, Page Width: 202mm, No. of Columns (Display): 2
Copy instructions: Copy Date: 4 weeks prior to publication date
Average advertising content per issue: 40%
BUSINESS: CONSTRUCTION

BRIDGE FOR DESIGN
1859320U4B-192

Editorial Address: Unit 16, Millbrook Trading Estate, Sybron Way, CROWBOROUGH, TN6 3DZ **Tel:** 01732 461090
Email: vivien@bridge4design.com
Web site: http://www.bridge4design.com
Publisher: Bridge For Design
Date Established: 2003
Frequency: Quarterly
Cover Price: £3.50
Circulation: 35,000 (Publisher's Statement)
Editor: Vivien Brockwell
Summary of Content: Interior design magazine.
Readership/Target Audience: Aimed at interior designers, hotel specifiers and architects.
BUSINESS: ARCHITECTURE & BUILDING: Interior Design & Flooring

BRIGHT FUTURES
40980U62A-120

Formerly: Education Now
Editorial Address: Council House Extension, Margaret Street, BIRMINGHAM, B3 3BU **Tel:** 0121 675 2243
Fax: 0121 303 2387
Email: cypfcomms@birmingham.gov.uk
Advertising Address: As above. **Tel:** 0121 464 2387
Email: julie.hammonds@birmingham.gov.uk
Web site: http://www.birmingham.gov.uk/brighterfutures
Publisher: Birmingham City Council Children's Services
Frequency: 6 issues yearly
Free to qualifying individuals
Circulation: 6,000 (Publisher's Statement)
Usual Pagination: 28
Editor: Julie Hammonds; **Advertising Manager:** Julie Hammonds

Summary of Content: Bulletin covering all aspects of children's services in Birmingham, including good practice in schools and upcoming educational events.
Readership/Target Audience: Aimed at people interested in children's services in Birmingham. Distributed in schools, early years settings, children's homes and offices and other educational establishments in the area.
ADVERTISING RATES:
Full Page Colour £400.00
Mechanical Data: Film: Digital, Trim Size: 297 x 210mm
Copy instructions: Copy Date: 4 weeks prior to publication date
BUSINESS: CHURCH & SCHOOL EQUIPMENT & EDUCATION: Education

BRISTOL BRIEFING
1851573U44-3058
Editorial Address: The Law Library, Bristol Law Courts, Small Street, BRISTOL, BS1 1DA **Tel:** 01225 427791
Email: nigel@bud.uk.com
Web site: http://www.bristollawsociety.com
Publisher: Bud UK
Date Established: 2008
Frequency: 11 issues yearly - Combined issue July/August
Free to qualifying individuals
Circulation: 2,500 (Publisher's Statement)
Usual Pagination: 24
Editor: Anna Webb
Summary of Content: Member magazine for the Bristol Law Society featuring law society news, people profiles, CSR news, health and well-being, food and drink, jobs and courses and a social diary.
Readership/Target Audience: Aimed at members of the Bristol Law Society.
BUSINESS: LEGAL

BRITISH AIRWAYS NEWS
36425U6F-80
Editorial Address: Waterside (HCB3), PO Box 365, Harmondsworth, WEST DRAYTON, UB7 0GB
Tel: 020 8738 5100
Email: ian.lynch@ba.com
Advertising Address: Publicom Ltd, Battersea Studios, 80 Silverthorne Road, LONDON, SW8 3HE **Tel:** 020 7978 2544
Email: dsandells@publicon.uk.com
Web site: http://www.ba.com
Publisher: British Airways Communications Department
Frequency: Weekly
Free to qualifying individuals
Annual Sub.: £35.00
Circulation: 40,000 (Publisher's Statement)
Usual Pagination: 18
Editor: Ian Lynch; **Managing Editor:** Ian Lynch
Summary of Content: Publication covering news, events and all aspects of British Airways operations.
Readership/Target Audience: Read by the media, employees and retired staff of British Airways.
ADVERTISING RATES:
Full Page Mono £2500.00
Full Page Colour £2500.00
SCC £18.00
Agency Commission: 10%
Mechanical Data: Col Length: 370mm, Type Area: 370 x 274mm, Page Width: 274mm, Film: Digital
Copy instructions: Copy Date: Friday 1pm prior to publication date
Average advertising content per issue: 50%
BUSINESS: AVIATION & AERONAUTICS: Airlines

BRITISH AND IRISH ORTHOPTIC JOURNAL
40413U56E-110
Formerly: British Orthoptic Journal
Editorial Address: Tavistock House North, Tavistock Square, LONDON, WC1H 9HX **Tel:** 020 7387 7992
Fax: 020 7383 2584
Email: bios@orthoptics.org.uk
Advertising Address: As above.
Email: membership@orthoptics.org.uk
ISSN: 0068-2314
Publisher: British and Irish Orthoptic Society
Date Established: 1939
Frequency: Annual
Annual Sub.: £55.00
Circulation: 1,700 (Publisher's Statement)
Usual Pagination: 100
Editor: Sarah Shea
Summary of Content: Journal about orthoptics, binocular vision, ocular motility, paediatric ophthalmology, visual assessment in children and strabismus.
Readership/Target Audience: Aimed at orthoptists, paediatric ophthalmologists, researchers in vision and binocular vision.
ADVERTISING RATES:
Full Page Mono £700.00
Mechanical Data: Trim Size: 297 x 210mm, Type Area: 270 x 180mm, Col Length: 270mm, Page Width: 180mm, Film: Digital, Bleed Size: +3mm

Copy instructions: Copy Date: 31st March prior to publication date
BUSINESS: HEALTH & MEDICAL: Optics

BRITISH BAKER
36457U8A-70
Editorial Address: Broadfield Park, CRAWLEY, RH11 9RT
Tel: 01293 846593 **Fax:** 01293 846538
Email: bb@william-reed.co.uk
Advertising Address: As above. **Tel:** 01293 613400
Email: chris.duffett@william-reed.co.uk
Web site: http://www.bakerinfo.co.uk
ISSN: 0007-0300
Publisher: William Reed Business Media
Date Established: 1885
Frequency: 25 issues yearly
Cover Price: £2.75
Annual Sub.: £62.50
Circulation: 7,189 (ABC 01/01/2008 to 31/12/2008)
Usual Pagination: 44
Editor: Sylvia Macdonald; **Features Editor:** Andrew Williams
Summary of Content: Magazine which covers all aspects of the baking and snack food industry in the UK.
Readership/Target Audience: Read by plant bakers, supermarket in-store bakers, independent bakers and confectioners, manufacturers and suppliers of ingredients, plant and equipment and wholesale distributors.
ADVERTISING RATES:
Full Page Colour £1925.00
Agency Commission: 10%
Mechanical Data: Page Width: 145mm, Type Area: 220 x 145mm, Col Length: 220mm, Film: Digital, Bleed Size: 246 x 171mm, Trim Size: 240 x 165mm
Copy instructions: Copy Date: 1 week prior to publication date
Supplement(s): Bake-Off News - 2xY, Health and Special Diet - 1xY, Plant Baking - 1xY
BUSINESS: BAKING & CONFECTIONERY: Baking

BRITISH BUILDER & DEVELOPER
35886U4E-404
Editorial Address: 4th Floor, Geneva House, Park Road, PETERBOROUGH, PE1 2UX **Tel:** 01733 756555
Fax: 01733 760505
Email: bbd@onecoms.co.uk
Advertising Address: As above.
Email: stacey.kirton@onecoms.co.uk
Web site: http://www.onecoms.co.uk
Publisher: Media One Communications Ltd.
Frequency: Monthly - Published in the 3rd week of the month prior to cover month
Free to qualifying individuals
Circulation: 12,000 (Publisher's Statement)
Usual Pagination: 30
Editor: Karyn Reidy; **Publisher:** Robert Nisbet
Summary of Content: Magazine covering all aspects of building.
Readership/Target Audience: Aimed at builders, architects, property developers, builders merchants and larger suppliers of building materials.
ADVERTISING RATES:
Full Page Colour £565.00
Agency Commission: 10%
Mechanical Data: Type Area: 380 x 270mm, Col Length: 380mm, Film: Digital, Page Width: 270mm, Bleed Size: 426 x 303mm, Trim Size: 420 x 297mm
Copy instructions: Copy Date: 1 week prior to publication date
BUSINESS: ARCHITECTURE & BUILDING: Building

BRITISH COMMERCIAL AGENTS REVIEW
37228U14R-35
Editorial Address: 5A Cheltenham Mount, HARROGATE, HG1 1DW **Tel:** 01423 560608 **Fax:** 01423 561204
Email: info@agentsregister.com
Advertising Address: As above.
Email: info@agentsregister.com
Web site: http://www.agentsregister.com
Publisher: British Agents Register
Date Established: 1967
Frequency: Monthly
Annual Sub.: £45.00
Circulation: 4,000 (Publisher's Statement)
Usual Pagination: 12
Editor: Andrew Turner; **Advertising Manager:** Andrew Turner
Summary of Content: Journal promoting the services of manufacturers agents in the UK and providing a recruitment service for principals.
Readership/Target Audience: Aimed at commercial sales agents throughout the UK.
ADVERTISING RATES:
Full Page Mono £560.00
Agency Commission: 10%

Mechanical Data: Trim Size: 297 x 210mm, Page Width: 178mm, Film: Digital, Type Area: 266 x 178mm, Col Length: 266mm
Copy instructions: Copy Date: 22nd of month prior to publication date
Average advertising content per issue: 85%
BUSINESS: COMMERCE, INDUSTRY & MANAGEMENT: Commerce Related

BRITISH DAIRYING
37825U21C-150
Editorial Address: 12 Ashfield Road, CHORLEY, PR7 1LH
Tel: 01257 232694
Email: mike@dairyindustrynewsletter.co.uk
Advertising Address: 8 Oakhill Drive, WELWYN, AL6 9NW
Tel: 01438 716220 **Fax:** 01438 716230
Email: malcolm.bridges@btinternet.com
ISSN: 1356-1561
Publisher: WB Publishing Ltd
Frequency: Monthly
Cover Price: £4.20
Free to qualifying individuals
Annual Sub.: £50.00
Circulation: 16,847 (Publisher's Statement)
Usual Pagination: 46
Editor: Mike Green; **Publisher:** Malcolm Bridges
Summary of Content: Magazine covering news, independent business articles and technical information.
Readership/Target Audience: Aimed at dairy farmers.
ADVERTISING RATES:
Full Page Mono £1615.00
Full Page Colour £2403.00
SCC £16.50
Agency Commission: 10%
Mechanical Data: Film: Digital, No. of Columns (Display): 4, Col Length: 270mm, Type Area: 270 x 190mm, Bleed Size: 303 x 213mm, Trim Size: 297 x 210mm, Col Widths (Display): 44mm, Page Width: 190mm, Print Process: web-fed offset
Copy instructions: Copy Date: 1st of the cover month
Average advertising content per issue: 50%
BUSINESS: AGRICULTURE & FARMING: Dairy Farming

BRITISH DEALER NEWS
623987U31B-20
Editorial Address: Caddsdown Business Centre, Caddsdown Industrial Park, Clovelly Road, BIDEFORD, EX39 3DX **Tel:** 01237 422660 **Fax:** 01237 422661
Email: editorial@dealernews.co.uk
Advertising Address: As above.
Email: adsales@dealernews.co.uk
Web site: http://www.dealernewsonline.co.uk
Publisher: Mayo Media Ltd
Date Established: 2001
Frequency: Monthly
Cover Price: Free
Circulation: 9,818 (ABC 01/07/2008 to 30/06/2009)
Usual Pagination: 64
Editor: Rick Kemp; **Advertising Manager:** Paul Baggott
Summary of Content: Magazine focusing on the British motorcycle and scooter industry.
Readership/Target Audience: Aimed at dealers, importers, distributors, wholesalers, parts and accessory manufacturers.
ADVERTISING RATES:
Full Page Mono £1360.00
Full Page Colour £1360.00
Agency Commission: 10%
Mechanical Data: Bleed Size: 354 x 249mm, Film: Digital, Trim Size: 350 x 245mm
Copy instructions: Copy Date: 2 weeks prior to publication date
Average advertising content per issue: 60%
BUSINESS: MOTOR TRADE: Motorcycle Trade

THE BRITISH DENTAL NURSES' JOURNAL
40376U56D-27
Editorial Address: PO Box 4, Room 200, Hillhouse International Business Centre, THORNTON-CLEVELEYS, FY5 4QD **Tel:** 01253 338360
Email: editor@badn.org.uk
Advertising Address: Purple Media Solutions, 2nd Floor, 207-215 High Street, ORPINGTON, BR6 0PF
Tel: 01689 899177
Email: ed.hunt@purplems.com
Web site: http://www.badn.org.uk
ISSN: 1356-3807
Publisher: British Association of Dental Nurses
Date Established: 1947
Frequency: Quarterly
Free to qualifying individuals
Annual Sub.: £120.00
Circulation: 7,500 (Publisher's Statement)
Usual Pagination: 32
Editor: Pamela Swain
Summary of Content: Journal containing articles of interest to dental nurses and other members of the dental team.

Business Magazines

Readership/Target Audience: Aimed at all those working in the dental profession.
ADVERTISING RATES:
Full Page Colour £800.00
Mechanical Data: Bleed Size: 216 x 303mm, Trim Size: 190 x 277mm, Film: Digital
Copy instructions: Copy Date: 15th of the month prior to publication date
BUSINESS: HEALTH & MEDICAL: Dental

BRITISH FARMER AND GROWER
22601U21A-1102

Editorial Address: Stoneleigh Park, STONELEIGH, CV8 2TZ
Tel: 024 7685 8674 **Fax:** 024 7685 8651
Email: martin.stanhope@nfu.org.uk
Advertising Address: Agriculture House, North Gate, Uppingham, OAKHAM, LE15 9PL **Tel:** 01572 824600
Fax: 01572 824731
Email: david.leach-davies@associa.co.uk
Web site: http://www.nfuonline.com
Publisher: Associa Ltd
Date Established: 2002
Frequency: Monthly - Published last Friday of the month prior to cover month
Annual Sub.: £55.00
Circulation: 49,200 (ABC 01/01/2008 to 31/12/2008)
Usual Pagination: 68
Editor: Martin Stanhope
Summary of Content: Official magazine of the NFU, covering all aspects of farming and agriculture including legal, political and technical information.
Readership/Target Audience: Aimed at those within the farming and agricultural sector.
ADVERTISING RATES:
Full Page Mono £2040.00
Full Page Colour £2550.00
Agency Commission: 10%
Mechanical Data: Type Area: 263 x 182mm, Col Length: 263mm, Page Width: 182mm, Trim Size: 297 x 210mm, Film: Digital
Copy instructions: Copy Date: 4 weeks prior to publication date
Average advertising content per issue: 40%
BUSINESS: AGRICULTURE & FARMING

BRITISH FOOD JOURNAL
37998U22C-10

Editorial Address: Howard House, Wagon Lane, BINGLEY, BD16 1WA **Tel:** 01274 777700 **Fax:** 01274 785200
Email: cgriffith@uwic.ac.uk
Web site: http://www.emeraldinsight.com
ISSN: 0007-070X
Publisher: Emerald Group Publishing Ltd
Date Established: 1898
Frequency: 11 issues yearly
Annual Sub.: £5749.00
Usual Pagination: 70
Editor: Chris Griffith; **Publisher:** Kate Snowden
Summary of Content: Journal containing news on food quality, processing and manufacturing.
Readership/Target Audience: Aimed at academic researchers in the food area.
ADVERTISING: No Advertising taken
BUSINESS: FOOD: Food Processing & Packaging

BRITISH GOAT SOCIETY MONTHLY JOURNAL
37792U21A-130

Editorial Address: 34-36 Fore Street, Bovey Tracey, NEWTON ABBOT, TQ13 9AD **Tel:** 01626 833168
Email: secretary@allgoats.com
Advertising Address: As above. **Fax:** 01626 834536
Email: secretary@allgoats.com
ISSN: 0953-8070
Publisher: British Goat Society
Frequency: 11 issues yearly
Annual Sub.: £18.00
Circulation: 1,500 (Publisher's Statement)
Usual Pagination: 32
Editor: Sue Knowles; **Advertising Manager:** Sue Knowles
Summary of Content: Journal containing general news about the goat world, including show results and various reports.
Readership/Target Audience: Aimed at goat breeders and keepers.
ADVERTISING: Rates on application
Average advertising content per issue: 20%
BUSINESS: AGRICULTURE & FARMING

BRITISH GOAT SOCIETY YEAR BOOK
37853U21D-155

Editorial Address: 34-36 Fore Street, Bovey Tracey, NEWTON ABBOT, TQ13 9AD **Tel:** 01626 833168
Fax: 01626 834536
Email: secretary@allgoats.com
Advertising Address: As above.

Email: secretary@allgoats.com
Publisher: British Goat Society
Frequency: Annual - Published in March or April
Circulation: 3,000 (Publisher's Statement)
Editor: Sue Knowles; **Advertising Manager:** Sue Knowles
Summary of Content: Journal containing general topics of interest including breeding results, advertising, reports and general committee news.
Readership/Target Audience: Aimed at goat breeders and keepers.
ADVERTISING: Rates on application
BUSINESS: AGRICULTURE & FARMING: Livestock

BRITISH HOSPITALITY: TRENDS AND DEVELOPMENTS
1703359U11A-212

Formerly: BHA Trends and Statistics
Editorial Address: PO Box 2513, Farnham Royal, SLOUGH, SL2 3WZ **Tel:** 01753 645636 **Fax:** 01753 669402
Email: mq@wordsmith-and-co.demon.co.uk
ISSN: 1465-2854
Publisher: British Hospitality Association
Date Established: 1997
Frequency: Annual - Published in October
Free to qualifying individuals
Annual Sub.: £250.00
Circulation: 1,250 (Publisher's Statement)
Usual Pagination: 88
Editor: Miles Quest
Summary of Content: Magazine featuring UK tourism statistics, hotel openings, hotel sales and purchases, hotel and catering operating statistics and employment statistics.
Readership/Target Audience: Aimed at industry decision makers, ministers and government officials, media, senior industry executives, proprietors and major operators in the hotel, restaurant and catering industry.
ADVERTISING: No Advertising taken
BUSINESS: CATERING: Catering, Hotels & Restaurants

THE BRITISH JOURNAL FOR THE PHILOSOPHY OF SCIENCE
30839U55-9009

Editorial Address: Department of Philosophy, University of Bristol, 9 Woodland Road, BRISTOL, BS8 1TB
Tel: 0117 928 7826 **Fax:** 0117 928 7825
Email: bjps@bristol.ac.uk
Advertising Address: Great Clarendon Street, OXFORD, OX2 6DP **Tel:** 01865 353329
Email: jnlsadvertising@oxfordjournals.org
Web site: http://www.oup.co.uk/jnls
ISSN: 0007-0882
Publisher: OUP
Date Established: 1951
Frequency: Quarterly
Annual Sub.: £79.00
Circulation: 1,400 (Publisher's Statement)
Usual Pagination: 204
Editor: Alexander Bird
Summary of Content: Journal covering the application of philosophical techniques to issues raised by natural and human sciences.
Readership/Target Audience: Aimed at academics and those in the field of science philosophy.
ADVERTISING RATES:
Full Page Mono £340.00
Agency Commission: 10%
Mechanical Data: Film: Digital, Page Width: 130mm, Type Area: 200 x 130mm, Col Length: 200mm
Copy instructions: Copy Date: Middle of the month prior to publication date
BUSINESS: APPLIED SCIENCE & LABORATORIES

BRITISH JOURNAL OF BIOMEDICAL SCIENCE
39954U55-41

Editorial Address: Foxgloves, Sutton St. Nicholas, HEREFORD, HR1 3AY **Tel:** 01432 882077
Email: brnation@ukonline.co.uk
Web site: http://www.bjbs-online.org
ISSN: 0967-4845
Publisher: Step Publishing Ltd
Frequency: Quarterly
Free to qualifying individuals
Annual Sub.: £169.00
Circulation: 18,000 (Publisher's Statement)
Usual Pagination: 60
Editor: Brian Nation; **Publisher:** Trevor Moon
Summary of Content: Journal containing articles and book reviews on all aspects of biomedical science.
Readership/Target Audience: Aimed at scientists in universities and industry working in laboratory medicine in the NHS and around the world.
ADVERTISING: No Advertising taken
BUSINESS: APPLIED SCIENCE & LABORATORIES

BRITISH JOURNAL OF CARDIOLOGY
24806U56A-51_70

Editorial Address: 9 Langton Street, LONDON, SW10 0JL
Tel: 020 7823 3315 **Fax:** 020 8785 4603
Email: production@bjcardio.co.uk
Advertising Address: 42 Avondale Avenue, Hinchley Wood, ESHER, KT10 0DA **Tel:** 020 8339 0300 **Fax:** 020 8398 3361
Email: michael-young@btconnect.com
Web site: http://www.bjcardio.co.uk
ISSN: 0969-6113
Publisher: MediNews Cardiology Ltd.
Date Established: 1993
Frequency: 6 issues yearly
Free to qualifying individuals
Annual Sub.: £92.00
Circulation: 15,000 (Publisher's Statement)
Usual Pagination: 64
Editor: Henry Purcell; **Advertising Manager:** Michael Young
Summary of Content: Peer-reviewed journal linking primary and secondary care focusing on cardiovascular matters. Contains clinical reports, therapeutics, guidelines, policy, book reviews, case studies, news, analysis of new studies and features on cardiology practice.
Readership/Target Audience: Aimed at hospital cardiologists and GPs with an interest in cardiology.
ADVERTISING RATES:
Full Page Mono £1000.00
Full Page Colour £1400.00
Agency Commission: 10%
Mechanical Data: Type Area: 257 x 186mm, Bleed Size: 286 x 222mm, Trim Size: 280 x 216mm, Print Process: Sheet-fed offset litho, Film: Digital, Col Length: 257mm, Page Width: 186mm
Copy instructions: Copy Date: 6 weeks prior to publication date
Average advertising content per issue: 40%
BUSINESS: HEALTH & MEDICAL

BRITISH JOURNAL OF COMMUNITY NURSING
40294U56B-10

Editorial Address: St. Judes Church, Dulwich Road, LONDON, SE24 0PB **Tel:** 020 7738 5454
Fax: 020 7978 8316
Email: bjcn@markallengroup.com
Advertising Address: As above. **Tel:** 020 7501 6726
Fax: 020 7978 8319
Email: a.kerr@markallengroup.com
Web site: http://www.bjcn.co.uk
ISSN: 1362-4407
Publisher: M A Healthcare
Date Established: 1996
Frequency: Monthly - Published on the 1st Monday of the cover month
Annual Sub.: £105.00
Circulation: 5,000 (Publisher's Statement)
Usual Pagination: 48
Editor: Jonathan Dawes; **Managing Director:** Mark Allen; **Publisher:** Tom Pollard
Summary of Content: Clinical and professional Journal for the district nurse team.
Readership/Target Audience: Aimed at district nurses and community staff nurses, and their team members.
ADVERTISING RATES:
Full Page Colour £2000.00
Agency Commission: 10%
Mechanical Data: Type Area: 270 x 190mm, Col Length: 270mm, Page Width: 190mm, Trim Size: 292 x 215mm, Bleed Size: 302 x 225mm, No. of Columns (Display): 4, Film: Digital
Copy instructions: Copy Date: 20th of the month prior to publication date
Average advertising content per issue: 30%
Supplement(s): Oedema - 2xY, Wound Care - 4xY
BUSINESS: HEALTH & MEDICAL: Nursing

THE BRITISH JOURNAL OF CRIMINOLOGY
25864U44-3075

Editorial Address: Goldsmiths College, University of London, New Cross, LONDON, SE14 6NW
Tel: 020 7919 7839 **Fax:** 020 7919 7839
Email: bjced@gold.ac.uk
Advertising Address: 60 Upper Broadmoor Road, CROWTHORNE, RG45 7DE **Tel:** 01344 779945
Fax: 01344 779945
Email: lhann@lhms.fsnet.co.uk
Web site: http://www.oup.co.uk/jnls
ISSN: 0007-0955
Publisher: OUP
Date Established: 1950
Frequency: 6 issues yearly
Cover Price: £10.00
Annual Sub.: £55.00
Usual Pagination: 96
Editor: Pat Carlen; **Editor-in-Chief:** Pat Carlen
Summary of Content: Journal that focuses on British and international criminology including social deviances.

Readership/Target Audience: Aimed at professionals working in the field of criminology.
ADVERTISING RATES:
Full Page Mono £360.00
Agency Commission: 10%
Mechanical Data: Film: Digital, Page Width: 130mm, Type Area: 200 x 130mm, Col Length: 200mm
BUSINESS: LEGAL

BRITISH JOURNAL OF DERMATOLOGY
24448U56A-51_85
Editorial Address: BAD House, 4 Fitzroy Square, LONDON, W1T 5HQ **Tel:** 020 7383 0266 **Fax:** 020 7387 0240
Email: bjd@bad.org.uk
Advertising Address: 9600 Garsington Road, Cowley, OXFORD, OX4 2DQ **Tel:** 01865 776868
Email: mia.scot-ruddock@oxon.blackwellpublishing.com
Web site: http://www.blackwellpublishing.com/journal. asp?ref=0007-0963
Publisher: Wiley-Blackwell Publishing
Date Established: 1888
Frequency: Monthly
Annual Sub.: £482.00
Circulation: 3,500 (Publisher's Statement)
Usual Pagination: 200
Editor: John English; **Advertising Manager:** Mia Scott-Ruddock
Summary of Content: Journal covering experimental and clinical ethical research, articles on the biology and pathology of the skin and reviews on laboratory research.
Language(s): English; Italian; Portuguese
Readership/Target Audience: Aimed at clinicians, academics and research workers in dermatology.
ADVERTISING RATES:
Full Page Mono £582.00
Full Page Colour £1461.00
Agency Commission: 10%
Mechanical Data: Type Area: 245 x 180mm, Col Length: 245mm, Trim Size: 276 x 210mm, Film: Digital, Bleed Size: 282 x 216mm, Page Width: 180mm
Copy instructions: Copy Date: 5 weeks prior to publication date
BUSINESS: HEALTH & MEDICAL

BRITISH JOURNAL OF DEVELOPMENT PSYCHOLOGY
40501U56N-2
Editorial Address: St. Andrews House, 48 Princess Road East, LEICESTER, LE1 7DR **Tel:** 0116 252 9580
Fax: 0116 227 1314
Email: journals@bps.org.uk
Advertising Address: As above. **Fax:** 0116 247 0787
Email: journals@bps.org.uk
Web site: http://www.bps.org.uk
ISSN: 0261-510X
Publisher: The British Psychological Society
Frequency: Quarterly
Annual Sub.: £45.00
Circulation: 1,700 (Publisher's Statement)
Usual Pagination: 160
Editor: Margaret Harris; **Advertising Manager:** Claire Shinfield
Summary of Content: Journal publishing empirical, conceptual and review articles relating to all areas of development.
Readership/Target Audience: Aimed at academics in university departments and researchers.
ADVERTISING RATES:
Full Page Mono £320.00
Agency Commission: 10%
Mechanical Data: Film: Digital, Type Area: 210 x 135mm, Col Length: 210mm, Trim Size: 247 x 174mm, Bleed Size: 253 x 180mm, Page Width: 135mm
Copy instructions: Copy Date: 12 weeks prior to publication date
Average advertising content per issue: 1%
BUSINESS: HEALTH & MEDICAL: Mental Health

THE BRITISH JOURNAL OF DIABETES & VASCULAR DISEASE
761897U56A-213
Editorial Address: 1 Oliver's Yard, 55 City Road, LONDON, EC1Y 1SP **Tel:** 020 7324 8500 **Fax:** 020 7324 8600
ISSN: 1474-6514
Publisher: Sage Publications
Frequency: 6 issues yearly
Editor: Clifford Bailey; **Executive Editor:** Caroline Day
Summary of Content: Journal focusing on diabetes and vascular disease, insulin resistance, hyperinsulinaemia, obesity, hypertension, dyslipidaemia, antherosclerosis, hyperglycaemia and thrombosis.
Readership/Target Audience: Aimed at general practitioners and specialists in diabetes and cardiology.
BUSINESS: HEALTH & MEDICAL

BRITISH JOURNAL OF EDUCATIONAL PSYCHOLOGY
41130U62R-30
Editorial Address: St. Andrews House, 48 Princess Road East, LEICESTER, LE1 7DR **Tel:** 0116 252 9580
Fax: 0116 227 1314
Email: journals@bps.org.uk
Advertising Address: As above. **Fax:** 0116 247 0787
Email: journals@bps.org.uk
Web site: http://www.bps.org.uk
ISSN: 0007-0998
Publisher: The British Psychological Society
Date Established: 1931
Frequency: Quarterly
Annual Sub.: £165.00
Circulation: 2,200 (Publisher's Statement)
Usual Pagination: 180
Editor: Andy Tolmie; **Advertising Manager:** Julie Neason
Summary of Content: Journal containing educational research, empirical and theoretical, making a significant contribution to the understanding and practice of education.
Readership/Target Audience: Aimed at academic and professional educators.
ADVERTISING RATES:
Full Page Mono £375.00
Agency Commission: 10%
Mechanical Data: Bleed Size: +3mm, Type Area: 210 x 135mm, Col Length: 210mm, Page Width: 135mm, Film: Digital, Trim Size: 247 x 174mm
Copy instructions: Copy Date: 6 weeks prior to publication date
Average advertising content per issue: 2%
BUSINESS: CHURCH & SCHOOL EQUIPMENT & EDUCATION: Education Related

THE BRITISH JOURNAL OF FORENSIC PRACTICE
601557U32G-18
Editorial Address: Richmond House, Richmond Road, BRIGHTON, BN2 3RL **Tel:** 01273 623222
Fax: 01273 625526
Email: david.ndegwa@slam.nhs.uk
Web site: http://www.pavpub.com
ISSN: 1463-6646
Publisher: Pavilion Journals (Brighton) Ltd
Date Established: 1999
Frequency: Quarterly
Annual Sub.: £55.00
Circulation: 400 (Publisher's Statement)
Usual Pagination: 44
Editor: David Ndegwa
Summary of Content: Journal covering multi-disciplinary and multi-agency issues in relation to people in secure environments.
Readership/Target Audience: Aimed at commissioners, planners, managers, staff, police, solicitors and probation officers.
ADVERTISING: No Advertising taken
BUSINESS: LOCAL GOVERNMENT, LEISURE & RECREATION: Community Care & Social Services

BRITISH JOURNAL OF GENERAL PRACTICE
40144U56A-52
Editorial Address: 14 Princes Gate, LONDON, SW7 1PU **Tel:** 020 7581 3232 **Fax:** 020 7584 6716
Email: journal@rcgp.org.uk
Advertising Address: As above. **Fax:** 020 7225 0629
Email: advertising@rcgp.org.uk
Web site: http://www.rcgp.org.uk
ISSN: 0960-1643
Publisher: Royal College of General Practitioners
Date Established: 1953
Frequency: Monthly
Free to qualifying individuals
Annual Sub.: £133.00
Circulation: 35,000 (Publisher's Statement)
Usual Pagination: 88
Editor: David Jewell; **Advertising Manager:** Brenda Laurent
Summary of Content: Journal containing discussion papers, correspondence, book and video reviews, research papers, articles featuring new ideas and reporting on studies on the biological and behavioural aspects of medicine.
Readership/Target Audience: Aimed at members of the Royal College, GPs and those interested or involved in primary healthcare.
ADVERTISING RATES:
Full Page Mono £1150.00
Full Page Colour £1815.00
Agency Commission: 10%
Mechanical Data: Film: Digital, Bleed Size: 301 x 214mm, Trim Size: 297 x 210mm, Col Length: 248mm, Page Width: 182mm, Type Area: 248 x 182mm
Copy instructions: Copy Date: 3 weeks prior to publication date
Average advertising content per issue: 15%
BUSINESS: HEALTH & MEDICAL

BRITISH JOURNAL OF GUIDANCE & COUNSELLING
40285U56A-52_10
Editorial Address: 4 Park Square, Milton Park, ABINGDON, OX14 4RN **Tel:** 020 7017 6000 **Fax:** 020 7017 6336
Email: samantha.cragg@tandf.co.uk
Web site: http://www.informaworld.com/cbjg
ISSN: 0306-9885
Publisher: Routledge, Taylor & Francis
Date Established: 1973
Frequency: Quarterly
Annual Sub.: £140.00
Circulation: 600 (Publisher's Statement)
Usual Pagination: 152
Editor: Samantha Cragg
Summary of Content: Journal providing a forum for debate between academics, trainers and practitioners in the field, publishing high-quality, international contributions in the theory and practice of guidance and counselling, the provision of guidance and counselling services, training and professional issues.
Readership/Target Audience: Aimed at UK academics, trainers and practitioners within the relevant field.
ADVERTISING: No Advertising taken
BUSINESS: HEALTH & MEDICAL

THE BRITISH JOURNAL OF HEALTHCARE ASSISTANTS
1808732U56B-295
Editorial Address: St. Judes Church, Dulwich Road, LONDON, SE24 0PB **Tel:** 020 7738 5454
Fax: 020 7978 8316
Email: bjhca@markallengroup.com
Advertising Address: As above. **Fax:** 020 7733 2325
Email: tom.w@markallengroup.com
Web site: http://www.healthcare-assistants.co.uk
ISSN: 1753-1586
Publisher: MA Health Care Ltd
Date Established: 2007
Frequency: Monthly - 2nd Thursday of the month
Cover Price: £3.50
Annual Sub.: £72.00
Circulation: 12,000 (Publisher's Statement)
Usual Pagination: 52
Editor: Julie Smith; **Advertising Manager:** Tom Wallmer
Summary of Content: Magazine focusing on continuing professional development, enabling readers to improve skills and provide support for patients.
Readership/Target Audience: Aimed at healthcare assistants and assistant practitioners.
ADVERTISING RATES:
Full Page Colour £2000.00
Agency Commission: 10%
Mechanical Data: Type Area: 245 x 186mm, Bleed Size: 298 x 221mm, Trim Size: 292 x 215mm, Col Length: 245mm, Page Width: 186mm, Col Widths (Display): 43mm, No. of Columns (Display): 4, Film: Digital
Average advertising content per issue: 5%
BUSINESS: HEALTH & MEDICAL: Nursing

BRITISH JOURNAL OF HEALTHCARE MANAGEMENT
40344U56C-42_50
Editorial Address: St. Judes Church, Dulwich Road, LONDON, SE24 0PB **Tel:** 020 7738 5454
Fax: 020 7978 8316
Email: bjhcm@markallengroup.com
Advertising Address: As above. **Fax:** 020 7733 2325
Email: abdul.h@markallengroup.com
Web site: http://www.bjhcm.co.uk
ISSN: 1358-0574
Publisher: M A Healthcare
Date Established: 1995
Frequency: Monthly - Published second Monday of the month
Annual Sub.: £193.00
Circulation: 4,000 (Publisher's Statement)
Usual Pagination: 32
Editor: Rosalind Hill; **Managing Director:** Mark Allen; **Publisher:** Adrian Johnston
Summary of Content: Journal containing peer reviewed management papers, practical advice for managers, analytical news features, policy analysis, political coverage and opinion features.
Readership/Target Audience: Aimed at senior managers in healthcare and influential policy and political figures.
ADVERTISING RATES:
Full Page Colour £1800.00
Agency Commission: 10%
Mechanical Data: Col Length: 260mm, Bleed Size: 299 x 222mm, Trim Size: 292 x 215mm, Film: Digital, Type Area: 260 x 190mm, Page Width: 190mm
Copy instructions: Copy Date: 1 week prior to publication date
Average advertising content per issue: 25%
BUSINESS: HEALTH & MEDICAL: Hospitals

Business Magazines

THE BRITISH JOURNAL OF HOSPITAL MEDICINE
40360U56C-338

Formerly: Hospital Medicine
Editorial Address: St. Judes Church, Dulwich Road, LONDON, SE24 0PB **Tel:** 020 7738 5454
Fax: 020 7733 2325
Email: bjhm@markallengroup.com
Advertising Address: As above.
Email: adrian.j@markallengroup.com
Web site: http://www.bjhm.co.uk
ISSN: 1462-3935
Publisher: M A Healthcare
Date Established: 1966
Frequency: Monthly - Published on the 2nd Wednesday of each month
Annual Sub.: £110.00
Circulation: 2,174 (Publisher's Statement)
Usual Pagination: 84
Editor: Rebecca Linssen; **Editor-in-Chief:** Jack Tinker; **Publisher:** Adrian Johnston
Summary of Content: Journal containing clinical reviews of new developments in hospital medicine.
Readership/Target Audience: Read by doctors, surgeons and nurses.
ADVERTISING RATES:
Full Page Mono £1550.00
Full Page Colour £2350.00
Agency Commission: 10%
Mechanical Data: Page Width: 190mm, Type Area: 270 x 190mm, Col Length: 270mm, Bleed Size: 299 x 222mm, Trim Size: 292 x 215mm, Film: Digital
Copy instructions: Copy Date: 1 week prior to publication date
Supplement(s): Modernising Medical Careers - 12xY
BUSINESS: HEALTH & MEDICAL: Hospitals

BRITISH JOURNAL OF INDUSTRIAL RELATIONS
36902U14B-90

Editorial Address: Houghton Street, LONDON, WC2A 2AE
Tel: 020 7955 7931 **Fax:** 020 7955 7424
Email: s.roesch@lse.ac.uk
Advertising Address: 9600 Garsington Road, Cowley, OXFORD, OX4 2DQ **Tel:** 01865 776868 **Fax:** 01865 471267
Email: craig.pickett@oxon.blackwellpublishing.com
Web site: http://www.blackwellpublishers.co.uk
ISSN: 0007-1080
Publisher: Wiley-Blackwell Publishing
Frequency: Quarterly
Annual Sub.: £51.00
Circulation: 2,000 (Publisher's Statement)
Editor: Sylvia Roesch; **Managing Editor:** Sylvia Roesch
Summary of Content: Academic articles on all aspects of industrial relations.
Readership/Target Audience: Aimed at academics and practitioners.
ADVERTISING RATES:
Full Page Mono £420.00
Agency Commission: 10%
Mechanical Data: Page Width: 112mm, Type Area: 190 x 112mm, Col Length: 190mm
BUSINESS: COMMERCE, INDUSTRY & MANAGEMENT: Industry & Factories

BRITISH JOURNAL OF INTENSIVE CARE
40345U56C-50

Editorial Address: 106 Earls Court Road, Kensington, LONDON, W8 6EG **Tel:** 020 7937 6233
Email: mail@greycoatpublishing.co.uk
Advertising Address: As above. **Tel:** 020 8882 7199
Email: r.sloan@greycoatpublishing.co.uk
Web site: http://www.greycoatpublishing.co.uk
ISSN: 0961-7930
Publisher: Greycoat Publishing Ltd
Date Established: 1991
Frequency: Quarterly
Cover Price: Free
Circulation: 12,967 (Publisher's Statement)
Usual Pagination: 36
Editor: Elizabeth Duff; **Advertising Manager:** Robert Sloan
Summary of Content: Journal containing original papers, review articles, case reports and news of new products and developments in the intensive care field.
Readership/Target Audience: Read by anaesthetists, intensivists, accident and emergency specialists, cardiothoracic surgeons, general surgeons, microbiologists, cardiologists, biochemists, critical care pharmacists and critical care nurses.
ADVERTISING RATES:
Full Page Mono £1080.00
Full Page Colour £1455.00
Mechanical Data: Type Area: 267 x 186mm, Col Length: 267mm, Page Width: 186mm, Trim Size: 297 x 210mm, Bleed Size: 303 x 216mm, Film: Digital
BUSINESS: HEALTH & MEDICAL: Hospitals

BRITISH JOURNAL OF MATHEMATICAL & STATISTICAL PSYCHOLOGY
48765U62R-468

Editorial Address: St. Andrews House, 48 Princess Road East, LEICESTER, LE1 7DR **Tel:** 0116 252 9580
Fax: 0116 247 0787
Email: journals@bps.org.uk
Advertising Address: As above. **Tel:** 0116 252 9586
Email: claire.shinfield@bps.org.uk
Web site: http://www.bps.org.uk/publications/journals
ISSN: 0007-1102
Publisher: The British Psychological Society
Frequency: Half-yearly - Published in May and November
Cover Price: £170.00
Circulation: 700 (Publisher's Statement)
Usual Pagination: 200
Editor: Thom Bagueley; **Advertising Manager:** Claire Shinfield
Summary of Content: Journal covering substantive psychological issues, mathematical, statistical and other format aspects.
Readership/Target Audience: Aimed at academics and researchers in universities, government departments and industry.
ADVERTISING RATES:
Full Page Mono £250.00
Agency Commission: 10%
Mechanical Data: Trim Size: 247 x 174mm, Film: Digital, Type Area: 210 x 135mm
BUSINESS: CHURCH & SCHOOL EQUIPMENT & EDUCATION: Education Related

BRITISH JOURNAL OF MIDWIFERY
40295U56B-20

Formerly: BJM
Editorial Address: St. Judes Church, Dulwich Road, LONDON, SE24 0PB **Tel:** 020 7738 5454
Fax: 020 7978 8316
Email: bjm@markallengroup.com
Advertising Address: As above. **Fax:** 020 7733 2325
Email: roger@markallengroup.com
Web site: http://www.intermid.co.uk
ISSN: 0969-4900
Publisher: M A Healthcare
Date Established: 1993
Frequency: Monthly - Published in the 1st week of the cover month
Annual Sub.: £99.00
Circulation: 3,173 (ABC 01/01/2008 to 31/12/2008)
Usual Pagination: 64
Editor: Victoria Clift-Matthews; **Publisher:** Matthew Chianfarani
Summary of Content: Journal promoting excellence in midwifery and women's health.
Readership/Target Audience: Aimed at midwives.
ADVERTISING RATES:
Full Page Mono £995.00
Full Page Colour £1900.00
Agency Commission: 10%
Mechanical Data: Type Area: 287 x 220mm, Col Length: 287mm, Bleed Size: 303 x 236mm, Trim Size: 297 x 230mm, Film: Digital, Page Width: 220mm
Copy instructions: Copy Date: 3 weeks prior to publication date
Average advertising content per issue: 25%
BUSINESS: HEALTH & MEDICAL: Nursing

BRITISH JOURNAL OF NURSING
40296U56B-30

Editorial Address: St. Judes Church, Dulwich Road, LONDON, SE24 0PB **Tel:** 020 7738 5454
Fax: 020 7978 8316
Email: bjn@markallengroup.com
Advertising Address: As above. **Fax:** 020 7733 2325
Email: a.kerr@markallengroup.com
Web site: http://www.britishjournalofnursing.com
ISSN: 0966-0461
Publisher: M A Healthcare
Date Established: 1992
Frequency: 22 issues yearly
Cover Price: £4.99
Annual Sub.: £142.00
Circulation: 3,888 (ABC 01/01/2008 to 31/12/2008)
Usual Pagination: 68
Editor: Tom Pollard; **Advertising Manager:** Anthony Kerr; **Publisher:** Tom Pollard
Summary of Content: Clinical research based journal for all specialities of nursing.
Readership/Target Audience: Read by nurses in hospitals and in the community.
ADVERTISING RATES:
Full Page Colour £2000.00
Agency Commission: 10%
Mechanical Data: Type Area: 287 x 220mm, Col Length: 287mm, Bleed Size: 303 x 236mm, Trim Size: 297 x 230mm, Film: Digital, Page Width: 220mm
Copy instructions: Copy Date: 1 week prior to publication date

Average advertising content per issue: 25%
Supplement(s): Continence - 1xY, Infection Control - 1xY, IV Therpay - 1xY, Stoma Care - 2xY, Tissue Viability - 4xY
BUSINESS: HEALTH & MEDICAL: Nursing

BRITISH JOURNAL OF OPHTHALMOLOGY
40146U56A-52_80

Editorial Address: BMA House, Tavistock Square, LONDON, WC1H 9JR **Tel:** 020 7387 4499
Fax: 020 7383 6418
Email: bjo@bmjgroup.com
Advertising Address: As above. **Fax:** 020 7383 6556
Email: ecurrer@bmj.
Web site: http://www.bjophthalmol.com
ISSN: 0007-1161
Publisher: BMJ Publishing Group
Frequency: Monthly
Annual Sub.: £116.00
Circulation: 2,370 (Publisher's Statement)
Usual Pagination: 138
Editor: Gavin Stewart; **Advertising Manager:** Euan Currer
Summary of Content: Journal concerned with all aspects of eye disorders and their treatment.
Readership/Target Audience: Read by ophthalmologists and opticians.
ADVERTISING RATES:
Full Page Mono £910.00
Full Page Colour £1610.00
Agency Commission: 10%
Mechanical Data: Type Area: 260 x 175mm, Col Length: 260mm, Bleed Size: 303 x 216mm, Trim Size: 297 x 210mm, Film: Digital, Page Width: 175mm
Copy instructions: Copy Date: 20th of 2 months prior to publication date
Average advertising content per issue: 10%
BUSINESS: HEALTH & MEDICAL

BRITISH JOURNAL OF PHOTOGRAPHY
38786U38-10

Editorial Address: 32-34 Broadwick Street, LONDON, W1A 2HG **Tel:** 020 7316 9000
Email: bjp.news@bjphoto.co.uk
Advertising Address: As above. **Fax:** 020 7316 9257
Email: bjpsales@incisivemedia.co.uk
Web site: http://www.bjp-online.com
ISSN: 0007-1196
Publisher: Incisive Media
Date Established: 1854
Frequency: Weekly
Cover Price: £2.20
Annual Sub.: £90.00
Circulation: 5,157 (ABC 01/07/2008 to 31/12/2008)
Usual Pagination: 52
Editor: Olivier Laurent; **News Editor:** Olivier Laurent; **Publisher:** Fotoulla Michael
Summary of Content: Magazine covering the professional photographic market: social, press, commercial, documentary, fine art and scientific. Contains advanced technical reviews, technology reports, interviews, award winners and market reports.
Readership/Target Audience: Read by full-time professional photographers, photography students and serious amateurs along with related occupations such as picture editors, art buyers and photo retailers.
ADVERTISING RATES:
Full Page Mono £1025.00
Full Page Colour £1300.00
SCC £50.00
Agency Commission: 10%
Mechanical Data: Trim Size: 300 x 220mm, Bleed Size: 306 x 226mm, Film: Digital, Type Area: 265 x 200mm, Col Length: 265mm, Page Width: 200mm
Copy instructions: Copy Date: 1 week prior to publication date
Average advertising content per issue: 25%
Supplement(s): Digital Update - 2xY, Lab Topics - 12xY, Lighting - 12xY, Social Photography - 2xY
BUSINESS: PHOTOGRAPHIC TRADE

THE BRITISH JOURNAL OF PRIMARY CARE NURSING
1645674U32G-169

Editorial Address: 3 Duchess Place, BIRMINGHAM, B16 8NH **Tel:** 0121 454 4114 **Fax:** 0121 454 1190
Email: susanmayor@mac.com
Advertising Address: 42 Avondale Avenue, Hichley Wood, ESHER, KT10 0DA **Tel:** 020 8339 0300 **Fax:** 020 8398 3361
Email: michael-young@btconnect.com
Web site: http://www.bjpcn.com
Publisher: Sherborne Gibbs
Date Established: 2004
Frequency: Quarterly
Free to qualifying individuals
Circulation: 10,000 (Publisher's Statement)
Editor: Susan Mayor; **Advertising Manager:** Michael Young; **Managing Editor:** Susan Mayor

Summary of Content: Journal covering cardiovascular and diabetes medicine.
Readership/Target Audience: Aimed at primary care nurses.
ADVERTISING RATES:
Full Page Mono £650.00
Full Page Colour £1200.00
Mechanical Data: Type Area: 257 x 186mm, Bleed Size: 286 x 222mm, Trim Size: 280 x 216mm, Col Length: 257mm, Page Width: 186mm, Print Process: Sheet-fed offset litho, Film: Digital
BUSINESS: LOCAL GOVERNMENT, LEISURE & RECREATION: Community Care & Social Services

THE BRITISH JOURNAL OF PRIMARY CARE NURSING - RESPIRATORY DISEASES AND ALLERGY
1789773U56B-298
Editorial Address: 3 Duchess Place, BIRMINGHAM, B16 8NH **Tel:** 0121 454 4114 **Fax:** 0121 454 1190
Email: mgibbs@sherbornegibbs.co.uk
Advertising Address: 42 Avondale Avenue, Hinchley Wood, ESHER, KT10 0DA **Tel:** 020 8339 300 **Fax:** 020 8398 3361
Email: michael-young@btconnect.com
Web site: http://www.bjpcn.co.uk
ISSN: 1752-4385
Publisher: Sherborne Gibbs
Date Established: 2007
Frequency: Quarterly
Cover Price: Free
Circulation: 7,000 (Publisher's Statement)
Usual Pagination: 40
Editor: Michael Gibbs; **Advertising Manager:** Michael Young; **Publisher:** Michael Gibbs
Summary of Content: Journal featuring practical reviews and updated research on respiratory diseases including asthma and COPD as well as allergies.
Readership/Target Audience: Aimed at practice care nurses with a special interest in respiratory medicine.
ADVERTISING: Rates on application
BUSINESS: HEALTH & MEDICAL: Nursing

THE BRITISH JOURNAL OF PSYCHIATRY
40481U56N-4
Editorial Address: 17 Belgrave Square, LONDON, SW1X 8PG **Tel:** 020 7235 2351 **Fax:** 020 7259 6507
Email: bjp@rcpsych.ac.uk
Advertising Address: PTM Publishers Ltd, Westmead Road, 123 Westmead Road, SUTTON, SM1 4JH
Tel: 020 8642 0162 **Fax:** 020 8643 2275
Email: jan@ptmpublishers.com
Web site: http://www.rcpsych.ac.uk
ISSN: 0007-1250
Publisher: Royal College of Psychiatrists
Frequency: Monthly
Annual Sub.: £188.00
Circulation: 13,645 (Publisher's Statement)
Usual Pagination: 100
Editor: Peter Tyrer; **Advertising Manager:** Jan Pointing
Summary of Content: Journal of the Royal College of Psychiatrists. Containing research papers, small articles and reports on matters of clinical significance and all aspects of psychiatry and mental health.
Readership/Target Audience: Aimed at psychiatrists, clinical psychologists and those within the mental health profession.
ADVERTISING RATES:
Full Page Mono £715.00
Full Page Colour £1495.00
Agency Commission: 10%
Mechanical Data: Type Area: 241 x 183mm, Col Length: 241mm, Page Width: 183mm, Trim Size: 297 x 210mm, Bleed Size: 303 x 216mm, Film: Digital
BUSINESS: HEALTH & MEDICAL: Mental Health

BRITISH JOURNAL OF PSYCHOLOGY
24503U56A-168
Editorial Address: St. Andrews House, 48 Princess Road East, LEICESTER, LE1 7DR **Tel:** 0116 254 9568
Fax: 0116 227 1314
Email: journals@bps.org.uk
Advertising Address: As above. **Tel:** 0116 252 9580
Fax: 0116 247 0787
Email: claire.shinfield@bps.org.uk
Web site: http://www.bps.org.uk
ISSN: 0007-1269
Publisher: The British Psychological Society
Date Established: 1902
Frequency: Quarterly
Annual Sub.: £270.00
Circulation: 2,000 (Publisher's Statement)
Usual Pagination: 180
Editor: Julie Neason; **Advertising Manager:** Claire Shinfield
Summary of Content: Journal containing reports of empirical studies likely to further our understanding of

psychology and critical reviews of the literature and theoretical contributions.
Readership/Target Audience: Read by people interested in psychology and researchers in experimental cognitive and general psychology.
ADVERTISING RATES:
Full Page Mono £375.00
Agency Commission: 10%
Mechanical Data: Film: Digital, Type Area: 210 x 135mm, Col Length: 210mm, Trim Size: 247 x 174mm, Page Width: 135mm
BUSINESS: HEALTH & MEDICAL

BRITISH JOURNAL OF RENAL MEDICINE
40147U56A-52_90
Editorial Address: 8-10 Dryden Street, Covent Garden, LONDON, WC2E 9NA **Tel:** 020 7240 4493
Fax: 020 7240 4479
Email: edit@hayward.co.uk
Web site: http://www.hayward.co.uk
ISSN: 1365-5604
Publisher: Hayward Medical Communications Ltd
Date Established: 1996
Frequency: Quarterly
Free to qualifying individuals
Editor: Joel Barrick; **Publisher:** Christopher Tidman
Summary of Content: Journal covering the multidisciplinary nature of renal healthcare provision.
Readership/Target Audience: Aimed at healthcare professionals and doctors.
ADVERTISING: No Advertising taken
BUSINESS: HEALTH & MEDICAL

BRITISH JOURNAL OF SCHOOL NURSING
1793313U56B-294
Editorial Address: St. Judes Church, Dulwich Road, LONDON, SE24 0PB **Tel:** 020 7738 5454
Email: bjsn@markallengroup.com
Advertising Address: As above. **Fax:** 020 7733 2325
Email: roger@markallengroup.com
Web site: http://www.school-nursing.co.uk
Publisher: MA Health Care Ltd
Frequency: 10 issues yearly
Editor: Jane Dudeney; **Advertising Director:** Roger Allen
Summary of Content: Journal covering all aspects of children's and public health.
Readership/Target Audience: Aimed at school nurses.
ADVERTISING: Rates on application
BUSINESS: HEALTH & MEDICAL: Nursing

THE BRITISH JOURNAL OF SOCIAL WORK
38451U32G-20
Editorial Address: Centre for Applied Childhood Studies, University of Huddersfield, Queensgate, HUDDERSFIELD, HD1 3DH **Tel:** 01865 353907 **Fax:** 01865 353485
Email: s.m.hanson@hud.ac.uk
Advertising Address: 60 Upper Broadmoor Road, CROWTHORNE, RG45 7DE **Tel:** 01344 779945
Fax: 01344 779945
Email: lhann@lhms.fsnet.co.uk
Web site: http://www.oup.co.uk/jnls
ISSN: 0045-3102
Publisher: OUP
Date Established: 1971
Frequency: 8 issues yearly
Annual Sub.: £175.00
Circulation: 1,600 (Publisher's Statement)
Usual Pagination: 200
Editor: Sue Hanson
Summary of Content: International journal of the British Association of Social Workers, covering research studies and theoretical articles.
Readership/Target Audience: Read by social workers, administrators and social work educators.
ADVERTISING RATES:
Full Page Mono £340.00
Agency Commission: 10%
Mechanical Data: Type Area: 200 x 130mm, Col Length: 200mm, Page Width: 130mm, Film: Digital
Copy instructions: Copy Date: 1 month prior to publication date
BUSINESS: LOCAL GOVERNMENT, LEISURE & RECREATION: Community Care & Social Services

BRITISH JOURNAL OF SPECIAL EDUCATION
41121U62G-40
Editorial Address: Faculty of Education, 184 Hills Road, CAMBRIDGE, CB2 8PQ **Tel:** 01223 767627
Fax: 01223 767602
Email: rb218@cam.ac.uk
Advertising Address: Nasen House, 4-5 Amber Business Village, Amber Close, Amington, TAMWORTH, B77 4RP
Tel: 01827 311500 **Fax:** 01827 313005
Email: seans@nasen.org.uk

Web site: http://www.blackwellpublishers.co.uk
ISSN: 0952-3383
Publisher: Wiley-Blackwell Publishing
Frequency: Quarterly
Free to qualifying individuals
Annual Sub.: EUR65.00
Circulation: 9,000 (Publisher's Statement)
Usual Pagination: 54
Editor: Richard Byers; **Advertising Manager:** Sean Stockdale
Summary of Content: Journal covering all aspects of the education of children and young people with special educational needs.
Readership/Target Audience: Aimed at teachers and other concerned professionals.
ADVERTISING RATES:
Full Page Mono £600.00
Mechanical Data: Type Area: 250 x 170mm, Col Length: 250mm, Page Width: 170mm, Col Widths (Display): 84mm, No. of Columns (Display): 2, Print Process: Offset litho, Film: Digital
Copy instructions: Copy Date: Beginning of the month prior to publication date
BUSINESS: CHURCH & SCHOOL EQUIPMENT & EDUCATION: Special Needs Education

THE BRITISH JOURNAL OF SURGERY
40346U56C-55
Editorial Address: The Atrium, Southern Gate, CHICHESTER, PO19 8SQ **Tel:** 01243 779777
Fax: 01243 775878
Advertising Address: 9600 Garsington Road, Cowley, OXFORD, OX4 2DQ **Tel:** 01865 776868
Email: mia.scott-ruddock@wiley.com
Web site: http://www.bjs.co.uk
ISSN: 1365-1323
Publisher: John Wiley & Sons Ltd
Frequency: Monthly
Circulation: 12,000 (Publisher's Statement)
Editor: Bryony Urquhart; **Managing Editor:** Bryony Urquhart
Summary of Content: Journal focusing on developments in surgical practice, with articles on clinical and laboratory based research on all aspects of general surgery and related topics.
Readership/Target Audience: Aimed at general and vascular surgeons.
ADVERTISING: Rates on application
BUSINESS: HEALTH & MEDICAL: Hospitals

THE BRITISH JOURNAL OF VISUAL IMPAIRMENT
40454U56L-7
Editorial Address: c/o Visual Impairment Centre for Teaching and Rese, School of Education, University of Birmingham, BIRMINGHAM, B15 2TT **Tel:** 0121 414 6733
Email: edu-bjvieditors@adf.bham.ac.uk
Advertising Address: 1 Oliver's Yard, 55 City Road, LONDON, EC1Y 1SP **Tel:** 020 7324 8500
Fax: 020 7324 8600
Email: sheena.karim@sagepub.co.uk
Web site: http://www.sagepub.co.uk
ISSN: 0264-6196
Publisher: Sage Publications
Date Established: 1983
Frequency: 3 issues yearly - Published in January, May and September
Cover Price: £13.00
Free to qualifying individuals
Annual Sub.: £35.00
Usual Pagination: 44
Editor: Steve McCall; **Advertising Manager:** Sheena Karim
Summary of Content: Journal providing a national forum for all views on related subjects.
Readership/Target Audience: Read by those professionally concerned with children and adults who have a visual impairment.
ADVERTISING: Rates on application
BUSINESS: HEALTH & MEDICAL: Disability & Rehabilitation

BRITISH JOURNALISM REVIEW
35603U2B-10
Editorial Address: 1 Oliver's Yard, 55 City Road, LONDON, EC1Y 1SP **Tel:** 020 7324 8500 **Fax:** 020 7324 8600
Email: editor@bjr.org.uk
Advertising Address: As above.
Email: tamara.haq@sagepub.co.uk
Web site: http://www.bjr.org.uk
ISSN: 0956-5758
Publisher: Sage Publications
Date Established: 1989
Frequency: Quarterly
Usual Pagination: 80
Editor: Bill Hagerty; **Managing Editor:** Brian Bass
Summary of Content: Journal containing articles on current journalism issues in the print and broadcast media, plus research and analysis of media trends.
Readership/Target Audience: Read by professional journalists, media consultants, politicians and civil servants.

Business Magazines

ADVERTISING RATES:
Full Page Mono £200.00
Agency Commission: 10%
Mechanical Data: Type Area: 205 x 125mm, Col Length: 205mm, Page Width: 125mm
Copy instructions: Copy Date: 12 weeks prior to publication date
BUSINESS: COMMUNICATIONS, ADVERTISING & MARKETING: Press

BRITISH MARINE NEWS   1739863U45R-375
Editorial Address: Marine House, Thorpe Lea Road, EGHAM, TW20 8BF **Tel:** 01784 223678 **Fax:** 01784 439678
Email: rjackson@britishmarine.co.uk
Advertising Address: As above.
Email: bmn@britishmarine.co.uk
Web site: http://www.britishmarine.co.uk
Publisher: British Marine Federation
Frequency: Monthly
Free to qualifying individuals
Circulation: 5,500 (Publisher's Statement)
Editor: Rebecca Jackson; **Advertising Manager:** Joe Roel
Summary of Content: Newsletter covering marine industry news and forthcoming events.
Readership/Target Audience: Aimed at members of the British Marine Federation.
ADVERTISING RATES:
Full Page Colour £1600.00
Mechanical Data: Bleed Size: 296 x 209mm, Film: Digital
BUSINESS: MARINE & SHIPPING: Marine Related

BRITISH NUTRITION FOUNDATION NEWS   38039U22R-10
Editorial Address: High Holborn House, 52-54 High Holborn, LONDON, WC1V 6RQ **Tel:** 020 7404 6504
Fax: 020 7404 6747
Email: postbox@nutrition.org.uk
Web site: http://www.nutrition.org.uk
Publisher: British Nutrition Foundation
Date Established: 1994
Frequency: 3 issues yearly - Published in April, September and December
Cover Price: Free
Circulation: 2,000 (Publisher's Statement)
Usual Pagination: 4
Editor: Bridget Aisbitt
Summary of Content: Journal covering nutrition and health issues.
Readership/Target Audience: Read by nutritionists, dieticians, teachers and scientists working in the food industry.
ADVERTISING: No Advertising taken
BUSINESS: FOOD: Food Related

BRITISH PLASTICS & RUBBER   38816U39-5
Editorial Address: 233 Farleigh Road, WARLINGHAM, CR6 9EL **Tel:** 07860 484643 **Fax:** 01829 770047
Email: ken@britishplastics.co.uk
Advertising Address: Unit 2, Chowley Court, Chowley Oak Lane, CHESTER, CH3 9GA **Tel:** 01829 770037
Fax: 01829 770047
Email: andrew@mcmpublishing.co.uk
Web site: http://www.britishplastics.co.uk
ISSN: 0307-6164
Publisher: Euro Publishing Consultancy
Date Established: 1976
Frequency: 10 issues yearly
Cover Price: £8.00
Free to qualifying individuals
Annual Sub.: £80.00
Circulation: 10,420 (ABC 01/01/2008 to 31/12/2008)
Usual Pagination: 52
Editor: Ken Grace; **Advertising Manager:** Andrew Rostron;
Publisher: Mark Blezard
Summary of Content: Magazine covering technical news of the plastics and rubber processing industry.
Readership/Target Audience: Read by managers with specifying and purchasing influence.
ADVERTISING RATES:
Full Page Mono £1190.00
Full Page Colour £1800.00
Agency Commission: 10%
Mechanical Data: Col Length: 265mm, Film: Digital, Type Area: 265 x 190mm, Bleed Size: +5mm, Trim Size: 297 x 210mm, No. of Columns (Display): 3, Page Width: 190mm, Print Process: Sheet fed litho
Average advertising content per issue: 40%
BUSINESS: PLASTICS & RUBBER

BRITISH STYLE   39481U47A-15
Formerly: British Style Trader
Editorial Address: Beacon House, 2 Beacon Hill, LONDON, N7 9LY **Tel:** 020 7609 5100 **Fax:** 020 7700 5103
Email: scotay@gmail.com

Advertising Address: As above. **Fax:** 020 7609 5103
Email: scotay@gmail.com
Web site: http://www.savilerow-style.com
ISSN: 0963-9438
Publisher: Scott Taylor Publishing Ltd
Date Established: 1988
Frequency: Half-yearly - Published in June and November
Cover Price: Free
Circulation: 6,000 (Publisher's Statement)
Editor: Marie Scott; **Managing Director:** Marie Scott;
Advertising Manager: Evelyn Bainsfair; **Circulation Manager:** Angela Tuck
Summary of Content: Publication containing features, photographs and information on British up-market merchandise.
Language(s): Chinese; English; Japanese; Korean
Readership/Target Audience: Read by high quality trade buyers worldwide and consumers at British promotions overseas.
BUSINESS: CLOTHING & TEXTILES

BRITISH SUGAR BEET REVIEW   37928U21R-140
Editorial Address: Sugar Way, PETERBOROUGH, PE2 9AY **Tel:** 01733 422278 **Fax:** 01733 422080
Email: beetreview@britishsugar.co.uk
Advertising Address: As above.
Email: beetreview@britishsugar.co.uk
Web site: http://www.beetreview.co.uk
Publisher: British Sugar plc
Frequency: Quarterly
Cover Price: Free
Circulation: 6,600 (Publisher's Statement)
Usual Pagination: 56
Editor: Denise Chandler; **Advertising Manager:** Denise Chandler
Summary of Content: Journal covering sugar beet research, machine technology, and crop husbandry.
Readership/Target Audience: Read by scientists and sugar beet growers.
ADVERTISING RATES:
Full Page Mono £1961.00
Full Page Colour £2226.00
Mechanical Data: Type Area: 265 x 185mm, Print Process: Litho, Film: Positive, right reading, emulsion side down. Digital, Page Width: 185mm, Bleed Size: 303 x 216mm, Trim Size: 297 x 210mm, Col Length: 265mm
Copy instructions: Copy Date: 6 weeks prior to publication date
Average advertising content per issue: 28%
BUSINESS: AGRICULTURE & FARMING: Agriculture & Farming Related

---

BRITISH TAX REVIEW   35402U1M-10
Editorial Address: 100 Avenue Road, Swiss Cottage, LONDON, NW3 3PF **Tel:** 020 7393 7000 **Fax:** 020 7393 7030
Email: jayne.chippendale@thomsonreuters.com
Web site: http://www.sweetandmaxwell.co.uk
ISSN: 0007-1870
Publisher: Sweet & Maxwell Ltd
Date Established: 1956
Frequency: 6 issues yearly
Annual Sub.: £448.00
Usual Pagination: 128
Editor: Victoria Cowan
Summary of Content: Journal containing information on draft legislation and in-depth comment on specialist law topics.
Readership/Target Audience: Aimed at those who work in all aspects of tax work.
ADVERTISING: No Advertising taken
BUSINESS: FINANCE & ECONOMICS: Taxation

BROADBAND   37336U18A-40
Formerly: CTE Cable Telecommunication Engineering
Editorial Address: Communications House, 41A Market Street, WATFORD, WD18 0PN **Tel:** 01923 815500
Fax: 01923 803203
Email: sara.waddington@scte.org.uk
Advertising Address: As above. **Fax:** 01923 818018
Email: sara.waddington@scte.org.uk
Web site: http://www.scte.org.uk
Publisher: The Society of Cable and Telecommunication Engineers
Date Established: 1945
Frequency: 3 issues yearly - Published in April, August and December
Free to qualifying individuals
Circulation: 3,000 (Publisher's Statement)
Usual Pagination: 44
Editor: Sara Waddington; **Advertising Manager:** Sara Waddington; **Managing Editor:** Sara Waddington
Summary of Content: Magazine covering cable telecommunication engineering and featuring reviews on new products.

Readership/Target Audience: Read by members of the Society of Cable Telecommunication Engineers and other qualified persons.
ADVERTISING: Rates on application
BUSINESS: ELECTRONICS

BROADCAST   35662U2D-53
Editorial Address: Greater London House, Hampstead Road, LONDON, NW1 7EJ **Tel:** 020 7728 5542
Fax: 020 7728 5555
Email: will.hurrell@emap.com
Advertising Address: As above. **Tel:** 020 7728 5000
Fax: 020 7505 8020
Email: andrew.shelley@emap.com
Web site: http://www.broadcastnow.co.uk
Publisher: EMAP Communications Ltd
Frequency: Weekly
Cover Price: £4.25
Circulation: 8,082 (ABC 01/07/2008 to 30/06/2009)
Usual Pagination: 32
Editor: Chris Curtis; **News Editor:** Chris Curtis; **Features Editor:** Emily Booth; **Advertising Manager:** Andy Shelley
Summary of Content: Magazine of the television and radio industry covering all aspects of television, radio, cable and satellite.
Readership/Target Audience: Aimed at decision makers in the broadcasting industry.
ADVERTISING RATES:
Full Page Colour £3800.00
Agency Commission: 10%
Mechanical Data: Page Width: 266mm, Type Area: 367 x 266mm, Trim Size: 390 x 290mm, Bleed Size: 396 x 296mm, Col Length: 367mm, Film: Digital
Copy instructions: Copy Date: 1 week prior to publication date
Average advertising content per issue: 40%
Supplement(s): Broadcast International - 2xY
BUSINESS: COMMUNICATIONS, ADVERTISING & MARKETING: Broadcasting

---

THE BROKER   35105U1D-20
Editorial Address: 8th Floor, John Stow House, 18 Bevis Marks, LONDON, EC3A 7JB **Tel:** 020 7397 0223
Fax: 020 7626 9676
Email: burtrandl@biba.org.uk
Advertising Address: As above.
Email: burtrandl@biba.org.uk
Web site: http://www.biba.org.uk
Publisher: British Insurance Brokers Association
Date Established: 1985
Frequency: Quarterly
Cover Price: Free
Circulation: 3,000 (Publisher's Statement)
Usual Pagination: 36
Editor: Leighann Burtrand; **Advertising Manager:** Leighann Burtrand
Summary of Content: Publication covering all matters relating to insurance broking.
Readership/Target Audience: Read by members of BIBA only.
ADVERTISING RATES:
Full Page Colour £1045.00
Agency Commission: 10%
Mechanical Data: Trim Size: 297 x 210mm, Film: Digital, Bleed Size: +3mm
Copy instructions: Copy Date: 1st week of month prior to publication date
BUSINESS: FINANCE & ECONOMICS: Insurance

BROWNFIELD BRIEFING   1744893U4D-408
Editorial Address: The Chapel, Wellington Road, LONDON, NW10 5LJ **Tel:** 020 8969 1008 **Fax:** 020 8969 1334
Email: editorial@brownfieldbriefing.com
Advertising Address: As above.
Email: emmacharter@newzeye.com
Web site: http://www.brownfieldbriefing.com
ISSN: 1474-2098
Publisher: Newzeye Ltd
Date Established: 2001
Frequency: Monthly
Annual Sub.: £395.00
Circulation: 5,000 (Publisher's Statement)
Usual Pagination: 20
Editor: Ian Grant; **Managing Editor:** Ian Grant
Summary of Content: Newsletter focusing on all aspects of previously developed land including contamination, remediation, regeneration and legal developments.
Readership/Target Audience: Aimed at all those with an interest in the brownfield and remediation sector including environmental consultants, local authorities and developers, amongst others.
ADVERTISING RATES:
Full Page Mono £1450.00
Full Page Colour £1750.00
Agency Commission: 10%
Mechanical Data: Type Area: 267 x 180mm, Col Length: 267mm, Page Width: 180mm, Film: Digital

Copy instructions: Copy Date: 10th of the month prior to publication date

Average advertising content per issue: 10%

BUSINESS: ARCHITECTURE & BUILDING: Planning & Housing

BRUSHWORK
37229U14R-40

Editorial Address: 59-61 The Broadway, HAYWARDS HEATH, RH16 3AS **Tel:** 01444 440188 **Fax:** 01444 414813

Email: info@airstream.co.uk

Advertising Address: As above.

Email: b.a.may@airstream.co.uk

Web site: http://www.brushwork.com

Publisher: Airstream Communications Ltd

Date Established: 1989

Frequency: 7 issues yearly - Published in the 2nd week of the 1st cover month

Annual Sub.: £100.00

Circulation: 2,200 (Publisher's Statement)

Usual Pagination: 48

Editor: Roland Ravenhill; **Managing Director:** Brian Hall; **Advertising Manager:** Belinda May; **Publisher:** Brian Hall

Summary of Content: Independent magazine for the brush trade.

Language(s): English; German

Readership/Target Audience: Aimed at brush manufacturers and suppliers to the trade.

ADVERTISING RATES:

Full Page Colour £1400.00

Agency Commission: 10%

Mechanical Data: Bleed Size: 303 x 216mm, Trim Size: 297 x 210mm, Film: Digital

Average advertising content per issue: 40%

Supplement(s): Brushwork Catalogue - 1xY

BUSINESS: COMMERCE, INDUSTRY & MANAGEMENT: Commerce Related

BSD BUILDING SUSTAINABLE DESIGN
35754U3B-9

Formerly: Building Services Journal

Editorial Address: 3rd Floor, Ludgate House, 245 Blackfriars Road, LONDON, SE1 9UY **Tel:** 020 7921 5000

Fax: 020 7560 4020

Email: andy.pearson@ubm.com

Advertising Address: As above. **Tel:** 020 7560 4100

Email: nicole.rinaldi@ubm.com

Web site: http://www.bsdlive.co.uk

ISSN: 1365-5671

Publisher: UBM Information Ltd

Frequency: Monthly - Published on the 1st Monday of the cover month

Cover Price: £5.50

Annual Sub.: £80.00

Circulation: 19,030 (Publisher's Statement)

Usual Pagination: 110

Editor: Andy Pearson; **Managing Director:** Adrian Barrick

Summary of Content: Journal of the Chartered Institution of Building Services Engineers, containing in-depth news analysis, design and technical guidance.

Readership/Target Audience: Aimed at members and building services engineers.

ADVERTISING RATES:

Full Page Mono £3320.00

Full Page Colour £4734.00

Agency Commission: 10%

Mechanical Data: Page Width: 178mm, Trim Size: 297 x 210mm, Type Area: 254 x 178mm, Col Length: 254mm, Bleed Size: 303 x 216mm, Film: Digital

Copy instructions: Copy Date: 3rd week of the month prior to publication date

Average advertising content per issue: 40%

BUSINESS: HEATING & VENTILATION: Industrial Heating & Ventilation

BT TODAY
37417U18B-360

Editorial Address: Post Point A5E, 81 Newgate Street, LONDON, EC1A 7AJ **Tel:** 020 7356 6543

Fax: 020 7356 6546

Email: debbie.mayhew@bt.com

Advertising Address: Landmark Publishing Services, 2 Windmill Street, LONDON, W1T 2HX **Tel:** 020 7692 9292

Fax: 020 7692 9393

Email: sharon@lps.co.uk

Web site: http://www.bt.com

Publisher: British Telecommunications plc

Frequency: 6 issues yearly

Cover Price: Free

Annual Sub.: £18.00

Circulation: 180,000 (Publisher's Statement)

Usual Pagination: 32

Editor: Debbie Mayhew

Summary of Content: Newspaper focusing on BT products, developments and company news.

Readership/Target Audience: Read by British Telecommunications personnel.

ADVERTISING RATES:

Full Page Colour £7000.00

SCC £45.00

Agency Commission: 10%

Mechanical Data: Type Area: 272 x 180mm, Trim Size: 297 x 210mm, Bleed Size: 303 x 216mm, Col Length: 272mm, Page Width: 180mm, Film: Digital

BUSINESS: ELECTRONICS: Telecommunications

THE BUILDER
35887U4E-41_75

Editorial Address: McDermott Chambers, 2 The Green, Kings Norton, BIRMINGHAM, B38 8SD **Tel:** 0121 451 3037

Fax: 0121 433 3461

Email: oliver.james@mcdermottpublishing.com

Advertising Address: As above. **Fax:** 0121 459 2179

Email: david.steade@mcdermottpublishing.com

Web site: http://www.mcdermottpublishing.com/about_the_builder.html

Publisher: McDermott Publishing Ltd

Frequency: 11 issues yearly - Published on the 26th of the cover month

Free to qualifying individuals

Annual Sub.: £23.50

Circulation: 23,627 (Publisher's Statement)

Usual Pagination: 50

Editor: Oliver James; **Managing Director:** Lawrence McDermott; **Publisher:** Lawrence McDermott

Summary of Content: Magazine containing product information concerning the building trade.

Readership/Target Audience: Aimed at builders, contractors, residential and light commercial property developers, architects, building and quantity surveyors.

ADVERTISING RATES:

Full Page Colour £1695.00

Agency Commission: 10%

Mechanical Data: Page Width: 190mm, Type Area: 270 x 190mm, Trim Size: 297 x 210mm, Col Length: 270mm, Bleed Size: 303 x 216mm, Film: Digital

Copy instructions: Copy Date: 4 weeks prior to publication date

Average advertising content per issue: 60%

BUSINESS: ARCHITECTURE & BUILDING: Building

BUILDER & ENGINEER
35890U4E-44

Editorial Address: Portland Buildings, 127-129 Portland Street, MANCHESTER, M1 4PZ **Tel:** 0161 236 2782

Fax: 0161 236 2783

Email: claire.stapleton@excelpublishing.co.uk

Advertising Address: As above.

Email: terry.hanlon@excelpublishing.co.uk

Web site: http://www.builderandengineer.co.uk

Publisher: Excel Publishing Company Ltd

Frequency: 11 issues yearly - Published around the 25th of the cover month

Cover Price: £2.50

Circulation: 13,061 (ABC 01/07/2008 to 30/06/2009)

Usual Pagination: 70

Editor: Claire Stapleton; **Managing Director:** Patrick Rafter

Summary of Content: Magazine containing information relating to the building and engineering trades.

Twitter: http://twitter.com/TheEngineerUK.

Readership/Target Audience: Aimed at construction professionals, contractors and developers throughout the UK.

ADVERTISING RATES:

Full Page Colour £1995.00

Agency Commission: 10%

Mechanical Data: Type Area: 266 x 185mm, Bleed Size: 303 x 216mm, Trim Size: 297 x 210mm, Film: Digital, Col Length: 266mm, Page Width: 185mm

Copy instructions: Copy Date: 1st of the month prior to publication date

Average advertising content per issue: 40%

BUSINESS: ARCHITECTURE & BUILDING: Building

BUILDERS' MERCHANTS NEWS
35892U4E-45

Editorial Address: Hereford House, Bridle Path, CROYDON, CR9 4NL **Tel:** 020 8680 4200 **Fax:** 020 8680 8400

Email: lisa@bmpublications.co.uk

Advertising Address: As above.

Email: dvw@bmpublications.co.uk

Web site: http://www.buildersmerchantsnews.co.uk

ISSN: 0141-2035

Publisher: Hemming Information Services

Date Established: 1977

Frequency: Monthly - Published in the 3rd week of the cover month

Annual Sub.: £52.00

Circulation: 7,304 (ABC 01/07/2008 to 30/06/2009)

Usual Pagination: 60

Editor: Lisa Arcangeli; **Managing Editor:** Lisa Arcangeli

Summary of Content: Magazine covering new products and developments in the building industry.

Readership/Target Audience: Read by senior management.

ADVERTISING RATES:

Full Page Mono 1945.00

Full Page Colour £2670.00

Agency Commission: 10%

Mechanical Data: Type Area: 370 x 265mm, Trim Size: 400 x 285mm, Film: Digital, Print Process: Sheet-fed litho, Page Width: 265mm, Col Length: 370mm, Bleed Size: 406 x 291mm, Col Widths (Display): 40mm, No. of Columns (Display): 6

Copy instructions: Copy Date: 6 weeks prior to publication date

Average advertising content per issue: 50%

BUSINESS: ARCHITECTURE & BUILDING: Building

BUILDING
35893U4E-60

Editorial Address: 3rd Floor, Ludgate House, 245 Blackfriars Road, LONDON, SE1 9UY **Tel:** 020 7560 4000

Fax: 020 7560 4004

Advertising Address: As above. **Tel:** 020 7560 4100

Fax: 020 7560 4408

Email: lucy.morphew@ubm.com

Web site: http://www.building.co.uk

ISSN: 0007-3318

Publisher: UBM Information Ltd

Date Established: 1843

Frequency: Weekly - Published on Friday

Cover Price: £2.90

Annual Sub.: £132.00

Circulation: 23,645 (ABC 01/07/2008 to 30/06/2009)

Editor: Joey Gardiner; **News Editor:** Joey Gardiner; **Features Editor:** Sarah Richardson; **Managing Director:** Jonathan Newby; **Advertising Manager:** Lucy Morphew

Summary of Content: Magazine containing news of major development in the building industry.

Twitter: http://twitter.com/buildingnews.

Readership/Target Audience: Read by senior managers and designers.

ADVERTISING RATES:

Full Page Mono £2249.00

Full Page Colour £3117.00

Agency Commission: 10%

Mechanical Data: Type Area: 245 x 192mm, Trim Size: 285 x 225mm, Film: Digital, Col Length: 245mm, Page Width: 192mm, Bleed Size: 291 x 231mm

Copy instructions: Copy Date: 1 week prior to publication date

Average advertising content per issue: 30%

BUSINESS: ARCHITECTURE & BUILDING: Building

BUILDING & CONSTRUCTION
38963U42A-7_50

Editorial Address: Kentons House, 24 Blendon Road, BEXLEY, DA5 1BW **Tel:** 0870 701 3536

Email: buildingandconstruction@ntlworld.com

Advertising Address: As above.

Email: buildingandconstruction@ntlworld.com

Publisher: Direct Publishing Ltd

Date Established: 1996

Frequency: Quarterly

Cover Price: £2.75

Free to qualifying individuals

Annual Sub.: £45.00

Circulation: 4,700 (Publisher's Statement)

Usual Pagination: 24

Editor: Phil Brown; **Advertising Manager:** Alan Puttock; **Publisher:** Phil Brown

Summary of Content: Magazine containing news, technical features and product editorial on developments in the building and construction industry.

Readership/Target Audience: Aimed at senior managers and directors within construction companies, civil engineering companies, plant hire companies, architects and local government departments.

ADVERTISING RATES:

Full Page Mono £1295.00

Full Page Colour £1395.00

SCC £28.00

Agency Commission: 10%

Mechanical Data: Type Area: 270 x 210mm, Bleed Size: 303 x 216mm, Trim Size: 297 x 210mm, Film: Digital, Col Length: 270mm, Page Width: 210mm

Copy instructions: Copy Date: Middle of the month prior to publication date

BUSINESS: CONSTRUCTION

BUILDING AND FACILITIES MANAGEMENT
35955U4R-355

Editorial Address: Northern Regional Office, 46 Charlecote Road, Poynton, STOCKPORT, SK12 1DL **Tel:** 01625 630152

Fax: 01625 630154

Email: alan@abbeypublishing.co.uk

Advertising Address: As above.

Email: alan@abbeypublishing.co.uk

Web site: http://www.abbeypublishing.co.uk

ISSN: 1470-5281

Publisher: Abbey Publishing

Date Established: 1992

Section 4 (b) Business Magazines

Frequency: 11 issues yearly - Published at the beginning of the 3rd week of the cover month
Cover Price: £5.00
Free to qualifying individuals
Annual Sub.: £50.00
Circulation: 8,500 (Publisher's Statement)
Editor: Alan Ashton; **Managing Director:** Ralph Scrivens;
Advertising Manager: Alan Ashton; **Publisher:** Ralph Scrivens
Summary of Content: Magazine covering all aspects of building management, maintenance and facilities management within the public sector.
Readership/Target Audience: Read by facilities managers, buyers and specifiers in the public sector and members of the IMBM.
ADVERTISING RATES:
Full Page Mono £1000.00
Full Page Colour £1500.00
Agency Commission: 10%
Mechanical Data: Col Length: 270mm, Film: Digital, No. of Columns (Display): 3, Type Area: 270 x 180mm, Print Process: Offset litho, Bleed Size: 307 x 220mm, Trim Size: 297 x 210mm, Page Width: 180mm
Copy instructions: Copy Date: Last Friday of the month prior to publication date
Supplement(s): Energy Solutions - 12xY
BUSINESS: ARCHITECTURE & BUILDING: Building Related

BUILDING AND FACILITIES NEWS
1804996U4R-623
Editorial Address: Suite 4.4B, 4th Floor, Maybrook House, Queensway, HALESOWEN, B63 4AH **Tel:** 0121 504 3671
Fax: 0121 550 7482
Email: bafn@btconnect.com
Advertising Address: As above. **Fax:** 0121 550 5819
Email: bafn@btconnect.com
Web site: http://www.buildingandfacilitiesnews.co.uk
Publisher: Building and Facilities News
Frequency: Monthly - Published around the last Friday of the cover month
Annual Sub.: £180.00
Circulation: 5,000 (Publisher's Statement)
Usual Pagination: 36
Editor: Andre Laurent; **Advertising Manager:** Andre Laurent
Summary of Content: Magazine featuring asset management, best practice, green issues, facilities news, support services, vending, lighting and interiors, document security and show reviews.
Readership/Target Audience: Aimed at facilities managers, directors and senior buyers.
ADVERTISING RATES:
Full Page Colour £2000.00
Agency Commission: 10%
Mechanical Data: Type Area: 420 x 297mm, Col Length: 420mm, Page Width: 297mm, Film: Digital
Average advertising content per issue: 20%
BUSINESS: ARCHITECTURE & BUILDING: Building Related

BUILDING CONSERVATION JOURNAL
1695528U4R-618
Editorial Address: 12 Great George Street, Parliament Square, LONDON, SW1P 3AD **Tel:** 020 7695 1554
Fax: 020 7334 3768
Email: jambrose@rics.org
Advertising Address: 45-47 Clerkenwell Green, LONDON, EC1R 0ED **Tel:** 020 7490 5644 **Fax:** 020 7490 4957
Email: mei@atompublishing.co.uk
Web site: http://www.rics.org
Publisher: Royal Institution of Chartered Surveyors
Frequency: Quarterly
Free to qualifying individuals
Circulation: 1,000 (Publisher's Statement)
Editor: Jan Ambrose
Summary of Content: Journal focusing on building conservation techniques, topical issues, legislation, case studies, building conservation related courses and updates from forum board members involved in high-profile projects.
Readership/Target Audience: Aimed at RICS members.
ADVERTISING RATES:
Full Page Colour £630.00
Agency Commission: 10%
Mechanical Data: Type Area: 280 x 190mm, Col Length: 280mm, Page Width: 190mm, Film: Digital
BUSINESS: ARCHITECTURE & BUILDING: Building Related

BUILDING CONTROL JOURNAL
35894U4E-70
Editorial Address: 12 Great George Street, Parliament Square, LONDON, SW1P 3AD **Tel:** 020 7695 1554
Fax: 020 7695 1526
Email: jambrose@rics.org
Advertising Address: Atom Publishing, 45-47 Clerkenwell Green, LONDON, EC1R 0EB **Tel:** 020 7490 5632
Fax: 020 7490 4957
Email: mei@atompublishing.co.uk
Web site: http://www.rics.org
Publisher: Royal Institution of Chartered Surveyors

Date Established: 1974
Frequency: 10 issues yearly - Published at the end of each month prior to cover date
Free to qualifying individuals
Annual Sub.: £82.50
Circulation: 4,000 (Publisher's Statement)
Usual Pagination: 32
Editor: Jan Ambrose
Summary of Content: Journal of the Royal Institute of Chartered Surveyors' Building Control Forum. Covers news and all aspects of building and surveying.
Readership/Target Audience: Aimed at building control surveyors.
ADVERTISING RATES:
Full Page Mono £1470.00
Full Page Colour £1660.00
Agency Commission: 10%
Mechanical Data: Type Area: 280 x 190mm, Col Length: 280mm, Page Width: 190mm, No. of Columns (Display): 4, Film: Digital
BUSINESS: ARCHITECTURE & BUILDING: Building

BUILDING DESIGN
35794U4A-95
Editorial Address: Ludgate House, 245 Blackfriars Road, LONDON, SE1 9UY **Tel:** 020 7921 8560 **Fax:** 020 7921 8244
Email: katherine.hayes@ubm.com
Advertising Address: As above. **Tel:** 020 7921 8203
Email: lucy.morphew@ubm.com
Web site: http://www.bdonline.co.uk
ISSN: 0007-3423
Publisher: UBM Information Ltd
Date Established: 1970
Frequency: 47 issues yearly - Published on Friday
Free to qualifying individuals
Annual Sub.: £105.00
Circulation: 19,778 (ABC 01/07/2008 to 30/06/2009)
Usual Pagination: 32
Editor: Amanda Baillieu; **News Editor:** Will Hurst;
Advertising Manager: Lucy Morphew
Summary of Content: Magazine containing articles about construction, design and building.
Readership/Target Audience: Aimed at architects, building contractors, architectural technicians and other designers and specifiers.
ADVERTISING RATES:
Full Page Mono £2249.00
Full Page Colour £3117.00
Mechanical Data: Type Area: 380 x 272mm, Col Length: 380mm, Page Width: 272mm, Trim Size: 404 x 293mm, Bleed Size: 408 x 296mm, No. of Columns (Display): 6, Col Widths (Display): 42mm, Print Process: Web-fed offset litho, Film: Digital
Copy instructions: Copy Date: 2 weeks prior to publication date
Supplement(s): Concrete Quarterly - 4xY
BUSINESS: ARCHITECTURE & BUILDING: Architecture

BUILDING ENGINEER
35795U4A-110
Editorial Address: Lutyens House, Billing Brook Road, NORTHAMPTON, NN3 8NW **Tel:** 01604 404121
Fax: 01604 784220
Email: editor@abe.org.uk
Advertising Address: As above. **Tel:** 01604 773948
Email: editor@abe.org.uk
Web site: http://www.abe.org.uk
ISSN: 0969-8213
Publisher: Association of Building Engineers
Date Established: 1993
Frequency: Monthly - Published on the 1st of the cover month
Cover Price: £5.00
Free to qualifying individuals
Annual Sub.: £40.00
Circulation: 6,500 (Publisher's Statement)
Usual Pagination: 64
Editor: Carol Langham; **Advertising Manager:** Carol Langham
Summary of Content: Journal of The Association of Building Engineers covering all aspects of building regulations, products and technical articles.
Readership/Target Audience: Read by building engineers, surveyors, architects and others involved in the technology of building.
ADVERTISING RATES:
Full Page Mono £670.00
Full Page Colour £1050.00
Agency Commission: 10%
Mechanical Data: Col Length: 267mm, No. of Columns (Display): 3, Type Area: 267 x 180mm, Trim Size: 297 x 210mm, Bleed Size: 303 x 216mm, Page Width: 180mm, Film: Positive, right reading, emulsion side down. Digital
Copy instructions: Copy Date: 3 weeks prior to publication date
Average advertising content per issue: 25%
BUSINESS: ARCHITECTURE & BUILDING: Architecture

BUILDING FOR EDUCATION
35799U4A-112
Formerly: Educational Building
Editorial Address: St. James House, 118 Greys Road, HENLEY-ON-THAMES, RG9 1QW **Tel:** 01491 411848
Fax: 01491 411416
Email: sales@schoolspublishing.co.uk
Advertising Address: As above.
Email: sales@schoolspublishing.co.uk
Web site: http://www.b4e.co.uk
Publisher: Schools Publishing Limited
Date Established: 1998
Frequency: Monthly - Published around the 14th of the cover month
Cover Price: £3.00
Free to qualifying individuals
Annual Sub.: £30.00
Circulation: 8,000 (Publisher's Statement)
Usual Pagination: 36
Editor: James Eves
Summary of Content: Magazine covering building related matters that affect the education market place, including latest news, special features, case studies and new products and services.
Readership/Target Audience: Aimed at a cross section in the education sector, including educational architects, independent and grant maintained schools, colleges and nurseries.
ADVERTISING RATES:
Full Page Mono £1100.00
Full Page Colour £1265.00
SCC £8.50
Agency Commission: 10%
Mechanical Data: Film: Digital, Type Area: 270 x 180mm, Col Length: 270mm, Bleed Size: +3mm, Page Width: 180mm, Trim Size: 297 x 210mm
Copy instructions: Copy Date: 1 week prior to publication date
Average advertising content per issue: 35%
BUSINESS: ARCHITECTURE & BUILDING: Architecture

BUILDING FOR LEISURE
35896U4E-75
Editorial Address: SBC House, Restmor Way, WALLINGTON, SM6 7AH **Tel:** 020 8288 1080
Fax: 020 8288 1099
Email: richard@buildingforleisure.co.uk
Advertising Address: As above.
Email: julian@buildingforleisure.co.uk
Web site: http://www.bflmagazine.co.uk
Publisher: Stable Publishing Ltd
Frequency: 10 issues yearly - Published around the middle of the cover month
Free to qualifying individuals
Annual Sub.: £36.00
Circulation: 11,444 (Publisher's Statement)
Usual Pagination: 76
Editor: Richard Sutton; **Group Editor:** Richard Sutton;
Publisher: Toby Filby
Summary of Content: Magazine covering all aspects of the public and private sector leisure build market. Includes articles on the building of hotels, pubs, leisure centres, restaurants, cinemas, universities, schools and parks.
Readership/Target Audience: Aimed at specifiers and buyers involved in leisure build projects, architects, quantity surveyors, contractors and local authority building departments.
ADVERTISING RATES:
Full Page Colour £1945.00
Agency Commission: 10%
Mechanical Data: Type Area: 265 x 180mm, Bleed Size: 303 x 216mm, Trim Size: 297 x 210mm, Col Length: 265mm, Film: Digital, Page Width: 180mm
Copy instructions: Copy Date: 4 weeks prior to publication date
Average advertising content per issue: 40%
BUSINESS: ARCHITECTURE & BUILDING: Building

BUILDING INNOVATIONS
1629415U4E-409
Editorial Address: 16 Parker Court, Dyson Way, Staffordshire Technology Park, STAFFORD, ST18 0WP
Tel: 01785 330635 **Fax:** 0845 862 8639
Email: info@link2media.co.uk
Advertising Address: As above. **Tel:** 01785 711591
Fax: 01785 711592
Email: david@link2media.co.uk
Web site: http://www.link2media.co.uk
Publisher: Link2.Media Business Publishing Ltd
Date Established: 2003
Frequency: Quarterly
Cover Price: Free
Circulation: 7,000 (Publisher's Statement)
Usual Pagination: 84
Editor: David Broadfield; **Advertising Manager:** David Broadfield
Summary of Content: Magazine covering the architectural and construction industry.
Readership/Target Audience: Aimed at architects and technologists.

ADVERTISING RATES:
Full Page Colour £795.00
Agency Commission: 10%
Copy instructions: Copy Date: 6 weeks prior to publication date
Average advertising content per issue: 10%
BUSINESS: ARCHITECTURE & BUILDING: Building

BUILDING LAW MONTHLY
39125U44-165
Editorial Address: Telephone House, 69-77 Paul Street, LONDON, EC2A 4LQ **Tel:** 020 7017 6762
Fax: 020 7017 5274
Email: jessica.westwood@informa.com
Web site: http://www.informalaw.com
ISSN: 0266-1628
Publisher: Informa PLC
Frequency: 10 issues yearly
Usual Pagination: 12
Editor: Jessica Westwood; **Advertising Manager:** Caroline Gasking
Summary of Content: Newsletter providing updates on building regulations and case law.
Readership/Target Audience: Aimed at law practitioners and legal buildings experts.
ADVERTISING: No Advertising taken
BUSINESS: LEGAL

BUILDING NEWS
35913U4E-283
Formerly: The Merchant
Editorial Address: McDermott Chambers, 2 The Green, Kings Norton, BIRMINGHAM, B38 8SD **Tel:** 0121 451 3037
Fax: 0121 459 2179
Email: lee.butler@buildingnews.co.uk
Advertising Address: As above.
Email: lee.butler@buildingnews.co.uk
Web site: http://www.buildingnews.co.uk
Publisher: Butler Publishing Ltd
Date Established: 2003
Frequency: 11 issues yearly - Published on the 15th of the cover month
Cover Price: £4.00
Free to qualifying individuals
Annual Sub.: £23.00
Circulation: 15,250 (Publisher's Statement)
Usual Pagination: 56
Editor: Lee Butler; **Advertising Manager:** Lee Butler; **Publisher:** Lee Butler
Summary of Content: Publication covering products, regulations, application and safety issues relevant to the building trade.
Readership/Target Audience: Aimed at builders, contractors, architects, merchants and stockists including retailers and DIY outlets.
ADVERTISING RATES:
Full Page Colour £1330.00
Agency Commission: 10%
Mechanical Data: Type Area: 375 x 280mm, Col Length: 375mm, Trim Size: 395 x 300mm, Bleed Size: 401 x 306mm, Page Width: 280mm, Film: Digital
Copy instructions: Copy Date: 1st of the cover month
Average advertising content per issue: 40%
BUSINESS: ARCHITECTURE & BUILDING: Building

BUILDING POWER SCOTLAND
38965U42A-9
Editorial Address: PO Box 6, HADDINGTON, EH41 3NQ
Tel: 01620 822578 **Fax:** 01620 822578
Email: allscotnews@btinternet.com
Advertising Address: As above. **Fax:** 01620 825079
Email: allscotnews@btinternet.com
Publisher: Rae-Lin Communications
Frequency: Monthly
Annual Sub.: £30.00
Usual Pagination: 36
Editor: Richard Brown
Summary of Content: Magazine covering the latest developments and issues affecting the construction industry in Scotland.
Readership/Target Audience: Aimed at those involved in the construction industry.
BUSINESS: CONSTRUCTION

BUILDING PRODUCTS
35900U4E-134
Editorial Address: 6th Floor, Davis House, 2 Robert Street, CROYDON, CR0 1QQ **Tel:** 020 8253 4606
Fax: 020 8253 4603
Email: editorial@buildingproducts.co.uk
Advertising Address: As above. **Tel:** 020 8253 4602
Email: simon.higginbottom@metropolis.co.uk
Web site: http://www.buildingproducts.co.uk
Publisher: Metropolis International Group Ltd
Date Established: 1978
Frequency: Monthly
Cover Price: £6.00
Free to qualifying individuals
Annual Sub.: £55.00

Circulation: 26,850 (ABC 01/07/2008 to 30/06/2009)
Usual Pagination: 76
Editor: James Parker; **Advertising Manager:** Simon Higginbottom
Summary of Content: Magazine containing information on products and services available in the UK building industry together with technical advice and current issues.
Readership/Target Audience: Aimed at architects, architectural technologists, surveyors, engineers and property developers in the public and private sector.
ADVERTISING RATES:
Full Page Mono £2895.00
Full Page Colour £2895.00
Agency Commission: 10%
Mechanical Data: Type Area: 254 x 178mm, Trim Size: 297 x 210mm, Bleed Size: 303 x 216mm, Film: Digital, Col Length: 254mm, Page Width: 178mm, Col Widths (Display): 86mm, No. of Columns (Display): 2
Average advertising content per issue: 45%
BUSINESS: ARCHITECTURE & BUILDING: Building

BUILDING SCOTLAND
767359U4E-403
Editorial Address: Unit N4, Chorley Business & Technology Centre, Euxton Lane, Euxton, CHORLEY, PR7 6TE
Tel: 01257 231900 **Fax:** 01257 249389
Email: edit@esengroup.co.uk
Advertising Address: As above. **Tel:** 01204 386363
Fax: 01204 543590
Email: mblackmore@esengroup.co.uk
Web site: http://www.esengroup.co.uk
Publisher: ESEN Group
Date Established: 2002
Frequency: 6 issues yearly
Annual Sub.: £75.00
Circulation: 3,502 (ABC 01/07/2007 to 30/06/2008)
Editor: Victoria Lee; **Advertising Manager:** Mathew Blackmore
Summary of Content: Magazine for the building and construction industry.
Readership/Target Audience: Aimed at home builders, professional team members, housing associations, local councils, main contractors, large engineering companies and health trusts.
ADVERTISING RATES:
Full Page Colour £1695.00
Agency Commission: 10%
Mechanical Data: Type Area: 266 x 185mm, Bleed Size: 307 x 216mm, Trim Size: 297 x 210mm, Film: Digital, Col Length: 266mm, Page Width: 185mm
BUSINESS: ARCHITECTURE & BUILDING: Building

BUILDING SERVICES & ENVIRONMENTAL ENGINEER
35753U3B-7
Editorial Address: 15A London Road, MAIDSTONE, ME16 8LY **Tel:** 01733 266990 **Fax:** 01733 266990
Email: trushtonthorpe@datateam.co.uk
Advertising Address: As above. **Tel:** 01622 687031
Fax: 01622 757646
Email: rgouge@datateam.co.uk
Web site: http://www.bsee.co.uk
Publisher: Datateam Publishing Ltd
Date Established: 1978
Frequency: Monthly - Published in the middle of the month prior to cover date
Cover Price: Free
Circulation: 21,248 (ABC 01/01/2008 to 31/12/2008)
Usual Pagination: 40
Editor: Tracey Rushton-Thorpe; **Publisher:** Andrew Castle
Summary of Content: Journal covering all aspects of services in buildings.
Readership/Target Audience: Read by professional building services engineers.
ADVERTISING RATES:
Full Page Mono £2309.00
Full Page Colour £2990.00
SCC £29.00
Agency Commission: 10%
Mechanical Data: Type Area: 362 x 260mm, Col Length: 362mm, Bleed Size: 386 x 286mm, Page Width: 260mm, Trim Size: 380 x 280mm, Film: Digital
Copy instructions: Copy Date: 2 weeks prior to publication date
Average advertising content per issue: 20%
BUSINESS: HEATING & VENTILATION: Industrial Heating & Ventilation

BULK DISTRIBUTOR
39630U49C-20
Editorial Address: Oakhill House, 22 Williams Grove, SURBITON, KT6 5RN **Tel:** 020 8398 9048
Fax: 0870 762 0434
Email: pwh@oakhillmedia.com
Advertising Address: As above.
Email: anne.bulkd@btinternet.com
Web site: http://www.bulkdistributor.co.uk
ISSN: 0269-7726
Publisher: Oakhill Media Ltd

Date Established: 1990
Frequency: 6 issues yearly - Published in the middle of the 1st cover month
Annual Sub.: £150.00
Circulation: 5,476 (Publisher's Statement)
Usual Pagination: 20
Editor: Patrick Hicks; **Managing Editor:** Neil Madden; **Advertisement Director:** Anne Williams
Summary of Content: Magazine covering the full distribution chain and all bulk commodities. Focusing on storage, transportation and handling.
Readership/Target Audience: Read by shippers, their representatives and service providers to the bulk cargo industry.
ADVERTISING RATES:
Full Page Colour £2850.00
Agency Commission: 10%
Mechanical Data: Trim Size: 420 x 297mm, Bleed Size: 426 x 303mm, Film: Digital
Copy instructions: Copy Date: 2 weeks prior to publication date
Average advertising content per issue: 46%
BUSINESS: TRANSPORT: Freight

BULK MATERIALS INTERNATIONAL
36523U10-15
Editorial Address: Northbank House, 5 Bridge Street, LEATHERHEAD, KT22 8BL **Tel:** 01372 375511
Fax: 01372 370111
Email: awilkinson@wcnpublishing.com
Web site: http://www.bulkmaterialsinternational.com
ISSN: 0955-3754
Publisher: WCN Publishing
Date Established: 1994
Frequency: 6 issues yearly - Published at the end of the 2nd month
Annual Sub.: £135.00
Circulation: 6,739 (Publisher's Statement)
Usual Pagination: 20
Editor: Anne Wilkinson
Summary of Content: News magazine reporting on the bulk handling, transport and storage of materials such as coal, fertilisers, animal feeds, ores, cement, aggregates and grain etc., looking at it from a port and transport interface.
Readership/Target Audience: Aimed at companies involved in bulk handling of materials.
ADVERTISING: No Advertising taken
BUSINESS: MATERIALS HANDLING

BULK SOLIDS TODAY
36524U10-20
Editorial Address: Apex House, 28 Ruskin Avenue, WALTHAM ABBEY, EN9 3BP **Tel:** 0845 652 1012
Email: james@abbeypublishing.co.uk
Advertising Address: As above.
Email: james@bulksolidstoday.co.uk
Web site: http://www.bulksolidstoday.co.uk
ISSN: 1365-7119
Publisher: Abbey Publishing
Date Established: 1996
Frequency: 6 issues yearly - Published in the 2nd week of the cover month
Cover Price: £5.00
Free to qualifying individuals
Annual Sub.: £35.00
Circulation: 8,500 (Publisher's Statement)
Usual Pagination: 44
Editor: James Scrivens; **Managing Director:** Ralph Scrivens; **Advertising Manager:** James Scrivens
Summary of Content: Journal concerning the storage, movement, processing and control of powders and granular materials.
Readership/Target Audience: Aimed at key buyers and specifiers of loose materials handling storage and processing equipment throughout the industry.
ADVERTISING RATES:
Full Page Colour £1000.00
Agency Commission: 10%
Mechanical Data: Bleed Size: 303 x 215mm, Trim Size: 297 x 210mm, Type Area: 270 x 180mm, Col Length: 270mm, Film: Digital, Print Process: Web-fed offset, Page Width: 180mm
Average advertising content per issue: 85%
BUSINESS: MATERIALS HANDLING

THE BULLETIN
38026U22E-50
Formerly: British Frozen Food Federation Bulletin
Editorial Address: Warwick House, Unit 7, Long Bennington Business Park, Long Bennington, NEWARK, NG23 5JR
Tel: 01400 283090 **Fax:** 01400 283097
Email: bulletineditorial@bfff.co.uk
Advertising Address: As above.
Email: janj@dewberryredpoint.co.uk
Web site: http://www.bfff.co.uk
Publisher: Dewberry Redpoint Ltd

Business Magazines

Frequency: 10 issues yearly - Published the 1st Monday of the cover month. Double issues are the 1st Monday of the 2nd cover month
Free to qualifying individuals
Circulation: 600 (Publisher's Statement)
Usual Pagination: 30
Editor: Graeme Day; **Advertising Manager:** Graeme Day
Summary of Content: Publication representing the quick frozen food industry.
Readership/Target Audience: Aimed at retail and food service buyers.
ADVERTISING RATES:
Full Page Colour £990.00
Agency Commission: 10%
Mechanical Data: Type Area: 260 x 176mm, Bleed Size: 303 x 216mm, Trim Size: 297 x 210mm, Film: Digital, Col Length: 260mm, Page Width: 176mm
Average advertising content per issue: 30%
BUSINESS: FOOD: Frozen Food

THE BULLETIN
40623U57-6
Editorial Address: 48 Thornton Close, Girton, CAMBRIDGE, CB3 0NG **Tel:** 01223 700993
Email: bulletin@britishecologicalsociety.org
Advertising Address: 26 Blades Court, Deodar Road, LONDON, SW15 2NU **Tel:** 020 8871 9797
Fax: 020 8871 9779
Email: bill@britishecologicalsociety.org
Web site: http://www.britishecologicalsociety.org
ISSN: 0306-8307
Publisher: The British Ecological Society
Frequency: Quarterly
Free to qualifying individuals
Annual Sub.: £35.00
Circulation: 3,600 (Publisher's Statement)
Usual Pagination: 68
Editor: Alan Crowden; **Advertising Manager:** Bill Bewes
Summary of Content: Publication containing news and views from The British Ecological Society and informative features on ecological issues.
Readership/Target Audience: Aimed at members of The British Ecological Society.
ADVERTISING RATES:
Full Page Mono £450.00
Full Page Colour £900.00
Mechanical Data: Film: Digital
Copy instructions: Copy Date: 1st of the month prior to publication date
Average advertising content per issue: 1%
BUSINESS: ENVIRONMENT & POLLUTION

BULLETIN OF NORTHERN IRELAND LAW
23603U44-185
Editorial Address: 50 Malone Road, BELFAST, BT9 5BS
Tel: 028 9066 7711 **Fax:** 028 9032 6308
Web site: http://www.sls.qub.ac.uk
Publisher: SLS Legal Publications (NI)
Date Established: 1981
Frequency: 10 issues yearly
Annual Sub.: £210.00
Circulation: 600 (Publisher's Statement)
Usual Pagination: 45
Editor: Deborah McBride
Summary of Content: Journal covering legal cases and issues in Northern Ireland.
Readership/Target Audience: Aimed at those within the legal profession.
ADVERTISING: No Advertising taken
BUSINESS: LEGAL

THE BULLETIN OF THE BRITISH POLIO FELLOWSHIP
40455U56L-8
Editorial Address: Unit A, Eagle Office Centre, The Runway, SOUTH RUISLIP, HA4 6SE **Tel:** 0800 018 0586
Fax: 0845 450 0226
Email: info@britishpolio.org.uk
Advertising Address: As above.
Email: info@britishpolio.org.uk
Web site: http://www.britishpolio.org.uk
Publisher: British Polio Fellowship
Frequency: 6 issues yearly
Free to qualifying individuals
Annual Sub.: £12.00
Circulation: 9,000 (Publisher's Statement)
Usual Pagination: 32
Editor: Nicola Hill; **Advertising Manager:** Jackie Ball
Summary of Content: Magazine covering all aspects of polio, new and existing product information, reviews and entertainment.
Readership/Target Audience: Aimed at polio survivors and those who work with them.
ADVERTISING: Rates on application
BUSINESS: HEALTH & MEDICAL: Disability & Rehabilitation

BULLETIN OF THE ROYAL COLLEGE OF SPEECH AND LANGUAGE THERAPISTS
40456U56L-8_50
Formerly: Bulletin Supplement of the Royal College of Speech and Language Therapists
Editorial Address: 2 White Hart Yard, LONDON, SE1 1NX
Tel: 020 7378 3004 **Fax:** 020 7403 7261
Email: bulletin@rcslt.org
Web site: http://www.rcslt.org
ISSN: 0953-6086
Publisher: RCSLT
Date Established: 1945
Frequency: Monthly
Free to qualifying individuals
Annual Sub.: £90.00
Circulation: 13,500 (Publisher's Statement)
Usual Pagination: 36
Editor: Steven Harulow
Summary of Content: Bulletin containing news, features, reviews and notices of forthcoming events of interest to speech and language therapists.
Readership/Target Audience: Aimed at speech and language therapists and others with an interest in the field.
ADVERTISING: No Advertising taken
BUSINESS: HEALTH & MEDICAL: Disability & Rehabilitation

THE BULLETIN OF THE SCHOOL OF ORIENTAL AND AFRICAN STUDIES
25410U62R-36
Editorial Address: School Of Oriental & African Studies, University of London, Thornhaugh Street, Russell Square, LONDON, WC1H 0XG **Tel:** 01223 312393
Fax: 01223 315052
Email: bulletin@soas.ac.uk
Advertising Address: The Edinburgh Building, Shaftesbury Road, CAMBRIDGE, CB2 2RU **Tel:** 01223 326070
Fax: 01223 315052
Email: ad_sales@cambridge.org
Web site: http://uk.cambridge.org/journals/bso
ISSN: 0041-977X
Publisher: Cambridge University Press
Date Established: 1917
Frequency: 3 issues yearly - Published in February, June and October
Annual Sub.: £165.00
Editor: Theodore Proferes
Summary of Content: Refereed journal containing contributions to the knowledge of Asian languages, culture, history and literature.
Readership/Target Audience: Aimed at academics and researchers.
ADVERTISING RATES:
Full Page Mono £425.00
Agency Commission: 10%
Mechanical Data: Page Width: 135mm, Film: Digital, Type Area: 200 x 135mm, Col Length: 200mm
BUSINESS: CHURCH & SCHOOL EQUIPMENT & EDUCATION: Education Related

THE BURNING ISSUE
1743722U54A-232
Editorial Address: Goss Chambers, Goss Street, CHESTER, CH1 2BG **Tel:** 01244 624022 **Fax:** 01244 624023
Email: info@theburningissue.co.uk
Advertising Address: As above.
Email: sales@theburningissue.co.uk
Web site: http://www.theburningissue.co.uk
Publisher: United Awareness Publishing Ltd
Date Established: 2003
Frequency: 6 issues yearly
Cover Price: Free
Cover Price: £3.99
Circulation: 12,000 (Publisher's Statement)
Editor: Brett Tudor; **Advertising Manager:** Brett Tudor
Summary of Content: Publication that highlights the awareness campaigns of the Fire and Rescue Service and related organisations. Providing a forum for good practice within the services.
Readership/Target Audience: Aimed at all employees of the Fire and Rescue Service nationwide.
ADVERTISING RATES:
Full Page Colour £995.00
Mechanical Data: Bleed Size: 303 x 216mm, Trim Size: 297 x 210mm, Film: Digital
Copy instructions: Copy Date: 4 weeks prior to publication date
BUSINESS: SAFETY & SECURITY: Fire Fighting

BUS & COACH BUYER
39607U49B-2
Editorial Address: The Publishing Centre, 1 Woolram Wygate, SPALDING, PE11 1NU **Tel:** 01775 711777
Fax: 01775 711737
Email: stuart@busandcoachbuyer.com
Advertising Address: As above.
Email: bcbsales@busandcoachbuyer.com
Web site: http://www.busandcoachbuyer.com

Publisher: Glen-Holland Ltd
Date Established: 1989
Frequency: Weekly
Free to qualifying individuals
Annual Sub.: £115.00
Circulation: 7,200 (Publisher's Statement)
Usual Pagination: 50
Editor: Stuart Jones; **Advertising Manager:** Sallyanne Bellerby
Summary of Content: Magazine covering all aspects of buying and selling buses, coaches, mini-buses and related items.
Readership/Target Audience: Aimed at coach, minibus and bus company operators, manufacturers and dealers.
ADVERTISING RATES:
Full Page Mono £781.00
Full Page Colour £1309.00
Agency Commission: 10%
Mechanical Data: Col Length: 270mm, Bleed Size: 307 x 220mm, Trim Size: 297 x 210mm, Type Area: 270 x 190mm, Film: Digital, Page Width: 190mm
Copy instructions: Copy Date: Tuesday prior to publication date
BUSINESS: TRANSPORT: Bus & Coach Transport

BUS & COACH PRESERVATION
39608U49B-5
Formerly: Bus and Coach Preservation incorporating Preserved Bus
Editorial Address: PO Box 636, PORTSMOUTH, PO2 9XR
Tel: 023 9265 5224
Email: presbusps@aol.com
Advertising Address: As above.
Email: presbusps@aol.com
Web site: http://www.ianallanpub.co.uk
ISSN: 1462-1886
Publisher: PressBus Publishing Services
Date Established: 1998
Frequency: Monthly
Cover Price: £3.25
Annual Sub.: £39.00
Usual Pagination: 64
Editor: Philip Lamb; **Advertising Manager:** Sandra Lamb
Summary of Content: Magazine containing news, features and technical advice on older buses and coaches.
Readership/Target Audience: Aimed at companies running restored coaches and buses, as well as private owners.
ADVERTISING RATES:
Full Page Mono £120.00
Full Page Colour £120.00
Agency Commission: 10%
Mechanical Data: Type Area: 265 x 185mm, Col Length: 265mm, Page Width: 185mm, No. of Columns (Display): 2, Bleed Size: 303 x 216mm, Trim Size: 297 x 210mm, Film: Digital
Copy instructions: Copy Date: 2 weeks prior to publication date
Average advertising content per issue: 20%
BUSINESS: TRANSPORT: Bus & Coach Transport

BUS AND COACH PROFESSIONAL
39610U49B-6
Editorial Address: Suite 1, Cornerstone House, Stafford Park 13, TELFORD, TF3 3AZ **Tel:** 01952 204920
Fax: 01952 204929
Email: steve.rooney@busandcoach.com
Advertising Address: As above.
Email: jo.taylor@busandcoach.com
Web site: http://www.busandcoach.com
Publisher: Plum Publishing Limited
Date Established: 1998
Frequency: 25 issues yearly
Annual Sub.: £55.00
Circulation: 5,100 (Publisher's Statement)
Editor: Steve Rooney; **News Editor:** Stewart Brown; **Managing Editor:** Steve Rooney
Summary of Content: Magazine containing news briefings, analysis, media reviews, professional profiles, technology, government policies and articles covering topical issues.
Readership/Target Audience: Aimed mainly at bus and coach operators.
ADVERTISING RATES:
Full Page Colour £990.00
Agency Commission: 10%
Mechanical Data: Col Length: 273mm, Film: Digital, Type Area: 273 x 186mm, Bleed Size: 303 x 216mm, Trim Size: 297 x 210mm, Page Width: 186mm
Average advertising content per issue: 40%
BUSINESS: TRANSPORT: Bus & Coach Transport

BUS FAYRE
39609U49B-10
Editorial Address: 42 Coniston Avenue, Queensbury, BRADFORD, BD13 2JD **Tel:** 01274 881640
Fax: 0870 094 0075
Email: keith@autobus-review.co.uk
Advertising Address: As above. **Fax:** 08700 940075
Email: keith@autobus-review.co.uk

Web site: http://www.autobus-review.co.uk
ISSN: 1043-9162
Publisher: Autobus Review Publications Ltd
Date Established: 1978
Frequency: 6 issues yearly
Cover Price: £3.40
Annual Sub.: £20.40
Circulation: 5,500 (Publisher's Statement)
Usual Pagination: 32
Editor: Keith Jenkinson; Managing Director: Keith Jenkinson; Advertising Manager: Keith Jenkinson
Summary of Content: Magazine examining the past and present bus and coach industry with bus group and regional news.
Readership/Target Audience: Read by bus and coach enthusiasts, historians and professionals.
ADVERTISING RATES:
Full Page Mono £150.00
Full Page Colour £375.00
Agency Commission: 15%
Mechanical Data: Col Length: 270mm, Col Widths (Display): 83mm, No. of Columns (Display): 2, Print Process: Offset, Page Width: 210mm, Type Area: 270 x 210mm, Film: Digital
Copy instructions: Copy Date: 25th of the month prior to publication date
Average advertising content per issue: 10%
BUSINESS: TRANSPORT: Bus & Coach Transport

BUSES
39611U49B-8
Editorial Address: PO Box 14644, LEVEN, KY9 1WX
Tel: 01333 340637 Fax: 01333 340608
Email: buseseditor@btconnect.com
Advertising Address: Foundry Road, STAMFORD, PE9 2PP
Tel: 01780 484632 Fax: 01780 763388
Email: david.lane@ianallanpublishing.co.uk
Web site: http://www.busesmag.com
ISSN: 0007-6392
Publisher: Ian Allan Publishing Ltd
Date Established: 1949
Frequency: Monthly
Cover Price: £3.80
Annual Sub.: £45.60
Circulation: 19,000 (Publisher's Statement)
Usual Pagination: 84
Editor: Alan Millar; Managing Director: Iain Aitken; Publisher: Paul Appleton
Summary of Content: Magazine containing information and news on bus fleets, operators and manufacturers.
Readership/Target Audience: Read by bus industry professionals and enthusiasts worldwide.
ADVERTISING RATES:
Full Page Mono £450.00
Full Page Colour £600.00
Mechanical Data: Trim Size: 297 x 210mm, Film: Digital
BUSINESS: TRANSPORT: Bus & Coach Transport

THE BUSINESS
41277U63B-415
Editorial Address: Blundell's Corner, Beverley Road, HULL, HU3 1XS Tel: 01482 315360 Fax: 01482 315477
Email: n.glaves@mailnewsmedia.co.uk
Advertising Address: As above. Tel: 01482 327111
Fax: 01482 315456
Email: d.peat@mailnewsmedia.co.uk
Web site: http://www.thisishull.co.uk
Publisher: Mail News & Media Ltd
Frequency: Weekly
Cover Price: £0.32
Usual Pagination: 16
Editor: Nick Glaves
Summary of Content: Regional business newspaper for the Hull and East Riding of Yorkshire area. Includes local business news, features, property and motors page.
Readership/Target Audience: Aimed at those in the Hull and East Riding of Yorkshire area.
ADVERTISING: Rates on application
Agency Commission: 10%
Copy instructions: Copy Date: Thursday 2pm prior to publication date
Supplement to: Hull Daily Mail
BUSINESS: REGIONAL BUSINESS: Regional Business English Counties

BUSINESS 7
1825928U63D-725
Editorial Address: Onesixty, 160 Dundee Street, EDINBURGH, EH11 1DQ Tel: 0131 535 5550
Fax: 0131 220 1203
Email: editor@business7.co.uk
Web site: http://www.business7.co.uk
Publisher: Scottish Daily Record & Sunday Mail Ltd
Date Established: 2007
Frequency: Weekly - Published on Friday
Cover Price: Free
Circulation: 20,000 (Publisher's Statement)
Usual Pagination: 24
Editor: Alasdair Northrop

Summary of Content: Magazine focusing on Scottish company news, finance and the economy, company results and trends.
Readership/Target Audience: Aimed at middle managers and leading decision makers.
BUSINESS: REGIONAL BUSINESS: Regional Business Scotland

BUSINESS AFRICA
36928U14C-32_60
Editorial Address: 26 Red Lion Square, LONDON, WC1R 4HQ Tel: 020 7576 8000 Fax: 020 7576 8485
Email: janemorley@eiu.com
Web site: http://www.eiu.com
ISSN: 0968-4468
Publisher: Economist Intelligence Unit
Date Established: 1992
Frequency: 22 issues yearly
Annual Sub.: £725.00
Circulation: 500 (Publisher's Statement)
Usual Pagination: 12
Editor: Jane Morley
Summary of Content: Newsletter containing business commentary on current events throughout Africa.
Readership/Target Audience: Read by managers of African operations.
ADVERTISING: No Advertising taken
BUSINESS: COMMERCE, INDUSTRY & MANAGEMENT: International Commerce

BUSINESS & INDUSTRY TODAY
1666667U14A-542
Editorial Address: Suite 4.4B, 4th Floor, Maybrook House, HALESOWEN, B63 4AH Tel: 0121 550 5445
Fax: 0121 550 7940
Email: bait@btconnect.com
Advertising Address: 5th Floor, Scala House, Holloway Circus, BIRMINGHAM, B1 1EQ Tel: 0121 687 1044
Fax: 0121 687 1051
Email: freshmediasales@aol.com
Web site: http://www.businessandindustrytoday.co.uk
Publisher: Business and Industry Today Ltd
Date Established: 2004
Frequency: 26 issues yearly
Free to qualifying individuals
Annual Sub.: £150.00
Circulation: 5,000 (Publisher's Statement)
Usual Pagination: 32
Editor: Andre Laurent; Advertising Manager: Ian Bird
Summary of Content: Magazine focusing on news, product reviews, company profiles, awards, appointments, exhibitions and monthly themed features.
Readership/Target Audience: Aimed at senior managers, purchasers and company directors.
ADVERTISING RATES:
Full Page Mono £1500.00
Full Page Colour £2016.00
SCC £7.00
Agency Commission: 10%
Mechanical Data: Type Area: 360 x 262mm, Col Length: 360mm, Page Width: 262mm, No. of Columns (Display): 8, Print Process: Web offset, Film: Digital
Copy instructions: Copy Date: Friday prior to publication date
Average advertising content per issue: 20%
BUSINESS: COMMERCE, INDUSTRY & MANAGEMENT

BUSINESS BRIEF
41369U63B-2482
Editorial Address: 33 Middle Meadow Avenue, BIRMINGHAM, B32 1NU Tel: 07803 053056
Email: businessbrief32@aol.com
Advertising Address: As above.
Email: businessbrief32@aol.com
Publisher: Business Brief Ltd
Frequency: 26 issues yearly
Free to qualifying individuals
Annual Sub.: £50.00
Circulation: 5,000 (Publisher's Statement)
Usual Pagination: 12
Editor: Andre Laurent; Advertising Manager: Andre Laurent
Summary of Content: Magazine covering new products and corporate and financial news.
Readership/Target Audience: Aimed at businesses in the Midlands area and the surrounding areas.
ADVERTISING RATES:
Full Page Colour £1800.00
Agency Commission: 10%
Mechanical Data: No. of Columns (Display): 8, Type Area: 360 x 260mm, Col Length: 360mm, Page Width: 260mm
Copy instructions: Copy Date: Thursday prior to publication date
Average advertising content per issue: 39%
BUSINESS: REGIONAL BUSINESS: Regional Business English Counties

BUSINESS BRIEF CHANNEL ISLANDS
41459U63F-50
Formerly: Business Brief (Jersey)
Editorial Address: PO Box 582, JERSEY, JE4 8XQ
Tel: 01534 611611 Fax: 01534 611610
Email: pbody@msppublishing.com
Advertising Address: As above. Tel: 01534 611740
Fax: 01534 611737
Email: cjenkins@jerseyeveningpost.com
Web site: http://www.thisisjersey.com
Publisher: MSP Publishing
Frequency: Monthly - Published in the 3rd week of the cover month
Cover Price: Free
Circulation: 6,000 (Publisher's Statement)
Editor: Peter Body; Advertising Manager: Paul Rebours
Summary of Content: Magazine covering all aspects of industry, commerce and financial services in the Channel Islands.
Readership/Target Audience: Read by people in the industry and commerce business.
ADVERTISING: Rates on application
Copy instructions: Copy Date: 2 weeks prior to publication date
BUSINESS: REGIONAL BUSINESS: Regional Business Channel Islands

BUSINESS BRIEF/CONFIDENTIAL
41460U63F-60
Editorial Address: PO Box 582, JERSEY, JE4 8XQ
Tel: 01534 611611 Fax: 01534 611610
Email: editorial@msppublishing.com
Advertising Address: As above. Tel: 01534 611744
Fax: 01534 611737
Email: nmontgomery@jerseyeveningpost.com
Web site: http://www.thisisjersey.com
Publisher: MSP Publishing
Frequency: Monthly
Free to qualifying individuals
Annual Sub.: £120.00
Circulation: 2,000 (Publisher's Statement)
Usual Pagination: 45
Editor: Peter Body; Advertising Manager: Norma Montgomery
Summary of Content: Directory including debt judgements, loan registrations and property transactions within the Channel Islands.
Readership/Target Audience: Read by subscribers to Business Brief Channel Islands.
ADVERTISING RATES:
Full Page Mono £1115.00
Full Page Colour £2000.00
Agency Commission: 10%
Mechanical Data: Trim Size: 297 x 210mm, Type Area: 265 x 182mm, Col Length: 265mm, Page Width: 182mm, Bleed Size: +3mm, Film: Digital
Average advertising content per issue: 40%
BUSINESS: REGIONAL BUSINESS: Regional Business Channel Islands

BUSINESS CONNECTION$
21992U14C-32_40
Editorial Address: 6 Querrin Street, LONDON, SW6 2SJ
Tel: 07050 600420
Advertising Address: As above.
Email: davidbp@msn.com
Publisher: Business Connexion$
Date Established: 1985
Frequency: Monthly
Annual Sub.: £48.00
Circulation: 15,000 (Publisher's Statement)
Usual Pagination: 112
Editor: David Bach-Price; Advertising Manager: David Bach-Price
Summary of Content: Magazine covering the traditional links between UK businesses and foreign markets, with reports on the impact of information services and IT communications on industries worldwide.
Readership/Target Audience: Aimed at directors and senior management.
ADVERTISING RATES:
Full Page Mono £1850.00
Full Page Colour £2500.00
Agency Commission: 15%
Mechanical Data: Trim Size: 297 x 210mm, No. of Columns (Display): 4, Film: Positive, right reading, emulsion side down. Digital
Copy instructions: Copy Date: 30 days prior to publication date
BUSINESS: COMMERCE, INDUSTRY & MANAGEMENT: International Commerce

BUSINESS CONTINUITY JOURNAL
1790659U1R-379
Editorial Address: PO Box 1393, HUDDERSFIELD, HD1 9TN Tel: 01484 300750

Business Magazines

Email: editor@businesscontinuityjournal.com
Web site: http://www.businesscontinuityjournal.com
ISSN: 1752-4539
Publisher: Portal Publishing Ltd
Date Established: 2006
Frequency: Quarterly
Circulation: 500 (Publisher's Statement)
Usual Pagination: 80
Editor: David Honour
Summary of Content: Peer reviewed academic journal covering all aspects of the business continuity profession.
Readership/Target Audience: Aimed at business continuity, disaster recovery, information security and business risk planners.
ADVERTISING: No Advertising taken
BUSINESS: FINANCE & ECONOMICS: Financial Related

BUSINESS CORNWALL
1817438U63B-2582
Editorial Address: The Old Farmhouse, Nancemellin, CAMBORNE, TR14 0DW **Tel:** 01209 718688
Email: nick@businesscornwall.co.uk
Advertising Address: As above.
Email: toni@businesscornwall.co.uk
Web site: http://www.businesscornwall.co.uk
Publisher: Tonick Business Publishing Ltd
Date Established: 2005
Frequency: 10 issues yearly - Double issues published in August/September and December/January
Cover Price: Free
Circulation: 4,000 (Publisher's Statement)
Usual Pagination: 32
Editor: Nick Eyriey
Summary of Content: Magazine focusing on business issues, featuring key stories and analysis, information about people moves, interviews with major business people and profiles of upcoming business talent.
Readership/Target Audience: Aimed at managers of SMEs in Cornwall.
ADVERTISING RATES:
Full Page Colour £775.00
Mechanical Data: Bleed Size: 303 x 216mm, Trim Size: 297 x 210mm
Copy instructions: Copy Date: 18th of the month prior to publication date
BUSINESS: REGIONAL BUSINESS: Regional Business English Counties

BUSINESS DESTINATIONS
1794991U50-232
Editorial Address: 37-42 Compton Street, LONDON, EC1V 0AP **Tel:** 020 7014 0330 **Fax:** 020 7014 0331
Email: nathan@wnmedia.com
Advertising Address: As above. **Fax:** 020 7014 0301
Email: stuart@wnmedia.com
Web site: http://www.businessdestinations.co.uk
Publisher: World News Media
Date Established: 2006
Frequency: 6 issues yearly
Annual Sub.: £48.00
Editor: Nathan May; **Features Editor:** Nathan May; **Advertising Manager:** Stuart Stone
Summary of Content: Magazine combining up-to-date country and city guides, interviews and industry comment.
Readership/Target Audience: Aimed at business travellers.
ADVERTISING RATES:
Full Page Colour EUR7000.00
Agency Commission: 10%
Mechanical Data: Bleed Size: 288 x 218mm, Trim Size: 280 x 210mm, Film: Digital
Copy instructions: Copy Date: 4 weeks prior to publication date
Average advertising content per issue: 40%
BUSINESS: TRAVEL & TOURISM

BUSINESS EAST
41280U63B-1590
Formerly: Business Scene
Editorial Address: Press House, 30 Lower Brook Street, IPSWICH, IP4 1AN **Tel:** 01473 324670 **Fax:** 01473 324776
Email: duncan.brodie@eadt.co.uk
Advertising Address: As above. **Tel:** 01473 230023
Fax: 01473 324626
Email: julian.evans@archant.co.uk
Web site: http://www.eadt.co.uk
Publisher: Archant Suffolk
Frequency: Weekly
Cover Price: £0.50
Circulation: 32,208 (Publisher's Statement)
Usual Pagination: 12
Editor: Duncan Brodie; **Advertising Manager:** Julian Evans
Summary of Content: Newspaper containing business news, profiles and advice.
Readership/Target Audience: Aimed at businesses in Essex and Suffolk.
ADVERTISING RATES:
Full Page Mono £2522.88
Full Page Colour £3532.03
SCC £8.76

Agency Commission: 10%
Mechanical Data: Type Area: 360 x 270mm, Col Length: 360mm, Col Widths (Display): 32mm, No. of Columns (Display): 8, Screen: 40 lpc, Film: Digital, Page Width: 270mm
Copy instructions: Copy Date: Tuesday 1 week prior to publication date
Supplement to: East Anglian Daily Times
BUSINESS: REGIONAL BUSINESS: Regional Business English Counties

BUSINESS EAST MIDLANDS
1638243U63B-2500
Formerly: BFEM - Business & Finance East Midlands
Editorial Address: Old Guild House, 1 New Market Street, BIRMINGHAM, B3 2NH **Tel:** 0845 602 2816
Email: amanda.woolley@bemmag.co.uk
Advertising Address: As above.
Email: enquires@bemmag.co.uk
Web site: http://www.bem-mag.com
Publisher: Business Magazine Publishing
Date Established: 2002
Frequency: 6 issues yearly
Annual Sub.: £49.00
Circulation: 7,000 (Publisher's Statement)
Usual Pagination: 68
Editor: Amanda Woolley; **Advertising Manager:** Andrew Shelton; **Publisher:** Andrew Shelton
Summary of Content: Magazine covering business news and information on the key issues affecting the East Midlands economy.
Readership/Target Audience: Aimed at chief executives, senior directors, managers and senior partners.
ADVERTISING RATES:
Full Page Colour £2150.00
Agency Commission: 10%
Mechanical Data: Type Area: 267 x 180mm, Bleed Size: 303 x 216mm, Trim Size: 297 x 210mm, Col Length: 267mm, Page Width: 180mm, Film: Digital
BUSINESS: REGIONAL BUSINESS: Regional Business English Counties

THE BUSINESS ECONOMIST
34911U1A-50
Editorial Address: 11 Baytree Walk, WATFORD, WD17 4RX
Tel: 01923 237287
Email: journal@sbe.co.uk
Advertising Address: Dean House, Vernham Dean, ANDOVER, SP11 0JZ **Tel:** 01264 737552
Email: admin@sbe.co.uk
Web site: http://www.sbe.co.uk
ISSN: 0306-5049
Publisher: Society of Business Economists
Date Established: 1969
Frequency: 3 issues yearly - Published in February/March, June/July and October/November
Free to qualifying individuals
Annual Sub.: £40.00
Circulation: 750 (Publisher's Statement)
Usual Pagination: 76
Editor: Jim Hirst; **Advertising Manager:** Katie Abberton; **Managing Editor:** Adam Chester
Summary of Content: Magazine covering developments in UK and world economics. Includes applied economic theory, and analysis of individual industries.
Readership/Target Audience: Read by accountants and business economists, financial institutions and governments.
ADVERTISING RATES:
Full Page Mono £400.00
Mechanical Data: Page Width: 110mm, Film: Digital, Type Area: 170 x 110mm, Trim Size: 210 x 148mm, Col Length: 170mm, Bleed Size: 216 x 154mm
BUSINESS: FINANCE & ECONOMICS

BUSINESS EDGE
41359U63B-1690
Editorial Address: Winchester Court, 1 Forum Place, Fiddlebridge Lane, HATFIELD, AL10 0RN **Tel:** 01707 273999
Fax: 01707 276555
Email: james.lancaster@trmg.co.uk
Advertising Address: As above. **Tel:** 01273 711555
Fax: 01273 778294
Email: stephen.chambers@trmg.co.uk
Web site: http://www.sussexenterprise.co.uk
ISSN: 0968-2910
Publisher: TRMG Ltd
Date Established: 2002
Frequency: 10 issues yearly - Combined issues December/January, July/August
Cover Price: £3.50
Free to qualifying individuals
Annual Sub.: £30.00
Circulation: 10,000 (Publisher's Statement)
Usual Pagination: 50
Editor: James Lancaster
Summary of Content: Business lifestyle magazine containing business advice, news and legislation relating to business in Sussex.

Readership/Target Audience: Aimed at members of The Chamber of Commerce for Sussex and businesses in Sussex.
ADVERTISING RATES:
Full Page Colour £2000.00
Agency Commission: 10%
Mechanical Data: Bleed Size: 281 x 216mm, Trim Size: 275 x 210mm, Film: Digital
Copy instructions: Copy Date: 2 weeks prior to publication date
BUSINESS: REGIONAL BUSINESS: Regional Business English Counties

BUSINESS EUROPE
36929U14C-33
Editorial Address: 26 Red Lion Square, LONDON, WC1R 4HQ **Tel:** 020 7576 8000 **Fax:** 020 7576 8500
Email: tessatoone@eiu.com
Web site: http://www.eiu.com
ISSN: 1351-8755
Publisher: Economist Intelligence Unit
Frequency: 22 issues yearly
Annual Sub.: £835.00
Circulation: 350 (Publisher's Statement)
Usual Pagination: 12
Editor: Tessa Toone
Summary of Content: Newsletter on the European Union. Contains analysis of European cross-border business issues, commercial opportunities, comparative statistics and practical case studies.
Readership/Target Audience: Aimed at managers of European operations.
ADVERTISING: No Advertising taken
BUSINESS: COMMERCE, INDUSTRY & MANAGEMENT: International Commerce

BUSINESS EYE
626307U14A-36
Editorial Address: Upper Newtownards Road, BELFAST, BT4 3JF **Tel:** 028 9047 4490 **Fax:** 028 9047 4495
Email: richard@businesseye.co.uk
Advertising Address: As above.
Email: claire@businesseye.co.uk
Web site: http://www.businesseye.co.uk
ISSN: 1468-1498
Publisher: Buckley Publications
Date Established: 1999
Frequency: 10 issues yearly - Published at the end of the cover month
Cover Price: £2.25
Annual Sub.: £30.00
Circulation: 7,261 (Publisher's Statement)
Usual Pagination: 100
Editor: Richard Buckley; **Advertising Manager:** Claire Dickson
Summary of Content: Magazine covering training, leadership and the latest developments within the business sector.
Readership/Target Audience: Aimed at senior business managers and directors.
ADVERTISING RATES:
Full Page Mono £1150.00
Full Page Colour £1800.00
Agency Commission: 15%
Mechanical Data: Type Area: 270 x 183mm, Col Length: 270mm, Trim Size: 297 x 210mm, Bleed Size: 305 x 215mm, Film: Digital, Print Process: Litho, Page Width: 183mm
Copy instructions: Copy Date: 3 weeks prior to publication date
Average advertising content per issue: 33%
BUSINESS: COMMERCE, INDUSTRY & MANAGEMENT

BUSINESS FIRST
1664776U63E-503
Editorial Address: Suite 60, Enterprise House, Balloo Avenue, BANGOR, BT19 7QT **Tel:** 028 9147 2119
Fax: 028 9147 0738
Email: info@twworks.co.uk
Advertising Address: As above. **Tel:** 028 9147 0739
Email: mervyn@twworks.co.uk
Publisher: The Word Works Partnership Limited
Date Established: 2005
Frequency: 6 issues yearly
Cover Price: Free
Circulation: 5,000 (Publisher's Statement)
Usual Pagination: 80
Editor: Gavin Walker
Summary of Content: Official publication of the Northern Ireland Chamber of Commerce, including business issues and company profiles.
Readership/Target Audience: Aimed at members of the Northern Ireland Chamber of Commerce.
ADVERTISING RATES:
Full Page Colour £1550.00
Mechanical Data: Type Area: 245 x 190mm, Trim Size: 265 x 210mm, Bleed Size: 271 x 216mm, Col Length: 245mm, Page Width: 190mm, Film: Digital
BUSINESS: REGIONAL BUSINESS: Regional Business Northern Ireland

BUSINESS FIRST MAGAZINE
1837015U63B-2589

Editorial Address: Unit 84, Mackley Industrial Estate, Small Dole, HENFIELD, BN5 9XE **Tel:** 01903 885191
Email: nick.peters@businessfirstmagazine.co.uk
Advertising Address: As above.
Email: nick.hall@businessfirstmagazine.co.uk
Web site: http://www.businessfirstmagazine.co.uk
Publisher: Business First
Date Established: 2008
Frequency: Quarterly
Free to qualifying individuals
Circulation: 10,000 (Print Run)
Editor: Nick Peters
Summary of Content: Magazine covering general business to business topics including banking, finance and motoring.
Readership/Target Audience: Aimed at managing directors, financial directors and marketing directors of companies with a turnover of 5 million pounds in the South East.
ADVERTISING RATES:
Full Page Colour £3925.00
Mechanical Data: Type Area: 261 x 197mm, Bleed Size: 307 x 230mm, Trim Size: 297 x 225mm, Col Length: 261mm, Page Width: 197mm, Film: Digital
BUSINESS: REGIONAL BUSINESS: Regional Business English Counties

BUSINESS FOCUS
1789530U14A-582

Editorial Address: 123 Sutherland Street, COVENTRY, CV5 7NH **Tel:** 0560 132 6260 **Fax:** 0871 733 5046
Email: editor@business-focus.net
Advertising Address: As above.
Email: info@business-focus.net
Web site: http://www.business-focus.net
Publisher: Proteus Media
Date Established: 2002
Frequency: 6 issues yearly - Frequency sometimes changes to 8 times per year
Annual Sub.: £30.00
Circulation: 15,000 (Publisher's Statement)
Usual Pagination: 48
Editor: Alan Bramton; **Features Editor:** Louise Wilding;
Advertising Manager: Ashley Campbell
Summary of Content: Magazine covering management, marketing, finance, legislation, IT, law, telecommunications, commercial property, energy and environment, government and trade, human resources, exhibitions and events, transportation and logistics.
Readership/Target Audience: Circulated to an ABC1 readership including owner-managers, managing directors, chief executives, finance directors, senior managers and entrepreneurs. All of whom are in a position to make or directly influence the purchasing decisions.
ADVERTISING RATES:
Full Page Colour £850.00
Agency Commission: 10%
Mechanical Data: Type Area: 297 x 210mm, Col Length: 297mm, Page Width: 210mm, Film: Digital
Copy instructions: Copy Date: 3 weeks prior to publication date
BUSINESS: COMMERCE, INDUSTRY & MANAGEMENT

BUSINESS FRANCHISE
36733U14A-38

Editorial Address: Carlton Plaza, 111 Upper Richmond Road, LONDON, SW15 2TJ **Tel:** 020 8394 5216
Email: alison.ledger@businessfranchise.com
Advertising Address: As above. **Tel:** 020 8394 5229
Email: michael@businessfranchise.com
Web site: http://www.businessfranchise.com
ISSN: 0955-789X
Publisher: Venture Marketing Group
Date Established: 1997
Frequency: 10 issues yearly
Cover Price: £3.60
Free to qualifying individuals
Annual Sub.: £25.00
Circulation: 20,000 (Publisher's Statement)
Usual Pagination: 140
Editor: Alison Ledger
Summary of Content: Official magazine of the British Franchise Association, covering aspects of franchising as a method of starting your own business, including industry news, company profiles and legal & financial advice.
Readership/Target Audience: Aimed at those involved with franchising and those who want to know more.
ADVERTISING RATES:
Full Page Colour £1600.00
Agency Commission: 10%
Mechanical Data: Col Length: 271mm, Page Width: 187mm, Type Area: 271 x 187mm, Bleed Size: 307 x 220mm, Trim Size: 297 x 210mm, Film: Digital
Copy instructions: Copy Date: 5 weeks prior to publication date
BUSINESS: COMMERCE, INDUSTRY & MANAGEMENT

BUSINESS HISTORY
21711U14A-40

Editorial Address: 4 Park Square, Milton Park, ABINGDON, OX14 4RN **Tel:** 020 7017 6000 **Fax:** 020 7017 6336
Email: enquiry@tandf.co.uk
Web site: http://www.tandf.co.uk/journals/titles/00076791.asp
ISSN: 0007-6791
Publisher: Routledge, Taylor & Francis
Date Established: 1958
Frequency: 6 issues yearly
Annual Sub.: £486.00
Circulation: 700 (Publisher's Statement)
Usual Pagination: 200
Editor: John Wilson
Summary of Content: Journal concerned with business history and in particular with the long-run evolution and contemporary operation of business systems and enterprises.
Readership/Target Audience: Aimed at business and economic historians, management specialists and economists.
ADVERTISING: No Advertising taken
BUSINESS: COMMERCE, INDUSTRY & MANAGEMENT

BUSINESS IN FOCUS
767734U14H-407

Editorial Address: Enterprise House, 127 Bute Street, CARDIFF, CF10 5LE **Tel:** 029 2045 0532 **Fax:** 029 2045 0533
Email: info@citypublications.org
Advertising Address: As above.
Email: info@citypublications.org
Web site: http://www.citypublications.org
Publisher: City Publications
Frequency: Quarterly
Cover Price: Free
Circulation: 98,000 (Publisher's Statement)
Usual Pagination: 16
Editor: Adrian Stone
Summary of Content: Magazine covering legal matters, advice and small business success stories.
Readership/Target Audience: Aimed at those starting up or expanding their business, as well as readers of The Western Mail (Cardiff) and the South Wales Echo.
ADVERTISING RATES:
SCC £9.75
Agency Commission: 10%
Mechanical Data: Type Area: 350 x 277mm, Col Length: 350mm, Film: Digital, Page Width: 277mm, No. of Columns (Display): 8, Col Widths (Display): 31.5mm
Copy instructions: Copy Date: 3 weeks prior to publication date
Average advertising content per issue: 40%
BUSINESS: COMMERCE, INDUSTRY & MANAGEMENT: Small Business

BUSINESS IN WALES
41430U63C-20

Editorial Address: 6 Park Street, CARDIFF, CF10 1XR
Tel: 029 2022 3333
Email: chris.kelsey@mediawales.co.uk
Advertising Address: As above. **Fax:** 029 2022 4144
Email: scott.cunningham@mediawales.co.uk
Web site: http://www.walesonline.co.uk
Publisher: Media Wales Ltd
Frequency: 6 issues yearly
Annual Sub.: £20.00
Circulation: 10,500 (Publisher's Statement)
Usual Pagination: 84
Editor: Chris Kelsey
Summary of Content: Welsh business news for industry, commerce and local government.
Readership/Target Audience: Read by managing directors of companies in Wales.
ADVERTISING RATES:
Full Page Colour £1480.00
Agency Commission: 10%
Mechanical Data: Trim Size: 265 x 175mm
Copy instructions: Copy Date: 8th of the month prior to publication date
Average advertising content per issue: 30%
BUSINESS: REGIONAL BUSINESS: Regional Business Wales

BUSINESS INDEPENDENT
41370U63B-1787

Editorial Address: Suite 1, 2nd Floor, 26-32 Hill Street, POOLE, BH15 1NR **Tel:** 01202 666602
Email: info@businessindependent.com
Advertising Address: As above.
Email: info@businessindependent.com
Publisher: Business Independent Publishing
Date Established: 1997
Frequency: Monthly
Free to qualifying individuals
Annual Sub.: £30.00
Circulation: 15,000 (Publisher's Statement)
Usual Pagination: 28
Editor: John Thompson; **Advertising Manager:** Nigel Watson; **Publisher:** Nigel Watson

Summary of Content: Newspaper covering business to business news, corporate company profiles, special features, regional economic development, inward investment reviews and business banking.
Readership/Target Audience: Read by local business decision-makers throughout the East and West Midlands and Home Counties areas.
ADVERTISING: Rates on application
Agency Commission: 10%
Copy instructions: Copy Date: 7 working days prior to publication date
Average advertising content per issue: 50%
BUSINESS: REGIONAL BUSINESS: Regional Business English Counties

BUSINESS INFO MAGAZINE
38643U34-21

Editorial Address: 4 New Cottages, Green Farm Lane, Shorne, GRAVESEND, DA12 3HQ **Tel:** 01962 771862
Email: info@binfo.co.uk
Advertising Address: As above. **Tel:** 01474 824711
Email: jamesg@binfo.co.uk
Web site: http://www.binfo.co.uk
ISSN: 1464-8814
Publisher: Kingswood Media Ltd
Date Established: 1998
Frequency: 11 issues yearly - Published on the 20th of the cover month
Cover Price: £3.50
Free to qualifying individuals
Annual Sub.: £40.00
Circulation: 6,000 (Publisher's Statement)
Usual Pagination: 52
Editor: James Goulding; **Advertising Manager:** Ethan White
Summary of Content: Magazine covering all aspects of office equipment and IT.
Readership/Target Audience: Aimed at companies employing between 20 and 350 office based staff.
ADVERTISING RATES:
Full Page Colour £3000.00
Agency Commission: 10%
Mechanical Data: Bleed Size: 307 x 220mm, Film: Digital, Page Width: 185mm, Type Area: 260 x 185mm, Trim Size: 297 x 210mm, Col Length: 260mm
Copy instructions: Copy Date: 1st of the month prior to publication
Average advertising content per issue: 45%
Supplement(s): Pen 2 Paper - 4xY, PrintIT - 6xY, Sustainable Times - 4xY, Voice2Data - 6xY
BUSINESS: OFFICE EQUIPMENT

BUSINESS INFORMATION REVIEW
40813U60A-61

Editorial Address: 1 Oliver's Yard, 55 City Road, LONDON, EC1Y 1SP **Tel:** 020 7324 8500 **Fax:** 020 7324 8600
Web site: http://www.sagepub.co.uk
ISSN: 0266-3821
Publisher: Sage Publications
Frequency: Quarterly
Cover Price: £48.00
Annual Sub.: £15.00
Editor: Gwenda Sippings
Summary of Content: Journal devoted entirely to business information, including publications and databases about companies and markets.
Readership/Target Audience: Aimed at business professionals.
ADVERTISING: No Advertising taken
BUSINESS: PUBLISHING: Publishing & Book Trade

BUSINESS INFORMATION SEARCHER
40885U60B-13_60

Editorial Address: PO Box 171, GRIMSBY, DN35 0TP
Tel: 01472 816660 **Fax:** 01472 816660
Email: bis@dataresources.co.uk
Advertising Address: As above.
Email: bis@dataresources.co.uk
Web site: http://www.dataresources.co.uk
ISSN: 1365-5760
Publisher: Effective Technology Marketing Ltd
Date Established: 1991
Frequency: Quarterly
Annual Sub.: £95.00
Circulation: 500 (Publisher's Statement)
Usual Pagination: 24
Editor: Anthony Wood; **Advertising Manager:** Alan Baldwin;
Publisher: Alan Baldwin
Summary of Content: Journal providing news and developments on the on-line information industry.
Readership/Target Audience: Aimed at people in the on-line information industry, librarians and information managers.
ADVERTISING RATES:
Full Page Mono £195.00
Full Page Colour £295.00
Agency Commission: 15%

Mechanical Data: Film: Digital, Bleed Size: +3mm, Trim Size: 297 x 210mm
Copy instructions: Copy Date: 15th of the month prior to publication date
Average advertising content per issue: 5%
BUSINESS: PUBLISHING: Libraries

BUSINESS INFORMER
37120U14H-22

Editorial Address: 2 West Street, Blackhall, HARTLEPOOL, TS27 4LJ **Tel:** 0191 518 4281
Email: editor@thebusinessinformer.co.uk
ISSN: 0266-8297
Publisher: Deneholme Publishing
Date Established: 1984
Frequency: 6 issues yearly
Annual Sub.: £48.00
Circulation: 225,000 (Publisher's Statement)
Usual Pagination: 8
Editor: Alan Roxborough
Summary of Content: Newsletter covering UK and EU business legislation and associated business information for small businesses.
Readership/Target Audience: Read by small business owners and managers, business librarians and local government officers.
ADVERTISING: No Advertising taken
BUSINESS: COMMERCE, INDUSTRY & MANAGEMENT: Small Business

BUSINESS INSURANCE
35106U1D-30

Editorial Address: 21 St. Thomas Street, LONDON, SE1 9RY **Tel:** 020 7457 1400 **Fax:** 020 7457 1440
Email: sveysey@crain.com
Advertising Address: 711 3rd Avenue, NEW YORK, NY 10017 **Tel:** 212 21 00 133
Email: braidt@businessinsurance.com
Web site: http://www.businessinsurance.com
Publisher: Crain Communications Ltd
Frequency: Weekly
Annual Sub.: $209.00
Circulation: 53,255 (Publisher's Statement)
Editor: Michael Bradford
Summary of Content: Journal covering the latest developments in risk management, insurance and reinsurance, employee benefit and health care within the USA and worldwide.
Readership/Target Audience: Aimed at insurance professionals.
ADVERTISING RATES:
Full Page Mono $18270.00
Full Page Colour $20745.00
BUSINESS: FINANCE & ECONOMICS: Insurance

BUSINESS INTELLIGENCE
41278U63B-420

Editorial Address: 34-38 Beverley Road, HULL, HU3 1YE **Tel:** 01482 324976 **Fax:** 01482 213962
Email: press@hull-humber-chamber.co.uk
Advertising Address: 2 Earl's Court, Fifth Avenue, Team Valley Trading Estate, GATESHEAD, NE11 0HF
Tel: 0191 499 4200
Email: emma.lindsay@tenalpspublishing.com
Web site: http://www.hull-humber-chamber.co.uk
Publisher: Hull & Humber Chamber of Commerce Industry & Shipping
Date Established: 1997
Frequency: 6 issues yearly - Published around the 26th of the cover month
Cover Price: £2.00
Free to qualifying individuals
Circulation: 2,000 (Publisher's Statement)
Usual Pagination: 28
Editor: Bruce Massie
Summary of Content: Chamber of Commerce newsletter covering news and issues of interest to commerce and industry.
Readership/Target Audience: Read by Chamber of Commerce Members in and around the Humber region.
ADVERTISING RATES:
Full Page Mono £1777.00
Full Page Colour £1777.00
Mechanical Data: Col Length: 280mm, Page Width: 180mm, Bleed Size: 297 x 210mm, Type Area: 280 x 180mm, Film: Digital
Copy instructions: Copy Date: 11th of the month prior to publication date
Average advertising content per issue: 33%
BUSINESS: REGIONAL BUSINESS: Regional Business English Counties

BUSINESS ISSUES FOR LEICESTERSHIRE
1611063U63B-2491

Formerly: Business Issues
Editorial Address: Leicestershire Chamber of Commerce, Charnwood Court, 5B New Walk, LEICESTER, LE1 6TE
Tel: 0116 204 6609 **Fax:** 0116 247 0430
Email: farmer.s@chamberofcommerce.co.uk
Advertising Address: 11 Swan Courtyard, Yardley, BIRMINGHAM, B26 1BU **Tel:** 0121 765 4144
Fax: 0121 706 3491
Email: farmer.s@chamberofcommerce.co.uk
Publisher: Kemps Publishing Ltd
Date Established: 2002
Frequency: 6 issues yearly - Published in the 2nd week of 1st cover month
Free to qualifying individuals
Circulation: 8,000 (Publisher's Statement)
Usual Pagination: 32
Editor: Suzanne Farmer; **Advertising Manager:** Suzanne Farmer
Summary of Content: Magazine covering all aspects of business in Leicestershire including regeneration, professional training and corporate hospitality as well as retail, legal and financial issues.
Readership/Target Audience: Aimed at leading businesses in Leicestershire.
ADVERTISING: Rates on application
BUSINESS: REGIONAL BUSINESS: Regional Business English Counties

BUSINESS JET INTERIORS INTERNATIONAL
1833010U6R-159

Editorial Address: Abinger House, Church Street, DORKING, RH4 1DF **Tel:** 01306 743744 **Fax:** 01306 742525
Email: aircraftinteriors@ukintpress.com
Advertising Address: As above.
Email: aircraftinteriors@ukintpress.com
Web site: http://www.ukipme.com
Publisher: UKIP Media & Events Ltd
Date Established: 2007
Frequency: Quarterly - Published in the 3rd week of the cover month
Annual Sub.: £60.00
Circulation: 8,000 (Publisher's Statement)
Editor: Anthony James; **Advertising Manager:** Simon Hughes
Summary of Content: Magazine focusing on VIP and business jet interiors, covering aircraft designs, technologies, products and services, market trends and analysis, materials, craftsmanship, tailoring, concepts, seating, flooring, ambient lighting and bespoke fittings.
Readership/Target Audience: Aimed at major and minor private charter operators, corporate fleet operators and multiple independent owners.
ADVERTISING RATES:
Full Page Colour £3925.00
Mechanical Data: Type Area: 276 x 200mm, Bleed Size: 306 x 236mm, Trim Size: 300 x 230mm, Col Length: 276mm, Page Width: 200mm, Film: Digital
BUSINESS: AVIATION & AERONAUTICS: Aviation Related

BUSINESS LAW INTERNATIONAL
622899U44-190

Editorial Address: 10th Floor, 1 Stephen Street, LONDON, W1T 1AT **Tel:** 020 7691 6868 **Fax:** 020 7691 6544
Email: adam.smith@int-bar.org
Advertising Address: As above.
Email: advertising@int-bar.org
Web site: http://www.ibanet.org
ISSN: 0143-7453
Publisher: International Bar Association
Date Established: 1947
Frequency: 3 issues yearly
Cover Price: £80.00
Free to qualifying individuals
Annual Sub.: £195.00
Circulation: 16,000 (Publisher's Statement)
Usual Pagination: 150
Editor: Adam Smith
Summary of Content: Magazine covering key international business law issues and analysis.
Readership/Target Audience: Aimed at international commercial lawyers.
ADVERTISING RATES:
Full Page Mono £1200.00
Mechanical Data: Type Area: 202 x 134mm, Bleed Size: 251 x 173mm, Trim Size: 245 x 170mm, Col Length: 202mm, Page Width: 134mm, Film: Digital
BUSINESS: LEGAL

BUSINESS LAW REVIEW
39129U44-200

Editorial Address: 250 Waterloo Road, LONDON, SE1 8RD
Tel: 020 7981 0656 **Fax:** 020 7981 0587
Email: simon.bellamy@kluwerlaw.com
Web site: http://www.kluwerlaw.com

ISSN: 0143-6295
Publisher: Kluwer Law International
Frequency: 11 issues yearly
Annual Sub.: EUR673.00
Circulation: 1,000 (Publisher's Statement)
Usual Pagination: 28
Editor: Simon Bellamy; **Publisher:** Simon Bellamy
Summary of Content: Publication containing articles on all aspects of business law. Includes sections which provide information on UK, EC and international law.
Readership/Target Audience: Read by business lawyers, academic lawyers, solicitors and students.
ADVERTISING: No Advertising taken
BUSINESS: LEGAL

BUSINESS LINK (YORKSHIRE & LINCOLNSHIRE)
41394U63B-2095

Editorial Address: Armstrong House, Armstrong Street, GRIMSBY, DN31 2QE **Tel:** 01472 310305
Fax: 01472 310317
Email: s.williams@blmgroup.co.uk
Advertising Address: As above. **Tel:** 01472 310310
Fax: 01472 310312
Email: k.collins@blmgroup.co.uk
Web site: http://www.blmgroup.co.uk
ISSN: 1462-2092
Publisher: Haychart Ltd
Date Established: 1988
Frequency: Monthly - Published in the 1st week of the cover month
Free to qualifying individuals
Annual Sub.: £30.00
Circulation: 13,500 (Publisher's Statement)
Usual Pagination: 60
Editor: Steve Williams; **Managing Director:** Steve Fisher; **Publisher:** Steve Fisher
Summary of Content: Business to business magazine covering the latest topical issues in business and industry.
Readership/Target Audience: Mailed to senior executives and company principals on request, in industry and commerce throughout the Yorkshire and Lincolnshire region.
ADVERTISING RATES:
Full Page Mono £1325.00
Full Page Colour £1625.00
Agency Commission: 10%
Mechanical Data: Col Length: 277mm, Film: Digital, Trim Size: 297 x 210mm, Type Area: 277 x 190mm, Page Width: 190mm
Copy instructions: Copy Date: 3 weeks prior to publication date
BUSINESS: REGIONAL BUSINESS: Regional Business English Counties

THE BUSINESS MAGAZINE
41237U63B-156

Formerly: The Business Magazine (Thames Valley)
Editorial Address: 2 The Courtyard, The Old Dairy House, Dark Lane, Maidenhatch, Pangbourne, READING, RG8 8HP
Tel: 0118 974 5580 **Fax:** 0118 974 4110
Email: editorial@elcot.co.uk
Advertising Address: As above. **Tel:** 0118 974 5330
Email: sales@elcot.co.uk
Web site: http://www.businessmag.co.uk
Publisher: Elcot Publications Ltd
Date Established: 1993
Frequency: 10 issues yearly
Cover Price: £2.50
Free to qualifying individuals
Annual Sub.: £35.00
Circulation: 15,000 (Publisher's Statement)
Editor: David Murray; **Managing Editor:** David Murray
Summary of Content: Magazine containing business news and features of interest to directors and business executives.
Readership/Target Audience: Read by company directors and principles of owner managed businesses in the South East and South West of England.
ADVERTISING: Rates on application
Agency Commission: 10%
Mechanical Data: Type Area: 274 x 188mm, Col Length: 274mm, Page Width: 188mm, Trim Size: 297 x 210mm, Bleed Size: 303 x 216mm, No. of Columns (Display): 4, Film: Digital
Copy instructions: Copy Date: 2 weeks prior to publication date
Average advertising content per issue: 35%
Editions:
The Business Magazine (Gatwick)
The Business Magazine (Solent & South Central)
The Business Magazine (Thames Valley)
BUSINESS: REGIONAL BUSINESS: Regional Business English Counties

BUSINESS MANAGEMENT
1733461U14A-564

Editorial Address: Queen Square House, 18-21 Queen Square, BRISTOL, BS1 4NH **Tel:** 0117 921 4000
Fax: 0117 926 7444

Email: bthompson@gdspublishing.com
Advertising Address: As above.
Email: richard.owen@gdsinternational.com
Web site: http://www.busmanagement.com
Publisher: GDS Publishing
Frequency: Quarterly
Cover Price: $4.95
Circulation: 32,038 (Publisher's Statement)
Usual Pagination: 144
Editor: Ben Thompson; **Advertising Manager:** Richard Stirk
Summary of Content: Magazine focusing on business management issues including executive education and training.
Readership/Target Audience: Aimed at senior management.
ADVERTISING RATES:
Full Page Colour EUR14500.00
BUSINESS: COMMERCE, INDUSTRY & MANAGEMENT

BUSINESS MATTERS
1808728U14H-436
Editorial Address: 17 Ensign House, Canary Wharf, LONDON, E14 9XQ **Tel:** 020 7148 3861
Email: editorial.bm@cbmeg.co.uk
Advertising Address: As above. **Tel:** 0870 116 2853
Fax: 0845 638 0341
Email: acarty@cbmeg.co.uk
Web site: http://www.bmmagazine.co.uk
ISSN: 1754-3096
Publisher: Capital Business Media
Date Established: 1987
Frequency: Monthly - Published around the 1st Friday of the cover month
Cover Price: £3.00
Free to qualifying individuals
Annual Sub.: £30.00
Circulation: 41,500 (Publisher's Statement)
Usual Pagination: 68
Editor: Richard Alvin; **Advertising Manager:** Anthony Carty; **Managing Editor:** Richard Alvin
Summary of Content: Magazine containing news and briefings, details of government-led initiatives for small and medium businesses, high profile interviews, new software, best practice, advice and tips.
Readership/Target Audience: Aimed at owners and managers of small businesses and those hoping to start a new business.
ADVERTISING RATES:
Full Page Colour £2350.00
Agency Commission: 10%
Mechanical Data: Bleed Size: 307 x 220mm, Trim Size: 297 x 204mm, Film: Digital
Copy instructions: Copy Date: 10 working days prior to publication date
Average advertising content per issue: 22%
BUSINESS: COMMERCE, INDUSTRY & MANAGEMENT: Small Business

BUSINESS MK
41252U63B-237_30
Editorial Address: Suite 433C, Midsummer House, Midsummer Boulevard, MILTON KEYNES, MK9 3BN
Tel: 01908 394501 **Fax:** 01908 394502
Email: news@businessmk.co.uk
Advertising Address: As above.
Email: sales@businessmk.co.uk
Web site: http://www.businessmk.co.uk
Publisher: Woburn Media Ltd
Date Established: 1999
Frequency: Monthly
Cover Price: Free
Annual Sub.: £30.00
Circulation: 4,546 (Publisher's Statement)
Usual Pagination: 32
Editor: Andrew Gibbs; **Managing Director:** Andrew Gibbs
Summary of Content: Publication containing news on companies in Milton Keynes and North Buckinghamshire. Covers management, business developments and achievements, personal finance, commercial property and motoring.
Readership/Target Audience: Aimed at business people and Chamber of Commerce members in North Buckinghamshire.
ADVERTISING RATES:
Full Page Colour £2275.00
Agency Commission: 10%
Mechanical Data: Type Area: 300 x 263mm, Col Length: 300mm, No. of Columns (Display): 9, Page Width: 263mm, Bleed Size: 335 x 292mm, Film: Digital
Copy instructions: Copy Date: 2nd Friday of month prior to publication date
Average advertising content per issue: 50%
BUSINESS: REGIONAL BUSINESS: Regional Business English Counties

BUSINESS MONEY
35071U1C-83
Editorial Address: Bowdens Business Centre, Hambridge, LANGPORT, TA10 0BP **Tel:** 01458 253536
Fax: 01458 253538

Email: editor@business-money.com
Advertising Address: As above.
Email: advertising@business-money.com
Web site: http://www.business-money.com
ISSN: 1350-1038
Publisher: Business Money Ltd
Date Established: 1993
Frequency: Monthly - Published in the last week of the cover month
Annual Sub.: £129.00
Circulation: 14,237 (Publisher's Statement)
Usual Pagination: 100
Editor: Robert Lefroy; **Group Editor:** Robert Lefroy
Summary of Content: Industry journal covering commercial finance and business banking.
Readership/Target Audience: Aimed at accountants, legal practitioners, brokers and IFAs, as well as major banks, factors, trade finance houses, all asset finance providers and commercial lenders.
ADVERTISING RATES:
Full Page Colour £2090.00
Agency Commission: 10%
Mechanical Data: Bleed Size: 303 x 216mm, Trim Size: 297 x 210mm
Average advertising content per issue: 29%
BUSINESS: FINANCE & ECONOMICS: Banking

BUSINESS MONEYFACTS
34912U1A-55
Editorial Address: Moneyfacts House, 66-70 Thorpe Road, NORWICH, NR1 1BJ **Tel:** 0870 225 0561
Fax: 0870 225 0201
Email: ltillcock@moneyfacts.co.uk
Advertising Address: As above. **Tel:** 0870 225 0520
Email: advertising@moneyfacts.co.uk
Web site: http://www.moneyfacts.co.uk
ISSN: 1355-8218
Publisher: Moneyfacts Group
Date Established: 1994
Frequency: Monthly
Annual Sub.: £87.50
Circulation: 4,000 (Publisher's Statement)
Usual Pagination: 100
Editor: Lee Tillcock; **Group Editor:** John Woods
Summary of Content: Guide to business finance. Covers buy to let mortgages, investment accounts, business current account tariffs, commercial business charge and credit cards, venture capital and factoring.
Readership/Target Audience: Aimed at accountants, financial advisors, solicitors and any other business finance intermediary.
ADVERTISING RATES:
Full Page Mono £1300.00
Full Page Colour £1690.00
Agency Commission: 10%
Mechanical Data: Type Area: 285 x 195mm, Trim Size: 297 x 210mm, Col Length: 285mm, Film: Digital, Page Width: 195mm
BUSINESS: FINANCE & ECONOMICS

BUSINESS MONTHLY
1893308U63B-2592
Editorial Address: 48 Bell Street, MAIDENHEAD, SL6 1HX
Tel: 01628 417834 **Fax:** 01628 678245
Email: carlad@baylismedia.co.uk
Web site: http://www.maidenhead-advertiser.co.uk
Publisher: Baylis & Co.
Date Established: 2007
Frequency: Monthly - Published on the last Thursday of each month
Cover Price: Free
Editor: Carla Delaney
Summary of Content: Magazine covering news, features, commercial property and tips for businesses.
Readership/Target Audience: Aimed at the business community.
Supplement to: Maidenhead Advertiser Series
BUSINESS: REGIONAL BUSINESS: Regional Business English Counties

BUSINESS NETWORK
37122U14H-421
Editorial Address: Sir Frank Whittle Way, Blackpool Business Park, BLACKPOOL, FY4 2FE **Tel:** 01253 336000
Fax: 0131 449 7060
Email: editorial@businessnetworkmagazine.com
Advertising Address: As above. **Tel:** 01536 747333
Fax: 01536 746565
Email: nicky@businessnetworkmagazine.com
Web site: http://www.businessnetworkmagazine.com
Publisher: FSB Publications
Date Established: 1998
Frequency: 6 issues yearly
Cover Price: £2.00
Free to qualifying individuals
Annual Sub.: £25.00
Circulation: 201,476 (ABC 01/07/2008 to 30/06/2009)
Usual Pagination: 48
Editor: Nigel Duncan; **Advertising Manager:** Nicky Peacock

Summary of Content: Business magazine including new product information and features on IT, finance and legal matters.
Readership/Target Audience: Aimed at decision-makers in small, medium-sized and micro businesses.
ADVERTISING RATES:
Full Page Mono £2400.00
Full Page Colour £2400.00
Agency Commission: 10%
Mechanical Data: Type Area: 264 x 180mm, Bleed Size: 303 x 216mm, Trim Size: 297 x 210mm, Col Length: 264mm, Film: Digital, Page Width: 180mm
Copy instructions: Copy Date: 17th of the month prior to publication date
Average advertising content per issue: 60%
BUSINESS: COMMERCE, INDUSTRY & MANAGEMENT: Small Business

BUSINESS NEWS
41392U63B-2040
Formerly: Business Essentials
Editorial Address: Lantern House, Lodge Drove, Woodfalls, SALISBURY, SP5 2NH **Tel:** 01725 512200
Email: amanda@phoenix-2.co.uk
Web site: http://www.businesslink.gov.uk/southeast
ISSN: 1471-9487
Publisher: Business Link
Date Established: 1986
Frequency: Quarterly
Cover Price: Free
Circulation: 80,000 (Publisher's Statement)
Usual Pagination: 12
Editor: Amanda Walker
Summary of Content: Journal containing news, products and advice for small businesses.
Readership/Target Audience: Aimed at senior business people in the South East.
ADVERTISING: No Advertising taken
BUSINESS: REGIONAL BUSINESS: Regional Business English Counties

BUSINESS NEWS (SOUTH EAST HAMPSHIRE)
41296U63B-594_75
Editorial Address: Regional Business Centre, Harts Farm Way, HAVANT, PO9 1HR **Tel:** 023 9244 9449
Fax: 023 9244 9444
Email: businessnews@chamber.org.uk
Advertising Address: As above.
Email: traci.baker@chamber.org.uk
Web site: http://www.chamber.org.uk
Publisher: Portsmouth & South East Hampshire Chamber of Commerce
Date Established: 1971
Frequency: 10 issues yearly
Cover Price: £3.00
Free to qualifying individuals
Circulation: 1,100 (Publisher's Statement)
Usual Pagination: 30
Editor: Traci Baker; **Managing Editor:** Maureen Frost
Summary of Content: Magazine containing local business news.
Readership/Target Audience: Aimed at members of the Portsmouth and South East Hampshire Chamber of Commerce and other key local decision makers.
ADVERTISING RATES:
Full Page Colour £480.00
Agency Commission: 10%
Mechanical Data: Trim Size: 297 x 210mm, Bleed Size: 303 x 216mm, Film: Digital
Copy instructions: Copy Date: 8th of the month prior to publication date
Average advertising content per issue: 25%
BUSINESS: REGIONAL BUSINESS: Regional Business English Counties

BUSINESS NORTH WEST MAGAZINE
1873498U63B-2602
Editorial Address: West Hill House, West Hill, DARTFORD, DA1 2EU **Tel:** 07956 231078
Email: bnw.pr.press@mellormedia.co.uk
Web site: http://www.bnw-magazine.co.uk
Publisher: Mellor Media Ltd
Date Established: 2009
Frequency: 6 issues yearly
Free to qualifying individuals
Circulation: 10,461 (Publisher's Statement)
Editor: Sue Watts
Summary of Content: Magazine covering business issues, with a focus on a particular area of the North West of England in each issue.
Readership/Target Audience: Aimed at all businesses based in the North West of England.
BUSINESS: REGIONAL BUSINESS: Regional Business English Counties

Business Magazines

BUSINESS POWER SCOTLAND
41439U63D-47

Editorial Address: PO Box 6, HADDINGTON, EH41 3NQ
Tel: 01620 822578 **Fax:** 01620 822578
Email: allscotnews@btinternet.com
Advertising Address: As above.
Email: allscotnews@btinternet.com
Publisher: Rae-Lin Communications
Frequency: 6 issues yearly
Usual Pagination: 24
Editor: Richard Brown; **Advertising Manager:** Richard
Brown
Summary of Content: Regional magazine covering all
aspects of business.
Readership/Target Audience: Read by managing directors,
company directors, government organisations and
businessmen.
ADVERTISING: Rates on application
BUSINESS: REGIONAL BUSINESS: Regional Business
Scotland

BUSINESS RATIO
36737U14A-52

Formerly: Business Ratio Plus
Editorial Address: Field House, 72 Oldfield Road,
HAMPTON, TW12 2HQ **Tel:** 020 8481 8742
Fax: 020 8783 0049
Email: nbarn@keynote.co.uk
Web site: http://www.keynote.co.uk
Publisher: Keynote
Frequency: 150 issues yearly
Cover Price: £295.00
Editor: Navjit Barn
Summary of Content: Publication reporting on UK
companies, credit check information and business analysis.
Readership/Target Audience: Aimed at business
executives.
ADVERTISING: No Advertising taken
BUSINESS: COMMERCE, INDUSTRY & MANAGEMENT

BUSINESS REPORT (BLACK COUNTRY)
1895881U63B-2598

Editorial Address: The Creative Industries Centre, Glaisher
Drive, Wolverhampton Science Park, WOLVERHAMPTON,
WV10 9TG **Tel:** 01902 710078 **Fax:** 01902 663400
Email: jason@businessreport.co.uk
Web site: http://www.businessreport.co.uk
Publisher: Business Report Ltd
Frequency: 6 issues yearly
Cover Price: Free
Circulation: 25,000 (Publisher's Statement)
Editor: Jason Pitt; **Publisher:** Jason Pitt
Summary of Content: Newspaper profiling local business
success stories in the area. Featuring news, legal update,
property and podcasts.
Readership/Target Audience: Aimed at business decision
makers.
ADVERTISING: Rates on application
Editions:
Business Report (Birmingham)
BUSINESS: REGIONAL BUSINESS: Regional Business
English Counties

BUSINESS REVIEW UK
1858422U4R-629

Editorial Address: 2nd Floor, Churchill House, Hagley
Street, HALESOWEN, B63 4RH **Tel:** 0121 550 4593
Email: businessreview@btconnect.com
Web site: http://www.businessandleisurereview.co.uk
Publisher: Business Review UK
Frequency: Monthly
Cover Price: Free
Circulation: 15,000 (Publisher's Statement)
Editor: Kathy McKernan
Summary of Content: Magazine covering facilities
management, construction and building.
Readership/Target Audience: Aimed at facilities managers,
directors and building distributors.
BUSINESS: ARCHITECTURE & BUILDING: Building Related

BUSINESS STANDARDS
36739U14A-57

Editorial Address: 198 Kings Road, LONDON, SW3 5XP
Email: kr2@caspianpublishing.co.uk
Web site: http://www.businessstandards.com
ISSN: 1366-5650
Publisher: Caspian Publishing
Frequency: Quarterly
Circulation: 31,436 (Publisher's Statement)
Usual Pagination: 36
Editor: Keith Ryan; **Group Editor:** Keith Ryan
Summary of Content: Business magazine focusing on
standards and quality management.
Readership/Target Audience: Aimed at members of the
British Standards Institution and decision-makers within
industry.

ADVERTISING: No Advertising taken
BUSINESS: COMMERCE, INDUSTRY & MANAGEMENT

BUSINESS STRATEGY AND THE ENVIRONMENT
40624U57-7

Editorial Address: The Atrium, Southern Gate,
CHICHESTER, PO19 8SQ **Tel:** 01243 779777
Email: aobrien@wiley.com
Advertising Address: As above. **Fax:** 01243 770432
Email: adsales@wiley.co.uk
Web site: http://www.wileyeurope.com
ISSN: 0964-4733
Publisher: Wiley-Blackwell
Frequency: 8 issues yearly
Annual Sub.: £180.00
Circulation: 500 (Publisher's Statement)
Usual Pagination: 72
Editor: Anna O'Brien; **Editor-in-Chief:** Richard Welford
Summary of Content: Journal about the major
environmental issues facing industry.
Readership/Target Audience: Aimed at strategic planners,
senior environmental managers and researchers.
ADVERTISING RATES:
Full Page Mono £1175.00
Full Page Colour £2350.00
Agency Commission: 10%
Mechanical Data: Print Process: Sheet-fed offset litho, Film:
Digital, Type Area: 230 x 170mm, Trim Size: 260 x 200mm,
Col Length: 230mm, Page Width: 170mm
BUSINESS: ENVIRONMENT & POLLUTION

THE BUSINESS, THE INDEPENDENT MAGAZINE (DORSET, WEST HANTS & SOUTH WILTSHIRE)
41273U63B-390

Formerly: The Business, The Independent Magazine (Dorset
& South Wiltshire)
Editorial Address: 9 Gainsborough Road, Ashley Heath,
RINGWOOD, BH24 2HY **Tel:** 01425 471500
Fax: 01425 475600
Email: mail@bizmag.co.uk
Advertising Address: As above.
Email: mail@bizmag.co.uk
Web site: http://www.bizmag.co.uk
ISSN: 1354-3806
Publisher: The Business (Dorset) Ltd
Date Established: 1994
Frequency: 9 issues yearly - Published on the 8th of the
cover month
Free to qualifying individuals
Annual Sub.: £35.00
Circulation: 4,500 (Publisher's Statement)
Usual Pagination: 36
Editor: Gill Bevis; **Advertising Manager:** Gill Bevis;
Publisher: Gill Bevis
Summary of Content: Magazine focusing on different
aspects of commercial life in Dorset, neighbouring
Hampshire towns and South Wiltshire.
Readership/Target Audience: Read by managing directors,
owners and chief executives. Individually mailed to named
business people at companies throughout Dorset and South
Wiltshire.
ADVERTISING RATES:
Full Page Mono £465.00
Full Page Colour £650.00
SCC £12.00
Agency Commission: 10%
Mechanical Data: Trim Size: 297 x 210mm, Bleed Size:
+5mm, Film: Digital
Copy instructions: Copy Date: 15th of the month prior to
publication date
Average advertising content per issue: 30%
BUSINESS: REGIONAL BUSINESS: Regional Business
English Counties

BUSINESS TIMES
41337U63B-1260

Editorial Address: 16 York Road, NORTHAMPTON, NN1
5QG **Tel:** 01604 259900 **Fax:** 01604 259901
Email: news@business-times.co.uk
Advertising Address: As above.
Email: news@business-times.co.uk
Publisher: The Publishing Partnership
Date Established: 1991
Frequency: Monthly - Published in the 1st week of cover
month
Cover Price: Free
Circulation: 9,500 (Publisher's Statement)
Usual Pagination: 52
Editor: Tony Rowen; **Advertising Manager:** Julie Barnes-
Ward; **Publisher:** Alan Spooner
Summary of Content: Magazine containing news and
information on business strategy in the area.
Readership/Target Audience: Aimed at business managers
in Northamptonshire.
ADVERTISING RATES:
Full Page Mono £1425.00
Agency Commission: 10%

ADVERTISING: No Advertising taken
BUSINESS: COMMERCE, INDUSTRY & MANAGEMENT

Mechanical Data: Type Area: 360 x 251mm, Col Length:
360mm, Page Width: 251mm, No. of Columns (Display): 6,
Film: Digital
Copy instructions: Copy Date: 3rd week of month prior to
publication date
BUSINESS: REGIONAL BUSINESS: Regional Business
English Counties

BUSINESS TO BUSINESS
41231U63B-126

Formerly: Bedfordshire and Luton Business to Business
Editorial Address: Suite 433C, Midsummer House,
Midsummer Boulevard, MILTON KEYNES, MK9 3BN
Tel: 01908 394501 **Fax:** 01908 394502
Email: news@businessmk.co.uk
Advertising Address: As above.
Email: sales@businessmk.co.uk
Web site: http://www.businessmk.co.uk
Publisher: Woburn Media Ltd
Date Established: 1992
Frequency: Monthly
Cover Price: Free
Annual Sub.: £30.00
Circulation: 4,059 (Publisher's Statement)
Usual Pagination: 32
Editor: Andrew Gibbs; **Managing Director:** Andrew Gibbs;
Advertising Manager: Andrew Gibbs
Summary of Content: Newspaper covering finance, law,
local news, company profiles, lifestyle and comment.
Readership/Target Audience: Aimed at businesses in
Bedfordshire.
ADVERTISING RATES:
Full Page Mono £1417.50
Full Page Colour £1417.50
SCC £5.25
Agency Commission: 10%
Mechanical Data: Type Area: 290 x 262mm, No. of
Columns (Display): 9, Col Length: 290mm, Col Widths
(Display): 25mm, Print Process: Web-fed offset litho, Page
Width: 262mm
Copy instructions: Copy Date: 2nd Friday of the month
prior to publication date
Average advertising content per issue: 50%
BUSINESS: REGIONAL BUSINESS: Regional Business
English Counties

BUSINESS TO BUSINESS MARKETING APPOINTMENTS
35557U2A-52_30

Editorial Address: 22 John Street, LONDON, WC1N 2BY
Tel: 020 7419 7999 **Fax:** 020 7419 7282
Email: robert@electricmarketing.co.uk
Advertising Address: As above.
Web site: http://www.electricmarketing.co.uk
ISSN: 1369-7714
Publisher: Electric Marketing
Date Established: 1992
Frequency: Monthly
Annual Sub.: £355.00
Usual Pagination: 10
Editor: Robert Bingham
Summary of Content: Journal containing details of recently
appointed decision makers in business to business, hi-tech
and industrial marketing.
Readership/Target Audience: Read by new business
managers, sales, marketing managers and directors.
ADVERTISING: No Advertising taken
BUSINESS: COMMUNICATIONS, ADVERTISING &
MARKETING

BUSINESS TODAY
1693793U14A-590

Editorial Address: Trinity House, Trinity Street,
LEAMINGTON SPA, CV32 5YN **Tel:** 01926 359844
Fax: 01926 337193
Email: info@mediatodayonline.co.uk
Advertising Address: As above.
Email: andy@mediatodayonline.co.uk
Web site: http://www.mediatodayonline.co.uk
Publisher: Media Today South Ltd
Date Established: 2002
Frequency: 26 issues yearly
Editor: Andrew Simpson; **Advertising Manager:** Andrew
Simpson
Summary of Content: Magazine covering business,
property, manufacturing, training, recruitment and
conferences.
Readership/Target Audience: Aimed at senior directors
within SME and blue chip companies.
ADVERTISING RATES:
Full Page Mono £3000.00
Full Page Colour £3600.00
Mechanical Data: Type Area: 360 x 330mm, Col Length:
360mm, Page Width: 330mm, Film: Digital
Copy instructions: Copy Date: 3rd week of the month
BUSINESS: COMMERCE, INDUSTRY & MANAGEMENT

Section 4 (b) Business Magazines

THE BUSINESS TRAVEL MAGAZINE

1779188U50-229

Editorial Address: Suffolk House, George Street, CROYDON, CR9 1SR **Tel:** 020 8649 7233
Fax: 020 8649 7234
Email: andy.hoskins@bmipublications.com
Advertising Address: As above.
Email: david.clare@bmipublications.com
Web site: http://www.thebusinesstravelmag.com
Publisher: BMI Publications Ltd
Date Established: 2006
Frequency: 6 issues yearly
Cover Price: Free
Circulation: 19,000 (Print Run)
Usual Pagination: 76
Editor: Andy Hoskins; **Advertising Manager:** David Clare;
Managing Editor: Alan Orbell; **Publisher:** David Clare
Summary of Content: Publication covering a mix of news, views and in-depth analysis of the most relevant business travel topics. Content ranges from back-to-basics guides to reports and topical debate.
Readership/Target Audience: Aimed at business travel and meetings arrangers, PAs, secretaries, finance managers, purchase organisers and business travel agents.
ADVERTISING RATES:
Full Page Colour £3750.00
Agency Commission: 10%
Mechanical Data: Type Area: 277 x 190mm, Bleed Size: 303 x 216mm, Trim Size: 297 x 210mm, Col Length: 277mm, Page Width: 190mm
Average advertising content per issue: 40%
BUSINESS: TRAVEL & TOURISM

BUSINESS UPDATE

1775641U63B-2562

Formerly: Business In Brief
Editorial Address: 5th Floor, Scala House, Holloway Circus, BIRMINGHAM, B1 1EQ **Tel:** 0121 687 1041
Fax: 0121 687 1051
Email: freshmediacopy@aol.com
Advertising Address: As above.
Email: freshmediauk@aol.com
Web site: http://www.businessupdateuk.co.uk
Publisher: Fresh Media UK Ltd
Frequency: 24 issues yearly
Cover Price: Free
Circulation: 5,000 (Publisher's Statement)
Usual Pagination: 20
Editor: Ian Bird; **Advertising Manager:** Ian Bird
Summary of Content: Magazine covering items of interest to businesses across the Midlands including new product launches, company and individual profiles and exhibition reviews.
Readership/Target Audience: Aimed at decision makers within businesses and industrial based organisations.
ADVERTISING: Rates on application
Copy instructions: Copy Date: 3 days prior to publication date
BUSINESS: REGIONAL BUSINESS: Regional Business English Counties

BUSINESS UPDATE MAGAZINE

1601725U63B-2489

Editorial Address: Blakemere Craft Centre, Unit 21, Chester Road, Sandiway, NORTHWICH, CW8 2EB
Tel: 01606 888111 **Fax:** 01606 882266
Email: info@profilecommunication.com
Advertising Address: As above.
Email: sarah@profilecommunication.com
Web site: http://www.profilecommunication.com
Publisher: Profile Communication UK Ltd
Date Established: 2002
Frequency: 6 issues yearly
Cover Price: £1.00
Free to qualifying individuals
Circulation: 8,000 (Publisher's Statement)
Usual Pagination: 16
Editor: Lucy Beaumont
Summary of Content: Magazines (two separate editions) covering stories and features on businesses in Mid and South Cheshire.
Readership/Target Audience: Aimed at managing directors and leading business people.
ADVERTISING RATES:
Full Page Mono £900.00
Agency Commission: 10%
Mechanical Data: Trim Size: 297 x 210mm
Average advertising content per issue: 40%
BUSINESS: REGIONAL BUSINESS: Regional Business English Counties

BUSINESS VOICE

36743U14A-63

Formerly: Business Voice (North Derbyshire)
Editorial Address: 198 Kings Road, LONDON, SW3 5XP
Tel: 020 7368 7100 **Fax:** 020 7368 7201
Email: edit@businessvoice.co.uk

Advertising Address: As above. **Tel:** 020 7368 7111
Fax: 020 7368 7112
Email: jw2@caspianpublishing.co.uk
Web site: http://www.caspianpublishing.co.uk
ISSN: 1468-9162
Publisher: Caspian Publishing
Date Established: 1999
Frequency: 10 issues yearly
Cover Price: £3.00
Free to qualifying individuals
Annual Sub.: £30.00
Circulation: 20,997 (ABC 01/07/2007 to 30/06/2008)
Usual Pagination: 60
Editor: Peter Curtis; **Advertising Manager:** Jonathan Wood;
Publisher: Mike Bokaie
Summary of Content: Magazine focusing on strategic and management best practice issues facing top bosses.
Readership/Target Audience: Readership largely includes chairmen, managing directors, chief executives, heads of division and business leaders with the power to make strategic and policy decisions.
ADVERTISING RATES:
Full Page Mono £3400.00
Full Page Colour £4200.00
Agency Commission: 15%
Mechanical Data: Col Length: 255mm, Page Width: 195mm, Type Area: 255 x 195mm, Bleed Size: 281 x 221mm, Trim Size: 275 x 215mm, Film: Digital
Average advertising content per issue: 40%
BUSINESS: COMMERCE, INDUSTRY & MANAGEMENT

BUSINESS VOICE THAMES VALLEY CHAMBER OF COMMERCE

41239U63B-157

Editorial Address: 467 Malton Avenue, SLOUGH, SL1 4QU
Tel: 01753 870500 **Fax:** 01753 870501
Email: mariannecreaney@thamesvalleychamber.co.uk
Advertising Address: 2 Earls Court, Fifth Avenue Business Park, Team Valley Trading Estate, GATESHEAD, NE11 0HF
Tel: 0191 499 4200 **Fax:** 0191 499 4205
Email: liz.hughes@tenalpspublishing.com
Publisher: Ten Alps Publishing
Frequency: 6 issues yearly
Cover Price: £4.00
Free to qualifying individuals
Circulation: 4,000 (Publisher's Statement)
Usual Pagination: 40
Editor: Marianne Creaney
Summary of Content: Official magazine of the Thames Valley Chamber of Commerce covering business and economic issues.
Readership/Target Audience: Aimed at directors and senior managers in the Thames Valley region.
ADVERTISING: Rates on application
BUSINESS: REGIONAL BUSINESS: Regional Business English Counties

BUSINESS WEEKLY

41332U63B-1215

Formerly: Business Weekly Eastern England
Editorial Address: The Old Horse Yard, Toft, CAMBRIDGE, CB23 2RY **Tel:** 01223 264864 **Fax:** 01223 264665
Email: news@businessweekly.co.uk
Advertising Address: As above.
Email: sales@businessweekly.co.uk
Web site: http://www.businessweekly.co.uk
Publisher: Q Communications Ltd
Date Established: 1990
Frequency: 38 issues yearly
Cover Price: £0.65
Annual Sub.: £62.50
Circulation: 28,500 (Publisher's Statement)
Usual Pagination: 32
Editor: Lautaro Vargas; **Features Editor:** Alan Johnson;
Managing Director: Tony Quested; **Advertising Manager:** Alan Johnson
Summary of Content: Newspaper combining the latest business news with in-depth reports and analysis on issues of importance to companies involved in manufacturing and services to industry. Also features lifestyle features and stories.
Readership/Target Audience: Aimed at senior executives and decision makers in businesses throughout the East and South East of England.
ADVERTISING RATES:
Full Page Mono £1380.00
Full Page Colour £1560.00
SCC £6.50
Agency Commission: 10%
Mechanical Data: Col Widths (Display): 39mm, No. of Columns (Display): 6, Type Area: 375 x 265mm, Col Length: 375mm, Page Width: 265mm
Copy instructions: Copy Date: 1 week prior to publication date
Average advertising content per issue: 30%
Supplement(s): Business Space - 12xY
BUSINESS: REGIONAL BUSINESS: Regional Business English Counties

BUSINESS WEST

1894244U63B-2593

Editorial Address: Portland Street, 127-129 Portland Street, MANCHESTER, M1 4PZ **Tel:** 0161 236 2782
Email: johnny@imprintpub.co.uk
Advertising Address: As above. **Tel:** 0161 443 5077
Email: johnny@imprintpub.co.uk
Web site: http://www.westlondon.com
Publisher: Excel Publishing Company Ltd
Frequency: Quarterly
Free to qualifying individuals
Editor: Johnny Gupta
Summary of Content: Official West London Business Chamber of Commerce magazine featuring business activities and its successes, business services and events.
Readership/Target Audience: Aimed at members of the West London Business Chamber of Commerce.
ADVERTISING RATES:
Full Page Colour £1755.00
Mechanical Data: Type Area: 267 x 180mm, Bleed Size: 303 x 216mm, Trim Size: 297 x 210mm, Col Length: 267mm, Page Width: 180mm, Film: Digital
BUSINESS: REGIONAL BUSINESS: Regional Business English Counties

BUSINESS WORLD

21801U63B-1796

Editorial Address: Building D, Templar Business Park, off Torrington Avenue, COVENTRY, CV4 9AP
Tel: 024 7646 5000
Email: businessworlduk@btconnect.com
Advertising Address: As above. **Fax:** 024 7646 2694
Email: businessworlduk@btconnect.com
Web site: http://www.bizworldonline.com
Publisher: Artfeks Publishing
Date Established: 1996
Frequency: 11 issues yearly
Circulation: 25,000 (Publisher's Statement)
Usual Pagination: 36
Editor: Peter Marshall; **Advertising Manager:** Paul Clark
Summary of Content: Newspaper covering every facet of local business activity in the Midlands and the North of England region.
Readership/Target Audience: Aimed at the business community.
ADVERTISING RATES:
Full Page Mono £1560.00
Full Page Colour £1872.00
SCC £5.00
Agency Commission: 10%
Mechanical Data: Film: Digital, No. of Columns (Display): 8, Col Widths (Display): 30mm
Copy instructions: Copy Date: 15th of the month prior to publication date
Average advertising content per issue: 40%
Supplement(s): Corporate Solutions - 11xY, Manufacturing Solutions - 11xY
BUSINESS: REGIONAL BUSINESS: Regional Business English Counties

BUSINESS XL

761851U14H-29_70

Editorial Address: Octavia House, 50 Banner Street, LONDON, EC1Y 8ST **Tel:** 020 7250 7010
Fax: 020 7250 7011
Email: marc.barber@vitessemedia.co.uk
Advertising Address: As above.
Email: fraser.owen@vitessemedia.co.uk
Web site: http://www.businessxl.co.uk
Publisher: Vitesse Media plc
Date Established: 2002
Frequency: 10 issues yearly - Published 10th of the cover month
Cover Price: £3.50
Free to qualifying individuals
Circulation: 31,461 (ABC 01/07/2008 to 30/06/2009)
Usual Pagination: 66
Editor: Marc Barber; **Editor-in-Chief:** Leslie Copeland
Summary of Content: Business magazine containing four sections covering: financing the business, expanding the business, selling the business and floating the business.
Readership/Target Audience: Aimed at owner-managers and entrepreneurs behind fast growing, small to medium businesses.
ADVERTISING RATES:
Full Page Colour £3950.00
Agency Commission: 10%
Mechanical Data: Film: Digital, Col Length: 245mm, Page Width: 175mm, Type Area: 245 x 175mm, Bleed Size: 280 x 209mm, Trim Size: 274 x 203mm, Print Process: Web-fed offset litho
Copy instructions: Copy Date: 1 week prior to publication date
Average advertising content per issue: 35%
BUSINESS: COMMERCE, INDUSTRY & MANAGEMENT: Small Business

BUSINESSCAR
39577U49A-113

Formerly: Fleet Week
Editorial Address: Progressive House, 2 Maidstone Road, Foots Cray, SIDCUP, DA14 5HZ **Tel:** 020 8269 7741
Email: editorial@businesscar.co.uk
Advertising Address: As above. **Tel:** 020 8269 7700
Email: dwallace@businesscar.co.uk
Web site: http://www.businesscar.co.uk
ISSN: 0968-0144
Publisher: Progressive Media Publications
Date Established: 2006
Frequency: 25 issues yearly
Cover Price: £4.00
Free to qualifying individuals
Annual Sub.: £92.00
Circulation: 17,968 (ABC 01/01/2008 to 31/12/2008)
Usual Pagination: 32
Editor: Paul Barker; **Editor-in-Chief:** Tristan Young
Summary of Content: Magazine covering current news and trends affecting business cars.
Readership/Target Audience: Aimed at fleet managers and other senior management involved in running company cars.
ADVERTISING RATES:
Full Page Mono £3330.00
Full Page Colour £3330.00
Agency Commission: 10%
Mechanical Data: Type Area: 281 x 210mm, Film: Digital, Trim Size: 297 x 230mm, Col Length: 281mm, Page Width: 210mm, Bleed Size: 303 x 236mm
Copy instructions: Copy Date: 1 week prior to publication date
Average advertising content per issue: 50%
BUSINESS: TRANSPORT

BUTLER GROUP REVIEW
1683719U5R-680

Editorial Address: Shire Thorne House, 37-43 Prospect Street, HULL, HU2 8PX **Tel:** 01482 586149
Fax: 01482 323577
Email: maxine.holt@butlergroup.com
Web site: http://www.butlergroup.com
Publisher: Ovum
Date Established: 2002
Frequency: 10 issues yearly
Free to qualifying individuals
Circulation: 2,000 (Publisher's Statement)
Editor: Sophie Danby
Summary of Content: Journal providing analysis on industry developments and technology trends within the IT industry.
Readership/Target Audience: Aimed at IT managers and CEOs.
ADVERTISING: No Advertising taken
BUSINESS: COMPUTERS & AUTOMATION: Computers Related

THE BUYER
37020U14D-30

Editorial Address: Informa House, 30-32 Mortimer Street, LONDON, W1W 7RE **Tel:** 020 7017 4600
Fax: 020 7017 5274
Email: victoria.ophield@informa.com
Web site: http://www.informa.com
ISSN: 0141-6796
Publisher: Informa PLC
Frequency: 10 issues yearly
Annual Sub.: £255.00
Usual Pagination: 8
Editor: Victoria Ophield
Summary of Content: Publication covering key procurement and contract news, law and cases.
Readership/Target Audience: Read by lawyers, solicitors, buyers and legal departments of large companies.
ADVERTISING: No Advertising taken
BUSINESS: COMMERCE, INDUSTRY & MANAGEMENT: Purchasing

BUYING BUSINESS TRAVEL
1638080U50-208

Editorial Address: Cardinal House, 39-40 Albemarle Street, LONDON, W1S 4TE **Tel:** 020 7647 6330 **Fax:** 020 7647 6331
Email: editor@buyingbusinesstravel.com
Advertising Address: As above.
Web site: http://www.buyingbusinesstravel.com
Publisher: Panacea Publishing
Date Established: 2003
Frequency: 6 issues yearly - Published the 1st week of the 1st cover month
Cover Price: Free
Circulation: 16,000 (Publisher's Statement)
Usual Pagination: 78
Editor: Mike Toynbee; **Executive Editor:** Bob Papworth; **Managing Director:** Julian Gregory; **Advertising Manager:** Chris Mihalop; **Publisher:** Chris Mihalop
Summary of Content: Magazine covering the latest news, product information and updates within the corporate travel industry.
Readership/Target Audience: Aimed at corporate travel buyers and arrangers including meetings and events.

ADVERTISING RATES:
Full Page Colour £4500.00
Agency Commission: 10%
Mechanical Data: Trim Size: 297 x 210mm, Bleed Size: +3mm, Type Area: 265 x 187mm, Col Length: 265mm, Page Width: 187mm, Film: Digital
Copy instructions: Copy Date: 13th of month prior to publication date
BUSINESS: TRAVEL & TOURISM

BUY-SIDE TECHNOLOGY
1640277U1F-583

Formerly: Buyside Technology
Editorial Address: Haymarket House, 28-29 Haymarket, LONDON, SW1Y 4RX **Tel:** 020 7484 9799
Email: victor.anderson@incisivemedia.com
Advertising Address: As above. **Tel:** 020 7484 9700
Fax: 020 7484 9932
Email: dan.morgan@incisivemedia.com
Web site: http://www.buysidetechnology.net/
Publisher: Incisive Media Investments
Date Established: 1994
Frequency: Monthly
Annual Sub.: £575.00
Circulation: 2,750 (Publisher's Statement)
Editor: Victor Anderson; **Advertising Manager:** Dan Morgan
Summary of Content: Magazine covering news and analysis on the business and technology trends and processes shaping the hedge fund, investment management and asset management industries.
Readership/Target Audience: Aimed at asset managers, risk officers, technology vendors and chief technical managers.
ADVERTISING RATES:
Full Page Colour £3255.00
Agency Commission: 15%
Mechanical Data: Film: Digital, Bleed Size: 256 x 216mm, Trim Size: 250 x 210mm
Copy instructions: Copy Date: 20th of the month prior to publication date
Average advertising content per issue: 20%
BUSINESS: FINANCE & ECONOMICS: Investment

BVRLA NEWS
35382U31R-37

Formerly: Motive
Editorial Address: River Lodge, Badminton Court, AMERSHAM, HP7 0DD **Tel:** 01494 434747
Fax: 01494 434499
Email: toby@bvrla.co.uk
Advertising Address: Century One Publishing Ltd, Arquen House, 4-6 Spicer Street, ST. ALBANS, AL3 4PQ **Tel:** 01727 893894 **Fax:** 01727 893895
Email: ollie@centuryonepublishing.ltd.uk
Web site: http://www.bvrla.co.uk
Publisher: BVRLA
Date Established: 1972
Frequency: 10 issues yearly
Free to qualifying individuals
Annual Sub.: £30.00
Circulation: 3,500 (Publisher's Statement per month)
Usual Pagination: 8
Editor: Toby Poston; **Advertising Manager:** Oliver Kirkman
Summary of Content: Official publication of the British Vehicle, Rental and Leasing Association. Covers motoring and transport issues, used-car market, vehicle security, topical news, environment-related issues, safety, insurance and current legislation and e-commerce.
Readership/Target Audience: Read by senior executives in member companies, as well as government departments, MPs and MEPs.
ADVERTISING RATES:
Full Page Colour £2100.00
Agency Commission: 10%
Mechanical Data: Trim Size: 297 x 210mm, Type Area: 276 x 186mm, Col Length: 276mm, Film: Digital, Bleed Size: 303 x 216mm, Page Width: 186mm
Copy instructions: Copy Date: 10 days prior to publication date
Average advertising content per issue: 40%
BUSINESS: MOTOR TRADE: Motor Trade Related

C & C BUSINESS MAGAZINE
1745412U63A-255

Editorial Address: Suite 7, Sherwood House, 89 Lillie Road, LONDON, SW6 1UD **Tel:** 020 7385 6486
Fax: 020 7117 1563
Email: info@candcbusiness.com
Advertising Address: As above.
Email: info@candcbusiness.com
Web site: http://www.candcbusiness.com
Publisher: C & C Business UK Ltd
Date Established: 2006
Frequency: Quarterly
Annual Sub.: £150.00
Circulation: 1,500 (Publisher's Statement)
Usual Pagination: 62
Editor: Constantin Juhasz; **Advertising Manager:** Constantin Juhasz; **Publisher:** Constantin Juhasz

Summary of Content: Publication covering business issues such as marketing, human resources, revenue forecasting, general management and foreign exchange.
Readership/Target Audience: Aimed at the managerial level within small to medium sized businesses in London.
ADVERTISING RATES:
Full Page Colour £1750.00
Copy instructions: Copy Date: 2 weeks prior to publication date
BUSINESS: REGIONAL BUSINESS: Regional Business Greater London

C2M
1700423U2D-148

Editorial Address: 3rd Floor, Armstrong House, 38 Market Square, UXBRIDGE, UB8 1TG **Tel:** 01895 421111
Fax: 01895 431252
Email: joe.o'halloran@rbi.co.uk
Advertising Address: As above.
Email: clare_s@btl-business.com
Web site: http://www.c2m.com
Publisher: BPL Business Media Ltd
Date Established: 2006
Frequency: Quarterly
Cover Price: Free
Circulation: 5,277 (Publisher's Statement)
Usual Pagination: 36
Editor: Joe O'Halloran; **Advertising Manager:** Clare Sturzaker; **Managing Editor:** Neil Nixon; **Publisher:** Clare Sturzaker
Summary of Content: Magazine dedicated to the mobile TV market and future developments in broadcasting.
Readership/Target Audience: Aimed at content creators and owners, operational support and billing support firms, handset manufacturers and technology suppliers.
ADVERTISING RATES:
Full Page Mono £2370.00
Full Page Colour £3150.00
Agency Commission: 10%
Mechanical Data: Type Area: 265x 185mm, Bleed Size: 303 x 216mm, Trim Size: 297 x 210mm, Col Length: 265mm, Page Width: 185mm, Film: Digital
BUSINESS: COMMUNICATIONS, ADVERTISING & MARKETING: Broadcasting

C & W IN BUSINESS
41378U63B-1810

Formerly: Coventry and Warwickshire Enterprise
Editorial Address: Oak Tree Court, Binley Business Park, Harry Weston Road, COVENTRY, CV3 2UN **Tel:** 024 7665 4321 **Fax:** 024 7665 4318
Email: news@cw-chamber.co.uk
Advertising Address: Houldsworth Mill, South Mill, Reddish, STOCKPORT, SK5 6DA **Tel:** 0161 442 2576
Fax: 0161 443 2382
Email: murray@imprintpub.co.uk
Web site: http://www.cw-chamber.co.uk
Publisher: Excell Publishing
Frequency: 6 issues yearly
Cover Price: Free
Circulation: 5,000 (Publisher's Statement)
Usual Pagination: 28
Editor: Sally Glarvey; **Advertising Manager:** Murray Hobson; **Publisher:** Murray Hobson
Summary of Content: Regional business newspaper for the Central Midlands.
Readership/Target Audience: Aimed at decision makers.
ADVERTISING RATES:
Full Page Colour £1955.00
SCC £10.00
Agency Commission: 10%
Mechanical Data: No. of Columns (Display): 6, Print Process: Web-fed offset litho, Bleed Size: 346 x 251mm
Average advertising content per issue: 25%
BUSINESS: REGIONAL BUSINESS: Regional Business English Counties

C+MW
1696529U2C-510

Editorial Address: Faraday House, 39 Thornton Road, Wimbledon, LONDON, SW19 4NQ **Tel:** 020 8971 8282
Fax: 020 8971 8283
Email: pcolston@mashmedia.net
Advertising Address: As above.
Email: kteague@mashmedia.net
Web site: http://www.mashmedia.net
Publisher: Mash Media
Date Established: 2005
Frequency: Monthly - Online versions available monthly on request
Free to qualifying individuals
Circulation: 7,500 (Publisher's Statement)
Editor: Paul Colston; **Advertising Manager:** Amelie Lambert; **Publisher:** Roisin Sullens
Summary of Content: Magazine focusing on the issues facing organisers of international events.
Readership/Target Audience: Aimed at those working in the international conference and meetings industry.

ADVERTISING RATES:
Full Page Colour £2995.00
Agency Commission: 10%
Mechanical Data: Type Area: 270 x 190mm, Bleed Size: 303 x 216mm, Trim Size: 297 x 210mm, Col Length: 270mm, Page Width: 190mm, Film: Digital
Copy instructions: Copy Date: 15th of the month prior to publication date
Average advertising content per issue: 15%
BUSINESS: COMMUNICATIONS, ADVERTISING & MARKETING: Conferences & Exhibitions

---

CA MAGAZINE
35033U1B-82

Editorial Address: Studio 2001, Mile End, PAISLEY, PA1 1JS **Tel:** 0141 561 0300 **Fax:** 0141 561 0400
Email: carnag@connectcommunications.co.uk
Advertising Address: Suite 4/2 Great Michael House, 14 Links Place, EDINBURGH, EH6 7EZ **Tel:** 0131 561 0020
Fax: 0131 553 1193
Email: jenn@connectcommunications.co.uk
Web site: http://www.camagonline.co.uk
ISSN: 1352-9021
Publisher: Connect Communications
Date Established: 1897
Frequency: Monthly - Published on the 1st of the cover month
Cover Price: £3.75
Annual Sub.: £45.00
Circulation: 22,362 (ABC 01/07/2008 to 30/06/2009)
Usual Pagination: 84
Editor: Robert Outram; **Managing Director:** David Cameron
Summary of Content: Journal of the Institute of Chartered Accountants of Scotland. Contains articles covering management, strategy, finance and funding issues, also includes the latest trends in business practice as well as articles on human resources and IT.
Readership/Target Audience: Read by financial directors, managing directors, owner managers, chief executives, chairmen, lawyers, surveyors, stockbrokers and bankers.
ADVERTISING RATES:
Full Page Mono £2197.00
Full Page Colour £2977.00
Agency Commission: 15%
Mechanical Data: Film: Positive, right reading, emulsion side down, Type Area: 272 x 185mm, Trim Size: 297 x 210mm, Bleed Size: 303 x 216mm, Col Length: 272mm, Page Width: 185mm
Copy instructions: Copy Date: 3 weeks prior to publication date
Average advertising content per issue: 45%
Supplement(s): Who's Who In Corporate Finance - 1xY
BUSINESS: FINANCE & ECONOMICS: Accountancy

THE CAB DRIVER
41516U64G-250

Editorial Address: PO Box 3472, BARNET, EN5 9HF
Tel: 020 8440 3333
Email: cabdriver@btconnect.com
Advertising Address: As above.
Web site: http://www.thecabdriver.co.uk
Publisher: DJA Design
Date Established: 1921
Frequency: 26 issues yearly
Free to qualifying individuals
Annual Sub.: £20.00
Circulation: 15,000 (Publisher's Statement)
Usual Pagination: 24
Editor: Dave Allen; **Managing Director:** Dave Allen;
Advertising Manager: Dave Allen
Summary of Content: Publication covering taxi trade affairs, plus articles on tourism, travel, vehicles, restaurants, holidays, theatre, night-life and sport.
Readership/Target Audience: Aimed at taxi and private hire drivers.
ADVERTISING RATES:
Full Page Colour £1200.00
Agency Commission: 15%
Mechanical Data: Film: Digital, Type Area: 380 x 285mm, Col Length: 380mm, No. of Columns (Display): 6, Col Widths (Display): 38mm, Page Width: 285mm
Copy instructions: Copy Date: 4 weeks prior to publication date
Average advertising content per issue: 50%
BUSINESS: OTHER CLASSIFICATIONS: Taxi Trade

CAB TRADE NEWS
41517U64G-441

Editorial Address: Transport House, 128 Theobalds Road, LONDON, WC1X 8TN **Tel:** 020 8518 1274
Email: joancolin_williams@hotmail.com
Advertising Address: 13 Ford End, Woodford Green, WOODFORD GREEN, IG8 0EG **Tel:** 07903 525520
Email: peterjrose@cabtradenews.co.uk
Publisher: C.T.N
Date Established: 1930
Frequency: Monthly
Cover Price: Free
Circulation: 11,500 (Publisher's Statement)
Usual Pagination: 12

Editor: Colin Williams; **Advertising Manager:** Peter Rose
Summary of Content: Newspaper covering trade and union news, plus features on theatre, hotels, films and events.
Readership/Target Audience: Read by garage fleet drivers, owner drivers, fleet owners and taxi cab drivers.
ADVERTISING RATES:
Full Page Colour £380.00
Agency Commission: 10%
Mechanical Data: Col Length: 378mm, Type Area: 378 x 260mm, Page Width: 260mm, No. of Columns (Display): 4, Film: Digital
BUSINESS: OTHER CLASSIFICATIONS: Taxi Trade

CABINET MAKER
38055U23A-10

Editorial Address: The Irwin Centre, Scotland Road, Dry Drayton, CAMBRIDGE, CB3 8AR **Tel:** 01954 212906
Fax: 01954 212105
Email: editorial@manpublishing.co.uk
Advertising Address: As above.
Email: ed@manpublishing.co.uk
Web site: http://www.cabinet-maker.co.uk
ISSN: 0007-9278
Publisher: Manning Publishing Ltd
Date Established: 1880
Frequency: Weekly - Published every Friday
Cover Price: £2.50
Annual Sub.: £125.00
Circulation: 2,841 (ABC 01/01/2007 to 31/12/2007)
Usual Pagination: 40
Editor: George Cooper; **News Editor:** George Cooper;
Features Editor: Stephen Bevan; **Publisher:** Chris Manning
Summary of Content: Magazine covering furniture and furnishings, bedding and upholstery retailing.
Readership/Target Audience: Aimed at retailers working within the furniture industry.
ADVERTISING RATES:
Full Page Colour £3050.00
Agency Commission: 10%
Mechanical Data: Film: Digital, Col Length: 277mm, Type Area: 277 x 207mm, Print Process: Sheet-fed offset litho, Bleed Size: 303 x 231mm, Trim Size: 297 x 225mm, Page Width: 207mm
Copy instructions: Copy Date: 2 weeks prior to publication date
Average advertising content per issue: 40%
BUSINESS: FURNISHINGS & FURNITURE

CABLETALK
37291U17-256

Editorial Address: Waterloo Chambers, 19 Waterloo Street, GLASGOW, G2 6AY **Tel:** 0141 222 2100 **Fax:** 0141 222 2177
Email: glove@55north.com
Advertising Address: As above. **Tel:** 0141 222 5387
Email: gbryans@55north.com
Web site: http://www.55north.com
ISSN: 1365-3288
Publisher: 55 North
Date Established: 1977
Frequency: Monthly - Published at the end of the 1st full week of cover month
Cover Price: £3.50
Free to qualifying individuals
Annual Sub.: £28.00
Circulation: 5,400 (Publisher's Statement)
Usual Pagination: 46
Editor: Georgia Love
Summary of Content: Official journal of Electrical Contractors Association of Scotland containing product features, international and association news and articles on health and safety. Also covers new products, training, business news and environmental issues.
Readership/Target Audience: Read by contractors, specifiers, consulting engineers, architects, HVCA, local authorities, property managers, communication and security companies.
ADVERTISING RATES:
Full Page Colour £1575.00
Agency Commission: 10%
Mechanical Data: Bleed Size: 303 x 216mm, Trim Size: 297 x 210mm, Film: Digital
Copy instructions: Copy Date: 1 week prior to publication date
Average advertising content per issue: 40%
BUSINESS: ELECTRICAL

CAFÉ BUSINESS
1615673U11A-219

Formerly: EuroBev News
Editorial Address: Rephoto House, Plough Road, Smallfield, HORLEY, RH6 9EZ **Tel:** 01342 844444
Fax: 01342 844488
Email: amanda-roberts@btconnect.com
Advertising Address: As above.
Email: ian.kitchener@rephotopublishing.co.uk
Web site: http://www.cafe-business.com
Publisher: Rephoto Publishing Ltd
Frequency: 11 issues yearly - Published at the end of 1st week of cover month. Combined issues published at the end of 1st week of 2nd cover month

---

Circulation: 7,500 (Publisher's Statement)
Editor: Amanda Roberts
Summary of Content: Magazine covering the out-of-home, non alcoholic beverage service sector and all aspects of the beverage service industry from the equipment manufacturers to the high street outlets. Includes news and reviews about beverage making equipment, ingredients and ancillaries.
Readership/Target Audience: Aimed at those working in the beverage industry, managers of high street coffee shops, golf clubs and leisure venues, contract caterers, catering managers in the workplace and others who make decisions about beverages.
ADVERTISING RATES:
Full Page Colour £995.00
Agency Commission: 10%
Mechanical Data: Film: Digital, Type Area: 270 x 190mm, Bleed Size: 303 x 216mm, Trim Size: 297 x 210mm, Col Length: 270mm, Page Width: 190mm
Copy instructions: Copy Date: 2 weeks prior to publication date
Average advertising content per issue: 40%
BUSINESS: CATERING: Catering, Hotels & Restaurants

CAFÉ CULTURE
601200U22R-15

Formerly: Real Coffee
Editorial Address: Association House, 18C Moor Street, CHEPSTOW, NP16 5DB **Tel:** 01291 636336
Fax: 01291 630402
Email: clare@jandmgroup.co.uk
Advertising Address: As above. **Tel:** 01291 636333
Email: paul@jandmgroup.co.uk
Web site: http://www.cafeculturemagazine.co.uk
Publisher: J & M Group Ltd.
Date Established: 2000
Frequency: 6 issues yearly
Free to qualifying individuals
Annual Sub.: £25.00
Circulation: 7,000 (Publisher's Statement)
Usual Pagination: 48
Editor: Clare Benfield; **Managing Director:** Jim Winship;
Advertising Manager: Paul Steer
Summary of Content: Magazine covering news, views, equipment and product reviews and events coverage of the coffee and hot beverage market and the cafe scene that surrounds it.
Readership/Target Audience: Aimed at key buyers in the multiple retail sector, major catering and hotel groups, coffee bars and sandwich and snack outlets.
ADVERTISING RATES:
Full Page Colour £1200.00
Agency Commission: 10%
Mechanical Data: Type Area: 268 x 184mm, Bleed Size: 303 x 216mm, Trim Size: 297 x 210mm, Film: Digital, Col Length: 268mm, Page Width: 184mm
Average advertising content per issue: 35%
BUSINESS: FOOD: Food Related

CALL CENTRE EUROPE
37424U18B-440

Editorial Address: PO Box 220, WALTON-ON-THAMES, KT12 1YQ **Tel:** 01932 254400 **Fax:** 01932 240294
Email: editor@call-centre-europe.com
Advertising Address: As above.
Email: advertising@call-centre-europe.com
Web site: http://www.call-centre-europe.com
ISSN: 1357-4868
Publisher: Stanworth Communications
Date Established: 1992
Frequency: 6 issues yearly - Published around the middle of the cover month
Free to qualifying individuals
Annual Sub.: £18.00
Circulation: 7,443 (ABC 01/07/2007 to 30/06/2008)
Usual Pagination: 46
Editor: Paul Liptrot; **Advertising Manager:** Paul Liptrot;
Publisher: Paul Liptrot
Summary of Content: Publication covering all aspects of managing inbound and outbound telephone call centres, customer service departments, reservation centres and help desks.
Readership/Target Audience: Read by decision makers and managers within the industry.
ADVERTISING RATES:
Full Page Mono £1943.00
Full Page Colour £2310.00
Agency Commission: 10%
Mechanical Data: Type Area: 270 x 190mm, Bleed Size: 303 x 216mm, Trim Size: 297 x 210mm, Page Width: 190mm, Col Length: 270mm, No. of Columns (Display): 4, Film: Digital
Copy instructions: Copy Date: 2 weeks prior to publication date
Average advertising content per issue: 45%
BUSINESS: ELECTRONICS: Telecommunications

Business Magazines

CALL SIGN
41518U64G-450

Editorial Address: 25 Hillview Crescent, Gants Hill, ILFORD, IG1 3QD **Tel:** 07976 294463 **Fax:** 020 7250 0581
Email: callsignmag@aol.com
Advertising Address: As above.
Email: callsignmag@aol.com
Web site: http://www.dac-callsign.com
Publisher: Dial-a-Cab
Date Established: 1964
Frequency: 11 issues yearly - No June issue
Cover Price: Free
Circulation: 2,200 (Publisher's Statement)
Usual Pagination: 40
Editor: Alan Fisher; **Advertising Manager:** Alan Fisher
Summary of Content: Magazine covering products and services for London's licensed taxi trade, coming events, letters and general news. Also contains by-lined articles.
Readership/Target Audience: Read by taxi drivers and related staff.
ADVERTISING RATES:
Full Page Mono £200.00
Full Page Colour £300.00
Mechanical Data: Trim Size: 297 x 210mm, No: of Columns (Display): 3, Film: Positive, right reading, emulsion side down. Digital
Copy instructions: Copy Date: 16th of the month prior to publication date
Average advertising content per issue: 10%
BUSINESS: OTHER CLASSIFICATIONS: Taxi Trade

CAM
768066U56A-167

Editorial Address: The Old Dairy, Hudsons Farm, Fieldgate Lane, Ugley Green, BISHOP'S STORTFORD, CM22 6HJ
Tel: 01279 816300 **Fax:** 01279 816496
Email: editor@cam-mag.com
Advertising Address: As above.
Email: info@targetpublishing.com
Web site: http://www.cam-mag.com
ISSN: 1475-9403
Publisher: Target Publishing Ltd
Date Established: 2001
Frequency: Monthly
Cover Price: £6.00
Free to qualifying individuals
Annual Sub.: £65.00
Circulation: 6,500 (Publisher's Statement)
Editor: Sally-Ann Dobson; **Managing Director:** David Cann
Summary of Content: Magazine covering the latest news, research and political developments in complementary and alternative medicine including nutrition, diet, herbal medicine, naturopathy, bodywork, homeopathy, acupuncture and the therapeutic application of mind-body research.
Readership/Target Audience: Aimed at practitioners.
ADVERTISING RATES:
Full Page Colour £2226.00
Agency Commission: 10%
Mechanical Data: Type Area: 268 x 180mm, Col Length: 268mm, Trim Size: 297 x 210mm, Film: Digital, Page Width: 180mm, Bleed Size: 303 x 216mm
Copy instructions: Copy Date: 3 weeks prior to publication date
Average advertising content per issue: 40%
BUSINESS: HEALTH & MEDICAL

CAMBRIDGE JOURNAL OF ECONOMICS
601479U62A-28

Editorial Address: Faculty of Economics and Politics, Sidgwick Avenue, CAMBRIDGE, CB3 9DD
Tel: 01223 335266 **Fax:** 01233 335299
Email: apn1000@econ.cam.ac.uk
Advertising Address: 60 Upper Broadmoor Road, CROWTHORNE, RG45 7DE **Tel:** 01344 779945
Fax: 01344 779945
Email: lhann@lhms.fsnet.co.uk
Web site: http://www.cje.oupjournals.org
ISSN: 0309-166X
Publisher: OUP
Date Established: 1977
Frequency: 6 issues yearly
Circulation: 1,800 (Publisher's Statement)
Usual Pagination: 164
Editor: Jacqui Lagrue; **Managing Editor:** Jacqui Lagrue
Summary of Content: Journal which features theoretical and applied articles on major contemporary issues, with a strong emphasis on the provision and use of empirical evidence and on the formulation of economics policies.
Readership/Target Audience: Read by political economists world-wide.
ADVERTISING RATES:
Full Page Mono £340.00
Agency Commission: 10%
Mechanical Data: Film: Digital, Type Area: 200 x 130mm, Col Length: 200mm, Page Width: 130mm
BUSINESS: CHURCH & SCHOOL EQUIPMENT & EDUCATION: Education

THE CAMBRIDGE LAW JOURNAL
1851524U44-3054

Editorial Address: The Edinburgh Building, Shaftesbury Road, CAMBRIDGE, CB2 8RU **Tel:** 01223 326070
Fax: 01223 325150
Advertising Address: As above.
Email: ad_sales@cambridge.org
Web site: http://www.journals.cambridge.org
ISSN: 0008-1973
Publisher: Cambridge University Press
Frequency: 3 issues yearly - Published in March, July and November
Annual Sub.: £70.00
Editor: David Ibbetson
Summary of Content: Journal featuring articles on all aspects of law.
Readership/Target Audience: Aimed at practitioners, students, teachers, judges and administrators.
ADVERTISING RATES:
Full Page Mono £465.00
Copy instructions: Copy Date: 8 weeks prior to publication date
BUSINESS: LEGAL

THE CAMBRIDGE QUARTERLY
47518U62R-460

Editorial Address: Clare College, CAMBRIDGE, CB2 1TL
Tel: 01223 352540
Email: apn1000@cantab.net
Advertising Address: Great Clarendon Street, OXFORD, OX2 6DP **Tel:** 01865 353329
Email: jnlsadvertising@oxfordjournals.org
Web site: http://www3.oup.co.uk/camquj
ISSN: 0008-199X
Publisher: OUP
Date Established: 1964
Frequency: Quarterly
Cover Price: £11.00
Annual Sub.: £36.00
Usual Pagination: 108
Editor: Ann Newton; **Managing Editor:** Ann Newton
Summary of Content: Journal containing literary criticism and critical articles on painting, sculpture, music and cinema.
Readership/Target Audience: Read by academics in the field of literature and the arts, as well as those with a general interest in the topic.
ADVERTISING RATES:
Full Page Mono £310.00
Agency Commission: 10%
Mechanical Data: Film: Digital, Type Area: 175 x 100mm, Col Length: 175mm, Page Width: 100mm
BUSINESS: CHURCH & SCHOOL EQUIPMENT & EDUCATION: Education Related

CAMPAIGN
35479U2A-55

Editorial Address: 174 Hammersmith Road, LONDON, W6 7JP **Tel:** 020 8267 4683 **Fax:** 020 8267 4927
Email: campaign@haymarket.com
Advertising Address: 161 Hammersmith Road, LONDON, W6 8SD **Tel:** 020 8267 4683 **Fax:** 020 8267 4927
Email: andrea.thomas@haymarket.com
Web site: http://www.campaignlive.co.uk/
Publisher: Haymarket Business Media Ltd
Frequency: Weekly
Cover Price: £3.20
Annual Sub.: £125.00
Circulation: 9,005 (ABC 01/07/2008 to 30/06/2009)
Usual Pagination: 30
Editor: Claire Beale; **News Editor:** Larissa Vince; **Executive Editor:** Caroline Marshall; **Managing Editor:** Michael Porter;
Advertising Director: Andrea Thomas
Summary of Content: Publication covering people and account moves, advertising campaigns, marketing strategies, finance management and the media.
Readership/Target Audience: Read by media owners, personnel in advertising agencies and marketing departments.
ADVERTISING RATES:
Full Page Colour £6442.00
Agency Commission: 10%
Mechanical Data: Type Area: 356 x 248mm, Bleed Size: 389 x 277mm, Trim Size: 381 x 273mm, Col Length: 356mm, Page Width: 248mm, Film: Digital
Copy instructions: Copy Date: 1 week prior to publication date
Average advertising content per issue: 25%
Supplement(s): A-List - 1xY, Top 100 - 1xY
BUSINESS: COMMUNICATIONS, ADVERTISING & MARKETING

CAMPDEN FB
768399U14H-408

Formerly: Families in Business
Editorial Address: 1 St. John's Square, LONDON, EC1M 4PN **Tel:** 020 7214 0500 **Fax:** 020 7214 0501
Email: fb@campden.com

Advertising Address: As above. **Tel:** 020 7214 0565
Fax: 020 7214 0586
Email: andyjames@campden.com
Web site: http://www.campdenfb.com
Publisher: Campden Publishing Ltd
Date Established: 2001
Frequency: 6 issues yearly
Free to qualifying individuals
Annual Sub.: £210.00
Circulation: 7,500 (Publisher's Statement)
Usual Pagination: 88
Editor: Marc Smith; **Editor-in-Chief:** Bruce Love;
Advertising Manager: Andy James
Summary of Content: Publication covering all issues relating to HNW family business including news, research and reviews, articles on business and private wealth management.
Readership/Target Audience: Read by family offices, academics and family business owners.
ADVERTISING RATES:
Full Page Colour £6950.00
Agency Commission: 10%
Mechanical Data: Trim Size: 297 x 210mm, Bleed Size: 303 x 216mm, Film: Digital
Average advertising content per issue: 20%
BUSINESS: COMMERCE, INDUSTRY & MANAGEMENT: Small Business

CANCER DRUG NEWS
38727U37-15

Editorial Address: Lincoln House, City Fields Business Park, City Fields Way, Tangmere, CHICHESTER, PO20 2FS
Tel: 01243 533322 **Fax:** 01243 533418
Email: healthcare@espicom.com
Web site: http://www.espicom.com/cdn
ISSN: 1462-656X
Publisher: Espicom Ltd
Frequency: Weekly
Annual Sub.: £575.00
Circulation: 1,500 (Publisher's Statement)
Usual Pagination: 20
Editor: Matthew Dennis
Summary of Content: Newsletter providing business information on developments in research and development, products and agreements within the global anticancer drug market.
Readership/Target Audience: Aimed at pharmaceutical executives.
ADVERTISING: No Advertising taken
BUSINESS: PHARMACEUTICAL & CHEMISTS

THE CANMAKER
38144U27-

Editorial Address: Durand House, Manor Royal, CRAWLEY RH10 9PY **Tel:** 01293 435100 **Fax:** 01293 619988
Email: monicah@sayers-publishing.com
Advertising Address: As above.
Email: joelh@sayers-publishing.com
Web site: http://www.canmaker.com
ISSN: 1354-5396
Publisher: Sayers Publishing Group Ltd
Date Established: 1988
Frequency: Monthly - Published on the 1st of the cover month
Annual Sub.: £260.00
Circulation: 2,500 (Publisher's Statement)
Usual Pagination: 80
Editor: Daniel Searle; **Managing Director:** Christina Kerr
Summary of Content: Journal covering the worldwide metal packaging industry.
Readership/Target Audience: Read by top executives in the metal packaging industry worldwide.
ADVERTISING RATES:
Full Page Colour £2297.0
Agency Commission: 15%
Mechanical Data: Film: Digital, Page Width: 179mm, Type Area: 244 x 179mm, Col Length: 244mm, Trim Size: 280 x 210mm, Bleed Size: 283 x 213mm
Copy instructions: Copy Date: 10th of the month prior to publication date
Average advertising content per issue: 50%
Supplement(s): The Canmaker Innovations - 1xY
BUSINESS: METAL, IRON & STEEL

CANTECH INTERNATIONAL
714998U22C-2

Editorial Address: The Maltings, 57 Bath Street, GRAVESEND, DA11 0DF **Tel:** 01474 532202
Fax: 01474 532203
Email: suzanne@bellpublishing.com
Advertising Address: As above.
Email: davidm@bellpublishing.com
Web site: http://www.cantechonline.com
Publisher: Bell Publishing Ltd
Frequency: 7 issues yearly - Published at the beginning of the 2nd cover month
Free to qualifying individuals
Annual Sub.: $120.00

Editor: Suzanne Christiansen; **Managing Editor:** Suzanne Christiansen; **Publisher:** Neil McRitchie
Summary of Content: Journal covering all aspects of metal packaging from the raw material supplier to the can maker and the filler, including news on the latest technologies and developments, world news, plant and company profiles, machinery and equipment updates.
Readership/Target Audience: Read by top decision makers in the can making and filling industries.
ADVERTISING RATES:
Full Page Colour EUR3335.00
Agency Commission: 10%
Mechanical Data: Bleed Size: 306 x 231mm, Type Area: 280 x 200mm, Col Length: 280mm, Page Width: 200mm, Trim Size: 300 x 225mm, Print Process: Sheet-fed litho, Film: Positive, right reading, emulsion side down. Digital, Col Widths (Display): 50mm, No. of Columns (Display): 4
Copy instructions: Copy Date: 1 week prior to publication date
BUSINESS: FOOD: Food Processing & Packaging

CAP MONITOR
1664991U21A-1113
Editorial Address: 80 Calverley Road, TUNBRIDGE WELLS, TN1 2UN **Tel:** 020 7017 7500 **Fax:** 020 7017 7599
Email: marketing@agra-net.com
Web site: http://www.agra-net.com
ISSN: 0142-5633
Publisher: Agra Informa Ltd
Frequency: Continuously updated, no fixed frequency
Annual Sub.: £1669.00
Summary of Content: Loose-leaf reference and guide to the common agricultural policy of the European Union. Includes statistics for European agriculture and contact details for important personnel in the European Commission, European Parliament and agricultural organisations.
Readership/Target Audience: Aimed at agribusiness, food companies and institutions.
ADVERTISING: No Advertising taken
BUSINESS: AGRICULTURE & FARMING

CAPACITY
708164U18B-465
Editorial Address: 9B Millennium House, 21 Eden Street, KINGSTON UPON THAMES, KT1 1BL **Tel:** 020 8549 2449
Fax: 020 8549 1249
Email: matthew.whalley@capacitymedia.com
Advertising Address: As above.
Email: paul.collinson@capacitymedia.com
Web site: http://www.capacitymedia.com
ISSN: 1471-762X
Publisher: Capacity Media
Date Established: 2000
Frequency: 11 issues yearly - Combined issues July/August
Free to qualifying individuals
Annual Sub.: £60.00
Circulation: 5,000 (Publisher's Statement)
Usual Pagination: 48
Editor: Matthew Whalley; **Editor-in-Chief:** Mark Kemp; **Managing Editor:** Eira Hayward
Summary of Content: Magazine covering the latest market developments and technological challenges in wholesale telecommunications capacity, includes practical techniques, strategies and processes.
Readership/Target Audience: Aimed at senior executives with telecommunications companies and trading and financial institutions who are responsible for the buying and selling of network capacity.
ADVERTISING RATES:
Full Page Mono £5330.00
Full Page Colour £5995.00
Agency Commission: 15%
Mechanical Data: Type Area: 273 x 186mm, Trim Size: 297 x 210mm, Bleed Size: 303 x 216mm, Film: Digital, Col Length: 273mm, Page Width: 186mm
Copy instructions: Copy Date: 3 weeks prior to publication date
Average advertising content per issue: 40%
BUSINESS: ELECTRONICS: Telecommunications

CAPTIVE REVIEW
1656920U1D-408
Formerly: Captive & ART Review
Editorial Address: 1st Floor, Dunstan House, 14A St. Cross Street, LONDON, EC1N 8XA **Tel:** 020 7269 7575
Fax: 020 7269 7570
Email: g.bradshaw@pageantmedia.com
Advertising Address: As above.
Email: n.morgan@pageantmedia.com
Web site: http://www.captivereview.com
ISSN: 1742-2469
Publisher: Pageant Media Ltd
Date Established: 1999
Frequency: 11 issues yearly
Annual Sub.: £510.00
Circulation: 5,200 (Publisher's Statement)
Usual Pagination: 52
Editor: Gavin Bradshaw; **Advertising Manager:** Nick Morgan

Summary of Content: Magazine covering all aspects of the alternative risk transfer insurance market.
Readership/Target Audience: Aimed at CEOs, CFOs and Risk Transfer Managers.
ADVERTISING RATES:
Full Page Colour £3300.00
Agency Commission: 10%
Mechanical Data: Film: Digital, Type Area: 252 x 177mm, Bleed Size: 303 x 216mm, Trim Size: 297 x 210mm, Col Length: 252mm, Page Width: 177mm
Average advertising content per issue: 40%
BUSINESS: FINANCE & ECONOMICS: Insurance

CAR DEALER
1835441U31A-398
Editorial Address: PO Box 227, GOSPORT, PO12 9DE
Tel: 023 9252 2434
Email: james@blackballmedia.co.uk
Advertising Address: As above. **Tel:** 07936 778599
Email: jon@blackballmedia.com
Web site: http://www.cardealermagazine.co.uk
Publisher: Blackball Media Ltd
Date Established: 2008
Frequency: Monthly
Free to qualifying individuals
Circulation: 13,000 (Print Run)
Editor: James Baggott; **Advertising Director:** Jon Baggott
Summary of Content: Magazine featuring industry news, car reviews, products, features on the motor trade and expert comment from industry leaders.
Readership/Target Audience: Aimed at all members of the motor trade from small independent dealers to multi franchise and multi outlets.
ADVERTISING RATES:
Full Page Colour £2695.00
BUSINESS: MOTOR TRADE: Motor Trade Accessories

CAR MECHANICS
46307U31R-55
Editorial Address: PO Box 978, PETERBOROUGH, PE1 9FL **Tel:** 01733 347559 **Fax:** 01733 891342
Email: cm.ed@kelseypb.co.uk
Advertising Address: Broadway Court, Broadway, PETERBOROUGH, PE1 1RP **Tel:** 01733 347559
Fax: 01733 891342
Email: natasha.lewis@kelseypb.co.uk
Web site: http://www.carmechanicsmag.co.uk
ISSN: 0008-6037
Publisher: Kelsey Publishing Ltd
Date Established: 1958
Frequency: Monthly
Cover Price: £3.85
Annual Sub.: £42.00
Circulation: 30,000 (Publisher's Statement)
Usual Pagination: 100
Editor: Martyn Knowles; **Managing Editor:** Peter Simpson
Summary of Content: Magazine covering everything from servicing to repairing major accident damage. Includes the latest news and views from the motor trade.
Readership/Target Audience: Read by the motor trade and enthusiastic DIY mechanics.
ADVERTISING RATES:
Full Page Colour £1995.00
Agency Commission: 10%
Mechanical Data: Page Width: 188mm, Film: Digital, Type Area: 272 x 188mm, Trim Size: 297 x 210mm, Bleed Size: 303 x 216mm, Col Length: 272mm
Copy instructions: Copy Date: 8 weeks prior to publication date
Average advertising content per issue: 20%
BUSINESS: MOTOR TRADE: Motor Trade Related

CARAVAN INDUSTRY AND PARK OPERATOR
38419U32D-75
Editorial Address: 30 Diamond Ridge, CAMBERLEY, GU15 4LD **Tel:** 01276 686654 **Fax:** 01276 63307
Email: teamwork@ukonline.co.uk
Advertising Address: 8A High Street, EPSOM, KT19 8AD **Tel:** 01280 847038 **Fax:** 01372 744493
Email: sue@aemorgan.co.uk
ISSN: 1359-1223
Publisher: A.E. Morgan Publications Ltd
Date Established: 1968
Frequency: Monthly - Published on the 1st Thursday of the cover month
Cover Price: £3.00
Annual Sub.: £19.90
Circulation: 2,600 (Publisher's Statement)
Usual Pagination: 32
Editor: David Ritchie; **Managing Director:** Terence Morgan; **Advertising Manager:** Doreen Reed; **Publisher:** Terence Morgan
Summary of Content: Journal covering all aspects of the caravan industry.
Readership/Target Audience: Aimed at caravan park owners and managers, caravan manufacturers, dealers and suppliers to the industry.

ADVERTISING RATES:
Full Page Mono £620.00
Full Page Colour £860.00
SCC 7.70
Agency Commission: 10%
Mechanical Data: Type Area: 270 x 182mm, Bleed Size: 305 x 213mm, Trim Size: 297 x 210mm, Film: Digital, No. of Columns (Display): 4, Col Length: 270mm, Page Width: 182mm
Copy instructions: Copy Date: 15th of the month prior to publication date
Average advertising content per issue: 50%
BUSINESS: LOCAL GOVERNMENT, LEISURE & RECREATION: Parks

CARAVAN INDUSTRY SUPPLIES & SERVICES DIRECTORY
38423U32D-76
Editorial Address: 8A High Street, EPSOM, KT19 8AD
Tel: 01372 741411 **Fax:** 01372 744493
Email: teamwork@ukonline.co.uk
Advertising Address: As above.
Email: sue@aemorgan.co.uk
Publisher: A.E. Morgan Publications Ltd
Date Established: 1972
Frequency: Annual
Cover Price: £12.50
Circulation: 2,500 (Publisher's Statement)
Usual Pagination: 160
Editor: David Ritchie; **Advertising Manager:** Doreen Reed
Summary of Content: Directory listing manufacturers, dealers and suppliers to the caravan industry.
Readership/Target Audience: Aimed at distributors, suppliers, retail outlets, service organisations and park operators.
ADVERTISING RATES:
Full Page Mono £515.00
Agency Commission: 10%
Mechanical Data: Trim Size: 190 x 120mm, Print Process: Sheet-fed litho, Film: Digital
Copy instructions: Copy Date: 1 month prior to publication date
BUSINESS: LOCAL GOVERNMENT, LEISURE & RECREATION: Parks

CARBOHYDRATE POLYMERS
38040U22R-20
Editorial Address: The Boulevard, Langford Lane, KIDLINGTON, OX5 1GB **Tel:** 01865 843000
Fax: 01865 843960
Email: w.hurp@elsevier.com
Advertising Address: 32 Jamestown Road, LONDON, NW1 7BY **Tel:** 020 7424 4400 **Fax:** 01865 853136
Email: j.kenney@elsevier.com
Web site: http://www.elsevier.com/locate/carbpol
ISSN: 0144-8617
Publisher: Elsevier
Date Established: 1981
Frequency: 16 issues yearly
Annual Sub.: EUR2868.00
Usual Pagination: 140
Editor: Wendy Hurp; **Publisher:** Lyndon Driscoll
Summary of Content: Papers on industrial applications of carbohydrate polymers in food, textiles, paper, wood, adhesives, pharmaceuticals and chemistry.
Readership/Target Audience: Read by university and industrial research institutes, users and manufacturers of carbohydrate polymers.
ADVERTISING RATES:
Full Page Mono EUR1020.00
Full Page Colour EUR2160.00
Mechanical Data: Page Width: 180mm, Type Area: 250 x 180mm, Col Length: 250mm, Trim Size: 280 x 210mm, Bleed Size: 286 x 216mm
BUSINESS: FOOD: Food Related

CARBON FINANCE
1799194U57-153
Editorial Address: 22-24 Corsham Street, LONDON, N1 6DR **Tel:** 020 7251 9151 **Fax:** 020 7251 9161
Email: katie.kouchakji@environmental-finance.com
Web site: http://www.carbon-financeonline.com
Publisher: Fulton Publishing
Date Established: 2003
Frequency: 11 issues yearly
Annual Sub.: £525.00
Circulation: 6,000 (Publisher's Statement)
Usual Pagination: 24
Editor: Katie Kouchakji
Summary of Content: Newsletter providing in-depth coverage of global markets in greenhouse gas emissions, providing news and analysis of developments in the sector.
Readership/Target Audience: Aimed at directors and managers of industrial companies, financial institutions, government officials, lawyers and market intermediaries.
ADVERTISING: No Advertising taken
BUSINESS: ENVIRONMENT & POLLUTION

Business Magazines

CARCINOGENESIS
24443U56A-56

Editorial Address: Great Clarendon Street, OXFORD, OX2 6DP **Tel:** 01865 353907 **Fax:** 01865 353985
Advertising Address: As above. **Fax:** 01865 353774
Email: steve.simmonds@oxfordjournals.org
Web site: http://www.oup.co.uk/jnls
ISSN: 0143-3334
Publisher: OUP
Date Established: 1980
Frequency: Monthly
Cover Price: £32.00
Annual Sub.: £315.00
Usual Pagination: 208
Editor: Curtis Harris; **Executive Editor:** Curtis Harris
Summary of Content: Journal containing multi-disciplinary research in the areas of viral, physical and chemical carcinogenesis mutagenesis.
Readership/Target Audience: Aimed at members of the National Cancer Institute.
ADVERTISING RATES:
Full Page Mono £646.00
Full Page Colour £1076.00
Agency Commission: 10%
Mechanical Data: Type Area: 255 x 178mm, Trim Size: 279 x 216mm, Bleed Size: 285 x 222mm, Film: Positive, right reading, emulsion side down. Digital, Col Length: 255mm, Print Process: Litho, Page Width: 178mm
BUSINESS: HEALTH & MEDICAL

CARD TECHNOLOGY TODAY
35340U1G-14

Editorial Address: The Boulevard, Langford Lane, KIDLINGTON, OX5 1GB **Tel:** 01865 843000
Fax: 01865 843971
Email: m.lockie@btopenworld.com
Web site: http://www.compseconline.com
ISSN: 0965-2590
Publisher: Elsevier Ltd
Frequency: 10 issues yearly
Annual Sub.: $895.00
Usual Pagination: 16
Editor: Mark Lockie
Summary of Content: International newsletter about smart card technology and applications.
Readership/Target Audience: Aimed at integrators, manufacturers and investors.
ADVERTISING: No Advertising taken
BUSINESS: FINANCE & ECONOMICS: Credit Trading

CARD WORLD
35074U1C-87

Formerly: Card World Independent
Editorial Address: 3A Market Place, UPPINGHAM, LE15 9QH **Tel:** 01572 820088 **Fax:** 01572 820099
Email: amcintosh@cm-media.net
Web site: http://www.cardworldonline.com
ISSN: 0954-8564
Publisher: C&M Publications Ltd
Date Established: 1988
Frequency: Monthly
Annual Sub.: £435.00
Circulation: 2,000 (Publisher's Statement)
Usual Pagination: 16
Editor: Annich McIntosh; **Managing Editor:** Annich McIntosh
Summary of Content: Newsletter which focuses on the international market for plastic cards for all uses, including financial, access, identity, transit and loyalty prepaid, mobile payments, contactless schemes. Also includes information about the associated technology.
Readership/Target Audience: Read by those working in financial services, banking, the credit card industry, retail, transit, government and major corporations.
ADVERTISING: No Advertising taken
BUSINESS: FINANCE & ECONOMICS: Banking

CARD WORLD AND FRAUD WATCH USER GUIDE DIRECTORY
35073U1C-86

Editorial Address: 3A Market Place, UPPINGHAM, LE15 9QH **Tel:** 01572 820088 **Fax:** 01572 820099
Email: candmpubs@aol.com
Web site: http://www.cardworldonline.com
ISSN: 0967-8026
Publisher: C&M Publications Ltd
Date Established: 1989
Frequency: Annual - Published in January/February
Free to qualifying individuals
Annual Sub.: £50.00
Circulation: 12,000 (Publisher's Statement)
Usual Pagination: 100
Editor: Annich McIntosh; **Managing Editor:** Annich McIntosh
Summary of Content: Annual directory covering the payment card industry, with predictions and suggested trends for the next year, a glossary of terms, directory of companies, company profiles and articles covering the major sector of the card industry, including EMV smart card migration, security and ID, fraud prevention and control,

card processing and management, mobile and electronic payments and loyalty and gift cards.
Readership/Target Audience: Aimed at card issuers and acquirers (bankers and those involved in card schemes) across all sectors and geographical regions.
ADVERTISING: No Advertising taken
BUSINESS: FINANCE & ECONOMICS: Banking

CARDIFF UNIVERSITY NEWS
41182U62R-40

Editorial Address: Public Relations and Communications Division, Cardiff University, Park Place, CARDIFF, CF10 3AT **Tel:** 029 2087 5596 **Fax:** 029 2087 0104
Email: newsletter@cardiff.ac.uk
Web site: http://www.cardiff.ac.uk/news/cardiff_news
ISSN: 1335-3127
Publisher: Cardiff University
Date Established: 1993
Frequency: 10 issues yearly
Cover Price: Free
Circulation: 8,600 (Publisher's Statement)
Usual Pagination: 12
Editor: Stephen Rouse
Summary of Content: Newsletter containing news on university research, staff achievements, corporate announcements and recruitment information.
Readership/Target Audience: Read by academics, research sponsors, school, industry, government contacts and university staff.
ADVERTISING: No Advertising taken
BUSINESS: CHURCH & SCHOOL EQUIPMENT & EDUCATION: Education Related

CARDIOLOGY NEWS
40243U56A-56_50

Editorial Address: 9 Gayfield Square, EDINBURGH, EH1 3NT **Tel:** 0131 478 8403 **Fax:** 0131 557 4701
Email: jennifer@pinpoint-scotland.com
Advertising Address: As above.
Email: cardiologynews@pinpoint-scotland.com
Web site: http://www.pinpointmedical.com
Publisher: Pinpoint Scotland Ltd
Date Established: 1997
Frequency: 6 issues yearly
Free to qualifying individuals
Annual Sub.: £15.00
Circulation: 5,000 (Publisher's Statement)
Usual Pagination: 44
Editor: Jennifer Fallon; **Managing Director:** Caroline Elder
Summary of Content: Reviews of papers in the major cardiology journals, plus lead and feature articles.
Readership/Target Audience: Aimed at cardiologists, cardiothoracic surgeons, technicians, academics, nurses and GPs with a special interest in cardiology.
ADVERTISING RATES:
Full Page Mono £980.00
Full Page Colour £1367.00
Agency Commission: 10%
Mechanical Data: Type Area: 280 x 180mm, Bleed Size: 303 x 216mm, Trim Size: 297 x 210mm, Col Length: 280mm, Page Width: 180mm
Copy instructions: Copy Date: 3 weeks prior to publication date
Average advertising content per issue: 45%
BUSINESS: HEALTH & MEDICAL

CARDIOVASCULAR DRUG NEWS (CVDN)
1799524U37-429

Editorial Address: Lincoln House, City Fields Business Park, City Fields Way, Tangmere, CHICHESTER, PO20 2FS **Tel:** 01243 533322 **Fax:** 01243 533418
Email: healthcare@espicom.com
Web site: http://www.espicom.com
Publisher: Espicom Ltd
Date Established: 2000
Frequency: Monthly
Annual Sub.: £560.00
Circulation: 300 (Publisher's Statement)
Editor: Johanna Shiu
Summary of Content: Newsletter monitoring the companies, products, strategic alliances and research developments in the cardiovascular market. Features coronary artery disease, dyslipidaemia, heart failure, arrhythmia, hypertension, hypotension, ischaemia, thrombosis, embolism and fibrinolysis. Includes general news and a conference diary.
Readership/Target Audience: Aimed at senior executives in pharmaceutical companies.
ADVERTISING: No Advertising taken
BUSINESS: PHARMACEUTICAL & CHEMISTS

CARDS INTERNATIONAL
35339U1G-13

Editorial Address: The Colonnades, 34 Porchester Road, LONDON, W2 6ES **Tel:** 020 7563 5600 **Fax:** 020 7563 5702
Email: vicky.conroy@vrlknowledgebank.com
Web site: http://www.vrlpublishing.com
ISSN: 0956-5558

Publisher: VRL Knowledge Bank Ltd
Frequency: 20 issues yearly
Annual Sub.: £1257.00
Usual Pagination: 28
Editor: Victoria Conroy
Summary of Content: Publication covering card operations in banks and retail outlets.
Readership/Target Audience: Aimed at senior executives in banks and retailing organisations, technology suppliers, card processors and personnel within payment systems companies.
ADVERTISING: No Advertising taken
BUSINESS: FINANCE & ECONOMICS: Credit Trading

CARE AND NURSING ESSENTIALS
713774U56B-45

Editorial Address: 150 Burnley Road, ACCRINGTON, BB5 6DW **Tel:** 01254 390066 **Fax:** 01254 390077
Email: editorial@euromedia-al.com
Advertising Address: Unit 8, Chorley West Business Park, Ackhurst Road, CHORLEY, PR7 1NL **Tel:** 0870 444 8955
Fax: 0870 444 8956
Email: ads@euromedia-al.co.uk
Publisher: Euromedia Associates Ltd
Date Established: 1999
Frequency: 6 issues yearly
Free to qualifying individuals
Annual Sub.: £16.80
Circulation: 7,000 (Publisher's Statement)
Usual Pagination: 70
Editor: Richard Cheesbrough
Summary of Content: Magazine covering all aspects of healthcare management, including property, finance, training and recruitment, bathrooms and fittings, contract furnishing and flooring, laundries and sluice rooms, catering and kitchen equipment, cleaning and hygiene, bed and bedding, products and services, transport, mobility, holidays and days out.
Readership/Target Audience: Aimed at nursing and care homes proprietors and workers in related industries.
ADVERTISING RATES:
Full Page Colour £1200.00
Mechanical Data: Type Area: 280 x 190mm, Col Length: 280mm, Page Width: 190mm, Film: Digital
Copy instructions: Copy Date: 4 weeks prior to publication date
BUSINESS: HEALTH & MEDICAL: Nursing

CARE APPOINTMENTS
1685484U56A-188

Formerly: Care Appointments Scotland
Editorial Address: 70 West Regent Street, GLASGOW, G2 2QZ **Tel:** 0141 333 6665 **Fax:** 0141 333 1116
Email: bigmac@careappointments.co.uk
Advertising Address: As above.
Email: advertising@careappointments.co.uk
Web site: http://www.careappointments.co.uk
Publisher: Career Media Ltd
Date Established: 2005
Frequency: Monthly
Free to qualifying individuals
Annual Sub.: £30.00
Circulation: 20,000 (Publisher's Statement)
Usual Pagination: 48
Editor: Iain MacDonald; **Advertising Director:** Iain McDonald
Summary of Content: Magazine featuring jobs and opportunities, courses, training, advice, news, features and interviews.
Readership/Target Audience: Aimed at care sector workers.
ADVERTISING RATES:
Full Page Mono £3295.00
Full Page Colour £4495.00
Agency Commission: 10%
Mechanical Data: Type Area: 254 x 180mm, Col Length: 254mm, Page Width: 180mm, No. of Columns (Display): 4, Col Widths (Display): 43.5mm, Trim Size: 297 x 210mm, Bleed Size: 303 x216mm
Average advertising content per issue: 30%
BUSINESS: HEALTH & MEDICAL

CARE MANAGEMENT MATTERS
1642362U32G-168

Editorial Address: Valley Court Offices, ROYSTON, SG8 0HF **Tel:** 01223 207770 **Fax:** 01223 207135
Email: editor@caremanagementmatters.co.uk
Advertising Address: 4 Valley Court, Lower Road, Croydon, ROYSTON, SG8 0HF **Tel:** 01223 207770 **Fax:** 01223 207108
Email: cmm@carechoices.co.uk
Web site: http://www.caremanagementmatters.co.uk
Publisher: Care Choices Ltd
Date Established: 2003
Frequency: 10 issues yearly
Cover Price: £4.00
Free to qualifying individuals
Annual Sub.: £50.00

Circulation: 18,021 (ABC 01/01/2008 to 31/12/2008)
Usual Pagination: 60
Editor: Emma Morriss; **Advertising Manager:** Mia Campbell
Summary of Content: Magazine covering all aspects of senior management, finance, marketing, property, legal and training and recruiting matters for the UK care sector.
Readership/Target Audience: Aimed at care home owners and managers.
ADVERTISING RATES:
Full Page Mono £1600.00
Full Page Colour £1600.00
Agency Commission: 10%
Mechanical Data: Trim Size: 297 x 210mm, Bleed Size: 303 x 216mm, Film: Digital, Type Area: 277 x 190mm, Col Length: 277mm, Page Width: 190mm
Copy instructions: Copy Date: End of first week of month prior to publication date
Average advertising content per issue: 40%
BUSINESS: LOCAL GOVERNMENT, LEISURE & RECREATION: Community Care & Social Services

CARE OF THE CRITICALLY ILL   40298U56B-52
Editorial Address: 26 Brickfields Close, Lychpit, BASINGSTOKE, RG24 8UX **Tel:** 01256 352221
Fax: 01256 352221
Email: thetapress@btinternet.com
Advertising Address: As above.
Email: thetapress@btinternet.com
Web site: http://www.thetapress.com
ISSN: 0266-9070
Publisher: Theta Press
Date Established: 1985
Frequency: 6 issues yearly
Annual Sub.: £65.00
Circulation: 4,100 (Publisher's Statement)
Usual Pagination: 48
Editor: Harry Holt; **Advertising Manager:** Harry Holt; **Publisher:** Harry Holt
Summary of Content: Magazine providing in-depth coverage of a particular aspect of critical care as well as reliable information on the wide range of new and increasingly sophisticated equipment used in different specialities.
Readership/Target Audience: Readership includes doctors, technicians and nurses who run ITUs, CCUs, SCBUs and A&EUs, as well as those who treat the critically ill before they reach hospital.
ADVERTISING RATES:
Full Page Mono £730.00
Full Page Colour £1450.00
Agency Commission: 10%
Mechanical Data: Type Area: 270 x 175mm, Col Length: 270mm, Bleed Size: 303 x 213mm, Trim Size: 297 x 210mm, No. of Columns (Display): 2, Print Process: Litho, Film: Digital, Page Width: 175mm
Copy instructions: Copy Date: Middle of month prior to publication date
Average advertising content per issue: 5%
BUSINESS: HEALTH & MEDICAL: Nursing

CARE ON THE ROAD   39862U54B-10
Editorial Address: Edgbaston Park, 353 Bristol Road, Edgbaston, BIRMINGHAM, B5 7ST **Tel:** 0121 248 2000
Fax: 0121 248 2001
Email: coreditor@rospa.com
Advertising Address: As above.
Email: safetyadvertising@rospa.com
Web site: http://www.rospa.org.uk
Publisher: Royal Society for the Prevention of Accidents
Frequency: 6 issues yearly
Free to qualifying individuals
Annual Sub.: £19.50
Circulation: 10,000 (Publisher's Statement)
Usual Pagination: 16
Editor: Janice Cave; **Advertising Manager:** Susan Philo; **Managing Editor:** Janice Cave
Summary of Content: Magazine covering vehicle and product design, all aspects of road safety, driver training, new legislation and road safety statistics.
Readership/Target Audience: Aimed at road safety officers, police, teachers and advanced drivers who are members of ROSPA Advanced Drivers Association.
ADVERTISING RATES:
Full Page Mono £895.00
Agency Commission: 10%
Mechanical Data: Page Width: 262mm, Film: Digital, Type Area: 365 x 262mm, Col Length: 365mm
Copy instructions: Copy Date: 1st of the month prior to publication date
Average advertising content per issue: 20%
BUSINESS: SAFETY & SECURITY: Safety

CAREER DEVELOPMENT INTERNATIONAL   37029U14F-8_60
Editorial Address: Howard House, Wagon Lane, BINGLEY, BD16 1WA **Tel:** 01274 777700 **Fax:** 01274 785200
Email: nrolph@emeraldinsight.com

Web site: http://www.emeraldinsight.com/cdi.htm
ISSN: 1362-0436
Publisher: Emerald Group Publishing Ltd
Date Established: 1995
Frequency: 7 issues yearly
Annual Sub.: £5419.00
Usual Pagination: 96
Editor: Nancy Rolph; **Publisher:** Nancy Rolph
Summary of Content: Scholarly journal publishing international research on Careers and Development.
Readership/Target Audience: Aimed at researchers and educators working in the areas of Careers and Development.
ADVERTISING: No Advertising taken
BUSINESS: COMMERCE, INDUSTRY & MANAGEMENT: Training & Recruitment

THE CARER   1841401U56B-299
Editorial Address: Suite 4, Roddis House, Old Christchurch Road, BOURNEMOUTH, BH1 1LG **Tel:** 01202 552333
Fax: 01202 552666
Email: sales@thecareruk.com
Advertising Address: As above.
Email: sales@thecareruk.com
Web site: http://www.thecareruk.com
Publisher: RBC Publishing Limited
Date Established: 2008
Frequency: Quarterly - Published on the 3rd Monday of the month of publication
Free to qualifying individuals
Circulation: 15,000 (Print Run)
Usual Pagination: 32
Editor: Peter Adams; **Advertising Manager:** Sylvia Mawson
Summary of Content: Magazine covering industry news, general news and new products.
Readership/Target Audience: Aimed at proprietors and managers of residential nursing and care homes.
ADVERTISING: Rates on application
BUSINESS: HEALTH & MEDICAL: Nursing

CARGO SECURITY INTERNATIONAL
1642446U49C-502
Editorial Address: Petrospot House, Somerville Court, Trinity Way, Adderbury, BANBURY, OX17 3SN
Tel: 01295 814455 **Fax:** 01295 814466
Email: ian@petrospot.com
Advertising Address: As above.
Email: ian@petrospot.com
Web site: http://www.cargosecurityinternational.com
Publisher: Petrospot Limited
Date Established: 2003
Frequency: 6 issues yearly
Annual Sub.: £95.00
Circulation: 7,000 (Publisher's Statement)
Usual Pagination: 56
Editor: Ian Taylor; **Managing Director:** Llewellyn Bankes-Hughes; **Advertising Manager:** Ian Taylor
Summary of Content: Magazine covering intermodal cargo and transportation security.
Readership/Target Audience: Aimed at transportation companies, government bodies and transport service providers.
ADVERTISING RATES:
Full Page Colour £1200.00
Mechanical Data: Type Area: 272 x 190mm, Bleed Size: 303 x 216mm, Trim Size: 297 x 210mm, Col Length: 272mm, Film: Digital, Page Width: 190mm
BUSINESS: TRANSPORT: Freight

CARGO SYSTEMS   39631U49C-24
Editorial Address: Telephone House, 69-77 Paul Street, LONDON, EC2A 4LQ **Tel:** 020 7017 5000
Fax: 020 7017 4172
Email: benedict.young@informa.com
Advertising Address: As above. **Tel:** 020 7017 4240
Email: peter.marpuri@informa.com
Web site: http://www.cargosystems.net
ISSN: 0306-0985
Publisher: Informa Cargo Information
Date Established: 1974
Frequency: 10 issues yearly - Published at the end of the month prior to cover month
Free to qualifying individuals
Annual Sub.: £191.00
Circulation: 5,283 (ABC 01/01/2008 to 31/12/2008)
Usual Pagination: 60
Editor: Ben Young; **Advertising Manager:** Peter Marpuri
Summary of Content: Magazine covering all aspects of port development and privatisation, container handling, container technology and intermodalism.
Language(s): Chinese; English
Readership/Target Audience: Readership includes ship operators, consulting engineers and container repairers.
ADVERTISING RATES:
Full Page Colour £3459.00
Agency Commission: 10%

Mechanical Data: Type Area: 275 x 190mm, Col Length: 275mm, Trim Size: 297 x 210mm, Bleed Size: 303 x 216mm, Film: Digital, Page Width: 190mm
Copy instructions: Copy Date: 20th of the month prior to publication date
Average advertising content per issue: 45%
Supplement(s): Americas - 2xY, Chinese Language - 2xY, Top 100 Container Ports - 1xY
BUSINESS: TRANSPORT: Freight

CARIBBEAN INSIGHT   36935U14C-46
Editorial Address: 2 Belgrave Square, LONDON, SW1X 8PJ
Tel: 020 7235 9484 **Fax:** 020 7823 1370
Email: cbrogan@aol.com
Web site: http://www.caribbean-insight.com
ISSN: 0142-4742
Publisher: Caribbean Council
Frequency: 45 issues yearly
Annual Sub.: £225.00
Usual Pagination: 6
Editor: Chris Brogan; **Managing Director:** David Jessop; **Publisher:** David Jessop
Summary of Content: Journal containing information on politics and economics in the Caribbean.
Readership/Target Audience: Aimed at government, business, academic and international institutions.
ADVERTISING: No Advertising taken
BUSINESS: COMMERCE, INDUSTRY & MANAGEMENT: International Commerce

CARING   622518U32G-28
Editorial Address: 20 Great Dover Street, LONDON, SE1 4LX **Tel:** 020 7490 8818 **Fax:** 020 7490 8824
Email: caring@carersuk.org
Advertising Address: As above.
Email: matt.hill@carersuk.org
Web site: http://www.carersuk.org
ISSN: 1469-137X
Publisher: Carers UK
Date Established: 1999
Frequency: Quarterly
Free to qualifying individuals
Annual Sub.: £30.00
Circulation: 12,000 (Publisher's Statement)
Usual Pagination: 16
Editor: Matt Hill; **Advertising Manager:** Matt Hill
Summary of Content: Magazine focusing on key issues and information on matters relevant to unpaid carers.
Readership/Target Audience: Aimed at unpaid carers and families of disabled people.
ADVERTISING RATES:
Full Page Colour £1250.00
Agency Commission: 10%
Mechanical Data: Print Process: Web-fed litho, Type Area: 270 x 182mm, Bleed Size: 300 x 213mm, Trim Size: 297 x 210mm, Screen: 60 lpc, Col Length: 270mm, Film: Digital, Page Width: 182mm
Average advertising content per issue: 15%
BUSINESS: LOCAL GOVERNMENT, LEISURE & RECREATION: Community Care & Social Services

CARING BUSINESS   38499U32G-130
Formerly: This Caring Business
Editorial Address: Ludgate House, 245 Blackfriars Road, LONDON, SE1 9UY **Tel:** 020 7921 8502
Email: olufunmi.majekodunmi@ubm.com
Advertising Address: As above. **Fax:** 020 7921 8131
Email: chris.edwards@ubm.com
Web site: http://www.caringbusiness.co.uk
ISSN: 0268-4047
Publisher: UBM Information Ltd
Date Established: 1985
Frequency: Monthly
Free to qualifying individuals
Annual Sub.: £64.00
Circulation: 20,843 (ABC 01/07/2006 to 30/06/2007)
Usual Pagination: 48
Editor: Olufunmi Majekodunmi; **Advertising Manager:** Chris Edwards
Summary of Content: Magazine containing information and product news on the private and voluntary sectors of nursing and residential care, sheltered housing and independent hospitals.
Readership/Target Audience: Aimed at owners and managers of private and voluntary residential homes, nursing homes and independent hospitals, local health authority registrations and inspection and purchasing officers, major business finance houses, architects, equipment suppliers and manufacturers.
ADVERTISING RATES:
Full Page Colour £3200.00
SCC £22.00
Agency Commission: 10%
Mechanical Data: Type Area: 350 x 267mm, Film: Digital, Col Length: 350mm, Page Width: 267mm, Bleed Size: 396 x 303mm, Trim Size: 390 x 297mm

Business Magazines

Copy instructions: Copy Date: 1 week prior to publication date
Average advertising content per issue: 50%
BUSINESS: LOCAL GOVERNMENT, LEISURE & RECREATION: Community Care & Social Services

CARING TIMES
38453U32G-28_80
Formerly: Caring Times Incorporating Homecare Professional
Editorial Address: 2nd Floor, Culvert House, Culvert Road, Battersea, LONDON, SW11 5DH Tel: 020 7720 2108
Email: caringtimes@foxpound.co.uk
Advertising Address: As above. Fax: 020 7498 3023
Email: caroline@hawkerpublications.com
Web site: http://www.careinfo.org
ISSN: 0953-4873
Publisher: Hawker Publications
Date Established: 1988
Frequency: 11 issues yearly - Combined issue published in July/August
Free to qualifying individuals
Annual Sub.: £70.00
Circulation: 16,782 (ABC 01/07/2008 to 30/06/2009)
Usual Pagination: 52
Editor: Geoff Hodgson; Advertisement Director: Caroline Bowern
Summary of Content: Magazine containing news, features and products for the long term social care sector.
Readership/Target Audience: Aimed at owners, corporate managers and managers of organisations which operate residential or nursing homes within the private and local authority sectors.
ADVERTISING RATES:
Full Page Mono £1925.00
Full Page Colour £2485.00
Agency Commission: 10%
Mechanical Data: Type Area: 276 x 207mm, Bleed Size: 304 x 234mm, Trim Size: 298 x 228mm, Col Length: 276mm, Page Width: 207mm, Film: Digital, No. of Columns (Display): 4
Copy instructions: Copy Date: Beginning of the month prior to publication date
Average advertising content per issue: 60%
BUSINESS: LOCAL GOVERNMENT, LEISURE & RECREATION: Community Care & Social Services

CARING UK
38455U32G-29_5
Editorial Address: 47 Church Street, BARNSLEY, S70 2AS Tel: 01226 734333 Fax: 01226 734478
Email: dm@whpl.net
Advertising Address: As above. Fax: 01226 734477
Email: jb@whpl.net
Web site: http://www.caring-uk.co.uk
Publisher: Wharncliffe Publishing Ltd
Frequency: Monthly
Annual Sub.: £50.00
Circulation: 20,251 (ABC 01/07/2008 to 30/06/2009)
Usual Pagination: 44
Editor: Dominic Musgrave; Group Editor: Andrew Harrod
Summary of Content: Business to business magazine containing news, interviews, features, editorial insights and product information about the UK residential care and elderly nursing home sector, also covering sheltered housing and domiciliary care.
Readership/Target Audience: Distributed to independent sector residential care and nursing specialist homes for older people, people with learning difficulties and the disabled; domiciliary care agencies, social services departments and health authorities.
ADVERTISING RATES:
Full Page Colour £2600.00
Agency Commission: 10%
Mechanical Data: Trim Size: 420 x 297mm, Film: Digital
Copy instructions: Copy Date: 3 weeks prior to publication date
Supplement(s): Homecare - 12xY
BUSINESS: LOCAL GOVERNMENT, LEISURE & RECREATION: Community Care & Social Services

CARITAS MAGAZINE
1846559U1P-285
Editorial Address: 6-14 Underwood Street, LONDON, N1 7JQ Tel: 020 7324 2322 Fax: 020 7324 8238
Email: cdann@caritasdata.co.uk
Web site: http://www.charitiesdirect.com
Publisher: Waterlow
Frequency: Monthly
Annual Sub.: £145.00
Circulation: 8,000 (Publisher's Statement)
Editor: Clarissa Dann
Summary of Content: Magazine covering strategy, management and leadership.
Readership/Target Audience: Aimed at senior contacts in all voluntary organisations with an income of a million pounds or more. This includes members of the Charity Finance Directors Group and Association of Chief Executives in voluntary organisations.
BUSINESS: FINANCE & ECONOMICS: Fundraising

CARPET & FLOORING REVIEW
38069U23B-509
Formerly: CFR
Editorial Address: 4 Red Barn Mews, High Street, BATTLE, TN33 0AG Tel: 01424 774982 Fax: 01424 774321
Email: paul@gearingmediagroup.com
Advertising Address: As above. Fax: 01424 775077
Email: andrew@gearingmediagroup.com
Web site: http://www.cfr-magazine.com
ISSN: 1471-8162
Publisher: Gearing Media Group
Date Established: 1946
Frequency: Monthly - Published around the beginning of the cover month
Free to qualifying individuals
Annual Sub.: £75.00
Circulation: 3,903 (ABC 01/01/2008 to 31/12/2008)
Usual Pagination: 64
Editor: Hannah Frackiewicz; Advertising Manager: Andrew Wilson
Summary of Content: Magazine covering the carpets and floor coverings industry, includes features on manufacturing, wholesaling and retailing.
Readership/Target Audience: Aimed at flooring retailers and wholesalers, floor layers, interior designers, architects and specifiers.
ADVERTISING RATES:
Full Page Colour £1445.00
Mechanical Data: Bleed Size: 303 x 222mm, Trim Size: 297 x 216mm, Film: Digital
Copy instructions: Copy Date: Middle of the month prior to cover date
BUSINESS: FURNISHINGS & FURNITURE: Furnishings, Carpets & Flooring

CASENOTES
711521U62A-347
Formerly: Parents and Schools
Editorial Address: 8 The Moorings, NORWICH, NR3 3AX Tel: 01603 623336 Fax: 01603 624767
Email: contact@campaignforstateeducation.org.uk
Web site: http://www.campaignforstateeducation.org.uk
Publisher: Campaign for State Education
Date Established: 1963
Frequency: 6 issues yearly
Annual Sub.: £15.00
Circulation: 1,000 (Publisher's Statement)
Usual Pagination: 4
Editor: Stephen Adamson
Summary of Content: Magazine of the Campaign for State Education. Includes information on all aspects of education.
Readership/Target Audience: Read by parents, teachers and governors.
ADVERTISING: No Advertising taken
BUSINESS: CHURCH & SCHOOL EQUIPMENT & EDUCATION: Education

CASH & CARRY MANAGEMENT INC. CASH & CARRY WHOLESALER
37996U22B-10
Editorial Address: PO Box 366, EAST GRINSTEAD, RH19 4ZE Tel: 01342 303042 Fax: 01342 303052
Email: mail.winlove@btconnect.com
Advertising Address: As above.
Email: mail.winlove@btconnect.com
ISSN: 1352-254X
Publisher: Winlove Publications Ltd
Frequency: 11 issues yearly - Published around the 14th of the cover month (except Jan/Feb: pub end of Jan)
Cover Price: £5.00
Free to qualifying individuals
Annual Sub.: £46.00
Circulation: 4,559 (ABC 01/07/2008 to 30/06/2009)
Usual Pagination: 44
Editor: Mervyn Gilbert; Advertising Manager: Martin Lovell; Managing Editor: Kirsti Sharratt
Summary of Content: Journal carrying details of new products, campaigns, and industry news and analysis.
Readership/Target Audience: Read by directors, managers and buyers within cash and carry and delivered wholesale head offices and depots.
ADVERTISING RATES:
Full Page Colour £1092.00
Agency Commission: 10%
Mechanical Data: Film: Digital, Type Area: 267 x 190mm, Bleed Size: 303 x 213mm, Trim Size: 297 x 210mm, No. of Columns (Display): 4, Col Length: 267mm, Page Width: 190mm
Copy instructions: Copy Date: 1st day of the cover month
Average advertising content per issue: 45%
BUSINESS: FOOD: Cash & Carry

CASINO & GAMING INTERNATIONAL
1667707U64A-178
Editorial Address: Woodland Place, Hurricane Way, Wickford Business Park, WICKFORD, SS11 8YB
Tel: 01268 766515 Fax: 01268 766516
Email: info@casinoandgaming.net
Advertising Address: As above.
Email: info@casinoandgaming.net
Web site: http://www.casinoandgaming.net
Publisher: Champ Media Group
Date Established: 2005
Frequency: Quarterly
Cover Price: £107.00
Circulation: 7,200 (Publisher's Statement)
Editor: Stephen Lawton
Summary of Content: Publication focusing on issues facing the casino and gaming industry.
Readership/Target Audience: Aimed at senior executives and management personnel worldwide, throughout the entire casino and gaming industry.
ADVERTISING RATES:
Full Page Colour £3450.00
BUSINESS: OTHER CLASSIFICATIONS: Amusement Trade

CASINO INTERNATIONAL
601099U64A-180
Editorial Address: 15A London Road, MAIDSTONE, ME16 8LY Tel: 01622 687031 Fax: 01622 757646
Email: jonbruford@yahoo.co.uk
Advertising Address: As above.
Email: casino@datateam.co.uk
Web site: http://www.casinointernational-online.com
ISSN: 1467-9175
Publisher: Datateam Publishing Ltd
Frequency: 11 issues yearly - Published at the beginning of the cover month
Annual Sub.: £55.00
Circulation: 4,449 (Publisher's Statement)
Usual Pagination: 44
Editor: Jon Bruford; Advertising Manager: Paul Ryder; Managing Editor: Jon Bruford
Summary of Content: Magazine covering news, products and issues in the gaming industry.
Readership/Target Audience: Read by purchasers of casino equipment and decision makers in the casino field.
ADVERTISING RATES:
Full Page Colour £2100.00
Mechanical Data: Type Area: 278 x 202mm, No. of Columns (Display): 5, Col Length: 278mm, Page Width: 202mm, Trim Size: 306 x 229mm, Bleed Size: 312 x 235mm
Copy instructions: Copy Date: 3 weeks prior to publication date
BUSINESS: OTHER CLASSIFICATIONS: Amusement Trade

CASINO LIFE
1704335U64A-180
Editorial Address: 4 Carriers Place, Blackham, TUNBRIDGE WELLS, TN3 9UQ Tel: 01892 740869 Fax: 0870 762 8112
Email: admin@casinolifemagazine.com
Advertising Address: As above.
Email: pwhite@casinolifemagazine.com
Web site: http://www.casinolifemagazine.com
Publisher: Ace Publishing
Date Established: 2005
Frequency: 6 issues yearly
Free to qualifying individuals
Annual Sub.: EUR40.00
Circulation: 2,394 (Publisher's Statement)
Usual Pagination: 48
Editor: Glyn Thomas
Summary of Content: Magazine covering all aspects of running a casino. Also features articles of interest to casino managers including personal development, lifestyle, travel and entertainment.
Readership/Target Audience: Aimed at casino managers and key casino equipment manufacturers.
ADVERTISING RATES:
Full Page Colour £2000.00
Agency Commission: 15%
Mechanical Data: Trim Size: 238 x 170mm, Bleed Size: 248 x 180mm, Film: Digital
Copy instructions: Copy Date: 25th of the month prior to publication date
BUSINESS: OTHER CLASSIFICATIONS: Amusement Trade

CAST METAL & DIECASTING TIMES
629542U27-22
Editorial Address: Gresham House, 54 High Street, SHOREHAM-BY-SEA, BN43 5DB Tel: 01273 453033
Fax: 01273 453085
Email: sueives@mmcpublications.co.uk
Advertising Address: As above.
Email: sueives@mmcpublications.co.uk
Web site: http://www.mmcpublications.co.uk
Publisher: Modern Media Communications Ltd
Frequency: 5 issues yearly - Published around the end of the 2nd week of the 1st cover month

Cover Price: £9.00
Free to qualifying individuals
Annual Sub.: £50.00
Circulation: 5,250 (Publisher's Statement)
Usual Pagination: 34
Editor: Sue Ives; **Advertising Manager:** Sue Ives
Summary of Content: Magazine reporting on new developments in the machinery field with company profiles, new contracts, news and up to date installation features.
Readership/Target Audience: Aimed at managers of diecasting foundries throughout Europe and South America.
ADVERTISING RATES:
Full Page Colour £1350.00
Agency Commission: 10%
Mechanical Data: Page Width: 185mm, Film: Digital, Type Area: 265 x 185mm, Col Length: 265mm, Trim Size: 297 x 210mm, Bleed Size: 303 x 213mm
Copy instructions: Copy Date: 3 weeks prior to publication date
Average advertising content per issue: 40%
BUSINESS: METAL, IRON & STEEL

CASTINGS BUYER
1646068U27-202

Editorial Address: I C M E, National Metalforming Centre, 47 Birmingham Road, WEST BROMWICH, B70 6PY
Tel: 0121 601 6979 **Fax:** 0121 601 6981
Email: lynn@icme.org.uk
Advertising Address: River Media, Brockington Studios, Bodenham, HEREFORD, HR1 3HT **Tel:** 01568 797111
Fax: 01568 797197
Email: les@rivers-media.co.uk
Web site: http://www.foundrytradejournal.com
ISSN: 0265-8321
Publisher: The Institute of Cast Metals Engineers
Date Established: 1987
Frequency: Annual
Free to qualifying individuals
Circulation: 4,000 (Publisher's Statement)
Usual Pagination: 32
Editor: Lynn Postle
Summary of Content: Magazine covering all aspects of the cast metals industry.
Readership/Target Audience: Aimed at buyers of castings and specifiers in all sectors of engineering.
ADVERTISING RATES:
Full Page Colour £1925.00
Mechanical Data: Type Area: 265 x 185mm, Col Length: 265mm, Film: Digital, Trim Size: 297 x 210mm, Page Width: 185mm
BUSINESS: METAL, IRON & STEEL

CAT (CAR & ACCESSORY TRADER)
38296U31A-40

Editorial Address: Teddington Studios, Broom Road, TEDDINGTON, TW11 9BE **Tel:** 020 8267 5906
Fax: 020 8267 5993
Email: emma.butcher@haymarket.com
Advertising Address: As above. **Tel:** 020 8943 5868
Fax: 020 8943 5855
Email: martin.lee@haymarket.com
Web site: http://www.catmag.co.uk
Publisher: Haymarket Media Group Ltd
Date Established: 1979
Frequency: Monthly - Published at the end of the month prior to cover date
Annual Sub.: £44.00
Circulation: 17,008 (ABC 01/07/2008 to 30/06/2009)
Usual Pagination: 60
Editor: Emma Butcher; **Publisher:** Jim Foster
Summary of Content: Magazine dedicated to the distribution of components and accessories. Contains news, views, features and product category features.
Readership/Target Audience: Aimed at motor factors, retailers, franchised dealer parts departments and cash and carry outlets.
ADVERTISING RATES:
Full Page Colour £3000.00
Agency Commission: 10%
Mechanical Data: Col Length: 277mm, Film: Digital, No. of Columns (Display): 2, Bleed Size: 303 x 216mm, Trim Size: 297 x 210mm, Type Area: 277 x 190mm, Page Width: 190mm
Copy instructions: Copy Date: 14th of the month prior to publication date
Average advertising content per issue: 50%
BUSINESS: MOTOR TRADE: Motor Trade Accessories

CAT - CIVIL AVIATION TRAINING
36334U6A-76

Editorial Address: Pembroke House, 8 St. Christophers Place, FARNBOROUGH, GU14 0NH **Tel:** 01252 532000
Fax: 01252 512714
Email: cat@halldale.com
Advertising Address: As above.
Email: jeremy@halldale.com
Web site: http://www.halldale.com/cat
ISSN: 1960-9024

Publisher: Halldale Media Ltd
Frequency: 6 issues yearly
Free to qualifying individuals
Annual Sub.: £65.00
Circulation: 14,184 (Publisher's Statement)
Usual Pagination: 54
Editor: Fiona Greenyer; **News Editor:** Fiona Greenyer;
Editor-in-Chief: Chris Lehman; **Managing Editor:** Alan Emmings
Summary of Content: Journal covering training, simulation and education in the field of commercial aerospace.
Readership/Target Audience: Aimed at chief pilots, training captains, engineering training managers, cabin crew training staff and senior management of all regional and international airlines.
ADVERTISING RATES:
Full Page Mono £4315.00
Full Page Colour £5600.00
Agency Commission: 10%
Mechanical Data: Type Area: 254 x 178mm, Bleed Size: 277 x 206mm, Page Width: 178mm, Col Length: 254mm, Film: Digital
Average advertising content per issue: 40%
BUSINESS: AVIATION & AERONAUTICS

CATALOGUE E-BUSINESS
39794U53-35

Formerly: Catalogue/e-business
Editorial Address: 151 High Street, ILFRACOMBE, EX34 9EZ **Tel:** 01271 866221
Email: edit@catalog-biz.com
Advertising Address: As above. **Tel:** 01271 866112
Fax: 01271 866040
Email: info@catalog-biz.com
Web site: http://www.catalog-biz.com
ISSN: 1362-2315
Publisher: Catalogue Development Centre Ltd
Date Established: 1995
Frequency: Monthly - Published in the 1st week of the cover month
Annual Sub.: £85.00
Circulation: 8,500 (Publisher's Statement)
Usual Pagination: 36
Editor: Miri Thomas; **Managing Director:** Jane Revell-Higgins; **Publisher:** Jane Revell-Higgins
Summary of Content: Magazine containing features on marketing, creative merchandising and operations within the catalogue and e-commerce sector.
Readership/Target Audience: Aimed at senior managers within catalogue, home shopping and retail businesses.
ADVERTISING RATES:
Full Page Mono £1465.00
Full Page Colour £2465.00
Agency Commission: 10%
Mechanical Data: Type Area: 311 x 220mm, Bleed Size: 326 x 236mm, Trim Size: 320 x 230mm, Col Length: 311mm, Film: Digital, Page Width: 220mm, No. of Columns (Display): 4, Print Process: web-fed offset litho
Average advertising content per issue: 50%
BUSINESS: RETAILING & WHOLESALING

CATCARE
41527U64H-157

Formerly: Feline Advisory Bureau Journal
Editorial Address: Taeselbury, High Street, Tisbury, SALISBURY, SP3 6LD **Tel:** 0870 742 2278
Fax: 01747 871873
Email: claire@fabcats.org
Advertising Address: As above.
Email: esfm@fabcats.org
Web site: http://www.fabcats.org
Publisher: FAB
Date Established: 1957
Frequency: Quarterly
Free to qualifying individuals
Annual Sub.: £26.00
Circulation: 3,000 (Publisher's Statement)
Usual Pagination: 32
Editor: Claire Bessant; **Advertising Manager:** Marilyn Peters
Summary of Content: Journal of the Feline Advisory Bureau which promotes health and welfare of cats.
Readership/Target Audience: Aimed at vets, veterinary nurses, cattery and cat owners.
ADVERTISING RATES:
Full Page Mono £200.00
Full Page Colour £500.00
Agency Commission: 10%
Mechanical Data: Trim Size: 297 x 210mm, Film: Digital, Bleed Size: 303 x 216mm
Copy instructions: Copy Date: 6 weeks prior to publication date
BUSINESS: OTHER CLASSIFICATIONS: Veterinary

CATERER AND HOTELKEEPER
36556U11A-20

Formerly: Caterer & Hotelkeeper
Editorial Address: Quadrant House, The Quadrant, SUTTON, SM2 5AS **Tel:** 020 8652 3500 **Fax:** 020 8652 8973

Email: caterernews@rbi.co.uk
Advertising Address: As above. **Fax:** 020 8652 8213
Email: gillian.cumming@rbi.co.uk
Web site: http://www.caterersearch.com
ISSN: 0008-7777
Publisher: Reed Business Information
Date Established: 1874
Frequency: Weekly - Published on Thursday
Cover Price: £3.00
Annual Sub.: £135.00
Circulation: 13,944 (ABC 01/07/2008 to 30/06/2009)
Usual Pagination: 120
Managing Editor: James Aufenast
Summary of Content: Magazine focusing on all aspects of the hospitality industry. Featuring catering news, letters to the editor, news from the industry and forthcoming events.
Readership/Target Audience: Aimed at people in all sectors of the catering industry, particularly staff in hotels, restaurants, pubs and the contract catering sector.
ADVERTISING RATES:
Full Page Colour £3975.00
Agency Commission: 10%
Mechanical Data: Page Width: 180mm, Type Area: 270 x 180mm, Col Length: 270mm, Trim Size: 297 x 210mm, Bleed Size: 303 x 216mm, Film: Digital
Copy instructions: Copy Date: 1 week prior to publication date
Average advertising content per issue: 40%
Supplement(s): Buy It! - 12xY, Careers Guide - 1xY, Education Month - 1xY, Green Month - 1xY, Healthy Eating - 1xY, Inside Beverages - 4xY, Inside Education - 2xY, Inside Kitchens - 3xY, Working World - 1xY
BUSINESS: CATERING: Catering, Hotels & Restaurants

CATERER AND HOTELKEEPER DIRECTORY
36557U11A-25

Editorial Address: Windsor Court, East Grinstead House, London Road, EAST GRINSTEAD, RH19 1XA
Tel: 01342 335861 **Fax:** 01342 336113
Email: phewson@reedinfo.co.uk
Advertising Address: As above. **Tel:** 01342 335779
Email: hosborn@reedinfo.co.uk
Web site: http://www.caterer-directory.com
Publisher: Reed Business Information
Date Established: 1997
Frequency: Annual - Published in December
Usual Pagination: 450
Editor: Pat Hewson; **Advertising Manager:** Harvey Osborn; **Publisher:** Richard Price
Summary of Content: Directory providing information about the catering and hotel trade.
Readership/Target Audience: Aimed at suppliers and decision-makers within the catering industry.
ADVERTISING: Rates on application
BUSINESS: CATERING: Catering, Hotels & Restaurants

THE CATERER, LICENSEE & HOTELIER NEWS GROUP
628960U22A-58

Formerly: The Caterer and Licensee News Group
Editorial Address: Suite 4, Roddis House, Old Christchurch Road, BOURNEMOUTH, BH1 1LG **Tel:** 01202 552333
Fax: 01202 552666
Email: padams@catererlicensee.com
Advertising Address: As above.
Email: sales@catererlicensee.com
Web site: http://www.catererlicensee.com
Publisher: RBC Publishing Limited
Date Established: 2000
Frequency: Monthly - Published on the 1st Monday of the cover month
Free to qualifying individuals
Annual Sub.: £20.00
Circulation: 20,000 (Publisher's Statement)
Usual Pagination: 36
Editor: Peter Adams
Summary of Content: Magazine covering industry news.
Readership/Target Audience: Aimed at proprietors, managers, chefs and licensees for catering, hospitality and licensed industries.
ADVERTISING RATES:
Full Page Colour £2200.00
Agency Commission: 10%
Mechanical Data: Col Length: 370mm, Col Widths (Display): 31mm, No. of Columns (Display): 8, Page Width: 274mm, Film: Digital, Type Area: 370 x 274mm, Trim Size: 395 x 290mm, Bleed Size: 405 x 300mm
Copy instructions: Copy Date: 1 week prior to publication date
Average advertising content per issue: 60%
Editions:
Caterer & Licensee Heart of England
Caterer, Licensee & Hotelier East of England Edition
The Caterer, Licensee & Hotelier South East Edition
The Caterer, Licensee & Hotelier Wales Edition
The Caterer, Licensee & Hotelier Westcountry Edition
BUSINESS: FOOD

Business Magazines

CATERING IN SCOTLAND
36562U11A-194

Editorial Address: 45 Queen Street, EDINBURGH, EH2 3NH
Tel: 0870 011 5020 **Fax:** 0131 225 6317
Email: alex@cateringinscotland.com
Advertising Address: 216 St. Vincent Street, GLASGOW, G2 5SG **Tel:** 0141 243 2871
Email: gordon@cateringinscotland.com
Web site: http://www.cateringinscotland.com
Publisher: DriveMedia Ltd
Date Established: 1986
Frequency: 6 issues yearly
Free to qualifying individuals
Annual Sub.: £23.50
Usual Pagination: 52
Editor: Alex Buchanan
Summary of Content: Journal covering catering, hospitality and tourism in Scotland.
Readership/Target Audience: Aimed at decision makers and buyers in hotels, restaurants, catering companies, wine bars, pubs, clubs, sports clubs, guest houses, facilities management firms and others in the catering industry.
ADVERTISING RATES:
Full Page Colour £1310.00
Agency Commission: 10%
Mechanical Data: Bleed Size: +3mm, Film: Digital
Copy instructions: Copy Date: 1 week prior to publication date
Average advertising content per issue: 35%
BUSINESS: CATERING: Catering, Hotels & Restaurants

CATERING MANAGER
36559U11A-63_25

Editorial Address: The Derwent Business Centre, Clarke Street, DERBY, DE1 2BU **Tel:** 01332 290460
Fax: 01332 345680
Email: admin@cateringmgr.co.uk
Advertising Address: As above.
Email: admin@cateringmgr.co.uk
Web site: http://www.newtonmann.co.uk
Publisher: Newton Mann Ltd
Frequency: Quarterly
Free to qualifying individuals
Annual Sub.: £12.00
Circulation: 3,000 (Publisher's Statement)
Usual Pagination: 16
Editor: Gail Mann; **Managing Director:** Charles Mann;
Publisher: Charles Mann
Summary of Content: Journal for catering managers in commercial, industrial, local and national government service.
Readership/Target Audience: Aimed at catering managers.
ADVERTISING RATES:
Full Page Mono £200.00
Full Page Colour £420.00
Agency Commission: 10%
Mechanical Data: Type Area: 260 x 180mm, Print Process: Sheet-fed litho, Bleed Size: 305 x 215mm, Trim Size: 297 x 210mm, Col Length: 260mm, Page Width: 180mm, Film: Digital
Copy instructions: Copy Date: 3 weeks prior to publication date
BUSINESS: CATERING: Catering, Hotels & Restaurants

CAYMAN FUNDS
1835238U1F-646

Editorial Address: 15-17 Newton Way, Woolsthorpe By Colsterworth, GRANTHAM, NG33 5NR **Tel:** 020 8290 4943
Fax: 020 7681 1248
Email: nlipinski@newtonmedia.co.uk
Advertising Address: As above. **Tel:** 020 8313 3967
Email: nlipinski@newtonmedia.co.uk
Web site: http://www.caymanfundsmagazine.com
Publisher: Newton Media Ltd
Frequency: Half-yearly - Published in spring and autumn
Circulation: 5,000 (Publisher's Statement)
Editor: Nicholas Lipinski; **Advertising Manager:** Nicholas Lipinski; **Publisher:** Nicholas Lipinski
Summary of Content: Publication for the funds industry in Cayman. Covering best practice in the industry as well as promoting Cayman as a domicile.
Readership/Target Audience: Aimed at International fund managers, institutional investors, administrators and service providers.
ADVERTISING RATES:
Full Page Colour £4650.00
Mechanical Data: Type Area: 270 x 185mm, Col Length: 270mm, Page Width: 185mm, Bleed Size: 303 x 216mm, Trim Size: 297 x 210mm, Film: Digital
BUSINESS: FINANCE & ECONOMICS: Investment

CCF
37425U18B-460

Editorial Address: 7th Floor, Ludgate House, 245 Blackfriars Road, LONDON, SE1 9UY **Tel:** 020 7921 8515
Email: claudia.hathway@ubm.com
Advertising Address: Ludgate House, 245 Blackfriars Road, LONDON, SE1 9UY **Tel:** 020 7921 8507
Fax: 020 7921 8549
Email: simon.thorpe@ubm.com

Web site: http://www.callcentre.co.uk
ISSN: 1353-5439
Publisher: UBM Information Ltd
Date Established: 1995
Frequency: Monthly - Published in the last week of the month prior to cover month
Free to qualifying individuals
Annual Sub.: £99.00
Circulation: 8,716 (Publisher's Statement)
Usual Pagination: 68
Editor: Claudia Hathway
Summary of Content: Magazine providing information on products and services for call centres and the telebusiness industry.
Readership/Target Audience: Aimed at call centre managers and other senior level call/contact centre staff and CEOs and any managers involved in the customer service industry.
ADVERTISING RATES:
Full Page Colour £3775.00
Agency Commission: 10%
Mechanical Data: Type Area: 273 x 186mm, Bleed Size: 279 x 192mm, Trim Size: 297 x 210mm, Col Length: 273mm, Film: Digital, Page Width: 186mm
Copy instructions: Copy Date: 2 weeks prior to publication date
Average advertising content per issue: 50%
BUSINESS: ELECTRONICS: Telecommunications

CCTV IMAGE
1640095U54C-309

Editorial Address: PO Box 795A, SURBITON, KT5 8YB
Tel: 020 8255 5007 **Fax:** 020 8255 5003
Email: tom@cctvimage.com
Advertising Address: PO Box 5231, LICHFIELD, WS14 4EB
Tel: 01543 250456 **Fax:** 01543 415044
Email: advertising@cctvimage.com
Web site: http://www.cctvimage.com
Publisher: CCTV Media Ltd
Date Established: 2004
Frequency: 6 issues yearly
Free to qualifying individuals
Annual Sub.: £24.00
Circulation: 8,500 (Publisher's Statement)
Usual Pagination: 56
Editor: Tom Reeve; **Advertising Manager:** Peter Mawson
Summary of Content: Magazine covering all aspects of the CCTV industry. Covers technology, case studies, legal, management issues, control room operations and products.
Readership/Target Audience: Aimed at CCTV control managers, consultants and manufacturers.
ADVERTISING RATES:
Full Page Mono £1200.00
Full Page Colour £1800.00
Agency Commission: 10%
Mechanical Data: Film: Positive, right reading, emulsion side down. Digital
Copy instructions: Copy Date: 3 weeks prior to publication date
BUSINESS: SAFETY & SECURITY: Security

CDC NEWS
39613U49B-26

Formerly: CDC News Incorporating Coach Monthly
Editorial Address: 37 Tyndall Court, Commerce Road, Lynch Wood, PETERBOROUGH, PE2 6LR
Tel: 01733 405738 **Fax:** 01733 405745
Email: frank.forster@coachdriversclub.com
Advertising Address: As above. **Tel:** 01733 405730
Email: lauren.kirt@coachdriversclub.com
Web site: http://www.coachdriversclub.com
Publisher: Expo Publishing
Date Established: 1982
Frequency: Monthly - Published on the 2nd Thursday of the cover month
Free to qualifying individuals
Circulation: 7,000 (Publisher's Statement)
Usual Pagination: 60
Editor: Frank Forster; **Advertising Manager:** Lauren Kirt;
Publisher: Tony West
Summary of Content: Magazine covering coaches and coach tours, including planning guidance for group visits.
Readership/Target Audience: Read by coach operators, drivers, group organisers and tour planners in the UK.
ADVERTISING RATES:
Full Page Colour £525.00
Agency Commission: 10%
Mechanical Data: Type Area: 272 x 190mm, Bleed Size: 303 x 216mm, Trim Size: 297 x 210mm, Col Length: 272mm, Page Width: 190mm, Print Process: Offset litho, Film: Digital
Copy instructions: Copy Date: 1 week prior to publication date
Average advertising content per issue: 50%
Supplement(s): Coach Drivers Club Yearbook - 1xY
BUSINESS: TRANSPORT: Bus & Coach Transport

CEBIT ASIA NEWS
768779U5R-655

Editorial Address: PO Box 107, BICESTER, OX25 4WA
Tel: 01869 347644

Email: cebitasia@xsmail.com
Advertising Address: 212 Carnegie Center, PRINCETON, NJ 08540 **Tel:** 609 987 0056 **Fax:** 609 987 0318
Email: info@cebitnews.com
Web site: http://www.cebit-asia.com
Publisher: CeBIT News Media Network
Date Established: 2001
Frequency: Annual - Published in September
Cover Price: Free
Circulation: 50,000 (Publisher's Statement)
Usual Pagination: 56
Editor: Philip Gallagher; **Advertising Manager:** Jim Charos
Summary of Content: Official newspaper of CeBIT Asia trade fair covering telecommunications, IT hardware, software, services, ebusiness and Internet solutions.
Language(s): Chinese; English
Readership/Target Audience: Aimed at professional infotech buyers from multiple industries attending the CeBIT Asia Exhibition in Shanghai, also technology industry executives, analysts and media.
ADVERTISING: Rates on application
BUSINESS: COMPUTERS & AUTOMATION: Computers Related

CEBIT NEWS HANNOVER
759852U5R-5

Editorial Address: PO Box 107, BICESTER, OX25 4WA
Tel: 01869 347644
Email: edit@cebitnews.com
Advertising Address: 212 Carnegie Center, PRINCETON, NJ 08540 **Tel:** 609 987 0056 **Fax:** 609 987 0318
Email: info@cebitnews.com
Web site: http://www.cebitnews.com
ISSN: 1543-9186
Publisher: CeBIT News Media Network
Date Established: 1986
Frequency: Annual - Published in March
Cover Price: Free
Circulation: 180,000 (Publisher's Statement)
Usual Pagination: 128
Editor: Philip Gallagher
Summary of Content: Official English language newspaper of the CeBIT Hannover, the annual IT and Telecoms trade fair.
Readership/Target Audience: Read by professional buyers from industries of all types, infotech executives, technology analysts and the media.
ADVERTISING RATES:
Full Page Colour EUR11760.00
Agency Commission: 15%
Mechanical Data: Trim Size: 301 x 225mm, Bleed Size: +4mm, Film: Digital
Copy instructions: Copy Date: 15th of February prior to publication date
BUSINESS: COMPUTERS & AUTOMATION: Computers Related

CEMA CONSUMER ELECTRONICS
37335U18A-45

Editorial Address: PO Box 107, BICESTER, OX25 4WA
Tel: 01869 347644
Email: cemanewsletters@xsmail.com
Publisher: Cores Publications Inc.
Date Established: 1986
Frequency: Monthly
Annual Sub.: £2000.00
Circulation: 1,000 (Publisher's Statement)
Usual Pagination: 20
Editor: Philip Gallagher
Summary of Content: Newsletter covering all aspects of consumer electronics, including market news and analysis.
Language(s): English; Japanese
Readership/Target Audience: Aimed at senior executives in manufacturing and distribution companies across Europe and in East Asia.
ADVERTISING: No Advertising taken
BUSINESS: ELECTRONICS

CENTRAL
41221U63A-70

Editorial Address: 13 College Approach, Greenwich, LONDON, SE10 9HY **Tel:** 020 8858 9771
Email: central@dma.eclipse.co.uk
Web site: http://www.iod.com/clb
Publisher: DMA Ltd
Date Established: 1991
Frequency: Quarterly - Published on the first working day of each quarter
Cover Price: £3.50
Free to qualifying individuals
Circulation: 8,000 (Publisher's Statement)
Usual Pagination: 8
Editor: David Twigge-Molecey
Summary of Content: Newsletter of the Central London Branch of the Institute of Directors. Contains news, reviews and notices of forthcoming events.
Readership/Target Audience: Read by Members of the Central London Branch of the Institute of Directors.

ADVERTISING: No Advertising taken
BUSINESS: REGIONAL BUSINESS: Regional Business Greater London

CENTRAL AND EASTERN EUROPE TEXTILE BUSINESS REVIEW
1708404U47A-582

Editorial Address: 2A Bridge Street, Silsden, KEIGHLEY, BD20 9NB **Tel:** 01535 656489 **Fax:** 0870 094 0863
Email: gfisher@textilemedia.com
Web site: http://www.textilemedia.com
ISSN: 1748-7765
Publisher: Textile Media Services Ltd
Date Established: 2005
Frequency: Annual - Published in October
Cover Price: £315.00
Circulation: 100 (Publisher's Statement)
Usual Pagination: 80
Editor: Geoff Fisher; **Publisher:** Judy Holland
Summary of Content: Publication featuring statistical information and analysis on the textile and clothing industries in Central and Eastern Europe and the former Soviet Union.
Readership/Target Audience: Aimed at companies looking for market information on the clothing and textile industry in the merging region.
ADVERTISING: No Advertising taken
BUSINESS: CLOTHING & TEXTILES

CENTRAL BANKING
35075U1C-100

Editorial Address: Haymarket House, 28-29 Haymarket, LONDON, SW1Y 4RX **Tel:** 020 7004 7404
Fax: 020 7484 9758
Email: info@centralbanking.co.uk
Advertising Address: As above. **Tel:** 020 7484 9700
Fax: 020 7388 9040
Email: marketing@centralbanking.co.uk
Web site: http://www.centralbanking.co.uk
ISSN: 0960-6319
Publisher: Incisive Media Investments
Date Established: 1990
Frequency: Quarterly
Annual Sub.: £300.00
Circulation: 2,000 (Publisher's Statement)
Usual Pagination: 100
Editor: Robert Pringle; **Managing Director:** Robert Pringle
Summary of Content: Journal reporting and commenting on the activities of the central banks. Covers monetary policy, reserve management, exchange rate policy, bank supervision, human resource development and training.
Readership/Target Audience: Read by central bankers, research and financial institutions.
ADVERTISING RATES:
Full Page Colour £2950.00
Mechanical Data: Bleed Size: 276 x 196mm, Trim Size: 270 x 190mm, Film: Digital
Copy instructions: Copy Date: 3 weeks prior to publication date
BUSINESS: FINANCE & ECONOMICS: Banking

CENTRAL GOVERNMENT
1687354U32R-493

Editorial Address: Ebenezer House, Ryecroft, NEWCASTLE-UNDER-LYME, ST5 2UB **Tel:** 01782 740088
Fax: 01782 740066
Email: lcarnwell@publicservice.co.uk
Advertising Address: As above. **Tel:** 01782 620088
Fax: 01782 625533
Email: gmellor@publicservice.co.uk
Web site: http://www.publicservice.co.uk
ISSN: 1470-5257
Publisher: PSCA International Ltd
Date Established: 2000
Frequency: Half-yearly - Published in April and October
Free to qualifying individuals
Circulation: 9,256 (ABC 01/07/2008 to 30/06/2009)
Usual Pagination: 226
Editor: Lisa Carnwell; **Managing Editor:** Lisa Carnwell
Summary of Content: Publication providing an overview of the policy and projects of major government departments.
Readership/Target Audience: Aimed at government ministers, chief executives, finance directors, senior civil servants, senior officers, procurement, project, HR, IT, transport and energy managers.
ADVERTISING RATES:
Full Page Colour £3995.00
Mechanical Data: Film: Digital
Copy instructions: Copy Date: 6 weeks prior to publication date
Average advertising content per issue: 50%
BUSINESS: LOCAL GOVERNMENT, LEISURE & RECREATION: Local Government Related

CENTRE CIRCLE
713542U32H-475

Formerly: Football Business International
Editorial Address: 16 Butlers & Colonial Wharf, LONDON, SE1 2PX **Tel:** 020 7403 4110
Email: admin@soccerinvestor.com
Advertising Address: As above.
Email: admin@soccerinvestor.com
Web site: http://www.soccerinvestor.com
ISSN: 1476-2447
Publisher: Soccer Investor Ltd
Frequency: Quarterly
Free to qualifying individuals
Circulation: 5,000 (Publisher's Statement)
Usual Pagination: 40
Editor: Brian Sturgess; **Advertising Manager:** Brian Sturgess; **Publisher:** Brian Sturgess
Summary of Content: Magazine focusing on commercial issues affecting the worldwide football industry.
Readership/Target Audience: Aimed at commercial and marketing directors' of professional football clubs and leagues.
ADVERTISING RATES:
Full Page Colour £1000.00
Agency Commission: 10%
Average advertising content per issue: 50%
BUSINESS: LOCAL GOVERNMENT, LEISURE & RECREATION: Leisure, Recreation & Entertainment

CEO
1663207U14A-539

Editorial Address: Brunel House, 55-57 North Wharf Road, LONDON, W2 1LA **Tel:** 020 7915 9600 **Fax:** 020 7915 9776
Email: michaeljones@spgmedia.com
Advertising Address: As above. **Fax:** 020 7915 9958
Email: sanjeevdole@spgmedia.com
Web site: http://www.the-chiefexecutive.com
Publisher: SPG Media Ltd
Frequency: Half-yearly - Published in March and September
Free to qualifying individuals
Circulation: 10,400 (ABC 01/07/2008 to 30/06/2009)
Usual Pagination: 100
Editor: Michael Jones
Summary of Content: Magazine covering analysis, case studies and interviews covering key issues impacting the CEO's mission and responsibilities.
Readership/Target Audience: Aimed at C-level decision makers within large organisations.
ADVERTISING RATES:
Full Page Colour £7900.00
Copy instructions: Copy Date: 6 weeks prior to publication date
BUSINESS: COMMERCE, INDUSTRY & MANAGEMENT

CEPHALALGIA
623257U56A-57_20

Editorial Address: Cephalagia Editorial Office, 6 Ardleigh Gardens, Hutton, BRENTWOOD, CM13 1QR
Tel: 01277 215940 **Fax:** 01865 714591
Email: chaedoffice@wiley.com
Advertising Address: 9600 Garsington Road, Cowley, OXFORD, OX4 2DQ **Tel:** 01865 776868
Email: nchesher@wiley.com
Web site: http://www.manuscriptcentral.com/cephalalgia
ISSN: 0333-1024
Publisher: Wiley-Blackwell Publishing
Date Established: 1981
Frequency: Monthly
Annual Sub.: £209.00
Circulation: 2,100 (Publisher's Statement)
Usual Pagination: 80
Editor: Emma Missen; **Editor-in-Chief:** David Dodick; **Publisher:** Gavin Sharrock
Summary of Content: Journal of the International Headache Society. Provides the latest news on clinical research applied to the study of headaches.
Readership/Target Audience: Aimed at neurologists, headache specialists and pharmaceutical companies.
ADVERTISING RATES:
Full Page Mono £582.00
Full Page Colour £1367.00
Agency Commission: 10%
Mechanical Data: Type Area: 245 x 180mm, Col Length: 245mm, Trim Size: 276 x 210mm, Bleed Size: 282 x 216mm, Film: Digital, Page Width: 180mm
BUSINESS: HEALTH & MEDICAL

CERAMIC REVIEW
36611U12A-25

Editorial Address: 25 Fouberts Place, LONDON, W1F 7QF
Tel: 020 7439 3377 **Fax:** 020 7287 9954
Email: editorial@ceramicreview.com
Advertising Address: As above.
Email: advertising@ceramicreview.com
Web site: http://www.ceramicreview.com
ISSN: 0144-1825
Publisher: Ceramic Review Publishing Ltd
Frequency: 6 issues yearly
Cover Price: £5.95
Annual Sub.: £34.00

Circulation: 10,000 (Publisher's Statement)
Usual Pagination: 74
Editor: Emmanuel Cooper; **Advertising Manager:** Paul Cuthill
Summary of Content: Magazine providing articles on ceramic production, history and exhibitions.
Readership/Target Audience: Read by professional and amateur potters, collectors and suppliers and those based within art colleges, schools, galleries and art centres.
ADVERTISING RATES:
Full Page Colour £1010.00
Agency Commission: 10%
Mechanical Data: Film: Positive, right reading, emulsion side down. Digital, Type Area: 284 x 200mm, Bleed Size: 306 x 226mm, Col Length: 284mm, Trim Size: 300 x 220mm, Page Width: 200mm
Copy instructions: Copy Date: 1st Monday 2 months prior to publication date
Average advertising content per issue: 20%
BUSINESS: CERAMICS, POTTERY & GLASS: Ceramics & Pottery

CERN COURIER
39955U55-41_80

Editorial Address: Dirac House, Temple Back, BRISTOL, BS1 6BE **Tel:** 0117 929 7481 **Fax:** 0117 930 1178
Email: cern.courier@cern.ch
Advertising Address: As above.
Email: edward.jost@iop.org
Web site: http://cerncourier.com
ISSN: 0374-2288
Publisher: IOP Publishing
Date Established: 1958
Frequency: 10 issues yearly - Combined January/Febuary and July/August issues
Cover Price: Free
Circulation: 21,500 (Publisher's Statement)
Usual Pagination: 48
Editor: Jo Nicholas; **Advertising Manager:** Edward Jost; **Publisher:** Jo Nicholas
Summary of Content: International journal of high-energy physics. Contains product and technology news and views, and updates on software, hardware, components and inventions.
Language(s): English; French
Readership/Target Audience: Read by the scientific community associated with CERN (European Centre for Nuclear Research) and physicists inhabiting major research sites throughout the world who wish to keep updated with fundamental physics research.
ADVERTISING RATES:
Full Page Mono £3239.00
Full Page Colour £4258.00
Agency Commission: 10%
Mechanical Data: Type Area: 282 x 213mm, Bleed Size: 288 x 219mm, Film: Digital, Col Length: 282mm, Page Width: 213mm
Average advertising content per issue: 30%
BUSINESS: APPLIED SCIENCE & LABORATORIES

CFJ CONTRACT FLOORING JOURNAL
38068U23B-40

Editorial Address: 102 Queens Road, TUNBRIDGE WELLS, TN4 9JU **Tel:** 01892 680816 **Fax:** 01892 543064
Email: alancfj@btconnect.com
Advertising Address: The Oast, Great Danegate, Eridge, TUNBRIDGE WELLS, TN3 9HU **Tel:** 01892 752400
Fax: 01892 752405
Email: sales@contractflooringjournal.co.uk
Web site: http://www.contractflooringjournal.co.uk
ISSN: 1263-4236
Publisher: Kick-Start Publishing Ltd
Date Established: 1989
Frequency: Monthly
Annual Sub.: £48.00
Circulation: 6,888 (ABC 01/07/2008 to 30/06/2009)
Usual Pagination: 80
Editor: Alan Bakalor; **Advertising Director:** Stuart Bourne
Summary of Content: Official journal of The Contract Flooring Association, covering news, product information, interviews, survey and case histories relating to the commercial flooring market.
Readership/Target Audience: Aimed at manufacturers, distributors, retailers, architects, specifiers, facilities and property managers and cleaning and flooring contractors.
ADVERTISING RATES:
Full Page Mono £1390.00
Full Page Colour £1390.00
Agency Commission: 10%
Mechanical Data: Film: Digital, Type Area: 268 x 185mm, Bleed Size: 303 x 213mm, Trim Size: 297 x 210mm, Col Length: 268mm, Page Width: 185mm
Average advertising content per issue: 40%
Supplement(s): Flooring Industry Awards - 1xY
BUSINESS: FURNISHINGS & FURNITURE: Furnishings, Carpets & Flooring

Business Magazines

THE CHAMBER
41355U63B-1659

Formerly: The Chamber (Surrey CoC)
Editorial Address: 5th Floor, Hollywood House, Church Street East, Woking, SURREY, GU21 6HJ
Tel: 01483 726655 **Fax:** 01483 740217
Email: info@surrey-chambers.co.uk
Advertising Address: 8th Floor, Bridgewater House, 60 Whitworth Street, MANCHESTER, M1 6LT
Tel: 0161 838 2596 **Fax:** 0161 832 4176
Email: paul.lyon@tenalpspublishing.com
Web site: http://www.surrey-chambers.co.uk
Publisher: Ten Alps Publishing
Frequency: 6 issues yearly
Cover Price: Free
Circulation: 5,000 (Publisher's Statement)
Usual Pagination: 32
Editor: Rachel Cherryman
Summary of Content: Official newspaper of Surrey Chambers of Commerce.
Readership/Target Audience: Aimed at members of the Chamber of Commerce, business support organisations, MPs and local councillors.
ADVERTISING: Rates on application
BUSINESS: REGIONAL BUSINESS: Regional Business English Counties

CHAMBER BULLETIN
1732050U63B-2556

Formerly: Chamber Matters
Editorial Address: 2 Genesis Park, Sheffield Road, ROTHERHAM, S60 1DX **Tel:** 01709 386200
Email: andrew.denniff@brchamber.org.uk
Advertising Address: As above. **Fax:** 01709 839271
Email: fhall@brchamber.co.uk
Web site: http://www.brchamber.co.uk
Publisher: Barnsley and Rotherham Chamber of Commerce
Date Established: 2008
Frequency: 6 issues yearly
Cover Price: Free
Circulation: 3,500 (Publisher's Statement)
Usual Pagination: 44
Editor: Francis Hall; **Advertising Manager:** Francis Hall
Summary of Content: Official Publication of the Barnsley & Rotherham Chamber of Commerce. Includes local business news, chamber news and events.
Readership/Target Audience: Aimed at members of the Barnsley & Rotherham Chamber of Commerce and other local businesses.
ADVERTISING RATES:
Full Page Colour £650.00
Copy instructions: Copy Date: 4 weeks prior to publication date
BUSINESS: REGIONAL BUSINESS: Regional Business English Counties

CHAMBER NEWS
41426U63B-2153

Editorial Address: Charnwood Court, 5B New Walk, LEICESTER, LE1 6TE **Tel:** 0116 247 1800
Fax: 0116 247 0430
Email: farmer.s@chamberofcommerce.co.uk
Advertising Address: As above.
Email: leics@chamberofcommerce.co.uk
Web site: http://www.chamberofcommerce.co.uk
Publisher: Leicestershire Chamber of Commerce
Frequency: 11 issues yearly - Published at the end of each month
Free to qualifying individuals
Circulation: 1,500 (Publisher's Statement)
Usual Pagination: 8
Editor: Suzanne Farmer; **Advertising Manager:** Sharon Jeffrey
Summary of Content: Newsletter containing information about Chamber activities.
Readership/Target Audience: Aimed at Chamber Membership and media contacts.
ADVERTISING: Rates on application
BUSINESS: REGIONAL BUSINESS: Regional Business English Counties

CHAMBERLINK
41374U63B-1800

Editorial Address: Birmingham Chamber of Commerce & Industry, 75 Harborne Road, Edgbaston, BIRMINGHAM, B15 3DH **Tel:** 0121 454 6171 **Fax:** 0121 450 4221
Email: j.lamb@birminghamchamber.org.uk
Advertising Address: Kemps Publishing, 11 Swan Courtyard, Charles Edward Road, BIRMINGHAM, B26 1BU
Tel: 0121 765 4144
Email: maria.notton@kempspublishing.co.uk
Web site: http://www.birmingham-chamber.com
Publisher: Kemps Publishing Ltd
Frequency: 10 issues yearly - Published around the 1st week of the cover month
Cover Price: £2.00
Free to qualifying individuals
Annual Sub.: £24.50
Circulation: 9,000 (Publisher's Statement)

Usual Pagination: 56
Editor: John Lamb; **Advertising Manager:** Maria Notton
Summary of Content: Publication for the Birmingham Chamber of Commerce and Industry and a business audience generally.
Readership/Target Audience: Aimed at senior decision makers within business.
ADVERTISING RATES:
Full Page Mono £1650.00
Full Page Colour £1898.00
Agency Commission: 10%
Mechanical Data: Type Area: 265 x 190mm, Bleed Size: + 3mm, Trim Size: 297 x 210mm, Col Length: 265mm, Page Width: 190mm, Film: Digital
Supplement(s): Business Connections - 10xY
BUSINESS: REGIONAL BUSINESS: Regional Business English Counties

CHAMBERS CLIENT REPORT
39132U44-230

Formerly: Commercial Lawyer
Editorial Address: 23 Long Lane, LONDON, EC1A 9HL
Tel: 020 7606 1300 **Fax:** 020 7606 0906
Advertising Address: As above. **Tel:** 020 7778 1300
Fax: 020 7600 1168
Email: biancam@chambersandpartners.co.uk
Web site: http://www.chambersandpartners.co.uk
ISSN: 1744-6392
Publisher: Chambers & Partners
Date Established: 2004
Frequency: Quarterly
Annual Sub.: £300.00
Circulation: 9,584 (Publisher's Statement)
Editor: David Robinson; **Publisher:** Michael Chambers
Summary of Content: Magazine covering all areas of business law.
Readership/Target Audience: Aimed at business lawyers, solicitors and barristers within Europe and the USA.
ADVERTISING RATES:
Full Page Mono £2950.00
Full Page Colour £2950.00
Mechanical Data: Type Area: 268 x 199mm, Col Length: 268mm, Page Width: 199mm
Average advertising content per issue: 45%
BUSINESS: LEGAL

THE CHANNEL
637989U2D-58

Editorial Address: PO Box 141, CRANBROOK, TN17 9AJ
Tel: 020 7993 2557 **Fax:** 020 7993 8043
Email: gunda.cannon@aib.org.uk
Advertising Address: Century One Publishing, Arquen House, 4-6 Spicer Street, ST. ALBANS, AL3 4PQ
Tel: 01727 739184 **Fax:** 01727 893895
Email: ollie@centuryonepublishing.ltd.uk
Web site: http://www.aib.org.uk
ISSN: 1477-8718
Publisher: The AIB-Association for International Broadcasting
Date Established: 1996
Frequency: 3 issues yearly
Free to qualifying individuals
Annual Sub.: £12.75
Circulation: 7,000 (Publisher's Statement)
Usual Pagination: 50
Editor: Gunda Cannon; **Executive Editor:** Alison Feary
Summary of Content: Magazine covering cross-border broadcasting news, strategy, programming, technology, engineering and appointments with technology reports and listings of shows and conferences.
Readership/Target Audience: Read by senior executives in the media and related industries - broadcasting companies, equipment manufacturers and distribution companies, service providers and consultants involved in cross-border broadcasting.
ADVERTISING RATES:
Full Page Mono £750.00
Full Page Colour £1225.00
Agency Commission: 10%
Mechanical Data: Type Area: 277 x 190mm, Bleed Size: 303 x 216mm, Trim Size: 297 x 210mm, Col Length: 277mm, Page Width: 190mm, Print Process: Web-fed offset litho, Film: Digital
Average advertising content per issue: 25%
BUSINESS: COMMUNICATIONS, ADVERTISING & MARKETING: Broadcasting

CHANNEL 21 INTERNATIONAL
1896758U2D-158

Editorial Address: 2nd Floor, 148 Curtain Road, LONDON, EC2A 3AT **Tel:** 020 7729 7460 **Fax:** 020 7490 7461
Email: david@c21media.net
Web site: http://www.c21media.net
Publisher: C21 Media Ltd
Frequency: 10 issues yearly
Annual Sub.: £120.00
Circulation: 6,500 (Publisher's Statement)
Editor: David Jenkinson

Summary of Content: Television business magazine covering programming development and International business information.
Readership/Target Audience: Aimed at those producing, co-producing, acquiring, distributing and managing content to all types of channels from TV stations to internet portals.
BUSINESS: COMMUNICATIONS, ADVERTISING & MARKETING: Broadcasting

CHANNEL INFO
38645U34-23

Editorial Address: Progressive House, Maidstone Road, Foots Cray, SIDCUP, DA14 5HZ **Tel:** 020 8269 7700
Fax: 020 8269 7877
Email: cbentley@progressivemediagroup.com
Advertising Address: As above.
Email: swight@progressivemediagroup.com
Web site: http://www.channelinfo.net
ISSN: 1467-0593
Publisher: Office Solutions Media Limited
Date Established: 1999
Frequency: 10 issues yearly
Free to qualifying individuals
Annual Sub.: £63.00
Circulation: 6,002 (ABC 01/07/2008 to 30/06/2009)
Usual Pagination: 68
Editor: Caron Bentley; **Advertising Manager:** Sue Wight
Summary of Content: Magazine covering the broad spectrum of the office market, including stationery, furniture, equipment, telecoms, supplies, and IT products and services. Contains industry news, case studies, profiles, new product information, market analysis, benchmarking, features and events coverage.
Readership/Target Audience: Aimed at dealers, distributors, wholesalers and resellers of all products for the office environment.
ADVERTISING RATES:
Full Page Mono £1947.00
Full Page Colour £1947.00
Agency Commission: 10%
Mechanical Data: Type Area: 272 x 185mm, Col Length: 272mm, Page Width: 185mm, Film: Positive, right reading, emulsion side down. Digital, Trim Size: 297 x 210mm, Bleed Size: 303 x 216mm, Print Process: Sheet-fed litho
Copy instructions: Copy Date: 20th of the month prior to publication date
Average advertising content per issue: 50%
BUSINESS: OFFICE EQUIPMENT

CHARITIES MANAGEMENT
35435U1P-40

Editorial Address: PO Box 29, SOUTH PETHERTON, TA13 5WE **Tel:** 01460 241106 **Fax:** 01460 241091
Email: charitiesman@btconnect.com
Advertising Address: As above.
Email: charitiesman@btconnect.com
Web site: http://www.charitiesmanagement.com
ISSN: 0964-9093
Publisher: Mitre House Publishing Ltd
Date Established: 1993
Frequency: 6 issues yearly
Annual Sub.: £48.00
Circulation: 5,000 (Publisher's Statement)
Usual Pagination: 56
Editor: Richard Blausten; **Managing Director:** Richard Blausten; **Advertising Manager:** Richard Blausten; **Publisher:** Richard Blausten
Summary of Content: Journal covering news, issues and management features.
Readership/Target Audience: Readership includes chief executives, finance directors, fundraising managers, administrators and solicitors.
ADVERTISING RATES:
Full Page Mono £1100.00
Full Page Colour £1700.00
Agency Commission: 10%
Mechanical Data: Type Area: 262 x 181mm, Col Length: 262mm, Film: Digital, Page Width: 181mm, Bleed Size: 303 x 216mm, Trim Size: 297 x 210mm
BUSINESS: FINANCE & ECONOMICS: Fundraising

THE CHARITY BUYERS GUIDE
35436U1P-5

Editorial Address: 6th Floor, 3 London Wall Buildings, LONDON, EC2M 5PD **Tel:** 020 7562 2401
Fax: 020 7374 2701
Email: andrew.holt@perspectivepublishing.com
Advertising Address: As above.
Email: cerys.mclean@charitytimes.com
Web site: http://www.cbg.org.uk
ISSN: 1460-115X
Publisher: Perspective Publishing Ltd
Frequency: Annual - Published in June
Annual Sub.: £39.95
Usual Pagination: 150
Editor: Andrew Holt; **Advertising Manager:** Cerys Mclean
Summary of Content: Guide to products and services available to charities.
Readership/Target Audience: Read by professional charity buyers, fund raising directors and managing directors.

ADVERTISING RATES:
Full Page Colour £3172.00
Agency Commission: 10%
Mechanical Data: Type Area: 262 x 181mm, Bleed Size: 303 x 216mm, Trim Size: 297 x 210mm, Col Length: 262mm, Film: Digital, Page Width: 181mm
BUSINESS: FINANCE & ECONOMICS: Fundraising

CHARITY FINANCE
34954U1A-70
Formerly: NGO Finance Incorporating Charity
Editorial Address: 15 Prescott Place, LONDON, SW4 6BS
Tel: 020 7819 1200 **Fax:** 020 7819 1210
Email: info@charityfinance.co.uk
Advertising Address: As above. **Tel:** 020 7819 1209
Fax: 020 7819 1219
Email: phil@plazapublishing.co.uk
Web site: http://www.charityfinance.co.uk
ISSN: 0963-0295
Publisher: Plaza Publishing Ltd
Date Established: 1990
Frequency: 10 issues yearly
Annual Sub.: £90.00
Circulation: 5,500 (Publisher's Statement)
Usual Pagination: 68
Editor: Ian Allsop
Summary of Content: Publication covering all aspects of accounting, tax, investment, banking, property, IT and law. Shows those involved in charities how to manage them in the proper way.
Readership/Target Audience: Aimed at finance managers and chief executives of UK charities.
ADVERTISING RATES:
Full Page Mono £1995.00
Full Page Colour £2395.00
Agency Commission: 10%
Mechanical Data: Film: Digital, Type Area: 257 x 185mm, Bleed Size: 303 x 216mm, Trim Size: 297 x 210mm, Col Length: 257mm, Page Width: 185mm
Copy instructions: Copy Date: 3 weeks prior to publication date
Average advertising content per issue: 50%
BUSINESS: FINANCE & ECONOMICS

CHARITY FUNDING REPORT
1841370U1P-284
Editorial Address: 6-14 Underwood Street, LONDON, N1 7JQ **Tel:** 020 7324 2322 **Fax:** 020 7566 8238
Email: cdann@caritasdata.co.uk
Web site: http://www.caritasdata.co.uk
Publisher: Waterlow
Frequency: Monthly
Annual Sub.: £166.00
Circulation: 3,500 (Publisher's Statement)
Editor: Clarissa Dann
Summary of Content: Publication covering fundraising, grant seeking and social investment.
Readership/Target Audience: Aimed at social enterprise and grant seekers.
BUSINESS: FINANCE & ECONOMICS: Fundraising

CHARITY TIMES
35437U1P-73
Editorial Address: 6th Floor, 3 London Wall Buildings, LONDON, EC2M 5PD **Tel:** 020 7562 2401
Fax: 020 7374 2701
Email: andrew.holt@charitytimes.com
Advertising Address: As above. **Tel:** 020 7562 2424
Email: richard.dove@charitytimes.com
Web site: http://www.charitytimes.com
ISSN: 1355-4573
Publisher: Perspective Publishing Ltd
Date Established: 1995
Frequency: 6 issues yearly - Published in the 1st week of the cover month
Annual Sub.: £119.00
Circulation: 10,373 (ABC 01/07/2008 to 30/06/2009)
Usual Pagination: 68
Editor: Andrew Holt; **Managing Director:** John Woods; **Advertising Manager:** Richard Dove
Summary of Content: Magazine covering all areas of financial, business and fundraising management for charities.
Readership/Target Audience: Read by decision-makers in voluntary groups.
ADVERTISING RATES:
Full Page Colour £3041.00
Agency Commission: 10%
Mechanical Data: Film: Digital, Type Area: 262 x 181mm, Trim Size: 297 x 210mm, Bleed Size: 303 x 216mm, Col Length: 262mm, Page Width: 181mm
Copy instructions: Copy Date: 2 weeks prior to publication date
Average advertising content per issue: 40%
BUSINESS: FINANCE & ECONOMICS: Fundraising

CHART & COMPASS
39322U45A-30
Editorial Address: 350 Shirley Road, SOUTHAMPTON, SO15 3HY **Tel:** 023 8051 5950 **Fax:** 023 8051 5951
Email: jwebber@sailors-society.org
Advertising Address: As above.
Email: events@sailors-society.org
Web site: http://www.sailors-society.org
Publisher: Sailors' Society
Date Established: 1879
Frequency: 3 issues yearly - Published in January, July and November.
Cover Price: Free
Circulation: 11,000 (Publisher's Statement)
Usual Pagination: 8
Editor: Jan Webber; **Advertising Manager:** Karen Watts
Summary of Content: Magazine of the British & International Sailors' Society, a charity for seafarers, including news, articles on the year's events and marine industry information.
Readership/Target Audience: Read by members, seafarers and the marine industry.
ADVERTISING RATES:
Full Page Mono £445.00
Full Page Colour £595.00
Mechanical Data: Film: Digital
Average advertising content per issue: 10%
BUSINESS: MARINE & SHIPPING

CHART BREAKOUT
35226U1F-120
Editorial Address: PO Box 1638, LONDON, W8 4QR
Tel: 020 7937 7879 **Fax:** 020 7937 7364
Email: qlumsden@bloomberg.net
Publisher: Letterprint Ltd
Date Established: 1984
Frequency: Monthly
Annual Sub.: £99.50
Usual Pagination: 16
Editor: Quentin Lumsden
Summary of Content: Journal covering the stock market covering fundamental and technical analysis and recommendations on shares.
Readership/Target Audience: Read by private investors, asset management companies and bankers.
ADVERTISING: No Advertising taken
BUSINESS: FINANCE & ECONOMICS: Investment

THE CHARTERED ARCHITECT
35797U4A-115
Editorial Address: 15 Rutland Square, EDINBURGH, EH1 2BE **Tel:** 0131 229 7545 **Fax:** 0131 228 2188
Email: smccord@rias.org.uk
Advertising Address: As above.
Email: smccord@rias.org.uk
Web site: http://www.rias.org.uk
Publisher: RIAS
Frequency: Quarterly
Free to qualifying individuals
Annual Sub.: £15.00
Circulation: 3,900 (Publisher's Statement)
Usual Pagination: 16
Editor: Sharon McCord; **Advertising Manager:** Sharon McCord
Summary of Content: Newsletter of the Royal Incorporation of Architects in Scotland.
Readership/Target Audience: Aimed at architects and students of architecture.
ADVERTISING: Rates on application
BUSINESS: ARCHITECTURE & BUILDING: Architecture

CHARTERED BANKER
35092U1C-350
Formerly: The Scottish Banker
Editorial Address: The Loft, Bonnington Mill, Newhaven Road, EDINBURGH, EH6 5QG **Tel:** 0131 467 2502
Fax: 0131 476 2672
Email: john@editions.co.uk
Advertising Address: As above. **Tel:** 0131 476 7607
Email: tony@editions.co.uk
Web site: http://www.charteredbanker.com
Publisher: Editions Publishing Ltd
Date Established: 1987
Frequency: 6 issues yearly - Published around the 5th of the cover month
Free to qualifying individuals
Circulation: 11,000 (Publisher's Statement)
Usual Pagination: 52
Editor: John Cooper; **Advertising Manager:** Tony Dixon
Summary of Content: Journal of the Chartered Institute of Banking in Scotland covering banking and financial service practitioners' professional development.
Readership/Target Audience: Aimed at banking and finance professionals.
ADVERTISING RATES:
Full Page Colour £1600.00
Agency Commission: 10%

Mechanical Data: Film: Digital, Trim Size: 297 x 210mm, Bleed Size: 305 x 218mm, Type Area: 260 x 178mm, Col Length: 260mm, Page Width: 178mm
Copy instructions: Copy Date: 3 weeks prior to publication date
Average advertising content per issue: 20%
BUSINESS: FINANCE & ECONOMICS: Banking

CHARTERED FORESTER
1828543U46-148
Editorial Address: 59 George Street, EDINBURGH, EH2 2JG **Tel:** 0131 240 1425 **Fax:** 0131 240 1424
Email: icf@charteredforesters.org
Advertising Address: Contact Publicity, 15 Newton Terrace, GLASGOW, G3 7PJ **Tel:** 0141 204 2042
Email: info@contactpublicity.co.uk
Web site: http://www.charteredforesters.org
Publisher: Institute of Chartered Foresters
Frequency: Quarterly
Cover Price: Free
Circulation: 1,300 (Publisher's Statement)
Editor: Allison Lock
Summary of Content: Journal covering news and articles related to the forestry and arboriculture professions.
Readership/Target Audience: Aimed at members of the Institute of Chartered Foresters.
ADVERTISING RATES:
Full Page Colour £400.00
Agency Commission: 10%
Mechanical Data: Trim Size: 297 x 210mm, Film: Digital
Average advertising content per issue: 20%
BUSINESS: TIMBER, WOOD & FORESTRY

CHARTERED SECRETARY
37112U14G-10
Editorial Address: 16 Park Crescent, LONDON, W1B 1AH
Tel: 020 7612 7020 **Fax:** 020 7612 7034
Email: chartsec@icsa.co.uk
Advertising Address: Homelands, Exford, SOMERSET, TA24 7NY **Tel:** 01643 831635 **Fax:** 01643 831015
Email: penelope.barker@btinternet.com
Web site: http://www.charteredsecretary.net
ISSN: 1363-5905
Publisher: ICSA Information and Training
Date Established: 1898
Frequency: Monthly
Annual Sub.: £80.00
Circulation: 18,079 (ABC 01/07/2008 to 30/06/2009)
Usual Pagination: 68
Editor: Kevin Eddy; **Advertising Director:** Penny Barker
Summary of Content: Magazine containing features and news of interest to chartered and company secretaries and other business professionals in company, charity and local government administration. Focusing on corporate governance, legal compliance and business law and ethics.
Readership/Target Audience: Read by chartered and company secretaries, company directors and senior managers, local government and charity managers and administration workers and other business professionals in all sectors.
ADVERTISING RATES:
Full Page Mono £2837.00
Agency Commission: 10%
Mechanical Data: Type Area: 259 x 188mm, Bleed Size: 303 x 216mm, Trim Size: 297 x 210mm, Col Length: 259mm, Page Width: 188mm, Film: Digital
Copy instructions: Copy Date: 2 weeks prior to publication date
Average advertising content per issue: 33%
Supplement(s): Chartered Secretary Careers - 1xY, Chartered Secretary Focus - 4xY, ICSA Connect - 4xY
BUSINESS: COMMERCE, INDUSTRY & MANAGEMENT: Company Secretaries

CHEMICAL AND ENGINEERING NEWS
36647U13-25
Editorial Address: 41 Galveston Road, LONDON, SW15 2RZ **Tel:** 020 8870 6884 **Fax:** 020 8874 4633
Email: p_short@acs.org
Advertising Address: Hallmark House, 25 Downham Road, RAMSDEN HEATH, CM11 1PU **Tel:** 01268 711560
Fax: 01268 711567
Email: ieaco@aol.com
Web site: http://www.cen-online.org
Publisher: The American Chemical Society
Date Established: 1924
Frequency: Weekly
Annual Sub.: $203.00
Circulation: 160,000 (Publisher's Statement)
Editor: Patricia Short; **Advertising Manager:** Paul Barrett
Summary of Content: Magazine containing news and information on the chemical enterprise, from academic research through industrial application and operations.
Readership/Target Audience: Read by chemists and those involved in analysis, management and regulation of chemical developments.
ADVERTISING RATES:
Full Page Colour $11440.00

Business Magazines

Agency Commission: 15%
Mechanical Data: Type Area: 254 x 178mm, Col Length: 254mm, Trim Size: 276 x 203mm, Bleed Size: 283 x 210mm, Film: Digital, Page Width: 178mm
Average advertising content per issue: 33%
BUSINESS: CHEMICALS

CHEMICAL BIOLOGICAL WARFARE REVIEW
1667828U40-431

Editorial Address: Global House, 47A Tottenham Lane, LONDON, N8 9BD **Tel:** 020 8347 6406 **Fax:** 020 8347 6427
Email: info@global-defence.com
Advertising Address: As above.
Email: tina.hill@global-defence.co.uk
Web site: http://www.cbwreview.com
ISSN: 1744-0440
Publisher: GDR Publications Ltd
Date Established: 2004
Frequency: Annual - Published in June
Free to qualifying individuals
Annual Sub.: £10.00
Circulation: 8,500 (Publisher's Statement)
Usual Pagination: 86
Editor: David Oliver; **Advertising Manager:** Tina Hill
Summary of Content: Magazine featuring in-depth articles on the battle against potential chemical and biological terrorism threats. Includes contributions by International chemical and biological defence companies plus news updates on programmes and products.
Readership/Target Audience: Aimed at those working in the defence industry.
ADVERTISING RATES:
Full Page Colour £3500.00
Agency Commission: 10%
Mechanical Data: Type Area: 282 x 180mm, Bleed Size: +4mm, Trim Size: 297 x 210mm, Col Length: 282mm, Page Width: 180mm, Film: Digital, Print Process: Litho
Average advertising content per issue: 30%
BUSINESS: DEFENCE

CHEMICAL COMMUNICATIONS
1659600U13-196

Editorial Address: Thomas Graham House, Science Park, Milton Road, CAMBRIDGE, CB4 0WF **Tel:** 01223 420066
Fax: 01223 420247
Email: chemcomm@rsc.org
Advertising Address: As above. **Tel:** 01223 432246
Fax: 01223 426017
Email: advertising@rsc.org
Web site: http://www.rsc.org/chemcomm
ISSN: 1359-7345
Publisher: Royal Society of Chemistry
Date Established: 1964
Frequency: Weekly
Annual Sub.: £1595.00
Circulation: 3,000 (Publisher's Statement)
Editor: Sarah Thomas; **Advertising Manager:** Ian Swain
Summary of Content: Journal covering news and analysis on important developments within the chemical sciences.
Readership/Target Audience: Aimed at academics and industrial chemists.
ADVERTISING RATES:
Full Page Colour £890.00
Agency Commission: 10%
Mechanical Data: Type Area: 252 x 188mm, Bleed Size: 287 x 222mm, Trim Size: 281 x 216mm, Col Length: 252mm, Page Width: 188mm, Film: Digital
BUSINESS: CHEMICALS

CHEMICAL ENGINEERING RESEARCH AND DESIGN
36688U13-37

Formerly: The Chemical Engineer
Editorial Address: Davis Building, 165-189 Railway Terrace, RUGBY, CV21 3HQ **Tel:** 01788 578214 **Fax:** 01788 560833
Email: ccliffe@icheme.org
Advertising Address: Mainline Media Ltd, The Barn, Oakley Hay Lodge, Great Fold Road, CORBY, NN18 9AS
Tel: 01536 747333
Email: jayne.stewart@mainlinemedia.co.uk
Web site: http://www.icheme.org/cherd
ISSN: 0263-8762
Publisher: Institution of Chemical Engineers
Date Established: 1922
Frequency: Monthly
Annual Sub.: £816.00
Circulation: 630 (Publisher's Statement)
Usual Pagination: 144
Editor: Jacqui Cressey; **Advertising Manager:** Jayne Stewart; **Managing Editor:** Catherine Cliffe
Summary of Content: International academic journal covering core subjects in chemical engineering.
Readership/Target Audience: Aimed at both academic and industrial based researchers.
ADVERTISING RATES:
Full Page Colour £895.00

Mechanical Data: Type Area: 240 x 175mm, Col Length: 240mm, Page Width: 175mm, Film: Digital
Copy instructions: Copy Date: 2 weeks prior to publication date
Average advertising content per issue: 5%
BUSINESS: CHEMICALS

CHEMICAL HAZARDS IN INDUSTRY
36650U13-40

Editorial Address: Thomas Graham House, Science Park, Milton Road, CAMBRIDGE, CB4 0WF **Tel:** 01223 420066
Fax: 01223 423623
Email: hazards@rsc.org
Advertising Address: As above. **Tel:** 01223 432246
Fax: 01223 426017
Email: advertising@rsc.org
Web site: http://www.rsc.org/chi
ISSN: 0265-5721
Publisher: Royal Society of Chemistry
Date Established: 1983
Frequency: Monthly
Advertising Manager: Ian Swain
Summary of Content: Newsletter and database containing topical information about health and safety in the chemical sector, includes legislation and precautions for the prevention and containment of chemical and biological hazards.
Readership/Target Audience: Aimed at those involved in the health and safety side of the chemical sector.
ADVERTISING RATES:
Full Page Mono £890.00
Mechanical Data: Col Length: 252mm, Page Width: 188mm, Bleed Size: 281 x 216mm, Type Area: 252 x 188mm, Trim Size: 275 x 210mm
BUSINESS: CHEMICALS

CHEMICAL MATTERS
36652U13-52

Editorial Address: Chapel House, 7 Schoolbell Mews, Arbery Road, LONDON, E3 5BZ **Tel:** 020 8981 3309
Email: hilfra@chemicalmatters.net
Publisher: Chemical Matters Ltd
Date Established: 1982
Frequency: Monthly
Usual Pagination: 16
Editor: Hilfra Tandy
Summary of Content: Newsletter providing independent analysis of the global chemical industry.
Readership/Target Audience: Aimed at board level executives within the mainstream chemical industry, service and logistics providers, bankers, consultants and analysts.
ADVERTISING: No Advertising taken
BUSINESS: CHEMICALS

CHEMICAL SAFETY BRIEFING
1641994U13-193

Editorial Address: 145 London Road, KINGSTON UPON THAMES, KT2 6SR **Tel:** 020 8547 3333 **Fax:** 020 8549 7275
Email: simon.gallagher@croner.co.uk
Web site: http://www.croner.co.uk
ISSN: 1742-9277
Publisher: Wolters Kluwer (UK) Ltd
Date Established: 2004
Frequency: Monthly
Usual Pagination: 8
Editor: Louise Faramus
Summary of Content: Magazine covering substances hazardous to health and the environment, occupational health, and the transport of dangerous substances.
Readership/Target Audience: Aimed at health and safety advisors, environmental protection officers, dangerous goods safety advisors and occupational health professionals.
BUSINESS: CHEMICALS

CHEMICAL SOCIETY REVIEWS
21638U55-44

Editorial Address: Thomas Graham House, Science Park, Milton Road, CAMBRIDGE, CB4 0WF **Tel:** 01223 420066
Fax: 01223 423429
Email: csr@rsc.org
Advertising Address: As above. **Tel:** 01223 432246
Fax: 01223 426017
Email: advertising@rsc.org
Web site: http://www.rsc.org/csr
ISSN: 1460-4744
Publisher: Royal Society of Chemistry
Date Established: 1972
Frequency: Monthly
Annual Sub.: £395.00
Circulation: 1,900 (Publisher's Statement)
Editor: Robert Eagling; **Advertising Manager:** Ian Swain; **Managing Editor:** Robert Eagling
Summary of Content: Journal providing overviews of topics of current interest across the chemical sciences.
Readership/Target Audience: Aimed at students about to embark on a career in research, experienced researchers

and chemists wanting to keep up with advances outside their own immediate interests.
ADVERTISING RATES:
Full Page Mono £890.00
Mechanical Data: Type Area: 252 x 188mm, Col Length: 252mm, Page Width: 188mm, Bleed Size: 281 x 216mm, Trim Size: 275 x 210mm
BUSINESS: APPLIED SCIENCE & LABORATORIES

CHEMICAL WEEK
36655U13-57

Editorial Address: 24-25 Scala Street, LONDON, W1T 2HP
Tel: 020 7436 7676 **Fax:** 020 7436 3749
Email: nalperowicz@chemweek.com
Advertising Address: As above. **Tel:** 020 7692 5278
Email: vcurzio@chemweek.com
Web site: http://www.chemweek.com
ISSN: 0009-272X
Publisher: Access Intelligence LLC
Date Established: 1914
Frequency: 42 issues yearly
Annual Sub.: $499.00
Circulation: 20,112 (BPA Worldwide)
Usual Pagination: 46
Editor: Natasha Alperowicz; **Executive Editor:** Natasha Alperowicz; **Editor-in-Chief:** Robert Westervelt; **Publisher:** Lyn Tattum
Summary of Content: Magazine providing worldwide coverage of the news and issues affecting the global chemical industry.
Readership/Target Audience: Aimed at business executives and decision makers throughout the chemical industry.
ADVERTISING RATES:
Full Page Mono $10193.00
Full Page Colour $13862.00
Mechanical Data: Type Area: 254 x 178mm, Col Length: 254mm, Bleed Size: 279 x 206mm, Trim Size: 273 x 200mm, Film: Digital, Page Width: 178mm
Copy instructions: Copy Date: 3 weeks prior to publication date
Supplement(s): Investment Locations - 1xY, Pharmaceutical Ingredients - 4xY
BUSINESS: CHEMICALS

CHEMIST+DRUGGIST
38728U37-20

Formerly: Chemist & Druggist
Editorial Address: Riverbank House, Angel Lane, TONBRIDGE, TN9 1SE **Tel:** 01732 364422
Fax: 01732 367065
Email: chemdrug@cmpmedica.com
Advertising Address: Ludgate House, 245 Blackfriars Road, LONDON, SE1 9UY **Tel:** 020 7921 5000
Fax: 020 7921 8136
Email: dspruytenburg@cmpmedica.com
Web site: http://www.chemistanddruggist.co.uk
ISSN: 0009-3033
Publisher: UBM Information (Tonbridge)
Date Established: 1859
Frequency: Weekly - Published every Saturday
Circulation: 13,263 (ABC 01/01/2008 to 31/12/2008)
Usual Pagination: 40
Editor: Gary Paragpuri; **News Editor:** Max Gosney; **Features Editor:** Fiona Salvage; **Advertising Manager:** Daniel Spruytenburg
Summary of Content: Journal covering NHS and pharmacy news, business management, OTC medicines, clinical pharmacy, toiletries, cosmetics and health foods.
Readership/Target Audience: Aimed at retail pharmacists and at the pharmaceutical, cosmetics and toiletries industries.
ADVERTISING RATES:
Full Page Colour £4176.00
Agency Commission: 10%
Mechanical Data: Type Area: 272 x 190mm, Bleed Size: 303 x 213mm, Trim Size: 297 x 210mm, Col Length: 272mm, Page Width: 190mm, Film: Digital
Copy instructions: Copy Date: 10 days prior to publication date
Supplement(s): C&D Generics - 2xY, C&D Price List - 12xY, Guide to OTC Medicine - 2xY, Over The Counter - 12xY, Winter Remedies - 1xY
BUSINESS: PHARMACEUTICAL & CHEMISTS

CHEMISTRY & INDUSTRY
36656U13-58

Editorial Address: 9 Savoy Street, LONDON, WC2E 7HR
Tel: 020 7878 2300
Email: patrick.walter@tenalpspublishing.com
Web site: http://www.chemistryandindustry.com
ISSN: 0009-3068
Publisher: Ten Alps Publishing
Date Established: 1881
Frequency: 24 issues yearly
Free to qualifying individuals
Annual Sub.: £200.00
Circulation: 6,214 (Publisher's Statement)
Usual Pagination: 42

Editor: Patrick Walter; **News Editor:** Patrick Walter; **Features Editor:** Cath O'Driscoll
Summary of Content: Contains news and information on the fine chemicals, pharmaceutical, biotechnology and life science businesses. Includes articles on food, the environment, chemistry, water, biotechnology and energy.
Readership/Target Audience: Read by chemical, pharmaceutical, biotechnology, life science industry executives, research managers, academics and government officials.
ADVERTISING: No Advertising taken
BUSINESS: CHEMICALS

CHEMISTRY WORLD
36657U13-60
Formerly: Chemistry in Britain
Editorial Address: Thomas Graham House, Science Park, Milton Road, CAMBRIDGE, CB4 0WF **Tel:** 01223 420066
Fax: 01223 426017
Email: chemistryworld@rsc.org
Advertising Address: As above. **Tel:** 01223 432246
Email: advertising@rsc.org
Web site: http://www.chemistryworld.org
ISSN: 1473-7604
Publisher: Royal Society of Chemistry
Date Established: 1965
Frequency: Monthly - Published on the 1st of the month
Cover Price: £55.00
Free to qualifying individuals
Annual Sub.: £612.00
Circulation: 47,042 (ABC 01/01/2008 to 31/12/2008)
Usual Pagination: 84
Editor: James Mitchell Crow; **Features Editor:** James Mitchell Crow; **Advertising Manager:** Ian Swain
Summary of Content: News magazine of the Royal Society of Chemistry covering global developments of the chemical sciences.
Readership/Target Audience: Read by chemists and chemical scientists.
ADVERTISING RATES:
Full Page Colour £3050.00
Mechanical Data: Type Area: 252 x 188mm, Bleed Size: 281 x 216mm, Trim Size: 275 x 210mm, Col Length: 252mm, Page Width: 188mm
BUSINESS: CHEMICALS

CHILD ABUSE REVIEW
38458U32G-29_20
Editorial Address: Newcomen Centre, Guys Hospital, St. Thomas Street, LONDON, SE1 9RT **Tel:** 01243 779777
Fax: 01243 770201
Email: nstanley@uclan.ac.uk
Advertising Address: The Atrium, Southern Gate, CHICHESTER, PO19 8SQ **Tel:** 01243 770254
Fax: 01243 770432
Email: adsales@wiley.com
Web site: http://www.baspcan.org.uk
ISSN: 0952-9136
Publisher: John Wiley & Sons Ltd
Date Established: 1992
Frequency: 6 issues yearly
Annual Sub.: £80.00
Circulation: 2,500 (Publisher's Statement)
Usual Pagination: 75
Editor: Nicky Stanley
Summary of Content: Journal covering practice developments, research findings, training initiatives and policy issues in the field of child protection.
Readership/Target Audience: Aimed at researchers, clinical psychologists, social workers, health and legal professionals.
ADVERTISING RATES:
Full Page Mono £1175.00
Full Page Colour £2575.00
Mechanical Data: Trim Size: 260 x 200mm
BUSINESS: LOCAL GOVERNMENT, LEISURE & RECREATION: Community Care & Social Services

CHILD AND FAMILY LAW QUARTERLY
39131U44-225
Editorial Address: 21 St. Thomas Street, BRISTOL, BS1 6JS **Tel:** 0117 918 1529 **Fax:** 0117 925 0486
Email: cflq_editor@familylaw.co.uk
Web site: http://www.familylaw.co.uk
ISSN: 1358-8184
Publisher: Jordan Publishing Ltd
Date Established: 1988
Frequency: Quarterly
Annual Sub.: £125.00
Circulation: 500 (Publisher's Statement)
Usual Pagination: 125
Editor: Charlotte Potter; **Managing Director:** Caroline Vandridge-Ames; **Publisher:** Caroline Vandridge-Ames
Summary of Content: Journal covering major legislative and judicial developments, as well as current research. Provides comment and information on all areas of child law and family law.
Readership/Target Audience: Aimed at legal professionals.

ADVERTISING: No Advertising taken
BUSINESS: LEGAL

CHILD CARE
1687134U62C-729
Formerly: Practical Professional Child Care
Editorial Address: St. Jude's Church, Dulwich Road, LONDON, SE24 0PB **Tel:** 020 7501 6770
Fax: 020 7978 8319
Email: amy.g@markallengroup.com
Advertising Address: As above. **Tel:** 020 7738 5454
Fax: 020 7733 2325
Email: farhad.b@markallengroup.com
Web site: http://www.professionalchildcare.co.uk
Publisher: Step Forward Publishing Ltd
Date Established: 2004
Frequency: Monthly
Cover Price: £3.99
Circulation: 5,000 (Publisher's Statement)
Usual Pagination: 50
Editor: Amy Griggs; **Publisher:** Mark Allen
Summary of Content: Magazine covering all aspects of care and management including practical guidance on activities and care for all those who are paid to look after other peoples children.
Readership/Target Audience: Aimed at all those who work with children in their homes as childminders, in day care centres and nurseries, in the children's own homes as nannies and in holiday play schemes and after-school clubs.
ADVERTISING RATES:
Full Page Colour £850.00
Agency Commission: 10%
Mechanical Data: Film: Digital
Copy instructions: Copy Date: 2 weeks prior to publication date
Average advertising content per issue: 10%
BUSINESS: CHURCH & SCHOOL EQUIPMENT & EDUCATION: Junior Education

CHILD EDUCATION PLUS
41081U62C-726
Formerly: Child Education
Editorial Address: Villiers House, Clarendon Avenue, LEAMINGTON SPA, CV32 5PR **Tel:** 01926 887799
Fax: 01926 883331
Email: childed@scholastic.co.uk
Advertising Address: As above.
Email: jsmith@scholastic.co.uk
Web site: http://magazines.scholastic.co.uk/mags
ISSN: 0009-3947
Publisher: Scholastic UK Ltd
Date Established: 1923
Frequency: Monthly - Published around the 2nd week of the month prior to cover month
Cover Price: £4.25
Annual Sub.: £42.50
Circulation: 15,078 (ABC 01/07/2006 to 30/06/2007)
Usual Pagination: 64
Editor: Helen Freeman
Summary of Content: Magazine for teachers packed with practical activities, lesson plans and resources for reception and KS1 children.
Readership/Target Audience: Aimed at teachers of children aged 4 to 7 years.
ADVERTISING RATES:
Full Page Mono £1540.00
Full Page Colour £1740.00
Agency Commission: 10%
Mechanical Data: Type Area: 266 x 186mm, Bleed Size: 303 x 216mm, Trim Size: 297 x 210mm, Page Width: 186mm, Col Length: 266mm, Film: Digital
Copy instructions: Copy Date: 3 weeks prior to publication date
Average advertising content per issue: 40%
Supplement(s): Best Books - 1xY, Education Show Guide - 1xY, ICT - 1xY
BUSINESS: CHURCH & SCHOOL EQUIPMENT & EDUCATION: Junior Education

CHILDHOOD
48737U62R-470
Editorial Address: 1 Oliver's Yard, 55 City Road, LONDON, EC1Y 1SP **Tel:** 020 7324 8500 **Fax:** 020 7324 8600
Email: info@sagepub.co.uk
Advertising Address: As above.
Email: advertising@sagepub.co.uk
Web site: http://www.sagepub.co.uk
ISSN: 0907-5682
Publisher: Sage Publications
Frequency: Quarterly
Annual Sub.: £48.00
Circulation: 450 (Publisher's Statement)
Editor: Virginia Morrow
Summary of Content: Journal focusing on child research. Includes articles, reviews and research on children's culture, economics, language, health and social networks.
Readership/Target Audience: Aimed at people working in sociological research and child development.

ADVERTISING RATES:
Full Page Mono £400.00
Agency Commission: 5%
Mechanical Data: Col Length: 205mm, Page Width: 130mm, Type Area: 205 x 130mm, Film: Digital
BUSINESS: CHURCH & SCHOOL EQUIPMENT & EDUCATION: Education Related

CHILDMINDING
39562U32G-29_30
Editorial Address: 7 Melville Terrace, STIRLING, FK8 2ND **Tel:** 01786 445377 **Fax:** 01786 449062
Email: leigh.mcewan@childminding.org
Advertising Address: As above.
Email: kevin.croall@childminding.org
Web site: http://www.childminding.org
Publisher: Scottish Childminding Association
Frequency: Quarterly
Cover Price: Free
Circulation: 5,500 (Publisher's Statement)
Usual Pagination: 24
Editor: Leigh McEwan; **Advertising Manager:** Kevin Croall
Summary of Content: Childminding magazine covering numerous topics including child development, best practice in registered childminding, personal and home safety, health and wellbeing, equal opportunities, training, self-development, arts and crafts, literature and resources, food and hygiene.
Readership/Target Audience: Read by registered childminders, social workers and parents of children who are looked after by childminders.
ADVERTISING RATES:
Full Page Colour £395.00
Mechanical Data: Film: Digital, Bleed Size: 303 x 213mm, Trim Size: 297 x 210mm
Average advertising content per issue: 10%
BUSINESS: LOCAL GOVERNMENT, LEISURE & RECREATION: Community Care & Social Services

CHILDREN & YOUNG PEOPLE NOW
47290U32G-167
Formerly: Young People Now
Editorial Address: 174 Hammersmith Road, LONDON, W6 7JP **Tel:** 020 8267 4706
Advertising Address: As above. **Tel:** 020 8267 4210
Fax: 020 8267 4013
Email: elliot.thomas@haymarket.com
Web site: http://www.cypnow.co.uk
ISSN: 0956-2842
Publisher: Haymarket Professional Publications Ltd
Date Established: 1989
Frequency: Weekly
Cover Price: £2.25
Annual Sub.: £85.00
Usual Pagination: 60
Editor: Ruth Smith; **News Editor:** Ruth Smith; **Advertising Manager:** Elliot Thomas
Summary of Content: Magazine produced in partnership with the National Youth Agency and the NCB. Covers articles on youth work, young people and those working with young people, features on the public sector, voluntary sector and private sector and children's organisations.
Readership/Target Audience: Aimed at professionals that work with children and young people, including youth workers, youth justice workers, policymakers, teachers and those involved in personal and social education and the voluntary sector, workers in children's services from education and health to social work.
ADVERTISING RATES:
Full Page Mono £2340.00
Full Page Colour £2660.00
Agency Commission: 10%
Mechanical Data: Film: Digital, Type Area: 260 x 207mm, Col Length: 260mm, Page Width: 207mm, Trim Size: 295 x 225mm, Bleed Size: 301 x 231mm
Copy instructions: Copy Date: Friday 2pm prior to publication date
Average advertising content per issue: 40%
BUSINESS: LOCAL GOVERNMENT, LEISURE & RECREATION: Community Care & Social Services

CHILDRIGHT
38459U32G-193
Editorial Address: University of Essex, Wivenhoe Park, COLCHESTER, CO4 3SQ **Tel:** 01206 872466
Fax: 01206 874026
Email: dominicb@essex.ac.uk
Web site: http://www.childrenslegalcentre.com
ISSN: 0265-1458
Publisher: The Children's Legal Centre Ltd
Date Established: 1983
Frequency: 10 issues yearly
Annual Sub.: £60.00
Circulation: 1,600 (Publisher's Statement)
Usual Pagination: 36
Summary of Content: Journal of law and policy affecting children and young people in England and Wales.

Business Magazines

Readership/Target Audience: Read by lawyers, academics, children's charities, councils, social services and youth workers.
ADVERTISING: No Advertising taken
BUSINESS: LOCAL GOVERNMENT, LEISURE & RECREATION: Community Care & Social Services

CHINA BRITAIN BUSINESS REVIEW
36938U14C-48

Formerly: China Britain Trade Review
Editorial Address: 1 Warwick Row, LONDON, SW1E 5ER
Tel: 020 7802 2000 **Fax:** 020 7802 2029
Email: janet.kealey@cbbc.org
Advertising Address: As above.
Email: fiona.huo@cbbc.org
Web site: http://www.cbbc.org
ISSN: 0583-4279
Publisher: China-Britain Business Council
Date Established: 1964
Frequency: 10 issues yearly - Published in the 1st week of the cover month
Free to qualifying individuals
Annual Sub.: £75.00
Circulation: 5,000 (Publisher's Statement)
Usual Pagination: 24
Editor: Janet Kealey; **Advertising Manager:** Fiona Huo
Summary of Content: Magazine containing news on the latest developments in China's industry, together with information on UK company activities in China.
Readership/Target Audience: Aimed at companies and organisations doing business in China.
ADVERTISING RATES:
Full Page Colour £2000.00
Mechanical Data: Trim Size: 297 x 210mm
Copy instructions: Copy Date: 1 week prior to publication date
BUSINESS: COMMERCE, INDUSTRY & MANAGEMENT: International Commerce

CHINA CHEMICALS
36659U13-76

Editorial Address: Quadrant House, The Quadrant, SUTTON, SM2 5AS **Tel:** 020 8652 3153 **Fax:** 020 8652 3375
Email: john.baker@icis.com
Advertising Address: As above. **Tel:** 020 8652 3500
Fax: 020 8652 8918
Email: paul.shapiro@icis.com
Web site: http://www.icis.com
Publisher: Reed Business Information
Date Established: 1994
Frequency: 6 issues yearly
Free to qualifying individuals
Circulation: 7,101 (BPA Worldwide 01/07/2007 to 31/12/2007)
Usual Pagination: 72
Editor: John Baker; **Advertising Manager:** Paul Shapiro
Summary of Content: Magazine covering all aspects of the chemical industry.
Language(s): Chinese
Readership/Target Audience: Read by companies in China.
ADVERTISING RATES:
Full Page Mono $2925.00
Full Page Colour $3775.00
Mechanical Data: Page Width: 179mm, Type Area: 246 x 179mm, Col Length: 246mm, Trim Size: 285 x 210mm, Bleed Size: 291 x 216mm, Film: Digital
Copy instructions: Copy Date: 4 weeks prior to publication date
BUSINESS: CHEMICALS

THE CHINA QUARTERLY
21879U14C-352

Editorial Address: Department of Political Studies, School of Oriental and African Studies, Thornhaugh Street, Russell Square, LONDON, WC1H 0XG **Tel:** 01223 312393
Fax: 01223 315052
Email: chinaq@soas.ac.uk
Advertising Address: The Edinburgh Building, Shaftesbury Road, CAMBRIDGE, CB2 2RU **Tel:** 01223 312393
Fax: 01223 315052
Email: ad_sales@cambridge.org
Web site: http://uk.cambridge.org/journals/cqy/
ISSN: 0009-4439
Publisher: Cambridge University Press
Date Established: 1959
Frequency: Quarterly
Annual Sub.: £93.00
Circulation: 2,700 (Publisher's Statement)
Editor: Julia Strauss
Summary of Content: Magazine covering all aspects of issues relating to the People's Republic of China, Taiwan, Macao, and Hong Kong with information concerning politics, economics, commerce, arts and literature, international affairs, social change and demography.
Readership/Target Audience: Aimed at diplomats, journalists, members of the business community, financiers, academics and researchers.

ADVERTISING RATES:
Full Page Mono £465.00
Agency Commission: 10%
Mechanical Data: Type Area: 200 x 135mm, Col Length: 200mm, Page Width: 135mm, Film: Digital
Copy instructions: Copy Date: 8 weeks prior to publication date
Average advertising content per issue: 20%
BUSINESS: COMMERCE, INDUSTRY & MANAGEMENT: International Commerce

CHOCOLATE & CONFECTIONERY INTERNATIONAL
36463U8B-40

Editorial Address: 80 Calverley Road, TUNBRIDGE WELLS, TN1 2UN **Tel:** 020 7017 7500 **Fax:** 020 7017 7599
Email: marketing@agra-net.com
Web site: http://www.agra-net.com
ISSN: 1369-8699
Publisher: Agra Informa Ltd
Frequency: Monthly
Annual Sub.: £332.00
Usual Pagination: 24
Summary of Content: Newsletter reviewing the global chocolate and confectionery industry. Contains information on legislation, new products and packaging, research and development.
Readership/Target Audience: Read by industry executives who need to keep up-to-date with the industry as a whole.
ADVERTISING: No Advertising taken
BUSINESS: BAKING & CONFECTIONERY: Confectionery Manufacturing

CHP PACKER INTERNATIONAL
38663U35-10

Editorial Address: Attwood House, Mansfield Park, Four Marks, ALTON, GU34 5PZ **Tel:** 01420 568900
Fax: 01420 565995
Email: editorial@binstedgroup.com
Advertising Address: As above.
Email: andrew.flew@binstedgroup.com
Web site: http://www.binstedgroup.com
Publisher: The Binsted Group plc
Frequency: Quarterly
Cover Price: £9.00
Annual Sub.: £55.00
Circulation: 4,050 (Publisher's Statement)
Usual Pagination: 46
Editor: Julie Foskett
Summary of Content: Magazine covering all aspects of packaging machinery, materials for the cosmetics, healthcare and pharmaceutical industries.
Readership/Target Audience: Aimed at individuals responsible for purchasing, technical and production directors, packaging buyers and senior management.
ADVERTISING RATES:
Full Page Colour £1535.00
Agency Commission: 10%
Mechanical Data: No. of Columns (Display): 2, Col Widths (Display): 83mm, Film: Digital, Type Area: 229 x 178mm, Col Length: 229mm, Trim Size: 280 x 210mm, Bleed Size: 286 x 216mm, Page Width: 178mm
Average advertising content per issue: 35%
BUSINESS: PACKAGING & BOTTLING

CHRISTIAN LIBRARIAN
40887U60B-14_50

Editorial Address: 34 Thurlestone Avenue, Seven Kings, ILFORD, IG3 9DU **Tel:** 020 8599 1310
Email: graham@hedges96.freeserve.co.uk
Web site: http://www.librarianscf.org.uk
ISSN: 0309-4170
Publisher: Librarians' Christian Fellowship
Date Established: 1976
Frequency: Quarterly
Cover Price: £3.50
Circulation: 500 (Publisher's Statement)
Usual Pagination: 48
Editor: Graham Hedges
Summary of Content: Journal of the Librarians' Christian Fellowship, containing articles on librarianship, books, publishing, and communications, written from the standpoint of the Christian faith.
Readership/Target Audience: Read by Christians in library work, other librarians and members of the Christian church.
ADVERTISING: No Advertising taken
BUSINESS: PUBLISHING: Libraries

CHRISTMAS TREE NEWSLETTER
39453U46-5

Editorial Address: 13 Wolrige Road, EDINBURGH, EH16 6HX **Tel:** 0131 664 1100 **Fax:** 0131 664 2669
Email: rogermhay@btinternet.com
Advertising Address: As above.
Email: rogermhay@btinternet.com
Web site: http://www.christmastree.org.uk
Publisher: BCTGA
Date Established: 1982
Frequency: Half-yearly - Published in April and October

Cover Price: £5.00
Free to qualifying individuals
Circulation: 1,000 (Publisher's Statement)
Usual Pagination: 20
Editor: Roger Hay; **Advertising Manager:** Roger Hay
Summary of Content: Journal containing product information, advice, research, market trends, decoration product news and industry news.
Readership/Target Audience: Read by Christmas tree growers and consultants in the UK.
ADVERTISING RATES:
Full Page Mono £250.00
Full Page Colour £400.00
Mechanical Data: Bleed Size: 303 x 216mm, Trim Size: 297 x 210mm
Average advertising content per issue: 10%
BUSINESS: TIMBER, WOOD & FORESTRY

CHROMATOGRAPHY TODAY
1899490U37-435

Editorial Address: Oak Court, Sandridge Park, Porters Wood, ST. ALBANS, AL3 6PH **Tel:** 01727 731812
Fax: 01727 833014
Email: chromatographytoday@designs4you.biz
Web site: http://www.chromatographytoday.com
Publisher: Designs for You Ltd
Date Established: 2007
Frequency: Quarterly
Cover Price: Free
Circulation: 8,500 (Publisher's Statement)
Editor: Bernie Monaghan
Summary of Content: Journal featuring in-depth articles and application notes exploring the most current issues within chromatography as well as industry news and information on the very latest products, training courses, exhibitions & conferences. News from the Chromatographic Society and biographies of ChromSoc medal winners are also included.
Readership/Target Audience: Aimed at attracting lab managers, analysts and quality control and research & development departments within the pharmaceutical industry.
BUSINESS: PHARMACEUTICAL & CHEMISTS

CHT CLEANING & HYGIENE TODAY
35950U4F-22

Editorial Address: Sparta Works, 487 Blackfen Road, SIDCUP, DA15 9NP **Tel:** 020 8298 6490 **Fax:** 020 8301 5304
Email: annabel.hilder@mpp.co.uk
Advertising Address: As above.
Email: paul@mpp.co.uk
Web site: http://www.cleanpoint.com
ISSN: 1362-4776
Publisher: MPP Ltd
Date Established: 1989
Frequency: Monthly - Published on the last day of the month prior to cover month
Free to qualifying individuals
Annual Sub.: £68.00
Circulation: 12,519 (ABC 01/01/2008 to 31/12/2008)
Usual Pagination: 90
Editor: Annabel Hilder; **Group Editor:** Wayne Cyrus
Summary of Content: Magazine covering products, services, market trends, trade news and events relevant to the UK cleaning industry.
Readership/Target Audience: Aimed at personnel with purchasing and specifying authority for cleaning and hygiene equipment, supplies, services and those that have an interest in the cleaning industry, as well as executives working for the NHS within Estates & Facilities.
ADVERTISING RATES:
Full Page Mono £1490.00
Full Page Colour £2250.00
Agency Commission: 10%
Mechanical Data: Col Length: 273mm, Type Area: 273 x 187mm, Bleed Size: 307 x 220mm, Trim Size: 297 x 210mm, Page Width: 187mm
Copy instructions: Copy Date: 4 weeks prior to publication date
Average advertising content per issue: 60%
Supplement(s): FloorCare - 1xY, Washroom Hygiene - 1xY
BUSINESS: ARCHITECTURE & BUILDING: Cleaning & Maintenance

CHURCH BUILDING
35902U4E-157

Editorial Address: 4th Floor, Landmark House, Station Road, Cheadle Hulme, CHEADLE, SK87JH
Tel: 0161 488 1700
Email: joseph.kelly@churchbuilding.co.uk
Advertising Address: As above. **Fax:** 01785 660544
Email: carolj.malpass@ntlworld.com
ISSN: 0268-912X
Publisher: Gabriel Communications Ltd
Frequency: 6 issues yearly - Published in the 1st week of the month
Cover Price: £4.00
Annual Sub.: £31.00

Circulation: 4,500 (Publisher's Statement)
Usual Pagination: 84
Editor: Joseph Kelly; **Advertising Manager:** Carol Malpass
Summary of Content: International journal covering the design, construction and maintenance of churches, religious buildings and their furnishings, worldwide.
Readership/Target Audience: Read by architects, crafts persons and clergy.
ADVERTISING RATES:
Full Page Mono £1084.00
Full Page Colour £1480.00
SCC £9.54
Agency Commission: 10%
Mechanical Data: Trim Size: 297 x 210mm, Film: Digital, Type Area: 277 x 190mm, Col Length: 277mm, Page Width: 190mm, Bleed Size: 303 x 216mm, No. of Columns (Display): 3
Copy instructions: Copy Date: 2 weeks prior to publication date
Average advertising content per issue: 30%
BUSINESS: ARCHITECTURE & BUILDING: Building

CIA
38182U27-177
Formerly: Wire & Cable Bulletin
Editorial Address: 31 Mount Pleasant, LONDON, WC1X 0AD **Tel:** 020 7903 2000
Email: glynn.stainthorpe@crugroup.com
Web site: http://www.crugroup.com
ISSN: 1368-4191
Publisher: CRU International Ltd
Date Established: 1997
Frequency: Monthly
Annual Sub.: £595.00
Usual Pagination: 8
Editor: Glynn Stainthorpe
Summary of Content: Bulletin containing analysis behind what is happening in the wire and cable business.
Readership/Target Audience: Read by manufacturers and users of cables, harnesses, cable assemblies and related components.
ADVERTISING: No Advertising taken
BUSINESS: METAL, IRON & STEEL

CIBSE JOURNAL
1895663U4E-456
Editorial Address: PR by email only **Tel:** 01223 273520
Email: editor@cibsejournal.com
Web site: http://www.cibsejournal.com
Publisher: Chartered Institute of Building Services Engineers
Date Established: 2009
Frequency: Monthly
Free to qualifying individuals
Circulation: 19,851 (ABC 01/02/2009 to 30/04/2009)
Editor: Bob Cervi
Summary of Content: Magazine containing news and analysis, design, technical and practical guidance, new product information, continuous professional development content and legislation.
Readership/Target Audience: Aimed at members of the Chartered Institution of Building Services Engineers as well as building engineers and their associates.
BUSINESS: ARCHITECTURE & BUILDING: Building

CIE
37340U18A-55
Editorial Address: 8-10 Dryden Street, LONDON, WC2E 9NA **Tel:** 07545 927528
Email: neil.tyler@cieonline.co.uk
Advertising Address: As above. **Tel:** 020 7618 3456
Fax: 020 7618 3467
Email: sat.dhillon@cieonline.co.uk
Web site: http://www.cieonline.co.uk
Publisher: Specialist Business Media
Date Established: 1986
Frequency: 10 issues yearly - Published on the 15th of the cover month. Double issues July/August and December/January
Free to qualifying individuals
Annual Sub.: £61.00
Circulation: 14,000 (ABC 01/01/2008 to 31/12/2008)
Usual Pagination: 52
Editor: Neil Tyler; **Advertising Manager:** Sat Dhillon;
Publisher: Robin Shoot
Summary of Content: Journal covering technical articles, applications, product information and designer issues.
Readership/Target Audience: Aimed at personnel who design, specify or purchase electronic components, related products and services.
ADVERTISING RATES:
Full Page Colour £2796.00
Agency Commission: 10%
Mechanical Data: Type Area: 275 x 254mm, Bleed Size: 300 x 286mm, Trim Size: 295 x 280mm, Col Length: 275mm, Film: Digital, Page Width: 254mm
Copy instructions: Copy Date: Last week of the month prior to publication date
Average advertising content per issue: 54%

Supplement(s): Distributor Directory - 1xY, PCIM - 1xY, Southern Electronics - 1xY
BUSINESS: ELECTRONICS

CINEMA BUSINESS
1659568U64K-645
Editorial Address: 359 Kennington Lane, LONDON, SE11 5QY **Tel:** 0845 270 7871
Email: mark.moran@landor.co.uk
Advertising Address: CJPL Consultants Ltd, Suite 17, Spice Court, Ivory Square, Plantation Wharf, LONDON, SW11 3UE **Tel:** 020 7924 1415 **Fax:** 020 7924 4565
Email: frankkingaby@cjplconsultants.com
Web site: http://www.cinemabusiness.co.uk
Publisher: Landor Publishing
Date Established: 2004
Frequency: Monthly
Annual Sub.: £53.00
Circulation: 2,400 (Publisher's Statement)
Usual Pagination: 44
Editor: Mark Moran; **Advertising Manager:** Frank Kingaby
Summary of Content: Magazine covering news, admissions and box office figures, profiles of circuits and venues, A-Z of current releases, previews of new films and trends and festival dates.
Readership/Target Audience: Aimed at those who show, distribute and market films.
ADVERTISING RATES:
Full Page Colour £1000.00
Agency Commission: 10%
Mechanical Data: Bleed Size: 306 x 226mm, Trim Size: 300 x 220mm, Film: Digital, Type Area: 280 x 195mm, Col Length: 280mm, Page Width: 195mm
Average advertising content per issue: 25%
BUSINESS: OTHER CLASSIFICATIONS: Cinema Entertainment

CINEMA TECHNOLOGY
1611049U64K-642
Editorial Address: 17 Winterslow Road, Porton, SALISBURY, SP4 0LW **Tel:** 01980 610544
Fax: 01980 590611
Email: jim.slater@slaterelectronics.com
Advertising Address: Caixa Postal 2011, Vale da Telha, 8670-156 ALJEZUR **Tel:** 282 997 050
Email: bobcavanagh@sapo.pt
Web site: http://www.bksts.com
ISSN: 0995-2251
Publisher: British Kinematograph, Sound & Television Society
Frequency: Quarterly - Published in the 1st week of the cover month
Annual Sub.: £85.00
Circulation: 4,000 (Publisher's Statement)
Usual Pagination: 48
Editor: Jim Slater; **Advertising Manager:** Bob Cavanagh; **Managing Editor:** Jim Slater
Summary of Content: Magazine covering all aspects of technology of interest to the cinema exhibition industry with an emphasis on projectors.
Readership/Target Audience: Aimed at cinema managerial and technical staff.
ADVERTISING RATES:
Full Page Mono £1500.00
Full Page Colour £1500.00
Agency Commission: 10%
Mechanical Data: Type Area: 260 x 178mm, Bleed Size: 303 x 213mm, Trim Size: 297 x 210mm, Col Length: 260mm, Page Width: 178mm, Film: Digital
Copy instructions: Copy Date: 12th of the month prior to publication date
Average advertising content per issue: 20%
BUSINESS: OTHER CLASSIFICATIONS: Cinema Entertainment

CIO CHIEF INFORMATION OFFICER
758571U5B-115
Formerly: MIS Managing Information Strategies
Editorial Address: 4th Floor, 101 Euston Road, LONDON, NW1 2RA **Tel:** 020 7756 2807
Email: martin_veitch@idg.co.uk
Advertising Address: As above. **Tel:** 020 7756 2800
Fax: 020 7756 2838
Email: greg_whitehead@idg.co.uk
Web site: http://www.cio.co.uk
ISSN: 1471-275X
Publisher: IDG (International Data Group)
Date Established: 2000
Frequency: 10 issues yearly
Free to qualifying individuals
Annual Sub.: £60.00
Circulation: 21,068 (BPA Worldwide 01/01/2008 to 30/06/2008)
Usual Pagination: 68
Editor: Martin Veitch; **Managing Director:** Kit Gould
Summary of Content: Magazine covering all aspects of IT management including business news, analysis, strategies, training and user issues.

Readership/Target Audience: Read by CIOs, IT directors and senior IT professionals.
ADVERTISING RATES:
Full Page Colour £5450.00
Agency Commission: 10%
Mechanical Data: Trim Size: 275 x 208mm, Film: Digital, Type Area: 253 x 183mm, Bleed Size: 281 x 214mm, Col Length: 253mm, Page Width: 183mm
Copy instructions: Copy Date: 1 week prior to publication date
Average advertising content per issue: 30%
BUSINESS: COMPUTERS & AUTOMATION: Data Processing

CIO CONNECT
1616382U14A-511
Editorial Address: 21 Whitefriars Street, LONDON, EC4Y 8JJ **Tel:** 020 7842 7999 **Fax:** 020 7842 7998
Email: magazine@cio-connect.com
Advertising Address: As above.
Email: magazine@cio-connect.com
Web site: http://www.cio-connect.com
Publisher: CIO Connect
Date Established: 2003
Frequency: Quarterly
Cover Price: Free
Circulation: 5,763 (ABC 01/01/2008 to 31/12/2008)
Usual Pagination: 54
Editor: Mark Samuels; **Advertising Manager:** Sonia Kaur
Summary of Content: Magazine providing support for the key leadership role of CIOs in bringing together the requirements of business and technology.
Readership/Target Audience: Aimed at senior IT executives.
ADVERTISING RATES:
Full Page Colour £3500.00
Mechanical Data: Film: Digital, Trim Size: 297 x 210mm, Bleed Size: 303 x 216mm, Type Area: 267 x 187mm, Col Length: 267mm, Page Width: 187mm
Copy instructions: Copy Date: 3 weeks prior to publication date
BUSINESS: COMMERCE, INDUSTRY & MANAGEMENT

C-IQ
1863501U1G-109
Editorial Address: PR by email only
Email: susan.hicks@contactless-intelligence.com
Web site: http://www.contactless-intelligence.com
Publisher: Contactless Intelligence
Frequency: Quarterly - Plus weekly news feed
Cover Price: Free
Editor: Susan Hicks
Summary of Content: Publication concentrating on business-to-business within the contactless industry. Covers cards, passports, software, system integration and data handling.
Readership/Target Audience: Aimed at the contactless industry.
BUSINESS: FINANCE & ECONOMICS: Credit Trading

CIRCLE UPDATE
36512U9C-20
Editorial Address: 34 Frobisher Court, Sydenham Rise, LONDON, SE23 3XH **Tel:** 020 8699 3173
Email: budmac@btinternet.com
Web site: http://www.winewriters.org
Publisher: Circle of Wine Writers
Date Established: 1991
Frequency: 5 issues yearly
Annual Sub.: £60.00
Circulation: 1,000 (Publisher's Statement)
Usual Pagination: 50
Editor: Jim Budd
Summary of Content: The newsletter of the Circle of Wine Writers containing news and views on wine and the wine trade and also beer and spirits news.
Readership/Target Audience: Aimed at the wine trade, wine writers and the drinks industry.
ADVERTISING: No Advertising taken
BUSINESS: DRINKS & LICENSED TRADE: Licensed Trade, Wines & Spirits

CIRCUIT WORLD
1615250U18A-9007
Editorial Address: Howard House, Wagon Lane, BINGLEY, BD16 1WA **Tel:** 01274 777700 **Fax:** 01274 785200
Email: jhling@talktalk.net
Web site: http://www.emeraldinsight.com
ISSN: 0305-6120
Publisher: Emerald Group Publishing Ltd
Date Established: 1974
Frequency: Quarterly
Annual Sub.: £1009.00
Usual Pagination: 74
Editor: John Ling; **Publisher:** Harry Colson
Summary of Content: Journal covering standards, design, analysis, materials, process, reliability and manufacturing.

Business Magazines

Readership/Target Audience: Aimed at academics, researchers, practitioners and managers within the electronics engineering industry.
ADVERTISING: No Advertising taken
BUSINESS: ELECTRONICS

CIRCULATION FACTORS
35605U2B-15

Editorial Address: 49 New Road, LITTLEHAMPTON, BN17 5AT **Tel:** 01903 733569
Email: rjm@mediafinancial.co.uk
Web site: http://www.mediafinancial.co.uk
ISSN: 1351-2463
Publisher: Circulation Factors
Date Established: 1993
Frequency: Monthly
Annual Sub.: £225.00
Circulation: 700 (Publisher's Statement)
Usual Pagination: 32
Editor: Roger Melody; **Publisher:** Roger Melody
Summary of Content: Newsletter providing financial analysis of the publishing and news trade sector.
Readership/Target Audience: Aimed at publishers, circulation managers and directors.
ADVERTISING: No Advertising taken
BUSINESS: COMMUNICATIONS, ADVERTISING & MARKETING: Press

CITY BUSINESS
1696782U63E-504

Editorial Address: Sinclair House, 2nd Floor, 95-101 Royal Avenue, BELFAST, BT1 1FE **Tel:** 028 9024 2111
Fax: 028 9023 0809
Email: info@belfastcentre.com
Advertising Address: BPC, 3 Wellington Park, BELFAST, BT9 6DJ **Tel:** 028 9092 3347 **Fax:** 028 9092 3348
Email: slogue@bpcni.com
Web site: http://www.belfastcentre.com
Publisher: Belfast City Centre Management & Belfast Chamber of Trade & Commerce
Frequency: Quarterly
Cover Price: £2.75
Free to qualifying individuals
Annual Sub.: £15.00
Circulation: 8,000 (Publisher's Statement)
Usual Pagination: 64
Editor: Peter Mann; **Advertising Manager:** Sarah Logue
Summary of Content: Magazine focusing on business news in Belfast including finance, small business, regeneration, investment and recruitment.
Readership/Target Audience: Aimed at those working in the private sector.
ADVERTISING RATES:
Full Page Colour £1300.00
Agency Commission: 10%
Mechanical Data: Type Area: 274 x 180mm, Bleed Size: 301 x 214mm, Trim Size: 297 x 210mm, Col Length: 274mm, Page Width: 180mm, Film: Digital
Copy instructions: Copy Date: 2 weeks prior to publication date
BUSINESS: REGIONAL BUSINESS: Regional Business Northern Ireland

CITY PLANNING
35848U4D-40

Editorial Address: 8 Crane Grove, LONDON, N7 8LE
Tel: 020 7017 2934
Email: leemallett@btinternet.com
Web site: http://www.greaterlondonpublishing.com
Publisher: Greater London Publishing
Frequency: 10 issues yearly
Annual Sub.: £235.00
Circulation: 100 (Publisher's Statement)
Usual Pagination: 12
Editor: Lee Mallett
Summary of Content: Newsletter reporting the activities of the City of London Corporation Planning Committee.
Readership/Target Audience: Read by architects, surveyors, property agents, developers and institutions.
ADVERTISING: No Advertising taken
BUSINESS: ARCHITECTURE & BUILDING: Planning & Housing

CITY SECURITY
39897U54C-307

Editorial Address: 17 Station Road, NEW BARNET, EN5 7NW **Tel:** 020 8275 3303 **Fax:** 020 8275 3301
Email: eugene@berkoffdesign.co.uk
Advertising Address: 182 Bishopsgate, LONDON, EC2M 4NP **Tel:** 020 7601 2063 **Fax:** 020 7601 2323
Email: csb@city-of-london.police.uk
Publisher: Berkoff Design & Communications
Date Established: 1992
Frequency: Quarterly
Cover Price: Free
Circulation: 3,500 (Publisher's Statement)
Usual Pagination: 32
Editor: Eugene O'Mahony

Summary of Content: Magazine covering every aspect of security and the City of London in general.
Readership/Target Audience: Aimed at businesses operating within the City and all Force Crime Prevention Officers throughout the UK.
BUSINESS: SAFETY & SECURITY: Security

CITYWIRE FUNDS INSIDER
1640372U1F-604

Editorial Address: 1st Floor, 87 Vauxhall Walk, LONDON, SE11 5HJ **Tel:** 020 7840 2250
Email: funds@citywire.co.uk
Advertising Address: As above. **Fax:** 020 7840 2251
Email: pjohnson@citywire.co.uk
Web site: http://www.citywire.co.uk
Publisher: Citywire
Frequency: Weekly
Free to qualifying individuals
Circulation: 6,298 (Publisher's Statement)
Editor: Gavin Lumsden; **Editor-in-Chief:** Gavin Lumsden; **Advertising Manager:** Piers Johnson
Summary of Content: Magazine providing fund manager performance tables, recommendations, profiles and analysis.
Readership/Target Audience: Aimed at IFAs, fund managers and stock brokers.
ADVERTISING RATES:
Full Page Colour £3900.00
Agency Commission: 10%
Copy instructions: Copy Date: Middle of the month prior to publication date
Average advertising content per issue: 40%
BUSINESS: FINANCE & ECONOMICS: Investment

CIVIL ENFORCEMENT NOW
1819918U49R-402

Formerly: Civil Enforcement News
Editorial Address: Stuart House, 41-43 Perrymount Road, HAYWARDS HEATH, RH16 3BN **Tel:** 01444 447300
Fax: 01444 447311
Email: editor@civilenforcementnow.com
Advertising Address: Richard Langrish Communications, Rose Cottage, Taybridge Road, ABERFELDY, PH15 2BH
Tel: 01887 820533 **Fax:** 01887 820533
Email: richard.l@britishparking.co.uk
Web site: http://www.civilenforcementnow.com
Publisher: British Parking Association
Date Established: 2006
Frequency: Quarterly
Annual Sub.: £25.00
Circulation: 5,000 (Publisher's Statement)
Editor: Simon Burgess
Summary of Content: Magazine covering feature articles, news, products and the latest technology, parking, health and safety, debt collection and insolvency.
Readership/Target Audience: Aimed at those working in civil enforcement and local council.
ADVERTISING RATES:
Full Page Mono £700.00
Full Page Colour £1000.00
Agency Commission: 10%
Mechanical Data: Type Area: 277 x 190mm, Bleed Size: 303 x 213mm, Trim Size: 297 x 210mm, Col Length: 277mm, Page Width: 190mm, Film: Digital
Copy instructions: Copy Date: 10 days prior to publication date
Average advertising content per issue: 40%
BUSINESS: TRANSPORT: Transport Related

CIVIL ENGINEERING
38968U42A-11_50

Editorial Address: Thomas Telford House, 1 Heron Quay, LONDON, E14 4JD **Tel:** 020 7665 2448 **Fax:** 020 7538 9620
Email: journals@ice.org.uk
Advertising Address: The Warners Group, The Maltings, West Street, BOURNE, PE10 9PH **Tel:** 01778 391108
Fax: 01778 392079
Email: michaelt@warnersgroup.com
Web site: http://www.ice.org.uk
ISSN: 0965-089X
Publisher: Thomas Telford Ltd
Date Established: 1991
Frequency: 6 issues yearly
Annual Sub.: £85.00
Circulation: 62,000 (Publisher's Statement)
Usual Pagination: 48
Editor: Simon Fullalove; **Publisher:** Leon Heward-Mills
Summary of Content: International journal with refereed papers and articles on innovations and developments in civil engineering.
Readership/Target Audience: Aimed at civil engineers and members of the Institution of Civil Engineers (ICE).
ADVERTISING RATES:
Full Page Colour £1950.00
Mechanical Data: Type Area: 275 x 190mm, Bleed Size: 303 x 216mm, Trim Size: 297 x 210mm, Col Length: 275mm, Page Width: 190mm, Digital: Digital
BUSINESS: CONSTRUCTION

CIVIL ENGINEERING SURVEYOR
38969U42A-12

Editorial Address: Dominion House, Sibson Road, SALE, M33 7PP **Tel:** 0161 972 3110 **Fax:** 0161 972 3118
Email: editor@ices.org.uk
Advertising Address: As above. **Fax:** 0161 972 3119
Email: sales@ices.org.uk
Web site: http://www.ices.org.uk
ISSN: 0266-139X
Publisher: SURCO Ltd
Frequency: 10 issues yearly - Published on the 1st of the cover month
Free to qualifying individuals
Annual Sub.: £38.00
Circulation: 4,000 (Publisher's Statement)
Usual Pagination: 40
Editor: Darrell Smart; **Advertising Manager:** Alan Lees
Summary of Content: Technical journal covering the civil engineering industry.
Readership/Target Audience: Aimed at measurement engineers and quantity and land surveyors.
ADVERTISING RATES:
Full Page Mono £1028.00
Full Page Colour £1285.00
SCC £12.00
Agency Commission: 10%
Mechanical Data: Film: Digital, Type Area: 267 x 180mm, Print Process: Sheet-fed offset litho, Col Widths (Display): 86mm, No. of Columns (Display): 4, Bleed Size: 303 x 216mm, Trim Size: 297 x 210mm, Col Length: 267mm, Page Width: 180mm
Copy instructions: Copy Date: 15th of the month prior to publication date
Average advertising content per issue: 30%
Supplement(s): Construction Law Review - 1xY, Professional Constructor - 1xY
BUSINESS: CONSTRUCTION

CIVIL SOCIETY IT
1895069U5R-697

Editorial Address: 15 Prescott Place, LONDON, SW4 6BS
Tel: 020 7819 1200 **Fax:** 020 7819 1201
Email: tania@plazapublishing.co.uk
Web site: http://www.civilsocietyit.co.uk
Publisher: Plaza Publishing Ltd
Date Established: 2008
Frequency: Quarterly
Annual Sub.: £59.00
Editor: Tania Mason; **Publisher:** Daniel Phelan
Summary of Content: Magazine covering the effective use of IT in all kinds of not-for-profit organisations.
Readership/Target Audience: Aimed at those who influences, specifies or procures IT equipment or expertise.
ADVERTISING: Rates on application
BUSINESS: COMPUTERS & AUTOMATION: Computers Related

CIWM
38411U32B-240

Formerly: Wastes Management
Editorial Address: 9 Saxon Court, St. Peter's Gardens, NORTHAMPTON, NN1 1SX **Tel:** 01604 620426
Fax: 01604 604467
Email: ben.wood@ciwm.co.uk
Advertising Address: As above.
Email: james.stanton@ciwm.co.uk
Web site: http://www.ciwm.co.uk
ISSN: 1751-5602
Publisher: IWM Business Services Ltd
Date Established: 1910
Frequency: Monthly - Published around the 10th of the cover month
Free to qualifying individuals
Annual Sub.: £84.00
Circulation: 7,800 (Publisher's Statement)
Usual Pagination: 72
Editor: Ben Wood
Summary of Content: Journal focusing on the disposal, collection and treatment of household and commercial solid wastes.
Readership/Target Audience: Aimed at those involved in the collection, treatment and disposal of solid waste from both the public and private sectors.
ADVERTISING RATES:
Full Page Colour £1540.00
Agency Commission: 10%
Mechanical Data: Trim Size: 276 x 210mm, Bleed Size: +3mm, Film: Digital
Copy instructions: Copy Date: 3 weeks prior to publication date
Average advertising content per issue: 20%
Supplement(s): CIWM Scientific & Technical Review - 3xY
BUSINESS: LOCAL GOVERNMENT, LEISURE & RECREATION: Public Health & Cleaning

CJM
39143U44-450

Formerly: Criminal Justice Management
Editorial Address: 9th Floor, St. James's Buildings, Oxford Street, MANCHESTER, M1 6PP **Tel:** 0161 211 3000
Fax: 0161 211 3008
Email: editorial@govnet.co.uk
Advertising Address: 4th Floor, St. James's Buildings, Oxford Street, MANCHESTER, M1 6PP **Tel:** 0161 211 3000
Fax: 0161 211 3008
Email: ed.irving@govnet.co.uk
Web site: http://www.govnet.co.uk
ISSN: 1465-4547
Publisher: GovNet Communications
Date Established: 1997
Frequency: 6 issues yearly
Free to qualifying individuals
Circulation: 7,493 (ABC 01/07/2008 to 30/06/2009)
Usual Pagination: 64
Editor: Natalie Quinn; **Advertising Manager:** Ed Irving
Summary of Content: Journal containing an insight into politics, policy, strategic and operational management issues in the criminal justice arena.
Readership/Target Audience: Aimed at strategic decision-makers and operational managers in criminal justice agencies and their associated central and local government partnerships.
ADVERTISING RATES:
Full Page Colour £3595.00
Agency Commission: 10%
Mechanical Data: Trim Size: 297 x 210mm, Film: Digital
Average advertising content per issue: 40%
BUSINESS: LEGAL

CLASS MAGAZINE
36474U9A-37

Editorial Address: Gainsborough House, 2 Sheen Road, RICHMOND, TW9 1AE **Tel:** 020 8973 2611
Email: sean@alchemymedia.co.uk
Advertising Address: As above. **Fax:** 020 8288 7444
Email: ollie@alchemymedia.co.uk
ISSN: 1464-0430
Publisher: Alchemy Media
Date Established: 1997
Frequency: 10 Issues yearly - Published around the 28th of the month
Cover Price: £3.00
Annual Sub.: £35.00
Circulation: 9,617 (ABC 01/07/2006 to 30/06/2007)
Usual Pagination: 100
Editor: Tom Sandham
Summary of Content: Magazine containing bar reviews, profiles of those within the industry and tasting of wines, beers and spirits. Also includes the latest news, advice on making quality cocktails and features on music, bar design and equipment.
Readership/Target Audience: Aimed at bar owners, managers and all those in the drinks business.
ADVERTISING RATES:
Full Page Colour £3295.00
Mechanical Data: Bleed Size: 293 x 228mm, Type Area: 253 x 186mm, Col Length: 253mm, Page Width: 186mm, Print Process: Web-offset, Film: Digital, Trim Size: 285 x 220mm
Copy instructions: Copy Date: 2 weeks prior to publication date
Average advertising content per issue: 35%
BUSINESS: DRINKS & LICENSED TRADE: Drinks, Licensed Trade, Wines & Spirits

THE CLASSICAL QUARTERLY
47880U62R-459

Editorial Address: The Edinburgh Building, Shaftesbury Road, CAMBRIDGE, CB2 8RU **Tel:** 01223 325809
Fax: 01223 325801
Email: ad_sales@cambridge.org
Advertising Address: As above. **Tel:** 01223 326070
Fax: 01223 325150
Email: ad_sales@cambridge.org
ISSN: 0009-8388
Publisher: Cambridge University Press
Date Established: 1906
Frequency: Half-yearly - Published in May and December
Cover Price: £43.00
Annual Sub.: £68.00
Circulation: 1,800 (Publisher's Statement)
Usual Pagination: 320
Editor: Rhiannon Ash
Summary of Content: Journal covering language, literature, history and philosophy.
Readership/Target Audience: Aimed at academics, students and teachers.
ADVERTISING RATES:
Full Page Mono £385.00
Mechanical Data: Film: Digital, Type Area: 200 x 135mm, Col Length: 200mm, Page Width: 135mm
BUSINESS: CHURCH & SCHOOL EQUIPMENT & EDUCATION: Education Related

THE CLASSICAL REVIEW
47556U62R-462

Editorial Address: The Edinburgh Building, Shaftesbury Road, CAMBRIDGE, CB2 2RU **Tel:** 01223 325809
Fax: 01223 325801
Email: ad_sales@cambridge.org
Advertising Address: Great Clarendon Street, OXFORD, OX2 6DP **Tel:** 01865 353329
Email: jnlsadvertising@oxfordjournals.org
Web site: http://journals.cambridge.org
ISSN: 0009-840X
Publisher: Cambridge University Press
Date Established: 1886
Frequency: Half-yearly - Published in April and November
Cover Price: £46.00
Annual Sub.: £74.00
Circulation: 1,800 (Publisher's Statement)
Usual Pagination: 352
Editor: Roy Gibson
Summary of Content: Journal featuring reviews of books on Graeco-Roman antiquity.
Readership/Target Audience: Aimed at members of the Classical Association.
ADVERTISING RATES:
Full Page Mono £385.00
Agency Commission: 10%
Mechanical Data: Film: Digital, Page Width: 110mm, Type Area: 195 x 110mm, Col Length: 195mm
BUSINESS: CHURCH & SCHOOL EQUIPMENT & EDUCATION: Education Related

CLASSROOM MUSIC
1695160U62B-1408

Editorial Address: 241 Shaftesbury Avenue, LONDON, WC2H 8TF **Tel:** 020 7333 1714 **Fax:** 020 7333 1765
Email: classroom@rhinegold.co.uk
Advertising Address: As above. **Tel:** 020 7333 1748
Fax: 020 7333 1736
Email: natasha@rhinegold.co.uk
Web site: http://www.rhinegold.co.uk
Publisher: Rhinegold Publishing Ltd
Date Established: 2004
Frequency: 6 issues yearly
Cover Price: £12.50
Annual Sub.: £67.50
Circulation: 2,500 (Publisher's Statement)
Usual Pagination: 66
Editor: Chris Elcombe; **Advertising Manager:** Natasha Cowley
Summary of Content: Magazine providing product reviews, new ideas and lesson plans.
Readership/Target Audience: Aimed at music and non-specialist teachers.
ADVERTISING RATES:
Full Page Mono £1220.00
Full Page Colour £1480.00
Agency Commission: 10%
Mechanical Data: Type Area: 272 x 184mm, Bleed Size: 303 x 216mm, Trim Size: 297 x 210mm, Col Length: 272mm, Page Width: 184mm, Film: Digital
Average advertising content per issue: 12%
BUSINESS: CHURCH & SCHOOL EQUIPMENT & EDUCATION: Education Teachers

CLAY MINERALS
36619U12A-30

Editorial Address: Department of Engineering, University of Exeter, Harrison Building, North Park Road, EXETER, EX4 4QF **Tel:** 020 8891 6600 **Fax:** 020 8891 6599
Email: kevin@minersoc.org
Web site: http://www.minersoc.org
ISSN: 0009-8558
Publisher: Mineralogical Society
Date Established: 1948
Frequency: Quarterly
Cover Price: £232.00
Circulation: 500 (Publisher's Statement)
Usual Pagination: 160
Editor: Kevin Murphy
Summary of Content: Journal about clay minerals and fine particle science.
Readership/Target Audience: Aimed at those with a professional interest in clay minerals.
ADVERTISING: No Advertising taken
BUSINESS: CERAMICS, POTTERY & GLASS: Ceramics & Pottery

CLAY TECHNOLOGY
36612U12A-35

Editorial Address: 1 Carlton House Terrace, LONDON, SW1Y 5DB **Tel:** 020 7451 7314
Email: ctnews@iom3.org
Advertising Address: Mongoose Media Ltd, Mongoose House, Lonsdale Road, LONDON, NW6 6RD
Tel: 020 7306 0300 **Fax:** 020 7306 0301
Email: iom3@mongoosemedia.com
Web site: http://www.iom3.org/claytechnology
ISSN: 0954-6146
Publisher: IOM Communications Ltd
Date Established: 1988

Frequency: 6 issues yearly
Annual Sub.: £45.00
Circulation: 1,000 (Publisher's Statement)
Usual Pagination: 28
Editor: Katherine Williams; **News Editor:** Rupal Mehta; **Advertising Manager:** James Priest
Summary of Content: Magazine of the Institute of Clay Technology. Contains matters affecting the construction products industries, especially heavy clay products.
Readership/Target Audience: Aimed at members of the Institute of Clay Technology, managers and suppliers within the heavy clay sector.
ADVERTISING RATES:
Full Page Mono £500.00
Full Page Colour £802.00
Agency Commission: 10%
Mechanical Data: Col Length: 255mm, Type Area: 255 x 180mm, Bleed Size: 305 x 215mm, Trim Size: 297 x 210mm, Film: Digital, Page Width: 180mm
Copy instructions: Copy Date: 4 weeks prior to publication date
Average advertising content per issue: 25%
BUSINESS: CERAMICS, POTTERY & GLASS: Ceramics & Pottery

CLEAN SLATE
1825720U1A-345

Editorial Address: PR by email only **Tel:** 020 7639 5120
Email: newsdesk@bestadvice.net
Advertising Address: Denvilles House, 33 Emsworth Road, HAVANT, PO9 2SN **Tel:** 020 7828 4794
Email: gustavo@bestadvice.net
Publisher: Bestadvice.net
Date Established: 2007
Frequency: Quarterly
Cover Price: £2.95
Free to qualifying individuals
Circulation: 12,000 (Publisher's Statement)
Usual Pagination: 48
Editor: Kevin Rose; **Advertising Director:** Gustavo Inocencio
Summary of Content: Magazine and online news service focusing on debt mediation, debt solutions, IVAs, bankruptcy and personal insolvencies.
Readership/Target Audience: Aimed at insolvency practitioners, master brokers and mortgage brokers dealing with debt.
ADVERTISING: Rates on application
BUSINESS: FINANCE & ECONOMICS

CLEANING & MAINTENANCE
35949U4F-23

Editorial Address: Armstrong House, 38 Market Square, UXBRIDGE, UB8 1LH **Tel:** 01409 241166 **Fax:** 01895 454643
Email: nnixon@btconnect.com
Advertising Address: As above. **Tel:** 01895 454600
Email: claireullyart@quartzltd.com
Web site: http://www.cleaningmag.com
Publisher: Quartz Publishing
Date Established: 1953
Frequency: Monthly - Published on the 6th of the cover month
Free to qualifying individuals
Annual Sub.: £80.00
Circulation: 11,096 (ABC 01/01/2008 to 31/12/2008)
Usual Pagination: 32
Editor: Neil Nixon; **Advertising Manager:** Claire Ullyart; **Publisher:** Martin Scott
Summary of Content: Magazine providing the cleaning news, articles and product information concerning the cleaning industry.
Readership/Target Audience: Aimed at anyone involved in the cleaning, maintenance and management of buildings and their upkeep.
ADVERTISING RATES:
Full Page Colour £2848.00
SCC £35.00
Agency Commission: 10%
Mechanical Data: Type Area: 390 x 260mm, Bleed Size: 426 x 300mm, Trim Size: 420 x 297mm, Col Length: 390mm, Film: Digital, Page Width: 260mm
Copy instructions: Copy Date: 20th of the month prior to publication date
Supplement(s): Machine Guide - 1xY
BUSINESS: ARCHITECTURE & BUILDING: Cleaning & Maintenance

CLEANING MATTERS
623195U4F-24

Editorial Address: 33-35 Cantelupe Road, EAST GRINSTEAD, RH19 3BE **Tel:** 01342 333721
Fax: 01342 333701
Email: gcoyne@progressive-media.co.uk
Advertising Address: As above. **Tel:** 01342 314300
Email: lnelson@progressive-media.co.uk
Web site: http://www.cleaning-matters.co.uk
Publisher: Progressive Media
Date Established: 2000
Frequency: 6 issues yearly - Published at the end of the 1st cover month
Cover Price: Free

Circulation: 15,061 (ABC 01/01/2008 to 31/12/2008)
Usual Pagination: 92
Editor: Gerardine Coyne
Summary of Content: Magazine covering news, views, features, new products, service information, testing and surveys.
Readership/Target Audience: Aimed at buyers, specifiers manufacturers, distributors, cleaning and maintenance contractors, local authorities, facilities managers and those involved in cleaning products, services and equipment.
ADVERTISING RATES:
Full Page Mono £1470.00
Full Page Colour £1970.00
Agency Commission: 10%
Mechanical Data: Type Area: 287 x 200mm, Bleed Size: +3mm, Col Length: 287mm, Page Width: 200mm, Trim Size: 297 x 210mm, Film: Digital
Copy instructions: Copy Date: 4 weeks prior to publication date
Average advertising content per issue: 40%
Supplement(s): Green Cleaning - 1xY, Industrial Focus - 1xY, Industry Guide - 1xY, Practical Cleaning Solutions - 1xY
BUSINESS: ARCHITECTURE & BUILDING: Cleaning & Maintenance

CLEANROOM TECHNOLOGY   39957U55-46

Editorial Address: Paulton House, 8 Shepherdess Walk, LONDON, N1 7LB **Tel:** 020 7490 0049 **Fax:** 020 7549 8622
Email: hilarya@hpcimedia.com
Advertising Address: As above.
Email: abadr@wilmington.co.uk
Web site: http://www.cleanroom-technology.co.uk
ISSN: 1365-553X
Publisher: HPCi Media Ltd
Date Established: 1995
Frequency: 10 issues yearly
Annual Sub.: £154.00
Circulation: 7,200 (Publisher's Statement)
Usual Pagination: 36
Editor: Hilary Ayshford; **Managing Editor:** Hilary Ayshford
Summary of Content: European journal of contamination control.
Readership/Target Audience: Aimed at engineers, managers and consultants in cleanroom and contamination-control industries throughout Europe.
ADVERTISING RATES:
Full Page Colour £2540.00
Agency Commission: 10%
Mechanical Data: No. of Columns (Display): 5, Film: Digital, Type Area: 269 x 195mm, Col Length: 269mm, Trim Size: 297 x 210mm, Page Width: 195mm
Copy instructions: Copy Date: 4 weeks prior to publication date
Average advertising content per issue: 45%
BUSINESS: APPLIED SCIENCE & LABORATORIES

CLEANTECH   1926499U1F-683

Editorial Address: PO Box 63865, LONDON, SE1 3SN
Tel: 020 7394 7110 **Fax:** 020 7252 0910
Email: editor@cleantechinvestor.com
Web site: http://www.cleantechinvestor.com
Publisher: Cleantech Investor
Date Established: 2007
Frequency: 6 issues yearly
Free to qualifying individuals
Editor: Anne McIvor
Summary of Content: Magazine featuring news on deals and fundraising in the sector, both on quoted markets and in the private equity and venture capital space.
Readership/Target Audience: Aimed at investors.
BUSINESS: FINANCE & ECONOMICS: Investment

CLEARVIEW   1620655U12B-78

Editorial Address: Office F2-F3, Holme Suite, Oaks Business Park, Oaks Lane, BARNSLEY, S71 1HT
Tel: 01226 321450 **Fax:** 01226 240202
Email: editor@clearview-uk.com
Advertising Address: As above.
Email: sheilah@clearview-uk.com
Web site: http://www.clearview-uk.com
ISSN: 1745-0985
Publisher: Zine Media Publishing Ltd
Date Established: 2001
Frequency: Monthly - Published around the 7th of the cover month
Cover Price: £3.00
Free to qualifying individuals
Circulation: 15,000 (Publisher's Statement)
Usual Pagination: 64
Editor: Sheilah Reed; **Features Editor:** Sheilah Reed; **Group Editor:** James Snow
Summary of Content: Magazine featuring specialist solutions for the glass and glazing industry.
Readership/Target Audience: Read by fabricators and installers, architects, housing developers, local authority professionals, shop fitters and glass manufacturers.

ADVERTISING RATES:
Full Page Colour £1195.00
Agency Commission: 10%
Mechanical Data: Trim Size: 297 x 210mm, Film: Digital, Bleed Size: 220 x 151mm, No. of Columns (Display): 3
Copy instructions: Copy Date: 1 week prior to publication date
Average advertising content per issue: 60%
Editions:
Clearview Midlands
Clearview North & Scotland
Clearview South
BUSINESS: CERAMICS, POTTERY & GLASS: Glass

THE CLERK   38372U32A-40

Editorial Address: 19-21 Main Street, Keyworth, NOTTINGHAM, NG12 5AA **Tel:** 0115 937 6506
Email: elliottnews@btconnect.com
Advertising Address: James Pembroke Publishing Ltd, 90 Walcot Street, BATH, BA1 5BG **Tel:** 0125 337777
Fax: 01225 339977
Email: charlest@jppublishing.co.uk
Web site: http://www.slcc.co.uk
Publisher: James Pembroke Publishing Ltd
Date Established: 1974
Frequency: 6 issues yearly - Published on the 1st of the month
Free to qualifying individuals
Annual Sub.: £20.00
Circulation: 3,800 (Publisher's Statement)
Usual Pagination: 50
Editor: Mike Elliott; **Advertising Manager:** Charles Troy
Summary of Content: Journal of the Society of Local Council Clerks. Includes information and news on new products, services and equipment.
Readership/Target Audience: Aimed at parish and town clerks.
ADVERTISING RATES:
Full Page Colour £625.00
Agency Commission: 10%
Mechanical Data: Type Area: 277 x 190mm, Trim Size: 297 x 210mm, Bleed Size: 303 x 216mm, Col Length: 277mm, Page Width: 190mm, Film: Digital
Copy instructions: Copy Date: 15th of the month prior to publication date
BUSINESS: LOCAL GOVERNMENT, LEISURE & RECREATION: Local Government

CLERKS AND COUNCILS DIRECT   38373U32A-45

Editorial Address: Banklands, Ferry Lane, Wraysbury, STAINES, TW19 6HG **Tel:** 01784 483281 **Fax:** 01784 483600
Email: clerkscouncils@btinternet.com
Advertising Address: Willow Barns Farm, Redbrook Street, Woodchurch, ASHFORD, TN26 3QR **Tel:** 01233 861146
Fax: 01233 861035
Email: clerksads@btinternet.com
Web site: http://www.clerksandcouncilsdirect.co.uk/
Publisher: CommuniCorp
Date Established: 1999
Frequency: 6 issues yearly
Free to qualifying individuals
Annual Sub.: £12.00
Circulation: 11,000 (Publisher's Statement)
Usual Pagination: 32
Editor: Brian Lewis; **Managing Editor:** Carol Lee
Summary of Content: Magazine covering all matters affecting town, parish and community councils. Contains news, features and information on products and services. Also covers relations between all levels of local government in England and Wales.
Readership/Target Audience: Read by chief executives and chief officers of all principal local authorities, council clerks and councillors via members rooms.
ADVERTISING RATES:
Full Page Mono £1250.00
Full Page Colour £1445.00
Agency Commission: 10%
Mechanical Data: Col Length: 270mm, Type Area: 270 x 190mm, Trim Size: 297 x 210mm, Bleed Size: 303 x 216mm, Page Width: 190mm
Copy instructions: Copy Date: 10th of the month prior to publication date
Average advertising content per issue: 50%
BUSINESS: LOCAL GOVERNMENT, LEISURE & RECREATION: Local Government

CLI CLINICAL LABORATORY INTERNATIONAL   39956U55-48

Editorial Address: 2 Claridge Court, Lower Kings Road, BERKHAMSTED, HP4 2AF **Tel:** 01442 877777
Fax: 01442 870617
Email: bobw@lansdowne-media.co.uk
Advertising Address: As above.
Email: bobw@lansdowne-media.co.uk
Web site: http://www.cli-online.com
Publisher: Reed Business Information

Date Established: 1973
Frequency: 7 issues yearly
Cover Price: Free
Circulation: 22,499 (BPA Worldwide 01/01/2007 to 30/06/2007)
Usual Pagination: 42
Editor: Bob Warren; **Publisher:** Bernard Leger
Summary of Content: Publication which reports on new clinical laboratory instrumentation equipment and reagents which are marketed internationally.
Readership/Target Audience: Aimed at senior clinical biologists, hospital laboratory management and blood banking specialists in Europe, Middle East, Asia/Pacific and Latin America.
ADVERTISING RATES:
Full Page Mono EUR7750.00
Full Page Colour EUR9545.00
Agency Commission: 15%
Mechanical Data: Type Area: 276 x 206mm, Bleed Size: 312 x 232mm, Trim Size: 300 x 230mm, Col Length: 276mm, Page Width: 206mm, No. of Columns (Display): 3, Film: Positive, right reading, emulsion side down. Digital
Copy instructions: Copy Date: 2 weeks prior to publication date
Average advertising content per issue: 50%
BUSINESS: APPLIED SCIENCE & LABORATORIES

CLINICA WORLD MEDICAL TECHNOLOGY NEWS   40347U56C-60

Formerly: Clinica World Medical Device & Diagnostic News
Editorial Address: Telephone House, 69-77 Paul Street, LONDON, EC2A 4LQ **Tel:** 020 7017 5000
Fax: 020 7017 6975
Email: ashley.yeo@informa.com
Advertising Address: As above. **Fax:** 020 7017 6787
Email: jennifer.cheng@informa.com
Web site: http://www.pjbpubs.com/clinica/index.htm
ISSN: 0144-7777
Publisher: Informa Healthcare
Date Established: 1980
Frequency: Weekly
Annual Sub.: £1195.00
Circulation: 1,585 (Publisher's Statement)
Usual Pagination: 24
Editor: Ashley Yeo; **Advertising Manager:** Jennifer Cheng; **Publisher:** Phil Solomon
Summary of Content: Journal covering the global medical device and diagnostic industry.
Readership/Target Audience: Aimed at the healthcare business, government departments and service organisations.
ADVERTISING RATES:
Full Page Mono £1689.00
Full Page Colour £2359.00
Agency Commission: 10%
Mechanical Data: Type Area: 260 x 185mm, Bleed Size: 303 x 216mm, Trim Size: 297 x 210mm, Film: Digital, Page Width: 185mm, No. of Columns (Display): 2, Col Widths (Display): 88mm, Col Length: 260mm
Copy instructions: Copy Date: 3 days prior to publication date
BUSINESS: HEALTH & MEDICAL: Hospitals

CLINICAL & EXPERIMENTAL IMMUNOLOGY   40558U56R-5(

Editorial Address: Vintage House, 37 Albert Embankment, LONDON, SE1 7TL **Tel:** 020 3031 9800 **Fax:** 020 7582 2882
Email: CEI@immunology.org
Advertising Address: 9600 Garsington Road, Cowley, OXFORD, OX4 2DQ **Tel:** 01865 776868 **Fax:** 01865 471354
Email: medsaleseurope@oxon.blackwellpublishing.com
Web site: http://www.blackwellpublishing.com/cei
ISSN: 0009-9104
Publisher: Wiley-Blackwell Publishing
Date Established: 1966
Frequency: Monthly
Annual Sub.: £877.00
Circulation: 1,300 (Publisher's Statement)
Usual Pagination: 192
Editor: Sharon Tobin; **Editor-in-Chief:** Mark Peakman; **Advertising Manager:** Advertising Manager
Summary of Content: Primary research papers covering a wide range of immunological topics (immunological basis of disease, therapy, diagnosis) from basic research through to clinical work. Reviews on important immunological areas/discoveries.
Readership/Target Audience: Aimed at clinicians and academics working in the field of immunology based generally in universities, research institutions or hospitals.
BUSINESS: HEALTH & MEDICAL: Health Medical Related

CLINICAL CHILD PSYCHOLOGY & PSYCHIATRY   40496U56N-4_1

Editorial Address: 1 Oliver's Yard, 55 City Road, LONDON, EC1Y 1SP **Tel:** 020 7324 8500 **Fax:** 020 7324 8600
Email: market@sagepub.co.uk

Advertising Address: As above.
Email: advertising@sagepub.co.uk
Web site: http://www.sagepub.co.uk
ISSN: 1359-1045
Publisher: Sage Publications
Date Established: 1996
Frequency: Quarterly
Annual Sub.: £64.00
Usual Pagination: 160
Editor: Arlene Ventere; **Advertising Manager:** Sheena Karim
Summary of Content: Journal providing a forum for papers which focus on clinical and therapeutic aspects of child and adolescent psychology and psychiatry.
Readership/Target Audience: Aimed at professionals in the field.
ADVERTISING RATES:
Full Page Mono £450.00
Agency Commission: 5%
Mechanical Data: Type Area: 210 x 140mm, Col Length: 210mm, Page Width: 140mm, Film: Digital
Copy instructions: Copy Date: 12 weeks prior to publication date
BUSINESS: HEALTH & MEDICAL: Mental Health

CLINICAL FOCUS
40151U56A-59_10
Editorial Address: 73 Newman Street, LONDON, W1A 4PG
Tel: 020 7637 3544 **Fax:** 020 7580 7166
Email: admin@rila.co.uk
Advertising Address: As above.
Email: admin@rila.co.uk
Web site: http://www.rila.co.uk
Publisher: Rila Publications Ltd
Date Established: 1995
Frequency: 6 issues yearly
Cover Price: £15.00
Free to qualifying individuals
Circulation: 30,000 (Publisher's Statement)
Editor: Ram Dhillon; **Advertising Manager:** Ram Dhillon
Summary of Content: Magazine for general practitioners and hospital specialists to enhance their clinical skills.
Readership/Target Audience: Aimed at general practitioners and hospital specialists.
ADVERTISING: Rates on application
BUSINESS: HEALTH & MEDICAL

CLINICAL GOVERNANCE: AN INTERNATIONAL JOURNAL
40534U56R-30
Formerly: The British Journal of Clinical Governance
Editorial Address: Howard House, Wagon Lane, BINGLEY, BD16 1WA **Tel:** 01274 777700 **Fax:** 01274 785200
Email: j.lucas@bradford.ac.uk
Web site: http://www.emeraldinsight.com
ISSN: 1477-7274
Publisher: Emerald Group Publishing Ltd
Frequency: Quarterly
Annual Sub.: £439.00
Usual Pagination: 60
Editor: Alan Gillies; **Advertising Manager:** Liz Godden; **Publisher:** Nicola Codner
Summary of Content: Journal covering multi-professional healthcare auditing, evidence-based practice, fund monitoring and clinical effectiveness.
Readership/Target Audience: Read by clinical and non-clinical professionals in healthcare and community care, as well as those in purchasing and education.
ADVERTISING: No Advertising taken
BUSINESS: HEALTH & MEDICAL: Health Medical Related

CLINICAL MEDICINE
40188U56A-69_45
Formerly: Journal of the Royal College of Physicians of London
Editorial Address: 11 St Andrews Place, LONDON, NW1 4LE **Tel:** 020 7935 1174 **Fax:** 020 7486 5425
Email: clinicalmedicine@rcplondon.ac.uk
Advertising Address: As above.
Email: clinical.medicine@btinternet.com
Web site: http://www.rcplondon.ac.uk
ISSN: 1470-2118
Publisher: Royal College of Physicians
Date Established: 2000
Frequency: 6 issues yearly
Annual Sub.: £120.00
Circulation: 22,000 (Publisher's Statement)
Usual Pagination: 100
Editor: Robert Allen; **Advertising Manager:** David Cox
Summary of Content: Journal covering peer reviewed articles relevant to science and the practice of international medicine.
Readership/Target Audience: Read by members and fellows of the Royal College of Physicians.
ADVERTISING RATES:
Full Page Mono £944.00
Full Page Colour £1584.00
Agency Commission: 10%

Mechanical Data: Page Width: 178mm, Type Area: 248 x 178mm, Bleed Size: 286 x 216mm, Trim Size: 280 x 210mm, Film: Digital, Col Length: 248mm
Copy instructions: Copy Date: 6 weeks prior to publication date
Average advertising content per issue: 10%
BUSINESS: HEALTH & MEDICAL

CLINICAL ONCOLOGY
24444U56R-51
Formerly: Harcourt Health Sciences
Editorial Address: Mount Vernon Hospital, Rickmansworth Road, NORTHWOOD, HA6 2RN **Tel:** 01923 844568
Fax: 01923 844167
Email: elsie.arjune@nhs.net
Advertising Address: 32 Jamestown Road, LONDON, NW1 7BY **Tel:** 020 7424 4538 **Fax:** 020 7424 4433
Email: s.cahill@elsevier.com
Web site: http://intl.elsevierhealth.com/journals/clon
ISSN: 0936-6555
Publisher: Elsevier
Date Established: 1989
Frequency: 10 issues yearly
Annual Sub.: EUR145.00
Circulation: 5,286 (Publisher's Statement)
Usual Pagination: 80
Editor: Peter Hoskin
Summary of Content: Journal covering all aspects of the clinical management of cancer patients including multidisciplinary approach to therapy, articles on all types of malignant disease and all modalities used in cancer therapy.
Readership/Target Audience: Read by clinicians with an active interest in the treatment of cancer.
ADVERTISING RATES:
Full Page Mono EUR1116.00
Full Page Colour EUR2028.00
Agency Commission: 10%
Mechanical Data: Type Area: 250 x 180mm, Trim Size: 280 x 210mm, Bleed Size: 285 x 213mm, Col Length: 250mm, Film: Positive, right reading, emulsion side down. Digital, Page Width: 180mm
Copy instructions: Copy Date: 5 weeks prior to publication date
BUSINESS: HEALTH & MEDICAL: Health Medical Related

CLINICAL PHARMACIST
38735U56C-340
Formerly: Hospital Pharmacist
Editorial Address: 1 Lambeth High Street, LONDON, SE1 7JN **Tel:** 020 7572 2425 **Fax:** 020 7572 2504
Email: clinicalpharmacist@pharmj.org.uk
Advertising Address: As above. **Tel:** 020 7572 2222
Fax: 020 7572 2505
Email: stuart.thomas@rpsgb.org
Web site: http://www.pjonline.com
ISSN: 1352-7967
Publisher: RPS Publishing
Date Established: 1994
Frequency: 11 issues yearly
Cover Price: £14.00
Free to qualifying individuals
Annual Sub.: £120.00
Circulation: 9,936 (ABC 01/01/2008 to 31/12/2008)
Usual Pagination: 44
Summary of Content: Journal covering all aspects of hospital pharmacy.
Readership/Target Audience: Aimed at hospital pharmacists and pharmaceutical advisers.
ADVERTISING RATES:
Full Page Mono £3860.00
Full Page Colour £5165.00
Agency Commission: 10%
Mechanical Data: Type Area: 260 x 186mm, Bleed Size: 302 x 216mm, Trim Size: 297 x 210mm, Col Widths (Display): 44mm, No. of Columns (Display): 4, Page Width: 186mm, Col Length: 260mm, Film: Digital
Copy instructions: Copy Date: 8 days prior to publication date
Average advertising content per issue: 40%
BUSINESS: HEALTH & MEDICAL: Hospitals

CLINICAL REHABILITATION
24914U56L-9
Editorial Address: 1 Oliver's Yard, 55 City Road, LONDON, EC1Y 1SP **Tel:** 020 7324 8500 **Fax:** 020 7324 8600
Email: rowena.pagdin@sagepub.co.uk
Advertising Address: As above.
Email: sheena.karim@sagepub.co.uk
Web site: http://www.clinicalrehabilitation.com
ISSN: 0269-2155
Publisher: Sage Publications
Date Established: 1987
Frequency: Monthly
Annual Sub.: £169.00
Circulation: 1,600 (Publisher's Statement)
Usual Pagination: 104
Editor: Rowena Pagdin
Summary of Content: Academic publication providing a forum for the exchange of ideas and information for people

concerned with rehabilitation. The journal covers the whole field of disability and rehabilitation.
Readership/Target Audience: Aimed at those involved in rehabilitation and related areas such as physiotherapy, rehabilitation nursing, strokes and multiple sclerosis.
ADVERTISING RATES:
Full Page Mono £550.00
Agency Commission: 56%
Mechanical Data: Bleed Size: +4mm, Print Process: Sheet-fed litho, Film: Positive, right reading, emulsion side down. Digital, Type Area: 215 x 160mm, Trim Size: 246 x 189mm, Col Length: 215mm, Page Width: 160mm
Copy instructions: Copy Date: 12 weeks prior to publication date
BUSINESS: HEALTH & MEDICAL: Disability & Rehabilitation

CLINICAL RHEUMATOLOGY
40560U56R-52_20
Editorial Address: Ashbourne House, The Guildway, Old Portsmouth Road, Artington, GUILDFORD, GU3 1LP
Tel: 01483 734437 **Fax:** 01483 734411
Email: w.j.pontefract@sheffield.ac.uk
Web site: http://www.link.springer.de
ISSN: 0770-3198
Publisher: Springer
Frequency: Monthly
Annual Sub.: £198.00
Circulation: 1,000 (Publisher's Statement)
Usual Pagination: 130
Editor: Wendy Pontefract; **Executive Editor:** Christiane Notarmarco; **Editor-in-Chief:** Paul Davis; **Managing Editor:** Wendy Pontefract
Summary of Content: Journal containing original clinical investigation and research in the general field of rheumatology at postgraduate level.
Readership/Target Audience: Read by postgraduates.
ADVERTISING: No Advertising taken
BUSINESS: HEALTH & MEDICAL: Health Medical Related

THE CLINICAL SERVICES JOURNAL
1615878U56C-387
Editorial Address: Step House, North Farm Road, TUNBRIDGE WELLS, TN2 3DR **Tel:** 01892 518877
Fax: 01892 616177
Email: csj@stepcomms.com
Advertising Address: As above.
Email: geoffking@stepcomms.com
Web site: http://www.clinicalservicesjournal.com
ISSN: 1478-5641
Publisher: Step Communications Ltd
Date Established: 2002
Frequency: 10 issues yearly - Published on the 1st of the cover month
Cover Price: £14.00
Free to qualifying individuals
Annual Sub.: £93.00
Circulation: 11,328 (Publisher's Statement)
Usual Pagination: 76
Editor: Louise Frampton; **Advertising Manager:** Geoff King; **Managing Editor:** Nicholas Marshall
Summary of Content: Journal covering healthcare and clinical product news and developments as well as technical articles based on the application of products in clinical areas and a look at clinical products used within.
Readership/Target Audience: Aimed at key personnel within clinical departments in hospitals including operating theatres, intensive care, A&E and infection control.
ADVERTISING RATES:
Full Page Colour £1820.00
Agency Commission: 10%
Mechanical Data: Type Area: 254 x 180mm, Trim Size: 297 x 210mm, Bleed Size: 303 x 216mm, Film: Digital, Col Length: 254mm, Page Width: 180mm
Copy instructions: Copy Date: 10th of the month prior to publication date
Average advertising content per issue: 40%
BUSINESS: HEALTH & MEDICAL: Hospitals

CLOSE-UP
41398U63B-2155
Editorial Address: The Stable Block, Brewery Drive, Lockwood Park, HUDDERSFIELD, HD4 6EN
Tel: 0844 980 0045
Email: daphne.leach@mycci.co.uk
Advertising Address: As above.
Email: anne.gerard@mycci.co.uk
Web site: http://www.mycci.co.uk
Publisher: The Mid Yorkshire Chamber of Commerce
Date Established: 1985
Frequency: Quarterly
Cover Price: Free
Circulation: 5,000 (Publisher's Statement)
Usual Pagination: 32
Editor: Daphne Leach; **Advertising Manager:** Anne Gerard
Summary of Content: Journal of the Mid-Yorkshire Chamber of Commerce and Industry covering construction, property, finance, legal, environment, technology and health and safety contracts with general business news.

Business Magazines

Readership/Target Audience: Aimed at businesses throughout West Yorkshire.
ADVERTISING RATES:
Full Page Colour £450.00
Agency Commission: 10%
Mechanical Data: No. of Columns (Display): 6, Col Length: 287mm, Film: Digital, Type Area: 287 x 200mm, Bleed Size: 317 x 230mm, Trim Size: 297 x 210mm, Page Width: 200mm
Average advertising content per issue: 50%
BUSINESS: REGIONAL BUSINESS: Regional Business English Counties

CLUB HOUSE
1685614U64C-201

Editorial Address: Gainsborough House, 2 Sheen Road, RICHMOND, TW9 1AE **Tel:** 020 8973 2611
Email: sean@alchemymedia.co.uk
Advertising Address: As above. **Fax:** 020 8288 7444
Email: hugh@clubmirror.com
Web site: http://www.alchemymedia.com
Publisher: Alchemy Media
Date Established: 2005
Frequency: Monthly
Free to qualifying individuals
Circulation: 9,000 (Publisher's Statement)
Editor: Sean Ferris; **Managing Director:** Sean Ferris;
Advertisement Director: Hugh Jenkins
Summary of Content: Magazine covering all aspects of running a club house including food and drink, catering and events.
Readership/Target Audience: Aimed at key decision makers within golf clubs.
ADVERTISING RATES:
Full Page Colour £1950.00
Agency Commission: 10%
Mechanical Data: Type Area: 275 x 205mm, Bleed Size: 305 x 233mm, Trim Size: 297 x 230mm, Col Length: 275mm, Page Width: 205mm, Film: Digital
Average advertising content per issue: 35%
BUSINESS: OTHER CLASSIFICATIONS: Clubs

CLUB JOURNAL
41474U64C-3

Editorial Address: Unit 17, St. Peters Wharf, NEWCASTLE UPON TYNE, NE6 1TZ **Tel:** 0191 265 0040
Email: cj@powdene.com
Advertising Address: As above. **Fax:** 0191 275 2609
Email: club.journal@powdene.com
Web site: http://www.powdene.com
Publisher: Powdene Publicity Ltd
Date Established: 1876
Frequency: Monthly
Cover Price: £0.60
Free to qualifying individuals
Circulation: 26,254 (Publisher's Statement)
Usual Pagination: 24
Editor: Chris Brewis; **Advertising Manager:** Geraldine Oliver
Summary of Content: Official journal for Working Men's clubs.
Readership/Target Audience: Read by members of the Working Men's Club & Institute Union, secretaries and committee members.
ADVERTISING RATES:
Full Page Mono £1520.00
Full Page Colour £2250.00
Agency Commission: 10%
Mechanical Data: Page Width: 253mm, Bleed Size: 408 x 288mm, Type Area: 375 x 253mm, Trim Size: 400 x 280mm, Col Length: 375mm, Film: Digital
Copy instructions: Copy Date: 2 weeks prior to publication date
BUSINESS: OTHER CLASSIFICATIONS: Clubs

CLUB REPORT
1794073U64C-203

Editorial Address: Gainsborough House, 2 Sheen Road, RICHMOND, TW9 1AE **Tel:** 020 8973 2611
Email: sean@clubmirror.com
Advertising Address: As above.
Email: hugh@clubmirror.com
Web site: http://www.alchemymedia.co.uk
Publisher: Alchemy Media
Frequency: Annual - Published in December
Free to qualifying individuals
Circulation: 21,000 (Publisher's Statement)
Editor: Caroline Scoular; **Advertising Director:** Hugh Jenkins
Summary of Content: Publication providing an overview of the previous year's activities and a preview of the next year.
Readership/Target Audience: Aimed at club managers.
ADVERTISING RATES:
Full Page Colour £3295.00
Agency Commission: 10%
Mechanical Data: Type Area: 275 x 205mm, Bleed Size: 305 x 235mm, Trim Size: 297 x 230mm, Col Length: 275mm, Page Width: 205mm, Film: Digital
Copy instructions: Copy Date: End of November
BUSINESS: OTHER CLASSIFICATIONS: Clubs

CN FOCUS
1640394U22R-753

Formerly: CN Primary Care Review
Editorial Address: 6 Harforde Court, John Tate Road, Foxholes Business Park, HERTFORD, SG13 7NW
Tel: 01992 538001 **Fax:** 01992 538002
Email: info@cm-2.co.uk
Advertising Address: As above.
Email: dylan@cm-2.co.uk
Web site: http://www.nutrition2me.com
ISSN: 1479-3415
Publisher: Complete Media & Marketing Ltd
Date Established: 2002
Frequency: 3 issues yearly - Published in March, May and Spetember
Free to qualifying individuals
Circulation: 10,170 (Publisher's Statement)
Usual Pagination: 32
Editor: Faye Eagle; **Managing Director:** Mike Fryer;
Advertising Manager: Dylan Jenear; **Publisher:** Faye Eagle
Summary of Content: Magazine covering all areas of primary care nutrition, including articles on the latest news, products and research.
Readership/Target Audience: Aimed at GPs and practice nurses.
ADVERTISING RATES:
Full Page Colour £1450.00
Agency Commission: 10%
Mechanical Data: Type Area: 277 x 190mm, Col Length: 277mm, Page Width: 190mm, Bleed Size: 303 x 216mm, Trim Size: 297 x 210mm, Film: Digital
Copy instructions: Copy Date: 2 weeks prior to publication date
Average advertising content per issue: 20%
BUSINESS: FOOD: Food Related

CNBC EUROPEAN BUSINESS
1647210U14A-526

Formerly: European Business Magazine
Editorial Address: 141-143 Shoreditch High Street, LONDON, E1 6JE **Tel:** 020 7613 8777 **Fax:** 020 7613 8778
Email: richard.lofthouse@cnbceb.com
Advertising Address: As above.
Email: tina-louise.jackson@cnbceb.com
Web site: http://www.cnbceb.com
Publisher: Ink Publishing
Date Established: 2004
Frequency: 10 issues yearly
Cover Price: £3.25
Circulation: 96,477 (BPA Worldwide 2008)
Usual Pagination: 116
Editor: Richard Lofthouse; **Advertising Manager:** Tina-Louise Jackson; **Publisher:** Anna Szpunar
Summary of Content: Business magazine for Europe written by Europeans. Special attention paid to entrepreneurship and cross border enterprise and SMEs, but otherwise tackling business with a view to inspiring and educating Europe's business community. Also looks at CSR; the future low-carbon economy and social entrepreneurism.
Readership/Target Audience: Aimed at MDs, CEOs, COOs, entrepreneurs and senior executives of the fastest growing companies across Europe.
ADVERTISING RATES:
Full Page Colour £9240.00
Agency Commission: 15%
Mechanical Data: Bleed Size: 291 x 216mm, Trim Size: 285 x 210mm, Film: Digital
BUSINESS: COMMERCE, INDUSTRY & MANAGEMENT

CNS DRUG NEWS
1799446U37-424

Editorial Address: Lincoln House, City Fields Business Park, City Fields Way, Tangmere, CHICHESTER, PO20 2FS
Tel: 01243 756041 **Fax:** 01243 533418
Email: healthcare@espicom.com
Web site: http://www.espicom.com
Publisher: Espicom Ltd
Frequency: 22 issues yearly
Annual Sub.: £575.00
Editor: Lucy Vann
Summary of Content: Newsletter focusing on company and product developments in the treatment of central nervous system disorders, also features conference listings.
Readership/Target Audience: Aimed at executives in pharmaceutical companies.
ADVERTISING: No Advertising taken
BUSINESS: PHARMACEUTICAL & CHEMISTS

COACH AND BUS WEEK
39612U49B-25

Editorial Address: 3 The Office Village, Cygnet Park, Forder Way, Hampton, PETERBOROUGH, PE7 8GX
Tel: 01733 293240 **Fax:** 0845 280 2927
Email: cbwinbox@rouncymedia.co.uk
Advertising Address: As above.
Email: vicki.culverhouse@rouncymedia.co.uk
Web site: http://www.cbwonline.com
ISSN: 1351-3877
Publisher: Rouncy Media Ltd
Date Established: 1978

Frequency: Weekly
Cover Price: £2.50
Annual Sub.: £69.00
Circulation: 3,901 (Publisher's Statement)
Usual Pagination: 64
Editor: Andrew Sutcliffe; **Advertising Director:** Vicki Culverhouse
Summary of Content: News reports and in-depth articles on the public service vehicle industry.
Readership/Target Audience: Read by managers in the road transport industry and key contractors such as local authorities, traffic commissioners, government and decision makers at local and national operators.
ADVERTISING RATES:
Full Page Colour £1000.00
Agency Commission: 10%
Mechanical Data: Type Area: 270 x 190mm, Bleed Size: 307 x 220mm, Trim Size: 297 x 210mm, Col Length: 270mm, Col Widths (Display): 46mm, No. of Columns (Display): 4, Page Width: 190mm, Film: Digital
Copy instructions: Copy Date: Monday prior to publication date
Average advertising content per issue: 30%
Supplement(s): Coach & Bus Guide - 1xY, Coach Operators Handbook - 1xY, Minibus - 13xY, Out & About - 13xY
BUSINESS: TRANSPORT: Bus & Coach Transport

COACH MONTHLY
1657335U50-212

Formerly: Route One On Tour
Editorial Address: 37 Tyndall Court, Commerce Road, Lynch Wood, PETERBOROUGH, PE2 6LR
Tel: 01733 405746
Email: zoe.d@coachmonthly.com
Advertising Address: As above. **Tel:** 0870 758 6808
Email: sally.eyre@coachmonthly.com
Publisher: Expo Publishing
Date Established: 1982
Frequency: Monthly
Free to qualifying individuals
Circulation: 7,000 (Publisher's Statement)
Editor: Zoë Doyle
Summary of Content: Magazine covering news and features on coach tourism, attractions and destinations at home and abroad.
Readership/Target Audience: Aimed at coach tour operators, planners, managers and drivers.
ADVERTISING RATES:
Full Page Colour £1275.00
Agency Commission: 10%
Mechanical Data: Trim Size: 272 x 190mm, Bleed Size: 303 x 216mm, Film: Digital
Copy instructions: Copy Date: 2 weeks prior to publication date
Average advertising content per issue: 50%
BUSINESS: TRAVEL & TOURISM

COACH TOURING
1623381U50-206

Editorial Address: Publishing House, Windrush, Ash Lane, Hopwood, Alvechurch, BIRMINGHAM, B48 7TS
Tel: 0121 445 6961 **Fax:** 0121 445 4436
Email: beau.medialtd@btconnect.com
Advertising Address: As above.
Email: beau.medialtd@btconnect.com
Web site: http://www.coachtouringlive.co.uk
Publisher: Beau Business Media Ltd
Date Established: 2003
Frequency: Monthly - Published in the last week of the cover month
Free to qualifying individuals
Circulation: 4,000 (Publisher's Statement)
Usual Pagination: 64
Editor: Hugh Cairns; **Advertising Manager:** Hugh Cairns
Summary of Content: Magazine covering news and views about the coach tourism industry at home and abroad including legislation, driver hours, repatriation and insurance.
Readership/Target Audience: Aimed at coach operators and tour managers.
ADVERTISING RATES:
Full Page Colour £1400.00
Mechanical Data: Type Area: 290 x 190mm, Bleed Size: 303 x 216mm, Trim Size: 297 x 210mm, Col Length: 290mm, Page Width: 190mm, Film: Digital
Copy instructions: Copy Date: 3 weeks prior to publication date
BUSINESS: TRAVEL & TOURISM

COACH TOURISM PROFESSIONAL
1656083U49B-82

Editorial Address: Suite 1, Cornerstone House, Stafford Park 13, TELFORD, TF3 3AZ **Tel:** 01952 204920
Fax: 01952 204929
Email: steve.rooney@busandcoach.com
Advertising Address: As above.
Email: charlotte.hicks@busandcoach.com
Web site: http://www.busandcoach.com
Publisher: Plum Publishing Limited

Date Established: 1998
Frequency: 24 issues yearly
Annual Sub.: £55.00
Circulation: 5,300 (Publisher's Statement)
Usual Pagination: 64
Editor: Steve Rooney; **News Editor:** Stewart Brown;
Advertising Manager: Charlotte Hicks; **Managing Editor:** Steve Rooney
Summary of Content: Magazine focusing on the coach tourism industry.
Readership/Target Audience: Aimed at coach operators and group organisers.
ADVERTISING RATES:
Full Page Colour £975.00
Mechanical Data: Type Area: 273 x 186mm, Bleed Size: 303 x 216mm, Col Length: 273mm, Page Width: 186mm, Col Widths (Display): 41mm, Film: Digital, Trim Size: 297 x 210mm, No. of Columns (Display): 4
BUSINESS: TRANSPORT: Bus & Coach Transport

COACH TOURS UK
39717U50-15_50

Editorial Address: The Publishing Centre, 1 Woolram Wygate, SPALDING, PE11 1NU **Tel:** 01775 711777
Fax: 01775 711737
Email: karen.wright@coachtoursuk.com
Advertising Address: As above.
Email: sales@coachtoursuk.com
Web site: http://www.coachtoursuk.com
Publisher: Glen-Holland Ltd
Date Established: 1990
Frequency: Monthly
Cover Price: Free
Circulation: 7,000 (Publisher's Statement)
Usual Pagination: 50
Editor: Karen Wright; **Advertising Manager:** Matthew Inglis;
Publisher: Steve Cole
Summary of Content: Magazine containing features on potential tour and entertainment venues in the UK and Europe.
Readership/Target Audience: Read by coach tour operators.
ADVERTISING RATES:
Full Page Mono £1167.00
Full Page Colour £1645.00
Agency Commission: 10%
Mechanical Data: Type Area: 270 x 190mm, Col Length: 270mm, Film: Digital, No. of Columns (Display): 4, Print Process: Sheet-fed litho, Bleed Size: 309 x 220mm, Trim Size: 297 x 210mm, Page Width: 190mm
Average advertising content per issue: 60%
BUSINESS: TRAVEL & TOURISM

COACHING AT WORK
1843468U14F-267

Editorial Address: 151 The Broadway, LONDON, SW19 1JQ **Tel:** 020 8612 6200 **Fax:** 020 8612 6201
Email: c.suri@cipd.co.uk
Web site: http://www.cipd.co.uk/coachingatwork
ISSN: 1748-9113
Publisher: CIPD
Date Established: 2005
Frequency: 6 issues yearly
Annual Sub.: £90.00
Editor: Chan Suri
Summary of Content: Magazine covering coaching theory and practical advice on coaching and mentoring.
Readership/Target Audience: Aimed at those involved in coaching.
BUSINESS: COMMERCE, INDUSTRY & MANAGEMENT: Training & Recruitment

COACHING VENUES & EXCURSIONS GUIDE
601114U50-15

Formerly: Coaching Venues & Excursions
Editorial Address: PO Box 5122, MILTON KEYNES, MK15 8ZP **Tel:** 01908 613323 **Fax:** 01908 210656
Email: cveg@groupleisure.com
Advertising Address: As above.
Email: sarah.d@yandellmedia.com
Web site: http://www.yandellmedia.com/cveg
Publisher: Yandell Publishing Limited
Date Established: 1999
Frequency: Annual - Published in October
Cover Price: £30.00
Free to qualifying individuals
Circulation: 3,500 (Publisher's Statement)
Usual Pagination: 144
Editor: Rob Yandell; **Advertising Manager:** Sarah Danyi;
Managing Editor: Rob Yandell; **Publisher:** Rob Yandell
Summary of Content: Publication covering destinations for leisure groups travelling by coach in England, Scotland, Wales, Ireland and mainland Europe. Includes news, case studies, reviews and advice for planning group travel visits.
Readership/Target Audience: Read by group travel organisers and coach tour operators.
ADVERTISING: Rates on application
BUSINESS: TRAVEL & TOURISM

COAL INTERNATIONAL
38233U30-30

Formerly: Colliery Guardian
Editorial Address: British Fields, Ollerton Road, Tuxford, NEWARK, NG22 0PQ **Tel:** 01777 871007 **Fax:** 01777 872271
Email: info@coalinternational.co.uk
Advertising Address: As above.
Email: sales@tradelinkpub.co.uk
Web site: http://www.coalinternational.co.uk
ISSN: 1357-6941
Publisher: Tradelink Publications Ltd
Date Established: 1858
Frequency: 6 issues yearly - Published in the last week of the 1st cover month
Annual Sub.: £120.00
Circulation: 6,000 (Publisher's Statement)
Editor: Trevor Barratt; **Managing Director:** Trevor Barratt
Summary of Content: Journal covering news, developments and quarrying information in the coal mining industry.
Readership/Target Audience: Read by technical directors and managers of coal mines.
ADVERTISING RATES:
Full Page Colour £2400.00
Agency Commission: 10%
Mechanical Data: Page Width: 185mm, Type Area: 265 x 185mm, Bleed Size: 303 x 216mm, Trim Size: 297 x 210mm, Col Length: 265mm, Film: Digital
Copy instructions: Copy Date: 1 week prior to publication date
Average advertising content per issue: 30%
BUSINESS: MINING & QUARRYING

COALTRANS INTERNATIONAL
40741U58-26_50

Editorial Address: Northbank House, 5 Bridge Street, LEATHERHEAD, KT22 8BL **Tel:** 01372 375511
Fax: 01372 370111
Email: awilkinson@wcnpublishing.com
Advertising Address: As above.
Email: gtilbury@wcnpublishing.com
Web site: http://www.coaltransinternational.com
ISSN: 1472-197X
Publisher: WCN Publishing
Date Established: 1979
Frequency: 6 issues yearly
Annual Sub.: £130.00
Circulation: 3,372 (Publisher's Statement)
Usual Pagination: 48
Editor: Anne Wilkinson; **Advertisement Director:** Simon Peskett
Summary of Content: Magazine covering the coal chain from mine-head to end user, including coal trading, transportation and handling. Includes the latest developments in clean coal technology.
Readership/Target Audience: Read by coal end-users, coal producers, traders, institutions, terminal operators and equipment suppliers worldwide.
ADVERTISING RATES:
Full Page Colour £2255.00
Agency Commission: 10%
Mechanical Data: Bleed Size: 303 x 216mm, Film: Digital, Trim Size: 297 x 210mm
Copy instructions: Copy Date: 15th of the month prior to publication date
BUSINESS: ENERGY, FUEL & NUCLEAR

COATINGS COMET
1840540U16B-232

Editorial Address: 14 Castle Mews, High Street, HAMPTON, TW12 2NP **Tel:** 020 8487 0807
Fax: 020 8487 0801
Email: g.thisdell@pra-world.com
Web site: http://www.pra-world.com
Publisher: Paint Research Association
Date Established: 1992
Frequency: 10 issues yearly
Annual Sub.: £445.00
Circulation: 300 (Publisher's Statement)
Usual Pagination: 32
Editor: Glenda Thisdell
Summary of Content: Magazine covering paint, coatings and raw materials for paints and coating manufacturers.
Readership/Target Audience: Aimed at paint and coating manufacturers and the suppliers in the chemical industry.
ADVERTISING: No Advertising taken
BUSINESS: DECORATING & PAINT: Paint - Technical Manufacture

CODICIL
1846562U1P-286

Editorial Address: 6-14 Underwood Street, LONDON, N1 7JQ **Tel:** 020 7324 2322 **Fax:** 020 7324 8238
Email: cdann@caritasdata.co.uk
Publisher: Waterlow
Frequency: Quarterly
Free to qualifying individuals
Annual Sub.: £60.00
Circulation: 5,000 (Publisher's Statement)
Editor: Clarissa Dann

Summary of Content: Legacy magazine from SME and FORD.
Readership/Target Audience: Aimed at wills and trusts probate solicitors, legacy administrators, legacy fund raisers and undertakers.
BUSINESS: FINANCE & ECONOMICS: Fundraising

COFFEE AND COCOA INTERNATIONAL
38041U22R-30

Editorial Address: Office 8, Unit 1-2 Wyvern Estate, Beverley Way, NEW MALDEN, KT3 4PH **Tel:** 020 8949 0088
Fax: 020 8949 0160
Email: coffeemagazine@yahoo.co.uk
Advertising Address: As above.
Email: andrew@siemex.biz
Web site: http://www.coffeeandcocoa.net
ISSN: 0262-5938
Publisher: Siemex International Ltd
Date Established: 1974
Frequency: 6 issues yearly - Published in the 3rd week of the month prior to 1st cover month
Annual Sub.: £110.00
Circulation: 7,590 (ABC 01/01/2008 to 31/12/2008)
Usual Pagination: 52
Editor: David Foxwell; **Advertising Manager:** Andrew Kingsley
Summary of Content: Magazine containing international coffee and cocoa news, ICO and ICCO reports and articles on shipping, warehousing, processing, plant and machinery, profiles and trade events.
Readership/Target Audience: Aimed at those within the international coffee and cocoa trade.
ADVERTISING RATES:
Full Page Mono £2990.00
Full Page Colour £4150.00
Agency Commission: 10%
Mechanical Data: Trim Size: 297 x 210mm, Page Width: 185mm, Bleed Size: 303 x 216mm, Type Area: 265 x 185mm, Col Length: 265mm, Film: Digital
Copy instructions: Copy Date: 5th of the month prior to publication date
BUSINESS: FOOD: Food Related

COIL WINDING INTERNATIONAL AND ELECTRICAL INSULATION MAGAZINE
37338U18A-50

Editorial Address: East by North, Tudor Road, Newton, Alderney, GUERNSEY, GY9 3XP **Tel:** 01481 823292
Fax: 01202 736018
Email: office@coilwinding.e7even.com
Advertising Address: As above. **Tel:** 01202 743906
Email: marketing@coilwinding.e7even.com
Web site: http://www.coilwindingmagazine.com
Publisher: Coil Winding International Ltd
Date Established: 1976
Frequency: 6 issues yearly
Circulation: 8,000 (Publisher's Statement)
Usual Pagination: 40
Editor: Rachel Gale; **Advertising Manager:** Rachel Gale
Summary of Content: Magazine covering news and information on electric coil, transformer and electric motor production and repair.
Readership/Target Audience: Read by design and production engineers in the electrical and electronic industries.
ADVERTISING RATES:
Full Page Colour EUR1348.00
Agency Commission: 10%
Mechanical Data: Col Length: 273mm, Page Width: 185mm, Type Area: 273 x 185mm, Bleed Size: 305 x 214mm, Trim Size: 297 x 210mm, Film: Digital
BUSINESS: ELECTRONICS

COINSLOT INTERNATIONAL
41465U64A-130

Editorial Address: 50 Upper North Street, BRIGHTON, BN1 3FH **Tel:** 01204 438377 **Fax:** 01273 204827
Email: cm@sjc.co.uk
Advertising Address: Bolton Technology Exchange, 33 Queensbrook, BOLTON, BL1 4AY **Tel:** 01204 396397
Fax: 01204 392748
Email: jsullivan@gbmedia.eu
Web site: http://www.coinslot.co.uk
Publisher: ATE / Clarion Events
Frequency: Weekly
Annual Sub.: £79.00
Circulation: 4,300 (Publisher's Statement)
Usual Pagination: 26
Editor: Chris Murphy; **Advertising Manager:** John Sullivan;
Managing Editor: Ken Scott
Summary of Content: Journal focusing on coin-operated machines for amusement arcades, pubs and clubs. Also covers theme parks, bingo halls, casinos, licensed betting, Internet gaming and visitor attractions.
Readership/Target Audience: Read by members of the coin-operated amusement industry including manufacturers, operators and distributors.

Business Magazines

ADVERTISING RATES:
Full Page Colour £1460.00
Agency Commission: 10%
Mechanical Data: Trim Size: 340 x 240mm, Type Area: 312 x 219mm, Col Length: 312mm, Bleed Size: 346 x 246mm, No. of Columns (Display): 6, Col Widths (Display): 34mm, Page Width: 219mm, Film: Digital
Copy instructions: Copy Date: Thursday prior to publication date
Average advertising content per issue: 60%
BUSINESS: OTHER CLASSIFICATIONS: Amusement Trade

COLD CHAIN NEWS
35765U3C-25
Editorial Address: 7 Ship Street Gardens, BRIGHTON, BN1 1AJ **Tel:** 07796 297350
Email: johanna.thomson@coldchainnews.com
Advertising Address: As above. **Tel:** 01273 326569
Email: johanna.thomson@coldchainnews.com
Publisher: Cold Chain News Limited
Date Established: 1994
Frequency: 11 issues yearly - Published 3rd week of cover month
Annual Sub.: £48.00
Circulation: 4,500 (Publisher's Statement)
Usual Pagination: 16
Editor: Johanna Thomson; **Managing Director:** Johanna Thomson; **Advertising Manager:** Johanna Thomson
Summary of Content: Journal focusing on the manufacture and operation of specialist equipment to store, transport and distribute temperature-sensitive products.
Readership/Target Audience: Read by the manufacturers and operators of temperature sensitive equipment.
ADVERTISING RATES:
Full Page Mono £1000.00
Full Page Colour £1500.00
Agency Commission: 10%
Mechanical Data: Page Width: 275mm, Type Area: 390 x 275mm, Bleed Size: 430 x 307mm, Trim Size: 420 x 297mm, Col Length: 390mm, No. of Columns (Display): 4, Film: Positive, right reading, emulsion side down, Print Process: Offset litho
Average advertising content per issue: 50%
Supplement(s): Cold Store News - 3xY
BUSINESS: HEATING & VENTILATION: Refrigeration & Ventilation

COLORATION TECHNOLOGY
1685485U55-9015
Editorial Address: PO Box 244, Perkin House, 82 Grattan Road, BRADFORD, BD1 2JB **Tel:** 01274 725138
Fax: 01274 392888
Email: editorial@sdc.org.uk
Web site: http://www.sdc.org.uk
ISSN: 1472-3581
Publisher: Society of Dyers & Colourists
Date Established: 1884
Frequency: 6 issues yearly
Circulation: 2,000 (Publisher's Statement)
Editor: Carmel McNamara
Summary of Content: Journal focusing on dyes, pigments, colour measurements and colour substrates.
Readership/Target Audience: Aimed at colour scientists.
ADVERTISING: No Advertising taken
BUSINESS: APPLIED SCIENCE & LABORATORIES

THE COLUMN
40152U56A-59_20
Editorial Address: The Cottage, Hornsea Road, Atwick, DRIFFIELD, YO25 8DG **Tel:** 01964 534376
Email: js1sda@aol.com
Advertising Address: Linden Barns, Greens Norton Road, TOWCESTER, NN12 8AW **Tel:** 01327 358855
Email: nationalbackexch@btconnect.com
ISSN: 1461-0922
Publisher: National Back Exchange
Date Established: 1988
Frequency: 3 issues yearly
Cover Price: £10.00
Free to qualifying individuals
Circulation: 1,500 (Publisher's Statement)
Usual Pagination: 36
Editor: Jacqui Smith; **Advertising Manager:** Pat Lee
Summary of Content: Magazine covering back care issues and advice for the prevention of work related, musculoskeletal problems.
Readership/Target Audience: Aimed at professionals in ergonomics, physiotherapy, occupational health and nursing.
ADVERTISING: Rates on application
Copy instructions: Copy Date: 1 month prior to publication date
BUSINESS: HEALTH & MEDICAL

COMBAT AND SURVIVAL MAGAZINE
38856U40-32
Editorial Address: Revenue Chambers, St. Peters Street, HUDDERSFIELD, HD1 1DL **Tel:** 01484 435011
Fax: 01484 422177
Email: martialartsltd@btconnect.com
Advertising Address: As above.
Email: martialartsltd@btconnect.com
Web site: http://www.combatandsurvival.com
ISSN: 0955-9841
Publisher: MAI Publications
Date Established: 1989
Frequency: Monthly
Cover Price: £3.50
Circulation: 30,000 (Publisher's Statement)
Usual Pagination: 76
Editor: Bob Morrison; **Managing Director:** Roy Jessop
Summary of Content: Magazine containing the latest news and feature articles on military issues and products.
Readership/Target Audience: Aimed at serving soldiers, TAs, cadets, military enthusiasts and survivalists.
ADVERTISING RATES:
Full Page Mono £295.00
Full Page Colour £600.00
Agency Commission: 10%
Mechanical Data: Type Area: 271 x 186mm, Film: Positive, right reading, emulsion side down. Digital, Col Length: 271mm, Bleed Size: 303 x 216mm, Trim Size: 297 x 210mm, No. of Columns (Display): 3, Page Width: 186mm
Copy instructions: Copy Date: 10 weeks prior to publication date
Average advertising content per issue: 40%
BUSINESS: DEFENCE

COMMERCE & INDUSTRY
41329U63B-1065
Editorial Address: Upper Spring Street, GRIMSBY, DN31 1QP **Tel:** 01472 359036 **Fax:** 01472 599910
Email: editor@waltonspublications.com
Advertising Address: As above. **Tel:** 01472 359037
Email: ci@waltonspublications.com
Web site: http://www.commerceandindustryonline.co.uk
Publisher: W.M. Walton & Co Ltd
Date Established: 1990
Frequency: 10 issues yearly
Cover Price: Free
Circulation: 12,500 (Publisher's Statement)
Usual Pagination: 50
Editor: Nicole Tinmurth; **Managing Director:** T. Clive Aspinall; **Advertising Manager:** Hayley Jane Drinkell
Summary of Content: Journal featuring news of local company expansions, promotions and buy-outs. Also covers new products, legislative and parliamentary matters, EEC news, hotel and conference facilities and motoring.
Readership/Target Audience: Read by members of Chamber, company personnel and members of the public in Lincolnshire, Humberside, South Yorkshire and West Yorkshire.
ADVERTISING RATES:
Full Page Mono £1358.00
Full Page Colour £1703.00
Agency Commission: 10%
Mechanical Data: Col Length: 256mm, Film: Digital, Type Area: 256 x 192mm, Page Width: 192mm
BUSINESS: REGIONAL BUSINESS: Regional Business English Counties

COMMERCE GM
1775041U63B-2579
Editorial Address: Portland Buildings, 127-129 Portland Street, MANCHESTER, M1 4PZ **Tel:** 0161 236 2782
Email: sharpley@imprintpub.co.uk
Advertising Address: As above.
Email: deborah@imprintpub.co.uk
Web site: http://www.excelpublishing.co.uk
Publisher: Excel Publishing Company Ltd
Date Established: 2006
Frequency: 6 issues yearly - Published in the 1st week of the 1st cover month
Cover Price: £2.20
Free to qualifying individuals
Annual Sub.: £20.00
Circulation: 6,500 (Publisher's Statement)
Usual Pagination: 48
Editor: Danielle Regan
Summary of Content: Magazine containing interviews with leading business, academic and political figures, news and business updates.
Readership/Target Audience: Aimed at small and medium-sized businesses and large corporate businesses in the Greater Manchester area.
ADVERTISING RATES:
Full Page Colour £2000.00
Mechanical Data: Type Area: 300 x 230mm, Bleed Size: 346 x 251mm, Trim Size: 340 x 245mm, Col Length: 300mm, Page Width: 230mm, Film: Positive, right reading, emulsion side down. Digital, Screen: 60 lpc

Copy instructions: Copy Date: 2 weeks prior to publication date
BUSINESS: REGIONAL BUSINESS: Regional Business English Counties

COMMERCIAL CRIME INTERNATIONAL
39898U54C-26_50
Editorial Address: Cinnabar Wharf, 26 Wapping High Street, LONDON, E1W 1NG **Tel:** 020 7423 6960
Fax: 020 7423 6961
Email: ajholder@gmail.com
Web site: http://www.icc-ccs.org
ISSN: 0112-2710
Publisher: Commercial Crime Services Ltd
Date Established: 1982
Frequency: Monthly
Annual Sub.: £95.00
Circulation: 1,100 (Publisher's Statement)
Usual Pagination: 12
Editor: Andy Holder; **Publisher:** Pottengal Mukundan
Summary of Content: Publication that reports on all aspects of commercial crime, from piracy, insurance frauds, to bank fraud, counterfeiting and computer crime.
Readership/Target Audience: Aimed at worldwide members of the International Maritime Bureau, Commercial Crime Bureau and Counterfeiting Intelligence Bureau.
ADVERTISING: No Advertising taken
BUSINESS: SAFETY & SECURITY: Security

COMMERCIAL FOCUS
35606U2B-22
Formerly: Commercial Update
Editorial Address: St. Andrew's House, St. Andrew Street, LONDON, EC4A 3AY **Tel:** 020 7632 7400
Email: justin_fenton@newspapersoc.org.uk
Web site: http://www.newspapersoc.org.uk
Publisher: The Newspaper Society
Frequency: Quarterly
Free to qualifying individuals
Circulation: 600 (Publisher's Statement)
Editor: Justin Fenton
Summary of Content: Electronic newsletter covering the local and regional newspaper industry. Contains industry news, ideas, information on advertising ideas, newspaper sales and promotions managers, marketing managers and new media managers.
Readership/Target Audience: Aimed at advertising managers, newspaper sales and promotions managers, marketing managers and new media managers.
ADVERTISING: Rates on application
BUSINESS: COMMUNICATIONS, ADVERTISING & MARKETING: Press

THE COMMERCIAL GREENHOUSE GROWER
38114U26C-13
Editorial Address: Lion House, Church Street, MAIDSTONE, ME14 1EN **Tel:** 01622 695656
Fax: 01622 663733
Email: green@actpub.co.uk
Advertising Address: As above.
Email: jill@actpub.co.uk
Web site: http://www.actpub.co.uk
ISSN: 1355-4301
Publisher: ACT Publishing
Date Established: 1994
Frequency: Monthly - Published in the 3rd week of the cover month
Free to qualifying individuals
Annual Sub.: £30.00
Circulation: 4,300 (Publisher's Statement)
Usual Pagination: 36
Editor: Jill Williams; **Managing Director:** John Jarrett
Summary of Content: Magazine covering news, products, ideas and advice on flowers, plants and salads.
Readership/Target Audience: Aimed at professional growers.
ADVERTISING RATES:
Full Page Mono £1148.00
Full Page Colour £1840.00
Agency Commission: 10%
Mechanical Data: Type Area: 257 x 190mm, Col Length: 257mm, Col Widths (Display): 41mm, Film: Digital, No. of Columns (Display): 4, Bleed Size: 303 x 216mm, Trim Size: 297 x 210mm, Page Width: 190mm, Print Process: Sheet-fed litho
Copy instructions: Copy Date: 2 weeks prior to publication date
Average advertising content per issue: 35%
BUSINESS: GARDEN TRADE

COMMERCIAL INTERIORS
1825898U4B-186
Editorial Address: 4th Floor, Geneva House, Park Road, PETERBOROUGH, PE1 2UX **Tel:** 01733 756555
Fax: 01733 760505
Email: ci@onecoms.co.uk

Advertising Address: As above.
Email: stacey.channing@onecoms.co.uk
Web site: http://www.onecoms.co.uk
Publisher: Media One Communications Ltd.
Date Established: 2007
Frequency: 6 issues yearly - Published around the middle of the cover month
Circulation: 9,000 (Publisher's Statement)
Editor: Jade Tilley
Summary of Content: Journal featuring the latest commercial interior product lines and designs from around the world, industry news and case studies.
Readership/Target Audience: Aimed at designers and specifiers of commercial interiors from hotels and restaurants to offices and bars.
ADVERTISING RATES:
Full Page Mono £490.00
Full Page Colour £565.00
Agency Commission: 10%
Mechanical Data: Type Area: 280 x 190mm, Bleed Size: 303 x 216mm, Trim Size: 297 x 210mm, Film: Digital
Copy instructions: Copy Date: 3 weeks prior to publication date
BUSINESS: ARCHITECTURE & BUILDING: Interior Design & Flooring

COMMERCIAL LEASES
39133U44-232
Editorial Address: Telephone House, 69-77 Paul Street, LONDON, EC2A 4LQ **Tel:** 020 7017 6762
Fax: 020 7017 5274
Email: jessica.westwood@informa.com
Web site: http://www.informalaw.com
ISSN: 0951-0628
Publisher: Informa PLC
Frequency: 10 issues yearly
Editor: Jessica Westwood
Summary of Content: Newsletter covering the latest developments in landlord and tenant law.
Readership/Target Audience: Aimed at property and investment managers.
ADVERTISING: No Advertising taken
BUSINESS: LEGAL

COMMERCIAL MOTOR
39662U49D-40
Editorial Address: Quadrant House, The Quadrant, SUTTON, SM2 5AS **Tel:** 020 8652 3500 **Fax:** 020 8652 8971
Email: commercial.motor@rbi.co.uk
Advertising Address: As above. **Fax:** 020 8652 8960
Email: david.john.smith@rbi.co.uk
Web site: http://www.roadtransportmedia.co.uk
Publisher: Reed Business Information
Date Established: 1905
Frequency: Weekly
Annual Sub.: £97.00
Circulation: 15,918 (ABC 01/01/2008 to 31/12/2008)
Editor: Justin Stanton; **News Editor:** Christopher Walton; **Publisher:** Roger Williams
Summary of Content: Journal covering all aspects of the road transport industry with an emphasis on product reporting and regular vehicle road tests.
Readership/Target Audience: Aimed at commercial vehicle purchasing decision makers across all fleet sites who operate vehicles of 3.5 tonnes and above.
ADVERTISING RATES:
Full Page Colour £4000.00
Agency Commission: 10%
Mechanical Data: Type Area: 275 x 190mm, Film: Digital, Bleed Size: 303 x 229mm, Trim Size: 297 x 223mm, Col Length: 275mm, Page Width: 190mm
Copy instructions: Copy Date: 2 weeks prior to publication date
Average advertising content per issue: 60%
BUSINESS: TRANSPORT: Commercial Vehicles

COMMERCIAL MOVES
1902864U1E-409
Editorial Address: Talbot Hays Farm, WINCHFIELD, RG27 8BZ **Tel:** 01252 843566 **Fax:** 01252 843556
Email: rosalind.renshaw@googlemail.com
Publisher: The National Association of Estate Agents
Frequency: Quarterly
Editor: Rosalind Renshaw
Summary of Content: Magazine for the National Federation of Property Professionals covering the commercial property sector.
Readership/Target Audience: Aimed at those with an interest in the commercial property sector.
BUSINESS: FINANCE & ECONOMICS: Property

COMMERCIAL PROPERTY MONTHLY
35185U1E-100
Editorial Address: Challenge House, 616 Mitcham Road, CROYDON, CR9 3AU **Tel:** 020 8683 6422
Tel: 020 8683 6426
Email: editorial@commercialpropertymonthly.com

Advertising Address: As above.
Email: advertising@commercialpropertymonthly.com
Web site: http://www.commercialpropertymonthly.com
Publisher: MMP Fulfilment
Date Established: 1979
Frequency: 6 issues yearly
Free to qualifying individuals
Annual Sub.: £89.00
Circulation: 20,000 (Publisher's Statement)
Usual Pagination: 72
Editor: Kevin Phillips; **Features Editor:** Kevin Phillips;
Advertising Director: Kevin Philips
Summary of Content: Magazine covering retail, industrial and commercial property news.
Readership/Target Audience: Aimed at estate agents dealing with commercial properties.
ADVERTISING RATES:
Full Page Mono £985.00
Full Page Colour £1570.00
Agency Commission: 10%
Mechanical Data: Film: Digital, Type Area: 274 x 194mm, Col Length: 274mm, Bleed Size: 303 x 216mm, Page Width: 194mm, Trim Size: 297 x 210mm
Copy instructions: Copy Date: 1 week prior to publication date
Average advertising content per issue: 50%
BUSINESS: FINANCE & ECONOMICS: Property

COMMERCIAL PROPERTY REGISTER
1697071U1E-389
Editorial Address: Woodlands Annexe, 79 High Street, GREENHITHE, DA9 9RD **Tel:** 01322 387555
Fax: 01322 385444
Email: clive@eliotvale.fsnet.co.uk
Advertising Address: As above.
Email: jane@mapub.co.uk
Web site: http://www.martinaustinpublishing.co.uk
Publisher: Martin Austen Publishing Ltd
Frequency: 30 issues yearly
Cover Price: Free
Circulation: 120,000 (Publisher's Statement)
Editor: Clive Branson; **Publisher:** Charlie Potter
Summary of Content: Magazine focusing on the marketing of commercial, office and industrial premises.
Readership/Target Audience: Aimed at property agents and developers.
ADVERTISING RATES:
Full Page Colour £1225.00
Agency Commission: 10%
Mechanical Data: Type Area: 275 x 188mm, Bleed Size: 303 x 216mm, Trim Size: 297 x 210mm, Col Length: 275mm, Page Width: 188mm, Film: Digital
Editions:
Commercial Property Register Central London
Commercial Property Register Kent, Surrey & Essex
Commercial Property Register Midlands
Commercial Property Register North West
Commercial Property Register Northern Home Counties
Commercial Property Register Scotland
Commercial Property Register South Coast Central
Commercial Property Register South West
Commercial Property Register Thames Valley & Heathrow
Commercial Property Register Yorkshire
BUSINESS: FINANCE & ECONOMICS: Property

COMMERCIAL VEHICLE WORKSHOP
1666659U49D-361
Editorial Address: Regal House, Regal Way, WATFORD, WD24 4YF **Tel:** 01923 237799 **Fax:** 01923 246901
Email: cvw@hamerville.co.uk
Advertising Address: As above.
Email: cvwsales@hamerville.co.uk
Web site: http://www.hamerville-magazines.co.uk
Publisher: Hamerville Magazines Ltd
Date Established: 2004
Frequency: 11 issues yearly - Published in the last week of the month prior to the cover month
Cover Price: Free
Circulation: 10,013 (ABC 01/07/2008 to 30/06/2009)
Usual Pagination: 48
Editor: Sharon Clancy; **Advertising Manager:** Robert Gilham
Summary of Content: Magazine covering the commercial vehicle aftermarket. Includes articles on safety, product tests and training.
Readership/Target Audience: Aimed at independent repair workshops and in-house fleet workshops.
ADVERTISING RATES:
Full Page Colour £1990.00
Agency Commission: 10%
Mechanical Data: Type Area: 255 x 180mm, Col Length: 255mm, Page Width: 180mm, Film: Digital
Copy instructions: Copy Date: 4 weeks prior to publication date
Average advertising content per issue: 40%
BUSINESS: TRANSPORT: Commercial Vehicles

COMMODITIES NOW
35385U1L-3
Editorial Address: 39 Thurloe Place, LONDON, SW7 2HP
Tel: 020 7584 0000
Email: gish@commodities-now.com
Advertising Address: As above. **Fax:** 020 7584 0022
Email: james@commodities-now.com
Web site: http://www.commodities-now.com
ISSN: 1365-6953
Publisher: Isherwood Production
Date Established: 1997
Frequency: Quarterly
Free to qualifying individuals
Annual Sub.: £120.00
Circulation: 10,000 (Publisher's Statement)
Editor: Guy Isherwood
Summary of Content: Magazine providing analysis and information on trends in the commodities markets.
Readership/Target Audience: Read by commodities specialists.
ADVERTISING RATES:
Full Page Colour £3950.00
Agency Commission: 15%
Mechanical Data: Film: Digital, Type Area: 283 x 196mm, Trim Size: 297 x 210mm, Bleed Size: 303 x 216mm, Page Width: 196mm, Col Length: 283mm
Copy instructions: Copy Date: 3 weeks prior to publication date
BUSINESS: FINANCE & ECONOMICS: Commodities

COMMON LAW WORLD REVIEW
39122U44-235
Formerly: The Anglo American Law Review
Editorial Address: Bridge House, DALBY, IM5 3BP
Tel: 01624 844056 **Fax:** 01624 845043
Email: mlw@vathek.com
Advertising Address: As above.
Email: mlw@vathek.com
Web site: http://www.vathek.com
ISSN: 1473-7795
Publisher: Vathek Publishing
Date Established: 1971
Frequency: Quarterly
Annual Sub.: £168.00
Circulation: 400 (Publisher's Statement)
Usual Pagination: 108
Editor: Mairwen Lloyd-Williams; **Managing Director:** Mairwen Lloyd-Williams; **Advertising Manager:** Mairwen Lloyd-Williams; **Publisher:** Mairwen Lloyd-Williams
Summary of Content: Journal containing comment and analysis of developments in the common law world.
Readership/Target Audience: Read by academic lawyers.
ADVERTISING RATES:
Full Page Mono £100.00
Agency Commission: 15%
Mechanical Data: Type Area: 190 x 100mm, Col Length: 190mm, Trim Size: 243 x 165mm, Page Width: 100mm, Film: Digital
Average advertising content per issue: 5%
BUSINESS: LEGAL

COMMONWEALTH BROADCASTER
39102U43B-47
Editorial Address: 17 Fleet Street, LONDON, EC4Y 1AA
Tel: 020 7583 5550 **Fax:** 020 7583 5549
Email: cba@ba.org.uk
Advertising Address: Commonwealth Publications, The Studios, Portsmouth Road, THAMES DITTON, KT7 0SY
Tel: 020 8339 0081 **Fax:** 020 8181 6459
Email: broadcast@london.com
Web site: http://www.cba.org.uk
Publisher: Commonwealth Broadcasting Association
Date Established: 1960
Frequency: Quarterly
Free to qualifying individuals
Annual Sub.: £41.00
Circulation: 3,000 (Publisher's Statement)
Usual Pagination: 48
Editor: Elizabeth Smith; **Advertising Manager:** Andy Morgan
Summary of Content: Official journal of the Commonwealth Broadcasting Association, including news of editorial and technical developments in the broadcasting world.
Readership/Target Audience: Read by members of the CBA and leading broadcasting executives and engineers.
ADVERTISING RATES:
Full Page Colour £1195.00
Agency Commission: 10%
Mechanical Data: Trim Size: 297 x 210mm, Film: Digital, Type Area: 254 x 178mm, Page Width: 254mm, Col Length: 178mm
Copy instructions: Copy Date: 4 weeks prior to publication date
Average advertising content per issue: 15%
BUSINESS: ELECTRICAL RETAIL TRADE: Radio & Hi-Fi

Section 4 (b) Business Magazines

COMMS BUSINESS
600993U18B-473

Editorial Address: White House, Commercial Road, TUNBRIDGE WELLS, TN1 2RR **Tel:** 01892 538348
Email: ianh@cbmagazine.co.uk
Advertising Address: As above. **Fax:** 01892 515724
Email: mat@cbmagazine.co.uk
Web site: http://www.cbmagazine.co.uk
Publisher: Miles Publishing Ltd
Date Established: 1999
Frequency: Monthly - Published at the beginning of the 3rd week of the month prior to publication date
Cover Price: Free
Circulation: 11,115 (ABC 01/01/2008 to 31/12/2008)
Usual Pagination: 80
Editor: Ian Hunter; **Publisher:** Miles Bossom
Summary of Content: Magazine covering essential news and analysis, themed features, opinion pieces, interviews, appointments and contract news.
Readership/Target Audience: Aimed at manufacturers, distributors, dealers and resellers.
ADVERTISING RATES:
Full Page Colour £3250.00
Agency Commission: 10%
Mechanical Data: Type Area: 270 x 185mm, Col Length: 270mm, Trim Size: 297 x 210mm, Bleed Size: 303 x 216mm, Film: Positive, right reading, emulsion side down. Digital
Copy instructions: Copy Date: 2 weeks prior to publication date
BUSINESS: ELECTRONICS: Telecommunications

COMMS DEALER
37428U18B-475

Editorial Address: 3rd Floor, Armstrong House, 38 Market Square, UXBRIDGE, UB8 1TG **Tel:** 01895 421111
Fax: 01895 431252
Email: sgilroy@bpl-business.com
Advertising Address: As above.
Email: mobrien@bpl-business.com
Web site: http://www.comms-dealer.com
ISSN: 1366-5243
Publisher: Business Publications UK Ltd
Date Established: 1995
Frequency: Monthly - Published on the 1st of the cover month
Annual Sub.: £65.00
Circulation: 11,735 (ABC 01/01/2008 to 31/12/2008)
Usual Pagination: 72
Editor: Stuart Gilroy; **Advertising Manager:** Michael O'Brien; **Publisher:** Nigel Sergent
Summary of Content: Magazine covering industry news and information on telecommunications products.
Readership/Target Audience: Aimed at dealers and resellers in the telecommunications industry.
ADVERTISING RATES:
Full Page Colour £3710.00
Agency Commission: 10%
Mechanical Data: Page Width: 266mm, Film: Digital, Type Area: 380 x 266mm, Bleed Size: 426 x 303mm, Trim Size: 420 x 297mm, Col Length: 380mm
Copy instructions: Copy Date: 2 weeks prior to publication date
Average advertising content per issue: 60%
BUSINESS: ELECTRONICS: Telecommunications

COMMUNICATE MAGAZINE
1911508U2A-737

Editorial Address: 26-32 Voltaire Road, LONDON, SW4 6DH **Tel:** 020 7498 7008
Email: neil.gibbons@communicatemagazine.co.uk
Web site: http://www.communicatemagazine.co.uk
Publisher: Cravenhill Publishing
Frequency: Monthly
Annual Sub.: £90.00
Circulation: 11,000 (Publisher's Statement)
Editor: Neil Gibbons; **Publisher:** Andrew Thomas
Summary of Content: Magazine helping organisations present a consistent and coherent image to all stakeholders including the media, investors, employees, regulators and the communities in which they operate.
Readership/Target Audience: Aimed at professionals charged with the responsibility of their company's corporate communications.
ADVERTISING: Rates on application
BUSINESS: COMMUNICATIONS, ADVERTISING & MARKETING

COMMUNICATIONS AFRICA
37431U18B-540

Editorial Address: University House, 11-13 Lower Grosvenor Place, LONDON, SW1W 0EX **Tel:** 020 7834 7676
Fax: 020 7973 0076
Email: andrew.croft@alaincharles.com
Advertising Address: As above.
Email: stephen.thomas@alaincharles.com
Web site: http://www.alaincharles.com
ISSN: 0962-3841
Publisher: Alain Charles Publishing Ltd
Frequency: 6 issues yearly - Published around the middle of the 2nd cover month

---

Cover Price: $12.50
Annual Sub.: $78.00
Circulation: 6,198 (ABC 01/01/2008 to 31/12/2008)
Usual Pagination: 72
Editor: Andrew Croft; **Managing Director:** Nick Fordham;
Managing Editor: Andrew Croft; **Publisher:** Derek Fordham
Summary of Content: Magazine covering all aspects of communications technology relevant to Africa.
Language(s): English; French
Readership/Target Audience: Aimed at professionals in Africa.
ADVERTISING RATES:
Full Page Mono EUR3550.00
Full Page Colour EUR5220.00
Agency Commission: 15%
Mechanical Data: Type Area: 266 x 180mm, Bleed Size: 298 x 214mm, Trim Size: 292 x 208mm, Col Length: 266mm, Film: Digital, Page Width: 180mm
Copy instructions: Copy Date: 2 weeks prior to publication date
BUSINESS: ELECTRONICS: Telecommunications

COMMUNICATIONS LAW
39243U44-1861

Formerly: Tolley's Communications Law
Editorial Address: Maxwelton House, 41-43 Boltro Road, HAYWARDS HEATH, RH16 1BJ **Tel:** 01444 416119
Fax: 01444 440426
Web site: http://www.tottelpublishing.com
ISSN: 1746-7616
Publisher: Tottel Publishing
Date Established: 1996
Frequency: 6 issues yearly
Usual Pagination: 38
Editor: Linda Whittle
Summary of Content: Journal providing information on the law relating to information technology, communications and the entertainment industry.
Readership/Target Audience: Aimed at lawyers, academics and communications professionals.
ADVERTISING: No Advertising taken
BUSINESS: LEGAL

COMMUNICATOR
35737U2R-106

Editorial Address: Airport House, Purley Way, CROYDON, CR0 0XZ **Tel:** 020 8253 4506 **Fax:** 020 8253 4510
Email: journal.editor@istc.org.uk
Advertising Address: Tou-can Marketing, The Holly, 42 Heath Hill Road South, CROWTHORNE, RG45 7BW
Tel: 01344 466600 **Fax:** 01344 466601
Email: felicity@tou-can.co.uk
Web site: http://www.istc.org.uk/publications/communicator.htm
ISSN: 0953-3699
Publisher: ISTC
Date Established: 1968
Frequency: Quarterly
Free to qualifying individuals
Annual Sub.: £37.00
Circulation: 2,000 (Publisher's Statement)
Usual Pagination: 52
Editor: Andrew Marlow; **Advertising Manager:** Felicity Davie
Summary of Content: Journal of the Institute of Scientific and Technical Communicators (ISTC). Contains news and features of interest to authors, managers, consultants, educators, editors, illustrators and translators, involved in publishing technical and scientific information in all media.
Readership/Target Audience: Read by members of the ISTC, other related organisations and subscribers. Key specializations for readers are engineering, information technology, aerospace, defence, manufacturing, science, education, energy and banking/finance.
ADVERTISING RATES:
Full Page Mono £660.00
Full Page Colour £690.00
Mechanical Data: Type Area: 276 x 186mm, Bleed Size: 305 x 218mm, Trim Size: 297 x 210mm, Film: Digital, Col Length: 276mm, Page Width: 186mm
Copy instructions: Copy Date: 8 weeks prior to publication date
BUSINESS: COMMUNICATIONS, ADVERTISING & MARKETING: Communications Related

COMMUNICATORS
1614124U2R-182

Formerly: Communicator
Editorial Address: 4 Sandford Close, CLEVEDON, BS21 7UZ **Tel:** 01275 871925
Email: news@cib.uk
Advertising Address: As above.
Email: steve@knighttrain.co.uk
Web site: http://www.cib.uk.com
ISSN: 1741-2315
Publisher: British Association of Communicators in Business
Date Established: 2003
Frequency: 10 issues yearly
Free to qualifying individuals

Circulation: 1,400 (Publisher's Statement)
Usual Pagination: 20
Editor: Steve Knight; **Advertising Manager:** Steve Knight; **Managing Editor:** Kathie Jones
Summary of Content: Journal of the British Association of Communicators in Business, covering news about the communications industry.
Readership/Target Audience: Aimed at members and business communicators.
ADVERTISING RATES:
Full Page Mono £500.00
Full Page Colour £650.00
Mechanical Data: Type Area: 272 x 186mm, Col Length: 272mm, Page Width: 186mm, Film: Positive, right reading, emulsion side down. Digital, Print Process: Sheet-fed litho
Copy instructions: Copy Date: 10th of the month prior to publication date
BUSINESS: COMMUNICATIONS, ADVERTISING & MARKETING: Communications Related

COMMUNIQUÉ
1606315U37-403

Editorial Address: Vincent House, Vincent Lane, DORKING, RH4 3JD **Tel:** 01306 740777 **Fax:** 01306 741069
Email: kflack@pmlive.com
Advertising Address: As above.
Email: croy@pmlive.com
Web site: http://www.pmlive.com
Publisher: P M Group
Date Established: 1998
Frequency: Half-yearly - Published in June and December
Annual Sub.: £100.00
Circulation: 4,500 (Publisher's Statement)
Usual Pagination: 100
Editor: Kate Flack
Summary of Content: Magazine covering pharmaceutical PR and medical education, including professional relations, NICE and NHS, patient relations, DTC government relations and issues management.
Readership/Target Audience: Aimed at pharmaceutical manufacturers and marketers.
ADVERTISING RATES:
Full Page Colour £3100.00
Agency Commission: 10%
Mechanical Data: Film: Digital, Col Length: 270mm, Page Width: 185mm, Type Area: 270 x 185mm, Trim Size: 297 x 210mm, Bleed Size: 305 x 213mm
Copy instructions: Copy Date: 2 weeks prior to publication date
Average advertising content per issue: 40%
BUSINESS: PHARMACEUTICAL & CHEMISTS

COMMUNIQUE AIRPORT BUSINESS
36379U6B-142

Editorial Address: 3A Gatwick Metro Centre, Balcombe Road, HORLEY, RH6 9GA **Tel:** 01293 783851
Fax: 01293 782959
Email: ross@pps-publications.com
Advertising Address: As above.
Email: jenny@pps-publications.com
Web site: http://www.pps-publications.com
Publisher: PPS Publications Ltd
Date Established: 1991
Frequency: Quarterly
Free to qualifying individuals
Circulation: 10,000 (Publisher's Statement)
Usual Pagination: 100
Editor: Ross Falconer
Summary of Content: Journal covering policy, news and features on airport and associated industries.
Readership/Target Audience: Aimed at CEOs, CFOs, regulators, legislators and operations directors within the airport industry.
ADVERTISING RATES:
Full Page Mono £1738.00
Full Page Colour £2750.00
Agency Commission: 10%
Mechanical Data: Type Area: 270 x 188mm, Trim Size: 297 x 210mm, Page Width: 188mm, Col Length: 270mm, Bleed Size: 303 x 216mm, Film: Digital
Average advertising content per issue: 40%
BUSINESS: AVIATION & AERONAUTICS: Airports

COMMUNITY
38460U32G-29_7!

Editorial Address: 12-20 Baron Street, LONDON, N1 9LL **Tel:** 020 7837 7887 **Fax:** 020 7278 9253
Email: communitymatters@communitymatters.org.uk
Advertising Address: As above.
Email: annie.jenkins@communitymatters.org.uk
Web site: http://www.communitymatters.org.uk
Publisher: Community Matters
Date Established: 1979
Frequency: 6 issues yearly
Free to qualifying individuals
Annual Sub.: £15.00
Circulation: 1,200 (Publisher's Statement)
Usual Pagination: 16

Editor: David Tyler; **Advertising Manager:** Annie Jenkins
Summary of Content: Newspaper of Community Matters (The National Federation of Community Organisations). Contains news of legislation, current campaigns, funding information and matters of concern to community groups and community buildings.
Readership/Target Audience: Aimed at community group organisers and advisors.
ADVERTISING RATES:
Full Page Colour £500.00
Mechanical Data: Film: Digital, Trim Size: 297 x 210mm
Average advertising content per issue: 5%
BUSINESS: LOCAL GOVERNMENT, LEISURE & RECREATION: Community Care & Social Services

COMMUNITY CARE
38461U32G-30

Editorial Address: 2nd Floor, Quadrant House, The Quadrant, SUTTON, SM2 5AS **Tel:** 020 8652 3500
Fax: 020 8652 4739
Email: comcare.news@rbi.co.uk
Advertising Address: As above.
Web site: http://www.communitycare.co.uk
ISSN: 0307-5508
Publisher: Reed Business Information
Date Established: 1974
Frequency: Weekly
Cover Price: £2.25
Free to qualifying individuals
Annual Sub.: £85.00
Circulation: 42,052 (ABC 01/07/2008 to 30/06/2009)
Editor: Mithran Samuel; **News Editor:** Mithran Samuel; **Executive Editor:** Mark Ivory; **Managing Director:** Mark Kelsey; **Advertising Manager:** Nicky Davies; **Group Editor:** Bronagh Miskelly; **Publisher:** Trevor Parker
Summary of Content: Magazine covering news and features on all areas of social care, including health, housing and education.
Readership/Target Audience: Read by those associated with the provision of care.
ADVERTISING RATES:
Full Page Mono £2400.00
Full Page Colour £3000.00
Agency Commission: 10%
Mechanical Data: Bleed Size: 303 x 216mm, Trim Size: 297 x 210mm, No. of Columns (Display): 6, Type Area: 280 x 193mm, Col Length: 280mm, Film: Digital, Page Width: 193mm
Copy instructions: Copy Date: Thursday 1 week prior to publication end
BUSINESS: LOCAL GOVERNMENT, LEISURE & RECREATION: Community Care & Social Services

COMMUNITY CARE MARKET NEWS
38462U32G-32

Editorial Address: 29 Angel Gate, City Road, LONDON, EC1V 2PT **Tel:** 020 7841 0049 **Fax:** 020 7833 9129
Email: justin@laingbuisson.co.uk
Advertising Address: As above. **Tel:** 020 7833 9123
Fax: 020 7833 5349
Email: news@laingbuisson.co.uk
Web site: http://www.communitycaremarketnews.co.uk
ISSN: 1354-103X
Publisher: Laing & Buisson
Date Established: 1994
Frequency: 10 issues yearly - Double issues in December/January and August/September
Annual Sub.: £595.00
Circulation: 1,000 (Publisher's Statement)
Usual Pagination: 32
Editor: Justin Merritt; **Advertising Manager:** Karen Ogilvie; **Publisher:** William Laing
Summary of Content: Journal containing news, analysis and informed comment within the community care sector.
Readership/Target Audience: Read by senior managers and decision makers within social services.
ADVERTISING RATES:
Full Page Mono £1650.00
Mechanical Data: Type Area: 250 x 175mm, Col Length: 250mm, Bleed Size: 303 x 216mm, Trim Size: 297 x 210mm, Page Width: 175mm, Film: Digital
Copy instructions: Copy Date: 15th of the month prior to publication date
Average advertising content per issue: 10%
BUSINESS: LOCAL GOVERNMENT, LEISURE & RECREATION: Community Care & Social Services

COMMUNITY DEVELOPMENT JOURNAL
29409U14C-353

Editorial Address: Faculty of Health and Social Care, University of West of England, Glenside Campus, Blackberry Hill, Stapleton, BRISTOL, BS16 1DD **Tel:** 0117 328 8758
Fax: 0117 328 8437
Email: christopher.miller@uwe.ac.uk
Advertising Address: Great Clarendon Street, OXFORD, OX2 6DP **Tel:** 01865 353329
Email: jnlsadvertising@oxfordjournals.org
Web site: http://www.cdj.oupjournals.org

ISSN: 0010-3802
Publisher: OUP
Date Established: 1966
Frequency: Quarterly
Cover Price: £15.00
Annual Sub.: £47.00
Circulation: 1,250 (Publisher's Statement)
Usual Pagination: 108
Editor: Christopher Miller
Summary of Content: Journal covering community work and development in industrial and developing nations.
Readership/Target Audience: Aimed at academics, students and practitioners involved in development studies, policies, social planning and administration, charities and local government departments of health, education, community education and social services.
ADVERTISING RATES:
Full Page Mono £310.00
Agency Commission: 10%
Mechanical Data: Film: Digital, Page Width: 130mm, Type Area: 200 x 130mm, Col Length: 200mm
BUSINESS: COMMERCE, INDUSTRY & MANAGEMENT: International Commerce

COMMUNITY HEALTH & SOCIAL CARE
1827401U32G-180

Editorial Address: The Diary House, Rickett Street, LONDON, SW6 1RU **Tel:** 020 7386 6100 **Fax:** 020 7381 8890
Email: inbox@mar-media.com
Advertising Address: As above.
Email: julien.wildman@mar-media.com
Web site: http://www.chasc.co.uk
Publisher: Roxby Media Ltd
Date Established: 2007
Frequency: Annual - Published in April
Cover Price: Free
Circulation: 10,000 (Print Run)
Usual Pagination: 132
Editor: Jenny Sims; **Advertising Manager:** Julien Wildman
Summary of Content: Magazine covering the management and care of patients with long term conditions, focusing on services in the community.
Readership/Target Audience: Aimed at commissioners, procurers and providers of community and home care services.
ADVERTISING RATES:
Full Page Colour £7950.00
Agency Commission: 10%
Mechanical Data: Type Area: 254 x 178mm, Bleed Size: 303 x 216mm, Trim Size: 297 x 210mm, Col Length: 254mm, Page Width: 178mm, Print Process: Sheet-fed litho, Film: Digital
Copy instructions: Copy Date: May 1st
BUSINESS: LOCAL GOVERNMENT, LEISURE & RECREATION: Community Care & Social Services

COMMUNITY PRACTITIONER
38464U32G-39

Editorial Address: 33-37 Moreland Street, LONDON, EC1V 8HA **Tel:** 020 7780 4086 **Fax:** 020 7780 4141
Email: danny.ratnaike@tenalpspublishing.com
Web site: http://www.commprac.com
ISSN: 1462-2815
Publisher: Ten Alps Publishing
Frequency: Monthly
Annual Sub.: £99.50
Circulation: 20,500 (Publisher's Statement)
Usual Pagination: 52
Editor: Danny Ratnaike
Summary of Content: Official Journal of the Community Practitioners and Health Visitors Association. Includes professional reports and news features of people and events associated with community health and nursing.
Readership/Target Audience: Aimed at members of the Community Practitioners and Health Visitors Association and other community nursing specialists, including health visitors, school nurses, practice nurses, community paediatric nurses, community nursery nurses, as well as educational establishments and libraries.
ADVERTISING: No Advertising taken
BUSINESS: LOCAL GOVERNMENT, LEISURE & RECREATION: Community Care & Social Services

COMPANY CLOTHING
39484U47A-65

Editorial Address: 32 Vauxhall Bridge Road, LONDON, SW1V 2SS **Tel:** 020 7973 6400 **Fax:** 020 7233 4797
Email: l.debell@hgluk.com
Advertising Address: As above. **Tel:** 020 7973 4647
Fax: 020 7233 5057
Email: a.suttle@hgluk.com
Web site: http://www.companyclothing.co.uk
ISSN: 0967-2311
Publisher: Hemming Group Ltd
Date Established: 1991
Frequency: 10 issues yearly - Published on the 1st Monday of the cover month
Free to qualifying individuals

Annual Sub.: £30.00
Circulation: 5,000 (Publisher's Statement)
Usual Pagination: 60
Editor: Lotte Debell; **Publisher:** Graham Bond
Summary of Content: Journal covering all aspects of corporate wear, workwear and protective clothing industry, including manufacturing, design, distribution and services.
Readership/Target Audience: Read by corporate clothing buyers and specifiers and the manufacturers and suppliers of corporate clothing.
ADVERTISING RATES:
Full Page Colour £1990.00
Agency Commission: 10%
Mechanical Data: Type Area: 275 x 190mm, Bleed Size: 303 x 216mm, Trim Size: 297 x 210mm, Col Length: 275mm, Page Width: 190mm, Film: Digital
Copy instructions: Copy Date: 2 weeks prior to publication date
Average advertising content per issue: 40%
BUSINESS: CLOTHING & TEXTILES

COMPANY COMPLIANCE MONITOR
625471U44-238

Editorial Address: 100 Avenue Road, Swiss Cottage, LONDON, NW3 3PF **Tel:** 020 7393 7400 **Fax:** 020 7393 7434
Email: lian.boyle@thomson.com
Web site: http://www.consultgee.co.uk
ISSN: 0964-5578
Publisher: GEE Publishing Ltd
Date Established: 1986
Frequency: 22 issues yearly
Usual Pagination: 4
Editor: Lian Boyle; **Executive Editor:** Madeleine Cordes
Summary of Content: Newsletter providing legal and procedural requirements relating to the business of a company secretary.
Readership/Target Audience: Aimed at company secretaries.
ADVERTISING: No Advertising taken
BUSINESS: LEGAL

COMPARATIVE CLINICAL PATHOLOGY
40561U56R-52_30

Formerly: Comparative Haematology International
Editorial Address: Ashbourne House, The Guildway, Old Portsmouth Road, Artington, GUILDFORD, GU3 1LP
Tel: 01483 734620 **Fax:** 01483 734411
Email: christiane.notarmarco@springer.com
Advertising Address: As above. **Tel:** 01483 734622
Email: clare.colwell@springer.com
Web site: http://www.springer.com/medicine/pathology/journal/580
ISSN: 0938-7714
Publisher: Springer
Frequency: Quarterly
Circulation: 850 (Publisher's Statement)
Editor: Christiane Notarmarco; **Executive Editor:** Christiane Notarmarco; **Advertising Manager:** Clare Colwell
Summary of Content: Journal featuring reviews, research reports, technical notes and case histories covering all aspects of haematology and clinical chemistry in any species.
Readership/Target Audience: Aimed at all scientists with an interest in the field of comparative clinical pathology, research institutes, toxicology and pathology laboratories, medical and veterinary colleges and practices, zoological institutes, universities and teaching hospitals.
ADVERTISING RATES:
Full Page Mono £430.00
Full Page Colour £1144.00
Agency Commission: 10%
Mechanical Data: Type Area: 237 x 172mm, Col Length: 237mm, Bleed Size: 283 x 216mm, Page Width: 172mm, Trim Size: 279 x 210mm, Film: Digital
Copy instructions: Copy Date: 6 weeks prior to publication date
Average advertising content per issue: 1%
BUSINESS: HEALTH & MEDICAL: Health Medical Related

COMPEL
1750446U55-9025

Editorial Address: 14 Halfpenny Lane, KNARESBOROUGH, HG5 0PS **Tel:** 01423 866479 **Fax:** 01423 866479
Email: ksutcliffe@emeraldinsight.com
Web site: http://engineering.emeraldinsight.com/computation/journals/compel.htm
ISSN: 0332-1649
Publisher: Emerald Group Publishing Ltd
Date Established: 1981
Frequency: 5 issues yearly
Usual Pagination: 324
Editor: Kay Sutcliffe
Summary of Content: Publication includes academic, peer reviewed research papers on computational methods in electrical and electronic engineering.

Readership/Target Audience: Aimed at research engineers working in academia and industry, particularly in electrical and electronic engineering.
ADVERTISING: No Advertising taken
BUSINESS: APPLIED SCIENCE & LABORATORIES

COMPETITION LAW INSIGHT
39160U44-255
Formerly: Competition Law Insights
Editorial Address: Telephone House, 69-77 Paul Street, LONDON, EC2A 4LQ **Tel:** 020 7017 6762
Fax: 020 7017 5274
Email: jessica.westwood@informa.com
Advertising Address: As above. **Tel:** 020 7017 4600
Fax: 020 7017 5221
Email: christopher.dooley@informa.com
Web site: http://www.informa.com
ISSN: 1350-1968
Publisher: Informa PLC
Frequency: 20 issues yearly
Circulation: 600 (Publisher's Statement)
Usual Pagination: 16
Editor: Jessica Westwood; **Advertising Manager:** Christopher Dooley
Summary of Content: Newsletter pinpointing the implications for business of key developments in community law.
Readership/Target Audience: Aimed at business lawyers and managers.
ADVERTISING: Rates on application
BUSINESS: LEGAL

COMPLEMENTARY THERAPIES IN CLINICAL PRACTICE
24818U56A-59_35
Formerly: Complementary Therapies in Nursing & Midwifery
Editorial Address: PO Box 10, MACCLESFIELD, SK10 4HW
Tel: 01625 820898 **Fax:** 01625 820029
Email: drankinbox@compuserve.com
Web site: http://www.intl.elsevierhealth.com/journals/ctnm
ISSN: 1353-6117
Publisher: Elsevier Ltd
Date Established: 1995
Frequency: Quarterly
Annual Sub.: EUR84.00
Circulation: 600 (Publisher's Statement)
Usual Pagination: 68
Editor: Denise Rankin-Box
Summary of Content: Magazine covering news, educational issues and features on the integration of complementary therapies into conventional nursing practices. Includes book and product reviews and articles on aromatherapy, massage, acupuncture, reflexology and herbal medicine.
Readership/Target Audience: Read by nursing professionals, complementary medicine practitioners and other allied health professionals.
ADVERTISING: No Advertising taken
BUSINESS: HEALTH & MEDICAL

COMPLEMENTARY THERAPIES IN MEDICINE
40153U56A-59_30
Editorial Address: The Boulevard, Langford Lane, KIDLINGTON, OX5 1GB **Tel:** 01865 843884
Fax: 01865 843992
Email: ctm@elsevier.com
Web site: http://www.elsevier.com
ISSN: 0965-2299
Publisher: Elsevier Ltd
Date Established: 1993
Frequency: Quarterly
Annual Sub.: EUR119.00
Circulation: 1,000 (Publisher's Statement)
Usual Pagination: 80
Editor: Robbert Van Haselen
Summary of Content: Journal providing information on traditional health practices and complementary therapies including primary research, reviews and opinion pieces.
Readership/Target Audience: Aimed at GPs, nurses, physiotherapists and complementary therapists.
ADVERTISING: No Advertising taken
BUSINESS: HEALTH & MEDICAL

COMPLETE NUTRITION
711698U22F-113
Editorial Address: 6 Harforde Court, John Tate Road, Foxholes Business Park, HERTFORD, SG13 7NW
Tel: 01992 538001 **Fax:** 01992 538002
Email: info@cm-2.co.uk
Advertising Address: As above.
Email: info@cm-2.co.uk
Web site: http://www.nutrition2me.com
Publisher: Complete Media & Marketing Ltd
Date Established: 2001
Frequency: 6 issues yearly - Published at the beginning of the 2nd week of the cover month
Free to qualifying individuals

Annual Sub.: £45.00
Circulation: 6,700 (Publisher's Statement)
Usual Pagination: 64
Editor: Faye Eagle; **Publisher:** Mike Fryer
Summary of Content: Magazine covering medical nutrition news, views, peer reviewed articles and product information.
Readership/Target Audience: Aimed at health professionals including dieticians, gastroenterologists, nutrition nurses and pharmacists.
ADVERTISING RATES:
Full Page Colour £1450.00
Agency Commission: 10%
Mechanical Data: Film: Positive, right reading, emulsion side down. Digital, Type Area: 277 x 190mm, Col Length: 277mm, Print Process: Litho, Bleed Size: 303 x 216mm, Trim Size: 297 x 210mm, Page Width: 190mm
Copy instructions: Copy Date: 2 weeks prior to publication date
Average advertising content per issue: 30%
Supplement(s): Functional Nutrition - 6xY
BUSINESS: FOOD: Health Food

COMPLIANCE MONITOR
35229U1F-123
Editorial Address: Telephone House, 69-77 Paul Street, LONDON, EC2A 4LQ **Tel:** 020 7017 4214
Email: timon.molloy@informa.com
Web site: http://www.informaprofessional.com
ISSN: 0953-9239
Publisher: Informa PLC
Frequency: 10 issues yearly
Usual Pagination: 16
Editor: Timon Molloy
Summary of Content: Journal containing news and practitioner analysis of the UK financial services regulatory system.
Readership/Target Audience: Aimed at people specialising in UK financial services compliance and regulation.
ADVERTISING: No Advertising taken
BUSINESS: FINANCE & ECONOMICS: Investment

COMPLIANCE REPORTER
35230U1F-125
Editorial Address: Nestor House, Playhouse Yard, LONDON, EC4V 5EX **Tel:** 020 7303 1748
Email: hleask@euromoneyplc.com
Advertising Address: Institutional Investor Inc, 225 Park Avenue South, New York, NY 10003 **Tel:** 212 22 43 566
Fax: 212 22 43 493
Email: jwright@iinews.com
Web site: http://www.compliancereporter.com
Publisher: Euromoney Institutional Investor plc
Date Established: 1995
Frequency: Weekly
Editor: Hugh Leask; **Advertising Manager:** Jonathan Wright
Summary of Content: Newsletter reporting on global regulatory systems of financial service markets.
Readership/Target Audience: Aimed at finance managers and compliance officers.
ADVERTISING RATES:
Full Page Mono $5600.00
Full Page Colour $7700.00
Mechanical Data: Film: Digital
Copy instructions: Copy Date: 12 days prior to publication date
BUSINESS: FINANCE & ECONOMICS: Investment

COMPOSTING NEWS
1693770U57-138
Editorial Address: 3 Burystead Place, WELLINGBOROUGH, NN8 1AH **Tel:** 0870 160 3270
Fax: 0870 160 3280
Email: claudia@organics-recycling.org.uk
Advertising Address: As above.
Email: jenni@compost.org.uk
Web site: http://www.organics-recycling.org.uk
ISSN: 1369 3069
Publisher: Association for Organics Recycling
Date Established: 1995
Frequency: Quarterly
Free to qualifying individuals
Circulation: 1,000 (Publisher's Statement)
Usual Pagination: 64
Editor: Claudia Cahalane; **Advertising Manager:** Jenni Harris
Summary of Content: Magazine covering all aspects of the compost industry including features, policy and industry news.
Readership/Target Audience: Aimed at local authorities, academics, waste managers and the horticulture and agriculture trade.
ADVERTISING: Rates on application
Average advertising content per issue: 30%
BUSINESS: ENVIRONMENT & POLLUTION

COMPOUND SEMICONDUCTOR
1696851U55-9020
Editorial Address: Dirac House, Temple Back, BRISTOL, BS1 6BE **Tel:** 0117 929 7481
Email: michael.hatcher@iop.org
Advertising Address: As above. **Fax:** 0117 930 1178
Email: sales@compsemi.iop.org
Web site: http://www.compoundsemiconductor.net
Publisher: IOP Publishing
Date Established: 1995
Frequency: 8 issues yearly
Free to qualifying individuals
Circulation: 9,094 (BPA Worldwide 01/01/2007 to 30/06/2007)
Usual Pagination: 40
Editor: Michael Hatcher; **News Editor:** Andy Extance;
Features Editor: Richard Stevenson; **Circulation Manager:** Claire Webber
Summary of Content: Magazine focusing on current developments within the global compound semiconductor industry.
Readership/Target Audience: Aimed at engineers and corporate managers within the compound semiconductor industry.
ADVERTISING RATES:
Full Page Colour £3480.00
Agency Commission: 10%
Mechanical Data: Trim Size: 282 x 213mm, Film: Digital
Copy instructions: Copy Date: 2 weeks prior to publication date
Average advertising content per issue: 35%
BUSINESS: APPLIED SCIENCE & LABORATORIES

COMPUTER & TELECOMMUNICATIONS LAW REVIEW
25982U44-270
Editorial Address: The Hatchery, Hall Bank Lane, Mytholmroyd, HEBDEN BRIDGE, HX7 5HQ
Tel: 01422 888000 **Fax:** 01422 888002
Email: mike.radley@thomson.com
Web site: http://www.sweetandmaxwell.co.uk
ISSN: 1357-3128
Publisher: Sweet & Maxwell Ltd
Date Established: 1995
Frequency: 8 issues yearly
Annual Sub.: £440.00
Usual Pagination: 64
Editor: Michele Rennie
Summary of Content: Specialist law journal which analyses and reports on legal and regulatory developments in the telecommunications and computer industries. Provides coverage of significant cases and changes in legislation throughout the world and contains in-depth discussion of current issues relating to case law and regulation.
Readership/Target Audience: Aimed at specialist practitioners within the field.
ADVERTISING: No Advertising taken
BUSINESS: LEGAL

COMPUTER BUSINESS REVIEW
36284U5R-20
Formerly: Computer Business Review incorporating Information Strategy
Editorial Address: PR by email only **Tel:** 020 7336 5200
Email: jstamper@industryreview.com
Advertising Address: Boundary House, 91 Charterhouse Street, LONDON, EC1M 6HR **Tel:** 020 7336 5200
Email: arahman@progressivemediagroup.com
Web site: http://www.cbronline.com
ISSN: 1350-4665
Publisher: Progressive Media Publications
Date Established: 1993
Frequency: 10 issues yearly
Annual Sub.: £150.00
Circulation: 21,241 (BPA Worldwide 01/07/2007 to 31/12/2007)
Usual Pagination: 60
Editor: Jason Stamper; **Advertising Manager:** Aziz Rahman
Summary of Content: Magazine providing business orientated analysis of events, trends and companies in the IT industry.
Readership/Target Audience: Aimed at CIOs and other decision makers in IT, plus industry CEOs, VPs and market analysts.
ADVERTISING RATES:
Full Page Colour £4850.00
Agency Commission: 10%
Mechanical Data: Page Width: 178mm, Type Area: 254 x 178mm, Trim Size: 273 x 205mm, Bleed Size: 279 x 211mm, Col Length: 254mm
Copy instructions: Copy Date: 2 weeks prior to publication date
Average advertising content per issue: 40%
BUSINESS: COMPUTERS & AUTOMATION: Computers Related

COMPUTER FRAUD & SECURITY

39899U54C-27

Editorial Address: The Boulevard, Langofrd Lane, KIDLINGTON, OX5 1GB **Tel:** 01865 843695
Fax: 01865 843971
Email: cfseditor@elsevier.com
Web site: http://www.computerfraudandsecurity.com
ISSN: 1361-3723
Publisher: Elsevier Ltd
Frequency: Monthly
Annual Sub.: EUR1017.00
Usual Pagination: 20
Editor: Danny Bradbury
Summary of Content: Newsletter providing practical information on how to effectively manage and control computer information security within commercial organisations with information relating to detection of cyber crime, computer fraud and different investigation techniques.
Readership/Target Audience: Read by auditors, financial and corporate management in companies who use computers and rely on information integrity to do business.
ADVERTISING: No Advertising taken
BUSINESS: SAFETY & SECURITY: Security

THE COMPUTER LAW AND SECURITY REPORT

39135U44-300

Editorial Address: School of Law, The University of Southampton, Highfield, SOUTHAMPTON, SO17 1BJ
Tel: 023 8059 3404
Email: s.j.saxby@soton.ac.uk
Web site: http://www.compseconline.com
ISSN: 0267-3649
Publisher: Elsevier Ltd
Date Established: 1985
Frequency: 6 issues yearly
Annual Sub.: EUR979.00
Circulation: 1,000 (Publisher's Statement)
Usual Pagination: 80
Editor: Stephen Saxby
Summary of Content: Report on computer security and the law governing information technology and computer use.
Readership/Target Audience: Read by legal specialists and business managers, security advisers, consultants, government and non-governmental organisations, libraries and academic institutions.
ADVERTISING: No Advertising taken
BUSINESS: LEGAL

COMPUTER WEEKLY

36044U5B-50

Editorial Address: Quadrant House, The Quadrant, SUTTON, SM2 5AS **Tel:** 020 8652 3500 **Fax:** 020 8652 8979
Email: computer.weekly@rbi.co.uk
Advertising Address: As above. **Tel:** 020 8625 3500
Fax: 020 8652 4437
Email: tina.french@rbi.co.uk
Web site: http://www.computerweekly.com
ISSN: 0010-4787
Publisher: Reed Business Information
Date Established: 1966
Frequency: Weekly - Published on Tuesday
Cover Price: £3.15
Free to qualifying individuals
Annual Sub.: £132.00
Circulation: 139,122 (BPA Worldwide 01/06/2007 to 31/12/2007)
Usual Pagination: 48
News Editor: Bill Goodwin; **Executive Editor:** Tony Collins
Summary of Content: Magazine for IT decision makers in end-user companies, delivering news and analysis on topics that matter, from the latest technical developments to winning management strategies.
Twitter: http://twitter.com/computerweekly.
Readership/Target Audience: Aimed at IT directors, data processing managers, systems analysts and engineers.
ADVERTISING RATES:
Full Page Colour £7140.00
Agency Commission: 10%
Mechanical Data: Col Length: 280mm, Col Widths (Display): 49mm, Type Area: 280 x 206mm, Film: Digital, No. of Columns (Display): 4, Bleed Size: 310 x 236mm, Trim Size: 300 x 226mm, Page Width: 206mm
Average advertising content per issue: 50%
BUSINESS: COMPUTERS & AUTOMATION: Data Processing

COMPUTERS & LAW

39136U44-310

Editorial Address: The Coach House, Black Dog Hill, Studley, CALNE, SN11 9LT **Tel:** 01249 822400
Fax: 01249 822522
Email: lseastham@aol.com
Advertising Address: As above.
Email: lseastham@aol.com
Web site: http://www.scl.org
ISSN: 0140-3249
Publisher: The Society for Computers & Law

Date Established: 1974
Frequency: 6 issues yearly
Free to qualifying individuals
Annual Sub.: £95.00
Circulation: 1,650 (Publisher's Statement)
Usual Pagination: 40
Editor: Laurence Eastham; **Advertising Manager:** Laurence Eastham; **Publisher:** Ruth Baker
Summary of Content: Journal for members of the Society for Computers & Law. Deals with IT applications of interest to lawyers and IT law.
Readership/Target Audience: Aimed at all lawyers in the UK, particularly those with IT responsibilities and those practising IT law.
ADVERTISING RATES:
Full Page Colour £1100.00
Agency Commission: 10%
Mechanical Data: Bleed Size: 303 x 216mm, Trim Size: 297 x 210mm, Print Process: Offset litho, Film: Digital
Average advertising content per issue: 10%
BUSINESS: LEGAL

COMPUTING

36048U5B-55

Editorial Address: 32-34 Broadwick Street, LONDON, W1A 2HG **Tel:** 020 7316 9000 **Fax:** 020 7316 9160
Email: madeline.bennett@incisivemedia.com
Advertising Address:
Email: paul.harvey@incisivemedia.com
Web site: http://www.computing.co.uk
Publisher: Incisive Media
Date Established: 1973
Frequency: Weekly
Cover Price: £2.70
Free to qualifying individuals
Annual Sub.: £100.00
Circulation: 93,362 (BPA Worldwide 01/07/2008 to 31/12/2008)
Usual Pagination: 48
Editor: Bryan Glick; **Managing Director:** Graham Harman
Summary of Content: Newspaper covering information on developing and using business computing systems. Includes e-business, analysis, technology, statistics, enterprise and communications.
Twitter: https://twitter.com/computing_news.
Readership/Target Audience: Read by computer professionals and decision makers.
ADVERTISING RATES:
Full Page Colour £6995.00
Agency Commission: 10%
Mechanical Data: Type Area: 278 x 218mm, Col Length: 278mm, Trim Size: 335 x 270mm, Bleed Size: 306 x 248mm, Film: Digital, Page Width: 218mm
Copy instructions: Copy Date: 10 days prior to publication date
Supplement(s): Computing Business - 10xY
BUSINESS: COMPUTERS & AUTOMATION: Data Processing

COMPUTING AND COMMUNICATIONS AFRICA

36290U5R-15

Formerly: Computers + Telecommunications in Africa
Editorial Address: 8 High Street, Croxton, ST. NEOTS, PE19 6SX **Tel:** 01480 880774 **Fax:** 01480 880765
Email: seanm@aitecafrica.com
Advertising Address: As above.
Email: seanm@aitecafrica.com
Web site: http://www.aitecafrica.com
ISSN: 0953-3257
Publisher: Aitec
Date Established: 1987
Frequency: Quarterly
Cover Price: £1.50
Free to qualifying individuals
Annual Sub.: £20.00
Circulation: 8,000 (Publisher's Statement)
Usual Pagination: 48
Editor: Sean Moroney; **Managing Director:** Sean Moroney; **Advertising Manager:** Sean Moroney; **Publisher:** Sean Moroney
Summary of Content: Guide to information technology in Africa.
Readership/Target Audience: Aimed at the IT, telecommunications and business community in Africa.
ADVERTISING RATES:
Full Page Colour £1560.00
Agency Commission: 15%
Mechanical Data: Bleed Size: +4mm, Trim Size: 275 x 210mm, Film: Digital, Print Process: Offset litho
BUSINESS: COMPUTERS & AUTOMATION: Computers Related

COMPUTING BUSINESS

1703372U14A-559

Editorial Address: 32-34 Broadwick Street, LONDON, W1A 2HG **Tel:** 020 7316 9000 **Fax:** 020 7316 9160
Email: gareth.morgan@incisivemedia.com
Advertising Address: As above.

Email: paul.harvey@incisivemedia.com
Web site: http://www.computingbusiness.co.uk
Publisher: Incisive Media
Date Established: 2005
Frequency: 10 issues yearly
Free to qualifying individuals
Circulation: 35,000 (Publisher's Statement)
Editor: Gareth Morgan
Summary of Content: Magazine focusing on organisational and management issues.
Readership/Target Audience: Aimed at senior executives in the IT industry.
ADVERTISING RATES:
Full Page Colour £5395.00
Agency Commission: 10%
Mechanical Data: Type Area: 278 x 218mm, Bleed Size: 306 x 248mm, Trim Size: 335 x 270mm, Col Length: 278mm, Page Width: 218mm, Film: Digital
Copy instructions: Copy Date: 2 weeks prior to publication date
Average advertising content per issue: 35%
BUSINESS: COMMERCE, INDUSTRY & MANAGEMENT

COMPUTING SECURITY

1859384U5R-693

Editorial Address: 35 Station Square, Petts Wood, ORPINGTON, BR5 1LZ **Tel:** 01689 616000
Fax: 01689 826622
Email: ray.smyth@btc.co.uk
Web site: http://www.computing-security.co.uk
Publisher: Business & Technical Communications
Date Established: 2008
Frequency: Quarterly
Circulation: 10,000 (Publisher's Statement)
Editor: Ray Smyth
Summary of Content: Magazine dealing with the key issue that organisations face as they try to maintain secure networks in the face of new and old threats.
Readership/Target Audience: Aimed at those responsible for computer security including IT managers and directors, IT security, risk and compliance managers, managing directors, CEOs and partners.
BUSINESS: COMPUTERS & AUTOMATION: Computers Related

CONCEPT

1622640U62F-953

Editorial Address: 21 De Montfort Street, LEICESTER, LE1 7GE **Tel:** 0116 204 4200 **Fax:** 0116 285 4215
Email: david.shaw@niace.org.uk
Web site: http://www.niace.org.uk/publications/periodicals/concept
ISSN: 1359-1983
Publisher: National Institute of Adult Continuing Education
Date Established: 2002
Frequency: 3 issues yearly - Published in April, September and December
Annual Sub.: £22.00
Circulation: 250 (Publisher's Statement)
Editor: Mae Shaw
Summary of Content: The Journal of Contemporary Community Education Practice Theory.
Readership/Target Audience: Aimed at practitioners, academics and political commentators.
ADVERTISING: No Advertising taken
BUSINESS: CHURCH & SCHOOL EQUIPMENT & EDUCATION: Adult Education

CONCRETE

38970U42A-20

Editorial Address: Riverside House, 4 Meadows Business Park, Station Approach, Blackwater, CAMBERLEY, GU17 9AB **Tel:** 01276 607158 **Fax:** 01276 607141
Email: editorial@concrete.org.uk
Advertising Address: As above. **Tel:** 01572 824716
Fax: 01572 824731
Email: francesca.huggett@associa.co.uk
Web site: http://www.concrete.org.uk
ISSN: 0010-5317
Publisher: The Concrete Society
Date Established: 1967
Frequency: 11 issues yearly - Published around the 1st Monday of the cover month
Free to qualifying individuals
Annual Sub.: £130.00
Circulation: 5,000 (Publisher's Statement)
Usual Pagination: 48
Editor: James Luckey
Summary of Content: Journal covering all matters related to concrete technology, design and construction of concrete structures.
Readership/Target Audience: Read by consulting engineers, contractors, construction equipment and material manufacturers and suppliers.
ADVERTISING RATES:
Full Page Mono £1350.00
Full Page Colour £1835.00
Agency Commission: 10%

Business Magazines

Mechanical Data: Type Area: 265 x 186mm, Bleed Size: 303 x 216mm, Film: Digital, Page Width: 186mm, Col Length: 265mm, Trim Size: 297 x 210mm
Copy instructions: Copy Date: 4 weeks prior to publication date
Average advertising content per issue: 20%
Supplement(s): News and Views - 3xY
BUSINESS: CONSTRUCTION

CONCRETE ENGINEERING INTERNATIONAL
38971U42A-23

Formerly: Concrete Engineering
Editorial Address: Riverside House, 4 Meadows Business Park, Station Approach, Blackwater, CAMBERLEY, GU17 9AB **Tel:** 01276 607158 **Fax:** 01276 607141
Email: editorial@concreteengineering.com
Advertising Address: North Gate, Uppingham, OAKHAM, LE15 9PL **Tel:** 01572 824682 **Fax:** 01572 824731
Email: francesca.gourlay@associa.co.uk
Web site: http://www.concreteengineering.com
ISSN: 1742-352X
Publisher: The Concrete Society
Date Established: 1997
Frequency: Quarterly - Published in the middle of the cover months of March, June, September and December
Cover Price: £17.00
Free to qualifying individuals
Annual Sub.: £50.00
Circulation: 4,395 (Publisher's Statement)
Usual Pagination: 64
Editor: James Luckey
Summary of Content: Magazine about all matters relating to concrete, from design, applications and production to appearance and function also contains details of equipment for concrete technology.
Readership/Target Audience: Read by specifiers, engineers, contractors and suppliers.
ADVERTISING RATES:
Full Page Mono £1175.00
Full Page Colour £1795.00
Agency Commission: 10%
Mechanical Data: Type Area: 268 x 178mm, Bleed Size: 303 x 213mm, Trim Size: 297 x 210mm, Page Width: 178mm, Col Length: 268mm, Print Process: Offset litho, Film: Digital
Copy instructions: Copy Date: 27th of the month prior to publication date
Average advertising content per issue: 20%
BUSINESS: CONSTRUCTION

CONDITION MONITOR
37702U19R-150

Editorial Address: PO Box 72, CHIPPING NORTON, OX7 6UP **Tel:** 01451 830261 **Fax:** 01451 870261
Email: mail@coxmoor.com
Web site: http://www.coxmoor.com
ISSN: 0263-8050
Publisher: British Institute of Non-Destructive Testing
Date Established: 1986
Frequency: Monthly
Annual Sub.: £285.00
Circulation: 500 (Publisher's Statement)
Usual Pagination: 18
Editor: Simon Atkinson
Summary of Content: International newsletter covering techniques for failure analysis and implementation of condition monitoring in predictive maintenance programmes.
Readership/Target Audience: Aimed at those concerned with increasing machine life, planning for effective maintenance scheduling and avoiding machine failure.
ADVERTISING: No Advertising taken
BUSINESS: ENGINEERING & MACHINERY: Engineering Related

CONFECTIONERY PRODUCTION
36465U8B-100

Editorial Address: The Maltings, 57 Bath Street, GRAVESEND, DA11 0DF **Tel:** 01474 532202
Fax: 01474 532203
Email: katrine@bellpublishing.com
Advertising Address: As above. **Tel:** 01484 532202
Email: jon@bellpublishing.co.uk
Web site: http://www.confectioneryproduction.com
ISSN: 0010-5473
Publisher: Bell Publishing Ltd
Date Established: 1935
Frequency: 10 issues yearly - Published on the 20th of the cover month with double issues in Dec/Jan and Jul/Aug
Annual Sub.: £110.00
Circulation: 7,077 (Publisher's Statement)
Usual Pagination: 48
Editor: Katrine Kjoeller; **Advertising Manager:** Jon Pittock; **Publisher:** Neil McRitchie
Summary of Content: Publication covering machinery equipment, ingredients and packaging for the chocolate, bakery, ice cream and confectionery industries.

Readership/Target Audience: Read by works, development engineers, technicians, sales personnel, managers and directors.
ADVERTISING RATES:
Full Page Colour £2250.00
Agency Commission: 10%
Mechanical Data: Type Area: 270 x 185mm, Print Process: Sheet-fed offset litho, Bleed Size: 303 x 213mm, Trim Size: 297 x 210mm, Film: Digital, Col Length: 270mm, No. of Columns (Display): 3, Page Width: 185mm
Copy instructions: Copy Date: 15th of the month prior to publication date
Average advertising content per issue: 35%
BUSINESS: BAKING & CONFECTIONERY: Confectionery Manufacturing

THE CONFECTIONERY TRADE BUYER
1794884U8B-201

Formerly: Confectionery Buyer
Editorial Address: First Floor Offices, Stafford House, 16 East Street, TONBRIDGE, TN9 1HG **Tel:** 01732 371510
Fax: 01732 361385
Email: scallander@kennedys.co.uk
Advertising Address: As above.
Email: info@kennedys.co.uk
Publisher: Kennedy's Publications Ltd
Frequency: Annual - Published around the 10th of January
Free to qualifying individuals
Circulation: 7,200 (Publisher's Statement)
Usual Pagination: 140
Editor: Suzanne Callander; **Managing Director:** Angus Kennedy; **Advertising Manager:** Angus Kennedy
Summary of Content: Magazine covering all aspects of purchasing confectionery including marketing strategies and industry trends.
Readership/Target Audience: Aimed at purchasers of confectionery.
ADVERTISING RATES:
Full Page Mono £1500.00
Full Page Colour £1995.00
Agency Commission: 10%
Mechanical Data: Bleed Size: 307 x 220mm, Trim Size: 297 x 210mm, Film: Digital
Copy instructions: Copy Date: 8 weeks prior to publication date
Average advertising content per issue: 35%
BUSINESS: BAKING & CONFECTIONERY: Confectionery Manufacturing

CONFERENCE & INCENTIVE TRAVEL
35631U2C-39

Editorial Address: 174 Hammersmith Road, LONDON, W6 7JP **Tel:** 020 8267 4307 **Fax:** 020 8267 4192
Email: cit@haymarket.com
Advertising Address: As above. **Tel:** 020 8267 4016
Fax: 020 8267 4272
Email: alison.pitchford@haymarket.com
Web site: http://www.citmagazine.com
Publisher: Haymarket Specialist Publications
Frequency: 10 issues yearly - Published on the 1st Friday of the cover month
Cover Price: Free
Circulation: 18,176 (ABC 01/07/2008 to 30/06/2009)
Usual Pagination: 100
Editor: Yasmin Arrigo; **Features Editor:** Susie Harwood; **Advertising Director:** Alison Pitchford; **Publisher:** Paul Twite
Summary of Content: Magazine containing news and features on incentive travel and conference organisation.
Readership/Target Audience: Aimed at corporate buyers and professional organisers of conferences, exhibitions and incentive travel.
ADVERTISING RATES:
Full Page Colour £4420.00
Agency Commission: 10%
Mechanical Data: Type Area: 265 x 184mm, Film: Digital, Col Length: 265mm, Page Width: 184mm, Trim Size: 297 x 210mm, Bleed Size: 303 x 216mm
Copy instructions: Copy Date: 8 weeks prior to publication date
BUSINESS: COMMUNICATIONS, ADVERTISING & MARKETING: Conferences & Exhibitions

CONFERENCE & SEMINAR SELECTOR PACK
35652U2C-39_50

Editorial Address: PO Box 100, EDENBRIDGE, TN8 6ZN **Tel:** 01732 866122 **Fax:** 01732 866926
Email: simon@target-response.co.uk
Advertising Address: As above.
Email: simon@target-response.co.uk
Web site: http://www.target-response.co.uk
Publisher: Target Response
Date Established: 1986
Frequency: Half-yearly - Published May and October
Cover Price: Free
Circulation: 15,000 (Publisher's Statement)

Editor: Simon Tilley; **Managing Director:** Simon Tilley; **Advertising Manager:** Simon Tilley
Summary of Content: Journal listing conference products, venues and services.
Readership/Target Audience: Aimed at companies, associations and institutes.
ADVERTISING RATES:
Full Page Mono £1550.00
Full Page Colour £1750.00
Mechanical Data: Bleed Size: 303 x 216mm, Film: Digital, Trim Size: 297 x 210mm
Copy instructions: Copy Date: 1 month prior to publication date
BUSINESS: COMMUNICATIONS, ADVERTISING & MARKETING: Conferences & Exhibitions

CONFERENCE NEWS
1622770U2C-507

Editorial Address: Faraday House, 39 Thornton Road, Wimbledon, LONDON, SW19 4NQ **Tel:** 020 8971 8282
Fax: 020 8971 8283
Email: pcolston@mashmedia.net
Advertising Address: As above. **Fax:** 020 8971 8284
Email: kthomas@mashmedia.net
Web site: http://www.mashmedia.net
Publisher: Mash Media
Date Established: 2003
Frequency: Monthly - Published on the 2nd of the cover month
Free to qualifying individuals
Circulation: 7,514 (ABC 01/07/2007 to 30/06/2008)
Usual Pagination: 56
Editor: Paul Colston; **Publisher:** Roisin Sullens
Summary of Content: Magazine featuring the latest conference news, interviews with key market figures and industry analysis.
Readership/Target Audience: Aimed at organisers, venue owners and suppliers.
ADVERTISING RATES:
Full Page Colour £2995.00
Agency Commission: 10%
Mechanical Data: Trim Size: 297 x 210mm, Film: Digital, Type Area: 270 x 190mm, Bleed Size: 303 x 216mm, Col Length: 270mm, Page Width: 190mm
Copy instructions: Copy Date: 2 weeks prior to publication date
Average advertising content per issue: 50%
BUSINESS: COMMUNICATIONS, ADVERTISING & MARKETING: Conferences & Exhibitions

CONFERENCE WALES
35634U2C-52

Editorial Address: 6 Park Street, CARDIFF, CF10 1XR
Tel: 029 2022 3333
Email: mag.supps@mediawales.co.uk
Advertising Address: As above. **Tel:** 029 2022 2777
Email: emma.gough@mediawales.co.uk
Web site: http://www.icwales.co.uk
Publisher: Media Wales Ltd
Date Established: 1997
Frequency: Annual - Published in January
Cover Price: Free
Circulation: 10,000 (Publisher's Statement)
Usual Pagination: 100
Editor: Simon Farrington
Summary of Content: Guide to venues, facilities and services, including articles on corporate entertainment, education, training and accommodation.
Readership/Target Audience: Aimed at small, medium and large businesses.
ADVERTISING RATES:
Full Page Colour £750.00
Agency Commission: 10%
Mechanical Data: Bleed Size: 216 x 154mm, Trim Size: 195 x 130mm, Film: Digital
Copy instructions: Copy Date: 4 weeks prior to publication date
Average advertising content per issue: 68%
BUSINESS: COMMUNICATIONS, ADVERTISING & MARKETING: Conferences & Exhibitions

CONNECT
1805211U50-234

Editorial Address: 3rd Floor, 21 Great Sutton Street, LONDON, EC1V 0DY **Tel:** 020 7566 9910
Fax: 020 7490 1723
Email: shalene.varcoe@psprarepublishing.co.uk
Web site: http://www.psprarepublishing.co.uk
Publisher: PSP Rare Publishing
Date Established: 2006
Frequency: Quarterly
Cover Price: Free
Circulation: 6,000 (Publisher's Statement)
Usual Pagination: 52
Editor: Daska Davis; **Publisher:** Shalene Varcoe
Summary of Content: Carlson Wagonlit publication featuring corporate travel, including city reviews, hotels, airlines and conference venues.

Readership/Target Audience: Aimed at procurement managers, heads of purchasing, business travellers and travel bookers.
ADVERTISING: No Advertising taken
BUSINESS: TRAVEL & TOURISM

CONNECT
1800747U63B-2578

Editorial Address: 1st Floor, Heron House, Hale Wharf, Ferry Lane, LONDON, N17 9NF **Tel:** 020 8885 9200
Fax: 020 8493 8314
Email: connect@northlondonbusiness.com
Web site: http://www.northlondonbusiness.com
Publisher: Excel Publishing Company Ltd
Date Established: 2007
Frequency: 6 issues yearly
Cover Price: Free
Circulation: 6,000 (Publisher's Statement)
Usual Pagination: 44
Editor: Maria Taylor; **Advertising Manager:** Michelle Holmes
Summary of Content: Official publication of North London Business featuring business and company news, workplace issues, workforce development and skills. Aims to promote the economic development of the area.
Readership/Target Audience: Aimed at members of the business community in North London.
ADVERTISING: Rates on application
BUSINESS: REGIONAL BUSINESS: Regional Business English Counties

CONNECTED
37498U18B-1300

Formerly: Review
Editorial Address: 30 St. Georges Road, Wimbledon, LONDON, SW19 4BD **Tel:** 020 8971 6000
Fax: 020 8971 6002
Email: connected@connectuk.org
Advertising Address: As above.
Email: connected@connectuk.org
Web site: http://www.connectuk.org
Publisher: Connect
Date Established: 2004
Frequency: 8 issues yearly
Cover Price: £2.00
Free to qualifying individuals
Circulation: 22,000 (Publisher's Statement)
Usual Pagination: 24
Advertising Manager: Jane McCarten
Summary of Content: Magazine covering union and industry news, interviews, career advice and services.
Language(s): English; French; Italian
Readership/Target Audience: Read by members of Connect, the union for professionals in communications.
ADVERTISING RATES:
Full Page Colour £1250.00
Mechanical Data: Trim Size: 297 x 210mm
Average advertising content per issue: 20%
BUSINESS: ELECTRONICS: Telecommunications

CONNECTINGINDUSTRY.COM AUTOMATION
37683U19J-82

Formerly: Automation
Editorial Address: 15A London Road, MAIDSTONE, ME16 8LY **Tel:** 01622 687031 **Fax:** 01622 757646
Email: nmead@datateam.co.uk
Advertising Address: As above. **Tel:** 01622 699177
Email: jpilcher@datateam.co.uk
Web site: http://www.connectingindustry.com
ISSN: 1364-2561
Publisher: Dateam Publishing Ltd
Frequency: 10 issues yearly - Published in the 2nd week of the cover month
Free to qualifying individuals
Annual Sub.: £74.00
Circulation: 16,986 (ABC 01/01/2008 to 31/12/2008)
Usual Pagination: 52
Editor: Neil Mead
Summary of Content: Magazine covering all aspects of automation in production and engineering.
Readership/Target Audience: Aimed at manufacturing end users and machine designers.
ADVERTISING RATES:
Full Page Colour £2200.00
Agency Commission: 10%
Mechanical Data: Type Area: 272 x 191mm, Bleed Size: 303 x 216mm, Trim Size: 297 x 210mm, Col Length: 272mm, Page Width: 191mm, Film: Digital
Copy instructions: Copy Date: 14th of the month prior to publication date
Average advertising content per issue: 50%
Supplement(s): Machine Vision - 1xY
BUSINESS: ENGINEERING & MACHINERY: CAD & CIM (Computer Integrated Manufacture)

CONNECTINGINDUSTRY.COM DESIGN SOLUTIONS
37617U19B-110

Formerly: CONNECTINGINDUSTRY.COM/oem design
Editorial Address: 15A London Road, MAIDSTONE, ME16 8LY **Tel:** 01622 699171 **Fax:** 01622 757646
Email: rwinter@connectingindustry.com
Advertising Address: As above. **Tel:** 01622 699195
Email: khogg@datateam.co.uk
Web site: http://www.connectingindustry.com
ISSN: 1740-2654
Publisher: Dateam Publishing Ltd
Date Established: 1971
Frequency: 10 issues yearly - Published in the 2nd week of the cover month
Free to qualifying individuals
Annual Sub.: £74.00
Circulation: 17,850 (ABC 01/01/2008 to 31/12/2008)
Usual Pagination: 60
Editor: Rachael Winter; **Advertising Manager:** Damien Oxlee
Summary of Content: Magazine providing advice and information for solving design problems.
Readership/Target Audience: Aimed at design engineers, OEMs, machine builders.
ADVERTISING RATES:
Full Page Colour £2200.00
Agency Commission: 10%
Mechanical Data: Type Area: 254 x 178mm, Bleed Size: 303 x 215mm, Trim Size: 297 x 210mm, Col Length: 254mm, Page Width: 178mm, Film: Digital
Copy instructions: Copy Date: 14th of the month prior to publication date
Average advertising content per issue: 60%
BUSINESS: ENGINEERING & MACHINERY: Engineering - Design

CONNECTINGINDUSTRY.COM ELECTRONICS
37357U18A-56

Formerly: Electronic Product Review
Editorial Address: 15A London Road, MAIDSTONE, ME16 8LY **Tel:** 01843 866607 **Fax:** 01843 866607
Email: mwinny@datateam.co.uk
Advertising Address: As above. **Tel:** 01622 687031
Fax: 01622 757646
Email: mjennerhall@datateam.co.uk
Web site: http://www.connectingindustry.com/electronics
ISSN: 1472-1252
Publisher: Dateam Publishing Ltd
Frequency: Monthly - Published in the 2nd week of the cover month
Free to qualifying individuals
Annual Sub.: £54.00
Circulation: 16,882 (ABC 01/01/2006 to 31/12/2006)
Usual Pagination: 60
Editor: Michelle Winny
Summary of Content: A magazine aimed at OEM design engineers and procurement specialists, providing a helpful guide to the context behind the latest announcements in components, design tools, services, supply chain initiatives and legislation. Coverage comprises feature articles, news stories, opinion columns and product stories.
Readership/Target Audience: Aimed at buyers, specifiers and designers.
ADVERTISING RATES:
Full Page Colour £2200.00
Agency Commission: 10%
Mechanical Data: No. of Columns (Display): 4, Type Area: 272 x 191mm, Col Length: 272mm, Trim Size: 297 x 210mm, Bleed Size: 303 x 216mm, Film: Digital, Page Width: 191mm
Copy instructions: Copy Date: 14th of the month prior to publication date
Average advertising content per issue: 60%
BUSINESS: ELECTRONICS

CONNECTINGINDUSTRY.COM ENERGY MANAGEMENT
1795478U58-183

Editorial Address: 15A London Road, MAIDSTONE, ME16 8LY **Tel:** 01622 699193 **Fax:** 01622 757646
Email: jbush@datateam.co.uk
Advertising Address: As above. **Tel:** 01622 687031
Email: mjennerhall@datateam.co.uk
Web site: http://www.connectingindustry.com
Publisher: Dateam Publishing Ltd
Frequency: Quarterly - Published around the end of the 1st cover month
Cover Price: Free
Editor: Joe Bush; **Advertising Manager:** Kate Mustill
Summary of Content: Publication covering the managing energy process and providing an insight into the latest products, systems, services and methods available.
Readership/Target Audience: Aimed at senior managers and engineers involved in the specification, installation, maintenance and operation of plant, equipment and building services and those involved in energy procurement, distribution and use.
ADVERTISING RATES:
Full Page Colour £1700.00

SCC £20.00
Agency Commission: 10%
Mechanical Data: Type Area: 272 x 191mm, Bleed Size: 303 x 216mm, Trim Size: 297 x 210mm, Col Length: 272mm, Page Width: 191mm, Film: Digital
Copy instructions: Copy Date: 3 weeks prior to publication date
Average advertising content per issue: 40%
BUSINESS: ENERGY, FUEL & NUCLEAR

CONNECTINGINDUSTRY.COM INSTRUMENTATION
634056U14A-80

Editorial Address: 15A London Road, MAIDSTONE, ME16 8LY **Tel:** 01622 699171 **Fax:** 01622 757646
Email: rwinter@datateam.co.uk
Advertising Address: As above. **Tel:** 01622 699129
Email: kambrose@datateam.co.uk
Web site: http://www.connectingindustry.com
ISSN: 1472-1260
Publisher: Dateam Publishing Ltd
Date Established: 1968
Frequency: 10 issues yearly - Published in the 1st week of the cover month
Free to qualifying individuals
Annual Sub.: £74.00
Circulation: 14,909 (ABC 01/01/2006 to 31/12/2006)
Usual Pagination: 52
Editor: Rachael Winter; **Advertising Manager:** Kathryn Ambrose
Summary of Content: Journal covering control instruments, tests and measurements.
Readership/Target Audience: Aimed at buyers and specifiers.
ADVERTISING RATES:
Full Page Colour £2100.00
Agency Commission: 10%
Mechanical Data: Page Width: 191mm, Type Area: 272 x 191mm, Bleed Size: 303 x 216mm, Trim Size: 297 x 210mm, Col Length: 272mm, Film: Digital
Copy instructions: Copy Date: 2 weeks prior to publication date
BUSINESS: COMMERCE, INDUSTRY & MANAGEMENT

CONNECTINGINDUSTRY.COM IRISH MANUFACTURING
1663441U19A-553

Editorial Address: 15A London Road, MAIDSTONE, ME16 8LY **Tel:** 01622 699166 **Fax:** 01622 757646
Email: mlea@datateam.co.uk
Advertising Address: As above.
Email: lmontgomery@datateam.co.uk
Web site: http://www.connectingindustry.com/irishmanufacturing
ISSN: 1475-0783
Publisher: Dateam Publishing Ltd
Date Established: 2001
Frequency: Quarterly - Published in the 3rd week of the cover month
Free to qualifying individuals
Circulation: 9,500 (Publisher's Statement)
Editor: Michelle Lea; **Advertising Manager:** Les Montgomery
Summary of Content: Magazine covering all aspects of engineering, including electrical, electronics, factory, instrumentation, design and process engineering.
Readership/Target Audience: Aimed at engineers.
ADVERTISING RATES:
Full Page Colour £2885.00
Agency Commission: 10%
Mechanical Data: Type Area: 272 x 191mm, Bleed Size: 303 x 216mm, Trim Size: 297 x 210mm, Col Length: 272mm, Page Width: 191mm, Film: Digital
Copy instructions: Copy Date: 4 weeks prior to publication date
Average advertising content per issue: 40%
BUSINESS: ENGINEERING & MACHINERY

CONNECTINGINDUSTRY.COM PROCESS & CONTROL
37667U19F-103

Editorial Address: 15A London Road, MAIDSTONE, ME16 8LY **Tel:** 01622 687031 **Fax:** 01622 757646
Email: mlea@datateam.co.uk
Advertising Address: As above. **Tel:** 01622 699136
Email: lmontgomery@connectingindustry.com
Web site: http://www.connectingindustry.com
ISSN: 0306-0381
Publisher: Dateam Publishing Ltd
Date Established: 1980
Frequency: 11 issues yearly - Published in the 2nd week of the cover month
Free to qualifying individuals
Annual Sub.: £59.00
Circulation: 15,900 (ABC 01/01/2006 to 31/12/2006)
Usual Pagination: 60
Editor: Michelle Lea; **Advertising Manager:** Les Montgomery

Summary of Content: Journal concerned with economy, efficiency and safety in the processing of fluids and solids.
Readership/Target Audience: Read by senior management and engineers.
ADVERTISING RATES:
Full Page Mono £2100.00
Full Page Colour £3005.00
Agency Commission: 10%
Mechanical Data: Trim Size: 297 x 210mm, Bleed Size: 303 x 215mm, Type Area: 254 x 178mm, Col Length: 254mm, Page Width: 178mm
Copy instructions: Copy Date: 3 weeks prior to publication date
Average advertising content per issue: 55%
BUSINESS: ENGINEERING & MACHINERY: Production & Mechanical Engineering

CONNECTIONS
37322U17-165
Formerly: NICEIC Connections
Editorial Address: 17 Britton Street, LONDON, EC1M 5TP
Tel: 020 7880 6200 **Fax:** 020 7880 7553
Email: nick.martindale@niceicconnections.com
Advertising Address: As above.
Email: darren@niceic.co.uk
Web site: http://www.niceic.org.uk
Publisher: Redactive Media Group
Frequency: Quarterly
Free to qualifying individuals
Circulation: 37,000 (Publisher's Statement)
Usual Pagination: 32
Editor: Nick Martindale
Summary of Content: Newsletter of the National Inspection Council for Electrical Installation Contracting. Includes technical advice, guidance and information.
Readership/Target Audience: Aimed at approved contractors of NICEIC plus 7000 requested readers in commercial, industrial and architectural areas.
ADVERTISING RATES:
Full Page Colour £2900.00
Mechanical Data: Bleed Size: 313 x 216mm, Trim Size: 297 x 210mm, Film: Digital
Copy instructions: Copy Date: 4 weeks prior to publication date
Average advertising content per issue: 30%
BUSINESS: ELECTRICAL

CONSERVATORY INDUSTRIES
36626U12B-15
Editorial Address: 173 High Street, RICKMANSWORTH, WD3 1AY **Tel:** 01923 692660 **Fax:** 01923 692679
Email: m.downs@turretgroup.com
Advertising Address: As above.
Email: conservatories@turretgroup.com
Web site: http://www.turretgroup.com
Publisher: Turret Group Ltd.
Frequency: Quarterly
Free to qualifying individuals
Annual Sub.: £85.00
Circulation: 7,500 (Publisher's Statement)
Usual Pagination: 32
Editor: Matthew Downs
Summary of Content: Magazine containing news, views and information from the conservatory market.
Readership/Target Audience: Aimed at fabricators and installers of conservatories.
ADVERTISING RATES:
Full Page Mono £920.00
Full Page Colour £1465.00
SCC £25.00
Agency Commission: 10%
Mechanical Data: Trim Size: 297 x 210mm, Bleed Size: 303 x 216mm, Type Area: 254 x 178mm, Col Length: 254mm, Page Width: 178mm, Film: Digital, No. of Columns (Display): 4
Copy instructions: Copy Date: 4 weeks prior to publication date
Average advertising content per issue: 60%
BUSINESS: CERAMICS, POTTERY & GLASS: Glass

CONSERVATORY MAGAZINE
601449U12B-20
Editorial Address: Becket House, Vestry Road, SEVENOAKS, TN14 5EJ **Tel:** 01732 748000
Fax: 01732 748001
Email: dgill@unity-media.com
Advertising Address: As above.
Email: sknight@unity-media.com
Web site: http://www.consmag.com
Publisher: Unity Media plc
Date Established: 1999
Frequency: 6 issues yearly - Published in the middle of the 1st cover month
Cover Price: £5.00
Free to qualifying individuals
Circulation: 7,374 (ABC 01/01/2008 to 31/12/2008)
Usual Pagination: 72
Editor: Davinia Gill

Summary of Content: Magazine containing news, product and technical articles on all aspects of conservatories.
Readership/Target Audience: Aimed at suppliers and fitters of conservatories.
ADVERTISING RATES:
Full Page Colour £1400.00
Agency Commission: 10%
Mechanical Data: Film: Digital, Page Width: 190mm, Type Area: 265 x 190mm, Col Length: 265mm, Trim Size: 297 x 210mm, Bleed Size: 303 x 216mm
Copy instructions: Copy Date: 8th of the month prior to 1st cover month
Average advertising content per issue: 50%
BUSINESS: CERAMICS, POTTERY & GLASS: Glass

CONSPECTUS
36050U5B-57
Editorial Address: Cavendish House, Cavendish Court, 44-47 Hill Avenue, AMERSHAM, HP6 5FA **Tel:** 0870 908 8767
Fax: 0870 134 0931
Email: editor@ncc.co.uk
Advertising Address: As above.
Email: meera.butterworth@ncc.co.uk
Web site: http://www.conspectus.com
ISSN: 1363-6804
Publisher: NCC (UK) Ltd
Frequency: 11 issues yearly - Published in the middle of the cover month
Free to qualifying individuals
Circulation: 22,000 (Publisher's Statement)
Usual Pagination: 32
Editor: Tim Ring; **Publisher:** Steve Markwell
Summary of Content: Magazine covering developments in information technology, with each issue focusing on a separate IT topic.
Readership/Target Audience: Aimed at directors and decision makers.
ADVERTISING RATES:
Full Page Colour £3600.00
Mechanical Data: Trim Size: 297 x 210mm
Average advertising content per issue: 45%
BUSINESS: COMPUTERS & AUTOMATION: Data Processing

CONSTABULARY MAGAZINE
38429U32F-110
Editorial Address: PR only accepted via e-mail
Tel: 0870 350 1892
Email: chrislocke@constabularymagazine.co.uk
Advertising Address: Landmark Publishing Services, 2 Windmill Street, LONDON, W1T 2HX **Tel:** 020 7692 9292
Fax: 020 7692 9393
Email: sharon@lps.co.uk
Web site: http://www.constabulary.org.uk
Publisher: National Press Publishers Ltd
Date Established: 1979
Frequency: 10 issues yearly
Free to qualifying individuals
Circulation: 30,000 (Publisher's Statement)
Usual Pagination: 20
Editor: Chris Locke; **Editor-in-Chief:** Chris Locke
Summary of Content: Magazine featuring police news, product reviews, political interviews, IT section, training, celebrity interviews and articles on leisure, travel, finance, motoring and force profiles.
Readership/Target Audience: Read by members of the police force as well as retired members. Distributed internally via police stations plus 4000 mailed to key personnel and home addresses.
ADVERTISING RATES:
Full Page Mono £4900.00
Full Page Colour £4900.00
SCC £30.00
Agency Commission: 10%
Mechanical Data: Type Area: 420 x 297mm, No. of Columns (Display): 6, Col Length: 420mm, Page Width: 297mm, Film: Digital
Copy instructions: Copy Date: 2 weeks prior to publication date
Average advertising content per issue: 40%
BUSINESS: LOCAL GOVERNMENT, LEISURE & RECREATION: Police

CONSTRUCTION COMPUTING
1696778U42A-232
Formerly: Construction Computing Online
Editorial Address: 35 Station Square, Petts Wood, ORPINGTON, BR5 1LZ **Tel:** 01689 616000
Fax: 01689 826622
Email: david.chadwick@btc.co.uk
Advertising Address: As above.
Email: josh.bolton@btc.co.uk
Web site: http://www.construction-computing.com
Publisher: Business & Technical Communications
Date Established: 2005
Frequency: 6 issues yearly
Free to qualifying individuals
Circulation: 10,000 (Publisher's Statement)

Usual Pagination: 36
Editor: David Chadwick
Summary of Content: Magazine focusing on construction related IT products and services, including case studies, product reviews, interviews, research, analysis and training.
Readership/Target Audience: Aimed at construction IT professionals.
ADVERTISING RATES:
Full Page Colour £1250.00
Agency Commission: 10%
Copy instructions: Copy Date: 1 week prior to publication date
Average advertising content per issue: 50%
BUSINESS: CONSTRUCTION

CONSTRUCTION EQUIPMENT ASIA
1793972U42A-241
Editorial Address: The Courtyard, Sondes Road, DEAL, CT14 7BW **Tel:** 01304 368688 **Fax:** 01304 375181
Email: john.hooper@joempr.demon.co.uk
Advertising Address: As above.
Email: john.hooper@joempr.demon.co.uk
Web site: http://www.construction-equipment-asia.com
Publisher: Joem PR Far East
Frequency: Quarterly
Cover Price: Free
Circulation: 15,000 (Publisher's Statement)
Usual Pagination: 36
Editor: John Hooper; **Advertising Manager:** John Hooper
Summary of Content: Magazine covering equipment for civil engineering, infrastructure building, extraction industries, water and oil pipelines and ports construction.
Language(s): Chinese; English; Korean; Thai; Vietnamese
Readership/Target Audience: Aimed at key buyers and specifiers in the construction industry throughout South East Asia and China.
ADVERTISING RATES:
Full Page Colour £2200.00
Agency Commission: 15%
BUSINESS: CONSTRUCTION

CONSTRUCTION EUROPE
38975U42A-29_50
Editorial Address: Southfields, Southview Road, WADHURST, TN5 6TP **Tel:** 01892 784088
Fax: 01892 786257
Email: chris.sleight@khl.com
Advertising Address: As above. **Fax:** 01892 784086
Email: david.stowe@khl.com
Web site: http://www.khl.com
ISSN: 0964-0665
Publisher: KHL Group
Date Established: 1990
Frequency: Monthly - Published on the 15th of the cover month
Free to qualifying individuals
Annual Sub.: £140.00
Circulation: 13,795 (BPA Worldwide 01/07/2007 to 31/12/2007)
Usual Pagination: 76
Editor: Chris Sleight; **Advertising Manager:** David Stowe;
Publisher: James King
Summary of Content: News and features for the construction industry in Europe.
Language(s): English; French; German
Readership/Target Audience: Read by contractors, consultants and international authorities.
ADVERTISING RATES:
Full Page Colour £4250.00
Agency Commission: 10%
Mechanical Data: Page Width: 184mm, Type Area: 268 x 184mm, Col Length: 268mm, Trim Size: 297 x 210mm, Bleed Size: 303 x 216mm, Film: Digital
Copy instructions: Copy Date: 3 weeks prior to publication date
Average advertising content per issue: 60%
BUSINESS: CONSTRUCTION

CONSTRUCTION FORUM
767832U42A-212
Editorial Address: Bradford Buildings, 27 Mawdsley Street, BOLTON, BL1 1LN **Tel:** 01204 418866 **Fax:** 01204 418890
Email: gwinrow@forummedia.org
Advertising Address: As above.
Email: mail@forummedia.org
Web site: http://www.forummedia.org
ISSN: 1477-5875
Publisher: Forum Media Ltd
Date Established: 2002
Frequency: Monthly
Cover Price: £3.50
Annual Sub.: £64.00
Circulation: 21,000 (Publisher's Statement)
Usual Pagination: 100
Editor: Gareth Winrow; **Advertising Manager:** Gareth Winrow
Summary of Content: Magazine covering news and developments within the construction industry as well as

construction reports and architectural and civil engineering projects throughout the UK and Ireland.
Readership/Target Audience: Aimed at construction industry professionals, developers, main contractors, architects, consultants, local and central government, councils and housing associations, both in the UK and Ireland.
ADVERTISING RATES:
Full Page Colour £1625.00
Agency Commission: 10%
Mechanical Data: Bleed Size: +3mm, Trim Size: 297 x 210mm, No. of Columns (Display): 6, Print Process: Offset litho, Film: Digital
Copy instructions: Copy Date: 4 weeks prior to publication date
Average advertising content per issue: 25%
BUSINESS: CONSTRUCTION

CONSTRUCTION HOUSING 1732883U42A-235
Editorial Address: Brook House, Brook Street, Hazel Grove, STOCKPORT, SK7 4QX **Tel:** 0161 292 3432
Fax: 0161 292 3299
Email: editorial@networkmediagroup.co.uk
Advertising Address: Suite 6B, Blackfriars House, St. Mary's Parsonage, MANCHESTER, M3 2JA
Tel: 0161 830 4567 **Fax:** 0161 839 1443
Email: richard@networkmediagroup.co.uk
Web site: http://www.constructionhousing.co.uk
Publisher: Destination Maps & Media Ltd
Date Established: 2006
Frequency: Quarterly
Free to qualifying individuals
Editor: Chris Stokes; **Advertising Manager:** Richard Shepherd
Summary of Content: Magazine focusing on new build housing projects in the UK.
Readership/Target Audience: Aimed at architects, surveyors and consultant engineers.
ADVERTISING RATES:
Full Page Colour £1500.00
Agency Commission: 10%
Mechanical Data: Type Area: 266 x 185mm, Bleed Size: 295 x 215mm, Trim Size: 290 x 210mm, Col Length: 266mm, Page Width: 185mm, Film: Digital
Copy instructions: Copy Date: Beginning of the month prior to publication date
BUSINESS: CONSTRUCTION

CONSTRUCTION INDUSTRY LAW LETTER 39137U44-340
Editorial Address: Telephone House, 69-77 Paul Street, LONDON, EC2A 4LQ **Tel:** 020 7017 4600
Fax: 020 7017 5274
Email: jessica.westwood@informa.com
Web site: http://www.informalaw.com
ISSN: 0269-0039
Publisher: Informa PLC
Frequency: 10 issues yearly
Annual Sub.: £499.00
Circulation: 476 (Publisher's Statement)
Usual Pagination: 12
Editor: Jessica Westwood; **Publisher:** Victoria Ophield
Summary of Content: Newsletter summarising new developments in the law affecting the construction industry.
Readership/Target Audience: Read by people working in construction, planning and development.
ADVERTISING: No Advertising taken
BUSINESS: LEGAL

CONSTRUCTION INDUSTRY NEWS 1626198U4A-308
Editorial Address: 17 Old Leeds Road, HUDDERSFIELD, HD1 1SG **Tel:** 01484 441400 **Fax:** 01484 441421
Email: editorial@codebluegroup.co.uk
Advertising Address: As above. **Fax:** 01484 441401
Email: simon.thornhill@codebluegroup.co.uk
Web site: http://www.cinmagazine.co.uk
Publisher: Code Blue Publishing Limited
Frequency: Monthly
Cover Price: £2.95
Circulation: 6,000 (Publisher's Statement)
Editor: Nigel Martin
Summary of Content: Magazine covering all sectors of the building and construction industry.
Readership/Target Audience: Aimed at senior management.
ADVERTISING RATES:
Full Page Mono £1395.00
Full Page Colour £1965.00
Agency Commission: 10%
Mechanical Data: Type Area: 280 x 216mm, Col Length: 280mm, Page Width: 216mm, Film: Digital
Copy instructions: Copy Date: 7 days prior to publication date
Average advertising content per issue: 40%
BUSINESS: ARCHITECTURE & BUILDING: Architecture

CONSTRUCTION INDUSTRY NEWS IRELAND 1834633U4E-451
Editorial Address: 17 Old Leeds Road, HUDDERSFIELD, HD1 1SG **Tel:** 01484 441400 **Fax:** 01484 441421
Email: editorial@codebluegroup.co.uk
Advertising Address: As above. **Fax:** 01484 441401
Email: barry.smith@codebluegroup.co.uk
Publisher: Code Blue Publishing Limited
Date Established: 2008
Frequency: Monthly
Cover Price: £2.95
Circulation: 6,000 (Publisher's Statement)
Editor: Nigel Martin
Summary of Content: Magazine covering all sectors of the building and construction industry.
Readership/Target Audience: Aimed at senior management in the Irish Republic and Northern Ireland.
ADVERTISING RATES:
Full Page Mono EUR1848.00
Full Page Colour EUR2513.00
Agency Commission: 10%
Mechanical Data: Type Area: 280 x 216mm, Bleed Size: +3mm, Film: Digital
BUSINESS: ARCHITECTURE & BUILDING: Building

CONSTRUCTION IRELAND 38976U42A-32
Editorial Address: Unit N4, Chorley Business & Technology Centre, Euxton Lane, Euxton, CHORLEY, PR7 6TE
Tel: 01257 231900 **Fax:** 01257 249389
Email: edit@esengroup.co.uk
Advertising Address: As above. **Tel:** 01204 386363
Email: mblackmore@esengroup.co.uk
Web site: http://www.esengroup.co.uk
ISSN: 1461-2720
Publisher: ESEN Group
Date Established: 1997
Frequency: 6 issues yearly
Free to qualifying individuals
Annual Sub.: £75.00
Circulation: 4,004 (ABC 01/07/2007 to 30/06/2008)
Usual Pagination: 75
Editor: Victoria Lee; **Advertising Manager:** Mathew Blackmore
Summary of Content: Magazine focusing on the building and construction industry in Ireland. Includes articles on nationwide projects, legislation changes, EU edicts, training programmes and new products and services.
Readership/Target Audience: Aimed at local government, architects, quantity surveyors, mechanical, electrical and structural engineers and construction companies.
ADVERTISING RATES:
Full Page Colour £1695.00
Agency Commission: 10%
Mechanical Data: Type Area: 266 x 185mm, Col Length: 266mm, Bleed Size: 307 x 216mm, Trim Size: 297 x 210mm, Page Width: 185mm, Film: Digital
Copy instructions: Copy Date: 3 weeks prior to publication date
Average advertising content per issue: 45%
BUSINESS: CONSTRUCTION

CONSTRUCTION LAW REVIEW 39090U44-345
Editorial Address: Dominion House, Sibson Road, SALE, M33 7PP **Tel:** 0161 972 3110 **Fax:** 0161 972 3118
Email: editor@ices.org.uk
Web site: http://www.ices.org.uk
ISSN: 0266-139X
Publisher: Institution of Civil Engineering Surveyors
Date Established: 1996
Frequency: Annual - Published in July
Cover Price: £5.00
Free to qualifying individuals
Annual Sub.: £32.00
Circulation: 6,000 (Publisher's Statement)
Usual Pagination: 100
Editor: Darrell Smart; **Editor-in-Chief:** Darrell Smart
Summary of Content: Journal containing a major review of developments in construction law in the UK and overseas.
Readership/Target Audience: Aimed at surveyors, consulting engineers and lawyers working in construction.
ADVERTISING: Rates on application
Mechanical Data: Film: Positive, right reading, emulsion side down, Type Area: 267 x 180mm, Print Process: Sheet-fed offset litho, Screen: Mono: 40 lpc, Colour: 54 lpc, Col Length: 267mm, Page Width: 180mm, Bleed Size: 303 x 216mm, Trim Size: 297 x 210mm
Supplement to: Civil Engineering Surveyor
Supplement(s): Electronic Surveying - 1xY, GIS/GPS - 1xY, ICES Yearbook - 1xY
BUSINESS: LEGAL

CONSTRUCTION MAGAZINE 623164U42A-35
Editorial Address: 7 Bay Hall, Willow Lane, Birkby, HUDDERSFIELD, HD1 5EN **Tel:** 01484 321000
Fax: 01484 321001
Email: d.wilson@planet-group.co.uk

Advertising Address: As above.
Email: d.wilson@planet-group.co.uk
Web site: http://www.construction-online.net
Publisher: The Planet Group (UK) Ltd
Date Established: 1999
Frequency: Monthly
Cover Price: £2.50
Annual Sub.: £30.00
Circulation: 17,500 (Publisher's Statement)
Usual Pagination: 110
Editor: Rod Millington; **Advertising Manager:** Dennis Wilson
Summary of Content: Magazine covering the construction industry, contains news, project and company features, product news and profiles.
Readership/Target Audience: Aimed at the general construction industry.
ADVERTISING RATES:
Full Page Mono £1665.00
Full Page Colour £1905.00
Agency Commission: 10%
Mechanical Data: Bleed Size: 303 x 216, Trim Size: 297 x 210, Film: Digital
Copy instructions: Copy Date: 3rd Friday of the month prior to publication date
Average advertising content per issue: 35%
BUSINESS: CONSTRUCTION

CONSTRUCTION MANAGER 35904U4E-167
Formerly: Construction Manager inc. Construction Computing
Editorial Address: 3rd Floor, Ludgate House, 245 Blackfriars Road, LONDON, SE1 9UY **Tel:** 020 7560 4052
Email: elaine.knutt@ubm.com
Advertising Address: As above. **Tel:** 020 7560 4100
Fax: 020 7560 4008
Email: lucy.morphew@ubm.com
Web site: http://www.construction-manager.co.uk
ISSN: 1360-3566
Publisher: UBM Information Ltd
Date Established: 2000
Frequency: 10 issues yearly - Published in the 1st week of the cover month
Annual Sub.: £65.00
Circulation: 33,438 (ABC 01/07/2008 to 30/06/2009)
Usual Pagination: 60
Editor: Elaine Knutt; **Advertising Manager:** Lucy Morphew; **Publisher:** Nina Wright
Summary of Content: Magazine containing news and information about the building industry as well as articles about the C.I.O.B.
Readership/Target Audience: Aimed at project managers, quantity surveyors, property developers, site managers, engineers, local authorities and architects.
ADVERTISING RATES:
Full Page Mono £2249.00
Full Page Colour £2249.00
Agency Commission: 10%
Mechanical Data: Type Area: 254 x 178mm, Col Length: 254mm, Page Width: 178mm, Bleed Size: 303 x 216mm, Trim Size: 297 x 210mm, Film: Digital
Copy instructions: Copy Date: 3 weeks prior to publication date
Average advertising content per issue: 10%
BUSINESS: ARCHITECTURE & BUILDING: Building

CONSTRUCTION NATIONAL 38978U42A-38
Formerly: Construction Midlands
Editorial Address: Brook House, Brook Street, Hazel Grove, STOCKPORT, SK7 4QX **Tel:** 0161 292 3432
Fax: 0161 292 3299
Email: editorial@networkmediagroup.co.uk
Advertising Address: 14 Booth Street, SALFORD, M3 5DG
Tel: 0161 408 2395 **Fax:** 0161 830 4559
Email: richard@networkmediagroup.co.uk
Web site: http://www.constructionmagazine.net
Publisher: Destination Maps & Media Ltd
Frequency: Quarterly
Cover Price: £5.00
Free to qualifying individuals
Annual Sub.: £27.00
Circulation: 5,007 (Publisher's Statement)
Usual Pagination: 70
Editor: Chris Stokes; **Managing Director:** Stephen Foley
Summary of Content: Magazine containing the latest news on the construction industry.
Readership/Target Audience: Aimed at architects, surveyors, consulting engineers, property owners and personnel within government departments and health authorities.
ADVERTISING RATES:
Full Page Colour £1500.00
Agency Commission: 10%
Mechanical Data: Trim Size: 290 x 210mm, Bleed Size: 295 x 215mm, Film: Digital, Type Area: 266 x 185mm, Col Length: 266mm, Page Width: 185mm

Section 4 (b) Business Magazines

Business Magazines

Copy instructions: Copy Date: Beginning of the month prior to publication date
BUSINESS: CONSTRUCTION

CONSTRUCTION NEWS
38979U42A-40
Editorial Address: Greater London House, Hampstead Road, LONDON, NW1 7EJ **Tel:** 020 7391 3435
Fax: 020 7728 4400
Email: cneditorial@emap.com
Advertising Address: As above. **Tel:** 020 7728 5000
Fax: 020 7391 3435
Email: martin.sinclair@emap.com
Web site: http://www.cnplus.co.uk
ISSN: 0010-6860
Publisher: EMAP Inform
Date Established: 1871
Frequency: Weekly - Published every Thursday
Cover Price: £3.00
Annual Sub.: £99.00
Circulation: 16,523 (ABC 01/07/2008 to 30/06/2009)
Usual Pagination: 64
Editor: Nick Edwards; **Features Editor:** Lucy Handley;
Advertising Manager: Martin Sinclair
Summary of Content: Magazine containing the latest news for the building and construction industry.
Twitter: https://twitter.com/CONSTRUCTIONews.
Readership/Target Audience: Aimed at contractors, sub-contractors, materials manufacturers and suppliers, plant manufacturers and suppliers and plant hire services to the construction industry.
ADVERTISING RATES:
Full Page Mono £4300.00
Full Page Colour £4300.00
Agency Commission: 10%
Mechanical Data: Bleed Size: 353 x 254mm, Trim Size: 347 x 248mm, Film: Positive, right reading, emulsion side down. Digital
Copy instructions: Copy Date: 2 weeks prior to publication date
Average advertising content per issue: 50%
BUSINESS: CONSTRUCTION

THE CONSTRUCTION PLANT-HIRE ASSOCIATION BULLETIN
38981U42A-46
Editorial Address: 27-28 Newbury Street, Barbican, LONDON, EC1A 7HU **Tel:** 020 7796 3366
Fax: 020 7796 3399
Email: enquiries@cpa.uk.net
Advertising Address: As above.
Email: enquiries@cpa.uk.net
Web site: http://www.cpa.uk.net
Publisher: CPA
Date Established: 1941
Frequency: Quarterly
Free to qualifying individuals
Circulation: 2,000 (Publisher's Statement)
Usual Pagination: 32
Editor: Adam Godwin; **Advertising Manager:** Neil Levett
Summary of Content: Magazine providing articles on health and safety, employment law, training information and forthcoming events.
Readership/Target Audience: Circulated to construction plant hire companies in the UK.
ADVERTISING: Rates on application
BUSINESS: CONSTRUCTION

CONSTRUCTION RISKS SPECIAL REPORT
38983U42A-47_50
Formerly: Construction Risks
Editorial Address: 145 London Road, KINGSTON UPON THAMES, KT2 6SR **Tel:** 020 8247 1211 **Fax:** 020 8546 9374
Email: matthew.looker@croner.co.uk
Web site: http://www.croner.co.uk
Publisher: Wolters Kluwer (UK) Ltd
Frequency: 10 issues yearly
Editor: Matthew Looker
Summary of Content: Bulletin containing in-depth articles which cover a specific aspect of construction risk assessment in each issue.
Readership/Target Audience: Mainly read by contractors.
ADVERTISING: No Advertising taken
BUSINESS: CONSTRUCTION

CONSTRUCTION SAFETY BRIEFING
38984U42A-48
Editorial Address: 145 London Road, KINGSTON UPON THAMES, KT2 6SR **Tel:** 0870 240 4388 **Fax:** 020 8546 9374
Email: matthew.looker@croner.co.uk
Web site: http://www.croner.cch.co.uk
Publisher: Wolters Kluwer (UK) Ltd
Frequency: Monthly
Usual Pagination: 8
Editor: Matthew Looker

Summary of Content: Newsletter covering the latest developments within construction health and safety.
Readership/Target Audience: Read by contractors, client organisations, designers, planners and supervisors.
ADVERTISING: No Advertising taken
BUSINESS: CONSTRUCTION

CONSTRUCTION SCOTLAND
1840307U4E-453
Editorial Address: Portland Buildings, 127-129 Portland Street, MANCHESTER, M1 4PZ **Tel:** 0161 236 2782
Fax: 0161 236 2783
Email: paula.english@excelpublishing.co.uk
Advertising Address: As above.
Email: paula.english@excelpublishing.co.uk
Web site: http://www.construction-scotland.co.uk
Publisher: Excel Publishing Company Ltd
Date Established: 2008
Frequency: Quarterly - Published in the 2nd week of the cover month
Annual Sub.: £15.00
Circulation: 5,000 (Print Run)
Editor: Paula English
Summary of Content: Magazine covering construction in Scotland. Featuring news, legislation, education, training, recruitment and health and safety.
Readership/Target Audience: Aimed at RIAS architects in Scotland, all key Scottish main contractors, property developers, house builders, quantity surveyors, structural engineers and key subcontractors and installers.
ADVERTISING RATES:
Full Page Colour £995.00
Agency Commission: 10%
Mechanical Data: Type Area: 266 x 185mm, Bleed Size: 303 x 216mm, Trim Size: 297 x 210mm, Col Length: 266mm, Page Width: 185mm, Film: Digital
Copy instructions: Copy Date: 4 weeks prior to publication date
Average advertising content per issue: 40%
BUSINESS: ARCHITECTURE & BUILDING: Building

CONSTRUCTION TODAY
1639504U4E-411
Editorial Address: Unit 10, Cringleford Business Centre, Intwood Road, Cringleford, NORWICH, NR4 6AU
Tel: 01603 274130 **Fax:** 01603 274136
Email: libbie@schofieldpublishing.co.uk
Advertising Address: Cringleford Business Centre, Intwood Road, Cringleford, NORWICH, NR4 6AU **Tel:** 01603 274130
Fax: 01603 274136
Email: gallinson@schofieldpublishing.co.uk
Web site: http://www.schofield-media.com
Publisher: Schofield Publishing Ltd
Date Established: 2004
Frequency: 6 issues yearly - Published at the end of the 1st cover month
Cover Price: £3.95
Free to qualifying individuals
Circulation: 10,000 (Publisher's Statement)
Usual Pagination: 120
Editor: Libbie Hammond; **Advertising Manager:** Graham Allinson
Summary of Content: Magazine covering construction related topics including engineering, technology, project funding, labour and legal issues, equipment, IT and the environment.
Readership/Target Audience: Aimed at purchasing managers, contract managers and other executives in the construction industry.
ADVERTISING RATES:
Full Page Mono £2500.00
Full Page Colour £3265.00
Agency Commission: 10%
Mechanical Data: Bleed Size: 303 x 216mm, Trim Size: 297 x 210mm, Film: Digital
Copy instructions: Copy Date: 1 week prior to publication date
Average advertising content per issue: 30%
BUSINESS: ARCHITECTURE & BUILDING: Building

CONSTRUCTOR AND ARCHITECT
1647353U42A-216
Formerly: Constructor
Editorial Address: Barham Court, Teston, MAIDSTONE, ME18 5BZ **Tel:** 01622 618796 **Fax:** 01622 618793
Email: juliet@cimltd.co.uk
Advertising Address: As above. **Fax:** 01622 618653
Email: ross@cimltd.co.uk
Web site: http://www.constructorgroup.co.uk
Publisher: CIM LLP
Date Established: 2004
Frequency: Monthly - Published in the 3rd week of the cover month
Cover Price: Free
Cover Price: £2.99
Circulation: 20,000 (Publisher's Statement)
Usual Pagination: 68
Editor: Ross Ringham

Summary of Content: Magazine covering specialist features, company and personal profiles, equipment evaluation, product updates, information on new products and specification and trade events for the building and design industry.
Readership/Target Audience: Aimed at housebuilders, building and sub contractors, architects, specifiers, project and facilities managers, allied trades and all decision makers or who have purchasing power.
ADVERTISING RATES:
Full Page Colour £2200.00
Agency Commission: 10%
Mechanical Data: Type Area: 290 x 220mm, Bleed Size: 306 x 236mm, Trim Size: 300 x 230mm, Col Length: 290mm, Page Width: 220mm, Film: Digital
Copy instructions: Copy Date: 4 weeks prior to publication date
BUSINESS: CONSTRUCTION

CONSULTING ENGINEER
1832413U3B-45
Editorial Address: The Maltings, West Street, BOURNE, PE10 9PH **Tel:** 01778 391000 **Fax:** 01778 392079
Email: philc@warnersgroup.co.uk
Advertising Address: As above.
Email: julietg@warnersgroup.co.uk
Web site: http://www.consultingengineer-hvacr.co.uk
Publisher: Warners Group Publications plc
Date Established: 2007
Frequency: 6 issues yearly
Cover Price: Free
Circulation: 6,273 (Publisher's Statement)
Editor: Phil Creaney; **Publisher:** Simon Moody
Summary of Content: Magazine covering the heating, ventilation, air conditioning and refrigeration industry featuring companies, people, products and projects to bring news of innovation, legislation and best practice.
Readership/Target Audience: Aimed at heating, ventilation, air conditioning and refrigeration consultants, designers, specifiers and end-users.
ADVERTISING RATES:
Full Page Colour £1350.00
Mechanical Data: Bleed Size: 303 x 216mm, Type Area: 275 x 190mm, Col Length: 275mm, Page Width: 190mm, Film: Digital, Trim Size: 297 x 210mm
Copy instructions: Copy Date: 4 weeks prior to publication date
BUSINESS: HEATING & VENTILATION: Industrial Heating & Ventilation

CONSULTING ENGINEER REVIEW
1657615U19R-452
Editorial Address: 28A Jubilee Trade Centre, Jubilee Road, LETCHWORTH GARDEN CITY, SG6 1SP
Tel: 020 8942 8899 **Fax:** 020 8942 3477
Email: kirsty@specifierreview.info
Advertising Address: As above.
Email: sales@specifierreview.info
Web site: http://www.specifierreview.info
Publisher: First City Media
Date Established: 2000
Frequency: Quarterly
Cover Price: Free
Circulation: 12,000 (Publisher's Statement)
Usual Pagination: 24
Editor: Kirsty Hammond
Summary of Content: Magazine providing product references and reviews for the construction industry.
Readership/Target Audience: Aimed at civil, structural and consulting engineers.
ADVERTISING RATES:
Full Page Colour £1855.00
Agency Commission: 10%
Mechanical Data: Type Area: 278 x 182mm, Print Process: Sheet-fed litho, Film: Digital, Col Length: 278mm, Page Width: 182mm, Trim Size: 297 x 210mm
Copy instructions: Copy Date: 1st of the month prior to publication date
Average advertising content per issue: 100%
BUSINESS: ENGINEERING & MACHINERY: Engineering Related

CONSUMER LAW TODAY
39138U44-350
Editorial Address: Telephone House, 69-77 Paul Street, LONDON, EC2A 4LQ **Tel:** 020 7017 6762
Fax: 020 7017 5274
Email: jessica.westwood@informa.com
Advertising Address: As above. **Tel:** 020 7017 5000
Fax: 020 7436 8384
Email: mark.windsor@informa.com
Web site: http://www.informalaw.com
ISSN: 0266-0628
Publisher: Informa PLC
Frequency: 10 issues yearly
Editor: Jessica Westwood

Summary of Content: Magazine containing an advisory service on consumer protection, safety, fair trading practices, consumer credit and relevant EC developments.
Readership/Target Audience: Aimed at those concerned with consumer protection and fair trading practices.
ADVERTISING: Rates on application
BUSINESS: LEGAL

CONTACT (BRITISH CHIROPRACTIC ASSOCIATION)
40515U56Q-10

Editorial Address: 59 Castle Street, READING, RG1 7SN
Tel: 0118 950 5950 **Fax:** 0118 958 8946
Email: anne.barlow@chiropractic-uk.co.uk
Advertising Address: As above.
Email: anne.barlow@chiropractic-uk.co.uk
Web site: http://www.chiropractic-uk.co.uk
Publisher: British Chiropractic Association
Frequency: Quarterly - Published in March, June, September and December
Cover Price: £1.50
Free to qualifying individuals
Circulation: 2,200 (Publisher's Statement)
Usual Pagination: 44
Editor: Anne Barlow; **Advertising Manager:** Ann Goble
Summary of Content: Magazine of the British Chiropractic Association. Featuring reports on committees, articles and features relevant to the chiropractic and medical field.
Readership/Target Audience: Read by members of the British Chiropractic Association.
ADVERTISING RATES:
Full Page Mono £402.60
Full Page Colour £402.60
Mechanical Data: Trim Size: 297 x 210mm
Copy instructions: Copy Date: 1st of month prior to publication date
BUSINESS: HEALTH & MEDICAL: Chiropractic

CONTAGIOUS
1685811U2A-671

Editorial Address: 45 Fouberts Place, LONDON, W1F 7QH
Tel: 020 7575 1981 **Fax:** 020 7525 1918
Email: hello@contagiousmagazine.com
Advertising Address: As above. **Tel:** 020 7575 1880
Fax: 020 7575 1988
Email: richard@contagiousmagazine.com
Web site: http://www.contagiousmagazine.com
Publisher: Xtreme Information
Date Established: 2004
Frequency: Quarterly
Annual Sub.: £975.00
Circulation: 2,500 (Publisher's Statement)
Usual Pagination: 100
Editor: Emily Hare
Summary of Content: Magazine focusing on non-invasive approaches to re-defining the advertising business. Topics covered include retail design, technology, future trends, branded entertainment and online innovations.
Readership/Target Audience: Aimed at the global marketing community.
ADVERTISING RATES:
Full Page Colour £4500.00
Mechanical Data: Bleed Size: 326 x 246mm, Trim Size: 320 x 240mm, Film: Digital
Copy instructions: Copy Date: 3 weeks prior to publication date
Average advertising content per issue: 8%
BUSINESS: COMMUNICATIONS, ADVERTISING & MARKETING

CONTAINER MANAGEMENT
39394U45C-23

Editorial Address: Marshall House, 124 Middleton Road, MORDEN, SM4 6RW **Tel:** 020 8648 7113
Email: sidcass@onetel.com
Advertising Address: As above. **Fax:** 020 8687 4130
Email: marieanne.hoffer@container-mag.com
Web site: http://www.container-mag.com
ISSN: 0269-7726
Publisher: Container Management Ltd
Date Established: 1984
Frequency: 8 issues yearly - Published in the 2nd week of the 1st cover month
Free to qualifying individuals
Annual Sub.: £180.00
Circulation: 4,474 (Publisher's Statement)
Usual Pagination: 60
Editor: Sid Cass; **Publisher:** Stuart Fryer
Summary of Content: Magazine focusing on container ports, shipping, intermodal operations and management, including container leasing and asset management, handling technology and issues and industry trends and developments.
Readership/Target Audience: Read by senior managers in ports, shipping companies, intermodal transport operators and related industry service providers and suppliers.
ADVERTISING RATES:
Full Page Colour £2100.00
Agency Commission: 10%

Mechanical Data: Type Area: 265 x 190mm, Page Width: 190mm, Bleed Size: 303 x 216mm, Film: Digital, Col Length: 265mm, Trim Size: 297 x 210mm
Copy instructions: Copy Date: Middle of the month prior to publication month
Average advertising content per issue: 40%
Supplement(s): Latin American - 2xY, World Top Container Pools - 1xY
BUSINESS: MARINE & SHIPPING: Maritime Freight

CONTAINERISATION INTERNATIONAL
39634U49C-63

Editorial Address: Telephone House, 69 77 Paul Street, LONDON, EC2A 4LQ **Tel:** 020 7017 4891
Fax: 020 7017 4976
Advertising Address: As above. **Tel:** 020 7017 5000
Email: ed.andrews@informa.com
Web site: http://www.ci-online.co.uk
Publisher: Informa Cargo Information
Date Established: 1967
Frequency: Monthly - Published on the 1st of the cover month
Annual Sub.: £199.00
Circulation: 10,498 (BPA Worldwide 01/01/2007 to 30/06/2007)
Usual Pagination: 84
Editor: John Fossey; **Advertising Manager:** Edward Andrews; **Managing Editor:** Matthew Beddow
Summary of Content: Magazine covering international authority on inter-modal container transportation, shipping, rail and trucking services, freighting policy, finance, insurance and leasing.
Readership/Target Audience: Aimed at shippers, manufacturers, ports and terminals, leasing companies, research institutes, ocean carriers and financial institutions.
ADVERTISING RATES:
Full Page Mono £3700.00
Full Page Colour £4400.00
Agency Commission: 10%
Mechanical Data: Type Area: 254 x 180mm, Bleed Size: 279 x 214mm, Trim Size: 273 x 208mm, Col Length: 254mm, Page Width: 180mm, Film: Digital
Copy instructions: Copy Date: Middle of the month prior to publication date
Average advertising content per issue: 40%
BUSINESS: TRANSPORT: Freight

CONTAINERISATION INTERNATIONAL YEARBOOK
601154U45C-20

Formerly: CI Yearbook
Editorial Address: Informa House, 30-32 Mortimer Street, LONDON, W1W 7RE **Tel:** 020 7017 5000
Fax: 020 7017 4976
Email: jane.degerlund@informa.com
Advertising Address: As above.
Email: ed.andrews@informa.com
Web site: http://www.ci-online.co.uk
ISSN: 0305-7402
Publisher: Informa UK Limited
Date Established: 1970
Frequency: Annual - Published in January
Cover Price: £350.00
Circulation: 1,000 (Publisher's Statement)
Usual Pagination: 960
Editor: Jane Degerlund
Summary of Content: International directory of the freight container transport industry, including ports, liner operators, containership register and equipment.
Readership/Target Audience: Aimed at shipping lines, port authorities, freight forwarders, industry analysts and consultants.
ADVERTISING RATES:
Full Page Mono £3400.00
Full Page Colour £4100.00
Agency Commission: 10%
Mechanical Data: Type Area: 254 x 178mm, Bleed Size: 303 x 216mm, Trim Size: 297 x 210mm, Col Length: 254mm, No. of Columns (Display): 4, Film: Digital, Page Width: 178mm
Average advertising content per issue: 15%
BUSINESS: MARINE & SHIPPING: Maritime Freight

CONTEMPORARY ISSUES IN LAW
23665U44-355

Editorial Address: Office G18, Spinners Court, 55 West End, WITNEY, OX28 1NH **Tel:** 01993 706183
Fax: 01993 703410
Email: ltp@lawtext.com
Advertising Address: As above. **Fax:** 01993 709410
Email: ltp@lawtext.com
Web site: http://www.lawtext.com
ISSN: 1357-0374
Publisher: Lawtext Publishing Ltd
Frequency: Quarterly
Annual Sub.: £85.00

Editor: Nick Gingell; **Advertising Manager:** Nick Gingell; **Publisher:** Nick Gingell
Summary of Content: Journal covering topical issues for law academics, practitioners and students.
Readership/Target Audience: Read by all those involved in law including practitioners and students.
ADVERTISING: Rates on application
BUSINESS: LEGAL

CONTEMPORARY PHYSICS
39958U55-50

Editorial Address: 4 Park Square, Milton Park, ABINGDON, OX14 4RN **Tel:** 020 7017 6000 **Fax:** 020 7017 6336
Email: p.knight@imperial.ac.uk
Web site: http://www.informaworld.com/tcph
ISSN: 0010-7514
Publisher: Routledge, Taylor & Francis
Date Established: 1953
Frequency: 6 issues yearly
Annual Sub.: £165.00
Circulation: 1,000 (Publisher's Statement)
Usual Pagination: 100
Editor: Peter Knight
Summary of Content: Journal written by scientists, covering the latest developments in physics and related topics.
Readership/Target Audience: Readership includes researchers, educators, students and those employed in government or industrial establishments.
ADVERTISING: Rates on application
BUSINESS: APPLIED SCIENCE & LABORATORIES

CONTEXT
600795U32F-115

Editorial Address: PO Box 77, Hutton, PRESTON, PR4 5SB
Tel: 01772 412973 **Fax:** 01772 412478
Email: context@lancashire.pnn.police.uk
Web site: http://www.lancashire.police.uk
Publisher: Lancashire Constabulary
Date Established: 1998
Frequency: Monthly
Cover Price: Free
Circulation: 2,500 (Publisher's Statement)
Usual Pagination: 12
Editor: Sarah Airey
Summary of Content: In-house newspaper of the Lancashire Constabulary covering news and events relating to support staff and staff working in operational offices.
Readership/Target Audience: Read mainly by staff and some retired personnel.
ADVERTISING: No Advertising taken
BUSINESS: LOCAL GOVERNMENT, LEISURE & RECREATION: Police

CONTEXT NEWS MAGAZINE OF FAMILY THERAPY AND SYSTEMIC PRACTICE IN THE UK
38466U32G-44

Formerly: Context News Magazine of Family Therapy and Systemic Practice
Editorial Address: 7 Executive Suite, St James Court, Wilderspool Causeway, WARRINGTON, WA4 6PS
Tel: 01925 444414
Email: bcade@netspace.net.au
Advertising Address: As above.
Email: s.kennedy@aft.org.uk
Web site: http://www.aft.org.uk
ISSN: 0969-1936
Publisher: AFT Ltd
Date Established: 1972
Frequency: 6 issues yearly
Cover Price: £6.50
Free to qualifying individuals
Annual Sub.: £30.00
Circulation: 1,600 (Publisher's Statement)
Usual Pagination: 52
Editor: Louise Norris; **Advertising Manager:** Louise Norris
Summary of Content: Magazine focusing on family systems ideas, therapy and related work, including current events, politics and the arts.
Readership/Target Audience: Aimed at members of the Association for Family Therapy & Systematic Practice, professionals, voluntary workers and academics interested in how families and small groups operate. Also includes a job advertisement service.
ADVERTISING RATES:
Full Page Mono £500.00
Agency Commission: 10%
Mechanical Data: Page Width: 168mm, Col Length: 257mm, Type Area: 257 x 168mm, Trim Size: 297 x 210mm
Copy instructions: Copy Date: 1 month prior to publication date
Average advertising content per issue: 20%
BUSINESS: LOCAL GOVERNMENT, LEISURE & RECREATION: Community Care & Social Services

CONTINUITY, INSURANCE & RISK

35112U1D-58

Formerly: CIR Continuity Insurance & Risk
Editorial Address: 6th Floor, 3 London Wall Buildings, LONDON, EC2M 5PD **Tel:** 020 7562 2401
Fax: 020 7562 2701
Email: deborah.ritchie@cirmagazine.com
Advertising Address: As above. **Tel:** 020 7562 2400
Fax: 020 7374 2701
Email: murray.barber@cirmagazine.com
Web site: http://www.cirmagazine.com
ISSN: 1364-3606
Publisher: Perspective Publishing Ltd
Date Established: 1996
Frequency: 6 issues yearly - Published the 25th of the 1st cover month
Free to qualifying individuals
Annual Sub.: £189.00
Circulation: 8,584 (ABC 01/07/2007 to 30/06/2008)
Usual Pagination: 76
Editor: Deborah Ritchie; **Managing Director:** John Woods;
Advertising Manager: Murray Barber
Summary of Content: Magazine covering corporate risk industry news, risk analysis, insurance, legal rulings and health and safety issues. Includes IT security, market surveys, profiles and conference and events coverage.
Readership/Target Audience: Aimed at Risk Managers and insurance buyers in corporations, Business Continuity Managers, Heads of Risk and Compliance and Health and Safety Personnel.
ADVERTISING RATES:
Full Page Mono £2889.00
Full Page Colour £3756.00
Agency Commission: 10%
Mechanical Data: Page Width: 181mm, Trim Size: 297 x 210mm, Type Area: 262 x 181mm, Bleed Size: 303 x 216mm, Col Length: 262mm, Film: Digital
Copy instructions: Copy Date: 3 weeks prior to publication date
Average advertising content per issue: 33%
BUSINESS: FINANCE & ECONOMICS: Insurance

CONTRACT FLOORS

600845U23B-50

Editorial Address: Suite 3, Independent House, Imberhorne Lane, EAST GRINSTEAD, RH19 1TU **Tel:** 01342 300070
Fax: 01342 300060
Email: emma@floordata.com
Advertising Address: As above.
Email: hayley@floordata.com
Web site: http://www.floordata.com
ISSN: 1465-1459
Publisher: Networks Business Publications
Date Established: 1999
Frequency: Monthly - Published on the 1st of the cover month
Free to qualifying individuals
Annual Sub.: £75.00
Circulation: 7,747 (ABC 01/07/2006 to 30/06/2007)
Usual Pagination: 72
Editor: Emma Jamieson
Summary of Content: Magazine covering all aspects of flooring from sub-floors to floor coverings.
Readership/Target Audience: Aimed at flooring contractors, architects and specifiers.
ADVERTISING RATES:
Full Page Colour £1295.00
Agency Commission: 10%
Mechanical Data: Col Length: 287mm, No. of Columns (Display): 4, Bleed Size: 303 x 216mm, Print Process: Web-fed offset litho, Trim Size: 297 x 210mm, Page Width: 200mm, Film: Digital, Type Area: 287 x 200mm
Copy instructions: Copy Date: 2 weeks prior to publication date
Average advertising content per issue: 60%
Supplement(s): Wood and Laminates - 2xY
BUSINESS: FURNISHINGS & FURNITURE: Furnishings, Carpets & Flooring

CONTRACT FURNISHING CONCEPTS

1745609U23A-313

Editorial Address: Q1 Capital Park, Capital Business Park, Parkway, CARDIFF, CF3 2PU **Tel:** 029 2077 8918
Fax: 029 2079 3508
Email: mikes@smeuk.com
Advertising Address: As above.
Email: mikes@smeuk.com
Web site: http://www.thefurnishinggroup.co.uk/cfc/cfcfindex1.htm
ISSN: 1749-7779
Publisher: FUSS Limited
Date Established: 2006
Frequency: 6 issues yearly
Free to qualifying individuals
Annual Sub.: £21.00
Circulation: 3,500 (Publisher's Statement)
Usual Pagination: 36

Editor: Mike Spencer; **Editor-in-Chief:** Mike Spencer;
Advertising Manager: Mike Spencer
Summary of Content: Publication covering news, views and features on contract furniture, fabrics, materials, exhibitions, sector specific business issues, machinery, design and designers.
Readership/Target Audience: Aimed at architects, specifiers, contract furnishers, designers, hotels, interior designers, contract upholsterers and public procurement authorities.
ADVERTISING: Rates on application
BUSINESS: FURNISHINGS & FURNITURE

CONTRACT JOURNAL

38989U42A-60

Editorial Address: Quadrant House, The Quadrant, SUTTON, SM2 5AS **Tel:** 020 8652 3500 **Fax:** 020 8652 8958
Email: james.stagg@rbi.co.uk
Advertising Address: As above. **Fax:** 020 8652 4804
Email: tim.porter@rbi.co.uk
Web site: http://www.contractjournal.com
ISSN: 0010-7859
Publisher: Reed Business Information
Frequency: Weekly - Published on Wednesday
Cover Price: £3.35
Free to qualifying individuals
Annual Sub.: £139.00
Circulation: 21,232 (ABC 01/07/2008 to 31/12/2008)
Usual Pagination: 48
Editor: Aaron Morby
Summary of Content: Newspaper covering the latest news in the construction industry.
Readership/Target Audience: Aimed at staff working in civil engineering, project managers, building contractors, sub-contractors, construction engineers, plant hire companies, quality surveying practices and the extractive industries.
ADVERTISING RATES:
Full Page Colour £4060.00
Agency Commission: 10%
Mechanical Data: Type Area: 277 x 202mm, Col Length: 277mm, Trim Size: 300 x 226mm, Bleed Size: 306 x 232mm, Film: Digital, Page Width: 202mm
Copy instructions: Copy Date: 2 weeks prior to publication date
Average advertising content per issue: 55%
BUSINESS: CONSTRUCTION

CONTRACTING BULLETIN

37934U21R-160

Formerly: Update
Editorial Address: Samuelson House, 62 Forder Way, Hampton, PETERBOROUGH, PE7 8JB **Tel:** 0845 6448 748
Fax: 01733 362921
Email: jill.hewitt@naac.co.uk
Advertising Address: As above.
Email: jill.hewitt@naac.co.uk
Web site: http://www.naac.co.uk
Publisher: National Association of Agricultural Contractors
Date Established: 2001
Frequency: Monthly
Free to qualifying individuals
Circulation: 450 (Publisher's Statement)
Usual Pagination: 16
Editor: Jill Hewitt
Summary of Content: Journal of the National Association of Agricultural Contractors, covering all aspects of agricultural and amenity contracting operations.
Readership/Target Audience: Read by members of the National Association of Agricultural Contractors.
ADVERTISING: Rates on application
BUSINESS: AGRICULTURE & FARMING: Agriculture & Farming Related

CONTRASTS

35810U4A-120

Editorial Address: 157 Vicarage Road, Leyton, LONDON, E10 5DU **Tel:** 020 8539 3876 **Fax:** 020 8539 3876
Email: keys@fsmail.net
Publisher: Delane Press
Date Established: 1983
Frequency: Annual - Published in the autumn
Cover Price: Free
Editor: Ronald King
Summary of Content: Journal consists of a study of Pugin, Gothic architecture and medieval guilds.
Readership/Target Audience: Read by specialists in early Victorian architecture, arts and crafts.
ADVERTISING: No Advertising taken
BUSINESS: ARCHITECTURE & BUILDING: Architecture

CONTRAX WEEKLY

35460U1R-3_110

Editorial Address: 300 Glasgow Road, Rutherglen, GLASGOW, G73 1SQ **Tel:** 0141 332 8247
Fax: 0141 353 2151
Email: grahame.steed@bipsolutions.com
Web site: http://www.bipsolutions.com
Publisher: BIP Solutions Ltd

Frequency: Weekly
Annual Sub.: £880.00
Editor: Grahame Steed
Summary of Content: Magazine containing approximately four hundred contract notices per issue.
Readership/Target Audience: Read by contractors.
ADVERTISING: No Advertising taken
BUSINESS: FINANCE & ECONOMICS: Financial Related

CONTROL ENGINEERING EUROPE

1663521U19A-556

Editorial Address: Blair House, 184-186 High Street, TONBRIDGE, TN9 1BQ **Tel:** 01732 359990
Fax: 01732 770049
Email: michael.babb@imlgroup.co.uk
Advertising Address: As above.
Email: andrea.church@imlgroup.co.uk
Web site: http://www.controlengeurope.com
Publisher: IML Group plc
Frequency: 6 issues yearly - Published in the 1st week of the cover month
Cover Price: Free
Circulation: 16,527 (Publisher's Statement)
Usual Pagination: 52
Editor: Andrea Church; **Advertising Manager:** Andrea Church; **Publisher:** Andrea Church
Summary of Content: Magazine designed to help engineers increase the performance in manufacturing and processing plants across all industries.
Readership/Target Audience: Aimed at research and development, engineering and production professionals working in process manufacturing and original equipment manufacturing industries.
ADVERTISING RATES:
Full Page Colour £3680.00
Agency Commission: 15%
Mechanical Data: Type Area: 250 x 180mm, Bleed Size: 274 x 206mm, Trim Size: 268 x 200mm, Col Length: 250mm, Page Width: 180mm, Film: Digital
Copy instructions: Copy Date: 4 weeks prior to publication date
BUSINESS: ENGINEERING & MACHINERY

CONTROL ENGINEERING UK

1666073U19A-557

Formerly: Control Engineering Europe (UK Edition)
Editorial Address: Blair House, 184-186 High Street, TONBRIDGE, TN9 1BQ **Tel:** 01732 359990
Fax: 01732 770049
Email: anna.mitchell@imlgroup.co.uk
Advertising Address: As above.
Email: andrea.church@imlgroup.co.uk
Web site: http://www.controlenguk.com
Publisher: IML Group plc
Date Established: 2004
Frequency: 6 issues yearly - Published in the 1st week of the 1st cover month
Cover Price: Free
Circulation: 7,500 (Publisher's Statement)
Usual Pagination: 76
Editor: Anna Mitchell; **Advertising Manager:** Andrea Church
Summary of Content: Magazine designed to help engineers increase the performance in manufacturing and processing plants across all industries.
Readership/Target Audience: Aimed at research and development, engineering and production professionals working in process manufacturing and original equipment manufacturing industries.
ADVERTISING RATES:
Full Page Colour £1920.00
SCC £20.00
Agency Commission: 10%
Mechanical Data: Type Area: 250 x 180mm, Bleed Size: 274 x 206mm, Trim Size: 268 x 200mm, Col Length: 250mm, Page Width: 180mm, Film: Digital
Copy instructions: Copy Date: 4 weeks prior to publication date
Average advertising content per issue: 60%
BUSINESS: ENGINEERING & MACHINERY

CONVENIENCE STORE

39796U53-50

Editorial Address: Broadfield Park, CRAWLEY, RH11 9RT
Tel: 01293 613400 **Fax:** 01293 610340
Advertising Address: As above. **Fax:** 01293 610330
Email: tony.hawkes@william-reed.co.uk
Web site: http://www.thegrocer.co.uk/index.aspx?page=independents
ISSN: 0267-9361
Publisher: William Reed Business Media
Frequency: 26 issues yearly
Cover Price: £3.40
Free to qualifying individuals
Annual Sub.: £65.00
Circulation: 42,518 (ABC 01/07/2008 to 30/06/2009)
Usual Pagination: 72

Editor: Sarah Britton; **Features Editor:** Sarah Britton; **Managing Director:** Charles Reed
Summary of Content: Journal covering groceries, off-licensed trade, confectionery, tobacco, newsagents, petrol, lottery and all convenience store goods.
Readership/Target Audience: Read by convenience store owners, management and suppliers.
ADVERTISING RATES:
Full Page Colour £3535.00
Agency Commission: 10%
Mechanical Data: Type Area: 267 x 185mm, Bleed Size: 303 x 216mm, Trim Size: 297 x 210mm, Col Length: 267mm, Page Width: 185mm, Film: Digital
Copy instructions: Copy Date: 2 weeks prior to publication date
Average advertising content per issue: 50%
BUSINESS: RETAILING & WHOLESALING

CONVERGENCE
36890U14A-85
Editorial Address: School of Media, Art and Design, Park Square, LUTON, LU1 3JU **Tel:** 01582 489031
Fax: 01582 489212
Email: convergence@luton.ac.uk
Advertising Address: 1 Oliver's Yard, 55 City Road, LONDON, EC1Y 1SP **Tel:** 020 7324 8500
Fax: 020 7324 8600
Email: advertising@sagepub.co.uk
Web site: http://www.luton.ac.uk/convergence
ISSN: 1354-8565
Publisher: Sage Publications
Date Established: 1994
Frequency: Quarterly
Annual Sub.: £30.00
Circulation: 1,000 (Publisher's Statement)
Usual Pagination: 128
Editor: Julia Knight
Summary of Content: Journal of research into new media technologies covering the creative, social, political and pedagogical issues raised by its advent.
Readership/Target Audience: Aimed at researchers and practitioners in new media technologies.
ADVERTISING RATES:
Full Page Mono £400.00
Agency Commission: 5%
Mechanical Data: Film: Digital, Type Area: 210 x 140mm, Col Length: 210mm, Page Width: 140mm
Copy instructions: Copy Date: 12 weeks prior to publication date
BUSINESS: COMMERCE, INDUSTRY & MANAGEMENT

CONVERGENCE WORLD
1703698U18B-1967
Editorial Address: 71-73 Coval Lane, CHELMSFORD, CM1 1TG **Tel:** 01245 283984
Email: john.williamson20@btopenworld.com
Advertising Address: 2 Granger Row, CHELMSFORD, CM1 4WF **Tel:** 07734 315506
Email: terry.roll@marianamediagroup.com
Web site: http://www.convergenceworld.net
Publisher: Moriana Media Group
Date Established: 2005
Frequency: 6 issues yearly
Cover Price: Free
Circulation: 8,500 (Publisher's Statement)
Usual Pagination: 48
Editor: John Williamson
Summary of Content: Magazine covering the convergence of fixed and mobile communications.
Readership/Target Audience: Aimed at senior management in the fixed mobile telecommunications industry.
ADVERTISING RATES:
Full Page Colour £4490.00
Mechanical Data: Type Area: 255 x 187mm, Bleed Size: 281 x 213mm, Trim Size: 275 x 207mm, Col Length: 255mm, Page Width: 187mm, Film: Digital
BUSINESS: ELECTRONICS: Telecommunications

CONVERTER
38664U35-20
Editorial Address: Faversham House, 232A Addington Road, SOUTH CROYDON, CR2 8LE **Tel:** 01452 760900
Fax: 01452 760900
Email: convertermag@btopenworld.com
Advertising Address: As above. **Tel:** 020 8651 7100
Fax: 020 8651 7117
Email: ruth.feather@fav-house.com
Web site: http://www.converter-magazine.info
ISSN: 0010-8189
Publisher: Faversham House Group Ltd
Frequency: Monthly - Published in the 3rd week of the cover month
Annual Sub.: £65.00
Circulation: 5,507 (ABC 01/01/2008 to 31/12/2008)
Usual Pagination: 48
Editor: David Callinan; **Managing Director:** Amanda Barnes; **Publisher:** Chris Trayers

Summary of Content: Journal focusing on the techniques of converting paper, film, foil and board.
Readership/Target Audience: Aimed at key decision makers, purchasers and buyers within the industry.
ADVERTISING RATES:
Full Page Mono £1235.00
Full Page Colour £1756.00
Agency Commission: 10%
Mechanical Data: Type Area: 260 x 198mm, Col Length: 260mm, Bleed Size: 293 x 238mm, Trim Size: 285 x 230mm, Page Width: 198mm, Film: Digital
Copy instructions: Copy Date: 6 weeks prior to publication date
Average advertising content per issue: 50%
BUSINESS: PACKAGING & BOTTLING

CONVERTING TODAY
38666U35-21
Editorial Address: Progressive House, 2 Maidstone Road, Foots Cray, SIDCUP, DA14 5HZ **Tel:** 020 8269 7700
Fax: 020 8269 7874
Email: mtaylor@progressivemediagroup.com
Advertising Address: As above.
Email: rmolinari@progressivemediagroup.com
Web site: http://www.convertingtoday.co.uk
ISSN: 0264-715X
Publisher: Progressive Media Publications
Date Established: 1986
Frequency: 10 issues yearly - Published in the 3rd week of the cover month
Free to qualifying individuals
Annual Sub.: £76.50
Circulation: 6,423 (ABC 01/01/2008 to 31/12/2008)
Usual Pagination: 52
Editor: Sonali Advani
Summary of Content: Magazine containing news and features of interest to management within the plastics, film, foil, paper and board converting industries including flexo printing.
Readership/Target Audience: Aimed at buyers and specifiers throughout Europe.
ADVERTISING RATES:
Full Page Colour £2200.00
Agency Commission: 10%
Mechanical Data: Type Area: 280 x 185mm, Col Length: 280mm, Page Width: 185mm, Film: Digital, Trim Size: 300 x 230mm, Bleed Size: 306 x 236mm, Print Process: Litho
Copy instructions: Copy Date: 2 weeks prior to publication date
Average advertising content per issue: 60%
BUSINESS: PACKAGING & BOTTLING

THE CONVEYANCER & PROPERTY LAWYER
35187U1E-465
Editorial Address: The Hatchery, Hall Bank Lane, Mytholmroyd, HEBDEN BRIDGE, HX7 5HQ
Tel: 01422 889202 **Fax:** 01422 888002
Email: amy.1.thomas@thomsonreuters.com
Web site: http://www.sweetandmaxwell.co.uk
ISSN: 0010-8200
Publisher: Sweet & Maxwell Yorkshire
Frequency: 6 issues yearly
Annual Sub.: £279.00
Circulation: 1,500 (Publisher's Statement)
Usual Pagination: 90
Editor: Amy Thomas
Summary of Content: Journal containing the latest developments, authoritative articles, notes of recent cases, book reviews and correspondence.
Readership/Target Audience: Aimed at property companies, lawyers, conveyancing departments of large companies and academics.
ADVERTISING: No Advertising taken
BUSINESS: FINANCE & ECONOMICS: Property

COOLER INNOVATION
1705975U22R-762
Editorial Address: 7 Kingsmead Square, BATH, BA1 2AB
Tel: 01225 327861 **Fax:** 01225 327891
Email: medina.bailey@zipublishing.com
Advertising Address: As above. **Tel:** 01225 327890
Email: ruth.cole@zipublishing.com
Web site: http://www.foodbev.com/cooler
Publisher: Zenith International
Date Established: 2006
Frequency: 6 issues yearly - Published in the 2nd week of the 1st cover month
Circulation: 3,000 (Publisher's Statement)
Editor: Medina Bailey; **Advertising Manager:** Ruth Cole
Summary of Content: Magazine featuring news, views and analysis of both the bottled water cooler and point of use water cooler sectors.
Readership/Target Audience: Aimed at industry leaders and key decision makers.
ADVERTISING RATES:
Full Page Colour £1410.00
Mechanical Data: Bleed Size: 303 x 213mm, Trim Size: 297 x 210mm, Print Process: Sheet-fed litho, Film: Digital

Copy instructions: Copy Date: 2nd week of the cover month
BUSINESS: FOOD: Food Related

CO-OPERATIVE NEWS
40801U59-20
Editorial Address: Holyoake House, Hanover Street, MANCHESTER, M60 0AS **Tel:** 0161 214 0870
Fax: 0161 214 0878
Email: editorial@thenews.coop
Advertising Address: As above.
Email: advertising@thenews.coop
Web site: http://www.thenews.coop
Publisher: Co-operative Press Ltd
Date Established: 1871
Frequency: 26 issues yearly
Annual Sub.: £48.00
Circulation: 7,500 (Publisher's Statement)
Usual Pagination: 24
Editor: Dave Bowman; **Advertising Manager:** Geraldine Birtwistle; **Managing Editor:** Dave Bowman
Summary of Content: Retail trade newspaper covering news and features on the Co-operative movement.
Readership/Target Audience: Aimed at Co-op managers, supervisors and members.
ADVERTISING RATES:
Full Page Colour £1595.00
Agency Commission: 10%
Mechanical Data: Col Length: 345mm, Col Widths (Display): 35mm, No. of Columns (Display): 6, Type Area: 345 x 340mm, Trim Size: 340 x 245mm, Page Width: 340mm
Copy instructions: Copy Date: 2 weeks prior to publication date
Average advertising content per issue: 25%
BUSINESS: CO-OPERATIVES

CORPCOMMS
1702310U2A-678
Editorial Address: Churchill House, 142-146 Old Street, LONDON, EC1V 9BW **Tel:** 020 7250 0607
Fax: 020 3014 8612
Email: helen@corpcommsmagazine.co.uk
Advertising Address: As above. **Tel:** 020 7251 7500
Fax: 020 7490 4349
Email: alexa.clark@thecrossbordergroup.com
Web site: http://www.corpcommsmagazine.co.uk
Publisher: Hardy Media
Date Established: 2005
Frequency: 10 issues yearly - Published at the end of the month prior to the cover month
Annual Sub.: £75.00
Circulation: 6,000 (Publisher's Statement)
Usual Pagination: 48
Editor: Helen Dunne; **Advertising Manager:** David Sweet
Summary of Content: Magazine covering advice on managing and communicating corporate image and identity.
Readership/Target Audience: Aimed at agencies, corporate and corporate communications directors.
ADVERTISING RATES:
Full Page Colour £3850.00
Agency Commission: 10%
Mechanical Data: Type Area: 250 x 188mm, Bleed Size: 276 x 214mm, Trim Size: 270 x 208mm, Col Length: 250mm, Page Width: 188mm, Film: Digital
Copy instructions: Copy Date: 2 weeks prior to publication date
Average advertising content per issue: 40%
BUSINESS: COMMUNICATIONS, ADVERTISING & MARKETING

CORPORATE ADVISER
1750347U1F-615
Editorial Address: St. Giles House, 50 Poland Street, LONDON, W1F 7AX **Tel:** 020 7970 4819
Email: john.greenwood@centaur.co.uk
Advertising Address: As above. **Tel:** 020 7970 4000
Fax: 020 7943 8090
Email: will.bolton@centaur.co.uk
Publisher: Centaur Media Plc
Date Established: 2006
Frequency: Monthly - Published at the end of the month prior to cover date
Cover Price: £3.50
Free to qualifying individuals
Circulation: 6,094 (ABC 01/07/2008 to 30/06/2009)
Usual Pagination: 48
Editor: John Greenwood
Summary of Content: Magazine covering pensions, investments and employee benefits.
Readership/Target Audience: Aimed at corporate advisers going into the workplace.
ADVERTISING RATES:
Full Page Colour £2650.00
Agency Commission: 10%
Mechanical Data: Type Area: 253 x 184mm, Bleed Size: 290 x 220mm, Trim Size: 280 x 210mm, Col Length: 253mm, Page Width: 184mm, Film: Digital
Copy instructions: Copy Date: 2 weeks prior to publication date

Business Magazines

Average advertising content per issue: 33%
BUSINESS: FINANCE & ECONOMICS: Investment

CORPORATE BRIEFING
39140U44-400

Editorial Address: Telephone House, 69-77 Paul Street, LONDON, EC2A 4LQ **Tel:** 020 7017 6762
Fax: 020 7017 5274
Email: jessica.westwood@informa.com
Web site: http://www.informalaw.com
ISSN: 0950-6209
Publisher: Informa PLC
Frequency: 10 issues yearly
Editor: Jessica Westwood
Summary of Content: Newsletter covering news of legal and regulatory developments affecting company strategy.
Readership/Target Audience: Aimed at lawyers and legal professionals.
ADVERTISING: No Advertising taken
BUSINESS: LEGAL

CORPORATE CITIZENSHIP BRIEFING
35708U2E-51

Formerly: Community Affairs Briefing
Editorial Address: 5th Floor, Holborn Gate, 330 High Holborn, LONDON, WC1V 7QG **Tel:** 020 7861 1616
Fax: 020 7861 3908
Email: news@corporate-citizenship.co.uk
Web site: http://www.ccbriefing.co.uk
ISSN: 0964-8798
Publisher: Corporate Citizenship
Date Established: 1992
Frequency: 6 issues yearly
Annual Sub.: £240.00
Circulation: 300 (Publisher's Statement)
Usual Pagination: 24
Editor: Francesca Langdon
Summary of Content: Magazine covering the latest news, developments and trends in corporate social responsibility, community affairs and the third sector.
Readership/Target Audience: Aimed at the corporate sector, FTSE500, community affairs managers, CSR managers, corporate communications, PR, investor relations and human resources.
ADVERTISING: No Advertising taken
BUSINESS: COMMUNICATIONS, ADVERTISING & MARKETING: Public Relations

---

CORPORATE COMMUNICATIONS: AN INTERNATIONAL JOURNAL
35485U2A-61

Editorial Address: Howard House, Wagon Lane, BINGLEY, BD16 1WA **Tel:** 01274 777700 **Fax:** 01274 785200
Email: mlawrence@emeraldinsight.com
Web site: http://www.emeraldinsight.com/ccij.htm
ISSN: 1356-3289
Publisher: Emerald Group Publishing Ltd
Frequency: Quarterly
Usual Pagination: 64
Editor: Martyn Lawrence; **Publisher:** Martyn Lawrence
Summary of Content: Journal covering communications within organisations, between organisations and the public and how to implement a strategic communications plan.
Readership/Target Audience: Aimed at academics and practitioners interested in corporate communications.
ADVERTISING: No Advertising taken
BUSINESS: COMMUNICATIONS, ADVERTISING & MARKETING

CORPORATE FINANCIER
1641355U1A-303

Editorial Address: 25 Finsbury Business Centre, 40 Bowling Green Lane, LONDON, EC1R 0NE **Tel:** 020 7415 7101
Email: grant@heavensto.com
Advertising Address: ICAEW, Chartered Accountants Hall, PO Box 433, Moorgate Place, LONDON, EC2P 2BJ
Tel: 020 7920 8100
Email: ross.arthurs@icaew.com
Web site: http://www.icaew.com/corpfinfac
ISSN: 1367-4544
Publisher: Bladonmore
Date Established: 1997
Frequency: 10 issues yearly
Free to qualifying individuals
Annual Sub.: £120.00
Circulation: 7,000 (Publisher's Statement)
Usual Pagination: 24
Editor: Grant Murgatroyd
Summary of Content: Magazine covering the developments in the corporate finance market including mergers and acquisitions, private equity, capital markets, HR, legal and regulatory issues.
Readership/Target Audience: Aimed at investment bankers, private equity firms, bankers, lawyers, accountancy firms and stock brokers.
ADVERTISING RATES:
Full Page Colour £3000.00

Mechanical Data: Trim Size: 320 x 240mm, Film: Digital, Page Width: 240mm
Copy instructions: Copy Date: 3 weeks prior to publication date
BUSINESS: FINANCE & ECONOMICS

CORPORATE FINANCING WEEK
1851430U1A-347

Editorial Address: 3rd Floor, Mermaid House, 2 Puddle Dock, LONDON, EC4V 3DS **Tel:** 020 7248 0468
Fax: 020 7248 0467
Email: tsteel@businessmonitor.com
Web site: http://www.corporatefinancingweek.com
Publisher: Business Monitor International Ltd
Frequency: Weekly
Free to qualifying individuals
Usual Pagination: 12
Editor: Tiffany Steel
Summary of Content: Publication covering mergers and acquisition activity in North America, Europe and emerging markets. Also includes features on IPOs and privatisations, equity and debt financing.
Readership/Target Audience: Aimed at professionals and individuals in corporate finance and investment.
BUSINESS: FINANCE & ECONOMICS

CORPORATE IT UPDATE
36051U5B-57_20

Editorial Address: PR by email only **Tel:** 020 7047 0200
Email: m2pw@m2.com
Web site: http://www.m2.com
Publisher: M2 Communications Ltd
Frequency: Daily
Annual Sub.: £25.00
Editor: Jamie Ayres
Summary of Content: A news service that provides updates on the issues, products and technologies relevant to corporate organisations which emerge from the IT and telecoms marketplace.
Readership/Target Audience: Aimed at IT managers.
ADVERTISING: No Advertising taken
BUSINESS: COMPUTERS & AUTOMATION: Data Processing

THE CORPORATE REGISTER
36876U14A-288

Formerly: The Price Waterhouse Coopers Corporate Register
Editorial Address: Sophia House, 76-80 City Road, LONDON, EC1Y 2BJ **Tel:** 020 3326 2000
Email: s.bolton@capitalideasplc.co.uk
Web site: http://www.ccplcwebsite.co.uk
Publisher: Capital Ideas Financial Publishing Limited
Date Established: 1979
Frequency: Quarterly
Annual Sub.: £249.00
Circulation: 5,000 (Publisher's Statement)
Editor: Sarah Bolton; **Publisher:** Sarah Bolton
Summary of Content: Register of information on the structure and management of every UK quoted company.
Readership/Target Audience: Aimed at corporate management.
ADVERTISING: No Advertising taken
BUSINESS: COMMERCE, INDUSTRY & MANAGEMENT

CORPORATE UK
1687641U1A-314

Editorial Address: Charles House, 148-149 Great Charles Street Queensway, BIRMINGHAM, B3 3HT
Tel: 0121 236 0411 **Fax:** 0121 233 3874
Email: jamessweeney@corp-intl.com
Advertising Address: As above. **Tel:** 0121 237 8831
Email: jonathonrichards@corp-intl.com
Web site: http://www.corp-uk.com
Publisher: JRS Corporate Ltd
Date Established: 2005
Frequency: Monthly
Annual Sub.: £49.50
Circulation: 8,123 (Publisher's Statement)
Usual Pagination: 104
Editor: James Sweeney; **Advertising Manager:** Jonathon Richards
Summary of Content: Magazine focusing on corporate finance including industry analysis, deal coverage, boardroom advice, sector reviews, funding solutions, investment guidance and corporate governance procedures.
Readership/Target Audience: Aimed at company directors, legal partners and members of the British Venture Capitalist Association, members of the European Venture Capitalist Association, financial advisers, FTSE 350 directors, AIM listed business, plus listed boardroom level decision makers of private mid-market businesses.
ADVERTISING RATES:
Full Page Mono £1700.00
Full Page Colour £1700.00
Agency Commission: 10%

Mechanical Data: Type Area: 297 x 210mm, Col Length: 297mm, Page Width: 210mm, Film: Digital
Copy instructions: Copy Date: 1 week prior to publication date
Average advertising content per issue: 10%
BUSINESS: FINANCE & ECONOMICS

CORROSION ENGINEERING, SCIENCE & TECHNOLOGY
37622U19C-70

Formerly: British Corrosion Journal
Editorial Address: 1 Carlton House Terrace, LONDON, SW1Y 5AF **Tel:** 020 7451 7300 **Fax:** 020 7451 7307
Email: cest@materials.org.uk
Advertising Address: Suite 1C, Josephs Well, Hanover Walk, LEEDS, LS3 1AB **Tel:** 0113 243 2800
Fax: 0113 386 8178
Email: n.taylor@maney.co.uk
Web site: http://www.maney.co.uk
ISSN: 1482-422X
Publisher: Maney Publishing
Date Established: 1965
Frequency: Quarterly
Annual Sub.: £444.00
Circulation: 550 (Publisher's Statement)
Usual Pagination: 88
Editor: Mark Hull; **Advertising Manager:** Natalie Taylor; **Managing Editor:** Mark Hull
Summary of Content: Journal covering all aspects corrosion protection, corrosion control and in particular materials performance in service environments.
Readership/Target Audience: Read by managers, designers, engineers and researchers involved in the selection, use and protection of metallic materials.
ADVERTISING RATES:
Full Page Mono £500.00
Full Page Colour £1100.00
Agency Commission: 10%
Mechanical Data: Type Area: 266 x 188mm, Bleed Size: 305 x 215mm, Trim Size: 297 x 210mm, Film: Digital, Col Length: 266mm, Page Width: 188mm
Copy instructions: Copy Date: 15th of the month prior to publication date
BUSINESS: ENGINEERING & MACHINERY: Finishing

CORROSION MANAGEMENT
37623U19C-100

Editorial Address: 90 Totley Brook Road, SHEFFIELD, S17 3QT **Tel:** 0114 262 1873 **Fax:** 0114 235 6537
Email: jonathan@squareone.co.uk
Advertising Address: As above.
Email: jonathan@squareone.co.uk
Web site: http://www.icorr.org
Publisher: Square One Advertising and Design
Frequency: 6 issues yearly
Annual Sub.: £70.00
Circulation: 2,000 (Publisher's Statement)
Usual Pagination: 36
Editor: Jonathan Phillips; **Advertising Manager:** Jonathan Phillips; **Managing Editor:** Tony Cross; **Publisher:** Tony Cross
Summary of Content: Journal focusing on corrosion management, covering property, equipment and systems relating to coatings, cathodic protection, material selection and monitoring.
Readership/Target Audience: Aimed at members of the Institute of Corrosion and people involved in the control or prevention of corrosion.
ADVERTISING RATES:
Full Page Mono £450.00
Full Page Colour £830.00
Agency Commission: 10%
Mechanical Data: Bleed Size: 303 x 216mm, Trim Size: 297 x 210mm, Page Width: 188mm, Film: Digital, Col Length: 275mm, Type Area: 275 x 188mm, Print Process: Web-fed offset litho
Copy instructions: Copy Date: 2 weeks prior to publication date
Average advertising content per issue: 20%
BUSINESS: ENGINEERING & MACHINERY: Finishing

CORUS NEWS
38173U27-21

Formerly: Steel News Sections, Plates & Commercial Steels
Editorial Address: PO Box 1, Brigg Road, SCUNTHORPE, DN16 1BP **Tel:** 01724 402090 **Fax:** 01724 405383
Email: liz.brown@corusgroup.com
Web site: http://www.corusgroup.com
Publisher: Corus
Frequency: Quarterly
Cover Price: Free
Circulation: 1,000 (Publisher's Statement)
Usual Pagination: 28
Editor: Liz Brown
Summary of Content: Magazine covering Corus contracts, structural work and personnel.
Readership/Target Audience: Aimed at those involved with the company, both employees and customers, including

---

metal industries such as the construction, automotive, aerospace, packaging and domestic appliances industries.
ADVERTISING: No Advertising taken
BUSINESS: METAL, IRON & STEEL

COSMETICS INTERNATIONAL
37245U15A-20

Editorial Address: 209 Linen Hall, 162-168 Regent Street, LONDON, W1B 5TB **Tel:** 020 7434 1530 **Fax:** 020 7437 0915
Email: cosmeticsint@1530.com
Advertising Address: As above.
Email: cosint@1530.com
Web site: http://www.cosmeticsinternational.net
Publisher: Communications International Group
Date Established: 1974
Frequency: 22 issues yearly
Annual Sub.: £400.00
Circulation: 2,000 (Publisher's Statement)
Usual Pagination: 16
Editor: Vivienne Rudd; **Advertising Director:** Suzi Richardson
Summary of Content: Newsletter covering all aspects of cosmetics, perfumes and toiletries. Includes product launches, packaging, reports, market trends and Internet updates. Also covers raw materials, events and corporate news.
Readership/Target Audience: Aimed at the worldwide cosmetics industry.
ADVERTISING: Rates on application
Agency Commission: 10%
Average advertising content per issue: 5%
BUSINESS: COSMETICS & HAIRDRESSING: Cosmetics

COSMETICS PRODUCTS REPORT
37246U15A-18

Editorial Address: 207 Linen Hall, 162-168 Regent Street, LONDON, W1B 5TB **Tel:** 020 7434 1530 **Fax:** 020 7437 0915
Email: cosmeticsint@1530.com
Advertising Address: As above.
Email: liz.jones@1530.com
Web site: http://www.cosmeticsint.co.uk
Publisher: Communications International Group
Frequency: Monthly
Annual Sub.: £296.00
Circulation: 2,000 (Publisher's Statement)
Usual Pagination: 12
Editor: Liz Jones; **Advertising Manager:** Liz Jones
Summary of Content: Publication reporting on international new product launches in the beauty and toiletries market. Also includes packaging and design.
Readership/Target Audience: Aimed at a wide range of companies involved in the global beauty and toiletry industries.
ADVERTISING RATES:
Full Page Mono £1135.00
Full Page Colour £1545.00
BUSINESS: COSMETICS & HAIRDRESSING: Cosmetics

COSPP - COGENERATION AND ON-SITE POWER PRODUCTION
1622429U58-179

Editorial Address: Warlies Park House, Horseshoe Hill, Upshire, WALTHAM ABBEY, EN9 3SR **Tel:** 01992 656600
Email: cospp@pennwell.com
Advertising Address: As above. **Fax:** 01992 656700
Email: cosppadsales@pennwell.com
Web site: http://www.cospp.com
Publisher: PennWell Publications International Ltd
Date Established: 2000
Frequency: 6 issues yearly
Free to qualifying individuals
Annual Sub.: £60.00
Circulation: 17,000 (Publisher's Statement)
Usual Pagination: 96
Editor: David Appleyard; **News Editor:** David Appleyard
Summary of Content: Magazine providing international coverage of cogeneration and other distributed energy issues including technology, economics, deregulation and the environmental framework.
Readership/Target Audience: Aimed at cogeneration professionals and key buyers in both the private and public sectors.
ADVERTISING RATES:
Full Page Colour £3505.00
Mechanical Data: Type Area: 277 x 190mm, Bleed Size: 307 x 220mm, Trim Size: 297 x 210mm, Col Length: 277mm, Page Width: 190mm, Film: Digital
BUSINESS: ENERGY, FUEL & NUCLEAR

COST SECTOR CATERING
36564U11A-79

Editorial Address: Progressive House, 2 Maidstone Road, SIDCUP, DA14 5HZ **Tel:** 0845 000 2500
Email: davidf@dewberryredpoint.co.uk
Advertising Address: As above.
Email: jamier@dewred.co.uk
Web site: http://www.costsectorcatering.co.uk

Publisher: Dewberry Redpoint Ltd
Date Established: 1993
Frequency: Monthly - Published in the 1st week of the cover month
Cover Price: £4.00
Free to qualifying individuals
Circulation: 12,403 (ABC 01/07/2008 to 30/06/2009)
Usual Pagination: 84
Editor: David Foad; **Group Editor:** David Foad; **Publisher:** Andrew Archer
Summary of Content: Magazine providing information on all aspects of catering, including contracts, appointments and equipment for restaurants, schools, hospitals, prisons and airlines.
Readership/Target Audience: Aimed at managers, buyers and key decision makers.
ADVERTISING RATES:
Full Page Colour £3995.00
Agency Commission: 10%
Mechanical Data: Type Area: 268 x 186mm, Bleed Size: 303 x 216mm, Trim Size: 297 x 210mm, Page Width: 186mm, Col Length: 268mm, Film: Digital
Copy instructions: Copy Date: 4 weeks prior to publication date
Average advertising content per issue: 40%
BUSINESS: CATERING: Catering, Hotels & Restaurants

COTSWOLD BUSINESS NEWS
1745997U63B-2559

Formerly: CBN Cotswold Business News
Editorial Address: 45 Dyer Street, CIRENCESTER, GL7 2PP
Tel: 01285 650661 **Fax:** 01285 650620
Email: simon@cotswoldmedia.co.uk
Advertising Address: As above.
Email: barbara.eadon@caerpublishing.co.uk
Publisher: Caer Publishing Group
Date Established: 2005
Frequency: 10 issues yearly
Cover Price: Free
Circulation: 5,000 (Publisher's Statement)
Usual Pagination: 20
Editor: Simon Jefferson; **Advertising Manager:** Barbara Eadon
Summary of Content: Business magazine covering issues of interest to businesses in the Cotswolds. Provides details of the services and expertise available within the area and also relevant regional news.
Readership/Target Audience: Aimed at managers and directors of small to medium sized enterprises.
ADVERTISING RATES:
Full Page Colour £495.00
Agency Commission: 10%
Mechanical Data: Type Area: 255 x 190mm, Bleed Size: 303 x 216mm, Trim Size: 297 x 210mm, Col Widths (Display): 61.25mm, Print Process: Litho, Film: Digital, Col Length: 255mm, Page Width: 190mm
Average advertising content per issue: 50%
BUSINESS: REGIONAL BUSINESS: Regional Business English Counties

COTTON OUTLOOK
35386U1L-10

Editorial Address: Outlook House, 458 New Chester Road, Rock Ferry, BIRKENHEAD, CH42 2AE **Tel:** 0151 644 6400
Fax: 0151 644 8550
Email: editor@cotlook.com
Advertising Address: As above.
Email: advertising@cotlook.com
Web site: http://www.cotlook.com
Publisher: Cotlook Ltd
Date Established: 1923
Frequency: Weekly
Annual Sub.: £474.60
Usual Pagination: 24
Editor: Ray Butler; **Managing Director:** Ray Butler; **Advertising Manager:** Richard Butler
Summary of Content: Information on the growing, marketing and pricing of cotton and other textiles.
Language(s): English; Spanish
Readership/Target Audience: Aimed at buyers and sellers of raw cotton and those within the cotton textile industries.
ADVERTISING RATES:
Full Page Mono £965.00
Full Page Colour £1647.00
SCC £11.07
Mechanical Data: Film: Digital, Type Area: 218 x 182mm, Trim Size: 297 x 210mm, Col Length: 218mm, Bleed Size: 303 x 216mm, Col Widths (Display): 60mm, Page Width: 182mm
Copy instructions: Copy Date: 4 weeks prior to publication date
BUSINESS: FINANCE & ECONOMICS: Commodities

COUNCILLOR
622781U32A-25

Formerly: Briefing
Editorial Address: 22 Upper Woburn Place, LONDON, WC1H 0TB **Tel:** 020 7554 2800 **Fax:** 020 7554 2801

Email: cllr@lgiu.org.uk
Web site: http://www.lgiu.gov.uk
Publisher: Local Government Information Unit
Date Established: 2006
Frequency: 6 issues yearly
Cover Price: Free
Circulation: 10,500 (Publisher's Statement)
Usual Pagination: 20
Editor: Jane Sankarayya
Summary of Content: Journal covering topical issues from a councillor perspective.
Readership/Target Audience: Aimed at councillors.
ADVERTISING: No Advertising taken
BUSINESS: LOCAL GOVERNMENT, LEISURE & RECREATION: Local Government

COUNCILS, COMMITTEES & BOARDS
38400U32A-48

Editorial Address: Chancery House, 15 Wickham Road, BECKENHAM, BR3 5JS **Tel:** 020 8650 7745
Fax: 020 8650 0768
Email: cbd@cbdresearch.com
Web site: http://www.cbdresearch.com
ISSN: 0070-1211
Publisher: CBD Research Ltd
Date Established: 1970
Frequency: Published every two years
Cover Price: £163.00
Circulation: 2,000 (Publisher's Statement)
Editor: Cris Henderson
Summary of Content: Directory of the 1500 official and unofficial bodies in the UK.
Readership/Target Audience: Aimed at reference libraries - public and corporate, all media categories and all other business.
ADVERTISING: No Advertising taken
BUSINESS: LOCAL GOVERNMENT, LEISURE & RECREATION: Local Government

COUNSEL
39142U44-420

Editorial Address: 2 Addiscombe Road, CROYDON, CR9 5AF **Tel:** 020 8686 9141
Email: jane.maynard@lexisnexis.co.uk
Advertising Address: As above. **Tel:** 020 8662 2013
Fax: 020 8212 1970
Email: charlotte.witherden@lexisnexis.co.uk
Web site: http://www.barcouncil.org.uk
ISSN: 0268-3784
Publisher: LexisNexis
Date Established: 1985
Frequency: Monthly
Cover Price: £8.00
Annual Sub.: £74.00
Circulation: 21,000 (Publisher's Statement)
Usual Pagination: 56
Editor: Jane Maynard
Summary of Content: The Journal of the Bar of England and Wales.
Readership/Target Audience: Read by barristers, judges, solicitors and other legal advisers.
ADVERTISING RATES:
Full Page Colour £1990.00
Agency Commission: 10%
Mechanical Data: No. of Columns (Display): 3, Page Width: 185mm, Film: Digital, Col Widths (Display): 60mm, Type Area: 260 x 185mm, Col Length: 260mm, Trim Size: 297 x 210mm, Bleed Size: 303 x 216mm
Copy instructions: Copy Date: 2 weeks prior to publication date
Average advertising content per issue: 25%
BUSINESS: LEGAL

COUNSELLING AT WORK
38468U32G-47

Editorial Address: 15 St. John's Business Park, LUTTERWORTH, LE17 4HB **Tel:** 01455 883300
Fax: 01455 550243
Email: acw@bacp.co.uk
Advertising Address: BACP House, 15 St. Johns Business Park, Lutterworth, LEICESTERSHIRE, LE17 4HB
Tel: 0870 443 5225 **Fax:** 0870 443 5161
Email: kate.morris@bacp.co.uk
Web site: http://www.counsellingatwork.org.uk
ISSN: 1351-007X
Publisher: British Association for Counselling and Psychotherapy
Date Established: 1993
Frequency: Quarterly
Free to qualifying individuals
Annual Sub.: £30.00
Circulation: 1,700 (Publisher's Statement)
Usual Pagination: 40
Editor: Rick Hughes; **Advertising Manager:** Kate Morris
Summary of Content: Journal containing employee counselling services, organisational dynamics, communication skills, change of management and

Business Magazines

workplace issues, which includes bullying, stress, redundancy, conflict resolution and traumatic incident.
Readership/Target Audience: Read mainly by individual and organisational members of the Association for Counselling at Work and subscribers.
ADVERTISING RATES:
Full Page Mono £400.00
Full Page Colour £530.00
Agency Commission: 10%
Mechanical Data: Bleed Size: 303 x 216mm, Trim Size: 297 x 210mm, Page Width: 160mm, Film: Digital, Type Area: 240 x 160mm, Col Length: 240mm
BUSINESS: LOCAL GOVERNMENT, LEISURE & RECREATION: Community Care & Social Services

COUNTRYSIDE BUILDING   633885U4E-170
Editorial Address: 5A The Maltings, Stowupland Road, STOWMARKET, IP14 5AG **Tel:** 01449 677500
Fax: 01449 770028
Email: tony@ghyllhouse.co.uk
Advertising Address: As above.
Email: chris@ghyllhouse.co.uk
Web site: http://www.ridba.org.uk
ISSN: 1473-835X
Publisher: Ghyll House Publishing
Date Established: 2000
Frequency: Quarterly - Published in the last week of the cover month
Free to qualifying individuals
Annual Sub.: £20.00
Circulation: 8,000 (Publisher's Statement)
Usual Pagination: 40
Editor: Tony Hutchinson
Summary of Content: Magazine covering rural and industrial steel framed building projects, news, case studies and products.
Readership/Target Audience: Aimed at professionals within the building industry, suppliers, builders and farmers.
ADVERTISING RATES:
Full Page Colour £1255.00
Agency Commission: 10%
Mechanical Data: Type Area: 267 x 190mm, Col Length: 267mm, Page Width: 190mm
BUSINESS: ARCHITECTURE & BUILDING: Building

COURIER DIRECT   760596U49C-49_65
Editorial Address: Sybrig House, Ridge Way, Donibristle Industrial Park, Hillend, DUNFERMLINE, KY11 9JN
Tel: 0870 443 0270 **Fax:** 0870 443 0271
Email: editorial@courier-direct.co.uk
Advertising Address: As above.
Email: info@courier-direct.co.uk
Web site: http://www.courier-direct.co.uk
Publisher: Rainbow Media
Date Established: 2001
Frequency: Monthly
Cover Price: Free
Circulation: 9,000 (Publisher's Statement)
Usual Pagination: 40
Editor: Brian Regan; **Features Editor:** Tim Gilbert;
Advertising Manager: Alex Ellis
Summary of Content: Magazine covering industry updates, financial news, company profiles, IT developments, human interest articles and vehicle reviews.
Readership/Target Audience: Aimed at courier firms in the UK from one man businesses to multi-national fleet operators.
ADVERTISING RATES:
Full Page Colour £1195.00
Mechanical Data: Type Area: 273 x 186mm, Col Length: 273mm, Page Width: 186mm, Film: Digital
BUSINESS: TRANSPORT: Freight

COVER   35113U1D-59
Editorial Address: Haymarket House, 28-29 Haymarket, LONDON, SW1Y 4RX **Tel:** 020 7484 9700
Email: paul.robertson@incisivemedia.com
Advertising Address: As above. **Tel:** 020 7968 4623
Email: rachel.calvert@incisivemedia.com
Web site: http://www.cover-mag.co.uk
Publisher: Incisive Media Investments
Date Established: 1997
Frequency: Monthly - Published in the 1st week of the cover month
Free to qualifying individuals
Annual Sub.: £80.00
Circulation: 10,664 (ABC 01/07/2008 to 30/06/2009)
Usual Pagination: 68
Editor: Paul Robertson; **Advertising Manager:** Rachel Calvert
Summary of Content: Publication about insurance policies covering income protection, critical illness, PMI and long term care.
Readership/Target Audience: Aimed at advisers working in the protection market.
ADVERTISING RATES:
Full Page Colour £5000.00

Agency Commission: 10%
Mechanical Data: Page Width: 185mm, Type Area: 274 x 185mm, Bleed Size: 303 x 216mm, Trim Size: 297 x 210mm, Col Length: 274mm, Film: Digital
Copy instructions: Copy Date: 1 week prior to publication date
Average advertising content per issue: 40%
BUSINESS: FINANCE & ECONOMICS: Insurance

CPB CIVIC & PUBLIC BUILDING   39026U42A-11
Formerly: Civic & Public Building Specifier
Editorial Address: Cointronic House, Station Road, HEATHFIELD, TN21 8DF **Tel:** 01435 865797
Fax: 01435 863897
Email: editorial@netmagmedia.eu
Advertising Address: As above. **Tel:** 01435 863500
Web site: http://www.parker-ellis.co.uk
Publisher: Parker Ellis Publishing Ltd
Date Established: 1997
Frequency: 6 issues yearly - Published in the middle of the 1st cover month
Free to qualifying individuals
Annual Sub.: £48.00
Circulation: 10,000 (Publisher's Statement)
Usual Pagination: 40
Editor: Patricia Percival
Summary of Content: Magazine featuring projects, technical information, products and industry news.
Readership/Target Audience: Aimed at specifiers in the public building construction industry.
ADVERTISING RATES:
Full Page Colour £1425.00
Agency Commission: 10%
Mechanical Data: Type Area: 277 x 190mm, Bleed Size: 303 x 216mm, Trim Size: 297 x 210mm, Col Length: 277mm, Page Width: 190mm, Film: Digital
Copy instructions: Copy Date: 4 weeks prior to publication date
Average advertising content per issue: 50%
BUSINESS: CONSTRUCTION

CPO AGENDA   1668003U14A-544
Editorial Address: 17 Britton Street, LONDON, EC1M 5TP
Tel: 020 7324 2746 **Fax:** 020 7324 2791
Email: editorial@cpoagenda.com
Advertising Address: As above. **Tel:** 020 7880 7551
Fax: 020 7880 7553
Email: darren.ephrain@redactive.co.uk
Web site: http://www.cpoagenda.com
ISSN: 1745-9877
Publisher: Redactive Media Group
Date Established: 2005
Frequency: Quarterly
Annual Sub.: £90.00
Circulation: 4,000 (Publisher's Statement)
Usual Pagination: 68
Editor: Steve Bagshaw; **Advertising Manager:** Darren Ephrain
Summary of Content: Journal focusing on strategic procurement and supply chain management issues.
Readership/Target Audience: Aimed at chief procurement officers and senior purchasing executives in larger organisations globally.
ADVERTISING RATES:
Full Page Colour £3650.00
Agency Commission: 10%
Mechanical Data: Type Area: 247 x 180mm, Bleed Size: 282 x 221mm, Trim Size: 276 x 215mm, Col Length: 247mm, Page Width: 180mm, Film: Digital
Copy instructions: Copy Date: 4 weeks prior to publication date
Average advertising content per issue: 20%
BUSINESS: COMMERCE, INDUSTRY & MANAGEMENT

CR ADVISOR   622561U37-22_50
Editorial Address: PO Box 9, GUILDFORD, GU3 2WZ
Tel: 01483 811483 **Fax:** 01483 821163
Email: books@canarybooks.com
Advertising Address: As above. **Tel:** 01483 811383
Fax: 01483 812163
Email: info@canarybooks.com
Web site: http://www.canarybooks.com
ISSN: 1369-9407
Publisher: Canary Ltd
Date Established: 1998
Frequency: 20 issues yearly
Annual Sub.: £320.00
Circulation: 3,000 (Publisher's Statement)
Usual Pagination: 8
Editor: David Hutchinson; **Advertising Manager:** Neil Mountain
Summary of Content: Newsletter containing information and executive summaries of clinical research news, regulations and GCP implementation.
Readership/Target Audience: Read by clinical research professionals, regulators and investigators.

ADVERTISING RATES:
Full Page Mono £800.00
Mechanical Data: Trim Size: 297 x 210mm, Film: Digital, Type Area: 240 x 165mm, Col Length: 240mm, Page Width: 165mm
BUSINESS: PHARMACEUTICAL & CHEMISTS

CRAFT BUSINESS   1614155U53-675
Editorial Address: 25 Phoenix Court, Hawkins Road, COLCHESTER, CO2 8JY **Tel:** 01206 505983
Fax: 01206 505985
Email: elizabeth.sharp@aceville.co.uk
Advertising Address: 21-23 Phoenix Court, Hawkins Road, COLCHESTER, CO2 8JY **Tel:** 01206 505900
Fax: 01206 505945
Email: martin.lack@aceville.co.uk
Web site: http://www.craftbusiness.com
Publisher: Aceville Publications Ltd
Date Established: 2000
Frequency: 8 issues yearly - Extra Issue at Christmas
Cover Price: £3.50
Free to qualifying individuals
Circulation: 7,137 (ABC 01/07/2007 to 30/06/2008)
Usual Pagination: 40
Editor: Elizabeth Sharp; **Advertising Manager:** Sharon Butler
Summary of Content: Magazine covering current news, features, profiles and product showcase from within the craft industry.
Readership/Target Audience: Aimed at wholesalers, retailers and designers.
ADVERTISING RATES:
Full Page Colour £1450.00
Agency Commission: 10%
Mechanical Data: Col Length: 350mm, Col Widths (Display): 50mm, No. of Columns (Display): 5, Type Area: 350 x 267mm, Print Process: Web-fed offset litho, Bleed Size: 390 x 290mm, Trim Size: 380 x 280mm, Page Width: 267mm, Film: Digital
Copy instructions: Copy Date: 2 weeks prior to publication date
Average advertising content per issue: 50%
BUSINESS: RETAILING & WHOLESALING

CRAFT FOCUS MAGAZINE   1835432U53-703
Editorial Address: Broseley House, Newlands Drive, WITHAM, CM8 2UL **Tel:** 01376 514000 **Fax:** 01376 514555
Email: editor@craftfocus.com
Advertising Address: As above.
Email: tracyv@craftfocus.com
Web site: http://www.craftfocus.com
ISSN: 1758-0900
Publisher: Kline Davis Ltd
Date Established: 2007
Frequency: 6 issues yearly
Cover Price: Free
Circulation: 6,750 (Publisher's Statement)
Editor: Rebecca Winward
Summary of Content: Magazine covering all aspects of the craft industry including news, events, industry trends and craft products.
Readership/Target Audience: Aimed at the craft industry.
ADVERTISING RATES:
Full Page Colour £1100.00
Mechanical Data: Bleed Size: 303 x 216mm, Trim Size: 297 x 210mm, Film: Digital
BUSINESS: RETAILING & WHOLESALING

CRAIN'S MANCHESTER BUSINESS
1820990U63B-2585
Editorial Address: PR by email only **Tel:** 0161 209 5800
Fax: 0161 237 3711
Email: manchesternews@crain.com
Advertising Address: City Tower, Suite 22A, Piccadilly Plaza, MANCHESTER, M1 4BD **Tel:** 0161 209 5800
Email: ktoledano@crain.com
Web site: http://www.crainsmanchesterbusiness.co.uk
Publisher: Crain Communications Ltd
Date Established: 2007
Frequency: Weekly
Cover Price: £2.00
Annual Sub.: £79.00
Circulation: 13,693 (ABC 01/07/2008 to 30/06/2009)
Editor: Steve Brauner; **Advertising Director:** Kathryn Toledano; **Publisher:** Arthur Porter
Summary of Content: Business newspaper covering local business news for the Greater Manchester area.
Readership/Target Audience: Aimed at senior level executives and small business owners, and members of the professional and executives in finance.
ADVERTISING RATES:
Full Page Mono £5900.00
Full Page Colour £6550.00
Agency Commission: 10%

Mechanical Data: Type Area: 377 x 255mm, Bleed Size: 411 x 293mm, Trim Size: 403 x 285mm, Col Length: 377mm, Page Width: 255mm, Film: Digital
Copy instructions: Copy Date: 10 days prior to publication date
BUSINESS: REGIONAL BUSINESS: Regional Business English Counties

CRANES & ACCESS
39084U42R-102_50

Formerly: Cranes UK
Editorial Address: 18 Cross Lane, Helmdon, BRACKLEY, NN13 5QL **Tel:** 01295 768340 **Fax:** 01295 768223
Email: lws@vertikal.net
Advertising Address: PO Box 6998, BRACKLEY, NN13 5WY **Tel:** 0870 774 0436 **Fax:** 01295 768223
Email: info@vertikal.net
Web site: http://www.vertikal.net
ISSN: 1467-0852
Publisher: The Vertikal Press
Date Established: 1995
Frequency: 8 issues yearly - Published around the 1st of the cover month (combined issues: 1st of the 2nd cover month)
Cover Price: £8.00
Free to qualifying individuals
Annual Sub.: £40.00
Circulation: 8,500 (Publisher's Statement)
Usual Pagination: 68
Editor: Leigh Sparrow; **Publisher:** Leigh Sparrow
Summary of Content: Magazine covering UK and Irish crane news and information on access equipment.
Readership/Target Audience: Aimed at British and Irish buyers and users of cranes and access equipment.
ADVERTISING RATES:
Full Page Colour £2300.00
Agency Commission: 15%
Mechanical Data: Type Area: 268 x 184mm, Bleed Size: 304 x 216mm, Trim Size: 297 x 210mm, Print Process: Litho, Film: Positive, right reading, emulsion side down. Digital, Col Length: 268mm, Page Width: 184mm
Copy instructions: Copy Date: 3 weeks prior to publication date
Average advertising content per issue: 40%
BUSINESS: CONSTRUCTION: Construction Related

CRANES TODAY
39085U42R-103

Editorial Address: Progressive House, 2 Maidstone Road, Foots Cray, SIDCUP, DA14 5HZ **Tel:** 020 8269 7861
Fax: 020 8269 7803
Email: rhowes@cranestodaymagazine.com
Advertising Address: As above. **Tel:** 020 8269 7700
Email: mmccarthy@progressivemediagroup.com
Web site: http://www.cranestodaymagazine.com
ISSN: 0307-0018
Publisher: Progressive Media Publications
Date Established: 1972
Frequency: Monthly - Published the 1st day of the month of publication
Cover Price: £18.00
Free to qualifying individuals
Annual Sub.: £175.00
Circulation: 16,337 (ABC 01/07/2007 to 30/06/2008)
Usual Pagination: 72
Editor: Richard Howes; **Group Editor:** Richard Howes
Summary of Content: Magazine covering events within the international lifting industry. Provides information on all types of cranes used in a wide variety of industries.
Readership/Target Audience: Aimed at buyers and users within the crane and lifting industry, rental companies, engineers and consultants.
ADVERTISING RATES:
Full Page Mono £2365.00
Full Page Colour £3245.00
Agency Commission: 10%
Mechanical Data: Type Area: 264 x 184mm, Col Length: 264mm, Bleed Size: 293 x 216mm, Trim Size: 287 x 210mm, Film: Digital, Page Width: 184mm
Copy instructions: Copy Date: 20th of the month prior to publication date
Average advertising content per issue: 60%
Supplement(s): Cranes Today Buyers Guide - 1xY
BUSINESS: CONSTRUCTION: Construction Related

CRANES TODAY BUYERS GUIDE
39089U42R-110

Formerly: Cranes Today Handbook
Editorial Address: Progressive House, 2 Maidstone Road, Foots Cray, SIDCUP, DA14 5HZ **Tel:** 020 8269 7700
Fax: 020 8269 7874
Email: rhowes@cranestodaymagazine.com
Advertising Address: As above.
Email: benellefsen@boundarymedia.co.uk
Web site: http://www.cranestodaymagazine.com
Publisher: Progressive Media Publications
Frequency: Annual - Published in March
Annual Sub.: £69.00
Circulation: 3,000 (Publisher's Statement)

Usual Pagination: 200
Editor: Richard Howes; **Group Editor:** Richard Howes
Summary of Content: Handbook about manufacturers technical data on cranes, ancillary lifting equipment and industry directory.
Readership/Target Audience: Aimed at all crane users worldwide.
ADVERTISING RATES:
Full Page Mono £2365.00
Full Page Colour £3245.00
Agency Commission: 10%
Mechanical Data: Film: Digital, Type Area: 180 x 125mm, Bleed Size: 216 x 125mm, Trim Size: 210 x 148mm, Col Length: 180mm, Page Width: 125mm
Copy instructions: Copy Date: 2nd week of March prior to publication date
Average advertising content per issue: 18%
Supplement to: Cranes Today
BUSINESS: CONSTRUCTION: Construction Related

CREAM
1684374U2A-674

Editorial Address: 115 Southwark Bridge Road, LONDON, SE1 0AX **Tel:** 020 7367 6990
Email: alastair.ray@btinternet.com
Web site: http://www.cmdglobal.com
Publisher: C Squared Communications
Date Established: 2005
Frequency: Quarterly
Annual Sub.: £87.00
Circulation: 6,000 (Publisher's Statement)
Usual Pagination: 56
Editor: Alastair Ray; **Publisher:** Charlie Crowe
Summary of Content: Magazine focusing on the very best in creative media thinking across the world. Covers in-depth marketing initiatives, multimedia strategies, consumer insight studies and innovative media executions.
Readership/Target Audience: Aimed at marketing directors, media and creative agencies.
ADVERTISING: No Advertising taken
BUSINESS: COMMUNICATIONS, ADVERTISING & MARKETING

CREATIVE HEAD
712038U15B-10

Editorial Address: 21 The Timber Yard, Drysdale Street, LONDON, N1 6ND **Tel:** 020 7324 7540 **Fax:** 020 7739 7789
Email: cecily@headmag.co.uk
Advertising Address: As above. **Tel:** 020 7324 7544
Email: enquiries@headmag.co.uk
Web site: http://www.head1st.net
Publisher: Alfol Ltd
Date Established: 2000
Frequency: 11 issues yearly - Joint issues in July/August
Cover Price: £4.50
Free to qualifying individuals
Annual Sub.: £36.00
Circulation: 17,000 (Publisher's Statement)
Usual Pagination: 74
Editor: Cecily Bennett; **Advertising Manager:** Sophie Constantinou
Summary of Content: Magazine containing hairdressing industry news, fashion collections, features and comments on the hairdressing industry in the UK.
Readership/Target Audience: Aimed at hairdressing salon owners and managers, creative directors and senior stylists.
ADVERTISING RATES:
Full Page Colour £2100.00
Mechanical Data: Type Area: 280 x 210mm, Col Length: 280mm, Page Width: 210mm, Bleed Size: 306 x 236mm, Film: Digital, Trim Size: 300 x 230mm
Average advertising content per issue: 50%
Supplement(s): Space - 2xY
BUSINESS: COSMETICS & HAIRDRESSING: Hairdressing

CREATIVE REVIEW
35486U2A-66

Editorial Address: St. Giles House, 50 Poland Street, LONDON, W1F 7AX **Tel:** 020 7970 4000 **Fax:** 020 7970 6712
Email: patrick.burgoyne@centaur.co.uk
Advertising Address: As above. **Fax:** 020 7970 6713
Email: jonathan.cockley@centaur.co.uk
Web site: http://www.creativereview.co.uk
Publisher: Centaur Communications Ltd
Frequency: Monthly - Published around the 3rd Monday of the cover month
Cover Price: £5.00
Annual Sub.: £56.00
Circulation: 14,942 (ABC 01/07/2008 to 30/06/2009)
Editor: Patrick Burgoyne; **Publisher:** Jessica Macdermot
Summary of Content: Magazine focusing on graphics, new media design, video, film, computer animation and new packaging. Includes advertising, typography, photography and features on computer technology relating to design.
Readership/Target Audience: Aimed at those working in communications art.
ADVERTISING RATES:
Full Page Mono £4125.00
Full Page Colour £4125.00

Agency Commission: 10%
Mechanical Data: Bleed Size: 286 x 286mm, Film: Digital, No. of Columns (Display): 5, Trim Size: 280 x 280mm
Copy instructions: Copy Date: 1st week of the month prior to publication date
Average advertising content per issue: 53%
BUSINESS: COMMUNICATIONS, ADVERTISING & MARKETING

CREDIT
626553U1G-14_75

Editorial Address: Haymarket House, 28-29 Haymarket, LONDON, SW1Y 4RX **Tel:** 020 7484 9700
Email: matthew.attwood@creditmag.com
Advertising Address: As above.
Email: damian.clarke@incisivemedia.com
Web site: http://www.creditmag.com
Publisher: Incisive Media Investments
Date Established: 2000
Frequency: 11 issues yearly - Published in the 2nd week of the cover month
Annual Sub.: £875.00
Circulation: 10,000 (Publisher's Statement)
Usual Pagination: 56
Editor: Matthew Attwood; **Advertising Manager:** Damian Clarke; **Managing Editor:** Alex Krohn; **Publisher:** Robert Mannix
Summary of Content: Magazine covering European bond markets, news, analysis, comment and opinions.
Readership/Target Audience: Aimed at fixed income and commercial bankers, corporate borrowers, investors and financial, academic institutions, issuers, market professionals, technology and software vendors, law firms and regulators.
ADVERTISING RATES:
Full Page Colour £10450.00
Agency Commission: 10%
Mechanical Data: Film: Digital, Page Width: 177mm, Type Area: 228 x 177mm, Col Length: 228mm, Trim Size: 280 x 216mm, Bleed Size: 286 x 222mm
Copy instructions: Copy Date: 15th of the month prior to publication date
BUSINESS: FINANCE & ECONOMICS: Credit Trading

CREDIT COLLECTIONS AND RISK
1749970U1G-105

Editorial Address: 53 Harvey Gardens, LONDON, SE7 8AJ
Tel: 020 8858 4223
Email: stephen@ccrmagazine.com
Advertising Address: The Cellar, 81 Cambridge Road, SOUTHEND-ON-SEA, SS1 1EP **Tel:** 07785 268404
Fax: 01702 331026
Email: gary@ccrmagazine.co.uk
Web site: http://www.ccrmagazine.com
Publisher: GTS Media
Date Established: 2005
Frequency: Monthly
Annual Sub.: £200.00
Circulation: 10,051 (ABC 01/07/2008 to 30/06/2009)
Usual Pagination: 60
Editor: Stephen Kiely
Summary of Content: Publication covering all areas of interest to both consumer and commercial credit professionals on both the credit assessment and collections sides. Includes everything from new scoring and modelling technologies through to new ideas in debt selling and insolvency trends.
Readership/Target Audience: Aimed at credit professionals both consumer and commercial with an emphasis on more senior management such as credit managers and financial directors.
ADVERTISING RATES:
Full Page Mono £2000.00
Full Page Colour £2000.00
Agency Commission: 10%
Mechanical Data: Type Area: 267 x 180mm, Bleed Size: 303 x 216mm, Trim Size: 297 x 210mm, Col Length: 267mm, Page Width: 180mm, Film: Digital
Copy instructions: Copy Date: 15th of the month
Average advertising content per issue: 35%
BUSINESS: FINANCE & ECONOMICS: Credit Trading

CREDIT CONTROL
35341U1G-15

Editorial Address: 7 Greding Walk, Hutton, BRENTWOOD, CM13 2UF **Tel:** 01277 225402 **Fax:** 0870 137 5688
Email: carol.baker@creditcontrol.co.uk
Advertising Address: As above.
Email: carol.baker@creditcontrol.co.uk
Web site: http://www.creditcontrol.co.uk
ISSN: 0143-5329
Publisher: House of Words Ltd
Date Established: 1979
Frequency: 10 issues yearly
Annual Sub.: £635.00
Circulation: 16,386 (Publisher's Statement)
Usual Pagination: 108
Editor: Carol Baker; **Advertising Manager:** Carol Baker

Summary of Content: Journal of academic research dedicated to the advancement of asset and risk management, and credit management knowledge. It incorporates practical illustrations as well as theoretical analysis and empirical studies which address the key issues facing multinational corporations.
Readership/Target Audience: Read by chief executive officers, chief financial officers, finance directors, credit analysts, credit managers, controllers, analysts, accountants and academics.
ADVERTISING RATES:
Full Page Mono £650.00
Full Page Colour £1620.00
Agency Commission: 10%
Mechanical Data: Type Area: 243 x 167mm, Film: Digital, Col Length: 243mm, Page Width: 167mm, Print Process: Litho, Bleed Size: +3mm, Trim Size: 297 x 210mm
Copy instructions: Copy Date: 2nd Wednesday of the month prior to publication date
Average advertising content per issue: 8%
BUSINESS: FINANCE & ECONOMICS: Credit Trading

CREDIT MANAGEMENT
35342U1G-20
Editorial Address: The Water Mill, Station Road, South Luffenham, OAKHAM, LE15 8NB **Tel:** 01780 722910
Fax: 01780 721271
Email: editorial@icm.org.uk
Advertising Address: As above.
Email: editorial@icm.org.uk
Web site: http://www.icm.org.uk
ISSN: 0265-2099
Publisher: Institute of Credit Management
Date Established: 1946
Frequency: Monthly - Published on the 28th of the month prior to the cover month
Cover Price: £6.50
Annual Sub.: £55.00
Circulation: 8,791 (ABC 01/07/2008 to 30/06/2009)
Usual Pagination: 56
Editor: Rob Beddington; **Advertising Manager:** Rob Beddington
Summary of Content: Journal covering developments in trade, retail and export credit.
Readership/Target Audience: Aimed at credit professionals.
ADVERTISING RATES:
Full Page Colour £1525.00
Agency Commission: 10%
Mechanical Data: Type Area: 263 x 177mm, Col Length: 263mm, Film: Digital, Trim Size: 297 x 210mm, Bleed Size: 303 x 216mm, Page Width: 177mm
Copy instructions: Copy Date: 2 weeks prior to publication date
Average advertising content per issue: 25%
Supplement(s): Credit Supplements - 2xY
BUSINESS: FINANCE & ECONOMICS: Credit Trading

CREDIT RATINGS INTERNATIONAL
35344U1G-23
Editorial Address: Fitzroy House, 13-17 Epworth Street, LONDON, EC2A 4DL **Tel:** 020 7825 8000
Fax: 020 7825 8722
Email: steve.crisp@interactivedata.com
Advertising Address: As above. **Tel:** 020 7825 8100
Fax: 020 7608 2032
Email: arthur.evans@interactivedata.com
Web site: http://www.ftinteractivedata.com
ISSN: 0965-9331
Publisher: Interactive Data (Europe) Limited
Frequency: Quarterly
Summary of Content: Financial journal covering International credit news and features.
Readership/Target Audience: Read by investors, borrowers and those involved in the International credit markets.
ADVERTISING: Rates on application
BUSINESS: FINANCE & ECONOMICS: Credit Trading

CREDIT TODAY
35345U1G-28
Editorial Address: 1st Floor, Axe and Bottle Court, 70 Newcomen Street, LONDON, SE1 1YT **Tel:** 0844 477 4740
Fax: 020 7940 4843
Email: heather@credittoday.co.uk
Advertising Address: As above. **Tel:** 020 7940 4835
Email: thomas@credittoday.co.uk
Web site: http://www.credittoday.co.uk
ISSN: 1464-679X
Publisher: Athene Publishing
Date Established: 1998
Frequency: Monthly - Published around the beginning of the cover month
Annual Sub.: £195.00
Circulation: 13,694 (ABC 01/07/2008 to 30/06/2009)
Usual Pagination: 64
Editor: Heather Greig-Smith; **Publisher:** Kamala Panday
Summary of Content: Magazine covering all aspects of the commercial and consumer credit industry. Contains features

on credit granting, debt prevention and collecting, credit control and risk management.
Readership/Target Audience: Aimed at credit managers.
ADVERTISING RATES:
Full Page Mono £1785.00
Full Page Colour £2280.00
Agency Commission: 10%
Mechanical Data: Bleed Size: 303 x 216mm, Type Area: 267 x 180mm, Col Length: 267mm, Page Width: 180mm, Trim Size: 297 x 210mm, Film: Digital
Copy instructions: Copy Date: 17th of the month prior to publication date
Average advertising content per issue: 60%
BUSINESS: FINANCE & ECONOMICS: Credit Trading

CREDITFLUX
1657858U1G-102
Editorial Address: 2-6 Northburgh Street, LONDON, EC1V 0AY **Tel:** 020 7253 9510 **Fax:** 020 7253 3485
Email: editor@creditflux.com
Advertising Address: As above. **Fax:** 020 7253 5238
Email: tom.davidson@creditflux.com
Web site: http://www.creditflux.com
ISSN: 1475-0716
Publisher: Creditflux
Date Established: 2001
Frequency: Monthly
Annual Sub.: £850.00
Circulation: 1,500 (Publisher's Statement)
Usual Pagination: 32
Editor: Michael Peterson; **Advertising Manager:** Tom Davidson; **Managing Editor:** Michael Peterson; **Publisher:** Tom Davidson
Summary of Content: Journal covering news and analysis of the global credit derivatives market and structured credit markets.
Readership/Target Audience: Aimed at derivatives dealers, investment managers, insurance companies, commercial banks, lawyers, consultants and recruiters.
ADVERTISING RATES:
Full Page Colour £3500.00
Mechanical Data: Film: Digital, Type Area: 265 x 203mm, Bleed Size: 271 x 209mm, Col Length: 265mm, Page Width: 203mm
Copy instructions: Copy Date: 3rd week of the month prior to publication date
Average advertising content per issue: 25%
BUSINESS: FINANCE & ECONOMICS: Credit Trading

THE CREW REPORT
1842229U45E-373
Editorial Address: Lansdowne House, 3-7 Northcote Road, LONDON, SW11 1NG **Tel:** 020 7924 4004
Fax: 020 7924 1004
Email: newsdesk@theyachtreport.com
Advertising Address: As above.
Email: newsdesk@theyachtreport.com
Web site: http://www.yotcru.com
Publisher: TRP Magazines
Date Established: 2006
Frequency: 9 issues yearly
Free to qualifying individuals
Circulation: 20,000 (Publisher's Statement)
Editor: Natalie Vizard
Summary of Content: Magazine reporting on the serious issues that directly affect the manning and safe operation of large yachts.
Readership/Target Audience: Aimed at the crew of large yachts.
ADVERTISING RATES:
Full Page Colour £2645.00
BUSINESS: MARINE & SHIPPING: Boat Trade

CRIMINAL BEHAVIOUR & MENTAL HEALTH
38430U32F-120
Editorial Address: The Atrium, Southern Gate, CHICHESTER, PO19 8SQ **Tel:** 01243 779777
Email: rachel.o'kane@oxon.blackwellpublishing.com
Advertising Address: As above. **Tel:** 01243 770254
Fax: 01243 770432
Email: fpidduck@wiley.co.uk
Web site: http://www.wiley.co.uk
ISSN: 0957-9664
Publisher: John Wiley & Sons Ltd
Date Established: 1991
Frequency: Quarterly
Annual Sub.: £108.00
Usual Pagination: 80
Editor: Rachel O'Kane; **Publisher:** Rachel O'Kane
Summary of Content: Journal at the interface of psychiatry, psychology, crime and the law.
Readership/Target Audience: Read by psychiatrists, psychologists, lawyers, criminologists and other social scientists.
ADVERTISING RATES:
Full Page Mono £385.00

Full Page Colour £1120.00
BUSINESS: LOCAL GOVERNMENT, LEISURE & RECREATION: Police

CRIMINAL LAW REVIEW
39144U44-460
Editorial Address: 100 Avenue Road, LONDON, NW3 3PF
Tel: 020 7393 7000 **Fax:** 020 7393 7030
Email: fiona.keyte@thomsonreuters.com
Web site: http://www.sweetandmaxwell.co.uk
ISSN: 0011-135X
Publisher: Sweet & Maxwell Ltd
Frequency: Monthly
Annual Sub.: £254.00
Usual Pagination: 80
Editor: Ian Dennis; **Managing Director:** Peter Lake
Summary of Content: Journal containing case reports, articles, comment, book reviews and letters about criminal law.
Readership/Target Audience: Aimed at law practitioners and academics.
ADVERTISING: No Advertising taken
BUSINESS: LEGAL

CRITICAL POLICY ANALYSIS
1748512U32A-263
Editorial Address: University of Birmingham, Edgbaston, BIRMINGHAM, B15 2TT **Tel:** 0121 414 5015
Fax: 0121 414 4954
Email: p.thornington-jones@bham.ac.uk
Web site: http://www.inlogov.bham.ac.uk
ISSN: 1750-8762
Publisher: University of Birmingham
Date Established: 2006
Frequency: Quarterly
Cover Price: £90.00
Circulation: 200 (Publisher's Statement)
Editor: Carol Fowler; **Managing Editor:** Steven Griggs
Summary of Content: Journal covering the theory and practice of local government policy analysis.
Readership/Target Audience: Aimed at academics and policy analysists.
ADVERTISING: No Advertising taken
BUSINESS: LOCAL GOVERNMENT, LEISURE & RECREATION: Local Government

CRN
36179U5C-40
Editorial Address: 32-34 Broadwick Street, LONDON, W1A 2HG **Tel:** 020 7316 9000 **Fax:** 020 7316 9519
Email: sara.yirrell@incisivemedia.com
Advertising Address: As above. **Fax:** 020 7316 9451
Email: david.thomas@incisivemedia.com
Web site: http://www.channelweb.co.uk
Publisher: Incisive Media
Date Established: 1998
Frequency: Weekly
Free to qualifying individuals
Annual Sub.: £100.00
Circulation: 16,000 (BPA Worldwide 01/01/2007 to 24/06/2007)
Editor: Sara Yirrell; **News Editor:** Doug Woodburn; **Features Editor:** Fleur Doidge
Summary of Content: Magazine covering all aspects of the personal IT industry. Includes news and opinion, contract wins, tender information and product reviews.
Readership/Target Audience: Read by distributors, vendors and senior personnel in business computer dealerships.
ADVERTISING RATES:
Full Page Colour £3195.00
Agency Commission: 10%
Mechanical Data: Page Width: 212mm, Type Area: 280 x 212mm, Col Length: 280mm, Trim Size: 300 x 232mm, Bleed Size: 310 x 242mm
Copy instructions: Copy Date: 1 week prior to publication date
Average advertising content per issue: 40%
BUSINESS: COMPUTERS & AUTOMATION: Professional Personal Computers

CRONER TRADE INTERNATIONAL DIGEST
37716U20-70
Formerly: Trade International Digest
Editorial Address: 145 London Road, KINGSTON UPON THAMES, KT2 6SR **Tel:** 020 8547 3333 **Fax:** 020 8549 7275
Email: trade@croner.co.uk
Advertising Address: Old Byre House, East Knoyle, Wilts, SALISBURY, SP3 6AW **Tel:** 020 8247 1401
Fax: 01747 830691
Email: sabrina.croner@spmedia.co.uk
Web site: http://www.croner.co.uk
Publisher: Wolters Kluwer (UK) Ltd
Date Established: 1957
Frequency: Monthly - Published on the 15th of the cover month
Annual Sub.: £80.95

Usual Pagination: 40
Editor: Peter Tucker
Summary of Content: Magazine covering international trade, high profile export issues such as finance, customs, freight, logistics and documentation as well as country profiles, marketing tips, Q&A and buyer's guides. Also covers European and UK law, interviews and training.
Readership/Target Audience: Read by those involved in international trade including exporters, importers and freight forwarders.
ADVERTISING RATES:
Full Page Colour £2000.00
Agency Commission: 10%
Mechanical Data: Film: Digital, Type Area: 255 x 189mm, Trim Size: 297 x 210mm, Bleed Size: 300 x 215mm, Col Length: 255mm, Page Width: 189mm
Average advertising content per issue: 40%
BUSINESS: IMPORT & EXPORT

CRONER'S ENVIRONMENT BRIEFING

39145U57-15_30

Editorial Address: 145 London Road, KINGSTON UPON THAMES, KT2 6SR **Tel:** 020 8547 3333 **Fax:** 020 8549 7275
Email: laura.king@croner.co.uk
Web site: http://www.croner.co.uk
Publisher: Wolters Kluwer (UK) Ltd
Frequency: 10 issues yearly
Annual Sub.: £500.00
Usual Pagination: 8
Editor: Laura King
Summary of Content: Newsletter containing news, case law and policy guidance on environmental legislation.
Readership/Target Audience: Aimed at health and safety managers, environmental managers, environmental consultants and local authorities.
ADVERTISING: No Advertising taken
BUSINESS: ENVIRONMENT & POLLUTION

CRONER'S ENVIRONMENT MAGAZINE

40629U57-154

Formerly: Croner's Waste Management Magazine
Editorial Address: 145 London Road, KINGSTON UPON THAMES, KT2 6SR **Tel:** 020 8547 3333 **Fax:** 020 8546 9374
Email: kevin.whitten@croner.co.uk
Advertising Address: SP Media, Old Byre House, Millbrook Lane, East Knoyle, SALISBURY, SP3 6AW
Tel: 01747 830520 **Fax:** 01747 830691
Email: sabrina.croner@spmedia.co.uk
Web site: http://www.croner.co.uk
ISSN: 1472-5037
Publisher: Wolters Kluwer (UK) Ltd
Date Established: 2000
Frequency: Quarterly
Cover Price: £4.00
Circulation: 21,000 (Publisher's Statement)
Usual Pagination: 24
Editor: Kevin Whitten; **Advertising Manager:** Sabrina Sully
Summary of Content: Magazine reporting on UK and EU regulations affecting environmental, water, recycling, energy and waste management with topical news and analytical features commissioned from experts.
Readership/Target Audience: Aimed at managers and directors with a responsibility for environmental and waste management within companies, local authorities, health trusts and local government.
ADVERTISING RATES:
Full Page Colour £1450.00
Mechanical Data: Type Area: 255 x 189mm, Bleed Size: 300 x 215mm, Trim Size: 297 x 210mm, Col Length: 255mm, Page Width: 189mm, Film: Digital
Copy instructions: Copy Date: 3 weeks prior to publication date
BUSINESS: ENVIRONMENT & POLLUTION

CRONER'S GUIDE TO CREDIT MANAGEMENT

35349U1G-30

Editorial Address: 145 London Road, KINGSTON UPON THAMES, KT2 6SR **Tel:** 020 8247 5333 **Fax:** 020 8247 1184
Email: customerservices@cch.co.uk
Web site: http://www.croner.co.uk
Publisher: Wolters Kluwer (UK) Ltd
Date Established: 1992
Frequency: Quarterly
Annual Sub.: £528.59
Usual Pagination: 60
Editor: Melissa Prideaux
Summary of Content: A loose-leaf guide and newsletter dedicated to the development of professional credit control in UK businesses.
Readership/Target Audience: Aimed at credit managers and controllers.
ADVERTISING: No Advertising taken
BUSINESS: FINANCE & ECONOMICS: Credit Trading

CRONER'S HEALTH & SAFETY AT WORK

39893U54B-15

Editorial Address: 145 London Road, KINGSTON UPON THAMES, KT2 6SR **Tel:** 020 8547 3333 **Fax:** 020 8547 2638
Email: info@croner.co.uk
Web site: http://www.croner.co.uk
Publisher: Croner Group Ltd
Frequency: 24 issues yearly
Editor: Vicky McKay
Summary of Content: Publication containing an A-Z guide of health and safety information on compliance and best practice.
Readership/Target Audience: Aimed at health and safety co-ordinators, advisors, managers and any personnel with responsibilities in health and safety.
ADVERTISING: No Advertising taken
BUSINESS: SAFETY & SECURITY: Safety

CRONER'S IMPORTER'S BRIEFING

37730U20-89

Formerly: Croner's Reference Book for Importers
Editorial Address: 145 London Road, KINGSTON UPON THAMES, KT2 6SR **Tel:** 020 8547 3333 **Fax:** 020 8549 7275
Email: trade@croner.co.uk
Web site: http://www.croner.co.uk
Publisher: Wolters Kluwer (UK) Ltd
Frequency: 11 issues yearly - Not issued in August
Usual Pagination: 12
Editor: Peter Tucker
Summary of Content: Newsletter providing information on the numerous regulations covering the importing of goods into the UK and companies who provide services and products to UK importers.
Readership/Target Audience: Aimed at importers.
ADVERTISING: No Advertising taken
BUSINESS: IMPORT & EXPORT

CRONER'S OFFICE HEALTH & SAFETY

39894U54B-17

Editorial Address: 145 London Road, KINGSTON UPON THAMES, KT2 6SR **Tel:** 020 8547 3333
Email: veronica.fitzmaurice@croner.co.uk
Web site: http://www.croner.co.uk
Publisher: Wolters Kluwer (UK) Ltd
Date Established: 1993
Frequency: 10 issues yearly
Annual Sub.: £508.00
Editor: Veronica Fitzmaurice
Summary of Content: Publication focusing on the management of health and safety, display screen equipment, electricity, first aid, fire, manual handling, food hygiene, the workplace environment, training and human factors.
Readership/Target Audience: Aimed at personnel, health and safety, administration managers in private and public services and the service industry.
ADVERTISING: No Advertising taken
BUSINESS: SAFETY & SECURITY: Safety

CRONER'S PAY & BENEFITS SOURCEBOOK

37106U14F-8_86

Editorial Address: 145 London Road, KINGSTON UPON THAMES, KT2 6SR **Tel:** 020 8547 3333 **Fax:** 020 8547 3465
Email: info@croner.co.uk
Web site: http://www.croner.co.uk
Publisher: Croner Group Ltd
Date Established: 1992
Frequency: Monthly
Editor: Natalie Dunn
Summary of Content: Reference source for any manager in charge of pay policy and implementation and ensuring legal compliance within a company's pay system.
Readership/Target Audience: Aimed at directors, remuneration and benefits managers, HR managers, consultants and pay bargainers.
ADVERTISING: No Advertising taken
BUSINESS: COMMERCE, INDUSTRY & MANAGEMENT: Training & Recruitment

CRONER'S PERSONNEL ASSISTANT'S HANDBOOK

37107U14F-8_87

Editorial Address: 145 London Road, KINGSTON UPON THAMES, KT2 6SR **Tel:** 020 8247 1175 **Fax:** 020 8547 2637
Email: info@croner.co.uk
Web site: http://www.croner.co.uk
Publisher: Croner Group Ltd
Date Established: 1994
Frequency: Quarterly
Editor: Anne Powell
Summary of Content: Practical reference book for personnel assistants to run an efficient HR and personnel department.

Readership/Target Audience: Aimed at HR and personnel assistants.
ADVERTISING: No Advertising taken
BUSINESS: COMMERCE, INDUSTRY & MANAGEMENT: Training & Recruitment

CRONER'S PERSONNEL IN PRACTICE : RECORDS & PROCEDURES

37108U14F-8_89

Editorial Address: 145 London Road, KINGSTON UPON THAMES, KT2 6SR **Tel:** 020 8547 3333 **Fax:** 020 8549 7275
Email: gillian.fraser@croner.co.uk
Web site: http://www.croner.co.uk
ISSN: 0309-4995
Publisher: Wolters Kluwer (UK) Ltd
Date Established: 1992
Frequency: 26 issues yearly
Editor: Gillian Fraser
Summary of Content: Journal containing model procedures covering every area of employment with the contracts, records and forms needed to ensure their implementation.
Readership/Target Audience: Aimed at personnel managers.
ADVERTISING: No Advertising taken
BUSINESS: COMMERCE, INDUSTRY & MANAGEMENT: Training & Recruitment

CRONER'S ROAD TRANSPORT OPERATION: RECORDS & PROCEDURES

39601U49A-47

Editorial Address: 145 London Road, KINGSTON UPON THAMES, KT2 6SR **Tel:** 020 8547 3333
Email: michael.phillips@croner.co.uk
Web site: http://www.croner.co.uk
Publisher: Wolters Kluwer (UK) Ltd
Date Established: 1994
Frequency: Half-yearly
Usual Pagination: 50
Editor: Michael Phillips
Summary of Content: Guide to establishing an effective management system in the transport business.
Readership/Target Audience: Aimed at managers of transport companies, especially small and medium-sized.
ADVERTISING: No Advertising taken
BUSINESS: TRANSPORT

CROP PHYSIOLOGY ABSTRACTS

37800U21A-230

Editorial Address: Nosworthy Way, WALLINGFORD, OX10 8DE **Tel:** 01491 832111 **Fax:** 01491 829198
Email: cabi@cabi.org
Web site: http://www.cabi-publishing.org
ISSN: 0306-7556
Publisher: CABI
Frequency: 6 issues yearly
Annual Sub.: £785.00
Circulation: 50 (Publisher's Statement)
Editor: David Simpson
Summary of Content: Journal covering all aspects of physiology from germination to senescence of all higher plants of economic importance.
Readership/Target Audience: Aimed at academic and government research institutes, seed, agro-chemical and plant breeding companies.
ADVERTISING: No Advertising taken
BUSINESS: AGRICULTURE & FARMING

CROP PROTECTION MONTHLY

37802U21B-90

Editorial Address: Blacksmiths Cottage, Ashbocking Road, Henley, IPSWICH, IP6 0QX **Tel:** 01473 831645
Fax: 01473 832943
Email: mredbond@aol.com
Web site: http://www.crop-protection-monthly.co.uk
ISSN: 1366-5634
Publisher: Market Scope Europe Ltd
Date Established: 1989
Frequency: Monthly - Published at the end of each month and mid-December
Usual Pagination: 20
Editor: Martin Redbond
Summary of Content: International business newsletter reporting, analysing and commenting on developments in international crop protection markets and R&D, with the main focus on Europe. Regular coverage of American and Asian markets. Regular reports on the key international conferences.
Readership/Target Audience: Read by top business and research management.
ADVERTISING: No Advertising taken
BUSINESS: AGRICULTURE & FARMING: Agriculture - Supplies & Services

Business Magazines

CROPS
37755U21A-250

Editorial Address: Quadrant House, The Quadrant, SUTTON, SM2 5AS **Tel:** 020 8652 4081 **Fax:** 020 8652 4006
Email: crops@rbi.co.uk
Advertising Address: As above. **Tel:** 020 8652 4030
Fax: 020 8652 4043
Email: vic.bunby@rbi.co.uk
Web site: http://www.fwi.co.uk
ISSN: 1364-6559
Publisher: Reed Business Information
Frequency: 21 issues yearly
Annual Sub.: £61.50
Circulation: 14,795 (ABC 01/01/2008 to 31/12/2008)
Editor: Robert Harris; **Advertising Director:** Vic Bunby
Summary of Content: Journal covering practical and technical information on all aspects of arable farming.
Readership/Target Audience: Aimed at arable farmers, farm managers and advisors.
ADVERTISING: Rates on application
Copy instructions: Copy Date: 2 weeks prior to publication date
BUSINESS: AGRICULTURE & FARMING

CROSS & COCKADE INTERNATIONAL
36351U6A-86_50

Editorial Address: 4 Cliff Terrace, Easington, PETERLEE, SR8 3BL **Tel:** 0191 527 2163
Email: mickateasington@aol.com
Advertising Address: 6 Cowper Road, Southgate, LONDON, N14 5RP **Tel:** 020 8361 8482
Email: advertising.manager@crossandcockade.com
Web site: http://www.crossandcockade.com
ISSN: 1360-9009
Publisher: Cross & Cockade International
Date Established: 1969
Frequency: Quarterly
Annual Sub.: £24.00
Circulation: 1,400 (Publisher's Statement)
Usual Pagination: 60
Editor: Mick Davies
Summary of Content: Journal containing articles, photographs and scale drawings relating to all aspects of World War One Aviation.
Readership/Target Audience: Aimed at those interested in all aspects of World War One aviation.
ADVERTISING RATES:
Full Page Mono £100.00
Mechanical Data: Film: Digital, Type Area: 269 x 178mm, Col Length: 269mm, Page Width: 178mm, Trim Size: 297 x 210mm
BUSINESS: AVIATION & AERONAUTICS

CRU STEEL NEWS
38176U27-152

Formerly: Steel Week
Editorial Address: 31 Mount Pleasant, LONDON, WC1X 0AD **Tel:** 020 7903 2406 **Fax:** 020 7837 3558
Email: swnewsdesk@crugroup.com
Web site: http://www.steelweek.com
ISSN: 1359-1681
Publisher: CRU International Ltd
Date Established: 1995
Frequency: Weekly
Annual Sub.: £950.00
Usual Pagination: 26
Editor: John Quigley; **News Editor:** David Maitland
Summary of Content: Newsletter covering company news on global steel-making. Includes articles on stockholding, finance, regulation, scrap and markets.
Readership/Target Audience: Aimed at those involved in the steel industry.
ADVERTISING: No Advertising taken
BUSINESS: METAL, IRON & STEEL

CRUISE TRADE NEWS
626349U50-15_68

Formerly: Cruise & Ferry News
Editorial Address: 33 Pages Lane, Muswell Hill, LONDON, N10 1PU **Tel:** 020 8444 7819
Email: barry30551@aol.com
Advertising Address: 10 Tadorne Road, TADWORTH, KT20 5TD **Tel:** 01737 812411 **Fax:** 01737 819587
Email: kmellis@btinternet.com
Publisher: Webtrafix Ltd
Date Established: 2000
Frequency: 6 issues yearly
Cover Price: £2.00
Free to qualifying individuals
Annual Sub.: £15.00
Circulation: 5,500 (Publisher's Statement)
Usual Pagination: 20
Editor: Barry Cain; **News Editor:** Mark Ackerman
Summary of Content: Magazine containing cruise and ferry news and features.
Readership/Target Audience: Read by travel agents and executives in the cruise and ferry industry.

ADVERTISING RATES:
Full Page Colour £2200.00
Agency Commission: 10%
Mechanical Data: Film: Digital, Page Width: 275mm, Bleed Size: 412 x 306mm, Trim Size: 402 x 296mm, Col Length: 360mm, Type Area: 360 x 275mm
Copy instructions: Copy Date: 20th of the month prior to publication date
Average advertising content per issue: 40%
BUSINESS: TRAVEL & TOURISM

CSI CABLE & SATELLITE INTERNATIONAL
622575U2D-56

Formerly: Cable & Satellite International
Editorial Address: 6th Floor, 3 London Wall Buildings, LONDON, EC2M 5PD **Tel:** 020 7562 2401
Fax: 020 7374 2701
Email: goran.nastic@cable-satellite.com
Advertising Address: As above. **Tel:** 020 7562 2400
Email: tiro.bestonso@csimagazine.com
Web site: http://www.cable-satellite.com
ISSN: 1467-5935
Publisher: Perspective Publishing Ltd
Date Established: 1999
Frequency: 6 issues yearly
Free to qualifying individuals
Annual Sub.: £88.00
Circulation: 6,999 (BPA Worldwide)
Usual Pagination: 52
Editor: Goran Nastic
Summary of Content: Magazine covering key technology and product trends for the contribution, distribution, transport and delivery of content within the cable, satellite, terrestrial broadcast, IPTV and mobile TV industries.
Readership/Target Audience: Aimed at board level executives and senior technical management and personnel who specify, recommend or authorise technology purchases within cable, satellite, broadcast and IPTV and mobile TV service providers.
ADVERTISING RATES:
Full Page Colour £3200.00
Agency Commission: 10%
Mechanical Data: Bleed Size: 277 x210mm, Trim Size: 271 x 204mm, Film: Digital
Copy instructions: Copy Date: 1 week prior to publication date
Average advertising content per issue: 40%
Supplement(s): Product of the Year Awards - 2xY
BUSINESS: COMMUNICATIONS, ADVERTISING & MARKETING: Broadcasting

CSN COPY SHOP NEWS
38918U41A-21

Editorial Address: Colourfast Studio, 36 Cheltenham Place, BRIGHTON, BN1 4AB **Tel:** 01273 674321
Fax: 01273 609135
Email: editor@dpsnews.co.uk
Advertising Address: As above.
Email: editor@copyshopnews.co.uk
Web site: http://www.copyshopnews.co.uk
Publisher: Colourfast Group Ltd
Date Established: 1998
Frequency: 10 issues yearly - Combined issues July/August and Dec/Jan
Cover Price: £3.00
Free to qualifying individuals
Annual Sub.: £25.00
Circulation: 4,950 (Publisher's Statement)
Usual Pagination: 36
Editor: Peter Foulkes; **Advertising Manager:** Peter Foulkes
Summary of Content: Magazine containing digital print industry news, product information, business guidance and suppliers index.
Readership/Target Audience: Aimed at digital printers, copy and instant print bureaus, high street printers and in-house corporate print rooms.
ADVERTISING RATES:
Full Page Mono £600.00
Full Page Colour £1000.00
Agency Commission: 10%
Mechanical Data: Type Area: 210 x 190mm, Bleed Size: 301 x 214mm, Trim Size: 297 x 210mm, Col Length: 210mm, Film: Digital, No. of Columns (Display): 2, Page Width: 190mm, Print Process: Litho
Copy instructions: Copy Date: 3 weeks prior to publication date
Average advertising content per issue: 35%
Supplement(s): Digital Print Shop News - 10xY
BUSINESS: PRINTING & STATIONERY: Printing

CTA JOURNAL
39614U49B-80

Formerly: Community Transport
Editorial Address: Unit 4, 25A Vyner Street, LONDON, E2 9DG **Tel:** 020 8980 0236 **Fax:** 020 8983 1858
Email: julie@ctajournal.org
Advertising Address: Highbank, Halton Street, HYDE, SK14 2NY **Tel:** 0870 774 3581 **Fax:** 0870 774 3586
Email: ann@ctauk.org

Web site: http://www.ctauk.org
Publisher: Community Transport Association
Date Established: 1982
Frequency: 6 issues yearly
Free to qualifying individuals
Annual Sub.: £50.00
Circulation: 2,500 (Publisher's Statement)
Usual Pagination: 48
Editor: Julie Pybus; **Advertising Manager:** Diann Quinn; **Publisher:** Tim West
Summary of Content: Magazine covering community transport with essential news, reviews and features.
Readership/Target Audience: Aimed at community transport and other voluntary operators and local authority officers and academics working in this field.
ADVERTISING: Rates on application
Mechanical Data: Film: Positive, right reading, emulsion side down
BUSINESS: TRANSPORT: Bus & Coach Transport

CTO WORLD
1773220U18B-1971

Editorial Address: University House, 11-13 Lower Grosvenor Place, LONDON, SW1W 0EX **Tel:** 020 7834 7676
Fax: 020 7973 0076
Email: ctoworld@alaincharles.com
Advertising Address: As above. **Fax:** 020 7834 0076
Email: ctoworld@alaincharles.com
Web site: http://www.cto.int
Publisher: Alain Charles Publishing Ltd
Frequency: Quarterly
Cover Price: Free
Editor: Andrew Croft
Summary of Content: Publication representing the work of the Commonwealth Telecommunications Organisation in-support of the global application of information and communication technologies (ICT) with a strong emphasis on development issues.
Readership/Target Audience: Aimed at government offices and departments, communication enterprises and organisations.
ADVERTISING: Rates on application
BUSINESS: ELECTRONICS: Telecommunications

CUE ENTERTAINMENT
1626442U43A-68

Editorial Address: Hoadsbrook, Mockbeggar Lane, East End, BENENDEN, TN17 4BG **Tel:** 01580 243441
Email: samandrews@cueentertainment.com
Advertising Address: As above.
Email: samandrews@cueentertainment.com
Web site: http://www.cueentertainment.com
Publisher: Stills Audio Motion Ltd
Date Established: 2003
Frequency: Monthly
Annual Sub.: £60.00
Circulation: 4,000 (Publisher's Statement)
Usual Pagination: 36
Editor: Sam Andrews
Summary of Content: Magazine covering home entertainment including, DVD players, games, TV and video on demand.
Readership/Target Audience: Aimed at video games retailers, wholesalers and content owners in the home entertainment industry.
ADVERTISING RATES:
Full Page Colour £1500.00
Mechanical Data: Type Area: 340 x 240mm, Bleed Size: 346 x 246mm, Col Length: 340mm, Page Width: 240mm, Film: Digital
BUSINESS: ELECTRICAL RETAIL TRADE

CULTURAL GEOGRAPHIES
1786257U57-163

Editorial Address: 1 Oliver's Yard, 55 City Road, LONDON, EC1Y 1SP **Tel:** 020 7324 8500 **Fax:** 020 7324 8600
Email: market@sagepub.co.uk
Advertising Address: As above.
Email: advertising@sagepub.co.uk
Web site: http://www.sagepub.co.uk
ISSN: 1474-4740
Publisher: Sage Publications
Frequency: Quarterly
Annual Sub.: £66.00
Editor: Tim Cresswell; **Advertising Manager:** Sheena Karim; **Managing Editor:** Tim Cresswell
Summary of Content: Journal publishing scholary research on the cultural appropriation and politics of nature, environment, place and space.
Readership/Target Audience: Aimed at academics and students.
ADVERTISING RATES:
Full Page Mono £450.00
Agency Commission: 5%
Mechanical Data: Type Area: 210 x 140mm, Col Length: 210mm, Page Width: 140mm, Film: Digital
Copy instructions: Copy Date: 12 weeks prior to publication date
BUSINESS: ENVIRONMENT & POLLUTION

CUMBRIAN EXECUTIVE
41270U63B-332

Editorial Address: 3 Chatsworth Square, CARLISLE, CA1 1HB **Tel:** 01228 547144 **Fax:** 01228 514747
Email: editor@cumbriapress.co.uk
Advertising Address: As above.
Email: alan@cumbriapress.co.uk
Publisher: Cumbrian Press Group
Frequency: Quarterly
Cover Price: Free
Circulation: 5,000 (Publisher's Statement)
Editor: Tony Thornton; **Managing Director:** Alan Taylor;
Advertising Manager: Alan Taylor
Summary of Content: Regional business magazine for Cumbria.
Readership/Target Audience: Read by local business people.
ADVERTISING RATES:
Full Page Colour £945.00
Mechanical Data: Type Area: 265 x 185mm, Bleed Size: +3mm, Trim Size: 297 x 210mm, Col Length: 265mm, Print Process: Offset litho, Film: Digital, Page Width: 185mm
Copy instructions: Copy Date: 1 week prior to publication date
BUSINESS: REGIONAL BUSINESS: Regional Business English Counties

CUMBRIAN FARMING
37886U21J-67

Editorial Address: 3 Chatsworth Square, CARLISLE, CA1 1HB **Tel:** 01228 547144 **Fax:** 01228 514747
Email: editor@cumbriapress.co.uk
Advertising Address: As above.
Email: alan@cumbrianpress.co.uk
Publisher: Cumbrian Press Group
Frequency: 6 issues yearly
Cover Price: Free
Circulation: 5,000 (Publisher's Statement)
Editor: Tony Thornton; **Managing Director:** Alan Taylor;
Advertising Manager: Alan Taylor
Summary of Content: Magazine covering all aspects of the farming industry in Cumbria, with stories of country folk.
Readership/Target Audience: Aimed at farmers in Cumbria, rural initiatives and landowners.
ADVERTISING RATES:
Full Page Mono £495.00
Full Page Colour £795.00
Agency Commission: 10%
Mechanical Data: Trim Size: 210 x 150mm, Bleed Size: 216 x 156mm, Type Area: 190 x 130mm, Col Length: 190mm, No. of Columns (Display): 2, Print Process: Offset litho, Film: Digital, Page Width: 130mm
Average advertising content per issue: 50%
BUSINESS: AGRICULTURE & FARMING: Agriculture & Farming - Regional

CURRENCY NEWS
1702775U1R-372

Editorial Address: 2A High Street, SHEPPERTON, TW17 9AW **Tel:** 01932 269917 **Fax:** 01932 269918
Email: info@currencynews.info
Web site: http://www.currencynews.info
Publisher: Currency Publications Ltd
Date Established: 2003
Frequency: Monthly
Annual Sub.: £836.00
Usual Pagination: 12
Editor: Astrid Mitchell
Summary of Content: Newsletter covering all aspects of currency. Covers news, analysis, events, standards, companies, people and technologies shaping the developments of banknotes and coins around the world.
Readership/Target Audience: Aimed at those involved in specifying, issuing, producing or handling currency.
ADVERTISING: No Advertising taken
BUSINESS: FINANCE & ECONOMICS: Financial Related

CURRENT BRITISH DIRECTORIES
40829U60A-29

Editorial Address: Chancery House, 15 Wickham Road, BECKENHAM, BR3 5JS **Tel:** 020 8650 7745
Fax: 020 8650 0768
Email: cbd@cbdresearch.com
Web site: http://www.cbdresearch.com
ISSN: 0070-1858
Publisher: CBD Research Ltd
Date Established: 1953
Frequency: Annual
Cover Price: £165.00
Circulation: 1,500 (Publisher's Statement)
Usual Pagination: 300
Editor: Charlotte Willow-Edwards
Summary of Content: Book containing details of 4100 directories published in Britain and listed A-Z by title.
Readership/Target Audience: Aimed at reference libraries - public and corporate - all media categories and all other business.

ADVERTISING: No Advertising taken
BUSINESS: PUBLISHING: Publishing & Book Trade

CURRENT MEDICAL RESEARCH AND OPINION
1657333U56A-181

Editorial Address: 5th Floor, Telephone House, 69-77 Paul Street, LONDON, EC2A 4LQ **Tel:** 020 7017 6457
Fax: 020 7017 7831
Email: info@cmrojournal.com
Web site: http://www.cmrojournal.com
ISSN: 0300-7995
Publisher: Informa Healthcare
Date Established: 1972
Frequency: Monthly
Annual Sub.: £1470.00
Circulation: 4,000 (Publisher's Statement)
Usual Pagination: 304
Editor: Piers Allen; **Managing Editor:** Piers Allen
Summary of Content: Peer-reviewed international journal for the rapid publication of original research on new and existing drugs, medical devices and therapies.
Readership/Target Audience: Aimed at primary care and hospital physicians and clinical researchers, pharmacists and clinical pharmacologists and healthcare professionals in pharmaceutical medicine. Distributed to medical libraries, large GP practices and hospital pharmacists.
ADVERTISING: No Advertising taken
BUSINESS: HEALTH & MEDICAL

CURRENT OPINION IN NEUROLOGY
40604U56R-52_75

Editorial Address: 250 Waterloo Road, LONDON, SE1 8RD **Tel:** 020 7981 0600 **Fax:** 020 7981 0652
Email: daniel.hyde@wolterskluwer.com
Advertising Address: The Point of Difference, 4 Chase Side Avenue, LONDON, SW20 8LU **Tel:** 020 8542 3200
Fax: 020 8543 3810
Email: pointofdiff@btinternet.com
Web site: http://www.co-neurology.com/
ISSN: 1350-7540
Publisher: Lippincott Williams & Wilkins
Frequency: 6 issues yearly
Annual Sub.: £136.00
Circulation: 1,515 (Publisher's Statement)
Usual Pagination: 144
Editor: Daniel Hyde; **Advertising Manager:** Bill D'Sa;
Managing Editor: Daniel Hyde; **Advertising Director:** Dick Bower; **Publisher:** Ian Burgess
Summary of Content: Journal consists of a bibliography of world literature with review articles and recommended reading.
Readership/Target Audience: Aimed at clinicians, researchers, academics, lecturers and students in the field of neurology.
ADVERTISING RATES:
Full Page Mono $945.00
Full Page Colour $2195.00
Agency Commission: 15%
Mechanical Data: Col Length: 254mm, Trim Size: 276 x 207mm, Film: Digital, Type Area: 254 x 178mm, Page Width: 178mm, Bleed Size: 282 x 213mm
Copy instructions: Copy Date: 6 weeks prior to publication date
BUSINESS: HEALTH & MEDICAL: Health Medical Related

CURRENT SOCIOLOGY
40607U56R-52_80

Editorial Address: 1 Oliver's Yard, 55 City Road, LONDON, EC1Y 1SP **Tel:** 020 7324 8500 **Fax:** 020 7324 8600
Email: market@sagepub.com
Advertising Address: As above.
Web site: http://www.sagepub.co.uk
ISSN: 0011-3921
Publisher: Sage Publications
Date Established: 1970
Frequency: 6 issues yearly
Annual Sub.: £57.00
Usual Pagination: 160
Editor: Dennis Smith; **Advertising Manager:** Sheena Karim
Summary of Content: Focuses on the theory research and methodology of current international sociology. The journal also features short articles reviewing emergent and challenging issues. Contains abstracts of research papers in English, French and Spanish. Occasionally includes a research paper in French.
Readership/Target Audience: Aimed at sociologists.
ADVERTISING RATES:
Full Page Mono £250.00
Agency Commission: 5%
Mechanical Data: Type Area: 180 x 114mm, Col Length: 180mm, Page Width: 114mm
BUSINESS: HEALTH & MEDICAL: Health Medical Related

CURRY LIFE
1792871U11A-217

Editorial Address: Suite 9, 5 Durham Yard, Teesdale Street, LONDON, E2 6QF **Tel:** 020 7729 0999 **Fax:** 020 7729 0222
Email: info@currylife.com
Advertising Address: As above.
Email: info@currylife.com
Web site: http://www.currylife.com
Publisher: Curry Life Ltd
Frequency: 6 issues yearly
Cover Price: £1.50
Circulation: 10,000 (Publisher's Statement)
Editor: Syed Ahmed; **Editor-in-Chief:** Syed Pasha;
Advertising Manager: Syed Pasha
Summary of Content: Magazine covering the Indian and Bangladeshi curry industry covering industry news, restaurant reviews, food, food related services and issues in the catering and entertainment industry. Also includes lifestyle features on travel and motoring.
Language(s): Bengali; English
Readership/Target Audience: Aimed at people working within food related businesses.
ADVERTISING RATES:
Full Page Mono £1995.00
Full Page Colour £1995.00
Agency Commission: 15%
Mechanical Data: Type Area: 270 x 190mm, Bleed Size: +3mm, Trim Size: 297 x 210mm, Col Length: 270mm, Page Width: 190mm, Col Widths (Display): 85mm, Film: Digital, No. of Columns (Display): 2
Copy instructions: Copy Date: 2 weeks prior to publication date
Average advertising content per issue: 35%
BUSINESS: CATERING: Catering, Hotels & Restaurants

CUSTODIAL REVIEW
38558U32R-50

Formerly: HMP Review
Editorial Address: 1st Floor, Clifton House, 4A Goldington Road, BEDFORD, MK40 3NF **Nf:** 0870 7490220
Fax: 0870 749 0221
Email: custodialreview@pirnet.co.uk
Advertising Address: As above. **Tel:** 0870 749 0220
Email: derek.cooper@pirnet.co.uk
Web site: http://www.pirnet.co.uk
Publisher: The Bellmont Agency Ltd
Date Established: 1993
Frequency: Quarterly
Cover Price: Free
Circulation: 7,500 (Publisher's Statement)
Usual Pagination: 48
Editor: Derek Cooper; **Managing Director:** Steve Mitchell;
Advertising Manager: Derek Cooper; **Publisher:** Steve Mitchell
Summary of Content: Magazine dealing with security, communications, catering, building design and other subjects related to police, courts, immigration, customs & excise, prison work and management.
Readership/Target Audience: Aimed at chief constables, assistant chief constables, directors of finance, procurement managers, prison, customs and immigration personnel.
ADVERTISING RATES:
Full Page Colour £1095.00
Agency Commission: 10%
Mechanical Data: Film: Digital, Trim Size: 297 x 210mm
Copy instructions: Copy Date: 1st of the month prior to publication date
Average advertising content per issue: 50%
BUSINESS: LOCAL GOVERNMENT, LEISURE & RECREATION: Local Government Related

CUSTOM INSTALLER
39095U43A-20

Editorial Address: Rephoto House, Plough Road, Smallfield, HORLEY, RH6 9EZ **Tel:** 01342 844444
Fax: 01342 844488
Email: nicholas.clancy@rephotopublishing.co.uk
Advertising Address: As above.
Email: david.kitchener@rephotopublishing.co.uk
Web site: http://www.custominstaller.co.uk
Publisher: Rephoto Publishing Ltd
Date Established: 1998
Frequency: Monthly - Published on the 15th of the cover month
Free to qualifying individuals
Annual Sub.: £80.00
Circulation: 8,700 (Publisher's Statement)
Usual Pagination: 32
Editor: Nicholas Clancy; **Managing Director:** Phil Reynolds;
Advertising Manager: David Kitchener
Summary of Content: Magazine containing the latest news, views, insights and solutions within the key sectors of the custom install industry. Covers audio, video, lighting, Internet, telecoms, systems management, heating and air conditioning.
Readership/Target Audience: Read by manufacturers, retailers, suppliers, distributors, custom install specialists and architects.
ADVERTISING RATES:
Full Page Mono £1300.00
Full Page Colour £1300.00

Business Magazines

Agency Commission: 10%
Mechanical Data: Bleed Size: 303 x 216mm, Film: Digital, Trim Size: 297 x 210mm
Copy instructions: Copy Date: 2 weeks prior to publication date
BUSINESS: ELECTRICAL RETAIL TRADE

CUSTOMER STRATEGY
37156U14K-30

Formerly: Customer Management
Editorial Address: 7th Floor, Ludgate House, 245 Blackfriars Road, LONDON, SE1 9UY **Tel:** 020 7378 1188
Fax: 020 7378 1199
Email: steve.hurst@quest-media.com
Advertising Address: As above. **Fax:** 020 7921 8549
Email: ashley.williamson@ubm.com
Web site: http://www.customer-strategy.co.uk
ISSN: 1351-8321
Publisher: Quest Media Ltd
Date Established: 1992
Frequency: 6 issues yearly
Cover Price: £12.00
Annual Sub.: £54.00
Circulation: 10,100 (Publisher's Statement)
Usual Pagination: 96
Editor: Steve Hurst; **Publisher:** Mark Snell
Summary of Content: Magazine covering all aspects of customer service. Contains briefings, case studies, methodology, technology and opinions.
Readership/Target Audience: Aimed at quality and customer service directors and managers.
ADVERTISING RATES:
Full Page Colour £3097.00
Agency Commission: 10%
Mechanical Data: Bleed Size: 303 x 216mm, Print Process: Offset litho, Film: Digital, Trim Size: 297 x 210mm
Copy instructions: Copy Date: 1st week of month prior to publication date
Average advertising content per issue: 40%
BUSINESS: COMMERCE, INDUSTRY & MANAGEMENT: Quality Assurance

CUSTOMERFIRST
623312U14K-20

Formerly: Customer First
Editorial Address: 2 Castle Court, St. Peter's Street, COLCHESTER, CO1 1EW **Tel:** 01733 555880
Fax: 01733 555880
Email: gary.dawkes@icsmail.co.uk
Advertising Address: As above.
Email: customerfirst@deeson.co.uk
Web site: http://www.instituteofcustomerservice.com
Publisher: Institute of Customer Service
Date Established: 1998
Frequency: 6 issues yearly
Cover Price: £4.95
Free to qualifying individuals
Circulation: 13,000 (Publisher's Statement)
Usual Pagination: 64
Editor: Gary Dawkes; **Managing Editor:** Gary Dawkes
Summary of Content: Official magazine of the Institute of Customer Service, contains features on best practice issues and raising standards of customer service.
Readership/Target Audience: Aimed at board level decision-makers, middle management and primarily front line staff.
ADVERTISING RATES:
Full Page Colour £2500.00
Agency Commission: 10%
Mechanical Data: Bleed Size: 303 x 216mm, Trim Size: 297 x 210mm, Type Area: 267 x 180mm, Col Length: 267mm, Page Width: 180mm
Average advertising content per issue: 10%
BUSINESS: COMMERCE, INDUSTRY & MANAGEMENT: Quality Assurance

CV DEALER MONTHLY
1683722U49D-362

Editorial Address: 100 Bridge Street, PETERBOROUGH, PE1 1DY **Tel:** 01733 566933 **Fax:** 01733 566776
Email: jasonhodge@focuspublishing.co.uk
Advertising Address: As above.
Email: nuria.macdonald@cvdealer.co.uk
Web site: http://www.cvdealer.co.uk
Publisher: Focus Publishing Ltd
Date Established: 2001
Frequency: Monthly
Free to qualifying individuals
Annual Sub.: £35.00
Circulation: 8,000 (Publisher's Statement)
Usual Pagination: 32
Editor: Jason Hodge; **Advertising Manager:** Nuria Macdonald
Summary of Content: Magazine covering product news, people moves and industry news for the commercial vehicle sector.
Readership/Target Audience: Aimed at key players in the commercial vehicle dealer industry.

ADVERTISING RATES:
Full Page Colour £1150.00
Agency Commission: 10%
Mechanical Data: Trim Size: 273 x 189mm, Bleed Size: +15mm, Film: Digital
BUSINESS: TRANSPORT: Commercial Vehicles

CWB CHILDRENSWEAR BUYER
39482U47A-75

Formerly: Childrenswear Buyer
Editorial Address: The Old Town Hall, Lewisham Road, Slaithwaite, HUDDERSFIELD, HD7 5AL **Tel:** 01484 846069
Fax: 01484 846232
Email: laura@ras-publishing.com
Advertising Address: As above.
Email: alex.boyd@ras-publishing.com
Web site: http://www.ras-publishing.com
Publisher: RAS Publishing Ltd
Date Established: 1999
Frequency: 6 issues yearly
Annual Sub.: £50.00
Circulation: 3,000 (Publisher's Statement)
Managing Director: Colette Tebbutt; **Managing Editor:** Martin Wanless
Summary of Content: Magazine focusing on the teenage, children's and babies' branded fashion industry.
Readership/Target Audience: Readership includes buyers of children's wear in department stores, children's wear boutiques, multiple retailers, catalogue houses and wholesale warehouses.
ADVERTISING RATES:
Full Page Mono £2815.00
Full Page Colour £2815.00
Agency Commission: 10%
Mechanical Data: Page Width: 230mm, Type Area: 300 x 230mm, Col Length: 300mm, Trim Size: 300 x 230mm, No. of Columns (Display): 4, Film: Positive, right reading, emulsion side down. Digital
Average advertising content per issue: 40%
BUSINESS: CLOTHING & TEXTILES

CWU VOICE
37177U14L-140

Editorial Address: 150 The Broadway, LONDON, SW19 1RX **Tel:** 020 8971 7286 **Fax:** 020 8971 7437
Email: salford@cwu.org
Advertising Address: Century One Publishing, Arquin House, Spicer Street, ST. ALBANS, AL3 4PQ
Tel: 01727 739184 **Fax:** 01727 893895
Email: ollie@centuryonepublishing.ltd.uk
Web site: http://www.cwu.org
Publisher: Communication Workers Union
Frequency: 6 issues yearly
Cover Price: Free
Circulation: 260,000 (Publisher's Statement)
Usual Pagination: 16
Editor: Simon Alford; **Advertising Manager:** Oliver Kirkman
Summary of Content: Magazine covering issues related to the Post Office, British Telecom and engineering.
Readership/Target Audience: Read by members of the Communication Workers Union.
ADVERTISING RATES:
Full Page Colour £9500.00
Agency Commission: 10%
Mechanical Data: Type Area: 342 x 264mm, Bleed Size: 376 x 296mm, Trim Size: 370 x 290mm, Col Length: 342mm, Page Width: 264mm, Film: Digital
BUSINESS: COMMERCE, INDUSTRY & MANAGEMENT: Trade Unions

CXO (EUROPE)
1799352U14A-585

Editorial Address: Queen Square House, 18-21 Queen Square, BRISTOL, BS1 4NH **Tel:** 0117 921 4000
Fax: 0117 926 7444
Email: bthompson@gdspublishing.com
Advertising Address: 4th Floor, 3 Callaghan Square, CARDIFF, CF10 5BT **Tel:** 029 2066 7422
Fax: 029 2072 9301
Email: oliversmart@gdsinternational.com
Web site: http://www.cxo.eu
Publisher: GDS Publishing
Frequency: Quarterly
Editor: Diana Milne
Summary of Content: Magazine containing articles about business management, includes IT security, outsourcing, product lifecycle management, enterprise mobility, communications issues and service-orientated architecture.
Readership/Target Audience: Aimed at senior executives, including CEOs, CFOs and head of HR departments.
ADVERTISING RATES:
Full Page Colour EUR14500.00
Copy instructions: Copy Date: 4 weeks prior to publication date
BUSINESS: COMMERCE, INDUSTRY & MANAGEMENT

D & T NEWS
1674209U62B-1406

Formerly: DATANews
Editorial Address: 16 Wellesbourne House, Walton Road, Wellesbourne, WARWICK, CV35 9JB **Tel:** 01789 470007
Fax: 01789 841955
Email: neil@data.org.uk
Advertising Address: 64 Endcliffe Hall Avenue, SHEFFIELD, S10 3EL **Tel:** 0114 266 5377 **Fax:** 0114 266 5377
Email: noreenpleavin@onetel.com
Web site: http://www.data.org.uk
ISSN: 1365-7348
Publisher: The Design and Technology Association
Date Established: 1995
Frequency: 3 issues yearly
Free to qualifying individuals
Circulation: 5,000 (Publisher's Statement)
Usual Pagination: 48
Editor: Neil Whitton; **Advertising Manager:** Noreen Pleavin
Summary of Content: Magazine including up-to-date information on the D & T Association's activities, national and local developments, resources and news of interest to design and technology professionals.
Readership/Target Audience: Read by members of the Design and Technology Association.
ADVERTISING RATES:
Full Page Colour £495.00
Mechanical Data: Type Area: 277 x 190mm, Bleed Size: 303 x 216mm, Col Length: 277mm, Page Width: 190mm, Film: Digital, Trim Size: 297 x 210mm
Copy instructions: Copy Date: 6 weeks prior to publication date
Average advertising content per issue: 20%
BUSINESS: CHURCH & SCHOOL EQUIPMENT & EDUCATION: Education Teachers

D&T PRACTICE
41036U62B-630

Formerly: DATA Practice
Editorial Address: 16 Wellesbourne House, Walton Road, Wellesbourne, WARWICK, CV35 9JB **Tel:** 01789 470007
Fax: 01789 841955
Email: neil@data.org.uk
Advertising Address: 64 Endcliffe Hall Avenue, SHEFFIELD, S10 3EL **Tel:** 0114 266 5377 **Fax:** 0114 266 5377
Email: noreenpleavin@onetel.com
Web site: http://www.data.org.uk
ISSN: 1745-5448
Publisher: The Design and Technology Association
Date Established: 1985
Frequency: 6 issues yearly
Free to qualifying individuals
Circulation: 6,000 (Publisher's Statement)
Usual Pagination: 48
Editor: Neil Whitton; **Advertising Manager:** Noreen Pleavin
Summary of Content: Magazine containing information and features on teaching design and technology.
Readership/Target Audience: Read by members of the Design and Technology Association.
ADVERTISING RATES:
Full Page Colour £600.00
Mechanical Data: Bleed Size: 303 x 216mm, Trim Size: 297 x 210mm, Film: Digital, Type Area: 277 x 190mm, Col Length: 277mm, Page Width: 190mm
Copy instructions: Copy Date: 6 weeks prior to publication date
Average advertising content per issue: 20%
BUSINESS: CHURCH & SCHOOL EQUIPMENT & EDUCATION: Education Teachers

DABS
35798U4A-125

Editorial Address: McDermott Chambers, 2 The Green, Kings Norton, BIRMINGHAM, B38 8SD **Tel:** 0121 451 3037
Fax: 0121 433 3461
Email: charlie.hodgetts@mcdermottpublishing.com
Advertising Address: As above. **Fax:** 0121 459 2179
Email: maria.hodgetts@mcdermottpublishing.com
Web site: http://www.dabsmagazine.co.uk
Publisher: McDermott Publishing Ltd
Frequency: 11 issues yearly - Published around the 28th of the cover month
Cover Price: £2.50
Free to qualifying individuals
Annual Sub.: £23.00
Circulation: 26,626 (Publisher's Statement)
Usual Pagination: 50
Editor: Charlie Hodgetts; **Advertising Manager:** Maria Hodgetts; **Publisher:** Lawrence McDermott
Summary of Content: Magazine containing information on building products and services.
Readership/Target Audience: Aimed at architects and specifiers, building contractors and developers, quantity surveyors and interior designers.
ADVERTISING RATES:
Full Page Colour £1725.00
Agency Commission: 10%
Mechanical Data: Page Width: 200mm, Type Area: 270 x 200mm, Bleed Size: 303 x 233mm, Trim Size: 300 x 230mm, Film: Digital, Col Length: 270mm

Copy instructions: Copy Date: 3 weeks prior to publication date
Average advertising content per issue: 50%
BUSINESS: ARCHITECTURE & BUILDING: Architecture

DAIRY FARMER
37826U21C-210
Editorial Address: Riverbank House, Angel Lane, TONBRIDGE, TN9 1SE Tel: 01732 377273
Fax: 01732 377543
Email: peter.hollinshead@ubm.com
Advertising Address: As above. Tel: 01322 377273
Fax: 01322 449624
Email: mark.jackson@ubm.com
ISSN: 0011-5576
Publisher: UBM Information (Tonbridge)
Date Established: 1929
Frequency: Monthly - Published around the 5th of the cover month
Cover Price: £3.75
Free to qualifying individuals
Annual Sub.: £45.00
Circulation: 13,554 (ABC 01/01/2008 to 31/12/2008)
Usual Pagination: 64
Editor: Peter Hollinshead; Advertising Manager: Mark Jackson; Publisher: Jim Jones
Summary of Content: Magazine covering technical articles on all aspects of dairy farming.
Readership/Target Audience: Aimed at dairy farmers with 70 dairy cows and over.
ADVERTISING RATES:
Full Page Mono £1941.00
Full Page Colour £2810.00
Agency Commission: 10%
Mechanical Data: Type Area: 254 x 184mm, No. of Columns (Display): 4, Film: Digital, Col Length: 254mm, Page Width: 184mm, Bleed Size: 303 x 216mm, Trim Size: 297 x 210mm
Copy instructions: Copy Date: 2 weeks prior to publication date
Average advertising content per issue: 60%
BUSINESS: AGRICULTURE & FARMING: Dairy Farming

DAIRY INDUSTRIES INTERNATIONAL
37999U22C-50
Editorial Address: The Maltings, 57 Bath Street, GRAVESEND, DA11 0DF Tel: 01474 532202
Fax: 01474 532203
Email: suzanne@bellpublishing.com
Advertising Address: As above.
Email: david@bellpublishing.com
Web site: http://www.dairyindustries.com
ISSN: 0308-8197
Publisher: Bell Publishing Ltd
Date Established: 1936
Frequency: Monthly - Published on the 1st Monday of the cover month
Annual Sub.: £130.00
Circulation: 6,178 (Publisher's Statement)
Usual Pagination: 52
Editor: Suzanne Christiansen; Advertising Manager: David Cox; Managing Editor: Suzanne Christiansen
Summary of Content: Journal containing all aspects of dairy products processing and equipment worldwide.
Readership/Target Audience: Aimed at the international dairy processing industry.
ADVERTISING RATES:
Full Page Mono £1565.00
Full Page Colour £2059.00
SCC £34.00
Agency Commission: 10%
Mechanical Data: Col Length: 254mm, Col Widths (Display): 42mm, Film: Digital, No. of Columns (Display): 4, Type Area: 254 x 180mm, Print Process: Sheet-fed litho, Bleed Size: 303 x 213mm, Page Width: 180mm, Trim Size: 297 x 210mm
Copy instructions: Copy Date: 20th of the month prior to publication date
Average advertising content per issue: 50%
BUSINESS: FOOD: Food Processing & Packaging

DAIRY INDUSTRY NEWSLETTER
37878U21G-30
Editorial Address: 37 Valiant House, Vicarage Crescent, LONDON, SW11 3LU Tel: 020 7228 3674
Web site: http://www.dairyindustrynewsletter.com
ISSN: 0956-8131
Publisher: Eden Publishing Company
Frequency: 25 issues yearly
Annual Sub.: £1000.00
Circulation: 1,000 (Publisher's Statement)
Usual Pagination: 8
Editor: Barry Wilson
Summary of Content: Newsletter containing technical information, news and features about the dairy processing industry.

Readership/Target Audience: Aimed at technical and management personnel in processing, dairy and ice-cream plants in the UK.
ADVERTISING: No Advertising taken
BUSINESS: AGRICULTURE & FARMING: Milk

DAIRY INNOVATION
1692791U21G-93
Editorial Address: 59 Coleridge Close, HITCHIN, CG4 0CX
Tel: 01462 457813 Fax: 01462 457813
Email: geoff.platt@zipublishing.com
Advertising Address: 7 Kingsmead Square, BATH, BA1 2AB Tel: 01225 327890 Fax: 01225 327891
Email: duncan.wilde@zipublishing.com
Web site: http://www.foodbev.com
Publisher: Zenith International
Date Established: 2005
Frequency: 10 issues yearly - Published within the 1st week of the cover month
Free to qualifying individuals
Annual Sub.: £95.00
Circulation: 6,000 (Publisher's Statement)
Usual Pagination: 52
Editor: Geoff Platt
Summary of Content: Magazine focusing on milk processing including corporate news, products, ingredients, packaging and equipment.
Readership/Target Audience: Aimed at senior executives, dairy processors, retailers and trade organisations in the milk industry.
ADVERTISING RATES:
Full Page Colour £2435.00
Agency Commission: 10%
Mechanical Data: Bleed Size: 303 x 213mm, Trim Size: 297 x 210mm, Film: Digital
Copy instructions: Copy Date: 4 weeks prior to publication date
BUSINESS: AGRICULTURE & FARMING: Milk

DAIRY MARKETS
37827U21C-260
Formerly: Dairy Markets Weekly
Editorial Address: 80 Calverley Road, TUNBRIDGE WELLS, TN1 2UN Tel: 020 7017 7500 Fax: 020 7017 7599
Email: marketing@agra-net.com
Web site: http://www.agra-net.com
ISSN: 1475-0686
Publisher: Agra Informa Ltd
Date Established: 1989
Frequency: Weekly
Annual Sub.: £1257.00
Usual Pagination: 16
Circulation Manager: Barbara Mason
Summary of Content: Newsletter covering prices and production trends, as well as the immediate and long-term effect of EU, North American and International dairy policy.
Readership/Target Audience: Aimed at the International dairy industry.
ADVERTISING: No Advertising taken
BUSINESS: AGRICULTURE & FARMING: Dairy Farming

DAIRY SCIENCE ABSTRACTS
22650U21C-270
Editorial Address: Nosworthy Way, WALLINGFORD, OX10 8DE Tel: 01491 832111 Fax: 01491 833508
Email: m.djuric@cabi.org
Web site: http://www.cabi-publishing.org
Publisher: CABI
Date Established: 1939
Frequency: Monthly
Annual Sub.: £1120.00
Circulation: 320 (Publisher's Statement)
Usual Pagination: 120
Editor: Miroslav Djuric
Summary of Content: Publication covering on all aspects of dairy science. Includes articles on farming, milk production, secretion, processing and milk products.
Readership/Target Audience: Aimed at large dairy farmers, academics, research institutes and scientists. Also governmental organisations, food companies and dairy technical services.
ADVERTISING: No Advertising taken
BUSINESS: AGRICULTURE & FARMING: Dairy Farming

DATA CENTRE MANAGEMENT
1775545U14A-573
Editorial Address: 173 High Street, RICKMANSWORTH, WD3 1AY Tel: 01923 692660 Fax: 01923 692679
Email: j.hatcher@turretgroup.com
Advertising Address: As above.
Email: e.milton@turretgroup.com
Web site: http://www.datacentremanagement.com
ISSN: 1753-9897
Publisher: Turret Group Ltd.
Date Established: 2006
Frequency: 6 issues yearly - Published around the 15th of the 1st cover month

---

Cover Price: Free
Circulation: 6,000 (Publisher's Statement)
Usual Pagination: 40
Editor: John Hatcher
Summary of Content: Magazine containing news, views, analysis and information for the management of data centres.
Readership/Target Audience: Aimed at managers of data centres, IT directors and third party suppliers of data centre equipment and services including outsourcing.
ADVERTISING RATES:
Full Page Colour £2995.00
Agency Commission: 10%
Mechanical Data: Type Area: 248 x 186mm, Bleed Size: 285 x 222mm, Trim Size: 279 x 216mm, Col Length: 248mm, Page Width: 186mm, Film: Digital
Copy instructions: Copy Date: 4 weeks prior to publication date
Average advertising content per issue: 40%
BUSINESS: COMMERCE, INDUSTRY & MANAGEMENT

DATA STRATEGY
1655452U5B-9012
Editorial Address: St. Giles House, 50 Poland Street, LONDON, W1F 7AX Tel: 020 7970 4000 Fax: 020 7970 6710
Email: david.editor@btinternet.com
Advertising Address: As above. Fax: 020 7970 6711
Email: ed.tillotson@centaur.co.uk
Web site: http://www.data-strategy.co.uk
Publisher: Centaur Communications Ltd
Date Established: 2004
Frequency: Monthly - Published at the beginning of the cover month
Free to qualifying individuals
Circulation: 6,216 (ABC 01/07/2008 to 30/06/2009)
Editor: David Reed; Advertising Manager: Ed Tillotson
Summary of Content: Magazine covering application of data to business issues across the enterprise.
Readership/Target Audience: Aimed at data users and practitioners in every business function and at each level.
ADVERTISING RATES:
Full Page Mono £1725.00
Full Page Colour £1975.00
Agency Commission: 10%
Mechanical Data: Bleed Size: 281 x 221mm, Trim Size: 275 x 215mm, Film: Digital
Copy instructions: Copy Date: 4 days prior to publication date
Average advertising content per issue: 45%
BUSINESS: COMPUTERS & AUTOMATION: Data Processing

DATABASE AND NETWORK JOURNAL
36056U5B-65
Editorial Address: 58 Ryecroft Way, LUTON, LU2 7TU
Tel: 01582 722219
Email: smpluton@ntlworld.com
Web site: http://www.softwareworldpublication.com
ISSN: 0265-4490
Publisher: AP Publications Ltd
Date Established: 1969
Frequency: 6 issues yearly
Cover Price: £24.00
Annual Sub.: £135.00
Usual Pagination: 30
Editor: Steven Patterson
Summary of Content: Journal containing information about new database products.
Readership/Target Audience: Aimed at professionals involved in IT.
ADVERTISING: No Advertising taken
BUSINESS: COMPUTERS & AUTOMATION: Data Processing

DATABASE MARKETING
35489U2A-66_75
Editorial Address: Waterloo Chambers, 19 Waterloo Street, GLASGOW, G2 6AY Tel: 01412 222100 Fax: 01412 222177
Email: abegley@55north.com
Advertising Address: Suite 415, KG Business Centre, Kingsfield Way, NORTHAMPTON, NN5 7QS
Tel: 0845 686 0125 Fax: 0845 686 0249
Email: info@dmarket.co.uk
Web site: http://www.dmarket.co.uk
ISSN: 1465-2900
Publisher: 55 North
Date Established: 1998
Frequency: 11 issues yearly - Published on the 5th of the cover month
Free to qualifying individuals
Annual Sub.: £50.00
Circulation: 6,000 (Publisher's Statement)
Usual Pagination: 52
Editor: Antony Begley; Managing Editor: Antony Begley
Summary of Content: Magazine covering analysis techniques and IT tools in the field of direct marketing, customer management and business planning. Contains

Business Magazines

news, events, software reviews, case studies, interviews and discussion articles.
Readership/Target Audience: Aimed at database marketing managers, direct marketing managers, data planners, analysts, IT and marketing directors.
ADVERTISING RATES:
Full Page Mono £1185.00
Full Page Colour £1650.00
Agency Commission: 10%
Mechanical Data: Bleed Size: 307 x 220mm, Trim Size: 297 x 210mm, Print Process: Offset litho, Film: Digital
Copy instructions: Copy Date: 2 weeks prior to publication date
Average advertising content per issue: 40%
BUSINESS: COMMUNICATIONS, ADVERTISING & MARKETING

DATACENTREDYNAMICS FOCUS
624512U5E-65

Formerly: ZERODOWNTIME
Editorial Address: 70 Clifton Street, LONDON, EC2A 4HB
Tel: 020 7246 4846 **Fax:** 020 7377 9583
Email: andrew.mcnevin@datacenterdynamics.com
Advertising Address: As above. **Tel:** 020 7377 1907
Email: philip.brooks@datacenterdynamics.com
Web site: http://www.datacenterdynamics.com
ISSN: 1470-5974
Publisher: DataCenterDynamics Ltd
Date Established: 2000
Frequency: 6 issues yearly
Free to qualifying individuals
Annual Sub.: £120.00
Circulation: 18,000 (Publisher's Statement)
Usual Pagination: 68
Editor: Ambrose McNevin; **Advertising Manager:** Philip Brooks
Summary of Content: Magazine focusing on identification, understanding and assessment of vulnerability, risk and threats to IT business systems and applications, specifically those relating to IT, data, web and telecommunications infrastructure. Editorial content falls into two broad categories: companies that choose to outsource their 'mission-critical' business systems to independent data centres and companies that invest in their own data centres.
Readership/Target Audience: Aimed at those involved in the telecommunications, IT infrastructure and business continuity market.
ADVERTISING RATES:
Full Page Colour £3950.00
Agency Commission: 10%
BUSINESS: COMPUTERS & AUTOMATION: Data Transmission

Y DDOLEN
40888U60B-16

Editorial Address: Department of Information Studies, Llanbadarn Fawr, ABERYSTWYTH, SY23 3AS
Tel: 01970 622174 **Fax:** 01970 622190
Email: mdp@aber.ac.uk
Web site: http://www.cilip.org.uk/branches/byregion/wales
ISSN: 0261-3557
Publisher: CILIP
Frequency: 3 issues yearly - Published in Spring, Summer/ Autumn and Winter
Free to qualifying individuals
Circulation: 1,800 (Publisher's Statement)
Usual Pagination: 20
Editor: Mandy Powell
Summary of Content: Journal containing articles on librarianship and information work in Wales.
Language(s): English; Welsh
Readership/Target Audience: Aimed at librarians and information workers in Wales.
ADVERTISING: No Advertising taken
BUSINESS: PUBLISHING: Libraries

DDR DIGITAL DISPLAY FOR RETAIL
1613659U5B-9004

Editorial Address: 6 Laurence Pountney Hill, LONDON, EC4R 0BL **Tel:** 020 7933 8999 **Fax:** 01843 866607
Email: jt.jtcs@btconnect.com
Advertising Address: As above. **Fax:** 020 7933 8998
Email: tomw@stjohnpatrick.com
Web site: http://www.ddrmag.co.uk
Publisher: St. John Patrick Publishers Ltd
Frequency: 6 issues yearly - Published around the 10th of the 1st cover month
Cover Price: £4.95
Free to qualifying individuals
Circulation: 4,300 (Publisher's Statement)
Editor: John Taylor; **Managing Director:** Wayne Darroch; **Advertising Manager:** Tom Westaway
Summary of Content: Magazine focusing on the whole world of digital display, whether static or moving, for the fast changing and innovative retail sector.

Readership/Target Audience: Aimed at retailers, business strategists, marketing and advertising agencies and promotional and sales organisations.
ADVERTISING RATES:
Full Page Colour £2688.00
Agency Commission: 10%
Mechanical Data: Col Length: 248mm, Page Width: 199mm, Film: Digital, Type Area: 248 x 199mm, Bleed Size: 270 x 231mm, Trim Size: 274 x 225mm
Copy instructions: Copy Date: 2 weeks prior to publication date
BUSINESS: COMPUTERS & AUTOMATION: Data Processing

DEAF WORLDS: THE INTERNATIONAL JOURNAL OF DEAF STUDIES
40457U56L-10_25

Formerly: Deafworlds
Editorial Address: The New Building, Ellwood Road, Milkwall, COLEFORD, GL16 7LE **Tel:** 01594 833858
Fax: 01594 833446
Web site: http://www.forestbooks.com
ISSN: 1362-3125
Publisher: Douglas McLean Publishing
Date Established: 1996
Frequency: 3 issues yearly - Published in March, July and November
Annual Sub.: £28.00
Circulation: 500 (Publisher's Statement)
Usual Pagination: 96
Editor: Doug McLean; **Publisher:** Doug McLean
Summary of Content: Journal containing detailed reports and book reviews on deafness.
Readership/Target Audience: Aimed at professionals and others working in the field of deafness.
ADVERTISING: No Advertising taken
BUSINESS: HEALTH & MEDICAL: Disability & Rehabilitation

THE DEAL
624567U1A-84_50

Editorial Address: 107-111 Fleet Street, LONDON, EC4A 2AB **Tel:** 020 7936 9037
Email: lboard@thedeal.com
Advertising Address: As above. **Fax:** 020 7936 9100
Email: gmcqueen@thedeal.com
Web site: http://www.thedeal.com
Publisher: The Deal
Date Established: 1999
Frequency: 26 issues yearly
Circulation: 50,000 (Publisher's Statement)
Editor: Laura Board
Summary of Content: Publication covering mergers, acquisitions, stock market floatations, private equity and venture capital transactions.
Readership/Target Audience: Aimed at investment bankers, corporate lawyers, venture capitalists, fund managers and board level corporate executives.
ADVERTISING RATES:
Full Page Mono £12750.00
Full Page Colour £17400.00
Agency Commission: 15%
Mechanical Data: Film: Digital, Type Area: 260 x 190mm, Bleed Size: 280 x 225mm, Trim Size: 274 x 223mm, Col Length: 260mm, Page Width: 190mm
Average advertising content per issue: 30%
BUSINESS: FINANCE & ECONOMICS

DEALER SUPPORT
38647U34-30

Editorial Address: Suite 223, Business Design Centre, 52 Upper Street, LONDON, N1 0QH **Tel:** 020 7288 6833
Fax: 020 7288 6834
Email: julia.dennison@intelligentmedia.co.uk
Advertising Address: As above.
Email: matthew.moore@intelligentmedia.co.uk
Web site: http://www.dealersupport.co.uk
Publisher: Intelligent Media Solutions
Frequency: Monthly - Published in the 2nd week of the month
Free to qualifying individuals
Circulation: 5,299 (ABC 01/07/2007 to 30/06/2008)
Editor: Julia Dennison
Summary of Content: Business supplies trade journal. Contains news and business management information on the office products industry, dealers and small businesses.
Readership/Target Audience: Aimed at those involved with office supplies and equipment.
ADVERTISING RATES:
Full Page Colour £1675.00
Agency Commission: 10%
Mechanical Data: Page Width: 180mm, Type Area: 260 x 180mm, Col Length: 260mm, Trim Size: 297 x 210mm, Bleed Size: 303 x 216mm, Print Process: Offset litho, Film: Digital
Copy instructions: Copy Date: Last week of the month prior to publication
Average advertising content per issue: 40%
BUSINESS: OFFICE EQUIPMENT

DEALER UPDATE
1656523U31R-59

Editorial Address: 3rd-4th Floor, 41-47 Hartfield Road, LONDON, SW19 3RQ **Tel:** 020 8544 7000
Fax: 020 8879 1879
Email: keith.collantine@tradermedia.co.uk
Advertising Address: As above. **Tel:** 020 8544 7061
Email: ben.maguire@autotrader.co.uk
Publisher: TNT Publishing
Frequency: Monthly
Cover Price: Free
Circulation: 18,500 (Publisher's Statement)
Usual Pagination: 39
Editor: Keith Collantine; **Advertising Manager:** Ben Maguire
Summary of Content: Magazine covering trade news, research and opinions for the motoring trade.
Readership/Target Audience: Aimed at all dealerships throughout the UK.
ADVERTISING RATES:
Full Page Colour ....:......................... £1200.00
Agency Commission: 10%
Copy instructions: Copy Date: 18th of each month
Average advertising content per issue: 30%
BUSINESS: MOTOR TRADE: Motor Trade Related

DEALING WITH TECHNOLOGY
34970U1A-276_80

Formerly: Trading Technology Week
Editorial Address: Haymarket House, 28-29 Haymarket, LONDON, SW1Y 4RX **Tel:** 020 7484 9700
Email: cecilia.bergamaschi@incisivemedia.com
Advertising Address: As above. **Fax:** 020 7930 2238
Email: dan.morgan@incisivemedia.com
Web site: http://www.dealingwithtechnology.com
ISSN: 1096-2638
Publisher: Incisive Media Investments
Date Established: 1988
Frequency: Weekly
Annual Sub.: £1125.00
Circulation: 2,600 (Publisher's Statement)
Usual Pagination: 12
Editor: Cecilia Bergamaschi; **Advertising Manager:** Dan Morgan
Summary of Content: Magazine covering the latest IT innovations for sell-side and financial trading markets.
Readership/Target Audience: Aimed at IT managers and traders.
ADVERTISING RATES:
Full Page Colour £2785.00
Agency Commission: 10%
Mechanical Data: Bleed Size: 303 x 216mm, Trim Size: 297 x 210mm, Film: Digital, Type Area: 297 x 187mm, Col Length: 297mm, Page Width: 187mm
Copy instructions: Copy Date: Wednesday prior to publication date
Average advertising content per issue: 20%
BUSINESS: FINANCE & ECONOMICS

DECANTER
45247U9A-40

Editorial Address: Blue Fin Building, 110 Southwark Street, LONDON, SE1 0SU **Tel:** 020 3148 5000 **Fax:** 020 3148 8524
Email: editorial@decanter.com
Advertising Address: As above.
Email: rosemary_archer@ipcmedia.com
Web site: http://www.decanter.com
ISSN: 0954-4240
Publisher: IPC Inspire
Date Established: 1976
Frequency: Monthly
Cover Price: £3.70
Annual Sub.: £43.00
Circulation: 40,000 (Publisher's Statement)
Usual Pagination: 120
Editor: Guy Woodward
Summary of Content: Magazine containing features on wines and spirits, wine tasting and wine regions worldwide.
Readership/Target Audience: Aimed at wine enthusiasts, connoisseurs and wine trade professionals.
ADVERTISING RATES:
Full Page Mono £1455.00
Full Page Colour £3030.00
Agency Commission: 10%
Mechanical Data: Bleed Size: 303 x 216mm, Trim Size: 297 x 210mm, Type Area: 273 x 185mm, Col Length: 273mm, Page Width: 185mm, Film: Digital
Copy instructions: Copy Date: 6 weeks prior to publication date
BUSINESS: DRINKS & LICENSED TRADE: Drinks, Licensed Trade, Wines & Spirits

DECISION
41297U63B-598

Editorial Address: PO Box 49, HAYLING ISLAND, PO11 9YJ **Tel:** 023 9246 5631
Email: pr@decisionmagazine.co.uk
Advertising Address: As above.
Email: mail@decisionmagazine.co.uk
Web site: http://www.decisionmagazine.co.uk

Publisher: Corporate Publications
Date Established: 1988
Frequency: Quarterly
Free to qualifying individuals
Circulation: 18,000 (Publisher's Statement)
Usual Pagination: 128
Editor: Larry Dillner; **Advertising Manager:** Larry Dillner;
Publisher: Larry Dillner
Summary of Content: Magazine containing articles on companies or directors who are achieving over and above their market norm, focusing solely on companies which have their headquarters in Berkshire, Dorset, Hampshire, Surrey, Sussex and Wiltshire.
Readership/Target Audience: Read by directors and senior managers of companies with a turnover of £5 million and over in Berkshire, Dorset, Hampshire, Surrey, Sussex and Wiltshire.
ADVERTISING RATES:
Full Page Mono £2900.00
Full Page Colour £2900.00
Agency Commission: 10%
Mechanical Data: Bleed Size: +3mm, Film: Digital, Type Area: 342 x 242mm, Col Length: 342mm, Page Width: 242mm
Copy instructions: Copy Date: 1 week prior to publication date
Average advertising content per issue: 2%
BUSINESS: REGIONAL BUSINESS: Regional Business English Counties

DECORATING MATTERS
1754883U16A-112
Editorial Address: Pavilion 2, Players Road, Castlecraig Business Park, STIRLING, FK7 7SH **Tel:** 01786 448838
Fax: 01786 450541
Email: info@scottishdecorators.co.uk
Advertising Address: Portland Buildings, 127-129 Portland Street, MANCHESTER, M1 4PZ **Tel:** 0161 236 2782
Fax: 0161 236 2783
Email: paula.english@excelpublishing.co.uk
Web site: http://www.scottishdecorators.co.uk
Publisher: Excel Publishing Company Ltd
Frequency: Quarterly
Cover Price: £2.50
Free to qualifying individuals
Circulation: 5,000 (Publisher's Statement)
Editor: Ian Rogers
Summary of Content: Official magazine of the Scottish Decorators Federation covering industry news including employment and contractual law, investment, vehicles, techniques, applications and manufacturing news.
Readership/Target Audience: Aimed at the decorating industry including contractors, applicators, architects, surveyors, designers, housing associations, clients and federation members.
ADVERTISING RATES:
Full Page Colour £750.00
Agency Commission: 10%
Mechanical Data: Type Area: 266 x 185mm, Bleed Size: 303 x 216mm, Trim Size: 297 x 210mm, Col Length: 266mm, Page Width: 185mm, Film: Digital
Copy instructions: Copy Date: 1st of the month prior to publication date
Average advertising content per issue: 30%
BUSINESS: DECORATING & PAINT

THE DECORATOR
37270U16A-5
Editorial Address: 4 Kenwood Road, SHEFFIELD, S7 1NP
Tel: 0114 255 9686
Email: catherine.saint@yahoo.co.uk
Advertising Address: As above.
Email: catherine.saint@yahoo.co.uk
Web site: http://www.paintingdecoratingassociation.co.uk
Publisher: Catherine Saint Publicity
Frequency: 6 issues yearly - Published at the beginning of the cover date
Free to qualifying individuals
Annual Sub.: £24.00
Circulation: 4,200 (Publisher's Statement)
Usual Pagination: 56
Editor: Catherine Saint; **Advertising Manager:** Catherine Saint
Summary of Content: Official journal of the Painting and Decoration Association. Contains articles on decoration, architecture, finishing, paint and varnish production.
Readership/Target Audience: Read by Association members or those involved in both the technical and business side of painting and decorating.
ADVERTISING RATES:
Full Page Colour £750.00
Agency Commission: 10%
Mechanical Data: Film: Digital, Trim Size: 297 x 210mm
Copy instructions: Copy Date: 1st Monday of month prior to publication date
BUSINESS: DECORATING & PAINT

DEER FARMING
1638156U21D-1001
Editorial Address: PO Box 7522, MATLOCK, DE4 9BR
Tel: 0845 634 4758 **Fax:** 0845 634 4759
Email: info@bdfa.co.uk
Advertising Address: As above. **Tel:** 08456 344758
Fax: 08456 344759
Email: claire.parkinson@parallelassociates.co.uk
Web site: http://www.bdfa.co.uk
Publisher: British Deer Farmers Association
Frequency: 3 issues yearly - Published in January, May and September
Free to qualifying individuals
Annual Sub.: £40.00
Circulation: 500 (Publisher's Statement)
Editor: Claire Parkinson; **Advertising Manager:** Claire Parkinson
Summary of Content: Official magazine of the British Deer Farming Association, covering all aspects of deer farming such as legislation, husbandry and promotions.
Readership/Target Audience: Aimed at deer farmers.
ADVERTISING RATES:
Full Page Colour £300.00
Agency Commission: 10%
Mechanical Data: Film: Digital, Trim Size: 297 x 210mm
Copy instructions: Copy Date: 2 weeks prior to publication date
Average advertising content per issue: 40%
BUSINESS: AGRICULTURE & FARMING: Livestock

DEFENCE ANALYSIS
767020U40-417
Editorial Address: PO Box 29478, LONDON, NW1 8GF
Tel: 020 7284 0331
Email: ftusa@defenceanalysis.com
Publisher: Defence Analysis Ltd
Date Established: 1998
Frequency: Monthly
Annual Sub.: £352.50
Usual Pagination: 20
Editor: Francis Tusa
Summary of Content: Magazine containing independent analysis of European military defences, also covering the areas of the Middle East and Asia.
Readership/Target Audience: Aimed at members of the defence industry and European Ministries of Defence.
ADVERTISING: No Advertising taken
BUSINESS: DEFENCE

DEFENCE DIRECTOR
1639545U40-424
Editorial Address: 9th Floor, St. James's Buildings, Oxford Street, MANCHESTER, M1 6PP **Tel:** 0161 211 3000
Email: editorial@govnet.co.uk
Advertising Address: Golden Cross House, 8 Duncannon Street, LONDON, WC2N 4JF **Tel:** 020 7484 5085
Fax: 020 7484 5100
Email: paul.binder@govnet.co.uk
Web site: http://www.govnet.co.uk
Publisher: GovNet Communications
Date Established: 2003
Frequency: 6 issues yearly
Free to qualifying individuals
Circulation: 7,716 (ABC 01/01/2008 to 31/12/2008)
Usual Pagination: 64
Editor: Adam Baddeley; **Managing Editor:** Wesley Charnock
Summary of Content: Magazine including a forum for the public and commercial side of the defence community to exchange information and views.
Readership/Target Audience: Aimed at key strategic policy and decision makers, operational managers and budget holders across the broad spectrum of the global UK defence community.
ADVERTISING RATES:
Full Page Mono £3595.00
Full Page Colour £3595.00
Agency Commission: 10%
Mechanical Data: Trim Size: 275 x 210mm, Bleed Size: +3mm, Film: Digital
Average advertising content per issue: 38%
BUSINESS: DEFENCE

DEFENCE HELICOPTER
38858U40-80
Formerly: Defence and Public Service Helicopter
Editorial Address: 268 Bath Road, SLOUGH, SL1 4DX
Tel: 01753 727001 **Fax:** 01753 727002
Email: ad@shephard.co.uk
Advertising Address: As above.
Email: js@shephard.co.uk
Web site: http://www.shephard.co.uk
ISSN: 0963-116X
Publisher: The Shephard Group
Date Established: 1983
Frequency: 6 issues yearly
Free to qualifying individuals
Annual Sub.: £80.00
Circulation: 12,000 (Publisher's Statement)
Usual Pagination: 52

Editor: Andrew Drwiega; **Publisher:** Sandy Doyle
Summary of Content: Journal containing the latest news and in-depth coverage of military and public service helicopters.
Readership/Target Audience: Aimed at key decision makers within the defence industry, general officers, procurement officials, senior aircrew and maintainers and unit commanders.
ADVERTISING RATES:
Full Page Mono £3720.00
Full Page Colour £4735.00
Agency Commission: 10%
Mechanical Data: Type Area: 254 x 182mm, Bleed Size: 279 x 211mm, Trim Size: 273 x 205mm, Film: Digital, Col Length: 254mm, Page Width: 182mm
Average advertising content per issue: 40%
BUSINESS: DEFENCE

DEFENCE MANAGEMENT JOURNAL
625054U40-423
Editorial Address: Ebenezer House, Ryecroft, NEWCASTLE-UNDER-LYME, ST5 2UB **Tel:** 01782 740088
Fax: 01782 740066
Email: mdarcy@publicservice.co.uk
Advertising Address: As above. **Tel:** 01782 620088
Fax: 01782 619137
Email: pete@publicservice.co.uk
Web site: http://www.defencemanagement.com
ISSN: 1464-2646
Publisher: PSCA International Ltd
Date Established: 1998
Frequency: Quarterly
Free to qualifying individuals
Circulation: 14,000 (Publisher's Statement)
Usual Pagination: 150
Editor: Matthew D'Arcy; **Managing Editor:** Lisa Carnwell
Summary of Content: Journal analysing a range of practical management issues, including information and communication technology, procurement, logistics, national security, human resources and estates management as well as high-level political comment, articles from central government, defence agencies and private sector.
Readership/Target Audience: Read by the MOD personnel, DOD personnel, defence agencies and government ministers.
ADVERTISING RATES:
Full Page Colour £3995.00
Mechanical Data: Type Area: 279 x 192mm, Bleed Size: 303 x 216mm, Trim Size: 297 x 210mm, Col Length: 279mm, Page Width: 192mm, Film: Digital
Copy instructions: Copy Date: 20 days prior to publication date
Average advertising content per issue: 35%
BUSINESS: DEFENCE

DEMOLITION AND RECYCLING INTERNATIONAL
622838U42A-90
Editorial Address: Southfields, Southview Road, WADHURST, TN5 6TP **Tel:** 01892 784088
Fax: 01892 786257
Email: lindsay.gale@khl.com
Advertising Address: As above. **Fax:** 01892 784086
Email: lynn.collet@khl.com
Web site: http://www.khl.com
ISSN: 1465-9778
Publisher: KHL Group
Date Established: 1999
Frequency: 6 issues yearly - Published in the 3rd week of the 1st cover month
Free to qualifying individuals
Annual Sub.: £60.00
Circulation: 8,000 (Publisher's Statement)
Usual Pagination: 60
Editor: Lindsay Gale; **Advertising Manager:** Alister Williams; **Publisher:** James King
Summary of Content: International demolition and recycling magazine covering news and developments from around the world.
Readership/Target Audience: Aimed at professionals in the demolition and recycling industry worldwide.
ADVERTISING RATES:
Full Page Mono £2940.00
Full Page Colour £2940.00
Agency Commission: 10%
Mechanical Data: Page Width: 184mm, Type Area: 268 x 184mm, Col Length: 268mm, Trim Size: 297 x 210mm, Bleed Size: 303 x 216mm, Film: Digital
Copy instructions: Copy Date: 2 weeks prior to publication date
Average advertising content per issue: 60%
BUSINESS: CONSTRUCTION

DENTAL HEALTH
40380U56D-35
Editorial Address: 19 Cwrt-y-Vil Road, PENARTH, CF64 3HN **Tel:** 029 2071 0042 **Fax:** 029 2071 0042
Email: editorofdh@ntlworld.com

Business Magazines

Advertising Address: 54 Gladstone Road, Saltcoats, AYRSHIRE, KA21 5LF **Tel:** 01294 462653
Email: eagray@dias.uk.com
Publisher: The British Society of Dental Hygiene and Therapy
Date Established: 1949
Frequency: 6 issues yearly
Cover Price: £14.00
Annual Sub.: £90.00
Circulation: 2,800 (Publisher's Statement)
Usual Pagination: 44
Editor: Heather Lewis; **Advertising Manager:** Eveline Gray
Summary of Content: Journal containing scientific articles and news of interest to dental hygienists and therapists, with features on dental health education, prevention and periodontology, oral health and paediatric dentistry.
Readership/Target Audience: Aimed at dental hygienists, therapists and members of dental teams.
ADVERTISING RATES:
Full Page Mono £458.00
Full Page Colour £899.00
Agency Commission: 10%
Mechanical Data: Type Area: 267 x 186mm, Col Length: 267mm, Bleed Size: 303 x 213mm, Trim Size: 297 x 210mm, Film: Digital, Page Width: 186mm
Copy instructions: Copy Date: 1st of month prior to publication date
Average advertising content per issue: 20%
BUSINESS: HEALTH & MEDICAL: Dental

DENTAL PRACTICE
40382U56D-65

Editorial Address: 8A High Street, EPSOM, KT19 8AD **Tel:** 01372 741411 **Fax:** 01372 744493
Email: chrisr@aemorgan.co.uk
Advertising Address: As above.
Email: lesley@aemorgan.co.uk
Web site: http://www.dental-practice.org
Publisher: A.E. Morgan Publications Ltd
Date Established: 1962
Frequency: Monthly - Published on the 1st of the cover month
Cover Price: £3.50
Free to qualifying individuals
Annual Sub.: £32.50
Circulation: 22,414 (ABC 01/01/2008 to 31/12/2008)
Usual Pagination: 56
Editor: Chris Ritchie; **Executive Editor:** Chris Ritchie; **Managing Director:** Terence Morgan; **Advertising Manager:** Lesley Evans
Summary of Content: Publication covering clinical articles, legal matters, postgraduate courses, business practice, materials and services for all members of the dental team.
Readership/Target Audience: Aimed at practising dentists, dental health educators, dental technicians and hygienists.
ADVERTISING RATES:
Full Page Colour £2700.00
Agency Commission: 10%
Mechanical Data: Col Widths (Display): 60mm, Film: Digital, No. of Columns (Display): 4, Bleed Size: 411 x 291mm, Trim Size: 405 x 285mm
Copy instructions: Copy Date: 5 weeks prior to publication date
Average advertising content per issue: 50%
BUSINESS: HEALTH & MEDICAL: Dental

THE DENTAL TECHNICIAN
40384U56D-65_5

Editorial Address: 8A High Street, EPSOM, KT19 8AD **Tel:** 01372 741411 **Fax:** 01372 744493
Email: chrisr@aemorgan.co.uk
Advertising Address: As above.
Email: lesley@aemorgan.co.uk
Web site: http://www.dental-technician.org
Publisher: A.E. Morgan Publications Ltd
Date Established: 1948
Frequency: Monthly
Cover Price: £1.85
Annual Sub.: £19.90
Circulation: 4,000 (Publisher's Statement)
Usual Pagination: 24
Editor: Chris Ritchie; **Publisher:** Terence Morgan
Summary of Content: Magazine containing news, views and technical articles including finance and management.
Readership/Target Audience: Read by dental laboratory owners, managers and technicians in both private and public services.
ADVERTISING RATES:
Full Page Colour £1260.00
Agency Commission: 10%
Mechanical Data: Type Area: 310 x 228mm, Col Length: 310mm, Page Width: 228mm, Bleed Size: 346 x 251mm, Col Widths (Display): 54mm, No. of Columns (Display): 4, Print Process: Litho, Trim Size: 190 x 120mm, Film: Digital
Copy instructions: Copy Date: 5th of the month prior to publication date
BUSINESS: HEALTH & MEDICAL: Dental

DENTAL TRADER
1925413U56D-209

Editorial Address: The British Dental Trade Association, Mineral Lane, CHESHAM, HP5 1NL **Tel:** 01494 782873
Email: rebeccaevans@bdta.org.uk
Web site: http://www.bdta.org.uk
Publisher: The British Dental Trade Association
Frequency: Monthly
Cover Price: Free
Editor: Rebecca Evans
Summary of Content: Magazine covering news from the dental trade.
Readership/Target Audience: Aimed exclusively at members of the dental trade.
ADVERTISING: Rates on application
BUSINESS: HEALTH & MEDICAL: Dental

DENTAL TRIBUNE
1864834U56D-207

Editorial Address: 4th Floor, Treasure House, 19-21 Hatton Garden, LONDON, EC1N 8BA **Tel:** 020 7400 8979
Fax: 020 7400 8988
Email: lisa@dentaltribuneuk.com
Web site: http://www.dental-tribune.co.uk
Publisher: Dental Tribune International
Frequency: Weekly
Cover Price: Free
Editor: Lisa Townshend
Summary of Content: Magazine with news and information about materials, techniques, trends and events in the dental industry.
Readership/Target Audience: Aimed at dentists.
BUSINESS: HEALTH & MEDICAL: Dental

DENTAL UPDATE
40385U56D-66

Editorial Address: Unit 2, Riverview Business Park, Walnut Tree Close, GUILDFORD, GU1 4UX **Tel:** 01483 304944
Fax: 01483 303191
Email: astroud@georgewarman.co.uk
Advertising Address: As above.
Email: ghenson@georgewarman.co.uk
Web site: http://www.dental-update.co.uk
ISSN: 0305-5000
Publisher: George Warman Publications (UK) Ltd
Date Established: 1973
Frequency: 10 issues yearly
Annual Sub.: £97.00
Circulation: 6,704 (ABC 01/01/2008 to 31/12/2008)
Usual Pagination: 72
Editor: Angela Stroud; **Executive Editor:** Angela Stroud; **Advertising Manager:** Gary Henson
Summary of Content: Journal of clinical reference with review articles.
Readership/Target Audience: Aimed at post-graduate dental practitioners.
ADVERTISING RATES:
Full Page Mono £600.00
Full Page Colour £850.00
Agency Commission: 10%
Mechanical Data: Film: Digital, Type Area: 251 x 185mm, Bleed Size: 291 x 216mm, Trim Size: 285 x 210mm, Col Length: 251mm, Page Width: 185mm
Average advertising content per issue: 25%
BUSINESS: HEALTH & MEDICAL: Dental

DENTALLAB JOURNAL
40381U56D-40

Formerly: Dental Laboratory
Editorial Address: 44-46 Wollaton Road, Beeston, NOTTINGHAM, NG9 2NR **Tel:** 0115 925 4888
Fax: 0115 925 4800
Email: frances@dla.org.uk
Advertising Address: As above.
Email: frances@dla.org.uk
Web site: http://www.dla.org.uk
ISSN: 0957-5318
Publisher: Dental Laboratories Association Ltd
Date Established: 1975
Frequency: 10 issues yearly - Published on the 15th of the cover month
Cover Price: £3.95
Free to qualifying individuals
Annual Sub.: £40.00
Circulation: 3,000 (Publisher's Statement)
Usual Pagination: 76
Editor: Frances Szymczak; **Advertising Manager:** Frances Szymczak
Summary of Content: Journal that covers new products, employment reviews, legislation, financial planning, personnel management and dental politics.
Readership/Target Audience: Read by Dental Laboratory owners, dental technicians, clinical dental technicians, dental traders, dental surgeons, dental students/ lecturers and anyone with an interest in dental technology.
ADVERTISING RATES:
Full Page Colour £800.00

Mechanical Data: Bleed Size: 307 x 220mm, Col Length: 255mm, Page Width: 187mm, Film: Digital, Trim Size: 297 x 210mm, Type Area: 255 x 187mm
Average advertising content per issue: 30%
BUSINESS: HEALTH & MEDICAL: Dental

THE DENTIST
40386U56D-66_5

Editorial Address: Unit 2, Riverview Business Park, Walnut Tree Close, GUILDFORD, GU1 4UX **Tel:** 01483 304944
Fax: 01483 303191
Email: dentist-ed@georgewarman.co.uk
Advertising Address: As above.
Email: ghenson@georgewarman.co.uk
Web site: http://www.the-dentist.co.uk
Publisher: George Warman Publications (UK) Ltd
Frequency: 11 issues yearly - Published on the 1st of the month
Cover Price: Free
Circulation: 17,684 (ABC 01/01/2008 to 31/12/2008)
Usual Pagination: 108
Editor: Jenny Dyer
Summary of Content: Journal which concentrates on practice management, with articles on financial, legal and investment matters, analysis pages, news, clinical management and products.
Readership/Target Audience: Read by practising general dental practitioners.
ADVERTISING RATES:
Full Page Mono £1100.00
Full Page Colour £1675.00
SCC £14.00
Agency Commission: 10%
Mechanical Data: Type Area: 258 x 186mm, Trim Size: 285 x 210mm, Bleed Size: 291 x 216mm, Col Length: 258mm, Film: Digital, Page Width: 186mm
Copy instructions: Copy Date: 6 weeks prior to publication
Average advertising content per issue: 60%
Supplement(s): Dental Hygienist Update - 2xY
BUSINESS: HEALTH & MEDICAL: Dental

DENTISTRY
40387U56D-68

Formerly: Dentistry Monthly
Editorial Address: 1 Hertford House, Hugo Gryn Way, Farm Close, SHENLEY, WD7 9AB **Tel:** 01923 851777
Fax: 01923 851778
Email: guy.hiscott@fmc.co.uk
Advertising Address: As above.
Email: dan.cockerton@fmc.co.uk
Web site: http://www.dentistry.co.uk
ISSN: 1466-6044
Publisher: Finlayson Media Communications Ltd
Date Established: 1995
Frequency: 20 issues yearly
Free to qualifying individuals
Circulation: 19,928 (ABC 01/01/2008 to 31/12/2008)
Usual Pagination: 80
Editor: James Macdonald; **Executive Editor:** Julian English
Summary of Content: Magazine covering all aspects of the dental industry, including product updates and practical information.
Readership/Target Audience: Read by dental practitioners.
ADVERTISING RATES:
Full Page Colour £3150.00
Mechanical Data: Type Area: 391 x 269mm, Bleed Size: 426 x 303mm, Trim Size: 420 x 297mm, Col Length: 391mm, Page Width: 269mm, Film: Digital, No. of Columns (Display): 6
BUSINESS: HEALTH & MEDICAL: Dental

DEPARTMENT STORE BUYER
1684271U53-688

Editorial Address: 4th Floor, Geneva House, Park Road, PETERBOROUGH, PE1 2UX **Tel:** 01733 756555
Fax: 01733 760505
Email: dsb@onecoms.co.uk
Advertising Address: As above.
Email: donna@onecoms.co.uk
Web site: http://www.onecoms.co.uk
Publisher: Media One Communications Ltd.
Date Established: 2005
Frequency: 6 issues yearly - Published in the 2nd week of the cover month
Free to qualifying individuals
Circulation: 3,500 (Publisher's Statement)
Editor: Naomi Davis
Summary of Content: Magazine featuring news, products, shows and market trends for the UK department store retail sector.
Readership/Target Audience: Aimed at buyers, executives, decision makers and senior management from all of Britain's department stores and catalogue retailers.
ADVERTISING RATES:
Full Page Colour £565.00
Agency Commission: 10%
Mechanical Data: Type Area: 280 x 190mm, Bleed Size: 303 x 216mm, Trim Size: 297 x 210mm, Col Length: 280mm, Page Width: 190mm, Film: Digital

Copy instructions: Copy Date: 19th of the month prior to publication date
Average advertising content per issue: 20%
BUSINESS: RETAILING & WHOLESALING

DERIVATIVES WEEK
35388U1L-11

Editorial Address: Nestor House, Playhouse Yard, LONDON, EC4V 5EX **Tel:** 020 7779 8888
Fax: 020 7303 1707
Email: ichapple@euromoneyplc.com
Advertising Address: 225 Park Avenue South, 6th Floor, New York, 10003 NY **Tel:** 212 22 43 300 **Fax:** 212 22 43 493
Email: pbertucci@iinews.com
Web site: http://www.iiderivatives.com
Publisher: Euromoney Institutional Investor plc
Frequency: Weekly
Usual Pagination: 12
Editor: Robert McGlinchey; **Advertising Manager:** Patricia Bertucci; **Managing Editor:** Katy Burne
Summary of Content: Newsletter covering the over-the-counter derivatives market.
Readership/Target Audience: Read by top executives, derivatives traders and marketers at investment and commercial banks.
ADVERTISING RATES:
Full Page Mono $5600.00
Full Page Colour $7500.00
BUSINESS: FINANCE & ECONOMICS: Commodities

DERMATOLOGY IN PRACTICE
40155U56A-60

Editorial Address: 8-10 Dryden Street, Covent Garden, LONDON, WC2E 9NA **Tel:** 020 7240 4493
Fax: 020 7240 4479
Email: edit@hayward.co.uk
Web site: http://www.hayward.co.uk
ISSN: 0262-5504
Publisher: Hayward Medical Communications Ltd
Frequency: Quarterly
Free to qualifying individuals
Circulation: 19,000 (Publisher's Statement)
Usual Pagination: 32
Editor: Claire Robertson
Summary of Content: Publication covering all aspects of dermatology including treatment, drugs, prescriptions, skin reactions and advice for GPs.
Readership/Target Audience: Aimed at GPs, consultants, doctors, professors and experts in the field of dermatology.
ADVERTISING: No Advertising taken
BUSINESS: HEALTH & MEDICAL

DESIDER
1852122U40-444

Editorial Address: Spur 5, E Block, Ensleigh, BATH, BA1 5AB **Tel:** 01225 468719
Email: caroline.wickhamsmith139@mod.uk
Advertising Address: Ten Alps Publishing, 9 Savoy Street, LONDON, WC2E 7HR **Tel:** 020 7878 2300
Fax: 020 7379 7118
Email: david.lancaster@tenalpspublishing.co.uk
Web site: http://www.mod.co.uk
Publisher: Ministry of Defence
Date Established: 2008
Frequency: Monthly
Cover Price: Free
Circulation: 23,000 (Publisher's Statement)
Editor: Caroline Wickham-Smith
Summary of Content: Magazine covering stories and features about support to operations and equipment acquisition. Also covers the work of those in the DE&S and other corporate news and information.
Readership/Target Audience: Aimed at readers across defence equipment and support and the wider MOD and armed forces.
ADVERTISING RATES:
Full Page Mono £2967.00
Full Page Colour £3376.00
Mechanical Data: Type Area: 310 x 210mm, Bleed Size: 346 x 246mm, Col Length: 310mm, Page Width: 210mm, Film: Digital
BUSINESS: DEFENCE

DESIGN AND TECHNOLOGY EDUCATION: AN INTERNATIONAL JOURNAL
41030U62B-420

Editorial Address: 16 Wellesbourne House, Walton Road, Wellesbourne, WARWICK, CV35 9JB **Tel:** 01789 470007
Fax: 01789 841955
Email: neil@data.org.uk
Web site: http://www.data.org.uk/
ISSN: 1360-1431
Publisher: The Design and Technology Association
Date Established: 1995
Frequency: 3 issues yearly - Published in spring, summer and autumn
Free to qualifying individuals

Annual Sub.: £43.00
Circulation: 6,000 (Publisher's Statement)
Usual Pagination: 96
Editor: Neil Whitton; **Managing Editor:** Neil Whitton
Summary of Content: Journal of the Design and Technology Association, which represents and supports all those involved in design and technology education.
Readership/Target Audience: Read by members of the Design and Technology Association and teachers and trainee teachers of design and technology.
ADVERTISING: No Advertising taken
BUSINESS: CHURCH & SCHOOL EQUIPMENT & EDUCATION: Education Teachers

---

DESIGN BUY BUILD
1739811U4E-437

Editorial Address: Redfern House, 347 Margate Road, RAMSGATE, CT12 6SG **Tel:** 01843 592802
Fax: 01843 593214
Email: mike@designbuybuild.co.uk
Advertising Address: As above.
Email: maria@designbuybuild.co.uk
Web site: http://www.designbuybuild.co.uk
Publisher: MH Media Solutions Ltd
Date Established: 2006
Frequency: 6 issues yearly
Free to qualifying individuals
Circulation: 15,000 (Publisher's Statement)
Editor: Mike Hills
Summary of Content: Magazine covering new build projects including regulations, health and safety and products.
Readership/Target Audience: Aimed at builders, interior designers, contractors, developers and specifiers.
ADVERTISING RATES:
Full Page Colour £1495.00
Mechanical Data: Type Area: 277 x 190mm, Bleed Size: 317 x 230mm, Trim Size: 297 x 210mm, Col Length: 277mm, Page Width: 190mm, Film: Digital
Copy instructions: Copy Date: 3 weeks prior to publication date
BUSINESS: ARCHITECTURE & BUILDING: Building

DESIGN EXCHANGE
1900155U4B-195

Formerly: myspace design
Editorial Address: 366 Bethnal Green Road, LONDON, E2 0AH **Tel:** 020 7033 9410 **Fax:** 020 7739 1924
Email: editor@demagazine.co.uk
Web site: http://www.demagazine.co.uk
Publisher: LDI Media (UK)
Date Established: 2004
Frequency: Quarterly
Cover Price: £3.80
Circulation: 15,000 (Publisher's Statement)
Editor: Diana Biggs
Summary of Content: Printed and online magazine featuring the latest in innovation for designers.
Readership/Target Audience: Aimed at designers, architects, interior decorators, retailers, specifiers for hotels, restaurants, bars, galleries, museums, building contractors, property developers and all design conscious consumers.
BUSINESS: ARCHITECTURE & BUILDING: Interior Design & Flooring

---

DESIGN FOOTPRINT
1900152U4B-194

Editorial Address: 366 Bethnal Green Road, LONDON, E2 0AH **Tel:** 020 7033 9410 **Fax:** 020 7739 1924
Email: editor@designfootprintmag.com
Web site: http://www.designfootprintmag.com/
Publisher: LDI Media (UK)
Date Established: 2009
Frequency: Quarterly
Cover Price: £3.80
Circulation: 7,000 (Print Run)
Editor: Diana Biggs
Summary of Content: Magazine focusing on sustainable and ecological design.
Readership/Target Audience: Aimed at architects and designers.
BUSINESS: ARCHITECTURE & BUILDING: Interior Design & Flooring

---

DESIGN WEEK
37149U14J-78

Editorial Address: St. Giles House, 50 Poland Street, LONDON, W1F 7AX **Tel:** 020 7970 4000 **Fax:** 020 7970 6730
Email: angus.montgomery@centaur.com
Advertising Address: As above. **Tel:** 020 7970 6414
Fax: 020 7970 6732
Email: victoria.adams@centaur.co.uk
Web site: http://www.designweek.co.uk
ISSN: 0950-3676
Publisher: Centaur Communications Ltd
Date Established: 1986
Frequency: Weekly - Published on Thursday
Cover Price: £2.80

Annual Sub.: £85.00
Circulation: 6,598 (ABC 01/07/2008 to 30/06/2009)
Usual Pagination: 36
Editor: Emily Pacey; **News Editor:** Angus Montgomery
Summary of Content: Magazine offering a broad range of news and features about the design industry.
Twitter: https://twitter.com/Design_Week

Readership/Target Audience: Aimed at those in retail, graphic, product and interior design, both practising designers and clients.
ADVERTISING RATES:
Full Page Colour £2535.00
Agency Commission: 10%
Mechanical Data: Type Area: 316 x 230mm, Col Length: 316mm, Bleed Size: 341 x 256mm, Trim Size: 335 x 250mm, Film: Digital, Page Width: 230mm, No. of Columns (Display): 5, Col Widths (Display): 42mm
Copy instructions: Copy Date: 2 weeks prior to publication date
Average advertising content per issue: 55%
BUSINESS: COMMERCE, INDUSTRY & MANAGEMENT: Commercial Design

THE DESIGNER
37147U14J-60

Formerly: CSD: The Magazine of the Chartered Society of Designers
Editorial Address: 1 Cedar Court, Royal Oak Yard, Bermondsey Street, LONDON, SE1 3GA **Tel:** 020 7357 8088
Fax: 020 7407 9878
Email: thedesigner@csd.org.uk
Web site: http://www.csd.org.uk
Publisher: Chartered Society of Designers
Frequency: Quarterly
Free to qualifying individuals
Annual Sub.: £33.00
Circulation: 7,500 (Publisher's Statement)
Editor: Carmen Martinez-Lopez
Summary of Content: Journal of the Chartered Society of Designers. Contains news, training information, interviews, book reviews, exhibitions and events. Also covers interiors, graphics, fashion, textiles, products and multimedia.
Readership/Target Audience: Aimed at CSD members and consultancies.
ADVERTISING: No Advertising taken
BUSINESS: COMMERCE, INDUSTRY & MANAGEMENT: Commercial Design

THE DESIGNER
629391U23C-45

Formerly: The Kitchen and Bathroom Designer
Editorial Address: Ivy Lane Business Centre, 8A Victoria Road, DARTMOUTH, TQ6 9SA **Tel:** 01803 839399
Email: martin@thedesignermagazine.com
Advertising Address: As above. **Fax:** 01803 839398
Email: cindy@thedesignermagazinemagazine.com
Web site: http://www.thedesignermagazine.com
Publisher: 5th Element Publications Ltd
Date Established: 2000
Frequency: Monthly
Free to qualifying individuals
Annual Sub.: £60.00
Circulation: 9,987 (ABC 01/07/2008 to 30/06/2009)
Usual Pagination: 92
Editor: Martin Allen-Smith; **Advertising Manager:** Cindy Cooper
Summary of Content: Magazine focused on designers, products and design trends with particular reference to fitted kitchen and bathroom design.
Readership/Target Audience: Aimed at professional designers working with kitchens and bathrooms, in particular architects, housebuilders / developers interior designers, specialist kitchen and bathroom designers, retailers and manufacturers.
ADVERTISING RATES:
Full Page Colour £3095.00
SCC £20.00
Agency Commission: 10%
Mechanical Data: Type Area: 311 x 205mm, Col Length: 311mm, Film: Digital, Trim Size: 340 x 240mm, Bleed Size: 346 x 246mm
Copy instructions: Copy Date: 10th of the month prior to publication date
Average advertising content per issue: 40%
BUSINESS: FURNISHINGS & FURNITURE: Furnishings & Furniture - Kitchens & Bathrooms

---

DESIGNING
41018U62B-80

Editorial Address: 16 Wellesbourne House, Walton Road, Wellesbourne, WARWICK, CV35 9JB **Tel:** 01789 470007
Fax: 01789 841955
Email: neil@data.org.uk
Advertising Address: 64 Endcliffe Hall Avenue, SHEFFIELD, S10 3EL **Tel:** 0114 266 5377 **Fax:** 0114 266 5377
Email: noreenpleavin@onetel.com
Web site: http://www.data.org.uk
ISSN: 1464-6277

Business Magazines

Publisher: The Design and Technology Association
Date Established: 1998
Frequency: 3 issues yearly - Published February, May and October
Free to qualifying individuals
Annual Sub.: £24.00
Circulation: 7,500 (Publisher's Statement)
Usual Pagination: 32
Editor: Ian Punter; **Advertising Manager:** Noreen Pleavin; **Managing Editor:** Neil Whitton
Summary of Content: Publication covering all areas of design technology education at primary, secondary undergraduate and postgraduate levels.
Readership/Target Audience: Aimed at teachers and pupils of design.
ADVERTISING RATES:
Full Page Colour £1100.00
Mechanical Data: Film: Digital, Type Area: 400 x 277mm, Bleed Size: 426 x 303mm, Trim Size: 422 x 298mm, Col Length: 400mm, Page Width: 277mm
Copy instructions: Copy Date: 6 weeks prior to publication date
Average advertising content per issue: 12%
BUSINESS: CHURCH & SCHOOL EQUIPMENT & EDUCATION: Education Teachers

DESPATCH MANAGER
35490U49C-68
Editorial Address: 1A Circus Street, OXFORD, OX4 1JR
Tel: 01865 205522 **Fax:** 01865 205533
Email: despatchmanager@aol.com
Advertising Address: As above.
Email: despatchmanager@aol.com
Publisher: CW Publishing
Date Established: 1997
Frequency: 6 issues yearly
Cover Price: £2.50
Free to qualifying individuals
Annual Sub.: £15.00
Circulation: 10,000 (Publisher's Statement)
Usual Pagination: 32
Editor: Ian Ward; **Advertising Manager:** Ian Ward; **Publisher:** Ian Ward
Summary of Content: Publication covering news and information on the mailroom and postal/express parcels industries.
Readership/Target Audience: Read by mailroom managers and post room staff within large companies.
ADVERTISING RATES:
Full Page Colour £1950.00
Agency Commission: 10%
Mechanical Data: Page Width: 180mm, Type Area: 257 x 180mm, Bleed Size: 303 x 213mm, Trim Size: 297 x 210mm, Col Length: 257mm, Film: Digital, Print Process: Sheet-fed litho
Copy instructions: Copy Date: 3 weeks prior to publication date
Average advertising content per issue: 33%
BUSINESS: TRANSPORT: Freight

DESPATCHES
39698U49R-50
Editorial Address: Lamb's End House, 36 Church Road, Magdalen, KING'S LYNN, PE34 3DG **Tel:** 01553 813479
Fax: 01553 813479
Email: phil@despatch.co.uk
Advertising Address: 17 Finches Rise, GUILDFORD, GU1 2UW **Tel:** 01483 853338
Email: ken@despatch.co.uk
Web site: http://www.despatch.co.uk
Publisher: The Despatch Association
Frequency: 6 issues yearly
Free to qualifying individuals
Annual Sub.: £10.00
Circulation: 2,500 (Publisher's Statement)
Usual Pagination: 16
Editor: Phillip Stone; **Advertising Manager:** Ken Hansard; **Publisher:** Ken Hansard
Summary of Content: Official magazine of the Despatch Association, the premier trade association of the same-day courier industry. Carries news and features about the industry including technology, taxation, insurance, business news and vehicle reviews.
Readership/Target Audience: Aimed at proprietors, directors, partners and senior personnel within the same-day courier industry.
ADVERTISING RATES:
Full Page Colour £350.00
Mechanical Data: Film: Digital, Bleed Size: +3mm
Average advertising content per issue: 25%
BUSINESS: TRANSPORT: Transport Related

DESTINATION UK
1776544U50-228
Editorial Address: 47 Church Street, BARNSLEY, S70 2AS
Tel: 01226 734456 **Fax:** 01226 734705
Email: nl@whpl.net
Advertising Address: As above. **Tel:** 01226 734333
Fax: 01226 734477
Email: rw@whpl.net

Web site: http://www.destination.uk.com
Publisher: Wharncliffe Publishing Ltd
Date Established: 2006
Frequency: 6 issues yearly - Published at the end of the second cover month
Cover Price: £3.50
Free to qualifying individuals
Circulation: 11,902 (Publisher's Statement)
Usual Pagination: 32
Editor: Nicola Hyde
Summary of Content: Magazine promoting the UK travel and tourism industry covering the latest news and information, attractions across England, Wales and Scotland, in-depth features exploring special areas of interest, market trends and growth opportunities.
Readership/Target Audience: Aimed at travel trade professionals in Britain and abroad including group travel organisers, corporate travel specialists, independent travel agents, tour agents, coach tour companies, Internet travel companies and organisers of domestic travel and tourism.
ADVERTISING RATES:
Full Page Colour £1850.00
Agency Commission: 10%
Mechanical Data: Type Area: 320 x 220mm, Bleed Size: 346 x 246mm, Trim Size: 340 x 240mm, Col Length: 320mm, Page Width: 220mm, Film: Digital
Copy instructions: Copy Date: Middle of the month prior to publication
BUSINESS: TRAVEL & TOURISM

DEUTSCHE UNQUOTE
1750387U1F-616
Editorial Address: 4th Floor, Haymarket House, 28-29 Haymarket, LONDON, SW1Y 4RX **Tel:** 020 7004 7446
Email: mareen.goebel@incisivemedia.com
Advertising Address: Haymarket House, 28-29 Haymarket, LONDON, SW1Y 4RX **Tel:** 020 7484 9700
Fax: 020 7004 7548
Email: stephen.osullivan@incisivemedia.com
Web site: http://www.deutscheunquote.com
Publisher: Incisive Media Investments
Date Established: 1998
Frequency: 10 issues yearly
Annual Sub.: £1095.00
Editor: Mareen Goebel; **Advertising Manager:** Stephen O'Sullivan
Summary of Content: News concerning private equity transactions in the German speaking regions of Europe.
Language(s): English; German
Readership/Target Audience: Aimed at people in the private equity industry.
ADVERTISING RATES:
Full Page Mono £1650.00
Full Page Colour £3300.00
Agency Commission: 10%
Mechanical Data: Bleed Size: 286 x 222mm, Trim Size: 280 x 216mm, Film: Digital
BUSINESS: FINANCE & ECONOMICS: Investment

DEVELOP
36216U5E-185
Editorial Address: Saxon House, 6A St. Andrew Street, HERTFORD, SG14 1JA **Tel:** 01992 535646
Fax: 01992 535648
Email: michael.french@intentmedia.co.uk
Advertising Address: As above. **Tel:** 01992 535647
Email: kate.rawlings@intentmedia.co.uk
Web site: http://www.developmag.com
ISSN: 1365-7240
Publisher: Intent Media
Date Established: 2000
Frequency: 11 issues yearly
Cover Price: Free
Circulation: 8,000 (Publisher's Statement)
Usual Pagination: 48
Editor: Michael French; **Executive Editor:** Owain Bennallack; **Managing Director:** Stuart Dinsey; **Advertising Manager:** Katie Rawlings; **Publisher:** Stuart Dinsey
Summary of Content: International newsletter covering technical advice and coverage on business, political and educational issues affecting the interactive entertainment industry.
Readership/Target Audience: Aimed at game producers, designers and publishers.
ADVERTISING RATES:
Full Page Mono £1660.00
Full Page Colour £1660.00
Mechanical Data: Page Width: 212mm, Type Area: 295 x 212mm, Col Length: 295mm, Trim Size: 315 x 230mm, Bleed Size: 321 x 236mm, Film: Digital
BUSINESS: COMPUTERS & AUTOMATION: Data Transmission

DEVELOP 3D
1847238U19J-155
Editorial Address: 93A Rivington Street, LONDON, EC2A 3AY **Tel:** 020 3355 7310 **Fax:** 020 3355 7319
Email: greg@x3dmedia.com
Advertising Address: As above.
Email: tony@x3dmedia.com

Web site: http://www.develop3d.com
Publisher: X3D Media
Date Established: 2008
Frequency: 11 issues yearly
Free to qualifying individuals
Circulation: 15,000 (Publisher's Statement)
Usual Pagination: 68
Editor: Al Dean; **Advertising Manager:** Tony Baksh; **Managing Editor:** Greg Corke
Summary of Content: Magazine and website which tracks all the essential technologies used throughout the entire product development process.
Readership/Target Audience: Aimed at the product development and manufacturing community.
ADVERTISING RATES:
Full Page Colour £3000.00
Mechanical Data: Type Area: 280 x 190mm, Bleed Size: 303 x 216mm, Trim Size: 297 x 210mm, Col Length: 280mm, Page Width: 190mm, Film: Digital
BUSINESS: ENGINEERING & MACHINERY: CAD & CIM (Computer Integrated Manufacture)

DEVELOPMENT AND LEARNING IN ORGANIZATIONS
37093U14F-140
Formerly: Training Strategies for Tomorrow
Editorial Address: Howard House, Wagon Lane, BINGLEY, BD16 1WA **Tel:** 01274 777700 **Fax:** 01274 785200
Email: ryoung@emeraldinsight.com
Web site: http://www.emeraldinsight.com
ISSN: 1369-7234
Publisher: Emerald Group Publishing Ltd
Date Established: 1987
Frequency: 6 issues yearly
Annual Sub.: £1369.00
Usual Pagination: 36
Editor: Ruth Young; **Publisher:** Ruth Young
Summary of Content: Independent journal covering news and views on development and learning.
Readership/Target Audience: Read by development and learning managers and HR.
ADVERTISING: No Advertising taken
BUSINESS: COMMERCE, INDUSTRY & MANAGEMENT: Training & Recruitment

THE DIABETES REPORT
1799522U37-428
Editorial Address: Lincoln House, City Fields Business Park, City Fields Way, Tangmere, CHICHESTER, PO20 2FS
Tel: 01243 756016 **Fax:** 01243 533418
Email: healthcare@espicom.com
Web site: http://www.espicom.com
Publisher: Espicom Ltd
Frequency: Monthly
Annual Sub.: £545.00
Circulation: 40 (Publisher's Statement)
Editor: Johanna Shiu
Summary of Content: Newsletter containing R&D updates, product news and strategic agreements relating to the treatment of diabetes. Also contains conference listings.
Readership/Target Audience: Aimed at senior executives and researchers in pharmaceutical companies.
ADVERTISING: No Advertising taken
BUSINESS: PHARMACEUTICAL & CHEMISTS

DIABETIC MEDICINE
40156U56A-60_50
Editorial Address: 9600 Garsington Road, Cowley, OXFORD, OX4 2DQ **Tel:** 01865 776868 **Fax:** 01865 714591
Email: mpowell@wiley.com
Advertising Address: As above. **Tel:** 01865 476383
Fax: 01865 471383
Email: mia.scott-ruddock@oxon.blackwellpublishing.com
Web site: http://www.wiley.com
Publisher: Wiley-Blackwell Publishing
Frequency: Monthly
Editor: Matthew Powell
Summary of Content: Journal of Diabetes UK focusing on research into diabetes mellitus.
Readership/Target Audience: Aimed at the medical profession, endocrinologists, pathologists and people involved in the pharmaceutical industry.
ADVERTISING RATES:
Full Page Mono £582.00
Full Page Colour £1703.00
Agency Commission: 10%
Mechanical Data: Page Width: 180mm, Type Area: 245 x 180mm, Col Length: 245mm, Trim Size: 276 x 210mm, Film: Digital, Bleed Size: 282 x 216mm
Copy instructions: Copy Date: 1 month prior to publication date
BUSINESS: HEALTH & MEDICAL

DIAGNOSTIC ENGINEERING
35986U5A-72
Editorial Address: 7 Weir Road, Kibworth, LEICESTER, LE8 0LQ **Tel:** 0116 279 6772 **Fax:** 0116 279 6884
Email: admin@diagnosticengineers.org

Advertising Address: As above.
Email: admin@diagnosticengineers.org
Web site: http://www.diagnosticengineers.org.uk
ISSN: 0269-0225
Publisher: Institution of Diagnostic Engineers
Date Established: 1983
Frequency: 6 issues yearly
Free to qualifying individuals
Annual Sub.: £65.00
Circulation: 2,000 (Publisher's Statement)
Usual Pagination: 30
Editor: David Mullins; **Advertising Manager:** Karen Seiles
Summary of Content: Journal covering problem solving and fault finding.
Readership/Target Audience: Aimed at members of the Institute of Diagnostic Engineers and those engaged in the running of plant, machinery and structures of all kinds.
ADVERTISING RATES:
Full Page Mono £250.00
Full Page Colour £335.00
Agency Commission: 20%
Mechanical Data: Type Area: 255 x 185mm, Trim Size: 297 x 210mm, Col Length: 255mm, Page Width: 185mm
Copy instructions: Copy Date: 3 weeks prior to publication date
BUSINESS: COMPUTERS & AUTOMATION: Automation & Instrumentation

---

DIAL
39718U50-16

Editorial Address: 79 Essex Road, Islington, LONDON, N1 2SF **Tel:** 020 7354 5577 **Fax:** 020 7354 8827
Email: wendy.saunt@chandlergooding.co.uk
Advertising Address: Kingsgate House, 29-39 The Broadway, Middlesex, STANMORE, HA7 4AN
Tel: 020 7604 2765 **Fax:** 020 7624 4238
Email: ssmith@expotel.com
Web site: http://www.chandlergooding.co.uk
ISSN: 0961-737X
Publisher: Editorial Design Concepts
Date Established: 1973
Frequency: Quarterly
Cover Price: Free
Circulation: 22,000 (Publisher's Statement)
Usual Pagination: 100
Editor: Wendy Saunt; **Advertising Manager:** Sharon Smith; **Publisher:** Ken Whyne
Summary of Content: Customer publication of Expotel Hotel Reservations, corporate hotel reservations - corporate travel and conference venue booking agency. Covers personal and career development, PA-related and business travel, executive issues, hotel facilities (spas, sports facilities, restaurants and bedrooms), food and wine, business travel and hotel news, UK events listings, lifestyle, health and beauty issues, finance and regular reader giveaways.
Readership/Target Audience: Aimed at business travellers, PAs and corporate buyers who book bulk hotel accommodation through the agency Exportel and its partner hotel groups, excluding travel agents.
ADVERTISING RATES:
Full Page Colour £4000.00
Mechanical Data: Type Area: 277 x 190mm, Col Length: 277mm, Page Width: 190mm, Trim Size: 297 x 210mm, Bleed Size: 303 x 216mm
Average advertising content per issue: 33%
BUSINESS: TRAVEL & TOURISM

DIARY
39487U47A-90

Editorial Address: 30 Harcourt Street, LONDON, W1H 4AA
Tel: 020 7724 7770 **Fax:** 020 7724 7357
Email: info@diaryd.com
Advertising Address: As above.
Email: julia@diaryd.com
Web site: http://www.diarydirectory.com
ISSN: 1366-9591
Publisher: The Diary
Date Established: 1968
Frequency: Monthly
Annual Sub.: £700.00
Circulation: 2,000 (Publisher's Statement)
Usual Pagination: 38
Editor: Gail Raymonde; **Advertising Manager:** Sarah Lanburn
Summary of Content: Magazine covering all PR and media moves within the fashion, beauty, homes and interiors industries.
Readership/Target Audience: Aimed at PR companies and the press.
ADVERTISING RATES:
Full Page Colour £850.00
Mechanical Data: Col Length: 190mm, Page Width: 126mm, Trim Size: 210 x 148mm, Bleed Size: +3mm, Film: Digital, Type Area: 182 x 126mm
Supplement(s): Diary Directory - 4xY
BUSINESS: CLOTHING & TEXTILES

DIARY DIRECTORY
39524U47A-91

Editorial Address: For all contact details see main record, Diary
Publisher: The Diary
Frequency: Quarterly - See main record for circulation figure
ADVERTISING RATES:
Full Page Colour £900.00
Supplement to: Diary
BUSINESS: CLOTHING & TEXTILES

DIESEL & GAS TURBINE WORLDWIDE
40742U58-27

Editorial Address: 120 Long Acre, Covent Garden, LONDON, WC2E 9ST **Tel:** 020 7632 9580
Fax: 020 7632 9585
Email: icameron@dieselpub.com
Advertising Address: As above.
Email: sdoran@dieselpub.com
Web site: http://www.dieselpub.com
Publisher: Diesel & Gas Turbine Publications
Frequency: 10 issues yearly - Published on the 15th of the month prior to cover month
Free to qualifying individuals
Circulation: 21,349 (BPA Worldwide 01/01/2006 to 30/06/2006)
Usual Pagination: 80
Editor: Ian Cameron; **Advertising Manager:** Samantha Doran
Summary of Content: Magazine covering the design, production, installation, operation and maintenance of medium to high power output diesel, natural gas and gas turbine engines.
Readership/Target Audience: Aimed at OEMs and end users.
ADVERTISING RATES:
Full Page Colour £3240.00
Agency Commission: 15%
Mechanical Data: Type Area: 254 x 190mm, Bleed Size: 273 x 210mm, Col Length: 254mm, Page Width: 190mm, Trim Size: 267 x 203mm, Film: Digital
BUSINESS: ENERGY, FUEL & NUCLEAR

DIESEL PROGRESS INTERNATIONAL
37540U19A-110

Editorial Address: 120 Long Acre, Covent Garden, LONDON, WC2E 9ST **Tel:** 020 7632 9580
Fax: 020 7632 9585
Email: icameron@dieselpub.com
Advertising Address: As above.
Web site: http://www.dieselpub.com
Publisher: Diesel & Gas Turbine Publications
Frequency: 6 issues yearly - Published in the 2nd week of the 1st cover month
Cover Price: Free
Circulation: 12,135 (Publisher's Statement)
Usual Pagination: 82
Editor: Ian Cameron; **Advertising Manager:** Samantha Doran
Summary of Content: Magazine providing coverage of major technical developments specifically related to the vehicular, industrial and marine markets for volume produced high speed diesel engines.
Readership/Target Audience: Aimed at OEMs, service engineers, government designers and re-builders.
ADVERTISING RATES:
Full Page Mono £2900.00
Full Page Colour £2900.00
Agency Commission: 15%
Mechanical Data: Film: Digital, Print Process: Offset litho, Col Widths (Display): 54mm, Trim Size: 267 x 203mm, Bleed Size: 273 x 210mm
Average advertising content per issue: 40%
BUSINESS: ENGINEERING & MACHINERY

DIGITAL ARTS
36268U5F-230

Formerly: DIGIT
Editorial Address: 4th Floor, 101 Euston Road, LONDON, NW1 2RA **Tel:** 020 7756 2800
Email: neilb@digitalartsonline.co.uk
Advertising Address: As above. **Fax:** 020 7756 2838
Email: advertising@digitalartsonline.co.uk
Web site: http://www.digitalartsonline.co.uk
Publisher: IDG (International Data Group)
Date Established: 1998
Frequency: 13 issues yearly
Cover Price: £5.99
Annual Sub.: £49.99
Usual Pagination: 132
Editor: Neil Bennett; **Managing Director:** Kit Gould; **Advertising Manager:** Matthew Bennett; **Publisher:** Mustafa Mustafa
Summary of Content: Magazine covering the latest technologies and techniques in graphic arts, design and page layout. Includes features on multimedia, CD-ROM, digital video, 3D modelling, animation and image editing.

Readership/Target Audience: Aimed at those involved in the creative industry and decision makers who purchase and specify hardware.
ADVERTISING RATES:
Full Page Colour £2442.00
Agency Commission: 10%
Mechanical Data: Film: Digital, No. of Columns (Display): 4, Trim Size: 297 x 210mm
Average advertising content per issue: 40%
BUSINESS: COMPUTERS & AUTOMATION: Multimedia

DIGITAL DEMAND - THE JOURNAL OF PRINTING AND PUBLISHING TECHNOLOGY
40823U60A-32

Formerly: Publishing Technology Review
Editorial Address: Cleeve Road, LEATHERHEAD, KT22 7RU **Tel:** 01372 802080 **Fax:** 01372 802079
Email: sara.ver-bruggen@pira-international.com
Web site: http://www.intertechpira.com
ISSN: 1471-5694
Publisher: PIRA International
Date Established: 2000
Frequency: 10 issues yearly
Annual Sub.: £499.00
Circulation: 4,000 (Publisher's Statement)
Usual Pagination: 48
Editor: Sara Ver-Bruggen; **Publisher:** Rav Lally
Summary of Content: Journal providing information on digital technologies for printing and publishing.
Readership/Target Audience: Aimed at managers and production managers involved in prepress and print production.
ADVERTISING: No Advertising taken
BUSINESS: PUBLISHING: Publishing & Book Trade

DIGITAL PRINTER
1800446U41A-338

Editorial Address: 30 London Road, Southborough, TUNBRIDGE WELLS, TN4 0RE **Tel:** 01892 542099
Fax: 01892 546693
Email: susan.w@whitmar.co.uk
Advertising Address: As above. **Tel:** 01892 514437
Email: david.g@whitmar.co.uk
Web site: http://www.paperandprint.com
ISSN: 1746-7179
Publisher: Whitmar Publications Ltd
Date Established: 2006
Frequency: 8 issues yearly - Published on the 2nd Wednesday of the cover month
Free to qualifying individuals
Annual Sub.: £75.00
Circulation: 6,000 (Publisher's Statement)
Editor: Simon Eccles; **Advertising Manager:** Chris Rushton; **Managing Editor:** Susan Wright; **Publisher:** Rob Mulligan
Summary of Content: Magazine focusing on new developments in technology, featuring case studies from digital printers, markets and trends, finishing, software, RIPs, papers and speciality media. Covers laser printing, inkjet, electron beam imaging, magnetography and digital duplicating.
Readership/Target Audience: Aimed at printers, corporates and local government, also print generators or print companies considering moving into the sector.
ADVERTISING RATES:
Full Page Mono £1400.00
Full Page Colour £2200.00
Mechanical Data: Type Area: 268 x 186mm, Bleed Size: 303 x 216mm, Trim Size: 297 x 210mm, Col Length: 268mm, Page Width: 186mm, Print Process: Sheet-fed offset litho, Film: Digital
Copy instructions: Copy Date: 1 week prior to publication date
BUSINESS: PRINTING & STATIONERY: Printing

DIGITAL SHIP
629383U45A-34

Editorial Address: Drewry House, 213 Marsh Wall, LONDON, E14 9FJ **Tel:** 020 7510 0015 **Fax:** 020 7510 2344
Email: odwyer@thedigitalship.com
Advertising Address: As above. **Tel:** 020 7510 4931
Email: ria@thedigitalship.com
Web site: http://www.thedigitalship.com
Publisher: Digitalship Ltd
Date Established: 2000
Frequency: 10 issues yearly - Published in the 1st week of the cover month
Annual Sub.: £195.00
Circulation: 2,041 (ABC 01/01/2008 to 31/12/2008)
Usual Pagination: 32
Editor: Rob O'Dwyer; **Advertising Manager:** Ria Kontogeorgou
Summary of Content: Magazine covering maritime information technology, including onboard electronics, maritime software, ship to shore communications, e-procurement and e-chartering.
Readership/Target Audience: Aimed at people in the maritime industry interested in information technology.

Business Magazines

ADVERTISING RATES:
Full Page Mono £2500.00
Full Page Colour £3650.00
Mechanical Data: Type Area: 358 x 254mm, Col Length: 358mm, Page Width: 254mm, Trim Size: 420 x 297mm
Copy instructions: Copy Date: 2 weeks prior to publication date
BUSINESS: MARINE & SHIPPING

DIGITAL TV EUROPE
35668U2D-55

Formerly: Cable & Satellite Europe
Editorial Address: Mortimer House, 37-41 Mortimer Street, LONDON, W1T 3JH **Tel:** 020 7017 5314 **Fax:** 020 7017 4953
Email: stuart.thomson@informa.com
Advertising Address: As above.
Email: katrina.coyne@informa.com
Web site: http://www.digitaltveurope.net
Publisher: T&F Informa Group PLC
Date Established: 1983
Frequency: 10 issues yearly
Free to qualifying individuals
Circulation: 6,185 (BPA Worldwide 01/07/2007 to 31/12/2007)
Usual Pagination: 60
Editor: Stuart Thomson; **Managing Director:** Ian Hemming; **Advertisement Director:** Katrina Coyne; **Publisher:** Lydia Blackwood
Summary of Content: Magazine covering the international business of multi-channel television distribution.
Readership/Target Audience: Aimed at TV operators, equipment manufacturers, distributors, network providers, consultants, agencies and the government.
ADVERTISING RATES:
Full Page Colour £2675.00
Agency Commission: 10%
Mechanical Data: Trim Size: 297 x 210mm, Bleed Size: 303 x 213mm, Film: Digital, Type Area: 269 x 188mm, Col Length: 269mm, Page Width: 188mm
Copy instructions: Copy Date: 4 weeks prior to publication date
Average advertising content per issue: 40%
BUSINESS: COMMUNICATIONS, ADVERTISING & MARKETING: Broadcasting

DIRECT
35674U2D-61

Editorial Address: 4 Windmill Street, LONDON, W1T 2HZ
Tel: 020 7580 9131
Email: info@dggb.org
Advertising Address: As above.
Email: direct@dggb.org
Web site: http://www.dggb.org
Publisher: Directors Guild of Great Britain
Date Established: 1995
Frequency: Annual - Published in Spring
Cover Price: £6.00
Free to qualifying individuals
Circulation: 6,000 (Publisher's Statement)
Usual Pagination: 32
Advertising Manager: Iris Godding
Summary of Content: Magazine focusing on film, theatre, television, radio, commercial multi-media and opera direction.
Readership/Target Audience: Aimed at directors.
ADVERTISING: Rates on application
BUSINESS: COMMUNICATIONS, ADVERTISING & MARKETING: Broadcasting

DIRECT DISTRIBUTION NEWSLETTER
767337U35-356

Editorial Address: Unit 8, Netherhall Yard, Mill Lane, Newick, LEWES, BN8 4JL **Tel:** 01825 724623
Fax: 01825 724623
Email: c.dann@completecircmktg.co.uk
Advertising Address: As above.
Email: c.dann@completecircmktg.co.uk
Web site: http://www.completecircmktg.co.uk
Publisher: Complete Circulation and Marketing Ltd
Date Established: 2002
Frequency: 6 issues yearly
Cover Price: £12.00
Annual Sub.: £70.00
Circulation: 2,000 (Publisher's Statement)
Usual Pagination: 16
Editor: Colin Dann; **Advertising Manager:** Colin Dann
Summary of Content: Newsletter covering the wrapping and domestic and international postal distribution of magazines.
Readership/Target Audience: Aimed at circulation, production and distribution managers in UK magazine publishing companies.
ADVERTISING RATES:
Full Page Colour £464.00
Agency Commission: 10%
Mechanical Data: Type Area: 278 x 188mm, Print Process: Offset litho, Bleed Size: 303 x 216mm, Trim Size: 297 x 210mm, Col Length: 278mm, Page Width: 188mm

Copy instructions: Copy Date: 4 weeks prior to publication date
Average advertising content per issue: 55%
BUSINESS: PACKAGING & BOTTLING

DIRECT MARKETING INTERNATIONAL
35491U2A-68

Editorial Address: New Broad Street House, New Broad Street, LONDON, EC2 M1NH **Tel:** 020 7043 9008
Fax: 020 7023 4953
Email: sally@dmi-news.com
Advertising Address: As above.
Email: matt@dmi-news.com
Web site: http://www.dmionline.net
ISSN: 0969-6881
Publisher: Direct Marketing International Ltd
Date Established: 1982
Frequency: 10 issues yearly - Published at the end of the last week of the cover month. Combined issues are in Jan/Feb and Aug/Sep
Cover Price: £4.35
Free to qualifying individuals
Annual Sub.: £65.00
Circulation: 14,650 (Publisher's Statement)
Usual Pagination: 52
Editor: Sally Hooton; **Advertising Manager:** Matt Edgar; **Publisher:** Matt Edgar
Summary of Content: Journal covering all aspects of direct marketing worldwide.
Readership/Target Audience: Read by those involved in the direct marketing industry, including list users and database users.
ADVERTISING RATES:
Full Page Mono £1210.00
Full Page Colour £1935.00
SCC £15.00
Agency Commission: 10%
Mechanical Data: Film: Digital, Col Length: 260mm, Type Area: 260 x 180mm, Bleed Size: 303 x 216mm, Trim Size: 297 x 210mm, Page Width: 180mm
Copy instructions: Copy Date: 4 weeks prior to publication date
Average advertising content per issue: 50%
BUSINESS: COMMUNICATIONS, ADVERTISING & MARKETING

DIRECTOR
36746U14A-100

Editorial Address: 116 Pall Mall, LONDON, SW1Y 5ED
Tel: 020 7766 8950 **Fax:** 020 7766 8840
Email: director-ed@iod.com
Advertising Address: As above. **Tel:** 020 7766 8900
Email: director-ads@iod.com
Web site: http://www.director.co.uk
ISSN: 0012-3242
Publisher: Director Publications Ltd
Frequency: Monthly
Cover Price: £3.50
Free to qualifying individuals
Annual Sub.: £39.00
Circulation: 56,701 (ABC 01/07/2008 to 30/06/2009)
Usual Pagination: 74
Editor: Richard Cree; **Advertising Manager:** Ben Hammond
Summary of Content: Journal covering general issues including leadership, finance and business advice.
Readership/Target Audience: Aimed at company directors of small to medium-sized enterprises.
ADVERTISING RATES:
Full Page Colour £7675.00
Agency Commission: 15%
Mechanical Data: Col Length: 263mm, Page Width: 190mm, Type Area: 263 x 190mm, Bleed Size: 306 x 231mm, Trim Size: 300 x 225mm, Film: Digital
Copy instructions: Copy Date: 15th of the month prior to publication
Average advertising content per issue: 45%
BUSINESS: COMMERCE, INDUSTRY & MANAGEMENT

DIRECTORY OF CARDIOLOGY
601241U56A-60_75

Editorial Address: 86 Overdale, ASHTEAD, KT21 1PU
Tel: 01372 271692 **Fax:** 01372 817737
Email: ann.bennion@btinternet.com
Advertising Address: As above.
Email: ann.bennion@btinternet.com
Web site: http://www.mediahuset.se
Publisher: Mediahuset
Date Established: 1995
Frequency: Annual - Usually published between April/May
Cover Price: £55.00
Free to qualifying individuals
Circulation: 5,000 (Publisher's Statement)
Usual Pagination: 350
Editor: Ann Bennion; **Advertising Manager:** Ann Bennion
Summary of Content: Publication containing information about cardiologists and cardiothoracic surgeons, hospitals and the cardiovascular services they provide.

Readership/Target Audience: Aimed at cardiologists and cardiothoracic surgeons, and industries involved in cardiology and cardiothoracic surgery.
ADVERTISING: Rates on application
Agency Commission: 10%
BUSINESS: HEALTH & MEDICAL

DIRECTORY OF EXECUTIVE RECRUITMENT - INTERNATIONAL EDITION
601166U14A-179_50

Formerly: International Directory of Executive Recruitment Consultants
Editorial Address: New Barnes Mill, Cottonmill Lane, ST. ALBANS, AL1 2HA **Tel:** 01727 844335 **Fax:** 01727 844779
Email: editorial@executive-grapevine.co.uk
Advertising Address: As above.
Email: s.ponte@executive-grapevine.co.uk
Web site: http://www.askgrapevine.com
Publisher: Executive Grapevine International Ltd
Date Established: 1990
Frequency: Annual - Published in January
Cover Price: £249.00
Editor: Christine Lawler; **Advertising Manager:** Sabrina Ponte
Summary of Content: Directory containing details of all the major international recruitment networks plus individual country sections. Detailed profiles include company statistics, function and industry specialisation, method of recruitment, location of assignments and salary levels.
Readership/Target Audience: Aimed at human resource directors, managers, senior line managers and individual job hunters.
ADVERTISING RATES:
Full Page Colour £2500.00
Agency Commission: 10%
Mechanical Data: Type Area: 257 x 170mm, Bleed Size: 307 x 220mm, Trim Size: 297 x 210mm, Col Length: 257mm, Page Width: 170mm, Film: Digital
Copy instructions: Copy Date: 20th of the month prior to month of publication
Average advertising content per issue: 20%
BUSINESS: COMMERCE, INDUSTRY & MANAGEMENT

DIRECTORY OF GASTROENTEROLOGY
1824163U56A-209

Editorial Address: 86 Overdale, ASHTEAD, KT21 1PU
Tel: 01372 271692 **Fax:** 01372 817737
Email: ann.bennion@btinternet.com
Advertising Address: As above.
Email: ann.bennion@btinternet.com
Web site: http://www.mediahuset.se
Publisher: Mediahuset
Date Established: 2007
Frequency: Annual - Published in April/May
Cover Price: £55.00
Circulation: 5,000 (Publisher's Statement)
Usual Pagination: 350
Editor: Ann Bennion; **Advertising Manager:** Ann Bennion
Summary of Content: Publication containing information about gastroenterologists and gastric surgeons, hospitals and the gastroenterology services they provide.
Readership/Target Audience: Aimed at gastroenterologists and gastric surgeons and industries involved in all aspects of gastroenterology and hepatology.
ADVERTISING: Rates on application
BUSINESS: HEALTH & MEDICAL

DISABILITY AND REHABILITATION
40460U56L-13_21

Editorial Address: Suffolk New College, Rope Walk, IPSWICH, IP4 1LT **Tel:** 01473 296521 **Fax:** 01473 296616
Email: dave.muller@suffolk.ac.uk
Advertising Address: As above.
Web site: http://www.informaworld.com/smpp/disabilityandrehabilitation
ISSN: 0963-8288
Publisher: Informa Healthcare
Date Established: 1979
Frequency: 26 issues yearly
Annual Sub.: £1925.00
Circulation: 500 (Publisher's Statement)
Usual Pagination: 80
Editor: Dave Muller; **Advertising Manager:** Beverly Acreman; **Managing Editor:** Sally Howells
Summary of Content: Journal covering the psycho-social aspects of disablement, clinical studies and related topics.
Readership/Target Audience: Read by medical practitioners, occupational therapists, physiotherapists, speech and language therapists.
BUSINESS: HEALTH & MEDICAL: Disability & Rehabilitation

DISASTER PREVENTION AND MANAGEMENT
39931U54R-25

Editorial Address: Department of Cybernetics & Virtual Systems, University of Bradford, Richmond Road, BRADFORD, BD7 1DP **Tel:** 01274 777700
Fax: 01274 785200
Email: h.c.wilson@bradford.ac.uk
Web site: http://www.emeraldinsight.com/dpm.htm
ISSN: 0965-3562
Publisher: Emerald Group Publishing Ltd
Date Established: 1991
Frequency: 5 issues yearly
Usual Pagination: 80
Editor: Harry Wilson; **Publisher:** Nicola Codner
Summary of Content: International academic journal devoted to disaster management and contingency planning for large scale emergencies.
Readership/Target Audience: Aimed at academics.
ADVERTISING: No Advertising taken
BUSINESS: SAFETY & SECURITY: Safety Related

DISASTERS
39932U54R-30

Editorial Address: Overseas Development Institute, 111 Westminster Bridge Road, LONDON, SE1 7JD
Tel: 020 7922 0300 **Fax:** 020 7922 0399
Email: disasters@odi.org.uk
Web site: http://www.blackwellpublishers.co.uk/journals/disa
ISSN: 0361-3666
Publisher: Wiley-Blackwell Publishing
Date Established: 1977
Frequency: Quarterly
Annual Sub.: £49.00
Circulation: 1,000 (Publisher's Statement)
Usual Pagination: 96
Editor: Paul Harvey; **Managing Editor:** Paul Harvey
Summary of Content: Publication covering all aspects of disaster studies, policy and relief management internationally. Adopts a worldwide geographical perspective and contains a mix of academic papers, field studies and book reviews.
Readership/Target Audience: Aimed at academics, policy makers and practitioners.
ADVERTISING: No Advertising taken
BUSINESS: SAFETY & SECURITY: Safety Related

DISCOURSE & SOCIETY
40042U55-50_90

Editorial Address: 1 Oliver's Yard, 55 City Road, LONDON, EC1Y 1SP **Tel:** 020 7324 8500 **Fax:** 020 7324 8600
Email: journals@discourse-in-society.org
Advertising Address: As above.
Email: sheena.karim@sagepub.co.uk
Web site: http://www.sagepub.co.uk
ISSN: 0957-9265
Publisher: Sage Publications
Date Established: 1990
Frequency: 6 issues yearly
Cover Price: £10.00
Annual Sub.: £46.00
Editor: Teun Van Dijk; **Advertising Manager:** Sheena Karim
Summary of Content: Journal that explores the relevance of discourse analysis to the social sciences with a problem-orientated and critical approach.
Readership/Target Audience: Aimed at those in social science concerned with the political implications of discourse and communication.
ADVERTISING RATES:
Full Page Mono £400.00
Agency Commission: 5%
Mechanical Data: Col Length: 210mm, Page Width: 140mm, Film: Digital, Type Area: 210 x 140mm
BUSINESS: APPLIED SCIENCE & LABORATORIES

DISPENSING OPTICS
40405U56E-410

Editorial Address: PO Box 233, CROWBOROUGH, TN6 9BD **Tel:** 01892 667626 **Fax:** 01892 667626
Email: do@abdo.uk.com
Advertising Address: As above. **Fax:** 01892 668547
Email: shope@abdo.uk.com
Web site: http://www.abdo.org.uk
ISSN: 0954-3201
Publisher: ABDO
Date Established: 1986
Frequency: Monthly
Annual Sub.: £60.00
Circulation: 8,500 (Publisher's Statement)
Usual Pagination: 16
Editor: Sheila Hope; **News Editor:** Nicky Collinson; **Features Editor:** Ann Johnson; **Advertising Manager:** Sheila Hope
Summary of Content: Journal of the Association of British Dispensing Opticians containing news, updates and product reviews.
Readership/Target Audience: Read by dispensing opticians.

ADVERTISING RATES:
Full Page Colour £1100.00
Agency Commission: 10%
Mechanical Data: Type Area: 271 x 185mm, Bleed Size: 303 x 214mm, Trim Size: 297 x 210mm, Col Length: 271mm, Page Width: 185mm, Film: Digital
Copy instructions: Copy Date: 3 weeks prior to publication date
Average advertising content per issue: 20%
BUSINESS: HEALTH & MEDICAL: Optics

DISPLAY MONITOR
36062U5B-71

Editorial Address: 1 Blackdown Road, Deepcut, CAMBERLEY, GU16 6SH **Tel:** 01252 835385
Fax: 01252 838621
Email: displaymonitor@meko.co.uk
Web site: http://www.meko.co.uk
ISSN: 1356-109X
Publisher: Meko Ltd
Date Established: 1994
Frequency: Weekly
Annual Sub.: £749.00
Circulation: 130 (Publisher's Statement)
Usual Pagination: 24
Editor: Pete Gamby; **Managing Editor:** Pete Gamby
Summary of Content: Newsletter covering all aspects of the display business. Includes news, products, trends and events.
Readership/Target Audience: Aimed at those in the display business trade.
ADVERTISING: No Advertising taken
BUSINESS: COMPUTERS & AUTOMATION: Data Processing

DIVERSITY LEAGUE TABLE
1852124U44-3060

Editorial Address: c/o Webster Dixon, 4th Floor, Thavies Inn House, 3-4 Holborn Circus, LONDON, EC1N 2HA
Tel: 020 7366 6311
Email: bsn@satsumaconsultancy.co.uk
Advertising Address: Suite 9, St. Lukes Business Centre, 85 Tarling Road, Royal Docks, LONDON, E16 1HN
Tel: 020 7366 6311 **Fax:** 020 7511 9500
Email: godwin@satsumaconsultancy.co.uk
Web site: http://www.blacksolicitorsnetwork.co.uk
Publisher: The Black Solicitors Network
Date Established: 2006
Frequency: Annual - Published in October
Cover Price: £75.00
Free to qualifying individuals
Circulation: 5,000 (Controlled Circulation)
Usual Pagination: 84
Editor: Michael Webster
Summary of Content: The Diversity League Table is a comprehensive analysis of gender and ethnicity within the legal profession in England & Wales. It looks at some of the top 150 law firms in the UK. As well as providing an analysis of major international law firms with bases in the UK. The publication also carries limited editorial.
Readership/Target Audience: It is accessible to all of the top law firms in the UK. Additionally it can also be accessed by all law schools and colleges across the country and overseas. It is also read by procurement heads of major listed companies as means of comparing actual diversity performance against stated diversity policy within potential supplier companies.
ADVERTISING RATES:
Full Page Colour £2995.00
Agency Commission: 10%
Mechanical Data: Bleed Size: 303 x 216mm, Trim Size: 297 x 210mm
BUSINESS: LEGAL

DIY WEEK
38092U25-20

Editorial Address: Faversham House, 232A Addington Road, SOUTH CROYDON, CR2 8LE **Tel:** 020 8651 7100
Fax: 020 8651 7117
Email: will.parsons@fav-house.com
Advertising Address: As above. **Tel:** 020 8651 7081
Email: rachael.pearson@fav-house.com
Web site: http://www.diyweek.net
Publisher: Faversham House Group Ltd
Date Established: 1874
Frequency: 25 issues yearly
Free to qualifying individuals
Annual Sub.: £102.00
Circulation: 7,900 (ABC 01/01/2008 to 31/12/2008)
Usual Pagination: 24
Editor: Will Parsons; **Publisher:** Colin Petty
Summary of Content: Magazine covering new products, promotions and news in the hardware, garden, housewares and DIY markets.
Readership/Target Audience: Aimed at retailers, wholesalers and suppliers.
ADVERTISING RATES:
Full Page Mono £2200.00
Full Page Colour £2500.00
Agency Commission: 10%

Mechanical Data: Page Width: 217mm, Type Area: 288 x 217mm, Col Length: 288mm, Trim Size: 300 x 230mm, Bleed Size: 306 x 236mm, Film: Digital
Copy instructions: Copy Date: 10 days prior to publication date
Average advertising content per issue: 50%
Supplement(s): DIY Retail Leaders - 1xY, Garden Retail Leaders - 1xY, Wholesale Retail Leaders - 1xY
BUSINESS: HARDWARE

DOCUMENT MANAGER
38649U34-35

Editorial Address: 35 Station Square, Petts Wood, ORPINGTON, BR5 1LZ **Tel:** 01689 616000
Fax: 01689 616622
Email: mark.lyward@btc.co.uk
Advertising Address: As above.
Email: liam.norval@btc.co.uk
Web site: http://www.dmmagazine.com
Publisher: Business & Technical Communications
Date Established: 1992
Frequency: 6 issues yearly
Cover Price: £2.95
Free to qualifying individuals
Annual Sub.: £29.00
Circulation: 6,000 (Publisher's Statement)
Usual Pagination: 36
Editor: David Tyler; **News Editor:** Mark Lyward; **Publisher:** Stuart Leigh
Summary of Content: Magazine covering document management, imaging and workgroup computing.
Readership/Target Audience: Aimed at management in banking, local government, utilities, insurance, engineering and health sectors.
ADVERTISING RATES:
Full Page Colour £1850.00
Agency Commission: 10%
Mechanical Data: Type Area: 287 x 200mm, Col Length: 287mm, Page Width: 200mm, Film: Digital, Trim Size: 297 x 210mm, Bleed Size: 307 x 220mm
Copy instructions: Copy Date: 7 days prior to publication date
Average advertising content per issue: 40%
BUSINESS: OFFICE EQUIPMENT

DORSET BUSINESS
41274U63B-395

Formerly: Dorset Business South
Editorial Address: Richmond Hill, BOURNEMOUTH, BH2 6HH **Tel:** 01202 411300 **Fax:** 01202 551246
Email: tim.saunders@bournemouthecho.co.uk
Advertising Address: As above. **Tel:** 01202 411419
Fax: 01202 411447
Email: mark.whittam@bournemouthecho.co.uk
Web site: http://www.dorsetbusiness.co.uk
Publisher: Dorset Business - The Chamber of Commerce and Industry
Frequency: 10 issues yearly - Published in the 2nd week of the month
Cover Price: Free
Circulation: 5,000 (Publisher's Statement)
Usual Pagination: 72
Editor: Tim Saunders
Summary of Content: Magazine of the Dorset Chamber of Commerce and Industry. Contains business news, profiles and sections on motoring, health and fitness.
Readership/Target Audience: Aimed at businesses in Dorset.
ADVERTISING RATES:
Full Page Colour £550.00
Agency Commission: 10%
Mechanical Data: Type Area: 300 x 234.5mm, Col Length: 300mm, Page Width: 234.5mm, Film: Digital, Col Widths (Display): 28mm, No. of Columns (Display): 8
Copy instructions: Copy Date: 2 weeks prior to publication date
Average advertising content per issue: 50%
BUSINESS: REGIONAL BUSINESS: Regional Business English Counties

DOWNSTREAM
38576U33-1_40

Editorial Address: 6 Royal Court, Tatton Street, KNUTSFORD, WA16 6EN **Tel:** 01565 631313
Fax: 01565 631314
Email: downstream@fpsonline.co.uk
Advertising Address: The Old Pound, Ludford, LUDLOW, SY8 1PP **Tel:** 01584 877442 **Fax:** 01584 875416
Email: shirley.price@btconnect.com
Web site: http://www.fpsonline.co.uk
ISSN: 1473-5539
Publisher: Federation of Petroleum Suppliers
Date Established: 1998
Frequency: 5 issues yearly
Annual Sub.: £25.00
Circulation: 1,800 (Publisher's Statement)
Usual Pagination: 28
Editor: Susan Hancock; **Advertising Manager:** Shirley Price

Section 4 (b) Business Magazines

Business Magazines

Summary of Content: Magazine covering the downstream oil distribution industry including news, developments, legislation and environmental matters, tank and tanker manufacture and commercial vehicle updates.
Readership/Target Audience: Senior managers and decision makers in the oil distribution industry throughout Britain and Ireland.
ADVERTISING RATES:
Full Page Colour £1317.00
Agency Commission: 10%
Mechanical Data: Bleed Size: 300 x 213mm, Trim Size: 297 x 210mm, Film: Digital
Average advertising content per issue: 20%
BUSINESS: OIL & PETROLEUM

DPA
39606U19B-160

Formerly: Design Products & Applications
Editorial Address: Blair House, 184-186 High Street, TONBRIDGE, TN9 1BQ **Tel:** 01732 359990
Fax: 01732 770049
Email: les.hunt@imlgroup.co.uk
Advertising Address: As above.
Email: barrie.barradell@imlgroup.co.uk
Web site: http://www.dpaonthenet.net
ISSN: 0965-4745
Publisher: IML Group plc
Date Established: 1979
Frequency: Monthly - Published in the 1st week of the cover month
Cover Price: £11.00
Free to qualifying individuals
Annual Sub.: £109.00
Circulation: 21,883 (ABC 01/01/2008 to 31/12/2008)
Usual Pagination: 52
Editor: Les Hunt
Summary of Content: Magazine containing product information, application stories and case studies.
Readership/Target Audience: Aimed at design engineers.
ADVERTISING RATES:
Full Page Colour £3855.00
Agency Commission: 10%
Mechanical Data: Film: Digital, Print Process: Web-fed offset litho, Bleed Size: 306 x 216mm, Type Area: 283 x 198mm, No. of Columns (Display): 4, Col Length: 283mm, Page Width: 198mm, Trim Size: 300 x 213mm
Copy instructions: Copy Date: 2 weeks prior to publication date
Average advertising content per issue: 60%
Supplement(s): Drives and automation - 5xY
BUSINESS: ENGINEERING & MACHINERY: Engineering - Design

DPC
39405U45D-66

Editorial Address: 3rd Floor, Lombard House, 3 Princess Way, REDHILL, RH1 1UP **Tel:** 01737 379159
Fax: 01737 379159
Email: tony.slinn@lrfairplay.com
Advertising Address: As above. **Tel:** 01737 379000
Fax: 01737 379001
Email: daniel.goncalves@lrfairplay.com
Web site: http://www.dpcmagazine.com
ISSN: 0264-4835
Publisher: Lloyd's Register-Fairplay Ltd
Date Established: 1968
Frequency: Monthly - Published in the 3rd week of the month prior to cover month
Cover Price: £14.50
Annual Sub.: £180.00
Circulation: 3,500 (Publisher's Statement)
Usual Pagination: 52
Editor: Tony Slinn; **Editor-in-Chief:** Tony Slinn
Summary of Content: Magazine covering all aspects of the world port development industry with the accent on engineering techniques and dredging operations.
Readership/Target Audience: Read by marine civil engineering professionals and port managers globally.
ADVERTISING RATES:
Full Page Colour £2813.00
Agency Commission: 10%
Mechanical Data: Type Area: 261 x 185mm, Bleed Size: 303 x 216mm, Trim Size: 297 x 210mm, Col Length: 261mm, Page Width: 185mm, Film: Digital
Copy instructions: Copy Date: 10th of the month prior to publication date
Average advertising content per issue: 45%
Supplement(s): The INternational Directory of Dredging - 1xY
BUSINESS: MARINE & SHIPPING: Marine Engineering Equipment

DRAIN TRADER MAGAZINE
39053U42C-150

Editorial Address: Units 6-8, Home Farm, Quat Goose Lane, Swindon Village, CHELTENHAM, GL51 9RP
Tel: 01242 576777 **Fax:** 01242 577733
Email: info@draintraderltd.com
Advertising Address: As above.
Email: info@draintraderltd.com

Web site: http://www.draintraderltd.com
Publisher: Drain Trader Ltd
Date Established: 1998
Frequency: Monthly - Published on the 1st working day of the cover month
Free to qualifying individuals
Annual Sub.: £45.00
Circulation: 4,500 (Publisher's Statement)
Usual Pagination: 96
Editor: Lorraine Scale; **Managing Director:** Lorraine Scale;
Advertising Manager: Lorraine Scale
Summary of Content: Magazine covering all aspects of drainage, the latest trenchless technology, health and safety, training, environmental and water news, new products and finance.
Readership/Target Audience: Aimed at those within the drainage and sewage industry, including water boards and local authorities.
ADVERTISING RATES:
Full Page Mono £695.00
Full Page Colour £995.00
SCC £2.50
Agency Commission: 10%
Mechanical Data: Type Area: 264 x 182mm, Col Length: 264mm, Page Width: 182mm, Film: Digital, Bleed Size: +3mm, Trim Size: 297 x 210mm
Copy instructions: Copy Date: 20th of the month prior to publication date
Average advertising content per issue: 40%
BUSINESS: CONSTRUCTION: Water Engineering

DRAM - DRINKS RETAILING & MARKETING
36475U9A-50

Formerly: Dram
Editorial Address: Upper Floor, Finnieston House, 1 Stables Yard, 1103 Argyle Street, GLASGOW, G3 8ND
Tel: 0141 221 6965 **Fax:** 0141 221 7641
Email: susan@mediaworldltd.com
Advertising Address: As above.
Email: sales@mediaworldltd.com
Web site: http://www.dramscotland.co.uk
ISSN: 1470-241X
Publisher: Media World Ltd
Date Established: 1994
Frequency: Monthly - Published the first week of the month
Free to qualifying individuals
Annual Sub.: £42.00
Circulation: 8,000 (Publisher's Statement)
Usual Pagination: 40
Editor: Susan Young; **Advertising Manager:** Cheryl Beattie;
Publisher: Susan Young
Summary of Content: Trade magazine covering drinks, design, new bars and interviews with licensees.
Readership/Target Audience: Aimed at the licensed trade throughout Scotland.
ADVERTISING RATES:
Full Page Mono £1200.00
Full Page Colour £1500.00
Agency Commission: 10%
Mechanical Data: Trim Size: 265 x 210mm, Type Area: 238 X 188mm, Col Length: 238mm, Page Width: 188mm, Bleed Size: 271 x 216mm, Film: Digital
Copy instructions: Copy Date: 20th of the month prior to publication date
Average advertising content per issue: 50%
BUSINESS: DRINKS & LICENSED TRADE: Drinks, Licensed Trade, Wines & Spirits

DRAMA
41019U62B-100

Editorial Address: University of Strathclyde, Southbrae Drive, GLASGOW, G13 1PP **Tel:** 0141 950 3743
Fax: 020 7722 4730
Email: m.j.mcnaughton@strath.ac.uk
Advertising Address: Underwood, Wells Road, Rodney Stoke, CHEDDAR, BS27 3XB **Tel:** 01749 870239
Email: peter.wild@nationaldrama.co.uk
Web site: http://www.dramamagazine.co.uk
ISSN: 0967-4454
Publisher: National Drama Publications
Date Established: 1993
Frequency: Half-yearly - Published in January and July
Free to qualifying individuals
Annual Sub.: £18.00
Circulation: 1,250 (Publisher's Statement)
Usual Pagination: 52
Editor: Marie Jeanne McNaughton; **Advertising Manager:** Peter Wild
Summary of Content: Journal of National Drama covering theory and practice, key issues, research and analysis.
Readership/Target Audience: Aimed at members of National Drama, teachers and advisers for drama and English and theatre workers.
ADVERTISING: Rates on application
Agency Commission: 10%
Average advertising content per issue: 5%
BUSINESS: CHURCH & SCHOOL EQUIPMENT & EDUCATION: Education Teachers

DRAPERS
39488U47A-95

Formerly: Drapers Record
Editorial Address: Greater London House, Hampstead Road, LONDON, NW1 7EJ **Tel:** 020 7728 5000
Fax: 020 7828 3500
Email: drapers@emap.com
Advertising Address: As above. **Fax:** 020 7728 3500
Email: lucy.walsh@emap.com
Web site: http://www.drapersonline.com
ISSN: 0967-3776
Publisher: EMAP Inform
Date Established: 1887
Frequency: Weekly - Published on Saturday
Cover Price: £3.20
Annual Sub.: £120.00
Circulation: 10,536 (ABC 01/07/2008 to 30/06/2009)
Usual Pagination: 52
Editor: Jessica Price Brown; **News Editor:** Jessica Price Brown; **Features Editor:** Khabi Mirza; **Advertising Manager:** Lucy Walsh; **Managing Editor:** Jessica Price Brown
Summary of Content: Journal covering all aspects of the fashion industry.
Readership/Target Audience: Aimed at retailers of womenswear, childrenswear, menswear and footwear and their suppliers.
ADVERTISING RATES:
Full Page Colour £4624.00
Agency Commission: 10%
Mechanical Data: Col Length: 280mm, Page Width: 210mm, Film: Digital, Trim Size: 300 x 230mm, Type Area: 280 x 210mm, Bleed Size: 306 x 236mm
Copy instructions: Copy Date: 2 weeks prior to publication date
Supplement(s): Footwear and Accessories - 2xY, Menswear - 2xY, Seasons Preview - 2xY, Sports Jeans - 2xY, Womenswear - 2xY
BUSINESS: CLOTHING & TEXTILES

THE DRINKS BUSINESS
765019U9A-251

Editorial Address: Unit 222-223, 30 Great Guildford Street, LONDON, SE1 OHS **Tel:** 020 7803 2420 **Fax:** 020 7803 2421
Email: info@thedrinksbusiness.com
Advertising Address: As above.
Email: david.hennelly@thedrinksbusiness.com
Web site: http://www.thedrinksbusiness.com
Publisher: Union Press Ltd
Date Established: 2002
Frequency: Monthly
Cover Price: £5.50
Free to qualifying individuals
Circulation: 10,000 (Publisher's Statement)
Usual Pagination: 100
Editor: Patrick Schmitt; **News Editor:** Alan Lodge;
Advertising Manager: David Hennelly; **Publisher:** Charlotte Hey
Summary of Content: Magazine covering key business and marketing issues and major trends in the wine and spirits industry, including PR, finance and the city.
Readership/Target Audience: Aimed at CEOs, MDs, directors, buyers, marketing and PR managers and leading professionals within the wine and spirits industry.
ADVERTISING RATES:
Full Page Colour £3450.00
Agency Commission: 10%
Mechanical Data: Type Area: 262 x 190mm, Trim Size: 297 x 230mm, Bleed Size: 305 x 238mm, Col Length: 262mm, Page Width: 190mm, Film: Digital
Copy instructions: Copy Date: 2 weeks prior to publication date
Average advertising content per issue: 40%
BUSINESS: DRINKS & LICENSED TRADE: Drinks, Licensed Trade, Wines & Spirits

DRINKS INTERNATIONAL
36476U9A-65

Editorial Address: Gateway House, 42A East Park, CRAWLEY, RH10 6AS **Tel:** 01293 590046
Email: david.longfield@drinksint.com
Advertising Address: As above. **Tel:** 01293 590041
Fax: 01293 763200
Email: justin.smith@drinksint.com
Web site: http://www.drinksint.com
ISSN: 0012-625X
Publisher: Agile Media
Frequency: Monthly - Published in the 1st week of the cover month
Free to qualifying individuals
Annual Sub.: £105.00
Circulation: 5,901 (ABC 01/07/2008 to 30/06/2009)
Usual Pagination: 56
Editor: David Longfield; **News Editor:** Lucy Britner;
Publisher: Russell Dodd
Summary of Content: Magazine covering international alcoholic drink products, marketing and trends.
Readership/Target Audience: For international buyers, distributors and agents of wines and spirits and other alcoholic drinks.

ADVERTISING RATES:
Full Page Colour £3226.00
Agency Commission: 10%
Mechanical Data: Type Area: 250 x 203mm, Bleed Size: 291 x 236mm, Trim Size: 285 x 230mm, Col Length: 250mm, Page Width: 203mm, Film: Digital
Copy instructions: Copy Date: 2 weeks prior to publication date
Average advertising content per issue: 40%
BUSINESS: DRINKS & LICENSED TRADE: Drinks, Licensed Trade, Wines & Spirits

DRIVES & CONTROLS
37541U19A-120

Editorial Address: Cape House, 60A Priory Road, TONBRIDGE, TN9 2BL **Tel:** 01732 370340
Fax: 01732 360034
Email: tony@drives.co.uk
Advertising Address: As above.
Email: simon@dfamedia.co.uk
Web site: http://www.drives.co.uk
ISSN: 0950-5490
Publisher: DFA Media Ltd
Date Established: 1986
Frequency: 10 issues yearly - Published in the 1st week of the cover month
Free to qualifying individuals
Annual Sub.: £90.00
Circulation: 19,997 (ABC 01/01/2008 to 31/12/2008)
Usual Pagination: 80
Editor: Tony Sacks; **Advertising Manager:** Simon Langston
Summary of Content: Magazine covering power transmission and motion control equipment. Also includes electronics, electrical, hydraulic, pneumatic and mechanical drive equipment.
Readership/Target Audience: Read by specifiers and buyers.
ADVERTISING RATES:
Full Page Mono £1920.00
Full Page Colour £2670.00
Mechanical Data: Page Width: 178mm, Type Area: 261 x 178mm, Col Length: 261mm, Bleed Size: 298 x 216mm, Trim Size: 297 x 210mm, Film: Positive, right reading, emulsion side down. Digital, Print Process: Web-fed offset
Copy instructions: Copy Date: 4 weeks prior to publication date
Supplement(s): Annual Buyers Guide - 1xY
BUSINESS: ENGINEERING & MACHINERY

DRIVING INSTRUCTOR
23029U31D-4

Editorial Address: Safety House, Beddington Farm Road, CROYDON, CR0 4XZ **Tel:** 020 8665 5151
Fax: 020 8665 5565
Email: drivinginstructor@driving.org
Advertising Address: As above.
Email: davidbreary@aol.com
Web site: http://www.driving.org
Publisher: DIA International Ltd
Date Established: 1988
Frequency: 6 issues yearly
Annual Sub.: £15.00
Circulation: 18,000 (Publisher's Statement)
Usual Pagination: 20
Editor: Stephen Picton; **Advertising Manager:** David Breary; **Managing Editor:** Graham Fryer
Summary of Content: Magazine covering developments in the world of driving instruction, articles include political comments and road tests.
Readership/Target Audience: Aimed at members of the Driving Instructor Association and is also distributed to DSA Driving Test Centres.
ADVERTISING RATES:
Full Page Colour £2200.00
Agency Commission: 10%
Mechanical Data: Type Area: 333 x 265mm, Col Length: 333mm, Col Widths (Display): 64mm, Print Process: Sheet-fed litho, No. of Columns (Display): 4, Trim Size: 375 x 285mm, Page Width: 265mm, Film: Digital
Copy instructions: Copy Date: 2 weeks prior to publication date
Average advertising content per issue: 45%
BUSINESS: MOTOR TRADE: Driving Schools

DRIVING MAGAZINE
38360U31D-10

Editorial Address: Safety House, Beddington Farm Road, CROYDON, CR0 4XZ **Tel:** 020 8665 5151
Fax: 020 8665 5565
Email: drivingmagazine@driving.org
Advertising Address: As above. **Tel:** 020 8665 8027
Email: davidbreary@aol.com
Web site: http://www.driving.org
ISSN: 0265-7716
Publisher: DIA International Ltd
Date Established: 1978
Frequency: 6 issues yearly
Cover Price: £2.50
Annual Sub.: £53.50
Circulation: 15,000 (Publisher's Statement)

Usual Pagination: 60
Editor: Stephen Picton; **Advertising Manager:** David Breary; **Managing Editor:** Graham Fryer
Summary of Content: Magazine containing road safety facts, new legislation, driving techniques and car advice.
Readership/Target Audience: Aimed at advanced drivers, driving instructors, examiners and road safety educationalists.
ADVERTISING RATES:
Full Page Mono £2200.00
Full Page Colour £2200.00
SCC £25.00
Agency Commission: 10%
Mechanical Data: Type Area: 270 x 190mm, Bleed Size: 303 x 213mm, Trim Size: 297 x 210mm, No. of Columns (Display): 3, Col Length: 270mm, Page Width: 190mm, Film: Digital, Col Widths (Display): 65mm
Copy instructions: Copy Date: 2 weeks prior to publication date
Average advertising content per issue: 40%
BUSINESS: MOTOR TRADE: Driving Schools

DRUG & THERAPEUTICS BULLETIN
1655802U56A-177

Editorial Address: BMJ House, Tavistock Square, LONDON, WC1H 9JR **Tel:** 020 7383 6885
Fax: 020 7383 6668
Email: dtb@bmjgroup.com
Web site: http://www.dtb.org.uk
ISSN: 0012-6543
Publisher: BMJ Publishing Group
Date Established: 1962
Frequency: Monthly
Free to qualifying individuals
Annual Sub.: £49.00
Circulation: 130,000 (Publisher's Statement)
Editor: Michael Allen
Summary of Content: Magazine providing independent evaluations of, and practical advice on, individual treatments and the management of disease.
Readership/Target Audience: Aimed at doctors, pharmacists, nurses and other healthcare professionals.
ADVERTISING: No Advertising taken
BUSINESS: HEALTH & MEDICAL

DRUG DELIVERY INSIGHT
1614670U37-404

Editorial Address: Lincoln House, City Fields Business Park, City Fields Way, Tangmere, CHICHESTER, PO20 2FS **Tel:** 01243 533322 **Fax:** 01243 533418
Email: health@espicom.com
Web site: http://www.espicom.com
Publisher: Espicom Ltd
Date Established: 2001
Frequency: 26 issues yearly
Annual Sub.: £475.00
Circulation: 1,500 (Publisher's Statement)
Usual Pagination: 24
Editor: Laura Watson
Summary of Content: Newsletter covering global injection devices, infusion pumps, transdermal delivery, slow/controlled release, implantable and biotech related drug-delivery technology.
Readership/Target Audience: Aimed at personnel within drug delivery companies.
ADVERTISING: No Advertising taken
BUSINESS: PHARMACEUTICAL & CHEMISTS

DRUG DISCOVERY TODAY
38730U37-23

Editorial Address: 32 Jamestown Road, LONDON, NW1 7BY **Tel:** 020 7424 4314 **Fax:** 01865 853067
Email: ddt@drugdiscoverytoday.com
Advertising Address: As above. **Tel:** 020 7424 4400
Fax: 01865 853136
Email: j.kenney@elsevier.com
Web site: http://www.drugdiscoverytoday.com
ISSN: 1359-6446
Publisher: Elsevier London Ltd
Date Established: 1995
Frequency: Monthly - Published around the 1st of the cover month
Cover Price: EUR282.00
Free to qualifying individuals
Annual Sub.: EUR2321.00
Circulation: 1,000 (Publisher's Statement)
Usual Pagination: 104
Editor: Steve Carney
Summary of Content: Magazine covering news, reviews and current awareness in key areas of pharmaceutical and biotechnology research.
Readership/Target Audience: Read by pharmaceutical research scientists, both in industry and academia, including medicinal chemists and molecular biologists.
ADVERTISING RATES:
Full Page Colour $2745.00
Agency Commission: 10%

Mechanical Data: Page Width: 186mm, Type Area: 243 x 186mm, Col Length: 243mm, Trim Size: 280 x 216mm, Bleed Size: 290 x 226mm
Copy instructions: Copy Date: 3 weeks prior to publication date
Average advertising content per issue: 10%
BUSINESS: PHARMACEUTICAL & CHEMISTS

DRUG DISCOVERY WORLD
629264U37-24

Editorial Address: 39 Vineyard Path, Mortlake, LONDON, SW14 8ET **Tel:** 020 8487 5656 **Fax:** 020 8487 5666
Email: robert@rjcoms.com
Advertising Address: As above.
Email: damian@rjcoms.com
Web site: http://www.ddw-online.com
ISSN: 1469-4344
Publisher: RJ Communications & Media Ltd
Date Established: 2000
Frequency: Quarterly
Free to qualifying individuals
Annual Sub.: £85.00
Circulation: 15,000 (Publisher's Statement)
Usual Pagination: 92
Editor: Robert Jordan; **Features Editor:** Sue Denim; **Editor-in-Chief:** Robert Jordan; **Advertising Manager:** Damian Doherty; **Publisher:** Robert Jordan
Summary of Content: Magazine containing a business review of drug discovery and development.
Readership/Target Audience: Aimed at pharmaceutical research and development professionals.
ADVERTISING RATES:
Full Page Colour £4350.00
Agency Commission: 10%
Mechanical Data: Film: Digital, Bleed Size: 303 x 216mm, Trim Size: 297 x 210mm, Type Area: 253 x 177mm, Col Length: 253mm, Page Width: 177mm
Average advertising content per issue: 40%
BUSINESS: PHARMACEUTICAL & CHEMISTS

DRUGLINK
1664693U56L-125

Editorial Address: Prince Consort House, 109-111 Farringdon Road, LONDON, EC1R 3BW **Tel:** 020 7520 7550
Email: maxd@drugscope.org.uk
Advertising Address: As above. **Tel:** 020 7940 7500
Email: maxd@drugscope.org.uk
Web site: http://www.drugscope.org.uk
Publisher: Drugscope
Date Established: 1975
Frequency: 6 issues yearly
Annual Sub.: £55.00
Circulation: 2,000 (Publisher's Statement)
Editor: Max Daly; **Advertising Manager:** Harry Shapiro
Summary of Content: Magazine focusing on drug related issues including news, analysis and interviews.
Readership/Target Audience: Aimed at drugs professionals.
ADVERTISING RATES:
Full Page Mono £640.00
Full Page Colour £640.00
Mechanical Data: Type Area: 250 x 182mm, Trim Size: 297 x 210mm, Col Length: 250mm, Page Width: 182mm, No. of Columns (Display): 1, Print Process: Litho, Film: Digital
Average advertising content per issue: 15%
BUSINESS: HEALTH & MEDICAL: Disability & Rehabilitation

DRUGS AND ALCOHOL TODAY
1647180U56R-510

Editorial Address: Richmond House, Richmond Road, BRIGHTON, BN2 3RL **Tel:** 01273 623222
Fax: 01273 625526
Email: joannas@pavpub.com
Advertising Address: As above. **Tel:** 0870 890 1080
Fax: 0870 890 1080
Email: pauls@pavpub.com
Web site: http://www.pavpub.com
ISSN: 1475-0384
Publisher: Pavilion Journals (Brighton) Ltd
Date Established: 2001
Frequency: Quarterly
Annual Sub.: £40.00
Circulation: 400 (Publisher's Statement)
Usual Pagination: 48
Editor: Joanna Sharrocks; **Advertising Manager:** Paul Somerville
Summary of Content: Journal focusing on substance misuse, including articles on legislative matters, policy and news.
Readership/Target Audience: Aimed at professionals involved or affected by substance misuse.
ADVERTISING RATES:
Full Page Mono £350.00
Agency Commission: 10%
Mechanical Data: Type Area: 240 x 170mm, Col Length: 240mm, Page Width: 170mm
BUSINESS: HEALTH & MEDICAL: Health Medical Related

DRUGS IN CONTEXT
1616620U56A-174

Editorial Address: Suite 119, Eagle Tower, Montpellier Drive, CHELTENHAM, GL50 1TA **Tel:** 01242 223890
Email: enquiries@drugsincontext.com
Web site: http://www.drugsincontext.com
ISSN: 1745-1981
Publisher: CSF Medical Communications Ltd
Date Established: 2003
Frequency: 6 issues yearly
Cover Price: £14.95
Circulation: 50,000 (Publisher's Statement)
Usual Pagination: 96
Editor: Julian Grover
Summary of Content: Independent peer reviewed publication focusing on drug and disease management covering all of the major diseases and clinical conditions encountered, and the drugs available to help prevent and treat them, whilst taking into account differences in epidemiology, culture and medical practice.
Readership/Target Audience: Aimed at healthcare professionals worldwide.
ADVERTISING: No Advertising taken
BUSINESS: HEALTH & MEDICAL

THE DRUM
35465U2A-15

Formerly: Adline
Editorial Address: 5 Oak Street, Northern Quarter, MANCHESTER, M4 5JD **Tel:** 0161 819 5651
Email: richard.draycott@carnyx.com
Advertising Address: 4th Floor, Mercat Building, 26 Gallowgate, GLASGOW, G1 5AB **Tel:** 0141 552 5858
Fax: 0141 559 6050
Email: chris.morton@carnyx.com
Web site: http://www.thedrum.co.uk
ISSN: 1353-7318
Publisher: Rush Media Ltd
Date Established: 1980
Frequency: 26 issues yearly
Annual Sub.: £94.50
Circulation: 8,000 (Publisher's Statement)
Usual Pagination: 48
Editor: Gordon Young; **News Editor:** Stephen Lepitak;
Publisher: Gordon Young
Summary of Content: Magazine covering news and features about media, creative, marketing and advertising industries in England outside of the M25.
Readership/Target Audience: Aimed at decision makers in major client companies and their marketing agencies.
ADVERTISING RATES:
Full Page Colour £1450.00
Agency Commission: 10%
Mechanical Data: Type Area: 298 x 216mm, Trim Size: 330 x 240mm, Bleed Size: 333 x 243mm, Film: Digital, Col Length: 298mm, Page Width: 216mm
Copy instructions: Copy Date: Monday prior to publication date
Average advertising content per issue: 60%
BUSINESS: COMMUNICATIONS, ADVERTISING & MARKETING

THE DRUM
35493U2A-71

Editorial Address: 4th Floor, The Mercat Building, 26 Gallowgate, GLASGOW, G1 5AB **Tel:** 0141 552 5858
Email: thomas@carnyx.com
Advertising Address: As above. **Fax:** 0141 559 6050
Email: sales@carnyx.com
Web site: http://www.thedrum.co.uk
Publisher: Carnyx Group Ltd
Date Established: 1985
Frequency: 26 issues yearly - Published on Friday
Cover Price: £3.95
Circulation: 12,000 (Publisher's Statement)
Usual Pagination: 40
Editor: Thomas O'Neill; **News Editor:** Stephen Lepitak;
Managing Director: Diane Young; **Publisher:** Gordon Young
Summary of Content: Magazine covering all aspects of the media and marketing industry in Scotland.
Readership/Target Audience: Read by account managers and managing directors of companies within the marketing and media industries.
ADVERTISING RATES:
Full Page Colour £1150.00
Agency Commission: 10%
Mechanical Data: Page Width: 216mm, Type Area: 298 x 216mm, Col Length: 298mm, Trim Size: 330 x 240mm, Bleed Size: +3mm, Film: Digital
Copy instructions: Copy Date: 1 week prior to publication date
Average advertising content per issue: 40%
BUSINESS: COMMUNICATIONS, ADVERTISING & MARKETING

THE DRUM YEARBOOK
35553U2A-15_50

Editorial Address: 5 Oak Street, Northern Quarter, MANCHESTER, M4 5JD **Tel:** 0121 773 5000
Fax: 0121 773 3311
Advertising Address: 4th Floor, The Mercat Building, 26 Gallowgate, GLASGOW, G1 5AB **Tel:** 0141 552 5858
Fax: 0141 552 6050
Email: emma.stewart@carnyx.com
Publisher: Carnyx Group Ltd
Date Established: 1996
Frequency: Annual - Published in January
Cover Price: £45.00
Circulation: 10,500 (Publisher's Statement)
Usual Pagination: 116
Editor: Keith Price; **Advertising Manager:** Emma Stewart;
Publisher: Gordon Young
Summary of Content: Handbook for marketing directors and managers, with analysis on predicted trends and developments within each element of the marketing mix during the year ahead. Also contains a directory of creative agencies.
Readership/Target Audience: Aimed at marketing directors and managers in major client companies.
ADVERTISING RATES:
Full Page Colour £1350.00
Agency Commission: 10%
Mechanical Data: Type Area: 268 x 206mm, Bleed Size: 306 x 236mm, Film: Digital, Col Length: 268mm, Trim Size: 300 x 230mm, Page Width: 206mm
Average advertising content per issue: 90%
BUSINESS: COMMUNICATIONS, ADVERTISING & MARKETING

DRYDOCK
39406U45D-70

Editorial Address: Peel House, Upper South View, FARNHAM, GU9 7JN **Tel:** 01252 732220 **Fax:** 01252 732221
Email: mark.langdon@drydockmagazine.com
Advertising Address: As above.
Email: info@mpigroup.co.uk
Web site: http://www.mpigroup.co.uk/drydock/index.html
ISSN: 0143-5000
Publisher: MPI Group Ltd
Date Established: 1979
Frequency: Quarterly - Published in the middle of the cover month
Annual Sub.: £58.00
Circulation: 8,275 (Publisher's Statement)
Usual Pagination: 70
Editor: Mark Langdon; **Managing Director:** Andrew Deere;
Publisher: Andrew Deere
Summary of Content: International journal covering ship repair, maintenance and conversion.
Readership/Target Audience: Read by ship owners, managers, operators and repairers.
ADVERTISING RATES:
Full Page Mono £1575.00
Full Page Colour £2175.00
Agency Commission: 10%
Mechanical Data: Bleed Size: 302 x 218mm, Trim Size: 292 x 208mm, Film: Digital, Type Area: 250 x 172mm, Page Width: 172mm, Col Length: 250mm
Average advertising content per issue: 40%
BUSINESS: MARINE & SHIPPING: Marine Engineering Equipment

DUTY FREE NEWS INTERNATIONAL
39798U53-56

Editorial Address: 6th Floor, Davis House, 2 Robert Street, CROYDON, CR0 1QQ **Tel:** 020 8253 8609
Fax: 020 8253 4603
Email: bill.lumley@dfnionline.com
Advertising Address: As above. **Tel:** 020 8253 8612
Email: amanda.felix@metropolis.com
Web site: http://www.dfnionline.com
ISSN: 1357-7077
Publisher: Metropolis International Group Ltd
Date Established: 1987
Frequency: 13 issues yearly - Published around the 15th of the cover month
Annual Sub.: £445.00
Circulation: 2,300 (Publisher's Statement)
Usual Pagination: 60
Editor: Bill Lumley; **Managing Director:** Kevin Crook;
Advertising Manager: Amanda Felix; **Publisher:** Amanda Felix
Summary of Content: Magazine covering the duty free market worldwide.
Readership/Target Audience: Read by key decision makers in retail, distribution and manufacture of duty-free goods.
ADVERTISING RATES:
Full Page Colour £3720.00
Agency Commission: 10%
Mechanical Data: Col Length: 272mm, Page Width: 185mm, Film: Digital, Print Process: Offset litho, Bleed Size: 305 x 118mm, Trim Size: 297 x 210mm, Type Area: 272 x 185mm, No. of Columns (Display): 4
BUSINESS: RETAILING & WHOLESALING

DVD & BEYOND
749619U43D-8

Formerly: DVD Primer
Editorial Address: 26 Windridge Close, ST. ALBANS, AL3 4JP **Tel:** 01727 851761 **Fax:** 01727 753454
Email: jean-luc@dvd-intelligence.com
Advertising Address: As above.
Email: jean-luc@dvd-intelligence.com
Web site: http://www.dvd-intelligence.com
Publisher: Globalcom Ltd
Date Established: 1999
Frequency: Annual - Published at the end of June
Cover Price: Free
Circulation: 10,000 (Publisher's Statement)
Usual Pagination: 60
Editor: Jean-Luc Renaud; **Advertising Manager:** Jean-Luc Renaud; **Publisher:** Jean-Luc Renaud
Summary of Content: Magazine covering the global DVD market. Includes news, products and company profiles.
Readership/Target Audience: Aimed at European professionals with an interest in DVD products.
ADVERTISING RATES:
Full Page Colour £2000.00
Agency Commission: 15%
Mechanical Data: Trim Size: 297 x 210mm, Film: Digital
Copy instructions: Copy Date: End of May prior to publication date
BUSINESS: ELECTRICAL RETAIL TRADE: Video

DYSLEXIA
40564U56R-53

Formerly: Dyslexia - An International Journal of Research & Practice
Editorial Address: The Atrium, Southern Gate, CHICHESTER, PO19 8SQ **Tel:** 01243 779777
Fax: 01243 775878
Email: a.j.fawcett@swansea.ac.uk
Advertising Address: As above. **Fax:** 01243 770432
Email: adsales@wiley.co.uk
Web site: http://www.wiley.com
ISSN: 1076-9242
Publisher: John Wiley & Sons Ltd
Date Established: 1995
Frequency: Quarterly
Annual Sub.: £205.00
Usual Pagination: 64
Editor: A. Fawcett
Summary of Content: Journal reviews and reports authoritative studies of dyslexia.
Readership/Target Audience: Aimed at academic researchers in psychology, education and medicine, teachers, psychologists, speech therapists, counsellors, psychiatrists and GPs.
ADVERTISING RATES:
Full Page Mono £2000.00
Full Page Colour £4375.00
Agency Commission: 10%
Mechanical Data: Trim Size: 248 x 165mm, Type Area: 220 x 135mm, Col Length: 220mm, Page Width: 135mm
BUSINESS: HEALTH & MEDICAL: Health Medical Related

EADT SUFFOLK BUSINESS
41353U63B-1635

Formerly: Suffolk Business
Editorial Address: Press House, 30 Lower Brook Street, IPSWICH, IP4 1AN **Tel:** 01473 324674 **Fax:** 01473 324872
Email: sheline.clarke@archant.co.uk
Advertising Address: As above. **Tel:** 01473 323003
Fax: 01473 324626
Email: mark.gallant@archant.co.uk
Web site: http://www.eadt.co.uk
Publisher: Archant Suffolk
Frequency: Monthly
Cover Price: £1.00
Free to qualifying individuals
Circulation: 5,100 (Publisher's Statement)
Usual Pagination: 72
Editor: Sheline Clarke; **Advertising Manager:** Mark Gallant
Summary of Content: Magazine published in conjunction with the Ipswich & Suffolk Chamber of Commerce, Industry & Shipping.
Readership/Target Audience: Aimed at the local business community in Suffolk, including doctors, dentists and estate agents.
ADVERTISING RATES:
Full Page Colour £615.00
Mechanical Data: Film: Digital, Type Area: 270 x 185mm, Col Length: 270mm, Page Width: 185mm, No. of Columns (Display): 4, Bleed Size: 303 x 213mm
BUSINESS: REGIONAL BUSINESS: Regional Business English Counties

EARTHMATTERS
25102U57-131

Editorial Address: 26-28 Underwood Street, LONDON, N1 7JQ **Tel:** 020 7490 1555 **Fax:** 020 7490 0881
Email: info@foe.co.uk
Advertising Address: As above.
Email: rita.marcangelo@foe.co.uk
Web site: http://www.foe.co.uk

Publisher: Friends of the Earth
Frequency: 3 issues yearly - Published in February, June and October
Cover Price: Free
Circulation: 65,000 (Publisher's Statement)
Usual Pagination: 32
Advertising Manager: Rita Marcangelo
Summary of Content: Magazine covering the activities of the Friends of The Earth. Includes articles on climate change, food, waste, transport, resource use and corporate accountability.
Readership/Target Audience: Aimed at members of Friends of The Earth.
ADVERTISING RATES:
Full Page Colour £1850.00
Mechanical Data: Type Area: 268 x 192mm, Col Length: 268mm, Page Width: 192mm, Film: Digital, Bleed Size: 297 x 210mm
BUSINESS: ENVIRONMENT & POLLUTION

EARTHMOVERS
1642436U42A-213
Editorial Address: Sundial House, 17 Wickham Road, BECKENHAM, BR3 5JS **Tel:** 020 8639 4400
Fax: 020 8639 4411
Email: editor@earthmoversmagazine.co.uk
Advertising Address: As above.
Email: ads@sundialmagazines.co.uk
Web site: http://www.earthmoversmagazine.co.uk
Publisher: Sundial Magazines Ltd
Date Established: 2004
Frequency: Monthly
Cover Price: £3.50
Annual Sub: £37.00
Circulation: 15,500 (Publisher's Statement)
Usual Pagination: 100
Editor: Graham Black; **Advertising Manager:** Paul Cosgrove
Summary of Content: Magazine covering the latest developments in earth moving machinery including site tests, buyers guides, fleet reviews and technical developments.
Readership/Target Audience: Aimed at buyers and operators of earth moving and material handling machinery.
ADVERTISING RATES:
Full Page Mono £1195.00
Full Page Colour £1495.00
Agency Commission: 10%
Mechanical Data: Type Area: 272 x 188mm, Bleed Size: 303 x 213mm, Trim Size: 297 x 210mm, Col Length: 272mm, Page Width: 188mm, Film: Digital
Copy instructions: Copy Date: 2nd week of month, 2 months prior to publication date
Average advertising content per issue: 25%
BUSINESS: CONSTRUCTION

EARTHWISE
40636U57-18_50
Editorial Address: Kingsley Dunham Centre, Keyworth, NOTTINGHAM, NG12 5GG **Tel:** 0115 936 3100
Fax: 0115 936 3200
Email: earthwise@bgs.ac.uk
Web site: http://www.bgs.ac.uk/earthwise
ISSN: 0967-9669
Publisher: British Geological Survey
Date Established: 1991
Frequency: Half-yearly - Published in March and September
Cover Price: Free
Circulation: 6,000 (Publisher's Statement)
Usual Pagination: 40
Editor: David Bailey
Summary of Content: Newsletter describing the role of the British Geological Survey, in supporting wealth creation and the quality of life through earth sciences.
Readership/Target Audience: Aimed at professional geologists in industry, national and local government scientists and financial decision-makers, chambers of commerce, diplomatic missions in the UK and overseas, international organisations, science libraries, universities, colleges and the media.
ADVERTISING: No Advertising taken
BUSINESS: ENVIRONMENT & POLLUTION

EAS EUROPEAN ADHESIVES AND SEALANTS
36642U13-5
Formerly: Adhesive Technology
Editorial Address: Westgate House, 120-130 Station Road, REDHILL, RH1 1ET **Tel:** 01737 855277 **Fax:** 01737 855034
Email: gregmorris@dmgworldmedia.com
Web site: http://www.coatingsgroup.com
ISSN: 1462-0146
Publisher: DMG Business Media
Frequency: Quarterly
Annual Sub: £103.00
Circulation: 8,211 (Publisher's Statement)
Usual Pagination: 30
Editor: Sue Tyler

Summary of Content: Magazine covering manufacturing techniques, new applications, new raw materials and general news of the industry.
Readership/Target Audience: Read by users and manufacturers of adhesives and sealants.
ADVERTISING: Rates on application
Mechanical Data: Type Area: 265 x 185mm, Col Length: 265mm, Trim Size: 297 x 210mm, Bleed Size: 303 x 216mm, Film: Digital
Supplement to: PPCJ Polymers Paint Colour Journal
BUSINESS: CHEMICALS

EASTERN DIRECTOR
41259U63B-253
Editorial Address: 14 Middletons Road, Yaxley, PETERBOROUGH, PE7 3LR **Tel:** 01733 242312
Fax: 01733 244035
Email: carol@pridepublications.co.uk
Advertising Address: As above.
Email: maxine@pridepublications.co.uk
Web site: http://www.pridepublications.co.uk
Publisher: Pride Publications Ltd
Frequency: 10 issues yearly
Cover Price: £2.00
Circulation: 3,000 (Publisher's Statement)
Usual Pagination: 16
Editor: Carol Lawless; **Managing Director:** Carol Lawless; **Publisher:** Carol Lawless
Summary of Content: Independent business magazine for business leaders.
Readership/Target Audience: Aimed at senior CEOs and senior partners.
ADVERTISING RATES:
Full Page Mono £675.00
Full Page Colour £675.00
Agency Commission: 10%
Mechanical Data: No. of Columns (Display): 3, Type Area: 272 x 187mm, Col Length: 272mm, Page Width: 187mm, Trim Size: 297 x 210mm, Bleed Size: 303 x 213mm
Copy instructions: Copy Date: 1 week prior to publication date
Average advertising content per issue: 50%
BUSINESS: REGIONAL BUSINESS: Regional Business English Counties

EASTERN EUROPEAN WIRELESS COMMUNICATIONS
622570U18A-69
Editorial Address: 3rd Floor, Brassey House, New Zealand Avenue, WALTON-ON-THAMES, KT12 1QD
Tel: 01932 886537 **Fax:** 01932 886539
Email: rahieln@kadiumpublishing.com
Advertising Address: As above.
Email: richardl@kadiumpublishing.com
Web site: http://www.kadiumonline.net
Publisher: Kadium Ltd
Date Established: 1998
Frequency: 6 issues yearly
Free to qualifying individuals
Circulation: 7,000 (Publisher's Statement)
Usual Pagination: 40
Editor: Rahiel Nasir
Summary of Content: Magazine dedicated to all aspects of wireless and mobile communications in eastern and central Europe.
Readership/Target Audience: Aimed at the wireless communications industry, mobile network operators and volume users of wireless communications in the private and public sectors.
ADVERTISING RATES:
Full Page Colour £3695.00
Agency Commission: 10%
Mechanical Data: Type Area: 280 x 190mm, Col Length: 280mm, Bleed Size: 307 x 220mm, Trim Size: 297 x 210mm, Page Width: 190mm, Film: Digital
Copy instructions: Copy Date: 5 days prior to publication date
Average advertising content per issue: 40%
BUSINESS: ELECTRONICS

EAT OUT
1666397U11A-199
Editorial Address: Progressive House, 2 Maidstone Road, SIDCUP, DA14 5HZ **Tel:** 0845 000 2500
Email: lesl@dewberryredpoint.co.uk
Advertising Address: As above.
Email: danielh@dewberryredpoint.co.uk
Web site: http://www.eatoutmagazine.co.uk
Publisher: Dewberry Redpoint Ltd
Date Established: 2005
Frequency: Monthly - Published in the 1st week of the cover month
Circulation: 23,944 (ABC 01/07/2008 to 30/06/2009)
Editor: David Foad; **Publisher:** Andrew Archer
Summary of Content: Magazine covering news, case studies, analysis and in-depth articles for the modern day restaurateur.

Readership/Target Audience: Aimed at key buyers and decision makers from the growing hotel, restaurant, pub, travel and leisure sectors.
ADVERTISING RATES:
Full Page Colour £3995.00
Agency Commission: 10%
Mechanical Data: Type Area: 268 x 186mm, Bleed Size: 303 x 216mm, Trim Size: 297 x 210mm, Col Length: 268mm, Page Width: 186mm, Film: Digital
Copy instructions: Copy Date: 4 weeks prior to publication date
Average advertising content per issue: 40%
BUSINESS: CATERING: Catering, Hotels & Restaurants

ECCLESIASTICAL AND HERITAGE WORLD
35905U4E-175
Formerly: Heritage World
Editorial Address: Brook House, Brook Street, Hazel Grove, STOCKPORT, SK7 4QX **Tel:** 0161 292 3432
Fax: 0161 292 3299
Email: editorial@networkmediagroup.co.uk
Advertising Address: Suite 6B, Blackfriar House, St Mary's Parsonage, MANCHESTER, M3 2JA **Tel:** 0161 839 1420
Fax: 0161 830 4559
Email: richard@networkmediagroup.co.uk
Publisher: Destination Maps & Media Ltd
Date Established: 1998
Frequency: Quarterly
Cover Price: £5.00
Free to qualifying individuals
Annual Sub.: £18.00
Circulation: 4,420 (Publisher's Statement)
Usual Pagination: 60
Editor: Chris Stokes
Summary of Content: Magazine covering the design, construction, refurbishment and maintenance of churches, their stonework, furnishings, museums, galleries and the heritage sector.
Readership/Target Audience: Aimed at architects, restorers and craftspeople.
ADVERTISING RATES:
Full Page Colour £1500.00
Agency Commission: 10%
Mechanical Data: Page Width: 185mm, Type Area: 266 x 185mm, Col Length: 266mm, Bleed Size: 295 x 215mm, Trim Size: 290 x 210mm, Film: Digital
Copy instructions: Copy Date: 1st of the month prior to publication date
BUSINESS: ARCHITECTURE & BUILDING: Building

ECN ELECTRICAL CONTRACTING NEWS
37295U17-17
Editorial Address: Alexander House, Forehill, ELY, CB7 4ZA
Tel: 01353 616117 **Fax:** 01353 665619
Email: rob@terringtonltd.co.uk
Advertising Address: As above. **Tel:** 01353 616100
Email: ian@terringtonltd.co.uk
Web site: http://www.electricalcontractingnews.co.uk
ISSN: 0951-6867
Publisher: Terrington Publications Ltd
Date Established: 1983
Frequency: Monthly - Published in the middle of the month prior to the cover month
Cover Price: Free
Circulation: 13,000 (ABC 01/01/2008 to 31/12/2008)
Usual Pagination: 40
Editor: Rob Shepherd
Summary of Content: Magazine covering all aspects of the electrical contracting industry.
Readership/Target Audience: Aimed at electrical contractors.
ADVERTISING RATES:
Full Page Mono £2600.00
Full Page Colour £2600.00
Agency Commission: 10%
Mechanical Data: Type Area: 395 x 270mm, Bleed Size: 426 x 303mm, Trim Size: 420 x 297mm, Col Length: 395mm, Film: Digital, Page Width: 270mm
Copy instructions: Copy Date: 2nd of the month prior to publication date
Average advertising content per issue: 50%
Supplement(s): Product Link - 12xY
BUSINESS: ELECTRICAL

THE ECOLOGIST
40638U57-32_65
Editorial Address: Unit 102D Lana House Studios, 116-118 Commercial Street, Spitalfields, LONDON, E1 6NF
Tel: 020 7422 8100 **Fax:** 020 7422 8101
Email: editorial@theecologist.org
Advertising Address: As above.
Email: jenny@theecologist.org
Web site: http://www.theecologist.org
ISSN: 0261-3131
Publisher: Ecosystems Ltd
Date Established: 1970

Business Magazines

Frequency: 11 issues yearly - Double issues in December/January and July/August
Cover Price: £3.50
Annual Sub.: £28.00
Circulation: 25,000 (Publisher's Statement)
Usual Pagination: 100
Editor: Mark Anslow; **News Editor:** Mark Anslow;
Advertising Manager: Jenny Bryan; **Publisher:** Richard Coles
Summary of Content: Current affairs underlining root causes of news, events, risks to the environment, culture and personal health, case studies for best practice, personal profiles, new products encompassing articles on food, technology, household products, finance, marketing, babies and family, fashion and culture.
Readership/Target Audience: Aimed at well educated, independent 30-55 year olds concerned about health, social, environmental and geo-political issues.
ADVERTISING RATES:
Full Page Mono £1200.00
Full Page Colour £1200.00
Agency Commission: 10%
Mechanical Data: Type Area: 279 x 215mm, Col Length: 279mm, Page Width: 215mm, Bleed Size: +3mm; Film: Digital
Copy instructions: Copy Date: 4 weeks prior to publication date
Average advertising content per issue: 20%
BUSINESS: ENVIRONMENT & POLLUTION

ECOLOGY & ENVIRONMENTAL MANAGEMENT - IN PRACTICE   40639U57-20_25
Editorial Address: 43 Southgate Street, WINCHESTER, SO23 9EH **Tel:** 01962 868626 **Fax:** 01962 868625
Email: jasonreeves@ieem.net
Advertising Address: As above.
Email: mimozanushi@ieem.net
Web site: http://www.ieem.net
ISSN: 0966-2200
Publisher: Institute of Ecology and Environmental Management
Date Established: 1991
Frequency: Quarterly
Annual Sub.: £30.00
Circulation: 3,700 (Publisher's Statement)
Usual Pagination: 28
Editor: Jason Reeves; **Advertising Manager:** Jason Reeves
Summary of Content: Magazine dedicated to the implementation of professional standards in ecology and environmental practice.
Readership/Target Audience: Aimed at practitioners in ecology, plus students and researchers.
ADVERTISING RATES:
Full Page Colour £500.00
Mechanical Data: Trim Size: 297 x 210mm, Film: Digital
Copy instructions: Copy Date: 1st of month prior to publication date
BUSINESS: ENVIRONMENT & POLLUTION

E-COMMERCE LAW AND POLICY
623245U44-540
Editorial Address: 17 The Timber Yard, Drysdale Street, LONDON, N1 6ND **Tel:** 020 7012 1380 **Fax:** 020 7729 6093
Email: lindsey.greig@e-comlaw.com
Web site: http://www.e-comlaw.com
ISSN: 1466-013X
Publisher: Cecile Park Publishing Ltd
Date Established: 1999
Frequency: Monthly
Annual Sub.: £420.00
Circulation: 9,000 (Publisher's Statement)
Usual Pagination: 16
Editor: Lindsey Greig; **Managing Editor:** Lindsey Greig
Summary of Content: Newsletter focusing on the latest business, legal and regulatory developments in e-commerce.
Readership/Target Audience: Aimed at lawyers and business people interested in e-commerce.
ADVERTISING: No Advertising taken
BUSINESS: LEGAL

E-COMMERCE LAW REPORTS   762614U44-3003
Editorial Address: 17 The Timber Yard, Drysdale Street, LONDON, N1 6ND **Tel:** 020 7012 1380 **Fax:** 020 7729 6093
Email: lindsey.greig@e-comlaw.com
Web site: http://www.e-comlaw.com
Publisher: Cecile Park Publishing Ltd
Date Established: 2001
Frequency: 6 issues yearly
Annual Sub.: £360.00
Circulation: 3,500 (Publisher's Statement)
Usual Pagination: 24
Editor: Lindsey Greig; **Managing Editor:** Lindsey Greig
Summary of Content: Practitioners guide to e-commerce cases.

Readership/Target Audience: Aimed at lawyers and advisors to businesses involved in e-commerce.
ADVERTISING: No Advertising taken
BUSINESS: LEGAL

ECONOMIC AFFAIRS   35462U1R-40
Editorial Address: Institute of Economic Affairs, 2 Lord North Street, LONDON, SW1P 3LB **Tel:** 020 7799 8912
Fax: 020 7222 8347
Email: pbooth@iea.org.uk
Advertising Address: 9600 Garsington Road, Cowley, OXFORD, OX4 2DQ **Tel:** 01865 206206 **Fax:** 01865 471267
Email: craig.pickett@oxon.blackwellpublishing.com
Web site: http://www.iea.org.uk
ISSN: 0265-0665
Publisher: Wiley-Blackwell Publishing
Date Established: 1980
Frequency: Quarterly
Annual Sub.: £27.00
Circulation: 2,000 (Publisher's Statement)
Usual Pagination: 90
Editor: Richard Wellings; **Advertising Manager:** Craig Pickett
Summary of Content: Journal of the Institute of Economic Affairs. Covers the analysis of domestic and international economic issues and the effects of government policies.
Readership/Target Audience: Read by UK politicians, city financial professionals, academics, students and corporate heads.
ADVERTISING RATES:
Full Page Mono £445.00
Mechanical Data: Type Area: 265 x 180mm, Bleed Size: 303 x 216mm, Trim Size: 297 x 210mm, Col Length: 265mm, Film: Digital, Page Width: 180mm
Copy instructions: Copy Date: 6 weeks prior to publication date
BUSINESS: FINANCE & ECONOMICS: Financial Related

ECONOMIC FOCUS   1789329U14C-368
Editorial Address: 43 Upper Grosvenor Street, LONDON, W1K 2NJ **Tel:** 020 7235 4363 **Fax:** 020 7659 4878
Email: economicfocus@abcc.org.uk
Advertising Address: As above.
Email: economicfocus@abcc.org.uk
Web site: http://www.abcc.org.uk
Publisher: Arab-British Chamber of Commerce
Date Established: 2006
Frequency: Quarterly
Cover Price: Free
Circulation: 4,000 (Print Run)
Editor: David Morgan; **Advertising Manager:** David Morgan
Summary of Content: Publication looking at policy matters with in-depth reports on countries and specific sectors, plus interviews with policy makers and business people and cultural issues.
Language(s): Arabic; English
Readership/Target Audience: Aimed at British companies trading in the Middle East and Arab countries trading in the UK also chambers of commerce, public bodies, embassies and academics.
ADVERTISING: Rates on application
BUSINESS: COMMERCE, INDUSTRY & MANAGEMENT: International Commerce

THE ECONOMIC HISTORY REVIEW
1925262U14-3
Editorial Address: The Atrium, Southern Gate, CHICHESTER, PO19 8SQ **Tel:** 01243 779777
Web site: http://www.wiley.com/bw/journal. asp?ref=0013-0117
Publisher: Wiley-Blackwell
Frequency: Quarterly
Cover Price: Free
Usual Pagination: 800
Editor: Steve Hindle
Summary of Content: Journal covering all aspects of economic and social history.
Readership/Target Audience: Aimed at those interested in economic and social history.
BUSINESS: COMMERCE, INDUSTRY & MANAGEMENT

ECONOMIC OUTLOOK AND BUSINESS REVIEW   1667261U1A-308
Editorial Address: 4 Queen's Square, BELFAST, BT1 3DJ
Tel: 028 9032 5599 **Fax:** 028 9023 5480
Email: desmond.rea@aib.ie
Publisher: First Trust Bank
Frequency: Quarterly
Cover Price: Free
Editor: Desmond Rea
Summary of Content: Magazine focusing on the economic outlook for Northern Ireland and the United Kingdom including business reviews and special features.

Readership/Target Audience: Aimed at business people, civil servants, educationalists and public administrators.
ADVERTISING: No Advertising taken
BUSINESS: FINANCE & ECONOMICS

ECOTEXTILE NEWS   1846836U47A-592
Formerly: Eco Textile News
Editorial Address: 80 Featherstone Lane, Featherstone, PONTEFRACT, WF7 6LR **Tel:** 01977 708488
Fax: 0700 609 0531
Email: editor@ecotextile.com
Advertising Address: As above.
Email: editor@ecotextile.com
Web site: http://www.ecotextile.com
Publisher: Mowbray Communications Ltd
Date Established: 2007
Frequency: 10 issues yearly
Annual Sub.: £199.00
Circulation: 3,000 (Publisher's Statement)
Usual Pagination: 40
Editor: John Mowbray; **Advertising Manager:** Judy Holland
Summary of Content: Magazine covering sustainable textiles and clothing including recycled fabrics, organics and industry news.
Readership/Target Audience: Aimed at retailers and brands including fabric specifiers and textile mills.
ADVERTISING: Rates on application
BUSINESS: CLOTHING & TEXTILES

ECO-YOU BUSINESS   1849968U14A-592
Editorial Address: Publishing House, 3 Bridgebank Industrial Estate, Taylor Street, Horwich, BOLTON, BL6 7PD
Tel: 0161 909 0909 **Fax:** 0161 909 0919
Email: dave.beevers@bigspark.co.uk
Advertising Address: As above.
Publisher: The Big Spark
Date Established: 2008
Frequency: Monthly
Cover Price: Free
Circulation: 10,000 (Publisher's Statement)
Usual Pagination: 40
Editor: Dave Beevers; **Executive Editor:** Joanna Yarrow
Summary of Content: Business to business magazine covering green solutions and eco advice for British industry's. Features new products, schemes and initiative.
Readership/Target Audience: Aimed at decision makers in the manufacturing industry sector.
BUSINESS: COMMERCE, INDUSTRY & MANAGEMENT

EDB   1911481U4E-457
Editorial Address: SBC House, Restmor Way, WALLINGTON, SM6 7AH **Tel:** 020 8288 1080
Fax: 020 8288 1099
Email: info@edbmagazine.co.uk
Advertising Address: As above.
Email: julian@edbmagazine.co.uk
Web site: http://www.edbmagazine.co.uk
Publisher: Stable Publishing Ltd
Frequency: Quarterly
Free to qualifying individuals
Circulation: 8,440 (Publisher's Statement)
Editor: Richard Sutton; **Publisher:** Toby Filby
Summary of Content: Magazine showcasing the best ideas in building design and the most innovative use of materials and technology. Features news, views and in-depth analysis.
Readership/Target Audience: Aimed at local authorities, architects, contractors, universities, colleges and schools and client design advisers.
ADVERTISING RATES:
Full Page Colour £1685.00
Mechanical Data: Type Area: 265 x 180mm, Bleed Size: 303 x 216mm, Trim Size: 297 x 210mm, Col Length: 265mm, Page Width: 180mm
BUSINESS: ARCHITECTURE & BUILDING: Building

EDGE   37076U14F-63
Formerly: Progress
Editorial Address: 1 Giltspur Street, LONDON, EC1A 9DD
Tel: 020 7294 8038 **Fax:** 020 7294 2402
Email: editorial@i-l-m.com
Advertising Address: As above. **Tel:** 020 3177 1161
Fax: 020 7627 5026
Email: editorial@i-l-m.com
Web site: http://www.i-l-m.com
ISSN: 1464-0503
Publisher: Institute of Leadership & Management
Date Established: 1991
Frequency: 9 issues yearly - Published on the 1st of the cover month, combined issues: 10th of the 1st cover month
Cover Price: £3.50
Free to qualifying individuals
Circulation: 17,809 (ABC 01/07/2008 to 30/06/2009)
Usual Pagination: 56
Editor: Jennifer Churchill

Summary of Content: Magazine covering contemporary leadership and management issues. Includes the latest business news and features a strong section on both personal and professional self development. Other columns include book reviews, opinion and diary dates.
Readership/Target Audience: Read by practising or prospective members registered with ILM, managers and staff in management centres.
ADVERTISING RATES:
Full Page Mono £1890.00
Full Page Colour £1890.00
Mechanical Data: Bleed Size: 276 x 216mm, Type Area: 250 x 190mm, Col Length: 250mm, Film: Digital, Page Width: 190mm, Trim Size: 270 x 210mm
Copy instructions: Copy Date: 2 weeks prior to publication date
Average advertising content per issue: 20%
BUSINESS: COMMERCE, INDUSTRY & MANAGEMENT: Training & Recruitment

EDINBURGH GAZETTE   1693395U44-3020
Editorial Address: 71 Lothian Road, EDINBURGH, EH3 9AZ
Tel: 0131 622 1342 **Fax:** 0131 622 1391
Email: edinburgh@tso.co.uk
Web site: http://www.edinburgh-gazette.co.uk
Publisher: TSO
Date Established: 1695
Frequency: 104 issues yearly
Editor: Elliot George; **Managing Editor:** Richard Goodwin
Summary of Content: Publication covering statutory, legal, bankruptcy and liquidation notices relating to Scotland.
Readership/Target Audience: Aimed at government departments, libraries, solicitors and many large credit information firms.
ADVERTISING: No Advertising taken
BUSINESS: LEGAL

EDN EUROPE   37345U18A-70
Formerly: EDN
Editorial Address: Quadrant House, The Quadrant, SUTTON, SM2 5AS **Tel:** 0118 935 1650
Email: gprophet@reedbusiness.com
Advertising Address: 33 Pembury Road, BEXLEYHEATH, DA7 5LW **Tel:** 020 8312 4696 **Fax:** 020 8312 4657
Email: jwadds@compuserve.com
Web site: http://www.edn-europe.com
ISSN: 1534-5483
Publisher: Reed Business Information
Frequency: Monthly - Published in the 1st week of the cover month
Cover Price: Free
Circulation: 35,058 (BPA Worldwide 01/01/2008 to 30/06/2008)
Usual Pagination: 70
Editor: Graham Prophet; **Publisher:** Martin Savery
Summary of Content: Magazine focusing on the application of new electronic technology and associated products.
Readership/Target Audience: Aimed at designers and design management in the European market.
ADVERTISING RATES:
Full Page Colour EUR8220.00
Agency Commission: 15%
Mechanical Data: Page Width: 178mm, Type Area: 254 x 178mm, Col Length: 254mm, Trim Size: 267 x 200mm, Bleed Size: +5mm, Film: Digital
Copy instructions: Copy Date: 4 weeks prior to publication date
Average advertising content per issue: 60%
BUSINESS: ELECTRONICS

EDUCATION AND THE LAW   41148U62J-108
Editorial Address: Notre Dame University, London Law Centre, 1 Suffolk Street, LONDON, SW1Y 4HG
Tel: 020 7484 7822 **Fax:** 020 7484 7854
Email: bennett.24@nd.edu
Advertising Address: 4 Park Square, Milton Park, ABINGDON, OX14 4RN **Tel:** 01235 828600
Fax: 01235 829000
Email: jenna.johnston@tandf.co.uk
Web site: http://www.tandf.co.uk/journals
ISSN: 0953-9964
Publisher: Routledge, Taylor & Francis
Date Established: 1989
Frequency: Quarterly
Annual Sub.: £86.00
Circulation: 1,000 (Publisher's Statement)
Editor: Geoffrey Bennett; **Advertising Manager:** Jenna Johnston
Summary of Content: Magazine providing an independent and comprehensive source of information on legal guidelines and requirements affecting education.
Readership/Target Audience: Read by principals, head teachers and governors, local authority officers and lawyers.
ADVERTISING RATES:
Full Page Mono £300.00
Agency Commission: 10%
Mechanical Data: Trim Size: 210 x 130mm, Film: Digital

Copy instructions: Copy Date: 6 weeks prior to publication date
BUSINESS: CHURCH & SCHOOL EQUIPMENT & EDUCATION: Teachers & Education Management

EDUCATION & TRAINING   37036U14F-9
Editorial Address: Howard House, Wagon Lane, BINGLEY, BD16 1WA **Tel:** 01274 777700 **Fax:** 01274 785200
Email: md@emeraldinsight.com
Web site: http://www.emeraldinsight.com/et.htm
ISSN: 0040-0912
Publisher: Emerald Group Publishing Ltd
Date Established: 1959
Frequency: 9 issues yearly
Annual Sub.: £5509.00
Usual Pagination: 56
Editor: Kate Snowden; **Publisher:** Kate Snowden
Summary of Content: Publication containing news and articles on the interface between education and training, particularly in relation to 16 to 24 year olds. Includes features on the vocational education and career development of new graduates and young people.
Readership/Target Audience: Aimed at those involved in training and management, in particular, academics interested in the transition from education to work or graduate careers.
ADVERTISING: No Advertising taken
BUSINESS: COMMERCE, INDUSTRY & MANAGEMENT: Training & Recruitment

EDUCATION & TRAINING PARLIAMENTARY MONITOR   41133U62H-70
Editorial Address: Devonia House, 4 Union Terrace, CREDITON, EX17 3DY **Tel:** 01363 774455
Email: info@educationpublishing.com
Web site: http://www.educationpublishing.com
ISSN: 1358-4812
Publisher: The Education Publishing Co Ltd
Date Established: 1994
Frequency: Monthly
Annual Sub.: £225.00
Usual Pagination: 90
Editor: Demitri Coryton
Summary of Content: Publication which reports on education and training developments in parliament and government. A weekly electronic newsletter is also available.
Readership/Target Audience: Aimed at university libraries and senior executives at FE colleges, universities and those involved in post 16 education and training.
ADVERTISING: No Advertising taken
BUSINESS: CHURCH & SCHOOL EQUIPMENT & EDUCATION: Careers

EDUCATION BUSINESS   41155U62J-110
Editorial Address: 226 High Road, LOUGHTON, IG10 1ET
Tel: 020 8532 0055 **Fax:** 020 8532 0066
Email: editor@psp-media.co.uk
Advertising Address: As above.
Email: sales@educationbusinessuk.com
Web site: http://www.educationbusinessuk.com
Publisher: Public Sector Publishing Ltd
Frequency: 6 issues yearly
Free to qualifying individuals
Annual Sub.: £45.00
Circulation: 7,500 (Publisher's Statement)
Usual Pagination: 100
Editor: Sofie Lidefjard; **Advertising Manager:** Barry Doyle; **Publisher:** Carol Symons
Summary of Content: Magazine that deals with the business end of state and private education requirements.
Readership/Target Audience: Aimed at head teachers and bursars.
ADVERTISING RATES:
Full Page Colour £2495.00
Agency Commission: 10%
Mechanical Data: Col Length: 255mm, Page Width: 178mm, Film: Digital, Type Area: 255 x 178mm, Bleed Size: 303 x 214mm, Trim Size: 297 x 210mm
Copy instructions: Copy Date: 2 weeks prior to publication date
Average advertising content per issue: 40%
BUSINESS: CHURCH & SCHOOL EQUIPMENT & EDUCATION: Teachers & Education Management

EDUCATION EXECUTIVE   1665333U62J-1102
Editorial Address: Suite 223, Business Design Centre, 52 Upper Street, LONDON, N1 0QH **Tel:** 020 7288 6833
Fax: 020 7288 6834
Email: editor@edexec.co.uk
Advertising Address: As above.
Email: richard.johnson@intelligentmedia.co.uk
Web site: http://www.edexec.co.uk
Publisher: Intelligent Media Solutions
Date Established: 2005
Frequency: 11 issues yearly

Cover Price: Free
Circulation: 12,576 (Publisher's Statement)
Usual Pagination: 52
Editor: Matthew Jane
Summary of Content: Magazine focusing on best practice solutions, ICT and HR including information on how to secure funding and grants for schools.
Readership/Target Audience: Aimed at bursars and school business managers.
ADVERTISING RATES:
Full Page Colour £1875.00
Agency Commission: 10%
Mechanical Data: Type Area: 260 x 180mm, Bleed Size: 303 x 216mm, Trim Size: 297 x 210mm, Col Length: 260mm, Page Width: 180mm, Film: Digital
Copy instructions: Copy Date: 20th of the month prior to publication date
Average advertising content per issue: 30%
BUSINESS: CHURCH & SCHOOL EQUIPMENT & EDUCATION: Teachers & Education Management

EDUCATION FOR EVERYBODY   713775U56L-13_23
Editorial Address: Unit 8, Chorley West Business Park, Ackhurst Road, CHORLEY, PR7 1NL **Tel:** 0870 444 8955
Fax: 0870 444 8956
Email: paulturner836@btinternet.com
Advertising Address: Euromedia, 150 Burnley Road, ACCRINGTON, BB5 6DW **Tel:** 01254 390066
Email: euromedia@btconnect.com
Publisher: Euromedia Associates Ltd
Date Established: 2000
Frequency: Quarterly
Cover Price: £3.00
Free to qualifying individuals
Annual Sub.: £12.00
Circulation: 3,000 (Publisher's Statement)
Usual Pagination: 112
Editor: Gemma Winstanley; **Features Editor:** Shirley Chisnall; **Advertising Manager:** Elkie Jeffries
Summary of Content: Magazine covering education news and regular features on autism, visual impairment (including RNI), hearing impairment (including RND), dyslexia, ICT, sport and music.
Readership/Target Audience: Read by staff working in special needs schools throughout Great Britain.
ADVERTISING RATES:
Full Page Colour £1500.00
Agency Commission: 10%
Copy instructions: Copy Date: 2 weeks prior to publication date
Average advertising content per issue: 50%
BUSINESS: HEALTH & MEDICAL: Disability & Rehabilitation

EDUCATION FOR PRIMARY CARE   40522U56R-54
Editorial Address: 18 Marcham Road, ABINGDON, OX14 1AA **Tel:** 01235 528820 **Fax:** 01235 528830
Email: contact.us@radcliffemed.com
Advertising Address: As above.
Email: contact.us@radcliffemed.com
Web site: http://www.radcliffe-oxford.com/epc
ISSN: 1473-9879
Publisher: Radcliffe Publishing Ltd.
Date Established: 1989
Frequency: 6 issues yearly
Annual Sub.: £325.00
Circulation: 1,700 (Publisher's Statement)
Editor: Ed Peile; **Advertising Manager:** Dan Allen
Summary of Content: Journal of the Association of Course Organisers, the National Association of Primary Care Educators UK and the World Organisation of Family Doctors (WONCA). The Journal aims to support vocational training and interprofessional development.
Readership/Target Audience: Aimed at healthcare educators who are involved in organising and running educational activities across the primary care team.
ADVERTISING RATES:
Full Page Mono £400.00
Mechanical Data: Film: Digital, Type Area: 194 x 126mm, Col Length: 194mm, Trim Size: 240 x 168mm, Page Width: 126mm
BUSINESS: HEALTH & MEDICAL: Health Medical Related

EDUCATION IN CHEMISTRY   36660U13-80
Editorial Address: Burlington House, Piccadilly, LONDON, W1J 0BA **Tel:** 020 7440 3370 **Fax:** 020 7437 8883
Email: eic@rsc.org
Advertising Address: Thomas Graham House, Science Park, Milton Road, CAMBRIDGE, CB4 0WF
Tel: 01233 432246 **Fax:** 01223 426017
Email: advertising@rsc.org
Web site: http://www.rsc.org/EIC
ISSN: 0013-1350
Publisher: Royal Society of Chemistry
Frequency: 6 issues yearly

Business Magazines

Annual Sub.: £227.00
Circulation: 7,000 (Publisher's Statement)
Usual Pagination: 32
Editor: Kathryn Roberts; **Advertising Manager:** Ian Swain
Summary of Content: Publication covering the whole spectrum of chemistry teaching, from balanced science in secondary schools to degrees.
Readership/Target Audience: Aimed at teachers of chemistry at public examination level in secondary schools, HE and FE colleges and universities.
ADVERTISING RATES:
Full Page Mono £890.00
Mechanical Data: Type Area: 252 x 188mm, Trim Size: 275 x 210mm, Col Length: 252mm, Bleed Size: 281 x 216mm, Page Width: 188mm
BUSINESS: CHEMICALS

EDUCATION IN SCIENCE
41022U62B-190
Editorial Address: College Lane, HATFIELD, AL10 9AA
Tel: 01707 283000 **Fax:** 01707 266532
Email: janehanrott@ase.org.uk
Advertising Address: As above. **Tel:** 01254 283000
Email: rebecca@ase.org.uk
Web site: http://www.ase.org.uk
ISSN: 0013-1377
Publisher: The Association for Science Education
Date Established: 1963
Frequency: 5 issues yearly
Free to qualifying individuals
Annual Sub.: £55.00
Circulation: 15,000 (Publisher's Statement)
Usual Pagination: 36
Editor: Jane Hanrott; **Advertising Manager:** Rebecca Dixon-Watmough
Summary of Content: Magazine of the Association for Science Education, covering issues relating to science education and the activities of the ASE.
Readership/Target Audience: Read by primary and secondary science teachers and educationalists.
ADVERTISING RATES:
Full Page Colour £580.00
Agency Commission: 10%
Mechanical Data: Type Area: 270 x 186mm, Bleed Size: 303 x 216mm, Trim Size: 297 x 210mm, Col Length: 270mm, Page Width: 186mm
Average advertising content per issue: 15%
BUSINESS: CHURCH & SCHOOL EQUIPMENT & EDUCATION: Education Teachers

EDUCATION JOURNAL
41147U62J-120
Editorial Address: Devonia House, 4 Union Terrace, CREDITON, EX17 3DY **Tel:** 01363 774455
Email: info@educationpublishing.com
Advertising Address: As above. **Fax:** 01363 776592
Email: ads@educationpublishing.com
Web site: http://www.educationpublishing.com
ISSN: 1364-4505
Publisher: The Education Publishing Co Ltd
Date Established: 1996
Frequency: 11 issues yearly - Combined issue July and August
Annual Sub.: £39.00
Circulation: 4,860 (Publisher's Statement)
Usual Pagination: 48
Editor: Demitri Coryton; **Managing Director:** Demitri Coryton; **Advertising Manager:** Demitri Coryton; **Publisher:** Demitri Coryton
Summary of Content: Journal containing policy, management, research, opinions, leadership features, new documents digest, reviews and coverage of Parliament including answers to Parliamentary questions.
Readership/Target Audience: Aimed at heads and deputies in schools and senior LEA officers.
ADVERTISING RATES:
Full Page Mono £650.00
Full Page Colour £950.00
Mechanical Data: Type Area: 270 x 190mm, Col Length: 270mm, Page Width: 190mm, Trim Size: 297 x 210mm, Col Widths (Display): 57mm, Print Process: Sheet-fed offset litho, Film: Digital
Copy instructions: Copy Date: 3 weeks prior to publication date
BUSINESS: CHURCH & SCHOOL EQUIPMENT & EDUCATION: Teachers & Education Management

EDUCATION LAW MONITOR
39149U44-550
Editorial Address: Telephone House, 69-77 Paul Street, LONDON, EC2A 4LQ **Tel:** 020 7017 6762
Fax: 020 7017 5274
Email: jessica.westwood@informa.com
Advertising Address: As above. **Tel:** 020 7017 5200
Fax: 020 7323 1319
Email: mark.windsor@informa.com
Web site: http://www.informalaw.com
ISSN: 0135-1646
Publisher: Informa PLC
Frequency: 10 issues yearly

Editor: Jessica Westwood
Summary of Content: Newsletter reviewing the latest developments in law.
Readership/Target Audience: Aimed at people engaged in the field of education.
ADVERTISING: Rates on application
BUSINESS: LEGAL

EDUCATION LAW REPORTS
39259U44-551
Editorial Address: 21 St. Thomas Street, BRISTOL, BS1 6JS **Tel:** 0117 923 0600 **Fax:** 0117 925 0486
Email: elr@jordanpublishing.co.uk
ISSN: 1351-7570
Publisher: Jordan Publishing Ltd
Frequency: 6 issues yearly
Editor: Frances O'Sullivan; **Publisher:** Caroline Vandridge-Ames
Summary of Content: Legal journal containing reported cases.
Readership/Target Audience: Read by education law specialists, solicitors, barristers and government agencies.
ADVERTISING: No Advertising taken
BUSINESS: LEGAL

EDUCATION TODAY
41175U62K-210
Editorial Address: 15A London Road, MAIDSTONE, ME16 8LY **Tel:** 01622 687031 **Fax:** 01622 757646
Email: education@dateam.co.uk
Advertising Address: As above. **Tel:** 01622 699153
Email: education@dateam.co.uk
Web site: http://www.education-today.co.uk
ISSN: 1460-0463
Publisher: Dateam Publishing Ltd
Date Established: 1991
Frequency: 11 issues yearly - Published in 1st week of the cover month
Free to qualifying individuals
Annual Sub.: £32.50
Circulation: 21,500 (Publisher's Statement)
Usual Pagination: 60
Editor: Izzy Chase-Philmore; **Advertising Manager:** Sophie Furr
Summary of Content: Magazine containing features, news and product information.
Readership/Target Audience: Read by decision makers in the education sector.
ADVERTISING RATES:
Full Page Colour £1900.00
Agency Commission: 10%
Mechanical Data: Film: Digital, Type Area: 275 x 192mm, Bleed Size: 312 x 235mm, Trim Size: 306 x 229mm, Col Length: 275mm, No. of Columns (Display): 4, Page Width: 192mm, Print Process: Sheet-fed offset litho
Copy instructions: Copy Date: 3 weeks prior to publication date
Average advertising content per issue: 25%
BUSINESS: CHURCH & SCHOOL EQUIPMENT & EDUCATION: Church & School Equipment

EDUCATION TRAVEL MAGAZINE
41185U62R-130
Editorial Address: 11-15 Emerald Street, LONDON, WC1N 3QL **Tel:** 020 7440 4020 **Fax:** 020 7440 4033
Email: bethan@hothousemedia.com
Advertising Address: As above. **Tel:** 020 7440 4026
Email: nicola@hothousemedia.com
Web site: http://www.hothousemedia.com
ISSN: 1466-7436
Publisher: Hothouse Media
Date Established: 1998
Frequency: 10 issues yearly - Published 2nd Friday of the month prior to the cover month
Annual Sub.: £20.00
Circulation: 38,000 (Publisher's Statement)
Editor: Bethan Norris; **Managing Director:** Scott Wade
Summary of Content: Magazine providing coverage of travelling overseas to study at high school, college or university. Contains market analysis, features and news on courses abroad.
Readership/Target Audience: Aimed at education consultants and specialist travel agents worldwide.
ADVERTISING RATES:
Full Page Mono £2128.50
Full Page Colour £2480.00
Agency Commission: 10%
Mechanical Data: Type Area: 260 x 181mm, Col Length: 260mm, Page Width: 181mm, Bleed Size: +5mm, Trim Size: 297 x 190mm, Film: Digital
Average advertising content per issue: 40%
BUSINESS: CHURCH & SCHOOL EQUIPMENT & EDUCATION: Education Related

EFFECTIVE BUSINESS
1923417U14H-444
Editorial Address: PR by email only **Tel:** 01252 210540
Email: peter@prman.org.uk

Publisher: Effective Business Media
Frequency: 6 issues yearly
Cover Price: Free
Circulation: 50,000 (Print Run)
Editor: Peter Vezey
Summary of Content: Magazine covering all matters relevant to SMEs upward of one man bands including financial, leasing, HR, health and safety, VAT, insurance, transport, distribution and courier services, equipment, commercial property, leases, all marketing services, business consultancy, training, purchasing, discounting, business associations, networking, sales and marketing, security and day to day issues relating to setting up and running SMEs.
Readership/Target Audience: Aimed at small and medium sized enterprises and those with a membership of the EBGI.
ADVERTISING RATES:
Full Page Colour £3500.00
BUSINESS: COMMERCE, INDUSTRY & MANAGEMENT: Small Business

EFM
1666134U1F-596
Editorial Address: Homelands, Exford, MINEHEAD, TA24 7NY **Tel:** 01643 831635 **Fax:** 01643 831015
Email: penny@efmpublishing.com
Advertising Address: As above.
Email: penny@efmpublishing.com
Web site: http://www.efmpublishing.com
ISSN: 1365-3768
Publisher: Efm Publishing
Date Established: 1998
Frequency: Quarterly
Free to qualifying individuals
Annual Sub.: £175.00
Circulation: 9,500 (Publisher's Statement)
Usual Pagination: 26
Editor: Penny Barker; **Advertising Manager:** Penny Barker; **Publisher:** Penny Barker
Summary of Content: Magazine focusing on the pan-European funds business. Includes information on products, regulation, technology, markets and distribution.
Readership/Target Audience: Aimed at Fund and Asset Managers.
ADVERTISING RATES:
Full Page Mono £6010.00
Full Page Colour £6930.00
Mechanical Data: Type Area: 277 x 190mm, Bleed Size: 305 x 218mm, Trim Size: 297 x 210mm, Col Length: 277mm, Page Width: 190mm, Film: Digital
BUSINESS: FINANCE & ECONOMICS: Investment

EFOOD
1620653U22R-752
Editorial Address: Europa House, 13-17 Ironmonger Row, LONDON, EC1V 3QG **Tel:** 020 7253 2545
Fax: 020 7608 1600
Email: editorial@setform.com
Advertising Address: As above.
Email: jabey@setform.com
Web site: http://www.scientistlive.com
Publisher: Setform Ltd
Frequency: Half-yearly - Published in June and December
Free to qualifying individuals
Circulation: 12,000 (Publisher's Statement)
Editor: Paul Boughton; **Managing Director:** Mike Bishop; **Publisher:** David Washington
Summary of Content: Magazine containing technical articles written by senior scientists and journalists covering press control technology, plant equipment, refrigeration, hygiene and research.
Readership/Target Audience: Aimed at food scientists, technologists, process engineers and technical directors.
ADVERTISING RATES:
Full Page Colour £3950.00
Agency Commission: 10%
Mechanical Data: Trim Size: 297 x 210mm, Film: Digital, Type Area: 261 x 185mm, Bleed Size: 303 x 216mm, Col Length: 261mm, Page Width: 185mm
Average advertising content per issue: 35%
BUSINESS: FOOD: Food Related

EGAMING REVIEW
1655839U64A-176
Editorial Address: 1st Floor, Dunstan House, 14A St. Cross Street, LONDON, EC1N 8XA **Tel:** 020 7269 7575
Fax: 020 7269 7570
Email: j.pollard@pageantmedia.com
Advertising Address: As above.
Email: c.steele@pageantmedia.com
Web site: http://www.egrmagazine.com
ISSN: 1742-2450
Publisher: Pageant Media Ltd
Date Established: 2002
Frequency: Monthly
Circulation: 6,000 (Publisher's Statement)
Editor: Jake Pollard; **Advertising Manager:** Caroline Steele; **Publisher:** Seb Timpson

Summary of Content: Magazine covering all aspects of the online gaming and gambling industry. Includes articles on payment processing, legal issues, marketing strategies, regulation and technology.
Readership/Target Audience: Aimed at decision makers within the gambling industry.
ADVERTISING RATES:
Full Page Colour £4500.00
Mechanical Data: Type Area: 297 x 210mm, Col Length: 297mm, Page Width: 210mm, Film: Digital, Bleed Size: 303 x 216mm
BUSINESS: OTHER CLASSIFICATIONS: Amusement Trade

EIA STANDARD
1709122U2C-512
Formerly: Exhibition Standard
Editorial Address: 119 High Street, BERKHAMSTED, HP4 2DJ **Tel:** 01442 873331 **Fax:** 01442 875551
Email: jim@aeo.org.uk
Advertising Address: The Eventful Publishing Co. Ltd, 43 Tabernacle Street, LONDON, EC2A 4AA **Tel:** 020 7324 4800
Fax: 020 7324 4801
Email: beverley@eventfulpublishing.co.uk
Web site: http://www.aeo.org.uk
Publisher: AEO
Frequency: Quarterly
Free to qualifying individuals
Circulation: 1,500 (Publisher's Statement)
Editor: Jim Curry; **Advertising Manager:** Beverley Harper
Summary of Content: Magazine featuring news, legal articles, advice and reports on the events and exhibition industry.
Readership/Target Audience: Aimed at AEO members.
ADVERTISING RATES:
Full Page Colour £1100.00
Mechanical Data: Trim Size: 297 x 210mm, Film: Digital, Bleed Size: 303 x 216mm
Copy instructions: Copy Date: 4 weeks prior to publication date
Average advertising content per issue: 33%
BUSINESS: COMMUNICATIONS, ADVERTISING & MARKETING: Conferences & Exhibitions

EIBI ENERGY IN BUILDINGS & INDUSTRY
40746U58-27_50
Editorial Address: PO Box 825, GUILDFORD, GU4 8WQ
Tel: 01483 452854 **Fax:** 01483 452854
Email: mark.thrower@btinternet.com
Advertising Address: Suite 16-18, Hawkesyard Hall, Armitage Park, RUGELEY, WS15 1PU **Tel:** 01889 577222
Fax: 01889 579177
Email: info@eibi.co.uk
Web site: http://www.eibi.co.uk
ISSN: 0969-885X
Publisher: Pinede Publishing
Date Established: 1984
Frequency: 10 issues yearly - Published in the 2nd week of the cover month
Free to qualifying individuals
Circulation: 11,214 (ABC 01/01/2008 to 31/12/2008)
Usual Pagination: 52
Editor: Mark Thrower; **Managing Editor:** Mark Thrower
Summary of Content: Journal covering all aspects of energy efficiency in industrial, commercial and public buildings. Includes reports on purchasing utilities, water management, renewable energy, energy efficient lighting and sustainable energy sources.
Readership/Target Audience: Aimed at energy managers, architects, building and service engineers.
ADVERTISING RATES:
Full Page Mono £1910.00
Full Page Colour £1910.00
Agency Commission: 10%
Mechanical Data: No. of Columns (Display): 4, Col Widths (Display): 47mm, Page Width: 200mm, Type Area: 268 x 200mm, Trim Size: 297 x 230mm, Bleed Size: 303 x 236mm, Col Length: 268mm, Film: Digital
Copy instructions: Copy Date: 4 weeks prior to publication date
Average advertising content per issue: 40%
BUSINESS: ENERGY, FUEL & NUCLEAR

EIPR EUROPEAN INTELLECTUAL PROPERTY REVIEW
39148U44-552
Editorial Address: 100 Avenue Road, LONDON, NW3 3PF
Tel: 020 7393 7000 **Fax:** 020 7393 7030
Email: jacqui.mowbrey@thomsonreuters.com
Web site: http://www.sweetandmaxwell.co.uk
ISSN: 0142-0461
Publisher: Sweet & Maxwell Ltd
Date Established: 1979
Frequency: Monthly
Annual Sub.: £645.00
Usual Pagination: 74
Editor: Jacqui Mowbrey
Summary of Content: International journal concerning all aspects of intellectual property, offering coverage and

analysis of new developments and important litigation through articles and case studies of trade marks, patents, copyright and designs.
Readership/Target Audience: Aimed at intellectual property legal professionals.
ADVERTISING: No Advertising taken
BUSINESS: LEGAL

ELDERLY CLIENT ADVISER
39273U44-552_90
Editorial Address: 266-276 Upper Richmond Road, LONDON, SW15 6TQ **Tel:** 020 8785 2700
Fax: 020 8785 9373
Email: jlee@ark-group.com
Advertising Address: As above.
Email: jkearns@ark-group.com
Web site: http://www.ecadviser.com
ISSN: 1361-2700
Publisher: Ark Group Ltd
Frequency: 6 issues yearly
Annual Sub.: £265.00
Circulation: 4,000 (Publisher's Statement)
Editor: Joanna Lee; **Advertising Manager:** John Kearns
Summary of Content: Journal of legal, financial and professional comment, advice and guidance for all professionals advising elderly clients.
Readership/Target Audience: Read by lawyers, accountants, financial advisers, nursing home managers and financial institutions.
ADVERTISING RATES:
Full Page Colour £1596.00
Agency Commission: 10%
Mechanical Data: Type Area: 270 x 185mm, Bleed Size: 303 x 216mm, Trim Size: 297 x 210mm, Film: Digital, Col Length: 270mm, Page Width: 185mm
Copy instructions: Copy Date: 15th of the month prior to publication date
Average advertising content per issue: 10%
BUSINESS: LEGAL

E.LEARNING AGE
760625U14F-222
Editorial Address: 80-82 Chiswick High Road, LONDON, W4 1SY **Tel:** 020 8995 9345
Email: sarahu@bizmedia.co.uk
Advertising Address: Royal Station Court, Station Road, Twyford, READING, RG10 9NF **Tel:** 0118 960 2820
Fax: 0118 960 2821
Web site: http://www.elearningage.co.uk
ISSN: 1474-5127
Publisher: Bizmedia Ltd
Date Established: 2001
Frequency: 10 issues yearly - Published around the 15th of the cover month
Annual Sub.: £65.00
Circulation: 9,500 (Publisher's Statement)
Usual Pagination: 36
Editor: Sarah Underwood; **Advertising Manager:** Clive Snell; **Publisher:** Melanie Williams
Summary of Content: Magazine covering all aspects of e-learning including news, training, development and management.
Readership/Target Audience: Aimed at chief learning officers and training managers in e-learning, information technology, and human resources who organise and implement training courses.
ADVERTISING RATES:
Full Page Colour £2650.00
Agency Commission: 10%
Mechanical Data: Bleed Size: 303 x 216mm, Trim Size: 297 x 210mm, Film: Digital
Copy instructions: Copy Date: 10 days prior to publication date
BUSINESS: COMMERCE, INDUSTRY & MANAGEMENT: Training & Recruitment

E-LEARNING TODAY
41029U62B-380
Formerly: InteracTive
Editorial Address: 215 The Green House, Gibb Street, Digbeth, BIRMINGHAM, B9 4AA **Tel:** 0121 224 7599
Fax: 0121 224 7598
Email: lucy.busuttil@imaginitiveminds.co.uk
Advertising Address: As above. **Tel:** 0121 224 7576
Fax: 0121 224 7565
Email: advertising@imaginativeminds.co.uk
Web site: http://www.teachingtimes.com
ISSN: 1751-6110
Publisher: Imaginative Minds
Date Established: 1995
Frequency: 3 issues yearly - Published at beginning of cover months March, June and October
Annual Sub.: £32.00
Circulation: 5,000 (Publisher's Statement)
Usual Pagination: 64
Editor: Lucy Busuttil
Summary of Content: Curriculum magazine for schools covering educational and IT issues.

Readership/Target Audience: Aimed at primary and secondary school teachers and IT co-ordinators.
ADVERTISING RATES:
Full Page Colour £1200.00
Agency Commission: 10%
Mechanical Data: Type Area: 251 x 172mm, Bleed Size: 307 x 220mm, Trim Size: 297 x 210mm, Col Length: 251mm, Page Width: 172mm, Film: Digital
Copy instructions: Copy Date: 3 weeks prior to publication date
Average advertising content per issue: 40%
BUSINESS: CHURCH & SCHOOL EQUIPMENT & EDUCATION: Education Teachers

ELECTRIC & HYBRID VEHICLE TECHNOLOGY
39697U49F-100
Editorial Address: Abinger House, Church Street, DORKING, RH4 1DF **Tel:** 01306 743744 **Fax:** 01306 887546
Email: electric@ukintpress.com
Advertising Address: As above. **Fax:** 01306 742525
Email: s.edmands@ukintpress.com
Web site: http://www.ukintpress.com
ISSN: 1362-5217
Publisher: UKIP Media & Events Ltd
Frequency: Annual - Published in December
Free to qualifying individuals
Circulation: 10,000 (Publisher's Statement)
Editor: Dean Slavnich; **Advertising Manager:** Simon Edmands; **Publisher:** Tony Robinson
Summary of Content: Magazine providing technical information about vehicle design and technology. Includes details of current and forthcoming projects.
Readership/Target Audience: Read by automotive engineers.
ADVERTISING RATES:
Full Page Mono £3450.00
Full Page Colour £3450.00
Agency Commission: 15%
Mechanical Data: Page Width: 180mm, Type Area: 270 x 180mm, Col Length: 270mm, Trim Size: 297 x 210mm, Bleed Size: 303 x 216mm, Film: Digital
Copy instructions: Copy Date: End of October prior to publication date
Average advertising content per issue: 30%
BUSINESS: TRANSPORT: Electric Vehicles

ELECTRICAL & MECHANICAL CONTRACTOR
37297U17-20
Formerly: Electrical Contractor
Editorial Address: 3rd Floor, Ludgate House, 245 Blackfriars Road, LONDON, SE1 9UY **Tel:** 020 7560 4117
Fax: 020 7560 4020
Email: andrew.brister@ubm.com
Advertising Address: Ludgate House, 245 Blackfriars Road, LONDON, SE1 9UY **Tel:** 020 7560 4117
Fax: 020 7560 4020
Email: richard.tomlin@ubm.com
Web site: http://www.emconline.co.uk
ISSN: 1471-5635
Publisher: UBM Information Ltd
Date Established: 1901
Frequency: 10 issues yearly - Published in the 3rd week of the month prior to cover date
Free to qualifying individuals
Annual Sub.: £38.00
Circulation: 8,929 (ABC 01/01/2008 to 31/12/2008)
Usual Pagination: 72
Editor: Andrew Brister; **Advertising Manager:** Richard Tomlin
Summary of Content: Magazine containing features on new products, technologies, installation, innovation, business issues, education and training.
Readership/Target Audience: Aimed at mechanical and electrical installation engineers and those responsible for its maintenance.
ADVERTISING RATES:
Full Page Mono £2251.00
Full Page Colour £3443.00
Agency Commission: 10%
Mechanical Data: Trim Size: 297 x 210mm, Type Area: 254 x 178mm, Col Length: 254mm, Bleed Size: 303 x 216mm, Film: Digital, Page Width: 178mm
Copy instructions: Copy Date: 3 weeks prior to publication date
Average advertising content per issue: 50%
BUSINESS: ELECTRICAL

ELECTRICAL ENGINEERING
37298U17-8
Formerly: CONNECTINGINDUSTRY.COM/electrical engineering
Editorial Address: 15A London Road, MAIDSTONE, ME16 8LY **Tel:** 01622 687031 **Fax:** 01622 757646
Email: jbush@datateam.co.uk
Advertising Address: As above. **Tel:** 01622 699118
Email: hprice@datateam.co.uk
Web site: http://www.connectingindustry.com

ISSN: 1472-1287
Publisher: Datateam Publishing Ltd
Date Established: 1961
Frequency: 10 issues yearly - Published around the 10th of the cover month
Free to qualifying individuals
Annual Sub.: £74.00
Circulation: 17,180 (ABC 01/01/2006 to 31/12/2006)
Usual Pagination: 52
Editor: Joe Bush
Summary of Content: Journal containing news, features and information on electrical components and equipment for industrial and commercial electrical contractors, and electrical engineers.
Readership/Target Audience: Read by electrical engineers, designers, maintenance engineers and contractors.
ADVERTISING RATES:
Full Page Colour £2200.00
SCC £20.00
Agency Commission: 10%
Mechanical Data: Type Area: 272 x 191mm, Bleed Size: 303 x 216mm, Trim Size: 297 x 210mm, Col Length: 272mm, Film: Digital, Page Width: 191mm, No. of Columns (Display): 4, Col Widths (Display): 44mm
Copy instructions: Copy Date: 2nd of the cover month
Average advertising content per issue: 50%
BUSINESS: ELECTRICAL

ELECTRICAL REVIEW
37300U17-70
Editorial Address: 6 Laurence Pountney Hill, LONDON, EC4R 0BL **Tel:** 020 7933 8999 **Fax:** 020 7933 8998
Email: elinorem@stjohnpatrick.com
Advertising Address: As above.
Email: neilc@stjohnpatrick.com
Web site: http://www.electricalreview.co.uk
ISSN: 0013-4384
Publisher: St. John Patrick Publishers Ltd
Date Established: 1872
Frequency: 11 issues yearly - Published in the last week of the month prior to cover date
Free to qualifying individuals
Annual Sub.: £160.00
Circulation: 8,847 (ABC 01/01/2008 to 31/12/2008)
Usual Pagination: 36
Editor: Elinore Mackay
Summary of Content: Magazine covering features, news, analysis, comment and products concerning all aspects of the electrotechnical industry in the UK.
Readership/Target Audience: Read by electrical engineers and consultants.
ADVERTISING RATES:
Full Page Colour £3071.00
SCC £11.00
Agency Commission: 10%
Mechanical Data: Film: Digital, Type Area: 254 x 178mm, Col Length: 254mm, Page Width: 178mm, Trim Size: 290 x 210mm, Bleed Size: 296 x 216mm
Copy instructions: Copy Date: 15th of the publication month
Average advertising content per issue: 40%
BUSINESS: ELECTRICAL

ELECTRICAL TIMES
37301U17-90
Editorial Address: 2nd Floor, 207-215 High Street, ORPINGTON, BR6 0PF **Tel:** 01689 899170
Fax: 01689 899171
Email: ben.cronin@purplems.com
Advertising Address: As above.
Email: rachel.samways@purplems.com
Web site: http://www.electricaltimes.co.uk
ISSN: 0013-4414
Publisher: Purple Media Solutions Ltd
Frequency: 11 issues yearly - Published in the 1st week of the cover month
Free to qualifying individuals
Annual Sub.: £145.00
Circulation: 10,550 (ABC 01/01/2008 to 31/12/2008)
Usual Pagination: 52
Editor: Ben Cronin; **Advertising Manager:** Jill Harrington
Summary of Content: Journal covering technological and business developments in the electrical installation industry.
Readership/Target Audience: Readership includes electrical contractors, consultants and local authority specifiers.
ADVERTISING RATES:
Full Page Colour £3213.00
Agency Commission: 10%
Mechanical Data: Page Width: 178mm, Type Area: 254 x 178mm, Col Length: 254mm, Trim Size: 290 x 210mm, Bleed Size: 296 x 216mm, Film: Positive, right reading, emulsion side down. Digital
Copy instructions: Copy Date: 2 weeks prior to publication date
BUSINESS: ELECTRICAL

ELECTRICAL WHOLESALER
37302U17-100
Formerly: Electrical Wholesaler & Buyer
Editorial Address: 15A London Road, MAIDSTONE, ME16 8LY **Tel:** 01622 687031 **Fax:** 01622 757646
Email: trushtonthorpe@datateam.co.uk
Advertising Address: As above.
Email: mgammon@datateam.co.uk
Web site: http://www.datateam.co.uk
Publisher: Datateam Publishing Ltd
Frequency: Monthly - Published on the 20th of the month prior to cover date
Free to qualifying individuals
Circulation: 3,639 (ABC 01/01/2008 to 31/12/2008)
Usual Pagination: 52
Editor: Tracey Rushton-Thorpe
Summary of Content: Journal covering wholesale product news and features.
Readership/Target Audience: Aimed at executives working in the electrical wholesaling and bulk buying industry.
ADVERTISING RATES:
Full Page Colour £1720.00
Agency Commission: 10%
Mechanical Data: Type Area: 265 x 180mm, Col Length: 265mm, Trim Size: 297 x 210mm, Bleed Size: 303 x 216mm, Page Width: 180mm, Film: Digital
Copy instructions: Copy Date: 5th of the month prior to publication date
Average advertising content per issue: 40%
BUSINESS: ELECTRICAL

ELECTRO OPTICS
37349U18A-90
Editorial Address: The Spectrum Building, Michael Young Centre, Purbeck Road, CAMBRIDGE, CB2 8PD
Tel: 01223 211196 **Fax:** 01223 211107
Email: editor.electro@europascience.com
Advertising Address: 8-10 Whiteladies Road, BRISTOL, BS8 1PD **Tel:** 0117 906 4078 **Fax:** 0117 973 2022
Email: sales.electro@europascience.com
Web site: http://www.electrooptics.com
ISSN: 0013-4589
Publisher: Europa Science Ltd
Date Established: 1968
Frequency: 6 issues yearly
Free to qualifying individuals
Annual Sub.: £170.00
Circulation: 19,853 (Publisher's Statement)
Usual Pagination: 60
Editor: Warren Clark
Summary of Content: Magazine providing UK and European coverage of electro-optics, fibre-optics and image processing equipment and systems.
Readership/Target Audience: Read by those working in the electro-optics field.
ADVERTISING RATES:
Full Page Mono £2800.00
Full Page Colour £3750.00
Agency Commission: 10%
Mechanical Data: Type Area: 253 x 184mm, Print Process: Web-fed offset litho, Film: Digital, Bleed Size: 288 x 219mm, Trim Size: 270 x 200mm, No. of Columns (Display): 4, Col Length: 253mm, Page Width: 184mm
Average advertising content per issue: 40%
BUSINESS: ELECTRONICS

ELECTROFACTS
714993U17-105
Editorial Address: Unit 8, Chorley West Business Park, Ackhurst Road, CHORLEY, PR7 1NL **Tel:** 0870 444 8955
Fax: 0870 444 8956
Email: sales@euromedia-al.com
Advertising Address: As above.
Email: ads@euromedia-al.com
Web site: http://www.euromediaal.com
Publisher: Euromedia Associates Ltd
Date Established: 2001
Frequency: 5 issues yearly - Published in the 1st week of the 1st cover month
Cover Price: Free
Circulation: 9,786 (ABC 01/01/2008 to 31/12/2008)
Usual Pagination: 100
Editor: Emma Higham; **Publisher:** Rhone Hammer
Summary of Content: Magazine containing product and industry news for the electrical industry.
Readership/Target Audience: Read by electrical wholesalers, contractors and facilities management companies.
ADVERTISING RATES:
Full Page Colour £1800.00
Agency Commission: 10%
Mechanical Data: Bleed Size: 307 x 220mm, Trim Size: 297 x 210mm, Film: Digital
Copy instructions: Copy Date: 4 weeks prior to publication date
Average advertising content per issue: 40%
BUSINESS: ELECTRICAL

ELECTRONIC DESIGN EUROPE
1832621U18A-9040
Editorial Address: PR by email only **Tel:** 020 8859 1206
Email: paul.whytock@penton.com
Web site: http://europe.elecdesign.com
Publisher: Penton Media
Frequency: 26 issues yearly
Cover Price: Free
Circulation: 20,000 (Publisher's Statement)
Usual Pagination: 26
Editor: Paul Whytock; **Editor-in-Chief:** Paul Whytock
Summary of Content: Magazine containing information on new products and technologies that help professionals design products.
Readership/Target Audience: Aimed at design engineers, engineering management and chief technology officers.
BUSINESS: ELECTRONICS

THE ELECTRONIC LIBRARY
40858U60B-15
Editorial Address: Howard House, Wagon Lane, BINGLEY, BD16 1WA **Tel:** 01274 777700 **Fax:** 01274 785200
Email: ebreen@emeraldinsight.com
Web site: http://www.emeraldinsight.com/el.htm
ISSN: 0264-0473
Publisher: Emerald Group Publishing Ltd
Date Established: 1983
Frequency: 6 issues yearly
Annual Sub.: £389.00
Usual Pagination: 80
Editor: Eileen Breen; **Publisher:** Eileen Breen
Summary of Content: Magazine covering the use of computerised systems in libraries, online databases, CD-ROMS, latest developments in digital information resources, networking and the changing face of information.
Readership/Target Audience: Read by librarians and information managers.
ADVERTISING: No Advertising taken
BUSINESS: PUBLISHING: Libraries

ELECTRONIC PRODUCT DESIGN
37355U18A-130
Editorial Address: Blair House, 184-186 High Street, TONBRIDGE, TN9 1BQ **Tel:** 01732 359990
Fax: 01732 770049
Email: tim.fryer@imlgroup.co.uk
Advertising Address: As above.
Email: esther.waite@imlgroup.co.uk
Web site: http://www.epdonthenet.net
ISSN: 0263-1474
Publisher: IML Group plc
Date Established: 1980
Frequency: Monthly - Published in the middle of the month
Free to qualifying individuals
Annual Sub.: £105.00
Circulation: 18,373 (BPA Worldwide 01/01/2007 to 30/06/2007)
Usual Pagination: 60
Editor: Tim Fryer; **Advertising Manager:** Esther Waite; **Managing Editor:** Tim Fryer; **Publisher:** Neil Whitaker
Summary of Content: A technical business to business electronics magazine, with design news, ideas, technology reports and application features.
Readership/Target Audience: Aimed at senior design engineers and managers responsible for the design and development of electronic components, equipment and systems in manufacturing, broadcast, telecommunications and servicing establishments.
ADVERTISING RATES:
Full Page Colour £5000.00
Agency Commission: 10%
Mechanical Data: Bleed Size: 289 x 216mm, Trim Size: 283 x 100mm, Page Width: 178mm, Type Area: 252 x 178mm, Col Length: 252mm, Film: Digital
Copy instructions: Copy Date: 6 weeks prior to publication date
Average advertising content per issue: 60%
Supplement(s): Automotive Design - 2xY, Design in Communications - 3xY, Power Design - 3xY
BUSINESS: ELECTRONICS

ELECTRONIC PRODUCTION
37390U18A-9016
Formerly: Electronic Production & Test
Editorial Address: Kentons House, 24 Blendon Road, BEXLEY, DA5 1BW **Tel:** 0870 701 3536
Email: electronicproduction@ntlworld.com
Advertising Address: As above.
Email: electronicproduction@ntlworld.com
Web site: http://www.directpublishing.webeden.co.uk
Publisher: Direct Publishing Ltd
Date Established: 1972
Frequency: Quarterly
Free to qualifying individuals
Annual Sub.: £45.00
Circulation: 4,100 (Publisher's Statement)
Editor: Phil Brown; **Advertising Manager:** Phil Brown

Summary of Content: Magazine covering all aspects of electronic product testing.
Readership/Target Audience: Aimed at electronic assembly manufacturers.
ADVERTISING RATES:
Full Page Colour £1395.00
Agency Commission: 10%
Mechanical Data: Type Area: 263 x 186mm, Bleed Size: 303 x 216mm, Trim Size: 297 x 210mm, Col Length: 263mm, Page Width: 186mm, Film: Digital
BUSINESS: ELECTRONICS

ELECTRONICS EDUCATION
41023U62B-230

Editorial Address: Michael Faraday House, Six Hills Way, STEVENAGE, SG1 2AY **Tel:** 01438 313311
Fax: 01438 765526
Email: roger.dettmer@theiet.org
Advertising Address: As above. **Tel:** 01438 767351
Fax: 01438 765563
Email: lhall@theiet.org
Web site: http://www.theiet.org/ee
ISSN: 0957-2953
Publisher: The Institution of Engineering and Technology
Frequency: 3 issues yearly - Published in January, May and September
Cover Price: £4.00
Free to qualifying individuals
Annual Sub.: £12.00
Circulation: 12,500 (Publisher's Statement)
Usual Pagination: 38
Editor: Roger Dettmer
Summary of Content: Magazine covering electronics and computing in school, with articles about successful projects, courses and technical information on educational equipment.
Readership/Target Audience: Read by teachers in secondary schools in the UK, further education institutions and teacher training colleges.
ADVERTISING RATES:
Full Page Mono £610.00
Full Page Colour £960.00
Agency Commission: 15%
Mechanical Data: Page Width: 178mm, Film: Digital, Type Area: 270 x 178mm, Col Length: 270mm, Print Process: Web-fed offset litho, Trim Size: 297 x 210mm, Bleed Size: 303 x 213mm
Copy instructions: Copy Date: 1 month prior to publication date
BUSINESS: CHURCH & SCHOOL EQUIPMENT & EDUCATION: Education Teachers

ELECTRONICS MANUFACTURE & TEST
37360U18A-240

Editorial Address: Blair House, 184-186 High Street, TONBRIDGE, TN9 1BQ **Tel:** 01732 359990
Fax: 01732 770049
Email: tim.fryer@imlgroup.co.uk
Advertising Address: As above.
Email: keith.murray@imlgroup.co.uk
Web site: http://www.emtworldwide.com
ISSN: 0265-301X
Publisher: IML Group plc
Date Established: 1982
Frequency: Monthly - Published on the 15th of the cover month
Cover Price: Free
Circulation: 5,925 (ABC 01/01/2008 to 31/12/2008)
Usual Pagination: 48
Editor: Tim Fryer; **Advertising Manager:** Keith Murray
Summary of Content: Magazine covering articles on the production, testing and quality control of electronic printed circuit boards and products.
Readership/Target Audience: Aimed at people involved in the electronics production, quality assurance and test marketplace.
ADVERTISING RATES:
Full Page Mono £1757.00
Full Page Colour £2507.00
Agency Commission: 10%
Mechanical Data: Type Area: 265 x 185mm, Trim Size: 297 x 210mm, Bleed Size: 303 x 213mm, Col Length: 265mm, Page Width: 185mm, Film: Digital
Copy instructions: Copy Date: 4 weeks prior to publication date
Average advertising content per issue: 52%
Supplement(s): Electronics Outsourcing - 4xY, PXI Technology for Manufacturing Test - 1xY, The Shortlist - 1xY
BUSINESS: ELECTRONICS

ELECTRONICS SOURCING
1667069U18A-9025

Editorial Address: MMG House, Connors Yard, Beeches Road, CROWBOROUGH, TN6 2AH **Tel:** 01892 613400
Fax: 01892 613402
Email: jonb@electronics-sourcing.co.uk
Advertising Address: As above.
Email: mark.leary@mmgpublishing.co.uk
Web site: http://www.electronics-sourcing.co.uk

Publisher: MMG Publishing Limited
Date Established: 2005
Frequency: Monthly - Published around the 1st week of the cover month
Free to qualifying individuals
Annual Sub.: £60.00
Circulation: 8,716 (ABC 01/01/2008 to 31/12/2008)
Usual Pagination: 60
Editor: Jon Barrett; **Advertising Manager:** Mark Leary;
Managing Editor: Jon Barrett
Summary of Content: Magazine focusing on the electronics industry including news, case studies, industry innovations and developments.
Readership/Target Audience: Aimed at professionals who source and buy electronics components and services for their manufacturing facilities.
ADVERTISING RATES:
Full Page Colour £1770.00
Agency Commission: 10%
Mechanical Data: Type Area: 254 x 178mm, Bleed Size: 303 x 216mm, Trim Size: 297 x 210mm, Col Length: 254mm, Page Width: 178mm, No. of Columns (Display): 4, Film: Digital
Copy instructions: Copy Date: 3 weeks prior to publication date
Average advertising content per issue: 50%
BUSINESS: ELECTRONICS

ELECTRONICS WEEKLY
37365U18A-280

Editorial Address: Quadrant House, The Quadrant, SUTTON, SM2 5AS **Tel:** 020 8652 3500 **Fax:** 020 8652 8956
Email: richard.wilson@rbi.co.uk
Advertising Address: As above. **Tel:** 020 8652 3613
Fax: 020 8652 8938
Email: chris.martin@rbi.co.uk
Web site: http://www.electronicsweekly.com
ISSN: 0013-5224
Publisher: Reed Business Information
Date Established: 1960
Frequency: 47 issues yearly - Published on Wednesday
Circulation: 40,778 (BPA Worldwide 01/01/2008 to 30/06/2008)
Usual Pagination: 56
Editor: Richard Wilson
Summary of Content: Newspaper containing technical and business news of the electronics manufacturing and using industries.
Readership/Target Audience: Aimed at technical directors and other senior directors, engineers and engineering management and buyers working in the UK electronics industry.
ADVERTISING RATES:
Full Page Colour £3275.00
SCC £31.00
Agency Commission: 15%
Mechanical Data: Film: Positive, right reading, emulsion side down. Digital, Type Area: 280 x 206mm, Bleed Size: 310 x 236mm, Trim Size: 300 x 226mm, Col Length: 280mm, Page Width: 206mm
Copy instructions: Copy Date: 1 week prior to publication date
BUSINESS: ELECTRONICS

ELECTRONICS WORLD
37366U18A-285

Formerly: Electronics World + Wireless World
Editorial Address: 6 Laurence Pountney Hill, LONDON, EC4R 0BL
Email: svetlana.josifovska@stjohnpatrick.com
Advertising Address: As above. **Tel:** 020 7933 8980
Fax: 020 7933 8998
Email: matthew.dawe@stjohnpatrick.com
Web site: http://www.electronicsworld.co.uk
ISSN: 0959-8332
Publisher: St. John Patrick Publishers Ltd
Date Established: 1912
Frequency: Monthly - Published around the beginning of the cover month
Cover Price: £4.60
Circulation: 8,923 (Publisher's Statement)
Usual Pagination: 52
Editor: Svetlana Josifovska
Summary of Content: Magazine covering all areas of electronics design, presenting innovation, news, research methodologies and techniques.
Readership/Target Audience: Read by electronics professionals.
ADVERTISING RATES:
Full Page Colour £1081.00
SCC £17.00
Mechanical Data: Type Area: 265 x 186mm, Bleed Size: 303 x 216mm, Trim Size: 297 x 210mm, Col Length: 265mm, Film: Digital, Page Width: 186mm
Copy instructions: Copy Date: 6 weeks prior to publication date
BUSINESS: ELECTRONICS

ELEMENTS FOR ENVIRONMENTAL DECISIONS
629409U57-20_47

Editorial Address: Castlemead, Lower Castle Street, BRISTOL, BS1 3AG **Tel:** 0117 917 5310 **Fax:** 0117 917 5005
Email: nicola.martin@imsplc.com
Web site: http://www.elementsonline.org
ISSN: 1472-815X
Publisher: IMS Marketing Communications Group PLC
Date Established: 2000
Frequency: Quarterly
Annual Sub.: £30.00
Circulation: 2,000 (Publisher's Statement)
Usual Pagination: 28
Editor: Nicola Martin
Summary of Content: Membership magazine for The Environment Council with a focus on raising sustainability issues and highlighting environmental decision making.
Readership/Target Audience: Aimed at representatives from commercial, academic, governmental, statutory and not-for-profit sectors who have an interest in the environment.
ADVERTISING: No Advertising taken
BUSINESS: ENVIRONMENT & POLLUTION

ELEVATION MAGAZINE
35956U4R-365

Formerly: Elevation
Editorial Address: St Albans House, 98 East Hill, DARTFORD, DA1 1SB **Tel:** 01322 626550
Fax: 01322 228239
Email: ish@elevation.co.uk
Advertising Address: As above.
Email: ish@elevation.co.uk
Web site: http://www.elevation.co.uk
ISSN: 1366-2783
Publisher: Cyber Communications Ltd
Date Established: 1994
Frequency: Quarterly - Published in the first week of the cover month
Free to qualifying individuals
Annual Sub.: £60.00
Circulation: 2,000 (Publisher's Statement)
Usual Pagination: 120
Editor: Ish Buckingham; **Advertising Manager:** Ish Buckingham; **Managing Editor:** Ish Buckingham
Summary of Content: Magazine covering all aspects of the UK lift industry.
Readership/Target Audience: Read by property managers, architects, consultants and authorities.
ADVERTISING RATES:
Full Page Mono £610.00
Full Page Colour £1100.00
Agency Commission: 15%
Mechanical Data: Film: Positive, right reading, emulsion side down, Type Area: 242 x 177mm, Col Length: 242mm, Page Width: 177mm, Trim Size: 297 x 210mm
Copy instructions: Copy Date: 2 weeks prior to publication date
Average advertising content per issue: 30%
BUSINESS: ARCHITECTURE & BUILDING: Building Related

ELT JOURNAL
41021U62B-240

Editorial Address: Homerton House, Cawston Road, REEPHAM, NR10 4LT **Fax:** 01603 872955
Email: editor@eltj.org
Advertising Address: 60 Upper Broadmoor Road, CROWTHORNE, RG45 7DE **Tel:** 01344 779945
Fax: 01344 779945
Email: lhann@lhms.fsnet.co.uk
Web site: http://eltj.oupjournals.org
ISSN: 0951-0893
Publisher: OUP
Date Established: 1946
Frequency: Quarterly
Cover Price: £11.00
Annual Sub.: £92.00
Circulation: 3,850 (Publisher's Statement)
Usual Pagination: 100
Editor: Keith Morrow
Summary of Content: Academic journal containing articles on the effects of educational policy, aspects of management, the planning and development of projects and evaluation procedures in the teaching of English as a second language.
Readership/Target Audience: Aimed at teachers and teacher trainers of English as a foreign or second language.
ADVERTISING RATES:
Full Page Mono £630.00
Agency Commission: 10%
Mechanical Data: Type Area: 200 x 135mm, Film: Digital, Page Width: 135mm, Col Length: 200mm
Copy instructions: Copy Date: 2 months prior to publication date
BUSINESS: CHURCH & SCHOOL EQUIPMENT & EDUCATION: Education Teachers

Business Magazines

EMBEDDED CONTROL EUROPE
634874U5B-9002

Editorial Address: 36A Blackacre Road, Theydon Bois, EPPING, CM16 7LU **Tel:** 01992 813662 **Fax:** 01992 813662
Email: devrex@teyboyz.freeserve.co.uk
Advertising Address: Blue Sky Communications, Kent Innovation Centre, Thanet Reach Business Park, Millennium Way, BROADSTAIRS, CT10 2QQ **Tel:** 01843 609357
Fax: 01843 609358
Email: mc@blue-sky-communications.com
Web site: http://www.embedded-control-europe.com
Publisher: ICC Media
Date Established: 2000
Frequency: 10 issues yearly
Free to qualifying individuals
Circulation: 15,000 (Publisher's Statement)
Usual Pagination: 54
Editor: Tony Devereux; **Advertising Manager:** Malcolm Cameron
Summary of Content: Magazine providing detailed information on hardware, software, tools, services and technologies.
Readership/Target Audience: Aimed at design engineers and technical specialists.
ADVERTISING RATES:
Full Page Mono EUR3465.00
Full Page Colour EUR4630.00
Agency Commission: 15%
Mechanical Data: Page Width: 184mm, Bleed Size: 303 x 216mm, Print Process: Offset litho, Film: Positive, right reading, emulsion side down. Digital, Type Area: 247 x 184mm, Trim Size: 297 x 210mm, Col Length: 247mm
BUSINESS: COMPUTERS & AUTOMATION: Data Processing

EMBEDDED SYSTEM EUROPE
36072U5B-9022

Formerly: Embedded System Engineering
Editorial Address: PO Box 32444, LONDON, SE18 3ZP
Tel: 020 8319 1324
Email: cholland@techinsights.com
Advertising Address: X3D Media Ltd, 93A Rivington Street, LONDON, EC2A 3AY **Tel:** 020 3355 7310
Fax: 020 3355 7319
Email: steve@x3dmedia.com
Web site: http://www.embedded-europe.com
ISSN: 1350-1305
Publisher: Techinsights
Date Established: 1980
Frequency: 10 issues yearly - Published in the 2nd week of the month
Free to qualifying individuals
Circulation: 15,000 (Publisher's Statement)
Usual Pagination: 44
Editor: Colin Holland; **Features Editor:** Philip Ling
Summary of Content: Magazine covering news and features on hardware and software developments.
Readership/Target Audience: Read by electronic system designers in the embedded engineering community.
ADVERTISING RATES:
Full Page Mono £2000.00
Full Page Colour £2500.00
Agency Commission: 10%
Mechanical Data: Trim Size: 297 x 210mm, Film: Digital, Bleed Size: 303 x 216mm, Type Area: 280 x 190mm, Col Length: 280mm, Page Width: 190mm
Copy instructions: Copy Date: 3 weeks prior to publication date
BUSINESS: COMPUTERS & AUTOMATION: Data Processing

EMBEDDED SYSTEMS EUROPE
37368U18A-287

Formerly: Embedded Systems Design Europe
Editorial Address: PO Box 32444, LONDON, SE18 3ZP
Tel: 020 8319 1324
Email: cholland@techinsights.com
Advertising Address: Star Media Services, 1 East Street, TONBRIDGE, TN9 1HP **Tel:** 01732 366555
Fax: 01732 366052
Email: tim@starmediaservices.co.uk
Web site: http://www.embedded-europe.com
Publisher: European Business Press/TechInsights Europe
Date Established: 1997
Frequency: 10 issues yearly
Cover Price: Free
Circulation: 20,000 (Publisher's Statement)
Usual Pagination: 48
Editor: Colin Holland
Summary of Content: Magazine focusing on the electronics industry involved in the development, design or use of embedded systems.
Readership/Target Audience: Aimed at embedded systems designers and engineers.
ADVERTISING RATES:
Full Page Mono EUR4720.00
Full Page Colour EUR5680.00
Agency Commission: 15%

Mechanical Data: No. of Columns (Display): 3, Trim Size: 297 x 210mm, Print Process: Web offset, Film: Digital, Type Area: 275 x 180mm, Page Width: 180mm, Col Length: 275mm
Average advertising content per issue: 40%
BUSINESS: ELECTRONICS

EMBEDDED TECHNOLOGY JOURNAL
1799441U18A-9042

Editorial Address: 34 North View, WINCHESTER, SO22 5EH **Tel:** 01962 853781
Email: pr@techfocusmedia.com
Web site: http://www.embeddedtechjournal.com
Publisher: Techfocus Media, Inc
Frequency: Weekly
Cover Price: Free
Circulation: 36,000 (Publisher's Statement)
Editor: Dick Selwood
Summary of Content: Magazine covering embedded computing technology. Topics covered include applications, ASIC and FPGA, development and debug environments, hardware design, mobile devices, open source, peripherals and memory, personalities, processors, RTOS and middleware, software development, system-on-chip, technology trends and wireless.
Readership/Target Audience: Aimed at systems, hardware, and software engineers and engineering managers in systems companies developing electronic products involving embedded computing technology.
ADVERTISING: Rates on application
BUSINESS: ELECTRONICS

THE EMBO JOURNAL
25798U64F-20

Editorial Address: The Macmillan Building, 4 Crinan Street, LONDON, N1 9XW **Tel:** 020 7833 4000 **Fax:** 020 7843 4839
Email: contact@embojournal.org
Advertising Address: As above.
Email: d.bagshaw@natureny.com
Web site: http://www.nature.com/emboj/index.html
ISSN: 0261-4189
Publisher: Nature Publishing Group
Date Established: 1982
Frequency: 24 issues yearly
Annual Sub.: £178.00
Circulation: 2,200 (Publisher's Statement)
Usual Pagination: 352
Editor: Allison Lang; **Executive Editor:** Pernille Rorth; **Advertising Manager:** David Bagshaw
Summary of Content: Journal publishing full-length papers describing original research of general rather than specialist interest in molecular biology and related areas, including findings of wide biological significance in the areas of development, immunology, neuroscience, plant biology, structural biology, genomic and computational biology, genome stability and dynamics, chromatin and transcription, RNA, proteins, cellular metabolism, signal transduction, cell cycle, differentiation and death, membranes and transport, cell and tissue architecture, microbiology and pathogens and molecular biology of disease.
Readership/Target Audience: Read by molecular biologists from any of the above areas of research.
ADVERTISING RATES:
Full Page Mono £860.00
Full Page Colour £1730.00
Agency Commission: 10%
Mechanical Data: Col Length: 250mm, Trim Size: 280 x 210mm, Bleed Size: 286 x 216mm, Film: Digital, Type Area: 250 x 175mm, Page Width: 175mm
Copy instructions: Copy Date: 3 weeks prior to publication date
Average advertising content per issue: 5%
BUSINESS: OTHER CLASSIFICATIONS: Biology

THE EMC JOURNAL
37393U18A-287_40

Formerly: EMC & Compliance Journal
Editorial Address: Eddystone Court, De Lank Lane, St. Breward, BODMIN, PL30 4NQ **Tel:** 01208 851530
Fax: 01208 850871
Email: alan@nutwood.uk.co.uk
Advertising Address: As above.
Email: lynne@theemcjournal.com
Web site: http://www.theemcjournal.com
ISSN: 1464-7559
Publisher: Nutwood UK Ltd
Date Established: 1995
Frequency: 6 issues yearly
Cover Price: Free
Circulation: 13,000 (Publisher's Statement)
Usual Pagination: 44
Editor: Alan Hutley; **Advertisement Director:** Lynne Rowland
Summary of Content: Journal dedicated to all matters relating to electromagnetic compatibility, including low voltage directive, product safety and compliance with European directives.

Readership/Target Audience: Aimed at design engineers, technical management and consultants.
ADVERTISING RATES:
Full Page Colour £1550.00
Agency Commission: 10%
Mechanical Data: Type Area: 267 x 180mm, Bleed Size: 303 x 216mm, Trim Size: 297 x 210mm, Film: Digital, Page Width: 180mm, Col Length: 267mm, Print Process: Web-fed litho
BUSINESS: ELECTRONICS

EMEA FINANCE MAGAZINE
1836472U1R-381

Editorial Address: 3C Hillgate Place, LONDON, SW12 9ER
Tel: 020 8673 9666 **Fax:** 020 8673 8662
Email: cmoore@exportagroup.com
Advertising Address: As above.
Email: twhitehead@exportagroup.com
Web site: http://www.emeafinance.com
Publisher: Exporta Publishing & Events Ltd
Frequency: 6 issues yearly
Annual Sub.: £300.00
Circulation: 20,000 (Publisher's Statement)
Usual Pagination: 96
Editor: Chris Moore; **Publisher:** Chris Moore
Summary of Content: Information source for the finance industry in the EMEA region. Featuring financial events, profiles of financial personalities and industry news.
Readership/Target Audience: Aimed at the financial community, its customers and suppliers across the EMEA region.
ADVERTISING RATES:
Full Page Colour £6000.00
Mechanical Data: Trim Size: 297 x 210mm, Bleed Size: 307 x 220mm, Film: Digital
BUSINESS: FINANCE & ECONOMICS: Financial Related

EMERGENCY & URGENT CARE TODAY
40230U56A-144

Formerly: Today's Emergency
Editorial Address: Media House, 48 High Street, SWANLEY, BR8 8BQ **Tel:** 01322 660434 **Fax:** 01322 666539
Email: mediajournals@aol.com
Advertising Address: As above.
Email: mediajournals@aol.com
Web site: http://www.mediapublishingcompany.com
Publisher: Media Publishing
Date Established: 1994
Frequency: Quarterly
Free to qualifying individuals
Annual Sub.: £30.00
Circulation: 3,500 (Publisher's Statement)
Editor: K Murali; **Managing Director:** Terry Gardner; **Advertising Manager:** Terry Gardner
Summary of Content: Journal covering all aspects of emergency care.
Readership/Target Audience: Aimed at consultants in A&E medicine, senior personnel engaged in resuscitation and intensive care and major A&E departments.
ADVERTISING RATES:
Full Page Mono £800.00
Full Page Colour £1200.00
Agency Commission: 10%
Mechanical Data: Type Area: 270 x 185mm, Trim Size: 297 x 210mm, Bleed Size: 303 x 216mm, Film: Digital, Col Length: 270mm, Page Width: 185mm
BUSINESS: HEALTH & MEDICAL

EMERGENCY MEDICINE JOURNAL
40511U56P-20

Editorial Address: BMA House, Tavistock Square, LONDON, WC1H 9JR **Tel:** 020 7387 6170
Fax: 020 7383 6668
Email: emjeditorial@bmjgroup.com
Advertising Address: As above. **Tel:** 020 7387 4499
Fax: 020 7383 6556
Email: ecurrer@bmj.com
Web site: http://emj.bmj.com
ISSN: 1351-0622
Publisher: BMJ Publishing Group
Date Established: 1984
Frequency: Monthly
Free to qualifying individuals
Annual Sub.: £97.00
Circulation: 1,500 (Publisher's Statement)
Usual Pagination: 96
Editor: Claire Folkes
Summary of Content: Journal covering all aspects of emergency medicine.
Readership/Target Audience: Aimed at all specialists involved in emergency care in the hospital environment.
ADVERTISING RATES:
Full Page Mono £910.00
Full Page Colour £1610.00
Agency Commission: 10%

Mechanical Data: Type Area: 243 x 186mm, Col Length: 243mm, Bleed Size: 286 x 216mm, Trim Size: 280 x 210mm, Film: Digital, Page Width: 186mm
Copy instructions: Copy Date: 20th of 2 months prior to publication date
Average advertising content per issue: 10%
Supplement(s): Newsletter - 4xY
BUSINESS: HEALTH & MEDICAL: Casualty & Emergency

EMERGENCY NURSE
40302U56B-82
Editorial Address: The Heights, 59-65 Lowlands Road, HARROW, HA1 3AW **Tel:** 020 8423 1066
Fax: 020 8872 3198
Email: nick.lipley@rcnpublishing.co.uk
Advertising Address: As above. **Fax:** 020 8872 3197
Email: advertising@rcnpublishing.co.uk
Web site: http://www.emergencynurse.co.uk
ISSN: 1354-5752
Publisher: RCN Publishing Co Ltd
Date Established: 1993
Frequency: 10 issues yearly
Annual Sub.: £59.40
Circulation: 5,571 (ABC 01/01/2008 to 31/12/2008)
Usual Pagination: 40
Editor: Nick Lipley; **Editor-in-Chief:** Linda Thomas; **Managing Editor:** Nick Lipley
Summary of Content: Journal of the RCN Accident and Emergency Nursing Association. Covers news, products, views and issues.
Readership/Target Audience: Aimed at accident and emergency nurses and nurses who work in minor injuries units, NHS direct and walk-in centres.
ADVERTISING RATES:
Full Page Colour £1705.00
Agency Commission: 10%
Mechanical Data: Page Width: 178mm, Film: Digital, Col Length: 271mm, Type Area: 271 x 178mm, Bleed Size: 303 x 216mm, Trim Size: 297 x 210mm
BUSINESS: HEALTH & MEDICAL: Nursing

EMERGENCY SERVICES TIMES
629541U56P-24
Editorial Address: Gresham House, 54 High Street, SHOREHAM-BY-SEA, BN43 5DB **Tel:** 01273 453033
Fax: 01273 453085
Email: davidholden@mmcpublications.co.uk
Advertising Address: As above.
Email: davidbrown@mmcpublications.co.uk
Web site: http://www.mmcpublications.co.uk
ISSN: 1472-1090
Publisher: Modern Media Communications Ltd
Date Established: 2000
Frequency: Quarterly - Published in the 2nd week of the 2nd cover month
Cover Price: £20.00
Free to qualifying individuals
Annual Sub.: £100.00
Circulation: 6,000 (Publisher's Statement)
Usual Pagination: 120
Editor: David Holden; **Advertising Manager:** David Brown
Summary of Content: Journal covering news and developments within the emergency services.
Readership/Target Audience: Aimed at buyers and decision makers within the emergency services.
ADVERTISING RATES:
Full Page Mono £1400.00
Full Page Colour £1400.00
SCC £15.00
Agency Commission: 10%
Mechanical Data: Page Width: 185mm, Type Area: 265 x 185mm, Col Length: 265mm, Bleed Size: 305 x 213mm, Trim Size: 297 x 210mm, Print Process: Litho, Film: Positive, right reading, emulsion side down. Digital
Copy instructions: Copy Date: 3 weeks prior to publication date
Average advertising content per issue: 50%
BUSINESS: HEALTH & MEDICAL: Casualty & Emergency

EMERGING EUROPE MONITOR
36943U14C-54_25
Formerly: Eastern Europe Monitor
Editorial Address: Mermaid House, 2 Puddle Dock, LONDON, EC4V 3DS **Tel:** 020 7248 0468
Email: editorial@businessmonitor.com
Web site: http://www.businessmonitor.com
ISSN: 1469-5278
Publisher: Business Monitor International Ltd
Date Established: 1993
Frequency: Monthly
Annual Sub.: $300.00
Circulation: 1,100 (Publisher's Statement)
Usual Pagination: 12
Editor: Justin Patrie; **Managing Editor:** Justin Patrie
Summary of Content: Magazine containing reports on the economy and politics of business in Eastern Europe.

Readership/Target Audience: Aimed at Directors of multinational companies.
ADVERTISING: No Advertising taken
BUSINESS: COMMERCE, INDUSTRY & MANAGEMENT: International Commerce

THE EMERGING MARKETS MONITOR
36944U14C-54_50
Editorial Address: Mermaid House, 2 Puddle Dock, LONDON, EC4V 3DS **Tel:** 020 7246 5158
Fax: 020 7248 0467
Email: talexander@businessmonitor.com
Web site: http://www.businessmonitor.com
Publisher: Business Monitor International Ltd
Frequency: Weekly
Annual Sub.: $1895.00
Circulation: 1,000 (Publisher's Statement)
Usual Pagination: 24
Editor: Terry Alexander; **Managing Editor:** Terry Alexander
Summary of Content: Newsletter for global investors interested in emerging market economies and emerging financial markets in Latin America, the Middle East, Africa, Asia and emerging Europe analysing and forecasting foreign exchange, interest rates, fixed income, equity indices and commodities across global emerging markets. Also features reports on the investment activities of global funds including mutual funds, pension funds, hedge funds and asset managers.
Readership/Target Audience: Aimed at global investors.
ADVERTISING: No Advertising taken
BUSINESS: COMMERCE, INDUSTRY & MANAGEMENT: International Commerce

EMERGING MARKETS REPORT
1773226U1F-624
Editorial Address: 1st Floor, Rennie House, 57-60 Aldgate High Street, LONDON, EC3N 1AL **Tel:** 020 7680 5151
Fax: 020 7680 5155
Email: francesca@berlinguer.com
Advertising Address: As above.
Email: paul.spendiff@berlinguer.com
Web site: http://www.berlinguer.com
Publisher: Berlinguer Ltd
Frequency: 6 issues yearly
Annual Sub.: £597.00
Circulation: 14,000 (Publisher's Statement)
Editor: Francesca Carnevale; **Advertising Manager:** Paul Spendiff
Summary of Content: Newsletter providing an overview of events, issues and trends in the emerging markets including coverage of equity, debt, foreign exchange, project finance, trade finance, foreign direct investment and mergers and acquisitions.
Readership/Target Audience: Aimed at financiers, corporate and asset managers involved in emerging markets around the world.
ADVERTISING RATES:
Full Page Colour £4995.00
Mechanical Data: Trim Size: 297 x 210mm, Bleed Size: 307 x 220mm
Copy instructions: Copy Date: 2 weeks prior to publication date
BUSINESS: FINANCE & ECONOMICS: Investment

EMPLOYEE BENEFITS
35353U1H-20
Editorial Address: St. Giles House, 50 Poland Street, LONDON, W1F 7AX **Tel:** 020 7970 4000 **Fax:** 020 7943 8094
Email: eb.editorial@centaur.co.uk
Advertising Address: As above.
Email: suzanne.saunders@centaur.co.uk
Web site: http://www.employeebenefits.co.uk
ISSN: 1366-8722
Publisher: Centaur Media plc
Date Established: 1997
Frequency: Monthly
Cover Price: £4.95
Free to qualifying individuals
Annual Sub.: £45.00
Circulation: 9,940 (ABC 01/07/2008 to 30/06/2009)
Usual Pagination: 60
Editor: Debi O'Donovan; **News Editor:** Katrina McKeeve
Summary of Content: Magazine covering all aspects of employee benefits.
Readership/Target Audience: Read by personnel and finance directors, pension managers, compensation and benefit managers and those with responsibilities for buying and managing employee benefits.
ADVERTISING RATES:
Full Page Colour £2840.00
Agency Commission: 10%
Mechanical Data: Film: Digital, Bleed Size: 303 x 231mm, Trim Size: 297 x 225mm, Type Area: 280 x 205mm, Col Length: 280mm, Page Width: 205mm
Copy instructions: Copy Date: 3rd Wednesday of the month prior to publication date

Supplement(s): Financial Education - 1xY, Fleet Research - 1xY, Flexible Benefits - 2xY, Health Research - 2xY, International - 1xY, Motivation - 1xY, Pensions Research - 2xY, Total Reward - 1xY, Voluntary Benefits - 1xY
BUSINESS: FINANCE & ECONOMICS: Pensions

EMPLOYERS LAW
39150U44-555
Editorial Address: Quadrant House, The Quadrant, SUTTON, SM2 5AS **Tel:** 020 8652 3500
Email: elaw.editor@rbi.co.uk
Advertising Address: As above. **Tel:** 020 8652 4668
Fax: 020 8652 3793
Email: darren.ward@rbi.co.uk
Web site: http://www.employers-law.com
ISSN: 1364-9493
Publisher: Reed Business Information
Date Established: 1996
Frequency: 10 issues yearly
Annual Sub.: £97.00
Circulation: 1,800 (Publisher's Statement)
Usual Pagination: 30
Editor: John Charlton; **News Editor:** Louisa Peacock
Summary of Content: Journal covering all aspects of legislation relating to employment law.
Readership/Target Audience: Aimed at human resources professionals.
ADVERTISING RATES:
Full Page Mono £1025.00
Full Page Colour £1705.00
Agency Commission: 10%
Mechanical Data: Page Width: 181mm, Film: Digital, Type Area: 271 x 181mm, Col Length: 271mm, Bleed Size: 303 x 216mm, Trim Size: 297 x 210mm
Copy instructions: Copy Date: 2 weeks prior to publication date
Average advertising content per issue: 10%
BUSINESS: LEGAL

EMPLOYING DOCTORS & DENTISTS
622719U56R-54_50
Editorial Address: Gothic House, 3 The Green, RICHMOND, TW9 1PL **Tel:** 020 8334 4500
Fax: 020 8332 7201
Email: mail@chamberdunn.co.uk
Web site: http://www.chamberlaindunn.com
ISSN: 1462-0170
Publisher: Chamberlain Dunn Associates
Date Established: 1998
Frequency: 10 issues yearly
Annual Sub.: £295.00
Circulation: 800 (Publisher's Statement)
Usual Pagination: 16
Editor: Jeremy Davies
Summary of Content: Magazine containing information about good human resources management within the UK Health Service.
Readership/Target Audience: Read by human resource managers in health care, medical managers and directors.
ADVERTISING: No Advertising taken
Supplement(s): EDD Guide to Recruiting and Retaining Doctors - 1xY, Medical and Dental Workforce Data - 1xY
BUSINESS: HEALTH & MEDICAL: Health Medical Related

EMPLOYING NURSES & MIDWIVES
622730U56B-82_50
Editorial Address: Gothic House, 3 The Green, RICHMOND, TW9 1PL **Tel:** 020 8334 4500
Fax: 020 8332 7201
Email: mail@chamberdunn.co.uk
Web site: http://www.health-workforce.com
ISSN: 1368-969X
Publisher: Chamberlain Dunn Associates
Date Established: 1996
Frequency: 6 issues yearly
Annual Sub.: £95.00
Circulation: 900 (Publisher's Statement)
Usual Pagination: 8
Editor: Judith Chamberlain-Webber; **Editor-in-Chief:** Alison Dunn
Summary of Content: Magazine covering the practical issues of employing midwives and nursing staff.
Readership/Target Audience: Aimed at HR directors, nurse managers and recruitment agencies.
ADVERTISING: No Advertising taken
BUSINESS: HEALTH & MEDICAL: Nursing

EMS ENGINEERING MAINTENANCE SOLUTIONS
1833108U19A-568
Editorial Address: Cobalt House, Centre Court, Sir Thomas Longley Road, ROCHESTER, ME2 4BQ **Tel:** 01634 731646
Fax: 01634 242611
Email: editorial@engineeringmaintenance.info
Advertising Address: As above. **Tel:** 020 7993 3355
Email: paul@engineeringmaintenance.info

Business Magazines

Web site: http://www.engineeringmaintenance.info
Publisher: MSL Media
Date Established: 2007
Frequency: 6 issues yearly
Cover Price: Free
Circulation: 12,000 (Publisher's Statement)
Editor: Jon Barrett; **Publisher:** Michael Dominguez
Summary of Content: Magazine informing and educating directors, managers and engineers responsible for asset management.
Readership/Target Audience: Aimed at engineering and maintenance professionals.
ADVERTISING RATES:
Full Page Colour £1600.00
Agency Commission: 10%
Mechanical Data: Type Area: 261 x 178mm, Bleed Size: 303 x 213mm, Trim Size: 297 x 210mm, Col Length: 261mm, Page Width: 178mm, Film: Digital
Copy instructions: Copy Date: 2 weeks prior to publication date
Average advertising content per issue: 50%
BUSINESS: ENGINEERING & MACHINERY

EN THE MAGAZINE FOR ENTREPRENEURS (NORTH WEST)

41319U63B-520

Editorial Address: Portland Buildings, 127-129 Portland Street, MANCHESTER, M1 4PZ **Tel:** 0161 236 2782
Fax: 0161 236 2783
Email: stuart.anderson@excelpublishing.co.uk
Advertising Address: As above.
Email: en@excelpublishing.co.uk
Web site: http://www.enforbusiness.com
Publisher: Excel Publishing Company Ltd
Date Established: 1994
Frequency: 11 issues yearly
Free to qualifying individuals
Annual Sub.: £35.00
Circulation: 12,000 (Publisher's Statement)
Usual Pagination: 56
Editor: Stuart Anderson; **Managing Director:** Martin Regan;
Publisher: Patrick Rafter
Summary of Content: Magazine covering all the latest news issues, trends and ideas for entrepreneurs and businesses in the Northwest and Yorkshire regions.
Readership/Target Audience: Aimed at owner-managed businesses, company directors and major shareholders, professional advisors and senior public sector executives.
ADVERTISING RATES:
Full Page Colour £1650.00
Agency Commission: 10%
Mechanical Data: No. of Columns (Display): 2, Type Area: 243 x 188mm, Trim Size: 285 x 216mm, Bleed Size: 291 x 221mm, Col Length: 243mm, Page Width: 188mm, Film: Digital
Copy instructions: Copy Date: 1 week prior to publication date
Average advertising content per issue: 30%
BUSINESS: REGIONAL BUSINESS: Regional Business English Counties

ENDODONTIC PRACTICE

622749U56D-68_50

Editorial Address: 1 Hertford House, Hugo Gryn Way, Farm Close, SHENLEY, WD7 9AB **Tel:** 01923 851777
Fax: 01923 851778
Email: siobhan.lewney@fmc.co.uk
Advertising Address: As above.
Email: joe.lovett@fmc.co.uk
Web site: http://www.endodonticpracticejournal.com
ISSN: 1465-9417
Publisher: Finlayson Media Communications Ltd
Date Established: 1998
Frequency: Quarterly
Free to qualifying individuals
Annual Sub.: £95.00
Circulation: 3,000 (Publisher's Statement)
Usual Pagination: 60
Editor: Siobhan Lewney; **Editor-in-Chief:** Julian Webber;
Advertising Manager: Joe Lovett; **Managing Editor:** Siobhan Lewney
Summary of Content: Endodontic Journal containing a variety of peer reviewed clinical articles and case studies to promote excellence within the profession, as well as practice management features, courses and product details.
Readership/Target Audience: Aimed at general dental practitioners and specialists worldwide who perform root canal work.
ADVERTISING RATES:
Full Page Colour £2275.00
Mechanical Data: Type Area: 287 x 200mm, Col Length: 287mm, Page Width: 200mm, Trim Size: 297 x 210mm, Bleed Size: 303 x 216mm, Film: Digital
BUSINESS: HEALTH & MEDICAL: Dental

THE ENDS REPORT

40642U57-20_50

Editorial Address: 11-17 Wolverton Gardens, LONDON, W6 7DY **Tel:** 020 8267 8100 **Fax:** 020 8267 8150
Email: news@ends.co.uk
Web site: http://www.endsreport.com
ISSN: 0966-4076
Publisher: Haymarket Business Media Ltd
Date Established: 1978
Frequency: Monthly
Annual Sub.: £529.00
Circulation: 4,000 (Publisher's Statement)
Usual Pagination: 68
Editor: Nicholas Schoon
Summary of Content: Magazine covering UK and EU environmental developments, including news and analysis of business and legislation and government policy.
Readership/Target Audience: Aimed at environmental professionals in industry, consultancy, clean-up firms, government, regulatory authorities, environmental NGOs and academia.
ADVERTISING: No Advertising taken
BUSINESS: ENVIRONMENT & POLLUTION

ENERGY

1665500U58-193

Editorial Address: PO Box 43, Lang Stracht, Mastrick, ABERDEEN, AB15 6DF **Tel:** 01224 690222
Email: jeremy.cresswell@ajl.co.uk
Advertising Address: As above. **Fax:** 01224 694613
Email: cara.beamish@ajl.co.uk
Web site: http://energy.pressandjournal.co.uk
Publisher: Aberdeen Journals Ltd
Date Established: 2003
Frequency: 13 issues yearly - Published the first Monday of the month. See main record for circulation
Editor: Jeremy Cresswell
Summary of Content: Supplement featuring news, views, features and analysis of the oil, gas and renewable energy sector with an emphasis on upstream oil and gas.
ADVERTISING RATES:
Full Page Mono £3621.00
Full Page Colour £4888.00
SCC £17.75
Agency Commission: 10%
Mechanical Data: Type Area: 340 x 266mm, Col Length: 340mm, Page Width: 266mm, Print Process: Web-fed offset litho, No. of Columns (Display): 6, Col Widths (Display): 41mm, Film: Digital
Copy instructions: Copy Date: Last Friday of the month prior to publication date
Average advertising content per issue: 40%
Supplement to: The Press & Journal (Aberdeen)
BUSINESS: ENERGY, FUEL & NUCLEAR

ENERGY ACTION

40743U58-28

Editorial Address: St. Andrew's House, 90-92 Pilgrim Street, NEWCASTLE UPON TYNE, NE1 6SG
Tel: 0191 261 5677 **Fax:** 0191 261 6496
Email: info@nea.org.uk
Web site: http://www.nea.org.uk
ISSN: 0262-5296
Publisher: NEA
Frequency: 3 issues yearly - Published in March, July and November
Annual Sub.: £25.00
Circulation: 850 (Publisher's Statement)
Editor: Ronald Campbell
Summary of Content: Official magazine of the NEA. Contains news and features on fuel poverty and energy efficiency.
Readership/Target Audience: Aimed at MPs and peers, fuel utilities and their regulators, caring agencies, manufacturers of energy efficiency materials, contractors and installers of energy efficiency products, local authorities and housing agencies.
ADVERTISING: No Advertising taken
BUSINESS: ENERGY, FUEL & NUCLEAR

ENERGY BYTES

1642254U4D-402

Editorial Address: Beech House, Berkeley Close, Stoke Goldington, NEWPORT PAGNELL, MK16 8TE
Tel: 01908 551976 **Fax:** 01908 551977
Email: energybytes@btinternet.com
Web site: http://www.nher.co.uk
Publisher: National Energy Services
Date Established: 2003
Frequency: 3 issues yearly - Publication month varies
Cover Price: Free
Circulation: 3,500 (Publisher's Statement)
Usual Pagination: 8
Editor: Liz Male
Summary of Content: Newsletter covering news on the energy efficiency and environmental impact of private and public sector housing in UK, including the energy assessment, labelling and marketing of new homes, older properties and social housing stock.

Readership/Target Audience: Aimed at energy efficiency professionals working for house builders, housing associations and local authorities. Also distributed to energy efficiency/environmental lobby groups, policy makers and key Government officials.
BUSINESS: ARCHITECTURE & BUILDING: Planning & Housing

ENERGY ECONOMIST

40756U58-30_50

Formerly: Financial Times Energy Economist
Editorial Address: 1 St. Annes Gardens, LYMINGTON, SO41 9HT **Tel:** 01590 679989
Email: ross_mccracken@platts.com
Web site: http://www.platts.com
Publisher: Platts
Date Established: 1981
Frequency: Monthly
Usual Pagination: 48
Editor: Ross McCracken; **Managing Editor:** Paul Whitehead
Summary of Content: Newsletter containing an overview and analysis of factors affecting world energy trends, plus news and detailed energy markets coverage.
Readership/Target Audience: Read by energy economists, planners, strategists, energy specialists in the fields of banking and finance, top executives in the major oil companies, regulators and senior government officials.
ADVERTISING: No Advertising taken
BUSINESS: ENERGY, FUEL & NUCLEAR

ENERGY ENGINEERING

1732865U58-177

Editorial Address: 6A New Street, WARWICK, CV34 4RX
Tel: 01926 408242 **Fax:** 01926 408206
Email: steve@energyengineering.co.uk
Advertising Address: As above. **Tel:** 01926 408244
Email: steve@energyengineering.co.uk
Web site: http://www.energyengineering.co.uk
Publisher: Steve Welch Media
Date Established: 2005
Frequency: 6 issues yearly
Annual Sub.: £65.00
Circulation: 7,000 (Publisher's Statement)
Usual Pagination: 64
Editor: Steve Welch; **Advertising Manager:** Steve Welch;
Managing Editor: Steve Welch
Summary of Content: Magazine that covers the products and processes, innovation, technology and management of renewable energy in all its forms.
Readership/Target Audience: Aimed at middle to senior management in the energy industry.
ADVERTISING RATES:
Full Page Colour £1945.00
Mechanical Data: Type Area: 274 x 181mm, Bleed Size: 305 x 214mm, Trim Size: 297 x 210mm, Col Length: 274mm, Page Width: 181mm, Film: Digital
Copy instructions: Copy Date: 3 weeks prior to publication date
BUSINESS: ENERGY, FUEL & NUCLEAR

ENERGY IN EAST EUROPE

601019U58-67_75

Formerly: Power In East Europe
Editorial Address: 20 Canada Square, Canary Wharf, LONDON, E14 5LH **Tel:** 020 7176 7000 **Fax:** 020 7176 6670
Email: martin_burdett@platts.com
Web site: http://www.platts.com
ISSN: 1479-2982
Publisher: Platts
Date Established: 2002
Frequency: 24 issues yearly
Annual Sub.: $1495
Usual Pagination: 40
Editor: Martin Burdett
Summary of Content: Journal focusing on the electricity, natural gas and oil sectors of central and Eastern Europe.
Readership/Target Audience: Aimed at investment banks, energy utilities, law firms, research companies, consultancies, libraries and government ministries.
ADVERTISING: No Advertising taken
BUSINESS: ENERGY, FUEL & NUCLEAR

ENERGY MANAGEMENT BRIEFING

40747U58-31_30

Editorial Address: 145 London Road, KINGSTON UPON THAMES, KT2 6SR **Tel:** 020 8547 3333 **Fax:** 020 8549 7275
Email: hazel.winter@croner.co.uk
Web site: http://www.croner.co.uk
Publisher: Croner Group Ltd
Date Established: 1998
Frequency: Monthly
Usual Pagination: 8
Editor: Hazel Winter
Summary of Content: Newsletter providing practical guidance for those organisations wishing to reduce their energy costs in a structured and sustainable way.

Readership/Target Audience: Aimed at those responsible for managing energy in the workplace, including energy and facility managers.
ADVERTISING: No Advertising taken
BUSINESS: ENERGY, FUEL & NUCLEAR

ENERGY NOW
1858705U58-196

Editorial Address: PO Box 716, WORCESTER, WR2 4WN
Tel: 01905 429018
Email: roger@energy-now.co.uk
Advertising Address: As above.
Email: david@energy-now.co.uk
Web site: http://www.energy-now.co.uk
Publisher: DJ Media
Date Established: 2007
Frequency: 6 issues yearly
Annual Sub.: £36.00
Circulation: 15,000 (Publisher's Statement)
Usual Pagination: 44
Editor: Roger Abbott; **Advertising Manager:** David Jacobmeyer; **Publisher:** David Jacobmeyer
Summary of Content: Magazine focusing on the renewable energy options available to farmers and landowners. Features include news, interviews, case studies, company profiles, area reports, machinery, energy people and diary dates.
Readership/Target Audience: Aimed at farmers and landowners.
ADVERTISING RATES:
Full Page Colour £1320.00
Mechanical Data: Bleed Size: 303 x 216mm, Trim Size: 297 x 210mm, Film: Digital
BUSINESS: ENERGY, FUEL & NUCLEAR

ENERGY POLICY
40749U58-32

Editorial Address: The Boulevard, Langford Lane, KIDLINGTON, OX5 1GB **Tel:** 01865 843000
Fax: 01865 843010
Advertising Address: 32 Jamestown Road, LONDON, NW1 7BY **Tel:** 020 7424 4200 **Fax:** 01865 853136
Email: j.kenney@elsevier.com
Web site: http://www.elsevier.com/locate/enpol
Publisher: Elsevier Ltd
Date Established: 1973
Frequency: Monthly
Circulation: 600 (Publisher's Statement)
Usual Pagination: 100
Editor: N. France; **Publisher:** Henry Van Dorssen
Summary of Content: Journal covering all aspects of energy supply, demand, utilisation and policy making, including information on pricing policy and energy efficiency potential in the domestic sector.
Readership/Target Audience: Aimed at decision makers, managers, energy consultants, politicians, planners, energy researchers and economists.
ADVERTISING: Rates on application
BUSINESS: ENERGY, FUEL & NUCLEAR

ENERGY RISK
38577U33-1_48

Formerly: Energy & Power Risk Management
Editorial Address: Haymarket House, 28-29 Haymarket, LONDON, SW1Y 4RX **Tel:** 020 7484 9700
Fax: 020 7930 2238
Email: stella.farrington@incisivemedia.com
Advertising Address: As above.
Email: manish.makwana@incisivemedia.com
Web site: http://www.energyrisk.com
ISSN: 1742-4305
Publisher: Incisive Media Investments
Date Established: 1994
Frequency: Monthly - Published around the 1st of the cover month
Annual Sub.: £329.00
Circulation: 11,000 (Publisher's Statement)
Usual Pagination: 64
Editor: Stella Farrington; **Advertising Manager:** Manish Makwana; **Publisher:** Trevor Wilkins
Summary of Content: Journal covering the world's energy markets, with an emphasis on risk management.
Readership/Target Audience: Aimed at energy executives, risk managers and traders.
ADVERTISING RATES:
Full Page Mono £5768.00
Full Page Colour £7176.00
Agency Commission: 10%
Mechanical Data: Type Area: 239 x 175mm, Bleed Size: 286 x 281mm, Trim Size: 280 x 216mm, Film: Digital, Page Width: 175mm, Col Length: 239mm
Copy instructions: Copy Date: 23rd of the month prior to publication date
Average advertising content per issue: 30%
Supplement(s): Awards - 1xY, Credit Risk - 1xY, Electricity - 1xY, Enterprise-Wide Risk Management - 1xY, Environmental Risk - 1xY, Germany - 1xY, Natural Gas - 1xY, Petroleum - 1xY, Technology - 1xY, Weather Risk - 1xY
BUSINESS: OIL & PETROLEUM

ENERGY WORLD
40751U58-35

Editorial Address: 61 New Cavendish Street, LONDON, W1G 7AR **Tel:** 020 7467 7100 **Fax:** 020 7467 7171
Email: eworld@energyinst.org.uk
Web site: http://www.energyinst.org.uk
ISSN: 0307-7942
Publisher: Energy Institute
Date Established: 1973
Frequency: 11 issues yearly - Published around the 28th of the month prior to cover date
Annual Sub.: £158.00
Circulation: 5,000 (Publisher's Statement)
Usual Pagination: 28
Editor: Steve Hodgson
Summary of Content: Magazine of the Energy Institute, covering the international energy scene, focussing on alternative energies, climate change and energy security.
Readership/Target Audience: Aimed at members of The Energy Institute and engineers.
ADVERTISING: No Advertising taken
BUSINESS: ENERGY, FUEL & NUCLEAR

ENGAGE
1775098U10-219

Editorial Address: Waterfront Studios, 1 Dock Road, LONDON, E16 1AH **Tel:** 020 8350 9443 **Fax:** 020 7476 6655
Email: gloria@engagemagazine.co.uk
Advertising Address: As above.
Email: craig@engagemagazine.co.uk
Web site: http://www.engagemagazine.co.uk
Publisher: Engage UK Networks Limited
Date Established: 2006
Frequency: Quarterly
Free to qualifying individuals
Annual Sub.: £15.00
Circulation: 40,000 (Publisher's Statement)
Usual Pagination: 84
Editor: Gloria Wyse; **Advertising Manager:** Craig Cordice
Summary of Content: Publication that aims to support and promote supplier diversity in the UK with features on procurement opportunities, financial advice, BME and other minority owned businesses, recruitment and training.
Readership/Target Audience: Aimed at small and medium sized enterprises particularly minority owned businesses, large organisations from both private and public sector, entrepreneurs and graduates.
ADVERTISING RATES:
Full Page Mono £2450.00
Full Page Colour £3950.00
Agency Commission: 15%
Mechanical Data: Type Area: 270 x 195mm, Bleed Size: 306 x 231mm, Trim Size: 300 x 225mm, Col Length: 270mm, Page Width: 195mm, Film: Digital
Average advertising content per issue: 25%
BUSINESS: MATERIALS HANDLING

ENGAGE
1743229U14F-258

Editorial Address: 7 St. Martin's Place, LONDON, WC2N 4HA **Tel:** 020 7747 0700 **Fax:** 020 7747 0701
Email: sarah.bale@redwoodgroup.net
Web site: http://www.jobcentreplus.gov.uk
Publisher: Redwood
Date Established: 2005
Frequency: Half-yearly - Published in April and September
Cover Price: Free
Circulation: 80,000 (Publisher's Statement)
Usual Pagination: 24
Editor: Sarah Bale
Summary of Content: Magazine covering recruitment and employment issues including legislation, discrimination, case studies and human resources.
Readership/Target Audience: Aimed at employers, recruitment agencies and key industry organisations who use the jobcentre plus.
ADVERTISING: No Advertising taken
BUSINESS: COMMERCE, INDUSTRY & MANAGEMENT: Training & Recruitment

ENGAGE MAGAZINE
35442U1P-275

Formerly: VS magazine
Editorial Address: Regent's Wharf, 8 All Saints Street, LONDON, N1 9RL **Tel:** 020 7713 6161 **Fax:** 020 7713 6300
Email: contact@beengaged.org
Advertising Address: The Barn, Oakley Hay Lodge Business Park, Great Folds Road, Great Oakley, CORBY, NN18 9AS **Tel:** 01536 747333 **Fax:** 01536 746565
Email: advertising@voluntarysector.co.uk
Web site: http://www.beengaged.org
ISSN: 0955-2170
Publisher: NCVO
Frequency: 6 issues yearly
Free to qualifying individuals
Annual Sub.: £65.00
Circulation: 10,000 (Publisher's Statement)
Usual Pagination: 44
Editor: Maurice Mcleod; **Executive Editor:** Maurice Mcleod; **Advertising Manager:** Lynn Newman

Summary of Content: Magazine of the National Council for Voluntary Organisations. Covers news, features and issues from fundraising to management and governance.
Readership/Target Audience: Aimed at chief executives, trustees and senior managers of voluntary organisations.
ADVERTISING RATES:
Full Page Colour £1400.00
Agency Commission: 10%
Mechanical Data: Bleed Size: 303 x 216mm, Trim Size: 297 x 210mm, Film: Digital
Copy instructions: Copy Date: 18th of month prior to publication date
Average advertising content per issue: 16%
Supplement(s): ICT - 1xY, Strategy - 2xY
BUSINESS: FINANCE & ECONOMICS: Fundraising

ENGAGED INVESTOR
1660509U1F-590

Editorial Address: 30 Cannon Street, LONDON, EC4M 6YJ
Tel: 020 7618 3485 **Fax:** 020 7618 3499
Email: news@engaged-investor.com
Advertising Address: As above. **Tel:** 020 7618 3456
Fax: 020 7618 3490
Email: stuart.hall@engaged-investor.com
Web site: http://www.engagedinvestor.com
Publisher: Newsquest Specialist Media Ltd
Date Established: 2004
Frequency: 6 issues yearly
Free to qualifying individuals
Circulation: 10,067 (BPA Worldwide 01/07/2007 to 31/12/2007)
Editor: Bob Campion; **Executive Editor:** Maggie Williams
Summary of Content: Magazine designed to educate pension trustees about investment and long term financial planning.
Readership/Target Audience: Aimed at pension fund trustees, charities and investment professionals.
ADVERTISING RATES:
Full Page Colour £4800.00
Agency Commission: 10%
Mechanical Data: Type Area: 285 x 210mm, Bleed Size: 313 x 243mm, Trim Size: 309 x 239mm, Col Length: 285mm, Page Width: 210mm, Film: Digital
Copy instructions: Copy Date: 1st of the month prior to publication date
Average advertising content per issue: 40%
BUSINESS: FINANCE & ECONOMICS: Investment

ENGINE REPAIR & REMANUFACTURE
38299U31A-59

Editorial Address: Oakapple Cottage, Furnace Lane, Broad Oak Brede, RYE, TN31 6ES **Tel:** 01424 882702
Fax: 01424 882702
Email: info@rgoltd.co.uk
Advertising Address: As above.
Email: info@rgoltd.co.uk
Web site: http://www.rgoltd.co.uk
Publisher: RGO Exhibitions & Publications Ltd
Frequency: Quarterly
Annual Sub.: £20.00
Circulation: 2,500 (Publisher's Statement)
Usual Pagination: 68
Editor: Chris Hancock; **Advertising Manager:** Pam Bourne
Summary of Content: Magazine that provides a means of communication between the user and supplier of engine re-conditioning machinery, equipment and services.
Readership/Target Audience: Aimed at the automotive, commercial vehicle, industrial, marine, rail and aeronautical markets.
ADVERTISING RATES:
Full Page Mono £395.00
Full Page Colour £635.00
Agency Commission: 10%
Mechanical Data: Page Width: 126mm, Film: Digital, Type Area: 184 x 126mm, Col Length: 184mm, Trim Size: 212 x 150mm
Copy instructions: Copy Date: 2 weeks prior to publication date
Average advertising content per issue: 40%
BUSINESS: MOTOR TRADE: Motor Trade Accessories

ENGINE TECHNOLOGY INTERNATIONAL
38300U31A-62

Editorial Address: Abinger House, Church Street, DORKING, RH4 1DF **Tel:** 01306 743744 **Fax:** 01306 887546
Email: d.slavnich@ukintpress.com
Advertising Address: As above. **Fax:** 01306 742525
Email: s.edmands@ukintpress.com
Web site: http://www.ukipme.com
ISSN: 1460-9509
Publisher: UKIP Media & Events Ltd
Date Established: 1997
Frequency: Quarterly - Published in the 1st week of the cover month
Annual Sub.: £140.00
Circulation: 9,886 (BPA Worldwide 01/01/2008 to 30/06/2008)

Business Magazines

Usual Pagination: 100
Editor: Dean Slavnich; **Managing Director:** Graham Johnson; **Publisher:** Tony Robinson
Summary of Content: Magazine dealing with the future of power transmission.
Readership/Target Audience: Read by people working in the international engine technology industry.
ADVERTISING RATES:
Full Page Colour £3450.00
Agency Commission: 15%
Mechanical Data: Film: Digital
BUSINESS: MOTOR TRADE: Motor Trade Accessories

THE ENGINEER
37542U19A-180

Editorial Address: St. Giles House, 50 Poland Street, LONDON, W1F 7AX **Tel:** 020 7970 4000
Email: tepr@centaur.co.uk
Advertising Address: As above. **Fax:** 020 7970 4190
Email: lars.fiddy@centaur.co.uk
Web site: http://www.theengineer.co.uk
ISSN: 0013-7758
Publisher: Centaur Media plc
Date Established: 1856
Frequency: 25 issues yearly
Cover Price: £2.70
Annual Sub.: £69.00
Circulation: 31,538 (ABC 01/01/2008 to 31/12/2008)
Usual Pagination: 60
Editor: Jon Excell; **News Editor:** Jason Ford; **Features Editor:** Jon Excell; **Advertising Manager:** Lars Fiddy; **Publisher:** Sean Marshall
Summary of Content: Magazine providing news, comment and analysis on innovation and technology across all UK manufacturing sectors.
Twitter: https://twitter.com/TheEngineerUK.
Readership/Target Audience: Aimed at engineers and senior executives in technology-led sectors.
ADVERTISING RATES:
Full Page Colour £3950.00
Agency Commission: 10%
Mechanical Data: Type Area: 255 x 185mm, Col Length: 255mm, Bleed Size: 286 x 216mm, Trim Size: 280 x 210mm, Film: Digital, Page Width: 185mm
Copy instructions: Copy Date: Monday prior to publication date
Average advertising content per issue: 50%
BUSINESS: ENGINEERING & MACHINERY

ENGINEERING
37543U19A-200

Editorial Address: 6A New Street, WARWICK, CV34 4RX
Tel: 01926 408242 **Fax:** 01926 408206
Email: press@engineeringnet.co.uk
Advertising Address: As above. **Tel:** 01926 408244
Email: kate@engineeringnet.co.uk
Web site: http://www.engineeringnet.co.uk
ISSN: 0013-7782
Publisher: Engineering Magazine Ltd
Date Established: 1866
Frequency: 11 issues yearly - Published in the 3rd week of the cover month
Free to qualifying individuals
Annual Sub.: £99.00
Circulation: 16,789 (ABC 01/01/2007 to 31/12/2007)
Usual Pagination: 90
Editor: Steve Welch; **Advertising Manager:** Kate Ryan; **Managing Editor:** Steve Welch
Summary of Content: Magazine covering all aspects of the manufacturing industry. Includes articles covering concepts and innovations through the product lifecycle, from design to recycling.
Readership/Target Audience: Readership includes senior executives and engineers in manufacturing industries, nationalised industries.
ADVERTISING: Rates on application
Copy instructions: Copy Date: 4 weeks prior to publication date
BUSINESS: ENGINEERING & MACHINERY

ENGINEERING AND TECHNOLOGY
37311U17-130

Formerly: IEE Review
Editorial Address: Michael Faraday House, Six Hills Way, STEVENAGE, SG1 2AY **Tel:** 01438 313311
Fax: 01438 765526
Email: engtechmag@theiet.org
Advertising Address: As above. **Tel:** 01438 767351
Fax: 01438 318361
Email: lhall@theiet.org
Web site: http://www.theiet.org/engtechmag
ISSN: 0013-5127
Publisher: The Institution of Engineering and Technology
Frequency: 21 issues yearly
Free to qualifying individuals
Circulation: 151,178 (Publisher's Statement)
Usual Pagination: 96

Editor: Dominic Lenton; **News Editor:** Lorna Sharpe; **Features Editor:** Vitali Vitaliev; **Editor-in-Chief:** Dickon Ross; **Managing Editor:** Dominic Lenton
Summary of Content: Magazine of the Institution of Engineering and Technology covering industry news and technical information from the IET.
Readership/Target Audience: Read by members of the IET.
ADVERTISING RATES:
Full Page Colour £3883.00
Agency Commission: 15%
Mechanical Data: Col Widths (Display): 40mm, Page Width: 186mm, Film: Digital, Type Area: 270 x 186mm, Col Length: 270mm, Trim Size: 297 x 210mm, Bleed Size: 303 x 216mm
Copy instructions: Copy Date: 2 weeks prior to publication date
BUSINESS: ELECTRICAL

ENGINEERING & TECHNOLOGY
37544U19A-545

Editorial Address: Kentons House, 24 Blendon Road, BEXLEY, DA5 1BW **Tel:** 0870 701 3536 **Fax:** 0870 701 3537
Email: engineeringandtechnology@ntlworld.com
Advertising Address: As above.
Email: engineeringandtechnology@ntlworld.com
Publisher: Direct Publishing Ltd
Date Established: 1996
Frequency: Quarterly
Free to qualifying individuals
Annual Sub.: £45.00
Circulation: 4,100 (Publisher's Statement)
Usual Pagination: 24
Editor: Phil Brown; **Advertising Manager:** Phil Brown; **Publisher:** Phil Brown
Summary of Content: Magazine covering news, technology and product developments in engineering design and manufacture.
Readership/Target Audience: Read by senior managers and directors within manufacturing companies, involved in design, production, test, R&D and purchasing.
ADVERTISING RATES:
Full Page Colour £1395.00
Agency Commission: 10%
Mechanical Data: Bleed Size: +3mm, Film: Digital, Type Area: 297 x 210mm, Col Length: 297mm, Page Width: 210mm
Copy instructions: Copy Date: 8th of month prior to publication date
Average advertising content per issue: 40%
BUSINESS: ENGINEERING & MACHINERY

ENGINEERING CAPACITY
22453U19A-233

Editorial Address: The Old Mill, Lower Quay, FAREHAM, PO16 0RA **Tel:** 01329 825335 **Fax:** 01329 825330
Email: editor@engineeringcapacity.com
Advertising Address: As above.
Email: sales@engineeringcapacity.com
Web site: http://www.engineeringcapacity.com
ISSN: 0306-0179
Publisher: Mercator Media Ltd
Date Established: 1959
Frequency: Monthly - Published in the middle of the cover month
Cover Price: Free
Circulation: 10,098 (ABC 01/01/2008 to 31/12/2008)
Usual Pagination: 40
Editor: Andy Sandford
Summary of Content: News for UK manufacturing buyers about contract engineering/manufacturing services. In particular, news of the services offered by subcontract companies; their developments in core competences and performance improvements. Also, industry news of interest to UK manufacturers who outsource bespoke components and production services.
Readership/Target Audience: Aimed at UK buyers of contract engineering manufacturing services and bespoke components.
ADVERTISING RATES:
Full Page Mono £1505.00
Full Page Colour £2060.00
Agency Commission: 10%
Mechanical Data: Type Area: 201 x 140mm, Col Length: 201mm, Page Width: 140mm, Film: Digital, Bleed Size: 235 x 168mm, Trim Size: 229 x 162mm, No. of Columns (Display): 3, Col Widths (Display): 44mm
Copy instructions: Copy Date: 1st week of the month prior to publication date
Average advertising content per issue: 50%
BUSINESS: ENGINEERING & MACHINERY

ENGINEERING COMPUTATIONS
1750448U55-9026

Editorial Address: Department of Civil Engineering, University of Wales Swansea, Singleton Park, SWANSEA, SA2 8PP **Tel:** 01792 295624 **Fax:** 01792 295705
Web site: http://www.emeraldinsight.com/ec.htm
ISSN: 0264-4401

Publisher: Emerald Group Publishing Ltd
Date Established: 1983
Frequency: 8 issues yearly
Editor: Harry Colson; **Publisher:** Harry Colson
Summary of Content: Publication providing information on the latest developments and applications of new solution algorithms and innovative numerical methods.
Readership/Target Audience: Aimed at research engineers, numerical analysts and software developers in academic institutions and industry.
ADVERTISING: No Advertising taken
BUSINESS: APPLIED SCIENCE & LABORATORIES

ENGINEERING, CONSTRUCTION AND ARCHITECTURAL MANAGEMENT
1750464U42A-237

Editorial Address: Howard House, Wagon Lane, BINGLEY, BD16 1WA **Tel:** 01274 777700
Email: vrobillard@emeraldinsight.com
Web site: http://www.emeraldinsight.com/ecam.htm
ISSN: 0969-9988
Publisher: Emerald Group Publishing Ltd
Frequency: 6 issues yearly
Usual Pagination: 96
Editor: Valerie Robillard; **Publisher:** Valerie Robillard
Summary of Content: Journal which publishes research in all areas of construction; building, civil engineering, major infrastructure and maintenance. Construction management is also covered; project management including design and construction processes, the management of construction companies and architectural practices, and industry developments from a national and international perspective.
Readership/Target Audience: Aimed at those involved in all areas of construction and construction management.
ADVERTISING: No Advertising taken
BUSINESS: CONSTRUCTION

ENGINEERING DESIGNER
37607U19B-230

Editorial Address: Ewell House, Graveney Road, FAVERSHAM, ME13 8UP **Tel:** 01795 542435
Fax: 01795 535469
Email: editorial@engineeringdesigner.co.uk
Advertising Address: As above. **Tel:** 01795 542403
Email: paulh@engineeringdesigner.co.uk
Web site: http://www.engineeringdesigner.co.uk
ISSN: 0013-7858
Publisher: GTC
Date Established: 1951
Frequency: 6 issues yearly - Published in the first week of each cover month
Cover Price: £6.80
Annual Sub.: £37.00
Circulation: 13,000 (Publisher's Statement)
Usual Pagination: 36
Editor: Clare Swaffer; **Managing Director:** Dominic Deeson; **Advertising Manager:** Paul Holness
Summary of Content: Journal containing features on engineering and product design, related technology and other relevant subjects.
Readership/Target Audience: Read by engineering product designers and CAD operators.
ADVERTISING RATES:
Full Page Colour £875.00
Agency Commission: 10%
Mechanical Data: Film: Digital, Trim Size: 297 x 210mm, Bleed Size: 303 x 216mm, Type Area: 275 x 188mm, Col Length: 275mm, Page Width: 188mm
Average advertising content per issue: 10%
BUSINESS: ENGINEERING & MACHINERY: Engineering - Design

ENGINEERING INTEGRITY
37652U19F-106

Editorial Address: Amber Instruments Ltd, Dunston House, Dunston Road, CHESTERFIELD, S41 9QD
Tel: 01246 260250
Email: eis@amberinstruments.com
Advertising Address: 5 Wentworth Avenue, SHEFFIELD, S11 9QX **Tel:** 0114 262 1155
Email: catherine@cpinder.com
Web site: http://www.e-i-s.org.uk
ISSN: 1365-4101
Publisher: The Engineering Integrity Society
Date Established: 1997
Frequency: Half-yearly - Published in March and September
Free to qualifying individuals
Annual Sub.: £50.00
Circulation: 1,460 (Publisher's Statement)
Usual Pagination: 56
Editor: Paul Armstrong; **Advertising Manager:** Catherine Pinder; **Managing Editor:** Catherine Pinder
Summary of Content: Journal of the Engineering Integrity Society containing technical articles, information on conferences and meetings, industry news and reports by the three groups within the Society.
Readership/Target Audience: Read by members of the Engineering Integrity Society.

ADVERTISING RATES:
Full Page Mono £255.00
Full Page Colour £445.00
Agency Commission: 10%
Mechanical Data: Bleed Size: 303 x 216mm, Trim Size: 297 x 210mm, Film: Positive, right reading, emulsion side down. Digital
Copy instructions: Copy Date: 1st of the month prior to publication date
Average advertising content per issue: 15%
BUSINESS: ENGINEERING & MACHINERY: Production & Mechanical Engineering

ENGINEERING PRECISELY

35987U5A-72_50

Formerly: DMAC News
Editorial Address: The National Physical Laboratory, Hampton Road, TEDDINGTON, TW11 0LW
Tel: 020 8943 6936 **Fax:** 020 8943 7160
Email: sarah.purcell@npl.co.uk
Web site: http://www.npl.co.uk/publications/news/engineering_precisely
Publisher: National Physical Laboratory
Date Established: 2005
Frequency: 3 issues yearly - Varies
Cover Price: Free
Circulation: 8,000 (Publisher's Statement)
Usual Pagination: 12
Editor: Sarah Purcell
Summary of Content: Newsletter covering news and technical information in the field of dimensional metrology.
Readership/Target Audience: Aimed at users and equipment manufacturers.
ADVERTISING: No Advertising taken
BUSINESS: COMPUTERS & AUTOMATION: Automation & Instrumentation

ENGINEERING SUBCONTRACTOR

1813939U19A-565

Editorial Address: Triumph House, Station Approach, Sanderstead Road, SOUTH CROYDON, CR2 0PL
Tel: 020 8916 0022 **Fax:** 020 8916 0033
Email: roger@rbpublishing.co.uk
Advertising Address: As above.
Email: roger@rbpublishing.co.uk
Web site: http://www.rogerbarberpublishing.com
ISSN: 1742-5778
Publisher: Roger Barber Publishing
Date Established: 2004
Frequency: 10 issues yearly - Published at the beginning of the cover month
Cover Price: £6.00
Free to qualifying individuals
Annual Sub.: £60.00
Circulation: 10,010 (Publisher's Statement)
Usual Pagination: 60
Editor: Roger Barber; **Advertising Manager:** Roger Barber
Summary of Content: Magazine covering the latest products and applications in order to increase productivity.
Readership/Target Audience: Aimed at precision engineers and metal fabricators.
ADVERTISING RATES:
Full Page Colour £1500.00
Agency Commission: 10%
Mechanical Data: Type Area: 265 x 185mm, Bleed Size: 303 x 216mm, Trim Size: 297 x 210mm, Col Length: 265mm, Page Width: 185mm, Film: Digital
Copy instructions: Copy Date: 3 weeks prior to publication date
BUSINESS: ENGINEERING & MACHINERY

ENGINEERING SURVEYING SHOWCASE

35840U4C-140

Editorial Address: Suite L, 17 Park Place, STEVENAGE, SG1 1DU **Tel:** 01438 352617 **Fax:** 01438 351989
Email: editor@pvpubs.demon.co.uk
Advertising Address: As above.
Email: sharon@pvpubs.demon.co.uk
Web site: http://www.pvpubs.co.uk
Publisher: PV Publications Ltd.
Date Established: 1993
Frequency: Half-yearly - Published in April and October
Cover Price: Free
Circulation: 6,000 (Publisher's Statement)
Usual Pagination: 56
Editor: Stephen Booth; **Advertising Manager:** Sharon Howard
Summary of Content: Magazine highlighting the latest developments and applications in surveying technology and techniques.
Readership/Target Audience: Aimed at senior managers, engineers and surveyors.
ADVERTISING RATES:
Full Page Mono £1250.00
Full Page Colour £1995.00
Agency Commission: 10%

Mechanical Data: Type Area: 269.5 x 189mm, Col Length: 269.5mm, Page Width: 189mm, Trim Size: 297 x 210mm, Film: Digital
Copy instructions: Copy Date: 2 weeks prior to publication date
BUSINESS: ARCHITECTURE & BUILDING: Surveying

THE ENGLISH HISTORICAL REVIEW

30757U62R-467

Editorial Address: Great Clarendon Street, OXFORD, OX2 6DP **Tel:** 01865 353000
Email: anne.borg@oupjournals.org
Advertising Address: 60 Upper Broadmoor Road, CROWTHORNE, RG45 7DE **Tel:** 01344 779945
Fax: 01344 779945
Email: lhann@lhms.fsnet.co.uk
Web site: http://www3.oup.co.uk/enghis
ISSN: 0013-8266
Publisher: OUP
Date Established: 1886
Frequency: 5 issues yearly
Annual Sub.: £150.00
Circulation: 2,400 (Publisher's Statement)
Usual Pagination: 280
Editor: Bernard Gowers
Summary of Content: Journal covering British, European and world history since the classical era. It also deals with the history of the Americas, including foreign policy of the USA and her role in the wider world.
Readership/Target Audience: Aimed at scholars and students.
ADVERTISING RATES:
Full Page Mono £415.00
Agency Commission: 10%
Mechanical Data: Film: Digital, Page Width: 125mm, Type Area: 200 x 125mm, Col Length: 200mm
Copy instructions: Copy Date: 1 month prior to publication date
BUSINESS: CHURCH & SCHOOL EQUIPMENT & EDUCATION: Education Related

ENT NEWS

40160U56A-63_50

Editorial Address: 9 Gayfield Square, EDINBURGH, EH1 3NT **Tel:** 0131 478 8401 **Fax:** 0131 557 4701
Email: editorial@pinpoint-scotland.com
Advertising Address: As above. **Tel:** 0131 557 4184
Email: heather@pinpoint-scotland.com
Web site: http://www.pinpoint-scotland.com
ISSN: 1368-8944
Publisher: Pinpoint Scotland Ltd
Date Established: 1991
Frequency: 6 issues yearly - Published in the 1st week of the 1st cover month
Free to qualifying individuals
Annual Sub.: £17.00
Circulation: 18,000 (Publisher's Statement)
Usual Pagination: 180
Editor: Joe Crossland; **Managing Director:** Caroline Elder; **Advertising Manager:** Heather McLaughlin
Summary of Content: Journal covering news and the latest developments in the field of ear, nose and throat, audiology and oral and maxillo-facial medicine.
Readership/Target Audience: Read by otolaryngologists, audiologists, hospital managers, nurses and doctors, and plastic surgeons.
ADVERTISING RATES:
Full Page Colour £1428.00
Copy instructions: Copy Date: 4 weeks prior to publication date
BUSINESS: HEALTH & MEDICAL

ENTERPRISE AND SOCIETY: THE INTERNATIONAL JOURNAL OF BUSINESS HISTORY

601427U14R-75

Formerly: Business and Economic History
Editorial Address: Great Clarendon Street, OXFORD, OX2 6DP **Tel:** 01865 353907 **Fax:** 01865 353485
Advertising Address: 60 Upper Broadmoor Road, CROWTHORNE, RG45 7DE **Tel:** 01344 779945
Fax: 01344 779945
Email: lhann@lhms.fsnet.co.uk
Web site: http://www.es.oupjournals.org
ISSN: 1467-2227
Publisher: OUP
Date Established: 2000
Frequency: Quarterly
Cover Price: £36.00
Annual Sub.: £44.00
Circulation: 800 (Publisher's Statement)
Usual Pagination: 200
Editor: Philip Scranton
Summary of Content: Journal which contains articles that focus on individual firms and industries which are grounded in a broad historical framework. It offers a forum for debate on historical relations between businesses and their larger

political, cultural, institutional, social, and economic contexts.
Readership/Target Audience: Aimed at all members of the Business History Conference, including academics in history, economics, sociology, management, political science and corporate and industry analysts.
ADVERTISING RATES:
Full Page Mono £290.00
Agency Commission: 10%
Mechanical Data: Film: Digital, Type Area: 220 x 140mm, Col Length: 220mm, Page Width: 140mm
BUSINESS: COMMERCE, INDUSTRY & MANAGEMENT: Commerce Related

ENTERPRISE DEVELOPMENT AND MICROFINANCE

37137U14H-84_50

Formerly: Small Enterprise Development
Editorial Address: Bourton Hall, Bourton, RUGBY, CV23 9QZ **Tel:** 01926 634501 **Fax:** 01926 634502
Email: denise.hastings@practicalaction.org.uk
Advertising Address: As above.
Email: marketing@practicalaction.org.uk
Web site: http://www.practicalactionpublishing.org.uk
ISSN: 1755-1978
Publisher: Practical Action Publishing
Date Established: 1990
Frequency: Quarterly
Annual Sub.: £75.00
Circulation: 550 (Publisher's Statement)
Usual Pagination: 72
Editor: Denise Hastings; **Managing Director:** Toby Milner; **Managing Editor:** Clare Tawney
Summary of Content: Academic journal containing information on small enterprise development programmes in developing countries.
Readership/Target Audience: Aimed at academics, fieldworkers and policy-makers.
ADVERTISING RATES:
Full Page Mono £500.00
Full Page Colour £900.00
Mechanical Data: Type Area: 210 x 145mm, Col Length: 210mm, Page Width: 145mm, Film: Positive, right reading, emulsion side down
Copy instructions: Copy Date: 6 weeks prior to publication date
BUSINESS: COMMERCE, INDUSTRY & MANAGEMENT: Small Business

ENTERPRISING NEWS

1740077U63D-718

Formerly: Enterprising
Editorial Address: Suite 1019, Abbey Mill Business Centre, 12 Seedhill Road, PAISLEY, PA1 1JS **Tel:** 0141 889 6868
Fax: 0141 849 7301
Email: carrie@axismediagroup.co.uk
Advertising Address: 29 Main Street, Bothwell, GLASGOW, G71 8RD **Tel:** 01698 853000 **Fax:** 01698 854208
Email: patrick@straightlinepublishing.com
Web site: http://www.enterprisingnews.com
Publisher: Straight Line Publishing Ltd
Frequency: 6 issues yearly
Cover Price: Free
Circulation: 27,500 (Publisher's Statement)
Editor: Carrie Wallace; **Advertising Manager:** Patrick Bellew; **Managing Editor:** Patrick Bellew
Summary of Content: Scottish business magazine covering all issues affecting Scottish SMEs.
Readership/Target Audience: Aimed at Scottish SMEs.
ADVERTISING RATES:
SCC £22.00
Agency Commission: 10%
Mechanical Data: Type Area: 420 x 295mm, Col Length: 420mm, Page Width: 295mm, Col Widths (Display): 43mm, No. of Columns (Display): 6, Film: Digital
Average advertising content per issue: 40%
Supplement(s): Think Finance - 1xY, Think River Clyde Regeneration - 1xY, Think Training - 1xY
BUSINESS: REGIONAL BUSINESS: Regional Business Scotland

ENTERPRISING SCOTLAND

601086U63D-120

Editorial Address: 6 Freskyn Place, East Mains Industrial Estate, BROXBURN, EH52 5NF **Tel:** 01506 508001
Fax: 01506 508002
Email: editorial@enterprisingscotland.com
Advertising Address: As above.
Email: adverts@enterprisingscotland.com
Web site: http://www.capitalgroupuk.com
Publisher: Capital Publishing
Date Established: 1999
Frequency: Quarterly
Cover Price: £2.45
Free to qualifying individuals
Annual Sub.: £9.80
Circulation: 19,700 (Publisher's Statement)
Usual Pagination: 120

Editor: Katy Sheilds; **Advertising Manager:** Graeme Holloway; **Managing Editor:** Graeme Holloway; **Publisher:** Lawrence Service
Summary of Content: Magazine covering all aspects of business and economic developments in Scotland.
Readership/Target Audience: Read by managing directors and senior decision makers.
ADVERTISING RATES:
Full Page Mono £1495.00
Full Page Colour £1970.00
Agency Commission: 10%
Mechanical Data: Type Area: 268 x 188mm, Film: Positive, right reading, emulsion side down, Page Width: 188mm, Col Length: 268mm
Average advertising content per issue: 38%
BUSINESS: REGIONAL BUSINESS: Regional Business Scotland

ENTERTAINMENT LAW REVIEW 39152U44-560
Editorial Address: 100 Avenue Road, Swiss Cottage, LONDON, NW3 3PF **Tel:** 020 7393 7000 **Fax:** 020 7393 7010
Email: jacqui.mowbrey@thomsonreuters.com
Web site: http://www.sweetandmaxwell.co.uk
ISSN: 0959-3799
Publisher: Sweet & Maxwell Ltd
Date Established: 1988
Frequency: 8 issues yearly
Annual Sub.: £470.00
Editor: Jacqui Mowbrey
Summary of Content: Journal covering international developments in entertainment and media law, with particular emphasis on the legal protection and exploitation of creative talent.
Readership/Target Audience: Aimed at legal professionals and those involved in the entertainment business.
ADVERTISING: No Advertising taken
BUSINESS: LEGAL

ENTERTAINMENT NEWS 1894693U2A-705
Editorial Address: The Johnson Building, 77 Hatton Garden, LONDON, EC1N 8JS **Tel:** 020 7190 7777
Fax: 020 7190 7860
Email: editorial@entnews.co.uk
Web site: http://www.entnews.co.uk
Publisher: The Profile Group (UK) Ltd
Frequency: Weekly - Published on a Monday
Free to qualifying individuals
Summary of Content: Report detailing information on events taking place in the next nine months.
Readership/Target Audience: Aimed at media and industry professionals.
BUSINESS: COMMUNICATIONS, ADVERTISING & MARKETING

ENTERTAINMENT TECHNOLOGY 1609336U64K-643
Formerly: Entertainment Technology Magazine
Editorial Address: The Studio, High Green, Great Shelford, CAMBRIDGE, CB2 5EG **Tel:** 01223 550805
Fax: 01223 550806
Email: editor@etnow.com
Advertising Address: As above.
Email: editor@etnow.com
Web site: http://www.etnow.com
Publisher: Entertainment Technology Press Ltd
Date Established: 2001
Frequency: Monthly
Cover Price: Free
Circulation: 5,170 (Publisher's Statement)
Usual Pagination: 12
Editor: John Offord; **Managing Director:** Ken Sewell; **Advertising Manager:** John Offord
Summary of Content: Magazine covering news from within the entertainment technology industry, special features and reports, the etnow web directory, job listings and profiles of prominent professionals within the industry.
Readership/Target Audience: Aimed at those working in the entertainment and presentation technology sectors within the UK.
ADVERTISING RATES:
Full Page Colour £1295.00
SCC £19.50
Agency Commission: 10%
Mechanical Data: Type Area: 278 x 190mm, Bleed Size: 298 x 210mm, Col Length: 278mm, Page Width: 190mm, Film: Digital
Copy instructions: Copy Date: 21st of the month prior to publication date
Average advertising content per issue: 30%
BUSINESS: OTHER CLASSIFICATIONS: Cinema Entertainment

ENTOMOLOGIST'S GAZETTE 41547U64H-150
Editorial Address: 18 Bathurst Walk, IVER, SL0 9AZ
Tel: 01753 631114 **Fax:** 01753 631115

Email: publishing@pemberleybooks.com
Advertising Address: As above.
Email: publishing@pemberleybooks.com
ISSN: 0013-8894
Publisher: Pemberley Books
Date Established: 1950
Frequency: Quarterly
Annual Sub.: £35.00
Circulation: 400 (Publisher's Statement)
Usual Pagination: 76
Editor: Ian Johnson; **Advertising Manager:** Ian Johnson
Summary of Content: Devoted to palaearctic entomology. Contains articles on biology, ecology, distribution, taxonomy and systematics of all orders of insects, particularly lepidoptera.
Readership/Target Audience: Aimed at professional and amateur entomologists.
ADVERTISING RATES:
Full Page Mono £50.00
Full Page Colour £300.00
Mechanical Data: Col Length: 176mm, Film: Digital, Type Area: 176 x 110mm, Print Process: Offset litho, Trim Size: 210 x 148mm, Page Width: 110mm
Copy instructions: Copy Date: 15th of the month prior to publication date
Average advertising content per issue: 5%
BUSINESS: OTHER CLASSIFICATIONS: Veterinary

ENTOMOLOGIST'S MONTHLY MAGAZINE 41548U64H-151
Editorial Address: 18 Bathurst Walk, IVER, SL0 9AZ
Tel: 01753 631114 **Fax:** 01753 631115
Email: publishing@pemberleybooks.com
Advertising Address: As above.
Email: publishing@pemberleybooks.com
Web site: http://www.pemberleybooks.com
ISSN: 0013-8908
Publisher: Pemberley Books
Date Established: 1864
Frequency: Quarterly
Annual Sub.: £36.00
Circulation: 400 (Publisher's Statement)
Usual Pagination: 86
Editor: K.G. V. Smith; **Advertising Manager:** Ian Johnson; **Publisher:** Ian Johnson
Summary of Content: Contains original papers and notes on all orders of insects and terrestrial arthropods from any part of the world, specialising in groups other than lepidoptera.
Readership/Target Audience: Aimed at professional and serious amateur entomologists.
ADVERTISING RATES:
Full Page Mono £45.00
Full Page Colour £350.00
Mechanical Data: Col Length: 176mm, Type Area: 176 x 110mm, Print Process: Offset litho, Trim Size: 215 x 140mm, Page Width: 110mm, Film: Digital
Copy instructions: Copy Date: 15th of the month prior to publication date
Average advertising content per issue: 5%
BUSINESS: OTHER CLASSIFICATIONS: Veterinary

ENTOMOLOGIST'S RECORD & JOURNAL OF VARIATION 41549U64H-152
Editorial Address: 14 West Road, BISHOP'S STORTFORD, CM23 3QP **Tel:** 01279 507697 **Fax:** 01279 507697
Email: cpauk1@ntlworld.com
Web site: http://www.entrecord.com
ISSN: 0013-8916
Publisher: Entomologist's Record & Journal of Variation
Date Established: 1890
Frequency: 6 issues yearly
Annual Sub.: £28.00
Circulation: 700 (Publisher's Statement)
Usual Pagination: 48
Editor: Colin W. Plant
Summary of Content: Journal containing information about the identification, collection, variation and distribution of British and European lepidoptera and other insects.
Readership/Target Audience: Aimed at professional and amateur entomologists.
ADVERTISING: No Advertising taken
BUSINESS: OTHER CLASSIFICATIONS: Veterinary

ENVIRONMENT BULLETIN 36624U12A-40
Editorial Address: Queens Road, Penkhull, STOKE-ON-TRENT, ST4 7LQ **Tel:** 01782 764444 **Fax:** 01782 412331
Email: joanne.dawson@ceram.com
Web site: http://www.ceram.com
ISSN: 1369-376X
Publisher: CERAM Research Ltd
Date Established: 1997
Frequency: 6 issues yearly
Free to qualifying individuals
Circulation: 750 (Publisher's Statement)
Editor: Joanne Dawson

Summary of Content: Bulletin covering legislation and standards, guidance and best practice on the environment, health and safety and food contact materials relevant to the ceramics industry.
Readership/Target Audience: Aimed at the ceramics industry.
ADVERTISING: No Advertising taken
BUSINESS: CERAMICS, POTTERY & GLASS: Ceramics & Pottery

ENVIRONMENT IN BUSINESS 40646U57-22
Formerly: Environment Information Bulletin
Editorial Address: Tolley House, 2 Addiscombe Road, CROYDON, CR9 5AF **Tel:** 020 7739 5889
Email: paulsuff@mac.com
Web site: http://www.eibonline.co.uk
ISSN: 0964-5322
Publisher: LexisNexis UK
Date Established: 1991
Frequency: Monthly
Annual Sub.: £218.00
Circulation: 5,000 (Publisher's Statement)
Usual Pagination: 32
Editor: Paul Suff
Summary of Content: Magazine covering all key environmental developments relating to industry and business, in particular legislation, company policy and practice.
Readership/Target Audience: Aimed at environmental managers, health and safety professionals, lawyers and environmental health officers.
ADVERTISING: No Advertising taken
BUSINESS: ENVIRONMENT & POLLUTION

ENVIRONMENT INDUSTRY MAGAZINE 1864578U57-166
Editorial Address: 254A Bury New Road, Whitefield, MANCHESTER, M45 8QN **Tel:** 0161 796 7870
Fax: 0161 766 8997
Email: alex@enviromedia.ltd.uk
Advertising Address: As above.
Web site: http://www.enviromedia.ltd.uk
Publisher: Enviromedia Ltd
Date Established: 2009
Frequency: 6 issues yearly
Cover Price: Free
Circulation: 30,000 (Publisher's Statement)
Usual Pagination: 68
Editor: Alex Stacey
Summary of Content: Magazine focusing on networking and communications within the environmental sector.
Readership/Target Audience: Aimed at professionals working in the environmental industry.
ADVERTISING RATES:
Full Page Colour £2250.00
BUSINESS: ENVIRONMENT & POLLUTION

ENVIRONMENT JOURNAL 1668180U57-135
Formerly: East Journal
Editorial Address: The Studio, Denton, PETERBOROUGH, PE7 3SD **Tel:** 01733 246850 **Fax:** 01733 243322
Email: mark.williams@environmentmagazine.uk.com
Advertising Address: As above. **Tel:** 020 7043 8624
Fax: 020 7493 0588
Email: sophie.barrowman@climateandenvironmentmedia.com
Web site: http://www.environmentmagazine.uk.com
Publisher: Climate and Environment Media Ltd
Date Established: 2002
Frequency: 10 issues yearly
Free to qualifying individuals
Annual Sub.: £100.00
Circulation: 14,500 (Publisher's Statement)
Usual Pagination: 44
Editor: Mark Williams; **Managing Editor:** Mark Williams; **Publisher:** Chris Innis
Summary of Content: Journal focusing on environmental sustainable development.
Readership/Target Audience: Aimed at government staff at all levels including cabinet ministers, local authorities, MEPs, members of the house of lords and other government officials and industry.
ADVERTISING RATES:
Full Page Colour £2150.00
SCC £25.00
Agency Commission: 10%
Mechanical Data: Type Area: 297 x 210mm, Col Length: 297mm, Page Width: 210mm, Bleed Size: 310 x 220mm, No. of Columns (Display): 3, Film: positive, right reading, emulsion side down
Copy instructions: Copy Date: 4 weeks prior to publication date
Average advertising content per issue: 30%
BUSINESS: ENVIRONMENT & POLLUTION

ENVIRONMENT TIMES
40648U57-25

Editorial Address: 22 Warwick Street, Adlington, CHORLEY, PR7 4JQ **Tel:** 01257 481878 **Fax:** 01257 474975
Email: duncan@environmenttimes.co.uk
Advertising Address: As above.
Email: susanne@environmenttimes.co.uk
Web site: http://www.environmenttimes.co.uk
ISSN: 1350-4584
Publisher: Beckhouse Media Ltd
Date Established: 1993
Frequency: Quarterly
Free to qualifying individuals
Annual Sub.: £49.00
Circulation: 13,158 (Publisher's Statement)
Usual Pagination: 60
Editor: Duncan Ashcroft; **Advertising Manager:** Susanne Karmy; **Publisher:** Duncan Ashcroft
Summary of Content: Magazine covering environmental topics, business information, legal comment and equipment guides.
Readership/Target Audience: Read by industrialists, local authorities, waste management companies and the environmental service industry.
ADVERTISING RATES:
Full Page Mono £1350.00
Full Page Colour £1890.00
Agency Commission: 10%
Mechanical Data: Trim Size: 297 x 210mm
Average advertising content per issue: 40%
Supplement(s): Case Study Collections - 1xY
BUSINESS: ENVIRONMENT & POLLUTION

ENVIRONMENTAL EDUCATION
1895114U57-199

Editorial Address: NAEE University of Wolverhampton, Walsall Campus, Gorway, WALSALL, WS1 3BD
Tel: 01332 202422
Email: editor@naeeuk.plus.com
Advertising Address: As above.
Web site: http://www.naee.org.uk
Publisher: National Association for Environmental Education (UK)
Date Established: 2000
Frequency: 3 issues yearly - Printed at the begnning of each academic term - Winter/Spring/Summer
Cover Price: Free
Annual Sub.: £25.00
Circulation: 1,000 (Publisher's Statement)
Usual Pagination: 40
Editor: Philip Sainty; **News Editor:** Katie Scanlan
Summary of Content: Magazine covering environmental education from pre-school to higher education.
Readership/Target Audience: Teachers and educational professionals.
BUSINESS: ENVIRONMENT & POLLUTION

ENVIRONMENTAL ENGINEERING
40649U19A-572

Editorial Address: 1 Birdcage Walk, LONDON, SW1H 9JJ
Tel: 020 7304 6809 **Fax:** 020 7973 0462
Email: johnp@pepublishing.com
Advertising Address: As above. **Tel:** 020 7973 1299
Fax: 020 7799 2479
Email: nigelse@pepublishing.com
Web site: http://www.pepublishing.com
ISSN: 0954-5824
Publisher: Professional Engineering Publishing Ltd
Frequency: Quarterly
Annual Sub.: £70.00
Circulation: 7,000 (Publisher's Statement)
Usual Pagination: 48
Editor: Tristan Honeywill; **Publisher:** Paul Williams
Summary of Content: Official Journal of the Society of Environmental Engineers.
Readership/Target Audience: Aimed at engineers involved in manufacturing and all types of testing and measurement.
ADVERTISING RATES:
Full Page Colour £2300.00
Agency Commission: 10%
Mechanical Data: Trim Size: 297 x 210mm
Copy instructions: Copy Date: 3 weeks prior to publication date
Average advertising content per issue: 40%
BUSINESS: ENGINEERING & MACHINERY

ENVIRONMENTAL FINANCE
623253U1R-50

Editorial Address: 22-24 Corsham Street, LONDON, N1 6DR **Tel:** 020 7251 9151 **Fax:** 020 7251 9161
Email: info@environmental-finance.com
Advertising Address: As above.
Email: matthew.colvan@environmental-finance.com
Web site: http://www.environmental-finance.com
ISSN: 1468-8573
Publisher: Fulton Publishing
Date Established: 1999

Frequency: 10 issues yearly - Published in the 1st week of the cover month
Annual Sub.: £315.00
Circulation: 6,000 (Publisher's Statement)
Usual Pagination: 36
Editor: Mark Nicholls; **Publisher:** Graham Cooper
Summary of Content: Magazine covering environmental risk and impact on companies, especially emissions trading, socially responsible investment, weather derivatives, renewable energy, and corporate social responsibility.
Readership/Target Audience: Aimed at risk managers, insurance professionals, fund managers, brokers, environmental affairs managers and weather derivatives professionals.
ADVERTISING RATES:
Full Page Colour £4500.00
Agency Commission: 10%
Mechanical Data: Type Area: 254 x 178mm, Bleed Size: 303 x 216mm, Trim Size: 297 x 210mm, Col Length: 254mm, Page Width: 178mm, Film: Positive, right reading, emulsion side down. Digital, Print Process: Offset litho
Copy instructions: Copy Date: 1 week prior to publication date
Average advertising content per issue: 30%
BUSINESS: FINANCE & ECONOMICS: Financial Related

ENVIRONMENTAL HEALTH NEWS - EHN
38406U32B-70

Editorial Address: Chadwick Court, 15 Hatfields, LONDON, SE1 8DJ **Tel:** 020 7928 6006 **Fax:** 020 7827 5862
Email: ehn@chgl.com
Advertising Address: As above. **Tel:** 020 7827 6006
Fax: 020 7827 9930
Email: p.prior@cieh.org
Web site: http://www.cieh.org
ISSN: 0969-9856
Publisher: Chadwick House Group Ltd
Date Established: 1986
Frequency: Weekly
Free to qualifying individuals
Annual Sub.: £89.00
Circulation: 12,000 (Publisher's Statement)
Usual Pagination: 20
Editor: Will Hatchett; **Advertising Manager:** Paul Prior
Summary of Content: Magazine of the Chartered Institute of Environmental Health. It covers the full breadth of the environmental health profession: food safety, health and safety, housing, environmental protection, pest control and aspects of public health. It contains up-to-the-minute news coverage, in-depth analysis of national and local issues, legal coverage, letters page, opinion articles, best practice and all the latest private and public sector jobs. It also includes new sections for practitioners who work in the private sector and in public health.
Readership/Target Audience: Aimed at members of the Chartered Institute of Environmental Health, private sector corporate subscribers working as environmental health professionals and health and safety officers, employees of local authorities, consultancies, the NHS and bodies such as the Environment Agency and the Health Protection Agency.
ADVERTISING RATES:
Full Page Mono £1470.00
Full Page Colour £1470.00
SCC £43.00
Agency Commission: 10%
Mechanical Data: Page Width: 190mm, Film: Digital, Type Area: 280 x 190mm, Col Length: 280mm, Trim Size: 300 x 230mm, Bleed Size: 306 x 236mm
Copy instructions: Copy Date: Wednesday 3pm prior to publication date
Average advertising content per issue: 50%
BUSINESS: LOCAL GOVERNMENT, LEISURE & RECREATION: Public Health & Cleaning

ENVIRONMENTAL HEALTH PRACTITIONER
38405U32B-65

Formerly: Environmental Health Journal Practitioner
Editorial Address: Chadwick Court, 15 Hatfields, LONDON, SE1 8DJ **Tel:** 020 7827 5828
Email: ehp@cieh.org
Advertising Address: As above. **Tel:** 020 7827 5862
Fax: 020 7827 9930
Email: p.prior@cieh.org
Web site: http://www.ehp-online.com
Publisher: Chadwick House Group Ltd
Frequency: 10 issues yearly - Published on the 1st Friday of the month. Not published in August or December
Free to qualifying individuals
Annual Sub.: £82.00
Circulation: 10,145 (Publisher's Statement)
Usual Pagination: 40
Editor: Stuart Spear; **Advertising Manager:** Paul Prior
Summary of Content: Journal of the Chartered Institute of Environmental Health covering features, best practice, case studies and a product news section.
Readership/Target Audience: Read by officers and members.

ADVERTISING RATES:
Full Page Colour £1197.00
Agency Commission: 10%
Mechanical Data: Film: Digital, Type Area: 270 x 190mm, Bleed Size: 302 x 214mm, Trim Size: 296 x 208mm, Col Length: 270mm, No. of Columns (Display): 4, Page Width: 190mm
Copy instructions: Copy Date: 2 weeks prior to publication date
Average advertising content per issue: 30%
BUSINESS: LOCAL GOVERNMENT, LEISURE & RECREATION: Public Health & Cleaning

ENVIRONMENTAL LAW AND MANAGEMENT
39154U44-580

Editorial Address: Office G18, Spinners Court, 55 West End, WITNEY, OX28 1NH **Tel:** 01993 706183
Fax: 01993 709410
Email: ltp@lawtext.com
Web site: http://www.lawtext.com
ISSN: 1067-6058
Publisher: Lawtext Publishing Ltd
Date Established: 1988
Frequency: 6 issues yearly
Annual Sub.: £425.00
Editor: Rachel Caldin
Summary of Content: Law report on land management and environmental law, covering developing issues, case law, statute policy and analysis.
Readership/Target Audience: Aimed at all involved in the practical management of environmental issues, including environmental, commercial and planning lawyers.
ADVERTISING: No Advertising taken
BUSINESS: LEGAL

ENVIRONMENTAL LAW MONTHLY
39155U44-600

Editorial Address: 80 Calverley Road, TUNBRIDGE WELLS, TN1 2UN **Tel:** 020 7017 7500 **Fax:** 020 7017 7599
Email: marketing@agra-net.com
Web site: http://www.informalaw.com
ISSN: 0964-4794
Publisher: Agra Informa Ltd
Frequency: Monthly
Annual Sub.: £394.00
Summary of Content: Newsletter on major UK environmental legislation and regulation, EU developments and case law.
Readership/Target Audience: Aimed at environmental lawyers and others concerned with the environment.
ADVERTISING: No Advertising taken
BUSINESS: LEGAL

ENVIRONMENTAL LIABILITY
23750U44-609

Editorial Address: Office G18, Spinners Court, 55 West End, WITNEY, OX28 1NH **Tel:** 01993 706183
Fax: 01993 709410
Email: ltp@lawtext.com
Advertising Address: As above.
Email: rachel_caldin@lawtext.com
Web site: http://www.lawtext.com
ISSN: 0966-2030
Publisher: Lawtext Publishing Ltd
Frequency: 6 issues yearly
Annual Sub.: £325.00
Usual Pagination: 64
Editor: Rachel Caldin; **Advertising Manager:** Rachel Caldin
Summary of Content: Journal covering the impact on industry and business of national and international developments in environmental law and policy.
Readership/Target Audience: Aimed at environmental practitioners, lawyers involved in commercial and property transactions and insolvency practitioners.
ADVERTISING: Rates on application
BUSINESS: LEGAL

ENVIRONMENTAL POLITICS
1895920U57-201

Editorial Address: 4 Park Square, Milton Park, ABINGDON, OX14 4RN **Tel:** 020 7017 6000
Email: ntc1@york.ac.uk
Web site: http://www.tandf.co.uk/journals/titles/09644016.asp
ISSN: 0964-4016
Publisher: Routledge, Taylor & Francis
Frequency: 6 issues yearly
Editor: Neil Carter
Summary of Content: Journal covering the study of environmental politics.
Readership/Target Audience: Aimed at students and those with an interest in environmental politics.
BUSINESS: ENVIRONMENT & POLLUTION

ENVIRONMENTAL SCIENCE & POLICY

1896225U57-202

Editorial Address: Environmental Change Institute, School of Geography and the Environment, South Parks Road, OXFORD, OX1 3QY **Tel:** 01865 275848 **Fax:** 01865 275850
Email: esp@eci.ox.ac.uk
Web site: http://www.elsevier.com/wps/find/journaldescription.cws_home/601264/description
ISSN: 1462-9011
Publisher: Elsevier
Frequency: 8 issues yearly
Annual Sub.: EUR145.00
Circulation: 1,415 (Publisher's Statement)
Editor: J.C. Briden
Summary of Content: Journal covering environmental issues such as climate change, biodiversity, environmental pollution and wastes, renewable and non-renewable natural resources and the interaction between these issues.
Readership/Target Audience: Aimed at those instrumental in the solution of environmental problems.
BUSINESS: ENVIRONMENT & POLLUTION

ENVIROTEC

40656U57-30_26

Editorial Address: Bergius House, 20 Clifton Street, GLASGOW, G3 7LA **Tel:** 0141 567 6000 **Fax:** 0141 331 1395
Email: editorial@peeblesmedia.com
Advertising Address: As above. **Fax:** 0141 353 1784
Email: james.swan@peeblesmedia.com
Web site: http://www.peeblesmedia.com
Publisher: Peebles Media Group Ltd
Frequency: 6 issues yearly - Published on the 1st Friday of the month
Annual Sub.: £30.50
Circulation: 8,958 (ABC 01/07/2008 to 30/06/2009)
Usual Pagination: 52
Editor: Mike Travers; **Advertising Manager:** James Swan; **Group Editor:** Mike Travers
Summary of Content: Magazine covering water, waste, pollution technology, air quality, recycling and any industry subject concerned with environmental issues.
Readership/Target Audience: Aimed at those involved in the environment technology sector.
ADVERTISING RATES:
Full Page Colour £1650.00
Agency Commission: 10%
Mechanical Data: Type Area: 270 x 188mm, Col Length: 270mm, Bleed Size: 303 x 216mm, Trim Size: 297 x 210mm, Film: Digital, Page Width: 188mm
Copy instructions: Copy Date: 2 weeks prior to publication date
Average advertising content per issue: 40%
BUSINESS: ENVIRONMENT & POLLUTION

ENVIRO-TECH NEWS

40631U57-30_27

Editorial Address: 45 Weymouth Street, LONDON, W1G 8ND **Tel:** 020 7935 1675 **Fax:** 020 7486 3455
Email: info@eic-uk.co.uk
Web site: http://www.eic-uk.co.uk
ISSN: 1358-3417
Publisher: Environmental Industries Commission
Date Established: 1995
Frequency: Monthly
Annual Sub.: £150.00
Circulation: 600 (Publisher's Statement)
Usual Pagination: 10
Editor: Merlin Hyman
Summary of Content: Bulletin covering UK environmental legislation and strategic decisions in the environmental field.
Readership/Target Audience: Aimed at UK environmental industry.
ADVERTISING: No Advertising taken
BUSINESS: ENVIRONMENT & POLLUTION

EPA

37299U17-65

Formerly: Electrical Products and Applications
Editorial Address: Blair House, 184-186 High Street, TONBRIDGE, TN9 1BQ **Tel:** 01732 359990
Fax: 01732 770049
Email: richard.scott@imlgroup.co.uk
Advertising Address: As above. **Fax:** 01732 778540
Email: lee.cashman@imlgroup.co.uk
Web site: http://www.epaonthenet.net
ISSN: 0260-1656
Publisher: IML Group plc
Date Established: 1978
Frequency: Monthly - Published on the 20th of the month prior to cover date
Free to qualifying individuals
Annual Sub.: £99.00
Circulation: 18,471 (ABC 01/01/2008 to 31/12/2008)
Usual Pagination: 44
Editor: Richard Scott
Summary of Content: Magazine covering all electrical products including cables, distribution and installation equipment. Includes articles on electrical contracting and electrical wholesaling.
Readership/Target Audience: Read by electrical engineers, specifiers, wholesalers and contractors.
ADVERTISING RATES:
Full Page Colour £2100.00
Agency Commission: 10%
Mechanical Data: Type Area: 283 x 198mm, No. of Columns (Display): 4, Bleed Size: 303 x 216mm, Trim Size: 297 x 210mm, Col Length: 283mm, Film: Digital, Page Width: 198mm
Copy instructions: Copy Date: 4 weeks prior to publication date
Average advertising content per issue: 60%
BUSINESS: ELECTRICAL

EPN

1664436U18A-9019

Editorial Address: PR by email only **Tel:** 07775 740638
Email: chayes@reedbusiness.fr
Advertising Address: 9 Kingsland Road, HEMEL HEMPSTEAD, HP1 1QE **Tel:** 01442 243481
Email: nickjwalker@btopenworld.com
Web site: http://www.epn-online.com
Publisher: Reed Business Information
Frequency: Monthly
Cover Price: Free
Circulation: 60,000 (Publisher's Statement)
Editor: Caroline Hayes; **Editor-in-Chief:** Caroline Hayes;
Advertising Manager: Nick Walker
Summary of Content: Journal covering new electronic components and instruments from manufacturers worldwide.
Readership/Target Audience: Aimed at European electronics professionals.
ADVERTISING RATES:
Full Page Mono EUR14215.00
Full Page Colour EUR14215.00
Mechanical Data: Type Area: 242 x 337,5mm, Trim Size: 297 x 210mm, Col Length: 361mm, Page Width: 247mm, Film: Digital
Copy instructions: Copy Date: 4 weeks prior to publication date
BUSINESS: ELECTRONICS

EPN EUROPEAN PENSIONS & INVESTMENT NEWS

35354U1H-20_50

Formerly: European Pensions News
Editorial Address: 1 Southwark Bridge, LONDON, SE1 9HL
Tel: 020 7775 3000 **Fax:** 020 7775 6414
Email: spencer.anderson@ft.com
Advertising Address: As above. **Tel:** 020 7873 3000
Email: alex.wharton@ft.com
Web site: http://www.epn-magazine.com
ISSN: 1462-7973
Publisher: FT Group
Date Established: 1998
Frequency: 25 issues yearly - Published on the 1st of the cover month
Circulation: 3,000 (ABC 01/07/2006 to 30/06/2007)
Usual Pagination: 24
Editor: Spencer Anderson
Summary of Content: Magazine covering developments in the corporate pensions and asset new management markets, including new business opportunities, legislative, regulatory and tax changes and EU issues relevant to the pensions industry.
Readership/Target Audience: Aimed at pensions professionals, investment managers, consultants and lawyers across Europe.
ADVERTISING RATES:
Full Page Colour EUR8800.00
Agency Commission: 10%
Mechanical Data: Type Area: 266 x 178mm, Print Process: Sheet-fed litho, Bleed Size: 308 x 216mm, Trim Size: 297 x 210mm, Col Length: 266mm, Col Widths (Display): 86mm, No. of Columns (Display): 2, Page Width: 178mm
Copy instructions: Copy Date: 2 weeks prior to publication date
Average advertising content per issue: 15%
BUSINESS: FINANCE & ECONOMICS: Pensions

EQUAL OPPORTUNITIES REVIEW

37040U14F-23

Editorial Address: PO Box 61064, LONDON, SE1P 5BQ
Tel: 020 7953 8796
Email: sue@rubensteinpublishing.com
Web site: http://www.eordirect.co.uk
ISSN: 0268-7143
Publisher: Rubenstein Publishing
Date Established: 1985
Frequency: Monthly
Annual Sub.: £397.00
Circulation: 1,800 (Publisher's Statement)
Usual Pagination: 32
Editor: Sue Johnstone
Summary of Content: Magazine focusing on equal opportunities law and employment practice.
Readership/Target Audience: Read by those involved in discrimination law and equal opportunities policy. Aimed at HR managers, union officers, equal opportunities/diversity practitioners and consultants, lawyers specialising in discrimination law.
ADVERTISING: No Advertising taken
BUSINESS: COMMERCE, INDUSTRY & MANAGEMENT: Training & Recruitment

EQUESTRIAN TRADE NEWS

39548U48B-25

Editorial Address: Stockeld Park, WETHERBY, LS22 4AW
Tel: 01937 582111 **Fax:** 01937 582778
Email: editor@equestriantradenews.com
Advertising Address: As above.
Email: sales@equestriantradenews.com
Web site: http://www.equestriantradenews.com
Publisher: Equestrian Management Consultants Ltd
Date Established: 1978
Frequency: Monthly - Published in the 1st week of the cover month
Annual Sub.: £34.95
Circulation: 6,500 (Publisher's Statement)
Usual Pagination: 52
Editor: Deborah Haywood
Summary of Content: Magazine covering saddlery, harness, riding and outdoor clothing, equipment, feedstuffs and horse care products.
Readership/Target Audience: Read by retailers, wholesalers and manufacturers.
ADVERTISING RATES:
Full Page Colour £1290.00
Agency Commission: 10%
Mechanical Data: Col Length: 272mm, Type Area: 272 x 186mm, Page Width: 186mm, Bleed Size: 303 x 216mm, Trim Size: 297 x 210mm, Film: Digital
Copy instructions: Copy Date: 15th of the month prior to publication date
Average advertising content per issue: 40%
Supplement(s): Trade Suppliers Directory - 1xY
BUSINESS: TOY TRADE & SPORTS GOODS: Sports Goods

EQUINE VETERINARY EDUCATION

41525U64H-153

Editorial Address: Mulberry House, 31 Market Street, Fordham, CAMBRIDGESHIRE, CB7 5LQ **Tel:** 01638 720250
Fax: 01638 721868
Email: viv@evj.co.uk
Advertising Address: As above. **Tel:** 01463 831133
Fax: 01463 831144
Email: sedstown@aol.com
Web site: http://www.evj.co.uk
ISSN: 0957-7734
Publisher: Equine Veterinary Journal Ltd
Date Established: 1989
Frequency: Monthly
Annual Sub.: £83.00
Circulation: 9,000 (Publisher's Statement)
Editor: T. Mair; **Managing Director:** Rachel Hutchinson
Summary of Content: Journal containing information on equine problems. Consists of case reports accompanied by tutorials and satellite articles.
Readership/Target Audience: Aimed at veterinary surgeons and all those who treat horses.
ADVERTISING RATES:
Full Page Mono £700.00
Full Page Colour £1160.00
Agency Commission: 10%
Mechanical Data: Print Process: Litho, Bleed Size: 290 x 217mm, Trim Size: 284 x 214mm
Copy instructions: Copy Date: 1st of month prior to publication date
Average advertising content per issue: 20%
BUSINESS: OTHER CLASSIFICATIONS: Veterinary

EQUINE VETERINARY JOURNAL

41526U64H-155

Editorial Address: Mulberry House, 31 Market Street, Fordham, CAMBRIDGESHIRE, CB7 5LQ **Tel:** 01638 720250
Fax: 01638 721868
Email: viv@evj.co.uk
Advertising Address: As above.
Email: sedstown@aol.com
Web site: http://www.evj.co.uk
ISSN: 0425-1644
Publisher: Equine Veterinary Journal Ltd
Date Established: 1968
Frequency: 6 issues yearly
Annual Sub.: £95.00
Circulation: 2,800 (Publisher's Statement)
Usual Pagination: 88
Editor: Peter Rossdale; **Managing Director:** Rachel Hutchinson; **Advertising Manager:** Sandra Townsley

Summary of Content: Official Journal of the British Equine Veterinary Association, publishing scientific and clinical papers.
Readership/Target Audience: Aimed at equine veterinary professionals.
ADVERTISING RATES:
Full Page Mono £700.00
Full Page Colour £1160.00
Agency Commission: 10%
Mechanical Data: Print Process: Litho, Bleed Size: 290 x 217mm, Trim Size: 284 x 214mm
Copy instructions: Copy Date: 1st of month prior to publication date
Average advertising content per issue: 20%
BUSINESS: OTHER CLASSIFICATIONS: Veterinary

EQUIP
38991U42A-94

Editorial Address: 31A Hibernia Street, HOLYWOOD, BT18 9JE **Tel:** 028 9042 4924 **Fax:** 028 9042 7378
Email: equip@dnet.co.uk
Advertising Address: 29 Shore Road, HOLYWOOD, BT18 9HX **Tel:** 028 9042 4924 **Fax:** 028 9042 7378
Email: equip@dnet.co.uk
Publisher: Equipment Publications
Frequency: 10 issues yearly
Cover Price: £2.40
Annual Sub.: £24.00
Circulation: 5,500 (Publisher's Statement)
Usual Pagination: 48
Editor: Bryan Nelson; **Advertising Manager:** Alan Stewart; **Publisher:** Alan Stewart
Summary of Content: Journal covering all aspects of plant, quarrying, plant hire, materials handling, municipal and civil engineering.
Readership/Target Audience: Read by anyone interested in the construction industry.
ADVERTISING RATES:
Full Page Colour £1190.00
Agency Commission: 10%
Mechanical Data: Type Area: 270 x 183mm, Col Length: 270mm, Page Width: 183mm, Bleed Size: 305 x 215mm, Film: Digital, Trim Size: 297 x 210mm
Copy instructions: Copy Date: Last day of the month prior to publication date
Average advertising content per issue: 40%
BUSINESS: CONSTRUCTION

EQUIPMENT SERVICES
1837342U56G-59

Editorial Address: St. Judes Church, Dulwich Road, LONDON, SE24 0PB **Tel:** 020 7738 5454
Fax: 020,7978 8316
Email: rebecca.l@markallengroup.com
Advertising Address: Jesses Farm, Snow Hill, Dinton, SALISBURY, SP3 5HN **Tel:** 01722 716997
Fax: 01722 716926
Email: oliver.h@markallengroup.co.uk
Web site: http://www.naep.org.uk
Publisher: MA Healthcare
Date Established: 2004
Frequency: Quarterly
Free to qualifying individuals
Circulation: 10,000 (Publisher's Statement)
Editor: Rebecca Linssen; **Advertising Manager:** Oliver Howe
Summary of Content: Journal of the National Association Equipment Providers featuring information on equipment provision and the practicalities of the equipment.
Readership/Target Audience: Aimed at equipment store managers, loan store managers and members of the National Association Equipment Providers.
ADVERTISING: Rates on application
BUSINESS: HEALTH & MEDICAL: Medical Equipment

EQUITY JOURNAL
37180U14L-195

Editorial Address: Guild House, Upper St Martin's Lane, LONDON, WC2H 9EG **Tel:** 020 7670 0211
Fax: 020 7836 5976
Email: mmcgrath@equity.org.uk
Web site: http://www.equity.org.uk
Publisher: Equity
Date Established: 1931
Frequency: Quarterly
Cover Price: £3.00
Free to qualifying individuals
Annual Sub.: £12.00
Circulation: 45,000 (Publisher's Statement)
Usual Pagination: 24
Editor: Martin McGrath
Summary of Content: Journal of Equity containing advice for actors and performers and news from within the industry.
Readership/Target Audience: Aimed at members of Equity.
ADVERTISING: No Advertising taken
BUSINESS: COMMERCE, INDUSTRY & MANAGEMENT: Trade Unions

THE ERGONOMIST
39960U55-52, 50

Editorial Address: Elms Court, Elms Grove, LOUGHBOROUGH, LE11 1RG **Tel:** 01509 234904
Email: editor@egronomics.org.uk
Advertising Address: As above. **Fax:** 01509 235666
Email: tonykaye@compuserve.com
Web site: http://www.ergonomics.org.uk
ISSN: 0268-5639
Publisher: The Ergonomics Society
Date Established: 1960
Frequency: Monthly
Cover Price: Free
Circulation: 1,400 (Publisher's Statement)
Usual Pagination: 12
Editor: Tina Worthy; **Advertising Manager:** Tina Worthy
Summary of Content: Newsletter of the Ergonomics Society, which studies the relationship between man and his workplace and working environment.
Readership/Target Audience: Read by ergonomists.
ADVERTISING RATES:
Full Page Mono £1450.00
Full Page Colour £1750.00
Agency Commission: 10%
Mechanical Data: Type Area: 227 x 174mm, Col Length: 227mm, Film: Digital, Page Width: 174mm
Copy instructions: Copy Date: 25th of the month prior to publication date
BUSINESS: APPLIED SCIENCE & LABORATORIES

EROTIC TRADE ONLY
1655831U53-687

Editorial Address: Unit 15, Coed-Arian House, Oldbury Road, CWMBRAN, NP44 3JU **Tel:** 01633 877177
Email: editorial@erotictradeonly.com
Advertising Address: 2nd Floor, White House, 6 Queens Square, POULTON-LE-FYLDE, FY6 7BN **Tel:** 0870 750 6070
Email: advertising@erotictradeonly.com
Web site: http://www.erotictradeonly.com
Publisher: Media On Screen
Date Established: 2003
Frequency: Monthly
Free to qualifying individuals
Annual Sub.: £60.00
Circulation: 4,500 (Publisher's Statement)
Usual Pagination: 72
Editor: Dale Bradford; **Advertising Manager:** Jacinta Williams
Summary of Content: Magazine covering all aspects of the commercial adult industry.
Readership/Target Audience: Aimed at retailers within the adult industry.
ADVERTISING RATES:
Full Page Mono £1200.00
Full Page Colour £1200.00
Mechanical Data: Type Area: 340 x 245mm, Bleed Size: 350 x 255mm, Col Length: 340mm, Page Width: 245mm, Film: Digital
BUSINESS: RETAILING & WHOLESALING

ERT
39097U43A-40

Formerly: ERT Weekly
Editorial Address: Equitable House, Lyon Road, HARROW, HA1 2EW **Tel:** 020 8515 2000 **Fax:** 020 8515 6891
Email: simonking@ertgroup.co.uk
Advertising Address: As above. **Tel:** 020 8515 6880
Email: stephenblakebrough@ertgroup.co.uk
Web site: http://www.ertonline.co.uk
ISSN: 0013-4228
Publisher: Taylist Media
Date Established: 1890
Frequency: 26 issues yearly
Annual Sub.: £123.00
Circulation: 6,000 (ABC 01/01/2007 to 31/12/2007)
Usual Pagination: 36
Editor: Simon King; **News Editor:** Penny Williams
Summary of Content: Magazine containing the latest news on the electrical retailing industry.
Readership/Target Audience: Aimed at retailers, manufacturers, importers and wholesalers.
ADVERTISING RATES:
Full Page Colour £3444.00
Agency Commission: 10%
Mechanical Data: Bleed Size: 336 x 251mm, Type Area: 306 x 215mm, Trim Size: 330 x 245mm, Col Length: 306mm, Page Width: 215mm, Film: Digital
Copy instructions: Copy Date: 2 weeks prior to publication date
Average advertising content per issue: 40%
Supplement(s): Cooking - 1xY, Digital Home - 2xY, In-home Laundry - 1xY
BUSINESS: ELECTRICAL RETAIL TRADE

ERT IRELAND
1704338U43A-67

Editorial Address: Equitable House, Lyon Road, HARROW, HA1 2EW **Tel:** 020 8515 6885 **Fax:** 020 8515 6891
Email: simonking@taylistmedia.com
Advertising Address: As above. **Tel:** 020 8515 6882

Email: danielfay@taylistmedia.com
Publisher: Taylist Media
Frequency: 6 issues yearly
Cover Price: Free
Circulation: 2,250 (Publisher's Statement)
Editor: Simon King
Summary of Content: Magazine focusing on electrical retailing in Ireland. Includes industry news, analysis and product reviews with product-related supplements.
Readership/Target Audience: Aimed at retailers, manufacturers, importers, distributors and wholesalers.
ADVERTISING RATES:
Full Page Colour £1200.00
Agency Commission: 10%
Mechanical Data: Type Area: 279 x 186mm, Bleed Size: 303 x 216mm, Trim Size: 297 x 210mm, Col Length: 279mm, Page Width: 186mm, Film: Digital
Copy instructions: Copy Date: 2 weeks prior to publication date
Average advertising content per issue: 40%
BUSINESS: ELECTRICAL RETAIL TRADE

ESPRIT
37248U15A-24, 50

Editorial Address: 87 Roundwood Way, BANSTEAD, SM7 1EJ **Tel:** 01737 373099
Email: esprit@esprit-magazine.co.uk
Advertising Address: As above.
Email: jon@esprit-magazine.co.uk
Web site: http://www.esprit-magazine.co.uk
ISSN: 1364-9922
Publisher: Sandron Publishing Ltd
Date Established: 1988
Frequency: Monthly - Published around the 2nd of the cover month
Annual Sub.: £95.00
Circulation: 5,200 (Publisher's Statement)
Usual Pagination: 44
Editor: Lorraine Wilson Morris; **Advertising Manager:** Jonathan Charles; **Publisher:** Jonathan Charles
Summary of Content: Magazine covering perfumery, cosmetics and toiletries.
Readership/Target Audience: Readers include buyers, consultants, managing directors, sales directors and consultant training managers in department stores, independent chemists and cosmetic houses.
ADVERTISING RATES:
Full Page Mono £2800.00
Full Page Colour £2800.00
Agency Commission: 10%
Mechanical Data: Col Length: 255mm, Page Width: 174mm, Trim Size: 297 x 210mm, Film: Positive, right reading, emulsion side down. Digital, Bleed Size: 303 x 216mm, Type Area: 255 x 174mm
Copy instructions: Copy Date: 12th of the month prior to publication date
Average advertising content per issue: 50%
Supplement(s): Esprit Beauty Directory - 1xY
BUSINESS: COSMETICS & HAIRDRESSING: Cosmetics

ESSAYS IN CRITICISM
47562U62R-458

Editorial Address: 6A Rawlinson Road, OXFORD, OX2 6UE **Tel:** 01865 353907 **Fax:** 01865 353985
Email: seamus.perry@balliol.oxford.ac.uk
Advertising Address: Great Clarendon Street, OXFORD, OX2 6DP **Tel:** 01865 353329
Email: jnlsadvertising@oxfordjournals.org
Web site: http://eic.oupjournals.org/
ISSN: 0014-0856
Publisher: OUP
Date Established: 1951
Frequency: Quarterly
Cover Price: £16.00
Annual Sub.: £51.00
Usual Pagination: 100
Editor: Seamus Perry
Summary of Content: Contains literary criticism and book reviews in English literature.
Readership/Target Audience: Aimed at scholars and students of English literature worldwide.
ADVERTISING RATES:
Full Page Mono £260.00
Agency Commission: 10%
Mechanical Data: Film: Digital, Type Area: 190 x 110mm, Col Length: 190mm, Page Width: 110mm
BUSINESS: CHURCH & SCHOOL EQUIPMENT & EDUCATION: Education Related

---

THE ESSENTIAL BOOK: HIP! HEATING ENGINEERS, INSTALLERS AND PLUMBERS
1793303U3D-103

Editorial Address: Unit 22, Midsomer Enterprise Park, Radstock Road, Midsomer Norton, RADSTOCK, BA3 2BB **Tel:** 0870 774 3049 **Fax:** 0870 758 5906
Email: celia@sng-publishing.co.uk
Advertising Address: As above.
Email: celia@sng-publishing.co.uk

Business Magazines

Web site: http://www.hipstudent.co.uk
Publisher: SNG Publishing Ltd
Date Established: 2006
Frequency: Annual - Published in September
Free to qualifying individuals
Annual Sub.: £6.99
Circulation: 20,000 (Publisher's Statement)
Editor: Celia Matthews; Advertising Manager: Celia Matthews
Summary of Content: Publication covering features by industry experts, product information, useful tips and guidance for new plumbers and heating engineers, information on how to set up a plumbing and heating business, tips on finding a plumbing job and writing a CV. Includes advice from college lecturers and fun cartoons and competitions with plumbing tools and products as prizes.
Readership/Target Audience: Aimed at final year plumbing and heating students, also independent and national merchants.
ADVERTISING RATES:
Full Page Colour £2200.00
Mechanical Data: Type Area: 190 x 128mm, Col Length: 190mm, Page Width: 128mm, Film: Digital
BUSINESS: HEATING & VENTILATION: Heating & Plumbing

THE ESSENTIAL BOOK: SPARKS

1793305U14E-411

Formerly: The Essential Book: Electricians
Editorial Address: Unit 22, Midsomer Enterprise Park, Radstock Road, Midsomer Norton, RADSTOCK, BA3 2BB
Tel: 0870 774 3049 Fax: 0870 758 5906
Email: celia@sng-publishing.co.uk
Web site: http://www.sng-publishing.co.uk/publications/essential-elec.html
Publisher: SNG Publishing Ltd
Date Established: 2007
Frequency: Annual - Published in September
Cover Price: £6.99
Free to qualifying individuals
Circulation: 18,000 (Publisher's Statement)
Usual Pagination: 200
Editor: Celia Matthews
Summary of Content: Publication featuring articles written by industry experts, product information, tips and advice from college lecturers, cartoons and competitions.
Readership/Target Audience: Aimed at the next generation of electricians and electrical contractors.
BUSINESS: COMMERCE, INDUSTRY & MANAGEMENT: Work Study

THE ESSENTIAL BUILDING PRODUCT REVIEW

1629416U4E-416

Formerly: Commercial and Industrial Buildings Product Review
Editorial Address: 16 Parker Court, Dyson Way, Staffordshire Technology, STAFFORD, ST18 0WP
Tel: 01785 330635 Fax: 0845 862 8639
Email: david@link2media.co.uk
Advertising Address: As above. Tel: 01785 711591
Fax: 01785 711592
Email: info@link2media.co.uk
Web site: http://www.ebpr.co.uk
Publisher: Link2.Media Business Publishing Ltd
Date Established: 2002
Frequency: Quarterly
Cover Price: £3.75
Free to qualifying individuals
Annual Sub.: £12.50
Circulation: 7,000 (Publisher's Statement)
Editor: David Broadfield; Advertising Manager: Kieran Pritchard
Summary of Content: Magazine covering all aspects of the construction industry.
Readership/Target Audience: Aimed at building specifiers and property owners in the commercial, retail, leisure, corporate and manufacturing sector.
ADVERTISING RATES:
Full Page Colour £795.00
Mechanical Data: Trim Size: 297 x 210mm, Film: Digital
Copy instructions: Copy Date: 2 weeks prior to publication date
Average advertising content per issue: 10%
BUSINESS: ARCHITECTURE & BUILDING: Building

ESSENTIAL KITCHEN & BATHROOM BUSINESS

1704689U23C-95

Editorial Address: The Tower, Phoenix Square, Wyncolls Road, Severalls Industrial Park, COLCHESTER, CO4 9HU
Tel: 01206 851117 Fax: 01206 849078
Email: gae.ratcliffe@burdamagazines.co.uk
Advertising Address: As above. Fax: 01206 849079
Email: darren@essentialpublishing.co.uk
Web site: http://www.ekbbusiness.co.uk
Publisher: Hubert Burda Media UK
Date Established: 2006

Frequency: Monthly
Cover Price: Free
Circulation: 11,076 (ABC 01/01/2008 to 31/12/2008)
Usual Pagination: 80
Editor: Gae Ratcliffe; Advertising Manager: Darren Summerfield; Publisher: Darren Summerfield
Summary of Content: Magazine covering news and design, kitchen sinks and taps, cooking, washing and cooling appliances, worktops, flooring, lighting and furniture, as well as bathroom suites, brassware, shower, tiles, accessories and lighting.
Readership/Target Audience: Aimed at independent kitchen and bathroom retailers, manufacturers, new builds, designers, architects and specifiers.
ADVERTISING RATES:
Full Page Colour £3225.00
Mechanical Data: Type Area: 314 x 216mm, Bleed Size: 346 x 246mm, Trim Size: 340 x 240mm, Col Length: 314mm, Page Width: 216mm, Film: Digital
BUSINESS: FURNISHINGS & FURNITURE: Furnishings & Furniture - Kitchens & Bathrooms

ESSENTIALLY CATERING

1852994U11A-229

Editorial Address: The Studio, 5 Philpotts Yard, Beare Green, DORKING, RH5 4QU Tel: 0845 644 1870
Email: nic@essentiallycatering.co.uk
Web site: http://www.essentiallycatering.co.uk
Publisher: Bestway & Batleys Cash & Carry
Date Established: 2007
Frequency: Quarterly
Free to qualifying individuals
Circulation: 50,000 (Publisher's Statement)
Usual Pagination: 72
Editor: Nicola Belfrage; Advertising Manager: David Gilroy
Summary of Content: Magazine covering industry and business news, caterer and restaurant profiles, recipes, events, health and safety advice, marketing tips, competitions, special seasonal ideas and opportunities, drinks, regional profiles and equipment news.
Readership/Target Audience: Aimed at caterers.
BUSINESS: CATERING: Catering, Hotels & Restaurants

ESTATE AGENCY NEWS

35188U1E-145

Editorial Address: Keenans Mill, Lord Street, LYTHAM ST. ANNES, FY8 2ER Tel: 01253 783206 Fax: 01253 783217
Email: enquiries@estateagencynews.co.uk
Advertising Address: As above. Fax: 01253 783229
Email: adrian@estateagencynews.co.uk
Web site: http://www.estateagencynews.co.uk
Publisher: Estates Press Ltd
Date Established: 1986
Frequency: 11 issues yearly - Published on the 1st Tuesday of the month. Not published in January
Annual Sub.: £18.00
Circulation: 16,728 (Publisher's Statement)
Usual Pagination: 32
Editor: Tony Durkin; Managing Director: Glenn Oldroyd; Advertising Manager: Adrian Heywood
Summary of Content: Journal covering news, views and informed comment on the residential property scene.
Readership/Target Audience: Read by residential estate agents.
ADVERTISING RATES:
Full Page Colour £3378.00
SCC £27.00
Agency Commission: 10%
Mechanical Data: Film: Digital, Type Area: 400 x 288mm, Col Length: 400mm, Col Widths (Display): 40mm, No. of Columns (Display): 7, Page Width: 288mm
Average advertising content per issue: 50%
BUSINESS: FINANCE & ECONOMICS: Property

THE ESTATE AGENCY TIMES

1800721U1E-397

Editorial Address: Unit 6, 5 Durham Yard, Teesdale Street, LONDON, E2 6QF Tel: 0870 850 3586 Fax: 020 7749 1280
Email: mark@ddgm.co.uk
Web site: http://www.estateagencytimes.co.uk
Publisher: DDGM
Date Established: 2007
Frequency: Monthly
Cover Price: Free
Editor: Mark Burgess
Summary of Content: Magazine focusing on the professional property industry. Contains in-depth news and opinion about residential sales and lettings, the commercial market, world of finance, technology, employment, home improvement packs (HIPs) and related articles.
Readership/Target Audience: Aimed at estate agents.
ADVERTISING: Rates on application
BUSINESS: FINANCE & ECONOMICS: Property

THE ESTATE AGENT

35189U1E-407

Editorial Address: Talbot Hays Farm, WINCHFIELD, RG27 8BZ Tel: 01252 843566 Fax: 01252 843566
Email: rosalind.renshaw@googlemail.com

Advertising Address: As above. Tel: 0844 800 3085
Fax: 01825 731845
Email: g.manchester@btconnect.com
Web site: http://www.naea.co.uk
ISSN: 0260-1001
Publisher: The National Association of Estate Agents
Frequency: 10 issues yearly - July/August and December/January are combined issues
Free to qualifying individuals
Annual Sub.: £100.00
Circulation: 10,500 (Publisher's Statement)
Usual Pagination: 64
Editor: Rosalind Renshaw
Summary of Content: Magazine covering matters related to the UK property market, estate agency law and practice, employment and business.
Readership/Target Audience: Aimed at members of the National Association of Estate Agents and allied professionals.
ADVERTISING RATES:
Full Page Colour £1900.00
Agency Commission: 10%
Mechanical Data: Trim Size: 297 x 210mm, Film: Digital, Bleed Size: 303 x 216mm, Type Area: 267 x 180mm, Col Length: 267mm, Page Width: 180mm
Copy instructions: Copy Date: 1 month prior to publication date
BUSINESS: FINANCE & ECONOMICS: Property

ESTATES GAZETTE

35190U1E-160

Editorial Address: 1 Procter Street, LONDON, WC1V 6EU
Tel: 020 7911 1800 Fax: 020 7911 1900
Email: newsdesk@egi.co.uk
Advertising Address: As above. Tel: 020 7911 1733
Fax: 020 7911 1730
Email: anthony.hackett@rbi.co.uk
Web site: http://www.estatesgazettegroup.com
ISSN: 0014-1240
Publisher: Reed Business Information
Date Established: 1858
Frequency: Weekly - Published on Saturday
Cover Price: £4.30
Circulation: 25,643 (ABC 01/07/2008 to 30/06/2009)
Usual Pagination: 180
Editor: Newsdesk; News Editor: Sam McClary; Features Editor: Lucy Barnard; Managing Director: Dominic Feltham; Managing Editor: Rod George
Summary of Content: Journal covering expert comment on the commercial, industrial, agricultural and residential property markets. Includes reports on market deals, and technical and legal issues.
Readership/Target Audience: Read by estate agents, surveyors, property developers and construction companies. Also local authorities and government departments.
ADVERTISING RATES:
Full Page Mono £1880.00
Full Page Colour £3080.00
Mechanical Data: Type Area: 274 x 185mm, Bleed Size: 305 x 216mm, Col Length: 274mm, Page Width: 185mm, Trim Size: 297 x 210mm, Film: Positive, right reading, emulsion side down. Digital
Copy instructions: Copy Date: 2 weeks prior to publication date
BUSINESS: FINANCE & ECONOMICS: Property

THE ESTATES GAZETTE LAW REPORTS

35213U1E-162_50

Editorial Address: 1 Proctor Street, LONDON, WC1V 6EU
Tel: 020 7911 1825 Fax: 020 7911 1900
Email: sarah.jackman@rbi.co.uk
Web site: http://www.egi.co.uk
ISSN: 0951-9289
Publisher: The Estates Gazette
Frequency: 3 issues yearly - Published in January, May and October
Annual Sub.: £275.00
Usual Pagination: 220
Editor: Sarah Jackman
Summary of Content: Publication containing key property related law reports, including rating and lands tribunal cases.
Readership/Target Audience: Aimed at legal advisers and academics.
ADVERTISING: No Advertising taken
BUSINESS: FINANCE & ECONOMICS: Property

ESTATES REVIEW

35192U1E-163_50

Editorial Address: 37-42 Compton Street, LONDON, EC1V 0AP Tel: 020 7014 0300 Fax: 020 7014 0302
Email: barry@estatesreview.com
Advertising Address: As above. Fax: 020 7014 0301
Email: david@wnmedia.co.uk
Web site: http://www.estatesreview.com/
ISSN: 1473-2491
Publisher: Tower Business Media
Date Established: 1992
Frequency: 6 issues yearly

Section 4 (b) Business Magazines

Cover Price: £2.90
Annual Sub.: £120.00
Circulation: 33,000 (Publisher's Statement)
Usual Pagination: 124
Editor: Barry Kingcome; **Publisher:** James Angel
Summary of Content: British Journal of Real Estate Management and Economic Development.
Readership/Target Audience: Aimed at commercial property advisers.
ADVERTISING RATES:
Full Page Mono £2838.00
Full Page Colour £3552.00
Agency Commission: 10%
Mechanical Data: Bleed Size: 305 x 218mm, Trim Size: 297 x 210mm, Print Process: Litho, Film: Digital
Copy instructions: Copy Date: 2 months prior to publication date
Average advertising content per issue: 60%
BUSINESS: FINANCE & ECONOMICS: Property

ESTATES WEST BULLETIN   35193U1E-167

Editorial Address: 26 Wood Street, SWINDON, SN1 4AB
Tel: 01793 615393 **Fax:** 01793 488517
Email: info@swindon-business.net
Web site: http://www.swindon-business.net
Publisher: County Business Publishing Ltd
Frequency: 24 issues yearly
Annual Sub.: £165.00
Circulation: 85 (Publisher's Statement)
Editor: Lorne Barling; **Managing Director:** Lorne Barling; **Publisher:** Lorne Barling
Summary of Content: Newsletter covering commercial property on the M4 corridor, London to South Wales.
Readership/Target Audience: Aimed at business, industry and property people.
ADVERTISING: No Advertising taken
BUSINESS: FINANCE & ECONOMICS: Property

ESTETICA UK   37261U15B-20

Formerly: Cutting Edge
Editorial Address: 118 Piccadilly, Mayfair, LONDON, W1J 7NW **Tel:** 020 7569 6776 **Fax:** 020 7569 6778
Email: estetica.uk@lineone.net
Advertising Address: As above.
Email: estetica.uk@lineone.net
Web site: http://www.estetica.it
Publisher: Estetica UK
Date Established: 1946
Frequency: 6 issues yearly
Cover Price: £5.00
Circulation: 15,000 (Publisher's Statement)
Usual Pagination: 176
Editor: Gary Kelly; **Advertising Manager:** Gary Kelly
Summary of Content: Magazine featuring industry news, products and new innovations. Also lists exhibitions and conferences within the hairdressing industry.
Language(s): English; French; German; Italian; Spanish
Readership/Target Audience: Aimed at salon owners and professional hairdressers.
ADVERTISING RATES:
Full Page Colour £1950.00
Agency Commission: 10%
Mechanical Data: Film: Digital, Trim Size: 288 x 216mm, Bleed Size: 298 x 226mm
BUSINESS: COSMETICS & HAIRDRESSING: Hairdressing

ET BUSINESS   41256U63B-246

Formerly: BTR Business Telegraph Review
Editorial Address: New Telegraph House, 57 Priestgate, PETERBOROUGH, PE1 1JW **Tel:** 01733 555111
Fax: 01733 313147
Email: paul.grinnell@peterboroughtoday.co.uk
Advertising Address: As above. **Fax:** 01733 555188
Email: sasha.dean@peterboroughtoday.co.uk
Web site: http://www.peterboroughtoday.co.uk
Publisher: East Midlands Newspapers Ltd
Frequency: Weekly
Circulation: 29,419 (Publisher's Statement)
Usual Pagination: 12
Editor: Paul Grinnell; **Features Editor:** Julia Ogden; **Managing Director:** Amanda Davison-Young; **Advertising Manager:** Sasha Dean
Summary of Content: Newspaper containing news on small businesses, appointments, recruitment, motoring, property and commercial vehicles.
Readership/Target Audience: Aimed at local businesses and residents of Peterborough and surrounding area.
ADVERTISING RATES:
Full Page Mono £2601.00
Full Page Colour £3381.30
Agency Commission: 10%
Mechanical Data: Col Widths (Display): 27mm, Page Width: 270mm, Type Area: 340 x 270mm, Col Length: 340mm, No. of Columns (Display): 9, Film: Digital
Copy instructions: Copy Date: 10am Thursday prior to publication date

Supplement to: Evening Telegraph (Peterborough)
BUSINESS: REGIONAL BUSINESS: Regional Business English Counties

ETC, ETC   1881502U42B-253

Editorial Address: 15 Onslow Gardens, WALLINGTON, SM6 9QL **Tel:** 020 8254 9406 **Fax:** 020 8647 0045
Email: kevin@h3bmedia.com
Web site: http://www.thinkinghihgways.com
Publisher: H3B Media Ltd
Date Established: 2006
Frequency: Quarterly
Free to qualifying individuals
Annual Sub.: £30.00
Usual Pagination: 88
Editor: Kevin Borras; **News Editor:** Lucy Cone
Summary of Content: Magazine looking at not just the technology but also the policy, strategy, political, aesthetic, urban design, environmental, interoperability and public acceptance issues that make the electronic toll collection, road pricing and road user charging sector one of the most, if not the most, vibrant and rapidly evolving in the advanced transportation management industry.
Readership/Target Audience: Aimed at national and state transportation departments, highway authorities, ITS divisions of national, state and local authorities and agencies, electronic toll collection system suppliers, toll concessionaires, motorway authorities, Aimed at government agencies, thinkers, planners, manufacturers, consultants, systems specifiers, policy makers, politicians from all parties, traffic engineers, police departments, emergency responders, public transit authorities, homeland security officials, system integrators, universities, state, county and city traffic departments and car manufacturers.
BUSINESS: CONSTRUCTION: Roads

ETHICAL CORPORATION MAGAZINE   765050U14R-501

Editorial Address: 7-9 Fashion Street, LONDON, E1 6PX
Email: editor@ethicalcorp.com
Advertising Address: As above. **Tel:** 020 7375 7516
Fax: 020 7375 7511
Email: hayley.stamp@ethicalcorp.com
Web site: http://www.ethicalcorporation.com
Publisher: FC Publishing
Date Established: 2001
Frequency: 11 issues yearly
Free to qualifying individuals
Annual Sub.: EUR399.00
Circulation: 3,500 (Publisher's Statement)
Usual Pagination: 60
Editor: John Russell; **Managing Editor:** John Russell; **Publisher:** Toby Webb
Summary of Content: Magazine providing companies around the world with practical advice and examples of how to successfully integrate responsible corporate practice into their management systems. Also covers the social and environmental challenges facing multinational organisations.
Readership/Target Audience: Aimed at corporate, social and environmental responsibility managers, strategists and senior executives.
ADVERTISING RATES:
Full Page Colour £1800.00
Agency Commission: 10%
Mechanical Data: Bleed Size: 290 x 226mm, Trim Size: 280 x 216mm, Type Area: 270 x 206mm, Col Length: 270mm, Page Width: 206mm, Film: Digital
Copy instructions: Copy Date: 15th of the month prior to publication date
Average advertising content per issue: 10%
BUSINESS: COMMERCE, INDUSTRY & MANAGEMENT: Commerce Related

ETHICAL PERFORMANCE   37231U14R-90

Editorial Address: 30 Wynter Street, LONDON, SW11 2TZ
Tel: 01227 722227 **Fax:** 01227 787658
Email: newsdesk@ethicalperformance.com
Advertising Address: Stodmarsh Enterprise Centre, Stodmarsh, CANTERBURY, CT3 4BE **Tel:** 01227 722227
Fax: 01227 722638
Email: publisher@ethicalperformance.com
Web site: http://www.ethicalperformance.com
ISSN: 1464-6315
Publisher: Dunstans Publishing
Date Established: 1999
Frequency: 11 issues yearly
Annual Sub.: £315.00
Circulation: 600 (Publisher's Statement)
Usual Pagination: 12
Editor: Peter Mason; **Advertising Manager:** Peter Mason; **Publisher:** Alistair Townley
Summary of Content: Business newsletter focusing on corporate ethical performance. Covers social reporting, ethical codes of practice, community finance initiatives, ethical investments, corporate social responsibility, socially responsible investment and corporate governance.

Readership/Target Audience: Aimed at individuals with a corporate social responsibility, including sustainability directors, environment managers, risk directors and ethics directors.
ADVERTISING RATES:
Full Page Colour £385.00
Agency Commission: 15%
Copy instructions: Copy Date: 20th of the month prior to publication
Average advertising content per issue: 15%
Supplement(s): Ethical Performance Best Practice - 4xY
BUSINESS: COMMERCE, INDUSTRY & MANAGEMENT: Commerce Related

ETHNOGRAPHY   601437U62R-472

Editorial Address: 1 Oliver's Yard, 55 City Road, LONDON, EC1Y 1SP **Tel:** 020 7324 8500 **Fax:** 020 7324 8600
Email: info@sagepub.co.uk
Advertising Address: As above.
Email: advertising@sagepub.co.uk
Web site: http://www.sagepub.co.uk
ISSN: 1466-1381
Publisher: Sage Publications
Date Established: 2000
Frequency: Quarterly
Annual Sub.: £46.00
Circulation: 400 (Publisher's Statement)
Editor: Paul Willis; **Advertising Manager:** Sheena Karim
Summary of Content: Journal providing an interdisciplinary forum for the ethnographic study of social and cultural change.
Readership/Target Audience: Aimed at those interested in ethnography, theory and society.
ADVERTISING RATES:
Full Page Mono £350.00
Agency Commission: 5%
Mechanical Data: Col Length: 205mm, Page Width: 130mm, Film: Digital, Type Area: 205 x 130mm
Copy instructions: Copy Date: 12 weeks prior to publication date
BUSINESS: CHURCH & SCHOOL EQUIPMENT & EDUCATION: Education Related

ETS NEWS   1667830U40-433

Editorial Address: Global House, 47A Tottenham Lane, LONDON, N8 9BD **Tel:** 020 8347 6406 **Fax:** 020 8347 6427
Email: info@ets-news.com
Advertising Address: As above.
Email: info@ets-news.com
Web site: http://www.ets-news.com
ISSN: 1460-0617
Publisher: GDR Publications Ltd
Date Established: 1998
Frequency: Quarterly
Free to qualifying individuals
Circulation: 10,500 (Publisher's Statement)
Usual Pagination: 54
Editor: David Oliver; **Advertising Manager:** Geoff Farmer
Summary of Content: Magazine covering all aspects of military equipment, training and simulation including news, insight and analysis of new programmes, products and services.
Readership/Target Audience: Aimed at those working within the defence industry.
ADVERTISING RATES:
Full Page Mono £2500.00
Full Page Colour £3500.00
Agency Commission: 15%
Mechanical Data: Type Area: 282 x 180mm, Col Length: 282mm, Page Width: 180mm, Film: Digital, Bleed Size: +4mm
Copy instructions: Copy Date: 1 month prior to publication date
BUSINESS: DEFENCE

EU ENERGY   40754U58-35_50

Editorial Address: 20 Canada Square, Canary Wharf, LONDON, E14 5LH **Tel:** 020 7176 6267 **Fax:** 020 7176 6670
Email: gala_colover@platts.com
Web site: http://www.platts.com
ISSN: 0957-3666
Publisher: Platts
Frequency: 26 issues yearly
Annual Sub.: £645.00
Circulation: 600 (Publisher's Statement)
Usual Pagination: 26
Editor: Gala Colover; **Managing Editor:** Paul Whitehead
Summary of Content: Magazine containing information on European energy policy and industry trends.
Readership/Target Audience: Aimed at energy executives, lawyers and consultants.
ADVERTISING: No Advertising taken
BUSINESS: ENERGY, FUEL & NUCLEAR

EU FOOD LAW WEEKLY
1665014U22R-757

Editorial Address: 80 Calverley Road, TUNBRIDGE WELLS, TN1 2UN **Tel:** 020 7017 7500 **Fax:** 020 7017 7599
Email: marketing@agra-net.com
Web site: http://www.agra-net.com
ISSN: 1357-0277
Publisher: Agra Informa Ltd
Frequency: Weekly
Annual Sub.: £1216.00
Summary of Content: Report to monitor and analyse the implementation of EU directives in the member states, the latest progress in Brussels and the implications these hold for the food industry.
Readership/Target Audience: Aimed at executives in the food industry, government, national and international organisations.
ADVERTISING: No Advertising taken
BUSINESS: FOOD: Food Related

EURALEX
622560U37-25

Formerly: ERA News
Editorial Address: Telephone House, 69-77 Paul Street, LONDON, EC2A 4LQ **Tel:** 020 7017 6973
Fax: 020 7017 6968
Email: faraz.kermani@informa.com
Advertising Address: As above. **Tel:** 020 7017 5000
Fax: 020 7017 6787
Email: diane.mckenna@informa.com
Web site: http://www.euralex.co.uk
ISSN: 1462-3129
Publisher: Informa Pharma
Date Established: 1992
Frequency: Monthly
Annual Sub.: EUR1225.00
Circulation: 7,000 (Publisher's Statement)
Usual Pagination: 32
Editor: Faraz Kermani; **Advertising Manager:** Diane Mckenna
Summary of Content: Newsletter with a focus on European regulatory affairs and legal developments in the pharmaceutical, biotechnology, medical device and animal health industries. Includes news and analysis of topical European regulatory developments, directives and guidelines as well as court cases and rulings.
Readership/Target Audience: Aimed worldwide at those working in the human and veterinary pharmaceutical and medical device industries; also legal and financial professionals, educational institutions and government.
ADVERTISING RATES:
Full Page Mono £986.00
Full Page Colour £1527.00
Agency Commission: 10%
Mechanical Data: Type Area: 260 x 185mm, Bleed Size: 303 x 216mm, Trim Size: 297 x 210mm, Col Length: 260mm, Page Width: 185mm, Film: Digital
Copy instructions: Copy Date: 10th of the month prior to publication date
BUSINESS: PHARMACEUTICAL & CHEMISTS

EUREKA
37608U19B-255

Formerly: Innovative Engineering Design Eureka
Editorial Address: Hawley Mill, Hawley Road, DARTFORD, DA2 7TJ **Tel:** 01322 221144 **Fax:** 01322 221188
Email: jcunningham@findlay.co.uk
Advertising Address: As above.
Email: cmolloy@findlay.co.uk
Web site: http://www.eurekamagazine.co.uk
ISSN: 0261-2097
Publisher: Findlay Media Ltd
Date Established: 1980
Frequency: Monthly - Published on the 7th of the cover month
Free to qualifying individuals
Annual Sub.: £78.00
Circulation: 19,103 (ABC 01/01/2008 to 31/12/2008)
Usual Pagination: 56
Editor: Justin Cunningham; **Publisher:** Ed Tranter
Summary of Content: Magazine covering any new products which include examples of innovative engineering design together with materials technology advances.
Readership/Target Audience: Aimed at senior design managers, technical and engineering directors in the UK manufacturing industry and design-only organisations.
ADVERTISING RATES:
Full Page Colour £2850.00
Agency Commission: 10%
Mechanical Data: Page Width: 178mm, Type Area: 254 x 178mm, Col Length: 254mm, Trim Size: 286 x 210mm, Bleed Size: 292 x 216mm, Film: Digital
Copy instructions: Copy Date: 2 weeks prior to publication date
Average advertising content per issue: 40%
Supplement(s): Eureka on Campus - 3xY
BUSINESS: ENGINEERING & MACHINERY: Engineering - Design

EURO TECHNOLOGY
37654U19F-671

Editorial Address: 8 Matthew Wren Close, Little Downham, ELY, CB6 2UL **Tel:** 01353 699094 **Fax:** 01353 699094
Email: hammerton_william@hotmail.com
Advertising Address: As above.
Email: williamhammerton_thejournalofindustryandtechnology@hotmail.co.uk
Web site: http://www.thejournalofindustryandtechnology.biz
Publisher: Journal of Industry and Technology
Date Established: 1996
Frequency: Quarterly
Cover Price: £5.00
Free to qualifying individuals
Annual Sub.: £25.00
Circulation: 6,000 (Publisher's Statement)
Editor: Bill Hammerton; **Advertising Manager:** Bill Hammerton
Summary of Content: Journal covering all aspects of industrial developments in Europe.
Readership/Target Audience: Aimed at production managers, directors, executives and engineers.
ADVERTISING RATES:
Full Page Mono £1000.00
Full Page Colour £1250.00
Agency Commission: 15%
Mechanical Data: Col Length: 258mm, Film: Positive, right reading, emulsion side down. Digital, Type Area: 258 x 185mm, Print Process: Offset litho, Trim Size: 285 x 205mm, Page Width: 185mm
Average advertising content per issue: 50%
BUSINESS: ENGINEERING & MACHINERY: Production & Mechanical Engineering

EUROASIA SEMICONDUCTOR
37372U18A-290

Formerly: European Semiconductor
Editorial Address: Hannay House, 39 Clarendon Road, WATFORD, WD17 1JA **Tel:** 01923 690200
Fax: 01923 690201
Email: dr@angelbcl.co.uk
Advertising Address: As above. **Tel:** 01923 690207
Email: sw@angelbc.co.uk
Web site: http://www.euroasiasemiconductor.com
ISSN: 0265-6027
Publisher: Angel Business Communications Ltd
Date Established: 1979
Frequency: Monthly - Published on the 1st of the cover month
Cover Price: £4.50
Free to qualifying individuals
Annual Sub.: £99.00
Circulation: 5,186 (BPA Worldwide 01/01/2007 to 30/06/2007)
Usual Pagination: 60
Editor: David Ridsdale; **Editor-in-Chief:** David Ridsdale; **Publisher:** Jackie Cannon
Summary of Content: Magazine covering equipment and materials used in the design and manufacture of semiconductor devices. Also includes related European and Asian news and politics.
Readership/Target Audience: Read by personnel working in the semiconductor industry.
ADVERTISING RATES:
Full Page Colour £3460.00
Agency Commission: 10%
Mechanical Data: Film: Digital, Col Length: 269mm, Page Width: 185mm, Bleed Size: 303 x 216mm, Trim Size: 297 x 210mm, Type Area: 269 x 185mm
Copy instructions: Copy Date: 1st of month prior to publication date
BUSINESS: ELECTRONICS

EUROCHEM MONITOR
1665018U13-200

Editorial Address: 80 Calverley Road, TUNBRIDGE WELLS, TN1 2UN **Tel:** 020 7017 7500 **Fax:** 020 7017 7599
Email: marketing@agra-net.com
Web site: http://www.agra-net.com
ISSN: 0967-7844
Publisher: Agra Informa Ltd
Frequency: 10 issues yearly
Annual Sub.: £2538.00
Summary of Content: Loose-leaf publication containing the full and consolidated texts of EU legislation on the marketing and use of dangerous substances and preparations.
Readership/Target Audience: Aimed at chemical, pharmaceutical and industrial companies worldwide.
ADVERTISING: No Advertising taken
BUSINESS: CHEMICALS

EUROFOOD
37756U21A-285

Editorial Address: 80 Calverley Road, TUNBRIDGE WELLS, TN1 2UN **Tel:** 020 7017 7500 **Fax:** 020 7017 7599
Email: marketing@agra-net.com
Web site: http://www.agra-net.com
ISSN: 0955-5405
Publisher: Agra Informa Ltd

Date Established: 1989
Frequency: 25 issues yearly
Annual Sub.: £479.00
Usual Pagination: 24
Summary of Content: Newsletter covering all the food business news in Europe.
Readership/Target Audience: Read by food industry executives.
ADVERTISING: No Advertising taken
BUSINESS: AGRICULTURE & FARMING

EUROFOOD MONITOR
1665015U22R-758

Editorial Address: 80 Calverley Road, TUNBRIDGE WELLS, TN1 2UN **Tel:** 020 7017 7500 **Fax:** 020 7017 7599
Email: marketing@agra-net.com
Web site: http://www.agra-net.com
ISSN: 0960-7943
Publisher: Agra Informa Ltd
Frequency: Quarterly
Annual Sub.: £733.00
Summary of Content: Publication providing the complete and consolidated texts of European Union legislation on foodstuffs.
Readership/Target Audience: Aimed at those working in all aspects of the food industry worldwide.
ADVERTISING: No Advertising taken
BUSINESS: FOOD: Food Related

EUROFRUIT MAGAZINE
38115U26C-22

Editorial Address: 1 Nine Elms Lane, LONDON, SW8 5NQ **Tel:** 020 7501 3700 **Fax:** 020 7498 6472
Email: news@fruitnet.com
Advertising Address: As above.
Email: linda@fruitnet.com
Web site: http://www.fruitnet.com
Publisher: Market Intelligence Ltd
Date Established: 1973
Frequency: 11 issues yearly - Published in the 1st week of cover month Double issue in November/December
Annual Sub.: EUR200.00
Circulation: 8,000 (Publisher's Statement)
Usual Pagination: 126
Editor: Mike Knowles; **Managing Director:** Chris White; **Publisher:** Chris White
Summary of Content: Magazine covering the marketing of fresh fruit and vegetables in Europe from producer through to retailer.
Readership/Target Audience: Read by directors, managers and decision-makers at fruit and vegetable producers, suppliers, marketers, importers, exporters, retailers, wholesalers and associated service companies.
ADVERTISING RATES:
Full Page Mono EUR1545.00
Full Page Colour EUR2475.00
Agency Commission: 10%
Mechanical Data: Type Area: 260 x 170mm, Bleed Size: 303 x 216mm, Trim Size: 297 x 210mm, No. of Columns (Display): 3, Col Length: 260mm, Page Width: 170mm, Col Widths (Display): 54mm
Copy instructions: Copy Date: 4 weeks prior to publication date
Average advertising content per issue: 40%
Supplement(s): Biologic - 2xY, Trade France - 1xY, Trade Fresh-Cut - 1xY, Trade Latin America - 1xY, Trade Middle East - 1xY, Trade NZ - 1xY, Trade South Africa - 1xY, Trade Spain - 1xY
BUSINESS: GARDEN TRADE

EUROHEDGE
1645513U1F-628

Editorial Address: Nestor House, Playhouse Yard, LONDON, EC4V 5EX **Tel:** 020 7779 7330
Fax: 020 7779 7331
Email: info@hedgefundintelligence.com
Advertising Address: As above.
Email: jwillis@hedgefundintelligence.com
Web site: http://www.hedgefundintelligence.com
Publisher: Hedge Fund Intelligence
Frequency: 10 issues yearly
Annual Sub.: £995.00
Usual Pagination: 38
Editor: Nick Evans; **Features Editor:** Barry Cohen; **Advertising Manager:** John Willis; **Managing Editor:** Neil Wilson
Summary of Content: Newsletter providing news on all hedge fund managers based in Europe, an overview of the trends in the industry, names and strategies of promising new European funds as well as monitoring the performance of established managers and alerting service providers of potential business opportunities.
Readership/Target Audience: Aimed at investors, European funds, service providers and others wishing to be kept up to date with the latest development in the hedge fund industry.
ADVERTISING RATES:
Full Page Mono £5950.00

Copy instructions: Copy Date: 10th of the publication month
BUSINESS: FINANCE & ECONOMICS: Investment

EURO-INSIDER
1623351U1A-294

Editorial Address: PO Box 33874, LONDON, N8 7XN
Tel: 020 8340 4328
Email: editor@euro-insider.com
Advertising Address: As above.
Email: publisher@euro-insider.com
Web site: http://www.euro-insider.com
ISSN: 1473-3196
Publisher: Richard Betts
Date Established: 2003
Frequency: 10 issues yearly
Annual Sub.: £585.00
Circulation: 800 (Publisher's Statement)
Usual Pagination: 16
Editor: Michael Halls; **Advertising Manager:** Richard Betts;
Publisher: Richard Betts
Summary of Content: Newsletter featuring the latest information and analysis of the European Central Bank, the euro area economics zone and its politics.
Readership/Target Audience: Aimed at economists, treasurers, fund managers and research departments.
ADVERTISING: Rates on application
Copy instructions: Copy Date: 1 week prior to publication date
BUSINESS: FINANCE & ECONOMICS

EUROMARINA REVIEW
1623085U45A-503

Editorial Address: 52 Rickman Hill, COULSDON, CR5 3DP
Tel: 01737 551687 **Fax:** 01737 551687
Email: euromarina@skynet.be
Advertising Address: As above.
Email: euromarina@skynet.be
Web site: http://www.waypoints-international.com/form_euromarinareview.html
ISSN: 1740-3766
Publisher: Gemini Media International bvba/sprl
Date Established: 2002
Frequency: 6 issues yearly - Published in the 3rd week of the 1st cover month
Cover Price: Free
Circulation: 5,900 (Publisher's Statement)
Usual Pagination: 44
Editor: David Young; **Advertising Manager:** David Young;
Managing Editor: David Young
Summary of Content: Official magazine of the European Federation of Yachting Harbours. Covering news, legislation, products, services and issues of special interest to the European Marina industry.
Language(s): English; French
Readership/Target Audience: Aimed at members of Euromarina and owners, managers, operators and developers of European marinas and marina equipment manufacturers.
ADVERTISING RATES:
Full Page Colour EUR1800.00
Agency Commission: 15%
Mechanical Data: Type Area: 265 x 185mm, Trim Size: 297 x 210mm, Bleed Size: 303 x 216mm, Col Length: 265mm, Page Width: 185mm, Film: Digital
Copy instructions: Copy Date: 15th of the month prior to publication date
Average advertising content per issue: 50%
BUSINESS: MARINE & SHIPPING

EUROMEDIA
600842U2R-183

Editorial Address: 4th Floor, Unit 4.01, 71 Bondway, LONDON, SW8 1SQ **Tel:** 020 7793 8855 **Fax:** 020 7793 9955
Email: colin.mann@advanced-television.com
Advertising Address: As above.
Email: sanjeev@advanced-television.com
Web site: http://www.advanced-television.com
ISSN: 1477-8902
Publisher: Advanced Television Ltd
Date Established: 1999
Frequency: 6 issues yearly - Published at the beginning of the 2nd cover month
Free to qualifying individuals
Annual Sub.: EUR95.00
Circulation: 4,711 (BPA Worldwide 01/01/2006 to 30/06/2006)
Usual Pagination: 72
Editor: Colin Mann; **Editor-in-Chief:** Nick Snow; **Managing Editor:** Colin Mann
Summary of Content: Magazine covering business and financial news within the European communications industry including analysis of broadcast, telecoms, Internet, media sectors, content and broadband delivery platforms.
Readership/Target Audience: Aimed at senior professionals in the European media and communications market.
ADVERTISING RATES:
Full Page Mono £2400.00
Full Page Colour £3400.00

Agency Commission: 10%
Mechanical Data: Trim Size: 297 x 210mm, Bleed Size: 303 x 216mm
Copy instructions: Copy Date: 3rd week of the 1st cover month
Average advertising content per issue: 20%
BUSINESS: COMMUNICATIONS, ADVERTISING & MARKETING: Communications Related

EUROMONEY
35077U1C-155

Editorial Address: Nestor House, Playhouse Yard, LONDON, EC4V 5EX **Tel:** 020 7779 8888
Fax: 020 7779 8345
Email: chorwood@euromoney.com
Advertising Address: As above.
Email: schung@euromoney.com
Web site: http://www.euromoney.com
ISSN: 0014-2433
Publisher: Euromoney Institutional Investor plc
Frequency: Monthly - Published on the 10th of the cover month
Cover Price: £25.00
Annual Sub.: £329.00
Circulation: 25,427 (ABC 01/07/2008 to 30/06/2009)
Usual Pagination: 150
Editor: Clive Horwood; **Advertising Manager:** Sui Chung;
Managing Editor: Lawrence White; **Publisher:** Neil Osborn
Summary of Content: Publication covering world financial activity, capital markets and banking.
Readership/Target Audience: Read by bankers and those involved with international finance, including senior decision makers and strategic thinkers.
ADVERTISING RATES:
Full Page Colour £21559.00
Agency Commission: 15%
Mechanical Data: Page Width: 186mm, Type Area: 259 x 186mm, Bleed Size: 292 x 215mm, Trim Size: 286 x 210mm, Col Length: 259mm, Film: Digital
Copy instructions: Copy Date: 18th of the month prior to publication date
Average advertising content per issue: 20%
Supplement(s): Liquid Real Estate - 4xY
BUSINESS: FINANCE & ECONOMICS: Banking

EUROPEAN AUTOMOTIVE COMPONENTS NEWS
1697359U31A-390

Editorial Address: Abinger House, Church Street, DORKING, RH4 1DF **Tel:** 01306 743744 **Fax:** 01306 887546
Email: d.slavnich@ukintpress.com
Advertising Address: As above.
Email: s.willard@ukintpress.com
Web site: http://www.ukintpress.com
Publisher: UKIP Media & Events Ltd
Date Established: 2005
Frequency: 8 issues yearly
Free to qualifying individuals
Circulation: 15,000 (Publisher's Statement)
Editor: Dean Slavnich; **Editor-in-Chief:** Dean Slavnich;
Advertising Manager: Simon Willard
Summary of Content: Magazine highlighting the latest contract, appointment and project news, as well as featuring interviews with leading figures from major auto suppliers.
Readership/Target Audience: Aimed at automotive manufacturers and suppliers.
ADVERTISING RATES:
Full Page Colour £3250.00
Agency Commission: 15%
Mechanical Data: Trim Size: 297 x 210mm, Film: Digital
Copy instructions: Copy Date: 1 week prior to publication date
Average advertising content per issue: 20%
BUSINESS: MOTOR TRADE: Motor Trade Accessories

EUROPEAN AUTOMOTIVE DESIGN
38301U31A-65

Editorial Address: Hawley Mill, Hawley Road, DARTFORD, DA2 7TJ **Tel:** 01322 221144 **Fax:** 01322 421538
Email: ead@findlay.co.uk
Advertising Address: As above. **Fax:** 01322 221188
Email: bstyles@findlay.co.uk
Web site: http://www.europeanautomotivedesign.com
ISSN: 1368-552X
Publisher: Findlay Media Ltd
Date Established: 1997
Frequency: 10 issues yearly - Not published in July and December
Free to qualifying individuals
Annual Sub.: EUR165.00
Circulation: 24,097 (BPA Worldwide 01/01/2008 to 30/06/2008)
Usual Pagination: 60
Editor: Ed Tranter; **Advertising Manager:** Beau Styles;
Publisher: Beau Styles
Summary of Content: Magazine containing reports on technological developments in components systems and materials specified by senior research and development,

design engineers and purchasing managers, who work with European vehicle manufacturers and their tier one and two suppliers.
Readership/Target Audience: Aimed at engineers in vehicle engineering design and R&D centres throughout Europe.
ADVERTISING RATES:
Full Page Mono EUR7405.00
Full Page Colour EUR8965.00
Agency Commission: 15%
Mechanical Data: Type Area: 266 x 184mm, Col Length: 266mm, Trim Size: 297 x 210mm, Bleed Size: 303 x 216mm, Page Width: 184mm, Film: Digital
Copy instructions: Copy Date: Last Wednesday of the month prior to publication date
Average advertising content per issue: 50%
BUSINESS: MOTOR TRADE: Motor Trade Accessories

EUROPEAN BAKER
36458U8A-200

Editorial Address: 1st Floor Offices, 1-3 Station Road East, OXTED, RH8 0BD **Tel:** 01883 734582 **Fax:** 01883 713640
Email: andre@crier.co.uk
Advertising Address: As above.
Email: nthorp@crier.co.uk
Web site: http://www.crier.co.uk
ISSN: 1351-0762
Publisher: Crier Media Group
Date Established: 1996
Frequency: 6 issues yearly - Published in the last week of the 1st cover month
Free to qualifying individuals
Annual Sub.: EUR70.00
Circulation: 10,000 (Publisher's Statement)
Usual Pagination: 64
Editor: Andre Erasmus; **Managing Director:** John Whitbread; **Managing Editor:** Andre Erasmus; **Publisher:** Renato Vrebec
Summary of Content: Magazine concerned with market information, trends, technical and scientific information within the European bakery industry.
Readership/Target Audience: Aimed at senior management, production managers, project managers and owners of larger bakeries across Europe.
ADVERTISING RATES:
Full Page Colour EUR3500.00
Agency Commission: 10%
Mechanical Data: Trim Size: 297 x 210mm, Type Area: 270 x 186mm, Bleed Size: 303 x 218mm, Film: Digital, Col Length: 270mm, Page Width: 186mm
Copy instructions: Copy Date: 20th of the month prior to publication date
Average advertising content per issue: 30%
BUSINESS: BAKING & CONFECTIONERY: Baking

EUROPEAN BOATBUILDER
754773U45E-45

Editorial Address: Leon House, 233 High Street, CROYDON, CR9 1HZ **Tel:** 020 8726 8000
Email: dennis_o'neill@ipcmedia.com
Advertising Address: As above. **Tel:** 020 8726 8124
Fax: 020 8726 8196
Email: philip_pereira@ipcmedia.com
Web site: http://www.europeanboatbuilder.com
Publisher: IPC Inspire
Frequency: 6 issues yearly
Cover Price: Free
Circulation: 6,000 (Publisher's Statement)
Usual Pagination: 60
Editor: Dennis O'Neill; **Advertising Manager:** Philip Pereira;
Managing Editor: Ed Slack
Summary of Content: Magazine covering industry and product news, building and production techniques, developments in materials and composite engineering, the impact of changing legislation and company profiles.
Readership/Target Audience: Read by senior company executives, technical directors, production managers, purchasers, yacht designers and those engaged in building leisure boats.
ADVERTISING RATES:
Full Page Colour £2390.00
Agency Commission: 10%
Mechanical Data: Page Width: 179mm, Film: Positive, right reading, emulsion side down. Digital, Type Area: 260 x 179mm, Col Length: 260mm, Trim Size: 297 x 210mm, Bleed Size: 303 x 216mm, Print Process: Sheet-fed litho
Copy instructions: Copy Date: 6 weeks prior to publication date
Average advertising content per issue: 40%
BUSINESS: MARINE & SHIPPING: Boat Trade

EUROPEAN BUSINESS AIR NEWS
36338U6A-87

Editorial Address: 134 South Street, BISHOP'S STORTFORD, CM23 3BQ **Tel:** 01279 714505
Fax: 01279 714519
Email: rod@ebanmagazine.com
Advertising Address: As above.
Email: mark@ebanmagazine.com

Web site: http://www.ebanmagazine.com
ISSN: 0959-1311
Publisher: Stansted News Ltd
Date Established: 1989
Frequency: 11 issues yearly
Free to qualifying individuals
Annual Sub.: £35.00
Circulation: 6,869 (BPA Worldwide 01/06/2007 to 31/12/2007)
Usual Pagination: 16
Editor: Rod Smith; **Advertising Manager:** Mark Ranger;
Publisher: David Wright
Summary of Content: Magazine which provides information on every aspect of business aircraft operation in Europe and monitors the market in order to reflect operators' opinions.
Readership/Target Audience: Aimed at owners and operators of business aircraft and helicopters throughout Europe.
ADVERTISING RATES:
Full Page Colour $9988.00
SCC $82.00
Agency Commission: 15%
Mechanical Data: Col Length: 380mm, Film: Digital, Type Area: 380 x 273mm, Bleed Size: 426 x 303mm, No. of Columns (Display): 5, Col Widths (Display): 51mm, Trim Size: 420 x 297mm, Page Width: 273mm
Copy instructions: Copy Date: 10 days prior to publication date
Average advertising content per issue: 40%
BUSINESS: AVIATION & AERONAUTICS

EUROPEAN BUSINESS REVIEW 36948U14C-67
Editorial Address: Howard House, Wagon Lane, BINGLEY, BD16 1WA **Tel:** 01274 777700 **Fax:** 01274 785200
Email: mlawrence@emeraldinsight.com
Web site: http://www.emeraldinsight.com
ISSN: 0955-534X
Publisher: Emerald Group Publishing Ltd
Frequency: 6 issues yearly
Editor: Martyn Lawrence; **Publisher:** Martyn Lawrence
Summary of Content: Journal featuring all aspects of European review legislative and management covering EC markets, legislation and corporate taxation.
Readership/Target Audience: Aimed at all managers working in a business environment and academics researching the European scene.
ADVERTISING: No Advertising taken
BUSINESS: COMMERCE, INDUSTRY & MANAGEMENT: International Commerce

EUROPEAN CEO 1698044U14A-556
Editorial Address: 37-42 Compton Street, LONDON, EC1V 0AP **Tel:** 020 7014 0300 **Fax:** 020 7014 0302
Email: h.scholl@europeanceo.com
Advertising Address: As above. **Fax:** 020 7014 0301
Email: hamish@wnmedia.com
Web site: http://www.europeanceo.com
Publisher: Tower Business Media
Date Established: 1999
Frequency: 6 issues yearly
Cover Price: £3.50
Free to qualifying individuals
Circulation: 46,484 (Publisher's Statement)
Usual Pagination: 150
Editor: Simon Thomas; **Editor-in-Chief:** Helene Scholl
Summary of Content: Magazine covering news, analysis and guidance on business matters affecting European business leaders.
Readership/Target Audience: Aimed at CEOs, CFOs and Managing Directors.
ADVERTISING RATES:
Full Page Mono EUR11450.00
Full Page Colour EUR13850.00
Agency Commission: 10%
Mechanical Data: Type Area: 278 x 190mm, Bleed Size: 305 x 218mm, Trim Size: 297 x 210mm, Col Length: 278mm, Page Width: 190mm, Film: Digital
Copy instructions: Copy Date: 4 weeks prior to publication date
Average advertising content per issue: 20%
BUSINESS: COMMERCE, INDUSTRY & MANAGEMENT

EUROPEAN CHEMICAL ENGINEER 37276U16B-6
Editorial Address: Europa House, 13-17 Ironmonger Row, LONDON, EC1V 3QG **Tel:** 020 7253 2545
Fax: 020 7608 1600
Email: editorial@setform.com
Advertising Address: As above. **Tel:** 020 7454 7160
Email: jabey@setform.com
Web site: http://www.engineerlive.com
Publisher: Setform Ltd
Frequency: Half-yearly - Published in June and December
Cover Price: Free
Circulation: 12,000 (Publisher's Statement)

Editor: Paul Boughton; **Managing Director:** Mike Bishop;
Publisher: David Washington
Summary of Content: Magazine covering powders, coatings, pigments, elastomers, paints, resins, inks and finishes. Includes articles on plant and machinery, packaging, storage and distribution. Also covers health and safety, IT and polymer technology.
Readership/Target Audience: Read by senior design managers, technical and research directors and consulting engineers.
ADVERTISING RATES:
Full Page Mono £4150.00
Full Page Colour £5350.00
Agency Commission: 10%
Mechanical Data: Bleed Size: 303 x 216mm, Trim Size: 297 x 210mm
Copy instructions: Copy Date: 8 weeks prior to publication date
Average advertising content per issue: 35%
BUSINESS: DECORATING & PAINT: Paint - Technical Manufacture

EUROPEAN CLEANING JOURNAL 35951U4F-100
Editorial Address: PO Box 299, CHESHAM, HP5 1EP
Tel: 01494 791222 **Fax:** 01494 792223
Email: michelle@europeancleaningjournal.com
Advertising Address: As above.
Email: info@europeancleaningjournal.com
Web site: http://www.europeancleaningjournal.com
ISSN: 0968-901X
Publisher: Criterion Publishing Ltd
Date Established: 1993
Frequency: 6 issues yearly
Free to qualifying individuals
Annual Sub.: £60.00
Circulation: 22,255 (Publisher's Statement)
Usual Pagination: 80
Editor: Michelle Marshall; **Managing Director:** Chris Godman; **Advertising Manager:** Carole Dawson
Summary of Content: Magazine carrying news, analysis and in-depth features on the European cleaning industry.
Language(s): English; French; German; Italian
Readership/Target Audience: Aimed at buyers and key specifiers of cleaning equipment, chemicals and services.
ADVERTISING RATES:
Full Page Mono £1650.00
Full Page Colour £2275.00
Mechanical Data: Type Area: 275 x 185mm, Col Length: 275mm, Page Width: 185mm, Trim Size: 297 x 210mm, Film: Digital
BUSINESS: ARCHITECTURE & BUILDING: Cleaning & Maintenance

EUROPEAN COMMUNICATIONS 37444U18B-680
Editorial Address: 6 Laurence Pountney Hill, LONDON, EC4R 0BL **Tel:** 020 7933 8999 **Fax:** 020 7933 8998
Email: lyndmorley@mac.com
Advertising Address: As above.
Email: markb@eurocomms.com
Web site: http://www.eurocomms.com
ISSN: 1367-9996
Publisher: St. John Patrick Publishers Ltd
Date Established: 1988
Frequency: Quarterly
Free to qualifying individuals
Circulation: 16,000 (BPA Worldwide 01/01/2008 to 30/06/2008)
Usual Pagination: 108
Editor: Lynd Morley; **Advertising Manager:** Mark Bradbury
Summary of Content: Magazine with news and information of the communications industry within Europe.
Readership/Target Audience: Aimed at heads and deputies of PTTs, communication decision makers at government, OEMs, VARs and major end user companies.
ADVERTISING RATES:
Full Page Colour £8950.00
Agency Commission: 10%
Mechanical Data: Film: Digital, Trim Size: 275 x 210mm
BUSINESS: ELECTRONICS: Telecommunications

EUROPEAN COMPETITION LAW REVIEW - ECLR 36950U14C-68
Editorial Address: 100 Avenue Road, Swiss Cottage, LONDON, NW3 3PF **Tel:** 020 7393 7000 **Fax:** 020 7393 7030
Web site: http://www.sweetandmaxwell.co.uk
ISSN: 0144-3054
Publisher: Sweet & Maxwell Ltd
Date Established: 1980
Frequency: Monthly
Annual Sub.: £694.00
Usual Pagination: 144
Editor: Julian Maitland-Walker
Summary of Content: Journal providing up-to-date information covering developments in EC competition law,

as well as other major trading nations such as the USA, Australia and Japan.
Readership/Target Audience: Aimed at competition lawyers.
ADVERTISING: No Advertising taken
BUSINESS: COMMERCE, INDUSTRY & MANAGEMENT: International Commerce

EUROPEAN COMPUTER SUPPORT 36037U5C-910
Formerly: ECM European Computer Marketplace
Editorial Address: Suite 26, 151 High Street, SOUTHAMPTON, SO14 2BT **Tel:** 023 8046 4675
Fax: 023 8046 6677
Email: chantalr@wilsonmarketing.co.uk
Advertising Address: As above.
Email: chantalr@wilsonmarketing.co.uk
Publisher: Wilson Marketing Ltd
Frequency: Monthly
Free to qualifying individuals
Circulation: 6,000 (Publisher's Statement)
Editor: Chantal Rushton
Summary of Content: Magazine covering all aspects of the hardware support industry in Europe.
Readership/Target Audience: Aimed at end users, brokers and corporate clients.
ADVERTISING RATES:
Full Page Mono £625.00
Full Page Colour £625.00
Agency Commission: 10%
Mechanical Data: Type Area: 273 x 189mm, Bleed Size: 303 x 216mm, Trim Size: 297 x 210mm, Col Length: 273mm, Page Width: 189mm, Film: Digital
Copy instructions: Copy Date: 1 week prior to publication date
Average advertising content per issue: 73%
BUSINESS: COMPUTERS & AUTOMATION: Professional Personal Computers

EUROPEAN COSMETIC MARKETS 37249U15A-25
Editorial Address: Paulton House, 8 Shepherdess Walk, LONDON, N1 7LB **Tel:** 020 7549 8626 **Fax:** 020 7549 8622
Email: ecm@wilmington.co.uk
Advertising Address: As above. **Tel:** 020 7549 8635
Email: siobhanm@hpcimedia.com
Web site: http://www.cosmeticsbusiness.com
ISSN: 0957-1515
Publisher: Progressive Media Publications
Date Established: 1984
Frequency: Monthly - Published at the beginning of the cover month
Annual Sub.: £800.00
Circulation: 500 (Publisher's Statement)
Usual Pagination: 40
Editor: Katie Rodgers; **Managing Director:** Colin Bailey-Wood; **Managing Editor:** Clare Henderson
Summary of Content: Journal covering news and data on the European cosmetics and toiletries markets.
Readership/Target Audience: Aimed at marketing personnel and management.
ADVERTISING RATES:
Full Page Colour £2275.00
Agency Commission: 10%
Mechanical Data: Bleed Size: 303 x 216mm, Trim Size: 297 x 210mm, Type Area: 254 x 178mm, Film: Digital, Col Length: 254mm, Page Width: 178mm
Copy instructions: Copy Date: 15th of the month prior to publication date
Average advertising content per issue: 10%
BUSINESS: COSMETICS & HAIRDRESSING: Cosmetics

EUROPEAN DAILY ELECTRICITY MARKETS 37305U17-109
Editorial Address: 1 Procter Street, LONDON, WC1V 6EU
Tel: 020 7911 1920 **Fax:** 020 7911 1852
Email: info@icisheren.com
Advertising Address: As above.
Email: sales@icisheren.com
Web site: http://www.heren.com
ISSN: 1368-2989
Publisher: ICIS Heren
Frequency: 260 issues yearly
Annual Sub.: £1000.00
Usual Pagination: 10
Editor: Zoe Double
Summary of Content: Fax report covering the European electricity market-place. Also contains European power prices and associated news items.
Readership/Target Audience: Aimed at decision makers and traders within the power industry.
ADVERTISING RATES:
Full Page Colour £1000.00

Mechanical Data: Type Area: 250 x 160mm, Col Length: 250mm, Page Width: 160mm, Film: Digital, Bleed Size: 297 x 210mm, Trim Size: 257 x 176mm
BUSINESS: ELECTRICAL

EUROPEAN DESIGN ENGINEER

37609U19B-260

Editorial Address: Europa House, 13-17 Ironmonger Row, LONDON, EC1V 3QG Tel: 020 7253 2545
Fax: 020 7608 1600
Email: editorial@setform.com
Advertising Address: As above.
Email: jabey@setform.com
Web site: http://www.engineerlive.com
Publisher: Setform Ltd
Frequency: Half-yearly - Published in April and October
Cover Price: Free
Circulation: 15,000 (Publisher's Statement)
Usual Pagination: 160
Editor: Paul Boughton; Managing Director: Mike Bishop; Publisher: David Washington
Summary of Content: Magazine covering the latest technological developments within Europe.
Readership/Target Audience: Aimed at design engineers.
ADVERTISING RATES:
Full Page Colour £5350.00
Agency Commission: 10%
Mechanical Data: Film: Digital, Trim Size: 297 x 210mm
Copy instructions: Copy Date: 3rd week of 2 months prior to publication date
Average advertising content per issue: 35%
BUSINESS: ENGINEERING & MACHINERY: Engineering - Design

EUROPEAN ELECTRONICS ENGINEER

37370U18A-288_50

Editorial Address: Europa House, 13-17 Ironmonger Row, LONDON, EC1V 3QG Tel: 020 7253 2545
Fax: 020 7608 1600
Email: editorial@setform.com
Advertising Address: As above.
Email: jabey@setform.com
Web site: http://www.engineerlive.com
Publisher: Setform Ltd
Frequency: Half-yearly - Published in January and July
Cover Price: Free
Circulation: 15,000 (Publisher's Statement)
Usual Pagination: 108
Editor: Paul Boughton; Managing Director: Mike Bishop; Publisher: David Washington
Summary of Content: Magazine containing an international review of the electronic engineering industry, covering fourteen countries.
Language(s): English; French; German
Readership/Target Audience: Read by electronics engineers, technical directors, design engineers and production engineers.
ADVERTISING RATES:
Full Page Mono £4150.00
Full Page Colour £5350.00
Mechanical Data: Trim Size: 297 x 210mm, Film: Digital
BUSINESS: ELECTRONICS

EUROPEAN ELECTRONICS MARKETS FORECAST

37371U18A-289

Editorial Address: Harvard House, Grove Technology Park, WANTAGE, OX12 9FF Tel: 01235 227310
Fax: 01235 227322
Email: andrew.fletcher@rer.co.uk
Web site: http://www.rer.co.uk
ISSN: 1364-2197
Publisher: Reed Electronics Research
Date Established: 1996
Frequency: Monthly
Annual Sub.: £450.00
Usual Pagination: 18
Editor: Andrew Fletcher; Publisher: Andrew Fletcher
Summary of Content: Newsletter providing market analysis on key areas within the European electronics market. It also covers the latest business news, company results and their impact on the electronics market.
Readership/Target Audience: Aimed at senior management, market researchers, business developers, industry watchers, strategic planners and investment professionals.
ADVERTISING: No Advertising taken
BUSINESS: ELECTRONICS

EUROPEAN ENVIRONMENTAL LAW FOR INDUSTRY

1665017U57-132

Editorial Address: 80 Calverley Road, TUNBRIDGE WELLS, TN1 2UN Tel: 020 7017 7500 Fax: 020 7017 7599
Email: marketing@agra-net.com
Web site: http://www.agra-net.com

ISSN: 1353-3525
Publisher: Agra Informa Ltd
Frequency: 5 issues yearly
Annual Sub.: £523.00
Summary of Content: Reference guide to EU environment legislation. Contains complete texts of directives and amendments on air, water, waste, general issues, pollution from biotechnology, control of major industrial risks and integrated pollution prevention with regular updates.
Readership/Target Audience: Aimed at industry and government executives throughout Europe.
ADVERTISING: No Advertising taken
BUSINESS: ENVIRONMENT & POLLUTION

EUROPEAN FERRY SCENE

39324U45A-35

Editorial Address: Plovers, Ivychurch, ROMNEY MARSH, TN29 0HJ Tel: 01797 344090
Email: ferrypubs@manx.net
Advertising Address: La Fontanella, 3A Martello Road, Branksome Park, POOLE, BH13 7DQ Tel: 01202 701053
Fax: 01202 701053
Email: smacey4@btinternet.com
Web site: http://www.ferrypubs.co.uk
ISSN: 0958-1863
Publisher: Ferry Publications Ltd
Date Established: 1987
Frequency: Quarterly
Annual Sub.: £27.00
Circulation: 5,000 (Publisher's Statement)
Usual Pagination: 56
Editor: John Hendy; Advertising Manager: Stephen Macey
Summary of Content: Magazine focusing on the ferry industry, travel trade and shipping enthusiasts.
Readership/Target Audience: Aimed at industry and ferry enthusiasts.
ADVERTISING RATES:
Full Page Colour £300.00
Agency Commission: 10%
Mechanical Data: Film: Digital, Type Area: 267 x 185mm, Col Length: 267mm, Page Width: 185mm, Bleed Size: 303 x 216mm
Copy instructions: Copy Date: 8 weeks prior to publication date
Average advertising content per issue: 20%
BUSINESS: MARINE & SHIPPING

EUROPEAN GAS MARKETS

38077U24-5

Editorial Address: 1 Procter Street, LONDON, WC1V 6EU
Tel: 020 7911 1943 Fax: 020 7911 1852
Email: james.allpress@icisheren.com
Web site: http://www.heren.com
ISSN: 1360-4880
Publisher: ICIS Heren
Date Established: 1994
Frequency: 22 issues yearly
Annual Sub.: £1100.00
Usual Pagination: 16
Editor: James Allpress; Managing Editor: James Allpress
Summary of Content: Newsletter offering in-depth insight into the thinking behind the decisions that shape the commerce and politics of the European natural gas sector.
Readership/Target Audience: Aimed at those involved in the gas industry.
ADVERTISING: No Advertising taken
BUSINESS: GAS

EUROPEAN JOURNAL OF AMERICAN CULTURE

1696245U62R-498

Editorial Address: University of Exeter, EXETER, EX8 2AT
Email: marionh.gibson@exeter.ac.uk
Web site: http://www.intellectbooks.co.uk
ISSN: 1466-0407
Publisher: Intellect Ltd
Date Established: 2000
Frequency: 3 issues yearly - Published in April, August and December
Annual Sub.: £210.00
Circulation: 400 (Publisher's Statement)
Usual Pagination: 80
Editor: Marion Gibson
Summary of Content: Journal focusing on American culture including cinema, music, art and other cultural forms.
Readership/Target Audience: Aimed at academics.
ADVERTISING: No Advertising taken
BUSINESS: CHURCH & SCHOOL EQUIPMENT & EDUCATION: Education Related

EUROPEAN JOURNAL OF ARCHAEOLOGY

48846U62R-473

Editorial Address: 1 Oliver's Yard, 55 City Road, LONDON, EC1Y 1SP Tel: 020 7324 8500 Fax: 020 7324 8600
Email: info@sagepub.co.uk
Advertising Address: As above.
Email: advertising@sagepub.co.uk

Web site: http://www.sagepub.co.uk
ISSN: 1461-9571
Publisher: Sage Publications
Frequency: 3 issues yearly - Published in April, August and December
Annual Sub.: £279.00
Circulation: 1,000 (Publisher's Statement)
Editor: Alan Saville; Advertising Manager: Sheena Karim
Summary of Content: Journal of the European Association of Archaeologists covering news, debate and articles on all periods of archaeology.
Readership/Target Audience: Aimed at archaeologists.
ADVERTISING RATES:
Full Page Mono £400.00
Agency Commission: 5%
Mechanical Data: Type Area: 205 x 130mm, Col Length: 205mm, Page Width: 130mm, Film: Digital
BUSINESS: CHURCH & SCHOOL EQUIPMENT & EDUCATION: Education Related

EUROPEAN JOURNAL OF CARDIOVASCULAR PREVENTION AND REHABILITATION

40183U56A-69_5

Formerly: Journal of Cardiovascular Risk
Editorial Address: 250 Waterloo Road, LONDON, SE1 8RD
Tel: 020 7981 0676 Fax: 020 7981 0556
Email: phil.daly@wolterskluwer.com
Advertising Address: The Point of Difference, 4 Chase Side Avenue, LONDON, SW20 8LU Tel: 020 8542 3200
Fax: 020 8543 3810
Email: pointofdiff@btinternet.com
Web site: http://www.ejcpr.org
ISSN: 1350-6277
Publisher: Lippincott Williams & Wilkins
Date Established: 1994
Frequency: 6 issues yearly
Annual Sub.: $330.00
Circulation: 430 (Publisher's Statement)
Usual Pagination: 84
Editor: Phil Daly; Advertising Manager: Dick Bower; Publisher: Phil Daly
Summary of Content: Journal covering molecular and cell biology, haemodynamics, epidemiology, genetics, thrombosis, diabetes, exercise, tobacco use and other cardiovascular risk factors.
Readership/Target Audience: Aimed at cardiologists, practitioners and researchers.
ADVERTISING RATES:
Full Page Mono $765.00
Full Page Colour $1645.00
Agency Commission: 15%
Mechanical Data: Type Area: 254 x 178mm, Col Length: 254mm, Bleed Size: 282 x 213mm, Trim Size: 276 x 207mm, Page Width: 178mm, Film: Positive, right reading, emulsion side down. Digital
Copy instructions: Copy Date: 6 weeks prior to publication date
Average advertising content per issue: 5%
BUSINESS: HEALTH & MEDICAL

EUROPEAN JOURNAL OF COMMUNICATION

35749U2R-124

Editorial Address: 1 Oliver's Yard, 55 City Road, LONDON, EC1Y 1SP Tel: 020 7324 8500 Fax: 020 7324 8600
Advertising Address: As above.
Web site: http://www.sagepub.co.uk
ISSN: 0267-3231
Publisher: Sage Publications
Date Established: 1986
Frequency: Quarterly - Published in March, June, September and December
Cover Price: £19.00
Circulation: 800 (Publisher's Statement)
Usual Pagination: 128
Editor: Peter Golding; Advertising Manager: Sheena Karim
Summary of Content: Journal concerned with research and analysis of communications, especially mass media, prioritising work by European scholars or with a particular interest to readers mainly in Europe.
Readership/Target Audience: Aimed at scholars, academics and media professionals.
ADVERTISING RATES:
Full Page Mono £400.00
Agency Commission: 5%
Mechanical Data: Col Length: 205mm, Page Width: 130mm, Type Area: 205 x 130mm
BUSINESS: COMMUNICATIONS, ADVERTISING & MARKETING: Communications Related

EUROPEAN JOURNAL OF CULTURAL STUDIES

48847U62R-474

Editorial Address: 1 Oliver's Yard, 55 City Road, LONDON, EC1Y 1SP Tel: 020 7324 8500 Fax: 020 7324 8600
Email: info@sagepub.co.uk
Advertising Address: As above.

Business Magazines

Email: advertising@sagepub.co.uk
Web site: http://www.sagepub.co.uk
ISSN: 1367-5494
Publisher: Sage Publications
Frequency: Quarterly
Annual Sub.: £44.00
Circulation: 350 (Publisher's Statement)
Editor: Ann Gray; **Advertising Manager:** Sheena Karim
Summary of Content: Journal covering cultural studies. Includes articles on youth culture and class relations, gender, migration, popular culture and reviews of new work and current debates.
Readership/Target Audience: Aimed at academics and professionals with an interest in culture studies and related disciplines.
ADVERTISING RATES:
Full Page Mono £400.00
Mechanical Data: Col Length: 210mm, Film: Digital, Type Area: 210 x 140mm, Page Width: 140mm
Copy instructions: Copy Date: 12 weeks prior to publication date
Average advertising content per issue: 5%
BUSINESS: CHURCH & SCHOOL EQUIPMENT & EDUCATION: Education Related

EUROPEAN JOURNAL OF ECHOCARDIOGRAPHY
1881576U56A-219

Editorial Address: Great Clarendon Street, OXFORD, OX2 6DP **Tel:** 01865 353907 **Fax:** 01865 353774
Email: eje@oxfordjournals.org
Web site: http://ejechocard.oxfordjournals.org/
ISSN: 1525-2167
Publisher: OUP
Frequency: 6 issues yearly
Circulation: 2,822 (Publisher's Statement)
Editor: Willeke Korpershoek
Summary of Content: Journal published on behalf of the European Society of Cardiology. Publishes peer reviewed articles on the ultrasonic examination of the cardiovascular system, including ischaemic heart disease, valve disease, cardiomyopathy, congenital heart disease and vascular disease.
Readership/Target Audience: Aimed at cardiologists.
BUSINESS: HEALTH & MEDICAL

EUROPEAN JOURNAL OF GASTROENTEROLOGY & HEPATOLOGY
40566U56R-55

Editorial Address: 250 Waterloo Road, LONDON, SE1 8RD **Tel:** 020 7981 0676 **Fax:** 020 7981 0556
Email: lwweditorialoffice@wolterskluwer.com
Advertising Address: The Point of Difference, 4 Chase Side Avenue, WIMBLEDON, SW20 8LU **Tel:** 020 8542 3200
Fax: 020 8543 3810
Email: pointofdiff@btinternet.com
Web site: http://www.eurojgh.com
ISSN: 0954-691X
Publisher: Lippincott Williams & Wilkins
Date Established: 1988
Frequency: Monthly
Annual Sub.: £392.00
Circulation: 180 (Publisher's Statement)
Usual Pagination: 128
Editor: Didier Lebrec
Summary of Content: Journal containing original papers, in-depth reviews of developing areas, assessments of equipment, case reports and other features.
Readership/Target Audience: Aimed at the European Society of Gastroenterologists and Hepatologists and others.
ADVERTISING RATES:
Full Page Mono $750.00
Full Page Colour $1610.00
Agency Commission: 15%
Mechanical Data: Col Length: 254mm, Bleed Size: 282 x 213mm, Page Width: 178mm, Trim Size: 276 x 207mm, Type Area: 254 x 178mm, Film: Digital
Copy instructions: Copy Date: 6 weeks prior to month of publication
BUSINESS: HEALTH & MEDICAL: Health Medical Related

EUROPEAN JOURNAL OF INDUSTRIAL RELATIONS
37110U14F-23_20

Editorial Address: 1 Oliver's Yard, 55 City Road, LONDON, EC1Y 1SP **Tel:** 020 7324 8500 **Fax:** 020 7324 8600
Advertising Address: As above.
Email: advertising@sagepub.co.uk
Web site: http://www.sagepub.co.uk/journal.aspx?pid=105539
ISSN: 0959-6801
Publisher: Sage Publications
Frequency: 3 issues yearly - Published in March, July and November
Cover Price: £19.00
Annual Sub.: £44.00

Circulation: 650 (Publisher's Statement)
Editor: Richard Hyman; **Advertising Manager:** Sheena Karim
Summary of Content: English language forum for analysis of key developments, and their theoretical and practical implications, in industrial relations in Europe.
Readership/Target Audience: Aimed at students and scholars interested in European industrial relations.
ADVERTISING RATES:
Full Page Mono £400.00
Agency Commission: 5%
Mechanical Data: Col Length: 205mm, Page Width: 130mm, Type Area: 205 x 130mm, Film: Digital
BUSINESS: COMMERCE, INDUSTRY & MANAGEMENT: Training & Recruitment

EUROPEAN JOURNAL OF INTERNATIONAL LAW
601525U44-633

Editorial Address: Great Clarendon Street, OXFORD, OX2 6DP **Tel:** 01865 353907 **Fax:** 01865 353985
Email: anny.bremner@iue.it
Advertising Address: 60 Upper Broadmoor Road, CROWTHORNE, RG45 7DE **Tel:** 01344 779945
Fax: 01344 779945
Email: lhann@lhms.fsnet.co.uk
Web site: http://www.oup.co.uk/ejilaw
ISSN: 0938-5428
Publisher: OUP
Date Established: 1990
Frequency: 5 issues yearly
Cover Price: £11.00
Annual Sub.: £42.00
Usual Pagination: 212
Editor: Anny Bremner; **Editor-in-Chief:** Joseph Weiler; **Managing Editor:** Anny Bremner
Summary of Content: Journal features international contributions on the theory and practice of international law.
Readership/Target Audience: Aimed at academics, educators, researchers, practitioners and managers, social policy academics and researchers.
ADVERTISING RATES:
Full Page Mono £340.00
Agency Commission: 10%
Mechanical Data: Film: Digital, Type Area: 200 x 125mm, Col Length: 200mm, Page Width: 125mm
BUSINESS: LEGAL

THE EUROPEAN JOURNAL OF ORTHODONTICS
24857U56D-69

Editorial Address: Flat 20, 49 Hallam Street, LONDON, W1W 6JN **Tel:** 020 7935 2795 **Fax:** 020 7323 0410
Email: eoslondon@aol.com
Advertising Address: Great Clarendon Street, OXFORD, OX2 6DP **Tel:** 01865 354907
Email: steve.simmonds@oxfordjournals.org
Web site: http://www.oup.co.uk/jnls
ISSN: 0141-5387
Publisher: OUP
Date Established: 1979
Frequency: 6 issues yearly
Free to qualifying individuals
Usual Pagination: 132
Editor: Fraser McDonald
Summary of Content: Presents research or clinical papers.
Readership/Target Audience: Aimed at orthodontists.
ADVERTISING RATES:
Full Page Mono £779.00
Full Page Colour £1298.00
Agency Commission: 10%
Mechanical Data: Type Area: 232 x 171mm, Trim Size: 276 x 210mm, Bleed Size: 282 x 216mm, Print Process: Litho, Film: Digital, Col Length: 232mm, Page Width: 171mm
BUSINESS: HEALTH & MEDICAL: Dental

EUROPEAN JOURNAL OF PALLIATIVE CARE
40303U56B-85

Editorial Address: 8-10 Dryden Street, Covent Garden, LONDON, WC2E 9NA **Tel:** 020 7240 4493
Fax: 020 7240 4479
Email: edit@hayward.co.uk
Advertising Address: Hayward Medical Communications, The Pines, Fordham Road, NEWMARKET, CB8 7LG
Tel: 01638 723560 **Fax:** 01638 723561
Email: hmc@hayward.co.uk
Web site: http://www.ejpc.eu.com
Publisher: Hayward Medical Communications Ltd
Frequency: 6 issues yearly
Annual Sub.: £65.00
Editor: Anne-Claire Bouzanne; **Publisher:** Christopher Tidman
Summary of Content: Journal containing reports and articles on the latest treatments and developments within the field of palliative care.
Language(s): English; French

Readership/Target Audience: Aimed at hospice workers, general practitioners, medical and clinical oncologists, nurses and social workers.
ADVERTISING RATES:
Full Page Colour £1950.00
Agency Commission: 10%
Mechanical Data: Film: Digital, Trim Size: 297 x 210mm, Bleed Size: +3mm
BUSINESS: HEALTH & MEDICAL: Nursing

EUROPEAN JOURNAL OF PERSONALITY
40568U56R-55_50

Editorial Address: The Atrium, Southern Gate, CHICHESTER, PO19 8SQ **Tel:** 01243 779777
Fax: 01243 775878
Advertising Address: As above. **Tel:** 01243 770254
Fax: 01243 770432
Email: adsales@wiley.co.uk
Web site: http://www.wiley.co.uk
ISSN: 0890-2070
Publisher: John Wiley & Sons Ltd
Date Established: 1987
Frequency: 7 issues yearly
Usual Pagination: 80
Editor: Marco Perugini
Summary of Content: Journal reflecting all areas of current personality psychology, publishes original reports, theoretical analyses, methodological contributions and critical review papers.
Readership/Target Audience: Aimed at clinical, social and personality psychologists and researchers.
ADVERTISING RATES:
Full Page Mono £1175.00
Full Page Colour £2575.00
Agency Commission: 10%
Mechanical Data: Print Process: Sheet-fed offset litho, Film: Digital, Type Area: 248 x 165mm, Col Widths (Display): 220mm, Page Width: 135mm
BUSINESS: HEALTH & MEDICAL: Health Medical Related

EUROPEAN JOURNAL OF PROSTHODONTICS AND RESTORATIVE DENTISTRY
40388U56D-29

Editorial Address: 5 Battery Green Road, LOWESTOFT, NR32 1DE **Tel:** 01502 511522 **Fax:** 01502 583152
Email: j.m.thomason@newcastle.ac.uk
Advertising Address: As above.
Email: wdp@dbgp.co.uk
Web site: http://www.fdiworlddental.org/resources/4_4prosthodontics.html
ISSN: 0965-7452
Publisher: FDI World Dental Press Ltd
Date Established: 1992
Frequency: Quarterly
Free to qualifying individuals
Annual Sub.: £60.00
Circulation: 1,300 (Publisher's Statement)
Usual Pagination: 48
Editor: Mark Thomason; **Advertising Manager:** Dennis Barber
Summary of Content: Academic journal of the British Society for Restorative Dentistry.
Readership/Target Audience: Aimed at all dental practitioners, especially those who specialise in restorative dentistry and prosthodontics.
ADVERTISING RATES:
Full Page Colour £360.00
Mechanical Data: Bleed Size: 303 x 216mm, Trim Size: 297 x 210mm, Film: Digital, Type Area: 270 x 179mm, Col Length: 270mm, Page Width: 179mm
Copy instructions: Copy Date: 6 weeks prior to publication date
BUSINESS: HEALTH & MEDICAL: Dental

EUROPEAN JOURNAL OF SOCIAL PSYCHOLOGY
40565U56R-55_55

Editorial Address: The Atrium, Southern Gate, CHICHESTER, PO19 8SQ **Tel:** 01243 779777
Fax: 01243 775878
Advertising Address: As above. **Fax:** 01243 770432
Email: fpidduck@wiley.co.uk
Web site: http://www.interscience.wiley.com
ISSN: 0046-2772
Publisher: John Wiley & Sons Ltd
Date Established: 1971
Frequency: 6 issues yearly
Annual Sub.: £210.00
Usual Pagination: 150
Editor: Russell Spears
Summary of Content: Journal promoting communication between social psychology researchers worldwide and providing a bridge between European and other research traditions.
Readership/Target Audience: Aimed at social psychologists.

Section 4 (b) Business Magazines

ADVERTISING RATES:
Full Page Mono £1175.00
Full Page Colour £2575.00
Agency Commission: 10%
Mechanical Data: Type Area: 220 x 135mm, Trim Size: 248 x 165mm, Col Length: 220mm, Page Width: 135mm, Print Process: Sheet-fed litho, Film: Digital
BUSINESS: HEALTH & MEDICAL: Health Medical Related

EUROPEAN JOURNAL OF SOCIAL THEORY
48848U62R-475
Editorial Address: 1 Oliver's Yard, 55 City Road, LONDON, EC1Y 1SP **Tel:** 020 7324 8500 **Fax:** 020 7324 8600
Email: info@sagepub.co.uk
Advertising Address: As above.
Email: advertising@sagepub.co.uk
Web site: http://www.sagepub.co.uk
ISSN: 1368-4310
Publisher: Sage Publications
Date Established: 1998
Frequency: Quarterly
Annual Sub.: £48.00
Circulation: 350 (Publisher's Statement)
Usual Pagination: 148
Editor: Gerard Delanty; **Advertising Manager:** Sheena Karim
Summary of Content: Journal covering social theory. Includes articles on critical theory, postmodernism, critical realism and Marxism.
Readership/Target Audience: Aimed at social theorists and theoretically minded social scientists.
ADVERTISING RATES:
Full Page Mono £400.00
Agency Commission: 5%
Mechanical Data: Col Length: 205mm, Type Area: 205 x 130mm, Page Width: 130mm, Film: Digital
BUSINESS: CHURCH & SCHOOL EQUIPMENT & EDUCATION: Education Related

EUROPEAN LAW REPORTS
39317U44-635_50
Editorial Address: 16C Worcester Place, OXFORD, OX1 2JW **Tel:** 01865 517530 **Fax:** 01865 510710
Email: barbara@hartpub.co.uk
Advertising Address: As above.
Email: barbara@hartpub.co.uk
Web site: http://www.hartjournals.co.uk
ISSN: 1091-3297
Publisher: Hart Publishing Ltd
Date Established: 1997
Frequency: 6 issues yearly
Annual Sub.: £325.00
Circulation: 250 (Publisher's Statement)
Usual Pagination: 150
Editor: Barbara Darling
Summary of Content: Publication looking at case studies of community law.
Readership/Target Audience: Aimed at solicitors, barristers and judiciary.
ADVERTISING RATES:
Full Page Mono £250.00
Agency Commission: 10%
Mechanical Data: Type Area: 200 x 125mm, Col Length: 200mm, Page Width: 125mm, Film: Digital, Trim Size: 234 x 156mm
Copy instructions: Copy Date: Middle of the month prior to publication
BUSINESS: LEGAL

THE EUROPEAN LAWYER
624607U44-635_75
Editorial Address: Hereford House, 22-24 Smithfield Street, LONDON, EC1A 9LF **Tel:** 020 7332 2580
Fax: 020 7332 2599
Email: james@europeanlawyer.co.uk
Advertising Address: As above. **Tel:** 020 7332 2572
Email: accounts@europeanlawyer.co.uk
Web site: http://www.europeanlawyer.co.uk
Publisher: Polyview Media Ltd
Date Established: 2000
Frequency: 10 issues yearly - Published on the 1st of the cover month
Annual Sub.: £299.00
Circulation: 6,000 (Publisher's Statement)
Usual Pagination: 64
Editor: Jonathan Ames; **Advertising Manager:** Karina Baker
Summary of Content: Magazine providing relevant and incisive legal information. Includes reports on issues faced by business lawyers and up-to-date information on technical legal developments.
Readership/Target Audience: Aimed at senior partners within law firms, government departments, law faculties and legal service suppliers throughout Europe.
ADVERTISING RATES:
Full Page Colour £4390.00
Mechanical Data: Film: Digital, Type Area: 248 x 185mm, Bleed Size: 303 x 216mm, Trim Size: 297 x 210mm, Col Length: 248mm, Page Width: 185mm

Copy instructions: Copy Date: 4 weeks prior to publication date
Average advertising content per issue: 20%
BUSINESS: LEGAL

EUROPEAN LIFE SCIENCE
1861848U55-9029
Editorial Address: 8 Hollington Way, Monkspath, SOLIHULL, B90 4YD **Tel:** 0121 705 2120
Email: daveharvett@btconnect.com
Web site: http://www.life-science.se
Publisher: Thomas Industrial Media bvba
Frequency: Quarterly
Circulation: 7,000 (Publisher's Statement)
Editor: Dave Harvett
Summary of Content: Journal featuring research and researchers within the life science fields in Europe. Covering the research and development of human health and disease, advances in medicine, biotechnology, chemistry, drug discovery, genetics, material science, medical research, microbiology, molecular cell biology, neuroscience, pharmacology and physiology.
Readership/Target Audience: Aimed at scientists, science parks, universities and organisations working with life science issues.
BUSINESS: APPLIED SCIENCE & LABORATORIES

EUROPEAN MEDICAL DEVICE MANUFACTURER
623072U56G-56
Editorial Address: Kent House, Romney Place, MAIDSTONE, ME15 6LH **Tel:** 01622 661350
Fax: 01622 661687
Email: colin.martin@cancom.co.uk
Advertising Address: As above.
Email: colin.martin@cancom.co.uk
Web site: http://www.devicelink.com/emdm
Publisher: Canon Communications
Date Established: 1990
Frequency: 7 issues yearly - Published in the last week of the cover month
Free to qualifying individuals
Circulation: 18,540 (Publisher's Statement)
Usual Pagination: 100
Editor: Colin Martin; **Advertising Manager:** Colin Martin; **Group Editor:** Norbert Sparrow; **Publisher:** Colin Martin
Summary of Content: Magazine covering the medical device industry including articles on materials, components, equipment, and services.
Readership/Target Audience: Aimed at manufacturers of finished medical devices, in vitro diagnostics, pharmaceutical manufacturers, academics and consultants.
ADVERTISING RATES:
Full Page Mono $6400.00
Full Page Colour $8150.00
Agency Commission: 15%
Mechanical Data: Bleed Size: 264 x 368mm, Trim Size: 362 x 257mm, Print Process: Web-fed offset litho, Film: Digital
Copy instructions: Copy Date: 4 weeks prior to publication date
BUSINESS: HEALTH & MEDICAL: Medical Equipment

EUROPEAN OFFSHORE PETROLEUM NEWSLETTER
38582U33-2
Editorial Address: Quatro House, Lyon Way, FRIMLEY, GU16 7ER **Tel:** 01276 804508 **Fax:** 01276 804513
Email: shamlen@ogilviepub.com
Web site: http://www.ogilviepub.com
Publisher: Ogilvie Publishing Ltd
Frequency: Weekly
Annual Sub.: £745.00
Usual Pagination: 8
Editor: Steve Hamlen
Summary of Content: Newsletter covering offshore oil and gas activity in Europe and worldwide.
Readership/Target Audience: Aimed at the offshore service sector as well as operators in the UK and European oil and gas industry.
ADVERTISING: No Advertising taken
BUSINESS: OIL & PETROLEUM

EUROPEAN ORTHOPAEDIC PRODUCT NEWS
40433U56G-55
Formerly: Orthopaedic Product News
Editorial Address: 2 Cheltenham Mount, HARROGATE, HG1 1DL **Tel:** 01423 569676 **Fax:** 01423 569677
Email: richard@pelgrp.com
Advertising Address: As above.
Email: debbie@pelgrp.com
Web site: http://www.opnews.com
ISSN: 1478-7393
Publisher: Pelican Magazines Ltd
Date Established: 1987
Frequency: 8 issues yearly - Published in the middle of the cover month
Free to qualifying individuals

Annual Sub.: £40.00
Circulation: 8,000 (Publisher's Statement)
Usual Pagination: 60
Editor: Richard Redwin; **Group Editor:** Leslie Charneca
Summary of Content: Journal that contains the latest news on existing and new products, with feature articles on the growing surgical and orthopaedic market.
Readership/Target Audience: Read by orthopaedic surgeons, rheumatologists, nurses and plaster room personnel.
ADVERTISING RATES:
Full Page Mono £1100.00
Full Page Colour £1520.00
Agency Commission: 10%
Mechanical Data: Trim Size: 297 x 210mm, Bleed Size: 303 x 213mm, Film: Digital, Print Process: Offset litho
Copy instructions: Copy Date: 2 weeks prior to publication date
Average advertising content per issue: 40%
BUSINESS: HEALTH & MEDICAL: Medical Equipment

EUROPEAN PATENT OFFICE REPORTS
39162U44-640
Editorial Address: The Hatchery, Hall Bank Lane, Mytholmroyd, HEBDEN BRIDGE, HX7 5HQ
Tel: 01422 888000 **Fax:** 01422 888002
Web site: http://www.sweetandmaxwell.co.uk
ISSN: 0269-0802
Publisher: Sweet & Maxwell Ltd
Frequency: 8 issues yearly
Annual Sub.: £624.00
Usual Pagination: 72
Editor: Peter Colley
Summary of Content: Law reports of decisions of the legal Boards of Appeal at the European Patent office.
Readership/Target Audience: Aimed at European Intellectual Property lawyers.
ADVERTISING: No Advertising taken
BUSINESS: LEGAL

EUROPEAN PENSIONS
1808878U1H-96
Editorial Address: 6th Floor, 3 London Wall Buildings, LONDON, EC2M 5PD **Tel:** 020 7562 2409
Fax: 020 7374 2701
Email: graham.buck@europeanpensions.net
Advertising Address: As above. **Tel:** 020 7562 2401
Email: louise.fielden@europeanpensions.net
Web site: http://www.europeanpensions.net
Publisher: Perspective Publishing Ltd
Date Established: 2007
Frequency: 6 issues yearly
Circulation: 8,500 (ABC 01/07/2008 to 30/06/2009)
Usual Pagination: 60
News Editor: Sophie Baker; **Advertising Manager:** Louise Fielden
Summary of Content: Magazine featuring news analysis and features, pensions and investment news.
Readership/Target Audience: Aimed at European pension funds managers and advisers to the European pensions industry.
ADVERTISING RATES:
Full Page Mono £7500.00
Full Page Colour £7500.00
Agency Commission: 15%
Mechanical Data: Type Area: 245 x 180mm, Bleed Size: 277 x 210mm, Trim Size: 271 x 204mm, Col Length: 245mm, Page Width: 180mm, Film: Digital
Copy instructions: Copy Date: 20th of the month prior to publication date
Average advertising content per issue: 25%
BUSINESS: FINANCE & ECONOMICS: Pensions

EUROPEAN PHARMACEUTICAL CONTRACTOR
38731U37-26
Formerly: European BioPharmaceutical Review
Editorial Address: 16 Hampden Gurney Street, LONDON, W1H 5AL **Tel:** 020 7724 3456 **Fax:** 020 7724 2632
Email: danielle@samedanltd.com
Advertising Address: As above.
Email: neil@samedanltd.com
Web site: http://www.samedanltd.com
ISSN: 1364-369X
Publisher: Samedan Ltd
Date Established: 1997
Frequency: Quarterly
Free to qualifying individuals
Annual Sub.: £56.00
Circulation: 10,500 (Publisher's Statement)
Usual Pagination: 112
Editor: Danielle Levett; **Advertising Manager:** Neil Clarke
Summary of Content: Journal providing news and information about the Pan-European bio/ pharmaceutical contract market.
Readership/Target Audience: Aimed at laboratory and corporate management, pharmaceutical MDs, heads of research and development and heads of clinical supply.

Business Magazines

ADVERTISING RATES:
Full Page Colour £2750.00
Agency Commission: 15%
Mechanical Data: Col Length: 273mm, Trim Size: 297 x 210mm, No. of Columns (Display): 2, Page Width: 186mm, Type Area: 273 x 186mm, Film: Digital
Average advertising content per issue: 40%
BUSINESS: PHARMACEUTICAL & CHEMISTS

EUROPEAN PHARMACEUTICAL MANUFACTURER
749697U37-26_10

Editorial Address: Unit 2, Chowley Court, Chowley Oak Lane, Tattenhall, CHESTER, CH3 9GA **Tel:** 01829 770037 **Fax:** 01829 770047
Email: orla@rapidnews.com
Advertising Address: As above.
Email: sales@pharm-europe.com
Web site: http://www.pharm-europe.com
Publisher: Europublishing Consultancy Ltd
Date Established: 2001
Frequency: 8 issues yearly
Free to qualifying individuals
Circulation: 25,113 (Publisher's Statement)
Usual Pagination: 36
Editor: Aleksandra Wisniewski; **Managing Director:** Chris Young; **Advertising Manager:** Michael Taylor; **Publisher:** Chris Young
Summary of Content: Magazine covering all aspects of pharmaceutical manufacturing supplies. Covers industry news, equipment, services and new products.
Readership/Target Audience: Aimed at buyers, purchasing managers and professionals within the European pharmaceutical industry.
ADVERTISING RATES:
Full Page Mono £2470.00
Full Page Colour £3095.00
Agency Commission: 10%
Mechanical Data: Film: Digital, Trim Size: 420 x 297mm, Bleed Size: 430 x 302mm
BUSINESS: PHARMACEUTICAL & CHEMISTS

EUROPEAN PHARMACEUTICAL REVIEW
38732U37-26_20

Editorial Address: Court Lodge, Hogtrough Hill, Brasted, WESTERHAM, TN16 1NU **Tel:** 01959 563311
Fax: 01959 563317
Email: clancaster@russellpublishing.com
Advertising Address: As above. **Fax:** 01959 563123
Email: gking@russellpublishing.com
Web site: http://www.russellpublishing.com
ISSN: 1360-8606
Publisher: Russell Publishing Ltd
Frequency: 6 issues yearly - Published around the 2nd week of the cover month
Annual Sub.: £90.00
Circulation: 11,994 (ABC 01/01/2008 to 31/12/2008)
Usual Pagination: 96
Editor: Pippa McCartney
Summary of Content: Magazine concentrating on technology in the pharmaceutical industry. Covers business, manufacturing, processing, analysis and control, R and D, IT, outsourcing and packaging.
Readership/Target Audience: Aimed at senior decision makers in the pharmaceutical industry across Europe.
ADVERTISING RATES:
Full Page Colour £4937.00
Agency Commission: 10%
Mechanical Data: Type Area: 275 x 188mm, Bleed Size: +3mm, Trim Size: 297 x 210mm, Col Length: 275mm, Page Width: 188mm, Film: Digital
Copy instructions: Copy Date: 4 weeks prior to publication date
Average advertising content per issue: 38%
BUSINESS: PHARMACEUTICAL & CHEMISTS

EUROPEAN PHYSICAL EDUCATION REVIEW
38550U32H-80

Editorial Address: Department of Sport and Exercise Sciences, University College Chester, Parkgate Road, CHESTER, CH1 4BJ **Tel:** 01244 375444 **Fax:** 01244 392820
Email: kengreen@chester.ac.uk
Advertising Address: 1 Oliver's Yard, 55 City Road, LONDON, EC1Y 1SP **Tel:** 020 7324 8500
Fax: 020 7324 8600
Email: advertising@sagepub.co.uk
Web site: http://www.sagepub.co.uk
ISSN: 1356-336X
Publisher: Sage Publications
Frequency: 3 issues yearly - Published in February, June and October
Annual Sub.: £42.00
Circulation: 325 (Publisher's Statement)
Editor: Ken Green; **Advertising Manager:** Sheena Karim
Summary of Content: An international interdisciplinary journal that seeks to stimulate and present scholarly enquiry in the broad field of physical education.

Readership/Target Audience: Aimed at academics interested in the field of physical education.
ADVERTISING RATES:
Full Page Mono £400.00
Agency Commission: 5%
Mechanical Data: Col Length: 210mm, Page Width: 140mm, Film: Digital, Type Area: 210 x 140mm
BUSINESS: LOCAL GOVERNMENT, LEISURE & RECREATION: Leisure, Recreation & Entertainment

EUROPEAN PLANNING STUDIES
36994U14C-70_20

Editorial Address: 4 Park Square, Milton Park, ABINGDON, OX14 4RN **Tel:** 020 7017 6000 **Fax:** 020 7017 6336
Email: ginny.smith@tandf.co.uk
Advertising Address: As above. **Tel:** 01235 828600
Fax: 01235 829000
Email: marketing@carfax.co.uk
Web site: http://www.informaworld.com
ISSN: 0965-4313
Publisher: Routledge, Taylor & Francis
Date Established: 1993
Frequency: 10 issues yearly - Not published in March or December
Annual Sub.: £440.00
Circulation: 500 (Publisher's Statement)
Usual Pagination: 136
Editor: Philip Cooke; **Advertising Manager:** Claire Buckminster
Summary of Content: A forum for ideas and information about spatial planning/development processes and policies in Europe.
Readership/Target Audience: Aimed at academics, practitioners and policy makers in the field of spatial planning and development.
Copy instructions: Copy Date: 2 months prior to publication date
BUSINESS: COMMERCE, INDUSTRY & MANAGEMENT: International Commerce

EUROPEAN PLASTIC PRODUCT MANUFACTURER
600893U39-18

Editorial Address: Unit 2, Chowley Court, Chowley Oak Lane, Tattenhall, CHESTER, CH3 9GA **Tel:** 01829 770037 **Fax:** 01829 770047
Email: james@rapidnews.com
Advertising Address: EPPM House, 37 Raeburn Avenue, DARTFORD, DA1 3BQ **Tel:** 01322 410899
Email: scott@eppm.com
Web site: http://www.eppm.com
Publisher: Europublishing Consultancy Ltd
Date Established: 1999
Frequency: 9 issues yearly
Cover Price: Free
Circulation: 19,678 (Publisher's Statement)
Usual Pagination: 36
Editor: James Woodcock; **Advertising Manager:** Scott Colman; **Publisher:** Mark Blezard
Summary of Content: Magazine containing information on all products and services in the plastics material market.
Readership/Target Audience: Aimed at manufacturers and suppliers of plastic products and services.
ADVERTISING RATES:
Full Page Mono £2350.00
Full Page Colour £2945.00
Agency Commission: 15%
Mechanical Data: Col Length: 395mm, Page Width: 277mm, Type Area: 395 x 277mm, Trim Size: 420 x 297mm, Bleed Size: 430 x 302mm, Film: Digital
Average advertising content per issue: 60%
BUSINESS: PLASTICS & RUBBER

EUROPEAN PLASTICS NEWS
38817U39-20

Editorial Address: 4th Floor, Carolyn House, 26 Dingwall Road, CROYDON, CR0 9XF **Tel:** 020 8253 9600
Fax: 020 8253 9652
Email: chsmith@crain.com
Advertising Address: 19th Floor, Leon House, 233 High Street, CROYDON, CR0 9XT **Tel:** 020 8277 5511
Fax: 020 8277 5103
Email: khewitt@crain.com
Web site: http://www.europeanplasticsnews.com
ISSN: 0306-3534
Publisher: Crain Communications Ltd
Date Established: 1974
Frequency: 11 issues yearly - Published in the 1st week of the cover month
Cover Price: £20.00
Free to qualifying individuals
Annual Sub.: £205.00
Circulation: 13,695 (ABC 01/01/2008 to 31/12/2008)
Usual Pagination: 48
Editor: Chris Smith
Summary of Content: Magazine covering technology, management and business issues relevant to the plastics industry in Europe.

Readership/Target Audience: Aimed at commercial and technical managers and engineers operating in the polymer industry throughout Europe.
ADVERTISING RATES:
Full Page Colour EUR6880.00
Agency Commission: 10%
Mechanical Data: Page Width: 180mm, Type Area: 265 x 180mm, Col Length: 265mm, Trim Size: 297 x 210mm, Bleed Size: 303 x 216mm, Film: Digital
Copy instructions: Copy Date: 4 weeks prior to publication date
Average advertising content per issue: 40%
BUSINESS: PLASTICS & RUBBER

EUROPEAN POLICY ANALYST
36952U14C-70_30

Editorial Address: 26 Red Lion Square, LONDON, WC1R 4HQ **Tel:** 020 7576 8310 **Fax:** 020 7830 1083
Email: charlesjenkins@eiu.com
Web site: http://www.eiu.com
ISSN: 1364-2758
Publisher: Economist Intelligence Unit
Frequency: Quarterly
Annual Sub.: £615.00
Circulation: 800 (Publisher's Statement)
Usual Pagination: 70
Editor: Garrick Holmes; **Managing Director:** Nigel Ludlow
Summary of Content: An analysis of the evolution of European Union policies, the internal market, environmental legislation, EU external relations and competition policy. Also special reports and reference section.
Readership/Target Audience: Aimed at academics and media businesses.
ADVERTISING: No Advertising taken
BUSINESS: COMMERCE, INDUSTRY & MANAGEMENT: International Commerce

EUROPEAN POTATO MARKETS
22640U21B-981

Editorial Address: 80 Calverley Road, TUNBRIDGE WELLS, TN1 2UN **Tel:** 020 7017 7500 **Fax:** 020 7017 7599
Email: marketing@agra-net.com
Web site: http://www.agra-net.com
ISSN: 1360-4392
Publisher: Agra Informa Ltd
Frequency: Monthly
Annual Sub.: £658.00
Usual Pagination: 32
Summary of Content: Report providing analysis of the European potato industry and monitoring of the market trends. Includes comparative figures and tables for review of production, consumption, processing and prices for the major producing companies.
Readership/Target Audience: Aimed at food manufacturers, governments, trade associations and the Ministry of Agriculture.
ADVERTISING: No Advertising taken
BUSINESS: AGRICULTURE & FARMING: Agriculture - Supplies & Services

EUROPEAN POWER DAILY
37307U58-36_50

Formerly: Platts Daily Power Markets
Editorial Address: 20 Canada Square, Canary Wharf, LONDON, E14 5LH **Tel:** 020 7176 6158 **Fax:** 020 7176 6670
Email: power@platts.com
Web site: http://www.platts.com
Publisher: The McGraw-Hill Companies
Frequency: 300 issues yearly
Annual Sub.: $1200.00
Usual Pagination: 5
Editor: Claire Louise Isted; **Managing Editor:** Claire Louise Isted
Summary of Content: Newsletter available by fax-stream and email, covering the buying and selling of power.
Readership/Target Audience: Aimed at market analysts and executives within the power industry.
ADVERTISING: No Advertising taken
BUSINESS: ENERGY, FUEL & NUCLEAR

EUROPEAN PROCESS ENGINEER
37653U19F-112

Editorial Address: Europa House, 13-17 Ironmonger Row, LONDON, EC1V 3QG **Tel:** 020 7253 2545
Fax: 020 7608 1600
Email: editorial@setform.com
Advertising Address: As above.
Email: jabey@setform.com
Web site: http://www.engineerlive.com
ISSN: 1062-7987
Publisher: Setform Ltd
Frequency: Half-yearly - Published in May and November
Circulation: 15,000 (Publisher's Statement)
Usual Pagination: 108

Editor: Paul Boughton; **Managing Director:** Mike Bishop; **Advertising Manager:** John Abey; **Publisher:** David Washington
Summary of Content: Journal covering all aspects of process engineering throughout Europe.
Readership/Target Audience: Aimed at senior engineers within the major processing industries in Europe.
ADVERTISING RATES:
Full Page Mono £4150.00
Full Page Colour £5350.00
Mechanical Data: Trim Size: 297 x 210mm, Film: Digital
BUSINESS: ENGINEERING & MACHINERY: Production & Mechanical Engineering

EUROPEAN RAILWAY REVIEW
39676U49E-30
Editorial Address: Court Lodge, Hogtrough Hill, Brasted, WESTERHAM, TN16 1NU **Tel:** 01959 563311
Fax: 01959 563123
Email: cwaters@russellpublishing.com
Advertising Address: As above.
Email: bholliday@russellpublishing.com
Web site: http://www.europeanrailwayreview.com
ISSN: 1351-1599
Publisher: Russell Publishing Ltd
Date Established: 1994
Frequency: 6 issues yearly
Free to qualifying individuals
Annual Sub.: £70.00
Circulation: 7,494 (ABC 01/01/2008 to 31/12/2008)
Usual Pagination: 88
Editor: Craig Waters; **Managing Director:** Vivien Cotterill-Lee
Summary of Content: Magazine focusing on the railway industry, providing European coverage and comment, with a business bias on technological advances, new products and design developments.
Readership/Target Audience: Aimed at railway industry purchasing personnel throughout Europe.
ADVERTISING RATES:
Full Page Colour £3697.00
Agency Commission: 10%
Mechanical Data: Trim Size: 297 x 210mm, Film: Digital
Average advertising content per issue: 35%
BUSINESS: TRANSPORT: Railways

EUROPEAN RESELLER MAGAZINE
624029U5R-240
Formerly: Netcom Reseller Magazine
Editorial Address: Berkeley House, Barnet Road, London Colney, ST. ALBANS, AL2 1BG **Tel:** 01727 742975
Fax: 01727 742976
Email: andy@europeanreseller.com
Advertising Address: As above.
Email: ken@europeanreseller.com
Web site: http://www.europeanreseller.com
ISSN: 1471-0099
Publisher: European Reseller Ltd
Date Established: 2000
Frequency: Quarterly
Free to qualifying individuals
Annual Sub.: EUR90.00
Circulation: 17,000 (Publisher's Statement)
Usual Pagination: 80
Editor: Andy Brockhurst; **Advertising Manager:** Ken Kauder; **Managing Editor:** Geoff Marshall
Summary of Content: Channel magazine covering news and features on all aspects of the IT channel. Areas covered are hardware, software, audio visual, mobile computing, storage, Protection and security, IP convergence, networking, Data Capture, wireless solutions and imaging solutions.
Readership/Target Audience: Aimed at OEMs, distributors, VAD's, resellers, VAR's and system integrators.
ADVERTISING RATES:
Full Page Colour £3950.00
Mechanical Data: Film: Digital
Copy instructions: Copy Date: 2 weeks prior to publication date
BUSINESS: COMPUTERS & AUTOMATION: Computers Related

EUROPEAN RETAIL
39801U53-57
Editorial Address: Flat 8, Mowson Street, Gopsall Street, Hoxton, LONDON, N1 5HN **Tel:** 07941 103659
Email: euroretail@btinternet.com
ISSN: 0960-0191
Publisher: GFJ Publishing Ltd
Date Established: 1988
Frequency: 24 issues yearly
Annual Sub.: £1063.00
Usual Pagination: 12
Editor: Rajiv Desai; **Publisher:** Graham Forest-Jones; **Circulation Manager:** Philip Morton
Summary of Content: Magazine containing information about retail strategy news, information on market moves, European legislation and on-line retailing.

Readership/Target Audience: Read by the retail industry.
ADVERTISING: No Advertising taken
BUSINESS: RETAILING & WHOLESALING

EUROPEAN RUBBER JOURNAL
38818U39-20_50
Editorial Address: 3rd Floor, 21 St. Thomas Street, LONDON, SE1 9RY **Tel:** 020 7457 1408 **Fax:** 020 7457 1440
Email: dshaw@crain.com
Advertising Address: As above. **Tel:** 020 7457 1400
Email: pmitchell@crain.com
Web site: http://www.europeanrubberjournal.com
ISSN: 0266-4151
Publisher: Crain Communications Ltd
Date Established: 1882
Frequency: 6 issues yearly - Published at the beginning of the 2nd cover month
Annual Sub.: £100.00
Circulation: 6,954 (ABC 01/01/2008 to 31/12/2008)
Usual Pagination: 40
Editor: David Shaw; **Advertising Manager:** Paul Mitchell; **Publisher:** Paul Mitchell
Summary of Content: Pan-European journal covering developments in the international rubber industry.
Readership/Target Audience: Aimed at senior managers in the rubber industry.
ADVERTISING RATES:
Full Page Mono EUR2132.00
Full Page Colour EUR3016.00
Agency Commission: 10%
Mechanical Data: Type Area: 254 x 184mm, Bleed Size: 292 x 212mm, Trim Size: 286 x 209mm, Col Length: 254mm, Page Width: 184mm, Film: Digital
Copy instructions: Copy Date: 4 weeks prior to publication date
Average advertising content per issue: 44%
Supplement(s): Global Tyre Report - 1xY
BUSINESS: PLASTICS & RUBBER

EUROPEAN SPA
1895674U56-666
Editorial Address: 47-49 Borough High Street, LONDON, SE1 1NB **Tel:** 01353 649920
Email: sarah@spapublishing.com
Web site: http://www.thespaprcompany.com
Publisher: Spa Publishing
Frequency: 6 issues yearly
Annual Sub.: £24.00
Circulation: 5,000 (Publisher's Statement)
Editor: Sarah Ward; **Publisher:** Sarah Ward
Summary of Content: Magazine of the Spa PR Company. Focuses on spa industry news, interviews, spa reviews, new treatments and products, treatments and products, expert views and advice, trends and spa design.
Readership/Target Audience: Aimed at spa and wellness professionals.
BUSINESS: HEALTH & MEDICAL

EUROPEAN SUPPLY CHAIN MANAGEMENT
1703594U10-218
Editorial Address: Unit 10, Cringleford Business Centre, Intwood Road, Cringleford, NORWICH, NR4 6AU
Tel: 01603 274130 **Fax:** 01603 274131
Email: pkaur@schofieldpublishing.co.uk
Advertising Address: As above.
Email: dvalerga@schofieldpublishing.co.uk
Web site: http://www.europeansupplychainmanagement.co.uk
Publisher: Schofield Publishing Ltd
Date Established: 2005
Frequency: 6 issues yearly - Published at the end of the 2nd cover month
Cover Price: 3.50
Free to qualifying individuals
Circulation: 20,000 (Publisher's Statement)
Usual Pagination: 120
Editor: Pam Kaur; **Advertising Manager:** Daniel Valerga
Summary of Content: Magazine covering industry news, developments and company profiles. It also includes diary dates of events, seminars and exhibitions as well as gadget reviews.
Readership/Target Audience: Aimed at senior management in the European supply chain industry.
ADVERTISING RATES:
Full Page Mono £2500.00
Full Page Colour £3265.00
Mechanical Data: Trim Size: 297 x 210mm, Bleed Size: 303 x 216mm, Film: Digital
Copy instructions: Copy Date: 2 weeks prior to publication date
BUSINESS: MATERIALS HANDLING

EUROPEAN URBAN AND REGIONAL STUDIES
38557U32R-90
Editorial Address: Department of Geography, Durham University, South Road, DURHAM, DH1 3LE
Tel: 020 7324 8500 **Fax:** 020 7324 8600
Advertising Address: 1 Oliver's Yard, 55 City Road, LONDON, EC1Y 1SP **Tel:** 020 7324 8500
Fax: 020 7324 8600
Email: sheena.karim@sagepub.co.uk
Web site: http://www.sagepub.co.uk
ISSN: 0969-7764
Publisher: Sage Publications
Date Established: 1994
Frequency: Quarterly
Annual Sub.: £54.00
Circulation: 400 (Publisher's Statement)
Usual Pagination: 96
Editor: Ray Hudson; **Managing Editor:** Allan Williams
Summary of Content: International journal of research on European urban and regional development processes and policy issues.
Readership/Target Audience: Read by academics and policy makers.
ADVERTISING RATES:
Full Page Mono £400.00
Agency Commission: 5%
Mechanical Data: Page Width: 160mm, Type Area: 215 x 160mm, Col Length: 215mm, Film: Digital
BUSINESS: LOCAL GOVERNMENT, LEISURE & RECREATION: Local Government Related

EUROPEAN VENTURE CAPITAL AND PRIVATE EQUITY JOURNAL
35427U1N-15
Formerly: European Venture Capital Journal
Editorial Address: Aldgate House, 33 Aldgate High Street, LONDON, EC3N 1DL **Tel:** 020 7369 7768
Fax: 020 7369 7603
Email: amanda.palmer@thomsonreuters.com
Advertising Address: Global Private Equity Group, 3 Times Square, NEW YORK, NY 10036 **Tel:** 646 2236774
Fax: 646 2234473
Email: crystel.debs@thomsonreuters.com
Web site: http://www.evcj.com
ISSN: 0954-1675
Publisher: Thomson Reuters
Date Established: 1996
Frequency: 10 issues yearly - Published in the 1st week of the cover month
Annual Sub.: £866.00
Circulation: 6,708 (Publisher's Statement)
Usual Pagination: 84
Editor: Tom Allchorne
Summary of Content: Journal about venture capital and private equity investment activity in Europe.
Readership/Target Audience: Aimed at venture capitalists, lenders, institutional investors, accountancy firms, lawyers and investors.
ADVERTISING RATES:
Full Page Mono £2248.00
Full Page Colour £2998.00
Agency Commission: 15%
Mechanical Data: Type Area: 260 x 175mm, Col Length: 260mm, Page Width: 175mm, Print Process: Offset litho, Bleed Size: 303 x 216mm, Trim Size: 297 x 210mm, Film: Digital
Copy instructions: Copy Date: 10 days prior to publication date
Average advertising content per issue: 30%
BUSINESS: FINANCE & ECONOMICS: Venture Capital

EUROPROPERTY
35194U1E-169
Editorial Address: 1 Proctor Street, LONDON, WC1V 6EU
Tel: 020 7911 1845 **Fax:** 020 7911 1900
Email: mark.cooper@rbi.co.uk
Advertising Address: As above. **Tel:** 020 7911 1701
Fax: 020 7911 1730
Email: stuart.burgess@rbi.co.uk
Web site: http://www.europroperty.com
ISSN: 0967-1862
Publisher: Reed Business Information
Date Established: 1992
Frequency: 22 issues yearly - Published on the 1st and the 3rd Monday of the month. 3rd Monday only in January and August
Annual Sub.: £750.00
Circulation: 1,300 (Publisher's Statement)
Usual Pagination: 48
Editor: Mark Cooper; **Group Editor:** Mark Cooper; **Publisher:** Geoff Hadwick
Summary of Content: Newsletter covering all aspects of European commercial property. Includes news of major deals, investments and developments and surveys of property markets.
Readership/Target Audience: Aimed at property professionals with a pan-European remit. This includes fund managers, CEOs of property investors and developers as well as their advisers.

Business Magazines

ADVERTISING RATES:
Full Page Mono £2395.00
Full Page Colour £2395.00
Agency Commission: 12%
Mechanical Data: Bleed Size: 286 x 216mm, Trim Size: 280 x 210mm, Type Area: 250 x 180mm, Col Length: 250mm, Page Width: 180mm, Film: Positive, right reading, emulsion side down. Digital
Copy instructions: Copy Date: 2 weeks prior to publication date
Average advertising content per issue: 25%
BUSINESS: FINANCE & ECONOMICS: Property

EUROSLOT MAGAZINE
41466U64A-135
Formerly: EuroSlot
Editorial Address: 15A London Road, MAIDSTONE, ME16 8LY **Tel:** 01622 687031 **Fax:** 01622 757646
Email: euroslot@datateam.co.uk
Advertising Address: As above.
Email: euroslot@datateam.co.uk
Web site: http://www.euroslot-online.com
ISSN: 0966-0259
Publisher: Datateam Publishing Ltd
Date Established: 1986
Frequency: Monthly - Published on the 1st of the month on the cover date
Annual Sub.: £55.00
Circulation: 6,137 (Publisher's Statement)
Usual Pagination: 40
Editor: Steph Norbury; **Advertising Manager:** Roz Rustell
Summary of Content: European amusement magazine focusing exclusively on the coin-operated trade and family entertainment centres around the world and all their contributing industries and interests.
Readership/Target Audience: Read by members of the amusement and coin-operated industry.
ADVERTISING RATES:
Full Page Mono £1837.00
Full Page Colour £1995.00
Mechanical Data: Bleed Size: 312 x 235mm, Trim Size: 306 x 229mm, Type Area: 278 x 202mm, Film: Digital, Col Length: 278mm, Page Width: 202mm
BUSINESS: OTHER CLASSIFICATIONS: Amusement Trade

EUROTRANSPORT
1643658U49A-407
Editorial Address: Court Lodge, Hogtrough Hill, Brasted, WESTERHAM, TN16 1NU **Tel:** 01959 563311
Fax: 01959 563317
Email: cwaters@russellpublishing.com
Advertising Address: As above. **Fax:** 01959 563123
Email: wangood@russellpublishing.com
Web site: http://www.eurotransportmagazine.com
ISSN: 1478-8217
Publisher: Russell Publishing Ltd
Date Established: 2003
Frequency: 6 issues yearly
Annual Sub.: £90.00
Circulation: 11,794 (ABC 01/01/2008 to 31/12/2008)
Usual Pagination: 88
Editor: Karen Hutchinson
Summary of Content: Magazine covering European integrated transport, including articles on new technologies and developments within the transport industry.
Readership/Target Audience: Aimed at Transport Ministers, Local and Regional Government Decision Makers, Chief Executives, Procurement Directors and other Senior Purchasing Personnel.
ADVERTISING RATES:
Full Page Colour £4297.00
Mechanical Data: Bleed Size: 303 x 216mm, Trim Size: 297 x 210mm, Type Area: 277 x 190mm, Col Length: 277mm, Page Width: 190mm, Film: Digital
Copy instructions: Copy Date: 2 weeks prior to publication date
BUSINESS: TRANSPORT

EUROWEEK
34926U1A-90
Editorial Address: Thanet House, 232 The Strand, LONDON, WC2 R1DA **Tel:** 020 7440 6051
Fax: 020 7440 6087
Email: njacob@euroweek.com
Advertising Address: Nestor House, Playhouse Yard, LONDON, EC4V 5EX **Tel:** 020 7779 8888
Web site: http://www.euroweek.com
ISSN: 0952-7036
Publisher: Euromoney Institutional Investor plc
Frequency: Weekly - Published on Friday
Annual Sub.: £2950.00
Usual Pagination: 55
Editor: Nick Jacob; **Advertising Manager:** Daniel Elton; **Managing Editor:** Toby Fildes
Summary of Content: Publication providing hard news on deals, people, and the driving forces behind international capital markets.
Readership/Target Audience: Aimed at executives in the international capital markets.

ADVERTISING RATES:
Full Page Colour £6500.00
Supplement(s): Euroweek Review of the Year - 1xY
BUSINESS: FINANCE & ECONOMICS

EUROWIRE
38148U27-24
Editorial Address: 46 Holly Walk, LEAMINGTON SPA, CV32 4HY **Tel:** 01926 334137 **Fax:** 01926 314755
Email: gill@intras.co.uk
Advertising Address: As above.
Email: paul.b@intras.co.uk
Web site: http://www.read-eurowire.com
ISSN: 1463-2438
Publisher: Intras Ltd
Date Established: 1998
Frequency: 6 issues yearly
Free to qualifying individuals
Annual Sub.: £80.00
Circulation: 16,317 (Publisher's Statement)
Usual Pagination: 156
Editor: Gill Watson; **Publisher:** Caroline Sullens
Summary of Content: International trade magazine covering the wire and cable manufacturing industries.
Language(s): English; French; German; Italian; Russian; Spanish
Readership/Target Audience: Read by key decision-makers in wire, cable fibre-optic and wire products companies.
ADVERTISING RATES:
Full Page Mono £1612.00
Full Page Colour £2163.00
Agency Commission: 15%
Mechanical Data: Film: Digital, No. of Columns (Display): 3, Bleed Size: 303 x 214mm, Trim Size: 297 x 210mm, Type Area: 260 x 180mm, Col Length: 260mm, Page Width: 180mm
Copy instructions: Copy Date: 6 weeks prior to publication date
Average advertising content per issue: 37%
BUSINESS: METAL, IRON & STEEL

EVALUATION
48739U62R-476
Editorial Address: 1 Oliver's Yard, 55 City Road, LONDON, EC1Y 1SP **Tel:** 020 7324 8500 **Fax:** 020 7324 8600
Email: info@sagepub.co.uk
Advertising Address: As above. **Tel:** 020 7324 8578
Email: advertising@sagepub.co.uk
Web site: http://www.sagepub.co.uk
ISSN: 1356-3890
Publisher: Sage Publications
Date Established: 1995
Frequency: Quarterly
Annual Sub.: £54.00
Circulation: 1,000 (Publisher's Statement)
Editor: Elliot Stern; **Advertising Manager:** Sheena Karim
Summary of Content: Journal containing original evaluation research, both theoretical and empirical. Includes reviews of relevant literature and overviews of developments in evaluation policy and practice.
Readership/Target Audience: Read by evaluation specialists.
ADVERTISING RATES:
Full Page Mono £400.00
Agency Commission: 5%
Mechanical Data: Type Area: 210 x 140mm, Col Length: 210mm, Page Width: 140mm, Film: Digital
BUSINESS: CHURCH & SCHOOL EQUIPMENT & EDUCATION: Education Related

EVENT
35528U2A-75_30
Formerly: Event Magazine
Editorial Address: 174 Hammersmith Road, LONDON, W6 7JP **Tel:** 020 8267 4407 **Fax:** 020 8267 4442
Email: jeremy.king@haymarket.com
Advertising Address: As above. **Tel:** 020 8267 4511
Fax: 020 8267 4206
Email: victoria.chapman@haymarket.com
Web site: http://www.eventmagazine.co.uk
Publisher: Haymarket Brand Media
Date Established: 1997
Frequency: Monthly - Published on the 1st of the cover month
Free to qualifying individuals
Circulation: 15,055 (ABC 01/07/2008 to 30/06/2009)
Usual Pagination: 60
Editor: Jeremy King; **Features Editor:** Chantelle Thorley; **Advertising Manager:** Victoria Chapman
Summary of Content: Magazine aiming to convince marketers that successful events and exhibitions can bring brands and services to life.
Readership/Target Audience: Read by decision-makers involved in all types of marketing activity.
ADVERTISING RATES:
Full Page Mono £3678.00
Full Page Colour £3678.00
Agency Commission: 10%

Mechanical Data: Col Length: 265mm, Col Widths (Display): 43mm, No. of Columns (Display): 2, Bleed Size: 303 x 216mm, Trim Size: 297 x 210mm, Page Width: 184mm, Type Area: 265 x 184mm, Film: Digital
Copy instructions: Copy Date: 2 weeks prior to publication date
Average advertising content per issue: 50%
BUSINESS: COMMUNICATIONS, ADVERTISING & MARKETING

EVENT ORGANISER
35637U2C-70
Editorial Address: Association House, 18C Moor Street, CHEPSTOW, NP16 5DB **Tel:** 07764 420813
Fax: 01291 630402
Email: editorial@papa.org.uk
Advertising Address: As above. **Tel:** 01291 636334
Email: andrew@jandmgroup.co.uk
Web site: http://www.tesa.org.uk
Publisher: J & M Group Ltd.
Date Established: 1992
Frequency: Quarterly
Annual Sub.: £45.00
Circulation: 7,000 (Publisher's Statement)
Usual Pagination: 32
Editor: Simon Ambrose; **Advertising Manager:** Andrew Emery; **Managing Editor:** Simon Ambrose
Summary of Content: Magazine that contains news and features relating to the indoor and outdoor event industry.
Readership/Target Audience: Read by event organisers including, supply companies, contractors, local authorities and licensing authorities.
ADVERTISING RATES:
Full Page Colour £1375.00
SCC £18.00
Agency Commission: 15%
Mechanical Data: Page Width: 220mm, Type Area: 300 x 220mm, Col Length: 300mm, Trim Size: 330 x 240mm, Film: Digital, Bleed Size: 355 x 245mm
BUSINESS: COMMUNICATIONS, ADVERTISING & MARKETING: Conferences & Exhibitions

EVENT PLANNER'S GUIDE
35635U2C-53
Formerly: London - The Meeting Guide
Editorial Address: 6th Floor, 2 More London Riverside, LONDON, SE1 2RR **Tel:** 020 7234 5800 **Fax:** 020 7234 5750
Email: business@visitlondon.com
Advertising Address: Mongoose Media Ltd, 2 Lonsdale Road, LONDON, NW6 6RD **Tel:** 020 7306 0300
Fax: 020 7306 0301
Email: visitlondon@mongoosemedia.com
Web site: http://www.visitlondon.com/business
Publisher: Visit London
Frequency: Annual - Published in November
Cover Price: Free
Circulation: 20,000 (Publisher's Statement)
Usual Pagination: 114
Editor: Severine Ougier
Summary of Content: A guide to meeting, incentive and exhibition facilities.
Readership/Target Audience: Aimed at all event organisers.
ADVERTISING RATES:
Full Page Colour £5650.00
Agency Commission: 10%
Mechanical Data: Type Area: 278 x 186mm, Bleed Size: 303 x 216mm, Trim Size: 297 x 210mm, Film: Digital, Col Length: 278mm, Page Width: 186mm
Copy instructions: Copy Date: 6 weeks prior to publication date
Average advertising content per issue: 22%
BUSINESS: COMMUNICATIONS, ADVERTISING & MARKETING: Conferences & Exhibitions

EVIDENCE AND POLICY
1779304U32R-495
Editorial Address: Beacon House, 4th Floor, Queens Road, BRISTOL, BS8 1QU **Tel:** 0117 331 4054 **Fax:** 0117 331 4093
Email: tpp-info@bristol.ac.uk
Advertising Address: As above.
Email: jessica.hughes@bristol.ac.uk
Web site: http://www.policypress.org.uk
ISSN: 1744-2648
Publisher: The Policy Press
Frequency: Quarterly
Annual Sub.: £61.00
Editor: Kathryn King; **Advertising Manager:** Jessica Hughes
Summary of Content: Journal dedicated to comprehensive and critical treatment of the relationship between evidence and the concerns of policy makers and practitioners as well as researchers.
Readership/Target Audience: Aimed at those who provide public services, and those who provide the research base for evaluation and development across a wide range of social and public policy issues from social care to education and from public health to criminal justice.
ADVERTISING RATES:
Full Page Mono £200.00

Mechanical Data: Type Area: 203 x 120mm, Bleed Size: 258 x 178mm, Col Length: 203mm, Page Width: 120mm, Film: Digital
Copy instructions: Copy Date: 8 weeks prior to publication date
BUSINESS: LOCAL GOVERNMENT, LEISURE & RECREATION: Local Government Related

EXCHANGE
40461U56L-13_30
Editorial Address: Hill House, Highgate Hill, LONDON, N19 5NA **Tel:** 020 7281 3553
Web site: http://www.eczema.org
ISSN: 0951-9785
Publisher: National Eczema Society
Date Established: 1975
Frequency: Quarterly
Cover Price: £5.00
Free to qualifying individuals
Circulation: 11,000 (Publisher's Statement)
Usual Pagination: 48
Editor: Claire Moulds
Summary of Content: Journal of the National Eczema Society. Contains articles from professionals, news of Society activities, hints and tips from other members and details of developments in treatment.
Readership/Target Audience: Read by members of the National Eczema Society.
ADVERTISING: No Advertising taken
BUSINESS: HEALTH & MEDICAL: Disability & Rehabilitation

EXCHANGE TRADED FUNDS MAGAZINE
1895116U1F-666
Editorial Address: Haymarket House, 28-29 Haymarket, LONDON, SW1Y 4RX **Tel:** 020 7484 9700
Email: monica.woodley@incisivemedia.com
Web site: http://www.etfmonline.com
Publisher: Incisive Media Investments
Date Established: 2008
Frequency: Monthly
Free to qualifying individuals
(Controlled Circulation)
Editor: Monica Woodley; **Editor-in-Chief:** Alex Beveridge
Summary of Content: Magazine dedicated to exchange-traded funds. Includes news, industry profiles, comment, sector analysis and features.
Readership/Target Audience: Aimed at all users and providers of exchange traded funds as well as other ETF industry players.
BUSINESS: FINANCE & ECONOMICS: Investment

EXECUTIVE ACCOUNTANT
35038U1B-170
Editorial Address: Akhtar House, 2 Shepherds Bush Road, LONDON, W6 7PJ **Tel:** 020 8749 7126 **Fax:** 020 8749 7127
Email: icea@enta.net
Advertising Address: As above. **Tel:** 020 8746 1642
Fax: 020 8740 8358
Email: alam1948@aol.com
Web site: http://www.icea.enta.net
Publisher: Institute of Cost and Executive Accountants Educational Trust
Frequency: Quarterly
Annual Sub.: £12.00
Circulation: 5,000 (Publisher's Statement)
Editor: Mohammed Allam; **Advertising Manager:** Mohammed Alam
Summary of Content: Publication containing news of current developments in the accounting profession.
Readership/Target Audience: Aimed at members and registered students of the Institute of Cost and Executive Accountants and careers offices.
ADVERTISING: Rates on application
BUSINESS: FINANCE & ECONOMICS: Accountancy

EXECUTIVE COMPENSATION BRIEFING
1797548U14F-260
Editorial Address: 27 Parsons Green Lane, LONDON, SW6 4HH **Tel:** 020 7736 8180 **Fax:** 020 7504 3610
Advertising Address: As above. **Tel:** 020 8871 4019
Fax: 020 7801 9304
Email: stephen.harris@clearviewpublishing.com
Web site: http://www.executive-compensation-briefing.com
ISSN: 1743-7113
Publisher: ClearView Publishing
Frequency: Monthly
Annual Sub.: £495.00
Circulation: 300 (Publisher's Statement)
Usual Pagination: 14
Editor: Hugo Chamberlain; **Advertising Manager:** Stephen Harris; **Publisher:** Stephen Harris
Summary of Content: Newsletter containing expert advice on executive rewards and corporate governance.
Readership/Target Audience: Aimed at human resource managers and those focusing on executive rewards within large corporations, also lawyers working in the field.

ADVERTISING RATES:
Full Page Colour £1000.000
Mechanical Data: Bleed Size: 307 x 220mm, Trim Size: 297 x 210mm, Film: Digital
Copy instructions: Copy Date: 1 week prior to publication date
BUSINESS: COMMERCE, INDUSTRY & MANAGEMENT: Training & Recruitment

EXECUTIVE HIRE NEWS
35957U4R-370
Editorial Address: Hartham Park, CORSHAM, SN13 0RP **Tel:** 01249 700607 **Fax:** 01249 700235
Email: alan@executivehirenews.co.uk
Advertising Address: As above. **Fax:** 01249 700776
Email: nigel@executivehirenews.co.uk
Web site: http://www.executivehirenews.co.uk
Publisher: Executive Hire News Ltd
Date Established: 1993
Frequency: 11 issues yearly - Published in the 1st week of the cover month
Free to qualifying individuals
Annual Sub.: £48.00
Circulation: 6,128 (ABC 01/07/2008 to 30/06/2009)
Usual Pagination: 48
Editor: Alan Guthrie; **Publisher:** Robert Aplin
Summary of Content: Magazine covering business information within the power tools, small plant and equipment hire industry.
Readership/Target Audience: Aimed at hire company owners and management.
ADVERTISING RATES:
Full Page Mono £1420.00
Full Page Colour £1850.00
Mechanical Data: Col Length: 264mm, Page Width: 190mm, Trim Size: 297 x 210mm, Bleed Size: 303 x 216mm, Type Area: 264 x 190mm, Film: Digital
Copy instructions: Copy Date: 2 weeks prior to publication date
Supplement(s): Groundscare Hire News - 2xY
BUSINESS: ARCHITECTURE & BUILDING: Building Related

EXECUTIVE MAGAZINE
41444U63D-130
Formerly: Executive Life
Editorial Address: New Century House, Stadium Road, INVERNESS, IV1 1FF **Tel:** 01463 732222 **Fax:** 01463 732220
Email: editor@executive-magazine.co.uk
Advertising Address: As above. **Tel:** 01463 732212
Fax: 01463 732289
Email: info@executive-magazine.co.uk
Web site: http://www.executive-magazine.co.uk
Publisher: New Century Publishing Group
Date Established: 1982
Frequency: Monthly - Published 1st Friday of each month
Cover Price: Free
Circulation: 15,000 (Publisher's Statement)
Usual Pagination: 48
Editor: Katrina Ashford; **Advertising Manager:** Alison Maclean
Summary of Content: Business-to-business magazine covering regional news, business profiles and lifestyle.
Readership/Target Audience: Aimed at the business community in the area north of Perth.
ADVERTISING RATES:
Full Page Colour £980.00
Agency Commission: 10%
Mechanical Data: Type Area: 262 x 182mm, Bleed Size: 303 x 213mm, Page Width: 182mm, Col Length: 262mm, Film: Digital, Trim Size: 297 x 210mm
Copy instructions: Copy Date: 8 weeks prior to publication date
Average advertising content per issue: 50%
BUSINESS: REGIONAL BUSINESS: Regional Business Scotland

EXHIBITING
1601485U2C-502
Editorial Address: Faraday House, 39 Thornton Road, Wimbledon, LONDON, SW19 4NQ **Tel:** 020 8971 8282
Fax: 020 8971 8283
Email: pdavis@mashmedia.net
Advertising Address: As above. **Tel:** 020 8971 8288
Fax: 020 8971 8284
Email: pking@mashmedia.net
ISSN: 1479-0904
Publisher: Mash Media
Date Established: 2002
Frequency: 10 issues yearly
Free to qualifying individuals
Circulation: 10,010 (ABC 01/07/2008 to 30/06/2009)
Usual Pagination: 40
Editor: James Barrett; **Advertising Manager:** Paul King; **Publisher:** Roisin Sullens
Summary of Content: Magazine covering exhibition tips, statistics and comment with case studies, advice and analysis.
Readership/Target Audience: Aimed at regular exhibitors.

ADVERTISING RATES:
Full Page Colour £1900.00
Agency Commission: 10%
Mechanical Data: Type Area: 270 x 190mm, Col Length: 270mm, Page Width: 190mm, Bleed Size: +3mm, Trim Size: 297 x 210mm, Film: Digital
Copy instructions: Copy Date: 13th of the month prior to publication date
Average advertising content per issue: 50%
BUSINESS: COMMUNICATIONS, ADVERTISING & MARKETING: Conferences & Exhibitions

EXHIBITION BULLETIN
35638U2C-80
Editorial Address: Faraday House, 39 Thornton Road, Wimbledon, LONDON, SW19 4NQ **Tel:** 020 8971 8282
Fax: 020 8971 8283
Email: pcolston@mashmedia.net
Advertising Address: As above. **Tel:** 020 8971 8288
Fax: 020 8971 8284
Email: pking@mashmedia.net
Web site: http://www.expoabc.com
ISSN: 0014-4649
Publisher: Mash Media
Date Established: 1948
Frequency: Monthly
Annual Sub.: £125.00
Circulation: 6,000 (Publisher's Statement)
Usual Pagination: 300
Editor: Paul Colston; **Managing Editor:** Paul Colston; **Publisher:** Roisin Sullens
Summary of Content: Magazine containing details of exhibitions both in Britain and abroad.
Readership/Target Audience: Aimed at manufacturers, import and export companies, marketing, PR and advertising agencies, government and trade associations, venues, corporate companies, exhibition contractors and organisers.
ADVERTISING RATES:
Full Page Colour £1700.00
Agency Commission: 10%
Mechanical Data: Film: Digital, Page Width: 150mm, Type Area: 210 x 150mm, Col Length: 210mm, Bleed Size: 250 x 190mm, Trim Size: 244 x 184mm
Copy instructions: Copy Date: 15th of the month prior to publication date
BUSINESS: COMMUNICATIONS, ADVERTISING & MARKETING: Conferences & Exhibitions

EXHIBITION NEWS
601643U2C-84
Editorial Address: Faraday House, 39 Thornton Road, Wimbledon, LONDON, SW19 4NQ **Tel:** 020 8971 8282
Fax: 020 8971 8283
Email: rsullens@mashmedia.net
Advertising Address: As above.
Email: pking@mashmedia.net
Web site: http://www.mashmedia.net
ISSN: 1467-2014
Publisher: Mash Media
Date Established: 1998
Frequency: Monthly
Annual Sub.: £150.00
Circulation: 5,030 (ABC 01/07/2007 to 30/06/2008)
Usual Pagination: 48
Editor: Roisin Sullens; **Advertising Manager:** Paul King; **Managing Editor:** Paul Colston; **Publisher:** Roisin Sullens
Summary of Content: Magazine covering all aspects of organising exhibitions. Features news, comment, interviews and personnel moves within major exhibition companies.
Readership/Target Audience: Aimed at exhibition organisers, venues and suppliers.
ADVERTISING RATES:
Full Page Colour £1700.00
Agency Commission: 10%
Mechanical Data: Col Length: 270mm, Film: Digital, Type Area: 270 x 190mm, Bleed Size: 303 x 216mm, Page Width: 190mm, Trim Size: 297 x 210mm
Average advertising content per issue: 45%
BUSINESS: COMMUNICATIONS, ADVERTISING & MARKETING: Conferences & Exhibitions

EXPERIENCE BUILDING
1847237U19J-154
Editorial Address: 93A Rivington Street, LONDON, EC2A 3AY **Tel:** 020 3355 7310 **Fax:** 020 3355 7319
Email: greg@x3dmedia.com
Web site: http://www.experiencebuilding.com
Publisher: X3D Media
Date Established: 2008
Frequency: Quarterly
Free to qualifying individuals
Circulation: 60,000 (Publisher's Statement)
Usual Pagination: 52
Editor: Martyn Day; **Managing Editor:** Greg Corke
Summary of Content: Magazine keeping users up to speed with the fast changing world of products, technology and community surrounding Architecture and Building Information Modelling (BIM), Green Building Design, Civil

and Structural Engineering, Mechanical Electrical and Plumbing (MEP) systems and construction.
Language(s): Dutch; English; Swedish
Readership/Target Audience: Aimed at the Autodesk Architecture, Engineering and Construction (AEC) user community in Northern Europe.
BUSINESS: ENGINEERING & MACHINERY: CAD & CIM (Computer Integrated Manufacture)

EXPERIENCE MANUFACTURING

1847233U19J-156

Editorial Address: 93A Rivington Street, LONDON, EC2A 3AY **Tel:** 020 3355 7310 **Fax:** 020 3355 7319
Email: greg@x3dmedia.com
Web site: http://www.experiencemanufacturing.com
Publisher: X3D Media
Date Established: 2008
Frequency: Quarterly
Free to qualifying individuals
Circulation: 60,000 (Publisher's Statement)
Usual Pagination: 52
Editor: Martyn Day; **Managing Editor:** Greg Corke
Summary of Content: Publication keeping users up to speed with the fast changing world of products, technology and community surrounding digital prototyping, AutoCAD, Autodesk, Inventor, Autodesk AliasStudio and other industry leading solutions.
Language(s): Dutch; English; Swedish
Readership/Target Audience: Aimed at the Autodesk manufacturing solutions user community.
BUSINESS: ENGINEERING & MACHINERY: CAD & CIM (Computer Integrated Manufacture)

EXPERIMENTAL AGRICULTURE

37786U21A-286

Editorial Address: The Edinburgh Building, Shaftesbury Road, CAMBRIDGE, CB2 2RU **Tel:** 01223 325800
Fax: 01223 315052
Email: information@cup.cam.ac.uk
Advertising Address: As above. **Tel:** 01223 325757
Email: ad_sales@cambridge.org
Web site: http://www.cup.cam.ac.uk
ISSN: 0014-4797
Publisher: Cambridge University Press
Frequency: Quarterly - Published January, April, July and October
Annual Sub.: £190.00
Circulation: 700 (Publisher's Statement)
Editor: Dave Harris
Summary of Content: Journal publishing the results of new techniques in the production of crops for industrial use, human consumption and animal feed.
Readership/Target Audience: Aimed at students and teachers of agriculture, agricultural research stations in developing countries and agriculturalists involved in foreign aid.
ADVERTISING RATES:
Full Page Mono £465.00
Mechanical Data: Film: Digital, Type Area: 200 x 135mm, Col Length: 200mm, Page Width: 135mm
Copy instructions: Copy Date: 8 weeks prior to publication date
BUSINESS: AGRICULTURE & FARMING

THE EXPERT AND DISPUTE RESOLVER

39163U44-645

Editorial Address: 3 Gray's Inn Square, LONDON, WC1R 5AH **Tel:** 020 7430 0333 **Fax:** 020 7430 0666
Email: admin@academy-experts.org
Advertising Address: As above.
Web site: http://www.academy-experts.org
ISSN: 1751-987X
Publisher: Academy of Experts
Date Established: 1995
Frequency: 3 issues yearly - Published in April, September and December
Free to qualifying individuals
Annual Sub.: £60.00
Circulation: 2,000 (Publisher's Statement)
Usual Pagination: 36
Editor: Nicola Cohen; **Advertising Manager:** Nicola Cohen
Summary of Content: Journal covering developments in the law with regards to expert witnesses and alternative dispute resolution.
Readership/Target Audience: Circulated to members of The Academy of Experts and read by lawyers and members of the medical profession.
ADVERTISING RATES:
Full Page Colour £550.00
Agency Commission: 10%
Mechanical Data: Trim Size: 297 x 210mm, Film: Digital
Average advertising content per issue: 5%
BUSINESS: LEGAL

EXPERT INVESTOR EUROPE (EIE)

1894700U1F-665

Editorial Address: 4th Floor, 120 Moorgate, LONDON, EC2M 6SS **Tel:** 020 7065 7565
Email: dylan.emery@lastwordmedia.com
Web site: http://www.expertinvestoreurope.com
Publisher: Last Word Media
Date Established: 2009
Frequency: Quarterly
Free to qualifying individuals
Circulation: 3,000 (Publisher's Statement)
Editor: Dylan Emery
Summary of Content: Magazine focusing on key investment issues of interest to professional European investors. Covering asset allocation ideas, analysis of European economic issues and interviews with fund selectors and institutional investors from across Europe.
Readership/Target Audience: Aimed at fund selectors and institutional investors from banks, pension funds, insurance companies, fund of funds, family offices, distribution platforms and private banks.
BUSINESS: FINANCE & ECONOMICS: Investment

EXPERT OPINION ON DRUG DISCOVERY

1749932U37-421

Editorial Address: Telephone House, 69-77 Paul Street, LONDON, EC2A 4LQ **Tel:** 020 7017 5000
Fax: 020 7017 7667
Email: joris.roulleau@informa.com
Web site: http://www.expertopin.com
Publisher: Informa Healthcare
Frequency: Monthly
Annual Sub.: £2685.00
Editor: Joris Roulleau
Summary of Content: Review journal focusing on all the technology and disciplines involved in drug discovery and the strategic planning behind it.
Readership/Target Audience: Aimed at the pharmaceutical and biotechnology industry and academia.
ADVERTISING: No Advertising taken
BUSINESS: PHARMACEUTICAL & CHEMISTS

EXPLOSIVES ENGINEERING

38994U42A-96

Editorial Address: Wellington Hall, Cranfield University, Shrivenham Campus, SWINDON, SN6 8LA
Tel: 01729 840765 **Fax:** 01729 840765
Email: dianethall@aol.com
Advertising Address: Hatton Communications, Grooms Cottage, Chester Road, Tattenhall, CHESTER, CH3 9AH
Tel: 01829 771878 **Fax:** 01829 771878
Email: kate@hattoncommunications.co.uk
Web site: http://www.iexpe.org
Publisher: The Institute of Explosives Engineers
Date Established: 1983
Frequency: Quarterly
Cover Price: £5.00
Annual Sub.: £25.00
Circulation: 1,400 (Publisher's Statement)
Usual Pagination: 28
Editor: Diane Hall; **Advertising Manager:** Kate Hatton
Summary of Content: Official journal of the Institute of Explosives Engineers.
Readership/Target Audience: Aimed at researchers, manufacturers and users of all types of explosives.
ADVERTISING RATES:
Full Page Mono £500.00
Full Page Colour £800.00
Agency Commission: 10%
Mechanical Data: Type Area: 255 x 180mm, Bleed Size: 301 x 214mm, Trim Size: 297 x 210mm, Col Length: 255mm, Film: Digital, Page Width: 180mm
Copy instructions: Copy Date: 1st of the preceding month prior to publication date
Average advertising content per issue: 25%
BUSINESS: CONSTRUCTION

EXPORT & FREIGHT

39570U49A-100

Editorial Address: The Old Coach House, 12 Main Street, HILLSBOROUGH, BT26 6AE **Tel:** 028 9268 8888
Fax: 028 9268 8866
Email: helen@4squaremedia.net
Advertising Address: As above.
Email: info@4squaremedia.net
Web site: http://www.exportandfreight.com
Publisher: 4 Square Media
Date Established: 1975
Frequency: 7 issues yearly
Cover Price: £2.40
Annual Sub.: £25.00
Circulation: 8,500 (Publisher's Statement)
Usual Pagination: 80
Editor: Helen Beggs; **Advertising Manager:** Garfield Harrison; **Managing Editor:** Helen Beggs; **Publisher:** Helen Beggs

Summary of Content: Journal covering all aspects of the export trade, including handling and storage.
Readership/Target Audience: Read by exporters, manufacturers, hauliers, own account operators, transport suppliers and importers.
ADVERTISING RATES:
Full Page Colour £1300.00
Agency Commission: 10%
Mechanical Data: Trim Size: 297 x 210mm, Type Area: 267 x 180mm, Film: Digital, Col Length: 267mm, Page Width: 180mm, Bleed Size: 303 x 213mm, Col Widths (Display): 42mm
Copy instructions: Copy Date: 3 weeks prior to publication date
Average advertising content per issue: 40%
BUSINESS: TRANSPORT

THE EXPORT GUIDE

622600U20-306

Formerly: Export Buyers Guide
Editorial Address: 60 Churchill Square, Kings Hill, WEST MALLING, ME19 4YU **Tel:** 01732 525800
Fax: 01732 525801
Email: info@newconcept.co.uk
Advertising Address: As above.
Email: paul.curtis@exportbuyer.com
Web site: http://www.exportbuyer.com
ISSN: 1479-0440
Publisher: NCG Media
Frequency: Quarterly
Annual Sub.: £99.00
Circulation: 16,000 (Publisher's Statement)
Usual Pagination: 90
Editor: Paul Curtis; **Advertising Manager:** Paul Curtis
Summary of Content: Magazine providing advice for UK businesses either already exporting or looking to export.
Readership/Target Audience: Aimed at UK exporters.
ADVERTISING RATES:
Full Page Colour £2695.00
Agency Commission: 10%
Mechanical Data: Type Area: 270 x 190mm, Col Length: 270mm, Page Width: 190mm, Trim Size: 297 x 210mm, Film: Digital, Bleed Size: 303 x 216mm
Copy instructions: Copy Date: 6 weeks prior to publication date
Average advertising content per issue: 35%
BUSINESS: IMPORT & EXPORT

EXTERNAL ENVIRONMENT - PRODUCT REVIEW

1659647U4R-615

Formerly: Street, Landscape & Play Product Review
Editorial Address: The Oaks, Wesleyan Road, Ashley, MARKET DRAYTON, TF9 4JT **Tel:** 01630 673000
Fax: 01630 673247
Email: info@directcontactexhibitions.com
Advertising Address: As above.
Email: nick@directcontactexhibitions.com
Web site: http://www.directcontactexhibitions.com
Publisher: DCE Publications
Date Established: 1989
Frequency: Quarterly - Published at the beginning of the cover month
Cover Price: Free
Circulation: 16,555 (Publisher's Statement)
Usual Pagination: 48
Editor: Nick Downward; **Advertising Manager:** Nick Clowes
Summary of Content: Magazine covering product reviews on street furniture, landscape features and play areas.
Readership/Target Audience: Aimed at urban design professionals.
ADVERTISING RATES:
Full Page Colour £1395.00
Mechanical Data: Type Area: 275 x 198mm, Col Length: 275mm, Page Width: 198mm, Film: Digital
Copy instructions: Copy Date: 4 weeks prior to publication date
BUSINESS: ARCHITECTURE & BUILDING: Building Related

EXTERNAL FUNDING BULLETIN

35441U1P-83_50

Formerly: Lottery Monitor
Editorial Address: 33-41 Dallington Street, LONDON, EC1V 0BB **Tel:** 020 8871 1076
Email: jonathan.watson@yahoo.co.uk
Web site: http://www.external-funding.co.uk
ISSN: 1364-6737
Publisher: Optimus Education
Date Established: 1996
Frequency: 10 issues yearly
Annual Sub.: £290.00
Circulation: 700 (Publisher's Statement)
Usual Pagination: 12
Editor: Jonathan Watson; **Publisher:** Philip Savage
Summary of Content: Newsletter providing an independent perspective on government lottery and charitable funding of good causes. Includes expert analysis, original research and exclusive news about topics such as partnership funding,

assessment techniques and application criteria, as well as political developments and development in policies.
Readership/Target Audience: Aimed at people hoping to acquire funding including officers and policy advisers.
ADVERTISING: No Advertising taken
BUSINESS: FINANCE & ECONOMICS: Fundraising

EXTRACTION INDUSTRY IRELAND

708142U14B-110

Editorial Address: 90A Church Street, Portadown, CRAIGAVON, BT62 3AX **Tel:** 028 3835 2275
Fax: 028 3835 2276
Email: imqsyearbook@btinternet.com
Advertising Address: Bell Cottage, 205 Gilford Road, Portadown, CRAIGAVON, BT63 5LG **Tel:** 07789 757410
Email: quarry2007@btinternet.com
Publisher: Karen McAvoy Publishing Ltd
Frequency: Annual - Published in April
Cover Price: Free
Circulation: 5,450 (Publisher's Statement)
Usual Pagination: 200
Editor: Daryl Magee; **Advertising Manager:** Daryl Magee; **Publisher:** Andrew Crozier
Summary of Content: Publication with news of contracts and development plans within the Irish quarrying scene.
Readership/Target Audience: Aimed at those working in the extraction industry in Ireland.
ADVERTISING RATES:
Full Page Colour £950.00
Agency Commission: 10%
Mechanical Data: Trim Size: 297 x 210mm, No. of Columns (Display): 5, Film: Digital
Copy instructions: Copy Date: 4 weeks prior to publication date
Average advertising content per issue: 40%
BUSINESS: COMMERCE, INDUSTRY & MANAGEMENT: Industry & Factories

EYE

41082U62C-130

Formerly: EYE Early Years Educator
Editorial Address: St. Jude's Church, Dulwich Road, LONDON, SE24 0PB **Tel:** 020 7738 5454
Fax: 020 7326 4835
Email: neil@markallengroup.com
Advertising Address: As above. **Tel:** 020 7501 6735
Email: matt@markallengroup.com
Web site: http://www.earlyyearseducator.co.uk
ISSN: 1465-931X
Publisher: MA Education Ltd
Date Established: 1999
Frequency: Monthly - Published on the 1st Wednesday of the month prior to the cover month
Annual Sub.: £52.00
Circulation: 15,000 (Publisher's Statement)
Usual Pagination: 68
Editor: Neil Henty; **Advertising Manager:** Matt Govett
Summary of Content: Magazine for the 0-5 team, featuring a range of professional and practical articles. Topics include training, research, professional development, outdoor learning, in-depth analysis, focus on early years, foundation stage and reception year.
Readership/Target Audience: Aimed at the childcare workforce from early years teachers to nursery nurses in local authority schools, social services, children's centres, day care settings, extended schools, hospitals and the private sector.
ADVERTISING RATES:
Full Page Mono £995.00
Full Page Colour £995.00
SCC £27.50
Agency Commission: 10%
Mechanical Data: Type Area: 262 x 195mm, Bleed Size: 303 x 236mm, Trim Size: 297 x 230mm, No. of Columns (Display): 4, Page Width: 195mm, Film: Digital, Col Length: 262mm
Copy instructions: Copy Date: 2 weeks prior to publication date
Average advertising content per issue: 20%
BUSINESS: CHURCH & SCHOOL EQUIPMENT & EDUCATION: Junior Education

EYE NEWS

40163U56A-64_75

Editorial Address: 9 Gayfield Square, EDINBURGH, EH1 3NT **Tel:** 0131 557 4184 **Fax:** 0131 557 4701
Email: justin@pinpoint-scotland.com
Advertising Address: As above.
Email: eyenews@pinpoint-scotland.com
Web site: http://www.pinpointmedical.com
ISSN: 1368-8952
Publisher: Pinpoint Scotland Ltd
Date Established: 1994
Frequency: 6 issues yearly
Annual Sub.: £17.00
Circulation: 4,200 (Publisher's Statement)
Usual Pagination: 84
Editor: Justin Chater; **Advertising Manager:** Justin Chater

Summary of Content: Publication which presents reviews of articles from all the major international journals of ophthalmology.
Readership/Target Audience: Aimed at those specialising in ophthalmology.
ADVERTISING RATES:
Full Page Mono £990.00
Full Page Colour £1385.00
Agency Commission: 10%
BUSINESS: HEALTH & MEDICAL

EYE: THE INTERNATIONAL REVIEW OF GRAPHIC DESIGN

37151U14J-154

Editorial Address: Studio 6, The Lux Building, 2-4 Hoxton Square, LONDON, N1 6NU **Tel:** 020 7684 6530
Email: john.walters@eyemagazine.com
Advertising Address: As above.
Email: victoria.mcdougall@eyemagazine.com
Web site: http://www.eyemagazine.com
ISSN: 0960-779X
Publisher: Eye Magazine Ltd
Date Established: 1990
Frequency: Quarterly
Cover Price: £17.00
Annual Sub.: £68.00
Usual Pagination: 100
Editor: John Walters; **Advertising Manager:** Victoria McDougall; **Publisher:** Victoria McDougall
Summary of Content: Magazine covering the international graphic design and visual culture.
Readership/Target Audience: Aimed at graphic designers, typographers, academics, educators, advertising creatives, students, art directors, photographers, illustrators, writers and others in the field of graphic design and visual culture.
ADVERTISING RATES:
Full Page Colour £2185.00
Agency Commission: 10%
Mechanical Data: Type Area: 267 x 204mm, Col Length: 267mm, Page Width: 204mm, Trim Size: 297 x 237mm, Bleed Size: 303 x 243mm, Film: Digital
Copy instructions: Copy Date: 4 weeks prior to publication date
Average advertising content per issue: 20%
BUSINESS: COMMERCE, INDUSTRY & MANAGEMENT: Commercial Design

EYES

1666422U56E-581

Editorial Address: Unit 21, Highview, High Street, BORDON, GU35 0AX **Tel:** 01420 473716 **Fax:** 01420 487799
Email: bsaunders@rimsmedia.co.uk
Advertising Address: As above.
Email: sbradley@rimsmedia.co.uk
Publisher: RIMS Media
Date Established: 2005
Frequency: Monthly - Published in the 3rd week of the cover month
Cover Price: £3.00
Free to qualifying individuals
Annual Sub.: £35.25
Circulation: 7,300 (Publisher's Statement)
Usual Pagination: 36
Editor: Brenda Saunders; **Advertising Manager:** Sarah Bradley; **Publisher:** Brenda Saunders
Summary of Content: Magazine focusing on the optical retail industry including industry news, product information, business and educational features plus eyewear fashion.
Readership/Target Audience: Aimed at all UK optical retailers and those working in the industry.
ADVERTISING RATES:
Full Page Colour £1950.00
Mechanical Data: Page Width: 230mm, Type Area: 300 x 230mm, Bleed Size: +3mm, Col Length: 300mm, Film: Digital
Average advertising content per issue: 30%
Supplement(s): Healthy Eyes - 2xY
BUSINESS: HEALTH & MEDICAL: Optics

F2 FREELANCE PHOTOGRAPHER

38788U38-16

Formerly: F2 Freelance + Digital
Editorial Address: Finsbury Business Centre, 40 Bowling Green Lane, LONDON, EC1R 0NE **Tel:** 020 7415 7099
Email: mail@ec1publishing.com
Advertising Address: As above. **Tel:** 020 7692 9961
Fax: 020 7415 7133
Email: simon@eclpublishing.com
Publisher: ECI Publishing Limited
Frequency: 6 issues yearly
Annual Sub.: £29.50
Circulation: 3,500 (Publisher's Statement)
Usual Pagination: 64
Editor: Simon James; **Advertising Manager:** Simon James
Summary of Content: Magazine containing features, news, information, competitions and gallery exhibitions, trials, equipment tests, portfolios and profiles.

Readership/Target Audience: Aimed at direct subscribers and members of The Bureau of Freelance Photographers, direct subscribers and members of The Bureau of Freelance Photographers only.
ADVERTISING: Rates on application
Agency Commission: 10%
Copy instructions: Copy Date: 10th of the month prior to publication date
Average advertising content per issue: 30%
BUSINESS: PHOTOGRAPHIC TRADE

F & F MAGAZINE

1605014U14B-301

Editorial Address: PO Box 22894, LONDON, NW9 6ZE
Tel: 020 8905 9511 **Fax:** 020 8905 9512
Email: sarah@fastfixeuro.com
Advertising Address: As above.
Email: tony@fastfixeuro.com
Web site: http://www.fastfixeuro.com
Publisher: Fast Fix Euro Ltd
Frequency: Quarterly
Cover Price: Free
Circulation: 8,357 (Publisher's Statement)
Usual Pagination: 64
Editor: Sarah Beaumont; **Advertising Manager:** Tony Milbank; **Publisher:** Peter Draper
Summary of Content: Magazine covering industrial fasteners, tools and everything connected from raw materials to final applications.
Readership/Target Audience: Aimed at the European industrial fastener and fixing market including trade, industry, distributors, merchants, OEM and bulk buyers.
ADVERTISING RATES:
Full Page Mono £995.00
Full Page Colour £1295.00
Agency Commission: 10%
Mechanical Data: Type Area: 287 x 200mm, Col Length: 287mm, Film: Positive, right reading, emulsion side down. Digital, Screen: 70 lpc, Page Width: 200mm, Bleed Size: 307 x 220mm, Trim Size: 297 x 210mm
Average advertising content per issue: 50%
BUSINESS: COMMERCE, INDUSTRY & MANAGEMENT: Industry & Factories

THE FABRICATOR

36627U12B-25

Editorial Address: PR by email only **Tel:** 020 8505 6486
Fax: 020 8491 6728
Email: fabricator@profinder.eu
Advertising Address: PO Box 2087, WOODFORD GREEN, IG8 7LQ **Tel:** 01296 670018 **Fax:** 020 8491 6728
Email: steve.anthony@profinder.eu
Web site: http://www.profinder.eu
ISSN: 1752-2145
Publisher: Profinder Magazines Ltd
Date Established: 2005
Frequency: 11 issues yearly
Cover Price: Free
Circulation: 7,000 (Publisher's Statement)
Usual Pagination: 40
Editor: John Roper; **Advertisement Director:** Steve Anthony
Summary of Content: Product-orientated technical information, reporting on window and door systems and related products.
Readership/Target Audience: Aimed at manufacturers and specifiers of fenestration systems and products.
ADVERTISING RATES:
Full Page Colour £1050.00
SCC £19.00
Agency Commission: 10%
Mechanical Data: Type Area: 270 x 182mm, No. of Columns (Display): 4, Trim Size: 297 x 210mm, Film: Digital, Col Length: 270mm, Page Width: 182mm, Bleed Size: 303 x 216mm
Copy instructions: Copy Date: 7th of the month prior to publication date
Average advertising content per issue: 50%
BUSINESS: CERAMICS, POTTERY & GLASS: Glass

FABRICS & FURNISHINGS INTERNATIONAL

22834U23A-17

Editorial Address: 57 Keyes House, Dolphin Square, LONDON, SW1V 3NA **Tel:** 020 7834 5559
Fax: 020 7834 0600
Email: pgilmore@sipco.net
Advertising Address: As above.
Email: pgilmore@sipco.net
Web site: http://www.sipco.net
Publisher: Sipco Publications Inc
Date Established: 1991
Frequency: Quarterly
Annual Sub.: £130.00
Circulation: 8,376 (Publisher's Statement)
Usual Pagination: 70
Editor: Peter Gilmore; **Advertising Manager:** Peter Gilmore
Summary of Content: Publication containing reviews and previews of exhibitions worldwide, business to business

Business Magazines

news, company profiles, contract news, and interviews with leading figures within the home and contract furnishings industry.
Readership/Target Audience: Aimed at specifiers and buyers of fabrics and furnishings.
ADVERTISING RATES:
Full Page Colour $6800.00
Agency Commission: 15%
Mechanical Data: Bleed Size: 371 x 276mm, Trim Size: 365 x 270mm, Film: Digital
Average advertising content per issue: 60%
BUSINESS: FURNISHINGS & FURNITURE

FACILITIES
35962U4R-386

Editorial Address: Reader In Facilities Management, School of the Built Environment, Heriot-Watt University, EDINBURGH, EH14 4AS **Tel:** 01274 777700
Fax: 01274 785200
Email: e.finch@salford.ac.uk
Web site: http://www.emeraldinsight.com/f.htm
ISSN: 0263-2772
Publisher: Emerald Group Publishing Ltd
Frequency: 7 issues yearly
Annual Sub.: £5259.00
(Publisher's Statement)
Usual Pagination: 64
Editor: Edward Finch
Summary of Content: International journal covering research, news, information and comment on key issues regarding maximising building space resources.
Readership/Target Audience: Read by managers of building spaces and architects, designers, planners, directors of operations, administration, facilities managers, office service managers, premises consultants and property service managers.
ADVERTISING: No Advertising taken
BUSINESS: ARCHITECTURE & BUILDING: Building Related

FACILITIES MANAGEMENT
35963U4R-386_50

Editorial Address: Tolley House, 2 Addiscombe Road, CROYDON, CR9 5AF **Tel:** 020 8686 9141
Fax: 020 8686 3155
Email: jlpoidevin@aol.com
Web site: http://www.lexisnexis.co.uk
ISSN: 1315-668X
Publisher: LexisNexis UK
Date Established: 1993
Frequency: Monthly
Annual Sub.: £366.00
Usual Pagination: 28
Editor: Jackie Le Poidevin
Summary of Content: Magazine containing compliance and best practice information plus case studies relating to facilities management.
Readership/Target Audience: Read by estates, premises, property and facilities managers.
ADVERTISING: No Advertising taken
BUSINESS: ARCHITECTURE & BUILDING: Building Related

FACILITIES MANAGEMENT UK
35965U4R-386_80

Editorial Address: 3rd Floor, Hollinwood Business Centre, Albert Street, OLDHAM, OL8 3QL **Tel:** 0161 683 8000
Fax: 0161 683 8001
Email: john.kirkbride@worldsfair.co.uk
Advertising Address: As above.
Email: craig.mills@worldsfair.co.uk
Web site: http://www.fmuk-online.co.uk
Publisher: The World's Fair Ltd
Date Established: 1995
Frequency: 6 issues yearly
Annual Sub.: £69.00
Circulation: 12,800 (Publisher's Statement)
Usual Pagination: 60
Editor: John Kirkbride
Summary of Content: Magazine containing news and features of interest to facilities managers.
Readership/Target Audience: Aimed at facilities, estate and property managers.
ADVERTISING RATES:
Full Page Colour £1950.00
Agency Commission: 10%
Mechanical Data: Bleed Size: 303 x 216mm, Trim Size: 297 x 210mm, Film: Digital, Type Area: 274 x 185mm, Col Length: 274mm, Page Width: 185mm
BUSINESS: ARCHITECTURE & BUILDING: Building Related

FACILITIES-UK
36877U4R-386_95

Formerly: Premises Showcase
Editorial Address: Jesses Farm, Snow Hill, Dinton, SALISBURY, SP3 5HN **Tel:** 01722 716997
Fax: 01722 716926
Email: claire@markallengroup.co.uk
Advertising Address: As above. **Tel:** 01722 716996
Email: oliver.h@markallengroup.co.uk

Web site: http://www.facilities-uk.co.uk
Publisher: A & D Media Ltd
Date Established: 2001
Frequency: Monthly - Published on the 2nd Monday of the cover month
Free to qualifying individuals
Annual Sub.: £50.00
Circulation: 8,432 (Publisher's Statement)
Usual Pagination: 24
Editor: Claire White
Summary of Content: Magazine providing features on a range of subjects with relevance to facilities managers. Also containing reviews of existing products and services, case studies, what's new on the market and details of new contracts.
Readership/Target Audience: Aimed at owners, occupiers and managers of large buildings.
ADVERTISING RATES:
Full Page Colour £1500.00
Agency Commission: 10%
Mechanical Data: Film: Digital, Type Area: 400 x 277mm, Bleed Size: 426 x 303mm, Trim Size: 420 x 297mm, Col Length: 400mm, Page Width: 277mm
Copy instructions: Copy Date: 3 weeks prior to publication date
Average advertising content per issue: 90%
BUSINESS: ARCHITECTURE & BUILDING: Building Related

FACTORY EQUIPMENT
37655U19F-102

Formerly: Factory Equipment News
Editorial Address: 15A London Road, MAIDSTONE, ME16 8LY **Tel:** 01622 687031 **Fax:** 01622 757646
Email: nmead@datateam.co.uk
Advertising Address: As above.
Email: speters@datateam.co.uk
Web site: http://www.connectingindustry.com
ISSN: 1472-1295
Publisher: Datateam Publishing Ltd
Frequency: 10 issues yearly - Published in the 2nd week of the month
Free to qualifying individuals
Annual Sub.: £74.00
Circulation: 21,992 (ABC 01/01/2008 to 31/12/2008)
Usual Pagination: 68
Editor: Neil Mead
Summary of Content: Publication which contains regular features on factory and warehouse equipment, industry comment, technologies and case studies, products and services.
Readership/Target Audience: Aimed at purchasers and specifiers across all industrial sectors.
ADVERTISING RATES:
Full Page Colour £2400.00
Agency Commission: 10%
Mechanical Data: Type Area: 278 x 191mm, Col Length: 278mm, Trim Size: 297 x 210mm, Bleed Size: 303 x 216mm, Page Width: 191mm
Copy instructions: Copy Date: 14th of the month prior to publication date
Average advertising content per issue: 50%
Supplement(s): Compressed Air - 1xY, Health & Safety - 1xY, Maintenance Management - 1xY, Materials, Handling & Logistics - 6xY
BUSINESS: ENGINEERING & MACHINERY: Production & Mechanical Engineering

FACTORY: THE FILM INDUSTRY MAGAZINE
1664888U64K-647

Editorial Address: Flat 1, 30 Bramham Gardens, LONDON, SW5 0HF **Tel:** 020 7370 2430 **Fax:** 020 7370 2430
Email: howard.webster@factory-publishing.com
Advertising Address: As above.
Email: howard.webster@factory-publishing.com
Web site: http://www.factory-publishing.com
Publisher: Factory Publishing Ltd.
Date Established: 2003
Frequency: Quarterly
Free to qualifying individuals
Circulation: 10,000 (Publisher's Statement)
Usual Pagination: 100
Editor: Howard Webster; **Advertising Manager:** Howard Webster
Summary of Content: Magazine covering in-depth analysis of the issues affecting the global film industry. Includes photo shoots, information and insight into production, post production and writing.
Readership/Target Audience: Aimed at key decision makers within the Hollywood and global film industry.
ADVERTISING RATES:
Full Page Colour £5000.00
Mechanical Data: Type Area: 224 x 214mm, Bleed Size: 336 x 226mm, Trim Size: 330 x 220mm, Col Length: 224mm, Page Width: 214mm, Film: Digital
Supplement(s): Hollywood Rising Stars - 4xY
BUSINESS: OTHER CLASSIFICATIONS: Cinema Entertainment

FACTS
1665379U31A-384

Editorial Address: 34 Bernard Street, EDINBURGH, EH6 6PR **Tel:** 0131 554 1129 **Fax:** 0131 555 1622
Email: tony@belljohnstone.co.uk
Advertising Address: As above.
Email: esther@belljohnstone.co.uk
Web site: http://www.belljohnstone.co.uk
Publisher: Bell Johnstone Communications
Date Established: 2003
Frequency: Monthly - Published in the 1st week of the cover month
Free to qualifying individuals
Circulation: 7,500 (Publisher's Statement)
Editor: Tony Wood; **Managing Editor:** Tony Wood
Summary of Content: Magazine focusing on fleet, agriculture and commercial transport in Scotland.
Readership/Target Audience: Aimed at decision makers within the commercial transport industry.
ADVERTISING RATES:
Full Page Colour £1755.00
Agency Commission: 10%
Mechanical Data: Type Area: 270 x 190mm, Col Length: 270mm, Page Width: 190mm, Bleed Size: 303 x 216mm, Trim Size: 297 x 210mm, Film: Digital
Copy instructions: Copy Date: 5 working dates prior to publication date
Average advertising content per issue: 50%
BUSINESS: MOTOR TRADE: Motor Trade Accessories

FAIRPLAY INTERNATIONAL SHIPPING WEEKLY
39326U45A-40

Editorial Address: 3rd Floor, Lombard House, 3 Princess Way, REDHILL, RH1 1UP **Tel:** 01737 379140
Fax: 01737 379007
Email: editorial@fairplay.co.uk
Advertising Address: As above. **Tel:** 01737 379000
Fax: 01737 379001
Email: adam.foster@lrfairplay.co.uk
Web site: http://www.fairplay.co.uk
Publisher: Lloyd's Register-Fairplay Ltd
Date Established: 1883
Frequency: Weekly - Published on Thursday
Cover Price: £9.15
Circulation: 3,874 (ABC 01/01/2008 to 31/12/2008)
Usual Pagination: 52
Editor: Richard Clayton; **Advertising Manager:** Adam Foster; **Managing Editor:** Paul Gunton
Summary of Content: Magazine covering news and analysis of commercial shipping developments throughout the world.
Readership/Target Audience: Read by ship owners, operators and managers, port operators, bank personnel, lawyers, marine insurers, equipment manufacturers, shipyards and other technical organisations.
ADVERTISING RATES:
Full Page Mono £2337.00
Full Page Colour £2877.00
Agency Commission: 10%
Mechanical Data: Type Area: 252 x 194mm, Bleed Size: 281 x 216mm, Col Length: 252mm, Page Width: 194mm, Film: Digital
Copy instructions: Copy Date: 2 weeks prior to publication date
Average advertising content per issue: 35%
BUSINESS: MARINE & SHIPPING

FAIRPLAY SOLUTIONS
39327U45A-41

Editorial Address: 3rd Floor, Lombard House, 3 Princess Way, REDHILL, RH1 1UP **Tel:** 01737 379140
Fax: 01737 379007
Email: malcolm.latarche@fairplay.co.uk
Advertising Address: As above. **Tel:** 01737 379000
Fax: 01737 379001
Email: sales@lrfairplay.com
Web site: http://www.solutionsmagazine.co.uk
Publisher: Lloyd's Register-Fairplay Ltd
Frequency: Monthly - Published on the 1st Thursday of cover month
Circulation: 4,099 (ABC 01/01/2008 to 31/12/2008)
Usual Pagination: 72
Editor: Malcolm Latarche; **Managing Editor:** Paul Gunton
Summary of Content: Magazine offering technical solutions to commercial problems relating to shipping worldwide.
Readership/Target Audience: Read mainly by those involved in worldwide shipping.
ADVERTISING RATES:
Full Page Mono £2226.00
Full Page Colour £2740.00
Agency Commission: 10%
Mechanical Data: Page Width: 194mm, Type Area: 252 x 194mm, Bleed Size: 281 x 216mm, Film: Digital, Col Length: 252mm
Copy instructions: Copy Date: 2 weeks prior to publication date
BUSINESS: MARINE & SHIPPING

FAMILY & COMMUNITY HISTORY JOURNAL
1794032U32G-175

Editorial Address: 2 Elm Close, Ripley, WOKING, GU23 6LE **Tel:** 01483 224511
Email: angela.blaydon@fachrs.org.uk
Advertising Address: Suite 1C, Josephs Well, Hanover Walk, LEEDS, LS3 1AB **Tel:** 0113 243 2800
Fax: 0113 386 8178
Email: a.holgate@maney.co.uk
Web site: http://www.fachrs.com
ISSN: 1463-1180
Publisher: Maney Publishing
Date Established: 1998
Frequency: Half-yearly
Free to qualifying individuals
Usual Pagination: 80
Editor: Angela Blaydon; **News Editor:** Angela Blaydon;
Advertising Manager: Alison Holgate
Summary of Content: Academic journal covering family and community history.
Readership/Target Audience: Aimed at academics and any individuals interested in family and community history.
ADVERTISING RATES:
Full Page Mono £180.00
Mechanical Data: Type Area: 190 x 135mm, Col Length: 190mm, Page Width: 135mm, Film: Digital
Copy instructions: Copy Date: 4 weeks prior to publication date
BUSINESS: LOCAL GOVERNMENT, LEISURE & RECREATION: Community Care & Social Services

FAMILY LAW
39164U44-660

Editorial Address: 21 St. Thomas Street, BRISTOL, BS1 6JS **Tel:** 0117 918 1529 **Fax:** 0117 925 0486
Email: editor@familylaw.co.uk
Advertising Address: As above.
Email: sue_reynolds@jordanpublishing.co.uk
Web site: http://www.familylaw.co.uk
ISSN: 0014-7281
Publisher: Jordan Publishing Ltd
Date Established: 1971
Frequency: Monthly
Annual Sub.: £250.00
Circulation: 5,900 (Publisher's Statement)
Usual Pagination: 90
Editor: Elizabeth Walsh; **Managing Director:** Caroline Vandridge-Ames; **Advertising Manager:** Sue Reynolds
Summary of Content: Journal reviewing all aspects of the law as it affects families. Includes case reports and analysis, details of forthcoming legislation, book reviews and conference reports.
Readership/Target Audience: Read by judges, barristers, solicitors, JPs, law societies, divorce courts and local authorities.
ADVERTISING RATES:
Full Page Mono £730.00
Agency Commission: 10%
Mechanical Data: Col Length: 215mm, Film: Digital, No. of Columns (Display): 2, Type Area: 215 x 145mm, Bleed Size: 253 x 191mm, Trim Size: 247 x 185mm, Page Width: 145mm
Copy instructions: Copy Date: 10 days prior to publication date
BUSINESS: LEGAL

FAMILY LAW JOURNAL
39165U44-665

Editorial Address: Kensington Square House, 12-14 Ansdell Street, LONDON, W8 5BN **Tel:** 020 7396 9292
Fax: 020 7396 9300
Email: alec.johnson@legalease.co.uk
Advertising Address: As above. **Fax:** 020 7396 9302
Email: raju.mannk@legalease.co.uk
Web site: http://www.legalease.co.uk
ISSN: 1472-4944
Publisher: Legalease Ltd
Date Established: 2000
Frequency: 10 issues yearly - Double issues Jul/Aug and Dec/Jan
Annual Sub.: £135.00
Circulation: 500 (Publisher's Statement)
Usual Pagination: 24
Editor: Alec Johnson
Summary of Content: Magazine covering recent developments in family law.
Readership/Target Audience: Aimed at specialist lawyers and people concerned with family law.
ADVERTISING RATES:
Full Page Mono £950.00
Agency Commission: 10%
Mechanical Data: Bleed Size: 303 x 216mm, Type Area: 270 x 190mm, Col Length: 270mm, Page Width: 190mm, Film: Positive, right reading, emulsion side down, Trim Size: 297 x 210mm
Copy instructions: Copy Date: 13 days prior to publication date
Average advertising content per issue: 25%
BUSINESS: LEGAL

FAMILY PRACTICE
24720U56A-65_50

Editorial Address: Dept of Primary Care and General Practice, Primary Care Clinical Sciences Building, The University of Birmingham, BIRMINGHAM, B15 2TT
Tel: 0121 414 3765 **Fax:** 0121 414 6571
Email: v.tsimbili@gmail.com
Advertising Address: Great Clarendon Street, OXFORD, OX2 6DP **Tel:** 01865 353907 **Fax:** 01865 353774
Email: steve.simmonds@oxfordjournals.org
Web site: http://www.oup.co.uk/jnls
ISSN: 0263-2136
Publisher: OUP
Date Established: 1984
Frequency: 6 issues yearly
Cover Price: £44.00
Annual Sub.: £220.00
Usual Pagination: 116
Editor: Brendan Delaney
Summary of Content: Journal which intends to serve as a means of broadening the International base of family medicine in general practice. It covers healthcare delivery, epidemiology, public health and medical sociology.
Readership/Target Audience: Aimed at practitioners, teachers and researchers in the fields of family medicine, general practice and primary care in both developed and developing countries.
ADVERTISING RATES:
Full Page Mono £646.00
Full Page Colour £1076.00
Agency Commission: 10%
Mechanical Data: Type Area: 255 x 178mm, Col Length: 255mm, Trim Size: 279 x 216mm, Bleed Size: 285 x 222mm, Print Process: Litho, Page Width: Film: Digital
Copy instructions: Copy Date: 8 weeks prior to publication date
BUSINESS: HEALTH & MEDICAL

FANCY FOWL
37865U21F-300

Editorial Address: The Publishing House, Station Road, Framlingham, WOODBRIDGE, IP13 9EE **Tel:** 01728 622030
Fax: 01728 622031
Email: fancyfowl@todaymagazines.co.uk
Advertising Address: As above.
Email: fancyfowl@todaymagazines.co.uk
Web site: http://www.fancyfowl.com
Publisher: Today Magazines Ltd
Frequency: Monthly
Cover Price: £2.90
Annual Sub.: £29.00
Circulation: 6,000 (Publisher's Statement)
Usual Pagination: 40
Editor: Grant Brereton; **Managing Director:** Greg Davis;
Publisher: Kevin Davis
Summary of Content: Magazine featuring pure and rare breeds of poultry.
Readership/Target Audience: For people who keep pure and rare breeds of poultry as a hobby, including domestic waterfowl.
ADVERTISING RATES:
Full Page Colour £448.00
Agency Commission: 10%
Mechanical Data: Trim Size: 297 x 210mm, Bleed Size: 303 x 216mm, Col Length: 278mm, Type Area: 278 x 186mm, Film: Digital, Print Process: Sheet-fed litho, Page Width: 186mm
Copy instructions: Copy Date: 2 weeks prior to publication date
Average advertising content per issue: 20%
BUSINESS: AGRICULTURE & FARMING: Poultry

FANDB JOURNAL
1902462U15R-17

Editorial Address: 16 Camden Road, LONDON, NW1 9DP
Tel: 020 7485 8364
Email: iam@fandbjournal.co.uk
Web site: http://www.fandbjournal.co.uk
Cover Price: Free
Editor: Winnie Di Matos
Summary of Content: Journal bringing together ideas, experiences and opinions of those within the Fashion and Beauty industry.
Readership/Target Audience: Aimed at marketing and brand managers, media contacts and business owners.
BUSINESS: COSMETICS & HAIRDRESSING: Cosmetics & Hairdressing Related

FAR EASTERN AGRICULTURE
37757U21A-320

Editorial Address: University House, 11-13 Lower Grosvenor Place, LONDON, SW1W 0EX **Tel:** 020 7834 7676
Fax: 020 7973 0076
Email: andrew.croft@alaincharles.com
Advertising Address: As above.
Email: richard.rozelaar@alaincharles.com
Web site: http://www.alaincharles.com
Publisher: Alain Charles Publishing Ltd
Date Established: 1983

Frequency: 6 issues yearly - Published in the 2nd week of the 2nd cover month
Annual Sub.: £54.00
Circulation: 7,050 (ABC 01/01/2008 to 31/12/2008)
Usual Pagination: 36
Editor: Andrew Croft; **Managing Director:** Nick Fordham;
Advertising Manager: Richard Rozelaar; **Managing Editor:** Andrew Croft; **Publisher:** Derek Fordham
Summary of Content: Magazine covering all aspects of agriculture in Asia, including machinery, crop cultivation, livestock, feed, irrigation, agro-chemicals and biotechnology.
Readership/Target Audience: Read by people involved in public and private sector agricultural production and related organisations in Asia.
ADVERTISING RATES:
Full Page Mono £2400.00
Full Page Colour £3530.00
Agency Commission: 15%
Mechanical Data: Page Width: 180mm, Type Area: 255 x 180mm, Bleed Size: 282 x 216mm, Trim Size: 276 x 210mm, Col Length: 255mm
Average advertising content per issue: 35%
BUSINESS: AGRICULTURE & FARMING

FARADAY DISCUSSIONS
36695U13-91

Editorial Address: Thomas Graham House, Science Park, Milton Road, CAMBRIDGE, CB4 0WF **Tel:** 01223 420066
Fax: 01223 420247
Email: faraday@rsc.org
Web site: http://www.rsc.org/faraday_d
ISSN: 1359-6640
Publisher: Royal Society of Chemistry
Date Established: 1946
Frequency: 3 issues yearly
Annual Sub.: £470.00
Circulation: 600 (Publisher's Statement)
Usual Pagination: 450
Editor: Philip Earis
Summary of Content: Journal covering the broad aspects of physicochemical topics.
Readership/Target Audience: Read by scientists in the fields of physical chemistry, chemical physics and biophysical chemistry - in industry and in academic institutions.
ADVERTISING: No Advertising taken
BUSINESS: CHEMICALS

FARM AD (INCORPORATING AGRI ADS)
37863U21E-330

Formerly: Farm Ad
Editorial Address: Corporation Street, COVENTRY, CV1 1FP **Tel:** 024 7663 3633 **Fax:** 024 7655 0869
Email: christine.farn@coventrytelegraph.net
Advertising Address: As above. **Fax:** 024 7650 0499
Email: farm_ad@mrn.co.uk
Publisher: Midland Newspapers Ltd
Date Established: 1986
Frequency: Monthly
Cover Price: Free
Circulation: 6,850 (Publisher's Statement)
Usual Pagination: 48
Editor: Christine Farn; **Advertising Manager:** David Ford
Summary of Content: Publication covering information on farming machinery and supplies.
Readership/Target Audience: Aimed at farmers and those involved within the agricultural industry.
ADVERTISING RATES:
Full Page Colour £600.00
Agency Commission: 10%
Mechanical Data: Type Area: 240 x 160mm, Col Length: 240mm, Page Width: 160mm
Copy instructions: Copy Date: 20th of the month prior to publication date
Average advertising content per issue: 30%
BUSINESS: AGRICULTURE & FARMING: Agriculture - Machinery & Plant

FARM BRIEF
37759U21A-345

Editorial Address: 6 Cley Road, HOLT, NR25 6JD
Tel: 01263 711844 **Fax:** 01263 711845
Email: rb@farmbrief.com
Publisher: Lakebourne Ltd
Date Established: 1986
Frequency: 42 issues yearly
Annual Sub.: £270.00
Circulation: 2,000 (Publisher's Statement)
Usual Pagination: 8
Editor: Robert Bojduniak; **Publisher:** Robert Bojduniak
Summary of Content: Newsletter focusing on farming news, facts and figures.
Readership/Target Audience: Aimed at those involved in the farming industry.
ADVERTISING: No Advertising taken
BUSINESS: AGRICULTURE & FARMING

FARM BUSINESS
1605130U21R-1501

Editorial Address: Hendal Oast, Hendal Farm, Groombridge, KENT, TN3 9NU **Tel:** 01892 861770
Email: info@ghpublishing.co.uk
Advertising Address: As above.
Email: caroline@ghpublishing.co.uk
Web site: http://www.farmerbusiness.cc
ISSN: 1476-8607
Publisher: Grove House Publishing
Date Established: 2002
Frequency: 21 issues yearly
Cover Price: £2.85
Free to qualifying individuals
Annual Sub.: £60.00
Circulation: 15,813 (ABC 01/01/2008 to 31/12/2008)
Usual Pagination: 48
Editor: Andrew Watts; **Advertising Manager:** Caroline Calder-Smith; **Publisher:** Alan Whibley
Summary of Content: Magazine covering business information to assist farmers to produce food for the food chain.
Readership/Target Audience: Aimed at farm owners and managers and tenant farmers farming over 150 hectares as well as key influencers including vets, processors and retailers.
ADVERTISING RATES:
Full Page Colour £2530.00
Agency Commission: 10%
Mechanical Data: Trim Size: 297 x 210mm, Bleed Size: 303 x 216mm, Type Area: 280 x 194mm, Col Length: 280mm, Page Width: 194mm, Film: Digital
Copy instructions: Copy Date: 3 weeks prior to publication date
Average advertising content per issue: 40%
BUSINESS: AGRICULTURE & FARMING: Agriculture & Farming Related

FARM BUSINESS AGRONOMIST
1693352U21A-1115

Editorial Address: Hendal Oast, Hendal Farm, Groombridge, TUNBRIDGE WELLS, TN3 9NU
Tel: 01892 861993
Email: alan@ghpublishing.co.uk
Advertising Address: As above.
Email: keith@ghpublishing.co.uk
Web site: http://www.farmbusiness.cc
Publisher: Grove House Publishing
Date Established: 2005
Frequency: Quarterly
Free to qualifying individuals
Annual Sub.: £50.00
Circulation: 4,000 (Publisher's Statement)
Usual Pagination: 48
Editor: Alan Whibley; **Publisher:** Alan Whibley
Summary of Content: Magazine featuring business advice, industry news, research and developments, product reviews and interviews.
Readership/Target Audience: Aimed at agronomists and crop advisers.
ADVERTISING RATES:
Full Page Colour £1800.00
Mechanical Data: Type Area: 300 x 225mm, Bleed Size: 341 x 250mm, Trim Size: 335 x 244mm, Col Length: 300mm, Page Width: 225mm, Film: Digital
BUSINESS: AGRICULTURE & FARMING

FARM CONTRACTOR & LARGE SCALE FARMER
37855U21E-340

Editorial Address: Offices 2 & 3, Brixfield Farm, Sunrising Hill, Kineton, WARWICK, CV35 0ED **Tel:** 01926 691212
Fax: 01926 642060
Email: journals@acp-publishers.co.uk
Advertising Address: As above.
Email: journals@acp-publishers.co.uk
ISSN: 0144-0675
Publisher: ACP Publishers Ltd
Date Established: 1972
Frequency: Monthly - Published on the 1st of the cover month
Free to qualifying individuals
Annual Sub.: £25.00
Circulation: 9,570 (ABC 01/01/2008 to 31/12/2008)
Usual Pagination: 56
Editor: Malcolm Benjamin; **Publisher:** Malcolm Benjamin
Summary of Content: Journal covering agricultural machinery reviews, new product reports and management techniques. Includes agrochemical updates and agriculture show reports.
Readership/Target Audience: Aimed at professional agricultural contractors and large scale farmers who farm in excess of 1,200 acres.
ADVERTISING RATES:
Full Page Colour £1380.00
SCC £10.00
Agency Commission: 10%
Mechanical Data: Type Area: 270 x 190mm, Bleed Size: 305 x 216mm, Trim Size: 297 x 210mm, Film: Digital, No. of

Columns (Display): 4, Col Widths (Display): 43mm, Col Length: 270mm, Page Width: 190mm
Copy instructions: Copy Date: 13th of the month prior to publication date
Average advertising content per issue: 45%
Supplement(s): Farm Machinery Directory - 1xY
BUSINESS: AGRICULTURE & FARMING: Agriculture - Machinery & Plant

FARM LAW
39166U44-675

Editorial Address: 80 Calverley Road, TUNBRIDGE WELLS, TN1 2UN **Tel:** 020 7017 7500 **Fax:** 020 7017 7599
Email: marketing@agra-net.com
Web site: http://www.agra-net.com
ISSN: 0964-8488
Publisher: Agra Informa Ltd
Frequency: 11 issues yearly
Annual Sub.: £348.00
Usual Pagination: 20
Advertising Manager: Caroline Gasking
Summary of Content: Journal containing the latest legislation for agriculture and rural land with key extracts from legislation passed in Westminster, Brussels and Strasbourg. Also includes legal developments affecting all aspects of the business of food production and rural land use.
Readership/Target Audience: Aimed at professional advisers to rural business and large farming companies.
ADVERTISING: No Advertising taken
BUSINESS: LEGAL

FARM MACHINERY DIRECTORY
37861U21E-350

Editorial Address: Offices 2 & 3, Brixfield Farm, Sunrising Hill, Kineton, WARWICK, CV35 0ED **Tel:** 01926 691212
Fax: 01926 642060
Email: journals@acp-publishers.co.uk
Advertising Address: As above.
Email: journals@acp-publishers.co.uk
Publisher: ACP Publishers Ltd
Date Established: 1994
Frequency: Annual - Published in March
Cover Price: £12.00
Circulation: 7,500 (Publisher's Statement)
Usual Pagination: 84
Editor: Malcolm Benjamin
Summary of Content: Directory listing manufacturers details and a list of the products they manufacture within the agriculture industry.
Readership/Target Audience: Aimed at agricultural contractors and UK dealers.
ADVERTISING RATES:
Full Page Colour £1380.00
Agency Commission: 10%
Mechanical Data: Type Area: 270 x 190mm, Col Length: 270mm, Page Width: 190mm, Bleed Size: 305 x 216mm, Film: Digital, Trim Size: 297 x 210mm
Copy instructions: Copy Date: 2 weeks prior to publication date
Average advertising content per issue: 25%
BUSINESS: AGRICULTURE & FARMING: Agriculture - Machinery & Plant

FARM NORTH EAST
1642317U21A-1107

Editorial Address: 11 Sunnyside Gardens, Drumoak, BANCHORY, AB31 5EZ **Tel:** 01330 811616
Fax: 01330 811616
Email: eddie.gillanders@btopenworld.com
Advertising Address: As above.
Email: eddie.gillanders@btopenworld.com
Publisher: Agricultural Communications Ltd
Date Established: 2004
Frequency: 6 issues yearly
Cover Price: Free
Circulation: 5,000 (Publisher's Statement)
Usual Pagination: 40
Editor: Eddie Gillanders; **Advertising Manager:** Marion Gillanders; **Publisher:** Eddie Gillanders
Summary of Content: Magazine covering news and technical/business developments within the agri-food industry in North and North-East Scotland.
Readership/Target Audience: Aimed at the farmers in the North East of Scotland.
ADVERTISING RATES:
Full Page Mono £550.00
Full Page Colour £750.00
Agency Commission: 10%
Mechanical Data: Type Area: 310 x 212mm, Bleed Size: 341 x 241mm, Trim Size: 340 x 235mm, Col Length: 310mm, Page Width: 212mm, Film: Digital
Copy instructions: Copy Date: Middle of month prior to publication date
Average advertising content per issue: 40%
BUSINESS: AGRICULTURE & FARMING

FARM TAX BRIEF
35405U1M-30

Editorial Address: Telephone House, 69-77 Paul Street, LONDON, EC2A 4LQ **Tel:** 020 7017 5000
Fax: 020 7017 4135
Email: frida.fischer@informa.com
Web site: http://www.informafinance.com
ISSN: 0268-9865
Publisher: Informa PLC
Date Established: 1986
Frequency: 10 issues yearly
Annual Sub.: £230.00
Usual Pagination: 8
Editor: Frida Fischer; **Publisher:** Victoria Ophield
Summary of Content: Journal offering advice on effective tax planning and law relating to agricultural land.
Readership/Target Audience: Aimed at professionals in agriculture, commercial and service companies and solicitors. Also includes those involved in financial services and central government.
ADVERTISING: No Advertising taken
BUSINESS: FINANCE & ECONOMICS: Taxation

THE FARMER
37893U21J-125

Editorial Address: Waterloo Road, Ketley, TELFORD, TF1 5HU **Tel:** 01952 288889 **Fax:** 01952 254605
Email: thefarmer@shropshirestar.co.uk
Advertising Address: Chronicle House, Castle Foregate, SHREWSBURY, SY1 2DN **Tel:** 01743 248248
Fax: 01743 343350
Email: jphillips@shropshirestar.co.uk
Web site: http://www.thefarmer.com
Publisher: Shropshire Newspapers Ltd
Date Established: 1980
Frequency: Monthly - Published around the 2nd Friday of the cover month
Cover Price: £0.65
Free to qualifying individuals
Circulation: 15,000 (Publisher's Statement)
Usual Pagination: 24
Editor: Heather Jones; **Managing Director:** Steve Brown; **Advertising Manager:** John Phillips
Summary of Content: Magazine covering news and information on the regional, national and rural agricultural scene.
Readership/Target Audience: Aimed at regional farmers.
ADVERTISING RATES:
SCC £7.75
Copy instructions: Copy Date: 1 week prior to publication date
BUSINESS: AGRICULTURE & FARMING: Agriculture & Farming - Regional

FARMERS CLUB JOURNAL
37762U21A-407

Editorial Address: 3 Whitehall Court, LONDON, SW1A 2EL
Tel: 020 7930 3751 **Fax:** 020 7839 7864
Email: don.gomery@btinternet.com
Advertising Address: As above.
Email: don.gomery@btinternet.com
Web site: http://www.thefarmersclub.com
Publisher: Farmers Club Journal
Date Established: 1875
Frequency: 6 issues yearly
Cover Price: £2.00
Free to qualifying individuals
Annual Sub.: £12.00
Circulation: 6,000 (Publisher's Statement)
Usual Pagination: 24
Editor: Don Gomery; **Advertising Manager:** Don Gomery
Summary of Content: Journal covering Club meetings and events, supplemented by technical articles from leading authorities on agricultural matters.
Readership/Target Audience: Circulated to members of the Farmers' Club in the UK and overseas.
ADVERTISING RATES:
Full Page Colour £480.00
Mechanical Data: Type Area: 394 x 252mm, Col Length: 394mm, Page Width: 252mm, Trim Size: 296 x 207mm, Film: Digital
Copy instructions: Copy Date: 4 weeks prior to publication date
Average advertising content per issue: 5%
BUSINESS: AGRICULTURE & FARMING

FARMERS GUARDIAN
37895U21A-415

Editorial Address: Unit 4, Fulwood Business Park, Caxton Road, Fulwood, PRESTON, PR2 9NZ **Tel:** 01772 799411
Fax: 01772 654987
Email: fgeditorial@ubm.com
Advertising Address: As above. **Tel:** 0800 279 9428
Fax: 01772 655190
Email: angela.hughes@ubm.com
Web site: http://www.farmersguardian.com
Publisher: UBM Information (Preston)
Frequency: Weekly
Cover Price: £1.40
Annual Sub.: £52.00

Circulation: 51,668 (ABC 01/01/2008 to 31/12/2008)
Editor: Vickie Rogers; **News Editor:** Vickie Rogers;
Features Editor: Danusia Osiowy
Summary of Content: Newspaper covering all aspects of agriculture.
Twitter: https://twitter.com/FarmersGuardian.
Readership/Target Audience: Read by farmers and agriculturalists.
ADVERTISING RATES:
Full Page Mono £2320.00
Full Page Colour £2904.00
Agency Commission: 10%
Mechanical Data: Type Area: 330 x 262mm, Col Length: 330mm, Page Width: 262mm, Col Widths (Display): 42mm, No. of Columns (Display): 6, Film: Digital
Copy instructions: Copy Date: 2 weeks prior to publication date
Average advertising content per issue: 40%
BUSINESS: AGRICULTURE & FARMING

FARMERS GUIDE
37896U21J-140_30

Editorial Address: Parkside, London Road, IPSWICH, IP2 0SS **Tel:** 01473 691888 **Fax:** 01473 691886
Email: jane@farmersguide.co.uk
Advertising Address: As above.
Email: studio@farmersguide.co.uk
Web site: http://www.farmersguide.co.uk
Publisher: Earlybird Farming Publications Ltd
Date Established: 1979
Frequency: Monthly
Cover Price: Free
Circulation: 30,000 (Publisher's Statement)
Usual Pagination: 144
Editor: Jane Potts; **Advertising Manager:** Norma Ostler
Summary of Content: Publication covering farm machinery (including comprehensive used machinery section). Also carries regular grain, fertiliser, seed and agrochemical articles, together with topical and company profiles.
Readership/Target Audience: Aimed at those who work and buy within the agricultural industry from Yorkshire to the Channel, Herefordshire to the East Coast covering 27 counties in total.
ADVERTISING RATES:
Full Page Mono £729.00
Full Page Colour £850.00
SCC £7.30
Agency Commission: 10%
Mechanical Data: Type Area: 277 x 190mm, Col Length: 277mm, Bleed Size: 305 x 218mm, Trim Size: 297 x 210mm, Page Width: 190mm, Film: Digital
Average advertising content per issue: 70%
BUSINESS: AGRICULTURE & FARMING: Agriculture & Farming - Regional

FARMERS MART MAGAZINE
1804468U21A-1119

Editorial Address: Office 1, 40 Stockhill Road, BRADFORD, BD10 9AX **Tel:** 01274 610101 **Fax:** 01274 621730
Email: simone@farmers-mart.co.uk
Advertising Address: As above.
Email: benwalton@fencing-news.co.uk
Web site: http://www.farmers-mart.co.uk
Publisher: Little Red Marketing Ltd
Date Established: 2006
Frequency: Quarterly
Annual Sub.: £12.00
Circulation: 8,000 (Publisher's Statement)
Usual Pagination: 80
Editor: Simone Gallon
Summary of Content: Magazine featuring new products, machinery and show time diary. Each issue profiles winning farmers and leading auction marts.
Readership/Target Audience: Read by farmers, feed merchants and machinery dealers.
ADVERTISING RATES:
Full Page Colour £450.00
Mechanical Data: Type Area: 264 x 186mm, Col Length: 264mm, Page Width: 186mm, Film: Digital
BUSINESS: AGRICULTURE & FARMING

FARMERS WEEKLY
37763U21A-430

Editorial Address: Quadrant House, The Quadrant, SUTTON, SM2 5AS **Tel:** 020 8652 4911 **Fax:** 020 8652 4005
Email: farmers.weekly@rbi.co.uk
Advertising Address: As above. **Tel:** 020 8652 3500
Fax: 020 8652 4043
Email: vic.bunby@rbi.co.uk
Web site: http://www.fwi.co.uk
ISSN: 0014-8474
Publisher: Reed Business Information
Date Established: 1934
Frequency: Weekly - Published on Friday
Cover Price: £2.25
Annual Sub.: £116.00
Circulation: 68,461 (ABC 01/01/2008 to 31/12/2008)
Editor: Avril Samuel; **News Editor:** Jonathan Riley;
Advertisement Director: Vic Bunby

Summary of Content: Journal covering news, business advice and research within the agricultural industry.
Twitter: https://twitter.com/FarmersWeekly.
Readership/Target Audience: Aimed at farmers, farm managers and agricultural suppliers.
ADVERTISING RATES:
Full Page Colour £3750.00
Mechanical Data: Type Area: 271 x 190mm, Col Length: 271mm, Trim Size: 297 x 210mm, Bleed Size: 303 x 213mm, Film: Positive, right reading, emulsion side down. Digital, Page Width: 190mm
Copy instructions: Copy Date: 2 weeks prior to publication date
BUSINESS: AGRICULTURE & FARMING

THE FARMERS WEEKLY AGRICULTURAL REGISTER
37790U21A-431

Editorial Address: Windsor Court, East Grinstead House, EAST GRINSTEAD, RH19 1XA **Tel:** 01342 335861
Fax: 01342 336113
Email: agregisterenquiries@reedinfo.co.uk
Advertising Address: As above. **Fax:** 01342 335906
Email: harvey.osborn@reedinfo.co.uk
Web site: http://www.fwi.co.uk
Publisher: Reed Business Information
Date Established: 1996
Cover Price: £35.00
Circulation: 10,000 (Publisher's Statement)
Usual Pagination: 350
Editor: Pat Hewson; **Publisher:** Richard Price
Summary of Content: Buyers guide for the farming industry covering lists of suppliers and services.
Readership/Target Audience: Aimed at farmers within the top 10,000 farms.
ADVERTISING: Rates on application
Agency Commission: 10%
Copy instructions: Copy Date: 12 weeks prior to publication date
Average advertising content per issue: 20%
BUSINESS: AGRICULTURE & FARMING

FARMING LIFE
37764U21J-347

Editorial Address: 2 Esky Drive, Carn Industrial Estate, Portadown, CRAIGAVON, BT63 5YY **Tel:** 028 3839 5593
Fax: 028 3839 5599
Email: david.mccoy@farminglife.com
Advertising Address: As above. **Tel:** 028 3839 3939
Fax: 028 3839 3940
Email: kim.white@jpress.co.uk
Web site: http://www.farminglife.com
Publisher: Johnston Press
Frequency: 104 issues yearly - Published on Wednesday and Saturday
Cover Price: Free
Circulation: 42,000 (Publisher's Statement)
Usual Pagination: 70
Editor: David McCoy
Summary of Content: Magazine covering all aspects of the farming industry including development, news and advice.
Readership/Target Audience: Read by farmers in Northern Ireland.
ADVERTISING RATES:
SCC £9.55
Agency Commission: 10%
Mechanical Data: Col Widths (Display): 31.5mm, No. of Columns (Display): 8, Page Width: 265mm, Film: Digital, Type Area: 340 x 265mm, Col Length: 340mm
Copy instructions: Copy Date: Thursday 4pm prior to publication date
Average advertising content per issue: 50%
Supplement to: News Letter
BUSINESS: AGRICULTURE & FARMING: Agriculture & Farming - Regional

FARMING MONTHLY NATIONAL
37898U21A-1103

Formerly: Farming Monthly
Editorial Address: 15-17 Dugdale Street, NUNEATON, CV11 5QJ **Tel:** 024 7635 3537 **Fax:** 024 7635 3571
Email: editor@farmingmonthly.com
Advertising Address: As above.
Email: sales@farmingmonthly.com
Web site: http://www.farmingmonthly.com
Publisher: Farming Monthly Ltd
Date Established: 1997
Frequency: Monthly
Cover Price: Free
Circulation: 20,000 (Publisher's Statement)
Usual Pagination: 64
Editor: Melvyn Chapman; **Advertising Manager:** Shona Beedham; **Publisher:** Shona Beedham
Summary of Content: Journal covering all aspects of farming.
Readership/Target Audience: Aimed at farmers and associated industries.

ADVERTISING RATES:
Full Page Mono £740.00
Full Page Colour £740.00
Agency Commission: 10%
Mechanical Data: Trim Size: 280 x 200mm, Bleed Size: 286 x 206mm, Film: Digital
Copy instructions: Copy Date: 26th of the month prior to publication date
Average advertising content per issue: 50%
BUSINESS: AGRICULTURE & FARMING

FARMING SCOTLAND MAGAZINE
1789334U21A-1118

Editorial Address: Tolastadh, 18 Corsie Drive, Kinnoull, PERTH, PH2 7BU **Tel:** 01738 639747
Email: mail@farmingscotlandmagazine.com
Advertising Address: As above.
Web site: http://www.farmingscotlandmagazine.com
Publisher: Athole Design and Publishing Ltd
Date Established: 1984
Frequency: 6 issues yearly
Cover Price: Free
Circulation: 7,000 (Print Run)
Usual Pagination: 32
Editor: Athole Murray Fleming; **Advertising Manager:** Athole Murray Fleming
Summary of Content: Publication covering arable, livestock and machinery farming news with advisory columns, topical features and company profiles.
Readership/Target Audience: Aimed at the Scottish farming community.
ADVERTISING RATES:
Full Page Mono £525.00
Full Page Colour £675.00
Mechanical Data: Type Area: 276 x 188mm, Bleed Size: 303 x 213mm, Col Length: 276mm, Page Width: 188mm
BUSINESS: AGRICULTURE & FARMING

FARMING WALES YR AMAETHWR
37901U21J-142

Editorial Address: Agriculture House, Royal Welsh Showground, BUILTH WELLS, LD2 3TU **Tel:** 01982 554200
Fax: 01982 554201
Email: sarah.jones@nfu.org.uk
Advertising Address: Media Wales Ltd, Thomson House, Havelock Street, CARDIFF, CF10 1XR **Tel:** 029 2058 3651
Fax: 029 2058 3586
Email: abigail.nation@mediawales.co.uk
Web site: http://www.nfu-cymru.org.uk
Publisher: Associa Ltd
Frequency: 10 issues yearly
Free to qualifying individuals
Circulation: 14,000 (Publisher's Statement)
Usual Pagination: 36
Editor: Sarah Jones; **Advertising Manager:** Abigail Nation
Summary of Content: Newspaper of the National Farmers Union Wales.
Language(s): English; Welsh
Readership/Target Audience: Aimed at NFU members in Wales.
ADVERTISING: Rates on application
BUSINESS: AGRICULTURE & FARMING: Agriculture & Farming - Regional

FARMINGUK
1616347U21A-1104

Editorial Address: PO Box 75, BRIGHOUSE, HD6 3WF
Tel: 01484 400666 **Fax:** 01484 400661
Email: keith@farminguk.com
Advertising Address: As above.
Email: keith@farminguk.com
Web site: http://www.farminguk.com
Publisher: Breezi Publishing Ltd
Date Established: 2002
Frequency: Quarterly
Free to qualifying individuals
Circulation: 10,000 (Publisher's Statement)
Usual Pagination: 32
Editor: Keith Wild; **Advertising Manager:** Keith Wild;
Publisher: Keith Wild
Summary of Content: Magazine containing features, profiles, news and information on farmers and farming activities from shows to new machinery.
Readership/Target Audience: Aimed at farmers.
ADVERTISING RATES:
Full Page Colour £850.00
Agency Commission: 10%
Mechanical Data: Type Area: 196 x 138mm, Trim Size: 240 x 170mm, Col Length: 196mm, Page Width: 138mm, Film: Digital
Average advertising content per issue: 30%
BUSINESS: AGRICULTURE & FARMING

FARMLAND MARKET
37787U21A-465

Editorial Address: Quadrant House, The Quadrant, SUTTON, SM2 5AS **Tel:** 020 8652 4920 **Fax:** 020 8652 4926
Email: ian.ashbridge@rbi.co.uk
Advertising Address: As above. **Tel:** 020 8652 3500
Email: ian.ashbridge@rbi.co.uk
Publisher: Reed Business Information
Date Established: 1974
Frequency: Half-yearly - Spring and Autumn
Annual Sub.: £95.00
Circulation: 500 (Publisher's Statement)
Usual Pagination: 70
Editor: Ian Ashbridge; **Advertising Manager:** Ian Ashbridge;
Publisher: Trevor Parker
Summary of Content: Journal containing reports on the sales of farms and farmland and specific changes within the land market.
Readership/Target Audience: Aimed at surveyors, institutional bodies and pension fund managers, large acreage farmers and rural consultants.
ADVERTISING RATES:
Full Page Mono £1000.00
Full Page Colour £1000.00
Mechanical Data: Trim Size: 297 x 210mm, Film: Digital
BUSINESS: AGRICULTURE & FARMING

FARMWEEK
37769U21J-349

Editorial Address: 113-117 Donegall Street, BELFAST, BT1 2GE **Tel:** 028 9033 4480 **Fax:** 028 9033 4481
Email: fweditorial@farmweek.com
Advertising Address: As above.
Email: d.murphy@farmweek.com
Web site: http://www.farmweek.com
Publisher: Irish News Ltd
Date Established: 1961
Frequency: Weekly - Published on Friday
Cover Price: £1.00
Circulation: 10,528 (ABC 01/01/2008 to 31/12/2008)
Usual Pagination: 80
Editor: Robert Irwin; **Advertising Manager:** Diane Murphy
Summary of Content: Tabloid containing features on farming in Northern Ireland.
Readership/Target Audience: Aimed at the farming community and equestrian enthusiasts in Northern Ireland and the Border Counties of Ireland.
ADVERTISING RATES:
Full Page Colour £3032.00
Agency Commission: 15%
Mechanical Data: Film: Digital, Type Area: 340 x 265mm, Col Length: 340mm, Page Width: 265mm
Copy instructions: Copy Date: 1 week prior to publication date
BUSINESS: AGRICULTURE & FARMING: Agriculture & Farming - Regional

FASHION THEORY
39494U47A-130

Editorial Address: 1st Floor, Angel Court, 81 St. Clements Street, OXFORD, OX4 1AW **Tel:** 01865 245104
Fax: 01865 791165
Email: enquiry@bergpublishers.com
Advertising Address: As above.
Email: enquiry@bergpublishers.com
Web site: http://www.fashiontheory.com
ISSN: 1362-704X
Publisher: Berg Publishers
Date Established: 1997
Frequency: Quarterly
Annual Sub.: £46.00
Circulation: 1,000 (Publisher's Statement)
Usual Pagination: 200
Editor: Corina Kapinos; **Managing Director:** Kathryn Earle
Summary of Content: Journal of dress, body and culture, providing an interdisciplinary forum for the analysis of cultural phenomena.
Readership/Target Audience: Aimed at fashion historians, fashion students and those interested in fashion.
ADVERTISING RATES:
Full Page Mono £325.00
Mechanical Data: Trim Size: 230 x 160mm, Type Area: 218 x 150mm, Bleed Size: 244 x 172mm, Col Length: 218mm, Page Width: 150mm
Copy instructions: Copy Date: 3 months prior to publication date
Average advertising content per issue: 2%
BUSINESS: CLOTHING & TEXTILES

FAST FASTENING ADHESIVES ASSEMBLY & JOINING TECHNOLOGY
37610U19B-275

Editorial Address: Crendon House, Crendon Industrial Park, LONG CRENDON, HP18 9BB **Tel:** 01844 202027
Fax: 01844 202267
Email: editor@fastmagazine.co.uk
Advertising Address: As above.
Web site: http://www.fastmagazine.co.uk

Publisher: NewbyCom Ltd
Date Established: 1995
Frequency: Quarterly
Cover Price: Free
Circulation: 5,964 (Publisher's Statement)
Usual Pagination: 36
Editor: Bob Brooks; **Managing Director:** Mark Newby;
Advertising Manager: Mark Newby
Summary of Content: Magazine dedicated to fastening, adhesives, assembly and joining technology to aid design and production personnel in choosing fastening methods and types in all areas of manufacture from concept to design and production.
Readership/Target Audience: Aimed at the manufacturing industry.
ADVERTISING RATES:
Full Page Colour £1895.00
Agency Commission: 10%
Mechanical Data: Page Width: 187mm, Type Area: 267 x 187mm, Bleed Size: 303 x 216mm, Trim Size: 297 x 210mm, Col Length: 267mm, Film: Digital
Copy instructions: Copy Date: 3 weeks prior to publication date
BUSINESS: ENGINEERING & MACHINERY: Engineering - Design

FAST FERRY INTERNATIONAL
36405U6E-100

Editorial Address: 14 Marston Gate, WINCHESTER, SO23 7DS **Tel:** 01962 869842 **Fax:** 01962 843863
Email: fastferry@fastferryinfo.com
Advertising Address: As above.
Email: helen@fastferryinfo.com
Web site: http://www.fastferryinfo.com
ISSN: 0954-3988
Publisher: Fast Ferry Information Ltd
Date Established: 1961
Frequency: 10 issues yearly
Annual Sub.: £75.00 (UK & Europe)
Circulation: 1,000 (Publisher's Statement)
Usual Pagination: 40
Editor: Alan Blunden; **Advertising Manager:** Helen Bliault
Summary of Content: Magazine covering new fast ferry designs and components, fast ferry operations worldwide, company profiles, conference reports and annual statistics.
Readership/Target Audience: Aimed at senior management and professionals, fast ferry operators, builders, suppliers and consultants.
ADVERTISING RATES:
Full Page Mono £1230.00
Full Page Colour £1760.00
Agency Commission: 10%
Mechanical Data: Type Area: 260 x 180mm, Bleed Size: 303 x 216mm, Trim Size: 297 x 210mm, Film: Digital, Col Length: 260mm, Page Width: 180mm, Print Process: Offset litho
Copy instructions: Copy Date: 3 weeks prior to publication date
Average advertising content per issue: 20%
BUSINESS: AVIATION & AERONAUTICS: Hovercraft VTOL

FASTENER & FIXING MAGAZINE
633869U19A-275

Formerly: Fastener & Fixing Europe
Editorial Address: 18 Alban Park, Hatfield Road, ST. ALBANS, AL4 0JJ **Tel:** 01727 739150 **Fax:** 01727 831033
Email: editor@fastfair.net
Advertising Address: As above.
Email: jamie@fastfair.net
Web site: http://www.fastenerfair.com
Publisher: Fastener Fairs Limited
Date Established: 1998
Frequency: 6 issues yearly
Free to qualifying individuals
Annual Sub.: £60.00
Circulation: 13,500 (Print Run)
Usual Pagination: 120
Editor: Phil Matten; **Advertising Director:** Jamie Mitchell;
Publisher: Jeremy Ramsdale
Summary of Content: Magazine covering industry news for the European industrial fastener and fixing market, new products, trade fair reviews, factory profiles, technical articles and product applications including automotive, marine, aeronautical, construction, building, architectural, engineering and manufacturing.
Readership/Target Audience: Aimed at European trade readers involved or closely related to the industrial fastener, fixing and tool industry.
ADVERTISING RATES:
Full Page Colour £1550.00
Agency Commission: 10%
Mechanical Data: Type Area: 277 x 190mm, Col Length: 277mm, Page Width: 190mm, Trim Size: 297 x 210mm, Film: Digital, Bleed Size: +3mm
Copy instructions: Copy Date: 4 weeks prior to publication date
Average advertising content per issue: 50%
BUSINESS: ENGINEERING & MACHINERY

FASTFORWARD
1812713U10-220

Editorial Address: Roadway House, 35 Monument Hill, WEYBRIDGE, KT13 8RN **Tel:** 01932 814515
Fax: 01932 852516
Email: peter.shakespeare@rha.uk.net
Advertising Address: As above. **Tel:** 01932 841515
Fax: 01932 846989
Email: nick.payne@rha.uk.net
Web site: http://www.fastforwardcareers.co.uk
ISSN: 1753-190X
Publisher: Roadway Publishing
Date Established: 2007
Frequency: Quarterly
Free to qualifying individuals
Annual Sub.: £10.00
Circulation: 30,000 (Print Run)
Usual Pagination: 52
Editor: Peter Shakespeare; **Managing Editor:** Peter Shakespeare
Summary of Content: Magazine focusing on training, skills and careers within the UK's freight transport and logistics industry.
Readership/Target Audience: Aimed at the managerial levels within road haulage and logistics companies, training providers, recruitment companies, and HR professionals. Special supplements are aimed at school and college leavers, the unemployed and service personnel leaving the armed forces.
ADVERTISING RATES:
Full Page Colour £1200.00
Agency Commission: 10%
Mechanical Data: Type Area: 275 x 190mm, Bleed Size: 303 x 216mm, Trim Size: 297 x 210mm, Col Length: 275mm, Page Width: 190mm, Film: Digital
Copy instructions: Copy Date: 2 weeks prior to publication date
Average advertising content per issue: 40%
BUSINESS: MATERIALS HANDLING

FAULTLINE
1642085U5F-381

Editorial Address: 1 Wide Lane Close, BROCKENHURST, SO42 7TU **Tel:** 01590 624530 **Fax:** 020 7900 2225
Email: peter@rethinkresearch.biz
Web site: http://www.rethinkresearch.biz
Publisher: Rethink Research Associates
Date Established: 2003
Frequency: Weekly
Annual Sub.: £1000.00
Usual Pagination: 30
Editor: Peter White
Summary of Content: Magazine covering digital media, digital broadcasting, digital rights management, codecs, IP TV, HD TV, set-tops, online music services, games consoles, interactive TV and mobile entertainment.
Readership/Target Audience: Aimed at broadcasters, TV and film production companies, technology suppliers and consumer electronics companies.
ADVERTISING: No Advertising taken
BUSINESS: COMPUTERS & AUTOMATION: Multimedia

F.C. BUSINESS
1655665U32H-459

Editorial Address: Baltic Business Centre, Saltmeadows Road, GATESHEAD, NE8 3DA **Tel:** 0191 442 4001
Fax: 0191 442 4002
Email: ryan@fcbusiness.co.uk
Advertising Address: As above.
Email: paulfoster@fcbusiness.co.uk
Web site: http://www.fcbusiness.co.uk
Publisher: Baltic Publications Ltd
Date Established: 2004
Frequency: 8 issues yearly
Cover Price: £2.95
Free to qualifying individuals
Circulation: 45,000 (Publisher's Statement)
Usual Pagination: 60
Editor: Ryan McKnight
Summary of Content: Magazine focusing on good practices in all areas involved in running a football club.
Readership/Target Audience: Aimed at chairmen of football clubs and business people involved in football.
ADVERTISING RATES:
Full Page Colour £3995.00
Agency Commission: 10%
Mechanical Data: Film: Digital, Type Area: 277 x 190mm, Col Length: 277mm, Page Width: 190mm, Bleed Size: 303 x 216mm, Trim Size: 297 x 210mm, Print Process: Web offset litho
Average advertising content per issue: 50%
BUSINESS: LOCAL GOVERNMENT, LEISURE & RECREATION: Leisure, Recreation & Entertainment

FCS BULLETIN
36224U5E-350

Formerly: FCS
Editorial Address: Burnhill Business Centre, Provident House, Burrell Row, BECKENHAM, BR3 1AT
Tel: 020 8249 6363 **Fax:** 0844 870 5927

Email: jbrookes@fcs.org.uk
Advertising Address: As above. **Fax:** 0870 120 5927
Email: fcs@fcs.org.uk
Web site: http://www.fcs.org.uk
Publisher: The Federation of Communication Services Ltd
Date Established: 1990
Frequency: 3 issues yearly
Free to qualifying individuals
Circulation: 1,500 (Publisher's Statement)
Usual Pagination: 8
Editor: Jacqui Brookes; **Advertising Manager:** Christine Warwick
Summary of Content: Information bulletin detailing industry news.
Readership/Target Audience: Aimed at FCS members.
ADVERTISING: Rates on application
BUSINESS: COMPUTERS & AUTOMATION: Data Transmission

FD
1638552U22A-382

Editorial Address: Progressive House, 2 Maidstone Road, SIDCUP, DA14 5HZ **Tel:** 0845 000 2500
Email: sheilae@dewberryredpoint.co.uk
Advertising Address: As above.
Email: danielh@dewberryredpoint.co.uk
Web site: http://www.fdaonline.co.uk
Publisher: Dewberry Redpoint Ltd
Date Established: 2003
Frequency: Quarterly
Free to qualifying individuals
Annual Sub.: £40.00
Circulation: 5,000 (Publisher's Statement)
Editor: Sheila Eggleston; **Advertising Manager:** Daniel Hillman
Summary of Content: Magazine of the Food Development Association providing information on new trends, developments and activities in the food development industry.
Readership/Target Audience: Aimed at food and menu developers.
ADVERTISING RATES:
Full Page Colour £2500.00
Agency Commission: 10%
Mechanical Data: Bleed Size: 303 x 216mm, Trim Size: 297 x 210mm, Film: Digital, Type Area: 268 x 186mm, Col Length: 268mm, Page Width: 186mm
Copy instructions: Copy Date: 6 weeks prior to publication date
Average advertising content per issue: 40%
BUSINESS: FOOD

FD LEGAL
1792879U44-3046

Editorial Address: 266-276 Upper Richmond Road, LONDON, SW15 6TQ **Tel:** 020 8785 5938
Fax: 020 8785 9373
Email: jlee@ark-group.com
Advertising Address: As above. **Tel:** 020 8785 2700
Email: jadams@ark-group.com
Web site: http://www.fd-legal.com
ISSN: 1752-8011
Publisher: Ark Group Ltd
Date Established: 2006
Frequency: 6 issues yearly
Annual Sub.: £245.00
Circulation: 1,500 (Publisher's Statement)
Editor: Joanna Lee
Summary of Content: Publication containing case studies and articles covering all aspects of financial management in law firms.
Readership/Target Audience: Aimed at financial managers and finance departments within law firms.
ADVERTISING RATES:
Full Page Colour £1995.00
Agency Commission: 10%
Mechanical Data: Type Area: 235 x 175mm, Bleed Size: 271 x 211mm, Trim Size: 265 x 205mm, Col Length: 235mm, Page Width: 175mm, Film: Digital
Copy instructions: Copy Date: 10th of the month prior to publication date
Average advertising content per issue: 30%
BUSINESS: LEGAL

FDI
1656959U1F-585

Editorial Address: 1 Southwark Bridge, LONDON, SE1 9HL
Tel: 020 7873 3000
Email: courtney.fingar@ft.com
Advertising Address: As above.
Email: charlotte.lloyd@ft.com
Web site: http://www.fdimagazine.com
Publisher: FT Group
Date Established: 2001
Frequency: 6 issues yearly
Free to qualifying individuals
Circulation: 15,000 (ABC 01/07/2008 to 30/06/2009)
Editor: Courtney Fingar; **Editor-in-Chief:** Brian Caplen;
Advertising Manager: Charlotte Lloyd

Summary of Content: Magazine covering all aspects of foreign direct investment world-wide.
Readership/Target Audience: Aimed at senior company executives.
ADVERTISING RATES:
Full Page Colour £6950.00
Mechanical Data: Trim Size: 297 x 210mm, Film: Digital, Bleed Size: 303 x 216mm
Copy instructions: Copy Date: 25th of the month prior to publication date
BUSINESS: FINANCE & ECONOMICS: Investment

FE FOOTWEAR AND FASHION EXTRAS
39790U52D-25

Formerly: Fashion Extras
Editorial Address: The Old Town Hall, Lewisham Road, Slaithwaite, HUDDERSFIELD, HD7 5AL **Tel:** 01484 846069
Fax: 01484 846232
Email: christina@ras-publishing.com
Advertising Address: As above.
Email: sharon@ras-publishing.com
Web site: http://www.ras-publishing.com
ISSN: 0264-8555
Publisher: RAS Publishing Ltd
Date Established: 1917
Frequency: 10 issues yearly
Circulation: 5,000 (Publisher's Statement)
Editor: Christina Williams
Summary of Content: Magazine covering fashion accessories, leather goods, luggage, footwear, costume jewellery and all wearable accessories.
Readership/Target Audience: Aimed at retailers, manufacturers, distributors, agents, decision-makers and independent and multiple buyers within the fashion industry.
ADVERTISING RATES:
Full Page Colour £1932.00
SCC £22.00
Agency Commission: 10%
Mechanical Data: Film: Digital, Bleed Size: 322 x 249mm, Trim Size: 316 x 243mm, Type Area: 292 x 219mm, Col Length: 292mm, Page Width: 219mm, No. of Columns (Display): 4
Average advertising content per issue: 50%
BUSINESS: GIFT TRADE: Leather

FEED COMPOUNDER
37803U21B-150

Editorial Address: Station Road, Great Longstone, BAKEWELL, DE45 1TS **Tel:** 01629 640941
Fax: 01629 640588
Email: mail@pentlandspublishing.com
Advertising Address: As above.
Email: mail@feedcompounder.com
Web site: http://www.pentlandspublishing.com
ISSN: 0950-771X
Publisher: Pentlands Publishing Ltd
Date Established: 1981
Frequency: 11 issues yearly - Published on the 28th of the month prior to cover month
Cover Price: £10.00
Annual Sub.: £75.00
Circulation: 2,300 (Publisher's Statement)
Usual Pagination: 48
Editor: Andrew Mounsey
Summary of Content: Journal covering all aspects of the animal feed industry. Includes economics, transport, health, nutrition, plant and equipment.
Readership/Target Audience: Read by feed manufacturers of the animal industry and their suppliers.
ADVERTISING RATES:
Full Page Mono £850.00
Full Page Colour £1350.00
Agency Commission: 10%
Mechanical Data: Trim Size: 297 x 210mm, Bleed Size: 300 x 213mm, Col Length: 254mm, No. of Columns (Display): 3, Type Area: 254 x 178mm, Page Width: 178mm, Film: Digital
Average advertising content per issue: 25%
Supplement(s): Pet Food Supplement - 1xY
BUSINESS: AGRICULTURE & FARMING: Agriculture - Supplies & Services

FEED INTERNATIONAL
37804U21B-200

Editorial Address: Lavant House, Lavant Street, PETERSFIELD, GU32 3EL **Tel:** 01730 262200
Fax: 01730 262201
Email: pbest@wattnet.net
Advertising Address: Albast 25, 2719 TV ZOETERMEER
Tel: 79 32 30 782 **Fax:** 79 32 30 783
Email: driesmvd@xs4all.nl
Web site: http://www.feedindustrynetwork.com
ISSN: 0274-5771
Publisher: Watt Publishing Co
Date Established: 1981
Frequency: 10 issues yearly - Published in the 1st week of the cover month
Free to qualifying individuals
Circulation: 19,000 (Publisher's Statement)

Usual Pagination: 44
Editor: Peter Best
Summary of Content: Journal covering all aspects of the livestock and poultry feed industry.
Readership/Target Audience: Aimed at feed manufacturers and allied professionals.
ADVERTISING RATES:
Full Page Colour $7895.00
Mechanical Data: Type Area: 254 x 178mm, Bleed Size: 274 x 207mm, Trim Size: 267 x 200mm, Col Length: 254mm, Page Width: 178mm, Film: Digital
Copy instructions: Copy Date: 5th of the month prior to publication date
BUSINESS: AGRICULTURE & FARMING: Agriculture - Supplies & Services

FENCING AND LANDSCAPING NEWS
35967U4R-387

Editorial Address: Office 1, 40 Stockhill Road, BRADFORD, BD10 9AX **Tel:** 01274 610101 **Fax:** 01274 621730
Email: simone@fencing-news.co.uk
Advertising Address: As above.
Email: benwalton@fencing-news.co.uk
Web site: http://www.fencing-news.co.uk
Publisher: Little Red Marketing Ltd
Date Established: 1981
Frequency: 6 issues yearly
Cover Price: Free
Circulation: 8,000 (Publisher's Statement)
Usual Pagination: 80
Editor: Simone Gallon
Summary of Content: Magazine covering training, product developments, new products, health and safety and company profiles.
Readership/Target Audience: Read by fencing installers, contractors, merchants, retailers and manufacturers.
ADVERTISING RATES:
Full Page Colour £950.00
Agency Commission: 10%
Mechanical Data: Type Area: 265 x 180mm, Col Length: 265mm, Page Width: 180mm, Film: Digital
Copy instructions: Copy Date: 10th of the month prior to publication date
Average advertising content per issue: 60%
BUSINESS: ARCHITECTURE & BUILDING: Building Related

FERTILIZER FOCUS
36665U13-92

Editorial Address: FMB House, 6 Windmill Road, Hampton Hill, HAMPTON, TW12 1RH **Tel:** 020 8979 7866
Fax: 020 8979 4573
Email: mike.smith@fmb-group.co.uk
Advertising Address: As above.
Email: fmb@fmb-group.co.uk
Web site: http://www.fmb-group.co.uk
ISSN: 0951-1490
Publisher: FMB Consultants Ltd
Date Established: 1984
Frequency: 6 issues yearly - Published in the middle of the 1st cover month
Free to qualifying individuals
Annual Sub.: £245.00
Circulation: 2,780 (Publisher's Statement)
Usual Pagination: 52
Editor: Mike Smith; **Advertising Manager:** Mike Smith;
Managing Editor: Mike Smith
Summary of Content: Journal covering the fertilizer industry, production and use, technical and agronomic issues.
Readership/Target Audience: Aimed at fertilizer manufacturers, industrial users, intermediate suppliers, suppliers of raw materials, fertilizer purchasing organisations, trading companies and agents, financial institutions, research organisations, construction, engineering and processing companies and shipping, handling and storage companies.
ADVERTISING RATES:
Full Page Mono £1625.00
Full Page Colour £2420.00
Agency Commission: 15%
Mechanical Data: Type Area: 254 x 178mm, Film: Digital, Bleed Size: 303 x 216mm, Trim Size: 297 x 210mm, Col Length: 254mm, Page Width: 178mm
Copy instructions: Copy Date: Middle of month prior to 1st cover month
Average advertising content per issue: 30%
BUSINESS: CHEMICALS

FERTILIZER INDUSTRY DIRECTORY
37823U21B-215

Formerly: Fertilizer Yearbook
Editorial Address: Southbank House, Black Prince Road, LONDON, SE1 7SJ **Tel:** 020 7793 2567 **Fax:** 020 7793 2577
Email: tina.firman@bcinsight.com
Advertising Address: As above.
Email: tina.firman@bcinsight.com
Web site: http://www.bcinsight.com

Business Magazines

Publisher: BC Insight
Date Established: 1999
Frequency: Annual - Published in July
Annual Sub.: £205.00
Usual Pagination: 296
Editor: Tina Firman; **Advertising Manager:** Tina Firman
Summary of Content: Guide on the worlds fertilizer industry enabling you to locate the world's leading fertilizer manufacturers, discover the major fertilizer products and identifying fertilizer technology companies.
Readership/Target Audience: Aimed at all fertilizer companies.
ADVERTISING: Rates on application
BUSINESS: AGRICULTURE & FARMING: Agriculture - Supplies & Services

FERTILIZER INTERNATIONAL
36666U13-95

Editorial Address: Southbank House, Black Prince Road, LONDON, SE1 7SJ **Tel:** 020 7793 2567 **Fax:** 020 7793 2577
Email: mark.evans@bcinsight.com
Advertising Address: As above.
Email: tina.firman@bcinsight.com
Web site: http://www.britishsulphur.com
Publisher: BC Insight
Frequency: 6 issues yearly - Published in the 1st week of the 1st cover month
Annual Sub.: £270.00
Usual Pagination: 56
Editor: Mark Evans; **Advertising Manager:** Tina Firman
Summary of Content: Journal analysing news in the world fertilizer markets.
Readership/Target Audience: Aimed at manufacturers, transporters, traders, government departments and agronomic institutions.
ADVERTISING RATES:
Full Page Mono £1250.00
Full Page Colour £2000.00
Agency Commission: 15%
Mechanical Data: Col Length: 254mm, Page Width: 178mm, Film: Digital, Type Area: 254 x 178mm, Bleed Size: 304 x 216mm, Trim Size: 297 x 210mm
Copy instructions: Copy Date: 4 weeks prior to publication date
BUSINESS: CHEMICALS

FERTILIZERWEEK
36667U13-97

Editorial Address: 31 Mount Pleasant, LONDON, WC1X 0AD **Tel:** 020 7903 2421 **Fax:** 020 7903 2139
Email: natalie.noor-drugan@crugroup.com
Web site: http://www.fertilizerweek.com
ISSN: 0951-7472
Publisher: British Sulphur Publishing
Date Established: 1987
Frequency: Weekly
Annual Sub.: £1200.00
Circulation: 500 (Publisher's Statement)
Usual Pagination: 16
Editor: Natalie Noor-Drugan; **Editor-in-Chief:** Natalie Noor-Drugan; **Managing Editor:** Magnus Berge
Summary of Content: Newsletter focusing on industry news, markets and price information on global fertilizer trade.
Readership/Target Audience: Aimed at executives, analysts and trade in all sectors of the fertilizer industry.
ADVERTISING: No Advertising taken
BUSINESS: CHEMICALS

THE FESPA WORLD
38922U41A-23

Editorial Address: Association House, 7B West Street, REIGATE, RH2 9BL **Tel:** 01623 882398 **Fax:** 01737 240770
Email: elford@btconnect.com
Advertising Address: As above. **Tel:** 01737 240788
Fax: 01737 233734
Email: info@fespa.com
Web site: http://www.fespa.com
Publisher: FESPA
Date Established: 1989
Frequency: Quarterly - Published in the middle of the cover month
Annual Sub.: £45.00
Circulation: 5,000 (Publisher's Statement)
Usual Pagination: 74
Editor: Val Hirst
Summary of Content: Membership magazine of the Federation of European Screen Printing Associations.
Language(s): English; French; German; Spanish
Readership/Target Audience: Aimed at all users of screen printing and wide format digital imaging and pad printing.
ADVERTISING RATES:
Full Page Colour EUR3000.00
Agency Commission: 10%
Mechanical Data: Type Area: 250 x 175mm, Film: Digital, Col Length: 250mm, Bleed Size: +3mm, Trim Size: 297 x 210mm, Page Width: 175mm, Print Process: Offset
Copy instructions: Copy Date: 1st of the month prior to publication date

Average advertising content per issue: 20%
BUSINESS: PRINTING & STATIONERY: Printing

FIBRESYSTEMS EUROPE
39963U55-53_50

Formerly: FibreSystems Europe in association with Lightwave Europe
Editorial Address: Dirac House, Temple Back, BRISTOL, BS1 6BE **Tel:** 0117 929 7481 **Fax:** 0117 930 1178
Email: pauline.rigby@iop.org
Advertising Address: As above.
Email: mattias.persson@iop.org
Web site: www.fibresystems.org
ISSN: 1472-3638
Publisher: IOP Publishing
Date Established: 1996
Frequency: 6 issues yearly
Cover Price: Free
Circulation: 15,000 (Publisher's Statement)
Usual Pagination: 50
Editor: Pauline Rigby; **Publisher:** Susan Curtis
Summary of Content: European magazine dedicated to fibre optic and optical networking, covering components, modules and systems, along with associated industries like test and measurement and network installation.
Readership/Target Audience: Aimed at managers and engineers working in the optical communications industry within Western Europe.
ADVERTISING RATES:
Full Page Mono £2900.00
Full Page Colour £3900.00
Agency Commission: 10%
Mechanical Data: Type Area: 262 x 193mm, Bleed Size: 288 x 216mm, Trim Size: 282 x 213mm, No. of Columns (Display): 4, Col Length: 262mm, Film: Digital, Page Width: 193mm
Copy instructions: Copy Date: 6 weeks prior to publication date
Average advertising content per issue: 55%
BUSINESS: APPLIED SCIENCE & LABORATORIES

FIELD MARKETING AND BRAND X
1639728U2A-655

Formerly: Field Marketing
Editorial Address: 86 Sandyhurst Lane, ASHFORD, TN25 4NT **Tel:** 01233 622001
Email: frank@frankpublishing.com
Advertising Address: As above. **Tel:** 01303 812183
Fax: 01303 812634
Email: frank@frankpublishing.com
Web site: http://www.marketingchannel.co.uk
Publisher: Frank Publishing Ltd
Date Established: 2003
Frequency: Quarterly
Annual Sub.: £40.00
Circulation: 13,000 (Publisher's Statement)
Editor: Frank Wainwright; **Advertising Manager:** Frank Wainwright
Summary of Content: Magazine covering all aspects of field sales, outsourcing, merchandising and experiential marketing.
Readership/Target Audience: Aimed at sales and marketing brand managers.
ADVERTISING RATES:
Full Page Colour £2890.00
Agency Commission: 10%
Mechanical Data: Trim Size: 297 x 210mm, Bleed Size: 303 x 216mm, Type Area: 277 x 190mm, Col Length: 277mm, Page Width: 190mm, Film: Digital
Copy instructions: Copy Date: 15th of the month prior to publication date
Average advertising content per issue: 40%
BUSINESS: COMMUNICATIONS, ADVERTISING & MARKETING

FILM AND TV MONTHLY
623135U64K-558_50

Formerly: Film Monthly
Editorial Address: Zenith House, 155 Curtain Road, LONDON, EC2A 3QY **Tel:** 020 7613 2299
Fax: 020 7613 3822
Email: kerri@londonatlarge.com
Web site: http://www.londonatlarge.com
Publisher: London At Large Ltd
Frequency: Monthly
Cover Price: £40.00
Usual Pagination: 150
Editor: Kerri Darn
Summary of Content: Publication covering premieres, release dates, festivals and events for the coming year.
Readership/Target Audience: Aimed at film correspondents within the press and media.
ADVERTISING: No Advertising taken
BUSINESS: OTHER CLASSIFICATIONS: Cinema Entertainment

FILM EXTRUSION MATERIALS AND MARKETS BULLETIN
38668U35-23

Editorial Address: PO Box 14, DORKING, RH5 4YN
Tel: 01306 884473 **Fax:** 01306 884473
Email: info@datatranscripts.com
Web site: http://www.datatranscripts.com
ISSN: 1361-1623
Publisher: Data Transcripts
Date Established: 1986
Frequency: 10 issues yearly
Annual Sub.: £255.00
Circulation: 1,800 (Publisher's Statement)
Usual Pagination: 6
Editor: Lynda Crane; **Publisher:** Robert Higham;
Circulation Manager: Stella Roscoe
Summary of Content: Newsletter containing information on industry, companies, prices, film product news and supply and demand trends.
Readership/Target Audience: Aimed at packaging companies, film packaging producers in Europe and North America.
ADVERTISING: No Advertising taken
BUSINESS: PACKAGING & BOTTLING

FILTRATION+SEPARATION
37706U19R-320

Editorial Address: PO Box 150, KIDLINGTON, OX5 1AS
Tel: 01865 843000 **Fax:** 01865 843971
Email: n.dudley@elsevier.com
Advertising Address: As above. **Fax:** 01865 843973
Email: s.pye@elsevier.com
Web site: http://www.filtsep.com
ISSN: 0015-1882
Publisher: Elsevier Ltd
Date Established: 1963
Frequency: 6 issues yearly
Free to qualifying individuals
Annual Sub.: EUR258.00
Circulation: 14,093 (BPA Worldwide 01/07/2007 to 31/12/2007)
Usual Pagination: 48
Editor: Nova Dudley-Gough
Summary of Content: Magazine covering liquid, air and gas filtration and separation technologies, including industrial and product news, technical articles and trends features.
Readership/Target Audience: Read by worldwide users of filtration and separation equipment in the following market places; chemicals, pharmaceuticals, waste water treatment, fuel material extraction and processing, mining and mineral extraction and processing, food and beverage, wood pulp and paper, fresh water production, power generation and mechanical, electrical and electronic equipment production.
ADVERTISING RATES:
Full Page Colour EUR5000.00
Agency Commission: 10%
Mechanical Data: Type Area: 256 x 176mm, Col Length: 256mm, Page Width: 176mm, Trim Size: 297 x 210mm, Bleed Size: 303 x 216mm, Print Process: Sheet-fed litho, No. of Columns (Display): 4
Average advertising content per issue: 50%
Supplement(s): Desalination - 2xY, Filter Media - 2xY, Working with Water - 2xY, World Buyers' Guide & Directory - 1xY
BUSINESS: ENGINEERING & MACHINERY: Engineering Related

FILTRATION INDUSTRY ANALYST
37707U19R-330

Editorial Address: The Boulevard, Langford Lane, KIDLINGTON, OX5 1GB **Tel:** 01865 843695
Fax: 01865 843971
Email: r.reidy@elsevier.com
Web site: http://www.filtrationindustryanalyst.com
ISSN: 1365-6937
Publisher: Elsevier Ltd
Date Established: 1997
Frequency: Monthly
Annual Sub.: EUR1049.00
Usual Pagination: 16
Editor: Roisin Reidy
Summary of Content: Business newsletter containing business information on the filtration and separation industries worldwide.
Readership/Target Audience: Aimed at filtration and separation equipment manufacturers and industry analysts.
ADVERTISING: No Advertising taken
BUSINESS: ENGINEERING & MACHINERY: Engineering Related

FINANCE & CREDIT LAW
39167U44-676

Editorial Address: Telephone House, 69-77 Paul Street, LONDON, EC2A 4LQ **Tel:** 020 7017 5000
Fax: 020 7017 4135
Email: frida.fischer@informa.com
Web site: http://www.informafinance.com
ISSN: 0954-0857
Publisher: Informa PLC

Date Established: 1989
Frequency: 10 issues yearly
Annual Sub.: £599.00
Usual Pagination: 8
Editor: Frida Fischer
Summary of Content: Report containing analysis of the latest developments concerning commercial credit transactions.
Readership/Target Audience: For all those involved in credit transactions.
ADVERTISING: No Advertising taken
BUSINESS: LEGAL

FINANCE DIRECTOR EUROPE

36954U14C-70_61

Editorial Address: Brunel House, 55-57 North Wharf Road, LONDON, W2 1LA **Tel:** 020 7915 9660 **Fax:** 020 7915 9776
Email: michaeljones@spgmedia.com
Advertising Address: As above. **Fax:** 020 7915 9773
Email: sanjeevdole@spgmedia.com
Web site: http://www.the-financedirector.com
Publisher: SPG Media Ltd
Date Established: 1992
Frequency: Quarterly
Cover Price: £5.95
Free to qualifying individuals
Circulation: 11,000 (ABC 01/07/2008 to 30/06/2009)
Usual Pagination: 68
Editor: Michael Jones
Summary of Content: Magazine covering all aspects of corporate finance.
Readership/Target Audience: Aimed at financial directors and treasurers within Europe's largest corporations and banks.
ADVERTISING RATES:
Full Page Mono £6700.00
Full Page Colour £7920.00
Mechanical Data: Trim Size: 297 x 210mm
BUSINESS: COMMERCE, INDUSTRY & MANAGEMENT: International Commerce

FINANCE ON WINDOWS

601093U5B-84_30

Formerly: Insurance on Windows
Editorial Address: Tudor House, 6 Friar Lane, LEICESTER, LE1 5RA **Tel:** 0116 222 9900 **Fax:** 0116 222 9901
Email: editorial@tudor-rose.co.uk
Advertising Address: As above.
Email: info@tudor-rose.co.uk
Web site: http://www.onwindows.com
ISSN: 1473-2170
Publisher: Tudor Rose Holdings Ltd
Date Established: 2000
Frequency: Quarterly - Published in the middle of the cover month
Free to qualifying individuals
Annual Sub.: £30.00
Circulation: 15,000 (Publisher's Statement)
Usual Pagination: 50
Editor: Jacqui Griffiths; **Advertising Manager:** Amandip Singh
Summary of Content: Magazine covering industry views, advice and knowledge that highlights the business benefits for enterprise organisations using Microsoft technology.
Readership/Target Audience: Aimed at senior BDMs in enterprise organisations.
ADVERTISING RATES:
Full Page Mono £4250.00
Full Page Colour £4250.00
Agency Commission: 10%
Mechanical Data: Trim Size: 297 x 210mm, Film: Digital, Bleed Size: 303 x 216mm
Copy instructions: Copy Date: 2 weeks prior to publication date
Average advertising content per issue: 40%
BUSINESS: COMPUTERS & AUTOMATION: Data Processing

FINANCIAL ADVISER

34931U1A-140

Editorial Address: 1 Southwark Bridge, LONDON, SE1 9HL
Tel: 020 7775 3000
Email: hal.austin@ft.com
Advertising Address: As above. **Tel:** 020 7775 6614
Email: ben.bonney-james@ft.com
Web site: http://www.ftadviser.com
ISSN: 0953-5276
Publisher: FT Group
Date Established: 1987
Frequency: Weekly
Free to qualifying individuals
Annual Sub.: £99.00
Circulation: 30,957 (ABC 01/07/2008 to 30/06/2009)
Usual Pagination: 104
Editor: Hal Austin; **Features Editor:** Melanie Tringham; **Advertising Manager:** Ben Bonney-James; **Managing Editor:** Emma Ann Hughes

Summary of Content: Journal covering the life assurance, pensions, investment and mortgage markets, as well as financial regulations.
Twitter: https://twitter.com/financialtimes.
Readership/Target Audience: Aimed at professional financial advisers.
ADVERTISING RATES:
Full Page Colour £7064.00
Agency Commission: 10%
Mechanical Data: Film: Digital, Type Area: 370 x 266mm, Bleed Size: 394 x 303mm, Trim Size: 388 x 300mm, Col Length: 370mm, Page Width: 266mm
Copy instructions: Copy Date: Thursday prior to publication date
Supplement(s): FA Careers Extra - 12xY, FA Investment Extra - 12xY, FA Mortgage Extra - 24xY, FA Pensions Extra - 12xY, FA Protection Extra - 12xY
BUSINESS: FINANCE & ECONOMICS

FINANCIAL DIRECTOR

34932U1A-150

Editorial Address: 32-34 Broadwick Street, LONDON, W1A 2HG **Tel:** 020 7316 9000 **Fax:** 020 7316 9250
Email: andrew.sawers@incisivemedia.com
Advertising Address: As above. **Tel:** 020 7316 9119
Fax: 020 7316 9350
Email: preya.shah@incisivemedia.com
Web site: http://www.financialdirector.co.uk
ISSN: 0961-2556
Publisher: Incisive Media
Date Established: 1984
Frequency: 11 issues yearly
Free to qualifying individuals
Annual Sub.: £68.00
Circulation: 18,237 (ABC 01/07/2008 to 30/06/2009)
Usual Pagination: 70
Editor: Andrew Sawers; **Advertising Manager:** Preya Shah
Summary of Content: Magazine covering financial management issues, banking, accounting, regulation and corporate governance, stock markets and IT. Includes articles on general management and interviews with FTSE100/FTSE250 FDs or equivalent.
Readership/Target Audience: Aimed at financial directors, chief financial officers and financial controllers in UK companies.
ADVERTISING RATES:
Full Page Colour £4669.00
Agency Commission: 10%
Mechanical Data: Type Area: 260 x 240mm, Bleed Size: 306 x 236mm, Trim Size: 300 x 230mm, Col Length: 260mm, Film: Digital, Page Width: 240mm
Copy instructions: Copy Date: 2 weeks prior to publication date
Average advertising content per issue: 70%
BUSINESS: FINANCE & ECONOMICS

FINANCIAL I

1697204U1R-368

Editorial Address: 40 Bowling Green Lane, LONDON, EC1R 0NE **Tel:** 020 7415 7169 **Fax:** 020 7415 7172
Email: anita.hawser@financial-i.com
Advertising Address: As above.
Email: mo.isman@financial-i.com
Web site: http://www.financial-i.com
Publisher: Financial I Ltd
Frequency: Quarterly
Free to qualifying individuals
Circulation: 7,500 (Publisher's Statement)
Editor: Anita Hawser
Summary of Content: Magazine focusing on transaction banking including payment and security processing.
Readership/Target Audience: Aimed at banks, brokers, fund managers, regulators, CFOs and other corporate executives.
ADVERTISING RATES:
Full Page Mono £5000.00
Full Page Colour £6600.00
Agency Commission: 10%
Mechanical Data: Type Area: 240 x 170mm, Bleed Size: 286 x 216mm, Trim Size: 280 x 210mm, Col Length: 240mm, Page Width: 170mm, Film: Digital
Copy instructions: Copy Date: 3 weeks prior to publication date
Average advertising content per issue: 30%
BUSINESS: FINANCE & ECONOMICS: Financial Related

FINANCIAL INDUSTRY GAZETTE

765302U1R-353

Editorial Address: Room SA301, St. Andrews House, St. Andrews Street, NORWICH, NR2 4TP **Tel:** 01603 773722
Email: info@fignorfolk.com
Advertising Address: As above.
Email: admin@fignorfolk.com
Publisher: Financial Industry Gazette
Date Established: 2002
Frequency: Monthly
Cover Price: Free
Circulation: 20,000 (Publisher's Statement)
Usual Pagination: 16

Editor: Marjorie Eade; **Advertising Manager:** Marjorie Eade
Summary of Content: Magazine for the financial industry within the Norwich and Norfolk area.
Readership/Target Audience: Aimed at financial individuals, companies and service providers including training and recruitment companies.
ADVERTISING RATES:
Full Page Mono £500.00
Full Page Colour £1250.00
Mechanical Data: Type Area: 252 x 194mm, Col Length: 252mm, Page Width: 194mm, Trim Size: 297 x 210mm, Print Process: Offset litho, Film: Digital, Bleed Size: 303 x 216mm
Copy instructions: Copy Date: 4 weeks prior to publication date
BUSINESS: FINANCE & ECONOMICS: Financial Related

FINANCIAL INSTRUMENTS TAX & ACCOUNTING REVIEW

34934U1A-167

Editorial Address: Informa House, 30-32 Mortimer Street, LONDON, W1W 7RE **Tel:** 020 7017 4600
Fax: 020 7017 4135
Email: laura.brown@informa.com
Web site: http://www.informafinance.com
ISSN: 1361-3472
Publisher: Informa PLC
Date Established: 1996
Frequency: 10 issues yearly
Annual Sub.: £469.00
Circulation: 800 (Publisher's Statement)
Usual Pagination: 16
Editor: Laura Brown; **Publisher:** Nicola Whyke
Summary of Content: Newsletter focusing on the tax, accounting and regulatory aspects of treasury management.
Readership/Target Audience: Read by treasurers, tax specialists and financial directors in corporate and financial institutions.
ADVERTISING: No Advertising taken
BUSINESS: FINANCE & ECONOMICS

FINANCIAL MANAGEMENT

35044U1B-194

Formerly: Management Accounting
Editorial Address: 198 Kings Road, LONDON, SW3 5XP
Tel: 020 7368 7100 **Fax:** 020 7368 7201
Email: rp1@caspianpublishing.co.uk
Advertising Address: As above. **Tel:** 020 7368 7111
Fax: 020 7368 7112
Email: ep1@caspianpublishing.co.uk
Web site: http://www.cimaglobal.com
ISSN: 0025-1682
Publisher: Caspian Publishing
Frequency: 10 issues yearly
Free to qualifying individuals
Annual Sub.: £45.00
Circulation: 152,429 (ABC 01/07/2007 to 30/06/2008)
Usual Pagination: 64
Editor: Ruth Prickett; **Advertising Manager:** Ellen Pagliarulo
Summary of Content: Membership magazine for the chartered institute of Management Accountants. Contains articles on management accounting methods, corporate compliance/governance, ethics, technology and related issues that will enhance the knowledge and competence of financial managers in business.
Twitter: https://twitter.com/CIMA_News.
Readership/Target Audience: Aimed at part-qualified and qualified members of the Chartered Institute of Management Accountants.
ADVERTISING RATES:
Full Page Colour £5515.00
Agency Commission: 15%
Mechanical Data: Page Width: 195mm, Trim Size: 275 x 215mm, Bleed Size: 281 x 221mm, Type Area: 255 x 195mm, Col Length: 255mm, Film: Digital
Copy instructions: Copy Date: 2 weeks prior to publication date
BUSINESS: FINANCE & ECONOMICS: Accountancy

FINANCIAL NEWS

35235U1F-193

Editorial Address: 2nd Floor, Stapleton House, 29-33 Scrutton Street, LONDON, EC2A 4HU **Tel:** 020 7426 3333
Fax: 020 7426 3329
Email: news@efinancialnews.com
Advertising Address: As above.
Email: sdick@efinancialnews.com
Web site: http://www.efinancialnews.com
ISSN: 1461-1260
Publisher: Efinancialnews.com
Date Established: 1996
Frequency: Weekly
Cover Price: £6.00
Circulation: 19,772 (Publisher's Statement)
Usual Pagination: 44
Editor: Grant Clelland; **News Editor:** Dominic Elliott; **Features Editor:** Juliette Pearse; **Managing Director:** William Wright; **Advertising Manager:** Sean O'Callaghan

Summary of Content: Financial newspaper focusing on securities and investment banking.
Twitter: https://twitter.com/eFinancialNews.
Readership/Target Audience: Aimed at those involved in the securities and investment banking sector.
ADVERTISING RATES:
Full Page Colour £11600.00
Agency Commission: 10%
Mechanical Data: Type Area: 360 x 270mm, Col Length: 360mm, Page Width: 270mm, Film: Digital
Copy instructions: Copy Date: Wednesday prior to publication date
Supplement(s): Brummell - 6xY
BUSINESS: FINANCE & ECONOMICS: Investment

FINANCIAL PLANNER
1858770U1R-386

Editorial Address: Panstar House (1-2), 13-15 Swakeleys Road, UXBRIDGE, UB10 8DF **Tel:** 07725 038752
Email: newsdesk@portfoliopublishing.co.uk
Web site: http://www.portfoliopublishing.co.uk
Publisher: Portfolio Publishing, London
Date Established: 1987
Frequency: Monthly
Cover Price: £4.95
Free to qualifying individuals
Circulation: 5,246 (Publisher's Statement)
Usual Pagination: 52
Editor: Kevin O'Donnell; **Features Editor:** Stephanie Spicer; **Group Editor:** Kevin O'Donnell
Summary of Content: Official magazine of the Institute of Financial Planning.
Readership/Target Audience: Aimed at members of the Institute of Financial Planning and 3000 plus financial planners and wealth managers.
BUSINESS: FINANCE & ECONOMICS: Financial Related

FINANCIAL REGULATION INTERNATIONAL
35236U1F-195

Formerly: Financial Regulation Report
Editorial Address: Telephone House, 69-77 Paul Street, LONDON, EC2A 4LQ **Tel:** 020 7017 5000
Fax: 020 7017 4135
Email: frida.fischer@informa.com
Web site: http://www.informa.com
ISSN: 4173-3323
Publisher: Informa PLC
Frequency: 10 issues yearly
Annual Sub.: £804.00
Circulation: 300 (Publisher's Statement)
Usual Pagination: 20
Editor: Frida Fischer; **Publisher:** Victoria Ophield
Summary of Content: Publication reporting on worldwide regulatory developments and their implications for the financial services industry.
Readership/Target Audience: Read by compliance officers and law firms.
ADVERTISING: No Advertising taken
BUSINESS: FINANCE & ECONOMICS: Investment

FINANCIAL REGULATORY BRIEFING
34938U1A-174

Editorial Address: 2 Clifton Villas, LONDON, W9 2PH
Tel: 020 7289 9784 **Fax:** 020 7266 1991
Email: frb@synopsis.co.uk
Web site: http://www.frb.co.uk
ISSN: 0968-2651
Publisher: Weekend City Press Review Ltd
Date Established: 1993
Frequency: Monthly
Annual Sub.: £135.00
Circulation: 1,500 (Publisher's Statement)
Usual Pagination: 60
Editor: Lance Poynter
Summary of Content: Magazine focusing on factual statements, regulatory information and official pronouncements in the financial services sector.
Readership/Target Audience: Read by compliance officers in financial institutions and professionals involved in financial regulation.
ADVERTISING: No Advertising taken
BUSINESS: FINANCE & ECONOMICS

FINANCIAL SERVICES REVIEW
35024U1B-196

Formerly: ACCA Financial Services Newsletter
Editorial Address: 29 Lincoln's Inn Fields, LONDON, WC2A 3EE **Tel:** 020 7059 5700 **Fax:** 020 7059 5916
Email: lucy.calderwood@uk.accaglobal.com
Web site: http://www.accaglobal.com
Publisher: ACCA
Frequency: Quarterly
Cover Price: Free
Circulation: 7,000 (Publisher's Statement)
Usual Pagination: 20
Editor: Lucy Calderwood

Summary of Content: An internal newsletter covering all aspects of financial matters.
Readership/Target Audience: Aimed at members of the ACCA working in financial services.
ADVERTISING: No Advertising taken
BUSINESS: FINANCE & ECONOMICS: Accountancy

FINANCIAL SOLUTIONS
35372U1H-80

Formerly: Prospect
Editorial Address: 20 Aldermanbury, LONDON, EC2V 7HY
Tel: 020 7417 4430
Email: kevin.pratt@thepfs.org
Web site: http://www.thepfs.org
Publisher: Personal Finance Society
Date Established: 1974
Frequency: 6 issues yearly
Cover Price: £3.50
Free to qualifying individuals
Circulation: 23,000 (Publisher's Statement)
Usual Pagination: 52
Editor: Kevin Pratt
Summary of Content: Journal of the personal finance society. Provides news and comment from across the profession as well as articles on business issues, personal effectiveness, product innovations and exam preparation.
Readership/Target Audience: Aimed at members and professionals within the financial services sector.
BUSINESS: FINANCE & ECONOMICS: Pensions

FINANCIAL TIMES MANDATE
35237U1F-197

Editorial Address: 1 Southwark Bridge, LONDON, SE1 9HL
Tel: 020 7873 3000
Email: henry.smith@ft.com
Advertising Address: As above.
Email: ceri.williams@ft.com
Web site: http://www.ftmandate.com
ISSN: 1466-2469
Publisher: FT Group
Date Established: 1999
Frequency: 10 issues yearly - Published around the middle of the cover month
Free to qualifying individuals
Annual Sub.: £375.00
Circulation: 16,373 (ABC 01/07/2008 to 30/06/2009)
Usual Pagination: 24
Editor: Henry Smith; **Managing Director:** Caspar De Bono; **Publisher:** Peter Collins
Summary of Content: Newspaper providing news and commentary on new business wins in the asset management and global custody industry.
Readership/Target Audience: Aimed at buyers and sellers of asset management services.
ADVERTISING RATES:
Full Page Colour £8850.00
Agency Commission: 10%
Mechanical Data: Type Area: 370 x 266mm, Film: Digital, Bleed Size: 394 x 303mm, Col Length: 370mm, Page Width: 266mm
Copy instructions: Copy Date: 1 week prior to publication date
Average advertising content per issue: 75%
BUSINESS: FINANCE & ECONOMICS: Investment

FINANCIAL WORLD
35081U1C-170_30

Editorial Address: 5 Derby Street, LONDON, W1J 7AB
Tel: 020 7493 0173 **Fax:** 020 7493 0190
Email: editor@financialworld.co.uk
Web site: http://www.financialworld.co.uk
ISSN: 1360-4295
Publisher: The Institute of Financial Services
Date Established: 1998
Frequency: 10 issues yearly
Free to qualifying individuals
Annual Sub.: £75.00
Circulation: 27,530 (ABC 01/07/2007 to 30/06/2008)
Usual Pagination: 68
Editor: Jay Elwes; **Managing Editor:** Denise Smith
Summary of Content: Magazine containing news, features, interviews and case studies on the banking and financial services sector.
Readership/Target Audience: Aimed at members of The Chartered Institute of Bankers.
ADVERTISING: No Advertising taken
BUSINESS: FINANCE & ECONOMICS: Banking

FINE FOOD DIGEST
37966U22A-102

Formerly: Good Food Retailing
Editorial Address: Guild House, Station Road, Wincanton, SOMERSET, BA9 9FE **Tel:** 01963 824464
Fax: 01963 824651
Email: bob.farrand@finefoodworld.co.uk
Advertising Address: As above. **Tel:** 01963 822290
Email: sallie.james@finefoodworld.co.uk
Web site: http://www.finefoodworld.co.uk

Publisher: The Guild of Fine Food Ltd
Date Established: 1979
Frequency: 10 issues yearly - Published on the 1st Monday of the cover month
Free to qualifying individuals
Annual Sub.: £40.00
Circulation: 4,500 (Publisher's Statement)
Usual Pagination: 52
Editor: Mick Whitworth
Summary of Content: Business magazine for speciality food and drink retailers in the UK.
Readership/Target Audience: Aimed at owners, managers and buyers in independent delicatessens, food halls and upmarket farm shops.
ADVERTISING RATES:
Full Page Colour £1485.00
Agency Commission: 10%
Mechanical Data: Bleed Size: 321 x 236mm, Trim Size: 315 x 230mm, Type Area: 287 x 204mm, Col Length: 287mm, Page Width: 204mm, Film: Digital, Print Process: Litho
Copy instructions: Copy Date: 4 weeks prior to publication date
Average advertising content per issue: 30%
BUSINESS: FOOD

FINISHED VEHICLE LOGISTICS
1834446U31R-62

Editorial Address: Lamb House, Church Street, LONDON, W4 2PD **Tel:** 020 8987 0900 **Fax:** 020 8987 0948
Email: maxine.elkin@ultimamedia.com
Advertising Address: As above.
Email: matt.allard@ultimamedia.com
Web site: http://www.fvlmagazine.com
Publisher: Ultima Media Ltd
Date Established: 2005
Frequency: Quarterly
Cover Price: Free
Circulation: 9,000 (Publisher's Statement)
Editor: Christopher Ludwig; **Advertising Manager:** Matthew Allard
Summary of Content: Magazine covering outbound automotive logistics.
Readership/Target Audience: Aimed at carmakers.
ADVERTISING RATES:
Full Page Colour £5250.00
BUSINESS: MOTOR TRADE: Motor Trade Related

FINISHING
37625U19C-200

Editorial Address: 173 High Street, RICKMANSWORTH, WD3 1AY **Tel:** 01923 692660 **Fax:** 01923 692679
Email: j.hatcher@turretgroup.com
Advertising Address: As above.
Email: s.freshwater@turretgroup.com
Web site: http://www.finishingmagazine.co.uk
ISSN: 0264-2506
Publisher: Turret Group Ltd.
Date Established: 1898
Frequency: 6 issues yearly - Published at the end of the cover month
Free to qualifying individuals
Annual Sub.: £91.00
Circulation: 8,000 (Publisher's Statement)
Usual Pagination: 48
Editor: John Hatcher; **Advertising Manager:** Stewart Freshwater
Summary of Content: Journal dealing with all aspects of finishing including surface treatment, anodising, galvanising and spray coating. The magazine covers news, technical papers and product information.
Readership/Target Audience: Aimed at line managers through to chief executives within the trade metal finishing/surface coating industry, and production managers within manufacturing plants responsible for metal finishing and surface coating lines or the outsourcing of metal finishing. The magazine is also circulated to all members of the Surface Engineering Association (SEA).
ADVERTISING RATES:
Full Page Colour £1250.00
Agency Commission: 10%
Mechanical Data: Film: Digital, Trim Size: 297 x 210mm
Copy instructions: Copy Date: 1st Friday of publication month
BUSINESS: ENGINEERING & MACHINERY: Finishing

FIPP WORLD MAGAZINE TRENDS BOOK 2007/2008
601501U2A-75_62

Formerly: The FIPP/Zenith Optimedia World Magazine Trends Book
Editorial Address: Queens House, 55-56 Lincoln's Inn Fields, LONDON, WC2A 3LJ **Tel:** 020 7404 4169
Fax: 020 7404 4170
Email: info@fipp.com
Advertising Address: As above.
Email: andrew@fipp.com
Web site: http://www.fipp.com
ISSN: 1464-6463

Publisher: FIPP
Date Established: 1994
Frequency: Annual - Published in December
Annual Sub: £280.00
Usual Pagination: 280
Editor: Rolf Rohwer
Summary of Content: Covering a comprehensive collection of world data with extended business to business sections for the major markets. In addition to profiles of 54 countries it includes the regional summaries, international overviews, advertising expenditure forecasts and top 10 magazine titles.
Readership/Target Audience: Aimed at publishers, advertising agencies, financial and media analysts, investment bankers, knowledge institutions and students.
ADVERTISING RATES:
Full Page Colour £1200.00
Agency Commission: 10%
Mechanical Data: Film: Digital
Copy instructions: Copy Date: 4 weeks prior to publication date
Average advertising content per issue: 20%
BUSINESS: COMMUNICATIONS, ADVERTISING & MARKETING

FIRE
39844U54A-30
Editorial Address: PO Box 100, CHICHESTER, PO18 8HD
Tel: 01243 576444 **Fax:** 01243 576456
Email: andrew.lynch@keywaypublishing.com
Advertising Address: As above.
Email: victoria.evans@keywaypublishing.com
Web site: http://www.fire-magazine.com
ISSN: 0142-2510
Publisher: Keyways Publishing Limited
Date Established: 1908
Frequency: Monthly - Published around the 1st of the cover month
Cover Price: £10.30
Annual Sub: £76.00
Circulation: 3,000 (Publisher's Statement)
Usual Pagination: 68
Editor: Andrew Lynch; **Advertising Manager:** Victoria Evans
Summary of Content: The Journal of the Fire Prevention and Firefighting Profession containing columns from all main stakeholders, articles on fire brigades, fire politics, operational techniques, personnel moves, diary dates and letters. A feature on one particular area of fire safety is included in each issue.
Readership/Target Audience: Aimed at public and industrial fire services, fire prevention officers, building control officers and emergency planners. Also read by both local and central government politicians, fire consultants, surveyors, architects and MOD.
ADVERTISING RATES:
Full Page Mono £1576.00
Full Page Colour £2392.00
SCC £32.65
Agency Commission: 10%
Mechanical Data: Type Area: 265 x 185mm, Col Length: 265mm, Page Width: 185mm, Bleed Size: 303 x 216mm, Trim Size: 297 x 210mm, Film: Digital, No. of Columns (Display): 4
Average advertising content per issue: 20%
Supplement(s): Shout - 2xY
BUSINESS: SAFETY & SECURITY: Fire Fighting

FIRE & RESCUE
39845U54A-35
Editorial Address: 8 The Old Yarn Mills, SHERBORNE, DT9 3RQ **Tel:** 01935 816030 **Fax:** 01935 817200
Email: am.knegt@hisdorset.com
Advertising Address: 32 Vauxhall Bridge Road, LONDON, SW1V 2SS **Tel:** 020 7973 4666 **Fax:** 020 7233 5057
Email: k.francis@hgluk.com
Web site: http://www.hemmingfire.com
ISSN: 0964-9727
Publisher: Hemming Group Ltd
Date Established: 1992
Frequency: Quarterly - Published in the middle of the cover month
Free to qualifying individuals
Annual Sub: £40.00
Circulation: 6,721 (Publisher's Statement)
Usual Pagination: 80
Editor: Ann-Marie Knegt
Summary of Content: Magazine with worldwide coverage which reports on fire and rescue action, equipment, techniques, medical aspects and training issues for firefighters.
Readership/Target Audience: Read by chief fire officers, training officers and engineering officers in every major municipal fire department in over 150 countries worldwide.
ADVERTISING RATES:
Full Page Colour £2199.00
Agency Commission: 10%
Mechanical Data: Type Area: 275 x 185mm, Bleed Size: 303 x 216mm, Trim Size: 297 x 210mm, Col Length: 275mm, Page Width: 185mm, Film: Digital
Average advertising content per issue: 50%
BUSINESS: SAFETY & SECURITY: Fire Fighting

FIRE RISK MANAGEMENT
39849U54A-55
Formerly: Fire Prevention & Fire Engineers Journal
Editorial Address: London Road, MORETON-IN-MARSH, GL56 0RH **Tel:** 01608 812500 **Fax:** 01608 812501
Email: rgilbey@thefpa.co.uk
Advertising Address: As above.
Email: lsearle@thefpa.co.uk
Web site: http://www.frmjournal.com
ISSN: 1478-3576
Publisher: Fire Protection Association
Frequency: Monthly - Published on the 1st of the cover month
Annual Sub: £125.00
Circulation: 15,000 (Publisher's Statement)
Usual Pagination: 64
Editor: Rupert Gilbey
Summary of Content: Journal of the Fire Protection Association and The Institution of Fire Engineers. Includes guidance and feature articles on global fire industry, covering subjects such as fire engineering, risk management, fire service operations, new legislation, codes, standards and fire statistics.
Readership/Target Audience: Read by fire professionals in all disciplines of fire prevention, protection and firefighting.
ADVERTISING RATES:
Full Page Mono £1899.00
Full Page Colour £2499.00
Agency Commission: 10%
Mechanical Data: Type Area: 247 x 175mm, Bleed Size: 303 x 216mm, Trim Size: 297 x 210mm, Col Length: 247mm, Film: Digital, Page Width: 175mm
Copy instructions: Copy Date: 15th of the month prior to publication date
Average advertising content per issue: 25%
BUSINESS: SAFETY & SECURITY: Fire Fighting

FIRE TIMES
39853U54A-70
Editorial Address: Gresham House, 54 High Street, SHOREHAM-BY-SEA, BN43 5DB **Tel:** 01273 453033
Fax: 01273 453085
Email: davidholden@mmcpublications.co.uk
Advertising Address: As above.
Email: colinrobinson@mmcpublications.co.uk
Web site: http://www.mmcpublications.co.uk
ISSN: 1465-8798
Publisher: Modern Media Communications Ltd
Date Established: 1998
Frequency: 6 issues yearly - Published in the 1st week of the 1st cover month
Cover Price: £25.00
Free to qualifying individuals
Annual Sub: £73.00
Circulation: 5,000 (Publisher's Statement)
Usual Pagination: 64
Editor: David Holden
Summary of Content: Magazine covering firefighting products and services and fire prevention within the fire brigade and industrial companies.
Readership/Target Audience: Read by fire officers and fire prevention managers who are responsible for buying fire equipment.
ADVERTISING RATES:
Full Page Mono £1485.00
Full Page Colour £1485.00
Agency Commission: 10%
Mechanical Data: Col Length: 265mm, No. of Columns (Display): 3, Type Area: 265 x 185mm, Print Process: Litho, Bleed Size: 303 x 213mm, Trim Size: 297 x 210mm, Page Width: 185mm, Film: Digital
Copy instructions: Copy Date: 3 weeks prior to publication date
Average advertising content per issue: 45%
BUSINESS: SAFETY & SECURITY: Fire Fighting

FIREFIGHTER
37181U14L-210
Editorial Address: Bradley House, 68 Coombe Road, KINGSTON UPON THAMES, KT2 7AE **Tel:** 020 8541 1765
Fax: 020 8546 5187
Email: firefighter@fbu.org.uk
Web site: http://www.fbu.org.uk
Publisher: Fire Brigades Union
Frequency: 10 issues yearly
Cover Price: Free
Circulation: 50,000 (Publisher's Statement)
Usual Pagination: 24
Editor: Tom Gill
Summary of Content: Magazine covering all aspects of fire-fighting and fire prevention including trade union and labour movement issues.
Readership/Target Audience: Read by members of the FBU as well as some MPs and solicitors.
ADVERTISING: No Advertising taken
BUSINESS: COMMERCE, INDUSTRY & MANAGEMENT: Trade Unions

FIRES & FIREPLACES
35828U4B-112_50
Editorial Address: PO Box 206, DARLINGTON, DL2 2YN
Tel: 01325 720775 **Fax:** 01325 720775
Email: editor@fireplacemarketing.co.uk
Advertising Address: Haseley Manor, Birmingham Road, WARWICK, CV35 7LS **Tel:** 024 7624 7246
Fax: 024 7624 7266
Email: karen@fireplacemarketing.co.uk
Web site: http://www.fireplace.co.uk
ISSN: 1462-1738
Publisher: Fireplace Marketing Company Limited
Date Established: 1994
Frequency: 9 issues yearly
Free to qualifying individuals
Annual Sub: £60.00
Circulation: 6,500 (Publisher's Statement)
Usual Pagination: 60
Editor: Philip Malkin; **Advertising Manager:** Karen O'Riordan; **Publisher:** David Spencer
Summary of Content: Magazine for the fireplace and hearth products industry.
Readership/Target Audience: Aimed at retailers, merchants, manufacturers, suppliers, builders, architects and interior designers.
ADVERTISING RATES:
Full Page Colour £900.00
SCC £15.00
Agency Commission: 10%
Mechanical Data: Bleed Size: 303 x 216mm, Trim Size: 297 x 210mm, Film: Digital, Col Length: 272mm, Page Width: 187mm, Type Area: 272 x 187mm
Copy instructions: Copy Date: 4 weeks prior to publication date
Average advertising content per issue: 40%
BUSINESS: ARCHITECTURE & BUILDING: Interior Design & Flooring

FIRETRADE ASIA AND MIDDLE EAST
25992U54A-75
Formerly: FireTrade Asia
Editorial Address: 8 The Old Yarn Mills, SHERBORNE, DT9 3RQ **Tel:** 01935 816030 **Fax:** 01935 817200
Email: s.elder@hisdorset.com
Advertising Address: As above. **Fax:** 01935 816410
Email: a.hire@hisdorset.com
Web site: http://www.firedirectory.net
ISSN: 1357-8529
Publisher: Hemming Group Ltd
Frequency: Annual - Published in June
Annual Sub: £75.00
Circulation: 5,000 (Publisher's Statement)
Group Editor: Sylke Elder
Summary of Content: Directory of passive and active fire equipment.
Readership/Target Audience: Aimed at the Asian and Middle East markets.
ADVERTISING RATES:
Full Page Colour £2237.00
Agency Commission: 10%
Mechanical Data: Type Area: 263 x 185mm, Bleed Size: 303 x 216mm, Trim Size: 297 x 210mm, Col Length: 263mm, Page Width: 185mm, Film: Digital
Copy instructions: Copy Date: April 21st
BUSINESS: SAFETY & SECURITY: Fire Fighting

FIREWORKS
38524U32H-90
Editorial Address: PO Box 40, BEXHILL-ON-SEA, TN40 1GX **Tel:** 01424 733050 **Fax:** 01424 733050
Email: editor@fireworks-mag.org
Advertising Address: As above.
Email: editor@fireworks-mag.org
Web site: http://www.fireworks-mag.org
ISSN: 0264-9780
Publisher: Fireworks
Date Established: 1982
Frequency: Half-yearly - Published in July and February
Cover Price: £5.00
Annual Sub: £10.00
Circulation: 600 (Publisher's Statement)
Usual Pagination: 48
Editor: John Bennett; **Managing Director:** John Bennett; **Advertising Manager:** John Bennett; **Publisher:** John Bennett
Summary of Content: Magazine covering firework history, celebrations, news and book reviews, new fireworks and services and details of legislation.
Readership/Target Audience: Read by firework enthusiasts and those working in the firework trade.
ADVERTISING RATES:
Full Page Mono £140.00
Full Page Colour £280.00
Mechanical Data: No. of Columns (Display): 2, Trim Size: 297 x 210mm, Type Area: 280 x 267mm, Col Length: 280mm, Page Width: 267mm, Bleed Size: 307 x 220mm, Film: Digital
Copy instructions: Copy Date: May 1st and December 1st

Average advertising content per issue: 12.5%
BUSINESS: LOCAL GOVERNMENT, LEISURE &
RECREATION: Leisure, Recreation & Entertainment

FIRM SCOTLAND
625196U44-3012

Editorial Address: 4th Floor, The Mercat Building, 26
Gallowgate, GLASGOW, G1 5AB **Tel:** 0141 552 5858
Email: steven.raeburn@carnyx.com
Advertising Address: As above.
Email: gavin.bryans@carnyx.com
Web site: http://www.firmmagazine.com
Publisher: Carnyx Group Ltd
Date Established: 1999
Frequency: Monthly
Free to qualifying individuals
Circulation: 8,000 (Publisher's Statement)
Editor: Steven Raeburn; **Advertising Manager:** Gavin
Bryans
Summary of Content: Lifestyle magazine covering current
news and high-profile interviews with leading personalities
with resource section for marketing and technology.
Readership/Target Audience: Read by Scottish solicitors
and advocates.
ADVERTISING RATES:
Full Page Colour £1500.00
Mechanical Data: Type Area: 245 x 182mm, Bleed Size:
271 x 206mm, Trim Size: 265 x 200mm, Col Length: 245mm,
Page Width: 182mm, Film: Digital
BUSINESS: LEGAL

FIRST
36754U14A-115

Editorial Address: 56 Haymarket, LONDON, SW1Y 4RN
Tel: 020 7389 9650 **Fax:** 020 7389 9644
Email: publisher@firstmagazine.com
Advertising Address: As above.
Email: e.daly@firstmagazine.com
Web site: http://www.firstmagazine.com
Publisher: First Magazine Limited
Date Established: 1986
Frequency: Quarterly
Annual Sub.: £145.00
Circulation: 25,156 (Publisher's Statement)
Usual Pagination: 200
Editor: Eamonn Daly; **Advertising Manager:** Eamonn Daly;
Publisher: Alastair Harris
Summary of Content: Magazine covering world politics and
government policies affecting business.
Readership/Target Audience: Aimed at business, financial
and political leaders.
ADVERTISING RATES:
Full Page Mono EUR12500.00
Full Page Colour EUR15200.00
Mechanical Data: Film: Digital, Page Width: 177mm, Type
Area: 265 x 177mm, Col Length: 265mm, Trim Size: 297 x
220mm, Bleed Size: +3mm, Print Process: Sheet-fed litho
Copy instructions: Copy Date: 4 weeks prior to publication
date
Average advertising content per issue: 33%
BUSINESS: COMMERCE, INDUSTRY & MANAGEMENT

FIRST FIVE
41083U62C-160

Editorial Address: 21 Granville Street, GLASGOW, G3 7EE
Tel: 0141 221 4148 **Fax:** 0141 221 6043
Email: gwen.garner@sppa.org.uk
Advertising Address: As above.
Email: ian.williamson@sppa.org.uk
Web site: http://www.sppa.org.uk
ISSN: 1364-8659
Publisher: Scottish Pre-School Play Association
Date Established: 1996
Frequency: Quarterly
Free to qualifying individuals
Annual Sub.: £12.00
Circulation: 1,800 (Publisher's Statement)
Usual Pagination: 20
Editor: Gwen Garner; **Advertising Manager:** Ian Williamson
Summary of Content: Magazine of the Scottish Pre-school
Play Association covering child development, education and
matters of general interest to playworkers and carers of
children under five.
Readership/Target Audience: Aimed at those involved in
SPPA affiliated pre-school groups.
ADVERTISING RATES:
Full Page Mono £250.00
Full Page Colour £350.00
Agency Commission: 10%
Mechanical Data: Bleed Size: 303 x 216mm, Trim Size: 297
x 210mm, Film: Digital
Copy instructions: Copy Date: 3 weeks prior to publication
date
Average advertising content per issue: 20%
BUSINESS: CHURCH & SCHOOL EQUIPMENT &
EDUCATION: Junior Education

FIRST FOR BUSINESS
41395U63B-2165

Editorial Address: RMC House, Broadfield Court,
Broadfield Business Park, SHEFFIELD, S8 0XF
Tel: 0114 250 6300 **Fax:** 0114 250 6320
Email: andy.waple@regionalmagazine.co.uk
Advertising Address: As above.
Email: mandy.ogle@regionalmagazine.co.uk
Web site: http://www.northernlifestyle.com
Publisher: Regional Magazine Company
Date Established: 1992
Frequency: 11 issues yearly - Double issue in December/
January
Cover Price: Free
Circulation: 10,500 (Publisher's Statement)
Usual Pagination: 90
Editor: Andy Waple; **Managing Director:** John Murphy;
Advertising Manager: Mandy Ogle
Summary of Content: Official bulletin of the Sheffield
Chamber of Commerce and Industry and Sheffield First
Partnership.
Readership/Target Audience: Aimed at the business
market in Sheffield, South Yorkshire and the North Midlands.
ADVERTISING RATES:
Full Page Colour £1390.00
Agency Commission: 10%
Mechanical Data: Type Area: 260 x 185mm, Bleed Size:
303 x 216mm, Trim Size: 297 x 210mm, Col Length: 260mm,
Page Width: 185mm, Film: Digital
Copy instructions: Copy Date: 3 weeks prior to publication
date
Average advertising content per issue: 50%
BUSINESS: REGIONAL BUSINESS: Regional Business
English Counties

FIRST MOVE CONSTRUCTION
1674070U62H-422

Editorial Address: Portland Buildings, 127-129 Portland
Street, MANCHESTER, M1 4PZ **Tel:** 0161 661 4136
Fax: 0161 236 2783
Email: claire.stapleton@excelpublishing.co.uk
Advertising Address: Ground Floor, Houldsworth Mill,
Houldsworth Street, STOCKPORT, SK5 6DA
Tel: 0161 442 2576
Email: steve.gardner@excelpublishing.co.uk
Publisher: Excel Publishing Company Ltd
Date Established: 2005
Frequency: Annual - Published in September
Free to qualifying individuals
Circulation: 40,000 (Publisher's Statement)
Editor: Claire Stapleton; **Advertising Manager:** Steve
Gardner; **Publisher:** Steve Gardner
Summary of Content: Magazine covering careers advice,
industry intelligence and opportunities for those wishing to
enter the construction industry.
Readership/Target Audience: Aimed at graduates and
school leavers.
ADVERTISING RATES:
Full Page Colour £2550.00
Agency Commission: 10%
Mechanical Data: Type Area: 185 x 125mm, Bleed Size:
216 x 154mm, Trim Size: 210 x 148.5mm, Col Length:
185mm, Page Width: 125mm, Film: Digital
Average advertising content per issue: 30%
BUSINESS: CHURCH & SCHOOL EQUIPMENT &
EDUCATION: Careers

FIRST MOVE HEALTHCARE
1699358U56A-201

Editorial Address: Ground Floor, Houldsworth Mill,
Houldsworth Street, STOCKPORT, SK5 6DA
Tel: 0161 442 2576
Email: steve.gardner@excelpublishing.co.uk
Advertising Address: As above.
Email: steve.gardner@excelpublishing.co.uk
Web site: http://www.yourfirstmove.co.uk
Publisher: Excel Publishing Company Ltd
Date Established: 2006
Frequency: Annual
Circulation: 45,000 (Publisher's Statement)
Editor: Steve Gardner; **Advertising Manager:** Steve
Gardner; **Publisher:** Steve Gardner
Summary of Content: Magazine providing a guide to
careers in the healthcare sector.
Readership/Target Audience: Aimed at 16 to 18 year olds
in schools and universities as well as higher education
institutions.
ADVERTISING RATES:
Full Page Colour £2550.00
Mechanical Data: Type Area: 185 x 125mm, Bleed Size:
216 x 154mm, Trim Size: 210 x 148.5mm, Col Length:
185mm, Page Width: 125mm, Film: Digital
BUSINESS: HEALTH & MEDICAL

FIRST MOVE HOSPITALITY, LEISURE
AND TOURISM
1674073U62H-421

Formerly: First Move Hospitality
Editorial Address: Ground Floor, Houldsworth Mill,
Houldsworth Street, STOCKPORT, SK5 6DA
Tel: 0161 442 2576
Email: steve.gardner@excelpublishing.co.uk
Advertising Address: As above.
Email: steve.gardner@excelpublishing.co.uk
Web site: http://www.yourfirstmove.co.uk
Publisher: Excel Publishing Company Ltd
Date Established: 2002
Frequency: Annual - Published in March
Free to qualifying individuals
Circulation: 20,000 (Publisher's Statement)
Editor: Steve Gardner; **Advertising Manager:** Steve
Gardner; **Publisher:** Steve Gardner
Summary of Content: Magazine covering careers advice,
industry intelligence and opportunities for those wishing to
enter the hospitality industry.
Readership/Target Audience: Aimed at graduates.
ADVERTISING RATES:
Full Page Colour £2550.00
Agency Commission: 10%
Mechanical Data: Type Area: 185 x 125mm, Bleed Size:
216 x 154mm, Trim Size: 210 x 148.5mm, Page Width:
125mm, Film: Digital, Col Length: 185mm
Average advertising content per issue: 30%
BUSINESS: CHURCH & SCHOOL EQUIPMENT &
EDUCATION: Careers

FIRST MOVE NORTH WEST
1748207U62H-423

Editorial Address: Ground Floor, Houldsworth Mill,
Houldsworth Street, STOCKPORT, SK5 6DA
Tel: 0161 443 5075 **Fax:** 0161 442 2582
Email: steve.gardner@excelpublishing.co.uk
Advertising Address: As above.
Email: steve.gardner@excelpublishing.co.uk
Web site: http://www.yourfirstmove.co.uk
Publisher: Excel Publishing Company Ltd
Frequency: Annual - Published in December
Free to qualifying individuals
Circulation: 55,000 (Publisher's Statement)
Editor: Steve Gardner; **Advertising Manager:** Elizabeth
Attenborough; **Publisher:** Steve Gardner
Summary of Content: Publication covering graduate
recruitment and designed to promote opportunities for
graduates in the region, providing advice and intelligence on
the local economy and major employers.
Readership/Target Audience: Aimed at individuals in the
north west of England coming out of education and into the
employment market.
ADVERTISING RATES:
Full Page Colour £2550.00
Agency Commission: 10%
Mechanical Data: Type Area: 185 x 125mm, Bleed Size:
216 x 154mm, Trim Size: 210 x 148.5mm, Col Length:
185mm, Page Width: 125mm, Film: Digital
Copy instructions: Copy Date: 3 weeks prior to publication
date
Average advertising content per issue: 75%
BUSINESS: CHURCH & SCHOOL EQUIPMENT &
EDUCATION: Careers

FIRST VOICE OF BUSINESS
37128U14H-50

Formerly: First Voice of Small Business
Editorial Address: 275 Newmarket Road, CAMBRIDGE,
CB5 8JE **Tel:** 01223 477411 **Fax:** 01223 327356
Email: editorial@firstvoice.co.uk
Advertising Address: Mainline Media, The Barn, Oakley
Hay Lodge Business Park, Great Folds Road, Great Oakley,
NORTHANTS, NN18 9AS **Tel:** 01536 747333
Fax: 01536 746565
Email: nigel.stephens@mainlinemedia.co.uk
Web site: http://www.firstvoice.co.uk
ISSN: 1460-809X
Publisher: NFSE (Sales Ltd)
Date Established: 1974
Frequency: 6 issues yearly
Cover Price: £2.65
Annual Sub.: £25.00
Circulation: 202,111 (ABC 01/07/2008 to 30/06/2009)
Usual Pagination: 36
Editor: Mike Sewell
Summary of Content: Official magazine of the Federation of
Small Businesses. Offers advice on current legislation and
reforms, federation news, meeting dates and legal advice.
Readership/Target Audience: Read by members of
Parliament and the media, as well as members of the
Federation.
ADVERTISING RATES:
Full Page Colour £4500.00
Agency Commission: 10%
Mechanical Data: Film: Digital, Type Area: 264 x 180mm,
Bleed Size: 303 x 216mm, Trim Size: 297 x 210mm, Col
Widths (Display): 45mm, Col Length: 264mm, Page Width:
180mm

Copy instructions: Copy Date: 15th of the month prior to publication date
Supplement(s): FSB Conference - 1xY
BUSINESS: COMMERCE, INDUSTRY & MANAGEMENT: Small Business

FISH
39380U45B-22

Editorial Address: 22 Rushworth Avenue, West Bridgford, NOTTINGHAM, NG2 7LF **Tel:** 0115 982 2317
Fax: 0115 982 6150
Email: v.holt@ifm.org.uk
Advertising Address: As above.
Email: v.holt@ifm.org.uk
Web site: http://www.ifm.org.uk
Publisher: Institute of Fisheries Management
Date Established: 1975
Frequency: Quarterly
Free to qualifying individuals
Circulation: 1,000 (Publisher's Statement)
Usual Pagination: 56
Editor: Valerie Holt; **Advertising Manager:** Valerie Holt
Summary of Content: Official magazine of the Institute of Fisheries Management.
Readership/Target Audience: Read by members of the institute, fisheries managers and interested anglers.
ADVERTISING RATES:
Full Page Mono £175.00
Mechanical Data: Trim Size: 210 x 148mm, Film: Digital
Average advertising content per issue: 20%
BUSINESS: MARINE & SHIPPING: Commercial Fishing

FISH & CHIPS AND FAST FOOD
36606U11C-20

Editorial Address: 10 Queen Victoria Avenue, HOVE, BN3 6WN **Tel:** 01273 249751 **Fax:** 01273 264413
Email: wdurham@globalnet.co.uk
Advertising Address: As above.
Email: frazer@brighton-pearl.co.uk
Web site: http://www.brighton-pearl.co.uk
ISSN: 0969-2037
Publisher: Brighton Pearl
Date Established: 1993
Frequency: 8 issues yearly
Free to qualifying individuals
Annual Sub.: £28.00
Circulation: 10,200 (Publisher's Statement)
Usual Pagination: 48
Editor: Wendy Durham; **Advertising Manager:** Frazer Clifford; **Publisher:** Frazer Clifford
Summary of Content: Magazine containing industry news and views on the fish and fast food equipment, new products and quality assurance.
Readership/Target Audience: Aimed at owners and managers of fish and chip shops, restaurants and fast food outlets.
ADVERTISING: Rates on application
BUSINESS: CATERING: Fried Fish

FISH FARMER
39381U45B-25

Editorial Address: Craigcrook Castle, Craigcrook Road, EDINBURGH, EH4 3PE **Tel:** 0131 312 4550
Fax: 0131 312 4551
Email: editor@fishfarmer-magazine.com
Advertising Address: As above. **Tel:** 0131 312 4564
Email: wdowds@fishupdate.com
Web site: http://www.fishfarmer-magazine.com
ISSN: 0262-9615
Publisher: Special Publications
Date Established: 1976
Frequency: 6 issues yearly
Annual Sub.: £69.00
Circulation: 7,000 (Publisher's Statement)
Usual Pagination: 44
Editor: Malcolm Dickenson
Summary of Content: International magazine featuring articles on marketing, feed, husbandry, research and development, plus management of all farmed fish and shellfish species. Also contains a website with daily news, events, buyers guides and web classifieds.
Readership/Target Audience: Read by producers and suppliers of farmed seafood.
ADVERTISING RATES:
Full Page Mono £1100.00
Full Page Colour £1600.00
Agency Commission: 10%
Mechanical Data: Type Area: 297 x 210mm, Bleed Size: 303 x 216mm, Col Length: 297mm, Film: Digital, No. of Columns (Display): 4, Print Process: Sheet-fed offset litho, Page Width: 210mm, Col Widths (Display): 44mm
Copy instructions: Copy Date: 3 weeks prior to publication date
Average advertising content per issue: 35%
BUSINESS: MARINE & SHIPPING: Commercial Fishing

FISH FARMING INTERNATIONAL
39382U45B-30

Editorial Address: 6th Floor, Eldon House, 2 Eldon Street, LONDON, EC2M 7LS **Tel:** 01892 533813 **Fax:** 01892 544895
Email: press@agra-net.com
Advertising Address: As above. **Tel:** 020 7650 1008
Email: antonina.ferrara@fishfarminginternational.com
Web site: http://www.intrafish.no
ISSN: 0268-1293
Publisher: Agra Informa Ltd
Date Established: 1973
Frequency: Monthly - Published around the 1st Monday of the cover month
Annual Sub.: £100.00
Circulation: 5,941 (Publisher's Statement)
Usual Pagination: 44
Editor: Rachel Mutter; **Publisher:** Pål Korneliussen
Summary of Content: Newspaper covering the latest news and developments in fish and shellfish farming worldwide.
Readership/Target Audience: Read by decision makers in every aspect of aquaculture.
ADVERTISING RATES:
Full Page Colour £3180.00
Agency Commission: 10%
Mechanical Data: Col Widths (Display): 84mm, Page Width: 262mm, Film: Digital, Print Process: Offset litho, Type Area: 332 x 262mm, Col Length: 332mm, No. of Columns (Display): 6
Copy instructions: Copy Date: 4 weeks prior to publication date
Average advertising content per issue: 50%
BUSINESS: MARINE & SHIPPING: Commercial Fishing

FISH FRIERS REVIEW
36607U11C-30

Editorial Address: New Federation House, 4 Greenwood Mount, Meanwood, LEEDS, LS6 4LQ **Tel:** 0113 230 7044
Fax: 0113 230 7010
Advertising Address: As above.
Email: k.clark@federationoffishfriers.co.uk
Web site: http://www.federationoffishfriers.co.uk
Publisher: National Federation of Fish Friers
Date Established: 1925
Frequency: Monthly
Annual Sub.: £55.00
Circulation: 8,500 (Publisher's Statement)
Usual Pagination: 30
Editor: Karen Clark; **Advertising Manager:** Karen Clark
Summary of Content: Magazine containing information on pending legislation, trade trends, new products and promotions.
Readership/Target Audience: Aimed at fish and chip shops throughout the UK.
ADVERTISING RATES:
Full Page Colour £1600.00
Agency Commission: 10%
Mechanical Data: Film: Digital, Type Area: 265 x 215mm, Bleed Size: 303 x 216mm, Trim Size: 297 x 210mm, Col Length: 265mm, Page Width: 215mm
Copy instructions: Copy Date: 10th of the month prior to publication date
Average advertising content per issue: 50%
BUSINESS: CATERING: Fried Fish

FISHING NEWS
39386U45B-50

Editorial Address: 6th Floor, Eldon House, 2 Eldon Street, LONDON, EC2M 7LS **Fax:** 020 7650 1050
Email: tim.oliver@fishingnews.co.uk
Advertising Address: As above. **Tel:** 020 7650 1021
Email: vicky.reeves@fishingnews.co.uk
Web site: http://www.fishingnews.co.uk
ISSN: 0015-3036
Publisher: IntraFish Media AS
Date Established: 1913
Frequency: Weekly - Published on Friday
Cover Price: £1.85
Circulation: 8,101 (Publisher's Statement)
Usual Pagination: 24
Editor: Tim Oliver
Summary of Content: News and comment on important developments in the UK and Ireland commercial fishing industry.
Readership/Target Audience: Read by the commercial fishing industry.
ADVERTISING RATES:
Full Page Colour £2601.00
Agency Commission: 10%
Mechanical Data: Col Length: 360mm, No. of Columns (Display): 6, Print Process: Web-fed offset litho, Type Area: 360 x 262mm, Col Widths (Display): 44mm, Page Width: 262mm, Film: Digital
Copy instructions: Copy Date: Friday prior to publication date
Average advertising content per issue: 20%
BUSINESS: MARINE & SHIPPING: Commercial Fishing

FISHING NEWS INTERNATIONAL
39387U45B-60

Editorial Address: 6th Floor, Eldon House, 2 Eldon Street, LONDON, EC2M 7LS **Tel:** 020 7650 1031
Email: ian.strutt@fishingnewsinternational.com
Advertising Address: As above. **Tel:** 020 7650 1005
Email: emma.bates@fishingnewsinternational.com
Web site: http://www.fishingnewsinternational.com
ISSN: 0015-3044
Publisher: IntraFish Media AS
Date Established: 1961
Frequency: Monthly - Published at the end of the month prior to the cover date
Circulation: 6,189 (Publisher's Statement)
Usual Pagination: 44
Editor: Ian Strutt
Summary of Content: Newspaper containing news, features and technical reviews of the world's commercial fishing industries.
Readership/Target Audience: Read by the international fishing industry.
ADVERTISING RATES:
Full Page Mono £2135.00
Full Page Colour £2730.00
Agency Commission: 10%
Mechanical Data: Type Area: 332 x 262mm, Col Length: 332mm, Page Width: 262mm, Film: Digital
Copy instructions: Copy Date: 3 weeks prior to publication date
Average advertising content per issue: 50%
BUSINESS: MARINE & SHIPPING: Commercial Fishing

FITPRO
1657340U32H-460

Editorial Address: Kalbarri House, 107-113 London Road, LONDON, E13 0DA **Tel:** 020 8586 0101 **Fax:** 020 8586 0685
Email: heather.b@fitpro.com
Advertising Address: As above. **Tel:** 0870 513 3434
Email: beth.p@fitpro.com
Web site: http://www.fitpro.com
Publisher: Fitness Professionals Ltd
Frequency: 6 issues yearly - Published in the 1st week of the cover month
Annual Sub.: £35.00
Circulation: 12,000 (Publisher's Statement)
Editor: Helen Jones; **Managing Director:** Brent Hallo
Summary of Content: Magazine covering the latest industry research and trends within the fitness industry.
Readership/Target Audience: Aimed at group exercise instructors and personal trainers.
ADVERTISING RATES:
Full Page Colour £1700.00
Mechanical Data: Bleed Size: 303 x 213mm, Trim Size: 297 x 210mm, Film: Digital
Copy instructions: Copy Date: 5 weeks prior to publication date
Average advertising content per issue: 40%
BUSINESS: LOCAL GOVERNMENT, LEISURE & RECREATION: Leisure, Recreation & Entertainment

FITPRO BUSINESS
38525U32H-107

Editorial Address: Kalbarri House, 107-113 London Road, LONDON, E13 0DA **Tel:** 020 8586 0101 **Fax:** 020 8586 0685
Email: publish@fitpro.com
Advertising Address: As above.
Email: joanna.b@fitpro.com
Web site: http://www.fitpro.com
Publisher: Fitness Professionals Ltd
Date Established: 2003
Frequency: 6 issues yearly
Annual Sub.: £35.00
Circulation: 5,000 (Publisher's Statement)
Usual Pagination: 50
Editor: Helen Jones; **Managing Director:** Brent Hallo; **Advertising Manager:** Joanna Brunt
Summary of Content: Magazine covering information relating to the fitness industry e.g. sales, marketing, retention and business development.
Readership/Target Audience: Aimed at fitness professionals in both the public and private sector.
ADVERTISING RATES:
Full Page Colour £1500.00
Agency Commission: 10%
Mechanical Data: Trim Size: 297 x 210mm, Bleed Size: 303 x 213mm, Film: Digital
Copy instructions: Copy Date: 4 weeks prior to publication date
Average advertising content per issue: 20%
BUSINESS: LOCAL GOVERNMENT, LEISURE & RECREATION: Leisure, Recreation & Entertainment

FITPRO NETWORK
38526U32H-105

Formerly: Fitness Network
Editorial Address: Kalbarri House, 107-113 London Road, LONDON, E13 0DA **Tel:** 0870 513 3434 **Fax:** 020 8586 0685
Email: publish@fitpro.com
Advertising Address: As above. **Tel:** 020 8586 7334

Business Magazines

Email: publish@fitpro.com
Web site: http://www.fitpro.com
Publisher: Fitness Professionals Ltd
Date Established: 1996
Frequency: 6 issues yearly
Free to qualifying individuals
Circulation: 5,000 (Publisher's Statement)
Usual Pagination: 36
Editor: Christopher Henry; **Advertising Manager:** Joanna Brunt
Summary of Content: Magazine covering news, reports on sports science training, nutrition research, injury, exercise and physiology matters.
Readership/Target Audience: Aimed at fitness professionals, health clubs and leisure centres.
ADVERTISING RATES:
Full Page Colour £1610.00
Mechanical Data: Bleed Size: 303 x 213mm, Trim Size: 297 x 210mm, Film: Digital
Copy instructions: Copy Date: 4 weeks prior to publication date
Average advertising content per issue: 20%
BUSINESS: LOCAL GOVERNMENT, LEISURE & RECREATION: Leisure, Recreation & Entertainment

FIVE EIGHT
1749920U61-513
Editorial Address: c/o FRUKT, 56 Compton Street, LONDON, EC1V 0ET **Tel:** 020 7017 8181
Fax: 020 7017 8199
Email: giles@fruktmusic.com
Advertising Address: As above.
Web site: http://www.fiveeight.net
Publisher: FRUKT Music
Date Established: 2001
Frequency: Monthly
Annual Sub.: £295.00
Circulation: 1,500 (Publisher's Statement)
Usual Pagination: 24
Editor: Giles Fitzgerald
Summary of Content: Music business strategy publication and daily bulletin providing music industry news. The magazine includes interviews with key executives and by-lines from industry decision makers, it also covers issues including music downloading, mobile music, legal affairs in music, branding and music, and many other key industry issues.
Readership/Target Audience: Aimed at senior executives from the major record labels, music publishers, music broadcasters, music retailers. Also, the people who run music related businesses at mobile operators, technology companies, mobile handset manufacturers, law firms, accountancies and consumer brands.
ADVERTISING: No Advertising taken
BUSINESS: MUSIC TRADE

FLAVOUR & FRAGRANCE JOURNAL
38043U22R-110
Editorial Address: SIPBS, University of Strathclyde, 204 George Street, GLASGOW, G1 1XW
Email: j.r.piggott@strath.ac.uk
Advertising Address: The Atrium, Southern Gate, CHICHESTER, PO19 8SQ **Tel:** 01243 770254
Fax: 01243 770432
Email: fpidduck@wiley.co.uk
Web site: http://www.interscience.wiley.com/jpages/0882-5734
ISSN: 0882-5734
Publisher: John Wiley & Sons Ltd
Date Established: 1986
Frequency: 6 issues yearly
Annual Sub.: $905.00
Circulation: 550 (Publisher's Statement)
Usual Pagination: 64
Editor: John Piggott; **Editor-in-Chief:** John Piggott
Summary of Content: International journal about flavours and fragrances, essential oils and oleoresins.
Readership/Target Audience: Read by pharmacognosists, food scientists, flavour chemists and technologists, natural product and organic chemists, economic botanists, chromatographers, biochemists and toxicologists.
ADVERTISING RATES:
Full Page Mono £1175.00
Full Page Colour £2575.00
Agency Commission: 10%
Mechanical Data: Trim Size: 279 x 210mm, Type Area: 254 x 180mm, Col Length: 254mm, Page Width: 180mm, Film: Digital, Print Process: Sheet-fed litho
BUSINESS: FOOD: Food Related

FLEET NEWS
39574U49A-110
Editorial Address: Media House, Lynchwood, Peterborough Business Park, PETERBOROUGH, PE2 6EA
Tel: 01733 468306 **Fax:** 01733 468296
Email: julian.kirk@bauermedia.co.uk
Advertising Address: As above. **Tel:** 01733 468000
Fax: 01733 468350

Email: dan.atkin@bauermedia.co.uk
Web site: http://www.fleetnews.co.uk
ISSN: 0953-8526
Publisher: Bauer Media Ltd (Orton)
Date Established: 1978
Frequency: Weekly
Cover Price: £2.25
Free to qualifying individuals
Annual Sub.: £99.00
Circulation: 19,082 (ABC 01/01/2008 to 31/12/2008)
Usual Pagination: 36
Editor: Daniel Attwood; **News Editor:** Daniel Attwood
Summary of Content: Magazine covering developments in the company car and van markets, including new vehicle reviews, vehicle finance, accident management and running cost tables for 1500 new cars.
Readership/Target Audience: Aimed at fleet directors, finance directors, human resource directors, company secretaries and managing directors of fleets running ten or more vehicles.
ADVERTISING RATES:
Full Page Mono £6563.00
Full Page Colour £6563.00
Agency Commission: 10%
Mechanical Data: Page Width: 250mm, Col Length: 352mm, Type Area: 352 x 250mm, Trim Size: 380 x 280mm, Bleed Size: 386 x 286mm, No. of Columns (Display): 4
Copy instructions: Copy Date: 1 week prior to publication date
Average advertising content per issue: 50%
Supplement(s): The Cost - 4xY, Daily Rental Guide - 1xY, Fleet Funding - 1xY, Fleet News Awards - 1xY, Fleet News Europe Guide - 1xY, Fleet News Europe Year Book - 1xY, Fleet Van - 10xY, FN50 - 1xY, Hit for Six Conference - 2xY, Industry Conference - 1xY
BUSINESS: TRANSPORT

FLEET TIMES
1794230U49A-419
Editorial Address: Portland Buildings, 127-129 Portland Street, MANCHESTER, M1 4PZ **Tel:** 0161 236 2782
Fax: 0161 236 2783
Email: chris.newbould@excelpublishing.co.uk
Advertising Address: Imprint Publishing, Ground Floor, Houldsworth Street, South Mill, STOCKPORT, SK5 6DA
Tel: 0161 442 2576 **Fax:** 0161 443 2382
Email: gary@imprintpub.co.uk
Web site: http://www.excelpublishing.co.uk
Publisher: Excel Publishing Company Ltd
Frequency: 6 issues yearly - Published at the beginning of the 1st cover month
Cover Price: Free
Circulation: 6,000 (Publisher's Statement)
Editor: Chris Newbould; **Advertising Manager:** Gary Pollard
Summary of Content: Publication covering the issues affecting transportation management in the public sector providing a guide to new products and services and includes analysis of the latest technological developments in the motoring world.
Readership/Target Audience: Aimed at key personnel within the public sector, including transport managers, lease car co-ordinators, supplies and financial officers with a responsibility for fleets.
ADVERTISING RATES:
Full Page Mono £2000.00
Full Page Colour £2000.00
Agency Commission: 10%
Mechanical Data: Type Area: 250 x 192mm, Bleed Size: 284 x 216mm, Col Length: 250mm, Page Width: 192mm, Film: Digital
Copy instructions: Copy Date: 6th of the month prior to publication date
Average advertising content per issue: 30%
BUSINESS: TRANSPORT

FLEET VAN
39663U49D-55
Formerly: Commercials in Business
Editorial Address: Media House, Lynchwood, Peterborough Business Park, PETERBOROUGH, PE2 6EA
Tel: 01733 468000 **Fax:** 01733 468296
Email: trevor.gelken@bauermedia.co.uk
Advertising Address: As above. **Fax:** 01733 468350
Email: dee.kennedy@bauerconsumer.co.uk
Web site: http://www.fleetnews.co.uk
Publisher: Bauer Media Ltd (Orton)
Date Established: 1999
Frequency: 10 issues yearly
Cover Price: Free
Circulation: 13,053 (ABC 01/01/2008 to 31/12/2008)
Usual Pagination: 40
Editor: Trevor Gelken
Summary of Content: Magazine covering light commercial vehicles, up to 3.5 tonnes. Contains features on funding, taxation, legislation and vehicle product information.
Readership/Target Audience: Aimed at the smaller van operator.
ADVERTISING RATES:
Full Page Colour £2827.00
Agency Commission: 10%

Mechanical Data: Type Area: 265 x 185mm, Bleed Size: 303 x 216mm, Trim Size: 297 x 210mm, Col Length: 265mm, Page Width: 185mm, Film: Digital
Copy instructions: Copy Date: 2 weeks prior to publication date
Average advertising content per issue: 40%
Supplement to: Fleet News
BUSINESS: TRANSPORT: Commercial Vehicles

FLEET WORLD
39578U49A-114
Editorial Address: 18 Alban Park, Hatfield Road, ST. ALBANS, AL4 0JJ **Tel:** 01727 739160 **Fax:** 01727 739169
Email: editorial@fleetworldgroup.co.uk
Advertising Address: As above.
Email: anne@fleetworldgroup.co.uk
Web site: http://www.fleetworldgroup.co.uk
Publisher: Stag Publications Ltd
Date Established: 1998
Frequency: Monthly
Cover Price: Free
Circulation: 19,722 (ABC 01/01/2008 to 31/12/2008)
Usual Pagination: 44
Editor: Ross Durkin; **Managing Editor:** Ross Durkin
Summary of Content: Magazine containing management style features on cars and light commercial vehicles, plus features on other allied services.
Readership/Target Audience: Aimed at company car fleet operators.
ADVERTISING RATES:
Full Page Colour £3190.00
Agency Commission: 10%
Mechanical Data: Type Area: 265 x 190mm, Bleed Size: 303 x 213mm, Trim Size: 297 x 210mm, Film: Digital, Col Length: 265mm, Page Width: 190mm
Average advertising content per issue: 40%
BUSINESS: TRANSPORT

FLEXOTECH
38923U41A-24
Editorial Address: 30 London Road, Southborough, TUNBRIDGE WELLS, TN4 0RE **Tel:** 01892 514437
Fax: 01892 546693
Email: ft@whitmar.co.uk
Advertising Address: As above. **Tel:** 01892 542099
Email: lindsey.p@whitmar.co.uk
Web site: http://www.paperandprint.com
ISSN: 1356-9287
Publisher: Whitmar Publications Ltd
Date Established: 1994
Frequency: 8 issues yearly - Published on the 1st of the cover month
Free to qualifying individuals
Annual Sub.: £75.00
Circulation: 5,500 (Publisher's Statement)
Usual Pagination: 64
Editor: Martin White; **Advertising Manager:** Lindsey Pearson; **Publisher:** Rob Mulligan
Summary of Content: Journal for the flexographic printing industry.
Readership/Target Audience: Aimed at personnel involved in all aspects of design and production.
ADVERTISING RATES:
Full Page Colour £1900.00
Agency Commission: 10%
Mechanical Data: Film: Digital, Type Area: 268 x 186mm, Print Process: Sheet-fed offset litho, Bleed Size: 303 x 216mm, Trim Size: 297 x 210mm, Col Length: 268mm, Page Width: 186mm
Copy instructions: Copy Date: 2 weeks prior to publication date
Average advertising content per issue: 50%
BUSINESS: PRINTING & STATIONERY: Printing

FLEXPACK MATERIALS & MARKETS BULLETIN
38669U35-24
Editorial Address: PO Box 14, DORKING, RH5 4YN
Tel: 01306 884473 **Fax:** 01306 884473
Email: info@datatranscripts.com
Web site: http://www.flexpackworld.com
ISSN: 1361-1658
Publisher: Data Transcripts
Date Established: 1975
Frequency: 10 issues yearly
Annual Sub.: £255.00
Circulation: 3,200 (Publisher's Statement)
Usual Pagination: 6
Editor: Robert Higham; **Managing Director:** Robert Higham; **Circulation Manager:** Stella Roscoe
Summary of Content: International newsletter covering flexible packaging materials and market trends.
Readership/Target Audience: Read by professionals in the packaging industry.
ADVERTISING: No Advertising taken
BUSINESS: PACKAGING & BOTTLING

FLIGHT INTERNATIONAL
36339U6A-90

Editorial Address: Quadrant House, The Quadrant, SUTTON, SM2 5AS **Tel:** 020 8652 3842 **Fax:** 020 8652 3840
Email: flight.international@flightglobal.com
Advertising Address: As above. **Fax:** 020 8652 8923
Email: liz.devlin@rbi.co.uk
Web site: http://www.flightglobal.com
ISSN: 0015-3710
Publisher: Reed Business Information
Date Established: 1909
Frequency: Weekly
Cover Price: £2.85
Free to qualifying individuals
Annual Sub.: £97.00
Circulation: 42,016 (BPA Worldwide 01/07/2007 to 31/12/2007)
Editor: Andrew Doyle; **News Editor:** Dan Thisdell;
Managing Director: Jim Muttram; **Advertising Manager:** Shaun Barton; **Managing Editor:** Andrew Doyle; **Group Editor:** Kieran Daly
Summary of Content: Magazine covering aerospace industry news and features on commercial and military air transport.
Readership/Target Audience: Aimed at managers in airlines, corporate aviation departments, manufacturers, governments and the armed forces.
ADVERTISING RATES:
Full Page Mono £5770.00
Full Page Colour £7790.00
Agency Commission: 10%
Mechanical Data: Type Area: 246 x 181mm, Bleed Size: 273 x 200mm, Trim Size: 267 x 197mm, Film: Digital, Col Length: 246mm, Page Width: 181mm
Copy instructions: Copy Date: 1 week prior to publication date
BUSINESS: AVIATION & AERONAUTICS

FLIGHT SAFETY
36340U6A-95

Formerly: Flight Safety Bulletin
Editorial Address: Coombe Cottage, Colway Cross, Bishopsteignton, TEIGNMOUTH, TQ14 9TJ
Tel: 01626 776199 **Fax:** 01626 776199
Email: nigeleverett@btconnect.com
Advertising Address: 7 Avon Gardens, Bransgore, CHRISTCHURCH, BH23 8HA **Tel:** 01425 673386
Email: michaelharriss@hotmail.com
Web site: http://www.gasco.org.uk
ISSN: 0015-3737
Publisher: Jeremy Pratt
Date Established: 1964
Frequency: Quarterly
Free to qualifying individuals
Annual Sub.: £16.00
Circulation: 14,500 (Publisher's Statement)
Usual Pagination: 52
Editor: Nigel Everett; **Advertising Manager:** Michael Harriss
Summary of Content: Magazine covering general aviation flight safety (not including airline, airport or military flight safety), both in the air and on land. Includes Aviation Authority aircraft accident reports, summaries of safety leaflets and general aviation accident statistics.
Readership/Target Audience: Aimed at aeroplane, helicopter, microlight, glider, balloon and airfield owners, pilots and operators.
ADVERTISING RATES:
Full Page Mono £925.00
Full Page Colour £1029.00
Agency Commission: 10%
Mechanical Data: Type Area: 276 x 190mm, Col Length: 276mm, Film: Digital, Bleed Size: 303 x 216mm, Trim Size: 297 x 210mm, Page Width: 190mm
Copy instructions: Copy Date: 6 weeks prior to publication date
Average advertising content per issue: 40%
BUSINESS: AVIATION & AERONAUTICS

THE FLOORING MAGAZINE
35829U23B-505

Formerly: Flooring - The Magazine for Contractors & Specifiers
Editorial Address: Sparta Works, 487 Blackfen Road, SIDCUP, DA15 9NP **Tel:** 020 8298 6490 **Fax:** 020 8301 5304
Email: flooring@mpp.co.uk
Advertising Address: As above.
Email: dean.walford@mpp.co.uk
Web site: http://www.floorpoint.com
ISSN: 1461-3999
Publisher: MPP Ltd
Date Established: 1981
Frequency: Monthly - Published around the 10th of the cover month
Free to qualifying individuals
Annual Sub.: £68.00
Circulation: 8,515 (ABC 01/07/2006 to 30/06/2007)
Usual Pagination: 72
Editor: Jemma Tipping; **Publisher:** Laurence Allen
Summary of Content: Magazine covering products, services, market trends, trade news and events relevant to the UK contract flooring market.

Readership/Target Audience: Circulated on a controlled basis to flooring contractors, flooring stockists, building and architectural specifies, and specifies, specialist trades as well as facilities and property managers.
ADVERTISING RATES:
Full Page Mono £1100.00
Full Page Colour £1795.00
Agency Commission: 10%
Mechanical Data: Bleed Size: 307 x 220mm, Type Area: 273 x 187mm, Col Length: 273mm, Page Width: 187mm, Film: Digital, Trim Size: 297 x 210mm
Copy instructions: Copy Date: 6 weeks prior to publication date
Average advertising content per issue: 60%
Supplement(s): Flooring Industry Yearbook - 1xY
BUSINESS: FURNISHINGS & FURNITURE: Furnishings, Carpets & Flooring

THE FLORIST & WHOLESALE BUYER
38116U26C-25

Formerly: The Florist Trade Magazine & Wholesale Buyer
Editorial Address: 68 First Avenue, Mortlake, LONDON, SW14 8SR **Tel:** 020 8939 6470 **Fax:** 020 8878 9983
Email: austin@thewordhouse.co.uk
Advertising Address: As above.
Email: marion@thewordhouse.co.uk
Web site: http://www.fandwb.com
ISSN: 1466-3899
Publisher: The Wordhouse Publishing Group Ltd
Date Established: 1949
Frequency: 11 issues yearly - Published around the 7th of the cover month
Free to qualifying individuals
Annual Sub.: £50.00
Circulation: 8,522 (ABC 01/07/2008 to 30/06/2009)
Usual Pagination: 68
Editor: Austin Clark; **Managing Director:** Caroline Marshall-Foster; **Advertising Manager:** Marion Billett; **Publisher:** Caroline Marshall-Foster
Summary of Content: Journal covering industry news, business and retailing concepts, new varieties and products, company, people and shop profiles and seasonal items.
Readership/Target Audience: Aimed at retail buyers of flowers, plants and sundries, growers, importers, exporters and wholesalers.
ADVERTISING RATES:
Full Page Mono £1700.00
Full Page Colour £1700.00
Agency Commission: 10%
Mechanical Data: Type Area: 267 x 190mm, Bleed Size: 303 x 216mm, Trim Size: 297 x 210mm, Col Length: 267mm, Page Width: 190mm, Film: Digital
Copy instructions: Copy Date: 4 weeks prior to publication date
Average advertising content per issue: 50%
BUSINESS: GARDEN TRADE

FLUTEWISE
40940U61-14_50

Editorial Address: 8-9 Beaconsfield Road, PORTSLADE, BN41 1XA **Tel:** 01273 702367
Email: hello@flutewise.com
Advertising Address: As above. **Fax:** 01273 888864
Email: hello@flutewise.com
Web site: http://www.flutewise.com
ISSN: 1475-259X
Publisher: Flutewise Organisation
Date Established: 1989
Frequency: Quarterly
Annual Sub.: £20.00
Circulation: 2,031 (Publisher's Statement)
Usual Pagination: 56
Editor: Liz Goodwin; **Advertising Manager:** Tony Goodwin
Summary of Content: Magazine providing information on all aspects of flute playing. Covers events, workshops, competitions and professional players.
Readership/Target Audience: Aimed at flute players of all ages and standards, teachers, adult learners and anybody interested in the flute and flute playing, but with special emphasis on the young.
ADVERTISING RATES:
Full Page Mono £245.00
Full Page Colour £370.00
Agency Commission: 10%
Mechanical Data: Film: Negative, wrong reading, emulsion side up. Digital, Type Area: 255 x 185mm, Print Process: Offset litho, Bleed Size: 303 x 216mm, Trim Size: 297 x 210mm, Col Length: 255mm, Page Width: 185mm
Copy instructions: Copy Date: 6 weeks prior to publication date
Average advertising content per issue: 20%
BUSINESS: MUSIC TRADE

FM REPORT
1615572U4R-610

Editorial Address: Blair House, 184-186 High Street, TONBRIDGE, TN9 1BQ **Tel:** 01732 359990
Fax: 01732 770049
Email: jane.fenwick@imlgroup.co.uk

Advertising Address: As above.
Email: ian.webb@imlgroup.co.uk
Web site: http://www.pfmonthenet.net
Publisher: IML Group plc
Date Established: 1999
Frequency: 24 issues yearly
Cover Price: Free
Circulation: 10,500 (Publisher's Statement)
Editor: Jane Fenwick; **Advertising Manager:** Ian Webb; **Publisher:** Peter Middup
Summary of Content: Email newsletter containing news from the facilities management marketplace covering contract wins, relevant Government regulation and people moves.
Readership/Target Audience: Aimed at facilities managers in both the private and public sectors.
ADVERTISING RATES:
Full Page Mono £400.00
Full Page Colour £400.00
Agency Commission: 10%
Mechanical Data: Film: Digital, Type Area: 252 x 178mm, Col Length: 252mm, Page Width: 178mm
BUSINESS: ARCHITECTURE & BUILDING: Building Related

FM WORLD
626176U4R-613

Editorial Address: 17 Britton Street, LONDON, EC1M 5TP
Tel: 020 7880 6229 **Fax:** 020 7880 7691
Email: editorial@fm-world.co.uk
Advertising Address: As above. **Tel:** 020 7880 7660
Fax: 020 7880 7690
Email: munira@fm-world.co.uk
Web site: http://www.fm-world.co.uk
ISSN: 1743-8845
Publisher: Redactive Media Group
Date Established: 2004
Frequency: 25 issues yearly
Cover Price: £5.00
Free to qualifying individuals
Annual Sub.: £90.00
Circulation: 11,781 (ABC 01/07/2008 to 30/06/2009)
Usual Pagination: 50
Editor: Cathy Hayward; **News Editor:** Louisa Roberts
Summary of Content: Magazine covering all aspects of facilities management, includes news and views from a range of industry sectors.
Readership/Target Audience: Aimed at facilities managers in large companies, corporations and the members of the British Institute of Facilities Management.
ADVERTISING RATES:
Full Page Mono £2700.00
Agency Commission: 10%
Mechanical Data: Type Area: 272 x 190mm, Bleed Size: 303 x 216mm, Trim Size: 297 x 210mm, Film: Digital, Col Length: 272mm, Page Width: 190mm
Copy instructions: Copy Date: 2 weeks prior to publication date
Average advertising content per issue: 35%
BUSINESS: ARCHITECTURE & BUILDING: Building Related

FMCG
39804U53-671

Editorial Address: 17 Old Leeds Road, HUDDERSFIELD, HD1 1SG **Tel:** 01484 441420 **Fax:** 01484 441421
Email: editorial@codebluegroup.co.uk
Advertising Address: As above. **Tel:** 01484 441400
Fax: 01484 441401
Web site: http://www.codebluegroup.co.uk
Publisher: Code Blue Publishing Limited
Date Established: 1999
Frequency: Monthly - Published the last week of the month prior to cover date
Cover Price: £2.65
Free to qualifying individuals
Annual Sub.: £39.95
Circulation: 5,348 (Publisher's Statement)
Usual Pagination: 50
Editor: Nigel Martin
Summary of Content: Magazine containing UK and world news affecting the FMCG (Fast Moving Consumable Goods) industry. Focuses on the food and drink sector, chilled and frozen industry, manufacturing and grocery and produce sector.
Readership/Target Audience: Read by manufacturers, suppliers and those within the wholesale and retail trades.
ADVERTISING RATES:
Full Page Mono £1395.00
Full Page Colour £1965.00
Agency Commission: 10%
Mechanical Data: Type Area: 280 x 216mm, Col Length: 280mm, Page Width: 216mm, Bleed Size: 286 x 222mm, Film: Digital
Average advertising content per issue: 35%
BUSINESS: RETAILING & WHOLESALING

FMCG NEWS
1641779U53-706

Editorial Address: 4th Floor, Geneva House, Park Road, PETERBOROUGH, PE1 2UX **Tel:** 01733 756555
Fax: 01733 760505

Business Magazines

Email: fmcg@onecoms.co.uk
Advertising Address: As above.
Email: fmcg@onecoms.co.uk
Web site: http://www.onecoms.co.uk
Publisher: Media One Communications Ltd.
Frequency: 6 issues yearly
Cover Price: £3.75
Free to qualifying individuals
Editor: Karyn Reidy; **Advertising Manager:** Victoria Ellis
Summary of Content: Magazine covering fast moving consumer goods. Featuring news and information, analysis, product information and editorial on manufacturing, packaging, storage and handling, distribution and logistics.
Readership/Target Audience: Aimed at executives and decision makers in the fast moving consumer goods sector.
ADVERTISING RATES:
Full Page Colour £565.00
Mechanical Data: Type Area: 280 x 190mm, Col Length: 280mm, Page Width: 190mm, Bleed Size: 303 x 216mm, Trim Size: 297 x 210mm
BUSINESS: RETAILING & WHOLESALING

FMJ THE FACILITIES MANAGEMENT JOURNAL
35959U4R-387_90

Editorial Address: Sparta Works, 487 Blackfen Road, SIDCUP, DA15 9NP **Tel:** 020 8298 6490 **Fax:** 020 8301 5304
Email: wayne.cyrus@mpp.co.uk
Advertising Address: As above.
Email: stuart.attwood@mpp.co.uk
Web site: http://www.fmj.co.uk
ISSN: 1362-4768
Publisher: MPP Ltd
Date Established: 1992
Frequency: Monthly - Published the last working day of the month prior to cover month
Free to qualifying individuals
Annual Sub.: £68.00
Circulation: 12,008 (ABC 01/07/2008 to 30/06/2009)
Usual Pagination: 98
Editor: Wayne Cyrus
Summary of Content: Magazine providing reports and opinions on developments within the facilities management industry. Includes case studies and interviews.
Readership/Target Audience: Aimed at directors and senior executives concerned with property management.
ADVERTISING RATES:
Full Page Mono £1680.00
Full Page Colour £2280.00
SCC £25.00
Agency Commission: 10%
Mechanical Data: Bleed Size: 307 x 220mm, Film: Digital, Trim Size: 297 x 210mm, Type Area: 273 x 187mm, Col Length: 273mm, Page Width: 187mm
Copy instructions: Copy Date: 6 weeks prior to publication date
BUSINESS: ARCHITECTURE & BUILDING: Building Related

FMX
35961U4R-388_50

Formerly: FMX Facilities Management Excellence
Editorial Address: 91 Charterhouse Street, LONDON, EC1M 6HR **Tel:** 020 7336 5245 **Fax:** 020 7336 5201
Email: jgale@fmxmagazine.co.uk
Advertising Address: As above. **Tel:** 0845 155 1845
Email: mrigg@progressivemediagroup.com
Web site: http://www.fmxmagazine.co.uk
ISSN: 1462-0618
Publisher: Progressive Media
Date Established: 1998
Frequency: 10 issues yearly - Published around the 25th of the cover month (combined issues: 25th of the 1st cover month)
Free to qualifying individuals
Annual Sub.: £42.00
Circulation: 9,989 (ABC 01/07/2008 to 30/06/2009)
Usual Pagination: 120
Editor: John Gale
Summary of Content: Magazine covering all aspects of facilities management. Features technology, case studies, interviews, worldwide news and product specifications.
Readership/Target Audience: Aimed at facility managers, architects, building surveyors and buyers.
ADVERTISING RATES:
Full Page Colour £2450.00
Agency Commission: 10%
Mechanical Data: Page Width: 194mm, Film: Digital, Trim Size: 300 x 230mm, Bleed Size: 310 x 240mm, Type Area: 265 x 194mm, Col Length: 265mm, Print Process: Sheet-fed litho
Copy instructions: Copy Date: 2 weeks prior to publication date
Average advertising content per issue: 50%
BUSINESS: ARCHITECTURE & BUILDING: Building Related

F.O. LICHT'S INTERNATIONAL COFFEE REPORT
1665003U1L-84

Editorial Address: 80 Calverley Road, TUNBRIDGE WELLS, TN1 2UN **Tel:** 020 7017 7500 **Fax:** 020 7017 7599
Email: marketing@agra-net.com
Web site: http://www.agra-net.com
ISSN: 1434-2723
Publisher: Agra Informa Ltd
Frequency: 24 issues yearly
Annual Sub.: £1222.00
Summary of Content: Newsletter containing a complete overview of the world coffee market with international reports and detailed production, consumption and trade statistics.
Readership/Target Audience: Aimed at senior executives in the coffee industry worldwide.
ADVERTISING: No Advertising taken
BUSINESS: FINANCE & ECONOMICS: Commodities

F.O. LICHT'S INTERNATIONAL SUGAR & SWEETENER REPORT
1664999U1L-83

Editorial Address: 80 Calverley Road, TUNBRIDGE WELLS, TN1 2UN **Tel:** 020 7017 7500 **Fax:** 020 7017 7599
Email: marketing@agra-net.com
Web site: http://www.agra-net.com
ISSN: 0940-8541
Publisher: Agra Informa Ltd
Frequency: 36 issues yearly
Annual Sub.: £2380.00
Summary of Content: Newsletter covering unique news and analysis on the world sugar and sweetener markets, with production, consumption and trade statistics.
Readership/Target Audience: Aimed at senior executives in the sugar industry worldwide.
ADVERTISING: No Advertising taken
BUSINESS: FINANCE & ECONOMICS: Commodities

F.O. LICHT'S WORLD ETHANOL & BIOFUELS REPORT
1665002U13-202

Editorial Address: 80 Calverley Road, TUNBRIDGE WELLS, TN1 2UN **Tel:** 020 7017 7500 **Fax:** 020 7017 7599
Email: marketing@agra-net.com
Web site: http://www.agra-net.com
ISSN: 1478-5765
Publisher: Agra Informa Ltd
Frequency: 24 issues yearly
Annual Sub.: £1389.00
Summary of Content: Newsletter covering news and analysis reporting on fuel ethanol, industrial and beverage alcohol with production, consumption and trade statistics.
Readership/Target Audience: Aimed at Senior Executives in the ethanol and biofuels industry worldwide.
ADVERTISING: No Advertising taken
BUSINESS: CHEMICALS

F.O. LICHT'S WORLD GRAIN MARKETS REPORT
1665006U1L-86

Editorial Address: 80 Calverley Road, TUNBRIDGE WELLS, TN1 2UN **Tel:** 020 7017 7500 **Fax:** 020 7017 7599
Email: marketing@agra-net.com
Web site: http://www.agra-net.com
ISSN: 1745-2899
Publisher: Agra Informa Ltd
Frequency: 24 issues yearly
Annual Sub.: £1113.00
Summary of Content: Newsletter covering the latest market news and analysis, trade statistics and world production statistics for the international grains industry.
Readership/Target Audience: Aimed at senior industry Executives in the grain industry worldwide.
ADVERTISING: No Advertising taken
BUSINESS: FINANCE & ECONOMICS: Commodities

F.O. LICHT'S WORLD MOLASSES & FEED INGREDIENTS REPORT
1665001U1L-87

Editorial Address: 80 Calverley Road, TUNBRIDGE WELLS, TN1 2UN **Tel:** 020 7017 7500 **Fax:** 020 7017 7599
Email: marketing@agra-net.com
Web site: http://www.agra-net.com
ISSN: 1478-5773
Publisher: Agra Informa Ltd
Frequency: 24 issues yearly
Annual Sub.: £1232.00
Summary of Content: Newsletter covering news and analysis on molasses and special feed ingredients with production, consumption and trade statistics.
Readership/Target Audience: Aimed at senior executives in the molasses and special feed ingredients industry worldwide.
ADVERTISING: No Advertising taken
BUSINESS: FINANCE & ECONOMICS: Commodities

F.O. LICHT'S WORLD TEA MARKETS MONTHLY
1665005U1L-85

Editorial Address: 80 Calverley Road, TUNBRIDGE WELLS, TN1 2UN **Tel:** 020 7017 7500 **Fax:** 020 7017 7599
Email: marketing@agra-net.com
Web site: http://www.agra-net.com
ISSN: 1467-4920
Publisher: Agra Informa Ltd
Frequency: Monthly
Annual Sub.: £862.00
Summary of Content: Newsletter covering news, expert analysis, action reports and detailed statistical reports on the tea markets worldwide.
Readership/Target Audience: Aimed at senior executives in the tea industry worldwide.
ADVERTISING: No Advertising taken
BUSINESS: FINANCE & ECONOMICS: Commodities

FOCUS
40525U56R-58

Formerly: Health-Care Focus
Editorial Address: 111 Westminster Bridge Road, LONDON, SE1 7HR **Tel:** 020 7960 4360 **Fax:** 020 7960 4361
Email: daniel.jones@abhi.org.uk
Advertising Address: As above.
Email: enquiries@abhi.org.uk
Web site: http://www.abhi.org.uk
Publisher: Association of British Health-Care Industries
Frequency: Quarterly
Cover Price: Free
Circulation: 1,000 (Publisher's Statement)
Usual Pagination: 32
Editor: Daniel Jones; **Advertising Manager:** Daniel Jones
Summary of Content: Journal of the Association of British Health-Care Industries. Covers UK trade, international markets, healthcare and environmental legislation and standards, business opportunities, companies, new products and technology transfer opportunities.
Readership/Target Audience: Aimed at manufacturers and suppliers of health-care equipment (non-pharmaceutical).
ADVERTISING: Rates on application
BUSINESS: HEALTH & MEDICAL: Health Medical Related

FOCUS
1800725U63B-2576

Formerly: Staffordshire Focus
Editorial Address: Portland Buildings, 127-129 Portland Street, MANCHESTER, M1 4PZ **Tel:** 0161 661 4194
Fax: 0161 443 5099
Email: laurie.prescott@excelpublishing.co.uk
Advertising Address: Imprint Publishing, Houldsworth Mill, Reddish, STOCKPORT, SK5 6DA **Tel:** 0161 442 2576
Fax: 0161 443 2382
Email: lesley@imprintpub.co.uk
Publisher: Excel Publishing Company Ltd
Date Established: 2006
Frequency: 6 issues yearly
Free to qualifying individuals
Editor: Laurie Prescott; **Advertising Manager:** Lesley Vachre
Summary of Content: Magazine containing articles of interest to the business community, includes interviews and profiles.
Readership/Target Audience: Aimed at members of the Staffordshire Chambers of Commerce.
ADVERTISING RATES:
Full Page Mono £1795.00
Agency Commission: 10%
Mechanical Data: Type Area: 303 x 216mm, Col Length: 303mm, Page Width: 216mm
Copy instructions: Copy Date: Middle of the month prior to publication date
BUSINESS: REGIONAL BUSINESS: Regional Business English Counties

FOCUS ON CATALYSTS
36668U13-98_20

Editorial Address: Ei Cambridge, Block 6, Westbrook Centre, Milton Road, CAMBRIDGE, CB4 1YG
Tel: 01223 463160 **Fax:** 01223 463169
Email: cbnb@elsevier.com
Web site: http://www.ei.org
ISSN: 1351-4180
Publisher: Elsevier
Frequency: Monthly
Usual Pagination: 8
Editor: Alan Comyns
Summary of Content: International newsletter monitoring technical and commercial developments in the manufacture and use of catalysts in chemical processing.
Readership/Target Audience: Read by those involved in the chemical processing industry and catalyst development industry.
ADVERTISING: No Advertising taken
BUSINESS: CHEMICALS

FOCUS ON COMMERCIAL AVIATION SAFETY

36341U6A-96

Editorial Address: Graham Suite, Fairoaks Airport, Chobham, WOKING, GU24 8HX **Tel:** 01276 855193
Fax: 01276 855195
Email: admin@ukfsc.co.uk
Advertising Address: As above.
Email: admin@ukfsc.co.uk
Web site: http://www.ukfsc.co.uk
ISSN: 1355-1523
Publisher: The UK Flight Safety Committee
Date Established: 1960
Frequency: Quarterly
Annual Sub.: £16.60
Circulation: 12,500 (Publisher's Statement)
Usual Pagination: 26
Editor: Rich Jones; **Advertising Manager:** June Cox
Summary of Content: Official publication of The Flight Safety Committee. Covers news and articles on flight operations, air traffic control, simulators, meteorology and avionics.
Readership/Target Audience: Read by UK commercial pilots, flight engineers, maintenance organisations and air traffic control officers.
ADVERTISING RATES:
Full Page Colour £1950.00
Mechanical Data: Bleed Size: +5mm, Trim Size: 297 x 210mm, Film: Digital
Copy instructions: Copy Date: 4 weeks prior to publication date
Average advertising content per issue: 25%
BUSINESS: AVIATION & AERONAUTICS

FOCUS ON PIGMENTS

36670U13-98_60

Editorial Address: Ei Cambridge, Block 6, Westbrook Centre, Milton Road, CAMBRIDGE, CB4 1YG
Tel: 01223 463160 **Fax:** 01223 463169
Email: cbnb@elsevier.com
Web site: http://www.ei.org
Publisher: Elsevier
Frequency: Monthly
Usual Pagination: 8
Editor: Reg Adams
Summary of Content: Magazine containing an international monitoring service for all those who manufacture or use pigments.
Readership/Target Audience: Read by those in the pigment manufacturing industry including end users.
ADVERTISING: No Advertising taken
BUSINESS: CHEMICALS

FOCUS ON SURFACTANTS

36672U13-98_90

Editorial Address: Ei Cambridge, Block 6, Westbrook Centre, Milton Road, CAMBRIDGE, CB4 1YG
Tel: 01223 463160 **Fax:** 01233 463169
Email: cbnb@elsevier.com
Web site: http://www.ei.org
ISSN: 1351-4210
Publisher: Elsevier
Frequency: Monthly
Usual Pagination: 8
Editor: Caroline Edser
Summary of Content: International newsletter containing information on surface acting agents and their key market areas including detergents, toiletries and cosmetics.
Readership/Target Audience: Read by those involved in the detergents, toiletries and cosmetics industry.
ADVERTISING: No Advertising taken
BUSINESS: CHEMICALS

FOLDING CARTON INDUSTRY

38670U35-25

Editorial Address: 1 Salisbury Office Park, London Road, SALISBURY, SP1 3HP **Tel:** 01722 337038
Email: publications@brunton.co.uk
Advertising Address: As above.
Email: publications@brunton.co.uk
Web site: http://www.brunton.co.uk
Publisher: Brunton Business Publications Ltd
Frequency: 6 issues yearly - Published on the 10th of the cover month
Annual Sub.: £35.00
Circulation: 7,800 (Publisher's Statement)
Usual Pagination: 80
Editor: Michael Brunton; **Managing Director:** Michael Brunton; **Advertising Manager:** Michael Brunton; **Publisher:** Michael Brunton
Summary of Content: Magazine covering news on all aspects of carton manufacture including the latest techniques, new machinery and production lines.
Readership/Target Audience: Aimed at management in the carton industry and cartonboard mills.
ADVERTISING RATES:
Full Page Colour £1280.00
Agency Commission: 10%

Mechanical Data: Page Width: 178mm, Type Area: 229 x 178mm, Col Length: 229mm, Trim Size: 280 x 210mm, Bleed Size: 286 x 216mm, Film: Digital
Copy instructions: Copy Date: 2 weeks prior to publication date
BUSINESS: PACKAGING & BOTTLING

FOOD & AGRICULTURAL IMMUNOLOGY

37815U21B-260

Editorial Address: 4 Park Square, Milton Park, ABINGDON, OX14 4RN **Tel:** 020 7017 6000 **Fax:** 020 7017 6336
Email: fai@chester.ac.uk
Advertising Address: As above. **Tel:** 01235 828600
Fax: 01235 829000
Email: marketing@carfax.co.uk
Web site: http://www.informaworld.com/fai
ISSN: 0954-0105
Publisher: Routledge, Taylor & Francis
Date Established: 1989
Frequency: Quarterly
Annual Sub.: £754.00
Circulation: 300 (Publisher's Statement)
Usual Pagination: 96
Editor: Chris Smith; **Advertising Manager:** Simon Dunn; **Managing Editor:** Adam Wheeler
Summary of Content: Presents original immunological research with food, agricultural, environmental and veterinary applications.
Copy instructions: Copy Date: 2 months prior to publication date
BUSINESS: AGRICULTURE & FARMING: Agriculture - Supplies & Services

FOOD & BEVERAGE

1601401U22A-374

Editorial Address: Kentons House, 24 Blendon Road, BEXLEY, DA5 1BW **Tel:** 0870 701 3536
Email: foodandbeverage@ntlworld.com
Advertising Address: As above.
Email: foodandbeverage@ntlworld.com
Publisher: Direct Publishing Ltd
Date Established: 2003
Frequency: Quarterly
Free to qualifying individuals
Annual Sub.: £45.00
Circulation: 6,000 (Publisher's Statement)
Usual Pagination: 24
Editor: Phil Brown; **Advertising Manager:** Phil Brown; **Publisher:** Phil Brown
Summary of Content: Magazine covering food and drink, new products, distribution and manufacture.
Readership/Target Audience: Aimed at managers within the food and drink sector.
ADVERTISING RATES:
Full Page Colour £980.00
Agency Commission: 10%
Mechanical Data: Bleed Size: 196 x 134mm, Trim Size: 190 x 128mm, Print Process: Sheet-fed litho, Film: Digital
Copy instructions: Copy Date: 3 weeks prior to publication date
Average advertising content per issue: 40%
BUSINESS: FOOD

FOOD AND BEVERAGE INTERNATIONAL

1600939U22R-751

Editorial Address: Lodge House, Lodge Lane, Langham, COLCHESTER, CO4 5NE **Tel:** 01206 233156
Fax: 01206 233157
Email: c.rowan@foodandbeverageinternational.com
Advertising Address: As above.
Email: m.byrne@foodandbeverageinternational.com
Web site: http://www.foodandbev.com
ISSN: 1479-0823
Publisher: Zenith International Publishing
Date Established: 2002
Frequency: 6 issues yearly - Published around the 1st Monday of the cover month
Free to qualifying individuals
Annual Sub.: EUR150.00
Circulation: 13,208 (BPA Worldwide 01/01/2007 to 30/06/2007)
Usual Pagination: 50
Editor: Claire Rowan; **Executive Editor:** Maureen Byrne; **Advertising Manager:** Maureen Byrne; **Managing Editor:** Claire Rowan; **Publisher:** Maureen Byrne
Summary of Content: Magazine covering the latest food and beverage manufacturing news and technology, food and drink product formulation and launches and the latest technical developments in processing, packaging and ingredients. Also covers issues affecting the food and drink industry in Europe.
Readership/Target Audience: Aimed at food and beverage manufacturers across Europe.
ADVERTISING RATES:
Full Page Mono EUR4960.00
Full Page Colour EUR7200.00
Agency Commission: 15%

Mechanical Data: Film: Digital, Trim Size: 297 x 210mm, Type Area: 273 x 186mm, Bleed Size: 303 x 216mm, Col Length: 273mm, Page Width: 186mm
Copy instructions: Copy Date: 4 weeks prior to publication date
Average advertising content per issue: 50%
BUSINESS: FOOD: Food Related

FOOD & CATERING SOUTH WEST

36560U11A-64

Formerly: Catering & Food South West
Editorial Address: Tindle Suite, Webbs House, The Parade, LISKEARD, PL14 6AH **Tel:** 01579 342174
Fax: 01579 341852
Email: sales@foodandcateringsw.co.uk
Advertising Address: As above.
Email: foodandcateringsw@internet-today.co.uk
Web site: http://www.foodandcateringsw.co.uk
Publisher: Putnam Newspapers Ltd
Frequency: 6 issues yearly
Cover Price: Free
Circulation: 20,000 (Publisher's Statement)
Editor: John Noble
Summary of Content: Magazine featuring articles on running hotels, restaurants, pubs, fast food outlets and institutions in the South West of England.
Readership/Target Audience: Aimed at those involved in catering such as hotels, chefs and housekeepers.
ADVERTISING RATES:
Full Page Mono £1152.00
Full Page Colour £1152.00
SCC £4.00
Agency Commission: 10%
Mechanical Data: Col Widths (Display): 42.5mm, Film: Digital, No. of Columns (Display): 4, Type Area: 254 x 185mm, Col Length: 254mm, Page Width: 185mm
BUSINESS: CATERING: Catering, Hotels & Restaurants

FOOD & DRINK INTERNATIONAL

37952U22A-125_50

Editorial Address: Armstrong House, Armstrong Street, GRIMSBY, DN31 2QE **Tel:** 01472 310305
Fax: 01472 310317
Email: fdi@blmgroup.co.uk
Advertising Address: As above. **Tel:** 01472 310302
Fax: 01472 310312
Email: b.darnell@blmgroup.co.uk
Web site: http://www.foodanddrinkinternational.co.uk
Publisher: Haychart Ltd
Date Established: 1997
Frequency: Monthly - Published around the beginning of the cover month
Cover Price: £2.99
Annual Sub.: £26.91
Circulation: 17,500 (Publisher's Statement)
Usual Pagination: 60
Editor: Angela Sharman; **Publisher:** Stephen Fisher
Summary of Content: Magazine covering new products and services plus current legislation and issues facing food and drink.
Readership/Target Audience: Aimed at senior decision makers and buyers.
ADVERTISING RATES:
Full Page Mono £1240.00
Full Page Colour £1610.00
Agency Commission: 10%
Mechanical Data: Page Width: 190mm, Type Area: 277 x 190mm, Bleed Size: 303 x 216mm, Trim Size: 297 x 210mm, Col Length: 277mm, Film: Digital
Copy instructions: Copy Date: 2 weeks prior to publication date
Average advertising content per issue: 40%
BUSINESS: FOOD

FOOD & DRINK LAW MONTHLY

1665016U22R-759

Editorial Address: 80 Calverley Road, TUNBRIDGE WELLS, TN1 2UN **Tel:** 020 7017 7500 **Fax:** 020 7017 7599
Email: marketing@agra-net.com
Web site: http://www.agra-net.com
ISSN: 1479-537X
Publisher: Agra Informa Ltd
Frequency: Monthly
Annual Sub.: £405.00
Summary of Content: Newsletter providing coverage of legislative developments in the UK food and drink industries.
Readership/Target Audience: Aimed at professionals in the food and drink manufacturing, processing, packaging, labelling and retail sectors who need to keep up-to-date with all current legal and regulatory developments in the UK and EU.
ADVERTISING: No Advertising taken
BUSINESS: FOOD: Food Related

FOOD AND DRINK NETWORK UK

634519U22A-125_75

Editorial Address: Upper Spring Street, GRIMSBY, DN31 1QP **Tel:** 01472 599916 **Fax:** 01472 599910
Email: editor@waltonspublications.com
Advertising Address: As above. **Tel:** 01472 359036
Email: fd@waltonspublications.com
Publisher: W.M. Walton & Co Ltd
Date Established: 2001
Frequency: 10 issues yearly
Cover Price: Free
Usual Pagination: 56
Editor: Nicole Tinmurth; **Advertising Manager:** Kerry Foley
Summary of Content: Publication containing up-to-date news on the food and drink industry as well as information on the latest in technology, company profiles, product reviews, exhibitions and forthcoming events.
Readership/Target Audience: Aimed at food manufacturers, wholesalers and retailers, hotel groups and restaurants, caterers, breweries, food and drink consultants and researchers.
ADVERTISING RATES:
Full Page Mono £1426.00
Full Page Colour £1745.00
Agency Commission: 10%
Mechanical Data: Type Area: 270 x 186mm, Col Length: 270mm, Trim Size: 297 x 210mm, Bleed Size: 305 x 218mm, Page Width: 186mm
Copy instructions: Copy Date: 4 weeks prior to publication date
Average advertising content per issue: 40%
BUSINESS: FOOD

FOOD & DRINK NEWS

37953U22A-126

Editorial Address: 7 Bay Hall, Willow Lane, Birkby, HUDDERSFIELD, HD1 5EN **Tel:** 01484 321000
Fax: 01484 321001
Email: laura@planet-group.co.uk
Advertising Address: As above.
Email: laura@planet-group.co.uk
Web site: http://www.planet-group.net
Publisher: The Planet Group (UK) Ltd
Date Established: 1997
Frequency: Monthly - Published in the last week of the month prior to cover date
Cover Price: £4.75
Annual Sub.: £57.00
Circulation: 17,500 (Publisher's Statement)
Usual Pagination: 88
Editor: Laura Wojciechowski; **Editor-in-Chief:** Rod Millington; **Managing Director:** Edouard Rayner
Summary of Content: Magazine providing up-to-date news and views on all aspects of the food and drink industry.
Readership/Target Audience: Aimed at purchasing and sales directors within the industry.
ADVERTISING RATES:
Full Page Mono £1395.00
Full Page Colour £1750.00
Agency Commission: 10%
Mechanical Data: Type Area: 277 x 210mm, Bleed Size: 303 x 236mm, Trim Size: 297 x 230mm, Col Length: 277mm, Film: Digital, Page Width: 210mm
Copy instructions: Copy Date: 6 weeks prior to publication date
Average advertising content per issue: 35%
BUSINESS: FOOD

FOOD & DRINK TECHNOLOGY

714996U22A-252

Formerly: Liquid Food & Drink Technology
Editorial Address: The Maltings, 57 Bath Street, GRAVESEND, DA11 0DF **Tel:** 01474 532202
Fax: 01474 532203
Email: michelle@bellpublishing.com
Advertising Address: As above.
Email: katy@bellpublishing.com
Web site: http://www.bellpublishing.com
Publisher: Bell Publishing Ltd
Date Established: 2001
Frequency: 10 issues yearly - Published at the end of the month prior to cover month
Free to qualifying individuals
Annual Sub.: £95.00
Circulation: 8,500 (Publisher's Statement)
Editor: Michelle Maynard; **Advertising Manager:** Katy White; **Publisher:** Neil McRitchie
Summary of Content: Magazine covering ingredients, processing and packaging, includes technical and business news, analysis, comment, plant profiles, interviews and product development as well as geographic and industry sector reviews.
Readership/Target Audience: Aimed at major specifiers within the food industry.
ADVERTISING RATES:
Full Page Mono £1390.00
Full Page Colour £2165.00
Agency Commission: 10%

Mechanical Data: Bleed Size: 303 x 216mm, Type Area: 254 x 180mm, Trim Size: 297 x 210mm, Col Length: 254mm, Page Width: 180mm, Film: Digital
Copy instructions: Copy Date: 20th of the month prior to publication date
BUSINESS: FOOD

FOOD CHEMISTRY

38044U22R-120

Editorial Address: Food Biosciences, University of Reading, PO Box 226, READING, RG6 6AP **Tel:** 0118 931 8705
Fax: 0118 931 0080
Advertising Address: 32 Jamestown Road, LONDON, NW1 7BY **Tel:** 020 7424 4400 **Fax:** 01865 853136
Email: j.kenney@elsevier.com
Publisher: Elsevier Ltd
Frequency: 24 issues yearly
Circulation: 600 (Publisher's Statement)
Editor: Gordon Birch; **Managing Editor:** Gordon Birch; **Publisher:** Dan Lovegrove
Summary of Content: Papers on the chemical, sensory and nutritional properties of food.
Readership/Target Audience: Read by food technologists, scientists and chemists.
ADVERTISING RATES:
Full Page Mono £865.00
Full Page Colour £1885.00
Agency Commission: 15%
Copy instructions: Copy Date: 5 weeks prior to publication date
BUSINESS: FOOD: Food Related

FOOD MANUFACTURE

38002U22C-130

Editorial Address: Broadfield Park, CRAWLEY, RH11 9RT
Tel: 01293 613400 **Fax:** 01293 846538
Email: foodman@william-reed.co.uk
Advertising Address: As above. **Tel:** 01293 610275
Fax: 01293 610345
Email: chris.cross@william-reed.co.uk
Web site: http://www.foodmanufacture.co.uk
ISSN: 0015-6477
Publisher: William Reed Business Media
Date Established: 1927
Frequency: Monthly - Published on the 1st of the cover month
Cover Price: £8.00
Free to qualifying individuals
Annual Sub.: £81.00
Circulation: 14,694 (ABC 01/01/2008 to 31/12/2008)
Usual Pagination: 120
News Editor: Rod Addy; **Advertising Manager:** Chris Cross
Summary of Content: Publication covering ingredients, processing, machinery, packaging, handling and storage, process control and distribution.
Readership/Target Audience: Read by directors and senior management.
ADVERTISING RATES:
Full Page Colour ....:...... £2168.00
Agency Commission: 10%
Mechanical Data: Type Area: 267 x 185mm, Trim Size: 297 x 210mm, Bleed Size: 303 x 216mm, Film: Digital, Col Length: 267mm, Page Width: 185mm, Print Process: Web-offset
Average advertising content per issue: 40%
Supplement(s): Food Ingredients Health & Nutrition - 6xY, New Product Development (NPD) - 4xY
BUSINESS: FOOD: Food Processing & Packaging

FOOD PACKAGING BULLETIN

38671U35-30

Editorial Address: Grenville Court, Britwell Road, Burnham, SLOUGH, SL1 8DF **Tel:** 01628 600499 **Fax:** 01628 600488
Email: info@researchinformation.co.uk
Web site: http://www.researchinformation.co.uk
ISSN: 1355-0497
Publisher: Research Information Ltd
Frequency: 10 issues yearly
Annual Sub.: £425.00
Circulation: 200 (Publisher's Statement)
Usual Pagination: 12
Editor: Kumar Patel; **Publisher:** Kumar Patel; **Circulation Manager:** Richard Wood
Summary of Content: Newsletter covering all aspects of regulatory affairs in food packaging.
Readership/Target Audience: Aimed at regulatory managers, technical directors and senior managers in the food industry.
ADVERTISING: No Advertising taken
BUSINESS: PACKAGING & BOTTLING

FOOD PACKER AND PROCESSOR DIRECTORY

718527U35-353

Editorial Address: Attwood House, Mansfield Park, Four Marks, ALTON, GU34 5PZ **Tel:** 01420 568900
Fax: 01420 565995
Email: editorial@binstedgroup.com

Advertising Address: As above. **Fax:** 01420 565994
Web site: http://www.binstedgroup.com
Publisher: The Binsted Group plc
Date Established: 1988
Frequency: Annual - Published in October
Cover Price: £100.00
Usual Pagination: 220
Editor: Julie Foskett; **Advertising Manager:** Andrew Flew; **Circulation Manager:** Tracey Jarrold
Summary of Content: Directory containing information on suppliers of packaging machinery and materials, UK food companies with named personnel, contract packers and trade associations.
Readership/Target Audience: Read by top management, production directors, marketing and brand managers, packaging buyers and project teams from the food industry.
ADVERTISING RATES:
Full Page Mono £995.00
Full Page Colour £1535.00
Agency Commission: 10%
Mechanical Data: Type Area: 229 x 178mm, Film: Digital, Bleed Size: 286 x 216mm, Trim Size: 280 x 210mm, Col Length: 229mm, Page Width: 178mm
Copy instructions: Copy Date: 10th of month prior to publication date
BUSINESS: PACKAGING & BOTTLING

FOOD PACKER & PROCESSOR INTERNATIONAL

38672U35-35

Formerly: Food Packer International
Editorial Address: Attwood House, Mansfield Park, Four Marks, ALTON, GU34 5PZ **Tel:** 01420 568900
Fax: 01420 565995
Email: editorial@binstedgroup.com
Advertising Address: As above.
Email: andrew.flew@binstedgroup.com
Web site: http://www.binstedgroup.com
Publisher: The Binsted Group plc
Frequency: 6 issues yearly - Published on the 1st of the 1st cover month
Cover Price: £8.00
Annual Sub.: £55.00
Circulation: 5,960 (Publisher's Statement)
Usual Pagination: 72
Editor: Julie Foskett
Summary of Content: Magazine that deals with primary/ secondary packaging equipment and materials for the food industry.
Readership/Target Audience: Aimed at those responsible for specifying and buying packaging materials.
ADVERTISING RATES:
Full Page Mono £995.00
Full Page Colour £1535.00
Agency Commission: 10%
Mechanical Data: Page Width: 178mm, Film: Digital, Type Area: 229 x 178mm, Col Length: 229mm, Trim Size: 280 x 210mm, Bleed Size: 286 x 216mm
Copy instructions: Copy Date: 6 weeks prior to publication date
Average advertising content per issue: 35%
BUSINESS: PACKAGING & BOTTLING

FOOD PROCESSING

38004U22C-140

Editorial Address: Blair House, 184-186 High Street, TONBRIDGE, TN9 1BQ **Tel:** 01732 359990
Fax: 01732 770049
Email: david.strydom@imlgroup.co.uk
Advertising Address: As above. **Fax:** 01732 778542
Email: adam.garside@imlgroup.co.uk
Web site: http://www.fponthenet.net
ISSN: 0264-9462
Publisher: IML Group plc
Date Established: 1931
Frequency: Monthly - Published the last week of the month prior to cover date
Cover Price: £10.00
Free to qualifying individuals
Annual Sub.: £99.00
Circulation: 8,430 (ABC 01/01/2008 to 31/12/2008)
Usual Pagination: 72
Editor: David Strydom; **Advertising Manager:** Adam Garside
Summary of Content: Magazine covering technical news with features on packaging, hygiene, distribution, all aspects of food production and process control. Includes relevant business issues and legislative issues for the food industry.
Readership/Target Audience: Read by decision-makers in the food processing industry.
ADVERTISING RATES:
Full Page Mono £1500.00
Full Page Colour £1950.00
Agency Commission: 10%
Mechanical Data: Col Length: 254mm, Film: Positive, right reading, emulsion side down. Digital, Type Area: 254 x 178mm, Print Process: Web-fed offset, Bleed Size: 286 x 208mm, Trim Size: 280 x 205mm, Page Width: 178mm
Average advertising content per issue: 60%
BUSINESS: FOOD: Food Processing & Packaging

FOOD QUALITY AND PREFERENCE

38046U22R-160

Editorial Address: The Boulevard, Langford Lane, KIDLINGTON, OX5 1GB **Fax:** 0117 986 3590
Email: fqp@halmacfie.com
Web site: http://www.elsevier.nl/locate/foodqual
Publisher: Elsevier Ltd
Date Established: 1989
Frequency: 8 issues yearly
Annual Sub.: $819.00
Editor: H.J.H. MacFie
Summary of Content: Publishes peer-reviewed scientific articles on sensory and consumer sciences in relation to food and beverages. Interested in details of scientific meetings around the world.
Readership/Target Audience: Read by professionals employed in the food industry and in food and nutrition research.
ADVERTISING: No Advertising taken
BUSINESS: FOOD: Food Related

FOOD SCIENCE AND TECHNOLOGY

38047U22R-170

Formerly: Food Science and Technology Today
Editorial Address: 7 Miners Close, Long Ashton, BRISTOL, BS41 9DE **Tel:** 01275 395368 **Fax:** 01275 395368
Email: roger.atkin2@btopenworld.com
Advertising Address: Portland Buildings, 127-129 Portland Street, MANCHESTER, M1 4PZ **Tel:** 0161 661 2782
Fax: 0161 236 2783
Email: paula.english@excelpublishing.co.uk
Web site: http://www.ifst.org
ISSN: 0950-9623
Publisher: Excel Publishing Company Ltd
Date Established: 1987
Frequency: Quarterly
Annual Sub.: £101.00
Circulation: 4,000 (Publisher's Statement)
Usual Pagination: 64
Editor: Roger Atkin; **Executive Editor:** Elizabeth Donevan
Summary of Content: Journal of the Institute of Food Science and Technology, covering all aspects of food science and technology, including professional matters.
Readership/Target Audience: Aimed at industrial scientists, researchers, academics and consultants working in the field of food science technology and government scientists.
ADVERTISING RATES:
Full Page Colour £2950.00
Agency Commission: 10%
Mechanical Data: Film: Digital, Col Length: 266mm, Type Area: 266 x 185mm, Bleed Size: 303 x 216mm, Trim Size: 297 x 210mm, Page Width: 185mm, No. of Columns (Display): 4
Copy instructions: Copy Date: 1st of the month prior to publication date
Average advertising content per issue: 30%
BUSINESS: FOOD: Food Related

FOOD TECHNOLOGY & PACKAGING

37960U22A-170

Editorial Address: 7B Lower Ballinderry Road, Upper Ballinderry, LISBURN, BT28 2JB **Tel:** 028 9265 2773
Email: beryl@bebmedia.com
Advertising Address: As above.
Email: beryl@bebmedia.com
Publisher: BeB Media Ltd
Date Established: 1995
Frequency: Quarterly
Free to qualifying individuals
Annual Sub.: £18.00
Circulation: 2,786 (Publisher's Statement)
Usual Pagination: 48
Editor: Beryl Bickerstaff; **Advertising Manager:** Beryl Bickerstaff; **Publisher:** Beryl Bickerstaff
Summary of Content: Magazine covering all aspects of the food processing, packaging and related industries in Northern Ireland.
Readership/Target Audience: Aimed at trade in food processing, packaging, distribution and related industries in Northern Ireland.
ADVERTISING RATES:
Full Page Colour £1200.00
Agency Commission: 10%
Mechanical Data: Type Area: 265 x 180mm, Bleed Size: 297 x 210mm, Trim Size: 307 x 220mm, Col Length: 265mm, Page Width: 180mm
Average advertising content per issue: 40%
BUSINESS: FOOD

FOOD TRADE REVIEW

38005U22C-150

Editorial Address: Station House, Hortons Way, WESTERHAM, TN16 1BZ **Tel:** 01959 563944
Fax: 01959 561285
Email: info@foodtradereview.com

Advertising Address: As above.
Email: info@foodtradereview.com
Web site: http://www.foodtradereview.com
ISSN: 0015-6671
Publisher: Food Trade Press Ltd
Date Established: 1931
Frequency: Monthly - Published on the 20th of the cover month
Cover Price: £6.00
Annual Sub.: £60.00
Circulation: 5,012 (Publisher's Statement)
Usual Pagination: 72
Editor: Adrian Binsted; **Managing Director:** Adrian Binsted;
Advertising Manager: Adrian Binsted; **Publisher:** Adrian Binsted
Summary of Content: Contains news about the latest methods and techniques of food processing and manufacturing, as well as the latest trade news.
Readership/Target Audience: Aimed at production and technical managers in food manufacturing and processing companies.
ADVERTISING RATES:
Full Page Mono £1250.00
Full Page Colour £1400.00
Agency Commission: 10%
Mechanical Data: No. of Columns (Display): 3, Bleed Size: 303 x 216mm, Trim Size: 297 x 210mm, Col Length: 260mm, Page Width: 182mm, Col Widths (Display): 56mm, Type Area: 260 x 182mm
Copy instructions: Copy Date: 5th of the cover month
Average advertising content per issue: 35%
BUSINESS: FOOD: Food Processing & Packaging

FOOD TRADER FOR BUTCHERS

37962U22A-167

Formerly: Food Trader
Editorial Address: 1 Belgrove, TUNBRIDGE WELLS, TN1 1YW **Tel:** 01892 541412 **Fax:** 01892 535462
Email: graham@nfmft.co.uk
Advertising Address: As above. **Tel:** 0870 443 0217
Fax: 0870 443 0218
Email: robert_ftfb@tiscali.co.uk
Web site: http://www.nfmft.co.uk
ISSN: 1470-9775
Publisher: The National Federation of Meat and Food Traders
Date Established: 2000
Frequency: 10 issues yearly - Published around the 12th of the cover month
Free to qualifying individuals
Annual Sub.: £25.00
Circulation: 7,500 (Publisher's Statement)
Usual Pagination: 20
Editor: Graham Bidston; **Advertising Manager:** Robert Norman
Summary of Content: Official journal of the National Federation of Meat and Food Traders. Contains articles on news, products, promotions, features, events, and competitions in the meat industry.
Readership/Target Audience: Aimed at independent butchers, slaughter houses, cutting plants, factories, catering butchers and farm shops in the UK.
ADVERTISING RATES:
Full Page Colour £2400.00
SCC £14.00
Agency Commission: 10%
Mechanical Data: No. of Columns (Display): 4, Trim Size: 297 x 210mm, Type Area: 260 x 190mm, Col Length: 260mm, Bleed Size: 303 x 216mm, Page Width: 190mm, Film: Digital
Copy instructions: Copy Date: 15th of the month prior to publication date
Average advertising content per issue: 30%
BUSINESS: FOOD

FOOD WORKER

37182U14L-225

Editorial Address: Stanborough House, Great North Road, WELWYN GARDEN CITY, AL8 7TA **Tel:** 01707 260150
Fax: 01707 261570
Email: joe.marino@bfawu.org
Advertising Address: As above. **Tel:** 01707 260750
Web site: http://www.bfawu.org
Publisher: Bakers, Food and Allied Workers' Union
Date Established: 1898
Frequency: Quarterly
Cover Price: £1.00
Free to qualifying individuals
Circulation: 10,000 (Publisher's Statement)
Usual Pagination: 28
Editor: Joe Marino
Summary of Content: Journal of the Bakers, Food and Allied Workers' Union. Focusing on world issues, running bakeries and product news.
Readership/Target Audience: Read by members.
Supplement(s): Health and Safety Bulletin - 4xY
BUSINESS: COMMERCE, INDUSTRY & MANAGEMENT: Trade Unions

FOODCHAIN

652223U22A-130

Editorial Address: Unit 10, Cringleford Business Centre, Intwood Road, Cringleford, NORWICH, NR4 6AU
Tel: 01603 274130 **Fax:** 01603 274136
Email: libbie@schofieldpublishing.co.uk
Advertising Address: As above. **Fax:** 01603 274131
Email: pmonument@schofieldpublishing.co.uk
Web site: http://www.foodchain-magazine.com
ISSN: 1473-9321
Publisher: Schofield Publishing Ltd
Frequency: 6 issues yearly - Published in the 3rd week of the cover month
Cover Price: £3.95
Free to qualifying individuals
Usual Pagination: 130
Editor: Libbie Hammond; **Advertising Manager:** Phillip Monument
Summary of Content: Magazine containing articles on management issues and recent trends within the food and drink industry.
Readership/Target Audience: Read by MDs and senior level management in the food and drinks industry.
ADVERTISING RATES:
Full Page Mono £1995.00
Full Page Colour £2595.00
Agency Commission: 10%
Mechanical Data: Type Area: 420 x 258mm, Bleed Size: 466 x 306mm, Trim Size: 460 x 300mm, Col Length: 420mm, Film: Digital, Page Width: 258mm
Copy instructions: Copy Date: 1st week of the publication month
Average advertising content per issue: 42%
BUSINESS: FOOD

FOODNEWS

37956U22A-137

Editorial Address: 80 Calverley Road, TUNBRIDGE WELLS, TN1 2UN **Tel:** 020 7017 7500 **Fax:** 020 7017 7599
Email: marketing@agra-net.com
Advertising Address: As above. **Fax:** 020 7017 7594
Email: fnadvertising@agra-net.com
Web site: http://www.agra-net.com
ISSN: 0951-130X
Publisher: Agra Informa Ltd
Date Established: 1973
Frequency: Weekly
Annual Sub.: £578.00
Usual Pagination: 12
Summary of Content: Magazine covering weekly prices, production and trade news for the world markets for fruit juice and fruit juice concentrates, canned and frozen foods, tomato products, dairy products and dried fruit and nuts.
Readership/Target Audience: Read by decision makers in the International food trade.
ADVERTISING RATES:
Full Page Mono £1280.00
Full Page Colour £2425.00
Agency Commission: 15%
Mechanical Data: Type Area: 220 x 179mm, Film: Digital, Col Length: 220mm, Page Width: 179mm, Print Process: Litho, Trim Size: 260 x 202mm, Bleed Size: 266 x 205mm
Average advertising content per issue: 50%
BUSINESS: FOOD

FOODSERVICE UPDATE

1804690U11A-222

Editorial Address: Progressive House, 2 Maidstone Road, SIDCUP, DA14 5HZ **Tel:** 0845 000 2500
Email: saraha@dewberryredpoint.co.uk
Advertising Address: As above.
Email: danielh@dewberryredpoint.co.uk
Web site: http://www.foodserviceupdate.co.uk
ISSN: 1755-7658
Publisher: Dewberry Redpoint Ltd
Date Established: 2007
Frequency: 10 issues yearly - Double issues published in July/August and November/December
Free to qualifying individuals
Annual Sub.: £60.00
Circulation: 21,648 (ABC 01/07/2008 to 30/06/2009)
Usual Pagination: 64
Editor: Sarah Allen
Summary of Content: Publication covering catering products, food, presentation, equipment and furnishings.
Readership/Target Audience: Aimed at buyers and people influencing purchasing decisions in hotels, restaurants, pubs, wine bars and contract caterers.
ADVERTISING RATES:
Full Page Colour £3995.00
Agency Commission: 10%
Mechanical Data: Type Area: 268 x 186mm, Bleed Size: 303 x 216mm, Trim Size: 297 x 210mm, Col Length: 268mm, Page Width: 186mm, Film: Digital
Copy instructions: Copy Date: 4 weeks prior to publication date
Average advertising content per issue: 40%
BUSINESS: CATERING: Catering, Hotels & Restaurants

Business Magazines

FOOTBALL & SPORTS ARENA
38522U32H-78

Formerly: European Football Decision
Editorial Address: 11 Adria Road, Didsbury, MANCHESTER, M20 6SQ **Tel:** 0161 434 8194
Fax: 0161 613 9187
Email: mike.pepper48@ntlworld.com
Advertising Address: As above.
Email: mike.pepper48@ntlworld.com
Web site: http://www.fsarena.co.uk
Publisher: Grandflame Ltd
Frequency: 6 issues yearly - Published around the 7th of the cover month
Usual Pagination: 56
Editor: Mike Pepper
Summary of Content: Business magazine with features, news reviews and topics relating to the day to day management within the football and sports arena markets.
Readership/Target Audience: Aimed at directors and senior managers/department heads who are charged with the day to day running of the various departments within the football and sports arenas throughout the UK.
ADVERTISING RATES:
Full Page Mono £895.00
Full Page Colour £1250.00
Agency Commission: 10%
Mechanical Data: Bleed Size: 303 x 216mm, Trim Size: 297 x 210mm
Copy instructions: Copy Date: 4 weeks prior to publication date
Average advertising content per issue: 40%
BUSINESS: LOCAL GOVERNMENT, LEISURE & RECREATION: Leisure, Recreation & Entertainment

FOOTBALL AND STADIUM MANAGEMENT
38529U32H-107_50

Editorial Address: 3rd Floor, Hollinwood Business Centre, Albert Street, OLDHAM, OL8 3QL **Tel:** 0161 683 8000
Fax: 0161 683 8001
Email: lynne.whatmore@worldsfair.co.uk
Advertising Address: As above.
Email: craig.mills@worldsfair.co.uk
Web site: http://www.worldsfair.co.uk
ISSN: 1361-9500
Publisher: The World's Fair Ltd
Frequency: 6 issues yearly - Published on the 25th of the cover month
Free to qualifying individuals
Annual Sub.: £30.00
Usual Pagination: 48
Editor: Lynne Whatmore
Summary of Content: Independent business magazine for indoor and outdoor sports venues throughout the UK and Ireland.
Readership/Target Audience: Aimed at decision makers with buying authority in professional and semi-professional clubs, in football, both codes of rugby, athletics, cricket and tennis.
ADVERTISING RATES:
Full Page Colour £1550.00
Agency Commission: 10%
Mechanical Data: Bleed Size: 303 x 216mm, Trim Size: 297 x 210mm
Copy instructions: Copy Date: 16 days prior to publication date
Average advertising content per issue: 60%
BUSINESS: LOCAL GOVERNMENT, LEISURE & RECREATION: Leisure, Recreation & Entertainment

FOOTBALL INSIDER
1866239U32H-477

Editorial Address: 292 Vauxhall Bridge Road, LONDON, SW1V 1AE **Tel:** 020 7963 7888 **Fax:** 020 7963 7894
Email: rory.squires@pa-sport.com
Web site: http://www.pa-sport.com
Publisher: Press Association Sport Services
Frequency: Daily
Circulation: 5,000 (Publisher's Statement)
Usual Pagination: 50
Editor: Rory Squires; **Managing Editor:** Rory Squires
Summary of Content: Daily bulletin containing interviews with those running world football, plus analysis of trends and commercial issues within the game.
Readership/Target Audience: Aimed at commercial managers and directors of football league and county football clubs, as well as manufacturing and supply companies targeting the football business.
BUSINESS: LOCAL GOVERNMENT, LEISURE & RECREATION: Leisure, Recreation & Entertainment

FOOTWEAR NEWS
22934U29-52

Editorial Address: 8B Wallace Road, LONDON, N12 PG
Tel: 020 7226 7540
Email: elisa.anniss@virgin.net
Web site: http://www.footwearnews.com
Publisher: Fairchild Publications, Inc.
Frequency: Weekly
Cover Price: $10.00
Editor: Elisa Anniss
Summary of Content: Magazine covering products, trends and news in the footwear industry.
Readership/Target Audience: Aimed at footwear manufacturers, retailers and those involved in the footwear industry.
ADVERTISING: No Advertising taken
BUSINESS: FOOTWEAR

FOOTWEAR TODAY
38222U29-53

Formerly: Footwear and Leather Goods Today
Editorial Address: 15A London Road, MAIDSTONE, ME16 8LY **Tel:** 01622 687031 **Fax:** 01622 757646
Email: footwear@datateam.co.uk
Advertising Address: As above.
Email: footwear@datateam.co.uk
Web site: http://www.footweartoday.co.uk
Publisher: Datateam Publishing Ltd
Frequency: 10 issues yearly - Published around the 1st of the cover month
Annual Sub.: £50.00
Circulation: 6,228 (Publisher's Statement)
Usual Pagination: 68
Editor: Cheryl Taylor
Summary of Content: Magazine covering news, products, events, services and footwear industry information.
Readership/Target Audience: Aimed at footwear, leather goods and fashion retailers. Also mail order companies, manufacturers, distributors and those involved in associated services.
ADVERTISING RATES:
Full Page Colour £1350.00
SCC £15.00
Agency Commission: 10%
Mechanical Data: Page Width: 195mm, Type Area: 280 x 195mm, Bleed Size: 312 x 235mm, Trim Size: 306 x 229mm, Col Length: 280mm, Film: Positive, right reading, emulsion side down, Screen: 60 lpc
Copy instructions: Copy Date: 2 weeks prior to publication date
Average advertising content per issue: 40%
Supplement(s): Moda Footwear - 2xY
BUSINESS: FOOTWEAR

FORBES
1657294U14A-550

Editorial Address: 36-38 Piccadilly, LONDON, W1J 0DP
Tel: 020 7534 3900
Email: dweathers@forbes.com
Advertising Address: As above.
Email: cyardley@forbes.com
Web site: http://www.forbes.com
Publisher: Forbes Inc
Frequency: 26 issues yearly
Annual Sub.: $59.95
Circulation: 900,000 (Publisher's Statement)
Editor: Debbie Weathers; **Managing Director:** Charles Yardley; **Advertising Manager:** Charles Yardley
Summary of Content: Magazine focusing on management performance, technology, finance, marketing, law, tax, communications, investment and global business trends.
Readership/Target Audience: Aimed at business management professionals.
ADVERTISING RATES:
Full Page Mono $73100.00
Full Page Colour $107520.00
Agency Commission: 15%
Mechanical Data: Type Area: 254 x 178mm, Trim Size: 267 x 203mm, Bleed Size: 413 x 273mm, Col Length: 254mm, Page Width: 178mm, Print Process: Web-fed offset litho. Digital
Average advertising content per issue: 60%
BUSINESS: COMMERCE, INDUSTRY & MANAGEMENT

FORD NEWS
749337U31R-31

Editorial Address: Eagle Way, BRENTWOOD, CM13 3BW
Tel: 01277 252880 **Fax:** 01277 253097
Email: fnews@ford.com
Advertising Address: As above. **Tel:** 01277 254195
Email: fnews@ford.com
Publisher: Ford Motor Company Ltd
Date Established: 1942
Frequency: 10 issues yearly
Cover Price: Free
Circulation: 50,000 (Publisher's Statement)
Usual Pagination: 28
Editor: Jason Simms; **Advertising Manager:** Martin Hammond
Summary of Content: Magazine covering Ford company news.
Readership/Target Audience: Read by Ford employees and pensioners.
ADVERTISING RATES:
Full Page Mono £2200.00
Full Page Colour £2200.00
Agency Commission: 15%

Mechanical Data: Type Area: 259 x 184mm, Bleed Size: 288 x 218mm, Trim Size: 280 x 210mm, Col Length: 259mm, Page Width: 184mm, Film: Digital
Copy instructions: Copy Date: 2 weeks prior to publication date
Average advertising content per issue: 45%
BUSINESS: MOTOR TRADE: Motor Trade Related

FORECOURT
626067U53-75

Editorial Address: 201 Great Portland Street, LONDON, W1W 5AB **Tel:** 020 7580 9122 **Fax:** 020 7580 6376
Email: vaughanfreeman1@aol.com
Advertising Address: As above.
Email: rayrogers@rmif.co.uk
Web site: http://www.rmif.co.uk
Publisher: Retail Motor Industry Federation Ltd
Frequency: 10 issues yearly - Published in the middle of the cover month
Cover Price: Free
Circulation: 3,000 (Publisher's Statement)
Usual Pagination: 24
Editor: Vaughan Freeman; **Advertising Manager:** Ray Rogers
Summary of Content: Magazine that investigates and reports on all the latest news and views from the Government, regulatory bodies, retailers, shop suppliers and oil companies. Covers PRA activities, opinions, retailer contracts, fuel duty, pricing, warm fuel deliveries, shop products, smuggling and Government transport policy.
Readership/Target Audience: Aimed at independent, company owned, franchised and motorway retailers.
ADVERTISING RATES:
Full Page Mono £1175.00
Full Page Colour £1350.00
Agency Commission: 10%
Mechanical Data: Type Area: 260 x 180mm, Bleed Size: 305 x 216mm, Trim Size: 297 x 210mm, Col Length: 260mm, Page Width: 180mm, Film: Digital
Copy instructions: Copy Date: 1 week prior to publication date
Average advertising content per issue: 33%
BUSINESS: RETAILING & WHOLESALING

FORECOURT TRADER
39806U53-80

Editorial Address: Broadfield Park, CRAWLEY, RH11 9RT
Tel: 01293 613400 **Fax:** 01293 610330
Email: merril.boulton@william-reed.co.uk
Advertising Address: As above.
Email: james.bush@william-reed.co.uk
Web site: http://www.forecourttrader.co.uk
Publisher: William Reed Business Media
Frequency: Monthly - Published in the 1st week of the cover month
Circulation: 10,922 (ABC 01/07/2008 to 30/06/2009)
Usual Pagination: 60
Editor: Merril Boulton; **Features Editor:** Linda Harrison; **Managing Director:** Charles Reed; **Advertising Manager:** James Bush
Summary of Content: Journal containing the latest news, features, legal advice and the latest developments in products and equipment.
Readership/Target Audience: Read by retailers, major suppliers of forecourt equipment and oil company executives responsible for key purchasing decisions.
ADVERTISING RATES:
Full Page Colour £2650.00
SCC £33.00
Agency Commission: 10%
Mechanical Data: Type Area: 267 x 185mm, Col Length: 267mm, Trim Size: 298 x 210mm, Bleed Size: 304 x 216mm, Film: Digital, Page Width: 185mm
Copy instructions: Copy Date: 2 weeks prior to publication date
Average advertising content per issue: 50%
BUSINESS: RETAILING & WHOLESALING

FORESIGHT
37232U14R-110

Editorial Address: 13 High Street, Cottenham, CAMBRIDGE, CB4 8SA **Tel:** 01954 205278
Fax: 01954 209916
Email: colin.blackman@ntlworld.com
Web site: http://www.emeraldinsight.com
ISSN: 1463-6689
Publisher: Emerald Group Publishing Ltd
Date Established: 1999
Frequency: 6 issues yearly
Annual Sub.: £679.00
Usual Pagination: 96
Editor: Colin Blackman; **Publisher:** Claire Jackson
Summary of Content: Journal providing a forum for debate on the social, economic, political and technological issues which are shaping the future. Contains future studies, strategic thinking and policy.
Readership/Target Audience: Aimed at economic planners and policy makers within businesses and government and those who need to keep abreast of research and current thinking about the future.

ADVERTISING: No Advertising taken
BUSINESS: COMMERCE, INDUSTRY & MANAGEMENT: Commerce Related

FORESTRY
39457U46-12

Editorial Address: Institute of Chartered Foresters, 59 George Street, EDINBURGH, EH2 2JG **Tel:** 0131 240 1425
Fax: 0131 240 1424
Email: icf@charteredforesters.org
Advertising Address: Great Clarendon Street, OXFORD, OX2 6DP **Tel:** 01865 354637 **Fax:** 01865 353774
Email: steve.simmonds@oxfordjournals.org
Web site: http://forestry.oxfordjournals.org
ISSN: 0015-752X
Publisher: OUP
Date Established: 1927
Frequency: 5 issues yearly
Cover Price: £61.00
Annual Sub.: £242.00
Circulation: 620 (Publisher's Statement)
Editor: Allison Lock
Summary of Content: Journal covering all scientific and environmental aspects of forestry.
Readership/Target Audience: Read by those concerned with the fundamental study of forestry.
ADVERTISING RATES:
Full Page Mono £646.00
Full Page Colour £1076.00
Agency Commission: 10%
Mechanical Data: Page Width: 150mm, Type Area: 210 x 150mm, Col Length: 210mm, Trim Size: 246 x 189mm, Bleed Size: 252 x 195mm, Print Process: Litho, Film: Digital
BUSINESS: TIMBER, WOOD & FORESTRY

FORESTRY & TIMBER NEWS
39469U46-40

Formerly: Timber Grower
Editorial Address: Woodland Place, West Street, BELFORD, NE70 7QA **Tel:** 01668 213937
Fax: 01668 213555
Email: jane@apfs.demon.co.uk
Advertising Address: 27 Norwich Road, HALESWORTH, IP19 8BX **Tel:** 01986 834250 **Fax:** 01986 834255
Email: jo@micropress.co.uk
Web site: http://www.confor.org.uk
ISSN: 1476-8615
Publisher: BC Publications
Date Established: 2002
Frequency: 6 issues yearly
Free to qualifying individuals
Annual Sub.: £32.00
Circulation: 3,000 (Publisher's Statement)
Usual Pagination: 48
Editor: Jane Karthaus; **Publisher:** Simon Tooth
Summary of Content: Official magazine of the Confederation of Forest Industries.
Readership/Target Audience: Read by those working in the forestry and timber industry.
ADVERTISING RATES:
Full Page Colour £1345.05
SCC £8.60
Agency Commission: 10%
Mechanical Data: Page Width: 188mm, Film: Positive, right reading, emulsion side down. Digital, Type Area: 270 x 188mm, Col Length: 270mm, Trim Size: 290 x 210mm, Bleed Size: 305 x 214mm, No. of Columns (Display): 5
Copy instructions: Copy Date: 4 weeks prior to publication date
Average advertising content per issue: 40%
Supplement(s): Woodland Owner - 6xY
BUSINESS: TIMBER, WOOD & FORESTRY

FORESTRY JOURNAL
39456U46-11_50

Formerly: Forest Machine Journal
Editorial Address: PO Box 7570, DUMFRIES, DG2 8YD
Tel: 01387 880359 **Fax:** 01387 880359
Email: editor@forestryjournal.co.uk
Advertising Address: 23 Egerton Place, WHITCHURCH, SY13 1NU **Tel:** 01948 662825 **Fax:** 01948 662825
Email: anne@forestryjournal.co.uk
Web site: http://www.forestryjournal.co.uk
ISSN: 1356-1006
Publisher: Forest Machine Journal
Date Established: 1994
Frequency: Monthly - Published around the 1st of the cover month
Annual Sub.: £49.00
Circulation: 4,000 (Publisher's Statement)
Usual Pagination: 60
Editor: Mark Andrews; **Publisher:** Mark Andrews
Summary of Content: Magazine covering a wide range of subjects including woodland and forestry equipment, arboriculture, estate and amenity work, timber harvesting and extraction, planting, chipping, shredding, ground preparation, road making, sawmilling and timber haulage.
Language(s): English; French; German

Readership/Target Audience: Aimed at forestry contractors, machinery operators, estate workers, tree surgeons, woodland managers, arboriculturalists, manufacturers and dealers.
ADVERTISING RATES:
Full Page Mono £700.00
Full Page Colour £1100.00
Agency Commission: 10%
Mechanical Data: Film: Digital, Bleed Size: 303 x 212mm, Trim Size: 297 x 210mm, Type Area: 277 x 190mm, Col Length: 277mm, Page Width: 190mm
Copy instructions: Copy Date: 16th of the month prior to publication date
Average advertising content per issue: 25%
Supplement(s): essentailARB - 4xY
BUSINESS: TIMBER, WOOD & FORESTRY

FORGE
37837U21D-480

Editorial Address: The Derwent Business Centre, Clarke Street, DERBY, DE1 2BU **Tel:** 01332 290460
Fax: 01332 345680
Email: harris.gill@googlemail.com
Advertising Address: As above.
Email: sales@forgemagazine.co.uk
Web site: http://www.nafbae.org.uk
ISSN: 0955-5293
Publisher: Newton Mann Ltd
Frequency: 6 issues yearly
Annual Sub.: £42.00
Circulation: 3,700 (Publisher's Statement)
Usual Pagination: 32
Editor: Gill Harris; **Publisher:** Charles Mann
Summary of Content: Journal of the National Association of Farriers, Blacksmiths and Agricultural Engineers. Covers news, products, information, articles reports and results.
Readership/Target Audience: Read by farriers, blacksmiths, NAFBAE members and welding and fabricating engineers.
ADVERTISING RATES:
Full Page Mono £510.00
Full Page Colour £800.00
Agency Commission: 10%
Mechanical Data: Film: Digital, Trim Size: 297 x 210mm, Bleed Size: 305 x 215mm
Average advertising content per issue: 50%
BUSINESS: AGRICULTURE & FARMING: Livestock

FORMAL ASPECTS OF COMPUTING
36148U5B-85

Editorial Address: Ashbourne House, The Guildway, Old Portsmouth Road, Artington, GUILDFORD, GU3 1LP
Tel: 01483 734635 **Fax:** 01483 734411
Email: rhonda.lane@springer.com
Advertising Address: As above. **Tel:** 01483 734638
Email: rhonda.lane@springer.com
Web site: http://www.springer.com
ISSN: 0934-5043
Publisher: Springer
Date Established: 1988
Frequency: 6 issues yearly
Annual Sub.: £120.00
Usual Pagination: 104
Editor: Rhonda Lane; **Advertising Manager:** Rhonda Lane
Summary of Content: Journal dedicated to the growth of computer science, to show its relationship to practice and to stimulate applications of apposite formalisms.
Readership/Target Audience: Aimed at anyone involved in the formal aspects of computing.
ADVERTISING RATES:
Full Page Mono £460.00
Full Page Colour £1200.00
Agency Commission: 10%
Mechanical Data: Col Length: 237mm, Page Width: 172mm, Trim Size: 277 x 210mm, Type Area: 237 x 172mm, Film: Digital
Copy instructions: Copy Date: 4 weeks prior to publication date
BUSINESS: COMPUTERS & AUTOMATION: Data Processing

FORTUNE
36756U14A-118

Editorial Address: Blue Fin Building, 110 Southwark Street, LONDON, SE1 0SU **Tel:** 020 3148 3000
Email: peter_gumbel@fortunemail.com
Advertising Address: As above. **Fax:** 020 3148 8516
Email: charlotte_laycock@fortunemail.com
Web site: http://www.fortune.com
Publisher: Time Inc.
Date Established: 1930
Frequency: 25 issues yearly
Cover Price: £2.95
Circulation: 105,967 (ABC 01/07/2008 to 31/12/2008)
Usual Pagination: 150
Editor: Peter Gumbel
Summary of Content: Magazine focusing on business management, providing innovative ideas, solutions and

strategies for modern business drivers. Features include reports on investment trends, updates on the management behind the trends and analysis of the effects of current events on the business world.
Readership/Target Audience: Aimed at top management.
ADVERTISING RATES:
Full Page Mono $18100.00
Full Page Colour $25800.00
Agency Commission: 15%
Mechanical Data: Bleed Size: 283 x 210mm, Trim Size: 276 x 203mm
Average advertising content per issue: 60%
BUSINESS: COMMERCE, INDUSTRY & MANAGEMENT

FORUM FOR MODERN LANGUAGE STUDIES
41025U62B-280

Editorial Address: University of St Andrews, ST. ANDREWS, KY16 9AL **Tel:** 01334 462681
Fax: 01334 462655
Email: irj@st-and.ac.uk
Advertising Address: 60 Upper Broadmoor Road, CROWTHORNE, RG45 7DE **Tel:** 01344 779945
Fax: 01344 779945
Email: lhann@lhms.fsnet.co.uk
Web site: http://www.oup.co.uk/jnls
ISSN: 0015-8518
Publisher: OUP
Date Established: 1965
Frequency: Quarterly
Annual Sub.: £117.00
Circulation: 400 (Publisher's Statement)
Usual Pagination: 120
Editor: Mary Orr
Summary of Content: Journal featuring articles and book reviews on literary and linguistic studies from the Middle Ages to the present day.
Language(s): English; French; German; Italian; Russian; Spanish
Readership/Target Audience: Read by people involved with modern language studies.
ADVERTISING RATES:
Full Page Mono £270.00
Agency Commission: 10%
Mechanical Data: Film: Digital, Page Width: 130mm, Type Area: 200 x 130mm, Col Length: 200mm
Copy instructions: Copy Date: 1 month prior to publication date
BUSINESS: CHURCH & SCHOOL EQUIPMENT & EDUCATION: Education Teachers

FORWARD THOUGHT
38924U41A-24_50

Editorial Address: 25 Forward Drive, Christchurch Business Centre, HARROW, HA3 8NT **Tel:** 020 8861 6440
Fax: 020 8861 3134
Email: sales@allstar.co.uk
Web site: http://www.forwardthought.co.uk
Publisher: Allstar Services Ltd
Frequency: 3 issues yearly - Published in April, August and November
Cover Price: Free
Circulation: 3,800 (Publisher's Statement)
Usual Pagination: 4
Editor: Martin Warner
Summary of Content: Newsletter containing technical information about printing from disk, comment on current issues and articles on marketing and business ideas.
Readership/Target Audience: Aimed at middle and senior managers of companies involved in digitally printing manuals and documentation.
ADVERTISING: No Advertising taken
BUSINESS: PRINTING & STATIONERY: Printing

FORWARD WALES
622630U63C-27

Editorial Address: 6 Park Street, CARDIFF, CF10 1XR
Tel: 029 2022 3333
Email: sion.barry@mediawales.co.uk
Advertising Address: As above. **Fax:** 029 2024 4144
Email: liz.bedford@mediawales.co.uk
Web site: http://www.walesonline.co.uk
Publisher: Media Wales Ltd
Date Established: 1995
Frequency: Quarterly
Cover Price: Free
Circulation: 45,000 (Publisher's Statement)
Usual Pagination: 40
Editor: Robert Llewellyn-Jones; **Advertising Manager:** Elizabeth Bedford
Summary of Content: Magazine covering major developments, investments and business news stories in Wales.
Language(s): English; Welsh
Readership/Target Audience: Aimed at the public sector and businesses in Wales.
ADVERTISING: Rates on application
Copy instructions: Copy Date: 4 weeks prior to publication date

Business Magazines

Supplement(s): Wales Fast Growth 50 - 1xY, Wales Top 300 - 1xY, Who's Who in Welsh Business - 1xY
BUSINESS: REGIONAL BUSINESS: Regional Business Wales

FOSTER CARE MAGAZINE
38472U32G-51
Editorial Address: 87 Blackfriars Road, LONDON, SE1 8HA
Tel: 020 7620 6443 **Fax:** 020 7620 6401
Email: laurence.pollock@fostering.net
Web site: http://www.fostering.net
ISSN: 1477-0199
Publisher: The Fostering Network
Date Established: 1975
Frequency: Quarterly
Cover Price: £2.75
Free to qualifying individuals
Annual Sub.: £10.00
Circulation: 35,000 (Publisher's Statement)
Usual Pagination: 24
Editor: Laurence Pollock
Summary of Content: Publication containing news and features focusing on foster care and young people in care.
Readership/Target Audience: Aimed at all fostering professionals including foster carers, social workers and policy makers.
ADVERTISING: No Advertising taken
BUSINESS: LOCAL GOVERNMENT, LEISURE & RECREATION: Community Care & Social Services

FOUNDRY TRADE JOURNAL
38152U27-30
Editorial Address: National Metalforming Centre, 47 Birmingham Road, WEST BROMWICH, B70 6PY
Tel: 0121 601 6979 **Fax:** 0121 601 6981
Email: lynn@foundrytradejournal.com
Advertising Address: As above.
Email: terry.fendley@rivers-media.co.uk
Web site: http://www.foundrytradejournal.com
ISSN: 0015-9042
Publisher: The Institute of Cast Metals Engineers
Date Established: 1902
Frequency: 10 issues yearly
Cover Price: £26.00
Annual Sub.: £192.00
Circulation: 4,500 (Publisher's Statement)
Usual Pagination: 40
Editor: Lynn Postle; **Features Editor:** Jonathan Mitchell; **Advertising Manager:** Les Rivers
Summary of Content: Magazine covering all aspects of the international ferrous and non-ferrous foundry industry, including greensand, chemical bonded, carbon dioxide silicate, shell moulding, diecasting (gravity, low pressure, high pressure), investment casting, centrifugal and continuous.
Readership/Target Audience: Read by key foundry management and personnel, managing directors, foundry managers, chief metallurgists and technical directors.
ADVERTISING RATES:
Full Page Colour £2347.00
Agency Commission: 10%
Mechanical Data: Bleed Size: 305 x 216mm, Trim Size: 297 x 210mm, Col Length: 265mm, Page Width: 185mm, Film: Digital, Type Area: 265 x 185mm
Average advertising content per issue: 40%
BUSINESS: METAL, IRON & STEEL

FOW
35390U1L-13_50
Formerly: Futures & OTC World
Editorial Address: Nestor House, Playhouse Yard, LONDON, EC4V 5EX **Tel:** 020 7779 8888
Fax: 020 7779 8248
Email: jhay@fow.com
Advertising Address: As above. **Fax:** 020 7827 6413
Email: estinson@karengleason.com
Web site: http://www.fow.com
ISSN: 0953-6620
Publisher: Euromoney Institutional Investor plc
Date Established: 1982
Frequency: 10 issues yearly - Published around the 28th of the cover month
Annual Sub.: £280.00
Circulation: 8,081 (Publisher's Statement)
Usual Pagination: 80
Editor: Jon Hay; **Managing Editor:** Jon Hay
Summary of Content: Publication covering OTC and exchange trade derivatives, global risk management, including the financial and commodity markets.
Readership/Target Audience: Read by banks, brokers, dealers, exchanges and corporate treasurers. Also fund managers, systems houses and other support services and regulators.
ADVERTISING RATES:
Full Page Mono £4910.00
Full Page Colour £6320.00
Agency Commission: 10%
Mechanical Data: Col Length: 254mm, Page Width: 178mm, Type Area: 254 x 178mm, Print Process: Offset

Litho, Bleed Size: 307 x 220mm, Trim Size: 297 x 210mm, Film: Digital
Copy instructions: Copy Date: 5 weeks prior to publication date
Average advertising content per issue: 30%
BUSINESS: FINANCE & ECONOMICS: Commodities

FRANCHISE FOCUS
1648665U14A-529
Formerly: Franchiseek International
Editorial Address: 129A High Street, LYMINGTON, SO41 9AQ **Tel:** 01590 689755 **Fax:** 01590 688978
Email: news@franchiseek.com
Advertising Address: As above. **Fax:** 01590 677660
Email: news@franchiseek.com
Web site: http://www.franchiseek.com
ISSN: 1747-9476
Publisher: Franchiseek Limited
Date Established: 2004
Frequency: 6 issues yearly
Cover Price: Free
Circulation: 25,000 (Publisher's Statement)
Usual Pagination: 64
Editor: Trevor Hart; **Advertising Manager:** Trevor Hart
Summary of Content: Magazine covering products and services for UK franchisers, franchisees and start-up businesses.
Readership/Target Audience: Aimed at UK franchisers, franchisees and start-up businesses.
ADVERTISING RATES:
Full Page Colour £1000.00
Agency Commission: 10%
Mechanical Data: Print Process: Litho, Type Area: 277 x 190mm, Trim Size: 297 x 210mm, Col Length: 277mm, Page Width: 190mm, No. of Columns (Display): 2, Col Widths (Display): 92mm, Film: Digital
BUSINESS: COMMERCE, INDUSTRY & MANAGEMENT

THE FRANCHISE MAGAZINE
36759U14A-127
Editorial Address: Franchise House, 56 Surrey Street, NORWICH, NR1 3FD **Tel:** 01603 620301 **Fax:** 01603 630174
Email: editorial@fdsltd.com
Advertising Address: As above.
Email: enquiries@fdsltd.com
Web site: http://www.thefranchisemagazine.net
ISSN: 0268-8395
Publisher: Franchise Development Services Ltd
Date Established: 1985
Frequency: 8 issues yearly
Cover Price: £3.95
Circulation: 25,000 (Publisher's Statement)
Usual Pagination: 180
Editor: Derin Ibrahim; **Publisher:** Roy Seaman
Summary of Content: Journal promoting franchising in the UK.
Language(s): Chinese; English; Spanish
Readership/Target Audience: Aimed at prospective franchisees requiring advice and guidance and franchisers looking to franchise their business.
ADVERTISING RATES:
Full Page Colour £2085.00
Agency Commission: 10%
Mechanical Data: Type Area: 270 x 190mm, Bleed Size: 303 x 216mm, Trim Size: 297 x 210mm, Col Length: 270mm, Film: Digital, Page Width: 190mm
Copy instructions: Copy Date: 2 weeks prior to publication date
Average advertising content per issue: 75%
BUSINESS: COMMERCE, INDUSTRY & MANAGEMENT

FRANCHISE WORLD
36760U14A-130
Editorial Address: Highlands House, 165 The Broadway, LONDON, SW19 1NE **Tel:** 020 8605 2555
Fax: 020 8605 2556
Email: info@franchiseworld.co.uk
Advertising Address: As above.
Email: info@franchiseworld.co.uk
Web site: http://www.franchiseworld.co.uk
ISSN: 0144-0543
Publisher: Franchise World
Frequency: 6 issues yearly
Annual Sub.: £35.00
Circulation: 10,000 (Publisher's Statement)
Editor: Robert Riding; **Advertising Manager:** Nicholas Riding; **Publisher:** Robert Riding
Summary of Content: Journal advising on franchise opportunities and providing coverage of the British Franchise Association, legal advice and developments.
Readership/Target Audience: Aimed at potential and existing franchisees.
ADVERTISING RATES:
Full Page Colour £1700.00
Agency Commission: 10%
Mechanical Data: Type Area: 261 x 178mm, Bleed Size: 303 x 216mm, Trim Size: 297 x 210mm, Col Length: 261mm, Page Width: 178mm, Film: Digital

Copy instructions: Copy Date: 3 weeks prior to publication date
Average advertising content per issue: 60%
BUSINESS: COMMERCE, INDUSTRY & MANAGEMENT

FRANCOPHONIE
41050U62B-290
Editorial Address: 87 Wynford Road, LONDON, N1 9TY
Tel: 020 7837 0789 **Fax:** 020 7837 0789
Email: shirleylawes@aol.com
Advertising Address: University of Leicester, University Road, LEICESTER, LE1 7RH **Tel:** 0116 229 7453
Fax: 0116 229 7456
Email: info@all-languages.org.uk
Web site: http://www.all-languages.org.uk
ISSN: 0957-1744
Publisher: The Association for Language Learning
Date Established: 1990
Frequency: Half-yearly - Published in March and September
Free to qualifying individuals
Circulation: 5,000 (Publisher's Statement)
Usual Pagination: 32
Editor: Shirley Lawes; **Advertising Manager:** Linda Parker
Summary of Content: Magazine containing articles, reviews and information on the French language.
Language(s): English; French
Readership/Target Audience: Read by French language teachers.
ADVERTISING RATES:
Full Page Mono £550.00
BUSINESS: CHURCH & SCHOOL EQUIPMENT & EDUCATION: Education Teachers

FRAUD INTELLIGENCE
1862534U1R-387
Editorial Address: Telephone House, 69-77 Paul Street, LONDON, EC2A 4LQ **Tel:** 020 7017 4214
Email: timon.molloy@informa.com
Web site: http://www.informafinance.com
Publisher: Informa PLC
Frequency: 6 issues yearly
Usual Pagination: 16
Editor: Timon Molloy
Summary of Content: Specialist newsletter giving practical and probing solutions to fraud in corporate and business operations, how to recognise it, defend yourself against it and how to deal with it.
Readership/Target Audience: Aimed at those in corporate and business operations dealing with fraud in the workplace.
ADVERTISING: No Advertising taken
BUSINESS: FINANCE & ECONOMICS: Financial Related

FRAUD WATCH
35463U1R-100
Editorial Address: 3A Market Place, UPPINGHAM, LE15 9QH **Tel:** 01572 820088 **Fax:** 01572 820099
Email: amcintosh@cm-media.net
Web site: http://www.fraudwatchonline.com
ISSN: 0966-7334
Publisher: C&M Publications Ltd
Date Established: 1992
Frequency: 6 issues yearly
Annual Sub.: £295.00
Circulation: 2,000 (Publisher's Statement)
Usual Pagination: 12
Editor: Annich McIntosh; **Managing Editor:** Annich McIntosh
Summary of Content: Publication dealing with fraud and compliance issues within financial services across the world. Includes payment cards, counterfeiting, money laundering and internal audit fraud.
Readership/Target Audience: Aimed at all financial services.
ADVERTISING: No Advertising taken
BUSINESS: FINANCE & ECONOMICS: Financial Related

FREE PRESS
35608U2B-45
Editorial Address: Vi and Garner Smith House, 23 Orford Road, LONDON, E17 9NL **Tel:** 020 8521 5932
Email: freepress@cpbf.org.uk
Advertising Address: As above.
Email: freepress@cpbf.org.uk
Web site: http://www.cpbf.org.uk
ISSN: 1353-310X
Publisher: Campaign for Press & Broadcasting Freedom
Date Established: 1979
Frequency: 6 issues yearly
Cover Price: £1.00
Annual Sub.: £15.00
Circulation: 5,250 (Publisher's Statement)
Usual Pagination: 8
Editor: Julie Ann Davies; **Advertising Manager:** Barry White
Summary of Content: Journal of the Campaign for Press and Broadcasting Freedom. Covers current media issues from a radical perspective.
Readership/Target Audience: Read by journalists, media professionals and anyone else interested in media reform.

Section 4 (b) Business Magazines

ADVERTISING: Rates on application
BUSINESS: COMMUNICATIONS, ADVERTISING & MARKETING: Press

FREELANCE MARKET NEWS
38945U60R-105

Editorial Address: Sevendale House, 7 Dale Street, MANCHESTER, M1 1JB **Tel:** 0161 228 2362
Fax: 0161 228 3533
Email: fmn@writersbureau.com
Advertising Address: As above.
Email: fmna@writersbureau.com
Web site: http://www.freelancemarketnews.com
Publisher: The Writers Bureau
Date Established: 1968
Frequency: 11 issues yearly
Annual Sub.: £29.00
Usual Pagination: 16
Editor: Angela Cox
Summary of Content: Magazine containing market information, articles and advice for new and established freelance writers, photographers and poets.
Readership/Target Audience: Aimed at freelance writers, photographers and poets.
BUSINESS: PUBLISHING: Publishing Related

FREELANCE PHOTOGRAPHER'S MARKET HANDBOOK
38807U38-16_50

Editorial Address: Focus House, 497 Green Lanes, LONDON, N13 4BP **Tel:** 020 8882 3315 **Fax:** 020 8886 3933
Email: mail@thebfp.com
Publisher: BFP Books
Date Established: 1983
Frequency: Annual - Published in October
Cover Price: £14.95
Usual Pagination: 250
Editor: John Tracy
Summary of Content: Publication featuring listings of magazines, newspapers and picture agencies.
Readership/Target Audience: Aimed at freelance photographers.
ADVERTISING: No Advertising taken
BUSINESS: PHOTOGRAPHIC TRADE

FREIGHT
39637U49C-73

Editorial Address: Hermes House, St. Johns Road, TUNBRIDGE WELLS, TN4 9UZ **Tel:** 01892 526171
Fax: 01892 552352
Email: rmeczes@fta.co.uk
Advertising Address: As above. **Tel:** 01892 552211
Fax: 01892 552360
Email: nqueree@fta.co.uk
Web site: http://www.fta.co.uk
ISSN: 0964-1513
Publisher: Freight Transport Association
Date Established: 1964
Frequency: 11 issues yearly
Free to qualifying individuals
Circulation: 11,464 (ABC 01/01/2008 to 31/12/2008)
Usual Pagination: 32
Editor: Robin Meczes; **Advertising Manager:** Naomi Queree
Summary of Content: Journal for FTA members. Covers all modes of transport.
Readership/Target Audience: Read by transport managers and directors.
ADVERTISING RATES:
Full Page Mono £1250.00
Full Page Colour £2080.00
Agency Commission: 10%
Mechanical Data: Page Width: 195mm, Type Area: 270 x 195mm, Col Length: 270mm, Trim Size: 297 x 210mm, Bleed Size: 303 x 216mm, Film: Digital
Average advertising content per issue: 25%
BUSINESS: TRANSPORT: Freight

FREIGHT INDUSTRY TIMES
623411U49C-80

Editorial Address: Trelawney House, Chestergate, MACCLESFIELD, SK11 6DW **Tel:** 01625 613000
Fax: 01625 435078
Email: michael.parry@tenalpspublishing.com
Advertising Address: As above. **Tel:** 01625 667720
Fax: 01625 435076
Email: matthew.swindells@tenalpspublishing.com
Web site: http://www.freight-online.co.uk
Publisher: Ten Alps Publishing
Date Established: 2000
Frequency: Quarterly
Cover Price: £2.00
Free to qualifying individuals
Circulation: 5,000 (Publisher's Statement)
Usual Pagination: 28
Editor: Michael Parry; **Advertising Manager:** Matthew Swindells

Summary of Content: Magazine providing news on all sectors of the freight industry including road, sea, air and rail.
Readership/Target Audience: Aimed at managers, directors and owners of freight haulage companies and freight forwarders.
ADVERTISING RATES:
Full Page Mono £2590.00
Full Page Colour £3885.00
SCC £9.00
Agency Commission: 10%
Mechanical Data: Film: Digital, Type Area: 420 x 297mm, Col Length: 420mm, Page Width: 297mm
Copy instructions: Copy Date: 2 weeks prior to publication date
Average advertising content per issue: 33%
BUSINESS: TRANSPORT: Freight

FRENCH HISTORY
30783U62R-465

Editorial Address: School of History, Keele University, KEELE, ST5 5BG **Tel:** 01865 353907
Email: m.h.crook@his.keele.ac.uk
Advertising Address: 60 Upper Broadmoor Road, CROWTHORNE, RG45 7DE **Tel:** 01344 779945
Fax: 01344 779945
Email: lhann@lhms.fsnet.co.uk
Web site: http://www3.oup.co.uk/french
ISSN: 0269-1191
Publisher: OUP
Date Established: 1987
Frequency: Quarterly
Annual Sub.: £122.00
Circulation: 850 (Publisher's Statement)
Usual Pagination: 136
Editor: Malcolm Crook
Summary of Content: Journal of the Society for the Study of French history, contains articles from the early middle ages to the twentieth century and book reviews.
Readership/Target Audience: Read by scholars working in the field of French history.
ADVERTISING RATES:
Full Page Mono £310.00
Agency Commission: 10%
Mechanical Data: Film: Digital, Type Area: 200 x 130mm, Col Length: 200mm, Page Width: 130mm
BUSINESS: CHURCH & SCHOOL EQUIPMENT & EDUCATION: Education Related

FRENCH STUDIES
41051U62B-295

Editorial Address: Great Clarendon Street, OXFORD, OX2 6DP **Tel:** 01865 353907
Email: jnls.cust.serv@oxfordjournals.org
Advertising Address: 60 Upper Broadmoor Road, CROWTHORNE, RG45 7DE **Tel:** 01344 779945
Fax: 01344 779945
Email: lhann@lhms.fsnet.co.uk
Web site: http://www.oup.co.uk/jnls
ISSN: 0016-1128
Publisher: OUP
Date Established: 1946
Frequency: Quarterly
Annual Sub.: £83.00
Circulation: 1,400 (Publisher's Statement)
Usual Pagination: 172
Editor: Jean Duffy
Summary of Content: Journal containing articles of French literature and French language with an occasional contribution on other aspects of French culture.
Language(s): English; French; German; Italian
Readership/Target Audience: Aimed at enthusiasts of film, cultural studies and critical theory and those interested in french literature.
ADVERTISING RATES:
Full Page Mono £340.00
Agency Commission: 10%
BUSINESS: CHURCH & SCHOOL EQUIPMENT & EDUCATION: Education Teachers

FRESH PRODUCE JOURNAL
38118U26C-28_50

Editorial Address: 430-438 Market Towers, 1 Nine Elms Lane, New Covent Garden, LONDON, SW8 5NN
Tel: 020 7501 0300 **Fax:** 020 7720 2047
Email: editorial@fpj.co.uk
Advertising Address: As above. **Tel:** 020 7501 0315
Fax: 020 7720 8451
Email: advertising@fpj.co.uk
Web site: http://www.freshinfo.com
ISSN: 0967-6899
Publisher: Lockwood Press Ltd
Date Established: 1895
Frequency: Weekly - Published on Friday
Annual Sub.: £125.00
Circulation: 3,000 (Publisher's Statement)
Usual Pagination: 36
Editor: Laura Gould; **Features Editor:** Anna Sbuttoni;
Managing Director: Justin Hope-Mason; **Advertising Manager:** Ian Graham

Summary of Content: Journal covering all aspects of the fresh produce and flower trade including associated service industries such as transport, packaging and machinery.
Readership/Target Audience: Read by the fresh produce supply chain, from seed breeders through to in-store produce managers at major retailers.
ADVERTISING RATES:
Full Page Colour £1400.00
Agency Commission: 10%
Mechanical Data: Type Area: 306 x 216mm, Bleed Size: 340 x 250mm, Trim Size: 335 x 245mm, Col Length: 306mm, No. of Columns (Display): 4, Film: Digital, Page Width: 216mm, Print Process: Litho
Copy instructions: Copy Date: 1 week prior to publication date
Average advertising content per issue: 30%
Supplement(s): Bananas - 6xY, Citrus - 6xY, Grapes - 6xY, Organics - 6xY, Packaging - 6xY, Soft Fruit - 6xY, Stone Fruit - 6xY, Top Fruit - 6xY
BUSINESS: GARDEN TRADE

FRIENDS CONNECT
40528U56R-65

Formerly: The Hospital and Community Friend
Editorial Address: 11-13 Cavendish Square, LONDON, W1G 0AN **Tel:** 020 7307 2570 **Fax:** 020 7307 2571
Email: matt.kevan@attend.org.uk
Advertising Address: As above.
Email: matt.kevan@attend.org.uk
Web site: http://www.attend.org.uk
Publisher: Attend
Date Established: 2002
Frequency: Half-yearly
Free to qualifying individuals
Circulation: 5,000 (Publisher's Statement)
Usual Pagination: 16
Editor: Matt Kevan; **Advertising Manager:** Matt Kevan
Summary of Content: Magazine of Attend (formerly the National Association of Hospital and Community Friends). Contains news about the work of friends and other health care charities in the UK.
Readership/Target Audience: Read by those who run voluntary organisations supporting the NHS and other healthcare providers. Also aimed at general readers who may wish to support health care through charities.
ADVERTISING RATES:
Full Page Colour £750.00
Mechanical Data: Bleed Size: 220 x 307mm, Trim Size: 210 x 297mm, Film: Digital
BUSINESS: HEALTH & MEDICAL: Health Medical Related

FRONTIER
625100U53-672

Editorial Address: 6th Floor, Davis House, Robert Street, CROYDON, CR0 1QQ **Tel:** 020 8253 8393
Fax: 020 8253 8383
Email: frontier@metropolis.co.uk
Advertising Address: As above. **Tel:** 020 8253 8392
Fax: 020 8253 8380
Email: frontier@metropolis.co.uk
Web site: http://www.frontiermagazine.co.uk
Publisher: Metropolis International Group Ltd
Date Established: 1984
Frequency: 8 issues yearly - Published at the beginning of the cover month
Annual Sub.: £385.00
Circulation: 3,041 (Publisher's Statement)
Usual Pagination: 60
Editor: Marek Kolasinski; **Features Editor:** Jessica Harvey; **Managing Editor:** Marek Kolasinski
Summary of Content: Magazine covering all aspects of travel retail including news, products, industry interviews, regional reports and analysis of regions worldwide.
Readership/Target Audience: Aimed at international management of travel retail including directors, marketing and purchasing personnel and brand managers.
ADVERTISING RATES:
Full Page Colour £2700.00
Mechanical Data: Type Area: 270 x 184mm, Bleed Size: 303 x 216mm, Trim Size: 297 x 210mm, Col Length: 270mm, Page Width: 184mm, Film: Digital
Copy instructions: Copy Date: 6 weeks prior to publication date
Supplement(s): Frontier Brands - 3xY, New Frontier - 1xY
BUSINESS: RETAILING & WHOLESALING

FRONTIER BRANDS
37722U53-674

Editorial Address: 6th Floor, Davies House, Robert Street, CROYDON, CR0 1QQ **Tel:** 020 8253 8393
Fax: 020 8253 4603
Email: frontier@metropolis.co.uk
Advertising Address: As above. **Tel:** 020 8253 8600
Fax: 020 8253 8383
Email: frontier@metropolis.co.uk
Web site: http://www.frontiermagazine.co.uk
ISSN: 0969-2495
Publisher: Metropolis International (UK) Limited
Date Established: 1998

Business Magazines

Frequency: 3 issues yearly - Published in April, May and October
Annual Sub.: £385.00
Circulation: 3,992 (Publisher's Statement)
Editor: Marek Kolasinski; **Features Editor:** Jessica Harvey;
Managing Director: Kevin Crook; **Advertising Manager:** Jay Firmager
Summary of Content: Magazine covering product news of international brands both domestic and overseas, product marketing, promotion and design as well as a buyers guide.
Readership/Target Audience: Aimed at international buyers and marketing executives within the travel retail business.
ADVERTISING: Rates on application
Copy instructions: Copy Date: 2 weeks prior to publication date
Supplement to: Frontier
BUSINESS: RETAILING & WHOLESALING

FROZEN & CHILLED FOODS
38028U22E-170

Formerly: Frozen & Chilled Foods Europe
Editorial Address: PO Box 88, EDENBRIDGE, TN8 6ZW
Tel: 01732 868288 **Fax:** 01732 865874
Email: publisher@frozenandchilledfoods.com
Advertising Address: As above.
Email: martyn@frozenandchilledfoods.com
Web site: http://www.frozenandchilledfoods.com
ISSN: 1741-4172
Publisher: Sherwin Publications Ltd
Date Established: 1948
Frequency: 6 issues yearly - Published in the 1st week of the 2nd cover month
Free to qualifying individuals
Annual Sub.: £90.00
Circulation: 6,500 (Publisher's Statement)
Usual Pagination: 36
Editor: Richard Cogan; **Advertising Manager:** Martyn Cogan; **Publisher:** Richard Cogan
Summary of Content: Journal covering every aspect of temperature controlled foods and their uses including company profiles, exhibition reviews and previews, hygiene and safety, packaging, transport, storage and distribution.
Readership/Target Audience: Read by buyers, directors and product managers of manufacturers and processors of frozen and chilled foods, frozen food retail chains, multiple retail offices, symbol groups, cash and carries, co-operatives and wholesale distributors.
ADVERTISING RATES:
Full Page Mono £1120.00
Full Page Colour £1750.00
Agency Commission: 10%
Mechanical Data: Type Area: 265 x 185mm, Col Length: 265mm, Bleed Size: 303 x 216mm, Trim Size: 297 x 210mm, Film: Digital, Page Width: 185mm
Copy instructions: Copy Date: 21st of the month prior to publication date
Supplement(s): Frozen & CHilled Foods Yearbook - 1xY
BUSINESS: FOOD: Frozen Food

FRUIT AND VEGETABLE MARKETS
37770U21A-490

Editorial Address: 80 Calverley Road, TUNBRIDGE WELLS, TN1 2UN **Tel:** 020 7017 7500 **Fax:** 020 7017 7599
Email: marketing@agra-net.com
Web site: http://www.agra-net.com
ISSN: 0961-0464
Publisher: Agra Informa Ltd
Date Established: 1990
Frequency: 24 issues yearly
Annual Sub.: £623.00
Usual Pagination: 28
Circulation Manager: Sue Crouch
Summary of Content: Report on the international fresh and processed fruit and vegetable industry. Contains market prices, processing, new crop forecasts, trade and company news.
Readership/Target Audience: Aimed at traders, producers, processors and those connected with fresh and processed fruit and vegetables.
ADVERTISING: No Advertising taken
BUSINESS: AGRICULTURE & FARMING

THE FRUIT GROWER
38119U26C-29

Editorial Address: Lion House, Church Street, MAIDSTONE, ME14 1EN **Tel:** 01622 695656
Fax: 01622 663733
Email: chris@actpub.co.uk
Advertising Address: As above.
Email: chris@actpub.co.uk
Web site: http://www.actpub.co.uk
ISSN: 0953-2188
Publisher: ACT Publishing
Frequency: Monthly - Published in the 2nd week of the cover month
Annual Sub.: £27.00
Circulation: 2,400 (Publisher's Statement)

Editor: Chris Tanton; **Managing Director:** John Jarrett;
Advertising Manager: Chris Tanton
Summary of Content: Magazine covering news on all types of fruit, equipment, pest control and crop insurance.
Readership/Target Audience: Aimed specifically at the commercial grower.
ADVERTISING RATES:
Full Page Mono £990.00
Full Page Colour £1435.00
SCC £21.00
Agency Commission: 10%
Mechanical Data: Page Width: 190mm, Film: Digital, Type Area: 257 x 190mm, Trim Size: 297 x 210mm, Col Length: 257mm, Bleed Size: 303 x 216mm
Copy instructions: Copy Date: 10 days prior to publication date
Average advertising content per issue: 40%
BUSINESS: GARDEN TRADE

FRY MONTHLY
761402U22A-90

Formerly: The Frying Operator
Editorial Address: Suite 1, Bexley House, 77 Bexley High Street, BEXLEY, DA5 1JX **Tel:** 01322 526089
Fax: 01322 528172
Email: fryhelen@sky.com
Advertising Address: As above.
Email: info@fry-online.co.uk
Web site: http://www.fry-online.co.uk
Publisher: Pybus Events and Publications Limited
Frequency: Monthly - Published on the 14th of the cover month
Free to qualifying individuals
Annual Sub.: £39.00
Circulation: 15,500 (Publisher's Statement)
Usual Pagination: 68
Editor: Helen Edmonds; **Advertising Manager:** Reece Head; **Publisher:** Reece Head
Summary of Content: Magazine covering articles of interest to the fast food sector including fish and chips, burger bars, kebab shops and chicken and pizza outlets.
Readership/Target Audience: Aimed at shop owners and managers with purchasing power for their food and equipment products.
ADVERTISING RATES:
Full Page Colour £1892.00
SCC £10.00
Agency Commission: 10%
Mechanical Data: Film: Digital, Trim Size: 297 x 210mm, Bleed Size: 303 x 216mm, Type Area: 265 x 185mm, Col Length: 265mm, Print Process: Litho, Page Width: 185mm
Copy instructions: Copy Date: 27th of the month prior to publication date
Average advertising content per issue: 45%
Supplement(s): Buyers Guide to Frying Ranges and Refits - 1xY
BUSINESS: FOOD

FRYER & FAST FOOD
1646151U22A-385

Editorial Address: PO Box 1469, HUDDERSFIELD, HD1 9EB **Tel:** 01484 311089 **Fax:** 01484 311089
Email: keith.dixon6@btinternet.com
Advertising Address: As above.
Email: keith.dixon6@btinternet.com
Web site: http://www.fff-uk.co.uk
ISSN: 1745-0810
Publisher: Experience Press and PR
Date Established: 2004
Frequency: 10 issues yearly - Published around the 20th of the cover month. Not published in August and December
Free to qualifying individuals
Annual Sub.: £30.00
Circulation: 10,500 (Publisher's Statement)
Usual Pagination: 40
Editor: Keith Dixon; **Advertising Manager:** Keith Dixon; **Publisher:** Keith Dixon
Summary of Content: Magazine covering all aspects of the fast food and catering trade.
Readership/Target Audience: Read by the top 10001 fast food outlets in the UK by performance.
ADVERTISING RATES:
Full Page Colour £750.00
SCC £12.50
Agency Commission: 10%
Mechanical Data: Type Area: 272 x 190mm, Bleed Size: 220 x 307, Trim Size: 297 x 210mm, Col Length: 272mm, Page Width: 190mm, Film: Digital, No. of Columns (Display): 3
Copy instructions: Copy Date: 3 weeks prior to publication date
Average advertising content per issue: 60%
BUSINESS: FOOD

FSE
39851U54A-80

Editorial Address: Ludgate House, 245 Blackfriars Road, LONDON, SE1 9UY **Tel:** 020 7921 8056 **Fax:** 020 7921 8058
Email: fseeditor@ubm.com

Advertising Address: As above. **Tel:** 020 7921 8342
Fax: 020 7921 8059
Email: peter.poole@ubm.com
Web site: http://www.fseonline.co.uk
ISSN: 1352-2280
Publisher: UBM Information Ltd
Date Established: 1994
Frequency: 10 issues yearly - Published around the 7th of the cover month
Free to qualifying individuals
Annual Sub.: £76.00
Circulation: 7,687 (ABC 01/07/2008 to 30/06/2009)
Editor: Ron Alalouff; **Publisher:** Jonathon Collins
Summary of Content: Magazine covering all aspects of active and built-in fire protection, fire safety management, legislation and regulation.
Readership/Target Audience: Read by fire safety engineers, specifiers, installers, fire safety managers and facilities managers.
ADVERTISING RATES:
Full Page Colour £2090.00
Agency Commission: 10%
Mechanical Data: Col Length: 268mm, Page Width: 188mm, Bleed Size: 303 x 216mm, Trim Size: 297 x 210mm, Type Area: 268 x 188mm, Film: Digital
Copy instructions: Copy Date: 3 weeks prior to publication date
Average advertising content per issue: 40%
BUSINESS: SAFETY & SECURITY: Fire Fighting

FSP FIRE SAFETY PROFESSIONAL
39855U54A-228

Formerly: IFPO Journal
Editorial Address: Fair View, Wissett Road, HALESWORTH, IP19 8BT **Tel:** 01986 874526
Email: fspmagazine@aol.com
Advertising Address: BC Publications, 27 Norwich Road, HALESWORTH, IP19 8BX **Tel:** 01986 834250
Fax: 01986 834255
Email: david@micropress.co.uk
Web site: http://www.ifpo.org.uk
ISSN: 1363-4801
Publisher: FSP Fire Safety Professional
Date Established: 1996
Frequency: Quarterly
Free to qualifying individuals
Annual Sub.: £20.00
Circulation: 2,500 (Publisher's Statement)
Usual Pagination: 24
Editor: Fred Tingle; **Publisher:** Fred Tingle
Summary of Content: Magazine of the Institute of Fire Prevention Officers covering news and developments in fire safety.
Readership/Target Audience: Read by fire safety professionals in industry and the public sector.
ADVERTISING RATES:
Full Page Mono £1100.00
Full Page Colour £1100.00
Agency Commission: 10%
Mechanical Data: Type Area: 270 x 188mm, Bleed Size: 305 x 214mm, Trim Size: 297 x 210mm, Col Length: 270mm, Page Width: 188mm, Film: Digital
Copy instructions: Copy Date: 3 weeks prior to publication date
Average advertising content per issue: 35%
BUSINESS: SAFETY & SECURITY: Fire Fighting

FST FINANCIAL SECTOR TECHNOLOGY
36225U5E-360

Formerly: Financial Sector Technology
Editorial Address: 6th Floor, 3 London Wall Buildings, LONDON, EC2M 5PD **Tel:** 020 7562 2401
Fax: 020 7374 2701
Email: neil.ainger@fstech.co.uk
Advertising Address: As above. **Tel:** 020 7562 2400
Email: melanie.lovegrove@fstech.co.uk
Web site: http://www.fstech.co.uk
ISSN: 1358-8664
Publisher: Perspective Publishing Ltd
Frequency: 6 issues yearly - Published at the end of the 1st cover month
Free to qualifying individuals
Annual Sub.: £149.00
Circulation: 12,775 (ABC 01/01/2008 to 31/12/2008)
Usual Pagination: 60
Editor: Neil Ainger; **Managing Director:** John Woods;
Advertising Manager: Melanie Lovegrove; **Publisher:** Mark Evans
Summary of Content: Journal covering news, features and analysis on information technology within the financial sector.
Readership/Target Audience: Aimed at finance IT managers, CIOs, CTOs and other key IT decision makers.
ADVERTISING RATES:
Full Page Colour £3909.00
Agency Commission: 10%

Mechanical Data: Page Width: 181mm, Type Area: 262 x 181mm, Bleed Size: 303 x 216mm, Trim Size: 297 x 210mm, Col Length: 262mm, Film: Digital
Copy instructions: Copy Date: 2 weeks prior to publication date
Average advertising content per issue: 37%
BUSINESS: COMPUTERS & AUTOMATION: Data Transmission

FST FINANCIAL SERVICES TECHNOLOGY (EUROPE)   1775376U1C-356
Editorial Address: Queen Square House, 18-21 Queen Square, BRISTOL, BS1 4NH **Tel:** 0117 921 4000
Fax: 0117 926 7444
Email: huw.thomas@gdspublishing.com
Advertising Address: As above.
Email: jack.scott@fsteurope.com
Web site: http://www.fsteurope.com
Publisher: GDS Publishing
Frequency: Quarterly
Cover Price: Free
Circulation: 38,000 (Publisher's Statement)
Editor: Huw Thomas; **Advertising Manager:** Jack Scott
Summary of Content: IT focused magazine covering all sectors of the financial services industry including technology, risk management, ATMs, security issues and customer services.
Readership/Target Audience: Aimed at those in the financial services industry at decision-maker level.
ADVERTISING RATES:
Full Page Colour £9750.00
Mechanical Data: Trim Size: 297 x 210mm, Film: Digital
Copy instructions: Copy Date: 6 weeks prior to publication date
Average advertising content per issue: 30%
Editions:
FST Financial Services Technology (US)
BUSINESS: FINANCE & ECONOMICS: Banking

FST FINANCIAL SERVICES TECHNOLOGY (US)   1775631U1C-357
Editorial Address: For all contact details see main edition, FST Financial Services Technology (Europe)
Web site: http://www.usfst.com
Frequency: Quarterly
Cover Price: Free
Circulation: 36,092 (Publisher's Statement)
ADVERTISING RATES:
Full Page Colour $27000.00
Edition of: FST Financial Services Technology (Europe)
BUSINESS: FINANCE & ECONOMICS: Banking

FTFM   759866U1F-586
Editorial Address: 1 Southwark Bridge, LONDON, SE1 9HL
Tel: 020 7873 3000
Email: pauline.skypala@ft.com
Advertising Address: As above. **Fax:** 020 7873 4296
Email: emma.boyd@ft.com
Web site: http://www.ft.com/ftfm
Publisher: Financial Times
Frequency: Weekly - See main record for circulation figure
Usual Pagination: 28
Editor: Pauline Skypala; **Advertising Manager:** Johanna Mayer-Jones
Summary of Content: Magazine focusing on the global fund management industry. Includes people in the news, opinion page, weekly analysis of a fund managers portfolio and global investment issues.
Readership/Target Audience: Aimed at fund managers, specialist investors, pension fund trustees and investment consultants.
ADVERTISING RATES:
Full Page Colour £26093.00
Mechanical Data: No. of Columns (Display): 6, Col Widths (Display): 40mm, Film: Digital
Copy instructions: Copy Date: 4 days prior to publication date
Supplement to: Financial Times
BUSINESS: FINANCE & ECONOMICS: Investment

FTSE GLOBAL MARKETS   1697318U1F-611
Editorial Address: 1st Floor, Rennie House, 57-60 Aldgate High Street, LONDON, EC3N 1AL **Tel:** 020 7680 5151
Fax: 020 7680 5155
Email: francesca@berlinguer.com
Advertising Address: As above.
Email: paul.spendiff@berlinguer.com
Web site: http://www.ftse.com/Research_and_Publications/FTSE_Global_Markets.jsp
ISSN: 1742-6650
Publisher: Berlinguer Ltd
Date Established: 2004
Frequency: 8 issues yearly
Free to qualifying individuals

Annual Sub.: £399.00
Circulation: 19,619 (ABC 01/07/2008 to 30/06/2009)
Usual Pagination: 96
Editor: Francesca Carnevale
Summary of Content: Magazine covering comment and analysis on the world's financial markets, specialist investment services and key corporates.
Language(s): English; French; Italian; Polish
Readership/Target Audience: Aimed at fund and hedge fund managers, securities services providers, issuers, pension plan sponsors, investment bankers, brokers, stock exchanges and specialist financial data providers.
ADVERTISING RATES:
Full Page Colour £7595.00
Agency Commission: 10%
Mechanical Data: Type Area: 250 x 185mm, Bleed Size: 282 x 214mm, Trim Size: 272 x 204mm, Col Length: 250mm, Page Width: 185mm, Film: Digital
Copy instructions: Copy Date: 1 week prior to publication date
BUSINESS: FINANCE & ECONOMICS: Investment

FUCHSIA ANNUAL   38131U26D-40
Editorial Address: 55 Vicarage Meadow, FOWEY, PL23 1DZ
Email: editor@thebfs.org.uk
Advertising Address: As above. **Tel:** 01726 832567
Email: editor@thebfs.org.uk
Web site: http://www.thebfs.org.uk
ISSN: 0071-9730
Publisher: The British Fuchsia Society
Date Established: 1938
Frequency: 3 issues yearly - Published in February, June and November
Cover Price: £4.00
Free to qualifying individuals
Circulation: 3,000 (Publisher's Statement)
Usual Pagination: 80
Editor: Rhona Foster; **Advertising Manager:** Rhona Foster
Summary of Content: Journal containing information about the society, articles about plant growing and fuchsias in particular.
Readership/Target Audience: Aimed at members of the British Fuchsia Society.
ADVERTISING RATES:
Full Page Mono £100.00
Full Page Colour £200.00
Mechanical Data: Type Area: 185 x 125mm, Col Length: 185mm, Page Width: 125mm, No. of Columns (Display): 1
Average advertising content per issue: 15%
BUSINESS: GARDEN TRADE: Garden Trade Horticulture

FUEL OIL NEWS   38585U33-5
Formerly: Fuel Oil News & Road Tanker Transport
Editorial Address: Regent House, Bexton Lane, KNUTSFORD, WA16 9AB **Tel:** 01565 653283
Fax: 01565 755607
Email: mail@fueloilnews.co.uk
Advertising Address: As above.
Email: mail@fueloilnews.co.uk
Web site: http://www.fueloilnews.co.uk
Publisher: Fuel Oil News
Date Established: 1977
Frequency: Monthly - Published in the 1st week of the cover month
Annual Sub.: £82.00
Circulation: 1,200 (Publisher's Statement)
Usual Pagination: 24
Editor: Jane Hughes; **Managing Director:** James Smith;
Advertising Manager: Jane Hughes
Summary of Content: Magazine containing news and views on the downstream oil distribution sector, including legislation, environmental issues, developments in tanker sales, tank construction and pump and hose manufacture.
Readership/Target Audience: Aimed at the fuel oil distribution and tanker trade.
ADVERTISING RATES:
Full Page Mono £1290.00
Full Page Colour £1740.00
Agency Commission: 10%
Mechanical Data: Type Area: 270 x 190mm, Col Length: 270mm, Page Width: 190mm, Trim Size: 297 x 210mm, Film: Digital
Copy instructions: Copy Date: 4 weeks prior to publication date
Average advertising content per issue: 15%
BUSINESS: OIL & PETROLEUM

FULFILMENT AND E.LOGISTICS   623833U10-40_50
Editorial Address: 17 Spice Court, Plantation Wharf, Battersea, LONDON, SW11 3UE **Tel:** 020 7924 5885
Fax: 020 7924 1882
Email: peter@elogmag.com
Advertising Address: As above. **Tel:** 020 7924 1415
Email: cjpl@elogmag.com

Web site: http://www.elogmag.com
ISSN: 1468-7097
Publisher: Spice Court Publications Ltd
Date Established: 2000
Frequency: Quarterly - Published in the last week of the cover month
Free to qualifying individuals
Annual Sub.: £95.00
Circulation: 7,500 (Publisher's Statement)
Usual Pagination: 44
Editor: Peter Rowlands; **Advertising Manager:** Chris Propert-Lewis
Summary of Content: Magazine covering the operational strategy, technology and IT support underpinning home shopping, online selling and multi-channel fulfilment in general, primarily to consumers but also business to business with emphasis on internet fulfilment and home delivery services. Includes news and features on forecasting, warehouse management and supply chain execution, order picking and despatch, last mile deliveries and parcel delivery services, order tracking and real-time PODs, unattended delivery solutions and contact centre management with a strong IT theme throughout.
Readership/Target Audience: Aimed at directors and decision-makers within the manufacturing, retailing, carrier and fulfilment sectors.
ADVERTISING RATES:
Full Page Mono £1470.00
Full Page Colour £2580.00
Agency Commission: 10%
Mechanical Data: No. of Columns (Display): 2, Print Process: Sheet-fed, Type Area: 269 x 187mm, Trim Size: 297 x 210mm, Bleed Size: 303 x 216mm, Col Length: 269mm, Film: Digital, Page Width: 187mm
Average advertising content per issue: 25%
BUSINESS: MATERIALS HANDLING

FUNCTIONAL NUTRITION   718411U22F-15
Editorial Address: For all contact details see main record, Complete Nutrition
Date Established: 2002
Frequency: 6 issues yearly
Advertising Manager: Mike Fryer
ADVERTISING: Rates on application
Mechanical Data: Col Length: 277mm, Bleed Size: 303 x 216mm, Trim Size: 297 x 210mm, Film: Positive, right reading, emulsion side down. Digital, Print Process: Litho, Screen: 60 lpc, Type Area: 277 x 190mm, Page Width: 190mm
Supplement to: Complete Nutrition
BUSINESS: FOOD: Health Food

THE FUND BUSINESS   35289U1F-310
Formerly: Pi The Fund Business
Editorial Address: 30 Cannon Street, LONDON, EC4M 6YJ
Tel: 020 7618 3456 **Fax:** 020 7618 3499
Email: news@thefundbusiness.com
Advertising Address: As above. **Fax:** 020 7618 3420
Email: stuart.hall@thefundbusiness.com
Web site: http://www.thefundbusiness.com
ISSN: 0957-1973
Publisher: Newsquest Specialist Media Ltd
Date Established: 1986
Frequency: Quarterly
Annual Sub.: £159.00
Circulation: 10,141 (BPA Worldwide 01/04/2007 to 30/06/2007)
Usual Pagination: 56
Editor: Bob Campion; **Executive Editor:** Maggie Williams
Summary of Content: Magazine covering all aspects of the international and offshore investment marketplace.
Readership/Target Audience: Aimed at international high net worth advisory community.
ADVERTISING RATES:
Full Page Colour £4370.00
Agency Commission: 10%
Mechanical Data: Page Width: 210mm, Type Area: 285 x 210mm, Bleed Size: 313 x 243mm, Trim Size: 309 x 239mm, Film: Digital, Col Length: 285mm
Copy instructions: Copy Date: 2 weeks prior to publication date
Average advertising content per issue: 35%
BUSINESS: FINANCE & ECONOMICS: Investment

FUND MANAGER TODAY   1777331U1F-632
Editorial Address: 17 Ensign House, Canary Wharf, LONDON, E14 9XQ **Tel:** 020 7148 3861 **Fax:** 0845 638 0341
Email: editorial.fmt@cbmeg.co.uk
Advertising Address: As above.
Email: acarty@cbmeg.co.uk
Web site: http://www.fundmanagertoday.com
Publisher: Capital Business Media
Date Established: 1996
Frequency: 6 issues yearly
Free to qualifying individuals
Annual Sub.: £310.00

Circulation: 8,000 (Publisher's Statement)
Usual Pagination: 80
Editor: Richard Alvin; **Advertising Manager:** Anthony Carty;
Managing Editor: Richard Alvin
Summary of Content: Publication focusing on the financial markets and the key opinion makers and shakers and includes coverage of the goods and services for high net worth readers.
Readership/Target Audience: Aimed at European and global fund managers.
ADVERTISING RATES:
Full Page Colour £5995.00
Agency Commission: 10%
Mechanical Data: Trim Size: 297 x 210mm, Bleed Size: 307 x 220mm, Film: Digital
Copy instructions: Copy Date: 17 days prior to publication date
Average advertising content per issue: 15%
BUSINESS: FINANCE & ECONOMICS: Investment

FUND SELECTOR
1648462U1F-584
Formerly: Fund Manager International
Editorial Address: 1st Floor, 87 Vauxhall Walk, LONDON, SE11 5HJ **Tel:** 020 7840 2250
Email: afoote@citywire.co.uk
Advertising Address: As above. **Tel:** 020 7840 5105
Fax: 020 7840 2251
Email: cdelahunt@citywire.co.uk
Web site: http://www.citywire.co.uk/selector
Publisher: Citywire
Date Established: 2003
Frequency: Monthly
Free to qualifying individuals
Circulation: 2,500 (Publisher's Statement)
Editor: Angus Foote; **News Editor:** Philip Haddon;
Advertising Manager: Chris Delahunt
Summary of Content: Magazine covering all aspects of the European fund management industry, with a focus on fund manager performance.
Readership/Target Audience: Aimed at advisors and fund distributors.
ADVERTISING RATES:
Full Page Colour £3000.00
Agency Commission: 10%
Mechanical Data: Type Area: 255 x 180mm, Col Length: 255mm, Page Width: 180mm, Film: Digital, Bleed Size: 286 x 216mm, Trim Size: 280 x 210mm
Copy instructions: Copy Date: 4 weeks prior to publication date
Average advertising content per issue: 40%
BUSINESS: FINANCE & ECONOMICS: Investment

FUND STRATEGY
629666U1F-210_50
Editorial Address: St. Giles House, 50 Poland Street, LONDON, W1F 7AX **Tel:** 020 7970 4000 **Fax:** 020 7943 8090
Email: daniel.ben-ami@centaur.co.uk
Advertising Address: As above. **Tel:** 020 7943 4000
Fax: 020 7943 8099
Email: rory.wilson@centaur.co.uk
Web site: http://www.fundstrategy.co.uk
ISSN: 1472-3042
Publisher: Centaur Media plc
Date Established: 2000
Frequency: Weekly
Cover Price: £3.95
Free to qualifying individuals
Circulation: 6,049 (ABC 01/07/2008 to 30/06/2009)
Usual Pagination: 32
Editor: Daniel Ben-Ami; **Features Editor:** Will Jackson;
Advertising Manager: Richard Fletcher
Summary of Content: Magazine covering investment fund industry news and analysis. Also covers multi-manager and fund distribution.
Readership/Target Audience: Aimed at top end financial advisers in investment businesses, multi-managers and 'gatekeepers' in banks and other financial institutions.
ADVERTISING: Rates on application
BUSINESS: FINANCE & ECONOMICS: Investment

FUNDING FOR INDEPENDENT SCHOOLS
1774773U62E-421
Editorial Address: PO Box 4435, Cubbington, LEAMINGTON SPA, CV31 9EA **Tel:** 01926 339661
Email: info@pentastic.co.uk
Advertising Address: As above.
Email: info@pentastic.co.uk
Web site: http://www.fismagazine.co.uk
ISSN: 1751-7001
Publisher: Pentastic Ltd
Date Established: 2006
Frequency: 3 issues yearly - Published in January, April and September
Free to qualifying individuals
Annual Sub.: £95.00
Circulation: 4,500 (Print Run)
Usual Pagination: 44

Editor: Andrew Maiden; **Advertising Manager:** Andrew Maiden
Summary of Content: Magazine and termly emailed updates designed to help improve the effective management of independent schools through coverage of financial, strategic and fundraising issues.
Readership/Target Audience: Aimed at head teachers, bursars and governors of independent schools.
ADVERTISING RATES:
Full Page Colour £1550.00
Agency Commission: 10%
Mechanical Data: Trim Size: 297 x 210mm, Bleed Size: 303 x 216mm, Film: Digital
Copy instructions: Copy Date: 4 weeks prior to publication date
Average advertising content per issue: 20%
BUSINESS: CHURCH & SCHOOL EQUIPMENT & EDUCATION: Preparatory & Independent Schools

FUNDS EUROPE
763082U1F-574
Editorial Address: 4th Floor, Broadgate Court, 199 Bishopsgate, LONDON, EC2M 3TY **Tel:** 020 3178 5872
Fax: 020 3178 4002
Email: nick.fitzpatrick@funds-europe.com
Advertising Address: As above.
Email: andrew.chesney@funds-europe.com
Web site: http://www.funds-europe.com
ISSN: 1477-4453
Publisher: Funds Europe Limited
Date Established: 2002
Frequency: 11 issues yearly - Published in the 1st week of the cover month
Annual Sub.: EUR385.00
Circulation: 10,238 (ABC 01/07/2008 to 30/06/2009)
Usual Pagination: 88
Editor: Nick Fitzpatrick; **Advertising Manager:** Andrew Chesney; **Publisher:** Alan Chalmers
Summary of Content: Magazine providing in-depth analysis of all issues pertaining to the construction of a cross-border funds business in Europe including developments in Europe's retail and institutional investment fund markets.
Readership/Target Audience: Aimed at senior fund management and pension fund executives operating a Pan-European business.
ADVERTISING RATES:
Full Page Colour £7250.00
Agency Commission: 10%
Mechanical Data: Type Area: 267 x 190mm, Bleed Size: 293 x 216mm, Trim Size: 287 x 210mm, Col Length: 267mm, Page Width: 190mm, Film: Digital
Copy instructions: Copy Date: 19th of the month prior to publication date
Average advertising content per issue: 30%
BUSINESS: FINANCE & ECONOMICS: Investment

THE FUNERAL DIRECTOR MONTHLY
41578U64L-350
Editorial Address: 618 Warwick Road, SOLIHULL, B91 1AA
Tel: 0845 230 1343 **Fax:** 0121 711 1351
Email: su@nafd.org.uk
Advertising Address: Suite 209, 2nd Floor, Wellington House, Butt Road, COLCHESTER, CO3 3DA
Tel: 01206 767797 **Fax:** 01202 767532
Email: joemurgia@prnmediasales.co.uk
Web site: http://www.nafd.org.uk
ISSN: 0964-0398
Publisher: The National Association of Funeral Directors
Date Established: 1921
Frequency: Monthly
Free to qualifying individuals
Annual Sub.: £38.00
Circulation: 3,611 (ABC 01/07/2008 to 30/06/2009)
Usual Pagination: 68
Editor: Su Lewis; **Advertising Manager:** Joe Murgia
Summary of Content: Official magazine of the National Association of Funeral Directors, designed to keep funeral directors abreast of important industry developments by highlighting new initiatives, carrying updates on UK, European and International issues and reporting on key business subjects, such as Health and Safety and Employment Law.
Readership/Target Audience: Aimed at funeral directors, NAFD members and decision-makers in all areas of the business of providing services and products for funerals.
ADVERTISING RATES:
Full Page Mono £400.00
Full Page Colour £525.00
Agency Commission: 10%
Mechanical Data: Col Widths (Display): 85mm, No. of Columns (Display): 2, Trim Size: 297 x 210mm, Film: Digital
Copy instructions: Copy Date: 3 weeks prior to publication date
Average advertising content per issue: 40%
BUSINESS: OTHER CLASSIFICATIONS: Funeral Directors, Cemeteries & Crematoria

FUNERAL SERVICE JOURNAL
41579U64L-400
Editorial Address: 38 Great James Street, LONDON, WC1N 3HB **Tel:** 020 7242 2907 **Fax:** 020 7242 2907
Email: editor@fsj.co.uk
Advertising Address: The Media Centre, Garcia Estate, Canterbury Road, WORTHING, BN13 1EH
Tel: 01903 602104 **Fax:** 01903 537321
Email: advertising@fsj.co.uk
Web site: http://www.fsj.co.uk
ISSN: 0016-2809
Publisher: FSJ Communications
Date Established: 1886
Frequency: 11 issues yearly
Cover Price: £2.00
Annual Sub.: £19.00
Circulation: 2,100 (Publisher's Statement)
Usual Pagination: 144
Editor: Brian Parsons; **Advertising Manager:** Denise Walker
Summary of Content: Journal covering all aspects of undertaking and funeral direction.
Readership/Target Audience: Aimed at all personnel in the funeral trade including funeral directors, manufacturers and distributors, councils and corporations.
ADVERTISING RATES:
Full Page Mono £175.00
Full Page Colour £377.00
Agency Commission: 10%
Mechanical Data: Film: Digital, Type Area: 188 x 128mm, Print Process: Litho, Col Length: 188mm, No. of Columns (Display): 2, Trim Size: 193 x 132mm, Page Width: 128mm
Copy instructions: Copy Date: 1st of the month prior to publication date
Average advertising content per issue: 65%
BUSINESS: OTHER CLASSIFICATIONS: Funeral Directors, Cemeteries & Crematoria

FUNERAL SERVICE TIMES
1776546U64L-562
Editorial Address: Suite 209, 2nd Floor, Wellington House, Butt Road, COLCHESTER, CO3 3DA **Tel:** 01206 767797
Fax: 01206 767532
Email: tom@funeralservicetimes.co.uk
Advertising Address: As above.
Email: nick@funeralservicetimes.co.uk
Web site: http://www.funeralservicetimes.co.uk
Publisher: Mulberry Publications Ltd
Date Established: 2006
Frequency: Monthly
Cover Price: Free
Circulation: 6,000 (Publisher's Statement)
Usual Pagination: 48
Summary of Content: Magazine covering issues of concern or interest to the sector.
Readership/Target Audience: Aimed at funeral directors.
ADVERTISING RATES:
Full Page Mono £410.00
Full Page Colour £510.00
Agency Commission: 10%
Mechanical Data: Type Area: 287 x 200mm, Bleed Size: 303 x 216mm, Trim Size: 297 x 210mm, Col Length: 287mm, Page Width: 200mm, Film: Digital
Copy instructions: Copy Date: 2 weeks prior to publication date
Average advertising content per issue: 50%
BUSINESS: OTHER CLASSIFICATIONS: Funeral Directors, Cemeteries & Crematoria

FURNACES INTERNATIONAL
1697244U27-212
Editorial Address: 2nd Floor, Westgate House, 120-130 Station Road, REDHILL, RH1 1ET **Tel:** 01737 855000
Fax: 01737 855474
Email: timsmith@dmgworldmedia.com
Advertising Address: As above. **Tel:** 01276 470182
Fax: 01276 470182
Web site: http://www.furnacesinternational.com
ISSN: 1740-6501
Publisher: DMG Business Media
Date Established: 1926
Frequency: Quarterly
Free to qualifying individuals
Circulation: 9,000 (Publisher's Statement)
Editor: Tim Smith
Summary of Content: Magazine covering features, news, product stories, industry updates and events relating to the thermal processing of metals and materials.
Readership/Target Audience: Aimed at professionals working within the thermal processing and heat treatment industry.
ADVERTISING RATES:
Full Page Mono £1300.00
Full Page Colour £2100.00
Agency Commission: 10%
Mechanical Data: Type Area: 265 x 185mm, Bleed Size: 305 x 213mm, Trim Size: 297 x 210mm, Col Length: 265mm, Page Width: 185mm, Film: Positive, right reading, emulsion side down. Digital
Copy instructions: Copy Date: 4 weeks prior to publication date

Average advertising content per issue: 50%
BUSINESS: METAL, IRON & STEEL

FURNITURE AND CABINETMAKING

38059U23A-35

Editorial Address: 86 High Street, LEWES, BN7 1XN
Tel: 01273 477374 **Fax:** 01273 487692
Email: andreah@thegmcgroup.com
Advertising Address: As above. **Tel:** 01273 487535
Email: rhonab@thegmcgroup.com
Web site: http://www.gmcmags.com
ISSN: 1365-4292
Publisher: GMC Publications Ltd
Frequency: 13 issues yearly
Cover Price: £3.25
Free to qualifying individuals
Annual Sub.: £39.00
Usual Pagination: 94
Editor: Andrea Hargreaves; **Advertising Manager:** Rhona Bolger; **Publisher:** Simon McKeown
Summary of Content: Magazine providing news and features, equipment test reports and project ideas. Also covers current styles and up-and-coming designers.
Readership/Target Audience: Aimed at makers of bespoke fine furniture and at skilled hobbyists.
ADVERTISING RATES:
Full Page Colour £825.00
Agency Commission: 10%
Mechanical Data: Bleed Size: 284 x 233mm, Trim Size: 278 x 227mm, No. of Columns (Display): 4, Film: Digital
Copy instructions: Copy Date: 7 weeks prior to publication date
Average advertising content per issue: 40%
BUSINESS: FURNISHINGS & FURNITURE

FURNITURE HISTORY

38066U23A-37

Editorial Address: 1 Mercedes Cottages, St. Johns Road, HAYWARDS HEATH, RH16 4EH **Tel:** 01444 413845
Fax: 01444 413845
Email: furniturehistorysociety@hotmail.com
Web site: http://www.furniturehistorysociety.com
ISSN: 0016-3058
Publisher: The Furniture History Society
Date Established: 1965
Frequency: Annual - Published in November
Cover Price: £30.00
Free to qualifying individuals
Circulation: 1,800 (Publisher's Statement)
Usual Pagination: 250
Editor: Jonathan Marsden
Summary of Content: Journal containing articles concerning the history of furniture and furnishings. The scope of articles is worldwide but concentrated on Western Europe.
Readership/Target Audience: Aimed at academic, professional, trade and the general public interested in the history of furniture and furnishings.
ADVERTISING: No Advertising taken
BUSINESS: FURNISHINGS & FURNITURE

FURNITURE JOURNAL

38060U23A-50

Editorial Address: Napier House, 11 Surrey Street, LOWESTOFT, NR32 1LJ **Tel:** 01502 517115
Fax: 01502 517117
Email: barry@furniturejournal.co.uk
Advertising Address: As above.
Email: chris@furniturejournal.co.uk
Web site: http://www.craftsmanpublishing.co.uk
ISSN: 1353-8969
Publisher: CPC Ltd
Date Established: 1993
Frequency: 6 issues yearly
Free to qualifying individuals
Annual Sub.: £15.00
Circulation: 8,000 (Publisher's Statement)
Usual Pagination: 48
Editor: Chris Skwarka; **Advertising Manager:** Chris Skwarka
Summary of Content: Magazine covering technical articles and features which include new and existing products, company profiles and furniture and machinery showcases.
Readership/Target Audience: Read by UK furniture manufacturers.
ADVERTISING RATES:
Full Page Colour £1095.00
Agency Commission: 10%
Mechanical Data: Film: Digital, Type Area: 271 x 187mm, Bleed Size: 303 x 213mm, Trim Size: 297 x 210mm, Col Length: 271mm, Page Width: 187mm
Average advertising content per issue: 50%
BUSINESS: FURNISHINGS & FURNITURE

FURNITURE NEWS

39463U46-15_5

Formerly: Pine News International
Editorial Address: 4 Red Barn Mews, High Street, BATTLE, TN33 0AG **Tel:** 01424 776101 **Fax:** 01424 775077
Email: paul@gearingmediagroup.com
Advertising Address: As above. **Tel:** 01424 776104
Email: sam@gearingmediagroup.com
Web site: http://www.furniturenews.net
ISSN: 1475-3731
Publisher: Gearing Media Group
Date Established: 1988
Frequency: Monthly - Published on the 1st of the cover month
Annual Sub.: £50.00
Circulation: 8,155 (ABC 01/01/2008 to 31/12/2008)
Usual Pagination: 72
Editor: Paul Farley; **Publisher:** Nigel Gearing
Summary of Content: Publication containing news and analysis, editorial comment, show previews and reviews and features covering all domestic and contract interiors products.
Readership/Target Audience: Aimed at furniture retailers.
ADVERTISING RATES:
Full Page Colour £1569.00
Agency Commission: 10%
Mechanical Data: Type Area: 297 x 210mm, Film: Digital, Col Length: 297mm, Page Width: 210mm, Bleed Size: 346 x 243mm, Trim Size: 340 x 240mm
Copy instructions: Copy Date: 14th of the month prior to publication date
Average advertising content per issue: 60%
BUSINESS: TIMBER, WOOD & FORESTRY

FURNITURE PRODUCTION

38062U23A-80

Formerly: Furniture Production International
Editorial Address: 4 Red Barn Mews, High Street, BATTLE, TN33 0AG **Tel:** 01424 776104 **Fax:** 01424 775077
Email: john@gearingmediagroup.com
Advertising Address: As above. **Tel:** 01424 774982
Email: travis@gearingmediagroup.com
Web site: http://www.furnitureproduction.net
ISSN: 1364-9191
Publisher: Gearing Media Group
Date Established: 1990
Frequency: Monthly - Published on the 1st of the cover month
Free to qualifying individuals
Annual Sub.: £50.00
Circulation: 7,500 (Publisher's Statement)
Usual Pagination: 84
Editor: John Legg
Summary of Content: Magazine covering all aspects of the furniture and joinery manufacturing industry from product design to production systems.
Readership/Target Audience: Read by furniture and joinery manufacturers, kitchen and bathroom manufacturers and fitters, contract furniture manufacturers.
ADVERTISING RATES:
Full Page Colour £1376.00
Agency Commission: 10%
Mechanical Data: Col Length: 297mm, Page Width: 210mm, No. of Columns (Display): 4, Bleed Size: 346 x 243mm, Trim Size: 340 x 240mm, Type Area: 297 x 210mm, Film: Digital
Copy instructions: Copy Date: 4 weeks prior to publication date
Average advertising content per issue: 45%
BUSINESS: FURNISHINGS & FURNITURE

FURNITURE PRODUCTS

1647280U23A-306

Editorial Address: The Old Sun, Crete Hall Road, GRAVESEND, DA11 9AA **Tel:** 01474 536535
Fax: 01474 536552
Advertising Address: As above.
Email: donna@nelton.co.uk
Web site: http://www.nelton.co.uk
Publisher: Nelton Publications
Date Established: 2003
Frequency: Quarterly
Free to qualifying individuals
Annual Sub.: £10.00
Circulation: 10,048 (Publisher's Statement)
Editor: Donna Ludbrook; **Advertising Manager:** Donna Ludbrook
Summary of Content: Magazine covering all aspects of furniture products.
Readership/Target Audience: Aimed at furniture manufacturers.
ADVERTISING RATES:
Full Page Colour £375.00
Mechanical Data: Type Area: 190 x 128mm, Film: Digital, Col Length: 190mm, Page Width: 128mm
BUSINESS: FURNISHINGS & FURNITURE

FURTHER EDUCATION TODAY

41109U62F-200

Editorial Address: St. James House, 118 Greys Road, HENLEY-ON-THAMES, RG9 1QW **Tel:** 01491 411848
Fax: 01491 411416
Email: sales@schoolspublishing.co.uk
Advertising Address: As above.
Email: sales@schoolspublishing.co.uk
Publisher: Schools Publishing Limited
Date Established: 1993
Frequency: Monthly - Published around the 1st week of the cover month
Free to qualifying individuals
Annual Sub.: £30.00
Circulation: 6,000 (Publisher's Statement)
Usual Pagination: 32
Editor: Sarah Williams; **Advertising Manager:** Beverley Rees
Summary of Content: Journal containing articles and features relevant to further education, management and purchasing.
Readership/Target Audience: Aimed at educational institutions and all personnel within the teaching profession. Mailed to every 6th form college, FE college and university in the UK.
ADVERTISING RATES:
Full Page Mono £1391.00
Full Page Colour £1490.00
Agency Commission: 10%
Mechanical Data: Bleed Size: 303 x 216mm, Trim Size: 297 x 210mm, Film: Digital, Type Area: 267 x 190mm, Col Length: 267mm, Page Width: 190mm
Copy instructions: Copy Date: 1 week prior to publication date
Average advertising content per issue: 35%
BUSINESS: CHURCH & SCHOOL EQUIPMENT & EDUCATION: Adult Education

FUTURE AIRPORT

1625888U6B-353

Formerly: Airport Technology International
Editorial Address: Brunel House, 55-57 North Wharf Road, LONDON, W2 1LA **Tel:** 020 7915 9960 **Fax:** 020 7915 9958
Email: lucyschwerdtfeger@spgmedia.com
Advertising Address: As above. **Tel:** 020 7915 9600
Fax: 020 7262 9757
Email: info@spgmedia.com
Web site: http://www.futureairport.com
Publisher: SPG Media Ltd
Date Established: 1997
Frequency: Half-yearly - Published in February and August
Free to qualifying individuals
Circulation: 7,751 (ABC 01/01/2008 to 31/12/2008)
Editor: Lucy Schwerdtfeger; **Advertising Manager:** David Chai
Summary of Content: Magazine covering all aspects of airport technology, including projects, long term views and reviews.
Readership/Target Audience: Aimed at airport chief executives.
ADVERTISING RATES:
Full Page Mono £5800.00
Full Page Colour £6900.00
Agency Commission: 10%
Mechanical Data: Trim Size: 286 x 210mm, Film: Digital, Bleed Size: 292 x 216mm
Copy instructions: Copy Date: 6 weeks prior to publication date
Average advertising content per issue: 35%
BUSINESS: AVIATION & AERONAUTICS: Airports

FUTURE MATERIALS

761863U47A-561

Editorial Address: Perkin House, 1 Longlands Street, BRADFORD, BD1 2TP **Tel:** 01274 378800
Fax: 01274 378811
Email: athornton@world-textile.net
Advertising Address: As above.
Email: jwilson@world-textile.net
Web site: http://www.futurematerials.com
Publisher: World Textile Publications Ltd
Date Established: 2002
Frequency: Monthly
Annual Sub.: £255.00
Circulation: 6,000 (Publisher's Statement)
Editor: Jonathan Dyson; **Managing Director:** Mark Jarvis
Summary of Content: Magazine covering industrial and technical materials including technical textiles, nonwovens, paper and resin.
Readership/Target Audience: Read by European manufacturers and converters working in technical textiles, nonwovens, glass, films, composites and laminates.
ADVERTISING RATES:
Full Page Mono £1179.00
Full Page Colour £1850.00
Mechanical Data: Film: Digital, Trim Size: 297 x 210mm, Type Area: 264 x 179mm, Col Length: 264mm, Bleed Size: 303 x 216mm, Page Width: 179mm
BUSINESS: CLOTHING & TEXTILES

Business Magazines

FUTURE PRESCRIBER
623155U37-26_72

Editorial Address: The Atrium, Southern Gate, CHICHESTER, PO19 8SQ **Tel:** 01243 779777
Fax: 01243 770144
Email: futureprescriber@wiley.com
Advertising Address: As above.
Email: sripsher@wiley.com
Web site: http://www.escriber.com
ISSN: 1468-9871
Publisher: Wiley Interface Ltd
Date Established: 1999
Frequency: Quarterly
Free to qualifying individuals
Annual Sub: £40.00
Circulation: 7,000 (Publisher's Statement)
Usual Pagination: 28
Editor: Kerry Laundon; **Managing Editor:** Sarah Blagbrough; **Publisher:** Tim Dean
Summary of Content: Magazine covering new and pre-launched drugs and prescribing policies.
Readership/Target Audience: Aimed at prescribing advisers, heads of primary care trusts and those on therapeutic and drug committees.
ADVERTISING: Rates on application
Agency Commission: 10%
Copy instructions: Copy Date: 4 weeks prior to publication date
Average advertising content per issue: 10%
BUSINESS: PHARMACEUTICAL & CHEMISTS

FUTUREMEDIA
1896756U2D-157

Editorial Address: 2nd Floor, 148 Curtain Road, LONDON, EC2A 3AT **Tel:** 020 7729 7460 **Fax:** 020 7729 7461
Email: jonathan@c21media.net
Web site: http://www.c21media.net
Publisher: C21 Media Ltd
Frequency: 6 issues yearly
Annual Sub.: £30.00
Circulation: 11,000 (Publisher's Statement)
Editor: Jonathan Webdale; **Advertising Manager:** Peter Treacher
Summary of Content: Guide to the converging worlds of entertainment and technology, covering channel branding, programme promotion, internet TV and mobiles.
Readership/Target Audience: Aimed at content producers, distributors and broadcasters looking to develop digital strategies.
BUSINESS: COMMUNICATIONS, ADVERTISING & MARKETING: Broadcasting

FUTURES
37233U14R-120

Editorial Address: 1 Orchard Gate, LONDON, NW9 6HU
Tel: 020 8201 3193
Email: futures@ziasardar.com
Advertising Address: 32 Jamestown Road, LONDON, NW1 7BY **Tel:** 020 7424 4400 **Fax:** 01865 853136
Email: j.kenney@elsevier.com
Web site: http://www.elsevier.com
ISSN: 0016-3287
Publisher: Elsevier Ltd
Frequency: 10 issues yearly
Annual Sub.: EUR725.00
Circulation: 3,000 (Publisher's Statement)
Usual Pagination: 110
Editor: Zia Sardar; **Publisher:** Mary Malin
Summary of Content: International journal containing forecasting information.
Readership/Target Audience: Aimed at technical, industrial and socio-economic planning professionals.
ADVERTISING: Rates on application
BUSINESS: COMMERCE, INDUSTRY & MANAGEMENT: Commerce Related

FUTURES AND OPTIONS INTELLIGENCE
35389U1L-14_20

Formerly: FO Week
Editorial Address: Nestor House, Playhouse Yard, LONDON, EC4V 5EX **Tel:** 020 7779 8888
Fax: 020 7779 8355
Email: cpackham@fow.com
Advertising Address: As above. **Tel:** 020 7556 6024
Fax: 020 7337 8943
Email: ahezareh@fow.com
Web site: http://www.fointelligence.com
ISSN: 1361-8571
Publisher: Euromoney Institutional Investor plc
Date Established: 1992
Frequency: Weekly
Annual Sub.: £950.00
Circulation: 1,175 (Publisher's Statement)
Usual Pagination: 20
Editor: Colin Packham
Summary of Content: Newsletter covering news from the global exchange traded derivatives industry.

Readership/Target Audience: Read by brokers, lawyers, traders and service providers.
ADVERTISING RATES:
Full Page Mono £2720.00
Agency Commission: 10%
Mechanical Data: Type Area: 245 x 175mm, Col Length: 245mm, Page Width: 175mm, Bleed Size: 303 x 216mm, Trim Size: 297 x 210mm, Film: Digital
Copy instructions: Copy Date: Wednesday prior to publication date
Average advertising content per issue: 15%
BUSINESS: FINANCE & ECONOMICS: Commodities

FX
35826U4B-117

Editorial Address: 91 Charterhouse Street, LONDON, EC1M 6HR **Tel:** 020 7336 5200
Email: tdowling@fxmagazine.co.uk
Advertising Address: As above.
Email: jkilpatrick@progressivemediagroup.com
Web site: http://www.fxmagazine.co.uk
ISSN: 0966-0380
Publisher: Progressive Media Publications
Frequency: Monthly
Annual Sub.: £48.00
Circulation: 13,273 (ABC 01/07/2008 to 30/06/2009)
Usual Pagination: 200
Editor: Theresa Dowling
Summary of Content: Magazine focusing on design in the commercial sector. Includes articles on public sector, office, retail, hotel, lighting and leisure design.
Readership/Target Audience: Read by architects and designers.
ADVERTISING RATES:
Full Page Colour £2500.00
Agency Commission: 10%
Mechanical Data: Film: Digital, No. of Columns (Display): 4, Type Area: 265 x 194mm, Bleed Size: 310 x 240mm, Trim Size: 300 x 230mm, Print Process: Offset litho, Col Length: 265mm, Page Width: 194mm
Copy instructions: Copy Date: 6 weeks prior to publication date
Average advertising content per issue: 55%
BUSINESS: ARCHITECTURE & BUILDING: Interior Design & Flooring

FX & MM
20187U1C-175

Editorial Address: Court Lodge, Hogtrough Hill, Brasted, WESTERHAM, TN16 1NU **Tel:** 01959 563311
Fax: 01959 563123
Email: swills@russellpublishing.com
Advertising Address: As above.
Email: bbeaney@russellpublishing.com
Web site: http://www.fx-mm.com
ISSN: 1351-5195
Publisher: Russell Publishing Ltd
Frequency: 10 issues yearly - Published at the beginning of the cover month
Free to qualifying individuals
Annual Sub.: £277.00
Circulation: 6,000 (Publisher's Statement)
Usual Pagination: 64
Editor: Sarah Wills
Summary of Content: Journal covering all aspects of foreign exchange and trading instruments including political, economic and market conditions. Also covers treasury, technology and fund management.
Readership/Target Audience: Aimed at heads of foreign exchange and money markets, fund and investment managers, corporate treasurers, risk and compliance managers.
ADVERTISING RATES:
Full Page Colour £3797.00
Agency Commission: 10%
Mechanical Data: Bleed Size: 280 x 211mm, Trim Size: 274 x 205mm, Film: Digital
Copy instructions: Copy Date: 4 weeks prior to publication date
BUSINESS: FINANCE & ECONOMICS: Banking

FX WEEK
34928U1A-185

Editorial Address: Haymarket House, 28-29 Haymarket, LONDON, SW1Y 4RX **Tel:** 020 7484 9700
Fax: 020 7484 9991
Email: saima.farooqi@incisivemedia.com
Advertising Address: As above. **Fax:** 020 7930 2238
Email: stephen.couling@incisivemedia.com
Web site: http://www.fxweek.com
ISSN: 1050-0782
Publisher: Incisive Media Investments
Date Established: 1990
Frequency: Weekly
Annual Sub.: £1125.00
Usual Pagination: 14
Editor: Saima Farooqi; **Advertising Manager:** Stephen Couling; **Publisher:** Stephen Couling

Summary of Content: Newsletter that focuses exclusively on the business of foreign exchange and related short-term interest rate products.
Readership/Target Audience: Aimed at banks, brokerage houses and corporate personnel.
ADVERTISING RATES:
Full Page Mono £2475.00
Full Page Colour £3250.00
Agency Commission: 10%
Mechanical Data: Bleed Size: 303 x 216mm, Trim Size: 297 x 210mm, Film: Digital
Copy instructions: Copy Date: 1 week prior to publication date
Average advertising content per issue: 30%
BUSINESS: FINANCE & ECONOMICS

G3 GLOBAL GAMES & GAMING MAGAZINE
1640909U64A-174

Editorial Address: Samson House, 457 Manchester Road, MANCHESTER, M29 7BR **Tel:** 01942 879291
Fax: 01942 879291
Email: lewis.pek@hppublishing.co.uk
Advertising Address: 2 Loweswater Crescent, BURNLEY, BB12 8TW **Tel:** 01282 838371
Email: john.slattery@hppublishing.co.uk
Web site: http://www.g3-magazine.com
Publisher: HP Publishing Ltd.
Date Established: 2002
Frequency: Monthly
Annual Sub.: £80.00
Circulation: 5,250 (Publisher's Statement)
Editor: Lewis Pek; **Advertising Manager:** John Slattery
Summary of Content: Magazine covering the casino and amusement gaming industry with product features and country reports.
Readership/Target Audience: Aimed at operators and buyers within the games and casino business.
ADVERTISING RATES:
Full Page Colour £2095.00
Mechanical Data: Type Area: 270 x 190mm, Bleed Size: 307 x 216mm, Trim Size: 297 x 210mm, Film: Digital, Col Length: 270mm, Page Width: 190mm
Copy instructions: Copy Date: 17th of the month prior to publication date
Average advertising content per issue: 50%
BUSINESS: OTHER CLASSIFICATIONS: Amusement Trade

G M JOURNAL
40167U56A-66_10

Formerly: Geriatric Medicine
Editorial Address: 19th Floor, 1 Canada Square, Canary Wharf, LONDON, E14 5AP **Tel:** 020 7772 8300
Fax: 020 7772 8597
Email: gmsubmissions@oceanmedia.co.uk
Advertising Address: As above. **Tel:** 020 7772 8466
Email: peter.sayer@oceanmedia.co.uk
Web site: http://www.gerimed.co.uk
ISSN: 0268-201X
Publisher: Medpress
Date Established: 1970
Frequency: Monthly
Free to qualifying individuals
Annual Sub.: £101.00
Circulation: 25,000 (Publisher's Statement)
Usual Pagination: 68
Editor: Linne Kincaid; **Advertising Manager:** Peter Sayer; **Publisher:** Peter Sayer
Summary of Content: Clinical magazine regarding care of the elderly, clinical advances in drug development, modern prescribing, clinical bulletins and updates circulated to doctors with an interest in the older patient.
Readership/Target Audience: Aimed at GPs, physicians and other hospital doctors with an interest in geriatrics.
ADVERTISING RATES:
Full Page Mono £1615.00
Full Page Colour £2425.00
Agency Commission: 10%
Mechanical Data: Type Area: 260 x 180mm, Bleed Size: 286 x 206mm, Film: Digital, Print Process: Offset litho, Col Length: 260mm, Trim Size: 280 x 200mm, Page Width: 180mm
Copy instructions: Copy Date: 2 weeks prior to publication date
Average advertising content per issue: 50%
Supplement(s): Care of the Elderly - 12xY
BUSINESS: HEALTH & MEDICAL

GALLERIES
36448U7-180

Editorial Address: 54 Uxbridge Road, LONDON, W12 8LP
Tel: 020 8740 7020 **Fax:** 020 8740 7020
Email: features@galleries.co.uk
Advertising Address: As above.
Email: ads@galleries.co.uk
Web site: http://www.galleries.co.uk
ISSN: 0265-7511
Publisher: Barrington Publications
Date Established: 1983
Frequency: Monthly

Cover Price: £1.58
Annual Sub.: £24.00
Circulation: 20,000 (Publisher's Statement)
Usual Pagination: 80
Editor: Andrew Aitken; **Executive Editor:** Andrew Aitken;
Features Editor: Nicholas Usherwood; **Publisher:** Paul Hooper
Summary of Content: Listings guide of art galleries containing news, previews, Internet guide and maps.
Readership/Target Audience: Aimed at regular visitors of art galleries and museums.
ADVERTISING RATES:
Full Page Mono £550.00
Full Page Colour £940.00
Agency Commission: 10%
Mechanical Data: Type Area: 196 x 135mm, Col Length: 196mm, No. of Columns (Display): 2, Film: Digital, Bleed Size: +3mm, Col Widths (Display): 65mm, Page Width: 135mm, Trim Size: 214 x 151mm
Copy instructions: Copy Date: 1 month prior to publication date
Average advertising content per issue: 15%
BUSINESS: ANTIQUES

GALPIN SOCIETY JOURNAL   40966U61-16

Editorial Address: 13 Upland Park Road, OXFORD, OX2 7RU **Tel:** 01865 512807
Email: editor@galpinsociety.org
Advertising Address: 4 Princes Ride, Woodstock, OXFORD, OX20 1UP **Tel:** 01993 810035 **Fax:** 01993 810035
Email: cmm1@talktalk.net
Web site: http://www.galpinsociety.org
ISSN: 0072-0127
Publisher: The Galpin Society
Date Established: 1947
Frequency: Annual - Published in April
Annual Sub.: £22.00
Circulation: 800 (Publisher's Statement)
Usual Pagination: 380
Editor: Michael Fleming; **Advertising Manager:** Charles Mould
Summary of Content: Publication containing original research into the study of musical instruments, history, construction, development and use.
Readership/Target Audience: Aimed at amateur and professional makers, researchers, restorers and performers throughout the world.
ADVERTISING RATES:
Full Page Mono £120.00
Mechanical Data: Type Area: 240 x 160mm, Col Length: 240mm, Page Width: 160mm, No. of Columns (Display): 2
Copy instructions: Copy Date: January 31st
BUSINESS: MUSIC TRADE

GARAGE & MOT PROFESSIONAL

752836U31A-122

Formerly: MOT Professional
Editorial Address: 2 Crown Street, Wellington, TELFORD, TF1 1LP **Tel:** 01952 415334 **Fax:** 01952 245077
Email: chris.owen@ppmedia.co.uk
Advertising Address: As above.
Email: chris.owen@ppmedia.co.uk
Publisher: Partnership Publishing Limited
Frequency: 18 issues yearly
Cover Price: Free
Circulation: 18,500 (Publisher's Statement)
Usual Pagination: 48
Editor: Chris Owen; **Advertising Manager:** Chris Owen;
Managing Editor: David Gregory
Summary of Content: Magazine covering industry news and data, legal updates, human interest features, business profiles, product information and testing.
Readership/Target Audience: Aimed at professional technicians in the UK's MOT test stations.
ADVERTISING RATES:
Full Page Mono £1440.00
Full Page Colour £1800.00
Agency Commission: 10%
Mechanical Data: Bleed Size: 303 x 216mm, Trim Size: 297 x 210mm, Page Width: 186mm, Film: Digital, Type Area: 273 x 186mm, Col Length: 273mm, Col Widths (Display): 43.5mm, No. of Columns (Display): 4
Copy instructions: Copy Date: 1 week prior to publication date
Average advertising content per issue: 40%
BUSINESS: MOTOR TRADE: Motor Trade Accessories

GARAGE TRADER   38305U31A-70_50

Editorial Address: 5B Edgewater Business Park, Belfast Harbour Estate, BELFAST, BT3 9JQ **Tel:** 028 9078 3200
Fax: 028 9078 3210
Email: patburns@greerpublications.com
Advertising Address: As above.
Email: jackiestott@greerpublications.com
Publisher: Greer Publications Ltd
Frequency: Quarterly

Cover Price: Free
Circulation: 6,500 (Publisher's Statement)
Usual Pagination: 76
Editor: Jackie Stott; **Advertising Manager:** Jackie Stott;
Publisher: James Greer
Summary of Content: Magazine covering garage trade news for the Republic of Ireland and Northern Ireland.
Readership/Target Audience: Aimed at retailers, fleet operators, wholesalers and distributors within the garage trade.
ADVERTISING RATES:
Full Page Mono £880.00
Full Page Colour £980.00
Agency Commission: 10%
Mechanical Data: Type Area: 299 x 206mm, Bleed Size: 340 x 250mm, Col Length: 299mm, Trim Size: 330 x 240mm, Page Width: 206mm, Film: Digital
Average advertising content per issue: 40%
BUSINESS: MOTOR TRADE: Motor Trade Accessories

GARDEN AND HARDWARE NEWS

38103U26B-72

Editorial Address: 4th Floor, Geneva House, Park Road, PETERBOROUGH, PE1 2UX **Tel:** 01733 756555
Fax: 01733 760505
Email: ghn@onecoms.co.uk
Advertising Address: As above.
Web site: http://www.onecoms.co.uk
Publisher: Media One Communications Ltd.
Frequency: 6 issues yearly
Cover Price: £3.50
Free to qualifying individuals
Circulation: 12,500 (Publisher's Statement)
Editor: Naomi Davis; **Advertising Manager:** Donna Jenkins
Summary of Content: Magazine covering garden and hardware industry news including tools, security, planting and new product information.
Readership/Target Audience: Aimed at purchasers, garden centres, equipment dealers and wholesalers.
BUSINESS: GARDEN TRADE: Garden Trade Supplies

GARDEN & HORTICULTURE   1706499U26D-202

Editorial Address: Kentons House, 24 Blendon Road, BEXLEY, DA5 1BW **Tel:** 0870 701 3536
Email: gardenandhorticulture@ntlworld.com
Advertising Address: As above.
Email: gardenandhorticulture@ntlworld.com
Web site: http://www.directpublishing.webeden.co.uk
Publisher: Direct Publishing Ltd
Date Established: 2006
Frequency: Quarterly
Free to qualifying individuals
Circulation: 4,100 (Publisher's Statement)
Editor: Phil Brown; **Advertising Manager:** Phil Brown;
Publisher: Phil Brown
Summary of Content: Magazine featuring products and services for the garden and horticulture trade.
Readership/Target Audience: Aimed at industry professionals.
ADVERTISING RATES:
Full Page Colour £1395.00
Agency Commission: 10%
Mechanical Data: Type Area: 297 x 210mm, Col Length: 297mm, Page Width: 210mm, Bleed Size: 303 x 216mm
Copy instructions: Copy Date: 3 weeks prior to publication date
BUSINESS: GARDEN TRADE: Garden Trade Horticulture

GARDEN CENTRE MONTHLY   623066U26B-30

Formerly: Garden Centre Monthly incorporating Flower Business International
Editorial Address: Unit 4, 4 Stanhope Road, LONDON, N6 5LR **Tel:** 020 8341 0037
Email: info@rdbmedia.co.uk
Advertising Address: As above. **Fax:** 020 7851 8613
Email: jon@rdbmedia.co.uk
Web site: http://www.gardencentremonthly.co.uk
Publisher: RDB Media
Date Established: 1999
Frequency: Monthly - Published around the 15th of the cover month
Annual Sub.: £30.00
Circulation: 6,500 (Publisher's Statement)
Usual Pagination: 46
Editor: David McCairney; **Publisher:** Robert Bloch
Summary of Content: Magazine containing industry related events and news, profiles, interviews and product based features.
Readership/Target Audience: Aimed at garden centre growers, wholesalers and retailers.
ADVERTISING RATES:
Full Page Mono £1000.00
Full Page Colour £1350.00
Agency Commission: 10%

Mechanical Data: Type Area: 264 x 186mm, Col Length: 264mm, Trim Size: 297 x 210mm, Bleed Size: 303 x 216mm, Page Width: 186mm, Film: Digital
Copy instructions: Copy Date: 2 weeks prior to publication date
Average advertising content per issue: 40%
BUSINESS: GARDEN TRADE: Garden Trade Supplies

GARDEN CENTRE UPDATE   22869U26B-73

Editorial Address: 15A London Road, MAIDSTONE, ME16 8LY **Tel:** 01622 687031 **Fax:** 01622 757646
Email: garden@datateam.co.uk
Advertising Address: As above.
Email: garden@datateam.co.uk
Web site: http://www.gardencentreupdate.com
ISSN: 1475-8598
Publisher: Datateam Publishing Ltd
Date Established: 1994
Frequency: 11 issues yearly
Free to qualifying individuals
Annual Sub.: £60.00
Circulation: 6,000 (Publisher's Statement)
Editor: Phil Brown
Summary of Content: Magazine covering products available through garden centres.
Readership/Target Audience: Aimed at garden centre managers.
ADVERTISING RATES:
Full Page Colour £1350.00
Mechanical Data: Bleed Size: 312 x 235mm, Trim Size: 292 x 203mm, Film: Digital, Type Area: 265 x 195mm, Col Length: 265mm, Page Width: 195mm
Copy instructions: Copy Date: 4 weeks prior to publication date
BUSINESS: GARDEN TRADE: Garden Trade Supplies

GARDEN DESIGN JOURNAL   38133U26D-45

Editorial Address: 90 Walcot Street, BATH, BA1 5BG
Tel: 01225 337777 **Fax:** 01225 339977
Email: gdj@jppublishing.co.uk
Advertising Address: As above.
Email: charlest@jppublishing.co.uk
Web site: http://www.sgd.org.uk
ISSN: 1356-6458
Publisher: James Pembroke Publishing Ltd
Date Established: 1998
Frequency: Monthly - Published around the middle of the month prior to cover date
Annual Sub.: £45.00
Circulation: 3,500 (Publisher's Statement)
Usual Pagination: 50
Editor: Jackie Bennett; **Advertising Manager:** Charles Troy
Summary of Content: Journal containing inspiration and practical information for the professional garden designer.
Readership/Target Audience: Aimed at professional garden designers and members of the Society of Garden Designers.
ADVERTISING RATES:
Full Page Colour £1000.00
Agency Commission: 10%
Mechanical Data: Bleed Size: 306 x 213mm, Trim Size: 297 x 210mm, Type Area: 247 x 163mm, Col Length: 247mm, Page Width: 163mm
Copy instructions: Copy Date: 3 weeks prior to publication date
Average advertising content per issue: 30%
BUSINESS: GARDEN TRADE: Garden Trade Horticulture

GARDEN TRADE NEWS   38107U26B-45

Editorial Address: 4th Floor, Churchgate, New Road, PETERBOROUGH, PE1 1TT **Tel:** 01733 775700
Fax: 01733 775838
Email: editorial@gardentradenews.co.uk
Advertising Address: As above.
Email: clare.williams@gardentradenews.co.uk
Web site: http://www.gardentradenews.co.uk
Publisher: The Garden Communication & Media Company Ltd
Date Established: 1978
Frequency: Monthly
Free to qualifying individuals
Annual Sub.: £29.00
Circulation: 5,500 (Publisher's Statement)
Usual Pagination: 32
Editor: Mike Wyatt
Summary of Content: Journal providing news, features and business advice relating to the UK retail garden trade.
Readership/Target Audience: Read by retailers, wholesalers, distributors and manufacturers of garden and garden-related products worldwide.
ADVERTISING RATES:
Full Page Colour £1785.00
Agency Commission: 10%
Mechanical Data: Type Area: 276 x 192mm, Col Length: 276mm, Page Width: 192mm, Trim Size: 297 x210mm, Bleed Size: 302 x 215mm, Film: Digital, Print Process: Sheet-fed offset litho

Average advertising content per issue: 50%
BUSINESS: GARDEN TRADE: Garden Trade Supplies

THE GAS INSTALLER
35750U3A-35

Editorial Address: Unit 7, Oakridge Office Park, Southampton Road, Whaddon, SALISBURY, SP5 3HT
Tel: 01722 711332
Email: emcmanus@lyricalcomms.com
Advertising Address: 1 Elmwood, Crockford Lane, Chineham Business Park, Chineham, BASINGSTOKE, RG24 8WG **Tel:** 0870 401 2529 **Fax:** 0870 401 2626
Email: tdark@trustcorgi.com
Web site: http://www.trustcorgi.com
Publisher: Corgi
Frequency: Monthly - Published in the 1st week of the cover month
Annual Sub.: £50.00
Circulation: 74,913 (ABC 01/01/2008 to 31/12/2008)
Usual Pagination: 60
Editor: Eoin McManus; **Advertising Manager:** Tony Dark
Summary of Content: Journal for CORGI registered gas installers, includes technical features, industry news and a training and recruitment section.
Readership/Target Audience: Aimed at all Corgi registered companies and gas installers.
ADVERTISING RATES:
Full Page Colour £4520.00
Agency Commission: 10%
BUSINESS: HEATING & VENTILATION: Domestic Heating & Ventilation

GAS INTERNATIONAL (ENGINEERING AND MANAGEMENT)
38081U24-20

Formerly: International Gas Engineering and Management
Editorial Address: IGEM House, High Street, KEGWORTH, DE74 2DA **Tel:** 0844 375 4436
Email: rebecca@igem.org.uk
Advertising Address: As above.
Email: gemma@igem.org.uk
Web site: http://www.igem.org.uk
Publisher: Institution of Gas Engineers and Managers
Date Established: 1960
Frequency: 10 issues yearly - Published in the 1st week of the cover month
Free to qualifying individuals
Annual Sub.: £88.00
Circulation: 5,000 (Publisher's Statement)
Usual Pagination: 36
Editor: Rebecca Burnsall; **Advertising Manager:** Gemma Tunnicliffe
Summary of Content: Journal containing news and product information on the gas utility industries in the UK and internationally.
Readership/Target Audience: Aimed at executives, engineers and managers in the gas and utility industries.
ADVERTISING RATES:
Full Page Mono £1425.00
Full Page Colour £2040.00
Agency Commission: 10%
Mechanical Data: Page Width: 190mm, Type Area: 270 x 190mm, Col Length: 270mm, Film: Digital, Bleed Size: 305 x 218mm, Trim Size: 297 x 210mm
Copy instructions: Copy Date: 15th of the month prior to publication date
Average advertising content per issue: 25%
BUSINESS: GAS

GAS MATTERS
38082U24-35

Editorial Address: 35 New Bridge Street, LONDON, EC4V 6BW **Tel:** 020 7332 9920 **Fax:** 020 7332 9901
Email: info@gas-matters.com
Web site: http://www.gas-matters.com
ISSN: 0964-8496
Publisher: EconoMatters Ltd
Date Established: 1988
Frequency: Monthly
Annual Sub.: £735.00
Editor: John Elkins
Summary of Content: Newsletter covering news and information on the natural gas industry.
Readership/Target Audience: Aimed at those interested in the gas industry.
ADVERTISING: No Advertising taken
Supplement(s): Gas Briefing International - 12xY
BUSINESS: GAS

GAS TECHNOLOGY NEWS
1866421U24-104

Editorial Address: 47 Williamson Way, RICKMANSWORTH, WD3 8GL **Tel:** 01923 776690
Email: dave@gastechnologynews.net
Web site: http://gastechnologynews.net
Publisher: Gas Technology News Ltd
Date Established: 2009
Frequency: Quarterly

Annual Sub.: £30.00
Circulation: 2,000 (Print Run)
Usual Pagination: 52
Editor: Dave Williams; **Publisher:** Jonathan Preece
Summary of Content: Technical magazine containing features on fitting, fixing and fault-finding on gas appliances, as well as associated plumbing and heating issues.
Readership/Target Audience: Aimed at gas and heating engineers and trainees.
BUSINESS: GAS

GAS TURBINE WORLD
40759U58-43_12

Editorial Address: 8 Spencer Hill, Wimbledon, LONDON, SW19 4NY **Tel:** 020 8946 5347
Advertising Address: As above.
Web site: http://www.gtwbooks.com
ISSN: 0747-7988
Publisher: The Pequot Publishing Group
Date Established: 1970
Frequency: 6 issues yearly
Free to qualifying individuals
Annual Sub.: £90.00
Circulation: 10,500 (Publisher's Statement)
Usual Pagination: 48
Editor: Sally Donlevy; **Advertising Manager:** Sally Donlevy
Summary of Content: Magazine covering businesses and industries engaged in electric utility and non-utility power generation, oil and gas pipeline, production and transmission and related businesses. Contains global business news and features, on-site services and engineering.
Readership/Target Audience: Aimed at industrial and electric utility power engineers.
ADVERTISING RATES:
Full Page Mono £3220.00
Full Page Colour £4050.00
Agency Commission: 15%
Mechanical Data: Type Area: 254 x 178mm, Col Length: 254mm, Page Width: 178mm, Bleed Size: 283 x 210mm, Trim Size: 276 x 206mm, Film: Digital
Copy instructions: Copy Date: 3 weeks prior to publication date
Average advertising content per issue: 30%
Supplement(s): The Annual Gas Turbine World Handbook - 1xY, The Annual Gas Turbine World Performance Specification - 1xY
BUSINESS: ENERGY, FUEL & NUCLEAR

GASTROENTEROLOGY TODAY
40166U56A-66_4

Editorial Address: Media House, 48 High Street, SWANLEY, BR8 8BQ **Tel:** 01322 660434 **Fax:** 01322 666539
Email: mediajournals@aol.com
Advertising Address: As above.
Email: mediajournals@aol.com
Web site: http://www.mediapublishingcompany.com
Publisher: Media Publishing
Date Established: 1990
Frequency: Quarterly
Annual Sub.: £35.00
Circulation: 2,700 (Publisher's Statement)
Usual Pagination: 28
Editor: Martin Goldman; **Managing Director:** Terry Gardner; **Advertising Manager:** Terry Gardner; **Publisher:** Terry Gardner
Summary of Content: Journal containing original papers, audits, reviews, case reports, meetings reports, news, updates and topical material.
Readership/Target Audience: Aimed at hospital-based gastroenterologists at senior level plus all relevant major GI departments.
ADVERTISING RATES:
Full Page Mono £800.00
Full Page Colour £1200.00
Agency Commission: 10%
Mechanical Data: Type Area: 270 x 185mm, Trim Size: 297 x 210mm, Bleed Size: 303 x 216mm, Film: Positive, right reading, emulsion side down. Digital, Col Length: 270mm, Page Width: 185mm
BUSINESS: HEALTH & MEDICAL

GATELODGE
37187U14L-248

Editorial Address: Cronin House, 245 Church Street, LONDON, N9 9HW **Tel:** 020 8803 0255 **Fax:** 020 8803 1761
Email: gatelodge@poauk.org.uk
Advertising Address: The Maltings, West Street, BOURNE, PE10 0FR **Tel:** 01778 391000 **Fax:** 01778 392079
Email: julietg@warnersgroup.co.uk
Web site: http://www.poauk.org.uk
Publisher: The Prison Officers' Association
Frequency: 6 issues yearly
Free to qualifying individuals
Annual Sub.: £15.00
Circulation: 16,500 (Publisher's Statement)
Usual Pagination: 60
Editor: Glyn Travis

Summary of Content: Journal containing topical news and features of interest to Prison Officers.
Readership/Target Audience: Read by members of the Prison Officers' Association.
ADVERTISING RATES:
Full Page Colour £1200.00
Agency Commission: 10%
Mechanical Data: Type Area: 275 x 190mm, Col Length: 275mm, No. of Columns (Display): 3, Bleed Size: 303 x 216mm, Trim Size: 297 x 210mm, Page Width: 190mm
BUSINESS: COMMERCE, INDUSTRY & MANAGEMENT: Trade Unions

GATESHEAD COUNCIL NEWS
623420U32A-50

Editorial Address: Gateshead Service, Communications Office, Civic Centre, Regent Street, GATESHEAD, NE8 1HH
Tel: 0191 433 3444 **Fax:** 0191 477 5154
Email: dianebrennan@gateshead.gov.uk
Web site: http://www.gateshead.gov.uk
Publisher: Grey Moon Design
Date Established: 1990
Frequency: 6 issues yearly
Cover Price: Free
Circulation: 110,000 (Publisher's Statement)
Usual Pagination: 48
Editor: Diane Brennan
Summary of Content: Magazine covering local government issues including health, education, social services, art, sport and entertainment.
Readership/Target Audience: Aimed at Gateshead residents, businesses and visitors.
ADVERTISING: No Advertising taken
BUSINESS: LOCAL GOVERNMENT, LEISURE & RECREATION: Local Government

THE GATESHEAD HOUSING COMPANY NEWS
1639147U1E-360

Editorial Address: Keelman House, Fifth Avenue Business Park, Fifth Avenue, Team Valley Trading Estate, GATESHEAD, NE11 0XA **Tel:** 0191 433 5382
Fax: 0191 433 5354
Email: ianclarkin@gatesheadhousing.co.uk
Web site: http://www.gatesheadhousing.co.uk
Publisher: Grey Moon Design
Date Established: 2003
Frequency: Quarterly
Cover Price: Free
Circulation: 30,000 (Publisher's Statement)
Usual Pagination: 28
Editor: Ian Clarkin
Summary of Content: Magazine covering all aspects of housing issues and regeneration.
Readership/Target Audience: Aimed at council house and potential council house tenants.
ADVERTISING: No Advertising taken
BUSINESS: FINANCE & ECONOMICS: Property

GAVEL
1902862U1E-410

Editorial Address: Talbot Hays Farm, WINCHFIELD, RG27 8BZ **Tel:** 01252 843566 **Fax:** 01252 843566
Email: rosalind.renshaw@googlemail.com
Publisher: The National Association of Estate Agents
Frequency: Quarterly
Cover Price: Free
Editor: Rosalind Renshaw
Summary of Content: Magazine of the National Federation of Property Professionals covering investment property and property auctions.
Readership/Target Audience: Aimed at those looking to buy investment property.
BUSINESS: FINANCE & ECONOMICS: Property

EL GAZETTE
41020U62B-130

Editorial Address: 3 Constantine Court, Fairclough Street, LONDON, E1 1PW **Tel:** 020 7481 6700 **Fax:** 020 7488 9240
Email: editorial@elgazette.com
Advertising Address: As above. **Tel:** 020 7481 6714
Email: info@elgazette.com
Web site: http://www.elgazette.com
ISSN: 0732-5819
Publisher: EL Gazette New Media Ltd
Frequency: Monthly
Circulation: 5,000 (Publisher's Statement)
Usual Pagination: 20
Editor: Melanie Butler; **Managing Editor:** Melanie Butler
Summary of Content: Magazine covering all aspects of English language teaching.
Readership/Target Audience: Read by teachers of English as a foreign language and language school students.
ADVERTISING RATES:
Full Page Mono £2160.00
Full Page Colour £3240.00
Agency Commission: 10%

Mechanical Data: Type Area: 420 x 297mm, Col Length: 420mm, Page Width: 297mm, Film: Digital
Copy instructions: Copy Date: 3rd week of month prior to publication date
Average advertising content per issue: 40%
BUSINESS: CHURCH & SCHOOL EQUIPMENT & EDUCATION: Education Teachers

GC MAGAZINE
36082U5B-85_35

Editorial Address: 20-24 Kirby Street, LONDON, EC1N 8TS
Tel: 020 7061 3242
Email: gc@kable.co.uk
Advertising Address: As above. **Tel:** 020 7061 3220
Fax: 020 7061 3283
Email: roger.massey@kable.co.uk
Web site: http://www.kablenet.com
ISSN: 1462-2467
Publisher: Kable
Date Established: 1987
Frequency: 11 issues yearly
Free to qualifying individuals
Annual Sub.: £75.00
Circulation: 15,501 (ABC 01/01/2008 to 31/12/2008)
Usual Pagination: 40
Editor: Mark Say; **News Editor:** Steve Mathieson
Summary of Content: Journal covering reports and issues on all sections of IT and information management in the UK public sector.
Readership/Target Audience: Aimed at public sector professionals and those involved in IT for national and local government.
ADVERTISING RATES:
Full Page Colour £3520.00
Agency Commission: 10%
Mechanical Data: Film: Digital, Bleed Size: 303 x 216mm, Trim Size: 297 x 210mm
Average advertising content per issue: 50%
BUSINESS: COMPUTERS & AUTOMATION: Data Processing

GD PRO
1895426U41A-342

Editorial Address: PO Box 7574, BILLERICAY, CM12 9XF
Tel: 01277 650037
Email: mike@gdpro.co.uk
Web site: http://www.gdpro.co.uk
Publisher: Open House Publishing Ltd
Date Established: 2008
Frequency: 6 issues yearly
Free to qualifying individuals
Circulation: 4,000 (Publisher's Statement)
Editor: Mike Lyons
Summary of Content: Magazine containing reports on buying trends, market characteristics and emerging technologies and innovations as well as regular briefings from print associations FESPA and PRISM.
Readership/Target Audience: Aimed at specialist manufacturers, service providers and end-users and buyers within the screen printing and digital imaging spheres, sign and display manufacturers, vinyl, substrate and ink distributors, creatives and suppliers to the exhibition and display market.
BUSINESS: PRINTING & STATIONERY: Printing

THE GDP
40390U56D-78

Editorial Address: 61 Harley Street, LONDON, W1G 8QU
Tel: 020 7636 1072 **Fax:** 020 7636 1086
Email: farideh@uk-dentistry.org
Advertising Address: As above.
Email: info@uk-dentistry.org
Web site: http://www.uk-dentistry.org
ISSN: 0954-4186
Publisher: The Dental Practitioners' Association
Date Established: 1954
Frequency: 6 issues yearly - Published the 15th of the odd months
Free to qualifying individuals
Annual Sub.: £260.00
Circulation: 3,000 (Publisher's Statement)
Usual Pagination: 42
Editor: Farideh Ghassemian; **Advertising Manager:** Farideh Ghassemian
Summary of Content: Journal for members of the Dental Practitioners Association containing articles and news of interest to practising dentists. Also contains features on all aspects of the dental surgery including materials and dental work.
Readership/Target Audience: Aimed at Dentists in the UK with purchasing power on behalf of their practices and Dentists they employ. Dentists who need risk management advice and business consultancy, also employment advice.
ADVERTISING RATES:
Full Page Colour £625.00
Agency Commission: 10%
Mechanical Data: Type Area: 259 x 175mm, Bleed Size: 303 x 216mm, Trim Size: 297 x 210mm, Col Length: 259mm, Page Width: 175mm, Film: Digital

Copy instructions: Copy Date: 20th of the month prior to publication date
Average advertising content per issue: 60%
BUSINESS: HEALTH & MEDICAL: Dental

GEMS & JEWELLERY
39777U52A-70

Formerly: Gem & Jewellery News
Editorial Address: 27 Greville Street, LONDON, EC1N 8TN
Tel: 020 7404 3334 **Fax:** 020 7404 8843
Email: mary.burland@gem-a.com
Web site: http://www.gem-a.com
ISSN: 1746-8043
Publisher: Gemmological Association of Great Britain
Date Established: 1991
Frequency: 5 issues yearly
Annual Sub.: £72.50
Circulation: 3,500 (Publisher's Statement)
Usual Pagination: 32
Editor: Mary Burland; **Managing Editor:** Mary Burland
Summary of Content: Journal containing news and articles concerning gem and/or jewellery trade, meetings, books, history and research.
Readership/Target Audience: Aimed at anyone with an interest in gemstones jewellery, ranging from those working in the trade to those with an academic or hobby interest.
ADVERTISING: No Advertising taken
BUSINESS: GIFT TRADE: Jewellery

GENDER & DEVELOPMENT
35450U56R-508

Editorial Address: Oxfam House, John Smith Drive, Cowley, OXFORD, OX4 2JY **Tel:** 01865 472106
Email: gadeditor@oxfam.org.uk
Advertising Address: 274 Banbury Road, OXFORD, OX2 7DZ **Tel:** 01865 311311 **Fax:** 01865 312600
Email: rcornford@oxfam.org.uk
Web site: http://www.informaworld.com/gad
ISSN: 1355-2074
Publisher: Oxfam
Date Established: 1993
Frequency: 3 issues yearly
Annual Sub.: £46.00
Circulation: 700 (Publisher's Statement)
Usual Pagination: 100
Editor: Caroline Sweetman
Summary of Content: Journal containing thematic issues, addressing a particular aspect of gender relations as they affect the lives of women and men living in poverty.
Readership/Target Audience: Aimed at development researchers, policy makers and practitioners.
ADVERTISING: No Advertising taken
BUSINESS: HEALTH & MEDICAL: Health Medical Related

GENE THERAPY
40523U56R-56

Editorial Address: The Macmillan Building, 4 Crinan Street, LONDON, N1 9XW **Tel:** 020 7833 4000 **Fax:** 020 7843 4640
Email: genetherapy@btopenworld.com
Advertising Address: 25 First Street, Suite 104, Cambridge, MA 02141 **Tel:** 617 4759231
Email: a.anderson@boston.nature.com
Web site: http://www.nature.com/gt
ISSN: 0969-7128
Publisher: Nature Publishing Group
Frequency: 24 issues yearly
Annual Sub.: £226.00
Circulation: 1,000 (Publisher's Statement)
Usual Pagination: 80
Editor: Nick Lemoine; **Advertising Manager:** Alf Anderson
Summary of Content: International journal covering all aspects of the application of new genetic therapies to all areas of medicine.
Readership/Target Audience: Aimed at doctors and scientists.
ADVERTISING RATES:
Full Page Mono £750.00
Full Page Colour £1285.00
Mechanical Data: Type Area: 250 x 175mm, Col Length: 250mm, Bleed Size: 286 x 216mm, Trim Size: 280 x 210mm, Film: Digital, Page Width: 175mm
Copy instructions: Copy Date: 6 weeks prior to publication date
BUSINESS: HEALTH & MEDICAL: Health Medical Related

GENERAL AVIATION
36436U6R-148

Formerly: Light Aviation
Editorial Address: The Studio, Kettys Close, Withiel, BODMIN, PL30 5NR **Tel:** 01208 832975 **Fax:** 01208 832995
Email: pat@richmondaviation.co.uk
Advertising Address: 50A Cambridge Street, LONDON, SW1V 4QQ **Tel:** 020 7834 5631
Email: aopa@easynet.co.uk
Web site: http://www.aopa.co.uk
Publisher: Richmond Aviation
Date Established: 2002
Frequency: 6 issues yearly

Cover Price: £3.25
Free to qualifying individuals
Circulation: 5,500 (Publisher's Statement)
Usual Pagination: 44
Editor: Pat Malone; **Editor-in-Chief:** Pat Malone
Summary of Content: Official journal of the Aircraft Owners and Pilots' Association of the United Kingdom. Covers general aviation, private and club, training and business flying.
Readership/Target Audience: Aimed at pilot's license holders and organisations of the general aviation industry. Includes flying clubs, flying schools, professional and private pilots.
BUSINESS: AVIATION & AERONAUTICS: Aviation Related

GENERATION
1791188U14A-584

Editorial Address: St. Augustines Yard, Orchard Lane, BRISTOL, BS1 5DE **Tel:** 0117 314 5678 **Fax:** 0117 314 5679
Email: editor@generation-online.co.uk
Web site: http://www.generation-online.co.uk
ISSN: 1753-5891
Publisher: The International Centre for Families in Business
Date Established: 2006
Frequency: Quarterly
Annual Sub.: £40.00
Circulation: 20,000 (Print Run)
Usual Pagination: 52
Editor: Paul Andrews
Summary of Content: Magazine containing features, case studies and expert advice geared towards the challenges for anyone involved in family business.
Readership/Target Audience: Aimed at all levels of the sector from company executives to family stakeholders and professional advisers.
BUSINESS: COMMERCE, INDUSTRY & MANAGEMENT

GENERICS BULLETIN
1666009U37-410

Editorial Address: 54 Creynolds Lane, Shirley, SOLIHULL, B90 4ER **Tel:** 01564 777550 **Fax:** 01564 777524
Email: aidan.fry@generics-bulletin.com
Advertising Address: As above.
Email: ads@generics-bulletin.com
Web site: http://www.generics-bulletin.com
ISSN: 1742-0784
Publisher: OTC Publications Ltd
Date Established: 2003
Frequency: 20 issues yearly
Annual Sub.: £475.00
Editor: Aidan Fry; **Advertising Manager:** Val Davis
Summary of Content: Newsletter covering commercial and regulatory information for the global generics industry.
Readership/Target Audience: Aimed at those working within the generics medicine industry.
ADVERTISING RATES:
Full Page Mono £940.00
Full Page Colour £1410.00
SCC £30.00
Agency Commission: 10%
Mechanical Data: Type Area: 272 x 189mm, Col Length: 272mm, Page Width: 189mm, Print Process: Offset litho, Film: Digital, Bleed Size: 307 x 220mm, Trim Size: 297 x 210mm, Col Widths (Display): 90mm, No. of Columns (Display): 3
Copy instructions: Copy Date: 10 days prior to publication date
Average advertising content per issue: 10%
BUSINESS: PHARMACEUTICAL & CHEMISTS

GENETIC ENGINEERING NEWS
1696591U55-9019

Editorial Address: 36 Orchard Road, Hook Norton, BANBURY, OX15 5LX **Tel:** 01608 737084
Email: eurogennews@aol.com
Advertising Address: Impress International Media Ltd, Main Street, Carrington Kirk, Carrington, GOREBRIDGE, EH23 4LR **Tel:** 01875 825700 **Fax:** 01875 825701
Email: gen@impressmedia.com
Web site: http://www.genengnews.com
Publisher: Mary Ann Liebert, Inc.
Frequency: 24 issues yearly
Free to qualifying individuals
Circulation: 59,560 (BPA Worldwide 01/01/2007 to 30/06/2007)
Editor: Sophia Fox; **Managing Editor:** Tamlyn Oliver
Summary of Content: Magazine focusing on all aspects of the biotechnology industry.
Readership/Target Audience: Aimed at biotechnology professionals involved in research, technical and commercial management.
ADVERTISING: Rates on application
Copy instructions: Copy Date: 3 weeks prior to publication date
BUSINESS: APPLIED SCIENCE & LABORATORIES

Business Magazines

Section 4 (b) Business Magazines

GEO:CONNEXION INTERNATIONAL

36294U5R-100

Formerly: GEO:connexion
Editorial Address: PO Box 594, CAMBRIDGE, CB1 0FY
Tel: 01223 279151 **Fax:** 0870 134 6492
Email: roger@geoconnexion.com
Advertising Address: As above. **Tel:** 0114 268 1133
Fax: 0114 268 1155
Email: mickiknight@geoconnexion.com
Web site: http://www.geoconnexion.com
ISSN: 1476-8941
Publisher: GEO:connexion Limited
Date Established: 2002
Frequency: 10 issues yearly - Published on the 1st of the cover month
Free to qualifying individuals
Annual Sub.: £45.00
Circulation: 14,000 (Publisher's Statement)
Usual Pagination: 60
Editor: Roger Longhorn; **Advertising Manager:** Micki Knight; **Publisher:** Mai Ward
Summary of Content: Geographical technology magazine covering the uses of GIS, GPS, remote sensing, photogrammetry, surveying, cartography, image processing, telematics and Location Based Services.
Readership/Target Audience: Read by decision makers in both the public and private sectors.
ADVERTISING RATES:
Full Page Mono $2610.00
Full Page Colour $3960.00
Agency Commission: 10%
Mechanical Data: Bleed Size: 307 x 220mm, Col Widths (Display): 44mm, Trim Size: 297 x 210mm, Film: Digital
Average advertising content per issue: 30%
BUSINESS: COMPUTERS & AUTOMATION: Computers Related

GEO:CONNEXION UK

1639880U5R-667

Editorial Address: PO Box 594, CAMBRIDGE, CB1 0FY
Tel: 07816 893097 **Fax:** 01223 279148
Email: maria@geoconnexion.com
Advertising Address: As above. **Tel:** 01223 279151
Fax: 0114 268 1155
Email: mickiknight@geoconnexion.com
Web site: http://www.geoconnexion.com
Publisher: GEO:connexion Limited
Date Established: 2004
Frequency: 5 issues yearly - Published in the 1st week of the month
Annual Sub.: £25.00
Circulation: 8,000 (Publisher's Statement)
Usual Pagination: 44
Editor: Maria Pellegrini
Summary of Content: Magazine including news, features, comment, interviews, conference and event pages devoted to the UK's geo information industry.
Readership/Target Audience: Read by decision makers in both the public and private sectors.
ADVERTISING RATES:
Full Page Mono £990.00
Full Page Colour £1485.00
Agency Commission: 10%
Mechanical Data: Bleed Size: 303 x 220mm, Trim Size: 297 x 210mm, Film: Digital
Average advertising content per issue: 30%
BUSINESS: COMPUTERS & AUTOMATION: Computers Related

GEODRILLING INTERNATIONAL

38996U42A-100

Editorial Address: Albert House, 1 Singer Street, LONDON, EC2A 4BQ **Tel:** 020 7216 6060 **Fax:** 020 7216 6050
Email: luke.clancy@mining-journal.com
Advertising Address: As above.
Email: linda.winfield@mining-journal.com
Web site: http://www.mining-journal.com
ISSN: 0969-3769
Publisher: Aspermont
Date Established: 1993
Frequency: 10 issues yearly - Published in the 3rd week of the cover month
Annual Sub.: £69.00
Circulation: 4,000 (Publisher's Statement)
Usual Pagination: 44
Editor: Luke Clancy
Summary of Content: Journal covering all aspects of drilling in soils and rocks, including civil engineering, water well work, construction, piling, geotechnical, geothermal, coal bed methane, mineral resources exploration and environmental testing, quarrying, and open pit/underground mining.
Readership/Target Audience: Aimed at manufacturers of equipment, geotechnical contracting and consulting companies, governmental users and academics.
ADVERTISING RATES:
Full Page Colour £1641.00
Agency Commission: 10%

Mechanical Data: Type Area: 275 x 186mm, Bleed Size: 303 x 216mm, Trim Size: 297 x 210mm, Col Length: 275mm, No. of Columns (Display): 3, Print Process: Offset litho, Film: Digital, Page Width: 186mm, Col Widths (Display): 57mm
Copy instructions: Copy Date: 8th of the month prior to publication date
BUSINESS: CONSTRUCTION

GEOGRAPHY

41026U62B-310

Editorial Address: 160 Solly Street, SHEFFIELD, S1 4BF
Tel: 0114 296 0088 **Fax:** 0114 296 7176
Email: dturner@geography.org.uk
Advertising Address: As above.
Email: anna@geography.org.uk
Web site: http://www.geography.org.uk/journals
ISSN: 0016-7487
Publisher: The Geographical Association
Date Established: 1901
Frequency: 3 issues yearly - Published in autumn, spring and summer
Annual Sub.: £54.25
Circulation: 4,000 (Publisher's Statement)
Usual Pagination: 64
Editor: Dorcas Turner; **Advertising Manager:** Anna Grandfield
Summary of Content: Journal covering all matters relating to research and teaching.
Readership/Target Audience: Aimed at lecturers, teachers and students of geography.
ADVERTISING RATES:
Full Page Mono £390.00
Full Page Colour £760.00
Mechanical Data: Type Area: 215 x 146mm, Col Length: 215mm, Trim Size: 245 x 190mm, Bleed Size: +5mm, Page Width: 146mm, Film: Digital
BUSINESS: CHURCH & SCHOOL EQUIPMENT & EDUCATION: Education Teachers

GEOMATICS WORLD

35841U4C-150

Formerly: Surveying World
Editorial Address: Suite L, 17 Park Place, STEVENAGE, SG1 1DU **Tel:** 01438 352617 **Fax:** 01438 351989
Email: editor@pvpubs.demon.co.uk
Advertising Address: As above.
Email: sharon@pvpubs.demon.co.uk
Web site: http://www.pvpubs.com
ISSN: 1567-5882
Publisher: PV Publications Ltd.
Date Established: 1992
Frequency: 6 issues yearly
Free to qualifying individuals
Annual Sub.: £45.00
Circulation: 4,500 (Publisher's Statement)
Usual Pagination: 52
Editor: Stephen Booth; **Publisher:** Stephen Booth
Summary of Content: Magazine focusing on land, engineering and hydrographic surveying.
Readership/Target Audience: Aimed at RICS Geomatics Division members and all other professionals involved in using spatial data.
ADVERTISING RATES:
Full Page Mono £1200.00
Full Page Colour £1995.00
Agency Commission: 10%
Mechanical Data: Page Width: 189mm, Type Area: 269.5 x 189mm, Col Length: 269.5mm, Trim Size: 297 x 210mm, Film: Digital, Bleed Size: 303 x 216mm
Copy instructions: Copy Date: 2 weeks prior to publication date
Average advertising content per issue: 30%
BUSINESS: ARCHITECTURE & BUILDING: Surveying

GEOSCIENTIST

38236U30-35

Editorial Address: Unit 7, Brassmill Enterprise Centre, Brassmill Lane, BATH, BA1 3JN **Tel:** 01225 445046
Fax: 01225 442836
Email: ted.nield@geolsoc.org.uk
Advertising Address: DP Media, Suite 2.1, 30 Queen Charlotte Street, BRISTOL, BS1 4HJ **Tel:** 0117 904 1283
Fax: 0117 904 0085
Email: nick.goltan@dpmedia.org.uk
Web site: http://www.geolsoc.org.uk
ISSN: 0961-5628
Publisher: The Geological Society Publishing House
Date Established: 1990
Frequency: Monthly
Free to qualifying individuals
Annual Sub.: £95.00
Circulation: 9,600 (Publisher's Statement)
Usual Pagination: 32
Editor: Ted Nield
Summary of Content: Magazine covering news and developments in earth sciences.
Readership/Target Audience: Aimed at earth scientists involved in industry, education and government departments.

ADVERTISING RATES:
Full Page Mono £1320.00
Full Page Colour £1980.00
Agency Commission: 10%
Mechanical Data: Film: Digital, Type Area: 254 x 178mm, Trim Size: 297 x 210mm, Col Length: 254mm, Bleed Size: 303 x 216mm, Page Width: 178mm
Copy instructions: Copy Date: 7th of the month prior to publication date
Average advertising content per issue: 15%
BUSINESS: MINING & QUARRYING

GET CONNECTED MAGAZINE

1655551U43A-61

Editorial Address: Winchfield Lodge, Old Portbridge Road, Winchfield, HOOK, RG27 8TB **Tel:** 01252 849050
Fax: 01420 88633
Email: marlinda@gcmagazine.co.uk
Advertising Address: As above. **Tel:** 01252 849051
Email: adam@gcmagazine.co.uk
Web site: http://www.gcmagazine.co.uk
Publisher: Mud Hut Publishing
Date Established: 2004
Frequency: Monthly
Free to qualifying individuals
Annual Sub.: £88.00
Circulation: 6,228 (ABC 01/01/2008 to 31/12/2008)
Usual Pagination: 48
Editor: Marlinda Conway; **Editor-in-Chief:** Marlinda Conway; **Advertising Manager:** Adam Baker
Summary of Content: Magazine focusing on domestic electrical appliances. Includes articles on consumer electronics, major domestic appliances and small kitchen appliances.
Readership/Target Audience: Aimed at independent electrical retailers, selected multiple outlets, selected department stores, kitchen specialists, kitchen contractors and developers purchasing built in kitchen appliances.
ADVERTISING RATES:
Full Page Colour £1800.00
Agency Commission: 10%
Mechanical Data: Trim Size: 297 x 210mm, Bleed Size: 303 x 216mm, Film: Digital
Copy instructions: Copy Date: 21st of the month prior to publication date
Average advertising content per issue: 50%
BUSINESS: ELECTRICAL RETAIL TRADE

GETTING PAID

35350U1G-33

Editorial Address: 7 Greding Walk, Hutton, BRENTWOOD, CM13 2UF **Tel:** 01277 225402 **Fax:** 0870 137 5688
Email: carol.baker@creditcontrol.co.uk
Advertising Address: As above.
Email: carol.baker@creditcontrol.co.uk
Web site: http://www.creditcontrol.co.uk
ISSN: 1368-9320
Publisher: House of Words Ltd
Date Established: 1998
Frequency: 10 issues yearly
Free to qualifying individuals
Annual Sub.: £635.00
Circulation: 16,317 (Publisher's Statement)
Usual Pagination: 72
Editor: Carol Baker; **Advertising Manager:** Carol Baker
Summary of Content: Newsletter containing a mix of news, and legal and technical articles for corporations dealing with consumers, also carries sections on mortgages, E-billings, motor trade and credit cards.
Readership/Target Audience: Aimed at credit lenders, credit card operators, retailers, credit managers, managers, credit controllers and financial institutions.
ADVERTISING RATES:
Full Page Mono £680.00
Full Page Colour £1620.00
Agency Commission: 10%
Mechanical Data: Type Area: 243 x 167mm, Col Length: 243mm, Page Width: 167mm, Film: Digital, Bleed Size: +3mm
Copy instructions: Copy Date: 2nd Wednesday of the month prior to publication date
BUSINESS: FINANCE & ECONOMICS: Credit Trading

GIFT FOCUS

629112U52C-20

Formerly: Gift-Focus
Editorial Address: Broseley House, Newland Drive, WITHAM, CM8 2UL **Tel:** 01376 514000 **Fax:** 01376 514555
Email: editor@giftfocus.com
Advertising Address: As above. **Tel:** 01376 535609
Email: sharonc@giftfocus.com
Web site: http://www.giftfocus.com
Publisher: Kline Davis Ltd
Date Established: 1999
Frequency: 6 issues yearly
Cover Price: Free
Circulation: 6,757 (ABC 01/07/2007 to 30/06/2008)
Usual Pagination: 100
Editor: Sarah Reeve; **Managing Director:** Robert Clark; **Group Editor:** Demelza Rayner

Summary of Content: Magazine covering every aspect of the giftware industry including news, reviews and reports on trade fairs.
Readership/Target Audience: Aimed at buyers and retailers in the giftware industry.
ADVERTISING RATES:
Full Page Mono £1300.00
Full Page Colour £1300.00
Agency Commission: 10%
Mechanical Data: Trim Size: 297 x 210mm, Bleed Size: 303 x 216mm, Film: Digital
Average advertising content per issue: 45%
BUSINESS: GIFT TRADE: Fancy Goods

GIFTS AND HOUSEWARES MAGAZINE
1641778U52C-152

Editorial Address: 4th Floor, Geneva House, Park Road, PETERBOROUGH, PE1 2UX **Tel:** 01733 756555
Fax: 01733 760505
Email: ghm@onecoms.co.uk
Advertising Address: As above.
Email: donna@onecoms.co.uk
Web site: http://www.onecoms.co.uk
Publisher: Media One Communications Ltd.
Date Established: 2004
Frequency: Quarterly
Cover Price: £3.25
Free to qualifying individuals
Circulation: 9,500 (Publisher's Statement)
Usual Pagination: 24
Editor: Naomi Davis
Summary of Content: Magazine covering news, and the latest innovations and trends in the gifts and housewares market.
Readership/Target Audience: Aimed at buyers, executives and owners of gift and houseware retailers throughout the UK.
ADVERTISING RATES:
Full Page Colour £950.00
Agency Commission: 10%
Mechanical Data: Type Area: 280 x 190mm, Bleed Size: 303 x 216mm, Trim Size: 297 x 210mm, Col Length: 280mm, Page Width: 190mm, Film: Digital
BUSINESS: GIFT TRADE: Fancy Goods

GIFTS TODAY
39784U52C-30

Editorial Address: 1 Churchgates, The Wilderness, BERKHAMSTED, HP4 2AZ **Tel:** 01442 289930
Fax: 01442 289950
Email: phughes@lemapublishing.co.uk
Advertising Address: As above. **Fax:** 01422 289950
Email: markh@lemapublishing.co.uk
Publisher: Lema Publishing
Frequency: 8 issues yearly
Annual Sub: £45.00
Circulation: 7,142 (ABC 01/07/2008 to 30/06/2009)
Editor: Paul Hughes; **Advertising Manager:** Mark Horsnell; **Publisher:** Mark Naish
Summary of Content: Magazine containing information on gift products.
Readership/Target Audience: Aimed at all those involved in gift retailing and manufacturing.
ADVERTISING RATES:
Full Page Colour £1595.00
Agency Commission: 10%
Mechanical Data: Film: Digital, Col Length: 285mm, Page Width: 210mm, Type Area: 285 x 210mm, Trim Size: 315 x 240mm, Bleed Size: 321 x 246mm
Copy instructions: Copy Date: 3 weeks prior to publication date
Average advertising content per issue: 40%
Supplement(s): Exhibitions Diary - 1xY
BUSINESS: GIFT TRADE: Fancy Goods

GIFTWARE REVIEW
39786U52C-60

Editorial Address: Media House, Hallidays Yard, Radcliffe Road, STAMFORD, PE9 1ED **Tel:** 01780 765960
Fax: 01780 765904
Email: annette@giftwarereview.net
Advertising Address: As above.
Email: nicola@giftwarereview.net
Web site: http://www.giftwarereview.net
Publisher: Detail Extra Ltd
Date Established: 1997
Frequency: 5 issues yearly
Cover Price: Free
Circulation: 8,000 (Publisher's Statement)
Editor: Annette Harrison
Summary of Content: Newspaper focusing on new product news within the giftware industry.
Readership/Target Audience: Aimed at retailers.
ADVERTISING RATES:
Full Page Colour £999.00
Agency Commission: 10%

Mechanical Data: Type Area: 379 x 264mm, Col Length: 379mm, Film: Digital, Page Width: 264mm, Bleed Size: 417 x 299mm, Trim Size: 407 x 294mm
Copy instructions: Copy Date: 4 weeks prior to publication date
Average advertising content per issue: 95%
BUSINESS: GIFT TRADE: Fancy Goods

GIG
1668188U61-508

Editorial Address: 2nd Floor, Century House, 11 St. Peters Square, MANCHESTER, M2 3DN **Tel:** 0161 236 9526
Fax: 0161 247 7978
Email: clloyd@impromptupublishing.com
Advertising Address: As above.
Email: sabrina@impromptupublishing.com
Web site: http://www.gigmag.co.uk
Publisher: Impromptu Publishing Ltd
Date Established: 2005
Frequency: 24 issues yearly
Cover Price: £2.95
Annual Sub.: £70.80
Circulation: 24,000 (Publisher's Statement)
Usual Pagination: 32
Editor: Christian Lloyd; **Advertising Manager:** Sabrina Abdelhak
Summary of Content: Magazine covering news, recruitment, artist management, recording services, financial matters, policy and legal developments for the international performing arts industry, with a primary focus on classical music and opera.
Readership/Target Audience: Aimed at senior executives in the performing arts industry.
ADVERTISING RATES:
Full Page Colour £2495.00
Mechanical Data: Bleed Size: 348 x 248mm, Film: Digital, Trim Size: 340 x 240mm
Copy instructions: Copy Date: 10 days prior to publication date
BUSINESS: MUSIC TRADE

GIS PROFESSIONAL
1659644U4C-238

Editorial Address: Suite L, 17 Park Place, STEVENAGE, SG1 1DU **Tel:** 01438 352617 **Fax:** 01438 351989
Email: editor@pvpubs.demon.co.uk
Advertising Address: As above.
Email: sharon@pvpubs.demon.co.uk
Web site: http://www.gisprofessional.co.uk
Publisher: PV Publications
Date Established: 2004
Frequency: 6 issues yearly
Free to qualifying individuals
Circulation: 4,500 (Publisher's Statement)
Editor: Stephen Booth; **Publisher:** Stephen Booth
Summary of Content: Magazine covering case studies; reviews and impressions; peer-reviewed material; industry news; new products, systems and services.
Readership/Target Audience: Aimed at GIS users, managers, developers, consultants, data collectors, sensor and system developers, academics and researchers.
ADVERTISING RATES:
Full Page Mono £995.00
Full Page Colour £1595.00
Agency Commission: 10%
Mechanical Data: Type Area: 265 x 185mm, Trim Size: 297 x 210mm, Col Length: 265mm, Page Width: 185mm, Film: Digital
BUSINESS: ARCHITECTURE & BUILDING: Surveying

GKT GAZETTE
40351U56C-195

Editorial Address: 2nd Floor, Doyles House, 19 Newcomen Street, LONDON, SE1 1UL **Tel:** 020 7848 6983
Fax: 020 7848 6984
Email: editor@gktgazette.com
Advertising Address: As above.
Email: editor@gktgazette.com
Web site: http://www.gktgazette.com
ISSN: 0017-5870
Publisher: Committee of GKT Medical Schools
Date Established: 1872
Frequency: 10 issues yearly
Annual Sub.: £25.00
Usual Pagination: 64
Editor: Lowell Ling; **Advertising Manager:** Lowell Ling
Summary of Content: Magazine containing medical, dental and surgical news with relevant features, also covers websites and book reviews.
Readership/Target Audience: Read by supporters, staff and students at Guy's Hospital, St. Thomas's Hospital and Kings College Hospital.
ADVERTISING RATES:
Full Page Colour £300.00
Copy instructions: Copy Date: 1st of the cover month
BUSINESS: HEALTH & MEDICAL: Hospitals

GLASGOW BUSINESS
41447U63D-200

Formerly: Journal (Glasgow)
Editorial Address: 30 George Square, GLASGOW, G2 1EQ
Tel: 0141 204 2121 **Fax:** 0141 221 2336
Email: annemarie.hughes@glasgowchamber.org
Advertising Address: Excel Publishing, Ground Floor, Houldsworth Mill, Houldsworth Street, STOCKPORT, SK5 6DA **Tel:** 0161 442 2576 **Fax:** 0161 443 2382
Email: n.ackroyd@imprintpub.co.uk
Web site: http://www.glasgowchamber.org
Publisher: Excel Publishing Company Ltd
Frequency: 6 issues yearly
Annual Sub.: £45.00
Circulation: 5,000 (Publisher's Statement)
Usual Pagination: 32
Editor: Anne Marie Hughes; **Advertising Manager:** Nick Ackroyd
Summary of Content: Magazine of the Glasgow Chamber of Commerce.
Readership/Target Audience: Aimed at members of the Glasgow Chamber of Commerce.
ADVERTISING RATES:
Full Page Colour £2250.00
Mechanical Data: Type Area: 260 x 160mm, No. of Columns (Display): 4, Col Length: 260mm, Page Width: 160mm, Film: Digital
Copy instructions: Copy Date: 3 weeks prior to publication date
BUSINESS: REGIONAL BUSINESS: Regional Business Scotland

GLASS AND GLAZING PRODUCTS
36630U12B-45

Editorial Address: Becket House, Vestry Road, SEVENOAKS, TN14 5EJ **Tel:** 01732 748000
Fax: 01732 748001
Email: mgannon@unity-media.com
Advertising Address: As above.
Email: nluck@unity-media.com
Web site: http://www.ggpmag.com
Publisher: Unity Media plc
Frequency: Monthly - Published on the 15th of the cover month
Cover Price: £3.50
Free to qualifying individuals
Annual Sub.: £35.00
Circulation: 10,159 (ABC 01/01/2008 to 31/12/2008)
Usual Pagination: 150
Editor: Mike Gannon; **Advertising Manager:** Natalie Luck
Summary of Content: Journal providing news and information on the glass and fenestration industry.
Readership/Target Audience: Read by fabricators and installers working within the industry with a purchasing ability.
ADVERTISING RATES:
Full Page Colour £1690.00
Agency Commission: 10%
Mechanical Data: Type Area: 254 x 178mm, Bleed Size: 303 x 216mm, Trim Size: 297 x 210mm, No. of Columns (Display): 4, Print Process: Sheet-fed offset litho, Col Length: 254mm, Film: Digital, Page Width: 178mm
Copy instructions: Copy Date: 2 weeks prior to publication date
Average advertising content per issue: 60%
BUSINESS: CERAMICS, POTTERY & GLASS: Glass

GLASS INTERNATIONAL
36631U12B-50

Editorial Address: Westgate House, 120-130 Station Road, REDHILL, RH1 1ET **Tel:** 01737 855151 **Fax:** 01737 855463
Email: glass@dmgworldmedia.com
Advertising Address: As above. **Tel:** 01737 855000
Email: glass@dmgworldmedia.com
Web site: http://www.glassmediaonline.com
ISSN: 0143-7838
Publisher: DMG Business Media
Frequency: 10 issues yearly
Cover Price: £35.00
Annual Sub.: £167.00
Circulation: 7,000 (Publisher's Statement)
Usual Pagination: 72
Editor: Leanne Dennehy
Summary of Content: Magazine containing information on the latest technology in glass production and in-depth surveys on the location and activities of the glassmaking industries in countries around the world.
Readership/Target Audience: Read by production, technical and research personnel worldwide.
ADVERTISING RATES:
Full Page Mono £2980.00
Full Page Colour £3900.00
Agency Commission: 10%
Mechanical Data: Trim Size: 297 x 210mm, Type Area: 265 x 185mm, Col Length: 265mm, Bleed Size: 303 x 216mm, Film: Digital, positive, right reading, emulsion side down, Page Width: 185mm
Average advertising content per issue: 50%
BUSINESS: CERAMICS, POTTERY & GLASS: Glass

Business Magazines

GLASS TECHNOLOGY
36633U12B-55

Editorial Address: Unit 9, Twelve O'Clock Court, 21 Attercliffe Road, SHEFFIELD, S4 7WW **Tel:** 0114 263 4455 **Fax:** 0114 263 4411
Email: david@sgt.org
Advertising Address: As above.
Email: adverts@sgt.org
Web site: http://www.sgt.org
ISSN: 0017-1050
Publisher: Society of Glass Technology
Date Established: 1960
Frequency: 6 issues yearly - Published on the 1st Friday of the cover month
Free to qualifying individuals
Annual Sub.: £215.00
Circulation: 900 (Publisher's Statement)
Usual Pagination: 48
Editor: David Moore; **Advertising Manager:** David Moore; **Managing Editor:** David Moore
Summary of Content: Journal covering society and industry news relating to the glass industry.
Readership/Target Audience: Aimed at managers in the glass manufacturing industry, academic researchers and others working in the industry.
ADVERTISING RATES:
Full Page Mono £500.00
Full Page Colour £900.00
Agency Commission: 15%
Mechanical Data: Bleed Size: 305 x 213mm, Trim Size: 299 x 210mm, Type Area: 254 x 178mm, Col Length: 254mm, Page Width: 178mm, Film: Digital
Copy instructions: Copy Date: 3 weeks prior to publication date
Average advertising content per issue: 5%
BUSINESS: CERAMICS, POTTERY & GLASS: Glass

GLASS TIMES
1799704U12B-88

Editorial Address: PO Box 56916, LONDON, N10 1XQ
Tel: 020 8444 1302
Email: dominic@glasstimes.co.uk
Advertising Address: 18 Guildford Road, Urmston, MANCHESTER, M41 0SD **Tel:** 0161 747 8390
Email: andy@glasstimes.co.uk
Web site: http://www.glasstimes.co.uk
Publisher: Times Publishing Limited
Frequency: Monthly - Published around the 1st of the cover month
Annual Sub.: £66.00
Circulation: 10,163 (ABC 01/01/2008 to 31/12/2008)
Editor: Dominic Bentham; **Advertising Manager:** Andy Westhead
Summary of Content: Journal covering all aspects of the glass industry, containing articles on glass and glazing, industry news and product information.
Readership/Target Audience: Aimed at installers of windows and glass products, glass merchants and processors.
ADVERTISING RATES:
Full Page Colour £1930.00
Agency Commission: 10%
Mechanical Data: Type Area: 270 x 190mm, Bleed Size: 303 x 216mm, Trim Size: 297 x 210mm, Col Length: 270mm, Page Width: 190mm, Film: Digital
Copy instructions: Copy Date: 10th of the month prior to publication date
Average advertising content per issue: 40%
Supplement(s): Conservatory Times Supplement - 6xY
BUSINESS: CERAMICS, POTTERY & GLASS: Glass

GLOBAL BROKER & UNDERWRITER
1810698U1D-424

Formerly: Global Broker
Editorial Address: The Annexe, 7 Birchin Lane, LONDON, EC3V 9BW **Tel:** 020 7148 3688
Email: info@globalbrokermagazine.com
Advertising Address: As above.
Email: john.walsh@editorial-solutions.com
Web site: http://www.globalbrokermagazine.com
Publisher: Editorial Solutions Ltd
Date Established: 2007
Frequency: 6 issues yearly
Cover Price: Free
Circulation: 11,795 (ABC 01/07/2008 to 30/09/2008)
Usual Pagination: 40
Editor: Jon Guy; **Advertising Manager:** John Walsh
Summary of Content: Magazine covering insurance news from around the world, risk management, legal issues, technology, comment, features, profiles, analysis and a forum for discussion.
Readership/Target Audience: Aimed at high-end international brokers and underwriters working in the international insurance and reinsurance markets.
ADVERTISING RATES:
Full Page Colour £4995.00
Agency Commission: 10%
Copy instructions: Copy Date: 7 days prior to publication date

Average advertising content per issue: 30%
BUSINESS: FINANCE & ECONOMICS: Insurance

GLOBAL CEMENT MAGAZINE
38960U42A-103

Formerly: Global Cement and Lime Magazine
Editorial Address: 1st Floor, Adelphi Court, 1 East Street, EPSOM, KT17 1BB **Tel:** 01372 743837 **Fax:** 01372 743838
Email: joe.kellam@propubs.com
Advertising Address: As above.
Email: pgbrown@propubs.com
Web site: http://www.propubs.com
ISSN: 1473-1940
Publisher: PRo Publications International Ltd
Date Established: 1997
Frequency: 11 issues yearly - Published at the end of the cover month, double issue at end of 1st cover month
Annual Sub.: £100.00
Circulation: 2,567 (ABC 01/07/2007 to 30/06/2008)
Usual Pagination: 68
Editor: Robert McCaffrey
Summary of Content: Journal containing research and comment on trade and production issues within the global cement industry, as well as news and details of the latest technical advances in the field.
Readership/Target Audience: Read mainly by cement producers.
ADVERTISING RATES:
Full Page Mono EUR2280.00
Full Page Colour EUR3360.00
Agency Commission: 10%
Mechanical Data: Type Area: 274 x 184mm, Bleed Size: 303 x 216mm, Trim Size: 297 x 210mm, Col Length: 274mm, Page Width: 184mm, Film: Digital
Average advertising content per issue: 30%
BUSINESS: CONSTRUCTION

GLOBAL COMPETITION REVIEW
634888U44-723

Editorial Address: 87 Lancaster Road, LONDON, W11 1QQ
Tel: 020 7908 1184 **Fax:** 020 7229 6910
Email: editorial@lbresearch.com
Advertising Address: As above.
Email: subscriptions@globalcompetitionreview.com
Web site: http://www.globalcompetitionreview.com
ISSN: 1369-4561
Publisher: Law Business Research Ltd
Frequency: 10 issues yearly
Annual Sub.: £595.00
Circulation: 2,000 (Publisher's Statement)
Usual Pagination: 48
Editor: David Samuels; **Advertising Manager:** Helen Mitchell; **Managing Editor:** David Samuels
Summary of Content: Magazine covering competition (antitrust) policy and regulation, including news stories, feature articles, high-profile interviews and special reports.
Readership/Target Audience: Aimed at competition or antitrust lawyers, academics and enforcers worldwide.
ADVERTISING RATES:
Full Page Mono £1650.00
Full Page Colour £3000.00
Mechanical Data: Bleed Size: +3mm, Film: Digital
Copy instructions: Copy Date: 1 week prior to publication date
Average advertising content per issue: 10%
BUSINESS: LEGAL

GLOBAL CUSTODIAN
20295U1F-214

Editorial Address: 150 Borough High Street, LONDON, SE1 1LB **Tel:** 020 7148 4290 **Fax:** 020 7148 4292
Email: news@globalcustodian.com
Advertising Address: As above. **Tel:** 020 7939 9934
Email: gtsimitakopoulos@globalcustodian.com
Web site: http://www.globalcustodian.com
Publisher: Asset International
Date Established: 1989
Frequency: Quarterly - Published in the middle of the cover month
Annual Sub.: £275.00
Circulation: 20,000 (Publisher's Statement)
Usual Pagination: 140
Editor: Dominic Hobson; **News Editor:** Giles Turner; **Executive Editor:** Dominic Hobson; **Advertising Manager:** Gregory Tsimitakopoulos; **Publisher:** Gregory Tsimitakopoulos
Summary of Content: Magazine covering payment systems, fund management, CSDs, CCPs, ICSDs, securities lending, repo, collateral management, custody, off shore administration, mutual fund administration, prime brokerage/hedge funds, private equity and derivatives.
Readership/Target Audience: Aimed at people working on the operational side in custodian banks, CSDs, prime brokers, securities lending and financing, fund administrators, pension funds, insurance companies fund managers and exchangers.
ADVERTISING RATES:
Full Page Colour $12350.00

Agency Commission: 15%
Mechanical Data: Trim Size: 276 x 210mm, Bleed Size: 289 x 223mm, Film: Digital, Print Process: Web-fed offset litho, Type Area: 251 x 184mm, Col Length: 251mm, Page Width: 184mm
Copy instructions: Copy Date: 6 weeks prior to publication date
Average advertising content per issue: 40%
BUSINESS: FINANCE & ECONOMICS: Investment

GLOBAL DEFENCE REVIEW
1616145U40-432

Editorial Address: Global House, 47A Tottenham Lane, LONDON, N8 9BD **Tel:** 020 8347 6406 **Fax:** 020 8347 6427
Email: info@global-defence.com
Advertising Address: As above.
Email: geoff.farmer@global-defence.co.uk
Web site: http://www.global-defence.com
Publisher: GDR Publications Ltd
Frequency: Half-yearly - Published in January and June
Free to qualifying individuals
Annual Sub.: £30.00
Circulation: 10,000 (Publisher's Statement)
Editor: David Oliver; **Advertising Manager:** Geoff Farmer
Summary of Content: Magazine focusing on all aspects of the global defence industry including, air, land, sea, missiles, weapons, training and surveillance.
Readership/Target Audience: Aimed at those working in all sectors of the defence industry.
ADVERTISING RATES:
Full Page Colour £3500.00
Agency Commission: 10%
Mechanical Data: Type Area: 278 x 176mm, Bleed Size: +4mm, Trim Size: 297 x 210mm, Col Length: 278mm, Page Width: 176mm, Film: Digital
Copy instructions: Copy Date: 2 weeks prior to publication date
Average advertising content per issue: 40%
BUSINESS: DEFENCE

GLOBAL FINANCE
34941U1A-307

Editorial Address: 123-127 Cannon Street, LONDON, EC4N 5AX **Tel:** 020 7929 0777
Email: anita@gfinance.co.uk
Advertising Address: St. Mary Abchurch House, 123 Cannon Street, LONDON, EC4N 5AX **Tel:** 020 7929 0777 **Fax:** 020 7929 0757
Email: richard@gfinance.co.uk
Web site: http://www.gfmag.com
ISSN: 0896-4181
Publisher: Global Finance
Date Established: 1987
Frequency: 11 issues yearly
Circulation: 50,000 (Publisher's Statement)
Usual Pagination: 80
Editor: Anita Howser; **Advertising Manager:** Richard Scholtz
Summary of Content: Magazine covering global financial services. Contains analysis of e-business trends, news and features covering a wide range of subjects from around the world.
Readership/Target Audience: Aimed at senior managers, bankers, CFOs, treasurers, fund managers and finance executives.
ADVERTISING RATES:
Full Page Mono $26900.00
Full Page Colour $32000.00
Agency Commission: 15%
Mechanical Data: Page Width: 178mm, Col Widths (Display): 55mm, Film: Digital, Type Area: 254 x 178mm, Bleed Size: 279 x 206mm, Trim Size: 273 x 200mm, Col Length: 254mm
Copy instructions: Copy Date: 15th of the month prior to publication date
Average advertising content per issue: 20%
BUSINESS: FINANCE & ECONOMICS

GLOBAL GYPSUM MAGAZINE
38998U42A-104

Editorial Address: 1st Floor, Adelphi Court, 1 East Street, EPSOM, KT17 1BB **Tel:** 01372 743837 **Fax:** 01372 743838
Email: system@propubs.com
Advertising Address: As above.
Email: pgbrown@propubs.com
Web site: http://www.propubs.com
ISSN: 1463-9661
Publisher: PRo Publications International Ltd
Date Established: 1998
Frequency: 6 issues yearly - Published at the end of the cover month
Free to qualifying individuals
Annual Sub.: £150.00
Circulation: 3,000 (Publisher's Statement)
Usual Pagination: 36
Editor: Robert McCaffrey
Summary of Content: Magazine concentrating on the raw gypsum and plasterboard industry. Contains news, case studies, advances in technology, contract updates and conference and exhibition reports.

Readership/Target Audience: Aimed at gypsum rock extractors, plaster and plasterboard manufacturers, contractors, traders, equipment manufacturers, researchers and academics.
ADVERTISING RATES:
Full Page Mono EUR2280.00
Full Page Colour EUR3360.00
Agency Commission: 10%
Mechanical Data: Type Area: 274 x 184mm, Bleed Size: 303 x 216mm, Trim Size: 297 x 210mm, Col Length: 274mm, Film: Digital, Page Width: 184mm
Average advertising content per issue: 30%
BUSINESS: CONSTRUCTION

GLOBAL INVESTOR
35243U1F-221
Editorial Address: Nestor House, Playhouse Yard, LONDON, EC4V 5EX **Tel:** 020 7779 8888
Email: callen@euromoneyplc.com
Advertising Address: As above. **Tel:** 020 7779 8309
Fax: 020 7779 8792
Email: wbrowne@euromoneyplc.com
Web site: http://www.globalinvestormagazine.com
ISSN: 0951-3604
Publisher: Euromoney Institutional Investor plc
Frequency: 10 issues yearly - Published on the 1st of the cover month
Annual Sub.: £360.00
Circulation: 9,345 (Publisher's Statement)
Usual Pagination: 56
Editor: Caroline Allen
Summary of Content: Magazine covering the business of asset management, including strategies for success in the international investment management industry.
Readership/Target Audience: Read by institutional investors, intermediaries and fund managers worldwide.
ADVERTISING RATES:
Full Page Colour £8250.00
Agency Commission: 10%
Mechanical Data: Bleed Size: 276 x 211mm, Trim Size: 270 x 205mm, Type Area: 236 x 175mm, Page Width: 175mm, Col Length: 236mm, Film: Digital, Print Process: Litho
Copy instructions: Copy Date: 20th of the month prior to publication date
Average advertising content per issue: 20%
BUSINESS: FINANCE & ECONOMICS: Investment

GLOBAL MONEY MANAGEMENT
35244U1F-222
Editorial Address: Nestor House, Playhouse Yard, LONDON, EC4V 5EX **Tel:** 020 7303 1718
Fax: 020 7303 1707
Email: vbatistaamorim@euromoneyplc.com
Advertising Address: 7th Floor, 225 Park Avenue South, New York, 10003 NY **Tel:** 212 22 43 267 **Fax:** 212 22 43 142
Email: mjodice@iinews.com
Web site: http://www.globalmoneymanagement.com
Publisher: Euromoney Institutional Investor plc
Date Established: 1990
Frequency: Monthly
Annual Sub.: $2330.00
Circulation: 300 (Publisher's Statement)
Usual Pagination: 24
Editor: Venilia Batista Amorim; **Advertising Manager:** Maria Jodice; **Managing Editor:** Venilia Batista Amorim
Summary of Content: Newsletter covering the global institutional fund management industry.
Readership/Target Audience: Read by international money managers, consultants, pension fund administrators and insurance fund executives.
ADVERTISING RATES:
Full Page Mono $3300.00
Full Page Colour $4500.00
Agency Commission: 15%
Mechanical Data: Film: Digital
Copy instructions: Copy Date: 12 days prior to publication date
BUSINESS: FINANCE & ECONOMICS: Investment

GLOBAL PENSIONS
35245U1F-224
Editorial Address: Haymarket House, 28-29 Haymarket, LONDON, SW1Y 4RX **Tel:** 020 7484 9700
Email: alex.beveridge@incisivemedia.com
Advertising Address: As above. **Fax:** 020 7484 9886
Email: haydon.bambury@incisivemedia.com
Web site: http://www.globalpensions.com
Publisher: Incisive Media Investments
Date Established: 1999
Frequency: Monthly - Published on the 1st Monday of the cover month
Annual Sub.: $510.00
Circulation: 8,115 (ABC 01/07/2007 to 30/06/2008)
Usual Pagination: 56
Editor: Alex Beveridge; **News Editor:** Jonathan Stapleton; **Advertising Manager:** Haydon Bambury
Summary of Content: Magazine focusing on developments in the pension industry and international pension issues.

Readership/Target Audience: Aimed at professionals responsible for large retirement plans and service providers to the pensions industry.
ADVERTISING RATES:
Full Page Colour £8750.00
Agency Commission: 10%
Mechanical Data: Page Width: 226mm, Type Area: 332 x 226mm, Bleed Size: 356 x 256mm, Trim Size: 350 x 250mm, Col Length: 332mm, Film: Digital
Copy instructions: Copy Date: 18th of the month prior to publication date
Average advertising content per issue: 35%
BUSINESS: FINANCE & ECONOMICS: Investment

GLOBAL REINSURANCE
35122U1D-110
Editorial Address: 30 Cannon Street, LONDON, EC4M 6YJ **Tel:** 020 7618 3454 **Fax:** 020 7618 3457
Email: david.banks@globalreinsurance.com
Advertising Address: As above. **Tel:** 020 7618 3456
Fax: 020 7618 3420
Email: rajesh@globalreinsurance.com
Web site: http://www.globalreinsurance.com
ISSN: 1358-7420
Publisher: Newsquest Specialist Media Ltd
Date Established: 1990
Frequency: 10 issues yearly - Published in the 1st week of the cover month
Free to qualifying individuals
Annual Sub.: £236.00
Circulation: 9,278 (Publisher's Statement)
Usual Pagination: 56
Editor: David Sandham; **Advertising Manager:** Rajesh Sidhu; **Publisher:** Will Sanders
Summary of Content: Publication containing analysis of the international risk business, reinsurance sector, physical risk management and primary insurance topics from around the world.
Readership/Target Audience: Aimed at risk professionals.
ADVERTISING RATES:
Full Page Colour £5299.00
Agency Commission: 10%
Mechanical Data: Page Width: 180mm, Type Area: 267 x 180mm, Bleed Size: 303 x 216mm, Trim Size: 297 x 210mm, Col Length: 267mm, Film: Digital
Copy instructions: Copy Date: 4 weeks prior to publication date
Average advertising content per issue: 30%
Supplement(s): ERM - 1xY, European Run-Off - 1xY, Solvency 2 - 1xY
BUSINESS: FINANCE & ECONOMICS: Insurance

GLOBAL SMT AND PACKAGING
765854U18A-9045
Editorial Address: 8 Talbot Hill Road, BOURNEMOUTH, BH9 2JT **Tel:** 01202 388997
Email: news@globalsmt.net
Advertising Address: As above.
Email: akellard@globalsmt.net
Web site: http://www.globalsmt.net
ISSN: 1474-0893
Publisher: Trafalgar Publications Ltd
Date Established: 2001
Frequency: Monthly
Free to qualifying individuals
Annual Sub.: £185.00
Circulation: 13,000 (Publisher's Statement)
Usual Pagination: 60
Editor: Heather Lackey; **News Editor:** Jade Jo Kellard; **Editor-in-Chief:** Trevor Galbraith; **Advertising Manager:** Andy Kellard; **Managing Editor:** Heather Lackey
Summary of Content: Magazine covering in-depth technical articles and information on surface mount technology and advanced packaging from around the world.
Readership/Target Audience: Aimed at leading production engineers and technologists, OEMs, CEMs and assemblers within the electronics manufacturing industry.
ADVERTISING RATES:
Full Page Colour £2750.00
Agency Commission: 10%
Mechanical Data: Film: Digital, Type Area: 254 x 178mm, Bleed Size: 303 x 216mm, Trim Size: 275 x 203mm, Col Length: 254mm, Page Width: 178mm
BUSINESS: ELECTRONICS

GLOBAL SOLAR TECHNOLOGY
1923837U58-205
Editorial Address: 7 Castle Street, BRIDGWATER, TA6 3DT **Tel:** 07765 277677
Email: news@globalsolartechnology.com
Web site: http://globalsolartechnology.com
Publisher: Trafalgar Publications Ltd
Frequency: 6 issues yearly
Free to qualifying individuals
Editor: Trevor Galbraith

Summary of Content: Magazine featuring solution lead technical articles to enhance your manufacturing process, market news, previews and reports on the trade shows.
Readership/Target Audience: Aimed at manufacturers of solar panels and suppliers and distributors of equipment.
BUSINESS: ENERGY, FUEL & NUCLEAR

GLOBAL TELECOMS BUSINESS
37457U18B-820
Editorial Address: Nestor House, Playhouse Yard, LONDON, EC4V 5EX **Tel:** 020 7779 8518
Fax: 020 7779 8960
Email: gtb@euromoneyplc.com
Advertising Address: As above. **Tel:** 020 7779 8888
Email: gtb@euromoneyplc.com
Web site: http://www.globaltelecomsbusiness.com
ISSN: 0969-7500
Publisher: Euromoney Institutional Investor plc
Date Established: 1993
Frequency: 6 issues yearly - Published on the 30th of the cover month
Annual Sub.: £300.00
Circulation: 4,500 (Publisher's Statement)
Usual Pagination: 92
Editor: Alan Burkitt-Gray; **Advertising Manager:** Laurence Mackintosh; **Publisher:** Laurence Mackintosh
Summary of Content: Magazine covering funding and investment, business strategy and regulation of the telecommunications industry.
Readership/Target Audience: Read by CEOs of telecommunications, investment banks, analysts, regulators and leading manufacturers.
ADVERTISING RATES:
Full Page Colour £4500.00
Agency Commission: 15%
Mechanical Data: Type Area: 267 x 185mm, Col Length: 267mm, Page Width: 185mm, Bleed Size: 303 x 216mm, Trim Size: 297 x 210mm, Film: Digital
Copy instructions: Copy Date: 2 weeks prior to publication date
Average advertising content per issue: 35%
Supplement(s): Global Telecoms Business Guide to Satellite and Telecommunications Lawyers - 1xY, Global Telecoms Business Yearbook - 1xY
BUSINESS: ELECTRONICS: Telecommunications

GLOBAL TRADE REVIEW
1836471U14C-375
Editorial Address: 3C Hillgate Place, LONDON, SW12 9ER **Tel:** 020 8673 9666 **Fax:** 020 8673 8662
Email: rsayer@exportagroup.com
Web site: http://www.gtreview.com
ISSN: 1478-5269
Publisher: Exporta Publishing & Events Ltd
Date Established: 2002
Frequency: 6 issues yearly
Annual Sub.: £375.00
Circulation: 5,000 (Publisher's Statement)
Usual Pagination: 96
Editor: Rebecca Spong
Summary of Content: Magazine featuring the market's key banks, credit and political risk insurers, corporates, traders, law firms, brokers and consultants with news, leads and analysis on global emerging markets trade, commodity and export finance and risk.
Readership/Target Audience: Aimed at bankers, trade financiers, credit and political risk insurers, corporates, traders, law firms, brokers and consultants.
BUSINESS: COMMERCE, INDUSTRY & MANAGEMENT: International Commerce

GLOBAL WATER INTELLIGENCE
1666335U42C-756
Editorial Address: The Jam Factory, 27 Park End Street, OXFORD, OX1 1HU **Tel:** 01865 204208 **Fax:** 01865 204209
Email: ie@globalwaterintel.com
Advertising Address: As above.
Email: dw@globalwaterintel.com
Web site: http://www.globalwaterintel.com
ISSN: 1471-3322
Publisher: Media Analytics Ltd
Date Established: 2000
Frequency: Monthly
Annual Sub.: £795.00
Usual Pagination: 60
Editor: Ian Elkins; **Publisher:** Christopher Gasson
Summary of Content: Newsletter providing analysis and strategic data on the international water market.
Language(s): Chinese; English; French; German; Italian; Russian; Spanish
Readership/Target Audience: Aimed at water companies, investment banks, law firms, contractors, consultants and equipment suppliers.
ADVERTISING RATES:
Full Page Colour £3000.00

Business Magazines

Mechanical Data: Type Area: 277 x 190mm, Bleed Size: 303 x 213mm, Col Length: 277mm, Page Width: 190mm, Film: Digital, Trim Size: 297 x 210mm
BUSINESS: CONSTRUCTION: Water Engineering

GO PUBLIC
1800680U4A-319

Editorial Address: 16 Parker Court, Dyson Way, Staffordshire Business Park, STAFFORD, ST18 0WP **Tel:** 01785 330635 **Fax:** 0845 862 8639
Email: info@link2media.co.uk
Advertising Address: As above. **Tel:** 01785 711591
Fax: 01785 711592
Email: david@link2media.co.uk
Web site: http://www.link2media.co.uk
Publisher: Link2.Media Business Publishing Ltd
Date Established: 2006
Frequency: Quarterly
Cover Price: Free
Circulation: 7,000 (Publisher's Statement)
Editor: David Broadfield; **Advertising Manager:** David Broadfield
Summary of Content: Magazine covering building product and project news.
Readership/Target Audience: Aimed at architects working in the public sector and private practices.
ADVERTISING: Rates on application
BUSINESS: ARCHITECTURE & BUILDING: Architecture

GOLF CLUB MANAGEMENT
41477U64C-30

Editorial Address: Unit 222-223, 30 Great Guildford Street, LONDON, SE1 0HS **Tel:** 020 7803 2420 **Fax:** 020 7803 2421
Email: golf@unionpress.co.uk
Advertising Address: As above.
Email: shane.mortimer@unionpress.co.uk
Web site: http://www.agcs.org.uk
Publisher: Union Press Ltd
Frequency: Monthly - Published on the 15th of the cover month
Cover Price: £5.00
Annual Sub.: £45.00
Circulation: 5,500 (Publisher's Statement)
Usual Pagination: 72
Editor: Alistair Dunsmuir; **Managing Director:** Alan Chalmers; **Advertising Manager:** Shane Mortimer; **Publisher:** Anthony Hawser
Summary of Content: Official Journal of the Association of Golf Club Secretaries.
Readership/Target Audience: Aimed at decision makers in golf clubs.
ADVERTISING RATES:
Full Page Colour £2995.00
Agency Commission: 10%
Mechanical Data: Type Area: 247 x 180mm, Bleed Size: 286 x 226mm, Trim Size: 280 x 220mm, Col Length: 247mm, Page Width: 180mm, Print Process: Offset litho, Film: Digital
Copy instructions: Copy Date: 1st of the month prior to publication date
Average advertising content per issue: 35%
BUSINESS: OTHER CLASSIFICATIONS: Clubs

GOLF COURSE ARCHITECTURE
1833925U64D-95

Editorial Address: Tudor House, 6 Friar Lane, LEICESTER, LE1 5RA **Tel:** 0116 222 9900 **Fax:** 0116 222 9901
Email: news@golfcoursearchitecture.net
Advertising Address: As above.
Email: jemma.farley@golfcoursearchitecture.net
Web site: http://www.golfcoursearchitecture.net
Publisher: Tudor Rose Holdings Ltd
Date Established: 2005
Frequency: Quarterly
Cover Price: £4.95
Annual Sub.: £19.80
Circulation: 10,000 (Publisher's Statement)
Usual Pagination: 80
Editor: Adam Lawrence; **News Editor:** James Dodd;
Publisher: Toby Ingleton
Summary of Content: Magazine dedicated to golf course design and renovation.
Readership/Target Audience: Circulated to all European golf facilities, architects, developers and interested individuals, as well as leading clubs in the US and a range of golf industry influencers.
ADVERTISING RATES:
Full Page Colour £2250.00
Mechanical Data: Trim Size: 297 x 210mm, Film: Digital
Copy instructions: Copy Date: 3 weeks prior to publication date
BUSINESS: OTHER CLASSIFICATIONS: Course Maintenance

GOLF MANAGEMENT EUROPE
41479U64C-140

Editorial Address: Deben House, Main Road, Martlesham, WOODBRIDGE, IP12 4SE **Tel:** 01394 380800
Fax: 01394 380594
Email: editorial@portman.uk.com
Advertising Address: As above. **Tel:** 0870 241 4678
Email: sales@portman.uk.com
Web site: http://www.portman.uk.com
ISSN: 1368-7727
Publisher: Portman Publishing & Communications Ltd
Date Established: 1997
Frequency: 6 issues yearly
Cover Price: £5.00
Annual Sub.: £30.00
Circulation: 5,500 (Publisher's Statement)
Usual Pagination: 36
Editor: John Vinicombe; **News Editor:** David Bowers;
Managing Director: Michael Lenihan; **Advertising Manager:** Michael Lenihan; **Publisher:** Michael Lenihan
Summary of Content: Business magazine for the European golf industry.
Readership/Target Audience: Aimed at owners, groundstaff, directors and officials throughout Europe, Ireland and the UK.
ADVERTISING RATES:
Full Page Colour £1475.00
Agency Commission: 10%
Mechanical Data: No. of Columns (Display): 2, Trim Size: 297 x 210mm, Bleed Size: 303 x 216mm, Film: Digital
Copy instructions: Copy Date: Last Friday of month prior to publication date
Average advertising content per issue: 40%
BUSINESS: OTHER CLASSIFICATIONS: Clubs

GOLF RANGE NEWS
1665555U64D-91

Editorial Address: Polmood, Sissinghurst, CRANBROOK, TN17 2AJ **Tel:** 01580 715248 **Fax:** 01580 714516
Email: colin@golfrangenews.org
Advertising Address: As above.
Email: colin@golfrangenews.org
Web site: http://www.golfrangenews.org
Publisher: Golf Range News Ltd
Date Established: 2002
Frequency: Monthly
Cover Price: £50.00
Free to qualifying individuals
Circulation: 4,100 (Publisher's Statement)
Editor: Colin Jenkins; **Advertising Manager:** Colin Jenkins
Summary of Content: Magazine focusing on the golf range industry including golf development, golf based leisure and business tips.
Readership/Target Audience: Aimed at owners and operators of golf ranges.
ADVERTISING RATES:
Full Page Colour £900.00
Mechanical Data: Film: Digital, Type Area: 210 x 145mm, Col Length: 210mm, Page Width: 145mm
BUSINESS: OTHER CLASSIFICATIONS: Course Maintenance

THE GOOD BOOK GUIDE
40844U60A-43_50

Editorial Address: 29-30 Monument Business Park, CHALGROVE, OX44 7RW **Tel:** 01865 893434
Email: hfoakes@gbgdirect.com
Advertising Address: As above.
Web site: http://www.thegoodbookguide.com
Publisher: The Good Book Guide
Date Established: 1977
Frequency: Monthly
Cover Price: £2.85
Free to qualifying individuals
Annual Sub.: £24.99
Circulation: 15,000 (Publisher's Statement)
Usual Pagination: 40
Editor: Hilary Foakes; **Advertising Manager:** Hilary Foakes
Summary of Content: Magazine featuring book reviews, profiles, book recommendations, competitions and features on videos, DVDs and audiobooks, also contains a mail order book supply service.
Readership/Target Audience: Aimed at people who enjoy reading.
ADVERTISING: Rates on application
BUSINESS: PUBLISHING: Publishing & Book Trade

GOOD CHEESE
1665961U22A-389

Editorial Address: Guild House, Station Road, Wincanton, SOMERSET, BA9 9FE **Tel:** 01963 824464
Fax: 01963 824651
Email: mick.whitworth@finefoodworld.co.uk
Advertising Address: As above.
Email: becky.stacey@finefoodworld.co.uk
Web site: http://www.finefoodworld.co.uk
Publisher: The Guild of Fine Food Ltd
Frequency: Half-yearly - Published after the World Cheese Awards results
Cover Price: £3.50
Free to qualifying individuals
Circulation: 6,000 (Publisher's Statement)
Usual Pagination: 54
Summary of Content: Magazine covering fine cheeses and recipes.
Readership/Target Audience: Aimed at cheese buyers throughout the world and cheese lovers, suppliers and retailers.
ADVERTISING RATES:
Full Page Colour £1485.00
Mechanical Data: Type Area: 287 x 204mm, Bleed Size: 321 x 236mm, Trim Size: 315 x 230mm, Col Length: 287mm, Page Width: 204mm, Film: Digital
Copy instructions: Copy Date: 3 weeks prior to publication date
BUSINESS: FOOD

GOOD CLINICAL PRACTICE JOURNAL
40168U56A-66_15

Editorial Address: Telephone House, 69-77 Paul Street, LONDON, EC2A 4LQ **Tel:** 020 7017 5000
Fax: 020 7017 6968
Email: stefan.fritsch@informa.com
Advertising Address: As above. **Fax:** 020 7017 6787
Email: maryjane.riddell@informa.com
Web site: http://www.gcpj.com
ISSN: 1350-0961
Publisher: Informa Healthcare
Date Established: 1994
Frequency: Monthly - Published at the end of the month prior to cover month
Annual Sub.: £530.00
Circulation: 6,000 (Publisher's Statement)
Usual Pagination: 44
Editor: Stefan Fritsch
Summary of Content: Journal containing peer-reviewed articles that interpret international GCP standards and regulatory requirements and explains practical ways to comply with them in pharmaceutical clinical research.
Readership/Target Audience: Aimed at biopharmaceutical companies, clinical researchers, regulatory affairs and QA personnel.
ADVERTISING RATES:
Full Page Colour £2283.00
Agency Commission: 10%
Mechanical Data: Type Area: 260 x 185mm, Trim Size: 297 x 210mm, Bleed Size: 303 x 216mm, Col Length: 260mm, Page Width: 185mm, Film: Digital
Copy instructions: Copy Date: 5 weeks prior to publication date
Average advertising content per issue: 40%
BUSINESS: HEALTH & MEDICAL

GOVERNANCE
36762U14A-150

Editorial Address: Watchfield House, Watchfield, HIGHBRIDGE, TA9 4RD **Tel:** 01278 793300
Fax: 01278 783750
Email: lstephenson@governance.co.uk
Web site: http://www.governance.co.uk
ISSN: 1358-5142
Publisher: Governance Publishing and Information Services Ltd.
Date Established: 1992
Frequency: Monthly
Annual Sub.: £275.00
Circulation: 250 (Publisher's Statement)
Usual Pagination: 12
Editor: Lesley Stephenson; **Executive Editor:** Michelle Edkins; **Publisher:** Lesley Stephenson
Summary of Content: Publication focusing on corporate governance issues, shareholder activism and boardroom practice.
Readership/Target Audience: Aimed at directors, institutional investors, corporate advisers, regulatory authorities and research organisations.
ADVERTISING: No Advertising taken
BUSINESS: COMMERCE, INDUSTRY & MANAGEMENT

GOVERNANCE
1708612U44-3040

Editorial Address: 34 Whitehall Road, HARROW, HA1 3AJ **Tel:** 020 8426 6686
Email: dorothydalton@charitygovernance.co.uk
Advertising Address: 15 Prescott Place, LONDON, SW4 6BS **Tel:** 020 7819 1200 **Fax:** 020 7819 1219
Email: phil@plazapublishing.co.uk
Web site: http://www.plazapublishing.co.uk
Publisher: Plaza Publishing Ltd
Date Established: 2005
Frequency: 6 issues yearly
Annual Sub.: £145.00
Circulation: 11,000 (Publisher's Statement)
Usual Pagination: 24
Editor: Dorothy Dalton
Summary of Content: Magazine covering all aspects of charity governance including model documents, legal,

financial and charity commission updates, legal and financial matters and practical advice.
Readership/Target Audience: Aimed at trustees, CEs, company secretaries and others interested in charity governance.
ADVERTISING: Rates on application
BUSINESS: LEGAL

GOVERNMENT & PUBLIC SECTOR JOURNAL

1894330U32A-304

Editorial Address: UK Media House, 13 Bankside Avenue, Uppermill, OLDHAM, OL3 6JU **Tel:** 0845 345 5222
Fax: 01457 877244
Email: press@gpsj.co.uk
Web site: http://www.gpsj.co.uk
Frequency: Quarterly
Circulation: 26,000 (Publisher's Statement)
Editor: Stuart Littleford
Summary of Content: Journal covering news, latest developments, legislation, investment, PFI, PPP and building and engineering projects carried out in these sectors.
Readership/Target Audience: Aimed at those in local authorities, councils, NHS health trusts, government offices and agencies, rescue and emergency services, MOD, prison service, universities and colleges.
ADVERTISING RATES:
Full Page Colour £3500.00
BUSINESS: LOCAL GOVERNMENT, LEISURE & RECREATION: Local Government

GOVERNMENT AUCTION NEWS

36449U7-200

Editorial Address: 17 Fleet Street, LONDON, EC4Y 1AA
Tel: 020 7353 7300 **Fax:** 020 7353 6533
Email: info@ganews.co.uk
Web site: http://www.ganews.co.uk
ISSN: 0966-1034
Publisher: Wentworth Publishing Ltd
Date Established: 1992
Frequency: 10 issues yearly - Double issues in December/January and July/ August
Annual Sub.: £59.50
Circulation: 6,000 (Publisher's Statement)
Usual Pagination: 20
Editor: Stuart McLaren; **Publisher:** Justin Power
Summary of Content: Newsletter containing auction news, features, letters and queries and UK listings.
Readership/Target Audience: Aimed at those interested in purchasing or selling goods at auction.
ADVERTISING: No Advertising taken
BUSINESS: ANTIQUES

GOVERNMENT BUSINESS

38412U32C-50

Editorial Address: 226 High Road, LOUGHTON, IG10 1ET
Tel: 020 8532 0055 **Fax:** 020 8532 0066
Email: editor@psp-media.co.uk
Advertising Address: As above.
Email: clive@governmentbusinessuk.com
Web site: http://www.governmentbusinessuk.com
Publisher: Public Sector Publishing Ltd
Frequency: Monthly
Free to qualifying individuals
Annual Sub.: £95.00
Circulation: 12,000 (Publisher's Statement)
Usual Pagination: 76
Editor: Sofie Lidefjard
Summary of Content: Journal covering public sector and privatised utility financial and administrative issues.
Readership/Target Audience: Aimed at chief executives, finance directors, facilities managers and other senior executives within local and central government, health service and other regulated utilities.
ADVERTISING RATES:
Full Page Colour £2495.00
Agency Commission: 10%
Mechanical Data: Bleed Size: 303 x 216mm, Trim Size: 297 x 210mm, Film: Digital
Copy instructions: Copy Date: 3 weeks prior to publication date
Average advertising content per issue: 50%
BUSINESS: LOCAL GOVERNMENT, LEISURE & RECREATION: Local Government Finance

GOVERNMENT IT

36083U5B-85_40

Editorial Address: 9th Floor, St. James's Buildings, Oxford Street, MANCHESTER, M1 6PP **Tel:** 0161 211 3000
Fax: 0161 211 3025
Email: editorial@govnet.co.uk
Advertising Address: As above. **Fax:** 0161 211 3008
Email: sharon.randhawa@govnet.co.uk
Web site: http://www.govnet.co.uk
ISSN: 1464-3235
Publisher: GovNet Communications
Date Established: 1997
Frequency: 6 issues yearly

Free to qualifying individuals
Annual Sub.: £125.00
Circulation: 8,570 (ABC 01/07/2007 to 30/06/2008)
Usual Pagination: 64
Editor: Felicity King-Evans; **Managing Director:** Joanne Walsh
Summary of Content: Journal providing a critical analysis of both government policy, strategy and implementation of IT solutions across the entire UK public sector.
Readership/Target Audience: Aimed at information communication technology decision-makers in central government, local government, health, education, police, emergency services and executive agencies.
ADVERTISING RATES:
Full Page Colour £3595.00
Agency Commission: 10%
Mechanical Data: Trim Size: 297 x 210mm, Film: Digital
Average advertising content per issue: 35%
BUSINESS: COMPUTERS & AUTOMATION: Data Processing

GOVERNMENT OPPORTUNITIES

36847U32A-254

Editorial Address: 300 Glasgow Road, Rutherglen, GLASGOW, G73 1SQ **Tel:** 0141 332 8247
Fax: 0141 353 2151
Email: media@bipsolutions.com
Advertising Address: As above. **Fax:** 0141 331 2652
Email: advertising@bipsolutions.com
Web site: http://www.govopps.co.uk
ISSN: 1357-1001
Publisher: BIP Solutions Ltd
Frequency: 10 issues yearly - Published in the 1st week of the cover month
Free to qualifying individuals
Annual Sub.: £50.40
Circulation: 8,276 (ABC 01/07/2007 to 30/06/2008)
Usual Pagination: 80
Editor: Morven MacNeil; **Features Editor:** Morven MacNeil; **Advertising Manager:** Jenny Coombes; **Managing Editor:** Grahame Steed
Summary of Content: Publication advising how to improve communication between the public and private sectors particularly in relation to purchasing and supply. Contains news and features on public sector procurements, strategy, directives and developments, as well as articles by and interviews with government ministers, MPs and procurement officers.
Readership/Target Audience: Aimed at buyers within the public sector and suppliers to the public sector.
ADVERTISING RATES:
Full Page Colour £1500.00
Agency Commission: 10%
Mechanical Data: Trim Size: 297 x 210mm, Film: Digital, Bleed Size: +3mm
Copy instructions: Copy Date: 2 weeks prior to publication date
Average advertising content per issue: 25%
BUSINESS: LOCAL GOVERNMENT, LEISURE & RECREATION: Local Government

GOVERNMENT TECHNOLOGY

1659837U32R-490

Formerly: GT Government Technology
Editorial Address: 226 High Road, LOUGHTON, IG10 1ET
Tel: 020 8532 0055 **Fax:** 020 8532 0066
Email: editor@psp-media.co.uk
Advertising Address: As above.
Email: jesse@governmenttechnologyuk.com
Web site: http://www.governmenttechnologyuk.com
Publisher: Public Sector Publishing Ltd
Date Established: 1999
Frequency: Monthly
Free to qualifying individuals
Annual Sub.: £95.00
Circulation: 10,000 (Publisher's Statement)
Usual Pagination: 64
Editor: Sofie Lidefjard; **Advertising Manager:** Jesse Sand
Summary of Content: Magazine covering news and case studies that explain the administrative and commercial issues affecting IT and computing in central and local government.
Readership/Target Audience: Aimed at IT departments in local authorities.
ADVERTISING RATES:
Full Page Colour £2495.00
Agency Commission: 10%
Mechanical Data: Type Area: 255 x 178mm, Bleed Size: 303 x 216mm, Trim Size: 297 x 210mm, Col Length: 255mm, Page Width: 178mm, Film: Digital
Copy instructions: Copy Date: 4 weeks prior to publication date
BUSINESS: LOCAL GOVERNMENT, LEISURE & RECREATION: Local Government Related

GP INCORPORATING MEDECONOMICS

40165U56A-66_20

Formerly: GP General Practitioner
Editorial Address: 174 Hammersmith Road, LONDON, W6 7JP **Tel:** 020 8267 4850 **Fax:** 020 8267 4866
Email: gpnewspaper@haymarket.com
Advertising Address: As above. **Tel:** 020 8267 5000
Email: gemma.higgins@haymarket.com
Web site: http://www.healthcarerepublic.com
Publisher: Haymarket Medical Publications Ltd
Frequency: Weekly
Free to qualifying individuals
Annual Sub.: £150.00
Circulation: 39,018 (ABC 01/07/2006 to 30/06/2007)
Usual Pagination: 100
Editor: Neil Durham; **News Editor:** Nick Bostock; **Managing Director:** Peter Welland
Summary of Content: Newspaper containing medical news and matters of interest to the family doctor.
Readership/Target Audience: Aimed at general practitioners.
ADVERTISING RATES:
Full Page Colour £4410.00
Agency Commission: 10%
Mechanical Data: Type Area: 325 x 230mm, Bleed Size: 355 x 257mm, Trim Size: 345 x 247mm, Col Length: 325mm, Page Width: 230mm, Film: Digital, Print Process: Offset litho
Copy instructions: Copy Date: 9 days prior to publication date
BUSINESS: HEALTH & MEDICAL

GRAFIK

35501U2A-75_85

Formerly: Graphics International
Editorial Address: Third Floor, 104 Great Portland Street, LONDON, W1W 6PE **Tel:** 020 7637 5900
Email: hello@grafikmagazine.co.uk
Advertising Address: As above. **Fax:** 020 7839 6993
Email: stefan@grafikmagazine.co.uk
Web site: http://www.grafikmagazine.co.uk
ISSN: 1479-7534
Publisher: Grafik Ltd
Frequency: 11 issues yearly
Cover Price: £8.00
Circulation: 14,500 (Publisher's Statement)
Usual Pagination: 100
Editor: Caroline Roberts; **Advertising Manager:** Stefan Ketelsen
Summary of Content: Graphic design magazine featuring typography, packaging, multimedia, corporate identity, illustration work, exhibitions and books.
Readership/Target Audience: Read by design groups, illustrators, typographers, design students and advertising agency executives.
ADVERTISING RATES:
Full Page Colour £1875.00
Agency Commission: 10%
Mechanical Data: Col Length: 295mm, Page Width: 209mm, Type Area: 295 x 209mm, Bleed Size: 317 x 231mm, Trim Size: 311 x 225mm, Film: Digital
Average advertising content per issue: 10%
BUSINESS: COMMUNICATIONS, ADVERTISING & MARKETING

GRAIN & FEED MILLING TECHNOLOGY

37807U21B-300

Editorial Address: 7 St. Georges Terrace, St. James Square, CHELTENHAM, GL50 3PT **Tel:** 01242 267707
Fax: 01242 267701
Email: nickyb@gfmt.co.uk
Advertising Address: As above.
Email: carolinew@gfmt.co.uk
Web site: http://www.gfmt.co.uk
ISSN: 1466-3872
Publisher: Perendale
Date Established: 1891
Frequency: 6 issues yearly - Published on the 15th of the 2nd cover month
Annual Sub.: £70.00
Circulation: 5,500 (Publisher's Statement)
Usual Pagination: 48
Editor: Nicky Barnes; **Advertising Manager:** Caroline Wearn
Summary of Content: Magazine covering flour milling, animal feed compounding, grain processing and the storage handling industries. Covers news, product updates, diary dates, show guides and features.
Readership/Target Audience: Read by mill managers, port operators, production and technical staff. Also commodity buyers and QC managers.
ADVERTISING RATES:
Full Page Mono £1530.00
Full Page Colour £1530.00
Agency Commission: 7%
Mechanical Data: Trim Size: 298 x 210mm, Bleed Size: 304 x 216mm, Film: Digital
BUSINESS: AGRICULTURE & FARMING: Agriculture - Supplies & Services

Section 4 (b) Business Magazines

Business Magazines

THE GRAPEVINE
37045U14F-23_95

Formerly: The Executive Grapevine
Editorial Address: New Barnes Mill, Cottonmill Lane, ST. ALBANS, AL1 2HA **Tel:** 01727 844335 **Fax:** 01727 844779
Email: editorial@executive-grapevine.co.uk
Advertising Address: As above.
Email: d.bateman@executive-grapevine.co.uk
Web site: http://www.thegrapevinemagazine.com
Publisher: Executive Grapevine International Ltd
Date Established: 1999
Frequency: Monthly - Published on the 1st Wednesday of the cover month
Free to qualifying individuals
Annual Sub.: £99.00
Circulation: 7,000 (Publisher's Statement)
Usual Pagination: 54
Editor: Douglas Peck
Summary of Content: Magazine covering the relationship between corporate and professional recruiters.
Readership/Target Audience: Aimed at HR directors and recruitment consultants.
ADVERTISING RATES:
Full Page Colour £1800.00
Agency Commission: 10%
Mechanical Data: Type Area: 257 x 180mm, Bleed Size: 307 x 220mm, Trim Size: 297 x 210mm, Col Length: 257mm, Page Width: 180mm, Film: Digital
Copy instructions: Copy Date: 2 weeks prior to publication date
Average advertising content per issue: 40%
BUSINESS: COMMERCE, INDUSTRY & MANAGEMENT: Training & Recruitment

GRASS & FORAGE SCIENCE
40698U57-30_34

Editorial Address: 9600 Garsington Road, Cowley, OXFORD, OX4 2DQ **Tel:** 0131 226 7232 **Fax:** 01865 714591
Email: gfs@oxon.blackwellpublishing.com
Web site: http://www.blackwellpublishing.com
ISSN: 0142-5242
Publisher: Wiley-Blackwell Publishing
Frequency: Annual
Free to qualifying individuals
Annual Sub.: £247.50
Circulation: 1,490 (Publisher's Statement)
Usual Pagination: 96
Editor: John Milne
Summary of Content: Official journal of the British Grassland Society. Covers research on cultivated temperate grasslands including advances in all aspects of the production, management and utilisation of grass and forage crops.
Readership/Target Audience: Aimed at research workers, extension workers and teachers in the fields of agronomy and animal production.
ADVERTISING: No Advertising taken
BUSINESS: ENVIRONMENT & POLLUTION

GRASSLANDS & FORAGE ABSTRACTS
37785U21A-500

Editorial Address: Nosworthy Way, WALLINGFORD, OX10 8DE **Tel:** 01491 832111 **Fax:** 01491 829198
Email: cabi@cabi.org
Web site: http://www.cabi.org/
ISSN: 1350-9837
Publisher: CABI
Frequency: Monthly
Annual Sub.: £630.00
Circulation: 150 (Publisher's Statement)
Editor: David Simpson
Summary of Content: Abstract journal covering management, productivity, ecology and economics of grasslands.
Readership/Target Audience: Aimed at academic and government research institutes involved in grassland, rangeland, natural resources and animal nutrition research.
ADVERTISING: No Advertising taken
BUSINESS: AGRICULTURE & FARMING

GREECE & ROME
41116U62F-250

Editorial Address: St. Hilda's College, OXFORD, OX4 1DY **Tel:** 01223 326070 **Fax:** 01223 325150
Email: katherine.clarke@st-hildas.ox.ac.uk
Advertising Address: The Edinburgh Building, Shaftesbury Road, CAMBRIDGE, CB2 8RU **Tel:** 01223 326070
Email: ad_sales@cambridge.org
Web site: http://www.journals.cambridge.org/gar
ISSN: 0017-3835
Publisher: Cambridge University Press
Date Established: 1931
Frequency: Half-yearly - Published in April and October
Cover Price: £37.00
Annual Sub.: £60.00
Circulation: 1,300 (Publisher's Statement)
Usual Pagination: 140
Editor: Katherine Clarke

Summary of Content: Journal containing a literary evaluation of the major Greek and Roman authors, articles on ancient history, art, archaeology, the classical tradition and on the teaching of classics at the tertiary level.
Readership/Target Audience: Aimed at students, teachers and academics.
ADVERTISING RATES:
Full Page Mono £385.00
Agency Commission: 10%
Mechanical Data: Film: Digital, Type Area: 190 x 115mm, Col Length: 190mm, Page Width: 115mm
Copy instructions: Copy Date: Beginning of the month prior to publication
BUSINESS: CHURCH & SCHOOL EQUIPMENT & EDUCATION: Adult Education

GREEN BUILDING
623546U4E-74

Formerly: Building for a Future
Editorial Address: PO Box 32, LLANDYSUL, SA44 5ZA
Advertising Address: As above. **Tel:** 01208 895103
Email: jerry@greenbuildingpress.co.uk
Web site: http://www.greenbuildingpress.co.uk
ISSN: 1357-759X
Publisher: Green Building Press
Date Established: 1992
Frequency: Quarterly
Cover Price: £7.00
Annual Sub.: £20.00
Circulation: 4,500 (Publisher's Statement)
Usual Pagination: 76
Editor: Keith Hall; **Advertising Manager:** Jerry Clark
Summary of Content: Magazine covering news, developments, products, projects and reports from within the construction industry.
Readership/Target Audience: Aimed at architects, planners and builders.
ADVERTISING RATES:
Full Page Colour 1146.00
Agency Commission: 10%
Mechanical Data: Type Area: 270 x 208mm, Bleed Size: 302 x 234mm, Trim Size: 297 x 230mm, Col Length: 270mm, Film: Digital, Page Width: 208mm
Copy instructions: Copy Date: 1st of the month prior to publication date
Average advertising content per issue: 20%
Supplement(s): Green Building Bible - 1xY
BUSINESS: ARCHITECTURE & BUILDING: Building

GREEN CHEMISTRY
600999U57-30_35

Editorial Address: Thomas Graham House, Science Park, Milton Road, CAMBRIDGE, CB4 0WF **Tel:** 01223 432293
Fax: 01223 420247
Email: green@rsc.org
Advertising Address: As above. **Tel:** 01223 432246
Fax: 01223 426017
Email: advertising@rsc.org
Web site: http://www.rsc.org/greenchem
ISSN: 1463-9262
Publisher: Royal Society of Chemistry
Date Established: 1999
Frequency: Monthly
Annual Sub.: £525.00
Circulation: 650 (Publisher's Statement)
Usual Pagination: 200
Editor: Sarah Ruthven; **Advertising Manager:** Ian Swain
Summary of Content: Journal assessing the surge in research and development of clean technology systems. Includes items on the design of more eco-friendly chemicals, materials and technologies, measurement analysis systems, waste reduction options and news and legislative matters.
Readership/Target Audience: Aimed at academics, industrialists and government agencies dedicated to the use of clean, renewable and sustainable resources.
ADVERTISING RATES:
Full Page Mono £890.00
Mechanical Data: Type Area: 252 x 188mm, Trim Size: 275 x 210mm, Bleed Size: 281 x 216mm, Page Width: 188mm, Col Length: 252mm
BUSINESS: ENVIRONMENT & POLLUTION

GREEN FUTURES
40658U57-30_37

Editorial Address: Overseas House, 19-23 Ironmonger Row, LONDON, EC1V 3QN **Tel:** 020 7324 3660
Email: post@greenfutures.org.uk
Advertising Address: 9 Imperial Square, CHELTENHAM, GL50 1QB **Tel:** 01242 262729 **Fax:** 01242 262757
Email: ads@forumforthefuture.org.uk
Web site: http://www.greenfutures.org.uk
ISSN: 1366-4417
Publisher: Forum for the Future
Date Established: 1996
Frequency: Quarterly
Annual Sub.: £24.00
Circulation: 8,000 (Publisher's Statement)
Usual Pagination: 48

Editor: Anna Simpson; **Advertising Manager:** Lindsay Travis; **Managing Editor:** Hannah Bullock; **Publisher:** Anna Simpson
Summary of Content: Magazine providing positive sustainable solutions.
Readership/Target Audience: Read by decision-makers with responsibility for environmental matters in companies, public sector departments and the wider public.
ADVERTISING RATES:
Full Page Colour £1600.00
Agency Commission: 10%
Mechanical Data: Bleed Size: 305 x 214mm, Trim Size: 297 x 210mm, Film: Digital, Type Area: 257 x 178mm, Col Length: 257mm, Page Width: 178mm
Copy instructions: Copy Date: 3 weeks prior to publication date
BUSINESS: ENVIRONMENT & POLLUTION

GREEN I.T.
1859321U5R-692

Editorial Address: 35 Station Square, Petts Wood, ORPINGTON, BR5 1LZ **Tel:** 01689 616000
Fax: 01689 826622
Email: josh.boulton@btc.co.uk
Web site: http://www.greenitmagazine.com
Publisher: Business & Technical Communications
Date Established: 2008
Frequency: 6 issues yearly
Cover Price: £8.50
Circulation: 70,089 (Publisher's Statement)
Editor: Josh Boulton; **Advertising Manager:** Josh Boulton
Summary of Content: Magazine dedicated to improving the IT industries environmental performance. Featuring news and information from around the industry.
Readership/Target Audience: Aimed at IT professionals who are in charge of purchasing and using IT equipment.
BUSINESS: COMPUTERS & AUTOMATION: Computers Related

GREEN PAGES THE DIRECTORY OF AGRICULTURE FOR THE UK
37808U21B-320

Editorial Address: 229 Acton Lane, LONDON, W4 5DD
Tel: 020 8747 8028 **Fax:** 020 8747 8054
Web site: http://www.green-pages.co.uk
ISSN: 0963-1682
Publisher: Geraldine Flower Publications
Date Established: 1990
Frequency: Annual - Published in July
Cover Price: £25.00
Circulation: 20,000 (Publisher's Statement)
Usual Pagination: 724
Editor: Geraldine Flower; **Publisher:** Geraldine Flower
Summary of Content: Reference guide to agricultural products and services in the UK.
Readership/Target Audience: Read by farmers and the agricultural industry in the UK.
ADVERTISING: No Advertising taken
BUSINESS: AGRICULTURE & FARMING: Agriculture - Supplies & Services

GREEN PLACES INCORPORATING LANDSCAPE DESIGN
40672U57-36

Formerly: Landscape Design
Editorial Address: Ewell House, Graveney Road, FAVERSHAM, ME13 8UP **Tel:** 01795 542436
Fax: 01795 535469
Email: editorial@green-places.co.uk
Advertising Address: As above. **Tel:** 01795 535468
Email: ads@green-places.co.uk
Web site: http://www.landscape.co.uk
ISSN: 1742-3724
Publisher: GTC
Date Established: 2003
Frequency: 10 issues yearly - Published around the 1st of the cover month
Cover Price: £5.50
Annual Sub.: £49.00
Usual Pagination: 56
Editor: Melanie Armstrong; **Advertising Manager:** Melanie Richards
Summary of Content: Journal covering awareness of environmental, social, cultural and economic factors in the planning, development and management of public space in Britain and the rest of the world.
Readership/Target Audience: Readership includes garden and park planners, ecologists, landscape architects, architects, civil engineers and conservationists.
ADVERTISING RATES:
Full Page Mono £800.00
Full Page Colour £1200.00
SCC £34.10
Agency Commission: 10%
Mechanical Data: Col Length: 273mm, Type Area: 273 x 206mm, Bleed Size: 303 x 236mm, Trim Size: 297 x 230mm, Film: Digital, Page Width: 206mm
Copy instructions: Copy Date: 2 weeks prior to publication date

Average advertising content per issue: 30%
Supplement(s): Green Places News - 12xY
BUSINESS: ENVIRONMENT & POLLUTION

GREENFLEET
1786089U14A-577

Editorial Address: 226 High Road, LOUGHTON, IG10 1ET
Tel: 020 8532 0055 Fax: 020 8532 0066
Email: editor@psp-media.co.uk
Advertising Address: As above.
Email: colin@pse-events.co.uk
Web site: http://www.greenfleet.net
Publisher: Public Sector Publishing Ltd
Date Established: 2005
Frequency: 6 issues yearly
Cover Price: Free
Circulation: 5,700 (Publisher's Statement)
Usual Pagination: 44
Editor: Sofie Lidefjard
Summary of Content: Publication covering all aspects of fleet management from an environmental perspective including technology, management issues, law and government policy.
Readership/Target Audience: Aimed at fleet and procurement managers.
ADVERTISING RATES:
Full Page Colour £2495.00
Agency Commission: 10%
Mechanical Data: Bleed Size: 307 x 220mm, Trim Size: 297 x 210mm, Film: Digital
Copy instructions: Copy Date: 3 weeks prior to publication date
Average advertising content per issue: 40%
Supplement(s): Transport Business International - 6xY
BUSINESS: COMMERCE, INDUSTRY & MANAGEMENT

GREENKEEPER INTERNATIONAL
41483U64D-40

Editorial Address: Bigga House, Aldwark, Alne, YORK, YO61 1UF Tel: 01347 833800 Fax: 01347 833801
Email: melissa@bigga.co.uk
Advertising Address: As above. Fax: 01347 833802
Email: kirsten@bigga.co.uk
Web site: http://www.bigga.org.uk
Publisher: BIGGA
Date Established: 1990
Frequency: Monthly
Cover Price: £3.80
Circulation: 7,000 (Publisher's Statement)
Usual Pagination: 64
Summary of Content: Official publication of the British & International Golf Greenkeepers Association.
Readership/Target Audience: Aimed at Members of BIGGA and members of the fine turf industry as well as other related golfing associations.
ADVERTISING RATES:
Full Page Colour £1475.00
Agency Commission: 10%
Mechanical Data: Col Length: 260mm, Type Area: 260 x 180mm, Trim Size: 297 x 210mm, Page Width: 180mm, Film: Digital, Bleed Size: 303 x 213mm
Copy instructions: Copy Date: 20th of each month prior to publication date
Average advertising content per issue: 35%
BUSINESS: OTHER CLASSIFICATIONS: Course Maintenance

GREENPEACE BUSINESS
40661U57-30_50

Editorial Address: Canonbury Villas, LONDON, N1 2PN
Tel: 020 7865 8100 Fax: 020 7865 8203
Email: john.sauven@uk.greenpeace.org
Web site: http://www.greenpeace.org.uk
ISSN: 0962-9467
Publisher: Greenpeace Ltd
Frequency: Quarterly
Free to qualifying individuals
Annual Sub.: £99.00
Circulation: 10,000 (Publisher's Statement)
Usual Pagination: 12
Editor: John Sauven
Summary of Content: Newsletter explaining the thinking behind the Greenpeace campaign demands. Highlights sound industrial practices and exposes activities of companies, which harm the environment.
Readership/Target Audience: Aimed at businesses interested in Greenpeace campaigns.
ADVERTISING: No Advertising taken
BUSINESS: ENVIRONMENT & POLLUTION

GREENS WEEKLY DIGEST
39256U44-730

Editorial Address: 21 Alva Street, EDINBURGH, EH2 4PS
Tel: 0131 225 4879 Fax: 0131 225 2104
Email: slt-enquiries@wgreen.co.uk
Web site: http://www.wgreen.thomson.com
ISSN: 0955-4491
Publisher: W. Green Thomson Reuters

Date Established: 1986
Frequency: 40 issues yearly - Published weekly during court terms
Annual Sub.: £232.00
Usual Pagination: 12
Editor: Rebecca Standing; Managing Editor: Rebecca Standing
Summary of Content: Rapid information service to keep Scottish law practitioners abreast of judgements in Scottish courts.
Readership/Target Audience: Aimed at Scottish law practitioners, academics, students and other professionals.
ADVERTISING: No Advertising taken
BUSINESS: LEGAL

GREETINGS TODAY
38950U41B-30

Editorial Address: 1 Churchgates, The Wilderness, BERKHAMSTED, HP4 2UB Tel: 01442 289930
Fax: 01442 289950
Email: jo@lemapublishing.co.uk
Advertising Address: As above. Fax: 01442 289935
Email: jfurlong@lemapublishing.co.uk
Publisher: Lema Publishing
Frequency: 11 issues yearly - Published the 1st week of the month
Free to qualifying individuals
Annual Sub.: £45.00
Circulation: 6,516 (ABC 01/07/2008 to 30/06/2009)
Usual Pagination: 52
Editor: Jo Cooper; Advertising Manager: John Furlong
Summary of Content: Journal containing a mixture of news, developments and in-depth features on the greetings card industry.
Readership/Target Audience: Aimed at retailers and multiple department store buyers.
ADVERTISING RATES:
Full Page Colour £1375.00
Agency Commission: 10%
Mechanical Data: Print Process: Litho, Bleed Size: 315 x 240mm, Trim Size: 305 x 230mm, Film: Digital
Copy instructions: Copy Date: 5th of the month prior to publication date
Average advertising content per issue: 50%
BUSINESS: PRINTING & STATIONERY: Stationery

GRINDING AND SURFACE FINISHING
1626348U19C-701

Editorial Address: Triumph House, Station Approach, Sanderstead Road, SOUTH CROYDON, CR2 0PL
Tel: 020 8916 0022 Fax: 020 8916 0033
Email: roger@rbpublishing.co.uk
Advertising Address: As above.
Email: roger@rbpublishing.co.uk
Web site: http://www.rbpublishing.co.uk
ISSN: 1740-1100
Publisher: Roger Barber Publishing
Date Established: 2003
Frequency: 5 issues yearly - Published 2nd week of cover month
Cover Price: £6.00
Free to qualifying individuals
Circulation: 10,019 (Publisher's Statement)
Usual Pagination: 52
Editor: Roger Barber; Advertising Manager: Roger Barber
Summary of Content: Magazine covering production grinding, tool grinding, surface finishing tools and machinery.
Readership/Target Audience: Magazine aimed at the aerospace industry, motor vehicle manufacturers, medical device manufacturers, engineering subcontractors and engineering distributors.
ADVERTISING RATES:
Full Page Colour £1500.00
Agency Commission: 10%
Mechanical Data: Type Area: 265 x 185mm, Bleed Size: 303 x 216mm, Trim Size: 297 x 210mm, Col Length: 265mm, Page Width: 185mm, Film: Digital
Copy instructions: Copy Date: 3 weeks prior to publication date
Average advertising content per issue: 30%
BUSINESS: ENGINEERING & MACHINERY: Finishing

THE GROCER
37967U22A-190

Editorial Address: Broadfield Park, CRAWLEY, RH11 9RT
Tel: 01293 613400 Fax: 01293 610333
Email: katherine.barrack@william-reed.co.uk
Advertising Address: As above. Fax: 01293 610340
Email: grocer.display@william-reed.co.uk
Web site: http://www.thegrocer.co.uk
ISSN: 0017-4351
Publisher: William Reed Business Media
Date Established: 1862
Frequency: Weekly
Cover Price: £1.95
Annual Sub.: £82.50
Circulation: 30,724 (ABC 01/07/2007 to 30/06/2008)
Usual Pagination: 120

Editor: Katherine Barrack; News Editor: Ronan Hegarty; Features Editor: Alex Black; Managing Director: Charles Reed; Advertising Director: Jonathan Daniels
Summary of Content: Magazine containing news, finance, personnel, marketing and special features relating to the food industry.
Twitter: https://twitter.com/TheGrocer.
Readership/Target Audience: Aimed at retailers, manufacturers, suppliers and distributors in the food industry.
ADVERTISING RATES:
Full Page Mono £1370.00
Full Page Colour £3485.00
Agency Commission: 10%
Mechanical Data: Type Area: 267 x 185mm, Bleed Size: 303 x 216mm, Trim Size: 297 x 210mm, Film: Digital, Page Width: 185mm, Col Length: 267mm
Copy instructions: Copy Date: 2 weeks prior to publication date
Average advertising content per issue: 30%
BUSINESS: FOOD

THE GROCER DIRECTORY OF MANUFACTURERS & SUPPLIERS
39833U53-88

Editorial Address: Broadfield Park, CRAWLEY, RH11 9RT
Tel: 01293 613400 Fax: 01293 610322
Email: stephen.whitehead@william-reed.co.uk
Advertising Address: As above. Tel: 01293 610331
Fax: 01293 610384
Email: clare.dackombe@william-reed.co.uk
Web site: http://www.therightinfo.co.uk
ISSN: 1475-9772
Publisher: William Reed Business Media
Date Established: 2001
Frequency: Annual - Published in November
Annual Sub.: £297.00
Circulation: 5,000 (Publisher's Statement)
Usual Pagination: 900
Editor: Sarah Wibling; Advertising Manager: Clare Dackombe
Summary of Content: Directory listing over 9000 manufacturers, suppliers, wholesalers, distributors, agents and brokers of food, drink and non-food items for the grocery and retail trade.
Readership/Target Audience: Aimed at manufacturers, buyers and specifiers in grocery retailers and distributors, as well as service companies.
ADVERTISING RATES:
Full Page Colour £1850.00
Mechanical Data: Col Length: 214mm, Page Width: 138mm, Type Area: 214 x 138mm, Bleed Size: 258 x 186mm, Trim Size: 252 x 180mm, Film: Digital
BUSINESS: RETAILING & WHOLESALING

GROCER.ME
37975U22A-260

Formerly: Middle East Grocer
Editorial Address: 6 Tobin close, Livingstone Park, EPSOM, KT198AE Tel: 01372 742347
Email: pharmedia@aol.com
Advertising Address: As above. Fax: 01372 745187
Email: pharmedia@btconnect.com
Web site: http://www.pharmedia.co.uk
ISSN: 1368-5929
Publisher: Pharmedia International
Frequency: 6 issues yearly - Published around the middle of the cover month
Free to qualifying individuals
Annual Sub.: £35.00
Circulation: 11,500 (Publisher's Statement)
Usual Pagination: 36
Editor: Russ Finnerty; Advertising Manager: Russ Finnerty; Publisher: Russ Finnerty
Summary of Content: Journal covering branded product sales to the market, news, trends and developments affecting manufacturers, retailers and consumers.
Readership/Target Audience: Aimed at grocery retailers and managers in the Middle East region.
ADVERTISING RATES:
Full Page Colour £2750.00
Agency Commission: 15%
Mechanical Data: Type Area: 272 x 186mm, Bleed Size: 303 x 216mm, Trim Size: 297 x 210mm, Film: Digital, Page Width: 186mm
Copy instructions: Copy Date: 6 weeks prior to publication date
BUSINESS: FOOD

THE GROCERY TRADER
37968U22A-200

Editorial Address: Flame House, 12 Kings Park, Primrose Hill, KINGS LANGLEY, WD4 8ST Tel: 01923 272960
Fax: 01923 270760
Email: grocery@flame1.com
Advertising Address: As above.
Email: grocery@flame1.com
Web site: http://www.grocerytrader.co.uk

ISSN: 1355-5928
Publisher: Grandflame Ltd
Date Established: 1995
Frequency: Monthly - Published in the 1st week of the cover month
Free to qualifying individuals
Annual Sub.: £36.00
Circulation: 7,600 (Publisher's Statement)
Usual Pagination: 28
Editor: Charles Smith; **Advertising Manager:** Adam Dillon; **Publisher:** James Surridge
Summary of Content: Newsletter covering all aspects of the UK grocery trade including product information, market news and company news from retailers and suppliers.
Readership/Target Audience: Aimed at named individuals in the head offices of supermarkets, co-ops, wholesalers, buying groups and convenience retail groups, plus branch and depot managers at local level.
ADVERTISING RATES:
Full Page Mono £1150.00
Full Page Colour £1450.00
SCC £21.00
Agency Commission: 10%
Mechanical Data: Film: Digital, Type Area: 380 x 260mm, Bleed Size: 426 x 303mm, Trim Size: 420 x 297mm, Col Length: 380mm, Page Width: 260mm, Col Widths (Display): 52mm, No. of Columns (Display): 5
BUSINESS: FOOD

GROUND ENGINEERING
39000U42A-105
Editorial Address: Greater London House, Hampstead Road, LONDON, NW1 7EJ **Tel:** 020 7728 5000
Email: damon.schunmann@emap.com
Advertising Address: As above. **Fax:** 020 7728 4666
Email: roland.maybank@emap.com
Web site: http://www.geplus.co.uk
ISSN: 0017-4653
Publisher: EMAP Insight
Date Established: 1968
Frequency: Monthly - Published at the beginning of the month prior to cover month
Cover Price: £10.00
Annual Sub.: £56.00
Circulation: 4,000 (Publisher's Statement)
Usual Pagination: 48
Editor: Damon Schunmann
Summary of Content: Journal of the British Geotechnical Association. Concerned with the practical application of soil and rock mechanics in the construction of foundations, underground chambers and tunnels and engineering geology.
Readership/Target Audience: Read by geotechnical and geo-environmental engineers.
ADVERTISING RATES:
Full Page Colour £2285.00
SCC £45.00
Agency Commission: 10%
Mechanical Data: Page Width: 181mm, Film: Digital, Type Area: 254 x 181mm, Col Length: 254mm, Trim Size: 284 x 210mm, Bleed Size: 292 x 216mm
Copy instructions: Copy Date: 3 weeks prior to publication date
Supplement(s): European Foundations - 4xY, Geotechnical Services File - 1xY
BUSINESS: CONSTRUCTION

GROUND HANDLING INTERNATIONAL
36342U6A-96_25
Editorial Address: The Stables, Willow Lane, Paddock Wood, TONBRIDGE, TN12 6PF **Tel:** 01892 839200
Fax: 01892 839210
Email: alwyn@groundhandling.com
Advertising Address: As above.
Email: advertising@groundhandling.com
Web site: http://www.groundhandling.com
Publisher: Airports Publishing Network Ltd
Frequency: 6 issues yearly
Free to qualifying individuals
Annual Sub.: £55.00
Circulation: 6,179 (ABC 01/01/2008 to 31/12/2008)
Usual Pagination: 64
Editor: Alwyn Brice; **Publisher:** Tim Ornellas
Summary of Content: Magazine concentrating on the international ground handling industry. Covers handling issues including, health and safety, technology, legislation, new products and interviews with senior industry figures.
Readership/Target Audience: Aimed at airport, airline and independent ground handling organisations.
ADVERTISING RATES:
Full Page Mono £2600.00
Full Page Colour £3595.00
Agency Commission: 10%
Mechanical Data: Bleed Size: 303 x 216mm, Trim Size: 297 x 210mm, Type Area: 264 x 170mm, Film: Digital, Page Width: 170mm, Col Length: 264mm
BUSINESS: AVIATION & AERONAUTICS

THE GROUNDSMAN
38421U32D-145
Editorial Address: 64 James Street, Cellardyke, ANSTRUTHER, KY10 3AY **Tel:** 01795 506327
Advertising Address: The Deeson Group Ltd, Ewell House, FAVERSHAM, ME13 8UP **Tel:** 01795 542402
Fax: 01795 535469
Email: stevenr@thegroundsman.co.uk
Web site: http://www.iog.org
Publisher: GTC
Date Established: 1934
Frequency: Monthly - Published on the 10th of the cover month
Cover Price: £4.00
Free to qualifying individuals
Circulation: 7,500 (Publisher's Statement)
Usual Pagination: 60
Editor: Trevor Ledger
Summary of Content: Magazine covering grounds management, maintenance and care of leisure facilities, major stadiums and pitches in football, cricket and rugby, plus general landscaping, drainage and management of golf courses, bowling greens, horseracing circuits, polo pitches and artificial surfaces. Also covers management of school, college and university sports and horticultural facilities.
Readership/Target Audience: Read by members of the Institute of Groundsmanship, major sports organisers, landscape and sports ground contractors, sports clubs, local authority managers, machinery manufacturers and product suppliers.
ADVERTISING RATES:
Full Page Colour £1135.00
Agency Commission: 10%
Mechanical Data: Col Length: 275mm, Col Widths (Display): 42mm, Trim Size: 297 x 210mm, Bleed Size: 303 x 216mm, Film: Digital, No. of Columns (Display): 4, Type Area: 275 x 188mm, Page Width: 188mm
Copy instructions: Copy Date: 1 week prior to publication date
Average advertising content per issue: 40%
BUSINESS: LOCAL GOVERNMENT, LEISURE & RECREATION: Parks

GROUP ANALYSIS
40562U56R-57
Editorial Address: 1 Oliver's Yard, 55 City Road, LONDON, EC1Y 1SP **Tel:** 020 7324 8500 **Fax:** 020 7324 8600
Advertising Address: As above.
Email: sheena.karim@sagepub.co.uk
Web site: http://www.sagepub.co.uk
ISSN: 0533-3164
Publisher: Sage Publications
Date Established: 1986
Frequency: Quarterly
Cover Price: £18.00
Annual Sub.: £56.00
Usual Pagination: 144
Editor: Tom Ormay; **Advertising Manager:** Sheena Karim
Summary of Content: Journal centred upon the theory, practice and experience of analytic group psychotherapy.
Readership/Target Audience: Aimed at psychotherapists.
ADVERTISING RATES:
Full Page Mono £400.00
Agency Commission: 5%
Mechanical Data: Film: Digital, Col Length: 175mm, Page Width: 100mm, Type Area: 175 x 100mm
BUSINESS: HEALTH & MEDICAL: Health Medical Related

GROUP LEISURE
39720U50-16_17
Editorial Address: PO Box 5122, MILTON KEYNES, MK15 8ZP **Tel:** 01908 613323 **Fax:** 01908 210656
Email: editorial@groupleisure.com
Advertising Address: As above.
Email: rob.y@yandellmedia.com
Web site: http://www.groupleisure.com
ISSN: 1363-7797
Publisher: Yandell Publishing Limited
Date Established: 1995
Frequency: Monthly
Free to qualifying individuals
Annual Sub.: £40.00
Circulation: 10,819 (Publisher's Statement)
Usual Pagination: 84
Editor: Rob Yandell; **Managing Editor:** Rob Yandell; **Publisher:** Rob Yandell
Summary of Content: Magazine with news, information and features of interest to group travel organisers from clubs, societies and associations.
Readership/Target Audience: Aimed at decision makers and organisers in the group leisure and travel industry.
ADVERTISING RATES:
Full Page Colour £1800.00
Agency Commission: 10%
Mechanical Data: Type Area: 273 x 178mm, Film: Digital, Col Length: 273mm, Print Process: Sheet-fed offset litho, Page Width: 178mm
Copy instructions: Copy Date: 1st of the month prior to publication date
Average advertising content per issue: 50%
BUSINESS: TRAVEL & TOURISM

GROUP PROCESSES & INTERGROUP RELATIONS
40608U56R-57_20
Editorial Address: 1 Oliver's Yard, 55 City Road, LONDON, EC1Y 1SP **Tel:** 020 7324 8500 **Fax:** 020 7324 8600
Advertising Address: As above.
Email: sheena.karim@sagepub.co.uk
Web site: http://www.sagepub.co.uk
ISSN: 1368-4302
Publisher: Sage Publications
Date Established: 1998
Frequency: Quarterly
Cover Price: £15.00
Annual Sub.: £47.00
Usual Pagination: 104
Editor: Dominic Abrams; **Advertising Manager:** Sheena Karim
Summary of Content: International social psychology journal that focuses on basic and applied aspects of group and intergroup phenomena, ranging from small interactive groups to large scale social categories.
Readership/Target Audience: Aimed at social psychologists and researchers.
ADVERTISING RATES:
Full Page Mono £400.00
Agency Commission: 5%
Mechanical Data: Type Area: 210 x 140mm, Col Length: 210mm, Page Width: 140mm, Film: Digital
Copy instructions: Copy Date: 12 weeks prior to publication date
BUSINESS: HEALTH & MEDICAL: Health Medical Related

GROUP TRAVEL ORGANISER
39721U50-16_20
Editorial Address: 47 Wellington Square, HASTINGS, TN34 1PN **Tel:** 0845 166 8120 **Fax:** 01424 200478
Email: editorial@grouptravelorganiser.com
Advertising Address: As above.
Email: sales@grouptravelorganiser.com
Web site: http://www.grouptravelorganiser.com
ISSN: 0962-8266
Publisher: Group Travel Organiser Ltd
Date Established: 1988
Frequency: 10 issues yearly
Cover Price: £2.50
Free to qualifying individuals
Annual Sub.: £24.00
Circulation: 9,872 (ABC 01/07/2008 to 30/06/2009)
Usual Pagination: 60
Editor: Carrie Drage; **Advertising Manager:** Adrian Gates
Summary of Content: Magazine covering organisation and commissioning of travel arrangements on behalf of groups of 20 or more people.
Readership/Target Audience: Aimed at group travel organisers.
ADVERTISING RATES:
Full Page Mono £1240.00
Full Page Colour £1690.00
Agency Commission: 10%
Mechanical Data: Film: Digital, Trim Size: 297 x 210mm, Type Area: 267 x 187mm, Col Length: 267mm, Page Width: 187mm
Average advertising content per issue: 50%
BUSINESS: TRAVEL & TOURISM

GROUP TRAVEL TODAY
1805680U50-236
Editorial Address: 16 Ballencrieff Mill, Balmuir Road, BATHGATE, EH48 4LL **Tel:** 01506 636531
Fax: 01506 636531
Email: grouptraveltoday@uwclub.net
Advertising Address: Publishing House, Windrush, Ash Lane, Hopwood, Alvechurch, BIRMINGHAM, B48 7TS
Tel: 0121 445 6961 **Fax:** 0121 445 4436
Email: hughgrouptravel@btinternet.com
Web site: http://www.grouptraveltodaylive.co.uk
Publisher: Beau Business Media Ltd
Date Established: 2007
Frequency: 8 issues yearly
Cover Price: Free
Circulation: 8,000 (Publisher's Statement)
Usual Pagination: 64
Editor: Simon Walton; **Advertising Manager:** Hugh Cairns
Summary of Content: Magazine focusing on group travel, featuring areas and attractions keen to work with group organisers, advice from group travel experts, contributions from the Coach Tourism Council and a forum for the industry. Includes a diary of events and shows.
Readership/Target Audience: Aimed at group organisers, special interest groups, travel providers, transport operators, tour guides and professional chaperones.
ADVERTISING RATES:
Full Page Mono £1575.00
Full Page Colour £1575.00
Mechanical Data: Bleed Size: 303 x 216mm, Trim Size: 297 x 210mm, Film: Digital
Copy instructions: Copy Date: 3 weeks prior to publication date
BUSINESS: TRAVEL & TOURISM

GROUPS WELCOME
39619U49B-25_50

Formerly: Coaches & Parties Welcome
Editorial Address: The Old Police House, The Green, Tysoe, WARWICK, CV35 0SN **Tel:** 01295 688263
Fax: 01295 688263
Email: info@groupswelcome.co.uk
Advertising Address: As above.
Email: info@groupswelcome.co.uk
Web site: http://www.groupswelcome.co.uk
Publisher: Groups Welcome
Date Established: 1977
Frequency: Annual - Published in January
Cover Price: Free
Circulation: 17,000 (Publisher's Statement)
Usual Pagination: 128
Editor: Digby Norton; **Advertising Manager:** Digby Norton
Summary of Content: Directory of tourism venues and attractions, accommodation and others who welcome group bookers.
Readership/Target Audience: Aimed at party organisers, coach companies, sports and gardening clubs, pensioner groups, Age Concern and affinity groups.
ADVERTISING RATES:
Full Page Colour £1050.00
Agency Commission: 10%
Copy instructions: Copy Date: End of October
Average advertising content per issue: 65%
BUSINESS: TRANSPORT: Bus & Coach Transport

GROWING BUSINESS
752672U14H-51

Editorial Address: Westminster House, Kew Road, RICHMOND, TW9 2ND **Tel:** 020 8334 1653
Fax: 020 8334 1601
Email: editor@crimsonbusiness.co.uk
Advertising Address: As above. **Tel:** 020 8334 1600
Email: taraw@crimsonbusiness.co.uk
Web site: http://www.growingbusiness.co.uk
Publisher: Crimson Business Ltd
Date Established: 2001
Frequency: 10 issues yearly - Combined issues December/January and July/August
Cover Price: £3.00
Free to qualifying individuals
Circulation: 37,153 (ABC 01/07/2008 to 30/06/2009)
Usual Pagination: 64
Editor: Jon Card
Summary of Content: Magazine covering business practice including management, marketing, technology, finance and lifestyle.
Readership/Target Audience: Read by UK business entrepreneurs, and business leaders, as well as finance providers including VCs, angel investors and institutions, management consultants and other professional service providers to the sector.
ADVERTISING RATES:
Full Page Colour £4950.00
Agency Commission: 10%
Mechanical Data: Type Area: 275 x 184mm, Bleed Size: 303 x 216mm, Trim Size: 297 x 210mm, Col Length: 275mm, Page Width: 184mm, Film: Digital
Copy instructions: Copy Date: 2 weeks prior to publication date
Average advertising content per issue: 40%
BUSINESS: COMMERCE, INDUSTRY & MANAGEMENT: Small Business

GROWTH COMPANY INVESTOR
35302U1F-225

Formerly: Small Company Investor
Editorial Address: Octavia House, 50 Banner Street, LONDON, EC1Y 8ST **Tel:** 020 7250 7010
Fax: 020 7250 7011
Email: editorial@growthcompany.co.uk
Advertising Address: As above.
Email: darren.griffin@vitessemedia.co.uk
Web site: http://www.growthcompany.co.uk
Publisher: Vitesse Media plc
Date Established: 1996
Frequency: 10 issues yearly
Annual Sub.: £119.50
Circulation: 3,000 (Publisher's Statement)
Usual Pagination: 32
Editor: Oliver Haill; **News Editor:** Robert Tyerman; **Editor-in-Chief:** Leslie Copeland
Summary of Content: Magazine containing investment advice on small companies for private investors.
Readership/Target Audience: Aimed at investors interested in buying shares in smaller companies.
ADVERTISING RATES:
Full Page Colour £2950.00
Agency Commission: 10%
Mechanical Data: Bleed Size: 386 x 281mm, Trim Size: 380 x 275mm, Film: Digital
Copy instructions: Copy Date: 1 week prior to publication date
Average advertising content per issue: 15%
BUSINESS: FINANCE & ECONOMICS: Investment

GROWTHPOINT
48582U26D-55

Editorial Address: The Geoffrey Udall Centre, Beech Hill, READING, RG7 2AT **Tel:** 0118 988 5688 **Fax:** 0118 988 5677
Email: info@thrive.org.uk
Web site: http://www.thrive.org.uk
ISSN: 9051-7774
Publisher: Thrive
Date Established: 1979
Frequency: Quarterly
Cover Price: £5.00
Free to qualifying individuals
Circulation: 1,750 (Publisher's Statement)
Usual Pagination: 24
Editor: Janet Carruzzo
Summary of Content: Journal devoted to social and therapeutic horticulture. Includes the latest news, research and project profiles and is essential reading for those working in the fields of health, care, environment and education.
Language(s): English; Japanese
Readership/Target Audience: Aimed mainly at professionals working in the field of social and therapeutic horticulture: horticultural therapists, horticulturalists, occupational therapists and garden project managers running projects for disabled, disadvantaged and older people.
ADVERTISING: No Advertising taken
BUSINESS: GARDEN TRADE: Garden Trade Horticulture

GS MAGAZINE
36568U4B-193

Editorial Address: 19 Wharfdale Road, LONDON, N1 9SB
Tel: 020 7833 3772 **Fax:** 020 7833 3830
Email: editor@gsmagazine.co.uk
Advertising Address: As above.
Email: sales@gsmagazine.co.uk
Web site: http://www.gsmagazine.co.uk
Publisher: Stevenson Publications Ltd
Date Established: 1997
Frequency: Quarterly
Free to qualifying individuals
Annual Sub.: £16.00
Circulation: 10,000 (Publisher's Statement)
Usual Pagination: 68
Editor: Stirling Johnstone; **Advertising Manager:** Stirling Johnstone
Summary of Content: Independent magazine for the hospitality industry containing product reviews and design related articles.
Readership/Target Audience: Aimed at restaurateurs, hoteliers, theme bars, pub chains, hotel and leisure groups, designers and architects.
ADVERTISING RATES:
Full Page Mono £2950.00
Full Page Colour £2950.00
Agency Commission: 10%
Mechanical Data: Film: Digital, Bleed Size: 303 x 236mm, Trim Size: 230 x 207mm, Col Length: 262mm, Type Area: 262 x 200mm, Page Width: 200mm, Col Widths (Display): 95mm, No. of Columns (Display): 2, Print Process: Litho
Copy instructions: Copy Date: 4 weeks prior to publication date
Average advertising content per issue: 40%
BUSINESS: ARCHITECTURE & BUILDING: Interior Design & Flooring

GUIDE TO INDUSTRY & COMMERCE IN CUMBRIA
1657559U63B-2506

Editorial Address: 3 Chatsworth Square, CARLISLE, CA1 1HB **Tel:** 01228 547144
Email: editor@cumbriapress.co.uk
Advertising Address: As above. **Fax:** 01228 514747
Email: alan@cumbriapress.com
Publisher: Cumbrian Press Group
Frequency: 3 issues yearly
Cover Price: Free
Circulation: 5,000 (Publisher's Statement)
Editor: Tony Thornton; **Advertising Manager:** Alan Taylor
Summary of Content: Magazine covering current industrial affairs and business advice.
Readership/Target Audience: Aimed at businesses in Cumbria.
ADVERTISING RATES:
Full Page Colour £795.00
Agency Commission: 10%
Mechanical Data: Trim Size: 210 x 150mm, Bleed Size: 220 x 160mm
Average advertising content per issue: 45%
BUSINESS: REGIONAL BUSINESS: Regional Business English Counties

GUIDES TO INDUSTRIAL ESTATES IN NORTHERN IRELAND
628803U14B-120

Editorial Address: 90A Church Street, Portadown, CRAIGAVON, BT62 3AX **Tel:** 028 3835 2275
Fax: 028 3835 2275
Email: estates2007@btinternet.com

Advertising Address: As above.
Email: andrewcrozier@mainstreammagazines.co.uk
Publisher: Karen McAvoy Publishing Ltd
Frequency: Quarterly
Annual Sub.: £5.00
Circulation: 8,000 (Publisher's Statement)
Usual Pagination: 80
Editor: Andrew Crozier; **Advertising Manager:** Andrew Crozier
Summary of Content: Directories of Northern Ireland Industrial Estates, including maps and location details, company names, descriptions, contact names and addresses.
Readership/Target Audience: Read by companies who require information on industries within the area.
ADVERTISING: Rates on application
BUSINESS: COMMERCE, INDUSTRY & MANAGEMENT: Industry & Factories

GUILD NEWS
37121U14H-24

Formerly: Guild of Master Craftsmen News
Editorial Address: 86 High Street, LEWES, BN7 1XN
Tel: 01273 477374 **Fax:** 01273 487692
Email: richardw@thegmcgroup.com
Advertising Address: As above. **Tel:** 01273 402823
Email: rhonab@thegmcgroup.com
Web site: http://www.thegmcpubs.com
ISSN: 0965-9455
Publisher: GMC Publications Ltd
Date Established: 1991
Frequency: Quarterly
Cover Price: £4.95
Free to qualifying individuals
Circulation: 30,000 (Publisher's Statement)
Usual Pagination: 84
Editor: Richard Walsh; **Publisher:** Simon McKeown
Summary of Content: Official journal of the Guild of Master Craftsmen providing news, advice, information and features.
Readership/Target Audience: Aimed at small and medium expanding businesses.
ADVERTISING RATES:
Full Page Colour £750.00
Agency Commission: 10%
Mechanical Data: Film: Digital, Trim Size: 297 x 210mm
Copy instructions: Copy Date: 6 weeks prior to publication date
Average advertising content per issue: 50%
BUSINESS: COMMERCE, INDUSTRY & MANAGEMENT: Small Business

GUILD NEWS
37268U15R-5

Formerly: Guild News (Beauty)
Editorial Address: 3 Charnwood Street, DERBY, DE1 2GT
Tel: 01332 227683 **Fax:** 01332 227688
Email: melissa@beautyserve.net
Advertising Address: As above. **Tel:** 01332 227689
Email: ruth@beautyserve.net
Web site: http://www.beautyserve.com
Publisher: Guild Press Ltd
Date Established: 1997
Frequency: Monthly
Free to qualifying individuals
Annual Sub.: £30.00
Circulation: 18,949 (ABC 01/07/2007 to 30/06/2008)
Usual Pagination: 164
Editor: Melissa Dennis; **Group Editor:** Melissa Dennis
Summary of Content: Beauty trade magazine covering beauty, nails, tanning and holistic therapies. Also includes coverage of new product and equipment launches, industry news, training courses, business and marketing advice and information on health and safety.
Readership/Target Audience: Salon and spa owners, salon and spa managers, qualified beauty therapists and nail technicians, mobile and home-based therapists, holistic therapists, college lecturers and final year students.
ADVERTISING RATES:
Full Page Colour £1895.00
SCC £25.00
Agency Commission: 10%
Mechanical Data: Type Area: 270 x 186mm, Bleed Size: +3mm, Trim Size: 297 x 210mm, Col Length: 270mm, Film: Digital, Page Width: 186mm
Average advertising content per issue: 45%
Supplement(s): The Beauty Index - 1xY, BeautyUK Catalogue - 1xY, Holistic Health Catalogue, Scottish Beauty Catalogue - 1xY
BUSINESS: COSMETICS & HAIRDRESSING: Cosmetics & Hairdressing Related

GULF AFFAIRS JOURNAL
1808477U14C-369

Editorial Address: Davina House, 137-149 Goswell Road, LONDON, EC1V 7ET **Tel:** 020 7490 7101
Fax: 020 7490 7102
Email: gcss@btconnect.com
Web site: http://www.gcss.org.bh/web/myweb_magaz/index1.htm

Business Magazines

Publisher: Gulf Centre for Strategic Studies
Date Established: 1999
Frequency: Quarterly
Circulation: 1,500 (Publisher's Statement)
Editor: Omar Al Hassan; **Editor-in-Chief:** Omar Al Hassan
Summary of Content: Academic journal providing analysis of political, economic, social and military developments at Gulf, Arab and international levels.
Language(s): Arabic
Readership/Target Audience: Aimed at members of the business community, academics, the military and civil service.
ADVERTISING: No Advertising taken
BUSINESS: COMMERCE, INDUSTRY & MANAGEMENT: International Commerce

GULF CONSTRUCTION
39002U42A-110

Editorial Address: Crescent Court, 102 Victor Road, TEDDINGTON, TW11 8SS **Tel:** 020 8943 3630
Email: tculhane@hilal.co.uk
Advertising Address: As above.
Email: tculhane@hilal.co.uk
Web site: http://www.gulfconstructionworldwide.com
Publisher: Hilal International (UK) Ltd
Frequency: Monthly - Published on the 1st Monday of the cover month
Annual Sub.: $95.00
Circulation: 12,500 (Publisher's Statement)
Editor: Tara Culhane; **Advertising Manager:** Tara Culhane
Summary of Content: Journal containing news and information concerning building construction in the Middle East.
Readership/Target Audience: Read by civil engineers, public works authorities, building contractors, architects and related professions.
ADVERTISING RATES:
Full Page Colour $3730.00
Agency Commission: 15%
Mechanical Data: Type Area: 245 x 185mm, Col Length: 245mm, Trim Size: 282 x 210mm, Bleed Size: +5mm, Film: Digital, Page Width: 185mm
Copy instructions: Copy Date: 4 weeks prior to publication date
Average advertising content per issue: 40%
BUSINESS: CONSTRUCTION

GULF INDUSTRY
36903U14B-130

Formerly: Gulf Industry & Saudi Arabia Review
Editorial Address: Crescent Court, 102 Victor Road, TEDDINGTON, TW11 8SS **Tel:** 020 8943 3630
Email: tculhane@hilal.co.uk
Advertising Address: As above.
Email: mike@hilal.co.uk
Web site: http://www.gulfindustryonline.com
ISSN: 0965-2809
Publisher: Hilal International (UK) Ltd
Frequency: Monthly - Published at the beginning of the cover month
Annual Sub.: $68.00
Circulation: 11,000 (Publisher's Statement)
Usual Pagination: 200
Editor: James Webber; **Managing Director:** Tara Culhane; **Advertising Manager:** Mike Tanousis
Summary of Content: Publication focusing on industry and manufacturing in the Gulf.
Readership/Target Audience: Read by individuals with an involvement or interest in the industrial development of the region.
ADVERTISING RATES:
Full Page Colour $3730.00
Agency Commission: 15%
Mechanical Data: Type Area: 245 x 185mm, Col Length: 245mm, Trim Size: 282 x 210mm, Bleed Size: +5mm, Film: Digital, Page Width: 185mm
Copy instructions: Copy Date: 4 weeks prior to publication date
Average advertising content per issue: 40%
BUSINESS: COMMERCE, INDUSTRY & MANAGEMENT: Industry & Factories

GULF STATES NEWSLETTER
36956U14C-74

Editorial Address: PO Box 124, HASTINGS, TN34 1WP
Tel: 01424 721667 **Fax:** 01424 721721
Email: admin@gsn-online.com
Web site: http://www.gsn-online.com
ISSN: 0953-5411
Publisher: Cross-Border Information
Date Established: 1975
Frequency: 24 issues yearly
Annual Sub.: £695.00
Usual Pagination: 20
Editor: Eleanor Gillespie; **News Editor:** Eleanor Gillespie
Summary of Content: Newsletter containing news and analysis, focusing on political, security and economic affairs in the Gulf.

Readership/Target Audience: Read by decision makers in government, diplomacy, finance and industry.
ADVERTISING: No Advertising taken
BUSINESS: COMMERCE, INDUSTRY & MANAGEMENT: International Commerce

GUN TRADE NEWS
39551U48B-37

Editorial Address: Lawrence House, Morrell Street, LEAMINGTON SPA, CV32 5SZ **Tel:** 01926 339808
Fax: 01926 470400
Email: edit@blazepublishing.co.uk
Advertising Address: As above. **Fax:** 01926 421083
Email: info@blazepublishing.co.uk
Web site: http://www.blazepublishing.co.uk
Publisher: Blaze Publishing Limited
Date Established: 1993
Frequency: 6 issues yearly
Annual Sub.: £29.50
Circulation: 2,240 (Publisher's Statement)
Usual Pagination: 32
Editor: Rosie Fuller; **Publisher:** Wesley Stanton
Summary of Content: Magazine covering all aspects of the shooting industry.
Readership/Target Audience: Aimed at people involved in the shooting industry worldwide.
ADVERTISING RATES:
Full Page Mono £928.00
Full Page Colour £928.00
Agency Commission: 10%
Mechanical Data: Film: Digital, Trim Size: 420 x 290mm, Bleed Size: 426 x 296mm
Copy instructions: Copy Date: 4 weeks prior to publication date
Average advertising content per issue: 50%
BUSINESS: TOY TRADE & SPORTS GOODS: Sports Goods

H&V NEWS
35755U3B-14

Editorial Address: Greater London House, Hampstead Road, LONDON, NW1 7EJ **Tel:** 020 7728 5000
Fax: 020 7728 4400
Email: alex.hawkes@emap.com
Advertising Address: As above. **Fax:** 020 7728 3888
Email: mark.palmer@emap.com
Web site: http://www.hvnplus.co.uk
ISSN: 0962-1784
Publisher: EMAP Insight
Frequency: 40 issues yearly
Cover Price: £2.40
Free to qualifying individuals
Annual Sub.: £109.00
Circulation: 17,592 (ABC 01/01/2008 to 31/12/2008)
Usual Pagination: 20
Summary of Content: Newspaper covering all aspects of heating, ventilating and air conditioning.
Readership/Target Audience: Aimed at people working in the industry.
ADVERTISING RATES:
Full Page Colour £2997.00
Agency Commission: 10%
Mechanical Data: Film: Digital, Type Area: 350 x 255mm, Col Length: 350mm, Bleed Size: 384 x 280mm, Trim Size: 378 x 274mm, Page Width: 255mm
Copy instructions: Copy Date: 2 weeks prior to publication date
Average advertising content per issue: 40%
BUSINESS: HEATING & VENTILATION: Industrial Heating & Ventilation

HA HOUSING ASSOCIATION
35850U4D-100

Editorial Address: 11 Galena Close, Amington Industrial Estate, TAMWORTH, B77 4AS **Tel:** 01827 311800
Fax: 01827 301199
Email: press@wavcoms.co.uk
Advertising Address: As above. **Fax:** 01827 301186
Email: laurence@wavcoms.co.uk
Web site: http://www.wavcoms.co.uk
Publisher: Waverley Communications Ltd
Date Established: 1998
Frequency: 10 issues yearly - Published in the last week of the cover month combined issues for July/August and November/December
Cover Price: Free
Circulation: 10,636 (ABC 01/07/2008 to 30/06/2009)
Usual Pagination: 56
Editor: Gemma O'Rourke; **Advertising Manager:** Laurence Sands; **Publisher:** Kevin Edgeworth
Summary of Content: Magazine focusing on product features relating to housing associations and partnership contractors, including articles on exhibition previews, designs, specifications, energy efficiency, social housing and security.
Readership/Target Audience: Aimed at housing associations, surveyors, architects and contractors working in partnership with housing associations.
ADVERTISING RATES:
Full Page Colour £1985.00
Agency Commission: 10%

Mechanical Data: Col Length: 386mm, Page Width: 265mm, Film: Digital, Type Area: 386 x 265mm, Bleed Size: 410 x 295mm, Trim Size: 400 x 285mm
Copy instructions: Copy Date: 3 weeks prior to publication date
Average advertising content per issue: 60%
BUSINESS: ARCHITECTURE & BUILDING: Planning & Housing

THE HAIRDRESSER
37265U15B-200

Formerly: State Registered Hairdresser
Editorial Address: Dragon Marketing, Black House Road, Colgate, HORSHAM, RH13 6HS **Tel:** 01293 851101
Fax: 01293 851112
Email: francis@dragon-marketing.co.uk
Advertising Address: As above.
Email: francis@dragon-marketing.co.uk
Web site: http://www.haircouncil.org.uk
Publisher: Dragon Marketing for The Hairdressing Council
Date Established: 1986
Frequency: Quarterly
Cover Price: £3.25
Free to qualifying individuals
Circulation: 8,000 (Publisher's Statement)
Usual Pagination: 32
Editor: Francis Rowlands; **Advertising Manager:** Debbie Smith
Summary of Content: Official magazine for professionally qualified State Registered Hairdressers (SRHs) published by their statutory body, the Hairdressing Council. Contains news, education, business development, style and fashion items of interest to SRHs, hairdressers and trainees, product manufacturers and service suppliers to the hair and beauty industry in the UK, as well as colleges, educationalists and business support agencies.
Readership/Target Audience: Primarily aimed at State Registered Hairdressers worldwide.
ADVERTISING RATES:
Full Page Colour £1500.00
Agency Commission: 12%
Mechanical Data: Type Area: 267 x 180mm, Col Length: 267mm, Film: Digital, Page Width: 180mm, Bleed Size: +3mm, Trim Size: 297 x 210mm, Print Process: 4 colour Litho
Copy instructions: Copy Date: 2 weeks prior to publication date
Average advertising content per issue: 40%
BUSINESS: COSMETICS & HAIRDRESSING: Hairdressing

HAIRDRESSERS JOURNAL INTERNATIONAL
37262U15B-50

Editorial Address: Quadrant House, The Quadrant, SUTTON, SURREY, SM2 5AS **Tel:** 020 8652 3500
Fax: 020 8652 8937
Email: ruth.hunsley@rbi.co.uk
Advertising Address: As above. **Tel:** 020 8652 8273
Fax: 020 8652 3958
Email: jackie.h.mayes@rbi.co.uk
Web site: http://www.hji.co.uk
ISSN: 0143-6910
Publisher: Reed Business Information
Date Established: 1882
Frequency: Weekly
Cover Price: £2.25
Free to qualifying individuals
Annual Sub.: £90.00
Circulation: 13,340 (ABC 01/07/2008 to 30/06/2009)
Usual Pagination: 70
Editor: Ruth Hunsley; **News Editor:** Matthew Batham; **Editor-in-Chief:** Jayne Lewis-Orr; **Advertising Manager:** Jackie Mayes
Summary of Content: Journal containing industry related news, profiles and business advice, plus latest hair shots, techniques and products.
Readership/Target Audience: Aimed at hair salon partners, managers, stylists, juniors, trainees and students.
ADVERTISING RATES:
Full Page Colour £2127.00
Agency Commission: 10%
Mechanical Data: Col Length: 280mm, Type Area: 280 x 210mm, Bleed Size: 306 x 236mm, Trim Size: 300 x 230mm, Page Width: 210mm, Film: Digital
Copy instructions: Copy Date: 2 weeks prior to publication date
Supplement(s): Beauty - 1xY, Business Extra - 12xY, Extensions - 2xY, The Hair & Beauty Directory - 1xY, Interiors - 2xY, Retail Therapy - 2xY, Salon Catalogue - 1xY, Winning Collections - 1xY
BUSINESS: COSMETICS & HAIRDRESSING: Hairdressing

HALI
36450U7-220

Editorial Address: Studio 30, Liddell Road, LONDON, NW6 2EW **Tel:** 020 7578 7201 **Fax:** 020 7578 7222
Email: info@hali.com
Advertising Address: St. Giles House, 50 Poland Street, LONDON, W1F 7AX **Tel:** 020 7578 7209 **Fax:** 020 7578 7221
Email: david.young@centaur.co.uk

Web site: http://www.hali.com
ISSN: 0142-0789
Publisher: Hali Publications Ltd
Date Established: 1978
Frequency: Quarterly
Cover Price: £17.00
Annual Sub.: £92.00
Circulation: 5,000 (Publisher's Statement)
Usual Pagination: 180
Editor: Ben Evans; **Executive Editor:** Daniel Shaffer;
Publisher: Sebastian Ghandchi
Summary of Content: Magazine focusing on international carpet, textile and Islamic art.
Readership/Target Audience: Aimed at professional traders, academics, museum curators, collectors, amateur enthusiasts and designers.
ADVERTISING RATES:
Full Page Colour £1570.00
Mechanical Data: Type Area: 280 x 203mm, Col Length: 280mm, Bleed Size: 310 x 235mm, Trim Size: 300 x 225mm, Page Width: 203mm, Film: Digital
BUSINESS: ANTIQUES

HANDBOOK OF FEED ADDITIVES
37817U21B-400

Editorial Address: Rye House, 47 Oakfield Avenue, Somersall, CHESTERFIELD, S40 3LE **Tel:** 01246 569967
Fax: 01246 567932
Email: simon@simonmounsey.com
Web site: http://www.simonmounsey.com
ISSN: 0956-8220
Publisher: Simon Mounsey Ltd
Date Established: 1982
Frequency: Annual
Cover Price: £85.00
Circulation: 2,000 (Publisher's Statement)
Usual Pagination: 380
Editor: Simon Mounsey; **Managing Director:** Simon Mounsey
Summary of Content: Compendium of additives for inclusion in livestock feed and drinking water.
Readership/Target Audience: Aimed at animal feed manufacturers, veterinary surgeons, home-mixers, pharmaceutical companies, trading standards and environmental health officers.
ADVERTISING: No Advertising taken
BUSINESS: AGRICULTURE & FARMING: Agriculture - Supplies & Services

THE HANDBOOK OF WORLD STOCK DERIVATIVES & COMMODITY EXCHANGES
1777046U1L-89

Formerly: The World Stock, Commodity & Derivative Exchanges
Editorial Address: 3rd Floor, Baird House, 15-17 St. Cross Street, LONDON, EC1N 8UW **Tel:** 020 7404 1940
Fax: 020 7040 1942
Email: michael.bulmer@exchange-handbook.com
Web site: http://www.mondovisione.com
Publisher: Mondo Visione Ltd
Frequency: Annual - Published in June
Annual Sub.: £450.00
Circulation: 4,800 (Publisher's Statement)
Editor: Michael Bulmer
Summary of Content: Handbook covering equities, futures and options covering 265 exchanges in more than 120 countries.
Readership/Target Audience: Aimed at fund managers, traders on both buy or sell side, custodians and analysts, exchange professionals and a wide range of other roles throughout the banking community.
ADVERTISING: No Advertising taken
BUSINESS: FINANCE & ECONOMICS: Commodities

HANDLING & STORAGE SOLUTIONS
36529U10-48

Editorial Address: 33-35 Cantelupe Road, EAST GRINSTEAD, RH19 3BE **Tel:** 01342 314300
Fax: 01342 333700
Email: bcoyne@western-bp.co.uk
Advertising Address: As above. **Tel:** 01342 836275
Email: alyus@western-bp.co.uk
Web site: http://www.hsssearch.co.uk
ISSN: 1460-7344
Publisher: Western Business Publishing
Frequency: 6 issues yearly - Published at the end of the cover month
Free to qualifying individuals
Circulation: 18,079 (ABC 01/01/2008 to 31/12/2008)
Usual Pagination: 80
Editor: Brendan Coyne; **Managing Director:** Neill Western; **Publisher:** Neill Western
Summary of Content: Magazine covering products and services related to materials, handling, storage, conveying, packaging, health and safety and premises management.

Readership/Target Audience: Read by works operations managers, directors and warehouse and distribution managers.
ADVERTISING RATES:
Full Page Mono £1935.00
Full Page Colour £1935.00
SCC £70.00
Agency Commission: 10%
Mechanical Data: Film: Digital, Type Area: 287 x 200mm, Col Length: 287mm, Trim Size: 297 x 210mm, Bleed Size: 303 x 216mm, Page Width: 200mm, Col Widths (Display): 44mm, No. of Columns (Display): 4
Copy instructions: Copy Date: 2 weeks prior to publication date
Average advertising content per issue: 50%
Supplement(s): Lift Trucks - 1xY, Logistics and Distribution - 1xY, The Supply Chain - 1xY
BUSINESS: MATERIALS HANDLING

HAPPENINGS
40467U56L-14

Formerly: Foundation News
Editorial Address: Leatherhead Court, LEATHERHEAD, KT22 0BN **Tel:** 01372 841100 **Fax:** 01372 844657
Email: caroline.barratt@qef.org.uk
Web site: http://www.qef.org.uk
Publisher: Queen Elizabeth's Foundation for Disabled People
Frequency: Half-yearly - Published in spring and autumn
Cover Price: Free
Circulation: 22,000 (Publisher's Statement)
Usual Pagination: 6
Editor: Caroline Barratt
Summary of Content: Magazine covering the work of Queen Elizabeth's Foundation for Disabled People containing information of fundraising events and updates of new centres opening.
Readership/Target Audience: Aimed at sponsors and those that donate to the foundation.
ADVERTISING: No Advertising taken
BUSINESS: HEALTH & MEDICAL: Disability & Rehabilitation

THE HARBOURMASTER
39328U45A-43

Editorial Address: Maritime Centre, F5 Northney Marina, HAYLING ISLAND, PO11 0NH **Tel:** 023 9246 0111
Fax: 023 9246 0123
Email: editor.ihma@harbourmaster.org
Web site: http://www.harbourmaster.org
ISSN: 1470-7233
Publisher: International Harbour Masters' Association
Date Established: 1996
Frequency: Quarterly
Free to qualifying individuals
Circulation: 3,000 (Publisher's Statement)
Usual Pagination: 12
Editor: Peter Moth; **Publisher:** Peter Moth
Summary of Content: Official newsletter of the International Harbour Masters Association. Focuses on international maritime legislation and regulation, safety, security, IMO news, industry news, association news, port and harbour operations and management.
Readership/Target Audience: Aimed at harbour masters and senior port officials throughout the maritime world, in ports large and small, publicly and privately owned.
ADVERTISING: No Advertising taken
BUSINESS: MARINE & SHIPPING

HARDCOPY
1693235U5C-911

Editorial Address: 7 Unity Street, BRISTOL, BS1 5HH
Tel: 0117 930 0255
Email: dnj@mattmags.com
Advertising Address: Grey Matter, 2 Prigg Meadow, Ashburton, NEWTON ABBOT, TQ13 7DF **Tel:** 0870 366 5566
Fax: 01364 654200
Email: jona@greymatter.com
Web site: http://www.hardcopymag.com
Publisher: Matt Publishing
Frequency: Quarterly
Free to qualifying individuals
Circulation: 27,000 (Publisher's Statement)
Usual Pagination: 36
Editor: Matt Nicholson; **Advertising Manager:** Jon Anderson
Summary of Content: Grey Matter customer magazine that focuses on software development including product reviews.
Readership/Target Audience: Aimed at software professionals.
ADVERTISING RATES:
Full Page Colour £3200.00
Mechanical Data: Type Area: 287 x 200mm, Bleed Size: 303 x 216mm, Trim Size: 297 x 210mm, Col Length: 287mm, Page Width: 200mm, Film: Digital
Average advertising content per issue: 20%
BUSINESS: COMPUTERS & AUTOMATION: Professional Personal Computers

HARDWARE & GARDEN REVIEW
38093U25-30

Editorial Address: Faversham House, 232A Addington Road, SOUTH CROYDON, CR2 8LE **Tel:** 020 8651 7100
Fax: 020 8651 7117
Email: paul.fanning@fav-house.com
Advertising Address: As above.
Email: chrisc@fav-house.com
ISSN: 0266-0539
Publisher: Faversham House Group Ltd
Frequency: Quarterly
Free to qualifying individuals
Annual Sub.: £67.00
Circulation: 7,000 (ABC 01/01/2008 to 31/12/2008)
Usual Pagination: 20
Editor: Paul Fanning; **Advertising Manager:** Chris Carnevale
Summary of Content: Journal covering trade news, product innovations, business articles and features.
Readership/Target Audience: Aimed at independent retailers in the DIY and garden industry.
ADVERTISING RATES:
Full Page Colour £2095.00
Agency Commission: 10%
Mechanical Data: No. of Columns (Display): 4, Type Area: 270 x 180mm, Col Length: 270mm, Trim Size: 297 x 210mm, Bleed Size: 303 x 216mm, Film: Digital, Page Width: 180mm
Copy instructions: Copy Date: 14th of the month prior to publication date
Average advertising content per issue: 30%
Supplement(s): 120 Things You Need To Know - 1xY, Did You See at Glee? - 1xY, Did You See at the DIY & Garden Show? - 1xY, Hot Products - 1xY, Make the Most of Glee - 1xY, Make the Most of the DIY & Garden Show - 1xY, Sell More Gardening - 2xY, Top Shops - 1xY
BUSINESS: HARDWARE

HARDWARE TODAY
38094U25-37

Editorial Address: Entrance B, Level 1, Salamander Quay West, Park Lane, HAREFIELD, UB9 6NZ **Tel:** 0870 205 2924
Fax: 0870 205 2534
Email: hardwaretoday@indices.co.uk
Advertising Address: As above. **Fax:** 0870 205 2934
Email: kevintoole@indices.co.uk
Web site: http://www.indices.co.uk
Publisher: BHF Publishing
Frequency: Monthly - Published on the 1st of the cover month
Cover Price: Free
Circulation: 10,000 (Publisher's Statement)
Usual Pagination: 40
Editor: Michael Weedon; **Advertising Manager:** Kevin Toole
Summary of Content: Journal featuring news on the British Hardware Federation. Covers legal information, IT articles and developments within the industry.
Readership/Target Audience: Read by independent hardware and DIY retailers.
ADVERTISING RATES:
Full Page Mono £975.00
Full Page Colour £1495.00
SCC £10.00
Agency Commission: 10%
Mechanical Data: Film: Digital, Type Area: 264 x 190mm, Bleed Size: 303 x 213mm, Trim Size: 297 x 210mm, Col Length: 264mm, Page Width: 190mm
Copy instructions: Copy Date: 17th of the month prior to publication date
Average advertising content per issue: 40%
BUSINESS: HARDWARE

HARPERS WINE AND SPIRIT
36514U9C-90

Formerly: Harpers The Wine and Spirit Weekly
Editorial Address: Broadfield Park, CRAWLEY, RH11 9RT
Tel: 01293 613400
Email: richard.siddle@william-reed.co.uk
Advertising Address: As above. **Tel:** 01322 613400
Email: kevin.moore@harpers.co.uk
Web site: http://www.harpers.co.uk
ISSN: 1367-9082
Publisher: William Reed Business Media
Date Established: 1878
Frequency: 26 issues yearly - Published every 2nd Friday
Cover Price: £2.95
Annual Sub.: £115.00
Circulation: 5,000 (Publisher's Statement)
Usual Pagination: 52
Editor: Richard Siddle; **News Editor:** Eamonn Houston; **Managing Editor:** Claire Hu
Summary of Content: Journal containing news and information about the wine and spirit trade.
Readership/Target Audience: Aimed at multiple and specialist retailers, sommeliers, restaurateurs, hoteliers and those involved in the wine and spirit trade.
ADVERTISING RATES:
Full Page Colour £2830.00
Agency Commission: 10%
Mechanical Data: Type Area: 253 x 196mm, Col Length: 253mm, Page Width: 196mm, Bleed Size: 303 x 231mm, Trim Size: 297 x 225mm, Film: Digital

Section 4 (b) Business Magazines

Copy instructions: Copy Date: 1 week prior to publication date
Average advertising content per issue: 40%
BUSINESS: DRINKS & LICENSED TRADE: Licensed Trade, Wines & Spirits

---

HAZARDEX: THE JOURNAL   1655344U54R-332

Editorial Address: Blair House, 184-186 High Street, TONBRIDGE, TN9 1BQ **Tel:** 01732 359990
Fax: 01732 770049
Email: paul.gay@imlgroup.co.uk
Advertising Address: As above.
Email: russell.goater@imlgroup.co.uk
Web site: http://www.hazardexonthenet.net
ISSN: 1476-7376
Publisher: IML Group plc
Date Established: 2002
Frequency: 6 issues yearly - Published on the 1st of the cover month
Cover Price: £16.00
Free to qualifying individuals
Annual Sub.: £76.00
Circulation: 8,200 (Publisher's Statement)
Usual Pagination: 52
Editor: Paul Gay; **Advertising Manager:** Russell Goater
Summary of Content: Journal focusing on the issues affecting the safe installation and operation of plant and equipment within potentially explosive atmospheres.
Readership/Target Audience: Aimed at engineering managers and safety officers responsible for their company's hazardous areas.
ADVERTISING RATES:
Full Page Colour £1838.00
Agency Commission: 10%
Mechanical Data: Type Area: 254 x 178mm, Bleed Size: 286 x 208mm, Trim Size: 280 x 205mm, Col Length: 254mm, Page Width: 178mm, Film: Digital
Copy instructions: Copy Date: 6 weeks prior to publication date
Average advertising content per issue: 50%
BUSINESS: SAFETY & SECURITY: Safety Related

HAZARDOUS AREA INTERNATIONAL   1775697U54R-335

Editorial Address: Blair House, 184-186 High Street, TONBRIDGE, TN9 1BQ **Tel:** 01732 359990
Fax: 01732 770049
Email: paul.gay@imlgroup.co.uk
Advertising Address: As above.
Email: lee.cashman@imlgroup.co.uk
Web site: http://www.hazardexonthenet.net
ISSN: 1751-780X
Publisher: IML Group plc
Date Established: 2006
Frequency: Quarterly - Published in the middle of the 1st cover month
Free to qualifying individuals
Annual Sub.: £151.00
Circulation: 25,707 (Publisher's Statement)
Editor: Paul Gay
Summary of Content: Journal focusing on the issues affecting the safe installation and operation of plant and equipment within potentially explosive atmospheres includes coverage of international legislation.
Readership/Target Audience: Aimed at engineering managers and safety officers responsible for their companies' hazardous areas.
ADVERTISING RATES:
Full Page Colour £1800.00
Mechanical Data: Type Area: 254 x 178mm, Bleed Size: 286 x 208mm, Trim Size: 280 x 205mm, Col Length: 254mm, Page Width: 178mm, Film: Digital
Copy instructions: Copy Date: 6 weeks prior to publication date
BUSINESS: SAFETY & SECURITY: Safety Related

HAZARDOUS CARGO BULLETIN   39641U49C-95

Editorial Address: Informa House, 30-32 Mortimer Street, LONDON, W1W 7RE **Tel:** 020 7017 5000
Fax: 020 7017 4592
Email: peter.mackay@informa.com
Advertising Address: Telephone House, 69-77 Paul Street, LONDON, EC2A 4LQ **Tel:** 020 7017 4374
Fax: 020 7017 4592
Email: kalpesh.patel@informa.com
Web site: http://www.hazardouscargo.com
ISSN: 0143-6864
Publisher: Informa Cargo Information
Date Established: 1980
Frequency: Monthly - Published on the 12th of the cover month
Annual Sub.: £229.00
Circulation: 7,000 (Publisher's Statement)
Usual Pagination: 80
Editor: Peter Mackay; **Managing Editor:** Peter Mackay

Summary of Content: International journal dealing with the handling, storage and transport of hazardous materials by all modes.
Readership/Target Audience: Read by shippers and carriers of hazardous materials, regulatory authorities and safety experts.
ADVERTISING RATES:
Full Page Colour EUR3700.00
Agency Commission: 10%
Mechanical Data: Page Width: 180mm, Col Length: 254mm, Type Area: 254 x 180mm, Bleed Size: 279 x 214mm, Trim Size: 273 x 208mm, Film: Digital
Copy instructions: Copy Date: 1 week prior to publication date
Average advertising content per issue: 20%
BUSINESS: TRANSPORT: Freight

HAZARDS   39865U54B-33

Editorial Address: PO Box 4042, Kent Road, SHEFFIELD, S8 9RL **Tel:** 0114 201 4265
Email: editor@hazards.org
Advertising Address: As above.
Email: sub@hazards.org
Web site: http://www.hazards.org
ISSN: 0267-7296
Publisher: Hazards Publications Ltd
Frequency: Quarterly
Annual Sub.: £28.00
Circulation: 8,500 (Publisher's Statement)
Usual Pagination: 36
Editor: Rory O'Neill; **Advertising Manager:** Jawad Qasrawi
Summary of Content: Magazine focusing on workplace health and safety.
Readership/Target Audience: Aimed at trade union safety representatives.
ADVERTISING RATES:
Full Page Mono £850.00
Copy instructions: Copy Date: 8 weeks prior to publication date
Average advertising content per issue: 10%
BUSINESS: SAFETY & SECURITY: Safety

HB HEALTH BUSINESS   765004U56R-502

Editorial Address: 226 High Road, LOUGHTON, IG10 1ET
Tel: 020 8532 0055 **Fax:** 020 8532 0066
Email: editor@psp-media.com
Advertising Address: As above. **Fax:** 020 8502 3830
Email: benita@healthbusinessuk.com
Web site: http://www.healthbusinessuk.com
Publisher: Public Sector Publishing Ltd
Frequency: 6 issues yearly
Free to qualifying individuals
Annual Sub.: £45.00
Circulation: 6,500 (Publisher's Statement)
Usual Pagination: 88
Editor: Sofie Lidefjard; **Advertising Manager:** Benita Lester; **Publisher:** Benita Lester
Summary of Content: Magazine covering health sector management.
Readership/Target Audience: Aimed at decision makers within the primary care trusts and healthcare establishments.
ADVERTISING RATES:
Full Page Colour £2200.00
Mechanical Data: Trim Size: 297 x 210mm, Film: Digital
BUSINESS: HEALTH & MEDICAL: Health Medical Related

HCD   1639087U43D-103

Formerly: Home Cinema Digest
Editorial Address: BCM Compulsion, LONDON, WC1N 3XX
Tel: 0870 011 8168 **Fax:** 0870 011 8168
Email: jamie@hcdmag.com
Advertising Address: As above.
Email: theresa@hcdmag.com
Web site: http://www.hcdmag.com
Publisher: Compulsion Media
Date Established: 2003
Frequency: 10 issues yearly
Cover Price: Free
Usual Pagination: 56
Editor: Jamie Carter; **Managing Director:** Janis Brealey; **Advertising Manager:** Theresa Jackaman; **Publisher:** Rob Lane
Summary of Content: Magazine covering the home cinema trade.
Readership/Target Audience: Aimed at AV dealers and installers, AV manufacturers, relevant architects and designers, newspapers and related consumer publications.
ADVERTISING: Rates on application
BUSINESS: ELECTRICAL RETAIL TRADE: Video

HEADLINES   35609U2B-53

Editorial Address: 8 Sovereign Park, Cleveland Way, HEMEL HEMPSTEAD, HP2 7DA **Tel:** 01442 233656
Fax: 01442 258853
Email: gary@cullumpublishing.co.uk

Advertising Address: As above.
Email: gary@cullumpublishing.co.uk
Web site: http://www.newstech.co.uk
ISSN: 0954-9021
Publisher: Cullum Publishing
Date Established: 1988
Frequency: 6 issues yearly - Published in the 1st week of the month
Annual Sub.: £25.00
Circulation: 3,000 (Publisher's Statement)
Editor: Gary Cullum; **Advertising Manager:** Gary Cullum; **Publisher:** Gary Cullum
Summary of Content: Magazine focusing on the marketing of regional newspapers. Each issue profiles key figures in the industry and covers news of Newspaper Society Award winners and new media developments.
Readership/Target Audience: Read by advertising agency executives, company marketing directors, regional newspaper publishers and editors.
ADVERTISING RATES:
Full Page Colour £900.00
Agency Commission: 10%
Mechanical Data: Type Area: 320 x 270mm, Bleed Size: 350 x 300mm, Trim Size: 340 x 290mm, Film: Digital, Col Length: 320mm, Page Width: 270mm
Average advertising content per issue: 25%
BUSINESS: COMMUNICATIONS, ADVERTISING & MARKETING: Press

HEADTEACHER UPDATE   41181U62J-1103

Formerly: Teacher Update
Editorial Address: Unit 1, Crumplin's Business Court, Odiham, HAMPSHIRE, RG29 1DU **Tel:** 01256 704288
Fax: 01256 703447
Email: pclarke@rapportlearning.com
Advertising Address: As above.
Email: kevin@rapportlearning.com
Web site: http://www.rapportgroup.com
ISSN: 1478-5307
Publisher: Rapport Learning Ltd
Date Established: 2001
Frequency: 6 issues yearly
Free to qualifying individuals
Annual Sub.: £48.00
Circulation: 25,000 (Publisher's Statement)
Usual Pagination: 36
Editor: Peter Clarke; **Advertising Manager:** Kevin North
Summary of Content: Magazine containing management and leadership issues including information on products and resources.
Readership/Target Audience: Aimed at UK primary school head teachers with responsibility for purchasing resources.
ADVERTISING RATES:
Full Page Mono £3410.00
Full Page Colour £3850.00
Agency Commission: 10%
Mechanical Data: Bleed Size: 303 x 216mm, Trim Size: 297 x 210mm, Film: Digital, Type Area: 267 x 186mm, Col Length: 267mm, Page Width: 186mm, Col Widths (Display): 43.5mm, No. of Columns (Display): 4
Average advertising content per issue: 40%
BUSINESS: CHURCH & SCHOOL EQUIPMENT & EDUCATION: Teachers & Education Management

---

THE HEALING HAND   40585U56R-57_80

Editorial Address: 7 Washington Lane, EDINBURGH, EH11 2HA **Tel:** 0131 313 3828 **Fax:** 0131 313 4662
Email: info@emms.org
Web site: http://www.emms.org
ISSN: 0017-8829
Publisher: EMMS International
Date Established: 1943
Frequency: 3 issues yearly - Published in March, July and November
Cover Price: £1.00
Free to qualifying individuals
Circulation: 5,000 (Publisher's Statement)
Usual Pagination: 12
Editor: James Wells
Summary of Content: Reports and articles on medical mission and the work of the EMMS International.
Readership/Target Audience: Aimed at supporters of the society and those interested in medical mission.
ADVERTISING: No Advertising taken
BUSINESS: HEALTH & MEDICAL: Health Medical Related

HEALTH   40273U56A-66_50

Editorial Address: 1 Oliver's Yard, 55 City Road, LONDON, EC1Y 1SP **Tel:** 020 7324 8500 **Fax:** 020 7324 8600
Advertising Address: As above.
Email: sheena.karim@sagepub.co.uk
Web site: http://www.sagepub.co.uk
ISSN: 1363-4593
Publisher: Sage Publications
Date Established: 1997
Frequency: Quarterly

Cover Price: £15.00
Annual Sub.: £45.00
Usual Pagination: 128
Editor: Michael Traynor; **Advertising Manager:** Sheena Karim
Summary of Content: A broad ranging interdisciplinary journal related to health and social science, focusing on the changing place of health matters in modern society. The journal provides an international forum for original articles and review essays from around the world.
Readership/Target Audience: Aimed at academic and applied social scientists working in the field of health.
ADVERTISING RATES:
Full Page Mono £400.00
Agency Commission: 5%
Mechanical Data: Film: Digital, Page Width: 114mm, Type Area: 200 x 130mm, Col Length: 189mm
BUSINESS: HEALTH & MEDICAL

HEALTH & BEAUTY SALON
37269U15R-10
Editorial Address: Quadrant House, The Quadrant, SUTTON, SM2 5AS **Tel:** 020 8652 3500 **Fax:** 020 8652 8937
Email: moira.paulusz@rbi.co.uk
Advertising Address: As above. **Fax:** 020 8652 3958
Email: steve.james@rbi.co.uk
Web site: http://www.healthandbeautysalon.uk.com
ISSN: 0261-4146
Publisher: Reed Business Information
Frequency: Monthly - Published in the third week of the month prior to the cover date
Annual Sub.: £45.00
Circulation: 12,702 (ABC 01/07/2008 to 30/06/2009)
Usual Pagination: 100
Editor: Moira Paulusz; **Editor-in-Chief:** Jayne Lewis-Orr; **Publisher:** Jayne Lewis-Orr
Summary of Content: Magazine providing news and information from the beauty, spa and nail industry. Contains features on innovative treatments, new techniques, men's health and alternative therapies. Also offering advice on salon management with promotional and marketing ideas, plus employment issues.
Readership/Target Audience: Aimed at beauty therapists, salon owners and suppliers.
ADVERTISING RATES:
Full Page Colour £1930.00
Agency Commission: 10%
Mechanical Data: Page Width: 210mm, Film: Digital, Type Area: 290 x 210mm, Col Length: 290mm, Trim Size: 296 x 216mm
Copy instructions: Copy Date: 4 weeks prior to publication date
BUSINESS: COSMETICS & HAIRDRESSING: Cosmetics & Hairdressing Related

HEALTH & HYGIENE
40421U56F-60
Editorial Address: 28 Portland Place, LONDON, W1B 1DE
Tel: 020 7291 8358 **Fax:** 020 7580 6157
Email: health.hygiene@riph.org.uk
Advertising Address: As above. **Tel:** 020 7580 2731
Email: health.hygiene@riph.org.uk
Web site: http://www.riph.org.uk
ISSN: 0140-2986
Publisher: The Royal Institute of Public Health
Date Established: 1977
Frequency: 3 issues yearly
Free to qualifying individuals
Annual Sub.: £50.00
Circulation: 2,500 (Publisher's Statement)
Usual Pagination: 20
Editor: Nicole Seeff; **Advertising Manager:** Nicole Seeff
Summary of Content: Journal covering all aspects of public health, food safety and hygiene, home hygiene and nutrition.
Readership/Target Audience: Read by food hygienists and safety specialists, nutritionists, public health professionals and all members of The Royal Institute of Public Health.
ADVERTISING RATES:
Full Page Colour £450.00
Mechanical Data: Bleed Size: 303 x 216mm, Trim Size: 297 x 210mm, Film: Positive, right reading, emulsion side down. Digital
Average advertising content per issue: 5%
BUSINESS: HEALTH & MEDICAL: Health Education

HEALTH AND SAFETY AT WORK
39868U54B-45
Editorial Address: 2 Addiscombe Road, CROYDON, CR9 5AF **Tel:** 020 8686 9141 **Fax:** 020 8212 1910
Email: hsw@lexisnexis.co.uk
Advertising Address: As above. **Tel:** 020 8212 1995
Fax: 020 8212 1970
Email: laura.thompson@lexisnexis.co.uk
Web site: http://www.healthandsafetyprofessional.co.uk
ISSN: 0141-8246
Publisher: LexisNexis UK
Date Established: 1978
Frequency: Monthly - Published on the 15th of the cover month
Cover Price: £8.25

Annual Sub.: £110.00
Circulation: 23,051 (ABC 01/01/2008 to 31/12/2008)
Usual Pagination: 48
Editor: Louis Wustemann
Summary of Content: Magazine containing coverage of occupational health and safety in all public and private sectors, including working environment matters in the UK and Europe.
Readership/Target Audience: Read by health and safety managers, consultants, safety representatives and facilities/environment managers.
ADVERTISING RATES:
Full Page Mono £1505.00
Full Page Colour £2025.00
Agency Commission: 10%
Mechanical Data: Page Width: 200mm, Type Area: 270 x 200mm, Col Length: 270mm, Bleed Size: 303 x 231mm, Trim Size: 297 x 225mm, Film: Digital
Copy instructions: Copy Date: 1st of the publication month
Average advertising content per issue: 30%
Supplement(s): Construction - 1xY, Personal Protective Equipment - 1xY, Training - 2xY, Work at Height - 1xY
BUSINESS: SAFETY & SECURITY: Safety

HEALTH & SAFETY AT WORK ACT NEWSLETTER
39869U54B-47
Editorial Address: 70 Chancellors Road, LONDON, W6 9RS
Tel: 020 8741 1231 **Fax:** 020 8741 0835
Email: publications@britsafe.org
Web site: http://www.britishsafetycouncil.org
Publisher: British Safety Council
Frequency: Monthly
Annual Sub.: £200.00
Circulation: 1,000 (Publisher's Statement)
Usual Pagination: 12
Editor: Brian Shillibeer
Summary of Content: Newsletter providing a summary of safety directives and legislation.
Readership/Target Audience: Aimed at directors, managers and anyone with responsibility for workplace health and safety.
ADVERTISING: No Advertising taken
BUSINESS: SAFETY & SECURITY: Safety

HEALTH AND SAFETY AT WORK NEWSLETTER
39870U54B-48
Editorial Address: Maxwelton House, 41-43 Boltro Road, HAYWARDS HEATH, RH16 1BJ **Tel:** 01444 416119
Fax: 01444 440426
ISSN: 1464-1569
Publisher: Tottel Publishing
Date Established: 1993
Frequency: 6 issues yearly
Usual Pagination: 8
Editor: Linda Whittle
Summary of Content: Business newsletter containing coverage of legal developments.
Readership/Target Audience: Aimed at safety professionals.
ADVERTISING: No Advertising taken
BUSINESS: SAFETY & SECURITY: Safety

HEALTH AND SAFETY INTERNATIONAL
1604979U54B-98
Editorial Address: 1st Floor, Suite One, St. Albans Chambers, 15-16 St. Alban Street, WEYMOUTH, DT4 8PY
Tel: 01305 785199 **Fax:** 01305 772722
Email: info@bay-publishing.com
Advertising Address: As above.
Email: nick@bay-publishing.com
Web site: http://www.hsimagazine.com
ISSN: 1478-8829
Publisher: Bay Publishing Ltd
Date Established: 2002
Frequency: Quarterly - Published in the 2nd week of the cover month
Annual Sub.: £65.00
Circulation: 10,725 (ABC 01/07/2008 to 31/12/2008)
Usual Pagination: 84
Editor: Nigel Fellows; **Advertising Manager:** Nick Limm; **Publisher:** Nigel Fellows
Summary of Content: Magazine covering news, views and product information relating to safe working practices and employee health and safety.
Readership/Target Audience: Aimed at health and safety directors and managers.
ADVERTISING RATES:
Full Page Colour £2700.00
Agency Commission: 10%
Mechanical Data: Type Area: 270 x 180mm, Col Length: 270mm, Bleed Size: 303 x 216mm, Trim Size: 297 x 210mm, Film: Digital, Page Width: 180mm
Average advertising content per issue: 40%
BUSINESS: SAFETY & SECURITY: Safety

HEALTH & SAFETY MATTERS
626070U54B-37
Editorial Address: 33-35 Cantelupe Road, EAST GRINSTEAD, RH19 3BE **Tel:** 01342 314300
Fax: 01342 333700
Email: gbisby@western-bp.co.uk
Advertising Address: As above.
Email: swood@western-bp.co.uk
Web site: http://www.hsmsearch.co.uk
ISSN: 1471-0463
Publisher: Western Business Publishing
Date Established: 2000
Frequency: 6 issues yearly - Published the Monday of the 2nd week of the cover month
Free to qualifying individuals
Circulation: 18,024 (ABC 01/01/2008 to 31/12/2008)
Usual Pagination: 72
Editor: Georgina Bisby
Summary of Content: Magazine containing product news and features on all matters relating to health and safety in the industrial manufacturing work place.
Readership/Target Audience: Aimed at those with specific health and safety responsibility such as health and safety managers and those who find health and safety part of their overall responsibility.
ADVERTISING RATES:
Full Page Colour £1950.00
Agency Commission: 10%
Mechanical Data: Type Area: 287 x 200mm, Film: Digital, Bleed Size: +3mm, Trim Size: 297 x 210mm, Col Length: 287mm, Page Width: 200mm
Copy instructions: Copy Date: Last week of the month prior to publication date
Average advertising content per issue: 50%
BUSINESS: SAFETY & SECURITY: Safety

HEALTH AND SAFETY NEWSLETTER
1779667U54B-111
Editorial Address: The Health and Safety Executive, 5N.1 Redgrave Court, Merton Road, BOOTLE, L20 7HS
Tel: 0151 951 3450
Email: newsletter@hse.gsi.gov.uk
Web site: http://www.hse.gov.uk
Publisher: HSE Books
Frequency: 6 issues yearly
Free to qualifying individuals
Annual Sub.: £20.00
Circulation: 12,000 (Publisher's Statement)
Usual Pagination: 16
Editor: Colette Manning
Summary of Content: Newsletter covering news, issues and features pertinent to Health and Safety.
Readership/Target Audience: Aimed at small to medium sized businesses, health and safety professionals and local authorities.
ADVERTISING: No Advertising taken
BUSINESS: SAFETY & SECURITY: Safety

HEALTH & SAFETY SPECIFIER
39867U54B-97_53
Formerly: Safety Specifier
Editorial Address: 32 Portland Street, CHELTENHAM, GL52 2PE **Tel:** 01242 236336 **Fax:** 01242 222331
Email: specifier@btconnect.com
Advertising Address: As above.
Email: specifier@btconnect.com
Publisher: Specifier Publishing
Date Established: 1975
Frequency: 6 issues yearly - Published at the end of the 1st week of the 2nd cover month
Cover Price: £5.00
Annual Sub.: £30.00
Circulation: 14,000 (Publisher's Statement)
Usual Pagination: 32
Editor: Linda Brindley; **Features Editor:** Linda Brindley; **Advertising Manager:** David Constantine; **Publisher:** David Constantine
Summary of Content: Magazine covering health and safety in the industrial market place, commercial and public sectors.
Readership/Target Audience: Aimed at local authorities, local government departments, manufacturing and service sectors.
ADVERTISING RATES:
Full Page Mono £650.00
Full Page Colour £950.00
SCC £95.00
Mechanical Data: Type Area: 277 x 190mm, Bleed Size: 303 x 216mm, Trim Size: 297 x 210mm, Col Widths (Display): 45mm, No. of Columns (Display): 4, Print Process: Litho, Film: Digital, Col Length: 277mm, Page Width: 190mm
BUSINESS: SAFETY & SECURITY: Safety

HEALTH CARE RISK REPORT
40352U56C-205
Editorial Address: 3 The Green, RICHMOND, TW9 1PL
Tel: 020 8334 4500 **Fax:** 020 8332 7201
Email: pat@leonarda.co.uk

Web site: http://www.healthcareriskreport.com
ISSN: 1356-0611
Publisher: IRS
Date Established: 1994
Frequency: 10 issues yearly
Annual Sub.: £398.00
Usual Pagination: 24
Editor: Pat Anderson
Summary of Content: Magazine covering developments in medical negligence, clinical risk management and governance, and litigation in the NHS.
Readership/Target Audience: Aimed at senior health service risk managers.
ADVERTISING: No Advertising taken
BUSINESS: HEALTH & MEDICAL: Hospitals

HEALTH CARE UPDATE FOR EASTERN & CENTRAL EUROPE
40170U56A-66_55

Editorial Address: Sahara House, 38 Greyhound Road, LONDON, W6 8NX **Tel:** 020 7610 1387 **Fax:** 020 7610 0078
Email: sahara@btconnect.com
Advertising Address: As above.
Email: sahara@btconnect.com
Web site: http://www.saharapublications.com
Publisher: Sahara Publications
Date Established: 1991
Frequency: Quarterly
Cover Price: Free
Usual Pagination: 48
Editor: M. Butros; **Managing Director:** Abed Najjar;
Advertising Manager: Thomas Eros; **Publisher:** Abed Najjar
Summary of Content: Magazine featuring articles about the latest product developments within the healthcare industry in Eastern Europe.
Readership/Target Audience: Aimed at doctors, surgeons and consultants in hospitals, universities, medical training institutions in Central and Eastern Europe.
ADVERTISING RATES:
Full Page Mono £995.00
Full Page Colour £1495.00
Agency Commission: 10%
Mechanical Data: Print Process: Offset litho, Bleed Size: 309 x 216mm, Trim Size: 297 x 210mm, No. of Columns (Display): 3, Film: Digital
Average advertising content per issue: 40%
BUSINESS: HEALTH & MEDICAL

HEALTH CLUB MANAGEMENT
38531U32H-140

Editorial Address: Portmill House, Portmill Lane, HITCHIN, SG5 1DJ **Tel:** 01462 431385 **Fax:** 01462 433909
Email: healthclub@leisuremedia.com
Advertising Address: As above.
Email: displaysales@leisuremedia.com
Web site: http://www.health-club.co.uk
ISSN: 1361-3510
Publisher: The Leisure Media Company Ltd
Date Established: 1995
Frequency: 11 issues yearly - Published at the beginning of the cover month
Annual Sub.: £36.00
Circulation: 9,000 (Publisher's Statement)
Usual Pagination: 84
Editor: Kate Cracknell; **News Editor:** Tom Walker;
Advertising Manager: Jan Williams; **Publisher:** Jan Williams
Summary of Content: Magazine covering all aspects of health and fitness affecting the owner, operator, developer or manager of a private or public facility.
Language(s): English; German
Readership/Target Audience: Aimed at middle and senior management and professionals in health and fitness throughout the UK and Europe.
ADVERTISING RATES:
Full Page Colour £1680.00
Agency Commission: 10%
Mechanical Data: Type Area: 260 x 172mm, Col Length: 260mm, Trim Size: 297 x 210mm, Bleed Size: 303 x 213mm, Page Width: 172mm
Copy instructions: Copy Date: 19th of the month prior to publication date
Average advertising content per issue: 40%
Supplement(s): Health Club World - 2xY
BUSINESS: LOCAL GOVERNMENT, LEISURE & RECREATION: Leisure, Recreation & Entertainment

---

HEALTH DIRECTOR
1615361U56R-507

Editorial Address: 4th Floor, St. James's Building, Oxford Street, MANCHESTER, M1 6PP **Tel:** 0161 211 3000
Fax: 0161 211 3008
Email: editorial@govnet.co.uk
Advertising Address: Golden Cross House, 8 Duncannon Street, LONDON, WC2N 4JF **Tel:** 020 7484 5085
Fax: 020 7484 4950
Email: richard.holloway@govnet.co.uk
Web site: http://www.govnet.co.uk
Publisher: GovNet Communications

Date Established: 2002
Frequency: 6 issues yearly
Free to qualifying individuals
Circulation: 7,422 (ABC 01/01/2008 to 31/12/2008)
Usual Pagination: 78
Editor: Natalie Quinn
Summary of Content: Magazine covering healthcare provision and high level policy and strategic decision making.
Readership/Target Audience: Aimed at directors and managers involved in health care provision and policy and decision making throughout the NHS and healthcare sector as well as organisations operating or supplying the public service area.
ADVERTISING RATES:
Full Page Mono £3595.00
Full Page Colour £3595.00
Agency Commission: 10%
Mechanical Data: Type Area: 272 x 205mm, Bleed Size: 298 x 231mm, Col Length: 272mm, Page Width: 205mm, Film: Digital
Copy instructions: Copy Date: 2 weeks prior to publication date
Average advertising content per issue: 40%
BUSINESS: HEALTH & MEDICAL: Health Medical Related

HEALTH EDUCATION
40419U56F-68

Editorial Address: Howard House, Wagon Lane, BINGLEY, BD16 1WA **Tel:** 01274 777700 **Fax:** 01274 785200
Email: jbennett@emeraldinsight.com
Web site: http://www.emeraldinsight.com/he.htm
ISSN: 0965-4283
Publisher: Emerald Group Publishing Ltd
Date Established: 1971
Frequency: 6 issues yearly
Annual Sub.: £1499.00
Usual Pagination: 76
Editor: Katherine Weare; **Publisher:** Kelly Dutton
Summary of Content: Journal focusing on all aspects of health awareness and education.
Readership/Target Audience: Aimed at personnel in hospitals, health authorities, local government, education authorities, medical centres, schools and family health centres.
ADVERTISING: No Advertising taken
BUSINESS: HEALTH & MEDICAL: Health Education

THE HEALTH EDUCATION JOURNAL
40420U56F-70

Editorial Address: 1 Oliver's Yard, 55 City Road, LONDON, EC1Y 1SP **Tel:** 020 7324 8500
Email: ablinkhorn@usyd.edu.au
Advertising Address: School of Dentistry, University of Manchester, Higher Cambridge Street, MANCHESTER, M15 6FH **Tel:** 0161 275 6610 **Fax:** 0161 275 6299
Web site: http://www.sagepub.com/journalsProdDesc.nav?prodId=Journal201777
ISSN: 0017-8969
Publisher: Sage Publications
Frequency: Quarterly
Annual Sub.: £47.00
Circulation: 2,200 (Publisher's Statement)
Editor: Anthony Blinkhorn; **Advertising Manager:** Anthony Blinkhorn; **Managing Editor:** Maggie Palmer
Summary of Content: Journal that covers a wide range of subjects of interest to people with a professional involvement in health promotion, research and practice.
Readership/Target Audience: Aimed at those with an interest in public health improvement including health authorities and professionals working in the NHS and research.
ADVERTISING: Rates on application
BUSINESS: HEALTH & MEDICAL: Health Education

HEALTH EDUCATION RESEARCH
24722U56A-66_56

Formerly: Health Education Research: Theory and Practice
Editorial Address: 42 Moseley Wood Lane, LEEDS, LS16 7EP **Tel:** 01865 353907 **Fax:** 01865 353985
Advertising Address: Great Clarendon Street, OXFORD, OX2 6DP **Tel:** 01865 353329 **Fax:** 01865 353774
Email: elisabetta.sheffield@oxfordjournals.org
Web site: http://www.oup.co.uk/jnls
ISSN: 0268-1153
Publisher: OUP
Date Established: 1986
Frequency: 6 issues yearly
Cover Price: £21.00
Annual Sub.: £108.00
Usual Pagination: 128
Summary of Content: Journal promoting understanding of the processes, rationale and philosophy underlying the work of health educators in the international forum.
Readership/Target Audience: Aimed at those interested in health education and promotion worldwide.

ADVERTISING RATES:
Full Page Mono £646.00
Agency Commission: 10%
Mechanical Data: Type Area: 203 x 150mm, Bleed Size: 252 x 195mm, Trim Size: 246 x 189mm, Col Length: 203mm, Print Process: Litho, Film: Digital, Page Width: 150mm
Copy instructions: Copy Date: 8 weeks prior to publication date
BUSINESS: HEALTH & MEDICAL

HEALTH ESTATE JOURNAL
40438U56H-20

Editorial Address: Step House, North Farm Road, TUNBRIDGE WELLS, TN2 3DR **Tel:** 01892 518877
Fax: 01892 616177
Email: nicholasmarshall@stepcomms.com
Advertising Address: As above.
Email: waynebanks@stepex.com
Web site: http://www.healthestatejournal.com
ISSN: 0957-7742
Publisher: Step Communications Ltd
Frequency: 10 issues yearly
Annual Sub.: £72.00
Circulation: 4,387 (Publisher's Statement)
Editor: Nicholas Marshall; **Advertising Manager:** Wayne Banks; **Managing Editor:** Nicholas Marshall; **Publisher:** Trevor Moon
Summary of Content: The Journal of the Institute of Healthcare Engineering and Estate Management, providing information on the latest technical advances and current issues affecting the health estate.
Readership/Target Audience: Aimed at estate directors, managers, healthcare engineers, private consultants, architects and construction companies.
ADVERTISING RATES:
Full Page Colour £1610.00
SCC £31.69
Agency Commission: 10%
Mechanical Data: Trim Size: 297 x 210mm, Print Process: Sheet-fed offset litho, Film: Digital, Page Width: 180mm, Col Length: 254mm, No. of Columns (Display): 2, Type Area: 254 x 180mm
Copy instructions: Copy Date: 17th of the month prior to publication date
Average advertising content per issue: 35%
BUSINESS: HEALTH & MEDICAL: Medical Engineering Technology

HEALTH FOOD BUSINESS
38031U22F-20

Editorial Address: The Old Dairy, Hudsons Farm, Fieldgate Lane, Ugley Green, BISHOP'S STORTFORD, CM22 6HJ **Tel:** 01279 816300 **Fax:** 01279 816496
Email: rachel.symonds@targetpublishing.com
Advertising Address: As above.
Email: ruth.dodsley@targetpublishing.com
Web site: http://www.healthfoodbusiness.co.uk
Publisher: Target Publishing Ltd
Date Established: 1985
Frequency: Monthly - Published around the 20th of the month prior to publication date
Free to qualifying individuals
Annual Sub.: £54.00
Circulation: 3,205 (Publisher's Statement)
Usual Pagination: 52
Editor: Rachel Symonds; **Managing Director:** David Cann
Summary of Content: UK trade magazine for the independent natural health market providing information and advice on matters relating to alternative and complimentary health markets, such as legislation, new products, market analysis, training & education and retailing for natural health food products.
Readership/Target Audience: Read by retail buyers and employees of independent health food stores, multiple health chains, specialist chemists, wholesalers and manufacturers.
ADVERTISING RATES:
Full Page Colour £2445.00
Agency Commission: 10%
Mechanical Data: Type Area: 268 x 180mm, Bleed Size: 303 x 216mm, Trim Size: 297 x 210mm, Col Length: 268mm, Page Width: 180mm
Copy instructions: Copy Date: 3 weeks prior to publication date
Average advertising content per issue: 40%
BUSINESS: FOOD: Health Food

HEALTH INFORMATION AND LIBRARIES JOURNAL
40859U60B-17

Formerly: Health Libraries Review
Editorial Address: 9600 Garsington Road, Cowley, OXFORD, OX4 2DQ **Tel:** 01865 476540 **Fax:** 01865 471540
Email: dhollings@wiley.com
Advertising Address: As above. **Tel:** 01865 476271
Fax: 01865 471271
Email: joanna.baker@oxon.blackwellpublishing.com
Web site: http://www.blackwellpublishing.com
ISSN: 0265-6647
Publisher: Wiley-Blackwell Publishing

Frequency: Quarterly
Circulation: 800 (Publisher's Statement)
Usual Pagination: 80
Editor: Danielle Hollings
Summary of Content: Official journal of the Health Libraries Group of the Chartered Institute of Library and Information Professionals. Covers news, ideas, articles on current practice and new developments. Includes book reviews and reports of meetings.
Readership/Target Audience: Read by medical, health and welfare librarians and information managers.
ADVERTISING RATES:
Full Page Mono £550.00
Full Page Colour £950.00
Agency Commission: 10%
Mechanical Data: Type Area: 230 x 170mm, Col Length: 230mm, Film: Digital, Trim Size: 276 x 210mm, Page Width: 170mm
Copy instructions: Copy Date: 6 weeks prior to publication date
BUSINESS: PUBLISHING: Libraries

HEALTH INSURANCE & PROTECTION
35124U1D-134

Formerly: Health Insurance
Editorial Address: Telephone House, 69-77 Paul Street, LONDON, EC2A 4LQ **Tel:** 020 7017 5000
Fax: 020 7017 4194
Email: news@hi-mag.com
Advertising Address: Informa House, 30-32 Mortimer Street, LONDON, W1W 7RE **Tel:** 020 7017 4000
Fax: 020 7017 4194
Email: matt.dias@informa.com
Web site: http://www.hi-mag.com
Publisher: Informa PLC
Date Established: 1997
Frequency: Monthly
Free to qualifying individuals
Annual Sub.: £205.00
Circulation: 10,003 (ABC 01/07/2008 to 30/06/2009)
Usual Pagination: 40
Editor: David Sawers; **Advertising Manager:** Matt Dias
Summary of Content: Magazine covering all aspects of healthcare insurance.
Readership/Target Audience: Aimed at the professional intermediary.
ADVERTISING RATES:
Full Page Colour £6566.00
Agency Commission: 10%
Mechanical Data: Type Area: 265 x 190mm, Bleed Size: 303 x 216mm, Trim Size: 297 x 210mm, Col Length: 265mm, Film: Digital, Page Width: 190mm
Copy instructions: Copy Date: 3 weeks prior to publication date
Average advertising content per issue: 35%
BUSINESS: FINANCE & ECONOMICS: Insurance

HEALTH MANAGEMENT
40171U56A-66_59

Editorial Address: 17 Eaton Road, Rocester, UTTOXETER, ST14 5LL
Email: vicky.burman@ashridgecommunications.com
Advertising Address: Berkhamsted House, 121 High Street, BERKHAMSTED, HP4 2DJ **Tel:** 01753 714999
Email: mark.wilkins@ashridgecommunications.com
Web site: http://www.ihm.org.uk
Publisher: Ashridge Communications
Date Established: 2001
Frequency: 6 issues yearly
Free to qualifying individuals
Annual Sub.: £55.00
Circulation: 10,500 (Publisher's Statement)
Usual Pagination: 36
Editor: Vicky Burman
Summary of Content: Official journal of the Institute of Healthcare Management.
Readership/Target Audience: Aimed at health and social care managers in the NHS, independent and voluntary sectors.
ADVERTISING RATES:
Full Page Colour £2500.00
Agency Commission: 10%
Mechanical Data: Type Area: 275 x 190mm, Col Length: 275mm, Page Width: 190mm, Bleed Size: 303 x 216mm, Trim Size: 297 x 210mm, Film: Digital
Copy instructions: Copy Date: 3 weeks prior to publication date
Average advertising content per issue: 35%
BUSINESS: HEALTH & MEDICAL

HEALTH POLICY & PLANNING
23070U32B-90

Editorial Address: London School of Hygiene & Tropical Medicine, Keppel (Gower) Street, LONDON, WC1E 7HT
Tel: 01865 353907 **Fax:** 01865 353485
Email: tamsin.kelk@lshtm.ac.uk
Advertising Address: Great Clarendon Street, OXFORD, OX2 6DP **Tel:** 01865 353329 **Fax:** 01865 353774

Email: elisabetta.sheffield@oxfordjournals.org
Web site: http://www.heapol.oupjournals.org
ISSN: 0268-1080
Publisher: OUP
Date Established: 1986
Frequency: 6 issues yearly
Cover Price: £20.00
Annual Sub.: £94.00
Circulation: 720 (Publisher's Statement)
Usual Pagination: 80
Editor: Richard Coker
Summary of Content: Publication covering health policies and planning.
Readership/Target Audience: Aimed at those interested in modern international health care.
ADVERTISING RATES:
Full Page Mono £646.00
Full Page Colour £1076.00
Agency Commission: 10%
Mechanical Data: Type Area: 255 x 178mm, Trim Size: 279 x 216mm, Bleed Size: 285 x 222mm, Film: Digital, Page Width: 178mm, Col Length: 255mm
BUSINESS: LOCAL GOVERNMENT, LEISURE & RECREATION: Public Health & Cleaning

HEALTH SERVICE JOURNAL
40174U56A-66_65

Editorial Address: Greater London House, Hampstead Road, LONDON, NW1 7EJ **Tel:** 020 7728 3750
Fax: 020 7728 3700
Email: hsjnews@emap.com
Advertising Address: As above. **Tel:** 020 7728 5000
Fax: 020 7728 3866
Email: patrick.kearns@emap.com
Web site: http://www.hsj.co.uk
ISSN: 0952-2271
Publisher: EMAP Inform
Date Established: 1892
Frequency: Weekly - Published on Thursday
Cover Price: £2.80
Circulation: 17,651 (ABC 01/01/2008 to 31/12/2008)
Editor: Richard Vize; **Features Editor:** Ingrid Torjesen
Summary of Content: Magazine focusing on all aspects of health policy and management. Containing news and features, special reports and political commentary.
Readership/Target Audience: Read by managers predominantly working in the NHS.
ADVERTISING RATES:
Full Page Colour £4460.00
Agency Commission: 10%
Mechanical Data: Type Area: 275 x 205mm, Bleed Size: 306 x 236mm, Trim Size: 300 x 230mm, Col Length: 275mm, Page Width: 205mm, Print Process: Web-fed offset litho, Film: Digital
Copy instructions: Copy Date: 1 week prior to publication date
BUSINESS: HEALTH & MEDICAL

HEALTHCARE HYGIENE MANAGEMENT
1859580U4F-110

Editorial Address: Sparta Works, 487 Blackfen Road, SIDCUP, DA15 9NP **Tel:** 020 8298 6490 **Fax:** 020 8301 5304
Email: wayne.cyrus@mpp.co.uk
Publisher: MPP Ltd
Date Established: 2008
Frequency: Quarterly
Free to qualifying individuals
Circulation: 6,500 (Print Run)
Editor: Wayne Cyrus
Summary of Content: Magazine covering healthcare hygiene in trust managements and the NHS.
Readership/Target Audience: Aimed at facilities managers and in house domestic managers.
BUSINESS: ARCHITECTURE & BUILDING: Cleaning & Maintenance

HEALTHCARE INSURANCE REPORT
35123U1D-120

Editorial Address: Bank House, Great Rissington, CHELTENHAM, GL54 2LP **Tel:** 01451 821982
Fax: 01451 821972
Email: info@andycouchman.com
Web site: http://www.andycouchman.com
ISSN: 1461-5746
Publisher: Bank House Communications Ltd
Date Established: 1998
Frequency: 10 issues yearly - Published the 28th of the month prior to cover month
Annual Sub.: £365.00
Usual Pagination: 16
Editor: Andy Couchman; **Publisher:** Andy Couchman
Summary of Content: Newsletter containing news and updated information on health, protection and care insurance.
Readership/Target Audience: Aimed at those concerned with health, protection and care insurance.

ADVERTISING: No Advertising taken
BUSINESS: FINANCE & ECONOMICS: Insurance

HEALTHCARE MARKET NEWS
40509U56P-30

Editorial Address: 29 Angel Gate, City Road, LONDON, EC1V 2PT **Tel:** 020 7833 9123 **Fax:** 020 7833 9129
Email: maria@laingbuisson.co.uk
Advertising Address: As above.
Email: kate@laingbuisson.co.uk
Web site: http://www.healthcaremarketnews.co.uk
ISSN: 1360-9378
Publisher: Laing & Buisson
Frequency: 10 issues yearly
Annual Sub.: £410.00
Circulation: 800 (Publisher's Statement)
Usual Pagination: 24
Editor: Maria Davies; **Advertising Manager:** Kate Rudlin
Summary of Content: Newsletter reporting news and developments in the provision and funding of acute and primary healthcare. Includes analysis of companies in the sector, plus reports on the NHS, primary care and trends in private medical insurance.
Readership/Target Audience: Aimed at independent healthcare operators, NHS organisations, insurance companies, financial institutions and health economists.
ADVERTISING RATES:
Full Page Mono £1650.00
Full Page Colour £1950.00
Agency Commission: 10%
Mechanical Data: Film: Digital
Copy instructions: Copy Date: 1 week prior to publication date
Average advertising content per issue: 15%
BUSINESS: HEALTH & MEDICAL: Casualty & Emergency

HEALTHCARE TODAY
1777374U56B-293

Editorial Address: 45 Centurion House, Centurion Way, Leyland Business Park, Farington, LEYLAND, PR25 3GR
Tel: 01772 459418
Email: judith@flyingstartmagazine.co.uk
Advertising Address: As above.
Email: julie@flyingstartmagazine.co.uk
Web site: http://www.healthcaretoday.org.uk
Publisher: Magenta Press Ltd
Date Established: 2006
Frequency: Annual - Published in August
Cover Price: Free
Circulation: 15,000 (Publisher's Statement)
Usual Pagination: 64
Editor: Judith McKay
Summary of Content: Publication covering news, views and up to date articles regarding the healthcare sector and includes a product and services directory.
Readership/Target Audience: Aimed at healthcare managers and staff, care homes with nursing and NHS trusts.
ADVERTISING RATES:
Full Page Mono £800.00
Full Page Colour £850.00
Mechanical Data: Bleed Size: 307 x 220mm, Trim Size: 297 x 210mm, Film: Digital
Copy instructions: Copy Date: 3 weeks prior to publication date
Average advertising content per issue: 50%
BUSINESS: HEALTH & MEDICAL: Nursing

HEALTHINVESTOR
1657402U1F-591

Editorial Address: 6th Floor, Greener House, 66-68 Haymarket, LONDON, SW1Y 4RF **Tel:** 020 7451 7066
Fax: 020 7451 7051
Email: editorial@healthinvestor.co.uk
Advertising Address: As above. **Tel:** 020 7451 7058
Email: matt.purnell@healthinvestor.co.uk
Web site: http://www.healthinvestor.co.uk
ISSN: 1742-884X
Publisher: Healthinvestor
Date Established: 2004
Frequency: 10 issues yearly
Free to qualifying individuals
Annual Sub.: £350.00
Usual Pagination: 36
Editor: Alex Beaumont
Summary of Content: Magazine covering the commercial implications of recent developments in primary care, property, dentistry, pharmacy, foundation hospitals, PFI, mergers and acquisitions and private equity. Also includes company and fund profiles, European news and company results.
Readership/Target Audience: Aimed at Venture Capital Investors, private equity and institutional fund managers, healthcare service providers, NHS trust managers, Government policy makers, property developers and premises managers, financial analysts and corporate finance professionals.
ADVERTISING RATES:
Full Page Colour £1500.00
Agency Commission: 10%

Mechanical Data: Film: Digital, Trim Size: 297 x 210mm
Copy instructions: Copy Date: 1 month prior to publication date
Average advertising content per issue: 35%
BUSINESS: FINANCE & ECONOMICS: Investment

HEALTHY FOODS AND SNACKS

1794885U8B-202

Editorial Address: First Floor Offices, Stafford House, 16 East Street, TONBRIDGE, TN9 1HG **Tel:** 01732 371510
Fax: 01732 361385
Email: scallander@kennedys.co.uk
Advertising Address: As above.
Email: mneilson@kennedys.co.uk
Web site: http://www.kennedys.co.uk
ISSN: 1753-2337
Publisher: Kennedy's Publications Ltd
Frequency: 3 issues yearly - Published around the middle of the 1st cover month
Cover Price: Free
Circulation: 7,200 (Publisher's Statement)
Usual Pagination: 36
Editor: Suzanne Callander; **Advertising Manager:** Mark Neilson; **Publisher:** Angus Kennedy
Summary of Content: Magazine covering the production, formulation and marketing of healthy foods and snacks.
Readership/Target Audience: Aimed at snacks and healthy foods manufacturers.
ADVERTISING RATES:
Full Page Colour £1995.00
Agency Commission: 10%
Mechanical Data: Type Area: 251 x 176mm, Bleed Size: 303 x 216mm, Trim Size: 297 x 210mm, Col Length: 251mm, Page Width: 176mm, Film: Digital
Copy instructions: Copy Date: 1st of the month prior to publication date
Average advertising content per issue: 40%
BUSINESS: BAKING & CONFECTIONERY: Confectionery Manufacturing

HEATING & PLUMBING MONTHLY

35758U3B-17

Editorial Address: Becket House, Vestry Road, SEVENOAKS, TN14 5EJ **Tel:** 01732 748000
Fax: 01732 748001
Email: twood@unity-media.com
Advertising Address: As above.
Email: jwallace@unity-media.com
Web site: http://www.unity-media.com
Publisher: Unity Media plc
Date Established: 1983
Frequency: 11 issues yearly - Published in the 1st week of the cover month
Free to qualifying individuals
Annual Sub.: £50.00
Circulation: 30,043 (ABC 01/01/2008 to 31/12/2008)
Usual Pagination: 92
Editor: Nichola Farrugia; **Advertising Manager:** Jenny Wallace
Summary of Content: Magazine providing up-to-date information on the latest equipment, developments, methods, product testing plus technical advice on installation and specification.
Readership/Target Audience: Read by heating engineers and plumbers working in the domestic and light commercial sectors.
ADVERTISING RATES:
Full Page Colour £2400.00
SCC £16.00
Agency Commission: 10%
Mechanical Data: Page Width: 190mm, Trim Size: 297 x 210mm, Bleed Size: 303 x 216mm, Film: Digital, Type Area: 265 x 190mm, Col Length: 265mm
Copy instructions: Copy Date: Middle of the month prior to publication date
Average advertising content per issue: 60%
BUSINESS: HEATING & VENTILATION: Industrial Heating & Ventilation

THE HEDGE FUND JOURNAL

1659571U1F-625

Editorial Address: 31 Davies Street, LONDON, W1K 4LW
Tel: 020 7409 0888 **Fax:** 020 7629 7272
Email: simon.kerr@thehedgefundjournal.com
Advertising Address: As above. **Fax:** 020 7409 0905
Email: rod.sparks@thehedgefundjournal.com
Web site: http://www.thehedgefundjournal.com
Publisher: Hedge Fund Publishing Ltd
Date Established: 2004
Frequency: 10 issues yearly
Annual Sub.: £895.00
Circulation: 3,000 (Publisher's Statement 2007)
Usual Pagination: 80
News Editor: John Clayman; **Advertising Manager:** Rod Sparks; **Publisher:** Rod Sparks
Summary of Content: Journal covering news, features and technical analysis relating to hedge fund investment.
Readership/Target Audience: Aimed at managers of hedge funds and investors.
ADVERTISING: Rates on application
BUSINESS: FINANCE & ECONOMICS: Investment

HEDGE FUNDS REVIEW

707905U1F-228_50

Editorial Address: Haymarket House, 28-29 Haymarket, LONDON, SW1Y 4RX **Tel:** 020 7484 9889
Fax: 020 7484 9932
Email: margie.lindsay@incisivemedia.com
Advertising Address: As above.
Email: luther.rahman@incisivemedia.com
Web site: http://www.hedgefundsreview.com
Publisher: Incisive Media Investments
Date Established: 2000
Frequency: Monthly - Published around the beginning of the cover month
Annual Sub.: £795.00
Circulation: 4,500 (Publisher's Statement)
Usual Pagination: 56
Editor: Margie Lindsay; **Managing Director:** Matthew Crabbe
Summary of Content: Magazine covering all aspects of the hedge fund industry. Includes news, analysis, technical features and articles on fund launches and markets. Hedge Funds Review also has a website (www.hedgefundsreview.com) updated daily with a news email shot sent out to all subscribers twice weekly.
Readership/Target Audience: Aimed at investors, hedge fund professionals and service providers assisting them.
ADVERTISING RATES:
Full Page Colour £6000.00
Agency Commission: 10%
Mechanical Data: Type Area: 280 x 205mm, Bleed Size: 316 x 241mm, Trim Size: 310 x 235mm, Film: Digital, Col Length: 280mm, Page Width: 205mm
Copy instructions: Copy Date; Last Friday of the month prior to publication date
Supplement(s): Auditing and accounting - 1xY, British Virgin Islands - 1xY, Cayman Islands - 1xY, Channel Islands - 1xY, Ireland - 1xY, Legal Services - 1xY, Prime Brokerage - 1xY, Roundtables - 1xY, Technology - 1xY
BUSINESS: FINANCE & ECONOMICS: Investment

HELICOPTER INTERNATIONAL

36406U6E-133

Editorial Address: 75 Elm Tree Road, Locking, WESTON-SUPER-MARE, BS24 8EL **Tel:** 01934 822524
Fax: 01934 822400
Email: editorial@aviapress.fsnet.co.uk
Advertising Address: As above.
Email: helicopterinternational@aviapress.fsnet.co.uk
Web site: http://www.helidata.rotor.com
ISSN: 0143-1005
Publisher: Avia Press Associates
Date Established: 1977
Frequency: 6 issues yearly - Published on the 1st of the month
Cover Price: £3.00
Circulation: 25,000 (Publisher's Statement per year)
Usual Pagination: 40
Editor: Elfan ap Rees; **Editor-in-Chief:** Elfan ap Rees; **Managing Editor:** Claire ap Rees; **Publisher:** Elfan ap Rees
Summary of Content: Journal covering safety, international defence, new civil sales, accidents and offshore European operations.
Readership/Target Audience: Aimed at commercial, military and private operators worldwide.
ADVERTISING RATES:
Full Page Mono £3152.00
Full Page Colour £4355.00
Agency Commission: 15%
Mechanical Data: Type Area: 250 x 175mm, Bleed Size: 281 x 209mm, Trim Size: 275 x 203mm, Film: Digital, Col Length: 250mm, Page Width: 175mm
Average advertising content per issue: 43%
Supplement(s): Asia Pacific Operators Directory - 1xY, European Helicopter Operators - 1xY, World Military Helicopter Inventory - 1xY
BUSINESS: AVIATION & AERONAUTICS: Hovercraft VTOL

HELIDATA NEWS & CLASSIFIED

36408U6E-137

Editorial Address: 75 Elm Tree Road, Locking, WESTON-SUPER-MARE, BS24 8EL **Tel:** 01934 822524
Fax: 01934 822400
Email: helidata@aviapress.fsnet.co.uk
Advertising Address: As above.
Email: helidata@aviapress.fsnet.co.uk
Web site: http://www.helidata.rotor.com
ISSN: 0951-9904
Publisher: Avia Press Associates
Date Established: 1980
Frequency: 26 issues yearly
Annual Sub.: £250.00
Circulation: 11,530 (Publisher's Statement)
Usual Pagination: 16
Editor: Elfan ap Rees; **Managing Director:** Elfan ap Rees; **Managing Editor:** Claire ap Rees; **Publisher:** Elfan ap Rees
Summary of Content: Publication containing news and information about both civil and military rotorcraft.
Readership/Target Audience: Aimed at helicopter owners, operators and companies in over 180 countries worldwide.
ADVERTISING RATES:
Full Page Mono £1030.00
Full Page Colour £1432.00
SCC £9.00
Agency Commission: 10%
Mechanical Data: Type Area: 254 x 182mm, Trim Size: 297 x 210mm, Bleed Size: 303 x 216mm, Film: Digital, Col Length: 254mm, Page Width: 182mm
Copy instructions: Copy Date: 1 week prior to publication date
Average advertising content per issue: 70%
BUSINESS: AVIATION & AERONAUTICS: Hovercraft VTOL

HELIDATA SHOW DAILY

36343U6A-96_50

Editorial Address: 75 Elm Tree Road, Locking, WESTON-SUPER-MARE, BS24 8EL **Tel:** 01934 822524
Fax: 01934 822400
Email: helidata@aviapress.fsnet.co.uk
Advertising Address: As above.
Email: helidata@aviapress.fsnet.co.uk
Web site: http://www.helidata.rotor.com
ISSN: 0951-9904
Publisher: Avia Press Associates
Date Established: 1980
Frequency: Quarterly
Free to qualifying individuals
Annual Sub.: £20.00
Circulation: 15,500 (Publisher's Statement per year)
Usual Pagination: 16
Editor: Elfan ap Rees; **Editor-in-Chief:** Elfan ap Rees; **Managing Editor:** Claire ap Rees; **Publisher:** Elfan ap Rees
Summary of Content: Publication covering, reports, exhibitor and travel details for specific helicopter trade shows. Includes coverage of Helitech and HeliExpo, Farnborough and Paris Air Shows.
Readership/Target Audience: Aimed at visitors and industry members worldwide.
ADVERTISING RATES:
Full Page Mono £1164.00
Full Page Colour £1832.00
SCC £9.00
Agency Commission: 10%
Mechanical Data: Type Area: 254 x 182mm, Bleed Size: 279 x 208mm, Film: Digital, Col Length: 254mm, Print Process: Offset litho, Trim Size: 273 x 205mm, Page Width: 182mm
Copy instructions: Copy Date: 7 days prior to publication date
Average advertising content per issue: 75%
BUSINESS: AVIATION & AERONAUTICS

THE HERALD BUSINESS MAGAZINE

1663864U63D-716

Editorial Address: 200 Renfield Street, GLASGOW, G2 3QB
Tel: 0141 302 7000 **Fax:** 0141 302 7227
Email: colin.cardwell@virgin.net
Advertising Address: As above. **Fax:** 0141 302 6363
Email: daniel.mccomiskey@glasgow.newsquest.co.uk
Publisher: Newsquest Herald & Times Ltd
Frequency: 10 issues yearly - For circulation see main record
Cover Price: Free
Usual Pagination: 40
Editor: Colin Cardwell; **Advertising Manager:** Danny McComiskey
Summary of Content: Magazine focusing on entrepreneurial and investment issues with lifestyle features.
Readership/Target Audience: Aimed at readers with an interest in business matters.
ADVERTISING RATES:
Full Page Colour £2000.00
Agency Commission: 15%
Mechanical Data: Type Area: 270 x 204mm, Bleed Size: 303 x 233mm, Trim Size: 295 x 230mm, Col Length: 270mm, Page Width: 204mm, Col Widths (Display): 48mm, No. of Columns (Display): 4, Film: Digital
Copy instructions: Copy Date: 10 days prior to publication date
Average advertising content per issue: 15%
Supplement to: The Herald (Glasgow)
BUSINESS: REGIONAL BUSINESS: Regional Business Scotland

HERD BOOK

37854U21D-600

Editorial Address: 34-36 Fore Street, Bovey Tracey, NEWTON ABBOT, TQ13 9AD **Tel:** 01626 833168
Fax: 01626 834536
Email: secretary@allgoats.com
Web site: http://www.allgoats.com
Publisher: British Goat Society
Frequency: Annual - Published in April
Circulation: 1,000 (Publisher's Statement)
Editor: Sue Knowles

Summary of Content: Journal about goat registers, owners, breeders and awards.
Readership/Target Audience: Aimed at members of the society and anyone interested in the breeding of goats.
ADVERTISING: No Advertising taken
BUSINESS: AGRICULTURE & FARMING: Livestock

THE HERTFORDSHIRE BUSINESS INDEPENDENT
767655U63B-2484

Formerly: Business Independent
Editorial Address: Simon James House, 17A Mill Lane, WELWYN, AL6 9EU **Tel:** 01438 841310 **Fax:** 01438 841311
Email: lynda.seaton@businessindependent.co.uk
Advertising Address: As above.
Email: lynda.seaton@businessindependent.co.uk
Web site: http://www.businessindependent.co.uk
Publisher: The Hertfordshire Business Independent
Date Established: 2002
Frequency: Monthly - Published around the beginning of the cover month
Cover Price: Free
Circulation: 15,000 (Publisher's Statement)
Usual Pagination: 36
Editor: Lynda Seaton; **Advertising Manager:** Lynda Seaton
Summary of Content: Newspaper covering business to business related news and feature articles in the Hertfordshire and Bedfordshire areas.
Readership/Target Audience: Aimed at named businesses and decision makers within companies in the Hertfordshire and Bedfordshire regions.
ADVERTISING RATES:
Full Page Mono £800.00
Full Page Colour £800.00
Agency Commission: 10%
Mechanical Data: Type Area: 320 x 260mm, Trim Size: 372 x 290mm, Col Widths (Display): 40mm, Print Process: Sheet-fed, No. of Columns (Display): 6, Page Width: 260mm, Col Length: 320mm, Film: Digital
Copy instructions: Copy Date: 1 week prior to publication date
BUSINESS: REGIONAL BUSINESS: Regional Business English Counties

HERTS DIRECTOR
712555U63B-750

Editorial Address: 14 Middletons Road, Yaxley, PETERBOROUGH, PE7 3LR **Tel:** 01733 242312
Fax: 01733 244035
Email: carol@pridepublications.co.uk
Advertising Address: As above.
Email: maxine@pridepublications.co.uk
Web site: http://www.pridepublications.co.uk
Publisher: Pride Publications Ltd
Date Established: 1999
Frequency: 6 issues yearly
Circulation: 3,500 (Publisher's Statement)
Editor: Carol Lawless; **Managing Director:** Carol Lawless; **Advertisement Director:** Maxine Coward; **Publisher:** Carol Lawless
Summary of Content: Magazine covering local news, views and general interest features.
Readership/Target Audience: Aimed at chief executives and directors of companies with a turnover exceeding £250,000.
ADVERTISING RATES:
Full Page Mono £675.00
Full Page Colour £675.00
Agency Commission: 10%
Mechanical Data: Type Area: 272 x 187mm, Bleed Size: 309 x 218mm, Trim Size: 303 x 212mm, Col Length: 272mm, Page Width: 187mm, Film: Digital
Copy instructions: Copy Date: 1 week prior to publication date
Average advertising content per issue: 40%
BUSINESS: REGIONAL BUSINESS: Regional Business English Counties

HFM WEEK
1668186U1F-600

Editorial Address: HFM Week, Dunstan House, 14A St. Cross Street, LONDON, EC1N 8XA **Tel:** 020 7269 6401
Fax: 020 7269 7570
Email: g.roberts@hfmweek.com
Advertising Address: 1st Floor, Dunstan House, 14A St. Cross Street, LONDON, EC1N 8XA **Tel:** 020 7269 7585
Fax: 020 7269 7570
Email: d.hood@hfmweek.com
Web site: http://www.hfmweek.com
Publisher: Pageant Media Ltd
Frequency: 40 issues yearly
Annual Sub.: £895.00
Editor: Gwyn Roberts; **News Editor:** Zaki Abushal; **Features Editor:** Elise Coroneos; **Advertising Manager:** David Hood
Summary of Content: Magazine providing up-to-date commentary, features and insight for the alternative investment industry. Including news on trends within the industry, fund launches, searches and senior people moves.

Readership/Target Audience: Aimed at the international hedge fund community.
ADVERTISING RATES:
Full Page Colour £3950.00
Agency Commission: 10%
Mechanical Data: Type Area: 253 x 183mm, Bleed Size: 279 x 209mm, Trim Size: 273 x 203mm, Col Length: 253mm, Page Width: 183mm, Film: Digital
Copy instructions: Copy Date: 1 week prior to publication date
Average advertising content per issue: 40%
BUSINESS: FINANCE & ECONOMICS: Investment

HIGH DEFINITION
1642070U2D-138

Editorial Address: The Studio, 64 Old Station Road, NEWMARKET, CB8 8AA **Tel:** 01638 662287
Fax: 01638 601937
Email: mike@definitionmagazine.com
Advertising Address: As above.
Email: julian@definitionmagazine.com
Web site: http://www.definitionmagazine.com
Publisher: Media Maker Publishing Ltd
Date Established: 2003
Frequency: 6 issues yearly
Free to qualifying individuals
Annual Sub.: £25.00
Circulation: 7,280 (Publisher's Statement)
Usual Pagination: 68
Editor: Michael Brennan; **Advertising Manager:** Nicki Mills; **Publisher:** Julian Mitchell
Summary of Content: Magazine covering equipment reviews, production techniques and industry news.
Readership/Target Audience: Aimed at cinematographers, broadcasters and those involved in production and post production.
ADVERTISING RATES:
Full Page Colour £1100.00
Agency Commission: 10%
Mechanical Data: Film: Digital, Bleed Size: 303 x 236mm, Trim Size: 297 x 230mm, Type Area: 277 x 210mm, Col Length: 277mm, Page Width: 210mm
Copy instructions: Copy Date: 2 weeks prior to publication date
Average advertising content per issue: 40%
BUSINESS: COMMUNICATIONS, ADVERTISING & MARKETING: Broadcasting

HIGH NET WORTH MAGAZINE
1819106U1F-644

Editorial Address: 1 Southwark Bridge, LONDON, SE1 9HL
Tel: 020 7873 3000
Email: padraig.floyd@ft.com
Advertising Address: As above.
Email: pierre.tachot@ft.com
Publisher: Financial Times
Frequency: 5 issues yearly
Cover Price: Free
Circulation: 5,010 (ABC 01/07/2006 to 30/06/2007)
Editor-in-Chief: Pádraig Floyd
Summary of Content: Magazine featuring news and features on pensions and investments.
Readership/Target Audience: Read by IFA's and advisors working with high net worth.
ADVERTISING RATES:
Full Page Colour £3000.00
Agency Commission: 10%
BUSINESS: FINANCE & ECONOMICS: Investment

HIGH PERFORMANCE PLASTICS
38822U39-22

Editorial Address: 9A Victoria Square, DROITWICH, WR9 8DE **Tel:** 0870 165 7211 **Fax:** 0870 165 7212
Email: hpp@intnews.com
Web site: http://www.performance-materials.net
ISSN: 0264-7753
Publisher: International Newsletters
Frequency: Monthly
Annual Sub.: £467.00
Usual Pagination: 12
Editor: Nick Butler
Summary of Content: Newsletter about high performance plastics: materials, products, applications, business and markets.
Readership/Target Audience: Aimed at design, production, processing and management, R&D, manufacturing and management in plastics and polymers.
ADVERTISING: No Advertising taken
BUSINESS: PLASTICS & RUBBER

HIGHER EDUCATION REVIEW
41111U62F-400

Editorial Address: 1 Poplar Close, BRIGHTON, BN1 6PR
Tel: 01273 556238
Email: j.pratt@uel.ac.uk
Web site: http://www.highereducationreview.com
ISSN: 0018-1609
Publisher: Tyrrell Burgess Associates
Date Established: 1968

Frequency: 3 issues yearly - Published in February, June and October
Annual Sub.: £56.00
Circulation: 1,000 (Publisher's Statement)
Usual Pagination: 96
Editor: John Pratt
Summary of Content: Academic journal covering policy and practice in post compulsory education affecting those engaged in teaching, research and administration.
Readership/Target Audience: Aimed at all institutions of post school education.
ADVERTISING: No Advertising taken
BUSINESS: CHURCH & SCHOOL EQUIPMENT & EDUCATION: Adult Education

HIGHWAY ELECTRICAL NEWS
1799995U17-268

Editorial Address: Bowden House, 1 Church Street, HENFIELD, BN5 9NS **Tel:** 01273 491462 **Fax:** 01273 495832
Email: hen@highlec.co.uk
Advertising Address: As above.
Email: hen@highlec.co.uk
Web site: http://www.highlec.co.uk
Publisher: Highlec Publishing
Date Established: 1996
Frequency: 6 issues yearly
Annual Sub.: £40.00
Circulation: 1,000 (Publisher's Statement)
Usual Pagination: 28
Editor: Vas Siantonas; **Advertising Manager:** Vas Siantonas
Summary of Content: Magazine focusing on the highway electrical industry; examines lamp replacement policies, CCT, best values, infrastructure, health and safety issues. Includes products and company news, private companies, contractors, manufacturers and suppliers.
Readership/Target Audience: Aimed at county surveyors, directors of technical services, heads of highways and transport sections and lighting engineers in county councils, London and metropolitan boroughs, district authorities and UAs in England, Scotland and Wales, also manufacturers and suppliers.
ADVERTISING RATES:
Full Page Mono £400.00
Full Page Colour £850.00
Mechanical Data: Film: Digital
BUSINESS: ELECTRICAL

HIGHWAYS
39048U42B-15

Editorial Address: 168 St. John's Hill, Severnoaks, KENT, TN13 3PF **Tel:** 01732 459683
Email: highwaysmagazine@googlemail.com
Advertising Address: As above. **Fax:** 01732 455837
Email: neil@aladltd.co.uk
Web site: http://www.highways-mag.co.uk
ISSN: 0142-6168
Publisher: Alad Ltd
Frequency: 10 issues yearly - Published in the 2nd week of the cover month
Free to qualifying individuals
Annual Sub.: £65.00
Circulation: 6,813 (ABC 01/07/2007 to 30/06/2008)
Editor: Grant Prior; **Advertising Manager:** Neil Levett; **Publisher:** Neil Levett
Summary of Content: Journal focusing on the road building, maintenance, traffic control, street management and utility works industries.
Readership/Target Audience: Aimed at county, borough and district councils, civil engineering and highways contractors, consulting engineers and personnel within government departments.
ADVERTISING RATES:
Full Page Mono £1417.00
Full Page Colour £2110.00
Agency Commission: 10%
Mechanical Data: Type Area: 264 x 181mm, Bleed Size: 303 x 216mm, Trim Size: 297 x 210mm, Col Length: 264mm, Page Width: 181mm, Film: Digital
Copy instructions: Copy Date: 17th of the month prior to publication date
Average advertising content per issue: 40%
BUSINESS: CONSTRUCTION: Roads

THE HIP! MAGAZINE: HEATING ENGINEERS, INSTALLERS AND PLUMBERS
1793304U3D-102

Editorial Address: Unit 22, Midsomer Enterprise Park, Radstock Road, Midsomer Norton, RADSTOCK, BA3 2BB
Tel: 0870 774 3049 **Fax:** 0870 758 5906
Email: celia@sng-publishing.co.uk
Advertising Address: As above.
Email: celia@sng-publishing.co.uk
Web site: http://www.sng-publishing.co.uk
Publisher: SNG Publishing Ltd
Date Established: 2007
Frequency: 3 issues yearly - Published in February, May and November
Free to qualifying individuals

Circulation: 14,072 (ABC 01/01/2007 to 01/07/2007)
Usual Pagination: 84
Editor: Celia Matthews; **Advertising Manager:** Celia Matthews; **Publisher:** Celia Matthews
Summary of Content: Publication covering topics to assist the next generation entering the plumbing and heating industry. Includes features written by industry experts (including manufacturers and trade associations), useful product information, tips on product installations, business advice and essential guidance from college lecturers, as well as fun cartoons and competitions to help the students build up their tool kits.
Readership/Target Audience: Aimed at level 2 and level 3 plumbing and heating trainees.
ADVERTISING RATES:
Full Page Colour £1320.00
Mechanical Data: Type Area: 275 x 180mm, Bleed Size: 303 x 216mm, Trim Size: 297 x 210mm, Col Length: 275mm, Page Width: 180mm, Film: Digital
Copy instructions: Copy Date: 2 weeks prior to publication date
BUSINESS: HEATING & VENTILATION: Heating & Plumbing

HISTORY OF THE HUMAN SCIENCES
24406U55-56_30
Editorial Address: 1 Oliver's Yard, 55 City Road, LONDON, EC1Y 1SP **Tel:** 020 7324 8500 **Fax:** 020 7324 8600
Advertising Address: As above.
Email: advertising@sagepub.co.uk
Web site: http://www.sagepub.co.uk
ISSN: 0952-6951
Publisher: Sage Publications
Date Established: 1992
Frequency: Quarterly
Cover Price: £49.00
Circulation: 350 (Publisher's Statement)
Editor: James Good; **Advertising Manager:** Sheena Karim
Summary of Content: Journal providing a forum for contemporary social science research that examines its own historical origins and interdisciplinary influences in an effort to review current practice.
Readership/Target Audience: Read by historians of ideas, scholars in the humanities and social science fields and those with an interest in historical and theoretical research across the social sciences sectors.
ADVERTISING RATES:
Full Page Mono £400.00
Agency Commission: 5%
Mechanical Data: Type Area: 205 x 130mm, Col Length: 205mm, Film: Digital, Page Width: 130mm
BUSINESS: APPLIED SCIENCE & LABORATORIES

HISTORY WORKSHOP JOURNAL
601528U62R-150
Formerly: History Workshop Journal: A Journal of Socialist Historians
Editorial Address: PO Box 60305, LONDON, WC1E 7WX **Tel:** 01865 353907 **Fax:** 01865 353985
Advertising Address: Great Clarendon Street, OXFORD, OX2 6DP **Tel:** 01865 353329
Email: jnlsadvertising@oxfordjournals.org
Web site: http://www.oup.co.uk/jnls
ISSN: 1363-3554
Publisher: OUP
Date Established: 1975
Frequency: Half-yearly - Published in April and October
Cover Price: £21.00
Annual Sub.: £37.00
Circulation: 1,200 (Publisher's Statement)
Usual Pagination: 320
Editor: Carmen Mangion
Summary of Content: Journal featuring innovative historical writing and research.
Readership/Target Audience: Aimed at scholars and students in research institutes and universities, teachers and students in colleges of adult education, teachers and students in schools and non-specialists with a lay-interest in history.
ADVERTISING RATES:
Full Page Mono £340.00
Agency Commission: 10%
BUSINESS: CHURCH & SCHOOL EQUIPMENT & EDUCATION: Education Related

HI-TECH SCOTLAND
1694986U5C-912
Editorial Address: 13 Coaledge, FIFE, KY4 8HB
Tel: 0141 632 0830
Email: michael@hi-techscotland.com
Advertising Address: As above. **Tel:** 0141 416 4055
Email: brian@hi-techscotland.com
Web site: http://www.hi-techscotland.com
Publisher: Feelgood Media
Date Established: 2005
Frequency: 10 issues yearly - Published in the 1st week of the cover month
Free to qualifying individuals

Annual Sub.: £44.00
Circulation: 8,000 (Publisher's Statement)
Usual Pagination: 24
Editor: Michael Feeley; **Advertising Manager:** Brian Halferty; **Publisher:** Brian Halferty
Summary of Content: Magazine focusing on ICT business services and support, digital media, networking, security, storage and communications technology.
Readership/Target Audience: Aimed at ICT companies and users both in the public and private sector.
ADVERTISING RATES:
Full Page Colour £2750.00
Agency Commission: 10%
Mechanical Data: Type Area: 360 x 260mm, Bleed Size: 396 x 296mm, Trim Size: 390 x 290mm, Col Length: 360mm, Page Width: 260mm, Film: Digital
Copy instructions: Copy Date: End of the month prior to publication date
BUSINESS: COMPUTERS & AUTOMATION: Professional Personal Computers

HIV MEDICINE
623256U56A-66_91
Editorial Address: 1 Mountview Court, 310 Friern Barnet Lane, LONDON, N20 0LD **Tel:** 020 8446 8898
Fax: 020 8446 9194
Email: editorial@mediscript.ltd.uk
Advertising Address: 9600 Garsington Road, Cowley, OXFORD, OX4 2DQ **Tel:** 01865 476354 **Fax:** 01865 471354
Email: mia.scott-ruddock@wiley.com
Web site: http://www.wiley.com
ISSN: 1464-2662
Publisher: Wiley-Blackwell Publishing
Frequency: Monthly
Annual Sub.: £133.00
Circulation: 1,900 (Publisher's Statement)
Usual Pagination: 68
Editor: Brian Gazzard
Summary of Content: The official journal of the British HIV Association, Australian Society for HIV Medicine and the European AIDS Clinical Society containing international research papers in the field of HIV medicine, embracing clinical, pharmacological, epidemiological, preclinical and in vitro studies. It also focuses on evidence-based medicine as the mainstay for the successful management of HIV and AIDS.
Readership/Target Audience: Read by researchers and clinicians who are responsible for treating HIV seropositive patients.
ADVERTISING: Rates on application
Agency Commission: 10%
Copy instructions: Copy Date: 2 months prior to publication date
BUSINESS: HEALTH & MEDICAL

HIV TREATMENT UPDATE
40133U56A-7
Formerly: AIDS Treatment Update
Editorial Address: Lincoln House, 1 Brixton Road, LONDON, SW9 6DE **Tel:** 020 7840 0050 **Fax:** 020 7735 5351
Email: info@nam.org.uk
Web site: http://www.aidsmap.com
ISSN: 1756-7890
Publisher: Nam Publications
Date Established: 1991
Frequency: 10 issues yearly
Free to qualifying individuals
Annual Sub.: £75.00
Circulation: 7,900 (Publisher's Statement)
Usual Pagination: 16
Editor: Gus Cairns
Summary of Content: Newsletter on treatment for HIV and AIDS. Reports on treatment developments, clinical trials and research.
Readership/Target Audience: Aimed at people living with or affected by HIV and associated professionals.
ADVERTISING: No Advertising taken
BUSINESS: HEALTH & MEDICAL

HM HEALTH MATTERS
38030U22F-22
Editorial Address: Suite 207, Linen Hall, 162-168 Regent Street, LONDON, WIB 5TB **Tel:** 07834 357965
Email: paul.newbon@1530.com
Advertising Address: As above. **Tel:** 020 7534 7216
Fax: 020 7437 0915
Email: rich@hm-magazine.com
Publisher: Edge Media and Research
Date Established: 1999
Frequency: 6 issues yearly - Published in the 3rd week of the cover month
Annual Sub.: £56.00
Circulation: 4,581 (Publisher's Statement)
Usual Pagination: 32
Editor: Paul Newbon; **Advertising Manager:** Richard Roe; **Publisher:** Richard Roe
Summary of Content: Magazine covering industry and product news, book reviews and features on alternative therapies, retailing and research.

Readership/Target Audience: Aimed at retailers of health foods and complementary health products.
ADVERTISING RATES:
Full Page Colour £2400.00
Agency Commission: 10%
Copy instructions: Copy Date: 2 weeks prior to publication date
Average advertising content per issue: 40%
BUSINESS: FOOD: Health Food

HNW JOURNAL
1656347U1R-365
Formerly: Stash Magazine
Editorial Address: 3rd Floor, Deansgate Court, Milton Hall, 244 Deansgate, MANCHESTER, M3 4BQ
Tel: 0161 832 7222 **Fax:** 0161 832 8414
Advertising Address: As above.
Email: melissa@hnwjournal.com
Web site: http://www.hnwjournal.com
Publisher: Stash Publications
Date Established: 2004
Frequency: Monthly
Cover Price: £3.50
Free to qualifying individuals
Circulation: 9,905 (Publisher's Statement)
Usual Pagination: 24
Editor: Hamayun Ahmed; **Managing Editor:** Hamayun Ahmed; **Publisher:** Hamayun Ahmed
Summary of Content: Magazine focusing on the trust, estates and wealth management sector including articles and news stories written by professionals within the industry as well as features on lifestyle, health and the arts.
Readership/Target Audience: Aimed at those working in the trust and estates sector worldwide including CEOs, partners and board members of major international and local companies.
ADVERTISING RATES:
Full Page Mono £2160.00
Full Page Colour £3000.00
Mechanical Data: Trim Size: 297 x 210mm, Type Area: 267 x 185mm, Bleed Size: 303 x 216mm, Col Length: 267mm, Page Width: 185mm, Film: Digital
Copy instructions: Copy Date: 10 days prior to publication date
Average advertising content per issue: 60%
BUSINESS: FINANCE & ECONOMICS: Financial Related

HOIST
39086U42R-120
Editorial Address: Progressive House, 2 Maidstone Road, Foots Cray, SIDCUP, DA14 5HZ **Tel:** 020 8269 7700
Fax: 020 8269 7874
Email: rhowes@progressivemediagroup.com
Advertising Address: As above. **Tel:** 020 8269 7746
Fax: 020 8269 7803
Email: mbridger@progressivemediagroup.com
Web site: http://www.hoistmagazine.com
Publisher: Progressive Media Publications
Date Established: 1998
Frequency: 10 issues yearly
Annual Sub.: £63.00
Circulation: 8,700 (Publisher's Statement)
Usual Pagination: 44
Editor: Richard Howes
Summary of Content: Magazine containing news, views and articles on procuring, supplying, using, maintaining, upgrading and repairing EOT and factory cranes from around the world.
Readership/Target Audience: Aimed at distributors and the larger industrial crane users, including automotive, transportation, manufacturers and specialist consultants in steel plants, paper mills, ports and docks.
ADVERTISING RATES:
Full Page Colour £2125.00
Agency Commission: 10%
Mechanical Data: Type Area: 254 x 178mm, Bleed Size: 303 x 215mm, Trim Size: 297 x 210mm, Film: Digital, Col Length: 254mm, Page Width: 178mm
Copy instructions: Copy Date: 28th of the month prior to publication date
Average advertising content per issue: 60%
BUSINESS: CONSTRUCTION: Construction Related

THE HOLLYWOOD REPORTER
41561U64K-560
Editorial Address: 5th Floor, Endeavour House, 189 Shaftesbury Avenue, LONDON, WC2H 8TJ
Tel: 020 7420 6004 **Fax:** 020 7420 6054
Email: london_one@thr.com
Advertising Address: As above. **Tel:** 020 7420 6000
Fax: 020 7420 6015
Email: alison.smith@thr.com
Web site: http://www.thr.com
Publisher: Nielsen Business Media
Frequency: 252 issues yearly
Cover Price: £5.50
Circulation: 63,006 (Publisher's Statement)
Usual Pagination: 20
Editor: Stuart Kemp

Summary of Content: Magazine containing news and reviews related to the television and film industry.
Readership/Target Audience: Aimed at those involved in the entertainment trade.
ADVERTISING RATES:
Full Page Mono $8016.00
Full Page Colour $13914.00
Mechanical Data: Type Area: 257 x 190mm, Bleed Size: 284 x 219mm, Trim Size: 278 x 212mm, Film: Digital, Col Length: 257mm, Page Width: 190mm
Copy instructions: Copy Date: 3 days prior to publication date
BUSINESS: OTHER CLASSIFICATIONS: Cinema Entertainment

HOLOCAUST AND GENOCIDE STUDIES
601530U62R-160
Editorial Address: Great Clarendon Street, OXFORD, OX2 6DP Tel: 01865 353907 Fax: 01865 353985
Email: jnls.cust.serv@oxfordjournals.org
Advertising Address: 60 Upper Broadmoor Road, CROWTHORNE, RG45 7DE Tel: 01344 779945
Fax: 01344 779945
Email: lhann@lhms.fsnet.co.uk
Web site: http://www.oup.co.uk/jnls
ISSN: 8756-6538
Publisher: OUP
Date Established: 1986
Frequency: 3 issues yearly - Published in April, July and November
Cover Price: £10.00
Annual Sub.: £115.00
Circulation: 1,100 (Publisher's Statement)
Usual Pagination: 172
Editor: Richard Breitman; Editor-in-Chief: Richard Breitman
Summary of Content: Journal features a major forum for work in the extensive body of literature and documentation on the Holocaust.
Readership/Target Audience: Read by historians and scholars.
ADVERTISING RATES:
Full Page Mono £290.00
Agency Commission: 10%
BUSINESS: CHURCH & SCHOOL EQUIPMENT & EDUCATION: Education Related

THE HOLOCENE
25152U57-33
Editorial Address: 1 Oliver's Yard, 55 City Road, LONDON, EC1Y 1SP Tel: 020 7324 8500 Fax: 020 7324 8600
Email: market@sagepub.co.uk
Advertising Address: As above.
Email: advertising@sagepub.co.uk
Web site: http://www.sagepub.co.uk
ISSN: 0959-6836
Publisher: Sage Publications
Date Established: 1991
Frequency: 8 issues yearly
Annual Sub.: £875.00
Usual Pagination: 160
Editor: John Matthews; Advertising Manager: Sheena Karim
Summary of Content: Academic publication focusing on scientific research into environmental changes over the last 10000 years, including past, present and future changes on local, regional and global scales.
Readership/Target Audience: Aimed at the International community of scientists working in the area.
ADVERTISING RATES:
Full Page Mono £500.00
Agency Commission: 5%
Mechanical Data: Trim Size: 297 x 210mm, Page Width: 180mm, Type Area: 265 x 180mm, Col Length: 265mm
Copy instructions: Copy Date: 12 weeks prior to publication date
BUSINESS: ENVIRONMENT & POLLUTION

HOLOGRAPHY NEWS
1702774U5F-382
Editorial Address: 2A High Street, SHEPPERTON, TW17 9AW Tel: 01932 269917 Fax: 01932 269918
Email: info@holographynews.info
Web site: http://www.holographynews.info
Publisher: Reconnaissance International Ltd
Date Established: 1986
Frequency: Monthly
Annual Sub.: £409.00
Usual Pagination: 8
Editor: Astrid Mitchell
Summary of Content: Magazine covering news, analysis and commentary on the holography industry.
Readership/Target Audience: Aimed at hologram producers, suppliers, converters and users.
ADVERTISING: No Advertising taken
BUSINESS: COMPUTERS & AUTOMATION: Multimedia

HOLSTEIN JOURNAL
37828U21C-355
Editorial Address: Scotsbridge House, Scots Hill, RICKMANSWORTH, WD3 3BB Tel: 01923 695200
Fax: 01923 695345
Email: simongee@holstein-uk.org
Advertising Address: As above.
Email: info@holstein-uk.org
Web site: http://www.holstein-uk.org
ISSN: 1467-0526
Publisher: Holstein UK
Date Established: 1919
Frequency: 6 issues yearly
Free to qualifying individuals
Annual Sub.: £30.00
Circulation: 8,500 (Publisher's Statement)
Usual Pagination: 96
Editor: Simon Gee; Advertising Manager: Simon Gee
Summary of Content: Journal containing news and technical information on pedigree Holstein Friesians and promoting the services of Holstein UK.
Readership/Target Audience: Read by British dairy farmers.
ADVERTISING RATES:
Full Page Colour £600.00
Mechanical Data: Type Area: 255 x 180mm, Film: Right reading, emulsion side down. Digital, Bleed Size: 306 x 219mm, Trim Size: 275 x 210mm, Page Width: 180mm, Col Length: 255mm, No. of Columns (Display): 2
Copy instructions: Copy Date: 3 weeks prior to publication date
Average advertising content per issue: 60%
BUSINESS: AGRICULTURE & FARMING: Dairy Farming

HOME & INTERIOR WORLD
1703373U4B-182
Editorial Address: Kentons House, 24 Blendon Road, BEXLEY, DA5 1BW Tel: 0870 701 3536
Email: hiworld@ntlworld.com
Advertising Address: As above. Fax: 01634 256798
Email: bljournals@tiscali.co.uk
Publisher: Direct Publishing Ltd
Frequency: Quarterly
Free to qualifying individuals
Circulation: 7,490 (Publisher's Statement)
Usual Pagination: 24
Editor: Phil Brown; Advertising Manager: Dave Peters
Summary of Content: Magazine covering news and product reviews on the interiors and DIY market.
Readership/Target Audience: Aimed at designers, architects, refurbishment specialists, property speculation specialists and senior managers involved in residential, retail and commercial construction.
ADVERTISING RATES:
Full Page Colour £895.00
Agency Commission: 10%
Mechanical Data: Type Area: 200 x 138mm, Bleed Size: 216 x 154mm, Trim Size: 210 x 148mm, Col Length: 200mm, Page Width: 138mm, Film: Digital
Copy instructions: Copy Date: 2 weeks prior to publication date
Average advertising content per issue: 15%
BUSINESS: ARCHITECTURE & BUILDING: Interior Design & Flooring

HOME DECOR & FURNISHINGS
37271U16A-70
Editorial Address: 1st Floor, Entrance B, Salamander Quay West, Park Lane, HAREFIELD, UB9 6NZ Tel: 0870 205 2924
Fax: 0870 205 2934
Email: michaelweedon@indices.co.uk
Advertising Address: As above.
Email: simongreen@indices.co.uk
Web site: http://www.indices.co.uk
Publisher: Indices Publications Ltd
Date Established: 1955
Frequency: 6 issues yearly
Annual Sub.: £49.50
Circulation: 8,200 (Publisher's Statement)
Usual Pagination: 36
Editor: Michael Weedon; Advertising Manager: Simon Green
Summary of Content: Magazine containing product and retail news from within the home decoration market.
Readership/Target Audience: Read by retailers of paint, fabrics, accessories, wall coverings, associated decorative products, also manufacturers, distributors, merchants and interior designers within the trade.
ADVERTISING RATES:
Full Page Mono £1150.00
Full Page Colour £1495.00
Agency Commission: 10%
Mechanical Data: Col Length: 264mm, Page Width: 190mm, Type Area: 264 x 190mm, Bleed Size: 303 x 213mm, Trim Size: 297 x 210mm, Film: Digital
BUSINESS: DECORATING & PAINT

THE HOME INSPECTOR
1642255U4C-237
Editorial Address: Beech House, Berkeley Close, Stoke Goldington, NEWPORT PAGNELL, MK16 8TE
Tel: 01908 551976 Fax: 01908 551977
Email: thehomeinspector@btinternet.com
Publisher: SAVA
Date Established: 2004
Frequency: 6 issues yearly
Cover Price: Free
Circulation: 5,000 (Publisher's Statement)
Usual Pagination: 10
Editor: Liz Male
Summary of Content: Newsletter covering all aspects of the market for home inspectors and energy assessors. Includes articles on legislation, statistics, estate agency news, interviews, book reviews, events, training and recruitment.
Readership/Target Audience: Aimed at home inspectors, domestic energy assessors, residential property surveyors, building engineers, estate agents, architects, building maintenance professionals and building control officers.
ADVERTISING: No Advertising taken
BUSINESS: ARCHITECTURE & BUILDING: Surveying

HOMECARER
38475U32G-67
Editorial Address: 2nd Floor, Group House, 52 Sutton Court Road, SUTTON, SM1 4SL Tel: 020 8288 5291
Fax: 020 8288 5290
Email: enquiries@ukhca.co.uk
Advertising Address: As above.
Email: enquiries@ukhca.co.uk
Web site: http://www.ukhca.co.uk
Publisher: United Kingdom Home Care Association Ltd
Frequency: 6 issues yearly
Cover Price: Free
Circulation: 3,000 (Publisher's Statement)
Usual Pagination: 20
Editor: Carole Broughton; Advertising Manager: Ruth Wainwright
Summary of Content: Newsletter of the United Kingdom Home Care Association containing news and reviews on current issues affecting organisations who provide homecare to private clients and others.
Readership/Target Audience: Read by those providing private home care.
ADVERTISING: Rates on application
Copy instructions: Copy Date: 1st of the month prior to publication date
Average advertising content per issue: 10%
BUSINESS: LOCAL GOVERNMENT, LEISURE & RECREATION: Community Care & Social Services

THE HOMEOPATH
40177U56A-66_93
Editorial Address: 11 Brookfield, Duncan Close, Moulton Park Industrial Estate, NORTHAMPTON, NN3 6WL
Tel: 0845 450 6611 Fax: 0845 450 6622
Email: francis_treuherz@homeopathy-soh.org
Advertising Address: As above.
Email: pamela_stevens@homeopathy-soh.org
Web site: http://www.homeopathy-soh.com
ISSN: 0263-3256
Publisher: Society of Homeopaths
Date Established: 1997
Frequency: Quarterly
Annual Sub.: £41.00
Circulation: 2,700 (Publisher's Statement)
Usual Pagination: 46
Editor: Francis Treuherz; Advertising Manager: Pamela Stevens
Summary of Content: Journal of the Society of Homeopaths. Covers reviews, new remedies and case histories.
Readership/Target Audience: Read by practitioners of homeopathy.
ADVERTISING RATES:
Full Page Mono £303.00
Full Page Colour £349.00
Mechanical Data: Trim Size: 297 x 210mm, Type Area: 262 x 180mm, Col Length: 262mm, Page Width: 180mm, Film: Digital
BUSINESS: HEALTH & MEDICAL

HOMEOPATHY
40284U56A-51_40
Formerly: British Homeopathic Journal
Editorial Address: The Faculty of Homeopathy, Hahnemann House, 29 Park Street West, LUTON, LU1 3BE
Tel: 0870 444 3955 Fax: 0870 444 3960
Email: journal@trusthomeopathy.org
Advertising Address: 32 Jamestown Road, LONDON, NW1 7BY Tel: 020 7424 4200 Fax: 020 7424 4433
Email: t.mpiyakhe@elsevier.com
Web site: http://intl.elsevierhealth.com/journals/homp
ISSN: 1475-4916
Publisher: Elsevier Ltd
Date Established: 1911
Frequency: Quarterly
Annual Sub.: EUR137.00

Business Magazines

Circulation: 1,800 (Publisher's Statement)
Usual Pagination: 80
Editor: Peter Fisher
Summary of Content: International journal dedicated to improving the understanding of homeopathy and clinical practice of homeopathy. Includes peer-reviewed articles on clinical and basic research and evidence based practice homeopathy. Also covers literature, meetings, debate and reviews.
Readership/Target Audience: Aimed at health professionals practicing homeopathy and at doctors, veterinarians, dentists, pharmacists and scientists using traditional medicine.
ADVERTISING RATES:
Full Page Mono EUR579.00
Full Page Colour EUR1053.00
Agency Commission: 10%
Mechanical Data: Page Width: 180mm, Film: Digital, Type Area: 267 x 180mm, Col Length: 267mm, Trim Size: 297 x 210mm, Bleed Size: 306 x 216mm
Copy instructions: Copy Date: 1 month prior to publication date
BUSINESS: HEALTH & MEDICAL

HOROLOGICAL JOURNAL   39780U52B-20
Editorial Address: Upton Hall, Main Street, Upton, NEWARK, NG23 5TE Tel: 01636 817601 Fax: 01636 812258
Email: hj@bhi.co.uk
Advertising Address: As above. Tel: 01636 813795
Email: jayne@bhi.co.uk
Web site: http://www.bhi.co.uk
ISSN: 0018-5108
Publisher: The British Horological Institute
Date Established: 1858
Frequency: Monthly
Annual Sub.: £80.00
Circulation: 3,800 (Publisher's Statement)
Usual Pagination: 44
Editor: Jayne Hall; Advertising Manager: Jayne Hall
Summary of Content: Journal covering all aspects of horology, containing technical articles about watches and clocks with trade news and adverts.
Readership/Target Audience: Circulated only to members of the British Horological Institute both UK and overseas.
ADVERTISING RATES:
Full Page Mono £415.00
Full Page Colour £622.50
SCC £9.00
Agency Commission: 10%
Mechanical Data: Bleed Size: +3mm, Trim Size: 297 x 210mm, Film: Digital, Type Area: 262 x 183mm, Col Length: 262mm, Page Width: 183mm
Copy instructions: Copy Date: 1st of month prior to publication date
Average advertising content per issue: 20%
BUSINESS: GIFT TRADE: Clocks & Watches

HORSE HEALTH   1698969U64H-244
Editorial Address: 47 Church Street, BARNSLEY, S70 2AS
Tel: 01226 734734 Fax: 01226 734705
Email: editorial@horsehealthmagazine.co.uk
Advertising Address: As above. Tel: 01226 734456
Fax: 01226 734478
Email: sales@horsehealthmagazine.co.uk
Web site: http://www.horsehealthmagazine.co.uk
Publisher: Wharncliffe Publishing Ltd
Date Established: 2005
Frequency: 6 issues yearly - Published in the 1st full week of the cover month
Free to qualifying individuals
Circulation: 10,110 (Publisher's Statement)
Usual Pagination: 36
Editor: Louise Cordell; Advertising Manager: Claire Mclean; Group Editor: Andrew Harrod
Summary of Content: Magazine focusing on the healthcare and management of horses.
Readership/Target Audience: Aimed at horse care professionals.
ADVERTISING RATES:
Full Page Colour £1200.00
Agency Commission: 10%
Mechanical Data: Col Widths (Display): 52mm, No. of Columns (Display): 4, Type Area: 320 x 220mm, Bleed Size: 346 x 246mm, Trim Size: 340 x 240mm, Col Length: 320mm, Page Width: 220mm, Film: Digital
Copy instructions: Copy Date: 2 weeks prior to publication date
Average advertising content per issue: 30%
BUSINESS: OTHER CLASSIFICATIONS: Veterinary

HORTICULTURE WEEK   38109U26B-55
Editorial Address: 22 Bute Gardens, LONDON, W6 7HN
Tel: 020 8267 4977 Fax: 020 8267 4987
Email: hortweek@haymarket.com
Advertising Address: 174 Hammersmith Road, LONDON, W6 7JP Tel: 020 8267 5000 Fax: 020 8267 4651
Email: jennie.meynell@haymarket.com

Web site: http://www.hortweek.com
ISSN: 0269-9478
Publisher: Haymarket Business Media Ltd
Date Established: 1841
Frequency: Weekly - Published on Friday
Cover Price: £2.10
Annual Sub.: £83.00
Circulation: 9,451 (ABC 01/07/2008 to 30/06/2009)
Usual Pagination: 52
Editor: Matthew Appleby; Features Editor: Gavin McEwan; Managing Director: Stephen Farish; Advertising Manager: Jennie Meynell; Managing Editor: Gemma Spence
Summary of Content: Magazine featuring horticultural news with business advice and technical features.
Readership/Target Audience: Aimed at commercial and retail nurseries, garden centres and landscapers, colleges, arboriculturists, the turf market and local authority parks managers.
ADVERTISING RATES:
Full Page Mono £1995.00
Full Page Colour £2950.00
Agency Commission: 10%
Mechanical Data: Bleed Size: 288 x 214mm, Trim Size: 280 x 210mm, Film: Digital, Type Area: 255 x 185mm, Col Length: 255mm, Page Width: 185mm
Copy instructions: Copy Date: 1 week prior to publication date
Average advertising content per issue: 40%
Supplement(s): Garden Retail - 6xY
BUSINESS: GARDEN TRADE: Garden Trade Supplies

THE HORTICULTURIST   38124U26D-60
Editorial Address: 9 Red Lion Court, LONDON, EC4A 3EF
Tel: 020 7936 5957 Fax: 020 7936 5958
Email: ioh@horticulture.org.uk
Advertising Address: As above.
Email: ioh@horticulture.org.uk
Web site: http://www.horticulture.org.uk
ISSN: 0964-8992
Publisher: The Institute of Horticulture
Date Established: 1992
Frequency: Quarterly
Annual Sub.: £84.00
Circulation: 2,500 (Publisher's Statement)
Usual Pagination: 32
Editor: Barbara Segall
Summary of Content: Journal containing articles on all aspects of professional horticulture including book reviews.
Readership/Target Audience: Aimed at professional horticulturists.
ADVERTISING RATES:
Full Page Colour £1000.00
Mechanical Data: Film: Digital, Trim Size: 297 x 210mm
Copy instructions: Copy Date: 3rd of the month prior to publication date
Average advertising content per issue: 10%
BUSINESS: GARDEN TRADE: Garden Trade Horticulture

HOSPITAL BULLETIN   40355U56C-324_80
Editorial Address: 1 Friary Chambers, Whitefriargate, HULL, HU1 2HA Tel: 01482 585735 Fax: 01482 229593
Email: info@hospital-bulletin.co.uk
Advertising Address: As above.
Email: info@hospital-bulletin.co.uk
Web site: http://www.hospital-bulletin.co.uk
Publisher: David Publishing Ltd
Date Established: 1997
Frequency: 6 issues yearly - Published on the 15th of the 1st cover month
Free to qualifying individuals
Annual Sub.: £50.00
Circulation: 6,771 (ABC 01/01/2008 to 31/12/2008)
Usual Pagination: 80
Editor: Debbie Cox; Managing Director: David Adamson; Advertising Manager: David Stephenson
Summary of Content: Magazine containing a wide range of articles about products and projects, plus development information.
Readership/Target Audience: Aimed at hospital estate and facilities management teams.
ADVERTISING RATES:
Full Page Colour £1650.00
Agency Commission: 10%
Mechanical Data: Type Area: 274 x 190mm, Bleed Size: 303 x 216mm, Trim Size: 297 x 210mm, Print Process: Litho, Film: Positive, right reading, emulsion side down. Digital, Col Length: 274mm, Page Width: 190mm
Copy instructions: Copy Date: 3 weeks prior to publication date
Average advertising content per issue: 40%
BUSINESS: HEALTH & MEDICAL: Hospitals

HOSPITAL CATERER   36573U11A-97
Editorial Address: 11-12 School House, Second Avenue, Trafford Park Village, MANCHESTER, M17 1DZ
Tel: 0161 872 6667 Fax: 0161 872 6668
Email: judy@lansdownepublishing.com

Advertising Address: As above.
Email: hca@lansdownepublishing.com
Web site: http://www.hospitalcaterers.org
Publisher: Lansdowne Publishing Partnership Ltd
Frequency: 6 issues yearly - Published in the 2nd week of the cover month
Annual Sub.: £30.00
Circulation: 1,500 (Publisher's Statement)
Usual Pagination: 32
Editor: Judy Sykes; Advertising Manager: Adrian Wright; Publisher: Adrian Wright
Summary of Content: Official journal of the Hospital Caterers Association.
Readership/Target Audience: Aimed at ASSOL members who are key buyers in the hospital catering industry.
ADVERTISING RATES:
Full Page Colour £1095.00
Agency Commission: 10%
Mechanical Data: Trim Size: 297 x 210mm, Film: Digital
Copy instructions: Copy Date: 3 weeks prior to publication date
Average advertising content per issue: 40%
BUSINESS: CATERING: Catering, Hotels & Restaurants

HOSPITAL DECISIONS   1660044U56R-513
Editorial Address: Lyndhurst, 10 Squires Lane, LONDON, N3 2AT Tel: 020 8343 4860 Fax: 020 8343 3756
Email: deanna@londonweb.net
Advertising Address: 32 Woodstock Grove, LONDON, W12 8LE Tel: 020 7616 0800 Fax: 020 7616 0810
Email: kbell@sovereign-publications.com
Web site: http://www.hospital-decisions.com
Publisher: Sovereign Publications Ltd
Date Established: 2001
Frequency: Half-yearly - Published in Summer and Winter
Free to qualifying individuals
Annual Sub.: £25.00
Circulation: 10,000 (Publisher's Statement)
Editor: Deanna Wilson; Advertising Manager: Kevin Bell
Summary of Content: Magazine covering the advances in medicine that are likely to have an impact on hospitals.
Readership/Target Audience: Aimed at hospital clinicians and management.
ADVERTISING RATES:
Full Page Mono £6900.00
Full Page Colour £7900.00
Mechanical Data: Trim Size: 297 x 210mm, Film: Digital
BUSINESS: HEALTH & MEDICAL: Health Medical Related

HOSPITAL IMAGING & RADIOLOGY EUROPE   1792965U56J-101
Editorial Address: 1 St. John's Square, LONDON, EC1M 4PN Tel: 020 7214 0500 Fax: 020 7214 0573
Email: hire@campden.com
Advertising Address: As above. Fax: 020 7214 0586
Email: manussetbrimicombe@campden.com
Web site: http://www.campden.com
ISSN: 1748-1082
Publisher: Campden Publishing Ltd
Date Established: 2006
Frequency: Quarterly
Cover Price: Free
Circulation: 10,000 (Publisher's Statement)
Usual Pagination: 52
Editor: Jacob Lonsdale; Publisher: Stephen Taylor
Summary of Content: Publication including clinical, technical and professional news, reviews, features and case studies.
Readership/Target Audience: Aimed at hospital radiologists, and other imaging professionals and IT support teams.
ADVERTISING RATES:
Full Page Colour £4450.00
Agency Commission: 10%
Mechanical Data: Bleed Size: 303 x 216mm, Trim Size: 297 x 210mm, Film: Digital
Copy instructions: Copy Date: 2 weeks prior to publication date
Average advertising content per issue: 30%
BUSINESS: HEALTH & MEDICAL: Radiography

HOSPITAL MANAGEMENT   40359U56C-337
Formerly: Hospital Management Today
Editorial Address: The Old Vicarage, Beck Hill, BARTON-UPON-HUMBER, DN18 5EY Tel: 01652 661510
Fax: 01652 661512
Email: joanne@hcpublications.fsworld.co.uk
Advertising Address: As above.
Email: joanne@hcpublications.fsworld.co.uk
Publisher: Health Care Publications
Frequency: 10 issues yearly - Published on the last day of the 1st cover month
Free to qualifying individuals
Annual Sub.: £50.00
Circulation: 7,850 (Publisher's Statement)
Usual Pagination: 40

Editor: Tracey Armitage; **Advertising Manager:** Joanne Dunderdale; **Publisher:** John Hughes
Summary of Content: Magazine covering all aspects of hospital management.
Readership/Target Audience: Aimed at those with an interest in works or estate matters in NHS and private hospitals in the UK.
ADVERTISING RATES:
Full Page Mono £1200.00
Full Page Colour £1700.00
Agency Commission: 10%
Mechanical Data: Trim Size: 297 x 210mm, Bleed Size: +3mm, Film: Digital
Copy instructions: Copy Date: 20th of the month prior to publication date
BUSINESS: HEALTH & MEDICAL: Hospitals

HOSPITAL PHARMACY EUROPE
1606337U56C-386

Formerly: HPE Hospital Pharmacy Europe
Editorial Address: 1 St. John's Square, LONDON, EC1M 4PN **Tel:** 020 7214 0556 **Fax:** 020 7214 0501
Email: hpe@campden.com
Advertising Address: As above. **Tel:** 020 7214 0515
Email: richardibbotson@campden.com
Web site: http://www.pharmacyeurope.net
ISSN: 1477-1896
Publisher: Campden Publishing Ltd
Date Established: 2002
Frequency: 6 issues yearly
Free to qualifying individuals
Annual Sub.: £75.00
Circulation: 10,000 (Publisher's Statement)
Usual Pagination: 80
Editor: Jacob Lonsdale; **Advertising Manager:** Richard Ibbotson; **Managing Editor:** Jacob Lonsdale; **Publisher:** Stephen Taylor
Summary of Content: Review journal covering developments in drug therapy, technology, healthcare policy and pharmacy practice.
Readership/Target Audience: Aimed at hospital pharmacists throughout Europe.
ADVERTISING RATES:
Full Page Mono £3500.00
Full Page Colour £4450.00
Agency Commission: 10%
Mechanical Data: Page Width: 190mm, Bleed Size: 303 x 216mm, Trim Size: 297 x 210mm, Type Area: 277 x 190mm, Col Length: 277mm, Film: Positive, right reading, emulsion side down. Digital
Average advertising content per issue: 30%
BUSINESS: HEALTH & MEDICAL: Hospitals

HOSPITALITY
36574U11A-100

Editorial Address: Trinity Court, 34 West Street, SUTTON, SM1 1SH **Tel:** 020 8661 4900 **Fax:** 020 8661 4901
Email: editor@instituteofhospitality.org
Advertising Address: As above.
Email: wally@hospitalitymagazine.co.uk
Web site: http://www.instituteofhospitality.org
ISSN: 0144-3704
Publisher: Institute of Hospitality
Date Established: 1980
Frequency: Quarterly
Free to qualifying individuals
Annual Sub.: £44.00
Circulation: 15,000 (Publisher's Statement)
Usual Pagination: 56
Editor: Ben Walker
Summary of Content: Magazine for hospitality, leisure and tourism management professionals.
Readership/Target Audience: Produced for members of the Hotel and Catering International Management Association and independent subscribers.
ADVERTISING RATES:
Full Page Colour £2250.00
Agency Commission: 10%
Mechanical Data: Bleed Size: 303 x 216mm, Trim Size: 297 x 210mm, Type Area: 270 x 180mm, Col Length: 270mm, Page Width: 180mm, Film: Digital
Copy instructions: Copy Date: 5 weeks prior to publication date
Average advertising content per issue: 25%
BUSINESS: CATERING: Catering, Hotels & Restaurants

HOSPITALITY & EVENTS NORTH
1810042U2C-516

Editorial Address: Host Media Centre, Savile Mount, LEEDS, LS7 3HZ **Tel:** 0845 052 2911 **Fax:** 0845 052 2912
Email: adam@media-mad.co.uk
Advertising Address: As above.
Email: elliot@media-mad.co.uk
Web site: http://www.media-mad.co.uk
Publisher: Media Mad
Date Established: 2007
Frequency: 6 issues yearly

Cover Price: Free
Circulation: 15,000 (Print Run)
Usual Pagination: 44
Editor: Adam Freedman; **Advertising Manager:** Elliot Landy
Summary of Content: Magazine covering conferencing, meetings, events, exhibitions and team building events.
Readership/Target Audience: Aimed at managing directors, commercial directors, HR managers, PAs and organisers looking to purchase hospitality events.
ADVERTISING RATES:
Full Page Mono £1000.00
Agency Commission: 10%
Mechanical Data: Type Area: 260 x 180mm, Col Length: 260mm, Page Width: 180mm, Bleed Size: +3mm, Film: Digital
Average advertising content per issue: 50%
BUSINESS: COMMUNICATIONS, ADVERTISING & MARKETING: Conferences & Exhibitions

HOSPITALITY INTERIORS
1655342U23A-307

Editorial Address: The Old Bakery, 31 Huntly Grove, PETERBOROUGH, PE1 4DJ **Tel:** 01733 890777
Fax: 01733 890711
Email: adrian@hospitality-interiors.com
Advertising Address: As above.
Email: rebecca@hospitality-interiors.co.uk
Web site: http://www.hospitality-interiors.com
Publisher: Carter Roe Ltd
Date Established: 2004
Frequency: 6 issues yearly
Cover Price: £6.50
Free to qualifying individuals
Annual Sub.: £30.00
Circulation: 7,500 (Publisher's Statement)
Usual Pagination: 84
Editor: Adrian Carter
Summary of Content: Magazine covering interior furnishings for the contract sector.
Readership/Target Audience: Aimed at architects, designers and specifiers in the hotel, restaurant, bar, pub and leisure industries.
ADVERTISING RATES:
Full Page Colour £1495.00
Agency Commission: 10%
Mechanical Data: Type Area: 276 x 191mm, No. of Columns (Display): 4, Col Length: 276mm, Page Width: 191mm
BUSINESS: FURNISHINGS & FURNITURE

HOSPITALITY REVIEW NI
36471U9A-30

Formerly: Catering & Licensing Review
Editorial Address: 5B Edgewater Business Park, Belfast Harbour Estate, BELFAST, BT3 9JQ **Tel:** 028 9078 3200
Fax: 028 9078 3210
Email: emmacowan@greerpublications.com
Advertising Address: As above.
Email: christineanderson@greerpublications.com
Web site: http://www.hospitalityreviewni.com
Publisher: Greer Publications Ltd
Date Established: 1977
Frequency: 11 issues yearly
Free to qualifying individuals
Annual Sub.: £27.50
Circulation: 4,308 (ABC 01/07/2006 to 30/06/2007)
Usual Pagination: 76
Editor: Emma Cowan; **Advertising Manager:** Christine Anderson; **Publisher:** James Greer
Summary of Content: Official publication of the Federation Of The Retail Licensed Trade Northern Ireland, the Northern Ireland Hotels Federation and the Northern Ireland Association of Chefs and Cooks. Covers industry news and comment.
Readership/Target Audience: Aimed at all sectors of the hospitality industry and licensed trade.
ADVERTISING RATES:
Full Page Colour £1860.00
Agency Commission: 10%
Mechanical Data: Film: Digital, Bleed Size: 340 x 245mm, Trim Size: 330 x 240mm, Type Area: 299 x 206mm, Col Length: 299mm, Page Width: 206mm
Copy instructions: Copy Date: 2 weeks prior to publication date
Average advertising content per issue: 40%
BUSINESS: DRINKS & LICENSED TRADE: Drinks, Licensed Trade, Wines & Spirits

HOTEL BUSINESS
36579U11A-106

Formerly: Hotel Magazine
Editorial Address: 25 Phoenix Court, Hawkins Road, COLCHESTER, CO2 8JY **Tel:** 01206 505983
Email: elizabeth.sharp@aceville.co.uk
Advertising Address: 2nd Floor, Ewer House, 44-46 Crouch Street, COLCHESTER, CO3 3HH **Tel:** 01206 506250
Fax: 01206 500228
Email: jenny@mspublications.co.uk
Web site: http://www.hotel-magazine.co.uk
ISSN: 1361-9454

Publisher: MS Publications (2001) Ltd
Date Established: 1991
Frequency: 10 issues yearly
Free to qualifying individuals
Annual Sub.: £35.00
Circulation: 8,063 (ABC 01/07/2006 to 30/06/2007)
Usual Pagination: 32
Editor: Elizabeth Sharp; **Advertising Manager:** Jenny O'Neil; **Group Editor:** Nicola Mallett
Summary of Content: Magazine covering all aspects of the hotel industry. Includes catering, refurbishment, recruitment, property, food and drink and topical news.
Readership/Target Audience: Aimed at management and staff in the accommodation sector.
ADVERTISING RATES:
Full Page Colour £1725.00
Agency Commission: 10%
Mechanical Data: Type Area: 359 x 254mm, Trim Size: 385 x 280mm, Col Length: 359mm, Page Width: 254mm, Bleed Size: 395 x 290mm, Film: Digital
Average advertising content per issue: 30%
BUSINESS: CATERING: Catering, Hotels & Restaurants

HOTEL MANAGEMENT INTERNATIONAL
21601U11A-118

Editorial Address: Brunel House, 55-57 North Wharf Road, LONDON, W2 1LA **Tel:** 020 7915 9600
Email: christopherkanal@spgmedia.com
Advertising Address: As above. **Tel:** 020 7753 4222
Fax: 020 7915 9773
Email: monicapalmas@spgmedia.com
Web site: http://www.hotelmanagement-network.com
Publisher: SPG Media Ltd
Frequency: Quarterly
Free to qualifying individuals
Circulation: 10,811 (ABC 01/07/2008 to 30/06/2009)
Usual Pagination: 176
Editor: Christopher Kanal
Summary of Content: Management publication for the hospitality industry in Europe.
Readership/Target Audience: Aimed at four and five star hoteliers and management companies.
ADVERTISING RATES:
Full Page Colour £5900.00
Agency Commission: 15%
Mechanical Data: Trim Size: 286 x 210mm, Film: Digital, Bleed Size: 292 x 216mm
Copy instructions: Copy Date: 12 weeks prior to publication date
Average advertising content per issue: 40%
BUSINESS: CATERING: Catering, Hotels & Restaurants

HOTEL REPORT
1640281U11A-193

Editorial Address: Broadfield Park, CRAWLEY, RH11 9RT **Tel:** 01293 613400 **Fax:** 01293 846577
Email: katherine.doggrell@william-reed.co.uk
Web site: http://www.hotelreport.co.uk
Publisher: William Reed Business Media
Frequency: Monthly
Annual Sub.: £485.00
Usual Pagination: 24
Editor: Katherine Doggrell; **News Editor:** Martyn Leek
Summary of Content: Magazine featuring intelligence and analysis for the hospitality industry.
Readership/Target Audience: Aimed at senior executives in the hotel sector.
ADVERTISING: No Advertising taken
BUSINESS: CATERING: Catering, Hotels & Restaurants

HOTEL SPEC
1645896U4B-177

Editorial Address: 2nd Floor, 207-215 High Street, ORPINGTON, BR6 0PF **Tel:** 01689 899170
Fax: 01689 899171
Email: gordon.green@purplems.com
Advertising Address: As above.
Email: gordon.green@purplems.com
Web site: http://www.hotelspeconline.com
Publisher: Purple Media Solutions Ltd
Date Established: 1986
Frequency: Annual - Published in January
Annual Sub.: £75.00
Circulation: 16,000 (Publisher's Statement)
Usual Pagination: 300
Editor: Gordon Green; **Advertising Manager:** Gordon Green
Summary of Content: Publication covering hotel interior design and specification.
Readership/Target Audience: Aimed at purchasing agents, project managers, design directors, managing directors and hotel owners.
ADVERTISING RATES:
Full Page Colour £3305.00
Mechanical Data: Film: Digital
Supplement(s): Premier Suppliers Supplement - 1xY
BUSINESS: ARCHITECTURE & BUILDING: Interior Design & Flooring

Business Magazines

HOTEL SPORT & LEISURE BUILDING & INTERIORS
1606126U4R-608

Editorial Address: Grosvenor House, Central Park, TELFORD, TF2 9TW **Tel:** 01952 234000 **Fax:** 01952 234003
Email: katie@tspltd.co.uk
Advertising Address: As above.
Email: marc@tspltd.co.uk
Web site: http://www.tspltd.co.uk
Publisher: Tanner Stiles Publishing Ltd
Frequency: Quarterly - Published in the 3rd week of the cover month
Cover Price: Free
Circulation: 10,698 (Publisher's Statement)
Usual Pagination: 44
Editor: Katie Wilcox; **Advertising Manager:** Marc Cooper
Summary of Content: Magazine covering news and product developments plus regular features on floors and floor coverings, catering equipment, interior furniture and furnishing, bathroom, washroom and changing room equipment, security and fire protection, exterior furniture and landscaping, sports and gym equipment, building services and refurbishment.
Readership/Target Audience: Aimed at hoteliers, facilities, sport and leisure managers, architects and interior designers.
ADVERTISING RATES:
Full Page Colour £1800.00
Agency Commission: 10%
Mechanical Data: Film: Digital, Bleed Size: 306 x 236mm, Trim Size: 300 x 230mm
Copy instructions: Copy Date: 2 weeks prior to publication date
Average advertising content per issue: 50%
BUSINESS: ARCHITECTURE & BUILDING: Building Related

HOTSHOE INTERNATIONAL
38789U38-17

Editorial Address: 29-31 Saffron Hill, LONDON, EC1N 8SW **Tel:** 020 7421 6000 **Fax:** 020 7421 6006
Email: melissa@hotshoeinternational.com
Advertising Address: As above.
Email: melissa@hotshoeinternational.com
Web site: http://www.hotshoeinternational.com
ISSN: 0959-6933
Publisher: World Illustrated Ltd
Frequency: 6 issues yearly
Cover Price: £4.50
Annual Sub.: £23.00
Circulation: 5,000 (Publisher's Statement)
Usual Pagination: 100
Editor: Melissa DeWitt; **Advertising Manager:** Fergus Elphinstone; **Publisher:** Charles Taylor
Summary of Content: Contemporary magazine featuring art, documentary and creative photography including portfolios and interviews along with book, exhibition and gear reviews as well as listings.
Readership/Target Audience: Aimed at individuals and businesses with an interest in professional and contemporary photography.
ADVERTISING RATES:
Full Page Colour £995.00
Agency Commission: 10%
Mechanical Data: Bleed Size: 250 x 178mm, Trim Size: 240 x 168mm, Page Width: 148mm, Film: Digital, Type Area: 214 x 148mm, Col Length: 214mm
Copy instructions: Copy Date: 4 weeks prior to publication date
Average advertising content per issue: 10%
BUSINESS: PHOTOGRAPHIC TRADE

HOUSEBUILDER
35851U4D-117

Editorial Address: 7-9 St. James's Street, LONDON, SW1A 1EE **Tel:** 020 7960 1630 **Fax:** 020 7960 1631
Email: suzie.mayes@house-builder.co.uk
Advertising Address: As above. **Tel:** 020 7960 1635
Email: chris.hart@house-builder.co.uk
Web site: http://www.house-builder.co.uk
ISSN: 0951-1334
Publisher: Housebuilder Media
Date Established: 1940
Frequency: 10 issues yearly - Published on the 1st Wednesday of the cover month
Cover Price: £7.00
Free to qualifying individuals
Annual Sub.: £77.00
Circulation: 17,709 (ABC 01/07/2008 to 30/06/2009)
Usual Pagination: 80
Editor: Suzie Mayes; **Advertising Manager:** Tim Mullin; **Managing Editor:** Ben Roskrow
Summary of Content: Trade journal covering specialist services and products, financial and economic issues, design land and planning matters.
Readership/Target Audience: Aimed at private sector house-builders and received by all NHBC registered house-builders.
ADVERTISING RATES:
Full Page Mono £2400.00
Full Page Colour £2400.00
Agency Commission: 10%

Mechanical Data: Type Area: 270 x 190mm, Bleed Size: 303 x 216mm, Trim Size: 297 x 210mm, Col Length: 270mm, Col Widths (Display): 44mm, Page Width: 190mm
Copy instructions: Copy Date: 10th of the month prior to publication date
Average advertising content per issue: 55%
Supplement(s): Britain's Biggest Housebuilders - 1xY
BUSINESS: ARCHITECTURE & BUILDING: Planning & Housing

HOUSEBUILDER & DEVELOPER
35908U4E-220

Formerly: housebuilder & developers datafile
Editorial Address: Cointronic House, Station Road, HEATHFIELD, TN21 8DF **Tel:** 01435 865797
Fax: 0870 855 5491
Email: editorial@netmagmedia.eu
Advertising Address: As above. **Tel:** 01435 863500
Fax: 01435 863897
Web site: http://www.hbdonline.eu
Publisher: Parker Ellis Publishing Ltd
Frequency: 6 issues yearly - Published around the beginning of the second cover month
Cover Price: £5.50
Free to qualifying individuals
Annual Sub.: £48.00
Circulation: 14,984 (ABC 01/07/2008 to 30/06/2009)
Usual Pagination: 40
Editor: Patricia Percival
Summary of Content: Magazine covering interiors, kitchens, bathrooms, floors and floor coverings, heating, plumbing, landscaping, timber and joinery, electrical supply, roofing and all products involved in house building.
Readership/Target Audience: Aimed at developers and specifiers associated with Housing Associations.
ADVERTISING RATES:
Full Page Mono £1225.00
Full Page Colour £1225.00
SCC £17.00
Agency Commission: 10%
Mechanical Data: Page Width: 190mm, Bleed Size: 303 x 216mm, Type Area: 277 x 190mm, Col Length: 277mm, Trim Size: 297 x 210mm, Film: Digital
Copy instructions: Copy Date: 4 weeks prior to publication date
Average advertising content per issue: 80%
BUSINESS: ARCHITECTURE & BUILDING: Building

HOUSEWARES DIRECTORY
601585U25-50

Formerly: Hayward Home Trade Directory
Editorial Address: Faversham House, 232A Addington Road, SOUTH CROYDON, CR2 8LE **Tel:** 020 8651 7100
Fax: 020 8651 7117
Email: clare.turner@fav-house.com
Advertising Address: As above.
Email: laurie.marrington@fav-house.com
Publisher: Faversham House Group Ltd
Date Established: 1999
Frequency: Annual - Published in March
Cover Price: £47.00
Free to qualifying individuals
Usual Pagination: 100
Editor: Clare Turner; **Publisher:** Colin Petty
Summary of Content: Guide covering all aspects of housewares.
Readership/Target Audience: Aimed at buyers and retailers.
ADVERTISING RATES:
Full Page Colour £1000.00
Agency Commission: 10%
Mechanical Data: No. of Columns (Display): 4, Bleed Size: 303 x 216mm, Trim Size: 297 x 210mm, Film: Digital
Copy instructions: Copy Date: 4 weeks prior to publication date
Average advertising content per issue: 50%
BUSINESS: HARDWARE

HOUSEWARES MAGAZINE
38097U25-170

Editorial Address: Faversham House, 232A Addington Road, SOUTH CROYDON, CR2 8LE **Tel:** 020 8651 7100
Fax: 020 8651 7117
Email: clare.turner@fav-house.com
Advertising Address: As above.
Email: laurie.marrington@fav-house.com
Web site: http://www.houswareslive.net
ISSN: 0264-8563
Publisher: Faversham House Group Ltd
Date Established: 1983
Frequency: 8 issues yearly - Published in the middle of the cover month
Free to qualifying individuals
Annual Sub.: £68.00
Circulation: 5,000 (ABC 01/07/2008 to 30/06/2009)
Editor: Clare Turner; **Publisher:** Colin Petty
Summary of Content: Magazine covering cookware, tabletop, small appliances and kitchenware.

Readership/Target Audience: Aimed at retailers of housewares.
ADVERTISING RATES:
Full Page Colour £2300.00
Agency Commission: 10%
Mechanical Data: Bleed Size: 303 x 216mm, Type Area: 270 x 180mm, Col Length: 270mm, Trim Size: 297 x 210mm, Film: Digital, Page Width: 180mm
Copy instructions: Copy Date: 3 weeks prior to publication date
BUSINESS: HARDWARE

HOUSING ACTIVE
1657699U4R-614

Formerly: Building, Repair and Maintenance
Editorial Address: PO Box 627, RICKMANSWORTH, WD3 0BQ **Tel:** 0870 766 1653 **Fax:** 0870 766 8529
Email: john.cowie@housingactive.co.uk
Advertising Address: As above.
Email: john@trade-mags.co.uk
Web site: http://www.trade-mags.co.uk
Publisher: Active Magazines Ltd
Date Established: 2002
Frequency: 3 issues yearly - No set months of publication
Free to qualifying individuals
Circulation: 25,000 (Publisher's Statement)
Usual Pagination: 52
Editor: John Cowie; **Advertising Manager:** John Cowie
Summary of Content: Magazine covering articles on the building, repair and maintenance of domestic and commercial property.
Readership/Target Audience: Aimed at trade professionals.
ADVERTISING RATES:
Full Page Mono £1750.00
Full Page Colour £1750.00
Agency Commission: 10%
Mechanical Data: Type Area: 254 x 178mm, Bleed Size: 303 x 216mm, Trim Size: 297 x 210mm, Col Length: 254mm, Page Width: 178mm, Film: Digital
Copy instructions: Copy Date: 3 weeks prior to publication date
Average advertising content per issue: 30%
BUSINESS: ARCHITECTURE & BUILDING: Building Related

HOUSING ASSOCIATION BUILDING & MAINTENANCE
35854U4D-124

Editorial Address: Regal House, Regal Way, WATFORD, WD24 4YF **Tel:** 01923 237799 **Fax:** 01923 246901
Email: habm@hamerville.co.uk
Advertising Address: As above.
Email: chris@hamerville.co.uk
Web site: http://www.habmonline.net
Publisher: Hamerville Magazines Ltd
Date Established: 1991
Frequency: 11 issues yearly - Published in the 2nd week of the cover month
Free to qualifying individuals
Annual Sub.: £20.00
Circulation: 11,723 (ABC 01/07/2008 to 30/06/2009)
Usual Pagination: 64
Editor: Ian Aubusson; **Managing Editor:** Terry Smith; **Publisher:** Bryan Shannon
Summary of Content: Magazine containing features on the types of work carried out on housing association properties.
Readership/Target Audience: Aimed at building officers in housing associations, architects, surveyors, housing managers, tenant representatives, building contractors and specifiers.
ADVERTISING RATES:
Full Page Colour £1850.00
Agency Commission: 10%
Mechanical Data: Type Area: 255 x 189mm, Film: Digital, Col Length: 255mm, Page Width: 189mm, Trim Size: 297 x 210mm
Copy instructions: Copy Date: 4 weeks prior to publication date
Average advertising content per issue: 50%
BUSINESS: ARCHITECTURE & BUILDING: Planning & Housing

HOUSING, CARE & SUPPORT
601094U32G-68

Editorial Address: Richmond House, Richmond Road, BRIGHTON, BN2 3RL **Tel:** 01273 623222
Fax: 01273 625526
Email: joannas@pavpub.com
Advertising Address: As above. **Tel:** 0870 890 1080
Fax: 0870 8901081
Email: pauls@pavpub.com
Web site: http://www.pavpub.com
ISSN: 1460-8790
Publisher: Pavilion Journals (Brighton) Ltd
Date Established: 1998
Frequency: Quarterly
Annual Sub.: £112.00
Circulation: 400 (Publisher's Statement)
Usual Pagination: 36

Editor: Gary Lashko
Summary of Content: Journal covering all aspects of housing support and community care. Includes descriptions of projects planned throughout the country, housing association news, advice on housing policies, events and book reviews.
Readership/Target Audience: Aimed at social landlords, care providers, local authorities, independent and voluntary organisations.
ADVERTISING RATES:
Full Page Mono £350.00
Mechanical Data: Type Area: 220 x 170mm, Col Length: 220mm, Page Width: 170mm, Film: Digital
BUSINESS: LOCAL GOVERNMENT, LEISURE & RECREATION: Community Care & Social Services

HOUSING MAGAZINE
35852U4D-404
Editorial Address: Octovia House, Westwood Way, COVENTRY, CV4 8JP **Tel:** 024 7685 1780
Fax: 024 7669 5110
Email: press@cih.org
Advertising Address: 1 Canada Square, 19th Floor, Canary Wharf, LONDON, E14 5AP **Tel:** 020 7772 8300
Fax: 020 7772 8590
Email: chris.softly@insidehousing.co.uk
Web site: http://www.cih.org
Publisher: Ocean Media Group Ltd
Frequency: 6 issues yearly
Free to qualifying individuals
Circulation: 19,000 (Publisher's Statement)
Usual Pagination: 16
Editor: Jill Dwyer
Summary of Content: Journal of the Chartered Institute of Housing. Includes features on all aspects of local authority housing departments, housing associations and the private sector.
Readership/Target Audience: Aimed at senior housing staff in local authorities and housing associations, members of the Institute and subscribers.
ADVERTISING RATES:
Full Page Mono £2282.00
Full Page Colour £2828.00
Agency Commission: 10%
Mechanical Data: Type Area: 280 x 210mm, Bleed Size: 306 x 236mm, Trim Size: 300 x 230mm, Col Length: 280mm, Page Width: 210mm, Film: Digital
Copy instructions: Copy Date: Wednesday 10.00am prior to publication date
Average advertising content per issue: 35%
BUSINESS: ARCHITECTURE & BUILDING: Planning & Housing

HOUSING SCOTLAND
1644557U4D-403
Editorial Address: Pegasus House, 375 West George Street, GLASGOW, G2 4LW **Tel:** 0141 332 8113
Fax: 0141 332 9684
Email: editor@housingscotland.co.uk
Advertising Address: 15 Newton Terrace, GLASGOW, G3 7PJ **Tel:** 0141 204 2042 **Fax:** 0141 204 2043
Email: l.grant@contactpublishing.co.uk
Publisher: SFHA
Date Established: 2004
Frequency: 10 issues yearly
Free to qualifying individuals
Circulation: 3,800 (Publisher's Statement)
Usual Pagination: 32
Editor: Claire Munro
Summary of Content: Magazine covering the Scottish housing sector. Covers news on major housing projects, changes in legislation, exhibitions and events.
Readership/Target Audience: Aimed at local authorities, associate members, landlords and tenants.
ADVERTISING RATES:
Full Page Colour £950.00
Mechanical Data: Type Area: 260 x 180mm, Film: Digital
Copy instructions: Copy Date: 2 weeks prior to publication
BUSINESS: ARCHITECTURE & BUILDING: Planning & Housing

HOUSING TECHNOLOGY
1829344U4D-421
Editorial Address: 24 Cardinal Crescent, Coombeside, NEW MALDEN, KT3 3EF **Tel:** 01386 700195
Email: news@housing-technology.com
Web site: http://www.housing-technology.com
Publisher: The Intelligent Business Company
Date Established: 2008
Frequency: 6 issues yearly
Cover Price: Free
Circulation: 7,500 (Publisher's Statement)
Usual Pagination: 28
Editor: Alastair Tweedie
Summary of Content: Magazine providing IT, technology and telco news and information to those responsible for technology strategy and business decision-making in the UK social housing sector, housing associations and local government.

Readership/Target Audience: Aimed at those responsible for technology strategy and business decision making in housing associations, the UK housing sector and local government.
BUSINESS: ARCHITECTURE & BUILDING: Planning & Housing

THE HOVERCRAFT NEWSLETTER
36409U6E-142
Formerly: The Hovercraft Bulletin
Editorial Address: Argus Gate, Broom Way, Lee on Solent, GOSPORT, PO13 9NY **Tel:** 023 9255 2090
Fax: 023 9255 2090
Email: enquiries@hovercraft-museum.org
Advertising Address: As above.
Email: chris@hovercraft-museum.org
Publisher: The Hovercraft Museum
Date Established: 1971
Frequency: Quarterly
Annual Sub.: £25.00
Circulation: 500 (Publisher's Statement)
Usual Pagination: 24
Editor: Warwick Jacobs; **Advertising Manager:** Warwick Jacobs
Summary of Content: Magazine covering all hovercraft activities, past present and future.
Readership/Target Audience: Read by members of the Hovercraft Society, Friends of the Hovercraft Museum Trust and organisations with an interest.
ADVERTISING RATES:
Full Page Mono £150.00
Full Page Colour £250.00
Agency Commission: 10%
Mechanical Data: Film: Digital, Bleed Size: 303 x 216mm, Trim Size: 297 x 210mm
Average advertising content per issue: 10%
BUSINESS: AVIATION & AERONAUTICS: Hovercraft VTOL

HRM HOTEL & RESTAURANT MANAGER
36580U11A-125
Editorial Address: Unit 24, Eldon Business Park, Eldon Road, Attenborough, NOTTINGHAM, NG9 6DZ
Tel: 0115 925 5227 **Fax:** 0115 922 9645
Email: hrm@btconnect.co.uk
Advertising Address: As above.
Email: hrm@btconnect.co.uk
Web site: http://www.nationalbartender.co.uk
Publisher: Emtrad
Date Established: 1999
Frequency: 6 issues yearly
Cover Price: Free
Circulation: 18,000 (Publisher's Statement)
Usual Pagination: 24
Editor: Simon Butler; **Advertising Manager:** Eddie Morris
Summary of Content: Magazine covering all aspects of the hotel and restaurant industries, including catering products and equipment, safety and security issues, general health and safety matters and features on fixtures and fittings for all areas of hotels and restaurants.
Readership/Target Audience: Aimed at owners, operators and managers of independent hotels and restaurants in England and Wales.
ADVERTISING RATES:
Full Page Colour £1900.00
SCC £10.00
Agency Commission: 10%
Mechanical Data: Col Length: 265mm, Film: Digital, Type Area: 265 x 185mm, Bleed Size: 303 x 216mm, Trim Size: 297 x 210mm, Page Width: 185mm
Average advertising content per issue: 45%
BUSINESS: CATERING: Catering, Hotels & Restaurants

HUMAN GIVENS
40596U56R-92_1
Formerly: The New Therapist
Editorial Address: The Barn, Church Farm, Chalvington, HAILSHAM, BN27 3TD **Tel:** 01323 811662
Fax: 01323 811486
Email: the-editor@humangivens.com
Web site: http://www.humangivens.com
ISSN: 1467-5676
Publisher: HG Publishing
Date Established: 1993
Frequency: Quarterly
Annual Sub.: £30.00
Circulation: 5,000 (Publisher's Statement)
Usual Pagination: 48
Editor: Denise Winn
Summary of Content: International journal containing multi-disciplinary articles relating to psychology and the human givens approach.
Readership/Target Audience: Aimed at therapeutic practitioners from all disciplines, including mental and physical health, welfare and education.
ADVERTISING: No Advertising taken
BUSINESS: HEALTH & MEDICAL: Health Medical Related

HUMAN MOLECULAR GENETICS
25737U64F-42
Editorial Address: Department of Physiology, Anatomy and Genetics, University of Oxford, South Parks Road, OXFORD, OX1 3QX **Tel:** 01865 272416 **Fax:** 01865 272427
Email: hmgjournal@anat.ox.ac.uk
Advertising Address: Great Clarendon Street, OXFORD, OX2 6DP **Tel:** 01865 353907
Email: steve.simmonds@oxfordjournals.org
Web site: http://www.hmg.oupjournals.org
ISSN: 0962-6906
Publisher: OUP
Date Established: 1992
Frequency: 26 issues yearly
Cover Price: £13.00
Annual Sub.: £280.00
Usual Pagination: 192
Editor: K. E. Davies
Summary of Content: Journal containing full-length research papers covering a wide range of topics in all aspects of human molecular genetics.
Readership/Target Audience: Aimed at human geneticists, molecular biologists, medical geneticists and human genome project researchers at universities, medical research institutes and pharmaceutical research departments.
ADVERTISING RATES:
Full Page Mono £646.00
Full Page Colour £1076.00
Agency Commission: 15%
Mechanical Data: Trim Size: 280 x 215mm, Bleed Size: 286 x 221mm, Film: Digital, Col Length: 255mm, Page Width: 178mm, Print Process: Litho, Type Area: 255 x 178mm
BUSINESS: OTHER CLASSIFICATIONS: Biology

HUMAN RELATIONS
601450U56R-66_50
Editorial Address: 1 Oliver's Yard, 55 City Road, LONDON, EC1Y 1SP **Tel:** 020 7324 8500 **Fax:** 020 7324 8600
Advertising Address: As above.
Email: advertising@sagepub.co.uk
Web site: http://www.sagepub.co.uk
ISSN: 0018-7267
Publisher: Sage Publications
Frequency: Monthly
Annual Sub.: £73.00
Editor-in-Chief: Stephen Deery; **Advertising Manager:** Sheena Karim; **Managing Editor:** Claire Castle
Summary of Content: Journal covering features and ideas in social sciences. Includes articles on theory and practice, book reviews and research advances.
Readership/Target Audience: Aimed at those interested in social sciences.
ADVERTISING RATES:
Full Page Mono £400.00
Agency Commission: 5%
Mechanical Data: Page Width: 140mm, Type Area: 210 x 140mm, Col Length: 210mm
Copy instructions: Copy Date: 12 weeks prior to publication date
BUSINESS: HEALTH & MEDICAL: Health Medical Related

HUMAN REPRODUCTION
24571U56A-68_10
Editorial Address: Editorial Office, ESHRE Journals, Childerley, CAMBRIDGE, CB23 8BA **Tel:** 01954 212404
Fax: 01954 212359
Email: editorial@humanreproduction.co.uk
Advertising Address: Great Clarendon Street, OXFORD, OX2 6DP **Tel:** 01865 353907
Email: steve.simmonds@oxfordjournals.org
Web site: http://www.oup.co.uk/jnls
ISSN: 0268-1161
Publisher: OUP
Date Established: 1986
Frequency: Monthly
Annual Sub.: £665.00
Usual Pagination: 250
Managing Editor: Helen Beard
Summary of Content: Publication covering all aspects of human reproduction research.
Readership/Target Audience: Aimed at scientists and clinicians working in international human reproduction research and practise.
ADVERTISING RATES:
Full Page Mono £742.00
Full Page Colour £1236.00
Agency Commission: 10%
Mechanical Data: Page Width: 178mm, Type Area: 255 x 178mm, Bleed Size: 286 x 222mm, Trim Size: 280 x 216mm, Col Length: 255mm, Film: Digital, Print Process: Litho
BUSINESS: HEALTH & MEDICAL

HUMAN REPRODUCTION & GENETIC ETHICS: AN INTERNATIONAL JOURNAL
40580U56R-66_60
Formerly: Human Reproduction & Genetic Ethics
Editorial Address: 191 Leith Walk, EDINBURGH, EH6 8NX
Tel: 0131 554 8869

Business Magazines

Email: bioethics@europe.com
Advertising Address: As above.
Email: bioethics@europe.com
Web site: http://www.geneticsethics.org
ISSN: 1028-7825
Publisher: The Bioethics Press Ltd
Date Established: 1995
Frequency: Half-yearly - Published in February and October
Annual Sub.: £24.00
Circulation: 500 (Publisher's Statement)
Usual Pagination: 44
Editor: Calum MacKellar; **Advertising Manager:** Calum MacKellar; **Managing Editor:** Carol Marlin
Summary of Content: Journal of human reproduction and genetic ethics.
Readership/Target Audience: Aimed at those working in the fields of medicine, nursing, law, philosophy, psychology, theology, politics, and science.
ADVERTISING RATES:
Full Page Mono £100.00
Agency Commission: 10%
Mechanical Data: Trim Size: 297 x 210mm, Film: Digital
Average advertising content per issue: 10%
BUSINESS: HEALTH & MEDICAL: Health Medical Related

HUMAN REPRODUCTION UPDATE
601533U56R-66_70

Editorial Address: Editorial Office, ESHRE Journals, 5 Mill Yard, Childerley, CAMBRIDGE, CB23 8BA
Tel: 01954 212404 **Fax:** 01954 212359
Email: editorial@humanreproduction.co.uk
Advertising Address: Great Clarendon Street, OXFORD, OX2 6DP **Tel:** 01865 354637
Email: steve.simmonds@oxfordjournals.org
Web site: http://www.oup.co.uk/jnls
ISSN: 1355-4786
Publisher: OUP
Date Established: 1963
Frequency: 6 issues yearly
Cover Price: £31.00
Annual Sub.: £168.00
Usual Pagination: 108
Editor: J. Collins; **Editor-in-Chief:** J. Collins; **Managing Editor:** H. Beard
Summary of Content: Journal featuring comprehensive review service of research within the field of human reproduction.
Readership/Target Audience: Read by members of the European Society of Human Reproduction and Embryology.
ADVERTISING RATES:
Full Page Mono £742.00
Full Page Colour £1236.00
Agency Commission: 10%
Mechanical Data: Type Area: 255 x 178mm, Trim Size: 280 x 216mm, Bleed Size: 286 x 222mm, Film: Digital, Page Width: 178mm, Col Length: 255mm, Print Process: Litho
Copy instructions: Copy Date: 6 weeks prior to publication date
BUSINESS: HEALTH & MEDICAL: Health Medical Related

HUMAN RESOURCES
36764U14A-155

Editorial Address: 22 Bute Gardens, LONDON, W6 7HN
Tel: 020 8267 4828
Email: human.resources@haymarket.com
Advertising Address: 174 Hammersmith Road, LONDON, W6 7JP **Tel:** 020 8267 5000 **Fax:** 020 8267 4554
Email: rebecca.nolan@haymarket.com
Web site: http://www.hrmagazine.co.uk
ISSN: 0964-8380
Publisher: Haymarket Business Media Ltd
Frequency: Monthly - Published around the beginning of the cover month
Free to qualifying individuals
Annual Sub.: £89.00
Circulation: 17,050 (ABC 01/07/2008 to 30/06/2009)
Usual Pagination: 84
Editor: Peter Crush
Summary of Content: Management magazine covering strategic human resource issues.
Readership/Target Audience: Read by chairmen, chief executive officers and managing and human resource directors of multinational and blue chip companies, public sector and charities.
ADVERTISING RATES:
Full Page Mono £4100.00
Full Page Colour £4950.00
Agency Commission: 10%
Mechanical Data: Page Width: 186mm, Trim Size: 280 x 210mm, Type Area: 235 x 186mm, Col Length: 235mm, Film: Digital
Copy instructions: Copy Date: Middle of the month prior to publication date
Supplement(s): HR Directors Year book - 1xY
BUSINESS: COMMERCE, INDUSTRY & MANAGEMENT

HVP HEATING, VENTILATING & PLUMBING
35757U3B-16

Editorial Address: 32 Vauxhall Bridge Road, LONDON, SW1V 2SS **Tel:** 020 7973 6400 **Fax:** 020 7233 5051
Email: edit@hvpmag.co.uk
Advertising Address: As above. **Tel:** 020 8680 4200
Fax: 020 8681 5049
Email: info@hvpmag.co.uk
Web site: http://www.hvpmag.co.uk
ISSN: 0265-4571
Publisher: Hemming Group Ltd
Date Established: 1984
Frequency: 10 issues yearly - Published in the 1st week of the cover month
Free to qualifying individuals
Annual Sub.: £48.00
Circulation: 35,238 (ABC 01/01/2008 to 31/12/2008)
Usual Pagination: 110
Editor: Jennie Ward
Summary of Content: Magazine covering heating, plumbing and ventilation in all forms for the domestic and light commercial markets. Includes supplements on gas, controls, bathrooms, training and the Institute of Plumbing and Heating Engineering.
Readership/Target Audience: Aimed at domestic and light commercial heating and plumbing installers, specifiers, buyers, merchants, manufacturers of heating, ventilating and plumbing equipment, purchasing executives, estate developers, local government specifiers and educational and research establishments.
ADVERTISING RATES:
Full Page Colour £2800.00
Agency Commission: 10%
Mechanical Data: Type Area: 254 x 178mm, Bleed Size: 303 x 216mm, Col Length: 254mm, Page Width: 178mm, Film: Digital, Trim Size: 297 x 210mm
Copy instructions: Copy Date: 4 weeks prior to publication date
Average advertising content per issue: 40%
Supplement(s): Bathroom - 1xY
BUSINESS: HEATING & VENTILATION: Industrial Heating & Ventilation

HVR
35759U3B-40

Formerly: Heating & Ventilating Review
Editorial Address: Faversham House, 232A Addington Road, SOUTH CROYDON, CR2 8LE **Tel:** 020 8651 7100
Fax: 020 8651 7117
Email: hvreditorial@fav-house.com
Advertising Address: As above.
Email: jan.thorpe@fav-house.com
Web site: http://www.heatingandventilating.net
ISSN: 0017-0396
Publisher: Faversham House Group Ltd
Date Established: 1960
Frequency: Monthly
Free to qualifying individuals
Annual Sub.: £57.00
Circulation: 13,275 (ABC 01/01/2008 to 31/12/2008)
Usual Pagination: 48
Editor: Paul Braithwaite; **Publisher:** Jan Thorpe
Summary of Content: Journal focusing on the commercial and industrial heating, air conditioning and ventilating market, local authority specifiers and multi-unit new builds.
Readership/Target Audience: Aimed at HVAC contractors, consultants, specifiers and end users.
ADVERTISING RATES:
Full Page Mono £1500.00
Full Page Colour £2000.00
Agency Commission: 10%
Mechanical Data: Page Width: 180mm, Type Area: 270 x 180mm, Col Length: 270mm, Trim Size: 297 x 210mm, Bleed Size: 303 x 216mm, Print Process: Sheet-fed offset, Film: Digital
Copy instructions: Copy Date: 3 weeks prior to publication date
Average advertising content per issue: 40%
BUSINESS: HEATING & VENTILATION: Industrial Heating & Ventilation

HYDRAULICS & PNEUMATICS
37634U19D-350

Editorial Address: Cape House, 60A Priory Road, TONBRIDGE, TN9 2BL **Tel:** 01892 615806
Fax: 01732 360034
Email: ed@dfamedia.co.uk
Advertising Address: As above. **Tel:** 01732 370340
Email: ryan@dfamedia.co.uk
Web site: http://www.hpmag.co.uk
ISSN: 1366-1981
Publisher: DFA Media Ltd
Date Established: 1996
Frequency: 8 issues yearly
Cover Price: Free
Circulation: 12,996 (ABC 01/01/2008 to 31/12/2008)
Usual Pagination: 52
Editor: Ed Holden
Summary of Content: Journal covering all aspects of fluid power equipment and systems.

Readership/Target Audience: Aimed at machine designers, purchasers, specifiers, engineers and other decision makers.
ADVERTISING RATES:
Full Page Mono £1220.00
Full Page Colour £1975.00
Agency Commission: 10%
Mechanical Data: Type Area: 264 x 178mm, Bleed Size: 303 x 216mm, Trim Size: 297 x 210mm, Col Length: 264mm, Page Width: 178mm, Film: Digital
Average advertising content per issue: 40%
BUSINESS: ENGINEERING & MACHINERY: Hydraulic Power

HYDROCARBON ENGINEERING
38588U33-9

Formerly: The International Journal of Hydrocarbon Engineering
Editorial Address: 15 South Street, FARNHAM, GU9 7QU
Tel: 01252 718999 **Fax:** 01252 718992
Email: james.little@hydrocarbonengineering.com
Advertising Address: As above.
Email: chris.atkin@hydrocarbonengineering.com
Web site: http://www.hydrocarbonengineering.com
ISSN: 1468-9340
Publisher: Palladian Publications Ltd
Date Established: 1996
Frequency: Monthly
Free to qualifying individuals
Annual Sub.: £105.00
Circulation: 10,141 (ABC 01/01/2008 to 31/12/2008)
Usual Pagination: 88
Editor: James Little; **Advertising Manager:** Chris Atkin; **Managing Editor:** James Little; **Publisher:** Nigel Hardy
Summary of Content: Journal containing technical information related to hydrocarbon engineering.
Readership/Target Audience: Aimed at technical directors and managers, plant and project managers and senior process engineers within oil refineries, gas processing plants and petrochemical plants worldwide.
ADVERTISING RATES:
Full Page Colour £3150.00
Agency Commission: 10%
Mechanical Data: Type Area: 268 x 178mm, Col Length: 268mm, Bleed Size: 303 x 216mm, Trim Size: 297 x 210mm, Page Width: 178mm, Print Process: Offset litho, Film: Digital
Copy instructions: Copy Date: 15th of the month prior to the cover month
Average advertising content per issue: 30%
Supplement(s): LNG Industry - 4xY
BUSINESS: OIL & PETROLEUM

HYDROLOGICAL PROCESSES
39093U55-35

Editorial Address: Editorial Office, University of Bristol, University Road, BRISTOL, BS8 1SS
Email: hp-journal@bristol.ac.uk
Advertising Address: The Atrium, Southern Gate, CHICHESTER, PO19 8SQ **Tel:** 01243 770254
Fax: 01243 770432
Email: fpidduck@wiley.com
Web site: http://www.interscience.wiley.com
ISSN: 0885-6087
Publisher: John Wiley & Sons Ltd
Date Established: 1987
Frequency: 26 issues yearly
Annual Sub.: $2590.00
Editor: Fiona Murphy; **Executive Editor:** Fiona Murphy
Summary of Content: Journal containing original scientific and technical papers in hydrology.
Readership/Target Audience: Aimed at hydrologists, geologists, environmental scientists and water engineers.
ADVERTISING RATES:
Full Page Mono £1175.00
Full Page Colour £2575.00
Agency Commission: 10%
Mechanical Data: Print Process: Sheet-fed litho, Film: Digital, Type Area: 270 x 180mm, Trim Size: 297 x 210mm, Col Length: 270mm, Page Width: 180mm
BUSINESS: APPLIED SCIENCE & LABORATORIES

THE HYGIENIST
40581U56R-67

Editorial Address: Shalimar, The Weavers, Farndon Road, NEWARK ON TRENT, NG24 4RY **Tel:** 01636 682 941
ISSN: 0018-8263
Publisher: British Natural Hygiene Society
Date Established: 1959
Frequency: Quarterly
Annual Sub.: £15.00
Circulation: 350 (Publisher's Statement)
Usual Pagination: 24
Editor: Keki Sidhwa
Summary of Content: International magazine advocating a healthier lifestyle, enhancing the human potential for health of body, mind and spirit.
Readership/Target Audience: Aimed at members of the British National Hygiene Society and members of the general public.

ADVERTISING: No Advertising taken
BUSINESS: HEALTH & MEDICAL: Health Medical Related

IAI INSTITUTIONAL ALTERNATIVE INVESTMENT
1810532U1F-641

Editorial Address: 337 City Road, LONDON, EC1V 1LJ
Tel: 020 7713 8748 **Fax:** 020 7837 7346
Email: fieldhouse@ifiglobal.com
Advertising Address: As above.
Email: hallett@ifiglobal.com
Web site: http://www.ifilive.com
Publisher: International Fund Investment
Frequency: 10 issues yearly
Free to qualifying individuals
Annual Sub.: £450.00
Circulation: 1,162 (Publisher's Statement)
Managing Director: Simon Osborn
Summary of Content: Magazine providing news on allocations made to alternatives by pension funds, insurance funds and banks. Covers art, currencies, commodities, energy, hedge funds, private equity, real estate, wine and all other forms of alternative investment activity.
Readership/Target Audience: Aimed at institutional investors.
ADVERTISING RATES:
Full Page Mono £2000.00
Full Page Colour £3000.00
Mechanical Data: Type Area: 254 x 178mm, Bleed Size: 286 x 216mm, Trim Size: 280 x 210mm, Col Length: 254mm, Page Width: 178mm, Film: Digital
Supplement(s): Institutional Alternative Investment Bulletin IAIB - 50xY
BUSINESS: FINANCE & ECONOMICS: Investment

IALA BULLETIN
39433U45R-60

Editorial Address: No 3 The Green, Ketton, STAMFORD, PE9 3RA **Tel:** 01780 721628 **Fax:** 01780 721980
Email: pridgway@globalnet.co.uk
Web site: http://www.iala-aism.org
ISSN: 0379-2811
Publisher: International Assoc. of Marine Aids to Navigation and Lighthouse Authorities
Date Established: 1957
Frequency: Quarterly
Circulation: 750 (Publisher's Statement)
Editor: Paul Ridgway
Summary of Content: Magazine of the International Association of Marine Aids to Navigation and Lighthouse Authorities.
Language(s): English; French
Readership/Target Audience: Read mainly by international marine navigators and those involved in the lighthouse authorities.
ADVERTISING: No Advertising taken
BUSINESS: MARINE & SHIPPING: Marine Related

IBD MEMBERS HANDBOOK
36503U9A-95

Formerly: IBD Company Directory
Editorial Address: 33 Clarges Street, LONDON, W1J 7EE
Tel: 020 7499 8144 **Fax:** 020 7499 1156
Email: enquiries@ibd.org.uk
Advertising Address: Clock House Studio, Clock House Lane, Bramley, GUILDFORD, GU5 0AP **Tel:** 01483 893100
Fax: 01483 894500
Email: enquiries@carlingpartnership.co.uk
Web site: http://www.ibd.org.uk
ISSN: 0309-7625
Publisher: Institute of Brewing & Distilling
Date Established: 2001
Frequency: Annual - Published in October
Free to qualifying individuals
Circulation: 4,000 (Publisher's Statement)
Usual Pagination: 200
Advertising Manager: Sally Carter
Summary of Content: Journal containing lists of IBD Members, trade, industry and educational contracts, details of IBD membership categories, training, examinations, awards and past winners. Lists standing committees, council representatives, section representatives, past presidents, upcoming dates, staff contact details, articles and byelaws.
Readership/Target Audience: Aimed at members of the IBD, who consist of allied traders and the brewing and distilling industry.
ADVERTISING RATES:
Full Page Mono £675.00
Full Page Colour £1050.00
Agency Commission: 10%
Mechanical Data: Type Area: 200 x 120mm, Bleed Size: 230 x 155mm, Print Process: Offset litho, Film: Digital, Col Length: 200mm, Page Width: 120mm
Copy instructions: Copy Date: 6 weeks prior to publication date
Average advertising content per issue: 30%
BUSINESS: DRINKS & LICENSED TRADE: Drinks, Licensed Trade, Wines & Spirits

IBE INTERNATIONAL BROADCAST ENGINEER
35676U2D-63

Editorial Address: 3rd Floor, Armstrong House, 38 Market Square, UXBRIDGE, UB8 1TG **Tel:** 01409 241166
Email: nnixon@btconnect.com
Advertising Address: As above. **Tel:** 01895 421111
Email: csturzaker@bpl-business.com
Web site: http://www.ibeweb.com
ISSN: 0220-6229
Publisher: BPL Business Media Ltd
Date Established: 1964
Frequency: 6 issues yearly
Cover Price: Free
Circulation: 10,105 (BPA Worldwide 01/01/2008 to 30/06/2008)
Usual Pagination: 40
Editor: Neil Nixon; **Advertising Manager:** Clare Sturzaker; **Publisher:** Clare Sturzaker
Summary of Content: Independent journal devoted to the design, manufacture and operation of professional television and radio equipment.
Readership/Target Audience: Read by senior broadcast engineers and operational staff within television and radio production and transmission facilities worldwide.
ADVERTISING RATES:
Full Page Mono £2370.00
Full Page Colour £3150.00
Agency Commission: 10%
Mechanical Data: Type Area: 265 x 185mm, Col Length: 265mm, Page Width: 185mm, Trim Size: 297 x 210mm, Bleed Size: 303 x 216mm, Film: Digital
Average advertising content per issue: 46%
BUSINESS: COMMUNICATIONS, ADVERTISING & MARKETING: Broadcasting

IBI INTERNATIONAL BOAT INDUSTRY
39421U45E-65

Editorial Address: Leon House, 233 High Street, CROYDON, CR9 1HZ **Tel:** 020 8726 8134
Fax: 020 8726 8196
Email: ed_slack@ipcmedia.com
Advertising Address: As above. **Tel:** 020 8726 8000
Email: philip_pereira@ipcmedia.com
Web site: http://www.ibinews.com
Publisher: IPC Inspire
Frequency: 7 issues yearly
Free to qualifying individuals
Circulation: 10,700 (Publisher's Statement)
Editor: Ed Slack; **Advertising Manager:** Philip Pereira
Summary of Content: Magazine covering market reports, industry news, company profiles, trade opinions, trade events, new products, technical developments and export and import opportunities.
Readership/Target Audience: Aimed at executives in the marine industry.
ADVERTISING RATES:
Full Page Colour £3460.00
Mechanical Data: Print Process: Sheet-fed litho, Type Area: 260 x 179mm, Col Length: 260mm, Film: Digital, Trim Size: 297 x 210mm, Bleed Size: 303 x 216mm, Page Width: 179mm
Copy instructions: Copy Date: 3 weeks prior to publication date
BUSINESS: MARINE & SHIPPING: Boat Trade

ICE CREAM MAGAZINE
38029U22E-225

Formerly: Ice Cream and Cafe Society
Editorial Address: 3 Melbourne Court, Pride Park, DERBY, DE24 8LZ **Tel:** 01332 203333 **Fax:** 01332 203420
Email: info@ice-cream.org
Advertising Address: As above.
Email: leslie@ice-cream.org
Web site: http://www.ice-cream.org
ISSN: 1356-0948
Publisher: Ice Cream Alliance Ltd
Date Established: 1942
Frequency: 11 issues yearly
Free to qualifying individuals
Annual Sub.: £130.00
Circulation: 900 (Publisher's Statement)
Usual Pagination: 48
Editor: Zelica Carr
Summary of Content: Journal focusing on ice cream manufacturing and vending.
Readership/Target Audience: Aimed at members of the Ice Cream Alliance and key ice cream buyers within the UK.
ADVERTISING RATES:
Full Page Mono £300.00
Full Page Colour £520.00
Mechanical Data: Type Area: 267 x 184mm, Bleed Size: 303 x 216mm, Trim Size: 297 x 210mm, Col Length: 267mm, Page Width: 184mm
BUSINESS: FOOD: Frozen Food

ICIS CHEMICAL BUSINESS
36663U13-90

Editorial Address: Quadrant House, The Quadrant, SUTTON, SM2 5AS **Tel:** 020 8652 3500 **Fax:** 020 8652 3375
Email: icbeditorial@icis.com
Advertising Address: As above. **Fax:** 020 8652 8918
Email: maarten.dubbeld@icis.com
Web site: http://www.icis.com
Publisher: Reed Business Information
Frequency: 47 issues yearly
Circulation: 23,358 (BPA Worldwide 01/01/2008 to 30/06/2008)
Usual Pagination: 48
Editor: Will Beecham
Summary of Content: Magazine containing news and features concerning the chemical industry.
Readership/Target Audience: Aimed at senior managers and key executives in chemical manufacturing, distribution, transportation and storage.
ADVERTISING RATES:
Full Page Mono EUR4660.00
Full Page Colour EUR5990.00
Agency Commission: 10%
Mechanical Data: Type Area: 246 x 175mm, Trim Size: 267 x 197mm, Col Length: 246mm, Page Width: 175mm, Bleed Size: 273 x 200mm, Film: Digital
Copy instructions: Copy Date: 2 weeks prior to publication date
Average advertising content per issue: 40%
BUSINESS: CHEMICALS

ICNM JOURNAL
1902435U56R-531

Editorial Address: Can Mezzanine, 32-36 Loman Street, LONDON, SE1 0EH **Tel:** 020 7922 7980 **Fax:** 020 7922 7981
Email: yvonne.wilcox@icnm.org.uk
Web site: http://www.icnm.org.uk
Publisher: Institute for Complementary Medicine
Frequency: Quarterly
Free to qualifying individuals
Circulation: 1,200 (Publisher's Statement)
Usual Pagination: 14
Editor: Joanne Flack; **Managing Editor:** Yvonne Wilcox
Summary of Content: Journal covering complementary and natural medicine.
Readership/Target Audience: Aimed at complementary practitioners.
BUSINESS: HEALTH & MEDICAL: Health Medical Related

ICON
1615423U4A-306

Editorial Address: National House, 121-123 High Street, EPPING, CM16 4BD **Tel:** 01992 570030 **Fax:** 01992 570031
Email: johanna@icon-magazine.co.uk
Advertising Address: As above.
Email: matt@icon-magazine.co.uk
Web site: http://www.iconeye.com
Publisher: Media 10
Date Established: 2003
Frequency: Monthly
Cover Price: £4.50
Free to qualifying individuals
Annual Sub.: £47.40
Circulation: 25,895 (Publisher's Statement)
Usual Pagination: 170
Editor: Justin McGuirk; **Advertising Manager:** Matt Clarke
Summary of Content: Magazine covering design, architecture, interior design, buildings, furniture and furnishings. Features interviews with leading international practitioners.
Readership/Target Audience: Aimed at architects and design professionals plus members of the public who are interested in contemporary architecture and design.
ADVERTISING RATES:
Full Page Colour £3200.00
Agency Commission: 10%
Mechanical Data: Film: Digital
Copy instructions: Copy Date: 10th of the month prior to publication date
Average advertising content per issue: 45%
BUSINESS: ARCHITECTURE & BUILDING: Architecture

ICON NEWS
41589U64P-30

Formerly: Conservation News
Editorial Address: Institute of Conservation, 3rd Floor, Downstream Building, 1 London Bridge, LONDON, SE1 9BG
Tel: 020 7785 3805 **Fax:** 020 7785 3806
Email: news@icon.org.uk
Advertising Address: Suite 2.1, 30 Queen Charlotte Street, BRISTOL, BS1 4HJ **Tel:** 0117 904 1283 **Fax:** 0117 904 0085
Email: jed.wells@dpmedia.co.uk
Web site: http://www.icon.org.uk
ISSN: 1749-8988
Publisher: DP Media
Date Established: 2005
Frequency: 6 issues yearly
Free to qualifying individuals
Circulation: 3,000 (Publisher's Statement)
Usual Pagination: 52

Business Magazines

Editor: Lynette Gill
Summary of Content: Magazine of the Institute for Conservation. Includes new methods and techniques, general essays on the role of the conservator, reviews of books, conferences, seminars and other training events, recruitment, letters news from the institute, information about professional standards and ethics and a calendar of events.
Readership/Target Audience: Read by members of the Institute for Conservation in the UK, promoting public understanding of, and access to, all the diverse elements of cultural heritage, preservation and raising public, political and professional awareness of the importance of caring for it.
ADVERTISING RATES:
Full Page Mono £655.00
Full Page Colour £875.00
Agency Commission: 10%
Mechanical Data: Type Area: 270 x 190mm, Bleed Size: +3mm, Trim Size: 297 x 210mm, Col Length: 270mm, Page Width: 190mm, Film: Digital
Copy instructions: Copy Date: 4 weeks prior to publication date
Average advertising content per issue: 20%
BUSINESS: OTHER CLASSIFICATIONS: Museums

ICT FOR EDUCATION
1644032U5R-661
Editorial Address: 116 Galton Road, Bearwood, SMETHWICK, B67 5JS **Tel:** 07974 641520
Email: joseph.devo@limapublishing.com
Advertising Address: 9 Pump Place, Old Stratford, MILTON KEYNES, MK19 6DL **Tel:** 01908 562433 **Fax:** 01983 568844
Email: ian.loosemore@limapublishing.com
Web site: http://www.ictforeducation.co.uk
Publisher: Lima Publishing
Date Established: 2004
Frequency: 6 issues yearly
Annual Sub.: £25.00
Circulation: 12,003 (ABC 01/01/2008 to 31/12/2008)
Usual Pagination: 48
Editor: Joseph Devo
Summary of Content: Magazine covering hardware, software and equipment reviews to help teachers.
Readership/Target Audience: Aimed at ICT co-ordinators and heads of ICT responsible for purchasing technology for schools.
ADVERTISING RATES:
Full Page Colour £2740.00
Mechanical Data: Type Area: 260 x 187mm, Bleed Size: 281 x 211mm, Trim Size: 275 x 205mm, Col Length: 260mm, Page Width: 187mm, Film: Digital
BUSINESS: COMPUTERS & AUTOMATION: Computers Related

ID INNER DESIGN
1917804U4B-198
Editorial Address: Redfern House, 347 Margate Road, Northwood, RAMSGATE, CT12 6SG **Tel:** 01843 592802
Fax: 01843 593145
Email: martin@inner-design.co.uk
Web site: http://www.inner-design.co.uk
Publisher: Inner Design
Frequency: 6 issues yearly
Free to qualifying individuals
Circulation: 30,349 (Publisher's Statement)
Editor: Martin Reynold
Summary of Content: Printed and interactive digital magazine featuring the UK's leading designers and manufactures within the industry and looking at the latest news, features and case studies for the whole interior design industry.
Readership/Target Audience: Aimed at interior designers, architects, contract furnishers, hotels and leisure establishments and healthcare furnishing buyers and specifiers.
BUSINESS: ARCHITECTURE & BUILDING: Interior Design & Flooring

---

IDFX
35832U4B-129
Editorial Address: 1st Floor, Boundry House, 91 Charterhouse Street, LONDON, EC1M 6HR
Tel: 020 7336 5200 **Fax:** 020 7336 5201
Email: kburnett@idfxmagazine.com
Advertising Address: As above.
Email: dboulter@idfxmagazine.com
Web site: http://www.idfxmagazine.com
ISSN: 1462-060X
Publisher: Progressive Media Publications
Date Established: 1998
Frequency: Monthly
Cover Price: £4.50
Free to qualifying individuals
Annual Sub.: £54.00
Circulation: 10,000 (Publisher's Statement)
Usual Pagination: 132
Editor: Kate Burnett

Summary of Content: Magazine containing new product information.
Readership/Target Audience: Aimed at the residential interior design market.
ADVERTISING RATES:
Full Page Colour £2450.00
Agency Commission: 10%
Mechanical Data: Col Length: 265mm, Page Width: 194mm, Bleed Size: 310 x 240mm, Trim Size: 300 x 230mm, Type Area: 265 x 194mm, Film: Digital
Copy instructions: Copy Date: 6 weeks prior to publication date
Average advertising content per issue: 55%
BUSINESS: ARCHITECTURE & BUILDING: Interior Design & Flooring

---

IDMI
38651U34-37
Formerly: The Green Sheet
Editorial Address: 13 Caird's Wynd, BANCHORY, AB31 5XU **Tel:** 024 7625 4957 **Fax:** 024 7638 2319
Email: johnbaker@idmionline.com
Advertising Address: As above.
Email: johnbaker@idmionline.com
Web site: http://www.idmionline.com
ISSN: 1476-3842
Publisher: Green Sheet Media
Date Established: 2002
Frequency: 6 issues yearly - Published at the beginning of the 1st cover month
Annual Sub.: £60.00
Circulation: 3,500 (Publisher's Statement)
Usual Pagination: 32
Editor: John Baker; **Advertising Manager:** John Baker; **Managing Editor:** John Baker
Summary of Content: Magazine containing news of document management in all forms.
Readership/Target Audience: Aimed at imaging service bureaus and departments of banks, building societies and Local Government.
ADVERTISING RATES:
Full Page Mono £650.00
Full Page Colour £650.00
Agency Commission: 10%
Mechanical Data: Type Area: 275 x 190mm, Bleed Size: 303 x 216mm, Trim Size: 297 x 210mm, Col Length: 275mm, Print Process: Litho, Page Width: 190mm, Film: Positive right reading emulsion side down. Digital
Copy instructions: Copy Date: 2 weeks prior to publication date
Average advertising content per issue: 50%
BUSINESS: OFFICE EQUIPMENT

IDPR INTERNATIONAL DEVELOPMENT PLANNING REVIEW
35874U4D-265
Formerly: TWPR Third World Planning Review
Editorial Address: Dept of Civic Design, University of Liverpool, 74 Bedford Street South, LIVERPOOL, L69 7ZQ
Tel: 0151 794 3118 **Fax:** 0151 794 3125
Email: sandrob@liverpool.ac.uk
Advertising Address: 4 Cambridge Street, LIVERPOOL, L69 7ZU **Tel:** 0151 794 2233 **Fax:** 0151 794 2235
Email: janmar@liv.ac.uk
Web site: http://www.liverpool-unipress.co.uk
ISSN: 1474-6743
Publisher: Liverpool University Press
Date Established: 1979
Frequency: Quarterly
Annual Sub.: £60.00
Circulation: 500 (Publisher's Statement)
Usual Pagination: 120
Editor: Sandra Robinson; **Publisher:** Anthony Cord
Summary of Content: Journal covering urban and regional planning issues in developing countries.
Readership/Target Audience: Read by academics, planning practitioners, policy-makers and students.
ADVERTISING RATES:
Full Page Colour £280.00
Agency Commission: 5%
Mechanical Data: Trim Size: 202 x 127mm
BUSINESS: ARCHITECTURE & BUILDING: Planning & Housing

IDS BRIEF
39287U44-770
Editorial Address: 23 College Hill, LONDON, EC4R 2RP
Tel: 020 7429 6800 **Fax:** 020 7393 8081
Email: ids@incomesdata.co.uk
Web site: http://www.incomesdata.co.uk
ISSN: 0308-9312
Publisher: Incomes Data Services
Frequency: 24 issues yearly
Annual Sub.: £614.78
Editor: Annabel Rutherford
Summary of Content: Magazine containing coverage of employment law developments.
Readership/Target Audience: Aimed at personnel specialists, lawyers and trade union officials.

ADVERTISING: No Advertising taken
BUSINESS: LEGAL

IDS EXECUTIVE COMPENSATION REVIEW
37100U14F-24_65
Formerly: IDS Management Pay Review
Editorial Address: 23 College Hill, LONDON, EC4R 2RP
Tel: 020 7429 6800 **Fax:** 020 7393 8081
Email: ids@incomesdata.co.uk
Advertising Address: As above.
Web site: http://www.incomesdata.co.uk
ISSN: 1351-4954
Publisher: Incomes Data Services
Frequency: Monthly
Editor: Adam Elston
Summary of Content: Magazine providing essential information on salaries, benefits and the labour market for managers and professionals.
Readership/Target Audience: Aimed at compensation and benefit specialists, HR staff involved in remuneration, consultancies and recruitment firms.
ADVERTISING: No Advertising taken
BUSINESS: COMMERCE, INDUSTRY & MANAGEMENT: Training & Recruitment

---

IDS HR STUDIES
37101U14F-24_75
Formerly: IDS Studies
Editorial Address: 23 College Hill, LONDON, EC4R 2RP
Tel: 020 7429 6800 **Fax:** 020 7398 8081
Email: ids.general@thomson.com
Web site: http://www.incomesdata.co.uk
ISSN: 0308-9339
Publisher: Incomes Data Services
Date Established: 1971
Frequency: 24 issues yearly
Editor: John Robertson
Summary of Content: Journal examining personnel policy and practice and wider developments in the employment field.
Readership/Target Audience: Aimed at personnel specialists, trade union officials, government departments and academics.
ADVERTISING: No Advertising taken
BUSINESS: COMMERCE, INDUSTRY & MANAGEMENT: Training & Recruitment

---

IDS PENSIONS BULLETIN
35357U1H-25
Formerly: IDS Pensions Service Bulletin
Editorial Address: 23 College Hill, LONDON, EC4R 2RP
Tel: 020 7429 6800 **Fax:** 020 7393 8081
Email: helen.sudell@thomsonreuters.com
Advertising Address: PO Box 57091, 77 Bastwick Street, LONDON, EC1P 1DB
Web site: http://www.incomesdata.co.uk
ISSN: 1748-0981
Publisher: Incomes Data Services
Date Established: 1986
Frequency: 10 issues yearly
Annual Sub.: £350.00
Usual Pagination: 12
Editor: Helen Sudell
Summary of Content: Journal providing news and information on changes in pension policy, legislation, pension companies and pension schemes.
Readership/Target Audience: Aimed at personnel and remuneration specialists, pension and benefit consultants, pension scheme managers and trustees.
ADVERTISING: No Advertising taken
BUSINESS: FINANCE & ECONOMICS: Pensions

IDS PENSIONS LAW REPORTS
39306U44-780
Formerly: Pensions Law Reports
Editorial Address: 23 College Hill, LONDON, EC4R 2RP
Tel: 020 7429 6800 **Fax:** 020 7393 8081
Email: ids@incomesdata.co.uk
Web site: http://www.incomesdata.co.uk
ISSN: 0959-8014
Publisher: Incomes Data Services
Date Established: 1989
Frequency: Monthly
Annual Sub.: £518.93
Editor: Andrew Powell
Summary of Content: Full text of key pension court judgements plus commentary.
Readership/Target Audience: Aimed at pensions specialists, pension advisers and lawyers.
ADVERTISING: No Advertising taken
BUSINESS: LEGAL

IEICE TRANSACTIONS ON ELECTRONICS

601536U18A-325

Formerly: IEICE Transactions of Electronics
Editorial Address: Great Clarendon, OXFORD, OX2 6DP **Tel:** 01865 353907 **Fax:** 01865 353485
Web site: http://www3.oup.co.uk/ietele
ISSN: 0916-8524
Publisher: OUP
Date Established: 1976
Frequency: Monthly
Cover Price: £15.00
Annual Sub.: £94.00
Usual Pagination: 100
Editor: Hidetoshi Onodera; **Editor-in-Chief:** Hidetoshi Onodera
Summary of Content: Publication of The Institute of Electronics, Information and Communication Engineers. Includes features on integrated circuits, semiconductor materials and devices, quantum electronics, opto-electronics, superconductive electronics, electronic displays, microwave and millimeter wave technologies, vacuum and beam technologies, recording and memory technologies and electromagnetic theory.
Language(s): English; Japanese
Readership/Target Audience: Aimed at members.
ADVERTISING: No Advertising taken
BUSINESS: ELECTRONICS

IEICE TRANSACTIONS ON FUNDAMENTALS OF ELECTRONICS, COMMUNICATIONS & COMPUTER SCIENCE

601537U18A-326

Editorial Address: Great Clarendon Street, OXFORD, OX2 6DP **Tel:** 01865 353907 **Fax:** 01865 353985
Email: sengoku@ie.niigata-u.ac.jp
Web site: http://www.oup.co.uk/ietfec
ISSN: 0916-8508
Publisher: OUP
Date Established: 1976
Frequency: Monthly
Cover Price: £15.00
Annual Sub.: £94.00
Usual Pagination: 150
Editor: Masakazu Sengoku; **Editor-in-Chief:** Masakazu Sengoku
Summary of Content: Publication of the Institute of Electronics, Information and Communication Engineers. Includes features on acoustics, algorithms, CAD, circuit theory, cryptography, digital signal processing, information security, information theory and coding, modelling and simulation, neural networks, non-linear circuits and systems and VLSI design.
Language(s): English; Japanese
Readership/Target Audience: Aimed at Members of the Institute of Electronics, Information and Communication Engineers.
ADVERTISING: No Advertising taken
BUSINESS: ELECTRONICS

IEICE TRANSACTIONS ON INFORMATION AND SYSTEMS

601539U5R-135

Editorial Address: Great Clarendon Street, OXFORD, OX2 6DP **Tel:** 01865 353907 **Fax:** 01865 353985
Email: wada@nitech.ac.jp
Web site: http://www3.oup.co.uk/ietisy
ISSN: 0916-8532
Publisher: OUP
Date Established: 1976
Frequency: Monthly
Cover Price: £15.00
Annual Sub.: £94.00
Editor: Koichi Wada; **Editor-in-Chief:** Koichi Wada
Summary of Content: Publication of the Institute of Electronics, Information and Communication Engineers. Includes features on automata, languages and theory of computing, algorithm and computational complexity, computer hardware and design, computer systems, software theory, software systems, databases, computer networks, fault tolerant computing and information security.
Language(s): English; Japanese
Readership/Target Audience: Read by Members of the Institute of Electronics, Information and Communication Engineers.
ADVERTISING: No Advertising taken
BUSINESS: COMPUTERS & AUTOMATION: Computers Related

THE IET STUDENT & YOUNG PROFESSIONAL MAGAZINE

1601514U17-251

Formerly: The IET Student & Graduate Magazine
Editorial Address: Michael Faraday House, Six Hills Way, STEVENAGE, SG1 2AY **Tel:** 01438 765534
Fax: 01438 742856
Email: holbytla@tiscali.co.uk
Web site: http://www.theiet.org/students

ISSN: 1745-0934
Publisher: The Institution of Engineering and Technology
Date Established: 2003
Frequency: 3 issues yearly
Free to qualifying individuals
Circulation: 17,000 (Publisher's Statement)
Usual Pagination: 48
Editor: Jane Maltby
Summary of Content: Magazine covering careers information including personal profiles, technical articles and features related to engineering and technology, topical technologies, industry news, reviews, issues, trends and developments.
Readership/Target Audience: Aimed at members of the IET who are engineering students, researchers, apprentices, recent graduates and those in their first jobs in engineering or technology related fields.
ADVERTISING: No Advertising taken
BUSINESS: ELECTRICAL

IFR BUYOUTS EUROPE

1659708U1A-302

Editorial Address: Aldgate House, 33 Aldgate High Street, LONDON, EC3N 1DL **Tel:** 020 7369 7845
Email: henry.gibbon@thomsonreuters.com
Web site: http://www.buyoutseurope.com
Publisher: Thomson Reuters
Date Established: 2004
Frequency: 26 issues yearly
Editor: Henry Gibbon
Summary of Content: Newsletter covering all aspects of the European buyouts business.
Readership/Target Audience: Aimed at private equity investors.
ADVERTISING: No Advertising taken
Copy instructions: Copy Date: 2 days prior to publication date
BUSINESS: FINANCE & ECONOMICS

IFR INTERNATIONAL FINANCING REVIEW

34945U1A-200

Editorial Address: Aldgate House, 33 Aldgate High Street, LONDON, EC3N 1DL **Tel:** 020 7369 7000
Fax: 020 7369 7482
Email: peoplemarkets@thomsonreuters.com
Advertising Address: As above. **Tel:** 020 7369 7539
Fax: 020 7369 7364
Email: ann.worsley@thomson.com
Web site: http://www.ifre.com
ISSN: 0953-0223
Publisher: Thomson Reuters
Frequency: Weekly
Cover Price: £3203.00
Circulation: 7,050 (Publisher's Statement)
Usual Pagination: 100
Editor-in-Chief: Keith Mullin; **Advertising Manager:** Ann Worsley
Summary of Content: International financing magazine covering global capital markets.
Readership/Target Audience: Aimed at investment and commercial banks, treasurers in corporations, government borrowing agencies and finance ministries, stock and derivative exchanges, risk insurance, fund managers and investors.
ADVERTISING RATES:
Full Page Mono £5900.00
Full Page Colour £8600.00
Agency Commission: 15%
Mechanical Data: Type Area: 270 x 184mm, Bleed Size: 303 x 216mm, Trim Size: 297 x 210mm, Col Length: 270mm, Film: Digital, Page Width: 184mm, Print Process: Offset litho
Copy instructions: Copy Date: Thursday prior to publication date
Average advertising content per issue: 20%
BUSINESS: FINANCE & ECONOMICS

IGAMING BUSINESS

1623304U64A-181

Editorial Address: 3rd Floor, 33-41 Dallington Street, LONDON, EC1V 0BB **Tel:** 020 7954 3412
Fax: 020 7954 3511
Email: ian@igamingbusiness.com
Advertising Address: As above.
Email: alex@igamingbusiness.com
Web site: http://www.igamingbusiness.com
Publisher: Lyceum Publishing
Date Established: 2003
Frequency: 6 issues yearly
Annual Sub.: £150.00
Circulation: 7,000 (Publisher's Statement)
Editor: Ian Larcombe; **Advertising Manager:** Alex Pratt
Summary of Content: Magazine covering the online gambling industry.
Readership/Target Audience: Aimed at key decision makers from online gambling operators.
ADVERTISING RATES:
Full Page Colour £3075.00
Agency Commission: 10%

Copy instructions: Copy Date: 4 weeks prior to publication date
Average advertising content per issue: 45%
BUSINESS: OTHER CLASSIFICATIONS: Amusement Trade

IMA JOURNAL OF APPLIED MATHEMATICS

29975U62A-505

Editorial Address: School of Mathematics, The University of Birmingham, Edgbaston, BIRMINGHAM, B15 2TT
Tel: 01865 353907 **Fax:** 01865 353485
Email: needhamd@for.mat.bham.ac.uk
Advertising Address: Great Clarendon Street, OXFORD, OX2 6DP **Tel:** 01865 353329 **Fax:** 01865 353774
Email: elisabetta.shefiled@oxfordjournals.org
Web site: http://www3.oup.co.uk/imamat
ISSN: 0272-4960
Publisher: OUP
Date Established: 1981
Frequency: 6 issues yearly
Cover Price: £81.00
Annual Sub.: £388.00
Circulation: 590 (Publisher's Statement)
Editor: David Needham
Summary of Content: Publishes papers in all areas of the application of mathematics.
Readership/Target Audience: Aimed at members of the Institute of Mathematics and its Applications.
ADVERTISING RATES:
Full Page Mono £646.00
Full Page Colour £1227.00
Agency Commission: 10%
Mechanical Data: Film: Digital, Type Area: 181 x 139mm, Bleed Size: 252 x 195mm, Trim Size: 246 x 189mm, Col Length: 181mm, Page Width: 139mm
BUSINESS: CHURCH & SCHOOL EQUIPMENT & EDUCATION: Education

IMA JOURNAL OF MANAGEMENT MATHEMATICS

29976U62A-506

Editorial Address: Department of Mathematical Sciences, Brunel University, UXBRIDGE, UB8 3PH **Tel:** 01865 353907
Fax: 01865 353485
Email: kenneth.darby-dowman@brunel.ac.uk
Advertising Address: Great Clarendon Street, OXFORD, OX2 6DP **Tel:** 01865 353329
Email: elisabetta.sheffield@oxfordjournals.org
Web site: http://www3.oup.co.uk/imaman
ISSN: 0953-0061
Publisher: OUP
Date Established: 1986
Frequency: Quarterly
Cover Price: £73.00
Annual Sub.: £233.00
Circulation: 231 (Publisher's Statement)
Editor: Kenneth Darby-Dowman; **Advertising Manager:** Elisabetta Palanghi Sheffield
Summary of Content: Publication covering new mathematical theories related to any class of management problems and practical case studies.
Readership/Target Audience: Aimed at departments of business studies, business schools and departments of industrial engineering, as well as mathematics departments with special interest in financial mathematics.
ADVERTISING RATES:
Full Page Mono £646.00
Agency Commission: 10%
Mechanical Data: Print Process: Litho, Col Length: 181mm, Film: Digital, Type Area: 181 x 139mm, Bleed Size: 254 x 182mm, Trim Size: 249 x 176mm, Page Width: 139mm
BUSINESS: CHURCH & SCHOOL EQUIPMENT & EDUCATION: Education

IMA JOURNAL OF MATHEMATICAL CONTROL & INFORMATION

40043U55-56_40

Editorial Address: Dept. of Automatic Control and Systems Engineering, University of Sheffield, Mappin Street, SHEFFIELD, S1 4DU **Tel:** 0114 222 2000
Advertising Address: Great Clarendon Street, OXFORD, OX2 6DP **Tel:** 01865 353329 **Fax:** 01865 353774
Email: elisabetta.sheffield@oxfordjournals.org
Web site: http://imamci.oupjournals.org
ISSN: 0265-0754
Publisher: OUP
Date Established: 1984
Frequency: Quarterly
Cover Price: £70.00
Annual Sub.: £233.00
Usual Pagination: 104
Editor: Sarah Spurgeon
Summary of Content: Journal covering mathematical control theory, systems theory and allied information sciences.
Readership/Target Audience: Aimed at members of the Institute of Mathematics and its Applications.
ADVERTISING RATES:
Full Page Mono £646.00

Full Page Colour £1076.00
Agency Commission: 10%
Mechanical Data: Print Process: Litho, Bleed Size: 255 x 182mm, Film: Digital, Page Width: 125mm, Trim Size: 249 x 176mm, Type Area: 210 x 125mm, Col Length: 210mm
Copy Date: Beginning of the 2nd week of the month prior to publication date
BUSINESS: APPLIED SCIENCE & LABORATORIES

IMA JOURNAL OF NUMERICAL ANALYSIS

29978U62A-508

Editorial Address: Atlas Centre, Rutherford Appleton Laboratory, OXFORD, OX11 0QX **Tel:** 01865 353485 **Fax:** 01865 353485
Advertising Address: Great Clarendon Street, OXFORD, OX2 6DP **Tel:** 01865 353329 **Fax:** 01865 353774
Email: elisabetta.sheffield@oxfordjournals.org
Web site: http://www3.oup.co.uk/imanum
ISSN: 0272-4979
Publisher: OUP
Date Established: 1981
Frequency: Quarterly
Cover Price: £85.00
Annual Sub.: £273.00
Circulation: 660 (Publisher's Statement)
Editor: A. Iserles
Summary of Content: Publication covering theoretical and practical aspects of numerical analysis.
Readership/Target Audience: Aimed at members of the Institute of Mathematics and its Applications.
ADVERTISING RATES:
Full Page Mono £646.00
Full Page Colour £1076.00
Agency Commission: 10%
Mechanical Data: Page Width: 139mm, Type Area: 181 x 139mm, Print Process: Litho, Bleed Size: 252 x 195mm, Trim Size: 246 x 189mm, Col Length: 181mm, Film: Digital
Copy instructions: Copy Date: Beginning of the month prior to publication date
BUSINESS: CHURCH & SCHOOL EQUIPMENT & EDUCATION: Education

IMAGE

38790U38-20

Editorial Address: 81 Leonard Street, LONDON, EC2A 4QS **Tel:** 020 7739 6669
Email: image@aophoto.co.uk
Advertising Address: As above. **Fax:** 020 7739 8707
Email: image@aophoto.co.uk
Web site: http://www.the-aop.org
Publisher: Association of Photographers
Date Established: 1975
Frequency: 6 issues yearly
Cover Price: £2.00
Free to qualifying individuals
Annual Sub.: £24.00
Circulation: 3,000 (Publisher's Statement)
Usual Pagination: 40
Editor: Helena Rhodes; **Advertising Manager:** Anna Roberts
Summary of Content: Publication containing features on all aspects of fashion, advertising and editorial photography.
Readership/Target Audience: Aimed at photographers, photographers' agents, model agencies and anyone interested in the world of photography.
ADVERTISING RATES:
Full Page Colour £1050.00
Agency Commission: 10%
Mechanical Data: Bleed Size: 256 x 216mm, Trim Size: 250 x 210mm, Film: Digital
Copy instructions: Copy Date: 16th of the month prior to publication date
Average advertising content per issue: 35%
BUSINESS: PHOTOGRAPHIC TRADE

IMAGE REPORTS

38791U38-30

Editorial Address: 6 Laurence Pountney Hill, LONDON, EC4R 0BL **Tel:** 020 7933 8977
Email: lesley.simpson@imagereportsmag.co.uk
Advertising Address: As above. **Tel:** 020 7933 8999
Fax: 020 7933 8998
Email: tomw@stjohnpatrick.co.uk
Web site: http://www.imagereportsmag.co.uk
Publisher: St. John Patrick Publishers Ltd
Date Established: 1994
Frequency: Monthly - Published on the 1st of the cover month
Cover Price: £2.50
Free to qualifying individuals
Circulation: 9,319 (ABC 01/01/2008 to 31/12/2008)
Usual Pagination: 60
Executive Editor: Melony Rocque-Hewitt; **Advertising Manager:** Tom Westaway; **Publisher:** Chris Cooke
Summary of Content: Magazine reporting on the latest products and services for the digital print industry.

Readership/Target Audience: Read by printers, bureaux, corporate buying groups, publishers, advertising designers and the sign and screen printing industries.
ADVERTISING RATES:
Full Page Mono £2688.00
Full Page Colour £2688.00
Agency Commission: 10%
Mechanical Data: Page Width: 204mm, Film: Digital, Type Area: 274 x 204mm, Col Length: 274mm, Trim Size: 300 x 230mm, Bleed Size: 306 x 236mm
Copy instructions: Copy Date: 14th of the month prior to publication date
Average advertising content per issue: 50%
BUSINESS: PHOTOGRAPHIC TRADE

IMAGES

39496U47A-167

Editorial Address: 9A Kings Road, Flitwick, BEDFORD, MK45 1ED **Tel:** 01525 718890 **Fax:** 01525 718026
Email: mail@images-magazine.com
Advertising Address: As above.
Email: mail@images-magazine.com
Web site: http://www.images-magazine.com
Publisher: CN Publishing
Date Established: 1992
Frequency: 8 issues yearly
Free to qualifying individuals
Annual Sub.: £40.00
Circulation: 5,000 (Publisher's Statement)
Usual Pagination: 104
Editor: Neil Bunyan; **Advertising Manager:** Cathy Hobson
Summary of Content: Journal covering textile screen printing, embroidery and garment decoration.
Readership/Target Audience: Aimed at textile printers, embroiderers, promotion companies, suppliers, manufacturers and designers.
ADVERTISING: Rates on application
BUSINESS: CLOTHING & TEXTILES

IMAGINE

766733U64K-651

Editorial Address: Unit 2.4, Paintworks, Bath Road, BRISTOL, BS4 3EH **Tel:** 0117 902 9977 **Fax:** 0117 902 9978
Email: frank@imagineanimation.net
Advertising Address: As above.
Email: ruth.morris@wildfirecomms.co.uk
Web site: http://www.imagineanimation.net
Publisher: Wildfire Communications
Date Established: 2001
Frequency: 6 issues yearly
Annual Sub.: £12.00
Circulation: 7,000 (Publisher's Statement)
Editor: Frank Grimshaw; **Advertising Manager:** Ruth Morris
Summary of Content: Magazine covering traditional animation through to the latest developments in digital design and production. Includes company and individual profiles, product news, reviews, retrospectives, causes, campaigns, training and education developments.
Readership/Target Audience: Aimed at the animation and convergent media industry including creators, suppliers, educators and those involved in creative media content.
ADVERTISING RATES:
Full Page Colour £1250.00
Copy instructions: Copy Date: 2 weeks prior to publication date
Average advertising content per issue: 25%
BUSINESS: OTHER CLASSIFICATIONS: Cinema Entertainment

IMAGING AND MACHINE VISION EUROPE

1657691U18A-9013

Formerly: Imaging and Machine Vision
Editorial Address: The Spectrum Building, Michael Young Centre, Purbeck Road, CAMBRIDGE, CB2 8PD **Tel:** 01223 211170 **Fax:** 01223 211170
Email: editor.imaging@europascience.com
Advertising Address: 8-10 Whiteladies Road, Clifton, BRISTOL, BS8 1PD **Tel:** 0117 906 4075 **Fax:** 0117 973 2022
Email: sales.imaging@europascience.com
Web site: http://www.europascience.com
Publisher: Europa Science Ltd
Date Established: 2002
Frequency: 6 issues yearly - Published in the 1st week of the 1st cover month
Free to qualifying individuals
Annual Sub.: £170.00
Editor: Warren Clark
Summary of Content: Magazine covering product news and applications for the machine vision and industrial image processing sector.
Readership/Target Audience: Aimed at design and production engineers working within the scientific imaging and machine vision markets.
ADVERTISING RATES:
Full Page Mono £2800.00
Full Page Colour £3750.00
Agency Commission: 10%

Mechanical Data: Type Area: 253 x 184mm, Bleed Size: 288 x 219mm, Trim Size: 270 x 200mm, Col Length: 253mm, Page Width: 184mm, Film: Digital
Average advertising content per issue: 60%
BUSINESS: ELECTRONICS

THE IMAGING SCIENCE JOURNAL

38792U38-40

Editorial Address: Suite 1C, Josephs Well, Hanover Walk, LEEDS, LS3 1AB **Tel:** 0113 243 2800 **Fax:** 0113 386 8178
Email: r.b.jenkin@rmcs.cranfield.ac.uk
Web site: http://www.maney.co.uk/journals/ims
ISSN: 1368-2199
Publisher: Maney Publishing
Frequency: 6 issues yearly
Annual Sub.: £229.00
Circulation: 1,000 (Publisher's Statement)
Editor: Juliet Rasen; **Executive Editor:** Robin Jenkin
Summary of Content: Industry/academic journal detailing research in medical photography, forensic applications and other advances in photographic technology, including chemistry and physics, imaging systems and applications.
Readership/Target Audience: Aimed at researchers in academia and industry.
ADVERTISING: No Advertising taken
BUSINESS: PHOTOGRAPHIC TRADE

IMBIBE

1828598U9A-263

Editorial Address: Quadrant House, 250 Kennington Lane, LONDON, SE11 5RD **Tel:** 020 7840 6268
Fax: 020 7582 5444
Email: hannah@imbibemagazine.co.uk
Web site: http://www.imbibemagazine.co.uk
Publisher: Monomax Ltd
Date Established: 2007
Frequency: 6 issues yearly
Cover Price: £3.40
Free to qualifying individuals
Circulation: 11,429 (ABC 01/09/2007 to 30/11/2007)
Usual Pagination: 140
Editor: Hannah Tovey; **Publisher:** Hannah Tovey
Summary of Content: Magazine covering premium wine, spirits, beer, water, coffee, soft drinks and all non-liquid topics relevant to the premium on-trade wine and drink buyers.
Readership/Target Audience: Aimed at drink buyers for the premium, on-trade sommeliers and bar tenders.
ADVERTISING RATES:
Full Page Colour £3134.00
BUSINESS: DRINKS & LICENSED TRADE: Drinks, Licensed Trade, Wines & Spirits

IMIS JOURNAL

36088U5B-87_90

Editorial Address: 5 Kingfisher House, New Mill Road, ORPINGTON, BR5 3QG **Tel:** 0700 002 3456
Fax: 0700 002 3023
Email: central@imis.org.uk
Advertising Address: Xenogamy Limited, 55A Belmont Road, WALLINGTON, SM6 8TE **Tel:** 020 8773 3404
Fax: 020 8773 3704
Email: rick@xenogamy-plc.co.uk
Web site: http://www.imis.org.uk
ISSN: 1369-4189
Publisher: IMIS
Frequency: 6 issues yearly
Cover Price: £19.00
Free to qualifying individuals
Circulation: 13,000 (Publisher's Statement)
Usual Pagination: 34
Editor: Deirdre Pointer; **Advertising Manager:** Rick Smith
Summary of Content: Journal of the Institute for the Management of Information Systems. Covers articles on education, training, research and information.
Readership/Target Audience: Aimed at members.
ADVERTISING RATES:
Full Page Colour £1300.00
Agency Commission: 10%
Mechanical Data: Type Area: 262 x 187mm, Col Length: 262mm, Bleed Size: 303 x 216mm, Trim Size: 297 x 210mm, Film: Positive, right reading, emulsion side down. Digital, Page Width: 187mm
BUSINESS: COMPUTERS & AUTOMATION: Data Processing

IMPACT (JOURNAL OF THE CAREER DEVELOPMENT GROUP)

40860U60B-18

Formerly: Impact
Editorial Address: Contact by email only
Email: cheneygardner@googlemail.com
Advertising Address: As above.
Email: cheneygardner@googlemail.com
Web site: http://www.careerdevelopmentgroup.org.uk
ISSN: 1468-1625

Publisher: Chartered Institute of Library & Information Professionals
Date Established: 1998
Frequency: Quarterly
Annual Sub.: £38.85
Circulation: 5,000 (Publisher's Statement)
Usual Pagination: 20
Editor: Cheney Gardner; **Advertising Manager:** Cheney Gardner
Summary of Content: Official journal of the Career Development Group containing important issues in the library and information sector. Also features articles and letters on current views and debates.
Readership/Target Audience: Aimed at library and information professionals at all levels working in public, academic and commercial sectors.
ADVERTISING: Rates on application
BUSINESS: PUBLISHING: Libraries

IMPROVING SCHOOLS
40981U62A-200
Editorial Address: 1 Oliver's Yard, 55 City Road, LONDON, EC1Y 1SP **Tel:** 020 7324 8500 **Fax:** 020 7324 8600
Email: terry.wrigley@ed.ac.uk
Advertising Address: As above.
Email: sheena.karim@sagepub.co.uk
Web site: http://www.sagepub.co.uk
ISSN: 1365-4802
Publisher: Sage Publications
Date Established: 1998
Frequency: 3 issues yearly - Published in March, July and November
Annual Sub.: £45.00
Circulation: 200 (Publisher's Statement)
Usual Pagination: 64
Editor: Terry Wrigley
Summary of Content: Magazine covering research, educational practice and policy making in the field of school improvement.
Readership/Target Audience: Aimed at practitioners, researchers and others in the educational community.
ADVERTISING RATES:
Full Page Mono £450.00
Agency Commission: 5%
Mechanical Data: Type Area: 210 x 140mm, Col Length: 210mm, Page Width: 140mm, Film: Digital
BUSINESS: CHURCH & SCHOOL EQUIPMENT & EDUCATION: Education

IN ATTENDANCE
39856U54A-175
Editorial Address: 260 Picton Road, Wavertree, LIVERPOOL, L15 4LP **Tel:** 0151 734 3038
Fax: 0151 734 2860
Email: info@inattendance.co.uk
Advertising Address: As above.
Email: inatt@gatepress.demon.co.uk
Publisher: Gateacre Press
Frequency: Quarterly
Annual Sub.: £16.00
Circulation: 10,000 (Publisher's Statement)
Usual Pagination: 32
Editor: Zane Bilall; **Advertising Manager:** Zane Bilall;
Publisher: Zane Billal
Summary of Content: Magazine containing articles on vehicles, equipment and fire incidents.
Readership/Target Audience: Read by British firefighters.
ADVERTISING RATES:
Full Page Mono £650.00
Full Page Colour £1150.00
Agency Commission: 10%
Mechanical Data: Film: Digital, Col Length: 262mm, Type Area: 262 x 175mm, Print Process: Offset litho, Bleed Size: 302 x 215mm, Trim Size: 297 x 210mm, Page Width: 175mm
Copy instructions: Copy Date: 3 weeks prior to publication date
Average advertising content per issue: 40%
BUSINESS: SAFETY & SECURITY: Fire Fighting

IN BRIEF
40478U56M-30
Formerly: Contraceptive Education Bulletin
Editorial Address: 50 Featherstone Street, LONDON, EC1Y 8QU **Tel:** 020 7608 5240 **Fax:** 0845 123 2349
Web site: http://www.fpa.org.uk
ISSN: 1368-0048
Publisher: Family Planning Association
Date Established: 1996
Frequency: Quarterly
Free to qualifying individuals
Annual Sub.: £30.00
Circulation: 1,500 (Publisher's Statement)
Usual Pagination: 6
Editor: Anna Nesbitt
Summary of Content: Bulletin covering the latest research and medical information from the contraception and sexual health field.

Readership/Target Audience: Read by GPs, family planning advisors, those dealing with health education and FPA members.
ADVERTISING: No Advertising taken
BUSINESS: HEALTH & MEDICAL: Family Planning

IN BUSINESS
41340U63B-1450
Formerly: Network
Editorial Address: Commerce House, 2 Victoria Way, Pride Park, DERBY, DE24 8AN **Tel:** 01322 851280
Fax: 01332 851284
Email: roland.curtis@dncc.co.uk
Web site: http://www.dncc.co.uk
Publisher: Bradgate Publishing
Date Established: 2000
Frequency: 10 issues yearly - Combined issues in July/August and December/January
Cover Price: £2.95
Free to qualifying individuals
Circulation: 7,000 (Print Run)
Usual Pagination: 48
Editor: Roland Curtis
Summary of Content: Business magazine containing news, features and company profiles.
Readership/Target Audience: Distributed to business organisation members.
ADVERTISING: No Advertising taken
BUSINESS: REGIONAL BUSINESS: Regional Business English Counties

IN BUSINESS EAST ENGLAND
1777104U63B-2565
Editorial Address: 14 Pierpoint Street, WORCESTER, WR1 1TA **Tel:** 01905 731985 **Fax:** 01905 731986
Email: eastsales@inbuspub.plus.com
Advertising Address: As above. **Fax:** 01905 721986
Email: eastsales@inbuspub.plus.com
Web site: http://www.inbusinesspublishing.com
Publisher: In Business Publishing
Frequency: Monthly
Annual Sub.: £112.00
Usual Pagination: 18
Editor: Rosemary Davies; **Advertising Manager:** Rosemary Davies
Summary of Content: Magazine focusing on successful businesses including company profiles, relocations, expansions, changes of ownership and awards.
Readership/Target Audience: Aimed at business owners in Eastern England.
ADVERTISING RATES:
Full Page Mono £1000.00
Full Page Colour £1250.00
Agency Commission: 10%
Mechanical Data: Bleed Size: 364 x 264mm, Trim Size: 360 x 260mm, Film: Digital
Copy instructions: Copy Date: 2 days prior to publication date
Average advertising content per issue: 50%
BUSINESS: REGIONAL BUSINESS: Regional Business English Counties

IN BUSINESS MIDLANDS
1777103U63B-2588
Editorial Address: 14 Pierpoint Street, WORCESTER, WR1 1TA **Tel:** 01905 20500 **Fax:** 01905 20370
Email: swsales@inbuspub.plus.com
Advertising Address: As above. **Tel:** 01905 20343
Fax: 01905 20376
Email: ibpublishing@ukonline.co.uk
Publisher: In Business Publishing
Frequency: Monthly
Annual Sub.: £78.00
Circulation: 45,000 (Publisher's Statement)
Editor: Hayden Jordon; **Managing Director:** Craig Taylor;
Advertising Manager: Hayden Jordon
Summary of Content: Magazine focusing on successful businesses including company profiles, relocations, expansions, changes of ownership and awards.
Readership/Target Audience: Aimed at business owners in the East and West Midlands.
ADVERTISING RATES:
Full Page Mono £1052.00
Full Page Colour £1276.00
BUSINESS: REGIONAL BUSINESS: Regional Business English Counties

IN BUSINESS NORTH WEST
1777102U63B-2568
Editorial Address: 14 Pierpoint Street, WORCESTER, WR1 1TA **Tel:** 01905 20500 **Fax:** 01905 20376
Email: swsales@inbuspub.plus.com
Advertising Address: As above. **Tel:** 01905 20343
Email: swsales@inbuspub.plus.com
Web site: http://www.inbusinesspublishing.com
Publisher: In Business Publishing
Frequency: Monthly - Last working day of the month

Free to qualifying individuals
Annual Sub.: £78.00
Circulation: 45,000 (Publisher's Statement)
Usual Pagination: 16
Editor: Hayden Jordon; **Managing Director:** Craig Taylor;
Advertising Manager: Darryen Tafft
Summary of Content: Magazine focusing on successful businesses in the North West including company profiles, relocations, expansions, changes of ownership and awards.
Readership/Target Audience: Aimed at business owners in the North West.
ADVERTISING RATES:
Full Page Mono £1052.00
Full Page Colour £1276.00
Agency Commission: 10%
Mechanical Data: Type Area: 350 x 268mm, Col Length: 350mm, Page Width: 268mm, Film: Digital
Copy instructions: Copy Date: 3 days prior to publication date
BUSINESS: REGIONAL BUSINESS: Regional Business English Counties

IN BUSINESS SOUTH WEST
1695585U63B-2550
Editorial Address: 14 Pierpoint Street, WORCESTER, WR1 1TA **Tel:** 01905 20332 **Fax:** 01905 20374
Email: swsales@inbuspub.plus.com
Advertising Address: As above. **Tel:** 01905 20355
Email: swsales@inbuspub.plus.com
Web site: http://www.inbusinesspublishing.com
Publisher: In Business Publishing
Date Established: 2001
Frequency: 13 issues yearly
Free to qualifying individuals
Circulation: 45,000 (Publisher's Statement)
Usual Pagination: 16
Editor: Hayden Jordon
Summary of Content: Magazine focusing on successful businesses including company profiles, relocations, expansions, change of ownership and awards.
Readership/Target Audience: Aimed at business owners in the South West.
ADVERTISING RATES:
Full Page Colour £1250.00
Mechanical Data: Type Area: 360 x 270mm, Col Length: 360mm, Page Width: 270mm, Film: Digital
Copy instructions: Copy Date: 1 month prior to publication date
BUSINESS: REGIONAL BUSINESS: Regional Business English Counties

IN BUSINESS THE OXFORD TIMES
26049U63B-1500
Editorial Address: Newspaper House, Osney Mead, OXFORD, OX2 0EJ **Tel:** 01865 425460 **Fax:** 01865 425554
Email: business@nqo.com
Advertising Address: As above. **Tel:** 01865 425262
Fax: 01865 425557
Email: advertising@nqo.com
Web site: http://www.oxfordtimes.co.uk
Publisher: Newsquest (Oxfordshire) Ltd
Frequency: Monthly
Circulation: 30,542 (Publisher's Statement)
Usual Pagination: 72
Editor: Andrew Smith; **Managing Director:** Shamus Donald;
Advertising Manager: Julian Richings
Summary of Content: Magazine containing local and Business Link news, interviews, company profiles, commercial property, training, personal finance and the Internet.
Readership/Target Audience: Aimed at people running small, medium and large enterprises in the Oxfordshire area.
ADVERTISING RATES:
Full Page Colour £855.00
Agency Commission: 10%
Mechanical Data: Type Area: 280 x 210mm, Col Length: 280mm, Page Width: 210mm, Film: Digital
Copy instructions: Copy Date: Friday of the last week of the month prior to publication date
Average advertising content per issue: 40%
Supplement to: The Oxford Times
BUSINESS: REGIONAL BUSINESS: Regional Business English Counties

IN CONTROL
760257U56A-69_60
Editorial Address: The Old Vicarage, Beck Hill, BARTON-UPON-HUMBER, DN18 5EY **Tel:** 01652 661510
Fax: 01652 661512
Email: joanne@hcpublications.fsworld.co.uk
Advertising Address: As above.
Email: an@hcpublications.fsworld.co.uk
Web site: http://www.apic.uk.org
Publisher: Health Care Publications
Date Established: 2002
Frequency: Quarterly
Annual Sub.: £50.00
Circulation: 7,000 (Publisher's Statement)

Business Magazines

Usual Pagination: 70
Editor: Joanne Dunderdale; **Advertising Manager:** John Hughes
Summary of Content: Journal covering infection control in all areas of hospital care.
Readership/Target Audience: Aimed at consultants, food hygiene and catering managers, health and safety officers, infection control managers, nurses, microbiologists, pathologists, laboratory, sterile services ward and housekeeping managers, care home proprietors and all members of the Infection Control Association.
ADVERTISING RATES:
Full Page Mono £1450.00
Full Page Colour £1950.00
Agency Commission: 10%
Mechanical Data: Bleed Size: 303 x 216mm, Trim Size: 297 x 210mm, Film: Digital
Copy instructions: Copy Date: 25th of the month prior to publication
Average advertising content per issue: 30%
BUSINESS: HEALTH & MEDICAL

IN DESIGN
1785629U4A-318
Formerly: Architect and Designer
Editorial Address: Barham Court, Teston, MAIDSTONE, ME18 5BZ **Tel:** 01622 618796 **Fax:** 01622 618653
Email: zoe@cimltd.co.uk
Advertising Address: As above.
Email: sam@cimltd.co.uk
Web site: http://www.constructorgroup.co.uk
Publisher: CIM LLP
Frequency: Monthly - Published in the 2nd week of the cover month
Cover Price: Free
Circulation: 10,000 (Publisher's Statement)
Editor: Zoe Revell
Summary of Content: Publication focusing on the latest design trends, products, ideas and innovations.
Readership/Target Audience: Aimed at architects, specifiers, interior and landscape designers.
ADVERTISING RATES:
Full Page Colour £2090.00
Agency Commission: 10%
Mechanical Data: Type Area: 300 x 230mm, Bleed Size: +3mm, Col Length: 300mm, Page Width: 230mm, Film: Digital
Copy instructions: Copy Date: 4 weeks prior to publication date
Average advertising content per issue: 40%
BUSINESS: ARCHITECTURE & BUILDING: Architecture

IN PRACTICE
41528U64H-158
Editorial Address: 7 Mansfield Street, LONDON, W1G 9NQ
Tel: 020 7908 6320 **Fax:** 020 7908 6329
Email: editorial@bva-edit.co.uk
Web site: http://www.bvapublications.com
ISSN: 0263-841X
Publisher: British Veterinary Association
Date Established: 1979
Frequency: 10 issues yearly
Annual Sub.: £126.00
Circulation: 11,000 (Publisher's Statement)
Usual Pagination: 64
Editor: Susan Cumming
Summary of Content: Magazine covering clinical developments and management issues relating to veterinary practice.
Readership/Target Audience: Aimed at all members of the British Veterinary Association and veterinary surgeons in practice.
ADVERTISING: No Advertising taken
BUSINESS: OTHER CLASSIFICATIONS: Veterinary

INAVATE
1708230U2D-149
Editorial Address: Blair House, 184-186 High Street, TONBRIDGE, TN9 1BQ **Tel:** 01732 359990
Fax: 01732 770049
Email: inavate@imlgroup.co.uk
Advertising Address: As above.
Email: simon.nana@imlgroup.co.uk
Web site: http://www.inavateonthenet.net
ISSN: 1749-8503
Publisher: IML Group plc
Date Established: 2005
Frequency: 10 issues yearly
Free to qualifying individuals
Annual Sub.: £99.00
Circulation: 11,500 (Publisher's Statement)
Usual Pagination: 68
Editor: Chris Fitzsimmons; **Advertising Manager:** Simon Nana; **Publisher:** Dan Jago
Summary of Content: Magazine covering the latest news, views, product reviews and market analysis on audio visual technology.

Readership/Target Audience: Aimed at designers, consultants, installers, contractors and end users of audio visual technologies within commercial environments.
ADVERTISING RATES:
Full Page Colour £2500.00
Agency Commission: 10%
Mechanical Data: Type Area: 270 x 205mm, Bleed Size: 306 x 251mm, Trim Size: 300 x 245mm, Col Length: 270mm, Page Width: 205mm
Copy instructions: Copy Date: 2 weeks prior to publication date
Average advertising content per issue: 50%
BUSINESS: COMMUNICATIONS, ADVERTISING & MARKETING: Broadcasting

INBLOOM
1846324U26C-83
Editorial Address: British Teleflower Service Ltd, Unit 35, Romsey Industrial Estate, Greatbridge Road, ROMSEY, SO51 0HR **Tel:** 01794 526445 **Fax:** 01794 511199
Email: lucy.calvert@teleflorist.co.uk
Advertising Address: As above. **Fax:** 01794 526489
Email: lucy.calvert@teleflorist.co.uk
Web site: http://www.teleflorist.co.uk/inbloom
Publisher: Lyrical Communications
Date Established: 2008
Frequency: 6 issues yearly
Cover Price: £2.95
Free to qualifying individuals
Circulation: 2,000 (Publisher's Statement)
Usual Pagination: 28
Editor: Lucy Calvert; **Advertising Manager:** Lucy Calvert
Summary of Content: Magazine covering news, marketing ideas, tips, inspirational designs and floristry products.
Readership/Target Audience: Aimed at retail florists and floristry.
ADVERTISING RATES:
Full Page Colour £950.00
Mechanical Data: Type Area: 277 x 190mm, Bleed Size: 303 x 216mm, Trim Size: 297 x 210mm, Col Length: 277mm, Page Width: 190mm, Film: Digital
BUSINESS: GARDEN TRADE

INBUSINESS
624134U63B-1798
Formerly: CBI West Midlands Business Update
Editorial Address: CBI, West Midlands Region, Number 1, Hagley Road, BIRMINGAM, B16 8TG **Tel:** 0121 450 8976
Fax: 0121 456 1634
Email: pauline.chadaway@cbi.org.uk
Advertising Address: Trelawney House, Chestergate, MACCLESFIELD, SK11 6DW **Tel:** 0121 608 2300
Fax: 0121 608 2220
Email: graham.hesp@openboxpublishing.co.uk
Web site: http://www.cbi.org.uk/westmidlands
Publisher: Ten Alps Publishing
Frequency: Quarterly
Cover Price: Free
Circulation: 5,000 (Publisher's Statement)
Usual Pagination: 32
Editor: Pauline Chadaway; **Advertising Manager:** Graham Hesp
Summary of Content: Newspaper of the West Midlands CBI. Covers regional business news as well as European and international affairs, transport, economics, e-business, technology, regulation, best practice, skills, planning and property.
Readership/Target Audience: Read by members of the West Midlands CBI and other decision makers in local business, MPs and MEPs.
ADVERTISING RATES:
Full Page Colour £4435.00
Mechanical Data: Type Area: 360 x 267mm, Col Length: 360mm, Page Width: 267mm
BUSINESS: REGIONAL BUSINESS: Regional Business English Counties

INBUSINESS
1775581U63D-721
Editorial Address: PO Box 5512, INVERNESS, IV2 3ZE
Tel: 01463 718131 **Fax:** 01463 231523
Email: paula@inverness-chamber.co.uk
Advertising Address: As above.
Email: paula@inverness-chamber.co.uk
Web site: http://www.inverness-chamber.co.uk
Publisher: Inverness Chamber of Commerce
Frequency: Quarterly
Cover Price: Free
Circulation: 10,000 (Publisher's Statement)
Editor: Paula Nicol; **Advertising Manager:** Paula Nicol
Summary of Content: Magazine of Inverness Chamber of Commerce which aims to keep businesses in touch with the economic developments within the region.
Readership/Target Audience: Aimed at managers of Highland businesses.
ADVERTISING: Rates on application
BUSINESS: REGIONAL BUSINESS: Regional Business Scotland

INCAMERA
41563U64K-582
Editorial Address: Kodak Business Centre, Hemel One, Boundary Way, HEMEL HEMPSTEAD, HP2 7YU
Tel: 01442 846945 **Fax:** 01422 846594
Email: laura.watson@kodak.com
Web site: http://www.kodak.com/go/motion
Publisher: Kodak Limited & Eastman Kodak Company
Frequency: Quarterly
Cover Price: Free
Circulation: 65,000 (Publisher's Statement)
Usual Pagination: 48
Editor: Laura Watson
Summary of Content: Magazine covering news and features on film making.
Readership/Target Audience: Aimed at professionals in the motion picture industry.
ADVERTISING: No Advertising taken
BUSINESS: OTHER CLASSIFICATIONS: Cinema Entertainment

INCENTIVE TRAVEL & CORPORATE MEETINGS
39723U50-16_75
Editorial Address: Market House, 19-21 Market Place, WOKINGHAM, RG40 1AP **Tel:** 0118 979 3277
Fax: 0118 979 3499
Email: itcm@incentivetravel.co.uk
Advertising Address: As above.
Email: tim@incentivetravel.co.uk
Web site: http://www.incentivetravel.co.uk
Publisher: ITCM Limited
Date Established: 1988
Frequency: 6 issues yearly - Published on the 10th of the month
Free to qualifying individuals
Annual Sub.: £36.00
Circulation: 7,365 (ABC 01/07/2008 to 30/06/2009)
Usual Pagination: 68
Editor: Sydney Paulden; **Advertising Manager:** Tim Manning; **Publisher:** Tim Manning
Summary of Content: Magazine aimed at keeping buyers up-to-date on incentive travel and corporate meetings facilities worldwide.
Readership/Target Audience: Aimed at UK conference and exhibition organisers, directors and marketing directors.
ADVERTISING RATES:
Full Page Colour £1975.00
Agency Commission: 10%
Mechanical Data: Type Area: 265 x 185mm, Bleed Size: 303 x 216mm, Trim Size: 297 x 210mm, Col Length: 265mm, Page Width: 185mm, Print Process: Sheet-fed offset litho, Film: Digital
Copy instructions: Copy Date: 15th of the month prior to publication date
Average advertising content per issue: 40%
BUSINESS: TRAVEL & TOURISM

INDEPENDENT BUSINESS TODAY
36768U14A-164
Editorial Address: 95 Kipling Avenue, Goring-by-Sea, WORTHING, BN12 6LJ **Tel:** 01903 530439
Fax: 01903 241585
Email: church@semple.org.uk
ISSN: 1470-5141
Publisher: Institute for Independent Business
Date Established: 1997
Frequency: Quarterly
Annual Sub.: £18.00
Circulation: 7,000 (Publisher's Statement)
Usual Pagination: 36
Editor: Churchill Semple
Summary of Content: Journal of the Institute for Independent Business with articles and features on management methodology.
Readership/Target Audience: Aimed at chief executives and higher management.
ADVERTISING: No Advertising taken
BUSINESS: COMMERCE, INDUSTRY & MANAGEMENT

THE INDEPENDENT COMMUNITY PHARMACIST
38736U37-27
Editorial Address: 207 Linen Hall, 162-168 Regent Street, LONDON, W1B 5TB **Tel:** 020 7434 1530 **Fax:** 020 7437 0915
Email: rebecca.derrington@1530.com
Advertising Address: As above.
Email: julian.bruxelles@1530.com
Web site: http://www.independentpharmacist.co.uk
ISSN: 0963-0759
Publisher: Communications International Group
Date Established: 1990
Frequency: Monthly - Published around the 12th of the cover month
Free to qualifying individuals
Annual Sub.: £65.00
Circulation: 6,506 (ABC 01/01/2008 to 31/12/2008)
Usual Pagination: 68

Editor: Rebecca Derrington; **Advertisement Director:** Julian de Bruxelles
Summary of Content: Magazine containing pharmaceutical news relating to business, finance, merchandising, category management and marketing.
Readership/Target Audience: Aimed at independent pharmacists.
ADVERTISING RATES:
Full Page Colour £3045.00
Agency Commission: 10%
Mechanical Data: Page Width: 184mm, Film: Digital, Type Area: 267 x 184mm, Col Length: 267mm, Trim Size: 297 x 210mm, Bleed Size: 303 x 216mm, No. of Columns (Display): 3, Col Widths (Display): 58.5mm
Copy instructions: Copy Date: 4 weeks prior to publication date
Average advertising content per issue: 30%
BUSINESS: PHARMACEUTICAL & CHEMISTS

INDEPENDENT EDUCATION TODAY

41101U62E-180

Editorial Address: St. James House, 118 Greys Road, HENLEY-ON-THAMES, RG9 1QW **Tel:** 01491 411848
Fax: 01491 411416
Email: sales@schoolspublishing.co.uk
Advertising Address: As above.
Email: sales@schoolspublishing.co.uk
Web site: http://www.ie-today.co.uk
Publisher: Schools Publishing Limited
Date Established: 1995
Frequency: 10 issues yearly - Published around the 9th of the cover month
Free to qualifying individuals
Annual Sub.: £30.00
Circulation: 7,000 (Publisher's Statement)
Usual Pagination: 48
Editor: Sarah Williams; **Advertising Director:** Neil Pauksztello
Summary of Content: National journal for independent schools, covering news from schools and features relevant to school management and purchasing.
Readership/Target Audience: Aimed at Head Teachers, Bursars and the staff room.
ADVERTISING RATES:
Full Page Mono £1100.00
Full Page Colour £1265.00
SCC £8.50
Agency Commission: 10%
Mechanical Data: Bleed Size: +3mm, Trim Size: 297 x 210mm, Film: Digital, Type Area: 270 x 180mm, Page Width: 180mm, Col Length: 270mm
Copy instructions: Copy Date: 1 week prior to publication date
Average advertising content per issue: 35%
BUSINESS: CHURCH & SCHOOL EQUIPMENT & EDUCATION: Preparatory & Independent Schools

THE INDEPENDENT ELECTRICAL RETAILER

39098U43A-60

Editorial Address: 15A London Road, MAIDSTONE, ME16 8LY **Tel:** 020 8429 5871 **Fax:** 01622 757646
Email: aryland@datateam.co.uk
Advertising Address: As above. **Tel:** 01622 687031
Email: tcurtiss@datateam.co.uk
Web site: http://www.independentelectricalretailer.co.uk
Publisher: Datateam Publishing Ltd
Date Established: 1990
Frequency: Monthly - Published two weeks prior to cover month
Free to qualifying individuals
Annual Sub.: £65.00
Circulation: 6,894 (ABC 01/01/2008 to 31/12/2008)
Usual Pagination: 44
Editor: Anna Ryland; **Advertising Manager:** Tom Curtiss
Summary of Content: Journal covering all processes involved in the retail and manufacture of electrical appliances.
Readership/Target Audience: Aimed at senior management in user and vendor organisations.
ADVERTISING RATES:
Full Page Colour £3200.00
Agency Commission: 10%
Mechanical Data: Type Area: 267 x 184mm, Bleed Size: 303 x 216mm, Trim Size: 297 x 210mm, Col Length: 267mm, Page Width: 184mm, Film: Digital
Copy instructions: Copy Date: 2 weeks prior to publication date
Average advertising content per issue: 40%
BUSINESS: ELECTRICAL RETAIL TRADE

INDEPENDENT EXAMINER

760265U1B-200

Editorial Address: ACIE, Bentley Resource Centre, High Street, Bentley, DONCASTER, DN5 0AA **Tel:** 01302 828338
Email: info@acie.org.uk
Web site: http://www.acie.org.uk
ISSN: 1470-3041
Publisher: Association of Charity Independent Examiners

Date Established: 1998
Frequency: 3 issues yearly - Published in February, June and October
Free to qualifying individuals
Annual Sub.: £50.00
Circulation: 600 (Publisher's Statement)
Usual Pagination: 12
Editor: Fiona Gordon
Summary of Content: Newsletter of the ACIE (Association of Charity Independent Examiners) covering charity accounting issues and specific issues for those acting as independent examiners and auditors of charity accounts.
Readership/Target Audience: Aimed at charity independent examiners including professional accountants specialising in charities and voluntary sector finance personnel from other backgrounds.
ADVERTISING: No Advertising taken
BUSINESS: FINANCE & ECONOMICS: Accountancy

INDEPENDENT NURSE

1663298U56B-283

Editorial Address: 174 Hammersmith Road, LONDON, W6 7JP **Tel:** 020 8267 4532 **Fax:** 020 8267 4841
Email: independentnurse@haymarket.com
Advertising Address: As above. **Tel:** 020 8267 5000
Fax: 020 8267 4878
Email: andrew.prentice@haymarket.com
Web site: http://www.healthcarepublic.com
Publisher: Haymarket Medical Publications Ltd
Date Established: 2005
Frequency: 26 issues yearly
Cover Price: £2.95
Free to qualifying individuals
Circulation: 12,122 (ABC 01/01/2008 to 31/12/2008)
Usual Pagination: 56
Editor: Nick Bostock; **News Editor:** Nick Bostock; **Features Editor:** Sarah Wild
Summary of Content: Magazine covering issues affecting primary care and community nurses, including news and features both clinical and non clinical.
Readership/Target Audience: Aimed at primary care and community nurses.
ADVERTISING RATES:
Full Page Colour £1648.00
Agency Commission: 10%
Mechanical Data: Type Area: 282 x 207mm, Bleed Size: 305 x 235mm, Trim Size: 295 x 225mm, Col Length: 282mm, Page Width: 207mm, No. of Columns (Display): 4, Film: Digital, Col Widths (Display): 51mm
Copy instructions: Copy Date: 2 weeks prior to publication date
Average advertising content per issue: 50%
BUSINESS: HEALTH & MEDICAL: Nursing

INDEPENDENT RETAIL NEWS

37969U22A-240

Editorial Address: 6th Floor, 2 Robert Street, CROYDON, CR0 1QQ **Tel:** 020 8253 8704 **Fax:** 020 8253 8727
Email: david.shrimpton@metropolis.co.uk
Advertising Address: As above. **Tel:** 01322 660070
Fax: 01322 616375
Email: paul.abbott@nexusmedia.com
Web site: http://www.talkingretail.com
ISSN: 1357-2660
Publisher: Metropolis International Group Ltd
Date Established: 1995
Frequency: 25 issues yearly
Free to qualifying individuals
Annual Sub.: £115.00
Circulation: 39,709 (ABC 01/07/2008 to 30/06/2009)
Editor: David Shrimpton; **Features Editor:** Mike Dennis
Summary of Content: Journal providing retail news and product information.
Readership/Target Audience: Aimed at independent retailers.
ADVERTISING RATES:
Full Page Colour £2995.00
Agency Commission: 10%
Mechanical Data: Type Area: 267 x 185mm, Trim Size: 291 x 203mm, Bleed Size: 297 x 209mm, Col Length: 267mm, Page Width: 185mm, Film: Digital, No. of Columns (Display): 4
Copy instructions: Copy Date: 10 days prior to publicaion
Average advertising content per issue: 50%
BUSINESS: FOOD

INDEPENDENT SCHOOLS MAGAZINE

1844718U62E-422

Editorial Address: PO Box 4136, Upper Basildon, READING, RG8 6BS **Tel:** 01491 671998
Email: mail@independentschoolsmagazine.co.uk
Advertising Address: As above.
Email: mail@independentschoolsmagazine.co.uk
Web site: http://www.independentschoolsmagazine.co.uk
Publisher: Bull Nelson Ltd
Date Established: 2007
Frequency: 10 issues yearly - Not published in July or August

Free to qualifying individuals
Annual Sub.: £20.00
Circulation: 2,800 (Publisher's Statement)
Usual Pagination: 60
Editor: Kimble Earl; **Advertising Manager:** Jeff Rice
Summary of Content: Magazine covering the latest trends and surveys, interviews, independent schools news, classroom ideas and initiatives, product and services as well as legal, financial, educational and marketing updates.
Readership/Target Audience: Aimed at decision makers in independent schools including governors, heads, bursars and departmental managers.
ADVERTISING RATES:
Full Page Colour £1100.00
BUSINESS: CHURCH & SCHOOL EQUIPMENT & EDUCATION: Preparatory & Independent Schools

INDUSTRIAL ANALYTICAL INSTRUMENTATION

39965U55-9003

Editorial Address: 8 Matthew Wren Close, Little Downham, ELY, CB6 2UL **Tel:** 01353 699094 **Fax:** 01353 699094
Email: hammerton_william@hotmail.com
Advertising Address: As above.
Email: hammerton_william@hotmail.com
Web site: http://www.thejournalofindustryandtechnology.biz
Publisher: Journal of Industry and Technology
Date Established: 1982
Frequency: 6 issues yearly
Cover Price: Free
Circulation: 6,000 (Publisher's Statement)
Usual Pagination: 160
Editor: Bill Hammerton; **Advertising Manager:** Bill Hammerton
Summary of Content: Journal covering biotechnology, chromatography, laboratory robotics, laser and fibre optics.
Readership/Target Audience: Aimed at key executives in research, scientific and industrial laboratories. Also those involved in universities and hospitals.
ADVERTISING RATES:
Full Page Mono £1000.00
Full Page Colour £1250.00
Agency Commission: 15%
Mechanical Data: Type Area: 258 x 185mm, Trim Size: 285 x 205mm, No. of Columns (Display): 3, Col Length: 258mm, Film: Positive, right reading, emulsion side down, Print Process: Web-fed litho, Page Width: 185mm
Average advertising content per issue: 35%
BUSINESS: APPLIED SCIENCE & LABORATORIES

INDUSTRIAL & COMMERCIAL TRAINING

37053U14F-25

Editorial Address: Howard House, Wagon Lane, BINGLEY, BD16 1WA **Tel:** 01274 777700 **Fax:** 01274 785200
Email: bryan.smith@easynet.co.uk
Web site: http://www.emeraldinsight.com/ict.htm
Publisher: Emerald Group Publishing Ltd
Frequency: 7 issues yearly
Annual Sub.: £6179.00
Usual Pagination: 44
Editor: Bryan Smith; **News Editor:** David Pollitt; **Publisher:** Kim Foster
Summary of Content: Journal containing news reports, articles, case studies and information on training in the UK. Includes the results of training activities.
Readership/Target Audience: Read by training practitioners in the field and researchers interested in the practical aspects of employee training.
ADVERTISING: No Advertising taken
BUSINESS: COMMERCE, INDUSTRY & MANAGEMENT: Training & Recruitment

INDUSTRIAL & CORPORATE CHANGE

22196U14R-125

Editorial Address: SPRU, Freeman Centre, University of Sussex, Mantell Building, Falmer, BRIGHTON, BN1 9QE **Tel:** 01273 877315 **Fax:** 01273 685865
Advertising Address: Great Clarendon Street, OXFORD, OX2 6DP **Tel:** 01865 353329
Email: jnlsadvertising@oxfordjournals.org
Web site: http://www.icc.oupjournals.org
ISSN: 0960-6491
Publisher: OUP
Date Established: 1991
Frequency: 6 issues yearly
Cover Price: £61.00
Annual Sub.: £295.00
Usual Pagination: 200
Editor: Nick von Tunzelmann; **Publisher:** James Green
Summary of Content: Magazine covering industrial organisations, the history of technologies, the nature of competition and new research on businesses worldwide, particularly as they are affected by change.
Readership/Target Audience: Aimed at academics and professionals with an interest in business economics, strategic management, industrial history, organisational sociology and industrial economics.

Business Magazines

ADVERTISING RATES:
Full Page Mono £310.00
Agency Commission: 10%
Mechanical Data: Film: Digital, Type Area: 210 x 135mm,
Col Length: 210mm, Page Width: 135mm
BUSINESS: COMMERCE, INDUSTRY & MANAGEMENT:
Commerce Related

INDUSTRIAL & MANUFACTURING ENGINEER

37554U19A-300

Editorial Address: 5B Edgewater Business Park, Belfast
Harbour Estate, BELFAST, BT3 9JQ **Tel:** 028 9078 3200
Fax: 028 9078 3210
Email: davidelliott@greerpublications.com
Advertising Address: As above.
Email: carolinemcclean@greerpublications.com
Web site: http://www.greerpublications.com
Publisher: Greer Publications Ltd
Date Established: 1991
Frequency: Quarterly
Free to qualifying individuals
Annual Sub.: £18.00
Circulation: 4,000 (Publisher's Statement)
Usual Pagination: 56
Editor: David Elliott
Summary of Content: Journal covering in-depth news,
features, interviews, company and personal profiles and
general information from the engineering, energy,
environmental and manufacturing industries.
Readership/Target Audience: Aimed at engineers in
industry and manufacturing with purchasing authority in
Ireland.
ADVERTISING RATES:
Full Page Mono £840.00
Full Page Colour £1200.00
Agency Commission: 10%
Mechanical Data: Type Area: 267 x 180mm, Col Length:
267mm, Page Width: 180mm, Trim Size: 297 x 210mm,
Bleed Size: 307 x 220mm, Col Widths (Display): 57mm, Film:
Digital
BUSINESS: ENGINEERING & MACHINERY

INDUSTRIAL AUTOMATION INSIDER

35997U5A-130

Formerly: SCADA Insider
Editorial Address: Vine House, Church Road, Harrietsham,
MAIDSTONE, ME17 1HJ **Tel:** 01622 858251
Fax: 0870 052 6044
Email: editorial@iainsider.co.uk
Web site: http://www.iainsider.co.uk
ISSN: 1147-3034
Publisher: Andrew Bond
Date Established: 1997
Frequency: Monthly
Annual Sub.: £250.00
Usual Pagination: 12
Editor: Andrew Bond; **Publisher:** Andrew Bond
Summary of Content: Newsletter covering news and
developments on systems technologies. Includes articles on
safety, field devices and hardware and software.
Readership/Target Audience: Aimed at developers,
vendors, system integrators and end users of industrial
automation systems.
ADVERTISING: No Advertising taken
BUSINESS: COMPUTERS & AUTOMATION: Automation &
Instrumentation

INDUSTRIAL DIAMOND REVIEW

37642U19E-252

Editorial Address: Odeon House, 146 College Road,
HARROW, HA1 1BH **Tel:** 020 8863 2767 **Fax:** 020 8863 3917
Email: martin.jennings@idr-online.com
Advertising Address: As above.
Web site: http://www.idr-online.com
ISSN: 0019-8145
Publisher: Lamda Publicity Ltd
Date Established: 1940
Frequency: Quarterly
Cover Price: Free
Circulation: 10,000 (Publisher's Statement)
Editor: Martin Jennings; **Advertising Manager:** Martin
Jennings
Summary of Content: Publication covering developments in
new types of industrial diamond and cubic boron nitride
products, tools and their applications.
Readership/Target Audience: Aimed at diamond tool
makers and users and technical, scientific and commercial
libraries.
BUSINESS: ENGINEERING & MACHINERY: Machinery,
Machine Tools & Metalworking

INDUSTRIAL ENGINEERING NEWS EUROPE

37643U19E-255

Formerly: Industrial Engineering News
Editorial Address: 2 Claridge Court, Lower Kings Road,
BERKHAMSTED, HP4 2AF **Tel:** 01442 877777
Fax: 01442 870617
Email: editor@ien.eu
Advertising Address: As above. **Fax:** 01442 840617
Email: daveharvett@btconnect.com
Web site: http://www.ien.eu
Publisher: Thomas Industrial Media bvba
Date Established: 1974
Frequency: 10 issues yearly
Cover Price: Free
Circulation: 53,061 (BPA Worldwide 01/01/2007 to
30/06/2007)
Usual Pagination: 34
Editor: Dave Harvett; **Advertising Manager:** Dave Harvett
Summary of Content: Journal containing information on
new industrial products, equipment and technologies with an
emphasis on the high-tech sector.
Readership/Target Audience: Aimed at product and
system design engineers, production and engineering
managers and general corporate managers.
ADVERTISING RATES:
Full Page Mono EUR13300.00
Full Page Colour EUR13950.00
Agency Commission: 15%
Mechanical Data: Trim Size: 376 x 265mm, Type Area: 358
x 247mm, Film: Digital, Col Length: 358mm, Page Width:
247mm
Copy instructions: Copy Date: 20 days prior to publication
date
Average advertising content per issue: 40%
BUSINESS: ENGINEERING & MACHINERY: Machinery,
Machine Tools & Metalworking

INDUSTRIAL FIRE JOURNAL

39857U54A-200

Editorial Address: 8 The Old Yarn Mills, SHERBORNE, DT9
3RQ **Tel:** 01935 816030 **Fax:** 01935 817200
Email: am.knegt@hisdorset.com
Advertising Address: 32 Vauxhall Bridge Road, LONDON,
SW1V 2SS **Tel:** 020 7973 6651 **Fax:** 020 7233 5057
Email: l.bentley@hgluk.com
Web site: http://www.hemmingfire.com
ISSN: 0964-9719
Publisher: Hemming Group Ltd
Date Established: 1990
Frequency: Quarterly
Annual Sub.: £40.00
Circulation: 6,906 (Publisher's Statement)
Usual Pagination: 88
Editor: Ann-Marie Knegt
Summary of Content: Journal reporting worldwide to
industrial fire professionals within the oil, gas, chemical,
power and other high risk industries in 153 countries.
Readership/Target Audience: Read by industrial
firefighters, fire protection chiefs, fire engineers, architects,
surveyors, buyers and specifiers of industrial fire equipment.
ADVERTISING RATES:
Full Page Colour £2199.00
Agency Commission: 10%
Mechanical Data: Film: Digital, Type Area: 263 x 185mm,
Bleed Size: 303 x 213mm, Col Length: 263mm, Trim Size:
297 x 210mm, Page Width: 185mm
Copy instructions: Copy Date: 4 weeks prior to publication
date
Average advertising content per issue: 50%
BUSINESS: SAFETY & SECURITY: Fire Fighting

INDUSTRIAL LAW JOURNAL

39178U44-820

Editorial Address: Law Department, London School of
Economics & Poloitical Science, Houghton Street, Aldwych,
LONDON, WC2A 2AE **Tel:** 020 7955 7268
Fax: 020 7955 7366
Email: p.l.davies@lse.ac.uk
Advertising Address: 60 Upper Broadmoor Road,
CROWTHORNE, RG45 7DE **Tel:** 01344 779945
Fax: 01344 779945
Email: lhann@lhms.fnset.co.uk
Web site: http://www.oup.co.uk/indlaw
ISSN: 0305-9332
Publisher: OUP
Date Established: 1972
Frequency: Quarterly
Cover Price: £22.00
Annual Sub.: £71.00
Usual Pagination: 110
Editor: Paul Davies
Summary of Content: Journal covering analysis and
information on all aspects of labour law. Includes a section
on the impact of EC labour law in the UK.
Readership/Target Audience: Aimed at lawyers,
academics and lay industrial relations experts.
ADVERTISING RATES:
Full Page Mono £340.00
Agency Commission: 10%
BUSINESS: LEGAL

INDUSTRIAL LUBRICATION & TRIBOLOGY

38587U33-10

Editorial Address: The White House, Marsh Lane, Bolton
Percy, YORK, YO23 7BA **Tel:** 01274 777700
Fax: 01274 785200
Email: john@cjtaylor.net
Web site: http://www.emeraldinsight.com/ilt.htm
Publisher: Emerald Group Publishing Ltd
Frequency: 6 issues yearly
Annual Sub.: £4459.00
Usual Pagination: 50
Editor: John Taylor; **Publisher:** Harry Colson
Summary of Content: Journal about industrial and
automotive lubricants, lubricating and hydraulic equipment
and wear prevention by materials selection, design and
maintenance.
Readership/Target Audience: Read by professionals
working in the field of lubrication research.
ADVERTISING: No Advertising taken
BUSINESS: OIL & PETROLEUM

INDUSTRIAL MANAGEMENT & DATA SYSTEMS

36904U14B-145

Editorial Address: Howard House, Wagon Lane, BINGLEY,
BD16 1WA **Tel:** 01274 777700 **Fax:** 01274 785200
Email: dheath@emeraldinsight.com
Web site: http://www.emeraldinsight.com
ISSN: 0263-5577
Publisher: Emerald Group Publishing Ltd
Frequency: 9 issues yearly
Annual Sub.: £5539.00
Editor: Diane Heath; **Editor-in-Chief:** Binshan Lin;
Publisher: Diane Heath
Summary of Content: Magazine covering management
information and data systems. Also contains industry
surveys, news stories and features on industrial
management.
Readership/Target Audience: Aimed at managers who
wish to gain an understanding of key issues in technology
and application.
ADVERTISING: No Advertising taken
BUSINESS: COMMERCE, INDUSTRY & MANAGEMENT:
Industry & Factories

INDUSTRIAL MINERALS

35392U1L-40

Editorial Address: Nestor House, Playhouse Yard,
LONDON, EC4V 5EX **Tel:** 020 7827 9977
Fax: 020 7827 6441
Email: edit@indmin.com
Advertising Address: 16 Lower Marsh, LONDON, SE1 7RJ
Tel: 020 7827 9977 **Fax:** 020 8224 0639
Email: iclarke@indmin.com
Web site: http://www.indmin.com
ISSN: 0019-8544
Publisher: Industrial Minerals Information
Date Established: 1967
Frequency: Monthly - Published around the last Thursday of
the cover month
Annual Sub.: £375.75
Circulation: 1,810 (ABC 01/01/2008 to 31/12/2008)
Usual Pagination: 84
Editor: Mike O'Driscoll; **Advertising Manager:** Ismene
Clarke
Summary of Content: Magazine covering non-fuel and non-
metallic minerals. Includes business news, mineral
production, processing, surveys and trade statistics.
Readership/Target Audience: Read by companies in all
sectors of the non-fuel and non-metallic business.
ADVERTISING RATES:
Full Page Mono £1750.00
Full Page Colour £2670.00
Agency Commission: 10%
Mechanical Data: Type Area: 254 x 178mm, Trim Size: 297
x 210mm, Bleed Size: 303 x 216mm, Page Width: 178mm,
Film: Digital, Col Length: 254mm
BUSINESS: FINANCE & ECONOMICS: Commodities

INDUSTRIAL PRODUCT & SERVICE BULLETIN

37658U19F-247

Editorial Address: 307 Bridge Road, Sutton Bridge,
SPALDING, PE12 9SL **Tel:** 01406 359390
Fax: 01406 351899
Email: mail@hijpublishing.com
Advertising Address: As above. **Tel:** 0870 350 0280
Fax: 0870 350 0281
Email: mail@hijpublishing.com
Web site: http://www.hijpublishing.com
Publisher: HIJ Publishing Ltd
Date Established: 1998
Frequency: Quarterly
Cover Price: Free
Circulation: 5,000 (Publisher's Statement)
Usual Pagination: 30
Editor: Ian Cashmore; **Features Editor:** Jo Hill; **Advertising
Manager:** Ian Cashmore; **Publisher:** Ian Cashmore

Summary of Content: Journal dedicated to the UK materials handling and bulk handling industry. Covers new products and services as well as case studies and application stories.
Readership/Target Audience: Read by managers and decision makers within influential companies.
ADVERTISING RATES:
Full Page Mono £825.00
Full Page Colour £1200.00
Agency Commission: 10%
Mechanical Data: Bleed Size: 303 x 216mm, Trim Size: 297 x 210mm, Type Area: 277 x 190mm, Col Length: 277mm, Page Width: 190mm, No. of Columns (Display): 3, Film: Digital
Copy instructions: Copy Date: Middle of the month prior to publication date
Average advertising content per issue: 40%
BUSINESS: ENGINEERING & MACHINERY: Production & Mechanical Engineering

THE INDUSTRIAL ROBOT
37659U19F-248
Editorial Address: 17 Old Lane, Low Mill Village, Addingham, ILKLEY, LS29 0SA **Tel:** 01943 830399
Fax: 01943 831876
Email: news@engineeringfirst.com
Web site: http://www.emeraldinsight.com/ir.htm
ISSN: 0143-991X
Publisher: Emerald Group Publishing Ltd
Frequency: 6 issues yearly
Annual Sub.: £4999.00
Editor: Clive Loughlin; **Publisher:** Harry Colson
Summary of Content: Magazine giving in-depth technical and managerial coverage on industrial robotics on an international basis.
Readership/Target Audience: Read by industrialists and academics.
ADVERTISING: No Advertising taken
BUSINESS: ENGINEERING & MACHINERY: Production & Mechanical Engineering

INDUSTRIAL TECHNOLOGY
37613U19B-320
Editorial Address: PO Box 342, TONBRIDGE, TN10 4WD
Tel: 01732 773268 **Fax:** 0161 374 6436
Email: mark.simms@itmagazine.uk.com
Advertising Address: Hesketh House, 3 School Road, SALE, M33 7XY **Tel:** 0161 374 5615 **Fax:** 0161 374 6436
Email: it.info@itmagazine.uk.com
Web site: http://www.industrialtechnology.co.uk
ISSN: 0967-5787
Publisher: New Wave Publishing
Date Established: 1988
Frequency: 10 issues yearly - Published on the 1st Thursday of the cover month
Free to qualifying individuals
Circulation: 20,811 (ABC 01/01/2008 to 31/12/2008)
Editor: Mark Simms; **Advertising Manager:** George Bennett
Summary of Content: Publication covering mechanical, electrical engineering and computer aided design.
Readership/Target Audience: Read by product design engineers and machine builders.
ADVERTISING RATES:
Full Page Mono £3120.00
Full Page Colour £3120.00
Agency Commission: 10%
Mechanical Data: Type Area: 290 x 220mm, Col Length: 290mm, Page Width: 220mm, Trim Size: 310 x 240mm, Bleed Size: 320 x 250mm, Film: Digital
Copy instructions: Copy Date: 1st of the month prior to publication date
Average advertising content per issue: 55%
BUSINESS: ENGINEERING & MACHINERY: Engineering - Design

INDUSTRIAL WOODWORKER
39460U46-17
Editorial Address: 29 High Street, RYE, TN31 7JG
Tel: 01797 224816
Email: post@willowe.demon.co.uk
Advertising Address: As above.
Email: bill@willowe.demon.co.uk
Web site: http://www.willowe.co.uk
Publisher: Willowe Magazines Limited
Date Established: 1991
Frequency: Monthly - Published on the 2nd Friday of the cover month. Combined issues 2nd Friday of the 2nd cover month
Cover Price: £3.00
Free to qualifying individuals
Circulation: 13,500 (Publisher's Statement)
Usual Pagination: 20
Editor: Bill Lowe; **Managing Director:** Bill Lowe;
Advertising Manager: Bill Lowe
Summary of Content: Journal covering all aspects of the woodwork industry.
Readership/Target Audience: Aimed at joinery manufacturers, cabinet makers, furniture makers, kitchen specialists, door and window manufacturers and exhibition stand contractors.

ADVERTISING RATES:
Full Page Colour £995.00
Agency Commission: 10%
Mechanical Data: Type Area: 389 x 275mm, Col Length: 389mm, Page Width: 275mm, Trim Size: 420 x 297mm, Film: Digital
Average advertising content per issue: 50%
Supplement(s): Woodwaste & Dust Extraction - 4xY
BUSINESS: TIMBER, WOOD & FORESTRY

INDUSTRY EUROPE
36958U14C-83
Formerly: Industry and European Market
Editorial Address: Alkmaar House, Alkmaar Way, NORWICH, NR6 6BF **Tel:** 01603 414444 **Fax:** 01603 406543
Email: peter@industryeurope.net
Advertising Address: As above.
Email: mh@industryeurope.net
Web site: http://www.industryeurope.net
Publisher: Positive Publications Ltd
Date Established: 1990
Frequency: 10 issues yearly
Cover Price: Free
Circulation: 5,535 (Publisher's Statement)
Usual Pagination: 250
Editor: Peter Mercer; **Advertising Manager:** Matthew Howe
Summary of Content: Magazine reporting on European manufacturing.
Readership/Target Audience: Aimed at senior managers across Europe.
ADVERTISING RATES:
Full Page Colour EUR4480.00
Agency Commission: 10%
Mechanical Data: Bleed Size: 303 x 216mm, Trim Size: 297 x 210mm, Film: Digital
Copy instructions: Copy Date: 15th of the month prior to publication date
BUSINESS: COMMERCE, INDUSTRY & MANAGEMENT: International Commerce

INDUSTRY UK
1781913U14A-574
Editorial Address: 17 Old Leeds Road, HUDDERSFIELD, HD1 1SG **Tel:** 01484 441420 **Fax:** 01484 441429
Email: editorial@codebluegroup.co.uk
Advertising Address: As above.
Email: jacquit@codebluegroup.co.uk
Web site: http://www.codebluegroup.co.uk
Publisher: Code Blue Publishing Limited
Date Established: 2006
Frequency: Monthly
Cover Price: £2.90
Free to qualifying individuals
Circulation: 6,000 (Publisher's Statement)
Usual Pagination: 50
Editor: Nigel Martin; **Advertising Manager:** Jacqui Tillotson
Summary of Content: Publication covering all areas of UK industry with a strong focus on environmental issues.
Readership/Target Audience: Aimed at key decision makers within all sectors of UK industry.
ADVERTISING: Rates on application
Copy instructions: Copy Date: 3 weeks prior to publication date
Average advertising content per issue: 50%
BUSINESS: COMMERCE, INDUSTRY & MANAGEMENT

INFANT
40311U56B-178
Editorial Address: 134 South Street, BISHOP'S STORTFORD, CM23 3BQ **Tel:** 01279 714511
Fax: 01279 714519
Email: publishing@infantgrapevine.co.uk
Advertising Address: As above. **Tel:** 01279 714509
Email: mark@infantgrapevine.co.uk
Web site: http://www.infantgrapevine.co.uk
ISSN: 1745-1205
Publisher: Stansted News Ltd
Date Established: 2005
Frequency: 6 issues yearly
Free to qualifying individuals
Annual Sub.: £45.00
Circulation: 5,000 (Publisher's Statement)
Usual Pagination: 48
Editor: Christine Bishop; **Publisher:** Christine Bishop
Summary of Content: Review journal containing articles with a clinical or practical bias written by experts in the field.
Readership/Target Audience: Aimed at the multidisciplinary team caring for vulnerable, sick or premature babies in their first year of life, including neonatal nurses, neonatologists, paediatric intensive care nurses and doctors, paediatric A & E personnel and midwives.
ADVERTISING RATES:
Full Page Mono £1078.00
Full Page Colour £1634.00
Agency Commission: 10%
Mechanical Data: Type Area: 268 x 178mm, Trim Size: 297 x 210mm, Bleed Size: 303 x 216mm, Film: Digital, Print Process: Sheet-fed offset litho, Page Width: 178mm, Col Length: 268mm

Copy instructions: Copy Date: 2 weeks prior to publication date
Average advertising content per issue: 30%
BUSINESS: HEALTH & MEDICAL: Nursing

INFO
36959U14C-86
Editorial Address: Lincoln House, 300 High Holborn, LONDON, WC1V 7JH **Tel:** 020 7304 7023
Fax: 020 7304 7034
Email: publications@ccfgb.co.uk
Advertising Address: As above. **Tel:** 020 7092 6651
Fax: 020 7092 6601
Email: coddo@ccfgb.co.uk
Web site: http://www.ccfgb.co.uk
Publisher: French Chamber of Commerce in Great Britain
Date Established: 1883
Frequency: 6 issues yearly
Annual Sub.: £45.00
Circulation: 10,000 (Publisher's Statement)
Usual Pagination: 36
Editor: Delphine Dewulf; **Advertising Manager:** Capucine Oddo
Summary of Content: Official journal of the French Chamber of Commerce in Great Britain.
Language(s): English; French
Readership/Target Audience: Read by senior executives in the Franco-British business world.
ADVERTISING RATES:
Full Page Colour £2010.00
Agency Commission: 10%
Mechanical Data: Page Width: 210mm, Type Area: 285 x 210mm, Col Length: 285mm, Film: Digital
Copy instructions: Copy Date: 4 weeks prior to publication date
BUSINESS: COMMERCE, INDUSTRY & MANAGEMENT: International Commerce

INFO
37462U18B-915
Editorial Address: Howard House, Wagon Lane, BINGLEY, BD16 1WA **Tel:** 01274 777700 **Fax:** 01274 785200
Email: kpycroft@emeraldinsight.com
Web site: http://www.emeraldinsight.com/info/journals/info/info.htm
ISSN: 1463-6697
Publisher: Emerald Group Publishing Ltd
Date Established: 1999
Frequency: 6 issues yearly
Annual Sub.: £679.00
Usual Pagination: 72
Editor: Colin Blackman
Summary of Content: Journal covering policy, regulation and strategy for telecommunications, information services and the media.
Readership/Target Audience: Aimed at those concerned with corporate strategy and planning including regulatory bodies and government departments.
ADVERTISING: No Advertising taken
BUSINESS: ELECTRONICS: Telecommunications

INFOPLUS+
1772593U2R-186
Formerly: ISTC Newsletter
Editorial Address: Airport House, Purley Way, CROYDON, CR0 0XZ **Tel:** 020 8253 4506 **Fax:** 020 8253 4510
Email: newsletter.editor@istc.org.uk
Advertising Address: Tou-can Marketing, The Holly, 42 Heath Hill Road South, CROWTHORNE, RG45 7BW
Tel: 01344 466600 **Fax:** 01344 466601
Email: felicity@tou-can.co.uk
Web site: http://www.istc.org.uk
Publisher: ISTC
Frequency: Monthly
Cover Price: Free
Circulation: 1,500 (Publisher's Statement)
Usual Pagination: 10
Advertising Manager: Felicity Davie; **Managing Editor:** Bob Hewitt
Summary of Content: Newsletter covering developments, current trends and training for technical and scientific communicators.
Readership/Target Audience: Aimed at technical and scientific communicators.
ADVERTISING RATES:
Full Page Mono £485.00
Full Page Colour £485.00
Mechanical Data: No. of Columns (Display): 3, Type Area: 260 x 170mm, Col Length: 260mm, Page Width: 170mm, Film: Digital
Copy instructions: Copy Date: 25th of the month prior to publication date
BUSINESS: COMMUNICATIONS, ADVERTISING & MARKETING: Communications Related

INFORM
41400U63B-2180
Editorial Address: Victoria House, 2 Victoria Place, LEEDS, LS11 5AE **Tel:** 0113 394 9707 **Fax:** 0113 243 9211

Business Magazines

Email: theresa.lindsay@yorkshire-forward.com
Advertising Address: As above. **Tel:** 0113 394 9600
Email: theresa.lindsay@yorkshire-forward.com
Web site: http://www.yorkshire-forward.com
Publisher: Yorkshire Forward
Date Established: 2000
Frequency: Quarterly
Cover Price: Free
Circulation: 10,000 (Publisher's Statement)
Usual Pagination: 12
Editor: Theresa Lindsay; **Advertising Manager:** Michelle Staveley
Summary of Content: Newsletter of Yorkshire Forward, the regional development agency for Yorkshire and Humberside, covering economic business and investment news.
Readership/Target Audience: Aimed at members, regional supporters, foreign owned companies and businesses based in the region.
ADVERTISING: Rates on application
BUSINESS: REGIONAL BUSINESS: Regional Business English Counties

INFORMATION AGE
36098U5B-89_50
Editorial Address: Octavia House, 50 Banner Street, LONDON, EC1Y 8ST **Tel:** 020 7250 7010
Fax: 020 7250 7011
Email: iaeditorial@vitessemedia.co.uk
Advertising Address: As above.
Email: john.bromley@vitessemedia.co.uk
Web site: http://www.information-age.com
ISSN: 1359-4214
Publisher: Vitesse Media plc
Date Established: 2000
Frequency: Monthly - Published in the 2nd week of the cover month
Circulation: 24,031 (BPA Worldwide 01/01/2007 to 30/06/2007)
Editor: Pete Swabey
Summary of Content: Magazine covering news, information and corporate IT issues.
Readership/Target Audience: Aimed at those involved in IT management and policy.
ADVERTISING RATES:
Full Page Colour £5050.00
Agency Commission: 10%
Mechanical Data: Type Area: 254 x 185mm, Bleed Size: 279 x 211mm, Trim Size: 273 x 205mm, Col Length: 254mm, Page Width: 185mm, No. of Columns (Display): 3, Film: Digital
Copy instructions: Copy Date: 1 week prior to publication date
Average advertising content per issue: 40%
BUSINESS: COMPUTERS & AUTOMATION: Data Processing

INFORMATION MANAGEMENT & TECHNOLOGY
1866240U60B-306
Editorial Address: University of Hertfordshire, Innovation Centre, College Lane, HATFIELD, AL10 9AB
Tel: 01707 281060 **Fax:** 01707 281061
Email: r.n.broadhurst@herts.ac.uk
Web site: http://www.cimtech.co.uk
Publisher: CIMTECH Ltd
Frequency: 10 issues yearly
Annual Sub.: £80.00
Circulation: 800 (Publisher's Statement)
Usual Pagination: 48
Editor: Roger Broadhurst
Summary of Content: Electronic journal covering news, topical issues, articles, case studies, product reviews and events within electronic document, content and record management.
Readership/Target Audience: Aimed at information management professionals including document managers, content managers, records managers, archivists, librarians, information officers, product and services suppliers.
BUSINESS: PUBLISHING: Libraries

INFORMATION SECURITY TECHNICAL REPORT
39905U54C-54
Editorial Address: The Boulevard, Langford Lane, KIDLINGTON, OX5 1GB **Tel:** 01865 843259
Fax: 01865 843971
Email: m.lamine@elsevier.com
Web site: http://www.compseconline.com
ISSN: 1363-4127
Publisher: Elsevier Ltd
Date Established: 1996
Frequency: Quarterly
Annual Sub.: $1720.00
Editor: Monique Lamine; **Editor-in-Chief:** Fred Piper;
Managing Editor: Monique Lamine
Summary of Content: Technical report covering a particular aspect of information security in each issue. Contains articles on smartcards, information warfare, cryptography, forensic investigation and platform security.

Readership/Target Audience: Aimed at IT security managers.
ADVERTISING: No Advertising taken
BUSINESS: SAFETY & SECURITY: Security

INFORMATION TECHNOLOGY LAW REPORTS
633808U44-825
Editorial Address: Office G18, Spinners Court, 55 West End, WITNEY, OX28 1NH **Tel:** 01993 706183
Fax: 01993 709410
Email: ltp@lawtext.com
Advertising Address: As above.
Web site: http://www.lawtext.com
ISSN: 1365-8559
Publisher: Lawtext Publishing Ltd
Date Established: 1997
Frequency: 6 issues yearly
Annual Sub.: £295.00
Usual Pagination: 90
Editor: Rachel Caldin; **Advertising Manager:** Nick Gingell
Summary of Content: Report containing headnotes on decisions and other materials on legal disputes, relating to computers, telecommunications and data protection.
Readership/Target Audience: Aimed at legal academics, institutions, libraries and information technology and litigation lawyers.
ADVERTISING: Rates on application
BUSINESS: LEGAL

INFORMATION WORLD REVIEW
37463U18B-920
Editorial Address: 80-82 Chiswick High Road, LONDON, W4 1SY **Tel:** 020 8995 9345
Email: peterw@bizmedia.co.uk
Advertising Address: As above. **Tel:** 020 7316 9000
Fax: 020 7316 9313
Email: john.steward@incisivemedia.com
Web site: http://www.iwr.co.uk
ISSN: 0950-9879
Publisher: Biz Media
Date Established: 1978
Frequency: 10 issues yearly - Published on the 2nd Monday of the cover month
Free to qualifying individuals
Annual Sub.: £47.00
Circulation: 10,000 (Publisher's Statement)
Usual Pagination: 32
Editor: Peter Williams; **Advertising Manager:** John Steward
Summary of Content: Newspaper with detailed analysis and in brief news from the online information industry, reporting on the latest trends and technologies and how they relate to the information world. Also examines views of producers and users of electronic information in a specific industry sector.
Readership/Target Audience: Read by sales and marketing, information and IT professionals.
ADVERTISING RATES:
Full Page Colour £3270.00
Agency Commission: 10%
Mechanical Data: Film: Digital, Bleed Size: 341 x 276mm, Type Area: 315 x 250mm, Trim Size: 335 x 270mm, Col Length: 315mm, Page Width: 250mm
Copy instructions: Copy Date: 3 weeks prior to publication date
BUSINESS: ELECTRONICS: Telecommunications

INFORME LATINOAMERICANO
601232U14C-87
Editorial Address: 61 Old Street, LONDON, EC1V 9HW
Tel: 020 7251 0012 **Fax:** 020 7253 8193
Email: subs@latinnews.com
Web site: http://www.latinnews.com
ISSN: 1741-7317
Publisher: Intelligence Research Ltd
Date Established: 1979
Frequency: Weekly
Annual Sub.: £610.00
Usual Pagination: 16
Editor: Jon Farmer
Summary of Content: Magazine covering politics, economics and finance. Spanish version of Latin American Weekly Report.
Language(s): Spanish
Readership/Target Audience: Aimed at senior businessmen, diplomats, government officials, academics, financial institutions and bankers.
ADVERTISING: No Advertising taken
BUSINESS: COMMERCE, INDUSTRY & MANAGEMENT: International Commerce

INFORMED
1664279U1R-362
Editorial Address: Bedford House, 3 Bedford Street, LONDON, WC2E 9HD **Tel:** 020 7379 1763
Fax: 020 7240 1320
Email: michael.mitchell@irs.org.uk

Advertising Address: 211 Linton House, 164-180 Union Street, LONDON, SE1 0LH **Tel:** 020 7928 7770
Fax: 020 7928 7780
Email: sveal@silverdart.co.uk
Web site: http://www.irs.org.uk
Publisher: Silverdart Publishing
Date Established: 1994
Frequency: Quarterly
Cover Price: £5.00
Free to qualifying individuals
Circulation: 2,000 (Publisher's Statement)
Usual Pagination: 36
Editor: Michael Mitchell; **Publisher:** Alex Murray
Summary of Content: Magazine covering topical stories, viewpoints on latest investor relations issues and an update on the regulatory framework.
Readership/Target Audience: Aimed at investor relation professionals.
ADVERTISING RATES:
Full Page Colour £1390.00
Mechanical Data: Type Area: 265 x 180mm, Col Length: 265mm, Page Width: 180mm, Trim Size: 297 x 210mm, Film: Digital
Copy instructions: Copy Date: 2 weeks prior to publication date
BUSINESS: FINANCE & ECONOMICS: Financial Related

INFOSECURITY
26037U54C-310
Formerly: Infosecurity Today
Editorial Address: The Boulevard, Langford Lane, KIDLINGTON, OX5 1GB **Tel:** 01865 843656
Email: editorial.infosecurity@elsevier.com
Advertising Address: As above. **Tel:** 01865 843000
Email: r.disanto@husonmedia.com
Web site: http://www.infosecurity-magazine.com
ISSN: 1754-4548
Publisher: Elsevier Ltd
Date Established: 2004
Frequency: 8 issues yearly - Published at the end of the month prior to the cover month
Free to qualifying individuals
Annual Sub.: EUR163.00
Circulation: 27,000 (Publisher's Statement)
Usual Pagination: 48
Editor: Eleanor Dallaway
Summary of Content: Magazine covering news, products and issues relevant to the IT security market.
Readership/Target Audience: Aimed at IT security professionals.
ADVERTISING RATES:
Full Page Colour £3114.00
Agency Commission: 10%
Mechanical Data: Page Width: 185mm, Type Area: 243 x 185mm, Bleed Size: 286 x 222mm, Col Length: 243mm, Film: Digital, Trim Size: 280 x 216mm
Average advertising content per issue: 30%
BUSINESS: SAFETY & SECURITY: Security

IN-HOUSE LAWYER
39174U44-830
Formerly: The In-House Lawyer Yearbook
Editorial Address: Kensington Square House, 12-14 Ansdell Street, LONDON, W8 5BN **Tel:** 020 7396 9292
Fax: 020 7396 9303
Email: ihl@legalease.co.uk
Advertising Address: As above. **Fax:** 020 7396 9302
Email: matthew.todd@legalease.co.uk
Web site: http://www.legalease.co.uk
ISSN: 0966-8012
Publisher: Legalease Ltd
Frequency: 10 issues yearly
Annual Sub.: £145.00
Circulation: 5,500 (Publisher's Statement)
Usual Pagination: 80
Editor: Eduardo Reyes; **Editor-in-Chief:** John Pritchard;
Advertising Manager: Matthew Todd
Summary of Content: Magazine providing the latest in-house legal information from UK and Europe with regular features on international issues and deals.
Readership/Target Audience: Aimed at in-house lawyers in the UK and non-lawyer executives who have been identified as key individuals in legal purchasing decisions.
ADVERTISING RATES:
Full Page Colour £3095.00
Agency Commission: 10%
Mechanical Data: Film: Positive, right reading, emulsion side down. Digital, No. of Columns (Display): 4, Type Area: 255 x 205mm, Bleed Size: 307 x 250mm, Trim Size: 297 x 240mm, Page Width: 205mm, Col Length: 255mm
Copy instructions: Copy Date: 25th of the month prior to publication date
BUSINESS: LEGAL

INJURY
40510U56P-40
Editorial Address: The Boulevard, Langford Lane, KIDLINGTON, OX5 1GB **Tel:** 01865 843380
Fax: 01865 883992

Section 4 (b) Business Magazines

Email: editor@injuryjournal.com
Advertising Address: 32 Jamestown Road, LONDON, NW1 7BY **Tel:** 020 7424 4280 **Fax:** 020 7424 4433
Email: k.mccormack@elsevier.com
Web site: http://www.injuryjournal.com
ISSN: 0020-1383
Publisher: Elsevier Ltd
Date Established: 1969
Frequency: Monthly
Free to qualifying individuals
Annual Sub.: EUR168.00
Circulation: 1,111 (Publisher's Statement)
Usual Pagination: 129
Editor: Suzanne Peedell; **Advertising Manager:** Katie McCormack; **Publisher:** Anne Lloyd
Summary of Content: International Journal of the Care of the Injured. Contains developments in accident and trauma surgery and management.
Readership/Target Audience: Read by accident and emergency, trauma and orthopaedic surgeons, anaesthetists, intensive care specialists, nursing staff, physical therapists, radiographers and paramedics.
ADVERTISING RATES:
Full Page Mono EUR1116.00
Full Page Colour EUR2028.00
Agency Commission: 10%
Mechanical Data: Type Area: 250 x 180mm, Col Length: 250mm, Trim Size: 280 x 210mm, Bleed Size: 286 x 216mm, Film: Digital, Page Width: 180mm
Copy instructions: Copy Date: 6 weeks prior to publication date
BUSINESS: HEALTH & MEDICAL: Casualty & Emergency

INK PELLET
622685U62B-370
Editorial Address: Kettle Chambers, 21 Stone Street, CRANBROOK, TN17 3HF **Tel:** 01580 713993
Fax: 01580 715983
Email: info@inkwellpress.co.uk
Advertising Address: As above.
Email: hayley.biddulph@inkpellet.co.uk
Web site: http://www.inkpellet.co.uk
Publisher: The Inkwell Press Limited
Date Established: 1998
Frequency: 6 issues yearly
Cover Price: Free
Annual Sub.: £8.00
Circulation: 10,386 (Publisher's Statement)
Usual Pagination: 36
Editor: Julie Simpson; **Publisher:** Julie Simpson
Summary of Content: Arts magazine containing information on the arts, literature, equipment and services, plus book, theatre and software reviews.
Readership/Target Audience: Aimed at English and drama teachers in secondary schools. Secondary copy also sent into schools for the staffroom and teachers of other subject areas.
ADVERTISING RATES:
Full Page Mono £660.00
Full Page Colour £860.00
Mechanical Data: Bleed Size: +3mm, Page Width: 210mm, Type Area: 297 x 210mm, Col Length: 297mm
BUSINESS: CHURCH & SCHOOL EQUIPMENT & EDUCATION: Education Teachers

INNOVATIONS IN FOOD TECHNOLOGY
38048U22R-190
Editorial Address: 17 Ashcroft Court, BURNHAM, SL1 8JT
Tel: 01628 666176 **Fax:** 01628 666176
Email: innft@aol.com
Advertising Address: As above.
Email: innft@aol.com
Web site: http://www.innovationsfood.com.com
ISSN: 1465-0460
Publisher: Print Workshop Publications
Date Established: 1998
Frequency: Quarterly - Published the beginning of the cover month
Free to qualifying individuals
Annual Sub.: £50.00
Circulation: 10,000 (Publisher's Statement)
Usual Pagination: 116
Editor: Terry Prior; **Advertising Manager:** David Copperfield
Summary of Content: Ingredients magazine covering the latest developments and innovations taking place within the food ingredients technology industry.
Readership/Target Audience: Read by R and D, food technologists, scientists, senior management and marketing personnel.
ADVERTISING RATES:
Full Page Mono £1050.00
Full Page Colour £2400.00
Agency Commission: 10%
Mechanical Data: Film: Digital, Page Width: 184mm, Type Area: 265 x 184mm, Col Length: 265mm, No. of Columns (Display): 4, Print Process: Sheet-fed litho, Bleed Size: 303 x 216mm, Trim Size: 297 x 210mm
BUSINESS: FOOD: Food Related

INNOVATIONS IN PHARMACEUTICAL TECHNOLOGY
758600U37-27_50
Editorial Address: 16 Hampden Gurney Street, LONDON, W1H 5AL **Tel:** 020 7724 3456 **Fax:** 020 7724 2632
Email: editor@iptonline.com
Advertising Address: As above.
Email: sales@iptonline.com
Web site: http://www.iptonline.com
ISSN: 1471-7204
Publisher: Samedan Pharmaceutical Publishers Ltd
Date Established: 1997
Frequency: 3 issues yearly - Published in April, August and December. Publishing months depends on trade shows
Annual Sub.: $150.00
Circulation: 10,000 (Publisher's Statement)
Usual Pagination: 130
Editor: Pamela Barnacal
Summary of Content: Magazine covering new technologies and innovations and the impact they have on how drugs are researched, developed and manufactured. Includes technical information, views, services and solutions.
Readership/Target Audience: Aimed at those involved in pharmaceutical companies; buyers, suppliers and manufacturers.
ADVERTISING RATES:
Full Page Colour £2850.00
Agency Commission: 10%
Mechanical Data: Film: Digital
Copy instructions: Copy Date: 2 weeks prior to publication date
Average advertising content per issue: 30%
BUSINESS: PHARMACEUTICAL & CHEMISTS

INNOVATIONS IN PROCESSING AND PACKAGING
1835709U35-367
Editorial Address: 17 Ashcroft Court, Burnham, SLOUGH, SL1 8JT **Tel:** 01628 666176 **Fax:** 01628 666176
Email: innovations@tinyworld.co.uk
Tel: 4 66 58 05 62
Email: innft@aol.com
Web site: http://www.innovfoodtech.com
Publisher: Print Workshop Publications
Date Established: 2007
Frequency: Quarterly
Annual Sub.: £50.00
Circulation: 10,000 (Publisher's Statement)
Usual Pagination: 36
Editor: Terry Prior
Summary of Content: Processing and packaging magazine that covers these sectors within the food technology industry.
Readership/Target Audience: Read by R and D, food technologists, scientists, senior management and marketing personnel.
ADVERTISING RATES:
Full Page Mono £1050.00
Full Page Colour £2400.00
SCC £9.91
BUSINESS: PACKAGING & BOTTLING

INPUBLISHING
1637492U10-205
Formerly: InCirculation
Editorial Address: Hawthorns, Station Road, Eynsford, DARTFORD, DA4 0EJ **Tel:** 01322 865984
Email: editorial@inpublishing.co.uk
Advertising Address: As above. **Tel:** 020 7924 5885
Fax: 01895 239999
Email: sales@inpublishing.co.uk
Web site: http://www.inpublishing.co.uk
Publisher: InPublishing Ltd
Frequency: 6 issues yearly
Free to qualifying individuals
Circulation: 5,481 (ABC 01/07/2007 to 30/06/2008)
Editor: James Evelegh
Summary of Content: Magazine covering marketing, circulation and distribution of newspapers and magazines.
Readership/Target Audience: Aimed at corporate management and marketing, promotion, distribution and circulation directors and managers.
ADVERTISING RATES:
Full Page Colour £1450.00
Agency Commission: 10%
Mechanical Data: Type Area: 273 x 187mm, Bleed Size: 307 x 226mm, Trim Size: 297 x 210mm, Col Length: 273mm, Page Width: 187mm, Film: Digital
Copy instructions: Copy Date: 2nd Friday of the month prior to month of publication
BUSINESS: MATERIALS HANDLING

INSIDE BUSINESS MILTON KEYNES
41253U63B-237_60
Editorial Address: 151 Silbury Boulevard, MILTON KEYNES, MK9 1LH **Tel:** 01908 545380 **Fax:** 01908 545389
Email: alan@insidebusiness.co.uk

Advertising Address: As above.
Email: sales@insidebusiness.co.uk
Web site: http://www.insidebusiness.co.uk
ISSN: 1464-2468
Publisher: Inside Business
Frequency: 6 issues yearly
Cover Price: £3.00
Free to qualifying individuals
Annual Sub.: £18.00
Circulation: 6,500 (Publisher's Statement)
Usual Pagination: 64
Editor: Alan Price
Summary of Content: Magazine containing Milton Keynes business news, IT, business profiles, Chamber of Commerce news, law, finance, events and motoring.
Readership/Target Audience: Aimed at all commercial business premises in Milton Keynes. Includes small one-man band to large blue chip corporate businesses, partners in all firms of solicitors, accountants and bank managers, The Milton Keynes Chamber of Commerce Federation of Small Business, and The Institute of Directors.
ADVERTISING RATES:
Full Page Colour £600.00
Agency Commission: 10%
Mechanical Data: Print Process: Sheet-fed litho, Type Area: 275 x 190mm, Bleed Size: 303 x 216mm, Trim Size: 297 x 210mm, Col Length: 275mm, Page Width: 190mm, Film: Digital
Copy instructions: Copy Date: 3 weeks prior to publication date
Average advertising content per issue: 50%
BUSINESS: REGIONAL BUSINESS: Regional Business English Counties

INSIDE BUSINESS READING
1623143U63B-2502
Editorial Address: 151 Silbury Boulevard, MILTON KEYNES, MK9 1LH **Tel:** 01908 545380
Email: alan@insidebusiness.co.uk
Web site: http://www.insidebusiness.co.uk
Publisher: Inside Business
Date Established: 2003
Frequency: 6 issues yearly
Cover Price: Free
Circulation: 38,000 (Publisher's Statement)
Usual Pagination: 32
Editor: Alan Price; **Publisher:** Alan Price
Summary of Content: Magazine covering the business community in Reading.
Readership/Target Audience: Aimed at key decision makers in Reading and the surrounding areas.
BUSINESS: REGIONAL BUSINESS: Regional Business English Counties

INSIDE HOSPITALS
40363U56C-342
Editorial Address: 1 Friary Chambers, Whitefriargate, HULL, HU1 2HA **Tel:** 01482 585735 **Fax:** 01482 229593
Email: sheri@inside-hospitals.co.uk
Advertising Address: As above.
Email: sheri@inside-hospitals.co.uk
Web site: http://www.inside-hospitals.co.uk
Publisher: David Publishing Ltd
Date Established: 2000
Frequency: 6 issues yearly
Free to qualifying individuals
Annual Sub.: £60.00
Circulation: 7,525 (Publisher's Statement)
Usual Pagination: 68
Editor: Sheridan O'Neill; **Advertising Manager:** Sheridan O'Neill
Summary of Content: Journal focusing on nursing and clinical support services. Contains features on new products, operating theatres, infection control and sterile services.
Readership/Target Audience: Aimed at nursing, infection control nurses and clinical and medical support teams.
ADVERTISING RATES:
Full Page Colour £1650.00
Agency Commission: 10%
Mechanical Data: Type Area: 274 x 190mm, Col Length: 274mm, Trim Size: 297 x 210mm, Bleed Size: 303 x 216mm, Film: Digital, Page Width: 190mm
Copy instructions: Copy Date: 3 weeks prior to publication date
Average advertising content per issue: 40%
BUSINESS: HEALTH & MEDICAL: Hospitals

INSIDE HOUSING
35857U4D-135
Editorial Address: 1 Canada Square, 19th Floor, Canary Wharf, LONDON, E14 5AP **Tel:** 020 7772 8364
Fax: 020 7772 8591
Email: editorial@insidehousing.co.uk
Advertising Address: As above. **Fax:** 020 7772 8590
Email: alex.haughton@insidehousing.co.uk
Web site: http://www.insidehousing.co.uk
ISSN: 0950-3358
Publisher: Ocean Media Group Ltd

Business Magazines

Date Established: 1984
Frequency: Weekly
Annual Sub.: £90.00
Circulation: 26,343 (ABC 01/07/2008 to 30/06/2009)
Usual Pagination: 45
Editor: Martin Hilditch; **News Editor:** Martin Hilditch;
Features Editor: Caroline Thorpe
Summary of Content: Magazine covering news on all aspects of housing, including local government housing, housing association housing, private accommodation, housing benefits and homelessness.
Readership/Target Audience: Read by members and student members of the Chartered Institute of Housing, local authority housing departments, housing associations and the private sector.
ADVERTISING RATES:
Full Page Colour £2828.00
Agency Commission: 10%
Mechanical Data: Film: Digital, Trim Size: 270 x 208mm, Bleed Size: +3mm
Copy instructions: Copy Date: Tuesday prior to publication date
Average advertising content per issue: 13%
BUSINESS: ARCHITECTURE & BUILDING: Planning & Housing

INSIDE KNOWLEDGE
1645926U5C-906
Formerly: EI & IK
Editorial Address: 266-276 Upper Richmond Road, LONDON, SW15 6TQ **Tel:** 020 8785 5938
Fax: 020 8785 9373
Email: kclifton@ark-group.com
Advertising Address: As above. **Tel:** 020 8785 2700
Email: jadams@ark-group.com
Web site: http://www.ikmagazine.com
ISSN: 1369-1368
Publisher: Ark Group Ltd
Date Established: 2004
Frequency: 10 issues yearly - Published on the 1st of the cover month
Annual Sub.: £345.00
Circulation: 5,000 (Publisher's Statement)
Usual Pagination: 52
Editor: Kate Clifton; **Managing Editor:** Kate Clifton
Summary of Content: Magazine covering developments within the content management and portal markets. Includes articles on management systems, intranets and web technologies.
Readership/Target Audience: Aimed at intranet, extranet and enterprise portal professionals.
ADVERTISING RATES:
Full Page Colour £1595.00
Agency Commission: 10%
Mechanical Data: Type Area: 250 x 190mm, Bleed Size: 281 x 221mm, Trim Size: 275 x 215mm, Col Length: 250mm, Page Width: 190mm, Film: Digital
Copy instructions: Copy Date: 10th of the month prior to publication date
Average advertising content per issue: 30%
BUSINESS: COMPUTERS & AUTOMATION: Professional Personal Computers

INSIDE LEARNING TECHNOLOGIES
622924U5E-440
Editorial Address: 19 Hurst Park, MIDHURST, GU29 0BP
Tel: 01730 817600 **Fax:** 01730 817602
Email: editor@learningtechnologies.co.uk
Web site: http://www.learningtechnologies.co.uk
Publisher: Principal Media Ltd
Date Established: 2000
Frequency: 3 issues yearly - Published in September, November and January
Cover Price: Free
Circulation: 12,000 (Publisher's Statement)
Usual Pagination: 84
Editor: Ben Chai; **Publisher:** Mark Penton
Summary of Content: Magazine focusing on IT skills, e-learning, training and development management. Includes features on knowledge management, e-commerce and faster network infrastructures.
Readership/Target Audience: Aimed at those involved in technology management and training.
ADVERTISING: No Advertising taken
BUSINESS: COMPUTERS & AUTOMATION: Data Transmission

INSIDE NRC
622551U58-55
Editorial Address: PR by email only
Email: david_stellfox@platts.com
Web site: http://www.platts.com
Publisher: Platts
Frequency: 26 issues yearly
Usual Pagination: 18
Editor: David Stellfox

Summary of Content: Publication covering all aspects of regulating the nuclear industry worldwide, with particular emphasis on the U.S regulator NRC.
Readership/Target Audience: Aimed at nuclear regulators, governments, NGOs and nuclear companies.
ADVERTISING: No Advertising taken
BUSINESS: ENERGY, FUEL & NUCLEAR

INSIDE OR
36794U14A-270
Formerly: Operational Research Newsletter
Editorial Address: Seymour House, 12 Edward Street, BIRMINGHAM, B1 2RX **Tel:** 0121 233 9300
Fax: 0121 233 0321
Email: newsletter@theorsociety.com
Advertising Address: As above.
Email: hilary.wilkes@orsoc.org.uk
Web site: http://www.theorsociety.com
Publisher: The Operational Research Society
Date Established: 1971
Frequency: Monthly - Published on the 22nd of the cover month
Annual Sub.: £60.00
Circulation: 3,000 (Publisher's Statement)
Usual Pagination: 40
Editor: Hilary Wilkes; **Advertising Manager:** Hilary Wilkes
Summary of Content: Newsletter concerned with management science including e-commerce and business topics, customer relationship management, database marketing and call centre issues.
Readership/Target Audience: Aimed at business professionals in medium to large enterprises.
ADVERTISING RATES:
Full Page Mono £1750.00
Full Page Colour £2045.00
Agency Commission: 10%
Mechanical Data: Type Area: 245 x 160mm, Col Length: 245mm, Page Width: 160mm
Copy instructions: Copy Date: 10th of the month prior to publication date
BUSINESS: COMMERCE, INDUSTRY & MANAGEMENT

INSIDE REFERENCE DATA
1773014U5B-9017
Editorial Address: Haymarket House, 28-29 Haymarket, LONDON, SW1Y 4RX **Tel:** 020 7484 9700
Email: tine.thoresen@incisivemedia.com
Advertising Address: As above.
Email: ird@incisivemedia.com
Web site: http://www.irdonline.com
ISSN: 1750-8517
Publisher: Incisive Media Investments
Date Established: 2006
Frequency: Monthly
Cover Price: £649.00
Usual Pagination: 24
Editor: Tine Thoresen; **Advertising Manager:** Lee Hartt;
Publisher: Lee Hartt
Summary of Content: Magazine covering the global, financial reference data industry.
Readership/Target Audience: Aimed at senior management involved in data management at global investment banks, institutions and financial services firms.
ADVERTISING: Rates on application
Agency Commission: 15%
BUSINESS: COMPUTERS & AUTOMATION: Data Processing

INSIDE TRACK
38559U32R-210
Editorial Address: Corporate Communication Unit, Home Office, 1st Floor, Peel Block, 2 Marsham Street, LONDON, SW1P 4DF **Tel:** 020 7035 4072
Publisher: Story Worldwide
Frequency: 10 issues yearly
Cover Price: Free
Circulation: 15,000 (Publisher's Statement)
Usual Pagination: 8
Editor: Gillian Hudson; **Advertising Manager:** Gaynor Garton
Summary of Content: Newspaper providing a round-up of news about Home Office staff and events.
Readership/Target Audience: Read by Home Office and agency staff.
ADVERTISING: No Advertising taken
BUSINESS: LOCAL GOVERNMENT, LEISURE & RECREATION: Local Government Related

INSIDER (NORTH WEST BUSINESS INSIDER)
41291U63B-525
Editorial Address: Boulton House, 17-21 Chorlton Street, MANCHESTER, M1 3HY **Tel:** 0161 907 9711
Fax: 0161 236 9862
Email: insider@newsco.com
Advertising Address: As above. **Tel:** 0161 907 9720
Email: insider@newsco.com
Web site: http://www.newsco.com

ISSN: 1362-5049
Publisher: Newsco Insider Ltd
Date Established: 1991
Frequency: Monthly - Published around the 10th of the cover month
Cover Price: £5.00
Annual Sub.: £50.00
Circulation: 14,802 (ABC 01/07/2008 to 30/06/2009)
Usual Pagination: 96
Editor: Michael Taylor
Summary of Content: Magazine containing in-depth coverage of major issues and analytical business information in the Northwest.
Readership/Target Audience: Aimed at senior executives and directors in industry and key professionals in finance and property.
ADVERTISING RATES:
Full Page Colour £2600.00
Agency Commission: 10%
Mechanical Data: Bleed Size: 286 x 216mm, Trim Size: 280 x 210mm, Film: Digital
Copy instructions: Copy Date: 4 weeks prior to publication date
Average advertising content per issue: 40%
BUSINESS: REGIONAL BUSINESS: Regional Business English Counties

INSIDER (SOUTH WEST BUSINESS INSIDER)
1819875U63B-2584
Editorial Address: Maxet House, 28 Baldwin Street, BRISTOL, BS1 1NG **Tel:** 0117 925 7342
Email: rob.rodgerson@newsco.com
Advertising Address: As above. **Tel:** 0117 906 5901
Fax: 0844 406 0025
Email: rob.rodgerson@newsco.com
Web site: http://www.insidermagazine.co.uk
Publisher: Newsco Insider Ltd
Date Established: 2007
Frequency: Monthly
Cover Price: £5.00
Circulation: 8,000 (Publisher's Statement)
Advertising Manager: Rob Rodgerson
Summary of Content: Magazine covering issues affecting South West businesses. Includes trends, profiles and advice.
Readership/Target Audience: Aimed at senior managers, decision makers and organisations.
ADVERTISING RATES:
Full Page Colour £2400.00
Agency Commission: 10%
Mechanical Data: Type Area: 267 x 174mm, Bleed Size: 303 x 216mm, Trim Size: 297 x 210mm, Col Length: 267mm, Page Width: 174mm, Film: Digital
BUSINESS: REGIONAL BUSINESS: Regional Business English Counties

INSIGHT
39966U55-56_80
Editorial Address: 1 Spencer Parade, NORTHAMPTON, NN1 5AA **Tel:** 01604 630124 **Fax:** 01604 231489
Email: insight@bindt.org
Advertising Address: As above.
Email: insight@bindt.org
Web site: http://www.bindt.org
ISSN: 1354-2575
Publisher: British Institute of Non-Destructive Testing
Date Established: 1994
Frequency: Monthly - Published on the 1st of the cover month
Annual Sub.: £120.00
Circulation: 3,000 (Publisher's Statement)
Editor: David Gilbert; **Advertising Manager:** David Gilbert
Summary of Content: Journal of the British Institute of Non-Destructive Testing. Contains meeting and conference reports, product updates and Institute news.
Readership/Target Audience: Aimed at members of the British Institute of Non-Destructive Testing and other engineers, technicians, practitioners, scientists and technologists with interests in NDT, condition monitoring and materials testing.
ADVERTISING RATES:
Full Page Mono £475.00
Full Page Colour £1025.00
Agency Commission: 10%
Mechanical Data: Film: Digital, Type Area: 254 x 184mm, Bleed Size: 303 x 213mm, Trim Size: 297 x 210mm, Page Width: 184mm, Col Length: 254mm
Supplement(s): NDT News - 12xY
BUSINESS: APPLIED SCIENCE & LABORATORIES

INSIGHT MAGAZINE
1789735U4E-440
Editorial Address: SIG Roofing Supplies Group, Harding Way, ST. IVES, PE27 3YJ **Tel:** 01480 302862
Fax: 01480 302881
Email: editor@insightmag.co.uk
Advertising Address: As above.
Email: editor@insightmag.co.uk
Web site: http://www.insightmag.co.uk

Section 4 (b) Business Magazines

Publisher: Insight Magazine
Date Established: 2007
Frequency: Quarterly
Cover Price: Free
Circulation: 22,000 (Publisher's Statement)
Usual Pagination: 35
Editor: Rachael Orchard; **Advertising Manager:** Rachael Orchard
Summary of Content: Roofing information services magazine covering all aspects of the roofing industry with features on roofing legislation, products, industry news and views.
Readership/Target Audience: Aimed at roofing contractors, builders, suppliers, manufacturers and architects.
ADVERTISING: Rates on application
BUSINESS: ARCHITECTURE & BUILDING: Building

INSITE
711587U4E-230
Editorial Address: 55 Tufton Street, LONDON, SW1P 3QL **Tel:** 01332 865084
Email: marketing@builders.org.uk
Advertising Address: Portland Buildings, 127-129 Portland Street, MANCHESTER, M1 4PZ **Tel:** 0161 832 6000
Fax: 0161 832 4176
Email: paul.mcmahon@excelpublishing.co.uk
Web site: http://www.builders.org.uk
Publisher: Excel Publishing Company Ltd
Date Established: 2000
Frequency: Quarterly
Cover Price: Free
Circulation: 5,000 (Publisher's Statement)
Usual Pagination: 60
Editor: Kathy Hunt
Summary of Content: Membership Magazine of the National Federation of Builders. Covers all aspects of building and construction.
Readership/Target Audience: Read by small, medium and large building contractors and housebuilders.
ADVERTISING RATES:
Full Page Colour £1495.00
Agency Commission: 10%
Mechanical Data: Bleed Size: 303 x 216mm, Trim Size: 297 x 210mm, Film: Digital, Type Area: 266 x 185mm, Col Length: 266mm, Page Width: 185mm
Copy instructions: Copy Date: 4 weeks prior to publication date
Average advertising content per issue: 40%
BUSINESS: ARCHITECTURE & BUILDING: Building

INSOLVENCY INTELLIGENCE
39180U44-850
Editorial Address: The Hatchery, Hall Bank Lane, Mytholmroyd, HEBDEN BRIDGE, HX7 5HQ
Tel: 01422 888000 **Fax:** 01422 888001
Email: stephanie.askham@thomsonreuters.com
Web site: http://www.sweetandmaxwell.co.uk
ISSN: 0950-2645
Publisher: Sweet & Maxwell Yorkshire
Frequency: 10 issues yearly
Annual Sub.: £245.00
Usual Pagination: 8
Editor: Stephanie Askham
Summary of Content: Journal covering news and views on all aspects of insolvency law.
Readership/Target Audience: Read by lawyers and accountants.
ADVERTISING: No Advertising taken
BUSINESS: LEGAL

INSOLVENCY LAW & PRACTICE
39181U44-860
Editorial Address: Halsbury House, 35 Chancery Lane, LONDON, WC2A 1EL **Tel:** 020 7400 2500
Email: ilp@lexisnexis.co.uk
Web site: http://www.lexisnexis.co.uk
ISSN: 0267-0771
Publisher: LexisNexis
Date Established: 1993
Frequency: 6 issues yearly
Annual Sub.: £190.00
Usual Pagination: 44
Editor: Sarah Hubert
Summary of Content: Journal covering all aspects of insolvency law.
Readership/Target Audience: Read by legal practitioners in insolvency law, legal students and accountants involved in insolvency.
ADVERTISING: No Advertising taken
BUSINESS: LEGAL

INSTALLATION EUROPE
714043U18A-326_75
Editorial Address: Ludgate House, 245 Blackfriars Road, LONDON, SE1 9UY **Tel:** 020 7921 8317 **Fax:** 020 7921 8302
Email: paddy.baker@ubm.com
Advertising Address: As above. **Tel:** 020 7921 8600
Tel: 020 7921 8339

Email: cara.turner@ubm.com
Web site: http://www.installationeurope.com
Publisher: UBM Information Ltd
Date Established: 1999
Frequency: Monthly
Cover Price: £5.00
Free to qualifying individuals
Annual Sub.: £60.00
Circulation: 9,823 (Publisher's Statement)
Usual Pagination: 64
Editor: Paddy Baker; **Advertising Manager:** Cara Turner
Summary of Content: Magazine covering design and integration within the audio, video and lighting industries. Includes business and product news and features on management.
Readership/Target Audience: Aimed at systems integrators, installers, architects and project consultants.
ADVERTISING RATES:
Full Page Colour £2440.00
Agency Commission: 10%
Mechanical Data: Type Area: 314 x 228mm, Bleed Size: 340 x 250mm, Trim Size: 335 x 245mm, Col Length: 314mm, Page Width: 228mm, Film: Digital
Copy instructions: Copy Date: 3 weeks prior to publication date
Average advertising content per issue: 50%
BUSINESS: ELECTRONICS

THE INSTALLER
36634U12B-60
Editorial Address: PO Box 587, BOREHAMWOOD, WD6 1HQ **Tel:** 020 8381 5511 **Fax:** 020 8386 4725
Email: installer@profinder.eu
Advertising Address: 7 Plover Close, FRINTON-ON-SEA, CO13 0UY **Tel:** 01255 673311
Email: steve.anthony@profinder.eu
Web site: http://www.profinder.eu
ISSN: 1369-8753
Publisher: Profinder Magazines Ltd
Date Established: 1998
Frequency: Monthly - Published on the 7th of the month
Free to qualifying individuals
Annual Sub.: £56.00
Circulation: 7,596 (Publisher's Statement)
Usual Pagination: 48
Editor: Brian Shillibeer; **Publisher:** John Roper
Summary of Content: Magazine providing trade fabricators of windows, conservatories and related building systems with a direct route to their end users. Includes information on the latest developments in the market sector.
Readership/Target Audience: Aimed at retail and commercial window installers, buyers and designers.
ADVERTISING RATES:
Full Page Colour £900.00
Agency Commission: 10%
Mechanical Data: Type Area: 255 x 178mm, Bleed Size: 303 x 216mm, Trim Size: 297 x 210mm, Film: Digital, Col Length: 255mm, Page Width: 178mm, Print Process: sheet litho
Copy instructions: Copy Date: 4 weeks prior to publication date
Average advertising content per issue: 50%
BUSINESS: CERAMICS, POTTERY & GLASS: Glass

INSTITUTIONAL INVESTOR
35250U1F-245
Editorial Address: Nestor House, Playhouse Yard, LONDON, EC4V 5EX **Tel:** 020 7303 1700
Fax: 020 7303 1710
Email: ladamson@iilondon.com
Advertising Address: As above. **Tel:** 020 7779 8888
Email: swicks@iilondon.com
Web site: http://www.institutionalinvestor.com
ISSN: 0192-5660
Publisher: Euromoney Institutional Investor plc
Date Established: 1967
Frequency: 10 issues yearly - Published in the 3rd week of the cover month
Annual Sub.: £47.00
Circulation: 136,000 (Publisher's Statement)
Editor: Loch Adamson; **Advertising Manager:** Spencer Wicks; **Publisher:** Spencer Wicks
Summary of Content: Journal covering all aspects of finance, including features on money management, pensions, corporate finance, banking, insurance, securities and technology.
Readership/Target Audience: Aimed at professional investors and senior management.
ADVERTISING RATES:
Full Page Colour EUR26700.00
Agency Commission: 15%
Mechanical Data: Trim Size: 297 x 210mm
Copy instructions: Copy Date: 15th of the month prior to publication date
Average advertising content per issue: 38%
BUSINESS: FINANCE & ECONOMICS: Investment

INSULATION - THE ENERGY EFFICIENCY NEWSLETTER
35909U4E-250
Formerly: Essential Energy Efficiency
Editorial Address: 6 Helmsman Rise, ST. LEONARDS-ON-SEA, TN38 8BQ **Tel:** 01424 854337
Email: m.corliss@netmatters.co.uk
Advertising Address: Unit 8, Netherhall Yard, Mill Lane, Newick, LEWES, BN8 4JL **Tel:** 01825 724623
Fax: 01825 724623
Email: c.dann@completecircmktg.co.uk
Publisher: Complete Circulation and Marketing Ltd
Frequency: 6 issues yearly - Published in the middle of each month
Annual Sub.: £88.00
Circulation: 2,000 (Publisher's Statement)
Usual Pagination: 24
Editor: Mark Corliss; **Advertising Manager:** Colin Dann; **Publisher:** Colin Dann
Summary of Content: Magazine containing news and views about new products and developments in the insulation industry.
Readership/Target Audience: Read by manufacturers, specifiers and contractors.
ADVERTISING RATES:
Full Page Colour £565.00
Agency Commission: 10%
Mechanical Data: Film: Positive, right reading, emulsion side down, Type Area: 278 x 188mm, Print Process: Sheet-fed offset litho, Bleed Size: 303 x 216mm, Trim Size: 297 x 210mm, Col Length: 278mm, Page Width: 188mm
Copy instructions: Copy Date: 14 days prior to publication date
BUSINESS: ARCHITECTURE & BUILDING: Building

INSURANCE AGE
35127U1D-170
Editorial Address: 32-34 Broadwick Street, LONDON, W1A 2HG **Tel:** 020 7316 9000 **Fax:** 020 7316 9313
Email: martin.friel@incisivemedia.com
Advertising Address: As above. **Fax:** 020 7316 9257
Email: james.murray@incisivemedia.com
Web site: http://www.insuranceage.com
ISSN: 0142-6265
Publisher: Incisive Media
Date Established: 1979
Frequency: Monthly - Published the 1st week of the cover month
Cover Price: £5.00
Free to qualifying individuals
Circulation: 15,880 (ABC 01/07/2008 to 30/06/2009)
Usual Pagination: 56
Editor: Martin Friel; **Publisher:** Alex Broad
Summary of Content: Magazine containing insurance-related issues in personal and commercial insurance, loss adjusting, risk and claims management.
Readership/Target Audience: Read by general insurance brokers based within the United Kingdom.
ADVERTISING RATES:
Full Page Mono £5506.00
Full Page Colour £5506.00
Agency Commission: 10%
Mechanical Data: Page Width: 228mm, Film: Digital, Type Area: 280 x 228mm, Bleed Size: 321 x 256mm, Trim Size: 315 x 250mm, Col Length: 280mm
Copy instructions: Copy Date: 1 week prior to publication date
Average advertising content per issue: 45%
Supplement(s): Insurance Age Directory - 1xY, Top 100 Brokers - 1xY, UK Broker Awards - 1xY
BUSINESS: FINANCE & ECONOMICS: Insurance

INSURANCE BROKERS' MONTHLY
35128U1D-180
Formerly: Insurance Brokers' Monthly & Insurance Adviser
Editorial Address: The Retreat, Collier Street, Tonbridge, STOURBRIDGE, TN12 9RL **Tel:** 01892 730539
Email: info@brokersmonthly.co.uk
Advertising Address: 7 Stourbridge Road, Lye, STOURBRIDGE, DY9 7DG **Tel:** 01384 895228
Fax: 01384 893666
Email: info@brokersmonthly.co.uk
Web site: http://www.brokersmonthly.co.uk
ISSN: 0260-2385
Publisher: Insurance Publishing & Printing Co
Date Established: 1950
Frequency: Monthly - Published on the 1st of the cover month
Annual Sub.: £68.00
Circulation: 7,500 (Publisher's Statement)
Usual Pagination: 40
Editor: John Sadler; **Advertising Manager:** Jeni Hall; **Publisher:** John Sadler
Summary of Content: Publication covering features on motor insurance, business questions, computer systems, broker problems and instructional articles on insurance.
Readership/Target Audience: Aimed at insurance brokers.
ADVERTISING RATES:
Full Page Colour £2070.00

Business Magazines

Agency Commission: 10%
Mechanical Data: Col Length: 260mm, Type Area: 260 x 181mm, Bleed Size: 303 x 214mm, Trim Size: 297 x 210mm, Col Widths (Display): 90mm, No. of Columns (Display): 2, Page Width: 181mm, Film: Digital
Copy instructions: Copy Date: 19th of the month prior to publication date
Average advertising content per issue: 40%
BUSINESS: FINANCE & ECONOMICS: Insurance

INSURANCE DIRECTORY
35180U1D-186

Editorial Address: Priory Park, Beech Green Lane, Withyham, HARTFIELD, TN7 4DB **Tel:** 01892 771047
Fax: 01892 771048
Email: insurance@boundaryimedia.co.uk
Advertising Address: As above.
Email: benellefsen@boundaryimedia.co.uk
Web site: http://www.insurance-directories.com
Publisher: Boundary I Media
Date Established: 1842
Frequency: Annual - Published in February
Annual Sub.: £299.00
Circulation: 1,300 (Publisher's Statement)
Usual Pagination: 648
Editor: Ben Martin; **Advertising Manager:** Ben Ellefsen
Summary of Content: Directory covering insurance companies, brokers, loss adjusters and assessors, legal and specialist service suppliers, associations and societies.
Readership/Target Audience: Circulated to insurance companies, brokers, loss adjusters and assessors, legal and specialist service suppliers, associations, societies and reference libraries.
ADVERTISING RATES:
Full Page Colour £2100.00
Agency Commission: 10%
Mechanical Data: Film: Digital, Type Area: 190 x 178mm, Bleed Size: 226 x 216mm, Trim Size: 220 x 210mm, Col Length: 190mm, Page Width: 178mm
Copy instructions: Copy Date: December 15th
Average advertising content per issue: 15%
BUSINESS: FINANCE & ECONOMICS: Insurance

THE INSURANCE INSIDER
35150U1D-198

Formerly: The London Insurance Insider
Editorial Address: 2nd Floor, Asia House, 31-33 Lime Street, LONDON, EC3M 7HT **Tel:** 020 7397 0618
Fax: 020 7397 0616
Email: info@insuranceinsider.com
Advertising Address: As above.
Web site: http://www.insuranceinsider.com
ISSN: 1472-2526
Publisher: Insider Publishing Ltd
Date Established: 1996
Frequency: Monthly
Annual Sub.: £645.00
Circulation: 1,000 (Publisher's Statement)
Usual Pagination: 24
Editor: David Bull; **Managing Editor:** David Bull
Summary of Content: Newsletter focusing on international insurance and reinsurance markets.
Readership/Target Audience: Aimed at insurance professionals.
ADVERTISING: No Advertising taken
BUSINESS: FINANCE & ECONOMICS: Insurance

INSURANCE NEWS 24
35132U1D-190

Formerly: Evansdale's Insurance News 24
Editorial Address: Telephone House, 69-77 Paul Street, LONDON, EC2A 4LQ **Tel:** 020 7017 4100
Fax: 020 7017 4092
Email: peter.birks@informa.com
Web site: http://www.informa.com
Publisher: Informa PLC
Frequency: 240 issues yearly
Annual Sub.: £2345.00
Usual Pagination: 4
Editor: Peter Birks
Summary of Content: Newsletter covering the international insurance market, including intelligence on strategic moves, product launches, interim and full results, court cases, personalities, high-level job changes, legislation, regulation, takeovers and mergers.
Readership/Target Audience: Aimed at those working or interested in the insurance market.
ADVERTISING: No Advertising taken
BUSINESS: FINANCE & ECONOMICS: Insurance

INSURANCE PROFESSIONAL MAGAZINE
1832702U1D-428

Editorial Address: 9 Savoy Street, LONDON, WC2E 7HR
Tel: 020 7878 2300
Email: amanda.jarvis@tenalpspublishing.com
Publisher: Ten Alps Publishing plc
Date Established: 2008

Frequency: Quarterly
Cover Price: Free
Circulation: 12,000 (Publisher's Statement)
Usual Pagination: 44
Editor: Amanda Jarvis
Summary of Content: Magazine covering news, analysis and features for the insurance broker market.
Readership/Target Audience: Aimed at insurance brokers.
ADVERTISING: No Advertising taken
BUSINESS: FINANCE & ECONOMICS: Insurance

INSURANCE REGULATION & ACCOUNTING
1616397U1D-406

Editorial Address: Informa House, 69-77 Paul Street, LONDON, EC2A 4LQ **Tel:** 020 7017 4020
Fax: 020 7436 8384
Email: graham.village@informa.com
ISSN: 1740-5262
Publisher: Informa Plc
Date Established: 2004
Frequency: Monthly
Annual Sub.: £1034.00
Usual Pagination: 20
Editor: Graham Village; **Publisher:** Graham Village
Summary of Content: Magazine providing an understanding of impending trading and financial reporting changes, a timetable of forthcoming legislation and regulatory developments, case studies of major insurance organisations and advice and views from leading industry figures.
Readership/Target Audience: Aimed at those working in insurance organizations and their professional advisers.
ADVERTISING: No Advertising taken
BUSINESS: FINANCE & ECONOMICS: Insurance

INSURANCE TIMES
35140U1D-230

Editorial Address: 30 Cannon Street, LONDON, EC4M 6YJ
Tel: 020 7618 3456 **Fax:** 020 7618 3499
Email: news@instimes.co.uk
Advertising Address: As above. **Fax:** 020 7618 3400
Email: tom.sinclair@instimes.co.uk
Web site: http://www.insurancetimes.co.uk
ISSN: 1466-8149
Publisher: Newsquest Specialist Media Ltd
Frequency: Weekly
Free to qualifying individuals
Annual Sub.: £340.00
Circulation: 19,997 (ABC 01/07/2008 to 30/06/2009)
Usual Pagination: 40
Editor: Michael Faulkner; **News Editor:** Saxon East;
Features Editor: Lauren MacGillivray; **Managing Director:** Tim Whitehouse
Summary of Content: Magazine covering news of and from the personal and commercial insurance world.
Readership/Target Audience: Aimed at insurance brokers and those involved in general insurance companies.
ADVERTISING RATES:
Full Page Colour £5561.00
Agency Commission: 10%
Mechanical Data: Page Width: 210mm, Type Area: 283 x 210mm, Bleed Size: 306 x 236mm, Trim Size: 300 x 230mm, Col Length: 283mm, Film: Digital
Copy instructions: Copy Date: 1 week prior to publication date
BUSINESS: FINANCE & ECONOMICS: Insurance

INTELLECTUAL ASSET MANAGEMENT
1638963U44-3010

Editorial Address: New Hibernia House, Winchester Walk, LONDON, SE1 9AG **Tel:** 020 7234 0606 **Fax:** 020 7234 0808
Email: jwild@iam-magazine.com
Advertising Address: As above.
Email: gstewart@iam-magazine.com
Web site: http://www.iam-magazine.com
ISSN: 1741-1424
Publisher: Globe White Page Ltd
Date Established: 2003
Frequency: 6 issues yearly
Annual Sub.: £435.00
Circulation: 2,500 (Publisher's Statement)
Editor: Joff Wild; **Advertising Manager:** Gavin Stewart
Summary of Content: Magazine covering business issues surrounding intellectual property and assets.
Readership/Target Audience: Aimed at CEOs, finance directors, CIOs, in-house lawyers, analysts and investors.
ADVERTISING RATES:
Full Page Colour £3000.00
Agency Commission: 10%
Mechanical Data: Type Area: 250 x 186mm, Col Length: 250mm, Bleed Size: 286 x 222mm, Trim Size: 280 x 216mm, Page Width: 186mm
Supplement(s): Brands In The Boardroom - 1xY, From Innovation To Commercialisation - 1xY, IP Value Yearbook - 1xY, Licensing In The Boardroom - 1xY, Pattents In Europe - 1xY
BUSINESS: LEGAL

INTENSIVE AND CRITICAL CARE NURSING
24790U56B-90

Editorial Address: The Boulevard, Langford Lane, KIDLINGTON, OX5 1GB **Tel:** 01865 843628
Fax: 01865 843997
Email: iccn@elsevier.com
Advertising Address: Jamestown Road, Camden Town, LONDON, NW1 7BY **Tel:** 020 7424 4274
Email: k.mccormack@elsevier.com
Web site: http://www.elsevier.com
ISSN: 0964-3397
Publisher: Elsevier Ltd
Frequency: 6 issues yearly
Annual Sub.: EUR85.00
Circulation: 700 (Publisher's Statement)
Usual Pagination: 64
Editor: Debra Mileham; **Editor-in-Chief:** Carol Ball;
Publisher: Sarah Davies
Summary of Content: Journal focusing on updates and reviews. Features articles on relevant clinical research including educational, psychological and technical aspects.
Readership/Target Audience: Aimed at those within the nursing profession.
ADVERTISING RATES:
Full Page Mono £520.00
Full Page Colour £985.00
Agency Commission: 10%
Mechanical Data: Page Width: 180mm, Type Area: 250 x 180mm, Trim Size: 280 x 210mm, Bleed Size: 286 x 216mm, Col Length: 250mm, Film: Positive, right reading, emulsion side down. Digital
Copy instructions: Copy Date: 5 weeks prior to publication date
BUSINESS: HEALTH & MEDICAL: Nursing

INTERFACE
37179U14L-180

Formerly: DTI News
Editorial Address: 1 Victoria Street, LONDON, SW1H 0ET
Tel: 020 7215 5245
Email: interface@berr.gsi.gov.uk
Advertising Address: Landmark Publishing Services, 2 Windmill Street, LONDON, W1T 2HX **Tel:** 020 7692 9292
Fax: 020 7692 9393
Email: sharon@lps,co.uk
Publisher: Department for Business
Date Established: 1972
Frequency: 6 issues yearly
Cover Price: Free
Circulation: 10,000 (Publisher's Statement)
Usual Pagination: 24
Editor: Adian Steer
Summary of Content: Newspaper of the Department of Trade and Industry.
Readership/Target Audience: Aimed at DTI employees, present and former also others with a professional interest in the department's activities.
ADVERTISING RATES:
Full Page Colour £750.00
Agency Commission: 10%
Mechanical Data: Type Area: 320 x 246mm, Col Length: 320mm, Page Width: 246mm, Bleed Size: +3mm, Film: Digital
BUSINESS: COMMERCE, INDUSTRY & MANAGEMENT: Trade Unions

INTERGAME
41467U64A-140

Editorial Address: Office Block 1 Southlink Business Park, Hamilton Street, OLDHAM, OL4 1DE **Tel:** 0161 633 0100
Fax: 0161 627 0009
Email: editorial@intergame.ltd.uk
Advertising Address: Unit 1 Southlink Business Park, Hamilton Street, OLDHAM, OL4 1DE **Tel:** 0161 633 0100
Fax: 0161 627 0009
Email: susan@intergame.ltd.uk
Web site: http://www.intergameonline.com
ISSN: 1356-966X
Publisher: InterGame Ltd
Date Established: 1994
Frequency: Monthly - Published at the end of the month prior to cover month
Annual Sub.: £100.00
Circulation: 5,500 (Publisher's Statement)
Usual Pagination: 80
Editor: Phil Clegg; **Editor-in-Chief:** Phil Clegg; **Managing Director:** Christine Butterworth; **Publisher:** Christine Butterworth
Summary of Content: International magazine containing news from the coin-operated games and leisure industries.
Readership/Target Audience: Aimed at personnel within family entertainment centres and people involved in the coin-operated games and casino industries.
ADVERTISING RATES:
Full Page Mono £1495.00
Full Page Colour £1995.00
Agency Commission: 10%
Mechanical Data: Trim Size: 297 x 210mm, Bleed Size: 307 x 216mm, Type Area: 285 x 194mm, Col Length: 285mm, Page Width: 194mm, Film: Digital

Copy instructions: Copy Date: 2 weeks prior to publication date
Average advertising content per issue: 60%
BUSINESS: OTHER CLASSIFICATIONS: Amusement Trade

INTERGAMING
41468U64A-142

Editorial Address: Office Block 1 Southlink Business Park, Hamilton Street, OLDHAM, OL4 1DE **Tel:** 0161 633 0100
Fax: 0161 627 0009
Email: simonl@intergame.ltd.uk
Advertising Address: Unit 1 Southlink Business Park, Hamilton Street, OLDHAM, OL4 1DE **Tel:** 0161 633 0100
Fax: 0161 633 0009
Email: terry@intergame.ltd.uk
Web site: http://www.intergameonline.com
ISSN: 1357-7891
Publisher: InterGame Ltd
Date Established: 1995
Frequency: Monthly
Free to qualifying individuals
Annual Sub.: £100.00
Circulation: 4,313 (Publisher's Statement)
Usual Pagination: 48
Editor: Simon Liddle; **Editor-in-Chief:** Phil Clegg;
Publisher: Christine Butterworth
Summary of Content: Magazine containing international casino industry news, including new casino projects, changes in legislation, new products, supplier activity and in-depth features on industry trends, technology and legal issues.
Readership/Target Audience: Aimed at casino operators and executives and those involved in the supply of equipment to casinos.
ADVERTISING RATES:
Full Page Mono £1495.00
Full Page Colour £2195.00
Agency Commission: 10%
Mechanical Data: Trim Size: 297 x 210mm, Bleed Size: 307 x 216mm, Type Area: 285 x 194mm, Col Length: 285mm, Film: Digital, Page Width: 194mm
Average advertising content per issue: 50%
BUSINESS: OTHER CLASSIFICATIONS: Amusement Trade

INTERIOR DESIGN TODAY
1633159U4B-176

Editorial Address: 4th Floor, Geneva House, Park Road, PETERBOROUGH, PE1 2UX **Tel:** 01733 756555
Fax: 01733 760505
Email: idt@onecoms.co.uk
Advertising Address: As above.
Email: donna@onecoms.co.uk
Web site: http://www.onecoms.co.uk
Publisher: Media One Communications Ltd.
Date Established: 2003
Frequency: 6 issues yearly
Cover Price: £2.30
Free to qualifying individuals
Circulation: 9,500 (Publisher's Statement)
Usual Pagination: 32
Editor: Jade Tilley
Summary of Content: Magazine covering products, news, applications and features regarding the interior design industry.
Readership/Target Audience: Aimed at interior designers, architects, soft furnishings retailers, furniture retailers, department stores and mail order companies.
ADVERTISING RATES:
Full Page Colour £565.00
Agency Commission: 10%
Mechanical Data: Type Area: 280 x 190mm, Bleed Size: 303 x 216mm, Trim Size: 297 x 210mm, Col Length: 280mm, Page Width: 190mm, Film: Digital
Copy instructions: Copy Date: 4 weeks prior to publication date
Average advertising content per issue: 30%
BUSINESS: ARCHITECTURE & BUILDING: Interior Design & Flooring

INTERIOR MOTIVES
759791U31R-33

Editorial Address: Lamb House, Church Street, LONDON, W4 2PD **Tel:** 020 8987 0900
Email: euan.sey@ultimamedia.com
Advertising Address: As above. **Fax:** 020 8987 0948
Email: abel.sampson@ultimamedia.com
Web site: http://www.interiormotivesmagazine.com
Publisher: Ultima Media Ltd
Date Established: 2002
Frequency: Quarterly - Published every 3 months
Free to qualifying individuals
Annual Sub.: £67.00
Circulation: 2,500 (BPA Worldwide 01/07/2007 to 31/12/2007)
Usual Pagination: 68
Editor: Euan Sey; **Advertising Manager:** Abel Sampson;
Publisher: Abel Sampson
Summary of Content: Magazine covering automotive interior, design, material and purchasing.

Readership/Target Audience: Read by designers, buyers, product planners, vehicle line executives and high tier suppliers.
ADVERTISING RATES:
Full Page Colour £5950.00
Agency Commission: 10%
Mechanical Data: Trim Size: 297 x 230mm, Film: Digital
Copy instructions: Copy Date: 4 weeks prior to publication date
Average advertising content per issue: 10%
BUSINESS: MOTOR TRADE: Motor Trade Related

INTERIORS FOCUS
622563U4B-140

Editorial Address: Olton Bridge, 245 Warwick Road, SOLIHULL, B92 7AH **Tel:** 0121 707 0077
Fax: 0121 706 1949
Email: interiorsfocus@ais-interiors.org.uk
Advertising Address: As above.
Email: interiorsfocus@ais-interiors.org.uk
Web site: http://www.ais-interiors.org.uk
Publisher: Association of Interior Specialists
Date Established: 1998
Frequency: Half-yearly - Published in April and October
Cover Price: Free
Circulation: 26,000 (Publisher's Statement)
Usual Pagination: 72
Editor: Jane Cook; **Advertising Manager:** Jane Cook
Summary of Content: Official publication of the Association of Interior Specialists. Content is predominantly concerned with interior fit-outs and refurbishment in the retail, commercial and public sectors, including partitioning, suspended ceilings, access floors, operable walls, drylining, wall and floor coverings, glass and glazing.
Readership/Target Audience: Aimed at interior designers, architects, facilities managers and other specifiers.
ADVERTISING RATES:
Full Page Colour £2098.00
Mechanical Data: Type Area: 245 x 192mm, Bleed Size: 291 x 231mm, Trim Size: 285 x 225mm, Col Length: 245mm, Page Width: 192mm, Print Process: Offset litho, Film: Digital
Copy instructions: Copy Date: 4 weeks prior to publication date
BUSINESS: ARCHITECTURE & BUILDING: Interior Design & Flooring

INTERIORS MONTHLY
1826684U4B-187

Editorial Address: 124 Pembury Road, TONBRIDGE, TN9 2JJ **Tel:** 01732 766333 **Fax:** 01732 352063
Email: akidd@interiorsmonthly.co.uk
Advertising Address: As above.
Email: tboden@interiorsmonthly.co.uk
Web site: http://www.interiorsmonthly.co.uk
ISSN: 1756-2236
Publisher: Interiors Media
Date Established: 2007
Frequency: Monthly - Published around the 6th of the cover month
Free to qualifying individuals
Annual Sub.: £25.00
Circulation: 6,000 (Print Run)
Usual Pagination: 84
Editor: Andrew Kidd; **Advertising Director:** Tim Boden
Summary of Content: Magazine covering furniture, flooring, interiors and retailing.
Readership/Target Audience: Aimed at interior retailers.
ADVERTISING RATES:
Full Page Colour £2400.00
Mechanical Data: Bleed Size: 303 x 216mm, Trim Size: 297 x 190mm, Film: Digital
Copy instructions: Copy Date: 1 week prior to publication date
BUSINESS: ARCHITECTURE & BUILDING: Interior Design & Flooring

INTERLENDING & DOCUMENT SUPPLY
40864U60B-19_50

Editorial Address: 11 Regina Drive, LEEDS, LS7 4LR
Tel: 01274 777700 **Fax:** 01274 785200
Email: mike@mikemcgrath.org.uk
Web site: http://www.emeraldinsight.com
ISSN: 0264-1615
Publisher: Emerald Group Publishing Ltd
Date Established: 1973
Frequency: Quarterly
Annual Sub.: £619.00
Usual Pagination: 60
Editor: Mike McGrath; **Publisher:** Eileen Breen
Summary of Content: Covers activities related to document supply, including traditional methods and technological innovations.
Readership/Target Audience: Aimed at senior librarians and professionals in the field.
ADVERTISING: No Advertising taken
BUSINESS: PUBLISHING: Libraries

INTERNAL AUDITING
35040U1B-218

Formerly: Internal Auditing & Business Risk
Editorial Address: Smith De Wint, 95 Harlaxton Drive, NOTTINGHAM, NG7 1JD **Tel:** 01797 253888
Email: neil@sdw.co.uk
Advertising Address: Mongoose Media, Mongoose House, 2 Lonsdale Road, LONDON, NW6 6RD **Tel:** 020 7306 0300
Fax: 020 7306 0301
Email: iia@mongoosemedia.com
Web site: http://www.iia.org.uk
Publisher: Institute of Internal Auditors (UK)
Date Established: 1977
Frequency: Monthly - Published the 2nd of the month
Annual Sub.: £120.00
Circulation: 10,000 (Publisher's Statement)
Usual Pagination: 72
Editor: Neil Baker; **Advertising Manager:** Robin Fox
Summary of Content: Corporate governance and internal control magazine of the Institute of Internal Auditors.
Readership/Target Audience: Aimed at internal and external auditors and risk managers in the UK and Ireland.
ADVERTISING RATES:
Full Page Mono £1636.00
Full Page Colour £2033.00
Agency Commission: 10%
Mechanical Data: Film: Digital, Type Area: 284 x 203mm, Bleed Size: 296 x 219mm, Trim Size: 290 x 213mm, Col Length: 284mm, Page Width: 203mm
Copy instructions: Copy Date: 3 weeks prior to publication date
Average advertising content per issue: 35%
BUSINESS: FINANCE & ECONOMICS: Accountancy

INTERNAL COMMUNICATION
37054U14F-28

Editorial Address: 80 Rosebery Road, EPSOM, KT18 6AA
Tel: 01372 277377
Email: gforestj@yahoo.co.uk
Advertising Address: As above. **Fax:** 020 8542 4420
Email: admin@gfjpublishing.co.uk
Publisher: GFJ Publishing Ltd
Date Established: 1991
Frequency: 10 issues yearly
Annual Sub.: £622.00
Usual Pagination: 24
Editor: Graham Forest-Jones; **Advertising Manager:** Graham Forest-Jones; **Publisher:** Graham Forest-Jones
Summary of Content: Journal including academic articles, case studies and survey results.
Readership/Target Audience: Read by internal communications, human resources managers, marketing directors and those concerned with employee communications.
ADVERTISING RATES:
Full Page Colour £1150.00
Agency Commission: 15%
Mechanical Data: Trim Size: 297 x 210mm, Film: Digital
Copy instructions: Copy Date: 2 weeks prior to publication date
BUSINESS: COMMERCE, INDUSTRY & MANAGEMENT: Training & Recruitment

INTERNATIONAL ACCOUNTANT
1644777U1B-318

Editorial Address: Staithes 3, The Watermark, Metro Riverside, NEWCASTLE UPON TYNE, NE11 9SN
Tel: 0191 493 0262 **Fax:** 0191 493 0278
Email: editor@aiaworldwide.com
Advertising Address: As above.
Email: media@aiaworldwide.com
Web site: http://www.aiaworldwide.com
ISSN: 1465-5144
Publisher: AIA
Date Established: 1994
Frequency: 6 issues yearly
Cover Price: £3.00
Free to qualifying individuals
Annual Sub.: £50.00
Circulation: 15,000 (Publisher's Statement)
Usual Pagination: 52
Editor: Rachel Rutherford; **Managing Editor:** Nicola Perry
Summary of Content: Magazine covering news of accountancy innovations, developments, economic and management issues.
Readership/Target Audience: Aimed at all those working in accountancy, auditing, finance, business, and economics.
ADVERTISING RATES:
Full Page Colour £3000.00
Mechanical Data: Trim Size: 297 x 210mm, Bleed Size: 317 x 230mm, Film: Positive, right reading, emulsion side down. Digital
Average advertising content per issue: 40%
BUSINESS: FINANCE & ECONOMICS: Accountancy

Business Magazines

INTERNATIONAL ACCOUNTING BULLETIN
35041U1B-224

Editorial Address: The Colonnades, 34 Porchester Road, LONDON, W2 6ES **Tel:** 020 7563 5631 **Fax:** 020 7563 5601
Email: arvind.hickman@vrlknowledgebank.com
Web site: http://www.worldaccountingintelligence.com
ISSN: 0265-0223
Publisher: VRL Knowledge Bank Ltd
Frequency: 20 issues yearly
Annual Sub.: £1297.00
Usual Pagination: 16
Editor: Arvind Hickman
Summary of Content: Business intelligence journal for accounting firms worldwide, coverage of medium-and smaller-sized firms. Each issue has country surveys of local accountancy industries with detailed firm-specification data.
Readership/Target Audience: Aimed at accountants worldwide.
ADVERTISING: No Advertising taken
BUSINESS: FINANCE & ECONOMICS: Accountancy

INTERNATIONAL ADVISER
1806074U1F-638

Editorial Address: 4th Floor, 120 Moorgate, LONDON, EC2M 6SS **Tel:** 020 7065 7567
Email: iam@lastwordmedia.com
Advertising Address: As above. **Tel:** 020 7065 7573
Fax: 020 7638 6354
Email: ben.wiseman@lastwordmedia.com
Web site: http://www.lastwordmedia.com
Publisher: Last Word Media
Date Established: 2006
Frequency: Monthly
Free to qualifying individuals
Annual Sub.: £125.00
Circulation: 10,000 (Publisher's Statement)
Editor: Daniel Judge; **Advertising Manager:** Ben Wiseman
Summary of Content: News magazine covering the latest on changes to tax, new investment trends, regulatory developments and portfolio strategy advice as they affect investors in offshore products.
Readership/Target Audience: Aimed at those who distribute international and offshore fund, life and banking products to high net worth individuals, families and trusts.
ADVERTISING RATES:
Full Page Colour £5550.00
Agency Commission: 10%
Mechanical Data: Bleed Size: 306 x 236mm, Trim Size: 300 x 230mm, Film: Digital
Copy instructions: Copy Date: Tuesday prior to publication date
Average advertising content per issue: 30%
BUSINESS: FINANCE & ECONOMICS: Investment

INTERNATIONAL AID + TRADE REVIEW
1808881U1P-283

Editorial Address: Trans-World House, 100 City Road, LONDON, EC1Y 2BP **Tel:** 020 7871 0123
Fax: 020 7871 0101
Email: sbruce@aidandtrade.org
Advertising Address: As above.
Email: mlewis@henleypublishinggroup.com
Web site: http://www.aidandtrade.org
Publisher: Henley Media Group Ltd.
Date Established: 2005
Frequency: Annual - Published in September
Free to qualifying individuals
Annual Sub.: £39.99
Circulation: 5,000 (Publisher's Statement)
Usual Pagination: 100
Editor: Sula Bruce
Summary of Content: Publication containing articles about disaster response and relief, peace and conflict, education, health and medical aid, water, sanitation and tools for development.
Readership/Target Audience: Aimed at aid agencies, UN organisations, NGOs, business and government.
ADVERTISING RATES:
Full Page Colour £5200.00
Mechanical Data: Type Area: 281 x 194mm, Bleed Size: 303 x 216mm, Trim Size: 297 x 210mm, Col Length: 281mm, Page Width: 194mm, Film: Digital
BUSINESS: FINANCE & ECONOMICS: Fundraising

INTERNATIONAL AIRPORT REVIEW
36382U6B-210

Editorial Address: Court Lodge, Hogtrough Hill, Brasted, WESTERHAM, TN16 1NU **Tel:** 01959 563311
Fax: 01959 563123
Email: rpiper@russellpublishing.com
Advertising Address: As above.
Email: dquinn@russellpublishing.com
Web site: http://www.internationalairportreview.com
ISSN: 1366-6339
Publisher: Russell Publishing Ltd
Date Established: 1996

Frequency: 6 issues yearly
Annual Sub.: £90.00
Circulation: 10,994 (ABC 01/01/2008 to 31/12/2008)
Usual Pagination: 88
Editor: Temi Adebo
Summary of Content: Magazine carrying in-depth articles on technological advancements and business strategies that affect the running of commercial airports worldwide.
Readership/Target Audience: Aimed at airport managers.
ADVERTISING RATES:
Full Page Colour £4517.00
Agency Commission: 10%
Mechanical Data: Bleed Size: 303 x 216mm, Trim Size: 297 x 210mm, Type Area: 277 x 190mm, Col Length: 277mm, Page Width: 190mm, Film: Digital
Average advertising content per issue: 40%
BUSINESS: AVIATION & AERONAUTICS: Airports

INTERNATIONAL AND COMPARATIVE LAW QUARTERLY
39191U44-893

Editorial Address: Charles Clore House, 17 Russell Square, LONDON, WC1B 5JP **Tel:** 020 7862 5151
Fax: 020 7862 5152
Email: iclq@biicl.org
Advertising Address: Cambridge University Press, Shaftesbury Road, CAMBRIDGE, CB2 8RA
Tel: 01223 326070 **Fax:** 01223 315051
Email: ad_sales@cambridge.org
Web site: http://www.biicl.org
ISSN: 0020-5893
Publisher: Cambridge University Press
Date Established: 1951
Frequency: Quarterly
Annual Sub.: £125.00
Circulation: 2,500 (Publisher's Statement)
Usual Pagination: 250
Editor: Orla Fee
Summary of Content: The ICLQ covers public and private international law, comparative law including human rights, European law and Commonwealth law.
Readership/Target Audience: Aimed at legal professionals and academics who specialise in international and comparative law.
ADVERTISING RATES:
Full Page Mono £465.00
Agency Commission: 10%
Mechanical Data: Film: Digital, Type Area: 200 x 130mm, Col Length: 200mm, Page Width: 130mm
Copy instructions: Copy Date: 1st of the month prior to publication date
BUSINESS: LEGAL

INTERNATIONAL AQUAFEED
38035U22G-75

Formerly: Aquafeed International
Editorial Address: 7 St. Georges Terrace, St. James Square, CHELTENHAM, GL50 3PT **Tel:** 01242 267706
Fax: 01242 267701
Email: mikem@aquafeed.co.uk
Advertising Address: As above.
Email: carolinew@aquafeed.co.uk
Web site: http://www.aquafeed.co.uk
Publisher: Perendale
Date Established: 1998
Frequency: 5 issues yearly - Published on the 1st of the 2nd cover month
Annual Sub.: £43.00
Circulation: 5,000 (Publisher's Statement)
Editor: Mike Martin; **Advertising Manager:** Caroline Wearn
Summary of Content: Magazine covering the design, production and delivery of feed to farmed aquatic species.
Readership/Target Audience: Aimed at fish food manufacturers.
ADVERTISING RATES:
Full Page Colour £1851.00
Agency Commission: 10%
Mechanical Data: Type Area: 270 x 190mm, Film: Digital, Trim Size: 297 x 210mm, Bleed Size: 303 x 216mm, Col Length: 270mm, Page Width: 190mm
BUSINESS: FOOD: Fish Trade

THE INTERNATIONAL BANKING SYSTEMS JOURNAL
36106U5B-95

Formerly: International Banking Systems
Editorial Address: 8 Stade Street, HYTHE, CT21 6BE
Tel: 01303 262636 **Fax:** 01303 262646
Email: martinw@ibspublishing.com
Advertising Address: As above.
Email: paulm@ibspublishing.com
Web site: http://www.ibspublishing.com
ISSN: 0965-674X
Publisher: IBS Publishing
Date Established: 1992
Frequency: 10 issues yearly
Annual Sub.: £440.00
Usual Pagination: 40

Editor: Martin Whybrow; **Managing Director:** Martin Whybrow; **Publisher:** Martin Whybrow
Summary of Content: Journal covering news and features on computer systems used in international banking.
Readership/Target Audience: Aimed at bank office system suppliers, consultants, bankers and IT operators.
ADVERTISING RATES:
Full Page Colour £2145.00
Mechanical Data: Bleed Size: 303 x 216mm, Trim Size: 297 x 210mm
Copy instructions: Copy Date: 16th of the month prior to publication date
Average advertising content per issue: 30%
BUSINESS: COMPUTERS & AUTOMATION: Data Processing

INTERNATIONAL BAR NEWS
39184U44-896

Editorial Address: 10th Floor, 1 Stephen Street, LONDON, W1T 1AT **Tel:** 020 7691 6868 **Fax:** 020 7691 6544
Email: editor@int-bar.org
Advertising Address: As above.
Email: andrew.webster-dunn@int-bar.org
Web site: http://www.ibanet.org
ISSN: 0143-7453
Publisher: International Bar Association
Date Established: 1947
Frequency: 6 issues yearly
Free to qualifying individuals
Annual Sub.: £99.00
Circulation: 20,000 (Publisher's Statement)
Usual Pagination: 40
Editor: Jackie Davis
Summary of Content: Magazine for members of the International Bar Association.
Readership/Target Audience: Read by international lawyers.
ADVERTISING RATES:
Full Page Colour £2000.00
Mechanical Data: Type Area: 267 x 180mm, Bleed Size: 303 x 216mm, Trim Size: 297 x 210mm, Col Length: 267mm, Page Width: 180mm, Film: Digital
Copy instructions: Copy Date: 15th of the month two months prior to publication
BUSINESS: LEGAL

INTERNATIONAL BOTTLER & PACKER
38674U35-50

Editorial Address: Attwood House, Mansfield Park, Four Marks, ALTON, GU34 5PZ **Tel:** 01420 568900
Fax: 01420 565995
Email: editorial@binstedgroup.com
Advertising Address: As above.
Email: andrew.flew@binstedgroup.com
Publisher: The Binsted Group plc
Date Established: 1927
Frequency: Monthly
Annual Sub.: £57.00
Circulation: 5,840 (Publisher's Statement)
Usual Pagination: 75
Editor: Julie Foskett
Summary of Content: Journal covering all aspects of the bottling and packaging industry including news, financial pages, features, appointments and in-depth surveys.
Readership/Target Audience: Aimed at production managers, project teams buyers and sales and marketing directors involved in the bottling and brewing sectors.
ADVERTISING RATES:
Full Page Mono £1055.00
Full Page Colour £1605.00
Agency Commission: 10%
Mechanical Data: No. of Columns (Display): 2, Col Widths (Display): 83mm, Page Width: 178mm, Film: Digital, Type Area: 229 x 178mm, Col Length: 229mm, Bleed Size: 286 x 216mm, Trim Size: 280 x 210mm
Average advertising content per issue: 35%
BUSINESS: PACKAGING & BOTTLING

INTERNATIONAL BULK JOURNAL
36532U10-70

Editorial Address: 7B High Street, BARNET, EN5 5UE
Tel: 020 8275 5561
Email: giles.large@ibj-online.com
Advertising Address: As above. **Fax:** 020 8275 5554
Email: ray.girvan@ibj-online.com
Web site: http://www.ibj-online.com
ISSN: 0206-1087
Publisher: Glenbuck Publishing Ltd
Date Established: 1981
Frequency: 6 issues yearly - Published in the 1st week of the cover month
Free to qualifying individuals
Annual Sub.: £195.00
Circulation: 7,673 (Publisher's Statement)
Usual Pagination: 60
Editor: Giles Large; **Advertising Manager:** Ray Girvan; **Publisher:** Ray Girvan

Summary of Content: Magazine providing information concerning the dry bulk trade transportation and handling industry.
Readership/Target Audience: Aimed at decision makers in industry in the UK and overseas.
ADVERTISING RATES:
Full Page Colour £2995.00
Agency Commission: 10%
Mechanical Data: Trim Size: 297 x 210mm, Film: Digital, Bleed Size: 303 x 216mm, Type Area: 275 x 185mm, Col Length: 275mm, Page Width: 185mm
Copy instructions: Copy Date: 26th of the month prior to publication date
Average advertising content per issue: 30%
Supplement(s): Bulker Services and Care - 1xY, Coal Handling Directory - 1xY, Storage Solutions - 1xY
BUSINESS: MATERIALS HANDLING

INTERNATIONAL BUSINESS OPPORTUNITIES
36772U14A-179
Editorial Address: Suite 207, Parkway House, Sheen Lane, LONDON, SW14 8LS **Tel:** 020 8392 1122
Fax: 020 8392 1422
Email: busopps@eapgroup.com
Advertising Address: As above.
Email: busopps@eapgroup.com
Web site: http://www.busopps.org
ISSN: 1463-3841
Publisher: EAP Group Business Media
Date Established: 1998
Frequency: 6 issues yearly
Annual Sub.: £80.00
Circulation: 9,000 (Publisher's Statement)
Usual Pagination: 64
Editor: Sajid Rizvi; **Advertising Manager:** Sybil Bernier-Hart; **Publisher:** Sajid Rizvi
Summary of Content: Business magazine which highlights areas for potential new investment, business and commerce. Contains industry news, events, interviews, new technology, finance and company profiles.
Readership/Target Audience: Aimed at the business community including bankers, corporators and independent businessmen.
ADVERTISING RATES:
Full Page Mono £1450.00
Full Page Colour £2450.00
Agency Commission: 10%
Mechanical Data: Type Area: 250 x 180mm, Bleed Size: 303 x 216mm, Trim Size: 297 x 210mm, Col Length: 250mm, Page Width: 180mm, Film: Digital
Copy instructions: Copy Date: 2 weeks prior to publication date
Average advertising content per issue: 33%
BUSINESS: COMMERCE, INDUSTRY & MANAGEMENT

INTERNATIONAL CARPET BULLETIN
38070U23B-100
Editorial Address: Perkin House, 1 Longlands Street, BRADFORD, BD1 2TP **Tel:** 01274 378800
Fax: 01274 378811
Email: info@world-textile.net
Advertising Address: As above.
Email: jwilson@world-textile.net
Web site: http://www.inteletex.com
Publisher: World Textile Publications Ltd
Date Established: 1970
Frequency: 6 issues yearly
Annual Sub.: £105.00
Circulation: 6,000 (Publisher's Statement)
Usual Pagination: 48
Editor: Philip Owen; **Managing Director:** Mark Jarvis
Summary of Content: Magazine covering all aspects of the carpet manufacturing industry.
Readership/Target Audience: Read by carpet manufacturers.
ADVERTISING RATES:
Full Page Mono £1303.00
Full Page Colour £2077.00
Mechanical Data: Trim Size: 297 x 210mm, Page Width: 179mm, Film: Digital, Type Area: 264 x 179mm, Col Length: 264mm, Bleed Size: 303 x 216mm
BUSINESS: FURNISHINGS & FURNITURE: Furnishings, Carpets & Flooring

INTERNATIONAL CEMENT REVIEW
39003U42A-115
Editorial Address: Old Kings Head Court, 15 High Street, DORKING, RH4 1AR **Tel:** 01306 740363 **Fax:** 01306 740660
Email: info@cemnet.co.uk
Advertising Address: As above.
Email: info@cemnet.co.uk
Web site: http://www.cemnet.co.uk
ISSN: 0959-6038
Publisher: Tradeship Publications Ltd
Frequency: Monthly - Published in the 1st week of the cover month

Annual Sub.: £150.00
Circulation: 4,020 (Publisher's Statement)
Usual Pagination: 86
Editor: David Hargreaves; **Advertising Manager:** Gary Morton; **Managing Editor:** David Hargreaves
Summary of Content: Journal covering the storage, shipping and trading of cement, clinker and allied materials worldwide.
Readership/Target Audience: Aimed at cement producers, terminal operators and distributors.
ADVERTISING RATES:
Full Page Mono EUR2000.00
Full Page Colour EUR3000.00
Agency Commission: 10%
Mechanical Data: Type Area: 274 x 184mm, Bleed Size: 303 x 216mm, Trim Size: 297 x 210mm, Film: Digital, Col Length: 274mm, Page Width: 184mm
Copy instructions: Copy Date: 2 weeks prior to publication date
Average advertising content per issue: 20%
BUSINESS: CONSTRUCTION

INTERNATIONAL COAL REPORT
40740U58-45
Formerly: Coal Week International
Editorial Address: 20 Canada Square, Canary Wharf, LONDON, E14 5LH **Tel:** 020 7176 6661 **Fax:** 020 7176 6657
Email: coal@platts.com
Web site: http://www.platts.com
Publisher: Platts
Frequency: Weekly
Editor: James O'Connell; **Managing Editor:** James O'Connell
Summary of Content: Newsletter covering world trade in metallurgical and steam coal.
Readership/Target Audience: Aimed at executives in the coal industry.
ADVERTISING: No Advertising taken
BUSINESS: ENERGY, FUEL & NUCLEAR

INTERNATIONAL COMMUNICATION GAZETTE
37524U18B-787
Formerly: Gazette
Editorial Address: 1 Oliver's Yard, 55 City Road, LONDON, EC1Y 1SP **Tel:** 020 7324 8500 **Fax:** 020 7324 8600
Advertising Address: As above.
Web site: http://www.sagepub.co.uk
ISSN: 0016-5492
Publisher: Sage Publications
Date Established: 1997
Frequency: 6 issues yearly
Annual Sub.: £56.00
Editor: Cees J. Hamelink; **Editor-in-Chief:** Cees J. Hamelink; **Advertising Manager:** Sheena Karim
Summary of Content: Journal featuring a variety of articles from the international community of communication scholars, focusing on modern mass media, the traditional media, community and alternative media, telecommunications and information and communication technologies.
Readership/Target Audience: Aimed at academics, communication scholars and those with a professional interest in media, telecommunications and communication technologies.
ADVERTISING RATES:
Full Page Mono £400.00
Agency Commission: 5%
Mechanical Data: Col Length: 197mm, Page Width: 118mm, Film: Digital, Type Area: 197 x 118mm
BUSINESS: ELECTRONICS: Telecommunications

INTERNATIONAL CONSTRUCTION
39004U42A-120
Editorial Address: Southfields, Southview Road, WADHURST, TN5 6TP **Tel:** 01892 784088
Fax: 01892 786257
Email: chris.sleight@khl.com
Advertising Address: As above. **Fax:** 01892 784086
Email: alister.williams@khl.com
Web site: http://www.khl.com
Publisher: KHL Group
Date Established: 1962
Frequency: Monthly - Published on the 20th of the cover month (combined issues: 20th of 1st cover month)
Annual Sub.: £140.00
Circulation: 24,134 (BPA Worldwide 01/07/2007 to 31/12/2007)
Editor: Chris Sleight; **Advertising Manager:** Alister Williams; **Publisher:** James King
Summary of Content: News of technological developments and techniques within the international construction industry.
Readership/Target Audience: Read by contractors, engineers and managers operating in the international construction industry.
ADVERTISING RATES:
Full Page Colour £4700.00
Agency Commission: 10%

Mechanical Data: Page Width: 184mm, Film: Digital, Type Area: 268 x 184mm, Col Length: 268mm, Bleed Size: 303 x 216mm, Trim Size: 297 x 210mm
Copy instructions: Copy Date: 15th of the month prior to publication date
Average advertising content per issue: 60%
BUSINESS: CONSTRUCTION

INTERNATIONAL CONSTRUCTION LAW REVIEW
39087U42R-130
Editorial Address: Telephone House, 69-71 Paul Street, LONDON, EC2A 4LQ **Tel:** 020 7017 4600
Fax: 020 7017 5274
Email: victoria.ophield@informa.com
Advertising Address: As above.
Web site: http://www.informalaw.com
ISSN: 0265-1416
Publisher: Informa PLC
Date Established: 1984
Frequency: Quarterly
Circulation: 600 (Publisher's Statement)
Usual Pagination: 150
Editor: Jessica Westwood; **Publisher:** Victoria Ophield
Summary of Content: Journal for all those interested in the legal aspects of international construction.
Readership/Target Audience: Aimed at legal professionals and construction managers.
ADVERTISING: No Advertising taken
BUSINESS: CONSTRUCTION: Construction Related

INTERNATIONAL CRANES AND SPECIALIZED TRANSPORT
39088U42R-140
Formerly: International Cranes
Editorial Address: Southfields, Southview Road, WADHURST, TN5 6TP **Tel:** 01892 784088
Fax: 01892 786257
Email: mail@khl.com
Advertising Address: As above. **Tel:** 01892 786220
Fax: 01892 786258
Email: john.austin@khl.com
Web site: http://www.khl.com
ISSN: 0967-8034
Publisher: KHL Group
Date Established: 1992
Frequency: Monthly - Published in the 1st week of the cover month
Free to qualifying individuals
Annual Sub.: £98.00
Circulation: 17,456 (BPA Worldwide 01/06/2007 to 31/12/2007)
Editor: Alex Dahm; **Advertising Manager:** John Austin
Summary of Content: Magazine containing practical advice and information on the effective use of cranes and lifting equipment.
Language(s): English; French; German; Spanish
Readership/Target Audience: Read by buyers and users of lifting equipment worldwide.
ADVERTISING RATES:
Full Page Colour £4200.00
Agency Commission: 10%
Mechanical Data: Page Width: 184mm, Type Area: 268 x 184mm, Col Length: 268mm, Trim Size: 297 x 210mm, Bleed Size: 303 x 216mm, Film: Digital, No. of Columns (Display): 3
Copy instructions: Copy Date: 1 week prior to publication date
Average advertising content per issue: 60%
Supplement(s): World Crane Guide - 1xY
BUSINESS: CONSTRUCTION: Construction Related

INTERNATIONAL CUSTODY AND FUND ADMINISTRATION
35252U1F-247_50
Editorial Address: Haymarket House, 28-29 Haymarket, LONDON, SW1Y 4RX **Tel:** 020 7484 9700
Email: kris.devasabai@incisivemedia.com
Advertising Address: As above. **Fax:** 020 7484 9990
Email: katie.wildeman@incisivemedia.com
Web site: http://www.icfamagazine.com
Publisher: Incisive Media Investments
Date Established: 1997
Frequency: 11 issues yearly
Annual Sub.: £220.00
Circulation: 7,078 (Publisher's Statement)
Usual Pagination: 100
Editor: Kris Devasabai
Summary of Content: Magazine covering custody, sub-custodial and fund administration issues affecting institutional and retail money managers around the world.
Readership/Target Audience: Aimed at securities industry investment and operations decision makers worldwide.
ADVERTISING RATES:
Full Page Colour £8251.00
Agency Commission: 10%
Mechanical Data: Page Width: 200mm, Type Area: 259 x 200mm, Bleed Size: 285 x 226mm, Trim Size: 279 x 220mm, Col Length: 259mm, Film: Digital

Copy instructions: Copy Date: 2 weeks prior to publication date
Average advertising content per issue: 40%
BUSINESS: FINANCE & ECONOMICS: Investment

INTERNATIONAL DAIRY TOPICS
718642U21C-365

Editorial Address: PO Box 4, DRIFFIELD, YO25 9DJ
Tel: 01377 241724 **Fax:** 01377 253640
Email: neh@positiveaction.co.uk
Advertising Address: As above.
Email: cf@positiveaction.co.uk
Publisher: Positive Action Publications Ltd
Date Established: 2001
Frequency: 6 issues yearly - Published at the end of the cover month
Free to qualifying individuals
Annual Sub.: £50.00
Circulation: 20,000 (Publisher's Statement)
Usual Pagination: 36
Editor: Colin Foster; **Managing Director:** Nigel Horrox;
Advertising Manager: Colin Foster
Summary of Content: Journal covering health, breeding, forage production, nutrition and milking equipment for dairy cattle.
Readership/Target Audience: Aimed at leading dairy farmers, breeders and A1 professionals, dairy veterinarians, dairy nutritionists, professional dairy advisors, statutory personnel, research and laboratory managers and dairy trainers and educators.
ADVERTISING RATES:
Full Page Mono £3027.00
Full Page Colour £3557.00
Agency Commission: 15%
Mechanical Data: Type Area: 255 x 180mm, Bleed Size: 303 x 216mm, Trim Size: 297 x 210mm, Col Length: 255mm, Page Width: 180mm, Film: Digital
Copy instructions: Copy Date: 1st week of the month prior to publication date
Average advertising content per issue: 50%
BUSINESS: AGRICULTURE & FARMING: Dairy Farming

INTERNATIONAL DEALER NEWS
38353U31B-30

Editorial Address: Kenwood House, 1 Upper Grosvenor Road, TUNBRIDGE WELLS, TN1 2DU **Tel:** 01892 511516
Fax: 01892 511517
Email: idn@dealer-world.com
Advertising Address: As above.
Email: idn@dealer-world.com
Web site: http://www.dealer-world.com
ISSN: 1354-4047
Publisher: Dealer-World Ltd
Date Established: 1997
Frequency: Monthly
Free to qualifying individuals
Circulation: 11,000 (Publisher's Statement)
Usual Pagination: 48
Editor: Alan Franck
Summary of Content: Motorcycle trade journal providing an international link between parts and accessories dealers and the industry that serves them all.
Readership/Target Audience: Aimed at the motorcycle parts and accessory trade.
ADVERTISING RATES:
Full Page Colour £1895.00
SCC £30.00
Mechanical Data: Bleed Size: 303 x 216mm, Trim Size: 297 x 190mm
Copy instructions: Copy Date: 30 days prior to publication date
Average advertising content per issue: 50%
BUSINESS: MOTOR TRADE: Motorcycle Trade

INTERNATIONAL DENTAL JOURNAL
40393U56D-32

Editorial Address: 5 Battery Green Road, LOWESTOFT, NR32 1DE **Tel:** 01502 511522 **Fax:** 01502 583152
Email: shancocks@aol.com
Advertising Address: As above.
Email: dennis@dbgp.co.uk
Web site: http://www.fdi.org.uk
ISSN: 0020-6539
Publisher: FDI World Dental Press Ltd
Date Established: 1950
Frequency: 6 issues yearly
Annual Sub.: £110.00
Circulation: 3,000 (Publisher's Statement)
Usual Pagination: 60
Editor: Dennis Barber; **Advertising Manager:** Evan Carr;
Publisher: Dennis Barber
Summary of Content: Scientific journal focusing on clinical dentistry.
Readership/Target Audience: Read by dental professionals worldwide.

ADVERTISING RATES:
Full Page Mono £825.00
Full Page Colour £1485.00
Mechanical Data: Bleed Size: 303 x 216mm, Trim Size: 297 x 210mm, Film: Positive, right reading, emulsion side down. Digital
Copy instructions: Copy Date: 1st week of the month prior to publication date
Average advertising content per issue: 8%
BUSINESS: HEALTH & MEDICAL: Dental

INTERNATIONAL DYER
39499U47A-195

Editorial Address: Perkin House, 1 Longlands Street, BRADFORD, BD1 2TP **Tel:** 01274 378800
Fax: 01274 378811
Email: jscrimshaw@world-textile.net
Advertising Address: As above.
Email: djagger@world-textile.net
Web site: http://www.international-dyer.com
ISSN: 0020-658X
Publisher: World Textile Publications Ltd
Date Established: 1881
Frequency: 11 issues yearly
Annual Sub.: £285.00
Circulation: 6,300 (Publisher's Statement)
Usual Pagination: 52
Editor: John Scrimshaw
Summary of Content: Magazine containing specialised information on all areas of textile dyeing, finishing, printing and coating.
Readership/Target Audience: Aimed at the textile dyeing, finishing and printing industry world-wide.
ADVERTISING RATES:
Full Page Mono £1240.00
Full Page Colour £2059.00
Agency Commission: 10%
Mechanical Data: Type Area: 259 x 186mm, Print Process: Sheet-fed offset litho, Bleed Size: 303 x 216mm, Trim Size: 297 x 210mm, Film: Digital, Col Length: 259mm, Page Width: 186mm
BUSINESS: CLOTHING & TEXTILES

INTERNATIONAL ENDODONTIC JOURNAL
40394U56D-84

Editorial Address: Cardiff University, School of Dentistry, Heath Park, CARDIFF, CF14 4XY **Tel:** 029 2074 2088
Fax: 029 2074 2088
Email: iejeditor@cardiff.ac.uk
Advertising Address: 9600 Garsington Road, Cowley, OXFORD, OX4 2DQ **Tel:** 01865 776868 **Fax:** 01865 714591
Email: martin.nielsen@mks.blackwellpublishing.com
Web site: http://www.blackwell-science.com/iej
ISSN: 0143-2885
Publisher: Wiley-Blackwell Publishing
Frequency: Monthly
Annual Sub.: £180.00
Usual Pagination: 85
Editor: Paul Dummer
Summary of Content: Journal containing original scientific articles, review articles, book reviews, clinical articles and case reports. Also features news on endodontology, the branch of dental sciences dealing with health, injuries and diseases of the dental pulp and periradicular region.
Readership/Target Audience: Aimed at dental professionals.
ADVERTISING RATES:
Full Page Mono £600.00
Full Page Colour £1000.00
Agency Commission: 15%
Mechanical Data: Type Area: 230 x 170mm, Col Length: 230mm, Trim Size: 276 x 210mm, Bleed Size: 282 x 216mm, Film: Positive, right reading, emulsion side down, Print Process: Litho, Screen: Mono: 48 lpc, Colour: 54 lpc, Page Width: 170mm
Copy instructions: Copy Date: 6 weeks prior to publication date
BUSINESS: HEALTH & MEDICAL: Dental

INTERNATIONAL ENERGY LAW REVIEW
39225U44-940

Formerly: International Energy Law & Taxation Review
Editorial Address: 100 Avenue Road, Swiss Cottage, LONDON, NW3 3PF **Tel:** 020 7393 7000 **Fax:** 020 7393 7010
Email: amanda.strange@thomsonreuters.com
Web site: http://www.sweetandmaxwell.co.uk
ISSN: 1472-4529
Publisher: Sweet & Maxwell Ltd
Frequency: 8 issues yearly
Annual Sub.: £965.00
Usual Pagination: 30
Editor: Amanda Strange
Summary of Content: Journal covering legislation, court decisions and fiscal developments.
Readership/Target Audience: For energy lawyers, tax and financial advisers and accountants.

ADVERTISING: No Advertising taken
BUSINESS: LEGAL

INTERNATIONAL ENVIRONMENTAL TECHNOLOGY
40667U57-33_40

Editorial Address: Oak Court Business Centre, Sandridge Park, Porters Wood, ST. ALBANS, AL3 6PH
Tel: 01727 858840 **Fax:** 01727 840310
Email: info@envirotechpubs.com
Advertising Address: As above.
Email: info@envirotechpubs.com
Web site: http://www.iet-pub.com
Publisher: Environmental Technology Publications Ltd
Date Established: 1990
Frequency: 6 issues yearly
Annual Sub.: £55.00
Circulation: 39,239 (Publisher's Statement)
Usual Pagination: 84
Editor: Marcus Pattison; **Managing Director:** Marcus Pattison; **Advertising Manager:** Marcus Pattison;
Publisher: Marcus Pattison
Summary of Content: Journal detailing the latest equipment, instruments and services available for environmental monitoring, pollution control and safety.
Readership/Target Audience: Read by environmental health officers, environmental scientists, safety officers and water industries personnel.
ADVERTISING RATES:
Full Page Mono £5195.00
Full Page Colour £6190.00
Agency Commission: 10%
Mechanical Data: Trim Size: 400 x 280mm, Type Area: 370 x 250mm, Bleed Size: 406 x 286mm, Col Length: 370mm, Page Width: 250mm, Film: Digital
Copy instructions: Copy Date: 5th of the month prior to publication date
Average advertising content per issue: 65%
BUSINESS: ENVIRONMENT & POLLUTION

INTERNATIONAL FINANCIAL LAW REVIEW
39187U44-960

Editorial Address: Nestor House, Playhouse Yard, LONDON, EC4V 5EX **Tel:** 020 7779 8251
Fax: 020 7779 8665
Email: scrompton@iflr.com
Advertising Address: As above. **Tel:** 020 7779 8888
Fax: 020 7246 5206
Email: ctan@iflr.com
Web site: http://www.iflr.com
ISSN: 0262-6969
Publisher: Euromoney Institutional Investor plc
Date Established: 1982
Frequency: Monthly
Annual Sub.: $750.00
Circulation: 17,000 (Publisher's Statement)
Usual Pagination: 68
Editor: Simon Crompton
Summary of Content: Magazine covering developments in financial law, banking law and capital markets, structured finance and M&A.
Readership/Target Audience: Aimed at private practice lawyers, in-house counsel, bankers and corporate officers involved in international capital markets and banking.
ADVERTISING RATES:
Full Page Mono EUR2781.00
Full Page Colour EUR3855.00
Agency Commission: 10%
Mechanical Data: Trim Size: 296 x 210mm, Bleed Size: 303 x 216mm, Film: Positive, right reading, emulsion side down. Digital, Type Area: 266 x 184mm, Col Length: 266mm, Page Width: 184mm
Copy instructions: Copy Date: 15th of the month prior to publication
Average advertising content per issue: 25%
BUSINESS: LEGAL

INTERNATIONAL FINANCIAL LAW REVIEW 1000
754596U44-785

Editorial Address: Nestor House, Playhouse Yard, LONDON, EC4V 5EX **Tel:** 020 7779 8888
Fax: 020 7779 8665
Email: blewis@iflr.com
Advertising Address: As above. **Fax:** 020 7779 7984
Email: rvalmarana@legalmediagroup.com
Web site: http://www.iflr1000.com
Publisher: Euromoney Institutional Investor plc
Date Established: 1990
Frequency: Annual - Published in October
Free to qualifying individuals
Annual Sub.: $440.00
Circulation: 6,000 (Publisher's Statement)
Usual Pagination: 1300
Editor: Ben Lewis; **Advertising Manager:** Richard Valmarana

Summary of Content: Publication containing a legislation guide and an overview of recommended law firms for international corporate finance work in over 100 jurisdictions.
Readership/Target Audience: Read by in-house and private practice lawyers.
ADVERTISING RATES:
Full Page Mono £5000.00
Mechanical Data: Trim Size: 297 x 210mm, Film: Digital
BUSINESS: LEGAL

THE INTERNATIONAL FIRE BUYERS' GUIDE
24213U54A-227

Formerly: International Fire Buyer
Editorial Address: 60 Churchill Square, Kings Hill, WEST MALLING, ME19 4YU **Tel:** 01732 525800
Fax: 01732 525801
Email: mike.weer@firebuyer.com
Advertising Address: As above.
Email: info@firebuyer.com
Web site: http://www.firebuyer.com
ISSN: 1476-7228
Publisher: NCG Media
Frequency: Quarterly
Free to qualifying individuals
Annual Sub.: £99.00
Circulation: 20,000 (Publisher's Statement)
Usual Pagination: 148
Editor: Michael Weer; **Advertising Manager:** Michael Weer
Summary of Content: Guide covering product and industry news, articles and a guide to relevant companies and services.
Readership/Target Audience: Aimed at purchasers and specifiers within the fire protection industry worldwide.
ADVERTISING RATES:
Full Page Colour £3950.00
Mechanical Data: Trim Size: 297 x 210mm, Type Area: 277 x 190mm, Col Length: 277mm, Bleed Size: 303 x 216mm, Film: Digital, Page Width: 190mm
Copy instructions: Copy Date: 8 weeks prior to publication date
Average advertising content per issue: 60%
BUSINESS: SAFETY & SECURITY: Fire Fighting

INTERNATIONAL FIRE FIGHTER
1644517U54A-229

Editorial Address: The Abbey Manor Business Centre, The Abbey, Preston Road, YEOVIL, BA20 2EN
Tel: 01935 426428 **Fax:** 01935 426926
Email: mark.bathard@iffmag.com
Advertising Address: As above.
Email: mark.bathard@iffmag.com
Web site: http://www.mdmpublishing.com
Publisher: MDM Publishing Ltd
Date Established: 2004
Frequency: Quarterly - Published in the middle of the cover month
Free to qualifying individuals
Annual Sub.: £35.00
Circulation: 7,000 (Publisher's Statement)
Usual Pagination: 68
Editor: Mark Bathard; **Advertising Manager:** Mark Bathard; **Publisher:** Mark Seton
Summary of Content: Magazine covering municipal and industrial fire training.
Readership/Target Audience: Aimed at training officers, fire chiefs and fire training schools and colleges.
ADVERTISING RATES:
Full Page Colour £1750.00
Agency Commission: 10%
Mechanical Data: Type Area: 275 x 185mm, Bleed Size: 303 x 216mm, Trim Size: 297 x 210mm, Col Length: 275mm, Page Width: 185mm, Film: Digital
Copy instructions: Copy Date: 6 weeks prior to publication date
Average advertising content per issue: 60%
BUSINESS: SAFETY & SECURITY: Fire Fighting

INTERNATIONAL FIRE PROTECTION
634417U54A-225

Editorial Address: The Abbey Manor Business Centre, The Abbey, Preston Road, YEOVIL, BA20 2EN
Tel: 01935 426428 **Fax:** 01935 426926
Email: dave.staddon@ifpmag.com
Advertising Address: As above.
Email: dave.staddon@ifpmag.com
Web site: http://www.mdmpublishing.com
ISSN: 1468-3873
Publisher: MDM Publishing Ltd
Date Established: 2000
Frequency: Quarterly - Published in the 3rd week of the cover month
Annual Sub.: £35.00
Circulation: 7,138 (Publisher's Statement)
Usual Pagination: 90
Editor: David Staddon; **Advertising Manager:** David Staddon; **Publisher:** David Staddon

Summary of Content: Magazine providing information concerning the international fire protection industry.
Readership/Target Audience: Aimed at specifiers, fire and safety officers, contractors, architects, building and design engineers, installers, end users and manufacturers.
ADVERTISING RATES:
Full Page Colour £1750.00
Agency Commission: 10%
Mechanical Data: Type Area: 275 x 216mm, Col Length: 275mm, Bleed Size: 303 x 216mm, Trim Size: 297 x 210mm, Film: Digital, Page Width: 216mm
Copy instructions: Copy Date: 4 weeks prior to publication date
Average advertising content per issue: 40%
BUSINESS: SAFETY & SECURITY: Fire Fighting

INTERNATIONAL FLEET WORLD
1616395U49A-406

Editorial Address: 18 Alban Park, Hatfield Road, ST. ALBANS, AL4 0JJ **Tel:** 01727 739160 **Fax:** 01727 739169
Email: ross@fleetworldgroup.co.uk
Advertising Address: As above.
Email: anne@fleetworldgroup.co.uk
Web site: http://www.fleetworldgroup.co.uk
Publisher: Stag Publications Ltd
Date Established: 2002
Frequency: 6 issues yearly
Free to qualifying individuals
Circulation: 11,000 (Publisher's Statement)
Editor: Ross Durkin; **Advertising Manager:** Anne Dopson; **Managing Editor:** Ross Durkin
Summary of Content: Magazine covering strategic fleet purchasing and policy issues. Includes articles on human resources, market information and finance.
Readership/Target Audience: Aimed at companies running pan European or global fleets.
ADVERTISING RATES:
Full Page Mono £3410.00
Full Page Colour £3410.00
Agency Commission: 10%
Mechanical Data: Col Length: 265mm, Page Width: 190mm, Type Area: 265 x 190mm, Trim Size: 297 x 210mm, Bleed Size: 303 x 213mm, Film: Digital
Average advertising content per issue: 30%
BUSINESS: TRANSPORT

INTERNATIONAL FOOD HYGIENE
38049U22R-200

Editorial Address: PO Box 4, DRIFFIELD, YO25 9DJ
Tel: 01377 241724 **Fax:** 01377 253640
Email: db@positiveaction.co.uk
Advertising Address: As above.
Email: db@positiveaction.co.uk
Web site: http://www.positiveaction.co.uk
ISSN: 0961-2831
Publisher: Positive Action Publications Ltd
Date Established: 1990
Frequency: 8 issues yearly - Published around the 25th of the cover month
Annual Sub.: £50.00
Circulation: 10,000 (Publisher's Statement)
Usual Pagination: 36
Editor: Derrick Blunden; **Managing Director:** Nigel Horrox; **Advertising Manager:** Derrick Blunden; **Publisher:** Nigel Horrox
Summary of Content: Journal covering all aspects of safety and hygiene in the production, processing and handling of food.
Readership/Target Audience: Aimed at those responsible for producing and distributing high quality, safe food and drink which is marketed around the world. Also technical staff working within the food processing sector including retail and catering.
ADVERTISING RATES:
Full Page Colour £2292.00
Agency Commission: 10%
Mechanical Data: No. of Columns (Display): 4, Type Area: 255 x 180mm, Bleed Size: 303 x 213mm, Trim Size: 297 x 210mm, Col Length: 255mm, Film: Digital, Col Widths (Display): 60mm, Page Width: 180mm
Copy instructions: Copy Date: 10 days prior to publication date
Average advertising content per issue: 50%
BUSINESS: FOOD: Food Related

INTERNATIONAL FOOD INGREDIENTS
37971U22A-244

Editorial Address: Ludgate House, 245 Blackfriars Road, LONDON, SE1 9UY **Tel:** 020 7921 5000
Email: camilla.edwards@ubm.com
Advertising Address: UBM International Media, Postbus 200, NL-3600 AE MAARSSEN **Tel:** 346 55 94 58
Fax: 346 57 38 11
Email: rene.striekwold@ubm.com
Web site: http://www.ingredientsnetwork.co.uk
ISSN: 0924-5863

Publisher: UBM Information Ltd
Date Established: 1988
Frequency: 6 issues yearly
Free to qualifying individuals
Annual Sub.: EUR100.00
Circulation: 10,721 (BPA Worldwide)
Usual Pagination: 60
Editor: Camilla Edwards; **Publisher:** Nik Rudge
Summary of Content: Magazine containing international news and developments in the food and ingredients industry. Covers new products, industry trends and new technology.
Readership/Target Audience: Aimed at professionals in the food industry.
ADVERTISING RATES:
Full Page Colour EUR5480.00
Agency Commission: 10%
Mechanical Data: Trim Size: 286 x 210mm, Bleed Size: 292 x 216mm, Type Area: 254 x 178mm, Col Length: 254mm, Page Width: 178mm, Film: Digital
Average advertising content per issue: 35%
BUSINESS: FOOD

INTERNATIONAL FORESTRY REVIEW
39454U46-142

Editorial Address: The Crib, Dinchope, CRAVEN ARMS, SY7 9JJ **Tel:** 01588 672868 **Fax:** 0870 011 6645
Email: cfa@cfa-international.org
Advertising Address: As above.
Email: cfa@cfa-international.org
Web site: http://www.cfa-international.org
ISSN: 0010-3381
Publisher: Commonwealth Forestry Association
Date Established: 1921
Frequency: Quarterly
Circulation: 1,000 (Publisher's Statement)
Editor: Alan Pottinger; **Advertising Manager:** Alan Pottinger
Summary of Content: Journal covering current science, research, conservation and policy in forestry.
Readership/Target Audience: Aimed at foresters, forestry institutions and academics worldwide.
ADVERTISING RATES:
Full Page Mono £260.00
Mechanical Data: Film: Digital
Copy instructions: Copy Date: 6 weeks prior to publication date
BUSINESS: TIMBER, WOOD & FORESTRY

INTERNATIONAL FREIGHTING WEEKLY
39643U49C-105

Editorial Address: Telephone House, 69-77 Paul Street, LONDON, EC2A 4LQ **Tel:** 020 7017 5000
Email: gavin.vanmarle@informa.com
Advertising Address: As above. **Fax:** 020 7017 4172
Email: marc.young@informa.com
Web site: http://www.ifw-net.com
Publisher: Informa Cargo Information
Date Established: 1971
Frequency: Weekly - Published on Monday
Cover Price: £5.40
Free to qualifying individuals
Annual Sub.: £270.00
Circulation: 10,065 (ABC 01/10/2008 to 31/12/2008)
Usual Pagination: 20
Editor: Gavin van Marle; **Executive Editor:** Will Waters; **Features Editor:** Isabel Lesto; **Advertising Manager:** Marc Young
Summary of Content: Journal featuring information and advice on the freight industry. Includes articles on ports, airports, road hauliers, shipping lines and the express sector.
Readership/Target Audience: Aimed at all people concerned with the freight industry.
ADVERTISING RATES:
Full Page Colour £5840.00
Agency Commission: 10%
Mechanical Data: Film: Digital, Type Area: 380 x 275mm, Col Length: 380mm, No. of Columns (Display): 6, Bleed Size: 411 x 303mm, Trim Size: 405 x 297mm, Page Width: 275mm, Col Widths (Display): 44mm
Copy instructions: Copy Date: 10 days prior to publication date
Average advertising content per issue: 40%
BUSINESS: TRANSPORT: Freight

INTERNATIONAL FUND INVESTMENT
35254U1F-248_30

Editorial Address: 337 City Road, LONDON, EC1V 1LJ
Tel: 020 7713 8748 **Fax:** 020 7837 7346
Email: fieldhouse@ifiglobal.com
Advertising Address: As above. **Tel:** 020 7713 8834
Email: hallett@ifiglobal.com
Web site: http://www.iailive.com
Publisher: International Fund Investment
Date Established: 1992

Business Magazines

Frequency: Quarterly - Published in the 1st week of the cover month
Annual Sub.: £95.00
Circulation: 2,002 (ABC 01/07/2008 to 30/06/2009)
Usual Pagination: 72
Managing Editor: Simon Osborn
Summary of Content: Magazine covering developments in fund management around the world.
Readership/Target Audience: Aimed at institutional investors and fund managers.
ADVERTISING RATES:
Full Page Mono £5000.00
Full Page Colour £5500.00
Agency Commission: 10%
Mechanical Data: Print Process: Web-fed offset litho, Bleed Size: 286 x 216mm, Trim Size: 280 x 210mm, Type Area: 254 x 178mm, Col Length: 254mm, Page Width: 178mm
Copy instructions: Copy Date: 3 weeks prior to publication date
Average advertising content per issue: 30%
BUSINESS: FINANCE & ECONOMICS: Investment

INTERNATIONAL GAS REPORT
38084U24-53

Editorial Address: 20 Canada Square, Canary Wharf, LONDON, E14 5LH **Tel:** 020 7176 6282 **Fax:** 020 7176 6667
Email: william_powell@platts.com
Web site: http://www.platts.com
ISSN: 0266-9382
Publisher: Platts
Date Established: 1984
Frequency: 24 issues yearly
Usual Pagination: 44
Editor: William Powell; **Managing Editor:** Paul Whitehead
Summary of Content: Newsletter carrying analysis, news and market information about gas worldwide.
Readership/Target Audience: Read by gas producers and utilities, major users, contractors and equipment manufacturers. Also suppliers, investors and analysts.
ADVERTISING: No Advertising taken
BUSINESS: GAS

INTERNATIONAL GUIDE TO THE COALFIELDS
601356U30-38

Editorial Address: British Fields, Ollerton Road, Tuxford, NEWARK, NG22 0PQ **Tel:** 01777 871007 **Fax:** 01777 872271
Email: info@coalinternational.co.uk
Advertising Address: As above.
Email: sales@tradelinkpub.co.uk
Web site: http://www.coalinternational.co.uk
ISSN: 1364-7512
Publisher: Tradelink Publications Ltd
Date Established: 1947
Frequency: Annual - Published in August
Cover Price: £150.00
Circulation: 5,000 (Publisher's Statement)
Usual Pagination: 220
Editor: Trevor Barratt; **Managing Director:** Trevor Barratt
Summary of Content: Journal covering news and information on coal mining and supporting engineering services.
Readership/Target Audience: Aimed at buyers, engineers and project managers within the industry.
ADVERTISING RATES:
Full Page Colour £2200.00
Agency Commission: 10%
Mechanical Data: Type Area: 265 x 185mm, Bleed Size: 303 x 216mm, Trim Size: 297 x 210mm, Col Length: 265mm, Page Width: 185mm, Film: Digital
Copy instructions: Copy Date: June 1st
BUSINESS: MINING & QUARRYING

INTERNATIONAL HATCHERY PRACTICE
37866U21F-500

Editorial Address: PO Box 4, DRIFFIELD, YO25 9DJ
Tel: 01377 241724 **Fax:** 01377 253640
Email: info@positiveaction.co.uk
Advertising Address: As above.
Email: cf@positiveaction.co.uk
Web site: http://www.positiveaction.co.uk
ISSN: 0959-9363
Publisher: Positive Action Publications Ltd
Frequency: 8 issues yearly - Published on the 1st of the cover month
Free to qualifying individuals
Annual Sub.: £50.00
Circulation: 13,000 (Publisher's Statement)
Usual Pagination: 40
Editor: Colin Foster; **Advertising Manager:** Colin Foster; **Publisher:** Nigel Horrox
Summary of Content: Journal covering all aspects of hatching and poultry breeding, incubating and hatching.
Readership/Target Audience: Aimed at poultry breeder farms, hatcheries, veterinarians and nutritionists.
ADVERTISING RATES:
Full Page Colour £2854.00
Mechanical Data: Film: Digital, Trim Size: 297 x 210mm

Copy instructions: Copy Date: 1st week of the month prior to publication
BUSINESS: AGRICULTURE & FARMING: Poultry

INTERNATIONAL INSOLVENCY REVIEW
39300U44-970

Editorial Address: The Atrium, Southern Gate, CHICHESTER, PO19 8SQ **Tel:** 01243 779777
Fax: 01243 775878
Email: i.f.fletcher@ucl.ac.uk
Advertising Address: As above. **Tel:** 01243 770254
Fax: 01243 770432
Email: adsales@wiley.co.uk
Web site: http://www.interscience.wiley.com/journal/iir
ISSN: 1180-0518
Publisher: John Wiley & Sons Ltd
Date Established: 1992
Frequency: 3 issues yearly - Published in April, August and November
Annual Sub.: £455.00
Circulation: 500 (Publisher's Statement)
Usual Pagination: 72
Editor: Ian Fletcher; **Publisher:** Graham Russel
Summary of Content: Official journal of the International Association of Insolvency Practitioners (INSOL International), providing authoritative analysis and commentary on key insolvency issues across major jurisdictions in Europe and the EC, Eastern Europe, the US, the Far East, Asia and Australia.
Readership/Target Audience: Aimed at insolvency lawyers, accountants, bankers, governmental regulators, judges and academics.
ADVERTISING: Rates on application
BUSINESS: LEGAL

INTERNATIONAL JOURNAL OF ADHESION & ADHESIVES
38823U39-23

Editorial Address: The Boulevard, Langford Lane, KIDLINGTON, OX5 1GB **Tel:** 01865 843000
Fax: 01865 843973
Email: authorsupport@elsevier.com
Advertising Address: 32 Jamestown Road, LONDON, NW1 7BY **Tel:** 020 7424 4400 **Fax:** 01865 853136
Email: j.kenney@elsevier.com
Web site: http://www.elsevier.com
ISSN: 0143-7496
Publisher: Elsevier Ltd
Frequency: 8 issues yearly
Annual Sub.: EUR963.00
Editor: Amy Tobin
Summary of Content: Journal publishing original research on adhesion and the development of adhesives, methods of testing, test data, new adhesive materials, sealants, design of bonded joints and manufacturing technology.
Readership/Target Audience: Read by adhesion scientists, chemists, civil design, mechanical engineers and manufacturers of adhesives and dispensing equipment.
ADVERTISING RATES:
Full Page Mono £835.00
Full Page Colour £1815.00
Agency Commission: 15%
Mechanical Data: Page Width: 180mm, Type Area: 250 x 180mm, Col Length: 250mm, Trim Size: 280 x 210mm, Bleed Size: +3mm, Digital: Digital
Copy instructions: Copy Date: 5 weeks prior to publication date
Average advertising content per issue: 5%
BUSINESS: PLASTICS & RUBBER

THE INTERNATIONAL JOURNAL OF CLINICAL LEADERSHIP
40349U56C-90

Formerly: Clinician in Management
Editorial Address: University of Warwick, Gibbet Hill Road, COVENTRY, CV4 7AL **Tel:** 01247 615 0453
Fax: 01247 652 8375
Email: p.c.spurgeon@warwick.ac.uk
Advertising Address: 18 Marcham Road, ABINGDON, OX14 1AA **Tel:** 01235 528820 **Fax:** 01235 528830
Email: contact.us@radcliffemed.com
Web site: http://www.radcliffe-oxford.com\cl
ISSN: 1757-207X
Publisher: Radcliffe Publishing Ltd.
Date Established: 1992
Frequency: Quarterly
Annual Sub.: £325.00
Circulation: 500 (Publisher's Statement)
Usual Pagination: 64
Editor: Dan Allen; **Advertising Manager:** Susan Rabson
Summary of Content: Journal of clinical leadership and management which seeks to encourage a constructive dialogue between doctors, other clinicians and managers in health systems leading to improved patient care.
ADVERTISING RATES:
Full Page Mono £400.00

Mechanical Data: Page Width: 157mm, Type Area: 240 x 157mm, Col Length: 240mm, Trim Size: 297 x 210mm, Film: Digital
BUSINESS: HEALTH & MEDICAL: Hospitals

INTERNATIONAL JOURNAL OF CLINICAL PRACTICE
40531U56R-68

Editorial Address: 9600 Garsington Road, Cowley, OXFORD, OX4 2DQ **Tel:** 01865 476327 **Fax:** 0872 115 8547
Email: ijcp_editorial@wiley.com
Web site: http://www.ijcp.org
ISSN: 1368-5031
Publisher: Wiley-Blackwell Publishing
Date Established: 1947
Frequency: Monthly
Free to qualifying individuals
Annual Sub.: £208.00
Circulation: 7,300 (Publisher's Statement)
Usual Pagination: 160
Editor: Chris Graf; **Publisher:** Chris Graf
Summary of Content: Journal containing review articles, editorials, original papers, preliminary communications, discussion papers, papers on the history of medicine, case reports, meeting reports, lectures, student studies, letters and book reviews.
Readership/Target Audience: Read by doctors involved in research worldwide and scientists in the worldwide pharma industry.
ADVERTISING: No Advertising taken
BUSINESS: HEALTH & MEDICAL: Health Medical Related

INTERNATIONAL JOURNAL OF CONTEMPORARY HOSPITALITY MANAGEMENT
36587U11A-140

Editorial Address: Howard House, Wagon Lane, BINGLEY, BD16 1WA **Tel:** 01274 777700 **Fax:** 01274 785200
Web site: http://www.emeraldinsight.com/ijchm.htm
ISSN: 0959-6119
Publisher: Emerald Group Publishing Ltd
Date Established: 1989
Frequency: 7 issues yearly
Annual Sub.: £4849.00
Usual Pagination: 108
Editor: Fevzi Okumus; **Publisher:** Valerie Robillard
Summary of Content: Database product with journal attached, for use by management within the hospitality, tourism and leisure professions.
Readership/Target Audience: Read by researchers and educators in the field of hospitality and tourism, as well as practicing managers within the hotel and catering industries.
ADVERTISING: No Advertising taken
BUSINESS: CATERING: Catering, Hotels & Restaurants

INTERNATIONAL JOURNAL OF CONTROL
37400U18A-327

Editorial Address: 4 Park Square, Milton Park, ABINGDON, OX14 4RN **Tel:** 020 7017 6000 **Fax:** 020 7017 6336
Email: info@tandf.co.uk
Advertising Address: As above. **Fax:** 020 7017 6714
Email: jenna.johnston@tandf.co.uk
Web site: http://www.tandf.co.uk
ISSN: 0020-7179
Publisher: Routledge, Taylor & Francis
Frequency: Monthly
Circulation: 750 (Print Run)
Editor: Rachel Jeffcoat; **Advertising Manager:** Jenna Johnston
Summary of Content: Covers areas of control theory and control applications. Aims to promote the increasingly important topics of intelligent control, robotics, automation, controller implementation and knowledge based controllers.
Readership/Target Audience: Aimed at development engineers, research workers and teachers of automatic control as well as applied mathematicians and physicists working in this area.
ADVERTISING RATES:
Full Page Mono £350.00
Full Page Colour £750.00
Agency Commission: 10%
Mechanical Data: Type Area: 240 x 190mm, Trim Size: 297 x 210mm, Col Length: 240mm, Page Width: 190mm, Film: Digital
BUSINESS: ELECTRONICS

INTERNATIONAL JOURNAL OF CULTURAL STUDIES
48849U62R-477

Editorial Address: 1 Oliver's Yard, 55 City Road, LONDON, EC1Y 1SP **Tel:** 020 7324 8500 **Fax:** 020 7324 8600
Advertising Address: As above.
Email: advertising@sagepub.co.uk
Web site: http://www.sagepub.co.uk
ISSN: 1367-8779
Publisher: Sage Publications

Date Established: 1998
Frequency: Quarterly
Annual Sub.: £44.00
Circulation: 350 (Publisher's Statement)
Usual Pagination: 128
Editor: John Hartley; **Advertising Manager:** Sheena Karim
Summary of Content: Academic journal which promotes the investigation of issues of culture and media in a global context and from a post-disciplinary perspective.
Readership/Target Audience: Aimed at researchers of cultural studies worldwide.
ADVERTISING RATES:
Full Page Mono £400.00
Agency Commission: 5%
Mechanical Data: Type Area: 205 x 130mm, Col Length: 205mm, Page Width: 130mm
BUSINESS: CHURCH & SCHOOL EQUIPMENT & EDUCATION: Education Related

INTERNATIONAL JOURNAL OF THE ECONOMICS OF BUSINESS
35000U1A-205

Editorial Address: 4 Park Square, Milton Park, ABINGDON, OX14 4RN **Tel:** 020 7017 6000 **Fax:** 020 7017 6336
Email: collette.teasdale@tandf.co.uk
Web site: http://www.informaworld.com/ijeb
ISSN: 1357-1516
Publisher: Routledge, Taylor & Francis
Frequency: 3 issues yearly - Published in February, July and November
Annual Sub.: £113.00
Usual Pagination: 160
Editor: Collette Teasdale; **Advertising Manager:** Claire Buckminster; **Publisher:** Dan Trinder
Summary of Content: Journal covering research in economics applicable to business or related public policy problems or issues and encompasses public and private sector-governmental, private non-profit and cooperative organizations, as well as profit-seeking enterprises.
Readership/Target Audience: Aimed at those with an academic interest in business.
ADVERTISING: No Advertising taken
BUSINESS: FINANCE & ECONOMICS

INTERNATIONAL JOURNAL OF EDUCATION THROUGH ART
1696246U62R-497

Editorial Address: University of Surrey Roehampton, Froebel College, Roehampton Lane, LONDON, SW15 5PJ
Tel: 020 8392 3009 **Fax:** 020 8392 3268
Email: r.mason@roehampton.ac.uk
Web site: http://www.intellect.co.uk
ISSN: 1743-5234
Publisher: Intellect Ltd
Date Established: 2005
Frequency: 3 issues yearly - Published in April, August and December
Annual Sub.: £180.00
Circulation: 1,000 (Publisher's Statement)
Usual Pagination: 80
Editor: Rachel Mason
Summary of Content: Journal that promotes relationships between art and education. Consists of refereed texts in the form of critical essays, articles, exhibition reviews and image-text features.
Readership/Target Audience: Aimed at academics.
ADVERTISING: No Advertising taken
BUSINESS: CHURCH & SCHOOL EQUIPMENT & EDUCATION: Education Related

INTERNATIONAL JOURNAL OF ELECTRONICS
1776313U17-266

Editorial Address: 4 Park Square, Milton Park, ABINGDON, OX14 4RN **Tel:** 020 7017 6000 **Fax:** 020 7017 6336
Email: rachel.moore@tandf.co.uk
Web site: http://www.informaworld.com/electronics
ISSN: 0020-7217
Publisher: Routledge, Taylor & Francis
Date Established: 1955
Frequency: Monthly
Annual Sub.: £1744.00
Usual Pagination: 112
Editor: Ian Hunter; **Managing Editor:** Rachel Moore
Summary of Content: Academic journal publishing original papers in experimental and theoretical aspects of electronics.
Readership/Target Audience: Aimed at academics in universities.
ADVERTISING: No Advertising taken
BUSINESS: ELECTRICAL

INTERNATIONAL JOURNAL OF EPIDEMIOLOGY
24579U56A-68_78

Editorial Address: Department of Social Medicine, University of Bristol, Canynge Hall, Whiteladies Road, BRISTOL, OX2 2PR **Tel:** 0117 928 7370 **Fax:** 0117 928 7222

Advertising Address: Great Clarendon Street, OXFORD, OX2 6DP **Tel:** 01865 354637 **Fax:** 01865 353774
Email: steve.simmonds@oxfordjournals.org
Web site: http://www.oup.co.uk/jnls
ISSN: 0300-5771
Publisher: OUP
Date Established: 1972
Frequency: 6 issues yearly
Cover Price: £59.00
Annual Sub.: £310.00
Usual Pagination: 260
Editor: George Davey Smith
Summary of Content: Journal of epidemiology covering infectious and non-infectious diseases.
Readership/Target Audience: Aimed at those working in social and preventive medicine.
ADVERTISING RATES:
Full Page Mono £742.00
Full Page Colour £1236.00
Agency Commission: 10%
Mechanical Data: Page Width: 178mm, Type Area: 255 x 178mm, Trim Size: 279 x 216mm, Bleed Size: 285 x 222mm, Col Length: 255mm, Film: Digital, Print Process: Litho
Copy instructions: Copy Date: 4 weeks prior to publication date
BUSINESS: HEALTH & MEDICAL

INTERNATIONAL JOURNAL OF FRANCOPHONE STUDIES
41205U62R-170

Editorial Address: School of Modern Languages & Cultures, University of Leeds, LEEDS, LS2 9JT **Tel:** 0113 343 3501
Fax: 0113 343 3477
Email: k.salhi@leeds.ac.uk
Web site: http://www.intellectbooks.co.uk/journals.php
ISSN: 1368-2679
Publisher: Intellect Ltd
Date Established: 1997
Frequency: 3 issues yearly
Free to qualifying individuals
Annual Sub.: £30.00
Usual Pagination: 120
Editor: Kamal Salhi
Summary of Content: Journal focusing on colonial and post-colonial periods, language, literature, film, society, politics, the arts and media studies, with an emphasis on contemporary aspects of Francophone and Post-colonial studies.
Language(s): English; French
Readership/Target Audience: Aimed at an academic audience and those interested in all aspects of the French-speaking world (France and outside France).
ADVERTISING: No Advertising taken
BUSINESS: CHURCH & SCHOOL EQUIPMENT & EDUCATION: Education Related

INTERNATIONAL JOURNAL OF HEALTH CARE QUALITY ASSURANCE
40532U56R-68_7

Editorial Address: Howard House, Wagon Lane, BINGLEY, BD16 1WA **Tel:** 01274 777700 **Fax:** 01274 785200
Email: vrobillard@emeraldinsight.com
Web site: http://www.emeraldinsight.com
ISSN: 0952-6862
Publisher: Emerald Group Publishing Ltd
Frequency: 7 issues yearly
Annual Sub.: £5449.00
Usual Pagination: 44
Editor: Keith Hurst; **Publisher:** Valerie Robillard
Summary of Content: Journal about quality assurance in the health sector covering management development, improving communications, defining standards, organisational structures and budgeting.
Readership/Target Audience: Aimed at healthcare managers, academics and researchers.
ADVERTISING: No Advertising taken
BUSINESS: HEALTH & MEDICAL: Health Medical Related

INTERNATIONAL JOURNAL OF HEALTH PLANNING & MANAGEMENT
40278U56F-110

Editorial Address: The Atrium, Southern Gate, CHICHESTER, PO19 8SQ **Tel:** 01243 779777
Fax: 01243 775878
Email: c.paton@keele.ac.uk
Advertising Address: As above. **Tel:** 01243 770254
Fax: 01243 770432
Email: adsales@wiley.co.uk
Web site: http://www.wiley.com
ISSN: 0749-6753
Publisher: John Wiley & Sons Ltd
Frequency: Quarterly
Editor: Calum Paton
Summary of Content: Journal covers the examination of the role of planning and management in the development of health delivery systems.
Readership/Target Audience: Aimed at health planners, administrators, policy makers and social policy administrators.

ADVERTISING RATES:
Full Page Mono £1135.00
Full Page Colour £2505.00
Agency Commission: 10%
Mechanical Data: Print Process: Sheet-fed litho, Film: Digital, Type Area: 220 x 135mm, Col Length: 220mm, Page Width: 135mm, Trim Size: 248 x 165mm
Copy instructions: Copy Date: 6 weeks prior to publication date
BUSINESS: HEALTH & MEDICAL: Health Education

INTERNATIONAL JOURNAL OF HUMANITIES AND ARTS COMPUTING
41027U62B-350

Formerly: History and Computing
Editorial Address: 22 George Square, EDINBURGH, EH8 9LF **Tel:** 0131 650 4223 **Fax:** 0131 662 0053
Email: journals@eup.ed.ac.uk
Advertising Address: As above. **Tel:** 0131 650 4222
Email: journals@eup.ed.ac.uk
Web site: http://www.eupjournals.com
ISSN: 1753-8545
Publisher: Edinburgh University Press Ltd
Date Established: 2008
Frequency: Half-yearly
Annual Sub.: £31.00
Editor: Wendy Gardiner; **Advertising Manager:** Wendy Gardiner
Summary of Content: Peer reviewed forum for research on all aspects of arts and humanities computing.
Readership/Target Audience: Aimed at historians using computers for research and those with an interest of history.
ADVERTISING RATES:
Full Page Mono £250.00
Mechanical Data: Type Area: 210 x 160mm, Col Length: 210mm, Page Width: 160mm, Film: Digital
BUSINESS: CHURCH & SCHOOL EQUIPMENT & EDUCATION: Education Teachers

INTERNATIONAL JOURNAL OF IBERIAN STUDIES
37742U62R-172

Editorial Address: Department of Politics, International Relations an, Loughborough University, Ashby Road, LOUGHBOROUGH, LE11 3TU **Tel:** 01509 222981
Fax: 01509 223917
Email: m.threlfall@lboro.ac.uk
Web site: http://www.intellectbooks.com/journals
ISSN: 1364-971X
Publisher: Intellect Ltd
Date Established: 1996
Frequency: 3 issues yearly
Annual Sub.: £30.00
Usual Pagination: 75
Editor: Monica Threlfall
Summary of Content: Journal focusing on Spanish and Portuguese politics and society, economics, ideologies, national and social identities, sub-national and ethnic issues, media, gender education, cultural and language issues and policies.
Language(s): English; Portuguese; Spanish
Readership/Target Audience: Aimed at the worldwide academic and scholarly community working on the above mentioned fields. Read mainly in the UK, USA, Spain and Portugal.
ADVERTISING: No Advertising taken
BUSINESS: CHURCH & SCHOOL EQUIPMENT & EDUCATION: Education Related

INTERNATIONAL JOURNAL OF INTENSIVE CARE
40365U56C-343

Editorial Address: 106 Earls Court Road, LONDON, W8 6EG **Tel:** 020 7937 6233 **Fax:** 020 7937 0933
Email: mail@greycoatpublishing.co.uk
Advertising Address: As above.
Email: a.wallis@greycoatpublishing.co.uk
Web site: http://www.greycoatpublishing.co.uk
ISSN: 1350-2794
Publisher: Greycoat Publishing Ltd
Date Established: 1994
Frequency: Quarterly
Cover Price: Free
Circulation: 15,000 (Publisher's Statement)
Usual Pagination: 36
Editor: Guy Wallis; **Advertising Manager:** Ashley Wallis; **Publisher:** Ashley Wallis
Summary of Content: Journal created to facilitate the rapid exchange of current thinking and practice in intensive and critical care throughout the world.
Readership/Target Audience: Aimed at practitioners who specialise in critical and emergency care, coronary and neonatal care.
ADVERTISING RATES:
Full Page Mono £1870.00
Full Page Colour £2375.00

Mechanical Data: Type Area: 267 x 186mm, Bleed Size: 303 x 216mm, Trim Size: 297 x 210mm, Col Length: 267mm, Page Width: 186mm, Film: Digital
BUSINESS: HEALTH & MEDICAL: Hospitals

INTERNATIONAL JOURNAL OF LANGUAGE AND COMMUNICATION DISORDERS
40249U56A-68_90

Editorial Address: Telephone House, 69-77 Paul Street, LONDON, EC2A 4LQ **Tel:** 020 7017 5000
Web site: http://www.informaworld.com/ijlcd
ISSN: 1368-2822
Publisher: Informa Healthcare
Date Established: 1966
Frequency: 6 issues yearly
Annual Sub.: £530.00
Editor: Katherine Sole; **Managing Editor:** Katherine Sole
Summary of Content: Features disorders of communication and language pathology.
Readership/Target Audience: Aimed at speech and language therapists, pathologists and students in the relevant disciplines.
ADVERTISING: Rates on application
- **BUSINESS:** HEALTH & MEDICAL

INTERNATIONAL JOURNAL OF LAW, POLICY & THE FAMILY
39290U44-990

Editorial Address: Pembroke College, St. Aldates, OXFORD, OX1 1DW **Tel:** 01865 276429 **Fax:** 01865 276418
Email: john.eekelaar@law.ox.ac.uk
Advertising Address: Great Clarendon Street, OXFORD, OX2 6DP **Tel:** 01865 353329
Email: jnlsadvertising@oxfordjournals.org
Web site: http://www.oup.co.uk/lawfam
ISSN: 1360-9933
Publisher: OUP
Date Established: 1987
Frequency: 3 issues yearly - Published in April, August and December
Cover Price: £26.00
Annual Sub.: £63.00
Circulation: 725 (Publisher's Statement)
Usual Pagination: 132
Editor: John Eekelaar
Summary of Content: Journal containing family law and sociological literature concerning the family.
Readership/Target Audience: Aimed at lawyers and social scientists.
ADVERTISING RATES:
Full Page Mono £270.00
Agency Commission: 10%
Mechanical Data: Type Area: 200 x 130mm, Film: Digital, Col Length: 200mm, Page Width: 130mm
BUSINESS: LEGAL

INTERNATIONAL JOURNAL OF LEXICOGRAPHY
30105U62R-455

Editorial Address: Great Clarendon Street, OXFORD, OX2 6DP **Tel:** 01865 353907 **Fax:** 01865 353485
Email: p.bogaards@let.leidenuniv.nl
Advertising Address: As above. **Tel:** 01865 353329
Email: jnlsadvertising@oxfordjournals.org
Web site: http://www.oup.co.uk/lexico
ISSN: 0950-3846
Publisher: OUP
Date Established: 1988
Frequency: Quarterly
Cover Price: £41.00
Annual Sub.: £131.00
Usual Pagination: 120
Editor: Paul Bogaards
Summary of Content: Journal covering theoretical, practise, diachronic and synchronic aspects of lexicography. Includes articles on Lexicology, terminology, semantics and pragmatics.
Readership/Target Audience: Aimed at lexicographers.
ADVERTISING RATES:
Full Page Mono £310.00
Agency Commission: 10%
Mechanical Data: Film: Digital, Type Area: 200 x 125mm, Col Length: 195mm, Page Width: 115mm
BUSINESS: CHURCH & SCHOOL EQUIPMENT & EDUCATION: Education Related

INTERNATIONAL JOURNAL OF MACHINE TOOLS AND MANUFACTURE
37644U19E-270

Editorial Address: School of Manufacturing and Mechanical Engineering, University of Birmingham, EDGBASTON, B15 2TT **Tel:** 0121 414 4176 **Fax:** 0121 414 3958
Email: witherca@bham.ac.uk
Advertising Address: 32 Jamestown Road, LONDON, NW1 7BY **Tel:** 020 7424 4400 **Fax:** 01865 853136

Email: j.kenney@elsevier.com
Web site: http://www.elsevier.com
ISSN: 0890-6955
Publisher: Elsevier Ltd
Frequency: Monthly
Circulation: 800 (Publisher's Statement)
Editor: Trevor Dean; **Editor-in-Chief:** Trevor Dean
Summary of Content: Journal publishing papers dealing with design, research and development of technologies and hardware also management systems apply to manufacturing using metals and non metals.
Readership/Target Audience: Aimed at research workers, educationalists and practical engineers involved in the development of manufacturing technologies, hardware and management systems.
ADVERTISING RATES:
Full Page Mono £865.00
Full Page Colour £1885.00
Mechanical Data: Film: Digital, Type Area: 250 x 180mm, Col Length: 250mm, Page Width: 180mm, Trim Size: 280 x 210mm, Bleed Size: 286 x 216mm, Print Process: Sheet-fed offset litho
Copy instructions: Copy Date: 4 weeks prior to publication date
BUSINESS: ENGINEERING & MACHINERY: Machinery, Machine Tools & Metalworking

INTERNATIONAL JOURNAL OF MANPOWER
36773U14A-180

Editorial Address: Howard House, Wagon Lane, BINGLEY, BD16 1WA **Tel:** 01274 777700 **Fax:** 01274 785200
Email: zidera@mail.biu.ac.il
Web site: http://www.emeraldinsight.com/ijm.htm
ISSN: 0143-7720
Publisher: Emerald Group Publishing Ltd
Frequency: 8 issues yearly
Annual Sub.: £7969.00
Usual Pagination: 76
Editor: Adrian Ziderman; **Publisher:** Nancy Rolph
Summary of Content: Publication covering issues in manpower resources management and labour economics at all levels of corporate local, national and international perspective.
Readership/Target Audience: Aimed at academics and researchers and to those who set policies and strategies relating to workforce issues.
ADVERTISING: No Advertising taken
BUSINESS: COMMERCE, INDUSTRY & MANAGEMENT

INTERNATIONAL JOURNAL OF MEDIA AND CULTURAL POLITICS
1696248U62R-500

Editorial Address: University of Leeds, Institute of Communications Studies, Houldsworth Building, LEEDS, LS2 9JT
Email: n.a.blain@stir.ac.uk
Web site: http://www.intellectbooks.co.uk
ISSN: 1740-8296
Publisher: Intellect Ltd
Date Established: 2005
Frequency: 3 issues yearly - Published in April, August and December
Annual Sub.: £180.00
Circulation: 300 (Publisher's Statement)
Editor: Katherine Sarikakis
Summary of Content: Journal committed to analysing the politics of communications and cultural processes.
Readership/Target Audience: Aimed at academics.
ADVERTISING: No Advertising taken
BUSINESS: CHURCH & SCHOOL EQUIPMENT & EDUCATION: Education Related

THE INTERNATIONAL JOURNAL OF METEOROLOGY
765189U64N-81

Formerly: The Journal of Meteorology
Editorial Address: PO Box 972, Thelwall, WARRINGTON, WA4 9DP **Tel:** 07813 075509 **Fax:** 0870 706 1858
Email: sam@ijmet.org
Advertising Address: As above.
Email: advertise@ijmet.org
Web site: http://www.ijmet.org
ISSN: 0307-5966
Publisher: Artetech Publishing Company
Date Established: 1975
Frequency: 10 issues yearly
Cover Price: £3.50
Free to qualifying individuals
Annual Sub.: £38.00
Circulation: 10,000 (Publisher's Statement)
Usual Pagination: 40
Editor: Samantha Hall
Summary of Content: International journal for those interested in weather and climate, in particular severe weather research and their influence on the human and physical environment.

Readership/Target Audience: Aimed at professional meteorologists, academics, amateur weather enthusiasts and students worldwide.
ADVERTISING RATES:
Full Page Mono £200.00
Full Page Colour £400.00
Agency Commission: 10%
Mechanical Data: Type Area: 180 x 130mm, Col Length: 180mm, Page Width: 130mm, Bleed Size: +2mm, Film: Digital
Copy instructions: Copy Date: 30th of the month prior to publication date
Average advertising content per issue: 5%
BUSINESS: OTHER CLASSIFICATIONS: Weather

INTERNATIONAL JOURNAL OF MICROGRAPHICS & OPTICAL TECHNOLOGY
38650U34-40_5

Editorial Address: Grenville Court, Britwell Road, Burnham, SLOUGH, SL1 8DF **Tel:** 01628 600499 **Fax:** 01628 600488
Email: info@researchinformation.co.uk
Web site: http://www.researchinformation.co.uk
ISSN: 0958-9961
Publisher: Research Information Ltd
Frequency: 6 issues yearly
Annual Sub.: £295.00
Circulation: 300 (Publisher's Statement)
Usual Pagination: 20
Editor: Bob Yorke; **Publisher:** Kumar Patel; **Circulation Manager:** Richard Wood
Summary of Content: Newsletter covering micrography and emerging technologies such as CD-ROM, magneto-optical, high performance image capture, text recognition, storage, indexing and retrieval.
Readership/Target Audience: Aimed at public libraries, company libraries and those who manufacture products in that field.
ADVERTISING: No Advertising taken
BUSINESS: OFFICE EQUIPMENT

INTERNATIONAL JOURNAL OF NUMERICAL METHODS FOR HEAT & FLUID FLOW
1750451U55-9024

Editorial Address: Department of Civil Engineering, University of Wales Swansea, Singleton Park, SWANSEA, SA2 8PP **Tel:** 01274 295624 **Fax:** 01792 295705
Web site: http://www.emeraldinsight.com/hff.htm
ISSN: 0961-5539
Publisher: Emerald Group Publishing Ltd
Frequency: 8 issues yearly
Editor: Harry Colson; **Publisher:** Harry Colson
Summary of Content: Publication providing information on the development of computer based numerical techniques for solving problems in heat and fluid flow.
Readership/Target Audience: Aimed at applied mathematicians, engineers and scientists.
ADVERTISING: No Advertising taken
BUSINESS: APPLIED SCIENCE & LABORATORIES

INTERNATIONAL JOURNAL OF PALLIATIVE NURSING
40306U56B-140

Editorial Address: St. Judes Church, Dulwich Road, LONDON, SE24 0PB **Tel:** 020 7738 5454
Fax: 020 7978 8316
Email: peter.b@markallengroup.com
Advertising Address: As above. **Fax:** 020 7733 2325
Email: roger@markallengroup.com
Web site: http://www.ijpn.co.uk
ISSN: 1357-6321
Publisher: MA Health Care Ltd
Date Established: 1995
Frequency: Monthly - Published on the 4th Friday of the cover month
Annual Sub.: £115.00
Circulation: 2,500 (Publisher's Statement)
Usual Pagination: 52
Editor: Peter Black; **Managing Director:** Mark Allen; **Advertising Director:** Roger Allen; **Publisher:** Mark Allen
Summary of Content: Journal covering the full range of subjects encompassed in palliative care, including nursing, clinical, research, educational, ethical and professional issues.
Readership/Target Audience: Aimed at palliative care nurses and other health professionals working in palliative care.
ADVERTISING RATES:
Full Page Mono £990.00
Full Page Colour £1800.00
Agency Commission: 10%
Mechanical Data: Type Area: 270 x 190mm, Col Length: 270mm, Bleed Size: 299 x 220mm, Trim Size: 292 x 215mm, Film: Digital, Page Width: 190mm
Copy instructions: Copy Date: 1 week prior to publication date

Average advertising content per issue: 25%
BUSINESS: HEALTH & MEDICAL: Nursing

INTERNATIONAL JOURNAL OF PERFORMANCE ARTS AND DIGITAL MEDIA
1696514U62R-503

Editorial Address: School of Intermedia and Performance Arts, Doncaster College, High Melton, DONCASTER, DN5 7SZ
Web site: http://www.intellectbooks.co.uk
ISSN: 1479-4713
Publisher: Intellect Ltd
Date Established: 2005
Frequency: 3 issues yearly - Published in April, August and December
Annual Sub.: £180.00
Circulation: 300 (Publisher's Statement)
Usual Pagination: 80
Editor: David Collins
Summary of Content: Journal covering the interface of new technology with performance arts.
Readership/Target Audience: Aimed at lecturers, researchers and students in performance-based arts.
ADVERTISING: No Advertising taken
BUSINESS: CHURCH & SCHOOL EQUIPMENT & EDUCATION: Education Related

INTERNATIONAL JOURNAL OF PRODUCTIVITY & PERFORMANCE MANAGEMENT
37023U14E-410

Formerly: Work Study
Editorial Address: Warwick Business School, The University of Warwick, COVENTRY, CV4 7AL
Tel: 01274 777700 **Fax:** 01274 785200
Email: zoe.radnor@wbs.ac.uk
Web site: http://www.emeraldinsight.com
ISSN: 1741-0401
Publisher: Emerald Group Publishing Ltd
Frequency: 8 issues yearly
Annual Sub.: £4759.00
Usual Pagination: 48
Editor: Zoe Radnor; **Publisher:** Lucy Sootheran
Summary of Content: Publication containing productivity through time and motion study, job evaluation and process control.
Readership/Target Audience: Aimed at human resources management and quality managers.
ADVERTISING: No Advertising taken
BUSINESS: COMMERCE, INDUSTRY & MANAGEMENT: Work Study

INTERNATIONAL JOURNAL OF PROJECT MANAGEMENT
36961U14C-92

Editorial Address: EuroProjex, Wildwood, Manor Close, East Horsley, LEATHERHEAD, KT24 6SA **Tel:** 01483 282344
Fax: 01483 281281
Email: rodneyturner@europrojex.co.uk
Advertising Address: 32 Jamestown Road, LONDON, NW1 7BY **Tel:** 020 7424 4400 **Fax:** 01865 853136
Email: j.kenney@elsevier.com
Web site: http://www.elsevier.com/locate/ijproman
ISSN: 0263-7863
Publisher: Elsevier Ltd
Date Established: 1984
Frequency: 8 issues yearly
Circulation: 3,000 (Publisher's Statement)
Usual Pagination: 80
Editor: Rodney Turner
Summary of Content: Journal covering all aspects of project management worldwide. Publishes refereed papers and case studies.
Readership/Target Audience: Read by project managers.
ADVERTISING RATES:
Full Page Mono £1465.00
Full Page Colour £2380.00
BUSINESS: COMMERCE, INDUSTRY & MANAGEMENT: International Commerce

THE INTERNATIONAL JOURNAL OF PSYCHOANALYSIS
40583U56R-68_8

Editorial Address: 9600 Garsington Road, Cowley, OXFORD, OX4 2DQ **Tel:** 01865 776868 **Fax:** 0870 164 0124
Email: ijpaoffice@oxon.blackwellpublishing.com
Advertising Address: As above. **Fax:** 01865 714591
Email: craig.pickett@wiley.com
Web site: http://www.blackwellpublishing.com/ijpa
ISSN: 0020-7578
Publisher: Wiley-Blackwell Publishing
Date Established: 1920
Frequency: 6 issues yearly
Annual Sub.: £163.00
Circulation: 6,500 (Publisher's Statement)
Usual Pagination: 286

Editor: Carol Saunders; **Managing Editor:** Carol Saunders
Summary of Content: Journal featuring articles on subjects including psychoanalytic theory and technique, methodology, the history of psychoanalysis, clinical communications, research and life-cycle development, education and professional issues, psychoanalytic psychotherapy and interdisciplinary studies.
Readership/Target Audience: Aimed at all mental health practitioners, principally psychoanalysts, psychotherapists, counsellors, psychologists and psychiatric social workers, as well as film and literary critics.
ADVERTISING RATES:
Full Page Mono £595.00
Agency Commission: 10%
Mechanical Data: Trim Size: 247 x 173mm, Film: Digital
Copy instructions: Copy Date: 8th of the month prior to publication date
BUSINESS: HEALTH & MEDICAL: Health Medical Related

INTERNATIONAL JOURNAL OF RETAIL & DISTRIBUTION MANAGEMENT
1898614U53-711

Editorial Address: Howard House, Wagon Lane, BINGLEY, BD16 1WA **Tel:** 01274 777700 **Fax:** 01274 785201
Email: emerald@emeraldinsight.com
Web site: http://www.emeraldinsight.com
ISSN: 0959-0552
Publisher: Emerald Group Publishing Ltd
Frequency: Monthly
Editor: John Fernie; **Publisher:** Lucy Sootheran
Summary of Content: Journal covering case studies and industry reports, information and reviews and research institute papers.
Readership/Target Audience: Aimed at consultants, retail managers and retail strategists, researchers and students.
BUSINESS: RETAILING & WHOLESALING

INTERNATIONAL JOURNAL OF TECHNOLOGY AND HUMAN INTERACTION
1914770U5B-9045

Editorial Address: Room G5.80A, De Montfort University, The Gateway, LEICESTER, LE1 9BH **Tel:** 0116 207 8252
Fax: 0116 207 8159
Email: bstahl@dmu.ac.uk
Publisher: IGI Global
Frequency: Quarterly
Editor: Bernd Carsten Stahl
Summary of Content: Journal providing a platform for leading research that addresses issues of human and technology interaction.
BUSINESS: COMPUTERS & AUTOMATION: Data Processing

INTERNATIONAL JOURNAL OF TECHNOLOGY MANAGEMENT AND SUSTAINABLE DEVELOPMENT
1696518U62R-502

Editorial Address: David Livingstone Institute, University of Strathclyde, Rottenrow East, GLASGOW, G4 0NG
Email: g.zawdie@strath.ac.uk
Web site: http://www.intellectbooks.co.uk
ISSN: 1474-2748
Publisher: Intellect Ltd
Date Established: 2002
Frequency: 3 issues yearly - Published in April, August and December
Annual Sub.: £180.00
Circulation: 400 (Publisher's Statement)
Usual Pagination: 80
Editor: Girma Zawdie
Summary of Content: Journal covering issues arising from the relationship between technology and development.
Readership/Target Audience: Aimed at policy makers, academics, planners, international development agencies, business, industry and non-governmental organisations.
ADVERTISING: No Advertising taken
BUSINESS: CHURCH & SCHOOL EQUIPMENT & EDUCATION: Education Related

INTERNATIONAL JOURNAL OF THERAPY AND REHABILITATION
40453U56L-6_75

Formerly: British Journal of Therapy and Rehabilitation
Editorial Address: St. Judes Church, Dulwich Road, LONDON, SE24 0PB **Tel:** 020 7501 6747
Fax: 020 7978 8316
Email: olivia.w@markallengroup.com
Advertising Address: As above. **Tel:** 020 7738 5454
Fax: 020 7733 2325
Email: laura.d@markallengroup.com
Web site: http://www.ijtr.co.uk
ISSN: 1741-1645

Publisher: M A Healthcare
Date Established: 1994
Frequency: Monthly - Published on the 2nd Wednesday of the cover month
Annual Sub.: £123.00
Circulation: 3,000 (Publisher's Statement)
Usual Pagination: 44
Editor: Olivia Wood; **Editor-in-Chief:** Alison Rushton; **Advertising Manager:** Adrian Johnston; **Managing Editor:** Olivia Wood; **Publisher:** Adrian Johnston
Summary of Content: Peer-reviewed clinical journal featuring original research and analysis articles on a wide range of interdisciplinary and discipline specific topics in therapy and rehabilitation.
Readership/Target Audience: Aimed at physiotherapists, occupational therapists, speech and language therapists, rehabilitation nurses, occupational therapists, dieticians and podiatrists.
ADVERTISING RATES:
Full Page Mono £945.00
Full Page Colour £1400.00
SCC £35.00
Agency Commission: 10%
Mechanical Data: Page Width: 190mm, Type Area: 270 x 190mm, Col Length: 270mm, Bleed Size: 299 x 220mm, Trim Size: 292 x 215mm, Film: Digital
Copy instructions: Copy Date: 1 week prior to publication date
Average advertising content per issue: 30%
BUSINESS: HEALTH & MEDICAL: Disability & Rehabilitation

INTERNATIONAL JOURNALIST
1695152U2B-202

Editorial Address: 33 Oakhurst Avenue, BARNET, EN4 8DN
Tel: 020 8368 4997 **Fax:** 020 8368 4997
Email: kjb@intercarb.org
Web site: http://www.cioj.co.uk
Publisher: The Chartered Institute of Journalists
Frequency: 5 issues yearly
Cover Price: Free
Usual Pagination: 8
Editor: Kenneth Brookes
Summary of Content: Journal focusing on news and features of interest to journalists.
Readership/Target Audience: Aimed at journalists (members of CIoJ).
ADVERTISING: No Advertising taken
BUSINESS: COMMUNICATIONS, ADVERTISING & MARKETING: Press

INTERNATIONAL LABMATE
39968U55-63

Editorial Address: Oak Court Business Centre, Sandridge Park, Porters Wood, ST. ALBANS, AL3 6PH
Tel: 01727 855574 **Fax:** 01727 855722
Email: pr@intlabmate.com
Advertising Address: As above. **Fax:** 01727 841694
Email: chris@intlabmate.com
Web site: http://www.internationallabmate.com
ISSN: 0143-5140
Publisher: International LABMATE Ltd
Frequency: 7 issues yearly - Published in the 3rd week of the cover month
Circulation: 29,887 (ABC 01/01/2008 to 31/12/2008)
Usual Pagination: 80
Editor: Tamsyn Hicks; **Features Editor:** Tamsyn Hicks; **Managing Director:** Michael Pattison; **Advertising Manager:** Chris Jarvis; **Publisher:** Michael Pattison
Summary of Content: Magazine featuring the latest instrumentation and applications from exporters in the UK and abroad.
Readership/Target Audience: Aimed at chemists, biochemists, biologists, lab technicians and managers.
ADVERTISING RATES:
Full Page Mono £5825.00
Full Page Colour £6820.00
Agency Commission: 10%
Mechanical Data: Film: Digital, Trim Size: 297 x 210mm, Bleed Size: 303 x 216mm
Copy instructions: Copy Date: 3 weeks prior to publication date
Average advertising content per issue: 60%
BUSINESS: APPLIED SCIENCE & LABORATORIES

INTERNATIONAL LEATHER GUIDE
714173U52D-35

Formerly: Leather International Buyer's Guide
Editorial Address: Priory Park, Beech Green Lane, Withyham, HARTFIELD, TN7 4DB **Tel:** 01892 771047
Fax: 01892 771048
Email: ilg@boundaryimedia.co.uk
Advertising Address: Progressive Media Markets, Progressive House, 2 Maidstone Road, SIDCUP, DA14 5HZ
Tel: 020 8269 7700 **Fax:** 020 8269 7881
Email: jreynolds@progressivemediagroup.com
Web site: http://www.leathermag.com
Publisher: Boundary I Media

Section 4 (b) Business Magazines

Date Established: 1968
Frequency: Annual - Published in September
Annual Sub.: £98.00
Circulation: 600 (Publisher's Statement)
Usual Pagination: 400
Editor: Peter Morris; **Advertising Manager:** Jemma Reynolds
Summary of Content: Directory containing international listings of leather companies and their products.
Readership/Target Audience: Read by tanners, traders, those working in abattoirs, trade associations, chemical suppliers, footwear designers, upholstery manufacturers and companies from every other aspect of the leather industry.
ADVERTISING: Rates on application
BUSINESS: GIFT TRADE: Leather

INTERNATIONAL MILLING DIRECTORY

38018U22C-300

Editorial Address: 7 St. Georges Terrace, St. James Square, CHELTENHAM, GL50 3PT **Tel:** 01242 267703
Fax: 01242 267701
Email: info@internationalmilling.com
Advertising Address: As above. **Tel:** 01242 267700
Email: bena@internationalmilling.com
Web site: http://www.internationalmilling.com
ISSN: 1464-0147
Publisher: Perendale
Date Established: 1991
Frequency: Annual - Published in April
Cover Price: £85.00
Free to qualifying individuals
Circulation: 12,500 (Publisher's Statement)
Usual Pagination: 200
Editor: Ben Adsett; **Advertising Manager:** Ben Adsett
Summary of Content: Directory containing comprehensive global reference source for the flour and feed milling industries worldwide.
Readership/Target Audience: Aimed at nutritionists, mill managers and production directors in the major flour and feed milling companies.
ADVERTISING: Rates on application
BUSINESS: FOOD: Food Processing & Packaging

INTERNATIONAL MINING

1699370U30-157

Editorial Address: 2 Claridge Court, Lower Kings Road, BERKHAMSTED, HP4 2AF **Tel:** 01442 870829
Fax: 01442 870617
Email: emma@im-mining.com
Advertising Address: As above.
Email: phil@im-mining.com
Web site: http://www.im-mining.com
Publisher: Team Publishing
Date Established: 2005
Frequency: Monthly - Published in the 1st week of the cover month
Free to qualifying individuals
Circulation: 13,000 (Publisher's Statement)
Editor: John Chadwick
Summary of Content: Magazine focusing on all aspects of the mining industry.
Readership/Target Audience: Aimed at mine managers, process plant managers and mining company executives.
ADVERTISING RATES:
Full Page Mono £2430.00
Full Page Colour £3440.00
Agency Commission: 10%
Mechanical Data: Type Area: 270 x 190mm, Bleed Size: 307 x 215mm, Trim Size: 297 x 210mm, Col Length: 270mm, Page Width: 190mm, Film: Digital
Copy instructions: Copy Date: 20th of the month prior to publication date
Average advertising content per issue: 40%
BUSINESS: MINING & QUARRYING

INTERNATIONAL OCEAN SYSTEMS

39434U45R-67

Formerly: International Ocean Systems Design
Editorial Address: 55 High Street, TEDDINGTON, TW11 8HA **Tel:** 020 8943 4288 **Fax:** 020 8943 4312
Email: daniel@divermag.co.uk
Advertising Address: As above.
Email: astrid@divermag.co.uk
Web site: http://www.intoceansys.co.uk
ISSN: 1471-0188
Publisher: Underwater World Publications Ltd
Date Established: 1979
Frequency: 6 issues yearly - Published on the last day of the month prior to publication date
Free to qualifying individuals
Annual Sub.: £80.00
Circulation: 10,000 (Publisher's Statement)
Usual Pagination: 44
Editor: Daniel Johnson; **Advertising Manager:** Astrid Powell; **Publisher:** Astrid Powell

Summary of Content: Magazine covering ocean data gathering, underwater surveying and instrumentation worldwide.
Readership/Target Audience: Aimed at people working in the commercial oceanology market.
ADVERTISING RATES:
Full Page Mono £1545.00
Full Page Colour £2075.00
Agency Commission: 10%
Mechanical Data: Type Area: 267 x 184mm, Bleed Size: 303 x 216mm, Trim Size: 297 x 210mm, Col Length: 267mm, Print Process: Offset litho, Page Width: 184mm, Film: Digital
Average advertising content per issue: 50%
BUSINESS: MARINE & SHIPPING: Marine Related

INTERNATIONAL OIL & GAS ENGINEER

713579U33-3

Editorial Address: Europa House, 13-17 Ironmonger Row, LONDON, EC1V 3QG **Tel:** 020 7253 2545
Fax: 020 7608 1600
Email: editorial@setform.com
Web site: http://www.engineerlive.com
Publisher: Setform Ltd
Frequency: Half-yearly - Published in February and August
Free to qualifying individuals
Circulation: 12,000 (Publisher's Statement)
Usual Pagination: 80
Editor: Paul Boughton
Summary of Content: Magazine covering exploration and drilling, production and processing, instrumentation, safety, environment and communications.
Readership/Target Audience: Read by oil and gas engineers.
ADVERTISING: No Advertising taken
BUSINESS: OIL & PETROLEUM

INTERNATIONAL PAPER BOARD INDUSTRY

38709U36-10

Editorial Address: 1 Salisbury Office Park, London Road, SALISBURY, SP1 3HP **Tel:** 01722 337038
Fax: 01722 337109
Email: publications@brunton.co.uk
Advertising Address: As above.
Email: publications@brunton.co.uk
Web site: http://www.brunton.co.uk
Publisher: Brunton Business Publications Ltd
Frequency: Monthly - Published at the beginning of the cover month
Cover Price: £3.00
Annual Sub.: £38.00
Circulation: 11,500 (Publisher's Statement)
Usual Pagination: 84
Editor: Dan Brunton; **Managing Director:** Michael Brunton; **Advertising Manager:** Dan Brunton
Summary of Content: Magazine covering news, trade and developments in the corrugated packaging industry.
Readership/Target Audience: Aimed at production managers and plant managers.
ADVERTISING RATES:
Full Page Colour £1500.00
Agency Commission: 10%
Mechanical Data: Bleed Size: 286 x 216mm, Type Area: 229 x 178mm, Col Length: 229mm, Page Width: 178mm, Trim Size: 280 x 210mm, Film: Digital
Copy instructions: Copy Date: 20th of the month prior to publication date
BUSINESS: PAPER

INTERNATIONAL PAYMENTS

1913515U1C-362

Editorial Address: Telephone House, 69-77 Paul Street, LONDON, EC2A 4LQ **Tel:** 020 7017 4600
Email: mckenzieheather@hotmail.co.uk
Web site: http://www.informaprofessional.com/publications/newsletter/international_payment
Publisher: Informa PLC
Frequency: Monthly
Annual Sub.: £985.00
Editor: Heather McKenzie
Summary of Content: Newsletter covering payments industry news, providing commentary and strategic analysis.
Readership/Target Audience: Aimed at the global payments community.
ADVERTISING: No Advertising taken
BUSINESS: FINANCE & ECONOMICS: Banking

INTERNATIONAL PEST CONTROL

37809U21B-560

Editorial Address: Grenville Court, Britwell Road, Burnham, SLOUGH, SL1 8DF **Tel:** 01628 600499 **Fax:** 01628 600488
Email: info@researchinformation.co.uk
Advertising Address: As above.
Email: info@researchinformation.co.uk
Web site: http://www.researchinformation.co.uk
ISSN: 0020-8256

Publisher: Research Information Ltd
Date Established: 1958
Frequency: 6 issues yearly - Published at the end of the 2nd cover month
Cover Price: £24.00
Annual Sub.: £148.00
Circulation: 2,000 (Publisher's Statement)
Usual Pagination: 48
Editor: Rebecca Murphy; **Advertising Manager:** Ras Patel; **Publisher:** Kumar Patel
Summary of Content: Journal covering the problem of pest eradication and prevention in all its aspects.
Readership/Target Audience: Read by manufacturers, suppliers, operators and researchers involved in the pest control industry.
ADVERTISING RATES:
Full Page Colour £995.00
SCC £25.00
Agency Commission: 10%
Mechanical Data: Type Area: 254 x 178mm, Film: Digital, Col Length: 254mm, Trim Size: 297 x 210mm, Page Width: 178mm, Bleed Size: 303 x 216mm
Copy Date: End of the 1st cover month
Average advertising content per issue: 25%
BUSINESS: AGRICULTURE & FARMING: Agriculture - Supplies & Services

INTERNATIONAL PIG TOPICS

37838U21D-640

Editorial Address: PO Box 4, DRIFFIELD, YO25 9DJ **Tel:** 01377 241724 **Fax:** 01377 253640
Email: neh@positiveaction.co.uk
Advertising Address: As above.
Email: gh@positiveaction.co.uk
Web site: http://www.positiveaction.co.uk
ISSN: 0963-5866
Publisher: Positive Action Publications Ltd
Frequency: 8 issues yearly - Published in the 1st week of the cover month
Free to qualifying individuals
Annual Sub.: £50.00
Circulation: 17,000 (Publisher's Statement)
Usual Pagination: 40
Editor: Colin Foster; **Advertising Manager:** Colin Foster; **Publisher:** Nigel Horrox
Summary of Content: Journal focusing on modern pig breeding and pork production.
Readership/Target Audience: Read by professional pork producers, pig farmers, nutritionists, veterinarians and those in the trade.
ADVERTISING RATES:
Full Page Mono £2081.00
Full Page Colour £2611.00
Mechanical Data: Type Area: 255 x 180mm, Bleed Size: 303 x 213mm, Trim Size: 297 x 210mm, Col Length: 255mm, Page Width: 180mm, Film: Digital
Copy instructions: Copy Date: 1st week of the month prior to publication date
BUSINESS: AGRICULTURE & FARMING: Livestock

INTERNATIONAL POLYMER SCIENCES & TECHNOLOGY

38840U39-23_50

Editorial Address: RAPRA Technology Ltd, Shawbury, SHREWSBURY, SY4 4NR **Tel:** 01939 252455
Fax: 01939 251118
Email: kmevans@rapra.net
Web site: http://www.rapra.net/journals
ISSN: 0307-174X
Publisher: Rapra Technology Ltd
Date Established: 1974
Frequency: Monthly
Annual Sub.: £1060.00
Circulation: 350 (Publisher's Statement)
Usual Pagination: 100
Editor: Kate Evans
Summary of Content: International journal containing translated articles from Eastern European and Japanese rubber and plastics journals.
Readership/Target Audience: Aimed at the plastics and rubber industries.
ADVERTISING: No Advertising taken
BUSINESS: PLASTICS & RUBBER

INTERNATIONAL POULTRY PRODUCTION

37867U21F-550

Editorial Address: PO Box 4, DRIFFIELD, YO25 9DJ **Tel:** 01377 241724 **Fax:** 01377 253640
Email: info@positiveaction.co.uk
Advertising Address: As above.
Email: info@positiveaction.co.uk
Web site: http://www.positiveaction.co.uk
ISSN: 1364-565X
Publisher: Positive Action Publications Ltd
Frequency: 8 issues yearly - Published at the beginning of the cover month
Free to qualifying individuals
Annual Sub.: £50.00

Circulation: 18,000.(Publisher's Statement)
Usual Pagination: 40
Editor: Colin Foster; **Advertising Manager:** Colin Foster;
Publisher: Nigel Horrox
Summary of Content: Magazine covering modern poultrymeat and egg production from the farm to the consumer.
Readership/Target Audience: Aimed at poultrymeat and egg producers, as well as nutritionists and those in the veterinarian trade.
ADVERTISING RATES:
Full Page Mono £2747.00
Full Page Colour £3226.00
Agency Commission: 15%
Mechanical Data: Trim Size: 297 x 210mm, Film: Digital, Type Area: 255 x 180mm, Col Length: 255mm, Page Width: 180mm, Bleed Size: 303 x 216mm
Copy instructions: Copy Date: 1st week of the month prior to publication date
BUSINESS: AGRICULTURE & FARMING: Poultry

INTERNATIONAL RAILWAY JOURNAL
39677U49E-115
Editorial Address: 46 Killigrew Street, FALMOUTH, TR11 3PP **Tel:** 01326 313945 **Fax:** 01326 211576
Email: irj@railjournal.co.uk
Advertising Address: Suite K5 and K6, The Priory, Syresham Gardens, HAYWARDS HEATH, RH16 3LB
Tel: 01444 416368 **Fax:** 01444 458185
Email: de@railjournal.co.uk
Web site: http://www.railjournal.com
ISSN: 0744-5326
Publisher: Simmons-Boardman Publishing Corporation
Date Established: 1960
Frequency: Monthly - Published at the beginning of the cover month
Free to qualifying individuals
Annual Sub.: £75.00
Circulation: 10,096 (BPA Worldwide 01/01/2008 to 30/06/2008)
Usual Pagination: 56
Editor: Keith Barrow; **Editor-in-Chief:** David Briginshaw
Summary of Content: Journal focusing on railway and transit systems worldwide, including managerial, technical and engineering articles.
Readership/Target Audience: Read by senior managers and engineers of the world's railways, metros and light rail systems, ministers of transport, railway equipment manufacturers and suppliers and consultants.
ADVERTISING RATES:
Full Page Mono £2600.00
Full Page Colour £3600.00
Agency Commission: 10%
Mechanical Data: Type Area: 254 x 181mm, Bleed Size: 296 x 216mm, Trim Size: 290 x 210mm, Col Length: 254mm, Col Widths (Display): 57mm, No. of Columns (Display): 4, Page Width: 181mm
Copy instructions: Copy Date: 3 weeks prior to publication date
Average advertising content per issue: 50%
BUSINESS: TRANSPORT: Railways

INTERNATIONAL RENTAL NEWS
714154U17-115
Formerly: European Rental News
Editorial Address: Southfields, Southview Road, WADHURST, TN5 6TP **Tel:** 01892 784088
Fax: 01892 786257
Email: murray.pollok@khl.com
Advertising Address: As above. **Tel:** 01892 786227
Fax: 01892 784086
Email: guy.harris@khl.com
Web site: http://www.khl.com
ISSN: 1470-7940
Publisher: KHL Group
Date Established: 2000
Frequency: 9 issues yearly - Published at the beginning of the 1st cover month. Combined issues: Published at the end of the 1st cover month
Cover Price: £10.00
Free to qualifying individuals
Annual Sub.: £60.00
Circulation: 9,000 (Publisher's Statement)
Usual Pagination: 60
Editor: Murray Pollok; **Publisher:** James King
Summary of Content: Magazine covering the International equipment rental industry, including tool hire and construction equipment rental, events and party rentals, plus specialist rental sectors such as temporary accommodation, power and temperature control equipment and aerial platforms.
Language(s): English; French; German; Italian; Spanish
Readership/Target Audience: Aimed at managers and owners of equipment rental companies Worldwide.
ADVERTISING RATES:
Full Page Colour £3100.00
Agency Commission: 10%

Mechanical Data: Page Width: 184mm, Type Area: 268 x 184mm, Col Length: 268mm, Trim Size: 297 x 210mm, Bleed Size: 303 x 216mm, Film: Digital
Copy instructions: Copy Date: 3 weeks prior to publication date
BUSINESS: ELECTRICAL

INTERNATIONAL REVIEW FOR THE SOCIOLOGY OF SPORT
41065U62B-400
Editorial Address: 1 Oliver's Yard, 55 City Road, LONDON, EC1Y 1SP **Tel:** 020 7324 8500 **Fax:** 020 7324 8600
Advertising Address: As above.
Email: sheena.karim@sagepub.co.uk
Web site: http://www.sagepub.co.uk
ISSN: 1012-6902
Publisher: Sage Publications
Date Established: 1997
Frequency: Quarterly
Annual Sub.: £50.00
Circulation: 650 (Publisher's Statement)
Editor: John Sugden; **Advertising Manager:** Sheena Karim
Summary of Content: Contains information on research and scholarship on sport throughout the international academic community.
Readership/Target Audience: Aimed at a wide range of academics and scholars, including anthropologists, geographers, historians and sociologists.
ADVERTISING RATES:
Full Page Mono £400.00
Agency Commission: 5%
Mechanical Data: Type Area: 210 x 140mm, Col Length: 210mm, Page Width: 140mm, Film: Digital
Copy instructions: Copy Date: 12 weeks prior to publication date
BUSINESS: CHURCH & SCHOOL EQUIPMENT & EDUCATION: Education Teachers

INTERNATIONAL REVIEW OF PSYCHIATRY
40582U56N-24
Editorial Address: Telephone House, 69-77 Paul Street, LONDON, EC2A 4LQ **Tel:** 020 7017 5000
Fax: 020 7017 6955
Email: rupal.malde@informa.com
Advertising Address: Taylor & Francis, 4 Park Square, Milton Park, ABINGDON, OX14 4RN **Tel:** 020 7017 5000
Fax: 020 7017 6413
Email: jenna.johnston@tandf.co.uk
Web site: http://www.informaworld.com/cirp
ISSN: 0954-0261
Publisher: Informa Healthcare
Date Established: 1989
Frequency: 6 issues yearly
Annual Sub.: £300.00
Circulation: 600 (Publisher's Statement)
Usual Pagination: 104
Advertising Manager: Jenna Johnston
Summary of Content: A thematic journal with a guest editor of each issue providing a comprehensive and modern account of a subject of interest to all psychiatrists.
Readership/Target Audience: Aimed at postgraduate students and general psychiatric professionals.
ADVERTISING RATES:
Full Page Mono £250.00
Agency Commission: 10%
Mechanical Data: Trim Size: 280 x 215mm, Film: Digital
Copy instructions: Copy Date: 6 weeks prior to publication date
BUSINESS: HEALTH & MEDICAL: Mental Health

INTERNATIONAL RIG REPORT
38589U33-10_5
Editorial Address: Bon Accord House, Riverside Drive, ABERDEEN, AB11 7SL **Tel:** 01224 572247
Fax: 01224 580320
Email: general@ods-petrodata.com
Web site: http://www.ods-petrodata.com
Publisher: ODS-Petrodata UK Ltd
Frequency: Monthly
Annual Sub.: $3000.00
Circulation: 100 (Publisher's Statement)
Editor: Paul Dear; **Managing Editor:** Paul Dear
Summary of Content: Analytical publication containing reviews and forecasts for international rig markets (excluding the North Sea and the Gulf of Mexico).
Readership/Target Audience: Aimed at oil operators, drilling contractors and financial analysts.
ADVERTISING: No Advertising taken
BUSINESS: OIL & PETROLEUM

INTERNATIONAL SANDWICH & SNACK NEWS
38052U22R-340
Formerly: Sandwich & Snack News
Editorial Address: Association House, 18C Moor Street, CHEPSTOW, NP16 5DB **Tel:** 01291 628103
Fax: 01291 630402

Email: editorial@papa.org.uk
Advertising Address: As above.
Email: paul@jandmgroup.co.uk
Web site: http://www.sandwich.org.uk/
Publisher: J & M Group Ltd.
Frequency: 8 issues yearly
Annual Sub.: £55.00
Circulation: 7,000 (Publisher's Statement)
Usual Pagination: 72
Editor: Simon Ambrose; **Advertising Manager:** Paul Steer;
Managing Editor: Simon Ambrose
Summary of Content: Official journal of the British Sandwich Association covering news, features and product information.
Readership/Target Audience: Read by sandwich makers, including bakers, sandwich bars, sandwich manufacturers and retail buyers.
ADVERTISING RATES:
Full Page Colour £1450.00
Agency Commission: 10%
Mechanical Data: Type Area: 260 x 182mm, Bleed Size: 303 x 216mm, Col Length: 260mm, Page Width: 182mm, Film: Digital, Trim Size: 297 x 210mm
Copy instructions: Copy Date: 2 weeks prior to publication date
Average advertising content per issue: 40%
BUSINESS: FOOD: Food Related

INTERNATIONAL SECURITISATION REPORT
35259U1F-256
Editorial Address: Aldgate House, 33 Aldgate High Street, LONDON, EC3N 1DL **Tel:** 020 7369 7573
Fax: 020 7369 7483
Email: helen.wray@thomsonreuters.com
Advertising Address: As above. **Tel:** 020 7369 7000
Fax: 020 7369 7766
Email: francesca.colombo@thomson.com
Web site: http://www.isr-e.com
ISSN: 0968-929X
Publisher: Thomson Reuters
Date Established: 1993
Frequency: Monthly
Annual Sub.: £787.00
Circulation: 4,055 (Publisher's Statement)
Editor: Helen Wray; **Advertising Director:** Francesca Colombo
Summary of Content: Magazine containing authoritative and independent news and the latest mandates and deals, as well as in-depth country and asset class surveys on securitisation.
Readership/Target Audience: Aimed at those involved in or interested in international securitisation.
ADVERTISING RATES:
Full Page Colour £6400.00
Agency Commission: 10%
Mechanical Data: Page Width: 192mm, Type Area: 278 x 192mm, Bleed Size: 303 x 216mm, Trim Size: 297 x 210mm, Col Length: 278mm, Film: Digital
Copy instructions: Copy Date: 20th of the month prior to publication date
BUSINESS: FINANCE & ECONOMICS: Investment

THE INTERNATIONAL SECURITY BUYERS GUIDE
39909U54C-58
Editorial Address: 60 Churchill Square, Kings Hill, WEST MALLING, ME19 4YU **Tel:** 01732 525800
Fax: 01732 525801
Email: info@newconcept.co.uk
Advertising Address: As above. **Tel:** 01732 525807
Email: anthony.parker@securitybuyer.com
Web site: http://www.securitybuyer.com
ISSN: 1476-7236
Publisher: NCG Media
Date Established: 1996
Frequency: Quarterly
Free to qualifying individuals
Annual Sub.: £99.00
Circulation: 14,000 (Publisher's Statement)
Usual Pagination: 160
Editor: Mark Fermor; **Managing Director:** David Rossiter;
Advertising Manager: Anthony Parker
Summary of Content: International buyers' guide for the security industry. Features on manufacturers of security products and services, news, interviews, product information and details on exhibitions and conferences.
Readership/Target Audience: Aimed at decision makers, buying authorities and purchasing officers in the security industry.
ADVERTISING RATES:
Full Page Colour £2495.00
Agency Commission: 10%
Mechanical Data: Type Area: 270 x 190mm, Bleed Size: 303 x 216mm, Trim Size: 297 x 210mm, Col Length: 270mm, Page Width: 190mm, Film: Digital
Average advertising content per issue: 40%
BUSINESS: SAFETY & SECURITY: Security

Section 4 (b) Business Magazines

Business Magazines

INTERNATIONAL SHEEPDOG NEWS

37851U21D-1000

Formerly: Working Sheepdog News
Editorial Address: 5 Vale Crescent, Bishop Wilton, YORK, YO42 1SU **Tel:** 01759 368577 **Fax:** 01759 368577
Email: workingsheepdog@googlemail.com
Advertising Address: 1 Hattonhill, HUMBIE, EH36 2PR
Tel: 01875 833321
Email: sheepdogads@hotmail.com
Web site: http://www.workingsheepdog.org
Publisher: Working Sheepdog News
Frequency: 6 issues yearly
Cover Price: £3.75
Free to qualifying individuals
Annual Sub.: £36.00
Circulation: 5,000 (Publisher's Statement)
Editor: Andrew Hall; **Publisher:** Andrew Hall
Summary of Content: Journal focusing on sheepdog training, care, handling and nutrition with reports and dates of sheepdog trials.
Readership/Target Audience: Aimed at sheepdog handlers, trainers and enthusiasts.
ADVERTISING RATES:
Full Page Mono £229.00
Full Page Colour £299.00
Agency Commission: 10%
Mechanical Data: Type Area: 267 x 180mm, Trim Size: 297 x 210mm, Bleed Size: +3mm, Col Length: 267mm, No. of Columns (Display): 3, Page Width: 180mm, Print Process: Litho, Film: Digital, Col Widths (Display): 53mm
Copy instructions: Copy Date: 3 weeks prior to publication date
Average advertising content per issue: 15%
BUSINESS: AGRICULTURE & FARMING: Livestock

INTERNATIONAL SHEET METAL REVIEW

26076U27-42

Editorial Address: Winchester Court, 1 Forum Place, Fiddlebridge Lane, HATFIELD, AL10 0RN **Tel:** 01707 273999
Fax: 01707 269333
Email: sara.waddington@trmg.co.uk
Advertising Address: As above.
Email: arfanq@trmg.co.uk
Web site: http://www.sheetmetalplus.com
ISSN: 1471-6542
Publisher: TRMG Ltd
Date Established: 1999
Frequency: 6 issues yearly
Free to qualifying individuals
Annual Sub.: £60.00
Circulation: 11,000 (Publisher's Statement)
Usual Pagination: 92
Editor: Sara Waddington; **Advertising Manager:** Arfan Qureshi
Summary of Content: Magazine providing insight into the technology of sheet metal processing. Contains a mix of in-depth technical articles, equipment profiles, news, views, application reports and business information.
Readership/Target Audience: Aimed at technical, production and managing directors.
ADVERTISING RATES:
Full Page Colour £2900.00
Agency Commission: 10%
Mechanical Data: Trim Size: 297 x 210mm
Copy instructions: Copy Date: 5 weeks prior to publication date
Average advertising content per issue: 40%
BUSINESS: METAL, IRON & STEEL

INTERNATIONAL SIGN MAGAZINE

1655129U64S-371

Editorial Address: PO Box 7574, BILLERICAY, CM12 9XF
Tel: 01277 650037 **Fax:** 0870 762 1039
Email: editorial@intersignmag.com
Advertising Address: As above.
Email: sales@intersignmag.com
Web site: http://www.intersignmag.com
Publisher: Open House Publishing Ltd
Date Established: 2003
Frequency: 6 issues yearly
Annual Sub.: £90.00
Circulation: 6,000 (Publisher's Statement)
Usual Pagination: 50
Editor: Mike Lyons; **Publisher:** Mike Lyons
Summary of Content: Magazine covering all aspects of the visual communications industry, including sign technology and digital printing.
Language(s): English; French; German
Readership/Target Audience: Aimed at specifiers, distributors and end users.
ADVERTISING RATES:
Full Page Colour £1495.00
Agency Commission: 10%
Mechanical Data: Type Area: 277 x 190mm, Col Length: 277mm, Page Width: 190mm, Bleed Size: 305 x 218mm, Trim Size: 297 x 210mm, Film: Digital

Copy instructions: Copy Date: 4 weeks prior to publication date
Average advertising content per issue: 60%
BUSINESS: OTHER CLASSIFICATIONS: Shop Equipment

INTERNATIONAL SOCIAL WORK

38509U32G-72_80

Editorial Address: London Metropolitan University, Department of Applied Social Sciences, Ladbroke House, 62-66 Highbury Grove, LONDON, N5 2AD
Tel: 020 7133 5029 **Fax:** 020 7753 5763
Email: k.lyons@londonmet.ac.uk
Advertising Address: 1 Oliver's Yard, 55 City Road, LONDON, EC1Y 1SP **Tel:** 020 7324 8500
Fax: 020 7324 8600
Email: sheena.karim@sagepub.co.uk
Web site: http://www.sagepub.com
ISSN: 0020-8728
Publisher: Sage Publications
Frequency: 6 issues yearly
Annual Sub.: £53.00
Circulation: 750 (Publisher's Statement)
Editor: Karen Lyons; **Editor-in-Chief:** Karen Lyons;
Advertising Manager: Sheena Karim
Summary of Content: Designed to extend knowledge and promote communication in the field of social development, social welfare and human services.
Readership/Target Audience: Aimed at people interested in the field of social development, social welfare and human services.
ADVERTISING RATES:
Full Page Mono £400.00
Agency Commission: 5%
Mechanical Data: Page Width: 105mm, Film: Digital, Type Area: 185 x 105mm, Col Length: 185mm
Copy instructions: Copy Date: 12 weeks prior to publication date
BUSINESS: LOCAL GOVERNMENT, LEISURE & RECREATION: Community Care & Social Services

INTERNATIONAL STEEL STATISTICS

38191U27-43

Editorial Address: 1 Carlton House Terrace, LONDON, SW1Y 5DB **Tel:** 020 7343 3916 **Fax:** 020 7343 3903
Email: p.hunt@issb.co.uk
Web site: http://www.issb.co.uk
Publisher: ISSB Ltd (Iron and Steel Statistics Bureau)
Date Established: 1972
Frequency: Annual
Cover Price: £195.00
Circulation: 12 (Publisher's Statement)
Usual Pagination: 60
Editor: Phil Hunt
Summary of Content: Guide showing production, materials consumed, apparent consumption and detailed imports and exports of 195 iron and steel products by quality and market.
Readership/Target Audience: Aimed at the steel industry, steel traders and producers. Also aimed at consultant libraries worldwide.
ADVERTISING: No Advertising taken
BUSINESS: METAL, IRON & STEEL

INTERNATIONAL SUGAR JOURNAL

37931U21R-355

Editorial Address: 80 Calverley Road, TUNBRIDGE WELLS, TN1 2UN **Tel:** 020 7017 7500 **Fax:** 020 7017 7599
Email: marketing@agra-net.com
Advertising Address: As above. **Fax:** 020 7017 7593
Email: advertising@world-sugar.com
Web site: http://www.agra-net.com
ISSN: 0020-8841
Publisher: Agra Informa Ltd
Frequency: Monthly
Annual Sub.: £236.00
Usual Pagination: 40
Summary of Content: Journal featuring technical, analytical and research articles on beet and cane sugar production, processing and technology.
Readership/Target Audience: Read by those involved in the International sugar industry.
ADVERTISING RATES:
Full Page Mono £1170.00
Full Page Colour £2110.00
Agency Commission: 15%
Mechanical Data: Col Length: 267mm, Film: Digital, No. of Columns (Display): 2, Type Area: 267 x 185mm, Bleed Size: 303 x 216mm, Trim Size: 297 x 210mm, Page Width: 185mm, Print Process: Sheet-fed offset litho, Col Widths (Display): 88mm
Copy instructions: Copy Date: 15th of the month prior to publication date
Average advertising content per issue: 30%
BUSINESS: AGRICULTURE & FARMING: Agriculture & Farming Related

INTERNATIONAL SUPERMARKET NEWS

37973U22A-247

Editorial Address: 3-4 Marshall's Court, Spring Garden, LINCOLNSHIRE, DN21 2AG **Tel:** 01427 616444
Email: editorial@internationalsupermarketnews.com
Advertising Address: As above. **Tel:** 01427 811825
Email: editorial@internationalsupermarketnews.com
Web site: http://www.internationalsupermarketnews.com
Publisher: International Trade Publications
Date Established: 1998
Frequency: Monthly - Published in the 1st week of the cover month
Free to qualifying individuals
Circulation: 22,300 (Publisher's Statement)
Usual Pagination: 132
Editor: Dennis Martin; **Advertising Manager:** Dennis Martin
Summary of Content: Magazine covering all aspects of the supermarket and hardware retail industry.
Readership/Target Audience: Aimed at CEOs, MDs, key decision makers, senior buyers of supermarkets, cash and carries, hypermarkets, wholesalers, garden centres and hardware retailers via a named mailing database.
ADVERTISING RATES:
Full Page Colour £2900.00
Agency Commission: 10%
Mechanical Data: Bleed Size: 303 x 216mm, Type Area: 289 x 196mm, Col Length: 289mm, Page Width: 196mm, Trim Size: 297 x 210mm, Film: Digital
Copy instructions: Copy Date: 10th of the month prior to publication date
Average advertising content per issue: 30%
BUSINESS: FOOD

INTERNATIONAL TAX REPORT

35406U1M-36

Editorial Address: Telephone House, 69-77 Paul Street, LONDON, EC2A 4LQ **Tel:** 020 7017 5000
Fax: 020 7017 4135
Email: frida.fischer@informa.com
Web site: http://www.informa.com
ISSN: 0300-1628
Publisher: Informa PLC
Frequency: 10 issues yearly
Annual Sub.: £560.00
Circulation: 2,000 (Publisher's Statement)
Usual Pagination: 12
Editor: Frida Fischer; **Publisher:** Victoria Ophield
Summary of Content: Publication reporting on tax planning opportunities worldwide.
Readership/Target Audience: Aimed at tax specialists, lawyers and senior accountants.
ADVERTISING: No Advertising taken
BUSINESS: FINANCE & ECONOMICS: Taxation

INTERNATIONAL TAX REVIEW

35407U1M-37

Editorial Address: Nestor House, Playhouse Yard, LONDON, EC4V 5EX **Tel:** 020 7779 8308
Fax: 020 7779 8500
Email: rcunningham@euromoneyplc.com
Advertising Address: As above. **Tel:** 020 7779 8385
Email: owatkins@euromoneyplc.com
Web site: http://www.internationaltaxreview.com
ISSN: 0958-7594
Publisher: Euromoney Institutional Investor plc
Frequency: 10 issues yearly - Published on first of each month
Usual Pagination: 56
Editor: Ralph Cunningham; **Advertising Manager:** Oliver Watkins; **Managing Editor:** Ralph Cunningham; **Publisher:** Oliver Watkins
Summary of Content: Journal covering reviews of international tax law and tax structuring techniques.
Readership/Target Audience: Aimed at tax directors within multinationals, tax lawyers and finance directors, partners of legal or accounting and academics.
ADVERTISING RATES:
Full Page Mono EUR3740.00
Full Page Colour EUR4785.00
Mechanical Data: Page Width: 190mm, Type Area: 277 x 190mm, Bleed Size: 303 x 216mm, Trim Size: 297 x 210mm, Col Length: 277mm, Film: Digital
Copy instructions: Copy Date: 12th of the month prior to publication date
Supplement(s): Asia Transfer Pricing - 1xY, Benelux - 1xY, Capital Markets - 1xY, Germany - 1xY, India - 1xY, Indirect Tax - 1xY, Italy - 1xY, Latin America - 1xY, Mergers and Acquisitions Yearbook - 1xY, North America - 1xY, Transfer Pricing - 1xY, World Tax - 1xY
BUSINESS: FINANCE & ECONOMICS: Taxation

INTERNATIONAL THERAPIST

40533U56R-69

Editorial Address: 18 Shakespeare Business Centre, Hathaway Close, EASTLEIGH, SO50 4SR
Tel: 0844 875 2022 **Fax:** 023 8062 4398
Email: kyoung@fht.org.uk
Advertising Address: Associa Ltd, North Gate, Uppingham, Oakham, RUTLAND, LE15 9PL **Tel:** 01572 824700

Email: seema.parmar@associa.co.uk
Web site: http://www.fht.org.uk
Publisher: Federation of Holistic Therapists
Date Established: 1994
Frequency: 6 issues yearly
Free to qualifying individuals
Circulation: 20,478 (ABC 01/07/2008 to 30/06/2009)
Usual Pagination: 60
Editor: Melanie Prince; **Advertising Manager:** Mandy Frisby
Summary of Content: Journal covering beauty, complementary and sport therapies including aromatherapy, reflexology and remedial massage.
Readership/Target Audience: Read by members of The Federation of Holistic Therapists, therapy lecturers, trainers and employers.
ADVERTISING RATES:
Full Page Mono £1365.00
Full Page Colour £1575.00
SCC £25.00
Mechanical Data: Bleed Size: 303 x 216mm, Trim Size: 297 x 210mm, Film: Digital, Type Area: 271 x 186mm
Copy instructions: Copy Date: 3 weeks prior to publication date
BUSINESS: HEALTH & MEDICAL: Health Medical Related

INTERNATIONAL TRADE FINANCE

34948U1A-210
Editorial Address: Informa House, 30-32 Mortimer Street, LONDON, W1W 7RE **Tel:** 020 7017 4600
Fax: 020 7017 4135
Email: laura.brown@informa.com
Web site: http://www.informafinance.com/itf
ISSN: 1365-3512
Publisher: Informa PLC
Frequency: 22 issues yearly
Annual Sub.: £679.00
Usual Pagination: 20
Editor: Laura Brown; **Publisher:** Nicola Whyke
Summary of Content: Newsletter covering the latest news and analysis of trade finance and export credit insurance developments worldwide.
Readership/Target Audience: Aimed at company managers and risk analysts.
ADVERTISING: No Advertising taken
BUSINESS: FINANCE & ECONOMICS

INTERNATIONAL TRADE FOCUS

1695441U14C-360
Formerly: Export Focus
Editorial Address: South Fens Conference Centre, Fenton Way, Chatteris, CAMBRIDGESHIRE, PE16 6TT
Tel: 01354 695599 **Fax:** 05600 495621
Email: info@internationaltradefocus.co.uk
Advertising Address: As above. **Tel:** 01354 651666
Email: info@marchpublishing.co.uk
Web site: http://www.exportfocus.co.uk
Publisher: March Publishing Ltd
Frequency: Quarterly
Free to qualifying individuals
Circulation: 6,000 (Publisher's Statement)
Editor: Roy Chegwin; **Advertising Manager:** Jeff Tucker;
Publisher: Jeff Tucker
Summary of Content: Magazine dedicated to international trade matters. Includes articles on export events, news and industry updates.
Readership/Target Audience: Aimed at those involved in international trade in the UK.
ADVERTISING RATES:
Full Page Colour £3995.00
Agency Commission: 10%
Mechanical Data: Bleed Size: +3mm, Trim Size: 297 x 210mm, Film: Digital
Copy instructions: Copy Date: 2 weeks prior to publication date
Average advertising content per issue: 25%
BUSINESS: COMMERCE, INDUSTRY & MANAGEMENT: International Commerce

INTERNATIONAL TUG & SALVAGE

39332U45A-78_50
Editorial Address: The Barn, Ford Barn, Bradford Leigh, BRADFORD-ON-AVON, BA15 2RP **Tel:** 01225 868821
Fax: 01225 868831
Email: dawn@tugandsalvage.com
Advertising Address: 4 The Coppice, Vicarage Lane, Scaynes Hill, HAYWARDS HEATH, RH17 7PD
Tel: 01444 831788
Email: nickie@tugandsalvage.com
Web site: http://www.tugandsalvage.com
ISSN: 1463-1555
Publisher: ABR Co Ltd
Date Established: 1995
Frequency: 6 issues yearly
Annual Sub.: £65.00
Circulation: 5,200 (Publisher's Statement)

Usual Pagination: 76
Editor: Dawn Gorman; **Managing Editor:** Andy Smith;
Advertisement Director: Nickie Hoddinott
Summary of Content: Magazine covering the international tug and salvage industry.
Readership/Target Audience: Aimed at tug owners, operators, builders and salvage contractors.
ADVERTISING RATES:
Full Page Colour £1500.00
Agency Commission: 10%
Mechanical Data: Col Length: 262mm, Page Width: 184mm, Type Area: 262 x 184mm, No. of Columns (Display): 3
Copy instructions: Copy Date: 5 weeks prior to publication date
Average advertising content per issue: 50%
BUSINESS: MARINE & SHIPPING

INTERNATIONAL TURFGRASS BULLETIN

41484U64D-50
Editorial Address: St. Ives Estate, BINGLEY, BD16 1AU
Tel: 01274 565131 **Fax:** 01274 561891
Email: anne.wilson@stri.co.uk
Advertising Address: As above.
Email: info@stri.co.uk
Web site: http://www.stri.co.uk
ISSN: 1362-9255
Publisher: STRI
Date Established: 1929
Frequency: Quarterly
Annual Sub.: £58.00
Circulation: 4,000 (Publisher's Statement)
Usual Pagination: 36
Editor: Anne Wilson; **Managing Director:** Gordon McKillop;
Advertising Manager: Anne Wilson
Summary of Content: International magazine covering the golf sports and amenity turf industries. Contains news of the latest innovations and regular features.
Language(s): Danish; Dutch; English
Readership/Target Audience: Aimed at golf and sports clubs, greenkeepers, grounds personnel, local authorities, education research, libraries, leisure services, related trade industries, turf growers, seed producers and landscape contractors.
ADVERTISING RATES:
Full Page Colour £1300.00
Agency Commission: 10%
Mechanical Data: Bleed Size: 303 x 216mm, Trim Size: 297 x 210mm, Col Length: 267mm, Film: Digital, No. of Columns (Display): 2, Type Area: 267 x 185mm, Print Process: Web-fed litho, Page Width: 185mm
Copy instructions: Copy Date: 4 weeks prior to publication date
Average advertising content per issue: 33%
Supplement(s): Green Matters - 4xY
BUSINESS: OTHER CLASSIFICATIONS: Course Maintenance

INTERNATIONAL UROGYNAECOLOGY JOURNAL

24592U56A-69
Editorial Address: Ashbourne House, The Guildway, Old Portsmouth Road, Artington, GUILDFORD, GU3 1LP
Tel: 01483 734437 **Fax:** 01483 734411
Email: clare.colwell@springer.com
Web site: http://www.springer.com
ISSN: 0937-3462
Publisher: Springer
Date Established: 1990
Frequency: Monthly
Annual Sub.: £276.00
Circulation: 2,700 (Publisher's Statement)
Usual Pagination: 64
Editor: Clare Colwell
Summary of Content: Journal containing research, results and clinically relevant material in the field of urogynaecology and pelvic disorders.
Readership/Target Audience: Read by urologists, gynaecologists, nurses and basic scientists working in this field.
ADVERTISING: No Advertising taken
BUSINESS: HEALTH & MEDICAL

INTERNATIONAL WATER POWER & DAM CONSTRUCTION

39056U42C-300
Editorial Address: Progressive House, 2 Maidstone Road, Foots Cray, SIDCUP, DA14 5HZ **Tel:** 020 8269 7777
Fax: 020 8269 7804
Email: cstocks@progressivemediagroup.com
Advertising Address: As above. **Tel:** 020 8269 7864
Email: sgalvin@progressivemediagroup.com
Web site: http://www.waterpowermagazine.com
ISSN: 0306-400X
Publisher: Progressive Media Publications
Date Established: 1949
Frequency: Monthly - Published around the middle of the cover month

Annual Sub.: £220.00
Circulation: 4,141 (ABC 01/01/2008 to 31/12/2008)
Usual Pagination: 52
Editor: Carrieann Stocks
Summary of Content: Magazine featuring the latest developments in the water power and dam construction industry. Includes news, views, industry insights and technical developments.
Readership/Target Audience: Aimed at those involved in the hydro-electric and dam industry and those in business and finance.
ADVERTISING RATES:
Full Page Mono $1750.00
Full Page Colour $2490.00
Agency Commission: 10%
Mechanical Data: Film: Digital, Type Area: 254 x 178mm, Print Process: Sheet-fed litho, Bleed Size: 303 x 216mm, Trim Size: 297 x 210mm, Col Length: 254mm, Page Width: 178mm
Copy instructions: Copy Date: 3 weeks prior to publication date
Average advertising content per issue: 20%
BUSINESS: CONSTRUCTION: Water Engineering

INTERNET RETAILING

1779365U53-698
Editorial Address: 6 Laurence Pountney Hill, LONDON, EC4R 0BL **Tel:** 020 7933 8999 **Fax:** 020 7933 8998
Email: press@internetretailing.net
Advertising Address: As above.
Email: annai@stjohnpatrick.com
Web site: http://www.internetretailing.net
Publisher: St. John Patrick Publishers Ltd
Date Established: 2006
Frequency: 6 issues yearly - Published around the 7th of the cover month
Cover Price: Free
Circulation: 5,000 (Print Run)
Usual Pagination: 44
Editor: Emma Herrod; **Advertising Manager:** Anna Idoyatova
Summary of Content: Magazine and web portal providing insight and analysis into retailing in the UK from the focus point of the online business. It provides a source of ideas, competitive intelligence and briefing for both internet only and multi-channel retailers. Every aspect of the business is covered from strategy and marketing to IT and delivery.
Readership/Target Audience: Aimed at managing directors and heads of departments of internet and multi-channel retailers.
ADVERTISING RATES:
Full Page Colour £2995.00
Agency Commission: 10%
Mechanical Data: Type Area: 271 x 184mm, Bleed Size: 303 x 216mm, Trim Size: 297 x 210mm, Col Length: 271mm, Page Width: 184mm, Film: Digital
Copy instructions: Copy Date: 3 weeks prior to publication date
BUSINESS: RETAILING & WHOLESALING

INTERPARK

41469U64A-143
Editorial Address: 8 Bowden Lane, Chapel-en-Le-Frith, HIGH PEAK, SK23 0JQ **Tel:** 01298 813148
Fax: 01298 814344
Email: editorial@interpark.co.uk
Advertising Address: As above. **Fax:** 01298 813148
Email: johnintergame@hotmail.com
Web site: http://www.interpark.co.uk
ISSN: 1359-6284
Publisher: InterGame Ltd
Date Established: 1995
Frequency: 5 issues yearly
Annual Sub.: £65.00
Circulation: 3,555 (Publisher's Statement)
Usual Pagination: 48
Editor: Adrian Lennox; **Features Editor:** Beth Whittaker;
Editor-in-Chief: Andrew Mellor; **Publisher:** John Fosbrooke
Summary of Content: Magazine dedicated to the international theme parks and family entertainment centre industry, covering news, projects and upgrades worldwide.
Readership/Target Audience: Aimed at ride manufacturers, operators and park managers.
ADVERTISING RATES:
Full Page Colour £1795.00
Mechanical Data: Trim Size: 297 x 210mm, Bleed Size: 307 x 216mm, Type Area: 285 x 194mm, Col Length: 285mm, Film: Digital, Page Width: 194mm
Average advertising content per issue: 50%
BUSINESS: OTHER CLASSIFICATIONS: Amusement Trade

INTERSEC

39911U54C-63
Editorial Address: Albany Villas, 74 Eastworth Road, CHERTSEY, KT16 8DR **Tel:** 020 8247 3790
Fax: 0870 486 9204
Email: rob@intersec.co.uk
Advertising Address: As above.
Email: sales@intersec.co.uk
Web site: http://www.intersec.co.uk

ISSN: 0963-0058
Publisher: Albany Media
Date Established: 1991
Frequency: 10 issues yearly - Published in the 1st week of the cover month
Annual Sub.: £102.00
Circulation: 10,510 (Publisher's Statement)
Usual Pagination: 48
Editor: Robert de le Poer
Summary of Content: Magazine covering risk assessment, explosives and drug detection, terrorism, advanced access and perimeter technology, maritime security, international policing issues, fraud and computer and communications security.
Readership/Target Audience: Aimed at senior management within government and industry.
ADVERTISING RATES:
Full Page Mono £2095.00
Full Page Colour £3190.00
Agency Commission: 10%
Mechanical Data: Type Area: 270 x 185mm, Page Width: 185mm, Col Length: 270mm, Trim Size: 297 x 210mm, Bleed Size: 303 x 216mm, Print Process: Sheet-fed litho, Film: Digital
Copy instructions: Copy Date: 2 weeks prior to publication date
Average advertising content per issue: 40%
BUSINESS: SAFETY & SECURITY: Security

INVEST IN SUCCESS   1658919U1F-587

Editorial Address: The Rookery, Belyars Lane, ST. IVES, TR26 2DA **Tel:** 01736 793363
Email: john@wordsthatwork.uk.com
Advertising Address: EMP House, 2 Pembroke Road, LONDON, N10 2HR **Tel:** 020 8444 3401 **Fax:** 020 8888 9504
Email: nigelwinter@empmedia.co.uk
Web site: http://www.investbritain.co.uk
Publisher: EMP Media
Frequency: Annual
Cover Price: Free
Editor: John Hancock
Summary of Content: Magazine highlighting the values and benefits of locating a business in a particular UK region.
Readership/Target Audience: Aimed at inward investors.
ADVERTISING: Rates on application
BUSINESS: FINANCE & ECONOMICS: Investment

INVEST IN THE UK   1660272U1F-647

Editorial Address: Banklands, Ferry Lane, Wraysbury, STAINES, TW19 6HG **Tel:** 01784 481784 **Fax:** 01784 483600
Email: enquiries@invest-in-the-uk.com
Advertising Address: As above.
Email: enquiries@invest-in-the-uk.com
Web site: http://www.invest-in-the-uk.com
Publisher: CommuniCorp
Date Established: 1990
Frequency: Annual - Published in December
Cover Price: $30.00
Free to qualifying individuals
Circulation: 12,240 (Publisher's Statement)
Usual Pagination: 92
Editor: Carol Lee
Summary of Content: Articles containing factual information to help foreign companies set up successfully in the UK and listings of the organisations which will help them locate in the UK.
Readership/Target Audience: Aimed at executives in foreign corporations which are planning to locate to the UK.
ADVERTISING RATES:
Full Page Colour £4950.00
Agency Commission: 10%
Mechanical Data: Type Area: 270 x 187mm, Col Length: 270mm, Page Width: 187mm
BUSINESS: FINANCE & ECONOMICS: Investment

INVESTHEDGE   1645515U1F-626

Editorial Address: Nestor House, Playhouse Yard, LONDON, EC4V 5EX **Tel:** 020 7779 7330
Fax: 020 7779 7331
Email: info@hedgefundintelligence.com
Advertising Address: As above.
Email: jwillis@hedgefundintelligence.com
Web site: http://www.hedgefundintelligence.com
Publisher: Hedge Fund Intelligence
Frequency: 10 issues yearly - July/August and December/January are joint issues
Annual Sub.: £1050.00
Usual Pagination: 60
Editor: Niki Natarajan; **Features Editor:** Barry Cohen;
Advertising Manager: John Willis
Summary of Content: Newsletter providing breaking news on new fund launches, mandate awards, institutional investor profiles and performance data for nearly 2700 funds.
Readership/Target Audience: Aimed at institutional investors and wealth management advisors who want to use

multi-managers and fund of funds to access hedge funds, multi-managers and professional hedge fund investors who need to know what their competitors are doing and hedge fund managers who need to keep abreast of developments amongst their clients and prospective clients.
ADVERTISING RATES:
Full Page Mono £5950.00
Mechanical Data: Type Area: 244 x 185mm, Bleed Size: 278 x 211mm, Trim Size: 272 x 205mm, Col Length: 244mm, Page Width: 185mm, Film: Digital
Copy instructions: Copy Date: 21st of the month prior to publication date
BUSINESS: FINANCE & ECONOMICS: Investment

INVESTING FOR GROWTH   35268U1F-256_60

Formerly: Jim Slater Investing for Growth
Editorial Address: 3rd Floor, Sophia House, 76-80 City Road, LONDON, EC1Y 2BJ **Tel:** 020 7324 5419
Web site: http://www.investing-for-growth.co.uk
Publisher: Independent Investor Services Ltd
Date Established: 1998
Frequency: Monthly
Annual Sub.: £199.00
Usual Pagination: 16
Editor: Pam Spooner; **Publisher:** Stuart Kinner
Summary of Content: Investment newsletter focusing on recommended UK growth shares. Contains advice, updates, company profiles and searches on top company performers.
Readership/Target Audience: Read by private investors.
ADVERTISING: No Advertising taken
BUSINESS: FINANCE & ECONOMICS: Investment

INVESTMENT ADVISER   35260U1F-257

Editorial Address: 1 Southwark Bridge, LONDON, SE1 9HL **Tel:** 020 7873 3000
Email: jim.robinson@ft.com
Advertising Address: As above.
Email: chris.sansom@ft.com
Web site: http://www.ftadviser.com/InvestmentAdviser
ISSN: 1361-1593
Publisher: FT Group
Frequency: Weekly
Free to qualifying individuals
Annual Sub.: £90.00
Circulation: 13,585 (ABC 01/07/2008 to 30/06/2009)
Usual Pagination: 80
Editor: Jim Robinson; **Features Editor:** Laura Hughes;
Advertising Manager: Chris Sansom
Summary of Content: Newspaper providing objective information on investment funds and related products.
Readership/Target Audience: Aimed at top financial intermediaries.
ADVERTISING RATES:
Full Page Mono £5816.00
Full Page Colour £5816.00
Agency Commission: 10%
Mechanical Data: Type Area: 370 x 266mm, Bleed Size: 394 x 303mm, Trim Size: 388 x 300mm, Col Length: 370mm, Film: Digital, Page Width: 266mm
Copy instructions: Copy Date: Thursday prior to publication date
BUSINESS: FINANCE & ECONOMICS: Investment

INVESTMENT & PENSIONS EUROPE   35358U1H-27

Editorial Address: 320 Great Guildford House, 30 Great Guildford Street, LONDON, SE1 0HS **Tel:** 020 7261 0666
Fax: 020 7928 3332
Email: julie.henderson@ipe.com
Web site: http://www.ipe.com
ISSN: 1369-3727
Publisher: IPE International Publishers Limited
Date Established: 1997
Frequency: 11 issues yearly
Cover Price: Free
Circulation: 10,292 (ABC 01/07/2008 to 30/06/2009)
Usual Pagination: 64
Editor: Julie Henderson; **News Editor:** Julie Henderson;
Publisher: Piers Diacre
Summary of Content: Magazine covering international investment opportunities for European pension funds.
Readership/Target Audience: Aimed at institutional and European Pension Fund investors.
ADVERTISING: Rates on application
Editions:
Investment & Pensions Nederland
BUSINESS: FINANCE & ECONOMICS: Pensions

INVESTMENT, LIFE & PENSIONS MONEYFACTS   35269U1F-278

Formerly: Life & Pensions Moneyfacts
Editorial Address: Moneyfacts House, 66-70 Thorpe Road, NORWICH, NR1 1BJ **Tel:** 0870 225 0476
Fax: 0870 225 0201

Email: reagling@moneyfacts.co.uk
Advertising Address: As above. **Tel:** 0845 168 9655
Fax: 01603 476017
Email: advertising@moneyfacts.co.uk
Web site: http://www.moneyfacts.co.uk
ISSN: 1355-4980
Publisher: Moneyfacts Group
Frequency: Monthly
Annual Sub.: £144.50
Circulation: 3,765 (Publisher's Statement)
Usual Pagination: 160
Editor: Richard Eagling; **Group Editor:** John Woods
Summary of Content: Publication providing editorial and data on life assurance, pensions, annuities, unit trusts, investment trusts and ISAs. Includes information on premium rates, plan details, fund performance and commission.
Readership/Target Audience: Read by financial advisors and financial institutions including IFAs, banks, building societies, accountants, solicitors, life companies and investment houses.
ADVERTISING RATES:
Full Page Colour £1500.00
Mechanical Data: Type Area: 285 x 195mm, Col Length: 285mm, Page Width: 195mm, Trim Size: 297 x 210mm
BUSINESS: FINANCE & ECONOMICS: Investment

INVESTMENT NOW   38392U32A-215

Formerly: Regional Development International
Editorial Address: 70 Singer Way, Woburn Road Industrial Estate, KEMPSTON, MK42 7PU **Tel:** 01234 843905
Fax: 01234 843901
Email: patw@investmentnow.co.uk
Advertising Address: As above.
Email: patw@investmentnow.co.uk
Web site: http://www.investmentnow.co.uk
ISSN: 1475-0813
Publisher: Lawn Graphics Ltd
Date Established: 1970
Frequency: Monthly - Published on the 28th of the cover month
Cover Price: £5.00
Annual Sub.: £50.00
Circulation: 23,000 (Publisher's Statement)
Usual Pagination: 40
Editor: Patricia Waller; **Managing Director:** Martin Howard Quince; **Advertising Manager:** Patricia Waller
Summary of Content: Publication containing news from European regions, counties and districts pinpointing business opportunities and locational advantages available to companies seeking to expand, relocate or start up.
Readership/Target Audience: Read by local authority and private sector decision makers in manufacturing and service companies looking to reallocate or form joint ventures, fund managers, local authority and private sector decision makers.
ADVERTISING RATES:
Full Page Mono £1425.00
Full Page Colour £1825.00
Agency Commission: 10%
Mechanical Data: Film: Digital, Page Width: 185mm, Type Area: 274 x 185mm, Col Length: 274mm, Bleed Size: 305 x 216mm, Trim Size: 297 x 210mm
Copy instructions: Copy Date: 2 weeks prior to publication date
Average advertising content per issue: 40%
BUSINESS: LOCAL GOVERNMENT, LEISURE & RECREATION: Local Government

INVESTMENT WEEK   35264U1F-262

Editorial Address: Haymarket House, 28-29 Haymarket, LONDON, SW1Y 4RX **Tel:** 020 7484 9700
Email: hysni.kaso@incisivemedia.com
Advertising Address: As above.
Email: paul.douglass@incisivemedia.com
Web site: http://www.investmentweek.co.uk
Publisher: Incisive Media Investments
Frequency: Weekly - Published on Monday
Free to qualifying individuals
Annual Sub.: £95.00
Circulation: 14,600 (ABC 01/07/2007 to 30/06/2008)
Editor: Hysni Kaso; **News Editor:** Hysni Kaso; **Managing Director:** Nick Rapley; **Advertising Manager:** Paul Douglass
Summary of Content: Magazine covering investment and product news.
Readership/Target Audience: Aimed at independent investment advisers.
ADVERTISING RATES:
Full Page Colour £7407.00
Agency Commission: 10%
Mechanical Data: Film: Digital, Trim Size: 350 x 250mm
Copy instructions: Copy Date: 1 week prior to publication date
Average advertising content per issue: 50%
BUSINESS: FINANCE & ECONOMICS: Investment

INVESTOR SERVICES JOURNAL

1666473U1F-597

Editorial Address: 16-17 Little Portland Street, LONDON, W1W 8BP **Tel:** 020 7299 7700
Email: ben@2ipartners.com
Advertising Address: As above.
Email: jon@2ipartners.com
Web site: http://www.isj.tv
ISSN: 1744-151X
Publisher: 2i Media plc
Date Established: 2004
Frequency: 10 issues yearly - Published at the end of the 2nd week of cover month
Free to qualifying individuals
Annual Sub.: £195.00
Circulation: 10,485 (Publisher's Statement)
Usual Pagination: 80
Summary of Content: Magazine focusing on the global securities services and treasury services, industry including articles on fund administration, information and data providers, technology, corporate actions, STP, trading services and outsourcing, hedge funds (administration & compliance), prime brokerage, custody; settlement and clearing, pensions, transition management, securities financing/lending and legal and compliance-related issues.
Readership/Target Audience: Aimed at pension fund managers, asset managers, financial lawyers, consultants, fund administrators and custodians.
ADVERTISING RATES:
Full Page Mono £5950.00
Full Page Colour £5950.00
Agency Commission: 10%
Mechanical Data: Type Area: 247 x 183mm, Bleed Size: 273 x 209mm, Trim Size: 267 x 203mm, Col Length: 247mm, Page Width: 183mm, Print Process: Web offset, Film: Digital
Copy instructions: Copy Date: 1 week prior to publication date
Average advertising content per issue: 28%
BUSINESS: FINANCE & ECONOMICS: Investment

INVESTORS CHRONICLE

34949U1A-219

Editorial Address: 1 Southwark Bridge, LONDON, SE1 9HL
Tel: 020 7873 3000
Email: rosie.carr@ft.com
Advertising Address: As above.
Email: beth.gordon-smith@ft.com
Web site: http://www.investorschronicle.co.uk
ISSN: 0261-3115
Publisher: FT Group
Frequency: Weekly
Cover Price: £3.35
Circulation: 30,027 (ABC 01/01/2009 to 30/06/2009)
Usual Pagination: 92
Editor: Rosemary Carr; **News Editor:** Graeme Davies;
Managing Director: Caspar De Bono; **Advertising Manager:** Beth Gordon-Smith; **Publisher:** Jonathan Church
Summary of Content: Magazine covering direct stock market investment offering news, advice and analysis. Includes features on areas of personal finance.
Readership/Target Audience: Aimed at UK stock market investors.
ADVERTISING RATES:
Full Page Colour £4000.00
Agency Commission: 10%
Mechanical Data: No. of Columns (Display): 4, Page Width: 181mm, Type Area: 240 x 181mm, Bleed Size: 276 x 211mm, Trim Size: 270 x 205mm, Col Length: 240mm, Film: Digital, Col Widths (Display): 54mm
Copy instructions: Copy Date: Monday prior to publication date
Average advertising content per issue: 25%
Supplement(s): Masterclass - 12xY
BUSINESS: FINANCE & ECONOMICS

IOD HERTFORDSHIRE

754337U63B-2498

Editorial Address: 16 Peakes Place, Granville Road, ST. ALBANS, AL1 5AY **Tel:** 01727 838321
Email: stephen@assimilating-talent.com
Advertising Address: Suite 12B, Pixmore Centre, Pixmore Avenue, LETCHWORTH GARDEN CITY, SG6 1JG
Tel: 01462 686985 **Fax:** 01462 681185
Email: sales@venturer.co.uk
Web site: http://www.iod.com
Publisher: Clickworks Ltd
Date Established: 2003
Frequency: Quarterly
Cover Price: £1.75
Free to qualifying individuals
Circulation: 3,500 (Publisher's Statement)
Usual Pagination: 16
Editor: Stephen Havard Davis; **Executive Editor:** Stephen Havard Davis
Summary of Content: Journal of the Institute of Directors for the Hertfordshire area covering regional and business news and features.
Readership/Target Audience: Read by members of the Institute of Directors, chief executive officers, managing directors and senior directors.

ADVERTISING RATES:
Full Page Colour £800.00
Mechanical Data: Trim Size: 297 x 210mm, Film: Digital, Type Area: 254 x 190mm, Col Length: 254mm, Page Width: 190mm
Average advertising content per issue: 40%
BUSINESS: REGIONAL BUSINESS: Regional Business English Counties

IOV FOCUS

39111U43D-10

Editorial Address: PO Box 625, LOUGHTON, IG10 3GZ
Tel: 020 8502 3817 **Fax:** 020 8508 9211
Email: martin.baker@iov.co.uk
Advertising Address: As above. **Tel:** 020 8508 3817
Email: kevin.cook@iov.co.uk
Web site: http://www.iov.co.uk
Publisher: IOV Focus Ltd
Date Established: 1995
Frequency: Monthly
Annual Sub.: £45.00
Circulation: 2,400 (Publisher's Statement)
Usual Pagination: 32
Editor: Kevin Cook; **News Editor:** Martin Baker;
Advertising Manager: Kevin Cook
Summary of Content: Official publication of the Institute of Videography.
Readership/Target Audience: Read by professional videographers.
ADVERTISING RATES:
Full Page Colour £1100.00
Agency Commission: 10%
Mechanical Data: Bleed Size: 302 x 215mm, Trim Size: 297 x 210mm, Film: Positive, right reading, emulsion side down. Digital
Copy instructions: Copy Date: 12th of the month prior to publication date
Average advertising content per issue: 40%
BUSINESS: ELECTRICAL RETAIL TRADE: Video

IP&E INDUSTRIAL PLANT & EQUIPMENT

37656U19F-249

Editorial Address: 33-35 Cantelupe Road, EAST GRINSTEAD, RH19 3BE **Tel:** 01342 314300
Fax: 01342 333700
Email: vkealey@western-bp.co.uk
Advertising Address: As above.
Email: jdiamond@western-bp.co.uk
Web site: http://www.ipesearch.com
ISSN: 0964-8321
Publisher: Western Business Publishing
Date Established: 1992
Frequency: 6 issues yearly - Published around the 28th of the cover month
Free to qualifying individuals
Circulation: 22,975 (ABC 01/01/2008 to 31/12/2008)
Usual Pagination: 160
Group Editor: Tim McManan-Smith; **Publisher:** Neill Western
Summary of Content: Journal covering plant, works, maintenance processes, production and electrical engineering, buildings management, health and safety, materials handling.
Readership/Target Audience: Aimed at engineers, managers and key executives in manufacturing, engineering and production environments.
ADVERTISING RATES:
Full Page Colour £2500.00
Agency Commission: 10%
Mechanical Data: Trim Size: 297 x 210mm, Film: Digital
Copy instructions: Copy Date: 2 weeks prior to publication date
Average advertising content per issue: 50%
Supplement(s): Compressed Air User - 1xY, Efficiency & Maintenance - 1xY, Energy Management - 1xY, Handling & Storing - 1xY, Health & Safety at Work - 1xY, Premises Management & Maintenance - 1xY
BUSINESS: ENGINEERING & MACHINERY: Production & Mechanical Engineering

IP REVIEW

1852287U44-3059

Editorial Address: The Pall Mall Deposit, 124-128 Barlby Road, LONDON, W10 6BL **Tel:** 020 8962 3020
Fax: 020 8962 8689
Email: emma@thinkpublishing.co.uk
Web site: http://www.ipreview.com
Publisher: Think Publishing Ltd
Date Established: 2003
Frequency: Quarterly
Cover Price: Free
Annual Sub.: £129.00
Circulation: 12,000 (Publisher's Statement)
Usual Pagination: 44
Editor: Emma Jones; **Publisher:** Ian McAuliffe
Summary of Content: Magazine covering trends, challenges and legal updates in the field of intellectual property, including patents, trademarks, domain names,

copyright and other forms of intangible assets such as know-how and databases.
Readership/Target Audience: Aimed at intellectual property professionals working for law firms and in-house at corporations.
BUSINESS: LEGAL

IP&E INDUSTRIAL PLANT & EQUIPMENT IRELAND

1872529U19F-687

Editorial Address: 33-35 Cantelupe Road, EAST GRINSTEAD, RH19 3BE **Tel:** 01342 314300
Fax: 01342 333700
Email: tmcsmith@western-bp.co.uk
Web site: http://www.ipesearch.com
Publisher: Western Business Publishing
Date Established: 2009
Frequency: Quarterly
Free to qualifying individuals
Editor: Tim McManan-Smith
Summary of Content: Publication providing information concerning the products, services and technologies available to assist with the running of an industrial site. Covering new products, technologies and case studies about the Irish market.
Readership/Target Audience: Aimed at engineers, managers and directors in manufacturing, engineering and production environments.
BUSINESS: ENGINEERING & MACHINERY: Production & Mechanical Engineering

IPA BULLETIN

36766U14A-187

Formerly: IPA Magazine
Editorial Address: 42 Colebrooke Row, LONDON, N1 8AF
Tel: 020 7354 8040 **Fax:** 020 7354 8041
Email: involve@ipa-involve.com
Web site: http://www.ipa-involve.com
Publisher: Involvement & Participation Association
Frequency: 10 issues yearly
Free to qualifying individuals
Annual Sub.: £58.75
Circulation: 2,500 (Publisher's Statement)
Usual Pagination: 4
Editor: Sarah Dawson
Summary of Content: Magazine containing news, analysis, comment and discussion about all areas of employee involvement and participation. Published by the Involvement and Participation Association, which is financially and politically independent, and promotes partnership at the workplace.
Readership/Target Audience: Aimed at management, employees and their representatives.
ADVERTISING: No Advertising taken
BUSINESS: COMMERCE, INDUSTRY & MANAGEMENT

IPE REAL ESTATE

1772589U1F-621

Editorial Address: 320 Great Guildford House, 30 Great Guildford Street, LONDON, SE1 0HS **Tel:** 020 7261 4623
Fax: 020 7928 3332
Email: martin.hurst@ipe.com
Advertising Address: As above. **Tel:** 020 7261 0666
Email: eric.davis@ipe.com
Web site: http://www.iperealestate.com
Publisher: IPE International Publishers Limited
Frequency: 6 issues yearly
Free to qualifying individuals
Annual Sub.: £245.00
Circulation: 10,553 (ABC 01/07/2008 to 30/06/2009)
Editor: Martin Hurst; **News Editor:** Julie Henderson;
Advertisement Director: Eric Davis
Summary of Content: Magazine covering institutional investment in real estate.
Readership/Target Audience: Aimed at investment managers within pension funds and insurance companies.
ADVERTISING RATES:
Full Page Colour £8147.00
Agency Commission: 10%
Mechanical Data: Type Area: 290 x 210mm, Bleed Size: 341 x 251mm, Trim Size: 335 x 245mm, Col Length: 290mm, Page Width: 210mm, Film: Digital
Average advertising content per issue: 30%
BUSINESS: FINANCE & ECONOMICS: Investment

IPTV INTERNATIONAL

1708438U2R-185

Editorial Address: 4th Floor, Unit 4.01, 71 Bondway, LONDON, SW8 1SQ **Tel:** 020 7793 8855 **Fax:** 020 7793 9955
Email: colin.mann@advanced-television.com
Advertising Address: As above.
Email: sanjeev@advanced-television.com
Web site: http://www.advanced-television.com
ISSN: 1477-7242
Publisher: Advanced Television Ltd
Date Established: 2005
Frequency: Quarterly
Free to qualifying individuals

Circulation: 5,500 (Publisher's Statement)
Usual Pagination: 46
Editor: Colin Mann; **Editor-in-Chief:** Nick Snow; **Managing Editor:** Colin Mann
Summary of Content: Magazine covering the strategies, companies and people involved in the developments of internet protocol television.
Readership/Target Audience: Aimed at broadcasters, producers, and network operators and anyone who supplies them the tools or know-how to deliver their viewers and subscribers the new services enabled by IPTV.
ADVERTISING RATES:
Full Page Colour £3000.00
Agency Commission: 10%
Mechanical Data: Bleed Size: 303 x 213mm, Trim Size: 297 x 210mm, Film: Digital
Average advertising content per issue: 40%
BUSINESS: COMMUNICATIONS, ADVERTISING & MARKETING: Communications Related

IQ
633899U1D-246_20

Editorial Address: Second Floor, Asia House, 31-33 Lime Street, LONDON, EC3M 7HT **Tel:** 020 7397 0618
Fax: 020 7397 0616
Email: david@theinsider.co.uk
Advertising Address: As above. **Tel:** 020 7397 0619
Email: spencer@theinsider.co.uk
Web site: http://www.insiderquarterly.com
Publisher: Insider Publishing Ltd
Date Established: 2002
Frequency: Quarterly
Free to qualifying individuals
Annual Sub.: £199.00
Circulation: 6,779 (ABC 01/07/2008 to 30/06/2009)
Usual Pagination: 44
Editor: David Bull; **Managing Editor:** David Bull
Summary of Content: Magazine containing information and intelligence on the international insurance and reinsurance markets.
Readership/Target Audience: Aimed at insurance professionals and related industries.
ADVERTISING RATES:
Full Page Colour £3500.00
Agency Commission: 10%
Mechanical Data: Trim Size: 297 x 210mm, Bleed Size: 303 x 216mm, Film: Digital
Copy instructions: Copy Date: 3 days prior to publication date
Average advertising content per issue: 30%
BUSINESS: FINANCE & ECONOMICS: Insurance

IQ EDUCATION
628939U62A-175

Editorial Address: Trelawney House, Chestergate, MACCLESFIELD, SK11 6DW **Tel:** 01625 613000
Fax: 01625 435078
Email: cathy.baldwin@tenalpspublishing.com
Advertising Address: 8th Floor, Bridgewater House, Whitworth Street, MANCHESTER, M1 6LT
Tel: 0161 832 6000 **Fax:** 0161 832 4176
Email: simon.smith@tenalpspublishing.com
Web site: http://www.iqmedia.co.uk
Publisher: Ten Alps Publishing
Frequency: 3 issues yearly - Published in January, April and September
Cover Price: Free
Circulation: 20,000 (Publisher's Statement)
Usual Pagination: 24
Editor: Cathy Baldwin; **News Editor:** Julie Nightingale; **Advertising Manager:** Simon Smith
Summary of Content: Magazine covering educational issues with an emphasis on ICT.
Readership/Target Audience: Aimed at educational professionals in both primary and secondary schools, heads of department and heads of school.
ADVERTISING RATES:
Full Page Colour £1950.00
Agency Commission: 10%
Mechanical Data: Film: Digital, Type Area: 306 x 256mm, Col Length: 306mm, Page Width: 256mm, No. of Columns (Display): 2
Copy instructions: Copy Date: 3 weeks prior to publication date
BUSINESS: CHURCH & SCHOOL EQUIPMENT & EDUCATION: Education

IR MAGAZINE
35265U1F-265

Formerly: Investor Relations Magazine
Editorial Address: Churchill House, 142-146 Old Street, LONDON, EC1V 9BW **Tel:** 020 7251 7510
Fax: 020 7490 4349
Email: clare.harrison@thecrossbordergroup.com
Advertising Address: As above. **Tel:** 020 7251 7500
Email: alexa.clark@thecrossbordergroup.com
Web site: http://www.irmagazine.com
ISSN: 0958-6679
Publisher: Cross Border Ltd

Frequency: Monthly - Published around the 25th of the month prior to the cover month
Free to qualifying individuals
Annual Sub.: £150.00
Circulation: 15,000 (Publisher's Statement)
Usual Pagination: 86
Editor: Clare Harrison; **Executive Editor:** Neil Stewart; **Managing Director:** Janet Dignan; **Advertising Manager:** Alexa Clark; **Publisher:** Ian Richman
Summary of Content: Magazine covering all matters of interest to investor relations professionals.
Readership/Target Audience: Read by investor relations professionals including IR officers, CFOs and corporate secretaries and the relevant service providers.
ADVERTISING RATES:
Full Page Colour £4195.00
Agency Commission: 10%
Mechanical Data: Type Area: 250 x 188mm, Bleed Size: 276 x 214mm, Trim Size: 270 x 208mm, Col Length: 250mm, Film: Digital, Page Width: 188mm
Average advertising content per issue: 40%
BUSINESS: FINANCE & ECONOMICS: Investment

IRELAND'S FORECOURT AND CONVENIENCE RETAILER
1616495U53-682

Formerly: Forecourt and Convenience Retailer
Editorial Address: Penton House, 38 Heron Road, Sydenham Business Park, BELFAST, BT3 9LE
Tel: 028 9045 7457 **Fax:** 028 9045 6622
Email: sharon.moody@pentonpublications.co.uk
Advertising Address: As above.
Email: brenda.courtney@pentonpublications.co.uk
Web site: http://www.pentongroup.com
Publisher: Penton Publications Ltd
Date Established: 2003
Frequency: 6 issues yearly
Cover Price: Free
Circulation: 4,331 (ABC 01/07/2008 to 30706/2009)
Usual Pagination: 72
Editor: Sharon Moody; **Advertising Manager:** Brenda Courtney
Summary of Content: Magazine covering all aspects of forecourt retailing, including interviews and news.
Readership/Target Audience: Aimed at forecourt owners and oil company executives.
ADVERTISING RATES:
Full Page Colour £1895.00
Agency Commission: 10%
Mechanical Data: Bleed Size: 303 x 216mm, Trim Size: 297 x 210mm, Film: Digital
Copy instructions: Copy Date: 1 week prior to publication date
Average advertising content per issue: 50%
BUSINESS: RETAILING & WHOLESALING

THE IRIS YEAR BOOK
38134U26D-65

Editorial Address: Edgebolton, Shawbury, Shrewsbury, SHROPSHIRE, SY4 4EL **Tel:** 01939 251173
Fax: 01939 251311
Email: enquiries@claireaustin-hardyplants.co.uk
Advertising Address: As above.
Web site: http://www.claireaustin-hardyplants.co.uk
Publisher: British Iris Society
Date Established: 1930
Frequency: Annual - Published in December
Free to qualifying individuals
Circulation: 550 (Publisher's Statement)
Usual Pagination: 128
Editor: Claire Austin
Summary of Content: Journal containing horticultural and scientific articles and reports for UK and overseas.
Readership/Target Audience: Aimed at amateur, professional and student horticulturists and botanists.
ADVERTISING: No Advertising taken
BUSINESS: GARDEN TRADE: Garden Trade Horticulture

IRISH BEAUTY
1659842U15R-11

Editorial Address: 3 Charnwood Street, DERBY, DE1 2GT
Tel: 01332 227683
Email: melissa@beautyserve.net
Advertising Address: As above. **Tel:** 01332 227689
Email: ruth@beautyserve.net
Web site: http://www.irishbeauty.com
Publisher: Fairtrade Media
Date Established: 2004
Frequency: 10 issues yearly
Free to qualifying individuals
Annual Sub.: EUR42.00
Circulation: 8,416 (Publisher's Statement)
Usual Pagination: 68
Editor: Melissa Dennis; **Advertising Manager:** Ruth Naylor; **Publisher:** Dave Horton
Summary of Content: Magazine covering all aspects of the Irish beauty, nails and spa industry, including news, product reviews and competitions.

Readership/Target Audience: Aimed at industry professionals.
ADVERTISING RATES:
Full Page Colour £845.00
Agency Commission: 10%
Mechanical Data: Trim Size: 223 x 168mm, Type Area: 203 x 148mm, Bleed Size: 233 x 178mm, Col Length: 203mm, Page Width: 148mm, Film: Digital
Copy instructions: Copy Date: 4 weeks prior to publication date
Average advertising content per issue: 30%
BUSINESS: COSMETICS & HAIRDRESSING: Cosmetics & Hairdressing Related

IRISH DENTIST
40395U56D-85

Editorial Address: 1 Hertford House, Hugo Gryn Way, Farm Close, SHENLEY, WD7 9AB **Tel:** 01923 851777
Fax: 01923 851778
Email: nicola.kramer@fmc.co.uk
Advertising Address: As above.
Email: alice.moody@fmc.co.uk
Web site: http://www.irishdentist.ie
ISSN: 1466-0679
Publisher: Finlayson Media Communications Ltd
Frequency: 10 issues yearly - Published in the last week of the month prior to the cover
Cover Price: Free
Circulation: 2,800 (Publisher's Statement)
Usual Pagination: 84
Editor: Siobhan Lewney; **Advertising Manager:** Alice Moody
Summary of Content: Journal covering all aspects of dental practice in Ireland including current affairs, opinion pieces, business and product information.
Readership/Target Audience: Aimed at dental professionals in Ireland.
ADVERTISING RATES:
Full Page Colour £2450.00
Agency Commission: 10%
Mechanical Data: Type Area: 287 x 200mm, Bleed Size: 303 x 216mm, Trim Size: 297 x 210mm, Col Length: 287mm, Page Width: 200mm, Film: Digital
Copy instructions: Copy Date: 6 weeks prior to publication date
Average advertising content per issue: 50%
BUSINESS: HEALTH & MEDICAL: Dental

IRISH FARMERS JOURNAL (NORTHERN IRELAND)
1694373U21A-1116

Editorial Address: 69 Ballyrainey Road, NEWTOWNARDS, BT23 5AF **Tel:** 07802 458987
Email: farmersjournal@btinternet.com
Advertising Address: The Mount Business & Conference Centre, 2 Woodstock Link, BELFAST, BT6 8DD
Tel: 028 9065 6407 **Fax:** 028 9067 1877
Email: gmcneill@farmersjournal.ie
Web site: http://www.farmersjournal.ie
Publisher: The Agricultural Trust
Frequency: Weekly - Published on Thursday
Cover Price: £1.30
Circulation: 6,000 (Publisher's Statement)
Usual Pagination: 112
Editor: James Campbell; **Advertising Manager:** Gill McNeill
Summary of Content: Magazine covering all aspects of agriculture.
Readership/Target Audience: Aimed at those working within the agriculture industry.
ADVERTISING RATES:
Full Page Mono EUR9288.00
Full Page Colour EUR14040.00
Agency Commission: 10%
Mechanical Data: Type Area: 340 x 262mm, Trim Size: 360 x 290mm, Col Length: 340mm, Page Width: 262mm, Col Widths (Display): 40mm, No. of Columns (Display): 6, Print Process: Web-fed offset litho, Film: Digital
Copy instructions: Copy Date: 1 week prior to publication date
BUSINESS: AGRICULTURE & FARMING

THE IRISH FRANCHISE MAGAZINE
1691292U14A-547

Editorial Address: Franchise House, 56 Surrey Street, NORWICH, NR1 3FD **Tel:** 01603 620301 **Fax:** 01603 630174
Email: stuarta@fdsltd.com
Advertising Address: As above.
Email: enquiries@fdsltd.com
Web site: http://www.irishfranchisemagazine.net
ISSN: 1463-0354
Publisher: Franchise Development Services Ltd
Date Established: 1999
Frequency: Half-yearly - Published in April and December
Cover Price: £3.50
Free to qualifying individuals
Editor: Stuart Anderson; **Advertising Manager:** Stuart Anderson

Summary of Content: Magazine covering advice and guidance to perspective and existing franchisees.
Readership/Target Audience: Aimed at individuals seeking to operate a franchise.
ADVERTISING RATES:
Full Page Colour £1465.00
Agency Commission: 10%
Mechanical Data: Type Area: 270 x 190mm, Bleed Size: 303 x 213mm, Trim Size: 297 x 210mm, Col Length: 270mm, Page Width: 190mm, Film: Digital
Copy instructions: Copy Date: 2 weeks prior to publication date
Average advertising content per issue: 75%
BUSINESS: COMMERCE, INDUSTRY & MANAGEMENT

IRISH WOODWORKING & FURNITURE NEWS
39477U46-18_50

Editorial Address: The Old Sun, Crete Hall Road, GRAVESEND, DA11 9AA **Tel:** 01474 536535
Fax: 01474 536552
Email: publications@nelton.co.uk
Advertising Address: As above.
Email: iwfn@nelton.co.uk
Web site: http://www.nelton.co.uk
ISSN: 1745-2198
Publisher: Nelton Publications
Date Established: 1997
Frequency: Quarterly
Free to qualifying individuals
Annual Sub.: £25.00
Circulation: 4,500 (Publisher's Statement)
Usual Pagination: 40
Editor: Neil Herbert-Smith; **Advertising Manager:** Donna Ludbrook
Summary of Content: News of machinery, components and services to the woodworking and furniture industries in Eire and Northern Ireland.
Readership/Target Audience: Aimed at manufacturers of joinery, furniture and other timber based products.
ADVERTISING RATES:
Full Page Mono EUR901.00
Full Page Colour EUR1350.00
SCC EUR13.70
Agency Commission: 10%
Mechanical Data: Page Width: 189mm, Type Area: 277 x 189mm, Bleed Size: 305 x 216mm, Trim Size: 297 x 210mm, Film: Positive, right reading, emulsion side down. Digital, Print Process: Sheet-fed litho, Screen: Mono 40 lpc Colour 54 lpc, Col Length: 277mm
BUSINESS: TIMBER, WOOD & FORESTRY

IRON & STEEL TODAY
1861847U27-215

Editorial Address: Gresham House, 54 High Street, SHOREHAM-BY-SEA, BN43 5DB **Tel:** 01273 453033
Fax: 01273 453085
Email: paulbinns@mmcpublications.co.uk
Web site: http://www.mmcpublications.co.uk
Publisher: Iron & Steel Publishing (MMC)
Date Established: 2007
Frequency: 5 issues yearly
Cover Price: £16.00
Free to qualifying individuals
Annual Sub.: £49.00
Circulation: 5,000 (Publisher's Statement)
Usual Pagination: 48
Editor: Paul Binns; **Publisher:** Paul Binns
Summary of Content: Magazine featuring news, contracts and people, commercial and technical features, product information, website reviews and a buyers guide.
Readership/Target Audience: Aimed at managers involved in the purchase of plant equipment, raw materials, finished steel products, steel producing, processing, trading and stockholding companies.
BUSINESS: METAL, IRON & STEEL

IRONMAKING AND STEELMAKING INCORPORATING STEEL WORLD
38154U27-45

Editorial Address: 1 Carlton House Terrace, LONDON, SW1Y 5AF **Tel:** 020 7451 7300 **Fax:** 020 7451 7307
Email: irs@materials.org.uk
Advertising Address: Suite 1C, Josephs Well, Hanover Walk, LEEDS, LS3 1AB **Tel:** 0113 243 2800
Fax: 0113 386 8178
Email: n.taylor@maney.co.uk
Web site: http://www.maney.co.uk
ISSN: 0301-9233
Publisher: Maney Publishing
Date Established: 1974
Frequency: 6 issues yearly
Annual Sub.: £445.00
Circulation: 900 (Publisher's Statement)
Usual Pagination: 88
Editor: Mark Hull; **Executive Editor:** David Price;
Advertising Manager: Natalie Taylor; **Managing Editor:** Mark Hull

Summary of Content: Journal covering all aspects of iron and steel-making, and of steel products and applications.
Readership/Target Audience: Aimed at those involved in the iron and steel-making industry, including scientists and product development companies.
ADVERTISING RATES:
Full Page Mono £1000.00
Full Page Colour £1600.00
Agency Commission: 10%
Mechanical Data: Type Area: 266 x 188mm, Bleed Size: 305 x 215mm, Trim Size: 297 x 210mm, Film: Digital, Col Length: 266mm, Page Width: 188mm
Copy instructions: Copy Date: 1st of the month prior to publication date
BUSINESS: METAL, IRON & STEEL

IRRV BENEFIT
1659808U32C-301

Editorial Address: 41 Doughty Street, LONDON, WC1N 2LF
Tel: 020 7691 8972 **Fax:** 01843 290919
Email: jcroberts54@hotmail.com
Advertising Address: Tregartha Dinnie Ltd, Chancery House, 199 Silbury Boulevard, MILTON KEYNES, MK9 1JL
Tel: 01908 306500 **Fax:** 01908 306505
Email: ads@tregartha-dinnie.co.uk
Web site: http://www.irrv.org.uk
Publisher: IRRV
Date Established: 1996
Frequency: 6 issues yearly
Annual Sub.: £495.00
Circulation: 2,000 (Publisher's Statement)
Usual Pagination: 28
Editor: John Roberts; **Advertising Manager:** Victoria Foskett; **Managing Editor:** John Roberts
Summary of Content: Magazine covering all aspects of housing, council tax and welfare benefits.
Readership/Target Audience: Aimed at housing benefits officers within local authorities.
ADVERTISING RATES:
Full Page Mono £325.00
Full Page Colour £620.00
Agency Commission: 10%
Mechanical Data: Type Area: 277 x 190mm, Bleed Size: 303 x 216mm, Trim Size: 297 x 210mm, Col Length: 277mm, Page Width: 190mm, Film: Digital
Copy instructions: Copy Date: 15th of the month prior to publication date
Average advertising content per issue: 40%
BUSINESS: LOCAL GOVERNMENT, LEISURE & RECREATION: Local Government Finance

IRRV INSIGHT
38413U32C-70

Editorial Address: 41 Doughty Street, LONDON, WC1N 2LF
Tel: 020 7831 3505 **Fax:** 01843 290919
Email: jcroberts54@hotmail.com
Advertising Address: Tregartha Dinnie Ltd, Chancery House, 199 Silbury Boulevard, MILTON KEYNES, MK9 1JL
Tel: 01908 306500 **Fax:** 01908 306505
Email: ads@tregartha-dinnie.co.uk
Web site: http://www.irrv.org.uk
ISSN: 1361-1305
Publisher: IRRV
Date Established: 1995
Frequency: 11 issues yearly
Cover Price: £5.50
Free to qualifying individuals
Circulation: 5,500 (Publisher's Statement)
Usual Pagination: 36
Editor: John Roberts; **Managing Editor:** John Roberts
Summary of Content: Publication containing articles on land and property valuations, local authority revenue collection, council tax, business rate collection and local authority benefits administration.
Readership/Target Audience: Read by members of the Institute of Revenues, Rating and Valuation, plus people in government and business.
ADVERTISING RATES:
Full Page Mono £846.00
Full Page Colour £1615.00
Agency Commission: 10%
Mechanical Data: Page Width: 190mm, Trim Size: 297 x 210mm, Type Area: 277 x 190mm, Col Length: 277mm, Bleed Size: 303 x 216mm, Film: Digital
Copy instructions: Copy Date: 5 weeks prior to publication date
BUSINESS: LOCAL GOVERNMENT, LEISURE & RECREATION: Local Government Finance

IRRV VALUER
761864U32C-300

Editorial Address: 41 Doughty Street, LONDON, WC1N 2LF
Tel: 020 7831 3505 **Fax:** 01843 290919
Email: jcroberts54@hotmail.com
Web site: http://www.irrv.org.uk
ISSN: 1361-1305
Publisher: IRRV
Date Established: 2002
Frequency: Quarterly
Cover Price: £10.00

Free to qualifying individuals
Circulation: 2,000 (Publisher's Statement)
Usual Pagination: 32
Editor: John Roberts; **Managing Editor:** John Roberts
Summary of Content: Magazine of the Institute of Revenues, Rating and Valuation covering services and developments in land and property valuation, in particular in relation to rating.
Readership/Target Audience: Read by members, practitioners and valuation professionals.
ADVERTISING: No Advertising taken
BUSINESS: LOCAL GOVERNMENT, LEISURE & RECREATION: Local Government Finance

IRS PAY INTELLIGENCE
34946U1A-225

Editorial Address: Quadrant House, The Quadrant, SUTTON, SM2 5AS **Tel:** 020 8652 2251 **Fax:** 020 8652 4394
Email: sheila.attwood@rbi.co.uk
Web site: http://www.xperthr.co.uk
ISSN: 1360-8711
Publisher: Reed Business Information
Frequency: Monthly
Annual Sub.: £276.00
Usual Pagination: 12
Editor: Sheila Attwood
Summary of Content: Magazine providing regular updates on pay and inflation.
Readership/Target Audience: Read by pay specialists, union employers and economic forecasting organisations.
ADVERTISING: No Advertising taken
BUSINESS: FINANCE & ECONOMICS

IS OPPORTUNITIES
35726U2F-41

Editorial Address: 3rd Floor, Hollinwood Business Centre, Albert Street, OLDHAM, OL8 3QL **Tel:** 0161 683 8000
Fax: 0161 683 8001
Email: john.kirkbride@worldsfair.co.uk
Advertising Address: As above.
Email: craig.mills@worldsfair.co.uk
Web site: http://www.isopps.com
ISSN: 1367-4684
Publisher: The World's Fair Ltd
Frequency: Monthly
Cover Price: Free
Editor: John Kirkbride
Summary of Content: Magazine providing the latest industry news, surveys, problem solving pieces and "how to" features for IT salespeople and marketing professionals.
Readership/Target Audience: Aimed at sales and marketing personnel within the IT industry.
ADVERTISING RATES:
Full Page Colour £1650.00
Agency Commission: 10%
Mechanical Data: Trim Size: 297 x 210mm, Type Area: 274 x 185mm, Bleed Size: 303 x 216mm, Col Length: 274mm, Page Width: 185mm, Film: Digital
Copy instructions: Copy Date: 2 weeks prior to publication date
BUSINESS: COMMUNICATIONS, ADVERTISING & MARKETING: Selling

ISF INTERNATIONAL SECURITIES FINANCE
35258U1F-275

Formerly: International Securities Lending
Editorial Address: Nestor House, Playhouse Yard, LONDON, EC4V 5EX **Tel:** 020 7779 8990
Fax: 020 7779 8792
Email: cmacdonald@euromoneyplc.com
Advertising Address: As above. **Tel:** 020 7779 8888
Email: jhodder@euromoneyplc.com
Web site: http://www.isfmagazine.com
Publisher: Euromoney Institutional Investor plc
Frequency: 6 issues yearly
Annual Sub.: £345.00
Circulation: 7,185 (Publisher's Statement)
Editor: Craig MacDonald; **Advertising Manager:** Jonathan Hodder; **Publisher:** Jonathan Hodder
Summary of Content: Magazine focusing on the expanding market for international debt and equity financing via stock lending, repo and swaps. Includes reports on market developments, participants, tax and regulatory issues.
Readership/Target Audience: Aimed at repo traders, stock lenders and departments within banks.
ADVERTISING RATES:
Full Page Colour £7850.00
Agency Commission: 15%
Mechanical Data: Page Width: 175mm, Type Area: 236 x 175mm, Bleed Size: 276 x 211mm, Trim Size: 270 x 205mm, Col Length: 236mm, Print Process: Offset litho, Film: Positive, right reading, emulsion side down. Digital
Average advertising content per issue: 30%
BUSINESS: FINANCE & ECONOMICS: Investment

Business Magazines

ISLAMIC BANKER

1882349U1C-361

Editorial Address: 30 Chelmsford Square, LONDON, NW10 3AR **Tel:** 020 8459 4310
Email: islambank@aol.com
Publisher: Mushtak Parker Associates
Frequency: Monthly
Annual Sub: £380.00
Circulation: 2,000 (Publisher's Statement)
Editor: Mushtak Parker
Summary of Content: Magazine featuring news, analysis and comment about the financial sector with a special focus on Islamic banking.
Readership/Target Audience: Aimed at government agencies, regulators, bankers, corporates, lawyers and accountants.
BUSINESS: FINANCE & ECONOMICS: Banking

ISLAMIC BANKING AND FINANCE

1616396U1C-351

Editorial Address: 69 Grand Parade, BRIGHTON, BN2 9TS **Tel:** 05601 169695
Email: david@islamicbankingandfinance.com
Advertising Address: Suite 3, 20 Old Steine, BRIGHTON, BN1 1EL **Tel:** 05601 169695 **Fax:** 0700 603 4010
Email: advertising@islamicbankingandfinance.com
Web site: http://www.islamicbankingandfinance.com
ISSN: 1752-2749
Publisher: New Millennium Publishing
Date Established: 2003
Frequency: 6 issues yearly
Free to qualifying individuals
Annual Sub.: £30.00
Circulation: 8,000 (Publisher's Statement)
Editor: David Williams; **Advertising Manager:** David Williams
Summary of Content: Magazine reporting on Shariah compliant financial products.
Readership/Target Audience: Aimed at decision makers within Islamic banks.
ADVERTISING RATES:
Full Page Mono £2995.00
Full Page Colour £2995.00
Agency Commission: 10%
Mechanical Data: Type Area: 269 x 190mm, Col Length: 269mm, Page Width: 190mm, Bleed Size: 303 x 216mm, Film: Digital
Copy instructions: Copy Date: 7 days prior to publication date
Average advertising content per issue: 35%
BUSINESS: FINANCE & ECONOMICS: Banking

ISLAND BUSINESS

41301U63B-618

Editorial Address: Mill Court, Furrlongs, NEWPORT, PO30 2AA **Tel:** 01983 520777 **Fax:** 01983 554555
Email: chamber@iwchamber.co.uk
Advertising Address: The Sixty Mile Publishing Co Ltd, 31 Cambridge Road, EAST COWES, PO32 6AH
Tel: 01983 209892
Email: production@60mile.co.uk
Web site: http://www.iwchamber.co.uk
Publisher: IW Chamber of Commerce
Frequency: Monthly - Published at the beginning of the cover month
Cover Price: £2.25
Free to qualifying individuals
Circulation: 2,000 (Publisher's Statement)
Usual Pagination: 36
Editor: Kevin Wilson; **Managing Editor:** Zoe Stroud
Summary of Content: Magazine covering national business news and reports relating to businesses in and around the Isle of Wight.
Readership/Target Audience: Aimed at chamber members and passengers on ferries between Cowes and Southampton.
ADVERTISING RATES:
Full Page Colour £775.00
Mechanical Data: Type Area: 267 x 180mm, Col Length: 267mm, Page Width: 180mm, Bleed Size: 303 x 216mm, Trim Size: 297 x 210mm, Film: Digital
Copy instructions: Copy Date: 10 days prior to publication date
BUSINESS: REGIONAL BUSINESS: Regional Business English Counties

IT ADVISER

1659743U5R-666

Editorial Address: National Computing Centre, Oxford Road, MANCHESTER, M1 7ED **Tel:** 0161 242 2170
Fax: 0161 242 2499
Email: ian.jones@ncc.co.uk
Advertising Address: As above. **Tel:** 0161 242 2118
Email: sonia.kaur@ncc.co.uk
Web site: http://www.ncc.co.uk
ISSN: 1745-8730
Publisher: The National Computing Centre
Date Established: 2001
Frequency: Quarterly

Free to qualifying individuals
Circulation: 10,076 (Publisher's Statement)
Usual Pagination: 36
Editor: Michelle O'Toole; **Advertising Manager:** Sonia Kaur; **Publisher:** Ian Jones
Summary of Content: Magazine promoting the effective use of technology within businesses.
Readership/Target Audience: Aimed at IT directors, IT managers and key decision makers in business and IT.
ADVERTISING RATES:
Full Page Colour £2750.00
Agency Commission: 10%
Mechanical Data: Bleed Size: 303 x 216mm, Trim Size: 297 x 210mm, Film: Digital
BUSINESS: COMPUTERS & AUTOMATION: Computers Related

IT EUROPA

36296U5R-140

Formerly: Systems Europa
Editorial Address: 3rd Floor, Armstrong House, 38 Market Square, UXBRIDGE, UB8 1LH **Tel:** 01895 454595
Fax: 01895 454598
Email: john.garratt@iteuropa.com
Web site: http://www.iteuropa.com
Publisher: BPL Business Media Ltd
Frequency: 20 issues yearly
Annual Sub.: £495.00
Circulation: 5,000 (Publisher's Statement)
Usual Pagination: 40
Editor: John Garratt
Summary of Content: Newsletter providing information and analysis on Europe's IT and consumer electronics channels including enterprise, SME and consumer sectors in Europe. Includes features on ISVs assemblers, distributors retailers, system integrators, VARs, outsourcing firms and IT service companies.
Readership/Target Audience: Aimed at senior managers and directors within the IT industry.
ADVERTISING: No Advertising taken
BUSINESS: COMPUTERS & AUTOMATION: Computers Related

IT RESELLER

36298U5R-157

Formerly: IT Reseller Magazine
Editorial Address: Latimer House, 189 High Street, POTTERS BAR, EN6 5DA **Tel:** 01707 664200
Fax: 01707 664800
Email: editor@ibcpub.com
Advertising Address: As above.
Email: davidlee@ibcpub.com
Web site: http://www.itrportal.com
ISSN: 1369-880X
Publisher: Interactive Business Communications Ltd
Date Established: 1997
Frequency: 5 issues yearly
Cover Price: Free
Circulation: 10,000 (Publisher's Statement)
Usual Pagination: 92
Editor: Ed Holden; **Advertising Manager:** David Lee; **Publisher:** David Lee
Summary of Content: Magazine dealing with issues affecting companies in the European IT Channel, including a feature section on automatic identification bar code and RFID, printing and labelling, document management, network technology for LANs and WANs, wired and wireless, including security products and UPS.
Readership/Target Audience: Aimed at IT re-sellers, VARs, distributors, system integrators and OEMs.
ADVERTISING RATES:
Full Page Colour £3950.00
Agency Commission: 10%
Mechanical Data: Bleed Size: 303 x 213mm, Trim Size: 297 x 210mm
Copy instructions: Copy Date: 2 weeks prior to publication date
Average advertising content per issue: 35%
BUSINESS: COMPUTERS & AUTOMATION: Computers Related

IT TRAINING

37052U14F-24_93

Editorial Address: 1st Floor, Block D, North Star House, North Star Avenue, SWINDON, SN2 1FA **Tel:** 01793 417417
Fax: 01793 417444
Email: helen.boddy@hq.bcs.org.uk
Advertising Address: Mongoose Media, 2 Lonsdale Road, LONDON, NW6 6RD **Tel:** 020 7306 0300
Fax: 020 7306 0301
Email: ittraining@mongoosemedia.com
Web site: http://www.bcs.org/ittraining
ISSN: 0954-7940
Publisher: British Computer Society
Date Established: 1988
Frequency: Quarterly
Free to qualifying individuals
Circulation: 13,000 (Publisher's Statement)
Usual Pagination: 36

Editor: Helen Boddy; **Managing Editor:** Brian Runciman
Summary of Content: Independent magazine for training and development, specialising in information technology training and skills development.
Readership/Target Audience: Aimed at purchasers and specifiers of IT training products and services within corporate organisations.
ADVERTISING RATES:
Full Page Mono £3000.00
Full Page Colour £3000.00
Agency Commission: 10%
Mechanical Data: Type Area: 235 x 186mm, Bleed Size: 286 x 216mm, Trim Size: 280 x 210mm, Col Length: 235mm, Page Width: 186mm, Film: Digital
Copy instructions: Copy Date: 4 weeks prior to publication date
BUSINESS: COMMERCE, INDUSTRY & MANAGEMENT: Training & Recruitment

ITIJ INTERNATIONAL TRAVEL INSURANCE JOURNAL

1609380U1D-403

Editorial Address: 43 Colston Street, BRISTOL, BS1 5AX **Tel:** 0117 922 6600 **Fax:** 0117 925 2040
Email: mail@itij.co.uk
Advertising Address: As above. **Tel:** 0117 925 5151
Fax: 0117 929 2023
Email: dave@itij.co.uk
Web site: http://www.itij.co.uk
ISSN: 1743-1522
Publisher: Voyageur Publishing
Date Established: 1999
Frequency: Monthly - Published around the beginning of the cover month
Cover Price: Free
Circulation: 29,500 (Publisher's Statement)
Usual Pagination: 40
Editor: Mandy Aitchison; **Editor-in-Chief:** Ian Cameron; **Advertising Manager:** David Fitzpatrick
Summary of Content: Journal covering the travel insurance industry including news, reviews and information on markets around the world.
Readership/Target Audience: Aimed at those working in the travel insurance industry: insurers, underwriters, intermediaries, air ambulance providers, hospitals and clinics, assistance companies, cost containment companies and PPO's.
ADVERTISING RATES:
Full Page Colour £2400.00
Agency Commission: 10%
Mechanical Data: Type Area: 363 x 273mm, Bleed Size: 404 x 303mm, Trim Size: 363 x 273mm, Col Length: 363mm, Film: Digital, Page Width: 273mm
Copy instructions: Copy Date: 1 week prior to publication date
Average advertising content per issue: 30%
BUSINESS: FINANCE & ECONOMICS: Insurance

ITNOW

35999U5A-52

Formerly: The Computer Bulletin
Editorial Address: 1st Floor, Block D, North Star House, North Star Avenue, SWINDON, SN2 1FA **Tel:** 01793 417417
Fax: 01793 417444
Email: editor@bcs.org.uk
Advertising Address: Mongoose Media Ltd, 2 Lonsdale Road, LONDON, NW6 6RD **Tel:** 020 7306 0300
Fax: 020 7306 0301
Email: bcs@mongoosemedia.com
Web site: http://www.bcs.org/publications
ISSN: 0010-4531
Publisher: BCS
Date Established: 1957
Frequency: 6 issues yearly - Published on the 15th of the cover month
Free to qualifying individuals
Annual Sub.: £92.00
Circulation: 65,000 (Publisher's Statement)
Usual Pagination: 36
Editor: Brian Runciman; **Managing Editor:** Brian Runciman
Summary of Content: Magazine containing features on the latest developments in information systems, IT innovation and technological developments.
Readership/Target Audience: Aimed at IT professionals, heads of IT, directors, software systems engineering, IT consultants, university researchers, programmers and designers.
ADVERTISING RATES:
Full Page Mono £1715.00
Full Page Colour £2285.00
Agency Commission: 10%
Mechanical Data: Type Area: 258 x 180mm, Col Length: 258mm, Film: Digital, Page Width: 180mm, Bleed Size: 297 x 210mm, Trim Size: 303 x 210mm
Average advertising content per issue: 17%
BUSINESS: COMPUTERS & AUTOMATION: Automation & Instrumentation

ITS INTERNATIONAL
39581U49A-134

Editorial Address: Horizon House, Azalea Drive, SWANLEY, BR8 8JR **Tel:** 01322 612055 **Fax:** 0870 751 8327
Email: jbarnes@ropl.com
Advertising Address: As above. **Fax:** 01322 612060
Email: media@ropl.com
Web site: http://www.itsinternational.com
ISSN: 1463-6344
Publisher: Route One Publishing Ltd
Date Established: 1995
Frequency: 6 issues yearly - Published at the end of the 1st cover month
Free to qualifying individuals
Annual Sub.: £165.00
Circulation: 21,749 (BPA Worldwide 01/01/2008 to 30/06/2008)
Usual Pagination: 64
Editor: Jason Barnes; **News Editor:** James Foster; **Managing Director:** Andrew Barriball; **Advertising Manager:** Andrew Barriball; **Publisher:** Andrew Barriball
Summary of Content: International journal of advanced technology for traffic management and urban mobility.
Readership/Target Audience: Aimed at ITS (intelligent transport systems) professionals in over 140 countries.
ADVERTISING RATES:
Full Page Colour £4005.00
Agency Commission: 10%
Mechanical Data: Trim Size: 297 x 210mm, Film: Digital, Type Area: 256 x 187mm, Col Length: 256mm, Page Width: 187mm
Copy instructions: Copy Date: 4 weeks prior to publication date
Average advertising content per issue: 40%
BUSINESS: TRANSPORT

IT'S OUR BUSINESS
35267U1F-277

Editorial Address: 2 Ridgmount Street, LONDON, WC1E 7AA **Tel:** 020 7436 9936 **Fax:** 020 7580 0016
Email: fhackworth@hurlstons.com
Web site: http://www.mhcc.co.uk/esop
Publisher: Employee Share Ownership Centre
Date Established: 1988
Frequency: Monthly
Free to qualifying individuals
Annual Sub.: £175.00
Circulation: 200 (Publisher's Statement)
Usual Pagination: 4
Editor: Fred Hackworth
Summary of Content: Official newsletter of the Employee Share Ownership Scheme, focusing on employee share and share option plans, executive remuneration and methods of funding domestic and global share plans such as derivatives.
Readership/Target Audience: Aimed at accountants, bankers, corporate lawyers, consultants, trustees and HR specialists.
ADVERTISING: No Advertising taken
BUSINESS: FINANCE & ECONOMICS: Investment

IVCA UPDATE
39112U43D-12

Editorial Address: 19 Pepper Street, Glengall Bridge, LONDON, E14 9RP **Tel:** 020 7512 0571 **Fax:** 020 7512 0591
Email: info@ivca.org
Advertising Address: As above.
Email: davecomley@ivca.org
Web site: http://www.ivca.org
Publisher: International Visual Communication Association
Frequency: 6 issues yearly
Cover Price: Free
Circulation: 2,000 (Publisher's Statement)
Usual Pagination: 16
Editor: Philip Fey
Summary of Content: Newsletter of the International Visual Communications Association.
Readership/Target Audience: Aimed at people involved in corporate visual communication, including members of the IVCA and relevant companies and organisations.
ADVERTISING RATES:
Full Page Colour £1300.00
Mechanical Data: Film: Digital, Bleed Size: 303 x 216mm, Trim Size: 297 x 210mm
Average advertising content per issue: 10%
BUSINESS: ELECTRICAL RETAIL TRADE: Video

IVT INTERNATIONAL
37612U19B-340

Formerly: IVT Europe
Editorial Address: Abinger House, Church Street, DORKING, RH4 1DF **Tel:** 01306 743744 **Fax:** 01306 887546
Email: ivt@ukintpress.com
Advertising Address: As above. **Fax:** 01306 743755
Email: k.barrett@ukintpress.com
Web site: http://www.ukintpress.com
ISSN: 1471-115X
Publisher: UKIP Media & Events Ltd
Date Established: 1997

Frequency: 6 issues yearly - Published at the end of the 1st cover month
Free to qualifying individuals
Annual Sub.: £105.00
Circulation: 11,972 (ABC 01/01/2008 to 31/12/2008)
Usual Pagination: 96
Editor: Richard Carr; **Advertising Manager:** Kevin Barrett
Summary of Content: Magazine covering design and engineering of materials handling, construction, agricultural and specialist vehicles and their components.
Readership/Target Audience: Aimed at designers, engineers and purchasing managers of industrial vehicle OEMs worldwide.
ADVERTISING: Rates on application
Agency Commission: 15%
Copy instructions: Copy Date: 4 weeks prior to publication date
Average advertising content per issue: 40%
BUSINESS: ENGINEERING & MACHINERY: Engineering - Design

IWO JOURNAL
39055U42C-370

Editorial Address: 4 Carlton Court, Team Valley, GATESHEAD, NE11 0AZ **Tel:** 0191 422 0088
Fax: 0191 422 0087
Email: lyndsey@iwo.org.uk
Advertising Address: Distinctive Publishing, 24 Lancaster Street, Somerhill, NEWCASTLE UPON TYNE, NE4 6EU
Tel: 0191 298 3571 **Fax:** 0191 298 3561
Email: john.nielson@distinctivepublishing.co.uk
Web site: http://www.iwo.org.uk
Publisher: IWO (Institution of Water Officers)
Date Established: 1950
Frequency: Quarterly
Free to qualifying individuals
Annual Sub.: £30.00
Circulation: 2,000 (Publisher's Statement)
Usual Pagination: 36
Editor: Lyndsey Campbell
Summary of Content: Journal containing technical articles, product launches, engineering section, environmental section, IWO area news reports and water industry related news. Includes section dedicated to products and services, highlighting products, equipment and services both established and new to the water industry market.
Readership/Target Audience: Aimed at members, senior management, engineers, key personnel and decision makers within the water and waste industries and subscribers as well as manufacturers of equipment and suppliers of services to the industry.
ADVERTISING RATES:
Full Page Colour £1000.00
Agency Commission: 10%
Mechanical Data: Type Area: 275 x 182mm, Bleed Size: 303 x 216mm, Trim Size: 297 x 210mm, Film: Digital, Col Length: 275mm, Page Width: 182mm
Average advertising content per issue: 10%
BUSINESS: CONSTRUCTION: Water Engineering

THE IWSR DRINKS RECORD
1849451U9C-101

Formerly: The IWSR (International Wine & Spirits Record)
Editorial Address: 254-258 Goswell Road, LONDON, EC1V 7EB **Tel:** 020 7689 6841 **Fax:** 020 7689 6827
Email: alsmith@iwsr.co.uk
Web site: http://www.iwsr.co.uk
ISSN: 1749-3331
Publisher: System Three Communications
Frequency: 11 issues yearly - Combined issue December/January
Annual Sub.: £195.00
Circulation: 10,000 (Publisher's Statement)
Usual Pagination: 32
Editor: Alex Smith
Summary of Content: Magazine covering wines and spirits with the latest trends, market insights and news, company interviews and category and company reports.
Readership/Target Audience: Aimed at international drinks groups, medium sized and smaller independent drinks companies as well as investment analysts, management consultants and packaging companies.
BUSINESS: DRINKS & LICENSED TRADE: Licensed Trade, Wines & Spirits

JANE'S AERO-ENGINES
36355U6A-97_130

Formerly: Jane's Aeroengines
Editorial Address: Sentinel House, 163 Brighton Road, COULSDON, CR5 2YH **Tel:** 020 8700 3700
Fax: 020 8763 1005
Email: info@janes.com
Advertising Address: As above. **Fax:** 020 8700 1005
Email: marion.ball@janes.com
Web site: http://jae.janes.com
Publisher: Jane's Information Group
Date Established: 1996
Frequency: Monthly - Also available quarterly and every 6 months

Annual Sub.: £905.00
Editor: Mark Daly; **Advertising Manager:** Marion Ball
Summary of Content: Publication containing specialised information on almost every gas-turbine engine in flight. Contains profiles of engines for airliners, military aircraft, helicopters and business aircraft.
Readership/Target Audience: Aimed at the civil air industry, defence industry, ministries of defence, transport ministries, civil operators and armed forces.
ADVERTISING RATES:
Full Page Mono £2370.00
Full Page Colour £3955.00
Mechanical Data: Type Area: 263 x 185mm, Col Length: 263mm, Trim Size: 297 x 210mm, Bleed Size: 303 x 216mm, Film: Digital, Page Width: 185mm
BUSINESS: AVIATION & AERONAUTICS

JANE'S AIR TRAFFIC CONTROL
36388U6B-215

Editorial Address: Sentinel House, 163 Brighton Road, COULSDON, CR5 2YH **Tel:** 020 8700 3700
Fax: 020 7700 3715
Email: yearbook@janes.com
Advertising Address: As above. **Fax:** 020 8763 1005
Email: info@janes.com
Web site: http://jatc.janes.com
Publisher: Jane's Information Group
Frequency: Monthly
Annual Sub.: £1035.00
Circulation: 25,856 (Publisher's Statement)
Editor: Jenny Beechener; **Advertising Manager:** Marion Ball
Summary of Content: Publication containing information on the very latest technology in air traffic control operations.
Readership/Target Audience: Aimed at senior airport management in authorities, air traffic controllers, ATC and airport organisations, consultants and aviation support services.
ADVERTISING RATES:
Full Page Mono £4250.00
Full Page Colour £7080.00
BUSINESS: AVIATION & AERONAUTICS: Airports

JANE'S AIRCRAFT COMPONENT MANUFACTURERS
36404U6D-500

Editorial Address: Sentinel House, 163 Brighton Road, COULSDON, CR5 2YH **Tel:** 020 8700 3700
Fax: 020 8763 1006
Email: press.releases@janes.com
Advertising Address: As above. **Tel:** 020 8700 3000
Fax: 020 8763 1005
Email: transadsales@janes.com
Web site: http://jacm.janes.com
Publisher: Jane's Information Group
Frequency: Monthly - Also available quarterly
Annual Sub.: £1990.00
Editor: Kylie Bull; **Advertising Manager:** Janine Boxall
Summary of Content: Detailed information on manufacturers of materials used for the completion of aircraft.
Readership/Target Audience: Aimed at businesses, manufacturers, defence ministries and governments.
ADVERTISING: Rates on application
BUSINESS: AVIATION & AERONAUTICS: Aviation Engineering Equipment

JANE'S AIRCRAFT UPGRADES
36356U6A-99_40

Editorial Address: Sentinel House, 163 Brighton Road, COULSDON, CR5 2YH **Tel:** 020 8700 3700
Fax: 020 8763 3788
Email: info@janes.com
Advertising Address: As above. **Fax:** 020 8763 1005
Email: info@janes.com
Web site: http://jau.janes.com
Publisher: Jane's Information Group
Frequency: Monthly - Also available quarterly and every 6 months
Annual Sub.: £1175.00
Editor: Jamie Hunter; **Advertising Manager:** Marion Ball
Summary of Content: Journal focusing on out-of-production aircraft that are still in service. Covers civil and military aircraft and lists upgrade programmes for all aircraft in and out of production.
Readership/Target Audience: Aimed at the civil and defence aircraft industry, governments, decision makers, businesses, universities and those who work in the military.
ADVERTISING RATES:
Full Page Mono £3795.00
Full Page Colour £6320.00
BUSINESS: AVIATION & AERONAUTICS

JANE'S AIRPORT REVIEW
36347U6A-99_50

Editorial Address: Sentinel House, 163 Brighton Road, COULSDON, CR5 2YH **Tel:** 020 8700 3700
Fax: 020 8763 1005

Email: jar@janes.com
Advertising Address: As above.
Email: info@janes.co.uk
Web site: http://jar.janes.com
ISSN: 0954-7649
Publisher: Jane's Information Group
Date Established: 1989
Frequency: 10 issues yearly
Cover Price: £140.00
Annual Sub.: £560.00
Circulation: 11,216 (BPA Worldwide 01/01/2008 to 30/06/2008)
Editor: Ben Vogel; **Publisher:** Chris Bridge
Summary of Content: Magazine covering every significant event in the airports, air traffic control and ground operations market worldwide.
Readership/Target Audience: Aimed at senior managers and decision makers worldwide working in the air transport business.
ADVERTISING RATES:
Full Page Mono £4250.00
Full Page Colour £7080.00
Agency Commission: 15%
Mechanical Data: Type Area: 263 x 185mm, Bleed Size: 303 x 216mm, Trim Size: 297 x 210mm, Film: Digital, Page Width: 185mm, Col Length: 263mm
BUSINESS: AVIATION & AERONAUTICS

JANE'S AIRPORTS AND HANDLING AGENTS
36387U6B-213
Editorial Address: Sentinel House, 163 Brighton Road, COULSDON, CR5 2YH **Tel:** 020 8700 3787
Fax: 020 8700 3715
Email: adam.harding@janes.com
Advertising Address: As above. **Tel:** 020 8700 3700
Fax: 020 8763 1005
Email: info@janes.com
Web site: http://jaha.janes.com
Publisher: Jane's Information Group
Date Established: 1987
Frequency: Monthly
Annual Sub.: £2180.00
Editor: Adam Harding; **Advertising Manager:** Marion Ball
Summary of Content: International series providing information on operational data for the world's airports and the handling agents and FBOs that operate at them.
Readership/Target Audience: Aimed at air charter companies and airlines, pilots, handling agents and business aircraft associations.
ADVERTISING RATES:
Full Page Mono £1455.00
Full Page Colour £2255.00
Mechanical Data: Type Area: 190 x 128mm, Col Length: 190mm, Page Width: 128mm, Bleed Size: 216 x 154mm, Trim Size: 210 x 154mm, Film: Digital
BUSINESS: AVIATION & AERONAUTICS: Airports

JANE'S AIRPORTS, EQUIPMENT & SERVICES
36386U6B-214
Editorial Address: Sentinel House, 163 Brighton Road, COULSDON, CR5 2YH **Tel:** 020 8700 3700
Fax: 020 8700 3715
Email: info@janes.com
Advertising Address: As above. **Fax:** 020 8700 3744
Email: airportgroup@janes.com
Web site: http://jaes.janes.com
Publisher: Jane's Information Group
Frequency: Monthly - Also available quarterly and annually
Annual Sub.: £1090.00
Editor: David Rider
Summary of Content: Publication providing a reference to all categories of equipment needed to run the modern commercial airport or military airbase.
Readership/Target Audience: Aimed at airport authorities and management, airlines, ground handlers and service suppliers.
ADVERTISING RATES:
Full Page Mono £3570.00
Full Page Colour £5705.00
Mechanical Data: Type Area: 263 x 185mm, Trim Size: 297 x 210mm, Bleed Size: 303 x 216mm, Col Length: 263mm, Film: Digital, Page Width: 185mm
BUSINESS: AVIATION & AERONAUTICS: Airports

JANE'S ALL THE WORLD'S AIRCRAFT
36357U6A-99_60
Editorial Address: Sentinel House, 163 Brighton Road, COULSDON, CR5 2YH **Tel:** 020 8700 3700
Fax: 020 8763 1007
Email: info@janes.com
Advertising Address: As above. **Fax:** 020 8763 1005
Email: info@janes.com
Web site: http://jawa.janes.com
Publisher: Jane's Information Group
Date Established: 1909
Frequency: Annual - Published in May

Annual Sub.: £555.00
Circulation: 276,890 (Publisher's Statement)
Editor: Paul Jackson; **Advertising Manager:** Marion Ball
Summary of Content: Journal of international civil and military aircraft in production.
Readership/Target Audience: Aimed at the defence and commercial industry, ministries of defence, armed forces and academic institutions worldwide.
ADVERTISING RATES:
Full Page Mono £4250.00
Full Page Colour £7080.00
Mechanical Data: Type Area: 279 x 185mm, Bleed Size: 324 x 222mm, Trim Size: 318 x 216mm, Col Length: 279mm, Film: Digital, Page Width: 185mm
Copy instructions: Copy Date: 26th March
BUSINESS: AVIATION & AERONAUTICS

JANE'S AMMUNITION HANDBOOK
23425U40-407
Editorial Address: Sentinel House, 163 Brighton Road, COULSDON, CR5 2YH **Tel:** 020 8700 3700
Fax: 020 8763 1005
Email: info@janes.com
Advertising Address: As above.
Email: defadsales@janes.com
Web site: http://jah.janes.com
ISSN: 1369-7277
Publisher: Jane's Information Group
Frequency: Quarterly
Annual Sub.: £1080.00
Editor: Leland Ness; **Advertising Manager:** Marion Ball
Summary of Content: Journal containing information on small arms, cannons, air defence guns, tanks artillery, naval guns, mortars, grenades and artillery rockets.
Readership/Target Audience: Aimed at the defence industry, government decision makers, military, ministries of defence, businesses and universities.
ADVERTISING RATES:
Full Page Mono £3860.00
Full Page Colour £6450.00
Mechanical Data: Type Area: 279 x 185mm, Bleed Size: 324 x 222mm, Trim Size: 318 x 216mm, Col Length: 279mm, Page Width: 185mm, Film: Digital
BUSINESS: DEFENCE

JANE'S ARMOUR & ARTILLERY
23426U40-404
Editorial Address: Sentinel House, 163 Brighton Road, COULSDON, CR5 2YH **Tel:** 020 8700 3700
Fax: 020 8763 1006
Email: info@janes.com
Advertising Address: As above. **Fax:** 020 8700 3744
Email: defadsales@janes.com
Web site: http://jaa.janes.com
Publisher: Jane's Information Group
Frequency: Quarterly
Annual Sub.: £1285.00
Editor: Christopher Foss
Summary of Content: Magazine containing information resource focused on MBTs, armoured fighting vehicles and artillery, major and medium level artillery systems.
Readership/Target Audience: Aimed at the defence industry, ministries of defence, armed forces and academic institutions worldwide.
ADVERTISING RATES:
Full Page Mono £4095.00
Full Page Colour £6840.00
Mechanical Data: Type Area: 246 x 182mm, Bleed Size: 279 x 211mm, Trim Size: 273 x 205mm, Col Length: 246mm, Page Width: 182mm, Film: Digital
BUSINESS: DEFENCE

JANE'S ARMOUR & ARTILLERY UPGRADES
23427U40-408
Editorial Address: Sentinel House, 163 Brighton Road, COULSDON, CR5 2YH **Tel:** 020 8700 3700
Fax: 020 8763 1006
Email: info@janes.com
Advertising Address: As above. **Tel:** 020 8700 3000
Fax: 020 8763 1005
Email: info@janes.co.uk
Web site: http://jaau.janes.com
Publisher: Jane's Information Group
Frequency: Quarterly
Annual Sub.: £1070.00
Editor: Richard Stickland; **Advertising Manager:** Marion Ball
Summary of Content: Journal containing details regarding upgrade packages available to upgrade older artillery and armoured vehicles to current technical standards.
Readership/Target Audience: Aimed at the defence industry, ministries of defence, armed forces and academic institutions worldwide.
ADVERTISING RATES:
Full Page Mono £4095.00
Full Page Colour £6840.00
BUSINESS: DEFENCE

JANE'S AVIONICS
36358U6A-99_70
Editorial Address: Sentinel House, 163 Brighton Road, COULSDON, CR5 2YH **Tel:** 020 8700 3700
Fax: 020 8763 1005
Email: info@janes.com
Advertising Address: As above. **Tel:** 020 8700 3000
Fax: 020 8700 3859
Email: info@janes.com
Web site: http://jav.janes.com
Publisher: Jane's Information Group
Frequency: Monthly
Annual Sub.: £1190.00
Circulation: 34,000 (Publisher's Statement)
Editor: Edward Downs; **Advertising Manager:** Marion Ball
Summary of Content: International publication providing coverage of civil and military airborne electronics.
Readership/Target Audience: Aimed at the defence industry, ministries of defence, armed forces and academic institutions worldwide.
ADVERTISING RATES:
Full Page Mono £4015.00
Full Page Colour £6700.00
Mechanical Data: Type Area: 279 x 185mm, Bleed Size: 324 x 222mm, Trim Size: 318 x 216mm, Col Length: 279mm, Page Width: 185mm, Film: Digital
BUSINESS: AVIATION & AERONAUTICS

JANE'S C4I SYSTEMS
23429U40-405
Editorial Address: Sentinel House, 163 Brighton Road, COULSDON, CR5 2YH **Tel:** 020 8700 3700
Fax: 020 8763 1006
Email: info@janes.com
Advertising Address: As above. **Fax:** 020 8700 1006
Email: info@janes.co.uk
Web site: http://jc4i.janes.com
Publisher: Jane's Information Group
Frequency: Quarterly
Annual Sub.: £1125.00
Editor: Giles Ebbutt; **Advertising Manager:** Marion Ball
Summary of Content: Journal containing detailed information on the communication and intelligence gathering capabilities of the world's armed forces.
Readership/Target Audience: Aimed at the defence industry, ministries of defence, armed forces and academic institutions worldwide.
ADVERTISING RATES:
Full Page Mono £4015.00
Full Page Colour £6700.00
Mechanical Data: Type Area: 279 x 185mm, Bleed Size: 324 x 222mm, Trim Size: 318 x 216mm, Page Width: 185mm, Col Length: 279mm, Film: Digital
Copy instructions: Copy Date: 8th March prior to publication date
BUSINESS: DEFENCE

JANE'S DEFENCE INDUSTRY
38859U40-90
Formerly: Defence Industry
Editorial Address: Sentinel House, 163 Brighton Road, COULSDON, CR5 2YH **Tel:** 020 8700 3700
Fax: 020 8763 1007
Email: guy.anderson@janes.com
Web site: http://jdin.janes.com
ISSN: 1363-271X
Publisher: Jane's Information Group
Frequency: Monthly
Annual Sub.: £770.00
Usual Pagination: 16
Editor: Guy Anderson; **Publisher:** Chris Bridge
Summary of Content: Newsletter covering news, developments and commentary concerning the defence industry.
Readership/Target Audience: Aimed at defence professionals.
ADVERTISING: No Advertising taken
BUSINESS: DEFENCE

JANE'S DEFENCE WEEKLY
38869U40-160
Editorial Address: Sentinel House, 163 Brighton Road, COULSDON, CR5 2YH **Tel:** 020 8700 3700
Fax: 020 8763 1007
Email: jdw@janes.com
Advertising Address: As above. **Fax:** 020 8763 1005
Email: marion.ball@janes.com
Web site: http://jdw.janes.com
ISSN: 0265-3818
Publisher: Jane's Information Group
Date Established: 1984
Frequency: Weekly
Annual Sub.: £245.00
Usual Pagination: 34
Editor: Peter Felstead; **Features Editor:** Tony Skinner; **Advertising Manager:** Marion Ball
Summary of Content: Magazine focusing on international defence, containing regular news, analysis, business, technology information as well as special reports on defence topics.

Readership/Target Audience: Aimed at the military and government.
ADVERTISING RATES:
Full Page Mono £3420.00
Full Page Colour £4955.00
Agency Commission: 15%
Mechanical Data: Type Area: 246 x 182mm, Bleed Size: 279 x 211mm, Trim Size: 273 x 205mm, Film: Digital, Col Length: 246mm, Page Width: 182mm
BUSINESS: DEFENCE

JANE'S EXPLOSIVE ORDNANCE DISPOSAL
762772U40-411
Editorial Address: Sentinel House, 163 Brighton Road, COULSDON, CR5 2YH **Tel:** 020 8700 3700
Fax: 020 8763 1006
Email: info@janes.com
Advertising Address: As above. **Tel:** 020 8700 3738
Fax: 020 8763 3859
Email: nicky.eakins@janes.com
Web site: http://jeod.janes.com
Publisher: Jane's Information Group
Date Established: 2001
Frequency: Quarterly
Annual Sub.: £1035.00
Editor: Colin King; **Advertising Manager:** Nicky Eakins
Summary of Content: Guide to the identification and assessment of unexploded ordnance, including coverage of the technical threat together with details of the associated equipment and services, EOD techniques, equipment and identification of explosives.
Readership/Target Audience: Read by EOD, mine clearance operatives, trainers, EOD and mine clearance manufacturers and industry, government, military institutions and non-profit organisations.
ADVERTISING RATES:
Full Page Mono £3860.00
Full Page Colour £6450.00
Agency Commission: 15%
Mechanical Data: Type Area: 279 x 185mm, Col Length: 279mm, Page Width: 185mm, Bleed Size: 324 x 222mm, Trim Size: 318 x 216mm, Film: Digital
BUSINESS: DEFENCE

JANE'S FIGHTING SHIPS
38896U40-161
Editorial Address: Sentinel House, 163 Brighton Road, COULSDON, CR5 2YH **Tel:** 020 8700 3700
Fax: 020 8763 1006
Email: info@janes.com
Advertising Address: As above. **Fax:** 020 8700 1006
Email: info@janes.com
Web site: http://jfs.janes.com
Publisher: Jane's Information Group
Date Established: 1898
Frequency: Monthly
Annual Sub.: £1285.00
Circulation: 222,947 (Publisher's Statement)
Editor: Stephen Saunders; **Advertising Manager:** Marion Ball
Summary of Content: International guide to the world's navies.
Readership/Target Audience: Aimed at the defence industry, ministries of defence, armed forces and academic institutions worldwide.
ADVERTISING RATES:
Full Page Mono £4250.00
Full Page Colour £7080.00
Mechanical Data: Type Area: 279 x 185mm, Col Length: 279mm, Bleed Size: 324 x 222mm, Trim Size: 318 x 216mm, Film: Digital, Page Width: 185mm
Copy instructions: Copy Date: May 8th
BUSINESS: DEFENCE

JANE'S HELICOPTER MARKETS & SYSTEMS
36414U6E-160
Editorial Address: Sentinel House, 163 Brighton Road, COULSDON, CR5 2YH **Tel:** 020 8700 3700
Fax: 020 8763 1006
Email: gunter.endres@btopenworld.com
Advertising Address: As above. **Fax:** 020 8700 1006
Email: info@janes.com
Web site: http://jhms.janes.com
Publisher: Jane's Information Group
Frequency: Monthly - Also available quarterly and every 6 months
Annual Sub.: £1480.00
Editor: David Oliver; **Advertising Manager:** Marion Ball
Summary of Content: Source containing intelligence information on airframe and engine programmes, civil and military helicopter operators, sales forecasts, prices and numbers in service around the world.
Readership/Target Audience: Aimed at the civil air industry, defence industry, ministries of defence, transport ministries, civil operators, armed forces, and consultants.
ADVERTISING RATES:
Full Page Mono £2370.00

Full Page Colour £3955.00
Mechanical Data: Type Area: 263 x 185mm, Col Length: 263mm, Trim Size: 297 x 210mm, Bleed Size: 303 x 216mm, Film: Digital, Page Width: 185mm
Copy instructions: Copy Date: 18th July
BUSINESS: AVIATION & AERONAUTICS: Hovercraft VTOL

JANE'S INFANTRY WEAPONS
23434U40-418
Editorial Address: Sentinel House, 163 Brighton Road, COULSDON, CR5 2YH **Tel:** 020 8700 3700
Fax: 020 8763 1005
Email: info@janes.com
Advertising Address: As above. **Fax:** 020 8700 3744
Email: defadsales@janes.co.uk
Web site: http://jiw.janes.com
Publisher: Jane's Information Group
Frequency: Monthly
Annual Sub.: £1275.00
Editor: Richard Jones; **Advertising Manager:** Marion Ball
Summary of Content: An international source of man-portable and self propelling weapons.
Readership/Target Audience: Aimed at the defence industry, ministries of defence, armed forces and academic institutions worldwide.
ADVERTISING RATES:
Full Page Mono £4095.00
Full Page Colour £6840.00
Mechanical Data: Page Width: 185mm, Type Area: 279 x 185mm, Col Length: 279mm, Film: Digital, Bleed Size: 324 x 222mm, Trim Size: 318 x 216mm
BUSINESS: DEFENCE

JANE'S INTELLIGENCE REVIEW
38870U40-162
Editorial Address: Sentinel House, 163 Brighton Road, COULSDON, CR5 2YH **Tel:** 020 8700 3700
Fax: 020 7287 7765
Email: christian.lemiere@janes.com
Advertising Address: As above. **Fax:** 020 8763 1005
Email: info@janes.com
Web site: http://jir.janes.com
ISSN: 1350-6226
Publisher: Jane's Information Group
Frequency: Monthly
Annual Sub.: £310.00
Circulation: 2,559 (Publisher's Statement)
Usual Pagination: 56
Editor: Christian LeMiere; **Advertising Manager:** Marion Ball; **Publisher:** James Green
Summary of Content: Magazine providing a reliable source of information and threat assessment for defence analysts and the intelligence community.
Readership/Target Audience: Read by corporate strategic planners, law enforcement personnel, defence institutes, ministries of defence, armed forces, academic and research institutes and commercial risk assessors.
ADVERTISING RATES:
Full Page Mono £1860.00
Full Page Colour £2805.00
BUSINESS: DEFENCE

JANE'S INTERNATIONAL ABC AEROSPACE DIRECTORY
36354U6A-99_80
Formerly: International ABC Aerospace Directory
Editorial Address: Sentinel House, 163 Brighton Road, COULSDON, CR5 2YH **Tel:** 020 8700 3700
Fax: 020 8700 3816
Email: directories@janes.com
Advertising Address: As above. **Fax:** 020 8700 3859
Email: defadsales@janes.com
Web site: http://abc.janes.com
Publisher: Jane's Information Group
Date Established: 1936
Frequency: Monthly - Also available quarterly and annually
Annual Sub.: £1110.00
Editor: Peter Partridge; **Advertising Manager:** Marion Ball
Summary of Content: International publication featuring a comprehensive directory of phone and fax numbers, e-mail and web sites, addresses and contact names for aerospace and air transport people, companies, organisations, products and services.
ADVERTISING RATES:
Full Page Mono £4015.00
Full Page Colour £6700.00
Mechanical Data: Type Area: 263 x 185mm, Col Length: 263mm, Bleed Size: 303 x 216mm, Trim Size: 297 x 210mm, Film: Digital, Page Width: 185mm
BUSINESS: AVIATION & AERONAUTICS

JANE'S INTERNATIONAL DEFENCE DIRECTORY
38897U40-162_50
Editorial Address: Sentinel House, 163 Brighton Road, COULSDON, CR5 2YH **Tel:** 020 8700 3700
Fax: 020 8700 3816
Email: directories@janes.com

Advertising Address: As above. **Fax:** 020 8700 3744
Email: defadsales@janes.co.uk
Web site: http://idd.janes.com
Publisher: Jane's Information Group
Date Established: 1985
Frequency: Annual
Annual Sub.: £1025.00
Editor: Peter Partridge; **Advertising Manager:** Marion Ball; **Publisher:** Sara Morgan
Summary of Content: An international directory of phone numbers, fax numbers, email and web sites, addresses, contact names, products and services for companies and organisations within the defence industry.
Readership/Target Audience: Read by those in the defence industry.
ADVERTISING RATES:
Full Page Mono £4015.00
Full Page Colour £6700.00
Mechanical Data: Type Area: 263 x 185mm, Bleed Size: 303 x 216mm, Trim Size: 297 x 210mm, Film: Digital, Col Length: 263mm, Page Width: 185mm
BUSINESS: DEFENCE

JANE'S INTERNATIONAL DEFENCE REVIEW
38866U40-162_53
Formerly: International Defense Review
Editorial Address: Sentinel House, 163 Brighton Road, COULSDON, CR5 2YH **Tel:** 020 8700 3700
Fax: 020 8700 3846
Email: nick.brown@janes.com
Advertising Address: As above. **Fax:** 020 8763 1005
Email: defadsales@janes.com
Web site: http://idr.janes.com
ISSN: 0020-6513
Publisher: Jane's Information Group
Frequency: Monthly
Annual Sub.: £340.00
Circulation: 19,672 (BPA Worldwide 01/01/2008 to 30/06/2008)
Editor: Nick Brown; **Advertising Manager:** Marion Ball; **Publisher:** Sara Morgan
Summary of Content: Magazine featuring original, full-length articles on key strategic, tactical and defence technology subjects from around the world.
Readership/Target Audience: Read by those in the military and defence industries as well as government departments.
ADVERTISING RATES:
Full Page Mono £5055.00
Full Page Colour £7630.00
Agency Commission: 15%
Mechanical Data: Type Area: 246 x 182mm, Bleed Size: 279 x 211mm, Trim Size: 273 x 205mm, Film: Digital, Col Length: 246mm, Page Width: 182mm
BUSINESS: DEFENCE

JANE'S LAND-BASED AIR DEFENCE
23435U40-406
Editorial Address: Sentinel House, 163 Brighton Road, COULSDON, CR5 2YH **Tel:** 020 8700 3700
Fax: 020 8763 1006
Email: info@defence-analyst.co.uk
Advertising Address: As above. **Tel:** 020 8700 3738
Fax: 020 8700 3859
Email: nicky.eakins@janes.com
Web site: http://jlad.janes.com
Publisher: Jane's Information Group
Frequency: Quarterly
Annual Sub.: £1150.00
Editor: Jim O'Halloran; **Advertising Manager:** Nicky Eakins
Summary of Content: A guide containing information on anti-aircraft gun and missile systems in service with the world's armies and air forces.
Readership/Target Audience: Aimed at the defence industry, ministries of defence, armed forces and academic institutions worldwide.
ADVERTISING RATES:
Full Page Mono £4095.00
Full Page Colour £6840.00
Mechanical Data: Type Area: 279 x 185mm, Bleed Size: 324 x 222mm, Trim Size: 318 x 216mm, Col Length: 279mm, Page Width: 185mm, Film: Digital
BUSINESS: DEFENCE

JANE'S MARINE PROPULSION
39417U45D-80
Editorial Address: Sentinel House, 163 Brighton Road, COULSDON, CR5 2YH **Tel:** 020 8700 3700
Fax: 020 8763 1006
Email: info@janes.com
Advertising Address: As above. **Tel:** 020 8700 3853
Fax: 020 8700 3859
Email: defadsales@janes.com
Web site: http://jmp.janes.com
Publisher: Jane's Information Group
Frequency: Monthly
Annual Sub.: £1265.00
Editor: Keith Henderson; **Publisher:** Sara Morgan

Summary of Content: Publication containing details of construction performance and applications of almost all marine engines in production, military and civic.
Readership/Target Audience: Aimed at propeller manufacturers, engine manufacturers, navies, the commercial shipping industry and shipbuilders.
ADVERTISING RATES:
Full Page Mono £2370.00
Full Page Colour £3955.00
BUSINESS: MARINE & SHIPPING: Marine Engineering Equipment

JANE'S MERCHANT SHIPS   23437U40-162_60
Editorial Address: Sentinel House, 163 Brighton Road, COULSDON, CR5 2YH **Tel:** 020 8700 3700
Fax: 020 8763 1006
Email: info@janes.com
Advertising Address: As above. **Tel:** 020 8700 3963
Fax: 020 8700 3744
Email: defadsales@janes.com
Web site: http://jms.janes.com
Publisher: Jane's Information Group
Frequency: Quarterly
Annual Sub.: £1005.00
Editor: David Greenman
Summary of Content: A comprehensive directory for recognition purposes of the world's merchant ships.
Readership/Target Audience: Aimed at Naval personnel.
ADVERTISING RATES:
Full Page Mono £3795.00
Full Page Colour £6320.00
BUSINESS: DEFENCE

JANE'S MILITARY COMMUNICATIONS
                                    23438U40-409
Editorial Address: Sentinel House, 163 Brighton Road, COULSDON, CR5 2YH **Tel:** 020 8700 3700
Fax: 020 8763 1006
Email: info@janes.com
Advertising Address: As above.
Email: defadsales@janes.co.uk
Web site: http://jmc.janes.com
Publisher: Jane's Information Group
Frequency: Annual - Published in March
Annual Sub.: £1125.00
Editor: John Williamson; **Advertising Manager:** Marion Ball
Summary of Content: An international resource on tactical and satellite communication technology.
Readership/Target Audience: Aimed at the defence industry, ministries of defence, armed forces and academic institutions worldwide.
ADVERTISING RATES:
Full Page Mono ....٨.... £4095.00
Full Page Colour £6840.00
Agency Commission: 15%
Mechanical Data: Type Area: 279 x 185mm, Bleed Size: 324 x 222mm, Trim Size: 318 x 216mm, Col Length: 279mm, Page Width: 185mm, Film: Digital
BUSINESS: DEFENCE

JANE'S MILITARY VEHICLES & LOGISTICS
                                    23439U40-410
Editorial Address: Sentinel House, 163 Brighton Road, COULSDON, CR5 2YH **Tel:** 020 8700 3700
Fax: 020 8763 1006
Email: info@janes.com
Advertising Address: As above.
Email: defadsales@janes.com
Web site: http://jmvl.janes.com
Publisher: Jane's Information Group
Frequency: Quarterly
Annual Sub.: £1145.00
Editor: Shaun Connors; **Advertising Manager:** Marion Ball
Summary of Content: An international resource on military transporters, equipment and transport systems.
Readership/Target Audience: Aimed at the defence industry, ministries of defence, army forces and academic institutions worldwide.
ADVERTISING RATES:
Full Page Mono £4015.00
Full Page Colour £6700.00
Agency Commission: 15%
Mechanical Data: Page Width: 185mm, Film: Digital, Type Area: 279 x 185mm, Bleed Size: 324 x 222mm, Trim Size: 318 x 216mm, Col Length: 279mm
Copy instructions: Copy Date: 7th February
BUSINESS: DEFENCE

JANE'S MINES & MINE CLEARANCE
                                    23440U40-402
Editorial Address: Sentinel House, 163 Brighton Road, COULSDON, CR5 2YH **Tel:** 020 8700 3700
Fax: 020 8763 1006
Email: info@janes.com

Advertising Address: As above.
Email: marion.ball@janes.co.uk
Web site: http://jmmc.janes.com
Publisher: Jane's Information Group
Frequency: Quarterly
Annual Sub.: £1045.00
Editor: Colin King; **Advertising Manager:** Marion Ball
Summary of Content: A comprehensive information source on mine threat assessment, mine clearance techniques and equipment.
Readership/Target Audience: Read by defence, military procurement officers, trainers and trainees and the defence industry.
ADVERTISING RATES:
Full Page Mono £3795.00
Full Page Colour £6320.00
Mechanical Data: Page Width: 185mm, Film: Digital, Type Area: 279 x 185mm, Bleed Size: 324 x 222mm, Trim Size: 318 x 216mm, Col Length: 279mm
BUSINESS: DEFENCE

JANE'S MISSILES & ROCKETS   38875U40-176
Formerly: Missiles & Rockets
Editorial Address: Sentinel House, 163 Brighton Road, COULSDON, CR5 2YH **Tel:** 020 8700 3700
Fax: 01279 793056
Email: derichardson@textrix.co.uk
Web site: http://jmr.janes.com
Publisher: Jane's Information Group
Frequency: Monthly
Annual Sub.: £315.00
Editor: Doug Richardson; **Managing Editor:** Damian Kemp; **Publisher:** Sara Morgan
Summary of Content: Magazine covering all aspects of land, sea and air missile technology.
Readership/Target Audience: Aimed at technology decision makers in the armed forces and defence. Also read by aviation and aerospace manufacturers.
ADVERTISING: No Advertising taken
BUSINESS: DEFENCE

JANE'S NAVAL WEAPONS SYSTEMS
                                    38898U40-162_80
Editorial Address: Sentinel House, 163 Brighton Road, COULSDON, CR5 2YH **Tel:** 020 8700 3700
Fax: 020 8763 1006
Email: sara.morgan@janes.com
Advertising Address: As above. **Tel:** 020 8700 3738
Fax: 020 8700 3859
Email: nicky.eakins@janes.com
Web site: http://jnws.janes.com
Publisher: Jane's Information Group
Frequency: Monthly
Annual Sub.: £1480.00
Editor: Malcolm Fuller; **Advertising Manager:** Nicky Eakins; **Publisher:** Sara Morgan
Summary of Content: Guide containing comprehensive profiles of every naval weapon in service or under development. Gives systematic analysis of each system.
Readership/Target Audience: Aimed at the defence industry, ministries of defence, armed forces and academic institutions worldwide.
ADVERTISING RATES:
Full Page Mono £2370.00
Full Page Colour £3955.00
Agency Commission: 15%
Mechanical Data: Type Area: 279 x 185mm, Bleed Size: 324 x 222mm, Trim Size: 318 x 216mm, Col Length: 279mm, Page Width: 185mm, Film: Digital
BUSINESS: DEFENCE

JANE'S NAVY INTERNATIONAL   38871U40-163
Editorial Address: Sentinel House, 163 Brighton Road, COULSDON, CR5 2YH **Tel:** 020 8700 3700
Fax: 020 8763 1423
Email: jon.rosamond@janes.com
Advertising Address: As above. **Fax:** 020 8763 1005
Email: info@janes.co.uk
Web site: http://jni.janes.com
ISSN: 0144-3194
Publisher: Jane's Information Group
Date Established: 1895
Frequency: 10 issues yearly
Annual Sub.: £160.00
Usual Pagination: 32
Editor: Jon Rosamond; **Advertising Manager:** Marion Ball; **Publisher:** Sara Morgan
Summary of Content: Journal covering naval affairs, defence, strategy, equipment, naval operations, ships, submarines, naval weapon systems and amphibious warfare.
Readership/Target Audience: Aimed at senior naval officers, ministry of defence personnel and civil servants of all nations.
ADVERTISING RATES:
Full Page Mono £2320.00

Full Page Colour £3505.00
Agency Commission: 15%
Mechanical Data: Type Area: 246 x 182mm, Bleed Size: 279 x 211mm, Trim Size: 273 x 205mm, Film: Digital, Col Length: 246mm, Page Width: 182mm
BUSINESS: DEFENCE

JANE'S NUCLEAR, BIOLOGICAL AND CHEMICAL DEFENCE   23441U40-163_20
Formerly: Jane's NBC Defence Systems
Editorial Address: Sentinel House, 163 Brighton Road, COULSDON, CR5 2YH **Tel:** 020 8700 3700
Fax: 020 8763 1006
Email: info@janes.com
Advertising Address: As above. **Tel:** 020 8700 3853
Fax: 020 8700 3744
Email: nicky.eakins@janes.com
Web site: http://jnbc.janes.com
Publisher: Jane's Information Group
Frequency: Quarterly
Annual Sub.: £1055.00
Editor: Andy Oppenheimer; **Publisher:** Sara Morgan
Summary of Content: Journal containing detailed intelligence on each nation's declared NBC policy and weapons capabilities, testing and research for each country in the world.
Readership/Target Audience: Aimed at the defence industry, ministries of defence, armed forces and academic institutions worldwide.
ADVERTISING RATES:
Full Page Mono £3860.00
Full Page Colour £6450.00
Agency Commission: 15%
BUSINESS: DEFENCE

JANE'S POLICE & HOMELAND SECURITY EQUIPMENT   38899U40-163_50
Formerly: Jane's Police & Security Equipment
Editorial Address: Sentinel House, 163 Brighton Road, COULSDON, CR5 2YH **Tel:** 020 8700 3700
Fax: 020 8763 1006
Email: mike.mcbride@interramp.co.uk
Advertising Address: As above. **Fax:** 020 8763 1005
Email: defadsales@janes.com
Web site: http://jpse.janes.com
Publisher: Jane's Information Group
Date Established: 1976
Frequency: Quarterly
Annual Sub.: £980.00
Editor: Mike McBride
Summary of Content: Guide to law enforcement equipment.
Readership/Target Audience: Aimed at the defence industry, ministries of defence, armed forces, academic institutions, police forces and security forces worldwide.
ADVERTISING RATES:
Full Page Mono £1610.00
Full Page Colour £2685.00
Agency Commission: 15%
Mechanical Data: Type Area: 279 x 185mm, Bleed Size: 324 x 222mm, Trim Size: 318 x 216mm, Col Length: 279mm, Film: Digital, Page Width: 185mm
BUSINESS: DEFENCE

JANE'S POLICE REVIEW   38440U32F-420
Editorial Address: 1st Floor, The Quadrangle, 180 Wardour Street, LONDON, W1F 8FY **Tel:** 020 8276 4701
Fax: 020 7287 7765
Email: policereviewnews@janes.com
Advertising Address: As above. **Tel:** 020 8700 3700
Email: lawadsales@janes.com
Web site: http://www.policereview.com
ISSN: 0309-1414
Publisher: Jane's Information Group
Date Established: 1893
Frequency: Weekly
Annual Sub.: £92.00
Circulation: 9,605 (BPA Worldwide 01/01/2007 to 30/06/2007)
Usual Pagination: 50
Editor: Chris Herbert
Summary of Content: Magazine containing expert briefings on the latest news affecting British police forces and their operational officers.
Readership/Target Audience: Aimed at all police ranks, security and allied organisations.
ADVERTISING RATES:
Full Page Mono £1350.00
Full Page Colour £1350.00
Agency Commission: 10%
Mechanical Data: Bleed Size: 303 x 216mm, Trim Size: 297 x 210mm, Type Area: 267 x 180mm, Col Length: 267mm, Film: Digital, Page Width: 180mm
Copy instructions: Copy Date: Monday midday prior to publication date

Average advertising content per issue: 30%
BUSINESS: LOCAL GOVERNMENT, LEISURE &
RECREATION: Police

JANE'S RADAR AND ELECTRONIC WARFARE

762768U40-413

Editorial Address: Sentinel House, 163 Brighton Road,
COULSDON, CR5 2YH **Tel:** 020 8700 3700
Fax: 020 8763 1007
Email: info@janes.com
Advertising Address: As above. **Tel:** 020 8700 3963
Fax: 020 8700 3744
Web site: http://jrew.janes.com
Publisher: Jane's Information Group
Frequency: Quarterly
Annual Sub.: £1285.00
Editor: Martin Streetly; **Advertising Manager:** Marion Ball
Summary of Content: Magazine focusing on military radars
and EW systems, including the role, format, capabilities,
status and specifications of each system. Also includes
contractor details to support procurement and market
intelligence.
Readership/Target Audience: Read by the army, navy, air
forces, intelligence operatives, governments, military
installations and institutions.
ADVERTISING RATES:
Full Page Mono £4095.00
Full Page Colour £6840.00
Mechanical Data: Page Width: 185mm, Film: Digital, Bleed
Size: 324 x 222mm, Trim Size: 318 x 216mm, Type Area: 279
x 185mm, Col Length: 279mm
BUSINESS: DEFENCE

JANE'S SPACE SYSTEMS AND INDUSTRY

21453U6A-201

Formerly: Jane's Space Directory
Editorial Address: Sentinel House, 163 Brighton Road,
COULSDON, CR5 2YH **Tel:** 020 8700 3700
Fax: 020 8763 1007
Email: info@janes.com
Advertising Address: As above. **Tel:** 020 8700 3738
Fax: 020 8700 3859
Email: nicky.eakins@janes.com
Web site: http://jsd.janes.com
Publisher: Jane's Information Group
Frequency: Monthly
Cover Price: £1145.00
Circulation: 58,581 (Publisher's Statement)
Editor: Peter Bond; **Advertising Manager:** Nicky Eakins
Summary of Content: Contains reference work for all space
related issues.
Readership/Target Audience: Aimed at engineers,
scientists, universities, government agencies, military
libraries and consultants.
ADVERTISING RATES:
Full Page Mono £3860.00
Full Page Colour £6450.00
Agency Commission: 15%
Mechanical Data: Type Area: 279 x 185mm, Trim Size: 318
x 216mm, Bleed Size: 324 x 222mm, Col Length: 279mm,
Page Width: 185mm, Film: Digital
Copy instructions: Copy Date: May 6th
BUSINESS: AVIATION & AERONAUTICS

JANE'S TERRORISM & SECURITY MONITOR

39928U54C-300

Formerly: Terrorism & Security Monitor
Editorial Address: The Quadrangle, 180 Wardour Street,
LONDON, W1A 4YG **Tel:** 020 8700 3700 **Fax:** 020 7287 4765
Email: jeremy.binnie@janes.com
Web site: http://jtsm.janes.com
ISSN: 1367-0409
Publisher: Jane's Information Group
Date Established: 1996
Frequency: 10 issues yearly
Annual Sub.: £249.00
Usual Pagination: 16
Editor: Jeremy Binnie; **Publisher:** James Green
Summary of Content: Publication containing a review of
global terrorism and security issues.
Readership/Target Audience: Aimed at people with a
professional interest in current affairs and security issues.
ADVERTISING: No Advertising taken
BUSINESS: SAFETY & SECURITY: Security

JANE'S TRANSPORT FINANCE

39700U49R-290

Formerly: Transport Finance
Editorial Address: Sentinel House, 163 Brighton Road,
COULSDON, CR5 2YH **Tel:** 020 8700 3794
Email: tfjimsmith@aol.com
Advertising Address: As above. **Tel:** 020 8700 3700
Fax: 020 8700 3744
Email: mat.stevens@janes.com
Web site: http://jtf.janes.com

ISSN: 1351-1211
Publisher: Jane's Information Group
Frequency: 24 issues yearly
Annual Sub.: £1270.00
Circulation: 12,000 (Publisher's Statement)
Editor: Jim Smith; **Advertising Manager:** Mat Stevens;
Publisher: Chris Bridge
Summary of Content: Newsletter reporting on aircraft, ship
and rail finance deals.
Readership/Target Audience: Read by international
bankers, lawyers, transport companies and government
agencies.
ADVERTISING RATES:
Full Page Mono £2375.00
Full Page Colour £3160.00
Agency Commission: 15%
Mechanical Data: Type Area: 263 x 185mm, Col Length:
263mm, Trim Size: 297 x 210mm, Bleed Size: 303 x 216mm,
Film: Digital, Page Width: 185mm
Copy instructions: Copy Date: 3 days prior to publication
date
Average advertising content per issue: 20%
BUSINESS: TRANSPORT: Transport Related

JANE'S UNDERWATER WARFARE SYSTEMS

38902U40-163_80

Editorial Address: Sentinel House, 163 Brighton Road,
COULSDON, CR5 2YH **Tel:** 020 8700 3700
Fax: 020 8763 1006
Email: yearbook@janes.com
Advertising Address: As above. **Fax:** 020 8700 3859
Email: defadsales@janes.com
Web site: http://www.janes.com
Publisher: Jane's Information Group
Frequency: Annual - Published in February
Cover Price: £335.00
Editor: Cliff Funnell; **Advertising Manager:** Marion Ball
Summary of Content: An international underwater warfare
systems yearbook.
Readership/Target Audience: Aimed at the defence
industry, ministries of defence, armed forces and academic
institutions worldwide and sea and shore based naval
personnel.
ADVERTISING RATES:
Full Page Mono £4015.00
Full Page Colour £6700.00
Mechanical Data: Page Width: 185mm, Type Area: 279 x
185mm, Col Length: 279mm, Bleed Size: 324 x 222mm, Trim
Size: 318 x 216mm, Film: Digital
BUSINESS: DEFENCE

JANE'S UNMANNED AERIAL VEHICLES & TARGETS

38903U40-164

Editorial Address: Sentinel House, 163 Brighton Road,
COULSDON, CR5 2YH **Tel:** 020 8700 3700
Fax: 020 8763 1007
Email: info@janes.com
Advertising Address: As above. **Tel:** 020 8700 3963
Fax: 020 8700 3744
Email: defadsales@janes.com
Web site: http://juav.janes.com
Publisher: Jane's Information Group
Date Established: 1995
Frequency: Monthly
Annual Sub.: £1545.00
Advertising Manager: Marion Ball; **Publisher:** Sara Morgan
Summary of Content: Contains specialised information on
the world's UAV technology, specifications, power plants,
launch and recovery systems.
Readership/Target Audience: Aimed at the defence
industry, ministries of defence, armed forces and academic
institutions worldwide.
ADVERTISING RATES:
Full Page Mono £2370.00
Full Page Colour £3955.00
Mechanical Data: Page Width: 185mm, Type Area: 279 x
185mm, Trim Size: 318 x 216mm, Bleed Size: 324 x 222mm,
Col Length: 279mm, Film: Digital
BUSINESS: DEFENCE

JANE'S URBAN TRANSPORT SYSTEMS

39598U49A-137

Editorial Address: Sentinel House, 163 Brighton Road,
COULSDON, CR5 2YH **Tel:** 020 8700 3700
Fax: 020 8700 3715
Email: info@janes.com
Advertising Address: As above. **Fax:** 020 8700 3744
Email: transadsales@janes.com
Web site: http://juts.janes.com
Publisher: Jane's Information Group
Date Established: 1982
Frequency: Annual - Published in April
Annual Sub.: £1140.00
Circulation: 50,341 (Publisher's Statement)
Editor: Mary Webb

Summary of Content: An all-in-one guide to city transport
systems, manufacturers and products worldwide.
Readership/Target Audience: Aimed at public transport
managers, transport planners, government transport
departments, financial institutions and consultants.
ADVERTISING RATES:
Full Page Mono £3750.00
Full Page Colour £5985.00
Mechanical Data: Type Area: 263 x 185mm, Bleed Size:
303 x 216mm, Trim Size: 297 x 210mm, Col Length: 263mm,
Film: Digital, Page Width: 185mm
BUSINESS: TRANSPORT

JANE'S WORLD AIR FORCES

38904U40-164_50

Editorial Address: Sentinel House, 163 Brighton Road,
COULSDON, CR5 2YH **Tel:** 020 8700 3700
Fax: 020 8700 3788
Email: info@janes.com
Web site: http://jwaf.janes.com
Publisher: Jane's Information Group
Date Established: 1996
Frequency: Monthly
Annual Sub.: £1345.00
Editor: Lindsay Peacock
Summary of Content: A complete analysis and order of
battle breakdowns of the air forces of the world.
Readership/Target Audience: Aimed at the defence
industry, ministries of defence, armed forces and academic
institutions worldwide.
ADVERTISING: No Advertising taken
BUSINESS: DEFENCE

JANE'S WORLD AIRLINES

36431U6F-160

Editorial Address: Sentinel House, 163 Brighton Road,
COULSDON, CR5 2YH **Tel:** 020 8700 3814
Fax: 020 8700 3715
Email: adam.harding@janes.com
Advertising Address: As above. **Tel:** 020 8700 3700
Fax: 020 8700 3744
Email: airportgroup@janes.co.uk
Web site: http://jwa.janes.com
Publisher: Jane's Information Group
Frequency: Monthly - Also available quarterly and every 6
months
Annual Sub.: £1235.00
Editor: David Pratt
Summary of Content: Resource providing comprehensive
up-to-date information on the structure and operations of
over 500 airlines worldwide, both scheduled and non-
scheduled cargo and passenger.
Readership/Target Audience: Aimed at operators
worldwide, businesses, decision makers in the airline
industry, manufacturers and governments.
ADVERTISING: Rates on application
BUSINESS: AVIATION & AERONAUTICS: Airlines

JANE'S WORLD ARMIES

38905U40-164_60

Editorial Address: Sentinel House, 163 Brighton Road,
COULSDON, CR5 2YH **Tel:** 020 8700 3700
Fax: 020 8763 1006
Email: info@janes.com
Web site: http://jwar.janes.com
Publisher: Jane's Information Group
Frequency: Monthly
Cover Price: £1345.00
Editor: Eleanor Keymer; **Publisher:** Sara Morgan
Summary of Content: Contains a complete analysis and
order of battle breakdowns on the armies of the world.
Readership/Target Audience: Aimed at the defence
industry, ministries of defence, armed forces and academic
institutions worldwide.
ADVERTISING: No Advertising taken
BUSINESS: DEFENCE

JANE'S WORLD INSURGENCY & TERRORISM

38906U40-164_70

Editorial Address: Sentinel House, 163 Brighton Road,
COULSDON, CR5 2YH **Tel:** 020 8700 3700
Fax: 020 8763 1005
Email: info@janes.com
Web site: http://jwit.janes.com
Publisher: Jane's Information Group
Date Established: 1997
Frequency: Monthly - Published in March and September
Annual Sub.: £1335.00
Editor: Will Hartley; **Managing Editor:** Will Hartley;
Publisher: James Green
Summary of Content: A complete detailed listing of over
190 insurgent and terrorist organisations worldwide
including group leader profiles.
Readership/Target Audience: Aimed at the police, armed
forces, governments, defence ministries and businesses.
ADVERTISING: No Advertising taken
BUSINESS: DEFENCE

JANE'S WORLD RAILWAYS

39694U49E-118

Editorial Address: Sentinel House, 163 Brighton Road, COULSDON, CR5 2YH **Tel:** 020 8700 3700
Fax: 020 8700 3715
Advertising Address: As above. **Fax:** 020 8763 1005
Email: transadsales@janes.com
Web site: http://jwr.janes.com
Publisher: Jane's Information Group
Frequency: Annual - Published in November
Annual Sub.: £1200.00
Circulation: 69,183 (Publisher's Statement)
Editor: Ken Harris; **Advertising Manager:** Marion Ball;
Publisher: Sara Morgan
Summary of Content: Covers all aspects of the international rail industry from systems to manufacturers.
Readership/Target Audience: Aimed at the railway industry, technical and operations executives, transport planners, transport ministries, associations and consultants.
ADVERTISING RATES:
Full Page Colour £5985.00
Mechanical Data: Type Area: 279 x 185mm, Bleed Size: 324 x 222mm, Trim Size: 318 x 216mm, Col Length: 279mm, Film: Digital, Page Width: 185mm
Copy instructions: Copy Date: October 7th
BUSINESS: TRANSPORT: Railways

JERSEY ALMANAC AND TRADES DIRECTORY

31151U14R-130

Editorial Address: PO Box 582, JERSEY, JE4 8XQ
Tel: 01534 611740 **Fax:** 01534 611610
Email: editorial@msppublishing.com
Advertising Address: As above.
Email: jvarcoe@msppublishing.com
Web site: http://www.thisisjersey.com
Publisher: MSP Publishing
Frequency: Annual - Published in December
Cover Price: £22.50
Circulation: 5,000 (Publisher's Statement)
Usual Pagination: 192
Editor: Peter Body; **Advertising Manager:** John Varcoe
Summary of Content: Publication containing useful information on Jersey and its commercial activities. An index of all house owners is also listed.
Readership/Target Audience: Aimed at businesses and residents in Jersey.
ADVERTISING RATES:
Full Page Mono £625.00
Full Page Colour £695.00
Agency Commission: 10%
Mechanical Data: Bleed Size: +3mm, Trim Size: 297 x 210mm, Film: Digital
BUSINESS: COMMERCE, INDUSTRY & MANAGEMENT: Commerce Related

THE JERSEY Q

37829U21C-375

Formerly: The Jersey
Editorial Address: Higher Moorlake Cottage, Moorlake, CREDITON, EX17 5EL **Tel:** 07968 182896
Fax: 01363 774992
Email: info@ukjerseys.com
Advertising Address: As above. **Tel:** 01363 776623
Email: aba@adelabooth.co.uk
Web site: http://www.jerseycattle.org
Publisher: Jersey Cattle Society of the United Kingdom
Frequency: Quarterly
Free to qualifying individuals
Circulation: 2,000 (Publisher's Statement)
Usual Pagination: 72
Editor: Roger Trewhella; **Advertising Manager:** Roger Trewhella
Summary of Content: Journal covering dairy farming, milk trade and stock breeding.
Readership/Target Audience: Read by members of the Jersey Cattle Society.
ADVERTISING: Rates on application
BUSINESS: AGRICULTURE & FARMING: Dairy Farming

THE JEWELLER

707096U52A-90

Editorial Address: 78A Luke Street, LONDON, EC2A 4XG
Tel: 020 7613 4445 **Fax:** 020 7613 4450
Email: joslyoung@gmail.com
Advertising Address: Cube Communications, 103 Farrington Road, LONDON, EC1R 3BS **Tel:** 020 7833 5500
Fax: 020 7833 5526
Email: ian@cube-uk.com
Web site: http://www.jewellers-online.org
Publisher: The National Association of Goldsmiths
Date Established: 1997
Frequency: 6 issues yearly
Cover Price: £4.95
Circulation: 4,000 (Publisher's Statement)
Usual Pagination: 64
Editor: Jo Young

Summary of Content: Magazine covering all aspects of the jewellery, watch and giftware industry. Covers news, features and new products.
Readership/Target Audience: Aimed at jewellery, watch and gift retailers and members of the jewellery industry and British Jewellers Association.
ADVERTISING RATES:
Full Page Colour £950.00
Agency Commission: 10%
Mechanical Data: Type Area: 260 x 182mm, Bleed Size: 303 x 216mm, Trim Size: 297 x 210mm, Film: Digital, Col Length: 260mm, Page Width: 182mm
Copy instructions: Copy Date: 5th of the month prior to publication date
BUSINESS: GIFT TRADE: Jewellery

JEWELLERY FOCUS

1708234U52A-121

Editorial Address: Suite 209, 2nd Floor, Wellington House, Butt Road, COLCHESTER, CO3 3DA **Tel:** 01206 767797
Fax: 01206 767532
Email: tom@jewelleryfocus.co.uk
Advertising Address: As above.
Email: jennifer@jewelleryfocus.co.uk
Web site: http://www.jewelleryfocus.co.uk
Publisher: Mulberry Publications Ltd
Date Established: 2006
Frequency: Monthly - Published in the 1st week of the cover month
Free to qualifying individuals
Circulation: 9,000 (Publisher's Statement)
Usual Pagination: 60
Advertising Manager: Kelly Smith
Summary of Content: Magazine focusing on the jewellery trade including industry news, interviews and product reviews.
Readership/Target Audience: Aimed at retailers in the jewellery trade.
ADVERTISING RATES:
Full Page Colour £2110.00
Agency Commission: 10%
Mechanical Data: Bleed Size: 303 x 216mm, Trim Size: 297 x 210mm, Film: Digital
Copy instructions: Copy Date: 4 weeks prior to publication date
BUSINESS: GIFT TRADE: Jewellery

JEWELLERY IN BRITAIN

625846U52A-100

Editorial Address: 10 Vyse Street, BIRMINGHAM, B18 6LT
Tel: 0121 237 1112 **Fax:** 0121 237 1113
Email: lindsey.straughton@jewelleryinbritain.org.uk
Web site: http://www.bja.org.uk
Publisher: EMAP Inform
Date Established: 2000
Frequency: Quarterly
Cover Price: Free
Circulation: 7,000 (Publisher's Statement)
Usual Pagination: 20
Editor: Lindsey Straughton
Summary of Content: Magazine covering trade association news, recent technologies, product trends and innovations within jewellery manufacture.
Readership/Target Audience: Read by companies involved in all aspects of jewellery and silverware production.
ADVERTISING: No Advertising taken
BUSINESS: GIFT TRADE: Jewellery

THE JOB

38433U32F-180

Editorial Address: Sea Containers House, 20 Upper Ground, LONDON, SE1 9PD **Tel:** 020 7775 5777
Email: jon.watkins@sevensquared.co.uk
Advertising Address: Square 7 Media Ltd, 1st Floor, 3 More London Riverside, LONDON, SE1 2RE **Tel:** 020 3283 4055
Email: gaynor@square7media.co.uk
Web site: http://www.met.police.uk/jobs
Publisher: Seven Squared
Frequency: Monthly
Free to qualifying individuals
Circulation: 19,500 (Publisher's Statement)
Usual Pagination: 32
Editor: Jon Watkins; **Advertising Manager:** Gaynor Garton;
Publisher: Sian Dudley
Summary of Content: Newspaper covering Metropolitan Police news, information and events.
Readership/Target Audience: Read by Metropolitan Police staff.
ADVERTISING RATES:
Full Page Colour £3500.00
Agency Commission: 10%
Mechanical Data: Trim Size: 260 x 225mm
BUSINESS: LOCAL GOVERNMENT, LEISURE & RECREATION: Police

JOBS AND CAREERS

48669U14F-230

Formerly: Appointments
Editorial Address: Newspaper House, Osney Mead, OXFORD, OX2 0EJ **Tel:** 01865 425475 **Fax:** 01865 425554
Email: ghedge@nqo.com
Advertising Address: As above. **Tel:** 01865 425342
Fax: 01865 425347
Email: brand@nqo.com
Web site: http://www.thisisoxfordshire.co.uk
Publisher: Newsquest (Oxfordshire) Ltd
Frequency: Weekly - Published on Saturday
Cover Price: £1.50
Circulation: 6,000 (Publisher's Statement)
Usual Pagination: 45
Editor: Geoffrey Hedge; **Managing Director:** Shamus Donald
Summary of Content: Newspaper covering the Thames Valley area, with job advertisements and features on the employment market.
Readership/Target Audience: Read by professionals looking for new jobs and careers advice.
ADVERTISING RATES:
Full Page Mono £459.00
Agency Commission: 10%
Mechanical Data: Type Area: 340 x 298mm, Col Length: 340mm, Col Widths (Display): 26.9mm, No. of Columns (Display): 9, Film: Digital, Page Width: 298mm
Copy instructions: Copy Date: Thursday prior to publication date
Average advertising content per issue: 75%
BUSINESS: COMMERCE, INDUSTRY & MANAGEMENT: Training & Recruitment

JOBS & CAREERS WEEKLY LONDON & ESSEX

30925U14F-34_42

Editorial Address: Unecol House, 819 London Road, SUTTON, SM3 9BN **Tel:** 020 8329 9244
Email: davidjsmith@london.newsquest.co.uk
Advertising Address: As above.
Email: mfoker@london.newsquest.co.uk
Web site: http://www.yourlocalguardian.co.uk
Publisher: Newsquest Media Group
Frequency: Weekly
Cover Price: £2.50
Annual Sub.: £78.00
Circulation: 3,208 (Publisher's Statement)
Usual Pagination: 80
Editor: David Smith; **Advertising Manager:** Mark Foker
Summary of Content: Newspaper covering job vacancies in Greater London, Kent, Hertfordshire, Buckinghamshire, Surrey, Middlesex, Sussex and Essex.
Readership/Target Audience: Aimed at people looking for a change in career.
ADVERTISING: Rates on application
BUSINESS: COMMERCE, INDUSTRY & MANAGEMENT: Training & Recruitment

JORS-JOURNAL OF THE OPERATIONAL RESEARCH SOCIETY

37234U14R-140

Formerly: Journal of the Operational Research Society
Editorial Address: Seymour House, 12 Edward Street, BIRMINGHAM, B1 2RX **Tel:** 0121 233 9300
Fax: 0121 233 0321
Email: sarah.parry@theorsociety.com
Advertising Address: As above.
Email: hilary.wilkes@theorsociety.com
Web site: http://www.theorsociety.com
Publisher: Palgrave MacMillan Ltd
Date Established: 1950
Frequency: Monthly
Free to qualifying individuals
Annual Sub.: £946.00
Circulation: 3,000 (Publisher's Statement)
Usual Pagination: 50
Editor: Sarah Parry; **Advertising Manager:** Hilary Wilkes
Summary of Content: Journal covering the theory and practice of operational research.
Readership/Target Audience: Read by members of the Operational Research Society.
ADVERTISING RATES:
Full Page Mono £1750.00
Full Page Colour £2045.00
Mechanical Data: Col Length: 245mm, Page Width: 160mm, Film: Digital, Type Area: 245 x 160mm
Copy instructions: Copy Date: 10th of the month prior to publication date
BUSINESS: COMMERCE, INDUSTRY & MANAGEMENT: Commerce Related

THE JOURNAL

35610U2B-55

Editorial Address: 2 Dock Offices, Surrey Quays Road, LONDON, SE16 2XU **Tel:** 020 7252 1187
Fax: 020 7232 2302
Email: editor@cioj.co.uk
Advertising Address: As above.

Email: editor@cioj.co.uk
Web site: http://www.cioj.co.uk
Publisher: The Chartered Institute of Journalists
Date Established: 1912
Frequency: Quarterly
Cover Price: Free
Circulation: 2,000 (Publisher's Statement)
Usual Pagination: 24
Editor: Andy Smith; **Advertising Manager:** Andy Smith
Summary of Content: Official publication of the Chartered Institute of Journalists. Contains news, features and reviews relevant to journalists and the journalistic profession, as well as news about the Chartered Institute of Journalists and its partner organisations.
Readership/Target Audience: Aimed at journalists, media executives and broadcasters. Also read by PR consultants and Internet communicators.
ADVERTISING: Rates on application
BUSINESS: COMMUNICATIONS, ADVERTISING & MARKETING: Press

JOURNAL - BRITISH HOLIDAY & HOME PARKS ASSOCIATION
39726U50-17_80

Editorial Address: 6 Pullman Court, Great Western Road, GLOUCESTER, GL1 3ND **Tel:** 01452 526911
Fax: 01452 508508
Email: s.duggan@bhhpa.org.uk
Advertising Address: As above.
Email: n.clark@bhhpa.org.uk
Web site: http://www.ukparks.com
Publisher: British Holiday and Home Parks Association
Date Established: 1950
Frequency: 6 issues yearly
Free to qualifying individuals
Circulation: 3,200 (Publisher's Statement)
Usual Pagination: 90
Editor: Sharon Duggan; **Advertising Manager:** Neil Clark
Summary of Content: Journal of the representative body of the holiday homes and caravan parks industry, including park homes, caravans, tents and all types of self catering accommodation.
Readership/Target Audience: Read by owners of caravan parks and their suppliers.
ADVERTISING RATES:
Full Page Colour £995.00
Mechanical Data: Bleed Size: +3mm, Film: Digital, Trim Size: 297 x 210mm
Average advertising content per issue: 20%
BUSINESS: TRAVEL & TOURISM

THE JOURNAL OF ADULT CONTINUING EDUCATION
1622642U62F-952

Editorial Address: Renaissance House, 20 Princess Road West, LEICESTER, LE1 6TP **Tel:** 0116 204 4200
Fax: 0116 204 4262
Email: alec.mcaulay@niace.org.uk
Web site: http://archive.niace.org.uk/Publications/Periodicals/JACE/Default.htm
ISSN: 1477-9714
Publisher: National Institute of Adult Continuing Education
Date Established: 2001
Frequency: Half-yearly - Published in April and October
Annual Sub.: £30.00
Circulation: 2,800 (Publisher's Statement)
Editor: Mike Osborne
Summary of Content: Journal containing theoretical and empirical works in the fields of adult, community and continuing education.
Readership/Target Audience: Aimed at academics, researchers, professionals and practitioners.
ADVERTISING: No Advertising taken
BUSINESS: CHURCH & SCHOOL EQUIPMENT & EDUCATION: Adult Education

THE JOURNAL OF ADULT PROTECTION
601110U32G-72_90

Editorial Address: Richmond House, Richmond Road, BRIGHTON, BN2 3RL **Tel:** 01273 623222
Fax: 01273 625526
Email: joannas@pavpub.com
Advertising Address: As above. **Tel:** 0870 890 1080
Fax: 0870 890 1081
Email: pauls@pavpub.com
Web site: http://www.pavpub.com
ISSN: 1466-8203
Publisher: Pavilion Journals (Brighton) Ltd
Date Established: 1999
Frequency: Quarterly
Annual Sub.: £129.00
Circulation: 550 (Publisher's Statement)
Usual Pagination: 48
Editor: Paul Kingston; **Advertising Manager:** Paul Somerville
Summary of Content: Academic journal covering all aspects of adult protection, from sexual to financial abuse.

Contains information on practice, policy, implementation and local government projects.
Readership/Target Audience: Read by managers in health and social care, researchers and policy makers.
ADVERTISING RATES:
Full Page Mono £350.00
Mechanical Data: Page Width: 150mm, Trim Size: 297 x 210mm, No. of Columns (Display): 2, Col Widths (Display): 72mm, Col Length: 225mm, Type Area: 225 x 150mm, Film: Digital
Average advertising content per issue: 10%
BUSINESS: LOCAL GOVERNMENT, LEISURE & RECREATION: Community Care & Social Services

JOURNAL OF ADVANCED NURSING
40308U56B-150

Editorial Address: 9600 Garsington Road, Cowley, OXFORD, OX4 2DQ **Tel:** 01865 476518 **Fax:** 01865 471519
Email: jan@oxon.blackwellpublishing.com
Advertising Address: As above. **Tel:** 01865 776868
Fax: 01865 471271
Email: joanna.baker@oxon.blackwellpublishing.com
Web site: http://www.journalofadvancednursing.com
ISSN: 0309-2402
Publisher: Wiley-Blackwell Publishing
Frequency: 24 issues yearly
Annual Sub.: £119.00
Circulation: 2,150 (Publisher's Statement)
Usual Pagination: 112
Editor: Elizabeth Phillamore; **Executive Editor:** Christine Webb; **Editor-in-Chief:** Alison Tierney; **Publisher:** Griselda Campbell
Summary of Content: Journal containing scholarly literature on nursing, midwifery and health visiting.
Readership/Target Audience: Aimed at senior nurses, midwives, health visitors and nursing students.
ADVERTISING RATES:
Full Page Mono £550.00
Full Page Colour £950.00
Agency Commission: 10%
Mechanical Data: Page Width: 170mm, Type Area: 230 x 170mm, Col Length: 230mm, Trim Size: 276 x 210mm, Bleed Size: 282 x 216mm, Film: Digital
Copy instructions: Copy Date: 6 weeks prior to publication date
BUSINESS: HEALTH & MEDICAL: Nursing

JOURNAL OF AFRICAN ECONOMIES
19995U1A-226

Editorial Address: CSAE, Department of Economics, University of Oxford, Manor Building, Manor Road, OXFORD, OX1 3UQ **Tel:** 01865 271084 **Fax:** 01865 281447
Email: csaepub@economics.ox.ac.uk
Advertising Address: Great Clarendon Street, OXFORD, OX2 6DP **Tel:** 01865 353329
Email: jnlsadvertising@oxfordjournals.org
Web site: http://www.oup.co.uk/jnls
ISSN: 0963-8024
Publisher: OUP
Date Established: 1992
Frequency: 5 issues yearly
Cover Price: £17.00
Annual Sub.: £67.00
Usual Pagination: 172
Editor: Suzanne George; **Managing Editor:** Michael Bleaney
Summary of Content: Journal that focuses on the continent of Africa. It publishes applied research papers, together with book reviews and a listing of current working papers from around the world.
Readership/Target Audience: Aimed at those interested in Africa's economic development.
ADVERTISING RATES:
Full Page Mono £235.00
Agency Commission: 10%
Mechanical Data: Film: Digital, Col Length: 200mm, Type Area: 200 x 130mm, Page Width: 130mm
Copy instructions: Copy Date: Middle of the month prior to publication date
BUSINESS: FINANCE & ECONOMICS

JOURNAL OF ANALYTICAL ATOMIC SPECTROMETRY
1625999U55-9008

Editorial Address: Thomas Graham House, Science Park, Milton Road, CAMBRIDGE, CB4 0WF **Tel:** 01223 420066
Fax: 01223 420247
Email: jaas@rsc.org
Advertising Address: As above. **Tel:** 01223 432246
Fax: 01223 426017
Email: advertising@rsc.org
Web site: http://www.rsc.org/jaas
ISSN: 0267-9477
Publisher: Royal Society of Chemistry
Frequency: Monthly
Annual Sub.: £1349.00
Circulation: 700 (Publisher's Statement)

Editor: Niamh O'Connor; **Advertising Manager:** Ian Swain
Summary of Content: Journal covering all aspects of development and applications of analytical atomic spectrometry.
Readership/Target Audience: Aimed at research scientists, manufacturers and users of spectrometric equipment.
ADVERTISING RATES:
Full Page Mono £890.00
Mechanical Data: Type Area: 252 x 188mm, Col Length: 252mm, Bleed Size: 281 x 216mm, Trim Size: 275 x 210mm, Page Width: 188mm
BUSINESS: APPLIED SCIENCE & LABORATORIES

THE JOURNAL OF ANTIMICROBIAL CHEMOTHERAPY
601540U56A-69_3

Editorial Address: JAC Editorial Office, 11 The Wharf, 16 Bridge Street, BIRMINGHAM, B1 2JS
Advertising Address: Great Clarendon Street, OXFORD, OX2 6DP **Tel:** 01865 354637 **Fax:** 01865 353774
Email: steve.simmonds@oxfordjournals.org
Web site: http://www.oup.co.uk/jnls
ISSN: 0305-7453
Publisher: OUP
Date Established: 1975
Frequency: Monthly
Annual Sub.: £374.00
Circulation: 3,891 (Publisher's Statement)
Editor: C. Drummond
Summary of Content: Journal containing peer-reviewed articles on the laboratory aspects and clinical use of all antimicrobials, including antibacterial, antiviral, antifungal and antiprotozoal.
Readership/Target Audience: Aimed at all members of British Society for Antimicrobial Chemotherapy, representatives from academia, industry and health services and those who are influential in formulary decisions.
ADVERTISING RATES:
Full Page Mono £742.00
Full Page Colour £1236.00
Agency Commission: 10%
Mechanical Data: Type Area: 238 x 182mm, Trim Size: 276 x 210mm, Bleed Size: 286 x 220mm, Col Length: 238mm, Film: Digital, Print Process: Litho, Page Width: 182mm
Copy instructions: Copy Date: 4 weeks prior to publication date
BUSINESS: HEALTH & MEDICAL

JOURNAL OF APPLIED RESEARCH IN INTELLECTUAL DISABILITY
40589U56R-69_55

Editorial Address: Tizard Centre, University of Kent, CANTERBURY, CT2 7LZ **Tel:** 01227 764000
Fax: 01227 763674
Email: g.h.murphy@kent.ac.uk
Advertising Address: 9600 Garsington Road, Cowley, OXFORD, OX4 2DQ **Tel:** 01865 776868 **Fax:** 01865 714591
Email: craig.pickett@wiley.com
Web site: http://www.blackwellpublishing.com/jarid
ISSN: 1360-2322
Publisher: Wiley-Blackwell Publishing
Date Established: 1988
Frequency: Quarterly
Annual Sub.: £57.00
Circulation: 600 (Publisher's Statement)
Usual Pagination: 94
Editor: Glynis Murphy
Summary of Content: Designed to draw together the findings of applied research in intellectual disabilities undertaken in the UK and overseas.
Readership/Target Audience: Aimed at research psychologists and professionals from all disciplines concerned with the care, treatment and rehabilitation of people with learning disabilities.
ADVERTISING RATES:
Full Page Mono £450.00
Full Page Colour £850.00
Agency Commission: 10%
Mechanical Data: Trim Size: 276 x 210mm, Bleed Size: +3mm, Film: Digital
Copy instructions: Copy Date: 6 weeks prior to publication date
BUSINESS: HEALTH & MEDICAL: Health Medical Related

JOURNAL OF ARCHITECTURAL COATINGS
1664683U19C-702

Editorial Address: 26 Chatsworth Road, SUTTON, SM3 8PN **Tel:** 020 8644 9977 **Fax:** 020 8644 9937
Email: brianpce@aol.com
Advertising Address: 2100 Wharton Street, Suite 310, PITTSBURGH PA 15203 **Tel:** 412 431 8300
Email: ekapp@protectivecoatings.com
Web site: http://www.paintsquare.com
Publisher: Technology Publishing Company
Date Established: 2005
Frequency: 6 issues yearly
Cover Price: $10.00
Free to qualifying individuals

Annual Sub.: $24.00
Circulation: 20,000 (Publisher's Statement)
Usual Pagination: 72
Editor: Brian Goldie; **Advertising Manager:** Emma Kapp
Summary of Content: Journal covering the practical aspects of architectural coatings.
Readership/Target Audience: Aimed at architects, specifiers, building managers, contractors, dealers and suppliers.
ADVERTISING RATES:
Full Page Mono $3543.00
Full Page Colour $4796.00
Agency Commission: 15%
Mechanical Data: Type Area: 254 x 183mm, Bleed Size: 282 x 212mm, Trim Size: 276 x 206mm, Col Length: 254mm, Page Width: 183mm, Film: Digital
BUSINESS: ENGINEERING & MACHINERY: Finishing

JOURNAL OF ASSET MANAGEMENT

759747U1F-277_35

Editorial Address: 4 Crinan Street, LONDON, N1 9XW
Tel: 020 7843 4684 **Fax:** 020 7843 4601
Email: b.rouse@palgrave.com
Advertising Address: As above.
Email: b.rouse@palgrave.com
Web site: http://www.palgrave.com
ISSN: 1470-8272
Publisher: Palgrave Macmillan Ltd
Date Established: 2000
Frequency: 6 issues yearly
Annual Sub.: £355.00
Usual Pagination: 72
Editor: Brenda Rouse; **Advertising Manager:** Brenda Rouse; **Managing Editor:** Stephen Satchell
Summary of Content: Journal covering new investment techniques, methodologies and strategies, new products and technologies, empirical studies, regulatory and legal developments, best practice and emerging trends in the asset management industry.
Readership/Target Audience: Read by asset managers, heads of research, CEOs, pension fund managers, risk managers, actuarial consultants, corporate treasurers, investment strategists, heads of pensions, quantitative analysts, investment consultants, chief investment officers and professors of economics.
ADVERTISING RATES:
Full Page Mono £500.00
Mechanical Data: Trim Size: 270 x 210mm, Film: Digital
BUSINESS: FINANCE & ECONOMICS: Investment

JOURNAL OF AUTOMATED METHODS & MANAGEMENT IN CHEMISTRY

36673U13-102

Editorial Address: Arthur House, Crayfields Industrial Park, Main Road, St Pauls Cray, ORPINGTON, BR5 3HP
Tel: 01689 891211 **Fax:** 01689 896009
Email: pbs@psanalytical.com
ISSN: 1463-9246
Publisher: Hindawi Publishing Corporation
Date Established: 1978
Frequency: 6 issues yearly
Annual Sub.: £112.00
Circulation: 1,000 (Publisher's Statement)
Usual Pagination: 36
Editor: Peter Stockwell; **Editor-in-Chief:** Peter Stockwell
Summary of Content: Journal covering all aspects of automation in the analytical, clinical and industrial environments.
Readership/Target Audience: Read by clinical, analytical, industrial and environmental chemists, laboratory managers and manufacturers.
ADVERTISING: Rates on application
BUSINESS: CHEMICALS

JOURNAL OF BIOLOGICAL EDUCATION

41494U64F-50

Editorial Address: 9 Red Lion Court, LONDON, EC4A 3EF
Tel: 020 7936 5900 **Fax:** 020 7936 5901
Email: jbe@iob.org
Advertising Address: As above.
Email: info@iob.org
Web site: http://www.iob.org
ISSN: 0021-9266
Publisher: Institute of Biology
Date Established: 1967
Frequency: Quarterly
Annual Sub.: £57.00
Circulation: 2,000 (Publisher's Statement)
Usual Pagination: 52
Editor: Simon Napper; **Features Editor:** Simon Napper
Summary of Content: Journal specialising in biological education.
Readership/Target Audience: Aimed at all workers in biology education including both teachers and researchers.
ADVERTISING: Rates on application

Copy instructions: Copy Date: 1st of the month prior to publication date
BUSINESS: OTHER CLASSIFICATIONS: Biology

JOURNAL OF BONE & JOINT SURGERY (BRITISH VOLUME)

40271U56A-69_4

Editorial Address: 22 Buckingham Street, LONDON, WC2N 6ET **Tel:** 020 7782 0010 **Fax:** 020 7782 0995
Email: edit@jbjs.org.uk
Advertising Address: Admedica, Stevenson, HADDINGTON, EH41 4PU **Tel:** 01620 823383
Fax: 01620 823325
Email: pnoble@admedica.co.uk
Web site: http://www.jbjs.org.uk
ISSN: 0301-620X
Publisher: British Editorial Society of Bone and Joint Surgery
Date Established: 1948
Frequency: Monthly
Annual Sub.: £80.00
Circulation: 15,000 (Publisher's Statement)
Usual Pagination: 160
Editor: James Scott; **Advertising Manager:** Pam Noble; **Publisher:** Stephen Bishop
Summary of Content: Official international journal covering all aspects of orthopaedics, sports injury and trauma.
Language(s): English; French; German; Italian; Polish; Romanian; Spanish
Readership/Target Audience: Aimed at trainee orthopaedic surgeons, orthopaedic surgeons and associated professions.
ADVERTISING RATES:
Full Page Mono £1380.00
Full Page Colour £2400.00
Agency Commission: 10%
Mechanical Data: Film: Digital, Type Area: 254 x 178mm, Bleed Size: 281 x 219mm, Trim Size: 275 x 213mm, Col Length: 254mm, Page Width: 178mm
Copy instructions: Copy Date: 1st of the month prior to publication date
Average advertising content per issue: 15%
BUSINESS: HEALTH & MEDICAL

THE JOURNAL OF BRAND MANAGEMENT

35507U2A-107_35

Editorial Address: The Macmillan Building, 4 Crinan Street, LONDON, N1 9XW **Tel:** 020 7843 4684 **Fax:** 020 7843 4601
Email: b.rouse@palgrave.com
Advertising Address: Museum House, 25 Museum Street, LONDON, WC1A 1JT **Tel:** 01256 329242 **Fax:** 01256 330688
Web site: http://www.palgrave.com
ISSN: 1350-231X
Publisher: Palgrave Macmillan Ltd
Date Established: 1993
Frequency: 8 issues yearly
Annual Sub.: £370.00
Circulation: 1,500 (Publisher's Statement)
Usual Pagination: 72
Editor: Brenda Rouse; **Advertising Manager:** Rosalind Pyne; **Managing Editor:** Brenda Rouse
Summary of Content: Journal providing a forum for the launch, development, management and evaluation of brands.
Readership/Target Audience: Read by marketing directors, managers, consultants and academics.
ADVERTISING: Rates on application
Mechanical Data: Trim Size: 270 x 210mm, Film: Digital, Type Area: 240 x 180mm, Col Length: 240mm, Page Width: 180mm
Copy instructions: Copy Date: 4 weeks prior to publication date
BUSINESS: COMMUNICATIONS, ADVERTISING & MARKETING

JOURNAL OF BUSINESS LAW

39192U44-1080

Editorial Address: The Hatchery, Hall Bank Lane, HEBDEN BRIDGE, HX7 5HQ **Tel:** 01422 888000 **Fax:** 01422 888002
Email: stephanie.askham@thomsonreuters.com
Web site: http://www.sweetandmaxwell.co.uk
ISSN: 0021-9460
Publisher: Sweet & Maxwell Ltd
Frequency: 8 issues yearly
Annual Sub.: £255.00
Circulation: 1,300 (Publisher's Statement)
Editor: Stephanie Askham
Summary of Content: Journal containing regular features on British, American, European and overseas business law, including recent and impending developments.
Readership/Target Audience: Read by high level practitioners including solicitors, legal advisers of large companies and financial institutions, accountants, economists and lecturers.
ADVERTISING: No Advertising taken
BUSINESS: LEGAL

THE JOURNAL OF BUSINESS STRATEGY

1641398U14A-517

Editorial Address: Howard House, Wagon Lane, BINGLEY, BD16 1WA **Tel:** 01274 777700 **Fax:** 01274 785200
Email: kfoster@emeraldinsight.com
Web site: http://www.emeraldinsight.com/jbs.htm
ISSN: 0275-6668
Publisher: Emerald Group Publishing Ltd
Frequency: 6 issues yearly
Usual Pagination: 64
Editor: Kim Foster; **Publisher:** Kim Foster
Summary of Content: Journal focusing on practical applications of business theory covering areas such as strategy, planning and business intelligence. Also includes columns on marketing, career development and partnerships.
Readership/Target Audience: Aimed at presidents, CEOs, board members or senior managers in any industry.
ADVERTISING: No Advertising taken
BUSINESS: COMMERCE, INDUSTRY & MANAGEMENT

JOURNAL OF CHANGE MANAGEMENT

762880U14A-504

Editorial Address: School of Business, Enterprise and Management, Queen Margaret University, EDINBURGH, MK43 OAL **Tel:** 0131 474 0000
Email: rby@qmu.ac.uk
Advertising Address: 4 Park Square, Milton Park, ABINGDON, OX14 4RN **Tel:** 020 7017 6000
Fax: 020 7017 6713
Email: enquiry@tandf.co.uk
Web site: http://www.informaworld.com/rjcm
ISSN: 1469-7017
Publisher: Routledge, Taylor & Francis
Date Established: 2000
Frequency: Quarterly
Annual Sub.: £237.00
Circulation: 900 (Publisher's Statement)
Usual Pagination: 96
Editor: Rune Todnem By; **Advertising Manager:** Jenna Johnston
Summary of Content: Journal covering business in changing markets including structure, processes, resources, technology and culture.
Readership/Target Audience: Read by change managers, human resources directors, strategic planners, CEOs, managing directors, project managers, business development managers, consultants, operations directors and heads of innovation.
ADVERTISING RATES:
Full Page Mono £250.00
Mechanical Data: Trim Size: 280 x 215mm, Film: Digital, Type Area: 250 x 195mm, Col Length: 250mm, Page Width: 195mm
BUSINESS: COMMERCE, INDUSTRY & MANAGEMENT

JOURNAL OF CHEMICAL TECHNOLOGY AND BIOTECHNOLOGY

39971U55-67

Editorial Address: The Atrium, Southern Gate, CHICHESTER, PO19 8SQ **Tel:** 01243 770200
Fax: 01243 770432
Email: jctb@wiley.com
Advertising Address: As above. **Tel:** 01243 770254
Email: adsales@wiley.co.uk
Web site: http://www.interscience.wiley.com/journal/jctb
ISSN: 0268-2575
Publisher: John Wiley & Sons Ltd
Date Established: 1979
Frequency: Monthly
Annual Sub.: $2205.00
Editor: Jenny Garratt
Summary of Content: Journal covering developments in chemical technology and biotechnology and their effect on commercial products and processes, including sustainable technology. It publishes peer-reviewed front matter articles (reviews, perspectives) as well as research papers.
Readership/Target Audience: Readership includes biochemists, biotechnologists, chemical and process engineers, biochemical engineers and biologists.
ADVERTISING RATES:
Full Page Mono £1175.00
Full Page Colour £2575.00
Agency Commission: 10%
Mechanical Data: Trim Size: 297 x 210mm, Type Area: 270 x 180mm, Col Length: 270mm, Page Width: 180mm, Print Process: Sheet-fed litho, Film: Digital
BUSINESS: APPLIED SCIENCE & LABORATORIES

THE JOURNAL OF CHINESE MEDICINE

40184U56A-69_10

Editorial Address: 22 Cromwell Road, HOVE, BN3 3EB
Tel: 01273 777760 **Fax:** 01273 748588
Email: info@jcm.co.uk
Advertising Address: As above.
Email: info@jcm.co.uk

Web site: http://www.jcm.co.uk
ISSN: 0143-8042
Publisher: The Journal of Chinese Medicine
Date Established: 1979
Frequency: 3 issues yearly - Published in February, June and October
Annual Sub.: £35.00
Circulation: 3,000 (Publisher's Statement)
Usual Pagination: 80
Editor: Peter Deadman; **Managing Director:** Peter Deadman; **Advertising Manager:** Susan Truce; **Publisher:** Peter Deadman
Summary of Content: International academic journal about Chinese medicine, acupuncture, herbal medicine and qigong.
Readership/Target Audience: Aimed at students and practitioners of Chinese medicine.
ADVERTISING RATES:
Full Page Mono £450.00
Full Page Colour £575.00
Agency Commission: 10%
Mechanical Data: Col Length: 260mm, No. of Columns (Display): 2, Type Area: 260 x 177mm, Trim Size: 297 x 210mm, Film: Digital, Bleed Size: 303 x 216mm, Col Widths (Display): 86mm, Page Width: 177mm
Copy instructions: Copy Date: 1st of the month prior to publication date
Average advertising content per issue: 10%
BUSINESS: HEALTH & MEDICAL

JOURNAL OF CLINICAL PHARMACY & THERAPEUTICS
38738U56R-69_80
Editorial Address: 9600 Garsington Road, Cowley, OXFORD, OX4 2DQ **Tel:** 01865 776868 **Fax:** 01865 714951
Web site: http://www.blackwell-science.com/jcp
ISSN: 0269-4727
Publisher: Wiley-Blackwell Publishing
Frequency: 6 issues yearly
Free to qualifying individuals
Circulation: 335 (Publisher's Statement)
Usual Pagination: 80
Editor: Alain Li Wan Po
Summary of Content: Journal containing information about rational therapeutics, evidence based practice, safety, cost effectiveness and clinical efficacy of drugs, drug prescribing and regulatory affairs.
Readership/Target Audience: For researchers, clinicians, pharmacologists and hospital pharmacists.
ADVERTISING: No Advertising taken
BUSINESS: HEALTH & MEDICAL: Health Medical Related

JOURNAL OF COMMONWEALTH LITERATURE
40903U60B-303
Editorial Address: English and American Studies, University of East Anglia, Earlham Road, NORWICH, NR4 7TJ
Tel: 020 7324 8500 **Fax:** 020 7324 8600
Email: johnthierne@aol.com
Web site: http://www.sagepub.co.uk
ISSN: 0021-9894
Publisher: Sage Publications
Frequency: Quarterly
Cover Price: £22.00
Annual Sub.: £69.00
Editor: John Thieme
Summary of Content: Journal acts as a critical and bibliographical forum on Commonwealth writing.
Readership/Target Audience: Aimed at libraries, students and researchers.
ADVERTISING: No Advertising taken
BUSINESS: PUBLISHING: Libraries

JOURNAL OF COMMUNICATION MANAGEMENT
35600U2A-107_37
Editorial Address: Howard House, Wagon Lane, BINGLEY, BD16 1WA **Tel:** 01274 777700 **Fax:** 01274 785200
Email: agregory@leedsmet.co.uk
Web site: http://www.emeraldinsight.com/info/journals/jcom/JCOM.htm
ISSN: 1363-254X
Publisher: Emerald Group Publishing Ltd
Date Established: 1996
Frequency: Quarterly
Annual Sub.: £209.00
Usual Pagination: 96
Editor: Magda Pieczka; **Editor-in-Chief:** Anne Gregory; **Publisher:** Martyn Lawrence
Summary of Content: Journal covering the latest developments, practice and thinking in the management of internal and external communications. Includes referenced articles and case studies.
Readership/Target Audience: Aimed at heads of communications, senior practitioners, academics, consultants and researchers.
ADVERTISING: No Advertising taken
BUSINESS: COMMUNICATIONS, ADVERTISING & MARKETING

JOURNAL OF COMMUNITY NURSING
40310U56B-170
Editorial Address: Westmead House, 123 Westmead Road, SUTTON, SM1 4JH **Tel:** 020 8642 0162 **Fax:** 020 8661 5879
Email: joanna.issa@ptmpublishers.com
Advertising Address: As above. **Fax:** 020 8643 2275
Email: joanna.issa@ptmpublishers.com
Web site: http://www.jcn.co.uk
ISSN: 0263-4465
Publisher: PTM Publishers Ltd
Date Established: 1977
Frequency: Monthly
Free to qualifying individuals
Annual Sub.: £65.00
Circulation: 23,000 (Publisher's Statement)
Usual Pagination: 44
Editor: Joanna Issa; **Advertising Director:** Joanna Issa; **Publisher:** Stephen Mell
Summary of Content: Magazine containing original scientific papers, review articles, case reports and drugs news.
Readership/Target Audience: Specifically for community nurses/midwives/health visitors and regional and district health authorities/primary care trusts.
ADVERTISING RATES:
Full Page Mono £1110.00
Full Page Colour £1730.00
Agency Commission: 10%
Mechanical Data: Type Area: 252 x 184mm, Trim Size: 297 x 210mm, Bleed Size: 303 x 216mm, Print Process: Sheet-fed litho, Film: Digital, Col Length: 252mm, Page Width: 184mm
Average advertising content per issue: 50%
BUSINESS: HEALTH & MEDICAL: Nursing

JOURNAL OF CONFLICT AND SECURITY LAW
601465U44-1085
Editorial Address: The University of Sheffield, SHEFFIELD
Tel: 01865 353907 **Fax:** 01865 353485
Email: jnls.cust.serv@oupjournals.org
Advertising Address: Great Clarendon Street, OXFORD, OX2 6DP **Tel:** 01865 353329
Email: jnlsadvertising@oxfordjournals.org
Web site: http://www.oup.co.uk/jconsl
ISSN: 1467-7954
Publisher: OUP
Date Established: 1995
Frequency: 3 issues yearly - Published in March, July and November
Cover Price: £13.00
Annual Sub.: £32.00
Usual Pagination: 138
Editor: Nigel White
Summary of Content: Journal covering all aspects relating to the international law of armed conflict, including international humanitarian law, the law of war, the law governing the use of armed forces in international relations, the law relating to collective and defence organisations; the legal principals and development of peacekeeping forces, the peaceful settlement of armed conflict in international law, together with issues of military law and other aspects of municipal law affected by armed conflict.
Readership/Target Audience: Aimed at all people who are involved in law, war, international law, military law, armed conflict, international relations, humanitarian law and peacekeeping.
ADVERTISING RATES:
Full Page Mono £235.00
Agency Commission: 10%
Mechanical Data: Film: Digital, Page Width: 130mm, Type Area: 200 x 130mm, Col Length: 200mm
BUSINESS: LEGAL

JOURNAL OF CONSTRUCTIONAL STEEL RESEARCH
38155U27-60
Editorial Address: The University of Surrey, GUILDFORD, GU2 7XH **Tel:** 01483 689544 **Fax:** 01483 300803
Email: g.parke@surrey.ac.uk
ISSN: 0143-974X
Publisher: Elsevier Ltd
Frequency: Monthly
Editor: Gerry Parke
Summary of Content: Journal about steel construction such as bridges, buildings and offshore structures.
Readership/Target Audience: Aimed at research workers, designers and engineers in the civil, structural and construction engineering fields.
ADVERTISING: No Advertising taken
BUSINESS: METAL, IRON & STEEL

JOURNAL OF CONSUMER BEHAVIOUR
711712U2F-41_50
Editorial Address: The Atrium, Southern Gate, CHICHESTER, PO19 8SQ **Tel:** 01243 775878

Advertising Address: As above. **Tel:** 01243 770254
Fax: 01243 770432
Email: fpidduck@wiley.co.uk
Web site: http://www.interscience.wiley.com/journal/cb
ISSN: 1472-0817
Publisher: John Wiley & Sons Ltd
Date Established: 2001
Frequency: 6 issues yearly
Annual Sub.: £224.00
Circulation: 600 (Publisher's Statement)
Usual Pagination: 96
Editor: Graham Russel
Summary of Content: Academic journal including practitioner papers based around all aspects of consumer behaviour.
Readership/Target Audience: Read by marketing academics and managers, market research managers, accounts directors, customer relations managers, marketing communications managers, media directors and planners.
ADVERTISING RATES:
Full Page Mono .... £1175..00
Full Page Colour £2575.00
Agency Commission: 10%
Mechanical Data: Bleed Size: 276 x 216mm, Trim Size: 297 x 210mm, Film: Digital, Type Area: 270 x 180mm, Col Length: 270mm, Page Width: 180mm
BUSINESS: COMMUNICATIONS, ADVERTISING & MARKETING: Selling

THE JOURNAL OF CONSUMER MARKETING
35508U2A-107_38
Editorial Address: Howard House, Wagon Lane, BINGLEY, BD16 1WA **Tel:** 01274 777700 **Fax:** 01274 785200
Email: rwhitfield@emeraldinsight.com
Web site: http://www.emeraldinsight.com
Publisher: Emerald Group Publishing Ltd
Frequency: 7 issues yearly
Editor: Richard Whitfield; **Publisher:** Richard Whitfield
Summary of Content: Journal covering consumer views, market segmentation, high technology and features on brand building. Includes articles on value analysis, demographics and other consumer marketing issues.
Readership/Target Audience: Read by academics in the marketing field.
ADVERTISING: No Advertising taken
BUSINESS: COMMUNICATIONS, ADVERTISING & MARKETING

JOURNAL OF CONTEMPORARY HISTORY
48850U62R-173
Editorial Address: 4 Devonshire Street, LONDON, W1W 5BH **Tel:** 020 7324 8500 **Fax:** 020 7324 8600
Advertising Address: 1 Oliver's Yard, 55 City Road, LONDON, EC1Y 1SP **Tel:** 020 7324 8500
Fax: 020 7324 8600
Email: rehannah.karim@sagepub.co.uk
Web site: http://www.sagepub.co.uk
ISSN: 0022-0094
Publisher: Sage Publications
Date Established: 1966
Frequency: Quarterly
Annual Sub.: £51.00
Circulation: 1,400 (Publisher's Statement)
Usual Pagination: 192
Editor: Richard Evans; **Advertising Manager:** Rehannah Karim
Summary of Content: An international forum for the analysis and discussion of 20th century history: the people, periods, places and critical issues.
Readership/Target Audience: Aimed at academic historians and students of contemporary history.
ADVERTISING RATES:
Full Page Mono £400.00
Agency Commission: 5%
Mechanical Data: Page Width: 130mm, Film: Digital, Type Area: 205 x 130mm, Col Length: 205mm
BUSINESS: CHURCH & SCHOOL EQUIPMENT & EDUCATION: Education Related

JOURNAL OF CORPORATE REAL ESTATE
1750462U1E-393
Editorial Address: Howard House, Wagon Lane, BINGLEY, BD16 1WA **Tel:** 01274 777700
Email: vrobillard@emeraldinsight.com
Web site: http://www.emeraldinsight.com/jcre.htm
ISSN: 1463-001X
Publisher: Emerald Group Publishing Ltd
Date Established: 1999
Frequency: Quarterly
Annual Sub.: £399.00
Usual Pagination: 96
Editor: Valerie Robillard; **Publisher:** Valerie Robillard
Summary of Content: Publication dedicated to corporate real estate providing guidance on best practice, new developments, applied research and case studies on key strategic issues.

Business Magazines

Readership/Target Audience: Aimed at corporate real estate executives.
ADVERTISING: No Advertising taken
BUSINESS: FINANCE & ECONOMICS: Property

JOURNAL OF DATABASE MARKETING & CUSTOMER STRATEGY MANAGEMENT

35509U2A-107_40

Formerly: Journal of Database Marketing
Editorial Address: Macmillan Building, 4 Crinan Street, LONDON, N1 9XW **Tel:** 020 7843 4684 **Fax:** 020 7843 4601
Email: b.rouse@palgrave.com
Advertising Address: Brunel Road, Houndmills, BASINGSTOKE, RG21 6XS **Tel:** 01256 329242
Fax: 01256 353774
Email: h.russell@palgrave.com
Web site: http://www.palgrave.com
ISSN: 1350-2328
Publisher: Palgrave Macmillan Ltd
Date Established: 1995
Frequency: Quarterly
Annual Sub.: £349.00
Circulation: 1,500 (Publisher's Statement)
Usual Pagination: 96
Editor: Brenda Rouse; **Advertising Manager:** Hannah Russell; **Managing Editor:** John Ozimek
Summary of Content: Journal covering refereed articles on building databases, analysis, data protection, data warehousing and mining.
Readership/Target Audience: Read by marketing directors, managers, consultants and academics.
ADVERTISING RATES:
Full Page Mono £500.00
Full Page Colour £1000.00
Mechanical Data: Trim Size: 270 x 210mm, Film: Digital
Copy instructions: Copy Date: 6 weeks prior to publication date
BUSINESS: COMMUNICATIONS, ADVERTISING & MARKETING

THE JOURNAL OF DEMENTIA CARE

38478U32G-73

Editorial Address: 2nd Floor, Culvert House, Culvert Road, Battersea, LONDON, SW11 5DH **Tel:** 020 7720 2108
Fax: 020 7498 3023
Email: sue@hawkerpublications.com
Advertising Address: As above.
Email: caroline@hawkerpublications.com
Web site: http://www.careinfo.org/dementiacare
ISSN: 1351-8372
Publisher: Hawker Publications
Date Established: 1993
Frequency: 6 issues yearly
Annual Sub.: £63.00
Circulation: 4,900 (Publisher's Statement)
Usual Pagination: 40
Editor: Sue Benson; **Editor-in-Chief:** Richard Hawkins; **Managing Director:** Richard Hawkins; **Advertising Director:** Caroline Bowern; **Publisher:** Pat Petker
Summary of Content: Journal containing news and features on education, care practice, training and research as well as debate about practical, moral and ethical issues in dementia care.
Readership/Target Audience: For professionals caring for people with dementia.
ADVERTISING RATES:
Full Page Mono £765.00
Full Page Colour £1105.00
Agency Commission: 10%
Mechanical Data: Type Area: 276 x 190mm, Col Length: 276mm, Bleed Size: 304 x 216mm, Trim Size: 298 x 210mm, Film: Digital, Page Width: 190mm
Average advertising content per issue: 15%
BUSINESS: LOCAL GOVERNMENT, LEISURE & RECREATION: Community Care & Social Services

JOURNAL OF DERIVATIVES AND HEDGE FUNDS

759749U1F-129

Formerly: Derivatives Use, Trading and Regulation
Editorial Address: The Macmillan Building, 4 Crinan Street, LONDON, N1 9XW **Tel:** 020 7843 4684 **Fax:** 020 7843 4601
Email: b.rouse@palgrave.com
Advertising Address: As above. **Tel:** 020 7323 2916
Email: b.rouse@palgrave.com
Web site: http://www.palgrave.com
ISSN: 1357-0927
Publisher: Palgrave Macmillan Ltd
Date Established: 1995
Frequency: Quarterly
Annual Sub.: £172.00
Usual Pagination: 96
Editor: Brenda Rouse; **Advertising Manager:** Brenda Rouse; **Managing Editor:** Stephen Satchell

Summary of Content: Journal covering international financial and commodity derivatives with case studies, empirical studies, comments, book and website reviews.
Readership/Target Audience: Read by those working within the derivatives market.
ADVERTISING RATES:
Full Page Mono £400.00
Full Page Colour £800.00
Agency Commission: 10%
Copy instructions: Copy Date: 6 weeks prior to publication date
BUSINESS: FINANCE & ECONOMICS: Investment

JOURNAL OF DESIGN HISTORY

37153U62R-174

Editorial Address: University College Falmouth, Tremough, PENRYN, TR10 9EZ **Tel:** 01865 353907 **Fax:** 01865 353985
Email: jnls.cust.serv@oxfordjournals.org
Advertising Address: 60 Upper Broadmoor Road, CROWTHORNE, RG45 7DE **Tel:** 01344 779945
Fax: 01344 779945
Email: lhann@lhms.fsnet.co.uk
Web site: http://jdh.oxfordjournals.org/
ISSN: 0952-4649
Publisher: OUP
Date Established: 1988
Frequency: Quarterly
Cover Price: £14.00
Annual Sub.: £48.00
Circulation: 900 (Publisher's Statement)
Usual Pagination: 95
Editor: Tim Putnam
Summary of Content: Journal focusing on reviews of specialist archives and collections. Reports on new educational initiatives, debates and a book review section.
Readership/Target Audience: Aimed at academics and students of art and design history and design studies, museum curators, professional designers and members of the Design History Society.
ADVERTISING RATES:
Full Page Mono £310.00
Agency Commission: 10%
Mechanical Data: Col Length: 220mm, Type Area: 220 x 150mm, Page Width: 150mm, Film: Digital
Copy instructions: Copy Date: 16th of the month prior to publication date
BUSINESS: CHURCH & SCHOOL EQUIPMENT & EDUCATION: Education Related

JOURNAL OF ECONOMIC GEOGRAPHY

623980U1A-227

Editorial Address: Department of Geography, University of Southampton, SOUTHAMPTON, SO17 1BJ
Tel: 01865 353907 **Fax:** 01865 353485
Email: n.wrigley@soton.ac.uk
Advertising Address: Great Clarendon Street, OXFORD, OX2 6DP **Tel:** 01865 353329
Email: jnlsadvertising@oxfordjournals.org
Web site: http://www.oup.co.uk/jnls
ISSN: 1468-2702
Publisher: OUP
Date Established: 2000
Frequency: Quarterly
Cover Price: £13.00
Annual Sub.: £240.00
Circulation: 350 (Publisher's Statement)
Usual Pagination: 104
Editor: Neil Wrigley
Summary of Content: Journal publishing new work in the field of economic geography. Particularly interested in topics at the intersection of economics and geography: spatial agglomeration, regional patterns of growth and specialisation, globalisation and the future of cities and regions. Provides a forum for the exchange of ideas between the two disciplines.
Readership/Target Audience: Aimed at geographers and economists.
ADVERTISING RATES:
Full Page Mono £290.00
Agency Commission: 10%
Mechanical Data: Film: Digital, Page Width: 140mm, Type Area: 210 x 140mm, Col Length: 210mm
BUSINESS: FINANCE & ECONOMICS

JOURNAL OF EDUCATION AND WORK

41135U62H-220

Editorial Address: Department of Education, University of Bath, BATH, BA2 7AY **Tel:** 01225 386236
Fax: 01225 386113
Email: h.lauder@bath.ac.uk
Web site: http://www.tandf.co.uk/journals
ISSN: 1363-9080
Publisher: Routledge, Taylor & Francis
Date Established: 1987
Frequency: 5 issues yearly
Annual Sub.: £65.00

Circulation: 200 (Publisher's Statement)
Usual Pagination: 128
Editor: Hugh Lauder
Summary of Content: Journal which focuses on the relationship between all aspects of the education system and the world of work and employment. Also covers issues relating to training.
Readership/Target Audience: Read by key practitioners, advisers, organisers, academics and administrators.
ADVERTISING: No Advertising taken
BUSINESS: CHURCH & SCHOOL EQUIPMENT & EDUCATION: Careers

JOURNAL OF ELECTRON MICROSCOPY

40056U55-67_50

Editorial Address: H.H. Wills Physics Laboratory, Bristol University, Tyndall Avenue, BRISTOL, BS8 1TL
Tel: 01865 353907 **Fax:** 01865 353485
Email: jnls.cust.serv@oxfordjournals.org
Advertising Address: Oxford University Press, Great Clarendon Street, OXFORD, OX2 6DP **Tel:** 01865 354637
Fax: 01865 353774
Email: steve.simmonds@oxfordjournals.org
Web site: http://jmicro.oupjournals.org
ISSN: 0022-0744
Publisher: OUP
Date Established: 1953
Frequency: 6 issues yearly
Cover Price: £26.00
Annual Sub.: £133.00
Usual Pagination: 100
Editor: Hideki Ichinose; **Managing Editor:** Eisaku Katayama
Summary of Content: Official journal of the Japanese Society of Electron Microscopy. The journal is an international forum, for publishing papers and articles on advanced electron microscopy and new scanning probe microscopy. Articles cover theories, methods, techniques and instrumentation, as well as their applications to life and material sciences.
Readership/Target Audience: Aimed at scientists in the field of microscopy.
ADVERTISING RATES:
Full Page Mono £742.00
Full Page Colour £1236.00
Agency Commission: 10%
Mechanical Data: Page Width: 178mm, Col Length: 255mm, Film: Digital, Type Area: 255 x 178mm, Bleed Size: 285 x 222mm, Trim Size: 279 x 216mm, Print Process: Litho
Copy instructions: Copy Date: 8 weeks prior to publication date
BUSINESS: APPLIED SCIENCE & LABORATORIES

JOURNAL OF ENERGY & NATURAL RESOURCES LAW

23754U44-1090

Editorial Address: 10th Floor, 1 Stephen Street, LONDON, W1T 2AT **Tel:** 020 7691 6868 **Fax:** 020 7691 6544
Email: editor@int-bar.org
Advertising Address: As above.
Email: andrew.webster-dunn@int-bar.org
Web site: http://www.ibanet.org
ISSN: 0264-6811
Publisher: International Bar Association
Date Established: 1982
Frequency: Quarterly
Cover Price: £78.00
Free to qualifying individuals
Annual Sub.: £295.00
Circulation: 2,000 (Publisher's Statement)
Usual Pagination: 112
Editor: Tom Maguire; **Managing Editor:** Kath Farrell
Summary of Content: Journal of the International Bar Association's containing sections on energy and natural resources law. Covers legal issues dealing with natural resources, energy, development, trade, transport and finance.
Readership/Target Audience: Aimed at in-house lawyers and lawyers in practice specialising in energy.
ADVERTISING RATES:
Full Page Mono £800.00
Mechanical Data: Film: Digital, Page Width: 134mm, Type Area: 202 x 134mm, Col Length: 202mm, Trim Size: 245 x 170mm, Bleed Size: 251 x 173mm
BUSINESS: LEGAL

JOURNAL OF ENGINEERING DESIGN

37620U19B-345

Editorial Address: 4 Park Square, Milton Park, ABINGDON, OX14 4RN **Tel:** 01235 828600 **Fax:** 01235 829008
Email: jed@metronet.co.uk
Advertising Address: 11 New Fetter Lane, LONDON, EC4P 4EF **Tel:** 020 842 2436 **Fax:** 020 842 2373
Email: kerry.christian@tandf.co.uk
Web site: http://www.informaworld.com/jed
ISSN: 0954-4828
Publisher: Routledge, Taylor & Francis
Date Established: 1990

Frequency: 6 issues yearly
Annual Sub.: $493.00
Usual Pagination: 128
Editor: Alex Duffy; **Publisher:** Meloney Bartlett
Summary of Content: Journal presenting current research into the improvement of design processes, practices in industry and the creation of advanced engineering products, alongside academic studies and review papers on design principles, practice and methodologies in the field of engineering design.
Readership/Target Audience: Aimed at practitioners and academics in the field of engineering design.
BUSINESS: ENGINEERING & MACHINERY: Engineering - Design

JOURNAL OF ENVIRONMENTAL LAW

40669U57-34_50

Editorial Address: Great Clarendon Street, OXFORD, OX2 6DP **Tel:** 01865 353907 **Fax:** 01865 353485
Email: c.j.hilson@reading.ac.uk
Advertising Address: As above. **Tel:** 01865 353329
Email: jnlsadvertising@oxfordjournals.org
Web site: http://jel.oupjournals.org
ISSN: 0952-8873
Publisher: OUP
Date Established: 1989
Frequency: 3 issues yearly - Published in April, July and September
Usual Pagination: 168
Editor: Chris Hilson; **Editor-in-Chief:** Chris Hilson
Summary of Content: Journal providing informed analysis in the field of legal study.
Readership/Target Audience: Aimed at lawyers, scientists, planners and others concerned with the environment and current legislation.
ADVERTISING RATES:
Full Page Mono £310.00
Agency Commission: 10%
Mechanical Data: Type Area: 220 x 150mm, Film: Digital, Col Length: 220mm, Page Width: 150mm
Copy instructions: Copy Date: 24th of the month prior to publication date
BUSINESS: ENVIRONMENT & POLLUTION

JOURNAL OF ENVIRONMENTAL MONITORING

600997U57-34_75

Editorial Address: Thomas Graham House, Science Park, Milton Road, CAMBRIDGE, CB4 0WF **Tel:** 01223 432293
Fax: 01223 420247
Email: jem@rsc.org
Advertising Address: As above. **Tel:** 01223 432246
Fax: 01223 426017
Email: advertising@rsc.org
Web site: http://www.rsc.org/jem
ISSN: 1464-0325
Publisher: Royal Society of Chemistry
Date Established: 1999
Frequency: Monthly
Circulation: 700 (Publisher's Statement)
Usual Pagination: 120
Editor: Harp Minhas; **Advertising Manager:** Ian Swain
Summary of Content: Journal acting as a single source for all relevant information on environmental monitoring issues, including primary papers, news and legislative material. Assesses exposure and health risks through the latest developments in measurement science and places special emphasis on the interface of analytical science with related disciplines.
Readership/Target Audience: Aimed at environmental and health professionals in industry and officials in governmental and regulatory agencies, as well as research scientists interested in the environment.
ADVERTISING RATES:
Full Page Colour £890.00
Mechanical Data: Type Area: 252 x 188mm, Trim Size: 275 x 210mm, Page Width: 188mm, Bleed Size: 281 x 216mm, Col Length: 252mm
BUSINESS: ENVIRONMENT & POLLUTION

JOURNAL OF THE EUROPEAN CERAMIC SOCIETY

36614U12A-60

Editorial Address: University of Oxford, Department of Materials, Parks Road, OXFORD, OX1 3PH
Tel: 01865 843000 **Fax:** 01865 843905
Email: richard.brook@materials.oxford.ac.uk
Advertising Address: 32 Jamestown Road, LONDON, NW1 7BY **Tel:** 020 7424 4400 **Fax:** 01865 853 136
Email: j.kenney@elsevier.com
Web site: http://www.elsevier.com
ISSN: 0955-2219
Publisher: Elsevier Ltd
Date Established: 1989
Frequency: 16 issues yearly
Annual Sub.: EUR2415.54

Summary of Content: Journal publishing the results of original research relating to the structure, properties and processing of ceramic materials.
Readership/Target Audience: Aimed ceramicists and materials scientists.
ADVERTISING RATES:
Full Page Mono EUR1020.00
Full Page Colour EUR2160.00
Agency Commission: 15%
Mechanical Data: Film: Digital, Type Area: 250 x 180mm, Col Length: 250mm, Page Width: 180mm, Trim Size: 280 x 210mm, Bleed Size: 286 x 216mm
Copy instructions: Copy Date: 4 weeks prior to publication date
Average advertising content per issue: 5%
BUSINESS: CERAMICS, POTTERY & GLASS: Ceramics & Pottery

JOURNAL OF EXPERIMENTAL BIOLOGY

41509U64F-55

Editorial Address: Bidder Building, 140 Cowley Road, CAMBRIDGE, CB4 0DL **Tel:** 01223 425525
Fax: 01223 423520
Email: kathryn@biologists.com
Advertising Address: As above. **Tel:** 01223 426164
Fax: 01223 423353
Email: nick@biologists.com
Web site: http://jeb.biologists.org
ISSN: 0022-0949
Publisher: The Company of Biologists Ltd
Frequency: 24 issues yearly
Circulation: 1,350 (Publisher's Statement)
Usual Pagination: 200
Editor: Kathryn Phillips; **News Editor:** Kathryn Phillips;
Advertising Manager: Nick Birch
Summary of Content: Publication containing reviews of new developments in comparative physiology and brief discussions of the latest news and techniques at the forefront of biology.
Readership/Target Audience: Aimed at academics interested in animal physiology.
ADVERTISING: Rates on application
BUSINESS: OTHER CLASSIFICATIONS: Biology

JOURNAL OF EXPERIMENTAL BOTANY

24290U55-67_60

Editorial Address: School of Biosciences, Faculty of Science, Room A03 Plant Sciences, Sutton Bonington, LOUGHBOROUGH, LE12 5RD
Advertising Address: Great Clarendon Street, OXFORD, OX2 6DP **Tel:** 01865 354637
Email: steve.simmonds@oxfordjournals.org
Web site: http://jxb.oupjournals.org
ISSN: 0022-0957
Publisher: OUP
Date Established: 1950
Frequency: 14 issues yearly
Cover Price: £69.00
Annual Sub.: £763.00
Usual Pagination: 200
Editor: Jerry Roberts; **Advertising Manager:** Steve Simmonds
Summary of Content: Journal presents papers in the fields of plant physiology, biochemistry, biophysics, molecular biology and related topics.
Readership/Target Audience: Aimed at academics interested in plant science.
ADVERTISING RATES:
Full Page Mono £742.00
Full Page Colour £1236.00
Agency Commission: 10%
Mechanical Data: Page Width: 178mm, Type Area: 255 x 178mm, Col Length: 255mm, Trim Size: 279 x 216mm, Bleed Size: 285 x 222mm, Print Process: Litho, Film: Digital
Copy instructions: Copy Date: 6 weeks prior to publication date
BUSINESS: APPLIED SCIENCE & LABORATORIES

JOURNAL OF FAMILY HEALTH CARE

40331U56B-173

Formerly: Professional Care of Mother & Child
Editorial Address: PO Box 100, CHICHESTER, PO18 8HD
Tel: 01243 576444 **Fax:** 01243 576456
Email: sarah.monger@keywayspublishing.com
Advertising Address: As above.
Email: sarah.monger@keywayspublishing.com
Web site: http://www.jfhc.co.uk
ISSN: 0964-4156
Publisher: Keyways Publishing Limited
Date Established: 1980
Frequency: 6 issues yearly
Annual Sub.: £28.00
Circulation: 6,000 (Publisher's Statement)
Usual Pagination: 36
Editor: Pat Scowen; **Advertising Manager:** Sarah Monger;
Publisher: Sarah Harkness

Summary of Content: Family health care journal with clinical and general articles.
Readership/Target Audience: Aimed at community health professionals, especially health visitors and their teams, midwives, practice nurses, school nurses, paediatric dieticians, community dieticians and paediatric/ district nurses.
ADVERTISING RATES:
Full Page Colour £1240.00
SCC £10.50
Agency Commission: 10%
Mechanical Data: Bleed Size: 300 x 213mm, Trim Size: 297 x 210mm, Type Area: 260 x 180mm, Print Process: Sheet-fed litho, Film: Positive, right reading, emulsion side down. Digital, Screen: 60 lpc, Col Length: 260mm, Page Width: 180mm
Copy instructions: Copy Date: 3 weeks prior to publication date
Average advertising content per issue: 40%
Supplement(s): Family Healthcare Bulletin - 3xY
BUSINESS: HEALTH & MEDICAL: Nursing

THE JOURNAL OF FAMILY PLANNING AND REPRODUCTIVE HEALTH CARE

40477U56M-300

Formerly: British Journal of Family Planning
Editorial Address: 27 Sussex Place, Regent's Place, LONDON, NW1 4RG **Tel:** 020 7724 5681
Fax: 020 7723 5333
Email: journal@fsrh.org
Advertising Address: PO Box 100, CHICHESTER, PO18 8HD **Tel:** 01243 576444 **Fax:** 01243 576456
Email: sarah.monger@keywayspublishing.com
Web site: http://www.fsrh.org
ISSN: 1471-1893
Publisher: Keyways Publishing Group
Date Established: 1975
Frequency: Quarterly
Free to qualifying individuals
Annual Sub.: £80.00
Circulation: 12,000 (Publisher's Statement)
Usual Pagination: 64
Editor: Anne Szarewski; **Editor-in-Chief:** Anne Szarewski
Summary of Content: Journal that aims to raise awareness of contraception and reproductive health issues including methods, treatments and service delivery and foster continuing professional development and future research.
Readership/Target Audience: Readership includes GPs, gynaecologists, nurses, doctors and other healthcare professionals who have a special interest in reproductive and sexual health.
ADVERTISING RATES:
Full Page Mono £750.00
Full Page Colour £1250.00
Agency Commission: 10%
Mechanical Data: Col Length: 260mm, Film: Digital, Type Area: 260 x 180mm, Bleed Size: 303 x 213mm, Trim Size: 297 x 210mm, No. of Columns (Display): 4, Page Width: 180mm
Copy instructions: Copy Date: 6 weeks prior to publication date
Average advertising content per issue: 20%
BUSINESS: HEALTH & MEDICAL: Family Planning

JOURNAL OF FELINE MEDICINE & SURGERY

41529U64H-158_50

Formerly: Feline Focus
Editorial Address: Taeselbury, High Street, Tisbury, SALISBURY, SP3 6LD **Tel:** 01747 871872
Fax: 01747 871873
Email: jfms@fabcats.org
Advertising Address: 32 Jamestown Road, LONDON, NW1 7BY **Tel:** 020 7424 4200 **Fax:** 020 7424 4433
Email: m.sibson@elsevier.com
Web site: http://intl.elsevierhealth.com
ISSN: 1098-612X
Publisher: Elsevier London Ltd
Date Established: 1999
Frequency: 6 issues yearly
Annual Sub.: £90.00
Circulation: 3,500 (Publisher's Statement)
Usual Pagination: 104
Editor: Marilyn Peters; **Advertising Manager:** Martin Sibson
Summary of Content: Official Journal of the European Society of Feline Medicine. Includes articles on all aspects of feline medicine and surgery, basic research and reviews.
Readership/Target Audience: Aimed at all members of the European Society of Feline Medicine who receive the journal as part of their membership subscription.
ADVERTISING RATES:
Full Page Mono EUR902.00
Full Page Colour EUR1638.00
Mechanical Data: Type Area: 250 x 170mm, Bleed Size: 286 x 216mm, Trim Size: 280 x 210mm, Col Length: 250mm, Film: Positive, right reading, emulsion side down. Digital, Page Width: 170mm
BUSINESS: OTHER CLASSIFICATIONS: Veterinary

Business Magazines

JOURNAL OF FINANCIAL SERVICES MARKETING
601128U1R-180

Editorial Address: Brunel Road, Houndmills, BASINGSTOKE, RG21 6XS **Tel:** 01256 302959
Advertising Address: As above. **Tel:** 01256 302971
Email: advertising@palgrave.com
Web site: http://www.palgrave-journals.com/fsm
ISSN: 1363-0539
Publisher: Palgrave Macmillan Ltd
Frequency: Quarterly
Annual Sub.: £374.00
Circulation: 600 (Publisher's Statement)
Usual Pagination: 96
Editor: Tina Harrison; **Advertising Manager:** Rosalind Pyne
Summary of Content: Journal containing articles on recent developments, latest management thinking and best practice.
Readership/Target Audience: Aimed at financial services marketing practitioners and academic researchers.
ADVERTISING RATES:
Full Page Mono £500.00
Full Page Colour £1000.00
Mechanical Data: Type Area: 270 x 210mm, Col Length: 270mm, Page Width: 210mm, Bleed Size: 276 x 216mm, Film: Digital
Copy instructions: Copy Date: 6 weeks prior to publication date
BUSINESS: FINANCE & ECONOMICS: Financial Related

JOURNAL OF FISH BIOLOGY
1732046U64F-502

Editorial Address: 9600 Garsington Road, Cowley, OXFORD, OX4 2DQ **Tel:** 01865 476516 **Fax:** 01865 471516
Email: silvana.marciano@oxon.blackwellpublishing.com
Advertising Address: As above. **Tel:** 01865 776868
Fax: 01865 471267
Email: craig.pickett@oxon.blackwellpublishing.com
Publisher: Wiley-Blackwell Publishing
Frequency: 20 issues yearly
Circulation: 1,400 (Publisher's Statement)
Usual Pagination: 336
Editor: Silvana Marciano; **Publisher:** Silvana Marciano
Summary of Content: Journal focusing on aquaculture, behaviour, biochemistry, diseases, distribution, ecology, genetics, growth, immunology, migration, morphology, parasitology, pollution, population studies, reproduction, taxonomy and toxicology.
Readership/Target Audience: Aimed at scientists in all aspects of fish and fisheries research.
ADVERTISING RATES:
Full Page Mono £450.00
Full Page Colour £850.00
Agency Commission: 10%
Mechanical Data: Trim Area: 246 x 171mm, Film: Digital
Copy instructions: Copy Date: 1 week prior to publication date
BUSINESS: OTHER CLASSIFICATIONS: Biology

JOURNAL OF FORENSIC AND LEGAL MEDICINE
40588U56R-69_60

Formerly: Journal of Clinical Forensic Medicine
Editorial Address: 19 Speldhurst Road, LONDON, E9 7EH
Fax: 01621 772200
Email: jasonpaynejames@aol.com
Advertising Address: Elsevier, 32 Jamestown Road, LONDON, NW1 7BY **Tel:** 020 7424 4383 **Fax:** 020 7424 4433
Email: n.dunwell@elsevier.com
Web site: http://www.elsevier.com
ISSN: 1353-1131
Publisher: Elsevier Ltd
Date Established: 1994
Frequency: 6 issues yearly
Circulation: 1,400 (Publisher's Statement)
Usual Pagination: 64
Editor: Jason Payne-James; **Editor-in-Chief:** Jason Payne-James; **Advertising Manager:** Fiona Macnab
Summary of Content: The official journal of the Association of Forensic Physicians, the Australia and New Zealand Forensic Medicine Society Inc. and the British Association in Forensic Medicine.
Readership/Target Audience: Aimed at police surgeons and forensic medical scientists.
ADVERTISING: Rates on application
Agency Commission: 10%
Mechanical Data: Page Width: 180mm, Type Area: 250 x 180mm, Col Length: 250mm, Trim Size: 280 x 210mm, Bleed Size: 286 x 216mm, Film: Digital
Copy instructions: Copy Date: 5 weeks prior to publication date
BUSINESS: HEALTH & MEDICAL: Health Medical Related

THE JOURNAL OF GEMMOLOGY
38268U30-42

Editorial Address: 27 Greville Street, LONDON, EC1N 8TN
Tel: 020 7404 3334 **Fax:** 020 7404 8843
Email: mary.burland@gem-a.com
Web site: http://www.gem-a.com

ISSN: 1355-4565
Publisher: Gemmological Association of Great Britain
Date Established: 1947
Frequency: Half-yearly - Published in April and October
Annual Sub.: £172.00
Circulation: 4,000 (Publisher's Statement)
Usual Pagination: 120
Editor: Mary Burland
Summary of Content: Official publication of the GAGTL. Provides a forum for presentation and discussion of the latest developments in gemmology. Papers are refereed by an international board of Associate Editors with trade, educational and laboratory expertise.
Readership/Target Audience: Aimed at those with interests in the gemological, mineralogical, lapidary and jewellery fields.
ADVERTISING: No Advertising taken
BUSINESS: MINING & QUARRYING

JOURNAL OF HEALTH, ORGANISATION AND MANAGEMENT
40535U56R-71

Formerly: Journal of Management in Medicine
Editorial Address: Howard House, Wagon Lane, BINGLEY, BD16 1WA **Tel:** 01274 777700 **Fax:** 01274 785200
Email: n.h.harding@bradford.ac.uk
Web site: http://www.emeraldinsight.com/info/journals/jhom/jhom.jsp
ISSN: 1477-7266
Publisher: Emerald Group Publishing Ltd
Frequency: 6 issues yearly
Free to qualifying individuals
Annual Sub.: £3749.00
Usual Pagination: 80
Editor: Valerie Robillard; **Publisher:** Valerie Robillard
Summary of Content: Journal acting as a forum for the exchanging of ideas, experiences and information relating to management issues in health care and providing practical approaches to enhance their work. Covers customer service, IT, decision-making, purchasing, management training and quality assurance.
Readership/Target Audience: Aimed at those interested in the management of health care.
ADVERTISING: No Advertising taken
BUSINESS: HEALTH & MEDICAL: Health Medical Related

JOURNAL OF HEALTH PSYCHOLOGY
40506U56N-24_50

Editorial Address: 1 Oliver's Yard, 55 City Road, LONDON, EC1Y 1SP **Tel:** 020 7324 8500 **Fax:** 020 7324 8600
Advertising Address: As above.
Email: advertising@sagepub.co.uk
Web site: http://www.sagepub.co.uk
ISSN: 1359-1053
Publisher: Sage Publications
Date Established: 1996
Frequency: 6 issues yearly
Cover Price: £10.00
Annual Sub.: £44.00
Editor: David Marks
Summary of Content: An international forum for the best research in health psychology from around the world.
Readership/Target Audience: Aimed at professionals working in the area of health psychology.
ADVERTISING RATES:
Full Page Mono £400.00
Agency Commission: 5%
Mechanical Data: Type Area: 210 x 140mm, Col Length: 210mm, Page Width: 140mm, Film: Digital
Copy instructions: Copy Date: 12 weeks prior to publication date
BUSINESS: HEALTH & MEDICAL: Mental Health

JOURNAL OF HERITAGE TOURISM
1779861U50-243

Editorial Address: 4 Park Square, Milton Park, ABINGDON, OX14 4RN **Tel:** 020 7017 6000
Email: jane.buffham@tandf.co.uk
ISSN: 1743-873X
Publisher: Routledge, Taylor & Francis
Frequency: Half-yearly
Annual Sub.: £64.00
Editor: Jane Buffham
Summary of Content: Peer reviewed, international journal focusing on all aspects of heritage tourism.
Readership/Target Audience: Aimed at undergraduates, postgraduates and researchers interested in tourism heritage.
ADVERTISING: No Advertising taken
BUSINESS: TRAVEL & TOURISM

JOURNAL OF THE HISTORY OF COLLECTIONS
30817U62R-463

Editorial Address: Ashmolean Museum, Beaumont Street, OXFORD, OX1 2PH **Tel:** 01865 278000 **Fax:** 01865 278018
Advertising Address: 60 Upper Broadmoor Road, CROWTHORNE, RG45 7DE **Tel:** 01344 779945
Fax: 01344 779945
Email: lhann@lhms.fsnet.co.uk
Web site: http://www3.oup.co.uk/hiscol
ISSN: 0954-6650
Publisher: OUP
Date Established: 1989
Frequency: Half-yearly - Published in June and November
Annual Sub.: £114.00
Circulation: 900 (Publisher's Statement)
Usual Pagination: 152
Editor: Arthur MacGregor; **Publisher:** Clare Morton
Summary of Content: Journal covering the study of collections and their collectors. Includes listings of forthcoming events, conferences, and reviews of relevant publications and exhibitions.
Readership/Target Audience: Aimed at art historians, art dealers, antique dealers and museum curators.
ADVERTISING RATES:
Full Page Mono £310.00
Agency Commission: 10%
BUSINESS: CHURCH & SCHOOL EQUIPMENT & EDUCATION: Education Related

JOURNAL OF IMMIGRATION ASYLUM AND NATIONALITY LAW
39245U44-1880

Formerly: Tolley's Immigration, Asylum and Nationality Law Journal
Editorial Address: Maxwelton House, 41-43 Boltro Road, HAYWARDS HEATH, RH16 1BJ **Tel:** 01444 416119
Fax: 01444 440426
Web site: http://www.tottelpublishing.com
ISSN: 0269-5774
Publisher: Tottel Publishing
Frequency: Quarterly
Usual Pagination: 72
Editor: Linda Whittle
Summary of Content: Official Journal of the Immigration Law Practitioners' Association. Contains news, court and immigration appeal tribunal decisions, ECHR case reports and original articles with a domestic and European focus.
Readership/Target Audience: Aimed at immigration law practitioners.
ADVERTISING: No Advertising taken
BUSINESS: LEGAL

THE JOURNAL OF INDUSTRY AND TECHNOLOGY
37660U19F-672

Editorial Address: 8 Matthew Wren Close, Little Downham, ELY, CB6 2UL **Tel:** 01353 699094 **Fax:** 01353 699094
Email: hammerton_william@hotmail.com
Advertising Address: As above.
Email: williamhammerton_thejournalofindustryandtechnology@ hotmail.co.uk
Web site: http://www.thejournalofindustryandtechnology.biz
Publisher: Journal of Industry and Technology
Date Established: 1978
Frequency: Quarterly
Cover Price: £5.00
Free to qualifying individuals
Annual Sub.: £25.00
Circulation: 6,000 (Publisher's Statement)
Usual Pagination: 48
Editor: Bill Hammerton; **Advertising Manager:** Bill Hammerton
Summary of Content: Journal covering news on the latest industrial developments. Includes articles on equipment, technology, general engineering, quality control and management practices.
Readership/Target Audience: Aimed at managing and production directors, design staff and chief, plant, works and production engineers.
ADVERTISING RATES:
Full Page Mono £1000.00
Full Page Colour £1250.00
SCC £200.00
Agency Commission: 15%
Mechanical Data: Page Width: 180mm, Type Area: 268 x 180mm, Film: Digital, No. of Columns (Display): 2, Col Widths (Display): 120mm, Col Length: 268mm, Trim Size: 285 x 205mm
Copy instructions: Copy Date: 4 weeks prior to publication date
Average advertising content per issue: 40%
BUSINESS: ENGINEERING & MACHINERY: Production & Mechanical Engineering

JOURNAL OF INFECTION PREVENTION

1614541U56B-281

Formerly: The British Journal of Infection Control
Editorial Address: 1 Oliver's Yard, 55 City Road, LONDON, EC1Y 1SP **Tel:** 020 7324 8500 **Fax:** 020 7324 8600
Email: claire.minto@sagepub.co.uk
Advertising Address: As above. **Tel:** 020 7324 5800
Email: matt.schlag@sagepub.co.uk
Web site: http://jip.sagepub.com
ISSN: 1757-1774
Publisher: Sage Publications
Date Established: 2000
Frequency: 6 issues yearly
Annual Sub.: £74.00
Circulation: 2,250 (Publisher's Statement)
Usual Pagination: 36
Editor: Claire Minto
Summary of Content: Journal covering hospital acquired infections.
Readership/Target Audience: Aimed at all Infection Control Nurses in the UK.
ADVERTISING RATES:
Full Page Mono £1012.00
Full Page Colour £1653.00
Agency Commission: 10%
Mechanical Data: Col Length: 254mm, Page Width: 178mm, Bleed Size: 303 x 213mm, Trim Size: 297 x 210mm, Type Area: 254 x 178mm, Film: Digital
Average advertising content per issue: 40%
BUSINESS: HEALTH & MEDICAL: Nursing

JOURNAL OF INTEGRATED CARE

601111U32G-77

Formerly: Managing Community Care
Editorial Address: Richmond House, Richmond Road, BRIGHTON, BN2 3RL **Tel:** 01273 623222
Fax: 01273 625526
Email: peter@whg.org.uk
Advertising Address: As above. **Tel:** 0870 890 1080
Email: pauls@pavpub.com
Web site: http://www.pavpub.com
ISSN: 1461-5436
Publisher: Pavilion Journals (Brighton) Ltd
Date Established: 1992
Frequency: 6 issues yearly
Annual Sub.: £195.00
Circulation: 400 (Publisher's Statement)
Usual Pagination: 48
Editor: Peter Shistlethwaite; **Advertising Manager:** Paul Somerville
Summary of Content: Journal covering new policies, practical issues and news in integrated care.
Readership/Target Audience: Aimed at managers, practitioners and academics.
ADVERTISING RATES:
Full Page Mono £350.00
Agency Commission: 10%
Mechanical Data: Type Area: 215 x 165mm, Col Length: 215mm, Page Width: 165mm
BUSINESS: LOCAL GOVERNMENT, LEISURE & RECREATION: Community Care & Social Services

JOURNAL OF INTELLECTUAL DISABILITIES

601455U62A-250

Formerly: Journal of Learning Disabilities
Editorial Address: 1 Oliver's Yard, 55 City Road, LONDON, EC1Y 1SP **Tel:** 020 7324 8500 **Fax:** 020 7324 8600
Advertising Address: As above.
Email: matt.schlag@sagepub.co.uk
Web site: http://www.sagepub.co.uk
ISSN: 1744-6295
Publisher: Sage Publications
Date Established: 2000
Frequency: Quarterly
Annual Sub.: £44.00
Circulation: 450 (Publisher's Statement)
Editor: Sheena Karim
Summary of Content: Journal covering academic and professional disciplines from education, social and health settings to bring about advancement of services for people with learning disabilities.
Readership/Target Audience: Aimed at professionals and academics in the education, social and health professions for people with learning difficulties.
ADVERTISING RATES:
Full Page Mono £400.00
Agency Commission: 5%
Mechanical Data: Type Area: 210 x 140mm, Col Length: 210mm, Page Width: 140mm, Film: Digital
BUSINESS: CHURCH & SCHOOL EQUIPMENT & EDUCATION: Education

JOURNAL OF INTERNATIONAL BANKING LAW AND REGULATION

35085U1C-210

Formerly: Journal of International Banking Law
Editorial Address: The Hatchery, Hall Bank Lane, Mytholmroyd, HEBDON, HX7 5HQ **Tel:** 01422 888000
Fax: 01422 888002
Email: hannah.buckroyd@thomsonreuters.com
Web site: http://www.sweetandmaxwell.co.uk
ISSN: 0267-937X
Publisher: Sweet & Maxwell Ltd
Frequency: Monthly
Annual Sub.: £645.00
Editor: Hannah Buckroyd
Summary of Content: Journal covering the latest developments in international banking law. Includes a comprehensive news section covering developments from 30 jurisdictions.
Readership/Target Audience: Aimed at city solicitors and in-house banking counsel.
ADVERTISING: No Advertising taken
BUSINESS: FINANCE & ECONOMICS: Banking

JOURNAL OF INTERNATIONAL ECONOMIC LAW

39292U44-1092

Editorial Address: Great Clarendon Street, OXFORD, OX2 6DP **Tel:** 01865 353907 **Fax:** 01865 353985
Email: jiel@law.georgetown.edu
Advertising Address: As above. **Tel:** 01865 353329
Email: jnlsadvertising@oxfordjournals.org
Web site: http://www3.oup.co.uk/jielaw/
ISSN: 1369-3034
Publisher: OUP
Date Established: 1998
Frequency: Quarterly
Cover Price: £16.00
Annual Sub.: £50.00
Usual Pagination: 236
Editor: John Jackson
Summary of Content: Covers the growing area of legal issues concerning economic activity that crosses national borders.
Readership/Target Audience: Aimed at academics and researchers, legal professionals and professionals in areas related to economic law.
ADVERTISING RATES:
Full Page Mono £310.00
Agency Commission: 10%
Mechanical Data: Type Area: 220 x 150mm, Film: Digital, Col Length: 220mm, Page Width: 150mm
Copy instructions: Copy Date: 1 month prior to publication date
BUSINESS: LEGAL

JOURNAL OF INTERNATIONAL MARITIME LAW

23752U44-1020

Formerly: International Maritime Law
Editorial Address: Office G18, Spinners Court, 55 West End, WITNEY, OX28 1NH **Tel:** 01993 706183
Fax: 01993 709410
Email: ltp@lawtext.com
Advertising Address: As above.
Email: jiml@lawtext.com
Web site: http://www.lawtext.com
ISSN: 1353-551X
Publisher: Lawtext Publishing Ltd
Frequency: 6 issues yearly
Annual Sub.: £315.00
Editor: Rachel Caldin; **Advertising Manager:** Rachel Caldin
Summary of Content: Journal covering developments in shipping and transport law, enabling practitioners and academics to acquire essential details and read detailed articles on recent decisions, new legislation and regulations.
Readership/Target Audience: Aimed at shipping lawyers, P & I clubs, legal academics, government agencies, freight and demurrage and defence departments.
ADVERTISING: Rates on application
BUSINESS: LEGAL

JOURNAL OF ISLAMIC STUDIES

29928U62R-451

Editorial Address: Oxford Centre for Islamic Studies, George Street, OXFORD, OX1 2AR **Tel:** 01865 278730
Fax: 01865 248942
Email: publications@oxcis.ac.uk
Advertising Address: 60 Upper Broadmoor Road, CROWTHORNE, RG45 7DE **Tel:** 01344 779945
Fax: 01344 779945
Email: lhann@lhms.fsnet.co.uk
Web site: http://jis.oxfordjournals.org
ISSN: 0955-2340
Publisher: OUP
Date Established: 1990
Frequency: 3 issues yearly - Published in January, May and September

Cover Price: £19.00
Annual Sub.: £47.00
Usual Pagination: 136
Editor: Farhan Ahmad Nizami
Summary of Content: Journal covering all aspects of Islam and the Islamic world.
Readership/Target Audience: Aimed at those interested in Islam.
ADVERTISING RATES:
Full Page Mono £270.00
Agency Commission: 10%
Mechanical Data: Film: Digital, Type Area: 200 x 130mm, Col Length: 200mm, Page Width: 130mm
Copy instructions: Copy Date: 1 month prior to publication date
BUSINESS: CHURCH & SCHOOL EQUIPMENT & EDUCATION: Education Related

THE JOURNAL OF LAW, ECONOMICS AND ORGANISATION

601486U44-1095

Editorial Address: Great Clarendon Street, OXFORD, OX2 6DP **Tel:** 01865 353907 **Fax:** 01865 353985
Email: jleo@pantheon.yale.edu
Advertising Address: Oxford Journals Advertising, PO Box 347, ABINGDON, OX14 1GJ **Tel:** 01235 201904
Web site: http://jleo.oupjournals.org
ISSN: 8756-6222
Publisher: OUP
Date Established: 1984
Frequency: Half-yearly - Published in March and September
Cover Price: £41.00
Annual Sub.: £66.00
Usual Pagination: 224
Editor: Ian Ayers
Summary of Content: Journal containing legal-economic scholarship with other social science disciplines such as political science and sociology.
Readership/Target Audience: Aimed at public and private institutions.
BUSINESS: LEGAL

JOURNAL OF THE LAW SOCIETY OF SCOTLAND

39193U44-1100

Editorial Address: Studio 2001, Mile End, PAISLEY, PA1 1JF **Tel:** 0141 561 0300 **Fax:** 0141 561 0400
Email: journal@connectcommunications.co.uk
Advertising Address: As above.
Email: elliot@connectcommunications.co.uk
Web site: http://www.journalonline.co.uk
ISSN: 0458-8711
Publisher: The Law Society of Scotland
Date Established: 1956
Frequency: Monthly
Free to qualifying individuals
Annual Sub.: £84.00
Circulation: 10,712 (ABC 01/07/2008 to 30/06/2009)
Editor: Peter Nicholson
Summary of Content: Official journal covering Scottish law.
Readership/Target Audience: Aimed at Scottish solicitors; also advocates, judiciary, universities and law departments of colleges, government departments and other professionals.
ADVERTISING RATES:
Full Page Colour £1785.00
Agency Commission: 10%
Mechanical Data: Type Area: 272 x 185mm, Bleed Size: 303 x 216mm, Trim Size: 297 x 210mm, Col Length: 272mm, Page Width: 185mm, Film: Digital
Average advertising content per issue: 40%
BUSINESS: LEGAL

JOURNAL OF LIBRARIANSHIP & INFORMATION SCIENCE

40904U60B-302

Editorial Address: Department of Information Science, Loughborough University, LOUGHBOROUGH, LE11 3TU
Tel: 020 7324 8500 **Fax:** 020 7324 8600
Web site: http://www.sagepub.co.uk
ISSN: 0961-0006
Publisher: Sage Publications
Frequency: Quarterly
Cover Price: £15.00
Annual Sub.: £48.00
Usual Pagination: 64
Editor: Anne Goulding
Summary of Content: An international academic review of library and information science, research and theory.
Readership/Target Audience: Aimed at librarians.
ADVERTISING: No Advertising taken
BUSINESS: PUBLISHING: Libraries

JOURNAL OF LOGIC & COMPUTATION

21067U5B-99_2

Editorial Address: Department of Computer Science, Kings College London, Strand, LONDON, WC2R 2LS
Tel: 01865 353907 **Fax:** 01865 353485
Email: jlc@dcs.kcl.ac.uk
Advertising Address: Great Clarendon Street, OXFORD, OX2 6DP **Tel:** 01865 354767
Email: jnlsadvertising@oxfordjournals.org
Web site: http://www3.oup.co.uk/logcom
ISSN: 0955-792X
Publisher: OUP
Date Established: 1990
Frequency: 6 issues yearly
Cover Price: £43.00
Annual Sub.: £206.00
Usual Pagination: 200
Editor: Dov Gabbay
Summary of Content: Journal promoting the growth of logic and computing.
Readership/Target Audience: Read by library and research institutes.
ADVERTISING RATES:
Full Page Mono £646.00
Agency Commission: 10%
Mechanical Data: Type Area: 210 x 130mm, Bleed Size: 254 x 180mm, Trim Size: 248 x 174mm, Print Process: Litho, Col Length: 210mm, Page Width: 130mm, Film: Digital
Copy instructions: Copy Date: 6 weeks prior to publication date
BUSINESS: COMPUTERS & AUTOMATION: Data Processing

JOURNAL OF MATERIAL CULTURE

48794U62R-478

Editorial Address: 1 Oliver's Yard, 55 City Road, LONDON, EC1Y 1SP **Tel:** 020 7324 8500 **Fax:** 020 7324 8600
Email: market@sagepub.co.uk
Advertising Address: As above.
Email: advertising@sagepub.co.uk
Web site: http://www.sagepub.co.uk
ISSN: 1359-1835
Publisher: Sage Publications
Date Established: 1996
Frequency: 3 issues yearly - Published in March, July and November
Annual Sub.: £42.00
Circulation: 550 (Publisher's Statement)
Editor: Christopher Pinney; **Managing Editor:** Christopher Pinney
Summary of Content: Publication exploring the relationship between artefacts and social relations.
Readership/Target Audience: Aimed at those interested in anthropology, archaeology, design studies, history, human geography and museology.
ADVERTISING RATES:
Full Page Mono £450.00
Agency Commission: 5%
Mechanical Data: Type Area: 205 x 130mm, Col Length: 205mm, Page Width: 130mm, Film: Digital
Copy instructions: Copy Date: 12 weeks prior to publication date
BUSINESS: CHURCH & SCHOOL EQUIPMENT & EDUCATION: Education Related

JOURNAL OF MEDIA PRACTICE

629958U62B-425

Editorial Address: Dept of Media Arts, Royal Holloway, University of London, Egham Hill, EGHAM, TW20 0EX
Tel: 01784 414034 **Fax:** 01784 443832
Email: lina.khatib@rhul.ac.uk
Web site: http://www.intellectbooks.co.uk/journals.php?issn=14682753
ISSN: 1468-2753
Publisher: Intellect Ltd
Date Established: 2000
Frequency: 3 issues yearly - Published in February, June and October
Annual Sub.: £30.00
Circulation: 180 (Publisher's Statement)
Usual Pagination: 76
Editor: Lina Khatib
Summary of Content: Journal addressing practical work in media teaching and research. Contains articles which profile established and innovative practical approaches to teaching and research.
Readership/Target Audience: Aimed at teachers, researchers and media practitioners.
ADVERTISING: No Advertising taken
BUSINESS: CHURCH & SCHOOL EQUIPMENT & EDUCATION: Education Teachers

JOURNAL OF MOLLUSCAN STUDIES

41504U64F-70

Editorial Address: Great Clarendon Street, OXFORD, OX2 6DP **Tel:** 01865 556767 **Fax:** 01865 267485
Email: jnls.cust.serv@oxfordjournals.org
Advertising Address: As above. **Tel:** 01865 353329
Email: elisabetta.sheffield@oxfordjournals.org
Web site: http://www.oup.co.uk/jnls
ISSN: 0260-1230
Publisher: OUP
Date Established: 1990
Frequency: Quarterly
Cover Price: £74.00
Annual Sub.: £248.00
Circulation: 500 (Publisher's Statement)
Editor: D. Reid; **Advertising Manager:** Elisabetta Palanghi Sheffield
Summary of Content: Journal covering neurophysiological and behavioural research using molluscs as experimental material and natural populations.
Readership/Target Audience: Aimed at people interest in the biology of molluscs.
ADVERTISING RATES:
Full Page Mono £1227.00
Agency Commission: 10%
Mechanical Data: Type Area: 255 x 178mm, Col Length: 255mm, Trim Size: 279 x 216mm, Bleed Size: 285 x 222mm, Print Process: Litho, Page Width: 178mm, Film: Digital
BUSINESS: OTHER CLASSIFICATIONS: Biology

JOURNAL OF NATURAL HISTORY

40030U55-70

Editorial Address: 4 Park Square, Milton Park, ABINGDON, OX14 4RN **Tel:** 020 7017 6000 **Fax:** 020 7017 6336
Email: adam.wheeler@informa.com
Advertising Address: 11 New Fetter Lane, LONDON, EC4P 4EE **Tel:** 01235 401000 **Fax:** 01235 401550
Email: info@tandf.co.uk
Web site: http://www.informaworld.com/jnh
ISSN: 0022-2933
Publisher: Routledge, Taylor & Francis
Date Established: 1841
Frequency: Monthly
Annual Sub.: £4804.00
Circulation: 350 (Publisher's Statement)
Usual Pagination: 112
Editor: Adam Wheeler; **Advertising Manager:** Di Owen; **Managing Editor:** Adam Wheeler
Summary of Content: An international journal publishing original research, reviews, opinions and correspondence in systematics and evolutionary and interactive biology.
Language(s): English; French
Readership/Target Audience: Aimed at systematists, behaviourists, ecologists, entomologists, parasitologists, agriculturalists, aquaculturalists, marine biologists, evolutionary biologists, geneticists, conservationists and environmental scientists.
BUSINESS: APPLIED SCIENCE & LABORATORIES

THE JOURNAL OF NAVIGATION

39435U45R-70

Editorial Address: The Royal Insitute of Navigation, The Royal Geographical Society, 1 Kensington Gore, LONDON, SW7 2AT **Tel:** 020 7591 3133 **Fax:** 020 7591 3131
Email: editor@rin.org.uk
Web site: http://journals.cambridge.org/action/displayJournal?jid=NAV
ISSN: 0373-4633
Publisher: Cambridge University Press
Frequency: 3 issues yearly - Published in January, April and July
Annual Sub.: £264.00
Editor: Norman Hughes
Summary of Content: Journal containing original papers contributing to the science of navigation over land and sea and through air and space, a record of navigational work, book reviews and other matters of concern.
Readership/Target Audience: Read by members of the Royal Institute of Navigation, professional and amateur navigators at sea, in the air or on land, executives of companies involved in the operation of airlines, shipping fleets or trucks, engineers working in navigation, government departments responsible for the safety of air, marine and road traffic and military personnel concerned with communications, command, control and information.
ADVERTISING: No Advertising taken
BUSINESS: MARINE & SHIPPING: Marine Related

JOURNAL OF NURSING MANAGEMENT

40312U56B-180

Editorial Address: 9600 Garsington Road, Cowley, OXFORD, OX4 2DQ **Tel:** 01865 476518 **Fax:** 01865 471519
Email: m.a.jasper@swansea.ac.uk
Advertising Address: As above. **Tel:** 01865 476271
Fax: 01865 471271
Email: joanne.baker@oxon.blackwellpublishing.com

Web site: http://www.blackwellpublishing.com/jnm
ISSN: 0966-0429
Publisher: Wiley-Blackwell Publishing
Frequency: 8 issues yearly
Usual Pagination: 96
Editor: Melanie Jasper
Summary of Content: Journal containing case studies, training news, information and advice on new practices and staff management.
Readership/Target Audience: Read by leaders and managers in the nursing profession.
ADVERTISING RATES:
Full Page Mono £550.00
Full Page Colour £950.00
Agency Commission: 10%
Mechanical Data: Type Area: 230 x 170mm, Col Length: 230mm, Trim Size: 276 x 210mm, Film: Digital, Page Width: 170mm
Copy instructions: Copy Date: 6 weeks prior to publication date
BUSINESS: HEALTH & MEDICAL: Nursing

JOURNAL OF NUTRITIONAL & ENVIRONMENTAL MEDICINE

40591U56R-71_7

Editorial Address: Telephone House, 69-77 Paul Street, LONDON, EC2A 4LQ **Tel:** 020 7017 5000
Fax: 020 7017 6955
Email: rupal.malde@informa.com
Web site: http://www.informaworld.com/tjne
ISSN: 1359-0847
Publisher: Informa Healthcare
Date Established: 1991
Frequency: Quarterly
Annual Sub.: £626.00
Circulation: 800 (Publisher's Statement)
Usual Pagination: 96
Summary of Content: A peer reviewed medical journal presenting original research and reports.
Readership/Target Audience: Aimed at physicians, surgeons, dieticians, nutritionists, clinical biochemists and clinical physiologists.
ADVERTISING: No Advertising taken
BUSINESS: HEALTH & MEDICAL: Health Medical Related

JOURNAL OF OBSTETRICS & GYNAECOLOGY

40536U56R-72

Editorial Address: 3rd Floor Ham House, Hammersmith Hospital, Du Cane Road, LONDON, W12 0NN
Tel: 020 8383 3920 **Fax:** 020 8383 2342
Web site: http://www.informaworld.com/smpp/title~content=g770390435~db=all
ISSN: 0144-3615
Publisher: Informa Healthcare
Date Established: 1980
Frequency: 8 issues yearly
Annual Sub.: £470.00
Circulation: 1,500 (Publisher's Statement)
Usual Pagination: 114
Editor: MacLean; **Publisher:** Didi Peng
Summary of Content: Journal containing reviews, case reports and articles about practical obstetrics, clinical and laboratory research and other aspects of obstetrics and gynaecology. Also includes book reviews and a conference diary.
Readership/Target Audience: Read by obstetricians, gynaecologists, midwives, nurses and student doctors.
ADVERTISING: Rates on application
BUSINESS: HEALTH & MEDICAL: Health Medical Related

THE JOURNAL OF ONE DAY SURGERY

40186U56A-69_17

Editorial Address: Directorate of Anaesthesia, University Hospital of North Staffordshire, Newcastle Road, STOKE-ON-TRENT, ST4 6QG **Tel:** 01782 553054
Fax: 01782 719754
Email: damsmith@btinternet.com
Advertising Address: British Association of Day Surgery, 35-43 Lincoln's Inn, LONDON, WC2A 3PN
Tel: 020 7973 0708 **Fax:** 020 7973 0314
Email: johnptoman@aol.com
Web site: http://www.bads.co.uk
ISSN: 0963-5386
Publisher: BLACK DOG
Date Established: 1991
Frequency: Quarterly
Annual Sub.: £22.00
Circulation: 2,000 (Publisher's Statement)
Usual Pagination: 24
Editor: Ian Smith; **Advertising Manager:** John Toman; **Circulation Manager:** Peter Mann
Summary of Content: Publication covering case reports, original articles, reviews, debates, preliminary and projected studies and extracts of relevant research papers.

Readership/Target Audience: Read by nurses, doctors, managers and others involved in day surgery.
BUSINESS: HEALTH & MEDICAL

JOURNAL OF ORGANIZATIONAL CHANGE MANAGEMENT   21761U14A-567
Editorial Address: Howard House, Wagon Lane, BINGLEY, BD16 1WA **Tel:** 01274 777700 **Fax:** 01274 785200
Email: kfoster@emeraldinsight.com
Web site: http://www.emeraldinsight.com/jocm.htm
ISSN: 0953-4814
Publisher: Emerald Group Publishing Ltd
Date Established: 1980
Frequency: 6 issues yearly
Annual Sub.: £5989.00
Usual Pagination: 128
Editor: Kim Foster; **Publisher:** Kim Foster
Summary of Content: Journal offering analysis and discussion on the philosophies and practices which underpin successful organizational change.
Readership/Target Audience: Aimed at academics, libraries, consultants, general managers, government agencies, organization development professionals, personnel and training specialists.
ADVERTISING: No Advertising taken
BUSINESS: COMMERCE, INDUSTRY & MANAGEMENT

JOURNAL OF ORTHODONTICS   24856U56D-87
Editorial Address: Suite 1C, Josephs Well, Hanover Walk, LEEDS, LS3 1AB **Tel:** 0113 386 8163 **Fax:** 0113 386 8178
Email: jorthod@sheffield.ac.uk
Advertising Address: British Orthodontic Society, 12 Bridewell Place, LONDON, EC4V 6AP **Tel:** 020 7353 8680
Fax: 020 7353 8682
Email: office@bos.org.uk
Web site: http://www.maney.co.uk/journals/orthodontics
ISSN: 1465-3125
Publisher: Maney Publishing
Date Established: 1974
Frequency: Quarterly
Annual Sub.: £203.00
Circulation: 2,700 (Publisher's Statement)
Usual Pagination: 96
Editor: Mark Simon; **Advertising Manager:** Ann Wright
Summary of Content: Journal containing original articles, reviews, critical commentaries, editorial and correspondence on features of orthodontic practice, teaching and research.
Readership/Target Audience: Aimed at practicing orthodontists and academic researchers.
ADVERTISING RATES:
Full Page Mono £460.00
Full Page Colour £1020.00
Agency Commission: 10%
Mechanical Data: Film: Digital, Type Area: 240 x 175mm, Col Length: 240mm, Page Width: 175mm, Trim Size: 276 x 215mm, Bleed Size: 282 x 221mm
Copy instructions: Copy Date: Last week of 2 months prior to publication date
Average advertising content per issue: 10%
BUSINESS: HEALTH & MEDICAL: Dental

JOURNAL OF PERIOPERATIVE PRACTICE   40297U56B-40
Formerly: British Journal of Perioperative Nursing
Editorial Address: Daisy Ayris House, 6 Grove Park Court, HARROGATE, HG1 4DP **Tel:** 01423 856557
Fax: 01423 531613
Email: editor@afpp.org.uk
Advertising Address: As above. **Tel:** 01423 856559
Email: advertising@afpp.org.uk
Web site: http://www.afpp.org.uk
ISSN: 1467-1026
Publisher: Association for Perioperative Practice
Date Established: 1963
Frequency: Monthly
Annual Sub.: £68.00
Circulation: 9,000 (Publisher's Statement)
Usual Pagination: 48
Editor: Luisa Prentice; **Advertising Manager:** Luisa Prentice; **Managing Editor:** Chris Wiles
Summary of Content: Journal covering information, advice and research on anaesthetics, perioperative (surgical) care management, recovery, surgical operations, sterilisation and decontamination issues.
Readership/Target Audience: Aimed at nurses, operating department practitioners, student nurses and other health care workers working in perioperative practice.
ADVERTISING RATES:
Full Page Colour £1100.00
Agency Commission: 10%
Mechanical Data: Trim Size: 296 x 210mm, Film: Digital, Bleed Size: +3mm
Copy instructions: Copy Date: 1st of the month prior to publication date
Average advertising content per issue: 22%
BUSINESS: HEALTH & MEDICAL: Nursing

JOURNAL OF PETROLEUM GEOLOGY   23209U33-10_7
Editorial Address: PO Box 21, BEACONSFIELD, HP9 1NS
Tel: 01494 675139 **Fax:** 01494 670155
Email: ct@jpg.co.uk
Web site: http://www.jpg.co.uk
Publisher: Scientific Press Ltd
Frequency: Quarterly
Annual Sub.: £190.00
Circulation: 3,500 (Publisher's Statement)
Usual Pagination: 120
Editor: Christopher Tiratsoo
Summary of Content: Journal publishing original science concerning the geology of hydrocarbons (oil and natural gas).
Readership/Target Audience: Aimed at petroleum geologists, academics and research institutes.
ADVERTISING: No Advertising taken
BUSINESS: OIL & PETROLEUM

JOURNAL OF PLANKTON RESEARCH   40054U55-71
Editorial Address: Ecology Research Unit, School of Biological Sciences, University of Wales, SWANSEA, SA2 8PP
Advertising Address: Great Clarendon Street, OXFORD, OX2 6DP **Tel:** 01865 354767 **Fax:** 01865 353774
Email: jnlsadvertising@oxfordjournals.co.uk
Web site: http://www.oxfordjournals.org
ISSN: 0142-7873
Publisher: OUP
Date Established: 1979
Frequency: Monthly
Cover Price: £23.00
Annual Sub.: £234.00
Usual Pagination: 128
Editor: Roger Harris; **Editor-in-Chief:** Roger Harris; **Managing Editor:** Lulu Stader
Summary of Content: Journal covering both zoo and phytoplankton in all environments.
Readership/Target Audience: Aimed at academics interested in the area of plankton research.
ADVERTISING RATES:
Full Page Mono £646.00
Full Page Colour £1076.00
Agency Commission: 10%
Mechanical Data: Col Length: 255mm, Type Area: 255 x 178mm, Trim Size: 279 x 216mm, Bleed Size: 285 x 222mm, Film: Digital, Print Process: Litho, Page Width: 178mm
Copy instructions: Copy Date: 4 weeks prior to publication date
BUSINESS: APPLIED SCIENCE & LABORATORIES

JOURNAL OF PLANNING & ENVIRONMENT LAW   23619U44-1097
Editorial Address: The Hatchery, Hall Bank Lane, Mytholmroyd, HEBDEN BRIDGE, HX7 5HQ
Tel: 020 7449 1111 **Fax:** 020 7449 1144
Email: amelia.clarke@thomson.com
Web site: http://www.sweetandmaxwell.co.uk
ISSN: 0307-4870
Publisher: Sweet & Maxwell Yorkshire
Date Established: 1948
Frequency: Monthly
Annual Sub.: £255.00
Circulation: 3,300 (Publisher's Statement)
Usual Pagination: 150
Editor: Michael Purdue
Summary of Content: Journal focusing on developments in planning and environmental law, compulsory purchase and related issues.
Readership/Target Audience: Read by lecturers, planning and law solicitors and planning consultants.
ADVERTISING: No Advertising taken
BUSINESS: LEGAL

JOURNAL OF PSYCHIATRIC AND MENTAL HEALTH NURSING   40483U56N-25
Editorial Address: University of Leeds, School of Healthcare, Baines Wing, LEEDS, LS2 9JT
Tel: 0113 343 6295 **Fax:** 0113 343 6296
Email: jpmhn@leeds.ac.uk
Advertising Address: 9600 Garsington Road, Cowley, OXFORD, OX4 2DQ **Tel:** 01865 776868 **Fax:** 01865 471271
Email: joanna.baker@oxon.blackwellpublishing.com
Web site: http://www.blackwellpublishing.com/jpm
ISSN: 1351-0126
Publisher: Wiley-Blackwell Publishing
Date Established: 1994
Frequency: 10 issues yearly
Free to qualifying individuals
Annual Sub.: £104.00
Usual Pagination: 112
Editor: Dawn Freshwater

Summary of Content: Journal providing an international forum for all professionals in the field of psychiatric and mental health nursing.
Readership/Target Audience: Read by advanced practitioners, primary carers, service users, accomplished researchers and student thesis writers.
ADVERTISING RATES:
Full Page Mono £550.00
Full Page Colour £950.00
Mechanical Data: Page Width: 170mm, Type Area: 230 x 170mm, Col Length: 230mm, Trim Size: 276 x 210mm, Film: Digital
Copy instructions: Copy Date: 6 weeks prior to publication date
BUSINESS: HEALTH & MEDICAL: Mental Health

THE JOURNAL OF PUBLIC MENTAL HEALTH   601104U56N-16
Formerly: The Journal of Mental Health Promotion
Editorial Address: Richmond House, Richmond Road, BRIGHTON, BN2 3RL **Tel:** 01273 623222
Fax: 01273 625526
Email: joannas@pavpub.com
Advertising Address: As above. **Tel:** 0870 890 1080
Fax: 0870 890 1081
Email: pauls@pavpub.com
Web site: http://www.pavpub.com
ISSN: 1475-9535
Publisher: Pavilion Journals (Brighton) Ltd
Date Established: 2002
Frequency: Quarterly
Annual Sub.: £45.00
Circulation: 300 (Publisher's Statement)
Usual Pagination: 48
Editor: Joanna Sharrocks
Summary of Content: Journal covering all aspects of the mental health field. Contains news and articles written by people involved in the health and social care industry.
Readership/Target Audience: Read by those involved in promoting mental health, academics and clinical staff.
ADVERTISING RATES:
Full Page Mono £350.00
Agency Commission: 10%
Mechanical Data: Type Area: 220 x 150mm, Col Length: 220mm, Page Width: 150mm
Average advertising content per issue: 10%
BUSINESS: HEALTH & MEDICAL: Mental Health

THE JOURNAL OF RISK FINANCE INCORPORATING BALANCE SHEET   34908U1A-42
Formerly: Balance Sheet
Editorial Address: Howard House, Wagon Lane, BINGLEY, BD16 1WA **Tel:** 01274 777700 **Fax:** 01274 785200
Email: kdutton@emeraldinsight.com
Web site: http://www.emeraldinsight.com/jrf.htm
ISSN: 1526-5943
Publisher: Emerald Group Publishing Ltd
Frequency: 5 issues yearly
Usual Pagination: 52
Editor: Kelly Dutton; **Publisher:** Kelly Dutton
Summary of Content: Magazine looking at risk, balance sheet and asset liability management.
Readership/Target Audience: Aimed at those involved in the financial management of a company.
ADVERTISING: No Advertising taken
BUSINESS: FINANCE & ECONOMICS

JOURNAL OF THE ROYAL ANTHROPOLOGICAL INSTITUTE (INC. MAN)   48693U62R-177
Editorial Address: 50 Fitzroy Street, LONDON, W1T 5BT
Tel: 020 7387 0455 **Fax:** 020 7388 8817
Advertising Address: 9600 Garsington Road, Cowley, OXFORD, OX4 2DQ **Tel:** 01865 776868 **Fax:** 01865 471267
Email: craig.pickett@oxon.blackwellpublishing.com
Web site: http://www.therai.org.uk
ISSN: 0025-1696
Publisher: Royal Anthropological Institute
Date Established: 1872
Frequency: Quarterly
Free to qualifying individuals
Circulation: 3,200 (Publisher's Statement)
Usual Pagination: 650
Editor: Simon Coleman
Summary of Content: Journal of the Royal Anthropological Institute covering all aspects of anthropology, as well as correspondence and book reviews.
Readership/Target Audience: Read by social, cultural and physical anthropologists, ethnographers and students of linguistics.
ADVERTISING RATES:
Full Page Colour £420.00
Agency Commission: 10%

Mechanical Data: Type Area: 212 x 121mm, Film: Digital, Col Length: 212mm, Page Width: 121mm, Bleed Size: +3mm
Copy instructions: Copy Date: 4 weeks prior to publication date
Average advertising content per issue: 15%
BUSINESS: CHURCH & SCHOOL EQUIPMENT & EDUCATION: Education Related

JOURNAL OF THE ROYAL COLLEGE OF PHYSICIANS OF EDINBURGH
40218U56A-117

Formerly: Journal of the Royal College of Physicians Edinburgh
Editorial Address: 9 Queen Street, EDINBURGH, EH2 1JQ
Tel: 0131 225 7324 **Fax:** 0131 226 6124
Email: editorial@rcpe.ac.uk
Advertising Address: As above.
Email: auxia@btinternet.com
Web site: http://www.rcpe.ac.uk
ISSN: 1478-2715
Publisher: Royal College of Physicians of Edinburgh
Date Established: 2003
Frequency: Quarterly
Cover Price: £15.00
Free to qualifying individuals
Annual Sub.: £60.00
Circulation: 7,800 (Publisher's Statement)
Usual Pagination: 96
Editor: Graeme McAlister; **Advertising Manager:** David Cox
Summary of Content: Journal containing clinical, medical and historical medical articles.
Readership/Target Audience: Aimed at all medical professions.
ADVERTISING RATES:
Full Page Colour £400.00
Mechanical Data: Trim Size: 297 x 210mm
BUSINESS: HEALTH & MEDICAL

JOURNAL OF THE ROYAL HIGHLAND FUSILIERS
38873U40-166

Editorial Address: 518 Sauchiehall Street, GLASGOW, G2 3LW **Tel:** 0141 332 0961 **Fax:** 0141 353 1493
Email: reg.sec@rhf.org.uk
Web site: http://www.rhf.org.uk
Publisher: Royal Highland Fusiliers
Frequency: Annual - Published in March
Circulation: 1,500 (Publisher's Statement)
Editor: Robert Steele
Summary of Content: Regimental journal of the Royal Highland Fusiliers covering news, features and activities.
Readership/Target Audience: Distributed to all elements of the regiment.
ADVERTISING: No Advertising taken
BUSINESS: DEFENCE

THE JOURNAL OF THE ROYAL SOCIETY OF MEDICINE
40190U56A-69_70

Editorial Address: 1 Wimpole Street, LONDON, W1G 0AE
Tel: 020 7290 2900 **Fax:** 020 7290 2929
Email: jrsmeditorial@rsm.ac.uk
Advertising Address: PRC Associates Ltd, The Annexe, 6, Knowles Manor, Chessington Road, Ewell, EPSOM, KT17 1TF **Tel:** 020 8786 7376 **Fax:** 020 8786 7262
Email: sue@prcassoc.co.uk
Web site: http://www.jrsm.rsmjournals.com
ISSN: 0141-0768
Publisher: The Royal Society of Medicine Press Ltd
Date Established: 1972
Frequency: Monthly
Free to qualifying individuals
Annual Sub.: £233.00
Circulation: 25,000 (Publisher's Statement)
Usual Pagination: 64
Editor: Kamran Abbasi; **Managing Director:** Peter Richardson
Summary of Content: General medical journal reflecting current thinking and practice across the range of specialities. Includes original reports, editorials and reviews.
Readership/Target Audience: Aimed at academics, dentists and doctors.
ADVERTISING RATES:
Full Page Mono £660.00
Full Page Colour £1430.00
Agency Commission: 10%
Mechanical Data: Trim Size: 280 x 210mm, Bleed Size: 286 x 216mm, Film: Digital, Type Area: 250 x 180mm, Page Width: 180mm, Col Length: 250mm
Copy instructions: Copy Date: 4 weeks prior to publication date
Average advertising content per issue: 1%
BUSINESS: HEALTH & MEDICAL

JOURNAL OF THE SCIENCE OF FOOD AND AGRICULTURE
37974U22A-248

Editorial Address: Publications Department, Society of Chemical Industry, 14-15 Belgrave Square, LONDON, SW1X 8PS **Tel:** 020 7598 1550 **Fax:** 020 7235 0887
Email: jsfa@soci.org
Web site: http://www.interscience.wiley.com
ISSN: 0022-5142
Publisher: John Wiley & Sons Ltd
Date Established: 1950
Frequency: 15 issues yearly
Annual Sub.: $3355.00
Editor: Sarah Cooney
Summary of Content: Interdisciplinary journal covering agriculture and food science.
Readership/Target Audience: Readership includes people in industry, academia and government agencies.
ADVERTISING: No Advertising taken
BUSINESS: FOOD

JOURNAL OF SEMANTICS
30083U62R-456

Editorial Address: Great Clarendon Street, OXFORD, OX2 6DP **Tel:** 01865 353907 **Fax:** 01865 353485
Email: bart.geurts@phil.ru.nl
Advertising Address: As above. **Tel:** 01865 353329
Email: jnlsadvertising@oxfordjournals.org
Web site: http://www3.oup.co.uk/semant
ISSN: 0167-5133
Publisher: OUP
Date Established: 1982
Frequency: Quarterly
Cover Price: £17.00
Annual Sub.: £55.00
Usual Pagination: 116
Editor: Bart Geurts
Summary of Content: Journal covering information on the integration of philosophical, psychological and linguistic semantics as well as work done in artificial intelligence.
Readership/Target Audience: Aimed at those interested in the semantics of natural language.
ADVERTISING RATES:
Full Page Mono £270.00
Agency Commission: 10%
Mechanical Data: Type Area: 200 x 135mm, Col Length: 200mm, Page Width: 135mm, Film: Digital
BUSINESS: CHURCH & SCHOOL EQUIPMENT & EDUCATION: Education Related

JOURNAL OF SEMITIC STUDIES
29851U62R-453

Editorial Address: Dept of Middle Eastern Studies, University of Manchester, Oxford Road, MANCHESTER, M13 9PL **Tel:** 0161 275 3551 **Fax:** 0161 275 3551
Email: jss@man.ac.uk
Advertising Address: Great Clarendon Street, OXFORD, OX2 6DP **Tel:** 01865 353329
Email: jnlsadvertising@oxfordjournals.com
Web site: http://jss.oupjournals.org
ISSN: 0022-4480
Publisher: OUP
Date Established: 1955
Frequency: Half-yearly - Published in June and November
Cover Price: £29.00
Annual Sub.: £48.00
Usual Pagination: 216
Editor: George Brooke
Summary of Content: Journal which addresses the modern and ancient Near East, with emphasis on research into the languages and literature of the area.
Readership/Target Audience: Read by orientalists, Biblical scholars and linguistics scholars.
ADVERTISING RATES:
Full Page Mono £310.00
Agency Commission: 10%
BUSINESS: CHURCH & SCHOOL EQUIPMENT & EDUCATION: Education Related

THE JOURNAL OF SERVICES MARKETING
35510U2A-107_65

Editorial Address: Howard House, Wagon Lane, BINGLEY, BD16 1WA **Tel:** 01274 777700 **Fax:** 01274 785200
Email: rwhitfield@emeraldinsight.com
Web site: http://www.emeraldinsight.com
ISSN: 0887-6045
Publisher: Emerald Group Publishing Ltd
Frequency: 7 issues yearly
Annual Sub.: £5049.00
Editor: Charles Martin; **Publisher:** Richard Whitfield
Summary of Content: Journal covering all aspects of services marketing. Includes features on planning, marketing, customer services and policies.
Readership/Target Audience: Read by academics in the marketing field.

ADVERTISING: No Advertising taken
BUSINESS: COMMUNICATIONS, ADVERTISING & MARKETING

JOURNAL OF SMALL ANIMAL PRACTICE
41530U64H-159

Editorial Address: Woodrow House, 1 Telford Way, GLOUCESTER, GL2 2AV **Tel:** 01452 726700
Fax: 01452 726701
Email: jsap@bsava.com
Advertising Address: 9600 Garsington Road, Cowley, OXFORD, OX4 2DQ **Tel:** 01865 776868 **Fax:** 01865 471272
Email: julie.gribben@wiley.com
Web site: http://www.bsava.com
ISSN: 0022-4510
Publisher: BSAVA
Frequency: Monthly - Published the 1st week of the month
Circulation: 7,500 (Publisher's Statement)
Usual Pagination: 60
Editor: Ben Dales; **Advertising Manager:** Julie Gribben; **Publisher:** Katie Dunn
Summary of Content: Official journal of the British Small Animal Veterinary Association and the World Small Animal Veterinary Association featuring editorials, clinical papers and news.
Readership/Target Audience: Aimed at veterinary practitioners specialising in small animals.
ADVERTISING RATES:
Full Page Colour £1300.00
Agency Commission: 10%
Mechanical Data: Col Length: 253mm, Page Width: 177mm, Type Area: 253 x 177mm, Bleed Size: 303 x 213mm, Trim Size: 297 x 210mm, Print Process: Offset litho, Film: Digital
Copy instructions: Copy Date: 5 weeks prior to publication date
BUSINESS: OTHER CLASSIFICATIONS: Veterinary

THE JOURNAL OF SOCIAL WELFARE & FAMILY LAW
38561U44-1115

Editorial Address: Department of Social Sciences and Humanities, University of Bradford, BRADFORD, BD7 1DP
Tel: 01274 233502 **Fax:** 01274 235295
Email: j.a.goddard@bradford.ac.uk
Web site: http://www.tandf.co.uk/journals
ISSN: 0964-9069
Publisher: Routledge, Taylor & Francis
Frequency: Quarterly
Annual Sub.: £60.00
Circulation: 750 (Publisher's Statement)
Editor: James Goddard
Summary of Content: Journal providing practical commentary on social welfare law, family law and related areas.
Readership/Target Audience: Read by social policy and legal professionals.
ADVERTISING: No Advertising taken
BUSINESS: LEGAL

JOURNAL OF STORED PRODUCTS RESEARCH
37937U21R-700

Editorial Address: School of Biological Sciences, Royal Holloway, University of London, EGHAM, TW20 0EX
Tel: 01784 443767 **Fax:** 01784 414224
Email: p.credland@rhul.ac.uk
Web site: http://www.elsevier.com
ISSN: 0022-474X
Date Established: 1964
Frequency: Quarterly
Annual Sub.: $901.00
Usual Pagination: 116
Editor: P. F. Credland
Summary of Content: Scientific journal providing an international medium for the publication of both reviews and original results from laboratory and field studies on stored products. These include food, foodstuffs and durable items including materials such as timber and museum artefacts.
Readership/Target Audience: Aimed at researchers in biology, ecology, physiology and genetics of the insects, mites and fungi associated with stored products.
ADVERTISING: No Advertising taken
BUSINESS: AGRICULTURE & FARMING: Agriculture & Farming Related

JOURNAL OF TARGETING, MEASUREMENT AND ANALYSIS FOR MARKETING
35511U2A-107_80

Editorial Address: The Macmillan Building, 4 Crinan Street, LONDON, N1 9XW **Tel:** 020 7843 4684
Email: b.rouse@palgrave.com
Advertising Address: As above.
Email: b.rouse@palgrave.com
Web site: http://www.palgrave.com
ISSN: 0967-3237

Publisher: Palgrave Macmillan Ltd
Date Established: 1992
Frequency: Quarterly
Annual Sub.: £135.00
Usual Pagination: 96
Editor: Brenda Rouse; **Advertising Manager:** Brenda Rouse
Summary of Content: Journal containing advice on how to apply techniques, achieve practical solutions, improve performance and increase profitability.
Readership/Target Audience: Aimed at marketing directors, database marketers, agency directors, marketing managers, researchers, managers, consultants and academics.
ADVERTISING RATES:
Full Page Mono £500.00
Full Page Colour £1000.00
Agency Commission: 10%
Mechanical Data: Trim Size: 270 x 210mm, Film: Digital
BUSINESS: COMMUNICATIONS, ADVERTISING & MARKETING

JOURNAL OF TELECOMMUNICATIONS MANAGEMENT
1828248U18B-1976
Editorial Address: Little Russell House, 28-30 Little Russell Street, LONDON, WC1A 2HN **Tel:** 020 7404 3040
Fax: 020 7404 2081
Email: daryn@hspublications.co.uk
Web site: http://www.henrystewart.com/jtm
ISSN: 1754-1662
Publisher: Henry Stewart Publications
Date Established: 2008
Frequency: Quarterly
Annual Sub.: £250.00
Circulation: 1,250 (Publisher's Statement)
Usual Pagination: 100
Editor: Daryn Moody; **Publisher:** Daryn Moody
Summary of Content: Journal reviewing the impact of the new technologies, products, services and standards that are emerging on how telecommunications companies are managed, the business models used and the markets they serve. Covering strategy and business development, operations, network services and development, content and product management, service provision, marketing, pricing, standards regulation and law, finance and investment and billing and security.
Readership/Target Audience: Aimed at management at telecom operators and service providers, suppliers, content providers, software suppliers, telecom consultants and researchers.
ADVERTISING: No Advertising taken
BUSINESS: ELECTRONICS: Telecommunications

THE JOURNAL OF THE TEXTILE INSTITUTE
39523U47A-220
Editorial Address: 1st Floor, St. James's Building, Oxford Street, MANCHESTER, M1 6FQ **Tel:** 0161 237 1188
Fax: 0161 236 1991
Email: pashworth@textileinst.org.uk
Web site: http://www.textileinstitute.org
ISSN: 0400-5000
Publisher: Routledge, Taylor & Francis
Date Established: 1900
Frequency: 6 issues yearly
Annual Sub.: £211.00
Circulation: 700 (Publisher's Statement)
Editor: Rebecca Unsworth
Summary of Content: Journal presenting the results of recent textile research featuring articles on fibre science and textile technology, textile economics management and marketing.
Readership/Target Audience: Aimed at professionals within the textile industry.
ADVERTISING: No Advertising taken
BUSINESS: CLOTHING & TEXTILES

THE JOURNAL OF THE INSTITUTE OF TELECOMMUNICATIONS PROFESSIONALS
37419U18B-957
Formerly: The Journal of the Communication Network
Editorial Address: Gainsborough House, 2 Sheen Road, RICHMOND, TW9 1AE **Tel:** 020 8973 2611
Fax: 01932 785205
Email: thejournal@theitp.org
Advertising Address: As above. **Tel:** 01932 788861
Email: marketing@theitp.org
Web site: http://www.theITP.org
ISSN: 1477-4739
Publisher: Alchemy Media
Date Established: 1908
Frequency: Quarterly
Free to qualifying individuals
Annual Sub.: £112.00
Circulation: 11,000 (Publisher's Statement)
Usual Pagination: 100

Editor: Caroline Schoular; **Advertising Manager:** Shara Spear; **Managing Editor:** Brendan O'Mahony
Summary of Content: The Journal of The Institute of Telecommunications Professionals is a technical publication for the ICT and Telecommunications industry.
Readership/Target Audience: International readership of operations managers and engineers within the ICT and Telecommunications industry, Universities, research institutes and libraries around the world.
ADVERTISING RATES:
Full Page Mono £2500.00
Full Page Colour £4500.00
Mechanical Data: Type Area: 263 x 176mm, Bleed Size: 303 x 216mm, Trim Size: 297 x 210mm, Col Length: 263mm, Page Width: 176mm, Film: Digital
BUSINESS: ELECTRONICS: Telecommunications

JOURNAL OF THE SOCIETY OF LEATHER TECHNOLOGISTS AND CHEMISTS
36675U13-107
Editorial Address: 49 North Park Street, DEWSBURY, WF13 4LZ **Tel:** 01924 460864 **Fax:** 01924 460864
Email: m.leafe@tiscali.co.uk
Advertising Address: As above.
Email: malcolm.leafe@btopenworld.com
Web site: http://www.sltc.org
ISSN: 0144-0322
Publisher: Society of Leather Technologists and Chemists
Date Established: 1897
Frequency: 6 issues yearly
Cover Price: £11.00
Annual Sub.: £63.00
Circulation: 500 (Publisher's Statement)
Usual Pagination: 48
Editor: Malcolm Leafe; **Advertising Manager:** J.S. Leafe
Summary of Content: Journal focusing on technical papers, as well as trade news and original research.
Readership/Target Audience: Aimed at technologists, managers and engineers in the leather and allied industries.
ADVERTISING RATES:
Full Page Mono £210.00
Full Page Colour £2350.00
Agency Commission: 10%
Mechanical Data: Film: Negative, right reading, emulsion side down, Digital, Type Area: 254 x 178mm, Bleed Size: 305 x 213mm, Trim Size: 297 x 210mm, Col Length: 254mm, Col Widths (Display): 85mm, Page Width: 178mm
Copy instructions: Copy Date: 6 weeks prior to publication date
Average advertising content per issue: 10%
BUSINESS: CHEMICALS

JOURNAL OF THE WARBURG AND COURTAULD INSTITUTES
48797U64P-91
Editorial Address: The Warburg Institute, University of London, Woburn Square, LONDON, WC1H 0AB
Tel: 020 7862 8949
Email: jwci@sas.ac.uk
Web site: http://warburg.sas.ac.uk/journal
ISSN: 0075-4390
Publisher: Warburg Institute
Date Established: 1937
Frequency: Annual - Published date varies from year to year
Cover Price: £105.00
Circulation: 1,500 (Publisher's Statement)
Usual Pagination: 300
Editor: Jenny Boyle; **Circulation Manager:** Elizabeth Witchell
Summary of Content: Journal covering new research of a documentary and analytical character, in the field of cultural and intellectual history. The subject matter includes art and architecture, religion, science and literature as well as intellectual, political and social life. Often with emphasis on their relation to the civilisation of antiquity.
Readership/Target Audience: Aimed at academic cultural historians.
ADVERTISING: No Advertising taken
BUSINESS: OTHER CLASSIFICATIONS: Museums

JOURNAL OF THEOLOGICAL STUDIES
29855U62R-454
Editorial Address: St. Stephens House, 16 Marston Street, OXFORD, OX4 1JX **Tel:** 01865 432301
Advertising Address: 60 Upper Broadmoor Road, CROWTHORNE, RG45 7DE **Tel:** 01344 779945
Fax: 01344 779945
Email: lhann@lhms.fsnet.co.uk
Web site: http://www.oup.co.uk/theolj
ISSN: 0022-5185
Publisher: OUP
Date Established: 1899
Frequency: Half-yearly - Published in April and September
Annual Sub.: £45.00
Usual Pagination: 450
Editor: Allen Yeh

Summary of Content: Journal containing original articles covering the entire range of theological research and also an extensive book review section.
Readership/Target Audience: Read by scholars in the field of theology, clergy, academic institution, libraries and theological college libraries.
ADVERTISING RATES:
Full Page Mono £340.00
Agency Commission: 10%
BUSINESS: CHURCH & SCHOOL EQUIPMENT & EDUCATION: Education Related

JOURNAL OF TRANSPORT ECONOMICS & POLICY
39599U49A-139
Editorial Address: University of Bath, The Avenue, Claverton Down, BATH, BA2 7AY **Tel:** 01225 386302
Fax: 01225 386767
Email: jtep@management.bath.ac.uk
Web site: http://www.jtep.com
ISSN: 0022-5258
Publisher: University of Bath & London School of Economics
Date Established: 1967
Frequency: 3 issues yearly - Published in January, May, and September
Annual Sub.: £137.00
Circulation: 1,000 (Publisher's Statement)
Usual Pagination: 128
Editor: Lachmi Bose; **Editor-in-Chief:** Steven Morrison
Summary of Content: International publication covering all modes and aspects of transport economics, including a section of contributions on the latest policy developments worldwide.
Readership/Target Audience: Aimed at government departments, libraries, academics and research consultants.
ADVERTISING: No Advertising taken
BUSINESS: TRANSPORT

JOURNAL OF TROPICAL PAEDIATRICS
24628U56A-62_3
Editorial Address: Great Clarendon Street, OXFORD, OX2 6DP **Tel:** 01865 353907 **Fax:** 01865 353485
Advertising Address: As above. **Tel:** 01865 354767
Email: jnlsadvertising@oxfordjournals.org
Web site: http://www.oup.co.uk/jnls
ISSN: 0142-6338
Publisher: OUP
Date Established: 1954
Frequency: 6 issues yearly
Annual Sub.: £93.00
Editor: D. Simkiss; **Advertising Manager:** Elisabetta Palanghi Sheffield
Summary of Content: Journal covers all aspects of child health nutrition, including the locality and quality of environment.
Readership/Target Audience: Aimed at people who work or have an interest in the field of tropical paediatrics in children.
ADVERTISING RATES:
Full Page Mono £1227.00
Full Page Colour £2046.00
Agency Commission: 10%
Mechanical Data: Type Area: 254 x 178mm, Col Length: 254mm, Trim Size: 277 x 210mm, Bleed Size: 280 x 216mm, Print Process: Litho, Film: Digital, Page Width: 178mm
Copy instructions: Copy Date: 5 weeks prior to publication date
BUSINESS: HEALTH & MEDICAL

JOURNAL OF VISUAL ARTS PRACTICE
1696519U62R-493
Editorial Address: London Metropolitan University, Sir John Cass Dept of Art, Media and Design, 59-63 Whitechapel High Street, LONDON, E1 7PF **Tel:** 020 7320 1950
Email: c.d.smith@londonmet.ac.uk
Web site: http://www.intellectbooks.co.uk
ISSN: 1470-2029
Publisher: Intellect Ltd
Date Established: 2001
Frequency: 3 issues yearly - Published in April, August and December
Annual Sub.: £180.00
Circulation: 400 (Publisher's Statement)
Usual Pagination: 80
Editor: Chris Smith
Summary of Content: Journal covering issues in fine arts education.
Readership/Target Audience: Aimed at educators and academics in fine arts.
ADVERTISING: No Advertising taken
BUSINESS: CHURCH & SCHOOL EQUIPMENT & EDUCATION: Education Related

Business Magazines

JOURNAL OF VISUAL COMMUNICATION IN MEDICINE
1696015U56R-517

Editorial Address: Department of Medical Illustration, Selly Oak Hospital, BIRMINGHAM, B29 7EX **Tel:** 0121 627 8545
Email: kathy.mcfall@northglasgow.scot.nhs.uk
Web site: http://www.tandf.co.uk/journals/titles/17453054.asp
ISSN: 1745-3054
Publisher: Routledge, Taylor & Francis
Frequency: Quarterly
Annual Sub.: £113.00
Circulation: 600 (Publisher's Statement)
Usual Pagination: 48
Editor: Carly Betton
Summary of Content: Journal focusing on the production, manipulation, storage and transport of images for medical education, records and research.
Readership/Target Audience: Aimed at those involved in media production within the healthcare setting.
ADVERTISING: No Advertising taken
BUSINESS: HEALTH & MEDICAL: Health Medical Related

THE JOURNAL OF WATER LAW
39252U44-2090

Formerly: Water Law
Editorial Address: Office G18, Spinners Court, 55 West End, WITNEY, OX28 1NH **Tel:** 01993 706183
Fax: 01993 709410
Email: ltp@lawtext.com
Advertising Address: As above.
Email: ltp@lawtext.com
Web site: http://www.lawtext.com
ISSN: 0959-9754
Publisher: Lawtext Publishing Ltd
Frequency: 6 issues yearly
Annual Sub.: £460.00
Usual Pagination: 44
Editor: Rachel Caldin; **Advertising Manager:** Rachel Caldin
Summary of Content: Journal covering legal issues relating to the water industry.
Readership/Target Audience: Aimed at environmental and commercial lawyers, legal academics and water company managers.
ADVERTISING: Rates on application
BUSINESS: LEGAL

JOURNAL OF WORKPLACE LEARNING
37058U14F-39

Editorial Address: Howard House, Wagon Lane, BINGLEY, BD16 1WA **Tel:** 01274 777700 **Fax:** 01274 785201
Email: lsootheran@emeraldinsight.com
Web site: http://www.emeraldinsight.com/jwl.htm
ISSN: 1366-5626
Publisher: Emerald Group Publishing Ltd
Frequency: 7 issues yearly
Annual Sub.: £5449.00
Usual Pagination: 44
Editor: Lucy Sootheran; **Managing Editor:** Lucy Sootheran
Summary of Content: Journal covering the growth of the individual within an organisation.
Readership/Target Audience: Aimed at professionals and academics.
ADVERTISING: No Advertising taken
BUSINESS: COMMERCE, INDUSTRY & MANAGEMENT: Training & Recruitment

JOURNAL OF WOUND CARE
40313U56B-195

Editorial Address: St. Jude's Church, Dulwich Road, LONDON, SE24 0PB **Tel:** 020 7738 5454
Fax: 020 7978 8316
Email: tracy.c@markallengroup.com
Advertising Address: As above. **Fax:** 020 7733 2325
Email: a.kerr@markallengroup.com
Web site: http://www.journalofwoundcare.com
ISSN: 0969-0700
Publisher: MA Healthcare
Date Established: 1990
Frequency: Monthly
Annual Sub.: £60.00
Circulation: 5,000 (Publisher's Statement)
Usual Pagination: 52
Editor: Tracy Cowan; **Publisher:** Tom Pollard
Summary of Content: Journal providing a forum for the exchange of information and research in wound care.
Readership/Target Audience: Aimed at doctors, nurses, podiatrists, physiotherapists and other allied health professionals involved in wound care.
ADVERTISING RATES:
Full Page Colour £2000.00
Agency Commission: 10%
Mechanical Data: Trim Size: 280 x 210mm, Bleed Size: 290 x 220mm, Film: Digital, Type Area: 255 x 180mm, Col Length: 255mm, Page Width: 180mm
Copy instructions: Copy Date: 2nd week of the month prior to publication date

Average advertising content per issue: 20%
BUSINESS: HEALTH & MEDICAL: Nursing

JOURNAL OF ZOOLOGY
25790U64F-90

Editorial Address: The Zoological Society of London, Regents Park, LONDON, NW1 4RY **Tel:** 01865 476236
Email: lucinda.haines@zsl.org
Advertising Address: 9600 Garsington Road, Cowley, OXFORD, OX4 2DQ **Tel:** 01223 325757 **Fax:** 01223 315052
Web site: http://www.blackwellpublishing.com/jzo
ISSN: 0952-8369
Publisher: Wiley-Blackwell Publishing
Date Established: 1830
Frequency: Monthly
Annual Sub.: £935.00
Circulation: 900 (Publisher's Statement)
Editor: Lucinda Haines
Summary of Content: Journal containing original research papers and reviews within the field of zoology.
Readership/Target Audience: Read by members of the Zoological Society of London, zoologists, ecologists, conservation biologists, policy makers and students.
ADVERTISING: Rates on application
Agency Commission: 10%
Copy instructions: Copy Date: 3 weeks prior to publication date
Average advertising content per issue: 10%
BUSINESS: OTHER CLASSIFICATIONS: Biology

JOURNALISM
601456U2R-129

Editorial Address: 1 Oliver's Yard, 55 City Road, LONDON, EC1Y 1SP **Tel:** 020 7324 8500 **Fax:** 020 7324 8600
Email: h.tumber@city.ac.uk
Advertising Address: As above.
Email: matt.schlag@sagepub.co.uk
Web site: http://www.sagepub.co.uk
ISSN: 1464-8849
Publisher: Sage Publications
Date Established: 2000
Frequency: 6 issues yearly - Published in February, April, June, August, October and December
Cover Price: £15.00
Annual Sub.: £47.00
Editor: Howard Tumber
Summary of Content: An international and interdisciplinary journal which will contribute to the social, economic, political, cultural and practical understanding of journalism, covering current developments and historical changes within the field.
Readership/Target Audience: Aimed at academic researchers and critical practitioners.
ADVERTISING RATES:
Full Page Mono £400.00
Agency Commission: 5%
Mechanical Data: Col Length: 205mm, Page Width: 130mm, Type Area: 205 x 130mm
BUSINESS: COMMUNICATIONS, ADVERTISING & MARKETING: Communications Related

THE JOURNALIST
37190U14L-375

Editorial Address: Headland House, 308 Gray's Inn Road, LONDON, WC1X 8DP **Tel:** 020 7278 7916
Fax: 020 7837 8143
Email: journalist@nuj.org.uk
Advertising Address: Landmark Publishing Services, 2 Windmill Street, LONDON, W1T 2HX **Tel:** 020 7692 9292
Fax: 020 7692 9393
Email: sharon@lps.co.uk
Web site: http://www.nuj.org.uk
ISSN: 0022-5541
Publisher: National Union of Journalists
Date Established: 1908
Frequency: 10 issues yearly - Not produced in January or August
Cover Price: £2.00
Free to qualifying individuals
Annual Sub.: £20.00
Circulation: 37,000 (Publisher's Statement)
Usual Pagination: 32
Editor: Tim Gopsill
Summary of Content: Official journal of the NUJ. Contains coverage of all media issues from the viewpoint of working journalists.
Readership/Target Audience: Aimed at NUJ members including reporters, photographers, press officers and designers.
ADVERTISING RATES:
Full Page Colour £1500.00
SCC £12.00
Agency Commission: 10%
Mechanical Data: Type Area: 272 x 183mm, Col Widths (Display): 48mm, Film: Digital, Col Length: 272mm, Page Width: 183mm
BUSINESS: COMMERCE, INDUSTRY & MANAGEMENT: Trade Unions

JUNIOR EDUCATION PLUS
41085U62C-300

Formerly: Junior Education
Editorial Address: Villiers House, Clarendon Avenue, LEAMINGTON SPA, CV32 5PR **Tel:** 01926 887799
Fax: 01926 883331
Email: juniored@scholastic.co.uk
Advertising Address: As above. **Tel:** 01926 333307
Email: jsmith@scholastic.co.uk
Web site: http://www.scholastic.co.uk/magazines
ISSN: 0309-3484
Publisher: Scholastic UK Ltd
Date Established: 1977
Frequency: Monthly
Cover Price: £3.99
Circulation: 10,563 (ABC 01/07/2006 to 30/06/2007)
Usual Pagination: 68
Editor: Michelle Guy; **Advertising Director:** Jason Smith
Summary of Content: Magazine covering the latest in education news, product reviews plus study packs and curriculum articles.
Readership/Target Audience: Aimed at junior and middle school teachers.
ADVERTISING RATES:
Full Page Mono £1120.00
Full Page Colour £1320.00
Agency Commission: 10%
Mechanical Data: Type Area: 266 x 186mm, Col Length: 266mm, Trim Size: 297 x 210mm, Bleed Size: 303 x 216mm, Film: Digital, Page Width: 186mm
Copy instructions: Copy Date: 4th Thursday of the month prior to publication date
Supplement(s): Best Books - 1xY
BUSINESS: CHURCH & SCHOOL EQUIPMENT & EDUCATION: Junior Education

JUSTICE OF THE PEACE
39194U44-1120

Editorial Address: Halsbury House, 35 Chancery Lane, LONDON, WC2A 1EL **Tel:** 020 7400 2828
Email: diana.rose@lexisnexis.co.uk
Advertising Address: 2 Addiscombe Road, CROYDON, CR9 5AF **Tel:** 020 8212 1929 **Fax:** 020 8212 1970
Email: charlotte.witherden@lexisnexis.co.uk
Web site: http://www.lexisnexis.com
ISSN: 1741-4555
Publisher: LexisNexis
Date Established: 1837
Frequency: Weekly
Annual Sub.: £251.00
Circulation: 4,000 (Publisher's Statement)
Usual Pagination: 20
Editor: Diana Rose
Summary of Content: Journal covering practice, criminal and local government law.
Readership/Target Audience: Read by solicitors, magistrates, barristers, clerks to the justices, senior police officers and professionals in the probation and prison services.
ADVERTISING RATES:
Full Page Mono £900.00
Full Page Colour £1050.00
Agency Commission: 10%
Mechanical Data: Col Length: 260mm, Page Width: 185mm, Film: Digital, Type Area: 260 x 185mm, Trim Size: 297 x 210mm, Bleed Size: 303 x 216mm
Copy instructions: Copy Date: 3 days prior to publication date
Average advertising content per issue: 10%
BUSINESS: LEGAL

KBBREVIEW
38075U23C-40

Editorial Address: Equitable House, Lyon Road, HARROW, HA1 2EW **Tel:** 020 8515 2000 **Fax:** 020 8515 2080
Email: kbbreview@taylistmedia.com
Advertising Address: As above. **Tel:** 020 8515 2008
Fax: 020 8515 2006
Email: maggielister@taylistmedia.com
Web site: http://www.kbbreview.com
Publisher: Taylist Media
Date Established: 1985
Frequency: Monthly
Free to qualifying individuals
Annual Sub.: £25.00
Circulation: 12,104 (ABC 01/01/2008 to 31/12/2008)
Usual Pagination: 48
Editor: Andrew Davies; **Advertising Manager:** Maggie Lister
Summary of Content: Journal reviewing trends in the kitchen, bedroom and bathroom industry.
Readership/Target Audience: Aimed at independent specialist retailers.
ADVERTISING RATES:
Full Page Colour £3200.00
Agency Commission: 10%
Mechanical Data: Bleed Size: 346 x 246mm, Trim Size: 340 x 240mm, Film: Digital, Type Area: 315 x 220mm, Col Length: 315mm, Page Width: 220mm
Copy instructions: Copy Date: 3 weeks prior to publication date

Average advertising content per issue: 45%
BUSINESS: FURNISHINGS & FURNITURE: Furnishings & Furniture - Kitchens & Bathrooms

KEEP IT REAL
1894844U34-206

Editorial Address: Suite 223, Business Design Centre, 52 Upper Street, LONDON, N1 0QH **Tel:** 020 7288 6833
Fax: 020 7288 6834
Email: julia.dennison@intelligentmedia.co.uk
Publisher: Intelligent Media Solutions
Frequency: 6 issues yearly
Free to qualifying individuals
Editor: Julia Dennison
Summary of Content: Magazine educating and informing sales people within resellers and dealers with regard to opportunities within the consumable sector.
Readership/Target Audience: Aimed at those working in sales.
BUSINESS: OFFICE EQUIPMENT

KENNEDY'S CONFECTION
36464U8B-200

Formerly: Confection
Editorial Address: First Floor Offices, Stafford House, 16 East Street, TONBRIDGE, TN9 1HG **Tel:** 01732 371510
Fax: 01732 361385
Email: scallander@kennedys.co.uk
Advertising Address: As above. **Fax:** 01732 352438
Email: post@kennedys.co.uk
Web site: http://www.kennedysconfection.com
ISSN: 1461-4324
Publisher: Kennedy's Publications Ltd
Date Established: 1890
Frequency: Monthly - Published in the 2nd week of the cover month
Annual Sub.: £99.00
Circulation: 5,881 (ABC 01/07/2008 to 30/06/2009)
Usual Pagination: 64
Editor: Suzanne Callander; **Advertising Manager:** Mark Neilson
Summary of Content: Specialised international trade publication specifically targeting manufacturers of chocolate, sugar confectionery, bakery and ice cream products.
Language(s): English; French; German; Italian; Spanish
Readership/Target Audience: Aimed at executives in the chocolate, sugar confectionery, chewing gum, ice cream and bakery manufacturing industries.
ADVERTISING RATES:
Full Page Colour £1995.00
Agency Commission: 10%
Mechanical Data: Trim Size: 297 x 210mm, Bleed Size: 303 x 216mm, Type Area: 251 x 176mm, Col Length: 251mm, Page Width: 176mm, Film: Digital
Copy instructions: Copy Date: 1st week of the month prior to publication date
BUSINESS: BAKING & CONFECTIONERY: Confectionery Manufacturing

KENNEL AND CATTERY MANAGEMENT
41486U64E-50

Editorial Address: PO Box 523, HORSHAM, RH12 4WL
Tel: 01293 871201 **Fax:** 01293 871301
Email: kennelandcattery@aol.com
Advertising Address: As above.
Email: kennelandcattery@aol.com
Web site: http://www.kennelandcattery.com
Publisher: Albatross Publications
Date Established: 1983
Frequency: 6 issues yearly - Published the end of the 1st full week of the cover month
Annual Sub.: £20.00
Circulation: 3,000 (Publisher's Statement)
Usual Pagination: 24
Editor: Carol Andrews; **Advertising Manager:** Carol Andrews
Summary of Content: Magazine covering all aspects of managing kennels and catteries.
Readership/Target Audience: Aimed at those involved in the care of dogs and cats.
ADVERTISING RATES:
Full Page Mono £495.00
Full Page Colour £650.00
Agency Commission: 10%
Mechanical Data: Page Width: 179mm, Type Area: 265 x 179mm, Bleed Size: 303 x 213mm, Trim Size: 297 x 210mm, Col Length: 265mm, Film: Digital, Print Process: Litho
Copy instructions: Copy Date: 4 weeks prior to publication date
Average advertising content per issue: 10%
BUSINESS: OTHER CLASSIFICATIONS: Pet Trade

KENT BUSINESS
41312U63B-926

Editorial Address: Messenger House, New Hythe Lane, Larkfield, AYLESFORD, ME20 6SG **Tel:** 01622 717880
Fax: 01622 715225
Email: businesseditor@thekmgroup.co.uk

Advertising Address: 43 High Street, SITTINGBOURNE, ME10 4AW **Tel:** 01795 435452 **Fax:** 01795 420885
Email: ggault@thekmgroup.co.uk
Web site: http://www.kentonline.co.uk/business
Publisher: Kent Messenger Group
Date Established: 1993
Frequency: Monthly - Published on the last Friday of the month prior to cover date
Cover Price: £2.00
Free to qualifying individuals
Annual Sub.: £20.00
Circulation: 165,000 (Publisher's Statement)
Usual Pagination: 48
Editor: Trevor Sturgess; **Advertising Manager:** George Gault; **Publisher:** Morag Welham
Summary of Content: Business newspaper covering county business and financial news.
Readership/Target Audience: Aimed at all key decision makers.
ADVERTISING RATES:
Full Page Colour £5984.00
Agency Commission: 10%
Mechanical Data: No. of Columns (Display): 8, Type Area: 340 x 276mm, Col Length: 340mm, Page Width: 276mm
Copy instructions: Copy Date: 10 days prior to publication date
Average advertising content per issue: 40%
BUSINESS: REGIONAL BUSINESS: Regional Business English Counties

KENT DIRECTOR
41314U63B-929

Editorial Address: 14 Middletons Road, Yaxley, PETERBOROUGH, PE7 3LR **Tel:** 01733 242312
Fax: 01733 244035
Email: carol@pridepublications.co.uk
Advertising Address: As above.
Email: maxine@pridepublications.co.uk
Web site: http://www.pridepublications.co.uk
Publisher: Pride Publications Ltd
Frequency: 10 issues yearly
Cover Price: £2.00
Circulation: 3,600 (Publisher's Statement)
Usual Pagination: 24
Editor: Carol Lawless; **Managing Director:** Carol Lawless; **Publisher:** Carol Lawless
Summary of Content: Business magazine containing local news items, views and features of general interest.
Readership/Target Audience: Read by senior directors, senior partners and chief executives.
ADVERTISING RATES:
Full Page Mono £675.00
Full Page Colour £675.00
Agency Commission: 10%
Mechanical Data: Type Area: 212 x 187mm, Bleed Size: 218 x 309mm, Trim Size: 212 x 303mm, No. of Columns (Display): 3, Film: Digital, Col Length: 212mm, Page Width: 187mm
Copy instructions: Copy Date: 1 week prior to publication date
Average advertising content per issue: 50%
BUSINESS: REGIONAL BUSINESS: Regional Business English Counties

KEYSTONE IRELAND
35910U4E-256

Formerly: Keystone
Editorial Address: 48-50 York Street, BELFAST, BT15 1AS
Tel: 028 9031 9008 **Fax:** 028 9072 7804
Email: ksnewscopy@flagshipmedia.co.uk
Advertising Address: As above. **Fax:** 028 9072 7800
Email: mboyd@flagshipmedia.co.uk
Publisher: Flagship Media Group Ltd
Frequency: Monthly - Published in the 3rd week of the cover month
Cover Price: Free
Circulation: 15,000 (Publisher's Statement)
Usual Pagination: 72
Editor: Noel Slevin; **Managing Director:** Derek Carstairs; **Publisher:** Derek Carstairs
Summary of Content: Newspaper covering all aspects of the construction industry. Includes project features and new product information.
Readership/Target Audience: Aimed at those involved in the construction industry.
ADVERTISING RATES:
Full Page Colour £2005.00
Agency Commission: 15%
Mechanical Data: Col Length: 330mm, Page Width: 261mm, Trim Size: 420 x 297mm, Film: Digital, Type Area: 330 x 261mm
BUSINESS: ARCHITECTURE & BUILDING: Building

KEYWAYS
39912U54C-70

Editorial Address: 71-73 Edleston Road, CREWE, CW2 7HP **Tel:** 01270 505902 **Fax:** 01270 501148
Email: simon@holdfast.co.uk

Advertising Address: 5D Great Central Way, Woodford Halse, DAVENTRY, NN11 3PZ **Tel:** 01327 262255
Fax: 01327 262539
Email: enquiries@locksmiths.co.uk
Web site: http://www.locksmiths.co.uk
Publisher: The Master Locksmiths Association
Frequency: 6 issues yearly
Cover Price: Free
Circulation: 2,000 (Publisher's Statement)
Usual Pagination: 40
Editor: Simon Griffiths; **Advertising Manager:** Simon Griffiths
Summary of Content: Official Journal of the Master Locksmiths Association, covering information and news about security, locks, bolts and safes.
Readership/Target Audience: Read by master locksmiths, retailers, installers, security officers, ironmongers, surveyors and insurance assessors.
ADVERTISING RATES:
Full Page Colour £650.00
Agency Commission: 10%
Mechanical Data: Bleed Size: +3mm, Film: Digital, Type Area: 180 x 124mm, Col Length: 180mm, Trim Size: 210 x 148mm, Page Width: 124mm
Copy instructions: Copy Date: 15th of preceding month of publication date
Average advertising content per issue: 20%
BUSINESS: SAFETY & SECURITY: Security

KIRKLEES BUSINESS NEWS
41402U63B-2190

Editorial Address: Huddersfield Examiner, Queen Street South, HUDDERSFIELD, HD1 2DU **Tel:** 01484 430000
Fax: 01484 437789
Email: henryk.zientek@examiner.co.uk
Advertising Address: As above. **Fax:** 01484 437730
Web site: http://www.examiner.co.uk
Publisher: Trinity Mirror Huddersfield Ltd
Date Established: 1989
Frequency: Monthly
Cover Price: Free
Circulation: 6,800 (Publisher's Statement)
Usual Pagination: 28
Editor: Henryk Zientek; **Advertising Manager:** Anne Barrett
Summary of Content: Magazine covering transport, manufacturing and distribution industries and business service companies.
Readership/Target Audience: Aimed at executives in the manufacturing, transport, distribution and construction industries as well as commercial and business service companies.
ADVERTISING RATES:
Full Page Mono £1496.00
Full Page Colour £2019.00
Agency Commission: 10%
Mechanical Data: Type Area: 342 x 272mm, Col Length: 342mm, Page Width: 272mm, No. of Columns (Display): 8, Film: Digital
Copy instructions: Copy Date: 1 week prior to publication date
BUSINESS: REGIONAL BUSINESS: Regional Business English Counties

KITCHEN JOURNAL
623102U23C-50

Editorial Address: Napier House, 11 Surrey Street, LOWESTOFT, NR32 1LJ **Tel:** 01502 517115
Fax: 01502 517117
Email: editor@kitchenjournal.co.uk
Advertising Address: As above.
Email: owen@kitchenjournal.co.uk
Web site: http://www.craftsman.co.uk
ISSN: 1468-6775
Publisher: CPC Ltd
Date Established: 2000
Frequency: 6 issues yearly
Free to qualifying individuals
Annual Sub.: £15.00
Circulation: 7,726 (Publisher's Statement)
Usual Pagination: 40
Editor: Jan Orchard; **Advertising Manager:** Eoin Costen
Summary of Content: Magazine looking at products and developments in the kitchen furniture industry covering appliances, accessories, components and technical features.
Readership/Target Audience: Read by kitchen retail specialists, builders merchants, appliance stockists and manufacturers.
ADVERTISING RATES:
Full Page Colour £1295.00
Agency Commission: 10%
Mechanical Data: Page Width: 187mm, Film: Digital, Type Area: 271 x 187mm, Col Length: 271mm, Trim Size: 297 x 210mm, Bleed Size: 303 x 213mm
Average advertising content per issue: 35%
BUSINESS: FURNISHINGS & FURNITURE: Furnishings & Furniture - Kitchens & Bathrooms

Business Magazines

KITCHEN MAKER
623162U23C-70

Editorial Address: 29 High Street, RYE, TN31 7JG
Tel: 01797 224816
Email: bill@willowe.demon.co.uk
Advertising Address: As above.
Email: bill@willowe.demon.co.uk
Publisher: Willowe Magazines Limited
Date Established: 1999
Frequency: Quarterly - Published on the 2nd Friday of the cover month
Cover Price: £5.00
Free to qualifying individuals
Annual Sub.: £10.00
Circulation: 7,500 (Publisher's Statement)
Usual Pagination: 52
Editor: Bill Lowe; **Managing Director:** Bill Lowe;
Advertising Manager: John Emslie; **Publisher:** Bill Lowe
Summary of Content: Magazine covering all aspects of kitchen manufacturing including machinery, tools, products and accessories.
Readership/Target Audience: Aimed at kitchen manufacturers and producers.
ADVERTISING RATES:
Full Page Mono £700.00
Full Page Colour £900.00
Agency Commission: 10%
Mechanical Data: Page Width: 205mm, Type Area: 275 x 205mm, Trim Size: 295 x 225mm, Bleed Size: 301 x 231mm, Col Length: 275mm, Film: Positive, right reading, emulsion side down. Digital
Average advertising content per issue: 20%
BUSINESS: FURNISHINGS & FURNITURE: Furnishings & Furniture - Kitchens & Bathrooms

KITCHEN SPECIALIST MAGAZINE
629085U23C-90

Formerly: KSA
Editorial Address: Unit L4A, Pleasley Vale Business Park, Severalls Industrial Park, MANSFIELD, NG19 8RL
Tel: 01623 818808 **Fax:** 01206 849078
Email: natalie.kelly@burdamagazines.co.uk
Web site: http://www.kbsa.co.uk
Publisher: Hubert Burda Media UK
Date Established: 1998
Frequency: Quarterly
Cover Price: Free
Summary of Content: Magazine focusing on the professional kitchen trade, providing information for traders and consumers.
Readership/Target Audience: Aimed at retailers and consumers.
ADVERTISING: Rates on application
BUSINESS: FURNISHINGS & FURNITURE: Furnishings & Furniture - Kitchens & Bathrooms

KITCHENS & BATHROOMS NEWS
1695023U23C-94

Formerly: Kitchens and Bathrooms Journal
Editorial Address: Regal House, Regal Way, WATFORD, WD24 4YF **Tel:** 01923 237799 **Fax:** 01293 246901
Email: pturrell@hamerville.co.uk
Advertising Address: As above. **Fax:** 01923 246901
Email: ascott@hamerville.co.uk
Web site: http://www.hamerville.co.uk
Publisher: Hamerville Magazines Ltd
Date Established: 2006
Frequency: 11 issues yearly - Published on the 1st of the cover month
Free to qualifying individuals
Annual Sub.: £30.00
Circulation: 19,223 (ABC 01/01/2008 to 31/12/2008)
Usual Pagination: 80
Editor: Philippa Turrell
Summary of Content: Magazine covering new products, guides, case studies and specification features on kitchens and bathrooms.
Readership/Target Audience: Aimed at bathroom and kitchen specialists, house builders, interior designers, builders, plumbers, local authorities and housing associations.
ADVERTISING RATES:
Full Page Colour £2350.00
Mechanical Data: Type Area: 255 x 180mm, Bleed Size: 295 x 216mm, Trim Size: 289 x 210mm, Col Length: 255mm, Page Width: 180mm, Film: Digital
Copy instructions: Copy Date: 3 weeks prior to publication date
BUSINESS: FURNISHINGS & FURNITURE: Furnishings & Furniture - Kitchens & Bathrooms

KNITTING INTERNATIONAL
39540U47C-193

Editorial Address: Perkin House, 1 Longlands Street, BRADFORD, BD1 2TP **Tel:** 01274 378800
Fax: 01274 378811
Email: mcurtis@world-textile.net
Advertising Address: As above.

Email: info@world-textile.net
Web site: http://www.knittinginternational.com
ISSN: 0266-9364
Publisher: World Textile Publications Ltd
Date Established: 1894
Frequency: 11 issues yearly
Annual Sub.: £285.00
Circulation: 8,000 (Publisher's Statement)
Usual Pagination: 56
Editor: Marianne Curtis; **Managing Director:** Mark Jarvis; **Advertising Manager:** Ross Barker
Summary of Content: Magazine that covers the latest trends and technological developments in all areas of knitting and hosiery.
Readership/Target Audience: Read by professionals in the textiles, knitting and hosiery industries.
ADVERTISING RATES:
Full Page Mono £1208.00
Full Page Colour £1675.00
Agency Commission: 10%
Mechanical Data: Type Area: 270 x 200mm, Trim Size: 300 x 230mm, Bleed Size: 306 x 236mm, Film: Digital, Col Length: 270mm, Page Width: 200mm
Average advertising content per issue: 40%
BUSINESS: CLOTHING & TEXTILES: Knitwear

KNOWLEDGE MANAGEMENT REVIEW
36778U14A-194_15

Editorial Address: 322B King Street, LONDON, W6 0AX
Tel: 020 8600 4670 **Fax:** 020 8741 9975
Email: jessica.twentyman@melcrum.com
Web site: http://www.melcrum.com
ISSN: 1369-7633
Publisher: Melcrum Publishing Ltd
Date Established: 1998
Frequency: 6 issues yearly - Published around the 1st week of the 1st cover month
Annual Sub.: £265.00
Usual Pagination: 36
Editor: Jessica Twentyman
Summary of Content: Journal containing corporate case studies, special reports, reviews and practical tips.
Readership/Target Audience: Read by senior managers with responsibility for organisational knowledge and information management in large organisations.
ADVERTISING: No Advertising taken
BUSINESS: COMMERCE, INDUSTRY & MANAGEMENT

LAB ASIA
39975U55-75

Editorial Address: Oak Court Business Centre, Sandridge Park, Porters Wood, ST. ALBANS, AL3 6PH
Tel: 01727 855574 **Fax:** 01727 841694
Email: pr@intlabmate.com
Advertising Address: As above.
Email: sales@intlabmate.com
Web site: http://www.labasia.net
ISSN: 1355-8625
Publisher: International LABMATE Ltd
Date Established: 1994
Frequency: 6 issues yearly - Published at the end of the 2nd cover month
Free to qualifying individuals
Circulation: 24,755 (Publisher's Statement)
Usual Pagination: 40
Editor: Tamsyn Hicks; **Features Editor:** Tamsyn Hicks;
Managing Director: Michael Pattison; **Publisher:** Michael Pattison
Summary of Content: Scientific and laboratory journal covering industry news and views, technical information and new products.
Readership/Target Audience: Aimed at decision-makers in hospital, government and university laboratories.
ADVERTISING RATES:
Full Page Mono £4730.00
Full Page Colour £5725.00
Agency Commission: 10%
Mechanical Data: Type Area: 254 x 180mm, No. of Columns (Display): 4, Film: Digital, Col Length: 254mm, Page Width: 180mm
Copy instructions: Copy Date: Last week of month prior to 1st cover date
Average advertising content per issue: 65%
BUSINESS: APPLIED SCIENCE & LABORATORIES

LAB INTERNATIONAL
39977U55-92

Formerly: LabPlus International
Editorial Address: 2 Claridge Court, Lower Kings Road, BERKHAMSTED, HP4 2AF **Tel:** 01442 877777
Fax: 01442 870617
Email: bobw@lansdowne-media.co.uk
Advertising Address: As above.
Email: bobw@lansdowne-media.co.uk
Web site: http://www.labplusinternational.com
Frequency: 6 issues yearly
Cover Price: Free
Circulation: 24,608 (BPA Worldwide)

Editor: Bob Warren; **Advertising Manager:** Bob Warren
Summary of Content: Reports on new instruments and technology used in industrial and research laboratories, provided they are marketed on a European basis.
Readership/Target Audience: Readership includes laboratory management and R&D personnel worldwide.
ADVERTISING RATES:
Full Page Mono EUR6144.00
Full Page Colour EUR8139.00
Agency Commission: 15%
Mechanical Data: Type Area: 254 x 182mm, Col Length: 254mm, Page Width: 182mm, Trim Size: 276 x 210mm, Bleed Size: 288 x 222mm, Film: Digital
Average advertising content per issue: 25%
BUSINESS: APPLIED SCIENCE & LABORATORIES

LAB ON A CHIP
707052U13-109

Editorial Address: Thomas Graham House, Science Park, Milton Road, CAMBRIDGE, CB4 0WF **Tel:** 01223 432293
Fax: 01233 420247
Email: minhash@rsc.org
Advertising Address: As above. **Tel:** 01223 432246
Fax: 01223 426017
Email: advertising@rsc.org
Web site: http://www.rsc.org/loc
ISSN: 1473-0197
Publisher: Royal Society of Chemistry
Date Established: 2001
Frequency: 24 issues yearly
Annual Sub.: £1040.00
Circulation: 500 (Publisher's Statement)
Usual Pagination: 150
Editor: Harp Minhas; **Advertising Manager:** Ian Swain;
Managing Editor: Harp Minhas
Summary of Content: Magazine examining miniaturisation research, technology and its applications in chemistry, biology, physics, electronics, clinical chemistry, fabrication, engineering and materials science, aiding communication and collaboration across disciplines.
Readership/Target Audience: Aimed at scientists in these fields.
ADVERTISING RATES:
Full Page Mono £890.00
Mechanical Data: Bleed Size: 281 x 216mm, Type Area: 252 x 188mm, Col Length: 252mm, Page Width: 188mm, Trim Size: 275 x 210mm
BUSINESS: CHEMICALS

LABELS & LABELLING INTERNATIONAL
38676U35-60

Editorial Address: 9th Floor, Metro Building, 1 Butterwick, Hammersmith, LONDON, W6 8DW **Tel:** 020 8846 2700
Fax: 020 8846 2801
Email: athomas@tarsus.co.uk
Advertising Address: 1 Butterwick, Hammersmith, LONDON, W6 8DW **Tel:** 020 8846 2700 **Fax:** 020 8846 2801
Email: sales@labelsandlabelling.com
Web site: http://www.labelsandlabelling.com
ISSN: 1478-7520
Publisher: Tarsus Group plc
Frequency: 6 issues yearly
Annual Sub.: £50.00
Circulation: 25,000 (Publisher's Statement)
Usual Pagination: 120
Editor: Andy Thomas; **Managing Director:** Douglas Emslie;
Publisher: Roger Pellow
Summary of Content: Magazine offering information on all aspects of the international label industry, including materials, printing and technology, application and usage.
Readership/Target Audience: Aimed at the labelling industry.
ADVERTISING RATES:
Full Page Colour EUR5743.00
Agency Commission: 10%
Mechanical Data: Type Area: 277 x 190mm, Bleed Size: 301 x 214mm, Trim Size: 297 x 210mm, Col Length: 277mm, Page Width: 190mm, Film: Digital
Copy instructions: Copy Date: 3 weeks prior to publication date
Average advertising content per issue: 50%
BUSINESS: PACKAGING & BOTTLING

LABMATE UK & IRELAND
24305U55-80

Editorial Address: Oak Court Business Centre, Sandridge Park, Porters Wood, ST. ALBANS, AL3 6PH
Tel: 01727 855574 **Fax:** 01727 841694
Email: pr@intlabmate.com
Advertising Address: As above.
Email: chris@intlabmate.com
Web site: http://www.labmate-online.com
ISSN: 0143-5140
Publisher: International LABMATE Ltd
Date Established: 1974
Frequency: 10 issues yearly - Published in the last week of the cover month
Cover Price: Free

Circulation: 8,686 (ABC 01/01/2008 to 31/12/2008)
Usual Pagination: 40
Editor: Tamsyn Hicks; **Features Editor:** Tamsyn Hicks;
Managing Director: Michael Pattison; **Advertising
Manager:** Chris Jarvis; **Publisher:** Michael Pattison
Summary of Content: Magazine covering industry news
and views, latest products and problem-solving articles.
Readership/Target Audience: Read by scientists.
ADVERTISING RATES:
Full Page Mono £1555.00
Full Page Colour £1995.00
Agency Commission: 10%
Mechanical Data: Film: Digital
Average advertising content per issue: 60%
BUSINESS: APPLIED SCIENCE & LABORATORIES

LABORATORY EQUIPMENT FOR THE MIDDLE EAST & EASTERN EUROPE

1691330U55-9018

Editorial Address: Sahara House, 38 Greyhound Road,
LONDON, W6 8NX **Tel:** 020 7610 1387 **Fax:** 020 7610 0078
Email: sahara@btconnect.com
Advertising Address: As above.
Email: sahara@btconnect.com
Web site: http://www.saharapublications.com
Publisher: Sahara Publications
Frequency: Annual - Published in November
Free to qualifying individuals
Circulation: 23,500 (Publisher's Statement)
Editor: Abed Najjar
Summary of Content: Publication providing a reference to
international suppliers and manufacturers of laboratory
equipment.
Readership/Target Audience: Aimed at lab technicians,
purchasing managers, research scientists and distributors.
ADVERTISING: Rates on application
Agency Commission: 10%
Mechanical Data: Bleed Size: +3mm, Type Area: 270 x
190mm, Trim Size: 297 x 210mm, Film: Digital, Col Length:
270mm, Page Width: 190mm
Copy instructions: Copy Date: 4 weeks prior to publication
date
Average advertising content per issue: 100%
BUSINESS: APPLIED SCIENCE & LABORATORIES

LABORATORY HAZARDS BULLETIN

39978U55-82

Editorial Address: Thomas Graham House, Science Park,
Milton Road, CAMBRIDGE, CB4 0WF **Tel:** 01223 420066
Email: hazards@rsc.org
Advertising Address: As above. **Tel:** 01223 432310
Fax: 01223 426017
Email: advertising@rsc.org
Web site: http://www.rsc.org/lhb
ISSN: 0261-2917
Publisher: Royal Society of Chemistry
Date Established: 1981
Frequency: Monthly
Circulation: 200 (Publisher's Statement)
Editor: Stephen Wilkes; **Advertising Manager:** Ian Swain;
Publisher: Graham McCann
Summary of Content: Publication reporting on any issue
which may affect health and safety in a laboratory.
Readership/Target Audience: Read by laboratory workers
in chemical and allied environments.
ADVERTISING RATES:
Full Page Colour £890.00
SCC £26.00
Agency Commission: 10%
Mechanical Data: Bleed Size: 281 x 216mm, Type Area:
252 x 188mm, Col Length: 252mm, Page Width: 188mm,
Trim Size: 275 x 210mm
BUSINESS: APPLIED SCIENCE & LABORATORIES

LABORATORY NEWS

39979U55-85

Editorial Address: 6th Floor, Davis House, 2 Robert Street,
CROYDON, CR0 1QQ **Tel:** 020 8253 8600
Fax: 020 8253 4609
Email: alexandra.bailey@laboratorynews.co.uk
Advertising Address: As above. **Tel:** 020 8253 8378
Email: dominic.moon@laboratorynews.co.uk
Web site: http://www.labnews.co.uk
ISSN: 0266-7169
Publisher: Metropolis International Group Ltd
Date Established: 1971
Frequency: Monthly - Published on the 1st of the cover
month
Free to qualifying individuals
Annual Sub.: £80.00
Circulation: 10,696 (ABC 01/01/2008 to 31/12/2008)
Usual Pagination: 60
Editor: Alexandra Bailey; **Managing Director:** Kevin Crook
Summary of Content: Magazine covering current news,
industry trends, latest developments in products and their
applications and health and safety.

Readership/Target Audience: Aimed at senior laboratory
personnel in the industrial, medical, education and
government sectors.
ADVERTISING RATES:
Full Page Mono £2699.00
Full Page Colour £2699.00
Agency Commission: 10%
Mechanical Data: Bleed Size: 395 x 288mm, Film: Digital
Copy instructions: Copy Date: 4 weeks prior to publication
date
Average advertising content per issue: 40%
BUSINESS: APPLIED SCIENCE & LABORATORIES

LABOUR RESEARCH

36908U14B-200

Editorial Address: 78 Blackfriars Road, LONDON, SE1 8HF
Tel: 020 7928 3649 **Fax:** 020 7928 0621
Email: info@lrd.org.uk
Advertising Address: As above.
Email: snavaz@lrd.org.uk
Web site: http://www.lrd.org.uk
ISSN: 0023-7000
Publisher: LRD Publications Ltd
Date Established: 1917
Frequency: Monthly
Annual Sub.: £37.50
Circulation: 5,000 (Publisher's Statement)
Usual Pagination: 28
Editor: Nathalie Towner; **Advertising Manager:** Shanaz
Nevaz
Summary of Content: Journal containing trade union,
employment, economic and political news, information and
research.
Readership/Target Audience: Aimed at trade unionists and
labour movement activists and sympathisers.
ADVERTISING RATES:
Full Page Mono £1000.00
Full Page Colour £1500.00
Agency Commission: 10%
Mechanical Data: Type Area: 267 x 180mm, Col Length:
267mm, Page Width: 180mm, Film: Digital
BUSINESS: COMMERCE, INDUSTRY & MANAGEMENT:
Industry & Factories

LAMP

629415U45C-808

Editorial Address: 3 Exeter Road, DAWLISH, EX7 9JD
Tel: 01626 888868
Email: longships@aol.com
Advertising Address: 116 Abbeyfield Drive, FAREHAM,
PO15 5PQ **Tel:** 01329 843883
Email: secretary@alk.org.uk
Web site: http://www.lighthouse.fsnet.co.uk
ISSN: 1468-0998
Publisher: Association of Lighthouse Keepers
Date Established: 1989
Frequency: Quarterly
Cover Price: £2.50
Annual Sub.: £16.00
Circulation: 450 (Publisher's Statement)
Usual Pagination: 24
Editor: Steven Winter; **Advertising Manager:** Keith Morton
Summary of Content: Magazine covering current news and
historical information relating to lighthouses, lightships and
other navigational aids. Also includes recollections of
keepers' lifestyles.
Readership/Target Audience: Aimed at maritime
enthusiasts, pharologists and serving and retired personnel
of general lighthouse authorities.
ADVERTISING RATES:
Full Page Mono £100.00
Full Page Colour £300.00
Agency Commission: 10%
Mechanical Data: Type Area: 270 x 190mm, Col Length:
270mm, Page Width: 190mm, Bleed Size: 303 x 216mm,
Trim Size: 297 x 210mm
Copy instructions: Copy Date: 1st of the month prior to
publication date
Average advertising content per issue: 10%
BUSINESS: MARINE & SHIPPING: Maritime Freight

LANCASHIRE BUSINESS VIEW

1685476U63B-2539

Editorial Address: East Park Lodge, East Park Road,
BLACKBURN, BB1 8DW **Tel:** 01254 297870
Fax: 01254 295581
Email: editorial@lancashirebusinessview.co.uk
Advertising Address: As above. **Tel:** 01254 295580
Email: advertising@lancashirebusinessview.co.uk
Web site: http://www.lancashirebusinessview.co.uk
Publisher: North Point Publishing
Date Established: 2005
Frequency: 6 issues yearly
Cover Price: £3.95
Circulation: 8,000 (Publisher's Statement)
Editor: Tim Aldred; **Advertising Manager:** Stephen Bolton;
Publisher: Richard Slater

Summary of Content: Magazine including coverage of
major issues and analytical business information in
Lancashire.
Readership/Target Audience: Aimed at business owners
and managers.
ADVERTISING RATES:
Full Page Colour £1475.00
Agency Commission: 10%
Mechanical Data: Type Area: 265 x 186mm, Col Length:
265mm, Page Width: 186mm, Trim Size: 297 x 210mm,
Bleed Size: 303 x 216mm, Film: Digital
Copy instructions: Copy Date: 2 weeks prior to publication
date
Average advertising content per issue: 25%
BUSINESS: REGIONAL BUSINESS: Regional Business
English Counties

THE LANCET

40191U56A-70

Editorial Address: 32 Jamestown Road, LONDON, NW1
7BY **Tel:** 020 7424 4910 **Fax:** 020 7424 4911
Email: editorial@lancet.com
Advertising Address: As above.
Email: f.macnab@elsevier.com
Web site: http://www.thelancet.com
ISSN: 0140-6736
Publisher: Elsevier Health Sciences
Date Established: 1823
Frequency: Weekly
Annual Sub.: £126.00
Circulation: 33,000 (Publisher's Statement)
Usual Pagination: 100
Editor-in-Chief: Richard Horton; **Managing Editor:**
Stephanie Clark
Summary of Content: Journal containing clinical research
reports and comments on medical topics.
Readership/Target Audience: Aimed at hospital-based
clinicians and research academics.
ADVERTISING RATES:
Full Page Colour £1350.00
Agency Commission: 10%
Mechanical Data: Bleed Size: 292 x 270mm, Trim Size: 282
210mm, Film: Digital, Type Area: 260 x 186mm, Col Length:
260mm, Page Width: 186mm
Copy instructions: Copy Date: 10 days prior to publication
date
BUSINESS: HEALTH & MEDICAL

THE LANCET INFECTIOUS DISEASES

712543U56A-70_50

Editorial Address: 32 Jamestown Road, LONDON, NW1
7BY **Tel:** 020 7424 4950 **Fax:** 020 7424 4911
Email: ideditorial@lancet.com
Advertising Address: As above.
Web site: http://infection.thelancet.com
ISSN: 1473-3099
Publisher: The Lancet Publishing Group
Date Established: 2001
Frequency: Monthly
Annual Sub.: £96.00
Circulation: 1,195 (BPA Worldwide 01/01/2008 to
30/06/2008)
Usual Pagination: 64
Editor: John McConnell; **Publisher:** Richard Horton
Summary of Content: Publication containing review articles
written by specialists, comment and debate on hot topics in
the field, interviews with top names in infectious diseases
and news from around the world.
Readership/Target Audience: Read by clinical
microbiologists, virologists and infectious diseases
specialists from a wide range of subspecialities.
BUSINESS: HEALTH & MEDICAL

THE LANCET ONCOLOGY

624515U56A-71

Editorial Address: 32 Jamestown Road, LONDON, NW1
7BY **Tel:** 020 7424 4200 **Fax:** 020 7424 4557
Email: david.collingridge@lancet.com
Advertising Address: As above. **Fax:** 020 7424 4433
Email: s.cahill@elsevier.com
Web site: http://www.thelancet.com/journals/lanonc
ISSN: 1470-2045
Publisher: Elsevier Health Sciences
Date Established: 2000
Frequency: Monthly
Annual Sub.: £116.00
Circulation: 1,539 (BPA Worldwide 01/01/2007 to
30/06/2007)
Usual Pagination: 100
Editor: David Collingridge
Summary of Content: Publication which includes any
original research that advocates change in, or illuminates,
oncological clinical practice. The journal also publishes
interesting and informative reviews, opinion pieces, news,
letters, and media reviews on any topic connected with
oncology.

Readership/Target Audience: Aimed at clinicians and researchers specialising in oncology, oncology-associated specialities and trainee physicians.
ADVERTISING RATES:
Full Page Mono £624.00
Full Page Colour £1839.00
Agency Commission: 10%
Mechanical Data: Type Area: 260 x 186mm, Bleed Size: 292 x 220mm, Trim Size: 282 x 210mm, Col Length: 260mm, Page Width: 186mm, Film: Digital
BUSINESS: HEALTH & MEDICAL

LAND AND LIBERTY
38378U32A-86
Editorial Address: 212 Piccadilly, LONDON, W1J 9HG
Tel: 020 7377 8885 **Fax:** 020 8881 4429
Email: editor@landandliberty.net
Web site: http://www.landandliberty.net
ISSN: 0023-7574
Publisher: Henry George Foundation of Great Britain Ltd
Date Established: 1894
Frequency: Quarterly
Annual Sub.: £15.00
Circulation: 1,000 (Publisher's Statement)
Usual Pagination: 24
Editor: Peter Gibb; **Executive Editor:** Lars Rindsig
Summary of Content: Journal aiming to explore how our common wealth should be used and to demonstrate that this is the key to building the bridge of sustainability between private life, the public sector and our resources; between the individual, the community and the environment.
Readership/Target Audience: Aimed at politicians, civil servants, public policy makers, industrialists, academics and other influential people.
ADVERTISING: No Advertising taken
BUSINESS: LOCAL GOVERNMENT, LEISURE & RECREATION: Local Government

LAND CONTAMINATION & RECLAMATION
40670U57-35
Editorial Address: 6 Eastbourne Road, LONDON, W4 3EB
Tel: 020 8400 1601
Email: enquiries@epppublications.com
Advertising Address: As above. **Fax:** 020 8747 9663
Email: enquiries@epppublications.com
Web site: http://www.epppublications.com
ISSN: 0967-0513
Publisher: EPP Publications
Date Established: 1993
Frequency: Quarterly
Annual Sub.: £99.00
Circulation: 600 (Publisher's Statement)
Usual Pagination: 100
Editor: Rupert Hough; **Advertising Manager:** Marc Pomel; **Publisher:** Marc Pomel
Summary of Content: Journal dealing with land contamination and reclamation issues.
Readership/Target Audience: Aimed at environmental consultants, civil engineers, regulators and academics.
ADVERTISING RATES:
Full Page Mono £100.00
Agency Commission: 10%
Mechanical Data: Bleed Size: 303 x 216mm, Trim Size: 297 x 210mm, Film: Digital
Copy instructions: Copy Date: 1st of the month prior to publication date
Average advertising content per issue: 5%
BUSINESS: ENVIRONMENT & POLLUTION

LAND MOBILE
37470U18B-960
Editorial Address: PO Box 190, REDHILL, RH1 6FU
Tel: 01737 771877 **Fax:** 0870 288 5828
Email: richard@landmobile.co.uk
Advertising Address: PO Box 700, GREAT MISSENDEN, HP16 9JA **Tel:** 01494 862104 **Fax:** 01494 890788
Email: ianm@landmobile.co.uk
Web site: http://www.landmobile.co.uk
ISSN: 1352-2701
Publisher: Symposium Ltd
Date Established: 1993
Frequency: 11 issues yearly - Published at the end of the 1st week of cover month
Free to qualifying individuals
Annual Sub.: £50.00
Circulation: 9,500 (Publisher's Statement)
Usual Pagination: 40
Editor: Richard Lambley; **Advertising Manager:** Ian MacFarlaine; **Publisher:** Eileen Laybourn
Summary of Content: Magazine dedicated to wireless communications for business. It spans the whole spectrum of business radio applications from cellular phones and large-scale private networks through to on-site radio, wireless LANs and low-power, licence-free systems.
Readership/Target Audience: Read by people involved in the mobile communications industry, major users and specifiers.

ADVERTISING RATES:
Full Page Mono £1785.00
Full Page Colour £2242.00
Agency Commission: 10%
Mechanical Data: Page Width: 190mm, Type Area: 270 x 190mm, Bleed Size: 303 x 216mm, Trim Size: 297 x 210mm, Col Length: 270mm, Film: Positive, right reading, emulsion side down. Digital, Screen: 60 lpc
Copy instructions: Copy Date: 20th of the month prior to publication date
Average advertising content per issue: 33%
BUSINESS: ELECTRONICS: Telecommunications

LANDSCAPE & AMENITY PRODUCT UPDATE
22872U26B-61
Editorial Address: Grosvenor House, Central Park, TELFORD, TF2 9TW **Tel:** 01952 234000 **Fax:** 01952 234003
Email: katie@tspltd.co.uk
Advertising Address: As above.
Email: neilh@tspltd.co.uk
Web site: http://www.landscapeandamenity.com
Publisher: Tanner Stiles Publishing Ltd
Date Established: 1998
Frequency: 10 issues yearly - Published around the 3rd week of the cover month
Cover Price: Free
Circulation: 16,676 (ABC 01/07/2007 to 30/06/2008)
Usual Pagination: 32
Editor: Neil Hancock; **Publisher:** David Stiles
Summary of Content: Newspaper covering news, advice and features on products and services.
Readership/Target Audience: Aimed at local authorities, landscape architects, landscape contractors, sports clubs, golf courses, amenity managers, parks and theme park officers.
ADVERTISING RATES:
Full Page Mono £2735.00
Full Page Colour £4320.00
SCC £18.00
Agency Commission: 10%
Mechanical Data: Col Widths (Display): 42mm, No. of Columns (Display): 6, Page Width: 185mm, Type Area: 254 x 185mm, Col Length: 254mm, Trim Size: 292 x 210mm, Bleed Size: 303 x 216mm
Copy instructions: Copy Date: 3rd Friday of the month prior to publication date
Average advertising content per issue: 60%
BUSINESS: GARDEN TRADE: Garden Trade Supplies

LANDSCAPE MAGAZINE
1637927U4A-317
Editorial Address: Walmar House, 296 Regent Street, LONDON, W1B 3AW **Tel:** 020 7016 2555
Fax: 020 7907 4820
Email: landscapenews@wardour.co.uk
Advertising Address: 33 Great Portland Street, LONDON, W1W 8QG **Tel:** 020 7299 4500 **Fax:** 020 7636 7151
Email: peterb@landscapeinstitute.org
Web site: http://www.landscapeinstitute.org
Publisher: Wardour Publishing and Design
Date Established: 2004
Frequency: 11 issues yearly
Free to qualifying individuals
Annual Sub.: £50.00
Circulation: 5,100 (Publisher's Statement)
Usual Pagination: 56
Editor: Tim Coulthard; **Advertising Manager:** Peter Beecroft
Summary of Content: Journal published for the Landscape Institute. Covers all aspects of landscape architecture, urban design, planning, public space usage, materials science, environmental issues and regeneration.
Readership/Target Audience: Aimed at urban planners, policy makers and landscape architects.
ADVERTISING RATES:
Full Page Mono £1350.00
Full Page Colour £1350.00
Agency Commission: 10%
Mechanical Data: Type Area: 277 x 200mm, Bleed Size: 303 x 236mm, Trim Size: 297 x 230mm, Col Length: 277mm, Page Width: 200mm, Col Widths (Display): 44mm, Film: Digital
Copy instructions: Copy Date: 1 week prior to publication date
Average advertising content per issue: 40%
BUSINESS: ARCHITECTURE & BUILDING: Architecture

LANDSCAPE NEWS
40673U26B-62
Editorial Address: Landscape House, Stoneleigh Park, KENILWORTH, CV8 2LG **Tel:** 024 7669 0333
Fax: 024 7669 0077
Email: contact@bali.org.uk
Advertising Address: As above.
Email: contact@bali.org.uk
Web site: http://www.bali.org.uk
Publisher: The British Association of Landscape Industries
Frequency: Quarterly
Cover Price: Free

Circulation: 800 (Publisher's Statement)
Usual Pagination: 32
Editor: Daljeet Billing; **Advertising Manager:** Denise Ewbank
Summary of Content: Official publication of the British Association of Landscape Industries, featuring articles on landscape gardening, industry news, advice and jobs.
Readership/Target Audience: Read by landscape contractors in the UK.
ADVERTISING RATES:
Full Page Colour £1200.00
Mechanical Data: Type Area: 265 x 180mm, Col Length: 265mm, Page Width: 180mm, Bleed Size: +2mm, Trim Size: 297 x 210mm, Film: Digital
Copy instructions: Copy Date: 2 weeks prior to publication date
Average advertising content per issue: 25%
BUSINESS: GARDEN TRADE: Garden Trade Supplies

THE LANDSCAPER
622585U26D-73
Editorial Address: 6th Floor, Davis House, 2 Robert Street, CROYDON, CR0 1QQ **Tel:** 0870 730 1632
Email: david.curtis@metropolis.co.uk
Advertising Address: As above. **Tel:** 0870 730 1692
Fax: 020 8253 4603
Email: ray.ibrahim@metropolis.co.uk
Web site: http://www.landscapermagazine.com
Publisher: Metropolis International Group Ltd
Frequency: Monthly - Published around the 2nd week of the cover month
Free to qualifying individuals
Annual Sub.: £38.00
Circulation: 7,000 (Publisher's Statement)
Usual Pagination: 52
Editor: David Curtis
Summary of Content: Magazine covering all aspects of landscaping industry news, products and machinery.
Readership/Target Audience: Read by landscape and garden architects and designers, senior groundsmen and arborists.
ADVERTISING RATES:
Full Page Colour £1364.00
Agency Commission: 10%
Mechanical Data: Page Width: 150mm, Col Length: 218mm, Trim Size: 240 x 170mm, Bleed Size: 246 x 176mm, Type Area: 218 x 150mm, Film: Positive
Copy instructions: Copy Date: 2 weeks prior to publication date
Average advertising content per issue: 30%
BUSINESS: GARDEN TRADE: Garden Trade Horticulture

LANDWARDS
37857U21E-450
Editorial Address: Barton Road, Silsoe, BEDFORD, MK45 4FH **Tel:** 01525 861096 **Fax:** 01525 861660
Email: secretary@iagre.org
Advertising Address: As above.
Email: secretary@iagre.org
Web site: http://www.iagre.org
ISSN: 1363-8300
Publisher: The Institution of Agricultural Engineers
Frequency: Quarterly
Cover Price: £15.00
Annual Sub.: £15.00
Circulation: 2,500 (Publisher's Statement)
Usual Pagination: 36
Editor: Chris Biddle; **Advertising Manager:** Christopher Whetnall
Summary of Content: Journal covering all areas of engineering which relate to agriculture, horticulture, food processing, forestry, soil and water.
Readership/Target Audience: Read by engineers, scientists, technologists and managers.
ADVERTISING RATES:
Full Page Mono £400.00
Full Page Colour £650.00
Mechanical Data: Bleed Size: 303 x 216mm, Trim Size: 297 x 210mm, Type Area: 270 x 185mm, Col Length: 270mm, Page Width: 185mm, Film: Digital
Copy instructions: Copy Date: The 1st of the month prior to publication date
Average advertising content per issue: 15%
BUSINESS: AGRICULTURE & FARMING: Agriculture - Machinery & Plant

LANDWORKER
1633015U14L-931
Editorial Address: 35 King Street, LONDON, WC2E 8JG
Tel: 020 7420 8900 **Fax:** 020 7611 2735
Email: amanda.campbell@unitetheunion.com
Advertising Address: Biggs Press Organisation, 57 Eylewood Road, LONDON, SE27 9LZ **Tel:** 07792 718925
Web site: http://www.tgwu.org.uk
Publisher: Unite the Union
Date Established: 1919
Frequency: 6 issues yearly
Cover Price: Free
Circulation: 15,000 (Publisher's Statement)
Usual Pagination: 8

Editor: Amanda Campbell; **Advertising Manager:** Laurence Cade
Summary of Content: Newspaper covering food safety, the environment and the protection of working conditions.
Readership/Target Audience: Aimed at the rural and food industry.
ADVERTISING RATES:
Full Page Colour £900.00
Agency Commission: 10%
Copy instructions: Copy Date: 1 month prior to publication date
Average advertising content per issue: 33%
BUSINESS: COMMERCE, INDUSTRY & MANAGEMENT: Trade Unions

LANGUAGE AND LITERATURE 41216U62R-180
Editorial Address: School of English, Queen's University of Belfast, BELFAST, BT7 1NN **Tel:** 020 7324 8500
Fax: 020 7324 8600
Advertising Address: 1 Oliver's Yard, 55 City Road, LONDON, EC1Y 1SP **Tel:** 020 7324 8500
Fax: 020 7324 8600
Email: sheena.karim@sagepub.co.uk
Web site: http://www.sagepub.co.uk
ISSN: 0963-9470
Publisher: Sage Publications
Date Established: 1992
Frequency: Quarterly
Cover Price: £12.00
Annual Sub.: £48.00
Circulation: 400 (Publisher's Statement)
Usual Pagination: 96
Editor: Paul Simpson; **Advertising Manager:** Sheena Karim
Summary of Content: An international journal covering the latest developments in stylistic analysis, the linguistic analysis of literature and related areas.
Readership/Target Audience: Aimed at academics.
ADVERTISING RATES:
Full Page Mono £400.00
Agency Commission: 5%
Mechanical Data: Col Length: 215mm, Page Width: 145mm, Film: Digital, Type Area: 215 x 145mm
BUSINESS: CHURCH & SCHOOL EQUIPMENT & EDUCATION: Education Related

LANGUAGE CULTURE & CURRICULUM
41059U62B-441
Editorial Address: 4 Park Square, Milton Park, ABINGDON, OX14 4RN **Tel:** 020 7017 6000 **Fax:** 020 7017 6699
Email: victoria.quantrell@tandf.co.uk
Web site: http://www.informaworld.com
ISSN: 0790-8318
Publisher: Routledge, Taylor & Francis
Date Established: 1987
Frequency: 3 issues yearly - Published in April, August and December
Cover Price: £259.00
Usual Pagination: 96
Editor: Vicky Quantrell; **Managing Editor:** Vicky Quantrell
Summary of Content: The journal of the Linguistic Institute of Ireland. Journal covering practical guidelines for the design and implementation of language curricula with cultural objectives.
Readership/Target Audience: Aimed at Academics interested in language and linguistics.
ADVERTISING: No Advertising taken
BUSINESS: CHURCH & SCHOOL EQUIPMENT & EDUCATION: Education Teachers

LANGUAGE LEARNING JOURNAL
41060U62B-450
Editorial Address: Institute of Education, University of London, LONDON, WC1H 0AL **Tel:** 020 7612 6712
Fax: 020 7612 6534
Email: n.pachler@ioe.ac.uk
Advertising Address: Taylor and Francis, 4 Park Square, Milton Park, ABINGDON, OX14 4RM **Tel:** 020 7017 6000
Email: jenna.johnston@tandf.co.k
Web site: http://www.all-languages.org.uk
ISSN: 0957-1736
Publisher: Routledge Cavendish Publishing Ltd
Date Established: 1990
Frequency: Half-yearly
Free to qualifying individuals
Annual Sub.: £48.00
Circulation: 5,000 (Publisher's Statement)
Usual Pagination: 82
Editor: Norbert Pachler; **Advertising Manager:** Jenna Johnston
Summary of Content: Contains articles on teaching and learning of languages, language policy, current and topical issues, and ideas on and experiences of practical classroom teaching.
Readership/Target Audience: Aimed at foreign language teachers in all school sectors, lecturers in higher, further and

adult education, advisors and inspectors, teacher trainers, business language trainers and interested language learners.
ADVERTISING RATES:
Full Page Mono £615.00
Mechanical Data: Col Length: 250mm, Col Widths (Display): 73mm, No. of Columns (Display): 2, Type Area: 250 x 185mm, Page Width: 185mm, Trim Size: 297 x 210mm, Bleed Size: 303 x 216mm
Copy instructions: Copy Date: 6 weeks prior to publication date
BUSINESS: CHURCH & SCHOOL EQUIPMENT & EDUCATION: Education Teachers

LANGUAGE TEACHING RESEARCH
41063U62B-460
Editorial Address: 1 Oliver's Yard, 55 City Road, LONDON, EC1Y 1SP **Tel:** 020 7324 8500 **Fax:** 020 7324 8600
Email: market@sagepub.co.uk
Advertising Address: As above.
Email: sheena.karim@sagepub.co.uk
Web site: http://www.sagepub.co.uk
ISSN: 1362-1688
Publisher: Sage Publications
Date Established: 1997
Frequency: Quarterly
Annual Sub.: £250.00
Usual Pagination: 128
Editor: Rod Ellis; **Advertising Manager:** Sheena Karim
Summary of Content: Features language teaching issues, programmes, syllabus and material designs, methodology and the reading of specific skills. Focus on the area of second or foreign language teaching.
Readership/Target Audience: Aimed at researchers in language teaching.
ADVERTISING RATES:
Full Page Mono £400.00
Agency Commission: 10%
Mechanical Data: Print Process: Sheet-fed litho, Type Area: 180 x 120mm, Trim Size: 234 x 156mm, Film: Positive, right reading, emulsion side down. Digital, Col Length: 180mm, Page Width: 120mm
Average advertising content per issue: 5%
BUSINESS: CHURCH & SCHOOL EQUIPMENT & EDUCATION: Education Teachers

LANGUAGE TRAVEL MAGAZINE 39727U50-20
Editorial Address: 11-15 Emerald Street, LONDON, WC1N 3QL **Tel:** 020 7440 4020 **Fax:** 020 7440 4033
Email: amy@hothousemedia.com
Advertising Address: As above. **Tel:** 020 7440 4026
Email: nicola@hothousemedia.com
Web site: http://www.hothousemedia.com
Publisher: Hothouse Media
Date Established: 1989
Frequency: Monthly - Published at the end of the cover month
Free to qualifying individuals
Annual Sub.: £35.00
Circulation: 36,000 (Publisher's Statement)
Usual Pagination: 48
Editor: Amy Baker; **Managing Director:** Scott Wade;
Publisher: Scott Wade
Summary of Content: Magazine for the language training industry and those involved in education, training and volunteer work experience overseas.
Readership/Target Audience: Read by overseas agents and education consultants, staff and students of language teaching institutions and relevant industry bodies.
ADVERTISING RATES:
Full Page Colour £2480.00
Agency Commission: 10%
Mechanical Data: Film: Digital, Trim Size: 297 x 210mm
Average advertising content per issue: 30%
BUSINESS: TRAVEL & TOURISM

LAPV LOCAL AUTHORITY PLANT & VEHICLES 38374U32A-97
Editorial Address: 8 The Old Yarn Mills, Westbury, SHERBORNE, DT9 3RQ **Tel:** 01935 816030
Fax: 01935 817200
Email: am.knegt@hisdorset.com
Advertising Address: Letsrecycle.com, Elizabeth House, 39 York Road, LONDON, SE1 7NQ **Tel:** 020 7633 4505
Fax: 020 7633 4519
Email: sales@letsrecycle.com
Web site: http://www.lapv.co.uk
ISSN: 1472-2607
Publisher: Hemming Group Ltd
Date Established: 1972
Frequency: Quarterly
Cover Price: Free
Circulation: 4,505 (Publisher's Statement)
Editor: Ann-Marie Knegt; **Managing Director:** Graham Bond
Summary of Content: Magazine covering local authority waste and environmental issues and the purchase and

specification of plant, vehicles and grounds maintenance equipment.
Readership/Target Audience: Aimed at local authority and public utility executives and waste transport officers.
ADVERTISING RATES:
Full Page Mono £1200.00
Full Page Colour £1200.00
Agency Commission: 10%
Copy instructions: Copy Date: 2 weeks prior to publication date
Average advertising content per issue: 50%
BUSINESS: LOCAL GOVERNMENT, LEISURE & RECREATION: Local Government

LATIN AMERICAN REGIONAL REPORT - BRAZIL AND SOUTHERN CONE REPORT
601211U14A-194_45
Formerly: Latin American Regional Report - Brazil Report
Editorial Address: 61 Old Street, LONDON, EC1V 9HW
Tel: 020 7251 0012 **Fax:** 020 7253 8193
Email: subs@latinnews.com
Web site: http://www.latinnews.com
ISSN: 1741-4423
Publisher: Intelligence Research Ltd
Date Established: 1979
Frequency: Monthly
Annual Sub.: £175.00
Usual Pagination: 16
Editor: Jon Farmer
Summary of Content: Magazine which examines in depth the economic, financial and current events in the region.
ADVERTISING: No Advertising taken
BUSINESS: COMMERCE, INDUSTRY & MANAGEMENT

LATIN AMERICAN REGIONAL REPORT - CARIBBEAN & CENTRAL AMERICA REPORT
601212U14C-94
Editorial Address: 61 Old Street, LONDON, EC1V 9HW
Tel: 020 7251 0012 **Fax:** 020 7253 8193
Email: subs@latinnews.com
Web site: http://www.latinnews.com
ISSN: 0968-2732
Publisher: Intelligence Research Ltd
Date Established: 1993
Frequency: Monthly
Annual Sub.: £175.00
Usual Pagination: 16
Editor: Sarah Sheldon
Summary of Content: Magazine examining the problems and opportunities of the Caribbean and Central America.
Readership/Target Audience: Aimed at business people with investments in Latin America.
ADVERTISING: No Advertising taken
BUSINESS: COMMERCE, INDUSTRY & MANAGEMENT: International Commerce

LATIN AMERICAN REGIONAL REPORT - MEXICO & NAFTA REPORT 601231U14C-94_1
Editorial Address: 61 Old Street, LONDON, EC1V 9HW
Tel: 020 7251 0012 **Fax:** 020 7253 8193
Email: info@latinnews.com
Web site: http://www.latinnews.com
ISSN: 0968-2724
Publisher: Intelligence Research Ltd
Date Established: 1979
Frequency: Monthly
Annual Sub.: £175.00
Usual Pagination: 16
Editor: Will Ollard
Summary of Content: Magazine focusing on economic, financial and current affairs in Mexico, contains in-depth coverage of the North American free trade agreement.
Readership/Target Audience: Aimed at investors and bankers in the US and Europe.
ADVERTISING: No Advertising taken
BUSINESS: COMMERCE, INDUSTRY & MANAGEMENT: International Commerce

LATIN AMERICAN REGIONAL REPORTS - ANDEAN GROUP REPORT 601229U14C-94_15
Editorial Address: 61 Old Street, LONDON, EC1V 9HW
Tel: 020 7251 0012 **Fax:** 020 7253 8193
Email: info@latinnews.com
Web site: http://www.latinnews.com
ISSN: 0143-5248
Publisher: Intelligence Research Ltd
Date Established: 1979
Frequency: Monthly
Annual Sub.: £175.00
Usual Pagination: 16
Editor: Jon Farmer

Business Magazines

Section 4 (b) Business Magazines

Summary of Content: Publication containing reports on the Andean region, looking at political and economic development.
Readership/Target Audience: Aimed at investors and bankers in the US and Europe.
ADVERTISING: No Advertising taken
BUSINESS: COMMERCE, INDUSTRY & MANAGEMENT: International Commerce

LATIN AMERICAN WEEKLY REPORT
36965U14C-96

Editorial Address: 61 Old Street, LONDON, EC1V 9HW
Tel: 020 7251 0012 **Fax:** 020 7253 8193
Email: info@latinnews.com
Web site: http://www.latinnews.com
ISSN: 0143-5280
Publisher: Intelligence Research Ltd
Date Established: 1967
Frequency: Weekly
Annual Sub.: £695.00
Usual Pagination: 16
Editor: Jon Farmer
Summary of Content: Newsletter providing analysis of news as it breaks in Latin America, covering the economic and political scene, long-term trends and the effects for business organisations.
Language(s): English; Spanish
Readership/Target Audience: Directed at businesses with interests in Latin America including bankers, businessmen, corporate planners, diplomats, politicians and academics.
ADVERTISING: No Advertising taken
BUSINESS: COMMERCE, INDUSTRY & MANAGEMENT: International Commerce

LATIN LAWYER
1829777U44-3052

Editorial Address: 87 Lancaster Road, LONDON, W11 1QQ
Tel: 020 7908 1184 **Fax:** 020 7229 6910
Email: briefing@latinlawyer.com
Web site: http://www.latinlawyer.com
Publisher: Law Business Research Ltd
Date Established: 2001
Frequency: 10 issues yearly
Annual Sub.: £400.00
Usual Pagination: 50
Editor: Sarah Wright; **Publisher:** Richard Davey
Summary of Content: Business law magazine for Latin America covering economic, legal regulatory and political issues affecting the practice of law in the region. A email briefing published twice weekly is also available.
Readership/Target Audience: Aimed at providers and users of legal services in Latin America.
BUSINESS: LEGAL

LATTE
1809259U62B-1410

Editorial Address: Boston House, 214 High Street, Boston Spa, WETHERBY, LS23 6AD **Tel:** 0844 800 0085
Fax: 01937 529236
Email: jimriley@tutor2u.net
Advertising Address: As above.
Email: jimriley@tutor2u.net
Web site: http://www.tutor2u.net
Publisher: Tutor2u Ltd
Date Established: 2006
Frequency: Half-yearly
Cover Price: Free
Circulation: 7,500 (Publisher's Statement)
Usual Pagination: 44
Editor: Jim Riley; **Managing Director:** Jim Riley; **Advertising Manager:** Jim Riley
Summary of Content: Magazine featuring tips and advice for teachers, learning support, personalised learning, competitions and awards.
Readership/Target Audience: Aimed at business studies and economics teachers.
ADVERTISING RATES:
Full Page Colour £1200.00
Agency Commission: 10%
Mechanical Data: Trim Size: 297 x 210mm, Film: Digital
Average advertising content per issue: 15%
BUSINESS: CHURCH & SCHOOL EQUIPMENT & EDUCATION: Education Teachers

LAUNDRY & CLEANING NEWS
38216U28-81

Editorial Address: Progressive House, 2 Maidstone Road, Foots Cray, SIDCUP, DA14 5HZ **Tel:** 020 8269 7786
Fax: 020 8269 7802
Email: jtaylor@laundryandcleaningnews.com
Web site: http://www.connectinglaundry.com
ISSN: 0142-9442
Publisher: Progressive Media Publications
Frequency: Monthly - Published on the 1st Monday of the cover month
Annual Sub.: £59.00
Circulation: 5,416 (ABC 01/07/2008 to 30/06/2009)
Usual Pagination: 48

Editor: Janet Taylor
Summary of Content: News and features for laundry, dry cleaning, textile rental and on-premises laundries.
Readership/Target Audience: Aimed at proprietors, managers and supervisors of laundry and dry cleaning companies.
ADVERTISING: No Advertising taken
BUSINESS: LAUNDRY & DRY CLEANING

LAUNDRY & CLEANING TODAY
38217U28-80

Editorial Address: 54 Crockhamwell Road, Woodley, READING, RG5 3LB **Tel:** 0118 969 5008
Email: enquiries@laundryandcleaningtoday.com
Advertising Address: As above. **Tel:** 0118 901 4471
Fax: 0118 962 8982
Email: enquiries@laundryandcleaningtoday.com
Web site: http://www.laundryandcleaningtoday.com
Publisher: Marketskil Ltd
Date Established: 1993
Frequency: 10 issues yearly - Published in the last week of the month prior to month of publication
Annual Sub.: £20.00
Circulation: 3,000 (Publisher's Statement)
Usual Pagination: 32
Editor: Carole Wright; **Advertising Director:** Tina Gleed; **Publisher:** Jack Fowler
Summary of Content: Newspaper covering news and articles on textile rental, all forms of textile care, laundry and dry cleaning.
Readership/Target Audience: Read by launderers, dry cleaners, textile rental operatives and launderette owners.
ADVERTISING RATES:
Full Page Colour £1911.50
SCC £9.00
Agency Commission: 10%
Mechanical Data: Type Area: 370 x 262mm, Col Length: 370mm, Page Width: 262mm, Col Widths (Display): 40mm, No. of Columns (Display): 6, Print Process: Sheet-fed litho
Copy instructions: Copy Date: 21 days prior to publication date
Average advertising content per issue: 40%
Supplement(s): Annual Buyers Guide - 1xY
BUSINESS: LAUNDRY & DRY CLEANING

LAW QUARTERLY REVIEW
39198U44-1180

Editorial Address: The Hatchery, Hall Bank Lane, Mytholmroyd, HEBDEN BRIDGE, HX7 5HQ
Tel: 01422 888000 **Fax:** 01422 888001
Web site: http://www.sweetandmaxwell.co.uk/lqr
ISSN: 0023-933X
Publisher: Sweet & Maxwell Yorkshire
Frequency: Quarterly
Annual Sub.: £138.00
Usual Pagination: 170
Editor: Sarah Mullins
Summary of Content: Journal containing an informative and critical perspective on all aspects of the law.
Readership/Target Audience: Aimed at barristers, solicitors, judges and academics.
ADVERTISING: No Advertising taken
BUSINESS: LEGAL

LAW SOCIETY GAZETTE
39170U44-1200

Formerly: Law Society's Gazette
Editorial Address: 113 Chancery Lane, LONDON, WC2A 1PL **Tel:** 020 7841 5555 **Fax:** 020 7841 5513
Email: gazette-editorial@lawsociety.org.uk
Advertising Address: As above. **Tel:** 020 7242 1222
Fax: 020 7841 5509
Email: gazette-advertising@lawsociety.org.uk
Web site: http://www.lawgazette.co.uk
ISSN: 0262-1495
Publisher: The Law Society
Date Established: 1903
Frequency: Weekly
Cover Price: £4.50
Free to qualifying individuals
Annual Sub.: £139.00
Circulation: 118,927 (ABC 01/07/2007 to 30/06/2008)
Usual Pagination: 80
Editor: Catherine Baksi; **Features Editor:** Rupert White; **Editor-in-Chief:** Paul Rogerson
Summary of Content: Journal providing law related news, commentary and analysis, features, and new city coverage. Twitter:https://twitter.com/lawsocgazette
Readership/Target Audience: Aimed at the legal profession.
ADVERTISING RATES:
Full Page Mono £3472.00
Full Page Colour £5006.00
Agency Commission: 10%
Mechanical Data: Page Width: 192mm, Trim Size: 297 x 230mm, Bleed Size: 303 x 236mm, Type Area: 270 x 210mm, Col Length: 268mm, Film: Digital
Copy instructions: Copy Date: 2 weeks prior to publication date
Average advertising content per issue: 25%

Supplement(s): Continuing Professional Development - 1xY, Guide to Expert Witnesses - 1xY
BUSINESS: LEGAL

THE LAWYER
39200U44-1240

Editorial Address: St. Giles House, 50 Poland Street, LONDON, W1F 7AX **Tel:** 020 7970 4000 **Fax:** 020 7970 4640
Email: editorial@thelawyer.com
Advertising Address: As above. **Tel:** 020 7970 4658
Fax: 020 7970 4668
Email: ian.sinclair@thelawyer.com
Web site: http://www.thelawyer.com
ISSN: 0953-7902
Publisher: Centaur Media Plc
Frequency: Weekly - Published every Monday of the week
Cover Price: £2.65
Free to qualifying individuals
Annual Sub.: £80.00
Circulation: 28,221 (ABC 01/07/2008 to 30/06/2009)
Usual Pagination: 54
Editor: Margaret Taylor; **News Editor:** Margaret Taylor; **Features Editor:** Matt Byrne; **Advertising Manager:** Ian Sinclair; **Publisher:** Libby Child
Summary of Content: Magazine reporting on legal news and opinions. Includes surveys, conferencing, network opportunities, management section and special reports. Twitter: https://twitter.com/completelawyer.
Readership/Target Audience: Read by commercial lawyers, corporate directors and decision makers in the legal profession.
ADVERTISING RATES:
Full Page Colour £4125.00
Agency Commission: 10%
Mechanical Data: Type Area: 340 x 254mm, Trim Size: 375 x 280mm, Bleed Size: 381 x 286mm, Page Width: 254mm, Film: Digital, Col Length: 340mm
Copy instructions: Copy Date: Wednesday prior to publication date
Supplement(s): UK 200 - 1xY
BUSINESS: LEGAL

LCA•GC EUROPE
39973U55-94_50

Formerly: LC•GC Europe
Editorial Address: Advanstar House, Park West, Sealand Road, CHESTER, CH1 4RN **Tel:** 01244 378888
Fax: 01244 370011
Email: amatheson@advanstar.com
Advertising Address: As above. **Fax:** 01244 383356
Email: lnoyes@advanstar.com
Web site: http://www.chromatographyonline.com
ISSN: 1471-6577
Publisher: Advanstar Communications (U.K.) Ltd
Date Established: 1988
Frequency: Monthly - Published around the middle of the cover month
Cover Price: Free
Usual Pagination: 60
Editor: Felicity Thomas
Summary of Content: Journal concerning separation science and analytical chemistry.
Readership/Target Audience: Aimed at chromatography users across Europe in all types of industry.
ADVERTISING RATES:
Full Page Colour £5598.00
Agency Commission: 10%
Mechanical Data: Type Area: 254 x 177mm, Bleed Size: 279 x 209mm, Trim Size: 273 x 203mm, Col Length: 254mm, Page Width: 177mm, Film: Digital
Average advertising content per issue: 45%
Supplement(s): The Applications Handbook - 4xY
BUSINESS: APPLIED SCIENCE & LABORATORIES

LCN LICENSED & CATERING NEWS
36487U9A-120

Editorial Address: Penton House, 38 Heron Road, Sydenham Business Park, BELFAST, BT3 9LE
Tel: 028 9045 7457 **Fax:** 028 9045 6611
Email: tara.craig@pentonpublications.co.uk
Advertising Address: As above.
Email: adam.kempster@pentonpublications.co.uk
Publisher: Penton Publications Ltd
Date Established: 1944
Frequency: 11 issues yearly - Published in the 1st week of the cover month
Free to qualifying individuals
Annual Sub.: £45.00
Circulation: 5,584 (ABC 01/07/2008 to 30/06/2009)
Usual Pagination: 48
Editor: Tara Craig
Summary of Content: Magazine for the licensed trade and the hospitality industry in Northern Ireland. News on the local industry including product launches, marketing campaigns, wine, refurbishment, premises, catering and hospitality. Also includes profiles of local players in the drinks, hotels, tourism and catering scenes.

Readership/Target Audience: Aimed at all buyers and decision makers in the hospitality and leisure industry in Northern Ireland, including pubs, clubs, hotels and restaurants.
ADVERTISING RATES:
Full Page Colour £1895.00
Agency Commission: 10%
Mechanical Data: Page Width: 248mm, Film: Digital, Type Area: 353 x 248mm, Col Length: 353mm, Trim Size: 381 x 273mm, Bleed Size: 387 x 279mm
Copy instructions: Copy Date: 1 week prior to publication date
Average advertising content per issue: 40%
BUSINESS: DRINKS & LICENSED TRADE: Drinks, Licensed Trade, Wines & Spirits

LDP BUSINESS
41330U63B-1160
Formerly: Business Week
Editorial Address: PO Box 48, Old Hall Street, LIVERPOOL, L69 3EB **Tel:** 0151 227 2000 **Fax:** 0151 330 4982
Email: billgleeson@dailypost.co.uk
Advertising Address: As above.
Email: julie.cowley@liverpool.com
Web site: http://www.ldpbusiness.co.uk
Publisher: Liverpool Daily Post & Echo Ltd
Frequency: Monthly - Published on Wednesdays
Cover Price: Free
Circulation: 20,000 (Publisher's Statement)
Usual Pagination: 16
Editor: Bill Gleeson; **Features Editor:** Barry Turnbull
Summary of Content: Regional business supplement containing the latest news and developments.
Readership/Target Audience: Read by businessmen and members of the Chamber of Commerce & Industry in Cheshire, Merseyside and parts of Lancashire.
ADVERTISING RATES:
SCC £10.48
Agency Commission: 10%
Mechanical Data: No. of Columns (Display): 8, Col Widths (Display): 31mm, Film: Digital, Type Area: 360 x 272mm, Col Length: 360mm, Page Width: 272mm, Bleed Size: +3mm
Copy instructions: Copy Date: Monday 4pm prior to publication date
Supplement to: Liverpool Daily Post
BUSINESS: REGIONAL BUSINESS: Regional Business English Counties

LEADER
41153U62J-325
Formerly: Headlines
Editorial Address: 130 Regent Road, LEICESTER, LE1 7PG
Tel: 0116 299 1122 **Fax:** 0116 299 1123
Advertising Address: As above.
Email: angela@ascl.org.uk
Web site: http://www.leadermagazine.co.uk
Publisher: Association of School and College Leaders
Date Established: 2005
Frequency: 9 issues yearly
Cover Price: £6.00
Free to qualifying individuals
Circulation: 13,500 (Publisher's Statement)
Usual Pagination: 36
Editor: Sara Gadzik; **Advertising Manager:** Angela Stewart
Summary of Content: Journal of the Association of School College Leaders, the professional association and trade union for secondary school and college leadership teams.
Readership/Target Audience: Read by secondary school and college leaders including heads, deputies, assistant heads, principals, vice-principals, business managers and others with whole school or college responsibility.
ADVERTISING RATES:
Full Page Colour £2400.00
Agency Commission: 10%
Mechanical Data: Type Area: 267 x 185mm, Col Length: 267mm, Page Width: 185mm, Film: Digital, Trim Size: 297 x 210mm, Bleed Size: 303 x 216mm
Copy instructions: Copy Date: 3 weeks prior to publication date
BUSINESS: CHURCH & SCHOOL EQUIPMENT & EDUCATION: Teachers & Education Management

LEADERSHIP FOCUS
41151U62J-600
Formerly: The Head Teachers Review
Editorial Address: 1 Heath Square, Boltro Road, HAYWARDS HEATH, RH16 1BL **Tel:** 01444 472474
Fax: 01444 472476
Email: info@naht.org.uk
Advertising Address: As above. **Tel:** 01444 472472
Fax: 01444 472491
Email: publications@naht.org.uk
Web site: http://www.naht.org.uk
ISSN: 1472-6181
Publisher: National Association of Head Teachers
Frequency: 6 issues yearly
Cover Price: £5.00
Circulation: 27,835 (ABC 01/07/2008 to 30/06/2009)
Usual Pagination: 80

Editor: Robert Sanders; **Managing Editor:** Steve Smethurst
Summary of Content: Magazine providing a forum for the exchange of educational ideas.
Readership/Target Audience: Read by NAHT members, retired life members, school inspectors and advisers.
ADVERTISING: Rates on application
BUSINESS: CHURCH & SCHOOL EQUIPMENT & EDUCATION: Teachers & Education Management

LEARNING DISABILITY PRACTICE
40484U56N-32
Editorial Address: The Heights, 59-65 Lowlands Road, HARROW, HA1 3AW **Tel:** 020 8423 1066
Fax: 020 8872 3198
Email: colin.parish@rcnpublishing.co.uk
Advertising Address: As above.
Email: advertising@rcnpublishing.co.uk
Web site: http://www.learningdisabilitypractice.co.uk
ISSN: 3605-8712
Publisher: RCN Publishing Co Ltd
Date Established: 1998
Frequency: 10 issues yearly
Annual Sub.: £75.80
Circulation: 4,067 (ABC 01/01/2008 to 31/12/2008)
Usual Pagination: 40
Editor: Helen Hyland
Summary of Content: Publication focusing on recent fundamental changes in the field of learning disabilities. Covers the areas of practice, policy, research and education, as well as carrying profiles of prominent people within the field.
Readership/Target Audience: Read by members of the Royal College of Nursing and people working in the learning disability field.
ADVERTISING RATES:
Full Page Colour £1705.00
Mechanical Data: Type Area: 271 x 178mm, Bleed Size: 303 x 216mm, Trim Size: 297 x 210mm, Col Length: 271mm, Page Width: 178mm, Film: Digital
Copy instructions: Copy Date: 2 weeks prior to publication date
BUSINESS: HEALTH & MEDICAL: Mental Health

LEARNING DISABILITY TODAY
717789U32G-76
Formerly: Living Well
Editorial Address: Richmond House, Richmond Road, BRIGHTON, BN2 3RL **Tel:** 01273 623222
Fax: 01273 625526
Email: joannas@pavpub.com
Advertising Address: As above. **Tel:** 0870 890 1080
Fax: 0870 890 1081
Email: helenc@pavpub.com
Web site: http://www.pavpub.com
ISSN: 1474-5178
Publisher: Pavilion Journals (Brighton) Ltd
Date Established: 2001
Frequency: Quarterly
Annual Sub.: £75.00
Circulation: 300 (Publisher's Statement)
Usual Pagination: 32
Editor: Barbara McIntosh; **Advertising Manager:** Helen Charlton
Summary of Content: Journal promoting inclusive lifestyles for people with learning disabilities including work, education, leisure and lifestyle as well as covering policy, practice and research discussions, events, resources and network information.
Readership/Target Audience: Aimed at managers, carers, social workers, GPs, residential care staff, community nurses and those in associated professions.
ADVERTISING RATES:
Full Page Mono £800.00
Full Page Colour £800.00
Agency Commission: 10%
Mechanical Data: Bleed Size: +5mm, Type Area: 260 x 180mm, Col Length: 260mm, Page Width: 180mm
Average advertising content per issue: 10%
BUSINESS: LOCAL GOVERNMENT, LEISURE & RECREATION: Community Care & Social Services

LEARNING SUPPORT
1691863U62C-728
Editorial Address: 38 High Street, BISHOPS CASTLE, SY9 5BQ
Email: info@learningsupport.co.uk
Advertising Address: As above.
Email: advertising@learningsupport.co.uk
Web site: http://www.learningsupport.co.uk
ISSN: 1747-1990
Publisher: Brightday
Date Established: 2005
Frequency: 6 issues yearly
Annual Sub.: £49.00
Circulation: 5,000 (Publisher's Statement)
Usual Pagination: 32
Editor: Frances Rickford; **Advertising Manager:** Frances Rickford

Summary of Content: Magazine providing information, ideas and resources for primary school teaching assistants.
Readership/Target Audience: Aimed at teaching assistants, learning support assistants, learning mentors, mealtime and playground supervisors.
ADVERTISING RATES:
Full Page Colour £780.00
Mechanical Data: Type Area: 218 x 146.5mm, Col Length: 218mm, Page Width: 146.5mm, Trim Size: 245 x 170mm, Bleed Size: +3mm, Film: Digital
Copy instructions: Copy Date: 3 weeks prior to publication date
Average advertising content per issue: 10%
BUSINESS: CHURCH & SCHOOL EQUIPMENT & EDUCATION: Junior Education

LEASING LIFE
35381U1K-120
Editorial Address: 39 Thorney Road, Capel St. Mary, IPSWICH, IP9 2HL **Tel:** 01473 311983
Email: briancrogerson@btinternet.com
Advertising Address: 34 Porchester Road, LONDON, W2 6ES **Tel:** 020 7563 5600 **Fax:** 020 7563 5601
Email: daniel.greenwood@financialnews.com
Web site: http://www.leasinglife.com
ISSN: 1351-3826
Publisher: VRL Knowledge Bank Ltd
Date Established: 1993
Frequency: Monthly - Published in the last week of the cover month
Annual Sub.: £295.00
Circulation: 1,100 (Publisher's Statement)
Usual Pagination: 48
Editor: Brian Rogerson; **Advertising Manager:** Daniel Greenwood
Summary of Content: News magazine covering the leasing and asset finance industry and related regulatory issues.
Readership/Target Audience: Aimed at leasing professionals, dealers, manufacturers and leaseholders.
ADVERTISING RATES:
Full Page Colour £2300.00
Agency Commission: 10%
Mechanical Data: Film: Digital, Type Area: 261 x 186mm, Col Length: 261mm, Page Width: 186mm, Bleed Size: 303 x 216mm, Trim Size: 297 x 210mm
Copy instructions: Copy Date: 2 weeks prior to publication date
BUSINESS: FINANCE & ECONOMICS: Rental Leasing

LEATHER INTERNATIONAL
39791U52D-50
Formerly: Leather
Editorial Address: Progressive House, 2 Maidstone Road, Foots Cray, SIDCUP, DA14 5HZ **Tel:** 020 8269 7700
Fax: 020 8269 7880
Email: mricker@leathermag.com
Advertising Address: As above. **Fax:** 020 8269 7840
Email: mcolyer@leathermag.com
Web site: http://www.leathermag.com
ISSN: 1473-6314
Publisher: Progressive Media Publications
Date Established: 1867
Frequency: 9 issues yearly - Published in the middle of the cover month
Cover Price: £10.00
Annual Sub.: £123.00
Circulation: 4,239 (Publisher's Statement)
Usual Pagination: 60
Editor: Martin Ricker
Summary of Content: International magazine covering everything in the leather world, from raw materials, through scientific and technological matters, to finished leather.
Readership/Target Audience: Read by tanners, hide and skin traders and other international leather industry professionals.
ADVERTISING RATES:
Full Page Mono EUR2950.00
Full Page Colour EUR4053.00
Agency Commission: 10%
Mechanical Data: Type Area: 280 x 192mm, Trim Size: 297 x 210mm, Bleed Size: 303 x 216mm, Col Length: 280mm, Page Width: 192mm, Film: Positive, right reading, emulsion side down. Digital, Print Process: Litho
Copy instructions: Copy Date: 3rd week of the month prior to publication date
Average advertising content per issue: 50%
Supplement(s): Leather Brazil - 1xY, Leather China - 3xY, What's New In Leather Chemicals - 1xY
BUSINESS: GIFT TRADE: Leather

LEDS MAGAZINE
1794336U17-267
Editorial Address: 16 Arlington Villas, Clifton, BRISTOL, BS8 2EG **Tel:** 0117 946 7262
Email: leds@pennwell.com
Advertising Address: As above.
Email: joanna@ledsmagazine.com
Web site: http://www.ledsmagazine.com
Publisher: Pennwell Corporation
Frequency: 6 issues yearly

Editor: Tim Whitaker; **Advertising Manager:** Joanna Hook
Summary of Content: Magazine and website covering the application and uses of high brightness LEDs and the technology of building LED based systems.
Readership/Target Audience: Aimed at people who build systems and end products such as lighting fixtures and displays that use LEDs.
ADVERTISING RATES:
Full Page Colour £1750.00
Agency Commission: 10%
Mechanical Data: Type Area: 262 x 193mm, Bleed Size: 288 x 219mm, Trim Size: 282 x 213mm, Col Length: 262mm, Page Width: 193mm, Film: Digital
BUSINESS: ELECTRICAL

THE LEEDS & YORKSHIRE LAWYER

39126U44-1255

Formerly: The Bulletin
Editorial Address: Barker Brooks House, 4 Greengate, Cardale Park, HARROGATE, HG3 1GY **Tel:** 01423 851150
Fax: 01423 851151
Email: emma.waddingham@barkerbrooks.co.uk
Advertising Address: As above.
Email: kate.mckittrick@barkerbrooks.co.uk
Web site: http://www.barkerbrooks.co.uk
Publisher: Barker Brooks Media
Date Established: 1997
Frequency: 10 issues yearly
Cover Price: Free
Circulation: 10,000 (Publisher's Statement)
Usual Pagination: 32
Editor: Emma Waddingham; **Advertising Manager:** Kate Mckittrick; **Managing Editor:** James Ratcliff
Summary of Content: Journal of the Leeds Law Society containing news and features relating to the legal profession and the law both nationally and in the Yorkshire region.
Readership/Target Audience: Read by registered members of the Leeds Law Society including qualified and trainee lawyers, partners, senior managers and other lawyers in the county.
ADVERTISING RATES:
Full Page Colour £1600.00
Agency Commission: 10%
Mechanical Data: Trim Size: 297 x 210mm, Film: Digital, Bleed Size: 303 x 216mm, Type Area: 275 x 185mm, Col Length: 275mm, Page Width: 185mm
Average advertising content per issue: 40%
BUSINESS: LEGAL

LEEDS BUSINESS UPDATE

1656924U63B-2505

Editorial Address: White Rose House, 28A York Place, LEEDS, LS1 2EZ **Tel:** 0113 247 0000 **Fax:** 0113 247 1111
Email: marketing@leedschamber.co.uk
Advertising Address: As above.
Email: marketing@leedschamber.co.uk
Web site: http://www.leedschamber.co.uk
Publisher: Yorkshire Post Newspapers Ltd
Frequency: 6 issues yearly
Cover Price: Free
Circulation: 4,000 (Publisher's Statement)
Editor: Amit Joshi; **Advertising Manager:** Amit Joshi
Summary of Content: Official publication of the Leeds Chamber of Commerce, covering issues affecting businesses in Leeds. Includes articles on policy, property, technology and retail.
Readership/Target Audience: Aimed at Leeds Chamber of Commerce members.
ADVERTISING RATES:
Full Page Colour £500.00
Agency Commission: 10%
Mechanical Data: Type Area: 300 x 228mm, Col Length: 300mm, Page Width: 228mm, Film: Digital
Average advertising content per issue: 40%
BUSINESS: REGIONAL BUSINESS: Regional Business English Counties

LEGAL ABACUS

35042U1B-230

Editorial Address: 2nd Floor, Marlowe House, 109 Station Road, SIDCUP, DA15 7ET **Tel:** 020 8302 5458
Fax: 020 8302 7481
Email: kiran.chita@ilca.org.uk
Advertising Address: As above.
Email: kiran.chita@ilca.org.uk
Web site: http://www.ilca.org.uk
ISSN: 0960-0647
Publisher: The Institute of Legal Cashiers and Administrators
Date Established: 1990
Frequency: 6 issues yearly
Cover Price: £5.00
Annual Sub.: £30.00
Circulation: 3,500 (Publisher's Statement)
Usual Pagination: 36
Editor: Kiran Chita; **Advertising Manager:** Kiran Chita

Summary of Content: Journal of the Institute of Legal Cashiers & Administrators. Reports on matters of finance and administration in a solicitor's practice.
Readership/Target Audience: Aimed at legal cashiers, bookkeepers, financial controllers, administrators and people within legal accounting.
ADVERTISING RATES:
Full Page Mono £495.00
Full Page Colour £685.00
Agency Commission: 10%
Mechanical Data: Film: Digital, Trim Size: 297 x 210mm
Copy instructions: Copy Date: 3 weeks prior to publication date
Average advertising content per issue: 30%
Supplement(s): Listed Legal Software Suppliers Guide - 1xY
BUSINESS: FINANCE & ECONOMICS: Accountancy

LEGAL ACTION

39203U44-1260

Editorial Address: 242 Pentonville Road, LONDON, N1 9UN
Tel: 020 7833 2931 **Fax:** 020 7837 6094
Email: lag@lag.org.uk
Advertising Address: 2 Windmill Street, LONDON, W1T 2HX **Tel:** 020 7692 9292 **Fax:** 020 7692 9393
Email: sharon@lps.co.uk
Web site: http://www.lag.org.uk
ISSN: 0306-7693
Publisher: LAG Education & Service Trust Ltd
Date Established: 1972
Frequency: Monthly
Cover Price: £7.16
Annual Sub.: £86.00
Circulation: 5,000 (Publisher's Statement)
Usual Pagination: 36
Editor: Valerie Williams
Summary of Content: Magazine giving practical advice on legal aid, housing law, criminal law, litigation and one's rights and civil liberties.
Readership/Target Audience: Aimed at lawyers, legal aid practitioners and advice workers.
ADVERTISING RATES:
Full Page Colour £950.00
Mechanical Data: Trim Size: 297 x 210mm, Type Area: 264 x 186mm, Col Length: 264mm, Page Width: 186mm, Film: Digital
Copy instructions: Copy Date: 2 weeks prior to publication date
BUSINESS: LEGAL

LEGAL & MEDICAL

1850116U44-3053

Editorial Address: Barker Brooks House, 4 Greengate, Cardale Park, HARROGATE, HG3 1GY **Tel:** 01423 851150
Email: emma.waddingham@barkerbrooks.co.uk
Web site: http://www.legal-medical.co.uk
Publisher: Barker Brooks Media
Frequency: 6 issues yearly
Annual Sub.: £90.00
Usual Pagination: 36
Editor: Emma Waddingham; **Managing Editor:** James Ratcliff
Summary of Content: Magazine and website for the personal injury industry, covering rehabilitation, regulation, personal injury, mediation, funding and insurance, forensics and clinical negligence.
Readership/Target Audience: Aimed at solicitors, barristers and medical professionals.
ADVERTISING: Rates on application
BUSINESS: LEGAL

LEGAL BUSINESS

39204U44-1280

Editorial Address: Kensington Square House, 12-14 Ansdell Street, LONDON, W8 5BN **Tel:** 020 7396 9292
Fax: 020 7396 9300
Advertising Address: As above. **Tel:** 020 7396 5618
Fax: 020 7396 9302
Email: helen.berwick@legalease.co.uk
Web site: http://www.legalease.co.uk
ISSN: 0958-4609
Publisher: Legalease Ltd
Date Established: 1990
Frequency: 10 issues yearly
Annual Sub.: £495.00
Circulation: 8,138 (ABC 01/07/2007 to 30/06/2008)
Usual Pagination: 90
News Editor: Mark McAteer; **Advertising Manager:** Helen Berwick
Summary of Content: Magazine covering the legal industry, with an emphasis on commercial law firms in the UK.
Readership/Target Audience: Aimed at top commercial lawyers in the UK and international firms.
ADVERTISING RATES:
Full Page Mono £3995.00
Full Page Colour £3995.00
Agency Commission: 10%
Mechanical Data: Type Area: 300 x 205mm, Bleed Size: 340 x 251mm, Trim Size: 340 x 245mm, Page Width: 205mm, Col Length: 300mm

Average advertising content per issue: 30%
BUSINESS: LEGAL

THE LEGAL EXECUTIVE

39205U44-1300

Formerly: Legal Executive Journal
Editorial Address: Kempston Manor, Kempston, BEDFORD, MK42 7AB **Tel:** 01234 845721
Fax: 01234 841999
Email: ipa@legal-executive-journal.co.uk
Advertising Address: As above. **Tel:** 01234 845737
Email: ipa@legal-executive-journal.co.uk
Web site: http://www.ilexjournal.com
Publisher: Institute of Legal Executives
Frequency: Monthly - Published on the last Wednesday of the cover month
Cover Price: £4.95
Annual Sub.: £57.00
Circulation: 22,184 (Publisher's Statement)
Usual Pagination: 46
Editor: Neil Rose; **Advertising Manager:** Sharon Bruty
Summary of Content: Journal of the Institute of Legal Executives. Contains news and information about the law and legal education.
Readership/Target Audience: Aimed at all members of the Institute, law libraries, the judiciary, MPs, banks and building societies.
ADVERTISING RATES:
Full Page Mono £796.00
Full Page Colour £871.00
Agency Commission: 10%
Mechanical Data: Type Area: 255 x 185mm, Col Length: 255mm, Page Width: 185mm, Bleed Size: 304 x 216mm, Trim Size: 298 x 210mm, No. of Columns (Display): 3, Print Process: Web litho, Film: Digital
Copy instructions: Copy Date: 2nd Monday of the cover month
Average advertising content per issue: 30%
Supplement(s): Student and Education - 1xY
BUSINESS: LEGAL

LEGAL INFORMATION MANAGEMENT

39197U44-1305

Formerly: Law Librarian
Editorial Address: The High Hall, St. Stephen's Road, STEETON, BD20 6SB **Tel:** 01535 657060
Fax: 01535 658442
Email: c.miskin@btinternet.com
Advertising Address: The Edinburgh Building, Shaftesbury Road, CAMBRIDGE, CB2 2RU **Tel:** 01223 325757
Fax: 01223 325801
Email: ad_sales@cambridge.org
Web site: http://www.biall.org.uk
ISSN: 0287-4903
Publisher: Cambridge University Press
Date Established: 1975
Frequency: Quarterly
Free to qualifying individuals
Annual Sub.: £73.00
Circulation: 1,400 (Publisher's Statement)
Usual Pagination: 64
Editor: Christine Miskin; **Advertising Manager:** Rebecca Roberts; **Publisher:** Ella Colvin
Summary of Content: Journal of the British and Irish Association of Law Librarians. Contains information on a wide variety of topics, including information technology of relevance to law librarians.
Readership/Target Audience: Aimed at legal information professionals in all types of institutions.
ADVERTISING RATES:
Full Page Mono £415.00
Full Page Colour £785.00
Agency Commission: 10%
Mechanical Data: Type Area: 250 x 170mm, Bleed Size: 286 x 216mm, Trim Size: 280 x 210mm, Col Length: 250mm, Page Width: 170mm
Copy instructions: Copy Date: 8 weeks prior to publication date
Average advertising content per issue: 10%
BUSINESS: LEGAL

LEGAL TECHNOLOGY INSIDER

39206U44-1310

Formerly: Legal Technology Media
Editorial Address: Oak Lodge, Darrow Green Road, Denton, HARLESTON, IP20 0AY **Tel:** 01986 788666
Fax: 01986 788808
Email: info@legaltechnology.com
Email: ads@legaltechnology.com
Web site: http://www.legaltechnology.com
ISSN: 1361-1240
Publisher: Legal Technology Insider
Date Established: 1995
Frequency: 11 issues yearly
Free to qualifying individuals
Annual Sub.: £140.00
Circulation: 6,500 (Publisher's Statement)
Usual Pagination: 12

Average advertising content per issue: 30%
BUSINESS: LEGAL

Editor: Charles Christian; **Publisher:** Charles Christian
Summary of Content: Newsletter containing information and guidance on law office computer systems.
Readership/Target Audience: Read by lawyers, software suppliers, IT consultants and practice managers.
ADVERTISING RATES:
Full Page Colour £350.00
BUSINESS: LEGAL

LEGAL WEEK
39207U44-1317

Editorial Address: 32-34 Broadwick Street, LONDON, W1A 2HG **Tel:** 020 7316 9000 **Fax:** 020 7316 9278
Email: alex.novarese@incisivemedia.com
Advertising Address: As above.
Email: anne-marie.judge@incisivemedia.com
Web site: http://www.legalweek.com
Publisher: Incisive Media
Frequency: Weekly
Cover Price: £5.00
Free to qualifying individuals
Annual Sub.: £130.00
Circulation: 25,895 (ABC 01/07/2008 to 30/06/2009)
Usual Pagination: 64
Editor: Georgina Stanley; **News Editor:** Georgina Stanley;
Features Editor: Charlotte Edmond; **Managing Director:** Graham Harman; **Publisher:** John Malpas
Summary of Content: Magazine covering news, views, analysis of the week's events and features on the legal profession.
Twitter: https://twitter.com/Legal_Week.
Readership/Target Audience: Aimed at the business lawyer.
ADVERTISING RATES:
Full Page Colour £4523.00
Agency Commission: 10%
Mechanical Data: Film: Digital, Type Area: 340 x 254mm, Bleed Size: 390 x 284mm, Trim Size: 384 x 278mm, Col Length: 340mm, Page Width: 254mm
Copy instructions: Copy Date: Friday 12 noon prior to publication date
Editions:
Legal Week Global
BUSINESS: LEGAL

LEICESTERSHIRE BUILDER MAGAZINE
715002U4E-259

Formerly: East Midlands Builder Magazine
Editorial Address: PO Box 8, MARKFIELD, LE67 9ZT
Tel: 01530 244069 **Fax:** 01530 249557
Email: info@buildermagazines.co.uk
Advertising Address: As above.
Email: info@buildermagazines.co.uk
Web site: http://www.buildermagazines.co.uk
Publisher: Builder Magazines
Date Established: 1997
Frequency: Monthly
Free to qualifying individuals
Annual Sub.: £20.00
Circulation: 3,500 (Publisher's Statement)
Usual Pagination: 36
Editor: Mike Wilkinson; **Advertising Manager:** Susan Hatton
Summary of Content: Magazine covering news of local building issues in Leicestershire and the East Midlands and nationwide, local developments planned, development sites and properties for sale, product news and local business news items.
Readership/Target Audience: Aimed at builders, contractors, architects, surveyors, estate agents and property developers in Leicestershire and the East Midlands.
ADVERTISING RATES:
Full Page Mono £190.00
Full Page Colour £290.00
Agency Commission: 10%
Mechanical Data: Trim Size: 297 x 210mm, Bleed Size: 303 x 216mm, Col Length: 268mm, No. of Columns (Display): 4, Print Process: Offset litho, Type Area: 268 x 194mm, Page Width: 194mm
Copy instructions: Copy Date: 15th of the month prior to publication date
Average advertising content per issue: 50%
BUSINESS: ARCHITECTURE & BUILDING: Building

LEISURE MANAGEMENT
38532U32H-190

Editorial Address: Portmill House, Portmill Lane, HITCHIN, SG5 1DJ **Tel:** 01462 431385 **Fax:** 01462 433909
Email: andreajezovit@leisuremedia.com
Advertising Address: As above. **Tel:** 01582 607970
Fax: 01582 604102
Email: johnchallinor@leisuremedia.com
Web site: http://www.leisuremanagement.co.uk
ISSN: 0266-9102
Publisher: The Leisure Media Company Ltd
Date Established: 1981
Frequency: Quarterly - Published around the 20th of the cover month

Annual Sub.: £36.00
Circulation: 9,000 (Publisher's Statement)
Usual Pagination: 64
Editor: Andrea Jezovit; **Managing Director:** Liz Terry;
Advertising Manager: John Challinor; **Publisher:** John Challinor
Summary of Content: Magazine catering for the information needs of leisure industry professionals.
Readership/Target Audience: Readership includes owners, operators, managers, policy makers, investors, consultants and architects in the International leisure industry.
ADVERTISING RATES:
Full Page Colour £1500.00
Agency Commission: 10%
Mechanical Data: Film: Digital, Bleed Size: 303 x 216mm, Trim Size: 297 x 210mm
Copy instructions: Copy Date: 20th of the month prior to publication date
Average advertising content per issue: 40%
BUSINESS: LOCAL GOVERNMENT, LEISURE & RECREATION: Leisure, Recreation & Entertainment

---

LEISURE OPPORTUNITIES
38535U32H-210

Editorial Address: Portmill House, Portmill Lane, HITCHIN, SG5 1DJ **Tel:** 01462 431385 **Fax:** 01462 433909
Email: tomwalker@leisuremedia.com
Advertising Address: As above.
Email: displaysales@leisuremedia.com
Web site: http://www.leisureopportunities.co.uk
ISSN: 0952-8210
Publisher: The Leisure Media Company Ltd
Date Established: 1982
Frequency: 26 issues yearly
Annual Sub.: £26.00
Circulation: 16,505 (ABC 01/07/2008 to 30/06/2009)
Usual Pagination: 56
Editor: Tom Walker; **Managing Director:** Liz Terry;
Managing Editor: Tom Walker; **Publisher:** Liz Terry
Summary of Content: Magazine containing news and recruitment information on current developments in the leisure sector.
Readership/Target Audience: Aimed at all those working in the leisure industry, including hotels, sports centres, museums, libraries, local authority and commercial operations.
ADVERTISING: Rates on application
BUSINESS: LOCAL GOVERNMENT, LEISURE & RECREATION: Leisure, Recreation & Entertainment

---

LEISURE, RECREATION & TOURISM ABSTRACTS
39754U50-20_2

Editorial Address: Nosworthy Way, WALLINGFORD, OX10 8DE **Tel:** 01491 829434 **Fax:** 01491 833508
Email: j.osborn@cabi.org
Web site: http://www.cabi.org/lrta
ISSN: 0261-1392
Publisher: CABI
Date Established: 1976
Frequency: Quarterly
Circulation: 300 (Publisher's Statement)
Editor: Janice Osborn
Summary of Content: Journal focusing on bringing together information for those interested in research and strategic development of leisure, recreation, sport, tourism and hospitality activities, facilities, products and services.
Readership/Target Audience: Aimed at academic libraries, universities and colleges of higher and further education, public libraries, government organisations, tourist boards and consultants.
ADVERTISING: No Advertising taken
BUSINESS: TRAVEL & TOURISM

LEISURE SCENE
622655U48B-40

Editorial Address: 7-8 Buckingham Place, Bellfield Road, HIGH WYCOMBE, HP13 5HW **Tel:** 01494 888433
Fax: 01494 888437
Email: ian.cooper@cssc.co.uk
Advertising Address: Square7 Media Ltd, 1st Floor, 3 More London Riverside, LONDON, SE1 2RE **Tel:** 020 3283 4055
Fax: 020 3283 4069
Email: gaynor@square7media.co.uk
Web site: http://www.cssc.co.uk
Publisher: CSSC Sports and Leisure
Date Established: 1996
Frequency: 3 issues yearly - Published in February, June and October
Free to qualifying individuals
Circulation: 700,000 (Publisher's Statement)
Usual Pagination: 20
Editor: Ian Cooper; **Advertising Manager:** Gaynor Garton
Summary of Content: Magazine for CSSC members in government departments and agencies, Royal Mail, BT and many other public bodies.
Readership/Target Audience: Aimed at government departments, government agencies, other public bodies and companies carrying out ex-civil service work.

ADVERTISING RATES:
Full Page Colour £3950.00
Agency Commission: 10%
Mechanical Data: Trim Size: 297 x 210mm, Film: Digital
BUSINESS: TOY TRADE & SPORTS GOODS: Sports Goods

LENDING STRATEGY
1700424U1A-337

Editorial Address: St. Giles House, 50 Poland Street, LONDON, W1F 7AX **Tel:** 020 7943 8096
Email: john.murray@centaur.co.uk
Advertising Address: As above. **Tel:** 020 7970 4000
Fax: 020 7973 8099
Email: scott.wendes@centaur.co.uk
ISSN: 1750-466X
Publisher: Centaur Communications Ltd
Date Established: 2006
Frequency: 10 issues yearly
Cover Price: £4.95
Free to qualifying individuals
Circulation: 3,000 (Publisher's Statement)
Usual Pagination: 54
Editor: John Murray
Summary of Content: Magazine focusing on commercial and retail mortgage lending. Includes news, analysis, legal developments and mergers.
Readership/Target Audience: Aimed at senior management in the mortgage lending industry.
ADVERTISING: Rates on application
Copy instructions: Copy Date: Last Wednesday of the month
BUSINESS: FINANCE & ECONOMICS

LETS FOCUS
1834565U1E-403

Formerly: eafocus
Editorial Address: Unit 6, 5 Durham Yard, Teesdale Street, LONDON, E2 6QF **Tel:** 0870 850 3586 **Fax:** 020 7749 1280
Email: editorial@ddgm.co.uk
Advertising Address: As above.
Email: markusrohmann@ddgm.co.uk
Web site: http://www.eafocus.co.uk
Publisher: DDGM
Date Established: 2007
Frequency: Monthly
Cover Price: £2.75
Annual Sub.: £33.00
Usual Pagination: 52
Editor: Mark Burgess
Summary of Content: Magazine covering all aspects within the estate agency industry including mortgages, lettings and sales.
Readership/Target Audience: Aimed at mortgage brokers, estate agents, lettings advisors, property developers and anyone interested in purchasing or renting properties.
ADVERTISING RATES:
Full Page Colour £775.00
BUSINESS: FINANCE & ECONOMICS: Property

LGC LOCAL GOVERNMENT CHRONICLE
38375U32A-104

Editorial Address: Greater London House, Hampstead Road, LONDON, NW1 7EJ **Tel:** 020 7728 5000
Fax: 020 7728 3700
Email: lgcnews@emap.com
Advertising Address: As above. **Tel:** 020 7874 0200
Fax: 020 7728 3866
Email: david.bentley@emap.com
Web site: http://www.lgcplus.com
ISSN: 0024-5534
Publisher: EMAP Inform
Date Established: 1855
Frequency: Weekly - Published every Thursday
Cover Price: £3.90
Annual Sub.: £125.00
Circulation: 6,485 (ABC 01/07/2008 to 30/06/2009)
Usual Pagination: 35
News Editor: Dan Drillsma-Milgrom
Summary of Content: Magazine covering news, analysis, comment and features on local government issues including policy, finance, personnel, law, compulsory competitive tendering, IT, Europe and housing.
Readership/Target Audience: Aimed at senior management, chief executives, heads of finance and members of the local government.
ADVERTISING RATES:
Full Page Mono £2505.00
Full Page Colour £3700.00
Agency Commission: 10%
Mechanical Data: Type Area: 299 x 225mm, Bleed Size: 329 x 251mm, Trim Size: 323 x 245mm, Col Length: 299mm, Page Width: 225mm, Print Process: Sheet-fed offset litho, Film: Digital
Copy instructions: Copy Date: 1 week prior to publication date
Average advertising content per issue: 30%

Supplement(s): LGC Finance - 5xY
BUSINESS: LOCAL GOVERNMENT, LEISURE &
RECREATION: Local Government

LIABILITY, RISK & INSURANCE 35149U1D-260

Editorial Address: Informa House, 30-32 Mortimer Street,
LONDON, W1W 7RE **Tel:** 020 7017 4100
Fax: 020 7553 1115
Email: tonydowding@blueyonder.co.uk
Web site: http://www.informa.com
ISSN: 0960-099X
Publisher: Informa PLC
Frequency: Monthly
Annual Sub.: £985.00
Usual Pagination: 20
Summary of Content: Newsletter covering all aspects of
managing liabilities and developing business strategy.
Readership/Target Audience: Aimed at liability
underwriters and lawyers.
ADVERTISING: No Advertising taken
BUSINESS: FINANCE & ECONOMICS: Insurance

THE LIBRARY 25306U60B-301

Editorial Address: Centre for the History of the Book and
School of L, The University of Edinburgh, 18 Buccleuch
Place, EDINBURGH, EH8 9LN **Tel:** 0131 650 4283
Email: b.bell@ed.ac.uk
Advertising Address: Oblong Creative Limited, 416B
Thorpe Arch, WETHERBY, LS23 7BJ **Tel:** 01937 849646
Email: mail@oblongcreative.co.uk
Web site: http://www.oup.co.uk/libraj
ISSN: 0024-2160
Publisher: OUP
Date Established: 1893
Frequency: Quarterly
Cover Price: £15.00
Annual Sub.: £49.00
Usual Pagination: 110
Editor: Bill Bell
Summary of Content: Official journal of the Bibliographical
Society of London, covering all aspects of the physical
production of books and manuscripts in history, including
the history of printing, publishing, bookselling and collecting,
analytical bibliography, and textual and manuscript studies.
Readership/Target Audience: Aimed at scholars of
bibliography, and anyone interested in the history of the
book.
ADVERTISING: Rates on application
BUSINESS: PUBLISHING: Libraries

LIBRARY + INFORMATION GAZETTE 1768600U60B-305

Editorial Address: 74 Marlborough Avenue, GLASGOW,
G11 7BH **Tel:** 0141 334 6019 **Fax:** 0141 334 6019
Email: debbyraven@btconnect.com
Advertising Address: 7 Ridgmount Street, LONDON, WC1E
7AE **Tel:** 020 7255 0550 **Fax:** 020 7255 0551
Email: gary.allman@cilip.org.uk
Web site: http://www.cilip.org.uk/publications/gazette
Publisher: Chartered Institute of Library & Information
Professionals
Date Established: 2004
Frequency: 25 issues yearly
Cover Price: Free
Circulation: 17,929 (ABC 01/07/2008 to 30/06/2009)
Usual Pagination: 28
Editor: Debby Raven; **Advertising Manager:** Gary Allman
Summary of Content: Magazine of the Chartered Institute
of Library and Information Professionals covering careers,
recruitment, products and services within the library and
information industry.
Readership/Target Audience: Aimed at those working in
public libraries, academic libraries, the information
technology sector and those in further and higher education.
ADVERTISING RATES:
Full Page Colour £3120.00
Agency Commission: 12.5%
Mechanical Data: Bleed Size: 316 x 234mm, Trim Size: 310
x 228mm, Film: Digital
Copy instructions: Copy Date: Wednesday prior to
publication date
Average advertising content per issue: 40%
BUSINESS: PUBLISHING: Libraries

LIBRARY & INFORMATION UPDATE 40866U60B-40

Editorial Address: 7 Ridgmount Street, LONDON, WC1E
7AE **Tel:** 020 7255 0500 **Fax:** 020 7255 0581
Email: update@cilip.org.uk
Web site: http://www.cilip.org.uk/update
ISSN: 1476-7171
Publisher: Chartered Institute of Library & Information
Professionals
Date Established: 2002

Frequency: 10 issues yearly - Combined issues Jan/Feb
and July/August
Free to qualifying individuals
Annual Sub.: £85.00
Circulation: 20,000 (Publisher's Statement)
Usual Pagination: 48
Editor: Matthew Mezey; **News Editor:** Matthew Mezey;
Managing Director: John Woolley; **Managing Editor:**
Rachel Middleton
Summary of Content: Magazine of the Chartered Institute
of Library and Information Professionals, containing news,
features, letters and regular columns.
Readership/Target Audience: Aimed at those working in
public libraries, academic libraries, the information
technology sector and those in further and higher education.
ADVERTISING: No Advertising taken
BUSINESS: PUBLISHING: Libraries

LIBRARY HI TECH NEWS 40872U60B-93

Editorial Address: Howard House, Wagon Lane, BINGLEY,
BD16 1WA **Tel:** 01274 777700 **Fax:** 01274 785200
Email: ebreen@emeraldinsight.com
Web site: http://www.emeraldinsight.com/lhtn.htm
ISSN: 0741-9058
Publisher: Emerald Group Publishing Ltd
Frequency: 10 issues yearly - Combined issues January/
February and July/August
Cover Price: £299.00
Usual Pagination: 40
Editor: Eileen Breen; **Publisher:** Eileen Breen
Summary of Content: Magazine reporting on items of
interest to users and providers of online databases.
Readership/Target Audience: Aimed at library and
information professionals and electronic publishers.
ADVERTISING: No Advertising taken
BUSINESS: PUBLISHING: Libraries

LIBRARY REVIEW 40868U60B-60

Editorial Address: The Andersonia Library, University of
Strathclyde, 101 St James Road, GLASGOW, G4 0NS
Tel: 01274 777700 **Fax:** 01274 785200
Email: n.c.joint@strath.ac.uk
Web site: http://www.emeraldinsight.com/info/journals/lr/lr.
jsp
ISSN: 0024-2535
Publisher: Emerald Group Publishing Ltd
Date Established: 1927
Frequency: 9 issues yearly
Annual Sub.: £5629.00
Usual Pagination: 48
Editor: David McMenemy; **Publisher:** Eileen Breen
Summary of Content: International journal covering library
news and information science.
Readership/Target Audience: Read by librarians.
ADVERTISING: No Advertising taken
BUSINESS: PUBLISHING: Libraries

LICENSE! GLOBAL 1625897U53-680

Formerly: License! Europe
Editorial Address: PR by e-mail only **Tel:** 020 8986 6683
Fax: 020 8986 6683
Email: josephine.collins@mac.com
Advertising Address: 500 Chiswick High Road, Suite 19,
LONDON, W4 5RG **Tel:** 020 8956 2669 **Fax:** 020 8956 2666
Email: rsimpson@advanstar.com
Web site: http://www.licensemag.com
Publisher: Advanstar Communications (UK) Ltd
Date Established: 2001
Frequency: Monthly
Free to qualifying individuals
Annual Sub.: £48.00
Circulation: 33,000 (Publisher's Statement)
Usual Pagination: 90
Editor: Josephine Collins
Summary of Content: Magazine of the Brand Licensing
exhibition covering the latest industry news, trend
forecasting, demographic data and analysis and product
news as well as licensed consumer product merchandising,
co-branding and brand extensions.
Readership/Target Audience: Aimed at senior executives
including retailers, licensees and manufacturers, sales
promotion agencies and consultancies.
ADVERTISING RATES:
Full Page Colour £3070.00
Mechanical Data: Trim Size: 247 x 203mm, Film: Digital,
Bleed Size: 279 x 234mm
Copy instructions: Copy Date: 1 week prior to publication
date
BUSINESS: RETAILING & WHOLESALING

LICENSING TODAY WORLDWIDE 761814U53-248

Editorial Address: 1 Churchgates, The Wilderness,
BERKHAMSTED, HP4 2UB **Tel:** 01442 289930
Fax: 01442 289950
Email: andy@lemapublishing.co.uk
Advertising Address: As above.
Email: rob@lemapublishing.co.uk
Publisher: Lema Publishing
Date Established: 1993
Frequency: Quarterly
Annual Sub.: £30.00
Circulation: 10,000 (Publisher's Statement)
Usual Pagination: 100
Editor: Andy Myall; **Publisher:** John Baulch
Summary of Content: Magazine covering articles and
features on new licensed products, developments,
promotional and marketing tools, news and statistics
worldwide.
Readership/Target Audience: Aimed at manufacturers of
consumer products, retail buyers and licensing agents.
ADVERTISING RATES:
Full Page Colour £2200.00
Agency Commission: 10%
Mechanical Data: Type Area: 300 x 225mm, Bleed Size:
321 246mm, Trim Size: 315 x 240mm, Col Length: 300mm,
Page Width: 225mm
Average advertising content per issue: 50%
BUSINESS: RETAILING & WHOLESALING

LIFE 623185U54R-330

Formerly: St. John Life
Editorial Address: St. John Ambulance, 27 St. John's Lane,
LONDON, EC1M 4BU **Tel:** 020 7324 4000
Fax: 020 7324 4001
Email: editor@stjohnlife.org.uk
Advertising Address: As above.
Email: editor@stjohnlife.org.uk
Web site: http://www.stjohnlife.org.uk
Publisher: Wordwide Communications
Date Established: 1999
Frequency: 3 issues yearly - Published in May, September
and January
Free to qualifying individuals
Annual Sub.: £9.00
Circulation: 37,000 (Publisher's Statement)
Usual Pagination: 32
Editor: Stephen Eastwood; **Advertising Manager:** Stephen
Eastwood
Summary of Content: Magazine covering news, articles on
first aid, medical procedures and health issues.
Readership/Target Audience: Read by members of St.
John Ambulance.
ADVERTISING: Rates on application
BUSINESS: SAFETY & SECURITY: Safety Related

A LIFE IN THE DAY 601113U56N-35

Editorial Address: Suite N4, The Old Market, Upper Market
Street, HOVE, BN3 1AS **Tel:** 01273 783720
Fax: 01273 6783723
Email: jos@pavilionjournals.com
Advertising Address: Richmond House, Richmond Road,
BRIGHTON, BN2 3RL **Tel:** 0870 890 1080
Fax: 0870 890 1081
Email: pauls@pavpub.com
Web site: http://www.pavilionjournals.com
ISSN: 1366-6282
Publisher: Pavilion Journals (Brighton) Ltd
Date Established: 1997
Frequency: Quarterly
Annual Sub.: £42.00
Circulation: 450 (Publisher's Statement)
Usual Pagination: 32
Editor: Joanna Sharrocks; **Advertising Manager:** Paul
Somerville
Summary of Content: Journal covering socially inclusive
work and daytime activities including benefits advice in the
mental health services.
Readership/Target Audience: Read by managers,
practitioners and service users in mental health.
ADVERTISING RATES:
Full Page Colour £350.00
Agency Commission: 10%
Mechanical Data: Type Area: 215 x 150mm, Col Length:
215mm, Page Width: 150mm
Average advertising content per issue: 4.5%
BUSINESS: HEALTH & MEDICAL: Mental Health

LIFE SCIENCE CLUSTERS 1847716U55-9027

Editorial Address: Global House, 13 Market Square,
HORSHAM, RH12 1EU **Tel:** 01403 220760
Fax: 01403 220761
Email: brian@life-science-clusters.com
Web site: http://www.life-science-clusters.com
Publisher: avakado Ltd

Date Established: 2007
Frequency: Quarterly
Free to qualifying individuals
Circulation: 8,894 (Publisher's Statement)
Usual Pagination: 48
Editor: Brian Cooper
Summary of Content: Magazine dedicated to the communication of information on location, development and finance for life science companies and linked enterprise.
Readership/Target Audience: Aimed at directors and owners of life science companies.
BUSINESS: APPLIED SCIENCE & LABORATORIES

THE LIFEBOAT
39934U54R-100

Editorial Address: West Quay Road, POOLE, BH15 1HZ
Tel: 01202 662254 **Fax:** 01202 663189
Email: thelifeboat@rnli.org.uk
Advertising Address: Landmark Publishing Services, 2 Windmill Street, LONDON, W1T 2HX **Tel:** 020 7692 9292
Email: sharon@lps.co.uk
Web site: http://www.rnli.org.uk
Publisher: Royal National Lifeboat Institution
Date Established: 1852
Frequency: Quarterly
Cover Price: Free
Circulation: 282,000 (Publisher's Statement)
Usual Pagination: 52
Editor: Liz Cook
Summary of Content: Magazine focusing on the Royal National Lifeboat Institution, including news of people and places within the institution and accounts of noteworthy rescues.
Readership/Target Audience: Read by RNLI members, supporters and people working at lifeboat stations and fundraising branches.
ADVERTISING RATES:
Full Page Colour £5000.00
BUSINESS: SAFETY & SECURITY: Safety Related

LIFESAVERS
39935U54R-115

Formerly: Lifeguard
Editorial Address: River House, High Street, Broom, ALCESTER, B50 4HN **Tel:** 01789 773994 **Fax:** 01789 773995
Email: lifesavers@rlss.org.uk
Advertising Address: As above.
Email: lifesavers@rlss.org.uk
Web site: http://www.lifesavers.org.uk
ISSN: 0968-7726
Publisher: The Royal Life Saving Society UK
Frequency: Quarterly
Cover Price: £2.50
Circulation: 15,500 (Publisher's Statement)
Usual Pagination: 24
Editor: Jane Cooper; **Advertising Manager:** Jane Cooper
Summary of Content: Magazine about lifeguard provision, sport, lifesaving, drowning prevention, water safety, life support and resuscitation training in the UK.
Readership/Target Audience: Aimed at members, pool operators, local education staff, leisure industry personnel and swimmers.
ADVERTISING: Rates on application
Agency Commission: 10%
Copy instructions: Copy Date: 6 weeks prior to publication date
Average advertising content per issue: 25%
BUSINESS: SAFETY & SECURITY: Safety Related

LIFESTYLES TODAY
1698554U14A-558

Formerly: Lifestyles for Business Today
Editorial Address: 26-28 Birmingham Street, OLDBURY, B69 4DS **Tel:** 0121 552 4321 **Fax:** 0121 552 4344
Email: info@lifestylestoday.co.uk
Advertising Address: 5th Floor, Scala House, Holloway Circus, BIRMINGHAM, B1 1EQ **Tel:** 0121 687 1044
Fax: 0121 687 1051
Email: freshmediasales@aol.com
Web site: http://www.lifestylestoday.co.uk
Publisher: Fresh Media UK Ltd
Date Established: 2005
Frequency: Weekly
Free to qualifying individuals
Annual Sub.: £65.00
Circulation: 5,000 (Publisher's Statement)
Usual Pagination: 24
Editor: Ian Bird; **Advertising Manager:** Ian Bird
Summary of Content: Magazine featuring lifestyle features and leisure time management. Topics covered include motoring, holidays and weddings.
Readership/Target Audience: Aimed at executives with a high level of expendable income.
ADVERTISING RATES:
Full Page Mono £495.00
Full Page Colour £795.00
Agency Commission: 10%

Mechanical Data: Type Area: 360 x 262mm, Bleed Size: +5mm, Col Length: 360mm, Page Width: 262mm, Film: Digital
Copy instructions: Copy Date: 1 week prior to publication date
Average advertising content per issue: 20%
BUSINESS: COMMERCE, INDUSTRY & MANAGEMENT

LIGHT HOVERCRAFT
36411U6E-180

Editorial Address: PR by email only
Email: magazine@hovercraft.org.uk
Tel: 01527 579700 **Fax:** 01425 650560
Email: magazine@hovercraft.org.uk
Web site: http://www.hovercraft.org.uk
Publisher: Hovercraft Club of Great Britain Ltd
Frequency: Monthly
Cover Price: £2.20
Free to qualifying individuals
Circulation: 400 (Publisher's Statement)
Usual Pagination: 24
Editor: Nick Drew; **Advertising Manager:** Simon Kemp
Summary of Content: Magazine covering all aspects of lightweight, and one to six seated leisure hovercraft.
Readership/Target Audience: Aimed at members of the Hover Club of Great Britain.
BUSINESS: AVIATION & AERONAUTICS: Hovercraft VTOL

LIGHTING
37316U17-150

Formerly: Lighting Equipment News
Editorial Address: Greater London House, Hampstead Road, LONDON, NW1 7EJ **Tel:** 020 7728 5000
Email: ray.molony@emap.com
Advertising Address: As above. **Fax:** 020 7728 4666
Email: steve.perry@emap.com
Web site: http://www.lighting.co.uk
ISSN: 0024-3418
Publisher: EMAP Inform
Date Established: 1967
Frequency: Monthly - Published on the 1st of the cover month
Cover Price: £7.00
Free to qualifying individuals
Annual Sub.: £48.00
Circulation: 9,958 (ABC 01/01/2008 to 31/12/2008)
Usual Pagination: 60
Editor: Ray Molony
Summary of Content: Business publication devoted solely to all aspects of commercial, industrial, public, decorative and architectural lighting.
Readership/Target Audience: Aimed at architects, consulting engineers, designers, retailers, contractors, wholesalers and end users of lighting.
ADVERTISING RATES:
Full Page Colour £2400.00
Agency Commission: 10%
Mechanical Data: Trim Size: 297 x 230mm, Bleed Size: 303 x 236mm, Film: Digital, Type Area: 272 x 200mm, Col Length: 272mm, Page Width: 200mm
Copy instructions: Copy Date: 2 weeks prior to publication date
Average advertising content per issue: 40%
Supplement(s): Lighting Directory - 1xY
BUSINESS: ELECTRICAL

LIGHTING & SOUND INTERNATIONAL
40943U61-17

Editorial Address: Redoubt House, 1 Edward Road, EASTBOURNE, BN23 8AS **Tel:** 01323 524120
Fax: 01323 524121
Email: news@plasa.org
Advertising Address: As above.
Email: barry@plasa.org
Web site: http://www.lsionline.co.uk
ISSN: 0268-7429
Publisher: Professional Lighting & Sound Association
Date Established: 1985
Frequency: 11 issues yearly - Combined issue in August/September
Cover Price: £3.50
Free to qualifying individuals
Annual Sub.: £30.00
Circulation: 9,877 (ABC 01/07/2008 to 30/06/2009)
Usual Pagination: 120
Editor: Lee Baldock; **Managing Director:** Matthew Griffiths; **Advertising Manager:** Barry Howse; **Publisher:** Matthew Griffiths
Summary of Content: Magazine covering the broad range of the professional lighting, audio, staging and audio-visual industry. Including the use of such equipment and services relating to professional entertainment, presentation, display, communication and architectural installation.
Readership/Target Audience: Aimed at designers, installers, specifers and venue managers working in entertainment, corporate presentation, leisure, architectural installation and communications markets.

ADVERTISING RATES:
Full Page Mono £1860.00
Full Page Colour £1860.00
Agency Commission: 10%
Mechanical Data: Bleed Size: 303 x 216mm, Trim Size: 297 x 210mm, Type Area: 277 x 190mm, Col Length: 277mm, Page Width: 190mm, Film: Digital
BUSINESS: MUSIC TRADE

THE LIGHTING JOURNAL
37317U17-152

Editorial Address: Regent House, Regent Place, RUGBY, CV21 2PN **Tel:** 020 7724 8543 **Fax:** 020 7723 8688
Email: lj@ile.org.uk
Advertising Address: Unit 5, Northfield Point, Cunliffe Drive, KETTERING, NN16 9QJ **Tel:** 01536 711684
Fax: 01536 711463
Email: ian@ile.org.uk
Web site: http://www.ile.org.uk
ISSN: 0950-4559
Publisher: Matrix Print
Date Established: 1935
Frequency: 6 issues yearly
Free to qualifying individuals
Annual Sub.: £40.00
Circulation: 4,500 (Publisher's Statement)
Usual Pagination: 64
Editor: Carl Gardner; **Advertising Manager:** Ian Marshall; **Publisher:** Gary Elliott
Summary of Content: Official journal of the Institution of Lighting Engineers. Contains information on technical developments, reports, product surveys and news on all aspects of public and commercial lighting.
Readership/Target Audience: Aimed at members of lighting authorities, lighting engineers, lighting design consultants, lighting manufacturers, architects, electricity companies and government departments.
ADVERTISING RATES:
Full Page Colour £950.00
Agency Commission: 10%
Mechanical Data: Film: Digital, Bleed Size: 303 x 216mm, Trim Size: 297 x 210mm
Average advertising content per issue: 33%
BUSINESS: ELECTRICAL

LINE UP
35681U2D-80

Editorial Address: PO Box 208, Havant, HAMPSHIRE, PO9 9BQ **Tel:** 01905 381725 **Fax:** 01905 381725
Email: editor@lineup.biz
Advertising Address: 7 The Leys, Adderbury, BANBURY, OX17 3ES **Tel:** 01295 812737 **Fax:** 01295 812434
Email: adverts@lineup.biz
Web site: http://www.lineup.biz
ISSN: 0953-6124
Publisher: Line Up Publications Ltd
Date Established: 1988
Frequency: Quarterly
Free to qualifying individuals
Annual Sub.: £50.00
Circulation: 6,023 (Publisher's Statement)
Usual Pagination: 44
Editor: Hugh Robjohns; **Advertising Manager:** Phil Guy
Summary of Content: Journal of the Institute of Broadcast Sound. Contains new developments in broadcast audio. Categories include radio, TV, live sound, post production and film.
Readership/Target Audience: Aimed at IBS members, senior operators, engineering and management staff responsible for audio in broadcast.
ADVERTISING RATES:
Full Page Mono £1240.00
Full Page Colour £1875.00
Agency Commission: 10%
Mechanical Data: Bleed Size: 305 x 215mm, Film: Digital, Trim Size: 297 x 210mm
Copy instructions: Copy Date: 2 weeks prior to publication date
Average advertising content per issue: 50%
BUSINESS: COMMUNICATIONS, ADVERTISING & MARKETING: Broadcasting

---

LINGERIE BUYER
39537U47B-100

Editorial Address: The Old Town Hall, Lewisham Road, Slaithwaite, HUDDERSFIELD, HD7 5AL **Tel:** 01484 846069
Fax: 01484 846232
Email: christina@ras-publishing.com
Advertising Address: 32 Vauxhall Bridge Road, LONDON, SW1V 2SS **Tel:** 020 7973 6400 **Fax:** 020 7233 5057
Email: e.sabin@hgluk.com
Web site: http://www.lingerie-buyer.co.uk
Publisher: Hemming Group Ltd
Date Established: 1992
Frequency: 8 issues yearly - Published around the middle of the cover month
Cover Price: £5.00
Annual Sub.: £53.00
Circulation: 3,000 (Publisher's Statement)
Usual Pagination: 60

Business Magazines

Editor: Christina Williams; **Editor-in-Chief:** Colette Tebbutt; **Advertising Manager:** Emma Sabin; **Managing Editor:** Martin Wanless; **Publisher:** Emma Sabin
Summary of Content: Magazine containing the latest news and information relevant to the lingerie industry.
Readership/Target Audience: Aimed at the lingerie, swimwear and hosiery trade.
ADVERTISING RATES:
Full Page Colour £2950.00
Agency Commission: 10%
Mechanical Data: Page Width: 235mm, Type Area: 290 x 235mm, Col Length: 290mm, Trim Size: 300 x 245mm, Film: Digital, Bleed Size: 308 x 253mm
Average advertising content per issue: 45%
BUSINESS: CLOTHING & TEXTILES: Lingerie, Hosiery/Swimwear

THE LINGUIST
41186U62R-190
Editorial Address: Saxon House, 48 Southwark Street, LONDON, SE1 1UN **Tel:** 020 7940 3100 **Fax:** 020 7940 3125
Email: linguist.editor@googlemail.com
Advertising Address: As above.
Email: djeffries@onlymedia.co.uk
Web site: http://www.iol.org.uk
ISSN: 0268-5965
Publisher: The Chartered Institute of Linguists
Date Established: 1915
Frequency: 6 issues yearly
Free to qualifying individuals
Annual Sub.: £39.00
Circulation: 10,000 (Publisher's Statement)
Usual Pagination: 32
Editor: Miranda Moore; **Advertising Manager:** David Jefferies
Summary of Content: Official journal of the Institute of Linguists. Contains articles for a more specialised readership, together with items of current and more popular interest in the field of language and culture.
Readership/Target Audience: Aimed at all members of the Institute, universities, libraries, active linguists and companies with international interests.
ADVERTISING RATES:
Full Page Mono £750.00
Full Page Colour £900.00
Agency Commission: 10%
Mechanical Data: Trim Size: 297 x 210mm
Copy instructions: Copy Date: 1 month prior to publication date
BUSINESS: CHURCH & SCHOOL EQUIPMENT & EDUCATION: Education Related

THE LINK
626629U44-1360
Editorial Address: 22 Station Road, Dunton Green, SEVENOAKS, TN13 2XA **Tel:** 01732 460457
Fax: 01732 462820
Email: editorial@pzpublishing.co.uk
Advertising Address: As above.
Email: sales@pzpublishing.co.uk
Web site: http://www.linkaws.co.uk
Publisher: PZ Publishing
Frequency: Quarterly
Cover Price: Free
Circulation: 40,000 (Publisher's Statement)
Usual Pagination: 52
Editor: Stephen Edwards; **Advertising Manager:** Stephen Edwards; **Publisher:** Stephen Edwards
Summary of Content: Magazine for the Association of Women Solicitors combining legal as well as social and lifestyle editorial.
Readership/Target Audience: Aimed at and distributed to female solicitors in the UK.
ADVERTISING RATES:
Full Page Colour £2750.00
Mechanical Data: Bleed Size: 303 x 216mm, Trim Size: 297 x 210mm, Film: Digital
Copy instructions: Copy Date: 3 weeks prior to publication date
Average advertising content per issue: 40%
BUSINESS: LEGAL

LINK
1667691U62R-479
Editorial Address: 2nd Floor, Century House, 11 St. Peters Square, MANCHESTER, M2 3DN **Tel:** 0161 236 9526
Fax: 0161 247 7978
Email: info@impromptupublishing.com
Advertising Address: As above.
Email: dino@impromptupublishing.com
Web site: http://www.linkmagazine.co.uk
ISSN: 1741-6140
Publisher: Impromptu Publishing Ltd
Date Established: 2004
Frequency: Quarterly
Cover Price: £3.95
Annual Sub.: £15.80
Circulation: 12,500 (Publisher's Statement)
Usual Pagination: 52
Editor: Tony Bush

Summary of Content: Magazine containing articles on all aspects of music teaching, from disability outreach and music therapy to early years learning and classroom teaching and training.
Readership/Target Audience: Aimed at practitioners working in community music, music education and outreach work.
ADVERTISING RATES:
Full Page Colour £1495.00
Agency Commission: 10%
Mechanical Data: Type Area: 270 x 202mm, Bleed Size: 298 x 240mm, Trim Size: 290 x 232mm, Col Length: 270mm, Page Width: 202mm, Film: Digital
Average advertising content per issue: 40%
BUSINESS: CHURCH & SCHOOL EQUIPMENT & EDUCATION: Education Related

LINUX USER & DEVELOPER
624235U5D-336
Formerly: Linux User
Editorial Address: Richmond House, 33 Richmond Hill, BOURNEMOUTH, BH2 6EZ **Tel:** 01202 586200
Email: dave.harfield@imagine-publishing.co.uk
Advertising Address: As above.
Web site: http://www.linuxuser.co.uk
ISSN: 1469-1434
Publisher: Imagine Publishing
Date Established: 2000
Frequency: Monthly
Cover Price: £5.99
Circulation: 36,000 (Publisher's Statement)
Usual Pagination: 100
Editor: David Harfield
Summary of Content: Magazine covering Linux-related news, opinion, features and reviews from a professional perspective.
Readership/Target Audience: Aimed at IT decision makers and professionals within organisations which use Linux or have expressed an interest in using Linux.
BUSINESS: COMPUTERS & AUTOMATION: Personal Computers

THE LION
38480U32G-75
Editorial Address: 3 Rosebank Road, West Mersea, COLCHESTER, CO5 8NH **Tel:** 01206 384663
Email: lionmag@editm.freeserve.co.uk
Advertising Address: The Maltings, West Street, BOURNE, PE10 9PH **Tel:** 01778 391158 **Fax:** 01778 392079
Email: rosso@warnersgroup.co.uk
Web site: http://www.lions.org.uk
Publisher: Warners Group Publications plc
Date Established: 1954
Frequency: 6 issues yearly
Cover Price: Free
Circulation: 20,000 (Publisher's Statement)
Usual Pagination: 56
Editor: Margaret Kimberley
Summary of Content: Magazine of The Lions of Great Britain and Ireland, covering events, club news and information on the latest projects.
Readership/Target Audience: Read by members of the Lions Clubs International Charity.
ADVERTISING RATES:
Full Page Mono £475.00
Full Page Colour £600.00
Agency Commission: 10%
Mechanical Data: Page Width: 184mm, Film: Digital, Type Area: 268 x 184mm, Bleed Size: 303 x 216mm, Col Length: 268mm, Trim Size: 297 x 210mm
Copy instructions: Copy Date: 4 weeks prior to publication date
BUSINESS: LOCAL GOVERNMENT, LEISURE & RECREATION: Community Care & Social Services

LIQUID REAL ESTATE
1824162U1C-359
Editorial Address: Nestor House, Playhouse Yard, LONDON, EC4V 5EX **Tel:** 020 7779 8888
Fax: 020 7779 8369
Email: liquid@euromoney.com
Advertising Address: As above.
Email: mdragoyevich@euromoney.com
Web site: http://www.euromoney.com
Publisher: Euromoney Institutional Investor plc
Date Established: 2007
Frequency: Quarterly
Editor: Rachel Wolcott; **Advertising Manager:** Mchael Dragoyevich; **Managing Editor:** Rachel Wolcott
Summary of Content: Magazine covering institutional investors and markets, industry sectors and analysis of deals.
Readership/Target Audience: Aimed at institutional investors, senior real estate advisers, bankers, developers and investors.
ADVERTISING RATES:
Full Page Mono £7500.00
Full Page Colour £10000.00

Mechanical Data: Type Area: 259 x 186mm, Bleed Size: 292 x 215mm, Trim Size: 286 x 210mm, Col Length: 259mm, Page Width: 186mm, Film: Digital
Supplement to: Euromoney
BUSINESS: FINANCE & ECONOMICS: Banking

LITERACY TIME PLUS
1840850U62C-743
Editorial Address: Villiers House, Clarendon Avenue, LEAMINGTON SPA, CV32 5PR **Tel:** 01926 887799
Email: littimefeedback@scholastic.co.uk
Web site: http://www.scholastic.co.uk/literacytime
Publisher: Scholastic UK Ltd
Frequency: 6 issues yearly
Annual Sub.: £72.00
Circulation: 7,764 (Publisher's Statement)
Usual Pagination: 24
Editor: Helen Watts
Summary of Content: Magazine covering the primary literacy curriculum with articles relating to teaching or literacy, children's stories and children's poetry.
Readership/Target Audience: Aimed at primary teachers and head teachers in the Commonwealth.
Editions:
Literacy Time PLUS Ages 5 to 7
Literacy Time PLUS Ages 7 to 9
Literacy Time PLUS Ages 9 to 11
BUSINESS: CHURCH & SCHOOL EQUIPMENT & EDUCATION: Junior Education

LITERACY TODAY
1726055U62R-505
Editorial Address: Devonia House, 4 Union Terrace, CREDITON, EX17 3DY **Tel:** 01363 774455
Email: info@educationpublishing.com
Advertising Address: As above.
Email: info@educationpublishing.com
Web site: http://www.educationpublishing.com
Publisher: The Education Publishing Co Ltd
Date Established: 1994
Frequency: Quarterly
Annual Sub.: £19.00
Circulation: 1,128 (Publisher's Statement)
Usual Pagination: 40
Editor: Michael Marshall; **Advertising Manager:** Demitri Coryton
Summary of Content: Magazine covering current literacy issues across practice, policy and research from early years to continuing education. Featuring articles, a research section, reviews of reports and conference reports.
Readership/Target Audience: Aimed at teachers.
ADVERTISING: Rates on application
Agency Commission: 10%
BUSINESS: CHURCH & SCHOOL EQUIPMENT & EDUCATION: Education Related

LITERARY AND LINGUISTIC COMPUTING
21367U5R-654
Editorial Address: Centre for Computing in the Humanities, Kings College London, The Strand, LONDON, WC2R 2LB **Tel:** 01865 353907 **Fax:** 01865 353485
Email: marilyn.deegan@kcl.ac.uk
Advertising Address: Great Clarendon Street, OXFORD, OX2 6DP **Tel:** 01865 353329
Email: jnlsadvertising@oxfordjournals.org
Web site: http://www.llc.oupjournals.org
ISSN: 0268-1145
Publisher: OUP
Date Established: 1986
Frequency: Quarterly
Cover Price: £49.00
Annual Sub.: £156.00
Usual Pagination: 112
Editor: Marilyn Deegan
Summary of Content: Journal covering all aspects of computing applied as to literature and language.
Readership/Target Audience: Aimed at members of the Association for Literary and Linguistic Computing, scholars of English language and literature and scholars involved in computing the humanities.
ADVERTISING RATES:
Full Page Mono £310.00
Agency Commission: 10%
BUSINESS: COMPUTERS & AUTOMATION: Computers Related

LITERATURE & THEOLOGY
29892U62R-452
Editorial Address: Dept of Religious Studies, University of Stirling, OXFORD, FK9 4LA **Tel:** 01786 466240
Fax: 01786 466233
Email: andrew.hass@stir.ac.uk
Advertising Address: Great Clarendon Street, OXFORD, OX2 6DP **Tel:** 01865 353329
Email: jnlsadvertising@oxfordjournals.org
Web site: http://litthe.oupjournals.org
ISSN: 0269-1205

Publisher: OUP
Date Established: 1987
Frequency: Quarterly
Cover Price: £13.00
Annual Sub.: £42.00
Usual Pagination: 124
Editor: Andrew Hass
Summary of Content: Journal features an interdisciplinary study of theology.
Readership/Target Audience: Aimed at theologians and students of literature.
ADVERTISING RATES:
Full Page Mono £310.00
Agency Commission: 10%
Mechanical Data: Page Width: 150mm, Type Area: 220 x 150mm, Col Length: 220mm
Copy instructions: Copy Date: 24th of the month prior to publication date
BUSINESS: CHURCH & SCHOOL EQUIPMENT & EDUCATION: Education Related

---

LITIGATION FUNDING
1777382U44-3044

Editorial Address: 19 Bell Yard, LONDON, WC2A 2JR
Tel: 020 7841 5550 **Fax:** 020 7841 5513
Email: neil.rose@writtenmedia.co.uk
Advertising Address: 113 Chancery Lane, LONDON, WC2A 1PL **Tel:** 020 7841 5442 **Fax:** 020 7841 5508
Email: peter.garner@lawsociety.org.uk
Publisher: The Law Society
Frequency: 6 issues yearly
Annual Sub.: £195.00
Circulation: 600 (Publisher's Statement)
Editor: Neil Rose
Summary of Content: Guide to the funding and costs of litigation.
Readership/Target Audience: Aimed at solicitors, law costs draftsmen and those involved in litigation and litigation funding.
ADVERTISING RATES:
Full Page Colour £1044.00
Agency Commission: 10%
Copy instructions: Copy Date: 2 weeks prior to publication date
Average advertising content per issue: 20%
BUSINESS: LEGAL

THE LITIGATION LETTER
39211U44-1380

Editorial Address: Telephone House, 69-77 Paul Street, LONDON, EC2A 4LQ **Tel:** 020 7017 6762
Fax: 020 7017 5274
Email: jessica.westwood@informa.com
Web site: http://www.informa.co.uk
ISSN: 0268-0653
Publisher: Informa PLC
Frequency: 10 issues yearly
Usual Pagination: 12
Editor: Jessica Westwood
Summary of Content: Newsletter covering all aspects of practice and procedure in civil litigation.
Readership/Target Audience: Aimed at legal professionals.
ADVERTISING: No Advertising taken
BUSINESS: LEGAL

LIVE UK
1779309U61-515

Editorial Address: 26 Dorset Street, LONDON, W1U 8AP
Tel: 020 7486 7007 **Fax:** 020 7486 2002
Email: steve@liveuk.com
Advertising Address: As above.
Email: martyn@liveuk.com
Web site: http://www.liveuk.com
Publisher: Audience Media Ltd
Frequency: Monthly
Cover Price: £5.85
Free to qualifying individuals
Circulation: 2,500 (Publisher's Statement)
Editor: Stephen Parker; **Managing Editor:** Stephen Parker
Summary of Content: Magazine covering the UK's contemporary live music industry providing news, features and tour information and examining the people, venues and services involved.
Readership/Target Audience: Aimed at the country's promoters, festival organisers, venues, artiste managers, booking agents of other live music-related sectors.
ADVERTISING RATES:
Full Page Colour £1300.00
Agency Commission: 10%
Mechanical Data: Type Area: 260 x 190mm, Bleed Size: 301 x 216mm, Trim Size: 295 x 210mm, Col Length: 260mm, Page Width: 190mm, Film: Digital
Copy instructions: Copy Date: 2 weeks prior to publication date
Average advertising content per issue: 50%
BUSINESS: MUSIC TRADE

LIVERPOOL LAW SOCIETY BULLETIN
39212U44-1390

Editorial Address: 25 Southworth Way, THORNTON-CLEVELEYS, FY5 2WW **Tel:** 01253 829431
Fax: 01253 829431
Email: j.baskerville@btconnect.com
Advertising Address: As above.
Email: j.baskerville@btconnect.com
Publisher: Julia Baskerville Publications
Date Established: 1994
Frequency: Monthly
Free to qualifying individuals
Circulation: 2,400 (Publisher's Statement)
Usual Pagination: 14
Editor: Julia Baskerville; **Advertising Manager:** Julia Baskerville; **Managing Editor:** Julia Baskerville
Summary of Content: Journal of the Liverpool Law Society containing news and features relating to the legal profession and the law.
Readership/Target Audience: Read by members of The Liverpool Law Society.
ADVERTISING RATES:
Full Page Mono £600.00
Full Page Colour £900.00
Agency Commission: 10%
Mechanical Data: Bleed Size: +5mm, Type Area: 270 x 185mm, Trim Size: 297 x 210mm, Col Length: 270mm, Page Width: 185mm, Film: Digital
BUSINESS: LEGAL

LIVERPOOL LINK
35440U1P-83

Editorial Address: 151 Dale Street, LIVERPOOL, L2 2AH
Tel: 0151 227 5177 **Fax:** 0151 237 3998
Email: link@lcvs.org.uk
Web site: http://www.lcvs.org.uk
ISSN: 0266-8750
Publisher: Liverpool Charity and Voluntary Services
Date Established: 1984
Frequency: Quarterly
Cover Price: Free
Circulation: 2,000 (Publisher's Statement)
Usual Pagination: 24
Editor: Minna Alanko
Summary of Content: Magazine containing features, reviews and listings about and for the third sector.
Readership/Target Audience: Aimed at the third sector on Merseyside.
ADVERTISING: No Advertising taken
BUSINESS: FINANCE & ECONOMICS: Fundraising

LIVESTOCK & MEAT
37839U21D-710

Editorial Address: 80 Calverley Road, TUNBRIDGE WELLS, TN1 2UN **Tel:** 020 7017 7500 **Fax:** 020 7017 7599
Email: marketing@agra-net.com
Web site: http://www.agra-net.com
ISSN: 1356-9139
Publisher: Agra Informa Ltd
Frequency: Monthly
Annual Sub.: £722.00
Usual Pagination: 26
Summary of Content: Report on the European livestock and meat market. Includes legislative changes, policy updates and statistics on price, consumption, slaughtering, livestock numbers and trade volumes.
Readership/Target Audience: Read by the European livestock and meat industry.
ADVERTISING: No Advertising taken
BUSINESS: AGRICULTURE & FARMING: Livestock

LIVING IT
1663955U14H-417

Editorial Address: Old Grammar School House, School Gardens, Castle Gates, SHREWSBURY, SY1 2AJ
Tel: 01743 248482
Email: stickleback@meredith.cix.co.uk
Advertising Address: Computer 2000, Hampshire House, Wade Road, BASINGSTOKE, RG24 8NE **Tel:** 0870 060 3344
Fax: 0870 401 0123
Email: nicci.mckenzie@computer2000.co.uk
Web site: http://www.living-it.co.uk
Publisher: Tech Data Group
Date Established: 2005
Frequency: Quarterly - Published at the end of the month
Cover Price: Free
Circulation: 19,000 (Publisher's Statement)
Usual Pagination: 40
Editor: Simon Meredith; **Advertising Manager:** Nicci McKenzie
Summary of Content: Magazine covering how to run small businesses using IT including products and solutions.
Readership/Target Audience: Aimed at small and medium businesses.
ADVERTISING RATES:
Full Page Colour £2900.00

Mechanical Data: Trim Size: 275 x 215mm, Film: Digital, Type Area: 245 x 185mm, Col Length: 245mm, Page Width: 185mm, Bleed Size: 281 x 221mm
BUSINESS: COMMERCE, INDUSTRY & MANAGEMENT: Small Business

LIVING STREETS
1646060U57-126

Editorial Address: 31-33 Bondway, LONDON, SW8 1SJ
Tel: 020 7820 1010
Email: lucy.abell@livingstreets.org.uk
Web site: http://www.livingstreets.org.uk
Publisher: Pedestrians Association
Date Established: 2004
Frequency: Half-yearly
Free to qualifying individuals
Circulation: 3,000 (Publisher's Statement)
Usual Pagination: 4
Editor: Lucy Abell
Summary of Content: Newsletter covering articles on walking, streets and public spaces, transport, planning, road safety and crime.
Readership/Target Audience: Aimed at members.
ADVERTISING: No Advertising taken
BUSINESS: ENVIRONMENT & POLLUTION

LLOYD'S CASUALTY WEEK
39936U54R-140

Editorial Address: Sheepen House, Sheepen Place, COLCHESTER, CO3 3LP **Tel:** 020 7017 5228
Fax: 01206 765284
Email: casualty@informa.com
Advertising Address: Telephone House, 69-77 Paul Street, LONDON, EC2A 4LQ **Tel:** 020 7017 5000
Fax: 020 7017 5007
Email: advertising@lloydsmiu.com
Web site: http://www.lloydsmiu.com
ISSN: 0047-4908
Publisher: Informa Cargo Information
Frequency: Weekly
Circulation: 1,000 (Publisher's Statement)
Usual Pagination: 32
Editor: Stephen Legall; **Advertising Manager:** Stephen Legall
Summary of Content: Newsletter covering marine and aviation casualties and reports on political situations and port conditions.
Readership/Target Audience: Aimed at shipowners, managers, insurance companies, brokers, and consultants.
ADVERTISING: Rates on application
BUSINESS: SAFETY & SECURITY: Safety Related

LLOYD'S LAW REPORTS
39213U44-1400

Editorial Address: Telephone House, 69-77 Paul Street, LONDON, EC2A 4LQ **Tel:** 020 7017 4600
Fax: 020 7017 5274
Email: victoria.ophield@informa.com
Web site: http://www.i-law.com
Publisher: Informa PLC
Date Established: 1919
Frequency: 24 issues yearly
Circulation: 2,500 (Publisher's Statement)
Usual Pagination: 64
Editor: Victoria Ophield
Summary of Content: Journal containing news about maritime and commercial law.
Readership/Target Audience: Aimed at lawyers, barristers, solicitors, and legal officials in business firms.
ADVERTISING: No Advertising taken
BUSINESS: LEGAL

LLOYD'S LIST
39334U45A-80

Editorial Address: Telephone House, 69-77 Paul Street, LONDON, EC2A 4LQ **Tel:** 020 7017 5531
Fax: 020 7017 4975
Email: editorial@lloydslist.com
Advertising Address: As above. **Tel:** 020 7017 5000
Fax: 020 7017 4969
Email: james.snowdon@informa.com
Web site: http://www.lloydslist.com
Publisher: Informa Cargo Information
Date Established: 1734
Frequency: 240 issues yearly
Cover Price: £1.80
Circulation: 6,886 (ABC 01/01/2008 to 31/12/2008)
Usual Pagination: 24
Editor: Chris Mayer; **News Editor:** Richard Meade; **Executive Editor:** Chris Mayer; **Advertising Manager:** James Snowdon
Summary of Content: Newspaper focusing on shipping, insurance, energy, trade and logistics.
Twitter: https://twitter.com/LloydsList.
Readership/Target Audience: Aimed at insurance underwriters, merchants and ship owners.
ADVERTISING RATES:
Full Page Mono £8902.95

Business Magazines

Full Page Colour £10198.65
Agency Commission: 10%
Mechanical Data: No. of Columns (Display): 5, Col Widths (Display): 54mm, Type Area: 440 x 286mm, Col Length: 440mm, Page Width: 286mm, Film: Digital
Copy instructions: Copy Date: 3 days prior to publication date
Average advertising content per issue: 30%
BUSINESS: MARINE & SHIPPING

LLOYD'S LOADING LIST
39396U45C-55

Editorial Address: Sheepen Place, COLCHESTER, CO3 3LP **Tel:** 020 7017 4846 **Fax:** 020 7017 5363
Email: kevin.willmott@informa.com
Advertising Address: As above. **Tel:** 020 7017 4870
Email: steve.carter@informa.com
Web site: http://www.lloydsloadinglist.com
ISSN: 0144-6681
Publisher: Informa UK Limited
Date Established: 1853
Frequency: Weekly - Published on Monday
Annual Sub.: £335.00
Circulation: 1,295 (Publisher's Statement)
Usual Pagination: 160
Editor: Kevin Willmott; **News Editor:** Kevin Willmott;
Advertising Manager: Steven Carter
Summary of Content: Magazine containing a directory of export services by sea, road, rail and air, from the UK to worldwide destinations, plus weekly news reviews, features and special reports. Also includes in-depth analysis of deep-sea liner trades.
Readership/Target Audience: Read by major manufacturing companies, freight forwarders, shipping lines, international road hauliers and airlines.
ADVERTISING RATES:
Full Page Mono £290.00
Full Page Colour £1600.00
Mechanical Data: Bleed Size: 303 x 216mm, Trim Size: 265 x 190mm, Film: Digital
Copy instructions: Copy Date: 2 weeks prior to publication date
Average advertising content per issue: 90%
Supplement(s): Lloyd's Loading List Yearbook - 1xY
BUSINESS: MARINE & SHIPPING: Maritime Freight

LLOYD'S MARITIME AND COMMERCIAL LAW QUARTERLY
39214U44-1420

Editorial Address: Mortimer House, 37-41 Mortimer Street, LONDON, W1T 3JH **Tel:** 020 7017 4600 **Fax:** 020 7017 4111
Email: iona.everson@informa.com
Web site: http://www.informa.com
ISSN: 0306-2945
Publisher: Informa PLC
Frequency: Quarterly
Annual Sub.: £450.00
Circulation: 1,500 (Publisher's Statement)
Usual Pagination: 180
Summary of Content: Contains case reports and articles by legal experts in maritime and commercial law.
Readership/Target Audience: Aimed at the practising lawyer or commercial legal executive.
ADVERTISING: No Advertising taken
BUSINESS: LEGAL

LLOYDS SHIP MANAGER
39333U45A-82

Formerly: LSM
Editorial Address: Telephone House, 69-77 Paul Street, LONDON, EC2A 4LQ **Tel:** 020 7017 5000
Fax: 020 7017 4165
Email: nigel@msn.com
Advertising Address: As above. **Fax:** 020 7017 4969
Email: john.bodill@informa.com
Web site: http://www.informa.com
ISSN: 0265-2455
Publisher: Informa Cargo Information
Frequency: 6 issues yearly - Published in the last week of the 1st cover month
Annual Sub.: £152.00
Circulation: 8,305 (Publisher's Statement)
Usual Pagination: 120
Editor: Nigel Kitchen; **Executive Editor:** Chris Mayer
Summary of Content: Publication containing worldwide coverage of ship management, technology and operations.
Readership/Target Audience: Read by ship-owners, managers, operators and providers of maritime services and those involved in the shipbuilding and ship repairing industries.
ADVERTISING RATES:
Full Page Mono £2840.00
Full Page Colour £2840.00
Agency Commission: 10%
Mechanical Data: Trim Size: 297 x 210mm, Film: Digital, Bleed Size: 303 x 216mm, Col Widths (Display): 90mm
Copy instructions: Copy Date: 2 weeks prior to publication date
Average advertising content per issue: 30%

Supplement(s): Marine Equipment Guide - 1xY, Maritime Build and Repair - 1xY, Maritime Bunkering Guide - 1xY, Maritime Management - 1xY, Maritime Training Guide - 1xY, Ship Registers Guide - 1xY
BUSINESS: MARINE & SHIPPING

LLOYD'S SHIPPING ECONOMIST
39397U45C-60

Editorial Address: Telephone House, 69-77 Paul Street, LONDON, EC2A 4LQ **Tel:** 020 7017 4709
Fax: 020 7017 4976
Email: steve.matthews@informa.com
Advertising Address: As above. **Tel:** 020 7017 5000
Email: dimitra.papachristou@informa.com
Web site: http://www.shipecon.com
Publisher: Informa Cargo Information
Date Established: 1979
Frequency: Monthly
Annual Sub.: £839.00
Circulation: 1,900 (Publisher's Statement)
Usual Pagination: 48
Editor: Steve Matthews; **Advertising Manager:** Dimitra Papachristou; **Publisher:** Nicola Whyke
Summary of Content: Magazine following trends and deals in the shipping finance market. Also contains research and comment on the international shipping industry, with ship price data and fleet supply and demand statistics.
Readership/Target Audience: Read by ship-owners, consultants, banks, finance houses, brokers, builders, repairers and government bodies.
ADVERTISING RATES:
Full Page Mono £2140.00
Full Page Colour £2950.00
Agency Commission: 10%
Mechanical Data: Type Area: 275 x 190mm, Trim Size: 297 x 210mm, Bleed Size: 303 x 216mm, Col Length: 275mm, Page Width: 190mm, Film: Digital
Average advertising content per issue: 10%
BUSINESS: MARINE & SHIPPING: Maritime Freight

LNG FOCUS
1698877U24-102

Editorial Address: 35 New Bridge Street, LONDON, EC4V 6BW **Tel:** 020 7332 9922
Email: info@gas-matters.com
Advertising Address: As above. **Tel:** 020 7332 9980
Fax: 020 7332 9901
Email: m.shelton@gas-matters.com
Web site: http://www.gas-matters.com
ISSN: 1745-3372
Publisher: EconoMatters Ltd
Date Established: 2004
Frequency: 6 issues yearly
Circulation: 1,000 (Publisher's Statement)
Usual Pagination: 36
Editor: Therse Robinson
Summary of Content: Publication focusing on the liquid natural gas industry including analytical articles and data.
Readership/Target Audience: Aimed at oil companies, law firms, government, banks and analysts involved in the LNG industry.
ADVERTISING RATES:
Full Page Colour £1700.00
Agency Commission: 10%
Mechanical Data: Film: Digital
BUSINESS: GAS

LNG JOURNAL
38085U24-53_50

Editorial Address: 213 Marsh Wall, LONDON, E14 9FJ
Tel: 020 7510 0015 **Fax:** 020 7510 2344
Email: editor@lngjournal.com
Advertising Address: As above.
Email: ads@lngjournal.com
Web site: http://www.lngjournal.com
ISSN: 1365-4314
Publisher: Tanker Operator Ltd
Date Established: 1986
Frequency: 10 issues yearly
Annual Sub.: £225.00
Circulation: 3,000 (Publisher's Statement)
Usual Pagination: 28
Editor: John McKay; **Managing Director:** Stuart Fryer;
Advertising Manager: Patrick Schweitezer; **Publisher:** Stuart Fryer
Summary of Content: Magazine containing articles on projects, trade, shipping, design and technology, safety, environmental impact, markets, pricing and new applications in the liquefied natural gas market.
Readership/Target Audience: Readership includes key personnel in processing, shipping, construction and project management.
ADVERTISING RATES:
Full Page Mono £1400.00
Full Page Colour £2100.00
Agency Commission: 10%

Mechanical Data: Page Width: 254mm, Type Area: 358 x 254mm, Col Length: 358mm, No. of Columns (Display): 3, Film: Digital, Print Process: Litho, Bleed Size: 392 x 288mm
Copy instructions: Copy Date: 2 weeks prior to publication date
BUSINESS: GAS

LNG MARKETS
1706834U24-103

Editorial Address: 1 Procter Street, LONDON, WC1V 6EU
Tel: 020 7911 1946 **Fax:** 020 9711 1852
Email: info@icisheren.com
Advertising Address: As above. **Tel:** 020 7911 1920
Email: doug@icisheren.com
Web site: http://www.heren.com
Publisher: ICIS Heren
Date Established: 2005
Frequency: Weekly
Editor: Simon Ellis; **Advertising Manager:** Douglas Strien
Summary of Content: Journal focusing on the marketing and trading of LNG.
Readership/Target Audience: Aimed at LNG producers, traders and buyers.
ADVERTISING RATES:
Full Page Mono £1000.00
Full Page Colour £1000.00
Agency Commission: 5%
Mechanical Data: Type Area: 250 x 160mm, Col Length: 250mm, Page Width: 160mm, Film: Digital
Copy instructions: Copy Date: 2 days prior to publication date
BUSINESS: GAS

LOCAL AUTHORITY BUILDING & MAINTENANCE
38379U32A-111

Editorial Address: Regal House, Regal Way, WATFORD, WD24 4YF **Tel:** 01923 237799 **Fax:** 01923 246901
Email: labm@hamerville.co.uk
Advertising Address: As above.
Email: dave@hamerville.co.uk
Web site: http://www.hamerville.co.uk
Publisher: Hamerville Magazines Ltd
Date Established: 1985
Frequency: 11 issues yearly - Published in the 1st week of the cover month. Combined issues: Published in the middle of the 1st cover month
Free to qualifying individuals
Annual Sub.: £27.00
Circulation: 17,755 (ABC 01/07/2008 to 30/06/2009)
Usual Pagination: 80
Editor: Claire Clutten; **Managing Director:** Bryan Shannon; **Managing Editor:** Terry Smith; **Publisher:** Bryan Shannon
Summary of Content: Journal containing news on technical issues concerning building materials and methods. Includes coverage of the Decent Homes Standard, housing refurbishment, school and hospital construction and all maintenance requirements and readers enquires.
Readership/Target Audience: Aimed at those in the public building sector responsible for maintaining buildings and specifying and purchasing building materials.
ADVERTISING RATES:
Full Page Colour £2500.00
Agency Commission: 10%
Mechanical Data: Type Area: 255 x 180mm, Bleed Size: 295 x 216mm, Trim Size: 289 x 210mm, Col Length: 255mm, Page Width: 180mm, Film: Digital
Copy instructions: Copy Date: 4 weeks prior to publication date
Average advertising content per issue: 45%
BUSINESS: LOCAL GOVERNMENT, LEISURE & RECREATION: Local Government

LOCAL AUTHORITY WASTE & RECYCLING
38408U32B-130

Formerly: Local Authority Waste & Environment (LAWE)
Editorial Address: Faversham House, 232A Addington Road, SOUTH CROYDON, CR2 8LE **Tel:** 020 8651 7100
Fax: 020 8651 7117
Email: lawr@fav-house.com
Advertising Address: As above.
Email: ella.westaway@fav-house.com
Web site: http://www.lawr.co.uk
ISSN: 0968-5533
Publisher: Faversham House Group Ltd
Date Established: 1993
Frequency: Monthly - Published in the 1st week of the cover month
Free to qualifying individuals
Annual Sub.: £72.00
Circulation: 6,515 (ABC 01/07/2008 to 30/06/2009)
Usual Pagination: 42
Editor: Maxine Perella; **Publisher:** Angela Himus
Summary of Content: Independent magazine covering news, products, plant, vehicles, services and articles on environmental protection and waste management and recycling for professionals across the public and private sectors. Includes features on air quality, street cleansing,

waste collection and disposal, recycling, landfill, contaminated land and sustainable energy.
Readership/Target Audience: Aimed at local authority and private sector professionals involved in pollution control, environmental regulation, waste management and recycling.
ADVERTISING RATES:
Full Page Mono £1250.00
Full Page Colour £1500.00
Agency Commission: 10%
Mechanical Data: Page Width: 180mm, Type Area: 270 x 180mm, Col Length: 270mm, Trim Size: 297 x 210mm, Bleed Size: 303 x 216mm, Film: Digital
Copy instructions: Copy Date: 4 weeks prior to publication date
Average advertising content per issue: 40%
BUSINESS: LOCAL GOVERNMENT, LEISURE & RECREATION: Public Health & Cleaning

LOCAL COUNCIL REVIEW
38380U32A-115

Editorial Address: 109 Great Russell Street, LONDON, WC1B 3LD **Tel:** 020 7290 0316 **Fax:** 020 7436 7451
Email: lcr@nalc.gov.uk
Advertising Address: Mongoose Media, Mongoose House, 2 Lonsdale Road, LONDON, NW6 6RD **Tel:** 020 7306 0300
Fax: 020 7328 8617
Email: alinton@mongoosemedia.com
Web site: http://www.nalc.gov.uk
Publisher: National Association of Local Councils
Date Established: 1947
Frequency: 6 issues yearly
Annual Sub.: £14.00
Circulation: 12,500 (Publisher's Statement)
Usual Pagination: 32
Editor: Alan Jones; **Advertising Manager:** Anthon Linton
Summary of Content: Official journal of the National Association of Local Councils. Contains news and features about the association, events concerning local councils and new legislation.
Readership/Target Audience: Aimed at those involved in town parish and community councils, including clerks, councillors and those interested in local council policy and budgets in England and Wales.
ADVERTISING RATES:
Full Page Colour £1950.00
Mechanical Data: Col Length: 314mm, Page Width: 220mm, Type Area: 314 x 220mm, Bleed Size: 297 x 210mm, Film: Digital
Average advertising content per issue: 15%
BUSINESS: LOCAL GOVERNMENT, LEISURE & RECREATION: Local Government

LOCAL GOVERNMENT EXECUTIVE
38382U32A-125_40

Formerly: Local Government & Health Executive
Editorial Address: Portland Buildings, 127-129 Portland Street, MANCHESTER, M1 4PZ **Tel:** 0161 236 2782
Fax: 0161 236 2783
Email: chris.newbould@excelpublishing.co.uk
Advertising Address: As above.
Email: louis@excelpublishing.co.uk
Web site: http://www.excelpublishing.co.uk
ISSN: 1350-2719
Publisher: Excel Publishing Company Ltd
Frequency: 6 issues yearly - Published in the 3rd week of the 1st cover month
Annual Sub.: £30.00
Circulation: 5,100 (Publisher's Statement)
Usual Pagination: 66
Editor: Chris Newbould; **Managing Editor:** Martin Regan; **Publisher:** Patrick Rafter
Summary of Content: Magazine covering all aspects of news, products and services of relevance to local government.
Readership/Target Audience: Aimed at key decision makers within the local government and healthcare sectors.
ADVERTISING RATES:
Full Page Colour £1495.00
Agency Commission: 10%
Mechanical Data: Bleed Size: 284 x 216mm, Trim Size: 278 x 210mm, Col Length: 256mm, Film: Digital, Type Area: 256 x 178mm, Page Width: 178mm
Copy instructions: Copy Date: 5 weeks prior to publication date
Average advertising content per issue: 40%
BUSINESS: LOCAL GOVERNMENT, LEISURE & RECREATION: Local Government

LOCAL GOVERNMENT FIRST
38385U32A-125_50

Editorial Address: Local Government House, Smith Square, LONDON, SW1P 3HZ **Tel:** 020 7664 3294
Fax: 020 7664 3250
Email: first@lga.gov.uk
Advertising Address: As above. **Tel:** 020 7664 3131
Fax: 020 7863 9158
Email: first@lga.gov.uk
Web site: http://www.lga.gov.uk/first
ISSN: 1468-3024

Publisher: The Local Government Association
Date Established: 1999
Frequency: 44 issues yearly
Free to qualifying individuals
Annual Sub.: £90.00
Circulation: 28,500 (Publisher's Statement)
Usual Pagination: 16
Editor: Karen Thornton; **Advertising Manager:** Richard Mole
Summary of Content: Magazine of the Local Government Association reporting on all issues affecting local government in England and Wales.
Readership/Target Audience: Read by local authority councillors in England and Wales, local government, chief executives and senior officers.
ADVERTISING RATES:
Full Page Mono £1100.00
Full Page Colour £1700.00
Mechanical Data: Type Area: 282 x 198mm, Bleed Size: 305 x 224mm, Trim Size: 299 x 218mm, Col Length: 282mm, Page Width: 198mm, Film: Digital
Copy instructions: Copy Date: Monday prior to publication date
Average advertising content per issue: 5%
BUSINESS: LOCAL GOVERNMENT, LEISURE & RECREATION: Local Government

LOCAL GOVERNMENT IT IN USE
38383U32A-126

Editorial Address: PO Box 2087, SHOREHAM-BY-SEA, BN43 5ZF **Tel:** 01273 273941
Email: helen@infopub.co.uk
Advertising Address: As above. **Tel:** 01983 812623
Fax: 01983 563340
Email: ann@infopub.co.uk
Web site: http://www.infopub.co.uk
ISSN: 1368-2660
Publisher: Informed Publications Ltd
Date Established: 1996
Frequency: 6 issues yearly
Cover Price: £49.00
Free to qualifying individuals
Circulation: 12,000 (Publisher's Statement)
Usual Pagination: 32
Editor: Helen Olsen; **Advertising Manager:** Ann-Marie Campbell-Smith; **Publisher:** Helen Olsen
Summary of Content: Journal focusing on the use of information technology and services within local government, and the development of local e-government.
Readership/Target Audience: Aimed at local government IT/IS decision makers, purchasers and end users.
ADVERTISING RATES:
Full Page Colour £2000.00
Agency Commission: 10%
Mechanical Data: Type Area: 270 x 178mm, Col Length: 270mm, Page Width: 178mm, Trim Size: 297 x 210mm, Bleed Size: 303 x 216mm, Film: Digital
Average advertising content per issue: 40%
BUSINESS: LOCAL GOVERNMENT, LEISURE & RECREATION: Local Government

LOCAL GOVERNMENT NEWS
38377U32A-108

Formerly: LGN Local Government News
Editorial Address: 32 Vauxhall Bridge Road, LONDON, SW1V 2SS **Tel:** 020 7973 6400
Email: l.sharman@hgluk.com
Advertising Address: As above. **Fax:** 020 7233 5057
Email: s.ellicott@hgluk.com
Web site: http://www.localgov.co.uk
ISSN: 0261-5185
Publisher: Hemming Group Ltd
Date Established: 1979
Frequency: 11 issues yearly - Published around the 10th of the cover month
Free to qualifying individuals
Annual Sub.: £55.00
Circulation: 18,006 (ABC 01/07/2006 to 30/06/2007)
Usual Pagination: 74
Editor: Laura Sharman
Summary of Content: Magazine covering all aspects of the built environment and the public realm.
Readership/Target Audience: Aimed at senior local government personnel in all departments.
ADVERTISING RATES:
Full Page Colour £2750.00
SCC £40.00
Agency Commission: 10%
Mechanical Data: Col Widths (Display): 45mm, No. of Columns (Display): 4, Page Width: 186mm, Type Area: 275 x 186mm, Trim Size: 297 x 210mm, Bleed Size: 307 x 220mm, Col Length: 275mm, Film: Digital
Copy instructions: Copy Date: 6 weeks prior to publication date
Average advertising content per issue: 40%
BUSINESS: LOCAL GOVERNMENT, LEISURE & RECREATION: Local Government

LOCAL GOVERNMENT REPORTS
25984U44-1435

Editorial Address: Halsbury House, 35 Chancery Lane, LONDON, WC2A 1EL **Tel:** 020 7400 2500
Fax: 020 7400 2988
Email: catherine.bayliss@lexisnexis.co.uk
Web site: http://www.lexisnexis.co.uk
ISSN: 1474-8657
Publisher: LexisNexis
Date Established: 1902
Frequency: 11 issues yearly
Annual Sub.: £341.00
Usual Pagination: 92
Editor: Catherine Bayliss
Summary of Content: Journal focusing on selected professional law reports relevant to local government.
Readership/Target Audience: Read by people interested in law and local government.
ADVERTISING: No Advertising taken
BUSINESS: LEGAL

LOCAL TRANSPORT TODAY
39701U49R-150

Editorial Address: 359 Kennington Lane, LONDON, SE11 5QY **Tel:** 0845 270 7875 **Fax:** 0845 270 7961
Email: ed.ltt@landor.co.uk
Advertising Address: As above. **Fax:** 0845 270 7960
Email: ads.ltt@landor.co.uk
Web site: http://www.lttonline.co.uk
ISSN: 0962-6220
Publisher: Landor Publishing
Date Established: 1989
Frequency: 26 issues yearly
Annual Sub.: £80.00
Circulation: 2,500 (Publisher's Statement)
Usual Pagination: 36
Editor: Andrew Forster; **Advertising Manager:** Sabrina Ayadassen; **Publisher:** Peter Stonham
Summary of Content: Publication focusing on urban and regional transport issues, with analysis of transport policies, plans and finance.
Readership/Target Audience: Aimed at professionals, students and technicians in all areas of transport.
ADVERTISING RATES:
Full Page Mono £4170.00
Full Page Colour £4670.00
SCC £37.00
Agency Commission: 10%
Mechanical Data: Type Area: 300 x 225mm, Film: Digital, Col Length: 300mm, No. of Columns (Display): 5, Page Width: 225mm
Copy instructions: Copy Date: Monday 12pm prior to publication date
Average advertising content per issue: 40%
BUSINESS: TRANSPORT: Transport Related

THE LOG
37194U14L-435

Editorial Address: BALPA House, 5 Heathrow Boulevard, 278 Bath Road, WEST DRAYTON, UB7 0DQ
Tel: 020 8476 4000 **Fax:** 020 8476 4077
Email: communications@balpa.org
Advertising Address: As above. **Tel:** 020 7692 9292
Fax: 020 7692 9393
Email: thelog@lps.co.uk
Web site: http://www.balpa.org
Publisher: B.A.L.P.A.
Date Established: 1937
Frequency: 6 issues yearly
Free to qualifying individuals
Annual Sub.: £26.50
Circulation: 13,500 (Publisher's Statement)
Usual Pagination: 50
Editor: Emma Chisholm; **Advertising Manager:** Emma Chisholm
Summary of Content: Official journal of the British Airline Pilots' Association containing aviation-related features, industry news, interviews, letters to the editor and technical information.
Readership/Target Audience: Aimed at members of the British Airline Pilots' Association.
ADVERTISING RATES:
Full Page Colour £1500.00
SCC £20.00
Agency Commission: 10%
Mechanical Data: Type Area: 274 x 185mm, No. of Columns (Display): 2, Col Length: 274mm, Film: Digital, Trim Size: 297 x 210mm, Page Width: 185mm
BUSINESS: COMMERCE, INDUSTRY & MANAGEMENT: Trade Unions

LOGIC JOURNAL OF IGPL
36311U5R-230

Editorial Address: Department of Computing, Imperial College, 180 Queens Gate, LONDON, SW7 2BZ
Tel: 020 7594 8205 **Fax:** 020 7594 8201
Email: dg@doc.ic.ac.uk
Web site: http://www3.oup.co.uk/igpl
ISSN: 1367-0751

Business Magazines

Publisher: OUP
Date Established: 1993
Frequency: 6 issues yearly
Cover Price: £45.00
Annual Sub.: £216.00
Usual Pagination: 140
Editor: Dov Gabbay; **Editor-in-Chief:** Dov Gabbay
Summary of Content: Journal covering all areas of pure and applied logic.
Readership/Target Audience: Read by members of the Interest Group in Pure and Applied Logic.
ADVERTISING: No Advertising taken
BUSINESS: COMPUTERS & AUTOMATION: Computers Related

LOGISTICS & TRANSPORT FOCUS

36535U10-77_15

Formerly: Logistics Focus
Editorial Address: Earlstrees Court, Earlstrees Court, CORBY, NN17 4AX **Tel:** 01536 740100 **Fax:** 01536 740103
Email: focus@ciltuk.org.uk
Advertising Address: As above.
Email: daryl.chesney@ciltuk.org.uk
Web site: http://www.ciltuk.org.uk
ISSN: 1466-836X
Publisher: The Chartered Institute of Logistics and Transport UK
Date Established: 1993
Frequency: Monthly - Published around the 1st of the cover month
Free to qualifying individuals
Annual Sub.: £15.00
Circulation: 16,992 (ABC 01/01/2008 to 31/12/2008)
Usual Pagination: 110
Editor: David Jinks; **Advertising Manager:** Daryl Chesney; **Publisher:** David Jinks
Summary of Content: Journal containing logistics, supply-chain management and distribution management, IT, passenger and commercial transport freight articles.
Readership/Target Audience: Aimed at management with overall responsibility in the supply chain covering purchasing, production, inventory control, warehousing and information management systems. Also, distribution, transportation, operations and general management.
ADVERTISING RATES:
Full Page Mono £1555.00
Full Page Colour £2300.00
Agency Commission: 10%
Mechanical Data: Page Width: 180mm, Col Length: 261mm, Film: Digital, No. of Columns (Display): 4, Type Area: 261 x 180mm, Trim Size: 297 x 210mm, Bleed Size: 303 x 216mm
Copy instructions: Copy Date: 3 weeks prior to publication date
Average advertising content per issue: 40%
BUSINESS: MATERIALS HANDLING

LOGISTICS BRIEFING

1620649U10-204

Editorial Address: Brinkworth House, Brinkworth, Wiltshire, CHIPPENHAM, SN15 5DF **Tel:** 01666 511880
Fax: 01666 511883
Email: newsdesk@transportintelligence.com
Web site: http://www.transportintelligence.com
Publisher: Transport Intelligence Ltd
Date Established: 2002
Frequency: Daily
Cover Price: Free
Circulation: 17,000 (Publisher's Statement)
Usual Pagination: 1
Editor: Thomas Cullen; **Executive Editor:** Mike Nordmann
Summary of Content: Newsletter covering analysis of daily events in the European and global freight transport and logistics industry.
Readership/Target Audience: Aimed at senior executives in the freight, transport and logistics industry.
ADVERTISING: No Advertising taken
BUSINESS: MATERIALS HANDLING

LOGISTICS BUSINESS IT

1818572U5E-9003

Editorial Address: The Anderson Centre, Unit D(A), Spitfire Close, Ermine Business Park, HUNTINGDON, PE29 6XY
Tel: 01480 455660 **Fax:** 01480 455661
Email: edit@logisticsbusinessit.com
Advertising Address: As above.
Email: mel@logisticsbusinessit.com
Web site: http://www.logisticsbusinessit.com
Publisher: Logistics Business Magazine Ltd
Date Established: 2007
Frequency: 5 issues yearly
Free to qualifying individuals
Circulation: 10,000 (Publisher's Statement)
Editor: Iestyn Armstrong-Smith; **Advertising Manager:** Mel Brill
Summary of Content: Magazine covering all aspects of technology and services spanning the entire supply chain. Focusing on business software as used throughout the

supply chain - including manufacturing, warehousing and transportation software solutions, automotive data capture (bar code and RFID), industrial mobile computing, and voice directed systems for warehouse operations such as picking.
Readership/Target Audience: Aimed at high-level logistics IT decision makers in major end-user companies, third party logistics specialists and providers as well as purchases, systems integrators, specifiers and practitioners in the supply chain and management IT fields.
ADVERTISING: Rates on application
BUSINESS: COMPUTERS & AUTOMATION: Data Transmission

LOGISTICS BUSINESS MAGAZINE

36536U10-77_25

Editorial Address: The Anderson Centre, Unit D(A), Spitfire Close, Ermine Business Park, HUNTINGDON, PE29 6XY
Tel: 01480 455660 **Fax:** 01480 455661
Email: edit@logisticsbusiness.com
Advertising Address: As above.
Email: sales@logisticsbusiness.com
Web site: http://www.logisticsbusiness.com
ISSN: 1367-0212
Publisher: Logistics Business Magazine Ltd
Date Established: 1997
Frequency: Quarterly - Published in the 2nd week of the 1st cover month
Free to qualifying individuals
Annual Sub.: £40.00
Circulation: 12,000 (Publisher's Statement)
Usual Pagination: 92
Editor: Chris Price-White; **Advertising Manager:** Mike Taylor; **Publisher:** David Priestman
Summary of Content: Publication containing articles on international materials handling, warehousing and logistics industries.
Language(s): English; French; German
Readership/Target Audience: Aimed at directors and management staff within the industry plus blue-chip end users.
ADVERTISING RATES:
Full Page Colour £3500.00
Agency Commission: 15%
Mechanical Data: Type Area: 254 x 178mm, Trim Size: 297 x 210mm, Bleed Size: 303 x 213mm, Col Length: 254mm, No. of Columns (Display): 4, Page Width: 178mm, Film: Digital
Average advertising content per issue: 35%
BUSINESS: MATERIALS HANDLING

LOGISTICS MANAGER - THE SUPPLY CHAIN BUSINESS

36539U10-85

Formerly: Logistics Manager
Editorial Address: St. Giles House, 50 Poland Street, LONDON, W1F 7AX **Tel:** 020 7970 4000 **Fax:** 020 7970 4493
Email: malory.davies@centaur.co.uk
Advertising Address: As above. **Fax:** 020 7970 4199
Email: selina.tickle@centaur.co.uk
Web site: http://www.logisticsmanager.com
ISSN: 1353-5595
Publisher: Centaur Communications Ltd
Date Established: 1994
Frequency: 11 issues yearly
Free to qualifying individuals
Annual Sub.: £55.00
Circulation: 13,988 (ABC 01/01/2007 to 31/12/2007)
Usual Pagination: 60
Editor: Malory Davies
Summary of Content: Journal covering all aspects of the supply chain from sourcing raw materials through to production, materials management, transport and distribution as well as new contracts, IT, electronic commerce and warehouse and property developments.
Readership/Target Audience: Read by logistics professionals in end-user industries.
ADVERTISING RATES:
Full Page Colour £2230.00
Agency Commission: 10%
Mechanical Data: Type Area: 267 x 189mm, Col Length: 267mm, Bleed Size: 303 x 216mm, Page Width: 189mm, Film: Digital, Trim Size: 297 x 210mm
Copy instructions: Copy Date: 4 weeks prior to publication date
Average advertising content per issue: 50%
BUSINESS: MATERIALS HANDLING

LONDON BULLETIN

752991U32A-218

Editorial Address: 59½ Southwark Street, LONDON, SE1 0AL **Tel:** 020 7934 9754
Email: ian.mitchell@londoncouncils.gov.uk
Advertising Address: As above. **Fax:** 020 7934 9769
Email: emma.stewart@londoncouncils.gov.uk
Web site: http://www.londoncouncils.gov.uk
Publisher: London Councils
Date Established: 2000
Frequency: 6 issues yearly

Free to qualifying individuals
Annual Sub.: £40.00
Circulation: 4,000 (Publisher's Statement)
Usual Pagination: 20
Editor: Ian Mitchell; **Editor-in-Chief:** Ian Mitchell;
Advertising Manager: Emma Stewart
Summary of Content: Magazine covering news on developments in London local government, especially London's boroughs, interviews with key local government figures and analysis of government policy.
Readership/Target Audience: Aimed at London councillors, chief officers, council officers, voluntary sector organisations, MPs and ministers.
ADVERTISING: Rates on application
Copy instructions: Copy Date: 3 weeks prior to publication date
Average advertising content per issue: 10%
BUSINESS: LOCAL GOVERNMENT, LEISURE & RECREATION: Local Government

LONDON BUSINESS MATTERS

41220U63A-110

Formerly: Business Matters
Editorial Address: 33 Queen Street, LONDON, EC4R 1AP
Tel: 020 7203 1897 **Fax:** 020 7203 1930
Advertising Address: Houldsworth Mill, South Mill, Reddish, STOCKPORT, SK5 6DA **Tel:** 0161 443 5084
Fax: 0161 443 5099
Email: alli@imprintpub.co.uk
Web site: http://www.londonchamber.co.uk
Publisher: Excell Publishing
Frequency: 10 issues yearly
Free to qualifying individuals
Circulation: 18,000 (Publisher's Statement)
Usual Pagination: 32
Editor: Peter Bishop; **Advertising Manager:** Alli Johnson
Summary of Content: Members' magazine of the London Chamber of Commerce and Industry. Contains local business and international news and articles on changes in legislation, seminars and new business opportunities.
Readership/Target Audience: Aimed at London Chamber of Commerce members and other businesses.
ADVERTISING RATES:
Full Page Colour £3400.00
Agency Commission: 10%
Mechanical Data: Type Area: 300 x 230mm, Bleed Size: 346 x 251mm, Film: Positive, right reading, emulsion side down. Digital, Col Length: 300mm, Page Width: 230mm
BUSINESS: REGIONAL BUSINESS: Regional Business Greater London

LONDON BUSINESS WORLD

714207U63A-115

Editorial Address: Building D, Templar Business Park, off Torrington Avenue, COVENTRY, CV4 9AP
Tel: 024 7646 5000
Email: petermarshall@bizworldonline.com
Advertising Address: As above.
Web site: http://www.bizworldonline.com
Publisher: Artfeks Publishing
Date Established: 2001
Frequency: 11 issues yearly
Circulation: 25,000 (Publisher's Statement)
Usual Pagination: 30
Editor: Peter Marshall; **Advertising Manager:** Adam Wall
Summary of Content: Newspaper covering all aspects of local business activity in London and the Home Counties.
Readership/Target Audience: Aimed at the business community.
ADVERTISING RATES:
Full Page Colour £1872.00
Agency Commission: 10%
Mechanical Data: Type Area: 390 x 260mm, No. of Columns (Display): 8, Col Length: 390mm, Page Width: 260mm, Film: Digital
Average advertising content per issue: 60%
BUSINESS: REGIONAL BUSINESS: Regional Business Greater London

LONDON CORN CIRCULAR

35394U1L-50

Editorial Address: The Palace Hall, Darthill Road, MARCH, PE15 8HP **Tel:** 07919 671194 **Fax:** 01733 560702
Email: andy@stylaprint.co.uk
Advertising Address: As above. **Tel:** 01354 661976
ISSN: 0024-6026
Publisher: London Corn Circular
Date Established: 1843
Frequency: Weekly
Annual Sub.: £80.00
Circulation: 1,000 (Publisher's Statement)
Usual Pagination: 8
Editor: John Bird; **Managing Director:** John Bird;
Advertising Manager: John Bird; **Publisher:** John Bird
Summary of Content: Magazine covering agricultural news and prices at home and abroad.
Readership/Target Audience: Aimed at agricultural merchants, farmers and traders worldwide.

Copy instructions: Copy Date: Tuesday prior to publication date
BUSINESS: FINANCE & ECONOMICS: Commodities

LONDON GAZETTE
1693393U44-3019

Editorial Address: PO Box 7923, LONDON, SE1 5ZH
Tel: 0870 600 3322 **Fax:** 020 7394 4572
Email: london.gazette@tso.co.uk
Web site: http://www.london-gazette.co.uk
Publisher: TSO
Date Established: 1665
Frequency: 260 issues yearly
Summary of Content: Publication covering statutory, legal, bankruptcy and liquidation notices relating to England.
Readership/Target Audience: Aimed at government departments, libraries, solicitors and many large credit information firms.
ADVERTISING: No Advertising taken
BUSINESS: LEGAL

THE LONDON PROPERTY REVIEW
1898835U4D-427

Editorial Address: 26 Store Street, LONDON, WC1E 7BT
Tel: 020 7636 4044
Email: niki.kernohan@thelpr.com
Advertising Address: 26 Stone Street, LONDON, WC1E 7BT **Tel:** 020 7636 4044
Email: niki.kernohan@thelpr.com
Web site: http://www.thelpr.com
Publisher: Pipers Publishing Ltd.
Frequency: Quarterly
Annual Sub.: £40.00
Circulation: 3,000 (Publisher's Statement)
Editor: David Taylor; **Publisher:** Nick McKeogh
Summary of Content: Magazine looking at the London property market.
Readership/Target Audience: Aimed at architects, developers and property consultants.
BUSINESS: ARCHITECTURE & BUILDING: Planning & Housing

THE LOOP MAGAZINE
1743032U57-148

Editorial Address: 57 Prince Street, BRISTOL, BS1 4QH
Tel: 0117 907 4107 **Fax:** 0117 907 7216
Email: theloop@resource.uk.com
Advertising Address: As above.
Email: marketing@resource.uk.com
Web site: http://www.larac.org.uk
Publisher: Resource Media Ltd
Frequency: Quarterly
Cover Price: Free
Circulation: 1,000 (Publisher's Statement)
Usual Pagination: 36
Editor: Leonie Butler; **Managing Editor:** Leonie Butler
Summary of Content: Magazine covering waste, particularly local authority issues.
Readership/Target Audience: Publication is only available to members of LARAC and selected individuals including local authority waste managers, recycling officers and government departments.
ADVERTISING RATES:
Full Page Colour £925.00
Agency Commission: 10%
Mechanical Data: Type Area: 265 x 185mm, Bleed Size: 303 x 216mm, Trim Size: 297 x 210mm, Col Length: 265mm, Page Width: 185mm, Film: Digital
Copy instructions: Copy Date: 2 weeks prior to publication date
Average advertising content per issue: 33%
BUSINESS: ENVIRONMENT & POLLUTION

LOSS PREVENTION BULLETIN
39874U54B-76

Editorial Address: Davis Building, 165-189 Railway Terrace, RUGBY, CV21 3HQ **Tel:** 01788 578214 **Fax:** 01788 560833
Email: tdonaldson@icheme.org
Web site: http://www.icheme.org
ISSN: 0260-9576
Publisher: Institution of Chemical Engineers
Date Established: 1974
Frequency: 6 issues yearly
Annual Sub.: £312.00
Circulation: 500 (Publisher's Statement)
Usual Pagination: 32
Editor: Tracey Donaldson
Summary of Content: Publication providing case studies and practical advice on specific chemical hazards.
Readership/Target Audience: Aimed at safety professionals within the process industries.
ADVERTISING: No Advertising taken
BUSINESS: SAFETY & SECURITY: Safety

LOW-FARE & REGIONAL AIRLINES
36348U6A-150

Formerly: Regional Airline World
Editorial Address: 268 Bath Road, SLOUGH, SL1 4DX
Tel: 01753 727001 **Fax:** 01753 727002
Email: bb@shephard.co.uk
Advertising Address: As above. **Tel:** 01753 727002
Email: dah@shephard.co.uk
Web site: http://www.shephard.co.uk
ISSN: 1753-0598
Publisher: The Shephard Group
Date Established: 1984
Frequency: 8 issues yearly - Published on the 1st of the cover month
Free to qualifying individuals
Annual Sub.: £80.00
Circulation: 10,600 (Publisher's Statement)
Usual Pagination: 40
Editor: Bernie Baldwin
Summary of Content: Magazine focusing on all business within the regional and low-fare airline industry worldwide.
Readership/Target Audience: Aimed at senior executives within regional airlines, low fare airlines, major airlines that operate regional aircraft and manufacturers and suppliers.
ADVERTISING RATES:
Full Page Colour £5080.00
Agency Commission: 15%
Mechanical Data: Type Area: 254 x 182mm, Col Length: 254mm, Page Width: 182mm, Col Widths (Display): 58mm, Trim Size: 273 x 205mm, Bleed Size: 279 x 208mm, Film: Digital, Print Process: Offset litho
Copy instructions: Copy Date: 4 weeks prior to publication date
Average advertising content per issue: 33%
Supplement(s): Low-Fare & Regional Aviation Handbook - 1xY
BUSINESS: AVIATION & AERONAUTICS

LP GAS
38086U24-54

Editorial Address: The Point, College Road, EASTBOURNE, BN21 4JJ **Tel:** 01323 646076 **Fax:** 01323 411050
Email: ppl@prgltd.co.uk
Advertising Address: As above.
Email: tracey@prgltd.co.uk
Web site: http://www.lpgasmagazine.co.uk
ISSN: 1362-7813
Publisher: PRG Ltd
Date Established: 1996
Frequency: 6 issues yearly - Published in the 2nd week of the 1st cover month
Cover Price: Free
Circulation: 5,000 (Publisher's Statement)
Usual Pagination: 28
Editor: Faye Spiers; **Publisher:** Raymond Groves
Summary of Content: Magazine covering industry news, product features, marketing initiatives and safety updates. Includes technical articles, features on liquefied petroleum gas utilisation and important events.
Readership/Target Audience: Read by those involved in the supply, distribution and use of LPG and associated equipment.
ADVERTISING RATES:
Full Page Mono £1470.00
Full Page Colour £2175.00
Agency Commission: 10%
Mechanical Data: Type Area: 265 x 189mm, Bleed Size: 303 x 213mm, Trim Size: 297 x 210mm, No. of Columns (Display): 4, Col Length: 265mm, Page Width: 189mm, Col Widths (Display): 43.5mm, Film: Digital
Copy instructions: Copy Date: 4 weeks prior to publication date
Average advertising content per issue: 40%
BUSINESS: GAS

LUBE
38592U33-10_8

Editorial Address: Berkhamsted House, 121 High Street, BERKHAMSTED, HP4 2DJ **Tel:** 01442 230589
Fax: 01442 259232
Email: lube@ukla.org.uk
Advertising Address: As above.
Email: lube@ukla.org.uk
Web site: http://www.ukla.org.uk
ISSN: 1744-5418
Publisher: UK Lubricants Association Limited
Date Established: 1988
Frequency: 6 issues yearly - Published around the beginning of the cover month
Free to qualifying individuals
Circulation: 5,000 (Publisher's Statement)
Usual Pagination: 32
Editor: Rod Parker; **Advertising Manager:** Rod Parker
Summary of Content: Magazine covering industry news on the lubricant market including legislation and technical information.
Readership/Target Audience: Read by members of the UK Lubricants Association and those in the lubricants industry in the UK and worldwide, plus allied industries, end users and interested third parties.

ADVERTISING RATES:
Full Page Mono £1638.00
Full Page Colour £1117.00
Agency Commission: 10%
Mechanical Data: Trim Size: 297 x 210mm, Film: Digital, Type Area: 277 x 190mm, Col Length: 277mm, Page Width: 190mm, Bleed Size: 303 x 216mm
Average advertising content per issue: 20%
BUSINESS: OIL & PETROLEUM

LUBRICATION SCIENCE
37576U19A-380

Editorial Address: The Atrium, Southern Gate, CHICHESTER, PO19 8SQ **Tel:** 01243 779777
Fax: 01243 775878
Email: fmarais@wiley.co.uk
Advertising Address: As above. **Tel:** 01243 770254
Fax: 01243 770432
Email: adsales@wiley.co.uk
Web site: http://www.interscience.wiley.com/lubricationscience
ISSN: 0954-0075
Publisher: John Wiley & Sons Ltd
Date Established: 1988
Frequency: 10 issues yearly
Annual Sub.: $1055.00
Usual Pagination: 88
Editor: Frea Marais; **Executive Editor:** Peter Mitchell
Summary of Content: Journal covering physics and chemistry of lubricants in tribological systems.
Readership/Target Audience: Aimed at chemical and lubricants engineers.
ADVERTISING RATES:
Full Page Mono £1175.00
Full Page Colour £2575.00
Agency Commission: 10%
Mechanical Data: Type Area: 230 170mm, Trim Size: 260 x 200mm, Col Length: 230mm, Page Width: 170mm
BUSINESS: ENGINEERING & MACHINERY

LUMINESCENCE
40119U55-66_50

Formerly: Journal of Bioluminescence & Chemiluminescence
Editorial Address: The Atrium, Southern Gate, CHICHESTER, PO19 8SQ **Tel:** 01243 779777
Fax: 01243 770437
Email: ptrevorr@wiley.com
Advertising Address: As above. **Fax:** 01243 770432
Email: fpidduck@wiley.co.uk
Web site: http://www.wiley.com
ISSN: 0884-3996
Publisher: John Wiley & Sons Ltd
Date Established: 1987
Frequency: 6 issues yearly
Cover Price: $1700.00
Circulation: 500 (Publisher's Statement)
Usual Pagination: 64
Editor: Paul Trevorrow
Summary of Content: Provides a forum for the publication of original scientific papers, short communications, technical notes and reviews on fundamental and applied aspects of all forms of luminescence.
Readership/Target Audience: Aimed at chemists, biochemists, clinical chemists and molecular biologists.
ADVERTISING RATES:
Full Page Mono £1175.00
Full Page Colour £2575.00
Agency Commission: 10%
Mechanical Data: Print Process: Sheet-fed litho, Film: Digital, Type Area: 254 x 180mm, Trim Size: 279 x 210mm, Col Length: 254mm, Page Width: 180mm
BUSINESS: APPLIED SCIENCE & LABORATORIES

LUXURY BRIEFING
39812U53-242

Formerly: Luxury Product & Service Briefing
Editorial Address: Coates House, Upper Largo, LEVEN, KY8 6JF **Tel:** 01333 360606 **Fax:** 01333 360607
Email: editorial@luxury-briefing.com
Web site: http://www.luxury-briefing.com
Publisher: Atlantic Publishing Company Ltd
Date Established: 1996
Frequency: 10 issues yearly - with two double issues
Annual Sub.: £395.00
Usual Pagination: 20
Editor: Catherine MacDonald-Keir; **Publisher:** James Ogilvy
Summary of Content: Magazine focusing on the luxury industry as a whole, as defined by the customer base, rather than the merchandise.
Readership/Target Audience: Read by luxury brands and those in surrounding industries including finance, property, marketing, advertising and PR.
ADVERTISING: No Advertising taken
BUSINESS: RETAILING & WHOLESALING

Business Magazines

Section 4 (b) Business Magazines

LUXURY MEETINGS
1864878U2C-524

Editorial Address: 22 Stephenson Way, LONDON, NW1 2HD **Tel:** 020 7380 3653
Email: jkeenan@luxury-meetings.com
Web site: http://www.luxury-meetings.com
Publisher: Big Publishing
Date Established: 2009
Frequency: 6 issues yearly
Circulation: 15,800 (Publisher's Statement)
Editor: John Keenan; **Managing Director:** Ned Dean
Summary of Content: Magazine looking at meeting destinations where readers actually place, or consider placing, their business.
Readership/Target Audience: Aimed at the buyers of luxury meetings and conferences throughout Europe.
ADVERTISING RATES:
Full Page Colour EUR6995.00
BUSINESS: COMMUNICATIONS, ADVERTISING & MARKETING: Conferences & Exhibitions

LUXURYFINANCE
1833004U1R-382

Editorial Address: 292 Vauxhall Bridge Road, LONDON, SW1V 1AE **Tel:** 020 7963 7680 **Fax:** 020 7963 7681
Email: anne-louise.fogtmann@pressassociation.co.uk
ISSN: 1352-6456
Publisher: PA Business
Date Established: 2008
Frequency: 11 issues yearly
Annual Sub.: £895.00
Usual Pagination: 36
Editor: Anne-Louise Fogtmann; **Managing Editor:** Oliver Cann
Summary of Content: Magazine covering leveraged buyouts, advisory appointments, mergers and acquisitions, project finance including ECA support, public and private placements of debt and equity, International business development opportunities, key joint ventures, IPO's and alliances and strategic stake sales.
Readership/Target Audience: Aimed at those interested in tracking competitor activity, forecasting market developments, identifying trends and forthcoming deals, establishing business contacts and discovering new business development opportunities.
BUSINESS: FINANCE & ECONOMICS: Financial Related

M&C REPORT
1640282U9A-253

Editorial Address: Broadfield Park, CRAWLEY, RH11 9RT
Tel: 01293 846549 **Fax:** 01293 846577
Email: mark.stretton@william-reed.co.uk
Web site: http://www.mcreport.com
Publisher: William Reed Business Media
Date Established: 1996
Frequency: Monthly
Annual Sub.: £485.00
Circulation: 500 (Publisher's Statement)
Editor: Mark Stretton; **News Editor:** Martyn Leek
Summary of Content: Newsletter covering business intelligence analysis for the licensed retail and leisure market.
Readership/Target Audience: Aimed at senior executives.
ADVERTISING: No Advertising taken
BUSINESS: DRINKS & LICENSED TRADE: Drinks, Licensed Trade, Wines & Spirits

M MAGAZINE
1927036U61-527

Editorial Address: Copyright House, 29-33 Berners Street, LONDON, W1T 3AB **Tel:** 020 7580 5544
Email: victoria.briggs@prsformusic.com
Web site: http://www.prsformusic.com
Publisher: Media 10
Date Established: 2005
Frequency: Quarterly
Free to qualifying individuals
Circulation: 50,000 (Publisher's Statement)
Usual Pagination: 60
Editor: Victoria Briggs
Summary of Content: Magazine covering music, featuring songwriter and composer profiles and interviews, music business news and issues.
Readership/Target Audience: Read by PRS for music members, songwriters, composers and music publishers.
BUSINESS: MUSIC TRADE

THE MAB BULLETIN
634808U64L-561

Formerly: The Bulletin
Editorial Address: 19 Heddon Street, LONDON, W1B 4BG
Tel: 020 7993 3833 **Fax:** 020 7437 4209
Email: mike@oneismore.com
Advertising Address: As above.
Email: katherineh@oneismore.com
Web site: http://www.oneismore.com
Publisher: One
Date Established: 1996

Frequency: 3 issues yearly - Published in April, August and November
Cover Price: Free
Circulation: 4,500 (Publisher's Statement)
Editor: Michael Dewar
Summary of Content: Magazine covering all aspects of the memorialisation industry.
Readership/Target Audience: Read by memorial masons, funeral directors and associated trades.
ADVERTISING: Rates on application
BUSINESS: OTHER CLASSIFICATIONS: Funeral Directors, Cemeteries & Crematoria

MACHINERY
37661U19F-385

Formerly: Machinery and Production Engineering
Editorial Address: Hawley Mill, Hawley Road, DARTFORD, DA2 7TJ **Tel:** 01322 221144 **Fax:** 01322 421549
Email: machinery@findlay.co.uk
Advertising Address: As above. **Fax:** 01322 221188
Email: jopitz@findlay.co.uk
Web site: http://www.machinery.co.uk
ISSN: 0024-919X
Publisher: Findlay Media Ltd
Date Established: 1912
Frequency: Monthly - Published around the 1st Friday of the cover month
Cover Price: £5.50
Free to qualifying individuals
Annual Sub.: £115.00
Circulation: 14,051 (ABC 01/01/2008 to 31/12/2008)
Usual Pagination: 68
Editor: Andrew Allcock
Summary of Content: Magazine covering new technology - machine tools, tooling, work holding, CADCAM - its development and applications. Also covering manufacturing business issues and the drivers that cause manufacturers to adopt new technology or working practices.
Readership/Target Audience: Aimed at production engineers, production managers and production directors in all companies plus managing directors in SME firms who have a more hands-on responsibility in terms of production matters.
ADVERTISING RATES:
Full Page Mono £2700.00
Full Page Colour £2700.00
SCC £30.00
Agency Commission: 10%
Mechanical Data: Page Width: 178mm, Type Area: 254 x 178mm, Bleed Size: 292 x 216mm, Trim Size: 286 x 210mm, No. of Columns (Display): 4, Film: Digital, Col Length: 254mm
Copy instructions: Copy Date: 10 days prior to publication date
Average advertising content per issue: 65%
BUSINESS: ENGINEERING & MACHINERY: Production & Mechanical Engineering

MACHINERY BUYERS' GUIDE
37648U19E-280

Editorial Address: Hawley Mill, Hawley Road, DARTFORD, DA2 7TJ **Tel:** 01322 221144 **Fax:** 01322 221188
Email: mbg@findlay.co.uk
Advertising Address: As above.
Email: mbg@findlay.co.uk
Web site: http://www.machinery.co.uk
ISSN: 0142-0658
Publisher: Findlay Media Ltd
Frequency: Annual - Published in May
Cover Price: £80.00
Circulation: 4,000 (Publisher's Statement)
Editor: Andrew Allcock; **Advertising Manager:** Stuart Tarrant
Summary of Content: Buyers' guide listing machine tools, production, mechanical engineering products, materials and contract manufacturing services.
Readership/Target Audience: Aimed at buyers of engineering equipment.
ADVERTISING RATES:
Full Page Mono £800.00
Full Page Colour £2500.00
Agency Commission: 10%
Mechanical Data: Type Area: 178 x 126mm, Trim Size: 210 x 145mm, Bleed Size: 216 x 149mm, Print Process: Offset litho, Film: Digital, Col Length: 178mm, Page Width: 126mm
Copy instructions: Copy Date: 6 weeks prior to publication date
Average advertising content per issue: 10%
BUSINESS: ENGINEERING & MACHINERY: Machinery, Machine Tools & Metalworking

MACHINERY CLASSIFIED
22525U19E-328

Editorial Address: Hawley Mill, Hawley Road, DARTFORD, DA2 7TJ **Tel:** 01322 221144 **Fax:** 01322 221188
Email: myclass@findlay.co.uk
Advertising Address: As above.
Email: myclass@findlay.co.uk
Web site: http://www.machineryclassified.co.uk
Publisher: Findlay Media Ltd

Frequency: Weekly
Free to qualifying individuals
Annual Sub.: £60.00
Circulation: 6,882 (ABC 01/01/2008 to 31/12/2008)
Editor: Andrew Allcock; **Publisher:** Peter Knutton
Summary of Content: Magazine covering new and used metalworking and associated machinery.
Readership/Target Audience: Aimed at purchasers of machine tools.
ADVERTISING RATES:
Full Page Colour £760.00
Agency Commission: 10%
Mechanical Data: Bleed Size: 296 x 216mm, Trim Size: 286 x 210mm, Film: Digital
Average advertising content per issue: 100%
BUSINESS: ENGINEERING & MACHINERY: Machinery, Machine Tools & Metalworking

MACHINERY CLASSIFIED INTERNATIONAL
37649U19E-330

Editorial Address: Hawley Mill, Hawley Road, DARTFORD, DA2 7TJ **Tel:** 01322 221144 **Fax:** 01322 221188
Email: myclass@findlay.co.uk
Advertising Address: As above. **Fax:** 01322 421548
Email: myclass@findlay.co.uk
Web site: http://www.mcworldwide.com
ISSN: 0953-9204
Publisher: Findlay Media Ltd
Date Established: 1994
Frequency: Quarterly
Circulation: 5,500 (Publisher's Statement)
Editor: Andrew Allcock; **Advertising Manager:** Fawad Minhas; **Publisher:** Peter Knutton
Summary of Content: Directory listing new and used machine tools for sale internationally.
Readership/Target Audience: Aimed at international machine tool dealers.
ADVERTISING RATES:
Full Page Colour £760.00
Agency Commission: 10%
Mechanical Data: Bleed Size: 292 x 216mm, Trim Size: 286 x 210mm, Page Width: 194mm, Col Length: 260mm, Film: Digital, Type Area: 260 x 194mm
Copy instructions: Copy Date: 1 week prior to publication date
Average advertising content per issue: 100%
BUSINESS: ENGINEERING & MACHINERY: Machinery, Machine Tools & Metalworking

MACHINERY MARKET
37556U19A-450

Editorial Address: Wadham House, 6 Blyth Road, BROMLEY, BR1 3RX **Tel:** 020 8460 4224
Fax: 020 8290 1668
Email: editorial@machinery-market.co.uk
Advertising Address: As above.
Email: advertising@machinery-market.co.uk
Web site: http://www.machinery-market.co.uk
ISSN: 0024-9211
Publisher: MM Publishing Ltd
Date Established: 1879
Frequency: Weekly
Cover Price: £2.25
Annual Sub.: £84.00
Circulation: 7,755 (ABC 01/01/2008 to 31/12/2008)
Usual Pagination: 80
Editor: Colin Granger; **News Editor:** Mark Green; **Advertising Manager:** Jean Young
Summary of Content: Publication focusing on general industrial plant and machine tools.
Readership/Target Audience: Aimed at machine tool users and other engineering equipment users.
ADVERTISING RATES:
Full Page Colour £715.00
SCC £6.60
Agency Commission: 10%
Mechanical Data: Film: Digital, Trim Size: 297 x 210mm, Type Area: 270 x 184mm, Col Length: 270mm, Print Process: Litho, Col Widths (Display): 45mm, Bleed Size: 303 x 216mm, Page Width: 184mm
Copy instructions: Copy Date: 2 weeks prior to publication date
Average advertising content per issue: 60%
BUSINESS: ENGINEERING & MACHINERY

MACHINERY TRADE INTERNATIONAL
1691333U19E-441

Editorial Address: Appleby House, Headley Road, LEATHERHEAD, KT22 8PT **Tel:** 01474 855505
Fax: 01372 373876
Email: enquiry@mti-online.com
Web site: http://www.mti-online.com
Publisher: MTI Ltd
Date Established: 2003
Frequency: Weekly
Free to qualifying individuals
Annual Sub.: £57.00

Circulation: 5,000 (ABC 01/01/2008 to 31/12/2008)
Editor: Steed Webzell
Summary of Content: Magazine covering the latest developments in global manufacturing, featuring news and used machine tool sales.
Readership/Target Audience: Aimed at dealers in machinery and machine tool buyers at manufacturing companies.
BUSINESS: ENGINEERING & MACHINERY: Machinery, Machine Tools & Metalworking

MACHINERY UPDATE
38677U35-65

Editorial Address: New Progress House, 34 Stafford Road, WALLINGTON, SM6 9AA **Tel:** 020 8773 8111
Fax: 020 8773 0022
Email: publishing@ppma.co.uk
Advertising Address: As above.
Email: publishing@ppma.co.uk
Web site: http://www.machineryupdate.co.uk
ISSN: 0969-4145
Publisher: PPMA Ltd
Date Established: 1989
Frequency: 6 issues yearly
Free to qualifying individuals
Annual Sub.: £35.00
Circulation: 9,000 (Publisher's Statement)
Editor: Janine Berriedale; **Advertising Manager:** David Chadd
Summary of Content: Journal of the Processing and Packaging Machinery Association.
Readership/Target Audience: Read by buyers and specifiers of processing and packaging machinery, senior engineers and design engineers and all member companies.
ADVERTISING RATES:
Full Page Mono £1070.00
Full Page Colour £1520.00
Agency Commission: 10%
Mechanical Data: Page Width: 180mm, Type Area: 270 x 180mm, Col Length: 270mm, Trim Size: 297 x 210mm, Bleed Size: 303 x 216mm, Film: Digital, Print Process: Sheet-fed litho
Average advertising content per issue: 45%
BUSINESS: PACKAGING & BOTTLING

MACHINERY WORLD
37646U19E-350

Editorial Address: 50 Queens Road, BUCKHURST HILL, IG9 5DD **Tel:** 020 8504 1661 **Fax:** 020 8505 4336
Email: machinery@sheenpublishing.co.uk
Advertising Address: As above.
Email: machinery@sheenpublishing.co.uk
Web site: http://www.sheenpublishing.co.uk
Publisher: Sheen Publishing Ltd
Date Established: 1982
Frequency: Monthly - Published around the 1st of the cover month
Cover Price: £3.50
Annual Sub.: £30.00
Circulation: 6,023 (Publisher's Statement)
Usual Pagination: 72
Editor: Carole Titmuss; **News Editor:** Pat Fairfax; **Features Editor:** Danielle Titmuss; **Managing Director:** Carole Titmuss; **Advertising Manager:** Tracy Chamberlain
Summary of Content: Magazine covering worldwide industry news, company profiles and product information.
Readership/Target Audience: Aimed at buyers and specifiers of new and used machinery in the UK, Western Europe and major developing countries.
ADVERTISING RATES:
Full Page Mono £420.00
Full Page Colour £520.00
Agency Commission: 10%
Mechanical Data: Film: Positive, right reading, emulsion side down, Type Area: 274 x 186mm, Bleed Size: 300 x 213mm, Trim Size: 297 x 210mm, Col Length: 274mm, Page Width: 186mm
Copy instructions: Copy Date: 20th of the month prior to publication date
BUSINESS: ENGINEERING & MACHINERY: Machinery, Machine Tools & Metalworking

MAGAZINE NEWS
35612U2B-60

Editorial Address: Queen's House, 28 Kingsway, LONDON, WC2B 6JR **Tel:** 020 7404 4166 **Fax:** 020 7404 4167
Email: hannah.trussell@ppa.co.uk
Advertising Address: As above. **Tel:** 020 7400 7519
Email: anne.ridyard@ppa.co.uk
Web site: http://www.ppa.co.uk
ISSN: 0956-9855
Publisher: PPA
Date Established: 1989
Frequency: Quarterly
Cover Price: Free
Circulation: 8,822 (Publisher's Statement)
Usual Pagination: 40
Editor: Hannnah Trussell

Summary of Content: Official magazine of the Periodical Publishers Association.
Readership/Target Audience: Aimed at publishers, media, marketing and advertising executives in the magazine publishing industry.
ADVERTISING RATES:
Full Page Colour £1584.00
Agency Commission: 10%
Mechanical Data: Film: Digital, Page Width: 187mm, Bleed Size: 302 x 215mm, Type Area: 273 x 187mm, Col Length: 273mm, Trim Size: 296 x 210mm
Copy instructions: Copy Date: 15th of the month prior to publication date
Average advertising content per issue: 40%
BUSINESS: COMMUNICATIONS, ADVERTISING & MARKETING: Press

MAGAZINE WORLD
35614U2B-65

Editorial Address: Queens House, 55-56 Lincoln's Inn Fields, LONDON, WC2A 3LJ **Tel:** 020 7404 4169
Fax: 020 7404 4170
Email: info@fipp.com
Advertising Address: As above.
Email: andrew@fipp.com
Web site: http://www.fipp.com
ISSN: 1359-1312
Publisher: FIPP
Date Established: 1998
Frequency: Quarterly
Free to qualifying individuals
Circulation: 6,000 (Publisher's Statement)
Usual Pagination: 52
Editor: Amy Duffin; **Advertising Manager:** Andrew Chidgey;
Publisher: Donald Kummerfeld
Summary of Content: Magazine of the International Federation of the Periodical Press (FIPP), reporting on changing magazine markets around the world. Features industry news, events, regional analysis and international commentary from specialist writers and leaders from media and business.
Readership/Target Audience: Read by publishers, editors, senior executives, national publishing associations, advertisers, agencies and executives.
ADVERTISING RATES:
Full Page Colour £1800.00
Agency Commission: 10%
Mechanical Data: Trim Size: 297 x 210mm, Type Area: 276 x 197mm, Bleed Size: 303 x 213mm, Film: Digital, Col Length: 276mm, Page Width: 197mm
Average advertising content per issue: 25%
BUSINESS: COMMUNICATIONS, ADVERTISING & MARKETING: Press

THE MAGISTRATE
39216U44-1440

Editorial Address: 1 Melbourne Road, NOTTINGHAM, NG2 5BG **Tel:** 01158 462040
Email: magistrate@ntlworld.com
Web site: http://www.magistrates-association.org.uk
Publisher: The Magistrates' Association
Date Established: 1920
Frequency: 10 issues yearly
Free to qualifying individuals
Annual Sub.: £28.00
Circulation: 30,000 (Publisher's Statement)
Usual Pagination: 32
Editor: Simon Hudson
Summary of Content: Official Journal of the Magistrates Association. Contents are intended to inform lay justices and others who work in the magistrates' courts in regard to law and practice.
Readership/Target Audience: Read by members, justice clerks, solicitors, probation officers and law school staff and students.
ADVERTISING: No Advertising taken
BUSINESS: LEGAL

MAIN EVENT
1698972U2C-511

Editorial Address: 47 Church Street, BARNSLEY, S70 2AS
Tel: 01226 734734 **Fax:** 01226 734705
Email: editorial@themaineventmagazine.co.uk
Advertising Address: As above. **Tel:** 01226 734456
Fax: 01226 734478
Email: sales@themaineventmagazine.co.uk
Web site: http://www.themaineventmagazine.co.uk
Publisher: Wharncliffe Publishing Ltd
Date Established: 2005
Frequency: Monthly - Published in the 1st week of the cover month
Free to qualifying individuals
Circulation: 15,000 (Publisher's Statement)
Editor: Andrew Harrod; **News Editor:** Nicola Hyde;
Advertising Manager: Paul Allott; **Group Editor:** Andrew Harrod
Summary of Content: Magazine focusing on all aspects of event management.
Readership/Target Audience: Aimed at event organisers.

ADVERTISING RATES:
Full Page Colour £1850.00
Agency Commission: 10%
Mechanical Data: Type Area: 320 x 220mm, Bleed Size: 346 x 246mm, Trim Size: 340 x 240mm, Col Length: 320mm, Page Width: 220mm, Film: Digital
Copy instructions: Copy Date: 1 week prior to publication date
Average advertising content per issue: 50%
BUSINESS: COMMUNICATIONS, ADVERTISING & MARKETING: Conferences & Exhibitions

MAINTENANCE AND ENGINEERING
704416U19F-246

Formerly: Industrial Maintenance and Engineering
Editorial Address: Monks Hill, Tilford, FARNHAM, GU10 2AJ **Tel:** 01252 783111
Email: info@maintenanceonline.co.uk
Advertising Address: As above. **Fax:** 01252 783143
Email: darrell@maintenanceonline.co.uk
Web site: http://www.maintenanceonline.co.uk
ISSN: 1472-9482
Publisher: Conference Communication
Date Established: 2001
Frequency: 6 issues yearly - Published at the end of the cover month
Free to qualifying individuals
Annual Sub.: £99.00
Circulation: 13,204 (ABC 01/01/2008 to 31/12/2008)
Usual Pagination: 84
Editor: David Willson; **Managing Editor:** David Willson;
Publisher: David Willson
Summary of Content: Magazine covering international issues on the industrial maintenance of plant, equipment and buildings, energy and environment management, health, safety, training and education relevant to maintenance professionals in industry, commerce and the public sector.
Readership/Target Audience: Aimed at maintenance professionals, directors, plant, works, factory, site and facilities managers.
ADVERTISING RATES:
Full Page Colour £1250.00
Agency Commission: 10%
Mechanical Data: Type Area: 260 x 178mm, Bleed Size: 303 x 213mm, Trim Size: 297 x 210mm, Col Length: 260mm, Page Width: 178mm, Film: Digital
Copy instructions: Copy Date: 2 weeks prior to publication date
Average advertising content per issue: 70%
BUSINESS: ENGINEERING & MACHINERY: Production & Mechanical Engineering

MAINTENANCE & EQUIPMENT NEWS FOR CHURCHES AND SCHOOLS
41178U62K-700

Editorial Address: PO Box 249, ASCOT, SL5 0BZ
Tel: 01344 459528 **Fax:** 01344 862569
Email: crownwood@btconnect.com
Advertising Address: As above.
Email: crownwood@btconnect.com
Web site: http://www.cwponline.com
Publisher: Crown Wood Publications Ltd
Date Established: 1959
Frequency: Quarterly
Free to qualifying individuals
Annual Sub.: £10.00
Circulation: 18,500 (Publisher's Statement)
Usual Pagination: 48
Editor: Christine Stevens; **Advertising Manager:** Madeline Whitney; **Publisher:** Madeline Whitney
Summary of Content: Magazine covering building, renovation, equipment, building contents, cleaning, heating, furnishings, lighting and landscaping for churches and church schools.
Readership/Target Audience: Aimed at church and diocesan advisory committees, theological colleges, churches, public and private schools, the Salvation Army and architects.
ADVERTISING RATES:
Full Page Mono £1165.00
Full Page Colour £1165.00
SCC £60.00
Agency Commission: 10%
Mechanical Data: Type Area: 188 x 134mm, Bleed Size: 217 x 155mm, Trim Size: 210 x 148mm, Print Process: Offset-litho, Film: Digital, Col Length: 188mm, Page Width: 134mm
Average advertising content per issue: 50%
BUSINESS: CHURCH & SCHOOL EQUIPMENT & EDUCATION: Church & School Equipment

MAKING MONEY
37115U14H-68

Formerly: All About Making Money
Editorial Address: 49 Old Steine, BRIGHTON, BN1 1NH
Tel: 01273 748675
Email: mmedit@partridgeltd.co.uk

Section 4 (b) Business Magazines

Advertising Address: Gloucester House, Gloucester Mews, South Street, EASTBOURNE, BN21 4XH **Tel:** 01323 636000 **Fax:** 01323 646144
Email: neil@partridgeltd.co.uk
Web site: http://www.makingmoney.co.uk
ISSN: 1366-2295
Publisher: Partridge Publications
Date Established: 1996
Frequency: Monthly - Published on the 3rd Friday of the month
Cover Price: £2.75
Annual Sub.: £17.50
Circulation: 25,000 (Publisher's Statement)
Usual Pagination: 100
Editor: Jeff James; **Group Editor:** Ted Rowe; **Publisher:** Matthew Tudor
Summary of Content: Magazine covering high street franchising through to network marketing with advice on finance, taxation and the law and small business technology.
Readership/Target Audience: Aimed at those looking to work for themselves.
ADVERTISING RATES:
Full Page Mono £2595.00
Full Page Colour £2595.00
Agency Commission: 10%
Mechanical Data: Type Area: 270 x 183mm, Bleed Size: 303 x 216mm, Trim Size: 297 x 210mm, No. of Columns (Display): 4, Film: Digital, Col Length: 270mm, Page Width: 183mm
Copy instructions: Copy Date: 3 weeks prior to publication date
Average advertising content per issue: 35%
BUSINESS: COMMERCE, INDUSTRY & MANAGEMENT: Small Business

MANAGEMENT CONSULTANTS NEWS
36783U14A-206

Editorial Address: Cavendish House, Cavendish Court, 44-47 Hill Avenue, AMERSHAM, HP6 5FA **Tel:** 0870 908 8767 **Fax:** 0870 134 0931
Email: editor@ncc.co.uk
Advertising Address: As above.
Web site: http://www.mconsultantsnews.com
ISSN: 1351-0894
Publisher: NCC (UK) Ltd
Date Established: 1989
Frequency: Quarterly
Free to qualifying individuals
Circulation: 11,000 (Publisher's Statement)
Usual Pagination: 4
Editor: Tim Ring; **Publisher:** Steve Markwell
Summary of Content: Publication containing news, trends and IT supplier updates.
Readership/Target Audience: Aimed at professional management consultants.
ADVERTISING: No Advertising taken
BUSINESS: COMMERCE, INDUSTRY & MANAGEMENT

MANAGEMENT IN PRACTICE
1750343U56R-522

Editorial Address: 1 St. John's Square, LONDON, EC1M 4PN **Tel:** 020 7214 0500 **Fax:** 020 7214 0501
Email: mip@campden.com
Advertising Address: As above. **Fax:** 020 7214 0586
Email: edwardburkle@campden.com
Web site: http://www.campden.com/mip
ISSN: 1747-9304
Publisher: Campden Publishing Ltd
Date Established: 2005
Frequency: Quarterly
Free to qualifying individuals
Circulation: 7,030 (ABC 01/01/2008 to 31/12/2008)
Usual Pagination: 60
Editor: Stuart Gidden; **Advertising Manager:** Edward Burkle; **Publisher:** Stephen Taylor
Summary of Content: Magazine covering news, features, reviews and views on all aspects of primary care practice management.
Readership/Target Audience: Aimed at primary care practice managers.
ADVERTISING RATES:
Full Page Mono £2950.00
Full Page Colour £2950.00
Agency Commission: 10%
Mechanical Data: Type Area: 277 x 190mm, Bleed Size: 303 x 216mm, Trim Size: 297 x 210mm, Col Length: 277mm, Page Width: 190mm, Film: Digital
Copy instructions: Copy Date: 3 weeks prior to publication date
Average advertising content per issue: 35%
BUSINESS: HEALTH & MEDICAL: Health Medical Related

MANAGEMENT LEARNING
37111U14F-45

Editorial Address: 1 Oliver's Yard, 55 City Road, LONDON, EC1Y 1SP **Tel:** 020 7324 8500 **Fax:** 020 7324 8600
Advertising Address: As above.
Email: sheena.karim@sagepub.co.uk

Web site: http://www.sagepub.co.uk/journal.aspx?pid=105708
ISSN: 1350-5076
Publisher: Sage Publications
Date Established: 1970
Frequency: 5 issues yearly
Annual Sub.: £51.00
Circulation: 500 (Publisher's Statement)
Usual Pagination: 128
Editor: Russ Vince; **Advertising Manager:** Sheena Karim
Summary of Content: Magazine concerned with issues of learning, change and development in organisations.
Readership/Target Audience: Aimed at educators, practitioners in organisational behaviour, organisational change and development, organisational psychology and human resource management.
ADVERTISING RATES:
Full Page Mono £500.00
Agency Commission: 5%
Mechanical Data: Col Length: 210mm, Page Width: 140mm, Type Area: 210 x 140mm
Copy instructions: Copy Date: 3 months prior to publication date
BUSINESS: COMMERCE, INDUSTRY & MANAGEMENT: Training & Recruitment

MANAGEMENT SERVICES
37022U14E-391

Editorial Address: Ewell House, Graveney Road, FAVERSHAM, ME13 8UP **Tel:** 01795 535468
Fax: 01795 535469
Email: editorial@msjournal.org.uk
Advertising Address: As above.
Email: ads@msjournal.org.uk
Web site: http://www.ims-productivity.com
ISSN: 0307-6768
Publisher: GTC
Date Established: 1946
Frequency: Quarterly
Cover Price: £4.00
Free to qualifying individuals
Annual Sub.: £15.00
Circulation: 4,000 (Publisher's Statement)
Usual Pagination: 44
Editor: Melanie Armstrong; **Advertising Manager:** Robert Aspin
Summary of Content: Official journal of the Institute of Management Services contains features on productivity improvement.
Readership/Target Audience: Read by members of the Institute and companies who subscribe.
ADVERTISING RATES:
Full Page Colour £540.00
SCC £14.00
Agency Commission: 10%
Mechanical Data: Col Length: 273mm, No. of Columns (Display): 4, Type Area: 273 x 186mm, Trim Size: 297 x 210mm, Bleed Size: 303 x 216mm, Film: Digital, Page Width: 186mm
Copy instructions: Copy Date: 25th of month prior to publication date
Average advertising content per issue: 10%
BUSINESS: COMMERCE, INDUSTRY & MANAGEMENT: Work Study

MANAGEMENT TODAY
36784U14A-210

Editorial Address: 174 Hammersmith Road, LONDON, W6 7JP **Tel:** 020 8267 4610 **Fax:** 020 8267 4976
Email: editorial@mtmagazine.co.uk
Advertising Address: As above. **Tel:** 020 8267 5000
Email: charlie.brewer@haymarket.com
Web site: http://www.managementtoday.com
ISSN: 0025-1925
Publisher: Haymarket Brand Media
Date Established: 1966
Frequency: Monthly
Cover Price: £3.90
Free to qualifying individuals
Annual Sub.: £46.80
Circulation: 100,016 (ABC 01/07/2008 to 30/06/2009)
Usual Pagination: 110
Editor: Matthew Gwyther; **Managing Director:** Martin Durham
Summary of Content: Publication covering features on modern business practice and trends.
Twitter: https://twitter.com/managementtoday.
Readership/Target Audience: Aimed at general management.
ADVERTISING RATES:
Full Page Colour £11600.00
Agency Commission: 15%
Mechanical Data: Page Width: 185mm, Film: Digital, Type Area: 245 x 185mm, Col Length: 245mm, Trim Size: 275 x 215mm, Bleed Size: 281 x 218mm
Copy instructions: Copy Date: Middle of the month prior to publication date
BUSINESS: COMMERCE, INDUSTRY & MANAGEMENT

MANAGER - THE INSTITUTE OF ADMINISTRATIVE MANAGEMENT
36786U14A-214_25

Formerly: Manager-The British Journal of Administrative Management
Editorial Address: PR by email only **Tel:** 020 7091 2600 **Fax:** 020 7091 2619
Email: roy.bass@ntlworld.com
Advertising Address: 6 Graphite Square, Vauxhall Walk, LONDON, SE11 5EE **Tel:** 020 7091 2600
Fax: 020 7091 2619
Email: richard.jane@instam.org
Web site: http://www.instam.org
ISSN: 1746-1278
Publisher: Method UK Ltd
Date Established: 1967
Frequency: Quarterly
Annual Sub.: £60.00
Circulation: 12,000 (Publisher's Statement)
Usual Pagination: 36
Editor: Roy Bass; **Advertising Manager:** Richard Jane
Summary of Content: Journal designed to promote and develop, for the public benefit, the science of administrative management.
Readership/Target Audience: Aimed at directors, managers and assistants of administration operations.
ADVERTISING RATES:
Full Page Colour £1250.00
Agency Commission: 10%
Mechanical Data: Trim Size: 297 x 210mm, Type Area: 275 x 190mm, Bleed Size: 303 x 216mm, Col Length: 275mm, Page Width: 190mm, Film: Digital
Copy instructions: Copy Date: 3 weeks prior to publication date
BUSINESS: COMMERCE, INDUSTRY & MANAGEMENT

MANAGING GROWTH
1824301U14R-510

Editorial Address: 134 Liverpool Road, LONDON, N1 1LA **Tel:** 020 7665 1111 **Fax:** 020 7609 5837
Email: editorial@cwcomms.com
Advertising Address: As above.
Email: andy.roberts@cwcomms.com
Web site: http://www.managinggrowth.net
Publisher: CW Publishing Group
Date Established: 2008
Frequency: Half-yearly - Published in March and October
Cover Price: Free
Circulation: 10,000 (Print Run)
Usual Pagination: 160
Editor: Trisha Doyle; **Advertising Manager:** Sema Demir
Summary of Content: Magazine giving advice on risk management, cash flow, corporate finance, human resources, taxation and business travel.
Readership/Target Audience: Aimed at business customers of PC World.
ADVERTISING: Rates on application
BUSINESS: COMMERCE, INDUSTRY & MANAGEMENT: Commerce Related

MANAGING INFORMATION
40870U60B-70

Editorial Address: The Holywell Centre, 1 Phipp Street, LONDON, EC2A 4PS **Tel:** 020 7253 3349
Fax: 020 7613 5080
Email: news@aslib.com
Advertising Address: Suite 2.1, 30 Queen Charlotte Street, BRISTOL, BS1 4HJ **Tel:** 0117 904 1283 **Fax:** 0117 904 0085
Email: nick.gaulton@dpmedia.co.uk
Web site: http://www.managinginformation.com
ISSN: 1352-0229
Publisher: ASLIB - Association for Information Management
Date Established: 1993
Frequency: 10 issues yearly - Published on the 1st Monday of the cover month
Free to qualifying individuals
Annual Sub.: £129.00
Circulation: 10,000 (Publisher's Statement)
Usual Pagination: 60
Editor: Graham Coult
Summary of Content: Magazine containing articles on all aspects of information and knowledge management, including electronic sources. Provides coverage of industry news and European Commission projects.
Readership/Target Audience: Aimed at people involved, or with an interest in, information and knowledge management around the world.
ADVERTISING RATES:
Full Page Colour £1700.00
Agency Commission: 10%
Mechanical Data: Trim Size: 297 x 210mm, Bleed Size: +3mm, Type Area: 265 x 178mm, Col Length: 265mm, Page Width: 178mm, Film: Digital
Copy instructions: Copy Date: 10th of the month prior to publication date
Average advertising content per issue: 50%
BUSINESS: PUBLISHING: Libraries

MANAGING INTELLECTUAL PROPERTY
39217U44-1460

Editorial Address: Nestor House, Playhouse Yard, LONDON, EC4V 5EX **Tel:** 020 7779 8685
Fax: 020 7779 8500
Email: jnurton@managingip.com
Advertising Address: As above. **Tel:** 020 7779 8888
Email: ajawad@managingip.com
Web site: http://www.managingip.com
ISSN: 0960-5002
Publisher: Euromoney Institutional Investor plc
Date Established: 1990
Frequency: 10 issues yearly - Published in the 1st week of the month. Double issues in July/August and December/January
Annual Sub.: £472.00
Circulation: 12,000 (Publisher's Statement)
Usual Pagination: 84
Editor: James Nurton; **Advertising Manager:** Ali Jawad; **Managing Editor:** James Nurton
Summary of Content: Magazine covering international patents, licensing, and trademark law as it applies to international corporations and their advisers.
Readership/Target Audience: Aimed at lawyers working in-house for multinational companies, senior intellectual property lawyers in private practice, trademark and patent agencies, government agencies and rights administration societies.
ADVERTISING RATES:
Full Page Mono EUR4205.00
Full Page Colour EUR5165.00
Agency Commission: 10%
Mechanical Data: Type Area: 255 x 217mm, Bleed Size: 303 x 216mm, Trim Size: 297 x 210mm, Col Length: 255mm, Page Width: 217mm, Film: Digital
Copy instructions: Copy Date: 15th of the month prior to publication date
Average advertising content per issue: 30%
Supplement(s): IP Contacts Yearbook - 1xY, IP Litigation Yearbook - 1xY, Patent Yearbook - 1xY, Trade Mark Yearbook - 1xY
BUSINESS: LEGAL

MANAGING PARTNER
26066U14A-217

Editorial Address: 266-276 Upper Richmond Road, Putney, LONDON, SW15 6TQ **Tel:** 020 8785 2700
Fax: 020 8785 9373
Email: rbrent@ark-group.com
Advertising Address: As above.
Email: jadams@ark-group.com
Web site: http://www.mpmagazine.com
ISSN: 1462-5571
Publisher: Ark Group Ltd
Date Established: 1998
Frequency: 10 issues yearly - Double issues July/August and December/January
Annual Sub.: £395.00
Circulation: 2,500 (Publisher's Statement)
Usual Pagination: 48
Editor: Richard Brent
Summary of Content: Journal covering strategic practice management in legal and accountancy firms. Article topics include e-commerce, risk management, change management, profitability, globalisation, CRM and culture.
Readership/Target Audience: Aimed at senior level management within law firms and those whose primary responsibility is the management of professional services firms.
ADVERTISING RATES:
Full Page Colour £1599.00
Agency Commission: 10%
Mechanical Data: Type Area: 267 x 180mm, Col Length: 267mm, Trim Size: 297 x 210mm, Bleed Size: 303 x 216mm, Film: Digital, Page Width: 180mm
Copy instructions: Copy Date: 10th of the month prior to publication date
Average advertising content per issue: 30%
BUSINESS: COMMERCE, INDUSTRY & MANAGEMENT

MANAGING RISK
758403U5R-41

Formerly: Cyber-Risks News
Editorial Address: 24 Carmarthen Way, RUSHDEN, NN10 0TN **Tel:** 01933 316488 **Fax:** 01933 316488
Email: RupertKendrick@aol.com
Advertising Address: As above.
Email: rupert@web4law.biz
Web site: http://www.web4law.biz
Publisher: Web4Law Ltd
Date Established: 2002
Frequency: Quarterly
Free to qualifying individuals
Annual Sub.: £25.00
Circulation: 500 (Publisher's Statement)
Usual Pagination: 16
Editor: Rupert Kendrick; **Advertising Manager:** Rupert Kendrick
Summary of Content: Quarterly magazine focusing on law firm risk management.

Readership/Target Audience: Aimed at lawyers, IT security solution providers, conference providers, events promoters, publishers, practice managers and risk managers.
ADVERTISING: Rates on application
Mechanical Data: Bleed Size: 303 x 216mm, Trim Size: 297 x 210mm, Film: Digital, No. of Columns (Display): 3
BUSINESS: COMPUTERS & AUTOMATION: Computers Related

THE MANCHESTER TEACHER
41068U62B-520

Editorial Address: NUT Office, Rackhouse Primary School, Yarmouth Drive, MANCHESTER, M23 0BT
Tel: 0161 945 5061 **Fax:** 0161 945 5061
Email: mtanut@tiscali.co.uk
Publisher: Manchester Teachers Association
Date Established: 1960
Frequency: Quarterly
Cover Price: Free
Circulation: 2,800 (Publisher's Statement)
Editor: George Strachan
Summary of Content: Newsletter of the National Union of Teachers in Manchester.
Readership/Target Audience: Aimed at N.U.T. members, serving and retired teachers, schools and other educational establishments in Manchester.
ADVERTISING: No Advertising taken
BUSINESS: CHURCH & SCHOOL EQUIPMENT & EDUCATION: Education Teachers

THE MANUFACTURER
36909U14B-250

Editorial Address: Elizabeth House, Block 2, Part 7th Floor, 39 York Road, LONDON, SE1 7NJ **Tel:** 020 7401 6033
Email: press@sayonemedia.com
Advertising Address: Britannia House, 45-53 Prince of Wales Road, NORWICH, NR1 1BL **Tel:** 01603 671300
Fax: 01603 618758
Email: m.chilton@sayonemedia.com
Web site: http://www.themanufacturer.com/uk
Publisher: SayOne Media
Date Established: 1998
Frequency: Monthly - Published in the 1st week of each month
Cover Price: £6.00
Free to qualifying individuals
Circulation: 16,216 (Publisher's Statement)
Usual Pagination: 128
Editor: Will Stirling; **Advertising Manager:** Matt Chilton
Summary of Content: Magazine containing national, corporate and legal manufacturing management, executive interview and coverage of manufacturing management issues in leadership and strategy, design and innovation, world class manufacturing, skills and productivity, information technology in manufacturing, logistics and supply chain and operations maintenance.
Readership/Target Audience: Aimed at board and management.
ADVERTISING RATES:
Full Page Colour £3495.00
Mechanical Data: Page Width: 178mm, Type Area: 271 x 178mm, Col Length: 271mm, Trim Size: 297 x 210mm, Film: Digital, Bleed Size: 303 x 216mm
Copy instructions: Copy Date: 3 weeks prior to publication date
Supplement(s): Materials Handling Today - 6xY
BUSINESS: COMMERCE, INDUSTRY & MANAGEMENT: Industry & Factories

MANUFACTURING AND LOGISTICS IT
36108U5B-100

Editorial Address: Latimer House, 189 High Street, POTTERS BAR, EN6 5DA **Tel:** 01707 664200
Fax: 01707 664800
Email: editor@ibcpub.com
Advertising Address: As above.
Email: dean@logisticsit.com
Web site: http://www.logisticsit.com
ISSN: 1463-1172
Publisher: Interactive Business Communications Ltd
Date Established: 1998
Frequency: 5 issues yearly
Cover Price: Free
Circulation: 10,000 (Publisher's Statement)
Usual Pagination: 72
Editor: Ed Holden; **Advertising Manager:** Dean Taylor
Summary of Content: Pan European magazine covering the use of IT throughout the supply chain, from raw materials to checkout. Covers articles on manufacturing and logistics software, automatic data capture and supply chain management.
Readership/Target Audience: Aimed mainly at IT managers in manufacturing, warehousing and the distribution industry.
ADVERTISING RATES:
Full Page Mono £3950.00
Full Page Colour £3950.00
Agency Commission: 10%

Mechanical Data: Page Width: 178mm, Trim Size: 297 x 210mm, Type Area: 254 x 178mm, Col Length: 254mm, Film: Digital, Bleed Size: 303 x 216mm
Copy instructions: Copy Date: 2 weeks prior to publication date
Average advertising content per issue: 40%
BUSINESS: COMPUTERS & AUTOMATION: Data Processing

MANUFACTURING CHEMIST
36676U13-110

Editorial Address: Paulton House, 8 Shepherdess Walk, LONDON, N1 7LB **Tel:** 020 7490 0049 **Fax:** 020 7549 8622
Email: hilarya@hpcimedia.com
Advertising Address: 6-14 Underwood Street, LONDON, N1 7JQ **Tel:** 020 7549 8719 **Fax:** 020 7566 5794
Email: kwaterfall@wilmington.co.uk
Web site: http://www.manufacturingchemist.com
ISSN: 0262-4230
Publisher: HPCi Media Ltd
Frequency: 10 issues yearly - Published in the 1st week of the cover month
Annual Sub.: £121.00
Circulation: 7,158 (ABC 01/01/2007 to 31/12/2007)
Editor: Hilary Ayshford; **Managing Editor:** Hilary Ayshford
Summary of Content: Magazine covering all aspects of the pharmaceutical industry, including development, formulation, processing and outsourcing.
Readership/Target Audience: Aimed at manufacturers of pharmaceuticals.
ADVERTISING RATES:
Full Page Mono £1650.00
Full Page Colour £2060.00
Agency Commission: 10%
Mechanical Data: Type Area: 254 x 178mm, Bleed Size: 292 x 216mm, Trim Size: 286 x 210mm, Film: Digital, Col Length: 254mm, Page Width: 178mm
Copy instructions: Copy Date: 2 weeks prior to publication date
Average advertising content per issue: 50%
BUSINESS: CHEMICALS

MANUFACTURING TODAY EUROPE
1638545U19F-674

Editorial Address: Unit 10, Cringleford Business Centre, Intwood Road, Cringleford, NORWICH, NR4 6AU
Tel: 01603 274130 **Fax:** 01603 274136
Email: libbie@schofieldpublishing.co.uk
Advertising Address: As above. **Fax:** 01603 274131
Email: mtulloch@schofieldpublishing.co.uk
Web site: http://www.schofield-media.com
Publisher: Schofield Publishing Ltd
Date Established: 2003
Frequency: 6 issues yearly - Published at the end of the cover month
Free to qualifying individuals
Circulation: 10,000 (Publisher's Statement)
Usual Pagination: 104
Editor: Libbie Hammond; **Advertising Manager:** Mike Tulloch
Summary of Content: Magazine covering best practice across the manufacturing industry. Includes articles on logistics, information technology, machine tool technology, case studies, interviews and news.
Readership/Target Audience: Aimed at top level management within the manufacturing industry in Europe.
ADVERTISING: Rates on application
Copy instructions: Copy Date: 2 weeks prior to publication date
BUSINESS: ENGINEERING & MACHINERY: Production & Mechanical Engineering

MARINA WORLD
1827154U45R-377

Editorial Address: 3 Brownlow Road, REDHILL, RH1 6AW
Tel: 01737 769175 **Fax:** 01737 773241
Email: carolfulford@marinaworld.com
Advertising Address: As above.
Email: juliahallam@marinaworld.co.uk
Web site: http://www.marinaworld.com
ISSN: 1471-5856
Publisher: Loud & Clear Publishing Ltd
Date Established: 2000
Frequency: 6 issues yearly
Free to qualifying individuals
Annual Sub.: £40.00
Circulation: 6,743 (ABC 01/07/2008 to 30/06/2009)
Editor: Carol Fulford; **Advertising Manager:** Julia Hallam
Summary of Content: Magazine featuring news led coverage on new marina developments, emerging marina markets and marinas around the world.
Readership/Target Audience: Aimed at marina planners, owners, managers and developers, equipment suppliers, key marine associations, municipal authorities developing waterfronts worldwide and marina service providers.
ADVERTISING RATES:
Full Page Colour £1840.00

Mechanical Data: Bleed Size: 432 x 303mm, Trim Size: 297 x 210mm, Film: Digital
BUSINESS: MARINE & SHIPPING: Marine Related

MARINE & PORTS REVIEW 1615571U45R-371

Editorial Address: Trelawney House, Chestergate, MACCLESFIELD, SK11 6DW **Tel:** 01625 613000
Fax: 01625 435078
Email: marie.roberts@tenalpspublishing.com
Web site: http://www.tenalpspublishing.com
Publisher: Ten Alps Publishing
Date Established: 2001
Frequency: Annual - Published in December
Free to qualifying individuals
Annual Sub.: £25.00
Usual Pagination: 80
Editor: Marie Roberts
Summary of Content: Publication covering a range of topics including port expansion and development as well as articles concerning topical issues within the industry.
Readership/Target Audience: Aimed at those working in and servicing the marine and ports industries.
ADVERTISING: No Advertising taken
BUSINESS: MARINE & SHIPPING: Marine Related

MARINE CONSERVATION 40674U57-36_60

Editorial Address: Unit 3, Wolf Business Park, ROSS-ON-WYE, HR9 5NB **Tel:** 01989 566017 **Fax:** 01989 567815
Email: info@mcsuk.org
Advertising Address: As above.
Email: info@mcsuk.org
Web site: http://www.mcsuk.org
ISSN: 0268-7666
Publisher: The Marine Conservation Society
Date Established: 1983
Frequency: Quarterly
Annual Sub.: £25.00
Circulation: 5,500 (Publisher's Statement)
Usual Pagination: 32
Editor: Richard Harrington; **Advertising Manager:** Richard Harrington
Summary of Content: Official magazine of the Marine Conservation Society, featuring articles on habitat and species conservation, education and project news.
Readership/Target Audience: Aimed at members of the Marine Conservation Society.
ADVERTISING RATES:
Full Page Colour £760.00
Mechanical Data: Type Area: 270 x 190mm, No. of Columns (Display): 2, Col Widths (Display): 90mm, Col Length: 270mm, Page Width: 190mm
Average advertising content per issue: 20%
BUSINESS: ENVIRONMENT & POLLUTION

MARINE PROPULSION & AUXILIARY MACHINERY

Editorial Address: 19 Rectory Green, BECKENHAM, BR3 4HX **Tel:** 020 8650 1573
Email: doug.woodyard@btconnect.com
Advertising Address: Mitre House, 66 Abbey Road, ENFIELD, EN1 2QN **Tel:** 020 8370 7013 **Fax:** 020 8364 1331
Email: john.labdon@rivieramm.com
Web site: http://www.mpropulsion.com
ISSN: 1742-2825
Publisher: Riviera Maritime Media
Frequency: 6 issues yearly - Published on the 10th of the 2nd cover month
Free to qualifying individuals
Circulation: 13,519 (ABC 01/01/2008 to 31/12/2008)
Editor: Doug Woodyard
Summary of Content: Magazine covering the latest developments in marine propulsion systems and auxiliary shipboard machinery.
Readership/Target Audience: Aimed at maritime engineers, ship operators, naval architects and consultants.
ADVERTISING RATES:
Full Page Colour £2365.00
Agency Commission: 10%
Mechanical Data: Type Area: 277 x 190mm, Bleed Size: 303 x 216mm, Trim Size: 297 x 210mm, Col Length: 277mm, Page Width: 190mm, Film: Digital
Copy instructions: Copy Date: 20th of the month prior to publication date
Average advertising content per issue: 40%
BUSINESS: MARINE & SHIPPING: Marine Engineering Equipment

THE MARINE SCIENTIST 1622487U45R-373

Editorial Address: 80 Coleman Street, LONDON, EC2R 5BJ
Tel: 020 7382 2600 **Fax:** 020 7382 2669
Email: john.butchers@imarest.org
Advertising Address: As above.
Email: alwyn.topliss@imarest.org
Web site: http://www.imarest.org
ISSN: 1478-1328

Publisher: IMarEST
Date Established: 2002
Frequency: Quarterly - Published on the 1st of the cover month
Annual Sub.: £40.00
Circulation: 4,500 (Publisher's Statement)
Usual Pagination: 56
Editor: John Butchers; **Publisher:** John Butchers
Summary of Content: Journal covering world news of hydrography, oceanography, metoceanology, fish conservation, ocean species and subsea developments. Also covers marine research and technology, marine conservation, marine renewables, marine environment and marine science conferences reports. Includes interviews with prominent marine scientists.
Readership/Target Audience: Aimed at marine science academics and students and all those interested in the 'deep blue' and technology disciplines including oceanographers, marine biologists, marine geologists, hydrographers and ecologists.
ADVERTISING RATES:
Full Page Mono £1210.00
Full Page Colour £1750.00
SCC £27.00
Agency Commission: 15%
Mechanical Data: Type Area: 280 x 195mm, Bleed Size: 307 x 220mm, Trim Size: 297 x 210mm, Col Length: 280mm, Page Width: 195mm, Film: Digital
Copy instructions: Copy Date: 22nd of the month prior to publication date
Average advertising content per issue: 45%
BUSINESS: MARINE & SHIPPING: Marine Related

MARINE TECHNOLOGY REPORTER
1743065U45D-408

Editorial Address: 12 Braehead, BO'NESS, EH51 0BZ
Tel: 01506 822240
Email: tony.r.stein@btinternet.com
Advertising Address: 215 NW 3rd Street, Boynton Beach, FLORIDA 33435 **Tel:** 561 732 4368 **Fax:** 561 732 6984
Email: howard@marinelink.com
Web site: http://www.seadiscovery.com
Publisher: New Wave Media Inc
Date Established: 2006
Frequency: 9 issues yearly - Published around the middle of the cover month
Free to qualifying individuals
Circulation: 22,529 (BPA Worldwide 01/01/2007 to 30/06/2007)
Usual Pagination: 56
Editor: Tony Stein
Summary of Content: Magazine covering the latest news, discoveries and technology in the fields of oceanography, hydrography, marine sciences, offshore drilling, underwater exploration and survey, diving, construction and undersea defence.
Readership/Target Audience: Aimed at business executives, technical personnel in industry, government and education as well as scientists and engineers who are actively engaged in the fields of oceanography, marine science, underwater exploration, offshore oil production, port and harbour security, diving and construction.
ADVERTISING RATES:
Full Page Mono $2784.00
Full Page Colour $3764.00
Agency Commission: 15%
Mechanical Data: Type Area: 270 x 206mm, Bleed Size: 283 x 219mm, Trim Size: 276 x 213mm, Col Length: 270mm, Page Width: 206mm, Film: Digital
BUSINESS: MARINE & SHIPPING: Marine Engineering Equipment

MARINE TRADER 39336U45A-86

Editorial Address: East Bridge House, East Street, COLCHESTER, CO1 2TX **Tel:** 01206 798900
Fax: 01206 798909
Email: info@impa.net
Advertising Address: As above.
Email: info@impa.net
Web site: http://www.impa.net
ISSN: 1027-0914
Publisher: International Marine Purchasing Association
Date Established: 1970
Frequency: 6 issues yearly
Free to qualifying individuals
Circulation: 2,000 (Publisher's Statement)
Usual Pagination: 40
Editor: Michael Bilonick; **Advertising Manager:** Michael Bilonick
Summary of Content: Journal of the International Marine Purchasing Association. Covers many aspects of the marine industry but with an emphasis on marine purchasing.
Readership/Target Audience: Read by members of the International Marine Purchasing Association.
ADVERTISING RATES:
Full Page Colour £1780.00
Agency Commission: 10%

Mechanical Data: Bleed Size: 303 x 216mm, Trim Size: 297 x 210mm, Film: Digital
Copy instructions: Copy Date: 24th of the month prior to publication date
Average advertising content per issue: 25%
BUSINESS: MARINE & SHIPPING

MARITIME CONTRACTS JOURNAL
23830U45A-88

Editorial Address: Maritime Centre, F5 Northney Marina, HAYLING ISLAND, PO11 0NH **Tel:** 023 9246 0111
Fax: 023 9246 0123
Email: editor@maritimecontracts.com
Web site: http://www.maritimecontracts.com
ISSN: 1466-9226
Publisher: Maritime Intelligence Ltd
Date Established: 1994
Frequency: 46 issues yearly
Annual Sub.: £480.00
Usual Pagination: 16
Editor: Peter Moth; **Publisher:** Peter Moth
Summary of Content: Business-to-business bulletin containing up to date information on business opportunities, invitations to tender and contracts covering the entire maritime sector.
Readership/Target Audience: Aimed at marine service and equipment providers and manufacturers, marine civil engineering contractors and those engaged in port, harbour and coastal areas of operation.
ADVERTISING: No Advertising taken
BUSINESS: MARINE & SHIPPING

MARITIME IT & ELECTRONICS 768460U45A-502

Editorial Address: 80 Coleman Street, LONDON, EC2R 5BJ
Tel: 020 7382 2600 **Fax:** 020 7382 2669
Email: bonita.nightingale@imarest.org
Advertising Address: As above.
Email: alwyn.topliss@imarest.org
Web site: http://www.imarest.org
ISSN: 1476-6027
Publisher: IMarEST
Date Established: 2002
Frequency: 5 issues yearly
Usual Pagination: 36
Editor: Bonita Nightingale; **Advertising Manager:** Alwyn Topliss
Summary of Content: Journal covering marine electronics and IT. Features include marine software/hardware, communications, navigation systems, machinery and systems control, monitoring and diagnostics, expert systems and computer-aided design and manufacture.
Language(s): Chinese; English; Japanese
Readership/Target Audience: Aimed at marine professionals interested in marine systems operation via hardware and software.
ADVERTISING RATES:
Full Page Colour £2705.00
Agency Commission: 10%
Mechanical Data: Type Area: 280 x 195mm, Col Length: 280mm, Print Process: Litho, Film: Negative, right reading, emulsion side down. Digital, Bleed Size: 307 x 220mm, Trim Size: 297 x 210mm, Col Widths (Display): 45mm, Page Width: 195mm
Copy instructions: Copy Date: 15th of the month prior to publication date
Average advertising content per issue: 40%
Supplement to: Shipping World & Shipbuilder
BUSINESS: MARINE & SHIPPING

MARITIME JOURNAL 39337U45A-90

Editorial Address: The Old Mill, Lower Quay, FAREHAM, PO16 0RA **Tel:** 01329 828335 **Fax:** 01329 825330
Email: editor@maritimejournal.com
Advertising Address: As above.
Email: lstewart@mercatormedia.com
Web site: http://www.maritimejournal.com
ISSN: 0957-7009
Publisher: Mercator Media Ltd
Date Established: 1987
Frequency: Monthly - Published in the 3rd week of the cover month
Free to qualifying individuals
Annual Sub.: £63.50
Circulation: 6,141 (ABC 01/01/2008 to 31/12/2008)
Usual Pagination: 100
Editor: Larz Bourne; **Managing Director:** Andrew Webster
Summary of Content: Magazine dedicated to the European, in-shore, off-shore coastal zone and short sea commercial maritime business.
Readership/Target Audience: Read mainly by ship owners, directors and proprietors as well as marine managers, harbour masters, operations managers, engineering and technical managers and general purchasing and sales staff.
ADVERTISING RATES:
Full Page Mono £1535.00
Full Page Colour £2050.00
Agency Commission: 10%

Mechanical Data: Trim Size: 297 x 210mm, Bleed Size: 303 x 216mm, Print Process: Web-fed offset litho, Film: Digital
Copy instructions: Copy Date: 4 weeks prior to publication date
Average advertising content per issue: 60%
BUSINESS: MARINE & SHIPPING

THE MARITIME PILOT
39343U45A-85

Formerly: The Marine Pilot
Editorial Address: Canterbury Gate House, Ash Road, SANDWICH, CT13 9HZ **Tel:** 01304 613020
Email: john@pilotmag.co.uk
Advertising Address: As above.
Email: john@pilotmag.co.uk
Web site: http://www.pilotmag.co.uk
Publisher: UKMPA
Date Established: 1884
Frequency: Quarterly
Free to qualifying individuals
Annual Sub.: £15.00
Circulation: 750 (Publisher's Statement)
Usual Pagination: 16
Editor: John Clandillon-Baker; **Advertising Manager:** John Clandillon-Baker
Summary of Content: Magazine of the United Kingdom Maritime Pilots Association. Covers news, features and items of interest to maritime pilots.
Readership/Target Audience: Read by working and retired marine pilots.
ADVERTISING RATES:
Full Page Mono £220.00
Mechanical Data: Trim Size: 297 x 210mm, Bleed Size: 303 x 216mm
Average advertising content per issue: 10%
BUSINESS: MARINE & SHIPPING

MARITIME REPORTER AND ENGINEERING NEWS
1640299U45A-504

Editorial Address: 12 Braehead, BO'NESS, EH51 0BZ
Tel: 01506 822240 **Fax:** 01506 822240
Email: tony.r.stein@btinternet.com
Advertising Address: As above.
Email: tony.r.stein@btinternet.com
Web site: http://www.marinelink.com
Publisher: New Wave Media Inc
Date Established: 1946
Frequency: Monthly - Published in the middle of the cover month
Free to qualifying individuals
Circulation: 38,004 (Publisher's Statement)
Usual Pagination: 66
Editor: Tony Stein; **Advertising Manager:** Tony Stein
Summary of Content: Magazine covering the commercial and naval maritime industry, vessel operations and management, offshore drilling operations, shipbuilding and repair, marine engineering, naval architecture and port authorities.
Readership/Target Audience: Aimed predominantly at shipowners, operators, management, marine superintendents, port captains, port engineers, naval architects, marine engineers, ship surveyors, project engineers and others employed aboard ships.
ADVERTISING RATES:
Full Page Mono $5277.00
Full Page Colour $6644.00
Agency Commission: 15%
Mechanical Data: Type Area: 305 x 241mm, Bleed Size: 353 x 283mm, Trim Size: 343 x 276mm, Film: Digital, Col Length: 305mm, Page Width: 241mm
Copy instructions: Copy Date: 4 weeks prior to publication date
Average advertising content per issue: 40%
BUSINESS: MARINE & SHIPPING

MARITIME RISK INTERNATIONAL
35156U1D-305

Formerly: P and I International
Editorial Address: Informa House, 30-32 Mortimer Street, LONDON, W1W 7RE **Tel:** 020 7017 4600
Fax: 020 7017 5274
Email: laura.brown@informa.com
Advertising Address: Telephone House, 69-77 Paul Street, LONDON, EC2A 4LQ **Tel:** 020 7017 4600
Fax: 020 7017 4098
Email: maxwell.harvey@informa.com
Web site: http://www.informalaw.com
ISSN: 0950-4044
Publisher: Informa PLC
Frequency: 10 issues yearly - Published on the 13th of the cover month
Annual Sub.: £763.13
Usual Pagination: 24
Editor: Laura Brown; **Advertising Manager:** Maxwell Harvey; **Publisher:** Victoria Ophield

Summary of Content: Magazine providing information and reports from around the world on legislation, case law, cargo, salvage and ship safety.
Readership/Target Audience: Aimed at people concerned with marine mutual insurance.
ADVERTISING RATES:
Full Page Mono £1400.00
Full Page Colour £1900.00
Mechanical Data: Film: Digital, Type Area: 240 x 170mm, Bleed Size: 297 x 210mm, Trim Size: 303 x 216mm, Col Length: 240mm, Page Width: 170mm
Copy instructions: Copy Date: 20th of the month prior to publication date
BUSINESS: FINANCE & ECONOMICS: Insurance

THE MARKET
35155U1D-287

Formerly: One Lime Street
Editorial Address: Walmour House, 296 Regent Street, LONDON, W1B 3AW **Tel:** 020 7016 2555
Fax: 020 7907 4820
Email: james@wardour.co.uk
Advertising Address: 24-30 Great Titchfield Street, LONDON, W1W 8BE
ISSN: 0969-7810
Publisher: Wardour Publishing and Design
Frequency: Quarterly
Circulation: 20,000 (Publisher's Statement)
Usual Pagination: 8
Editor: James Cash; **Managing Editor:** James Cash
Summary of Content: Journal focusing on insurance markets and new products. Includes information about Lloyds' syndicates.
Language(s): English; French; Italian
Readership/Target Audience: Aimed primarily at brokers across the world.
ADVERTISING: No Advertising taken
BUSINESS: FINANCE & ECONOMICS: Insurance

MARKET & MEDIAFACT POCKET BOOKS
601499U2A-109_32

Editorial Address: 24 Percy Street, LONDON, W1T 2BS
Tel: 020 7961 1196 **Fax:** 020 7961 1199
Email: publications@zenithoptimedia.com
Web site: http://www.zenithoptimedia.com
Publisher: Zenith Optimedia Group
Frequency: Annual - Published in November
Annual Sub.: £100.00
Usual Pagination: 250
Editor: Jonathan Barnard
Summary of Content: Pocket-sized books giving media statistics, including TV and radio audiences, press circulation and readership.
Readership/Target Audience: Aimed at advertising agencies, banks and consultancies.
ADVERTISING: No Advertising taken
BUSINESS: COMMUNICATIONS, ADVERTISING & MARKETING

MARKET LEADER THE JOURNAL OF THE MARKETING SOCIETY
35520U2A-109_40

Editorial Address: 1 Farm Road, HENLEY-ON-THAMES, RG9 1EJ **Tel:** 01491 411000 **Fax:** 01491 418600
Email: market_leader@warc.com
Advertising Address: 1 Ivory Square, Plantation Wharf, HENLEY-ON-THAMES, SW11 3UF **Tel:** 020 7326 8604
Email: diana.poundsford@warc.com
Web site: http://www.marketleadermagazine.com
ISSN: 1463-0877
Publisher: World Advertising Research Center
Date Established: 1998
Frequency: Quarterly
Free to qualifying individuals
Annual Sub.: £222.00
Circulation: 3,700 (Publisher's Statement)
Usual Pagination: 64
Editor: Judie Lannon
Summary of Content: Journal featuring articles covering leading edge business and marketing issues. Includes case studies, interviews and profiles of companies that have demonstrated innovative marketing and business strategies.
Readership/Target Audience: Aimed at senior management and board level directors.
ADVERTISING RATES:
Full Page Mono £1560.00
Full Page Colour £2520.00
Agency Commission: 10%
Mechanical Data: Page Width: 175mm, Type Area: 272 x 175mm, Bleed Size: 303 x 215mm, Trim Size: 297 x 210mm, Col Length: 272mm, Film: Positive, right reading, emulsion side down. Digital
Copy instructions: Copy Date: 4 weeks prior to publication date
Average advertising content per issue: 20%
BUSINESS: COMMUNICATIONS, ADVERTISING & MARKETING

MARKET NEWSLETTER
35615U38-183

Editorial Address: Focus House, 497 Green Lanes, LONDON, N13 4BP **Tel:** 020 8882 3315 **Fax:** 020 8886 3933
Email: info@thebfp.com
Advertising Address: As above.
Email: mail@thebfp.com
Web site: http://www.thebfp.com
Publisher: Bureau of Freelance Photographers
Date Established: 1965
Frequency: Monthly
Annual Sub.: £49.00
Circulation: 6,500 (Publisher's Statement)
Usual Pagination: 16
Editor: John Tracy; **News Editor:** Stewart Gibson; **Managing Director:** John Tracy; **Advertising Manager:** John Tracy; **Publisher:** John Tracy
Summary of Content: Newsletter covering up-to-date information on publications and other relevant matters.
Readership/Target Audience: Circulated to freelance photographers.
ADVERTISING: Rates on application
BUSINESS: PHOTOGRAPHIC TRADE

MARKET TRADER
38102U26A-50

Formerly: MT and Shopkeeper
Editorial Address: 3rd Floor, Hollinwood Business Centre, Albert Street, OLDHAM, OL8 3QL **Tel:** 0161 683 8032
Fax: 0161 683 8001
Email: john.kirkbride@worldsfair.co.uk
Advertising Address: As above. **Tel:** 0161 683 8000
Email: craig.mills@worldsfair.co.uk
Web site: http://www.worldsfair.co.uk
ISSN: 1361-9055
Publisher: The World's Fair Ltd
Date Established: 1922
Frequency: Weekly
Cover Price: £0.60
Circulation: 22,000 (Publisher's Statement)
Usual Pagination: 32
Editor: John Kirkbride
Summary of Content: National Newspaper covering information on retail marketing and wholesaling, indoor and outdoor markets.
Readership/Target Audience: Read by market traders and small shopkeepers.
ADVERTISING RATES:
Full Page Mono £560.00
Full Page Colour £725.00
Agency Commission: 10%
Mechanical Data: Col Length: 370mm, No. of Columns (Display): 6, Type Area: 370 x 262mm, Trim Size: 390 x 285mm, Page Width: 262mm, Film: Digital
Copy instructions: Copy Date: Friday, 4pm 1 week prior to publication date
Average advertising content per issue: 60%
Supplement to: World's Fair - 52xY
BUSINESS: GARDEN TRADE: Market Garden Traders

THE MARKETER
35526U2A-111_2

Formerly: Marketing Business
Editorial Address: 17-18 Britton Street, LONDON, EC1M 5TP **Tel:** 020 7324 2774
Email: editorial@themarketer.co.uk
Advertising Address: As above. **Tel:** 020 7880 6200
Fax: 020 7880 7690
Email: esther@themarketer.co.uk
Web site: http://www.themarketer.co.uk
ISSN: 1743-5528
Publisher: Redactive Media Group
Frequency: 10 issues yearly - Published around the 1st of the cover month
Cover Price: £10.00
Annual Sub.: £85.00
Circulation: 36,416 (ABC 01/07/2008 to 30/06/2009)
Usual Pagination: 50
Editor: Melody Bartlett
Summary of Content: Magazine of The Chartered Institute of Marketing, focusing on marketing as part of the wider business strategy, offering in depth features, comment, trends and analysis. Offers advise and information from the Institute's greatest gurus and plenty of real-word experiences from the best in the profession.
Readership/Target Audience: Read by marketing professionals around the world, members of the Chartered Institute of Marketing, and subscribers within the marketing discipline.
ADVERTISING RATES:
Full Page Mono £4500.00
Full Page Colour £4500.00
Agency Commission: 10%
Mechanical Data: Film: Digital, Type Area: 246 x 191mm, Col Length: 246mm, Trim Size: 270 x 215mm, Bleed Size: 276 x 221mm, Page Width: 191mm
Copy instructions: Copy Date: 3 weeks prior to publication date
Average advertising content per issue: 30%
BUSINESS: COMMUNICATIONS, ADVERTISING & MARKETING

Business Magazines

MARKETING
35523U2A-110

Editorial Address: 174 Hammersmith Road, LONDON, W6 8BS **Tel:** 020 8267 4567 **Fax:** 020 8267 4504
Email: edward.kemp@haymarket.com
Advertising Address: As above. **Tel:** 020 8267 5000
Fax: 020 8267 4333
Email: andrea.thomas@haymarket.com
Web site: http://www.marketingmagazine.co.uk
Publisher: Haymarket Specialist Publications
Date Established: 1931
Frequency: Weekly
Cover Price: £3.20
Free to qualifying individuals
Circulation: 35,615 (ABC 01/07/2008 to 30/06/2009)
Usual Pagination: 80
Editor: Edward Kemp; **News Editor:** Edward Kemp;
Managing Director: Jane Macken; **Advertising Director:** Andrea Thomas
Summary of Content: Magazine covering news and features on key marketing issues.
Twitter: https://twitter.com/MarketingB2B.
Readership/Target Audience: Read by marketing directors, brand and product managers and senior advertising agency personnel.
ADVERTISING RATES:
Full Page Colour £7196.00
Agency Commission: 10%
Mechanical Data: Type Area: 282 x 207mm, Bleed Size: 305 x 235mm, Trim Size: 295 x 225mm, Col Length: 282mm, Film: Digital, Col Widths (Display): 39mm, No. of Columns (Display): 5, Page Width: 207mm, Print Process: Web-fed offset litho
Copy instructions: Copy Date: 1 week prior to publication date
Average advertising content per issue: 60%
BUSINESS: COMMUNICATIONS, ADVERTISING & MARKETING

MARKETING TECHNOLOGY
1645907U2A-662

Formerly: Marketing Technology International
Editorial Address: Technology House, 8 Norroy Road, LONDON, SW15 1PF **Tel:** 0871 237 4787
Email: marketingtechnologymagazine@googlemail.com
Advertising Address: As above. **Tel:** 0871 237 4878
Email: marketingtechnology@hotmail.co.uk
Publisher: PAP Publications
Date Established: 2003
Frequency: 10 issues yearly - Published at the end of the month prior to 1st cover date
Annual Sub.: £50.00
Circulation: 15,000 (Publisher's Statement)
Usual Pagination: 20
Editor: Paul Phillips; **Advertising Manager:** Paul Phillips
Summary of Content: Magazine explaining how to use technology in marketing. Covering analytics, CRM, call centres, data, mobile, search, social media and security.
Readership/Target Audience: Aimed at CEOs, managing directors and sales and marketing directors.
ADVERTISING: Rates on application
Copy instructions: Copy Date: 1 week prior to publication date
BUSINESS: COMMUNICATIONS, ADVERTISING & MARKETING

MARKETING WEEK
35529U2A-115

Editorial Address: St. Giles House, 50 Poland Street, LONDON, W1F 7AX **Tel:** 020 7970 4000 **Fax:** 020 7970 6722
Email: mw.editorial@centaur.co.uk
Advertising Address: As above. **Fax:** 020 7963 8070
Email: richard.gordon@centaur.co.uk
Web site: http://www.marketingweek.co.uk
Publisher: Centaur Media plc
Date Established: 1978
Frequency: Weekly - Published on Thursday
Cover Price: £2.95
Free to qualifying individuals
Annual Sub.: £115.00
Circulation: 35,806 (ABC 01/07/2008 to 30/06/2009)
Usual Pagination: 100
Editor: Mark Choueke; **Publisher:** Sarah Gilchriest
Summary of Content: Magazine covering major marketing and advertising information.
Twitter: https://twitter.com/MarketingWeekEd.
Readership/Target Audience: Aimed at senior marketing executives with responsibility for marketing and advertising expenditure.
ADVERTISING RATES:
Full Page Colour £6335.00
Agency Commission: 10%
Mechanical Data: Film: Digital, Type Area: 254 x 190mm, Col Widths (Display): 44mm, Col Length: 254mm, Page Width: 190mm, Trim Size: 280 x 210mm
Copy instructions: Copy Date: 2 weeks prior to publication date
BUSINESS: COMMUNICATIONS, ADVERTISING & MARKETING

MASALA
712102U22A-255

Editorial Address: PO Box 5786, LEICESTER, LE5 5WL
Tel: 07930 422090
Email: masala04@aol.com
Advertising Address: 113 Fazeley Street, BIRMINGHAM, B5 5RX **Tel:** 0121 202 1586 **Fax:** 0121 685 1110
Email: jag@westpointmarketing.co.uk
ISSN: 1476-525X
Publisher: West Point Media Publications
Date Established: 1999
Frequency: Monthly
Free to qualifying individuals
Annual Sub.: £19.50
Circulation: 13,000 (Publisher's Statement)
Usual Pagination: 48
Editor: Hajra Makda
Summary of Content: Magazine covering Asian catering, hospitality and the restaurant trade within the UK, includes industry news, restaurant reviews, awards and competitions.
Readership/Target Audience: Aimed at those involved in the Asian restaurant and catering industry from chefs through to restaurant managers and owners.
ADVERTISING RATES:
Full Page Colour £1195.00
Agency Commission: 10%
Mechanical Data: Bleed Size: 303 x 216mm, Trim Size: 297 x 210mm, Film: Digital
Copy instructions: Copy Date: 2 weeks prior to publication date
BUSINESS: FOOD

MASONRY INTERNATIONAL
35911U4E-260

Editorial Address: Shermanbury, 6 Church Road, WHYTELEAFE, CR3 0AR **Tel:** 020 8660 3633
Fax: 020 8668 6983
Email: kenneth@fisher5053.fsnet.co.uk
Advertising Address: As above.
Web site: http://www.masonry.org.uk
Publisher: The International Masonry Society
Date Established: 1986
Frequency: 3 issues yearly
Annual Sub.: £60.00
Circulation: 500 (Publisher's Statement)
Usual Pagination: 44
Editor: Ken Fisher; **Advertising Manager:** Ken Fisher
Summary of Content: Journal Of The British Masonry Society covering masonry design, application and construction using concrete, clay, natural stone and other materials.
Readership/Target Audience: Read by members of The British Masonry Society. Also sent to university libraries and research centres worldwide.
ADVERTISING RATES:
Full Page Mono £200.00
Mechanical Data: Type Area: 259 x 178mm, Bleed Size: 303 x 216mm, Trim Size: 297 x 210mm, Col Length: 259mm, Page Width: 178mm
BUSINESS: ARCHITECTURE & BUILDING: Building

MASTER BUILDER
35912U4E-280

Editorial Address: The Maltings, West Street, BOURNE, PE10 9PH **Tel:** 01778 391000 **Fax:** 01778 394748
Email: nickyr@warnersgroup.co.uk
Advertising Address: As above. **Fax:** 01778 392079
Email: hayleyf@warnersgroup.co.uk
Publisher: Warners Group Publications plc
Frequency: Monthly - Published around the 25th of the month prior to cover month
Cover Price: £3.50
Free to qualifying individuals
Annual Sub.: £40.00
Circulation: 12,750 (ABC 01/07/2008 to 30/06/2009)
Usual Pagination: 56
Editor: Nicky Rogers; **Publisher:** Simon Moody
Summary of Content: Journal of the Federation of Master Builders. Includes features on all aspects of building, information on tools, fittings, building products and campaigning.
Readership/Target Audience: Aimed at small to medium builders and those involved in the construction industry.
ADVERTISING RATES:
Full Page Colour £1240.00
Agency Commission: 10%
Mechanical Data: Bleed Size: 303 x 216mm, Trim Size: 297 x 210mm, Film: Digital, Type Area: 272 x 190mm, Col Length: 272mm, Page Width: 190mm
Average advertising content per issue: 60%
BUSINESS: ARCHITECTURE & BUILDING: Building

MASTER CHEFS
764946U11A-186

Formerly: The Master's Table
Editorial Address: Woodmans, Brithem Bottom, CULLOMPTON, EX15 1NB **Tel:** 01884 35104
Email: masterchefs@msn.com
Advertising Address: As above. **Fax:** 01884 35105
Email: masterchefs@msn.com
Web site: http://www.masterchefs.co.uk
Publisher: The Master Chefs of Great Britain
Date Established: 1995
Frequency: Half-yearly - Published in April and October
Cover Price: £3.00
Circulation: 3,000 (Publisher's Statement)
Usual Pagination: 60
Editor: Susan McGeever; **Advertising Manager:** Susan McGeever
Summary of Content: Magazine published on behalf of the Master Chefs of Great Britain covering food, wine and real ale with chef profiles, travel articles, recipes and restaurant reviews.
Readership/Target Audience: Aimed at chefs, those working in the food and restaurant industry and individuals interested in fine food and wine.
ADVERTISING RATES:
Full Page Colour £1275.00
Agency Commission: 10%
Mechanical Data: Bleed Size: +3mm, Trim Size: 297 x 210mm, Film: Digital
Copy instructions: Copy Date: 4 weeks prior to publication date
Average advertising content per issue: 10%
BUSINESS: CATERING: Catering, Hotels & Restaurants

MASTER PHOTO DIGITAL
628350U38-42

Formerly: Master Digital
Editorial Address: Maxwell Place, Maxwell Lane, KELSO, TD5 7BB **Tel:** 01573 226032 **Fax:** 01573 226000
Email: iconmags@btconnect.com
Advertising Address: Abbeyfield House, 15 Brougham Place, HAWICK, TD9 9JU **Tel:** 01450 371169
Fax: 01450 373718
Email: adsales@btconnect.com
Web site: http://www.iconpublications.com
ISSN: 1740-3847
Publisher: Icon Publications Ltd
Date Established: 2004
Frequency: 10 issues yearly
Annual Sub.: £39.90
Circulation: 2,500 (Publisher's Statement)
Usual Pagination: 52
Editor: David Kilpatrick; **Advertising Director:** Richard Kilpatrick
Summary of Content: Magazine containing information and new products of interest to the professional photographer, including all aspects of digital imaging from processing to analysing.
Readership/Target Audience: Aimed at those who are interested in the more professional side of the digital imaging industry.
ADVERTISING RATES:
Full Page Colour £1350.00
Agency Commission: 10%
Mechanical Data: Trim Size: 297 x 210mm, Bleed Size: 303 x 216mm, Film: Digital
Copy instructions: Copy Date: 20th of the month prior to publication date
Average advertising content per issue: 30%
BUSINESS: PHOTOGRAPHIC TRADE

MASTERCLASS
1773129U14A-571

Editorial Address: Walmour House, 296 Regent Street, LONDON, W1B 3AW **Tel:** 020 7016 2555
Fax: 020 7970 4820
Email: molly.bennett@wardour.co.uk
Web site: http://www.masterclassmagazine.com
Publisher: Wardour
Date Established: 2006
Frequency: Half-yearly - Published in November and May
Cover Price: £3.95
Free to qualifying individuals
Circulation: 35,000 (Publisher's Statement)
Usual Pagination: 68
Editor: Molly Bennett
Summary of Content: Publication focusing on middle market business issues including funding, growth, expansion, exit, people and recruitment.
Readership/Target Audience: Aimed at financial directors, CEOs and non-executives of middle market companies and intermediaries such as PE houses, LLPs and banks.
ADVERTISING: No Advertising taken
BUSINESS: COMMERCE, INDUSTRY & MANAGEMENT

MATERIAL MATTERS MAGAZINE
1743029U57-149

Formerly: Cylchgrawn Magazine
Editorial Address: 57 Prince Street, BRISTOL, BS1 4QH
Tel: 0117 907 0698
Email: charles@resource.uk.com
Advertising Address: As above. **Tel:** 0117 907 4915
Fax: 0117 907 7216
Email: gemma@resource.uk.com
Web site: http://www.resourcepublishing.co.uk
Publisher: Resource Media Ltd

Frequency: Quarterly
Circulation: 750 (Publisher's Statement)
Editor: Charles Newman
Summary of Content: Magazine for Wales' sustainable waste management industry.
Language(s): English; Welsh
Readership/Target Audience: Aimed at local and national government officers working in waste and private and community waste sector companies.
ADVERTISING RATES:
Full Page Colour £660.00
Agency Commission: 10%
BUSINESS: ENVIRONMENT & POLLUTION

MATERIALS & DESIGN
37616U19B-400

Editorial Address: The Boulevard, Langford Lane, KIDLINGTON, OX5 1GB **Tel:** 01865 843000
Fax: 01865 843933
Advertising Address: 32 Jamestown Road, LONDON, NW1 7BY **Tel:** 020 7424 4400 **Fax:** 01865 853136
Email: j.kenney@elsevier.com
Web site: http://www.elsevier.com
ISSN: 0261-3069
Publisher: Elsevier Ltd
Frequency: 8 issues yearly
Circulation: 500 (Publisher's Statement)
Usual Pagination: 100
Editor: Kevin Edwards
Summary of Content: Journal reviewing developments in properties of materials, with an emphasis on research and design.
Readership/Target Audience: Aimed at engineers.
ADVERTISING RATES:
Full Page Mono £1465.00
Full Page Colour £2380.00
BUSINESS: ENGINEERING & MACHINERY: Engineering - Design

MATERIALS HANDLING WORLD MAGAZINE
1646439U10-207

Formerly: Materials Handling World
Editorial Address: PO BOX 222, DEWSBURY, WF13 3WN
Tel: 01924 437820 **Fax:** 01924 465828
Email: editorial@wprmedia.co.uk
Advertising Address: As above.
Email: advertising@wprmedia.co.uk
Web site: http://www.mhwmagazine.co.uk
Publisher: WPR Media
Date Established: 2003
Frequency: Quarterly
Cover Price: £4.00
Free to qualifying individuals
Circulation: 8,500 (Publisher's Statement)
Usual Pagination: 64
Editor: Barry Hemingway; **Advertising Manager:** David Ramsey
Summary of Content: Magazine covering all aspects of materials handling and logistics. Includes articles on forklift trucks, automated storage and retrieval systems, racking systems, waste management and health and safety.
Readership/Target Audience: Aimed at buyers, users and specifiers of materials handling equipment.
ADVERTISING RATES:
Full Page Mono £1140.00
Full Page Colour £1565.00
Agency Commission: 15%
Mechanical Data: Type Area: 277 x 190mm, Col Length: 277mm, Page Width: 190mm
Average advertising content per issue: 20%
BUSINESS: MATERIALS HANDLING

MATERIALS SCIENCE & TECHNOLOGY
22537U19F-440

Editorial Address: 1 Carlton House Terrace, LONDON, SW1Y 5DB **Tel:** 020 7451 7314 **Fax:** 020 7451 7307
Email: mark_hull@materials.org.uk
Advertising Address: Suite 1C, Josephs Well, Hanover Walk, LEEDS, LS3 1AB **Tel:** 0113 243 2800
Fax: 0113 386 8178
Email: n.taylor@maney.co.uk
Web site: http://www.materials.org.uk
ISSN: 0267-0836
Publisher: Maney Publishing
Date Established: 1984
Frequency: Monthly
Annual Sub.: £1204.00
Circulation: 1,000 (Publisher's Statement)
Editor: Mark Hull; **Advertising Manager:** Natalie Taylor; **Managing Editor:** Mark Hull
Summary of Content: Peer-reviewed publication concerned with original research and reviews on materials science, technology and engineering.
Readership/Target Audience: Designed for all those concerned with the production processing, structure and

properties of engineered materials and their future developments.
ADVERTISING RATES:
Full Page Mono £500.00
Full Page Colour £1100.00
Agency Commission: 10%
Mechanical Data: Type Area: 266 x 188mm, Bleed Size: 305 x 215mm, Trim Size: 297 x 210mm, Film: Digital, Col Length: 266mm, Page Width: 188mm
Copy instructions: Copy Date: 15th of month prior to publication date
BUSINESS: ENGINEERING & MACHINERY: Production & Mechanical Engineering

MATERIALS TODAY
39985U55-95_60

Editorial Address: The Boulevard, Langford Lane, KIDLINGTON, OX5 1GB **Tel:** 01865 843140
Fax: 01865 843987
Email: materialstoday@elsevier.com
Advertising Address: As above. **Tel:** 01865 843000
Fax: 01865 343973
Email: g.plowman@elsevier.com
Web site: http://www.materialstoday.com
ISSN: 1369-7021
Publisher: Elsevier Ltd
Date Established: 2001
Frequency: 10 issues yearly - Published in the last full week of the month prior to cover date
Free to qualifying individuals
Annual Sub.: EUR196.00
Circulation: 25,000 (BPA Worldwide 01/07/2007 to 31/12/2007)
Usual Pagination: 64
Editor: Maggy Heintz
Summary of Content: Magazine containing news and features covering developments in materials science.
Readership/Target Audience: Read by academic, government and industrial researchers involved in any area of materials science.
ADVERTISING RATES:
Full Page Colour $3840.00
Mechanical Data: Bleed Size: 286 x 222mm, Trim Size: 280 x 216mm
BUSINESS: APPLIED SCIENCE & LABORATORIES

MATERIALS WORLD
38157U27-80

Editorial Address: 1 Carlton House Terrace, LONDON, SW1Y 5DB **Tel:** 020 7451 7314 **Fax:** 020 7451 7406
Email: materials.world@iom3.org
Advertising Address: Mongoose Media Ltd, Mongoose House, Lonsdale Road, LONDON, NW6 6RD
Tel: 020 7306 0300 **Fax:** 020 7306 0301
Email: iom3@mongoosemedia.com
Web site: http://www.iom3.org
ISSN: 0967-8638
Publisher: IOM Communications Ltd
Date Established: 1993
Frequency: Monthly - Published around the 1st of the cover month
Free to qualifying individuals
Annual Sub.: £45.00
Circulation: 18,000 (Publisher's Statement)
Usual Pagination: 64
Editor: Katherine Williams; **News Editor:** Rupal Mehta;
Publisher: Bernard Rickinson
Summary of Content: Official magazine of the Institute of Materials, Minerals and Mining. Covering the latest developments in engineering materials worldwide. Includes metals, composites, ceramics, plastics and rubber. Also covers the primary extraction industries, minerals and mining industries and related technologies.
Readership/Target Audience: Read by members of the Institute as well as materials scientists, technologists and engineers in industry, research and education.
ADVERTISING RATES:
Full Page Mono £1470.00
Full Page Colour £2120.00
Agency Commission: 10%
Mechanical Data: Type Area: 255 x 180mm, Bleed Size: 305 x 215mm, Trim Size: 297 x 210mm, Film: Digital, Col Length: 255mm, Page Width: 180mm
Copy instructions: Copy Date: Beginning of the month prior to publication date
BUSINESS: METAL, IRON & STEEL

THE MATHEMATICAL GAZETTE
40059U55-95_64

Editorial Address: 259 London Road, LEICESTER, LE2 3BE
Tel: 0116 221 0013 **Fax:** 0116 212 2835
Email: gazette@m-a.org.uk
Advertising Address: As above.
Email: jcpadvertising@yahoo.co.uk
Web site: http://www.m-a.org.uk
ISSN: 0025-5572
Publisher: The Mathematical Association
Date Established: 1915

Frequency: 3 issues yearly - Published in March, July and November
Cover Price: £17.00
Annual Sub.: £55.00
Circulation: 4,500 (Publisher's Statement)
Usual Pagination: 192
Editor: Gerry Leversha; **Advertising Manager:** Janet Powell
Summary of Content: Journal containing articles, reviews and problems.
Readership/Target Audience: Aimed at teachers, lecturers and students.
ADVERTISING: Rates on application
BUSINESS: APPLIED SCIENCE & LABORATORIES

MATHEMATICAL MEDICINE AND BIOLOGY: A JOURNAL OF THE IMA
29977U62A-507

Formerly: IMA Journal of Mathematics Applied in Medicine & Biology
Editorial Address: School of Mathmatical Sciences, University of Nottingham, University Park, NOTTINGHAM, NG7 2RD **Tel:** 01865 353907 **Fax:** 01865 353485
Email: oliver.jensen@nottingham.ac.uk
Advertising Address: Great Clarendon Street, OXFORD, OX2 6DP **Tel:** 01865 353907 **Fax:** 01865 353774
Email: elisabetta.sheffield@oxfordjornals.org
Web site: http://www3.oup.co.uk/imammb
ISSN: 0265-0746
Publisher: OUP
Date Established: 1984
Frequency: Quarterly
Cover Price: £77.00
Annual Sub.: £233.00
Editor: Oliver Jensen
Summary of Content: Journal covering the uses of mathematics in medicine and biological research.
Readership/Target Audience: Aimed at members of the Institute of Mathematics and its Applications.
ADVERTISING RATES:
Full Page Mono £646.00
Full Page Colour £1076.00
Agency Commission: 10%
Mechanical Data: Film: Digital, Type Area: 181 x 139mm, Print Process: Litho, Bleed Size: 252 x 195mm, Trim Size: 246 x 189mm, Col Length: 181mm, Page Width: 139mm
BUSINESS: CHURCH & SCHOOL EQUIPMENT & EDUCATION: Education

MATHEMATICAL PIE
40060U55-95_65

Editorial Address: 259 London Road, LEICESTER, LE2 3BE
Tel: 0116 221 0013 **Fax:** 0116 212 2835
Email: wilransome@yahoo.co.uk
Web site: http://www.m-a.org.uk
ISSN: 0025-5602
Publisher: The Mathematical Association
Frequency: 3 issues yearly
Cover Price: £3.00
Circulation: 5,000 (Publisher's Statement)
Usual Pagination: 8
Editor: Wil Ransome
Summary of Content: International magazine containing a variety of problems and challenges to stimulate mathematical activity either individually or in groups. Also occasionally contains prize competitions.
Readership/Target Audience: Aimed at pupils aged between 10 and 15 years old.
ADVERTISING: No Advertising taken
BUSINESS: APPLIED SCIENCE & LABORATORIES

MATHEMATICS IN SCHOOL
41034U62B-540

Editorial Address: The Centre For Teaching Mathematics, The University of Plymouth, PLYMOUTH, PL4 8AA
Tel: 01458 851497
Email: mis@m-a.org.uk
Advertising Address: 259 London Road, LEICESTER, LE2 3BE **Tel:** 0116 221 0013 **Fax:** 0116 212 2835
Email: jcpadvertising@yahoo.co.uk
Web site: http://www.m-a.org.uk
ISSN: 0305-7259
Publisher: The Mathematical Association
Date Established: 1971
Frequency: 5 issues yearly
Free to qualifying individuals
Annual Sub.: £55.00
Circulation: 5,500 (Publisher's Statement)
Usual Pagination: 48
Editor: John Berry; **Advertising Manager:** Janet Powell
Summary of Content: Magazine covering the latest developments in mathematics education, looking at the development of the National Curriculum in mathematics.
Readership/Target Audience: Read by maths teachers, especially those who teach the 7 to 16 age range.
ADVERTISING RATES:
Full Page Mono £390.00
Full Page Colour £660.00

Mechanical Data: Type Area: 276 x 190mm, Col Length: 276mm, Bleed Size: 310 x 225m, Page Width: 190mm, Film: Digital
Copy instructions: Copy Date: 5 weeks prior to publication date
BUSINESS: CHURCH & SCHOOL EQUIPMENT & EDUCATION: Education Teachers

MATHEMATICS TODAY
40067U55-95_66

Editorial Address: Catherine Richards House, 16 Nelson Street, SOUTHEND-ON-SEA, SS1 1EF **Tel:** 01702 354020
Fax: 01702 354111
Email: post@ima.org.uk
Advertising Address: As above. **Tel:** 01702 356111
Email: gayna.leggott@ima.org.uk
Web site: http://www.ima.org.uk
ISSN: 1361-2042
Publisher: The Institute of Mathematics & its Applications
Frequency: 6 issues yearly
Annual Sub.: £93.00
Circulation: 5,000 (Publisher's Statement)
Usual Pagination: 32
Editor: Gayna Leggott; **Advertising Manager:** Gayna Leggott
Summary of Content: Journal containing articles of wide mathematical interest, mathematics in education, book reviews, conference reports, news of members as well as advertising for employment vacancies, financial services, new publications and software, conferences, symposia and courses.
Readership/Target Audience: Aimed at all members of the Institute of Mathematics and mathematics graduates in industry, commerce and education.
ADVERTISING RATES:
Full Page Mono £1000.00
Full Page Colour £1125.00
Agency Commission: 10%
Mechanical Data: Col Length: 258mm, Film: Digital, Bleed Size: 303 x 216mm, Trim Size: 297 x 210mm, Type Area: 258 x 182mm, Page Width: 182mm
Copy instructions: Copy Date: 4 weeks prior to publication date
BUSINESS: APPLIED SCIENCE & LABORATORIES

MATTERS ARISING
41150U62J-300

Formerly: Governors' News
Editorial Address: 2nd Floor SBQ1, 29 Smallbrook Queensway, BIRMINGHAM, B5 4HE **Tel:** 0121 643 5787
Fax: 0121 633 7141
Email: editor@nga.org.uk
Advertising Address: As above.
Email: governorhq@nga.org.uk
Web site: http://www.nga.org.uk
ISSN: 1352-8084
Publisher: Governors' Association
Date Established: 1979
Frequency: 6 issues yearly
Cover Price: £2.50
Free to qualifying individuals
Circulation: 40,000 (Publisher's Statement)
Usual Pagination: 32
Editor: Alison Murdoch; **Advertising Manager:** Dawn Pheasey
Summary of Content: Magazine providing advice, educational news and governors' issues.
Readership/Target Audience: Aimed at governors of state schools, members of the National Governors' Association.
ADVERTISING RATES:
Full Page Mono £1000.00
Mechanical Data: Type Area: 270 x 180mm, Bleed Size: 303 x 213mm, Trim Size: 297 x 210mm, Page Width: 180mm, Col Length: 270mm, Film: Digital
Copy instructions: Copy Date: 1 month prior to publication date
Average advertising content per issue: 25%
BUSINESS: CHURCH & SCHOOL EQUIPMENT & EDUCATION: Teachers & Education Management

MBM - METAL BULLETIN MONTHLY
38156U27-85

Editorial Address: Nestor House, Playhouse Yard, LONDON, EC4V 5EX **Tel:** 020 7827 9977
Fax: 020 7928 6892
Email: rbarrett@metalbulletin.com
Advertising Address: As above. **Fax:** 020 7827 5206
Email: sdinardo@metalbulletin.com
Web site: http://www.metalbulletin.com
ISSN: 0373-4064
Publisher: Euromoney Institutional Investor plc
Date Established: 1971
Frequency: 11 issues yearly - Published around the 1st of the cover month
Cover Price: £65.00
Free to qualifying individuals
Annual Sub.: £357.00
Circulation: 6,318 (ABC 01/01/2008 to 31/12/2008)

Usual Pagination: 56
Editor: Richard Barrett
Summary of Content: Magazine focusing on all aspects of the production and trade of ferrous and non-ferrous metals. Includes articles on the full supply chain from raw materials to end-use sectors.
Language(s): Chinese; English
Readership/Target Audience: Aimed at senior management in the steel and non-ferrous metals producing and trading industries. Also those involved in the semi-fabricating, raw materials and end user sectors.
ADVERTISING RATES:
Full Page Mono £2852.00
Full Page Colour £4314.00
Agency Commission: 10%
Mechanical Data: Bleed Size: 303 x 216mm, Trim Size: 297 x 210mm, Type Area: 254 x 178mm, Col Length: 254mm, No. of Columns (Display): 4, Film: Digital, Page Width: 178mm, Col Widths (Display): 42.5mm
Copy instructions: Copy Date: 1st of month prior to publication
Average advertising content per issue: 45%
Supplement(s): Aluminium - 1xY, Copper - 1xY, Ferro-Alloys - 1xY, London Metal Exchange - 1xY
BUSINESS: METAL, IRON & STEEL

MCCLOSKEY'S COAL REPORT
38237U30-43

Formerly: International Coal Report
Editorial Address: Unit 6, Rotherbrook Court, Bedford Road, PETERSFIELD, GU32 3QG **Tel:** 01730 265095
Fax: 01730 260044
Email: john.howland@mccloskeycoal.com
Web site: http://www.mccloskeycoal.com
Publisher: The McCloskey Group Ltd
Date Established: 2001
Frequency: 25 issues yearly
Annual Sub.: £1100.00
Circulation: 1,000 (Publisher's Statement)
Usual Pagination: 28
Editor: John Howland; **Managing Editor:** Gerard McCloskey; **Publisher:** Gerard McCloskey
Summary of Content: Newsletter featuring news and analysis for the international coal industry.
Readership/Target Audience: Read by people involved in producing, shipping, financing, consuming, buying and selling coal on the world market.
ADVERTISING: No Advertising taken
BUSINESS: MINING & QUARRYING

MCCLOSKEY'S COAL UK
40739U58-60

Formerly: Coal UK
Editorial Address: Unit 6, Rotherbrook Court, Bedford Road, PETERSFIELD, GU32 3QG **Tel:** 01730 265095
Fax: 01730 260044
Email: david.price@mccloskeycoal.com
Web site: http://www.mccloskeycoal.com
Publisher: The McCloskey Group Ltd
Date Established: 1992
Frequency: Monthly
Annual Sub.: £525.00
Usual Pagination: 24
Editor: David Price; **Managing Director:** Gerard McCloskey
Summary of Content: Newsletter covering UK coal, power generation and detailing purchases, production and market trends.
Readership/Target Audience: Read by coal producers, shippers, suppliers, power companies and steel companies.
ADVERTISING: No Advertising taken
BUSINESS: ENERGY, FUEL & NUCLEAR

MCCLOSKEY'S STEAM COAL FORECASTER
40799U58-62

Editorial Address: Unit 6, Rotherbrook Court, Bedford Road, PETERSFIELD, GU32 3QG **Tel:** 01730 265095
Fax: 01730 260044
Web site: http://www.mccloskeycoal.com
Publisher: The McCloskey Group Ltd
Date Established: 1995
Frequency: Quarterly
Annual Sub.: £1750.00
Usual Pagination: 70
Editor: David Price
Summary of Content: International steam coal forecasting service providing an analysis of market trends.
Readership/Target Audience: Aimed at buyers, coal producers, seller's agents, traders, merchant banks, shipping and barging companies, railroads and truck firms.
ADVERTISING: No Advertising taken
BUSINESS: ENERGY, FUEL & NUCLEAR

MCCLOSKEY'S UK POWERFOCUS
1641726U58-167

Editorial Address: Unit 6, Rotherbrook Court, Bedford Road, PETERSFIELD, GU32 3QG **Tel:** 01730 265095
Fax: 01730 260044
Email: scott.dendy@mccloskeycoal.com
Web site: http://www.ukpowerfocus.com
Publisher: The McCloskey Group Ltd
Date Established: 2001
Frequency: Monthly
Annual Sub.: £695.00
Circulation: 130 (Publisher's Statement)
Usual Pagination: 44
Editor: Scott Dendy
Summary of Content: Newsletter covering news and pricing data in the power industry.
Readership/Target Audience: Aimed at anyone following economic and pricing trends in the power industry. Targeted at more senior decision makers.
ADVERTISING: No Advertising taken
BUSINESS: ENERGY, FUEL & NUCLEAR

MCSS MATHEMATICS OF CONTROL, SIGNAL AND SYSTEMS
40066U55-95_67

Editorial Address: Ashbourne House, The Guildway, Old Portsmouth Road, Artington, GUILDFORD, GU3 1LP
Tel: 01483 734655 **Fax:** 01483 734429
Email: oliver.jackson@springer.com
Advertising Address: As above. **Tel:** 01483 734434
Email: anthony.doyle@springer.com
Web site: http://www.springer.com
ISSN: 0932-4194
Publisher: Springer
Frequency: Quarterly
Annual Sub.: $645.00
Usual Pagination: 80
Advertising Manager: Anthony Doyle
Summary of Content: Contains original and high quality research papers concerned with mathematically rigorous, system theoretical aspects of control and signal processing.
Readership/Target Audience: Aimed at academics and researchers in engineering and mathematics.
ADVERTISING: Rates on application
BUSINESS: APPLIED SCIENCE & LABORATORIES

MCV - THE MARKET FOR HOME COMPUTING & VIDEO GAMES
36273U5F-340

Formerly: MCV
Editorial Address: Saxon House, 6A St. Andrew Street, HERTFORD, SG14 1JA **Tel:** 01992 535646
Fax: 01992 535648
Email: lisa.foster@intentmedia.co.uk
Advertising Address: As above.
Email: lesley.blumson@intentmedia.co.uk
Web site: http://www.mcvuk.com
Publisher: Intent Media
Date Established: 1998
Frequency: Weekly
Cover Price: £3.25
Free to qualifying individuals
Annual Sub.: £150.00
Circulation: 8,833 (ABC 01/01/2008 to 31/12/2008)
Usual Pagination: 44
Editor: Lisa Foster; **Editor-in-Chief:** Michael French;
Managing Director: Stuart Dinsey; **Advertising Manager:** Lesley Blumson; **Managing Editor:** Lisa Foster; **Publisher:** Stuart Dinsey
Summary of Content: Magazine covering all aspects of the interactive entertainment industry with features on software development and international news.
Language(s): English; French; German
Readership/Target Audience: Aimed at all individuals working within the interactive entertainment marketplace and associated industries.
ADVERTISING RATES:
Full Page Colour £1960.00
Agency Commission: 10%
Mechanical Data: Film: Digital
Copy instructions: Copy Date: 7 days prior to publication date
Average advertising content per issue: 50%
BUSINESS: COMPUTERS & AUTOMATION: Multimedia

MEASUREMENT & CONTROL
35991U5A-185

Editorial Address: 87 Gower Street, LONDON, WC1E 6AF
Tel: 020 7387 4949 **Fax:** 020 7388 8431
Email: publications@instmc.org.uk
Advertising Address: As above.
Email: publications@instmc.org.uk
Web site: http://www.instmc.org.uk
ISSN: 0020-2940
Publisher: Institute of Measurement & Control
Frequency: 10 issues yearly - Published the 1st week of the cover month
Cover Price: £36.00

Annual Sub.: £237.00
Circulation: 4,000 (Publisher's Statement)
Usual Pagination: 32
Editor: Velda Wong; **Advertising Manager:** Velda Wong
Summary of Content: Journal of the Institute of Measurement and Control. Includes information, business news and features on technical advances.
Readership/Target Audience: Aimed at members and professional qualified engineers.
ADVERTISING RATES:
Full Page Mono £700.00
Full Page Colour £1100.00
Agency Commission: 10%
Mechanical Data: Type Area: 247 x 165mm, Trim Size: 297 x 210mm, Bleed Size: 303 x 216mm, Film: Digital, Print Process: Offset litho, Page Width: 165mm, Col Length: 247mm
Copy instructions: Copy Date: 1st of the month prior to publication date
Average advertising content per issue: 10%
BUSINESS: COMPUTERS & AUTOMATION: Automation & Instrumentation

MEASUREMENT SCIENCE & TECHNOLOGY
35992U5A-190
Editorial Address: Dirac House, Temple Back, BRISTOL, BS1 6BE **Tel:** 0117 929 7481 **Fax:** 0117 920 0669
Email: mst@iop.org
Advertising Address: As above. **Fax:** 0117 929 4318
Email: robert.fisher@iop.org
Web site: http://www.iop.org/journals/mst
ISSN: 0957-0233
Publisher: IOP Publishing
Date Established: 1923
Frequency: Monthly
Annual Sub.: £1032.00
Circulation: 1,000 (Publisher's Statement)
Usual Pagination: 250
Editor: Sharon D'Souza; **Publisher:** Sharon D'Souza
Summary of Content: Journal focusing on the theory and practice of measurement in engineering, chemistry, physics and related sciences.
Readership/Target Audience: Aimed at scientists and engineers.
ADVERTISING RATES:
Full Page Mono £715.00
Full Page Colour £1760.00
Agency Commission: 10%
Mechanical Data: Bleed Size: 303 x 216mm, Trim Size: 297 x 210mm
Copy instructions: Copy Date: 6 weeks prior to publication date
BUSINESS: COMPUTERS & AUTOMATION: Automation & Instrumentation

MEAT TRADES JOURNAL
38023U22D-280
Editorial Address: Broadfield Park, CRAWLEY, RH11 9RT
Tel: 01293 613400 **Fax:** 01293 846540
Email: ed.bedington@william-reed.co.uk
Advertising Address: As above. **Tel:** 01293 846572
Email: martin.goult@william-reed.co.uk
Web site: http://www.meatinfo.co.uk
Publisher: William Reed Business Media
Frequency: 26 issues yearly
Cover Price: £1.45
Annual Sub.: £65.00
Circulation: 5,633 (ABC 01/01/2008 to 31/12/2008)
Usual Pagination: 32
Editor: Ed Bedington
Summary of Content: Journal focusing on the meat trade in Great Britain, including poultry producers and abattoirs.
Readership/Target Audience: Read by those involved in the meat industry in Great Britain, including meat processors, retailers and manufacturers.
ADVERTISING RATES:
Full Page Colour £2500.00
Agency Commission: 10%
Mechanical Data: Type Area: 270 x 190mm, Bleed Size: 303 x 216mm, Col Length: 270mm, Page Width: 190mm, Trim Size: 297 x 210mm, Film: Digital
Copy instructions: Copy Date: 1 week prior to publication date
Average advertising content per issue: 30%
BUSINESS: FOOD: Meat Trade

MECHAID
37709U19R-360
Editorial Address: 41 High Street, Morcott, OAKHAM, LE15 9DN **Tel:** 01572 747472 **Fax:** 01572 747576
Email: editorial@mechaid.com
Advertising Address: As above. **Tel:** 01335 343545
Email: mechaid@mechaid.com
Web site: http://www.mechaid.com
Publisher: Special T Publishing
Date Established: 1994
Frequency: 6 issues yearly - Published on the 1st Monday of the cover month

---

Free to qualifying individuals
Annual Sub.: £24.00
Circulation: 8,000 (Publisher's Statement)
Usual Pagination: 48
Editor: Roger Ryan; **Managing Director:** Richard Hacker
Summary of Content: Business magazine covering tools, power tools, plant and equipment.
Readership/Target Audience: Read by buyers and specifiers of tools, plant and equipment in the hire industry, local authorities and public and private utilities.
ADVERTISING RATES:
Full Page Colour £1525.00
Agency Commission: 10%
Mechanical Data: Film: Digital, Type Area: 270 x 190mm, Col Length: 270mm, Page Width: 190mm, Print Process: Sheet-fed litho
Copy instructions: Copy Date: 4th of the month prior to publication date
Average advertising content per issue: 60%
BUSINESS: ENGINEERING & MACHINERY: Engineering Related

MEDIA, CULTURE & SOCIETY
40068U55-95_69
Editorial Address: 1 Oliver's Yard, 55 City Road, LONDON, EC1Y 1SP **Tel:** 020 7324 8500 **Fax:** 020 7324 8600
Advertising Address: As above.
Web site: http://www.sagepub.co.uk
ISSN: 0163-4437
Publisher: Sage Publications
Date Established: 1985
Frequency: 6 issues yearly
Cover Price: £11.00
Annual Sub.: £52.00
Advertising Manager: Sheena Karim
Summary of Content: An international forum for the presentation of research and discussion concerning the media.
Readership/Target Audience: Aimed at those concerned with information and communication technologies within their political, economic, cultural and historical contexts.
ADVERTISING RATES:
Full Page Mono £450.00
Mechanical Data: Type Area: 185 x 105mm, Col Length: 185mm, Page Width: 105mm
BUSINESS: APPLIED SCIENCE & LABORATORIES

MEDIA LAWYER
35616U2B-77
Editorial Address: 292 Vauxhall Bridge Road, LONDON, SW1V 1AE **Tel:** 020 7963 7132
Email: mike.dodd@pressassociation.com
Advertising Address: As above. **Tel:** 020 7963 7000
Fax: 020 7963 7199
Email: olja.pavlovsky@pabusiness.co.uk
Web site: http://www.medialawyer.press.net
ISSN: 1364-517X
Publisher: Press Association
Date Established: 1996
Frequency: 6 issues yearly
Circulation: 450 (Publisher's Statement)
Usual Pagination: 48
Editor: Mike Dodd
Summary of Content: Newsletter covering libel, contempt of court, reporting restrictions, data protection, privacy and other media law topics. The printed newsletter provides notes and reports on media law developments and cases in the UK in a two month period. The same material is uploaded on to the website as it happens.
Readership/Target Audience: Aimed at media lawyers, editors, journalists, journalism trainers and media academics.
ADVERTISING RATES:
Full Page Mono £1950.00
Mechanical Data: Film: Digital
BUSINESS: COMMUNICATIONS, ADVERTISING & MARKETING: Press

MEDIA MAGAZINE
1642080U2D-137
Editorial Address: 18 Compton Terrace, LONDON, N1 2UN
Tel: 020 7359 8080 **Fax:** 020 7354 0133
Email: jenny@englishandmedia.co.uk
Web site: http://www.mediamagazine.org.uk
Publisher: The English and Media Centre
Date Established: 2002
Frequency: Quarterly
Annual Sub.: £29.95
Circulation: 3,500 (Publisher's Statement)
Usual Pagination: 64
Editor: Jenny Grahame
Summary of Content: Educational magazine covering all aspects of film and media studies.
Readership/Target Audience: Aimed at A-level students and undergraduates of film and media studies.
ADVERTISING: Rates on application
BUSINESS: COMMUNICATIONS, ADVERTISING & MARKETING: Broadcasting

---

MEDIA WEEK
35618U2B-80
Editorial Address: 174 Hammersmith Road, LONDON, W6 7JP **Tel:** 020 8267 5000
Email: tristan.ocarroll@haymarket.com
Advertising Address: As above. **Fax:** 020 8267 8020
Email: chloe.lambert@haymarket.com
Web site: http://www.mediaweek.co.uk
ISSN: 0963-0023
Publisher: Haymarket Business Media Ltd
Date Established: 1985
Frequency: Weekly
Cover Price: £3.30
Free to qualifying individuals
Annual Sub.: £145.00
Circulation: 9,824 (ABC 01/07/2008 to 30/06/2009)
Usual Pagination: 36
Editor: Tristan O'Carroll; **News Editor:** Tristan O'Carroll; **Features Editor:** Harriet Dennys; **Managing Director:** Rufus Olins
Summary of Content: Magazine covering the business side of advertising, including media planning and buying, consumer magazines, radio, television, outdoor, national, regional and business press.
Readership/Target Audience: Read by senior marketing personnel in advertising companies, planner buyers in media agencies and media sales people.
ADVERTISING RATES:
Full Page Colour £5023.00
Agency Commission: 10%
Mechanical Data: Film: Digital, Type Area: 275 x 205mm, Col Length: 275mm, Page Width: 205mm, Trim Size: 295 x 225mm, Bleed Size: 301 x 231mm
Copy instructions: Copy Date: Friday 12pm prior to publication date
Average advertising content per issue: 40%
BUSINESS: COMMUNICATIONS, ADVERTISING & MARKETING: Press

MEDICAL DEVICE & DIAGNOSTICS INDUSTRY
1659595U56G-57
Editorial Address: Kent House, Romney Place, MAIDSTONE, ME15 6LH **Tel:** 01622 661350
Fax: 01622 661687
Email: colin.martin@cancom.co.uk
Advertising Address: As above. **Tel:** 01622 662511
Email: colin.martin@cancom.co.uk
Web site: http://www.devicelink.com/mddi
Publisher: Canon Communications
Date Established: 1979
Frequency: Monthly - Published in the 1st week of the cover month
Free to qualifying individuals
Circulation: 50,540 (BPA Worldwide 01/07/2006 to 31/12/2006)
Usual Pagination: 110
Editor: Colin Martin; **Advertising Manager:** Colin Martin; **Managing Editor:** Heather Thompson; **Publisher:** Colin Martin
Summary of Content: Magazine covering peer-reviewed articles by leading experts on specific technology issues and overviews of key business, industry, and regulatory topics.
Readership/Target Audience: Aimed at industry personnel involved in design, project and process engineering; research and development; production and manufacturing; quality assurance; regulatory and legal affairs and corporate management.
ADVERTISING RATES:
Full Page Mono $8250.00
Full Page Colour $9945.00
Agency Commission: 15%
Mechanical Data: Type Area: 255 x 180mm, Bleed Size: 280 x 210mm, Trim Size: 265 x 205mm, Col Length: 255mm, Page Width: 180mm, Print Process: Web-fed offset litho, Film: Digital
Copy instructions: Copy Date: 4 weeks prior to publication date
BUSINESS: HEALTH & MEDICAL: Medical Equipment

MEDICAL DEVICE COMPANIES ANALYSIS
40428U56G-47
Editorial Address: Lincoln House, City Fields Business Park, City Fields Way, Tangmere, CHICHESTER, PO20 2FS
Tel: 01243 533322 **Fax:** 01243 533418
Email: jayne_hardwell@espicom.com
Web site: http://www.espicom.com
Publisher: Espicom Ltd
Frequency: Monthly
Annual Sub.: £1575.00
Circulation: 1,000 (Publisher's Statement)
Usual Pagination: 70
Editor: Jayne Hardwell
Summary of Content: Newsletter containing individual worldwide medical device company profiles, including financial, corporate and international operations, R&D and products.
Readership/Target Audience: Aimed at people within the medical device industry.

ADVERTISING: No Advertising taken
BUSINESS: HEALTH & MEDICAL: Medical Equipment

THE MEDICAL DEVICE DECONTAMINATION
40362U56C-345

Formerly: The IDSc Journal
Editorial Address: Drumcross Hall, BATHGATE, EH48 4JT
Tel: 01506 811077 **Fax:** 01506 811477
Email: info@fitwise.co.uk
Advertising Address: As above.
Email: john@fitwise.co.uk
Web site: http://www.idsc-uk.org
ISSN: 1462-5156
Publisher: Fitwise
Frequency: Quarterly
Free to qualifying individuals
Annual Sub.: £24.00
Circulation: 1,250 (Publisher's Statement)
Usual Pagination: 48
Editor: Susan Meredith; **Advertising Manager:** John Matthews; **Publisher:** John Matthews
Summary of Content: Journal of the Institute of Decontamination Sciences containing features of interest to members.
Readership/Target Audience: Read by members of the Institute of Sterile Services Management, decontamination managers and technicians, sterile services managers and theatre managers.
ADVERTISING RATES:
Full Page Mono £315.00
Full Page Colour £760.00
Agency Commission: 10%
Mechanical Data: Type Area: 270 x 188mm, Bleed Size: 303 x 213mm, Trim Size: 297 x 210mm, Film: Digital, Print Process: Litho, Col Length: 270mm, Page Width: 188mm
Copy instructions: Copy Date: 1st of the month prior to publication date
Average advertising content per issue: 30%
BUSINESS: HEALTH & MEDICAL: Hospitals

MEDICAL DEVICE DEVELOPMENTS
601555U56A-80

Editorial Address: Brunel House, 55-57 North Wharf Road, LONDON, W2 1LA **Tel:** 020 7915 9879
Email: andrewtunnicliffe@spgmedia.com
Web site: http://www.medicaldevice-network.com
Publisher: SPG Media Ltd
Date Established: 2001
Frequency: Quarterly
Cover Price: Free
Circulation: 10,000 (ABC 01/01/2008 to 31/12/2008)
Usual Pagination: 136
Editor: Andrew Tunnicliffe
Summary of Content: Journal containing editorial about the development and manufacture of medical devices.
Readership/Target Audience: Aimed at medical device manufacturers.
ADVERTISING: No Advertising taken
BUSINESS: HEALTH & MEDICAL

MEDICAL DEVICE TECHNOLOGY
40429U56G-48

Editorial Address: Murlain Business Centre, Union Street, CHESTER, CH1 1QP **Tel:** 01244 357201 **Fax:** 01244 357246
Email: annie.ellerton@cancom.com
Advertising Address: Kent House, Romney Place, MAIDSTONE, ME15 6LH **Tel:** 01622 661350
Fax: 01622 661687
Email: colin.martin@cancom.co.uk
Web site: http://www.devicelink.com/mdt
ISSN: 1048-6690
Publisher: Canon Communications LLC
Date Established: 1990
Frequency: 7 issues yearly - Published in the 3rd week of the month prior to cover date
Free to qualifying individuals
Annual Sub.: £85.00
Circulation: 18,000 (BPA Worldwide 01/01/2006 to 30/06/2006)
Usual Pagination: 60
Editor: Annie Ellerton; **Editor-in-Chief:** Annie Ellerton; **Group Editor:** Norbert Sparrow; **Publisher:** Colin Martin
Summary of Content: Magazine containing practical articles on the design, development and manufacture of medical devices and in vitro diagnostic products.
Readership/Target Audience: Aimed at manufacturers of medical devices and in vitro diagnostic products in Europe.
ADVERTISING RATES:
Full Page Mono $6795.00
Full Page Colour $8545.00
Agency Commission: 10%
Mechanical Data: Trim Size: 285 x 225mm, Film: Digital
Copy instructions: Copy Date: 2 weeks prior to publication date
Average advertising content per issue: 40%
BUSINESS: HEALTH & MEDICAL: Medical Equipment

THE MEDICAL DIGEST MIDDLE EAST & N. AFRICA
40196U56A-81

Formerly: Medical Digest Middle East, N.Africa, India & Pakistan
Editorial Address: Sahara House, 38 Greyhound Road, LONDON, W6 8NX **Tel:** 020 7610 1387 **Fax:** 020 7610 0078
Email: sahara@btconnect.com
Advertising Address: As above.
Email: sahara@btconnect.com
Web site: http://www.saharapublications.com
Publisher: Sahara Publications
Date Established: 1990
Frequency: Quarterly
Editor: M. Butros; **Managing Director:** Abed Najjar;
Advertising Manager: Debbie Woolnoth; **Publisher:** Abed Najjar
Summary of Content: International journal focusing on new products and technology in the healthcare industry.
Readership/Target Audience: Read by healthcare professionals.
ADVERTISING RATES:
Full Page Mono £1395.00
Full Page Colour £2450.00
Agency Commission: 10%
Mechanical Data: Film: Digital, Bleed Size: 309 x 216mm, Trim Size: 297 x 210mm, No. of Columns (Display): 3
Average advertising content per issue: 45%
BUSINESS: HEALTH & MEDICAL

MEDICAL FUTURES
718532U56A-85

Editorial Address: The Royal Institution of Great Britain, 21 Albemarle Street, LONDON, W1S 4BS **Tel:** 0844 870 0056
Fax: 0844 540 0057
Email: mail@medicalfutures.co.uk
Advertising Address: As above. **Fax:** 0870 766 9483
Email: martine@medicalfutures.co.uk
Web site: http://www.medicalfutures.co.uk
Publisher: Medical Futures
Date Established: 2001
Frequency: Annual - Published in July
Cover Price: EUR5.75
Circulation: 90,000 (Publisher's Statement)
Usual Pagination: 82
Editor: Andy Goldberg; **Advertising Manager:** Martine Morris; **Publisher:** Andy Goldberg
Summary of Content: Magazine covering healthcare, business, medical and surgical innovation and entrepreneurship, technology, finance and articles on private practice. Includes interviews, issues and travel and lifestyle features.
Readership/Target Audience: Read by medical professionals, decision makers and key opinion leaders. In addition the magazine targets venture capitalists, angel investors and industry leaders interested in healthcare.
ADVERTISING RATES:
Full Page Colour £3500.00
Agency Commission: 15%
Mechanical Data: Type Area: 270 x 185mm, Col Length: 270mm, Bleed Size: 303 x 216mm, Trim Size: 297 x 210mm, Film: Digital, Page Width: 185mm
Copy instructions: Copy Date: 3 weeks prior to publication date
Average advertising content per issue: 20%
BUSINESS: HEALTH & MEDICAL

MEDICAL INDUSTRY WEEK
40430U56G-50

Editorial Address: Lincoln House, City Fields Business Park, City Fields Way, Tangmere, CHICHESTER, PO20 2FS
Tel: 01243 533322 **Fax:** 01243 533418
Email: healthcare@espicom.com
Web site: http://www.espicom.com
ISSN: 1462-8716
Publisher: Espicom Ltd
Date Established: 1998
Frequency: 44 issues yearly
Annual Sub.: £445.00
Circulation: 1,000 (Publisher's Statement)
Usual Pagination: 26
Editor: Lawrence Miller; **Publisher:** Eric Wigart
Summary of Content: Newsletter covering worldwide developments in medical device and equipment companies.
Readership/Target Audience: Aimed at people within the medical industry.
ADVERTISING: No Advertising taken
BUSINESS: HEALTH & MEDICAL: Medical Equipment

MEDICAL INFORMATICS AND THE INTERNET IN MEDICINE
40539U56R-90

Editorial Address: 4 Park Square, Milton Park, ABINGDON, OX14 4RN **Tel:** 020 7017 6000 **Fax:** 020 7017 6336
Email: susannah.douch@tandf.co.uk
Web site: http://www.tandf.co.uk
ISSN: 1463-9238
Publisher: Routledge, Taylor & Francis
Date Established: 1976

Frequency: Quarterly
Annual Sub.: £601.00
Circulation: 450 (Publisher's Statement)
Usual Pagination: 96
Editor: Steve Kay; **Advertising Manager:** Di Owen
Summary of Content: Journal promoting the application of analysis, inference and reasoning to medical information, including expert systems and the use of artificial intelligence techniques. Also contains organisation data and knowledge with applications to medical education.
Readership/Target Audience: Aimed at those involved with computing health care.
BUSINESS: HEALTH & MEDICAL: Health Medical Related

MEDICAL PRODUCTS MANUFACTURING NEWS
1659594U56G-58

Editorial Address: Kent House, Romney Place, MAIDSTONE, ME15 6LH **Tel:** 01622 662511
Fax: 01622 661687
Email: colin.martin@cancom.co.uk
Advertising Address: As above. **Tel:** 01622 662251
Email: colin.martin@cancom.co.uk
Web site: http://www.canonmediakit.com
Publisher: Canon Communications
Date Established: 1985
Frequency: 10 issues yearly - Published in the 1st week of the cover month
Circulation: 38,040 (Publisher's Statement)
Usual Pagination: 120
Editor: Colin Martin; **Advertising Manager:** Colin Martin; **Group Editor:** Norbert Sparrow
Summary of Content: Magazine providing information on new products and services available to medical device manufacturers.
Readership/Target Audience: Aimed at design engineers, manufacturers and specifying personnel.
ADVERTISING RATES:
Full Page Mono $6540.00
Full Page Colour $8170.00
Agency Commission: 15%
Mechanical Data: Trim Size: 394 x 268mm, Type Area: 380 x 255mm, Bleed Size: 414 x 285mm, Col Length: 380mm, Page Width: 255mm, Film: Digital
Copy instructions: Copy Date: 4 weeks prior to publication date
BUSINESS: HEALTH & MEDICAL: Medical Equipment

MEDICAL TEACHER
40199U56A-90

Editorial Address: Centre for Medical Education, Tay Park House, 484 Perth Road, DUNDEE, DD2 1LR
Tel: 01382 381994 **Fax:** 01382 381987
Email: medicalteacher@dundee.ac.uk
Web site: http://www.medicalteacher.org
ISSN: 0142-159X
Publisher: Routledge, Taylor & Francis
Date Established: 1973
Frequency: 10 issues yearly
Free to qualifying individuals
Annual Sub.: £178.00
Usual Pagination: 112
Editor: Morag Allan; **Managing Editor:** Pat Lilley
Summary of Content: Journal providing medical and healthcare information, including current research, practical guidelines, reviews and current awareness features. Covers undergraduate, postgraduate and continuing medical and healthcare professions education.
Readership/Target Audience: Aimed at medical and other healthcare professionals, teachers, administrators, curriculum developers, researchers and students.
ADVERTISING: Rates on application
BUSINESS: HEALTH & MEDICAL

MEDICAL TEXTILES
39502U47A-235

Editorial Address: 9A Victoria Square, DROITWICH, WR9 8DE **Tel:** 0870 165 7210 **Fax:** 0870 165 7212
Email: editorial@intnews.com
Web site: http://www.technical-textiles.net
ISSN: 0266-2078
Publisher: International Newsletters
Date Established: 1984
Frequency: Monthly
Annual Sub.: £417.00
Usual Pagination: 12
Editor: Geoff Fisher
Summary of Content: Newsletter covering textiles used in medical and hygiene applications.
Readership/Target Audience: Aimed at manufacturers, suppliers and users of textiles for medical applications.
ADVERTISING: No Advertising taken
BUSINESS: CLOTHING & TEXTILES

MEDICINE
40200U56A-95

Editorial Address: The Boulevard, Langford Lane, KIDLINGTON, OX5 1GB **Tel:** 01865 843000
Fax: 01865 843965

Email: medicine@medicinepublishing.co.uk
Advertising Address: As above. **Tel:** 01865 843154
Email: b.robinson@elsevier.com
Web site: http://www.medicinepublishing.co.uk
ISSN: 1357-3039
Publisher: The Medicine Publishing Company
Date Established: 1972
Frequency: Monthly
Annual Sub.: £116.00
Usual Pagination: 48
Editor: Vicky Hawkins; **Managing Editor:** Vicky Hawkins
Summary of Content: International journal of up-to-date medical information.
Readership/Target Audience: Aimed at junior doctors studying for MRCP examinations and qualified physicians keeping up-to-date.
ADVERTISING RATES:
Full Page Mono £863.00
Full Page Colour £1568.00
Mechanical Data: Type Area: 250 x 180mm, Bleed Size: 286 x 216mm, Trim Size: 280 x 210mm, Film: Digital, Col Length: 250mm, Page Width: 180mm
BUSINESS: HEALTH & MEDICAL

MEDISTAT
40431U56G-52
Editorial Address: Lincoln House, City Fields Business Park, City Fields Way, Tangmere, CHICHESTER, PO20 2FS
Tel: 01243 533322 **Fax:** 01243 533418
Email: andrew_crofts@espicom.com
Web site: http://www.espicom.com
ISSN: 1352-1179
Publisher: Espicom Ltd
Date Established: 1986
Frequency: Monthly
Annual Sub.: £1345.00
Circulation: 2,500 (Publisher's Statement)
Editor: Andrew Crofts; **Managing Director:** Eric Wigart;
Publisher: Eric Wigart; **Circulation Manager:** Carole Baker
Summary of Content: Journal providing hard data and analysis of the significant markets for medical devices and equipment around the world.
Readership/Target Audience: Aimed at members of the medical industry.
ADVERTISING: No Advertising taken
BUSINESS: HEALTH & MEDICAL: Medical Equipment

MEED
36966U14C-98
Formerly: MEED Middle East Economic Digest
Editorial Address: Greater London House, Hampstead Road, LONDON, NW1 7EJ **Tel:** 020 7728 5000
Email: richard.thompson@meed.com
Advertising Address: As above.
Email: sam.elbaire@meed.com
Web site: http://www.meed.com
ISSN: 0047-7238
Publisher: EMAP Communications Ltd
Date Established: 1957
Frequency: Weekly - Published on Friday
Annual Sub.: £562.26
Circulation: 5,993 (ABC 01/01/2007 to 31/12/2007)
Usual Pagination: 44
Editor: Dominic Dudley; **News Editor:** Dominic Dudley;
Features Editor: Sophie Evans
Summary of Content: Journal covering economics, business news and developments for trade and industry in the Middle East and North Africa.
Readership/Target Audience: Aimed at senior decision-makers in business and government, both in the Middle East and worldwide.
ADVERTISING RATES:
Full Page Mono EUR7176.00
Full Page Colour EUR9007.00
Agency Commission: 15%
Mechanical Data: Type Area: 250 x 186mm, Bleed Size: 285 x 216mm, Trim Size: 279 x 210mm, Col Length: 250mm, Page Width: 186mm, Film: Digital
Copy instructions: Copy Date: 10 days prior to publication date
BUSINESS: COMMERCE, INDUSTRY & MANAGEMENT: International Commerce

---

MEETINGS & INCENTIVE TRAVEL
35642U2C-100
Editorial Address: Kings House, Cantelupe Road, EAST GRINSTEAD, RH19 3BE **Tel:** 01342 306700
Fax: 01342 302547
Email: editorial@cat-publications.com
Advertising Address: As above.
Email: mbriggs@cat-publications.com
Web site: http://www.meetpie.com
ISSN: 0953-2803
Publisher: Conference & Travel Publications Ltd
Frequency: 10 issues yearly
Annual Sub.: £60.00
Circulation: 17,129 (ABC 01/07/2008 to 30/06/2009)

Editor: Rochelle Long; **Managing Director:** Martin Lewis;
Advertising Manager: Maxine Briggs; **Managing Editor:** Martin Lewis
Summary of Content: Magazine containing industry news, destination reports and articles on UK cities and country houses.
Readership/Target Audience: Aimed at event organisers.
ADVERTISING RATES:
Full Page Mono £2355.00
Full Page Colour £3195.00
Agency Commission: 10%
Mechanical Data: Bleed Size: 303 x 216mm, Trim Size: 297 x 210mm, Film: Digital
Average advertising content per issue: 33%
BUSINESS: COMMUNICATIONS, ADVERTISING & MARKETING: Conferences & Exhibitions

---

MEETINGS FILE
35643U2C-105
Editorial Address: 29A Market Square, BIGGLESWADE, SG18 8AQ **Tel:** 01767 316255 **Fax:** 01767 316430
Publisher: The Meetings Forum
Frequency: 10 issues yearly
Cover Price: £1.75
Circulation: 500 (Publisher's Statement)
Usual Pagination: 16
Editor: Peter Cotterell
Summary of Content: Newsletter containing news about events as well as offering views and advice.
Readership/Target Audience: Aimed at event organisers. Also distributed to all members of the Society of Event Organisers.
ADVERTISING: No Advertising taken
BUSINESS: COMMUNICATIONS, ADVERTISING & MARKETING: Conferences & Exhibitions

---

MEMBRANE TECHNOLOGY NEWSLETTER
36912U14B-260
Editorial Address: The Boulevard, Langford Lane, KIDLINGTON, OX5 1GB **Tel:** 01865 843239
Fax: 01865 843971
Email: s.barrett@elsevier.com
Web site: http://www.membrane-technology.com
ISSN: 0958-2118
Publisher: Elsevier Ltd
Date Established: 1990
Frequency: Monthly
Annual Sub.: EUR999.00
Usual Pagination: 16
Editor: Simon Atkinson
Summary of Content: Journal providing regular coverage of research, development and applications of membrane technology in a wide range of industries, including pharmaceuticals, food and beverage, industrial chemicals and gases, potable and industrial water, electronics and biotechnology.
Readership/Target Audience: Aimed at researchers, membrane producers and equipment manufacturers and industrial users of synthetic membranes.
ADVERTISING: No Advertising taken
BUSINESS: COMMERCE, INDUSTRY & MANAGEMENT: Industry & Factories

---

MENTAL HEALTH NURSING
40487U56N-45
Editorial Address: Ten Alps Publishing, 9 Savoy Street, LONDON, WC2E 7HR **Tel:** 07973 518682
Email: matt@pulzer.org
Publisher: Ten Alps Publishing
Frequency: 6 issues yearly
Free to qualifying individuals
Circulation: 5,000 (Publisher's Statement)
Usual Pagination: 24
Editor: Matthew Pulzer
Summary of Content: Journal of the Mental Health Nurses Association (MHNA).
Readership/Target Audience: Aimed at community psychiatric nurses.
ADVERTISING: No Advertising taken
BUSINESS: HEALTH & MEDICAL: Mental Health

MENTAL HEALTH PRACTICE
40488U56N-47
Editorial Address: The Heights, 59-65 Lowlands Road, HARROW, HA1 3AW **Tel:** 020 8423 1066
Fax: 020 8872 3198
Email: helen.hyland@rcnpublishing.co.uk
Advertising Address: As above. **Fax:** 020 8423 3196
Email: advertising@rcnpublishing.co.uk
Web site: http://www.mentalhealthpractice.co.uk
ISSN: 1465-8720
Publisher: RCN Publishing Co Ltd
Date Established: 1997
Frequency: 10 issues yearly
Annual Sub.: £59.40
Circulation: 11,232 (ABC 01/01/2008 to 31/12/2008)
Usual Pagination: 44

Editor: Helen Hyland
Summary of Content: Magazine covering mental health news, features, professional development articles and letters page.
Readership/Target Audience: Aimed at mental health nurses.
ADVERTISING RATES:
Full Page Colour £2299.00
Agency Commission: 10%
Mechanical Data: Type Area: 271 x 178mm, Trim Size: 297 x 210mm, Bleed Size: 303 x 216mm, Film: Digital, Col Length: 271mm, Page Width: 178mm
Copy instructions: Copy Date: 2 weeks prior to publication date
Average advertising content per issue: 15%
BUSINESS: HEALTH & MEDICAL: Mental Health

THE MENTAL HEALTH REVIEW JOURNAL
601106U56N-48
Formerly: The Mental Health Review
Editorial Address: Richmond House, Richmond Road, BRIGHTON, BN2 3RL **Tel:** 01273 623222
Fax: 01273 625526
Email: joannas@pavpub.com
Advertising Address: As above. **Tel:** 0870 890 1080
Fax: 0870 890 1081
Email: pauls@pavpub.com
Web site: http://www.pavpub.com
ISSN: 1361-9322
Publisher: Pavilion Journals (Brighton) Ltd
Date Established: 1996
Frequency: Quarterly
Annual Sub.: £49.00
Circulation: 450 (Publisher's Statement)
Usual Pagination: 40
Editor: Joanna Sharrocks; **Advertising Manager:** Paul Somerville
Summary of Content: Journal featuring case studies, communications updates, news and key developments in mental health policy.
Readership/Target Audience: Aimed at purchasers, policy analysts, provider managers, senior practitioners, social services and the independent sector.
ADVERTISING RATES:
Full Page Mono £350.00
Agency Commission: 10%
Mechanical Data: Type Area: 240 x 170mm, Col Length: 240mm, Film: Digital, Trim Size: 247 x 160mm, Page Width: 170mm
Average advertising content per issue: 10%
BUSINESS: HEALTH & MEDICAL: Mental Health

MENTAL HEALTH TODAY
40486U56N-49
Formerly: Mental Health & Learning Disabilities Care
Editorial Address: Richmond House, Richmond Road, BRIGHTON, BN2 3RL **Tel:** 01273 623222
Fax: 01273 625526
Email: mhtoday@pavpub.com
Advertising Address: As above. **Tel:** 0870 890 1080
Fax: 0870 890 1081
Email: helenc@pavpub.com
Web site: http://www.pavpub.com
ISSN: 1368-1230
Publisher: Pavilion Journals (Brighton) Ltd
Date Established: 1997
Frequency: 10 issues yearly
Cover Price: £3.95
Annual Sub.: £32.00
Circulation: 3,500 (Publisher's Statement)
Usual Pagination: 44
Editor: Lynn Eaton; **Advertising Manager:** Helen Charlton
Summary of Content: Magazine covering all aspects of mental health and social care.
Readership/Target Audience: Aimed at practitioners in the statutory, voluntary and independent sectors.
ADVERTISING RATES:
Full Page Mono £800.00
Full Page Colour £800.00
Agency Commission: 10%
Mechanical Data: Page Width: 180mm, Col Length: 260mm, Type Area: 260 x 180mm, Trim Size: 297 x 210mm, Bleed Size: 303 x 216mm, Film: Digital
BUSINESS: HEALTH & MEDICAL: Mental Health

MENTORING & TUTORING
41157U62J-680
Editorial Address: 4 Park Square, Milton Park, ABINGDON, OX14 4RN **Tel:** 020 7017 6000 **Fax:** 020 7017 6336
Web site: http://www.informaworld.com
ISSN: 1361-1267
Publisher: Routledge, Taylor & Francis
Frequency: Quarterly
Annual Sub.: £406.00
Usual Pagination: 112
Editor: Lannette Clifford
Summary of Content: Mentoring & Tutoring: Partnership in learning is an international refereed journal that has quickly

Business Magazines

Section 4 (b) Business Magazines

become the major resource to exchange information on mentoring and tutoring. The journal seeks to publish papers on all aspects of mentoring, tutoring and partnership in education, other disciplines and the professions. The journal is also playing an important role in burgeoning 'distance learning' programmes.
Readership/Target Audience: Academics, researchers and practitioners interested in all aspects of mentoring and tutoring.
BUSINESS: CHURCH & SCHOOL EQUIPMENT & EDUCATION: Teachers & Education Management

MER MARINE ENGINEERS REVIEW
39407U45D-140

Editorial Address: 80 Coleman Street, LONDON, EC2R 5BJ
Tel: 020 7382 2600 **Fax:** 020 7382 2672
Email: john.barnes@imarest.org
Advertising Address: As above. **Tel:** 020 7382 2672
Fax: 020 7382 2669
Email: alwyn.topliss@imarest.org
Web site: http://www.imarest.org/mer
ISSN: 0047-5955
Publisher: IMarEST
Date Established: 1967
Frequency: 10 issues yearly - Published on the 27th of the month prior to cover month
Free to qualifying individuals
Annual Sub.: £87.00
Circulation: 11,205 (ABC 01/01/2008 to 31/12/2008)
Usual Pagination: 52
Editor: John Barnes
Summary of Content: Journal covering shipbuilding, shipping, marine engineering, oil, gas and offshore technology.
Readership/Target Audience: Read by senior board managers, technical managers, consultants and surveyors.
ADVERTISING RATES:
Full Page Colour £2345.00
Agency Commission: 15%
Mechanical Data: Type Area: 280 x 195mm, Bleed Size: 307 x 220mm, Trim Size: 297 x 210mm, Print Process: Litho, Film: Digital, Col Length: 280mm, Page Width: 195mm
Copy instructions: Copy Date: 15th of the month prior to publication date
Average advertising content per issue: 45%
Supplement(s): Propulsion Incorporating the Directory of Marine Diesel Engines - 1xY
BUSINESS: MARINE & SHIPPING: Marine Engineering Equipment

MERCURY
38121U26C-65

Editorial Address: Interflora House, SLEAFORD, NG34 7TB
Tel: 01529 301468 **Fax:** 01529 414631
Email: catharine.brown@interflora.co.uk
Advertising Address: As above.
Email: catharine.brown@interflora.co.uk
Publisher: Interflora (BU) Ltd
Date Established: 1923
Frequency: 6 issues yearly
Free to qualifying individuals
Circulation: 3,500 (Publisher's Statement)
Usual Pagination: 52
Editor: Catharine Brown; **Advertising Manager:** Catharine Brown
Summary of Content: Magazine covering floristry, events and new products in the flower trade as well as information relating to the running of a small business.
Readership/Target Audience: Aimed at florists, wholesalers and those with an interest in floristry.
ADVERTISING RATES:
Full Page Colour £1000.00
Mechanical Data: Bleed Size: 303 x 216mm, Page Width: 185mm, Type Area: 270 x 185mm, Col Length: 270mm, Trim Size: 297 x 210mm, Film: Digital
BUSINESS: GARDEN TRADE

MERGERS & ACQUISITIONS MAGAZINE
34910U1A-241

Formerly: M&A
Editorial Address: Octavia House, 50 Banner Street, LONDON, EC1Y 8ST **Tel:** 020 7250 7066
Fax: 020 7250 7011
Email: patrizia.rossi@vitessemedia.co.uk
Advertising Address: As above. **Tel:** 0121 214 0880
Fax: 0121 236 9923
Email: martyn.black@vitessemedia.co.uk
Web site: http://www.vitessemedia.com
Publisher: Vitesse Media plc
Date Established: 1999
Frequency: Monthly - Published in the 1st week of cover month
Annual Sub.: £165.00
Circulation: 8,000 (Publisher's Statement)
Usual Pagination: 100
Editor: Patrizia Rossi; **Managing Editor:** Marc Barber

Summary of Content: Magazine providing news and features on corporate finance, and issues affecting growth companies.
Readership/Target Audience: Aimed at finance directors, CEOs and other company directors of large and small publicly quoted companies. The magazine is also targeted at a wide range of dealmakers including financial and legal advisers, banks, VCs and consultants.
ADVERTISING RATES:
Full Page Colour £1930.00
Agency Commission: 10%
Mechanical Data: Bleed Size: 303 x 216mm, Type Area: 257 x 180mm, Film: Digital, Trim Size: 297 x 210mm, Col Length: 257mm, Page Width: 180mm, Print Process: Sheet-fed litho
Copy instructions: Copy Date: 1st week of the month prior to publication date
Average advertising content per issue: 50%
BUSINESS: FINANCE & ECONOMICS

THE MESSENGER
39219U44-1474

Editorial Address: Rational House, 64 Bridge Street, MANCHESTER, M3 3BN **Tel:** 0161 831 7337
Fax: 0161 839 2631
Email: fran@manchesterlawsociety.org.uk
Advertising Address: 25 Southworth Way, THORNTON-CLEVELEYS, FY5 2WW **Tel:** 01253 829431
Fax: 01253 829431
Email: j.baskerville@btconnect.com
Web site: http://www.manchesterlawsociety.org.uk
Publisher: Julia Baskerville Publications
Date Established: 1994
Frequency: Monthly
Free to qualifying individuals
Circulation: 1,800 (Publisher's Statement)
Usual Pagination: 16
Editor: Fran Eccles; **Advertising Manager:** Julia Baskerville; **Publisher:** Julia Baskerville
Summary of Content: Journal of the Manchester Law Society covering news and features relating to the legal profession and the law.
Readership/Target Audience: Read by members of the Manchester Law Society.
ADVERTISING RATES:
Full Page Mono £600.00
Full Page Colour £900.00
Agency Commission: 10%
Mechanical Data: Type Area: 270 x 185mm, Trim Size: 297 x 210mm, Col Length: 270mm, Page Width: 185mm, Film: Digital, Bleed Size: +5mm
Copy instructions: Copy Date: 3 weeks prior to publication date
Average advertising content per issue: 50%
BUSINESS: LEGAL

METAL BULLETIN
38158U27-90

Editorial Address: 5-7 Ireland Yard, LONDON, EC4V 5EX
Tel: 020 7827 9977 **Fax:** 020 7928 6892
Email: editorial@metalbulletin.com
Advertising Address: 16 Lower Marsh, LONDON, SE1 7RJ
Tel: 020 7827 5220 **Fax:** 020 7827 5206
Email: advertising@metalbulletin.com
Web site: http://www.metalbulletin.com
ISSN: 0026-0533
Publisher: Euromoney Institutional Investor plc
Date Established: 1913
Frequency: Weekly
Annual Sub.: £1154.31
Circulation: 6,264 (ABC 01/01/2008 to 31/12/2008)
Usual Pagination: 36
Editor: Alex Harrison; **Managing Director:** Raju Daswani; **Advertising Manager:** Stefano Dinardo
Summary of Content: Magazine covering industry and market news and prices on steel, metals, ores and scrap.
Readership/Target Audience: Aimed at the steel, metals and scrap industry.
ADVERTISING RATES:
Full Page Mono £2308.00
Full Page Colour £3448.00
Agency Commission: 10%
Mechanical Data: Type Area: 250 x 184mm, Col Length: 250mm, Page Width: 184mm, Trim Size: 274 x 209mm, Bleed Size: 300 x 215mm, Film: Digital
Copy instructions: Copy Date: 10 days prior to publication date
Average advertising content per issue: 25%
BUSINESS: METAL, IRON & STEEL

METAL POWDER REPORT
38159U27-96

Editorial Address: The Boulevard, Langford Lane, KIDLINGTON, OX5 1GB **Tel:** 01865 843670
Fax: 01865 843971
Email: r.felton@elsevier.com
Advertising Address: 32 Jamestown Road, LONDON, NW1 7BY **Tel:** 020 7424 4200
Email: m.rami@elsevier.com
Web site: http://www.metal-powder.net

ISSN: 0026-0657
Publisher: Elsevier Ltd
Date Established: 1946
Frequency: 11 issues yearly - Published at the beginning of the cover month
Annual Sub.: EUR487.00
Circulation: 4,000 (Publisher's Statement)
Usual Pagination: 56
Editor: Richard Felton; **Publisher:** Greg Valero
Summary of Content: Magazine covering the powder metallurgy industry worldwide.
Readership/Target Audience: Aimed at management executives, design engineers, business analysts and research and academic establishments worldwide with an interest in PM technology.
ADVERTISING RATES:
Full Page Colour EUR4942.00
Agency Commission: 10%
Mechanical Data: Page Width: 185mm, Type Area: 285 x 185mm, Col Length: 285mm, Trim Size: 297 x 210mm, Bleed Size: 306 x 216mm, Film: Digital
Average advertising content per issue: 40%
BUSINESS: METAL, IRON & STEEL

METALWORKING PRODUCTION
37647U19E-440

Editorial Address: Unit 2, Sugarbrook Court, Aston Road, BROMSGROVE, B60 3EX **Tel:** 01992 587025
Email: mike.excell@centaur.co.uk
Advertising Address: As above. **Tel:** 01527 880803
Fax: 01527 880824
Email: laura.thornton@centaur.co.uk
Web site: http://www.mwponline.com
ISSN: 0026-1033
Publisher: Centaur Media Plc
Date Established: 1900
Frequency: 6 issues yearly - Published in the 1st week of the cover month
Cover Price: Free
Annual Sub.: £58.00
Circulation: 16,493 (Publisher's Statement)
Usual Pagination: 100
Editor: Mike Excell; **Advertising Manager:** Laura Thornton; **Publisher:** Mike Excell
Summary of Content: Journal focusing on current methods and ideas in modern engineering production, machine tools and other equipment.
Readership/Target Audience: Read by production engineers, general management, plant engineers, buyers, quality managers and designers.
ADVERTISING RATES:
Full Page Mono £1984.50
Full Page Colour £2205.00
Agency Commission: 10%
Mechanical Data: Film: Digital, Bleed Size: 292 x 213mm, Trim Size: 286 x 210mm, Page Width: 178mm, Type Area: 254 x 178mm, Col Length: 254mm
Copy instructions: Copy Date: 2 weeks prior to publication date
Average advertising content per issue: 60%
BUSINESS: ENGINEERING & MACHINERY: Machinery, Machine Tools & Metalworking

METHODS IN ORGANIC SYNTHESIS
21655U13-110_20

Editorial Address: Thomas Graham House, Science Park, Milton Road, CAMBRIDGE, CB4 0WF **Tel:** 01223 420066
Fax: 01223 420247
Email: mos@rsc.org
Web site: http://www.rsc.org/mos
ISSN: 0265-4245
Publisher: Royal Society of Chemistry
Frequency: Monthly
Annual Sub.: £625.00
Usual Pagination: 50
Editor: Sula Armstrong
Summary of Content: Alerting service for synthetic organic chemists covering organic chemistry in the fine and speciality chemical industries including pharmaceuticals, electronics, agrochemicals, intermediates and speciality polymers.
Readership/Target Audience: Aimed at industrial and academic chemists and chemical engineers.
ADVERTISING: No Advertising taken
BUSINESS: CHEMICALS

METROPOLITAN LIFE
1658506U32F-701

Editorial Address: Colchester Business Centre, 1 George Williams Way, COLCHESTER, CO1 2JS **Tel:** 01206 369448
Fax: 01206 369437
Email: info@policelife.net
Advertising Address: As above.
Email: info@policelife.net
Web site: http://www.police-life.co.uk
Publisher: Occucom Ltd
Date Established: 2004

Frequency: 11 issues yearly
Cover Price: Free
Circulation: 12,000 (Publisher's Statement)
Editor: Martin Herman; **Advertising Manager:** Ian Smith;
Publisher: Martin Herman
Summary of Content: Magazine covering news and lifestyle
articles relevant to police service personnel.
Readership/Target Audience: Aimed at the Metropolitan
police force.
ADVERTISING RATES:
Full Page Mono £1495.00
Full Page Colour £1495.00
Agency Commission: 10%
Mechanical Data: Type Area: 270 x 190mm, Col Length:
270mm, Page Width: 190mm, Film: Digital
Copy instructions: Copy Date: 14th of the month prior to
publication date
Average advertising content per issue: 50%
BUSINESS: LOCAL GOVERNMENT, LEISURE &
RECREATION: Police

MI PRO INCORPORATING MUSIC TRADE NEWS
713989U61-17_50
Formerly: MI Pro
Editorial Address: Saxon House, 6A St. Andrew Street,
HERTFORD, SG14 1JA **Tel:** 01992 535646
Fax: 01992 535648
Email: mipro@intentmedia.co.uk
Advertising Address: As above.
Email: ads@mi-pro.co.uk
Web site: http://www.mi-pro.co.uk
Publisher: Intent Media
Date Established: 1999
Frequency: Monthly
Cover Price: Free
Circulation: 7,400 (Publisher's Statement)
Usual Pagination: 96
Editor: Andy Barrett; **Advertising Manager:** Darrell Carter;
Managing Editor: Andy Barrett
Summary of Content: Magazine covering news, analysis
and opinion on the latest music instrument industry and pro
audio issues as well as an overview of stock not yet in the
market place.
Readership/Target Audience: Aimed at those within the
professional music instrument and professional audio
businesses.
ADVERTISING RATES:
Full Page Colour £1155.00
SCC £25.00
Agency Commission: 10%
Mechanical Data: Type Area: 290 x 206mm, Bleed Size:
321 x 236mm, Trim Size: 315 x 230mm, Col Length: 290mm,
Page Width: 206mm, Film: Digital
Average advertising content per issue: 50%
BUSINESS: MUSIC TRADE

MICRO MANUFACTURING MAGAZINE
1834342U19A-569
Editorial Address: Unit 2, Chowley Court, Chowley Oak
Lane, Tattenhall, CHESTER, CH3 9GA **Tel:** 01829 770037
Fax: 01829 770047
Email: chris@rapidnews.com
Web site: http://www.micromanu.com
Publisher: Rapid News Publications
Date Established: 2008
Frequency: 6 issues yearly
Free to qualifying individuals
Circulation: 35,000 (Print Run)
Editor: Chris Young
Summary of Content: Magazine dedicated to the world of
micro manufacturing and nano applications. Featuring news
from the sector, case studies and feature articles.
Readership/Target Audience: Aimed at manufacturers of
micro products and components and industrial nano scale
applications.
BUSINESS: ENGINEERING & MACHINERY

MICRO TECHNOLOGY EUROPE
36109U5B-110
Editorial Address: Prudence Place, Proctor Way, LUTON,
LU2 9PE **Tel:** 01582 722460
Email: steve.rogerson@journalist.co.uk
Advertising Address: As above.
Email: david@mtemag.com
Web site: http://www.mtemag.com
ISSN: 1352-7312
Publisher: MT Publications Ltd
Frequency: 11 issues yearly - Published in the 3rd week of
the cover month
Free to qualifying individuals
Annual Sub.: £55.00
Circulation: 12,500 (Publisher's Statement)
Usual Pagination: 32
Editor: Steve Rogerson; **Advertising Manager:** David
Williams; **Publisher:** David Williams
Summary of Content: Magazine covering all aspects of
system designing.

Readership/Target Audience: Aimed at key decision
makers involved in the design of industrial computing and
embedded systems.
ADVERTISING RATES:
Full Page Colour £2725.00
Agency Commission: 10%
Mechanical Data: Bleed Size: 341 x 251mm, Trim Size: 335
x 245mm, Film: Digital
Copy instructions: Copy Date: 4 weeks prior to publication
date
Average advertising content per issue: 40%
BUSINESS: COMPUTERS & AUTOMATION: Data
Processing

MICROBIOLOGY TODAY
41495U64F-100
Editorial Address: Marlborough House, Basingstoke Road,
Spencers Wood, READING, RG7 1AG **Tel:** 0118 988 1800
Fax: 0118 988 5656
Email: mtoday@sgm.ac.uk
Web site: http://www.sgm.ac.uk
ISSN: 1464-0570
Publisher: The Society for General Microbiology
Frequency: Quarterly
Free to qualifying individuals
Annual Sub.: £60.00
Circulation: 6,000 (Publisher's Statement)
Usual Pagination: 60
Editor: Janet Hurst; **Managing Editor:** Janet Hurst
Summary of Content: Magazine containing topical feature
articles, microbiological news and comment, membership
information and society news, meeting programmes, reports
and book reviews.
Readership/Target Audience: Aimed at academics,
industrial, medical and government microbiologists,
molecular biologists and biochemists, undergraduate and
postgraduate students and other society members.
ADVERTISING: No Advertising taken
BUSINESS: OTHER CLASSIFICATIONS: Biology

MICROELECTRONICS INTERNATIONAL
1615247U18A-9006
Editorial Address: The Reddings, Old Colwall, MALVERN,
WR13 6HH **Tel:** 01684 540957 **Fax:** 01684 540901
Email: jhling@talktalk.net
Web site: http://www.emeraldinsight.com
ISSN: 1356-5362
Publisher: Emerald Group Publishing Ltd
Frequency: 3 issues yearly - Published in January, May and
August
Annual Sub.: £619.00
Usual Pagination: 86
Editor: John Ling; **Managing Editor:** Sharon Parkinson
Summary of Content: Journal covering various
technologies, processes and current practices associated
with design, manufacture, assembly and various
applications of miniaturised electronic devices and
advanced packages.
Readership/Target Audience: Aimed at academics,
researchers, practitioners and managers within the
electronic engineering sector.
ADVERTISING: No Advertising taken
BUSINESS: ELECTRONICS

MICROSCOPE
36176U5C-160
Editorial Address: Quadrant House, The Quadrant,
SUTTON, SM2 5AS **Tel:** 020 8652 2088 **Fax:** 020 8652 8979
Email: microscope@rbi.co.uk
Advertising Address: As above. **Tel:** 020 8652 2000
Fax: 020 8652 2050
Email: lauren.reading@rbi.co.uk
Web site: http://www.microscope.co.uk
Publisher: Reed Business Information
Date Established: 1982
Frequency: Weekly - Published on Monday
Annual Sub.: £49.95
Circulation: 23,139 (BPA Worldwide 01/01/2007 to
30/06/2007)
Usual Pagination: 40
Editor: Simon Quicke; **Features Editor:** Simon Quicke;
Publisher: Paul Briggs
Summary of Content: Newspaper covering news and
information on all aspects of the computer trade.
Readership/Target Audience: Aimed at resellers and those
involved in the computer trade.
ADVERTISING RATES:
Full Page Colour £3043.00
Mechanical Data: Type Area: 280 x 206mm, Bleed Size:
310 x 236mm, Col Length: 280mm, Page Width: 206mm,
Trim Size: 300 x 226mm, Film: Digital
Copy instructions: Copy Date: 1 week prior to publication
date
BUSINESS: COMPUTERS & AUTOMATION: Professional
Personal Computers

MICROSCOPY AND ANALYSIS
39986U55-96_50
Editorial Address: The Atrium, Southern Gate,
CHICHESTER, PO19 8SQ **Tel:** 01243 779777
Fax: 01243 770432
Email: editor@microscopy-analysis.com
Advertising Address: As above. **Tel:** 01243 770254
Email: stephen.parkes@wiley.com
Web site: http://www.microscopy-analysis.com
ISSN: 0958-1952
Publisher: John Wiley & Sons Ltd
Date Established: 1987
Frequency: 6 issues yearly - Published in the 1st week of
the cover month
Free to qualifying individuals
Annual Sub.: £50.00
Circulation: 47,000 (Publisher's Statement)
Usual Pagination: 66
Editor: Victoria Regan; **Publisher:** Roy Opie
Summary of Content: Journal providing a forum for the
exchange of ideas and information about microscopes,
chemical analysis and imaging equipment.
Readership/Target Audience: Aimed at users who specify
microscopical, analytical and imaging equipment.
ADVERTISING RATES:
Full Page Mono £2120.00
Full Page Colour £3130.00
Agency Commission: 10%
Mechanical Data: Type Area: 264 x 190mm, Col Length:
264mm, Film: Digital, Bleed Size: 307 x 215mm, Trim Size:
297 x 210mm, Page Width: 190mm
Average advertising content per issue: 50%
BUSINESS: APPLIED SCIENCE & LABORATORIES

MICROSOFT CONNECTIONS IN COMMUNICATIONS
1833926U18B-1977
Editorial Address: Tudor House, 6 Friar Lane, LEICESTER,
LE1 5RA **Tel:** 0116 222 9900 **Fax:** 0116 222 9901
Email: adam.lawrence@tudor-rose.co.uk
Publisher: Tudor Rose Holdings Ltd
Frequency: Quarterly
Free to qualifying individuals
Circulation: 8,000 (Publisher's Statement)
Editor: Adam Lawrence; **News Editor:** James Dodd
Summary of Content: Magazine covering the use of
Microsoft technologies in the telecommunications, internet,
media and entertainment industries.
Readership/Target Audience: Aimed at senior executives
in telecommunications and media companies.
ADVERTISING: No Advertising taken
BUSINESS: ELECTRONICS: Telecommunications

MICROWAVE JOURNAL
37379U18A-390
Editorial Address: 16 Sussex Street, LONDON, SW1V 4RW
Tel: 020 7596 8787 **Fax:** 020 7596 8739
Email: rmumford@mwjournal.com
Advertising Address: As above. **Tel:** 020 7596 8730
Fax: 020 7596 8749
Email: rvaughan@horizonhouse.co.uk
Web site: http://www.mwjournal.com
ISSN: 0192-6225
Publisher: Horizon House Publications Ltd
Frequency: Monthly - Published at the beginning of the
cover month
Free to qualifying individuals
Circulation: 50,000 (BPA Worldwide 01/01/2008 to
30/06/2008)
Usual Pagination: 200
Editor: Richard Mumford
Summary of Content: Magazine for members of the
electronics industry involved in research, development and
design of instrumentation devices and systems in microwave
frequencies. Covers radar, microwave communications, test
and measurement, semiconductors, wireless technology,
electronic warfare and industry trends.
Readership/Target Audience: Read by manufacturers,
engineers, designers and researchers in the microwave
industry.
ADVERTISING RATES:
Full Page Colour $7540.00
Mechanical Data: Type Area: 254 x 178mm, Trim Size: 297
x 210mm, Col Length: 254mm, Col Widths (Display): 54mm,
Page Width: 178mm, Film: Digital
Copy instructions: Copy Date: 4 weeks prior to publication
date
Supplement(s): Cables and Connectors - 1xY, Military
Microwaves - 1xY, WiMAX and Emerging Technologies -
1xY
BUSINESS: ELECTRONICS

MICROWAVES AND RF MAGAZINE
1832622U18A-9041
Editorial Address: PR by email only **Tel:** 020 8859 1206
Email: paul.whytock@penton.com
Web site: http://www.mwrf.com
Publisher: Penton Media

Frequency: Monthly
Cover Price: Free
Editor: Paul Whytock; **Editor-in-Chief:** Nancy Friedrich
Summary of Content: Magazine featuring research, design development, application and use of devices, components, systems and techniques involving frequencies from kHz through light.
Readership/Target Audience: Aimed at those concerned with the research, design development, application and use of devices, components, systems and techniques involving frequencies from kHz through light.
BUSINESS: ELECTRONICS

MIDDLE EAST MONITOR
36969U14C-101
Editorial Address: Mermaid House, 2 Puddle Dock, LONDON, EC4V 3DS **Tel:** 020 7248 0468
Fax: 020 7248 0467
Email: mbrooks@businessmonitor.com
Web site: http://www.businessmonitor.com
ISSN: 0265-8724
Publisher: Business Monitor International Ltd
Frequency: Monthly
Cover Price: £325.00
Circulation: 702 (Publisher's Statement)
Editor: Elizabeth Martins
Summary of Content: Magazine covering the political risk, economy and business environment of the Middle East.
Readership/Target Audience: Read by heads of companies, financial advisors and business analysts.
ADVERTISING: No Advertising taken
BUSINESS: COMMERCE, INDUSTRY & MANAGEMENT: International Commerce

THE MIDDLE EAST REVIEW
37006U14C-102
Editorial Address: 11 Clarendon Street, CAMBRIDGE, CB1 1JU **Tel:** 01223 351584 **Fax:** 01223 351584
Email: suehewitt11@hotmail.com
Advertising Address: As above. **Tel:** 01799 521150
Email: sue@worldinformation.com
Web site: http://www.worldinformation.com
ISSN: 1351-4717
Publisher: World of Information
Date Established: 1974
Frequency: Annual - Published in spring
Annual Sub.: £55.00
Circulation: 7,500 (Publisher's Statement)
Usual Pagination: 220
Editor: Anthony Axon; **Advertising Manager:** Sue Hewitt; **Publisher:** Anthony Axon
Summary of Content: Journal containing economic and political profiles of Middle Eastern countries.
Readership/Target Audience: Aimed at the business, banking and industrial community, government and ngo.
ADVERTISING RATES:
Full Page Colour £4950.00
Agency Commission: 15%
Mechanical Data: Type Area: 235.5 x 172mm, Bleed Size: 276 x 216mm, Trim Size: 270 x 210mm, Col Length: 235.5mm, Page Width: 172mm, Print Process: Offset litho, Film: Digital
Copy instructions: Copy Date: End of September
Average advertising content per issue: 10%
BUSINESS: COMMERCE, INDUSTRY & MANAGEMENT: International Commerce

MIDIRS MIDWIFERY DIGEST
40314U56B-220
Editorial Address: 9 Elmdale Road, Clifton, BRISTOL, BS8 1SL **Tel:** 0117 925 1791 **Fax:** 0117 925 1792
Email: editor@midirs.org
Advertising Address: As above. **Tel:** 0117 907 7592
Email: faye@midirs.org
Web site: http://www.midirs.org
ISSN: 0961-5555
Publisher: Midwives Information and Resource Service
Date Established: 1985
Frequency: Quarterly
Cover Price: £44.00
Circulation: 12,500 (Publisher's Statement)
Usual Pagination: 152
Editor: Sally Marchant; **Advertising Manager:** Faye Duckers
Summary of Content: Journal of the Midwives Information and Resource Service.
Readership/Target Audience: Aimed at midwives in practice, research or education, student midwives and other health professionals concerned with women and infant health.
ADVERTISING RATES:
Full Page Colour £1625.00
Mechanical Data: Type Area: 255 x 165mm, Film: Digital, Col Length: 255mm, No. of Columns (Display): 2, Page Width: 165mm, Print Process: Web-fed offset
Average advertising content per issue: 3.5%
BUSINESS: HEALTH & MEDICAL: Nursing

MIDLANDS BUSINESS INSIDER
41379U63B-1830
Formerly: Finance Midlands Insider
Editorial Address: 4th Floor, Canterbury House, 85 Newhall Street, BIRMINGHAM, B3 1LH **Tel:** 0121 232 0980
Fax: 0121 232 0989
Email: andy.coyne@newsco.com
Advertising Address: As above.
Email: adrian.simcox@newsco.com
Web site: http://www.insidermedia.com
ISSN: 1475-9608
Publisher: Newsco Insider Ltd
Date Established: 1993
Frequency: Monthly - Published around the 20th of the month prior to cover month
Free to qualifying individuals
Annual Sub.: £48.00
Circulation: 12,942 (ABC 01/07/2008 to 30/06/2009)
Usual Pagination: 104
Editor: Andrew Coyne; **Managing Director:** Marlen Roberts
Summary of Content: Magazine containing news, developments and views affecting the success and prosperity of the Midlands business community.
Readership/Target Audience: Read by named financial decision makers of Midlands-based organisations with high turnovers.
ADVERTISING RATES:
Full Page Colour £2400.00
Agency Commission: 10%
Mechanical Data: Type Area: 267 x 178mm, Col Length: 267mm, Page Width: 178mm, Trim Size: 297 x 210mm, Bleed Size: 303 x 216mm, Film: Digital
Copy instructions: Copy Date: 3 weeks prior to publication date
Average advertising content per issue: 40%
BUSINESS: REGIONAL BUSINESS: Regional Business English Counties

MIDWIVES
40334U56B-278
Formerly: RCM Midwives Journal
Editorial Address: 17-18 Britton Street, LONDON, EC1M 5TP **Tel:** 020 7880 6200
Email: emma.godfrey@redactive.co.uk
Web site: http://www.rcm.org.uk/magazines
ISSN: 1479-2915
Publisher: Redactive Media Group
Date Established: 1998
Frequency: 6 issues yearly
Annual Sub.: £97.50
Circulation: 37,500 (Publisher's Statement)
Usual Pagination: 44
Editor: Emma Godfrey
Summary of Content: Official journal of the Royal College of Midwives. Contains research papers, review papers, news, book reviews, recruitment and letters to the editor.
Readership/Target Audience: Aimed at midwives, medical officers, obstetricians, gynaecologists and maternity care assistants.
ADVERTISING: No Advertising taken
BUSINESS: HEALTH & MEDICAL: Nursing

MIGRAINE ACTION NEWS
40258U56A-104_50
Editorial Address: 27 East Street, LEICESTER, LM1 6NB
Tel: 0116 275 8317 **Fax:** 0116 254 2023
Email: info@migraine.org.uk
Web site: http://www.migraine.org.uk
Publisher: Migraine Action Association
Date Established: 1962
Frequency: Quarterly
Free to qualifying individuals
Annual Sub.: £10.00
Circulation: 10,000 (Publisher's Statement)
Usual Pagination: 28
Editor: Demelza Burn
Summary of Content: Contains news of and views on research, developments, treatments both conventional and complementary, personal experiences and contacts.
Readership/Target Audience: Aimed at members of the Migraine Action Association and anyone affected by migraine.
ADVERTISING: No Advertising taken
BUSINESS: HEALTH & MEDICAL

MIGRAINE NEWS
40462U56L-16
Editorial Address: 2nd Floor, 55-56 Russell Square, LONDON, WC1B 4HP **Tel:** 020 7436 1336
Fax: 020 7436 2880
Email: education@migrainetrust.org
Web site: http://www.migrainetrust.org
Publisher: The Migraine Trust
Date Established: 1970
Frequency: 3 issues yearly - Published in February, June and September
Cover Price: Free
Circulation: 2,000 (Publisher's Statement)

Usual Pagination: 20
Editor: Alli Anthony
Summary of Content: Newsletter of the Migraine Trust. Covers the latest developments in medical research treatment and management of migraine.
Readership/Target Audience: Read by members of the Migraine Trust, UK researchers, selected GPs and health professionals.
ADVERTISING: No Advertising taken
BUSINESS: HEALTH & MEDICAL: Disability & Rehabilitation

MILITARY LOGISTICS INTERNATIONAL
1809295U40-438
Editorial Address: PO Box 29478, LONDON, NW1 8GF
Tel: 020 7284 0331
Email: ftusa@defenceanalysis.com
Advertising Address: ONE, Southbank House, Black Prince Road, LONDON, SE1 7SJ **Tel:** 020 7463 2020
Fax: 020 7463 2008
Email: rob@oneismore.com
Web site: http://www.mil-log.com
Publisher: Defence Analysis Ltd
Date Established: 2005
Frequency: 6 issues yearly
Free to qualifying individuals
Annual Sub.: £60.00
Circulation: 7,500 (Publisher's Statement)
Usual Pagination: 48
Editor: Francis Tusa; **Advertising Manager:** Rob Starbuck
Summary of Content: Magazine focusing on logistics, support, overhaul and maintenance.
Readership/Target Audience: Aimed at defence contractors and the armed services.
ADVERTISING RATES:
Full Page Colour £3000.00
Mechanical Data: Type Area: 277 x 200mm, Col Length: 277mm, Page Width: 200mm, Film: Digital
BUSINESS: DEFENCE

MILITARY TRAINING & SIMULATION NEWS
1616019U40-425
Editorial Address: PO Box 25, Clawton, HOLSWORTHY, EX22 6WZ **Tel:** 01409 271411 **Fax:** 01409 271414
Email: trevor@twpltd.com
Advertising Address: As above.
Email: sarahprew@twpltd.com
Web site: http://www.twpltd.com
Publisher: The Write Partnership
Date Established: 1999
Frequency: 6 issues yearly - Published at the beginning of the 2nd cover month
Free to qualifying individuals
Circulation: 9,766 (Publisher's Statement)
Editor: Trevor Nash; **Advertising Manager:** Sarah Prew
Summary of Content: Magazine covering international military organisations, the simulation and training industry, government, civil service, academic and other related industries.
Readership/Target Audience: Aimed at senior military officers, industry managers and engineers, industry sales persons, academics and other governmental officials involved in training and simulation.
ADVERTISING RATES:
Full Page Mono £2740.00
Full Page Colour £3600.00
Mechanical Data: Type Area: 275 x 184mm, Bleed Size: 303 x 216mm, Trim Size: 297 x 210mm, Col Length: 275mm, Film: Digital, Page Width: 184mm
Copy instructions: Copy Date: 4 weeks prior to publication date
BUSINESS: DEFENCE

MILK INDUSTRY
37880U21G-90
Formerly: Milk Industry International
Editorial Address: Ewell House, Graveney Road, FAVERSHAM, ME13 8UP **Tel:** 01795 535468
Email: editorial@milkindustrymag.co.uk
Advertising Address: As above. **Tel:** 01795 542419
Fax: 01795 535469
Email: stever@milkindustrymag.co.uk
Web site: http://www.milkindustry.com
ISSN: 1473-6381
Publisher: Dairy UK
Date Established: 1920
Frequency: 10 issues yearly
Cover Price: £6.00
Free to qualifying individuals
Annual Sub.: £70.00
Circulation: 2,000 (Publisher's Statement)
Usual Pagination: 32
Editor: Emma Abbott
Summary of Content: Journal of Dairy UK Ltd covering milk and dairy production, processing, marketing, retailing and technical matters.
Readership/Target Audience: Read by senior management in dairies and dairy product companies, bottled milk buyers,

research and development and dairy equipment manufacturers, dairy farmers and senior management in milk buying co-ops. Also aimed at retailers, executives in food and dairy organisations and politicians in the UK and Europe.
ADVERTISING RATES:
Full Page Colour £1000.00
SCC £15.00
Agency Commission: 10%
Mechanical Data: Col Length: 274mm, No. of Columns (Display): 2, Type Area: 274 x 190mm, Bleed Size: 303 x 213mm, Trim Size: 297 x 210mm, Film: Digital, Page Width: 190mm
Copy instructions: Copy Date: Middle of the month prior to publication date
Average advertising content per issue: 25%
BUSINESS: AGRICULTURE & FARMING: Milk

MILK PRODUCTS
1665010U21G-91

Editorial Address: 80 Calverley Road, TUNBRIDGE WELLS, TN1 2UN **Tel:** 020 7017 7500 **Fax:** 020 7017 7599
Email: marketing@agra-net.com
Web site: http://www.agra-net.com
ISSN: 0950-3730
Publisher: Agra Informa Ltd
Frequency: 10 issues yearly
Annual Sub.: £773.00
Summary of Content: Newsletter containing the latest European and international statistics on trade, production and prices for milk, butter and cheese.
Readership/Target Audience: Aimed at those in the global milk products industry.
ADVERTISING: No Advertising taken
BUSINESS: AGRICULTURE & FARMING: Milk

MILLENNIUM STEEL
704439U27-110

Editorial Address: 11 Clacton Road, LONDON, E17 8AP
Tel: 020 8509 3145 **Fax:** 020 8521 6999
Email: price.dj@virgin.net
Advertising Address: As above.
Email: millennium.steel@virgin.net
Web site: http://www.millennium-steel.com
Publisher: Millennium Steel Publishing
Date Established: 2000
Frequency: Annual - Published in May
Cover Price: Free
Circulation: 7,000 (Publisher's Statement)
Usual Pagination: 300
Editor: David Price; **Advertising Manager:** David Shatford
Summary of Content: Magazine covering process technology, plant and related subjects in the iron and steel industry.
Readership/Target Audience: Aimed at the iron and steel industry throughout the world.
ADVERTISING RATES:
Full Page Mono £3950.00
Full Page Colour £3950.00
Agency Commission: 15%
Mechanical Data: Type Area: 270 x 178mm, Col Length: 270mm, Page Width: 178mm, Trim Size: 297 x 210mm, Bleed Size: 303 x 216mm, Film: Digital
Copy instructions: Copy Date: 15th December prior to publication date
Average advertising content per issue: 40%
BUSINESS: METAL, IRON & STEEL

MILTON KEYNES BUSINESS CITIZEN
41251U63B-237

Formerly: Business Citizen
Editorial Address: Napier House, Auckland Park, Bond Avenue, Mount Farm, MILTON KEYNES, MK1 1BU
Tel: 01908 651241 **Fax:** 01908 632214
Email: carolyn.english@mkcitizen.co.uk
Advertising Address: As above. **Tel:** 01908 651221
Email: christine.rollason@mkcitizen.co.uk
Web site: http://www.miltonkeynes.co.uk
Publisher: Johnston Press plc
Date Established: 1994
Frequency: 11 issues yearly
Cover Price: Free
Circulation: 92,000 (Publisher's Statement)
Usual Pagination: 28
Editor: Carolyn English
Summary of Content: Newspaper containing news of Milton Keynes companies, company profiles and launches. Also covers motoring, commercial property and finance.
Readership/Target Audience: Read by businesses and residents in Milton Keynes and the surrounding area.
ADVERTISING RATES:
SCC £10.30
Agency Commission: 10%
Mechanical Data: Type Area: 340 x 268mm, Print Process: Web-fed offset litho, No. of Columns (Display): 9, Page Width: 268mm, Col Length: 340mm, Col Widths (Display): 28mm, Film: Digital
Copy instructions: Copy Date: 10 days prior to publication date

Average advertising content per issue: 50%
Supplement to: Milton Keynes Citizen Series
BUSINESS: REGIONAL BUSINESS: Regional Business English Counties

MIMS
40192U56A-105

Formerly: MIMS Monthly Index of Medical Specialities
Editorial Address: 174 Hammersmith Road, LONDON, W6 7JP **Tel:** 020 8267 4614 **Fax:** 020 8267 4866
Advertising Address: As above. **Tel:** 020 8267 4870
Fax: 020 8267 4878
Email: robert.nuzzaci@haymarket.com
Web site: http://www.mims.co.uk
ISSN: 0957-9095
Publisher: Haymarket Medical Publications Ltd
Date Established: 1959
Frequency: Monthly
Free to qualifying individuals
Annual Sub.: £165.00
Circulation: 39,388 (ABC 01/01/2008 to 31/12/2008)
Usual Pagination: 448
Editor: Jenny Gowans; **Managing Director:** Peter Welland
Summary of Content: Magazine covering prescription medicines for therapeutic use. Includes information on indications, dosage and warnings, new products reviews and licensing changes.
Readership/Target Audience: Aimed at doctors in general practice and consultants in hospitals.
ADVERTISING RATES:
Full Page Colour £4017.00
Agency Commission: 10%
Mechanical Data: Col Length: 185mm, Page Width: 130mm, Film: Digital, Bleed Size: 216 x 154mm, Trim Size: 210 x 148mm, Type Area: 185 x 130mm
Copy instructions: Copy Date: 2 weeks prior to publication date
BUSINESS: HEALTH & MEDICAL

MIND
30846U56N-201

Editorial Address: Department of Philosophy, University of York, YORK, YO10 5DD **Tel:** 01904 433257
Email: mind@york.ac.uk
Advertising Address: 60 Upper Broadmoor Road, CROWTHORNE, RG45 7DE **Tel:** 01344 779945
Fax: 01344 779945
Email: lhann@lhms.fsnet.co.uk
Web site: http://www.oup.co.uk/mind
ISSN: 0026-4423
Publisher: OUP
Date Established: 1876
Frequency: Quarterly
Cover Price: £8.00
Annual Sub.: £31.00
Usual Pagination: 276
Editor: Thomas Baldwin
Summary of Content: Journal focusing on philosophy with articles by leading philosophers, also contains a book review section.
Readership/Target Audience: Aimed at academics, students and teachers of philosophy.
ADVERTISING RATES:
Full Page Mono £475.00
Agency Commission: 10%
Mechanical Data: Film: Digital, Type Area: 200 x 130mm, Col Length: 200mm, Page Width: 130mm
Copy instructions: Copy Date: 10h of the month prior to publication date
BUSINESS: HEALTH & MEDICAL: Mental Health

MIND YOUR BUSINESS
1799610U63B-2573

Editorial Address: 438 Allesley Old Road, COVENTRY, CV5 8GF **Tel:** 024 7671 7707 **Fax:** 0845 128 0164
Email: martin@mindyour-biz.co.uk
Advertising Address: As above. **Tel:** 0845 128 0163
Email: mybnews@googlemail.com
Web site: http://www.mindyour-biz.co.uk
Publisher: ABC Media Group Ltd
Frequency: 6 issues yearly - Published around the 1st of the cover month
Free to qualifying individuals
Annual Sub.: £37.00
Circulation: 20,000 (Publisher's Statement)
Usual Pagination: 62
Editor: Tom Linstead; **Advertising Manager:** Sam Bhal; **Publisher:** Martin Whelan
Summary of Content: Magazine giving help, advice and updates as well as keeping you informed of all social activities within the region. It is a B2B magazine focusing on modern business and business lifestyle. Looking at local entrepreneurs on how they made it alongside interviews with some of the most recognised business people in Britain.
Readership/Target Audience: Aimed at directors and senior managers.
ADVERTISING RATES:
Full Page Mono £1200.00
Full Page Colour £1200.00
Agency Commission: 10%

Mechanical Data: Type Area: 267 x 180mm, Bleed Size: 303 x 216mm, Trim Size: 297 x 210mm, Col Length: 267mm, Page Width: 180mm, Film: Digital
Copy instructions: Copy Date: 1 week prior to publication date
Average advertising content per issue: 30%
BUSINESS: REGIONAL BUSINESS: Regional Business English Counties

MINERAL PLANNING
40677U57-37_50

Editorial Address: Suite1, Fullers Court, Lower Quay Street, GLOUCESTER, GL1 2LW **Tel:** 01452 835820
Fax: 01452 835822
Email: dcs@haymarket.com
Advertising Address: 11-17 Wolverton Gardens, LONDON, W6 7BY **Tel:** 020 8267 5000 **Fax:** 020 8267 4013
Email: paul.stone@haymarket.com
Web site: http://www.planningresource.co.uk/dcs
ISSN: 0267-1409
Publisher: Development Control Sevices Ltd
Date Established: 1979
Frequency: 6 issues yearly
Annual Sub.: £85.00
Circulation: 600 (Publisher's Statement)
Usual Pagination: 40
Editor: Tracey Flitcroft
Summary of Content: Journal reporting on the extraction and use of minerals and the environmental effects.
Readership/Target Audience: Aimed at local authorities, government departments, environmental pressure groups, the minerals industry, educational institutions, environmental consultants and lawyers.
ADVERTISING RATES:
Full Page Mono £278.00
Mechanical Data: Type Area: 260 x 183mm, Col Length: 260mm, Page Width: 183mm, Trim Size: 297 x 210mm
Copy instructions: Copy Date: 17th of the month prior to publication date
Average advertising content per issue: 7.5%
BUSINESS: ENVIRONMENT & POLLUTION

MINERAL PRICEWATCH
38243U30-52

Editorial Address: 16 Lower Marsh, LONDON, SE1 7RJ
Tel: 020 7827 9977 **Fax:** 020 7827 6441
Email: atran@indmin.com
Web site: http://www.indmin.com
ISSN: 1357-4795
Publisher: Industrial Minerals Information
Date Established: 1995
Frequency: Monthly
Annual Sub.: £477.00
Usual Pagination: 16
Editor: Alison Tran
Summary of Content: Newsletter covering pricing information, news and analysis on industrial minerals.
Readership/Target Audience: Aimed at professionals within the mineral industry.
ADVERTISING: No Advertising taken
BUSINESS: MINING & QUARRYING

MINING & QUARRY WORLD
1654969U30-152

Editorial Address: British Fields, Ollerton Road, Tuxford, NEWARK, NG22 0PQ **Tel:** 01777 871007 **Fax:** 01777 872271
Email: info@mqworld.com
Advertising Address: As above.
Email: sales@tradelinkpub.co.uk
Web site: http://www.mqworld.com
ISSN: 1463-6336
Publisher: Tradelink Publications Ltd
Date Established: 2004
Frequency: Quarterly
Free to qualifying individuals
Annual Sub.: £40.00
Circulation: 5,000 (Publisher's Statement)
Usual Pagination: 52
Editor: Jane Isaacs; **Advertising Manager:** Kevin Barratt; **Managing Editor:** Jane Isaacs
Summary of Content: Magazine focusing on hard-rock mining and quarrying.
Readership/Target Audience: Aimed at mining and mineral professionals.
ADVERTISING RATES:
Full Page Colour £2200.00
Agency Commission: 10%
Mechanical Data: Bleed Size: 303 x 216mm, Trim Size: 297 x 210mm, Film: Digital
Average advertising content per issue: 25%
BUSINESS: MINING & QUARRYING

MINING ENVIRONMENTAL MANAGEMENT
38245U30-57

Editorial Address: Albert House, 1 Singer Street, LONDON, EC2A 4BQ **Tel:** 020 7216 6060 **Fax:** 020 7216 6050
Email: mem@mining-journal.com
Advertising Address: As above.

Business Magazines

Section 4 (b) Business Magazines

Email: carmel.rodohan@mining-journal.com
Web site: http://www.mining-journal.com
ISSN: 0969-4218
Publisher: Aspermont
Date Established: 1994
Frequency: Quarterly - Published end of month
Annual Sub.: £85.00
Circulation: 3,000 (Publisher's Statement)
Usual Pagination: 32
Editor: Katherine Dixon; Advertising Manager: Carmel Rodohan; Publisher: Rob Barrowman
Summary of Content: Journal focusing on environmental management and sustainable development in the mining industry.
Readership/Target Audience: Aimed at mining corporations, consultants, financial and government bodies and environmental organisations. Global circulation to mining companies, ministries of mines, environmental ministries, EPAs and consultants.
ADVERTISING RATES:
Full Page Colour £2350.00
Agency Commission: 10%
Mechanical Data: Bleed Size: 303 x 216mm, Trim Size: 297 x 210mm, Film: Digital, Type Area: 275 x 186mm, Col Length: 275mm, Page Width: 186mm
Copy instructions: Copy Date: 1 week prior to publication date
Average advertising content per issue: 20%
BUSINESS: MINING & QUARRYING

MINING JOURNAL
38246U30-60

Editorial Address: Albert House, 1 Singer Street, LONDON, EC2A 4BQ Tel: 020 7216 6060 Fax: 020 7216 6050
Email: editorial@mining-journal.com
Advertising Address: As above.
Email: gabriella.kiss@mining-journal.com
Web site: http://www.mining-journal.com
ISSN: 0026-5225
Publisher: Aspermont
Date Established: 1835
Frequency: Weekly - Published Friday of each week
Annual Sub.: £360.00
Circulation: 2,926 (Publisher's Statement)
Usual Pagination: 30
Editor: Phil Halliday; Features Editor: Michelle Giglio; Advertising Manager: Gabriella Kiss
Summary of Content: Journal containing news and comments on global mining issues. Includes articles on exploration, development, production equipment, research development, marketing of metals, minerals and financial activities of mining companies.
Language(s): Chinese; English
Readership/Target Audience: Aimed at mining company management, company marketing executives, financial analysts and equipment manufacturers.
ADVERTISING RATES:
Full Page Colour £2350.00
Agency Commission: 10%
Mechanical Data: Type Area: 275 x 186mm, Bleed Size: 303 x 216mm, Trim Size: 297 x 210mm, Col Length: 275mm, Film: Digital, Page Width: 186mm
Copy instructions: Copy Date: 2 days prior to publication date
Average advertising content per issue: 40%
BUSINESS: MINING & QUARRYING

MINING MAGAZINE
38247U30-70

Editorial Address: Albert House, 1 Singer Street, LONDON, EC2A 4BQ Tel: 020 7216 6060 Fax: 020 7216 6050
Email: paul.moore@mining-journal.com
Advertising Address: As above.
Email: richard.dolan@mining-journal.com
Web site: http://www.mining-journal.com
ISSN: 0308-6631
Publisher: Aspermont
Date Established: 1909
Frequency: Monthly - Published on the 1st of the cover month
Cover Price: £8.00
Free to qualifying individuals
Annual Sub.: £69.00
Circulation: 12,731 (Publisher's Statement)
Usual Pagination: 56
Editor: Paul Moore; Advertising Manager: Richard Dolan
Summary of Content: Magazine containing product and processing updates, literature comments, mining coverage and exploration equipment reviews.
Readership/Target Audience: Aimed at suppliers of mining equipment.
ADVERTISING RATES:
Full Page Colour £3755.00
Agency Commission: 10%
Mechanical Data: Type Area: 254 x 178mm, Bleed Size: 282 x 208mm, Trim Size: 273 x 203mm, Col Length: 254mm, Film: Digital, Page Width: 178mm
Copy instructions: Copy Date: 2 weeks prior to publication date
BUSINESS: MINING & QUARRYING

MINING TIMES
1692323U30-154

Editorial Address: 5 Paxford Close, REDDITCH, B98 8RH
Tel: 01527 660940 Fax: 01527 660940
Email: miningtimes@goldmine.cix.co.uk
Web site: http://www.mine-on-line.com
Publisher: Marketing Support Services
Date Established: 2001
Frequency: 6 issues yearly
Cover Price: Free
Usual Pagination: 16
Editor: Paul Erlanger
Summary of Content: Newsletter covering mining project information and featured products and services.
Readership/Target Audience: Aimed at managers and specifiers in the mining industry.
ADVERTISING: No Advertising taken
BUSINESS: MINING & QUARRYING

MIR NEWS
40315U56B-225

Editorial Address: PO Box 44375, LONDON, SW19 8WA
Tel: 020 8739 0066 Fax: 020 8739 0077
Email: malpractice@btconnect.com
Advertising Address: As above.
Email: malpractice@btconnect.com
Web site: http://www.medicalindemnity.com
ISSN: 1468-6600
Publisher: Medical Indemnity Register
Date Established: 1990
Frequency: Quarterly
Free to qualifying individuals
Annual Sub.: £37.00
Circulation: 2,000 (Publisher's Statement)
Usual Pagination: 8
Editor: David Guest; Advertising Manager: David Guest
Summary of Content: Newsletter of the Medical Indemnity Register. Contains news, views and information on products and techniques connected with the world of immediate life support and pre-hospital care.
Readership/Target Audience: Read by first aiders, EMTs, ambulance personnel, paramedics, nurses, doctors and anyone else involved in PHLS (pre-hospital life support).
ADVERTISING RATES:
Full Page Mono £250.00
Mechanical Data: Page Width: 190mm, Type Area: 270 X 190mm, Col Length: 270mm
Average advertising content per issue: 20%
BUSINESS: HEALTH & MEDICAL: Nursing

MIX FUTURE INTERIORS
1849353U4B-189

Editorial Address: 1 Queen Anne Terrace, Sovereign Court, The Highway, LONDON, E1W 3HH Tel: 020 7481 1507
Fax: 020 7481 1548
Email: office@globalcolor.co.uk
Web site: http://www.globalcolor.co.uk
Publisher: Global Color Research
Frequency: Quarterly
Cover Price: £27.00
Annual Sub.: £129.00
Circulation: 7,500 (Publisher's Statement)
Editor: Carolina Calzada
Summary of Content: Magazine covering interiors design one year ahead of the season including fabrics, new products, materials, colour trends, exhibitions and shows.
Readership/Target Audience: Aimed at architects and interior designers.
BUSINESS: ARCHITECTURE & BUILDING: Interior Design & Flooring

MIX INTERIORS
624822U4B-183

Editorial Address: Wenden Court, Station Road, Wendens Ambo, SAFFRON WALDEN, CB11 4LB Tel: 01799 541841
Fax: 0870 762 8551
Email: mixinteriors@aol.com
Advertising Address: As above.
Email: mixinteriors@aol.com
Web site: http://www.mixinteriors.com
Publisher: Mix Media Ltd
Frequency: 10 issues yearly - Not published in August or December
Free to qualifying individuals
Annual Sub.: £45.00
Circulation: 10,000 (Publisher's Statement)
Usual Pagination: 72
Editor: Mick Jordan; Advertising Manager: Henry Pugh
Summary of Content: Magazine covering all aspects of office interior design, including profiles and case studies.
Readership/Target Audience: Aimed at architects, designers and facility managers.
ADVERTISING RATES:
Full Page Colour £1400.00
Agency Commission: 10%
Mechanical Data: Trim Size: 297 x 230mm, Film: Digital, Bleed Size: 303 x 236mm, Type Area: 270 x 208mm, Col Length: 270mm, Page Width: 208mm
Copy instructions: Copy Date: 20th of the month prior to publication date

Average advertising content per issue: 41%
BUSINESS: ARCHITECTURE & BUILDING: Interior Design & Flooring

THE MJ
38387U32A-150

Formerly: MJ Municipal Journal
Editorial Address: 32 Vauxhall Bridge Road, LONDON, SW1V 2SS Tel: 020 7973 6400 Fax: 020 7233 5051
Email: mjnews@hgluk.com
Advertising Address: As above. Fax: 020 7973 5053
Email: p.laverty@hgluk.com
Web site: http://www.localgov.co.uk
ISSN: 0143-4101
Publisher: Hemming Group Ltd
Date Established: 1893
Frequency: Weekly
Annual Sub.: £140.00
Circulation: 8,500 (ABC 01/07/2008 to 30/06/2009)
Usual Pagination: 36
Editor: Chris Smith; News Editor: Chris Smith
Summary of Content: Journal covering all aspects of local government, including tenders, contracts awarded and recruitment.
Readership/Target Audience: Aimed at top officers in local government and private sector companies working with the public sector.
ADVERTISING RATES:
Full Page Colour £2675.00
Agency Commission: 10%
Mechanical Data: Page Width: 219mm, Film: Digital, Type Area: 314 x 219mm, Col Length: 314mm, Trim Size: 340 x 245mm, Bleed Size: 350 x 255mm
Copy instructions: Copy Date: Monday 12pm prior to publication date
Average advertising content per issue: 25%
BUSINESS: LOCAL GOVERNMENT, LEISURE & RECREATION: Local Government

M.LOGISTICS
758617U5E-9001

Editorial Address: 17 Spice Court, Plantation Wharf, Battersea, LONDON, SW11 3UE Tel: 020 7924 1415
Fax: 020 7924 1882
Email: sharon@mlogmag.com
Advertising Address: As above. Tel: 020 7924 5885
Email: cjpl@mlogmag.com
Web site: http://www.mlogmag.com
Publisher: Spice Court Publications Ltd
Date Established: 2002
Frequency: 6 issues yearly
Free to qualifying individuals
Annual Sub.: £45.00
Circulation: 7,500 (Publisher's Statement)
Usual Pagination: 48
Editor: Sharon Clancy
Summary of Content: Magazine covering technology in logistics including laptop computers, handheld terminals and PDAs, voice and data communications, on-board computers, telematics and in-cab guidance systems, wireless networking, tracking, tracing and location, data capture and synchronisation, and field service support.
Readership/Target Audience: Aimed at directors, senior executives and line managers with strategic and practical responsibility for mobile supply-chain solutions.
ADVERTISING RATES:
Full Page Mono £1470.00
Full Page Colour £2580.00
Agency Commission: 10%
Mechanical Data: Col Length: 269mm, Page Width: 187mm, No. of Columns (Display): 2, Type Area: 269 x 187mm, Trim Size: 297 x 210mm, Bleed Size: 303 x 216mm, Film: Digital
Supplement(s): The Telematics and Mobile Data Guide - 1xY
BUSINESS: COMPUTERS & AUTOMATION: Data Transmission

MM MEDIA & MARKETING
35530U2A-117

Formerly: Media and Marketing
Editorial Address: 115 Southwark Bridge Road, LONDON, SE1 0AX Tel: 020 7367 6990
Email: pip@csquared.cc
Advertising Address: As above. Tel: 020 7613 9700
Fax: 020 7168 2292
Email: brice@csquared.cc
Web site: http://www.mandmglobal.com
ISSN: 1743-4920
Publisher: C Squared Communications
Date Established: 1989
Frequency: 11 issues yearly - Published the 1st week of the month
Free to qualifying individuals
Annual Sub.: EUR160.00
Circulation: 8,553 (BPA Worldwide 01/01/2008 to 30/06/2008)
Usual Pagination: 50
Editor: Pip Brooking

Summary of Content: Magazine covering news and information relating to the world of global media and advertising.
Readership/Target Audience: Aimed at global advertisers.
ADVERTISING RATES:
Full Page Colour £5500.00
Agency Commission: 10%
Mechanical Data: Bleed Size: 291 x 236mm, Trim Size: 285 x 230mm, Col Length: 246mm, Type Area: 246 x 195mm, Page Width: 195mm, Film: Digital
Copy instructions: Copy Date: 2 weeks prior to publication date
Average advertising content per issue: 33%
BUSINESS: COMMUNICATIONS, ADVERTISING & MARKETING

MMC
1696121U42A-221
Editorial Address: 11 Galena Close, Amington Industrial Estate, TAMWORTH, B77 4AS **Tel:** 01827 311800
Fax: 01827 301199
Email: press@wavcoms.co.uk
Advertising Address: As above.
Email: kedge@wavcoms.co.uk
Web site: http://www.wavcoms.co.uk
Publisher: Waverley Communications Ltd
Date Established: 2005
Frequency: Quarterly
Free to qualifying individuals
Circulation: 11,644 (ABC 01/07/2008 to 30/06/2009)
Usual Pagination: 44
Editor: Bruce Meechan; **Advertising Manager:** Kevin Edgeworth; **Publisher:** Kevin Edgeworth
Summary of Content: Magazine focusing on the latest developments in building and construction methods.
Readership/Target Audience: Aimed at architects, builders, developers, housing associations, health, education and local authorities.
ADVERTISING RATES:
Full Page Mono £1800.00
Full Page Colour £1800.00
Agency Commission: 10%
Mechanical Data: Type Area: 277 x 190mm, Bleed Size: 303 x 216mm, Trim Size: 297 x 210mm, Col Length: 277mm, Page Width: 190mm, No. of Columns (Display): 3, Print Process: Web-fed litho, Film: Digital, Col Widths (Display): 57mm
Copy instructions: Copy Date: 4 weeks prior to publication date
Average advertising content per issue: 40%
BUSINESS: CONSTRUCTION

MNS MICRO NANO SYSTEMS
1702777U19A-559
Formerly: MEMS Manufacturing
Editorial Address: Hannay House, 39 Clarendon Road, WATFORD, WD17 1JA **Tel:** 01923 690210
Fax: 01923 690201
Email: dr@angelbcl.co.uk
Advertising Address: As above.
Email: dt@angelbcl.co.uk
Web site: http://www.euroasiasemiconductor.com/mns.php
Publisher: Angel Business Communications Ltd
Frequency: Quarterly
Circulation: 15,000 (Publisher's Statement)
Editor: David Ridsdale; **Advertising Manager:** Darren Theodore; **Publisher:** Jackie Cannon
Summary of Content: Magazine focusing on the manufacturing of MEMS devices.
Readership/Target Audience: Aimed at manufacturers.
ADVERTISING: Rates on application
BUSINESS: ENGINEERING & MACHINERY

MOBILE
628892U18B-1030
Editorial Address: 14-16 Great Pulteney Street, LONDON, W1F 9ND **Tel:** 020 7440 3862 **Fax:** 020 7437 4250
Email: soheb.panja@nhmedia.co.uk
Advertising Address: As above. **Tel:** 020 7440 3866
Email: colin.white@nhmedia.co.uk
Web site: http://www.mobiletoday.co.uk
ISSN: 1472-0833
Publisher: Noble House Media Ltd
Date Established: 2000
Frequency: Weekly
Cover Price: £2.30
Annual Sub.: £115.00
Circulation: 6,190 (ABC 01/01/2008 to 31/12/2008)
Usual Pagination: 24
Editor: Soheb Panja; **Editor-in-Chief:** David Nunn; **Managing Editor:** Soheb Panja
Summary of Content: Magazine covering news, developments and product information.
Readership/Target Audience: Aimed at retailers, dealers, distributors and manufacturers of mobile phones and network operators.
ADVERTISING RATES:
Full Page Mono £2795.00
Full Page Colour £2795.00

Agency Commission: 10%
Mechanical Data: Film: Digital
Copy instructions: Copy Date: Monday 12 noon prior to publication date
Average advertising content per issue: 45%
BUSINESS: ELECTRONICS: Telecommunications

MOBILE & OUTSIDE CATERING
1622708U11A-192
Editorial Address: Association House, 89 Mappleborough Road, Shirley, SOLIHULL, B90 1AG **Tel:** 0121 603 2524
Fax: 0121 474 3938
Email: bob@ncass.org.uk
Advertising Address: As above.
Email: bob@ncass.org.uk
Web site: http://www.moca.org.uk
Publisher: Nationwide Caterers Association
Date Established: 1989
Frequency: Quarterly
Cover Price: Free
Circulation: 1,500 (Publisher's Statement)
Editor: Bob Fox; **Managing Director:** Bob Fox; **Advertising Manager:** Bob Fox
Summary of Content: Magazine of the Mobile and Outside Catering Association covering topics on mobile catering, including tips, legal issues, food hygiene and safety, cleaning, cooking and chilling.
Readership/Target Audience: Aimed at leisure businesses and mobile caterers.
ADVERTISING: Rates on application
Agency Commission: 10%
Average advertising content per issue: 25%
BUSINESS: CATERING: Catering, Hotels & Restaurants

MOBILE BUSINESS
37475U18B-1047
Editorial Address: White House, Commercial Road, TUNBRIDGE WELLS, TN1 2RR **Tel:** 01892 538348
Fax: 01892 538274
Email: miles@cbmagazine.co.uk
Advertising Address: As above.
Email: dlack@mbmagazine.co.uk
Web site: http://www.mbmagazine.co.uk
ISSN: 1466-4046
Publisher: Miles Publishing Ltd
Frequency: Monthly - Published 1st of each month
Free to qualifying individuals
Circulation: 6,000 (Publisher's Statement)
Usual Pagination: 60
Editor: Heather McLean; **Publisher:** Miles Bossom
Summary of Content: Business magazine for the mobile communications industry providing advice on all business and marketing issues.
Readership/Target Audience: Aimed at mobile communications dealers.
ADVERTISING: Rates on application
BUSINESS: ELECTRONICS: Telecommunications

MOBILE CHOICE
37476U18B-1055
Editorial Address: 14-16 Great Pulteney Street, LONDON, W1F 9ND **Tel:** 020 7440 3883 **Fax:** 020 7437 4250
Email: natasha.stokes@nhmedia.co.uk
Advertising Address: As above.
Email: richard.hemmings@nhmedia.co.uk
Web site: http://www.mobilechoiceuk.com
Publisher: Noble House Media Ltd
Frequency: 13 issues yearly
Cover Price: £3.95
Free to qualifying individuals
Annual Sub.: £24.00
Circulation: 20,170 (Publisher's Statement)
Usual Pagination: 88
Editor: Natasha Stokes; **Managing Director:** Debra Doran; **Publisher:** Debra Doran
Summary of Content: Magazine covering all aspects of mobile phones and mobile phone networks.
Readership/Target Audience: Aimed at general consumers and professionals choosing a mobile phone.
ADVERTISING RATES:
Full Page Colour £3096.00
Agency Commission: 10%
Mechanical Data: Type Area: 270 x 190mm, Col Length: 270mm, Trim Size: 297 x 210mm, Bleed Size: 305 x 214mm, Film: Digital, Page Width: 190mm
Copy instructions: Copy Date: 4 weeks prior to publication date
BUSINESS: ELECTRONICS: Telecommunications

MOBILE CHOICE FOR BUSINESS
1704180U18B-1965
Editorial Address: 14-16 Great Pulteney Street, LONDON, W1F 9ND **Tel:** 020 7440 3883
Email: huw.morgan@nhmedia.co.uk
Advertising Address: As above. **Tel:** 020 7440 3823
Email: richard.hemmings@nhmedia.co.uk

Web site: http://www.mc4b.co.uk
Publisher: Noble House Media Ltd
Date Established: 2006
Frequency: Quarterly
Free to qualifying individuals
Circulation: 25,000 (Publisher's Statement)
Editor: Huw Morgan; **Advertising Manager:** Richard Hemmings
Summary of Content: Magazine covering mobile solutions. Topics covered include tariffs, handsets and accessories.
Readership/Target Audience: Aimed at SMEs.
ADVERTISING RATES:
Full Page Colour £4375.00
Agency Commission: 10%
Mechanical Data: Bleed Size: 306 x 236mm, Trim Size: 300 x 230mm, Film: Digital
Copy instructions: Copy Date: 3 weeks prior to publication date
BUSINESS: ELECTRONICS: Telecommunications

MOBILE COMMUNICATIONS EUROPE
37477U18B-1060
Formerly: Mobile Communications
Editorial Address: Mortimer House, 37-41 Mortimer Street, LONDON, W1T 3JH **Tel:** 020 7017 5000
Email: gareth.willmer@informa.com
Web site: http://www.telecoms.com
ISSN: 0953-539X
Publisher: T&F Informa Group PLC
Frequency: 23 issues yearly
Annual Sub.: £1495.00
Usual Pagination: 14
Editor: Gareth Willmer
Summary of Content: Journal covering news and analysis of major events in the mobile communications industry in the Europe.
Readership/Target Audience: Aimed at operators, service providers, equipment manufacturers, investors, consultants, senior level executives and major users.
ADVERTISING: No Advertising taken
BUSINESS: ELECTRONICS: Telecommunications

MOBILE COMMUNICATIONS INTERNATIONAL
37478U18B-1080
Editorial Address: Mortimer House, 37-41 Mortimer Street, LONDON, W1T 3JH **Tel:** 020 7017 5201
Email: sean.jackson@informa.com
Advertising Address: As above. **Tel:** 020 7017 5000
Fax: 020 7017 5647
Email: tim.banham@informa.com
Web site: http://www.telecoms.com
ISSN: 1467-1034
Publisher: T&F Informa Group PLC
Date Established: 1988
Frequency: 10 issues yearly
Free to qualifying individuals
Circulation: 25,046 (BPA Worldwide 01/07/2007 to 31/12/2007)
Usual Pagination: 76
Editor: James Middleton; **News Editor:** James Middleton
Summary of Content: Magazine providing the latest news in the mobile communications industry.
Readership/Target Audience: Aimed at service providers, operators, distributors and manufacturers.
ADVERTISING RATES:
Full Page Colour £5800.00
Mechanical Data: Type Area: 257 x 184mm, Col Length: 257mm, Trim Size: 277 x 204mm, Bleed Size: 283 x 210mm, Print Process: Sheet-fed and web-fed offset litho, Film: Digital, Page Width: 184mm
Copy instructions: Copy Date: 3 weeks prior to publication date
BUSINESS: ELECTRONICS: Telecommunications

MOBILE ELECTRONICS NEWS
1685684U31A-388
Formerly: C.A.R
Editorial Address: 318C High Road, Off Meggison Way, BENFLEET, SS7 5HB **Tel:** 0870 444 3531
Fax: 01268 754429
Email: sarah.elson@creativemedialtd.co.uk
Advertising Address: As above.
Email: sarah.elson@creativemedialtd.co.uk
Web site: http://www.mobileelectronicsnews.co.uk
Publisher: Creative Media Ltd
Date Established: 2004
Frequency: Monthly
Cover Price: Free
Circulation: 6,000 (Publisher's Statement)
Usual Pagination: 56
Editor: Sarah Elson; **Advertising Manager:** Sarah Elson; **Publisher:** Charlotte Body
Summary of Content: Magazine covering car audio, security and multimedia.

Readership/Target Audience: Aimed at car audio dealers, manufacturers and retailers.
ADVERTISING RATES:
Full Page Colour £1100.00
Agency Commission: 10%
Mechanical Data: Film: Digital
Copy instructions: Copy Date: 2 weeks prior to publication date
Average advertising content per issue: 60%
BUSINESS: MOTOR TRADE: Motor Trade Accessories

MOBILE ENTERTAINMENT   1665481U18B-1962
Editorial Address: Saxon House, 6A St. Andrew Street, HERTFORD, SG14 1JA **Tel:** 01992 535646
Fax: 01992 535647
Email: stuart.obrien@intentmedia.co.uk
Advertising Address: As above. **Tel:** 01992 535647
Fax: 01992 535648
Email: tom.roberts@intentmedia.co.uk
Web site: http://www.mobile-ent.biz
Publisher: Intent Media
Date Established: 2005
Frequency: Monthly - Published in the 1st week of the cover month
Annual Sub.: £50.00
Circulation: 8,012 (Publisher's Statement)
Executive Editor: Tim Green; **Managing Editor:** Lisa Foster
Summary of Content: Magazine focusing on all aspects of the mobile content industry including distribution, development, retail, hardware and licensing.
Readership/Target Audience: Aimed at handset operators, games developers and broadcasters.
ADVERTISING RATES:
Full Page Colour £1495.00
Agency Commission: 10%
Mechanical Data: Type Area: 295 x 212mm, Bleed Size: 321 x 236mm, Trim Size: 315 x 230mm, Col Length: 295mm, Page Width: 212mm, Film: Digital
Average advertising content per issue: 50%
BUSINESS: ELECTRONICS: Telecommunications

MOBILE EUROPE   37479U18B-1100
Editorial Address: 6 Laurence Pountney Hill, LONDON, EC4R 0BL **Tel:** 020 7933 8999 **Fax:** 020 7933 8998
Email: keithd@mobileeurope.co.uk
Advertising Address: As above.
Email: shivad@mobileeurope.co.uk
Web site: http://www.mobileeurope.co.uk
ISSN: 1350-7362
Publisher: St. John Patrick Publishers Ltd
Date Established: 1990
Frequency: 10 issues yearly - Published around the 1st week of the cover month
Cover Price: Free
Circulation: 8,759 (BPA Worldwide 01/07/2007 to 31/12/2007)
Usual Pagination: 40
Editor: Keith Dyer
Summary of Content: Specialist mobile communications magazine providing news, views, product information, technology developments, policy updates and in-depth market reports.
Readership/Target Audience: Aimed at key decision makers on mobile communications throughout Europe.
ADVERTISING RATES:
Full Page Colour £4914.00
Agency Commission: 10%
Mechanical Data: Film: Positive, right reading, emulsion side down. Digital, Type Area: 275 x 180mm, Bleed Size: 303 x 216mm, Trim Size: 297 x 210mm, Col Length: 275mm, Page Width: 180mm
Copy instructions: Copy Date: 3 weeks prior to publication date
Average advertising content per issue: 60%
BUSINESS: ELECTRONICS: Telecommunications

MOBILE FRONTIERS   1804993U18B-1974
Editorial Address: JMR Associates, Manor Road, Towersey, THAME, OX9 3QR **Tel:** 01844 218778
Email: paul.rasmussen@informa.com
Advertising Address: Mortimer House, 37-41 Mortimer Street, LONDON, W1T 3JH **Tel:** 020 7017 5000
Fax: 020 7017 5647
Email: tim.banham@informa.com
Publisher: Informa Telecoms and Media Group
Date Established: 2003
Frequency: Quarterly
Free to qualifying individuals
Circulation: 18,000 (Publisher's Statement)
Usual Pagination: 64
Editor: Paul Rasmussen
Summary of Content: Magazine featuring the latest cellular tests, applications and services.
Readership/Target Audience: Aimed at people working in the cellular phone industry.

ADVERTISING: Rates on application
BUSINESS: ELECTRONICS: Telecommunications

MOBILE MEDIA   37469U18B-1106
Formerly: Mobile Internet
Editorial Address: Mortimer House, 37-41 Mortimer Street, LONDON, W1T 3JH **Tel:** 020 7017 4267 **Fax:** 020 7017 5698
Email: guillermo.escofet@informa.com
Web site: http://www.telecoms.com/mobilemedia
ISSN: 1470-8841
Publisher: T&F Informa Group PLC
Frequency: 23 issues yearly
Annual Sub.: £995.00
Usual Pagination: 16
Editor: Guillermo Escofet; **Managing Director:** Ian Hemming
Summary of Content: Newsletter covering the emerging market of mobile data. Looks at commerce contents and applications in mobile space including mobile messaging.
Readership/Target Audience: Readership includes equipment and software developers, service providers, network operators, consultants, analysts and regulators.
ADVERTISING: No Advertising taken
BUSINESS: ELECTRONICS: Telecommunications

MOBILE NEWS   37486U18B-1140
Editorial Address: 70-74 City Road, LONDON, EC1Y 2BJ **Tel:** 020 7324 3500 **Fax:** 020 7324 3529
Email: editorial@mobilenewscwp.co.uk
Advertising Address: As above. **Fax:** 020 7324 3511
Email: advertising@mobilenewscwp.co.uk
Web site: http://www.mobilenewscwp.co.uk
ISSN: 0964-9468
Publisher: Clark White Publications Ltd
Date Established: 1991
Frequency: 25 issues yearly
Cover Price: £2.75
Annual Sub.: £65.00
Circulation: 6,167 (ABC 01/01/2008 to 31/12/2008)
Usual Pagination: 52
Editor: James Blackman; **News Editor:** Marylou Costa
Summary of Content: Newspaper covering all aspects of the mobile communications industry.
Readership/Target Audience: Read by people working in the mobile communications and related industries.
ADVERTISING RATES:
Full Page Colour £3000.00
Agency Commission: 10%
Mechanical Data: Page Width: 245mm, Bleed Size: 406 x 281mm, Trim Size: 400 x 275mm, Type Area: 380 x 245mm, Col Length: 380mm, Film: Digital
Copy instructions: Copy Date: 2 weeks prior to publication date
Average advertising content per issue: 60%
BUSINESS: ELECTRONICS: Telecommunications

MODERN ASPHALTS   39049U42B-110
Editorial Address: Linden House, Linden Close, TUNBRIDGE WELLS, TN4 8HH **Tel:** 01892 524455
Fax: 01892 524456
Email: jon@barrett-byrd.com
Web site: http://www.modernasphalts.com
Publisher: Barrett, Byrd Associates
Date Established: 1997
Frequency: Half-yearly - Published in March and September
Cover Price: Free
Circulation: 15,000 (Publisher's Statement)
Usual Pagination: 16
Editor: Jon Masters
Summary of Content: Sponsored magazine providing information on the latest developments in the highways and airfields, asphalt pavement construction and maintenance sector.
Readership/Target Audience: Aimed at project managers, engineers and specifiers of the highways and airfields paving sector.
ADVERTISING: No Advertising taken
BUSINESS: CONSTRUCTION: Roads

MODERN BUILDING SERVICES   1640886U3B-43
Editorial Address: 1st Floor, Southgate House, St. George's Way, STEVENAGE, SG1 1HG **Tel:** 01438 759000
Fax: 01438 759007
Email: ksharpe@portico.uk.com
Advertising Address: As above.
Email: ckeel@portico.uk.com
Web site: http://www.modbs.co.uk
ISSN: 1743-6931
Publisher: Portico Publishing Ltd
Date Established: 2004
Frequency: Monthly - Published on the 5th of the cover month
Free to qualifying individuals
Annual Sub.: £40.00

Circulation: 21,816 (ABC 01/01/2008 to 31/12/2008)
Usual Pagination: 64
Editor: Ken Sharpe; **Advertising Manager:** Charles Keel
Summary of Content: Journal covering the entire supply and user chain in the building services industry.
Readership/Target Audience: Aimed at building designers, manufacturers and contractors and end users.
ADVERTISING RATES:
Full Page Colour £2369.00
Agency Commission: 10%
Mechanical Data: Bleed Size: 303 x 216mm, Type Area: 275 x 186mm, Trim Size: 297 x 210mm, Col Length: 275mm, Page Width: 186mm, Film: Digital
Copy instructions: Copy Date: 20th of the month prior to publication date
Average advertising content per issue: 45%
BUSINESS: HEATING & VENTILATION: Industrial Heating & Ventilation

MODERN CARPETS + TEXTILES   1692177U23B-504
Editorial Address: Studio 30, Liddell Road, LONDON, NW6 2EW **Tel:** 020 7578 7201 **Fax:** 020 7578 7221
Email: info@hali.com
Advertising Address: As above. **Tel:** 020 7578 7209
Email: david.young@hali.com
Web site: http://www.moderncarpetsandtextiles.com
Publisher: Hali Publications Ltd
Date Established: 2005
Frequency: Quarterly
Free to qualifying individuals
Editor: Ben Evans
Summary of Content: Magazine dedicated to high-end hand made carpets, textiles, art and design.
Readership/Target Audience: Aimed at carpet retailers, interior designers, architects and carpet and textile specifiers.
ADVERTISING RATES:
Full Page Colour £2990.00
Agency Commission: 10%
Mechanical Data: Type Area: 275 x 184mm, Bleed Size: 310 x 225mm, Trim Size: 300 x 215mm, Col Length: 275mm, Page Width: 184mm, Film: Digital
Average advertising content per issue: 50%
BUSINESS: FURNISHINGS & FURNITURE: Furnishings, Carpets & Flooring

THE MODERN LAW REVIEW   39220U44-1480
Editorial Address: London School of Economics, Houghton Street, LONDON, WC2A 2AE **Tel:** 020 7955 7687
Fax: 020 7955 7366
Web site: http://www.lse.ac.uk
ISSN: 0026-7961
Publisher: Wiley-Blackwell Publishing
Frequency: 6 issues yearly
Circulation: 1,900 (Publisher's Statement)
Editor: Bradley Barlow
Summary of Content: Publication carrying articles on social theory, economics, politics and government.
Readership/Target Audience: Aimed at the legal profession, academics and students.
ADVERTISING: No Advertising taken
BUSINESS: LEGAL

MODERN POWER SYSTEMS   40764U58-65_5
Editorial Address: Progressive House, 2 Maidstone Road, Foots Cray, SIDCUP, DA14 5HZ **Tel:** 020 8269 7700
Fax: 020 8269 7804
Email: jvarley@progressivemediagroup.com
Advertising Address: As above.
Email: ddipchan@progressivemediagroup.com
Web site: http://www.modernpowersystems.com
Publisher: Progressive Media Publications
Date Established: 1963
Frequency: Monthly - Published around the 25th of the month prior to publication date
Free to qualifying individuals
Annual Sub.: £111.00
Circulation: 11,926 (BPA Worldwide 01/07/2007 to 31/12/2007)
Usual Pagination: 48
Editor: James Varley; **Managing Editor:** James Varley
Summary of Content: Journal covering design, purchasing and operation of power generating, transmission and distribution systems.
Readership/Target Audience: Read by utilities, power and design engineers, consultants and government.
ADVERTISING RATES:
Full Page Mono £2730.00
Full Page Colour £3655.00
Agency Commission: 10%
Mechanical Data: Type Area: 254 x 178mm, Trim Size: 297 x 210mm, Col Length: 254mm, Bleed Size: 303 x 216mm, Film: Digital, Page Width: 178mm
Copy instructions: Copy Date: 2 weeks prior to publication date

Average advertising content per issue: 40%
BUSINESS: ENERGY, FUEL & NUCLEAR

MODERN RAILWAYS
39678U49E-120

Editorial Address: Transport Writing Services, PO Box 206, TUNBRIDGE WELLS, TN1 2XA **Tel:** 01892 525339
Fax: 01892 526256
Email: modern.railways@googlemail.com
Advertising Address: As above. **Tel:** 01303 267456
Fax: 01303 230028
Email: mrgto@tiscali.co.uk
Web site: http://www.ianallan.com/publishing/modrail
ISSN: 0026-8356
Publisher: Ian Allan Publishing Ltd
Date Established: 1947
Frequency: Monthly
Cover Price: £3.80
Circulation: 18,000 (Publisher's Statement)
Usual Pagination: 84
Editor: James Abbott; **Advertising Manager:** Paul Edwards
Summary of Content: Journal covering British and European railways, including business marketing and technical trends.
Readership/Target Audience: Aimed at railway professionals and enthusiasts.
ADVERTISING RATES:
Full Page Mono £915.00
Full Page Colour £1310.00
Mechanical Data: Type Area: 272 x 186mm, Bleed Size: 303 x 216mm, Trim Size: 297 x 210mm, Col Length: 272mm, Page Width: 186mm, Film: Digital
Copy instructions: Copy Date: 2 weeks prior to publication date
BUSINESS: TRANSPORT: Railways

MODERN UTILITY MANAGEMENT
1666511U58-174

Editorial Address: Unit 10, Cringleford Business Centre, Intwood Road, Cringleford, NORWICH, NR4 6AU
Tel: 01603 274130 **Fax:** 01603 274131
Email: libbie@schofieldpublishing.co.uk
Advertising Address: As above.
Web site: http://www.modernutilitymanagement.com
ISSN: 1479-1129
Publisher: Schofield Publishing Ltd
Date Established: 2003
Frequency: 6 issues yearly
Free to qualifying individuals
Circulation: 5,000 (Publisher's Statement)
Editor: Libbie Hammond; **Advertising Manager:** Dave King
Summary of Content: Magazine covering the development, maintenance and running of the UK's gas, electricity, water, telecommunications and renewable energy services. Includes news, case studies, company profiles and interviews.
Readership/Target Audience: Aimed at utility providers, contractors, suppliers, consultancies, trade associations, regulatory authorities and government departments.
ADVERTISING RATES:
Full Page Mono £1400.00
Full Page Colour £1800.00
Agency Commission: 10%
Mechanical Data: Type Area: 265 x 182mm, Bleed Size: 303 x 216mm, Trim Size: 297 x 210mm, Col Length: 265mm, Page Width: 182mm, Film: Digital
BUSINESS: ENERGY, FUEL & NUCLEAR

MODERNGOV
1604900U32R-491

Formerly: Modern Government
Editorial Address: 9th Floor, St. James's Buildings, Oxford Street, MANCHESTER, M1 6PP **Tel:** 0161 211 3000
Email: editorial@govnet.co.uk
Advertising Address: Golden Cross House, 8 Duncannon Street, LONDON, WC2N 4JF **Tel:** 020 7484 5246
Fax: 020 7484 4950
Email: richard.holloway@govnet.co.uk
Web site: http://www.govnet.co.uk/publications/moderngov
Publisher: GovNet Communications
Date Established: 2002
Frequency: 6 issues yearly
Free to qualifying individuals
Circulation: 7,500 (ABC 01/07/2008 to 30/06/2009)
Editor: Natalie Quinn; **Advertising Manager:** Maria Figgins
Summary of Content: Magazine covering topics affecting public sector officials including interviews with key policy makers.
Readership/Target Audience: Aimed at public sector professionals.
ADVERTISING RATES:
Full Page Colour £3595.00
Agency Commission: 10%
Mechanical Data: Type Area: 255 x 190mm, Bleed Size: 281 x 216mm, Trim Size: 275 x 210mm, Col Length: 255mm, Page Width: 190mm, Film: Digital
Copy instructions: Copy Date: 2 weeks prior to publication date

Average advertising content per issue: 50%
BUSINESS: LOCAL GOVERNMENT, LEISURE & RECREATION: Local Government Related

MOLECULAR HUMAN REPRODUCTION
25807U64F-110

Editorial Address: 4-5 Mill Yard, Dry Drayton, Childerley, CAMBRIDGE, CB23 8BA **Tel:** 01954 212404
Fax: 01954 212359
Email: editorial@humanreproduction.co.uk
Advertising Address: Great Clarendon Street, OXFORD, OX2 6DP **Tel:** 01865 353907 **Fax:** 01865 353774
Email: steve.simmonds@oxfordjournals.org
Web site: http://www.molehr.oxfordjournals.org
ISSN: 1360-9947
Publisher: OUP
Date Established: 1995
Frequency: 6 issues yearly
Cover Price: £41.00
Annual Sub.: £194.00
Usual Pagination: 180
Editor: Stephen Hillier; **Editor-in-Chief:** Stephen Hillier; **Managing Editor:** H. Beard
Summary of Content: Journal containing articles on the molecular aspects of human reproductive physiology, pathology and genetics.
Readership/Target Audience: Read by molecular biologists.
ADVERTISING RATES:
Full Page Mono £646.00
Full Page Colour £1076.00
Agency Commission: 10%
Mechanical Data: Type Area: 255 x 178mm, Trim Size: 279 x 216mm, Bleed Size: 285 x 222mm, Film: Digital, Print Process: Litho, Page Width: 178mm, Col Length: 255mm
Copy instructions: Copy Date: 4 weeks prior to publication date
BUSINESS: OTHER CLASSIFICATIONS: Biology

MOLECULAR PHYSICS
40049U55-97

Editorial Address: 4 Park Square, Milton Park, ABINGDON, OX14 4RN **Tel:** 020 7017 6370 **Fax:** 020 7017 6336
Email: richard.moore@tandf.co.uk
Advertising Address: 11 New Fetter Lane, LONDON, EC4P 4EE **Tel:** 01235 401000 **Fax:** 01235 401550
Email: info@tandf.co.uk
Web site: http://www.tandf.co.uk
ISSN: 0026-8976
Publisher: Routledge, Taylor & Francis
Date Established: 1958
Frequency: 24 issues yearly
Annual Sub.: £4304.00
Circulation: 1,000 (Publisher's Statement)
Usual Pagination: 172
Editor: Colin Bulpitt; **Managing Editor:** Richard Moore; **Publisher:** Colin Bulpitt
Summary of Content: Journal containing research papers on chemical physics including the structure and dynamics of individual molecules and molecular assemblies.
Readership/Target Audience: Aimed at research workers in university departments and research institutions in physical chemistry, theoretical chemistry, chemistry physics, biophysics and applied maths.
BUSINESS: APPLIED SCIENCE & LABORATORIES

MOMENTUM
601006U1F-294

Formerly: Momentum Investor
Editorial Address: 84 Addiscombe Road, CROYDON, CR0 5PP **Tel:** 020 8656 4648 **Fax:** 020 8656 0111
Email: georgina@scsw.co.uk
Web site: http://www.momentuminvestor.co.uk
Publisher: Equitylink Ltd
Date Established: 1998
Frequency: Monthly
Annual Sub.: £99.00
Usual Pagination: 8
Editor: Richard Welby
Summary of Content: Newsletter researching and focusing on all UK quoted companies showing relative strength against market averages, with an interest in a wide range of sectors.
Readership/Target Audience: Aimed at private and professional investors.
ADVERTISING: No Advertising taken
BUSINESS: FINANCE & ECONOMICS: Investment

MONDO*ARC
1651909U17-254

Editorial Address: Waterloo Place, Watson Square, STOCKPORT, SK1 3AZ **Tel:** 0161 476 8350
Fax: 0161 429 7214
Email: p.james@mondiale.co.uk
Advertising Address: As above. **Tel:** 0161 480 3344
Email: j.pennington@mondiale.co.uk
Web site: http://www.mondiale.co.uk
ISSN: 1753-5875

Publisher: Mondiale Publishing Ltd
Date Established: 2001
Frequency: 6 issues yearly
Annual Sub.: £24.00
Circulation: 10,651 (ABC 01/07/2007 to 30/06/2008)
Usual Pagination: 132
Editor: Paul James; **Advertising Manager:** Jason Pennington
Summary of Content: Magazine covering all aspects of architectural lighting.
Language(s): Chinese; English; French; German; Italian; Japanese; Spanish
Readership/Target Audience: Aimed at architects and lighting designers.
ADVERTISING RATES:
Full Page Colour £2100.00
Agency Commission: 10%
Mechanical Data: Type Area: 310 x 210mm, Bleed Size: 339 x 242mm, Trim Size: 333 x 236mm, Col Length: 310mm, Page Width: 210mm, Film: Digital
BUSINESS: ELECTRICAL

MONDO*DR
40962U61-17_60

Editorial Address: Waterloo Place, Watson Square, STOCKPORT, SK1 3AZ **Tel:** 0161 476 8340
Fax: 0161 429 7214
Email: p.brewis@mondiale.co.uk
Advertising Address: As above. **Tel:** 0161 476 5580
Email: j.perry@mondiale.co.uk
Web site: http://www.mondodr.com
Publisher: Mondiale Publishing Ltd
Date Established: 1990
Frequency: 7 issues yearly - Published around the 1st of the 1st cover month
Free to qualifying individuals
Annual Sub.: £30.00
Circulation: 13,000 (Publisher's Statement)
Usual Pagination: 180
Editor: Peter Brewis; **Advertising Manager:** Joel Perry
Summary of Content: Magazine providing worldwide coverage of developments in the entertainment technology equipment market.
Language(s): Chinese; English; French; German; Italian; Japanese; Russian; Spanish
Readership/Target Audience: Aimed at those working in the technology and entertainment markets.
ADVERTISING RATES:
Full Page Colour £2300.00
Mechanical Data: No. of Columns (Display): 2, Col Length: 310mm, Page Width: 210mm, Type Area: 310 x 210mm, Trim Size: 333 x 236mm, Bleed Size: 339 x 242mm, Film: Digital
BUSINESS: MUSIC TRADE

MONEY LAUNDERING BULLETIN
1862535U1R-388

Editorial Address: Telephone House, 69-77 Paul Street, LONDON, EC2A 4LQ **Tel:** 020 7017 4214
Email: timon.molloy@informa.com
Web site: http://www.informafinance.com
ISSN: 1462-141X
Publisher: Informa PLC
Frequency: 10 issues yearly
Usual Pagination: 18
Editor: Timon Molloy
Summary of Content: Newsletter giving information on money laundering schemes, methods, trends and policing.
Readership/Target Audience: Aimed at banks, investment trusts and houses, insurance companies, stock brokers, lawyers and accountants, money laundering reporting officers, government organisations, the police and other law enforcement agencies.
ADVERTISING: No Advertising taken
BUSINESS: FINANCE & ECONOMICS: Financial Related

MONEY MANAGEMENT
35274U1F-303

Editorial Address: 1 Southwark Bridge, LONDON, SE1 9HL
Tel: 020 7873 3000 **Fax:** 020 7775 6497
Email: janet.walford@ft.com
Advertising Address: As above. **Tel:** 020 7775 6607
Email: alex.michaels@ft.com
Web site: http://www.ftadviser.com
ISSN: 1463-1911
Publisher: FT Group
Date Established: 1962
Frequency: Monthly - Published on the 22nd of the month prior to cover date
Cover Price: £6.75
Annual Sub.: £71.50
Circulation: 9,667 (ABC 01/07/2008 to 30/06/2009)
Usual Pagination: 175
Editor: Janet Walford
Summary of Content: Magazine containing information on new products, new opportunities and analysis of new financial ideas, with highly detailed surveys. Covers tax,

insurance, investment, unit trusts, PEPs, pensions and all areas of personal finance.
Readership/Target Audience: Aimed at financial professionals.
ADVERTISING RATES:
Full Page Colour £4741.00
Agency Commission: 10%
Mechanical Data: Type Area: 266 x 178mm, Bleed Size: 303 x 216mm, Trim Size: 297 x 210mm, Col Length: 266mm, Film: Digital, Page Width: 178mm
Copy instructions: Copy Date: 3 weeks prior to publication date
Average advertising content per issue: 30%
BUSINESS: FINANCE & ECONOMICS: Investment

MONEY MARKETING
35275U1F-304

Editorial Address: St. Giles House, 50 Poland Street, LONDON, W1F 7AX **Tel:** 020 7943 8000 **Fax:** 020 7943 8097
Email: paul.mcmillan@centaur.co.uk
Advertising Address: As above. **Tel:** 020 7970 4000
Fax: 020 7943 8099
Email: danny.cormack@centaur.co.uk
Web site: http://www.moneymarketing.co.uk
ISSN: 0958-3769
Publisher: Centaur Communications Ltd
Frequency: Weekly - Published on Thursday
Cover Price: £1.95
Annual Sub.: £87.00
Circulation: 29,271 (ABC 01/07/2008 to 30/06/2009)
Usual Pagination: 88
Editor: Paul McMillan; **News Editor:** Paul McMillan; **Features Editor:** Gregor Watt; **Publisher:** David Cowan
Summary of Content: Magazine covering independent financial advisers, life assurance, news, pensions, mortgages, investments, products and information related to the financial services industry.
Readership/Target Audience: Aimed at professional intermediaries.
ADVERTISING RATES:
Full Page Mono £3888.00
Full Page Colour £5004.00
Agency Commission: 10%
Mechanical Data: Type Area: 360 x 266mm, Bleed Size: 395 x 298mm, Trim Size: 389 x 292mm, Film: Digital, Col Length: 360mm, Page Width: 266mm
Copy instructions: Copy Date: Thursday prior to publication date
BUSINESS: FINANCE & ECONOMICS: Investment

MONEY MEDIA
41462U63G-400

Editorial Address: Media House, Cronkbourne, DOUGLAS, IM4 4SB **Tel:** 01624 696590 **Fax:** 01624 625623
Email: simon.richardson@manninmedia.co.im
Advertising Address: As above. **Tel:** 01624 696551
Email: johntaylor@manninmedia.co.im
Web site: http://www.manninmedia.co.im
Publisher: Executive Publications
Frequency: Monthly
Cover Price: Free
Circulation: 12,000 (Publisher's Statement)
Usual Pagination: 52
Editor: Simon Richardson; **Advertising Manager:** John Taylor; **Managing Editor:** Simon Richardson
Summary of Content: Business magazine covering news, appointments, financial articles and political comment.
Readership/Target Audience: Aimed at potential offshore investors and the local finance sector.
ADVERTISING RATES:
Full Page Colour £745.00
Agency Commission: 10%
Mechanical Data: Trim Size: 297 x 210mm, Type Area: 266 x 188mm, Bleed Size: 303 x 216mm, Film: Digital, Col Length: 266mm, Page Width: 188mm
Copy instructions: Copy Date: 2 weeks prior to publication date
Average advertising content per issue: 40%
BUSINESS: REGIONAL BUSINESS: Regional Business Isle of Man

MONEY WEEK
629262U1F-304_37

Editorial Address: 7th Floor, Sea Containers House, 20 Upper Ground, LONDON, SE1 9JD **Tel:** 020 7633 3729
Fax: 020 7633 3740
Email: editor@moneyweek.com
Advertising Address: As above. **Fax:** 020 7633 3742
Email: simonc@moneyweek.com
Web site: http://www.moneyweek.com
Publisher: Fleet Street Publications Ltd
Date Established: 2000
Frequency: Weekly
Cover Price: £2.20
Circulation: 41,282 (ABC 01/01/2009 to 30/06/2009)
Usual Pagination: 48
Editor: John Stepek; **Advertising Manager:** Simon Cuff; **Publisher:** Bill Bonner

---

Summary of Content: Magazine containing a digest of financial and investment news taken from the British and foreign media, newsletters and websites.
Readership/Target Audience: Aimed at private investors and financial professionals.
ADVERTISING RATES:
Full Page Mono £4000.00
Full Page Colour £4000.00
Agency Commission: 10%
Mechanical Data: Trim Size: 297 x 210mm, Film: Digital, Bleed Size: 303 x 216mm
Copy instructions: Copy Date: 1 week prior to publication date
Average advertising content per issue: 30%
BUSINESS: FINANCE & ECONOMICS: Investment

MONEYFACTS
35273U1F-298

Editorial Address: Moneyfacts House, 66-70 Thorpe Road, NORWICH, NR1 1BJ **Tel:** 0845 168 9689
Fax: 0845 168 9690
Email: ltillcock@moneyfacts.co.uk
Advertising Address: As above. **Tel:** 0845 168 9690
Fax: 01603 476201
Email: advertising@moneyfacts.co.uk
Web site: http://www.moneyfacts.co.uk
ISSN: 0960-2704
Publisher: Moneyfacts Group
Date Established: 1988
Frequency: Monthly
Annual Sub.: £134.50
Circulation: 10,466 (ABC 01/07/2008 to 30/06/2009)
Usual Pagination: 112
Editor: Darren Cook
Summary of Content: Guide to UK savings, credit card, personal loan, current account and mortgage rates.
Readership/Target Audience: Read by IFAs, banks, building societies, solicitors, accountants and those interested in personal finance.
ADVERTISING RATES:
Full Page Colour £2860.00
Agency Commission: 10%
Mechanical Data: Page Width: 195mm, Type Area: 285 x 195mm, Trim Size: 297 x 210mm, Col Length: 285mm, Film: Digital
Copy instructions: Copy Date: 10 days prior to publication date
Average advertising content per issue: 20%
BUSINESS: FINANCE & ECONOMICS: Investment

MONTAGE
1842912U38-192

Editorial Address: 61 Forest Drive East, LONDON, E11 1JX
Tel: 020 8539 8547
Email: montage.ed@picture-research.org.uk
Web site: http://www.picture-research.org.uk
Publisher: Picture Research Association
Frequency: Quarterly
Free to qualifying individuals
Annual Sub.: £16.00
Circulation: 400 (Publisher's Statement)
Usual Pagination: 24
Editor: Diana Korchien
Summary of Content: Magazine covering the latest news in the image business including picture libraries, photographers, legal issues, software and book and exhibition reviews.
Readership/Target Audience: Aimed at members of the Picture Research Association and other image professionals.
BUSINESS: PHOTOGRAPHIC TRADE

MONTESSORI INTERNATIONAL
41103U62E-350

Editorial Address: 18 Balderton Street, LONDON, W1K 6TG
Tel: 020 7493 8300 **Fax:** 020 7493 9936
Email: amanda@montessori.org.uk
Advertising Address: As above.
Email: catherine@montessori.org.uk
Web site: http://www.montessorimagazine.com
ISSN: 1354-1498
Publisher: Montessori St Nicholas
Date Established: 1989
Frequency: Quarterly
Annual Sub.: £19.95
Circulation: 5,000 (Publisher's Statement)
Usual Pagination: 56
Editor: Amanda Engelbach; **Advertising Manager:** Catherine Bunbury
Summary of Content: Magazine focusing on Montessori education covering philosophy, new ideas, classroom activities, project ideas and international articles.
Readership/Target Audience: Aimed at lecturers and teachers, school owners, managers, students and parents.
ADVERTISING RATES:
Full Page Colour £775.00

Mechanical Data: Trim Size: 297 x 210mm, Bleed Size: 303 x 216mm, Film: Digital
BUSINESS: CHURCH & SCHOOL EQUIPMENT & EDUCATION: Preparatory & Independent Schools

---

MONTHLY OIL REPORT
23234U33-10_15

Editorial Address: 17 Knightsbridge, LONDON, SW1X 7LY
Tel: 020 7309 3610 **Fax:** 020 7235 4338
Email: marketing@cges.co.uk
Web site: http://www.cges.co.uk
ISSN: 1351-5365
Publisher: CGES
Date Established: 1990
Frequency: Monthly
Annual Sub.: £600.00
Usual Pagination: 6
Editor: Jenni Wilson
Summary of Content: Newsletter containing analysis of short to medium-term oil market analysis. Contains oil price forecasts, supply and demand fundamentals, expectations and the US futures markets, uncertainties and probabilities, projected scenarios, and an insight into OPEC and the Gulf countries.
Readership/Target Audience: Aimed at oil companies, banks, financiers, electricity and gas companies, shippers, refiners, airlines and governments.
ADVERTISING: No Advertising taken
BUSINESS: OIL & PETROLEUM

MORNING ADVERTISER
36488U9A-140

Formerly: The Licensee and Morning Advertiser
Editorial Address: Broadfield Park, CRAWLEY, RH11 9RT
Tel: 01293 613400 **Fax:** 01293 610317
Email: paul.charity@william-reed.co.uk
Advertising Address: As above.
Email: david.griffiths@william-reed.co.uk
Web site: http://www.morningadvertiser.co.uk
Publisher: William Reed Business Media
Frequency: Weekly - Published on Thursday
Cover Price: £1.75
Annual Sub.: £78.00
Circulation: 31,635 (ABC 01/07/2008 to 30/06/2009)
Usual Pagination: 52
Editor: Paul Charity; **News Editor:** John Harrington; **Features Editor:** Robyn Lewis; **Advertisement Director:** David Griffiths
Summary of Content: Newspaper containing marketing information and features on the pub, club and leisure industry.
Readership/Target Audience: Aimed at licensed trade professionals, nightclub owners, caterers and all leisure and hospitality outlets.
ADVERTISING RATES:
Full Page Colour £5350.00
Agency Commission: 10%
Mechanical Data: Type Area: 376 x 273mm, Film: Digital, Col Length: 376mm, Page Width: 273mm, Bleed Size: 406 x 303mm, Trim Size: 400 x 297mm
Copy instructions: Copy Date: 2 weeks prior to publication date
Average advertising content per issue: 50%
BUSINESS: DRINKS & LICENSED TRADE: Drinks, Licensed Trade, Wines & Spirits

---

MORTGAGE FINANCE GAZETTE
35377U1J-40

Editorial Address: 6th Floor, Davis House, 2 Robert Street, CROYDON, CR0 1QQ **Tel:** 020 8253 8618
Email: joanne.atkin@metropolis.co.uk
Advertising Address: As above. **Tel:** 020 8253 8604
Fax: 020 8253 4603
Email: daniel.miller@metropolis.co.uk
Web site: http://www.mfgonline.co.uk
ISSN: 0964-7988
Publisher: Metropolis International Group Ltd
Date Established: 1869
Frequency: Monthly - Published on the first week of the cover month
Cover Price: £5.00
Free to qualifying individuals
Annual Sub.: £60.00
Circulation: 5,630 (ABC 01/07/2006 to 30/06/2007)
Usual Pagination: 52
Editor: Joanne Atkin; **Managing Director:** Kevin Crook; **Advertising Manager:** Daniel Miller; **Publisher:** Daniel Miller
Summary of Content: Magazine covering issues in the mortgage market, including insurance, technology, lenders and legal matters.
Readership/Target Audience: Aimed at banks, building societies, insurance companies, management consultancies, systems providers and solicitors.
ADVERTISING RATES:
Full Page Colour £3095.00
Agency Commission: 10%
Mechanical Data: Bleed Size: 302 x 213mm, Type Area: 269 x 187mm, Col Length: 269mm, Page Width: 187mm, Trim Size: 297 x 210mm, Film: Digital

Copy instructions: Copy Date: 20th of the month prior to publication date
Supplement(s): BSA Annual Conference - 1xY, Council of Mortgage Lenders Conference - 2xY, European Mortgage Federation - 2xY
BUSINESS: FINANCE & ECONOMICS: Building Societies

MORTGAGE INTRODUCER
601393U1J-65

Editorial Address: Davina House, 137-149 Goswell Road, LONDON, EC1V 7ET **Tel:** 020 7490 0588
Fax: 020 7490 7069
Email: nia@thepublishinggroup.co.uk
Advertising Address: As above.
Email: ramesh@thepublishinggroup.co.uk
Web site: http://www.mortgageintroducer.com
Publisher: The Publishing Group Ltd
Frequency: 11 issues yearly - Published around the1st week of the cover month
Free to qualifying individuals
Annual Sub.: £50.00
Circulation: 10,000 (Publisher's Statement)
Usual Pagination: 56
Editor: Nia Williams; **Advertising Manager:** Ramesh Sharma; **Publisher:** Nia Williams
Summary of Content: Magazine providing mortgage product information, industry news and developments, Commercial mortgages and finance as well for the combined title Commercial Finance Introducer. Also protection news - products, developments etc in that industry.
Readership/Target Audience: Aimed at pre-qualified IFAs, mortgage brokers, accountants, solicitors, estate agents, tied agents and all types of mortgage advisers.
ADVERTISING RATES:
Full Page Colour £2800.00
Agency Commission: 10%
Mechanical Data: Bleed Size: 303 x 216mm, Trim Size: 297 x 210mm, Film: Digtal, No. of Columns (Display): 4, Type Area: 269 x 187mm, Col Length: 269mm, Page Width: 187mm
Copy instructions: Copy Date: 3 weeks prior to publication date
Average advertising content per issue: 40%
Supplement(s): Bridging Finance Introducer - 4xY, Buy-to-let Introducer - 2xY, Commercial Introducer - 4xY, Insurance Introducer - 2xY, Introducer, Loans - 6xY, Principal Introducer - 1xY, Protection Introducer, Technology Introducer - 2xY
BUSINESS: FINANCE & ECONOMICS: Building Societies

MORTGAGE SOLUTIONS
35378U1J-90

Editorial Address: Haymarket House, 28-29 Haymarket, LONDON, SW1Y 4RX **Tel:** 020 7484 9700
Fax: 020 7484 9990
Email: john.fitzsimons@incisivemedia.com
Advertising Address: As above. **Tel:** 020 7004 7496
Fax: 020 7004 7544
Email: james.prosser@incisivemedia.com
Web site: http://www.mortgagesolutions-online.co.uk
Publisher: Incisive Media Investments
Date Established: 1999
Frequency: Weekly
Free to qualifying individuals
Annual Sub.: £90.00
Circulation: 10,374 (Publisher's Statement)
Usual Pagination: 56
Editor: Jamie Obertelli
Summary of Content: Magazine covering all aspects of the mortgage market. Includes informative news, advice and regular features on technology, regulation and distribution for IFAs and mortgage brokers.
Readership/Target Audience: Read by mortgage brokers and independent financial advisers.
ADVERTISING RATES:
Full Page Colour £4700.00
Agency Commission: 10%
Mechanical Data: Type Area: 252 x 188mm, Col Length: 252mm, Page Width: 188mm, Bleed Size: 285 x 216mm, Col Widths (Display): 45mm, Trim Size: 297 x 210mm, Film: Digital
Copy instructions: Copy Date: 1 week prior to publication date
BUSINESS: FINANCE & ECONOMICS: Building Societies

MORTGAGE STRATEGY
714244U1J-95

Editorial Address: 79 Wells Street, LONDON, W1T 3QN
Tel: 020 7943 8098 **Fax:** 020 7943 8090
Email: robert.thickett@centaur.co.uk
Advertising Address: As above. **Tel:** 020 7970 4000
Fax: 020 7943 8099
Email: mortgagestrategy@centaur.co.uk
Web site: http://www.mortgagestrategy.co.uk
ISSN: 1475-651X
Publisher: Centaur Media Plc
Date Established: 2001
Frequency: Weekly
Cover Price: £3.95
Free to qualifying individuals

Circulation: 13,111 (Publisher's Statement)
Usual Pagination: 74
Editor: Robert Thickett; **Features Editor:** Christine Toner; **Publisher:** Anna Ruddock
Summary of Content: Magazine covering all aspects of mortgages. Includes news, in-depth analysis and trends.
Readership/Target Audience: Aimed at mortgage brokers and independent financial advisers.
ADVERTISING RATES:
Full Page Colour £3347.00
Agency Commission: 10%
Mechanical Data: Trim Size: 280 x 210mm, Film: Digital
Copy instructions: Copy Date: Tuesday prior to publication date
BUSINESS: FINANCE & ECONOMICS: Building Societies

MOT TESTING
38307U31A-125

Formerly: MOT Tester & Authorised Examiner
Editorial Address: PO Box 6118, OKHAM, LE15 6BR
Tel: 01753 646591 **Fax:** 01753 643555
Email: editor@motester.co.uk
Advertising Address: TRMG Ltd, Winchester Court, 1 Forum Place, Fiddlebridge Lane, HATFIELD, AL10 0RN
Tel: 01707 273999 **Fax:** 01707 252705
Email: stephen.chambers@trmg.co.uk
Web site: http://www.motester.co.uk
Publisher: Punters Publishing Ltd
Date Established: 1994
Frequency: Quarterly - Published in the 1st week of the cover month
Annual Sub.: £40.00
Circulation: 5,000 (Publisher's Statement)
Usual Pagination: 28
Editor: Stephen Chambers; **Managing Director:** Jim Punter; **Advertising Manager:** Stephen Chambers
Summary of Content: Journal covering all aspects of MOT testing and related subjects.
Readership/Target Audience: Aimed at MOT testing garage proprietors.
ADVERTISING RATES:
Full Page Colour £2160.00
Agency Commission: 10%
Mechanical Data: Film: Digital, No. of Columns (Display): 4, Type Area: 274 x 187mm, Trim Size: 297 x 210mm, Col Length: 274mm, Page Width: 187mm
Average advertising content per issue: 20%
BUSINESS: MOTOR TRADE: Motor Trade Accessories

MOTO TECH
1804994U31B-32

Editorial Address: 841 High Road, Finchley, LONDON, N12 8PT **Tel:** 020 8446 2100 **Fax:** 020 8446 2191
Email: william.kimberley@racetechmag.com
Advertising Address: As above.
Email: skimberley@racetechmag.com
Web site: http://www.racetechmag.com
ISSN: 1753-8866
Publisher: Racecar Graphic Ltd
Date Established: 2007
Frequency: 6 issues yearly
Cover Price: £3.95
Free to qualifying individuals
Annual Sub.: £24.00
Circulation: 25,000 (Publisher's Statement)
Usual Pagination: 90
Editor: William Kimberley; **Advertising Manager:** Soheila Kimberley
Summary of Content: Magazine focusing on the technology in high-performance road and racing bikes.
Readership/Target Audience: Aimed at engineers, manufacturers, suppliers, mechanics, team managers and riders.
ADVERTISING RATES:
Full Page Colour £2200.00
Agency Commission: 10%
Mechanical Data: Type Area: 277 x 190mm, Bleed Size: 303 x 216mm, Trim Size: 297 x 210mm, Col Length: 277mm, Page Width: 190mm, Film: Digital
BUSINESS: MOTOR TRADE: Motorcycle Trade

MOTOINFO
1851563U2A-698

Editorial Address: High View, Toothill Road, UTTOXETER, ST14 8JU **Tel:** 01889 568183
Email: chrislewis@motoinfo.co.uk
Web site: http://www.motoinfo.co.uk
Publisher: Chris Lewis
Date Established: 2002
Frequency: Monthly
Usual Pagination: 36
Editor: Chris Lewis
Summary of Content: Magazine covering information relevant to local and regional motor dealers and motor manufacturers national marketing initiatives.
Readership/Target Audience: Aimed at media and marketing sales staff.
BUSINESS: COMMUNICATIONS, ADVERTISING & MARKETING

MOTOR FACTOR
38310U31A-74

Editorial Address: Roydsdale Way, Euroway Industrial Estate, BRADFORD, BD4 6SE **Tel:** 01274 654600
Fax: 01274 654610
Email: trevor.watson@gau.co.uk
Advertising Address: As above.
Email: trevor.watson@gau.co.uk
Web site: http://www.gau.co.uk
Publisher: The Group Auto Union UK & Ireland Ltd
Date Established: 1980
Frequency: 10 issues yearly
Cover Price: Free
Circulation: 1,100 (Publisher's Statement)
Usual Pagination: 36
Editor: Trevor Watson; **Managing Director:** Jim Mazza; **Advertising Manager:** Trevor Watson
Summary of Content: Magazine covering all aspects of the supply of components, accessories and services to the specialist sectors of the independent after-market.
Readership/Target Audience: Aimed at independent motor factors, garages, parts manufacturers and distributors.
ADVERTISING RATES:
Full Page Colour £850.00
Mechanical Data: Type Area: 263 x 186mm, Col Length: 263mm, Page Width: 186mm, Trim Size: 297 x 210mm, Bleed Size: 303 x 216mm, Film: Digital
Copy instructions: Copy Date: 1st of the month prior to publication date
BUSINESS: MOTOR TRADE: Motor Trade Accessories

MOTOR FINANCE
34921U1A-84

Formerly: Credit & Car Finance
Editorial Address: 39 Thorney Road, Capel St. Mary, IPSWICH, IP9 2HL **Tel:** 01473 311983
Email: briancrogerson@btinternet.com
Advertising Address: 34 Porchester Road, LONDON, W2 6ES **Tel:** 020 7563 5604 **Fax:** 020 7563 5601
Email: daniel.greenwood@vrlknowledgebank.com
Web site: http://www.motorfinanceonline.com
ISSN: 1476-3079
Publisher: VRL Knowledge Bank Ltd
Date Established: 1998
Frequency: Monthly - Published around the 15th of the cover month
Annual Sub.: £295.00
Circulation: 1,300 (Publisher's Statement)
Usual Pagination: 24
Editor: Brian Rogerson
Summary of Content: Magazine focusing on UK and European credit finance news. Also covers personnel movements, corporate news, legal issues, commercial issues and new products.
Readership/Target Audience: Aimed at providers of consumer and motor finance including those which provide services to the industry.
ADVERTISING RATES:
Full Page Colour £1500.00
Agency Commission: 10%
Mechanical Data: Type Area: 270 x 190mm, Col Length: 270mm, Page Width: 190mm, Bleed Size: 307 x 220mm, Film: Digital, Trim Size: 297 x 210mm
Copy instructions: Copy Date: 10th of the month prior to publication date
Average advertising content per issue: 20%
BUSINESS: FINANCE & ECONOMICS

MOTOR INDUSTRY MAGAZINE
38311U31A-75

Formerly: Motor Industry Management
Editorial Address: Fanshaws, Brickendon, HERTFORD, SG13 8PQ **Tel:** 01992 511521 **Fax:** 01992 511548
Email: chrisp@motor.org.uk
Advertising Address: 6 Harforde Court, John Tate Road, HERTFORD, SG13 7NW **Tel:** 0870 300 0690
Fax: 0870 300691
Email: michael@leadmedia.co.uk
Web site: http://www.motor.org.uk
ISSN: 0265-0843
Publisher: The Institute of the Motor Industry
Frequency: 10 issues yearly - Published around the 1st of the cover month
Annual Sub.: £35.00
Circulation: 20,367 (ABC 01/07/2008 to 30/06/2009)
Usual Pagination: 40
Editor: Chris Phillips; **Advertising Manager:** Michael Linekar
Summary of Content: Magazine of the Institute of the Motor Industry containing news and covering subjects of concern to the industry.
Readership/Target Audience: Read by UK motor industry professionals within manufacturing, retailing, fleet operation, servicing and repairs.
ADVERTISING RATES:
Full Page Mono £1375.00
Full Page Colour £1890.00
Agency Commission: 10%
Mechanical Data: Type Area: 267 x 186mm, Bleed Size: 297 x 219mm, Trim Size: 291 x 216mm, Col Length: 267mm, Page Width: 186mm, Film: Digital

Copy instructions: Copy Date: 2 weeks prior to publication date
Average advertising content per issue: 40%
BUSINESS: MOTOR TRADE: Motor Trade Accessories

THE MOTOR SHIP
39338U45A-110

Editorial Address: The Old Mill, Lower Quay, FAREHAM, PO16 0RA **Tel:** 01329 825335 **Fax:** 01329 825330
Email: paul.vandyck@motorship.com
Advertising Address: As above.
Email: aoattes@motorship.com
Web site: http://www.motorship.com
ISSN: 0027-2000
Publisher: Mercator Media Ltd
Date Established: 1920
Frequency: 11 issues yearly - Published in the last week of the month prior to cover month
Free to qualifying individuals
Annual Sub: £121.00
Circulation: 7,124 (ABC 01/01/2008 to 31/12/2008)
Usual Pagination: 50
Editor: Bill Thomson
Summary of Content: Journal covering worldwide developments in marine technology.
Readership/Target Audience: Read by senior management in ship owning, operating and ship building companies.
ADVERTISING RATES:
Full Page Colour £2575.00
Agency Commission: 10%
Mechanical Data: Film: Digital, Type Area: 265 x 186mm, Bleed Size: 303 x 216mm, Trim Size: 297 x 210mm, Col Length: 265mm, Page Width: 186mm
Copy instructions: Copy Date: 1st of the month prior to publication date
Average advertising content per issue: 40%
BUSINESS: MARINE & SHIPPING

MOTOR TRADER
38312U31A-120

Editorial Address: 6th Floor, Davis House, 2 Robert Street, CROYDON, CR0 1QQ **Tel:** 020 8253 8711
Fax: 020 8253 8727
Email: john.kirwan@metropolis.co.uk
Advertising Address: As above. **Tel:** 01322 660070
Fax: 01322 616338
Email: mike.traylen@nexusmedia.com
Web site: http://www.talkingmotors.com
ISSN: 0027-2043
Publisher: Metropolis International Group Ltd
Date Established: 1905
Frequency: 47 issues yearly
Annual Sub.: £99.00
Circulation: 16,903 (ABC 01/07/2008 to 30/06/2009)
Usual Pagination: 24
Editor: John Kirwan; **Features Editor:** Waqas Qureshi
Summary of Content: Journal focusing on the automotive industry. Includes news and information on the latest developments within the industry.
Readership/Target Audience: Read by senior management in franchised dealerships, car manufacturers, importers and service and repair garages.
ADVERTISING RATES:
Full Page Colour £4095.00
Agency Commission: 10%
Mechanical Data: No. of Columns (Display): 5, Type Area: 313 x 228mm, Col Length: 313mm, Trim Size: 342 x 248mm, Bleed Size: 348 x 254mm, Page Width: 228mm, Film: Digital
Copy instructions: Copy Date: Wednesday prior to publication date
Average advertising content per issue: 50%
BUSINESS: MOTOR TRADE: Motor Trade Accessories

MOTOR TRANSPORT
39583U49A-140

Editorial Address: Quadrant House, The Quadrant, SUTTON, SM2 5AS **Tel:** 020 8652 3500 **Fax:** 020 8652 8957
Email: steve.hobson@rbi.co.uk
Advertising Address: As above.
Email: andrew.smith@rbi.co.uk
Web site: http://www.roadtransport.com
ISSN: 0027-206X
Publisher: Reed Business Information
Date Established: 1905
Frequency: 45 issues yearly
Cover Price: £3.05
Free to qualifying individuals
Annual Sub.: £107.00
Circulation: 20,376 (ABC 01/01/2008 to 31/12/2008)
Usual Pagination: 32
Editor: Steve Hobson; **News Editor:** Laura Hailstone
Summary of Content: Newspaper for the haulage and logistics industry, covering news of hauliers and supply chain companies, truck and technical news and management issues including communications, computers in haulage companies and distribution property.
Readership/Target Audience: Read by truck purchasers in transport operations running 11 or more commercial vehicles over 3.5 tonnes.

ADVERTISING RATES:
Full Page Colour £4000.00
Agency Commission: 10%
Mechanical Data: Col Length: 280mm, Page Width: 206mm, No. of Columns (Display): 4, Film: Digital, Bleed Size: 306 x 232mm, Trim Size: 300 x 226mm, Type Area: 280 x 206mm
Copy instructions: Copy Date: 10 days prior to publication date
Average advertising content per issue: 60%
BUSINESS: TRANSPORT

MOTORCYCLE TRADER
624219U31B-25

Editorial Address: 6 Kendal Court, Railway Road, NEWHAVEN, BN9 0AY **Tel:** 01273 616040
Fax: 01273 514417
Email: news@motorcycletrader.net
Advertising Address: As above.
Email: ads@motorcycletrader.net
Web site: http://www.motorcycletrader.net
Publisher: ME Publishing
Date Established: 1895
Frequency: Quarterly
Cover Price: Free
Circulation: 6,500 (Publisher's Statement)
Usual Pagination: 40
Editor: Andrew Foulkes; **Publisher:** Andrew Foulkes
Summary of Content: Magazine containing information about the motorcycle trade and industry covering issues of pricing, legality, new products and trade news.
Readership/Target Audience: Aimed at all those involved in the motorcycle trade and industry.
ADVERTISING RATES:
Full Page Colour £1000.00
Agency Commission: 10%
Mechanical Data: Type Area: 277 x 190mm, Bleed Size: 303 x 216mm, Trim Size: 297 x 210mm, Col Length: 277mm, Page Width: 190mm, Film: Digital
Copy instructions: Copy Date: 2 weeks prior to publication date
Average advertising content per issue: 40%
BUSINESS: MOTOR TRADE: Motorcycle Trade

MOULD TECHNOLOGY
761077U39-24_20

Editorial Address: PO Box 246, REIGATE, RH2 9FL
Tel: 01737 243433 **Fax:** 01737 888048
Email: media@mouldtechnology.co.uk
Advertising Address: As above.
Email: media@mouldtechnology.co.uk
Publisher: Profile Media Ltd
Date Established: 2000
Frequency: 6 issues yearly - Published in the last week of the 2nd cover month
Free to qualifying individuals
Annual Sub.: £75.00
Circulation: 6,000 (Publisher's Statement)
Usual Pagination: 40
Editor: Scott Unwin; **Advertising Manager:** Scott Unwin
Summary of Content: Magazine covering plastic injection moulding, case studies, news, technology and articles on mould making.
Readership/Target Audience: Aimed at managing directors, production managers and other professionals in the industry.
ADVERTISING RATES:
Full Page Mono £1645.00
Full Page Colour £1985.00
SCC £21.00
Agency Commission: 10%
Mechanical Data: Type Area: 267 x 180mm, Col Length: 267mm, Page Width: 180mm, Trim Size: 297 x 210mm, Bleed Size: 303 x 213mm, Col Widths (Display): 56mm, No. of Columns (Display): 3, Film: Digital
Copy instructions: Copy Date: 2 weeks prior to publication date
BUSINESS: PLASTICS & RUBBER

MQR (MINERALS, QUARRYING & RECYCLING)
38241U30-80

Editorial Address: 7 Regent Street, NOTTINGHAM, NG1 5BS **Tel:** 0115 945 3899 **Fax:** 0115 941 5658
Email: barry.wade@mqr.info
Advertising Address: As above. **Fax:** 0115 941 5685
Email: chris.cope@mqr.info
Web site: http://www.mqrmagazine.co.uk
ISSN: 1470-3289
Publisher: QMJ Publishing Ltd
Date Established: 1971
Frequency: 6 issues yearly - Published in the 2nd week of the 2nd cover month
Free to qualifying individuals
Annual Sub.: £37.00
Circulation: 5,396 (ABC 01/01/2006 to 31/12/2006)
Usual Pagination: 36
Editor: Barry Wade; **Editor-in-Chief:** Eric Bignell

Summary of Content: Magazine covering news on aggregates including quarrying and recycling. Also covers materials separation, demolition, waste and industrial minerals such as cement.
Readership/Target Audience: Aimed at senior management and site management.
ADVERTISING RATES:
Full Page Colour £1850.00
Agency Commission: 10%
Mechanical Data: Bleed Size: 396 x 281mm, Page Width: 254mm, Type Area: 343 x 254mm, Col Length: 343mm
Average advertising content per issue: 40%
Supplement(s): MQR Equipment Guide - 1xY, Product Recycle - 2xY
BUSINESS: MINING & QUARRYING

MRO MANAGEMENT
1654913U6D-504

Editorial Address: 16 Hampden Gurney Street, LONDON, W1H 5AL **Tel:** 020 7724 3456 **Fax:** 020 7724 2632
Email: ian@airtransportpubs.com
Web site: http://www.airtransportpubs.com
ISSN: 1446-6448
Publisher: Air Transport Publications Ltd
Date Established: 1999
Frequency: Quarterly
Free to qualifying individuals
Annual Sub.: £115.00
Circulation: 7,116 (BPA Worldwide 01/01/2007 to 30/06/2007)
Editor: Ian Harbison
Summary of Content: Magazine focusing on the aircraft maintenance, repair and overhaul sector.
Readership/Target Audience: Aimed at airline operators and third party service providers.
BUSINESS: AVIATION & AERONAUTICS: Aviation Engineering Equipment

---

MRW
40676U57-37

Editorial Address: Greater London House, Hampstead Road, LONDON, NW1 7EJ **Tel:** 020 7728 5000
Fax: 020 7728 4666
Email: mrw@emap.com
Advertising Address: As above.
Email: jason.winthrop@emap.com
Web site: http://www.mrw.co.uk
ISSN: 1354-8522
Publisher: EMAP Insight
Date Established: 1912
Frequency: Weekly - Published every Thursday of the month
Cover Price: £3.95
Annual Sub.: £130.00
Circulation: 3,455 (ABC 01/01/2008 to 31/12/2008)
Usual Pagination: 44
Editor: Paul Sanderson
Summary of Content: Journal covering the field of recycling and waste management.
Readership/Target Audience: Read by professional recyclers, environmental professionals, local authorities and government departments in the United Kingdom.
ADVERTISING RATES:
Full Page Colour £1950.00
Agency Commission: 10%
Mechanical Data: Film: Digital, Trim Size: 297 x 210mm, Type Area: 275 x 190mm, Bleed Size: 303 x 216mm, Col Length: 275mm, Page Width: 190mm
Copy instructions: Copy Date: 1 week prior to publication date
Average advertising content per issue: 60%
BUSINESS: ENVIRONMENT & POLLUTION

MS & T
623087U6A-130

Formerly: MST-Modern Simulation & Training
Editorial Address: Pembroke House, 8 St. Christophers Place, FARNBOROUGH, GU14 0NH **Tel:** 01252 532000
Fax: 01252 512714
Email: mst@halldale.com
Advertising Address: As above.
Email: jeremy@halldale.com
Web site: http://www.halldale.com/mst
ISSN: 1471-1052
Publisher: Halldale Media Ltd
Frequency: 6 issues yearly
Free to qualifying individuals
Annual Sub.: £65.00
Circulation: 14,745 (Publisher's Statement)
Usual Pagination: 54
Editor: Fiona Greenyer; **News Editor:** Fiona Greenyer;
Editor-in-Chief: Chris Lehman; **Advertising Manager:** Jeremy Humphreys; **Managing Editor:** Jeff Loube
Summary of Content: Journal focusing on military training, simulation and education.
Readership/Target Audience: Aimed at military simulation and training establishments and agencies. Also national defence ministries and administrations and procurement committees.

ADVERTISING RATES:
Full Page Mono £2525.00
Full Page Colour £4370.00
Agency Commission: 15%
Mechanical Data: Type Area: 254 x 178mm, Trim Size: 277 x 206mm, Bleed Size: 283 x 212mm, Col Length: 254mm, Film: Digital, Page Width: 178mm
Average advertising content per issue: 40%
BUSINESS: AVIATION & AERONAUTICS

MSA NEWSLINK
38362U31D-50
Editorial Address: 101 Wellington Road North, STOCKPORT, SK4 2LP **Tel:** 0161 429 9669
Fax: 0161 429 9779
Email: john.lepine@msagb.co.uk
Advertising Address: Houldsworth Mill, South Mill, Reddish, STOCKPORT, SK5 6DA **Tel:** 0161 443 5068
Fax: 0161 443 2382
Email: gary@imprintpub.co.uk
Web site: http://www.msagb.co.uk
Publisher: Excell Publishing
Date Established: 1989
Frequency: Monthly
Free to qualifying individuals
Circulation: 7,500 (Publisher's Statement)
Usual Pagination: 44
Editor: John Lepine; **Advertising Manager:** Gary Pollard
Summary of Content: Journal of the Motor Schools Association of Great Britain covering the driving, training and testing industry throughout Europe. Includes regulations, testing, events and research news.
Readership/Target Audience: Aimed at Britain's driving instructors, driving test centres, the Department for Transport and those interested in road or transport safety.
ADVERTISING RATES:
Full Page Colour £2000.00
Agency Commission: 10%
Mechanical Data: Trim Size: 300 x 230mm, Bleed Size: 346 x 251mm, Film: Digital
Copy instructions: Copy Date: 15th of the month prior to publication date
Average advertising content per issue: 40%
BUSINESS: MOTOR TRADE: Driving Schools

MT MATHEMATICS TEACHING INCORPORATING MICROMATH
41033U62B-550
Formerly: MT Mathematics Teaching
Editorial Address: Unit 7 Prime Industrial Park, Shaftesbury Street, DERBY, DE23 8YB **Tel:** 01332 346599
Fax: 01332 204357
Email: admin@atm.org.uk
Advertising Address: As above. **Tel:** 01322 346599
Fax: 01322 204357
Email: admin@atm.org.uk
Web site: http://www.atm.org.uk
ISSN: 0025-5785
Publisher: The Association of Teachers of Mathematics
Date Established: 1952
Frequency: 6 issues yearly
Free to qualifying individuals
Annual Sub.: £55.00
Circulation: 3,400 (Publisher's Statement)
Usual Pagination: 48
Editor: Helen Williams
Summary of Content: Journal seeking to relate mathematical education more closely to the abilities and needs of the learner.
Readership/Target Audience: Read by members of the Association of Teachers of Mathematics, teachers, advisors, students and consultants.
ADVERTISING RATES:
Full Page Mono £385.00
Full Page Colour £550.00
Mechanical Data: Type Area: 250 x 161mm, Col Length: 250mm, Page Width: 161mm
Copy instructions: Copy Date: 15th of the month prior to publication date
BUSINESS: CHURCH & SCHOOL EQUIPMENT & EDUCATION: Education Teachers

MTJ EXTRA
1774996U22D-281
Editorial Address: Broadfield Park, CRAWLEY, RH11 9RT
Tel: 01293 613400 **Fax:** 01293 846540
Email: ed.bedington@william-reed.co.uk
Web site: http://www.meatinfo.co.uk
Publisher: William Reed Business Media
Date Established: 2006
Frequency: Monthly
Circulation: 6,000 (Publisher's Statement)
Usual Pagination: 28
Editor: Keren Sall
Summary of Content: Publication covering the UK meat trade.
Readership/Target Audience: Aimed at Butchers.
BUSINESS: FOOD: Meat Trade

MULTICHANNEL MARKETING
1626386U53-681
Formerly: Catalogues Today
Editorial Address: Innovation Studios, 159 Shelbourne Road, BOURNEMOUTH, BH8 8RD **Tel:** 0845 838 6077
Fax: 0700 345 1606
Email: alan.scott@multichannelmarketing.co.uk
Advertising Address: As above.
Email: advertising@multichannelmarketing.co.uk
Web site: http://www.multichannelmarketing.co.uk
Publisher: The Catalogue E-tail Ltd
Frequency: 6 issues yearly
Annual Sub.: £55.00
Circulation: 7,500 (Publisher's Statement)
Usual Pagination: 36
Editor: Alan Scott; **Advertising Manager:** Mook Scott; **Publisher:** Alan Scott
Summary of Content: Magazine covering direct marketing, e-commerce, design, photography and print as well as practical advice and guides to help improve working practices and growth revenue in catalogue businesses.
Readership/Target Audience: Aimed at small to medium cataloguers.
ADVERTISING RATES:
Full Page Mono £1150.00
Full Page Colour £1400.00
SCC £12.00
Agency Commission: 10%
Mechanical Data: Trim Size: 297 x 210mm, Type Area: 287 x 200mm, Col Length: 287mm, Page Width: 200mm, Film: Digital
Copy instructions: Copy Date: 2 weeks prior to publication date
Average advertising content per issue: 40%
BUSINESS: RETAILING & WHOLESALING

MULTIMEDIA INFORMATION AND TECHNOLOGY
35683U2D-81_30
Formerly: Audiovisual Librarian: multimedia information
Editorial Address: 45 Gwenllian Morgan Court, Heol Gouesnou, BRECON, LD3 7EE **Tel:** 01874 610412
Email: lyndon.pugh@virgin.net
Advertising Address: As above. **Fax:** 01874 610412
Email: lyndon.pugh@virgin.net
Web site: http://www.cilip.org.uk/mmit
ISSN: 1466-190X
Publisher: Multimedia Information and Technology
Date Established: 1973
Frequency: Quarterly
Free to qualifying individuals
Annual Sub.: £70.00
Circulation: 4,000 (Publisher's Statement)
Usual Pagination: 32
Editor: Lyndon Pugh; **Advertising Manager:** Lyndon Pugh; **Managing Editor:** Lyndon Pugh
Summary of Content: Magazine covering all aspects of multi-media developments. Includes features on audiovisual materials and library equipment.
Readership/Target Audience: Read by librarians, resource managers, educational technologists, museum and archives professionals, academics, students and film and video professionals.
ADVERTISING RATES:
Full Page Mono £590.00
Full Page Colour £775.00
Agency Commission: 10%
Mechanical Data: Bleed Size: 303 x 216mm, Trim Size: 297 x 210mm, Film: Digital, Col Length: 188mm, Col Widths (Display): 60mm, No. of Columns (Display): 3, Page Width: 210mm, Type Area: 210 x 188mm
Copy instructions: Copy Date: 1st of month prior to publication date
Average advertising content per issue: 30%
BUSINESS: COMMUNICATIONS, ADVERTISING & MARKETING: Broadcasting

MULTIPLE SCLEROSIS
40261U56A-106
Editorial Address: 1 Oliver's Yard, 55 City Road, LONDON, EC1Y 1SP **Tel:** 020 7324 8500 **Fax:** 020 7324 8600
Email: claire.minto@sagepub.co.uk
Advertising Address: As above.
Email: advertising@sagepub.co.uk
Web site: http://www.sagepub.co.uk
ISSN: 1352-4585
Publisher: Sage Publications
Date Established: 1996
Frequency: Monthly
Annual Sub.: £889.00
Circulation: 700 (Publisher's Statement)
Usual Pagination: 144
Editor: Claire Minto; **Advertising Manager:** Sheena Karim
Summary of Content: Journal focusing on the aetiology and pathogenesis of demyelinating and inflammatory diseases of the central nervous system and on the application of such studies to scientifically based therapy.
Readership/Target Audience: Aimed at researchers in clinical neurology, pathology, genetics, epidemiology,

therapeutics, immunology, virology, psychology, rehabilitation, and clinicians involved in multiple sclerosis.
ADVERTISING: Rates on application
BUSINESS: HEALTH & MEDICAL

MUNICIPAL YEAR BOOK
38404U32A-160
Formerly: Municipal Year Book & Public Services Directory
Editorial Address: 32 Vauxhall Bridge Road, LONDON, SW1V 2SS **Tel:** 020 7973 4700 **Fax:** 020 7973 4794
Email: myb@hgluk.com
Advertising Address: Priory Park, Beech Green Lane, Withyham, HARTFIELD, TN7 4DB **Tel:** 01892 771047
Fax: 01892 771048
Email: myb@boundaryimedia.co.uk
Web site: http://www.localgov.co.uk
Publisher: Hemming Group Ltd
Date Established: 1897
Frequency: Annual - Published in October
Cover Price: £270.00
Circulation: 4,000 (Publisher's Statement)
Usual Pagination: 2100
Editor: Jackie Barker; **Managing Director:** Graham Bond
Summary of Content: Year Book containing full contact details of local government personnel throughout the UK, including central government and parliamentary information, statistics and other data on local authorities and local government.
Readership/Target Audience: Aimed at those involved or interested in local government, whether in the public or private sector.
ADVERTISING RATES:
Full Page Colour £2495.00
Agency Commission: 10%
Mechanical Data: Col Length: 230mm, Type Area: 230 x 160mm, Bleed Size: 258 x 186mm, Trim Size: 252 x 180mm, Page Width: 160mm
Supplement(s): Municipal Yearbook Update - 4xY
BUSINESS: LOCAL GOVERNMENT, LEISURE & RECREATION: Local Government

MUSEUM PRACTICE
41593U64P-65
Editorial Address: 24 Calvin Street, LONDON, E1 6NW
Tel: 020 7426 6920 **Fax:** 020 7426 6962
Email: javier@museumsassociation.org
Advertising Address: As above. **Tel:** 020 7426 6930
Email: adverts@museumsassociation.org
Web site: http://www.museumsassociation.org
Publisher: Museums Association
Date Established: 1996
Frequency: Quarterly
Annual Sub.: £120.00
Circulation: 8,000 (Publisher's Statement)
Usual Pagination: 68
Editor: Javier Pes
Summary of Content: Journal covering the practical and technical aspects of work in museums, galleries and historic buildings.
Readership/Target Audience: Aimed at museum and gallery professionals, curators, educators and designers.
ADVERTISING RATES:
Full Page Colour £1200.00
Agency Commission: 10%
Mechanical Data: Trim Size: 278 x 210mm, Bleed Size: 284 x 216mm, Film: Digital
Average advertising content per issue: 15%
BUSINESS: OTHER CLASSIFICATIONS: Museums

MUSEUMS & GALLERIES YEARBOOK
41596U64P-85
Formerly: Museums Yearbook
Editorial Address: 24 Calvin Street, LONDON, E1 6NW
Tel: 020 7426 6969 **Fax:** 020 7426 6962
Email: info@museumsassociation.org
Advertising Address: As above.
Email: adverts@museumsassociation.org
Web site: http://www.museumsassociation.org
ISSN: 0307-7675
Publisher: Museums Association
Frequency: Annual - Published in January
Cover Price: £110.00
Circulation: 2,500 (Publisher's Statement)
Usual Pagination: 300
Editor: Catrina Lucas
Summary of Content: A complete directory of museums and galleries in the UK and related information.
Readership/Target Audience: Read by curators in museums and galleries.
ADVERTISING RATES:
SCC £65.00
Agency Commission: 10%
Mechanical Data: Type Area: 267 x 200mm, Col Length: 267mm, Page Width: 200mm, Film: Digital, Bleed Size: 303 x236mm
Copy instructions: Copy Date: 1 week prior to publication date

Average advertising content per issue: 10%
BUSINESS: OTHER CLASSIFICATIONS: Museums

MUSEUMS & HERITAGE   48587U64P-96
Editorial Address: 8th Floor, Bridgewater House, Whitworth Street, MANCHESTER, M1 6LT **Tel:** 0161 832 6000
Fax: 0161 832 4176
Email: rachel.bridgewater@tenalpspublishing.com
Advertising Address: As above.
Email: lisa.hilton@tenalpspublishing.com
Web site: http://www.mandhlive.com
Publisher: Ten Alps Publishing
Date Established: 1993
Frequency: Quarterly
Cover Price: Free
Circulation: 5,000 (Publisher's Statement)
Usual Pagination: 54
Editor: Rachel Bridgewater
Summary of Content: Magazine covering the opening of museums with features on conservation, model making and display cases. Includes articles on conservation materials and case studies of recent restoration projects from around the United Kingdom.
Readership/Target Audience: Aimed at conservation bodies, architects, curators, libraries and local authority conservation departments.
ADVERTISING RATES:
Full Page Colour £1340.00
Agency Commission: 10%
Mechanical Data: Film: Digital, Trim Size: 297 x 210mm
Copy instructions: Copy Date: 8 weeks prior to publication date
Average advertising content per issue: 30%
BUSINESS: OTHER CLASSIFICATIONS: Museums

MUSEUMS JOURNAL   41594U64P-70
Editorial Address: 24 Calvin Street, LONDON, E1 6NW
Tel: 020 7426 6920 **Fax:** 020 7426 6962
Email: journal@museumsassociation.org
Advertising Address: As above.
Email: adverts@museumsassociation.org
Web site: http://www.museumsassociation.org
ISSN: 0027-416X
Publisher: Museums Association
Date Established: 1901
Frequency: Monthly - Published on the 3rd of each month
Cover Price: £5.00
Annual Sub.: £100.00
Circulation: 7,275 (ABC 01/07/2008 to 30/06/2009)
Usual Pagination: 64
Editor: Sharon Heal
Summary of Content: Journal covering all aspects of museum and gallery administration and policy.
Readership/Target Audience: Aimed at all museum and gallery workers.
ADVERTISING RATES:
Full Page Colour £1400.00
Agency Commission: 10%
Mechanical Data: Page Width: 198mm, Col Length: 267mm, Film: Digital, Type Area: 267 x 198mm, Bleed Size: 303 x 236mm, Trim Size: 297 x 230mm
Copy instructions: Copy Date: 19th of the month prior to publication date
Supplement(s): Museums Journal Jobs Extra - 12xY
BUSINESS: OTHER CLASSIFICATIONS: Museums

MUSIC & COPYRIGHT   40948U61-17_70
Editorial Address: Ivy House Farm, Weston Green Road, Weston Longville, NORWICH, NR9 5LB **Tel:** 01603 882002
Email: phil@hardy77.com
Web site: http://www.theviewfromtheboundary.com
ISSN: 0968-0322
Publisher: Informa PLC
Frequency: 23 issues yearly
Usual Pagination: 16
Editor: Phil Hardy
Summary of Content: Journal containing news and information on the music and copyright business worldwide.
Readership/Target Audience: Aimed at senior executives in the record and music publishing industry and related areas.
ADVERTISING: No Advertising taken
BUSINESS: MUSIC TRADE

MUSIC & LETTERS   46204U62R-457
Editorial Address: Department of Music, Kings College, Strand, LONDON, WC2R 2LS **Tel:** 020 7848 2384
Fax: 020 7848 2326
Email: musicandletters@kcl.ac.uk
Advertising Address: Great Clarendon Street, OXFORD, OX2 6DP **Tel:** 01865 353329
Email: jnlsadvertising@oxfordjournals.org
Web site: http://www3.oup.co.uk/musicj
ISSN: 0027-4224
Publisher: OUP

Date Established: 1920
Frequency: Quarterly
Cover Price: £12.00
Annual Sub.: £47.00
Circulation: 1,250 (Publisher's Statement)
Usual Pagination: 184
Editor: Daniel Grimley
Summary of Content: A musical enquiry, from the earliest times to present day.
Readership/Target Audience: Aimed at the leading British Journal of musical scholarship.
ADVERTISING RATES:
Full Page Mono £320.00
BUSINESS: CHURCH & SCHOOL EQUIPMENT & EDUCATION: Education Related

MUSIC JOURNAL   40951U61-20
Editorial Address: 10 Stratford Place, LONDON, W1C 1AA
Tel: 020 7629 4413 **Fax:** 020 7408 1538
Email: mj@ism.org
Advertising Address: Cabbell Publishing Ltd, Woodman Works, 204 Durnsford Road, LONDON, SW19 8DR
Tel: 020 8971 8474 **Fax:** 020 8971 8480
Email: lanabez@mailshack.com
Web site: http://www.ism.org
ISSN: 0951-5135
Publisher: Incorporated Society of Musicians (ISM)
Frequency: Monthly
Cover Price: £3.20
Free to qualifying individuals
Annual Sub.: £32.00
Circulation: 5,100 (Publisher's Statement)
Usual Pagination: 28
Editor: Deborah Annetts
Summary of Content: Journal of The Incorporated Society of Musicians. Covers news and I.S.M activities, focusing especially on classical music.
Readership/Target Audience: Read by all musicians including music students and amateurs.
ADVERTISING RATES:
Full Page Colour £1000.00
Agency Commission: 10%
Mechanical Data: Trim Size: 297 x 210mm, Film: Digital, Type Area: 271 x 185mm, Bleed Size: 303 x 216mm, Col Length: 271mm, Page Width: 185mm
Copy instructions: Copy Date: Middle of the month prior to publication month
Average advertising content per issue: 20%
BUSINESS: MUSIC TRADE

MUSIC TEACHER   41037U62B-670
Editorial Address: 239-241 Shaftesbury Avenue, LONDON, WC2H 8TF **Tel:** 020 7333 1747 **Fax:** 020 7333 1769
Email: music.teacher@rhinegold.co.uk
Advertising Address: As above. **Tel:** 020 7333 1733
Fax: 020 7333 1736
Email: ad.sales@rhinegold.co.uk
Web site: http://www.rhinegold.co.uk
Publisher: Rhinegold Publishing Ltd
Date Established: 1908
Frequency: Monthly
Cover Price: £4.95
Annual Sub.: £42.00
Circulation: 12,000 (Publisher's Statement)
Usual Pagination: 70
Editor: Clare Stevens; **Advertising Manager:** Natasha Cowley
Summary of Content: Magazine covering all aspects of the teaching of music.
Readership/Target Audience: Aimed at all those involved in music education particularly peripatetic teachers and those in private practice.
ADVERTISING RATES:
Full Page Mono £1575.00
Full Page Colour £1700.00
Agency Commission: 10%
Mechanical Data: Col Length: 274mm, Type Area: 274 x 186mm, Bleed Size: 303 x 216mm, Trim Size: 297 x 210mm, Film: Digital, Col Widths (Display): 45mm, No. of Columns (Display): 4, Page Width: 186mm
Copy instructions: Copy Date: 2 weeks prior to publication date
Average advertising content per issue: 40%
BUSINESS: CHURCH & SCHOOL EQUIPMENT & EDUCATION: Education Teachers

MUSIC WEEK   40952U61-25
Editorial Address: Ludgate House, 245 Blackfriars Road, LONDON, SE1 9UY
Email: ben@musicweek.com
Advertising Address: As above. **Tel:** 020 7921 5000
Fax: 020 7921 8339
Email: martina@musicweek.com
Web site: http://www.musicweek.com
ISSN: 0265-1548
Publisher: UBM Information Ltd
Frequency: Weekly

Cover Price: £3.80
Annual Sub.: £160.00
Circulation: 5,962 (ABC 01/07/2008 to 30/06/2009)
Usual Pagination: 40
Editor: Ben Cardew; **News Editor:** Ben Cardew; **Features Editor:** Chris Barrett; **Advertising Manager:** Billy Fahey
Summary of Content: Magazine covering all aspects of the music industry.
Readership/Target Audience: Aimed at those in the music industry, record companies and distributors.
ADVERTISING RATES:
Full Page Colour £3250.00
Agency Commission: 10%
Mechanical Data: Type Area: 315 x 225mm, Col Length: 315mm, Bleed Size: 340 x 250mm, Trim Size: 335 x 245mm, Page Width: 225mm
Copy instructions: Copy Date: Wednesday 12 noon 10 days prior to publication date
Average advertising content per issue: 35%
BUSINESS: MUSIC TRADE

MUSICIAN   37196U14L-480
Editorial Address: 60-62 Clapham Road, LONDON, SW9 0JJ **Tel:** 020 7582 5566 **Fax:** 020 7582 9805
Email: keith.ames@musiciansunion.org.uk
Advertising Address: 30 Monmouth Street, BATH, BA1 2BW **Tel:** 01225 442244 **Fax:** 01225 732380
Email: rosa.smith@futurenet.co.uk
Web site: http://www.musiciansunion.org.uk
Publisher: Future Publishing Ltd
Date Established: 1950
Frequency: Quarterly
Cover Price: Free
Circulation: 37,500 (Publisher's Statement)
Usual Pagination: 52
Editor: Keith Ames; **Advertising Manager:** Rosa Smith
Summary of Content: Journal of the Musicians Union, containing news, reviews, national events coverage, special notices and current issues relating to Musicians Union members.
Readership/Target Audience: Read by Musicians Union members, music journalists, members of parliament and industry contacts.
ADVERTISING RATES:
Full Page Colour £2000.00
Mechanical Data: Bleed Size: 303 x 216mm, Trim Size: 297 x 210mm, Page Width: 190mm, Type Area: 270 x 190mm, Col Length: 270mm, Film: Digital
Copy instructions: Copy Date: 4 weeks prior to publication date
Average advertising content per issue: 25%
BUSINESS: COMMERCE, INDUSTRY & MANAGEMENT: Trade Unions

MUTAGENESIS   24643U56A-106_50
Editorial Address: Institue of Cancer Research, Brookes Lawley Building, Cotswold Road, SUTTON, SM2 5NG
Tel: 01865 353907 **Fax:** 01865 353985
Email: jnls.cust.serv@oxfordjournals.org
Advertising Address: Great Clarendon Street, OXFORD, OX2 6DP **Tel:** 01865 354637 **Fax:** 01865 353774
Email: steve.simmonds@oxfordjournals.org
Web site: http://www.oup.co.uk/jnls
ISSN: 0267-8357
Publisher: OUP
Date Established: 1986
Frequency: 6 issues yearly
Annual Sub.: £486.00
Editor: David Phillips; **Editor-in-Chief:** David Phillips
Summary of Content: Journal containing information on genetic mutation studies, mutagenicity testing guidelines, test programme results, letters and reviews.
Readership/Target Audience: Aimed at academics concerned with the mechanisms of action of physical, chemical and biological agents capable of producing genetic change in living organisms and the study of the consequences of such changes.
ADVERTISING RATES:
Full Page Mono £646.00
Full Page Colour £1076.00
Agency Commission: 10%
Mechanical Data: Type Area: 255 x 178mm, Trim Size: 279 x 216mm, Bleed Size: 285 x 222mm, Film: Digital, Print Process: Litho, Col Length: 255mm, Page Width: 178mm
Copy instructions: Copy Date: 4 weeks prior to publication date
BUSINESS: HEALTH & MEDICAL

MWB MENSWEAR BUYER   39501U47A-245
Editorial Address: The Old Town Hall, Lewisham Road, Slaithwaite, HUDDERSFIELD, HD7 5AL **Tel:** 01484 846069
Fax: 01484 846232
Email: nick@ras-publishing.com
Advertising Address: As above.
Email: silvia@ras-publishing.com
Publisher: RAS Publishing Ltd
Date Established: 1994

Frequency: 11 issues yearly
Annual Sub.: £75.00
Circulation: 5,711 (Publisher's Statement)
Editor: Nicholas Cook; **Advertising Manager:** Silvia Collins;
Managing Editor: Martin Wanless
Summary of Content: Magazine covering news and fashion
in menswear.
Readership/Target Audience: Aimed at buyers,
manufacturers and agents in the menswear industry.
ADVERTISING RATES:
Full Page Colour £3235.00
Agency Commission: 10%
Mechanical Data: Trim Size: 336 x 243mm, Bleed Size: 342
x 249mm, Page Width: 219mm, Col Length: 312mm, Type
Area: 312 x 219mm, Film: Positive, right reading, emulsion
side down. Digital
BUSINESS: CLOTHING & TEXTILES

NAMNEWS
35730U2F-47
Editorial Address: Venture House, 2 Arlington Square,
Downshire Way, BRACKNELL, RG12 1WA
Tel: 01344 742816 **Fax:** 01344 742916
Email: mailbox@namnews.com
Web site: http://www.kamcity.com
ISSN: 1357-4418
Publisher: EMR-NAMNEWS Ltd
Frequency: Monthly
Annual Sub.: £120.00 (Paper edition - 12 issues)
Circulation: 2,000 (Publisher's Statement)
Editor: Mark Craft; **Managing Editor:** Brian Moore
Summary of Content: EC newsletter covering import and
export news, marketing, management and features on
FMCG brands.
Readership/Target Audience: Read by national account
managers.
ADVERTISING: No Advertising taken
BUSINESS: COMMUNICATIONS, ADVERTISING &
MARKETING: Selling

NANOTECHNOLOGY
600843U55-98
Editorial Address: Dirac House, Temple Back, BRISTOL,
BS1 6BE **Tel:** 0117 929 7481 **Fax:** 0117 929 4318
Email: nano@iop.org
Advertising Address: As above.
Email: jayne.osbourne@iop.org
Web site: http://www.iop.org/journals/nano
ISSN: 0957-4484
Publisher: IOP Publishing
Date Established: 1990
Frequency: Weekly
Annual Sub.: £309.00
Usual Pagination: 100
Editor: Nina Couzin; **Editor-in-Chief:** Mark Wellend;
Publisher: Nina Couzin
Summary of Content: Journal covering all aspects of
nanometre scale science and technology.
Readership/Target Audience: Aimed at physicists.
ADVERTISING RATES:
Full Page Mono £715.00
Full Page Colour £1760.00
Agency Commission: 10%
Mechanical Data: Trim Size: 297 x 210mm, Bleed Size: 303
x 216mm, Film: Digital
Copy instructions: Copy Date: 6 weeks prior to publication
date
BUSINESS: APPLIED SCIENCE & LABORATORIES

NAPO PROBATION DIRECTORY
38512U32G-79
Editorial Address: 23 Eaton Road, ILKLEY, LS29 9PU
Tel: 01943 602270
Email: o.r.wells@gmail.com
ISSN: 0142-1328
Publisher: Shaw & Sons Ltd
Date Established: 1972
Frequency: Annual - Published in January
Cover Price: £10.65
Circulation: 8,000 (Publisher's Statement)
Usual Pagination: 416
Editor: Owen Wells; **Publisher:** Crispin Williams
Summary of Content: Directory listing personnel in the
probation services of England, Wales, Eire and Scottish
social workers in criminal justice. Information on government
departments, the prison service and other areas of interest
to those in the criminal justice field.
Readership/Target Audience: Aimed at probation staff,
prison staff, lawyers, youth justice workers, personnel in
criminal justice system in UK and Irish Republic.
ADVERTISING: No Advertising taken
BUSINESS: LOCAL GOVERNMENT, LEISURE &
RECREATION: Community Care & Social Services

THE NATIONAL BARTENDER
36490U9A-141
Editorial Address: Unit 24, Eldon Business Park, Eldon
Road, Attenborough, NOTTINGHAM, NG9 6DZ
Tel: 0115 925 5227 **Fax:** 0115 922 9645

Email: nationalbartender@btconnect.com
Advertising Address: As above.
Email: nationalbartender@btconnect.com
Web site: http://www.nationalbartender.co.uk
Publisher: Emtrad
Date Established: 1993
Frequency: 10 issues yearly
Cover Price: Free
Circulation: 22,000 (Publisher's Statement)
Usual Pagination: 24
Editor: Chris Freer; **Advertising Manager:** Eddie Morris
Summary of Content: Magazine covering drinks, food,
fixtures and fittings, bar, kitchen and cellar equipment and
entertainment.
Readership/Target Audience: Read by free house pub
owners, operators and managers.
ADVERTISING RATES:
Full Page Colour £2200.00
Agency Commission: 10%
Mechanical Data: Col Length: 380mm, Col Widths (Display):
40mm, Film: Digital, No. of Columns (Display): 6, Type Area:
380 x 267mm, Bleed Size: 426 x 303mm, Trim Size: 420 x
297mm, Page Width: 267mm
Average advertising content per issue: 30%
BUSINESS: DRINKS & LICENSED TRADE: Drinks, Licensed
Trade, Wines & Spirits

NATIONAL FARMER
768344U21J-346
Editorial Address: Suite 1, 2nd Floor, 26-32 Hill Street,
POOLE, BH15 1NR **Tel:** 01202 666602
Email: info@nationalfarmer.net
Advertising Address: As above. **Fax:** 0844 443 1176
Email: info@nationalfarmer.net
Web site: http://www.nationalfarmer.net
Publisher: Business Independent Publishing
Date Established: 2003
Frequency: Monthly - Published in the 2nd week of the
cover month
Free to qualifying individuals
Annual Sub.: £20.00
Circulation: 20,864 (Publisher's Statement)
Usual Pagination: 40
Editor: John Thompson; **Advertising Manager:** Nigel
Watson
Summary of Content: Magazine covering the latest
agricultural independent news, product launches and special
features.
Readership/Target Audience: Aimed at arable, beef, dairy,
pig and sheep farmers and decision makers within the
farming community.
ADVERTISING RATES:
Full Page Colour £825.00
Agency Commission: 10%
Mechanical Data: Type Area: 250 x 170mm, Col Length:
250mm, Page Width: 170mm, Bleed Size: 290 x 210mm,
Trim Size: 280 x 200mm, Film: Digital
Copy instructions: Copy Date: 16th of the month prior to
publication date
Average advertising content per issue: 50%
BUSINESS: AGRICULTURE & FARMING: Agriculture &
Farming - Regional

NATIONAL GEOGRAPHIC MAGAZINE
40715U57-37_80
Editorial Address: PR by email only **Tel:** 01483 522068
Fax: 01483 522069
Email: vmattingley.ngs@btinternet.com
Advertising Address: NGTI Ltd, Shepherds Building East,
Richmond Way, Shepherds Bush, LONDON, W14 0DQ
Tel: 020 7751 7580 **Fax:** 020 7751 7556
Web site: http://www.nationalgeographic.com
Publisher: National Geographic Society
Date Established: 1888
Frequency: Monthly
Cover Price: £3.50
Annual Sub.: £29.00
Circulation: 340,264 (ABC 01/01/2009 to 30/06/2009)
Usual Pagination: 140
Editor: Valerie Mattingley
Summary of Content: Magazine covering geographical
subjects, natural history, environment, people and the way
they live, plus other world interests.
Language(s): Dutch; English; French; German; Greek;
Hebrew; Italian; Japanese; Korean; Polish; Russian; Spanish
Readership/Target Audience: Read by those interested in
world issues.
ADVERTISING RATES:
Full Page Mono £18740.00
Full Page Colour £22045.00
Agency Commission: 15%
Mechanical Data: Type Area: 235 x 156mm, Col Length:
235mm, Page Width: 156mm, Trim Size: 254 x 174mm,
Bleed Size: 260 x 182mm, Film: Digital
Copy instructions: Copy Date: 7 weeks prior to publication
date
BUSINESS: ENVIRONMENT & POLLUTION

NATIONAL HEALTH EXECUTIVE
1786328U56A-205
Formerly: National Health Professional
Editorial Address: Suite 102, International House, 82-86
Deansgate, MANCHESTER, M3 2ER **Tel:** 0161 833 6320
Fax: 0161 832 0571
Email: editorial@nationalhealthexecutive.com
Advertising Address: As above.
Email: royc@cognitivepublishing.com
Web site: http://www.nationalhealthexecutive.com
Publisher: Cognitive Publishing Ltd
Date Established: 2006
Frequency: 6 issues yearly - Published at the end of the 1st
cover month
Cover Price: Free
Circulation: 7,745 (ABC 01/07/2008 to 31/12/2008)
Usual Pagination: 64
Editor: Stephen Lewis
Summary of Content: The publication derives its editorial
from healthcare sources and includes additional reports and
comment from independent agencies and suppliers. Content
includes coverage of infection control, wound care,
cardiology, cancer therapies, mental health, quality
assurance, financial planning, alternative therapies, healthy
living, renal therapies, disabled access, urological therapies,
respiratory drugs and security.
Readership/Target Audience: Aimed at chief executives
and senior managers of the NHS and private healthcare.
ADVERTISING RATES:
Full Page Colour £1995.00
Agency Commission: 10%
Mechanical Data: Type Area: 270 x 184mm, Bleed Size:
303 x 216mm, Trim Size: 297 x 210mm, Col Length: 270mm,
Page Width: 184mm, Film: Digital
Copy instructions: Copy Date: 4th of the publication month
Average advertising content per issue: 40%
BUSINESS: HEALTH & MEDICAL

NATIONAL INSTITUTE ECONOMIC REVIEW
35003U1A-265
Editorial Address: 2 Dean Trench Street, Smith Square,
LONDON, SW1P 3HE **Tel:** 020 7222 7665
Fax: 020 7654 1900
Email: f.robinson@niesr.ac.uk
Advertising Address: 1 Oliver's Yard, 55 City Road,
LONDON, EC1Y 1SP **Tel:** 020 7324 8500
Fax: 020 7324 8600
Email: sheena.karim@sagepub.co.uk
Web site: http://www.niesr.ac.uk
ISSN: 0027-9501
Publisher: Sage Publications
Date Established: 1938
Frequency: Quarterly
Cover Price: £32.00
Annual Sub.: £98.00
Circulation: 1,000 (Publisher's Statement)
Usual Pagination: 120
Editor: Martin Weale; **Advertising Manager:** Sheena Karim
Summary of Content: Survey of economic situations,
prospects and articles on topical problems and underlying
trends.
Readership/Target Audience: Aimed at the academic,
business and financial sector and policy makers.
ADVERTISING: Rates on application
Agency Commission: 15%
Copy instructions: Copy Date: 2 months prior to publication
date
BUSINESS: FINANCE & ECONOMICS

NATM
39011U42A-124_50
Editorial Address: Unit 6A, Wharf Road, Ealand Industrial
Estate, EALAND, DN17 4JW **Tel:** 01724 712255
Fax: 01724 712266
Email: natm@fastmail.fm
Advertising Address: As above.
Email: natm@fastmail.fm
ISSN: 1364-5153
Publisher: NATM
Date Established: 1995
Frequency: 10 issues yearly - Published in the first week of
the cover month
Free to qualifying individuals
Annual Sub.: £47.00
Circulation: 10,984 (Publisher's Statement)
Usual Pagination: 86
Editor: Julie Durose; **Advertising Manager:** Julie Durose
Summary of Content: Journal containing contractual
information and news from within the UK construction
industry.
Readership/Target Audience: Aimed at specialist
contractors.
ADVERTISING RATES:
Full Page Mono £510.00
Full Page Colour £940.00
Agency Commission: 10%
Mechanical Data: Trim Size: 297 x 210mm, Film: Digital
BUSINESS: CONSTRUCTION

Business Magazines

NATURAL PRODUCT REPORT 36679U13-110_50
Formerly: Pesticide Outlook
Editorial Address: Thomas Graham House, Science Park, Milton Road, CAMBRIDGE, CB4 0WF **Tel:** 01223 420066
Fax: 01223 420247
Email: npr@rsc.org
Advertising Address: As above. **Tel:** 01223 432243
Fax: 01223 426017
Email: advertising@rsc.org
Web site: http://www.rsc.org/npr
ISSN: 0956-1250
Publisher: Royal Society of Chemistry
Date Established: 1984
Frequency: 6 issues yearly
Annual Sub.: £493.00
Usual Pagination: 100
Editor: Vikki Allen; **Advertising Manager:** Ian Swain
Summary of Content: Journal covering the study of natural products, bio-organic chemistry and chemical biology, includes features on the isolation, structure, biosynthesis, biological activity and chemistry of the major groups of natural products and other metabolites of marine, plant and microbial origins.
Readership/Target Audience: Aimed at those working within the agro-chemical industry and academic scientists.
ADVERTISING RATES:
Full Page Mono £890.00
SCC £26.00
Agency Commission: 10%
Mechanical Data: Type Area: 252 x 188mm, Bleed Size: 281 x 216mm, Col Length: 252mm, Page Width: 188mm, Trim Size: 275 x 210mm, Film: Digital
BUSINESS: CHEMICALS

NATURAL PRODUCTS 38033U22F-100
Formerly: Natural Products News
Editorial Address: Blenheim House, 119-120 Church Street, BRIGHTON, BN1 1UD **Tel:** 01273 645130
Fax: 01273 645169
Email: jmanson@divcom.co.uk
Advertising Address: As above. **Tel:** 01273 645110
Email: droberjot@divcom.co.uk
Web site: http://www.naturalproducts.co.uk
Publisher: Diversified Business Communications
Date Established: 1994
Frequency: 11 issues yearly - Published on the 1st Monday of the cover month
Annual Sub.: £59.00
Circulation: 5,594 (Publisher's Statement)
Usual Pagination: 50
Editor: Jim Manson; **Advertising Manager:** Dominic Roberjot
Summary of Content: Magazine covering news, views and trends from the health food industry.
Readership/Target Audience: Aimed at health store retailers and manufacturers.
ADVERTISING RATES:
Full Page Colour £2295.00
Agency Commission: 10%
Mechanical Data: Type Area: 261.5 x 205mm, Col Length: 261.5mm, Bleed Size: 303 x 231mm, Trim Size: 297 x 225mm, Page Width: 205mm, Film: Digital
Copy instructions: Copy Date: 15th of the month prior to publication date
Average advertising content per issue: 45%
Supplement(s): Natural Beauty - 1xY
BUSINESS: FOOD: Health Food

NATURAL STONE SPECIALIST 35914U4E-298
Editorial Address: 7 Regent Street, NOTTINGHAM, NG1 5BS **Tel:** 0115 945 3898 **Fax:** 0115 941 5685
Email: nss@qmj.co.uk
Advertising Address: As above. **Tel:** 0115 941 1315
Fax: 0115 958 2651
Email: anna.gibiino@qmj.co.uk
Web site: http://www.naturalstonespecialist.com
ISSN: 1356-5443
Publisher: QMJ Publishing Ltd
Date Established: 1966
Frequency: Monthly - Published in the 3rd week of the month
Annual Sub.: £42.00
Circulation: 4,000 (Publisher's Statement)
Usual Pagination: 44
Editor: Eric Bignell; **Advertising Manager:** Anna Gibiino
Summary of Content: Magazine covering all aspects of the use of natural stone, information on architecture and monumental masonry and equipment for extracting and working stone.
Readership/Target Audience: Aimed at architects, designers and the stone trades in the new build, conservation, restoration and RMI markets.
ADVERTISING RATES:
Full Page Colour £1024.00
SCC £12.75
Mechanical Data: Page Width: 182mm, Type Area: 255 x 182mm, Trim Size: 297 x 210mm, Col Length: 255mm, Film: Digital

Copy instructions: Copy Date: 2nd of each month of publication date
BUSINESS: ARCHITECTURE & BUILDING: Building

NATURALIST 40716U57-38_10
Editorial Address: Dept. of Geography & Environmental Science, University of Bradford, BRADFORD, BD7 1DP
Tel: 01274 234212 **Fax:** 01274 234231
Email: m.r.d.seaward@bradford.ac.uk
Advertising Address: As above.
Email: m.r.d.seaward@bradford.ac.uk
Web site: http://www.brad.ac.uk/acad/envisci
ISSN: 0028-0771
Publisher: Yorkshire Naturalists' Union
Date Established: 1875
Frequency: Quarterly
Annual Sub.: £20.00
Circulation: 5,000 (Publisher's Statement)
Usual Pagination: 40
Editor: M. Seaward; **Advertising Manager:** M. Seaward
Summary of Content: Journal covering natural history, botany, zoology, biology, ecology, conservation and the environment; particularly that relating to the North of England.
Readership/Target Audience: Read by naturalists, biologists and environmentalists, amateur and professional.
ADVERTISING RATES:
Full Page Mono £135.00
Agency Commission: 15%
Mechanical Data: Trim Size: 210 x 148mm, Type Area: 170 x 110mm, Col Length: 170mm, Page Width: 110mm
BUSINESS: ENVIRONMENT & POLLUTION

NATURE: INTERNATIONAL WEEKLY JOURNAL OF SCIENCE 39990U55-103
Editorial Address: The Macmillan Building, 4 Crinan Street, LONDON, N1 9XW **Tel:** 020 7833 4000 **Fax:** 020 7843 4596
Email: nature@nature.com
Advertising Address: As above. **Tel:** 020 7843 4960
Fax: 020 7843 4996
Email: salessupport@nature.com
Web site: http://www.nature.com
ISSN: 0028-0836
Publisher: Nature Publishing Group
Frequency: Weekly
Annual Sub.: £135.00
Circulation: 67,437 (Publisher's Statement)
Editor: Mark Peplow; **News Editor:** Mark Peplow; **Editor-in-Chief:** Philip Campbell; **Managing Director:** Annette Thomas
Summary of Content: Journal containing news and review articles together with original scientific research.
Readership/Target Audience: Aimed at those involved in scientific research and development.
ADVERTISING RATES:
Full Page Mono £4702.00
Full Page Colour £6022.00
SCC £66.00
Agency Commission: 15%
BUSINESS: APPLIED SCIENCE & LABORATORIES

NATURE MATERIALS 1647376U55-9011
Editorial Address: The Macmillan Building, 4 Crinan Street, LONDON, N1 9XW **Tel:** 020 7833 4000 **Fax:** 020 7843 4563
Email: materials@nature.com
Advertising Address: NPG, Suite 1453, 225 Bush Street, SAN FRANCISCO, CA 9034 **Tel:** 415 403 9034
Email: s.allardice@naturesf.com
Web site: http://www.nature.com/nmat
Publisher: Nature Publishing Group
Date Established: 2002
Frequency: Monthly
Editor: Vincent Dusastre; **Advertising Manager:** Simon Allardice
Summary of Content: Journal focusing on material sciences and engineering.
Readership/Target Audience: Aimed at academics.
ADVERTISING RATES:
Full Page Mono £1850.00
Full Page Colour £2250.00
Agency Commission: 15%
Mechanical Data: Type Area: 254 x 178mm, Bleed Size: 282 x 216mm, Trim Size: 276 x 210mm, Col Length: 254mm, Page Width: 178mm, Film: Digital
Copy instructions: Copy Date: 3 weeks prior to publication date
Average advertising content per issue: 10%
BUSINESS: APPLIED SCIENCE & LABORATORIES

NATURE REVIEWS DRUG DISCOVERY
1849935U37-434
Editorial Address: The Macmillan Building, 4 Crinan Street, LONDON, N1 9XW **Tel:** 020 7843 3620 **Fax:** 020 7843 3629
Email: naturereviews@nature.com

Web site: http://www.nature.com/nrd
ISSN: 1474-1776
Publisher: Nature Publishing Group
Date Established: 2002
Frequency: Monthly
Annual Sub.: $265.00
Editor: Peter Kirkpatrick
Summary of Content: Journal covering articles on the drug discovery spectrum from disease mechanisms and chemistry through to clinical development. Features research highlights, progress articles, reviews, analysis and perspectives.
Readership/Target Audience: Aimed at scientists and those working in the drug discovery and development areas.
BUSINESS: PHARMACEUTICAL & CHEMISTS

THE NAUTICAL MAGAZINE 39339U45A-120
Editorial Address: 4-10 Darnley Street, GLASGOW, G41 2SD **Tel:** 0141 429 1234 **Fax:** 0141 420 1694
Email: info@skipper.co.uk
Advertising Address: As above.
Email: info@skipper.co.uk
Web site: http://www.skipper.co.uk
ISSN: 0028-1336
Publisher: Brown, Son & Ferguson Ltd
Date Established: 1832
Frequency: Monthly
Annual Sub.: £39.00
Circulation: 600 (Publisher's Statement)
Usual Pagination: 80
Editor: Richard Brown; **Managing Director:** Leslie Ingram-Brown
Summary of Content: Journal covering ships, marine engineering, seamanship and port administration.
Readership/Target Audience: Aimed at the merchant navy and general sailors, ship-owners, ships' officers and harbour executives worldwide.
ADVERTISING RATES:
Full Page Mono £130.00
Agency Commission: 10%
Mechanical Data: Type Area: 192 x 118mm, Col Length: 192mm, Print Process: Litho, Page Width: 118mm
Copy instructions: Copy Date: 1st of the month prior to publication date
Average advertising content per issue: 2%
BUSINESS: MARINE & SHIPPING

NAUTILUS UK TELEGRAPH 37209U14L-490
Formerly: NUMAST Telegraph
Editorial Address: Oceanair House, 750-760 High Road, Leytonstone, LONDON, E11 3BB **Tel:** 020 8989 6677
Fax: 020 8530 1015
Email: telegraph@nautilusint.org
Advertising Address: Redactive Media Group, 17 Britton Street, LONDON, EC1M 5TP **Tel:** 020 7880 6200
Fax: 020 7880 7553
Email: claire.barber@redactive.co.uk
Web site: http://www.nautilusuk.org
ISSN: 0040-2575
Publisher: Nautilus UK
Date Established: 1876
Frequency: Monthly
Cover Price: £1.50
Free to qualifying individuals
Annual Sub.: £25.00
Circulation: 27,500 (Publisher's Statement)
Usual Pagination: 40
Editor: Andrew Linington
Summary of Content: Journal of Nautilus UK the union of maritime professionals. Covers international shipping industry and trade union news.
Readership/Target Audience: Aimed at the shipping industry and professional staff.
ADVERTISING RATES:
Full Page Mono £3975.00
Full Page Colour £3975.00
Agency Commission: 10%
Mechanical Data: No. of Columns (Display): 6, Type Area: 380 x 286mm, Col Length: 380mm, Page Width: 286mm, Film: Digital
Average advertising content per issue: 30%
BUSINESS: COMMERCE, INDUSTRY & MANAGEMENT: Trade Unions

THE NAVAL ARCHITECT 39410U45D-150
Editorial Address: 10 Upper Belgrave Street, LONDON, SW1X 8BQ **Tel:** 020 7235 4622 **Fax:** 020 7245 6959
Email: editorial@rina.org.uk
Advertising Address: As above. **Tel:** 020 7201 2404
Email: dbonner@rina-org.nl
Web site: http://www.rina.org.uk
ISSN: 0306-0209
Publisher: The Royal Institution of Naval Architects
Date Established: 1971
Frequency: 10 issues yearly - Published around the 15th of the cover month

Annual Sub.: £120.00
Circulation: 12,017 (ABC 01/01/2008 to 31/12/2008)
Usual Pagination: 68
Editor: Hugh O'Mahony; **Publisher:** Mark Staunton-Lambert
Summary of Content: International journal of the Royal Institution of Naval Architects.
Readership/Target Audience: Aimed at naval architects, marine superintendents, marine consultants, surveyors and other marine personnel worldwide.
ADVERTISING RATES:
Full Page Mono £1860.00
Full Page Colour £2375.00
Agency Commission: 10%
Mechanical Data: Film: Negative, right reading, emulsion side down, Type Area: 254 x 177mm, Print Process: Offset litho, Trim Size: 297 x 210mm, Bleed Size: 303 x 216mm, Col Length: 254mm, Page Width: 177mm
Copy instructions: Copy Date: 2 weeks prior to publication date
Average advertising content per issue: 50%
Supplement(s): Warship Technology - 5xY
BUSINESS: MARINE & SHIPPING: Marine Engineering Equipment

NAVIGATION NEWS
39440U45R-97
Editorial Address: Royal Institute of Navigation, 1 Kensington Gore, LONDON, SW7 2AT **Tel:** 020 7591 3130
Fax: 020 7591 3131
Email: editor@rin.org.uk
Advertising Address: The Old Mill, Lower Quay, FAREHAM, PO16 0RA **Tel:** 01329 825335 **Fax:** 01329 825330
Email: navnews@mercatormedia.com
Web site: http://www.rin.org.uk
ISSN: 0268-6317
Publisher: Mercator Media Ltd
Date Established: 1987
Frequency: 6 issues yearly
Free to qualifying individuals
Circulation: 3,500 (Publisher's Statement)
Usual Pagination: 32
Editor: Tony Fyler
Summary of Content: Magazine focusing on all forms of navigation: in space, in the air, on land and at sea.
Readership/Target Audience: Aimed at members of the Royal Institute of Navigation and anyone interested in navigation, from mariners and aviators to orienteers and rally drivers.
ADVERTISING RATES:
Full Page Mono £640.00
Full Page Colour £850.00
Agency Commission: 10%
Mechanical Data: Trim Size: 297 x 210mm, Film: Positive, right reading, emulsion side down. Digital
Average advertising content per issue: 10%
BUSINESS: MARINE & SHIPPING: Marine Related

NAVY NEWS
38877U40-210
Editorial Address: HMS Nelson, Queen Street, PORTSMOUTH, PO1 3HH **Tel:** 023 9229 4228
Fax: 023 9283 8845
Email: edit@navynews.co.uk
Advertising Address: As above. **Tel:** 023 9272 5062
Fax: 023 9283 0149
Email: advertising@navynews.co.uk
Web site: http://www.navynews.co.uk
Publisher: Navy News
Date Established: 1954
Frequency: Monthly
Cover Price: £1.40
Circulation: 60,000 (Publisher's Statement)
Usual Pagination: 48
Editor: Mike Gray; **News Editor:** Richard Hargreaves; **Advertising Manager:** Sarah Evemy
Summary of Content: Newspaper for the Royal Navy, Sea Cadets and the Royal Naval Association containing features and a kids club.
Readership/Target Audience: Aimed at the Royal Navy and the general public.
ADVERTISING RATES:
Full Page Mono £2449.00
SCC £15.20
Agency Commission: 10%
Mechanical Data: Col Length: 370mm, Col Widths (Display): 42mm, No. of Columns (Display): 6, Type Area: 370 x 273mm, Page Width: 273mm, Film: Digital
Copy instructions: Copy Date: 5th of the month prior to publication date
Average advertising content per issue: 30%
Supplement(s): Young Readers - 4xY
BUSINESS: DEFENCE

NCN NETWORK COMMUNICATIONS NEWS
37321U17-164
Formerly: NCN Network Cabling News
Editorial Address: Alexander House, Forehill, ELY, CB7 4ZA
Tel: 01353 616117 **Fax:** 01353 665619
Email: robshepherd@btconnect.com

Advertising Address: As above. **Tel:** 01353 616110
Email: ian@terringtonltd.co.uk
Web site: http://www.networkcommunicationsnews.co.uk
ISSN: 1465-2714
Publisher: Terrington Publications Ltd
Date Established: 1999
Frequency: Monthly - Published in the middle of the month prior to the cover month
Cover Price: Free
Circulation: 11,500 (Publisher's Statement)
Usual Pagination: 60
Editor: Rob Shepherd
Summary of Content: Magazine covering industry news, product reviews, applications and network installations.
Readership/Target Audience: Aimed at IT network infrastructure, integrators, consultants, end users and specifiers.
ADVERTISING RATES:
Full Page Colour £1750.00
SCC £25.00
Agency Commission: 10%
Mechanical Data: Page Width: 190mm, Type Area: 277 x 190mm, Bleed Size: 303 x 216mm, Trim Size: 297 x 210mm, Col Length: 277mm, Film: Digital
Copy instructions: Copy Date: 6 weeks prior to publication date
Average advertising content per issue: 40%
BUSINESS: ELECTRICAL

NDT & E INTERNATIONAL
39987U55-109
Editorial Address: The Boulevard, Langford Lane, KIDLINGTON, OX5 1GB **Tel:** 01865 843000
Fax: 01865 843010
Email: chimenti@iastate.edu
Advertising Address: 32 Jamestown Road, LONDON, NW1 7BY **Tel:** 020 7424 4400 **Fax:** 01865 853136
Email: j.kenney@elsevier.com
Web site: http://www.ees.elsevier.com/ndteint
ISSN: 0963-8695
Publisher: Elsevier Ltd
Frequency: 8 issues yearly
Annual Sub.: EUR610.00
Editor: D. Chimenti
Summary of Content: Publication covering the research and application of all aspects of non-destructive testing, including ultrasonic, x-ray, eddy-current and optical techniques.
Readership/Target Audience: Aimed at international engineering companies and academic establishments.
ADVERTISING RATES:
Full Page Mono £835.00
Full Page Colour £1815.00
Agency Commission: 15%
Mechanical Data: Film: Digital, Type Area: 250 x 180mm, Col Length: 250mm, Page Width: 180mm, Bleed Size: 216 x 286mm, Trim Size: 280 x 210mm
Copy instructions: Copy Date: 5 weeks prior to publication date
Average advertising content per issue: 5%
BUSINESS: APPLIED SCIENCE & LABORATORIES

NEEDLE & HANDICRAFTS
39541U47C-230
Formerly: Needle & Hobby Crafts
Editorial Address: 1 Castle Close, ROMFORD, RM3 7LN
Tel: 01708 379897 **Fax:** 01708 379804
Email: editorial@needlehandicrafts.co.uk
Advertising Address: As above.
Email: peter@needlehandicrafts.co.uk
Web site: http://www.needlehandicrafts.co.uk
ISSN: 1479-2842
Publisher: Needle & Handicrafts
Frequency: 6 issues yearly
Annual Sub.: £20.00
Circulation: 4,000 (Publisher's Statement)
Editor: Arthur Damery; **Advertising Manager:** Peter Damery; **Publisher:** Peter Damery
Summary of Content: Journal containing articles about the haberdashery, knitting and needlecrafts trade.
Readership/Target Audience: Read by manufacturers, wholesalers and retailers of knitting, haberdashery and needlecraft materials.
ADVERTISING RATES:
Full Page Mono £840.00
Full Page Colour £1260.00
Agency Commission: 10%
Mechanical Data: Page Width: 186mm, Type Area: 265 x 186mm, Col Length: 265mm, Trim Size: 297 x 210mm, Bleed Size: 303 x 213mm, Print Process: Sheet-fed litho, Film: Digital
Copy instructions: Copy Date: 1st of the month prior to publication date
BUSINESS: CLOTHING & TEXTILES: Knitwear

NEFTE COMPASS
38595U33-10_17
Editorial Address: 8th Floor, Holborn Tower, 137-144 High Holborn, LONDON, WC1V 6PW **Tel:** 020 7632 4700
Fax: 020 7404 1788

Email: mritchie@energyintel.com
Web site: http://www.energyintel.com
Publisher: Energy Intelligence Group
Date Established: 1992
Frequency: Weekly
Usual Pagination: 12
Editor: Mike Ritchie
Summary of Content: Publication focusing on the geopolitics of oil and gas in the former Soviet Union and Eastern Europe.
Readership/Target Audience: Read by people in the oil and gas industries and government officials.
ADVERTISING: No Advertising taken
BUSINESS: OIL & PETROLEUM

NEGOTIATOR
35197U1E-187
Editorial Address: 1 Canada Square, 19th Floor, Canary Wharf, LONDON, E14 5AP **Tel:** 020 7772 8300
Email: clare.betteley@oceanmedia.co.uk
Advertising Address: As above. **Tel:** 020 7772 8372
Fax: 020 7772 8584
Email: selan.cenan@oceanmedia.co.uk
Web site: http://www.negotiator-magazine.co.uk
Publisher: Ocean Media Group Ltd
Date Established: 1985
Frequency: 25 issues yearly
Free to qualifying individuals
Annual Sub.: £55.00
Circulation: 10,856 (ABC 01/07/2008 to 30/06/2009)
Usual Pagination: 72
Editor: Clare Betteley
Summary of Content: Magazine covering issues relating to residential property, lettings, property management and estate agency throughout the UK and increasingly, overseas.
Readership/Target Audience: Read by residential sales, letting, managing and property search agents.
ADVERTISING RATES:
Full Page Mono £1482.00
Full Page Colour £2074.80
Mechanical Data: Col Length: 278mm, Page Width: 190mm, Film: Digital, Type Area: 278 x 190mm, Bleed Size: 303 x 216mm, Trim Size: 297 x 210mm
Copy instructions: Copy Date: 1 week prior to publication date
BUSINESS: FINANCE & ECONOMICS: Property

NEIGHBOURHOOD RETAILER
39820U53-244
Formerly: Neighbourhood Retailer & Forecourt Technology
Editorial Address: Penton House, 38 Heron Road, Sydenham Business Park, BELFAST, BT3 9LE
Tel: 028 9045 7457 **Fax:** 028 9045 6622
Email: sarah.coburn@pentonpublications.co.uk
Advertising Address: As above. **Tel:** 028 9045 6611
Email: stephen.carson@pentonpublications.co.uk
Web site: http://www.neighbourhoodretailer.com
Publisher: Penton Publications Ltd
Date Established: 1995
Frequency: 11 issues yearly
Free to qualifying individuals
Annual Sub.: £25.00
Circulation: 4,849 (ABC 01/07/2008 to 30/06/2009)
Usual Pagination: 80
Editor: Sarah Coburn; **Advertising Manager:** Stephen Carson; **Managing Editor:** Bill Penton; **Publisher:** Bill Penton
Summary of Content: Magazine containing features and news about convenience stores and forecourt retailing.
Readership/Target Audience: Aimed at convenience retailers, independent grocers and garage forecourts in Northern Ireland.
ADVERTISING RATES:
Full Page Mono £1600.00
Full Page Colour £1895.00
Agency Commission: 10%
Mechanical Data: Trim Size: 297 x 210mm, Bleed Size: 303 x 216mm, Film: Digital
Copy instructions: Copy Date: Last week of the month prior to publication
Supplement(s): Neighbourhood Retailer Yearbook - 1xY
BUSINESS: RETAILING & WHOLESALING

NEPA NEWS
35533U2A-128
Editorial Address: Tynemouth House, 33 Preston Road, NORTH SHIELDS, NE29 0ND **Tel:** 0191 272 8283
Fax: 0191 272 8283
Email: nepa@kimmerston.co.uk
Advertising Address: As above.
Email: nepa@kimmerston.co.uk
Web site: http://www.nepaonline.org.uk
Publisher: Kimmerston Design
Date Established: 1929
Frequency: 11 issues yearly
Free to qualifying individuals
Annual Sub.: £150.00
Circulation: 1,500 (Publisher's Statement)
Usual Pagination: 16

Business Magazines

Editor: David Grey; **Advertising Manager:** David Grey
Summary of Content: Newsletter of the North East Publicity Association. Covers news, events and promotions, business, personnel, social and sports. Promotion and reviews of NEPA members events.
Readership/Target Audience: Read by people within the creative industries, advertising, design, marketing and PR agencies. Also TV and radio stations, publishers, media buyers, photographers, independent designers and printers in North East.
ADVERTISING RATES:
Full Page Colour £550.00
SCC £5.85
Mechanical Data: Col Widths (Display): 45mm, Page Width: 190mm, Col Length: 265mm, No. of Columns (Display): 4, Type Area: 265 x 190mm, Print Process: Litho, Bleed Size: 303 x 216mm, Trim Size: 297 x 210mm
Copy instructions: Copy Date: Last Tuesday of each month prior to publication date
Average advertising content per issue: 25%
BUSINESS: COMMUNICATIONS, ADVERTISING & MARKETING

NETWORK COMPUTING
36112U5B-134_10

Editorial Address: 35 Station Square, Petts Wood, ORPINGTON, BR5 1LZ **Tel:** 01689 616000
Fax: 01689 826622
Email: mark.lyward@btc.co.uk
Advertising Address: As above.
Email: david.bonner@btc.co.uk
Web site: http://www.networkcomputing.co.uk
Publisher: Business & Technical Communications
Date Established: 1990
Frequency: 6 issues yearly - Published in the middle of the 1st cover month
Free to qualifying individuals
Annual Sub.: £49.00
Circulation: 17,760 (Publisher's Statement)
Managing Director: John Jageurs; **Advertising Manager:** David Bonner
Summary of Content: Magazine covering networking interconnectivity. Includes news, advice, products and hardware and software reviews.
Readership/Target Audience: Read by decision makers, users and potential users.
ADVERTISING RATES:
Full Page Colour £1850.00
Agency Commission: 10%
Mechanical Data: Col Length: 287mm, Film: Digital, Type Area: 287 x 200mm, Bleed Size: 307 x 220mm, Trim Size: 297 x 210mm, Page Width: 200mm
Copy instructions: Copy Date: 4 weeks prior to publication date
Average advertising content per issue: 33%
BUSINESS: COMPUTERS & AUTOMATION: Data Processing

NETWORK HEALTH DIETITIANS
1776191U22F-112

Editorial Address: Suite 1 Freshfield Hall, The Square, Lewes Road, FOREST ROW, RH18 5ES **Tel:** 0845 450 2125
Fax: 0870 762 3713
Email: info@networkhealthgroup.co.uk
Advertising Address: Ad Plain Ltd, 7A Hithercroft Court, Lupton Road, WALLINGFORD, OX10 9BT
Tel: 01491 837117 **Fax:** 01491 837401
Email: leigh@theadplain.com
Web site: http://www.networkhealthgroup.co.uk
ISSN: 1756-9567
Publisher: NH Publishing Ltd
Date Established: 2005
Frequency: 10 issues yearly - Published on the 1st of the cover month
Free to qualifying individuals
Annual Sub.: £24.00
Circulation: 6,000 (Publisher's Statement)
Usual Pagination: 48
Editor: Geoff Weate; **Features Editor:** Ursula Arens; **Publisher:** Geoff Weate
Summary of Content: Magazine covering nutrition and dietetics featuring news, interviews, columns, features and letters.
Readership/Target Audience: Aimed at dietitians in the UK and Ireland.
ADVERTISING RATES:
Full Page Colour £1490.00
Agency Commission: 10%
Mechanical Data: Type Area: 277 x 190mm, Bleed Size: 303 x 216mm, Trim Size: 297 x 210mm, Col Length: 277mm, Page Width: 190mm, Film: Digital
Copy instructions: Copy Date: 3 weeks prior to publication date
BUSINESS: FOOD: Health Food

NETWORK NEW YORK/LONDON
36919U14C-106

Formerly: Network New York London
Editorial Address: 75 Brook Street, LONDON, W1K 4AD
Tel: 020 7290 9879 **Fax:** 020 7491 9172
Email: hholdroyd@babinc.org
Advertising Address: The Diary House, Rickett Street, LONDON, W6 1RU **Tel:** 020 7386 6100 **Fax:** 020 7381 8890
Email: brian.mawdsley@mar-media.com
Web site: http://www.babinc.org
Publisher: Roxby Media Ltd
Frequency: Quarterly
Cover Price: Free
Circulation: 6,000 (Publisher's Statement)
Usual Pagination: 24
Editor: Hannah Holdroyd; **Advertising Manager:** Brian Mawdsley
Summary of Content: Magazine of British-American Business Inc. Covers information on economic developments in the UK and US business scene. Includes news on US and UK trade, policy and development and a SME section.
Readership/Target Audience: Aimed at members of British-American Business Inc.
ADVERTISING: Rates on application
Agency Commission: 10%
Copy instructions: Copy Date: 1 month prior to publication date
Average advertising content per issue: 15%
BUSINESS: COMMERCE, INDUSTRY & MANAGEMENT: International Commerce

NETWORK SECURITY
39914U54C-85

Editorial Address: PO Box 150, KIDLINGTON, OX5 1AS
Tel: 01865 843239 **Fax:** 01865 843933
Email: s.barrett@elsevier.com
Web site: http://www.networksecuritynewsletter.com
ISSN: 1353-4858
Publisher: Elsevier Ltd
Frequency: Monthly
Annual Sub.: EUR992.00
Circulation: 2,500 (Publisher's Statement)
Usual Pagination: 20
Editor: Steve Barrett; **Publisher:** Henry Van Dorssen
Summary of Content: Network Security is devoted to solving network security problems in system-specific detail, now with even more news, information and solutions to network security problems. Filtering through the hype of non-stop vulnerability alerts and new malware, Network Security give the real threats to enterprises.
Readership/Target Audience: Aimed at technical IT security managers.
ADVERTISING: No Advertising taken
BUSINESS: SAFETY & SECURITY: Security

NETWORK WALES
38483U32G-80

Editorial Address: Baltic House, Mount Stuart Square, CARDIFF, CF10 5FH **Tel:** 029 2043 1700
Fax: 029 2043 1701
Email: lreynolds@wcva.org.uk
Advertising Address: As above. **Tel:** 029 2043 1718
Email: lreynolds@wcva.org.uk
Web site: http://www.wcva.org.uk
Publisher: Wales Council for Voluntary Action
Frequency: 21 issues yearly
Free to qualifying individuals
Circulation: 1,600 (Publisher's Statement)
Usual Pagination: 12
Editor: Lynne Reynolds; **Advertising Manager:** Lynne Reynolds
Summary of Content: Magazine covering updates for Wales Council for Voluntary Action. Includes news and funding information.
Language(s): English; Welsh
Readership/Target Audience: Aimed at WCVA membership national and regional charities, voluntary groups and agencies, local community groups, local authorities, members of parliament and assembly members.
ADVERTISING: Rates on application
BUSINESS: LOCAL GOVERNMENT, LEISURE & RECREATION: Community Care & Social Services

NETWORKING - CATHOLIC EDUCATION TODAY
624751U62B-675

Editorial Address: PO Box 8455, NEWARK, NG23 5WX
Tel: 01636 525607
Email: wpboylan@hotmail.com
Advertising Address: As above.
Email: johnclawson@xln.co.uk
ISSN: 1475-1666
Publisher: Bellcourt Limited
Date Established: 1999
Frequency: 5 issues yearly
Cover Price: £4.95
Circulation: 4,000 (Publisher's Statement)

Usual Pagination: 48
Editor: Peter Boylan; **Managing Director:** John Clawson; **Advertising Manager:** John Clawson
Summary of Content: Magazine covering news, research and development issues and achievement reports, with articles by eminent members of the teaching profession about Roman Catholic education today.
Readership/Target Audience: Aimed at Roman Catholic teachers and headteachers.
ADVERTISING: Rates on application
Agency Commission: 10%
Average advertising content per issue: 20%
BUSINESS: CHURCH & SCHOOL EQUIPMENT & EDUCATION: Education Teachers

NETWORKING +
36248U5E-9002

Editorial Address: Brassey House, New Zealand Avenue, WALTON-ON-THAMES, KT12 1QD **Tel:** 01932 886537
Fax: 01932 886539
Email: gregc@kadiumpublishing.com
Advertising Address: As above.
Email: danielm@kadiumpublishing.com
Web site: http://www.networkingplus.co.uk
Publisher: Kadium Ltd
Frequency: 11 issues yearly - Double edition published in July/August. Published in the middle of the cover month
Cover Price: Free
Circulation: 19,751 (ABC 01/07/2008 to 30/06/2009)
Usual Pagination: 24
Editor: Rahiel Nasir
Summary of Content: Magazine covering fixed and wireless voice and data networking, including industry news and views, technology developments, latest products, training, LAN, MAN and WAN services.
Readership/Target Audience: Aimed at voice and data managers and technical (ICT) professionals.
ADVERTISING RATES:
Full Page Mono £3360.00
Full Page Colour £3610.00
Agency Commission: 10%
Mechanical Data: Col Length: 325mm, Trim Size: 345 x 245mm, Type Area: 325 x 225mm, Page Width: 225mm
Copy instructions: Copy Date: 15th of the month prior to publication date
Average advertising content per issue: 60%
BUSINESS: COMPUTERS & AUTOMATION: Data Transmission

NEURAL COMPUTING & APPLICATIONS
36004U5R-241

Editorial Address: Ashbourne House, The Guildway, Old Portsmouth Road, Artington, GUILDFORD, GU3 1LP
Tel: 01483 734635
Email: rhonda.lane@springersbm.com
Advertising Address: As above. **Fax:** 01483 734411
Email: rhonda.lane@springer.com
Web site: http://www.springer.com
ISSN: 0941-0643
Publisher: Springer
Frequency: 8 issues yearly
Editor: Rhonda Lane; **Advertising Manager:** Rhonda Lane
Summary of Content: Journal containing original research and other information in the field of practical applications of neural computing.
Readership/Target Audience: Aimed at academics in that field.
ADVERTISING RATES:
Full Page Mono £440.00
Full Page Colour £1170.00
Agency Commission: 10%
Mechanical Data: Bleed Size: 283 x 216mm, Trim Size: 277 x 210mm, Type Area: 237 x 172mm, Col Length: 237mm, Page Width: 172mm, Film: Digital
Copy instructions: Copy Date: 4 weeks prior to publication date
BUSINESS: COMPUTERS & AUTOMATION: Computers Related

NEURO DRUG FOCUS (NDF)
1799521U37-427

Editorial Address: Lincoln House, City Fields Business Park, City Fields Way, Tangmere, CHICHESTER, PO20 2FS
Tel: 01243 756041 **Fax:** 01243 533418
Email: healthcare@espicom.com
Web site: http://www.espicom.com
Publisher: Espicom Ltd
Frequency: Monthly
Annual Sub.: £545.00
Editor: Lucy Vann
Summary of Content: Newsletter featuring the latest developments in neurodegenerative product registration, agreements and clinical trials. Summarises key research presented at international conferences and in journals. Covers Alzheimer's disease, multiple sclerosis, Parkinson's and other related disorders.
Readership/Target Audience: Aimed at senior executives in pharmaceutical companies.

ADVERTISING: No Advertising taken
BUSINESS: PHARMACEUTICAL & CHEMISTS

NEW BUSINESS
36793U14A-259

Editorial Address: 68 Lombard Street, LONDON, EC3V 9LJ
Tel: 020 3145 1240
Email: andrew.brown@newbusiness.co.uk
Advertising Address: As above.
Email: chris.bradshaw@newbusiness.co.uk
Web site: http://www.newbusiness.co.uk
Publisher: International Business Media Group Ltd.
Date Established: 1998
Frequency: Quarterly
Cover Price: £3.50
Free to qualifying individuals
Annual Sub.: £14.00
Circulation: 52,000 (Publisher's Statement)
Usual Pagination: 128
Editor: Andrew Brown; **Advertising Manager:** Chris
Bradshaw; **Publisher:** Gavin Cloake
Summary of Content: Magazine providing independent
information on how to achieve business success. Contains
advice, letters, interviews and features on a range of topics
including current business issues, IT, technology, planning,
banking and finance, legal, health and safety, marketing and
recruitment.
Readership/Target Audience: Aimed at entrepreneurs who
are looking to develop their companies.
ADVERTISING RATES:
Full Page Colour £5950.00
Agency Commission: 10%
Mechanical Data: Bleed Size: 303 x 216mm, Trim Size: 297
x 210mm, Film: Digital
Copy instructions: Copy Date: 3 weeks prior to publication
date
Average advertising content per issue: 40%
BUSINESS: COMMERCE, INDUSTRY & MANAGEMENT

NEW CINEMAS
1696522U62R-501

Editorial Address: School of Modern Languages and
Cultures, University of Leeds, Woodhouse Lane, LEEDS,
LS2 9JT
Email: p.cooke@leeds.ac.uk
Web site: http://www.intellectbooks.co.uk
ISSN: 1474-2756
Publisher: Intellect Ltd
Date Established: 2002
Frequency: 3 issues yearly - Published in April, August and
December
Annual Sub.: £180.00
Circulation: 300 (Publisher's Statement)
Usual Pagination: 80
Editor: Paul Cooke
Summary of Content: Journal covering issues in
contemporary film.
Readership/Target Audience: Aimed at those interested in
the academic study of contemporary film.
ADVERTISING: No Advertising taken
BUSINESS: CHURCH & SCHOOL EQUIPMENT &
EDUCATION: Education Related

NEW CIVIL ENGINEER
39012U42A-125

Editorial Address: Greater London House, Hampstead
Road, LONDON, NW1 7EJ **Tel:** 020 7728 5000
Email: nceedit@emap.com
Advertising Address: As above. **Fax:** 020 7391 3435
Email: john.coates@emap.com
Web site: http://www.nce.co.uk
ISSN: 0307-7683
Publisher: EMAP Insight
Date Established: 1972
Frequency: Weekly
Cover Price: £2.50
Annual Sub.: £107.00
Circulation: 54,747 (ABC 01/07/2008 to 30/06/2009)
Usual Pagination: 60
Editor: Antony Oliver; **Managing Director:** Fraser Murdoch
Summary of Content: Magazine covering construction
industry news and features and a diary of the Institution of
Civil Engineers.
Twitter: https://twitter.com/ncemagazine.
Readership/Target Audience: Read by qualified engineers
working in all areas of the construction industry.
ADVERTISING RATES:
Full Page Colour £4834.00
Agency Commission: 10%
Mechanical Data: Type Area: 275 x 190mm, Bleed Size:
303 x 216mm, Col Length: 275mm, Page Width: 190mm,
Film: Positive, right reading, emulsion side down. Digital
Copy instructions: Copy Date: 1 week prior to publication
date
BUSINESS: CONSTRUCTION

NEW CIVIL ENGINEER INTERNATIONAL
38967U42A-127

Formerly: Civil Engineer International
Editorial Address: 1st Floor, Greater London House,
Hampstead Road, LONDON, NW1 7EJ **Tel:** 020 7728 5000
Fax: 020 7728 4000
Email: nceedit@emap.com
Advertising Address: Greater London House, Hampstead
Road, LONDON, NW1 7EJ **Tel:** 020 7728 5000
Fax: 020 7728 4666
Email: gary.williams@emap.com
Web site: http://www.nce.co.uk
ISSN: 0307-7683
Publisher: EMAP Insight
Frequency: Monthly - Published on the 3rd Thursday of the
cover month
Cover Price: $10.00
Annual Sub.: $72.00
Circulation: 17,000 (Publisher's Statement)
Editor: Mark Hansford
Summary of Content: Magazine containing international
construction and civil engineering news, including site
reports and equipment developments.
Readership/Target Audience: Read by qualified civil
engineers working in all areas of the construction industry.
ADVERTISING RATES:
Full Page Colour £2955.00
Agency Commission: 10%
Mechanical Data: Type Area: 275 x 190mm, Bleed Size:
303 x 216mm, Col Length: 275mm, Page Width: 190mm,
Film: Digital
Copy instructions: Copy Date: 1 week prior to publication
date
Average advertising content per issue: 30%
BUSINESS: CONSTRUCTION

NEW DESIGN
623927U14J-550

Editorial Address: 6A New Street, WARWICK, CV34 4RX
Tel: 01926 408207 **Fax:** 01926 408206
Email: newdesignmagazine@googlemail.com
Advertising Address: As above.
Email: steve@newdesignmagazine.co.uk
Web site: http://www.newdesignmagazine.co.uk
ISSN: 1472-2674
Publisher: Newdesign Magazine Ltd
Date Established: 2000
Frequency: 10 issues yearly - Published in the 1st week of
the cover month
Annual Sub.: £65.00
Circulation: 7,000 (Publisher's Statement)
Usual Pagination: 84
Editor: Tanya Weaver; **Advertising Manager:** Steve Welch
Summary of Content: Magazine covering new product
news, technology, software, cultural studies, design
management and research looking at all aspects of product
and industrial design.
Readership/Target Audience: Aimed at industrial and
product designers, art and design directors, design
managers, consultants and design academics.
ADVERTISING RATES:
Full Page Colour £1950.00
Mechanical Data: Type Area: 245 x 195mm, Bleed Size:
281 x 231mm, Trim Size: 275 x 225mm, Col Length: 245mm,
Page Width: 195mm, Film: Digital
Copy instructions: Copy Date: 3 weeks prior to publication
date
BUSINESS: COMMERCE, INDUSTRY & MANAGEMENT:
Commercial Design

NEW DIRECTION
41307U63B-648

Editorial Address: Severn House, Prescott Drive, Warndon
Business Park, WORCESTER, WR4 9NE **Tel:** 0845 641 1524
Email: newdirection@hwchamber.co.uk
Advertising Address: As above. **Tel:** 0845 641 1522
Email: newdirection@hwchamber.co.uk
Web site: http://www.hwchamber.co.uk
Publisher: Chamber of Commerce Herefordshire and
Worcestershire
Date Established: 2001
Frequency: 6 issues yearly
Cover Price: Free
Circulation: 7,000 (Publisher's Statement)
Usual Pagination: 32
Editor: Corinna Parsons; **Advertising Manager:** Corinna
Rogers
Summary of Content: Magazine covering local news,
company and area profiles in Herefordshire and
Worcestershire.
Readership/Target Audience: Aimed at local businesses.
ADVERTISING: Rates on application
Copy instructions: Copy Date: Beginning of the month prior
to publication date
Average advertising content per issue: 20%
BUSINESS: REGIONAL BUSINESS: Regional Business
English Counties

NEW ELECTRONICS
37380U18A-400

Editorial Address: Hawley Mill, Hawley Road, DARTFORD,
DA2 7TJ **Tel:** 01322 221144 **Fax:** 01322 221188
Email: ne@findlay.co.uk
Advertising Address: As above.
Email: nesales@findlay.co.uk
Web site: http://www.newelectronics.co.uk
ISSN: 0047-9624
Publisher: Findlay Media Ltd
Date Established: 1968
Frequency: 22 issues yearly
Free to qualifying individuals
Annual Sub.: £106.00
Circulation: 17,988 (ABC 01/01/2008 to 31/12/2008)
Editor: Graham Pitcher; **Publisher:** Peter Ring
Summary of Content: Magazine covering electronics news,
product information, technology and developments with
technical articles, design briefings and case studies. Also
includes employment related issues and personal skills
development features.
Readership/Target Audience: Aimed at electronics
engineers and engineering management.
ADVERTISING RATES:
Full Page Colour £3200.00
Agency Commission: 10%
Mechanical Data: Type Area: 254 x 178mm, Bleed Size:
292 x 216mm, Trim Size: 286 x 210mm, Film: Digital, Page
Width: 178mm, Col Length: 254mm
Copy instructions: Copy Date: 1 week prior to publication
date
Average advertising content per issue: 50%
Supplement(s): New Electronics on Campus - 3xY
BUSINESS: ELECTRONICS

NEW ENERGY FINANCE BRIEFING
1846828U58-208

Formerly: New Energy Finance
Editorial Address: 2nd Floor, 283-288 High Holborn,
LONDON, WC1V 7HP **Tel:** 020 7092 8800
Fax: 020 7092 0801
Web site: http://www.newenergyfinance.com
Publisher: New Energy Finance
Frequency: Monthly
Annual Sub.: £1500
Editor: Angus McCrone
Summary of Content: Newsletter covering clean energy,
low carbon technologies and the carbon markets.
Readership/Target Audience: Aimed at investors,
corporations and governments.
BUSINESS: ENERGY, FUEL & NUCLEAR

NEW FOOD
37976U22A-265

Editorial Address: Court Lodge, Hogtrough Hill, Brasted,
WESTERHAM, TN16 1NU **Tel:** 01959 563311
Fax: 01959 563123
Email: hdifford@russellpublishing.com
Advertising Address: As above.
Email: tdean@russellpublishing.com
Web site: http://www.newfoodmagazine.com
ISSN: 1461-4642
Publisher: Russell Publishing Ltd
Date Established: 1997
Frequency: Quarterly
Annual Sub.: £60.00
Circulation: 13,750 (ABC 01/07/2008 to 30/06/2009)
Usual Pagination: 96
Editor: Helen Difford
Summary of Content: Magazine covering processing and
automation, analysis and control and QA/QC in the food and
beverage manufacturing industry.
Readership/Target Audience: Aimed at decision-makers in
the food industry throughout Europe.
ADVERTISING RATES:
Full Page Colour £4177.00
Agency Commission: 10%
Mechanical Data: Type Area: 257 x 180mm, Bleed Size:
303 x 216mm, Trim Size: 297 x 210mm, Col Length: 257mm,
Film: Digital, Page Width: 180mm
Copy instructions: Copy Date: 4 weeks prior to publication
date
Average advertising content per issue: 40%
BUSINESS: FOOD

NEW LAW JOURNAL
39222U44-1500

Editorial Address: Halsbury House, 35 Chancery Lane,
LONDON, WC2A 1EL **Tel:** 020 7400 2580
Fax: 020 7400 2583
Email: newlaw.journal@lexisnexis.co.uk
Advertising Address: 2 Addiscombe Road, CROYDON,
CR9 5AF **Tel:** 020 8662 2013 **Fax:** 020 8212 1970
Email: alain.demaurier@lexisnexis.co.uk
Web site: http://www.new-law-journal.co.uk
ISSN: 0306-6479
Publisher: LexisNexis
Frequency: Weekly
Annual Sub.: £230.00

Circulation: 6,600 (Publisher's Statement)
Usual Pagination: 36
Editor: Jan Miller
Summary of Content: Publication containing news on topical legal matters, law reports and comprehensive parliamentary coverage.
Readership/Target Audience: Aimed at solicitors, barristers, legal advisors, legal executives and law students.
ADVERTISING RATES:
Full Page Colour £1325.00
Agency Commission: 10%
Mechanical Data: No. of Columns (Display): 3, Page Width: 185mm, Film: Digital, Col Widths (Display): 60mm, Type Area: 260 x 185mm, Bleed Size: 303 x 216mm, Trim Size: 297 x 210mm, Col Length: 260mm
Copy instructions: Copy Date: 1 week prior to publication date
Average advertising content per issue: 30%
Supplement(s): ADR - 1xY, Arbitration - 1xY, Autumn Books - 1xY, Charities - 2xY, Education - 1xY, Employment - 2xY, Expert Witness - 4xY, Property - 2xY, Spring Books - 1xY, Summer Books - 1xY, Wills & Probate - 2xY, Winter Books - 1xY
BUSINESS: LEGAL

NEW LIBRARY WORLD
40871U60B-85

Editorial Address: School of Business Information, Faculty of Business and Law, Liverpool John Moores University, LIVERPOOL, L3 5UZ **Tel:** 0151 231 3425
Fax: 0151 707 0423
Email: l.s.ashcroft@ljmu.ac.uk
Web site: http://www.emeraldinsight.com/info/journals/nlw/nlw.jsp
ISSN: 0307-4803
Publisher: Emerald Group Publishing Ltd
Frequency: Monthly
Annual Sub.: £5169.00
Usual Pagination: 40
Editor: Linda Ashcroft; **Publisher:** Eileen Breen
Summary of Content: Magazine covering international information, commercial and technical libraries, information services, environmental information and charts new developments for the information profession. Covers the latest research and developments, new products and services, forthcoming events and software reviews.
Readership/Target Audience: Aimed at libraries and academics.
ADVERTISING: No Advertising taken
BUSINESS: PUBLISHING: Libraries

NEW MATERIALS ASIA
38164U27-118

Formerly: New Materials Japan
Editorial Address: 9A Victoria Square, DROITWICH, WR9 8DE **Tel:** 0870 165 7211 **Fax:** 0870 165 7212
Email: nma@intnews.com
Web site: http://www.performance-materials.net
ISSN: 0265-3443
Publisher: International Newsletters
Frequency: Monthly
Annual Sub.: £467.00
Usual Pagination: 12
Editor: Nick Butler
Summary of Content: International newsletter about advanced materials, products, applications, businesses and markets relating to Japan.
Readership/Target Audience: Aimed at those interested in business and investment in Asia.
ADVERTISING: No Advertising taken
BUSINESS: METAL, IRON & STEEL

NEW MEDIA AGE
36276U5F-367

Editorial Address: St. Giles House, 50 Poland Street, LONDON, W1F 7AX **Tel:** 020 7970 4000 **Fax:** 020 7970 4863
Email: justin.pearse@centaur.co.uk
Advertising Address: As above. **Fax:** 020 7970 4865
Email: bal.bhogal@centaur.co.uk
Web site: http://www.nma.co.uk
ISSN: 1364-7776
Publisher: Centaur Media Plc
Date Established: 1996
Frequency: Weekly
Annual Sub.: £99.00
Circulation: 6,600 (Publisher's Statement)
Usual Pagination: 48
Editor: Danielle Long; **News Editor:** Danielle Long;
Features Editor: Nic Howell; **Editor-in-Chief:** Michael Nutley; **Advertising Director:** Bal Bhogal
Summary of Content: Magazine covering the impact of new media on traditional media companies, advertising industries and marketing.
Readership/Target Audience: Read by strategists from advertisers, brand owners, agencies, consultancies, broadcasting and new media sectors.
ADVERTISING RATES:
Full Page Colour £3469.00

Mechanical Data: Type Area: 282 x 204mm, Col Length: 282mm, Trim Size: 300 x 225mm, Bleed Size: 310 x 235mm, Film: Digital, Page Width: 204mm
Copy instructions: Copy Date: Monday 5pm prior to publication date
BUSINESS: COMPUTERS & AUTOMATION: Multimedia

NEW MEDIA & SOCIETY
35596U2A-130

Editorial Address: 1 Oliver's Yard, 55 City Road, LONDON, EC1Y 1SP **Tel:** 020 7324 8500 **Fax:** 020 7324 8600
Advertising Address: As above.
Email: advertising@sagepub.co.uk
Web site: http://www.sagepub.co.uk
ISSN: 1461-4448
Publisher: Sage Publications
Date Established: 1999
Frequency: 8 issues yearly - Published in February, March, May, June, August, September, November and December
Cover Price: £8.00
Annual Sub.: £47.00
Usual Pagination: 32
Editor: Nicholas Jankowski; **Advertising Manager:** Sheena Karim
Summary of Content: International journal providing an interdisciplinary forum for the examination of the social dynamics of media and information change.
Readership/Target Audience: Aimed mainly at academics in media and sociology.
ADVERTISING RATES:
Full Page Mono £400.00
Agency Commission: 5%
Mechanical Data: Type Area: 205 x 130mm, Col Length: 205mm, Page Width: 130mm
BUSINESS: COMMUNICATIONS, ADVERTISING & MARKETING

NEW MEDIA MARKETS
35684U2D-82

Editorial Address: Mortimer House, 37-41 Mortimer Street, LONDON, W1T 3JH **Tel:** 020 7017 5000 **Fax:** 020 7017 4289
Email: julia.glotz@informa.com
Web site: http://www.informatm.com
ISSN: 0265-4717
Publisher: T&F Informa Group PLC
Date Established: 1983
Frequency: 46 issues yearly
Annual Sub.: £895.00
Usual Pagination: 12
Editor: Julia Glotz; **Publisher:** Simon Murray
Summary of Content: Newsletter covering news and analysis on the pay-television industry.
Readership/Target Audience: Aimed at industry professionals and city analysts.
ADVERTISING: No Advertising taken
BUSINESS: COMMUNICATIONS, ADVERTISING & MARKETING: Broadcasting

---

THE NEW MINERVA REPORT
35278U1F-304_60

Editorial Address: Kelston View, Corston, BATH, BA2 9AH
Tel: 01225 872300
Web site: http://www.minfm.com
ISSN: 0969-4986
Publisher: Minerva Fund Managers
Date Established: 1998
Frequency: Monthly
Annual Sub.: £90.00
Editor: Paul Warner
Summary of Content: Guide to unit trusts and OEICS.
Readership/Target Audience: Aimed at all investors.
ADVERTISING: No Advertising taken
BUSINESS: FINANCE & ECONOMICS: Investment

NEW MODEL ADVISER
1691860U1F-606

Editorial Address: 1st Floor, 87 Vauxhall Walk, LONDON, SE11 5HJ **Tel:** 020 7840 2500
Email: news@citywire.co.uk
Advertising Address: As above. **Tel:** 020 7840 2250
Fax: 020 7840 2251
Email: shone@citywire.co.uk
Web site: http://www.citywire.co.uk
Publisher: Citywire
Date Established: 2005
Frequency: Weekly
Free to qualifying individuals
Circulation: 6,146 (ABC 01/07/2008 to 30/06/2009)
Usual Pagination: 60
Executive Editor: Mark Battersby; **Editor-in-Chief:** Gavin Lumsden; **Advertising Manager:** Stuart Hone
Summary of Content: Magazine covering news and features for financial advisers trying to remodel their business and become professional, fee-based financial planners.
Readership/Target Audience: Aimed at upmarket, aspirational advisers.
ADVERTISING RATES:
Full Page Colour £5100.00

Agency Commission: 10%
Mechanical Data: Type Area: 369 x 280mm, Col Length: 369mm, Page Width: 280mm, Bleed Size: +3mm, Trim Size: 384 x 295mm, Film: Digital
Copy instructions: Copy Date: 1 week prior to publication date
Average advertising content per issue: 40%
BUSINESS: FINANCE & ECONOMICS: Investment

NEW NUTRITION BUSINESS
37977U22A-379

Editorial Address: Crown House, 72 Hammersmith Road, LONDON, W14 8TH **Tel:** 020 7617 7032 **Fax:** 020 7900 1937
Email: julian.mellentin@new-nutrition.com
Web site: http://www.new-nutrition.com
ISSN: 1464-3308
Publisher: The Centre for Food and Health Studies Ltd
Date Established: 1995
Frequency: 11 issues yearly
Annual Sub.: £525.00
Circulation: 1,050 (Publisher's Statement)
Usual Pagination: 40
Editor: Julian Mellentin
Summary of Content: Journal providing in-depth research, news and analysis of developments in foods, beverages, dietary supplements, ingredients, health and nutrition, including functional foods and nutraceuticals. It also covers consumers, brands, markets, claims, regulation, products, nutrition research and ingredients.
Readership/Target Audience: Aimed at those involved in the food industry.
ADVERTISING: No Advertising taken
BUSINESS: FOOD

NEW POWER
1912266U58-203

Editorial Address: Fair Snape, Gote Lane, RINGMER, BN8 5HT **Tel:** 01273 814795
Email: editorial@newpowerconsulting.com
Web site: http://www.newpowerconsulting.com
ISSN: 2040-5839
Publisher: New Power Consulting
Date Established: 2009
Frequency: Monthly
Usual Pagination: 50
Editor: Dominic Maclaine
Readership/Target Audience: Aimed at UK power station developers (CCGTS, coal, nuclear, renewables), energy and environmental regulators, energy financiers, UK power utility sector, transmission, supply and distribution companies.
BUSINESS: ENERGY, FUEL & NUCLEAR

NEW SCIENTIST
39992U55-105

Editorial Address: Lacon House, 84 Theobalds Road, LONDON, WC1X 8NS **Tel:** 020 7611 1200
Fax: 020 7611 1250
Email: news@newscientist.com
Advertising Address: As above. **Tel:** 020 7611 1294
Fax: 020 7611 1290
Email: jamie.labate@newscientist.com
Web site: http://www.newscientist.com
ISSN: 0262-4079
Publisher: Reed Business Information
Date Established: 1956
Frequency: Weekly
Cover Price: £2.70
Circulation: 160,633 (ABC 01/01/2009 to 30/06/2009)
Usual Pagination: 100
Editor: Claire Bowles; **News Editor:** Shaoni Bhattacharya; **Features Editor:** Graham Lawton; **Editor-in-Chief:** Jeremy Webb; **Managing Director:** Mark Kelsey; **Advertising Director:** Jamie Labate
Summary of Content: Magazine covering all fields of science and technology, focusing on developments in industry, the environment and everyday life.
Twitter: https://twitter.com/newscientist
Readership/Target Audience: Read by people in business, finance, government and industry.
ADVERTISING RATES:
Full Page Mono £6700.00
Full Page Colour £6700.00
Agency Commission: 15%
Mechanical Data: Type Area: 240 x 185mm, Trim Size: 267 x 203mm, Col Length: 240mm, Bleed Size: 273 x 219mm, Film: Digital, Page Width: 185mm
Copy instructions: Copy Date: 10 days prior to publication date
BUSINESS: APPLIED SCIENCE & LABORATORIES

NEW SECTOR
37237U14R-250

Editorial Address: 1 Red Hill Villas, DURHAM, DH1 4BA
Tel: 0191 375 0101 **Fax:** 0191 375 0202
Email: editor@newsector.co.uk
Advertising Address: As above.
Email: editor@newsector.co.uk
Web site: http://www.newsector.co.uk
ISSN: 0966-2197

Publisher: Community & Co-operative Publishind Limited
Date Established: 1981
Frequency: 6 issues yearly
Annual Sub.: £25.00
Circulation: 2,200 (Publisher's Statement)
Usual Pagination: 22
Editor: David Parker; **Advertising Manager:** David Parker
Summary of Content: Magazine promoting the principle of co-operative enterprise and common ownership.
Readership/Target Audience: Aimed at members of community businesses and people interested in local economic development.
ADVERTISING RATES:
Full Page Colour £860.00
Mechanical Data: Trim Size: 297 x 210mm, Type Area: 269 x 190mm, Bleed Size: +4mm, Film: Digital, Col Length: 269mm, Page Width: 190mm
Average advertising content per issue: 20%
BUSINESS: COMMERCE, INDUSTRY & MANAGEMENT: Commerce Related

NEW START
38484U32G-81
Editorial Address: The Workstation, Paternoster Row, SHEFFIELD, S1 2BX **Tel:** 0114 281 6133
Email: news@newstartmag.co.uk
Advertising Address: As above. **Tel:** 0114 281 6130
Fax: 0114 279 6522
Email: ad@newstartmag.co.uk
Web site: http://www.newstartmag.co.uk
ISSN: 1465-573X
Publisher: New Start Publishing Ltd
Date Established: 1999
Frequency: Monthly
Annual Sub.: £125.00
Circulation: 5,500 (Publisher's Statement)
Usual Pagination: 72
Editor: Austin Macauley; **Managing Director:** Jamie Veitch; **Advertising Manager:** Chloe Gray; **Publisher:** Jamie Veitch
Summary of Content: Magazine covering all aspects of sustainable communities and regeneration including development, community cohesion, urban design, education and housing.
Readership/Target Audience: Aimed at people working within local and health authorities, central government, regional development agencies, Housing associations, trusts, charities and voluntary organisations.
ADVERTISING RATES:
Full Page Mono £1545.00
Full Page Colour £1854.00
SCC £24.00
Agency Commission: 10%
Mechanical Data: Page Width: 213mm, Type Area: 270 x 213mm, Col Length: 270mm, Trim Size: 300 x 230mm, Bleed Size: 306 x 236mm, Film: Digital
Copy instructions: Copy Date: 3 days prior to publication date
Average advertising content per issue: 50%
BUSINESS: LOCAL GOVERNMENT, LEISURE & RECREATION: Community Care & Social Services

---

NEW START
1828230U63D-722
Editorial Address: 1019 Mile End, 12 Seedhill Road, PAISLEY, PA1 1JS **Tel:** 0141 889 6868 **Fax:** 0141 849 7301
Email: phil.hall@newstartexhibitions.com
Advertising Address: Brinkworth House, Brinkworth, CHIPPENHAM, SN15 5DF **Tel:** 0845 290 3190
Fax: 0845 290 3191
Email: phil.hall@newstartexhibitions.com
Web site: http://www.newstartscotland.com
Publisher: Insight Events
Date Established: 2007
Frequency: Quarterly
Cover Price: £4.00
Free to qualifying individuals
Circulation: 10,000 (Publisher's Statement)
Usual Pagination: 66
Editor: Phil Hall; **Advertising Manager:** Phil Hall
Summary of Content: Magazine taking an informal yet informative look at business issues affecting SMEs in Scotland.
Readership/Target Audience: Aimed at entrepreneurs looking to start or grow their business.
ADVERTISING RATES:
Full Page Colour £1250.00
Mechanical Data: Bleed Size: 246 x 171mm, Trim Size: 240 x 165mm, Film: Digital
Copy instructions: Copy Date: 2 weeks prior to publication date
BUSINESS: REGIONAL BUSINESS: Regional Business Scotland

NEW STEEL CONSTRUCTION
39013U42A-222
Editorial Address: Linden House, Linden Close, TUNBRIDGE WELLS, TN4 8HH **Tel:** 01323 422483
Fax: 01323 423496
Email: info@new-steel-construction.com

Advertising Address: As above. **Tel:** 01892 524455
Fax: 01474 834156
Email: sally@new-steel-construction.com
Web site: http://www.new-steel-construction.com
Publisher: Barrett, Byrd Associates
Frequency: 10 issues yearly
Free to qualifying individuals
Circulation: 8,000 (Publisher's Statement)
Usual Pagination: 44
Editor: Nick Barrett
Summary of Content: Magazine focusing on the use of steel in construction.
Readership/Target Audience: Aimed at structural engineers, steel work contractors and architectural surveyors.
ADVERTISING RATES:
Full Page Colour £1600.00
Mechanical Data: Type Area: 272 x 180mm, Col Length: 272mm, Trim Size: 297 x 210mm, Bleed Size: 303 x 216mm, Page Width: 180mm, Film: Digital
BUSINESS: CONSTRUCTION

NEW TRANSIT
39587U49A-220
Formerly: Transit
Editorial Address: 359 Kennington Lane, LONDON, SE11 5QY **Tel:** 0845 270 7954 **Fax:** 0845 270 7961
Email: ed.transit@landor.co.uk
Advertising Address: As above. **Tel:** 0845 270 7901
Fax: 0845 270 7960
Email: florence.branchu@landor.co.uk
Web site: http://www.transportxtra.com
ISSN: 1358-4766
Publisher: Landor Publishing
Date Established: 1995
Frequency: Monthly
Circulation: 5,000 (Publisher's Statement)
Usual Pagination: 68
Managing Editor: Robert Jack; **Publisher:** Peter Stonham
Summary of Content: Magazine providing analysis and information about public businesses in the UK.
Readership/Target Audience: Aimed at those in the world of passenger transport management, operation planning and customer relationships.
ADVERTISING RATES:
Full Page Mono £1275.00
Full Page Colour £1735.00
Agency Commission: 10%
Mechanical Data: Page Width: 226mm, Film: Digital, Type Area: 324 x 226mm, Col Length: 324mm, Bleed Size: 351 x 256mm, Trim Size: 345 x 250mm, Col Widths (Display): 44mm
Copy instructions: Copy Date: 4 days prior to publication date
Average advertising content per issue: 15%
BUSINESS: TRANSPORT

THE NEW WRITER
40927U60R-50
Editorial Address: PO Box 60, CRANBROOK, TN17 2ZR **Tel:** 01580 212626
Email: editor@thenewwriter.com
Advertising Address: As above. **Fax:** 01580 212041
Email: admin@thenewwriter.com
Web site: http://www.thenewwriter.com
ISSN: 1363-1667
Publisher: The New Writer
Date Established: 1996
Frequency: 6 issues yearly
Cover Price: £4.50
Annual Sub.: £27.00
Circulation: 2,000 (Publisher's Statement)
Usual Pagination: 56
Editor: Suzanne Ruthven; **Advertising Manager:** Merric Davidson; **Publisher:** Merric Davidson
Summary of Content: Magazine publishing fact, fiction, poetry and book reviews.
Readership/Target Audience: Aimed at would-be writers, authors, poetry and fiction readers.
ADVERTISING RATES:
Full Page Mono £150.00
Agency Commission: 10%
Mechanical Data: Type Area: 270 x 190mm, Trim Size: 297 x 210mm, Bleed Size: 303 x 216mm, Screen: 48 lpc, Col Length: 270mm, Film: Positive, right reading, emulsion side down, Page Width: 190mm
Copy instructions: Copy Date: 3 weeks prior to publication date
Average advertising content per issue: 5%
BUSINESS: PUBLISHING: Publishing Related

NEWBURY BUSINESS TODAY
41242U63B-160
Formerly: Newbury Business News
Editorial Address: Newspaper House, Faraday Road, NEWBURY, RG14 2DW **Tel:** 01635 564531
Fax: 01635 522922
Email: business.news@newburynews.co.uk

Advertising Address: As above. **Tel:** 01635 550444
Fax: 01635 46052
Email: advert@newburynews.co.uk
Web site: http://www.newburytoday.co.uk
Publisher: Newbury Weekly News (Printers) Ltd
Date Established: 1986
Frequency: Monthly - Published on the first Thursday of each month
Circulation: 24,000 (Publisher's Statement)
Usual Pagination: 20
Editor: Richard Maynard; **Managing Director:** Adrian Martin
Summary of Content: Regional business newspaper for Newbury and West Berkshire.
Readership/Target Audience: Read by residents and businesses in the West Berkshire area.
ADVERTISING RATES:
Full Page Mono £1572.30
Full Page Colour £1747.00
Agency Commission: 10%
Mechanical Data: No. of Columns (Display): 8, Type Area: 390 x 286mm, Col Length: 390mm, Page Width: 286mm, Col Widths (Display): 33.2mm, Film: Digital
Copy instructions: Copy Date: 2 weeks prior to publication date
Average advertising content per issue: 55%
Supplement to: Newbury Weekly News Series.
BUSINESS: REGIONAL BUSINESS: Regional Business English Counties

---

NEWHORIZON
35087U1C-300
Formerly: New Horizon
Editorial Address: 8 Stade Street, HYTHE, CT21 6BE
Tel: 01303 262636 **Fax:** 01303 262646
Email: editor@newhorizon-islamicbanking.com
Advertising Address: As above.
Email: paulm@ibspublishing.com
Web site: http://www.newhorizon-islamicbanking.com
ISSN: 0955-095X
Publisher: IBS Publishing
Date Established: 1991
Frequency: Quarterly
Free to qualifying individuals
Annual Sub.: £30.00
Circulation: 1,600 (Publisher's Statement)
Usual Pagination: 52
Editor: Tanya Andreasyan
Summary of Content: Journal covering Islamic banking and insurance with reports on international events and developments, interviews, in-depth analysis of various issues of Shari'ah-compliant finance, profiles of Islamic financial institutions, takaful operators and specialists of the industry.
Readership/Target Audience: Aimed at banks, investors, researchers, scholars, governments and business organisations.
ADVERTISING RATES:
Full Page Colour £2150.00
Mechanical Data: Film: Digital, Type Area: 285 x 222mm, Bleed Size: +3mm, Col Length: 285mm, Page Width: 222mm, Trim Size: 279 x 216mm
Copy instructions: Copy Date: 3 weeks prior to publication date
Average advertising content per issue: 25%
BUSINESS: FINANCE & ECONOMICS: Banking

NEWS FROM NEWSTRAID
40922U60C-80
Editorial Address: Barnetson Court, Braintree Road, DUNMOW, CM6 1HS **Tel:** 01371 874198 **Fax:** 01371 873816
Email: oldben@newstraid.org.uk
Web site: http://www.newstraid.org.uk
Publisher: NewstrAid Benelovent Fund
Frequency: Annual - Published in November
Cover Price: Free
Circulation: 59,000 (Publisher's Statement)
Usual Pagination: 16
Editor: Louise Fox
Summary of Content: Journal of the NewstrAid Benevolent Society, the charity for the newspaper industry. Provides information, advice and news on charity events.
Readership/Target Audience: Aimed at members of the Society and trade subscribers.
ADVERTISING: No Advertising taken
BUSINESS: PUBLISHING: Newsagents

NEWS IN CONSERVATION
1695432U64P-92
Formerly: IIC Bulletin
Editorial Address: 6 Buckingham Street, LONDON, WC2N 6BA **Tel:** 020 7839 5975 **Fax:** 020 7976 1564
Email: news@iiconservation.org
Web site: http://www.iiconservation.org
Publisher: IIC
Date Established: 1952
Frequency: 6 issues yearly
Free to qualifying individuals
Circulation: 3,000 (Publisher's Statement)
Usual Pagination: 8

Editor: Lucy Wrapson
Summary of Content: Bulletin covering items of interest to the conservation community including notices for IIC membership, events, courses and appointments.
Readership/Target Audience: Aimed at conservation professionals.
ADVERTISING: No Advertising taken
BUSINESS: OTHER CLASSIFICATIONS: Museums

NFU BRITISH FARMER AND GROWER (EAST ANGLIA)
37910U21J-350

Formerly: NFU Regional Journal East Anglia
Editorial Address: Agriculture House, Willie Snaith Road, NEWMARKET, CB8 7SN **Tel:** 01638 672100
Fax: 01638 672101
Email: brian.finnerty@nfu.org.uk
Advertising Address: As above. **Tel:** 01572 824679
Fax: 01572 824731
Email: david.leach@associa.co.uk
Web site: http://www.nfuonline.com
Publisher: Associa Ltd
Frequency: Monthly - Published on the last Friday of the cover month
Cover Price: Free
Circulation: 8,000 (Publisher's Statement)
Usual Pagination: 64
Editor: Brian Finnerty; **Advertising Manager:** David Leach-Davies
Summary of Content: Journal of the National Farmers Union covering all aspects of farming including legal, political and technical information.
Readership/Target Audience: Aimed at farmers in East Anglia.
ADVERTISING RATES:
Full Page Mono £435.00
Full Page Colour £560.00
Agency Commission: 10%
Mechanical Data: Bleed Size: 303 x 216mm, Trim Size: 297 x 210mm, Type Area: 263 x 182mm, Col Length: 263mm, Page Width: 182mm, Film: Digital
Copy instructions: Copy Date: 3 weeks prior to publication date
Average advertising content per issue: 40%
BUSINESS: AGRICULTURE & FARMING: Agriculture & Farming - Regional

NFU BRITISH FARMER AND GROWER (EAST MIDLANDS)
37890U21J-96

Formerly: East Midlands Farmer & Grower
Editorial Address: Agriculture House, North Gate, Uppingham, OAKHAM, LE15 9NX **Tel:** 01572 824250
Fax: 01572 824251
Email: alison.pratt@nfu.org.uk
Advertising Address: As above. **Tel:** 01572 824679
Fax: 01572 824731
Email: david.leach@associa.co.uk
Web site: http://www.nfuonline.com
Publisher: Associa Ltd
Date Established: 2002
Frequency: Monthly - Published on the last Friday of the cover month
Free to qualifying individuals
Annual Sub.: £55.00
Circulation: 7,584 (Publisher's Statement)
Editor: Alison Pratt; **Advertising Manager:** David Leach-Davies; **Publisher:** Mike Carr
Summary of Content: NFU regional journal covering all sectors of farming and agriculture including legal, political and technical information. Regional pages cover East Midlands, including North and North East Lincolnshire.
Readership/Target Audience: Read by NFU members.
ADVERTISING RATES:
Full Page Mono £435.00
Full Page Colour £560.00
Agency Commission: 10%
Mechanical Data: Bleed Size: 303 x 216mm, Type Area: 263 x 182mm, Col Length: 263mm, Page Width: 182mm, Film: Digital, Trim Size: 297 x 210mm
Copy instructions: Copy Date: 3 weeks prior to publication date
Average advertising content per issue: 40%
BUSINESS: AGRICULTURE & FARMING: Agriculture & Farming - Regional

NFU BRITISH FARMER AND GROWER (NORTH EAST)
37914U21J-201_50

Formerly: NFU North East British Farmer and Grower
Editorial Address: Agriculture House, 207 Tadcaster Road, YORK, YO24 1UD **Tel:** 01904 451550 **Fax:** 01904 451560
Email: rachael.gillbanks@nfu.org.uk
Advertising Address: As above. **Tel:** 01572 824600
Fax: 01572 824646
Email: carol.makepeace@associa.co.uk
Web site: http://www.nfuonline.com
Publisher: Associa Ltd

Frequency: Monthly - Published on the last Friday of the cover month
Cover Price: £3.50
Circulation: 6,000 (Publisher's Statement)
Usual Pagination: 66
Editor: Rachael Gillbanks
Summary of Content: Official journal of the National Farmers Union. Includes updates on policies as well as the technical, legal and promotional work which affects them.
Readership/Target Audience: Read by members of the NFU and their families in the North East of England.
ADVERTISING RATES:
Full Page Mono £435.00
Full Page Colour £560.00
Agency Commission: 10%
Mechanical Data: Bleed Size: 303 x 216mm, Type Area: 263 x 182mm, Col Length: 263mm, Page Width: 182mm, Film: Digital, Trim Size: 297 x 210mm
Copy instructions: Copy Date: 3 weeks prior to publication date
Average advertising content per issue: 40%
BUSINESS: AGRICULTURE & FARMING: Agriculture & Farming - Regional

NFU BRITISH FARMER AND GROWER (NORTH WEST)
37911U21J-202

Formerly: NFU North West Region
Editorial Address: Agriculture House, 1 Moss Lane View, SKELMERSDALE, WN8 9TL **Tel:** 01695 554900
Fax: 01695 554901
Email: carl.hudspith@nfu.org.uk
Advertising Address: As above. **Tel:** 01572 824600
Fax: 01572 824646
Email: carol.makepeace@associa.co.uk
Publisher: Associa Ltd
Frequency: Monthly - Published on the last Friday of the cover month
Free to qualifying individuals
Circulation: 7,000 (Publisher's Statement)
Usual Pagination: 18
Editor: Carl Hudspith
Summary of Content: Official journal of Cheshire, Cumbria and Lancashire NFU county branches.
Readership/Target Audience: Read by NFU members.
ADVERTISING RATES:
Full Page Mono £435.00
Full Page Colour £560.00
Agency Commission: 10%
Mechanical Data: Bleed Size: 303 x 216mm, Type Area: 263 x 182mm, Col Length: 263mm, Page Width: 182mm, Film: Digital, Trim Size: 297 x 210mm
Copy instructions: Copy Date: 3 weeks prior to publication date
Average advertising content per issue: 40%
BUSINESS: AGRICULTURE & FARMING: Agriculture & Farming - Regional

NFU BRITISH FARMER AND GROWER (SOUTH EAST)
37920U21J-310

Formerly: South East Region NFU Journal
Editorial Address: Unit 8, Ground Floor, Bedford Road, Petersfield, HAMPSHIRE, GU32 3QG **Tel:** 01730 711950
Fax: 01730 711951
Email: nfu.south.east@nfu.org.uk
Advertising Address: Agriculture House, North Gate, Uppingham, OAKHAM, LE15 9PL **Tel:** 01572 824642
Email: david.leach@associa.co.uk
Web site: http://www.nfuonline.co.uk
Publisher: Associa Ltd
Frequency: Monthly - Published on the last Friday of the cover month
Free to qualifying individuals
Circulation: 6,000 (Publisher's Statement)
Usual Pagination: 80
Editor: Sarah Acworth; **Advertising Manager:** David Leach-Davies
Summary of Content: Journal covering news of interest to all farmers in the South East.
Readership/Target Audience: Read by farmers and those involved in the agricultural industry.
ADVERTISING RATES:
Full Page Mono £435.00
Full Page Colour £560.00
Agency Commission: 10%
Mechanical Data: Type Area: 263 x 182mm, Bleed Size: 303 x 216mm, Trim Size: 297 x 210mm, Col Length: 263mm, Page Width: 182mm, Film: Digital
Copy instructions: Copy Date: 3 weeks prior to publication date
Average advertising content per issue: 50%
BUSINESS: AGRICULTURE & FARMING: Agriculture & Farming - Regional

NFU BRITISH FARMER AND GROWER (SOUTH WEST)
37909U21J-208

Formerly: NFU Regional Journal Devon
Editorial Address: Agriculture House, Pynes Hill, Rydon Lane, EXETER, EX2 5ST **Tel:** 01392 440700
Fax: 01392 440701
Email: ian.johnson@nfu.org.uk
Advertising Address: As above. **Tel:** 01572 824600
Fax: 01572 824646
Email: clive.marlow@associa.co.uk
Web site: http://www.nfu.org.uk
Publisher: Associa Ltd
Frequency: Monthly - Published on the last Friday of the month prior to cover month
Free to qualifying individuals
Circulation: 10,000 (Publisher's Statement)
Editor: Ian Johnson
Summary of Content: National Farmers Union magazine.
Readership/Target Audience: Read by members of the NFU.
ADVERTISING RATES:
Full Page Mono £660.00
Full Page Colour £825.00
Agency Commission: 10%
Mechanical Data: Bleed Size: 303 x 216mm, Type Area: 263 x 182mm, Col Length: 263mm, Page Width: 182mm, Film: Digital, Trim Size: 297 x 210mm
Copy instructions: Copy Date: 3 weeks prior to publication date
Average advertising content per issue: 40%
BUSINESS: AGRICULTURE & FARMING: Agriculture & Farming - Regional

NFU BRITISH FARMER & GROWER (WEST MIDLANDS)
37913U21J-218

Formerly: NFU Regional Journal West Midlands
Editorial Address: Agriculture House, Southwater Way, TELFORD, TF3 4NR **Tel:** 01952 400500 **Fax:** 01952 409380
Email: oliver.cartwright@nfu.org.uk
Advertising Address: As above. **Tel:** 01572 824679
Fax: 01572 824731
Email: david.leach@associa.co.uk
Web site: http://www.nfuonline.com
Publisher: Associa Ltd
Date Established: 2002
Frequency: Monthly - Published on the last Friday of the cover month
Free to qualifying individuals
Circulation: 8,500 (Publisher's Statement)
Usual Pagination: 40
Editor: Oliver Cartwright; **Advertising Manager:** David Leach-Davies
Summary of Content: Regional journal of the NFU, providing agricultural news and information.
Readership/Target Audience: Read by farmers in the West Midlands.
ADVERTISING RATES:
Full Page Mono £1920.00
Full Page Colour £2400.00
Agency Commission: 10%
Mechanical Data: Bleed Size: 303 x 216mm, Type Area: 263 x 182mm, Col Length: 263mm, Page Width: 182mm, Film: Digital, Trim Size: 297 x 210mm
Copy instructions: Copy Date: 3 weeks prior to publication date
Average advertising content per issue: 40%
BUSINESS: AGRICULTURE & FARMING: Agriculture & Farming - Regional

NFU HORTICULTURE
38125U26D-85

Editorial Address: Agriculture House, Stoneleigh Park, KENILWORTH, CV8 2LZ **Tel:** 024 7685 8674
Fax: 024 7685 8651
Email: martin.stanhope@nfu.org.uk
Web site: http://www.nfuonline.com
ISSN: 1465-4296
Publisher: Associa Ltd
Frequency: Quarterly
Circulation: 10,500 (Publisher's Statement)
Editor: Martin Stanhope
Summary of Content: Newsletter covering horticultural news, information and views.
Readership/Target Audience: Read by NFU horticultural members.
ADVERTISING: No Advertising taken
BUSINESS: GARDEN TRADE: Garden Trade Horticulture

NFU POULTRY FORUM MAGAZINE
37872U21F-700

Formerly: Poultry Forum
Editorial Address: Agriculture House, Stoneleigh Park, WARWICKSHIRE, CV8 2LZ **Tel:** 024 7685 8500
Email: alibone@btconnect.com
Web site: http://www.nfuonline.com
ISSN: 1354-2591

Publisher: Stephens & George Magazines
Frequency: 6 issues yearly
Free to qualifying individuals
Annual Sub.: £55.00
Circulation: 2,000 (Publisher's Statement)
Usual Pagination: 16
Editor: Alison Bone; **Advertising Manager:** Jan Riches
Summary of Content: Journal containing news associated with policy industry and services to NFU members. Includes features on poultry sectors (meat and eggs) with regard to new legislation, environment, health, feed, equipment and housing. Also features market information.
Readership/Target Audience: Aimed at NFU members with an interest in poultry meat and eggs.
ADVERTISING: No Advertising taken
BUSINESS: AGRICULTURE & FARMING: Poultry

NICHE COMMERCIAL FINANCE
1644549U1R-358
Editorial Address: PR by email only **Tel:** 020 7639 5120
Email: newsdesk@bestadvice.net
Advertising Address: PO Box 345, WATERLOOVILLE, PO7 9DR **Tel:** 07970 735054
Email: ed@bestadvice.net
Web site: http://www.ncfonline.co.uk
Publisher: Bestadvice.net
Date Established: 2003
Frequency: 10 issues yearly
Free to qualifying individuals
Circulation: 8,500 (Publisher's Statement)
Usual Pagination: 164
Editor: Kevin Rose; **Advertising Manager:** Ed Tackas
Summary of Content: Magazine covering property, factoring and invoice discounting, motor finance, trade finance, asset finance, export finance, business banking, regulation, qualifications and training.
Readership/Target Audience: Aimed at commercial finance brokers, commercial lenders and estate agents.
ADVERTISING: Rates on application
Copy instructions: Copy Date: 1 week prior to publication date
Supplement(s): Bridging Loans - 1xY, Commercial Mortgages - 1xY
BUSINESS: FINANCE & ECONOMICS: Financial Related

NICHOLAS HALL INSIGHT WESTERN EUROPE
38745U37-37
Formerly: OTC News & Market Report
Editorial Address: 35 Alexandra Street, SOUTHEND-ON-SEA, SS1 1BW **Tel:** 01702 220231 **Fax:** 01702 430787
Email: insight.europe@nicholashall.com
Advertising Address: As above. **Tel:** 01702 220200
Email: info@nicholashall.com
Web site: http://www.nicholashall.com
Publisher: Nicholas Hall & Company
Date Established: 1988
Frequency: Monthly - Published in the middle of the cover month
Annual Sub.: £1750.00
Circulation: 5,000 (Publisher's Statement)
Usual Pagination: 32
Editor: David Redford; **Advertising Manager:** Stacy Wootton
Summary of Content: Magazine covering market and business intelligence for the European OTC drugs industry.
Readership/Target Audience: Aimed at executives and decision makers.
ADVERTISING RATES:
Full Page Colour £1200.00
Mechanical Data: Film: Digital
Copy instructions: Copy Date: 4 weeks prior to publication date
Average advertising content per issue: 5%
BUSINESS: PHARMACEUTICAL & CHEMISTS

NIGHT MAGAZINE
40953U61-60
Editorial Address: Waterloo Place, Watson Square, STOCKPORT, SK1 3AZ **Tel:** 0161 429 7803
Fax: 0161 429 7214
Email: night@mondiale.co.uk
Advertising Address: As above. **Tel:** 0161 476 0456
Email: k.willett@mondiale.co.uk
Web site: http://www.nightmagazine.co.uk
ISSN: 1476-4059
Publisher: Mondiale Publishing Ltd
Date Established: 1984
Frequency: 13 issues yearly - Published in the 1st week of the cover month
Free to qualifying individuals
Annual Sub.: £20.00
Circulation: 10,499 (ABC 01/07/2007 to 30/06/2008)
Usual Pagination: 66
Editor: Rachel Esson; **Managing Director:** Justin Gawne; **Advertising Manager:** Katie Willett

Summary of Content: Magazine including hospitality industry news and reviews, industry news and information about technical equipment and design. Covers bars, clubs, restaurants, casinos and student unions.
Readership/Target Audience: Aimed at the light, sound and design industry, as well as late night entertainment operators.
ADVERTISING RATES:
Full Page Colour £1950.00
Agency Commission: 10%
Mechanical Data: Type Area: 270 x 208mm, Col Length: 270mm, Page Width: 208mm, Trim Size: 297 x 230mm, Bleed Size: 303 x 236mm, Film: Digital
Copy instructions: Copy Date: 1 week prior to publication date
Average advertising content per issue: 60%
BUSINESS: MUSIC TRADE

NIKON PRO
38795U38-49_50
Editorial Address: 85 Strand, LONDON, WC2R 0DW
Tel: 020 7550 8000
Email: sonja.klug@cedarcom.co.uk
Web site: http://www.cedarcom.co.uk
Publisher: Cedar Communications
Frequency: 3 issues yearly - Published in spring, summer and winter
Cover Price: EUR7.00
Free to qualifying individuals
Circulation: 65,000 (Publisher's Statement)
Usual Pagination: 50
Editor: Sonja Klug; **Managing Director:** Clare Broadbent
Summary of Content: Magazine featuring information on Nikon products and a showcase for the work of professional photographers.
Language(s): English; French; German; Italian; Spanish; Swedish
Readership/Target Audience: Aimed at professional photographers.
ADVERTISING: No Advertising taken
BUSINESS: PHOTOGRAPHIC TRADE

NITROGEN & SYNGAS
36677U13-112
Formerly: Nitrogen & Methanol
Editorial Address: Southbank House, Black Prince Road, LONDON, SE1 7SJ **Tel:** 020 7793 2567 **Fax:** 020 7793 2577
Email: richard.hands@bcinsight.com
Advertising Address: As above.
Email: tina.firman@bcinsight.com
Web site: http://www.bcinsight.com
Publisher: BC Insight
Date Established: 1959
Frequency: 6 issues yearly - Published in the middle of the 1st cover month
Annual Sub.: £425.00
Usual Pagination: 48
Editor: Richard Hands; **Advertising Manager:** Tina Firman
Summary of Content: Journal for the nitrogen fertiliser, methanol and related syngas-based chemical industries, covering both marketing and technical developments.
Readership/Target Audience: Aimed at those working within these industries.
ADVERTISING RATES:
Full Page Mono £1250.00
Full Page Colour £2000.00
Agency Commission: 15%
Mechanical Data: Col Length: 254mm, Page Width: 178mm, Trim Size: 297 x 210mm, Type Area: 254 x 178mm
Copy instructions: Copy Date: 1 week prior to publication date
BUSINESS: CHEMICALS

NOISE & VIBRATION WORLDWIDE
37710U19R-370
Editorial Address: 5 Wates Way, BRENTWOOD, CM15 9TB
Tel: 01277 224632 **Fax:** 01277 223453
Email: mscience@globalnet.co.uk
Advertising Address: As above.
Email: mscience@globalnet.co.uk
Web site: http://www.multi-science.co.uk
ISSN: 0957-4565
Publisher: Multi-Science Publishing Co Ltd
Date Established: 1961
Frequency: 11 issues yearly
Annual Sub.: £223.00
Circulation: 750 (Publisher's Statement)
Usual Pagination: 32
Editor: Bill Hughes; **Advertising Manager:** Bill Hughes
Summary of Content: International journal of noise and vibration control and diagnostic engineering.
Readership/Target Audience: Aimed at noise, vibration and condition monitoring specialists.
ADVERTISING RATES:
Full Page Mono £140.00
Full Page Colour £290.00
Agency Commission: 10%
Mechanical Data: Trim Size: 297 x 210mm, Film: Digital

Copy instructions: Copy Date: 15th of the month prior to publication date
Average advertising content per issue: 5%
BUSINESS: ENGINEERING & MACHINERY: Engineering Related

NONWOVENS REPORT INTERNATIONAL
39504U47A-255
Editorial Address: Perkin House, 1 Longlands Street, BRADFORD, BD1 2TP **Tel:** 01274 378800
Fax: 01274 378811
Email: adawilson@gmail.com
Advertising Address: As above.
Email: djagger@world-textile.net
Web site: http://www.world-textile.net
ISSN: 0953-1092
Publisher: World Textile Publications Ltd
Date Established: 1975
Frequency: 6 issues yearly
Annual Sub.: £160.00
Circulation: 6,000 (Publisher's Statement)
Editor: Adrian Wilson; **Managing Editor:** Adrian Wilson
Summary of Content: Publication covering the products, processes, equipment and commercial activities of the world's nonwovens industries.
Readership/Target Audience: Aimed at the nonwovens industry and its suppliers.
ADVERTISING RATES:
Full Page Mono £1158.00
Full Page Colour £1944.00
Agency Commission: 10%
Mechanical Data: Type Area: 264 x 179mm, Bleed Size: 303 x 216mm, Trim Size: 297 x 210mm, Film: Digital, Col Length: 264mm, Page Width: 179mm
BUSINESS: CLOTHING & TEXTILES

NONWOVENS REPORT INTERNATIONAL NEWSLETTER
1773982U47A-583
Editorial Address: Perkin House, 1 Longlands Street, BRADFORD, BD1 2TP **Tel:** 01274 378800
Fax: 01274 378811
Email: info@world-textile.net
Web site: http://www.inteletex.com
Publisher: World Textile Publications Ltd
Frequency: 6 issues yearly
Circulation: 10,000 (Publisher's Statement)
Editor: Adrian Wilson
Summary of Content: Newsletter containing news updates on all aspects of the global nonwovens industry.
Readership/Target Audience: Aimed at the nonwovens industry and its suppliers.
ADVERTISING: No Advertising taken
BUSINESS: CLOTHING & TEXTILES

NORDIC UNQUOTE"
1750388U1F-618
Editorial Address: 4th Floor, Haymarket House, 28-29 Haymarket, LONDON, SW1Y 4RX **Tel:** 020 7484 9824
Fax: 020 7004 7548
Email: rikke.lilla-eckhoff@incisivemedia.com
Advertising Address: Haymarket House, 28-29 Haymarket, LONDON, SW1Y 4RX **Tel:** 020 7484 9700
Fax: 020 7004 7548
Email: stephen.osullivan@incisivemedia.com
Web site: http://www.nordicunquote.com
Publisher: Incisive Media Investments
Date Established: 1999
Frequency: 10 issues yearly
Annual Sub.: £895.00
Usual Pagination: 50
Editor: Rikke Lilla Eckhoff; **Advertising Manager:** Stephen O'Sullivan
Summary of Content: Journal covering Nordic and Baltic private equity and venture capital news including transactions, portfolio management, funds and people moves.
Readership/Target Audience: Aimed at private equity and venture capital groups, adviser groups, law firms and banks.
ADVERTISING RATES:
Full Page Mono £1650.00
Full Page Colour £3300.00
Agency Commission: 10%
Mechanical Data: Bleed Size: 286 x 222mm, Trim Size: 280 x 216mm, Film: Digital
BUSINESS: FINANCE & ECONOMICS: Investment

NORTH AFRICA MONITOR
1641986U14C-354
Editorial Address: Mermaid House, 2 Puddle Dock, LONDON, EC4V 3DS **Tel:** 020 7248 0468
Fax: 020 7248 0467
Email: emartins@businessmonitor.com
Web site: https://www.businessmonitor.com
Publisher: Business Monitor International Ltd
Frequency: Monthly
Annual Sub.: £325.00

Circulation: 350 (Publisher's Statement)
Editor: Terry Alexander
Summary of Content: Publication covering economic and political developments in North Africa including government, economy, finance and the business environment.
Readership/Target Audience: Aimed at investors who have invested or are looking to invest in Africa.
ADVERTISING: No Advertising taken
BUSINESS: COMMERCE, INDUSTRY & MANAGEMENT: International Commerce

NORTH EAST BUSINESS
1741068U63B-2558

Editorial Address: 2 Earls Court, Fifth Avenue Business Park, Team Valley Trading Estate, GATESHEAD, NE11 0HF **Tel:** 0191 499 4200
Email: editorial@cameronpub.co.uk
Advertising Address: As above. **Fax:** 0191 499 4201
Email: angie.smith@tenalpspublishing.com
Publisher: Ten Alps Publishing
Date Established: 2006
Frequency: 10 issues yearly - Published around the beginning of the cover month
Cover Price: Free
Circulation: 15,000 (Publisher's Statement)
Editor: Mark Lane
Summary of Content: Business magazine covering business news and issues from the area including interviews with business personalities and opinion columns.
Readership/Target Audience: Aimed at managers and directors of small to medium sized companies in the north east of England.
ADVERTISING RATES:
Full Page Colour £1795.00
Agency Commission: 10%
Mechanical Data: Type Area: 247 x 190mm, Bleed Size: 276 x 216mm, Trim Size: 270 x 210mm, Col Length: 247mm, Page Width: 190mm, Film: Positive, right reading, emulsion side down. Digital
Copy instructions: Copy Date: 3rd of the month prior to publication date
Average advertising content per issue: 40%
BUSINESS: REGIONAL BUSINESS: Regional Business English Counties

NORTH EAST TIMES COUNTY MAGAZINE
46992U63B-2569

Editorial Address: 5-11 Causey Street, Gosforth, NEWCASTLE UPON TYNE, NE3 4DJ **Tel:** 0191 284 9994
Fax: 0191 284 9995
Email: richard.holmes@accentmagazines.co.uk
Advertising Address: Suite 2, 93-105 St. James Boulevard, NEWCASTLE UPON TYNE, NE1 4BW **Tel:** 0191 255 8888
Fax: 0191 261 9093
Email: jacqui.heath@accentmagazines.co.uk
Publisher: Accent Magazines Ltd
Date Established: 1983
Frequency: 11 issues yearly
Annual Sub.: £30.00
Circulation: 15,000 (Publisher's Statement)
Usual Pagination: 120
Editor: Richard Holmes; **Managing Director:** Michael Grahamslaw
Summary of Content: Magazine business news, features and advice as well as covering top social events, sport, motoring, fashion, profiles, property, weddings, wining and dining and travel.
Readership/Target Audience: Aimed at businesses in the North East and consumers with a high disposable income.
ADVERTISING RATES:
Full Page Mono £895.00
Full Page Colour £1250.00
Agency Commission: 10%
Mechanical Data: Type Area: 267 x 180mm, Film: Digital, Col Length: 267mm, Page Width: 180mm, Trim Size: 297 x 210mm, Bleed Size: 300 x 213mm
Copy instructions: Copy Date: 10th of the month prior to publication date
Average advertising content per issue: 60%
BUSINESS: REGIONAL BUSINESS: Regional Business English Counties

NORTH EAST VISION
41406U63B-2300

Formerly: Tees Valley Vision
Editorial Address: Gazette Buildings, 105-111 Borough Road, MIDDLESBROUGH, TS1 3AZ **Tel:** 01642 234307
Fax: 01642 247168
Email: northeastvision@eveninggazette.co.uk
Advertising Address: Groat Market, NEWCASTLE UPON TYNE, NE1 1ED **Tel:** 0191 201 6033 **Fax:** 0191 230 0241
Email: david.colburn@ncjmedia.co.uk
Web site: http://www.nebusiness.co.uk
Publisher: NCJ Media Ltd
Date Established: 2003
Frequency: Quarterly
Free to qualifying individuals
Circulation: 135,000 (Publisher's Statement)

Usual Pagination: 68
Editor: Sue Scott; **Advertising Manager:** David Colburn
Summary of Content: Regional business magazine for the North East of England.
Readership/Target Audience: Aimed at businesses located within the region and those interested in investing within the region.
ADVERTISING RATES:
Full Page Colour £2500.00
Agency Commission: 10%
Mechanical Data: Col Length: 330mm, Type Area: 330 x 245mm, Page Width: 245mm, Film: Digital
Copy instructions: Copy Date: 4 weeks prior to publication date
Average advertising content per issue: 40%
Supplement to: Evening Gazette (Middlesbrough)
BUSINESS: REGIONAL BUSINESS: Regional Business English Counties

NORTH SEA REPORTER
38597U33-10_20

Formerly: North Sea Letter
Editorial Address: PR by email only **Tel:** 020 7286 6055
Email: meg.leitch@klenergypublishing.com
Publisher: KL Energy Publishing Ltd
Date Established: 1974
Frequency: Weekly
Annual Sub.: £850.00
Usual Pagination: 26
Editor: Meg Leitch
Summary of Content: Newsletter providing a comprehensive picture of upstream oil and gas activity in the North Sea, including rig market and exploration activity, engineering, fabrication, field development, production figures and company news, such as deals and acquisitions.
Readership/Target Audience: Aimed at operators, suppliers, investors and advisers.
ADVERTISING: No Advertising taken
BUSINESS: OIL & PETROLEUM

NORTH SEA RIG REPORT
38599U33-10_27

Editorial Address: Second Floor, The Exchange, Market Street, ABERDEEN, AB11 5PJ **Tel:** 01224 597800
Fax: 01224 580320
Email: rsamsudin@ods-petrodata.com
Web site: http://www.ods-petrodata.com
ISSN: 0226-3112
Publisher: ODS-Petrodata UK Ltd
Frequency: Monthly
Annual Sub.: £1140.00
Circulation: 100 (Publisher's Statement)
Usual Pagination: 20
Editor: Rod Hutton; **Publisher:** David Bichard; **Circulation Manager:** Elsa Candlish
Summary of Content: Publication containing news, market analysis, and short-term supply and demand forecasts on the offshore mobile drilling rigs industry in Northwest Europe.
Readership/Target Audience: Aimed at oil, gas exploration and production companies, drilling contractors, oil industry service companies and the financial industry.
ADVERTISING: No Advertising taken
BUSINESS: OIL & PETROLEUM

NORTH WEST HOSPITALITY MAGAZINE
1804629U11A-220

Editorial Address: Halcyon House, Lowesby, Walton-le-Dale, PRESTON, PR5 4NF **Tel:** 0870 609 8045
Fax: 0871 522 7035
Email: editorial@my-hospitality.com
Advertising Address: As above. **Tel:** 0870 446 0635
Email: advertising@hospitality-magazines.co.uk
Web site: http://www.thgpublishing.co.uk
Publisher: THG Publishing
Date Established: 2007
Frequency: Monthly
Free to qualifying individuals
Circulation: 10,000 (Publisher's Statement)
Usual Pagination: 48
Editor: Shaun Turner; **Managing Director:** Shaun Turner; **Advertising Manager:** Marie Elvin; **Publisher:** Shaun Turner
Summary of Content: Magazine featuring hospitality industry trends, newest equipment, profiles of industry professionals, interviews, business, property, finance and legal issues.
Readership/Target Audience: Aimed at decision makers within the hospitality industry working in hotels, restaurants, bars and food destination pubs in the North West.
ADVERTISING RATES:
Full Page Colour £1295.00
Mechanical Data: Type Area: 277 x 190mm, Bleed Size: 303 x 216mm, Trim Size: 297 x 210mm, Col Length: 277mm, Page Width: 190mm, Film: Digital
BUSINESS: CATERING: Catering, Hotels & Restaurants

NORTH WORKS
1665383U63B-2535

Editorial Address: Aden House, Sunderland Road, GATESHEAD, NE8 3HU **Tel:** 0191 478 8300
Fax: 0191 298 3561
Email: john.graham@distinctivepublishing.co.uk
Advertising Address: As above.
Email: lydia.hughes@distinctivepublishing.co.uk
ISSN: 1746-4234
Publisher: Distinctive Publishing
Date Established: 2004
Frequency: 10 issues yearly
Cover Price: £3.00
Free to qualifying individuals
Annual Sub.: £25.00
Circulation: 32,000 (Publisher's Statement)
Usual Pagination: 76
Editor: John Graham
Summary of Content: Magazine covering leadership, strategy, workplace and technology affecting businesses in the North East.
Readership/Target Audience: Aimed at middle and senior management within businesses in the North East.
ADVERTISING RATES:
Full Page Mono £1400.00
Full Page Colour £1900.00
Agency Commission: 10%
Mechanical Data: Bleed Size: 281 x 222mm, Trim Size: 275 x 216mm, Film: Digital
Copy instructions: Copy Date: 4 weeks prior to publication date
Average advertising content per issue: 30%
BUSINESS: REGIONAL BUSINESS: Regional Business English Counties

NORTHERN AFRICAN WIRELESS COMMUNICATIONS
768341U18A-9001

Editorial Address: 3rd Floor, Brassey House, New Zealand Avenue, WALTON-ON-THAMES, KT12 1QD
Tel: 01932 886537 **Fax:** 01932 886539
Email: rahieln@kadiumpublishing.com
Advertising Address: As above.
Email: richardl@kadiumpublishing.com
Publisher: Kadium Ltd
Date Established: 2002
Frequency: 6 issues yearly - Published in the middle of the 2nd cover month
Annual Sub.: £105.00
Circulation: 7,000 (Publisher's Statement)
Usual Pagination: 36
Editor: Rahiel Nasir
Summary of Content: Magazine covering all aspects of wireless communications in northern equatorial Africa.
Readership/Target Audience: Aimed at mobile and wireless communications specialists and business managers.
ADVERTISING RATES:
Full Page Colour £3695.00
Agency Commission: 10%
Mechanical Data: Col Length: 280mm, Page Width: 190mm, Type Area: 280 x 190mm, Bleed Size: 307 x 220mm, Trim Size: 297 x 210mm, Film: Digital
Copy instructions: Copy Date: 1 week prior to publication date
Average advertising content per issue: 40%
BUSINESS: ELECTRONICS

NORTHERN BUILDER
35916U4E-302_60

Editorial Address: The Forge, 13B Lisburn Road, Moira, CRAIGAVON, BT67 0JR **Tel:** 028 9261 2990
Fax: 028 9261 2091
Email: northernbuilder@kmpltd.co.uk
Advertising Address: As above.
Email: diane@kmpltd.co.uk
Web site: http://www.northernbuilder.co.uk
Publisher: Karen McAvoy Publishing Ltd
Date Established: 1989
Frequency: Quarterly
Cover Price: Free
Circulation: 5,000 (Publisher's Statement)
Usual Pagination: 140
Editor: Alan Bailie; **Advertising Manager:** Diane Kerr
Summary of Content: Magazine with in-depth coverage on all sections of the building industry in Northern Ireland.
Readership/Target Audience: Read by architects, builders, quantity surveyors and specifiers.
ADVERTISING RATES:
Full Page Colour £1045.00
Agency Commission: 10%
Mechanical Data: Type Area: 270 x 185mm, Col Length: 270mm, Page Width: 185mm, Trim Size: 300 x 210mm, Film: Digital, Col Widths (Display): 60mm, No. of Columns (Display): 3, Bleed Size: 305 x 215mm
Average advertising content per issue: 50%
BUSINESS: ARCHITECTURE & BUILDING: Building

Section 4 (b) Business Magazines

NORTHERN FARMING GAZETTE
37916U21J-230

Editorial Address: Gazette House, King Street, Thorne, DONCASTER, DN8 5BA **Tel:** 01405 741382
Fax: 01405 741382
Email: northernfarming@thornetoday.co.uk
Advertising Address: As above. **Tel:** 01405 746070
Fax: 01405 740776
Email: jpeel@doncastertoday.co.uk
Publisher: Johnston Press plc
Date Established: 1991
Frequency: Monthly
Free to qualifying individuals
Annual Sub.: £8.00
Circulation: 20,000 (Publisher's Statement)
Usual Pagination: 14
Editor: Lambert Coverdale
Summary of Content: Journal covering all aspects of farming.
Readership/Target Audience: Aimed at farmers in the North East and East Midlands.
ADVERTISING RATES:
Full Page Mono £1005.21
Full Page Colour £1309.37
SCC £5.85
Agency Commission: 10%
Mechanical Data: No. of Columns (Display): 9, Trim Size: 420 x 297mm, Film: Digital
Copy instructions: Copy Date: 19th of the month prior to publication date
BUSINESS: AGRICULTURE & FARMING: Agriculture & Farming - Regional

NORTHERN HOUSING
35917U4E-302_70

Editorial Address: Portland Buildings, 127-129 Portland Street, MANCHESTER, M1 4PZ **Tel:** 0161 236 2782
Fax: 0161 236 2783
Email: michelle.mckenna@excelpublishing.co.uk
Advertising Address: As above. **Fax:** 0161 236 2793
Email: penni.pennington@excelpublishing.co.uk
Publisher: Excel Publishing Company Ltd
Frequency: 11 issues yearly - Published in the 1st week of the cover month
Cover Price: £2.00
Free to qualifying individuals
Annual Sub.: £25.00
Circulation: 6,000 (Publisher's Statement)
Usual Pagination: 60
Editor: Michelle McKenna; **Publisher:** Patrick Rafter
Summary of Content: Magazine covering news and articles on projects and companies within the construction industry, social housing and private residential sector.
Readership/Target Audience: Aimed at senior management in the construction industry.
ADVERTISING RATES:
Full Page Colour £1175.00
Agency Commission: 10%
Mechanical Data: Bleed Size: 303 x 284mm, Trim Size: 278 x 210mm, Film: Digital, Type Area: 256 x 178mm, Col Length: 256mm, Page Width: 178mm
Copy instructions: Copy Date: 17th of the month prior to publication
Average advertising content per issue: 50%
Editions:
Midlands Housing
Southern Housing
BUSINESS: ARCHITECTURE & BUILDING: Building

NORTHERN IRELAND LEGAL QUARTERLY
39223U44-1520

Editorial Address: School of Law, The Queen's University, 30 University Square, BELFAST, BT7 1NN
Tel: 028 9033 5224 **Fax:** 028 9032 6308
Email: s.wheeler@qub.ac.uk
ISSN: 0029-3105
Publisher: University Press
Date Established: 1936
Frequency: Quarterly
Annual Sub.: £75.00
Circulation: 500 (Publisher's Statement)
Usual Pagination: 130
Editor: Sally Wheeler
Summary of Content: Journal dedicated to legal matters in Northern Ireland and elsewhere.
Readership/Target Audience: Aimed at legal professionals.
ADVERTISING: No Advertising taken
BUSINESS: LEGAL

NORTHERN IRELAND MEDICAL REVIEW/LONDON CHEMIST REVIEW
40207U56A-107_29

Formerly: Northern Ireland Medical Review
Editorial Address: 10 Dargan Cresent, Duncrue Industrial Estate, BELFAST, BT3 9JP **Tel:** 028 9080 9090
Fax: 028 9080 9097

Email: eavan.murray@nimedical.info
Advertising Address: As above.
Email: eileen.boyle@nimedical.info
Web site: www.nimedical.info
Publisher: Medical Communications Ltd
Date Established: 2009
Frequency: 6 issues yearly
Cover Price: Free
Circulation: 14,000 (Publisher's Statement)
Usual Pagination: 76
Editor: Frances Privilage; **Managing Director:** Adrian Maginnis
Summary of Content: Magazine covering the politics and current affairs of GPs and hospital doctors. Also contains general news, views, business issues and articles on clinical and educational matters, human interest, finance, lifestyle, new products and current trials.
Readership/Target Audience: Aimed at GPs, consultants, hospital doctors and health-care professionals in Northern Ireland.
ADVERTISING RATES:
Full Page Mono £1595.00
Full Page Colour £1595.00
Agency Commission: 10%
Mechanical Data: Print Process: Litho, Film: Digital, Col Length: 267mm, Page Width: 180mm, Bleed Size: 307 x 220mm, Trim Size: 297 x 210mm, Type Area: 267 x 180mm, No. of Columns (Display): 5
Copy instructions: Copy Date: 4 weeks prior to publication date
Average advertising content per issue: 35%
BUSINESS: HEALTH & MEDICAL

NORTHERN IRELAND VETERINARY TODAY
41531U64H-159_30

Editorial Address: Penton House, 38 Heron Road, Sydenham Business Park, BELFAST, BT3 9LE
Tel: 028 9045 7457 **Fax:** 028 9045 6611
Email: sinead.doyle@pentonpublications.co.uk
Advertising Address: As above.
Email: nivttoday@pentonpublications.co.uk
Web site: http://www.pentongroup.com
Publisher: Penton Publications Ltd
Date Established: 1996
Frequency: Quarterly
Cover Price: Free
Circulation: 1,250 (Publisher's Statement)
Usual Pagination: 68
Editor: Sinead Doyle; **Managing Editor:** Bill Penton;
Publisher: Bill Penton
Summary of Content: Magazine carrying news, features and profiles on the veterinary profession.
Readership/Target Audience: Aimed at vets, veterinary nurses and final year students in Northern Ireland.
ADVERTISING RATES:
Full Page Mono £1100.00
Full Page Colour £1450.00
Agency Commission: 10%
Mechanical Data: Bleed Size: 303 x 216mm, Trim Size: 297 x 210mm, Film: Digital
Copy instructions: Copy Date: 2 weeks prior to publication date
Average advertising content per issue: 50%
BUSINESS: OTHER CLASSIFICATIONS: Veterinary

NORTHERN IRELANDS ELECTRICAL MAGAZINE
1691433U17-259

Editorial Address: The Forge, 13B Lisburn Road, Moira, CRAIGAVON, BT67 0JR **Tel:** 028 9261 2990
Fax: 028 9261 2091
Email: adam@kmpltd.co.uk
Advertising Address: As above.
Email: electrical@kmpltd.co.uk
Web site: http://www.kmpltd.co.uk
Publisher: Karen McAvoy Publishing Ltd
Date Established: 2005
Frequency: Quarterly - Published in the 1st week of the cover month
Free to qualifying individuals
Circulation: 5,100 (Publisher's Statement)
Editor: Janice Uprichard; **Advertising Manager:** Janice Uprichard
Summary of Content: Magazine focusing on the electrical trade including products, industry news, company profiles and legislation.
Readership/Target Audience: Aimed at specifiers, architects, builders, contractors, consultants, engineers, wholesalers and local government.
ADVERTISING RATES:
Full Page Colour £1045.00
Agency Commission: 10%
Mechanical Data: Type Area: 277 x 185mm, Bleed Size: 303 x 216mm, Trim Size: 297 x 210mm, Col Length: 277mm, Page Width: 185mm, Film: Digital
Copy instructions: Copy Date: 4 weeks prior to publication date
Average advertising content per issue: 40%
BUSINESS: ELECTRICAL

NOTTINGHAMSHIRE COMMERCIAL PROPERTY WEEKLY
41342U63B-1465

Editorial Address: Castle Wharf House, NOTTINGHAM, NG1 7EU **Tel:** 0115 948 2000 **Fax:** 0115 964 4032
Email: richard.tresidder@nottinghameveningpost.co.uk
Advertising Address: As above. **Tel:** 0115 964 2000
Fax: 0115 964 4099
Email: property@nottinghameveningpost.co.uk
Web site: www.thisisnottingham.co.uk
Publisher: Nottingham Post Media Group Ltd
Frequency: Weekly
Circulation: 60,000 (Publisher's Statement)
Usual Pagination: 8
Editor: Richard Tresidder; **Advertising Manager:** Joanne Lawson
Summary of Content: Newspaper covering business news and commercial property activity in the Nottinghamshire area.
Readership/Target Audience: Aimed at local businesses, commercial surveyors and potential developers.
ADVERTISING RATES:
Full Page Mono £4953.60
Full Page Colour £6133.00
Mechanical Data: Page Width: 277mm, Col Length: 360mm, No. of Columns (Display): 8, Type Area: 360 x 277mm
Copy instructions: Copy Date: Thursday 3pm prior to publication date
Average advertising content per issue: 75%
Supplement to: Nottingham Evening Post - 48x.Y.
BUSINESS: REGIONAL BUSINESS: Regional Business English Counties

NOW FOR HOSPITALS
40432U56G-53

Editorial Address: The Old Vicarage, Beck Hill, BARTON-UPON-HUMBER, DN18 5EY **Tel:** 01652 661510
Fax: 01652 661512
Email: sue@hcpublications.fsworld.co.uk
Advertising Address: As above.
Email: sue@hcpublications.fsworld.co.uk
Web site: www.healthcarepublications.co.uk
Publisher: Health Care Publications
Date Established: 1994
Frequency: Quarterly - Published around the last Monday of the cover month
Free to qualifying individuals
Annual Sub.: £50.00
Circulation: 7,300 (Publisher's Statement)
Usual Pagination: 48
Editor: Susan Hughes; **Advertising Manager:** John Hughes
Summary of Content: Magazine covering the very latest news on hospital-wide products, services and projects.
Readership/Target Audience: Aimed at purchasing consultants, clinical directors and service managers.
ADVERTISING RATES:
Full Page Mono £1200.00
Full Page Colour £1200.00
Agency Commission: 10%
Mechanical Data: Bleed Size: 303 x 216mm, Trim Size: 297 x 210mm, Film: Digital
Copy instructions: Copy Date: 4 weeks prior to publication date
BUSINESS: HEALTH & MEDICAL: Medical Equipment

NQ MAGAZINE
1667160U1B-324

Editorial Address: Fifth Floor, Central House, 142 Central Street, LONDON, EC1V 8AR **Tel:** 020 7216 6444
Email: graham@pqaccountant.com
Advertising Address: As above.
Email: polly@nqmagazine.com
Web site: http://www.pqmagazine.com
Publisher: PQ Publishing
Date Established: 2005
Frequency: 3 issues yearly - Published in March, June and September
Free to qualifying individuals
Circulation: 14,000 (Publisher's Statement)
Editor: Graham Hambly; **Advertising Manager:** Polly Thrasivoulou
Summary of Content: Magazine covering issues affecting newly qualified accountants.
Readership/Target Audience: Aimed at ICAEW, ICAS, CIMA, ACCA and CIPFAs.
ADVERTISING RATES:
Full Page Colour £5800.00
Agency Commission: 10%
Mechanical Data: Type Area: 278 x 192mm, Bleed Size: 303 x 216mm, Trim Size: 297 x 210mm, Col Length: 278mm, Page Width: 192mm, Film: Digital
BUSINESS: FINANCE & ECONOMICS: Accountancy

NUCLEAR ENGINEERING INTERNATIONAL
40768U58-66

Editorial Address: Progressive House, 2 Maidstone Road, Foots Cray, SIDCUP, DA14 5HZ **Tel:** 020 8269 7700
Fax: 020 8269 7804

Business Magazines

Email: editorial@neimagazine.com
Advertising Address: As above. **Fax:** 020 8269 7874
Email: sgalvin@progressivemediagroup.com
Web site: http://www.neimagazine.com
ISSN: 0029-5507
Publisher: Progressive Media Publications
Date Established: 1956
Frequency: Monthly - Published on the 1st of the cover month
Free to qualifying individuals
Annual Sub.: £254.00
Circulation: 2,488 (ABC 01/01/2008 to 31/12/2008)
Editor: Will Dalrymple
Summary of Content: Publication containing research and development, world news reviews, events and feature articles.
Readership/Target Audience: Aimed at buyers and specifiers within the nuclear engineering industry.
ADVERTISING RATES:
Full Page Mono £2160.00
Full Page Colour £2660.00
Agency Commission: 10%
Mechanical Data: Film: Digital, Type Area: 254 x 178mm, Print Process: Sheet-fed litho, Bleed Size: 303 x 216mm, Trim Size: 297 x 210mm, Col Length: 254mm, Page Width: 178mm
Copy instructions: Copy Date: 3 weeks prior to publication date
Average advertising content per issue: 20%
BUSINESS: ENERGY, FUEL & NUCLEAR

NUCLEAR FUEL
622553U58-66_30
Editorial Address: PR by email only
Email: david_stellfox@platts.com
Web site: http://www.platts.com
Publisher: Platts
Frequency: 26 issues yearly
Usual Pagination: 16
Editor: David Stellfox
Summary of Content: Publication covering the latest developments worldwide in nuclear fuel and nuclear non proliferation issues.
Readership/Target Audience: Aimed at nuclear executives, engineers, mining companies, nuclear consultants, governments and NGOs.
ADVERTISING: No Advertising taken
BUSINESS: ENERGY, FUEL & NUCLEAR

NUCLEAR FUTURE
40767U58-65_60
Editorial Address: 6 Yarde Hill Orchard, SIDMOUTH, EX10 9JZ **Tel:** 01395 516122 **Fax:** 01395 516122
Email: nuclear_future@btinternet.com
Advertising Address: As above.
Email: sandkpublishing@btinternet.com
Web site: http://www.nuclearfuture.info
ISSN: 1745-2058
Publisher: S and K Publishing Limited
Date Established: 2005
Frequency: 6 issues yearly - Published at the beginning of every odd numbered month
Annual Sub.: £200.00
Circulation: 3,300 (Publisher's Statement)
Usual Pagination: 52
Editor: Keith Simm; **Advertising Manager:** Keith Simm
Summary of Content: Journal of the Institution of Nuclear Engineer and the British Nuclear Energy Society. Includes articles of general interest and news and views from the nuclear world.
Readership/Target Audience: Aimed at nuclear engineers, scientists and those working in chemical, mechanical, electrical, electronic, civil and structural engineering.
ADVERTISING RATES:
Full Page Mono £470.00
Full Page Colour £850.00
Agency Commission: 15%
Mechanical Data: Type Area: 255 x 172mm, Col Length: 255mm, Trim Size: 297 x 210mm, Print Process: Litho, Film: Digital, Page Width: 172mm, Col Widths (Display): 75mm, No. of Columns (Display): 2
Copy instructions: Copy Date: 2 months prior to publication date
Average advertising content per issue: 5%
BUSINESS: ENERGY, FUEL & NUCLEAR

NUCLEIC ACIDS RESEARCH
25755U64F-125
Editorial Address: Great Clarendon Street, OXFORD, OX2 6DP **Tel:** 01865 353387 **Fax:** 01865 353985
Email: nar@neb.com
Advertising Address: As above. **Tel:** 01865 353907
Fax: 01865 353774
Email: steve.simmonds@oxfordjournals.org
Web site: http://nar.oxfordjournals.org/
ISSN: 0305-1048
Publisher: OUP
Date Established: 1974
Frequency: 24 issues yearly

Cover Price: £21.00
Annual Sub.: £395.00
Usual Pagination: 248
Executive Editor: Michael Gait
Summary of Content: Journal containing information on nucleic acids, constituents and analogue, RFLP sequencing reprints, sequence data, NMR assignment data and methods.
Readership/Target Audience: Aimed at professionals and academics within the relevant industry including molecular biologists and structural biologists.
ADVERTISING RATES:
Full Page Mono £742.00
Full Page Colour £1236.00
Agency Commission: 15%
Mechanical Data: Col Length: 255mm, Trim Size: 279 x 216mm, Film: Digital, Page Width: 178mm, Print Process: Litho, Type Area: 255 x 178mm, Bleed Size: 285 x 222mm
BUSINESS: OTHER CLASSIFICATIONS: Biology

NUCLEONICS WEEK
40769U58-66_40
Editorial Address: PR by email only
Email: david_stellfox@platts.com
Web site: http://www.platts.com
Publisher: Platts
Frequency: Weekly
Usual Pagination: 16
Editor: David Stellfox
Summary of Content: Publication reporting on the peaceful uses of nuclear energy, nuclear reactor developments and financial implications.
Readership/Target Audience: Aimed at nuclear industry executives, government officials, engineering contractors and NGOs.
ADVERTISING: No Advertising taken
BUSINESS: ENERGY, FUEL & NUCLEAR

NURSE EDUCATION TODAY
40316U56B-240
Editorial Address: PO Box 66, HULL, HU10 7XS
Tel: 01482 653828
Email: jtyldsley@jtyldsley.karoo.co.uk
Web site: http://www.nurseeducationtoday.com/
ISSN: 0260-6917
Publisher: Elsevier Health Sciences
Date Established: 1980
Frequency: 8 issues yearly
Annual Sub.: EUR126.00
Circulation: 1,000 (Publisher's Statement)
Usual Pagination: 124
Editor: Jill Tyldsley
Summary of Content: International journal covering all aspects of nursing education.
Readership/Target Audience: Read by nurses, nurse tutors and nursing academics within the UK.
ADVERTISING: No Advertising taken
BUSINESS: HEALTH & MEDICAL: Nursing

NURSEPRESCRIBING
1614220U56B-280
Editorial Address: St. Judes Church, Dulwich Road, LONDON, SE24 0PB **Tel:** 020 7738 5454
Fax: 020 7978 8316
Email: andrea.p@markallengroup.com
Advertising Address: As above. **Fax:** 020 7733 2325
Email: laura.d@markallengroup.com
Web site: http://www.nurseprescribing.com
ISSN: 1479-9189
Publisher: M A Healthcare
Date Established: 2003
Frequency: Monthly
Free to qualifying individuals
Annual Sub.: £84.00
Circulation: 13,000 (Publisher's Statement)
Usual Pagination: 44
Editor: Andrea Porter
Summary of Content: Magazine including articles on the clinical, practical, legal, professional and policy aspects of nurse prescribing as well as covering research.
Readership/Target Audience: Aimed at nurse prescribers, those who make clinical decisions that affect patient medication regimens and pharmacists.
ADVERTISING RATES:
Full Page Colour £1900.00
Agency Commission: 10%
Mechanical Data: Col Length: 270mm, Trim Size: 292 x 215mm, Bleed Size: 299 x 222mm, Type Area: 270 x 190mm, Page Width: 190mm, Film: Digital
Average advertising content per issue: 30%
BUSINESS: HEALTH & MEDICAL: Nursing

NURSERY EDUCATION PLUS
753133U62C-500
Formerly: Nursery Education
Editorial Address: Villiers House, Clarendon Avenue, LEAMINGTON SPA, CV32 5PR **Tel:** 01926 887799
Fax: 01926 883331
Email: earlyyears@scholastic.co.uk

Advertising Address: As above.
Email: jsmith@scholastic.co.uk
Web site: http://www.scholastic.co.uk/nurseryedplus
ISSN: 1472-1996
Publisher: Scholastic UK Ltd
Date Established: 1997
Frequency: Monthly - Published on the 2nd Thursday of the cover month
Cover Price: £4.25
Annual Sub.: £39.99
Circulation: 15,457 (ABC 01/07/2006 to 30/06/2007)
Usual Pagination: 40
Editor: Lesley Sudlow; **Advertising Manager:** Jason Smith
Summary of Content: Magazine covering all aspects of caring and educating children in the early years. Focus on planning, managing and delivering learning through play for the under 5s. Includes theme-based activities linked to the QCA Curriculum Guidance for the Foundation Stage.
Readership/Target Audience: Aimed at those working with children aged between 0 and 5 years old including nursery managers, reception teachers, nursery teachers, nursery nurses, pre-school workers, childminders and nannies.
ADVERTISING RATES:
Full Page Mono £950.00
Full Page Colour £1100.00
Agency Commission: 10%
Mechanical Data: Page Width: 186mm, Type Area: 266 x 186mm, Col Length: 266mm, Col Widths (Display): 43mm, Film: Digital, Bleed Size: 303 x 216mm, Trim Size: 297 x 210mm
Copy instructions: Copy Date: 5 weeks prior to publication date
Average advertising content per issue: 40%
BUSINESS: CHURCH & SCHOOL EQUIPMENT & EDUCATION: Junior Education

NURSERY INDUSTRY
39564U48C-70
Editorial Address: 15A London Road, MAIDSTONE, ME16 8LY **Tel:** 01622 687031 **Fax:** 01622 757646
Email: nursery@datateam.co.uk
Advertising Address: As above. **Tel:** 01622 699122
Email: nursery@datateam.co.uk
Web site: http://www.nursery-industry.co.uk
ISSN: 0967-4535
Publisher: Datateam Publishing Ltd
Frequency: Monthly - Published on the 7th of the cover month
Free to qualifying individuals
Annual Sub.: £39.00
Circulation: 3,483 (ABC 01/07/2007 to 30/06/2008)
Usual Pagination: 48
Editor: Becci Knowles; **Advertising Manager:** Mandy Reynolds
Summary of Content: Magazine featuring the latest information on baby products and the nursery trade.
Readership/Target Audience: Aimed at buyers, retailers and manufacturers.
ADVERTISING RATES:
Full Page Colour £1100.00
SCC £15.00
Agency Commission: 10%
Mechanical Data: Col Length: 280mm, Page Width: 195mm, Trim Size: 306 x 229mm, Bleed Size: 312 x 235mm, Type Area: 280 x 195mm, Film: Digital
Supplement(s): Baby and Child Fair - 1xY, Harrogate Nursery Fair - 1xY
BUSINESS: TOY TRADE & SPORTS GOODS: Toy Trade - Baby Goods

NURSERY MANAGEMENT TODAY
1739595U14A-566
Editorial Address: 2nd Floor, Culvert House, Culvert Road, Battersea, LONDON, SW11 5DH **Tel:** 020 7720 2108
Fax: 020 7498 3023
Email: alisonjgordon@googlemail.com
Advertising Address: Culvert House, Culvert Road, LONDON, SW11 5DH **Tel:** 01323 740701
Fax: 01323 740701
Email: chris.banner@dsl.pipex.com
ISSN: 1476-136X
Publisher: Hawker Publications
Date Established: 2001
Frequency: 6 issues yearly
Cover Price: £10.00
Annual Sub.: £60.00
Usual Pagination: 60
Editor: Alison Gordon; **Advertising Director:** Chris Banner
Summary of Content: Magazine covering business, property and management issues.
Readership/Target Audience: Aimed at senior managers and owners of nurseries on the private, voluntary and maintained sectors.
ADVERTISING RATES:
Full Page Colour £1185.00
Agency Commission: 10%
Mechanical Data: Type Area: 266 x 184mm, Trim Size: 297 x 210mm, Col Length: 266mm, Page Width: 184mm, Film: Digital

Copy instructions: Copy Date: 1st Thursday of the month prior to publication date
Average advertising content per issue: 40%
BUSINESS: COMMERCE, INDUSTRY & MANAGEMENT

NURSERY TODAY
39565U48C-120

Editorial Address: 1 Churchgates, The Wilderness, BERKHAMSTED, HP4 2UB **Tel:** 01442 289930
Fax: 01442 289950
Email: penny@lemapublishing.co.uk
Advertising Address: As above.
Email: christine@lemapublishing.co.uk
Web site: http://www.nursery-today.co.uk
Publisher: Lema Publishing
Date Established: 1997
Frequency: 9 issues yearly
Free to qualifying individuals
Annual Sub.: £35.00
Circulation: 4,315 (ABC 01/07/2008 to 30/06/2009)
Usual Pagination: 68
Editor: Christine Contreras; **Publisher:** John Baulch
Summary of Content: Magazine providing news, details of exhibitions, new product information and articles about the retail nursery trade.
Readership/Target Audience: Aimed at manufacturers and retailers of nursery products.
ADVERTISING RATES:
Full Page Mono £795.00
Full Page Colour £1195.00
Agency Commission: 10%
Mechanical Data: Bleed Size: 321 x 246mm, Type Area: 305 x 230mm, Col Length: 305mm, Page Width: 230mm, Film: Digital, Trim Size: 315 x 240mm
Average advertising content per issue: 40%
BUSINESS: TOY TRADE & SPORTS GOODS: Toy Trade - Baby Goods

NURSERY WORLD
41088U62C-490

Editorial Address: 174 Hammersmith Road, LONDON, W6 7JP **Tel:** 020 8267 8409
Email: news.nw@haymarket.com
Advertising Address: 22 Bute Gardens, LONDON, W6 7HN
Tel: 020 8267 5000
Email: elliot.thomas@haymarket.com
Web site: http://www.nurseryworld.co.uk
ISSN: 0029-6422
Publisher: Haymarket Business Media Ltd
Date Established: 1925
Frequency: Weekly
Cover Price: £1.50
Annual Sub.: £65.00
Circulation: 17,416 (ABC 01/07/2008 to 30/06/2009)
Usual Pagination: 40
Editor: Liz Roberts; **News Editor:** Catherine Gaunt;
Advertising Manager: Elliot Thomas
Summary of Content: Magazine covering all aspects of baby and child care, education and training.
Readership/Target Audience: Aimed at early years professionals, nursery managers, teachers, nursery nurses, nannies and child minders.
ADVERTISING RATES:
Full Page Mono £1690.00
Full Page Colour £1901.25
Agency Commission: 10%
Mechanical Data: Page Width: 186mm, Col Length: 267mm, Film: Digital, No. of Columns (Display): 4, Type Area: 267 x 186mm, Bleed Size: 304 x 218mm, Trim Size: 296 x 210mm
Copy instructions: Copy Date: 10 days prior to publication date
Average advertising content per issue: 40%
Supplement(s): Nursery Chains - 1xY, Nursery Management - 2xY, Training Today - 1xY
BUSINESS: CHURCH & SCHOOL EQUIPMENT & EDUCATION: Junior Education

NURSING AND RESIDENTIAL CARE
40318U56B-243

Editorial Address: St. Judes Church, Dulwich Road, LONDON, SE24 0PB **Tel:** 020 7738 5454
Fax: 020 7978 8316
Email: laura.do@markallengroup.com
Advertising Address: As above. **Fax:** 020 7733 2325
Email: chloe.m@markallengroup.com
Web site: http://www.nursingresidentialcare.co.uk
ISSN: 1465-9301
Publisher: M A Healthcare
Date Established: 1999
Frequency: Monthly
Annual Sub.: £136.00
Circulation: 5,000 (Publisher's Statement)
Usual Pagination: 52
Editor: Laura Dean-Osgood
Summary of Content: Journal covering up-to-date clinical reviews, NVQ in care, professional issues and

developments, care analysis, self directed learning, product focuses, jobs and courses.
Readership/Target Audience: Aimed at nursing and residential care staff, including nurses, managers and care assistants.
ADVERTISING RATES:
Full Page Colour £2000.00
Agency Commission: 10%
Mechanical Data: Type Area: 282 x 205mm, Col Length: 282mm, Bleed Size: 298 x 221mm, Trim Size: 292 x 215mm, Film: Digital, Page Width: 205mm
Average advertising content per issue: 25%
BUSINESS: HEALTH & MEDICAL: Nursing

NURSING IN CRITICAL CARE
40323U56B-248

Editorial Address: 9600 Garsington Road, Cowley, OXFORD, OX4 2DQ **Tel:** 01865 476540 **Fax:** 01865 471540
Email: samira.ceccarelli@wiley.com
Advertising Address: As above. **Tel:** 01865 776868
Fax: 01865 471271
Email: joanna.baker@oxon.blackwellpublishing.com
Web site: http://www.blackwellpublishing.com/journals/ncr
ISSN: 1362-1017
Publisher: Wiley-Blackwell Publishing
Frequency: 6 issues yearly
Usual Pagination: 56
Editor: Karen Hill; **News Editor:** Karen Hill
Summary of Content: Journal of the British Association of Critical Care Nurses. Contains clinical and research papers supporting critical and acute nursing.
Readership/Target Audience: Read by intensive and critical care nurses and nursing lecturers.
ADVERTISING RATES:
Full Page Mono £550.00
Full Page Colour £950.00
Agency Commission: 10%
Mechanical Data: Trim Size: 276 x 210mm, Film: Digital, Type Area: 230 x 170mm, Bleed Size: 282 x 216mm, Col Length: 230mm, Page Width: 170mm
Copy instructions: Copy Date: 6 weeks prior to publication date
BUSINESS: HEALTH & MEDICAL: Nursing

NURSING IN PRACTICE
711539U56B-252

Editorial Address: 1 St. John's Square, LONDON, EC1M 4PN **Tel:** 020 7214 0500 **Fax:** 020 7214 0501
Email: nip@campden.com
Advertising Address: As above. **Tel:** 020 7214 0526
Fax: 020 7214 0586
Email: edwardburkle@campden.com
Web site: http://www.nursinginpractice.com
ISSN: 1473-9445
Publisher: Campden Publishing Ltd
Date Established: 2001
Frequency: 6 issues yearly - Published in the 1st week of the 1st cover month
Free to qualifying individuals
Annual Sub.: £70.00
Circulation: 12,539 (ABC 01/01/2008 to 31/12/2008)
Usual Pagination: 88
Editor: Polly Moffat; **Advertising Manager:** Edward Burkle;
Publisher: Stephen Taylor
Summary of Content: Magazine providing clinical updates, news, views and features about primary care nursing. Includes features on asthma, diabetes, cardiology, wound care, neurology, clinical governance, travel medicine, vaccination, mother and baby, incontinence, allergy management and contraception.
Readership/Target Audience: Aimed at practice, district, school and community nurses, midwives and health visitors.
ADVERTISING RATES:
Full Page Mono £2950.00
Full Page Colour £3950.00
Agency Commission: 10%
Mechanical Data: Type Area: 277 x 190mm, Col Length: 277mm, Page Width: 190mm, Trim Size: 297 x 210mm, Bleed Size: 303 x 216mm, Film: Digital
Copy instructions: Copy Date: 3 weeks prior to publication date
Average advertising content per issue: 30%
BUSINESS: HEALTH & MEDICAL: Nursing

NURSING MANAGEMENT
40320U56B-250

Editorial Address: The Heights, 59-65 Lowlands Road, HARROW, HA1 3AW **Tel:** 020 8423 1066
Fax: 020 8423 3198
Email: nick.lipley@rcnpublishing.co.uk
Advertising Address: As above. **Fax:** 020 8423 9196
Email: neil.hobson@rcnpublishing.co.uk
Web site: http://www.nursingmanagement.co.uk
ISSN: 1354-5760
Publisher: RCN Publishing Co Ltd
Date Established: 1994
Frequency: 10 issues yearly
Cover Price: £4.65
Annual Sub.: £55.00
Circulation: 4,448 (ABC 01/01/2008 to 31/12/2008)

Usual Pagination: 40
Editor: Nick Lipley; **Publisher:** Linda Thomas
Summary of Content: Journal focusing on the management of trusts, hospitals, community care and the independent sector.
Readership/Target Audience: Aimed at nurses in leadership and managerial positions.
ADVERTISING RATES:
Full Page Colour £1705.00
Agency Commission: 10%
Mechanical Data: Col Length: 271mm, Type Area: 271 x 178mm, Bleed Size: 303 x 216mm, Trim Size: 297 x 210mm, Page Width: 178mm, Film: Digital
Copy instructions: Copy Date: 2 weeks prior to publication date
Average advertising content per issue: 10%
BUSINESS: HEALTH & MEDICAL: Nursing

NURSING OLDER PEOPLE
40301U56B-80

Formerly: Elderly Care
Editorial Address: The Heights, 59-65 Lowlands Road, HARROW, HA1 3AW **Tel:** 020 8423 1066
Fax: 020 8872 3198
Email: helen.hyland@rcnpublishing.co.uk
Advertising Address: As above. **Fax:** 020 8423 9196
Email: neil.hobson@rcnpublishing.co.uk
Web site: http://www.nursingolderpeople.co.uk
ISSN: 1472-0795
Publisher: RCN Publishing Co Ltd
Date Established: 1993
Frequency: 10 issues yearly - Published in the 4th week of the cover month
Annual Sub.: £66.00
Circulation: 7,505 (ABC 01/01/2008 to 31/12/2008)
Usual Pagination: 40
Editor: Lisa Berry; **Managing Director:** Linda Thomas;
Publisher: Linda Thomas
Summary of Content: Journal containing clinical articles, features and news.
Readership/Target Audience: Aimed at nursing staff working in hospitals, intermediate and rehabilitative care, the community and care homes.
ADVERTISING RATES:
Full Page Colour £2299.00
Mechanical Data: Type Area: 271 x 178mm, Col Length: 271mm, Page Width: 178mm, Trim Size: 297 x 210mm, Bleed Size: 303 x 216mm, Film: Digital
Copy instructions: Copy Date: 4 weeks prior to publication date
BUSINESS: HEALTH & MEDICAL: Nursing

NURSING STANDARD
40321U56B-255

Editorial Address: The Heights, 59-65 Lowlands Road, HARROW, HA1 3AW **Tel:** 020 8423 1066
Fax: 020 8423 3867
Email: news@rcnpublishing.co.uk
Advertising Address: As above. **Fax:** 020 8423 9196
Email: neil.hobson@rcnpublishing.co.uk
Web site: http://www.nursing-standard.co.uk
ISSN: 0029-6570
Publisher: RCN Publishing Co Ltd
Date Established: 1987
Frequency: Weekly - Published each Wednesday
Cover Price: £1.65
Annual Sub.: £74.00
Circulation: 68,046 (ABC 01/01/2008 to 31/12/2008)
Editor: Jean Gray; **News Editor:** Sarah Harrison; **Features Editor:** Charlotte Alderman; **Managing Director:** Linda Thomas; **Publisher:** Linda Thomas
Summary of Content: Specialist journal containing nursing news, clinical features, political comment and book reviews. Twitter: https://twitter.com/RCNPublishing.
Readership/Target Audience: Aimed at training and qualified nurses, health visitors and specialist advisors.
ADVERTISING RATES:
Full Page Colour £2495.00
Mechanical Data: Bleed Size: 283 x 191mm, Trim Size: 260 x 185mm, Type Area: 228 x 160mm, Col Length: 228mm, Page Width: 160mm, Film: Digital
Copy instructions: Copy Date: 1 week prior to publication date
Supplement(s): Tissue Viability - 4xY
BUSINESS: HEALTH & MEDICAL: Nursing

NURSING TIMES
40322U56B-260

Editorial Address: Greater London House, Hampstead Road, LONDON, NW1 7EJ **Tel:** 020 7728 5000
Fax: 020 7874 0505
Email: nt@emap.com
Advertising Address: As above. **Fax:** 020 7728 3866
Email: tim.verbrugge@emap.com
Web site: http://www.nursingtimes.net
ISSN: 0954-7762
Publisher: EMAP Public Sector
Date Established: 1905
Frequency: Weekly
Cover Price: £1.60

Annual Sub.: £67.50
Circulation: 30,923 (ABC 01/01/2008 to 31/12/2008)
Usual Pagination: 200
Editor: Alastair McLellan; **News Editor:** Steve Ford
Summary of Content: Journal containing news and features on management, clinical subjects and nursing education. Covers psychiatric, theatre and children's nursing, midwifery, community nursing and infection control.
Readership/Target Audience: Read by registered and student nurses, midwives and health visitors in hospitals and the community.
ADVERTISING RATES:
Full Page Colour £2625.00
Agency Commission: 10%
Mechanical Data: Type Area: 260 x 195mm, Bleed Size: 291 x 216mm, Trim Size: 285 x 210mm, Film: Digital, Col Length: 260mm, Page Width: 195mm
Copy instructions: Copy Date: 10 days prior to publication date
Average advertising content per issue: 60%
Supplement(s): Continence - 4xY, Infection Control - 4xY, Primary Care - 11xY, Respiratory Care - 4xY, Wound Care Nursing - 7xY
BUSINESS: HEALTH & MEDICAL: Nursing

NUSSL TN MAGAZINE
37224U14L-510

Formerly: NUSSL Trading News
Editorial Address: Snape Road, MACCLESFIELD, SK10 2NZ **Tel:** 01625 413200 **Fax:** 01625 413400
Email: agilhooley@nussl.co.uk
Advertising Address: As above.
Email: enquiries@nussl.co.uk
Web site: http://www.nussl.co.uk
Publisher: NUS Services Ltd
Date Established: 1996
Frequency: 11 issues yearly - Based upon the academic year
Free to qualifying individuals
Circulation: 1,400 (Publisher's Statement)
Usual Pagination: 48
Editor: Andy Gilhooley; **Advertising Manager:** Kate Gregory
Summary of Content: A membership magazine for all the student's unions in the UK. It is a commercial trade magazine which contains news from the retail and licensed trade and hospitality industry. It also contains feature articles of student's unions such as opening a new nightclub venue, shop or bar.
Readership/Target Audience: Aimed at all student union staff members and student officers in the UK.
ADVERTISING RATES:
Full Page Colour £600.00
Mechanical Data: Type Area: 277 x 190mm, Col Length: 277mm, Page Width: 190mm, Trim Size: 297 x 210mm, Bleed Size: 303 x 216mm, Film: Digital
Copy instructions: Copy Date: 4 weeks prior to publication date
Average advertising content per issue: 50%
BUSINESS: COMMERCE, INDUSTRY & MANAGEMENT: Trade Unions

NUTRACEUTICAL BUSINESS & TECHNOLOGY
1691514U22A-391

Editorial Address: 34 Loram Way, Alphington, EXETER, EX2 8GG **Tel:** 01392 202591 **Fax:** 01372 478961
Email: kevin@via-medialtd.com
Advertising Address: Oak House Mews, 43 The Parade, Claygate, ESHER, KT10 0PD **Tel:** 01392 202591
Fax: 01372 472862
Email: miranda@via-medialtd.com
Web site: http://www.nutraceuticalmag.com
ISSN: 1745-8307
Publisher: Via Media Ltd
Date Established: 2004
Frequency: 6 issues yearly
Free to qualifying individuals
Annual Sub.: £100.00
Circulation: 7,896 (Publisher's Statement)
Usual Pagination: 68
Editor: Kevin Robinson; **Advertising Manager:** Miranda Docherty
Summary of Content: Magazine focusing on the manufacture of neutraceutical and functional foods. Topics covered include compliance, health management, raw materials and regulatory affairs.
Readership/Target Audience: Aimed at key decision makers in the nutraceutical and functional foods industry.
ADVERTISING RATES:
Full Page Mono £2300.00
Full Page Colour £2800.00
Agency Commission: 15%
Mechanical Data: Type Area: 267 x 174mm, Bleed Size: 303 x 216mm, Trim Size: 297 x 210mm, Col Length: 267mm, Page Width: 174mm, Film: Digital
Copy instructions: Copy Date: 2 weeks prior to publication date
Average advertising content per issue: 35%
BUSINESS: FOOD

NUTRACEUTICALS INTERNATIONAL
38743U37-34_80

Editorial Address: Appleton House, 139 King Street, LONDON, W6 9JG **Tel:** 020 8735 6625 **Fax:** 020 8735 6688
Email: barbara@marketletter.com
Advertising Address: As above.
Email: rcardwell@marketletter.com
Web site: http://www.marketletter.com
ISSN: 1362-5411
Publisher: Marketletter (Publications) Ltd
Date Established: 1996
Frequency: Monthly
Annual Sub.: £399.00
Usual Pagination: 28
Editor: Barbara Obstoj; **Advertising Manager:** Robin Cardwell; **Publisher:** Barbara Obstoj
Summary of Content: Magazine containing a global perspective on nutraceuticals, dietary supplements and functional foods.
Readership/Target Audience: Read by senior executives in the industry, analysts and regulators.
ADVERTISING RATES:
Full Page Mono £1090.00
Full Page Colour £1780.00
Agency Commission: 10%
Mechanical Data: Type Area: 297 x 210mm, Trim Size: 297 x 210mm, Col Length: 297mm, Page Width: 210mm, Film: Digital, Bleed Size: +3mm
Copy instructions: Copy Date: 10th of the month prior to publication date
Average advertising content per issue: 7%
BUSINESS: PHARMACEUTICAL & CHEMISTS

NUTRITION & FOOD SCIENCE
38050U22R-297

Editorial Address: Denehurst, Newton Road, RUSHDEN, NN10 0SY **Tel:** 01274 777700 **Fax:** 01274 785200
Email: mabel@qmnds.demon.co.uk
Web site: http://www.emeraldinsight.com/nfs.htm
ISSN: 0034-6659
Publisher: Emerald Group Publishing Ltd
Date Established: 1970
Frequency: 6 issues yearly
Annual Sub.: £2319.00
Usual Pagination: 48
Editor: Mabel Blades; **Publisher:** Claire Jackson
Summary of Content: Educational journal concerned with all aspects of nutrition and food science. Also deals with home economics areas such as consumer issues, money matters and family health and welfare.
Readership/Target Audience: Academics and researchers in the field including dieticians, food company managers, food research institutes, health care professionals and nutritionists.
ADVERTISING: No Advertising taken
BUSINESS: FOOD: Food Related

NUTRITION BULLETIN
40209U56A-107_40

Editorial Address: High Holborn House, 52-54 High Holborn, LONDON, WC1V 6RQ **Tel:** 020 7404 6504
Fax: 020 7404 6747
Email: nbu@nutrition.org.uk
Advertising Address: 9600 Garsington Road, Cowley, OXFORD, OX4 2DQ **Tel:** 01865 776868 **Fax:** 01865 471267
Email: craig.pickett@oxon.blackwellpublishing.com
Web site: http://www.blackwellpublishing.com
ISSN: 1471-9827
Publisher: Wiley-Blackwell Publishing
Date Established: 1967
Frequency: Quarterly
Free to qualifying individuals
Annual Sub.: £72.00
Circulation: 4,000 (Publisher's Statement)
Usual Pagination: 96
Editor: Sara Stanner; **Publisher:** Joanna McMahon
Summary of Content: Official publication of the British Nutrition Foundation. Contains scientific reviews on aspects of nutrition and news of issues in the field of human nutrition.
Readership/Target Audience: Aimed at researchers and nutritionists working in universities and research institutes, public health nutritionists, dieticians and other health professionals, nutritionists, technologists and others in the food industry and teachers and journalists with an interest in nutrition.
ADVERTISING RATES:
Full Page Mono £550.00
Full Page Colour £950.00
Mechanical Data: Page Width: 170mm, Type Area: 230 x 170mm, Col Length: 230mm, Trim Size: 276 x 210mm, Film: Digital
Copy instructions: Copy Date: 6 weeks prior to publication date
BUSINESS: HEALTH & MEDICAL

THE NUTRITION PRACTITIONER
627295U22F-105

Editorial Address: Swift House, Market Place, WOKINGHAM, RG40 1AP **Tel:** 0118 979 8686
Fax: 0118 979 8786
Email: kate@cnelm.co.uk
Tel: 01480 385452 **Fax:** 01480 385452
Web site: http://www.ns3.co.uk
ISSN: 1472-0094
Publisher: NS3UK Ltd
Date Established: 1999
Frequency: 3 issues yearly
Cover Price: £16.25
Annual Sub.: £65.00
Circulation: 1,000 (Publisher's Statement)
Usual Pagination: 72
Editor: Kate Neil
Summary of Content: Magazine covering review articles, case histories, education, product news, drug and nutrient interactions, clinical tests and recipes.
Readership/Target Audience: Aimed at clinical nutritionists, all health professionals that use nutrition in their practice, scientists working in the food and health supplement industry, pharmacists, health writers and journalists.
BUSINESS: FOOD: Health Food

THE OBSERVATORY MAGAZINE
39994U55-120

Editorial Address: 16 Swan Close, Grove, WANTAGE, OX12 0QE **Tel:** 01235 767509
Email: manager@obsmag.org
Advertising Address: As above.
Email: manager@obsmag.org
Web site: http://www.ulo.ucl.ac.uk/obsmag
ISSN: 0029-7704
Publisher: The Editors of The Observatory
Date Established: 1877
Frequency: 6 issues yearly
Annual Sub.: £70.00
Circulation: 850 (Publisher's Statement)
Usual Pagination: 60
Editor: David Stickland; **Advertising Manager:** David Stickland; **Managing Editor:** David Stickland
Summary of Content: Publication reporting on meetings of the Royal Astronomical Society. Covers scientific papers, notes, book reviews and correspondence.
Readership/Target Audience: Read by astronomers, including many fellows of the RAS.
ADVERTISING RATES:
Full Page Mono £120.00
Mechanical Data: Film: Positive, right reading, emulsion side down. Digital, Trim Size: 210 x 148mm
Copy instructions: Copy Date: 2 months prior to publication date
BUSINESS: APPLIED SCIENCE & LABORATORIES

THE OBSTETRICIAN & GYNAECOLOGIST
623936U56R-92_10

Editorial Address: Publications Department RCOG, 27 Sussex Place, Regents Park, LONDON, NW1 4RG
Tel: 020 7772 6300 **Fax:** 020 7772 6273
Email: tog@rcog.org.uk
Advertising Address: As above.
Email: togads@rcog.org.uk
Web site: http://www.rcog.org.uk/tog
ISSN: 1467-2561
Publisher: RCOG Press
Date Established: 1999
Frequency: Quarterly
Free to qualifying individuals
Annual Sub.: £39.00
Circulation: 13,500 (Publisher's Statement)
Usual Pagination: 80
Editor: Susan Molony; **Advertising Manager:** Sarah Monger; **Managing Editor:** Susan Molony
Summary of Content: Journal for continuing professional development from The Royal College of Obstetricians & Gynaecologists containing information on current practice and research within the obstetric and gynaecology profession, including reviews, current papers, risk management, new developments, education articles, ethics articles and book reviews.
Readership/Target Audience: Aimed at all practising specialist obstetricians and gynaecologists, trainees and health professionals, including midwives and general practitioners.
ADVERTISING RATES:
Full Page Mono £945.00
Full Page Colour £1420.00
Agency Commission: 10%
Mechanical Data: Page Width: 185mm, Film: Digital, Bleed Size: 303 x 216mm, Trim Size: 297 x 210mm, Type Area: 254 x 185mm, Col Length: 254mm, No. of Columns (Display): 2
Copy instructions: Copy Date: 5 weeks prior to publication date
Average advertising content per issue: 10%
BUSINESS: HEALTH & MEDICAL: Health Medical Related

OCC COUNTRY
1696060U47A-581

Editorial Address: 1 The Square, WIMBORNE, BH21 1PS
Tel: 01202 841114 **Fax:** 01202 842314
Email: simon@occoutdoor.com
Advertising Address: Alibi Publishing Waggoner's Barn, Hunningham House, Long Itchington Road, Hunningham, LEAMINGTON SPA, CV33 9EW **Tel:** 01926 632583
Fax: 01926 632583
Email: lizzie@occoutdoor.com
Web site: http://www.occoutdoor.co.uk
Publisher: Alibi Publishing Ltd
Frequency: Quarterly
Cover Price: Free
Circulation: 2,800 (Publisher's Statement)
Usual Pagination: 32
Editor: Simon Baseley
Summary of Content: Magazine focusing on country clothing, goods and equipment.
Readership/Target Audience: Aimed at suppliers, retailers and distributors in the country trade.
ADVERTISING RATES:
Full Page Colour £1265.00
Agency Commission: 10%
Mechanical Data: Type Area: 280 x 225mm, Bleed Size: 311 x 256mm, Trim Size: 303 x 250mm, Col Length: 280mm, Page Width: 225mm, Film: Digital
Average advertising content per issue: 50%
BUSINESS: CLOTHING & TEXTILES

OCC OUTDOOR
39505U47A-257

Editorial Address: 1 The Square, WIMBORNE, BH21 1PS
Tel: 01202 841114 **Fax:** 01202 841314
Email: simon@occoutdoor.com
Advertising Address: Waggoners Cottage, Hunningham House Farm, Long Itchington Road, Hunningham, LEAMINGTON SPA, CV33 9EW **Tel:** 01926 632583
Fax: 01926 632583
Email: lizzie@occoutdoor.com
Web site: http://www.occoutdoor.com
Publisher: Alibi Publishing Ltd
Frequency: Monthly
Cover Price: Free
Circulation: 3,240 (Publisher's Statement)
Usual Pagination: 32
Editor: Simon Baseley; **Advertising Manager:** Lizzie Bendle
Summary of Content: Magazine focusing on outdoor clothing, goods and equipment.
Readership/Target Audience: Aimed at suppliers, retailers and distributors in the outdoor trade.
ADVERTISING RATES:
Full Page Colour £1265.00
Agency Commission: 10%
Mechanical Data: Type Area: 280 x 220mm, Bleed Size: 311 x 256mm, Trim Size: 303 x 244mm, Col Length: 280mm, Page Width: 220mm, Print Process: Sheet-fed litho, Film: Digital
Copy instructions: Copy Date: 2 weeks prior to publication date
BUSINESS: CLOTHING & TEXTILES

OCCUPATIONAL AND ENVIRONMENTAL MEDICINE
40544U56R-93

Editorial Address: BMA House, Tavistock Square, LONDON, WC1H 9JR **Tel:** 020 7383 6235
Fax: 020 7383 6668
Advertising Address: As above. **Tel:** 020 7387 4499
Fax: 020 7383 6556
Email: ecurrer@bmj.com
Web site: http://www.occenvmed.com
ISSN: 1351-0711
Publisher: BMJ Publishing Group
Date Established: 1943
Frequency: Monthly
Annual Sub.: £135.00
Circulation: 2,590 (Publisher's Statement)
Usual Pagination: 72
Editor: Francesca Grillo; **Advertising Manager:** Euan Currer
Summary of Content: Journal covering industrial, occupational and environmental medicine.
Readership/Target Audience: Aimed at doctors and specialists.
ADVERTISING RATES:
Full Page Mono £910.00
Full Page Colour £1610.00
Agency Commission: 10%
Mechanical Data: Type Area: 243 x 186mm, Col Length: 243mm, Bleed Size: 286 x 216mm, Trim Size: 280 x 210mm, Film: Digital, Page Width: 186mm
Copy instructions: Copy Date: 20th of 2 months prior to publication date
BUSINESS: HEALTH & MEDICAL: Health Medical Related

OCCUPATIONAL HEALTH AT WORK
1777115U54B-110

Editorial Address: 19 Bishops Avenue, Elstree, BOREHAMWOOD, WD6 3LZ **Tel:** 0845 017 6986
Fax: 020 8275 8469
Email: info@atworkpartnership.co.uk
Web site: http://www.atworkpartnership.co.uk
ISSN: 1744-2265
Publisher: The At Work Partnership Ltd
Date Established: 2004
Frequency: 6 issues yearly
Annual Sub.: £199.00
Usual Pagination: 44
Editor: John Ballard
Summary of Content: Journal covering the science, law and practice of occupational health.
Readership/Target Audience: Aimed at occupational health professionals including occupational physicians, OH nurses and hygienists.
ADVERTISING: No Advertising taken
BUSINESS: SAFETY & SECURITY: Safety

OCCUPATIONAL HEALTH JOURNAL
40324U56B-270

Editorial Address: Quadrant House, The Quadrant, SUTTON, SM2 5AS **Tel:** 020 8652 4669 **Fax:** 020 8652 8805
Email: oh.editor@rbi.co.uk
Advertising Address: As above. **Tel:** 020 8652 4668
Fax: 020 8652 4832
Email: mark.pickup@rbi.co.uk
Web site: http://www.personneltoday.com/occupational-health
ISSN: 0029-7917
Publisher: Reed Business Information
Frequency: Monthly
Annual Sub.: £120.00
Circulation: 4,669 (ABC 01/01/2008 to 31/12/2008)
Usual Pagination: 50
Editor: Noel O'Reilly
Summary of Content: Journal relating to employees healthcare within the workplace. Also articles with a safety aspect.
Readership/Target Audience: Aimed at occupational health practitioners, tutors and consultants.
ADVERTISING RATES:
Full Page Mono £1236.00
Full Page Colour £1622.00
Mechanical Data: Col Length: 260mm, Film: Digital, Type Area: 260 x 184mm, Bleed Size: 303 x 216mm, Trim Size: 297 x 210mm, Page Width: 184mm
BUSINESS: HEALTH & MEDICAL: Nursing

OCCUPATIONAL MEDICINE
40210U56A-107_50

Editorial Address: Society of Occupational Medicine, 6 St. Andrews Place, Regents Park, LONDON, NW1 4LB
Tel: 020 7486 2641
Email: omjournal@som.org.uk
Advertising Address: Oxford University Press, Great Clarendon Street, OXFORD, OX2 6DP **Tel:** 01865 354637
Fax: 01865 353774
Email: steve.simmonds@oxfordjournals.org
Web site: http://www.oup.co.uk/jnls
ISSN: 0962-7408
Publisher: OUP
Date Established: 1951
Frequency: 8 issues yearly
Cover Price: £23.00
Annual Sub.: £155.00
Usual Pagination: 72
Editor: John Hobson
Summary of Content: Journal covering all aspects of occupational medicine.
Readership/Target Audience: Aimed at full-time occupational physicians and GPs with a part-time appointment in industry.
ADVERTISING RATES:
Full Page Mono £742.00
Full Page Colour £1236.00
Agency Commission: 10%
Mechanical Data: Print Process: Litho, Type Area: 255 x 178mm, Col Length: 255mm, Trim Size: 279 x 216mm, Bleed Size: 285 x 222mm, Film: Digital, Page Width: 178mm
BUSINESS: HEALTH & MEDICAL

OCCUPATIONAL PENSIONS
35360U1H-40

Editorial Address: 15 Copper Beech Close, HEMEL HEMPSTEAD, HP3 0DG **Tel:** 01442 259349
Email: op@irseclipse.co.uk
Web site: http://www.lexisnexisconnect.co.uk
ISSN: 0952-231X
Publisher: LexisNexis
Date Established: 1987
Frequency: Monthly
Annual Sub.: £325.00
Usual Pagination: 20
Editor: Colin Sherwood

Summary of Content: Journal covering occupational pensions, specialising in case studies and surveys of named pension schemes.
Readership/Target Audience: Aimed at pensions, personnel and finance managers, company secretaries, trade union officials, professional advisers and trustees.
ADVERTISING: No Advertising taken
BUSINESS: FINANCE & ECONOMICS: Pensions

OCCUPATIONAL THERAPY NEWS
40543U56R-93_50

Editorial Address: 106-114 Borough High Street, LONDON, SE1 1LB **Tel:** 020 7450 2339 **Fax:** 020 7450 2350
Email: editorial@cot.co.uk
Advertising Address: As above. **Tel:** 020 7450 2341
Email: advertising@cot.co.uk
Web site: http://www.cot.co.uk
ISSN: 0969-5095
Publisher: The College of Occupational Therapists Ltd
Frequency: Monthly - Published on the 1st of the cover month
Cover Price: Free
Circulation: 29,000 (Publisher's Statement)
Usual Pagination: 64
Editor: Tracey Samuels; **Advertising Manager:** Steve Meertens
Summary of Content: Magazine containing news, features and up to date information relating to occupational therapy.
Readership/Target Audience: Aimed at full-time and part-time occupational therapists and students.
ADVERTISING RATES:
Full Page Mono £1100.00
Full Page Colour £1750.00
Agency Commission: 10%
Mechanical Data: Type Area: 265 x 186mm, Col Length: 265mm, Col Widths (Display): 42mm, Film: Digital, No. of Columns (Display): 4, Bleed Size: 297 x 210mm, Trim Size: 293 x 207mm, Page Width: 186mm
Copy instructions: Copy Date: 14th of the month prior to publication date
Average advertising content per issue: 40%
BUSINESS: HEALTH & MEDICAL: Health Medical Related

OCEAN CHALLENGE
40072U55-120_5

Editorial Address: Aurora Lodge, DITTSHAM, TQ6 0ES
Tel: 01803 722513
Email: a.m.colling@open.ac.uk
Advertising Address: National Oceanography Centre, Waterfront Campus, SOUTHAMPTON, SO14 3AH
Tel: 023 8059 6097 **Fax:** 023 8059 6149
Email: jxj@noc.soton.ac.uk
Web site: http://www.challenger-society.org.uk
ISSN: 0959-0161
Publisher: Challenger Society for Marine Science
Date Established: 1990
Frequency: 3 issues yearly - Published in January, May and November
Free to qualifying individuals
Annual Sub.: £40.00
Circulation: 600 (Publisher's Statement)
Usual Pagination: 32
Editor: Angela Colling; **Advertising Manager:** Jennifer Jones
Summary of Content: Official journal of the Challenger Society for Marine Science, containing feature articles, news, meeting reports and book reviews.
Readership/Target Audience: Aimed at those engaged in oceanographic and related studies worldwide and at non-professionals interested in the science of the sea.
ADVERTISING: Rates on application
BUSINESS: APPLIED SCIENCE & LABORATORIES

OE RETAILER
1705242U53-696

Editorial Address: The Old Dairy, Hudsons Farm, Fieldgate Lane, Ugley Green, BISHOP'S STORTFORD, CM22 6HJ
Tel: 01279 816300 **Fax:** 01279 816496
Email: rebecca.corbally@yahoo.co.uk
Advertising Address: As above.
Email: sallyjane.evans@oe-mag.com
Web site: http://www.oe-mag.com
Publisher: Target Publishing Ltd
Date Established: 2005
Frequency: Quarterly
Cover Price: Free
Circulation: 1,200 (Publisher's Statement)
Usual Pagination: 32
Editor: Rebecca Corbally; **Advertising Manager:** Sally-Jane Evans
Summary of Content: Magazine focusing on outdoor goods. Topics covered include news, interviews, market overviews, products, training, better retail practice and awards.
Readership/Target Audience: Aimed at retailers, agents, distributors and manufacturers.
ADVERTISING RATES:
Full Page Colour £1295.00

Business Magazines

Agency Commission: 10%
Mechanical Data: Film: Digital, Bleed Size: 303 x 216mm, Trim Size: 297 x 210mm
Average advertising content per issue: 35%
BUSINESS: RETAILING & WHOLESALING

OEN
38652U34-40_13

Editorial Address: Wilmington House, Maidstone Road, Foots Cray, SIDCUP, DA14 5HZ **Tel:** 020 8269 7785
Fax: 020 8269 7877
Email: michelle.ryder@clearercommunications.co.uk
Advertising Address: Progressive House, Maidstone Road, Foots Cray, SIDCUP, DA14 5HZ **Tel:** 020 8269 7700
Fax: 020 8269 7877
Email: swight@progressivemediagroup.com
Publisher: Office Solutions Media Limited
Date Established: 1956
Frequency: Monthly
Cover Price: £6.95
Free to qualifying individuals
Annual Sub.: £60.00
Circulation: 15,450 (Publisher's Statement)
Usual Pagination: 44
Editor: Michelle Ryder
Summary of Content: Journal providing essential information for buyers of office equipment, product services and supplies within large companies.
Readership/Target Audience: Aimed at purchasers and specifiers of office equipment, products, stationery and associated services within large corporate organisations.
ADVERTISING RATES:
Full Page Colour £2850.00
Agency Commission: 10%
Mechanical Data: Type Area: 272 x 185mm, Col Length: 272mm, Page Width: 185mm, Bleed Size: 303 x 216mm, Trim Size: 297 x 210mm, Film: Digital
Copy instructions: Copy Date: 4 weeks prior to publication date
Average advertising content per issue: 50%
BUSINESS: OFFICE EQUIPMENT

OFAS NEWSLETTER
1615452U34-202

Editorial Address: Manhattan House, 140 High Street, CROWTHORNE, RG45 7AY **Tel:** 01344 779438
Fax: 01344 779143
Email: ofas@ofas.org.uk
Web site: http://www.ofas.org.uk
Publisher: OFAS
Date Established: 1996
Frequency: Quarterly
Cover Price: Free
Circulation: 9,500 (Publisher's Statement)
Usual Pagination: 32
Editor: Margaret Haynes; **Managing Director:** Margaret Haynes
Summary of Content: Newsletter covering office furniture and related products.
Readership/Target Audience: Aimed at facilities managers, architects and design professionals and furniture managers, agents and dealers.
ADVERTISING: No Advertising taken
BUSINESS: OFFICE EQUIPMENT

OFF HIGHWAY ENGINEERING
1725811U19A-582

Editorial Address: Lee Farm, Fyfield, ESSEX, CM5 0RN
Tel: 01277 899476 **Fax:** 01277 899611
Email: stuart.birch@btopenworld.com
Web site: http://www.sae.org/mags/sohe/
Publisher: Society of Automotive Engineers Inc.
Date Established: 1993
Frequency: 8 issues yearly
Free to qualifying individuals
Circulation: 15,934 (BPA Worldwide 01/01/2009 to 30/06/2009)
Editor: Stuart Birch
Summary of Content: Magazine for the Global off-highway engineering community, delivering analysis and news.
Readership/Target Audience: Aimed at those in the International off-highway design and manufacturing field.
ADVERTISING: Rates on application
BUSINESS: ENGINEERING & MACHINERY

OFFICE PRODUCTS INTERNATIONAL
38655U34-70

Editorial Address: Diamond House, 36-38 Hatton Garden, LONDON, EC1N 8EB **Tel:** 020 7841 2950
Fax: 020 7841 2951
Email: stephen.white@opi.net
Advertising Address: As above.
Email: chris.turness@opi.net
Web site: http://www.opi.net
ISSN: 1360-8460
Publisher: Nelson Media Ltd
Date Established: 1991

Frequency: 10 issues yearly
Free to qualifying individuals
Annual Sub.: $295.00
Circulation: 12,096 (Publisher's Statement)
Usual Pagination: 80
Editor: Stephen White; **News Editor:** Rufus Jay; **Features Editor:** Andy Braithwaite; **Advertising Manager:** Chris Turness
Summary of Content: Guide to the international office products industry.
Readership/Target Audience: Aimed at senior executives and decision makers within the international office supplies and computer consumables business.
ADVERTISING RATES:
Full Page Colour £4000.00
Agency Commission: 10%
Mechanical Data: Type Area: 267 x 190mm, Bleed Size: 281 x 204mm, Trim Size: 277 x 200mm, Col Length: 267mm, Page Width: 190mm
Copy instructions: Copy Date: 2 weeks prior to publication date
Average advertising content per issue: 40%
BUSINESS: OFFICE EQUIPMENT

THE OFFICER
48703U40-220

Editorial Address: 19 Heddon Street, LONDON, W1B 4BG
Tel: 020 7993 3833 **Fax:** 020 7437 4209
Email: angelat@oneismore.com
Advertising Address: As above. **Fax:** 020 7793 4059
Email: jameslg@oneismore.com
Web site: http://www.theofficer.net
Publisher: One
Date Established: 1990
Frequency: 6 issues yearly
Free to qualifying individuals
Annual Sub.: £31.00
Circulation: 13,500 (Publisher's Statement)
Usual Pagination: 84
Editor: Michael Dewar; **Managing Director:** Michael Dewar; **Advertising Manager:** James Lyall Grant; **Publisher:** Michael Dewar
Summary of Content: Magazine covering strategy and defence related politics, lifestyle and re-settlement.
Readership/Target Audience: Aimed at serving and retired commissioned officers and senior non-commissioned officers in all the armed services.
ADVERTISING RATES:
Full Page Mono £1650.00
Full Page Colour £2000.00
Agency Commission: 10%
Mechanical Data: Film: Digital, Trim Size: 297 x 210mm, Type Area: 265 x 180mm, Col Length: 265mm, Page Width: 180mm
BUSINESS: DEFENCE

OFFSCREEN MAGAZINE
1892637U14J-551

Editorial Address: Michaelmas Cottage, Docking Road, Great Bircham, KING'S LYNN, PE31 6QP **Tel:** 01485 578571
Email: chris@offscreenmagazine.co.uk
Web site: http://www.offscreenmagazine.co.uk
Date Established: 2008
Frequency: 6 issues yearly
Cover Price: Free
Circulation: 3,000 (Publisher's Statement)
Usual Pagination: 36
Editor: Dominic Tolfts
Summary of Content: Magazine focusing on the art department and the art of production design. Covering television, film and theatre.
Readership/Target Audience: Aimed at television designers.
BUSINESS: COMMERCE, INDUSTRY & MANAGEMENT: Commercial Design

OFFSHORE
38601U33-10_30

Editorial Address: PO Box 32911, LONDON, SW19 5WL
Tel: 020 8946 7783 **Fax:** 020 8946 1543
Email: jeremyb@pennwell.com
Web site: http://www.offshore-mag.com
Publisher: PennWell Publishing Ltd
Frequency: Monthly - Published around the 20th of the cover month
Cover Price: Free
Circulation: 37,000 (Publisher's Statement)
Editor: Jeremy Beckman
Summary of Content: Journal containing information on innovative new technologies for offshore exploration, development and production activities worldwide.
Readership/Target Audience: Aimed at company managers, technicians, business analysts, suppliers, contractors and designers in the industry.
ADVERTISING: No Advertising taken
BUSINESS: OIL & PETROLEUM

OFFSHORE ENGINEER
38602U33-11

Editorial Address: The Arena, Stockley Park, UXBRIDGE, UB11 1AA **Tel:** 020 8899 1765
Email: dmorgan@offshore-engineer.com
Advertising Address: Alad Ltd, 168 St. Johns Hill, SEVENOAKS, TN13 3PF **Tel:** 01732 459683
Email: steve@aladltd.co.uk
Web site: http://www.offshore-engineer.com
ISSN: 9395-876X
Publisher: Atlantic Communications
Date Established: 1975
Frequency: Monthly - Published in the first week of the cover month
Free to qualifying individuals
Annual Sub.: £160.00
Circulation: 35,180 (Publisher's Statement)
Usual Pagination: 80
Editor: David Morgan; **Editor-in-Chief:** David Morgan; **Advertising Manager:** Steve Powell
Summary of Content: Journal about technical and international developments in the offshore oil and gas industry.
Readership/Target Audience: Aimed at operation managers and engineers in oil and gas organisations, supply companies and main and sub contractors.
ADVERTISING RATES:
Full Page Mono £6080.00
Full Page Colour £7680.00
Agency Commission: 10%
Mechanical Data: No. of Columns (Display): 3, Type Area: 255 x 180mm, Trim Size: 275 x 205mm, Col Length: 255mm, Bleed Size: 285 x 210mm, Page Width: 180mm, Film: Digital
Copy instructions: Copy Date: 14th of the month prior to publication date
Average advertising content per issue: 40%
BUSINESS: OIL & PETROLEUM

OFFSHORE INVESTMENT
35282U1F-305_50

Editorial Address: Lombard House, 10-20 Lombard Street, BELFAST, BT1 1BW **Tel:** 028 9032 8777 **Fax:** 028 9032 8555
Email: editorial@offshoreinvestment.com
Advertising Address: As above.
Email: advertising@offshoreinvestment.com
Web site: http://www.offshoreinvestment.com
ISSN: 0954-0628
Publisher: European Magazine Services Limited
Date Established: 1986
Frequency: 10 issues yearly - Published in the 1st week of the month
Annual Sub.: £320.00
Circulation: 10,000 (Publisher's Statement)
Usual Pagination: 48
Editor: Karen Wasson; **Editor-in-Chief:** Charles Cain; **Publisher:** Barry Bingham
Summary of Content: Journal covering all aspects of the offshore financial world. Includes trusts, private banking, managed funds, tax and estate planning, offshore leasing and other associated topics.
Readership/Target Audience: Aimed at professionals in the offshore world and their clients.
ADVERTISING RATES:
Full Page Mono £3990.00
Full Page Colour £5100.00
Agency Commission: 10%
Mechanical Data: Type Area: 267 x 175mm, Bleed Size: 303 x 216mm, Trim Size: 297 x 210mm, Page Width: 175mm, Col Length: 267mm, Film: Digital
Copy instructions: Copy Date: 3 weeks prior to publication date
Average advertising content per issue: 40%
BUSINESS: FINANCE & ECONOMICS: Investment

OFFSHORE MARINE MONTHLY
39340U45A-120_20

Formerly: Offshore Fleet Economics
Editorial Address: Bon Accord House, Riverside Drive, ABERDEEN, AB11 7SL **Tel:** 01224 597800
Fax: 01224 580320
Email: ods-petrodata.co.uk
Web site: http://www.ods-petrodata.com
ISSN: 0226-3112
Publisher: ODS-Petrodata UK Ltd
Frequency: Monthly
Usual Pagination: 20
Editor: David Bichard; **Publisher:** David Bichard
Summary of Content: Magazine covering marine activity for offshore markets. Includes latest newbuilds, market trends and fixtures of supply vessels and other support vessels. Also covers market information and analysis as well as issues facing supply vessel owners, such as crewing and equipment shortages.
Readership/Target Audience: Aimed at supply vessel owners and those involved in offshore fleet industry.
ADVERTISING: No Advertising taken
BUSINESS: MARINE & SHIPPING

OFFSHORE RED
1702772U1M-86

Editorial Address: 1 St. John's Square, LONDON, EC1M 4PN **Tel:** 020 7214 0500 **Fax:** 020 7214 0501
Email: offshorered@campden.com
Web site: http://www.campden.com
ISSN: 1465-2528
Publisher: Campden Publishing Ltd
Frequency: 10 issues yearly
Annual Sub: £495.00
Circulation: 400 (Publisher's Statement)
Usual Pagination: 24
Editor: Bob Reynolds
Summary of Content: Newsletter focusing on financial planning and international tax legislation.
Readership/Target Audience: Aimed at wealth managers and tax planners.
ADVERTISING: No Advertising taken
BUSINESS: FINANCE & ECONOMICS: Taxation

OFFSHORE TECHNOLOGY
1892655U33-93

Editorial Address: 80 Coleman Street, LONDON, EC2R 5BJ
Tel: 020 7382 2600 **Fax:** 020 7382 2669
Email: bruce.mcmichael@imarest.org
Publisher: IMarEST
Date Established: 2009
Frequency: Quarterly
Editor: Bruce McMichael
Summary of Content: Magazine covering offshore technology.
Readership/Target Audience: Aimed at professionals in the offshore sector.
BUSINESS: OIL & PETROLEUM

OIL AND ENERGY TRENDS
38611U33-34

Editorial Address: 9600 Garsington Road, Cowley, OXFORD, OX4 2DQ **Tel:** 01865 776868 **Fax:** 01865 714591
Email: akachkova@wiley.com
Web site: http://www.blackwellpublishing.com
ISSN: 0950-1045
Publisher: Wiley-Blackwell Publishing
Date Established: 1976
Frequency: Monthly - Published the 3rd Friday of the month
Annual Sub.: £1939.00
Circulation: 400 (Publisher's Statement)
Usual Pagination: 56
Editor: Anna Kachkova
Summary of Content: Journal containing international energy statistics and analysis of oil exploration and production, gas production, coal production, steel production, electricity production, refinery throughput, oil demand, oil prices, international commodities trade, tanker movements and freight rates.
Readership/Target Audience: Aimed at oil companies, research managers, directors, oil traders, government energy and petroleum departments, non-government organisations, think-tanks and universities.
ADVERTISING: No Advertising taken
Supplement(s): OET Annual Statistical Review - 1xY
BUSINESS: OIL & PETROLEUM

OIL & GAS NEWS
38607U33-30

Editorial Address: Crescent Court, 102 Victor Road, TEDDINGTON, TW11 8SS **Tel:** 020 8943 3630
Email: hilalmag@tradearabia.net
Advertising Address: As above. **Fax:** 020 8943 3701
Email: nhorne@hilal.co.uk
Web site: http://www.oilandgasnewsonline.com
ISSN: 0217-5541
Publisher: Hilal International (UK) Ltd
Date Established: 1983
Frequency: Weekly
Annual Sub.: $690.00
Circulation: 8,409 (Publisher's Statement)
Usual Pagination: 32
Editor: Nick Horne; **Advertising Manager:** Nick Horne
Summary of Content: Magazine containing news stories focusing on exploration, refining and petrochemicals.
Readership/Target Audience: Aimed at people working in the petroleum industry in Asia, the Middle East and the Pacific.
ADVERTISING RATES:
Full Page Mono $4690.00
Full Page Colour $6566.00
SCC $16.75
Agency Commission: 15%
Mechanical Data: Film: Positive, right reading, emulsion side down, Type Area: 400 x 275mm, Col Length: 400mm, Print Process: Sheet-fed offset litho, Trim Size: 420 x 290mm, Bleed Size: + 5mm, Col Widths (Display): 35mm, Page Width: 275mm, No. of Columns (Display): 7
Copy instructions: Copy Date: 3 weeks prior to publication date
BUSINESS: OIL & PETROLEUM

OIL & GAS TECHNOLOGY
1778658U33-87

Editorial Address: 15-19 Great Chapel Street, LONDON, W1F 8FN **Tel:** 020 7758 3040 **Fax:** 020 7758 3001
Email: b.avison@cavendishgroup.co.uk
Advertising Address: As above. **Tel:** 020 7758 3000
Email: j.mcbarek@cavendishgroup.co.uk
Publisher: Cavendish Group
Frequency: Quarterly
Free to qualifying individuals
Circulation: 8,162 (Publisher's Statement)
Editor: Martin Clark; **Editor-in-Chief:** Ben Avison;
Advertising Manager: Jamie McBarek
Summary of Content: Publication focusing on the key areas of the fossil fuel business. It addresses the technical challenges facing China's oil and gas sector examining the latest innovations developed in the west. Coverage includes topical developments and the latest technologies.
Readership/Target Audience: Aimed at those involved in the oil and gas industry within China.
ADVERTISING RATES:
Full Page Colour £5650.00
Agency Commission: 10%
Mechanical Data: Bleed Size: 218 x 292mm, Trim Size: 212 x 286mm, Film: Digital
Copy instructions: Copy Date: Middle of the month prior to publication date
Average advertising content per issue: 30%
BUSINESS: OIL & PETROLEUM

OIL CITY NEWS
38608U33-31

Editorial Address: PO Box 6, HADDINGTON, EH41 3NQ
Tel: 01620 822578 **Fax:** 01620 822578
Email: allscotnews@btinternet.com
Advertising Address: As above. **Fax:** 01620 825079
Publisher: Rae-Lin Communications
Frequency: Monthly
Usual Pagination: 48
Editor: Richard Brown; **Advertising Manager:** Angela Brown
Summary of Content: Magazine containing news and information on financial aspects, company mergers, take-overs and annual reports in the oil and gas industry worldwide.
Readership/Target Audience: Aimed at those in government, financial directors, shareholders and investors and company directors.
BUSINESS: OIL & PETROLEUM

OIL NEWS AND GAS INTERNATIONAL
38613U33-40

Editorial Address: PO Box 6, HADDINGTON, EH41 3NQ
Tel: 01620 822578 **Fax:** 01620 822578
Email: allscotnews@btinternet.com
Advertising Address: As above. **Fax:** 01620 825079
Email: allscottnews@btinternet.com
Publisher: Rae-Lin Communications
Frequency: Monthly
Annual Sub.: £30.00
Usual Pagination: 34
Editor: Richard Brown; **Advertising Manager:** Angela Brown
Summary of Content: Magazine containing news and information on oil and gas fields being explored, appraised and developed around the world.
Readership/Target Audience: Aimed at oil and gas companies around the world.
BUSINESS: OIL & PETROLEUM

OIL REVIEW MIDDLE EAST
38610U33-33_50

Editorial Address: University House, 11-13 Lower Grosvenor Place, LONDON, SW1W 0EX **Tel:** 020 7834 7676
Fax: 020 7973 0076
Email: oil@alaincharles.com
Advertising Address: As above.
Email: sales@alaincharles.co.uk
Web site: http://www.alaincharles.com
ISSN: 1464-9314
Publisher: Alain Charles Publishing Ltd
Date Established: 1997
Frequency: 7 issues yearly
Annual Sub.: £32.00
Circulation: 9,034 (ABC 01/01/2008 to 31/12/2008)
Usual Pagination: 98
Editor: David Clancy; **Managing Director:** Derek Fordham;
Managing Editor: David Clancy; **Publisher:** Derek Fordham
Summary of Content: Magazine featuring major projects, specific industry sector profiles, country reports, exhibition previews and product reviews.
Readership/Target Audience: Aimed at the regional oil, gas and petrochemicals industries and the companies supplying these industries.
ADVERTISING RATES:
Full Page Mono $4070.00
Full Page Colour $5990.00
Agency Commission: 15%

OIL & GAS TECHNOLOGY (right column top)
Mechanical Data: Type Area: 255 x 182mm, Page Width: 182mm, Col Length: 255mm, Trim Size: 276 x 210mm, Bleed Size: 282 x 216mm
Average advertising content per issue: 40%
BUSINESS: OIL & PETROLEUM

OILS & FATS INTERNATIONAL
35395U1L-55

Editorial Address: Westgate House, 120-130 Station Road, REDHILL, RH1 1ET **Tel:** 01737 855000 **Fax:** 01737 855034
Email: serenalim@dmgworldmedia.com
Advertising Address: As above.
Email: anitarevis@dmgworldmedia.com
Web site: http://www.oilsandfatsinternational.com
ISSN: 0267-8853
Publisher: DMG Business Media
Date Established: 1984
Frequency: 8 issues yearly
Cover Price: £28.00
Annual Sub.: £114.00
Circulation: 6,500 (Publisher's Statement)
Usual Pagination: 40
Editor: Serena Lim
Summary of Content: Publication containing general, biotechnology, transport/logistic and oleochemicals/surfactants news as well as a market review on production and supply and demand trends affecting oils and oilseeds trade.
Readership/Target Audience: Aimed at buyers and specifiers of a wide range of products and services relating to the edible oils and fats industry.
ADVERTISING RATES:
Full Page Mono £2549.00
Full Page Colour £3819.00
Mechanical Data: Bleed Size: 303 x 216mm, Trim Size: 297 x 210mm, Film: Digital, Type Area: 265 x 185mm, Col Length: 265mm, Page Width: 185mm
Copy instructions: Copy Date: 4 weeks prior to publication date
BUSINESS: FINANCE & ECONOMICS: Commodities

OLN OFF LICENCE NEWS
36520U9D-163

Editorial Address: Broadfield Park, CRAWLEY, RH11 9RT
Tel: 01293 613400 **Fax:** 01293 610317
Email: rosie.davenport@william-reed.co.uk
Advertising Address: As above.
Email: samantha.briney@william-reed.co.uk
Web site: http://www.offlicencenews.co.uk
ISSN: 0043-5775
Publisher: William Reed Business Media
Date Established: 1970
Frequency: 24 issues yearly - Published every other Friday
Cover Price: £3.25
Free to qualifying individuals
Annual Sub.: £65.00
Circulation: 13,318 (ABC 01/07/2008 to 30/06/2009)
Usual Pagination: 32
Editor: Rosie Davenport; **Features Editor:** Nicola Collenette; **Publisher:** Lee Sharkey
Summary of Content: Journal covering news from within major off licence outlets, including supermarkets, cash and carry stores and the wider drinks industry.
Readership/Target Audience: Read by managers and decision makers within major off licence outlets and head offices of drinks suppliers and producers.
ADVERTISING RATES:
Full Page Colour £3870.00
Agency Commission: 10%
Mechanical Data: Film: Digital, Bleed Size: 346 x 251mm, Trim Size: 340 x 245mm, Col Length: 315mm, Page Width: 232mm, Type Area: 315 x 232mm
Copy instructions: Copy Date: 10 days prior to publication date
Average advertising content per issue: 40%
BUSINESS: DRINKS & LICENSED TRADE: Off-Licence

ON TARGET
760252U2F-48_50

Editorial Address: Unit 4, Clarks Courtyard, 145 Granville Street, BIRMINGHAM, B1 1SB **Tel:** 0870 609 2834
Fax: 0870 609 2836
Email: chris.ross@healthpublishing.co.uk
Advertising Address: As above.
Email: james.gray@healthpublishing.co.uk
Web site: http://www.ontargetmag.com
Publisher: Health Sector Publishing
Frequency: 11 issues yearly
Cover Price: Free
Circulation: 7,000 (Publisher's Statement)
Usual Pagination: 32
Editor: Joel Lane; **Advertising Manager:** James Gray
Summary of Content: Magazine covering market access, sales and marketing issues within the medical devices and technologies industry, as well as features on new technology and companies, industry information and jobs.
Readership/Target Audience: Aimed at those in sales and marketing within the healthcare industry.
ADVERTISING RATES:
Full Page Mono £1500.00

Business Magazines

Full Page Colour £1650.00
SCC £45.00
Agency Commission: 10%
Mechanical Data: Trim Size: 285 x 210mm, Film: Digital, Type Area: 265 x 190mm, Col Length: 265mm, Page Width: 190mm, Bleed Size: 291 x 216mm
Copy instructions: Copy Date: 2 weeks prior to publication date
Average advertising content per issue: 40%
BUSINESS: COMMUNICATIONS, ADVERTISING & MARKETING: Selling

ON THE BELL
40513U56P-100

Editorial Address: 260 Picton Road, Wavertree, LIVERPOOL, L15 4LP **Tel:** 0151 734 3038
Fax: 0151 734 2860
Email: zane@onthebell.co.uk
Advertising Address: As above.
Email: otb@gatepress.demon.co.uk
Web site: http://www.onthebell.co.uk
Publisher: Gateacre Press
Date Established: 1986
Frequency: Quarterly
Free to qualifying individuals
Annual Sub.: £18.00
Circulation: 12,000 (Publisher's Statement)
Usual Pagination: 36
Editor: Zane Bilall; **Managing Director:** Christine Elliot; **Advertising Manager:** Zane Bilall; **Publisher:** Zane Billal
Summary of Content: Magazine about the emergency services including IT news, new products and related human interest stories.
Readership/Target Audience: Aimed at the emergency services, personnel and manufacturers of equipment for the services.
ADVERTISING RATES:
Full Page Mono £525.00
Full Page Colour £1050.00
Agency Commission: 10%
Mechanical Data: Col Length: 262mm, Page Width: 175mm, Type Area: 262 x 175mm, Bleed Size: 302 x 215mm, Trim Size: 297 x 210mm, Print Process: Offset litho, Film: Digital
Copy instructions: Copy Date: Beginning of 2nd week of the month prior to publication date
Average advertising content per issue: 40%
BUSINESS: HEALTH & MEDICAL: Casualty & Emergency

ON TRADE SCOTLAND
1639864U9A-252

Formerly: MA Scotland
Editorial Address: 2nd Floor, Waterloo Chambers, 19 Waterloo Street, GLASGOW, G2 6AY **Tel:** 0141 222 2100
Fax: 0141 222 2177
Email: kscott@55north.com
Advertising Address: As above.
Email: dstephenson@55north.com
Publisher: 55 North
Date Established: 2005
Frequency: Monthly
Cover Price: £2.75
Free to qualifying individuals
Annual Sub.: £38.00
Usual Pagination: 56
Editor: Kevin Scott; **Advertising Manager:** Donald Stephenson
Summary of Content: Magazine dedicated to helping the Scottish on-trade run profitable and responsible businesses.
Readership/Target Audience: Aimed at licensees managers of on-trade venues in Scotland.
ADVERTISING RATES:
Full Page Colour £2100.00
SCC £30.00
Agency Commission: 10%
Mechanical Data: Type Area: 267 x 185mm, Col Length: 267mm, Page Width: 185mm, Film: Digital, Bleed Size: 303 x 216mm, Trim Size: 297 x 210mm
Copy instructions: Copy Date: 25th of the month prior to publication date
Average advertising content per issue: 40%
BUSINESS: DRINKS & LICENSED TRADE: Drinks, Licensed Trade, Wines & Spirits

ONBOARD HOSPITALITY
36575U11A-102

Editorial Address: Suffolk House, George Street, CROYDON, CR9 1SR **Tel:** 020 8649 7233
Fax: 020 8649 7234
Email: jo.austin@bmipublications.com
Advertising Address: As above.
Email: sue.williams@bmipublications.com
Web site: http://www.onboardhospitality.com
Publisher: BMI Publications Ltd
Date Established: 1989
Frequency: 5 issues yearly - Published in the 2nd week of the month
Free to qualifying individuals
Annual Sub.: £60.00
Circulation: 6,000 (Publisher's Statement)

Usual Pagination: 72
Editor: Jo Austin; **Managing Director:** Martin Steady; **Advertising Manager:** Sue Williams; **Managing Editor:** Alan Orbell
Summary of Content: Magazine covering all aspects of the on board services industries for cruise, rail, airlines and ferries.
Readership/Target Audience: Aimed at decision-makers within the travel hospitality industry throughout the world.
ADVERTISING RATES:
Full Page Colour £2990.00
Agency Commission: 10%
Mechanical Data: Page Width: 177mm, Type Area: 237 x 177mm, Col Length: 237mm, Film: Digital, No. of Columns (Display): 4, Bleed Size: 266 x 201mm, Trim Size: 258 x 195mm
Copy instructions: Copy Date: 4 weeks prior to publication date
Average advertising content per issue: 33%
BUSINESS: CATERING: Catering, Hotels & Restaurants

ONE TO ONE
40954U61-100

Editorial Address: Ludgate House, 245 Blackfriars Road, LONDON, SE1 9UY **Tel:** 020 7921 8376 **Fax:** 020 7921 8302
Email: elizabeth.toppin@ubm.com
Advertising Address: As above. **Tel:** 020 7921 8000
Email: paul.reynolds@ubm.com
Web site: http://www.oto-online.com
ISSN: 0268-8786
Publisher: UBM Information Ltd
Date Established: 1985
Frequency: 8 issues yearly
Cover Price: £6.00
Free to qualifying individuals
Annual Sub.: £59.00
Circulation: 10,500 (Publisher's Statement)
Usual Pagination: 64
Editor: Elizabeth Toppin; **Managing Editor:** Jo Ruddock; **Group Editor:** Tim Frost; **Publisher:** Joe Hosken
Summary of Content: Journal about the audio, video and data mastering, replication and duplication industries.
Readership/Target Audience: Aimed at people working in the DVD and CD replication and authoring industries, and the video and audio duplication markets.
ADVERTISING RATES:
Full Page Colour EUR4110.00
Agency Commission: 10%
Mechanical Data: Type Area: 292 x 220mm, Col Length: 292mm, Page Width: 220mm, Trim Size: 334 x 244mm, Bleed Size: 340 x 250mm, Film: Digital
Copy instructions: Copy Date: 15th of month prior to publication date
Average advertising content per issue: 40%
BUSINESS: MUSIC TRADE

ONLINE INFORMATION REVIEW
36279U5F-380

Formerly: Online & CD-ROM Review
Editorial Address: Howard House, Wagon Lane, BINGLEY, BD16 1WA **Tel:** 01274 777700 **Fax:** 01274 785200
Email: ebreen@emeraldinsight.com
Web site: http://www.emeraldinsight.com
ISSN: 1353-2642
Publisher: Emerald Group Publishing Ltd
Frequency: 6 issues yearly
Annual Sub.: £499.00
Usual Pagination: 72
Editor: Eileen Breen; **Publisher:** Eileen Breen
Summary of Content: Magazine reviewing online information sources, systems and services. Includes features on digital information retrieval and use in the contexts of academic, corporate and scientific research.
Readership/Target Audience: Aimed at librarians, information professionals and researchers.
ADVERTISING: No Advertising taken
BUSINESS: COMPUTERS & AUTOMATION: Multimedia

ONLINE RECRUITMENT
623161U14F-50_67

Editorial Address: Imperial House, Imperial Park, 46-48 Towerfield Road, Shoeburyness, SOUTHEND-ON-SEA, SS3 9QT **Tel:** 0870 766 8530 **Fax:** 0870 766 9582
Email: editor@onrec.com
Advertising Address: As above.
Email: david@onrec.com
Web site: http://www.onrec.com
Publisher: DH Publishing Ltd
Date Established: 2000
Frequency: Monthly
Annual Sub.: £60.00 (UK)
Circulation: 7,000 (Publisher's Statement)
Usual Pagination: 28
Editor: David Hurst; **Managing Director:** David Hurst; **Advertising Manager:** Matt Burney
Summary of Content: Magazine covering all aspects of the Internet recruitment industry. Includes features, opinions, information on new sites, statistics, profiles and industry analysis.

Readership/Target Audience: Aimed at recruitment and HR professionals involved in Internet recruitment.
ADVERTISING RATES:
Full Page Colour £2000.00
Agency Commission: 10%
Mechanical Data: Page Width: 180mm, Type Area: 260 x 180mm, Col Length: 260mm, Trim Size: 295 x 208mm, Bleed Size: 305 x 218mm, Film: Digital
Copy instructions: Copy Date: 1 week prior to publication date
Average advertising content per issue: 40%
BUSINESS: COMMERCE, INDUSTRY & MANAGEMENT: Training & Recruitment

THE ONLINE REPORTER
1866241U5E-9005

Editorial Address: PO Box 2077, Verney Park, BUCKINGHAM, MK18 1WQ **Tel:** 01280 820560
Fax: 01280 820554
Email: simon@riderresearch.com
Web site: http://www.riderresearch.com
Publisher: Information Express
Frequency: Weekly
Annual Sub.: £395.00
Circulation: 2,000 (Publisher's Statement)
Editor: Simon Thompson; **Editor-in-Chief:** Charles Hall
Summary of Content: Electronically delivered newsletter covering digital rights management (DRM), audio and video enabling technologies, internet music, copyright, media asset management, merging of PCs and home entertainment, internet security, privacy and wireless networking relevant to digital media.
Readership/Target Audience: Aimed at professionals in the telecoms, consumer electronics and media industry.
BUSINESS: COMPUTERS & AUTOMATION: Data Transmission

ONOFFICE
1789977U4B-184

Editorial Address: National House, 121-123 High Street, EPPING, CM16 4BD **Tel:** 01992 570030 **Fax:** 01992 570031
Email: rachel@onofficemagazine.com
Advertising Address: As above.
Email: liam@onofficemagazine.com
Web site: http://www.onofficemagazine.com
Publisher: Media 10
Frequency: Monthly
Cover Price: Free
Circulation: 13,608 (ABC 01/01/2008 to 31/12/2008)
Usual Pagination: 60
Editor: Rachel Calton; **Managing Director:** Lee Newton; **Advertising Manager:** Liam Evans
Summary of Content: Magazine focusing on all aspects of workplace and office design including technology, green issues, furniture and interior design.
Readership/Target Audience: Aimed at architects, designers and facilities managers.
ADVERTISING RATES:
Full Page Colour £3000.00
Agency Commission: 10%
Mechanical Data: Bleed Size: 326 x 251mm, Trim Size: 320 x 245mm, Film: Digital
Copy instructions: Copy Date: 1st week of the month prior to publication
Average advertising content per issue: 45%
BUSINESS: ARCHITECTURE & BUILDING: Interior Design & Flooring

ONSHORE REPORT EUROPE/AFRICA
38614U33-40_25

Editorial Address: PO Box 2779, LONDON, W2 6ZW
Tel: 020 7386 5703
Email: info@offshore-intelligence.org.uk
Web site: http://www.offshore-intelligence.org.uk
Publisher: Offshore Intelligence
Frequency: Weekly
Annual Sub.: £1300.00
Editor: Steve Garner
Summary of Content: Report covering onshore oil and gas exploration in Europe and Africa.
Readership/Target Audience: Read by people working within oil companies and suppliers of oil and gas exploration companies.
ADVERTISING: No Advertising taken
BUSINESS: OIL & PETROLEUM

OOH (OUT OF HOME) MAGAZINE
1695651U22A-393

Editorial Address: Suite 1, Bexley House, 77 Bexley High Street, BEXLEY, DA5 1JX **Tel:** 01322 526089
Email: suedunk@dsl.pipex.com
Advertising Address: As above. **Fax:** 01322 528172
Email: rhona.manning@btconnect.com
Publisher: Pybus Events and Publications Limited
Date Established: 2005
Frequency: Monthly

Free to qualifying individuals
Annual Sub.: £49.00
Circulation: 12,000 (Publisher's Statement)
Usual Pagination: 68
Editor: Sue Dunk; **Advertising Manager:** Rhona Manning;
Managing Editor: Sue Dunk; **Publisher:** Rhona Manning
Summary of Content: Magazine focusing on the brunch, lunch and snacks market.
Readership/Target Audience: Aimed at bakers, sandwich manufacturers, contract caterers, coffee shops, tea rooms, forecourts, universities, school meal providers and supermarkets.
ADVERTISING RATES:
Full Page Colour £2200.00
Agency Commission: 10%
Mechanical Data: Type Area: 265 x 180mm, Bleed Size: 303 x 212mm, Trim Size: 297 x 210mm, Col Length: 265mm, Page Width: 180mm, Film: Digital
Copy instructions: Copy Date: 20th of the month prior to publication date
Average advertising content per issue: 40%
BUSINESS: FOOD

OPEN SPACE
40717U57-38_60

Editorial Address: 25A Bell Street, HENLEY-ON-THAMES, RG9 2BA **Tel:** 01491 573535 **Fax:** 01491 573051
Email: hq@oss.org.uk
Advertising Address: As above.
Email: hq@oss.org.uk
Web site: http://www.oss.org.uk
ISSN: 0265-8445
Publisher: Open Spaces Society
Date Established: 1927
Frequency: 3 issues yearly - Published in February, June and October
Cover Price: £3.50
Circulation: 2,800 (Publisher's Statement)
Usual Pagination: 16
Editor: Kate Ashbrook; **Advertising Manager:** Kate Ashbrook
Summary of Content: Magazine containing news, advice, correspondence and legal reports on common land, village greens, open spaces and rights of way.
Readership/Target Audience: Aimed at members of the Open Spaces Society.
ADVERTISING RATES:
Full Page Mono £200.00
Mechanical Data: Col Widths (Display): 60mm, No. of Columns (Display): 2
Average advertising content per issue: 5%
BUSINESS: ENVIRONMENT & POLLUTION

OPENINGS
35971U4R-540

Editorial Address: PO Box 271, ROCHDALE, OL12 7YS
Tel: 01706 861662 **Fax:** 01706 861673
Email: editor@ta-publishing.co.uk
Advertising Address: As above.
Email: advertising@ta-publications.co.uk
Web site: http://www.openingsid.com
Publisher: t a publishing Ltd
Date Established: 2002
Frequency: Quarterly
Cover Price: Free
Circulation: 4,800 (Publisher's Statement)
Usual Pagination: 80
Editor: Tony Edmondson; **Managing Director:** Tony Edmondson; **Advertising Manager:** Neil Williamson;
Managing Editor: Tony Edmondson
Summary of Content: Journal of The British Blind and Shutter Association. Covers news, products and information.
Readership/Target Audience: Aimed at those in the blind and shutter trades.
ADVERTISING RATES:
Full Page Colour £958.00
Agency Commission: 10%
Mechanical Data: Type Area: 262 x 180mm, Film: Digital, Trim Size: 297 x 210mm, Col Length: 262mm, Page Width: 180mm, No. of Columns (Display): 2
Copy instructions: Copy Date: 3 weeks prior to publication date
Average advertising content per issue: 60%
BUSINESS: ARCHITECTURE & BUILDING: Building Related

OPENMIND
40489U56N-50

Editorial Address: Granta House, 15-19 Broadway, LONDON, E15 4BQ **Tel:** 0844 448 4449 **Fax:** 020 8215 2269
Email: openmind@mind.org.uk
Advertising Address: As above. **Tel:** 020 8215 2301
Fax: 020 8221 9681
Email: openmind@mind.org.uk
Web site: http://www.openmindmagazine.org.uk
ISSN: 0265-511X
Publisher: Mind - The Mental Health Charity
Date Established: 1983
Frequency: 6 issues yearly - Published on the 1st Thursday of the cover month
Annual Sub.: £24.00

Circulation: 4,200 (Publisher's Statement)
Usual Pagination: 32
Editor: Kathryn Perry; **Executive Editor:** Sara Dunn;
Publisher: Bridget O'Connell
Summary of Content: Magazine covering news, background and analysis updates on medication, mental health research, legal and parliamentary progress, mental health issues and rights, campaigns for change in the mental health system and provides support and insight through first-hand accounts of mental distress.
Readership/Target Audience: Read by mental health professionals, users of the services and carers.
ADVERTISING RATES:
Full Page Mono £460.00
Full Page Colour £700.00
Agency Commission: 10%
Mechanical Data: Type Area: 250 x 175mm, Bleed Size: 303 x 216mm, Trim Size: 297 x 210mm, Screen: 60 lpc, Film: Positive, right reading, emulsion side down, Col Length: 250mm, Page Width: 175mm
BUSINESS: HEALTH & MEDICAL: Mental Health .

THE OPERA QUARTERLY
601468U64K-587

Editorial Address: Great Clarendon Street, OXFORD, OX2 6DP **Tel:** 01865 353907 **Fax:** 01865 353485
Email: opera.quarterly@oxfordjournals.org
Advertising Address: 60 Upper Broadmoor Road, CROWTHORNE, RG45 7DE **Tel:** 01344 779945
Fax: 01344 779945
Email: lhann@lhms.fsnet.co.uk
Web site: http://www.oup.co.uk/jnls
ISSN: 0736-0053
Publisher: OUP
Date Established: 1984
Frequency: Quarterly
Cover Price: £14.00
Annual Sub.: £46.00
Usual Pagination: 192
Editor: Tami Wysocki-Niimi; **Executive Editor:** David Levin;
Managing Editor: Tami Wysocki-Niimi
Summary of Content: Journal covering all aspects of opera including reviews, interviews and features on composers and singers.
Readership/Target Audience: Aimed at musicologists, historians, musicians, vocalists, theatre professionals, librarians, scholars and students.
ADVERTISING RATES:
Full Page Mono £390.00
Agency Commission: 10%
Mechanical Data: Film: Positive, right reading, emulsion side down, Screen: 54 lpc, Type Area: 200 x 125mm, Col Length: 200mm, Page Width: 125mm
BUSINESS: OTHER CLASSIFICATIONS: Cinema Entertainment

THE OPERATING THEATRE JOURNAL
40206U56A-107_25

Formerly: News Review - The Operating Theatre Journal
Editorial Address: PO Box 51, PONTYCLUN, CF72 9YY
Tel: 020 7100 2867 **Fax:** 07092 097696
Email: admin@lawrand.com
Advertising Address: As above.
Email: admin@lawrand.com
Web site: http://www.otjonline.com
ISSN: 1747-728X
Publisher: Lawrand Limited (Medical Publishing)
Date Established: 1987
Frequency: Monthly - Published on the 18th of each month
Free to qualifying individuals
Annual Sub.: £14.00
Circulation: 5,000 (Publisher's Statement)
Usual Pagination: 16
Editor: Lawrence Evans; **Advertising Manager:** Lawrence Evans
Summary of Content: Journal containing anaesthetic, surgical and medical news as well as equipment reviews and recruitment pages for specialist staff.
Readership/Target Audience: Aimed at operating theatre technicians, operating department assistants and practitioners, theatre, anaesthetic and recovery room nurses, anaesthetists, surgeons, hospital managers and employment agencies. Hospital Supplies Officers were added to the circulation list in early 2006.
ADVERTISING RATES:
Full Page Mono £475.00
Full Page Colour £575.00
SCC £22.00
Agency Commission: 10%
Mechanical Data: Page Width: 197mm, Col Length: 276mm, Print Process: Litho, No. of Columns (Display): 4, Type Area: 276 x 197mm, Film: Positive, right reading, emulsion side down. Digital
Copy instructions: Copy Date: 25th of the month prior to publication date
Average advertising content per issue: 60%
BUSINESS: HEALTH & MEDICAL

OPERATIONS MANAGEMENT
37230U14R-60

Formerly: Control
Editorial Address: CILT (UK) Earlstrees Court, Earlstrees Industrial Estate, CORBY, NN17 4AX **Tel:** 01536 740105
Fax: 01536 740103
Email: journal@iomnet.org.uk
Advertising Address: As above. **Fax:** 01536 740101
Email: diane.jones@iomnet.org.uk
Web site: http://www.iomnet.org.uk
ISSN: 0266-1713
Publisher: Institute of Operations Management
Date Established: 1985
Frequency: 6 issues yearly
Annual Sub.: £135.00
Circulation: 1,500 (Publisher's Statement)
Usual Pagination: 48
Editor: Leonie Edwards
Summary of Content: Journal of the Institute of Operations Management. Each issue contains technical articles and case studies, related to operations management, materials management, production control, logistics, manufacturing management, inventory control systems, lean and supply chain; as well as items on Institute news, educational information and book reviews.
Readership/Target Audience: Aimed at directors and senior management in the manufacturing and service industries. Operations Management is sent to all members of the Institute as one of the benefits of membership. Readership includes operations managers, stock controllers, production directors and materials managers, and is used in surveys and analysis with the Business Schools of Warwick and Coventry Universities.
ADVERTISING RATES:
Full Page Mono £200.00
Full Page Colour £300.00
Agency Commission: 10%
Mechanical Data: Type Area: 250 x 170mm, Col Length: 250mm, Trim Size: 297 x 210mm, Bleed Size: 309 x 217mm, Print Process: Offset litho, Film: Digital preferred, Page Width: 170mm
Copy instructions: Copy Date: 2 weeks prior to publication date
BUSINESS: COMMERCE, INDUSTRY & MANAGEMENT: Commerce Related

OPHTHALMOLOGY TIMES EUROPE
1894703U56A-222

Editorial Address: Advanstar House, Park West, Sealand Road, CHESTER, CH1 4RN **Tel:** 01244 378888
Fax: 01244 370011
Email: pbrook@advanstar.com
Web site: http://www.oteurope.com
Publisher: Advanstar Communications (U.K.) Ltd
Date Established: 2006
Frequency: 10 issues yearly
Free to qualifying individuals
Editor: Pamela Brook; **Managing Editor:** Fedra Pavlou
Summary of Content: Publication featuring news and information on clinical, social and political issues, developments within the ophthalmic industry and a focus on cataract, corneal and refractive surgery, glaucoma and vitreoretinal conditions.
Readership/Target Audience: Aimed at members of the European ophthalmology community.
BUSINESS: HEALTH & MEDICAL

OPRISK & COMPLIANCE
35296U1F-305_60

Formerly: Operational Risk
Editorial Address: Haymarket House, 28-29 Haymarket, LONDON, SW1Y 4RX **Tel:** 020 7484 7000
Fax: 020 7930 2238
Email: victoria.pennington@incisivemedia.com
Advertising Address: As above. **Tel:** 020 7484 9700
Email: rachel.white@incisivemedia.com
Web site: http://www.opriskandcompliance.com
ISSN: 1084-8096
Publisher: Incisive Media Investments
Frequency: Monthly
Annual Sub.: £575.00
Usual Pagination: 30
Editor: Ellen Davis
Summary of Content: Publication covering news on global, operational risk management in finance.
Readership/Target Audience: Aimed at the financial services industry.
ADVERTISING RATES:
Full Page Colour £4460.00
Mechanical Data: Type Area: 255 x 205mm, Col Length: 255mm, Page Width: 205mm, Bleed Size: 286 x 236mm, Trim Size: 280 x 230mm, Film: Digital
BUSINESS: FINANCE & ECONOMICS: Investment

OPTICAL WORLD
40409U56E-435

Editorial Address: 258A Fairfax Drive, WESTCLIFF-ON-SEA, SS0 9EJ **Tel:** 01702 345443 **Fax:** 01702 431806
Email: info@optical-world.co.uk

Advertising Address: As above.
Email: info@optical-world.co.uk
Web site: http://www.optical-world.co.uk
ISSN: 0969-1952
Publisher: Optical World Ltd
Date Established: 1972
Frequency: 9 issues yearly - Published around the 5th of the cover month
Annual Sub.: £80.00
Circulation: 4,500 (Publisher's Statement)
Usual Pagination: 52
Editor: Gerald Ward; **Managing Director:** Gerald Ward; **Advertising Manager:** Russell Ward; **Publisher:** Gerald Ward
Summary of Content: Magazine featuring equipment surveys, company profiles, optical exhibitions and new products section.
Readership/Target Audience: Aimed at manufacturers, distributors and users of optical equipment worldwide.
ADVERTISING RATES:
Full Page Colour £2625.00
Agency Commission: 10%
Mechanical Data: Type Area: 255 x 178mm, Bleed Size: 305 x 216mm, Trim Size: 297 x 210mm, Col Length: 255mm, Page Width: 178mm, No. of Columns (Display): 4
Copy instructions: Copy Date: 15th of the month prior to . publication date
BUSINESS: HEALTH & MEDICAL: Optics

OPTICIAN
40410U56E-440

Editorial Address: Quadrant House, The Quadrant, SUTTON, SM2 5AS **Tel:** 020 8652 8243 **Fax:** 020 8652 3062
Email: kay.hevey@rbi.co.uk
Advertising Address: As above. **Tel:** 020 8652 3500
Email: andrea.brunton@rbi.co.uk
Web site: http://www.opticianonline.net
ISSN: 0030-3968
Publisher: Reed Business Information
Date Established: 1896
Frequency: Weekly
Cover Price: £4.10
Annual Sub.: £192.00
Circulation: 6,467 (ABC 01/01/2008 to 31/12/2008)
Usual Pagination: 50
Editor: Perry Thakrar; **News Editor:** Perry Thakrar; **Features Editor:** Mike Hale; **Managing Director:** Robert Brighouse; **Managing Editor:** Rory Brogan; **Publisher:** Trevor Goodman
Summary of Content: Magazine containing news and features about all aspects of the optical industry.
Readership/Target Audience: Aimed at optometrists, dispensing opticians and manufacturing opticians.
ADVERTISING RATES:
Full Page Colour £2648.00
Agency Commission: 10%
Mechanical Data: Col Length: 270mm, Col Widths (Display): 60mm, Film: Positive, right reading, emulsion side down. Digital, Type Area: 270 x 188mm, Bleed Size: 303 x 216mm, Page Width: 188mm, Trim Size: 297 x 210mm
Copy instructions: Copy Date: 1 week prior to publication date
Average advertising content per issue: 40%
Supplement(s): Optician Student - 1xY
BUSINESS: HEALTH & MEDICAL: Optics

OPTICS & LASER EUROPE
39996U55-126

Formerly: Opto & Laser Europe
Editorial Address: Dirac House, Temple Back, BRISTOL, BS1 6BE **Tel:** 0117 929 7481 **Fax:** 0117 930 1178
Email: ole@iop.org
Advertising Address: As above. **Tel:** 0117 930 1193
Email: sales@optics.org
Web site: http://www.optics.org/ole
ISSN: 0966-9809
Publisher: IOP Publishing
Date Established: 1992
Frequency: 11 issues yearly
Cover Price: £12.00
Free to qualifying individuals
Annual Sub.: £125.00
Circulation: 23,304 (BPA Worldwide 01/01/2007 to 31/12/2007)
Usual Pagination: 48
Editor: Jacqueline Gage; **Publisher:** Joe McEntee
Summary of Content: Magazine covering the application of lasers, optical fibres, opto-electronic materials and related fields.
Readership/Target Audience: Aimed at scientists, engineers and technical managers in European industry and research.
ADVERTISING RATES:
Full Page Mono £4710.00
Full Page Colour £5210.00
Agency Commission: 10%
Mechanical Data: Film: Digital
Average advertising content per issue: 45%
BUSINESS: APPLIED SCIENCE & LABORATORIES

OR INSIGHT
36795U14A-275

Editorial Address: Seymour House, 12 Edward Street, BIRMINGHAM, B1 2RX **Tel:** 0121 233 9300
Fax: 0121 233 0321
Email: email@orsoc.org.uk
Web site: http://www.theorsociety.com
ISSN: 0953-5543
Publisher: The Operational Research Society
Frequency: Quarterly
Free to qualifying individuals
Circulation: 2,700 (Publisher's Statement)
Usual Pagination: 32
Editor: Brian Lehaney
Summary of Content: Magazine containing reports of operational research in action.
Readership/Target Audience: Aimed at members of the Operational Research Society.
ADVERTISING: No Advertising taken
BUSINESS: COMMERCE, INDUSTRY & MANAGEMENT

ORACLE
38552U14L-934

Formerly: Assessment Journal
Editorial Address: 160 Falcon Road, LONDON, SW11 2LN **Tel:** 020 7801 2884 **Fax:** 020 7801 2888
Email: coline@pcs.org.uk
Advertising Address: 17 Britton Street, LONDON, EC1M 5TP **Tel:** 020 7880 6219 **Fax:** 020 7880 7553
Email: leon.dominion@redactive.co.uk
Web site: http://www.pcs.org.uk
Publisher: Public and Commercial Services Union
Date Established: 1904
Frequency: 10 issues yearly - Combined issues in December / January and July / August
Free to qualifying individuals
Annual Sub.: £15.00
Circulation: 80,000 (Publisher's Statement)
Usual Pagination: 16
Editor: Colin Edwards
Summary of Content: Official journal of the Revenue and Customs group of the Public and Commercial Services Union featuring articles from members, negotiation officers, both PCS employees and lay elected officials.
Readership/Target Audience: Read by members.
ADVERTISING RATES:
Full Page Colour £1800.00
Agency Commission: 10%
Mechanical Data: Type Area: 277 x 180mm, Bleed Size: 303 x 216mm, Trim Size: 297 x 210mm, Page Width: 180mm, Film: Digital, Col Length: 277mm
Copy instructions: Copy Date: 5th of the month prior to publication date
Average advertising content per issue: 20%
BUSINESS: COMMERCE, INDUSTRY & MANAGEMENT: Trade Unions

ORGANIC & BIOMOLECULAR CHEMISTRY
36703U13-113_4

Formerly: Perkins Transactions 1
Editorial Address: Thomas Graham House, Science Park, Milton Road, CAMBRIDGE, CB4 0WF **Tel:** 01223 432100
Fax: 01223 420247
Email: obc@rsc.org
Advertising Address: As above. **Tel:** 01223 432246
Fax: 01223 426017
Email: advertising@rsc.org
Web site: http://www.rsc.org/obc
ISSN: 0300-922X
Publisher: Royal Society of Chemistry
Frequency: 24 issues yearly
Annual Sub.: £1053.00
Circulation: 2,200 (Publisher's Statement)
Editor: Vikki Allen; **Advertising Manager:** Ian Swain
Summary of Content: Journal covering news and information on organic chemistry.
Readership/Target Audience: Aimed at anyone in academia or within the pharmaceutical industry undertaking research in organic and biological chemistry.
ADVERTISING RATES:
Full Page Mono £890.00
Mechanical Data: Trim Size: 275 x 210mm, Bleed Size: 281 x 216mm, Type Area: 252 x 188mm, Col Length: 252mm, Page Width: 188mm
BUSINESS: CHEMICALS

ORGANIC AND NATURAL BUSINESS
626281U22F-110

Formerly: Organic Business
Editorial Address: The Old Dairy, Hudsons Farm, Fieldgate Lane, Ugley Green, BISHOP'S STORTFORD, CM22 6HJ **Tel:** 01279 816300
Email: rachel.symonds@targetpublishing.com
Advertising Address: As above. **Fax:** 01279 816496
Email: kathryn.howe@targetpublishing.com
Web site: http://www.organic-business.com
ISSN: 1475-7753

Publisher: Target Publishing Ltd
Date Established: 2000
Frequency: 6 issues yearly
Free to qualifying individuals
Annual Sub.: £54.00
Circulation: 7,000 (Publisher's Statement)
Usual Pagination: 40
Editor: Rachel Symonds
Summary of Content: Magazine devoted to keeping the global organic industry abreast of the latest news, views and market analysis within the organic financial market in the UK and abroad.
Readership/Target Audience: Aimed at organic retail buyers from independent and multiple stores, farm retailers, importers, wholesalers and distributors, trade commissions and chambers of commerce.
ADVERTISING RATES:
Full Page Colour £2326.00
Agency Commission: 10%
Mechanical Data: Bleed Size: 303 x 216mm, Trim Size: 297 x 210mm, Film: Digital, Type Area: 268 x 180mm, Col Length: 268mm, Page Width: 180mm
Copy instructions: Copy Date: 3 weeks prior to publication date
Average advertising content per issue: 50%
BUSINESS: FOOD: Health Food

ORGANIC FARMING
37776U21A-853

Editorial Address: South Plaza, Marlborough Street, BRISTOL, BS1 3NX **Tel:** 0117 314 5000 **Fax:** 0117 314 5001
Email: pmundy@soilassociation.org
Advertising Address: Think Publishing Ltd, 20-23 Woodside Place, GLASGOW, G3 7QF **Tel:** 0141 582 1280
Fax: 0141 582 1484
Email: john@thinkpublishing.co.uk
Web site: http://www.soilassociation.org/foodandfarming
ISSN: 1464-1224
Publisher: Soil Association
Date Established: 1983
Frequency: Quarterly
Annual Sub.: £20.00
Circulation: 7,000 (Publisher's Statement)
Usual Pagination: 52
Editor: Peter Mundy; **Advertising Manager:** John Innes
Summary of Content: Journal covering technical features and research on all aspects of organic farming.
Readership/Target Audience: Aimed at professional organic farmers and growers, and others interested in keeping abreast of developments in the UK organic farming sector.
ADVERTISING RATES:
Full Page Colour £1950.00
Agency Commission: 10%
Mechanical Data: Bleed Size: +3mm, Trim Size: 297 x 210mm, Type Area: 254 x 185mm, Col Length: 254mm, Page Width: 185mm, Film: Digital
Copy instructions: Copy Date: 6 weeks prior to publication date
Average advertising content per issue: 25%
BUSINESS: AGRICULTURE & FARMING

ORGANISATIONAL TRANSFORMATION AND SOCIAL CHANGE
1696515U62R-504

Editorial Address: Liverpool John Moores University, 98 Mount Pleasant, LIVERPOOL, L3 5UZ
Email: m.yolles@livjm.ac.uk
Web site: http://www.intellectbooks.co.uk
ISSN: 1477-9633
Publisher: Intellect Ltd
Date Established: 2004
Frequency: 3 issues yearly - Published in April, August and December
Annual Sub.: £180.00
Circulation: 300 (Publisher's Statement)
Usual Pagination: 80
Editor: Maurice Yolles
Summary of Content: Journal covering issues in research on organisational theory.
Readership/Target Audience: Aimed at academics in the fields of management, organisational behaviour, social psychology and development.
ADVERTISING: No Advertising taken
BUSINESS: CHURCH & SCHOOL EQUIPMENT & EDUCATION: Education Related

ORGANISATIONS & PEOPLE
1667728U14F-253

Editorial Address: 7-8 Roman Way, Small Business Park, London Road, Godmanchester, HUNTINGDON, PE29 2LN
Tel: 01480 459575
Email: amedoffice@amed.org.uk
Advertising Address: As above. **Fax:** 01480 450721
Email: amedoffice@amed.org.uk
Web site: http://www.amed.org.uk
ISSN: 1350-6269
Publisher: The Association for Management Education & Development

Frequency: Quarterly
Annual Sub.: £69.00
Circulation: 1,000 (Publisher's Statement)
Editor: Terry Gibson; **Advertising Manager:** Concepta Wayment; **Managing Editor:** Terry Gibson
Summary of Content: Journal focusing on management education and development for individuals, groups and organisations.
Readership/Target Audience: Aimed at development consultants, trainers, academics, researchers, management consultants and HR professionals.
ADVERTISING RATES:
Full Page Mono £650.00
Mechanical Data: Type Area: 255 x 130mm, Col Length: 255mm, Page Width: 130mm
Copy instructions: Copy Date: End of month prior to publication date
Average advertising content per issue: 3%
BUSINESS: COMMERCE, INDUSTRY & MANAGEMENT: Training & Recruitment

THE OSTEOPATH
40211U56A-107_70

Editorial Address: Osteopathy House, 176 Tower Bridge Road, LONDON, SE1 3LU **Tel:** 020 7357 6655
Fax: 020 7357 0011
Email: editor@osteopathy.org.uk
Advertising Address: Wealden Advertising Ltd, Cowden Close, Horns Road, Hawkhurst, CRANBROOK, TN18 4QT
Tel: 01580 753322 **Fax:** 01580 754104
Email: osteopath@wealdenads.co.uk
Web site: http://www.osteopathy.org.uk
ISSN: 1466-4984
Publisher: The General Osteopathic Council
Date Established: 1997
Frequency: 6 issues yearly
Cover Price: £3.50
Free to qualifying individuals
Annual Sub.: £24.00
Circulation: 4,600 (Publisher's Statement)
Usual Pagination: 44
Editor: Jodie Ward; **Advertising Manager:** Rebecca Hunt
Summary of Content: Official journal of the General Osteopathic Council. Covers news, issues concerning healthcare regulation, professional standards and guidance, the NHS, clinical updates, research, letters, media reviews and CPD resources.
Readership/Target Audience: Read by osteopaths and other health professionals and patients.
ADVERTISING RATES:
Full Page Colour £330.00
Agency Commission: 10%
Mechanical Data: Film: Digital, Type Area: 248 x 160mm, Col Length: 248mm, Trim Size: 297 x 210mm, Bleed Size: 303 x 216mm, Page Width: 160mm
Copy instructions: Copy Date: 3rd week of the month prior to publication date
Average advertising content per issue: 33%
BUSINESS: HEALTH & MEDICAL

OSTEOPOROSIS INTERNATIONAL
40212U56A-107_80

Editorial Address: Ashbourne House, The Guildway, Old Portsmouth Road, Artington, GUILDFORD, GU3 1LP
Tel: 01483 734437 **Fax:** 01483 734411
Email: clare.colwell@springer-sbm.com
Advertising Address: As above. **Fax:** 01483 734429
Email: clare.colwell@springer.com
Web site: http://www.springerlink.com
ISSN: 0937-941X
Publisher: Springer
Date Established: 1990
Frequency: Monthly
Annual Sub.: £792.00
Circulation: 4,000 (Publisher's Statement)
Usual Pagination: 80
Editor: Clare Colwell; **Advertising Manager:** Clare Colwell; **Publisher:** Christiane Notarmarco
Summary of Content: Journal of the International Osteoporosis Foundation and the National Osteoporosis Foundation covering the diagnosis, treatment and management of osteoporosis.
Readership/Target Audience: Readership includes all medical specialists working in the field including orthopaedic surgeons, gynaecologists, rheumatologists, endocrinologists, geriatricians, radiologists and nutritionists.
ADVERTISING RATES:
Full Page Mono £520.00
Full Page Colour £1397.00
Agency Commission: 10%
Mechanical Data: Type Area: 237 x 172mm, Col Length: 237mm, Film: Digital, Trim Size: 297 x 210mm, Bleed Size: 283 x 216mm, Page Width: 172mm
BUSINESS: HEALTH & MEDICAL

OT
40411U56E-30

Editorial Address: 61 Southwark Street, LONDON, SE1 0HL **Tel:** 020 7202 8165

Email: davidchallinor@optometry.co.uk
Web site: http://www.optometry.co.uk
ISSN: 0268-5485
Publisher: Ten Alps Publishing plc
Frequency: 24 issues yearly
Cover Price: £4.95
Free to qualifying individuals
Annual Sub.: £110.00
Circulation: 19,442 (ABC 01/01/2008 to 31/12/2008)
Usual Pagination: 60
Editor: David Challinor
Summary of Content: Magazine of the Association of Optometrists. Covers news, clinical, continuing education and training, technical and practice management.
Readership/Target Audience: Aimed at optometrists and dispensing opticians.
ADVERTISING: No Advertising taken
BUSINESS: HEALTH & MEDICAL: Optics

OTC BULLETIN
38744U37-35

Editorial Address: 54 Creynolds Lane, Shirley, SOLIHULL, B90 4ER **Tel:** 01564 777550 **Fax:** 01564 777524
Email: editor@otc-bulletin.com
Advertising Address: As above.
Email: val.davis@otc-bulletin.com
Web site: http://www.otc-bulletin.com
ISSN: 1350-1097
Publisher: OTC Publications Ltd
Date Established: 1993
Frequency: 20 issues yearly
Annual Sub.: £565.00
Circulation: 3,500 (Publisher's Statement)
Editor: Deborah Wilkes; **Advertising Manager:** Val Davis; **Publisher:** Deborah Wilkes
Summary of Content: Business newsletter covering all aspects of Europe's consumer healthcare industry.
Readership/Target Audience: Aimed at those with an interest in Europe's consumer healthcare industry.
ADVERTISING RATES:
Full Page Mono £940.00
Full Page Colour £1460.00
SCC £23.00
Agency Commission: 10%
Mechanical Data: Type Area: 272 x 189mm, Col Length: 272mm, Film: Digital, Print Process: Offset litho, Bleed Size: 307 x 220mm, Trim Size: 297 x 210mm, No. of Columns (Display): 3, Page Width: 189mm
Copy instructions: Copy Date: 10 days prior to publication date
Average advertising content per issue: 20%
Supplement(s): news@OTCbulletin - 45xY
BUSINESS: PHARMACEUTICAL & CHEMISTS

OUT ON A LIMB
623988U29-55

Editorial Address: 47 Church Street, BARNSLEY, S70 2AS
Tel: 01226 734734
Email: nl@whpl.net
Advertising Address: As above. **Tel:** 01226 734456
Fax: 01226 734478
Email: bg@whpl.net
Publisher: Wharncliffe Publishing Ltd
Date Established: 2000
Frequency: 6 issues yearly - Published at the beginning of the cover month
Free to qualifying individuals
Annual Sub.: £50.00
Circulation: 11,000 (Publisher's Statement)
Usual Pagination: 48
Editor: Louise Cordell; **News Editor:** Nicola Hyde;
Advertising Manager: Beverly Green
Summary of Content: Magazine covering news, research, product design and developments in the footwear and accessories industry. Includes articles on designer style, leisure and high street fashion worldwide.
Readership/Target Audience: Aimed at decision makers in the footwear industry.
ADVERTISING RATES:
Full Page Colour £1795.00
Agency Commission: 10%
Mechanical Data: Type Area: 312 x 219mm, Bleed Size: 346 x 253mm, Trim Size: 336 x 243mm, Col Length: 312mm, Page Width: 219mm, Film: Digital
Copy instructions: Copy Date: 3 weeks prior to publication date
Average advertising content per issue: 50%
Supplement(s): Kool for Kids - 2xY
BUSINESS: FOOTWEAR

OUTDOOR REVIEW
39552U48B-42

Editorial Address: Telford Way, Telford Way Industrial Estate, KETTERING, NN16 8UN **Tel:** 01536 382500
Fax: 01536 382501
Email: jtopenair@aol.com
Advertising Address: As above.
Email: paula.hearn@greenshirespublishing.com
Publisher: Greenshires Publishing Ltd

Date Established: 1997
Frequency: 3 issues yearly - Published in February, June and September
Cover Price: Free
Circulation: 4,000 (Publisher's Statement)
Usual Pagination: 32
Editor: John Traynor; **Advertising Manager:** Paula Hearn
Summary of Content: Magazine containing a business review of the outdoor leisure and snowsports trade.
Readership/Target Audience: Read by retail managers, buyers, suppliers, agents and reps.
ADVERTISING RATES:
Full Page Mono £730.00
Full Page Colour £1140.00
SCC £14.00
Agency Commission: 10%
Mechanical Data: Col Widths (Display): 45mm, Film: Digital, Page Width: 190mm, Type Area: 273 x 190mm, Col Length: 273mm, No. of Columns (Display): 4, Print Process: Sheet-fed litho, Trim Size: 297 x 210mm, Bleed Size: 303 x 216mm
Copy instructions: Copy Date: 8 weeks prior to publication date
Average advertising content per issue: 40%
BUSINESS: TOY TRADE & SPORTS GOODS: Sports Goods

OUTDOORS
1697633U62C-737

Formerly: Early Years Outdoors & Schoolgrounds UK
Editorial Address: 3rd Floor, Southside Offices, The Law Courts, WINCHESTER, SO23 9DL **Tel:** 01962 845811
Email: jbutterworth@ltl.org.uk
Web site: http://www.ltl.org.uk
Publisher: Learning Through Landscapes
Date Established: 2004
Frequency: 6 issues yearly
Free to qualifying individuals
Annual Sub.: £60.00
Circulation: 4,000 (Publisher's Statement)
Usual Pagination: 8
Editor: Spencer Butt
Summary of Content: Magazine focusing on outdoor space for play and learning. Topics covered include equipment, refurbishment and project planning.
Readership/Target Audience: Aimed at school staff and early years practitioners.
ADVERTISING: No Advertising taken
BUSINESS: CHURCH & SCHOOL EQUIPMENT & EDUCATION: Junior Education

OUTLOOK
1657339U32K-352

Editorial Address: Unit 8, Woodcock Hill Industrial Estate, Harefield Road, RICKMANSWORTH, WD3 1PQ
Tel: 01923 774111 **Fax:** 01923 721818
Email: richard.g@evolve-print.com
Publisher: Evolve
Date Established: 2000
Frequency: Half-yearly - Published in February and August
Free to qualifying individuals
Circulation: 105,000 (Publisher's Statement)
Usual Pagination: 6
Editor: Richard Gregory
Summary of Content: Magazine covering lifestyle, personal finance and health issues.
Readership/Target Audience: Aimed at employees of UK County Councils.
ADVERTISING: No Advertising taken
BUSINESS: LOCAL GOVERNMENT, LEISURE & RECREATION: Civil Service

OUTLOOK ON AGRICULTURE
37777U21A-855

Editorial Address: 258 Belsize Road, LONDON, NW6 4BT
Tel: 020 7316 1870
Email: outlookonagric@dsl.pipex.com
Web site: http://www.ippublishing.com
ISSN: 0030-7270
Publisher: IP Publishing Ltd
Date Established: 1971
Frequency: Quarterly
Usual Pagination: 64
Editor: David Lister; **Managing Director:** John Edmondson
Summary of Content: Journal containing analysis of developments in international agricultural science and associated disciplines.
Readership/Target Audience: Aimed at academics in agriculture and related disciplines.
ADVERTISING: No Advertising taken
BUSINESS: AGRICULTURE & FARMING

OUTLOOKS ON PEST MANAGEMENT
24314U55-126_70

Formerly: Pesticide Outlook
Editorial Address: Grenville Court, Britwell Road, Burnham, SLOUGH, SL1 8DF **Tel:** 01628 600499 **Fax:** 01628 600488
Email: info@researchinformation.co.uk
Advertising Address: As above.

Business Magazines

Email: raspatel@researchinformation.co.uk
Web site: http://www.pestoutlook.com
ISSN: 1743-1026
Publisher: Research Information Ltd
Frequency: 6 issues yearly
Annual Sub.: £575.00
Circulation: 300 (Publisher's Statement)
Editor: Leonard Copping
Summary of Content: Journal reporting on developments of synthetic and naturally occurring fungicides, herbicides, growth regulators, insecticides and rodenticides.
Readership/Target Audience: Aimed at academic and industrial chemists.
ADVERTISING: Rates on application
Agency Commission: 10%
Average advertising content per issue: 5%
BUSINESS: APPLIED SCIENCE & LABORATORIES

OUTSOURCE
1642454U14A-524
Editorial Address: EMP House, 2 Pembroke Road, LONDON, N10 2HR **Tel:** 01273 622249
Email: stuart.lauchlan@outsourcemagazine.co.uk
Advertising Address: As above. **Tel:** 020 8815 1540
Web site: http://www.outsourcemagazine.co.uk
Publisher: EMP Media
Date Established: 2004
Frequency: Quarterly
Annual Sub.: £39.00
Circulation: 10,500 (Publisher's Statement)
Editor: Stuart Lauchlan; **Managing Director:** Daniel Cuby
Advertising Manager: Nigel Winter; **Managing Editor:** Stuart Lauchlan; **Publisher:** Daniel Cuby
Summary of Content: Magazine covering all aspects of the outsourcing process. Includes articles on payroll, legal, IT and human resources.
Readership/Target Audience: Aimed at board level end users.
BUSINESS: COMMERCE, INDUSTRY & MANAGEMENT

OVER THE COUNTER
1659012U37-420
Editorial Address: Riverbank House, Angel Lane, TONBRIDGE, TN9 1SE **Tel:** 01732 377435
Fax: 01732 367065
Email: otc@ubm.com
Advertising Address: CMP Medica Ltd, Ludgate House, 245 Blackfriars Road, LONDON, SE1 9UY
Tel: 020 7921 5000 **Fax:** 020 7921 8136
Email: daniel.spruytenburg@ubm.com
Web site: http://www.otcmag.com
Publisher: UBM Information (Tonbridge)
Date Established: 1989
Frequency: Monthly
Annual Sub.: £210.00
Circulation: 11,576 (ABC 01/01/2008 to 31/12/2008)
Usual Pagination: 40
Editor: Fiona Salvage
Summary of Content: Magazine featuring news products and services on the pharmacy trade.
Readership/Target Audience: Aimed at pharmacy assistants and dispensing staff.
ADVERTISING RATES:
Full Page Colour £4055.00
Agency Commission: 10%
Mechanical Data: Type Area: 272 x 190mm, Bleed Size: 303 x 213mm, Trim Size: 297 x 210mm, Col Length: 272mm, Page Width: 190mm, Film: Digital
Copy instructions: Copy Date: 3 weeks prior to publication date
Average advertising content per issue: 30%
Supplement to: Chemist+Druggist
BUSINESS: PHARMACEUTICAL & CHEMISTS

OVER THE COUNTER
1792683U64H-246
Editorial Address: Hendal Oast, Hendal Farm, Groombridge, TUNBRIDGE WELLS, TN3 9NU
Tel: 01892 861664
Email: katherine@ghpublishing.co.uk
Advertising Address: As above. **Tel:** 01892 861667
Email: katherine@ghpublishing.co.uk
Web site: http://www.overthecounter.cc
ISSN: 1751-1275
Publisher: Grove House Publishing
Date Established: 2006
Frequency: 6 issues yearly
Free to qualifying individuals
Annual Sub.: £60.00
Circulation: 5,000 (Publisher's Statement)
Usual Pagination: 36
Editor: Katherine Openshaw; **News Editor:** Iona Walton;
Advertising Manager: Katherine Openshaw
Summary of Content: Publication designed as a practical and educational guide to small and large animal health practice and products. Provides guidance for advisors in the form of training and educational initiatives particularly on the sale of animal health products.

Readership/Target Audience: Read by AMTRA qualified SQPs, veterinary assistants and veterinary nurses, qualified advisers in country stores, wholesaler distributors and veterinary practices across the UK, also buyers, marketing directors and all those practices responsible for in-store product purchasing.
ADVERTISING RATES:
Full Page Colour £1700.00
Mechanical Data: Type Area: 300 x 225mm, Bleed Size: 341 x 250mm, Trim Size: 335 x 244mm, Col Length: 300mm, Page Width: 225mm, Film: Digital
Copy instructions: Copy Date: 2 weeks prior to publication date
BUSINESS: OTHER CLASSIFICATIONS: Veterinary

OVERSEAS LIVING
1614308U14A-508
Formerly: Total Business
Editorial Address: 37-42 Compton Street, LONDON, EC1V 0AP **Tel:** 020 7014 0355 **Fax:** 020 7014 0301
Email: jo@overseasliving.co.uk
Advertising Address: As above. **Tel:** 020 7014 0300
Fax: 020 7014 0302
Email: m.stevenson@overseasliving.co.uk
Web site: http://www.overseasliving.co.uk
Publisher: Tower Business Media
Date Established: 2008
Frequency: 6 issues yearly
Annual Sub.: £27.50
Circulation: 49,000 (Publisher's Statement)
Usual Pagination: 150
Editor: Jo Newsome; **Features Editor:** Nathan May;
Advertising Manager: Mathew Stevenson
Summary of Content: Magazine covering investment in real estate overseas, tourism and holidays.
Readership/Target Audience: Aimed at property investors.
ADVERTISING RATES:
Full Page Mono £4730.00
Full Page Colour £5920.00
Agency Commission: 10%
Mechanical Data: Trim Size: 280 x 210mm, Bleed Size: 288 x 218mm, Print Process: Litho, Film: Digital
Copy instructions: Copy Date: 8th of the month prior to publication date
BUSINESS: COMMERCE, INDUSTRY & MANAGEMENT

OVERSEAS PROPERTY PROFESSIONAL
1703505U1E-390
Editorial Address: 1 Red Lion Street, RICHMOND, TW9 1RE **Tel:** 020 8332 4600
Email: editor@opp.org.uk
Advertising Address: As above. **Fax:** 020 8332 4639
Email: sales@opp.org.uk
Web site: http://www.opp.org.uk
Publisher: PFI Media Ltd
Date Established: 2004
Frequency: Monthly
Free to qualifying individuals
Annual Sub.: £55.00
Circulation: 4,499 (ABC 01/07/2007 to 30/06/2008)
Usual Pagination: 92
Editor: Ben Dahlstrom; **News Editor:** Ben Dahlstrom;
Advertising Manager: David le Lacheur
Summary of Content: Magazine focusing on the sales and marketing of overseas property in the UK and Ireland: market trends, issues, news etc.
Readership/Target Audience: Aimed at managers, directors and owners of companies that target the multi-billion pound overseas property market in the UK and Ireland e.g. real estate agents, developers, IFAs etc.
ADVERTISING RATES:
Full Page Mono £2050.00
Full Page Colour £2050.00
Agency Commission: 10%
Mechanical Data: Bleed Size: 303 x 216mm, Trim Size: 297 x 210mm, Film: Digital
Copy instructions: Copy Date: 14th of the month prior to publication date
Average advertising content per issue: 45%
BUSINESS: FINANCE & ECONOMICS: Property

OXFORD ART JOURNAL
30048U62R-461
Editorial Address: Great Clarendon Street, OXFORD, OX2 6DP **Tel:** 01865 353907 **Fax:** 01865 353485
Advertising Address: As above. **Tel:** 01865 353329
Email: jnlsadvertising@oxfordjournals.org
Web site: http://www.oaj.oupjournals.org
ISSN: 0142-6540
Publisher: OUP
Date Established: 1978
Frequency: 3 issues yearly - Published in March, July and November
Annual Sub.: £111.00
Usual Pagination: 160
Editor: Constance Gounod
Summary of Content: Journal which addresses historical and philosophical issues concerning visual culture while

seeking to provide an alternative to mainstream art history journals.
Readership/Target Audience: Read by academics and art historians with an interest in historical and philosophical issues.
ADVERTISING RATES:
Full Page Mono £320.00
Agency Commission: 10%
Mechanical Data: Film: Digital, Type Area: 220 x 150mm, Col Length: 220mm, Page Width: 150mm
BUSINESS: CHURCH & SCHOOL EQUIPMENT & EDUCATION: Education Related

OXFORD JOURNAL OF LEGAL STUDIES
23642U44-1550
Editorial Address: Pembroke College, OXFORD, OX1 1DW
Tel: 01865 276429 **Fax:** 01865 276418
Email: ewan.mckendrick@lady-margaret-hall.oxford.ac.uk
Advertising Address: 60 Upper Broadmoor Road, CROWTHORNE, RG45 7DE **Tel:** 01344 779945
Fax: 01344 779945
Email: lhann@lhms.fsnet.co.uk
Web site: http://www.oup.co.uk/oxjlsj
ISSN: 0143-6503
Publisher: OUP
Date Established: 1981
Frequency: Quarterly
Cover Price: £20.00
Annual Sub.: £63.00
Circulation: 1,050 (Publisher's Statement)
Usual Pagination: 196
Editor: Ewan McKendrick
Summary of Content: Journal focusing on the examination of theory and issues arising from the relationship of law to other disciplines, with an emphasis on legal philosophy and history.
Readership/Target Audience: Aimed at leading law firms, legal scholars and philosophers of law and ethics.
ADVERTISING RATES:
Full Page Mono £335.00
Agency Commission: 10%
Mechanical Data: Page Width: 130mm, Film: Digital, Type Area: 210 x 130mm, Col Length: 210mm
Copy instructions: Copy Date: 21st of the month prior to publication date
BUSINESS: LEGAL

OXFORD REVIEW OF ECONOMIC POLICY
20476U1R-200
Editorial Address: Great Clarendon Street, OXFORD, OX2 6DP **Tel:** 01865 353907 **Fax:** 01865 353485
Email: econrev@herald.ox.ac.uk
Advertising Address: As above. **Tel:** 01865 353329
Email: jnlsadvertising@oxfordjournals.org
Web site: http://www.oup.co.uk/jnls
ISSN: 0266-903X
Publisher: OUP
Date Established: 1985
Frequency: Quarterly
Cover Price: £16.00
Annual Sub.: £50.00
Usual Pagination: 120
Editor: Christopher Allsopp; **Managing Editor:** Tim Jenkinson
Summary of Content: Journal featuring a review of economic policy, comprising of an assessment and a number of articles.
Readership/Target Audience: Aimed at academics and practitioners.
ADVERTISING RATES:
Full Page Mono £340.00
Agency Commission: 10%
Mechanical Data: Type Area: 260 x 160mm, Film: Digital, Col Length: 260mm, Page Width: 160mm
BUSINESS: FINANCE & ECONOMICS: Financial Related

P3
38767U37-60
Formerly: PPR
Editorial Address: 207 Linen Hall, 162-168 Regent Street, LONDON, W1B 5TB **Tel:** 020 7434 1530 **Fax:** 020 7437 0915
Email: carolyn.scott@1530.com
Advertising Address: As above.
Email: carrie.culbertson@1530.com
Web site: http://www.P3Pharmacy.co.uk
Publisher: Communications International Group
Date Established: 2006
Frequency: Monthly - Published in the 1st week of the cover month
Cover Price: £4.50
Free to qualifying individuals
Circulation: 13,178 (ABC 01/01/2008 to 31/12/2008)
Usual Pagination: 40
Editor: Carolyn Scott; **Managing Director:** Felim O'Brien;
Advertising Manager: Carrie Culbertson
Summary of Content: Magazine providing business management information for the entrepreneurial pharmacist.

Information includes news and analysis, category management guidance, an analysis of City trends, training modules, profiles plus an examination of over the counter pharmaceutical products and retail education.
Readership/Target Audience: Aimed at pharmacists in the UK and central buying offices.
ADVERTISING RATES:
Full Page Colour £3230.00
Agency Commission: 10%
Mechanical Data: Type Area: 279 x 202mm, Bleed Size: 303 x 216mm, Trim Size: 297 x 210mm, Col Length: 279mm, Page Width: 202mm, Film: Digital
Copy instructions: Copy Date: 2nd week of month prior to publication date
Average advertising content per issue: 35%
BUSINESS: PHARMACEUTICAL & CHEMISTS

PAC PALLET AND CASE INDUSTRY
38678U10-227
Editorial Address: The Old Sun, Crete Hall Road, GRAVESEND, DA11 9AA **Tel:** 01474 536535
Fax: 01474 536552
Email: pac@nelton.co.uk
Advertising Address: As above.
Email: pac@nelton.co.uk
Web site: http://www.nelton.co.uk
Publisher: Nelton Publications
Date Established: 1988
Frequency: Quarterly
Annual Sub.: £35.00
Circulation: 2,918 (Publisher's Statement)
Usual Pagination: 32
Editor: Neil Herbert-Smith; **Advertising Manager:** Donna Ludbrook
Summary of Content: Publication containing product news and information about services, machinery and legislation affecting the UK pallet and case industry.
Readership/Target Audience: Aimed at manufacturers of pallets and cases.
ADVERTISING RATES:
Full Page Mono £585.00
Full Page Colour £959.00
Agency Commission: 10%
Mechanical Data: Film: Digital, Trim Size: 297 x 210mm, Type Area: 277 x 189mm, Col Length: 277mm, Page Width: 189mm, Bleed Size: 305 x 216mm
Average advertising content per issue: 60%
BUSINESS: MATERIALS HANDLING

PACKAGING EUROPE
1693863U35-366
Editorial Address: Alkmaar House, Alkmaar Way, NORWICH, NR6 6BF **Tel:** 01603 414444 **Fax:** 01603 406543
Email: editor@packagingeurope.com
Advertising Address: As above.
Email: mm@packagingeurope.com
Web site: http://www.packagingeurope.com
Publisher: Positive Publications Ltd
Date Established: 2005
Frequency: 5 issues yearly
Cover Price: EUR12.00
Free to qualifying individuals
Circulation: 45,000 (Publisher's Statement)
Usual Pagination: 180
Editor: Elizabeth Skoda; **Advertising Manager:** Mac McCarthey
Summary of Content: Magazine covering all aspects of the packaging industry including equipment materials, events and environmental issues.
Readership/Target Audience: Aimed at decision makers in the packaging industry and user industries.
ADVERTISING RATES:
Full Page Mono EUR3800.00
Full Page Colour EUR4480.00
Agency Commission: 15%
Mechanical Data: Trim Size: 297 x 210mm
Copy instructions: Copy Date: 2 weeks prior to publication date
Average advertising content per issue: 30%
BUSINESS: PACKAGING & BOTTLING

PACKAGING GAZETTE
38684U35-357
Editorial Address: 4th Floor, Geneva House, Park Road, PETERBOROUGH, PE1 2UX **Tel:** 01733 756555
Fax: 01733 760505
Email: pg@onecoms.co.uk
Advertising Address: As above.
Email: donna@onecoms.co.uk
Web site: http://www.onecoms.co.uk
Publisher: Media One Communications Ltd.
Frequency: 6 issues yearly
Free to qualifying individuals
Circulation: 8,500 (Publisher's Statement)
Editor: Karyn Reidy; **Features Editor:** Donna Jenkins
Summary of Content: Magazine looking at all issues concerned with the packaging industry.

Readership/Target Audience: Aimed at those concerned with packaging purchasing across all industries.
ADVERTISING RATES:
Full Page Mono £880.00
Full Page Colour £960.00
Agency Commission: 10%
Mechanical Data: Type Area: 280 x 190mm, Col Length: 280mm, Page Width: 190mm, Film: Digital
Copy instructions: Copy Date: 19th of month prior to publication date
Average advertising content per issue: 25%
BUSINESS: PACKAGING & BOTTLING

PACKAGING MONTH
38675U35-55_110
Formerly: International Packaging Abstracts
Editorial Address: Cleeve Road, LEATHERHEAD, KT22 7RU **Tel:** 01372 802050 **Fax:** 01372 802239
Email: infocentre@pira-international.com
Web site: http://www.piranet.com
ISSN: 1475-598X
Publisher: PIRA International
Frequency: Monthly
Annual Sub.: £850.00
Editor: Gillian Micklewright
Summary of Content: Magazine covering the supply, design, conversion, use and application of every aspect of packaging. Coverage includes specialised areas as well as general packaging.
Readership/Target Audience: Read by the international packaging community.
ADVERTISING: No Advertising taken
BUSINESS: PACKAGING & BOTTLING

PACKAGING NEWS
38687U35-352
Editorial Address: 11-17 Wolverton Gardens, LONDON, W6 7DY **Tel:** 020 8267 8096
Email: packagingnews.editorial@haymarket.com
Advertising Address: 174 Hammersmith Road, LONDON, W6 7JP **Tel:** 020 8267 8093 **Fax:** 020 8267 8090
Email: james.fleetham@haymarket.com
Web site: http://www.packagingnews.co.uk
ISSN: 0030-9133
Publisher: Haymarket Business Media Ltd
Date Established: 1947
Frequency: Monthly
Cover Price: £6.99
Free to qualifying individuals
Annual Sub.: £79.00
Circulation: 13,919 (ABC 01/01/2008 to 31/12/2008)
Usual Pagination: 64
Editor: Josh Brooks; **Features Editor:** Catherine Dawes
Summary of Content: Magazine containing information on all aspects of the packaging industry including case studies.
Readership/Target Audience: Read by packaging buyers, technologists, engineers, designers, production directors and brand managers.
ADVERTISING RATES:
Full Page Colour £3675.00
Agency Commission: 10%
Mechanical Data: Film: Digital, Trim Size: 295 x 225mm, Type Area: 282 x 207mm, Col Length: 282mm, Page Width: 207mm, Bleed Size: 305 x 235mm
Average advertising content per issue: 50%
BUSINESS: PACKAGING & BOTTLING

THE PACKAGING PROFESSIONAL
762678U35-351
Editorial Address: 1 Carlton House Terrace, LONDON, SW1Y 5DB **Tel:** 020 7451 7300 **Fax:** 020 7451 7406
Email: pp@iom3.org
Advertising Address: Mongoose Media, 2 Lonsdale Road, LONDON, NW6 6RD **Tel:** 020 7306 0300
Fax: 020 7306 0301
Email: iom3@mongoosemedia.com
Web site: http://www.iom3.org/pp
ISSN: 1477-8467
Publisher: IOM Communications Ltd
Frequency: 6 issues yearly - Published in the 1st week of the 1st cover month
Cover Price: £4.50
Free to qualifying individuals
Circulation: 2,000 (Publisher's Statement)
Usual Pagination: 24
Editor: Rupal Mehta; **News Editor:** Rupal Mehta;
Advertising Manager: Robin Fox
Summary of Content: Magazine covering all aspects of packaging.
Readership/Target Audience: Aimed at members of IOP: The Packaging Society, a division of the Institute of Materials, Minerals and Mining.
ADVERTISING: Rates on application
Copy instructions: Copy Date: 6 weeks prior to publication date
BUSINESS: PACKAGING & BOTTLING

PACKAGING SCOTLAND
38688U35-130
Editorial Address: Bergius House, 20 Clifton Street, GLASGOW, G3 7LA **Tel:** 0141 567 6000 **Fax:** 0141 331 1395
Email: kim.mcallister@peeblesmedia.com
Advertising Address: As above. **Fax:** 0141 353 1784
Email: linda.scott@peeblesmedia.com
Web site: http://www.peeblesmedia.com
Publisher: Peebles Media Group Ltd
Frequency: Quarterly - Published in the middle of the month prior to the 1st cover month
Annual Sub.: £31.00
Circulation: 4,219 (ABC 01/01/2008 to 31/12/2008)
Usual Pagination: 48
Editor: Kim McAllister; **Managing Director:** Yvonne Bremner; **Advertising Manager:** Linda Scott; **Publisher:** Yvonne Bremner
Summary of Content: Magazine containing news and views of the packaging industry in Scotland.
Readership/Target Audience: Aimed at management in the packaging industry.
ADVERTISING RATES:
Full Page Colour £1475.00
Agency Commission: 10%
Mechanical Data: Type Area: 270 x 188mm, Col Length: 270mm, Trim Size: 297 x 210mm, Bleed Size: 303 x 213mm, Page Width: 188mm, Film: Digital
Copy instructions: Copy Date: 2 weeks prior to publication date
Average advertising content per issue: 50%
BUSINESS: PACKAGING & BOTTLING

PACKAGING TODAY
38690U35-135
Formerly: Packaging Today International
Editorial Address: Progressive House, 2 Maidstone Road, Foots Cray, SIDCUP, DA14 5HZ **Tel:** 020 8269 7700
Fax: 020 8269 7840
Email: sadvani@progressivemediagroup.com
Advertising Address: As above. **Fax:** 020 8269 7874
Email: rmolinari@progressivemediagroup.com
Web site: http://www.packagingtoday.co.uk
ISSN: 1470-6008
Publisher: Progressive Media Publications
Frequency: 10 issues yearly - Published in the 1st week of the cover month
Free to qualifying individuals
Annual Sub.: £133.00
Circulation: 14,470 (Publisher's Statement)
Usual Pagination: 72
Editor: Sonali Advani
Summary of Content: Journal containing news and features on all aspects of the packaging industry.
Readership/Target Audience: Aimed at the UK and European packaging industry.
ADVERTISING RATES:
Full Page Colour £2890.00
SCC £25.00
Agency Commission: 10%
Mechanical Data: Col Length: 277mm, No. of Columns (Display): 4, Trim Size: 297 x 210mm, Type Area: 277 x 192mm, Bleed Size: 303 x 216mm, Film: Digital, Page Width: 192mm
Copy instructions: Copy Date: 4 weeks prior to publication date
Average advertising content per issue: 60%
BUSINESS: PACKAGING & BOTTLING

PACKAGING, TRANSPORT, STORAGE AND SECURITY OF RADIOACTIVE MATERIAL
40762U58-47
Formerly: International Journal of Radioactive Materials Transport
Editorial Address: Suite 1C, Josephs Well, Hanover Walk, LEEDS, LS3 1AB **Tel:** 020 7451 7312 **Fax:** 0113 386 8178
Email: mark_hull@materials.org.uk
Advertising Address: As above. **Tel:** 0113 243 2800
Email: n.taylor@maney.co.uk
Web site: http://www.ntp.org.uk
ISSN: 0957-476X
Publisher: Maney Publishing
Date Established: 1990
Frequency: Quarterly
Annual Sub.: £156.00
Usual Pagination: 80
Editor: Mark Hull; **Advertising Manager:** Natalie Taylor; **Managing Editor:** Mark Hull
Summary of Content: Technical journal containing articles regarding the transport of radioactive materials, including regulatory safety, testing and operating experiences.
Readership/Target Audience: For designers, safety assessors, regulators and carriers of radioactive materials packages.
ADVERTISING RATES:
Full Page Colour £200.00
Mechanical Data: Type Area: 265 x 180mm, Col Length: 265mm, Page Width: 180mm, Film: Digital

Business Magazines

Copy instructions: Copy Date: 1st of the month prior to publication date
BUSINESS: ENERGY, FUEL & NUCLEAR

PAEDIATRIC NURSING
40326U56B-273

Editorial Address: The Heights, 59-65 Lowlands Road, HARROW, HA1 3AW **Tel:** 020 8423 1066
Fax: 020 8872 3198
Email: helen.hyland@rcnpublishing.co.uk
Advertising Address: As above. **Fax:** 020 8423 9196
Email: neil.hobson@rcnpublishing.co.uk
Web site: http://www.paediatricnursing.co.uk
ISSN: 0269-9079
Publisher: RCN Publishing Co Ltd
Date Established: 1988
Frequency: 10 issues yearly - Published in the last week of the month prior to the cover month
Annual Sub.: £86.00
Circulation: 13,354 (ABC 01/01/2008 to 31/12/2008)
Usual Pagination: 48
Editor: Chris Walker; **Managing Director:** Linda Thomas; **Publisher:** Linda Thomas
Summary of Content: Journal covering all aspects of child health and paediatric nursing with particular emphasis on clinical practice.
Readership/Target Audience: Aimed at paediatric nurses caring for children and young people in hospitals and in the community.
ADVERTISING RATES:
Full Page Colour £2299.00
Agency Commission: 10%
Mechanical Data: Bleed Size: 303 x 216mm, Trim Size: 297 x 210mm, Type Area: 271 x 178mm, Col Length: 271mm, Page Width: 178mm, Film: Digital
Copy instructions: Copy Date: 6 weeks prior to publication date
Average advertising content per issue: 30%
BUSINESS: HEALTH & MEDICAL: Nursing

PAEDIATRICS.ME
40202U56A-104

Formerly: Middle East Paediatrics
Editorial Address: 6 Tobin Close, Livingstone Park, EPSOM, KT19 8AE **Tel:** 01372 742347
Email: pharmedia@btconnect.com
Advertising Address: As above.
Email: pharmedia@aol.com
Web site: http://www.pharmedia.co.uk
ISSN: 1368-5937
Publisher: Pharmedia International
Frequency: Quarterly
Free to qualifying individuals
Annual Sub.: £35.00
Circulation: 9,200 (Publisher's Statement)
Editor: Pat Scowen; **Advertising Manager:** Russ Finnerty; **Managing Editor:** Pat Scowen; **Publisher:** Russ Finnerty
Summary of Content: International medical journal dedicated to childcare in the Middle East.
Readership/Target Audience: Aimed at paediatricians in the Middle East.
ADVERTISING RATES:
Full Page Colour £1900.00
Agency Commission: 15%
Mechanical Data: Trim Size: 297 x 210mm, Type Area: 272 x 186mm, Col Length: 272mm, Bleed Size: 303 x 216mm, Film: Digital, Page Width: 186mm
Copy instructions: Copy Date: 1 month prior to publication date
BUSINESS: HEALTH & MEDICAL

PAINT & RESIN TIMES
37280U16B-231

Formerly: Paint & Resin International
Editorial Address: Bannisters, Brightling, ROBERTSBRIDGE, TN32 5HL **Tel:** 01825 724623
Fax: 01825 724623
Email: prtimes@aol.com
Advertising Address: Unit 8, Netherhall Yard, Mill Lane, Newick, LEWES, BN8 4JL **Tel:** 01825 724623
Fax: 01825 724623
Email: c.dann@completecircmktg.co.uk
ISSN: 1476-0274
Publisher: Complete Circulation and Marketing Ltd
Date Established: 2001
Frequency: 6 issues yearly
Cover Price: £14.00
Annual Sub.: £89.00
Circulation: 2,000 (Publisher's Statement)
Usual Pagination: 20
Editor: Harriet Kinloch; **Advertising Manager:** Colin Dann
Summary of Content: Magazine covering information on all aspects of commercial and technical production and development of paint, varnish, adhesives and printing inks.
Readership/Target Audience: Aimed at paint, ink and coatings manufacturers based in Europe.
ADVERTISING RATES:
Full Page Colour £565.00
Agency Commission: 10%

Mechanical Data: Print Process: Sheet-fed offset litho, Film: Positive right reading emulsion side down. Digital, Type Area: 278 x 188mm, Trim Size: 297 x 210mm, Bleed Size: 303 x 216mm, Col Length: 278mm, Page Width: 188mm, Screen: Mono: 54 lpc, Colour: 70 lpc
Copy instructions: Copy Date: 14 days prior to publication date
BUSINESS: DECORATING & PAINT: Paint - Technical Manufacture

PALLIATIVE MEDICINE
24698U56A-108_55

Editorial Address: 1 Oliver's Yard, 55 City Road, LONDON, EC1Y 1SP **Tel:** 020 7324 8500 **Fax:** 020 7324 8600
Email: market@sagepub.co.uk
Advertising Address: As above.
Email: sheena.karim@sagepub.co.uk
ISSN: 0269-2163
Publisher: Sage Publications
Date Established: 1987
Frequency: 8 issues yearly
Annual Sub.: £780.00
Usual Pagination: 96
Editor: Geoff Hanks; **Advertising Manager:** Sheena Karim
Summary of Content: Journal covering all aspects of palliative care for patients with advanced diseases.
Readership/Target Audience: Aimed at doctors, nurses, physiotherapists, psychologists, social workers, occupational therapists and the clergy.
ADVERTISING RATES:
Full Page Mono £580.00
Full Page Colour £1885.00
Agency Commission: 10%
Mechanical Data: Print Process: Sheet-fed litho, Film: Positive, right reading, emulsion side down. Digital, Screen: Mono 52 lpc Colour 60 lpc, Trim Size: 280 x 210mm, Type Area: 248 x 174mm, Col Length: 248mm, Page Width: 174mm
BUSINESS: HEALTH & MEDICAL

PANEL & SYSTEM BUILDING
37325U17-165_35

Formerly: Panel Building and Panel Builder
Editorial Address: Blair House, 184-186 High Street, TONBRIDGE, TN9 1BQ **Tel:** 01732 359990
Fax: 01732 770049
Email: les.hunt@imlgroup.co.uk
Advertising Address: As above.
Email: barrie.barradell@imlgroup.co.uk
Web site: http://www.psbonthenet.net
ISSN: 1465-4717
Publisher: IML Group plc
Frequency: 8 issues yearly - Published in the 1st week of the cover month
Cover Price: £11.00
Free to qualifying individuals
Annual Sub.: £56.00
Circulation: 6,599 (ABC 01/01/2007 to 31/12/2007)
Usual Pagination: 44
Editor: Les Hunt; **Advertising Manager:** Barrie Barradell; **Publisher:** Andrew Quenault
Summary of Content: Publication providing information on the panel and systems building industry.
Readership/Target Audience: Read by panel builders, systems integrators, end users and component manufacturers.
ADVERTISING RATES:
Full Page Mono £1700.00
Full Page Colour £2100.00
Agency Commission: 10%
Mechanical Data: Type Area: 280 x 190mm, Bleed Size: 303 x 216mm, Trim Size: 297 x 210mm, Col Length: 280mm, Film: Digital, Page Width: 190mm
Copy instructions: Copy Date: 10th of the month prior to publication date
Average advertising content per issue: 60%
BUSINESS: ELECTRICAL

PANEL PRODUCTION
39462U46-19_50

Editorial Address: 23 Uvedale Road, ENFIELD, EN2 6HA **Tel:** 020 8366 3331 **Fax:** 020 8366 3331
Email: panelproduction@btconnect.com
Advertising Address: As above.
Email: panelproduction@btconnect.com
Web site: http://www.panelproduction.com
Publisher: EC Media Ltd.
Date Established: 1997
Frequency: 6 issues yearly - Published on the 24th of the cover month
Annual Sub.: £15.50
Circulation: 5,895 (Publisher's Statement)
Usual Pagination: 48
Editor: Ernie Hollister; **Advertising Manager:** Ernie Hollister; **Publisher:** Ernie Hollister
Summary of Content: Journal covering all aspects of the wood based panel industry.
Readership/Target Audience: Aimed at key decision makers involved in the production and manufacture of wood based products.

ADVERTISING RATES:
Full Page Colour £875.00
Agency Commission: 10%
Mechanical Data: Bleed Size: 303 x 216mm, Trim Size: 297 x 210mm, Type Area: 254 x 178mm, No. of Columns (Display): 2, Col Length: 254mm, Page Width: 178mm, Film: Digital
Copy instructions: Copy Date: 3 weeks prior to publication date
Average advertising content per issue: 25%
BUSINESS: TIMBER, WOOD & FORESTRY

PANEL, WOOD & SOLID SURFACES
1856400U4R-628

Editorial Address: Creative Media Centre, Robertson Street, HASTINGS, TN34 1HL **Tel:** 01424 205428
Fax: 01424 205436
Email: info@pawprintuk.co.uk
Advertising Address: As above.
Email: info@pawprintuk.co.uk
Web site: http://www.pawprintuk.co.uk
Publisher: Pawprint Publishing Ltd
Date Established: 2008
Frequency: Monthly
Free to qualifying individuals
Circulation: 6,060 (Publisher's Statement)
Editor: Pam Rowden
Summary of Content: Magazine covering joinery, shop fitting, kitchen fitting and allied trades.
Readership/Target Audience: Aimed at joiners, shop fitters, kitchen fitters and furniture manufacturers.
ADVERTISING RATES:
Full Page Colour £500.00
Agency Commission: 10%
Mechanical Data: Trim Size: 297 x 210mm, Bleed Size: 303 x 216mm, Film: Digital
BUSINESS: ARCHITECTURE & BUILDING: Building Related

PANSTADIA
629118U32H-248

Formerly: PanStadia International
Editorial Address: Head Office, Hall Farm House, 9 High Street, CASTLE DONINGTON, DE74 2PP **Tel:** 01332 814555
Fax: 01332 853410
Email: katie-mcintyre@panstadia.com
Advertising Address: As above.
Email: katie-mcintyre@panstadia.com
Web site: http://www.panstadia.com
ISSN: 1749-1983
Publisher: PanStadia Publishing Ltd
Date Established: 1993
Frequency: Quarterly
Annual Sub.: £100.00
Circulation: 21,000 (Publisher's Statement)
Usual Pagination: 150
Editor: Katie McIntyre; **Advertising Manager:** Katie McIntyre
Summary of Content: Magazine providing information and features about the international sports and entertainment facility industry from architecture, design and build, to fit out, maintenance, management and naming rights.
Readership/Target Audience: Aimed at stadium, arena and venue managers, sports federations, Olympics Committees, professional sports clubs and teams, architects and designers, product and service companies, conference and entertainment centre owners etc.
ADVERTISING RATES:
Full Page Colour £3141.00
Agency Commission: 10%
Mechanical Data: Type Area: 265 x 180mm, Bleed Size: 303 x 216mm, Trim Size: 297 x 210mm, Col Length: 265mm, Page Width: 180mm, Film: Digital
Copy instructions: Copy Date: 1 week prior to publication date
Average advertising content per issue: 25%
BUSINESS: LOCAL GOVERNMENT, LEISURE & RECREATION: Leisure, Recreation & Entertainment

PAPER MAKING & DISTRIBUTION
38712U36-26

Editorial Address: Tralee, Hillcrest Road, EDENBRIDGE, TN8 6JS **Tel:** 01732 505724 **Fax:** 01732 860052
Email: pmdmagazine@btinternet.com
Advertising Address: As above.
Email: pmdmagazine@btinternet.com
Web site: http://www.pmdmagazine.com
ISSN: 1479-3989
Publisher: Hartswood Media
Date Established: 1991
Frequency: 6 issues yearly - Published in the middle of the 1st cover month
Free to qualifying individuals
Annual Sub.: £110.00
Circulation: 11,813 (Publisher's Statement)
Usual Pagination: 40
Editor: Vince Maynard; **Advertising Manager:** Vince Maynard; **Publisher:** Paul Barrett

Summary of Content: Journal covering the production and conversion of pulp, paper, tissue and board.
Readership/Target Audience: Aimed at mill managers and superintendents, production managers, executives, engineers, chemists and logistics.
ADVERTISING RATES:
Full Page Colour £2995.00
Agency Commission: 10%
Mechanical Data: Page Width: 186mm, Type Area: 268 x 186mm, Bleed Size: 303 x 216mm, Trim Size: 297 x 210mm, Print Process: Offset litho, Col Length: 268mm, Film: Digital
Copy instructions: Copy Date: 1 week prior to publication date
Average advertising content per issue: 40%
BUSINESS: PAPER

PAPER MARKET DIGEST
38715U36-50
Editorial Address: PO Box 2002, WATFORD, WD25 9ZT
Tel: 01923 894777 **Fax:** 01923 897888
Email: enquiries@pplresearch.co.uk
Web site: http://www.pplresearch.co.uk
ISSN: 1358-0701
Publisher: PPL Research Ltd
Date Established: 1983
Frequency: Monthly
Annual Sub: £330.00
Circulation: 600 (Publisher's Statement)
Usual Pagination: 12
Editor: Lawrence Turk; **Managing Director:** Lawrence Turk; **Publisher:** Lawrence Turk; **Circulation Manager:** Anne Lovelock
Summary of Content: Publication containing data and analysis of the graphic papers market.
Readership/Target Audience: Aimed at professional buyers and suppliers of graphic papers.
ADVERTISING: No Advertising taken
BUSINESS: PAPER

PAPER TECHNOLOGY
38716U36-100
Editorial Address: 2 St Philip Street, LONDON, SW8 3SP
Tel: 020 7622 9269
Email: memarley@mac.com
Advertising Address: 5 Frecheville Court, BURY, BL9 0UF
Tel: 0161 764 5858 **Fax:** 0161 764 5353
Email: helen@pita.co.uk
Web site: http://www.pita.co.uk
ISSN: 0306-252X
Publisher: PITA
Date Established: 1920
Frequency: 10 issues yearly
Annual Sub: £100.00
Circulation: 2,300 (Publisher's Statement)
Usual Pagination: 64
Editor: Margaret Marley; **Advertising Manager:** Helen Dolan
Summary of Content: Official journal of The Paper Industry Technical Association. Contains information on new technology and developments in the pulp, papermaking, non-woven and converting industries.
Readership/Target Audience: Aimed at those associated with the paper industry.
ADVERTISING RATES:
Full Page Mono £1100.00
Full Page Colour £1900.00
Agency Commission: 10%
Mechanical Data: Page Width: 175mm, Type Area: 260 x 175mm, Bleed Size: 303 x 216mm, Trim Size: 297 x 210mm, Col Length: 260mm, Print Process: Offset litho, Film: Digital
Average advertising content per issue: 14%
BUSINESS: PAPER

PAPERBASE ABSTRACTS
38717U36-25
Editorial Address: Cleeve Road, LEATHERHEAD, KT22 7RU **Tel:** 01372 802000 **Fax:** 01372 802239
Email: jillian.low@pira-international.com
Web site: http://www.paperbase.org
ISSN: 1359-5156
Publisher: PIRA International
Date Established: 1968
Frequency: Monthly
Annual Sub: £850.00
Circulation: 40 (Publisher's Statement)
Editor: Jillian Low
Summary of Content: Publication covering information on key pulp and paper topics.
Readership/Target Audience: Aimed at those within the paper and board industry.
ADVERTISING: No Advertising taken
BUSINESS: PAPER

PARK WORLD
25712U64A-172
Editorial Address: 15A London Road, MAIDSTONE, ME16 8LY **Tel:** 01622 687031 **Fax:** 01622 757646
Email: parkworld@datateam.co.uk
Advertising Address: As above. **Tel:** 01622 699124

Email: parkworld@datateam.co.uk
Web site: http://www.parkworld-online.com
ISSN: 1462-4796
Publisher: Datateam Publishing Ltd
Frequency: 10 issues yearly - Published the 1st week of the cover month
Free to qualifying individuals
Annual Sub: £55.00
Circulation: 3,800 (Publisher's Statement)
Usual Pagination: 40
Editor: Owen Ralph; **Advertising Manager:** Mark Burgess; **Managing Editor:** Steph Norbury
Summary of Content: Magazine covering the theme and amusement park and family entertainment centre industry including new products, concepts, licensing and global trends.
Readership/Target Audience: Read by operators, developers, project managers and decision makers within the industry.
ADVERTISING RATES:
Full Page Colour ....: £1470.00
Mechanical Data: Trim Size: 306 x 229mm, Bleed Size: 312 x 235mm
Copy instructions: Copy Date: 3 weeks prior to publication date
BUSINESS: OTHER CLASSIFICATIONS: Amusement Trade

PARKING NEWS
39702U49R-175
Editorial Address: Stuart House, 41-43 Perrymount Road, HAYWARDS HEATH, RH16 3BN **Tel:** 01444 447300
Fax: 01444 447311
Email: simon.o@britishparking.co.uk
Advertising Address: Richard Langrish Communications, Rose Cottage, Taybridge Road, ABERFELDY, PH15 2BH
Tel: 01887 820533 **Fax:** 01887 820533
Email: richard.l@britishparking.co.uk
Web site: http://www.britishparking.co.uk
ISSN: 1470-8361
Publisher: British Parking Association
Date Established: 1969
Frequency: 11 issues yearly
Free to qualifying individuals
Circulation: 3,000 (Publisher's Statement)
Usual Pagination: 52
Editor: Simon O'Brien
Summary of Content: Journal covering all aspects of vehicle parking in the UK and abroad with feature articles, news, products and the latest technology.
Readership/Target Audience: Read by officials in local authorities, central government, hospitals and educational establishments who organise vehicle parking.
ADVERTISING RATES:
Full Page Mono £630.00
Full Page Colour £885.00
Agency Commission: 10%
Mechanical Data: Page Width: 190mm, Trim Size: 297 x 210mm, Type Area: 277 x 190mm, Col Length: 277mm, Film: Digital, Bleed Size: 303 x 216mm
Average advertising content per issue: 40%
BUSINESS: TRANSPORT: Transport Related

PARKING REVIEW
39703U49R-180
Editorial Address: 359 Kennington Lane, LONDON, SE11 5QY **Tel:** 0845 270 7871 **Fax:** 0845 270 7961
Email: ed.pr@landor.co.uk
Advertising Address: Suite 17, Spice Court, Plantation Wharf, LONDON, SW11 3UE **Tel:** 020 7924 5885
Fax: 020 7924 4565
Email: frankkingaby@cjplconsultants.com
Web site: http://www.parkingreview.co.uk
ISSN: 0962-3599
Publisher: Landor Publishing
Date Established: 1989
Frequency: Monthly - Published in the 1st week of the cover month
Annual Sub: £75.00
Circulation: 3,500 (Publisher's Statement)
Usual Pagination: 48
Editor: Mark Moran; **Managing Editor:** Mark Moran
Summary of Content: Magazine focusing on management and design of car parks and on-street enforcement worldwide.
Readership/Target Audience: Aimed at public and private parking authorities, car park designers, builders, contractors and equipment suppliers.
ADVERTISING RATES:
Full Page Colour £1900.00
Agency Commission: 10%
Mechanical Data: Type Area: 305 x 220mm, Col Length: 305mm, Film: Digital, Page Width: 220mm, Trim Size: 332 x 240mm, Bleed Size: 250 x 342mm
Copy instructions: Copy Date: Last week of the month prior to publication date
Average advertising content per issue: 50%
BUSINESS: TRANSPORT: Transport Related

THE PARLIAMENTARY MARITIME REVIEW
39342U45A-121
Editorial Address: No 3 The Green, Ketton, STAMFORD, PE9 3RA **Tel:** 01780 721628 **Fax:** 01780 721980
Email: pridgway@globalnet.co.uk
Advertising Address: As above.
Email: pridgway@globalnet.co.uk
ISSN: 1351-1351
Publisher: The Parliamentary Maritime Group
Frequency: 3 issues yearly - Published in March, July and December
Annual Sub: £20.00
Circulation: 850 (Publisher's Statement)
Usual Pagination: 12
Editor: Paul Ridgway; **Advertising Manager:** Paul Ridgway
Summary of Content: Journal of the all-party Parliamentary Maritime Group, with members in both houses, the EP and the marine industry.
Readership/Target Audience: Aimed at ship builders, oil, trade unions, defence, environment and people in the maritime industry.
ADVERTISING: Rates on application
Average advertising content per issue: 25%
BUSINESS: MARINE & SHIPPING

PARTY PARTY
1639846U52C-151
Editorial Address: 1 Churchgates, The Wilderness, BERKHAMSTED, HP4 2AZ **Tel:** 01442 289930
Fax: 01442 289950
Email: jacqui@lemapublishing.co.uk
Advertising Address: As above.
Email: rob@lemapublishing.co.uk
Publisher: Lema Publishing
Date Established: 2000
Frequency: 6 issues yearly
Cover Price: Free
Circulation: 4,500 (Publisher's Statement)
Usual Pagination: 46
Editor: Jacqui Parr; **Advertising Manager:** Rob Willis
Summary of Content: Magazine covering new products associations, new products, classified advertisements and general news concerned with the party industry.
Readership/Target Audience: Aimed at those within the party industry such as retailers, manufacturers and wholesalers of party products.
ADVERTISING RATES:
Full Page Colour £1395.00
Agency Commission: 10%
Mechanical Data: Type Area: 252 x 179mm, Bleed Size: 303 x 216mm, Trim Size: 297 x 210mm, Col Length: 252mm, Page Width: 179mm, Film: Digital
Average advertising content per issue: 40%
BUSINESS: GIFT TRADE: Fancy Goods

PASS
35046U1B-310
Editorial Address: 145 London Road, KINGSTON UPON THAMES, KT2 6SR **Tel:** 020 8247 1445 **Fax:** 020 8247 1424
Email: alex.miller@cch.co.uk
Advertising Address: As above. **Tel:** 020 8247 1350
Fax: 020 8247 1388
Email: elly.kiss@cch.co.uk
Web site: http://www.passmagazine.com
ISSN: 1352-8645
Publisher: Wolters Kluwer (UK) Ltd
Date Established: 1984
Frequency: Monthly - Published in the 1st week of the month
Cover Price: Free
Circulation: 40,000 (ABC 01/07/2007 to 30/06/2008)
Usual Pagination: 40
Editor: Alex Miller
Summary of Content: Magazine containing news and features relating to part-qualified accountants.
Readership/Target Audience: Aimed at part qualified accountants of the six major bodies of accountancy.
ADVERTISING RATES:
Full Page Mono £4530.00
Full Page Colour £5780.00
Agency Commission: 10%
Mechanical Data: Film: Positive, right reading, emulsion side down. Digital, Type Area: 270 x 200mm, Col Length: 270mm, Bleed Size: 303 x 216mm, Trim Size: 297 x 210mm, Page Width: 200mm
Copy instructions: Copy Date: 2 weeks prior to publication date
Average advertising content per issue: 60%
Supplement(s): Weblife - 1xY
BUSINESS: FINANCE & ECONOMICS: Accountancy

PASSENGER SHIP TECHNOLOGY
39356U45A-230
Formerly: Ferry Technology
Editorial Address: 6-7 Victoria Parade (top floor), TORQUAY, TQ1 2BB **Tel:** 01803 213148 **Fax:** 01803 213159
Email: clive.woodbridge@rivieramm.com

Business Magazines

Advertising Address: Miter House, 66 Abbey Road, ENFIELD, EN1 2QN **Tel:** 020 8364 1551 **Fax:** 020 8364 1331
Email: rob.gore@ferrytechnology.com
Web site: http://www.ferrytechnology.com
ISSN: 1359-4222
Publisher: Riviera Maritime Media
Date Established: 1995
Frequency: 6 issues yearly
Annual Sub.: £75.00
Circulation: 3,518 (ABC 01/01/2007 to 31/12/2007)
Editor: Clive Woodbridge; **Managing Editor:** Tony Wilson
Summary of Content: Journal covering all aspects of the worldwide ferry industry including construction, design, operation, safety, propulsion and including articles on future technology.
Readership/Target Audience: Read by ferry and fast ferry operators, shipbuilders, naval operators, equipment suppliers and naval architects and consultants.
ADVERTISING RATES:
Full Page Colour £2000.00
Agency Commission: 10%
Mechanical Data: Col Length: 264mm, Page Width: 190mm, Bleed Size: 303 x 216mm, Trim Size: 297 x 210mm, Type Area: 264 x 190mm, Film: Digital
Copy instructions: Copy Date: 3 weeks prior to publication date
Average advertising content per issue: 40%
BUSINESS: MARINE & SHIPPING

PASSENGER TERMINAL WORLD
39584U49A-170

Editorial Address: Abinger House, Church Street, DORKING, RH4 1DF **Tel:** 01306 743744 **Fax:** 01306 887546
Email: a.pickering@ukintpress.com
Advertising Address: As above. **Fax:** 01306 742525
Email: a.smith@ukintpress.com
Web site: http://www.passengerterminal-expo.com
ISSN: 1362-0770
Publisher: UKIP Media & Events Ltd
Date Established: 1995
Frequency: Quarterly - Published at the end of the cover month
Free to qualifying individuals
Annual Sub.: £140.00
Circulation: 10,509 (ABC 01/01/2008 to 31/12/2008)
Usual Pagination: 100
Editor: Andrew Pickering; **Advertising Manager:** Andrzej Smith
Summary of Content: Magazine dealing with all aspects of projects involving air, rail, sail and bus passenger terminals.
Readership/Target Audience: Aimed at decision makers within terminal projects.
ADVERTISING RATES:
Full Page Mono £3795.00
Full Page Colour £3795.00
Agency Commission: 10%
Mechanical Data: Bleed Size: 306 x 236mm, Trim Size: 300 x 230mm, Film: Digital, Type Area: 276 x 200mm, Col Length: 276mm, Page Width: 200mm
Copy instructions: Copy Date: 27th of the month prior to publication date
Average advertising content per issue: 33%
BUSINESS: TRANSPORT

PAST & PRESENT
48807U62R-466

Editorial Address: 175 Banbury Road, OXFORD, OX2 7AW **Tel:** 01865 353907 **Fax:** 01865 310080
Email: editors@pastandpresent.demon.co.uk
Advertising Address: 60 Upper Broadmoor Road, CROWTHORNE, RG45 7DE **Tel:** 01344 779945
Fax: 01344 779945
Email: lhann@lhms.fsnet.co.uk
Web site: http://past.oupjournals.org
ISSN: 0031-2746
Publisher: OUP
Date Established: 1952
Frequency: Quarterly
Annual Sub.: £104.00
Circulation: 3,200 (Publisher's Statement)
Usual Pagination: 240
Editor: Lyndal Roper
Summary of Content: Publication concerned with social, economic and cultural changes, their causes and consequences.
Readership/Target Audience: Aimed at scholars, teachers, students and non-specialists with an interest in history.
ADVERTISING RATES:
Full Page Mono £415.00
Agency Commission: 10%
Mechanical Data: Film: Digital, Type Area: 180 x 100mm, Col Length: 180mm, Page Width: 100mm
Copy instructions: Copy Date: 5th of the month prior to publication month
BUSINESS: CHURCH & SCHOOL EQUIPMENT & EDUCATION: Education Related

---

PATHFINDER
37069U14F-53

Editorial Address: Baltic Business Centre, Saltmeadows Road, GATESHEAD, NE8 3DA **Tel:** 0191 442 4001
Email: michaelbrash@pathfindermagazine.co.uk
Advertising Address: As above. **Tel:** 01294 232596
Email: helen@balticpublications.co.uk
Web site: http://www.pathfinder-one.com
Publisher: Baltic Publications Ltd
Date Established: 1991
Frequency: Monthly
Cover Price: Free
Annual Sub.: £20.00
Circulation: 40,000 (Publisher's Statement)
Usual Pagination: 56
Editor: Michael Brash
Summary of Content: Magazine covering all aspects of career transition and recruitment.
Readership/Target Audience: Aimed at serving and former members of the armed forces and defence related industries facing the transition to civilian employment and anyone dealing with redundancy or a career change.
ADVERTISING RATES:
Full Page Mono £3295.00
Full Page Colour £3995.00
Mechanical Data: Film: Digital, Trim Size: 297 x 210mm
BUSINESS: COMMERCE, INDUSTRY & MANAGEMENT: Training & Recruitment

---

PATROL
38435U32F-360

Editorial Address: Sussex Police HQ, Malling House, LEWES, BN7 2DZ **Tel:** 01273 404177 **Fax:** 01273 404280
Email: jill.pedersen@sussex.pnn.police.uk
Advertising Address: 7 Vectis Road, GOSPORT, PO12 2QD **Tel:** 023 9235 1920
Email: patrol@media3.co.uk
Web site: http://www.sussex.police.uk
Publisher: Sussex Police Press Office
Frequency: Monthly
Cover Price: Free
Circulation: 10,000 (Publisher's Statement)
Usual Pagination: 12
Editor: Jill Pedersen; **Advertising Manager:** Brian Seeney
Summary of Content: In-house newspaper covering news, information and activities of the Sussex Police force.
Readership/Target Audience: Aimed at police officers, police staff, retired officers and the general public at the front of a police station.
ADVERTISING RATES:
Full Page Colour £1100.00
Agency Commission: 10%
Mechanical Data: Col Widths (Display): 42mm, Film: Digital, No. of Columns (Display): 6, Type Area: 370 x 274mm, Col Length: 370mm, Page Width: 274mm
Copy instructions: Copy Date: 2 weeks prior to publication date
BUSINESS: LOCAL GOVERNMENT, LEISURE & RECREATION: Police

PATTERN ANALYSIS & APPLICATIONS
36002U5R-350

Editorial Address: Ashbourne House, The Guildway, Old Portsmouth Road, Artington, GUILDFORD, GU3 1LP
Tel: 01483 734635
Email: rhonda.lane@springer.com
Advertising Address: As above. **Tel:** 01483 734437
Fax: 01483 734411
Email: rhonda.lane@springer.com
Web site: http://www.springer.com
ISSN: 1433-7541
Publisher: Springer
Frequency: Quarterly
Editor: Rhonda Lane; **Advertising Manager:** Rhonda Lane
Summary of Content: Journal featuring articles concerning intelligent pattern analysis and applications in computer science and engineering.
Readership/Target Audience: Read by academics in that field.
ADVERTISING RATES:
Full Page Mono £380.00
Full Page Colour £1025.00
Agency Commission: 10%
Mechanical Data: Bleed Size: 283 x 216mm, Trim Size: 277 x 210mm, Type Area: 237 x 172mm, Col Length: 237mm, Page Width: 172mm, Film: Digital
Copy instructions: Copy Date: 4 weeks prior to publication date
Average advertising content per issue: 1%
BUSINESS: COMPUTERS & AUTOMATION: Computers Related

THE PAWNBROKER
39814U53-245

Formerly: The Pawn Broker
Editorial Address: Avenue Brooks, 5 The Avenue, LONDON, N8 0JR **Tel:** 020 8365 7313 **Fax:** 020 8365 7313
Email: peteroper@btconnect.com

Advertising Address: Chiltern Court, St. Peters Avenue, Caversham, READING, RG4 7DH **Tel:** 0845 612 0640
Email: des.milligan@thenpa.com
Web site: http://www.thenpa.com
Publisher: The National Pawnbrokers Association
Date Established: 2004
Frequency: Quarterly - Published in March, June, September and December
Cover Price: Free
Circulation: 1,500 (Publisher's Statement)
Usual Pagination: 24
Editor: Peter Roper; **Advertising Manager:** Des Milligan
Summary of Content: Magazine carrying news and legislative changes affecting the pawn broking industry.
Readership/Target Audience: Read by pawn brokers and affiliated organisations.
ADVERTISING RATES:
Full Page Colour £575.00
Mechanical Data: Film: Digital, Bleed Size: 303 x 216mm, Trim Size: 297 x 210mm
Copy instructions: Copy Date: 3 weeks prior to publication date
Average advertising content per issue: 15%
BUSINESS: RETAILING & WHOLESALING

PAY & BENEFITS MAGAZINE
34960U1A-273

Formerly: PHR: Payroll & Human Resources
Editorial Address: 2 Addiscombe Road, CROYDON, CR9 5AF **Tel:** 020 8662 2011 **Fax:** 020 8662 2041
Email: kavitha.siva@lexisnexis.co.uk
Advertising Address: As above. **Tel:** 020 8212 1925
Fax: 020 8212 1970
Email: dean.dalton@lexisnexis.co.uk
ISSN: 0950-8147
Publisher: LexisNexis
Frequency: Monthly - Published in the last week of the month prior to the cover month
Annual Sub.: £119.00
Circulation: 20,800 (Publisher's Statement)
Usual Pagination: 60
Editor: Kavitha Sivasubramaniam
Summary of Content: Magazine covering matters relating to payroll management and administration and HR.
Readership/Target Audience: Aimed at payroll managers, accountants and human resources managers.
ADVERTISING RATES:
Full Page Colour £1525.00
Agency Commission: 10%
Mechanical Data: Page Width: 185mm, Film: Digital, Type Area: 265 x 185mm, Bleed Size: 303 x 216mm, Trim Size: 297 x 210mm, Col Length: 265mm, No. of Columns (Display): 3
Copy instructions: Copy Date: 2 weeks prior to publication date
Average advertising content per issue: 40%
Supplement(s): P11D: A Guide to Completion - 1xY, Payroll and Personnel Systems: A Guide to Software - 1xY, Payroll Outsourcing - 1xY
BUSINESS: FINANCE & ECONOMICS

PAY MAGAZINE
34959U1A-271

Editorial Address: 145 London Road, KINGSTON UPON THAMES, KT2 6SR **Tel:** 020 8547 3333
Email: cathy.heys@cch.co.uk
Advertising Address: As above.
Email: jacqui.roughley@cch.co.uk
Web site: http://www.paymagazine.com
ISSN: 1465-3796
Publisher: CCH
Date Established: 1990
Frequency: Monthly - Published around the 3rd of the cover month
Free to qualifying individuals
Annual Sub.: £118.00
Circulation: 20,727 (ABC 01/07/2008 to 30/06/2009)
Usual Pagination: 56
Editor: Cathy Heys; **Advertising Manager:** Jacqui Roughley
Summary of Content: Magazine containing coverage of trends concerning pay, benefits, taxation and HR strategy.
Readership/Target Audience: Aimed at payroll, human resources and finance professionals.
ADVERTISING RATES:
Full Page Mono £2043.29
Full Page Colour £2705.29
Agency Commission: 10%
Mechanical Data: Page Width: 185mm, Type Area: 270 x 185mm, Bleed Size: 303 x 216mm, Trim Size: 297 x 210mm, Col Length: 270mm, Film: Digital
Copy instructions: Copy Date: 4 weeks prior to publication date
Average advertising content per issue: 45%
BUSINESS: FINANCE & ECONOMICS

PAYMENTS CARDS & MOBILE   35079U1C-157

Formerly: European Card Review
Editorial Address: The Granary, High Street, Blakeney, HOLT, NR25 7AL **Tel:** 01263 740396 **Fax:** 01263 741183
Email: anniet@paymentscm.com
Advertising Address: As above. **Tel:** 01263 741126
Email: wendy@europeancardreview.com
Web site: http://www.paymentscardsandmobile.com
ISSN: 1360-6069
Publisher: ECR Publishing Partnership
Date Established: 1995
Frequency: 6 issues yearly
Annual Sub.: £100.00
Circulation: 9,159 (Publisher's Statement)
Usual Pagination: 64
Editor: Annie Turner; **Advertising Manager:** Wendy Sanders; **Publisher:** Alex Rolfe
Summary of Content: Pan-European magazine covering all aspects of the European payment card industry, including smart cards, credit card programmes, loyalty cards, technology innovations and related management issues.
Readership/Target Audience: Aimed at bankers, credit card managers, manufacturers and private label card programme managers.
ADVERTISING RATES:
Full Page Mono £1750.00
Full Page Colour £2350.00
Agency Commission: 10%
Mechanical Data: Type Area: 280 x 200mm, No. of Columns (Display): 3, Bleed Size: 296 x 216mm, Trim Size: 290 x 210mm, Film: Digital, Col Length: 280mm, Page Width: 200mm
BUSINESS: FINANCE & ECONOMICS: Banking

PAYROLL PROFESSIONAL   34955U1A-268

Formerly: PAYadvice
Editorial Address: Shelley House, Farmhouse Way, Monkspath, SOLIHULL, B90 4EH **Tel:** 0121 712 1000
Fax: 0121 712 1001
Email: editor@payrollprofession.org
Advertising Address: As above.
Email: vickie.moss@payrollprofessional.org
Web site: http://www.payrollprofession.org
Publisher: Institute of Payroll Professionals
Frequency: 10 issues yearly - Published in the 1st week of each month
Annual Sub.: £100.00
Circulation: 5,000 (Publisher's Statement)
Usual Pagination: 44
Editor: Mike Nicholas; **Advertising Manager:** Vickie Moss
Summary of Content: Membership magazine of The Institute of Payroll Professionals, the professional body for the payroll and pensions profession in the UK.
Readership/Target Audience: Aimed at local governments and people who work in the payroll and pensions industry.
ADVERTISING RATES:
Full Page Colour £1490.00
Mechanical Data: Film: Digital, Trim Size: 297 x 210mm
BUSINESS: FINANCE & ECONOMICS

PAYROLL WORLD   765498U1A-287

Editorial Address: 1st Floor, 70 Newcomen Street, LONDON, SE1 1YT **Tel:** 020 7940 4801 **Fax:** 020 7940 4843
Email: editorial@payrollworld.com
Advertising Address: As above.
Email: advertising@payrollworld.com
Web site: http://www.payrollworld.com
ISSN: 1474-9068
Publisher: Maximvs
Date Established: 2001
Frequency: Monthly - Published around the 1st of the month
Annual Sub.: £75.00
Circulation: 13,000 (Publisher's Statement)
Usual Pagination: 48
Editor: Andrew Brown; **Publisher:** Chris Fitzgerald
Summary of Content: Magazine containing the latest payroll news and articles which are relevant to a busy payroll department.
Readership/Target Audience: Aimed at existing and newly appointed payroll managers.
ADVERTISING RATES:
Full Page Mono £1460.00
Full Page Colour £2085.00
Agency Commission: 10%
Mechanical Data: Bleed Size: 303 x 216mm, Trim Size: 297 x 210mm, Film: Digital, Type Area: 270 x 190mm, Col Length: 270mm, Page Width: 190mm
Copy instructions: Copy Date: 14th of the month prior to publication date
BUSINESS: FINANCE & ECONOMICS

PBW NEWS   41487U64E-55

Editorial Address: 6 The Rickyard, Clifton Reynes, OLNEY, MK46 5LQ **Tel:** 01234 714644 **Fax:** 01234 714633
Email: editor@pbwnews.com
Advertising Address: As above.

Email: sales@pbwnews.com
Web site: http://www.petbusinessworld.com
Publisher: Pickwick Swales Ltd
Date Established: 1951
Frequency: Monthly
Annual Sub.: £16.00
Circulation: 6,000 (Publisher's Statement)
Usual Pagination: 36
Editor: Karen Pickwick; **Advertising Manager:** Mark Lightfoot; **Publisher:** Karen Pickwick
Summary of Content: Magazine covering all aspects of the pet trade including market trends, product news, company and people profiles, exhibitions and conferences.
Readership/Target Audience: Read by all in the pet trade, retailers, wholesalers, distributors, manufacturers, groomers, vets and people who run kennels, catteries and garden centres.
ADVERTISING RATES:
Full Page Mono £925.00
Full Page Colour £925.00
SCC £18.00
Agency Commission: 10%
Mechanical Data: Page Width: 195mm, Type Area: 270 x 195mm, Bleed Size: 303 x 216mm, Trim Size: 297 x 210mm, Col Length: 270mm, Film: Digital
Copy instructions: Copy Date: 1 month prior to publication date
Average advertising content per issue: 40%
BUSINESS: OTHER CLASSIFICATIONS: Pet Trade

PC RETAIL INCORPORATING CTO

1623303U5R-658

Formerly: PC Retail
Editorial Address: Saxon House, 6A St. Andrew Street, HERTFORD, SG14 1JA **Tel:** 01992 535646
Fax: 01992 535648
Email: andrew.wooden@intentmedia.co.uk
Advertising Address: As above. **Tel:** 01992 535647
Email: katie.rawlings@intentmedia.co.uk
Web site: http://www.pcretailmag.com
Publisher: Intent Media
Date Established: 2003
Frequency: Monthly
Free to qualifying individuals
Circulation: 12,766 (ABC 01/01/2008 to 31/12/2008)
Usual Pagination: 64
Editor: Andrew Wooden; **Advertising Manager:** Katie Rawlings; **Managing Editor:** Lisa Foster; **Publisher:** Stuart Dinsey
Summary of Content: Magazine focusing on the computer retail industry. Features news and analysis of industry issues, company profiles and interviews with personalities in the industry. It is also an outlet for computer hardware and software product news and provides a general guide for retail buyers. Includes features on consumer computer retail products and games coverage.
Readership/Target Audience: Aimed at managers and staff of independent and multiple computer retail stores as well as online and catalogue retailers.
ADVERTISING RATES:
Full Page Colour £1155.00
Agency Commission: 10%
Mechanical Data: Type Area: 295 x 212mm, Col Length: 295mm, Page Width: 212mm, Film: Digital
BUSINESS: COMPUTERS & AUTOMATION: Computers Related

PCS VIEW   37198U14L-550

Editorial Address: 160 Falcon Road, LONDON, SW11 2LN
Email: alexf@pcs.org.uk
Advertising Address: 30 Monmouth Street, BATH, BA1 2BW **Tel:** 01225 442244
Email: rosa.smith@futurenet.co.uk
Web site: http://www.pcs.org.uk
ISSN: 1362-3737
Publisher: PCS
Date Established: 1998
Frequency: 10 issues yearly
Free to qualifying individuals
Annual Sub.: £18.00
Circulation: 320,000 (Publisher's Statement)
Usual Pagination: 32
Editor: Alex Flynn; **Advertising Manager:** Rosa Smith
Summary of Content: Journal covering news, features and information relating to the civil and public services.
Readership/Target Audience: Read by members of the Public and Commercial Services Union.
ADVERTISING RATES:
Full Page Colour £9500.00
Agency Commission: 10%
Mechanical Data: Type Area: 277 x 190mm, Bleed Size: 303 x 216mm, Trim Size: 297 x 210mm, Col Length: 277mm, Page Width: 190mm, Film: Digital
Copy instructions: Copy Date: 1st week of the month prior to publication date
Average advertising content per issue: 15%
BUSINESS: COMMERCE, INDUSTRY & MANAGEMENT: Trade Unions

PE AND SPORT TODAY   622900U62B-685

Editorial Address: 33-41 Dallington Street, LONDON, EC1V 0BB **Tel:** 020 7954 3400 **Fax:** 020 7251 9045
Email: ian.pickering@optimuseducation.co.uk
Advertising Address: As above.
Email: jon.pyser@electricwordplc.com
Web site: http://www.optimuspub.co.uk
ISSN: 1407-6121
Publisher: Optimus Education
Date Established: 1999
Frequency: Quarterly
Annual Sub.: £21.00
Circulation: 3,013 (Publisher's Statement)
Usual Pagination: 64
Editor: Ian Pickering
Summary of Content: Magazine providing information on all aspects of physical education.
Readership/Target Audience: Aimed at physical education and sports teachers, facility managers and LEA advisors.
ADVERTISING RATES:
Full Page Colour £1000.00
Copy instructions: Copy Date: 2 weeks prior to publication date
BUSINESS: CHURCH & SCHOOL EQUIPMENT & EDUCATION: Education Teachers

PECM PROCESS ENGINEERING, CONTROL & MAINTENANCE   1849423U19A-570

Editorial Address: Redfern House, 347 Margate Road, RAMSGATE, CT12 6SG **Tel:** 01843 592802
Fax: 01843 593214
Email: jessica@pecm.co.uk
Web site: http://www.pecm.co.uk
Publisher: MH Media Interactive Ltd
Date Established: 2007
Frequency: 6 issues yearly
Free to qualifying individuals
Annual Sub.: £24.00
Circulation: 70,000 (Publisher's Statement)
Usual Pagination: 36
Editor: Jessica Stokes
Summary of Content: Magazine covering the latest news and case studies of equipment in action as well as research and technology developments and opinion.
Readership/Target Audience: Aimed at key decision makers within the process and maintenance industries including process and chemical engineers, environmental and general engineers, companies and organisations in the food, dairy, beverage, brewing, semiconductor, pharmaceutical, biotechnology, chemical, petroleum and offshore industries.
BUSINESS: ENGINEERING & MACHINERY

PEDIATRIC ANESTHESIA   40213U56A-108

Editorial Address: 9600 Garsington Road, Cowley, OXFORD, OX4 2DQ **Tel:** 01865 776868 **Fax:** 01865 471326
Email: pan@oxon.blackwellpublishing.com
Advertising Address: As above. **Tel:** 01865 476383
Fax: 01865 471383
Email: neil.chesher@oxon.blackwellpublishing.com
Web site: http://www.blackwellpublishing.com
ISSN: 1155-5645
Publisher: Wiley-Blackwell Publishing
Frequency: Monthly
Annual Sub.: £150.00
Circulation: 990 (Publisher's Statement)
Usual Pagination: 96
Editor: Joseph Angelo; **Advertising Manager:** Rita Orban
Summary of Content: Magazine covering scientific and clinical research, case studies and articles relating to anaesthesia in newborns, infants and children.
Readership/Target Audience: Aimed at paediatric anaesthesiologists and those involved with paediatric anaesthesia.
ADVERTISING RATES:
Full Page Mono £582.00
Full Page Colour £1367.00
Agency Commission: 10%
Mechanical Data: Type Area: 245 x 180mm, Trim Size: 276 x 210mm, Col Length: 245mm, Bleed Size: 282 x 216mm, Film: Digital, Page Width: 180mm
Copy instructions: Copy Date: 5 weeks prior to publication date
BUSINESS: HEALTH & MEDICAL

PEM (PORT ENGINEERING MANAGEMENT)   39413U45D-200

Editorial Address: 131A Furtherwick Road, CANVEY ISLAND, SS8 7AT **Tel:** 01268 511300 **Fax:** 01268 510467
Email: shipaat@aol.com
Advertising Address: As above.
Email: shipaat@aol.com
Web site: http://www.portengineeringmanagement.com
ISSN: 0264-9783
Publisher: A&A Thorpe

Frequency: 6 issues yearly - Published in the 1st week of the 2nd cover month
Free to qualifying individuals
Annual Sub.: £55.00
Circulation: 4,000 (Publisher's Statement)
Usual Pagination: 36
Editor: Alan Thorpe; **Advertising Manager:** Alan Thorpe
Summary of Content: International journal of dredging, port development and ocean technology.
Readership/Target Audience: Aimed at executive, planning and operational personnel within major ports and harbours worldwide, as well as equipment suppliers, contractors, specialist shipowners, operators, consultants and funding agencies.
ADVERTISING RATES:
Full Page Mono £1250.00
Full Page Colour £1850.00
Agency Commission: 10%
Mechanical Data: Type Area: 274 x 190mm, Col Length: 274mm, Bleed Size: 303 x 213mm, Trim Size: 297 x 210mm, Page Width: 190mm, Film: Digital
Copy instructions: Copy Date: 3 weeks prior to publication date
BUSINESS: MARINE & SHIPPING: Marine Engineering Equipment

PEN 2 PAPER
1664669U41B-311

Editorial Address: 1 May Cottage, Cheriton, HAMPSHIRE, SO24 0PR **Tel:** 01474 824711
Email: jamesg@binfo.co.uk
Advertising Address: 4 New Cottages, Green Farm Lane, Shorne, GRAVESEND, DA12 3HQ **Tel:** 01474 824711
Email: ethan@binfo.co.uk
Web site: http://www.binfo.co.uk
Publisher: Kingswood Media Ltd
Date Established: 2002
Frequency: Quarterly
Free to qualifying individuals
Circulation: 5,000 (Publisher's Statement)
Usual Pagination: 32
Editor: James Goulding; **Advertising Manager:** Ethan White
Summary of Content: Magazine focusing on office stationery and business machines, including news, reviews and company profiles.
Readership/Target Audience: Aimed at directors of SMEs employing between 15 to 350 office based staff.
ADVERTISING RATES:
Full Page Colour £2200.00
Mechanical Data: Trim Size: 297 x 210mm, Film: Digital
Supplement to: Business Info Magazine
BUSINESS: PRINTING & STATIONERY: Stationery

THE PENSION SCHEME TRUSTEE
35363U1H-67

Editorial Address: Informa House, 30-32 Mortimer Street, LONDON, W1W 7RE **Tel:** 020 7017 4600
Fax: 020 7017 4135
Email: pensions@mac.com
Web site: http://www.informafinance.com
ISSN: 1353-1654
Publisher: Informa PLC
Frequency: Monthly
Usual Pagination: 8
Editor: Gregor Watt
Summary of Content: Newsletter which highlights the practical, legal and investment issues of pension schemes.
Readership/Target Audience: Aimed at pension scheme trustees.
ADVERTISING: No Advertising taken
BUSINESS: FINANCE & ECONOMICS: Pensions

PENSIONS AGE
35365U1H-71

Editorial Address: 6th Floor, 3 London Wall Buildings, LONDON, EC2M 5PD **Tel:** 020 7562 2401
Fax: 020 7374 2701
Email: marek.handzel@pensionsage.com
Advertising Address: As above. **Tel:** 020 7562 2400
Fax: 020 7274 2703
Email: james.pamplin@pensionsage.com
Web site: http://www.pensionsage.com
ISSN: 1366-8366
Publisher: Perspective Publishing Ltd
Date Established: 1997
Frequency: Monthly - Published in the middle of the 2nd week of the cover month
Annual Sub.: £99.00
Circulation: 14,193 (ABC 01/07/2007 to 30/06/2008)
Usual Pagination: 64
Editor: Marek Handzel; **News Editor:** Sophie Baker; **Managing Director:** John Woods
Summary of Content: Magazine covering news and information on the pensions industry. Includes articles on changes in UK and European law.
Readership/Target Audience: Aimed at pensions professionals.

ADVERTISING RATES:
Full Page Colour £3950.00
Agency Commission: 10%
Mechanical Data: Film: Digital, Type Area: 245 x 180mm, Bleed Size: 277 x 210mm, Trim Size: 271 x 204mm, Col Length: 245mm, Page Width: 180mm
Copy instructions: Copy Date: Last Friday of the month prior to publication
Average advertising content per issue: 50%
BUSINESS: FINANCE & ECONOMICS: Pensions

PENSIONS & INVESTMENTS
35364U1H-81

Editorial Address: 3rd Floor, 21 St. Thomas Street, LONDON, SE1 9RY **Tel:** 020 7457 1400 **Fax:** 020 7457 1440
Email: thua@pionline.com
Advertising Address: 711 Third Avenue, New York, NY, 10017-4036 **Tel:** 212 21 00 114 **Fax:** 212 21 00 117
Email: rscanlon@crain.com
Web site: http://www.pionline.com
Publisher: Crain Communications Ltd
Date Established: 1973
Frequency: 26 issues yearly
Cover Price: $12.00
Annual Sub.: $225.00
Circulation: 49,847 (Publisher's Statement)
Editor: Thao Hua; **Advertising Director:** Richard Scanlon
Summary of Content: News and information on the investment management of pension and institutional funds globally.
Readership/Target Audience: Aimed at pension plan sponsors, pension fund managers and consultants.
ADVERTISING RATES:
Full Page Colour $29830.00
Agency Commission: 15%
BUSINESS: FINANCE & ECONOMICS: Pensions

PENSIONS INSIGHT
1895659U1F-667

Editorial Address: 30 Cannon Street, LONDON, EC4M 6YJ **Tel:** 020 7618 3487
Email: maggie.williams@newsquestspecialistmedia.com
Web site: http://www.pensions-insight.co.uk
Publisher: Newsquest Specialist Media Ltd
Frequency: Monthly
Annual Sub.: £149.00
Circulation: 10,320 (ABC 01/07/2008 to 30/06/2009)
Editor: Bob Campion; **Executive Editor:** Maggie Williams
Summary of Content: Magazine featuring news digests and summaries of key developments, reports and briefings with analysis of what it means for pensions professionals.
Readership/Target Audience: Aimed at pension managers, senior administrative staff, investment, actuarial and legal advisers.
BUSINESS: FINANCE & ECONOMICS: Investment

PENSIONS MANAGEMENT
35367U1H-73

Editorial Address: 1 Southwark Bridge, LONDON, SE1 9HL **Tel:** 020 7873 3000
Email: pmnews@ft.com
Advertising Address: As above.
Email: andy.hill@ft.com
Web site: http://www.pensions-management.co.uk
ISSN: 0269-7505
Publisher: Financial Times
Date Established: 1985
Frequency: Monthly - Published on the 1st of the cover month
Free to qualifying individuals
Annual Sub.: £123.00
Circulation: 10,064 (ABC 01/07/2008 to 30/06/2009)
Usual Pagination: 96
Editor: Pádraig Floyd; **Editor-in-Chief:** Pádraig Floyd; **Managing Director:** Caspar De Bono; **Publisher:** Tim Baker
Summary of Content: Magazine covering statistics, features, interviews and news on the performance of most pension funds in the UK. Includes investment updates, interviews with experts, comments and analysis.
Readership/Target Audience: Read by intermediaries, pension fund managers, trustees and pension advisers. Also accountants, management consultants, corperorate and high net worth clients.
ADVERTISING RATES:
Full Page Colour £4200.00
Agency Commission: 10%
Mechanical Data: Type Area: 266 x 178mm, Film: Digital, Bleed Size: 303 x 216mm, Trim Size: 297 x 210mm, Col Length: 266mm, Page Width: 178mm
Copy instructions: Copy Date: 3 weeks prior to publication date
Average advertising content per issue: 40%
BUSINESS: FINANCE & ECONOMICS: Pensions

PENSIONS TODAY
35368U1H-74

Editorial Address: Informa House, 30-32 Mortimer Street, LONDON, W1W 7RE **Tel:** 020 7017 4600
Fax: 020 7017 4135

Email: pensions@mac.com
Advertising Address: As above.
Email: pauline.seymour@informa.com
Web site: http://www.informafinance.com
ISSN: 0140-8526
Publisher: Informa PLC
Frequency: 10 issues yearly
Usual Pagination: 8
Editor: Gregor Watt
Summary of Content: Advisory newsletter covering industry developments, legislative changes, regulations and information.
Readership/Target Audience: Aimed at pension scheme trustees, lawyers and independent financial advisers.
ADVERTISING: Rates on application
BUSINESS: FINANCE & ECONOMICS: Pensions

PENSIONS WEEK
35369U1H-74_50

Editorial Address: 1 Southwark Bridge, LONDON, SE1 9HL **Tel:** 020 7873 3000 **Fax:** 020 7775 6388
Email: david.rowley@ft.com
Advertising Address: As above.
Email: alex.wharton@ft.com
Web site: http://www.ftbusiness.com
ISSN: 1366-8765
Publisher: FT Group
Date Established: 1998
Frequency: Weekly
Free to qualifying individuals
Annual Sub.: £235.00
Circulation: 8,000 (ABC 01/07/2008 to 30/06/2009)
Usual Pagination: 32
Editor: David Rowley; **Editor-in-Chief:** Pádraig Floyd; **Publisher:** Tim Baker
Summary of Content: Magazine covering all aspects of the pensions industry. Includes company news, information, features on pension schemes and business and market reports.
Readership/Target Audience: Aimed at professionals running and advising on occupational pension schemes.
ADVERTISING RATES:
Full Page Colour £4000.00
SCC £40.00
Agency Commission: 10%
Mechanical Data: Col Length: 266mm, No. of Columns (Display): 4, Film: Digital, Type Area: 266 x 178mm, Bleed Size: 303 x 216mm, Trim Size: 297 x 210mm, Page Width: 178mm
Copy instructions: Copy Date: 1 week prior to publication date
Average advertising content per issue: 40%
BUSINESS: FINANCE & ECONOMICS: Pensions

PENSIONS WORLD
35370U1H-75

Editorial Address: 2 Addiscombe Road, CROYDON, CR9 5AF **Tel:** 020 8686 9141 **Fax:** 020 8212 1920
Email: stephanie.hawthorne@lexisnexis.co.uk
Advertising Address: As above. **Tel:** 020 8212 1925
Fax: 020 8212 1970
Email: andrew.gibson@lexisnexis.co.uk
Web site: http://www.pensionsworld.co.uk
ISSN: 0307-191X
Publisher: LexisNexis UK
Date Established: 1972
Frequency: Monthly - Published on the 1st of the cover month
Free to qualifying individuals
Annual Sub.: £119.00
Circulation: 8,429 (ABC 01/07/2008 to 30/06/2009)
Usual Pagination: 64
Editor: Stephanie Hawthorne
Summary of Content: Magazine covering pensions, investment, employee benefits and tax and law within the finance industry.
Readership/Target Audience: Aimed at company pension fund managers, trustees, investors and their advisors.
ADVERTISING RATES:
Full Page Colour £2920.00
Agency Commission: 10%
Mechanical Data: Film: Digital, Bleed Size: 303 x 231mm, Trim Size: 297 x 210mm, No. of Columns (Display): 4, Type Area: 270 x 200mm, Col Length: 270mm, Page Width: 200mm
Copy instructions: Copy Date: 14th of the month prior to publication date
Average advertising content per issue: 40%
BUSINESS: FINANCE & ECONOMICS: Pensions

PEOPLE & SCIENCE
48716U55-9010

Formerly: Science & Public Affairs
Editorial Address: 165 Queen's Gate, LONDON, SW7 5HD **Tel:** 0870 770 7101 **Fax:** 020 7019 4923
Email: wendy.barnaby@britishscienceassociation.org
Advertising Address: As above. **Tel:** 0870 241 0664
Fax: 020 7019 4924
Email: supporters@the-ba.net

Web site: http://www.britishscienceassociation.org/ps
ISSN: 0268-490X
Publisher: British Association for the Advancement of Science
Frequency: Quarterly
Cover Price: Free
Circulation: 4,000 (Publisher's Statement)
Usual Pagination: 32
Editor: Wendy Barnaby; Advertising Manager: Beena Parmar
Summary of Content: Magazine focusing on public engagement in science.
Readership/Target Audience: Aimed at decision-makers, opinion formers in government, NGOs, academics and members of the BA.
ADVERTISING RATES:
Full Page Colour £800.00
Mechanical Data: Trim Size: 297 x 210mm, Bleed Size: 303 x 216mm
BUSINESS: APPLIED SCIENCE & LABORATORIES

PEOPLE MANAGEMENT
37070U14F-55

Editorial Address: 17 Britton Street, LONDON, EC1M 5TP
Tel: 020 7880 6200 Fax: 020 7324 2791
Email: editorial@peoplemanagement.co.uk
Advertising Address: As above. Tel: 020 7880 7665
Fax: 020 7880 7690
Email: display@peoplemanagement.co.uk
Web site: http://www.peoplemanagement.co.uk
ISSN: 1358-6297
Publisher: Redactive Media Group
Date Established: 1995
Frequency: 25 issues yearly
Annual Sub.: £95.00
Circulation: 132,168 (ABC 01/07/2008 to 30/06/2009)
Usual Pagination: 116
Editor: Melanie Green; News Editor: James Brockett; Advertising Manager: Nick Marsh
Summary of Content: Magazine providing news, analysis and opinion on the latest developments in business, government and professional practice, focusing on HR.
Twitter: https://twitter.com/PeopleMgt.
Readership/Target Audience: Read by personnel and development professionals, academics and consultants.
ADVERTISING RATES:
Full Page Mono £5050.00
Full Page Colour £6125.00
Agency Commission: 10%
Mechanical Data: Type Area: 260 X 203mm, Col Length: 260mm, Bleed Size: 291 x 231mm, Trim Size: 288 x 225mm, Page Width: 203mm, Film: Digital
Copy instructions: Copy Date: 3 weeks prior to publication date
Average advertising content per issue: 60%
BUSINESS: COMMERCE, INDUSTRY & MANAGEMENT: Training & Recruitment

PERFORMANCE APPAREL MARKETS
766553U47A-564

Editorial Address: Suite 6, 1st Floor, Alderley House, Alderley Road, WILMSLOW, SK9 1AT Tel: 01625 536136
Fax: 01625 536137
Email: editorial@textilesintelligence.com
Advertising Address: As above.
Web site: http://www.textilesintelligence.com
ISSN: 1477-6456
Publisher: Textiles Intelligence Ltd
Date Established: 2002
Frequency: Quarterly
Annual Sub.: £595.00
Usual Pagination: 80
Editor: Belinda Carp
Summary of Content: Provides an overview of the sector for performance apparel and corporate wear. It provides market data and analysis of new and established markets for performance fibres, fabrics and clothing for executives who are working in or supplying this sector.
Readership/Target Audience: Aimed at executives in global and apparel markets.
ADVERTISING: No Advertising taken
BUSINESS: CLOTHING & TEXTILES

PERFUSION
24816U56B-273_50

Editorial Address: 1 Oliver's Yard, 55 City Road, LONDON, EC1Y 1SP Tel: 020 7324 8500 Fax: 020 7324 8600
Email: market@sagepub.co.uk
Advertising Address: As above.
Email: sheena.karim@sagepub.co.uk
Web site: http://www.sagepub.co.uk
ISSN: 0267-6591
Publisher: Sage Publications
Date Established: 1986
Frequency: 6 issues yearly
Annual Sub.: £799.00
Usual Pagination: 96
Editor: Prakesh Punjabi

Summary of Content: Academic publication providing current information about all aspects of perfusion, oxygenation and biocompatibility.
Readership/Target Audience: Aimed at cardiac surgeons, cardiologists, perfusionists, anaesthetists, bioengineers, biochemists, haematologists and all concerned with and interested in perfusion.
ADVERTISING RATES:
Full Page Mono £900.00
Full Page Colour £1995.00
Agency Commission: 15%
Mechanical Data: Type Area: 248 x 174mm, Trim Size: 280 x 210mm, Col Length: 248mm, Page Width: 174mm
Copy instructions: Copy Date: 15th of the month of publication
BUSINESS: HEALTH & MEDICAL: Nursing

PERIMETER SYSTEMS
35973U4R-550

Editorial Address: 19 Lincoln Croft, Shenstone, LICHFIELD, WS14 0ND Tel: 01543 480322 Fax: 01543 480864
Email: ps@eclipse.co.uk
Advertising Address: As above.
Email: ps@eclipse.co.uk
Publisher: Orton Associates
Date Established: 1984
Frequency: Quarterly
Free to qualifying individuals
Annual Sub.: £15.00 (Overseas)
Circulation: 6,275 (Publisher's Statement)
Usual Pagination: 20
Editor: Ian Law; Managing Director: Carol Law; Advertising Manager: Carol Law
Summary of Content: Magazine covering all aspects of the fencing industry and allied trades.
Readership/Target Audience: Aimed at fencing contractors, specifiers, manufacturers and allied industries supplying the industry.
ADVERTISING RATES:
Full Page Mono £902.00
Full Page Colour £1270.00
SCC £9.80
Agency Commission: 10%
Mechanical Data: Type Area: 300 x 220mm, Bleed Size: 336 x 243mm, Trim Size: 330 x 240mm, Col Length: 300mm, Col Widths (Display): 40mm, No. of Columns (Display): 5, Film: Digital, Page Width: 220mm
Copy instructions: Copy Date: 4 weeks prior to publication date
BUSINESS: ARCHITECTURE & BUILDING: Building Related

PERSONAL & UBIQUITOUS COMPUTING
36007U5R-360

Editorial Address: Ashbourne House, The Guildway, Old Portsmouth Road, Artington, GUILDFORD, GU3 1LP
Tel: 01483 734635
Email: rhonda.lane@springersbm.com
Advertising Address: As above. Fax: 01483 734411
Email: rhonda.lane@springer.com
Web site: http://www.springer.com
ISSN: 0949-2054
Publisher: Springer
Date Established: 1997
Frequency: 8 issues yearly
Annual Sub.: £76.00
Usual Pagination: 64
Editor: Rhonda Lane; Editor-in-Chief: Peter Thomas; Advertising Manager: Rhonda Lane
Summary of Content: Journal focusing on issues surrounding the innovation, design, use and evaluation of new generations of innovative handheld and mobile information appliances. Contains new developments and technical accounts.
Readership/Target Audience: Aimed at those with an interest in the development of personal technologies.
ADVERTISING RATES:
Full Page Mono £420.00
Full Page Colour £1128.75
Agency Commission: 10%
Mechanical Data: Trim Size: 277 x 210mm, Type Area: 237 x 172mm, Col Length: 237mm, Page Width: 172mm, Film: Digital, Bleed Size: 283 x 216mm
Copy instructions: Copy Date: 1 month prior to publication date
BUSINESS: COMPUTERS & AUTOMATION: Computers Related

PERSONNEL MANAGEMENT NEWSLETTER
37071U14F-59

Editorial Address: Far Side, 14 Faringdon Road, ABINGDON, OX14 1BB Tel: 01235 555260
Email: craig-gordon@supanet.com
Web site: http://www.croner.co.uk
Publisher: Wolters Kluwer (UK) Ltd
Date Established: 1985
Frequency: 22 issues yearly
Annual Sub.: £736.30
Usual Pagination: 8

Editor: Craig Gordon
Summary of Content: Newsletter covering all aspects of HR, personnel and employment law developments in the UK.
Readership/Target Audience: Aimed at personnel specialists.
ADVERTISING: No Advertising taken
BUSINESS: COMMERCE, INDUSTRY & MANAGEMENT: Training & Recruitment

PERSONNEL TODAY
37072U14F-62

Editorial Address: Quadrant House, The Quadrant, SUTTON, SM2 5AS Tel: 020 8652 3500 Fax: 020 8652 8805
Email: personneltoday@rbi.co.uk
Advertising Address: As above. Fax: 020 8652 3793
Email: richard.bennett@rbi.co.uk
Web site: http://www.personneltoday.com
ISSN: 0959-5848
Publisher: Reed Business Information
Date Established: 1988
Frequency: Weekly
Free to qualifying individuals
Annual Sub.: £99.00
Circulation: 43,633 (ABC 01/07/2008 to 30/06/2009)
Editor: Louisa Peacock; News Editor: Louisa Peacock; Features Editor: Helen Williams; Group Editor: Dawn Spalding
Summary of Content: Magazine containing news and information about personnel, recruitment and training.
Readership/Target Audience: Aimed at personnel and training professionals.
ADVERTISING RATES:
Full Page Colour £5342.00
Agency Commission: 10%
Mechanical Data: Page Width: 208mm, Film: Digital, Type Area: 268 x 208mm, Trim Size: 300 x 226mm, Bleed Size: 306 x 232mm, Col Length: 268mm
Copy instructions: Copy Date: 7 days prior to publication date
Average advertising content per issue: 30%
BUSINESS: COMMERCE, INDUSTRY & MANAGEMENT: Training & Recruitment

PERSPECTIVE
35802U4A-205

Editorial Address: 39 Boucher Road, BELFAST, BT12 6UT
Tel: 028 9066 3311 Fax: 028 9038 1915
Email: info@ulstertatler.com
Advertising Address: As above. Tel: 028 9072 1339
Fax: 028 9072 1339
Email: copy@ulstertatler.com
Web site: http://www.rsua.org.uk
ISSN: 0967-2176
Publisher: Ulster Journals Ltd
Date Established: 1992
Frequency: 6 issues yearly
Cover Price: £4.00
Free to qualifying individuals
Annual Sub.: £24.00
Circulation: 3,000 (Publisher's Statement)
Usual Pagination: 96
Editor: Christopher Sherry; Advertising Manager: Lorraine Gill
Summary of Content: Journal of the Royal Society of Ulster Architects covering architecture and the built environment in Northern Ireland, including finished projects, achievements, ideas and issues.
Readership/Target Audience: Aimed at members.
ADVERTISING RATES:
Full Page Colour £995.00
Agency Commission: 10%
Mechanical Data: Film: Digital, Bleed Size: 302 x 235mm, Trim Size: 297 x 230mm, Type Area: 267 x 190mm, Col Length: 267mm, Page Width: 190mm
Copy instructions: Copy Date: 20th of the month prior to publication date
Average advertising content per issue: 33%
Supplement(s): Queens - 1xY
BUSINESS: ARCHITECTURE & BUILDING: Architecture

PERSPECTIVE MAGAZINE
1837526U50-241

Editorial Address: 87 Station Road, ASHINGTON, NE63 8RS Tel: 07775 607903 Fax: 020 8113 2345
Email: sharon@timeshareperspective.com
Advertising Address: As above.
Email: sharon@timeshareperspective.com
Web site: http://www.theperspectivemagazine.com
Publisher: Perspective International Ltd
Frequency: Monthly - Not published in December
Free to qualifying individuals
Annual Sub.: £25.00
Circulation: 7,000 (Publisher's Statement)
Editor: Sharon Mattimoe; Advertising Manager: Sharon Mattimoe
Summary of Content: Magazine specialising in the timeshare and shared ownership industries.

Section 4 (b) Business Magazines

Readership/Target Audience: Aimed at upper management and CEOs.
ADVERTISING RATES:
Full Page Colour £1450.00
BUSINESS: TRAVEL & TOURISM

PERSUADER
1666376U14A-541
Editorial Address: 3 London Wall Buildings, LONDON, EC2M 5SY **Tel:** 020 7638 9571 **Fax:** 020 7628 3444
Web site: http://www.citigatedr.co.uk/persuader.html
Publisher: Citygate Dewe Rogerson
Frequency: 3 issues yearly
Free to qualifying individuals
Editor: Deborah Saw; **Publisher:** Deborah Saw
Summary of Content: Publication focusing on a theme or issue that has a critical impact on the way organisations interact with the wider world.
Readership/Target Audience: Aimed at senior UK and overseas journalists, politicians, academics and fund managers.
ADVERTISING: No Advertising taken
BUSINESS: COMMERCE, INDUSTRY & MANAGEMENT

PEST
37811U21B-900
Formerly: Professional Pest Controller
Editorial Address: Foxhill, Normanton Lane, Stanford on Soar, LOUGHBOROUGH, LE12 5PZ **Tel:** 01509 233219
Fax: 01509 211932
Email: frances@activesolutions.uk.com
Advertising Address: As above.
Email: frances@pestmagazine.co.uk
Web site: http://www.professionalpestcontroller.org
Publisher: British Pest Control Association
Date Established: 1993
Frequency: 6 issues yearly - Published in the middle of the 1st cover month
Cover Price: Free
Circulation: 4,000 (Publisher's Statement)
Usual Pagination: 28
Editor: Frances McKim; **Advertising Manager:** Frances McKim; **Publisher:** Oliver Madge
Summary of Content: Journal of the British Pest Control Association. Contains information on all forms of pest control, including new products and practices.
Readership/Target Audience: Aimed at all those working in professional pest control and public health.
ADVERTISING RATES:
Full Page Mono £850.00
Full Page Colour £1050.00
Copy instructions: Copy Date: 4 weeks prior to publication date
BUSINESS: AGRICULTURE & FARMING: Agriculture - Supplies & Services

PEST CONTROL NEWS
37810U21B-800
Editorial Address: PO Box 2, OSSETT, WF5 9NA
Tel: 01924 268400 **Fax:** 01924 264646
Email: editor@pestcontrolnews.com
Advertising Address: As above. **Fax:** 01924 267874
Email: ads@pestcontrolnews.com
Publisher: Pest Control News Ltd
Date Established: 1981
Frequency: Quarterly
Cover Price: Free
Circulation: 6,500 (Publisher's Statement)
Usual Pagination: 52
Editor: Emma Pemberton; **Advertising Manager:** Emma Pemberton
Summary of Content: Magazine covering all aspects of the public health and pest control industry.
Language(s): Dutch; English; German; Spanish
Readership/Target Audience: Aimed at all sectors of the public health and pest control industries.
ADVERTISING RATES:
Full Page Colour £1950.00
Mechanical Data: Bleed Size: 303 x 216mm, Trim Size: 297 x 210mm, Film: Digital
Average advertising content per issue: 18%
BUSINESS: AGRICULTURE & FARMING: Agriculture - Supplies & Services

PEST MANAGEMENT SCIENCE
36680U13-114_70
Formerly: Pesticide Science
Editorial Address: SCI, 14-15 Belgrave Square, LONDON, SW1X 8PS **Tel:** 020 7598 1556 **Fax:** 020 7598 1558
Email: pestmansci@soci.org
Advertising Address: The Atrium, Southern Gate, CHICHESTER, PO19 8SQ **Tel:** 01243 770254
Fax: 01243 770432
Email: adsales@wiley.co.uk
Web site: http://www.interscience.wiley.com/pestmanagementscience
ISSN: 1526-498X

Publisher: John Wiley & Sons Ltd
Frequency: Monthly
Annual Sub.: £740.00
Usual Pagination: 100
Editor: Tom Hopkinson; **Editor-in-Chief:** G. Brooks
Summary of Content: Journal about the research and development of products designed for pest control and crop, animal and public health protection.
Readership/Target Audience: Read by academics and people working within the pesticide industry.
ADVERTISING RATES:
Full Page Mono £2000.00
Full Page Colour £4375.00
Agency Commission: 10%
Mechanical Data: Type Area: 270 x 180mm, Col Length: 270mm, Page Width: 180mm, Trim Size: 297 x 210mm, Film: Digital, Print Process: Sheet-fed litho
BUSINESS: CHEMICALS

PETRO DAILY: EUROPEAN MARINE
39424U45E-200
Editorial Address: Bon Accord House, Riverside Drive, ABERDEEN, AB11 7SL **Tel:** 01224 597800
Fax: 01224 580320
Email: marinebase@ods-petrodata.com
Web site: http://www.ods-petrodata.com
Publisher: ODS-Petrodata UK Ltd
Frequency: 100 issues yearly
Annual Sub.: £2500.00
Circulation: 55 (Publisher's Statement)
Editor: David Bichard; **Managing Director:** David Bichard;
Publisher: David Bichard
Summary of Content: Magazine covering news, information and activities on North Sea supply vessels.
Readership/Target Audience: Read by people working in the oil supply vessel market, ship brokers and shipping companies.
ADVERTISING: No Advertising taken
BUSINESS: MARINE & SHIPPING: Boat Trade

PETRO DAILY: NORTH AMERICAN CONSTRUCTION
39020U42A-163_10
Editorial Address: Bon Accord House, Riverside Drive, ABERDEEN, AB11 7SL **Tel:** 01224 597800
Fax: 01224 580320
Email: info@ods-petrodata.com
Web site: http://www.ods-petrodata.com
Publisher: ODS-Petrodata UK Ltd
Frequency: 104 issues yearly
Usual Pagination: 2
Editor: David Bichard; **Publisher:** David Bichard
Summary of Content: Magazine covering industry and business news from contractors and suppliers in the offshore and marine markets in the Gulf of Mexico and Canada.
Readership/Target Audience: Aimed at contractors.
ADVERTISING: No Advertising taken
BUSINESS: CONSTRUCTION

PETRO INDUSTRY NEWS
633746U33-42
Editorial Address: Oak Court Business Centre, Sandridge Park, Porters Wood, ST. ALBANS, AL3 6PH
Tel: 01727 858840 **Fax:** 01727 840310
Email: marcus@envirotechpubs.com
Advertising Address: As above.
Email: david@pin-pub.com
Web site: http://www.pin-pub.com
ISSN: 1472-0590
Publisher: Environmental Technology Publications Ltd
Frequency: 6 issues yearly - Published at the end of the 1st cover month
Free to qualifying individuals
Annual Sub.: £25.00
Circulation: 33,133 (Publisher's Statement)
Usual Pagination: 52
Editor: Marcus Pattison; **Managing Director:** Marcus Pattison; **Publisher:** Marcus Pattison
Summary of Content: Magazine covering scientific research and processes relating to the petroleum industry.
Readership/Target Audience: Read by buyers and users of scientific instrumentation, safety control and automation products, condition monitoring and environmental compliance equipment in the oil related industries.
ADVERTISING RATES:
Full Page Mono £4650.00
Full Page Colour £5245.00
Agency Commission: 10%
Mechanical Data: Type Area: 353 x 252mm, Bleed Size: 408 x 285.5mm, Trim Size: 402 x 279.5mm, Col Length: 353mm, Page Width: 252mm, Film: Digital
Copy instructions: Copy Date: 5th of the month prior to publication date
Average advertising content per issue: 50%
BUSINESS: OIL & PETROLEUM

PETRODAILY NEWS: EUROPEAN CONSTRUCTION
38616U33-41_10
Editorial Address: Bon Accord House, Riverside Drive, ABERDEEN, AB11 7SL **Tel:** 01224 597800
Fax: 01224 580320
Email: newsdesk@ods-petrodata.com
Web site: http://www.ods-petrodata.com
Publisher: ODS-Petrodata UK Ltd
Frequency: 156 issues yearly
Annual Sub.: $3780.00
Circulation: 35 (Publisher's Statement)
Usual Pagination: 2
Editor: Mark Rae
Summary of Content: Magazine covering industry and business news from contractors and suppliers in Europe.
Readership/Target Audience: Aimed at oil companies, drilling contractors and oil industry service companies.
ADVERTISING: No Advertising taken
BUSINESS: OIL & PETROLEUM

PETRODAILY NEWS: INTERNATIONAL CONSTRUCTION
38618U33-41_20
Editorial Address: 2nd Floor, The Exchange, 62 Market Street, ABERDEEN, AB11 5PJ **Tel:** 01224 597800
Fax: 01224 850320
Email: mrae@ods-petrodata.com
Web site: http://www.ods-petrodata.com
Publisher: ODS-Petrodata UK Ltd
Frequency: 104 issues yearly
Usual Pagination: 4
Editor: Mark Rae
Summary of Content: Publication featuring news on surefield development and construction.
Readership/Target Audience: Aimed at oil companies, drilling contractors and oil industry service companies.
ADVERTISING: No Advertising taken
BUSINESS: OIL & PETROLEUM

PETRODAILY NEWS: INTERNATIONAL SUBSEA
38615U33-41
Formerly: Petrodaily News: International Diving
Editorial Address: Bon Accord House, Riverside Drive, ABERDEEN, AB11 7SL **Tel:** 01224 597800
Fax: 01224 580320
Email: sheywood@ods-petrodata.com
Web site: http://www.ods-petrodata.com
Publisher: ODS-Petrodata UK Ltd
Frequency: 156 issues yearly
Annual Sub.: $3600.00
Circulation: 50 (Publisher's Statement)
Editor: Shaun Heywood
Summary of Content: Newsletter reporting on all commercial aspects of the global, subsea and contracting markets.
Readership/Target Audience: Aimed at oil industry executives.
ADVERTISING: No Advertising taken
BUSINESS: OIL & PETROLEUM

PETRODAILY NEWS: NORTH AMERICAN CONSTRUCTION
38619U33-41_30
Editorial Address: 2nd Floor, The Exchange, Market Street, ABERDEEN, AB11 5PJ **Tel:** 01224 597800
Fax: 01224 580320
Email: info@ods-petrodata.com
Web site: http://www.ods-petrodata.com
Publisher: ODS-Petrodata UK Ltd
Frequency: 104 issues yearly
Editor: David Bichard; **Publisher:** David Bichard;
Circulation Manager: Elsa Candlish
Summary of Content: Publication covering drilling activities in the Gulf of Mexico.
Readership/Target Audience: Aimed at oil companies, drilling contractors and oil industry service companies.
ADVERTISING: No Advertising taken
BUSINESS: OIL & PETROLEUM

PETROLEUM ARGUS GAS CONNECTIONS
38622U33-44
Editorial Address: 175 St. John Street, LONDON, EC1V 4LW **Tel:** 020 7780 4200 **Fax:** 020 7780 4311
Email: agc@argusmediagroup.com
Web site: http://www.petroleumargus.com
ISSN: 1460-695X
Publisher: Argus Media Ltd
Frequency: 24 issues yearly
Annual Sub.: £1050.00
Usual Pagination: 16
Editor: Neil Campbell; **Managing Editor:** Cindy Galvin;
Publisher: Adrian Binks
Summary of Content: Newsletter covering gas and power generation in Europe. Includes upstream and downstream

news and features, industry and company developments, market analysis and monthly average prices.
Readership/Target Audience: Aimed at senior management of oil, gas and power companies.
ADVERTISING: No Advertising taken
BUSINESS: OIL & PETROLEUM

PETROLEUM ARGUS LPG WORLD

38623U33-44_50

Editorial Address: 175 St. John Street, LONDON, EC1V 4LW **Tel:** 020 7780 4200 **Fax:** 020 7780 4201
Email: lpgworld@argusmediagroup.com
Web site: http://www.argusmediagroup.com
ISSN: 1364-3711
Publisher: Argus Media Ltd
Date Established: 1995
Frequency: 24 issues yearly
Annual Sub.: £1010.00
Usual Pagination: 16
Editor: Nick Black; **Editor-in-Chief:** Ian Bourne; **Publisher:** Adrian Binks
Summary of Content: Newsletter covering the international liquified petroleum gas markets, including prices from all world centres, shipping, news and analysis.
Readership/Target Audience: Read by senior managers in the LPG industry, consultants involved in investment and bankers.
ADVERTISING: No Advertising taken
BUSINESS: OIL & PETROLEUM

PETROLEUM ECONOMIST

38624U33-45

Editorial Address: 69 Carter Lane, LONDON, EC4V 5EQ **Tel:** 020 7779 8800 **Fax:** 020 7779 8896
Email: editorial@petroleum-economist.com
Advertising Address: Nestor House, Playhouse Yard, LONDON, EC4V 5EX **Tel:** 020 7779 8855
Fax: 020 7779 8896
Email: jcorp@petroleum-economist.com
Web site: http://www.petroleum-economist.com
ISSN: 0306-395X
Publisher: Petroleum Economist Ltd
Date Established: 1934
Frequency: Monthly - Published on the 1st of the cover month
Annual Sub.: £625.00
Circulation: 2,000 (Publisher's Statement)
Usual Pagination: 48
Editor: Tom Nicholls; **Managing Director:** Crispian McCredie; **Advertising Manager:** John Corp
Summary of Content: Publication providing a worldwide analysis of the oil, gas, power and electricity sector.
Readership/Target Audience: Aimed at policy and decision makers in the energy industry, financial institutions, accountancy and legal practices and governmental departments and agencies.
ADVERTISING RATES:
Full Page Colour £5195.00
Agency Commission: 10%
Mechanical Data: Bleed Size: 303 x 216mm, Trim Size: 297 x 210mm, Print Process: Offset litho, Type Area: 254 x 181mm, No. of Columns (Display): 3, Film: Digital, Col Length: 254mm, Page Width: 181mm
Copy instructions: Copy Date: 12th of the month prior to publication date
Average advertising content per issue: 20%
BUSINESS: OIL & PETROLEUM

PETROLEUM REVIEW

38627U33-47

Editorial Address: 61 New Cavendish Street, LONDON, W1G 7AR **Tel:** 020 7467 7117 **Fax:** 020 7467 7171
Email: petrev@energyinst.org.uk
Web site: http://www.energyinst.org.uk
ISSN: 0020-3076
Publisher: Energy Institute
Date Established: 1899
Frequency: Monthly - Published on the 1st of the cover month
Cover Price: £22.00
Free to qualifying individuals
Annual Sub.: £250.00
Circulation: 5,663 (ABC 01/01/2008 to 31/12/2008)
Usual Pagination: 48
Editor: Kim Jackson
Summary of Content: Oil and gas magazine covering all aspects from exploration to the forecourt.
Readership/Target Audience: Read by subscribers in the oil and gas industry, members of the Energy Institute, technical libraries, learned bodies and the media.
ADVERTISING: No Advertising taken
Supplement(s): Future Energy - 1xY, Future Fuels, Future Refining - 1xY, Retail Marketing Survey - 1xY
BUSINESS: OIL & PETROLEUM

PFM (PREMISES & FACILITIES MANAGEMENT)

35972U4R-560

Editorial Address: Blair House, 184-186 High Street, TONBRIDGE, TN9 1BQ **Tel:** 01732 359990
Fax: 01732 770049
Email: pfm@imlgroup.co.uk
Advertising Address: As above.
Email: ian.webb@imlgroup.co.uk
Web site: http://www.pfmmagazine.co.uk
ISSN: 0965-4739
Publisher: IML Group plc
Date Established: 1986
Frequency: Monthly - Published in the middle of the cover month
Cover Price: £10.00
Free to qualifying individuals
Annual Sub.: £99.00
Circulation: 10,503 (ABC 01/07/2007 to 30/06/2008)
Usual Pagination: 56
Editor: Jane Fenwick; **Publisher:** Peter Middup
Summary of Content: Magazine containing news and information on facilities management, support services and buildings management.
Readership/Target Audience: Aimed at facilities managers of large buildings and major sites.
ADVERTISING RATES:
Full Page Mono £1580.00
Full Page Colour £1580.00
Agency Commission: 10%
Mechanical Data: Type Area: 254 x 178mm, Bleed Size: 286 x 208mm, Trim Size: 280 x 205mm, Col Length: 254mm, Film: Digital, Page Width: 178mm
Copy instructions: Copy Date: 25th of the month prior to publication date
Average advertising content per issue: 56%
BUSINESS: ARCHITECTURE & BUILDING: Building Related

PGRO PULSE MAGAZINE

37778U21A-860

Formerly: Pea and Bean Progress
Editorial Address: The Research Station, Great North Road, Thornhaugh, PETERBOROUGH, PE8 6HJ
Tel: 01780 782585
Advertising Address: As above.
Publisher: PGRO
Frequency: 3 issues yearly - Publication months vary
Circulation: 5,500 (Publisher's Statement)
Editor: Salvador Potter; **Advertising Manager:** Salvador Potter
Summary of Content: Magazine containing technical articles on vegetable crops grown specifically for processing.
Readership/Target Audience: Aimed at growers of vegetable and pulse crops.
ADVERTISING RATES:
Full Page Mono £750.00
Full Page Colour £1520.00
Mechanical Data: Trim Size: 297 x 210mm
Copy instructions: Copy Date: 4 weeks prior to publication date
Average advertising content per issue: 50%
BUSINESS: AGRICULTURE & FARMING

PHARMA

1691515U37-412

Editorial Address: Oak House Mews, 43 The Parade, Claygate, ESHER, KT10 0PD **Tel:** 01392 202591
Fax: 01372 478961
Email: kevin@via-medialtd.com
Advertising Address: As above. **Tel:** 01372 460117
Email: miranda@via-medialtd.com
Web site: http://www.pharma-mag.com
ISSN: 1746-174X
Publisher: Via Media Ltd
Date Established: 2005
Frequency: 6 issues yearly
Free to qualifying individuals
Circulation: 40,000 (Publisher's Statement)
Usual Pagination: 76
Editor: Kevin Robinson; **Advertising Manager:** Miranda Docherty
Summary of Content: Magazine for the pharmaceutical industry including articles on discovery and development, drug manufacture, labelling, distribution and business management issues.
Readership/Target Audience: Aimed at plant managers, MDs, lab scientists and production managers.
ADVERTISING RATES:
Full Page Colour £3825.00
Agency Commission: 15%
Mechanical Data: Film: Digital
Copy instructions: Copy Date: 2 weeks prior to publication date
Average advertising content per issue: 35%
BUSINESS: PHARMACEUTICAL & CHEMISTS

PHARMA AGREEMENT NEWS (PAN)

1799492U37-426

Editorial Address: Lincoln House, City Fields Business Park, City Fields Way, Tangmere, CHICHESTER, PO20 2FS
Tel: 01243 533322 **Fax:** 01243 533418
Email: healthcare@espicom.com
Web site: http://www.espicom.com
ISSN: 1469-9796
Publisher: Espicom Ltd
Date Established: 2000
Frequency: 24 issues yearly
Annual Sub.: £560.00
Circulation: 700 (Publisher's Statement)
Editor: Mike O'Harrow
Summary of Content: Newsletter focusing on collaborations in drug research, development, production and marketing.
Readership/Target Audience: Aimed at senior executives of pharmaceutical companies.
ADVERTISING: No Advertising taken
BUSINESS: PHARMACEUTICAL & CHEMISTS

PHARMA COMPANY INSIGHT

1795204U37-422

Editorial Address: Lincoln House, City Fields Business Park, City Fields Way, Tangmere, CHICHESTER, PO20 2FS
Tel: 01243 533322 **Fax:** 01243 533418
Email: healthcare@espicom.com
Web site: http://www.espicom.com
ISSN: 1464-2948
Publisher: Espicom Ltd
Date Established: 1998
Frequency: 44 issues yearly
Free to qualifying individuals
Annual Sub.: £560.00
Circulation: 1,000 (Publisher's Statement)
Usual Pagination: 24
Editor: Matthew Dennis
Summary of Content: Newsletter containing corporate and financial news. Includes details of new products and recent developments in R&D.
Readership/Target Audience: Aimed at professionals in the pharmaceutical industry.
ADVERTISING: No Advertising taken
BUSINESS: PHARMACEUTICAL & CHEMISTS

PHARMA MARKETLETTER

38750U37-61_50

Editorial Address: Appleton House, 139 King Street, LONDON, W6 9JG **Tel:** 020 8735 6625 **Fax:** 020 8735 6688
Email: editorial@marketletter.com
Advertising Address: As above.
Email: rcardwell@marketletter.com
Web site: http://www.marketletter.com
ISSN: 0951-3175
Publisher: Marketletter (Publications) Ltd
Date Established: 1974
Frequency: Weekly
Annual Sub.: £525.00
Usual Pagination: 28
Editor: Barbara Obstoj; **Advertising Manager:** Robin Cardwell; **Managing Editor:** Barbara Obstoj
Summary of Content: International publication covering worldwide market legislation, healthcare, environmental matters, company news, stock market commentaries, research and development and new product launches.
Readership/Target Audience: Read by senior executives and researchers in the pharmaceutical industry, financial analysts and regulatory bodies.
ADVERTISING RATES:
Full Page Mono £1090.00
Full Page Colour £1880.00
Agency Commission: 10%
Mechanical Data: Type Area: 297 x 210mm, Trim Size: 297 x 210mm, Film: Digital, Bleed Size: 303 x 216mm, Col Length: 297mm, Page Width: 210mm
Copy instructions: Copy Date: 10 days prior to publication date
Average advertising content per issue: 7%
BUSINESS: PHARMACEUTICAL & CHEMISTS

PHARMA PRICING & REIMBURSEMENT

1646013U37-407

Editorial Address: Unit 2 Quayside, Bridge Street, CAMBRIDGE, CB5 8AB **Tel:** 01223 273207
Fax: 01223 362742
Email: nturner@uk.imshealth.com
Web site: http://www.imshealth.com/pharmaquery.com
Publisher: IMS Health
Date Established: 1996
Frequency: Monthly
Annual Sub.: £1045.00
Usual Pagination: 36
Editor: Neil Turner
Summary of Content: Magazine focusing on international pharmaceutical pricing and reimbursement.

Readership/Target Audience: Aimed at key decision makers in industry, government and third party organisations involved in pricing and reimbursement.
ADVERTISING: No Advertising taken
BUSINESS: PHARMACEUTICAL & CHEMISTS

PHARMA TIMES
38760U37-61_57

Formerly: Pharmaceutical Times
Editorial Address: The Coach House, 173 Sheen Lane, East Sheen, LONDON, SW14 8NA **Tel:** 020 8878 8566
Fax: 020 8876 8834
Email: claire@pharmatimes.com
Advertising Address: As above.
Email: clare_newell@pharmatimes.com
Web site: http://www.pharmatimes.com
Publisher: Europharm Management Education Ltd
Date Established: 1988
Frequency: 11 issues yearly - Combined issue July/August
Cover Price: £6.00
Free to qualifying individuals
Circulation: 10,000 (Publisher's Statement)
Usual Pagination: 72
Editor: Claire Bowie; **Managing Editor:** Geoff Frew
Summary of Content: Magazine covering issues and developments in pharmaceutical management and marketing.
Readership/Target Audience: Read by senior managers in the pharmaceutical industry in the UK and Europe.
ADVERTISING RATES:
Full Page Colour £3500.00
Mechanical Data: Film: Digital, Bleed Size: 307 x 220mm
BUSINESS: PHARMACEUTICAL & CHEMISTS

PHARMACEUTICAL EXECUTIVE
38752U37-45_110

Editorial Address: 16 Littlewood, LONDON, SE13 6SD
Tel: 020 8297 0172
Email: sarah@owlmedia.co.uk
Advertising Address: 8th Floor, 641 Lexington Avenue, NEW YORK, NY 10022 **Tel:** 212 951 6604
Email: wcampbell@advanstar.com
Web site: http://www.pharmexec.com
Publisher: Advanstar Communications, Inc.
Frequency: Monthly
Free to qualifying individuals
Usual Pagination: 160
Editor: Sarah Houlton; **Managing Editor:** Matthew Kalash
Summary of Content: Magazine covering marketing and business issues in the global pharmaceutical industry.
Readership/Target Audience: Aimed at senior figures and suppliers within the industry.
ADVERTISING RATES:
Full Page Mono $5680.00
Full Page Colour $7780.00
Mechanical Data: Film: Digital
Copy instructions: Copy Date: 1 month prior to publication date
BUSINESS: PHARMACEUTICAL & CHEMISTS

PHARMACEUTICAL FIELD
601010U37-41

Formerly: PF
Editorial Address: Clark's Courtyard, 145 Granville Street, BIRMINGHAM, B1 1SB **Tel:** 0870 609 2834
Fax: 0870 609 2836
Email: diana.spencer@healthpublishing.co.uk
Advertising Address: 4 Clark's Courtyard, 145 Granville Street, BIRMINGHAM, B1 1SB **Tel:** 0870 609 2834
Fax: 0870 609 2836
Email: manjit.johal@healthpublishing.co.uk
Web site: http://www.pharmafield.co.uk
Publisher: Warners Group Publications plc
Date Established: 1999
Frequency: Monthly
Cover Price: Free
Circulation: 10,619 (Publisher's Statement)
Usual Pagination: 40
Editor: Diana Spencer; **Advertising Manager:** Heidi Sharland
Summary of Content: Publication looking at the environmental factors driving the market; from the NHS policy and reform shaping the industry's customer-base, to pharmaceutical innovations and corporate developments. It also looks at professional development providing insight, advice and analysis of how to progress a career in medical sales.
Readership/Target Audience: Aimed at field and head office based personnel within the pharmaceutical industry.
ADVERTISING RATES:
Full Page Mono £2052.00
Agency Commission: 10%
Mechanical Data: Type Area: 265 x 190mm, Bleed Size: 291 x 216mm, Trim Size: 285 x 210mm, Film: Digital, Col Length: 265mm, Page Width: 190mm
Copy instructions: Copy Date: 5 weeks prior to publication date
Average advertising content per issue: 40%

Supplement(s): pf Awards Brochure - 1xY
BUSINESS: PHARMACEUTICAL & CHEMISTS

THE PHARMACEUTICAL JOURNAL
38754U37-50

Editorial Address: 1 Lambeth High Street, LONDON, SE1 7JN **Tel:** 020 7572 2414 **Fax:** 020 7572 2504
Email: editor@pharmj.org.uk
Advertising Address: As above. **Fax:** 020 7572 2505
Email: stuart.thomas@rpsgb.org
Web site: http://www.pjonline.com
ISSN: 0031-6873
Publisher: RPS Publishing
Date Established: 1841
Frequency: Weekly
Free to qualifying individuals
Annual Sub: £210.00
Circulation: 56,963 (ABC 01/01/2008 to 31/12/2008)
Usual Pagination: 72
Editor: Olivia Timbs; **News Editor:** Harriet Adcock
Summary of Content: Official journal of the Royal Pharmaceutical Society of Great Britain. Contains news coverage on all aspects of pharmacy and research and articles on pharmaceutical and related subjects.
Readership/Target Audience: Read by pharmacists.
ADVERTISING RATES:
Full Page Mono £3860.00
Full Page Colour £5165.00
Agency Commission: 10%
Mechanical Data: Bleed Size: 303 x 216mm, Trim Size: 297 x 210mm, Film: Digital, Type Area: 260 x 186mm, Col Length: 260mm, Page Width: 186mm, Col Widths (Display): 45mm, No. of Columns (Display): 4
Copy instructions: Copy Date: 8 days prior to publication date
Average advertising content per issue: 35%
Supplement(s): Prescribing and Medicines - 4xY
BUSINESS: PHARMACEUTICAL & CHEMISTS

PHARMACEUTICAL MARKETING
38757U37-56

Editorial Address: Vincent House, Vincent Lane, DORKING, RH4 3JD **Tel:** 01306 740777 **Fax:** 01306 741069
Email: editor@pmlive.com
Advertising Address: As above.
Email: sales@pmlive.com
Web site: http://www.pmlive.com
ISSN: 0969-3963
Publisher: P M Group
Date Established: 1989
Frequency: Monthly
Free to qualifying individuals
Annual Sub.: £84.00
Circulation: 8,227 (ABC 01/01/2008 to 31/12/2008)
Usual Pagination: 84
Editor: Natalie Uhlarz; **Managing Director:** Mark Savage;
Publisher: Mark Savage
Summary of Content: Magazine containing features on all aspects of drug industry marketing, also includes a news, opinions and recruitment section.
Readership/Target Audience: Read by senior pharmaceutical marketers and sales personnel as well as advertising agencies, market research, recruitment, public relations, conference organisers, communications and other allied support services.
ADVERTISING RATES:
Full Page Mono £2850.00
Full Page Colour £3250.00
Agency Commission: 10%
Mechanical Data: Type Area: 270 x 185mm, Col Length: 270mm, Bleed Size: 303 x 213mm, Trim Size: 297 x 210mm, Page Width: 185mm, Film: Digital
Copy instructions: Copy Date: 20th of the month prior to publication date
Average advertising content per issue: 40%
BUSINESS: PHARMACEUTICAL & CHEMISTS

PHARMACEUTICAL MARKETING EUROPE
1795199U37-431

Editorial Address: Vincent House, Vincent Lane, DORKING, RH4 3JD **Tel:** 01306 740777 **Fax:** 01306 741069
Email: editor@pmlive.com
Advertising Address: As above.
Email: croy@pmlive.com
Web site: http://www.pmlive.com
Publisher: P M Group
Date Established: 2003
Frequency: 6 issues yearly
Free to qualifying individuals
Circulation: 6,248 (Publisher's Statement)
Usual Pagination: 80
Editor: Kerry Holmes; **Managing Director:** Mark Savage;
Publisher: Mark Savage
Summary of Content: Magazine focusing on pharmaceutical marketing within Europe. Provides news analysis and explanation about EU regulatory issues. Each

issue features a country report outlining challenges in marketing within individual countries including advertising, PR, medical education legislation, healthcare reforms and the economic environment.
Readership/Target Audience: Aimed at international marketing, brand and product management, international PR and communications executives, medical directors, regulatory personnel, MDs and other executives with multi-country responsibilities.
ADVERTISING RATES:
Full Page Colour £3100.00
Agency Commission: 10%
Copy instructions: Copy Date: 2 weeks prior to publication date
Average advertising content per issue: 40%
BUSINESS: PHARMACEUTICAL & CHEMISTS

PHARMACEUTICAL TECHNOLOGY EUROPE
38759U37-56_50

Editorial Address: Advanstar House, Park West, Sealand Road, CHESTER, CH1 4RN **Tel:** 01244 378888
Fax: 01244 370011
Email: ssutton@advanstar.com
Advertising Address: As above.
Email: ptesales@advanstar.com
Web site: http://www.ptemagazine.com
ISSN: 0164-6826
Publisher: Advanstar Communications (U.K.) Ltd
Date Established: 1989
Frequency: Monthly - Published in the middle of the cover month
Free to qualifying individuals
Annual Sub.: £95.00
Circulation: 18,000 (BPA Worldwide 01/01/2006 to 30/06/2006)
Usual Pagination: 76
Editor: Stephanie Sutton
Summary of Content: Publication carrying peer reviewed articles and regulatory updates on research and development, new products and manufacturing techniques for the industrial production of pharmaceuticals.
Readership/Target Audience: Read by qualified readers within the pharmaceutical and biopharmaceutical area.
ADVERTISING RATES:
Full Page Colour EUR6850.00
Agency Commission: 15%
Mechanical Data: Trim Size: 273 x 203mm, Print Process: Offset litho, Film: Digital, Bleed Size: 279 x 209mm
Copy instructions: Copy Date: 2nd week of the month prior to publication date
Average advertising content per issue: 40%
BUSINESS: PHARMACEUTICAL & CHEMISTS

PHARMACY BUSINESS
38764U37-59_25

Editorial Address: Garavi Gujarat House, 1 Silex Street, LONDON, SE1 0DW **Tel:** 020 7928 1234 **Fax:** 020 7261 0055
Email: editor@pharmacy.biz
Advertising Address: As above.
Email: ishan.tripathi@amg.biz
Web site: http://www.pharmacy.biz
Publisher: Asian Trade Publications Ltd
Date Established: 1998
Frequency: 11 issues yearly - Published at the beginning of the cover month
Cover Price: £3.00
Free to qualifying individuals
Annual Sub.: £45.00
Circulation: 9,419 (ABC 01/07/2007 to 30/06/2008)
Usual Pagination: 44
Editor: Shailesh Solanki; **Executive Editor:** Shailesh Solanki; **Advertising Manager:** Ishan Tripathi
Summary of Content: Magazine covering clinical and business news, news analysis, features, new products, ideas for developing front of shop, management, OTC products, profiles and social events.
Readership/Target Audience: Aimed at community pharmacists and pharmacy assistants in independent retail pharmacy outlets and pharmaceutical wholesalers.
ADVERTISING RATES:
Full Page Mono £2501.00
Full Page Colour £2501.00
Agency Commission: 10%
Mechanical Data: Trim Size: 297 x 210mm, Type Area: 280 x 195mm, Col Length: 280mm, Page Width: 195mm, Bleed Size: 303 x 216mm, Film: Digital
Copy instructions: Copy Date: 2 weeks prior to publication date
Average advertising content per issue: 40%
BUSINESS: PHARMACEUTICAL & CHEMISTS

PHARMACY IN FOCUS
1626347U37-406

Editorial Address: Unit 13 Ormeau Business Park, The Gasworks, Cromac Avenue, BELFAST, BT6 2JA
Tel: 028 9043 4112 **Fax:** 028 9043 4116
Email: laure@profilepublishing.com
Advertising Address: 10 Cromac Quay, The Gasworks, BELFAST, BT7 2JD **Tel:** 028 9043 4112 **Fax:** 028 9043 4116

Email: info@profilepublishing.com
Publisher: Profile Publishing & Design Ltd
Date Established: 2003
Frequency: 10 issues yearly - Published in the 1st week of the cover month
Free to qualifying individuals
Circulation: 3,400 (Publisher's Statement)
Usual Pagination: 52
Editor: Laure James; **Publisher:** Jason Andrews
Summary of Content: Magazine covering profiles, interviews, issues and news on the pharmacy industry in Northern Ireland.
Readership/Target Audience: Aimed at those involved within the pharmacy industry at all levels.
ADVERTISING RATES:
Full Page Colour £1550.00
Agency Commission: 10%
Mechanical Data: Type Area: 270 x 180mm, Bleed Size: 303 x 216mm, Trim Size: 297 x 210mm, Col Length: 270mm, No. of Columns (Display): 3, Print Process: Litho, Page Width: 180mm, Film: Digital
Copy instructions: Copy Date: 15th of the month prior to publication date
Average advertising content per issue: 40%
BUSINESS: PHARMACEUTICAL & CHEMISTS

PHARMACY MAGAZINE
38765U37-59_50
Editorial Address: 207 Linen Hall, 162-168 Regent Street, LONDON, W1B 5TB **Tel:** 020 7434 1530 **Fax:** 020 7437 0915
Email: pm@1530.com
Advertising Address: As above.
Email: martin.caldersmith@1530.com
Publisher: Communications International Group
Frequency: Monthly
Cover Price: Free
Circulation: 17,097 (ABC 01/01/2008 to 31/12/2008)
Usual Pagination: 56
Editor: Richard Thomas
Summary of Content: Magazine focusing on education, pharmacy news, product information, current affairs and features.
Readership/Target Audience: Aimed at pharmacists, locums and health care industry personnel.
ADVERTISING RATES:
Full Page Mono £3370.00
Full Page Colour £4565.00
Agency Commission: 10%
Mechanical Data: Type Area: 306 x 225mm, Bleed Size: 341 x 248mm, Trim Size: 335 x 245mm, Col Length: 306mm, Film: Digital, Page Width: 225mm
Average advertising content per issue: 40%
BUSINESS: PHARMACEUTICAL & CHEMISTS

PHARMACY PRODUCT GUIDE
38766U37-59_80
Formerly: Pharmacy Product News
Editorial Address: Graphic House, 46 Alcester Street, BIRMINGHAM, B12 0PH **Tel:** 0121 766 8830
Fax: 0121 766 8832
Email: kim@pharmacyproductguide.co.uk
Advertising Address: As above.
Email: vippharmacy@tiscali.co.uk
Web site: http://www.pharmacyproductguide.co.uk
ISSN: 1742-4291
Publisher: VIP Publishing
Date Established: 2000
Frequency: Quarterly
Free to qualifying individuals
Circulation: 11,500 (Publisher's Statement)
Usual Pagination: 20
Editor: Kim Johnson; **Advertising Manager:** Paul Sankey
Publisher: Paul Sankey
Summary of Content: Magazine containing pharmaceutical industry product focus and trade product news.
Readership/Target Audience: Read mainly by independent and small group pharmacy retailers.
ADVERTISING RATES:
Full Page Colour £800.00
Agency Commission: 15%
Mechanical Data: Trim Size: 345 x 240mm, Film: Digital, Bleed Size: +3mm, Type Area: 325 x 220mm, Col Length: 325mm, Page Width: 220mm
Copy instructions: Copy Date: 1 week prior to publication date
Average advertising content per issue: 100%
Supplement(s): Baby Times - 2xY
BUSINESS: PHARMACEUTICAL & CHEMISTS

PHARMACY.ME
38741U37-34
Formerly: Middle East Pharmacy
Editorial Address: 6 Tobin Close, Livingston Park, EPSOM, KT19 8AE **Tel:** 01372 742347
Email: pharmedia@aol.com
Advertising Address: As above.
Email: pharmedia@aol.com
Web site: http://www.pharmedia.co.uk
ISSN: 1368-5945

Publisher: Pharmedia International
Frequency: 6 issues yearly
Free to qualifying individuals
Annual Sub.: £35.00
Circulation: 11,230 (Publisher's Statement)
Usual Pagination: 36
Editor: Mike Fahey; **Advertising Manager:** Russ Finnerty
Summary of Content: Journal covering community pharmacy throughout the Middle East.
Readership/Target Audience: Aimed at community and hospital pharmacists.
ADVERTISING RATES:
Full Page Colour £2000.00
Agency Commission: 15%
Mechanical Data: Film: Digital, Page Width: 186mm, Type Area: 272 x 186mm, Col Length: 272mm, Trim Size: 297 x 210mm, Bleed Size: 303 x 216mm
Copy instructions: Copy Date: 1 month prior to publication date
BUSINESS: PHARMACEUTICAL & CHEMISTS

PHARMAFOCUS
38762U37-61_25
Editorial Address: The Atrium, Southern Gate, CHICHESTER, PO19 8SQ **Tel:** 01243 772050
Email: pharmafocus@wiley.co.uk
Advertising Address: As above. **Tel:** 01243 772010
Fax: 01243 772002
Email: bhaughey@wiley.co.uk
Web site: http://www.pharmafocus.com
ISSN: 1465-5403
Publisher: John Wiley & Sons Ltd
Date Established: 1999
Frequency: Monthly - Published in the 1st week of the cover month
Free to qualifying individuals
Annual Sub.: £110.00
Circulation: 6,500 (Publisher's Statement)
Usual Pagination: 32
Editor: Andrew McConaghie
Summary of Content: Newspaper style publication covering the UK ethical and pharmaceutical industry and NHS. Contains features on the NHS and supply sectors.
Readership/Target Audience: Aimed at product, marketing and sales managers, research and development personnel.
ADVERTISING RATES:
Full Page Mono £2895.00
Full Page Colour £3290.00
Agency Commission: 10%
Mechanical Data: Trim Size: 420 x 297mm, Bleed Size: 426 x 303mm, Print Process: Sheet-fed litho, Film: Digital
Copy instructions: Copy Date: 2 weeks prior to publication date
Average advertising content per issue: 50%
BUSINESS: PHARMACEUTICAL & CHEMISTS

PHARMATECHNOLOGY
1740588U56H-52
Editorial Address: 15-19 Great Chapel Street, LONDON, W1F 8FN **Tel:** 020 7758 3040 **Fax:** 020 7758 3001
Email: b.avison@cavendishgroup.co.uk
Advertising Address: As above. **Tel:** 020 7758 3000
Email: ekeazor@cavendishgroup.co.uk
Web site: http://www.cavendishgroup.co.uk/media/ind_pharma.html
Publisher: Cavendish Group
Frequency: Quarterly
Free to qualifying individuals
Circulation: 10,000 (Publisher's Statement)
Usual Pagination: 150
Editor: Ben Avison; **Advertising Manager:** Edward Keazor
Summary of Content: Magazine covering drug discovery, raw materials, clinical research, production processes and business development.
Language(s): Chinese; English
Readership/Target Audience: Aimed at pharmaceutical and biotech manufacturers and researchers in China.
ADVERTISING RATES:
Full Page Colour £5650.00
Agency Commission: 15%
Mechanical Data: Type Area: 258 x 186mm, Bleed Size: 292 x 218mm, Trim Size: 286 x 212mm, Col Length: 258mm, Page Width: 186mm, Film: Digital
Copy instructions: Copy Date: 4 weeks prior to publication date
Average advertising content per issue: 30%
BUSINESS: HEALTH & MEDICAL: Medical Engineering Technology

PHAROS INTERNATIONAL
41580U64L-550
Editorial Address: 1st Floor, Brecon House, 16-16A Albion Place, MAIDSTONE, ME14 5DZ **Tel:** 01622 688293
Fax: 01622 686698
Email: pharos.international@cremation.org.uk
Advertising Address: As above. **Tel:** 01622 688292
Email: pharos.international@cremation.org.uk
Web site: http://www.cremation.org.uk
Publisher: Pharos International

Date Established: 1937
Frequency: Quarterly
Annual Sub.: £31.00
Circulation: 1,000 (Publisher's Statement)
Usual Pagination: 52
Editor: Roger Arber; **Advertising Manager:** Julie Forrest
Summary of Content: Journal of the Cremation Society of Great Britain and the International Cremation Federation.
Readership/Target Audience: Aimed at crematoria personnel, government and local authority departments, libraries, press and funeral directors and anyone with an active interest in the death-care profession in the UK and overseas.
ADVERTISING RATES:
Full Page Mono £281.00
Full Page Colour £483.00
Agency Commission: 10%
Mechanical Data: Type Area: 265 x 180mm, Bleed Size: 305 x 218mm, Trim Size: 297 x 210mm, Col Length: 265mm, Page Width: 180mm, Film: Digital
Average advertising content per issue: 25%
BUSINESS: OTHER CLASSIFICATIONS: Funeral Directors, Cemeteries & Crematoria

PHE - PLANT HIRE EXECUTIVE
39016U42A-164
Editorial Address: Bakers House, 25 Bakers Road, UXBRIDGE, UB8 1RG **Tel:** 01895 819350
Fax: 01895 457457
Email: nick.johnson@phe.co.uk
Advertising Address: 10 Dovecote Road, DROITWICH SPA, WR9 7RN **Tel:** 01905 775572 **Fax:** 01905 776975
Email: david.holmes@phe.co.uk
Web site: http://www.phe.co.uk
ISSN: 1364-4890
Publisher: Executive Magazines Ltd
Date Established: 1987
Frequency: 11 issues yearly - Published in the middle of the cover month
Free to qualifying individuals
Annual Sub.: £40.00
Circulation: 6,402 (Publisher's Statement)
Usual Pagination: 40
Editor: Nick Johnson; **Advertising Manager:** David Holmes
Summary of Content: Magazine covering news, products and plant test reports for the UK plant hire industry.
Readership/Target Audience: Aimed at industry executives with responsibility for specifying plant and equipment.
ADVERTISING RATES:
Full Page Colour £1520.00
Agency Commission: 10%
Mechanical Data: Film: Digital, Type Area: 271 x 188mm, Bleed Size: 303 x 216mm, Trim Size: 297 x 210mm, Print Process: Sheet-fed litho, Col Length: 271mm, Page Width: 188mm
Copy instructions: Copy Date: 4 weeks prior to publication date
BUSINESS: CONSTRUCTION

PHILOSOPHICAL TRANSACTIONS OF THE ROYAL SOCIETY: BIOLOGICAL
41512U64F-130
Formerly: Proceedings of the Royal Society Series: Biological Sciences
Editorial Address: 6-9 Carlton House Terrace, LONDON, SW1Y 5AG **Tel:** 020 7451 2634 **Fax:** 020 7976 1837
Email: james.joseph@royalsoc.ac.uk
Web site: http://www.pubs.royalsoc.ac.uk/philtransb
ISSN: 0962-8436
Publisher: The Royal Society
Date Established: 1665
Frequency: 24 issues yearly - Published on the 12th and the 27th of each month
Annual Sub.: £1435.00
Circulation: 800 (Publisher's Statement)
Usual Pagination: 120
Editor: Claire Kingston
Summary of Content: Journal which focuses on a different specific area of the biological sciences each issue. This area will define a research frontier that is advancing rapidly, often bridging traditional disciplines.
Readership/Target Audience: Aimed at scientists working across the biological sciences.
ADVERTISING: No Advertising taken
BUSINESS: OTHER CLASSIFICATIONS: Biology

PHOENIX
41143U62H-420
Editorial Address: Millenium House, 30 Junction Road, SHEFFIELD, S11 8XB **Tel:** 0114 251 5750
Email: chris.jackson@agcas.org.uk
Advertising Address: As above. **Fax:** 0114 251 5751
Email: chris.jackson@agcas.org.uk
Web site: http://www.agcas.org.uk
Publisher: Graduate Prospects Ltd.
Date Established: 1970
Frequency: Quarterly
Free to qualifying individuals

Section 4 (b) Business Magazines

Business Magazines

Annual Sub.: £35.00
Circulation: 1,450 (Publisher's Statement)
Usual Pagination: 50
Editor: Chris Jackson; **Advertising Manager:** Chris Jackson
Summary of Content: Official journal of The Association of Graduate Careers Advisory Service. Contains current issues, events and trends in careers advice and graduate recruitment.
Readership/Target Audience: Aimed at members of the Association of Graduate Careers Advisory Services.
ADVERTISING: Rates on application
BUSINESS: CHURCH & SCHOOL EQUIPMENT & EDUCATION: Careers

PHOENIXFILE
761714U37-401
Editorial Address: Rivington Road, Whitehouse Industrial Estate, RUNCORN, WA7 3DJ **Tel:** 01928 750500
Fax: 01928 750555
Email: phoenixfile@phoenixmedical.co.uk
Web site: http://www.myp-i-n.co.uk
ISSN: 1470-3971
Publisher: Phoenix Medical Supplies Ltd
Date Established: 2001
Frequency: 7 issues yearly
Cover Price: Free
Circulation: 11,250 (Publisher's Statement)
Usual Pagination: 30
Editor: Lorna Atherton; **Advertising Manager:** Lorna Atherton
Summary of Content: Newsletter focusing on pharmacy, dispensing doctors, medicines, new products, retailing and own brands as well as merchandising and refits. Also covers pharmacy news and pharmacist and company profiles.
Readership/Target Audience: Aimed at independent pharmacists, dispensing doctors and staff.
ADVERTISING: No Advertising taken
BUSINESS: PHARMACEUTICAL & CHEMISTS

THE PHOTOGRAMMETRIC RECORD
38799U38-63
Editorial Address: 9 Merrytree Close, West Wellow, ROMSEY, SO51 6RB **Tel:** 01794 322993 **Fax:** 01794 322993
Email: photrec@rspsoc.org
Advertising Address: 9600 Garsington Road, Cowley, OXFORD, OX4 2DQ **Tel:** 01865 776868 **Fax:** 01865 476267
Email: Craig. Pickett@oxon.blackwellpublishing.com
Web site: http://www.rspsoc.org
ISSN: 0031-868X
Publisher: Blackwell Publishing and the Remote Sensing and Photogrammetry Society
Date Established: 1953
Frequency: Quarterly
Circulation: 2,000 (Publisher's Statement)
Usual Pagination: 1100
Editor: Paul Newby
Summary of Content: Journal of the Remote Sensing and Photogammetry Society. Contains articles about current photogammetric practice and research around the world.
Readership/Target Audience: Aimed at science, engineering and cultural heritage.
ADVERTISING RATES:
Full Page Mono £420.00
Agency Commission: 10%
Mechanical Data: Film: Digital, Type Area: 206 x 118mm, Col Length: 206mm, Page Width: 118mm
Copy instructions: Copy Date: 6 weeks prior to publication date
BUSINESS: PHOTOGRAPHIC TRADE

THE PHOTOGRAPHER
38800U38-65
Editorial Address: 18 Dove Close, BISHOP'S STORTFORD, CM23 4JD **Tel:** 01279 503871 **Fax:** 01279 503871
Email: editor@bipp.com
Advertising Address: Boland Advertising, 81 Castle Avenue, DOVER, CT16 1EZ **Tel:** 01304 202738
Email: barco@tiscali.co.uk
Web site: http://www.bipp.com
ISSN: 0031-8698
Publisher: BIPP
Frequency: Monthly
Cover Price: £4.25
Annual Sub.: £65.00
Circulation: 3,500 (Publisher's Statement)
Usual Pagination: 52
Editor: Jonathan Briggs; **Advertising Manager:** Barry Wadsworth-Smith
Summary of Content: Magazine covering business matters, news and updates, features on issues relating to photography, interviews with working photographers and product and service reviews.
Readership/Target Audience: Aimed at professionals in the photographic trade.
ADVERTISING RATES:
Full Page Mono £1195.00
Full Page Colour £1195.00
SCC £45.00

Agency Commission: 10%
Mechanical Data: Page Width: 190mm, Film: Digital, Type Area: 277 x 190mm, Col Length: 277mm, Trim Size: 297 x 210mm, Bleed Size: +3mm, Col Widths (Display): 43.75, No. of Columns (Display): 4
Copy instructions: Copy Date: 3rd week prior to publication date
Average advertising content per issue: 45%
BUSINESS: PHOTOGRAPHIC TRADE

PHOTOWORLD
38794U38-49
Formerly: Photo World
Editorial Address: Maxwell Place, Maxwell Lane, KELSO, TD5 7BB **Tel:** 01573 226032 **Fax:** 01573 226000
Email: iconmags@btconnect.com
Advertising Address: Abbey Field House, 15 Brougham Place, HAWICK, TD9 9JU **Tel:** 01450 371169
Fax: 01573 226000
Email: adsales@btconnect.com
Web site: http://www.photoclubalpha.com
Publisher: Icon Publications Ltd
Date Established: 1966
Frequency: Quarterly
Annual Sub.: £19.95
Circulation: 2,000 (Publisher's Statement)
Usual Pagination: 36
Editor: Shirley Kilpatrick; **Advertising Director:** Richard Kilpatrick
Summary of Content: Magazine containing news of interest to owners and users of Minolta, Konica Minolta and Sony Alpha still or video cameras.
Readership/Target Audience: Aimed at members of the Minolta Club of Great Britain.
ADVERTISING RATES:
Full Page Colour £1350.00
Agency Commission: 10%
Mechanical Data: Trim Size: 297 x 210mm, Bleed Size: 303 x 216mm, Print Process: Sheet-fed offset litho, Film: Digital
Average advertising content per issue: 20%
BUSINESS: PHOTOGRAPHIC TRADE

PHYSICAL CHEMISTRY CHEMICAL PHYSICS
36696U13-115
Editorial Address: Thomas Graham House, Science Park, Milton Road, CAMBRIDGE, CB4 0WF **Tel:** 01223 420066
Fax: 01223 420247
Email: pccp@rsc.org
Advertising Address: As above. **Tel:** 01223 432246
Fax: 01223 426017
Email: advertising@rsc.org
Web site: http://www.rsc.org/pccp
ISSN: 1463-9076
Publisher: Royal Society of Chemistry
Date Established: 1999
Frequency: Weekly
Annual Sub.: £2082.00
Circulation: 1,500 (Publisher's Statement)
Usual Pagination: 258
Editor: Kate McCallum; **Advertising Manager:** Ian Swain; **Managing Editor:** Philip Earis
Summary of Content: Journal containing new and original research and reviews, covering the areas of physical chemistry, chemical physics and biophysical chemistry.
Readership/Target Audience: Aimed at researchers and chemists across the physics and chemistry fields.
ADVERTISING RATES:
Full Page Colour £890.00
SCC £26.00
Agency Commission: 10%
Mechanical Data: Type Area: 252 x 188mm, Bleed Size: 281 x 216mm, Trim Size: 275 x 210mm, Col Length: 252mm, Page Width: 188mm, Film: Digital
BUSINESS: CHEMICALS

PHYSICAL EDUCATION MATTERS
38519U32H-30
Formerly: British Journal of Physical Education
Editorial Address: Building 25, London Road, READING, RG1 5AQ **Tel:** 0118 378 6240 **Fax:** 0118 378 6242
Email: enquiries@afpe.org.uk
Advertising Address: La Fontanella, 3A Martello Road, Branksome Park, POOLE, BH13 7DQ **Tel:** 01202 701053
Fax: 01202 701053
Email: stephensea@hotmail.com
Web site: http://www.afpe.org.uk
ISSN: 1751-0988
Publisher: Association for Physical Education
Date Established: 2006
Frequency: Quarterly
Free to qualifying individuals
Circulation: 3,500 (Publisher's Statement)
Usual Pagination: 72
Editor: Liz Taplin; **Advertising Manager:** Stephen Macey
Summary of Content: Publication covering news and features relating to physical education.

Readership/Target Audience: Aimed at teachers, lecturers, advisors and trainees.
ADVERTISING RATES:
Full Page Colour £720.00
Agency Commission: 10%
Mechanical Data: Trim Size: 297 x 210mm, Bleed Size: 303 x 216mm, Print Process: Sheet-fed offset litho, Film: Digital
Copy instructions: Copy Date: 4 weeks prior to publication date
Average advertising content per issue: 30%
BUSINESS: LOCAL GOVERNMENT, LEISURE & RECREATION: Leisure, Recreation & Entertainment

PHYSICS & CHEMISTRY OF GLASSES
36639U12B-70
Editorial Address: Unit 9, Twelve O'Clock Court, 21 Attercliffe Road, SHEFFIELD, S4 7WW **Tel:** 0114 263 4455
Fax: 0114 263 4411
Email: david@sgt.org
Web site: http://www.sgt.org
ISSN: 0031-9090
Publisher: Society of Glass Technology
Date Established: 1960
Frequency: 6 issues yearly - Published in the 1st week of the cover month
Annual Sub.: £220.00
Circulation: 700 (Publisher's Statement)
Usual Pagination: 64
Editor: David Moore; **Managing Editor:** David Moore
Summary of Content: Learned journal addressing advances in the understanding of glass. Contains reviews and original papers.
Readership/Target Audience: Aimed at learning institutes.
ADVERTISING: No Advertising taken
BUSINESS: CERAMICS, POTTERY & GLASS: Glass

PHYSICS WORLD
39998U55-127
Editorial Address: Dirac House, Temple Back, BRISTOL, BS1 6BE **Tel:** 0117 929 7481 **Fax:** 0117 925 1942
Email: pwld@iop.org
Advertising Address: As above.
Email: edward.jost@iop.org
Web site: http://www.physicsworld.com
ISSN: 0953-8585
Publisher: IOP Publishing
Date Established: 1988
Frequency: Monthly
Annual Sub.: EUR380.00
Circulation: 35,183 (ABC 01/01/2008 to 31/12/2008)
Usual Pagination: 70
Editor: Matin Durrani; **News Editor:** Michael Banks; **Features Editor:** Joao Medeiros; **Publisher:** Jo Nicholas
Summary of Content: Magazine of the Institute of Physics with news, features, reviews, readers' letters and regular columns.
Readership/Target Audience: Aimed at physicists and scientists with an interest in physics.
ADVERTISING RATES:
Full Page Mono £2990.00
Full Page Colour £3735.00
Agency Commission: 10%
Mechanical Data: Trim Size: 282 x 213mm, Bleed Size: 288 x 219mm, Type Area: 262 x 193mm, Col Length: 262mm, Page Width: 193mm
Copy instructions: Copy Date: 10 days prior to publication date
Average advertising content per issue: 25%
BUSINESS: APPLIED SCIENCE & LABORATORIES

PHYSIOTHERAPY
40546U56R-108_30
Editorial Address: The Boulevard, Langford Lane, KIDLINGTON, OX5 1GB **Tel:** 01865 842000
Fax: 01865 843997
Email: physiotherapy@elsevier.com
Advertising Address: 32 Jamestown Road, LONDON, NW1 7BY **Tel:** 020 7424 4200 **Fax:** 020 7483 2293
Email: e.steel@elsevier.com
Web site: http://www.physiotherapyjournal.com
ISSN: 0031-9406
Publisher: Elsevier
Date Established: 1915
Frequency: Quarterly
Annual Sub.: EUR93.00
Circulation: 49,000 (Publisher's Statement)
Usual Pagination: 96
Editor: Michele Harms; **Advertising Manager:** Emma Steel; **Publisher:** Stephen Wymbs
Summary of Content: Publication of the Chartered Society of Physiotherapy. Contains reviews and research concerned with the scientific basis and clinical application of physiotherapy, education of practitioners and management of services.
Readership/Target Audience: Aimed at physiotherapists.
ADVERTISING RATES:
Full Page Mono £744.00
Full Page Colour £1352.00

Agency Commission: 15%
Mechanical Data: Trim Size: 280 x 210mm, Bleed Size: 286 x 216mm, Film: Digital
Copy instructions: Copy Date: 6 weeks prior to publication date
BUSINESS: HEALTH & MEDICAL: Health Medical Related

PHYSIOTHERAPY FRONTLINE 40547U56R-120

Editorial Address: 14 Bedford Row, LONDON, WC1R 4ED
Tel: 020 7306 6664 **Fax:** 020 7306 6667
Email: frontline@csp.org.uk
Web site: http://www.csp.org.uk
ISSN: 1356-9791
Publisher: The Chartered Society of Physiotherapy
Date Established: 1995
Frequency: 23 issues yearly
Free to qualifying individuals
Annual Sub.: £65.00
Circulation: 46,500 (Publisher's Statement)
Usual Pagination: 108
Editor: Gary Henson; **News Editor:** Gary Henson; **Features Editor:** Catherine Hill
Summary of Content: Publication containing news and information about physiotherapy and chartered physiotherapists, physiotherapy assistants and students.
Readership/Target Audience: Aimed at chartered physiotherapists, physiotherapy assistants and students.
ADVERTISING: No Advertising taken
BUSINESS: HEALTH & MEDICAL: Health Medical Related

PHYTOCHEMICAL ANALYSIS 40126U55-128

Editorial Address: The Atrium, Southern Gate, CHICHESTER, PO19 8SQ **Tel:** 01243 779777
Fax: 01243 770432
Email: mrothlis@wiley.com
Advertising Address: As above.
Email: adsales@wiley.co.uk
Web site: http://www.interscience.wiley.com/journal/pca
ISSN: 0958-0344
Publisher: John Wiley & Sons Ltd
Date Established: 1989
Frequency: 6 issues yearly
Annual Sub.: $1770.00
Circulation: 300 (Print Run)
Usual Pagination: 96
Editor: Martin Rothlisberger; **Editor-in-Chief:** Barry Charlwood
Summary of Content: Scientific Research Journal which publishes original articles on the application of analytical methodology in the plant sciences. All forms of physical, chemical, biochemical, radiometric, electrometric and chromatographic investigations of plant products (monomoeric species as well as polymetric molecules such as nucleic acis, proteins, lipids and carbohydrates) will be included.
Readership/Target Audience: Aimed at plant, food and pharmaceutical scientists, agricultural and horticultural experts, flavour chemists and biochemists.
ADVERTISING RATES:
Full Page Mono £1175.00
Full Page Colour £2575.00
Agency Commission: 10%
Mechanical Data: Print Process: Sheet-fed litho, Film: Digital, Type Area: 270 x 180mm, Col Length: 270mm, Page Width: 180mm, Trim Size: 297 x 210mm
BUSINESS: APPLIED SCIENCE & LABORATORIES

PHYTOTHERAPY RESEARCH 601248U56A-108_80

Editorial Address: The Atrium, Southern Gate, CHICHESTER, PO19 8SQ **Tel:** 01243 779777
Fax: 01243 770133
Email: jwixon@wiley.co.uk
Advertising Address: As above. **Tel:** 01243 770254
Fax: 01243 770432
Email: adsales@wiley.co.uk
Web site: http://www.interscience.wiley.com
ISSN: 0951-418X
Publisher: John Wiley & Sons Ltd
Date Established: 1987
Frequency: Monthly
Annual Sub.: $2375.00
Usual Pagination: 104
Editor: Elizabeth Williamson; **Editor-in-Chief:** Elizabeth Williamson; **Managing Editor:** Rachael Bilginer
Summary of Content: Magazine covering original medical plant research, including biochemistry and molecular pharmacology, toxicology, pathology and the clinical applications of herbs and natural products to both human and animal medicine.
Readership/Target Audience: Aimed at biochemists, pharmacologists, toxicologists, medical chemists, pathologists, medical scientists, botanists, plant scientists and natural product chemists.
ADVERTISING RATES:
Full Page Mono £1175.00
Full Page Colour £2575.00

Agency Commission: 10%
Mechanical Data: Type Area: 270 x 180mm, Trim Size: 297 x 210mm, Col Length: 270mm, Page Width: 180mm, Print Process: Sheet-fed litho, Film: Digital
BUSINESS: HEALTH & MEDICAL

THE PICTURE BUSINESS 41598U64Q-300

Editorial Address: 1 Churchgates, The Wilderness, BERKHAMSTED, HP4 2UB **Tel:** 01442 289930
Fax: 01442 289950
Email: peter@lemapublishing.co.uk
Advertising Address: As above.
Email: jfurlong@lemapublishing.co.uk
ISSN: 1362-1238
Publisher: Lema Publishing
Date Established: 1984
Frequency: 6 issues yearly - Published on the 26th of the month prior to the cover month
Cover Price: £5.50
Annual Sub.: £36.00
Circulation: 5,300 (Publisher's Statement)
Usual Pagination: 52
Editor: Peter Hancocks; **Advertising Manager:** John Furlong
Summary of Content: Magazine covering news, trends and new products in art and framing and running a business.
Readership/Target Audience: Aimed at retailers who buy, frame and sell art, ranging from department stores to homewares and interiors retailers and independent galleries and framers.
ADVERTISING RATES:
Full Page Colour £2050.00
Agency Commission: 10%
Mechanical Data: Bleed Size: 321 x 246mm, Trim Size: 315 x 240mm, Film: Digital
Copy instructions: Copy Date: 20th of the month prior to publication date
Average advertising content per issue: 45%
BUSINESS: OTHER CLASSIFICATIONS: Framing

PIG INTERNATIONAL 37844U21D-835

Editorial Address: Lavant House, Lavant Street, PETERSFIELD, GU32 3EL **Tel:** 01730 262200
Fax: 01730 262201
Email: pbest@wattnet.net
Advertising Address: Albast 25, 2719 TV ZOETERMEER
Tel: 79 32 30 782 **Fax:** 79 32 30 783
Email: driesmvd@xs4all.nl
Web site: http://www.pig-international.com
ISSN: 0191-8834
Publisher: Watt Publishing Co
Frequency: 10 issues yearly - Published on the 15th of the cover month
Cover Price: $6.00
Free to qualifying individuals
Annual Sub.: $60.00
Circulation: 17,000 (Publisher's Statement)
Usual Pagination: 36
Editor: Peter Best
Summary of Content: Journal covering news, information and the latest advances in pig farming.
Readership/Target Audience: Aimed at pig producers and allied professionals.
ADVERTISING RATES:
Full Page Colour $7375.00
Agency Commission: 15%
Mechanical Data: Type Area: 254 x 178mm, Bleed Size: 274 x 207mm, Trim Size: 267 x 200mm, Col Length: 254mm, Page Width: 178mm, Film: Digital, Col Widths (Display): 54mm, No. of Columns (Display): 3
Copy instructions: Copy Date: 3 weeks prior to publication date
BUSINESS: AGRICULTURE & FARMING: Livestock

PIG MARKETING 1826479U21D-1006

Editorial Address: Hendel Oast, Hendal Farm, Groombridge, TUNBRIDGE WELLS, TN3 9NU
Tel: 01892 861664
Email: caroline@ghpublishing.co.uk
Advertising Address: As above.
Email: caroline@gnpublishing.co.uk
Web site: http://www.farmbusiness.cc
Publisher: Grove House Publishing
Date Established: 2007
Frequency: 5 issues yearly
Editor: Caroline Calder-Smith; **Advertising Manager:** Caroline Calder-Smith
Summary of Content: Magazine covering marketing within the food chain, increasing the competitiveness of UK farming, identifying future trends, anticipating customer demands and improving prices to the producer.
Readership/Target Audience: Aimed at producers, processors, vets, marketing groups and buyers.
ADVERTISING RATES:
Full Page Colour £1800.00

Mechanical Data: Type Area: 300 x 225mm, Bleed Size: 341 x 250mm, Trim Size: 335 x 244mm, Col Length: 300mm, Page Width: 225mm, Film: Digital
BUSINESS: AGRICULTURE & FARMING: Livestock

PIG NEWS & INFORMATION 37845U21D-840

Editorial Address: Nosworthy Way, WALLINGFORD, OX10 8DE **Tel:** 01491 832111 **Fax:** 01491 833508
Email: u.allen@cabi.org
Web site: http://www.cabi-publishing.org
ISSN: 0143-9014
Publisher: CABI
Frequency: Quarterly
Annual Sub.: £330.00
Circulation: 200 (Publisher's Statement)
Editor: Uma Sabapathy-Allen
Summary of Content: Magazine covering research summaries and reports, news, reprints of reviews (from Perspectives in Agriculture, Veterinary Science, Nutrition and Natural Resources) and 3500 abstracts of global literature (annually) on important developments in pig breeding, molecular genetics and pig health. Includes articles on nutrition, housing and management, environmental impact of production including waste management, carcass and meat, economics, welfare, reproduction and production.
Readership/Target Audience: Aimed at farmers and pig producers.
ADVERTISING: No Advertising taken
BUSINESS: AGRICULTURE & FARMING: Livestock

PIG WORLD 37846U21D-842

Editorial Address: PO Box 100, Benniworth, MARKET RASEN, LN8 6LE **Tel:** 01507 313798 **Fax:** 01507 313997
Email: sam@pigworld.co.uk
Advertising Address: As above.
Email: ann@benniworth.net
Web site: http://www.pigworld.co.uk
ISSN: 0966-3592
Publisher: Arnford Ltd
Frequency: Monthly - Published the middle of the month
Annual Sub.: £45.00
Circulation: 5,000 (Publisher's Statement)
Usual Pagination: 60
Editor: Sam Walton; **Advertising Manager:** Ann Scott
Summary of Content: Magazine containing national coverage of the pig industry.
Readership/Target Audience: Aimed at professional pig farmers.
BUSINESS: AGRICULTURE & FARMING: Livestock

PIGMENT & RESIN TECHNOLOGY 37281U16B-93

Editorial Address: Howard House, Wagon Lane, BINGLEY, BD16 1WA **Tel:** 01274 777700 **Fax:** 01274 785200
Email: hcolson@emeraldinsight.com
Web site: http://www.emeraldinsight.com/prt.htm
ISSN: 0369-9420
Publisher: Emerald Group Publishing Ltd
Frequency: 6 issues yearly
Annual Sub.: £1599.00
Usual Pagination: 90
Editor: Harry Colson; **Publisher:** Harry Colson
Summary of Content: Journal covering raw materials and plant used in the manufacture and formulation of paints, inks, dyes and adhesives.
Readership/Target Audience: Aimed at directors, buyers, technicians and scientists involved in the use and manufacture of paints and resins.
ADVERTISING: No Advertising taken
BUSINESS: DECORATING & PAINT: Paint - Technical Manufacture

PIPELINE & GAS JOURNAL 37674U19G-50

Editorial Address: PO Box 437, MAIDSTONE, ME14 4RB
Tel: 01622 721222 **Fax:** 01622 721333
Email: roger.kingswell@btinternet.com
Advertising Address: As above.
Email: roger.kingswell@btinternet.com
Web site: http://www.pipelineandgasjournal.com
Publisher: Oildom Publishing Co
Date Established: 1859
Frequency: Monthly - Published around the 15th of the cover month
Free to qualifying individuals
Annual Sub.: $70.00
Circulation: 26,878 (Publisher's Statement)
Usual Pagination: 90
Editor: Roger Kingswell; **Advertising Manager:** Roger Kingswell
Summary of Content: Technical journal about pipeline operations, planning, engineering, construction and maintenance worldwide, gas transmission and distribution, the storage and transportation of oil, gas, water and industrial products.

Business Magazines

Readership/Target Audience: Aimed at planning, engineering and operations management.
ADVERTISING RATES:
Full Page Mono $5530.00
Full Page Colour $6905.00
Agency Commission: 15%
Mechanical Data: Type Area: 260 x 184mm, Bleed Size: 280 x 203mm, Trim Size: 274 x 197mm, Film: Digital, Col Length: 260mm, Page Width: 184mm
Copy instructions: Copy Date: 17th of the month prior to publication date
Average advertising content per issue: 40%
BUSINESS: ENGINEERING & MACHINERY: Pipelines

PIR CARE HOME MANAGEMENT

1615297U56R-506

Formerly: PIR Healthcare Management
Editorial Address: 1st Floor, Clifton House, 4A Goldington Road, BEDFORD, MK40 3NF **Tel:** 0870 749 0220
Fax: 0870 749 0221
Email: tracy.cater@pirnet.co.uk
Advertising Address: As above.
Email: wasim.raja@pirnet.co.uk
Web site: http://www.pirnet.co.uk
Publisher: The Bellmont Agency Ltd
Frequency: Quarterly
Cover Price: Free
Circulation: 18,000 (ABC 01/07/2006 to 30/06/2007)
Editor: Tracy Cater
Summary of Content: Magazine covering topical issues within the healthcare industries.
Readership/Target Audience: Aimed at senior contacts in residential homes, clinics, doctors' practices, rest homes, hospitals and dentists.
ADVERTISING RATES:
Full Page Colour £1995.00
Agency Commission: 10%
Mechanical Data: Type Area: 280 x 205mm, Bleed Size: 303 x 216mm, Trim Size: 297 x 210mm, Col Length: 280mm, Page Width: 205mm, Film: Digital
Copy instructions: Copy Date: 2 weeks prior to publication date
Average advertising content per issue: 40%
BUSINESS: HEALTH & MEDICAL: Health Medical Related

PIR CONSTRUCTION

600923U4A-215

Editorial Address: 1st Floor, Clifton House, 4A Goldington Road, BEDFORD, MK40 3NF **Tel:** 0870 749 0220
Fax: 0870 749 0221
Email: derek.cooper@pirnet.co.uk
Advertising Address: As above.
Email: derek.cooper@pirnet.co.uk
Web site: http://www.pirnet.co.uk
Publisher: The Bellmont Agency Ltd
Date Established: 1997
Frequency: Quarterly
Cover Price: Free
Circulation: 22,670 (ABC 01/07/2007 to 30/06/2008)
Usual Pagination: 24
Editor: Derek Cooper; **Managing Director:** Steve Mitchell; **Advertising Manager:** Derek Cooper; **Publisher:** Steve Mitchell
Summary of Content: Magazine containing information on products and services for the building industry.
Readership/Target Audience: Aimed at architects, builders and the supply industry as well as local authorities and public utilities.
ADVERTISING RATES:
Full Page Colour £1995.00
Agency Commission: 10%
Mechanical Data: Type Area: 280 x 205mm, Bleed Size: 303 x 216mm, Trim Size: 297 x 210mm, Col Length: 280mm, Page Width: 205mm, Film: Digital
Copy instructions: Copy Date: 2 weeks prior to publication date
Average advertising content per issue: 100%
BUSINESS: ARCHITECTURE & BUILDING: Architecture

PIR EDUCATION

1615295U62A-503

Editorial Address: 1st Floor, Clifton House, 4A Goldington Road, BEDFORD, MK40 3NF **Tel:** 0870 749 0220
Fax: 0870 749 0221
Email: derek.cooper@pirnet.co.uk
Advertising Address: As above. **Tel:** 0870 7490 220
Fax: 0870 7490221
Email: derek.cooper@pirnet.co.uk
Web site: http://www.pirnet.co.uk
Publisher: The Bellmont Agency Ltd
Frequency: 6 issues yearly
Cover Price: Free
Circulation: 21,564 (ABC 01/07/2007 to 30/06/2008)
Editor: Derek Cooper; **Advertising Manager:** Derek Cooper
Summary of Content: Magazine covering the education sector.
Readership/Target Audience: Aimed at headteachers, bursars, principals and local education authorities.

ADVERTISING RATES:
Full Page Colour £1995.00
Agency Commission: 10%
Mechanical Data: Trim Size: 297 x 210mm, Film: Digital
Copy instructions: Copy Date: 2 weeks prior to publication date
Average advertising content per issue: 60%
BUSINESS: CHURCH & SCHOOL EQUIPMENT & EDUCATION: Education

PIR HOSPITALITY BUSINESS

38538U32H-235

Formerly: PIR Hotels, Sport & Leisure
Editorial Address: 1st Floor, Clifton House, 4A Goldington Road, BEDFORD, MK40 3NF **Tel:** 0870 749 0220
Fax: 0870 749 0221
Email: hotels@pirnet.co.uk
Advertising Address: As above. **Tel:** 01234 348878
Fax: 01234 352737
Email: admin@pirnet.co.uk
Web site: http://www.pirnet.co.uk
Publisher: The Bellmont Agency Ltd
Frequency: 6 issues yearly
Cover Price: Free
Circulation: 25,017 (ABC 01/07/2006 to 30/06/2007)
Usual Pagination: 30
Editor: Derek Cooper; **Advertising Manager:** Tony Heathfield
Summary of Content: Magazine focusing on the hotel and leisure industry. Contains information on products and services, as well as features on interiors, IT, computer management systems and health and safety.
Readership/Target Audience: Aimed at the sports, hotel, leisure and catering industries.
ADVERTISING RATES:
Full Page Colour £1795.00
Agency Commission: 10%
Mechanical Data: Film: Digital, Trim Size: 297 x 210mm, Type Area: 264 x 186mm, Bleed Size: 286 x 211mm, Col Length: 264mm, Page Width: 186mm
Copy instructions: Copy Date: 2 weeks prior to publication date
Average advertising content per issue: 80%
BUSINESS: LOCAL GOVERNMENT, LEISURE & RECREATION: Leisure, Recreation & Entertainment

PITCHCARE

1732044U64D-94

Editorial Address: The Technology Centre, Wolverhampton Science Park, WOLVERHAMPTON, WV10 9RU
Tel: 01902 440252 **Fax:** 01902 440253
Email: laurence@pitchcare.com
Advertising Address: 3 Pound Lane, SHAFTESBURY, SP7 8RZ **Tel:** 01747 855335 **Fax:** 01747 855335
Email: peter@pitchcare.com
Web site: http://www.pitchcare.com
Publisher: Pitchcare.com Limited
Frequency: 6 issues yearly
Free to qualifying individuals
Annual Sub.: £30.00
Circulation: 7,000 (Publisher's Statement)
Usual Pagination: 104
Editor: Laurence Gale; **Managing Director:** David Saltman; **Advertising Manager:** Peter Britton
Summary of Content: Magazine covering all aspects of the sports turf industry including news, products, education, training, health and safety and venues.
Readership/Target Audience: Aimed at groundsmen, greenkeepers, parks local authority managers, contractors, manufacturers, service providers and education colleges.
ADVERTISING RATES:
Full Page Colour £1200.00
Agency Commission: 10%
Mechanical Data: Bleed Size: 303 x 216mm, Trim Size: 297 x 210mm, Film: Digital
Copy instructions: Copy Date: 2 weeks prior to publication date
Average advertising content per issue: 25%
BUSINESS: OTHER CLASSIFICATIONS: Course Maintenance

PIXEL

38802U38-76

Editorial Address: Park View House, 19 The Avenue, EASTBOURNE, BN21 3YD **Tel:** 01323 411601
Fax: 01323 411654
Email: editorial@pixelmagazine.co.uk
Advertising Address: As above.
Email: jt@pixelmagazine.co.uk
Publisher: Park View Publishing Ltd
Date Established: 1989
Frequency: 37 issues yearly
Free to qualifying individuals
Circulation: 5,500 (Publisher's Statement)
Usual Pagination: 16
Editor: Laura Knight; **Managing Director:** Lee Mansfield; **Advertising Manager:** John Townsend
Summary of Content: News and views of the photography and video trade.

Readership/Target Audience: Read by high street retail executives.
ADVERTISING RATES:
Full Page Colour £1230.00
Agency Commission: 10%
Mechanical Data: Type Area: 275 x 198mm, Bleed Size: 323 x 230mm, Trim Size: 317 x 226mm, Col Length: 275mm, Page Width: 198mm, Print Process: Sheet-fed litho, Film: Digital
Copy instructions: Copy Date: 1 week prior to publication date
Average advertising content per issue: 40%
Editions:
infolab
BUSINESS: PHOTOGRAPHIC TRADE

PIZZA, PASTA & ITALIAN FOOD MAGAZINE

36590U11A-153

Editorial Address: Association House, 18C Moor Street, CHEPSTOW, NP16 5DB **Tel:** 01291 628103
Fax: 01291 630402
Email: clare@jandmgroup.co.uk
Advertising Address: As above. **Tel:** 01291 636334
Email: andrew@jandmgroup.co.uk
Web site: http://www.papa.org.uk
Publisher: J & M Group Ltd.
Frequency: 6 issues yearly
Free to qualifying individuals
Annual Sub.: £45.00
Circulation: 10,000 (Publisher's Statement)
Usual Pagination: 48
Editor: Clare Benfield; **Managing Editor:** Simon Ambrose
Summary of Content: Publication containing news and features relating to the pizza and pasta industry and the Italian food market.
Readership/Target Audience: Aimed at those within the industry from retail buyers and suppliers to service outlets including pizzerias, pasta stores, take-aways and home delivery also ingredient and equipment manufacturers.
ADVERTISING RATES:
Full Page Mono £975.00
Full Page Colour £1375.00
SCC £18.00
Agency Commission: 10%
Mechanical Data: Film: Digital, Type Area: 268 x 184mm, Bleed Size: 302 x 215mm, Trim Size: 297 x 210mm, Col Length: 268mm, Page Width: 184mm
Average advertising content per issue: 40%
BUSINESS: CATERING: Catering, Hotels & Restaurants

PLANNING

35859U4D-180

Editorial Address: 174 Hammersmith Road, LONDON, W6 7JP **Tel:** 020 8267 5000 **Fax:** 020 8267 4013
Email: planning@haymarket.com
Advertising Address: As above. **Fax:** 020 8267 4702
Email: julien.mealey@haymarket.com
Web site: http://www.planningresource.co.uk
ISSN: 1467-2073
Publisher: Haymarket Business Media Ltd
Date Established: 1972
Frequency: Weekly
Cover Price: £2.60
Free to qualifying individuals
Annual Sub.: £113.00
Circulation: 24,418 (ABC 01/07/2008 to 30/06/2009)
Usual Pagination: 16
Editor: Susanna Gillman; **News Editor:** Susanna Gillman; **Managing Director:** Stephen Farish; **Advertising Manager:** Julien Mealey; **Advertising Director:** Dom Lawrence-Jones
Summary of Content: Journal of the Royal Town Planning Institute. Carries news of transport, housing, regeneration, economic development, environment and changes in planning law.
Readership/Target Audience: Read by town and country planners.
ADVERTISING RATES:
Full Page Colour £4085.00
Agency Commission: 10%
Mechanical Data: Trim Size: 297 x 210mm, Bleed Size: 303 x 216mm, Film: Digital
Copy instructions: Copy Date: 1 week prior to publication date
Average advertising content per issue: 50%
BUSINESS: ARCHITECTURE & BUILDING: Planning & Housing

PLANNING IN LONDON

35860U4D-200

Editorial Address: Studio Crown & Gallery Reach, 149A Grosvenor Road, LONDON, SW1V 3JY **Tel:** 020 7834 9471
Fax: 020 7834 9470
Email: planninginlondon@mac.com
Advertising Address: As above.
Email: planninginlondon@mac.com
Web site: http://www.planninginlondon.com
ISSN: 1366-9672
Publisher: Land Research Unit Ltd
Date Established: 1992

Frequency: Quarterly - Published in January, April, July and October
Annual Sub.: £75.00
Circulation: 1,000 (Publisher's Statement)
Usual Pagination: 60
Editor: Brian Waters; **Advertising Manager:** Brian Waters;
Publisher: Lee Mallett
Summary of Content: Magazine focusing on the association with the London Planning Development Forum, bridging the gap between public and private sectors in planning London.
Readership/Target Audience: Read by anyone associated with the planning and development of London.
ADVERTISING RATES:
Full Page Mono £660.00
Full Page Colour £880.00
Agency Commission: 10%
Mechanical Data: Type Area: 266 x 192mm, Bleed Size: 303 x 216mm, Trim Size: 297 x 210mm, Col Length: 266mm, Page Width: 192mm, Print Process: Offset litho, Film: Digital
Copy instructions: Copy Date: 15th of the month prior to publication date
Average advertising content per issue: 8%
BUSINESS: ARCHITECTURE & BUILDING: Planning & Housing

PLANT & CIVIL ENGINEER
39021U42A-168_110

Editorial Address: The Old Coach House, 12 Main Street, HILLSBOROUGH, BT26 6AE **Tel:** 028 9268 8888
Fax: 028 9268 8866
Email: cathie@4squaremedia.net
Advertising Address: As above.
Email: cathie@4squaremedia.net
Web site: http://www.plantandcivilengineer.com
Publisher: 4 Square Media
Date Established: 1990
Frequency: 7 issues yearly
Cover Price: £2.40
Free to qualifying individuals
Annual Sub.: £21.00
Circulation: 5,508 (Publisher's Statement)
Usual Pagination: 80
Editor: Cathie Blackwood; **Advertising Manager:** Cathie Blackwood; **Publisher:** Helen Beggs
Summary of Content: Magazine focusing on the plant and civil engineering industry, covering quarrying, construction and recycling waste.
Readership/Target Audience: Aimed at plant and civil engineers and other construction industry professionals.
ADVERTISING RATES:
Full Page Colour £1200.00
Agency Commission: 10%
Mechanical Data: Type Area: 270 x 185mm, Bleed Size: 305 x 215mm, Trim Size: 297 x 210mm, Print Process: Offset litho, Film: Digital, Col Length: 270mm, Page Width: 185mm
Average advertising content per issue: 45%
BUSINESS: CONSTRUCTION

PLANT & WORKS ENGINEERING
37559U19A-506

Editorial Address: Cape House, 60A Priory Road, TONBRIDGE, TN9 2BL **Tel:** 01732 370340
Fax: 01732 360034
Email: aaron@dfamedia.co.uk
Advertising Address: As above.
Email: steve@dfamedia.co.uk
Web site: http://www.pwemag.co.uk
ISSN: 0262-0227
Publisher: DFA Media Ltd
Date Established: 1981
Frequency: 11 issues yearly - Published in the 1st week of the cover month
Free to qualifying individuals
Circulation: 9,958 (ABC 01/01/2008 to 31/12/2008)
Usual Pagination: 56
Editor: Aaron Blutstein
Summary of Content: Publication covering works, plant and maintenance engineering. Also includes application and feature stories.
Readership/Target Audience: Aimed at engineers and plant managers in commercial, industrial and government bodies who purchase equipment.
ADVERTISING RATES:
Full Page Mono £1550.00
Full Page Colour £1995.00
Mechanical Data: Page Width: 184mm, Type Area: 268 x 184mm, Col Length: 268mm, Trim Size: 297 x 210mm, Bleed Size: 303 x 216mm, Film: Digital
Copy instructions: Copy Date: 3 weeks prior to publication date
Supplement(s): Handling and Storage - 3xY, Health & Safety in Focus - 4xY
BUSINESS: ENGINEERING & MACHINERY

THE PLANT ENGINEER
37558U19A-500

Editorial Address: Hawley Mill, Hawley Road, DARTFORD, DA2 7TJ **Tel:** 01322 221144 **Fax:** 01322 221188
Email: btinham@findlay.co.uk
Advertising Address: As above. **Fax:** 01322 421546
Email: dwatson@findlay.co.uk
Web site: http://www.findlay.co.uk
ISSN: 0032-0838
Publisher: Findlay Media Ltd
Date Established: 1946
Frequency: 8 issues yearly - Published at the beginning of the 2nd cover month
Free to qualifying individuals
Annual Sub.: £45.00
Circulation: 9,705 (ABC 01/01/2008 to 31/12/2008)
Usual Pagination: 48
Editor: Brian Tinham; **Advertising Manager:** David Watson
Summary of Content: Magazine covering the specification, installation, operation and maintenance of all plant types for operations engineers in all industries (from manufacturing and process industries to utilities, power, transportation and the armed forces). Topics include energy efficiency, safety, education, plant equipment, plant design, inspection, process control, maintenance, repair and operations.
Readership/Target Audience: Aimed at plant engineers, operations engineers, project managers, maintenance engineers and safety officers.
ADVERTISING RATES:
Full Page Colour £1300.00
Agency Commission: 10%
Mechanical Data: Type Area: 264 x 178mm, Col Length: 264mm, Bleed Size: 302 x 200mm, Film: Digital, Page Width: 178mm, Trim Size: 296 x 210mm
Copy instructions: Copy Date: 2 weeks prior to publication date
BUSINESS: ENGINEERING & MACHINERY

PLANT GROWTH REGULATOR ABSTRACTS
37819U21B-805

Editorial Address: Nosworthy Way, WALLINGFORD, OX10 8DE **Tel:** 01491 832111 **Fax:** 01491 829198
Email: publishing@cabi.org
Web site: http://www.cabi-publishing.org
ISSN: 0305-9154
Publisher: CABI
Frequency: Quarterly
Annual Sub.: £670.00
Circulation: 75 (Publisher's Statement)
Editor: Debbie Cousins
Summary of Content: Abstracts of the world literature on the role of chemicals in plant growth regulation and in the modification of plant growth responses.
Readership/Target Audience: Aimed at academic and government research institutes, seed, agro-chemical and plant breeding companies.
ADVERTISING: No Advertising taken
BUSINESS: AGRICULTURE & FARMING: Agriculture - Supplies & Services

PLANT WORLD
39022U42A-170

Editorial Address: 50 Queens Road, BUCKHURST HILL, IG9 5DD **Tel:** 020 8504 1661 **Fax:** 020 8505 4336
Email: plant@sheenpublishing.co.uk
Advertising Address: As above.
Email: c.titmuss@sheenpublishing.co.uk
Web site: http://www.sheenpublishing.co.uk
Publisher: Sheen Publishing Ltd
Date Established: 1981
Frequency: 26 issues yearly
Cover Price: £3.50
Circulation: 12,000 (Publisher's Statement)
Usual Pagination: 196
Editor: Carole Titmuss; **Features Editor:** Danny Carter; **Managing Director:** Carole Titmuss; **Advertising Manager:** Carole Titmuss; **Publisher:** Carole Titmuss
Summary of Content: Magazine covering machinery and plant for construction and related industries.
Readership/Target Audience: Aimed at senior personnel who influence the buying and selling of construction plant and equipment worldwide.
ADVERTISING RATES:
Full Page Mono £160.00
Full Page Colour £180.00
Agency Commission: 10%
Mechanical Data: Type Area: 190 x 123mm, Col Length: 190mm, Trim Size: 210 x 148mm, Page Width: 123mm, Film: Digital
Copy instructions: Copy Date: 8 days prior to publication date
Average advertising content per issue: 90%
BUSINESS: CONSTRUCTION

THE PLANTSMAN
22890U26D-100

Formerly: The New Plantsman
Editorial Address: 4th Floor, Churchgate, New Road, PETERBOROUGH, PE1 1TT **Tel:** 01733 294636
Fax: 01733 341633
Email: theplantsman@rhspublications.co.uk
Web site: http://www.rhs.org.uk/plantsman
ISSN: 1352-4186
Publisher: RHS Media
Date Established: 1979
Frequency: Quarterly - Published on the first of the cover month
Annual Sub.: £32.00
Circulation: 3,500 (Publisher's Statement)
Usual Pagination: 68
Editor: Mike Grant; **News Editor:** Anisa Gress; **Advertising Manager:** Sarah Cottle
Summary of Content: Magazine dedicated to a deeper understanding and appreciation of garden plants. Covers plant groups and genera in detail, new plants entering cultivation, plant breeding, new cultivation and propagation techniques, developments in plant taxonomy, conservation of wild and cultivated plants, RHS science and plant trials, forthcoming events and book reviews.
Readership/Target Audience: Aimed at dedicated gardeners, professionals in horticulture and botanists.
BUSINESS: GARDEN TRADE: Garden Trade Horticulture

PLASTICS ADDITIVES & COMPOUNDING
26056U39-25

Editorial Address: The Boulevard, Langford Lane, KIDLINGTON, OX5 1GB **Tel:** 01865 843441
Fax: 01865 843973
Email: m.holmes@elsevier.com
Advertising Address: As above. **Tel:** 01865 843000
Email: n.reeves@elsevier.com
Web site: http://www.addcomp.com
Publisher: Elsevier Ltd
Date Established: 1999
Frequency: 6 issues yearly - Published in the middle of the 1st cover month
Free to qualifying individuals
Annual Sub.: EUR512.00
Circulation: 7,006 (Publisher's Statement)
Usual Pagination: 60
Editor: Mark Holmes
Summary of Content: Magazine covering plastics additives and compounding including news, materials, equipment and applications from around the world.
Readership/Target Audience: Aimed at users of plastics additives in compounding, finished parts and resin manufacture.
ADVERTISING RATES:
Full Page Colour £3905.00
Agency Commission: 10%
Mechanical Data: Trim Size: 280 x 216mm, Page Width: 185mm, Type Area: 243 x 185mm, Col Length: 243mm, Bleed Size: 286 x 222mm, Film: Digital
Copy instructions: Copy Date: 2 weeks prior to publication date
BUSINESS: PLASTICS & RUBBER

PLASTICS & BOARD INDUSTRIES FEDERATION MAGAZINE
38821U39-25_50

Editorial Address: 15A London Road, MAIDSTONE, ME16 8LY **Tel:** 01622 687031
Advertising Address: As above. **Tel:** 01622 699170
Fax: 01622 757646
Email: kbennett@datateam.co.uk
Publisher: Datateam Publishing Ltd
Date Established: 1987
Frequency: Quarterly
Free to qualifying individuals
Annual Sub.: £35.00
Circulation: 1,000 (Publisher's Statement)
Usual Pagination: 36
Editor: Jon Barrett
Summary of Content: Journal covering all aspects of converting plastics and board including high frequency welding with plastics.
Readership/Target Audience: Aimed at suppliers to and converters of the plastics and board industries, including those involved in the conversion of plastics and board including heat sealing, stitching, gluing and screen-printing.
ADVERTISING RATES:
Full Page Colour £975.00
Mechanical Data: Type Area: 280 x 195mm, Trim Size: 306 x 229mm, Col Length: 280mm, Bleed Size: 312 x 235mm, Film: Digital, Page Width: 195mm
Average advertising content per issue: 40%
BUSINESS: PLASTICS & RUBBER

PLASTICS & RUBBER ASIA
38825U39-26

Editorial Address: The Stables, Willow Lane, Paddock Wood, TONBRIDGE, TN12 6PF **Tel:** 01892 839200
Fax: 01892 839210

Section 4 (b) Business Magazines

Email: sherilee@plasticsandrubberasia.com
Advertising Address: As above.
Email: sherilee@plasticsandrubberasia.com
Web site: http://www.plasticsandrubberasia.com
ISSN: 1360-1245
Publisher: Plastics & Rubber Ltd
Date Established: 1985
Frequency: 8 issues yearly
Free to qualifying individuals
Annual Sub.: £132.00
Circulation: 9,269 (ABC 01/01/2008 to 31/12/2008)
Editor: Sherilee Clinch; **Advertising Manager:** Sherilee Clinch
Summary of Content: Magazine containing news and features about the plastics and rubber market.
Language(s): Chinese; English
Readership/Target Audience: Read by plastics producers, corporate managers and engineers involved in the Asian plastics industry.
ADVERTISING RATES:
Full Page Mono EUR4300.00
Full Page Colour EUR6020.00
Agency Commission: 15%
Mechanical Data: Bleed Size: 282 x 216mm, Trim Size: 276 x 210mm, Type Area: 245 x 190mm, Col Length: 245mm, Page Width: 190mm, Film: Digital
Copy instructions: Copy Date: 4 weeks prior to publication date
Average advertising content per issue: 40%
Supplement(s): Injection Moulding Asia - 4xY, Polyurethanes Asia - 2xY
BUSINESS: PLASTICS & RUBBER

PLASTICS ENGINEERING (EUROPEAN SECTION)
1614401U39-151
Formerly: Plastics Engineering Europe
Editorial Address: Bowmans Farmhouse, Perrymans Lane, Burwash, ETCHINGHAM, TN19 7DN **Tel:** 01435 882263
Advertising Address: PO Box 403, BROOKFIELD, CT 06804 **Tel:** 203 7405431 **Fax:** 203 7758490
Email: advertising@4spe.org
Web site: http://www.4spe.org
Publisher: Society of Plastic Engineers
Frequency: 10 issues yearly - Published at the beginning of the cover month
Cover Price: Free
Circulation: 40,000 (Publisher's Statement)
Usual Pagination: 60
Summary of Content: International magazine that includes specific coverage of the European plastics business, including materials, equipment and processing.
Readership/Target Audience: Read by members of SPE and others working in the European plastics industry, including many decision makers.
ADVERTISING: Rates on application
Average advertising content per issue: 40%
BUSINESS: PLASTICS & RUBBER

PLASTICS IN PACKAGING
749341U22C-450
Editorial Address: Durand House, Manor Royal, CRAWLEY, RH10 9PY **Tel:** 01293 435100 **Fax:** 01293 619988
Email: stevenp@sayers-publishing.com
Advertising Address: As above.
Email: joelh@sayers-publishing.com
Web site: http://www.plasticsinpackaging.com
ISSN: 1476-5241
Publisher: Sayers Publishing Group Ltd
Date Established: 2001
Frequency: Monthly - Published in the 1st week of the cover month
Annual Sub.: £125.00
Circulation: 11,000 (Publisher's Statement)
Usual Pagination: 40
Editor: Steven Pacitti; **Advertising Manager:** Joel Hibbert
Summary of Content: Journal covering the worldwide plastic packaging industry.
Language(s): Chinese; English
Readership/Target Audience: Read by top executives in food, beverage, cosmetic and pharmaceutical companies who deal with plastic packaging.
ADVERTISING RATES:
Full Page Colour £2297.00
Agency Commission: 15%
Mechanical Data: Type Area: 244 x 179mm, Col Length: 244mm, Trim Size: 280 x 210mm, Bleed Size: 286 x 216mm, Film: Digital, Page Width: 179mm
Copy instructions: Copy Date: 10th of the month prior to publication date
Average advertising content per issue: 40%
BUSINESS: FOOD: Food Processing & Packaging

PLATFORM
38630U33-50_50
Editorial Address: Woodburn Road, Blackburn Industrial Estate, Kinellar, ABERDEEN, AB21 0RX **Tel:** 01224 791123
Fax: 01224 791147
Email: sales@platform-media.co.uk

Advertising Address: As above. **Tel:** 01224 791117
Email: platformmedia@btconnect.com
Web site: http://www.platform-oilandgas.com
Publisher: Platform Media Ltd
Date Established: 1997
Frequency: Monthly - Published at the end of the cover month
Annual Sub.: £45.00
Circulation: 6,000 (Publisher's Statement)
Usual Pagination: 34
Editor: Alan Davies; **Managing Director:** Alan Davies;
Publisher: Alan Davies
Summary of Content: Publication reviewing the latest oil and gas technology and equipment. Covers people, contracts, local and international news and topical issues.
Readership/Target Audience: Aimed at middle management decision makers.
ADVERTISING RATES:
Full Page Mono £1450.00
Full Page Colour £1950.00
Agency Commission: 10%
Mechanical Data: No. of Columns (Display): 4, Film: Digital, Trim Size: 340 x 245mm, Bleed Size: +5mm, Type Area: 310 x 220mm, Col Length: 310mm, Page Width: 220mm
Copy instructions: Copy Date: 2 weeks prior to publication date
Average advertising content per issue: 30%
BUSINESS: OIL & PETROLEUM

PLATTS METALS WEEK
38165U27-124
Editorial Address: 20 Canada Square, Canary Wharf, LONDON, E14 5LH **Tel:** 020 7176 6189 **Fax:** 020 7176 6657
Email: stringer@platts.com
Web site: http://www.platts.com
Publisher: Platts
Frequency: Weekly - Published on a Monday
Annual Sub.: $1280.00
Usual Pagination: 20
Editor: Andy Blamey; **Managing Editor:** Andy Blamey
Summary of Content: Newsletter reporting on global nonferrous metals markets. Contains prices, industry news, analysis of the latest trends and developments, interviews and coverage of mining projects, legislation and joint-ventures.
Readership/Target Audience: Read by anybody with an interest in the metals markets including miners, producers and consumers.
ADVERTISING: No Advertising taken
BUSINESS: METAL, IRON & STEEL

PLATTS OILGRAM NEWS
23203U33-52
Editorial Address: 20 Canada Square, Canary Wharf, LONDON, E14 5LH **Tel:** 020 7176 7000 **Fax:** 020 7176 6172
Email: news@platts.com
Web site: http://www.platts.com
Publisher: The McGraw-Hill Companies
Date Established: 1923
Frequency: 250 issues yearly
Usual Pagination: 8
Editor: Richard Swan
Summary of Content: Newsletter containing news and information about the oil and gas industry and markets.
Readership/Target Audience: Aimed at industry executives worldwide.
ADVERTISING: No Advertising taken
BUSINESS: OIL & PETROLEUM

PLC CROSS-BORDER QUARTERLY
25979U44-725
Formerly: Global Counsel
Editorial Address: 19 Hatfields, LONDON, SE1 8DJ
Tel: 020 7202 1200 **Fax:** 020 7202 1211
Email: adam.frederickson@practicallaw.com
Advertising Address: As above. **Tel:** 020 7202 1223
Email: mark.eaton@practicallaw.com
Web site: http://www.practicallaw.com/crossborder
ISSN: 1364-8888
Publisher: Practical Law Company Ltd
Date Established: 1996
Frequency: Quarterly
Circulation: 5,000 (Publisher's Statement)
Usual Pagination: 58
Editor: Rossella Brambilla; **Advertising Manager:** Mark Eaton
Summary of Content: Magazine covering practical law and providing legal knowledge and news on the legal market. The magazine also summarises content that has been added to the website over the previous quarter.
Readership/Target Audience: Aimed at in-house and private practice lawyers.
ADVERTISING RATES:
Full Page Colour £2995.00
Agency Commission: 10%
Mechanical Data: Film: Digital, Type Area: 260 x 174mm, Bleed Size: 303 x 216mm, Trim Size: 297 x 210mm, Col Length: 260mm, Page Width: 174mm

Average advertising content per issue: 10%
BUSINESS: LEGAL

PLC MAGAZINE
39226U44-1630
Formerly: PLC Practical Law for Companies
Editorial Address: 19 Hatfields, LONDON, SE1 8DJ
Tel: 020 7202 1200 **Fax:** 020 7202 1211
Advertising Address: As above.
Email: mark.eaton@practicallaw.com
Web site: http://www.practicallaw.com
ISSN: 0959-9940
Publisher: Practical Law Company Ltd
Date Established: 1990
Frequency: 11 issues yearly
Annual Sub.: £495.00
Circulation: 8,500 (Publisher's Statement)
Usual Pagination: 96
Editor: Joanna Morris; **Advertising Manager:** Mark Eaton
Publisher: Robert Dow
Summary of Content: Magazine containing information on all aspects of company and business law in the UK.
Readership/Target Audience: Aimed at in-house lawyers, company commercial lawyers in practice, corporate financiers, and accountants.
ADVERTISING RATES:
Full Page Colour £2995.00
Agency Commission: 10%
Mechanical Data: Type Area: 260 x 174mm, Bleed Size: 303 x 216mm, Trim Size: 297 x 210mm, Col Length: 260mm, Page Width: 174mm, Film: Digital
Copy instructions: Copy Date: 3rd week of the month prior to publication date
Average advertising content per issue: 10%
BUSINESS: LEGAL

PLUMB HEAT
35774U3D-40
Editorial Address: 2 Walker Street, EDINBURGH, EH3 7LB
Tel: 0131 225 2255 **Fax:** 0131 226 7638
Email: info@snipef.org
Advertising Address: Portland Buildings, 127-129 Portland Street, MANCHESTER, M1 1PZ **Tel:** 0161 661 4113
Fax: 0161 236 2783
Email: info@excelpublishing.co.uk
Web site: http://www.snipef.org
Publisher: Excel Publishing Company Ltd
Frequency: Quarterly
Annual Sub.: £20.00
Circulation: 1,500 (Publisher's Statement)
Usual Pagination: 36
Editor: Alan Wilson; **Features Editor:** Alan Wilson;
Publisher: Paul Caunce
Summary of Content: Journal containing information for the Scottish and Northern Ireland Plumbing Employers Federation.
Readership/Target Audience: Read by members and local and national government departments.
ADVERTISING RATES:
Full Page Colour £950.00
Agency Commission: 10%
Mechanical Data: Type Area: 266 x 185mm, Col Length: 266mm, Bleed Size: 303 x 216mm, Film: Digital, Trim Size: 297 x 210mm, Page Width: 185mm
Copy instructions: Copy Date: 1st of the month prior to publication date
Average advertising content per issue: 30%
BUSINESS: HEATING & VENTILATION: Heating & Plumbing

PLUMBING & HEATING ENGINEERING MAGAZINE
35776U3D-80
Formerly: Plumbing and Heating Engineering
Editorial Address: The Chartered Institute of Plumbing & Heating Engi, 64 Station Lane, HORNCHURCH, RM12 6NB
Tel: 01708 472791 **Fax:** 01708 448987
Email: carolc@ciphe.org.uk
Web site: http://www.ciphe.org.uk
ISSN: 0032-1656
Publisher: Warners Group Publications plc
Date Established: 1970
Frequency: 6 issues yearly - Published around the middle of the 1st cover month
Free to qualifying individuals
Annual Sub.: £68.00
Circulation: 13,516 (Publisher's Statement)
Usual Pagination: 40
Editor: Joanne Morris
Summary of Content: Journal of the Institute of Plumbing and Heating Engineering containing technical articles and industry news, as well as Institute comment on plumbing matters.
Readership/Target Audience: Aimed at members of the Institute and other sectors of the industry including colleges, manufacturers, water companies, designers, specifiers and consultants.
ADVERTISING: No Advertising taken
BUSINESS: HEATING & VENTILATION: Heating & Plumbing

PLUMBING & HEATING IN NORTHERN IRELAND
759777U3D-65

Editorial Address: The Forge, 13B Lisburn Road, Moira, CRAIGAVON, BT67 0JR **Tel:** 028 9261 2990
Fax: 028 9261 2091
Email: adam@kmpltd.co.uk
Advertising Address: As above.
Email: jacqui@kmpltd.co.uk
Web site: http://www.niplumbingmagazine.co.uk
Publisher: Karen McAvoy Publishing Ltd
Frequency: Quarterly
Cover Price: Free
Circulation: 8,896 (Publisher's Statement)
Usual Pagination: 124
Editor: Jacqui Fairley; **Advertising Manager:** Jacqui Fairley
Summary of Content: Magazine covering new products, industry news, technical features, company profiles, testing tools and health and safety matters.
Readership/Target Audience: Read by heating engineers, plumbers, retailers and architects.
ADVERTISING RATES:
Full Page Colour £1045.00
Agency Commission: 10%
Mechanical Data: Col Length: 260mm, Film: Digital, Trim Size: 297 x 210mm, Type Area: 260 x 185mm, Bleed Size: 303 x 216mm, Col Widths (Display): 46mm
Average advertising content per issue: 40%
BUSINESS: HEATING & VENTILATION: Heating & Plumbing

PLUMBING, HEATING & AIR MOVEMENT NEWS
35775U3D-70

Editorial Address: 1B Station Square, Flitwick, BEDFORD, MK45 1DP **Tel:** 01525 716143 **Fax:** 01525 715316
Email: editor@phamnewsedit.co.uk
Advertising Address: Suite 16-18, Hawkesyard, Armitage Road, RUGELEY, WS15 1PU **Tel:** 01889 577222
Fax: 01889 579177
Email: info@phamnews.co.uk
Web site: http://www.phamnews.co.uk
ISSN: 1368-9061
Publisher: Pinede Publishing
Date Established: 1963
Frequency: 10 issues yearly - Published on 7th of the cover month
Free to qualifying individuals
Annual Sub.: £40.00
Circulation: 28,100 (ABC 01/01/2008 to 31/12/2008)
Usual Pagination: 76
Editor: Chris Jones; **Advertising Manager:** Russ Jackson; **Managing Editor:** Chris Jones
Summary of Content: Magazine containing product and trade news as well as technical and business articles.
Readership/Target Audience: Aimed at plumbers, heating contractors, installers and specifiers.
ADVERTISING RATES:
Full Page Mono £2255.00
Full Page Colour £2750.00
Agency Commission: 10%
Mechanical Data: Type Area: 356 x 274mm, Film: Digital, No. of Columns (Display): 6, Bleed Size: 400 x 302mm, Trim Size: 389 x 292mm, Col Length: 356mm, Col Widths (Display): 42mm, Page Width: 274mm
Copy instructions: Copy Date: 2 weeks prior to publication date
Average advertising content per issue: 50%
BUSINESS: HEATING & VENTILATION: Heating & Plumbing

+ PLASTIC ELECTRONICS
1837352U39-158

Editorial Address: Cleeve Road, LEATHERHEAD, KT22 7RU **Tel:** 01372 802000
Email: joe.thompson@pira-international.com
Publisher: PIRA International
Date Established: 2007
Frequency: 6 issues yearly
Annual Sub.: £100.00
Circulation: 7,000 (Publisher's Statement)
Editor: Joe Thompson
Summary of Content: Magazine covering all printed and organic electronic news.
Readership/Target Audience: Aimed at users and developers of finished products within the industry.
ADVERTISING: No Advertising taken
BUSINESS: PLASTICS & RUBBER

PMA MAGAZINE
38798U38-73

Formerly: Photo Marketing
Editorial Address: Wisteria House, 28 Fulling Mill Lane, WELWYN, AL6 9NS **Tel:** 0870 240 4542 **Fax:** 01438 716572
Email: tchapman@pmai.org
Advertising Address: PMAI, 3000 Picture Place, JACKSON, MI 49201 **Tel:** 202 2444131 **Fax:** 517 7888371
Email: jbyles@pmai.org
Web site: http://www.pmai.org
Publisher: Photo Marketing Association Intl. (UK) Ltd
Date Established: 1988

Frequency: Monthly
Free to qualifying individuals
Circulation: 1,500 (Publisher's Statement)
Usual Pagination: 8
Editor: Tracey Chapman; **Advertising Manager:** James Byles
Summary of Content: Magazine of the Photo Marketing Association International (UK) Ltd. Covers features on new technologies, profiles, news and advice.
Readership/Target Audience: Read by photo imaging retailers and processors.
ADVERTISING RATES:
Full Page Colour $3000.00
Agency Commission: 15%
Mechanical Data: Type Area: 250 x 175mm, Bleed Size: 280 x 210mm, Trim Size: 275 x 207mm, Col Length: 250mm, Page Width: 175mm, Film: Digital
BUSINESS: PHOTOGRAPHIC TRADE

PMI NEWS
35362U1H-76

Editorial Address: PMI House, 4-10 Artillery Lane, LONDON, E1 7LS **Tel:** 020 7247 1452 **Fax:** 020 7375 0603
Email: hsheridan@pensions-pmi.org.uk
Advertising Address: Inside Careers, Unit 6, The Quadrangle, 49 Atalanta Street, LONDON, SW6 6TU
Tel: 020 7565 7900 **Fax:** 020 7565 7938
Email: sales@pensioncareer.co.uk
Web site: http://www.pensions-pmi.org.uk
ISSN: 0969-2673
Publisher: Pensions Management Institute
Date Established: 1983
Frequency: Monthly - Published the 1st week of the month
Free to qualifying individuals
Circulation: 5,000 (Publisher's Statement)
Usual Pagination: 50
Editor: Holly Sheridan; **Advertising Manager:** Sean Morrissey
Summary of Content: Journal covering notification of the PMIs conferences and seminars. Includes news of pension legislation, student information and regional group news.
Readership/Target Audience: Read by the members of The Pensions Management Institute.
ADVERTISING RATES:
Full Page Colour £1750.00
Agency Commission: 10%
Mechanical Data: Film: Digital, Type Area: 270 x 186mm, Col Length: 270mm, Bleed Size: 303 x 216mm, Trim Size: 297 x 210mm, Page Width: 186mm
Copy instructions: Copy Date: 15th of the month prior to publication date
Average advertising content per issue: 25%
Supplement(s): PMI Technical News - 4xY
BUSINESS: FINANCE & ECONOMICS: Pensions

PMJ - PLANT MANAGERS JOURNAL
39017U42A-172

Editorial Address: Quadrant House, The Quadrant, SUTTON, SM2 5AS **Tel:** 020 8652 4858 **Fax:** 020 8652 8958
Email: colin.sowman@rbi.co.uk
Advertising Address: As above. **Fax:** 020 8652 4804
Email: tim.porter@rbi.co.uk
Web site: http://www.contractjournal.com
Publisher: Reed Business Information
Frequency: 7 issues yearly - Published on the 1st Thursday of the cover month
Free to qualifying individuals
Annual Sub.: £58.50
Circulation: 6,843 (ABC 01/07/2008 to 30/06/2009)
Editor: Colin Sowman
Summary of Content: Journal covering all aspects related to construction plant equipment and the plant hire industry.
Readership/Target Audience: Aimed at plant hire companies and all members of construction plant management teams.
ADVERTISING RATES:
Full Page Colour £2527.00
Agency Commission: 10%
Mechanical Data: Page Width: 186mm, Type Area: 265 x 186mm, Col Length: 265mm, Trim Size: 297 x 210mm, Bleed Size: 303 x 213mm, Film: Digital
Copy instructions: Copy Date: 15th of the month prior to publication date
BUSINESS: CONSTRUCTION

PMP DIGEST
39461U46-19

Formerly: PMP digest & MDF Monitor
Editorial Address: PO Box 14, DORKING, RH5 4YN
Tel: 01306 884473 **Fax:** 01306 884473
Email: info@datatranscripts.com
Web site: http://www.woodpanelsonline.com
ISSN: 1755-2664
Publisher: Data Transcripts
Date Established: 2003
Frequency: 6 issues yearly
Free to qualifying individuals
Annual Sub.: £169.00

Circulation: 1,700 (Publisher's Statement)
Usual Pagination: 6
Editor: Anne Browne; **Managing Director:** Robert Higham; **Circulation Manager:** Stella Roscoe
Summary of Content: Newsletter containing product news, financial information and general articles of interest to producers of wood panel products.
Readership/Target Audience: Aimed at people within the panel industry.
ADVERTISING: No Advertising taken
BUSINESS: TIMBER, WOOD & FORESTRY

PMPS PHARMACEUTICAL MANUFACTURING & PACKING SOURCER
38747U37-61_70

Editorial Address: 16 Hampden Gurney Street, LONDON, W1H 5AL **Tel:** 020 7724 3456 **Fax:** 020 7724 2632
Email: lucyw@samedanltd.com
Advertising Address: As above.
Email: info@samedanltd.com
Web site: http://www.samedanltd.com
ISSN: 1463-1245
Publisher: Samedan Ltd
Date Established: 1998
Frequency: Quarterly
Free to qualifying individuals
Annual Sub.: £62.00
Circulation: 7,500 (Publisher's Statement)
Usual Pagination: 130
Editor: Lucy Winder; **Managing Director:** Gulia Selby
Summary of Content: Journal containing worldwide coverage of the range of services from medical device trials, formulation development, clinical trial supplies, packing and production, technology, fine chemicals, laboratory analysis, warehousing, distribution, plant and machinery packing materials.
Readership/Target Audience: Aimed at senior decision makers within the manufacturing and packaging departments of pharmaceutical companies and their partners within contract organisations.
ADVERTISING RATES:
Full Page Colour £2750.00
Agency Commission: 10%
Mechanical Data: Film: Digital, Type Area: 273 x 186mm, Bleed Size: 303 x 213mm, Trim Size: 297 x 210mm, Col Length: 273mm, Page Width: 186mm
Copy instructions: Copy Date: 15th of the month prior to publication date
Average advertising content per issue: 89%
BUSINESS: PHARMACEUTICAL & CHEMISTS

PODIATRY NOW
40446U56K-20

Editorial Address: 1 Fellmongers Path, Tower Bridge Road, LONDON, SE1 3LY **Tel:** 0845 450 3720 **Fax:** 0845 450 3721
Email: cr@scpod.org
Advertising Address: PRN Media Ltd, Suite 209, 2nd Floor, Wellington House, Butt Road, COLCHESTER, CO3 3DA
Tel: 01206 767797 **Fax:** 01206 767532
Email: alan@mulberrypublications.net
Web site: http://www.feetforlife.org
ISSN: 1460-731X
Publisher: The Society of Chiropodists and Podiatrists
Date Established: 1998
Frequency: Monthly
Annual Sub.: £70.00
Circulation: 10,000 (Publisher's Statement)
Usual Pagination: 60
Editor: Clare Richards
Summary of Content: Journal of the Society of Chiropodists and Podiatrists. Contains news, political comment, legislative issues and continuing professional development.
Readership/Target Audience: Read by society members.
ADVERTISING RATES:
Full Page Mono £1055.00
Full Page Colour £1430.00
Agency Commission: 10%
Mechanical Data: Type Area: 264 x 175mm, Bleed Size: 303 x 216mm, Trim Size: 297 x 210mm, Film: Digital, Col Length: 264mm, Page Width: 175mm
Copy instructions: Copy Date: 3 weeks prior to publication date
Average advertising content per issue: 30%
BUSINESS: HEALTH & MEDICAL: Chiropody

PODIATRY REVIEW
40445U56K-10

Formerly: Chiropody Review
Editorial Address: 27 Wright Street, SOUTHPORT, PR9 0TL
Tel: 01704 546141 **Fax:** 01704 500477
Email: editor@iocp.org.uk
Advertising Address: As above.
Email: bernie@iocp.org.uk
Web site: http://www.iocp.org.uk
ISSN: 0009-4714
Publisher: The Institute of Chiropodists and Podiatrists
Frequency: 6 issues yearly

Free to qualifying individuals
Annual Sub.: £25.00
Circulation: 2,500 (Publisher's Statement)
Usual Pagination: 40
Editor: Roger Henry; **Advertising Manager:** Bernie Hawthorne
Summary of Content: Magazine containing news and views of the chiropodial/podiatric profession. Publishes clinical and academic articles and research, plus news of new products and equipment.
Readership/Target Audience: Read by chiropodists.
ADVERTISING: Rates on application
Agency Commission: 10%
BUSINESS: HEALTH & MEDICAL: Chiropody

THE POINT
1709111U1R-376
Editorial Address: 10-11 Percy Street, LONDON, W1T 1DA
Tel: 020 7631 1155 **Fax:** 020 7631 1444
Email: jonty.summers@bladonmore.com
Advertising Address: As above.
Email: jonty.summers@bladonmore.com
Web site: http://www.bladonmore.com
Publisher: Bladonmore
Date Established: 2002
Frequency: 3 issues yearly - Publication months vary
Free to qualifying individuals
Circulation: 8,000 (Publisher's Statement)
Usual Pagination: 36
Editor: Jonty Summers; **Editor-in-Chief:** Joanne Hart; **Managing Director:** Jonty Summers; **Advertising Manager:** Jonty Summers
Summary of Content: Magazine covering focusing on European private equity.
Readership/Target Audience: Aimed at finance professionals.
ADVERTISING RATES:
Full Page Colour £3000.00
Agency Commission: 10%
Mechanical Data: Type Area: 320 x 240mm, Bleed Size: 332 x 252mm, Film: Digital, Col Length: 320mm, Page Width: 240mm
Copy instructions: Copy Date: 2 weeks prior to publication date
Average advertising content per issue: 17%
BUSINESS: FINANCE & ECONOMICS: Financial Related

POLICE
38436U32F-380
Editorial Address: Federation House, Highbury Drive, SURREY, KT22 7UY **Tel:** 01372 352000
Email: syreeta.lund@polfed.org
Advertising Address: Landmark Publishing Services, 2 Windmill Street, LONDON, W1T 2HX **Tel:** 020 7692 9292
Fax: 020 7692 9393
Email: sharon@lps.co.uk
Web site: http://www.polfed.org
Publisher: Joint Central Cttee Police Federation (Eng./ Wales)
Date Established: 1968
Frequency: Monthly
Annual Sub.: £25.00
Circulation: 40,000 (Publisher's Statement)
Usual Pagination: 36
Editor: Syreeta Lund; **Advertising Manager:** Sharon Davies; **Managing Editor:** Metin Enver
Summary of Content: Official magazine of the Police Federation covering all aspects of policing.
Readership/Target Audience: Aimed at police forces throughout the UK, MPs and members of the House of Lords. Distributed nationally and internationally.
ADVERTISING RATES:
Full Page Mono £1500.00
Full Page Colour £1900.00
SCC £20.00
Agency Commission: 10%
Mechanical Data: Trim Size: 297 x 210mm, Page Width: 182mm, Film: Digital, Type Area: 270 x 182mm, Col Length: 270mm
Copy instructions: Copy Date: 1st of month prior to publication date
Average advertising content per issue: 40%
BUSINESS: LOCAL GOVERNMENT, LEISURE & RECREATION: Police

POLICE LIFE
711706U32F-400
Editorial Address: Colchester Business Centre, 1 George Williams Way, COLCHESTER, CO1 2JS **Tel:** 01206 369448
Fax: 01206 369437
Email: info@policelife.net
Advertising Address: As above.
Email: info@policelife.net
Web site: http://www.police-life.co.uk
Publisher: Occucom Ltd
Frequency: Monthly
Cover Price: Free
Circulation: 42,000 (Publisher's Statement)
Usual Pagination: 20

Editor: Martin Herman; **Publisher:** Martin Herman
Summary of Content: Newspaper covering news relevant to police service personnel and general lifestyle. Regular platforms and features including motoring, gardening, travel, overseas property, sports and leisure.
Readership/Target Audience: Read by police service professionals.
ADVERTISING RATES:
Full Page Colour £3200.00
SCC £24.00
Agency Commission: 10%
Mechanical Data: Type Area: 360 x 280mm, No. of Columns (Display): 7, Col Length: 360mm, Page Width: 280mm, Film: Digital
Copy instructions: Copy Date: 20th of the month prior to publication date
Average advertising content per issue: 50%
BUSINESS: LOCAL GOVERNMENT, LEISURE & RECREATION: Police

POLICE PROFESSIONAL
1725868U32F-705
Editorial Address: 7 Midshires Business Park, Smeaton Close, AYLESBURY, HP19 8HL **Tel:** 0845 057 0514
Fax: 01296 468549
Email: editor@policeprofessional.com
Advertising Address: As above. **Fax:** 01296 394245
Email: chrism@policeprofessional.com
Web site: http://www.policeprofessional.com
Publisher: Clarity Publishing Ltd
Date Established: 2004
Frequency: Weekly
Free to qualifying individuals
Annual Sub.: £110.00
Circulation: 12,266 (ABC 01/01/2008 to 30/06/2008)
Usual Pagination: 68
Editor: Paul Lander; **Advertising Manager:** Chris Meredith; **Managing Editor:** Paul Lander
Summary of Content: Publication covering guidance on law and best practice, forensics, career development and training, crime analysis, technology, management and operational issues.
Readership/Target Audience: Aimed at police officers, especially those from the rank of inspector to chief constable, heads of departments and specialists staff.
ADVERTISING RATES:
Full Page Colour £2765.00
Mechanical Data: Trim Size: 297 x 210mm
Copy instructions: Copy Date: Thursday 1 week prior to publication date
BUSINESS: LOCAL GOVERNMENT, LEISURE & RECREATION: Police

THE POLICE SERVICE GAZETTE INCORPORATING CONSTABULARY GAZETTE
38428U32F-100
Formerly: Constabulary Gazette
Editorial Address: 39 Boucher Road, BELFAST, BT12 6UT
Tel: 028 9068 1371 **Fax:** 028 9038 1915
Email: copy@psnigazette.co.uk
Advertising Address: As above. **Tel:** 028 9066 3311
Email: william@psnigazette.co.uk
Publisher: Ulster Journals Ltd
Frequency: Monthly
Cover Price: £1.50
Free to qualifying individuals
Circulation: 9,000 (Publisher's Statement)
Usual Pagination: 50
Editor: Billy Brown
Summary of Content: Publication covering police news, information and events.
Readership/Target Audience: Read by members of the Police Service of Northern Ireland.
ADVERTISING RATES:
Full Page Colour £750.00
Agency Commission: 15%
Mechanical Data: Bleed Size: 300 x 215mm, Trim Size: 297 x 210mm, Film: Digital
Copy instructions: Copy Date: 3 weeks prior to publication date
Average advertising content per issue: 60%
BUSINESS: LOCAL GOVERNMENT, LEISURE & RECREATION: Police

POLICING TODAY
38442U32F-470
Editorial Address: PO Box 100, CHICHESTER, PO18 8HD
Tel: 01243 576444 **Fax:** 01243 576456
Advertising Address: PO Box 86, WITNEY, OX28 5XA
Tel: 01993 709545 **Fax:** 01993 709580
Email: david.holden@keywayspublishing.com
Web site: http://www.pmh.uk.com
ISSN: 1355-4557
Publisher: Keyways Publishing Group
Frequency: 5 issues yearly
Free to qualifying individuals
Annual Sub.: £50.00
Circulation: 2,000 (Publisher's Statement)

Usual Pagination: 44
Editor: Peter Shipley
Summary of Content: Official journal of the Association of Chief Police Officers of England, Wales & Northern Ireland, covering policing strategies, technology, research and international matters.
Readership/Target Audience: Aimed at members of the ACPO and leading legislators, academics, senior officers in other law enforcement agencies, Government officials, the media and companies supplying goods and services to the police.
ADVERTISING RATES:
Full Page Mono £900.00
Full Page Colour £1700.00
Agency Commission: 10%
Mechanical Data: Bleed Size: 300 x 213mm, Trim Size: 297 x 210mm, Film: Positive, right reading, emulsion side down, Digital, Screen: 60 lpc
Average advertising content per issue: 25%
BUSINESS: LOCAL GOVERNMENT, LEISURE & RECREATION: Police

POLICY REVIEW MAGAZINE
1654977U32A-256
Editorial Address: PO Box 39976, LONDON, EC1M 5YT
Tel: 020 7324 4330 **Tel:** 020 7490 8830
Email: katrina.wright@neilstewartassociates.co.uk
Advertising Address: As above.
Email: katrina.wright@neilstewartassociates.co.uk
Web site: http://www.policyreview.co.uk
Publisher: Neil Stewart Associates
Date Established: 2003
Frequency: Quarterly
Free to qualifying individuals
Annual Sub.: £180.00
Circulation: 9,113 (Publisher's Statement)
Usual Pagination: 44
Editor: John O'Leary; **Advertising Manager:** Katrina Wright; **Publisher:** Neil Stewart
Summary of Content: Magazine covering analysis of public policy including criminal justice, education, local government, health and transport.
Readership/Target Audience: Aimed at public and private sector senior managers and policy makers.
ADVERTISING RATES:
Full Page Colour £1400.00
Agency Commission: 10%
Mechanical Data: Film: Digital, Bleed Size: 303 x 216mm, Trim Size: 297 x 210mm
BUSINESS: LOCAL GOVERNMENT, LEISURE & RECREATION: Local Government

POLICY STUDIES
37024U14E-402
Editorial Address: 4 Park Square, Milton Park, ABINGDON, OX14 4RN **Tel:** 020 7017 6000
Email: mge3@york.ac.uk
Advertising Address: PO Box 25, ABINGDON, OX14 3UE
Tel: 01235 401000 **Fax:** 01235 401550
Email: marketing@carfax.co.uk
ISSN: 0144-2872
Publisher: Routledge, Taylor & Francis
Frequency: Quarterly
Editor: Mark Evans; **Advertising Manager:** Claire Buckminster; **Managing Editor:** Jane Oakley
Summary of Content: Features articles on social and economic research related to policy.
Agency Commission: 10%
Copy instructions: Copy Date: 2 months prior to publication date
BUSINESS: COMMERCE, INDUSTRY & MANAGEMENT: Work Study

POLLUTION SOLUTIONS
1824596U57-159
Editorial Address: Oak Court Business Centre, Sandridge Park, Porters Wood, ST. ALBANS, AL3 6PH
Tel: 01727 858840 **Fax:** 01727 840310
Email: info@envirotechpubs.com
Advertising Address: As above.
Email: sam@ps-pubs.com
ISSN: 0963-7362
Publisher: Environmental Technology Publications Ltd
Date Established: 2008
Frequency: Quarterly
Cover Price: Free
Circulation: 50,465 (Print Run)
Editor: Marcus Pattison; **Publisher:** Marcus Pattison
Summary of Content: Magazine covering water and waste water equipment, air clean up, consultancy services, soil remediation and waste handling.
Readership/Target Audience: Aimed at the construction and utilities industry and governments.
ADVERTISING RATES:
Full Page Mono £4150.00
Full Page Colour £5145.00
BUSINESS: ENVIRONMENT & POLLUTION

POLYMER INTERNATIONAL
38829U39-47

Editorial Address: The Atrium, Southern Gate, CHICHESTER, PO19 8SQ **Tel:** 01243 779777
Email: polyint@wiley.com
Advertising Address: As above. **Tel:** 01243 770254
Fax: 01243 770432
Email: adsales@wiley.co.uk
Web site: http://www.interscience.wiley.com/polymerinternational
ISSN: 0959-8103
Publisher: John Wiley & Sons Ltd
Date Established: 1969
Frequency: Monthly
Annual Sub.: $1870.00
Usual Pagination: 200
Editor: Anne Pichon
Summary of Content: Contains original peer-reviewed mini-reviews, research papers, rapid reports and critical analysis.
Readership/Target Audience: Aimed at polymer and material scientists, engineers, strategists and opinion formers in academia and industry.
ADVERTISING RATES:
Full Page Mono £1135.00
Full Page Colour £2505.00
Agency Commission: 10%
Mechanical Data: Print Process: Sheet-fed offset litho, Film: Digital, Type Area: 270 x 180mm, Col Length: 270mm, Page Width: 180mm, Trim Size: 297 x 210mm
BUSINESS: PLASTICS & RUBBER

POLYMERS & POLYMER COMPOSITES
38844U39-48

Editorial Address: Shawbury, SHREWSBURY, SY4 4NR
Tel: 01939 252455 **Fax:** 01939 251118
Email: kmevans@rapra.net
Web site: http://www.rapra.net/journals
ISSN: 0967-3911
Publisher: Rapra Technology Ltd
Date Established: 1991
Frequency: 9 issues yearly
Annual Sub.: £595.00
Circulation: 300 (Publisher's Statement)
Usual Pagination: 70
Editor: Kate Evans
Summary of Content: Contains peer reviewed articles on science and technology of reinforced polymer materials.
Readership/Target Audience: Aimed at material scientists and students of material science.
ADVERTISING: No Advertising taken
BUSINESS: PLASTICS & RUBBER

POLYMERS FOR ADVANCED TECHNOLOGIES
601238U39-49

Editorial Address: The Atrium, Southern Gate, CHICHESTER, PO19 8SQ **Tel:** 01243 779777
Fax: 01243 775878
Email: amasmith@wiley.co.uk
Advertising Address: As above. **Fax:** 01243 770432
Email: f.pidduck@wiley.co.uk
Web site: http://www.interscience.wiley.com/journal/pat
ISSN: 1042-7147
Publisher: John Wiley & Sons Ltd
Date Established: 1990
Frequency: Monthly
Annual Sub.: $3045.00
Editor: Amanda Smith; **Editor-in-Chief:** Menachem Lewin; **Advertising Manager:** Faith Pidduck
Summary of Content: Research journal focusing on new areas of polymer research and development related to advanced technologies.
Readership/Target Audience: Aimed at industrial and academic scientists and engineers in the fields of materials and polymer science, inorganic, physical and organic chemistry, polymer physics, biochemistry, chemical, plastics and mechanical engineering, biotechnology, molecular modelling and design.
ADVERTISING RATES:
Full Page Mono £1175.00
Full Page Colour £2575.00
Agency Commission: 10%
Mechanical Data: Trim Size: 297 x 210mm, Type Area: 270 x 180mm, Print Process: Sheet-fed litho, Film: Digital, Col Length: 270mm, Page Width: 180mm
Copy instructions: Copy Date: 6 weeks prior to publication date
BUSINESS: PLASTICS & RUBBER

POOL AND SPA INDUSTRY
38427U32E-265

Editorial Address: 17 Sedgeway Business Park, Witchford, ELY, CB6 2HY **Tel:** 01353 666663 **Fax:** 01353 666664
Email: editorial@poolandspaindustry.co.uk
Advertising Address: As above.
Email: info@waterlandpublishing.co.uk
Web site: http://www.poolandspaindustry.co.uk
ISSN: 1356-1723
Publisher: Waterland Publishing Limited

Frequency: 6 issues yearly
Free to qualifying individuals
Annual Sub.: £20.00
Circulation: 9,000 (Publisher's Statement)
Usual Pagination: 100
Editor: Christina Connor; **Advertising Manager:** Christina Connor
Summary of Content: Magazine covering design and construction technology for domestic and commercial pools, saunas and spas.
Readership/Target Audience: Aimed at swimming pool builders, pool and spa retailers, architects, specifiers, local authorities, hotel chains and wet leisure facility operators.
ADVERTISING RATES:
Full Page Colour £1050.00
Agency Commission: 10%
Mechanical Data: Film: Digital, Bleed Size: 303 x 213mm, Trim Size: 297 x 210mm, Type Area: 264 x 182mm, Col Length: 264mm, Page Width: 182mm
Copy instructions: Copy Date: 4 weeks prior to publication date
Average advertising content per issue: 60%
BUSINESS: LOCAL GOVERNMENT, LEISURE & RECREATION: Swimming Pools

POPULAR ASTRONOMY
39999U55-129

Editorial Address: 7 Parc-An-Bre Drive, St. Dennis, ST. AUSTELL, PL26 8BH **Tel:** 0115 937 3610
Fax: 0115 937 3610
Email: editor@popastro.com
Advertising Address: As above.
Email: editor@popastro.com
Web site: http://www.popastro.com
ISSN: 0261-0892
Publisher: Society for Popular Astronomy
Date Established: 1953
Frequency: Quarterly
Cover Price: £2.99
Free to qualifying individuals
Annual Sub.: £16.00
Circulation: 3,000 (Publisher's Statement)
Usual Pagination: 48
Editor: Peter Grego; **Advertising Manager:** Peter Grego
Summary of Content: Official magazine of the Society for Popular Astronomy, covering astronomy news, local and national society news, general astronomy and space interest stories, astronomical observations and articles on all aspects of astronomy, space science and space exploration. Features reviews of books and astronomy related products, readers' letters and competitions.
Readership/Target Audience: Aimed primarily at members of the Society for Popular Astronomy, amateur astronomers and those interested in all aspects of space and it's exploration.
ADVERTISING RATES:
Full Page Mono £190.00
Full Page Colour £395.00
Mechanical Data: Col Length: 270mm, Col Widths (Display): 90mm, No. of Columns (Display): 2
Copy instructions: Copy Date: 2 months prior to publication date
Average advertising content per issue: 6%
BUSINESS: APPLIED SCIENCE & LABORATORIES

POPULAR MUSIC
40955U61-140

Editorial Address: The Edinburgh Building, Shaftesbury Road, CAMBRIDGE, CB2 8RU **Tel:** 01223 312393
Fax: 01223 325801
Advertising Address: As above. **Tel:** 01223 326070
Fax: 01223 325150
Email: ad_sales@cambridge.org
Web site: http://journals.cambridge.org/jid_pmu
ISSN: 0261-1430
Publisher: Cambridge University Press
Date Established: 1981
Frequency: 3 issues yearly - Published in January, May and October
Free to qualifying individuals
Annual Sub.: £42.00
Circulation: 1,500 (Publisher's Statement)
Usual Pagination: 200
Advertising Manager: Rebecca Roberts
Summary of Content: Academic journal covering the latest developments in popular music theories and methods. Includes book reviews and music titles from around the world.
Readership/Target Audience: Aimed at musicians, music journalists, students, teachers, researchers and music and humanities librarians.
ADVERTISING RATES:
Full Page Mono £470.00
Mechanical Data: Page Width: 170mm, Film: Digital, Type Area: 250 x 170mm, Col Length: 250mm
Copy instructions: Copy Date: 8 weeks prior to publication date
BUSINESS: MUSIC TRADE

PORT STRATEGY
1629421U45C-801

Editorial Address: The Old Mill, Lower Quay, FAREHAM, PO16 0RA **Tel:** 01329 825335 **Fax:** 01329 825330
Email: editor@portstrategy.com
Advertising Address: As above.
Email: sales@portstrategy.com
Web site: http://www.portstrategy.com
ISSN: 1740-2638
Publisher: Mercator Media Ltd
Date Established: 2003
Frequency: 10 issues yearly - Published in the 1st week of the cover month (combined issues 1st week of 2nd cover month)
Annual Sub.: £135.00
Circulation: 5,518 (ABC 01/07/2008 to 31/12/2008)
Usual Pagination: 52
Editor: Carly Fields; **Advertising Manager:** Rod Sessions; **Publisher:** Andrew Webster
Summary of Content: Magazine covering news and features on the key changes and opportunities within the international marine port industry. Includes regional surveys and articles on investment pricing, cargo handling, port engineering and management, vessel training, logistics, insurance and loss prevention.
Readership/Target Audience: Aimed at government strategists, port executives, maritime terminal operators and key port users.
ADVERTISING RATES:
Full Page Mono £2570.00
Full Page Colour £3250.00
Agency Commission: 15%
Mechanical Data: Type Area: 270 x 190mm, Bleed Size: 303 x 196mm, Trim Size: 297 x 210mm, Print Process: Sheet-fed offset litho, Col Length: 270mm, Page Width: 190mm
Copy instructions: Copy Date: 3 weeks prior to publication date
Average advertising content per issue: 25%
BUSINESS: MARINE & SHIPPING: Maritime Freight

PORT TECHNOLOGY INTERNATIONAL
766442U45A-501

Editorial Address: Trans-World House, 100 City Road, LONDON, EC1Y 2BP **Tel:** 020 7871 0123
Fax: 020 7871 0101
Email: adawson@porttechnology.org
Advertising Address: As above.
Email: mstewart@porttechnology.org
Web site: http://www.porttechnology.org
ISSN: 1358-1759
Publisher: Henley Media Group Ltd.
Date Established: 1995
Frequency: Quarterly
Cover Price: £25.00
Free to qualifying individuals
Annual Sub.: £100.00
Circulation: 15,500 (Publisher's Statement)
Usual Pagination: 200
Editor: Angus Dawson; **Advertising Manager:** Michael Stewart
Summary of Content: Preview and review of advanced technologies for ports, harbours and terminals worldwide.
Readership/Target Audience: Aimed at harbour masters, Port Authorities, terminal operators, industry associations and professionals.
ADVERTISING RATES:
Full Page Colour £4200.00
Agency Commission: 15%
Mechanical Data: Trim Size: 297 x 210mm, Bleed Size: 303 x 216mm
Average advertising content per issue: 30%
BUSINESS: MARINE & SHIPPING

PORTFOLIO ADVISER
1790453U1F-639

Editorial Address: 4th Floor, 120 Moorgate, LONDON, EC2M 6SS **Tel:** 020 7065 7566
Email: pam@lastwordmedia.com
Advertising Address: As above. **Tel:** 020 7065 7575
Email: daniel.gilmore@lastwordmedia.com
Web site: http://www.lastwordmedia.com/portfolio_adviser
Publisher: Last Word Media
Date Established: 2006
Frequency: Monthly
Free to qualifying individuals
Circulation: 5,000 (Publisher's Statement)
Editor: Gary Corcoran; **Advertising Manager:** Daniel Gilmore
Summary of Content: Publication covering investment strategies for professional advisers to help with clients' portfolio construction and asset allocation decisions.
Readership/Target Audience: Aimed at intermediaries and discretionary advisers who make investment decisions on behalf of their clients.
ADVERTISING RATES:
Full Page Colour £5550.00
Agency Commission: 10%
Mechanical Data: Bleed Size: 306 x 236mm, Trim Size: 300 x 230mm, Film: Digital

Business Magazines

Copy instructions: Copy Date: Tuesday prior to publication date
Average advertising content per issue: 30%
BUSINESS: FINANCE & ECONOMICS: Investment

PORTS & HARBORS
1732231U45A-515

Editorial Address: 3rd Floor, Lombard House, 3 Princess Way, REDHILL, RH1 1UP **Tel:** 01737 379000
Fax: 01737 379007
Email: penny.allen@lrfairplay.com
Advertising Address: As above.
Email: daniel.goncalves@lrfairplay.com
Web site: http://www.iaphworldports.org
Publisher: Lloyd's Register-Fairplay Ltd
Date Established: 1956
Frequency: 6 issues yearly - Published at the beginning of the cover month
Circulation: 3,600 (Publisher's Statement)
Usual Pagination: 48
Editor: Penny Allen
Summary of Content: Magazine covering views and opinions of port professionals and best practices across the world's ports and maritime industry.
Readership/Target Audience: Aimed at members of The International Association of Ports and Harbors.
ADVERTISING RATES:
Full Page Colour £2014.00
Agency Commission: 10%
Mechanical Data: Type Area: 268 x 188mm, Bleed Size: 303 x 216mm, Film: Digital, Col Length: 268mm, Page Width: 188mm
Copy instructions: Copy Date: 3 weeks prior to publication date
Average advertising content per issue: 30%
Official Journal of: The International Association of Ports and Harbors
BUSINESS: MARINE & SHIPPING

PORTUGUESE JOURNAL OF SOCIAL SCIENCE
1696520U62R-492

Editorial Address: The Mill, Parnall Road, Fishponds, BRISTOL, BS16 3JG **Tel:** 0117 958 9910
Email: pjss.editorial@gmail.com
Web site: http://www.intellectbooks.co.uk
ISSN: 1476-413X
Publisher: Intellect Ltd
Date Established: 2002
Frequency: 3 issues yearly - Published in April, August and December
Annual Sub.: £180.00
Circulation: 300 (Publisher's Statement)
Usual Pagination: 80
Editor: Freya Morris
Summary of Content: Journal covering Portuguese academic work in social services.
Readership/Target Audience: Aimed at academics and specialists in Latin America and Southern Europe with an interest in Portuguese social sciences.
ADVERTISING: No Advertising taken
BUSINESS: CHURCH & SCHOOL EQUIPMENT & EDUCATION: Education Related

POST MAGAZINE & INSURANCE WEEK
35158U1D-330

Editorial Address: 32-34 Broadwick Street, LONDON, W1A 2HG **Tel:** 020 7316 9000
Email: postmag@incisivemedia.com
Advertising Address: As above. **Fax:** 020 7316 9257
Email: sajeeda.merali@incisivemedia.com
Web site: http://www.postonline.co.uk
ISSN: 1365-4284
Publisher: Incisive Media
Date Established: 1840
Frequency: Weekly - Published on a Thursday
Cover Price: £4.80
Circulation: 5,245 (ABC 01/07/2008 to 30/06/2009)
Usual Pagination: 48
Editor: Jonathan Swift; **News Editor:** Mairi MacDonald; **Features Editor:** Stephanie Denton
Summary of Content: Magazine covering UK and International insurance industry news, opinions, analysis and technical features.
Readership/Target Audience: Read by all those involved in the insurance industry including insurance companies, brokers and intermediaries, corporate insurance buyers and service suppliers such as lawyers, IT companies and consultants.
ADVERTISING RATES:
Full Page Colour £4389.00
Agency Commission: 10%
Mechanical Data: Col Length: 286mm, Film: Digital, Type Area: 286 x 210mm, Bleed Size: 336 x 241mm, Trim Size: 330 x 235mm, Page Width: 210mm
Copy instructions: Copy Date: 1 week prior to publication date
BUSINESS: FINANCE & ECONOMICS: Insurance

POST NEWS
35347U1G-40

Editorial Address: STOKE-SUB-HAMDON, TA14 6BR
Tel: 01935 881245
Email: rb@epostnews.com
Publisher: Post News
Frequency: Monthly
Annual Sub.: £224.00
Usual Pagination: 14
Editor: Ron Brown
Summary of Content: Magazine that provides news, intelligence and analysis on point of sale terminals in banking, retailing and hotels.
Readership/Target Audience: Read by senior management.
ADVERTISING: No Advertising taken
BUSINESS: FINANCE & ECONOMICS: Credit Trading

POSTAL TECHNOLOGY INTERNATIONAL
1626204U10-206

Editorial Address: Abinger House, Church Street, DORKING, RH4 1DF **Tel:** 01306 743744 **Fax:** 01306 887546
Email: postaltech@ukintpress.com
Advertising Address: As above. **Fax:** 01306 742525
Email: h.blair@ukintpress.com
Web site: http://www.ukipme.com
ISSN: 1472-5274
Publisher: UKIP Media & Events Ltd
Date Established: 1996
Frequency: Quarterly
Free to qualifying individuals
Annual Sub.: £28.00
Circulation: 10,000 (Publisher's Statement)
Editor: Andrew Pickering; **Advertising Manager:** Helena Blair
Summary of Content: Magazine covering all aspects of postal technology, including product profiles, reviews and news.
Readership/Target Audience: Aimed at directors and senior managers of postal organisations.
ADVERTISING RATES:
Full Page Colour £4150.00
Agency Commission: 10%
Mechanical Data: Type Area: 270 x 180mm, Bleed Size: 303 x 216mm, Trim Size: 297 x 210mm, Col Length: 270mm, Page Width: 180mm, Film: Digital
Copy instructions: Copy Date: 3 weeks prior to publication date
Average advertising content per issue: 40%
BUSINESS: MATERIALS HANDLING

POSTGRADUATE MEDICAL JOURNAL
1739384U56A-203

Editorial Address: BMA House, Tavistock Square, LONDON, WC1H 9JR **Tel:** 020 7383 6439
Email: pmj@bmjgroup.com
Advertising Address: As above. **Tel:** 020 7387 4499
Fax: 020 7383 6556
Email: ecurrer@bmj.com
Web site: http://pmj.bmjjournals.com
Publisher: BMJ Publishing Group
Frequency: Monthly
Circulation: 1,400 (Publisher's Statement)
Editor: Fiona Moss
Summary of Content: Journal focusing on medical education.
Readership/Target Audience: Aimed at postgraduate tutors, clinical trainers and trainees, clinicians in any specialty and postgraduate nurses who wish to further their medical education.
ADVERTISING RATES:
Full Page Mono £910.00
Full Page Colour £1610.00
Agency Commission: 10%
Mechanical Data: Type Area: 243 x 186mm, Bleed Size: 286 x 216mm, Trim Size: 280 x 210mm, Col Length: 243mm, Page Width: 186mm, Film: Digital
Copy instructions: Copy Date: 20th of 2 months prior to publication date
Average advertising content per issue: 10%
BUSINESS: HEALTH & MEDICAL

POSTHARVEST NEWS AND INFORMATION
37779U21A-870

Editorial Address: Nosworthy Way, WALLINGFORD, OX10 8DE **Tel:** 01491 829359 **Fax:** 01491 833508
Email: a.rendell-dunn@cabi.org
Web site: http://www.cabi.org
ISSN: 0957-7505
Publisher: CABI
Date Established: 1990
Frequency: 6 issues yearly
Editor: Alexis Rendell-Dunn
Summary of Content: Journal containing abstracts, mini-reviews and conference papers on post-harvest research on grain, oilseeds, fruits, vegetables, ornamentals and other agricultural commodities.
Readership/Target Audience: Read by scientists and technical staff interested in drying, handling, grading, packing, storage, pests, spoilage, contamination and minimal processing of agricultural commodities.
ADVERTISING: No Advertising taken
BUSINESS: AGRICULTURE & FARMING

POTATO ABSTRACTS
37797U21A-880

Editorial Address: Nosworthy Way, WALLINGFORD, OX10 8DE **Tel:** 01491 832111 **Fax:** 01491 829198
Email: publishing@cabi.org
Web site: http://www.cabi.org
ISSN: 0308-7344
Publisher: CABI
Date Established: 1976
Frequency: Quarterly
Cover Price: £390.00
Circulation: 135 (Publisher's Statement)
Editor: Vicky Bornham
Summary of Content: Abstract journal featuring all aspects of production and uses of potatoes.
Readership/Target Audience: Aimed at academic and government research institutes, snack food and potato processing companies.
ADVERTISING: No Advertising taken
BUSINESS: AGRICULTURE & FARMING

POTATO MARKETS WEEKLY
26043U21R-1503

Editorial Address: 80 Calverley Road, TUNBRIDGE WELLS, TN1 2UN **Tel:** 020 7017 7500 **Fax:** 020 7017 7599
Email: marketing@agra-net.com
Web site: http://www.agra-net.com
ISSN: 0141-2221
Publisher: Agra Informa Ltd
Frequency: Weekly
Annual Sub.: £2274.00
Summary of Content: Newsletter for the potato industry. Includes monitoring, prices, production, processing and trade in the European and International markets.
Readership/Target Audience: Aimed at those in the global potato industry.
ADVERTISING: No Advertising taken
BUSINESS: AGRICULTURE & FARMING: Agriculture & Farming Related

POTATO PROCESSING INTERNATIONAL
38007U22C-500

Formerly: Potato Business World
Editorial Address: 1st Floor Offices, 1-3 Station Road East, OXTED, RH8 0BD **Tel:** 01883 734582 **Fax:** 01732 451383
Email: matthew@crier.co.uk
Advertising Address: As above.
Email: renato@crier.hr
Web site: http://www.potatobusiness.com
ISSN: 0968-7661
Publisher: Crier Media Group
Date Established: 1993
Frequency: 6 issues yearly - Published around the 3rd week of the cover month
Annual Sub.: £89.00
Circulation: 3,847 (Publisher's Statement)
Usual Pagination: 52
Editor: Andre Erasmus; **Advertising Manager:** Ivana Hromin
Summary of Content: Magazine about the international potato processing industry.
Readership/Target Audience: Aimed at those involved in the potato industry.
ADVERTISING RATES:
Full Page Colour EUR2750.00
Agency Commission: 10%
Mechanical Data: Page Width: 186mm, Type Area: 270 x 186mm, Bleed Size: 303 x 218mm, Trim Size: 297 x 210mm, Col Length: 270mm, Film: Digital
Copy instructions: Copy Date: 2 weeks prior to publication date
BUSINESS: FOOD: Food Processing & Packaging

POTATO REVIEW
37933U21R-897

Editorial Address: Docwras, Guestwick, DEREHAM, NR20 5AL **Tel:** 01362 684240
Email: edit@potatoreview.com
Advertising Address: 2 The Hill, Almondsbury, BRISTOL, BS32 4AE **Tel:** 01454 615118 **Fax:** 01454 202838
Email: ads@potatoreview.com
Web site: http://www.potatoreview.com
ISSN: 0961-7655
Publisher: AREMI LTD
Date Established: 1990
Frequency: 6 issues yearly
Free to qualifying individuals
Annual Sub.: £35.00

Circulation: 7,500 (Publisher's Statement)
Usual Pagination: 48
Editor: David Mossman; **Advertising Manager:** Hazel Hescott
Summary of Content: Journal covering in-depth review articles on market trends, technical and scientific developments and new products.
Readership/Target Audience: Read by potato growers, agronomists, major retailers, processors and merchants.
ADVERTISING RATES:
Full Page Colour £2180.00
Agency Commission: 10%
Mechanical Data: Page Width: 188mm, Type Area: 275 x 188mm, Bleed Size: 305 x 213mm, Trim Size: 297 x 210mm, Col Length: 275mm, Film: Digital
Copy instructions: Copy Date: 2 weeks prior to publication date
Average advertising content per issue: 40%
BUSINESS: AGRICULTURE & FARMING: Agriculture & Farming Related

POTATO STORAGE INTERNATIONAL

1657609U21R-1502

Editorial Address: 1st Floor Offices, 1-3 Station Road East, OXTED, RH8 0BD **Tel:** 01883 734582 **Fax:** 01883 713640
Email: andre@crier.co.uk
Advertising Address: As above.
Email: renato@crier.hr
Web site: http://www.potatobusiness.com
ISSN: 1745-2945
Publisher: Crier Media Group
Date Established: 2004
Frequency: Half-yearly - Published in the middle of the cover month. Published March and September
Circulation: 6,087 (Publisher's Statement)
Usual Pagination: 48
Editor: Andre Erasmus; **Advertising Manager:** Ivana Hromin
Summary of Content: Magazine focusing on the global potato storage industry.
Readership/Target Audience: Aimed at storage managers and decision makers involved with the large volume storage of potatoes.
ADVERTISING RATES:
Full Page Colour EUR2750.00
Agency Commission: 10%
Mechanical Data: Trim Size: 297 x 210mm, Film: Digital
Copy instructions: Copy Date: 2 weeks prior to publication date
Average advertising content per issue: 35%
BUSINESS: AGRICULTURE & FARMING: Agriculture & Farming Related

POULTRY GAZETTE

1804946U21F-883

Editorial Address: PO Box 75, BRIGHOUSE, HD6 3WF
Tel: 01484 400666 **Fax:** 01484 400661
Email: keith@farminguk.com
Advertising Address: As above.
Email: keith@farminguk.com
Web site: http://www.poultrygazette.com
Publisher: Breezi Publishing Ltd
Date Established: 2007
Frequency: Half-yearly - Published in June and December
Annual Sub.: £16.00
Circulation: 5,000 (Publisher's Statement)
Editor: Keith Wild; **Advertising Manager:** Keith Wild
Summary of Content: Magazine focusing on the poultry industry including meat and egg production by intensive, barn and free range methods.
Readership/Target Audience: Aimed at poultry farmers, suppliers and industry.
ADVERTISING RATES:
Full Page Colour £550.00
Agency Commission: 10%
Copy instructions: Copy Date: 1 week prior to publication date
Average advertising content per issue: 30%
BUSINESS: AGRICULTURE & FARMING: Poultry

POULTRY INTERNATIONAL

37873U21F-870

Editorial Address: Lavant House, Lavant Street, PETERSFIELD, GU32 3EL **Tel:** 07866 475388
Email: mclements@wattnet.net
Advertising Address: Albast 25, 2719 TV ZOETERMEER
Tel: 79 32 30 782 **Fax:** 79 32 30 783
Email: driesmvd@xs4all.nl
Web site: http://www.WATTpoultry.com
Publisher: Watt Publishing Co
Date Established: 1962
Frequency: Monthly - Published around the 1st of the cover month
Free to qualifying individuals
Annual Sub.: $144.00
Circulation: 20,076 (Publisher's Statement)
Usual Pagination: 52
Editor: Mark Clements

Summary of Content: Magazine covering all aspects of poultry production.
Readership/Target Audience: Aimed at poultry, meat and egg producers and processors.
ADVERTISING RATES:
Full Page Colour $7960.00
Agency Commission: 15%
Mechanical Data: Bleed Size: 207 x 274mm, Type Area: 254 x 188mm, Col Length: 254mm, Page Width: 188mm
Copy instructions: Copy Date: 4 weeks prior to publication date
BUSINESS: AGRICULTURE & FARMING: Poultry

POULTRY WORLD

37874U21F-880

Editorial Address: Quadrant House, The Quadrant, SUTTON, SM2 5AS **Tel:** 020 8652 4020 **Fax:** 020 8652 4006
Email: poultry.world@rbi.co.uk
Advertising Address: As above. **Tel:** 020 8652 3500
Fax: 020 8652 4043
Email: vic.bunby@rbi.co.uk
Web site: http://www.fwi.co.uk
ISSN: 0032-5813
Publisher: Reed Business Information
Date Established: 1874
Frequency: Monthly - Published on the 1st Friday of the month
Cover Price: £3.00
Circulation: 3,286 (ABC 01/01/2008 to 31/12/2008)
Usual Pagination: 44
Editor: Richard Allison; **Advertisement Director:** Vic Bunby;
Publisher: Trevor Parker
Summary of Content: Journal containing technical and statistical information as well as the latest news about the poultry industry.
Readership/Target Audience: Read by poultry farmers, breeders and suppliers to the industry, egg packers, poultry processors and wholesalers.
ADVERTISING RATES:
Full Page Colour £2500.00
Agency Commission: 10%
Mechanical Data: Type Area: 271 x 190mm, Col Length: 271mm, Page Width: 190mm, Bleed Size: 303 x 213mm, Trim Size: 297 x 210mm, Film: Positive, right reading, emulsion side down. Digital
Copy instructions: Copy Date: 3 weeks prior to publication date
Average advertising content per issue: 40%
BUSINESS: AGRICULTURE & FARMING: Poultry

POWDER METALLURGY

38166U27-128

Editorial Address: 1 Carlton House Terrace, LONDON, SW1Y 5DB **Tel:** 020 7451 7300 **Fax:** 020 7451 7307
Email: mark_hull@materials.org.uk
Advertising Address: Suite 1C, Josephs Well, Hanover Walk, LEEDS, LS3 1AB **Tel:** 0113 243 2800
Fax: 0114 386 8178
Email: n.taylor@maney.co.uk
Web site: http://www.maney.co.uk/journals/powder
ISSN: 0032-5899
Publisher: Maney Publishing
Date Established: 1958
Frequency: Quarterly
Annual Sub.: £363.00
Circulation: 1,000 (Publisher's Statement)
Usual Pagination: 96
Editor: Mark Hull; **Advertising Manager:** Natalie Taylor;
Managing Editor: Mark Hull
Summary of Content: Journal covering developments in metal, ceramic and hard-metal particulate science and engineering, including powder production and handling, consolidation and sintering, secondary processing and machining and the magnetics industry.
Readership/Target Audience: Read by professionals within the metal powder, hard materials and magnetics industry.
ADVERTISING RATES:
Full Page Mono £500.00
Full Page Colour £1100.00
Agency Commission: 10%
Mechanical Data: Type Area: 266 x 188mm, Bleed Size: 305 x 215mm, Trim Size: 297 x 210mm, Film: Digital, Col Length: 266mm, Page Width: 188mm
Copy instructions: Copy Date: 15th of the month prior to publication date
BUSINESS: METAL, IRON & STEEL

POWER ELECTRONICS EUROPE

622962U18A-9051

Editorial Address: Kildonan, St. Marys Road, Wrotham, SEVENOAKS, TN15 7AP **Tel:** 01732 886495
Fax: 01732 886149
Email: ian@power-mag.com
Web site: http://www.power-mag.com
Publisher: TechMedia International
Date Established: 1999
Frequency: 8 issues yearly
Free to qualifying individuals
Circulation: 16,000 (Publisher's Statement)

Usual Pagination: 50
Editor: Ian Atkinson; **Publisher:** Ian Atkinson
Summary of Content: Magazine covering all aspects of electronics including emerging technologies and the application of advanced components, sub-assemblies, systems and solutions.
Language(s): English; French; German
Readership/Target Audience: Aimed at engineers specialising in automotive, industrial and consumer electronics.
BUSINESS: ELECTRONICS

THE POWER ENGINEER

37638U19D-360

Editorial Address: Bedford Heights, Manton Lane, BEDFORD, MK4 7PH **Tel:** 01234 214340 **Fax:** 01234 355493
Email: enquiries@idgte.org
Advertising Address: As above.
Email: enquiries@idgte.org
Web site: http://www.idgte.org
ISSN: 1367-191X
Publisher: The Institution of Diesel & Gas Turbine Engineers
Date Established: 1997
Frequency: 5 issues yearly
Cover Price: £30.00
Annual Sub.: £150.00
Circulation: 600 (Publisher's Statement)
Editor: N. Pearce; **Advertising Manager:** Anne Youngman
Summary of Content: Publication containing technical papers and news items.
Readership/Target Audience: Aimed at those involved in diesel and gas turbine technology.
ADVERTISING RATES:
Full Page Mono £380.00
Full Page Colour £695.00
Mechanical Data: Trim Size: 297 x 210mm, Bleed Size: 303 x 216mm
Copy instructions: Copy Date: 1 month prior to publication date
Average advertising content per issue: 10%
BUSINESS: ENGINEERING & MACHINERY: Hydraulic Power

POWER ENGINEERING INTERNATIONAL

37327U17-165_48

Editorial Address: Warlies Park House, Horseshoe Hill, Upshire, WALTHAM ABBEY, EN9 3SR **Tel:** 01992 656600
Fax: 01992 656700
Email: peinews@pennwell.com
Advertising Address: As above.
Email: anthony@pennwell.com
Web site: http://www.peimagazine.com
ISSN: 1069-4994
Publisher: PennWell Publications International Ltd
Date Established: 1992
Frequency: 11 issues yearly - Published at the end of the 1st week of the cover month
Free to qualifying individuals
Annual Sub.: $130.00
Circulation: 12,500 (Publisher's Statement)
Usual Pagination: 68
Editor: Heather Johnstone; **Advertising Manager:** Anthony Orfeo
Summary of Content: Magazine covering global electric power generation and transmission, including news, technology, regulations and analysis.
Readership/Target Audience: Aimed at designers, specifiers and planners working in power generation companies and other allied fields.
ADVERTISING RATES:
Full Page Colour $8278.00
Agency Commission: 15%
Mechanical Data: Type Area: 267 x 180mm, Col Length: 267mm, Bleed Size: 307 x 220mm, Print Process: Web-fed offset litho, Film: Digital, Trim Size: 297 x 210mm, Col Widths (Display): 180mm
Copy instructions: Copy Date: 4 weeks prior to publication date
Average advertising content per issue: 45%
Supplement(s): Germany - 1xY
BUSINESS: ELECTRICAL

POWER IN ASIA

40771U58-67

Editorial Address: 20 Canada Square, Canary Wharf, LONDON, E14 5LH **Tel:** 020 7176 6207 **Fax:** 020 7176 6667
Email: martin_daniel@platts.com
Web site: http://www.platts.com
Publisher: Platts
Frequency: 24 issues yearly
Annual Sub.: $1440.00
Editor: Martin Daniel; **Managing Editor:** Henry Edwardes-Evans
Summary of Content: Magazine covering news and analysis on electricity related developments in Asia.
Readership/Target Audience: Read by equipment suppliers, utility companies, bankers, lawyers and consultants.

ADVERTISING: No Advertising taken
BUSINESS: ENERGY, FUEL & NUCLEAR

POWER IN EUROPE
40772U58-68

Editorial Address: 20 Canada Square, Canary Wharf, LONDON, E14 5LH **Tel:** 020 7176 6207 **Fax:** 020 7176 6667
Email: henry_edwardes-evans@platts.com
Web site: http://www.platts.com
ISSN: 0955-6079
Publisher: Platts
Date Established: 1987
Frequency: 24 issues yearly
Annual Sub.: $1660.00
Usual Pagination: 26
Editor: Henry Edwardes-Evans; **Managing Editor:** Henry Edwardes-Evans
Summary of Content: Publication covering all aspects of the European electricity industry, from power station to final consumer. Quarterly new power plant data set. Regular country profiles. Utility news, policy news, environmental and CO2/ETS analysis.
Readership/Target Audience: Aimed at utility executives in the electricity business, investment houses, consultants and policy makers.
ADVERTISING: No Advertising taken
BUSINESS: ENERGY, FUEL & NUCLEAR

POWERHOUSE
1790897U58-182

Editorial Address: 1st Floor, St. Georges House, St. Georges Street, WINCHESTER, SO23 8BG
Tel: 01962 890449
Email: jeremy@powerhousenews.biz
Advertising Address: PO Box 27, CHELTENHAM, GL53 0YH **Tel:** 01962 893847
Email: renewssales@btconnect.com
Web site: http://www.powerhousenews.biz
ISSN: 1751-181X
Publisher: ReNews Ltd
Date Established: 2005
Frequency: 24 issues yearly
Annual Sub.: £195.00
Usual Pagination: 10
Editor: Jeremy Dunning; **Publisher:** Dan Rigden
Summary of Content: Publication containing news and features on the microgeneration industry covering small scale renewable energy and low carbon building.
Readership/Target Audience: Aimed at the micro power industry, councils, utility companies and the building industry.
ADVERTISING: Rates on application
BUSINESS: ENERGY, FUEL & NUCLEAR

PPCJ POLYMERS PAINT COLOUR JOURNAL
37278U16B-65

Editorial Address: Westgate House, 120-130 Station Road, REDHILL, RH1 1ET **Tel:** 01737 855000
Email: suetyler@dmgworldmedia.com
Advertising Address: As above. **Tel:** 01737 855078
Fax: 01737 855034
Email: jeffmontgomery@dmgworldmedia.com
Web site: http://www.coatingsgroup.com
ISSN: 1357-731X
Publisher: DMG World Media
Date Established: 1879
Frequency: Monthly
Cover Price: £23.00
Free to qualifying individuals
Annual Sub.: £166.00
Circulation: 8,211 (Publisher's Statement)
Usual Pagination: 68
Editor: Sue Tyler
Summary of Content: Magazine containing news and features relevant to the paint and printing inks industries in Europe, The Middle East, the US and Africa.
Readership/Target Audience: Aimed at paint, ink and coatings manufacturers.
ADVERTISING RATES:
Full Page Mono £2511.00
Full Page Colour £4366.00
Agency Commission: 10%
Mechanical Data: Type Area: 265 x 185mm, Col Length: 265mm, Bleed Size: 306 x 216mm, Trim Size: 297 x 210mm, No. of Columns (Display): 2, Film: Digital, Page Width: 185mm
Average advertising content per issue: 42%
Supplement(s): EAS European Adhesives and Sealants - 4xY
BUSINESS: DECORATING & PAINT: Paint - Technical Manufacture

PPM PET PRODUCT MARKETING
41488U64E-75

Editorial Address: Bushfield House, Orton Centre, PETERBOROUGH, PE2 5UW **Tel:** 01733 237111
Fax: 01733 465820

Email: laura.wilcox@bauerconsumer.co.uk
Advertising Address: As above. **Fax:** 01733 288005
Email: helen.mccay@bauerconsumer.co.uk
Web site: http://www.petproductmarketing.co.uk
Publisher: Bauer Media Ltd (Orton)
Frequency: Monthly - Published on the 1st of the month
Cover Price: Free
Circulation: 5,520 (ABC 01/01/2008 to 31/12/2008)
Usual Pagination: 44
Editor: Laura Wilcox
Summary of Content: Magazine with features on products, legislation, business issues and merchandising.
Readership/Target Audience: Aimed at retailers, wholesalers and manufacturers in the pet industry.
ADVERTISING RATES:
Full Page Colour £1800.00
Agency Commission: 10%
Mechanical Data: Type Area: 370 x 275mm, Bleed Size: 401 x 301mm, Trim Size: 395 x 295mm, Col Length: 370mm, Film: Digital, Page Width: 275mm
Copy instructions: Copy Date: 2 weeks prior to publication date
Average advertising content per issue: 75%
BUSINESS: OTHER CLASSIFICATIONS: Pet Trade

PPP BULLETIN
34956U1A-273_10

Formerly: The PFI Intelligence Bulletin
Editorial Address: 20A Hillgate Place, LONDON, SW12 9ER
Tel: 020 8675 1233 **Fax:** 020 8675 0950
Email: anicholls@pppbulletin.com
Advertising Address: As above.
Email: bpoynton@pppbulletin.co.uk
Web site: http://www.pppbulletin.com
ISSN: 1363-0377
Publisher: Rockcliffe Ltd
Date Established: 1994
Frequency: 10 issues yearly - Published on the 1st of the cover month
Annual Sub.: £595.00
Circulation: 2,500 (Publisher's Statement)
Usual Pagination: 48
Editor: Amanda Nicholls; **Advertising Manager:** Brendan Poynton
Summary of Content: Magazine containing updates and case studies of projects under the Private Finance Initiative together with in-depth analysis of current issues and contributions from experts in the field.
Readership/Target Audience: Aimed at government bodies, bankers, contractors, lawyers and consultants.
ADVERTISING RATES:
Full Page Colour £995.00
Mechanical Data: Type Area: 268 x 180mm, Bleed Size: 303 x 213mm, Trim Size: 297 x 210mm, Col Length: 268mm, Page Width: 180mm
Average advertising content per issue: 2%
BUSINESS: FINANCE & ECONOMICS

THE PPP JOURNAL
34962U1A-273_30

Formerly: The Public Private Partnerships Journal
Editorial Address: 3rd Floor, City Wharf, New Bailey Street, SALFORD, M3 5ER **Tel:** 0161 835 1519
Email: mthame@publicservice.co.uk
Advertising Address: City Wharf, New Bailey Street, SALFORD, M3 5ER **Tel:** 0161 832 7387 **Fax:** 0161 832 7396
Email: cstubbs@publicservice.co.uk
Web site: http://www.publicservice.co.uk
ISSN: 1754-7415
Publisher: PSCA International Ltd
Date Established: 1995
Frequency: Quarterly
Free to qualifying individuals
Annual Sub.: £250.00
Circulation: 3,947 (ABC 01/01/2008 to 31/12/2008)
Usual Pagination: 100
Editor: Michael Thame; **Advertising Manager:** Craig Stubbs; **Managing Editor:** Lisa Carnwell
Summary of Content: Journal addressing all aspects of PFI and PPP. Contains articles and reports from high-profile individuals in the public and private sectors, examining latest trends and highlighting case studies of projects both in the UK and internationally.
Readership/Target Audience: Aimed at lawyers, financial advisors, contractors, accountants and public finance sector project managers, chief executives.
ADVERTISING RATES:
Full Page Colour £3995.00
Agency Commission: 10%
Mechanical Data: Film: Digital
Copy instructions: Copy Date: 4 weeks prior to publication date
BUSINESS: FINANCE & ECONOMICS

PQ MAGAZINE
1657144U1B-321

Editorial Address: 4th Floor, Central House, 142 Central Street, LONDON, EC1V 8AR **Tel:** 020 7216 6444
Fax: 020 7216 8556

Email: graham@pqaccountant.com
Advertising Address: As above.
Email: polly@pqaccountant.com
Web site: http://www.pqmagazine.co.uk
Publisher: PQ Publishing
Date Established: 2003
Frequency: Monthly
Free to qualifying individuals
Annual Sub.: £36.00
Circulation: 37,138 (ABC 01/07/2007 to 30/06/2008)
Usual Pagination: 44
Editor: Graham Hambly; **Advertising Manager:** Polly Thrasivoulou
Summary of Content: Magazine covering exam hints, independent career advice, tips and advice.
Readership/Target Audience: Aimed at part qualified accountants.
ADVERTISING RATES:
Full Page Colour £2895.00
Mechanical Data: Type Area: 278 x 192mm, Bleed Size: 303 x 216mm, Trim Size: 297 x 210mm, Col Length: 278mm, Page Width: 192mm, Film: Digital
BUSINESS: FINANCE & ECONOMICS: Accountancy

PR WEEK
35715U2E-70

Editorial Address: 174 Hammersmith Road, LONDON, W6 7JP **Tel:** 020 8267 5000 **Fax:** 020 8267 4509
Email: prweek@haymarket.com
Advertising Address: As above. **Tel:** 020 8267 4233
Fax: 020 8267 4189
Email: luke.burley@haymarket.com
Web site: http://www.prweek.com/uk
ISSN: 0267-6087
Publisher: Haymarket Brand Media
Frequency: Weekly - Published on Friday
Cover Price: £3.70
Annual Sub.: £114.00
Circulation: 14,818 (ABC 01/07/2008 to 30/06/2009)
Editor: David Singleton; **News Editor:** David Singleton; **Managing Director:** Stephen Farish; **Advertising Director:** Luke Burley; **Publisher:** Simon Lees
Summary of Content: Magazine covering all aspects of public relations and communications.
Readership/Target Audience: Aimed at executives in PR consultancies and in-house departments.
ADVERTISING RATES:
Full Page Colour £5269.00
Agency Commission: 10%
Mechanical Data: Page Width: 205mm, Trim Size: 295 x 225mm, Type Area: 275 x 205mm, Col Length: 275mm, Bleed Size: 301 x 231mm, Film: Digital
Copy instructions: Copy Date: 1 week prior to publication date
Supplement(s): Contact - 1xY, Power Book - 1xY, PR Week Black Book - 1xY, Top 150 PR Consultancies - 1xY
BUSINESS: COMMUNICATIONS, ADVERTISING & MARKETING: Public Relations

PR WEEK BLACK BOOK
35718U2E-40

Formerly: Contact
Editorial Address: 22 Bute Gardens, LONDON, W6 7HN
Tel: 020 8267 5000
Email: directories@haymarket.com
Web site: http://www.blueboomerang.com
Publisher: Haymarket Specialist Publications
Date Established: 1996
Frequency: Annual - Published in January
Cover Price: £90.00
Usual Pagination: 80
Editor: Felicity Mouat
Summary of Content: A guide to press contacts.
Readership/Target Audience: Aimed at journalists, PR professionals and their clients.
ADVERTISING: Rates on application
Supplement to: PR Week
BUSINESS: COMMUNICATIONS, ADVERTISING & MARKETING: Public Relations

THE PRA NEWSLETTER
38514U32G-85

Editorial Address: Bayford Mews, Bayford Street, LONDON, E8 3SF **Tel:** 020 8985 3570 **Fax:** 020 8986 1334
Email: mirellamanni@praservices.org.uk
Web site: http://www.praservices.org.uk
Publisher: Psychiatric Rehabilitation Association
Date Established: 1959
Frequency: Quarterly
Annual Sub.: £10.00
Circulation: 2,000 (Publisher's Statement)
Usual Pagination: 4
Editor: Mirella Manni
Summary of Content: Newsletter of the PRA. Contains information relating to community care for the mentally ill in East and North London.
Readership/Target Audience: Aimed at those involved with the rehabilitation of the mentally ill.

ADVERTISING: No Advertising taken
BUSINESS: LOCAL GOVERNMENT, LEISURE & RECREATION: Community Care & Social Services

PRACTICAL DIABETES INTERNATIONAL

40464U56L-20

Editorial Address: The Atrium, Southern Gate, CHICHESTER, PO19 8SQ **Tel:** 01243 770520
Fax: 01243 770144
Email: practical_diabetes@wiley.com
Advertising Address: As above. **Tel:** 01243 772018
Email: bhaughey@wiley.co.uk
Web site: http://www.interscience.wiley.com
ISSN: 1357-8170
Publisher: John Wiley & Sons Ltd
Frequency: 9 issues yearly - Combined issues Jan/Feb, Jul/Aug and Nov/Dec
Free to qualifying individuals
Annual Sub.: 86.00
Circulation: 18,000 (Publisher's Statement)
Usual Pagination: 56
Editor: Kenneth M. Shaw; **Executive Editor:** Sarah Blagbrough; **Editor-in-Chief:** Kenneth M. Shaw; **Managing Editor:** Caroline Birch
Summary of Content: Journal for the Diabetes Care Team, detailing information and features on the disease.
Readership/Target Audience: Aimed at those concerned with the care of people with diabetes.
ADVERTISING RATES:
Full Page Colour £2340.00
Agency Commission: 10%
Mechanical Data: Type Area: 270 x 175mm, Col Length: 270mm, Page Width: 175mm, Bleed Size: +6mm, Trim Size: 297 x 210mm, Film: Digital, Print Process: Web-fed offset litho
Copy instructions: Copy Date: 3 weeks prior to publication date
BUSINESS: HEALTH & MEDICAL: Disability & Rehabilitation

PRACTICAL FARM IDEAS QUARTERLY

37780U21A-900

Editorial Address: PO Box 1, WHITLAND, SA34 0HZ
Tel: 01994 240978 **Fax:** 01994 240978
Email: info@farmideas.co.uk
Advertising Address: As above.
Email: mike@farmideas.co.uk
Web site: http://www.farmideas.co.uk
Publisher: Mido Publications Ltd
Date Established: 1992
Frequency: Quarterly
Cover Price: £3.75
Annual Sub.: £14.85
Circulation: 8,400 (Publisher's Statement)
Usual Pagination: 48
Editor: Michael Donovan; **Advertising Manager:** Michael Donovan; **Publisher:** Michael Donovan
Summary of Content: Magazine covering machinery developments, new products and articles on money and time-saving ideas. Featuring machinery made and adapted by farmers for farmers.
Readership/Target Audience: Aimed at farmers, agricultural contractors and engineers, farm colleges and universities and those associated with agriculture.
ADVERTISING: Rates on application
Agency Commission: 10%
Average advertising content per issue: 2%
BUSINESS: AGRICULTURE & FARMING

PRACTICAL LAWYER

39229U44-1640

Editorial Address: Kensington Square House, 12-14 Ansdell Street, LONDON, W8 5BN **Tel:** 020 7396 9292
Fax: 020 7396 9300
Email: info@legalease.co.uk
Advertising Address: As above.
Web site: http://www.legalease.co.uk
ISSN: 0957-9281
Publisher: Legalease Ltd
Frequency: 10 issues yearly
Annual Sub.: £75.00
Circulation: 6,500 (Publisher's Statement)
Usual Pagination: 40
Editor: John Pritchard
Summary of Content: Digest of latest developments in the law, containing selected articles from a wide variety of magazines and journals.
Readership/Target Audience: Aimed at general practitioners and specialist legal professionals.
ADVERTISING: No Advertising taken
BUSINESS: LEGAL

PRACTICAL PATIENT CARE

1698860U56A-199

Formerly: International Review of Patient Care
Editorial Address: Brunel House, 55-57 North Wharf Road, LONDON, W2 1LA **Tel:** 020 7915 9789

Email: andrewtunnicliffe@spgmedia.com
Advertising Address: Sutton Place Business Centre, 49 Stoney Street, NOTTINGHAM, NG1 1LX **Tel:** 0115 989 5444
Fax: 0115 989 5445
Email: stuartmiller@spgmedia.com
Web site: http://www.hospitalmanagement.net
Publisher: SPG Media Ltd
Date Established: 2008
Frequency: Half-yearly - Published in March and September
Cover Price: £5.95
Circulation: 10,800 (ABC 01/07/2006 to 30/06/2007)
Usual Pagination: 110
Editor: Andrew Tunnicliffe
Summary of Content: Journal focusing on best practice for patient care, wound care management, patient monitoring and safety.
Readership/Target Audience: Aimed at physicians and medical specialists.
ADVERTISING RATES:
Full Page Colour £6900.00
Agency Commission: 15%
Mechanical Data: Type Area: 255 x 178mm, Bleed Size: 303 x 216mm, Trim Size: 297 x 210mm, Col Length: 255mm, Page Width: 178mm, Film: Digital
Average advertising content per issue: 40%
BUSINESS: HEALTH & MEDICAL

PRACTICAL PRE-SCHOOL

41089U62C-580

Editorial Address: St. Jude's Church, Dulwich Road, LONDON, SE24 0PB **Tel:** 020 7738 5454
Email: js@practicalpreschool.com
Advertising Address: As above. **Fax:** 020 7733 2325
Email: farhad.b@markallengroup.com
Web site: http://www.practicalpreschool.com
ISSN: 1366-610X
Publisher: Step Forward Publishing Ltd
Date Established: 1996
Frequency: Monthly - Published around the 1st of the cover month
Annual Sub.: £39.50
Circulation: 6,000 (Publisher's Statement)
Usual Pagination: 48
Editor: Sonali Hindmarch
Summary of Content: Magazine providing news, reviews of books and equipment, features, competitions and practical help and guidance.
Readership/Target Audience: Aimed at reception teachers, nursery teachers, managers, playgroups and pre-schools.
ADVERTISING RATES:
Full Page Colour £995.00
Agency Commission: 10%
Mechanical Data: Page Width: 186mm, Bleed Size: +4mm, Trim Size: 297 x 210mm, Film: Digital, Type Area: 262 x 186mm, Col Length: 262mm
Copy instructions: Copy Date: 3 weeks prior to publication date
Average advertising content per issue: 10%
BUSINESS: CHURCH & SCHOOL EQUIPMENT & EDUCATION: Junior Education

PRACTICE

38487U32G-86

Editorial Address: London Southbank University, 103 Borough Road, LONDON, SE1 0AA
Email: popplekj@lsbu.ac.uk
ISSN: 0950-3153
Publisher: Routledge, Taylor & Francis
Date Established: 1988
Frequency: Quarterly
Annual Sub.: £46.00
Usual Pagination: 72
Editor: Keith Popple
Summary of Content: Publication containing articles on social work and social care.
Readership/Target Audience: Aimed at social workers, practitioners, trainers, academics, policymakers, managers and anyone with professional interests or needs in the social work and social care field.
ADVERTISING: No Advertising taken
BUSINESS: LOCAL GOVERNMENT, LEISURE & RECREATION: Community Care & Social Services

PRACTICE BUSINESS

1748502U56R-521

Editorial Address: Suite 223, Business Design Centre, 52 Upper Street, LONDON, N1 0QH **Tel:** 020 7288 6833
Fax: 020 7288 6834
Email: suzannah.wright@intelligentmedia.co.uk
Advertising Address: As above.
Email: david.collingbourne@intelligentmedia.co.uk
Web site: http://www.practicebusiness.co.uk
Publisher: Intelligent Media Solutions
Date Established: 2006
Frequency: Monthly
Free to qualifying individuals
Circulation: 10,000 (Print Run)
Usual Pagination: 48

Editor: Suzannah Wright; **Advertising Manager:** David Collingbourne
Summary of Content: Magazine covering business management information for practice managers including industry specific news, views and opinions.
Readership/Target Audience: Aimed at primary care and general practice managers.
ADVERTISING RATES:
Full Page Colour £1875.00
Agency Commission: 10%
Mechanical Data: Type Area: 260 x 180mm, Bleed Size: 303 x 216mm, Trim Size: 297 x 210mm, Col Length: 260mm, Page Width: 180mm, Film: Digital
Average advertising content per issue: 35%
BUSINESS: HEALTH & MEDICAL: Health Medical Related

PRACTICE MANAGEMENT

40548U56R-185

Formerly: Primary Care Management Incorporating Practice Manager
Editorial Address: Unit 2, Riverview Business Park, Walnut Tree Close, GUILDFORD, GU1 4UX **Tel:** 01483 304944
Fax: 01483 303191
Email: jdyer@georgewarman.co.uk
Advertising Address: As above. **Fax:** 01433 303191
Email: ghenson@georgewarman.co.uk
Web site: http://www.primary-care-management.co.uk
ISSN: 1479-2818
Publisher: George Warman Publications (UK) Ltd
Date Established: 1990
Frequency: 10 issues yearly
Annual Sub.: £38.00
Circulation: 7,000 (Publisher's Statement)
Usual Pagination: 48
Editor: Jenny Dyer; **Managing Director:** Stuart Thompson; **Advertising Manager:** Gary Henson
Summary of Content: An educational resource concerned with the topic of advancing practice management.
Readership/Target Audience: Aimed at practice managers, primary care groups and trusts, GPs and health authorities.
ADVERTISING RATES:
Full Page Mono £650.00
Full Page Colour £950.00
SCC £19.00
Agency Commission: 10%
Mechanical Data: Type Area: 258 x 186mm, Trim Size: 285 x 210mm, Bleed Size: 291 x 216mm, Print Process: Sheet-fed, Film: Digital, Col Length: 258mm, Page Width: 186mm
Copy instructions: Copy Date: 2 weeks prior to publication date
Average advertising content per issue: 40%
BUSINESS: HEALTH & MEDICAL: Health Medical Related

PRACTICE NURSE

40327U56B-274

Editorial Address: The Boulevard, Langford Lane, KIDLINGTON, OX5 1GB **Tel:** 01865 843000
Fax: 01865 843965
Email: practice.nurse@elsevier.com
Advertising Address: 32 Jamestown Road, LONDON, NW1 7BY **Tel:** 020 7424 4200 **Fax:** 020 7424 4433
Email: b.keall@elsevier.com
Web site: http://www.practicenurse.net
ISSN: 0953-6612
Publisher: Elsevier Ltd
Date Established: 1988
Frequency: 22 issues yearly
Annual Sub.: £81.00
Circulation: 5,222 (ABC 01/01/2008 to 31/12/2008)
Usual Pagination: 80
Editor: Caley Montgomery; **News Editor:** Franchesca Robinson; **Advertising Manager:** Bethan Keall; **Managing Editor:** Caley Montgomery
Summary of Content: Journal covering clinical, professional, and prescribing news and information, with clinical features and educational articles.
Readership/Target Audience: Aimed at general practice nurses and all nurses in primary care from their first day in general practice through to highly specialised care.
ADVERTISING RATES:
Full Page Mono £1347.00
Full Page Colour £1659.00
Agency Commission: 10%
Mechanical Data: Film: Positive, right reading, emulsion side down. Digital, Type Area: 263 x 190mm, Print Process: Sheet-fed litho, Bleed Size: 286 x 216mm, Trim Size: 280 x 210mm, Col Length: 263mm, Page Width: 190mm
Copy instructions: Copy Date: 10 days prior to publication date
Average advertising content per issue: 30%
BUSINESS: HEALTH & MEDICAL: Nursing

PRACTICE NURSING

40328U56B-274_50

Editorial Address: St. Judes Church, Dulwich Road, LONDON, SE24 0PB **Tel:** 020 7738 5454
Fax: 020 7978 8316
Email: liam@markallengroup.com
Advertising Address: As above. **Fax:** 020 7733 2325
Email: matthewc@markallengroup.com

Web site: http://www.practicenursing.com
ISSN: 0964-9271
Publisher: M A Healthcare
Date Established: 1990
Frequency: Monthly
Annual Sub.: £114.00
Circulation: 5,498 (ABC 01/01/2008 to 31/12/2008)
Usual Pagination: 52
Editor: Liam Benison; **Publisher:** Matthew Cianfarani
Summary of Content: Magazine containing education, protocols, clinical and general articles.
Readership/Target Audience: Aimed at practice nurses.
ADVERTISING RATES:
Full Page Mono £2000.00
Full Page Colour £2000.00
Agency Commission: 10%
Mechanical Data: Type Area: 245 x 186mm, Bleed Size: 298 x 221mm, Trim Size: 292 x 215mm, Col Length: 245mm, Page Width: 186mm, Film: Digital
Average advertising content per issue: 30%
BUSINESS: HEALTH & MEDICAL: Nursing

THE PRACTISING MIDWIFE
40329U56B-274_55
Editorial Address: 54 Siward Road, BROMLEY, BR2 9JZ
Tel: 020 8464 0304 **Fax:** 0871 224 7390
Email: prac.mid@ntlworld.com
Advertising Address: As above. **Tel:** 01483 824094
Fax: 0870 163 9987
Email: margifloate@btinternet.com
Web site: http://www.thepractisingmidwife.com
ISSN: 1461-3123
Publisher: Elsevier Health Sciences
Date Established: 1998
Frequency: 11 issues yearly - Combined issue July/August
Annual Sub.: £55.00
Circulation: 5,005 (ABC 01/01/2008 to 31/12/2008)
Usual Pagination: 44
Editor: Laura Yeates; **Advertising Manager:** Margaret Floate; **Managing Editor:** Laura Yeates
Summary of Content: Journal containing news, reviews, methods, protocol and other features on midwifery.
Readership/Target Audience: Read by midwives and student midwives.
ADVERTISING RATES:
Full Page Mono £650.00
Full Page Colour £950.00
SCC £19.00
Agency Commission: 10%
Mechanical Data: Bleed Size: 286 x 216mm, Trim Size: 280 x 210mm, Type Area: 263 x 190mm, Col Length: 263mm, Page Width: 190mm
BUSINESS: HEALTH & MEDICAL: Nursing

PREMIER CONSTRUCTION
767102U42A-215
Editorial Address: 1 Livsey Street, ROCHDALE, OL16 1ST
Tel: 01706 719972 **Fax:** 0845 458 4446
Email: premierconstruction@romauk.net
Web site: http://www.romauk.net
Publisher: Roma Publications Ltd
Date Established: 1999
Frequency: Monthly
Annual Sub.: £39.50
Circulation: 15,000 (Publisher's Statement)
Editor: Lesley Coward
Summary of Content: Magazine covering news and developments within the construction industry.
Readership/Target Audience: Aimed at government authorities, housing associations, architects, main contractors, decision makers and investors.
ADVERTISING: No Advertising taken
BUSINESS: CONSTRUCTION

PRENATAL DIAGNOSIS
40550U56R-180
Editorial Address: The Atrium, Southern Gate, CHICHESTER, PO19 8SQ **Tel:** 01243 779777
Fax: 01243 770460
Email: rhughes@wiley.com
Advertising Address: As above. **Tel:** 01243 770254
Fax: 01243 770432
Email: adsales@wiley.co.uk
Web site: http://www.interscience.wiley.com
ISSN: 0197-3851
Publisher: John Wiley & Sons Ltd
Date Established: 1981
Frequency: 13 issues yearly
Annual Sub.: £945.00
Usual Pagination: 104
Editor: Richard Hughes
Summary of Content: Journal containing results from original research in a variety of clinical and scientific specialities concerned with in-utero diagnosis of foetal abnormality resulting from genetic and environmental factors.
Readership/Target Audience: Read by clinical geneticists, obstetricians, paediatricians and radiologists.

ADVERTISING RATES:
Full Page Mono £1175.00
Full Page Colour £2575.00
Agency Commission: 10%
Mechanical Data: Type Area: 270 x 180mm, Col Length: 270mm, Page Width: 180mm, Trim Size: 297 x 210mm, Print Process: Sheet-fed litho, Screen: 54 lpc, Film: Mono Negative, right reading, emulsion side down Colour Positive, right reading, emulsion side down. Digital
BUSINESS: HEALTH & MEDICAL: Health Medical Related

PREP SCHOOL
41104U62E-420
Editorial Address: Abbey Cottage, Blythburgh, HALESWORTH, IP19 9LQ **Tel:** 01502 478521
Email: david@dtytler.freeserve.co.uk
Advertising Address: 12 Deben Mill Business Centre, Melton, WOODBRIDGE, IP12 1BL **Tel:** 01394 389850
Fax: 01394 386893
Email: sales@johncatt.co.uk
Web site: http://www.prepschoolmag.co.uk
ISSN: 0963-8601
Publisher: John Catt Educational Ltd
Frequency: 3 issues yearly - Published in January, May and September
Free to qualifying individuals
Annual Sub.: £10.00
Circulation: 5,000 (Publisher's Statement)
Usual Pagination: 52
Editor: David Tytler
Summary of Content: Magazine covering news in junior independent education regarding teaching methods, equipment and current political thought.
Readership/Target Audience: Aimed at headteachers, staff, governors, parents and bursars.
ADVERTISING RATES:
Full Page Colour £1820.00
Agency Commission: 10%
Mechanical Data: Type Area: 267 x 188mm, Bleed Size: 303 x 216mm, Trim Size: 297 x 210mm, Col Length: 267mm, Page Width: 188mm, Print Process: Litho, Film: Digital
BUSINESS: CHURCH & SCHOOL EQUIPMENT & EDUCATION: Preparatory & Independent Schools

PRESCRIBER
40217U56A-115
Editorial Address: The Atrium, Southern Gate, CHICHESTER, PO19 8SQ **Tel:** 01243 770237
Fax: 01243 770144
Email: prescriber@wiley.com
Advertising Address: As above. **Tel:** 01243 779777
Email: sripsher@wiley.com
Web site: http://www.prescriber.co.uk
ISSN: 0959-6682
Publisher: Wiley Interface Ltd
Date Established: 1990
Frequency: 24 issues yearly
Cover Price: £9.00
Free to qualifying individuals
Annual Sub.: £93.00
Circulation: 21,923 (Publisher's Statement)
Editor: Tim Dean
Summary of Content: Journal containing commissioned articles about rational prescribing.
Readership/Target Audience: Aimed at general practitioners.
ADVERTISING RATES:
Full Page Mono £1380.00
Full Page Colour £1840.00
Agency Commission: 10%
Mechanical Data: Col Length: 243mm, Film: Digital, Type Area: 243 x 167mm, Bleed Size: 281 x 216mm, Trim Size: 275 x 210mm, Page Width: 167mm
Copy instructions: Copy Date: 2 weeks prior to publication date
Average advertising content per issue: 45%
BUSINESS: HEALTH & MEDICAL

PRESERVED MILK
26044U21G-92
Editorial Address: 80 Calverley Road, TUNBRIDGE WELLS, TN1 2UN **Tel:** 020 7017 7500 **Fax:** 020 7017 7599
Email: marketing@agra-net.com
Web site: http://www.agra-net.com
ISSN: 0141-223X
Publisher: Agra Informa Ltd
Frequency: 10 issues yearly
Annual Sub.: £879.00
Summary of Content: Report on European and international statistics on trade, production and prices for skimmed and whole milk powder, casein, whey and condensed milk.
Readership/Target Audience: Aimed at those in the global preserved milk industry.
ADVERTISING: No Advertising taken
BUSINESS: AGRICULTURE & FARMING: Milk

PRESS
714950U41A-143
Editorial Address: Cleeve Road, LEATHERHEAD, KT22 7RU **Tel:** 01372 802050 **Fax:** 01372 802239
Email: infocentre@pira-international.com
Web site: http://www.piranet.com
ISSN: 1475-0910
Publisher: PIRA International
Date Established: 2001
Frequency: Monthly
Annual Sub.: £850.00
Usual Pagination: 130
Editor: Gillian Micklewright
Summary of Content: Journal covering all aspects of the printing industry.
Readership/Target Audience: Aimed at those involved in the printing industry.
ADVERTISING: No Advertising taken
BUSINESS: PRINTING & STATIONERY: Printing

PRESS GAZETTE
35620U2B-207
Editorial Address: 7 Carmelite Street, LONDON, EC4Y 0DR
Tel: 020 7936 6432
Email: pged@pressgazette.co.uk
Advertising Address: As above.
Web site: http://www.pressgazette.co.uk
ISSN: 0041-5170
Publisher: Progressive Media Group
Date Established: 1965
Frequency: Monthly
Cover Price: £3.00
Annual Sub.: £115.00
Circulation: 6,000 (Publisher's Statement)
Usual Pagination: 64
Editor: Dominic Ponsford
Summary of Content: Magazine and website for all journalists and all those interested in UK journalism.
Readership/Target Audience: Aimed at newspaper, radio, TV and magazine journalists, also journalism managers, lawyers and PR contacts.
ADVERTISING: Rates on application
Supplement(s): Journalism Training Supplement - 1xY
BUSINESS: COMMUNICATIONS, ADVERTISING & MARKETING: Press

PRESSURE SENSITIVE INDUSTRY YEARBOOK
26077U35-210
Editorial Address: PO Box 14, DORKING, RH5 4YN
Tel: 01306 884473 **Fax:** 01306 884473
Email: info@datatranscripts.com
Web site: http://www.datatranscripts.com
ISSN: 1361-1631
Publisher: Data Transcripts
Date Established: 1998
Frequency: Annual - Published in December
Cover Price: £395.00
Circulation: 2,500 (Publisher's Statement)
Usual Pagination: 136
Editor: Lynda Crane; **Publisher:** Robert Higham
Summary of Content: Publication covering all aspects of tapes and labels.
Readership/Target Audience: Read by senior management in production, marketing and sales.
ADVERTISING: No Advertising taken
BUSINESS: PACKAGING & BOTTLING

PRESSWATCH COMPANY RANKINGS
35627U2B-180
Formerly: PressWatch Quarterly
Editorial Address: 66 Wilson Street, LONDON, EC2A 2JX
Tel: 020 7868 6080
Email: info@presswatch.com
Web site: http://www.presswatch.com
Publisher: TNS Media
Frequency: Quarterly
Cover Price: £300.00
Annual Sub.: £3595.00
Circulation: 90 (Publisher's Statement)
Usual Pagination: 60
Editor: Dominic Mills
Summary of Content: Reports assessing the top 2000 UK companies according to the negative or positive coverage they receive in the UK national press.
ADVERTISING: No Advertising taken
BUSINESS: COMMUNICATIONS, ADVERTISING & MARKETING: Press

PRESSWATCH FINANCIAL PRODUCTS
622925U1A-273_17
Editorial Address: 66 Wilson Street, LONDON, EC2A 2JX
Tel: 020 7868 6080
Email: info@presswatch.com
Web site: http://www.tnsmi.com
Publisher: TNS Media

Date Established: 1999
Frequency: Monthly
Cover Price: £300.00
Annual Sub.: £3595.00
Circulation: 80 (Publisher's Statement)
Usual Pagination: 60
Editor: Dominic Mills
Summary of Content: Report containing an independent ranking of financial service companies and their products.
Readership/Target Audience: Aimed at financial executives, public relations and marketing departments.
ADVERTISING: No Advertising taken
BUSINESS: FINANCE & ECONOMICS

PRESTIGE HOTEL AND HIGH STREET INTERIORS   41599U64S-200

Formerly: Prestige High Street Interiors
Editorial Address: PO Box 523, HORSHAM, RH12 4WL
Tel: 01293 871201 **Fax:** 01293 871301
Email: newsdesk123@aol.com
Advertising Address: As above.
Publisher: Albatross Publications
Frequency: 3 issues yearly - No set months of publication
Annual Sub.: £8.00
Circulation: 3,000 (Publisher's Statement)
Usual Pagination: 24
Editor: Carol Andrews; **Advertising Manager:** Carol Andrews
Summary of Content: Magazine of design for hotels and retail outlets.
Readership/Target Audience: Aimed at interior designers, hotel groups, hotels, retail outlets, banks and building societies.
ADVERTISING RATES:
Full Page Mono £495.00
Full Page Colour £650.00
Agency Commission: 10%
Mechanical Data: Trim Size: 297 x 210mm, Bleed Size: 300 x 213mm, Print Process: Litho, Type Area: 256 x 179mm, Col Length: 256mm, Page Width: 179mm, Film: Digital
Copy instructions: Copy Date: 4 weeks prior to publication date
Average advertising content per issue: 10%
BUSINESS: OTHER CLASSIFICATIONS: Shop Equipment

PREVENTIVE DENTISTRY   1790526U56D-205

Editorial Address: 1 Hertford House, Hugo Gryn Way, Farm Close, SHENLEY, WD7 9AB **Tel:** 01923 851777
Fax: 01923 851778
Email: thomas.roberts@fmc.co.uk
Advertising Address: As above.
Email: michelle.mchutchison@fmc.co.uk
Web site: http://www.preventivedentistry.co.uk
ISSN: 1748-8168
Publisher: Finlayson Media Communications Ltd
Date Established: 2006
Frequency: 6 issues yearly
Annual Sub.: £90.00
Circulation: 5,000 (Publisher's Statement)
Usual Pagination: 60
Editor: Thomas Roberts; **Advertising Manager:** Michelle McHutchison; **Managing Editor:** Thomas Roberts
Summary of Content: Journal covering items of interest for dental hygienists and therapists including oral health and periodontics, business, interviews and product news.
Readership/Target Audience: Aimed at dental hygienists and therapists.
ADVERTISING RATES:
Full Page Mono £2365.00
Full Page Colour £2365.00
Mechanical Data: Type Area: 287 x 200mm, Bleed Size: 303 x 216mm, Trim Size: 297 x 210mm, Col Length: 287mm, Page Width: 200mm, No. of Columns (Display): 8, Film: Digital
Copy instructions: Copy Date: 2 weeks prior to publication date
BUSINESS: HEALTH & MEDICAL: Dental

PREVIEW   1794074U64C-204

Editorial Address: Gainsborough House, 2 Sheen Road, RICHMOND, TW9 1AE **Tel:** 020 8973 2611
Email: justin@alchemymedia.co.uk
Advertising Address: As above.
Email: hugh@clubmirror.com
Web site: http://www.alchemymedia.co.uk
Publisher: Alchemy Media
Frequency: Monthly
Free to qualifying individuals
Circulation: 31,094 (Publisher's Statement)
Editor: Justin O'Regan; **Advertising Director:** Hugh Jenkins
Summary of Content: Magazine providing listings for Sky sports features and programmes and trade features.
Readership/Target Audience: Aimed at managers of pubs and clubs.
ADVERTISING RATES:
Full Page Colour £3925.00

SCC £22.00
Agency Commission: 10%
Mechanical Data: Type Area: 278 x 190mm, Bleed Size: 306 x 216mm, Trim Size: 297 x 210mm, Col Length: 278mm, Page Width: 190mm, Film: Digital
Copy instructions: Copy Date: 20th of the month prior to publication date
Average advertising content per issue: 10%
BUSINESS: OTHER CLASSIFICATIONS: Clubs

PRIMARY CARE TODAY   38488U32G-88

Editorial Address: Trelawney House, Chestergate, MACCLESFIELD, SK11 6DW **Tel:** 01625 667610
Fax: 01625 500286
Email: linda.towell@tenalpspublishing.com
Advertising Address: As above. **Tel:** 01625 613000
Fax: 01625 435076
Email: jim.kerr@tenalpspublishing.com
Web site: http://www.primarycaretoday.co.uk
Publisher: Ten Alps Publishing
Frequency: Quarterly - Published in the 1st week of the cover month
Cover Price: Free
Circulation: 35,000 (Publisher's Statement)
Usual Pagination: 20
Editor: Linda Towell; **News Editor:** Norma Beavers
Summary of Content: Newspaper covering management issues, including training, IT, clinical practice and information on running a surgery.
Readership/Target Audience: Aimed at GPs, health authorities, nurses and primary care trusts.
ADVERTISING RATES:
Full Page Colour £2500.00
Agency Commission: 10%
Mechanical Data: Film: Digital, Type Area: 360 x 267mm, Col Length: 360mm, Col Widths (Display): 32mm, Page Width: 267mm, No. of Columns (Display): 8
Copy instructions: Copy Date: 4 weeks prior to publication date
Average advertising content per issue: 30%
BUSINESS: LOCAL GOVERNMENT, LEISURE & RECREATION: Community Care & Social Services

PRIMARY HEALTH CARE   38489U32G-90

Editorial Address: The Heights, 59-65 Lowlands Road, HARROW, HA1 3AW **Tel:** 020 8423 1066
Fax: 020 8872 3198
Email: julie.sylvester@rcnpublishing.co.uk
Advertising Address: As above. **Fax:** 020 8423 9196
Email: neil.hobson@rcnpublishing.co.uk
Web site: http://www.primaryhealthcare.net
ISSN: 0264-5033
Publisher: RCN Publishing Co Ltd
Frequency: 10 issues yearly - Published in the 1st week of the cover month
Annual Sub.: £40.00
Circulation: 7,267 (ABC 01/01/2008 to 31/12/2008)
Usual Pagination: 52
Editor: Julie Sylvester; **Managing Director:** Linda Thomas
Summary of Content: Magazine focusing on news, views, opinions and clinical research in health care.
Readership/Target Audience: Read by staff in health centres, health clinics and major group practices in the UK.
ADVERTISING RATES:
Full Page Colour £2299.00
Agency Commission: 10%
Mechanical Data: Type Area: 271 x 178mm, Col Length: 271mm, Trim Size: 297 x 210mm, Bleed Size: 303 x 216mm, Film: Digital, Page Width: 178mm
Copy instructions: Copy Date: 6 weeks prior to publication date
Average advertising content per issue: 40%
BUSINESS: LOCAL GOVERNMENT, LEISURE & RECREATION: Community Care & Social Services

PRIMARY HEALTH CARE RESEARCH & DEVELOPMENT   623215U32G-91

Editorial Address: The Edinburgh Building, Shaftesbury Road, CAMBRIDGE, CB2 2RU **Tel:** 01223 326070
Fax: 01223 325150
Advertising Address: As above.
Email: ads_sales@cambridge.org
Web site: http://www.cambridge.org/uk/
ISSN: 1463-4326
Publisher: Cambridge University Press
Date Established: 2000
Frequency: Quarterly
Cover Price: £63.00
Usual Pagination: 96
Editor: Rosamund Bryar
Summary of Content: Journal covering all aspects of primary health care including policy and research developments, prevention, health promotion, education, clinical effectiveness and organizational, quality and management issues.

Readership/Target Audience: Aimed at practitioners and researchers in primary health care.
ADVERTISING: Rates on application
BUSINESS: LOCAL GOVERNMENT, LEISURE & RECREATION: Community Care & Social Services

PRIMARY MATHEMATICS   41096U62C-610

Editorial Address: 259 London Road, LEICESTER, LE2 3BE
Tel: 0116 221 0013 **Fax:** 0116 212 2835
Email: primarymaths@m-a.org.uk
Advertising Address: As above.
Email: jcpadvertising@yahoo.co.uk
Web site: http://www.m-a.org.uk
ISSN: 1465-0495
Publisher: The Mathematical Association
Frequency: 3 issues yearly - Published in Spring, Summer and Winter
Circulation: 1,300 (Publisher's Statement)
Usual Pagination: 28
Editor: Lynne McClure; **Advertising Manager:** Janet Powell
Summary of Content: Contains articles, notes and reviews.
Readership/Target Audience: Read by teachers in primary schools.
ADVERTISING: Rates on application
BUSINESS: CHURCH & SCHOOL EQUIPMENT & EDUCATION: Junior Education

PRIMARY MUSIC TODAY   41040U62B-830

Editorial Address: Faculty of Education, Edge Hill University, St. Helens Road, ORMSKIRK, L39 4QP
Tel: 01695 650998
Email: ian.shirley@edgehill.ac.uk
Advertising Address: Scout Bottom Farm, Mytholmroyd, HEBDEN BRIDGE, HX7 5JS **Tel:** 01422 886722
Fax: 01422 886157
Email: ian@recordermail.demon.co.uk
Web site: http://www.primarymusictoday.co.uk
ISSN: 1356-5745
Publisher: Peacock Press
Date Established: 1994
Frequency: 3 issues yearly - Published in February, May and October
Annual Sub.: £18.00
Circulation: 2,000 (Publisher's Statement)
Editor: Ian Shirley; **Advertising Manager:** Ian Davies; **Publisher:** Jeremy Burbidge
Summary of Content: Magazine providing help and advice for all those involved in music education in UK primary and nursery education.
Readership/Target Audience: Aimed at teachers involved with music in primary schools.
ADVERTISING RATES:
Full Page Mono £400.00
Agency Commission: 10%
Mechanical Data: Type Area: 264 x 180mm, Col Length: 264mm, Page Width: 180mm, Trim Size: 297 x 210mm
Copy instructions: Copy Date: 4 weeks prior to publication date
BUSINESS: CHURCH & SCHOOL EQUIPMENT & EDUCATION: Education Teachers

PRIMARY SCIENCE REVIEW   41043U62B-900

Editorial Address: College Lane, HATFIELD, AL10 9AA
Tel: 01707 283000
Email: helen.a.johnson@btinternet.com
Advertising Address: As above.
Email: rebecca@ase.org.uk
Web site: http://www.ase.org.uk
ISSN: 0269-2465
Publisher: The Association for Science Education
Date Established: 1986
Frequency: 5 issues yearly
Free to qualifying individuals
Annual Sub.: £53.00
Circulation: 3,000 (Publisher's Statement)
Usual Pagination: 40
Editor: Helen Johnson; **Executive Editor:** Helen Johnson; **Advertising Manager:** Rebecca Dixon-Watmough
Summary of Content: Refereed professional journal about science in primary education.
Readership/Target Audience: Aimed at primary teachers, advisers, teacher trainers, and student teachers.
ADVERTISING RATES:
Full Page Mono £400.00
Full Page Colour £400.00
Agency Commission: 10%
Mechanical Data: Type Area: 266 x 190mm, Bleed Size: 303 x 216mm, Trim Size: 297 x 210mm, Col Length: 266mm, Page Width: 190mm, Film: Digital
Copy instructions: Copy Date: 6 weeks prior to publication date
Average advertising content per issue: 5%
BUSINESS: CHURCH & SCHOOL EQUIPMENT & EDUCATION: Education Teachers

Business Magazines

PRINT AND PAPER BUYER
38929U41A-150

Editorial Address: Oxbrook Farm, Hoby Road, Thrussington, LEICESTER, LE7 4TH **Tel:** 01664 424752
Fax: 01664 424678
Email: editorial4ppb@aol.com
Advertising Address: As above.
Email: sales4ppb@aol.com
Web site: http://www.theprintandpaperbuyer.co.uk
ISSN: 0267-7644
Publisher: D. Riley Carrington & Co. Publications
Date Established: 1983
Frequency: 6 issues yearly
Annual Sub.: £45.00
Circulation: 6,750 (Publisher's Statement)
Usual Pagination: 24
Editor: Duncan Cook; **Advertising Manager:** Peter Williams
Summary of Content: Magazine containing features and news about the print, pre-press, paper and packaging industry.
Readership/Target Audience: Read by senior print buyers, contract managers and marketing directors of blue-chip corporates, advertising and design agencies, publishers and other related industries.
ADVERTISING RATES:
Full Page Mono £1295.00
Full Page Colour £1895.00
SCC £30.00
Agency Commission: 10%
Mechanical Data: Trim Size: 297 x 210mm
Copy instructions: Copy Date: 4 weeks prior to publication date
Average advertising content per issue: 60%
BUSINESS: PRINTING & STATIONERY: Printing

PRINT & PAPER MONTHLY
38713U36-150

Formerly: Print & Paper Europe
Editorial Address: 30 London Road, Southborough, TUNBRIDGE WELLS, TN4 0RE **Tel:** 01892 542099
Fax: 01892 546693
Email: susan.w@whitmar.co.uk
Advertising Address: As above. **Tel:** 01892 514991
Email: david.g@whitmar.co.uk
Web site: http://www.paperandprint.com
ISSN: 1746-7179
Publisher: Whitmar Publications Ltd
Date Established: 1989
Frequency: Monthly - Published in the 1st week of the cover month
Free to qualifying individuals
Annual Sub.: £110.00
Circulation: 11,967 (ABC 01/01/2008 to 31/12/2008)
Usual Pagination: 46
Editor: Susan Wright; **Managing Editor:** Susan Wright; **Publisher:** Rob Mulligan
Summary of Content: Magazine focusing on promoting the sale of paper and print products. Informs paper and print users of sources and supply developments within the European market.
Readership/Target Audience: Aimed at printers, buyers and specifiers of paper and print related products.
ADVERTISING RATES:
Full Page Colour £2999.00
Agency Commission: 10%
Mechanical Data: Type Area: 268 x 186mm, Print Process: Sheet-fed offset litho, Bleed Size: 303 x 216mm, Trim Size: 297 x 210mm, Col Length: 268mm, Page Width: 186mm, Film: Digital
Copy instructions: Copy Date: 2 weeks prior to publication date
Average advertising content per issue: 40%
BUSINESS: PAPER

THE PRINT BUSINESS
1703127U41A-337

Editorial Address: 28A Jubilee Trade Centre, Jubilee Road, LETCHWORTH GARDEN CITY, SG6 1SP **Tel:** 01462 678300
Fax: 01462 481622
Email: editorial@firstcitymedia.co.uk
Advertising Address: As above.
Email: jacqui.gray@firstcitymedia.co.uk
Web site: http://www.printmag.co.uk
Publisher: First City Media
Date Established: 2005
Frequency: Monthly
Cover Price: Free
Circulation: 12,909 (ABC 01/07/2007 to 30/06/2008)
Usual Pagination: 76
Editor: Gareth Ward
Summary of Content: Magazine covering the latest market intelligence, case studies, technology breakthroughs and customer insights.
Readership/Target Audience: Aimed at owners, executives, senior management, buyers and opinion formers within the print community.
ADVERTISING RATES:
Full Page Colour £2420.00
Agency Commission: 10%
Mechanical Data: Bleed Size: 303 x 216mm, Trim Size: 297 x 210mm, Film: Digital

Copy instructions: Copy Date: 1 week prior to publication date
Average advertising content per issue: 40%
BUSINESS: PRINTING & STATIONERY: Printing

PRINT MEDIA MANAGEMENT
766741U41A-326

Editorial Address: 28A Jubilee Trade Centre, Jubilee Road, LETCHWORTH GARDEN CITY, SG6 1SP **Tel:** 01462 678300
Fax: 01462 481622
Email: editorial@firstcitymedia.co.uk
Advertising Address: As above.
Email: james.hall@firstcitymedia.co.uk
Web site: http://www.printmediamag.co.uk
ISSN: 1745-5944
Publisher: First City Media
Date Established: 2002
Frequency: Monthly - Published around the beginning of the cover month
Cover Price: Free
Editor: Andy Knaggs; **Advertising Manager:** James Hall
Summary of Content: Magazine covering digital and print management, case studies, news and features on the print media industry.
Readership/Target Audience: Aimed at all those involved with the creation, processing and distribution of print in publishing, advertising and creative agencies, corporate and public sectors.
ADVERTISING RATES:
Full Page Colour £2755.00
Agency Commission: 10%
Mechanical Data: Type Area: 270 x 190mm, Bleed Size: 303 x 216mm, Trim Size: 297 x 210mm, Col Length: 270mm, Page Width: 190mm, Film: Digital
Copy instructions: Copy Date: 2 weeks prior to publication date
Average advertising content per issue: 40%
BUSINESS: PRINTING & STATIONERY: Printing

PRINT MONTHLY
768006U41A-327

Formerly: Repro-Link Magazine
Editorial Address: 1st Floor Offices, 27-31 Church Road, Lawrence Hill, BRISTOL, BS5 9JJ **Fax:** 0117 954 1476
Email: editor@printmonthly.co.uk
Advertising Address: As above. **Tel:** 0117 954 7370
Email: bevan@linkpublishing.co.uk
Publisher: Link Publishing
Date Established: 1992
Frequency: Monthly - Published in the 1st week of the cover month
Annual Sub.: £35.00
Circulation: 12,000 (Publisher's Statement)
Usual Pagination: 100
Editor: James Matthews-Paul
Summary of Content: Magazine covering the latest developments in printing.
Readership/Target Audience: Aimed at those working within the printing industry.
ADVERTISING RATES:
Full Page Colour £1675.00
Agency Commission: 10%
Mechanical Data: Film: Digital, Type Area: 267 x 180mm, Bleed Size: 303 x 216mm, Trim Size: 297 x 210mm, Col Length: 267mm, Page Width: 180mm
Copy instructions: Copy Date: 1 week prior to publication date
Average advertising content per issue: 70%
BUSINESS: PRINTING & STATIONERY: Printing

PRINTERS WORKSHOP
38935U41A-175_57

Editorial Address: Nithsdale House, 159 Cambridge Street, AYLESBURY, HP20 1BQ **Tel:** 01296 434381
Email: edit@printersworkshop.co.uk
Advertising Address: As above.
Email: pw@genesis-prepress.co.uk
Publisher: Genesis
Date Established: 1990
Frequency: 10 issues yearly - Published in the middle of the cover month
Free to qualifying individuals
Annual Sub.: £24.50
Circulation: 6,500 (Publisher's Statement)
Usual Pagination: 16
Editor: Tony Muir; **Advertising Manager:** Teresa Selfe; **Managing Editor:** Tony Muir; **Publisher:** Tony Muir
Summary of Content: Magazine containing news and information for the printing industry.
Readership/Target Audience: Aimed at people involved in the print industry.
ADVERTISING RATES:
Full Page Colour £870.00
SCC £16.50
Agency Commission: 10%
Mechanical Data: Trim Size: 297 x 210mm, Film: Digital, Type Area: 265 x 190mm, Col Length: 265mm, Page Width: 190mm
BUSINESS: PRINTING & STATIONERY: Printing

PRINTMAKING TODAY
1899395U41A-343

Editorial Address: 99-101 Kingsland Road, LONDON, E2 8AG, **Tel:** 020 7739 8645
Email: annedesmet@pt.cellopress.co.uk
Web site: http://www.cellopress.co.uk/celloweb
Publisher: Cello Press Limited
Date Established: 1990
Frequency: Quarterly - Published in March, June, September and December
Annual Sub.: £23.00
Editor: Anne Desmet
Summary of Content: Journal of the Royal Society of Painter-Printmakers.
Readership/Target Audience: Aimed at artists, curators and collectors.
BUSINESS: PRINTING & STATIONERY: Printing

PRINTVIEW
38658U34-82

Editorial Address: 28 Cotswold Close, BASINGSTOKE, RG22 5BA **Tel:** 968 97 06 51
Email: barryhickley@hotmail.com
Web site: http://www.intelligentview.info
Publisher: EP Market Intelligence
Date Established: 1993
Frequency: Monthly
Annual Sub.: £350.00
Circulation: 600 (Publisher's Statement)
Usual Pagination: 30
Editor: Barry Hickley; **Managing Director:** Barry Hickley
Summary of Content: European newsletter containing information and advice on electronic document production and management including imaging and process related software.
Readership/Target Audience: Aimed at people working in the print trade and organisations using printing systems.
ADVERTISING: No Advertising taken
BUSINESS: OFFICE EQUIPMENT

PRINTWEAR & PROMOTION
38938U41A-178

Editorial Address: 15A London Road, MAIDSTONE, ME16 8LY **Tel:** 01622 687031 **Fax:** 01622 757646
Email: nbarston@datateam.co.uk
Advertising Address: As above.
Email: rsmith@datateam.co.uk
Web site: http://www.printwearandpromotion.co.uk
ISSN: 0967-2486
Publisher: Datateam Publishing Ltd
Frequency: Monthly - Published on the 1st of the cover month
Free to qualifying individuals
Annual Sub.: £35.00
Circulation: 5,810 (ABC 01/01/2008 to 31/12/2008)
Usual Pagination: 120
Editor: Neill Barston; **Advertising Manager:** Richard Smith
Summary of Content: Magazine concentrating on screen-printing, heat transfers, digital printing and decorative embroidery for leisure and sportswear, workwear textiles and t-shirts. Also covers marketing, promotions and incentives.
Readership/Target Audience: Aimed at garment decorators in the leisurewear and promotional industry.
ADVERTISING RATES:
Full Page Colour £1549.00
Agency Commission: 10%
Mechanical Data: Type Area: 254 x 178mm, Trim Size: 297 x 210mm, Bleed Size: 303 x 216mm, Film: Digital, Col Length: 254mm, Page Width: 178mm
Average advertising content per issue: 50%
Supplement(s): Printwear Show Guide - 1xY, Yearbook - 1xY
BUSINESS: PRINTING & STATIONERY: Printing

PRINTWEAR TODAY
1809580U41A-339

Editorial Address: Mayer House, 70 Collington Avenue, BEXHILL-ON-SEA, TN39 3RA **Tel:** 01424 217888
Email: nick@mayerhouse.co.uk
Advertising Address: As above. **Fax:** 01424 211005
Email: nick@mayerhouse.co.uk
Web site: http://www.mayerhousebusinessmedia.co.uk
ISSN: 1753-2760
Publisher: Mayer House Business Media Limited
Date Established: 2007
Frequency: Monthly - Published around the 3rd week of the cover month
Cover Price: Free
Circulation: 6,112 (Publisher's Statement)
Usual Pagination: 48
Editor: Nick Carpenter; **News Editor:** Colin Gillman; **Features Editor:** Alison Bowie; **Managing Director:** Nick Carpenter; **Advertising Manager:** Nick Carpenter
Summary of Content: Magazine providing news, features and articles reflecting current and forward-thinking market conditions for the UK garment decorating industry.
Readership/Target Audience: Aimed at printers, embroiderers, garment decorators, manufacturers, distributors, wholesalers and suppliers.

ADVERTISING RATES:
Full Page Colour £1250.00
Agency Commission: 10%
Mechanical Data: Type Area: 258 x 179mm, Bleed Size: 303 x 213mm, Trim Size: 297 x 210mm, Col Length: 258mm, Page Width: 179mm, Film: Digital
Copy instructions: Copy Date: 2 weeks prior to publication date
Average advertising content per issue: 40%
BUSINESS: PRINTING & STATIONERY: Printing

PRINTWEEK
38934U41A-179

Editorial Address: 11-17 Wolverton Gardens, LONDON, W6 7DY **Tel:** 020 8267 4221 **Fax:** 020 8267 4455
Email: printweek.newsdesk@haymarket.com
Advertising Address: 174 Hammersmith Road, LONDON, W6 7JP **Tel:** 020 8267 4008 **Fax:** 020 8267 4521
Email: chrissie.roberts@haymarket.com
Web site: http://www.printweek.com
Publisher: Haymarket Business Media Ltd
Frequency: Weekly - Published on Friday
Cover Price: £2.95
Free to qualifying individuals
Annual Sub.: £97.00
Circulation: 16,536 (ABC 01/01/2008 to 31/12/2008)
Usual Pagination: 80
Editor: William Mitting; **News Editor:** William Mitting;
Executive Editor: Barney Cox; **Features Editor:** Simon Creasey
Summary of Content: Magazine covering printing news, technology and trends.
Readership/Target Audience: Aimed at those within the printing industry.
ADVERTISING RATES:
Full Page Mono £3479.00
Full Page Colour £3479.00
Agency Commission: 10%
Mechanical Data: Page Width: 190mm, Film: Digital, Type Area: 260 x 190mm, Col Length: 260mm, Trim Size: 280 x 210mm, Bleed Size: 288 x 216mm
Copy instructions: Copy Date: 1 week prior to publication date
Average advertising content per issue: 13%
Supplement(s): The Annual Buyers' Guide - 1xY
BUSINESS: PRINTING & STATIONERY: Printing

PRISON SERVICE NEWS
711365U32R-340

Editorial Address: Room 717, Cleland House, Page Street, LONDON, SW1P 4LN **Tel:** 020 7217 2118
Fax: 020 7217 2156
Email: psnmail@btconnect.com
Advertising Address: Mcmillan Scott plc, 10 Savoy Street, LONDON, WC2E 7HR **Tel:** 020 7240 2032
Fax: 020 7379 7118
Web site: http://www.hmprisonservice.gov.uk
ISSN: 0264-1461
Publisher: The Prison Service
Date Established: 1982
Frequency: 6 issues yearly
Cover Price: Free
Circulation: 21,000 (Publisher's Statement)
Usual Pagination: 40
Editor: Pete Huntingford
Summary of Content: Magazine focusing on news and views related to the management of prisons and their policies.
Readership/Target Audience: Aimed at prison officers, prison service staff and external partner agencies.
BUSINESS: LOCAL GOVERNMENT, LEISURE & RECREATION: Local Government Related

PRIVACY LAWS & BUSINESS
39308U44-1675

Editorial Address: 2nd Floor, Monument House, 215 Marsh Road, PINNER, HA5 5NE **Tel:** 020 8868 9200
Fax: 020 8868 5215
Email: laura.linkomies@privacylaws.com
Web site: http://www.privacylaws.com
ISSN: 0953-6795
Publisher: Privacy Laws and Business
Date Established: 1987
Frequency: 6 issues yearly
Annual Sub.: £275.00
Usual Pagination: 24
Editor: Laura Linkomies; **Publisher:** Stewart Dresner
Summary of Content: Newsletter on data protection laws and their impact on business operations.
Readership/Target Audience: Data protection managers and advisers in companies, government and other public sector organisations.
ADVERTISING: No Advertising taken
BUSINESS: LEGAL

PRIVATE BANKER INTERNATIONAL
601018U1C-314

Editorial Address: The Colonnades, 34 Porchester Road, LONDON, W2 6ES **Tel:** 020 7563 5600 **Fax:** 020 7563 5601
Email: john.evans@vrlknowledgebank.com
Web site: http://www.vrlknowledgebank.com
Publisher: VRL Knowledge Bank Ltd
Date Established: 1989
Frequency: Monthly
Annual Sub.: £1000.00
Usual Pagination: 16
Editor: William Cain
Summary of Content: Newsletter covering new private banking products and services, international marketing strategies, regulatory updates and industry trends.
Readership/Target Audience: Aimed at those with an interest in wealth management.
ADVERTISING: No Advertising taken
BUSINESS: FINANCE & ECONOMICS: Banking

PRIVATE DENTISTRY
1638414U56D-203

Editorial Address: 1 Hertford House, Hugo Gryn Way, Farm Close, SHENLEY, WD7 9AB **Tel:** 01923 851777
Fax: 01923 851778
Email: pd@fmc.co.uk
Advertising Address: As above.
Email: sonja.jelley@fmc.co.uk
Web site: http://www.privatedentistryjournal.com
Publisher: Finlayson Media Communications Ltd
Date Established: 1995
Frequency: 10 issues yearly
Annual Sub.: £95.00
Circulation: 5,000 (Publisher's Statement)
Usual Pagination: 140
Editor: James Macdonald; **Editor-in-Chief:** Ellis Paul;
Advertising Manager: Sonja Jelley; **Managing Editor:** Siobhan Lewney
Summary of Content: Journal focusing on private dental treatment and practice management.
Readership/Target Audience: Aimed at dentists.
ADVERTISING RATES:
Full Page Colour £2100.00
Agency Commission: 10%
Mechanical Data: Type Area: 287 x 200mm, Bleed Size: 303 x 216mm, Trim Size: 297 x 210mm, Col Length: 287mm, Page Width: 200mm, Film: Digital
Copy instructions: Copy Date: 6 weeks prior to publication date
Average advertising content per issue: 30%
BUSINESS: HEALTH & MEDICAL: Dental

PRIVATE EQUITY EUROPE
35428U1N-45

Editorial Address: Haymarket House, 28-29 Haymarket, LONDON, SW1Y 4RX **Tel:** 020 7484 9700
Email: kimberly.romaine@incisivemedia.com
Advertising Address: As above.
Email: stephen.osullivan@incisivemedia.com
Web site: http://www.unquote.com
ISSN: 1465-9719
Publisher: Incisive Media Investments
Date Established: 1988
Frequency: 10 issues yearly
Annual Sub.: £1095.00
Editor: Ashley Wassall; **Editor-in-Chief:** Kimberly Romaine;
Managing Director: Jonathan Whiteley
Summary of Content: Journal focusing on the Western European private equity market. Includes the latest news on fund structures and launches, investment news, geographic investor moves and pan-European strategic developments.
Readership/Target Audience: Aimed at private equity professionals, investment banks and advisors.
ADVERTISING RATES:
Full Page Mono £1650.00
Full Page Colour £3300.00
Agency Commission: 10%
Mechanical Data: Film: Digital, Type Area: 280 x 180mm, Col Length: 280mm, Page Width: 180mm, Trim Size: 297 x 230mm
Average advertising content per issue: 10%
BUSINESS: FINANCE & ECONOMICS: Venture Capital

PRIVATE EQUITY INTERNATIONAL
768537U1F-578

Editorial Address: Sycamore House, Sycamore Street, LONDON, EC1Y 0SG **Tel:** 020 7566 5434
Fax: 020 7566 5455
Email: philip.b@peimedia.com
Web site: http://www.privateequityonline.com
Publisher: PEI Media Ltd
Frequency: 10 issues yearly
Annual Sub.: £575.00
Circulation: 5,000 (Publisher's Statement)
Editor: Andy Thomson; **Executive Editor:** David Snow;
Publisher: David Hawkins

Summary of Content: Magazine focusing on the fundamental issues shaping the private equity industry.
Readership/Target Audience: Aimed at fund managers, financial intermediaries and institutional investors.
ADVERTISING: No Advertising taken
BUSINESS: FINANCE & ECONOMICS: Investment

PRIVATE EQUITY NEWS
1639384U1F-592

Editorial Address: 2nd Floor, Stapleton House, 29-33 Scrutton Street, LONDON, EC2A 4HU **Tel:** 020 7426 3333
Email: jmawson@efinancialnews.com
Web site: http://www.penews.com
Publisher: Efinancialnews.com
Date Established: 2003
Frequency: Weekly
Circulation: 8,000 (Publisher's Statement)
Editor: James Mawson; **News Editor:** Paul Hodkinson
Summary of Content: Magazine covering all aspects of private equity and venture capital activity in Europe.
Readership/Target Audience: Aimed at private equity professionals.
ADVERTISING: No Advertising taken
BUSINESS: FINANCE & ECONOMICS: Investment

PRIVATE HIRE AND TAXI MONTHLY
41520U64G-470

Formerly: Private Hire Monthly
Editorial Address: 8 Silver Street, BURY, BL9 0EX
Tel: 0161 280 2800 **Fax:** 0161 280 7787
Email: npha@btconnect.com
Advertising Address: PHTM House, 501 Oldham Road, Failsworth, MANCHESTER, M35 9AB **Tel:** 0161 688 7777
Fax: 0161 688 7788
Email: info@phtm.co.uk
Web site: http://www.phtm.co.uk
Publisher: Private Hire & Taxi Monthly Ltd
Date Established: 1993
Frequency: Monthly
Cover Price: £2.00
Free to qualifying individuals
Annual Sub.: £15.00
Circulation: 35,000 (Publisher's Statement)
Usual Pagination: 140
Editor: Bryan Roland; **Managing Director:** Liza Lipson;
Advertising Manager: Liza Lipson
Summary of Content: Magazine covering the private hire and taxi business.
Readership/Target Audience: Aimed at taxi and private hire operators and drivers.
ADVERTISING RATES:
Full Page Mono £995.00
Full Page Colour £1295.00
Agency Commission: 10%
Mechanical Data: Film: Digital, No. of Columns (Display): 6, Trim Size: 330 x 230mm
Copy instructions: Copy Date: 20th of the month prior to publication date
Average advertising content per issue: 60%
BUSINESS: OTHER CLASSIFICATIONS: Taxi Trade

PRIVATE LABEL UK MAGAZINE
1833011U53-702

Editorial Address: 7 Bay Hall, Willow Lane, Birkby, HUDDERSFIELD, HD1 5EN **Tel:** 01484 321000
Fax: 01484 321001
Email: laura@privatelabeluk.co.uk
Advertising Address: As above.
Email: laura@privatelabeluk.co.uk
Web site: http://www.privatelabeluk.co.uk
Publisher: The Planet Group (UK) Ltd
Date Established: 2007
Frequency: Quarterly
Cover Price: £12.00
Free to qualifying individuals
Annual Sub.: £48.00
Circulation: 5,000 (Publisher's Statement)
Usual Pagination: 80
Editor: Sonia Mortimer
Summary of Content: Magazine focusing on the private label sector providing a comprehensive source of information for the industry.
Readership/Target Audience: Aimed at manufacturers, buyers, marketeers, technologists and category managers.
ADVERTISING RATES:
Full Page Colour £3995.00
Agency Commission: 10%
Mechanical Data: Type Area: 277 x 190mm, Bleed Size: 303 x 216mm, Trim Size: 297 x 210mm, Col Length: 277mm, Page Width: 190mm, Film: Digital
Copy instructions: Copy Date: 4 weeks prior to publication date
Average advertising content per issue: 30%
BUSINESS: RETAILING & WHOLESALING

Business Magazines

PRO AUDIO ASIA
1695032U61-510

Editorial Address: 20 Clifton Road, BRIGHTON, BN1 3HN
Tel: 0870 787 1192 **Fax:** 0870 787 1193
Email: tgoodyer@proaudioasia.com
Advertising Address: Suite C, 30A Church Road, TUNBRIDGE WELLS, TN1 1JP **Tel:** 01892 676280
Fax: 01892 676282
Email: rlawn@proaudioasia.com
Web site: http://www.proaudioasia.com
Publisher: Blank Canvas (Publishing) Ltd
Date Established: 2002
Frequency: 6 issues yearly
Cover Price: Free
Circulation: 10,524 (BPA Worldwide per quarter)
Usual Pagination: 130
Editor: Tim Goodyer
Summary of Content: Magazine focusing on the live, installation, broadcast, post production and recording market throughout Asia.
Language(s): Chinese; English
Readership/Target Audience: Aimed at end-users, installers, manufacturers, suppliers and contractors.
ADVERTISING RATES:
Full Page Colour £2100.00
Mechanical Data: Type Area: 314 x 228mm, Bleed Size: 340 x 250mm, Trim Size: 335 x 245mm, Col Length: 314mm, Page Width: 228mm, Film: Digital
BUSINESS: MUSIC TRADE

PRO AUDIO MIDDLE EAST
1695030U61-509

Editorial Address: First Floor Office Suite, 20a Church Road, TUNBRIDGE WELLS, BN1 3HN **Tel:** 01892 676280
Fax: 01892 676282
Email: bjameson@proaudioasia.com
Advertising Address: Suite C, 30A Church Road, TUNBRIDGE WELLS, TN1 1JP **Tel:** 01892 676280
Fax: 01892 676282
Email: rlawn@proaudioasia.com
Web site: http://www.proaudio-central.com
Publisher: Blank Canvas (Publishing) Ltd
Date Established: 2004
Frequency: 6 issues yearly
Cover Price: Free
Circulation: 4,924 (Publisher's Statement)
Usual Pagination: 100
Advertising Manager: Sue Gould
Summary of Content: Magazine focusing on the live, installation, broadcast, post production and recording market throughout the Middle East and North Africa.
Readership/Target Audience: Aimed at end users, installers, manufacturers, specifies and contractors.
ADVERTISING RATES:
Full Page Colour £1680.00
Mechanical Data: Type Area: 314 x 228mm, Bleed Size: 340 x 250mm, Trim Size: 335 x 245mm, Col Length: 314mm, Page Width: 228mm, Film: Digital
BUSINESS: MUSIC TRADE

PRO SHOP EUROPE
39555U48B-45

Editorial Address: Jesses Farm, Snow Hill, Dinton, SALISBURY, SP3 5HN **Tel:** 01722 717026
Email: geraldine@markallengroup.co.uk
Advertising Address: As above. **Tel:** 01722 716996
Fax: 01722 716926
Email: mark.j@markallengroup.co.uk
Web site: http://www.proshopeurope.com
ISSN: 1355-2740
Publisher: A & D Media Ltd
Frequency: Monthly - Published in the 3rd week of the cover month
Free to qualifying individuals
Annual Sub.: £80.00
Circulation: 3,842 (Publisher's Statement)
Usual Pagination: 36
Editor: Geraldine Faulkner; **Managing Director:** Mark Allen;
Advertising Manager: Mark Jones; **Publisher:** Fiona Richards
Summary of Content: Journal containing news and information on the golf retail trade.
Readership/Target Audience: Aimed at those involved in the golf retail trade.
ADVERTISING RATES:
Full Page Colour £1750.00
SCC £25.00
Agency Commission: 10%
Mechanical Data: Page Width: 186mm, Trim Size: 297 x 210mm, Type Area: 273 x 186mm, Col Length: 273mm, Bleed Size: 303 x 216mm
Copy instructions: Copy Date: 2 weeks prior to publication date
Average advertising content per issue: 40%
BUSINESS: TOY TRADE & SPORTS GOODS: Sports Goods

PRO SOUND NEWS EUROPE
40956U61-150

Editorial Address: Ludgate House, 245 Blackfriars Road, LONDON, SE1 9UY **Tel:** 020 7921 8319 **Fax:** 020 7921 8302

Email: david.robinson@ubm.com
Advertising Address: As above. **Tel:** 020 7921 5000
Fax: 020 7921 8339
Email: steve.connolly@ubm.com
Web site: http://www.prosoundnewseurope.com
ISSN: 0269-4735
Publisher: UBM Information Ltd
Date Established: 1986
Frequency: Monthly
Cover Price: £4.00
Free to qualifying individuals
Annual Sub.: £39.00
Circulation: 6,876 (BPA Worldwide 01/07/2007 to 31/12/2007)
Usual Pagination: 90
Editor: David Robinson; **Advertising Manager:** Steve Connolly; **Managing Editor:** Jo Ruddock; **Publisher:** Joe Hosken
Summary of Content: News magazine covering all aspects of the professional audio industry.
Readership/Target Audience: Aimed at professionals in the European sound industry.
ADVERTISING RATES:
Full Page Colour £2510.00
Agency Commission: 10%
Mechanical Data: Film: Digital, Type Area: 314 x 228mm, Col Length: 314mm, Col Widths (Display): 42mm, No. of Columns (Display): 5, Bleed Size: 340 x 250mm, Trim Size: 335 x 245mm, Page Width: 228mm
Copy instructions: Copy Date: 15th of the month prior to publication date
Average advertising content per issue: 60%
BUSINESS: MUSIC TRADE

PRO VETERINARIO AUDIO MAGAZINE
41532U64H-159_50

Editorial Address: The White Cottage, The Street, Long Stratton, NORWICH, NR15 2XJ **Tel:** 0845 402 6527
Fax: 0845 402 6528
Email: roger@bhrcommunications.co.uk
Web site: http://www.bhrcommunications.co.uk
Publisher: BHR Communications
Date Established: 1984
Frequency: Quarterly
Free to qualifying individuals
Circulation: 4,500 (Publisher's Statement)
Editor: Roger Ranson; **Managing Director:** Roger Ranson
Summary of Content: Audio magazine featuring current topics and news for the veterinary profession.
Readership/Target Audience: Aimed at veterinary nurses and veterinary surgeons.
ADVERTISING: No Advertising taken
BUSINESS: OTHER CLASSIFICATIONS: Veterinary

PRO WHOLESALER
39816U53-247

Editorial Address: Broadfield Park, CRAWLEY, RH11 9RT **Tel:** 01293 613400 **Fax:** 01293 610330
Email: john.wood@william-reed.co.uk
Advertising Address: As above.
Email: karl.humphries@william-reed.co.uk
Web site: http://www.prowholesaler.co.uk
ISSN: 1746-8949
Publisher: William Reed Business Media
Date Established: 1991
Frequency: Monthly - Published on the 2nd Tuesday of the cover month
Free to qualifying individuals
Annual Sub.: £42.00
Circulation: 6,212 (ABC 01/07/2008 to 30/06/2009)
Usual Pagination: 72
Editor: John Wood; **Advertising Manager:** Karl Humphries
Summary of Content: Magazine covering all aspects of the grocery, alcohol and tobacco wholesale trade in both retail and catering.
Readership/Target Audience: Aimed at grocery wholesalers, both cash and carry, delivered and major suppliers.
ADVERTISING RATES:
Full Page Colour £1520.00
Agency Commission: 10%
Mechanical Data: Type Area: 267 x 185mm, Bleed Size: 303 x 216mm, Col Length: 267mm, Page Width: 185mm, Film: Digital, Trim Size: 297 x 210mm
Copy instructions: Copy Date: 2 weeks prior to publication date
BUSINESS: RETAILING & WHOLESALING

PRO WHOLESALER CASH & CARRY BIG BOOK
37997U22B-100

Editorial Address: Broadfield Park, CRAWLEY, RH11 9RT **Tel:** 01293 610289 **Fax:** 01293 610330
Email: john.wood@william-reed.co.uk
Advertising Address: As above. **Tel:** 01293 610439
Fax: 01293 610381
Email: karl.humphreys@william-reed.co.uk
Web site: http://www.william-reed.co.uk

Publisher: William Reed Business Media
Frequency: Annual - Published in September
Cover Price: £50.00
Free to qualifying individuals
Circulation: 6,042 (Publisher's Statement)
Editor: John Wood
Summary of Content: Annual year book focusing on the cash and carry industry profiling leading companies, information on product categories sold by cash and carries, and a directory of wholesalers and preferred suppliers.
Readership/Target Audience: Read by cash and carry managers, directors and staff.
ADVERTISING RATES:
Full Page Colour £1520.00
Agency Commission: 10%
Copy instructions: Copy Date: 4 weeks prior to publication date
Average advertising content per issue: 45%
BUSINESS: FOOD: Cash & Carry

PRO WHOLESALER DELIVERED BIG BOOK
39817U53-689

Editorial Address: Broadfield Park, CRAWLEY, RH11 9RT **Tel:** 01273 844345
Email: john.wood@william-reed.co.uk
Advertising Address: As above. **Tel:** 01293 613400
Fax: 01293 610330
Email: karl.humphreys@william-reed.co.uk
Publisher: William Reed Business Media
Frequency: Annual - Published in March
Free to qualifying individuals
Usual Pagination: 100
Editor: John Wood; **Advertising Manager:** Karl Humphreys
Summary of Content: Magazine covering data, company profiles, IT, marketing, new developments and partnerships.
Readership/Target Audience: Aimed at independent delivered wholesalers and their suppliers.
ADVERTISING RATES:
Full Page Colour £1520.00
Agency Commission: 10%
Mechanical Data: Type Area: 267 x 185mm, Bleed Size: 303 x 216mm, Trim Size: 297 x 210mm, Col Length: 267mm, Page Width: 185mm, Film: Digital
Copy instructions: Copy Date: 4 weeks prior to publication date
BUSINESS: RETAILING & WHOLESALING

PROBATION BULLETIN
29459U32G-92

Editorial Address: Shaway House, 21 Bourne Park, Bourne Road, CRAYFORD, DA1 4BZ **Tel:** 01322 621112
Fax: 01322 550991
Email: probation@shaws.co.uk
Advertising Address: As above.
Email: probation@shaws.co.uk
Web site: http://www.probationbulletin.co.uk
Publisher: Shaw & Sons Ltd
Frequency: 25 issues yearly - Published every other Monday
Cover Price: Free
Circulation: 2,000 (Publisher's Statement)
Usual Pagination: 16
Editor: Crispin Williams; **Advertising Manager:** Sarah Bruty
Summary of Content: Recruitment magazine for the probation service including information on courses and social events.
Readership/Target Audience: Aimed at those working within the probation service and related fields.
ADVERTISING RATES:
Full Page Mono £470.00
Agency Commission: 10%
Mechanical Data: Film: Digital, Page Width: 160mm, Type Area: 253 x 160mm, Col Length: 253mm
Copy instructions: Copy Date: Wednesday 11am prior to publication date
Average advertising content per issue: 95%
BUSINESS: LOCAL GOVERNMENT, LEISURE & RECREATION: Community Care & Social Services

PROBATION JOURNAL
38490U32G-95

Editorial Address: John Moores University, LIVERPOOL
Email: prbjournal@btinternet.com
Advertising Address: 1 Oliver's Yard, 55 City Road, LONDON, EC1Y 1SP **Tel:** 020 7324 8500
Fax: 020 7324 8600
Email: sheena.karim@sagepub.co.uk
Web site: http://www.sagepub.co.uk
ISSN: 0264-5505
Publisher: Sage Publications
Date Established: 1929
Frequency: Quarterly
Annual Sub.: £33.00
Circulation: 8,500 (Publisher's Statement)
Usual Pagination: 72
Editor: Lol Burke; **Advertising Manager:** Sheena Karim;
Managing Editor: Emma Cluley

Summary of Content: Publication covering probation practice, criminal justice, social work with offenders and family court welfare work. Also covers social policy and criminology.
Readership/Target Audience: Aimed at probation staff, probation and criminal justice academics and other criminal justice professionals.
ADVERTISING RATES:
Full Page Colour £450.00
Agency Commission: 5%
Mechanical Data: Type Area: 205 x 130mm, Col Length: 205mm, Page Width: 130mm
Copy instructions: Copy Date: 8 weeks prior to publication
BUSINESS: LOCAL GOVERNMENT, LEISURE & RECREATION: Community Care & Social Services

THE PROBE
40396U56D-90
Editorial Address: 2nd Floor, 207-215 High Street, ORPINGTON, BR6 0PF **Tel:** 01689 899170
Fax: 01689 899171
Email: sophie.odum@purplems.com
Advertising Address: As above. **Tel:** 01689 899177
Email: ed.hunt@purplems.com
Web site: http://www.purplems.com
ISSN: 1753-3589
Publisher: Purple Media Solutions Ltd
Date Established: 1959
Frequency: Monthly - Published in the 1st week of the cover month
Free to qualifying individuals
Circulation: 14,569 (ABC 01/01/2008 to 31/12/2008)
Usual Pagination: 32
Editor: Sophie Odum
Summary of Content: Journal covering practice management, clinical assessments of new techniques, previews of new materials and equipment, book reviews and dental news.
Readership/Target Audience: Aimed at dental practitioners.
ADVERTISING RATES:
Full Page Colour £2700.00
SCC £19.00
Agency Commission: 10%
Mechanical Data: Page Width: 228mm, Film: Digital, Type Area: 322 x 228mm, Col Length: 322mm, Trim Size: 338 x 244mm, Bleed Size: 346 x 252mm
Copy instructions: Copy Date: 1st of the month prior to publication date
Average advertising content per issue: 40%
BUSINESS: HEALTH & MEDICAL: Dental

PROCEEDINGS OF ICE, BRIDGE ENGINEERING
1831246U42A-246
Editorial Address: Thomas Telford House, 1 Heron Quay, LONDON, E14 4JD **Tel:** 020 7665 2453
Email: agnes.alvite@ice.org.uk
Advertising Address: Warners Group Publications plc, The Maltings, West Street, BOURNE, PE10 9PH
Tel: 01778 391000 **Fax:** 01778 392079
Email: julietg@warnersgroup.co.uk
Web site: http://www.bridgesjournal.com
ISSN: 1478-4637
Publisher: Thomas Telford Ltd
Date Established: 2003
Frequency: Quarterly
Annual Sub.: £216.00
Circulation: 500 (Publisher's Statement)
Editor: Agnes Alvite
Summary of Content: Publication covering developments in bridge engineering including the design, construction, maintenance, management, monitoring and upgrading of all types of bridge structures.
Readership/Target Audience: Aimed at practicing civil engineers and academics.
ADVERTISING RATES:
Full Page Mono £1375.00
Full Page Colour £1950.00
Mechanical Data: Type Area: 275 x 190mm, Bleed Size: 303 x 216mm, Trim Size: 297 x 210mm, Col Length: 275mm, Page Width: 190mm, Film: Digital
BUSINESS: CONSTRUCTION

PROCEEDINGS OF ICE, ENGINEERING HISTORY AND HERITAGE
1850011U19A-571
Editorial Address: Thomas Telford House, 1 Heron Quay, LONDON, E14 4JD **Tel:** 020 7987 6999
Email: simon.fullalove@ice.org.uk
Web site: http://www.engineeringhistoryandheritage.com
ISSN: 1757-9430
Publisher: Thomas Telford Ltd
Date Established: 2009
Frequency: Quarterly
Annual Sub.: £200.00
Editor: Simon Fullalove; **Publisher:** Leon Heward-Mills
Summary of Content: Journal providing historical perspective on engineering practice and engineering works

and how they developed into the profession today. Covering engineering disciplines, engineering science, design methods, construction firms and biographies.
Readership/Target Audience: Aimed at engineering historians as well as practitioners and researchers facing the challenge of maintaining or adapting infrastructure and engineering.
BUSINESS: ENGINEERING & MACHINERY

PROCEEDINGS OF ICE, GROUND IMPROVEMENT
39001U42A-107
Formerly: Ground Improvement
Editorial Address: Thomas Telford House, 1 Heron Quay, LONDON, E14 4JD **Tel:** 020 7665 2453 **Fax:** 020 7538 4101
Email: gi@ice.org.uk
Advertising Address: Warners Group Publications, The Maltings, West Street, BOURNE, PE10 9PH
Tel: 01778 391108 **Fax:** 01778 392079
Email: michaelt@warnersgroup.co.uk
Web site: http://www.thomastelford.com
ISSN: 1365-781X
Publisher: Thomas Telford Ltd
Date Established: 1997
Frequency: Quarterly
Annual Sub.: £186.00
Circulation: 2,000 (Publisher's Statement)
Usual Pagination: 48
Editor: Simon Fullalove; **Publisher:** Leon Heward-Mills
Summary of Content: Journal covering all aspects of geotechnical engineering. Contains papers and news articles on ground improvement, grouting and ground reinforcement.
Language(s): English; French
Readership/Target Audience: Aimed at civil and geotechnical engineers.
ADVERTISING RATES:
Full Page Colour £1950.00
Mechanical Data: Type Area: 275 x 190mm, Bleed Size: 303 x 216mm, Trim Size: 297 x 210mm, Col Length: 275mm, Page Width: 190mm, Film: Digital
BUSINESS: CONSTRUCTION

PROCEEDINGS OF ROYAL SOCIETY OF EDINBURGH (SECTION A, MATHS)
40091U55-129_70
Editorial Address: ICMS, 14 India Street, EDINBURGH, EH3 6EZ **Tel:** 0131 220 1777 **Fax:** 0131 220 1053
Email: proc.rse@icms.org.uk
Web site: http://www.royalsoced.org.uk
ISSN: 0208-2105
Publisher: The RSE Scotland Foundation
Frequency: 6 issues yearly
Annual Sub.: £260.00
Circulation: 700 (Publisher's Statement)
Usual Pagination: 256
Editor: A. Davie
Summary of Content: Peer reviewed scholarly papers in mathematics.
Readership/Target Audience: Aimed at researchers in mathematics.
ADVERTISING: No Advertising taken
BUSINESS: APPLIED SCIENCE & LABORATORIES

PROCEEDINGS OF THE EDINBURGH MATHEMATICAL SOCIETY
40082U55-9001
Editorial Address: The Edinburgh Building, Shaftesbury Road, CAMBRIDGE, CB2 8RU **Tel:** 01223 325800
Fax: 01223 325801
Email: icms.pems@ed.ac.uk
Advertising Address: As above. **Tel:** 01223 326070
Fax: 01223 325150
Email: ad_sales@cambridge.org
Web site: http://www.journals.cambridge.org
ISSN: 0013-0915
Publisher: Cambridge University Press
Frequency: 3 issues yearly - Published in February, June and October
Circulation: 850 (Publisher's Statement)
Editor: Rachel Eley; **Advertising Manager:** Rebecca Roberts
Summary of Content: Journal covering mathematical science, pure and applied.
Readership/Target Audience: Read by mathematicians and members of the Edinburgh Mathematical Society.
ADVERTISING RATES:
Full Page Mono £445.00
Mechanical Data: Film: Digital, Type Area: 200 x 135mm, Col Length: 200mm, Page Width: 135mm
Copy instructions: Copy Date: 8 weeks preceding 1st of publication month
BUSINESS: APPLIED SCIENCE & LABORATORIES

PROCEEDINGS OF THE LONDON MATHEMATICAL SOCIETY
24419U55-129_71
Editorial Address: Great Clarendon Street, OXFORD, OX2 6DP **Tel:** 01865 355146
Email: clive.hemingway@oxfordjournal.org
Web site: http://www.oxfordjournals.org
ISSN: 0024-6115
Publisher: OUP
Frequency: 6 issues yearly
Annual Sub.: £488.00
Circulation: 1,300 (Publisher's Statement)
Summary of Content: Journal covering complex analysis, differential equations and related areas, topology, geometry, logic, probability and statistics, algebra, number theory and combinational theory.
Readership/Target Audience: Aimed at mathematicians, researchers, university level students and members of the PLMS.
ADVERTISING: No Advertising taken
BUSINESS: APPLIED SCIENCE & LABORATORIES

PROCEEDINGS OF THE ROYAL SOCIETY SERIES: MATHS, PHYS. & ENG.SC.
40083U55-129_72
Editorial Address: 6-9 Carlton House Terrace, LONDON, SW1Y 5AG **Tel:** 020 7451 2634 **Fax:** 020 7976 1837
Email: joanna.harries@royalsociety.org
Web site: http://www.pubs.royalsoc.ac.uk
ISSN: 1364-5021
Publisher: The Royal Society
Date Established: 1854
Frequency: Monthly
Annual Sub.: £915.00
Circulation: 900 (Publisher's Statement)
Usual Pagination: 250
Editor: Joanna Harries
Summary of Content: Journal covering original scientific research papers on mathematics, physics, chemistry and engineering.
Language(s): Chinese; English
Readership/Target Audience: Aimed at scientists.
ADVERTISING: No Advertising taken
BUSINESS: APPLIED SCIENCE & LABORATORIES

PROCESS ENGINEERING
37666U19F-586
Editorial Address: St. Giles House, 50 Poland Street, LONDON, W1F 7AX **Tel:** 020 7970 4183 **Fax:** 020 7970 4493
Email: patrick.raleigh@centaur.co.uk
Advertising Address: As above. **Tel:** 020 7970 4000
Email: nick.collins@centaur.co.uk
Web site: http://www.processengineering.co.uk
ISSN: 0370-1859
Publisher: Centaur Media plc
Date Established: 1964
Frequency: 6 issues yearly
Free to qualifying individuals
Annual Sub.: £93.00
Circulation: 10,251 (ABC 01/01/2008 to 31/12/2008)
Usual Pagination: 60
Editor: Patrick Raleigh; **Advertising Manager:** Nick Collins; **Publisher:** Sean Marshall
Summary of Content: Editorial relates to practical applications of process plant, systems, equipment and management techniques.
Readership/Target Audience: Aimed at senior process and chemical engineers employed in UK process industries.
ADVERTISING RATES:
Full Page Colour £2495.00
Agency Commission: 10%
Mechanical Data: Page Width: 179mm, Type Area: 250 x 179mm, Bleed Size: 276 x 205mm, Trim Size: 270 x 199mm, Col Length: 250mm, No. of Columns (Display): 3, Film: Digital
Average advertising content per issue: 40%
BUSINESS: ENGINEERING & MACHINERY: Production & Mechanical Engineering

PROCESS INDUSTRY INFORMER
37668U19F-587_50
Formerly: Process Products
Editorial Address: Unit 40B, Passfield Business Centre, Lynchborough Road, LIPHOOK, GU30 7SB
Tel: 01428 751188 **Fax:** 01428 751199
Email: philblack@piimag.com
Advertising Address: As above.
Email: peterullmann@piimag.com
Web site: http://www.piimag.com
Publisher: Passfield Business Publications Ltd
Date Established: 1994
Frequency: 6 issues yearly
Cover Price: £5.00
Free to qualifying individuals
Annual Sub.: £15.00
Circulation: 14,000 (Publisher's Statement)
Usual Pagination: 52

Editor: Philip Black; **Advertising Manager:** Peter Ullmann
Summary of Content: Guide to process equipment and products.
Readership/Target Audience: Read by senior, middle management and engineers in the process industries.
ADVERTISING RATES:
Full Page Mono £1750.00
Full Page Colour £1850.00
SCC £2.95
Agency Commission: 10%
Mechanical Data: Col Length: 332mm, Col Widths (Display): 62mm, Film: Digital, No. of Columns (Display): 4, Type Area: 332 x 262mm, Page Width: 262mm, Bleed Size: 366 x 296mm, Trim Size: 360 x 290mm
Copy instructions: Copy Date: 2 weeks prior to publication date
Average advertising content per issue: 40%
BUSINESS: ENGINEERING & MACHINERY: Production & Mechanical Engineering

PRODUCE NEWS
1659446U22A-390

Editorial Address: 7 Bay Hall, Willow Lane, Birkby, HUDDERSFIELD, HD1 5EN **Tel:** 01484 321000
Fax: 01484 321001
Email: laura@planet-group.co.uk
Advertising Address: As above.
Email: producenews@planet-group.co.uk
Web site: http://www.planet-group.net
Publisher: The Planet Group (UK) Ltd
Date Established: 1999
Frequency: Monthly - Published in the last week of the month prior to cover date
Cover Price: £4.75
Annual Sub.: £57.00
Circulation: 17,500 (Publisher's Statement)
Usual Pagination: 62
Editor: Laura Wojciechowski; **Editor-in-Chief:** Rod Millington; **Advertising Manager:** Laura Wojciechowski
Summary of Content: Magazine focusing on the fresh produce and horticultural industries, including news, products and company features.
Readership/Target Audience: Aimed at senior management and buyers, multiples, farmers, growers, wholesalers, manufacturers, processors, caterers, importers, distributors, packers, the foodservice, nurseries and garden centres.
ADVERTISING RATES:
Full Page Mono £1395.00
Full Page Colour £1750.00
Agency Commission: 10%
Mechanical Data: Type Area: 277 x 210mm, Bleed Size: 303 x 236mm, Col Length: 277mm, Page Width: 210mm, Film: Digital
Average advertising content per issue: 30%
BUSINESS: FOOD

THE PRODUCER
35686U2D-83_15

Editorial Address: 26 Carnarvon Road, Redlands, BRISTOL, BS6 7DU **Tel:** 0117 942 6977 **Fax:** 0117 907 0717
Email: chris@smallworldpublishing.co.uk
Advertising Address: As above.
Email: ads@smallworldpublishing.co.uk
Web site: http://www.smallworldpublishing.co.uk
Publisher: Small World Publishing Ltd
Date Established: 1993
Frequency: 3 issues yearly - Published in spring, summer and autumn
Cover Price: £5.00
Free to qualifying individuals
Circulation: 16,000 (Publisher's Statement)
Usual Pagination: 20
Editor: Chris Dickinson; **Advertising Manager:** Abi Pears
Summary of Content: Magazine covering news and articles on broadcasters, commissioning editors and production techniques.
Readership/Target Audience: Aimed at producers, directors and cameramen.
ADVERTISING: Rates on application
BUSINESS: COMMUNICATIONS, ADVERTISING & MARKETING: Broadcasting

PRODUCT & IMAGE SECURITY INCORPORATING PACKAGE PRINT & CONVERTING
38695U54C-311

Formerly: Product & Image Security Magazine
Editorial Address: 81 Houting, Dosthill, TAMWORTH, B77 1PB **Tel:** 01827 281143 **Fax:** 01827 281143
Email: jeremyplimmer@aol.com
Advertising Address: White Cottage, 520 Bradgate Road, Newtown Linford, LEICESTER, LE6 0HB **Tel:** 01530 242232
Fax: 01827 281143
Email: dwillis@mailmight.com
Web site: http://www.productandimagesecurity.com
Publisher: Willis Plimmer Publishing Ltd
Date Established: 1997

Frequency: 6 issues yearly - Published in the 2nd week of the 1st cover month
Annual Sub.: £75.00
Circulation: 8,500 (Publisher's Statement)
Usual Pagination: 56
Editor: Jeremy Plimmer; **Advertising Manager:** Donna Willis
Summary of Content: Journal featuring all aspects of product and image security, including anti-counterfeiting, theft and product traceability. Also covering print on packaging for the food and drink, pharmaceutical and cosmetics industries. Includes flexible packaging and product labelling, packaging origination, print processes (both narrow and wide web) and materials and folding cartons.
Language(s): English; French
Readership/Target Audience: Aimed at users and suppliers of product and image security products, victims of forgery, counterfeiting and theft and package buyers, graphic designers, technicians, technologists and people working in repro origination, package printing, industrial equipment and supply.
ADVERTISING RATES:
Full Page Mono £1550.00
Full Page Colour £1550.00
Agency Commission: 10%
Copy instructions: Copy Date: 3 weeks prior to publication date
Average advertising content per issue: 10%
BUSINESS: SAFETY & SECURITY: Security

PRODUCTION ENGINEERING SOLUTIONS
37670U19F-600

Editorial Address: Featherstone House, 375 High Street, ROCHESTER, ME1 1DA **Tel:** 01634 830566
Fax: 01634 408488
Email: newsdesk@pesmag.co.uk
Advertising Address: As above.
Email: sales@pesmag.co.uk
Web site: http://www.pesmag.co.uk
Publisher: MIT Publishing
Date Established: 1997
Frequency: Monthly - Published in the middle of the month
Free to qualifying individuals
Circulation: 15,972 (ABC 01/01/2008 to 31/12/2008)
Usual Pagination: 40
Editor: Dave Tudor; **Advertising Director:** Andy Morley; **Publisher:** David Rose
Summary of Content: Magazine reporting on new machine tools and tooling, innovative CAD/CAM technology and applications in the metal working industry.
Readership/Target Audience: Aimed at production managers, engineers and senior buyers.
ADVERTISING RATES:
Full Page Colour £2420.00
SCC £44.00
Agency Commission: 10%
Mechanical Data: Bleed Size: 426 x 300mm, Type Area: 400 x 276mm, Col Length: 400mm, Page Width: 276mm, Col Widths (Display): 41mm, No. of Columns (Display): 6, Film: Digital, Trim Size: 420 x 297mm
Copy instructions: Copy Date: 12 days prior to publication date
Average advertising content per issue: 50%
BUSINESS: ENGINEERING & MACHINERY: Production & Mechanical Engineering

PRODUCTION JOURNAL
38939U41A-225

Editorial Address: 8 Sovereign Park, Cleveland Way, HEMEL HEMPSTEAD, HP2 7DA **Tel:** 01442 233656
Fax: 01442 258853
Email: gary@cullumpublishing.co.uk
Advertising Address: As above.
Email: donna@cullumpublishing.co.uk
Web site: http://www.newstech.co.uk
ISSN: 0032-9878
Publisher: Cullum Publishing
Date Established: 1958
Frequency: Monthly - Published at the end of the 1st week of cover month
Free to qualifying individuals
Annual Sub.: £40.00
Circulation: 3,500 (Publisher's Statement)
Usual Pagination: 28
Editor: Gary Cullum; **Managing Director:** Gary Cullum; **Advertising Manager:** Donna Flynn; **Publisher:** Gary Cullum
Summary of Content: Journal reviewing newspaper and new media technology.
Readership/Target Audience: Aimed at management personnel involved in newspaper and new media publishing.
ADVERTISING RATES:
Full Page Colour £1510.00
Agency Commission: 10%
Mechanical Data: Type Area: 380 x 270mm, Col Length: 380mm, Page Width: 270mm, Film: Digital
Copy instructions: Copy Date: 2 weeks prior to publication date
BUSINESS: PRINTING & STATIONERY: Printing

PROFESSIONAL ADVISER MAGAZINE
717668U1A-349

Editorial Address: Haymarket House, 28-29 Haymarket, LONDON, SW1Y 4RX **Tel:** 020 7484 9700
Email: rob.kingsbury@incisivemedia.com
Advertising Address: As above. **Tel:** 020 7484 9949
Fax: 020 7034 2751
Email: jon.seymour@incisivemedia.com
Web site: http://www.professionaladviser.co.uk
Publisher: Incisive Media Investments
Date Established: 2001
Frequency: Weekly
Free to qualifying individuals
Annual Sub.: £175.00
Circulation: 11,847 (ABC 01/07/2008 to 30/06/2009)
Editor: Robert Kingsbury; **Advertising Manager:** Jonathan Seymour
Summary of Content: Magazine covering financial markets including industry news and stock market analysis.
Readership/Target Audience: Aimed at independent financial advisers and brokers.
ADVERTISING RATES:
Full Page Colour £7054.00
Agency Commission: 10%
Mechanical Data: Type Area: 476 x 332mm, Bleed Size: 506 x 356mm, Trim Size: 350 x 250mm, Film: Digital, Col Length: 476mm, Page Width: 332mm
Copy instructions: Copy Date: 1 week prior to publication date
BUSINESS: FINANCE & ECONOMICS

PROFESSIONAL BEAUTY
37254U15A-85

Editorial Address: Greater London House, Hampstead Road, LONDON, NW1 7EJ **Tel:** 020 7728 3570
Email: professionalbeauty@emap.com
Advertising Address: As above. **Tel:** 020 7874 0200
Email: lyndsay.dixon@emap.com
Web site: http://www.professionalbeauty.co.uk
Publisher: EMAP Communications Ltd
Frequency: 11 issues yearly - Published in the 3rd week of the month prior to cover date
Cover Price: £3.50
Annual Sub.: £35.00
Circulation: 15,550 (ABC 01/07/2008 to 30/06/2009)
Usual Pagination: 136
Editor: Jenni Middleton
Summary of Content: Magazine covering all aspects of health and beauty treatment and therapy, including spas and beauty and nail salons.
Readership/Target Audience: Aimed at beauty/nail salon and spa managers and owners, beauty therapists, nail technicians and students.
ADVERTISING: Rates on application
Copy instructions: Copy Date: 3 weeks prior to publication date
BUSINESS: COSMETICS & HAIRDRESSING: Cosmetics

THE PROFESSIONAL BEAUTY DIRECTORY
37253U15A-80

Formerly: Professional Beauty Gold Book Directory
Editorial Address: Greater London Road, Hampstead Road, LONDON, NW1 7EJ **Tel:** 020 7728 5000
Email: jenni.middleton@emap.com
Advertising Address: Boundary I Media, Priory Park, Beech Green Lane, Withyham, HARTFIELD, TN7 4DB
Tel: 01892 771047 **Fax:** 01892 771048
Email: benellefsen@boundaryimedia.co.uk
Web site: http://www.professionalbeauty.co.uk
Publisher: EMAP Retail
Date Established: 1997
Frequency: Annual - Published in February
Free to qualifying individuals
Annual Sub.: £30.00
Circulation: 16,000 (Publisher's Statement)
Usual Pagination: 160
Editor: Jenni Middleton
Summary of Content: Directory providing reference material for the health and beauty sector.
Readership/Target Audience: Aimed at health and beauty professionals.
ADVERTISING RATES:
Full Page Colour £1960.00
Agency Commission: 10%
Mechanical Data: Col Length: 190mm, Page Width: 178mm, Film: Digital, Bleed Size: 230 x 220mm, Trim Size: 220 x 210mm, Type Area: 190 x 178mm
Copy instructions: Copy Date: End of October
BUSINESS: COSMETICS & HAIRDRESSING: Cosmetics

PROFESSIONAL BROKING
35159U1D-332

Editorial Address: 32-34 Broadwick Street, LONDON, W1A 2HG **Tel:** 020 7316 9000 **Fax:** 020 7316 9313
Email: andrew.tjaardstra@incisivemedia.com
Advertising Address: As above. **Fax:** 020 7316 9257
Email: oli.henry@incisivemedia.com

Web site: http://www.professionalbroking.co.uk
ISSN: 1355-0519
Publisher: Incisive Media
Frequency: Monthly - Published on the 1st Tuesday of the cover month
Free to qualifying individuals
Annual Sub.: £60.00
Circulation: 11,664 (ABC 01/07/2008 to 30/06/2009)
Usual Pagination: 48
Editor: Andrew Tjaardstra; **Publisher:** Alex Broad
Summary of Content: Magazine covering management and business issues relating to professional brokers of small to medium firms.
Readership/Target Audience: Read by the directors of brokers.
ADVERTISING RATES:
Full Page Colour £4120.00
Agency Commission: 10%
Mechanical Data: Film: Digital, Type Area: 212 x 170mm, Bleed Size: 266 x 216mm, Trim Size: 260 x 210mm, Col Length: 260mm, Page Width: 210mm
Copy instructions: Copy Date: 4 weeks prior to publication date
Average advertising content per issue: 45%
BUSINESS: FINANCE & ECONOMICS: Insurance

PROFESSIONAL BUILDER
35918U4E-305

Editorial Address: Regal House, Regal Way, WATFORD, WD24 4YF **Tel:** 01923 237799 **Fax:** 01923 246901
Email: pb@hamerville.co.uk
Advertising Address: As above.
Email: pbsales@hamerville.co.uk
Web site: http://www.hamerville.co.uk
Publisher: Hamerville Magazines Ltd
Date Established: 1980
Frequency: 11 issues yearly - Published on the 1st of the cover month
Free to qualifying individuals
Annual Sub.: £30.00
Circulation: 108,502 (ABC 02/07/2007 to 30/12/2007)
Usual Pagination: 160
Editor: Terry Smith; **Managing Director:** Bryan Shannon;
Managing Editor: Terry Smith; **Publisher:** Bryan Shannon
Summary of Content: Magazine covering news, products and information on building and roofing.
Readership/Target Audience: Read by professional builders throughout the UK and Europe.
ADVERTISING RATES:
Full Page Mono £3850.00
Full Page Colour £3850.00
Agency Commission: 10%
Mechanical Data: Type Area: 255 x 180mm, Film: Digital, Col Length: 255mm, Trim Size: 285 x 210mm, Bleed Size: 291 x 216mm, Page Width: 180mm
Copy instructions: Copy Date: 6 weeks prior to publication date
Average advertising content per issue: 55%
BUSINESS: ARCHITECTURE & BUILDING: Building

PROFESSIONAL BUILDERS MERCHANT
35919U4E-305_25

Editorial Address: Regal House, Regal Way, WATFORD, WD24 4YF **Tel:** 01923 237799 **Fax:** 01923 246901
Email: pbm@hamerville.co.uk
Advertising Address: As above.
Email: craig@hamerville.co.uk
Web site: http://www.hamerville.co.uk
Publisher: Hamerville Magazines Ltd
Date Established: 1991
Frequency: 11 issues yearly - Published on the 1st of the cover month
Free to qualifying individuals
Annual Sub.: £30.00
Circulation: 9,887 (ABC 01/07/2008 to 30/06/2009)
Usual Pagination: 72
Editor: Paul Davies; **Managing Editor:** Terry Smith;
Publisher: Bryan Shannon
Summary of Content: Magazine covering merchandising, marketing, new products, legal update and news relevant to the building materials supply trade.
Readership/Target Audience: Aimed at key builders merchant directors, buyers, managers and personnel.
ADVERTISING RATES:
Full Page Colour £2200.00
Agency Commission: 10%
Mechanical Data: Type Area: 255 x 180mm, Col Length: 255mm, Bleed Size: 295 x 213mm, Trim Size: 289 x 210mm, Page Width: 180mm, Film: Digital
Copy instructions: Copy Date: 4 weeks prior to publication date
Average advertising content per issue: 40%
BUSINESS: ARCHITECTURE & BUILDING: Building

PROFESSIONAL DEVELOPMENT TODAY
41160U62J-870

Editorial Address: 215 The Green House, Gibb Street, Digbeth, BIRMINGHAM, B9 4AA **Tel:** 0121 224 7576
Fax: 0121 224 7565
Email: lucy.busuttil@imaginitiveminds.co.uk
Web site: http://www.education-quest.com
ISSN: 1460-8340
Publisher: Imaginative Minds
Frequency: 3 issues yearly
Free to qualifying individuals
Annual Sub.: £45.00
Circulation: 5,000 (Publisher's Statement)
Usual Pagination: 48
Editor: Lucy Busuttil; **Managing Director:** Howard Sharron
Summary of Content: Journal covering professional development in the field of education.
Readership/Target Audience: Aimed at CPD co-ordinators.
ADVERTISING: No Advertising taken
BUSINESS: CHURCH & SCHOOL EQUIPMENT & EDUCATION: Teachers & Education Management

PROFESSIONAL DRIVER
1664190U64G-532

Formerly: The Chauffeur Magazine
Editorial Address: 1C The Courtyard, Market Square, WESTERHAM, TN16 1AZ **Tel:** 0845 290 3774
Email: paulwebb@prodrivermags.com
Advertising Address: As above.
Email: paulwebb@prodrivermags.com
Web site: http://www.prodrivermags.com
Publisher: London Road Media Limited
Date Established: 2003
Frequency: 10 issues yearly
Free to qualifying individuals
Annual Sub.: £24.95
Circulation: 10,318 (Publisher's Statement)
Usual Pagination: 84
Editor: Paul Webb; **Managing Director:** Simon Tozer;
Managing Editor: Mark Bursa; **Publisher:** Paul Webb
Summary of Content: Magazine covering all aspects of the chauffeuring industry including news and product reviews.
Readership/Target Audience: Aimed at chauffeurs.
ADVERTISING RATES:
Full Page Colour £925.00
BUSINESS: OTHER CLASSIFICATIONS: Taxi Trade

PROFESSIONAL ELECTRICIAN AND INSTALLER
37329U17-167

Editorial Address: Regal House, Regal Way, WATFORD, WD24 4YF **Tel:** 01923 237799 **Fax:** 01923 246901
Email: pe@hamerville.co.uk
Advertising Address: As above.
Email: pesales@hamerville.co.uk
Web site: http://www.hamerville.co.uk
Publisher: Hamerville Magazines Ltd
Frequency: 11 issues yearly - Published on the 1st of the cover month
Free to qualifying individuals
Annual Sub.: £30.00
Circulation: 66,117 (ABC 01/01/2007 to 01/07/2007)
Usual Pagination: 96
Editor: Jonathan Cole; **Advertising Manager:** Tim Benwell
Summary of Content: Journal covering business and technical articles and features on products.
Readership/Target Audience: Read by electricians, electrical contractors and maintenance engineers.
ADVERTISING RATES:
Full Page Mono £2975.00
Full Page Colour £2975.00
Agency Commission: 10%
Mechanical Data: Col Length: 255mm, Page Width: 180mm, Bleed Size: 291 x 213mm, Trim Size: 285 x 210mm, Type Area: 255 x 180mm, Film: Digital
Copy instructions: Copy Date: 5 weeks prior to publication date
Average advertising content per issue: 44%
BUSINESS: ELECTRICAL

PROFESSIONAL ENGINEERING
37671U19F-625

Editorial Address: 1 Birdcage Walk, LONDON, SW1H 9JJ
Tel: 020 7973 1299 **Fax:** 020 7973 0462
Email: pe@pepublishing.com
Advertising Address: As above. **Tel:** 020 7973 1700
Fax: 020 7799 2479
Email: nigelse@pepublishing.com
Web site: http://www.profeng.com
ISSN: 0953-6639
Publisher: Professional Engineering Publishing Ltd
Date Established: 1988
Frequency: 22 issues yearly
Free to qualifying individuals
Annual Sub.: £109.00
Circulation: 76,665 (ABC 01/01/2008 to 31/12/2008)
Usual Pagination: 100

Editor: John Pullin; **News Editor:** Ben Sampson;
Advertising Manager: Nigel Searle; **Managing Editor:** Lee Hibbert
Summary of Content: Publication covering management, business and technology in engineering.
Readership/Target Audience: Read by professional engineers many of whom are members of The Institution of Mechanical Engineers.
ADVERTISING RATES:
Full Page Mono £3494.00
Full Page Colour £4494.00
Agency Commission: 10%
Mechanical Data: Col Length: 255mm, No. of Columns (Display): 4, Film: Digital, Bleed Size: 303 x 216mm, Trim Size: 297 x 210mm, Page Width: 180mm, Type Area: 255 x 180mm
Copy instructions: Copy Date: 1 week prior to publication date
Average advertising content per issue: 40%
BUSINESS: ENGINEERING & MACHINERY: Production & Mechanical Engineering

PROFESSIONAL FUNDRAISING
35444U1P-100

Editorial Address: 15 Prescott Place, LONDON, SW4 6BS
Tel: 020 7819 1206 **Fax:** 020 7819 1210
Email: lucy@professionalfundraising.co.uk
Advertising Address: As above. **Tel:** 020 7819 1200
Fax: 020 7819 1219
Email: phil@plazapublishing.co.uk
Web site: http://www.professionalfundraising.co.uk
ISSN: 0961-5679
Publisher: Plaza Publishing Ltd
Date Established: 1990
Frequency: 11 issues yearly
Annual Sub.: £80.00
Circulation: 5,000 (Publisher's Statement)
Usual Pagination: 40
Editor: Lucy Harvey
Summary of Content: Magazine covering latest news, issues and debates in the fundraising sector.
Readership/Target Audience: Read by professional fundraisers and suppliers to the fundraising sector throughout the world.
ADVERTISING RATES:
Full Page Colour £1995.00
Agency Commission: 10%
Mechanical Data: Film: Digital, Col Length; 277mm, Type Area: 277 x 190mm, Bleed Size: 303 x 213mm, Page Width: 190mm
Copy instructions: Copy Date: 10 days prior to publication date
BUSINESS: FINANCE & ECONOMICS: Fundraising

THE PROFESSIONAL GARDENER
38127U26D-150

Editorial Address: 34 Fitz Road, COCKERMOUTH, CA13 0AN **Tel:** 01900 824377
Email: suetasker@sparker4.fsnet.co.uk
Advertising Address: PO Box 21, Heritage House, BALDOCK, SG7 5SH **Tel:** 01462 896688 **Fax:** 01462 896677
Email: bernadette@hall-mccartney.co.uk
Web site: http://www.pgg.org.uk
ISSN: 1366-5499
Publisher: Hall-McCartney Limited
Frequency: Quarterly - Published at the beginning of the cover month
Annual Sub.: £36.00
Circulation: 1,000 (Publisher's Statement)
Usual Pagination: 50
Editor: Sue Tasker; **Publisher:** David Lewis
Summary of Content: Journal of the Professional Gardeners' Guild.
Readership/Target Audience: Aimed at head gardeners, garden managers and those employed in private gardens.
ADVERTISING RATES:
Full Page Mono £385.00
Full Page Colour £470.00
SCC £15.00
Agency Commission: 10%
Mechanical Data: Page Width: 185mm, Film: Digital, Type Area: 270 x 185mm, Bleed Size: 303 x 213mm, Trim Size: 297 x 210mm, Col Length: 270mm, No. of Columns (Display): 4
Copy instructions: Copy Date: 6 weeks prior to publication date
Average advertising content per issue: 20%
BUSINESS: GARDEN TRADE: Garden Trade Horticulture

PROFESSIONAL HAIRDRESSER
1643863U15B-201

Formerly: Hairdressing & Beauty Magazine
Editorial Address: Regal House, Regal Way, WATFORD, WD24 4YF **Tel:** 01923 237799 **Fax:** 01923 246901
Email: nshannon@hamerville.co.uk
Advertising Address: As above.
Email: oshannon@hamerville.co.uk

Business Magazines

Publisher: Hamerville Magazines Ltd
Date Established: 2003
Frequency: 11 issues yearly
Free to qualifying individuals
Circulation: 17,668 (Publisher's Statement)
Usual Pagination: 104
Editor: Nicola Shannon
Summary of Content: Magazine covering the hairdressing industry. Includes articles on fashion, new products, education and training.
Readership/Target Audience: Aimed at salon owners and stylists.
ADVERTISING RATES:
Full Page Mono £1900.00
Full Page Colour £1900.00
Agency Commission: 10%
Mechanical Data: Type Area: 255 x 180mm, Bleed Size: 295 x 216mm, Trim Size: 289 x 210mm, Col Length: 255mm, Page Width: 180mm, Film: Digital
Copy instructions: Copy Date: 6 weeks prior to publication date
Average advertising content per issue: 60%
BUSINESS: COSMETICS & HAIRDRESSING: Hairdressing

PROFESSIONAL HEATING AND PLUMBING INSTALLER
35777U3D-100

Editorial Address: Regal House, Regal Way, WATFORD, WD24 4YF **Tel:** 01923 237799 **Fax:** 01923 246901
Email: phpi@hamerville.co.uk
Advertising Address: As above.
Email: astapleton@hamerville.co.uk
Web site: http://www.hamerville.co.uk
Publisher: Hamerville Magazines Ltd
Date Established: 1986
Frequency: 11 issues yearly - Published in the 1st week of the cover month
Free to qualifying individuals
Annual Sub.: £30.00
Circulation: 63,541 (ABC 02/07/2007 to 30/12/2007)
Usual Pagination: 76
Editor: Stuart Hamilton; **Managing Editor:** Terry Smith;
Publisher: Bryan Shannon
Summary of Content: Journal containing product, technical and business information.
Readership/Target Audience: Aimed at installers in the heating and plumbing industry.
ADVERTISING RATES:
Full Page Mono £2975.00
Full Page Colour £2975.00
Agency Commission: 10%
Mechanical Data: Type Area: 255 x 180mm, Bleed Size: 295 x 213mm, Trim Size: 289 x 210mm, Col Length: 255mm, Page Width: 180mm, Film: Positive, right reading, emulsion side down
Copy instructions: Copy Date: 4 weeks prior to publication date
Average advertising content per issue: 45%
BUSINESS: HEATING & VENTILATION: Heating & Plumbing

PROFESSIONAL HOUSEBUILDER & PROPERTY DEVELOPER
1824332U4E-449

Editorial Address: Regal House, Regal Way, WATFORD, WD24 4YF **Tel:** 01923 237799 **Fax:** 01923 246901
Email: phpd@hamerville.co.uk
Advertising Address: As above.
Email: cbland@hamerville.co.uk
Publisher: Hamerville Magazines Ltd
Date Established: 2007
Frequency: 9 issues yearly - Published in the 1st week of the cover month
Circulation: 21,214 (ABC 01/07/2008 to 30/06/2009)
Usual Pagination: 98
Editor: Jo Anne Wright
Summary of Content: Magazine covering housebuilding and developing.
Readership/Target Audience: Aimed at housebuilders and developers.
ADVERTISING RATES:
Full Page Mono £2600.00
Full Page Colour £2600.00
Agency Commission: 10%
Mechanical Data: Type Area: 255 x 180mm, Bleed Size: 295 x 216mm, Trim Size: 289 x 210mm, Col Length: 255mm, Page Width: 180mm, Film: Digital
Copy instructions: Copy Date: 20 days prior to publication date
Average advertising content per issue: 40%
BUSINESS: ARCHITECTURE & BUILDING: Building

PROFESSIONAL IMAGEMAKER PHOTOGRAPHIC MAGAZINE
1809960U38-190

Editorial Address: 6 Bath Street, RHYL, LL18 3EB
Tel: 01745 356935
Email: mikemcnamee@compuserve.com
Advertising Address: As above.
Email: cliveinsley@btinternet.com

Web site: http://www.swpp.co.uk/mag.htm
Publisher: SWPP & BPPA
Frequency: 6 issues yearly
Free to qualifying individuals
Annual Sub.: £30.00
Circulation: 8,750 (Publisher's Statement)
Editor: Mike McNamee; **News Editor:** Colin Jones;
Advertising Manager: Clive Insley
Summary of Content: Magazine featuring equipment reviews, digital capture, tutorials, photographer profiles, techniques, architectural photography, wedding and portrait tutorials, industry news and desk top publishing.
Readership/Target Audience: Aimed at professional photographers.
ADVERTISING RATES:
Full Page Mono £900.00
Full Page Colour £900.00
Agency Commission: 10%
Mechanical Data: Bleed Size: 303 x 216mm, Trim Size: 297 x 210mm, Film: Digital
Copy instructions: Copy Date: 3 weeks prior to publication date
Average advertising content per issue: 40%
Supplement(s): The Show Guide - 1xY
BUSINESS: PHOTOGRAPHIC TRADE

THE PROFESSIONAL INSTALLER
1703357U12B-87

Editorial Address: F1-F3 Holme Suite, Oaks Lane, Oaks Business Park, BARNSLEY, S71 1HT **Tel:** 01226 321450
Fax: 01226 240202
Email: sheilah@clearview-uk.com
Advertising Address: F2 Holme Suite, Oaks Lane, Oaks Business Park, BARNSLEY, S71 1HT **Tel:** 01226 321450
Fax: 01226 240202
Email: sheilah@zmpl.com
Publisher: Zine Media Publishing Ltd
Date Established: 2006
Frequency: 6 issues yearly - Published around the middle of the cover month
Free to qualifying individuals
Circulation: 6,000 (Publisher's Statement)
Usual Pagination: 40
Editor: Sheilah Reed; **Features Editor:** Sheilah Reed
Summary of Content: Magazine featuring product information and industry news on the glass and glazing industry.
Readership/Target Audience: Aimed at installers.
ADVERTISING RATES:
Full Page Colour £800.00
Agency Commission: 15%
Copy instructions: Copy Date: 10th of the cover month
Average advertising content per issue: 40%
BUSINESS: CERAMICS, POTTERY & GLASS: Glass

PROFESSIONAL INVESTOR
35290U1F-355

Editorial Address: 2nd Floor, 135 Cannon Street, LONDON, EC4N 5BP **Tel:** 020 7280 9623 **Fax:** 020 7796 3333
Advertising Address: As above. **Tel:** 020 7796 3000
Email: wgoodhart@cfauk.org
Web site: http://www.cfauk.org
ISSN: 0958-2541
Publisher: CFA UK
Frequency: Quarterly
Free to qualifying individuals
Annual Sub.: £145.00
Circulation: 14,500 (Publisher's Statement)
Usual Pagination: 80
Advertising Manager: Will Goodhart
Summary of Content: Journal of the UK Society of Investment Professionals. Covers news and investment features.
Readership/Target Audience: Aimed at members of the society, UK and European fund managers and investment analysts.
ADVERTISING RATES:
Full Page Colour £4500.00
Agency Commission: 10%
Mechanical Data: Film: Digital, Trim Size: 284 x 210mm, Type Area: 264 x 190mm, Bleed Size: 289 x 214mm, Col Length: 264mm, Page Width: 190mm
Copy instructions: Copy Date: 24th of the month prior to publication date
Average advertising content per issue: 25%
Supplement(s): Wincott Prize - 1xY
BUSINESS: FINANCE & ECONOMICS: Investment

PROFESSIONAL LANDSCAPER & GROUNDSMAN
40683U57-45

Formerly: Professional Landscaper
Editorial Address: PO Box 523, HORSHAM, RH12 4WL
Tel: 01293 871201 **Fax:** 01293 871301
Email: newsdesk123@aol.com
Advertising Address: As above.
Email: newsdesk123@aol.com
Web site: http://www.professional-landscaper.co.uk

Publisher: Albatross Publications
Frequency: Half-yearly - Published in March, July and November. Published around the 15th of the cover month
Annual Sub.: £6.00
Circulation: 3,000 (Publisher's Statement)
Usual Pagination: 24
Editor: Carol Andrews; **Advertising Manager:** Carol Andrews
Summary of Content: Magazine covering landscaping and groundsmanship.
Readership/Target Audience: Aimed at landscape contractors, architects, local authorities and groundsmen.
ADVERTISING RATES:
Full Page Mono £495.00
Full Page Colour £650.00
Agency Commission: 10%
Mechanical Data: Type Area: 265 x 179mm, Col Length: 265mm, Trim Size: 297 x 210mm, Bleed Size: 300 x 213mm, Print Process: Litho, Page Width: 179mm, Film: Digital
Copy instructions: Copy Date: 3 weeks prior to publication date
BUSINESS: ENVIRONMENT & POLLUTION

PROFESSIONAL MANAGER
36797U14F-257

Editorial Address: 3rd Floor, 2 Savoy Court, Strand, LONDON, WC2R 0EZ **Tel:** 020 7421 2710
Fax: 020 7497 0463
Email: professional.manager@managers.org.uk
Advertising Address: As above.
Email: barbara.kates@managers.org.uk
Web site: http://www.managers.org.uk/professionalmanager
ISSN: 0969-6695
Publisher: The Chartered Management Institute
Date Established: 1992
Frequency: 6 issues yearly - Published at the end of the month prior to cover date
Cover Price: £3.85
Annual Sub.: £23.10
Circulation: 81,977 (ABC 01/07/2008 to 30/06/2009)
Usual Pagination: 52
Editor: Sue Mann; **Advertising Manager:** Barbara Kates
Summary of Content: Journal covering developments in the management field.
Readership/Target Audience: Read by managerial personnel.
ADVERTISING RATES:
Full Page Mono £3965.00
Full Page Colour £4540.00
Agency Commission: 10%
Mechanical Data: Type Area: 263 x 205mm, Bleed Size: 306 x 236mm, Trim Size: 300 x 230mm, Col Length: 263mm, Page Width: 205mm, Film: Digital
Average advertising content per issue: 20%
BUSINESS: COMMERCE, INDUSTRY & MANAGEMENT: Training & Recruitment

PROFESSIONAL MARKETING
35537U2A-160

Editorial Address: Warnford Court, 29 Throgmorton Street, LONDON, EC2N 2AT **Tel:** 020 7786 9786
Fax: 020 7786 9799
Email: pm@pmint.co.uk
Advertising Address: As above.
Email: pm@pmint.co.uk
Web site: http://www.pmforum.co.uk
ISSN: 0969-1847
Publisher: Practice Management International LLP
Date Established: 1993
Frequency: 10 issues yearly - Not published in January or August
Circulation: 1,800 (Publisher's Statement)
Usual Pagination: 28
Editor: Nadia Cristina; **Advertising Manager:** Nadia Cristina; **Managing Editor:** Nadia Cristina
Summary of Content: Journal covering news, case studies and marketing techniques for those working in the professional services.
Readership/Target Audience: Aimed at those involved in professional services marketing.
ADVERTISING RATES:
Full Page Mono £800.00
Full Page Colour £1100.00
Mechanical Data: Film: Positive, right reading, emulsion side down, Type Area: 297 x 210mm, Col Length: 297mm, Page Width: 210mm
Copy instructions: Copy Date: 16 days prior to publication date
Average advertising content per issue: 7%
BUSINESS: COMMUNICATIONS, ADVERTISING & MARKETING

PROFESSIONAL MOTOR FACTOR
1791863U5A-235

Editorial Address: Regal House, Regal Way, WATFORD, WD24 4YF **Tel:** 01923 237799 **Fax:** 01923 246901
Email: bnoble@hamerville.co.uk

Advertising Address: As above.
Email: pmmsales@hamerville.co.uk
Web site: http://www.hamerville.co.uk/mag_pmf.htm
Publisher: Hamerville Magazines Ltd
Frequency: 6 issues yearly
Circulation: 3,167 (ABC 01/07/2008 to 30/06/2009)
Editor: Bernadette Noble
Summary of Content: Magazine providing coverage of key issues affecting factor business. Featuring information on all aspects of business, editorial coverage of product developments, new markets and industry news.
Readership/Target Audience: Aimed at key buyers and decision makers at branch level.
ADVERTISING: Rates on application
BUSINESS: COMPUTERS & AUTOMATION: Automation & Instrumentation

PROFESSIONAL MOTOR MECHANIC

624658U31A-129_75

Editorial Address: Regal House, Regal Way, WATFORD, WD24 4YF Tel: 01923 237799 Fax: 01923 246901
Email: pmm@hamerville.co.uk
Advertising Address: As above.
Email: pmmsales@hamerville.co.uk
Web site: http://www.hamerville.co.uk
Publisher: Hamerville Magazines Ltd
Date Established: 2000
Frequency: 11 issues yearly - Published in the 1st week of the cover month
Cover Price: Free
Circulation: 63,216 (ABC 01/01/2007 to 01/07/2007)
Usual Pagination: 60
Editor: Richard Bowler; Managing Editor: Terry Smith;
Publisher: Bryan Shannon
Summary of Content: Magazine containing news, business and technical advice, product information and mechanic profiles.
Readership/Target Audience: Aimed at those involved in the automotive services and body repair professionals.
ADVERTISING RATES:
Full Page Colour £2750.00
SCC £30.00
Agency Commission: 10%
Mechanical Data: Bleed Size: 291 x 213mm, Trim Size: 285 x 210mm, Film: Digital
Copy instructions: Copy Date: 6 weeks prior to publication date
Average advertising content per issue: 50%
BUSINESS: MOTOR TRADE: Motor Trade Accessories

PROFESSIONAL MOTORSPORT WORLD

1775354U32H-469

Editorial Address: Abinger House, Church Street, DORKING, RH4 1DF Tel: 01306 743744 Fax: 01306 887546
Email: motorsport@ukintpress.com
Advertising Address: As above. Fax: 01306 742525
Email: j.kesavan@ukintpress.com
Web site: http://www.ukipme.com
ISSN: 1748-9296
Publisher: UKIP Media & Events Ltd
Date Established: 2006
Frequency: Quarterly
Cover Price: £15.00
Free to qualifying individuals
Editor: Graham Heeps
Summary of Content: Publication covering the latest developments within the world of professional motor sport with news, interviews and articles covering technology, components, testing, transportation, marketing, politics, strategies and business operation.
Readership/Target Audience: Aimed at all people associated with professional motor sport including teams, drivers, promoters and support crews.
ADVERTISING RATES:
Full Page Colour £3400.00
Agency Commission: 15%
Mechanical Data: Type Area: 255 x 195mm, Trim Size: 275 x 215mm, Col Length: 255mm, Page Width: 195mm, Film: Digital
Average advertising content per issue: 30%
BUSINESS: LOCAL GOVERNMENT, LEISURE & RECREATION: Leisure, Recreation & Entertainment

THE PROFESSIONAL PAINTER & DECORATOR

37272U16A-110

Editorial Address: PO Box 419, FOLKESTONE, CT20 3GU
Tel: 01303 238002 Fax: 01303 237996
Email: davidpescod@aol.com
Advertising Address: The Barn, Stoney Lane, BOVINGDON, HP3 0LY Tel: 01442 832715
Fax: 01442 832715
Web site: http://www.paintshow.co.uk
Publisher: DPA Publishing
Date Established: 1986
Frequency: 6 issues yearly
Cover Price: £2.40

Annual Sub.: £18.00
Circulation: 23,000 (Publisher's Statement)
Usual Pagination: 72
Editor: David Pescod; Advertising Manager: Richard Daynes
Summary of Content: Official publication of the Painting & Decorating Federation.
Readership/Target Audience: Aimed at PDF members and all other contractors.
ADVERTISING RATES:
Full Page Mono £950.00
Full Page Colour £950.00
Agency Commission: 10%
Mechanical Data: Film: Digital, Bleed Size: 301 x 214mm, Trim Size: 297 x 210mm, Type Area: 272 x 190mm, Col Length: 272mm, Page Width: 190mm
Copy instructions: Copy Date: 2 weeks prior to publication date
Average advertising content per issue: 50%
BUSINESS: DECORATING & PAINT

PROFESSIONAL PENSIONS

35371U1H-78

Editorial Address: Haymarket House, 28-29 Haymarket, LONDON, SW1Y 4RX Tel: 020 7484 9700
Email: profpens@incisivemedia.com
Advertising Address: As above.
Email: john.waterson@incisivemedia.com
Web site: http://www.professionalpensions.co.uk
Publisher: Incisive Media Investments
Date Established: 1995
Frequency: Weekly - Published on Thursday
Free to qualifying individuals
Annual Sub.: £325.00
Circulation: 12,572 (ABC 01/07/2008 to 30/06/2009)
Editor: Jenna Towler; Features Editor: Helen Morrissey;
Editor-in-Chief: Alex Beveridge; Advertising Manager: John Waterson
Summary of Content: Magazine covering news and background on current issues in the pensions industry.
Readership/Target Audience: Aimed at pension scheme managers, trustees and pensions professionals.
ADVERTISING RATES:
Full Page Colour £6595.00
Agency Commission: 10%
Mechanical Data: Bleed Size: 356 x 256mm, Type Area: 332 x 226mm, Col Length: 332mm, Page Width: 226mm, Film: Digital, Trim Size: 350 x 250mm
Copy instructions: Copy Date: 1 week prior to publication date
Average advertising content per issue: 35%
BUSINESS: FINANCE & ECONOMICS: Pensions

PROFESSIONAL PHOTOGRAPHER

38803U38-80

Formerly: Professional Photographer & Digital Pro
Editorial Address: The Mill, Bearwalden Business Park, Wendens Ambo, SAFFRON WALDEN, CB11 4GB
Tel: 01799 544200 Fax: 01799 544201
Email: grant.scott@archant.co.uk
Advertising Address: As above. Tel: 01799 544219
Fax: 01799 544202
Email: ronnie.hagger@archant.co.uk
Web site: http://www.professionalphotographer.co.uk
Publisher: Archant Specialist Ltd (Saffron Walden)
Frequency: Monthly
Cover Price: £3.60
Annual Sub.: £35.40
Circulation: 12,300 (Publisher's Statement)
Usual Pagination: 100
Editor: Grant Scott
Summary of Content: Journal covering applied industrial, commercial, creative and social uses of photography using both conventional and digital equipment. Also photographic equipment and processing as well as features on the wider use of photography.
Readership/Target Audience: Aimed at professional and serious amateur photographers.
ADVERTISING RATES:
Full Page Colour £1930.00
Agency Commission: 10%
Mechanical Data: Col Length: 271mm, Page Width: 190mm, Bleed Size: 303 x 216mm, Trim Size: 297 x 210mm, Film: Digital, Type Area: 271 x 190mm
Copy instructions: Copy Date: 3 weeks prior to publication date
Average advertising content per issue: 40%
BUSINESS: PHOTOGRAPHIC TRADE

PROFESSIONAL RECOVERY

39704U49R-190

Formerly: Recovery Operator
Editorial Address: 2 Crown Street, Wellington, TELFORD, TF1 1LP Tel: 01952 415334 Fax: 01952 245077
Email: editor@ppmedia.co.uk
Advertising Address: As above.
Email: marie.dobson@ppmedia.co.uk
Web site: http://www.onlinerecovery.co.uk

Publisher: Partnership Publishing Limited
Date Established: 1999
Frequency: 18 issues yearly
Annual Sub.: £49.00
Circulation: 10,000 (Publisher's Statement)
Usual Pagination: 64
Editor: Martin Scholes; News Editor: Martin Scholes;
Advertising Manager: Marie Dobson; Managing Editor: David Gregory
Summary of Content: Journal containing news and features for the vehicle recovery industry.
Readership/Target Audience: Aimed at recovery operators.
ADVERTISING RATES:
Full Page Mono £700.00
Full Page Colour £1200.00
Agency Commission: 10%
Mechanical Data: Film: Digital, Bleed Size: 303 x 216mm, Trim Size: 297 x 210mm
Copy instructions: Copy Date: 1 week prior to publication date
Average advertising content per issue: 45%
BUSINESS: TRANSPORT: Transport Related

PROFESSIONAL SECURITY

39916U54C-90

Editorial Address: 4 Elms Lane, Shareshill, WOLVERHAMPTON, WV10 7JS Tel: 01922 415233
Fax: 01922 415208
Email: info@jtc.u-net.com
Advertising Address: As above.
Email: roy@jtc.u-net.com
Web site: http://www.professionalsecurity.co.uk
Publisher: JTC Associates Ltd
Date Established: 1990
Frequency: Monthly - Published in the last week of the cover month
Cover Price: £6.00
Annual Sub.: £40.00
Circulation: 11,200 (Publisher's Statement)
Usual Pagination: 120
Editor: Mark Rowe; Executive Editor: Mark Rowe; Editor-in-Chief: John Cully; Managing Director: Roy Cooper;
Advertising Manager: Steve Liddiard
Summary of Content: Magazine covering all aspects of the private security and CCTV industries including contributions from figures in the industry and information on new products and contracts.
Readership/Target Audience: Aimed at specifiers, end users, local and central government and system integrators.
ADVERTISING RATES:
Full Page Mono £2600.00
Full Page Colour £2900.00
SCC £86.00
Agency Commission: 10%
Mechanical Data: Type Area: 264 x 184mm, Col Length: 264mm, Bleed Size: 303 x 214mm, Trim Size: 297 X 210mm, Film: Digital, Page Width: 184mm
Copy instructions: Copy Date: Last week of the month prior to publication date
Average advertising content per issue: 40%
BUSINESS: SAFETY & SECURITY: Security

PROFESSIONAL SOCIAL WORK

38491U32G-100

Editorial Address: 16 Kent Street, BIRMINGHAM, B5 6RD
Tel: 0121 622 3911 Fax: 0121 622 4860
Email: j.devo@basw.co.uk
Web site: http://www.basw.co.uk
ISSN: 1352-3112
Publisher: British Association of Social Workers
Date Established: 1994
Frequency: Monthly
Free to qualifying individuals
Annual Sub.: £39.50
Circulation: 12,000 (Publisher's Statement)
Usual Pagination: 36
Editor: Joseph Devo; Publisher: Ian Johnston
Summary of Content: Journal of the British Association of Social Workers containing articles relevant to social workers and related professions also contains an employment section.
Readership/Target Audience: Aimed at social workers and related professions.
ADVERTISING: No Advertising taken
BUSINESS: LOCAL GOVERNMENT, LEISURE & RECREATION: Community Care & Social Services

PROFESSIONAL VAN & LIGHT TRUCK

1616004U49D-359

Editorial Address: 72 Carfin Street, MOTHERWELL, ML1 4JN Tel: 01698 833949 Fax: 01698 873873
Email: editor@vanandlighttruck.co.uk
Advertising Address: The Old Police Station, Golden Hill, LEYLAND, PR25 3NN Tel: 01772 433303
Fax: 01772 433772
Email: leah@campbelluk.com

Business Magazines

Web site: http://www.vanandlighttruck.co.uk
Publisher: Van UK ltd
Date Established: 2003
Frequency: 11 issues yearly
Cover Price: £3.50
Free to qualifying individuals
Circulation: 12,000 (Publisher's Statement)
Usual Pagination: 48
Editor: John Fife; **Advertising Manager:** Leah Halik;
Managing Editor: Tim Campbell; **Publisher:** Tim Campbell
Summary of Content: Magazine covering all aspects of the
Light Commercial Vehicle industry, appealing to all retail and
industry sectors from private buyers to fleet operators and
uniquely covers all light commercial vehicles, from car
derived vans all the way up to 7.5 tonne trucks, plus pickups
and 4x4s.
Readership/Target Audience: Aimed at drivers, private
buyers, small business users and fleet buyers as well as
industry professionals in the manufacturing and retail
sectors.
ADVERTISING RATES:
Full Page Colour £1745.00
Agency Commission: 10%
Mechanical Data: Type Area: 265 x 180mm, Col Length:
265mm, Page Width: 180mm, Film: Digital, Trim Size: 297 x
210mm, Bleed Size: 303 x 216mm
Copy instructions: Copy Date: 2 weeks prior to publication
date
Average advertising content per issue: 33%
BUSINESS: TRANSPORT: Commercial Vehicles

PROFESSIONAL WEALTH
MANAGEMENT   754736U1F-571
Editorial Address: 1 Southwark Bridge, LONDON, SE1 9HL
Tel: 020 7873 3000
Email: elisa.trovato@ft.com
Advertising Address: As above. **Tel:** 020 7775 6320
Email: andrew.campbell@ft.com
Web site: http://www.pwmnet.com
Publisher: FT Group
Date Established: 2001
Frequency: 10 issues yearly
Annual Sub.: £278.00
Circulation: 20,000 (Publisher's Statement)
Editor: Elisa Trovato; **Editor-in-Chief:** Yuri Bender;
Advertising Manager: Andrew Campbell; **Publisher:** Peter
Collins
Summary of Content: Magazine covering the mechanics,
application and benefits of product development including
investment strategies and techniques, management styles
and the benefits of using a variety of products. Also gives an
insight into wealth management market trends.
Readership/Target Audience: Aimed at private banks,
wealth management, institutions, fund management houses,
investment banks, family offices, consultants, brokers, IFAs,
retail banks and other distributors of wealth investment
products to wealthy individuals.
ADVERTISING RATES:
Full Page Colour £9250.00
Agency Commission: 10%
Mechanical Data: Trim Size: 297 x 210mm, Bleed Size: 308
x 216mm, Type Area: 266 x 178mm, Film: Digital, Col
Length: 266mm, Page Width: 178mm
Copy instructions: Copy Date: 15th of the month prior to
publication date
Average advertising content per issue: 30%
BUSINESS: FINANCE & ECONOMICS: Investment

PROFI INTERNATIONAL   37859U21E-580
Editorial Address: Goblands Farm, Court Lane, Hadlow,
TONBRIDGE, TN11 0EB **Tel:** 01732 852383
Fax: 01732 852488
Email: editorial@profi.com
Advertising Address: As above.
Email: mbrazier@profi.co.uk
Web site: http://www.profi.com
ISSN: 1430-6239
Publisher: Agri Publishing International Ltd
Date Established: 1996
Frequency: 11 issues yearly
Cover Price: £3.95
Annual Sub.: £51.50
Circulation: 12,890 (ABC 01/01/2008 to 31/12/2008)
Usual Pagination: 96
Editor: Andrew Faulkner; **Advertising Manager:** Mark
Brazier
Summary of Content: Magazine featuring independent
tests on farm machinery plus practical ideas and tips.
Language(s): English; German
Readership/Target Audience: Read by those involved in
the agricultural machinery industry, including farmers and
agricultural contractors.
ADVERTISING RATES:
Full Page Mono £1712.00
Full Page Colour £2396.00
SCC £16.88
Agency Commission: 10%

Mechanical Data: Type Area: 270 x 190mm, Bleed Size:
303 x 213mm, Trim Size: 297 x 210mm, No. of Columns
(Display): 4, Col Length: 270mm, Col Widths (Display):
46mm, Page Width: 190mm, Print Process: Offset, Film:
Digital
Copy instructions: Copy Date: 20 days prior to publication
date
Average advertising content per issue: 30%
BUSINESS: AGRICULTURE & FARMING: Agriculture -
Machinery & Plant

PROFILE   35711U2E-80
Formerly: The Institute of Public Relations Journal
Editorial Address: 32 St. James's Square, LONDON, SW1Y
4JR **Tel:** 020 7766 3364 **Fax:** 020 7766 3355
Email: amandaf@cipr.co.uk
Advertising Address: As above. **Tel:** 020 7766 3333
Email: advertising@cipr.co.uk
Web site: http://www.profile-extra.co.uk
ISSN: 0263-6166
Publisher: The Chartered Institute of Public Relations
Date Established: 1999
Frequency: 6 issues yearly
Cover Price: £4.75
Annual Sub.: £55.00
Circulation: 9,500 (Publisher's Statement)
Usual Pagination: 20
Editor: Charlotte Lindsay; **Advertising Manager:** Steve
Miller; **Publisher:** Ann Mealor
Summary of Content: Magazine containing news and
features from the Institute of Public Relations and the public
relations profession, covering IPR policies, work and PR
news, case studies and features.
Readership/Target Audience: Read by public affairs
managers, corporate communications heads, press officers
and publicity managers, directors and executives of public
relations consultancies.
ADVERTISING RATES:
Full Page Mono £2470.00
Full Page Colour £3660.00
Agency Commission: 10%
Mechanical Data: Type Area: 269 x 186mm, Bleed Size:
303 x 216mm, Trim Size: 297 x 210mm, Col Length: 269mm,
Page Width: 186mm, Film: Digital
Average advertising content per issue: 10%
BUSINESS: COMMUNICATIONS, ADVERTISING &
MARKETING: Public Relations

PROFILE   37188U14L-565
Formerly: The Bulletin
Editorial Address: New Prospect House, 8 Leake Street,
LONDON, SE1 7NN **Tel:** 020 7902 6654 **Fax:** 020 7902 6665
Email: charles.harvey@prospect.org.uk
Advertising Address: Century One Publishing, 4-6 Spicer
Street, ST. ALBANS, AL3 4PQ **Tel:** 01727 893894
Fax: 01727 893895
Email: claire@centuryonepublishing.ltd.uk
Web site: http://www.prospect.org.uk
ISSN: 0958-5222
Publisher: Prospect
Date Established: 1982
Frequency: 8 issues yearly
Free to qualifying individuals
Annual Sub.: £37.00
Circulation: 100,423 (ABC 01/07/2007 to 30/06/2008)
Usual Pagination: 32
Editor: Charles Harvey
Summary of Content: Magazine of Prospect Trade Union
covering work-related issues for professionals, scientists,
engineers and managers.
Readership/Target Audience: Aimed at scientists,
engineers and members of Prospect.
ADVERTISING RATES:
Full Page Colour £4830.00
Mechanical Data: Bleed Size: 303 x 216mm, Trim Size: 297
x 210mm, Film: Digital
Copy instructions: Copy Date: 4 weeks prior to publication
date
BUSINESS: COMMERCE, INDUSTRY & MANAGEMENT:
Trade Unions

PROFIT AND LOSS   624906U1F-360
Editorial Address: Suite 26, London Fruit Exchange,
Brushfield Street, LONDON, E1 6EU **Tel:** 020 7377 6716
Fax: 020 7426 0727
Email: colin_lambert@profit-loss.com
Advertising Address: As above. **Tel:** 020 7377 6383
Email: info@profit-loss.com
Web site: http://www.profit-loss.com
Publisher: P & L Services
Date Established: 1999
Frequency: 10 issues yearly - Published on the 17th of the
month
Annual Sub.: £275.00
Circulation: 12,000 (Publisher's Statement)
Usual Pagination: 60

Editor: Colin Lambert; **Editor-in-Chief:** Julie Ros;
Advertising Manager: Michelle Hemstedt; **Publisher:** Julie
Ros
Summary of Content: Magazine covering e-commerce
developments in the foreign exchange and derivatives
markets.
Readership/Target Audience: Aimed at bank treasurers,
traders and sales dealers, managers and corporate
treasurers.
ADVERTISING RATES:
Full Page Colour £4310.00
Agency Commission: 10%
Mechanical Data: Bleed Size: 303 x 216mm, Trim Size: 297
x 210mm, Film: Digital
Copy instructions: Copy Date: 10th of the month prior to
publication date
Average advertising content per issue: 25%
Editions:
Profit and Loss Squawkbox
BUSINESS: FINANCE & ECONOMICS: Investment

PROGRAM: ELECTRONIC LIBRARY AND
INFORMATION SYSTEMS   40874U60B-98
Editorial Address: Department of Information and Library
Studies, University of Wales, ABERYSTWYTH
Tel: 01274 777700 **Fax:** 01274 785200
Email: lat@aber.ac.uk
Web site: http://www.emeraldinsight.com/prog.htm
ISSN: 0033-0337
Publisher: Emerald Group Publishing Ltd
Date Established: 1967
Frequency: Quarterly
Free to qualifying individuals
Annual Sub.: £409.00
Usual Pagination: 70
Editor: Lucy A. Tedd; **Managing Editor:** Lucy A. Tedd;
Publisher: Eileen Breen
Summary of Content: Journal containing material on all
aspects of the use of information technology in libraries,
museums, art galleries and archives.
Readership/Target Audience: Read by libraries and
information professionals.
ADVERTISING: No Advertising taken
BUSINESS: PUBLISHING: Libraries

PROGRAMME NEWS BULLETIN
                              35688U2D-83_25
Formerly: Programme News
Editorial Address: 45 Fouberts Place, LONDON, W1F 7QH
Tel: 020 7575 1938 **Fax:** 020 7575 1931
Email: info@programmenews.co.uk
Web site: http://www.programmenews.co.uk
Publisher: Xtreme Information
Frequency: Monthly
Annual Sub.: £750.00
Usual Pagination: 150
Editor: Adam Hampton
Summary of Content: Magazine for forward planning, giving
advance details of TV and radio programmes in
development and production, as well as contact details for
production companies, commissioning editors and
broadcasters' PR contacts. Includes a forward-planning
diary of industry events and a news round-up.
Readership/Target Audience: Read by post-production
companies, facilities or rental houses, advertising agencies,
public relations companies, TV and radio production
companies, industry freelancers, facilities companies,
broadcasters and charities.
ADVERTISING: No Advertising taken
BUSINESS: COMMUNICATIONS, ADVERTISING &
MARKETING: Broadcasting

PROGRESS IN NEUROLOGY &
PSYCHIATRY   40490U56N-55
Editorial Address: The Atrium, Southern Gate,
CHICHESTER, PO19 8SQ **Tel:** 01243 779777
Fax: 01243 770144
Email: progress@wiley.com
Advertising Address: As above.
Email: sripsher@wiley.co.uk
Web site: http://www.progressnp.com
ISSN: 1367-7543
Publisher: John Wiley & Sons Ltd
Frequency: 9 issues yearly
Free to qualifying individuals
Circulation: 20,229 (Publisher's Statement)
Usual Pagination: 36
Editor: Steve Titmarsh; **Publisher:** Tim Dean
Summary of Content: Magazine covering advances in drug
use on patients with psychiatric and neurological problems.
Readership/Target Audience: Aimed at hospital
specialists, GPs, community psychiatric nurses and other
senior medical professionals.
ADVERTISING: Rates on application

Copy instructions: Copy Date: 6 weeks prior to publication date

BUSINESS: HEALTH & MEDICAL: Mental Health

PROGRESS IN PALLIATIVE CARE

40333U56B-277

Editorial Address: Suite 1C, Josephs Well, Hanover Walk, LEEDS, LS3 1AB
Email: davism6@ccf.org
Advertising Address: As above. **Tel:** 0113 243 2800
Fax: 0113 386 8178
Email: j.moore@maney.co.uk
Web site: http://www.maney.co.uk
ISSN: 0969-9260
Publisher: Maney Publishing
Date Established: 1995
Frequency: 6 issues yearly
Annual Sub.: £99.00
Circulation: 500 (Publisher's Statement)
Usual Pagination: 70
Editor: Juliet Moore; **Editor-in-Chief:** Mellar Davis;
Advertising Manager: Juliet Moore
Summary of Content: Journal covering the management of the problems of end-stage disease and issues pertinent to living with chronic or progressive diseases.
Readership/Target Audience: Aimed at clinicians in palliative care, nurses, hospice workers, health service managers and purchasers.
ADVERTISING RATES:
Full Page Mono £180.00
Mechanical Data: Film: Digital, Print Process: Litho, Type Area: 265 x 180mm, Col Length: 265mm, Page Width: 180mm
BUSINESS: HEALTH & MEDICAL: Nursing

PROGRESS IN PHOTOVOLTAICS

601237U58-68_44

Editorial Address: The Atrium, Southern Gate, CHICHESTER, PO19 8SQ **Tel:** 01243 779777
Fax: 01243 775878
Advertising Address: As above. **Fax:** 01243 770432
Email: adsales@wiley.co.uk
Web site: http://www.interscience.wiley.com
ISSN: 1062-7995
Publisher: John Wiley & Sons Ltd
Date Established: 1993
Frequency: 8 issues yearly
Annual Sub.: $1565.00
Usual Pagination: 96
Editor: James Hare
Summary of Content: Magazine covering the conversion of solar energy into electricity including photovoltaics - from research and advanced development to practical implementation, field testing, economic and environmental considerations.
Readership/Target Audience: Aimed at electrical and electronic engineers, scientists and engineers in the field of renewable energy and microelectronic engineers.
ADVERTISING RATES:
Full Page Mono £1175.00
Full Page Colour £2575.00
Agency Commission: 10%
Mechanical Data: Trim Size: 260 x 200mm, Type Area: 230 x 170mm, Col Length: 230mm, Page Width: 170mm
BUSINESS: ENERGY, FUEL & NUCLEAR

PROGRESS IN RUBBER, PLASTICS & RECYCLING TECHNOLOGY

38845U39-50

Formerly: Progress in Rubber & Plastics Technology
Editorial Address: Shawbury, SHREWSBURY, SY4 4NR
Tel: 01939 252455 **Fax:** 01939 251118
Email: kmevans@rapra.net
Web site: http://www.rapra.net/journals
ISSN: 1447-7606
Publisher: Rapra Technology Ltd
Date Established: 1983
Frequency: Quarterly
Annual Sub.: £415.00
Circulation: 275 (Publisher's Statement)
Usual Pagination: 70
Editor: Kate Evans
Summary of Content: Journal containing peer reviewed articles concerning rubber or plastics and recycling technology.
Readership/Target Audience: Polymner engineers and those involved in polymer technology.
ADVERTISING: No Advertising taken
BUSINESS: PLASTICS & RUBBER

PROGRESSIVE GIFTS & HOME WORLDWIDE

39789U52C-150

Editorial Address: United House, North Road, LONDON, N7 9DP **Tel:** 020 7700 6740 **Fax:** 020 7607 6411
Email: sue@sjbassoc.freeserve.co.uk

Advertising Address: As above.
Email: angieb@max-publishing.co.uk
Web site: http://www.max-publishing.co.uk
Publisher: Max Publishing Ltd
Frequency: 8 issues yearly
Annual Sub.: £45.00
Circulation: 5,996 (ABC 01/07/2008 to 30/06/2009)
Usual Pagination: 84
Editor: Sue Marks; **News Editor:** Sue Marks; **Features Editor:** Sue Marks; **Editor-in-Chief:** Jacqueline Brown;
Managing Director: Jacqueline Brown
Summary of Content: Magazine focusing on giftware and home accessories.
Readership/Target Audience: Aimed at giftware retailers, china and glassware outlets and department stores.
ADVERTISING RATES:
Full Page Mono £995.00
Full Page Colour £1395.00
Agency Commission: 10%
Mechanical Data: Type Area: 271 x 185mm, Bleed Size: 303 x 216mm, Trim Size: 297 x 210mm, Film: Positive, right reading, emulsion side down. Digital, Col Length: 271mm, Page Width: 185mm
Average advertising content per issue: 60%
Supplement(s): Greeting Cards for Gifts - 1xY, The Licensing Source Book - 4xY, Progressive Collectables - 1xY, Progressive Fragrance - 1xY, Progressive Jewellery - 1xY, Progressive Tableware - 1xY, Showtime Worldwide - 1xY
BUSINESS: GIFT TRADE: Fancy Goods

PROGRESSIVE GREETINGS WORLDWIDE

40923U60C-150

Editorial Address: United House, North Road, LONDON, N7 9DP **Tel:** 020 7700 6740 **Fax:** 020 7607 6411
Email: jw@max-publishing.co.uk
Advertising Address: As above. **Fax:** 020 7607 6007
Web site: http://www.progressivegreetings.co.uk
Publisher: Max Publishing Ltd
Date Established: 1990
Frequency: Monthly - Published in the 2nd week of the cover month
Annual Sub.: £50.00
Circulation: 4,979 (ABC 01/07/2008 to 30/06/2009)
Usual Pagination: 80
Editor: Jacqueline Brown; **Managing Director:** Warren Lomax; **Advertisement Director:** Warren Lomax
Summary of Content: Magazine covering all sectors of the greeting card industry including retailing, publishing, wholesaling, artists, news, products and features.
Readership/Target Audience: Read by manufacturers, retailers, department stores, gift shops, publishers, artists and agents.
ADVERTISING RATES:
Full Page Mono £1500.00
Full Page Colour £1500.00
Agency Commission: 10%
Mechanical Data: Type Area: 271 x 185mm, Bleed Size: 303 x 216mm, Trim Size: 297 x 210mm, Col Length: 271mm, Page Width: 185mm, Film: Digital
Copy instructions: Copy Date: 3 weeks prior to publication date
Supplement(s): Board! - 1xY, Brands, Sports and Licensing - 1xY, Focus on Art and Photographic - 1xY, Focus on Cute - 1xY, Focus on Humour - 1xY, Focus on Kids - 1xY, Focus on Weddings - 1xY, Focus on Words and Sentiments - 1xY, Focus on Wrappings - 1xY, Licensing Source Book - 1xY, Progressive Calendars - 3xY, Showtime Worldwide - 1xY, Source Book - 2xY, Trade Source Book - 1xY
BUSINESS: PUBLISHING: Newsagents

PROGRESSIVE HOUSEWARES

39807U53-246

Formerly: Gourmet Retailing
Editorial Address: United House, North Road, LONDON, N7 9DP **Tel:** 020 7700 6740 **Fax:** 020 7607 6411
Email: joh@max-publishing.co.uk
Advertising Address: Media Projects, Hazelbury, Horsted Lane, Isfield, UCKFIELD, TN22 5TX **Tel:** 01825 750784
Fax: 01825 750551
Email: mediap@aol.com
Web site: http://www.progressivehousewares.co.uk
Publisher: Max Publishing Ltd
Date Established: 1995
Frequency: 6 issues yearly
Annual Sub.: £45.00
Circulation: 4,008 (Publisher's Statement)
Usual Pagination: 80
Editor: Emma Cain; **Editor-in-Chief:** Jacqueline Brown;
Managing Director: Warren Lomax; **Advertising Manager:** Patrick Wade
Summary of Content: Magazine featuring house wares and kitchen and dining products, market reports, industry and retailer issues and news.
Readership/Target Audience: Aimed at kitchenware, cookware and general house ware and household product retailers.
ADVERTISING RATES:
Full Page Colour £1800.00

Agency Commission: 10%
Mechanical Data: Type Area: 271 x 185mm, Col Length: 271mm, Bleed Size: 303 x 216mm, Trim Size: 297 x 210mm, Film: Digital, Page Width: 185mm
Average advertising content per issue: 30%
BUSINESS: RETAILING & WHOLESALING

PROGRESSIVE PARTY

39788U52C-100

Formerly: Partytimes
Editorial Address: United House, North Road, LONDON, N7 9DP **Tel:** 020 7700 6740 **Fax:** 020 7607 6411
Email: susanfenton@btconnect.com
Advertising Address: As above.
Email: warren@max-publishing.co.uk
Web site: http://www.progressiveparty.co.uk
ISSN: 1462-2890
Publisher: Max Publishing Ltd
Frequency: 6 issues yearly - Published around the end of the 1st cover month
Annual Sub.: £30.00
Circulation: 5,000 (Publisher's Statement)
Editor: Sue Fenton; **Advertising Manager:** Warren Lomax;
Publisher: Warren Lomax
Summary of Content: Magazine containing news, research and specialist features with a focus on party planning.
Readership/Target Audience: Aimed at party shop retailers and party planners.
ADVERTISING RATES:
Full Page Colour £1500.00
Agency Commission: 10%
Mechanical Data: Trim Size: 297 x 210mm, Film: Digital, Bleed Size: +3mm
Average advertising content per issue: 50%
BUSINESS: GIFT TRADE: Fancy Goods

PROJECT

36799U14A-297

Editorial Address: Media House, 55 Old Road, LEIGHTON BUZZARD, LU7 2RB **Tel:** 01525 370013 **Fax:** 01525 382487
Email: info@impact-now.co.uk
Advertising Address: As above.
Email: vicki@impact-now.co.uk
ISSN: 0957-7033
Publisher: Impact!
Frequency: 10 issues yearly
Cover Price: £3.75
Circulation: 17,936 (ABC 01/07/2008 to 30/06/2009)
Usual Pagination: 48
Editor: James Simons
Summary of Content: Official magazine of the Association for Project Management. Focuses on all aspects of project and programme management across all industries and sectors.
Readership/Target Audience: Aimed at people concerned with project and programme management.
ADVERTISING RATES:
Full Page Mono £1320.00
Full Page Colour £1655.00
Agency Commission: 10%
Mechanical Data: Type Area: 272 x 185mm, Col Length: 272mm, Page Width: 185mm, Trim Size: 297 x 210mm, Film: Digital, Bleed Size: 305 x 218mm
Average advertising content per issue: 20%
BUSINESS: COMMERCE, INDUSTRY & MANAGEMENT

PROJECT CONTROL PROFESSIONAL

37703U19R-160

Formerly: The Cost Engineer
Editorial Address: Unit 12, Moor Place Farm, Plough Lane, Bramshill, HOOK, RG27 0RF **Tel:** 0118 932 6665
Fax: 0118 932 6663
Email: clive@projectmanagertoday.co.uk
Advertising Address: Wedgwood House, 11 Beauforts, ENGLEFIELD GREEN, TW20 0DW **Tel:** 01784 435677
Fax: 01784 435677
Email: petercookassoc@aol.com
Web site: http://www.acoste.org.uk
ISSN: 1750-371X
Publisher: Project Manager Today Publications
Date Established: 1962
Frequency: 6 issues yearly
Free to qualifying individuals
Annual Sub.: £50.00
Circulation: 2,000 (Publisher's Statement)
Usual Pagination: 28
Editor: Clive Wellings; **Advertising Manager:** Peter Cook
Summary of Content: Professional journal focusing on all aspects of the cost engineering profession. Covers project controls, planning and scheduling, resource and cost control, value engineering, estimating, quantity surveying, risk management and case studies.
Readership/Target Audience: Read by professional members of The Association of Cost Engineers.
ADVERTISING RATES:
Full Page Mono £400.00
Full Page Colour £550.00
Agency Commission: 10%

Mechanical Data: No. of Columns (Display): 4, Type Area: 256 x 178mm, Trim Size: 297 x 210mm, Col Length: 256mm, Bleed Size: 303 x 216mm, Page Width: 178mm, Film: Digital
Average advertising content per issue: 40%
BUSINESS: ENGINEERING & MACHINERY: Engineering Related

PROJECT FINANCE 36975U14C-110

Editorial Address: Nestor House, Playhouse Yard, LONDON, EC4V 5EX **Tel:** 020 7779 8888
Fax: 020 7779 7977
Email: psmith@euromoneyplc.com
Advertising Address: As above.
Email: nmahabir@euromoneyplc.com
Web site: http://www.projectfinancemagazine.com
ISSN: 1350-2700
Publisher: Euromoney Institutional Investor plc
Frequency: 10 issues yearly - Published the 1st of the month
Annual Sub.: £1200.00
Circulation: 2,500 (Publisher's Statement)
Editor: Paul Smith; **News Editor:** Paul Smith; **Advertising Manager:** Natasha Mahabir; **Managing Editor:** Sean Keating; **Publisher:** Gary Parker
Summary of Content: Magazine covering all aspects of project and investment financing for capital goods projects and privatisation programmes. Includes developer and sponsor profiles, capital market leasing and news from the telecommunications, gas and oil industries.
Readership/Target Audience: Aimed at project finance professionals.
ADVERTISING RATES:
Full Page Mono £7700.00
Full Page Colour £8500.00
Agency Commission: 15%
Mechanical Data: Type Area: 271 x 184mm, Bleed Size: 303 x 216mm, Col Length: 271mm, Page Width: 184mm, Print Process: Litho, Film: Digital, Trim Size: 297 x 210mm
Copy instructions: Copy Date: 1 week prior to publication date
Average advertising content per issue: 40%
Supplement(s): Asia Pacific - 1xY, Latin America - 1xY, Oil and Gas - 1xY, Power - 1xY, Transport - 1xY
BUSINESS: COMMERCE, INDUSTRY & MANAGEMENT: International Commerce

PROJECT FINANCE INTERNATIONAL 36976U14C-115

Editorial Address: Aldgate House, 33 Aldgate High Street, LONDON, EC3N 1DL **Tel:** 020 7369 7570
Fax: 020 7369 7482
Email: rod.morrison@thomsonreuters.com
Advertising Address: As above. **Tel:** 020 7369 7951
Fax: 020 7369 7766
Email: chris.keene@thomson.com
Web site: http://www.pfie.com
Publisher: Thomson Reuters
Date Established: 1992
Frequency: 24 issues yearly
Annual Sub.: £1450.00
Circulation: 2,500 (Publisher's Statement)
Editor: Rod Morrison; **Advertising Director:** Chris Keene; **Publisher:** Elly Hardwick
Summary of Content: Publication reporting on and analysing the financing of major projects world-wide.
Readership/Target Audience: Aimed at banks, sponsors of projects and lawyers.
ADVERTISING RATES:
Full Page Mono £4000.00
Full Page Colour £6000.00
Agency Commission: 10%
Mechanical Data: Type Area: 270 x 184mm, Bleed Size: 303 x 216mm, Trim Size: 297 x 210mm, Col Length: 270mm, Page Width: 184mm, Film: Digital, No. of Columns (Display): 4, Print Process: Digital
Copy instructions: Copy Date: 8 days prior to publication date
Average advertising content per issue: 30%
Supplement(s): Project Finance International Yearbook - 1xY
BUSINESS: COMMERCE, INDUSTRY & MANAGEMENT: International Commerce

PROJECT MANAGER TODAY 36801U14A-300

Editorial Address: Unit 12, Moor Place Farm, Plough Lane, Bramshill, HOOK, RG27 0RF **Tel:** 0118 932 6665
Fax: 0118 932 6663
Email: klane@projectmanagertoday.co.uk
Advertising Address: Wedgewood House, 11 Beauforts, ENGLEFIELD GREEN, TW20 0DW **Tel:** 01784 435677
Fax: 01784 435677
Email: petercookassoc@aol.com
Web site: http://www.pmtoday.co.uk
ISSN: 1366-6851
Publisher: Larchdrift Projects Ltd
Date Established: 1989
Frequency: Monthly
Free to qualifying individuals
Annual Sub.: £38.00
Circulation: 13,634 (ABC 01/07/2008 to 30/06/2009)
Usual Pagination: 48
Editor: Ken Lane; **Advertising Manager:** Peter Cook
Summary of Content: Magazine focusing on all aspects of project control, planning, costing and management throughout industry and commerce.
Readership/Target Audience: Read by project managers and directors involved in the planning, control and monitoring of projects in the UK and internationally.
ADVERTISING RATES:
Full Page Mono £1860.00
Full Page Colour £2510.00
Agency Commission: 10%
Mechanical Data: Film: Digital, Col Length: 260mm, Type Area: 260 x 190mm, Bleed Size: 303 x 216mm, Trim Size: 297 x 210mm, Page Width: 190mm
Average advertising content per issue: 50%
BUSINESS: COMMERCE, INDUSTRY & MANAGEMENT

PROJECT PLANT 39024U42A-175

Editorial Address: Bergius House, 20 Clifton Street, GLASGOW, G3 7LA **Tel:** 0141 567 6000 **Fax:** 0141 331 1395
Email: mike.travers@peeblesmedia.com
Advertising Address: As above. **Tel:** 0141 567 6007
Fax: 0141 332 2153
Email: terry.smith@peeblesmedia.com
Web site: http://www.peeblesmedia.com
Publisher: Peebles Media Group Ltd
Frequency: Quarterly - Published in the middle of the cover month
Annual Sub.: £25.00
Circulation: 5,330 (ABC 01/07/2008 to 30/06/2009)
Usual Pagination: 64
Editor: Mike Travers; **Advertising Manager:** Terry Smith; **Group Editor:** Mike Travers
Summary of Content: Journal covering news and features on construction equipment.
Readership/Target Audience: Aimed at those involved in construction, civil engineering and plant hire.
ADVERTISING RATES:
Full Page Colour £1525.00
Agency Commission: 10%
Mechanical Data: Type Area: 270 x 188mm, Col Length: 270mm, Trim Size: 297 x 210mm, Bleed Size: 303 x 213mm, Film: Digital, Page Width: 188mm
Copy instructions: Copy Date: 2 weeks prior to publication date
Average advertising content per issue: 40%
BUSINESS: CONSTRUCTION

PROJECT SCOTLAND 39025U4E-427

Editorial Address: Bergius House, 20 Clifton Street, GLASGOW, G3 7LA **Tel:** 0141 567 6000 **Fax:** 0141 331 1395
Email: mike.travers@peeblesmedia.com
Advertising Address: As above. **Tel:** 0141 567 6005
Fax: 0141 353 1784
Email: mark.griston@peeblesmedia.com
Web site: http://www.peeblesmedia.com
Publisher: Peebles Media Group Ltd
Frequency: Monthly - Published on the 1st Thursday of the cover month
Annual Sub.: £58.50
Circulation: 7,223 (ABC 01/07/2008 to 30/06/2009)
Usual Pagination: 36
Editor: Mike Travers; **Advertising Manager:** Mark Griston; **Group Editor:** Mike Travers
Summary of Content: Magazine containing articles on construction from major civil engineering works to housing and restoration projects, architecture, company profiles and site reports.
Readership/Target Audience: Read by architects, surveyors, engineers, council officers, government departments, contractors and sub-contractors.
ADVERTISING RATES:
Full Page Mono £2050.00
Full Page Colour £2600.00
SCC £12.00
Agency Commission: 10%
Mechanical Data: Page Width: 284mm, Film: Digital, Type Area: 380 x 284mm, Col Length: 380mm, Trim Size: 406 x 302mm, Bleed Size: 412 x 305mm
Copy instructions: Copy Date: 2 weeks prior to publication date
Average advertising content per issue: 50%
BUSINESS: ARCHITECTURE & BUILDING: Building

PROMOTIONS BUYER 35539U2A-697

Formerly: Promotions News
Editorial Address: 122 Warwick Street, LEAMINGTON SPA, CV32 4QY **Tel:** 01926 319930
Email: editorial@promotionsbuyer.co.uk
Advertising Address: As above.
Email: sales@promotionsbuyer.co.uk
Web site: http://www.bpma.co.uk
Publisher: Summersault Communications
Date Established: 2003
Frequency: 10 issues yearly - Published in the 1st week of the cover month
Cover Price: £4.95
Free to qualifying individuals
Circulation: 21,000 (Controlled Circulation)
Usual Pagination: 64
Editor: Aileen Lalor; **Advertising Manager:** Kyle Hadden; **Managing Editor:** Dan Bromage
Summary of Content: Magazine containing news and features on promotional merchandise, promotional marketing and business gifts.
Readership/Target Audience: Aimed at those who buy promotional merchandise and produced on behalf of the British Promotional Merchandise Association.
ADVERTISING RATES:
Full Page Mono £1720.00
Full Page Colour £1720.00
Agency Commission: 10%
Mechanical Data: Film: Digital, Trim Size: 297 x 210mm
Copy instructions: Copy Date: 2 weeks prior to publication date
Average advertising content per issue: 50%
BUSINESS: COMMUNICATIONS, ADVERTISING & MARKETING

PROPERTY DIRECT 718310U1E-265

Editorial Address: Ludgate House, 245 Blackfriars Road, LONDON, SE1 9UY **Tel:** 020 7921 8561 **Fax:** 020 7921 8394
Email: giles.barrie@ubm.com
Advertising Address: As above. **Tel:** 020 7921 8379
Fax: 020 7921 8392
Email: alex.segger@ubm.com
Web site: http://www.propertyweek.com
Publisher: UBM Information Ltd
Frequency: Weekly
Cover Price: Free
Circulation: 25,000 (Publisher's Statement)
Usual Pagination: 40
Editor: Hardeep Sandher; **Editor-in-Chief:** Giles Barrie; **Publisher:** Chris Kilby
Summary of Content: Magazine covering property issues that affect small to medium sized companies, including business rates, landlord and tenant relationships, leases and relocation.
Readership/Target Audience: Aimed at occupiers of small to medium sized office and industrial properties in the south of England.
ADVERTISING RATES:
Full Page Mono £1880.00
Full Page Colour £3080.00
Mechanical Data: Film: Digital, Type Area: 277 x 210mm, Bleed Size: 308 x 236mm, Trim Size: 302 x 230mm, Page Width: 210mm, Col Length: 277mm
Copy instructions: Copy Date: 2 weeks prior to publication date
Supplement to: Property Week
BUSINESS: FINANCE & ECONOMICS: Property

PROPERTY EAST MIDLANDS 1775858U1E-395

Editorial Address: The Old Guild House, 1 New Market Street, BIRMINGHAM, B3 2NH **Tel:** 0845 602 2816
Email: amanda.woolley@bemmag.co.uk
Advertising Address: As above. **Fax:** 0121 236 9962
Email: andrew.shelton@bemmag.co.uk
Web site: http://www.bem-mag.com
Publisher: Business Magazine Publishing
Date Established: 2006
Frequency: Quarterly
Annual Sub.: £20.00
Circulation: 5,000 (Publisher's Statement)
Editor: Amanda Woolley; **Advertising Manager:** Andrew Shelton; **Publisher:** Andrew Shelton
Summary of Content: Magazine covering new builds, architecture news, planning conditions and commercial law updates.
Readership/Target Audience: Aimed at construction companies, the commercial property industry and advisers.
ADVERTISING RATES:
Full Page Colour £1600.00
Mechanical Data: Type Area: 267 x 180mm, Bleed Size: 303 x 216mm, Trim Size: 297 x 210mm, Col Length: 267mm, Page Width: 180mm, Film: Digital
BUSINESS: FINANCE & ECONOMICS: Property

PROPERTY EXECUTIVE MAGAZINE 35199U1E-362

Formerly: The Property Executive
Editorial Address: 216 St. Vincent Street, GLASGOW, G2 5SG **Tel:** 0870 011 5010 **Fax:** 0141 221 8434
Email: jane@propertyexecutive.co.uk
Advertising Address: As above. **Tel:** 0141 243 2871
Email: gordon@propertyexecutive.co.uk
Web site: http://www.propertyexecutive.co.uk
Publisher: SGC Media Ltd
Date Established: 1992

Frequency: 6 issues yearly
Cover Price: £3.00
Annual Sub.: £30.00
Circulation: 5,600 (Publisher's Statement)
Usual Pagination: 68
Editor: Jane Ambrose
Summary of Content: Magazine covering commercial and
industrial property news. Includes interviews, appointments
and properties for sale and to let.
Readership/Target Audience: Read by property related
professionals throughout the UK and Ireland but pre-
dominantly Scotland.
ADVERTISING RATES:
Full Page Colour £1600.00
Agency Commission: 10%
Mechanical Data: Bleed Size: 303 x 216mm, Trim Size: 297
x 210mm, Film: Digital
Copy instructions: Copy Date: 1 week prior to publication
date
Average advertising content per issue: 35%
Editions:
Property Executive North
BUSINESS: FINANCE & ECONOMICS: Property

PROPERTY FORECAST
35200U1E-290

Editorial Address: 93 Popes Grove, TWICKENHAM, TW1
4JT **Tel:** 020 8892 2652 **Fax:** 020 8891 6172
Web site: http://www.propertyforecast.com
ISSN: 0955-8659
Publisher: Newzeye Ltd
Date Established: 1998
Frequency: Monthly
Annual Sub.: £250.00
Circulation: 700 (Publisher's Statement)
Usual Pagination: 16
Editor: Philip Marvin
Summary of Content: Newsletter providing intelligence on
future property trends.
Readership/Target Audience: Aimed at investors,
developers and financiers.
ADVERTISING: No Advertising taken
BUSINESS: FINANCE & ECONOMICS: Property

PROPERTY INVESTOR NEWS
1657247U1E-364

Editorial Address: 123-126 Trafalgar House, Grenville
Place, LONDON, NW7 3SA **Tel:** 020 8906 7772
Fax: 020 8906 7773
Email: info@property-investor-news.com
Advertising Address: As above.
Email: info@property-investor-news.com
Web site: http://www.property-investor-news.com
ISSN: 1478-9361
Publisher: Farscape Ltd
Date Established: 2002
Frequency: Monthly
Annual Sub.: £119.00
Circulation: 15,000 (Publisher's Statement)
Usual Pagination: 68
Editor: Donia O'Loughlin
Summary of Content: Magazine covering news, analysis
and research on property and direct investment - both
residential and commercial in the UK, Europe and overseas
markets.
Readership/Target Audience: Aimed at high net worth,
active private property investors and private residential
landlords.
ADVERTISING RATES:
Full Page Colour £2575.00
Agency Commission: 10%
Mechanical Data: Type Area: 262 x 181mm, Bleed Size:
303 x 216mm, Trim Size: 297 x 210mm, Col Length: 262mm,
Page Width: 181mm, Film: Digital
Average advertising content per issue: 30%
BUSINESS: FINANCE & ECONOMICS: Property

PROPERTY LAW JOURNAL
39310U44-1690

Editorial Address: Kensington Square House, 12-14 Ansdell
Street, LONDON, W8 5BN **Tel:** 020 7396 9292
Fax: 020 7396 9303
Email: legalease@legalease.co.uk
Advertising Address: As above. **Fax:** 020 7396 9302
Email: raju.mann@legalease.co.uk
Web site: http://www.legal500.com
ISSN: 1461-0752
Publisher: Legalease Ltd
Date Established: 1998
Frequency: 20 issues yearly
Annual Sub.: £192.00
Circulation: 900 (Publisher's Statement)
Usual Pagination: 24
Editor: Alec Johnson
Summary of Content: Journal updating UK lawyers on
developments and changes in property law.
Readership/Target Audience: Read by the legal profession
and other property professionals.

ADVERTISING RATES:
Full Page Mono £995.00
Agency Commission: 10%
Mechanical Data: Trim Size: 297 x 210mm, Type Area:
271.5 x 185mm, Bleed Size: 303 x 216mm, Col Length:
271.5mm, Page Width: 185mm, Film: Positive, right reading,
emulsion side down, Screen: 60 lpc
Copy instructions: Copy Date: 12 days prior to publication
date
Average advertising content per issue: 25%
BUSINESS: LEGAL

PROPERTY NEWS MIDLANDS
35206U1E-349

Editorial Address: Hereford House, 102-104 High Street,
COLESHILL, B46 3BL **Tel:** 01675 466100
Fax: 01675 466911
Email: mids@propnews.co.uk
Advertising Address: As above.
Email: mids@propnews.co.uk
Web site: http://www.propnews.co.uk
ISSN: 1351-2781
Publisher: Bennett Publishing Ltd
Date Established: 1993
Frequency: 11 issues yearly
Free to qualifying individuals
Annual Sub.: £30.00
Circulation: 8,105 (Publisher's Statement)
Usual Pagination: 28
Editor: Beverley Todd
Summary of Content: Journal focusing on the commercial
property market in the East and West Midlands.
Readership/Target Audience: Aimed at Surveyors,
Developers, Investors and companies who own or lease
property in the Midlands.
ADVERTISING RATES:
Full Page Mono £1060.00
Full Page Colour £1280.00
Agency Commission: 10%
Mechanical Data: Type Area: 275 x 185mm, Film: Digital,
Col Length: 275mm, Trim Size: 297 x 210mm, Bleed Size:
303 x 216mm, Page Width: 185mm
Average advertising content per issue: 50%
Supplement(s): Commercial Property Specialists Directory -
2xY
BUSINESS: FINANCE & ECONOMICS: Property

PROPERTY NEWS SOUTH
768343U1E-357

Editorial Address: 2-3 The Centre, WESTON-SUPER-
MARE, BS23 1US **Tel:** 01934 622000 **Fax:** 01934 622123
Email: enquiries@propnews.co.uk
Advertising Address: As above.
Email: enquiries@propnews.co.uk
Web site: http://www.propnews.co.uk
Publisher: Bennett Publishing Ltd
Date Established: 2002
Frequency: 6 issues yearly
Free to qualifying individuals
Annual Sub.: £30.00
Circulation: 7,100 (Publisher's Statement)
Usual Pagination: 20
Editor: Peter Bennett
Summary of Content: Magazine covering commercial
property in the south with views of the various markets,
availability of stock and advice from the legal profession,
developers, accountants and surveyors.
Readership/Target Audience: Aimed at property owners
and executives in large companies, commercial agents and
surveyors, developers, construction companies, investment
companies, insurance companies, banks, accountants,
solicitors and local and national government.
ADVERTISING RATES:
Full Page Mono £1005.00
Full Page Colour £1235.00
Agency Commission: 10%
Mechanical Data: Col Length: 275mm, Page Width:
185mm, Type Area: 275 x 185mm, Trim Size: 297 x 210mm,
Bleed Size: 303 x 216mm, Film: Digital
Average advertising content per issue: 50%
BUSINESS: FINANCE & ECONOMICS: Property

PROPERTY NEWS SOUTH WEST &
SOUTH WALES
35207U1E-351

Editorial Address: 2-3 The Centre, WESTON-SUPER-
MARE, BS23 1US **Tel:** 01934 622000 **Fax:** 01934 622123
Email: enquiries@propnews.co.uk
Advertising Address: As above.
Email: enquiries@propnews.co.uk
Web site: http://www.propnews.co.uk
ISSN: 0964-5209
Publisher: Bennett Publishing Ltd
Date Established: 1991
Frequency: Monthly
Cover Price: Free
Circulation: 7,100 (Publisher's Statement)
Usual Pagination: 24
Editor: Peter Bennett; **Publisher:** Peter Bennett

Summary of Content: Magazine providing information on
the commercial property market.
Readership/Target Audience: Aimed at professionals
throughout the United Kingdom involved in the commercial
property market in the South West and South Wales.
ADVERTISING RATES:
Full Page Mono £1005.00
Full Page Colour £1235.00
Agency Commission: 10%
Mechanical Data: Film: Digital, Type Area: 275 x 185mm,
Bleed Size: 303 x 216mm, Col Length: 275mm, Trim Size:
297 x 210mm, Page Width: 185mm
Average advertising content per issue: 50%
BUSINESS: FINANCE & ECONOMICS: Property

PROPERTY WEEK
35208U1E-351_75

Editorial Address: Ludgate House, 245 Blackfriars Road,
LONDON, SE1 9UY **Tel:** 020 7921 8600 **Fax:** 020 7921 8394
Email: laura.chesters@ubm.com
Advertising Address: As above. **Tel:** 020 7921 8558
Fax: 020 7921 8392
Email: carolyn.forde@ubm.com
Web site: http://www.propertyweek.com
ISSN: 1354-1471
Publisher: UBM Information Ltd
Frequency: Weekly
Annual Sub.: £120.00
Circulation: 23,146 (ABC 01/07/2008 to 30/06/2009)
Usual Pagination: 120
Editor: Laura Chesters; **News Editor:** Laura Chesters;
Features Editor: Mark Shepherd; **Advertising Manager:**
Carolyn Forde
Summary of Content: Magazine covering the latest news,
features and commentary on the UK and international
commercial property markets. Includes articles on law,
planning, auctions and finance.
Readership/Target Audience: Read by property
professionals.
ADVERTISING RATES:
Full Page Mono £1880.00
Full Page Colour £3080.00
Agency Commission: 10%
Mechanical Data: Type Area: 277 x 210mm, Bleed Size:
308 x 236mm, Trim Size: 302 x 230mm, Print Process: Web-
fed offset litho, Film: Digital, Col Length: 277mm, Page
Width: 210mm
Copy instructions: Copy Date: 2 weeks prior to publication
date
Supplement(s): Property Direct - 52xY
BUSINESS: FINANCE & ECONOMICS: Property

PROPERTY WEEK GLOBAL
1809384U1E-398

Editorial Address: Ludgate House, 245 Blackfriars Road,
LONDON, SE1 9UY **Tel:** 020 7921 5000 **Fax:** 020 7921 8394
Email: lucy.scott@ubm.com
Advertising Address: As above.
Email: grant.elrick@ubm.com
Web site: http://www.propertyweekglobal.com
Publisher: UBM Information Ltd
Date Established: 2007
Frequency: 10 issues yearly
Free to qualifying individuals
Circulation: 15,000 (Publisher's Statement)
Editor: Lucy Scott
Summary of Content: Magazine covering the latest news,
features and commentary on the UK and international
commercial property markets. Includes articles on law,
planning, auctions and finance.
Readership/Target Audience: Aimed at property
professionals.
ADVERTISING RATES:
Full Page Mono £1820.00
Full Page Colour £2990.00
Agency Commission: 10%
Mechanical Data: Type Area: 235 x 193mm, Bleed Size:
266 x 233mm, Trim Size: 260 x 230mm, Col Length: 235mm,
Page Width: 193mm, Film: Digital
Copy instructions: Copy Date: 10 days prior to publication
date
Average advertising content per issue: 40%
BUSINESS: FINANCE & ECONOMICS: Property

PROSPECT
35803U4A-220

Formerly: Prospect Architecture in Scotland
Editorial Address: 4th Floor, The Mercat Building, 26
Gallowgate, GLASGOW, G1 5AB **Tel:** 0141 552 5858
Email: gordon.young@carnyx.com
Advertising Address: As above.
Email: rachel.giddins@carnyx.com
Web site: http://www.prospectmagazine.com
ISSN: 0143-8883
Publisher: Carnyx Group Ltd
Frequency: Quarterly
Cover Price: £10.00
Free to qualifying individuals
Circulation: 4,000 (Publisher's Statement)
Usual Pagination: 64

Business Magazines

Editor: John Glenday; **Managing Director:** Diane Young; **Publisher:** Gordon Young

Summary of Content: Journal for architects in Scotland. Covering architecture in Scotland, North of England and abroad, current major projects in Scotland, interiors and design.

Readership/Target Audience: Aimed at all architects and other building professionals, planners, surveyors and engineers.

ADVERTISING RATES:
Full Page Colour £1400.00

Agency Commission: 10%

Mechanical Data: Type Area: 284 x 212mm, Trim Size: 300 x 228mm, Bleed Size: +3mm, Col Length: 284mm, Page Width: 212mm, Film: Digital

Copy instructions: Copy Date: 2 weeks prior to publication date

Average advertising content per issue: 40%

BUSINESS: ARCHITECTURE & BUILDING: Architecture

PROSPECTIVE IN PUBLIC HEALTH

40537U56R-73

Formerly: JRSH: The Journal of the Royal Society of Health

Editorial Address: 3rd Floor, 1 Nine Elms Lane, LONDON, SW8 5NQ **Tel:** 020 3177 1631 **Fax:** 020 3177 1601

Email: publications@rsph.org.uk

Web site: http://www.rsph.org.uk

ISSN: 1466-4240

Publisher: The Royal Society for Public Health

Date Established: 1880

Frequency: 6 issues yearly

Annual Sub.: £114.00

Circulation: 8,000 (Publisher's Statement)

Usual Pagination: 48

Editor: Caitlyn Donaldson; **Managing Editor:** Caitlyn Donaldson

Summary of Content: Journal covering developments in promotion of health and public health related subjects.

Readership/Target Audience: Aimed at members of the Society and others concerned with health related sciences.

ADVERTISING: No Advertising taken

BUSINESS: HEALTH & MEDICAL: Health Medical Related

PROSPER

41386U63B-1930

Editorial Address: Black County Chamber of Commerce, Ward Street, WALSALL, WS1 2AL **Tel:** 01902 750578

Fax: 01902 750578

Email: prosper@copestake-ltd.com

Advertising Address: Houldsworth Mill, Houldsworth Street, Southmill, STOCKPORT, SK5 6DA **Tel:** 0161 443 5081

Email: marie@imprintpub.co.uk

Web site: http://www.blackcountrychamber.co.uk

Publisher: Excell Publishing

Frequency: 6 issues yearly

Cover Price: Free

Circulation: 5,000 (Publisher's Statement)

Usual Pagination: 32

Editor: Kate Copestake; **Advertising Manager:** Marie Humphreys

Summary of Content: Magazine concentrating on Chamber of Commerce activities, national news affecting regional businesses, local business news, views and successes. Also contains profiles of local businessmen and women.

Readership/Target Audience: Aimed at Black Country Chamber of Commerce members, local businesses across the Black Country, opinion formers and local government.

ADVERTISING RATES:
Full Page Colour £1800.00

Agency Commission: 10%

Mechanical Data: No. of Columns (Display): 4, Trim Size: 300 x 230mm, Bleed Size: 346 x 251mm, Print Process: Sheet-fed, Film: Digital

Copy instructions: Copy Date: Middle of the month prior to publication date

Average advertising content per issue: 45%

BUSINESS: REGIONAL BUSINESS: Regional Business English Counties

PROTEIN ENGINEERING, DESIGN AND SELECTION

22818U22R-300

Formerly: Protein Engineering

Editorial Address: Great Clarendon Street, OXFORD, OX2 6DP **Tel:** 01865 353907 **Fax:** 01865 353985

Email: peds@editorialoffice.co.uk

Advertising Address: As above. **Tel:** 01865 354637

Fax: 01865 353774

Email: steve.simmonds@oxfordjournals.org

Web site: http://peds.oupjournals.org

ISSN: 0269-2139

Publisher: OUP

Date Established: 1986

Frequency: Monthly

Annual Sub.: £633.00

Usual Pagination: 372

Editor: Alan Fersht

Summary of Content: Journal describing the protein function and protein engineering through experimental studies.

Readership/Target Audience: Read by protein biochemists, biophysicists, drug designers, molecular biologists working on proteins, in universities and drug companies.

ADVERTISING RATES:
Full Page Mono £646.00
Full Page Colour £1076.00

Agency Commission: 10%

Mechanical Data: Type Area: 255 x 178mm, Trim Size: 279 x 216mm, Bleed Size: 285 x 222mm, Film: Digital, Col Length: 255mm, Print Process: Offset litho, Page Width: 178mm

Copy instructions: Copy Date: 4 weeks prior to publication date

BUSINESS: FOOD: Food Related

PRW PLASTICS & RUBBER WEEKLY

38824U39-24_30

Editorial Address: 4th Floor, Carolyn House, 26 Dingwall Road, CROYDON, CR0 9XF **Tel:** 020 8253 9610

Fax: 020 8253 9652

Email: prwnews@crain.com

Advertising Address: As above. **Tel:** 020 8253 9628

Fax: 020 8277 5103

Email: mabarber@crain.com

Web site: http://www.prw.com

ISSN: 0032-1168

Publisher: Crain Communications Ltd

Frequency: 25 issues yearly

Free to qualifying individuals

Annual Sub.: £120.00

Circulation: 11,778 (ABC 01/01/2008 to 31/12/2008)

Editor: David Eldridge; **News Editor:** Anthony Clark

Summary of Content: Magazine containing news from the UK and Europe on machinery, processes and materials.

Readership/Target Audience: Aimed at end users of plastics, materials and equipment manufacturers.

ADVERTISING RATES:
Full Page Mono £3309.00
Full Page Colour £4412.00

Agency Commission: 10%

Mechanical Data: Type Area: 322 x 228mm, Trim Size: 342 x 248mm, Col Length: 322mm, Page Width: 228mm, Bleed Size: 348 x 254mm, Film: Digital

Copy instructions: Copy Date: 1 week prior to publication date

BUSINESS: PLASTICS & RUBBER

PSA PEUGEOT CITROEN TIMES

23023U31A-129_50

Formerly: Peugeot Times

Editorial Address: Pinley House, 2 Sunbeam Way, COVENTRY, CV3 1ND **Tel:** 024 7688 4000

Fax: 024 7688 4288

Publisher: PSA Peugeot Citroen DRRH/DRHI

Date Established: 1932

Frequency: 6 issues yearly

Cover Price: Free

Circulation: 3,000 (Publisher's Statement)

Usual Pagination: 16

Editor: Phil Weare

Summary of Content: Magazine containing articles about the motor industry, employee and company news.

Readership/Target Audience: Aimed at employees, retired employees and Peugeot franchises.

ADVERTISING: No Advertising taken

BUSINESS: MOTOR TRADE: Motor Trade Accessories

PSI (PROFESSIONAL SECURITY INSTALLER)

39915U54C-92

Editorial Address: PO Box 332, DARTFORD, DA1 9FF

Tel: 01342 837897

Email: editorial@psimagazine.co.uk

Advertising Address: As above. **Tel:** 020 8295 1414

Fax: 020 8295 1401

Email: david.lewis@proactivpubs.co.uk

Web site: http://www.psimagazine.co.uk

ISSN: 1360-6476

Publisher: Pro-Activ Publications Ltd

Date Established: 1995

Frequency: Monthly

Free to qualifying individuals

Annual Sub.: £48.00

Circulation: 5,711 (ABC 01/07/2008 to 30/06/2009)

Editor: Pete Conway

Summary of Content: Magazine focusing on professional security equipment installation, covering industry news and views, product testing, technology based features, exhibition previews and new product launches.

Readership/Target Audience: Aimed at security installers.

ADVERTISING RATES:
Full Page Colour £2600.00

Agency Commission: 10%

Mechanical Data: Page Width: 190mm, Film: Digital, Col Length: 266mm, Type Area: 266 x 190mm, Bleed Size: 306 x 216mm, Trim Size: 300 x 213mm

Copy instructions: Copy Date: 12th of the month prior to publication date

BUSINESS: SAFETY & SECURITY: Security

PSLG BUILDING

38388U32A-205

Formerly: PSLG Public Sector And Local Government

Editorial Address: Becket House, Vestry Road, SEVENOAKS, TN14 5EJ **Tel:** 01732 748000

Fax: 01732 748001

Email: jwhite@unity-media.com

Advertising Address: As above.

Email: ssoffe@unity-media.com

Web site: http://www.pslgbuilding.com

ISSN: 0144-4212

Publisher: Unity Media plc

Frequency: 10 issues yearly - Published in the 1st week of the cover month. Combined issues: Published in the 1st week of the 2nd cover month

Cover Price: £3.50

Free to qualifying individuals

Annual Sub.: £35.00

Circulation: 15,703 (ABC 01/07/2007 to 30/06/2008)

Usual Pagination: 84

Editor: Jo White; **Publisher:** Colin Wilkinson

Summary of Content: Journal focusing on building methods and materials, maintenance and refurbishment in the public sector, including private companies involved in work for or with public sector and local and national government.

Readership/Target Audience: Read by decision makers in local authorities.

ADVERTISING RATES:
Full Page Colour £1950.00

Agency Commission: 10%

Mechanical Data: Col Length: 265mm, Page Width: 190mm, Type Area: 265 x 190mm, Trim Size: 297 x 210mm, Bleed Size: 303 x 216mm, Film: Digital

Copy instructions: Copy Date: 4 weeks prior to publication date

BUSINESS: LOCAL GOVERNMENT, LEISURE & RECREATION: Local Government

PSMG MAGAZINE

1645946U2A-660

Formerly: PSMG News Journal

Editorial Address: Suite E, The Business Village, Mersham Le Hatch, East Brabourne, ASHFORD, TN25 5NH

Tel: 01233 503200

Email: matt@coastcommunications.co.uk

Advertising Address: PO Box 131, SAFFRON WALDEN, CB11 4ZN **Tel:** 020 7907 9990

Email: marketing@psmg.co.uk

Web site: http://www.psmg.co.uk

Publisher: The Professional Services Marketing Group

Date Established: 1994

Frequency: 6 issues yearly

Free to qualifying individuals

Circulation: 1,000 (Publisher's Statement)

Usual Pagination: 28

Editor: Matt Baldwin; **Advertising Manager:** Michael Sugg

Summary of Content: Magazine covering all aspects of marketing and business development in the global professional services sector.

Readership/Target Audience: Aimed at marketing professionals in legal, accountancy, management consulting and property.

ADVERTISING: Rates on application

BUSINESS: COMMUNICATIONS, ADVERTISING & MARKETING

PSNC COMMUNITY PHARMACY NEWS

38748U37-62_20

Editorial Address: 59 Buckingham Street, AYLESBURY, HP20 2PJ **Tel:** 01296 432823 **Fax:** 01296 438427

Email: mike.king@psnc.org.uk

Web site: http://www.psnc.org.uk

Publisher: Pharmaceutical Services Negotiating Comm

Frequency: Monthly

Cover Price: Free

Circulation: 13,000 (Publisher's Statement)

Usual Pagination: 8

Editor: Michael King

Summary of Content: Newsletter of the Pharmaceutical Services Negotiating Committee. Covers NHS aspects of community pharmacy.

Readership/Target Audience: Aimed at chemist shops in England and Wales.

ADVERTISING: No Advertising taken

BUSINESS: PHARMACEUTICAL & CHEMISTS

PSYCHIATRIC BULLETIN

40491U56N-60

Editorial Address: 17 Belgrave Square, LONDON, SW1X 8PG **Tel:** 020 7235 2351 **Fax:** 020 7259 6507

Email: pb@rcpsych.ac.uk
Web site: http://pb.rcpsych.org
ISSN: 0955-6036
Publisher: Royal College of Psychiatrists
Frequency: Monthly
Annual Sub.: £86.00
Circulation: 9,000 (Publisher's Statement)
Usual Pagination: 40
Editor: Patricia Casey; **Publisher:** Dave Jago
Summary of Content: Publication of the Royal College of Psychiatrists.
Readership/Target Audience: Read by psychiatrists.
ADVERTISING: No Advertising taken
BUSINESS: HEALTH & MEDICAL: Mental Health

THE PSYCHOLOGIST
40494U56N-150

Editorial Address: St. Andrews House, 48 Princess Road East, LEICESTER, LE1 7DR **Tel:** 0116 252 9501
Fax: 0116 247 0787
Email: psychologist@bps.org.uk
Advertising Address: As above. **Tel:** 0116 252 9552
Email: psyadvert@bps.org.uk
Web site: http://www.thepsychologist.org.uk
ISSN: 0952-8229
Publisher: The British Psychological Society
Date Established: 1988
Frequency: Monthly
Free to qualifying individuals
Annual Sub.: £50.00
Circulation: 48,000 (Publisher's Statement)
Usual Pagination: 90
Editor: Debbie James; **Advertising Manager:** Sarah Stainton
Summary of Content: Newsletter of the British Psychological Society. Contains reviews, articles, conference reports and readers letters.
Readership/Target Audience: Aimed at psychologists at all levels and members of the British Psychological Society.
ADVERTISING RATES:
Full Page Colour £1050.00
Agency Commission: 10%
Mechanical Data: Film: Digital, Type Area: 248 x 190mm, Col Length: 248mm, Page Width: 190mm
Copy instructions: Copy Date: 5 weeks prior to publication date
Average advertising content per issue: 45%
BUSINESS: HEALTH & MEDICAL: Mental Health

PSYCHOLOGIST APPOINTMENTS
41140U62H-23

Formerly: BPS Appointments Memorandum
Editorial Address: St. Andrews House, 48 Princess Road East, LEICESTER, LE1 7DR **Tel:** 0116 252 9550
Fax: 0116 227 1314
Email: psychapp@bps.org.uk
Advertising Address: As above.
Email: psychapp@bps.org.uk
Web site: http://www.psychapp.co.uk
Publisher: The British Psychological Society
Frequency: Monthly
Free to qualifying individuals
Circulation: 45,000 (Publisher's Statement)
Usual Pagination: 20
Editor: Kirsty Wright; **Advertising Manager:** Kirsty Wright
Summary of Content: Magazine containing details of psychology related situations and editorial relating to employment issues and career opportunities.
Readership/Target Audience: Aimed at graduate psychologists and those on approved courses.
ADVERTISING RATES:
Full Page Mono £2450.00
Full Page Colour £2450.00
Agency Commission: 10%
Mechanical Data: Col Length: 248mm, Page Width: 190mm, Film: Digital, Type Area: 248 x 190mm
Average advertising content per issue: 100%
BUSINESS: CHURCH & SCHOOL EQUIPMENT & EDUCATION: Careers

PTA
41154U62J-940

Formerly: Home & School
Editorial Address: 15-17 Black Friars Lane, LONDON, EC4V 6ER **Tel:** 020 7236 1118 **Fax:** 020 7489 5809
Email: info@ncpta.org.uk
Advertising Address: As above.
Email: simon@solutionspublish.co.uk
Web site: http://www.ncpta.org.uk
ISSN: 0305-1536
Publisher: Solutions Publish Ltd
Frequency: 3 issues yearly - Published in February, May and September
Free to qualifying individuals
Circulation: 26,500 (Publisher's Statement)
Usual Pagination: 64
Editor: Natasha Reed

Summary of Content: Magazine covering news and information on key issues for members of the National Confederation of Parent Teacher Associations.
Readership/Target Audience: Read by members of the NCPTA, parents, head teachers and teachers.
ADVERTISING RATES:
Full Page Colour £2750.00
Agency Commission: 10%
Mechanical Data: Film: Digital, Type Area: 271 x 184mm, Bleed Size: 303 x 216mm, Trim Size: 297 x 210mm, Col Length: 271mm, Page Width: 184mm
Copy instructions: Copy Date: 4 weeks prior to publication date
Average advertising content per issue: 50%
BUSINESS: CHURCH & SCHOOL EQUIPMENT & EDUCATION: Teachers & Education Management

PTR
1657148U19F-675

Formerly: PT Review
Editorial Address: 22 Leydene Avenue, BOURNEMOUTH, BH8 9JG **Tel:** 01202 300033 **Fax:** 01202 399998
Email: tony@internalaffairs.co.uk
Advertising Address: As above.
Email: sandie@internalaffairs.co.uk
Web site: http://www.ptreview.co.uk
ISSN: 1474-4473
Publisher: IA Publications
Date Established: 2004
Frequency: 6 issues yearly
Cover Price: Free
Annual Sub.: £100.00
Circulation: 2,500 (Publisher's Statement)
Usual Pagination: 30
Editor: Tony Letts; **Advertising Manager:** Sandie Simmonds; **Managing Editor:** Tony Letts
Summary of Content: Magazine covering bearings, power transmissions, engineering and tooling and motion control.
Readership/Target Audience: Aimed at bearing distributors as well as OEM, designers and engineers.
ADVERTISING RATES:
Full Page Mono £389.00
Full Page Colour £431.00
Agency Commission: 10%
Mechanical Data: Type Area: 270 x 185mm, Bleed Size: 303 x 213mm, Trim Size: 297 x 210mm, Col Length: 270mm, Page Width: 185mm, No. of Columns (Display): 4, Print Process: Offset litho, Film: Digital, Col Widths (Display): 42mm
Copy instructions: Copy Date: 2 weeks prior to publication date
Average advertising content per issue: 70%
BUSINESS: ENGINEERING & MACHINERY: Production & Mechanical Engineering

PUBLIC AFFAIRS NEWS
38391U32A-213

Formerly: Public Affairs Newsletter
Editorial Address: Westminster Tower, 3rd Floor, 3 Albert Embankment, LONDON, SE1 7SP **Tel:** 020 7091 7522
Fax: 020 7091 7525
Email: ian.hall@publicaffairsnews.com
Web site: http://www.publicaffairsnews.com
Publisher: Dods
Frequency: Monthly
Annual Sub.: £155.00
Circulation: 3,000 (Publisher's Statement)
Usual Pagination: 48
Editor: Ian Hall; **Advertising Manager:** Philip Cronin
Summary of Content: Magazine focusing on lobbying in Westminster and Brussels.
Readership/Target Audience: Aimed at public affairs and government relations management and consultants.
Mechanical Data: Page Width: 186mm, Type Area: 247 x 186mm, Col Length: 247mm, Trim Size: 297 x 210mm, Bleed Size: +3mm, Film: Positive, right reading, emulsion side down
BUSINESS: LOCAL GOVERNMENT, LEISURE & RECREATION: Local Government

PUBLIC FINANCE
38414U32C-195

Editorial Address: 17 Britton Street, LONDON, EC1M 5TP
Tel: 020 7324 2768 **Fax:** 020 7324 2790
Email: judy.hirst@publicfinance.co.uk
Advertising Address: As above. **Tel:** 020 7543 5782
Fax: 020 7543 5889
Email: leon.willoughby@publicfinance.co.uk
Web site: http://www.publicfinance.co.uk
ISSN: 1352-9250
Publisher: Redactive Media Group
Frequency: Weekly
Annual Sub.: £100.00
Circulation: 18,163 (ABC 01/07/2008 to 30/06/2009)
Usual Pagination: 40
Editor: Judy Hirst
Summary of Content: Magazine focusing on public finance, covering central and local government, health, housing, charities and regulated utilities.

Readership/Target Audience: Read by finance directors, treasurers, pension managers and chief executives in the wider public and relevant private sectors.
ADVERTISING RATES:
Full Page Mono £2415.00
Full Page Colour £3465.00
SCC £66.00
Agency Commission: 10%
Mechanical Data: Type Area: 270 x 190mm, Bleed Size: 303 x 216mm, Trim Size: 297 x 210mm, Col Length: 270mm, Page Width: 190mm, Film: Digital
Copy instructions: Copy Date: 1 week prior to publication date
Average advertising content per issue: 40%
BUSINESS: LOCAL GOVERNMENT, LEISURE & RECREATION: Local Government Finance

THE PUBLIC LEDGER
35396U1L-60

Editorial Address: 80 Calverley Road, TUNBRIDGE WELLS, TN1 2UN **Tel:** 020 7017 7500 **Fax:** 020 7017 7599
Email: marketing@agra-net.com
Web site: http://www.public-ledger.com
ISSN: 1755-9847
Publisher: Agra Informa Ltd
Frequency: Weekly - Published on Monday
Annual Sub.: £659.00
Summary of Content: Magazine covering all factors influencing the world commodities market. Includes news, analysis and prices for commodities including grains, seeds and pulses, softs, edible nuts and dried fruit, oilseed, oils and fats, feed and exotics and minors.
Readership/Target Audience: Read by those needing the latest commodity prices and news.
ADVERTISING: No Advertising taken
BUSINESS: FINANCE & ECONOMICS: Commodities

PUBLIC LIBRARY JOURNAL
40875U60B-100

Editorial Address: PR by email only
Email: pljeditor@googlemail.com
Advertising Address: 4th Floor, Premier House, Station Road, SWINDON, SM1 1TZ **Tel:** 01793 466035
Fax: 01793 466485
Email: publiclibraryjournal@yahoo.co.uk
ISSN: 0286-893X
Publisher: Public Libraries Group of Cilip
Frequency: Quarterly
Free to qualifying individuals
Annual Sub.: £65.00
Circulation: 6,500 (Publisher's Statement)
Usual Pagination: 32
Editor: Simon Smith; **Advertising Manager:** Allyson Jordan; **Managing Editor:** Debby Raven
Summary of Content: Journal covering results of research and current practice in various aspects of public library issues.
Readership/Target Audience: Readership includes chief librarians, local government councillors, librarians and library staff at all levels.
ADVERTISING RATES:
Full Page Mono £700.00
Full Page Colour £800.00
Agency Commission: 10%
Mechanical Data: Bleed Size: 303 x 213mm, Trim Size: 297 x 210mm, Film: Digital
BUSINESS: PUBLISHING: Libraries

PUBLIC RELATIONS CONSULTANTS ASSOCIATION YEAR BOOK
35722U2E-85

Formerly: Public Relations Consultancy - the Public Relations Year Book
Editorial Address: Willow House, Willow Place, LONDON, SW1P 1JH **Tel:** 020 7233 6026 **Fax:** 020 7828 4797
Email: pressoffice@prca.org.uk
Advertising Address: As above.
Email: yearbook@prca.org.uk
Web site: http://www.prca.org.uk
Publisher: PRCA
Frequency: Annual - Published in May
Cover Price: £50.00
Circulation: 3,000 (Publisher's Statement)
Editor: Richard Ellis; **Advertising Manager:** Richard Ellis
Summary of Content: Directory providing comprehensive coverage of the public relations industry, also includes a listing of PRCA members.
Readership/Target Audience: Aimed at chief executives, sales and marketing and other directors, partners and executives in major companies, PR consultancies and advertising agencies, public relations, advertising and marketing managers.
ADVERTISING: Rates on application
BUSINESS: COMMUNICATIONS, ADVERTISING & MARKETING: Public Relations

Business Magazines

PUBLIC SECTOR BUILDING
35923U4E-307

Editorial Address: 2 Sugar Brook Court, Aston Road, BROMSGROVE, B60 3EX **Tel:** 01527 834400
Fax: 01527 574388
Email: angela.smith@centaur.co.uk
Advertising Address: As above. **Fax:** 01527 574399
Email: lyn.dignan@centaur.co.uk
Web site: http://www.psbmag.co.uk
Publisher: Centaur Special Interest Media
Date Established: 1991
Frequency: 6 issues yearly - Published at the beginning of the cover month
Cover Price: Free
Circulation: 12,000 (ABC 01/07/2008 to 30/06/2009)
Usual Pagination: 76
Editor: Angela Smith; **Publisher:** Derek Rogers
Summary of Content: Magazine covering detailed technical information on all aspects of public sector building.
Readership/Target Audience: Read by surveyors, architectural technicians, engineers, local authorities and housing associations.
ADVERTISING RATES:
Full Page Mono £1500.00
Full Page Colour £1500.00
Mechanical Data: Type Area: 267 x 190mm, Trim Size: 297 x 210mm, Bleed Size: 303 x 216mm, Col Length: 267mm, Page Width: 190mm
Copy instructions: Copy Date: 5th of the month prior to publication date
BUSINESS: ARCHITECTURE & BUILDING: Building

PUBLIC SECTOR CONSTRUCTION
1659648U42A-217

Editorial Address: Portland Buildings, 127-129 Portland Street, MANCHESTER, M1 4PZ **Tel:** 0161 236 2782
Fax: 0161 236 2783
Email: john.conway@excelpublishing.co.uk
Advertising Address: As above.
Email: matthew.baker@excelpublishing.co.uk
Web site: http://www.excelpublishing.co.uk
Publisher: Excel Publishing Company Ltd
Date Established: 2004
Frequency: 6 issues yearly
Editor: John Conway
Summary of Content: Magazine providing an overview of key public sector building developments throughout the UK.
Readership/Target Audience: Aimed at project directors, estates managers, architects, civil engineers, town planners, heads of private finance units and Chief Executives.
ADVERTISING RATES:
Full Page Colour £1495.00
Mechanical Data: Type Area: 256 x 178mm, Bleed Size: 284 x 216mm, Trim Size: 278 x 210mm, Col Length: 256mm, Page Width: 178mm, Film: Digital
Copy instructions: Copy Date: 4 weeks prior to publication date
BUSINESS: CONSTRUCTION

PUBLIC SECTOR EXECUTIVE
1601318U32A-253

Editorial Address: Suite 102, International House, 82-86 Deansgate, MANCHESTER, M3 2ER **Tel:** 0161 833 6320
Fax: 0161 832 0571
Email: newsdesk@publicsectorexecutive.com
Advertising Address: As above.
Email: royc@cognitivepublishing.com
Web site: http://www.publicsectorexecutive.com
ISSN: 1477-9331
Publisher: Cognitive Publishing Ltd
Frequency: 6 issues yearly - Published at the beginning of the 2nd cover month
Cover Price: Free
Circulation: 7,041 (ABC 01/07/2008 to 30/06/2009)
Usual Pagination: 80
Editor: Stephen Lewis; **Publisher:** Roy Rowlands
Summary of Content: Magazine covering issues relating to central and local government including urban management, finance, housing, recruitment, education, leisure services, e-government, conferences and exhibitions, risk and facilities management, products and services, human resource and development.
Readership/Target Audience: Aimed at senior managers and executives in local and central government and the health services.
ADVERTISING RATES:
Full Page Colour £1995.00
Agency Commission: 10%
Mechanical Data: Bleed Size: 303 x 216mm, Trim Size: 297 x 210mm, Film: Digital, No. of Columns (Display): 3, Col Widths (Display): 70mm, Type Area: 270 x 184mm, Col Length: 270mm, Page Width: 184mm
Copy instructions: Copy Date: 1 week prior to publication date
Average advertising content per issue: 20%
BUSINESS: LOCAL GOVERNMENT, LEISURE & RECREATION: Local Government

PUBLIC SECURITY
39917U54C-94

Editorial Address: PO Box 100, CHICHESTER, PO18 8HD
Tel: 01243 576444 **Fax:** 01243 576456
Email: cmowbr@aol.com
Advertising Address: PO Box 86, WITNEY, OX28 5XA
Tel: 01993 709545 **Fax:** 01993 709580
Email: david.holden@keywayspublishing.com
ISSN: 1461-3905
Publisher: Keyways Publishing Limited
Frequency: Quarterly
Free to qualifying individuals
Circulation: 6,000 (Publisher's Statement)
Usual Pagination: 40
Editor: David Holden; **Managing Director:** Peter Harkness;
Advertising Manager: David Holden; **Publisher:** Peter Harkness
Summary of Content: Official Journal of the Association of Police & Public Security Suppliers (APPSS), the trade body representing the UK's public security supply industry which exists to serve UK companies whose business is manufacturing equipment and supplying services, including training and consultancy, to public (government) security agencies world-wide.
Readership/Target Audience: Carefully delivered to a subscriber list that includes police forces, prisons, customs, border guards immigration, fire, airport and seaport authorities and all Government security agencies including those of the Defence ministries and military services concerned with public security and national resilience.
ADVERTISING RATES:
Full Page Colour £1650.00
Agency Commission: 10%
Mechanical Data: Trim Size: 297 x 210mm, Film: Digital, Bleed Size: +3mm
Average advertising content per issue: 25%
BUSINESS: SAFETY & SECURITY: Security

PUBLIC SERVANT
1645393U32K-351

Editorial Address: Ebenezer House, Ryecroft, NEWCASTLE-UNDER-LYME, ST5 2UB **Tel:** 01782 711000
Email: dcarroll@publicservant.co.uk
Advertising Address: As above. **Fax:** 01782 625533
Email: pete@publicservant.co.uk
Web site: http://www.publicservant.co.uk
Publisher: PSCA International Ltd
Date Established: 2004
Frequency: Monthly
Free to qualifying individuals
Circulation: 13,668 (ABC 01/01/2008 to 31/12/2008)
Usual Pagination: 60
Editor: Dean Carroll; **News Editor:** Dean Carroll; **Features Editor:** Alison Thomas; **Advertising Manager:** Peter Kelly
Summary of Content: Magazine covering major issues across the public sector and political spectrums.
Readership/Target Audience: Aimed at civil servants, other key public sector decision makers and private sector partners as well as senior politicians.
ADVERTISING RATES:
Full Page Colour £7995.00
Mechanical Data: Trim Size: 395 x 273mm, Bleed Size: 405 x 283mm, Film: Digital
Average advertising content per issue: 50%
BUSINESS: LOCAL GOVERNMENT, LEISURE & RECREATION: Civil Service

PUBLIC SERVICE MAGAZINE
38554U32K-350

Editorial Address: 8 Leake Street, LONDON, SE1 7NN
Tel: 020 7401 5555 **Fax:** 020 7401 5550
Email: psm@fda.org.uk
Advertising Address: Mongoose Media, 2 Lonsdale Road, LONDON, NW6 6RD **Tel:** 020 7306 0300
Fax: 020 7303 0310
Email: psm@mongoosemedia.com
Web site: http://www.fda.org.uk
ISSN: 1460-8936
Publisher: FDA
Date Established: 1998
Frequency: Quarterly
Cover Price: £4.00
Free to qualifying individuals
Annual Sub.: £16.00
Circulation: 18,856 (Publisher's Statement)
Usual Pagination: 40
Editor: Oliver Rowe
Summary of Content: Magazine covering business and current affairs in or affecting the public sector.
Readership/Target Audience: Aimed at senior managers and professionals in government and senior managers in the NHS.
ADVERTISING RATES:
Full Page Colour £2250.00
Agency Commission: 10%
Mechanical Data: Trim Size: 297 x 210mm, Film: Digital, Bleed Size: +3mm
Copy instructions: Copy Date: 4 weeks prior to publication date

Average advertising content per issue: 20%
BUSINESS: LOCAL GOVERNMENT, LEISURE & RECREATION: Civil Service

PUBLIC SERVICE REVIEW AND TRANSPORT
1655453U49C-504

Formerly: Freight Transport Review
Editorial Address: Ebenezer House, Ryecroft, NEWCASTLE-UNDER-LYME, ST5 2UB **Tel:** 01782 740088
Fax: 01782 740066
Email: jmiles@publicservice.co.uk
Advertising Address: As above. **Tel:** 01782 620088
Web site: http://www.publicservice.co.uk
ISSN: 1474-6505
Publisher: PSCA International Ltd
Date Established: 2000
Frequency: Quarterly
Free to qualifying individuals
Circulation: 6,114 (ABC 01/01/2007 to 31/12/2007)
Usual Pagination: 150
Editor: Jonathan Miles; **Advertising Manager:** Gerrod Mellor; **Managing Editor:** Lisa Carnwell
Summary of Content: Journal covering future developments within the freight transport industry.
Readership/Target Audience: Aimed at freight forwarders, haulage companies and relevant government departments.
ADVERTISING: Rates on application
BUSINESS: TRANSPORT: Freight

THE PUBLICAN
36495U9A-144

Formerly: The Publican Newspaper
Editorial Address: 1st Floor, Ludgate House, 245 Blackfriars Road, LONDON, SE1 9UY **Tel:** 020 7921 5000
Fax: 020 7955 3755
Email: news@thepublican.com
Advertising Address: Ludgate House, 245 Blackfriars Road, LONDON, SE1 9UY **Tel:** 020 7955 3746
Fax: 020 7955 3755
Email: escolding@thepublican.com
Web site: http://www.thepublican.com
ISSN: 1365-5817
Publisher: United Business Media International Limited
Date Established: 1975
Frequency: 42 issues yearly
Cover Price: £2.00
Free to qualifying individuals
Annual Sub.: £79.00
Circulation: 33,689 (ABC 01/07/2008 to 30/06/2009)
Usual Pagination: 55
Editor: Matt Eley; **News Editor:** Matt Eley; **Features Editor:** Phil Mellows; **Managing Editor:** Daniel Pearce
Summary of Content: News magazine containing pub industry news and features on the alcohol trade, pub food, catering, products and services.
Readership/Target Audience: Aimed at freehouse owners, pub tenants, managers and brewery management. Also targets headquarters of all retail pub chains.
ADVERTISING RATES:
Full Page Colour £3950.00
Agency Commission: 10%
Mechanical Data: Page Width: 214mm, Type Area: 280 x 214mm, Col Length: 280mm, Film: Digital, Bleed Size: 306 x 236mm, Trim Size: 300 x 230mm
Copy instructions: Copy Date: 10 days prior to publication date
Average advertising content per issue: 65%
BUSINESS: DRINKS & LICENSED TRADE: Drinks, Licensed Trade, Wines & Spirits

PULSE
601225U6R-156

Formerly: NATS News
Editorial Address: 4000 Parkway, WHITELY, P015 7FL
Tel: 01489 615804
Email: aarti.parajia@nats.co.uk
Web site: http://www.nats.co.uk
Publisher: National Air Traffic Services
Date Established: 1999
Frequency: 6 issues yearly
Cover Price: Free
Circulation: 6,000 (Publisher's Statement)
Usual Pagination: 12
Editor: Aarti Parajia
Summary of Content: Magazine covering all aspects of air traffic services and management.
Readership/Target Audience: Aimed at staff of the National Air Traffic Services.
ADVERTISING: No Advertising taken
BUSINESS: AVIATION & AERONAUTICS: Aviation Related

PULSE
40219U56A-120

Editorial Address: Ludgate House, 245 Blackfriars Road, LONDON, SE1 9UY **Tel:** 020 7921 8094 **Fax:** 020 7921 8133
Email: pulse@cmpmedica.com

Advertising Address: As above. **Tel:** 020 7921 5000
Fax: 020 7921 8136
Email: sbound@cmpmedica.com
Web site: http://www.pulsetoday.co.uk
ISSN: 0048-6000
Publisher: UBM Information Ltd
Date Established: 1961
Frequency: Weekly
Free to qualifying individuals
Annual Sub.: £160.00
Circulation: 28,218 (ABC 01/04/2009 to 30/06/2009)
Usual Pagination: 80
Editor: Richard Hoey; **News Editor:** Ian Quinn; **Advertising Manager:** Sue Bound; **Group Editor:** Jo Haynes
Summary of Content: Magazine covering medical, political and clinical news specifically relevant to general practice.
Readership/Target Audience: Aimed at general practitioners.
ADVERTISING RATES:
Full Page Mono £3465.00
Full Page Colour £4375.00
Agency Commission: 10%
Mechanical Data: Type Area: 377 x 271mm, Bleed Size: 406 x 290mm, Trim Size: 400 x 287mm, Col Length: 377mm, Page Width: 271mm, Col Widths (Display): 42mm, No. of Columns (Display): 6, Film: Digital
Copy instructions: Copy Date: 2 weeks prior to publication date
Average advertising content per issue: 55%
BUSINESS: HEALTH & MEDICAL

PULSE
40736U58-8
Formerly: Centre News
Editorial Address: Rosemary House, Lanwades Business Park, NEWMARKET, CB8 7PW **Tel:** 01638 751400
Fax: 01638 751801
Email: veronica.smart@eic.co.uk
Web site: http://www.eic.co.uk
Publisher: Energy Information Centre Ltd
Frequency: Quarterly
Free to qualifying individuals
Annual Sub.: £89.95
Circulation: 4,000 (Publisher's Statement)
Usual Pagination: 32
Editor: Veronica Smart
Summary of Content: Journal covering developments in the utilities markets for industrial, commercial and public sector electricity, gas, oil and water consumers.
Readership/Target Audience: Aimed at utilities professionals in the industrial and commercial sectors.
ADVERTISING: No Advertising taken
BUSINESS: ENERGY, FUEL & NUCLEAR

PUMP INDUSTRY ANALYST
37635U19D-550
Editorial Address: The Boulevard, Langford Lane, KIDLINGTON, OX5 1GB **Tel:** 01865 843695
Fax: 01865 843971
Email: r.reidy@elsevier.com
Web site: http://www.pumpindustryanalyst.com
ISSN: 1359-6128
Publisher: Elsevier Ltd
Date Established: 1996
Frequency: Monthly
Annual Sub.: EUR1049.00
Usual Pagination: 16
Editor: Roisin Reidy
Summary of Content: Business newsletter covering the international pump industry.
Readership/Target Audience: Aimed at senior management in the pump manufacturing industry, industry analysts and suppliers to the pump industry.
ADVERTISING: No Advertising taken
BUSINESS: ENGINEERING & MACHINERY: Hydraulic Power

PURE BEAUTY
37255U15A-87
Editorial Address: 34 Porchester Road, LONDON, W2 6ES
Tel: 020 7563 5664
Email: emily.miller@jldmedia.com
Advertising Address: As above. **Tel:** 020 7064 1234
Fax: 020 7064 1543
Email: sophiebatchelor@purebeauty.co.uk
Web site: http://www.purebeauty.co.uk
ISSN: 1478-162X
Publisher: JLD Media
Date Established: 1997
Frequency: 11 issues yearly
Cover Price: £9.00
Free to qualifying individuals
Annual Sub.: £85.00
Circulation: 15,208 (ABC 01/01/2008 to 31/12/2008)
Usual Pagination: 36
Editor: Emily Miller
Summary of Content: Magazine covering the beauty retail industry, from new products and promotions, to interviews and generic features.

Readership/Target Audience: Aimed at people who sell beauty products in multiple and independent pharmacies, supermarkets and department stores, as well as buyers and manufacturers.
ADVERTISING RATES:
Full Page Colour £2730.00
Agency Commission: 10%
Mechanical Data: Type Area: 270 x 183mm, Col Length: 270mm, Bleed Size: 303 x 216mm, Trim Size: 297 x 210mm, Film: Digital, Page Width: 183mm
Copy instructions: Copy Date: 4 weeks prior to publication date
Average advertising content per issue: 40%
Supplement(s): Fragrance - 1xY, Male Grooming - 1xY, Pure Beauty Book - 1xY, Skin Care - 1xY
BUSINESS: COSMETICS & HAIRDRESSING: Cosmetics

QA EDUCATION
41179U62K-800
Editorial Address: 150 Burnley Road, ACCRINGTON, BB5 6DW **Tel:** 01254 390066 **Fax:** 01254 390077
Email: paulturner836@btinternet.com
Advertising Address: Unit 8, Chorley West Business Park, Ackhurst Road, CHORLEY, PR7 1NL **Tel:** 0870 444 8955
Fax: 0870 447 8956
Email: sales@euromedia-al.com
Web site: http://www.euromedia-al.com
Publisher: Euromedia Associates Ltd
Date Established: 1997
Frequency: 6 issues yearly
Cover Price: Free
Circulation: 10,000 (Publisher's Statement)
Usual Pagination: 108
Editor: Paul Turner; **Advertising Manager:** Gemma Winstanley
Summary of Content: Guide containing information on cost-effective services and resources for schools.
Readership/Target Audience: Read by bursars, heads, senior managers, governors, head teachers and heads of departments.
ADVERTISING RATES:
Full Page Colour £1200.00
Agency Commission: 10%
Mechanical Data: Film: Digital, Bleed Size: 303 x 216mm, Trim Size: 297 x 210mm
Copy instructions: Copy Date: 2 weeks prior to publication date
Average advertising content per issue: 50%
BUSINESS: CHURCH & SCHOOL EQUIPMENT & EDUCATION: Church & School Equipment

QERCUS
36191U5D-30
Formerly: Acorn User
Editorial Address: 30 Finny Bank Road, SALE, M33 6LR
Tel: 0161 969 9820 **Fax:** 0870 051 9527
Email: editor@qercus.com
Advertising Address: As above.
Email: advertising@finnybank.com
Web site: http://www.qercus.com
ISSN: 1471-1001
Publisher: Finnybank Ltd
Date Established: 1982
Frequency: 9 issues yearly
Cover Price: £4.20
Annual Sub.: £49.95
Circulation: 6,000 (Publisher's Statement)
Usual Pagination: 76
Editor: John Cartmell; **Managing Director:** John Cartmell;
Advertising Manager: John Cartmell
Summary of Content: Magazine covering articles and information about 32-bit RISC OS computers.
Readership/Target Audience: Aimed at both home and business users of RISC OS equipment, as well as hardware and software developers.
ADVERTISING RATES:
Full Page Colour £320.00
Agency Commission: 10%
Mechanical Data: Bleed Size: +3mm, Film: Digital
Copy instructions: Copy Date: 4 weeks prior to publication date
Average advertising content per issue: 15%
BUSINESS: COMPUTERS & AUTOMATION: Personal Computers

QJM: AN INTERNATIONAL JOURNAL OF MEDICINE
24466U56A-122
Formerly: QJM Monthly Journal of the Association of Physicians
Editorial Address: PO Box 1130, OXFORD, OX2 9UR
Tel: 01865 248539 **Fax:** 01865 248540
Email: qjm.editorialoffice@oxfordjournals.org
Advertising Address: Great Clarendon Street, OXFORD, OX2 6DP **Tel:** 01865 354637
Email: steve.simmonds@oxfordjournals.org
Web site: http://www.oup.co.uk/jnls
ISSN: 1460-2725
Publisher: OUP

Date Established: 1907
Frequency: Monthly
Cover Price: £16.00
Annual Sub.: £166.00
Usual Pagination: 84
Editor: Wendy Moore
Summary of Content: Journal covering the whole field of medicine with emphasis on internal medicine.
Readership/Target Audience: Aimed at consultant physicians.
ADVERTISING RATES:
Full Page Mono £742.00
Full Page Colour £1236.00
Agency Commission: 10%
Mechanical Data: Type Area: 255 x 178 mm, Trim Size: 279 x 215 mm, Bleed Size: 285 x 218mm, Film: Digital, Col Length: 255mm, Page Width: 178mm
Copy instructions: Copy Date: 1 month prior to publication date
BUSINESS: HEALTH & MEDICAL

QSHEET
35689U2D-83_40
Formerly: Q Sheet
Editorial Address: Northburgh House, 10A Northburgh Street, LONDON, EC1V 0AT **Tel:** 020 7253 8888
Fax: 020 7253 8885
Email: info@qsheet.com
Advertising Address: As above.
Email: info@qsheet.com
Web site: http://www.qsheet.com
ISSN: 1369-2577
Publisher: markettiers4dc Publishing
Date Established: 1991
Frequency: Monthly
Cover Price: Free
Circulation: 2,100 (Publisher's Statement)
Usual Pagination: 64
Editor: Nik Harta; **Managing Director:** Howard Kosky;
Advertising Manager: Nik Harta
Summary of Content: Magazine containing programming support information for the radio industry.
Readership/Target Audience: Aimed at radio broadcasters and presenters.
ADVERTISING: Rates on application
BUSINESS: COMMUNICATIONS, ADVERTISING & MARKETING: Broadcasting

QUALITY ASSURANCE IN EDUCATION
37161U14K-490
Editorial Address: Howard House, Wagon Lane, BINGLEY, BD16 1WA **Tel:** 01274 777700 **Fax:** 01274 785200
Email: ksnowden@emeraldinsight.com
Web site: http://www.emeraldinsight.com
ISSN: 0968-4883
Publisher: Emerald Group Publishing Ltd
Frequency: Quarterly
Annual Sub.: £2659.00
Editor: Kate Snowden; **Publisher:** Kate Snowden
Summary of Content: Journal reporting on quality and related issues in education.
Readership/Target Audience: Aimed at educational managers, teachers, academics and academic libraries.
ADVERTISING: No Advertising taken
BUSINESS: COMMERCE, INDUSTRY & MANAGEMENT: Quality Assurance

QUALITY IN AGEING
717793U32G-103
Editorial Address: Richmond House, Richmond Road, BRIGHTON, BN2 3RL **Tel:** 01273 623222
Fax: 01273 625526
Email: joannas@pavpub.com
Advertising Address: As above. **Tel:** 0870 890 1080
Fax: 0870 890 1081
Email: pauls@pavpub.com
Web site: http://www.pavpub.com
ISSN: 1471-7794
Publisher: Pavilion Journals (Brighton) Ltd
Frequency: Quarterly
Annual Sub.: £119.00
Circulation: 250 (Publisher's Statement)
Usual Pagination: 48
Editor: Ron Iphofen; **Advertising Manager:** Paul Somerville
Summary of Content: Journal with a focus on real issues affecting older people and those who work with them, including quality of life and support services.
Readership/Target Audience: Aimed at carers, social workers, GPs, residential care staff and managers, community nurses and those in associated professions.
ADVERTISING RATES:
Full Page Mono £350.00
Agency Commission: 10%
Mechanical Data: Type Area: 240 x 150mm, Col Length: 240mm, Page Width: 150mm, Film: Digital
Average advertising content per issue: 10%
BUSINESS: LOCAL GOVERNMENT, LEISURE & RECREATION: Community Care & Social Services

Business Magazines

QUALITY IN PRIMARY CARE   714214U56R-69_70

Formerly: The Journal of Clinical Governance
Editorial Address: 18 Marcham Road, ABINGDON, OX14
1AA **Tel:** 01235 528820 **Fax:** 01235 528830
Email: contact.us@radcliffemed.com
Advertising Address: As above.
Email: dallen@radcliffemed.com
Web site: http://www.radcliffe-oxford.com/qpc
ISSN: 1467-5277
Publisher: Radcliffe Publishing Ltd.
Frequency: 6 issues yearly
Annual Sub.: £325.00
Circulation: 550 (Publisher's Statement)
Editor: Andrea Hargreaves; **Advertising Manager:** Dan
Allen
Summary of Content: Journal which informs those involved
or interested in quality about effective methods and
innovations and to stimulate discussion of topical issues.
The journal is particularly concerned with clinical governance
in primary care and at the interfaces between primary and
secondary, and primary and social care.
Readership/Target Audience: Aimed at leaders of clinical
and organisational teams in both secondary and primary
care, and also medical and healthcare libraries.
ADVERTISING RATES:
Full Page Mono £400.00
Mechanical Data: Page Width: 157mm, Type Area: 238 x
157mm, Col Length: 238mm, Trim Size: 297 x 210mm, Bleed
Size: +6mm
BUSINESS: HEALTH & MEDICAL: Health Medical Related

QUALITY MANUFACTURING TODAY
1894024U14B-302
Editorial Address: The Coach House, Angley Road,
CRANBROOK, TN17 2LE **Tel:** 01580 715152
Email: brendan.coyne@qmtmag.com
Web site: http://www.qmtmag.com
Publisher: Cranbrook Media Ltd
Frequency: 8 issues yearly
Cover Price: Free
Circulation: 4,000 (Publisher's Statement)
Editor: Brendan Coyne
Summary of Content: Print and on-line magazine promoting
improvements in manufacturing processes and products
through quality control and quality management, from
shopfloor to line and enterprise management.
Readership/Target Audience: Aimed at the quality
management and test industry.
BUSINESS: COMMERCE, INDUSTRY & MANAGEMENT:
Industry & Factories

QUALITYWORLD   37164U14K-660
Editorial Address: 12 Grosvenor Crescent, LONDON,
SW1X 7EE **Tel:** 020 7245 6676 **Fax:** 020 7245 6788
Email: editorial@thecqi.org
Advertising Address: Redactive Media Group, 17 Britton
Street, LONDON, EC1M 5TP **Tel:** 020 7880 6200
Fax: 020 7880 7553
Email: john.nahar@redactive.co.uk
Web site: http://www.thecqi.org
ISSN: 1352-8769
Publisher: Chartered Quality Institute
Date Established: 1974
Frequency: Monthly - Published on the 1st Monday of the
cover month
Annual Sub.: £66.00
Circulation: 10,940 (ABC 01/01/2008 to 31/12/2008)
Usual Pagination: 64
Editor: Felicity Francis
Summary of Content: Magazine of the Chartered Quality
Institute. Contains CQI news and a range of articles and
information on quality matters.
Readership/Target Audience: Read by quality
professionals in the UK and overseas.
ADVERTISING RATES:
Full Page Mono £1595.00
Full Page Colour £2060.00
Agency Commission: 10%
Mechanical Data: Type Area: 240 x 185mm, Col Length:
240mm, Trim Size: 274 x 210mm, Bleed Size: 280 x 216mm,
Page Width: 185mm, Film: Digital
Copy instructions: Copy Date: 3 weeks prior to publication
date
Average advertising content per issue: 42%
BUSINESS: COMMERCE, INDUSTRY & MANAGEMENT:
Quality Assurance

THE QUANTUM LEAP STOCKMARKET LETTER   35291U1F-375
Editorial Address: PO Box 1638, LONDON, W8 4QR
Tel: 020 7937 7879 **Fax:** 020 7937 7364
Email: qlumsden@bloomberg.net
Publisher: Letterprint Ltd
Date Established: 1984
Frequency: Monthly

Annual Sub.: £99.50
Editor: Quentin Lumsden
Summary of Content: Publication covering news, advice
and investment recommendations.
Readership/Target Audience: Aimed at private investors.
ADVERTISING: No Advertising taken
BUSINESS: FINANCE & ECONOMICS: Investment

QUARRY MANAGEMENT   38249U30-90
Editorial Address: 7 Regent Street, NOTTINGHAM, NG1
5BS **Tel:** 0115 945 3893 **Fax:** 0115 948 4035
Email: simon.chan@quarrymanagement.com
Advertising Address: As above. **Tel:** 0115 941 1315
Fax: 0115 941 5685
Email: jennie.reeves@quarrymanagement.com
Web site: http://www.quarrymanagement.com
ISSN: 0950-9526
Publisher: QMJ Publishing Ltd
Date Established: 1918
Frequency: Monthly - Published on the 1st of the cover
month
Cover Price: £4.00
Annual Sub.: £45.00
Circulation: 4,874 (ABC 01/01/2008 to 31/12/2008)
Usual Pagination: 76
Editor: Simon Chan; **Managing Director:** Jack Berridge
Summary of Content: Monthly journal for the quarry
products and associated industries.
Readership/Target Audience: Aimed at quarry managers,
executives and technologists.
ADVERTISING RATES:
Full Page Mono £1000.00
Full Page Colour £1775.00
Mechanical Data: Type Area: 263 x 175mm, Bleed Size:
303 x 216mm, Trim Size: 297 x 210mm, Col Length: 263mm,
Film: Positive, right reading, emulsion side down, Col Widths
(Display): 42mm, No. of Columns (Display): 4, Page Width:
175mm
Copy instructions: Copy Date: 15th of the month prior to
publication date
BUSINESS: MINING & QUARRYING

THE QUARTERLY   625433U41R-200
Editorial Address: 64 Nutbrook Street, LONDON, SE15 4LE
Tel: 020 7732 0125
Email: info@baph.org.uk
Web site: http://www.baph.org.uk
ISSN: 0957-4506
Publisher: BAPH Publications
Date Established: 1989
Frequency: Quarterly
Free to qualifying individuals
Annual Sub.: £30.00
Circulation: 500 (Publisher's Statement)
Usual Pagination: 48
Editor: Peter Bower
Summary of Content: Publication containing research
papers, letters and articles on the history of paper, its
making and usage.
Readership/Target Audience: Aimed at academics and
researchers in paper history and related fields.
ADVERTISING: No Advertising taken
BUSINESS: PRINTING & STATIONERY: Stationery &
Printing Related

QUARTERLY JOURNAL OF FORESTRY
39466U46-25
Editorial Address: Trinity Cottage, Buckingham Place, St.
Day, REDRUTH, TR16 5NT **Tel:** 01209 820733
Email: qjf@talktalk.net
Advertising Address: Cobbs Wood House, Chart Road,
ASHFORD, TN23 1EP **Tel:** 01233 633366
Fax: 01233 665713
Email: linda.body@geeringsprint.co.uk
Web site: http://www.rfs.org.uk
Publisher: Royal Forestry Society
Date Established: 1907
Frequency: Quarterly
Annual Sub.: £59.85
Circulation: 5,000 (Publisher's Statement)
Usual Pagination: 80
Editor: Lesley Trotter
Summary of Content: Journal of the Royal Forestry Society,
covering practice and methods in forestry both at home and
abroad.
Readership/Target Audience: Read by forest officers and
consultants, woodland owners, arboriculturalists, forestry
firms and land agents.
ADVERTISING RATES:
Full Page Mono £331.00
Full Page Colour £420.00
Agency Commission: 10%
Mechanical Data: Trim Size: 246 x 189mm, Bleed Size: 252
x 195mm, Type Area: 210 x 155mm, Col Length: 210mm,
Page Width: 155mm, Film: Digital

Copy instructions: Copy Date: 1st of the month prior to
publication date
Average advertising content per issue: 10%
Supplement(s): Education - 1xY
BUSINESS: TIMBER, WOOD & FORESTRY

THE QUARTERLY JOURNAL OF MATHEMATICS   30950U62A-420
Editorial Address: Mathematical Institute, 24-29 St Giles,
OXFORD, OX1 3LB **Tel:** 01865 353907 **Fax:** 01865 353985
Email: brian.steer@hertford.ox.ac.uk
Advertising Address: Great Clarendon Street, OXFORD,
OX2 6DP **Tel:** 01865 353329 **Fax:** 01865 353774
Email: elisabetta.sheffield@oxfordjournals.org
Web site: http://www.oup.co.uk/jnls
ISSN: 0033-5606
Publisher: OUP
Date Established: 1950
Frequency: Quarterly
Cover Price: £61.00
Annual Sub.: £204.00
Circulation: 730 (Publisher's Statement)
Editor: Brian Steer; **Executive Editor:** Brian Steer
Summary of Content: Journal covering pure mathematics,
including algebra, analysis, combinatorics and topology.
Readership/Target Audience: Read by academic
mathematicians.
ADVERTISING RATES:
Full Page Mono £646.00
Agency Commission: 10%
Mechanical Data: Type Area: 181 x 139mm, Col Length:
181mm, Film: Digital, Trim Size: 246 x 189mm, Bleed Size:
252 x 195mm, Page Width: 139mm
BUSINESS: CHURCH & SCHOOL EQUIPMENT &
EDUCATION: Education

QUARTERLY JOURNAL OF MECHANICS AND APPLIED MATHEMATICS   29982U62A-509
Editorial Address: Department of Mathematics, Imperial
College, Prince Consort Road, LONDON, SW7 2BZ
Tel: 01865 353907 **Fax:** 01865 353485
Email: r.craster@ma.ic.ac.uk
Advertising Address: Great Clarendon Street, OXFORD,
OX2 6DP **Tel:** 01865 354767
Email: jnlsadvertising@oxfordjournals.org
Web site: http://qjmam.oxfordjournals.org
ISSN: 0033-5614
Publisher: OUP
Date Established: 1948
Frequency: Quarterly
Cover Price: £89.00
Annual Sub.: £284.00
Usual Pagination: 168
Editor: R. Craster
Summary of Content: Journal covering original articles in
the general field of mechanics, particularly theoretical
mechanics, classical electromagnetism, nonlinear dynamics
and combined fields such as magneto hydro numerical
methods.
Readership/Target Audience: Aimed at academics,
students and teachers.
ADVERTISING RATES:
Full Page Mono £646.00
Agency Commission: 10%
Mechanical Data: Film: Digital, Col Length: 210mm, Type
Area: 210 x 125mm, Print Process: Litho, Bleed Size: 255 x
182mm, Trim Size: 249 x 176mm, Page Width: 125mm
Copy instructions: Copy Date: 8 weeks prior to publication
date
BUSINESS: CHURCH & SCHOOL EQUIPMENT &
EDUCATION: Education

QUARTERLY JOURNAL OF THE ROYAL METEOROLOGICAL SOCIETY   41585U64N-50
Editorial Address: 104 Oxford Road, READING, RG1 7LL
Tel: 0118 956 8500 **Fax:** 0118 956 8571
Email: qj@rmets.org
Advertising Address: Wiley Publishing, The Atrium,
Southern Gate, CHICHESTER, PO19 8SQ
Tel: 01243 770603 **Fax:** 01243 770432
Email: tturner@wiley.co.uk
Web site: http://www.rmets.org
ISSN: 0035-9009
Publisher: Royal Meteorological Society
Date Established: 1850
Frequency: 8 issues yearly
Annual Sub.: £480.00
Circulation: 1,000 (Publisher's Statement)
Usual Pagination: 350
Editor: Alison Hunter
Summary of Content: Journal covering atmospheric
sciences, applied meteorology and physical oceanography.
Readership/Target Audience: Aimed at professional
meteorologists and members of the Royal Meteorological
Society.

ADVERTISING RATES:
Full Page Mono £1175.00
Full Page Colour £2575.00
BUSINESS: OTHER CLASSIFICATIONS: Weather

QUAY NOTES
39347U45A-148
Editorial Address: F5 Northney Marina, HAYLING ISLAND, PO11 0NH **Tel:** 023 9246 0111 **Fax:** 023 9246 0123
Email: foreshore@mail.com
Advertising Address: Maritime Intelligence Ltd, Maritime Centre, F5 Northney Marina, HAYLING ISLAND, PO11 0NH
Tel: 023 9246 0111 **Fax:** 023 9246 0123
Email: foreshore@mail.com
Publisher: UK Harbour Masters Association
Date Established: 1993
Frequency: Quarterly
Cover Price: Free
Circulation: 450 (Publisher's Statement)
Usual Pagination: 8
Editor: Peter Moth; **Advertising Manager:** Peter Moth; **Publisher:** Peter Moth
Summary of Content: Newsletter of the UK Harbour Masters Association.
Readership/Target Audience: Read by harbour masters and senior port officials throughout the UK ports and harbours sector, including ports large and small, publicly and privately owned. Focuses on port legislation and regulation, operational practices, environmental news, industry news, association news, diary dates and book reviews.
ADVERTISING RATES:
Full Page Mono £475.00
Full Page Colour £475.00
Agency Commission: 10%
Mechanical Data: Type Area: 254 x 190mm, Bleed Size: 303 x 216mm, Trim Size: 297 x 210mm, Col Length: 254mm, Col Widths (Display): 60mm, No. of Columns (Display): 3, Page Width: 190mm, Print Process: Litho, Screen: 300
Average advertising content per issue: 10%
BUSINESS: MARINE & SHIPPING

QUBE MAGAZINE
35954U4R-595
Formerly: TFM-Total Facilities Management
Editorial Address: Wisteria House, Stump Cross Lane, Swineshead, BOSTON, PE20 3JJ **Tel:** 0845 388 0281
Fax: 0845 388 0283
Email: editor@qubeonline.co.uk
Advertising Address: As above.
Email: sales@qubeonline.co.uk
Web site: http://www.qubeonline.co.uk
Publisher: Clarke Design & Media Ltd
Date Established: 2001
Frequency: 6 issues yearly
Cover Price: £5.99
Free to qualifying individuals
Annual Sub.: £34.99
Circulation: 6,500 (Publisher's Statement)
Usual Pagination: 32
Editor: Shirley Clarke; **Advertising Manager:** Nigel Clarke; **Managing Editor:** Nigel Clarke; **Publisher:** Nigel Clarke
Summary of Content: Magazine covering building maintenance and facilities management. Includes industry news, case studies, building features, company profiles, equipment and articles on safety, security, new furnishings and lighting.
Readership/Target Audience: Aimed at building, estate and facilities management.
ADVERTISING RATES:
Full Page Colour £999.00
Agency Commission: 10%
Mechanical Data: Page Width: 190mm, Type Area: 267 x 190mm, Col Length: 267mm, Bleed Size: 303 x 276mm, Trim Size: 297 x 270mm, Film: Positive, right reading, emulsion side down, Screen: 150 lpc
Copy instructions: Copy Date: 1st week of the month prior to publication date
Average advertising content per issue: 60%
BUSINESS: ARCHITECTURE & BUILDING: Building Related

QUIDS IN
1899947U1R-391
Editorial Address: Derbyshire County Council, County Hall, MATLOCK, DE4 3AG **Tel:** 01629 760247
Email: contact.centre@derbyshire.gov.uk
Web site: http://www.derbyshire.gov.uk
Publisher: Derbyshire County Council
Cover Price: Free
Usual Pagination: 24
Summary of Content: Magazine aimed at helping you make the most of your money, tackle debt and get all the benefits you are entitled to.
Readership/Target Audience: Aimed at those in Derbyshire who are in debt or want some financial advice and options.
BUSINESS: FINANCE & ECONOMICS: Financial Related

R&D FOCUS
38770U37-62_40
Editorial Address: 7 Harewood Avenue, LONDON, NW1 6JB **Tel:** 020 3075 5847 **Fax:** 020 3075 5345
Email: rdfocus@uk.imshealth.com
Web site: http://www.imshealth.com/global
ISSN: 1350-1135
Publisher: IMS Health
Date Established: 1992
Frequency: Weekly
Annual Sub.: £500.00
Usual Pagination: 30
Editor: Carolyn Hughes; **Executive Editor:** Carolyn Hughes
Summary of Content: Monitors research and development within the pharmaceutical and biotechnology industries.
Readership/Target Audience: Aimed at pharmaceutical researchers, executives and financial analysts.
ADVERTISING: No Advertising taken
BUSINESS: PHARMACEUTICAL & CHEMISTS

RAC - REFRIGERATION AND AIR CONDITIONING
35768U3C-80
Editorial Address: Greater London House, Hampstead Road, LONDON, NW1 7EJ **Tel:** 020 7728 5000
Email: andrew.gaved@emap.com
Advertising Address: As above. **Fax:** 020 7391 3435
Email: david.gardner@emap.com
Web site: http://www.emap.com
ISSN: 0263-5739
Publisher: EMAP Insight
Date Established: 1898
Frequency: Monthly - Published on the 1st of the cover month
Annual Sub.: £55.00
Circulation: 5,151 (ABC 01/01/2008 to 31/12/2008)
Usual Pagination: 68
Editor: Andrew Gaved
Summary of Content: Journal covering the air conditioning and refrigeration industry.
Readership/Target Audience: Read by senior decision makers and buyers in the UK and overseas. Also aimed at installers, distributors, manufacturers and end users.
ADVERTISING RATES:
Full Page Colour £1780.00
SCC £18.00
Agency Commission: 10%
Mechanical Data: Page Width: 181mm, Type Area: 268 x 181mm, Col Length: 268mm, Trim Size: 297 x 210mm, Bleed Size: 303 x 216mm, Print Process: Litho, Film: Positive, right reading, emulsion side down
Copy instructions: Copy Date: 10th of the month prior to publication date
Average advertising content per issue: 54%
Supplement(s): RAC - Refrigeration and Air Conditioning Yearbook - 1xY, Service Engineer - 4xY
BUSINESS: HEATING & VENTILATION: Refrigeration & Ventilation

RACE ENGINE TECHNOLOGY
1806122U31A-397
Editorial Address: Whitfield House, Cheddar Road, WEDMORE, BS28 4EJ **Tel:** 01934 713811
Fax: 020 8497 2102
Email: ian@highpowermedia.com
Advertising Address: As above. **Fax:** 0844 545 8617
Email: simon@highpowermedia.com
Web site: http://www.highpowermedia.com
ISSN: 1740-6803
Publisher: High Power Media
Date Established: 2003
Frequency: 8 issues yearly
Cover Price: £10.00
Annual Sub.: £70.00
Circulation: 6,000 (Publisher's Statement)
Usual Pagination: 76
Editor: Ian Bamsey; **Advertising Manager:** Simon Moss; **Publisher:** Simon Moss
Summary of Content: Magazine covering all aspects of contemporary racing powertrain technology.
Readership/Target Audience: Aimed at design and development engineers, competition engine builders and enthusiastic amateurs.
ADVERTISING: Rates on application
BUSINESS: MOTOR TRADE: Motor Trade Accessories

RACE EQUALITY TEACHING
40982U62A-300
Formerly: Multicultural Teaching
Editorial Address: 28 Hillside Gardens, LONDON, N6 5ST
Tel: 020 8348 2174
Advertising Address: Westview House, 734 London Road, Oakhill, STOKE-ON-TRENT, ST4 5NP **Tel:** 01782 745567
Fax: 01782 745553
Email: tb@trentham-books.co.uk
Web site: http://www.trentham-books.co.uk
ISSN: 0263-0869
Publisher: Trentham Books Ltd
Date Established: 1982

Frequency: 3 issues yearly - Published in March, June and November
Annual Sub.: £35.00
Circulation: 1,500 (Publisher's Statement)
Usual Pagination: 56
Editor: Gillian Klein; **Advertising Manager:** Darren Green
Summary of Content: Journal covering the debate on race and education and reporting on new research, policy and best practice. Provides an information service on courses, conferences, events and new resources and also covers new initiatives, developments and publications.
Readership/Target Audience: Aimed at schools, LEA advisors, universities and college libraries.
ADVERTISING RATES:
Full Page Mono £280.00
Agency Commission: 10%
Mechanical Data: Print Process: Offset litho, Col Length: 260mm, No. of Columns (Display): 2, Film: Digital
Copy instructions: Copy Date: 15th of the month prior to publication date
Average advertising content per issue: 10%
BUSINESS: CHURCH & SCHOOL EQUIPMENT & EDUCATION: Education

RACECAR ENGINEERING
38317U31A-130
Editorial Address: Leon House, 233 High Street, CROYDON, CR9 1HZ **Tel:** 020 8726 8364
Fax: 020 8726 8398
Email: racecar@ipcmedia.com
Advertising Address: As above. **Tel:** 020 8726 8328
Fax: 020 8726 8399
Email: tony_tobias@ipcmedia.com
Web site: http://www.racecar-engineering.com
ISSN: 0961-1096
Publisher: IPC Inspire
Date Established: 1989
Frequency: Monthly
Cover Price: £4.99
Circulation: 22,000 (Publisher's Statement)
Usual Pagination: 108
Editor: Graham Jones; **Advertising Manager:** Tony Tobias
Summary of Content: Magazine covering all types of motor sports technology including four-wheeled competition vehicles such as Formula 1 cars, rally cars and touring cars.
Readership/Target Audience: Read by motor sport professionals, race car engineers, drivers, mechanics and the motor sports industry.
ADVERTISING RATES:
Full Page Colour £1500.00
Agency Commission: 10%
Mechanical Data: Col Widths (Display): 45mm, No. of Columns (Display): 4, Page Width: 190mm, Type Area: 277 x 190mm, Bleed Size: 303 x 216mm, Trim Size: 297 x 210mm, Col Length: 277mm, Film: Digital
Copy instructions: Copy Date: 2 weeks prior to publication date
Average advertising content per issue: 40%
BUSINESS: MOTOR TRADE: Motor Trade Accessories

RAD MAGAZINE
40443U56J-10
Editorial Address: PO Box 7861, BRAINTREE, CM7 4YZ
Tel: 01371 812960 **Fax:** 01371 812969
Email: info@radmagazine.co.uk
Advertising Address: As above.
Email: david@radmagazine.co.uk
Web site: http://www.radmagazine.co.uk
ISSN: 0264-6412
Publisher: Kingsmoor Publications Ltd
Date Established: 1974
Frequency: Monthly
Free to qualifying individuals
Circulation: 10,000 (Publisher's Statement)
Usual Pagination: 60
Editor: David Roberts; **Managing Director:** David Roberts; **Advertising Manager:** David Roberts
Summary of Content: Publication containing features relating to medical equipment, health and hygiene, radiology, radiography, radiotherapy, nuclear medicine and ultrasonics.
Readership/Target Audience: Read by radiologists, radiotherapists, medical physicists, and others working in CT, MR imaging and nuclear medicine.
ADVERTISING RATES:
Full Page Mono £1860.00
Full Page Colour £3660.00
SCC £9.60
Mechanical Data: Col Length: 380mm, Col Widths (Display): 42mm, Film: Digital, No. of Columns (Display): 6, Type Area: 380 x 268mm, Print Process: Sheet-fed litho, Bleed Size: 425 x 303mm, Trim Size: 419 x 297mm, Page Width: 268mm
Average advertising content per issue: 40%
BUSINESS: HEALTH & MEDICAL: Radiography

RADIATION PROTECTION DOSIMETRY
24272U55-134
Editorial Address: Great Clarendon Street, OXFORD, OX2 6DP **Tel:** 01865 353907 **Fax:** 01865 353985

Email: rpd@oupjournals.org
Advertising Address: As above. **Tel:** 01865 354637
Email: steve.simmonds@oxfordjournals.org
Web site: http://rpd.oupjournals.org
ISSN: 0144-8420
Publisher: OUP
Date Established: 1981
Frequency: 20 issues yearly
Annual Sub.: £655.00
Editor: E.P. Goldfinch; **Executive Editor:** E.P. Goldfinch
Summary of Content: Publication covering all aspects of personal and environmental dosimetry and monitoring, for both ionising and non-ionising radiations, including biological aspects, physical concepts, biophysical dosimetry, external and internal workplace monitoring and accident dosimetry.
Readership/Target Audience: Aimed at radiation protection practitioners and scientists in research, industry, universities, radiation dosimetrists, regulators, radiobiologists and environmentalists.
ADVERTISING RATES:
Full Page Mono £646.00
Full Page Colour £1076.00
Agency Commission: 10%
Mechanical Data: Type Area: 210 x 145mm, Col Length: 210mm, Page Width: 145mm, Film: Digital, Trim Size: 246 x 189mm, Bleed Size: 252 x 195mm, Print Process: Litho
BUSINESS: APPLIED SCIENCE & LABORATORIES

THE RADIO JOURNAL   1696527U62R-499
Editorial Address: Division of Media, Language and Leisure Management, Glasgow Caledonian University, Cowcaddens Road, GLASGOW, G4 0BA
Email: tim.wall@uce.ac.uk
Web site: http://www.intellectbooks.co.uk
ISSN: 1476-4504
Publisher: Intellect Ltd
Date Established: 2003
Frequency: 3 issues yearly - Published in April, August and December
Annual Sub.: £180.00
Circulation: 400 (Publisher's Statement)
Usual Pagination: 80
Editor: Tim Wall
Summary of Content: Journal covering research into contemporary radio.
Readership/Target Audience: Aimed at all those interested in research into the production, reception, texts and contexts of radio and audio media.
ADVERTISING: No Advertising taken
BUSINESS: CHURCH & SCHOOL EQUIPMENT & EDUCATION: Education Related

---

THE RADIO MAGAZINE   35690U2D-83_50
Editorial Address: 21 West St. Helen Street, ABINGDON, OX14 5BL **Tel:** 01536 418558 **Fax:** 01235 528121
Email: editor@theradiomagazine.co.uk
Advertising Address: As above. **Fax:** 01536 418539
Email: gay.schroeder@theradiomagazine.co.uk
Web site: http://www.theradiomagazine.co.uk
ISSN: 0996-7105
Publisher: Goldcrest Broadcasting Ltd
Date Established: 1992
Frequency: Weekly
Cover Price: £3.00
Free to qualifying individuals
Annual Sub.: £105.00
Circulation: 7,000 (Publisher's Statement)
Usual Pagination: 32
Editor: Collette Hillier
Summary of Content: Magazine covering news, job details, features and events.
Readership/Target Audience: Read by professionals within the UK radio services.
ADVERTISING RATES:
Full Page Mono £885.00
Full Page Colour £1240.00
Agency Commission: 10%
Mechanical Data: Col Widths (Display): 74mm, No. of Columns (Display): 2, Type Area: 240 x 170mm, Bleed Size: +5mm, Page Width: 170mm, Col Length: 240mm, Film: Digital
Average advertising content per issue: 40%
BUSINESS: COMMUNICATIONS, ADVERTISING & MARKETING: Broadcasting

---

RADNEWS   37282U16B-140
Editorial Address: 14 Castle Mews, High Street, HAMPTON, TW12 2NP **Tel:** 020 8487 0800
Fax: 020 8487 0801
Email: radnews@pra-world.com
Advertising Address: As above.
Email: radnews@pra-world.com
Web site: http://www.pra-world.com
ISSN: 0966-9698
Publisher: PRA

Frequency: Quarterly
Annual Sub.: £175.00
Usual Pagination: 36
Editor: Richard Kennedy; **Advertising Manager:** Richard Kennedy
Summary of Content: Newsletter covering worldwide news items on markets, products, companies, legislation, patents and literature as well as technical papers relating to radiation curing in the coating industry.
Readership/Target Audience: Aimed at the radiation curing industry.
ADVERTISING: Rates on application
BUSINESS: DECORATING & PAINT: Paint - Technical Manufacture

RAF NEWS   38879U40-422
Editorial Address: Royal Air Force Headquarters, Strike Command, Naphill, HIGH WYCOMBE, HP14 4UE
Tel: 01494 495566 **Fax:** 01494 495569
Email: editor@rafnews.co.uk
Advertising Address: Mongoose Media Ltd, 2 Lonsdale Road, LONDON, NW6 6RD **Tel:** 020 7306 0300
Fax: 020 7306 0301
Email: raf@mongoosemedia.com
Web site: http://www.rafnews.co.uk
Publisher: RAF
Date Established: 1961
Frequency: 25 issues yearly
Cover Price: £0.70
Annual Sub.: £17.50
Circulation: 24,000 (Publisher's Statement)
Usual Pagination: 28
Editor: Simon William
Summary of Content: News on RAF stations, aircraft, personnel and sport.
Readership/Target Audience: Aimed at RAF personnel, former members of the service and military enthusiasts.
ADVERTISING RATES:
Full Page Mono £2360.00
Full Page Colour £2990.00
Agency Commission: 10%
Mechanical Data: Col Widths (Display): 41.5mm, No. of Columns (Display): 6, Page Width: 274mm, Film: Digital, Print Process: Offset litho, Type Area: 370 x 274mm, Col Length: 370mm
Copy instructions: Copy Date: 10 days prior to publication date
BUSINESS: DEFENCE

RAIDER   1841365U40-442
Editorial Address: 2 Shaw Close, Peneden Heath, MAIDSTONE, ME14 5DN **Tel:** 01622 692885
Fax: 01622 683093
Email: paul@ai-mag.com
Advertising Address: As above. **Fax:** 01622 692885
Email: paul@ai-mag.com
Web site: http://www.raider-mag.com
Publisher: Ebcon Publishing
Date Established: 2008
Frequency: Monthly
Cover Price: £4.00
Annual Sub.: £45.00
Circulation: 15,000 (Publisher's Statement)
Editor: Paul Monaf; **Advertising Manager:** Paul Monaf
Summary of Content: Magazine for the professional soldier, covering technology, history, unit profiles and employment.
Readership/Target Audience: Aimed at British soldiers serving in Iraq and Afghanistan.
ADVERTISING RATES:
Full Page Colour £750.00
BUSINESS: DEFENCE

RAIL BUSINESS INTELLIGENCE
                                          39683U49E-160
Editorial Address: 9 Sutton Court Road, SUTTON, SM1 4SZ **Tel:** 020 8652 5200 **Fax:** 020 8652 5210
Email: robert.preston@railwaygazette.com
Web site: http://www.railwaygazette.com
ISSN: 1472-5428
Publisher: DVV Media UK Ltd
Date Established: 1995
Frequency: 24 issues yearly
Annual Sub.: £630.00
Usual Pagination: 8
Editor: Robert Preston; **Editor-in-Chief:** Chris Jackson; **Publisher:** Sheena Rennie
Summary of Content: Newsletter identifying new contracts and providing details of bids and bidders, plus analysis of the UK railway industry.
Readership/Target Audience: Aimed at professionals in the railway industry, including the financial, legal and regulatory sectors as well as manufacturers and operators.
ADVERTISING: No Advertising taken
BUSINESS: TRANSPORT: Railways

THE RAIL ENGINEER   1694354U49E-253
Editorial Address: Ashby House, Bath Street, ASHBY-DE-LA-ZOUCH, LE65 2FH **Tel:** 01530 560021
Fax: 01530 412166
Email: tre.news@railstaff.co.uk
Advertising Address: As above.
Email: adverts@railstaff.co.uk
Web site: http://www.railstaff.co.uk
Publisher: Rail Media Group
Date Established: 2004
Frequency: Monthly
Free to qualifying individuals
Circulation: 11,646 (Publisher's Statement)
Usual Pagination: 40
Editor: Grahame Taylor; **Advertising Manager:** Neil Ray
Summary of Content: Magazine focusing on all aspects of UK and European rail infrastructure.
Readership/Target Audience: Aimed at senior management and engineers within the rail industry.
ADVERTISING RATES:
Full Page Colour £1495.00
Agency Commission: 10%
Mechanical Data: Type Area: 307 x 220mm, Col Length: 307mm, Page Width: 220mm, Film: Digital
BUSINESS: TRANSPORT: Railways

RAIL PROFESSIONAL   39684U49E-163
Editorial Address: 275 Newmarket Road, CAMBRIDGE, CB5 8JE **Tel:** 01223 477411 **Fax:** 01223 327356
Email: editor@railpro.co.uk
Advertising Address: As above. **Tel:** 01223 477427
Email: advertising@railpro.co.uk
Web site: http://www.railpro.co.uk
ISSN: 1476-2196
Publisher: Rail Professional Ltd
Date Established: 1996
Frequency: Monthly
Free to qualifying individuals
Annual Sub.: £39.00
Circulation: 8,500 (Publisher's Statement)
Usual Pagination: 44
Editor: Katie Silvester; **Advertising Manager:** Rob Tidswell
Summary of Content: Contains information and support to all professionals working in the rail industry.
Readership/Target Audience: Read by rail business managers and directors and rail industry stake holders.
ADVERTISING RATES:
Full Page Colour £1895.00
Agency Commission: 10%
Mechanical Data: Trim Size: 297 x 210mm, Type Area: 265 x 185mm, Bleed Size: 303 x 216mm, Col Length: 265mm, Page Width: 185mm, Film: Digital
Average advertising content per issue: 30%
BUSINESS: TRANSPORT: Railways

RAIL TECHNOLOGY MAGAZINE
                                          755509U49E-213
Formerly: Railway Technology Magazine
Editorial Address: Suite 102, International House, 82-86 Deansgate, MANCHESTER, M3 2ER **Tel:** 0161 833 6320
Fax: 0161 832 0571
Email: editorial@railtechnologymagazine.com
Advertising Address: As above.
Email: royc@cognitivepublishing.com
Web site: http://www.railtechnologymagazine.com
ISSN: 1471-0668
Publisher: Cognitive Publishing Ltd
Date Established: 1999
Frequency: 6 issues yearly - Published at the end of the 1st cover month
Cover Price: £6.95
Free to qualifying individuals
Circulation: 8,000 (ABC 01/07/2008 to 31/12/2008)
Usual Pagination: 96
Editor: Stephen Lewis; **Publisher:** Roy Rowlands
Summary of Content: Journal covering commercial and political developments, latest technology, major projects and purchasing strategies within the rail industry.
Readership/Target Audience: Aimed at senior executives, directors, managers and engineers within the rail industry as well as government officials.
ADVERTISING RATES:
Full Page Colour £1995.00
Agency Commission: 10%
Mechanical Data: Type Area: 270 x 184mm, Print Process: Digital, Col Length: 270mm, Trim Size: 297 x 210mm, Page Width: 184mm, Bleed Size: 303 x 216mm
Copy instructions: Copy Date: 4th of the publication month
Average advertising content per issue: 40%
BUSINESS: TRANSPORT: Railways

RAILNEWS   39686U49E-162
Editorial Address: King's Cross Business Centre, Room 007, 180-186 King's Cross Road, LONDON, WC1X 9DE
Tel: 020 7278 6100 **Fax:** 020 7278 6145
Email: newsdesk@railnews.co.uk

Advertising Address: As above.
Email: advertising@railnews.co.uk
Web site: http://www.railnews.co.uk
ISSN: 0033-8745
Publisher: Railnews Ltd
Date Established: 1997
Frequency: Monthly
Cover Price: £1.95
Annual Sub: £23.40
Circulation: 63,000 (Publisher's Statement)
Usual Pagination: 40
Advertising Manager: Barry Smale
Summary of Content: Newspaper covering railway industry developments, changes of rail company policy and staff news.
Readership/Target Audience: Aimed at those working in the rail industry throughout the UK.
ADVERTISING RATES:
Full Page Mono £1945.00
Full Page Colour £2245.00
Agency Commission: 10%
Mechanical Data: Type Area: 345 x 274mm, Col Length: 345mm, Col Widths (Display): 42mm, No. of Columns (Display): 6, Page Width: 274mm, Film: Digital
Copy instructions: Copy Date: 3 days prior to publication date
BUSINESS: TRANSPORT: Railways

RAILSTAFF
1685612U49E-252
Editorial Address: Ashby House, Bath Street, ASHBY-DE-LA-ZOUCH, LE65 2FH **Tel:** 01530 560021
Fax: 01530 412166
Email: news@railstaff.co.uk
Advertising Address: As above.
Email: neilr@railstaff.co.uk
Web site: http://www.railstaff.co.uk
Publisher: Rail Media Group
Frequency: Monthly
Free to qualifying individuals
Circulation: 55,000 (Publisher's Statement)
Usual Pagination: 42
Editor: Andy Milne; **Advertising Manager:** Neil Ray;
Publisher: Paul O'Connor
Summary of Content: Magazine covering current news and issues affecting the UK rail industry.
Readership/Target Audience: Aimed at railway staff.
ADVERTISING RATES:
Full Page Colour £2295.00
Agency Commission: 10%
Mechanical Data: Type Area: 340 x 270mm, Col Length: 340mm, Page Width: 270mm, Film: Digital
BUSINESS: TRANSPORT: Railways

RAILWAY GAZETTE INTERNATIONAL
39687U49E-200
Editorial Address: 9 Sutton Court Road, SUTTON, SM2 4SZ **Tel:** 020 8652 5200 **Fax:** 020 8652 5210
Email: editor@railwaygazette.com
Advertising Address: As above. **Tel:** 020 8652 3278
Fax: 020 8652 3738
Email: sheena.rennie@railwaygazette.com
Web site: http://www.railwaygazette.com
ISSN: 0373-5346
Publisher: DVV Media UK Ltd
Date Established: 1835
Frequency: Monthly - Published in the last week of the month prior to cover month
Annual Sub: £88.00
Circulation: 10,614 (ABC 01/01/2008 to 31/12/2008)
Editor: Andrew Grantham; **News Editor:** Andrew Grantham;
Advertising Manager: Sheena Rennie
Summary of Content: Magazine featuring technical and operational articles and news about the international railway industry.
Readership/Target Audience: Read by railway management, railway operators and suppliers.
ADVERTISING RATES:
Full Page Mono £1875.00
Full Page Colour £2800.00
Agency Commission: 10%
Mechanical Data: Page Width: 178mm, Film: Digital, Type Area: 254 x 178mm, Bleed Size: 296 x 213mm, Trim Size: 290 x 210mm, Col Length: 254mm
Average advertising content per issue: 50%
Supplement(s): Metro Report - 4xY
BUSINESS: TRANSPORT: Railways

RAILWAY INTERIORS INTERNATIONAL
1697321U49E-255
Editorial Address: Abinger House, Church Street, DORKING, RH4 1DF **Tel:** 01306 743744 **Fax:** 01306 887546
Email: railwayinteriors@ukintpress.com
Advertising Address: As above. **Fax:** 01306 742525
Email: a.bayliss@ukintpress.com
Web site: http://www.ukipme.com
ISSN: 1744-2281

Publisher: UKIP Media & Events Ltd
Date Established: 2004
Frequency: Quarterly - Published around the 10th of the cover month
Free to qualifying individuals
Circulation: 7,500 (Publisher's Statement)
Usual Pagination: 72
Editor: Jonathan Lawson
Summary of Content: Magazine covering the latest trends and developments in the design, furnishing, equipment and management of passenger railway carriage interiors.
Readership/Target Audience: Aimed at rail operators and manufacturers.
ADVERTISING RATES:
Full Page Colour £3720.00
Agency Commission: 10%
Mechanical Data: Type Area: 255 x 195mm, Trim Size: 275 x 215mm, Col Length: 255mm, Page Width: 195mm, Film: Digital
BUSINESS: TRANSPORT: Railways

RAILWAY STRATEGIES
39690U49E-210
Editorial Address: Essex Technology & Innovation Centre, ONGAR, CM5 0GA **Tel:** 01277 368318 **Fax:** 01277 368291
Email: editor@railwaystrategies.co.uk
Advertising Address: As above.
Email: info@hartfordpublications.co.uk
Web site: http://www.railwaystrategies.co.uk
ISSN: 1467-0399
Publisher: Schofield Publishing Ltd
Date Established: 1999
Frequency: 6 issues yearly - Published around the 1st of the 2nd cover month
Cover Price: Free
Circulation: 5,600 (ABC 01/01/2008 to 31/12/2008)
Usual Pagination: 152
Editor: Martin Collier; **Publisher:** Mike Tulloch
Summary of Content: Magazine providing in-depth news and information on all aspects of railway management; reports on finance, contracts, franchise issues, safety, security, rolling stock, station developments, integrated transport, freight, appointments and trade exhibitions.
Readership/Target Audience: Aimed at directors and senior management within companies operating railway franchises, Government departments, official agencies, Network Rail and specialists with an interest in the development of railway systems.
ADVERTISING RATES:
Full Page Colour £1800.00
Agency Commission: 10%
Mechanical Data: Trim Size: 297 x 210mm, Film: Digital
Copy instructions: Copy Date: 5 weeks prior to publication date
Average advertising content per issue: 40%
BUSINESS: TRANSPORT: Railways

RAISING THE STANDARD
1655127U14F-240
Editorial Address: 7-10 Chandos Street, LONDON, W1G 9DQ **Tel:** 020 7467 1900 **Fax:** 020 7636 2386
Email: lucyh@iipuk.co.uk
Web site: http://www.investorsinpeople.co.uk
Publisher: Investors In People
Date Established: 2002
Frequency: Quarterly
Cover Price: Free
Circulation: 40,000 (Publisher's Statement)
Usual Pagination: 20
Summary of Content: Magazine focusing on the effective development of the human resource to achieve business objectives and the benefits of being an investor in people.
Readership/Target Audience: Aimed at human resource managers and directors.
ADVERTISING: No Advertising taken
BUSINESS: COMMERCE, INDUSTRY & MANAGEMENT: Training & Recruitment

RANGER
1804945U21F-882
Editorial Address: Po Box 75, BRIGHOUSE, HD6 3WF
Tel: 01484 400 666 **Fax:** 01484 400 661
Email: keith@farminguk.com
Advertising Address: The Breezi Publishing Co Ltd, PO Box 75, BRIGHOUSE, HD6 3WF **Tel:** 01484 400666
Fax: 01484 400661
Email: keith@farminguk.com
Web site: http://www.theranger.co.uk
Publisher: British Free Range Egg Producers Association
Frequency: Monthly
Free to qualifying individuals
Circulation: 1,000 (Publisher's Statement)
Editor: Keith Wild; **Advertising Manager:** Keith Wild
Summary of Content: Magazine containing news and features on free range egg production. Includes veterinary and husbandry information.
Readership/Target Audience: Aimed at members of the British Free Range Egg Producers Association.

ADVERTISING RATES:
Full Page Colour £200.00
Agency Commission: 10%
Copy instructions: Copy Date: 1 week prior to publication date
Average advertising content per issue: 30%
BUSINESS: AGRICULTURE & FARMING: Poultry

RAPID COMMUNICATIONS IN MASS SPECTROMETRY
40095U55-134_20
Editorial Address: The Atrium, Southern Gate, CHICHESTER, PO19 8SQ **Tel:** 01243 779777
Fax: 01243 775878
Email: ptrevorr@wiley.com
Advertising Address: As above.
Email: adsales@wiley.co.uk
Web site: http://www.interscience.wiley.com
ISSN: 0951-4198
Publisher: John Wiley & Sons Ltd
Date Established: 1987
Frequency: 24 issues yearly
Annual Sub: £5640.00
Circulation: 750 (Publisher's Statement)
Usual Pagination: 100
Editor: Paul Trevorrow
Summary of Content: Journal containing research ideas and results on all aspects of the science of gas-phase ions.
Readership/Target Audience: Aimed at analytical chemists, organic chemists, pharmaceutical chemists and spectroscopists.
ADVERTISING RATES:
Full Page Mono £1175.00
Full Page Colour £2575.00
Agency Commission: 10%
Mechanical Data: Type Area: 270 x 180mm, Col Length: 270mm, Page Width: 180mm, Bleed Size: 303 x 216mm, Trim Size: 297 x 210mm, Print Process: Sheet-fed offset litho, Film: Digital
Copy instructions: Copy Date: 4 weeks prior to publication date
BUSINESS: APPLIED SCIENCE & LABORATORIES

RAPID PROTOTYPING JOURNAL
37696U19J-150
Editorial Address: Loughborough University, Department of Design and Technology, LOUGHBOROUGH, LE11 3TU
Tel: 01509 228312 **Fax:** 01509 223999
Email: r.i.campbell@lboro.ac.uk
Web site: http://www.emeraldinsight.com
ISSN: 1355-2546
Publisher: Emerald Group Publishing Ltd
Date Established: 1994
Frequency: 3 issues yearly
Annual Sub: £1929.00
Usual Pagination: 64
Editor: Ian Campbell; **Publisher:** Harry Colson
Summary of Content: International journal covering the developments in rapid product development technologies.
Readership/Target Audience: Read by industrialists and academics.
ADVERTISING: No Advertising taken
BUSINESS: ENGINEERING & MACHINERY: CAD & CIM (Computer Integrated Manufacture)

RAPPORT
37225U14L-580
Editorial Address: Middleton Farmhouse, 37 Main Road, Middleton Cheney, BANBURY, OX17 2QT
Tel: 01295 710767 **Fax:** 01295 712580
Email: trose@ngsu.org.uk
Advertising Address: As above.
Email: ngsu@ngsu.org.uk
Web site: http://www.ngsu.org.uk
ISSN: 0961-3935
Publisher: Nationwide Group Staff Union
Date Established: 1990
Frequency: Quarterly
Cover Price: Free
Circulation: 13,000 (Publisher's Statement)
Usual Pagination: 16
Editor: Tim Rose; **Advertising Manager:** Lisa Wakefield
Summary of Content: Magazine containing staff union news, information and offers.
Readership/Target Audience: Aimed at staff union members, mainly females aged 25 to 55 years.
ADVERTISING: Rates on application
BUSINESS: COMMERCE, INDUSTRY & MANAGEMENT: Trade Unions

RAPPORT CYWU
37202U14L-600
Editorial Address: 211 Broad Street, BIRMINGHAM, B15 1AY **Tel:** 0121 643 6221 **Fax:** 0121 633 0184
Email: kev_henman@hotmail.com
Advertising Address: As above.
Email: kerry.jenkins@unitetheunion.com

Section 4 (b) Business Magazines

Business Magazines

Web site: http://www.cywu.org.uk
ISSN: 1462-8007
Publisher: CYWU/Unite The Union
Date Established: 1971
Frequency: 6 issues yearly
Free to qualifying individuals
Annual Sub.: £15.00
Circulation: 6,000 (Publisher's Statement)
Usual Pagination: 36
Editor: Kev Henman; **Advertising Manager:** Kerry Jenkins
Summary of Content: Official magazine of the Community and Youth Workers' Union. Contains professional, political and trade union issues within the youth community and playwork sectors.
Readership/Target Audience: Read by members of the Community and Youth Workers' Union, mentors and personal advisors.
ADVERTISING RATES:
Full Page Colour £450.00
Copy instructions: Copy Date: 3 weeks prior to publication date
Average advertising content per issue: 10%
BUSINESS: COMMERCE, INDUSTRY & MANAGEMENT: Trade Unions

RATING & VALUATION REPORTER
38416U32C-220
Editorial Address: 180 Fleet Street, LONDON, EC4A 2HG
Tel: 01483 233571 **Fax:** 01483 234804
Email: editor@rvr-online.co.uk
ISSN: 0048-6817
Publisher: Rating Publishers Limited
Date Established: 1924
Frequency: 11 issues yearly
Annual Sub.: £545.00
Editor: Christopher Lewsley
Summary of Content: Journal containing law reports on non-domestic rating, valuation of land for compulsory purchase, government finance and council tax.
Readership/Target Audience: Aimed at valuation officers, local authorities and surveyors.
ADVERTISING: No Advertising taken
BUSINESS: LOCAL GOVERNMENT, LEISURE & RECREATION: Local Government Finance

RATIONALITY & SOCIETY
40097U55-134_55
Editorial Address: 1 Oliver's Yard, 55 City Road, LONDON, EC1Y 1SP **Tel:** 020 7324 8500 **Fax:** 020 7324 8600
Advertising Address: As above.
Email: advertising@sagepub.co.uk
Web site: http://www.sagepub.co.uk/journalsProdDesc.nav?prodId=Journal200827&
ISSN: 1043-4631
Publisher: Sage Publications
Frequency: Quarterly
Cover Price: £17.00
Annual Sub.: £52.00
Editor: Douglas Heckathorn; **Advertising Manager:** Sheena Karim
Summary of Content: Journal focusing on the growing contributions of rational-action based theory, and the questions and controversies surrounding this growth.
Readership/Target Audience: Aimed at those concerned with rational choice theory in social sciences.
ADVERTISING RATES:
Full Page Mono £400.00
Agency Commission: 5%
Mechanical Data: Col Length: 185mm, Type Area: 185 x 105mm, Page Width: 105mm, Film: Digital
BUSINESS: APPLIED SCIENCE & LABORATORIES

RCI DIRECTORY
35944U4E-307_45
Editorial Address: Becket House, Vestry Road, SEVENOAKS, TN14 5EJ **Tel:** 01732 748000
Fax: 01732 748001
Email: kmanson@unity-media.com
Advertising Address: As above.
Email: tbrown@unity-media.com
Publisher: Unity Media plc
Date Established: 1986
Frequency: Annual
Cover Price: £75.00
Circulation: 7,687 (Publisher's Statement)
Usual Pagination: 212
Editor: Kathy Manson; **Advertising Manager:** Tony Brown; **Publisher:** Colin Wilkinson
Summary of Content: Directory for the RCI Industry.
Readership/Target Audience: Read by raters, specifiers, architects and local association building officers.
ADVERTISING RATES:
Full Page Colour £1075.00
Agency Commission: 10%
Mechanical Data: Type Area: 265 x 190mm, Bleed Size: 303 x 216mm, Trim Size: 297 x 210mm, Col Length: 265mm, Page Width: 190mm, Film: Digital

Copy instructions: Copy Date: 8 weeks prior to publication date
Average advertising content per issue: 55%
BUSINESS: ARCHITECTURE & BUILDING: Building

RCI (ROOFING, CLADDING & INSULATION)
35925U4E-307_50
Formerly: RCI Roofing, Cladding & Insulation
Editorial Address: Becket House, Vestry Road, SEVENOAKS, TN14 5EJ **Tel:** 01732 748000
Fax: 01732 748001
Email: kmanson@unity-media.com
Advertising Address: As above.
Web site: http://www.rcimag.co.uk
ISSN: 0951-6263
Publisher: Unity Media plc
Date Established: 1980
Frequency: Monthly - Published on the 15th of the cover month
Cover Price: £3.50
Free to qualifying individuals
Annual Sub.: £35.00
Circulation: 7,613 (ABC 01/07/2008 to 30/06/2009)
Usual Pagination: 84
Editor: Kathy Manson; **Advertising Manager:** Tony Brown; **Publisher:** Colin Wilkinson
Summary of Content: Journal covering roofing, weatherproofing and thermal insulation.
Readership/Target Audience: Aimed at architects, surveyors, specifiers, roofing, cladding and thermal insulation contractors and distributors of all roofing materials.
ADVERTISING RATES:
Full Page Colour £1020.00
Agency Commission: 10%
Mechanical Data: Film: Digital, Type Area: 265 x 190mm, Col Length: 265mm, Page Width: 190mm, Bleed Size: 306 x 216mm, Trim Size: 297 x 210mm
Copy instructions: Copy Date: 1st week of the month prior to publication date
Average advertising content per issue: 60%
BUSINESS: ARCHITECTURE & BUILDING: Building

RCI VENTURES
1660329U11A-196
Editorial Address: Kettering Parkway, KETTERING, NN15 6EY **Tel:** 01536 314266 **Fax:** 01536 314682
Email: helen.foster@rci.com
Advertising Address: Media Line Ltd, 23-25 Hockliffe Street, LEIGHTON BUZZARD, LU7 8EZ **Tel:** 0870 250 8701
Fax: 0870 250 9697
Email: nickyl@medialine.eu.com
Publisher: RCI Europe
Date Established: 2003
Frequency: Quarterly
Cover Price: Free
Circulation: 4,000 (Publisher's Statement)
Usual Pagination: 30
Editor: Helen Foster; **Advertising Director:** Nicky Lane
Summary of Content: Magazine covering the news and concerns of the hotel and shared holiday ownership industry and a showcase of ideas from the hospitality industry at large.
Readership/Target Audience: Aimed at hotel, time-share and high-end shared holiday ownership resort developers, managers, marketers and those associated with the industry, including hotel partners.
ADVERTISING RATES:
Full Page Mono £2300.00
Full Page Colour £2300.00
Agency Commission: 10%
Mechanical Data: Type Area: 240 x 171mm, Trim Size: 276 x 207mm, Bleed Size: 282 x 213mm, Col Length: 240mm, Page Width: 171mm, Film: Digital
BUSINESS: CATERING: Catering, Hotels & Restaurants

RDA NEWS
1706765U1R-373
Editorial Address: 32 Vauxhall Bridge Road, LONDON, SW1V 2SS **Tel:** 020 7973 6400 **Fax:** 020 7233 5051
Email: d.calpin@virgin.net
Advertising Address: As above. **Fax:** 020 7233 5053
Email: j.kitchen@hgluk.com
Web site: http://www.rdanews.co.uk
Publisher: Hemming Group Ltd
Date Established: 2001
Frequency: 11 issues yearly
Annual Sub.: £195.00
Usual Pagination: 16
Editor: Dermott Calpin; **Managing Editor:** Dermott Calpin
Summary of Content: Magazine featuring industry news and features on regional development.
Readership/Target Audience: Aimed at regional development agencies.
ADVERTISING RATES:
Full Page Mono £2295.00
Full Page Colour £2552.00
Agency Commission: 10%

Mechanical Data: Type Area: 266 x 184mm, Col Length: 266mm, Page Width: 184mm, Bleed Size: 307 x 220mm, Trim Size: 297 x 210mm, No. of Columns (Display): 4, Col Widths (Display): 45mm
Average advertising content per issue: 1%
BUSINESS: FINANCE & ECONOMICS: Financial Related

THE RE REPORT
35163U1D-339_50
Editorial Address: 69-77 Paul Street, LONDON, EC2A 4LQ
Tel: 020 7017 4600 **Fax:** 020 7436 8414
Email: graham.village@informa.com
Web site: http://www.informa.com
Publisher: Informa PLC
Frequency: 25 issues yearly
Annual Sub.: £1540.00
Editor: Graham Village
Summary of Content: Newsletter containing news and analysis of the international reinsurance industry as well as legal developments and corporate moves.
Readership/Target Audience: Aimed at professionals in the reinsurance and associated industries.
ADVERTISING: No Advertising taken
BUSINESS: FINANCE & ECONOMICS: Insurance

REACTIONS
35160U1D-336
Editorial Address: Nestor House, Playhouse Yard, LONDON, EC4V 5EX **Tel:** 020 7779 8193
Fax: 020 7779 8200
Email: mloney@institutionalinvestor.com
Advertising Address: As above. **Tel:** 020 7779 8000
Email: sabrown@euromoneyplc.com
Web site: http://www.reactionsnet.com
ISSN: 0953-5640
Publisher: Euromoney Institutional Investor plc
Frequency: 10 issues yearly - Published 1st week of month
Annual Sub.: £425.00
Circulation: 9,446 (ABC 01/07/2008 to 30/06/2009)
Usual Pagination: 60
Editor: Michael Loney; **News Editor:** Richard Crump; **Advertising Manager:** Stewart Brown
Summary of Content: Publication providing information, news and analysis on insurance and reinsurance worldwide.
Readership/Target Audience: Read by executives working in global insurance and reinsurance markets.
ADVERTISING RATES:
Full Page Mono $11032.00
Full Page Colour $12225.00
Agency Commission: 10%
Mechanical Data: Type Area: 271 x 186mm, Bleed Size: 303 x 216mm, Trim Size: 297 x 210mm, Film: Digital, Col Length: 271mm, Page Width: 186mm
Copy instructions: Copy Date: 10th of month prior to publication date
Supplement(s): Global Re Highlights - 1xY, Reactions Awards - 1xY
BUSINESS: FINANCE & ECONOMICS: Insurance

REAL BUSINESS
36802U14A-303
Editorial Address: 198 Kings Road, LONDON, SW3 5XP
Tel: 020 7368 7100
Email: editors@realbusiness.co.uk
Advertising Address: As above. **Fax:** 020 7368 7112
Email: mb5@caspianpublishing.co.uk
Web site: http://www.realbusiness.co.uk
ISSN: 1462-3064
Publisher: Caspian Publishing
Date Established: 1997
Frequency: 10 issues yearly
Annual Sub.: £35.00
Circulation: 40,982 (ABC 01/07/2007 to 30/06/2008)
Usual Pagination: 90
Editor: Kate Pritchard; **Advertising Manager:** Matthew Blore; **Managing Editor:** Kate Pritchard; **Group Editor:** Matthew Rock; **Publisher:** Mike Bokaie
Summary of Content: Magazine for those concerned with newly formed and growing companies.
Readership/Target Audience: Aimed at managing directors of growing companies employing between 10 and 500 people.
ADVERTISING RATES:
Full Page Mono £5190.00
Full Page Colour £5190.00
Agency Commission: 15%
Mechanical Data: Page Width: 163mm, Bleed Size: 261 x 189mm, Trim Size: 255 x 183mm, Type Area: 235 x 163mm, Col Length: 235mm, Film: Digital
Copy instructions: Copy Date: 3 weeks prior to publication date
Average advertising content per issue: 42%
BUSINESS: COMMERCE, INDUSTRY & MANAGEMENT

REAL DEALS
35429U1N-47
Editorial Address: 198 Kings Road, LONDON, SW3 5XP
Tel: 020 7368 7140 **Fax:** 020 7368 7178
Email: editorial@realdeals.eu.com

Advertising Address: As above. **Tel:** 020 7368 7111
Fax: 020 7368 7112
Email: dan@realdeals.eu.com
Web site: http://www.realdeals.eu.com
ISSN: 1468-9154
Publisher: Caspian Publishing
Date Established: 1999
Frequency: 26 issues yearly
Annual Sub: £375.00
Circulation: 3,110 (ABC 01/07/2007 to 30/06/2008)
Usual Pagination: 48
Editor: Clare Haughey; **Managing Editor:** Sam Barton;
Advertisement Director: Dan Brennan
Summary of Content: Magazine covering the European
private equity and venture capital industries with news
coverage, comments, features and analysis.
Readership/Target Audience: Aimed at venture capitalists,
investment bankers, lawyers, accountants, company
directors, and entrepreneurs.
ADVERTISING RATES:
Full Page Mono £2640.00
Full Page Colour £3630.00
Agency Commission: 10%
Mechanical Data: Col Length: 290mm, Page Width:
215mm, Film: Digital, No. of Columns (Display): 4, Trim Size:
310 x 325mm, Type Area: 290 x 215mm, Bleed Size: 316 x
241mm
Copy instructions: Copy Date: 8 days prior to publication
date
Average advertising content per issue: 25%
BUSINESS: FINANCE & ECONOMICS: Venture Capital

RECHARGE
1896204U58-200
Editorial Address: Eldon House, 2 Eldon Street, LONDON,
EC2M 7LS **Tel:** 020 7650 1060 **Fax:** 020 7650 1050
Email: editorial@rechargenews.com
Web site: http://www.rechargenews.com
Publisher: NHST Media Group
Date Established: 2009
Frequency: Weekly
Annual Sub: EUR350.00
Editor: Chris Hopson
Summary of Content: Publication featuring breaking
business, financial and contract news from the renewables
sector, technology news and insights, comment and
analysis, features and profiles.
Readership/Target Audience: Aimed at senior
management and executives in the Global renewables
industry.
BUSINESS: ENERGY, FUEL & NUCLEAR

RECOMMENDED COUNTRY HOTELS OF
BRITAIN
36602U11A-160
Editorial Address: Abbey Mill Business Centre, Seedhill,
PAISLEY, PA1 1TJ **Tel:** 0141 887 0428 **Fax:** 0141 889 7204
Email: admin@fhguides.co.uk
Advertising Address: As above.
Email: dorothy@fhguides.co.uk
Web site: http://www.holidayguides.com
Publisher: FHG Guides
Date Established: 1971
Frequency: Annual - Published in November
Cover Price: £6.99
Circulation: 15,000 (Publisher's Statement)
Usual Pagination: 176
Editor: Anne Cuthbertson; **Advertising Manager:** Dorothy
Clements
Summary of Content: Journal featuring articles on British
country hotels and country houses, accommodation choices
and places of historic interest.
Readership/Target Audience: Aimed at those planning a
holiday in the United Kingdom.
ADVERTISING RATES:
Full Page Colour £739.00
Agency Commission: 10%
Mechanical Data: Page Width: 118mm, Bleed Size: +3mm,
Trim Size: 210 x 145mm, Type Area: 190 x 118mm, Col
Length: 190mm, Film: Digital
Copy instructions: Copy Date: 10 weeks prior to
publication date
Average advertising content per issue: 50%
BUSINESS: CATERING: Catering, Hotels & Restaurants

RECORDS MANAGEMENT JOURNAL
40876U60B-110
Editorial Address: Howard House, Wagon Lane, BINGLEY,
BD16 1WA **Tel:** 01274 777700 **Fax:** 01274 785200
Email: julie.mcleod@northumbria.ac.uk
Web site: http://www.emeraldinsight.com/rmj.htm
ISSN: 0956-5698
Publisher: Emerald Group Publishing Ltd
Frequency: 3 issues yearly - Published in March, July and
October
Annual Sub: £229.00
Usual Pagination: 36
Editor: Julie McLeod

Summary of Content: Journal focusing on all aspects of
creating, processing, and the disposal and retention of
records whatever their form, emphasising the latest research
and current practice.
Readership/Target Audience: Aimed at document
managers and archivists.
ADVERTISING: No Advertising taken
BUSINESS: PUBLISHING: Libraries

RECOVERED FIBRE NEWS
INCORPORATING RECYCLING
MARKETS
38719U36-200
Formerly: Waste Paper News International incorporating
Recycling Markets
Editorial Address: 1 Salisbury Office Park, London Road,
SALISBURY, SP1 3HP **Tel:** 01722 337038
Email: publications@brunton.co.uk
Advertising Address: As above. **Fax:** 01722 337109
Email: subscriptions@brunton.co.uk
Web site: http://www.brunton.co.uk
Publisher: Brunton Business Publications Ltd
Frequency: Monthly - Published around the 10th of the
cover month
Annual Sub: £40.00
Circulation: 7,500 (Publisher's Statement)
Usual Pagination: 16
Editor: Bernard Stonestreet; **Managing Director:** Michael
Brunton
Summary of Content: Newsletter containing news and
prices of waste paper and packaging waste recovery notes
in Europe.
Readership/Target Audience: Aimed at managers of
waste-based paper mills, printers, brokers and publishers,
as well as personnel in local government, collection
authorities and supply chains.
ADVERTISING RATES:
Full Page Colour £525.00
Agency Commission: 10%
Mechanical Data: Type Area: 250 x 176mm, Col Length:
250mm, Page Width: 176mm, Trim Size: 275 x 197mm, Film:
Digital, No. of Columns (Display): 2, Col Widths (Display):
88mm
Copy instructions: Copy Date: 1st of the month prior to
publication date
Average advertising content per issue: 33%
BUSINESS: PAPER

RECOVERY
39233U44-1720
Editorial Address: The Barns, Preston Crowmarsh,
WALLINGFORD, OX10 6SL **Tel:** 01491 828939
Fax: 01491 833146
Email: sarah.houghton@groupgti.com
Advertising Address: As above. **Tel:** 01491 828920
Email: brendan.mcgrath@groupti.com
Web site: http://www.r3.org.uk
Publisher: GTI Specialist Publishers
Date Established: 1991
Frequency: Quarterly
Free to qualifying individuals
Annual Sub: £150.99
Circulation: 5,000 (Publisher's Statement)
Usual Pagination: 56
Editor: Sarah Houghton; **Advertising Manager:** Brendan
McGrath
Summary of Content: Professional journal containing
industry news, views and legal updates for the insolvency
profession.
Readership/Target Audience: Read by all those who work
with under performing businesses including insolvency
practitioners and turnaround professionals.
ADVERTISING RATES:
Full Page Colour £2230.00
Agency Commission: 10%
Mechanical Data: Film: Digital, Screen: 80 lpc, Trim Size:
297 x 210mm, Bleed Size: 303 x 216mm, Type Area: 277 x
190mm, Col Length: 277mm, Page Width: 190mm
Copy instructions: Copy Date: Beginning of the month prior
to publication date
Average advertising content per issue: 30%
BUSINESS: LEGAL

RECOVERY OPERATOR
1616250U49A-403
Editorial Address: 1 Bath Street, RUGBY, CV21 3JF
Tel: 01788 572850 **Fax:** 01788 572850
Email: garysatchwell@btconnect.com
Advertising Address: As above. **Tel:** 024 7647 4066
Fax: 08701 123827
Email: paul@twotone.co.uk
Web site: http://www.avrouk.com
Publisher: Recovery Operator Ltd.
Date Established: 2000
Frequency: 6 issues yearly
Cover Price: Free
Circulation: 12,000 (Publisher's Statement)
Usual Pagination: 32
Editor: Gary Satchwell

Summary of Content: Magazine covering the vehicle
recovery industry including suppliers of goods and services,
government legislation and road safety.
Readership/Target Audience: Aimed at members of AVRO,
IFRS, RRRA, IVR, VBRA, MVRA, RHA, motoring
organisations, police, government, insurance companies and
other subscribers.
ADVERTISING RATES:
Full Page Colour £495.00
Agency Commission: 10%
Average advertising content per issue: 40%
BUSINESS: TRANSPORT

RECREATION
38540U32H-260
Editorial Address: 275 Newmarket Road, CAMBRIDGE,
CB5 8JE **Tel:** 01223 477442 **Fax:** 01223 327356
Email: editor@isrm.co.uk
Advertising Address: As above. **Tel:** 01223 477427
Fax: 01223 304760
Email: advertising@isrm.co.uk
Web site: http://www.isrm.co.uk
Publisher: Cambridge Publishers Ltd
Date Established: 1931
Frequency: 10 issues yearly
Annual Sub: £40.00
Circulation: 4,500 (Publisher's Statement)
Usual Pagination: 56
Editor: Mike Sewell; **Executive Editor:** Jonathan Wilson;
Advertising Manager: Rob Tidswell
Summary of Content: Journal containing articles and
features on all aspects of recreation including safety,
training, marketing and sports development.
Readership/Target Audience: Read by managers of sport
and leisure facilities.
ADVERTISING RATES:
Full Page Colour £995.00
Agency Commission: 10%
Mechanical Data: Type Area: 264 x 185mm, Col Length:
264mm, Page Width: 185mm, Trim Size: 297 x 210mm,
Bleed Size: 303 x 216mm, Film: Digital
Copy instructions: Copy Date: 3 weeks prior to publication
date
Average advertising content per issue: 20%
BUSINESS: LOCAL GOVERNMENT, LEISURE &
RECREATION: Leisure, Recreation & Entertainment

RECRUITER
37075U14F-62_50
Formerly: Professional Recruiter
Editorial Address: St. Giles House, 50 Poland Street,
LONDON, W1F 7AX **Tel:** 020 7970 4000 **Fax:** 020 7970 4812
Email: recruiter.editorial@centaur.co.uk
Advertising Address: As above. **Tel:** 020 7970 4814
Email: kirsty.paterson@centaur.co.uk
Web site: http://www.recruiter.co.uk
ISSN: 1475-7478
Publisher: Centaur Communications Ltd
Date Established: 1998
Frequency: 25 issues yearly
Cover Price: Free
Circulation: 22,376 (ABC 01/07/2008 to 30/06/2009)
Usual Pagination: 68
Editor: Dee-Dee Doke
Summary of Content: Magazine providing coverage of the
recruitment sector across all recruitment offices, across all business and
industry sectors for permanent, temporary, contract and
search or selection assignments.
Readership/Target Audience: Aimed at all professionals
and managers working within the recruitment business.
ADVERTISING RATES:
Full Page Colour £2478.00
Agency Commission: 10%
Mechanical Data: Page Width: 190mm, Type Area: 277 x
190mm, Col Length: 277mm, Trim Size: 297 x 210mm, Bleed
Size: 303 x 216mm
Copy instructions: Copy Date: 1 week prior to publication
date
Average advertising content per issue: 50%
BUSINESS: COMMERCE, INDUSTRY & MANAGEMENT:
Training & Recruitment

RECRUITMENT CONSULTANT
765599U14F-226
Editorial Address: 112-114 High Street,
RICKMANSWORTH, WD3 1AQ **Tel:** 0845 094 8022
Email: editorial@rec-con.co.uk
Advertising Address: As above.
Email: sales@rec-con.co.uk
Web site: http://www.rec-con.co.uk
Publisher: Front Page Publishing
Date Established: 2002
Frequency: Monthly
Free to qualifying individuals
Circulation: 12,623 (Publisher's Statement)
Editor: Jim Tanfield; **Advertising Manager:** Gary King
Summary of Content: Magazine covering all recruitment,
staffing and HR issues.

Readership/Target Audience: Aimed at recruitment consultants, HR professionals, staff resources and any other suppliers to the industry.
ADVERTISING RATES:
Full Page Colour £1675.00
Agency Commission: 10%
Mechanical Data: Type Area: 277 x 190mm, Bleed Size: 303 x 216mm, Trim Size: 297 x 210mm, Col Length: 277mm, Page Width: 190mm
Average advertising content per issue: 30%
BUSINESS: COMMERCE, INDUSTRY & MANAGEMENT: Training & Recruitment

RECRUITMENT INTERNATIONAL
37077U14F-63_25
Editorial Address: 2nd Floor, Lynton House, Station Approach, WOKING, GU22 7PT **Tel:** 01483 740874
Email: david@recruitment-international.co.uk
Advertising Address: 13 High Road, Byfleet, WEST BYFLEET, KT14 7QH **Tel:** 01932 351144
Email: davidhead@dial.pipex.com
Web site: http://www.recruitment-international.co.uk
Publisher: Recruitment Publications Ltd.
Date Established: 1993
Frequency: Monthly - Published on the first Monday of the month
Cover Price: Free
Circulation: 7,000 (Publisher's Statement)
Usual Pagination: 64
Editor: David Head; **Managing Director:** David Head;
Advertising Manager: David Head; **Publisher:** David Head
Summary of Content: Magazine containing news, articles and information on recruitment and staffing issues.
Readership/Target Audience: Aimed at the owners of recruitment and staffing companies.
ADVERTISING RATES:
Full Page Mono £1400.00
Full Page Colour £1400.00
Agency Commission: 10%
Mechanical Data: Trim Size: 297 x 210mm, Film: Digital
Average advertising content per issue: 40%
BUSINESS: COMMERCE, INDUSTRY & MANAGEMENT: Training & Recruitment

RECRUITMENT MATTERS
1775696U14F-259
Editorial Address: 17 Britton Street, LONDON, EC1M 5TP
Tel: 020 7880 6200
Email: mick.james@redactive.co.uk
Advertising Address: As above. **Fax:** 020 7880 7690
Email: anne.sadler@redactive.co.uk
Web site: http://www.rec.uk.com
Publisher: Redactive Media Group
Date Established: 2005
Frequency: Quarterly
Cover Price: £3.50
Free to qualifying individuals
Circulation: 20,000 (Publisher's Statement)
Usual Pagination: 52
Editor: Mick James; **Advertising Manager:** Anne Sadler
Summary of Content: Publication covering recruitment industry news and information.
Readership/Target Audience: Aimed at recruitment professionals.
ADVERTISING RATES:
Full Page Colour £1980.00
Agency Commission: 10%
Mechanical Data: Type Area: 275 x 190mm, Bleed Size: 307 x 220mm, Trim Size: 297 x 210mm, Col Length: 275mm, Page Width: 190mm, Film: Digital
Copy instructions: Copy Date: 4 weeks prior to publication date
Average advertising content per issue: 30%
BUSINESS: COMMERCE, INDUSTRY & MANAGEMENT: Training & Recruitment

RECYCLER TRADE MAGAZINE
625517U41A-341
Editorial Address: 12 Spinners Court, West End, WITNEY, OX28 1NH **Tel:** 01993 899800 **Fax:** 01993 899801
Email: news@therecycler.com
Advertising Address: As above.
Email: markh@therecycler.com
Web site: http://www.therecycler.com
ISSN: 1467-0879
Publisher: The Recycler Ltd
Date Established: 1992
Frequency: Monthly
Annual Sub.: £50.00
Circulation: 5,000 (Publisher's Statement)
Usual Pagination: 132
Editor: Charlotte Hindle; **Managing Editor:** Charlotte Hindle;
Publisher: David Connett
Summary of Content: Magazine covering news and developments within the laser and inkjet printer cartridge recycling industry, includes new product information, company profiles and business advice.

Readership/Target Audience: Aimed at the printer cartridge remanufacturing industries.
ADVERTISING: Rates on application
Agency Commission: 10%
Copy instructions: Copy Date: 1st of the month prior to publication date
Average advertising content per issue: 50%
BUSINESS: PRINTING & STATIONERY: Printing

RECYCLING & WASTE WORLD MAGAZINE
40684U57-50
Formerly: Recycling World
Editorial Address: Jesses Farm, Snow Hill, Dinton, SALISBURY, SP3 5HN **Tel:** 020 7501 6773
Email: tom.f@markallengroup.com
Advertising Address: As above. **Tel:** 01722 716996
Fax: 01722 716887
Email: jane.k@markallengroup.co.uk
Web site: http://www.recyclingwasteworld.co.uk
Publisher: A & D Media Ltd
Date Established: 1987
Frequency: Weekly - Published weekly on Thursday
Cover Price: £2.00
Free to qualifying individuals
Annual Sub.: £92.00
Circulation: 3,500 (Publisher's Statement)
Usual Pagination: 12
Editor: Tom Freyberg; **Publisher:** Mark Allen
Summary of Content: Journal covering events, developments and news in the waste and recycling industry.
Readership/Target Audience: Aimed at local authorities, consultancies, material buyers and sellers, all recycling and waste management companies and energy from waste specialists.
ADVERTISING RATES:
Full Page Mono £1999.00
Full Page Colour £1999.00
SCC £25.00
Agency Commission: 10%
Mechanical Data: Film: Digital, Type Area: 400 x 277mm, Col Length: 400mm, Page Width: 277mm, Bleed Size: 426 x 303mm, Trim Size: 420 x 297mm
Average advertising content per issue: 40%
BUSINESS: ENVIRONMENT & POLLUTION

RECYCLING WORLD HANDBOOK
40719U57-52
Editorial Address: Jesses Farm, Snow Hill, Dinton, SALISBURY, SP3 5HN **Tel:** 020 7501 6773
Email: tom.f@markallengroup.com
Advertising Address: As above. **Tel:** 01722 716997
Fax: 01722 716926
Email: jane.k@markallengroup.co.uk
Web site: http://www.recyclingwasteworld.co.uk
Publisher: A & D Media Ltd
Frequency: Annual - Published in December
Cover Price: £50.00
Circulation: 6,000 (Publisher's Statement)
Usual Pagination: 270
Editor: Tom Freyberg; **Advertising Manager:** Jane Kennedy
Summary of Content: Journal containing information on all aspects of recycling, including ferrous, non-ferrous and precious metals, paper, glass, chemicals, textiles, composting and plastics. The journal also covers associations, legislation, specifications and testing, manufacturers and suppliers, also a merchants directory.
Readership/Target Audience: Aimed at local authorities, buyers and sellers within the recycling industry.
ADVERTISING: Rates on application
BUSINESS: ENVIRONMENT & POLLUTION

RED
1861537U53-709
Editorial Address: 91 Charterhouse Street, LONDON, EC1M 6HR **Tel:** 020 7336 5200
Email: dcassar@progressivemediagroup.com
Publisher: Progressive Media Publications
Frequency: Monthly
Free to qualifying individuals
Circulation: 14,000 (Publisher's Statement)
Editor: Dean Cassar
Summary of Content: Electronic newsletter focusing on the retail sector and design.
Readership/Target Audience: Aimed at shop fitters, architects and end users working in the retail industry.
BUSINESS: RETAILING & WHOLESALING

RED ALERT
35010U1A-274_50
Editorial Address: 7 Greding Walk, Hutton, BRENTWOOD, CM13 2UF **Tel:** 01277 225402 **Fax:** 0870 137 5688
Email: redalert@houseofwords.freeserve.co.uk
Advertising Address: As above.
Email: carol.baker@creditcontrol.co.uk
Web site: http://www.creditcontrol.co.uk
ISSN: 0956-6503

Publisher: House of Words Ltd
Date Established: 1989
Frequency: Weekly
Annual Sub.: £435.00
Circulation: 52,000 (Publisher's Statement)
Usual Pagination: 16
Editor: Carol Baker; **Advertising Manager:** Carol Baker;
Publisher: Gareth Price
Summary of Content: Contains details of companies going into liquidation; appointment of administrative receivers; and presentation of winding up petitions in England and Wales, plus insolvency news in brief.
Readership/Target Audience: Aimed at financial professionals, credit professionals, accountants and lawyers.
ADVERTISING RATES:
Full Page Colour £1320.00
Agency Commission: 10%
Mechanical Data: Film: Digital, Trim Size: 297 x 210mm, Bleed Size: + 3mm
Copy instructions: Copy Date: Wednesday prior to publication date
Average advertising content per issue: 5%
BUSINESS: FINANCE & ECONOMICS

RED HOT PENNY SHARES
20314U1F-634
Editorial Address: 7th Floor, Sea Containers House, 20 Upper Ground, LONDON, SE1 9JD **Tel:** 020 7633 3600
Fax: 020 7633 3740
Email: rhps@f-s-p.co.uk
Web site: http://www.fspinvest.co.uk
ISSN: 1475-4355
Publisher: Fleet Street Publications Ltd
Date Established: 1997
Frequency: Monthly
Annual Sub.: £29.00
Circulation: 15,000 (Publisher's Statement)
Editor: Garry White; **Managing Editor:** Garry White
Summary of Content: Print and online newsletter providing information on investments with recommendations of small cap shares also includes stock trading news and company analysis.
Readership/Target Audience: Aimed at investors.
ADVERTISING: No Advertising taken
BUSINESS: FINANCE & ECONOMICS: Investment

REFERENCE BOOK FOR EXPORTERS
762981U20-307
Editorial Address: 145 London Road, KINGSTON UPON THAMES, KT2 6SR **Tel:** 020 8547 3333 **Fax:** 020 8549 7275
Email: export@croner.co.uk
Web site: http://www.croner.co.uk
Publisher: Wolters Kluwer (UK) Ltd
Date Established: 1947
Frequency: Monthly
Cover Price: £54.95
Annual Sub.: £353.05
Editor: Peter Tucker
Summary of Content: Publication focusing on export procedures and country data, including advice and support on the carriage of dangerous goods, customs procedures, documents, export controls, financial, postal information, terminology/trade marks and country profiles.
Readership/Target Audience: Read by business managers in the United Kingdom.
ADVERTISING: No Advertising taken
BUSINESS: IMPORT & EXPORT

REFLEXIONS
764938U56A-166
Editorial Address: 5 Fore Street, TAUNTON, TA1 1HX
Tel: 01823 351010 **Fax:** 01823 336646
Email: dbucella@aor.org.uk
Advertising Address: 90 Walcot Street, BATH, BA1 5BG
Tel: 01225 337777 **Fax:** 01225 339977
Email: charlest@jppublishing.co.uk
Web site: http://www.aor.org.uk
ISSN: 1466-8092
Publisher: James Pembroke Publishing Ltd
Date Established: 1984
Frequency: Quarterly
Cover Price: £5.00
Free to qualifying individuals
Circulation: 8,000 (Publisher's Statement)
Usual Pagination: 40
Editor: Doreen Baker; **Advertising Manager:** Charles Troy
Summary of Content: Magazine covering reflexology news, reviews, case studies and information.
Readership/Target Audience: Read by members of the Association of Reflexologists.
ADVERTISING RATES:
Full Page Colour £550.00
Mechanical Data: Type Area: 264 x 190mm, Bleed Size: 303 x 216mm, Trim Size: 297 x 210mm, Col Length: 264mm, Page Width: 190mm
BUSINESS: HEALTH & MEDICAL

REFURB
35926U4E-308

Formerly: Refurb Projects
Editorial Address: 50 Queens Road, BUCKHURST HILL, IG9 5DD **Tel:** 020 8504 1661 **Fax:** 020 8505 4336
Email: refurb@sheenpublishing.co.uk
Advertising Address: As above.
Email: refurb@sheenpublishing.co.uk
Web site: http://www.sheenpublishing.co.uk
Publisher: Sheen Publishing Ltd
Frequency: 6 issues yearly - Published in the middle of the 1st cover month
Cover Price: £3.00
Annual Sub: £18.00
Circulation: 7,238 (Publisher's Statement)
Editor: Peter Ashmore; **News Editor:** John Grant;
Advertising Manager: Sue Watson; **Managing Editor:** Tony Prior
Summary of Content: Magazine covering the architectural maintenance and UK refurbishment markets.
Readership/Target Audience: Read by specifiers and builders.
ADVERTISING RATES:
Full Page Mono £800.00
Full Page Colour £1200.00
Agency Commission: 10%
Mechanical Data: Type Area: 260 x 184mm, Bleed Size: 300 x 218mm, Trim Size: 296 x 210mm, Film: Digital, Col Length: 260mm, Page Width: 184mm
Copy instructions: Copy Date: 5 weeks prior to publication date
Supplement(s): Secure Times - 3xY
BUSINESS: ARCHITECTURE & BUILDING: Building

REFURB & RENOVATION NEWS
1785630U4E-439

Editorial Address: Redfern House, 347 Margate Road, RAMSGATE, CT12 6SG **Tel:** 01843 592802
Fax: 01843 593214
Email: mike@randrnews.co.uk
Advertising Address: As above.
Email: carolyn@randrnews.co.uk
Web site: http://www.randrnews.co.uk
Publisher: MH Media Solutions Ltd
Date Established: 2006
Frequency: 6 issues yearly
Cover Price: £4.00
Free to qualifying individuals
Circulation: 14,537 (Publisher's Statement)
Usual Pagination: 48
Editor: Mike Hills
Summary of Content: Publication providing coverage of major UK refurbishment projects detailing the latest product and designer innovations as well as updates in health and safety, conservation and the latest regulations on a broad range of building aspects.
Readership/Target Audience: Aimed at specifiers of refurbishment projects.
ADVERTISING RATES:
Full Page Colour £1495.00
Agency Commission: 10%
Mechanical Data: Type Area: 277 x 190mm, Bleed Size: 317 x 230mm, Trim Size: 297 x 210mm, Col Length: 277mm, Page Width: 190mm, Film: Digital
Copy instructions: Copy Date: 3 weeks prior to publication date
Average advertising content per issue: 40%
BUSINESS: ARCHITECTURE & BUILDING: Building

REFURB & REGENERATION JOURNAL
1615239U4E-407

Editorial Address: 11 Galena Close, Amington Industrial Estate, TAMWORTH, B77 4AS **Tel:** 01827 311800
Fax: 01827 301199
Email: press@wavcoms.co.uk
Advertising Address: As above. **Fax:** 01827 301189
Email: sales@wavcoms.co.uk
Web site: http://www.wavcoms.co.uk
Publisher: Waverley Communications Ltd
Date Established: 2003
Frequency: 6 issues yearly - Published in the 1st week of the cover month
Cover Price: Free
Circulation: 10,539 (ABC 01/07/2008 to 30/06/2009)
Usual Pagination: 40
Editor: Diane Smith; **Advertising Manager:** Kevin Edgeworth; **Publisher:** Kevin Edgeworth
Summary of Content: Magazine covering news, appointments, in-depth articles and product information.
Readership/Target Audience: Aimed at builders, developers, health and education authorities, local authorities and housing associations.
ADVERTISING RATES:
Full Page Colour £1885.00
Agency Commission: 10%
Copy instructions: Copy Date: 7th of the month prior to publication date

Average advertising content per issue: 40%
BUSINESS: ARCHITECTURE & BUILDING: Building

REGENERATION AND RENEWAL
629372U4D-211_50

Editorial Address: 174 Hammersmith Road, LONDON, W6 7JP **Tel:** 020 8267 4381 **Fax:** 020 8267 4003
Email: regeneration@haymarket.com
Advertising Address: As above. **Tel:** 020 8267 4097
Fax: 020 8267 4244
Email: vicky.rule@haymarket.com
Web site: http://www.regen.net
ISSN: 1472-5053
Publisher: Haymarket Business Media Ltd
Date Established: 2000
Frequency: Weekly
Free to qualifying individuals
Annual Sub.: £95.00
Circulation: 10,238 (ABC 01/07/2008 to 30/06/2009)
Usual Pagination: 48
Editor: Jamie Carpenter; **News Editor:** Jamie Carpenter;
Features Editor: Adam Branson; **Advertising Manager:** Vicky Rule
Summary of Content: Magazine covering all aspects of regional economic development and social cohesion, including current projects, community renewal, physical regeneration, funding issues, opinion and analysis, careers and a diary of events.
Readership/Target Audience: Aimed at professionals working to regenerate towns, cities and rural areas of Britain including those in housing, education, health, crime prevention, marketing and planning, local authorities and voluntary organisations.
ADVERTISING RATES:
Full Page Mono £3035.00
Full Page Colour £3665.00
Agency Commission: 10%
Mechanical Data: Bleed Size: 301 x 231mm, Trim Size: 295 x 225mm, Type Area: 260 x 207mm, Film: Digital, Page Width: 270mm, Col Length: 260mm
Copy instructions: Copy Date: Monday 5pm prior to publication date
Supplement(s): A-Z of Funding - 1xY, Consultants Directory - 1xY, Focus On South-East England - 1xY, Guide to careers in Regeneration - 1xY, Regeneration and Renewal Awards Book - 1xY
BUSINESS: ARCHITECTURE & BUILDING: Planning & Housing

REGIONAL FILM & VIDEO
41567U64K-591

Editorial Address: 48-50 York Street, BELFAST, BT15 1AS **Tel:** 028 9031 9008 **Fax:** 028 9072 7804
Email: rfvnewscopy@flagshipmedia.co.uk
Advertising Address: As above. **Fax:** 028 9072 7800
Email: bodoherty@flagshipmedia.co.uk
Web site: http://www.4rfv.co.uk
Publisher: Flagship Media Group Ltd
Date Established: 1995
Frequency: Monthly
Cover Price: Free
Circulation: 12,000 (Publisher's Statement)
Usual Pagination: 64
Editor: Kirstin McAlpine; **Managing Director:** Derek Carstairs; **Publisher:** Derek Carstairs
Summary of Content: Newspaper providing general trade news about the film and video industry throughout the United Kingdom and Ireland.
Language(s): English; Gaelic; Welsh
Readership/Target Audience: Read by decision makers in film and video production companies.
ADVERTISING RATES:
Full Page Colour £1490.00
Agency Commission: 10%
Mechanical Data: Print Process: Web-fed offset litho, Film: Digital, Trim Size: 330 x 261mm
Copy instructions: Copy Date: 1 week prior to publication date
Average advertising content per issue: 60%
BUSINESS: OTHER CLASSIFICATIONS: Cinema Entertainment

REGISTER OF ARCHITECTS
35820U4A-230

Editorial Address: 8 Weymouth Street, LONDON, W1W 5BU **Tel:** 020 7580 5861 **Fax:** 020 7436 5269
Email: info@arb.org.uk
Web site: http://www.arb.org.uk
ISSN: 0306-6967
Publisher: The Architects' Registration Board
Frequency: Annual - Published in October
Circulation: 500 (Publisher's Statement)
Editor: Sue Young
Summary of Content: Directory of architects.
Readership/Target Audience: Aimed at members of the public.
ADVERTISING: No Advertising taken
BUSINESS: ARCHITECTURE & BUILDING: Architecture

REGISTERED GAS ENGINEER
1902979U24-105

Editorial Address: 11 Southwark Street, LONDON, SE1 1RQ **Tel:** 0845 071 4415
Email: editorial@registeredgasengineer.co.uk
Web site: http://www.registeredgasengineer.co.uk
Publisher: The Team
Date Established: 2009
Frequency: Monthly
Cover Price: Free
Circulation: 67,000 (Publisher's Statement)
Usual Pagination: 50
Editor: Nicki Shearer; **Managing Editor:** Natasha Dodds;
Publisher: Peter McCreary
Summary of Content: Magazine focusing on the in-depth knowledge of gas engineers, the issues that affect them, as well as the latest news and product tests.
Readership/Target Audience: Aimed at all Gas Safe registered engineers.
BUSINESS: GAS

THE REGULATORY AFFAIRS JOURNAL: DEVICES
40373U56C-370

Editorial Address: Telephone House, 69-77 Paul Street, LONDON, EC2A 4LQ **Tel:** 020 7017 5000
Email: maureen.kenny@informa.com
Advertising Address: As above. **Fax:** 020 7017 6787
Email: diane.mckenna@informa.com
Web site: http://www.rajdevices.com
ISSN: 0969-4129
Publisher: Informa Pharma
Date Established: 1993
Frequency: 6 issues yearly
Annual Sub.: £540.00
Usual Pagination: 72
Editor: Maureen Kenny; **Advertising Manager:** Diane Mckenna; **Publisher:** Phil Solomon
Summary of Content: Features articles on all aspects of regulatory affairs for the medical device industry worldwide.
Readership/Target Audience: Aimed at professionals and executives in the medical device industry and allied industries.
ADVERTISING RATES:
Full Page Mono £1043.00
Full Page Colour £1533.00
Agency Commission: 10%
Mechanical Data: Type Area: 250 x 178mm, Bleed Size: 303 x 216mm, Trim Size: 297 x 210mm, Col Length: 250mm, Page Width: 178mm, Film: Digital
BUSINESS: HEALTH & MEDICAL: Hospitals

REINFORCED PLASTICS
38831U39-60

Editorial Address: The Boulevard, Langford Lane, Kidlington, OXFORD, OX5 1GB **Tel:** 01865 843638
Fax: 01865 843973
Email: rp@elsevier.com
Advertising Address: As above. **Tel:** 01865 843271
Email: n.reeves@elsevier.com
Web site: http://www.reinforcedplastics.com
ISSN: 0034-3617
Publisher: Elsevier Ltd
Date Established: 1956
Frequency: 10 issues yearly - Published in the 1st week of the cover month
Free to qualifying individuals
Annual Sub.: EUR364.00
Circulation: 20,000 (BPA Worldwide 01/07/2007 to 31/12/2007)
Usual Pagination: 48
Editor: Amanda Jacob; **Advertising Manager:** Mark Sherman
Summary of Content: Magazine covering the latest business and technical developments in the polymer-based composites industry worldwide.
Readership/Target Audience: Read by designers and manufacturers of composite parts and end users of composite components worldwide.
ADVERTISING RATES:
Full Page Colour $5170.00
Agency Commission: 10%
Mechanical Data: Type Area: 243 x 185mm, Col Length: 243mm, Trim Size: 280 x 216mm, Bleed Size: 286 x 222mm, Page Width: 185mm, Film: Digital, Print Process: Sheet-fed litho
Copy instructions: Copy Date: 4 weeks prior to publication date
Average advertising content per issue: 40%
Editions:
Reinforced Plastics China
BUSINESS: PLASTICS & RUBBER

REINSURANCE
35161U1D-338

Editorial Address: 32-34 Broadwick Street, LONDON, W1A 2HG **Tel:** 020 7316 9000
Email: katherine.blackler@incisivemedia.com
Advertising Address: As above. **Fax:** 020 7316 9257
Email: martin.hughes@incisivemedia.com

Business Magazines

Web site: http://www.reinsurancemagazine.com
ISSN: 0048-7171
Publisher: Incisive Media
Date Established: 1969
Frequency: 10 issues yearly - Published on the 8th of the cover month
Cover Price: £23.00
Free to qualifying individuals
Annual Sub.: £225.00
Circulation: 8,177 (ABC 01/07/2008 to 30/06/2009)
Usual Pagination: 40
Editor: Katherine Blackler; **Advertising Manager:** Martin Hughes; **Publisher:** Martin Hughes
Summary of Content: Magazine dealing with all aspects of reinsurance.
Readership/Target Audience: Read by reinsurance buyers, brokers and service providers.
ADVERTISING RATES:
Full Page Colour £5170.00
Agency Commission: 10%
Mechanical Data: Page Width: 192mm, Col Length: 258mm, Type Area: 258 x 192mm, Bleed Size: 286 x 218mm, Trim Size: 280 x 215mm, Film: Digital
Copy instructions: Copy Date: 24th of the month prior to publication date
BUSINESS: FINANCE & ECONOMICS: Insurance

RELIEF & DEVELOPMENT (ASIA PACIFIC, MIDDLE EAST & AFRICA DIRECTORY)
1667706U1P-279
Formerly: Relief & Development (Asia Pacific & Africa Directory)
Editorial Address: Woodland Place, Hurricane Way, Wickford Business Park, WICKFORD, SS11 8YB
Tel: 01268 766515 **Fax:** 01268 766516
Email: info@reliefdevelopment.com
Advertising Address: As above.
Email: info@reliefdevelopment.com
Web site: http://www.reliefdevelopment.com
Publisher: Champ Media Group
Frequency: Annual - Published in September
Cover Price: £65.00
Circulation: 10,000 (Publisher's Statement)
Editor: Stephen Lawton
Summary of Content: Directory providing an up-to-date reference source, containing contact details and key information on all organisations involved in the provision of aid and development in the Asia-Pacific region.
Readership/Target Audience: Aimed at the international aid community.
ADVERTISING RATES:
Full Page Colour £4250.00
Mechanical Data: Type Area: 263 x 185mm, Col Length: 263mm, Page Width: 185mm, Bleed Size: 303 x 231mm, Trim Size: 297 x 225mm, Film: Digital
BUSINESS: FINANCE & ECONOMICS: Fundraising

RE:LOCATE
1643992U14F-251
Editorial Address: Spray Hill, Hastings Road, Lamberhurst, TUNBRIDGE WELLS, TN3 8JB **Tel:** 01892 891334
Fax: 01892 891336
Email: editorial@relocatemagazine.com
Advertising Address: As above.
Email: ads@relocatemagazine.com
Web site: http://www.relocatemagazine.com
Publisher: Profile Locations
Date Established: 2004
Frequency: Quarterly
Cover Price: £5.00
Free to qualifying individuals
Circulation: 15,000 (Publisher's Statement)
Usual Pagination: 32
Editor: Fiona Murchie; **Managing Editor:** Fiona Murchie
Summary of Content: Magazine covering key relocation issues to support domestic and individual employees and their families.
Readership/Target Audience: Aimed at HR professionals and relocation specialists.
ADVERTISING RATES:
Full Page Colour £2000.00
Agency Commission: 10%
Mechanical Data: Type Area: 273 x 186mm, Bleed Size: 307 x 220mm, Trim Size: 297 x 210mm, Col Length: 273mm, Page Width: 186mm, Film: Digital
BUSINESS: COMMERCE, INDUSTRY & MANAGEMENT: Training & Recruitment

REMOVALS & STORAGE
39706U49R-220
Editorial Address: 26 Swanwick Lane, Broughton Leys, MILTON KEYNES, MK10 9LD **Tel:** 01908 695500
Fax: 01908 690099
Email: rands@thewordsworkshop.co.uk
Advertising Address: As above.
Email: nikki@thewordsworkshop.co.uk
Web site: http://www.bar.co.uk
Publisher: The Words Workshop Ltd

Date Established: 1932
Frequency: Monthly
Cover Price: £3.00
Free to qualifying individuals
Annual Sub.: £36.00
Circulation: 4,000 (Publisher's Statement)
Usual Pagination: 64
Editor: Steve Jordan; **Advertising Manager:** Nikki Gee
Summary of Content: Journal of the British Association of Removers, providing information on transport, warehousing and shipping.
Readership/Target Audience: Aimed at managers in the removal and storage industry.
ADVERTISING RATES:
Full Page Mono £581.00
Full Page Colour £910.00
SCC £26.00
Agency Commission: 10%
Mechanical Data: Col Length: 275mm, Film: Digital, Type Area: 275 x 180mm, Bleed Size: 303 x 216mm, Trim Size: 297 x 210mm, Page Width: 180mm
Copy instructions: Copy Date: 10th of the month prior to publication date
Average advertising content per issue: 40%
BUSINESS: TRANSPORT: Transport Related

REMPLOY NEWS
40476U56L-21
Editorial Address: Stonecourt, Siskin Drive, COVENTRY, CV3 4FJ **Tel:** 024 7651 5870 **Fax:** 024 7651 5860
Email: shiona.williams@remploy.co.uk
Advertising Address: As above.
Email: jessie.perryman@remploy.co.uk
Web site: http://www.remploy.co.uk
Publisher: Remploy Ltd
Frequency: 6 issues yearly
Cover Price: Free
Circulation: 11,000 (Publisher's Statement)
Usual Pagination: 8
Editor: Shiona Williams; **Circulation Manager:** Christine Manning
Summary of Content: Newsletter about people, places and products from Britain's largest employer of disabled people.
Readership/Target Audience: Aimed at Remploy employees and placements.
ADVERTISING: Rates on application
BUSINESS: HEALTH & MEDICAL: Disability & Rehabilitation

RENEW
626382U4D-212
Formerly: Re:new
Editorial Address: 8th Floor, Anchorage House, East India Dock, 2 Clove Crescent, LONDON, E14 2BE
Tel: 020 7017 2011 **Fax:** 020 7017 2099
Email: communications@thames-gateway.org.uk
Web site: http://www.thames-gateway.org.uk
Publisher: Thames Gateway London Partnership
Date Established: 1999
Frequency: Quarterly
Cover Price: Free
Circulation: 4,500 (Publisher's Statement)
Usual Pagination: 12
Editor: Leon Panitzke
Summary of Content: Newsletter covering regeneration schemes, including urban renewal, economic development, social policy and projects in the Thames Gateway.
Readership/Target Audience: Aimed at regeneration agencies, private and public sector partners and community organisations in the Thames Gateway, London.
ADVERTISING: No Advertising taken
BUSINESS: ARCHITECTURE & BUILDING: Planning & Housing

RENEWABLE ENERGY FOCUS
704835U58-68_55
Formerly: Refocus
Editorial Address: The Boulevard, Langford Lane, KIDLINGTON, OX5 1GB **Tel:** 01865 843648
Fax: 01865 843971
Email: press_releases@renewableenergyfocus.com
Advertising Address: As above. **Tel:** 01865 843000
Fax: 01865 843973
Email: j.castle@elsevier.com
Web site: http://www.renewableenergyfocus.com
ISSN: 1471-0846
Publisher: Elsevier Ltd
Date Established: 2001
Frequency: 6 issues yearly
Free to qualifying individuals
Circulation: 28,000 (BPA Worldwide 01/07/2007 to 31/12/2007)
Usual Pagination: 64
Editor: Kari Larsen
Summary of Content: Magazine covering all aspects of clean power and renewable energy, including news, developments, new technology, the regulatory environment and commercialisation of renewable energy technology.
Language(s): Chinese; English

Readership/Target Audience: Aimed at renewable energy manufacturers, Public sector, utility companies, oil and gas industry, project and property developers, architects, energy consultants and those with an interest in using renewable energy.
ADVERTISING RATES:
Full Page Colour £2770.00
Agency Commission: 10%
Mechanical Data: Film: Digital, Type Area: 258 x 185mm, Bleed Size: 303 x 216mm, Trim Size: 297 x 210mm, Col Length: 258mm, Page Width: 185mm
Average advertising content per issue: 40%
Supplement(s): Fuel Cell Focus - 2xY, Green Building - 1xY, Renewable Energy - Asia Pacific - 1xY, Renewable Energy - EU - 1xY, Renewable Energy - USA - 1xY
BUSINESS: ENERGY, FUEL & NUCLEAR

RENEWABLE ENERGY INSTALLER
1858704U58-195
Editorial Address: Regent House, Bexton Lane, KNUTSFORD, WA16 9AB **Tel:** 01565 653283
Email: karen@keystonecomms.co.uk
Web site: http://www.ashleyanddumville.co.uk
Publisher: Ashley and Dumville Publishing Ltd
Date Established: 2008
Frequency: Quarterly
Free to qualifying individuals
Editor: Lu Quinney; **Features Editor:** Karen Fletcher
Summary of Content: Magazine for microgeneration covering renewable technologies for domestic and commercial buildings. Contains information on the latest products, legislation, training courses and case studies.
Readership/Target Audience: Aimed at installers and contractors and of interest to architects, specifiers, building control officers and local government housing professionals.
BUSINESS: ENERGY, FUEL & NUCLEAR

RENEWABLE ENERGY REPORT
600972U58-68_74
Editorial Address: 20 Canada Square, Canary Wharf, LONDON, E14 5LH **Tel:** 020 7176 6266 **Fax:** 020 7176 6670
Email: david_jones@platts.com
Web site: http://www.platts.com
ISSN: 1355-6258
Publisher: Platts
Date Established: 1999
Frequency: 24 issues yearly
Annual Sub.: £1030.00
Usual Pagination: 28
Editor: David Jones; **Managing Editor:** Paul Whitehead
Summary of Content: Newsletter covering the renewable energy industry world-wide. Contains analysis of global markets, finance and policy.
Readership/Target Audience: Aimed at those interested in the evolving renewables industry.
ADVERTISING: No Advertising taken
BUSINESS: ENERGY, FUEL & NUCLEAR

RENEWABLE ENERGY WORLD
40778U58-68_75
Editorial Address: Warlies Park House, Horseshoe Hill, Upshire, WALTHAM ABBEY, EN9 3SR **Tel:** 01992 656600
Fax: 01992 656700
Email: rew@pennwell.com
Advertising Address: As above.
Email: rewadsales@pennwell.com
Web site: http://www.renewableenergyworld.com
ISSN: 1462-6381
Publisher: PennWell Publications International Ltd
Date Established: 1998
Frequency: 6 issues yearly
Free to qualifying individuals
Annual Sub.: £60.00
Circulation: 17,467 (BPA Worldwide 01/07/2007 to 31/12/2007)
Usual Pagination: 144
Editor: David Appleyard; **Publisher:** David McConnell
Summary of Content: Magazine providing coverage of renewable energy issues, including conference and trade news, project developments, specialist area summaries and technology.
Readership/Target Audience: Read by professionals in the renewable energy industry.
ADVERTISING RATES:
Full Page Mono £2220.00
Full Page Colour £2645.00
Agency Commission: 10%
Mechanical Data: Type Area: 277 x 190mm, Bleed Size: 307 x 220mm, Trim Size: 297 x 210mm, Col Length: 277mm, Film: Digital, Page Width: 190mm
Copy instructions: Copy Date: 3rd week of the month prior to publication date
BUSINESS: ENERGY, FUEL & NUCLEAR

RENEWS

765303U58-162

Editorial Address: 1st Floor, St. Georges House, St. Georges Street, WINCHESTER, SO23 8BG
Tel: 01962 890449
Email: renews@btinternet.com
Advertising Address: As above. **Tel:** 01962 890440
Email: sales@renews.biz
Web site: http://www.renews.biz
ISSN: 1478-307X
Publisher: ReNews Ltd
Date Established: 2002
Frequency: 24 issues yearly
Annual Sub.: £340.00
Circulation: 2,000 (Publisher's Statement)
Usual Pagination: 10
Editor: Todd Westbrook; **Managing Director:** Dan Rigden;
Advertising Manager: Alison Softly
Summary of Content: Electronic newsletter focusing on the renewable energy sector.
Readership/Target Audience: Read by government agencies, engineering companies, suppliers, installation contractors and project developers.
ADVERTISING: Rates on application
BUSINESS: ENERGY, FUEL & NUCLEAR

REPORT

41162U62J-1000

Editorial Address: 7 Northumberland Street, LONDON, WC2N 5RD **Tel:** 020 7930 6441 **Fax:** 020 7930 1359
Email: report@atl.org.uk
Advertising Address: Archant Dialogue, Prospect House, Rouen Road, NORWICH, NR1 1XU **Tel:** 01603 772520
Fax: 01603 627823
Email: samantha.overton@archantdialogue.co.uk
Web site: http://www.atl.org.uk
ISSN: 0142-3134
Publisher: ATL
Date Established: 1978
Frequency: 9 issues yearly
Free to qualifying individuals
Annual Sub.: £15.50
Circulation: 160,000 (Publisher's Statement)
Editor: Alex Tomlin; **Managing Editor:** Victoria Poskitt
Summary of Content: Magazine covering key education issues and news which affect teachers, lecturers and educational support staff.
Readership/Target Audience: Aimed at members of the Association of Teachers and Lecturers.
ADVERTISING RATES:
Full Page Colour £2730.00
SCC £33.00
Agency Commission: 10%
Mechanical Data: Type Area: 277 x 187mm, Bleed Size: 303 x 216mm, Trim Size: 297 x 210mm, Film: Digital, Col Length: 277mm, No. of Columns (Display): 2, Col Widths (Display): 91mm, Print Process: Web-fed offset litho, Page Width: 187mm
Average advertising content per issue: 25%
BUSINESS: CHURCH & SCHOOL EQUIPMENT & EDUCATION: Teachers & Education Management

RESEARCH

35543U2A-167_80

Editorial Address: 15 Northburgh Street, LONDON, EC1V 0JR **Tel:** 020 7566 1864 **Fax:** 020 7251 0729
Email: news@researchmagazine.co.uk
Advertising Address: As above. **Tel:** 020 7490 4911
Fax: 020 7490 0509
Email: info@researchmagazine.co.uk
Web site: http://www.research-live.com
ISSN: 0969-6709
Publisher: The Market Research Society
Frequency: Monthly
Free to qualifying individuals
Annual Sub.: £130.00
Circulation: 10,314 (ABC 01/07/2008 to 30/06/2009)
Usual Pagination: 80
Editor: Brian Tarran; **News Editor:** Brian Tarran
Summary of Content: Magazine reporting on market research internationally.
Readership/Target Audience: Aimed at marketing directors, product and brand planning managers and researchers.
ADVERTISING RATES:
Full Page Mono £1495.00
Full Page Colour £2477.00
Agency Commission: 10%
Mechanical Data: Col Length: 262mm, Type Area: 262 x 175mm, Print Process: Web-fed offset litho, Page Width: 175mm, Bleed Size: 305 x 218mm, Trim Size: 297 x 210mm, Film: Digital
Copy instructions: Copy Date: 15th of the month prior to publication date
Average advertising content per issue: 40%
BUSINESS: COMMUNICATIONS, ADVERTISING & MARKETING

RESEARCH EUROPE

601112U55-134_70

Editorial Address: Unit 111, 134-146 Curtain Road, LONDON, EC2A 3AR **Tel:** 020 7216 6500
Fax: 020 7216 6501
Email: europe@researchresearch.com
Web site: http://www.researchresearch.com
ISSN: 1366-9885
Publisher: Research Research Ltd
Frequency: 22 issues yearly
Annual Sub.: EUR845.00
Circulation: 1,850 (Publisher's Statement)
Usual Pagination: 12
Editor: Colin Macilwain
Summary of Content: Publication covering news, analysis, funding opportunities, proposals and tenders on European research policy.
Readership/Target Audience: Read by researchers, scientists, policy and funding opportunities managers.
ADVERTISING: No Advertising taken
BUSINESS: APPLIED SCIENCE & LABORATORIES

RESEARCH FORTNIGHT

40002U55-135

Editorial Address: Unit 111, 134-146 Curtain Road, LONDON, EC2A 3AR **Tel:** 020 7216 6500
Fax: 020 7216 6501
Email: news@researchresearch.com
Advertising Address: As above.
Email: jt@researchresearch.com
Web site: http://www.researchresearch.com
ISSN: 1358-1198
Publisher: Research Research Ltd
Date Established: 1994
Frequency: 22 issues yearly
Annual Sub.: £495.00
Circulation: 1,850 (Publisher's Statement)
Usual Pagination: 24
Editor: Colin Macilwain
Summary of Content: Newsletter on research and technology policy in Britain and Europe.
Readership/Target Audience: Aimed at researchers within Britain and Europe.
ADVERTISING RATES:
Full Page Mono £3120.00
SCC £30.00
Agency Commission: 10%
Mechanical Data: Col Length: 260mm, Page Width: 190mm, Type Area: 260 x 190mm, No. of Columns (Display): 4, Trim Size: 285 x 210mm, Bleed Size: 291 x 216mm
Copy instructions: Copy Date: Thursday 4pm prior to publication date
Average advertising content per issue: 10%
BUSINESS: APPLIED SCIENCE & LABORATORIES

RESEARCH INFORMATION

1691335U60R-103

Editorial Address: The Spectrum Building, Michael Young Centre, Purbeck Road, CAMBRIDGE, CB2 8PD
Tel: 01223 211170 **Fax:** 01223 211107
Email: sian.harris@europascience.com
Advertising Address: As above.
Email: joe.galvin@europascience.com
Web site: http://www.researchinformation.info
Publisher: Europa Science Ltd
Frequency: 6 issues yearly - Published in the middle of the month prior to the 1st cover month
Free to qualifying individuals
Annual Sub.: £95.00
Circulation: 5,000 (Publisher's Statement)
Editor: Sian Harris
Summary of Content: Magazine focusing on current and future developments in the provision of online information in science, technology and medicine.
Readership/Target Audience: Aimed at electronic journal publishers, scientists, researchers and information professionals.
ADVERTISING RATES:
Full Page Colour £3750.00
Agency Commission: 10%
Mechanical Data: Type Area: 253 x 184mm, Bleed Size: 288 x 219mm, Trim Size: 270 x 200mm, Col Length: 253mm, Page Width: 184mm, Film: Digital
BUSINESS: PUBLISHING: Publishing Related

RESIDENTIAL PROPERTY INVESTOR

35862U4D-213

Editorial Address: Talbothays Farm, Station Road, Winchfield, HOOK, RG27 8BZ **Tel:** 01252 843566
Fax: 01252 843566
Email: rosalind.renshaw@talbothays.co.uk
Advertising Address: 1 Roebuck Lane, SALE, M33 7SY
Tel: 0845 666 5000 **Fax:** 0845 665 1845
Email: lisa_ebdy@hotmail.co.uk
Web site: http://www.rla.org.uk
Publisher: RLA Publishing Ltd
Frequency: 6 issues yearly
Cover Price: £3.50

Circulation: 6,400 (Publisher's Statement)
Usual Pagination: 32
Editor: Rosalind Renshaw; **Advertising Manager:** Lisa Ebdy
Summary of Content: Magazine providing news, advice and information on finance, property maintenance, market trends as well as legal and tax issues.
Readership/Target Audience: Read by landlords in the private sector.
ADVERTISING RATES:
Full Page Colour £995.00
Agency Commission: 10%
Mechanical Data: Type Area: 270 x 185mm, Col Length: 270mm, Page Width: 185mm, Film: Digital, Bleed Size: 303 x 216mm, Trim Size: 297 x 210mm
Copy instructions: Copy Date: 2 weeks prior to publication date
Average advertising content per issue: 50%
BUSINESS: ARCHITECTURE & BUILDING: Planning & Housing

RESIDENTIAL SYSTEMS EUROPE

1817439U18A-9036

Editorial Address: Ludgate House, 245 Blackfriars Road, LONDON, SE1 9UY **Tel:** 020 8656 4590
Advertising Address: As above. **Tel:** 020 7921 5000
Fax: 020 7921 8339
Email: cara.turner@ubm.com
Web site: http://www.residentialsystemseurope.com
Publisher: UBM Information Ltd
Date Established: 2007
Frequency: 6 issues yearly - Published around the middle of the 1st cover month (Jun/Jul beginning of 1st cover month)
Free to qualifying individuals
Circulation: 8,000 (Publisher's Statement)
Editor: Simon Croft
Summary of Content: Magazine focusing on European systems integration in the home, industry news, business analysis, new products and technology.
Readership/Target Audience: Aimed at custom electronics design and installation professionals.
ADVERTISING RATES:
Full Page Mono £2440.00
Full Page Colour £2440.00
Agency Commission: 10%
Mechanical Data: Type Area: 314 x 228mm, Bleed Size: 340 x 250mm, Trim Size: 335 x 245mm, Col Length: 314mm, Page Width: 228mm, Film: Digital
Copy instructions: Copy Date: 3 weeks prior to publication date
Average advertising content per issue: 40%
BUSINESS: ELECTRONICS

RESOURCE

1743031U57-147

Editorial Address: 57 Prince Street, BRISTOL, BS1 4QH
Tel: 0117 907 4107 **Fax:** 0117 907 7216
Email: news@resource.uk.com
Advertising Address: As above.
Email: sally@resource.uk.com
Web site: http://www.resourcepublishing.co.uk
Publisher: Resource Media Ltd
Date Established: 2001
Frequency: 6 issues yearly
Annual Sub.: £60.00
Circulation: 2,500 (Publisher's Statement)
Usual Pagination: 48
Editor: Leonie Butler
Summary of Content: Magazine covering sustainability, recycling, waste and environmental issues.
Readership/Target Audience: Aimed at the public waste industry, environmental professionals and government.
ADVERTISING RATES:
Full Page Colour £1050.00
Agency Commission: 10%
Mechanical Data: Type Area: 265 x 185mm, Bleed Size: 303 x 216mm, Trim Size: 297 x 210mm, Col Length: 265mm, Page Width: 185mm, Film: Digital
Copy instructions: Copy Date: 2 weeks prior to publication date
Average advertising content per issue: 25%
BUSINESS: ENVIRONMENT & POLLUTION

RESOURCE

40921U60B-110_50

Editorial Address: 22-26 George Street, EDINBURGH, EH2 2PQ **Tel:** 0131 240 5000 **Fax:** 0131 240 5024
Email: newsletter@royalsoced.org.uk
Web site: http://www.royalsoced.org.uk
ISSN: 1473-7841
Publisher: The RSE Scotland Foundation
Date Established: 1993
Frequency: Quarterly
Cover Price: Free
Circulation: 3,500 (Publisher's Statement)
Usual Pagination: 16
Editor: Jenny Liddell
Summary of Content: Newsletter of The RSE Edinburgh, with a focus on education, science and culture.

Business Magazines

Readership/Target Audience: Read by fellows of the Society.
ADVERTISING: No Advertising taken
BUSINESS: PUBLISHING: Libraries

RESOURCE MANAGEMENT AND RECOVERY
765137U57-122
Editorial Address: 154 Buckingham Palace Road, LONDON, SW1W 9TR **Tel:** 020 7633 4500
Fax: 020 7633 4519
Email: news@letsrecycle.com
Advertising Address: As above.
Email: steve.e@letsrecycle.com
ISSN: 1475-0791
Publisher: letsrecycle.com
Date Established: 2002
Frequency: 24 issues yearly - Published on the 1st and 3rd Friday of the month
Annual Sub.: £105.00
Circulation: 3,000 (Publisher's Statement)
Usual Pagination: 20
Editor: Steve Eminton; **News Editor:** Caelia Quinault
Summary of Content: Magazine about recycling and sustainable waste management.
Readership/Target Audience: Aimed at those who work in local government, industry and the community.
ADVERTISING RATES:
Full Page Mono £600.00
Full Page Colour £1000.00
Agency Commission: 10%
Mechanical Data: Type Area: 264 x 190mm, Col Length: 264mm, Bleed Size: 307 x 220mm, Trim Size: 297 x 210mm, Film: Digital, Page Width: 190mm
Copy instructions: Copy Date: Tuesday prior to publication date
Average advertising content per issue: 40%
BUSINESS: ENVIRONMENT & POLLUTION

RESPIRATORY MEDICINE
24454U56A-131
Editorial Address: The Boulevard, Langford Lane, KIDLINGTON, OX5 1GB **Tel:** 01865 843418
Email: r.garland@elsevier.com
Advertising Address: As above. **Tel:** 020 7424 4200
Fax: 020 7424 4431
Email: f.mcnab@elsevier.com
Web site: http://www.intl.elsevierhealth.com
ISSN: 0954-6111
Publisher: Elsevier Ltd
Date Established: 1907
Frequency: Monthly
Circulation: 600 (Publisher's Statement)
Usual Pagination: 160
Editor: Christian Virchow; **Editor-in-Chief:** Christian Virchow
Summary of Content: Journal containing information on respiratory medicine, including articles and topical reviews dealing with all aspects of respiratory diseases and therapy. Topics include paediatric and adult medicine, epidemiology, immunology and cell biology, physiology, occupational disorders and the role of allergens and pollutants.
Readership/Target Audience: Aimed at physicians working in the field of respiratory disease.
ADVERTISING RATES:
Full Page Mono EUR944.00
Full Page Colour EUR1716.00
Agency Commission: 10%
Mechanical Data: Type Area: 242 x 165mm, Col Length: 242mm, Trim Size: 280 x 210mm, Bleed Size: 286 x 216mm, Film: Digital, Page Width: 165mm
Copy instructions: Copy Date: 5 weeks prior to publication date
BUSINESS: HEALTH & MEDICAL

RESTAURANT
719350U11A-170
Editorial Address: Broadfield Park, CRAWLEY, RH11 9RT
Tel: 01293 613400
Email: editorial@restaurantmagazine.co.uk
Advertising Address: As above.
Email: tim.evans@william-reed.co.uk
Web site: http://www.bighospitality.co.uk
Publisher: William Reed Business Media
Date Established: 2001
Frequency: Monthly
Cover Price: £1.95
Circulation: 16,063 (ABC 01/07/2008 to 30/06/2009)
Usual Pagination: 68
Editor: Editorial Desk; **Features Editor:** Stefan Chomka
Summary of Content: Magazine covering industry news and developments with recruitment advertising.
Readership/Target Audience: Aimed at restaurateurs, food critics, industry employees and consumers.
ADVERTISING RATES:
Full Page Colour £2375.00
Agency Commission: 10%

Mechanical Data: Bleed Size: 306 x 226mm, Trim Size: 300 x 220mm, Type Area: 280 x 200mm, Col Length: 280mm, Page Width: 200mm, Film: Digital
Average advertising content per issue: 40%
BUSINESS: CATERING: Catering, Hotels & Restaurants

RESURGAM
41581U64L-560
Editorial Address: 5 Kenyon Lane, Highroad Well, HALIFAX, HX2 0AA **Tel:** 01422 372293 **Fax:** 01422 311482
Advertising Address: As above.
Email: paul.stubbs@calderdale.gov.uk
ISSN: 0034-5962
Publisher: Federation of Burial and Cremation Authorities
Date Established: 1958
Frequency: Quarterly
Free to qualifying individuals
Annual Sub.: £24.00
Circulation: 750 (Publisher's Statement)
Usual Pagination: 52
Editor: Paul Stubbs; **Advertising Manager:** Paul Stubbs
Summary of Content: Publication concerned with burial and cremation and crematoria. Covers equipment, management, operation, law and practice, horticulture relating to gardens of remembrance, ethics and commemoration.
Readership/Target Audience: Aimed at those involved in the burial and cremation service.
ADVERTISING RATES:
Full Page Mono £410.00
Full Page Colour £500.00
SCC £3.58
Mechanical Data: Bleed Size: 303 x 216mm, Trim Size: 297 x 210mm, Film: Positive, right reading, emulsion side down. Digital, No. of Columns (Display): 2
Copy instructions: Copy Date: 15th of the month 3 months prior to publication date
Average advertising content per issue: 35%
BUSINESS: OTHER CLASSIFICATIONS: Funeral Directors, Cemeteries & Crematoria

RETAIL & LEISURE INTERNATIONAL
1699018U53-695
Editorial Address: Suite 15, Hardmans Business Centre, New Hall Hey Road, ROSSENDALE, BB4 6HH
Tel: 01706 212200 **Fax:** 01706 211782
Email: andrew.climance@rli.uk.com
Advertising Address: As above.
Email: rli@paramountpublications.co.uk
Web site: http://www.rli.uk.com
ISSN: 1747-1354
Publisher: Paramount Publications
Date Established: 2005
Frequency: 11 issues yearly - Combined issue in July/ August
Cover Price: £4.00
Annual Sub.: £40.00
Circulation: 19,000 (Publisher's Statement)
Usual Pagination: 68
Editor: Andrew Climance; **Advertising Manager:** Jayne Rafter
Summary of Content: Magazine dedicated to the retail and leisure markets, incorporates global news, specialist features, profiles and regular sections including property, legal, design investment and technology.
Readership/Target Audience: Aimed at key decision makers, each of whom play a key role in the development of the retail and leisure sectors.
ADVERTISING RATES:
Full Page Colour £2250.00
Mechanical Data: Type Area: 266 x 185mm, Bleed Size: 303 x 216mm, Trim Size: 297 x 210mm, Col Length: 266mm, Page Width: 185mm, Film: Digital
BUSINESS: RETAILING & WHOLESALING

RETAIL BANKER INTERNATIONAL
35088U1C-325
Editorial Address: The Colonnades, 34 Porchester Road, LONDON, W2 6ES **Tel:** 020 7563 5629
Email: hugh.fasken@vrlknowledgebank.com
Advertising Address: 34 Porchester Road, LONDON, W2 6ES **Tel:** 020 7563 5629 **Fax:** 020 7563 5601
Email: lesley.fryer@vrlknowledgebank.com
Web site: http://www.vrlpublishing.com
Publisher: VRL Knowledge Bank Ltd
Frequency: 20 issues yearly
Annual Sub.: £1047.00
Usual Pagination: 16
Editor: Hugh Fasken; **Advertising Manager:** Lesley Fryer
Summary of Content: Newsletter covering the global consumer financial services sector.
Readership/Target Audience: Aimed at senior management in banking and finance.
ADVERTISING RATES:
Full Page Colour £3300.00
Agency Commission: 10%

Mechanical Data: Type Area: 287 x 200mm, Bleed Size: 303 x 216mm, Trim Size: 297 x 210mm, Col Length: 287mm, Page Width: 200mm, Film: Digital
Copy instructions: Copy Date: 4 days prior to publication date
Average advertising content per issue: 20%
BUSINESS: FINANCE & ECONOMICS: Banking

THE RETAIL DIRECTORY - UK
39838U53-296
Editorial Address: 32 Vauxhall Bridge Road, LONDON, SW1V 2SS **Tel:** 020 7973 6665 **Fax:** 020 7973 4798
Email: retail.directory@hgluk.com
Advertising Address: Priory Park, Beech Green Lane, Withyham, HARTFIELD, TN7 4DB **Tel:** 01892 771047
Fax: 01892 771048
Email: benellefsen@boundaryimedia.co.uk
Web site: http://www.theretaildirectory.co.uk
ISSN: 0305-4012
Publisher: Hemming Group Ltd
Date Established: 1939
Frequency: Annual - Published in October
Annual Sub.: £195.00
Usual Pagination: 1100
Editor: Dean Wanless; **Managing Editor:** Dean Wanless
Summary of Content: Directory detailing the names, addresses, types of trade, directors and buyers of department stores, multiple retailers, wholesalers, mail order and Internet companies in the UK.
Readership/Target Audience: Aimed at all those doing business with major retailers in the UK.
ADVERTISING RATES:
Full Page Mono £1000.00
Full Page Colour £2000.00
Agency Commission: 10%
Mechanical Data: Film: Digital, Col Length: 227mm, Trim Size: 247 x 175mm, Type Area: 227 x 155mm, Bleed Size: 253 x 181mm, Page Width: 155mm
Copy instructions: Copy Date: 8 weeks prior to publication date
BUSINESS: RETAILING & WHOLESALING

RETAIL EXPRESS
36467U8C-100
Editorial Address: 11 Angel Gate, City Road, LONDON, EC1V 2SD **Tel:** 020 7689 0600 **Fax:** 020 7689 0700
Email: lindsey.sharman@newtrade.co.uk
Advertising Address: As above. **Fax:** 020 7689 3384
Email: mike.baillie@newtrade.co.uk
Web site: http://www.newtrade.co.uk
Publisher: Newtrade Publishing Ltd
Date Established: 1998
Frequency: 25 issues yearly
Cover Price: Free
Circulation: 50,301 (ABC 01/01/2009 to 30/06/2009)
Usual Pagination: 32
Editor: Lindsay Sharman; **News Editor:** Lindsay Sharman; **Managing Director:** Nick Shanagher; **Advertising Manager:** Mike Baillie; **Publisher:** Paul Williams
Summary of Content: Publication covering all trade issues for impulse and convenience retailers. Features include latest product information, launches and promotions and related articles.
Readership/Target Audience: Aimed at management and staff in the retail business, including news retailers.
ADVERTISING RATES:
Full Page Colour £2995.00
Agency Commission: 10%
Mechanical Data: Trim Size: 339 x 260mm, Film: Digital
Copy instructions: Copy Date: 10 working days prior to publication date
Average advertising content per issue: 40%
BUSINESS: BAKING & CONFECTIONERY: Confectioners & Tobacconists

RETAIL FARMER
37782U21A-960
Editorial Address: 12 Southgate Street, WINCHESTER, SO23 9EF **Tel:** 0845 458 8420
Email: justask@farma.org.uk
Advertising Address: As above.
Email: rita@farma.org.uk
Web site: http://www.farma.org.uk
Publisher: Greenhouse Publishing
Date Established: 1995
Frequency: Quarterly
Cover Price: Free
Circulation: 2,500 (Publisher's Statement)
Usual Pagination: 24
Editor: Rita Exner; **Advertising Manager:** Rita Exner
Summary of Content: Magazine focusing on the sale of fresh and prepared products direct from farmers and producers distributing on a local scale, via farmers markets, farm shops, pick-your-own, box schemes, mail order and Internet sales.
Readership/Target Audience: Read by farmers and farm retailers.
ADVERTISING RATES:
Full Page Colour £495.00
Agency Commission: 10%

Mechanical Data: Bleed Size: +10mm, Trim Size: 310 x 228mm, Col Length: 320mm, Page Width: 238mm, Print Process: Sheet-fed offset litho, Film: Digital, Type Area: 320 x 238mm
Copy instructions: Copy Date: 2 weeks prior to publication date
Average advertising content per issue: 20%
BUSINESS: AGRICULTURE & FARMING

RETAIL FLOORS MAGAZINE   629687U23B-350
Editorial Address: Suite 3, Independent House, Imberhorne Lane, EAST GRINSTEAD, RH19 1TU **Tel:** 01342 300070
Fax: 01342 300060
Email: emma@floordata.com
Advertising Address: As above.
Email: dave@floordata.com
Web site: http://www.floordata.com
Publisher: Networks Business Publications
Frequency: Monthly - Published in the 1st week of the cover month
Annual Sub.: £75.00
Circulation: 6,135 (Publisher's Statement)
Usual Pagination: 52
Editor: Emma Jamieson; **Advertising Manager:** David Stroud; **Publisher:** David Stroud
Summary of Content: Magazine covering information, news, features and regular articles relevant to flooring retail.
Readership/Target Audience: Aimed at those in the carpet and flooring retail trade.
ADVERTISING RATES:
Full Page Mono £1395.00
Full Page Colour £1895.00
Agency Commission: 10%
Mechanical Data: Bleed Size: 336 x 239mm, Trim Size: 330 x 233mm, Film: Digital, Type Area: 320 x 223mm, Col Length: 320mm, Page Width: 223mm
Average advertising content per issue: 60%
Supplement(s): Carpet Review - 2xY, Industrial Floors - 2xY, Tile & Stain Review - 2xY, Wood and Laminate Review - 2xY
BUSINESS: FURNISHINGS & FURNITURE: Furnishings, Carpets & Flooring

RETAIL FRAUD   1862324U54C-338
Editorial Address: Imperial House, St. Nicholas Circle, LEICESTER, LE1 4LF **Tel:** 0116 242 4054
Fax: 0116 242 4048
Email: paul@retail-knowledge.com
Web site: http://www.retailevents.co.uk
Publisher: Retail Events
Date Established: 2008
Frequency: Quarterly
Annual Sub.: £23.80
Circulation: 5,000 (Publisher's Statement)
Usual Pagination: 40
Editor: John Wilson; **Managing Director:** Paul Bessant; **Advertising Manager:** Paul Bessant; **Publisher:** Simon Turton
Summary of Content: Magazine covering all matters related to the world of loss prevention and profit protection.
Readership/Target Audience: Aimed at heads of security and loss prevention directors of UK retail businesses.
BUSINESS: SAFETY & SECURITY: Security

RETAIL JEWELLER   39774U52A-120
Editorial Address: Greater London House, Hampstead Road, LONDON, NW1 7EJ **Tel:** 020 7728 5000
Email: retail.jeweller@emap.com
Advertising Address: As above. **Fax:** 020 7728 3600
Email: ash.allibhai@emap.com
Web site: http://www.retail-jeweller.com
ISSN: 0034-6063
Publisher: EMAP Retail
Date Established: 1960
Frequency: Monthly
Cover Price: £6.60
Annual Sub.: £79.00
Circulation: 3,848 (ABC 01/01/2008 to 31/12/2008)
Usual Pagination: 60
Editor: Sarah Carpin; **News Editor:** Rachael Taylor
Summary of Content: Magazine covering up-to-date business news, trends and new products in the jewellery, watch and objects market.
Readership/Target Audience: Aimed at jewellery and watch retailers and suppliers.
ADVERTISING RATES:
Full Page Colour £3302.00
Agency Commission: 10%
Mechanical Data: Col Length: 288mm, Type Area: 288 x 208mm, Bleed Size: 311 x 233mm, Trim Size: 305 x 230mm, Page Width: 208mm, Film: Digital
Copy instructions: Copy Date: 14 days prior to publication date
Average advertising content per issue: 50%
BUSINESS: GIFT TRADE: Jewellery

RETAIL MARKETING NEWS   1745535U2A-684
Formerly: Retail Media News
Editorial Address: HQ Bellway Court, WAKEFIELD, WF5 9TL **Tel:** 01924 230367 **Fax:** 01924 361146
Email: jmartin@bezier.co.uk
Web site: http://www.bezier.co.uk
Publisher: Bezier
Date Established: 2004
Frequency: Quarterly
Cover Price: Free
Circulation: 800 (Publisher's Statement)
Editor: Julie Martin
Summary of Content: Marketing and retail news magazine covering in-store marketing techniques and point of purchase activities. Also covers marketing and retail trends, innovations in retail, branding, retail technology, book reviews (branding, marketing) and retail design.
Readership/Target Audience: Aimed at marketing executives, directors and management within blue chip companies.
ADVERTISING: No Advertising taken
BUSINESS: COMMUNICATIONS, ADVERTISING & MARKETING

RETAIL NEWSAGENT   40924U60C-110
Editorial Address: 11 Angel Gate, City Road, LONDON, EC1V 2SD **Tel:** 020 7689 0600 **Fax:** 020 7689 0700
Email: editorial@newtrade.co.uk
Advertising Address: As above.
Email: mike.baillie@newtrade.co.uk
Web site: http://www.newtrade.co.uk
Publisher: Newtrade Publishing Ltd
Date Established: 1889
Frequency: Weekly - Published on Friday
Cover Price: £1.60
Annual Sub.: £100.00
Circulation: 14,465 (ABC 01/07/2008 to 30/06/2009)
Usual Pagination: 48
Editor: Caroline Cronin; **News Editor:** Stefan Appleby; **Features Editor:** Chris Rolfe; **Managing Director:** Nick Shanagher
Summary of Content: Magazine covering news, features and market information on the independent and multiple newsagent sector.
Readership/Target Audience: Aimed at the news industry, with a consumer focus, and independent news retailers.
ADVERTISING RATES:
Full Page Colour £2830.00
Agency Commission: 10%
Mechanical Data: Trim Size: 297 x 210mm, Bleed Size: 303 x 216mm, Type Area: 263 x 190mm, Col Length: 263mm, No. of Columns (Display): 4, Print Process: Web-fed litho, Film: Digital, Page Width: 190mm
Copy instructions: Copy Date: 2 weeks prior to publication date
Average advertising content per issue: 33%
Supplement(s): Best Sellers - 2xY, MarketFocus - 12xY
BUSINESS: PUBLISHING: Newsagents

RETAIL PACKAGING   38697U35-300
Editorial Address: 2nd Floor, Ewer House, 44-46 Crouch Street, COLCHESTER, CO3 3HH **Tel:** 01206 506249
Fax: 01206 500180
Email: retailpackaging@mspublications.co.uk
Advertising Address: As above.
Email: retailpackaging@mspublications.co.uk
Web site: http://www.retailpackagingmag.co.uk
Publisher: MS Publications (2001) Ltd
Date Established: 1995
Frequency: 6 issues yearly
Free to qualifying individuals
Annual Sub.: £20.00
Circulation: 6,307 (ABC 01/01/2008 to 31/12/2008)
Usual Pagination: 40
Editor: Bonnie Howard; **Publisher:** Tony Phelps
Summary of Content: Magazine covering news and features on retail packaging.
Readership/Target Audience: Aimed at directors, senior marketing, brand and sales management packaging designers, buyers, suppliers and individuals within converting and packaging equipment arenas.
ADVERTISING RATES:
Full Page Colour £925.00
SCC £9.00
Agency Commission: 10%
Mechanical Data: Film: Digital, Trim Size: 297 x 210mm, Bleed Size: 307 x 220mm, Type Area: 270 x 190mm, Col Length: 270mm, Page Width: 190mm
Average advertising content per issue: 50%
BUSINESS: PACKAGING & BOTTLING

RETAIL SECURITY FRAUD & LOSS PREVENTION   1862588U54C-339
Editorial Address: 4 Elms Lane, Shareshill, WOLVERHAMPTON, WV10 7JS **Tel:** 01922 415233
Fax: 01922 415208

Email: info@retailssecuritymagazine.co.uk
Advertising Address: As above.
Email: info@retailssecuritymagazine.co.uk
Web site: http://www.retailssecuritymagazine.co.uk
Publisher: CCS Publishing Ltd
Date Established: 2005
Frequency: 6 issues yearly - Published at the beginning of the cover month
Cover Price: £8.00
Circulation: 6,400 (Publisher's Statement)
Editor: Mark Rowe; **Managing Director:** Roy Cooper; **Advertising Manager:** Roy Cooper
Summary of Content: Magazine covering loss prevention, profit protection, fraud and security issues in the retail sector.
Readership/Target Audience: Aimed at the retail security and loss prevention sector, fraud managers, specialist installers and integrators working in retail environments such as banks, pubs and clubs, airports, shopping centres and forecourts.
ADVERTISING RATES:
Full Page Mono £1700.00
Full Page Colour £1900.00
Agency Commission: 10%
Mechanical Data: Type Area: 273 x 186mm, Trim Size: 297 x 210mm, Bleed Size: 303 x 216mm, Col Length: 273mm, Page Width: 186mm, Film: Digital
Copy instructions: Copy Date: 3 weeks prior to publication date
BUSINESS: SAFETY & SECURITY: Security

RETAIL SYSTEMS   36123U5B-157
Editorial Address: 6th Floor, 3 London Wall Buildings, LONDON, EC2M 5PD **Tel:** 020 7562 2401
Fax: 020 7374 2701
Email: scott.thompson@retail-systems.com
Advertising Address: As above. **Tel:** 020 7562 2400
Email: paul.copperwaite@retail-systems.com
Web site: http://www.retail-systems.com
ISSN: 1369-5037
Publisher: Perspective Publishing Ltd
Frequency: 6 issues yearly - Published in the last week of the 1st cover month
Free to qualifying individuals
Annual Sub.: £98.00
Circulation: 13,000 (ABC 01/01/2008 to 31/12/2008)
Usual Pagination: 60
Editor: Scott Thompson
Summary of Content: Magazine covering developments in technology for retailing.
Readership/Target Audience: Aimed at retail IT managers, directors, senior management and those who influence technology buying.
ADVERTISING RATES:
Full Page Colour £3349.00
Agency Commission: 10%
Mechanical Data: Type Area: 262 x 181mm, Bleed Size: 303 x 216mm, Trim Size: 297 x 210mm, Col Length: 262mm, Page Width: 181mm, Film: Digital
Copy instructions: Copy Date: 2 weeks prior to publication date
Average advertising content per issue: 40%
BUSINESS: COMPUTERS & AUTOMATION: Data Processing

RETAIL TECHNOLOGY   39824U53-450
Editorial Address: 3rd Floor, Armstrong House, 38 Market Square, UXBRIDGE, UB8 1TG **Tel:** 01895 421111
Fax: 01895 431252
Email: mknights@bpl-business.com
Advertising Address: As above.
Email: sturton@bpl-business.com
Web site: http://www.retailtechnology.co.uk
ISSN: 1359-0146
Publisher: BPL Business Media Ltd
Date Established: 1986
Frequency: 11 issues yearly
Free to qualifying individuals
Annual Sub.: £75.00
Circulation: 7,760 (ABC 01/01/2008 to 31/12/2008)
Usual Pagination: 44
Editor: Miya Knights; **Managing Director:** Chris Boeree; **Advertising Manager:** Simon Turton; **Publisher:** Simon Turton
Summary of Content: Magazine containing details of technology used by retailers and retail banks, in stores as well as remotely.
Readership/Target Audience: Aimed at IT specifiers and purchasers within medium to large UK retailers.
ADVERTISING RATES:
Full Page Mono £1600.00
Full Page Colour £2450.00
Agency Commission: 10%
Mechanical Data: Type Area: 253 x 179mm, Bleed Size: 303 x 213mm, Trim Size: 297 x 210mm, Page Width: 179mm, Col Length: 253mm, Film: Digital
Copy instructions: Copy Date: 3 weeks prior to publication date

Business Magazines

Average advertising content per issue: 30%
BUSINESS: RETAILING & WHOLESALING

RETAIL WEEK
39825U53-500
Editorial Address: Greater London House, Hampstead Road, LONDON, NW1 7EJ **Tel:** 020 7728 5000
Email: jennifer.creevy@emap.com
Advertising Address: As above. **Fax:** 020 7728 3500
Email: paul.titus@emap.com
Web site: http://www.retail-week.com
ISSN: 1360-8215
Publisher: EMAP Retail
Date Established: 1988
Frequency: Weekly
Cover Price: £2.75
Annual Sub.: £137.50
Circulation: 9,128 (ABC 01/07/2008 to 30/06/2009)
Usual Pagination: 36
Editor: Jennifer Creevy; **News Editor:** Jennifer Creevy
Summary of Content: Business magazine covering news and information on all aspects of retail.
Readership/Target Audience: Aimed at executives of large retail chains.
ADVERTISING RATES:
Full Page Colour £5700.00
Agency Commission: 10%
Mechanical Data: Trim Size: 347 x 250mm, Film: Digital
Copy instructions: Copy Date: 2 weeks prior to publication date
Average advertising content per issue: 50%
BUSINESS: RETAILING & WHOLESALING

THE RETAILER MAGAZINE
1775381U53-697
Formerly: BRC Solutions Magazine
Editorial Address: The Stationery Office, 24 Seward Street, City Central Two Estate, LONDON, EC1V 3PA
Tel: 01206 386736
Email: jonathan@doyleandco.net
Advertising Address: 8th Floor, Bridgewater House, 60 Whitworth Street, MANCHESTER, M1 6LT
Tel: 0161 832 6000
Email: katy.brown@tenalpspublishing.com
Web site: http://www.brc.org.uk
Publisher: TSO
Date Established: 2007
Frequency: 6 issues yearly - Published at the beginning of the cover month
Cover Price: £4.00
Free to qualifying individuals
Annual Sub.: £30.00
Circulation: 7,100 (Publisher's Statement)
Usual Pagination: 72
Editor: Jonathan Doyle; **Managing Editor:** Jonathan Doyle
Summary of Content: Publication for members and associate members of the British Retail Consortium. It aims to put operational and technological issues into a wider business context to help senior managers make informed decisions and includes retail industry news, business data and features.
Readership/Target Audience: Aimed at chief executives, chairmen, managing directors and senior managers of UK retailers.
ADVERTISING RATES:
Full Page Colour £2800.00
Agency Commission: 10%
Mechanical Data: Bleed Size: 303 x 216mm, Trim Size: 297 x 210mm, Film: Digital
Copy instructions: Copy Date: 3 weeks prior to publication date
Average advertising content per issue: 30%
BUSINESS: RETAILING & WHOLESALING

RETAILSPEAK
1779785U53-705
Editorial Address: Tudor House, 6 Friar Lane, LEICESTER, LE1 5RA **Tel:** 0116 222 9900 **Fax:** 0116 222 9901
Email: news@retailspeak.com
Advertising Address: As above.
Email: news@retailspeak.com
Web site: http://www.onwindows.com
Publisher: Tudor Rose Holdings Ltd
Frequency: Quarterly
Editor: James Dodd; **Publisher:** Andy Clayton-Smith
Summary of Content: Magazine covering the use of Microsoft technologies within the EMEA retail and hospitality sectors.
Readership/Target Audience: Aimed at business and IT decision makers within retail organisations.
ADVERTISING RATES:
Full Page Colour £3150.00
Mechanical Data: Trim Size: 297 x 210mm
BUSINESS: RETAILING & WHOLESALING

RETIREMENT PLANNER
1664290U1R-361
Editorial Address: Haymarket House, 28-29 Haymarket, LONDON, SW1Y 4RX **Tel:** 020 7484 9700

Email: helen.morrissey@incisivemedia.com
Advertising Address: As above.
Email: mick.hrabe@incisivemedia.com
Web site: http://www.retirement-planner.co.uk
ISSN: 1754-0496
Publisher: Incisive Media Investments
Date Established: 2004
Frequency: Monthly
Cover Price: Free
Circulation: 12,500 (Publisher's Statement)
Usual Pagination: 44
Editor: Helen Morrissey; **Advertising Manager:** Mick Hrabe
Summary of Content: Magazine covering retirement planning issues including fund management, tax planning, savings and investment management.
Readership/Target Audience: Aimed at independent financial advisers.
ADVERTISING RATES:
Full Page Colour £7054.00
Agency Commission: 10%
Mechanical Data: Type Area: 278 x 190mm, Bleed Size: 303 x 216mm, Trim Size: 297 x 210mm, Col Length: 278mm, Page Width: 190mm, Film: Digital
Copy instructions: Copy Date: 1 week prior to publication date
Average advertising content per issue: 30%
BUSINESS: FINANCE & ECONOMICS: Financial Related

RETODAY
41044U62B-950
Formerly: RE Today
Editorial Address: 1020 Bristol Road, Selly Oak, BIRMINGHAM, B29 6LB **Tel:** 0121 472 4242
Fax: 0121 472 7575
Email: lat@retoday.org.uk
Advertising Address: As above.
Email: membership@christianeducation.org.uk
Web site: http://www.retoday.org.uk
ISSN: 0226-7738
Publisher: Christian Education Publications
Frequency: 3 issues yearly - Published in January, April and September
Annual Sub.: £26.00
Circulation: 4,000 (Publisher's Statement)
Usual Pagination: 64
Editor: Lat Blaylock; **Advertising Manager:** Jennifer Smith
Summary of Content: Magazine focusing on modern religious education.
Readership/Target Audience: Aimed at teachers, advisers and governors.
ADVERTISING RATES:
Full Page Colour £713.00
Agency Commission: 10%
Mechanical Data: Type Area: 257 x 185mm, Col Length: 257mm, Film: Digital, Page Width: 185mm, Bleed Size: 3mm, Trim Size: 297 x 210mm, No. of Columns (Display): 3
Copy instructions: Copy Date: 8 weeks prior to publication date
Average advertising content per issue: 10%
BUSINESS: CHURCH & SCHOOL EQUIPMENT & EDUCATION: Education Teachers

REVIEW OF AFRICAN POLITICAL ECONOMY
37016U14C-117
Editorial Address: PO Box 678, SHEFFIELD, S1 1BF
Tel: 0114 229 0234 **Fax:** 0114 229 0233
Email: editor@roape.org
Advertising Address: 4 Park Square, Milton Park, ABINGDON, OX14 4RN **Tel:** 020 7017 6413
Fax: 020 7017 6713
Email: advertising@tandf.co.uk
Web site: http://www.roape.org
ISSN: 0305-6244
Publisher: Routledge, Taylor & Francis
Date Established: 1974
Frequency: Quarterly
Free to qualifying individuals
Circulation: 1,100 (Publisher's Statement)
Usual Pagination: 176
Editor: Jan Burgess; **Advertising Manager:** Alex Baker; **Managing Editor:** Jan Burgess
Summary of Content: Features comprehensive bibliographic referencing, information monitoring, statistical documentation and coverage of work-in-progress.
Language(s): English; French; Portuguese
Readership/Target Audience: Aimed at academics, activists and those interested in the field of African Politics and Economics.
ADVERTISING RATES:
Full Page Mono £400.00
Agency Commission: 10%
Mechanical Data: Type Area: 210 x 130mm, Col Length: 210mm, Page Width: 130mm, Film: Digital
Copy instructions: Copy Date: 2 weeks prior to publication date
Average advertising content per issue: 10%
BUSINESS: COMMERCE, INDUSTRY & MANAGEMENT: International Commerce

REVIEW OF AROMATIC AND MEDICINAL PLANTS
38138U26D-155
Editorial Address: Nosworthy Way, WALLINGFORD, OX10 8DE **Tel:** 01491 832111 **Fax:** 01491 829198
Email: d.cousins@cabi.org
Web site: http://www.cabi-publishing.org
ISSN: 1356-1421
Publisher: CABI
Date Established: 1994
Frequency: 6 issues yearly
Circulation: 245 (Publisher's Statement)
Editor: Debbie Cousins
Summary of Content: Journal covering all aspects of cultivated and wild, medicinal and culinary herbs and plants. Includes news, events, abstracts and literature plus articles on essential oils and spices.
Readership/Target Audience: Aimed at the research community working in universities and those in institutes specialising in medicinal and aromatic plants.
ADVERTISING: No Advertising taken
BUSINESS: GARDEN TRADE: Garden Trade Horticulture

THE REVIEW - WORLDWIDE REINSURANCE
35164U1D-340
Editorial Address: Telephone House, 69-77 Paul Street, LONDON, EC2A 4LQ **Tel:** 020 7017 4145
Fax: 020 7017 4197
Email: greg.dobie@informa.com
Advertising Address: As above. **Tel:** 020 7017 4600
Email: paul.clifton@informa.com
Web site: http://www.thereview.biz
ISSN: 0034-6349
Publisher: Informa PLC
Date Established: 1869
Frequency: 10 issues yearly - Published around the 1st of the cover month
Annual Sub.: £368.00
Circulation: 6,709 (ABC 01/07/2008 to 30/06/2009)
Editor: Greg Dobie; **Advertising Manager:** Paul Clifton
Summary of Content: International journal covering reinsurance and insurance.
Readership/Target Audience: Read by professionals and senior management in the insurance business.
ADVERTISING RATES:
Full Page Colour £5489.00
Agency Commission: 10%
Mechanical Data: Trim Size: 297 x 210mm, Film: Digital, Type Area: 265 x 180mm, Col Length: 265mm, Page Width: 180mm, Bleed Size: 303 x 216mm
Copy instructions: Copy Date: 3 weeks prior to publication date
BUSINESS: FINANCE & ECONOMICS: Insurance

REVIEWS IN CONSERVATION
1695437U64P-94
Editorial Address: 6 Buckingham Street, LONDON, WC2N 6BA **Tel:** 020 7839 5975
Email: iic@iiconservation.org
Advertising Address: As above.
Email: iic@iiconservation.org
Web site: http://www.iiconservation.org
Publisher: IIC
Frequency: Annual
Free to qualifying individuals
Circulation: 3,000 (Publisher's Statement)
Editor: Graham Voce; **Advertising Manager:** Graham Voce
Summary of Content: Peer reviewed journal devoted to the literature of conservation. Covers conservation treatments, materials, scientific research, technical art history, analytical techniques, training and ethics.
Readership/Target Audience: Aimed at conservation professionals.
ADVERTISING: Rates on application
BUSINESS: OTHER CLASSIFICATIONS: Museums

REVIEWS IN MEDICAL VIROLOGY
601224U56A-131_50
Editorial Address: Department of Virology, Royal Free and University College Medical School, Rowland Hill Street, LONDON, NW3 2PF **Tel:** 020 7830 2997 **Fax:** 020 7830 2854
Email: p.griffiths@medsch.ucl.ac.uk
Web site: http://www3.interscience.wiley.com/cgi-bin/jtoc/5616
ISSN: 1052-9276
Publisher: John Wiley & Sons Ltd
Date Established: 1991
Frequency: 6 issues yearly
Annual Sub.: £380.00
Circulation: 400 (Publisher's Statement)
Usual Pagination: 72
Editor: Paul Griffiths; **Editor-in-Chief:** Paul Griffiths
Summary of Content: Journal containing articles on conceptual or technological advances in the study of virology.

Readership/Target Audience: Aimed at clinicians, virologists, medical microbiologists, molecular biologists, infectious disease specialists and immunologists.
ADVERTISING: No Advertising taken
BUSINESS: HEALTH & MEDICAL

REVOLUTION
35545U2A-168

Editorial Address: 174 Hammersmith Road, LONDON, W6 7JP **Tel:** 020 8267 5000 **Fax:** 020 8267 4900
Email: gareth.jones@haymarket.com
Advertising Address: As above. **Tel:** 020 8267 4947
Fax: 020 8267 4113
Email: mark.gordon@haymarket.com
Web site: http://www.revolutionmagazine.com
ISSN: 1460-5953
Publisher: Haymarket Brand Media
Frequency: 11 issues yearly - Published on the 28th of the month prior to cover date
Free to qualifying individuals
Annual Sub.: £108.00
Circulation: 10,002 (ABC 01/07/2008 to 30/06/2009)
Usual Pagination: 84
Editor: Elizabeth Clifford-Marsh; **Features Editor:** Andy McCormick; **Advertisement Director:** Mark Gordon
Summary of Content: Magazine on marketing over digital channels including web, movie and ITV.
Readership/Target Audience: Aimed at brand marketers, their agencies and suppliers.
ADVERTISING RATES:
Full Page Colour £3048.00
Agency Commission: 10%
Mechanical Data: Type Area: 260 x 190mm, Col Length: 260mm, Page Width: 190mm, Trim Size: 280 x 210mm, Bleed Size: 286 x 216mm, Film: Digital
Copy instructions: Copy Date: 2 weeks prior to publication date
Average advertising content per issue: 40%
BUSINESS: COMMUNICATIONS, ADVERTISING & MARKETING

RHEUMATOLOGY
40551U56R-190

Editorial Address: Bride House, 18-20 Bride Lane, LONDON, EC4Y 8EE **Tel:** 020 7842 0900
Fax: 020 7842 0903
Email: editorial@rheumatology.org.uk
Advertising Address: Oxford University Press, Great Clarendon Street, OXFORD, OX2 6DP **Tel:** 01865 353329
Fax: 01865 353774
Email: elisabetta.sheffield@oxfordjournals.org
Web site: http://www.rheumatology.oupjournals.org
ISSN: 1462-0324
Publisher: OUP
Date Established: 1952
Frequency: Monthly
Annual Sub.: £452.00
Usual Pagination: 132
Editor: Robert Moots; **Managing Editor:** Serena Cubie
Summary of Content: Journal containing clinical and basic science research articles on rheumatology.
Language(s): English; Spanish
Readership/Target Audience: Read by basic research scientists, surgeons, rheumatologists, geriatricians and other health professionals in the field of rheumatology.
ADVERTISING RATES:
Full Page Mono £742.00
Full Page Colour £1236.00
Agency Commission: 10%
Mechanical Data: Type Area: 243 x 165mm, Col Length: 243mm, Trim Size: 279 x 210mm, Bleed Size: 285 x 216mm, Film: Digital, Print Process: Litho, Page Width: 165mm
Copy instructions: Copy Date: Last week of 2 months prior to publication date
BUSINESS: HEALTH & MEDICAL: Health Medical Related

RIBA JOURNAL
35804U4A-240

Editorial Address: 45-47 Clerkenwell Green, LONDON, EC1R 0EB **Tel:** 020 7490 5595
Email: hugh@atompublishing.co.uk
Advertising Address: As above.
Email: ian@atompublishing.co.uk
Web site: http://www.ribajournal.com
ISSN: 0953-6973
Publisher: Atom Publishing Ltd
Frequency: Monthly - Published at the beginning of the cover month
Cover Price: £5.50
Annual Sub.: £70.00
Circulation: 29,945 (ABC 01/07/2007 to 30/06/2008)
Usual Pagination: 120
Editor: Hugh Pearman; **Advertising Director:** Ian Christensen
Summary of Content: Official publication of the Royal Institute of British Architects, containing in-depth coverage of UK and international architecture, profiles of key personalities, technical and practice guidance, reviews, news of the institute, professional building studies, trade and product news.

Readership/Target Audience: Read by RIBA members and subscribers, including many overseas.
ADVERTISING RATES:
Full Page Mono £2249.00
Full Page Colour £3117.00
Agency Commission: 10%
Mechanical Data: Type Area: 260 x 194mm, Col Length: 260mm, Bleed Size: 291 x 226mm, Trim Size: 285 x 220mm, Film: Digital, Page Width: 194mm
Copy instructions: Copy Date: 2 weeks prior to publication date
BUSINESS: ARCHITECTURE & BUILDING: Architecture

RICS BUSINESS
35838U4C-100

Formerly: CSM
Editorial Address: 45-47 Clerkenwell Green, LONDON, EC1R 0EB **Tel:** 020 7490 5595 **Fax:** 020 7490 4957
Email: editor@atompublishing.co.uk
Advertising Address: As above. **Tel:** 020 7490 5638
Email: ian@atompublishing.co.uk
Web site: http://www.rics.org
Publisher: Atom Publishing Ltd
Frequency: 10 issues yearly
Annual Sub.: £45.00
Circulation: 96,033 (ABC 01/07/2008 to 30/06/2009)
Usual Pagination: 56
Editor: Duncan Johnson; **Advertising Director:** Ian Christensen
Summary of Content: Magazine of the Royal Institution of Chartered Surveyors.
Readership/Target Audience: Aimed at members and non-members with an interest in the chartered surveying profession.
ADVERTISING RATES:
Full Page Mono £2460.00
Full Page Colour £3270.00
SCC £46.00
Agency Commission: 10%
Mechanical Data: Trim Size: 297 x 210mm, Bleed Size: 303 x 216mm, Type Area: 258 x 182mm, Film: Digital, No. of Columns (Display): 4, Col Length: 258mm, Page Width: 182mm
Copy instructions: Copy Date: 15th of the month prior to publication date
Supplement(s): The Events Supplement - 3xY
BUSINESS: ARCHITECTURE & BUILDING: Surveying

THE RIDER'S DIGEST
35546U49C-220

Editorial Address: PO Box 45358, LONDON, SE14 5ZP **Tel:** 020 8677 4701
Email: editor@theridersdigest.co.uk
Advertising Address: As above.
Email: advertising@theridersdigest.co.uk
Web site: http://www.theridersdigest.co.uk
Publisher: Digest Publishing
Date Established: 1997
Frequency: Monthly
Cover Price: Free
Circulation: 32,000 (Publisher's Statement)
Usual Pagination: 52
Editor: Dave Gurman; **Advertising Manager:** John Newman; **Publisher:** John Newman
Summary of Content: Magazine containing London motorcycle news and transport, technical vehicle information and general motorcycling writing.
Readership/Target Audience: Read by London motorcyclists, including couriers, leisure motorcyclists and motorcycle industry management.
ADVERTISING RATES:
Full Page Colour £400.00
Mechanical Data: Trim Size: 210 x 148mm, Bleed Size: 216 x 154mm, Col Widths (Display): 40mm, No. of Columns (Display): 3, Film: Digital
Average advertising content per issue: 30%
BUSINESS: TRANSPORT: Freight

RISK
35089U1C-340

Editorial Address: Haymarket House, 28-29 Haymarket, LONDON, SW1Y 4RX **Tel:** 020 7484 9700
Fax: 020 7930 2238
Email: risk@incisivemedia.com
Advertising Address: As above.
Email: advert@incisivemedia.com
Web site: http://www.risk.net
ISSN: 0952-8776
Publisher: Incisive Media Investments
Date Established: 1987
Frequency: Monthly
Annual Sub.: £615.00
Circulation: 6,083 (BPA Worldwide 01/07/2007 to 31/12/2007)
Usual Pagination: 120
Editor: Nick Sawyer; **Advertising Manager:** Anthony Chambers

Summary of Content: Magazine covering news, analysis and developments in financial risk management and derivatives.
Readership/Target Audience: Read by money managers, academics, corporate treasurers, bankers and investment bankers.
ADVERTISING RATES:
Full Page Colour £14950.00
Agency Commission: 10%
Mechanical Data: Type Area: 265 x 198mm, Bleed Size: 303 x 236mm, Trim Size: 297 x 230mm, Film: Digital, Col Length: 265mm, Page Width: 198mm
Copy instructions: Copy Date: 15th of the month prior to publication date
BUSINESS: FINANCE & ECONOMICS: Banking

RISK MANAGEMENT PROFESSIONAL
1912821U1A-757

Editorial Address: 6th Floor, 3 London Wall Buildings, LONDON, EC2M 5PD **Tel:** 020 7562 2401
Fax: 020 7562 2701
Email: steve.good@perspectivepublishing.com
Publisher: Perspective Publishing Ltd
Date Established: 2009
Frequency: Quarterly
Editor: Graham Buck
Summary of Content: Magazine covering all areas of risk management with a particular emphasis on enterprise risk.
Readership/Target Audience: Aimed at all members of the Institute of Risk Management and at members of AIRMIC.
BUSINESS: FINANCE & ECONOMICS

RISK UK
1639145U54C-308

Editorial Address: PO Box 332, DARTFORD, DA1 9SF
Tel: 01354 680965 **Fax:** 020 8295 1401
Email: andy.clutton@risk-uk.com
Advertising Address: As above. **Tel:** 020 8295 1414
Email: paul.amura@proactvpubs.co.uk
Web site: http://www.risk-uk.com
ISSN: 1469-1469
Publisher: Pro-Activ Publications Ltd
Date Established: 2003
Frequency: Monthly - Published around the 11th of the cover month
Free to qualifying individuals
Circulation: 7,000 (Publisher's Statement)
Usual Pagination: 68
Editor: Andy Clutton
Summary of Content: Magazine covering all aspects of risk management, security, business continuity, health and safety and loss prevention.
Readership/Target Audience: Aimed at those responsible or security and risk management at the 7000 largest companies in the UK.
ADVERTISING RATES:
Full Page Colour £2100.00
Mechanical Data: Type Area: 275 x 185mm, Bleed Size: 303 x 216mm, Trim Size: 297 x 210mm, Col Length: 275mm, Page Width: 185mm, Film: Digital
Copy instructions: Copy Date: Last day of the month prior to publication date
BUSINESS: SAFETY & SECURITY: Security

RMT NEWS
22161U14L-615

Editorial Address: 39 Chalton Street, LONDON, NW1 1JD
Tel: 020 7387 4771 **Fax:** 020 7529 8808
Email: bdenny@rmt.org.uk
Advertising Address: Landmark Publishing, 2 Windmill Street, LONDON, W1T 2HX **Tel:** 020 7692 9292
Fax: 020 7692 9393
Email: sharon@lps.co.uk
Web site: http://www.rmt.org.uk
Publisher: RMT Publishing
Frequency: 10 issues yearly
Free to qualifying individuals
Annual Sub.: £24.00
Circulation: 80,000 (Publisher's Statement)
Usual Pagination: 32
Editor: Brian Denny; **Managing Editor:** Brian Denny; **Publisher:** Brian Denny
Summary of Content: Official journal of The National Union of Rail, Maritime and Transport Workers. Covers news, events and information on members.
Readership/Target Audience: Read by members of the shipping section of the RMT and London Underground workers.
ADVERTISING RATES:
Full Page Colour £2100.00
Agency Commission: 10%
Mechanical Data: Trim Size: 297 x 210mm, Film: Positive, right reading, emulsion side down. Digital
Copy instructions: Copy Date: 5th of the month prior to publication date
BUSINESS: COMMERCE, INDUSTRY & MANAGEMENT: Trade Unions

Business Magazines

ROADWAY
39644U49C-230

Editorial Address: Roadway House, 35 Monument Hill, WEYBRIDGE, KT13 8RN **Tel:** 01932 841515
Fax: 01932 838916
Email: peter.shakespeare@rha.uk.net
Advertising Address: As above. **Fax:** 01932 841516
Email: nick.payne@rha.uk.net
ISSN: 0035-7316
Publisher: Road Haulage Association Ltd
Date Established: 1945
Frequency: Monthly
Free to qualifying individuals
Annual Sub.: £36.00
Circulation: 9,261 (ABC 01/01/2008 to 31/12/2008)
Usual Pagination: 56
Editor: Peter Shakespeare
Summary of Content: Trade magazine published by the Road Haulage Association.
Readership/Target Audience: Read by owners and senior executives of road haulage and logistics companies, vehicle and equipment manufacturers, politicians, government agencies and industry bodies.
ADVERTISING RATES:
Full Page Mono £1282.00
Full Page Colour £1998.00
Agency Commission: 10%
Mechanical Data: Type Area: 275 x 190mm, Col Length: 275mm, Bleed Size: 303 x 216mm, Trim Size: 297 x 210mm, Print Process: Litho, Film: Digital, Page Width: 190mm
Copy instructions: Copy Date: 2 weeks prior to publication date
Average advertising content per issue: 40%
BUSINESS: TRANSPORT: Freight

ROBOTICA
35996U5A-215

Editorial Address: The Edinburgh Building, Shaftesbury Road, CAMBRIDGE, CB2 8RU **Tel:** 01223 326070
Fax: 01223 325150
Email: gregc@jhu.edu
Advertising Address: As above. **Tel:** 01223 325757
Fax: 01223 315052
Email: ad_sales@cambridge.org
Web site: http://www.cambridge.org/uk
ISSN: 0263-5747
Publisher: Cambridge University Press
Date Established: 1983
Frequency: 6 issues yearly
Annual Sub.: £135.00
Usual Pagination: 120
Editor: Gregory Chirikjian; **Editor-in-Chief:** Gregory Chirikjian
Summary of Content: Journal providing an international forum for the multidisciplinary subject of robotics, automation and artificial intelligence. Also encourages developments with regard to industry, education and research.
Readership/Target Audience: Read by academics and students in engineering, computer science, economics and information technology, health and rehabilitation and personnel in various industries.
ADVERTISING RATES:
Full Page Mono £510.00
Mechanical Data: Film: Digital, Type Area: 250 x 170mm, Col Length: 250mm, Page Width: 170mm
Copy instructions: Copy Date: 9 weeks prior to publication date
BUSINESS: COMPUTERS & AUTOMATION: Automation & Instrumentation

THE ROLLS ROYCE MAGAZINE
37589U19A-515

Editorial Address: 65 Buckingham Gate, LONDON, SW1E 6AT **Tel:** 020 7222 9020 **Fax:** 020 7227 9178
Email: david.howie@rolls-royce.com
Web site: http://www.rolls-royce.com
ISSN: 0142-9469
Publisher: Rolls-Royce plc
Date Established: 1979
Frequency: Quarterly
Cover Price: Free
Circulation: 11,000 (Publisher's Statement)
Usual Pagination: 32
Editor: David Howie
Summary of Content: Magazine containing features relating to power systems for civil aerospace, defence, marine and energy markets.
Readership/Target Audience: Aimed at customers, media, government, industry bodies, suppliers and Rolls-Royce personnel.
ADVERTISING: No Advertising taken
BUSINESS: ENGINEERING & MACHINERY

ROOF
35864U4D-220

Editorial Address: 88 Old Street, LONDON, EC1V 9HU
Tel: 0844 515 2000 **Fax:** 0844 515 2167
Email: roof@shelter.org.uk
Advertising Address: As above.

Email: lauren_mustill@shelter.org.uk
Web site: http://www.roofmag.org.uk
ISSN: 0307-6911
Publisher: Shelter
Date Established: 1975
Frequency: 6 issues yearly
Annual Sub.: £40.00
Circulation: 2,500 (Publisher's Statement)
Usual Pagination: 52
Editor: Bill Rashleigh
Summary of Content: Magazine covering the latest in housing and social policy, practice and homeless issues.
Readership/Target Audience: Read by professionals from housing associations and local authorities, advice workers and those developing housing policy.
ADVERTISING RATES:
Full Page Mono £1000.00
Full Page Colour £1000.00
Agency Commission: 10%
Mechanical Data: Trim Size: 280 x 210mm, Film: Digital, Bleed Size: 286 x 216mm
Average advertising content per issue: 15%
BUSINESS: ARCHITECTURE & BUILDING: Planning & Housing

ROOFING
35927U4E-310

Editorial Address: The Maltings, West Street, BOURNE, PE10 9PH **Tel:** 01778 391166 **Fax:** 01778 394748
Email: nickyr@warnersgroup.co.uk
Advertising Address: As above. **Tel:** 01778 391108
Fax: 01778 392079
Email: cassiec@warnersgroup.co.uk
Web site: http://www.roofingmag.com
Publisher: Warners Group Publications plc
Date Established: 1948
Frequency: 11 issues yearly - Combined issue in July/August and December/January
Cover Price: £3.00
Free to qualifying individuals
Annual Sub.: £30.00
Circulation: 6,499 (ABC 01/07/2008 to 30/06/2009)
Usual Pagination: 40
Editor: Nicky Rogers; **Managing Director:** Stephen Warner; **Publisher:** Juliet Goss
Summary of Content: Magazine covering news from leading industry bodies, products and information within the roofing, cladding and insulation trades.
Readership/Target Audience: Read by roofing and cladding contractors, specifiers, trade bodies, architects, manufacturers and civil servants.
ADVERTISING RATES:
Full Page Colour £1380.00
Agency Commission: 10%
Mechanical Data: Col Length: 275mm, Type Area: 275 x 190mm, Bleed Size: 303 x 216mm, Trim Size: 297 x 210mm, Page Width: 190mm, Print Process: Litho, Film: Positive, right reading, emulsion side down. Digital
Average advertising content per issue: 50%
BUSINESS: ARCHITECTURE & BUILDING: Building

ROOFING TODAY
1611046U4E-406

Editorial Address: 85-89 Duke Street, LIVERPOOL, L1 5AP
Tel: 0151 709 0904 **Fax:** 0151 709 0905
Email: editor@roofingtoday.co.uk
Advertising Address: As above.
Email: sales@roofingtoday.co.uk
Publisher: Roofing Today Magazine Ltd
Date Established: 2003
Frequency: 6 issues yearly
Cover Price: Free
Circulation: 7,800 (Publisher's Statement)
Usual Pagination: 44
Editor: Claire Griffiths
Summary of Content: Magazine covering all aspects of the roofing trade.
Readership/Target Audience: Aimed at decision makers, architects, specifiers, surveyors, roofing contractors, manufacturers and associations.
ADVERTISING RATES:
Full Page Colour £1300.00
Agency Commission: 10%
Mechanical Data: Bleed Size: 303 x 216mm, Trim Size: 297 x 210mm, Film: Digital
Average advertising content per issue: 45%
BUSINESS: ARCHITECTURE & BUILDING: Building

ROOFS, FLOORS & WALLS PRODUCT REVIEW
1666460U4R-616

Editorial Address: The Oaks, Wesleyan Road, Ashley, MARKET DRAYTON, TF9 4JT **Tel:** 01630 673000
Fax: 01630 673247
Email: info@directcontactexhibitions.com
Advertising Address: As above.
Email: info@directcontactexhibitions.com
Web site: http://www.directcontactexhibitions.com
Publisher: DCE Publications

Date Established: 1995
Frequency: Quarterly - Published in the 1st week of the cover month
Free to qualifying individuals
Circulation: 11,522 (Publisher's Statement)
Usual Pagination: 40
Editor: Steve Hilton; **Advertising Manager:** Andy Davies
Summary of Content: Magazine covering product reviews and services.
Readership/Target Audience: Aimed at builders, surveyors, architects and other related trades.
ADVERTISING RATES:
Full Page Colour £1395.00
Mechanical Data: Type Area: 275 x 198mm, Col Length: 275mm, Page Width: 198mm, Film: Digital
Copy instructions: Copy Date: 3 weeks prior to publication date
BUSINESS: ARCHITECTURE & BUILDING: Building Related

ROSKILL'S LETTER FROM JAPAN
38206U27-129_50

Editorial Address: 27A Leopold Road, LONDON, SW19 7BB **Tel:** 020 8944 0066 **Fax:** 020 8947 9568
Email: info@roskill.co.uk
Web site: http://www.roskill.co.uk
ISSN: 0143-4861
Publisher: Roskill Information Services Ltd
Frequency: Monthly
Annual Sub.: £320.00
Usual Pagination: 20
Editor: Matthew Davison; **Managing Director:** Judith Chegwidden
Summary of Content: Journal containing translations of metals and minerals information originally published in Japanese.
Readership/Target Audience: Aimed at mining companies, banks metal processing companies and electronics companies.
ADVERTISING: No Advertising taken
BUSINESS: METAL, IRON & STEEL

ROSKILL'S LITHIUM DIGEST
38207U27-129_60

Editorial Address: 27A Leopold Road, LONDON, SW19 7BB **Tel:** 020 8944 0066 **Fax:** 020 8947 9568
Email: info@roskill.co.uk
Web site: http://www.roskill.co.uk
ISSN: 0965-7711
Publisher: Roskill Information Services Ltd
Frequency: Quarterly
Annual Sub.: £240.00
Usual Pagination: 6
Editor: Trevor Williams
Summary of Content: Newsletter summarising recent developments in the lithium industry.
Readership/Target Audience: Aimed at the metals and minerals industry.
ADVERTISING: No Advertising taken
BUSINESS: METAL, IRON & STEEL

THE ROSPA OCCUPATIONAL SAFETY & HEALTH BULLETIN
39877U54B-92_5

Editorial Address: Edgbaston Park, 353 Bristol Road, Edgbaston, BIRMINGHAM, B5 7ST **Tel:** 0121 248 2000
Fax: 0121 248 2001
Email: eherbert@rospa.com
Advertising Address: As above.
Email: oshadvertising@rospa.com
Web site: http://www.rospa.com
ISSN: 1462-4958
Publisher: Royal Society for the Prevention of Accidents
Date Established: 1974
Frequency: Monthly
Cover Price: £5.75
Annual Sub.: £36.00
Circulation: 6,000 (Publisher's Statement)
Usual Pagination: 16
Editor: Elizabeth Herbert; **Managing Editor:** Rebbeca Spencer
Summary of Content: Journal of the Royal Society for the Prevention of Accidents (RoSPA). Contains features and updates on legal and research developments in the field of health and safety.
Readership/Target Audience: Aimed at professional health and safety personnel and senior managers, researchers, local government officers and those involved in the emergency, health and safety services.
ADVERTISING RATES:
Full Page Mono £800.00
Agency Commission: 10%
Mechanical Data: Type Area: 275 x 187mm, Bleed Size: 303 x 216mm, Trim Size: 297 x 210mm, Film: Digital, Col Length: 275mm, Page Width: 187mm
BUSINESS: SAFETY & SECURITY: Safety

THE ROSPA OCCUPATIONAL SAFETY & HEALTH JOURNAL

1613971U54B-100

Editorial Address: Edgbaston Park, 353 Bristol Road, Edgbaston, BIRMINGHAM, B5 7ST **Tel:** 0121 248 2000
Fax: 0121 248 2001
Email: rspencer@rospa.com
Advertising Address: Orchard Barn, The Green, Uffington, OXON, SN7 7SB **Tel:** 01367 820367 **Fax:** 01367 820367
Email: susanphilo@talktalk.net
Web site: http://www.rospa.com
ISSN: 1474-7952
Publisher: Royal Society for the Prevention of Accidents
Date Established: 1971
Frequency: Monthly
Annual Sub.: £82.00
Usual Pagination: 54
Editor: Rebbeca Spencer; **Advertising Manager:** Susan Philo; **Managing Editor:** Rebbeca Spencer
Summary of Content: Journal covering occupational health and safety issues.
Readership/Target Audience: Aimed at professional health and safety advisors and consultants across all industries.
ADVERTISING RATES:
Full Page Mono £900.00
Full Page Colour £1200.00
Mechanical Data: Type Area: 275 x 187mm, Bleed Size: 303 x 216mm, Trim Size: 297 x 210mm, Film: Digital, Col Length: 275mm, Page Width: 187mm.
BUSINESS: SAFETY & SECURITY: Safety

ROTARY TODAY

38493U32G-110

Formerly: Rotary Magazine
Editorial Address: Kinwarton Road, ALCESTER, B49 6PB
Tel: 01789 765411 **Fax:** 01789 765570
Email: editor@ribi.org
Advertising Address: County House, 9 Checkpoint Court, Sadler Road, LINCOLN, LN6 3PW **Tel:** 01522 513515
Fax: 01522 842000
Email: info@km-media.co.uk
Web site: http://www.rotary-ribi.org
Publisher: Rotary International in Great Britain and Ireland
Frequency: 6 issues yearly
Annual Sub.: £6.00
Circulation: 58,500 (Publisher's Statement)
Usual Pagination: 52
Editor: John Pike
Summary of Content: Official magazine of Rotary International in Great Britain and Ireland. Covers news of Rotary events, personalities, club and district activities, both domestic and international.
Readership/Target Audience: Read by Rotarians who are directors, managers and key executives in commerce, trade and industry and the professions.
ADVERTISING RATES:
Full Page Colour £1525.00
Agency Commission: 10%
Mechanical Data: Type Area: 272 x 185mm, Trim Size: 275 x 210mm, Col Length: 272mm, Bleed Size: +3mm, No. of Columns (Display): 4, Col Widths (Display): 44mm, Page Width: 185mm, Film: Digital
Copy instructions: Copy Date: 3 weeks prior to publication date
Average advertising content per issue: 40%
BUSINESS: LOCAL GOVERNMENT, LEISURE & RECREATION: Community Care & Social Services

ROUSTABOUT ENERGY INTERNATIONAL

38632U33-55

Formerly: Roustabout International Energy
Editorial Address: Suite 5, International Base, Greenwell Road, East Tullos, ABERDEEN, AB12 3AX
Tel: 01224 876582 **Fax:** 01224 879757
Email: editor@energyinternat.com
Advertising Address: As above.
Email: sales@energyinternat.com
Web site: http://www.energyinternat.com
Publisher: Roustabout Publications Ltd
Date Established: 1972
Frequency: Monthly - Published around the last working day of the cover month
Free to qualifying individuals
Annual Sub.: £55.00
Circulation: 10,000 (Publisher's Statement)
Usual Pagination: 64
Editor: Jo Barron; **Advertising Manager:** Drew Hamilton
Summary of Content: Journal focusing on technology, contracts and people in the international energy industry, with a business section featuring law, commercial property, finance and computers.
Readership/Target Audience: Read by energy industry professionals and business people.
ADVERTISING RATES:
Full Page Mono £1450.00
Full Page Colour £1950.00
Agency Commission: 10%

Mechanical Data: Col Length: 255mm, Page Width: 180mm, Type Area: 255 x 180mm, Bleed Size: 285x 215mm, Film: Digital, Trim Size: 275 x 205mm
Copy instructions: Copy Date: 10th of the month of publication date
Average advertising content per issue: 40%
BUSINESS: OIL & PETROLEUM

ROUTE ONE

1637682U49B-81

Editorial Address: 37 Tyndall Court, Commerce Road, Lynch Wood, PETERBOROUGH, PE2 6LR
Tel: 01733 405730 **Fax:** 01733 405745
Email: mike.morgan@route-one.net
Advertising Address: As above.
Email: sales@route-one.net
Web site: http://www.route-one.net
Publisher: Expo Publishing
Date Established: 2003
Frequency: Weekly
Free to qualifying individuals
Circulation: 5,894 (ABC 01/01/2008 to 31/12/2008)
Usual Pagination: 64
Editor: Mike Morgan; **Advertising Manager:** Daniel Lunn
Summary of Content: Magazine with news, legal coverage, European updates and operator relevant features.
Readership/Target Audience: Aimed at bus and coach operators.
ADVERTISING RATES:
Full Page Mono £597.00
Full Page Colour £773.00
SCC £12.63
Mechanical Data: Type Area: 257 x 189mm, Bleed Size: 303 x 216mm, Page Width: 189mm, Col Length: 257mm, Film: Digital
Copy instructions: Copy Date: Thursday prior to publication date
Average advertising content per issue: 50%
BUSINESS: TRANSPORT: Bus & Coach Transport

THE ROYAL AIR FORCE YEARBOOK

38880U40-251

Editorial Address: 25 Sabrina Way, BRISTOL, BS9 1ST
Tel: 0117 968 5193
Email: prmavia@blueyonder.co.uk
Advertising Address: Douglas Bader House, Horcott Hill, FAIRFORD, GL7 4RB **Tel:** 01285 713300 **Fax:** 01285 713268
Email: sales@rafcte.com
Web site: http://www.rafcte.co.uk
ISSN: 1465-5829
Publisher: Royal Air Force Charitable Trust Enterprises
Date Established: 1960
Frequency: Annual - Published in April
Annual Sub.: £4.99
Circulation: 60,000 (Publisher's Statement)
Usual Pagination: 96
Editor: Peter March; **Managing Editor:** Peter March
Summary of Content: Yearbook of the Royal Air Force containing news, events and features on training, RAF past and present and a look at new technology.
Readership/Target Audience: Aimed at RAF personnel and anybody interested in the RAF.
ADVERTISING: Rates on application
Mechanical Data: Type Area: 270 x 190mm, Trim Size: 297 x 210mm, Bleed Size: 303 x 216mm, Col Length: 270mm, Page Width: 190mm, Film: Digital
Copy instructions: Copy Date: 4 weeks prior to publication date
BUSINESS: DEFENCE

ROYAL ARMY DENTAL CORPS BULLETIN

38913U40-252

Editorial Address: Sutherland Press House, Main Street, GOLSPIE, KW10 6RA **Tel:** 01408 633871 **Fax:** 01408 633876
Email: magazinesales@methodpublishing.co.uk
Advertising Address: As above.
Email: magazinesales@methodpublishing.co.uk
Publisher: Method Publishing
Frequency: Annual - Published in November
Circulation: 1,500 (Publisher's Statement)
Editor: Linda Bennett
Summary of Content: Dental Magazine for armed forces.
Readership/Target Audience: Aimed at the Royal Army Dental Corps.
ADVERTISING RATES:
Full Page Colour £695.00
Agency Commission: 10%
Mechanical Data: Type Area: 266 x 186mm, Col Length: 266mm, Page Width: 186mm, Trim Size: 297 x 210mm, Bleed Size: 303 x 216mm, No. of Columns (Display): 4, Film: Digital
BUSINESS: DEFENCE

THE ROYAL CORNWALL

37917U21J-255

Editorial Address: PR by email only **Tel:** 01822 832548

Email: whitepaul@orange.fr
Advertising Address: Falmouth Business Park, Bickland Water Road, FALMOUTH, TR11 4SZ **Tel:** 01326 213302
Fax: 01326 212084
Email: patricia.curnow@packetseries.co.uk
Web site: http://www.royalcornwall.co.uk
Publisher: Packet Newspapers
Date Established: 1998
Frequency: Quarterly
Cover Price: £1.95
Free to qualifying individuals
Circulation: 7,000 (Publisher's Statement)
Editor: Paul White; **Advertising Manager:** Patricia Curnow
Summary of Content: Magazine of the Royal Cornwall Agricultural Association. Also covers finance, events, drink, arts and crafts, education, people, the countryside, gardening, property, book reviews and entertainment.
Readership/Target Audience: Read mainly by members of the association.
ADVERTISING RATES:
Full Page Mono £1882.50
Full Page Colour £2541.37
Agency Commission: 10%
Mechanical Data: Film: Digital, Trim Size: 297 x 210mm
Average advertising content per issue: 50%
BUSINESS: AGRICULTURE & FARMING: Agriculture & Farming - Regional

ROYAL MILITARY POLICE JOURNAL

38882U40-255

Editorial Address: Frogmore Farm House, Frogmore Lane, Sixpenny Handley, SALISBURY, SP5 5NY
Tel: 0845 768 2326
Email: editrmpj@tiscali.co.uk
Advertising Address: 19 Heddon Street, LONDON, W1B 4BG **Tel:** 020 7993 3833
Email: jameslg@oneismore.com
Web site: http://www.army.mod.uk/rhqrmp
Publisher: One
Date Established: 1950
Frequency: 3 issues yearly - Published in April, August and December
Annual Sub.: £5.50
Circulation: 3,500 (Publisher's Statement)
Usual Pagination: 64
Editor: Stuart McLean; **Advertising Manager:** James Lyall-Grant; **Managing Editor:** John Baber
Summary of Content: Magazine containing articles about the professional work of the Corps today and its history.
Readership/Target Audience: Aimed at serving and former Royal Military Police, Chief Constables, Commonwealth serving personnel and the Security Industry.
ADVERTISING RATES:
Full Page Colour £650.00
Agency Commission: 10%
Mechanical Data: Type Area: 265 x 180mm, Page Width: 180mm, Trim Size: 297 x 210mm, Bleed Size: 303 x 216mm, Col Length: 265mm, Film: Digital, Print Process: Sheet-fed litho
Copy instructions: Copy Date: 3 weeks prior to publication date
Average advertising content per issue: 10%
BUSINESS: DEFENCE

RPS JOURNAL

38801U38-85

Editorial Address: Finsbury Business Centre, 40 Bowling Green Lane, LONDON, EC1R 0NE **Tel:** 020 7415 7099
Fax: 020 7415 7133
Email: sue@ec1publishing.com
Advertising Address: As above. **Tel:** 020 7692 9961
Email: simon@eclpublishing.com
ISSN: 1468-8670
Publisher: The Royal Photographic Society
Date Established: 1853
Frequency: 10 issues yearly
Free to qualifying individuals
Annual Sub.: $110.00
Circulation: 10,000 (Publisher's Statement)
Usual Pagination: 52
Editor: Sue Harper; **Advertising Manager:** Simon James; **Publisher:** Simon James
Summary of Content: Magazine covering every field of photography for the amateur and professional.
Readership/Target Audience: Read by members of the Royal Photographic Society.
ADVERTISING RATES:
Full Page Colour £1295.00
Mechanical Data: Type Area: 260 x 175mm, Col Length: 260mm, Page Width: 175mm, Trim Size: 297 x 210mm, Bleed Size: 303 x 216mm, Film: Digital, Col Widths (Display): 40mm
Copy instructions: Copy Date: 10th of month prior to publication date
BUSINESS: PHOTOGRAPHIC TRADE

RUN OFF AND RESTRUCTURING

1655128U1D-407

Formerly: Run Off Business
Editorial Address: 153 Simpson, MILTON KEYNES, MK6
3AH **Tel:** 01908 660856 **Fax:** 01908 660856
Email: derek@runoffandrestructuring.com
Advertising Address: As above.
Email: helen@runoffandrestructuring.com
Web site: http://www.runoffandrestructuring.com
ISSN: 1753-772X
Publisher: BD Communications
Date Established: 2002
Frequency: Quarterly
Annual Sub.: £125.00
Circulation: 4,500 (Publisher's Statement)
Usual Pagination: 48
Editor: Derek Austin; **Advertising Manager:** Helen Perry
Summary of Content: Magazine covering all aspects of the
discontinued insurance business sector.
Readership/Target Audience: Aimed at run-off managers,
claims and reinsurance recovery specialists, lawyers,
accountants, insolvency practitioners, consultants and IT
specialists.
ADVERTISING: Rates on application
BUSINESS: FINANCE & ECONOMICS: Insurance

RURAL DEVELOPMENT ABSTRACTS

1779671U21A-1117

Editorial Address: Nosworthy Way, WALLINGFORD, OX10
8DE **Tel:** 01491 829434
Email: j.osborn@cabi.org
Web site: http://www.cabi-publishing.org
Publisher: CABI
Date Established: 1978
Frequency: Quarterly
Editor: Janice Osborn
Summary of Content: Publication covering all issues
relating to third world rural development.
Readership/Target Audience: Aimed at the academic
community, NGOs, consultants, government departments
and development specialists.
ADVERTISING: No Advertising taken
BUSINESS: AGRICULTURE & FARMING

RURAL EUROPE

1658851U57-130

Editorial Address: 80 Calverley Road, TUNBRIDGE WELLS,
TN1 2UN **Tel:** 020 7017 7500 **Fax:** 020 7017 7599
Email: marketing@agra-net.com
Web site: http://www.agra-net.com
ISSN: 1740-0503
Publisher: Agra Informa Ltd
Date Established: 2003
Frequency: Monthly
Annual Sub.: £550.00
Usual Pagination: 24
Summary of Content: Journal covering new EU rural
development and agri-environmental policy. Covers topics
ranging from rural regeneration and environmental
conservation to food processing, regional marketing, rural
tourism and the protection of jobs and services.
Readership/Target Audience: Aimed at rural
entrepreneurs, land managers, local authorities,
environmentalists, research institutes and non governmental
organisations.
ADVERTISING: No Advertising taken
BUSINESS: ENVIRONMENT & POLLUTION

RUSI DEFENCE SYSTEMS

1640366U40-426

Editorial Address: Whitehall, LONDON, SW1A 2ET
Tel: 01932 227827 **Fax:** 020 7747 2647
Email: bkincaid@rusi.org
Advertising Address: RUSI Defence Systems @ ONE, 19
Heddon Street, LONDON, W1B 4BG **Tel:** 020 7993 3840
Fax: 020 7437 4209
Email: rob@oneismore.com
Web site: http://www.rusi.org
Publisher: Royal United Services Institute For Defence &
Security Studies
Date Established: 1999
Frequency: 3 issues yearly - Published in June, October and
February
Free to qualifying individuals
Circulation: 5,000 (Publisher's Statement)
Usual Pagination: 120
Editor: Bill Kincaid; **Advertising Manager:** Rob Starbuck
Summary of Content: Journal covering military equipment
and acquisition issues.
Readership/Target Audience: Aimed at military officers,
government officials, politicians and those working in the
defence industry.
ADVERTISING RATES:
Full Page Colour £2450.00
Agency Commission: 10%
Mechanical Data: Trim Size: 266 x 186mm, Film: Digital,
Bleed Size: 303 x 216mm

Copy instructions: Copy Date: 3 weeks prior to publication
date
Average advertising content per issue: 30%
BUSINESS: DEFENCE

RUSI JOURNAL

38878U40-257

Editorial Address: Whitehall, LONDON, SW1A 2ET
Tel: 020 7930 5854 **Fax:** 020 7747 2647
Email: journal@rusi.org
Advertising Address: One, 19 Heddon Street, LONDON,
W1B 4BG **Tel:** 020 7793 3833 **Fax:** 020 7463 2008
Email: rob@oneismore.com
Web site: http://www.rusi.org/journal
Publisher: Royal United Services Institute For Defence &
Security Studies
Date Established: 1857
Frequency: 6 issues yearly
Annual Sub.: £100.00
Circulation: 5,000 (Publisher's Statement)
Usual Pagination: 96
Editor: Terence McNamee; **Advertising Manager:** Rob
Starbuck
Summary of Content: Journal containing features on the
promotion and advancement of military science,
international security, technology and defence procurement
and military history.
Readership/Target Audience: Read by military, defence
and defence based personnel, policy makers, academics,
media, diplomats and diplomatic staff.
ADVERTISING RATES:
Full Page Colour £2050.00
Agency Commission: 10%
Mechanical Data: Bleed Size: 303 x 216mm, Trim Size: 266
x 186mm, Film: Digital
Copy instructions: Copy Date: 3 weeks prior to publication
date
Average advertising content per issue: 25%
BUSINESS: DEFENCE

RUSSIAN INVESTMENT REVIEW

1626047U1F-582

Editorial Address: 3 Quayside Lodge, William Morris Way,
LONDON, SW6 2UZ **Tel:** 020 7183 2560 **Fax:** 020 7183 2561
Email: info@russiainvestors.com
Advertising Address: As above.
Email: info@russiainvestors.com
Web site: http://www.russiainvestors.com
Publisher: Eventica
Date Established: 2001
Frequency: Quarterly
Free to qualifying individuals
Annual Sub.: £75.00
Circulation: 10,000 (Publisher's Statement)
Usual Pagination: 64
Advertising Manager: Advertising Manager
Summary of Content: Magazine covering investment
opportunities and news.
Readership/Target Audience: Aimed at those interested in
investing in the Russian market.
ADVERTISING: Rates on application
BUSINESS: FINANCE & ECONOMICS: Investment

RUSSO-BRITISH CHAMBER OF COMMERCE BULLETIN

36927U14C-130

Editorial Address: 42 Southwark Street, LONDON, SE1
1UN **Tel:** 020 7403 1706 **Fax:** 020 7403 1245
Email: events@rbcc.co.uk
Advertising Address: As above.
Email: amelia.acland@rbcc.co.uk
Web site: http://www.rbcc.com
Publisher: The Russo-British Chamber of Commerce
Frequency: 10 issues yearly - Published on the 1st of each
cover month
Free to qualifying individuals
Annual Sub.: £200.00
Circulation: 6,000 (Publisher's Statement)
Usual Pagination: 48
Editor: Chalav Frim
Summary of Content: Journal containing information on
business opportunities in Britain and Russia, as well as
articles about political, economic and legal changes.
Language(s): English; Russian
Readership/Target Audience: Aimed at Russian
companies with business interests in Britain and British
companies with business in Russia.
ADVERTISING RATES:
Full Page Colour £1125.00
Mechanical Data: Film: Digital
Copy instructions: Copy Date: 13th of the month prior to
publication date
Average advertising content per issue: 25%
BUSINESS: COMMERCE, INDUSTRY & MANAGEMENT:
International Commerce

SAFER COMMUNITIES

1647179U54B-103

Formerly: Community Safety Journal
Editorial Address: Suite N4, The Old Market, Upper Market
Street, HOVE, BN3 1AS **Tel:** 01273 783720
Fax: 01273 783723
Email: jos@pavilionjournals.com
Advertising Address: As above. **Tel:** 01273 623222
Fax: 01273 625526
Email: pauls@pavpub.com
Web site: http://www.pavilionjournals.com
ISSN: 1477-5883
Publisher: Pavilion Journals (Brighton) Ltd
Date Established: 2002
Frequency: Quarterly
Annual Sub.: £40.00
Circulation: 400 (Publisher's Statement)
Usual Pagination: 48
Editor: Joanna Sharrocks; **Advertising Manager:** Paul
Somerville
Summary of Content: Magazine covering all aspects of
community safety including articles on training, legal
developments, policy and research.
Readership/Target Audience: Aimed at community safety
officers, police forces, probation services, magistrates,
community groups and academics.
ADVERTISING RATES:
Full Page Mono £350.00
Agency Commission: 10%
Mechanical Data: Type Area: 243 x 160mm, Col Length:
243mm, Page Width: 160mm
BUSINESS: SAFETY & SECURITY: Safety

SAFETY AND HEALTH PRACTITIONER

39881U54B-97_56

Editorial Address: Ludgate House, 245 Blackfriars Road,
LONDON, SE1 9UY **Tel:** 020 7921 8047 **Fax:** 020 7921 8060
Email: shpeditor@ubm.com
Advertising Address: As above. **Tel:** 020 7921 8048
Fax: 020 7921 8059
Email: kat.khoury@ubm.com
Web site: http://www.shponline.co.uk
ISSN: 0958-479X
Publisher: UBM Information Ltd
Date Established: 1983
Frequency: Monthly - Published around the 1st week of the
cover month
Free to qualifying individuals
Annual Sub.: £105.00
Circulation: 33,923 (ABC 01/01/2008 to 31/12/2008)
Usual Pagination: 100
Editor: Martina Weadick; **Publisher:** Adrian Newton
Summary of Content: Official magazine of the Institution of
Occupational Safety & Health. Contains the latest news and
information on occupational safety and health, covering risk
assessment, expert advice on health, safety and welfare
policies of employers and information about health and
safety equipment and legislation.
Readership/Target Audience: Read by members of IOSH
and safety professionals working in industry and commerce.
ADVERTISING RATES:
Full Page Colour £2280.00
Agency Commission: 10%
Mechanical Data: Type Area: 261 x 191mm, Col Length:
261mm, Page Width: 191mm, Film: Digital, Bleed Size: 291 x
222mm, Trim Size: 285 x 215mm
Copy instructions: Copy Date: 3 weeks prior to publication
date
Average advertising content per issue: 60%
BUSINESS: SAFETY & SECURITY: Safety

SAFETY & RELIABILITY

39882U54B-94

Editorial Address: Clayton House, 59 Piccadilly,
MANCHESTER, M1 2AQ **Tel:** 0161 228 7824
Fax: 0161 236 6977
Email: journal@sars.org.uk
Advertising Address: As above.
Email: journal@sars.org.uk
Web site: http://www.sars.org.uk
ISSN: 0961-7353
Publisher: The Safety & Reliability Society
Date Established: 1980
Frequency: Quarterly
Free to qualifying individuals
Annual Sub.: £55.00
Circulation: 800 (Publisher's Statement)
Usual Pagination: 48
Editor: Jacqui Christodoulou; **Advertising Manager:** Jacqui
Christodoulou
Summary of Content: Journal of the Safety and Reliability
Society. Contains peer-reviewed articles on new technology,
legislation and reliability centred maintenance.
Readership/Target Audience: Aimed at members of the
Safety and Reliability Society, safety and hazard assessment
engineers and safety related design engineers.
ADVERTISING RATES:
Full Page Mono £300.00

Mechanical Data: Trim Size: 210 x 148mm, Film: Negative, right reading, emulsion side down. Digital
BUSINESS: SAFETY & SECURITY: Safety

SAFETY AT SEA INTERNATIONAL
39883U54B-95

Editorial Address: 3rd Floor, Lombard House, 3 Princess Way, REDHILL, RH1 1UP **Tel:** 01737 379142
Fax: 01737 379007
Email: sas@lrfairplay.com
Advertising Address: As above. **Tel:** 01737 379700
Fax: 01737 379001
Email: nancy.oliver@lrfairplay.com
Web site: http://www.safetyatsea.net
ISSN: 0142-0666
Publisher: Lloyd's Register-Fairplay Ltd
Date Established: 1967
Frequency: Monthly - Published in the last week of the month prior to cover date
Annual Sub.: £175.00
Circulation: 5,074 (Publisher's Statement)
Usual Pagination: 40
Editor: Nick Blackmore; **Editor-in-Chief:** Tony Slinn; **Advertising Manager:** Daniel Goncalves; **Managing Editor:** Paul Gunton
Summary of Content: Magazine focusing on maritime and offshore safety.
Readership/Target Audience: Aimed at ship owners, operators and safety authorities.
ADVERTISING RATES:
Full Page Colour £2895.00
Agency Commission: 10%
Mechanical Data: Type Area: 258 x 185mm, Bleed Size: 303 x 216mm, Trim Size: 297 x 210mm, Col Length: 258mm, Page Width: 185mm, Film: Digital
Copy instructions: Copy Date: 3 weeks prior to publication date
Average advertising content per issue: 34%
BUSINESS: SAFETY & SECURITY: Safety

SAFETY EDUCATION
39884U54B-97

Editorial Address: Edgbaston Park, 353 Bristol Road, BIRMINGHAM, B5 7ST **Tel:** 0121 248 2025
Fax: 0121 248 2001
Advertising Address: Orchard Barn, The Green, Uffington, OXON, SN7 7SB **Tel:** 01367 820367 **Fax:** 01367 820367
Email: susanphilo@talktalk.net
Web site: http://www.rospa.co.uk
Publisher: Royal Society for the Prevention of Accidents
Frequency: 3 issues yearly - Published in January, June and September
Annual Sub.: £12.50
Circulation: 2,900 (Publisher's Statement)
Usual Pagination: 20
Editor: Janice Cave; **Managing Editor:** Janice Cave
Summary of Content: Journal covering news and information on teaching safety to children and occupational health and safety for teachers and other professionals in the education sector.
Readership/Target Audience: Read by teachers, overseas organisations and local education authorities.
ADVERTISING: Rates on application
Agency Commission: 10%
Copy instructions: Copy Date: 10th of the month prior to publication date
Average advertising content per issue: 5%
BUSINESS: SAFETY & SECURITY: Safety

SAFETY EXPRESS
39885U54B-97_10

Editorial Address: Edgbaston Park, 353 Bristol Road, Edgbaston, BIRMINGHAM, B5 7ST **Tel:** 0121 248 2088
Fax: 0121 248 2001
Email: lsmith@rospa.com
Advertising Address: Orchard Barn, The Green, Uffington, OXON, SN7 7SB **Tel:** 01367 820367 **Fax:** 01367 820367
Email: susanphilo@talktalk.net
Web site: http://www.rospa.com
Publisher: Royal Society for the Prevention of Accidents
Date Established: 1975
Frequency: 6 issues yearly - Published 1st of the month
Annual Sub.: £23.50
Circulation: 6,000 (Publisher's Statement)
Usual Pagination: 20
Editor: Lauren Smith; **Managing Editor:** Rebbeca Spencer
Summary of Content: Newspaper covering latest work-related health and safety news, health and safety in the workplace with coverage of court cases, new publications and videos, training courses, news from the trade unions plus features, competitions and a topical cartoon guide.
Readership/Target Audience: Aimed at safety workers in all occupations, trade union reps and line managers.
ADVERTISING RATES:
Full Page Mono £850.00
Agency Commission: 10%

Mechanical Data: Page Width: 233mm, Col Widths (Display): 44mm, Type Area: 346 x 233mm, Col Length: 346mm, Film: Digital
Copy instructions: Copy Date: 1st of the month prior to publication date
BUSINESS: SAFETY & SECURITY: Safety

SAFETY MANAGEMENT
39886U54B-97_50

Editorial Address: 70 Chancellors Road, LONDON, W6 9RS **Tel:** 020 8741 1231 **Fax:** 020 8741 0835
Email: publications@britsafe.org
Advertising Address: As above. **Tel:** 020 8600 5580
Email: publications@britsafe.org
Web site: http://www.britishsafetycouncil.org
ISSN: 0951-2624
Publisher: British Safety Council
Frequency: 11 issues yearly - Published on the 4th of the cover month
Annual Sub.: £60.00
Circulation: 15,087 (ABC 01/01/2008 to 31/12/2008)
Usual Pagination: 68
Editor: Brian Shillibeer
Summary of Content: Magazine covering current safety topics, key news stories, accidents and incidents that concern the safety industry, company profiles that examine specific industry areas and in-depth coverage of health and safety prosecutions.
Readership/Target Audience: Read by members of the British Safety Council, directors, senior executives and safety officers.
ADVERTISING RATES:
Full Page Mono £1445.00
Full Page Colour £1875.00
Agency Commission: 10%
Mechanical Data: Film: Digital, Print Process: Offset litho, Bleed Size: 303 x 216mm, Trim Size: 297 x 210mm, Type Area: 265 x 184mm, Col Length: 265mm, Page Width: 184mm
Copy instructions: Copy Date: 13th of the month prior to publication date
Average advertising content per issue: 40%
BUSINESS: SAFETY & SECURITY: Safety

SAFETY SPECIALIST
1833145U54B-113

Editorial Address: 18 High Street, Seal, SEVENOAKS, TN15 0AJ **Tel:** 01732 440389
Email: safetyspecialist@btinternet.com
Advertising Address: As above.
Email: safetyspecialist@btinternet.com
Web site: http://www.safetyspecialist.co.uk
Publisher: Safety Specialist (SOS) LTD
Date Established: 2007
Frequency: Quarterly
Cover Price: £3.00
Annual Sub.: £10.00
Circulation: 12,000 (Publisher's Statement)
Usual Pagination: 64
Editor: Tomarra Sunday; **Features Editor:** Tomarra Sunday;
Publisher: Joshuah Kalsi
Summary of Content: Magazine covering current issues and news within the health and safety arena.
Readership/Target Audience: Aimed at health and safety officers, safety consultants and advisors, safety engineers and facilities managers, environmental health officers, safety and fire training professionals and procurement and purchasing personnel.
ADVERTISING RATES:
Full Page Colour £1145.00
Mechanical Data: Type Area: 273 x 186mm, Bleed Size: 303 x 216mm, Trim Size: 297 x 210mm, Col Length: 273mm, Page Width: 186mm, Film: Digital
Supplement(s): Safety Specialist Plus - 4xY
BUSINESS: SAFETY & SECURITY: Safety

SALES PROMOTION
35734U2F-58

Editorial Address: Arena House, 66-68 Pentonville Road, LONDON, N1 9HS **Tel:** 020 7689 5572 **Fax:** 020 7837 5326
Email: editor@salespromo.co.uk
Advertising Address: As above. **Tel:** 020 7837 5340
Email: matt.s@salespromo.co.uk
Web site: http://www.salespromo.co.uk
ISSN: 0957-6193
Publisher: Sales Promotion Publishing Ltd
Date Established: 1971
Frequency: 11 issues yearly - Published in the middle of the cover month
Free to qualifying individuals
Annual Sub.: £49.00
Circulation: 7,821 (ABC 01/01/2008 to 30/06/2008)
Usual Pagination: 68
Editor: Martin Croft; **Advertising Manager:** Matthew Sullivan
Summary of Content: Magazine for clients, agencies and suppliers active in sales promotion, promotional marketing, incentives and motivation.
Language(s): English; French

Readership/Target Audience: Read by marketing directors, brand managers, marketing agencies, marketing services suppliers.
ADVERTISING RATES:
Full Page Colour £1690.00
SCC £20.00
Agency Commission: 10%
Mechanical Data: Type Area: 295 x 215mm, Film: Digital, Bleed Size: 325 x 240mm, Trim Size: 315 x 230mm, No. of Columns (Display): 4, Col Length: 295mm, Page Width: 215mm
Copy instructions: Copy Date: 1st week of the month of publication
Average advertising content per issue: 50%
Supplement(s): Sales Promotion Buyers Guide - 1xY, Sales Promotion Motivation Report - 1xY, Sales Promotion Technology Supplement - 1xY, Sales Promotion Voucher Report - 2xY
BUSINESS: COMMUNICATIONS, ADVERTISING & MARKETING: Selling

SALESFORCE
35733U2F-56

Editorial Address: 176 Swievelands Road, Biggin Hill, WESTERHAM, TN16 3QS **Tel:** 07020 957578
Email: beishon@salesforcemagazine.co.uk
Advertising Address: As above. **Tel:** 01959 572444
Fax: 0870 706 3074
Email: rapley@salesforcemagazine.co.uk
Web site: http://www.salesforcemagazine.co.uk
Publisher: Boadicea Publications Ltd
Date Established: 1995
Frequency: 10 issues yearly - Published on the 1st Friday of the month
Free to qualifying individuals
Annual Sub.: £30.00
Circulation: 16,008 (Publisher's Statement)
Editor: Marc Beishon; **Advertising Manager:** Elke Rapley
Summary of Content: Magazine focusing on IT/telecoms sales force management, development and personal development for sales people.
Readership/Target Audience: Aimed at IT and telecom sales professionals.
ADVERTISING RATES:
Full Page Mono £2280.00
Full Page Colour £2330.00
Agency Commission: 10%
Mechanical Data: Type Area: 265 x 190mm, Col Length: 265mm, Bleed Size: 303 x 216mm, Film: Digital, Trim Size: 297 x 210mm, Page Width: 190mm
Average advertising content per issue: 50%
BUSINESS: COMMUNICATIONS, ADVERTISING & MARKETING: Selling

SALON BUSINESS
622798U15B-80

Editorial Address: 223 Wickham Road, CROYDON, CR0 8TG **Tel:** 020 3253 0140
Email: sarah.andrews@salonbusiness.co.uk
Advertising Address: As above.
Email: info@salonbusiness.co.uk
Web site: http://www.salonbusiness.co.uk
Publisher: Salon Gold Publishing Ltd
Date Established: 2000
Frequency: 10 issues yearly
Cover Price: £3.95
Free to qualifying individuals
Annual Sub.: £39.95
Circulation: 14,000 (Publisher's Statement)
Usual Pagination: 116
Editor: Maria Weijers; **Advertising Manager:** Tracy Coupar-Fox
Summary of Content: Magazine covering product news, special offers and investigative features.
Readership/Target Audience: Aimed specifically at salon owners.
ADVERTISING RATES:
Full Page Colour £1950.00
Mechanical Data: Col Length: 300mm, Page Width: 230mm, Type Area: 300 x 230mm, Bleed Size: 306 x 236mm, Trim Size: 300 x 230mm, Film: Digital
Average advertising content per issue: 40%
BUSINESS: COSMETICS & HAIRDRESSING: Hairdressing

SALON FOCUS
37264U15B-75

Formerly: Headline News
Editorial Address: 1 Abbey Court, Fraser Road, Priory Business Park, BEDFORD, MK44 3WH **Tel:** 0845 345 6500
Fax: 01234 838875
Email: eileen.lawson@nhf.info
Advertising Address: As above.
Email: enquiries@nhf.info
Web site: http://www.nhf.biz
Publisher: National Hairdressers' Federation
Date Established: 1972
Frequency: 6 issues yearly
Free to qualifying individuals
Circulation: 8,000 (Publisher's Statement)
Usual Pagination: 36

Business Magazines

Editor: Eileen Lawson; **Advertising Manager:** Tina Beaumont-Goddard; **Publisher:** Eileen Lawson
Summary of Content: Newsletter of the National Hairdressers' Federation. Contains news and details on new legislation, new products and services.
Readership/Target Audience: Read mainly by members, all of whom own salons.
ADVERTISING RATES:
Full Page Colour £1195.00
Mechanical Data: Type Area: 200 x 138mm, Bleed Size: 226 x 161mm, Col Length: 200mm, Page Width: 138mm, Film: Digital
Copy instructions: Copy Date: 2 weeks prior to publication date
Average advertising content per issue: 50%
BUSINESS: COSMETICS & HAIRDRESSING: Hairdressing

THE SALON MAGAZINE
1794819U15R-16
Editorial Address: Barham Court, Teston, MAIDSTONE, ME18 5BZ **Tel:** 01622 618797 **Fax:** 01622 618793
Email: gemmaw@cimltd.co.uk
Advertising Address: As above. **Tel:** 01622 618792
Email: julieneill@cimltd.co.uk
Web site: http://www.thesalonmagazine.co.uk
Publisher: CIM LLP
Frequency: 10 issues yearly - Published at the beginning of the 1st cover month
Free to qualifying individuals
Annual Sub.: £18.00
Circulation: 9,500 (Publisher's Statement)
Usual Pagination: 60
Editor: Gemma Ward; **Advertising Manager:** Julie Neill
Summary of Content: Publication covering all aspects of the hair, beauty, nails and tanning industry.
Readership/Target Audience: Aimed at managers and owners of hair, beauty, nails and tanning salons.
ADVERTISING RATES:
Full Page Colour £1200.00
Agency Commission: 10%
Mechanical Data: Trim Size: 300 x 230mm, Bleed Size: 306 x 236mm, Film: Digital
Copy instructions: Copy Date: 3 weeks prior to publication date
Average advertising content per issue: 40%
BUSINESS: COSMETICS & HAIRDRESSING: Cosmetics & Hairdressing Related

SALON TODAY
1640730U15A-202
Editorial Address: 27 Old Gloucester Street, LONDON, WC1N 3XX **Tel:** 0870 850 3085
Email: info@salontoday.co.uk
Advertising Address: As above.
Email: info@salontoday.co.uk
Web site: http://www.salontoday.co.uk
Publisher: Viva Publishing Ltd
Date Established: 2003
Frequency: Quarterly
Free to qualifying individuals
Annual Sub.: £29.95
Circulation: 10,000 (Publisher's Statement)
Usual Pagination: 96
Editor: Fiona Bradshaw; **Advertising Manager:** Tim Morris
Summary of Content: Magazine covering all aspects of the health and beauty industry, including product reviews and celebrity interviews.
Readership/Target Audience: Aimed at salon and spa owners.
ADVERTISING RATES:
Full Page Colour £2450.00
Agency Commission: 10%
Mechanical Data: Type Area: 265 x 190mm, Bleed Size: 296 x 221mm, Trim Size: 290 x 215mm, Col Length: 265mm, Page Width: 190mm, Film: Digital
BUSINESS: COSMETICS & HAIRDRESSING: Cosmetics

THE SAPPER
38883U40-428
Editorial Address: RHQ RE, Brompton Barracks, CHATHAM, ME4 4UG **Tel:** 01634 822227
Fax: 01634 822397
Email: sappermag@royalengineers.mod.uk
Advertising Address: Crest Publications Ltd, 20 Moulton Business Park, Scirroco Close, NORTHAMPTON, NN3 6AP
Tel: 01604 495495 **Fax:** 01604 495465
Email: jayne@crestpublications.com
Web site: http://www.royalengineers.mod.uk
Publisher: Corps of Royal Engineers
Date Established: 1895
Frequency: 6 issues yearly
Free to qualifying individuals
Annual Sub.: £12.00
Circulation: 8,400 (Publisher's Statement)
Usual Pagination: 64
Editor: Charles Holman; **Advertising Manager:** Jayne Creer
Summary of Content: Magazine covering the activities of the serving and territorial Royal Engineers, branches of the

Royal Engineers Association, notices, calling old comrades, births, marriages, anniversaries and deaths.
Readership/Target Audience: Read by serving and retired Royal Engineers.
ADVERTISING RATES:
Full Page Mono £600.00
Full Page Colour £850.00
Agency Commission: 10%
Mechanical Data: Type Area: 236 x 176mm, Bleed Size: 244 x 184mm, Col Length: 236mm, Page Width: 176mm, Film: Digital, Trim Size: 240 x 180mm
Copy instructions: Copy Date: 15th of the month prior to publication date
Average advertising content per issue: 10%
BUSINESS: DEFENCE

SATELLITE FINANCE
35297U1F-395
Editorial Address: 292 Vauxhall Bridge Road, LONDON, SW1V 1AE **Tel:** 020 7963 7685 **Fax:** 0870 836 4301
Email: ed.ansell@satellitefinance.com
Advertising Address: As above. **Tel:** 020 7963 7680
Fax: 020 7963 7681
Email: yvonne.okagbue@telecomfinance.com
Web site: http://www.satellitefinance.com
ISSN: 1460-9754
Publisher: Press Association
Frequency: 11 issues yearly
Annual Sub.: £965.00
Circulation: 600 (Publisher's Statement)
Editor: Ed Ansell
Summary of Content: Journal covering debt and equity financing for the satellite industry.
Readership/Target Audience: Read by bankers, chief financial officers, business development professionals, lawyers and consultants.
ADVERTISING RATES:
Full Page Mono £2250.00
Full Page Colour £3250.00
Agency Commission: 10%
Mechanical Data: Bleed Size: 303 x 216mm, Trim Size: 297 x 210mm, Film: Digital
Copy instructions: Copy Date: 1 week prior to publication date
Average advertising content per issue: 10%
BUSINESS: FINANCE & ECONOMICS: Investment

SATRA BULLETIN
38221U29-50
Formerly: Satra Bulletin International
Editorial Address: SATRA House, Rockingham Road, KETTERING, NN16 9JH **Tel:** 01536 410000
Fax: 01536 313374
Web site: http://www.satra.co.uk
ISSN: 0966-7466
Publisher: SATRA Footwear Technology Centre
Date Established: 2005
Frequency: 11 issues yearly
Free to qualifying individuals
Circulation: 2,000 (Publisher's Statement)
Usual Pagination: 44
Editor: Stuart Morgan
Summary of Content: Magazine covering all aspects of the footwear and leather goods industry. Includes trade news, expert technical articles, machinery, materials and profiles.
Readership/Target Audience: Read by senior members of the international footwear industry.
ADVERTISING: No Advertising taken
BUSINESS: FOOTWEAR

SBT SUSSEX BUSINESS TIMES
41360U63B-1700
Formerly: SBT Southern Business Times
Editorial Address: Park View House, 19 The Avenue, EASTBOURNE, BN21 3YD **Tel:** 01323 411601
Fax: 01323 411654
Email: editorial@sbtmagazine.co.uk
Advertising Address: As above. **Tel:** 01323 433702
Fax: 01323 734909
Email: vanessa.souto@sbtmagazine.co.uk
Web site: http://www.sbtmagazine.co.uk
Publisher: Park View Publishing Ltd
Date Established: 1975
Frequency: 10 issues yearly - Published on the 3rd Monday of the cover month
Free to qualifying individuals
Annual Sub.: £30.00
Circulation: 24,000 (Publisher's Statement)
Usual Pagination: 48
Editor: Laura Knight; **Managing Director:** Lee Mansfield;
Advertising Manager: Vanessa Souto
Summary of Content: Magazine containing features on finance, law, commercial property, new technology, motoring, gadgets, lifestyle marketing and local business news.
Readership/Target Audience: Aimed at managers and directors in the South of England.

ADVERTISING RATES:
Full Page Colour £1270.00
Agency Commission: 10%
Mechanical Data: Type Area: 220 x 150mm, Col Length: 220mm, Bleed Size: 243 x 173mm, Trim Size: 240 x 170mm, Page Width: 150mm, Film: Digital
Copy instructions: Copy Date: 2 weeks prior to publication date
Average advertising content per issue: 50%
BUSINESS: REGIONAL BUSINESS: Regional Business English Counties

SC MAGAZINE
39919U54C-100
Editorial Address: 22 Bute Gardens, LONDON, W6 7HN
Tel: 020 8267 8017 **Fax:** 020 8267 4556
Email: sceditorial@haymarket.com
Advertising Address: 174 Hammersmith Road, LONDON, W6 7JP **Tel:** 020 8267 5000
Email: mhallett@westcoast.com
Web site: http://www.scmagazine.com/uk
ISSN: 1352-4097
Publisher: Haymarket Business Media Ltd
Date Established: 1994
Frequency: Monthly - Published in the 1st week of the cover month
Cover Price: £4.50
Annual Sub.: £45.00
Circulation: 11,051 (ABC 01/01/2008 to 31/12/2008)
Usual Pagination: 90
Editor: Paul Fisher; **Advertising Manager:** Rebecca Lockwood
Summary of Content: Magazine dedicated to providing an independent and authoritative view on all issues concerning computer and information security.
Readership/Target Audience: Aimed at network directors, managers and those who have a direct responsibility for information and network security within their organisation.
ADVERTISING RATES:
Full Page Colour £2800.00
Agency Commission: 10%
Mechanical Data: Type Area: 238 x 182mm, Film: Digital, Bleed Size: 281 x 212mm, Trim Size: 275 x 206mm, Col Length: 238mm, Page Width: 182mm
Copy instructions: Copy Date: 2 weeks prior to publication date
Average advertising content per issue: 30%
BUSINESS: SAFETY & SECURITY: Security

SCHOOL BUILDING
1911432U62R-508
Editorial Address: Waverley House, 11 Galena Close, Amington Heights, Amington Industrial Estate, STAFFORDSHIRE, B77 4AS **Tel:** 01827 301190
Email: press@wavcoms.co.uk
Advertising Address: As above.
Web site: http://www.waverleycommunications.co.uk/magazinesReaders/schoolbuildingpage.htm
Publisher: Waverley Communications Ltd
Frequency: Quarterly
Cover Price: Free
Editor: Gemma O'Rourke; **News Editor:** Gemma O'Rourke
Summary of Content: Online magazine looking at products and services relating to the School building industry.
Readership/Target Audience: Aimed at key decision makers and named specifiers within the school building industry.
BUSINESS: CHURCH & SCHOOL EQUIPMENT & EDUCATION: Education Related

SCHOOL FINANCIAL MANAGEMENT
623151U1P-83_45
Formerly: Lottery Cash for Schools
Editorial Address: 9 Throstle Nest Close, OTLEY, LS21 2RR
Tel: 020 7954 3407 **Fax:** 020 7251 9045
Email: brin@optimuseducation.co.uk
ISSN: 1465-8739
Publisher: Optimus Education
Date Established: 1999
Frequency: 10 issues yearly
Annual Sub.: £95.00
Usual Pagination: 12
Editor: Brin Best; **Managing Editor:** Charles Dietz
Summary of Content: Newsletter covering school funding issues, financial management and budget information.
Readership/Target Audience: Aimed at head and deputy head teachers, bursars, governors and those hoping to secure funding for an educational project.
ADVERTISING: No Advertising taken
BUSINESS: FINANCE & ECONOMICS: Fundraising

SCHOOL HEALTH
1826723U56F-112
Editorial Address: PO Box 100, CHICHESTER, PO18 8HD
Tel: 01243 576444 **Fax:** 01243 576456
Email: sarah.monger@keywayspublishing.com
Advertising Address: As above. **Tel:** 01243 816689
Email: sarah.monger@keywayspublishing.com

Web site: http://www.schoolhealthjournal.co.uk
ISSN: 1749-6098
Publisher: Keyways Publishing Limited
Date Established: 2007
Frequency: Quarterly
Cover Price: £5.00
Free to qualifying individuals
Annual Sub.: £30.00
Circulation: 6,000 (Publisher's Statement)
Usual Pagination: 16
Editor: Sarah Monger; **Publisher:** Sarah Harkness
Summary of Content: Journal that updates health care professionals on clinical and practical subjects relevant to the health of young people of school age.
Readership/Target Audience: Aimed at health care professionals, school nurses, social workers and health visitors.
ADVERTISING RATES:
Full Page Colour £1240.00
Agency Commission: 10%
Mechanical Data: Trim Size: 297 x 210mm, Bleed Size: +3mm
Average advertising content per issue: 40%
BUSINESS: HEALTH & MEDICAL: Health Education

SCHOOL LEADERSHIP
41152U62J-1050

Formerly: The Heads Legal Guide Magazine
Editorial Address: 145 London Road, KINGSTON UPON THAMES, KT2 6SR **Tel:** 020 8547 3333 **Fax:** 020 8549 7275
Email: samera.owusu.tutu@croner.co.uk.
Advertising Address: Old Byre House, Millbrook Lane, East Knoyle, SALISBURY, SP3 6AW **Tel:** 01747 830520
Fax: 01747 830691
Email: sabrina.croner@spmedia.co.uk
Web site: http://www.croner.co.uk
ISSN: 1460-3527
Publisher: Croner Group Ltd
Date Established: 1997
Frequency: 3 issues yearly - Published in January, May and September
Annual Sub.: £56.00
Circulation: 30,000 (Publisher's Statement)
Usual Pagination: 32
Editor: Samera Owusu-Tutu
Summary of Content: Magazine focusing on current issues of importance concerning education leadership.
Readership/Target Audience: Aimed at head and deputy head teachers, governors, SENCOs and management teams in all types of school.
ADVERTISING RATES:
Full Page Colour £1100.00
Agency Commission: 10%
Mechanical Data: Page Width: 189mm, Type Area: 255 x 189mm, Trim Size: 297 x 210mm, Bleed Size: 303 x 216mm, Col Length: 255mm, Film: Digital
Copy instructions: Copy Date: 2 weeks prior to publication date
Average advertising content per issue: 34%
BUSINESS: CHURCH & SCHOOL EQUIPMENT & EDUCATION: Teachers & Education Management

---

SCHOOL LEADERSHIP TODAY
41156U62J-650

Formerly: Managing Schools Today
Editorial Address: 215 The Green House, Gibb Street, Digbeth, BIRMINGHAM, B9 4AA **Tel:** 0121 224 7599
Fax: 0121 224 7598
Email: lucy.busuttil@imaginativeminds.co.uk
Advertising Address: As above. **Tel:** 0121 224 7576
Fax: 0121 224 7565
Email: aburgess@imaginativeminds.co.uk
Web site: http://www.teachingtimes.co.uk
ISSN: 0968-1558
Publisher: Imaginative Minds
Date Established: 1988
Frequency: 6 issues yearly - Published the 1st week of the month
Annual Sub.: £63.50
Circulation: 7,000 (Publisher's Statement)
Usual Pagination: 80
Editor: Lucy Busuttil
Summary of Content: Management magazine covering all aspects of running a school.
Readership/Target Audience: Aimed at head teachers, senior managers, governors and bursars.
ADVERTISING RATES:
Full Page Colour £1200.00
Agency Commission: 10%
Mechanical Data: Film: Digital, Type Area: 251 x 172mm, Bleed Size: 307 x 220mm, Trim Size: 297 x 210mm, Col Length: 251mm, Page Width: 172mm
Copy instructions: Copy Date: 2 weeks prior to publication date
Average advertising content per issue: 40%
BUSINESS: CHURCH & SCHOOL EQUIPMENT & EDUCATION: Teachers & Education Management

---

THE SCHOOL LIBRARIAN
40877U60B-125

Editorial Address: Unit 2, Lotmead Business Village, Lotmead Farm, Wanborough, SWINDON, SN4 0UY
Tel: 01793 791787 **Fax:** 01793 791786
Email: info@sla.org.uk
Advertising Address: Space Marketing, 10 Clayfield Mews, Newcomen Road, TUNBRIDGE WELLS, TN4 9PA
Tel: 01892 677740 **Fax:** 01892 677743
Email: brians@spacemarketing.co.uk
Web site: http://www.sla.org.uk
ISSN: 0036-6595
Publisher: School Library Association
Frequency: Quarterly
Cover Price: £45.00
Circulation: 4,000 (Publisher's Statement)
Usual Pagination: 56
Editor: Steve Hird; **Features Editor:** Steve Hird;
Advertising Manager: Brian Shilling
Summary of Content: Journal of the School Library Association covering the school library profession, reviews of books and children's literature.
Readership/Target Audience: Read by librarians, teachers, education advisory staff, publishers and book suppliers.
ADVERTISING RATES:
Full Page Colour £895.00
Agency Commission: 10%
Mechanical Data: Film: Digital, Trim Size: 297 x 210mm
Copy instructions: Copy Date: 4 weeks prior to publication date
BUSINESS: PUBLISHING: Libraries

SCHOOL PSYCHOLOGY INTERNATIONAL
40114U62A-440

Editorial Address: School of Education, University of Education, EXETER, EX4 4QJ **Tel:** 020 7324 8500
Fax: 020 7324 8600
Email: rlburden@exeter.ac.uk
Advertising Address: 1 Oliver's Yard, 55 City Road, LONDON, EC1Y 1SP **Tel:** 020 7324 8500
Fax: 020 7324 8600
Email: advertising@sagepub.co.uk
Web site: http://www.sagepub.co.uk
ISSN: 0143-0343
Publisher: Sage Publications
Date Established: 1979
Frequency: 5 issues yearly
Annual Sub.: £54.00
Circulation: 500 (Publisher's Statement)
Usual Pagination: 110
Editor: Robert Burden; **Advertising Manager:** Sheena Karim
Summary of Content: Journal covering mental health, educational, therapeutic and support services to schools and their communities.
Readership/Target Audience: Aimed at school psychologists, teachers, clinical and counselling psychologists and academic researchers.
ADVERTISING RATES:
Full Page Mono £400.00
Agency Commission: 5%
Mechanical Data: Type Area: 205 x 130mm, Film: Digital, Col Length: 205mm, Page Width: 130mm
Copy instructions: Copy Date: 12 weeks prior to publication date
BUSINESS: CHURCH & SCHOOL EQUIPMENT & EDUCATION: Education

SCHOOL SCIENCE REVIEW
40003U55-140

Editorial Address: College Lane, HATFIELD, AL10 9AA
Tel: 01707 283000 **Fax:** 01707 266532
Email: janehanrott@ase.org.uk
Advertising Address: As above. **Tel:** 01254 247764
Email: rebecca@ase.org.uk
Web site: http://www.ase.org.uk
ISSN: 0036-6811
Publisher: The Association for Science Education
Date Established: 1919
Frequency: Quarterly
Free to qualifying individuals
Annual Sub.: £92.00
Circulation: 14,000 (Publisher's Statement)
Usual Pagination: 144
Editor: Jane Hanrott; **Executive Editor:** Jane Welsh;
Advertising Manager: Rebecca Dixon Watmough
Summary of Content: Publication covering all subjects and pedagogic knowledge related to science teaching.
Readership/Target Audience: Aimed at science teachers and lecturers within 11-19 education in the independent and maintained sectors and those working in science teacher education and education research.
ADVERTISING RATES:
Full Page Mono £550.00
Full Page Colour £550.00
Agency Commission: 10%
Mechanical Data: Trim Size: 245 x 170mm, Bleed Size: 251 x 173mm, Type Area: 220 x 150mm, Film: Digital, Col Length: 220mm, Page Width: 150mm

---

Copy instructions: Copy Date: 2 weeks prior to publication date
Average advertising content per issue: 10%
BUSINESS: APPLIED SCIENCE & LABORATORIES

SCHOOL VISITS
41204U62R-400

Formerly: School Visits Guide
Editorial Address: Unit 1, Crumplin's Business Court, Odiham, HAMPSHIRE, RG29 1DU **Tel:** 01256 704288
Fax: 01256 703447
Email: schoolvisits@rapportgroup.com
Advertising Address: As above.
Email: jim@rapportlearning.com
Web site: http://www.school-visits.com
Publisher: Rapport Learning Ltd
Date Established: 1985
Frequency: Annual - Published in October
Cover Price: £9.50
Free to qualifying individuals
Circulation: 10,000 (Publisher's Statement)
Usual Pagination: 64
Editor: Peter Clarke
Summary of Content: Directory offering a comprehensive guide to locations suitable for school visits, tours, outings and holidays together with relevant suppliers such as insurance companies, bus, coach, train companies and airlines.
Readership/Target Audience: Aimed at teachers in UK schools organising visits outside the classroom and final year teaching students.
ADVERTISING RATES:
Full Page Mono £1420.00
Full Page Colour £2250.00
Agency Commission: 10%
Mechanical Data: Type Area: 267 x 175mm, Bleed Size: 303 x 216mm, Page Width: 175mm, Trim Size: 297 x 210mm, Col Length: 267mm, Film: Digital
Average advertising content per issue: 40%
BUSINESS: CHURCH & SCHOOL EQUIPMENT & EDUCATION: Education Related

---

SCHOOLS EQUIPMENT NEWS DIRECT
704441U62K-900

Formerly: Schools Equipment News Directory
Editorial Address: PO Box 249, ASCOT, SL5 0BZ
Tel: 01344 459528 **Fax:** 01344 862569
Email: crownwood@btconnect.com
Advertising Address: As above.
Email: crownwood@btconnect.com
Web site: http://www.cwponline.co.uk
Publisher: Crown Wood Publications Ltd
Date Established: 2000
Frequency: 3 issues yearly - Published in January, April and September. Published in the 1st week of the cover month
Cover Price: Free
Circulation: 9,000 (Publisher's Statement)
Usual Pagination: 40
Editor: Christine Stevens; **Advertising Manager:** Madeline Whitney; **Publisher:** Madeline Whitney
Summary of Content: Magazine covering schools equipment and furniture, details of exhibitions, travel and security, PA/sound systems, IT and anything to do with the upkeep of the building, contents and grounds.
Readership/Target Audience: Aimed at bursars, head teachers, principals, site managers, supply and facilities managers and architects.
ADVERTISING RATES:
Full Page Colour £745.00
Agency Commission: 10%
Mechanical Data: Film: Digital, Type Area: 188 x 134mm, Col Length: 188mm, Page Width: 134mm
Average advertising content per issue: 50%
BUSINESS: CHURCH & SCHOOL EQUIPMENT & EDUCATION: Church & School Equipment

---

SCIENCE
40004U55-150

Editorial Address: Science International, Bateman House, 82-88 Hills Road, CAMBRIDGE, CB2 1LQ
Tel: 01223 326500 **Fax:** 01223 326501
Email: science@science-int.co.uk
Advertising Address: As above.
Email: mfield@science-int.co.uk
Web site: http://www.scienceonline.org
ISSN: 0036-8075
Publisher: American Assoc. for the Advancement of Science
Date Established: 1880
Frequency: Weekly
Annual Sub.: $205.00
Circulation: 140,000 (Publisher's Statement)
Usual Pagination: 150
Editor: Eliot Marshall; **Advertising Manager:** Tracey Holmes
Summary of Content: Journal of the American Association for the Advancement of Science containing news, technical comment, research articles, letters, book reviews and new product information covering all areas of science.

Readership/Target Audience: Aimed at scientists and life science researchers.
ADVERTISING RATES:
Full Page Mono $8560.00
Full Page Colour $10310.00
Agency Commission: 15%
Mechanical Data: Bleed Size: 273 x 216mm, Trim Size: 266 x 209mm, Type Area: 254 x 178mm, Film: Digital, Col Length: 254mm, Page Width: 178mm, No. of Columns (Display): 3
Copy instructions: Copy Date: 3 weeks prior to publication date
Average advertising content per issue: 30%
BUSINESS: APPLIED SCIENCE & LABORATORIES

SCIENCE & JUSTICE
38443U32F-600
Editorial Address: 18A Mount Parade, HARROGATE, HG1 1BX **Tel:** 01423 566973 **Fax:** 01423 566391
Email: journal@forensic-science-society.org.uk
Advertising Address: Elsevier London Ltd, 32 Jamestown Road, LONDON, NW1 7BY **Tel:** 01423 566973
Email: n.dunwell@elsevier.com
Web site: http://www.forensic-science-society.org.uk
ISSN: 1355-0306
Publisher: The Forensic Science Society
Date Established: 1960
Frequency: Quarterly
Annual Sub.: EUR204.00
Circulation: 2,600 (Publisher's Statement)
Usual Pagination: 72
Editor: Tracey D'Alessandro-Rixon
Summary of Content: Journal of the Forensic Science Society covering the study, application and standing of forensic science including formal scientific papers.
Readership/Target Audience: Read by forensic scientists, police officers, scenes of crime officers, the legal profession, medico-legal and laboratory professions.
ADVERTISING RATES:
Full Page Mono EUR944.00
Full Page Colour EUR1716.00
Mechanical Data: Type Area: 250 x 180mm, Bleed Size: 286 x 216mm, Col Length: 250mm, Trim Size: 280 x 210mm, Page Width: 180mm
BUSINESS: LOCAL GOVERNMENT, LEISURE & RECREATION: Police

SCIENCE IN PARLIAMENT
1687237U55-9017
Editorial Address: 3 Birdcage Walk, LONDON, SW1H 9JJ **Tel:** 020 7222 7085 **Fax:** 020 7222 7189
Email: lloyda@pandsctte.demon.co.uk
Advertising Address: As above.
Email: lloyda@pandsctte.demon.co.uk
Web site: http://www.scienceinparliament.org.uk
ISSN: 0263-6271
Publisher: Parliamentary & Scientific Committee
Date Established: 1943
Frequency: Quarterly
Cover Price: £16.70
Annual Sub.: £66.80
Circulation: 1,300 (Publisher's Statement)
Usual Pagination: 64
Editor: Annabel Lloyd; **Advertising Manager:** Annabel Lloyd
Summary of Content: Journal providing the scientific community with an insight into the information and briefings supplied to members of Parliament on scientific subjects. Topics covered include policy issues and activities, legislation and selected debates.
Readership/Target Audience: Aimed at members of the House of Commons and the House of Lords, research organisations, universities, libraries and members of the EU Parliament.
ADVERTISING RATES:
Full Page Mono £480.00
Average advertising content per issue: 15%
BUSINESS: APPLIED SCIENCE & LABORATORIES

THE SCIENCE REPORTER
40127U55-155
Editorial Address: Wellcome Wolfson Building, 165 Queen's Gate, LONDON, SW7 5HE **Tel:** 0870 770 3361
Fax: 0870 770 7102
Email: press@kenward.eu
Advertising Address: As above.
Web site: http://www.absw.org.uk
Publisher: Association of British Science Writers - ABSW
Frequency: Quarterly
Free to qualifying individuals
Circulation: 800 (Publisher's Statement)
Usual Pagination: 4
Editor: Ted Nield
Summary of Content: Newsletter containing news, features and comment about science journalism.
Readership/Target Audience: Read by science communicators.
BUSINESS: APPLIED SCIENCE & LABORATORIES

SCIENTIFIC COMPUTING WORLD
36124U55-157
Editorial Address: The Spectrum Building, Michael Young Centre, Purbeck Road, CAMBRIDGE, CB2 8PD
Tel: 01223 211147 **Fax:** 01223 211107
Email: editor.scw@europascience.com
Advertising Address: As above.
Email: sales.scw@europascience.com
Web site: http://www.scientific-computing.com
ISSN: 1356-7853
Publisher: Europa Science Ltd
Date Established: 1994
Frequency: 6 issues yearly
Free to qualifying individuals
Annual Sub.: £95.00
Circulation: 15,475 (ABC 01/01/2008 to 31/12/2008)
Usual Pagination: 52
Summary of Content: Magazine covering the application of computing to questions facing researchers in science technology and medicine, especially physical, chemical, maths, statistics, engineering and life sciences.
Readership/Target Audience: Aimed at engineers, scientists, statisticians and mathematicians in industrial and academic environments across all areas of science, technology, medicine and life sciences.
ADVERTISING RATES:
Full Page Colour £3750.00
Agency Commission: 10%
Mechanical Data: Film: Digital, Type Area: 270 x 200mm, Col Length: 270mm, Page Width: 200mm, Bleed Size: 288 x 219mm, Trim Size: 282 x 213mm
Copy instructions: Copy Date: 7 days prior to publication date
Average advertising content per issue: 40%
BUSINESS: APPLIED SCIENCE & LABORATORIES

SCOOTER TRADE AND INDUSTRY
633782U31B-31
Editorial Address: 97 Front Street, Whickham, NEWCASTLE UPON TYNE, NE16 4JL **Tel:** 0191 488 1947
Email: office@tradeandindustry.net
Advertising Address: As above.
Email: kate@tradeandindustry.net
Web site: http://www.tradeandindustry.net
Publisher: KSA Partnership
Date Established: 2000
Frequency: 6 issues yearly
Cover Price: Free
Circulation: 2,600 (Publisher's Statement)
Editor: Peter Lumley; **Advertisement Director:** Kate Spencer; **Publisher:** Peter Lumley
Summary of Content: Magazine covering the news, developments and trends of the British scooter trade.
Readership/Target Audience: Aimed at retailers, distributors and manufacturers and sent as pdf to personal inboxes of executives all over the world.
ADVERTISING RATES:
Full Page Colour £1148.00
Agency Commission: 10%
Mechanical Data: Type Area: 260 x 183mm, Col Length: 260mm, Page Width: 183mm, Film: Digital
Copy instructions: Copy Date: Last week of the month prior to publication date
Average advertising content per issue: 40%
BUSINESS: MOTOR TRADE: Motorcycle Trade

SCOTS AUTO SCENE
1665350U31A-385
Editorial Address: 34 Bernard Street, EDINBURGH, EH6 6PR **Tel:** 0131 554 1129 **Fax:** 0131 555 1622
Email: tony@belljohnstone.co.uk
Advertising Address: As above. **Fax:** 0131 553 1622
Email: johnboyle@belljohnstone.co.uk
Web site: http://www.belljohnstone.co.uk
Publisher: Bell Johnstone Communications
Date Established: 2003
Frequency: Monthly - Published in the 1st week of the cover month
Free to qualifying individuals
Circulation: 7,500 (Publisher's Statement)
Editor: Tony Wood; **Managing Editor:** Tony Wood
Summary of Content: Magazine focusing on the automotive industry including sales, parts, manufacture and repair market.
Readership/Target Audience: Aimed at decision makers within the automotive industry.
ADVERTISING RATES:
Full Page Colour £1755.00
Agency Commission: 10%
Mechanical Data: Bleed Size: 303 x 216mm, Trim Size: 297 x 210mm, Film: Digital, Type Area: 270 x 190mm, Col Length: 270mm, Page Width: 190mm
Copy instructions: Copy Date: Last week of the month prior to publication
Average advertising content per issue: 55%
BUSINESS: MOTOR TRADE: Motor Trade Accessories

THE SCOTS LAW TIMES
39234U44-1740
Editorial Address: 21 Alva Street, EDINBURGH, EH2 4PS
Tel: 0131 225 4879 **Fax:** 0131 225 2104
Email: slt@wgreen.co.uk
Advertising Address: As above.
Email: alan.bett@thomson.com
Web site: http://www.wgreen.co.uk
ISSN: 0036-908X
Publisher: W. Green Thomson Reuters
Date Established: 1893
Frequency: 40 issues yearly
Annual Sub.: £730.00
Circulation: 700 (Publisher's Statement)
Usual Pagination: 48
Editor: Rebecca Standing; **Advertising Manager:** Alan Bett
Summary of Content: Law journal containing case reports, news, information and related articles.
Readership/Target Audience: Aimed at the legal profession in Scotland.
ADVERTISING RATES:
Full Page Mono £400.00
Agency Commission: 10%
Mechanical Data: Print Process: Litho, Film: Digital, Col Widths (Display): 76mm, No. of Columns (Display): 2, Type Area: 235 x 159mm, Col Length: 235mm, Page Width: 159mm
Copy instructions: Copy Date: Friday prior to publication date
Average advertising content per issue: 10%
BUSINESS: LEGAL

SCOTTISH BUSINESS INSIDER
41450U63D-710
Editorial Address: Onesixty, 160 Dundee Street, EDINBURGH, EH11 1DQ **Tel:** 0131 535 5555
Fax: 0131 220 1203
Email: research@insider.co.uk
Advertising Address: As above.
Email: sales@insider.co.uk
Web site: http://www.insider.co.uk
ISSN: 0952-1488
Publisher: Trinity Mirror
Date Established: 1984
Frequency: 11 issues yearly - Published in the 1st week of the cover month
Annual Sub.: £36.00
Circulation: 13,042 (ABC 01/07/2007 to 30/06/2008)
Usual Pagination: 88
Editor: Alasdair Northrop; **Advertising Manager:** David Hughes
Summary of Content: Magazine covering business and politics, corporate finance, IT, commercial property and management issues in Scotland.
Readership/Target Audience: Read by decision makers in the business and professional world.
ADVERTISING RATES:
Full Page Colour £2600.00
Agency Commission: 15%
Mechanical Data: Col Length: 273mm, Page Width: 178mm, Type Area: 273 x 178mm, Bleed Size: 305 x 218mm, Trim Size: 297 x 210mm, Film: Digital
Copy instructions: Copy Date: 4 weeks prior to publication date
Average advertising content per issue: 40%
BUSINESS: REGIONAL BUSINESS: Regional Business Scotland

SCOTTISH CHEMIST REVIEW
634842U37-62_50
Editorial Address: 10 Dargan Crescent, Duncrue Industrial Estate, BELFAST, BT3 9JP **Tel:** 028 9077 5500
Fax: 028 9055 6808
Email: kelly.eastwood@nimedical.info
Advertising Address: As above.
Email: donna.hosking@nimedical.info
Publisher: Medical Communications Ltd
Date Established: 2001
Frequency: 11 issues yearly - Published in the middle of the cover month
Free to qualifying individuals
Annual Sub.: £47.00
Circulation: 4,000 (Publisher's Statement)
Usual Pagination: 58
Editor: Kelly Jo Eastwood
Summary of Content: Journal covering news and developments within the pharmaceutical and healthcare industry.
Readership/Target Audience: Aimed at pharmacists in Scotland, decision makers in the Department of Health and Community Care, representatives of the industry, wholesalers, generic manufacturers and distributors in Scotland and England.
ADVERTISING RATES:
Full Page Colour £1565.00
Agency Commission: 10%
Mechanical Data: Col Length: 267mm, Page Width: 180mm, Bleed Size: 307 x 220mm, Trim Size: 297 x 210mm, Type Area: 267 x 180mm, Film: Digital

Copy instructions: Copy Date: 2 weeks prior to publication date
BUSINESS: PHARMACEUTICAL & CHEMISTS

SCOTTISH DENTIST
40397U56D-200

Editorial Address: 426 Drumoyne Road, GLASGOW, G51 4DA **Tel:** 0141 810 9003 **Fax:** 0141 810 9009
Email: editorial@inpositionmedia.co.uk
Advertising Address: As above. **Tel:** 0141 810 9001
Fax: 0141 810 9010
Email: advertising@inpositionmedia.co.uk
Web site: http://www.inpositionmedia.co.uk
ISSN: 0967-9537
Publisher: In Position Media Ltd
Frequency: 6 issues yearly
Free to qualifying individuals
Annual Sub.: £48.00
Circulation: 3,500 (Publisher's Statement)
Usual Pagination: 56
Editor: Bruce Oxley; **Managing Director:** Gary Friar
Summary of Content: Journal featuring clinical guidelines, news and advice, financial information, IT and product reviews.
Readership/Target Audience: Read mainly by dentists in Scotland.
ADVERTISING RATES:
Full Page Mono £500.00
Full Page Colour £750.00
Agency Commission: 10%
Mechanical Data: Type Area: 270 x 180mm, Col Length: 270mm, Bleed Size: 303 x 216mm, Trim Size: 297 x 210mm, Film: Digital, Page Width: 180mm
Copy instructions: Copy Date: End of 1st week prior to publication date
Average advertising content per issue: 50%
BUSINESS: HEALTH & MEDICAL: Dental

SCOTTISH EDUCATIONAL JOURNAL
40984U62A-450

Editorial Address: 46 Moray Place, EDINBURGH, EH3 6BH **Tel:** 0131 225 6244 **Fax:** 0131 220 3151
Email: bcooper@eis.org.uk
Advertising Address: As above.
Email: sharris@eis.org.uk
Web site: http://www.eis.org.uk
Publisher: Educational Institute of Scotland, Edinburgh
Frequency: 6 issues yearly
Cover Price: Free
Circulation: 64,000 (Publisher's Statement)
Usual Pagination: 32
Editor: Brian Cooper; **Advertising Manager:** Sheila Harris; **Managing Editor:** Simon Macaulay
Summary of Content: Magazine covering issues from nursery, primary, secondary and special schools through to further and higher education.
Readership/Target Audience: Read by teachers and lecturers in nursery, primary, secondary, special schools and further and higher education. Also read by MSPs, MPs, Local Authorities and others in education sector.
ADVERTISING RATES:
Full Page Colour £1917.00
Agency Commission: 10%
Mechanical Data: Film: Digital, Type Area: 269 x 186mm, Col Length: 269mm, Page Width: 186mm, Bleed Size: 303 x 216mm, Trim Size: 297 x 210mm
Copy instructions: Copy Date: 4 weeks prior to publication date
Average advertising content per issue: 15%
BUSINESS: CHURCH & SCHOOL EQUIPMENT & EDUCATION: Education

SCOTTISH EDUCATIONAL REVIEW
40997U62A-460

Editorial Address: The Stirling Institue of Education, University of Stirling, STIRLING, FK9 4LA **Tel:** 01786 467600
Fax: 01786 467633
Email: m.r.priestley@stir.ac.uk
ISSN: 0141-9072
Publisher: SER Editorial Board
Date Established: 1969
Frequency: Half-yearly - Published in May and November
Annual Sub.: £30.00
Circulation: 2,000 (Publisher's Statement)
Usual Pagination: 100
Editor: Mark Priestley
Summary of Content: Publication containing academic articles on all aspects of education, research reports, book reviews and regular reports on educational matters in the Scottish Parliament.
Readership/Target Audience: Aimed at those with an interest in education in universities, schools, local authorities and government.
ADVERTISING: No Advertising taken
BUSINESS: CHURCH & SCHOOL EQUIPMENT & EDUCATION: Education

THE SCOTTISH FARMER
37918U21J-270

Editorial Address: 200 Renfield Street, GLASGOW, G2 3QB
Tel: 0141 302 7732 **Fax:** 0141 302 7799
Email: alasdair.fletcher@thescottishfarmer.co.uk
Advertising Address: As above. **Tel:** 0141 302 7777
Fax: 0141 302 7796
Email: farmer.sales@thescottishfarmer.co.uk
Web site: http://www.thescottishfarmer.co.uk
ISSN: 0036-9195
Publisher: Newsquest (Herald and Times) Ltd
Date Established: 1893
Frequency: Weekly
Cover Price: £2.00
Annual Sub.: £90.00
Circulation: 18,755 (ABC 01/01/2008 to 31/12/2008)
Usual Pagination: 44
Editor: Ken Fletcher; **News Editor:** Gordon Davidson;
Advertising Manager: Susan Howie
Summary of Content: Journal covering new developments in livestock, arable and farm machinery.
Readership/Target Audience: Aimed at farmers in Scotland.
ADVERTISING RATES:
Full Page Mono £2400.00
Full Page Colour £2400.00
Agency Commission: 10%
Mechanical Data: Page Width: 272mm, Col Length: 365mm, Film: Digital, No. of Columns (Display): 6, Type Area: 365 x 272mm, Bleed Size: 396 x 300mm, Trim Size: 390 x 295mm
Copy instructions: Copy Date: 10 days prior to publication date
Average advertising content per issue: 50%
BUSINESS: AGRICULTURE & FARMING: Agriculture & Farming - Regional

SCOTTISH FARMING LEADER
37794U21A-970

Formerly: Scottish Farming Leader Update
Editorial Address: Rural Centre-West Mains, Ingliston, NEWBRIDGE, EH28 8LT **Tel:** 0131 472 4020
Fax: 0131 472 4010
Email: nfus@nfus.org.uk
Advertising Address: Associa Ltd, Agriculture House, North Gate, Uppingham, OAKHAM, LE15 9PL **Tel:** 01572 824600
Fax: 01572 824651
Email: david.leach-davies@associa.co.uk
Web site: http://www.nfus.org.uk
ISSN: 0967-5094
Publisher: NFU Scotland
Date Established: 1958
Frequency: Monthly
Cover Price: £2.95
Free to qualifying individuals
Circulation: 12,000 (Publisher's Statement)
Usual Pagination: 24
Editor: Anna Davies
Summary of Content: Magazine of the National Farmer's Union within Scotland.
Readership/Target Audience: Aimed at farmers.
ADVERTISING RATES:
Full Page Mono £660.00
Full Page Colour £825.00
Agency Commission: 10%
Mechanical Data: Type Area: 263 x 182mm, Col Length: 263mm, Page Width: 182mm, Bleed Size: +3mm, Trim Size: 297 x 210mm, Film: Digital
Copy instructions: Copy Date: 3 weeks prior to publication date
BUSINESS: AGRICULTURE & FARMING

SCOTTISH FORESTRY
39467U46-30

Editorial Address: Fowlers, Witney Lane, Stonesfield, WITNEY, OX29 8DN **Tel:** 01993 891872
Email: editor@rsfs.org.uk
Advertising Address: Impact Services Ltd, 2 Home farm, ARBROATH, DD11 4RW **Tel:** 01241 830373
Fax: 01241 830373
Email: rsfs@impactservicesltd.com
Web site: http://www.rsfs.org.uk
ISSN: 0036-9217
Publisher: Royal Scottish Forestry Society
Date Established: 1858
Frequency: Quarterly
Cover Price: £15.00
Free to qualifying individuals
Annual Sub.: £52.50
Circulation: 3,000 (Publisher's Statement)
Usual Pagination: 48
Editor: Gavin Strachan; **Advertising Manager:** Heather Murphy
Summary of Content: Magazine containing technical and news articles covering up-to-date developments in forestry relevant to Scotland.
Readership/Target Audience: Aimed at members of the Society, learned bodies and libraries.
ADVERTISING RATES:
Full Page Colour £600.00
Agency Commission: 10%

Mechanical Data: Type Area: 276 x 183mm, Col Length: 276mm, Trim Size: 297 x 210mm, Page Width: 183mm, Film: Digital, Bleed Size: 303 x 216mm
Copy instructions: Copy Date: Last day of the month prior to publication date
Average advertising content per issue: 30%
BUSINESS: TIMBER, WOOD & FORESTRY

THE SCOTTISH FRANCHISE MAGAZINE
1691299U14A-548

Editorial Address: Franchise House, 56 Surrey Street, NORWICH, NR1 3FD **Tel:** 01603 620301 **Fax:** 01603 630174
Email: stuarta@fdsltd.com
Advertising Address: As above.
Email: enquiries@fdsltd.com
Web site: http://www.scottishfranchisemagazine.net
Publisher: Franchise Development Services Ltd
Date Established: 2005
Frequency: Annual - Published in June
Free to qualifying individuals
Editor: Stuart Anderson; **Advertising Manager:** Stuart Anderson
Summary of Content: Magazine covering advice and guidance to perspective and existing franchisees.
Readership/Target Audience: Aimed at individuals seeking to operate a franchise.
ADVERTISING RATES:
Full Page Colour £995.00
Agency Commission: 10%
Mechanical Data: Type Area: 270 x 190mm, Bleed Size: 303 x 213mm, Trim Size: 297 x 210mm, Col Length: 270mm, Page Width: 190mm, Film: Digital
Copy instructions: Copy Date: 2 weeks prior to publication date
Average advertising content per issue: 75%
BUSINESS: COMMERCE, INDUSTRY & MANAGEMENT

SCOTTISH GROCER
37982U22A-300

Editorial Address: Bergius House, 20 Clifton Street, GLASGOW, G3 7LA **Tel:** 0141 567 6000 **Fax:** 0141 331 1395
Email: natalie.minnis@peeblesmedia.com
Advertising Address: As above. **Tel:** 0141 567 6021
Fax: 0141 353 1784
Email: lucie.cooney@peeblesmedia.com
Web site: http://www.peeblesmedia.com
Publisher: Peebles Media Group Ltd.
Frequency: Monthly - Published on the 1st Friday of the cover month
Free to qualifying individuals
Annual Sub.: £67.00
Circulation: 8,217 (ABC 01/07/2008 to 30/06/2009)
Usual Pagination: 100
Editor: Natalie Minnis; **Managing Director:** Yvonne Bremner; **Advertising Manager:** Lucie Cooney
Summary of Content: Magazine covering the Scottish independent retail sector, including comprehensive coverage of the take home drinks trade.
Readership/Target Audience: Read by the independent retail sector.
ADVERTISING RATES:
Full Page Colour £1620.00
Agency Commission: 10%
Mechanical Data: Type Area: 270 x 188mm, Bleed Size: 303 x 216mm, Trim Size: 297 x 210mm, Col Length: 270mm, Col Widths (Display): 47mm, No. of Columns (Display): 4, Page Width: 188mm, Film: Digital
Copy instructions: Copy Date: 3 weeks prior to publication date
Average advertising content per issue: 45%
Supplement(s): Fine Food Scotland - 4xY, Merchandising Scotland - 1xY
BUSINESS: FOOD

SCOTTISH JOURNAL OF GEOLOGY
38273U30-122

Editorial Address: Unit 7, Brassmill Enterprise Centre, Brassmill Lane, BATH, BA1 3JN **Tel:** 01225 445046
Fax: 01225 442836
Email: sally.oberst@geolsoc.org.uk
Web site: http://www.geolsoc.org.uk/pubs/journals/sjg.htm
ISSN: 0036-9276
Publisher: The Geological Society Publishing House
Frequency: Half-yearly
Annual Sub.: £160.00
Circulation: 1,500 (Publisher's Statement)
Usual Pagination: 96
Editor: Sally Oberst
Summary of Content: Journal containing review papers and papers on broader aspects of the earth sciences that cannot be discussed solely in terms of Scottish geology.
Readership/Target Audience: Aimed at professionals and academics in this field.
ADVERTISING: No Advertising taken
BUSINESS: MINING & QUARRYING

Business Magazines

THE SCOTTISH LAW DIRECTORY
39301U44-1750

Editorial Address: 2 Addiscombe Road, CROYDON, CR9 5AF **Tel:** 020 7400 4666 **Fax:** 020 7400 4697
Email: katrina.windett@lexisnexis.co.uk
Advertising Address: As above. **Tel:** 020 7400 2500
Email: richard.macey@lexisnexis.co.uk
ISSN: 0800-8083
Publisher: LexisNexis
Date Established: 1892
Frequency: Annual - Published in April
Cover Price: £62.95
Circulation: 4,500 (Publisher's Statement)
Usual Pagination: 1200
Editor: Katrina Windett
Summary of Content: Publication containing official lists of certificated solicitors practising in Scotland, by authority of the Law Society of Scotland.
Readership/Target Audience: Aimed at solicitors, central and local government, law courts and public companies.
ADVERTISING RATES:
Full Page Mono £875.00
Full Page Colour £1200.00
Mechanical Data: Type Area: 173 x 110mm, Film: Digital, Col Length: 173mm, Page Width: 110mm
Copy instructions: Copy Date: February 28th
BUSINESS: LEGAL

SCOTTISH LAW GAZETTE
39235U44-1760

Editorial Address: Dundee Business School, Old College, Bell Street, DUNDEE, DD1 1HG **Tel:** 01382 308401
Fax: 01382 308400
Email: ken@swinton98.freeserve.co.uk
Advertising Address: 166 Buchanan Street, GLASGOW, G1 2LW **Tel:** 0141 332 3536 **Fax:** 0141 353 3819
Email: secretary@slas.co.uk
Web site: http://www.slas.co.uk
ISSN: 0036-9314
Publisher: The Scottish Law Agents Society
Date Established: 1933
Frequency: 6 issues yearly
Free to qualifying individuals
Annual Sub.: £65.00
Circulation: 1,850 (Publisher's Statement)
Usual Pagination: 40
Editor: Kenneth Swinton; **Advertising Manager:** Michael Sheridan
Summary of Content: Journal of The Scottish Law Agents Society, containing articles on all aspects of Scottish law.
Readership/Target Audience: Aimed at Scottish solicitors, trainees and students of law.
ADVERTISING RATES:
Full Page Mono £220.00
Mechanical Data: Trim Size: 297 x 210mm, Film: Digital
Copy instructions: Copy Date: 4 weeks prior to publication date
Average advertising content per issue: 10%
BUSINESS: LEGAL

SCOTTISH LICENSED TRADE NEWS
36497U9A-158

Editorial Address: Bergius House, 20 Clifton Street, GLASGOW, G3 7LA **Tel:** 0141 567 6000 **Fax:** 0141 331 1395
Email: sltn@peeblesmedia.com
Advertising Address: As above. **Tel:** 0141 567 6021
Fax: 0141 353 1784
Email: lucie.cooney@peeblesmedia.com
Web site: http://www.peeblesmedia.com
Publisher: Peebles Media Group Ltd
Frequency: 24 issues yearly
Free to qualifying individuals
Annual Sub.: £62.00
Circulation: 17,340 (ABC 01/07/2008 to 30/06/2009)
Usual Pagination: 48
Editor: Scott Wright; **Advertising Manager:** Lucie Cooney; **Managing Editor:** Patrick Duffy
Summary of Content: Newspaper for the drinks retailing, hospitality and licensed leisure industries in Scotland. Containing news articles and features on licensing and other laws, licensed business issues, licensed trade representative groups, industry initiatives, products and promotions.
Readership/Target Audience: Aimed at licensees and staff in public houses, hotels, restaurants, entertainment venues, clubs off-sales outlets, licensed grocers and supermarkets in Scotland.
ADVERTISING RATES:
Full Page Colour £2620.00
SCC £14.00
Agency Commission: 10%
Mechanical Data: Type Area: 320 x 227mm, Film: Negative, wrong reading, emulsion side up. Digital, Bleed Size: 346 x 251mm, Trim Size: 340 x 245mm, Col Length: 320mm, Page Width: 227mm, Col Widths (Display): 41mm
Copy instructions: Copy Date: 1 week prior to publication date

Average advertising content per issue: 50%
BUSINESS: DRINKS & LICENSED TRADE: Drinks, Licensed Trade, Wines & Spirits

SCOTTISH LOCAL RETAILER (SLR)
1615661U53-676

Formerly: SLR Scottish Local Retailer
Editorial Address: 2nd Floor Waterloo Chambers, 19 Waterloo Street, GLASGOW, G2 6AY **Tel:** 0141 222 2100
Fax: 0141 222 2177
Email: abegley@55north.com
Advertising Address: As above.
Email: dstephenson@55north.com
Web site: http://www.55north.com
ISSN: 1740-2409
Publisher: William Reed Business Media
Date Established: 2003
Frequency: Monthly - Published in the 1st week of the cover month
Cover Price: Free
Circulation: 8,120 (ABC 01/07/2007 to 30/06/2008)
Usual Pagination: 64
Editor: Antony Begley; **Advertising Manager:** Donald Stephenson
Summary of Content: Magazine covering independent retail trade in Scotland, including product launches, marketplace analysis and ideas for retailers to improve their business.
Readership/Target Audience: Read by managers and owners of local retail stores.
ADVERTISING RATES:
Full Page Colour £1700.00
Agency Commission: 10%
Mechanical Data: Type Area: 267 x 185mm, Bleed Size: 303 x 216mm, Trim Size: 297 x 210mm, Col Length: 267mm, Page Width: 185mm, Film: Digital
Copy instructions: Copy Date: 15th of the month prior to publication date
Average advertising content per issue: 40%
BUSINESS: RETAILING & WHOLESALING

SCOTTISH MEDICAL JOURNAL
40225U56A-135

Editorial Address: Dept. of Surgical Paediatrics, Royal Hospital for Sick Children, York Hill, GLASGOW, G3 8SJ **Tel:** 0141 201 0170 **Fax:** 0141 201 0858
Email: r.carachi@clinmed.gla.ac.uk
Web site: http://www.smj.org.uk
Publisher: Royal College of Physicians and Surgeons of Glasgow
Frequency: Quarterly
Cover Price: £50.00
Circulation: 10,500 (Publisher's Statement)
Usual Pagination: 44
Editor: Robert Carachi
Summary of Content: Journal containing original articles, case reports and historical reports related to medicine.
Readership/Target Audience: Aimed at consultants and all other grades of hospital staff in Scotland.
ADVERTISING: No Advertising taken
BUSINESS: HEALTH & MEDICAL

SCOTTISH PLANNING AND ENVIRONMENTAL LAW
39236U44-1780

Editorial Address: Tontine House, 8 Gordon Street, GLASGOW, G1 3PL **Tel:** 0141 574 1900 **Fax:** 0141 574 1901
Email: tony.burton@idoxplc.com
Advertising Address: As above.
Email: morag.smith@idoxplc.com
Web site: http://www.idoxplc.com
ISSN: 1350-2808
Publisher: Idox
Date Established: 1980
Frequency: 6 issues yearly - Published on the 9th of the cover month
Annual Sub.: £145.00
Circulation: 450 (Publisher's Statement)
Usual Pagination: 24
Editor: Tony Burton; **Advertising Manager:** Morag Smith; **Managing Editor:** Tony Burton
Summary of Content: Publication covering new and impending legislation, regulations, court cases, circulars and government advice on town and country planning and the environment.
Readership/Target Audience: Aimed at lawyers, solicitors, advocates, planners, developers, surveyors, local authorities, public agencies, academics, land and property companies.
ADVERTISING: Rates on application
Copy instructions: Copy Date: 27th of the month prior to publication date
Average advertising content per issue: 20%
BUSINESS: LEGAL

SCOTTISH PRIMARY CARE
24577U56A-171

Editorial Address: 426 Drumoyne Road, GLASGOW, G51 4DA **Tel:** 0141 810 9000 **Fax:** 0141 810 9010
Email: editorial@inpositionmedia.co.uk
Advertising Address: As above. **Fax:** 0141 810 9009
Web site: http://www.inpositionmedia.co.uk
ISSN: 0967-9537
Publisher: In Position Media Ltd
Frequency: Monthly
Free to qualifying individuals
Annual Sub.: £48.00
Circulation: 4,000 (Publisher's Statement)
Usual Pagination: 24
Editor: Bruce Oxley
Summary of Content: Magazine covering clinical practice news and features with the aim of keeping Scottish GPs and primary care teams up to date with devolved healthcare issues in Scotland.
Readership/Target Audience: Aimed at GPs and other members of the primary care team in Scotland.
ADVERTISING RATES:
Full Page Mono £500.00
Full Page Colour £750.00
Agency Commission: 10%
Mechanical Data: Type Area: 270 x 180mm, Bleed Size: 303 x 216mm, Trim Size: 297 x 210mm, Print Process: Litho, Film: Digital, Col Length: 270mm, Page Width: 180mm
Copy instructions: Copy Date: 1st of month prior to publication date
Average advertising content per issue: 50%
BUSINESS: HEALTH & MEDICAL

SCOTTISH RECRUITMENT
22052U14F-67

Editorial Address: 34 Mackintosh Place, South Newmoor Industrial Estate, IRVINE, KA11 4JY **Tel:** 01294 218000
Fax: 01294 213982
Advertising Address: As above.
Email: dstevens@s-un.co.uk
Web site: http://www.scotcareers.co.uk
Publisher: Scottish & Universal Newspapers Ltd
Date Established: 1995
Frequency: Weekly
Cover Price: £1.20
Circulation: 3,500 (Publisher's Statement)
Usual Pagination: 24
Editor: Sheena Thomson; **Advertising Manager:** Sheena Thomson
Summary of Content: Magazine covering recruitment news, training, vocational education, employment law, inward investment, job vacancies and innovations in management.
Readership/Target Audience: Aimed at employers, investors and job seekers.
ADVERTISING RATES:
SCC £9.75
Agency Commission: 10%
Mechanical Data: Type Area: 340 x 265mm, Col Length: 340mm, Page Width: 265mm, No. of Columns (Display): 9, Film: Digital
Copy instructions: Copy Date: Friday 3pm prior to Wednesday publication
Average advertising content per issue: 100%
BUSINESS: COMMERCE, INDUSTRY & MANAGEMENT: Training & Recruitment

SCRATCH
1648837U15A-196

Editorial Address: 1 The Courtyard, Market Square, WESTERHAM, TN16 1AZ **Tel:** 01959 547000
Fax: 01959 565119
Email: helen.forster@scratchmagazine.co.uk
Advertising Address: As above. **Tel:** 01959 569867
Email: scott.derbyshire@scratchmagazine.co.uk
Web site: http://www.scratchmagazine.co.uk
Publisher: Seed Publishing Ltd
Date Established: 2003
Frequency: Monthly
Free to qualifying individuals
Annual Sub.: £30.00
Circulation: 13,230 (ABC 01/07/2008 to 30/06/2009)
Usual Pagination: 96
Editor: Helen Forster; **Advertising Manager:** Scott Derbyshire
Summary of Content: Magazine covering nail industry innovations, news, products, techniques and services. Treatments and services for hand, nail and foot grooming.
Readership/Target Audience: Aimed at nail professionals and beauty therapists.
ADVERTISING RATES:
Full Page Colour £1700.00
SCC £30.00
Agency Commission: 10%
Mechanical Data: Type Area: 276 x 185mm, Bleed Size: 303 x 216mm, Trim Size: 297 x 210mm, Col Length: 276mm, Page Width: 185mm, Film: Digital
Copy instructions: Copy Date: 10th of each month
Average advertising content per issue: 50%
BUSINESS: COSMETICS & HAIRDRESSING: Cosmetics

SCREEN DIGEST
41568U64K-593

Editorial Address: 30-31 Lyme Street, LONDON, NW1 0EE
Tel: 020 7424 2820 **Fax:** 020 7424 2838
Email: guy.bisson@screendigest.com
Web site: http://www.screendigest.com
ISSN: 1475-0171
Publisher: Screen Digest Ltd
Date Established: 1971
Frequency: Monthly
Annual Sub.: £425.00
Usual Pagination: 32
Editor: Guy Bisson; **News Editor:** Guy Bisson; **Executive Editor:** Ben Keen; **Managing Director:** Allan Hardy
Summary of Content: Magazine providing international news, market analysis, statistical research and intelligence on all screen-based entertainment and digital media. Includes film, cinema, video, DVD, television, cable and satellite, the Internet, interactive and other digital media.
Readership/Target Audience: Aimed at senior executives in the media, worldwide.
ADVERTISING: No Advertising taken
BUSINESS: OTHER CLASSIFICATIONS: Cinema Entertainment

SCREEN FINANCE
41569U64K-595

Editorial Address: Mortimer House, 37-41 Mortimer Street, LONDON, W1T 3JH **Tel:** 020 7017 4233 **Fax:** 020 7017 4289
Email: tim.adler@informa.com
Web site: http://www.informatm.com
Publisher: Informa Telecoms and Media Group
Date Established: 2000
Frequency: 23 issues yearly
Annual Sub.: £745.00
Usual Pagination: 12
Editor: Tim Adler
Summary of Content: Magazine covering European film and TV finance.
Readership/Target Audience: Read by accountants, banks and lawyers.
ADVERTISING: No Advertising taken
BUSINESS: OTHER CLASSIFICATIONS: Cinema Entertainment

SCREEN INTERNATIONAL
41570U64K-600

Editorial Address: Greater London House, Hampstead Road, LONDON, NW1 7EJ **Tel:** 020 7728 5000
Email: conor.dignam@emap.com
Advertising Address: As above. **Fax:** 020 7728 5555
Email: clare.bateman-king@emap.com
Web site: http://www.screendaily.com
ISSN: 0307-4617
Publisher: EMAP Inform
Frequency: Weekly - Published every Friday
Cover Price: £3.60
Annual Sub.: £160.00
Circulation: 6,306 (ABC 01/07/2008 to 30/06/2009)
Usual Pagination: 40
Editor: Conor Dignam
Summary of Content: Magazine containing news, statistics and analysis of the issues shaping the international film business.
Readership/Target Audience: Read by senior personnel within the entertainment business.
ADVERTISING RATES:
Full Page Colour £8331.00
Agency Commission: 10%
Mechanical Data: Type Area: 332 x 228mm, Trim Size: 342 x 248mm, Bleed Size: 348 x 254mm, Film: Digital, Col Length: 332mm, Page Width: 228mm
Copy instructions: Copy Date: 1 week prior to publication date
Average advertising content per issue: 55%
BUSINESS: OTHER CLASSIFICATIONS: Cinema Entertainment

SCREEN MEDIA MAGAZINE
1852996U53-708

Editorial Address: 6 Laurence Pountney Hill, LONDON, EC4R 0BL **Tel:** 020 7933 8999
Email: info@screens.tv
Web site: http://www.screens.tv
Publisher: St. John Patrick Publishers Ltd
Frequency: Quarterly
Cover Price: £3.50
Circulation: 6,400 (Publisher's Statement)
Editor: Barnaby Page
Summary of Content: Magazine covering digital signage.
Readership/Target Audience: Aimed at the retail sector, leisure and hospitality industry, transport and public sector, agencies, network owners and integrators.
BUSINESS: RETAILING & WHOLESALING

SCREEN PROCESS AND DIGITAL IMAGING
38943U41A-300

Formerly: Screen Process
Editorial Address: 15A London Road, MAIDSTONE, ME16 8LY **Tel:** 01622 687031 **Fax:** 01622 757646
Email: jbarrett@datateam.co.uk
Advertising Address: As above.
Email: kbyne@datateam.co.uk
Web site: http://www.datateam.co.uk
ISSN: 0953-3338
Publisher: Datateam Publishing Ltd
Frequency: Monthly - Published in the last week of the month prior to the cover month
Cover Price: £5.00
Free to qualifying individuals
Annual Sub.: £70.00
Circulation: 6,994 (ABC 01/01/2008 to 31/12/2008)
Usual Pagination: 48
Editor: Jon Barrett; **Managing Editor:** Jon Barrett
Summary of Content: Journal covering business and technical aspects of screen and digital printing.
Readership/Target Audience: Aimed at screen and digital printers and their suppliers.
ADVERTISING RATES:
Full Page Colour £1842.00
Agency Commission: 10%
Mechanical Data: Type Area: 280 x 195mm, Bleed Size: 312 x 235mm, Trim Size: 306 x 229mm, Col Length: 280mm, Page Width: 195mm
Copy instructions: Copy Date: 2 weeks prior to publication date
Average advertising content per issue: 40%
BUSINESS: PRINTING & STATIONERY: Printing

SCREENTRADE MAGAZINE
753033U64K-605

Editorial Address: PO Box 144, ORPINGTON, BR6 6LZ
Tel: 01689 833117 **Fax:** 01689 833117
Email: philip@screentrademagazine.com
Advertising Address: As above.
Email: advertising@screentrademagazine.com
Web site: http://www.screentrademagazine.co.uk
ISSN: 1476-198X
Publisher: Screentrade Media LTD
Date Established: 2002
Frequency: Quarterly
Cover Price: £7.50
Free to qualifying individuals
Annual Sub.: £29.95
Circulation: 4,600 (Publisher's Statement)
Usual Pagination: 80
Editor: Philip Turner; **Advertising Manager:** Les Waller;
Publisher: Philip Turner
Summary of Content: Magazine providing news, debate, features, opinion and nostalgia on the British and European cinema exhibition and film distribution industries.
Readership/Target Audience: Aimed at cinema management, film distributors, projectionists, floor staff, industry service providers, trade, film and cinema society members and other enthusiasts worldwide.
ADVERTISING RATES:
Full Page Colour £1500.00
Agency Commission: 10%
Mechanical Data: Trim Size: 297 x 230mm, Bleed Size: 303 x 236mm, Film: Digital
Copy instructions: Copy Date: 5th of the publication month
BUSINESS: OTHER CLASSIFICATIONS: Cinema Entertainment

SDUK
40659U57-30_38

Formerly: Green Government
Editorial Address: 9th Floor, St James's Building, Oxford Street, MANCHESTER, M1 6PP **Tel:** 0161 211 3000
Email: editorial@govnet.co.uk
Advertising Address: Golden Cross House, 8 Duncannon Street, LONDON, WC2N 4JF **Tel:** 020 7484 5246
Fax: 020 484 4950
Email: richard.holloway@govnet.co.uk
Web site: http://www.govnet.co.uk/publications/sduk/articles
ISSN: 1464-956X
Publisher: GovNet Communications
Date Established: 1997
Frequency: Quarterly
Free to qualifying individuals
Annual Sub.: £90.00
Circulation: 8,032 (ABC 01/01/2008 to 31/12/2008)
Usual Pagination: 64
Editor: Felicity King-Evans; **Managing Director:** Joanne Walsh; **Advertising Manager:** Maria Figgins
Summary of Content: Magazine with a focus on sustainability and environmental issues in all government policy and procedure. Also reports on management and technological issues in the environment and energy sectors.
Readership/Target Audience: Aimed at decision-makers throughout central, regional and local government.
ADVERTISING RATES:
Full Page Colour £3995.00

THE SEA
39348U45A-152

Editorial Address: St. Michael Paternoster Royal, College Hill, LONDON, EC4R 2RL **Tel:** 020 7248 5202
Fax: 020 7248 4761
Email: thesea@mtsmail.org
Web site: http://www.missiontoseafarers.org
Publisher: The Mission to Seafarers
Frequency: 6 issues yearly
Free to qualifying individuals
Annual Sub.: £1.50
Circulation: 29,500 (Publisher's Statement)
Usual Pagination: 8
Editor: Gillian Ennis
Summary of Content: Newspaper containing news and information about the shipping industry.
Language(s): Chinese; English; Russian; Spanish
Readership/Target Audience: Aimed at Merchant Navy seafarers of all nationalities.
ADVERTISING: No Advertising taken
BUSINESS: MARINE & SHIPPING

SEA BREEZES
39349U45A-152_50

Editorial Address: Media House, Cronkbourne, Douglas, ISLE OF MAN, IM4 4SB **Tel:** 01624 696573
Fax: 01624 661655
Email: seabreezes@manninmedia.co.im
Advertising Address: As above.
Email: seabreezes@manninmedia.co.im
Web site: http://www.seabreezes.co.im
ISSN: 0036-9977
Publisher: Sea Breezes Publications Ltd
Date Established: 1919
Frequency: Monthly
Cover Price: £3.25
Annual Sub.: £39.00
Circulation: 17,500 (Publisher's Statement)
Usual Pagination: 44
Editor: Andrew Douglas; **Advertising Manager:** Steve Robinson
Summary of Content: Publication containing marine historical and technical data, reports on merchant and naval ships and seamen and the sea.
Readership/Target Audience: Read by serving and former members of the Royal and Merchant Navy, plus those with a vocational interest in ships and the seas.
ADVERTISING RATES:
Full Page Mono £295.00
Full Page Colour £375.00
SCC £45.00
Agency Commission: 15%
Mechanical Data: Page Width: 186mm, Type Area: 270 x 186mm, Bleed Size: 305 x 215mm, Trim Size: 297 x 210mm, Col Length: 270mm, Film: Positive, right reading, emulsion side down. Digital, Screen: 60 lpc, Print Process: Offset litho
Copy instructions: Copy Date: 2 weeks prior to publication date
BUSINESS: MARINE & SHIPPING

SEAFOOD INTERNATIONAL
38036U22G-210

Editorial Address: 6th Floor, Eldon House, 2 Eldon Street, LONDON, EC2M 7LS **Tel:** 020 7650 1037
Email: jason.holland@intrafish.com
Advertising Address: As above. **Fax:** 020 7017 4536
Email: daniel.rich@intrafish.com
Web site: http://www.seafood-international.com
ISSN: 0268-1293
Publisher: IntraFish Media AS
Date Established: 1986
Frequency: Monthly - Published around the 1st of the cover month
Circulation: 6,153 (Publisher's Statement)
Usual Pagination: 52
Editor: Jason Holland
Summary of Content: Magazine with worldwide coverage on the fish trade and seafood industry. Includes news, reviews and reports on all aspects of the seafood industry.
Language(s): Chinese; English
Readership/Target Audience: Aimed at seafood professionals, from farming to supermarkets.
ADVERTISING RATES:
Full Page Mono £1665.00
Full Page Colour £2680.00
Agency Commission: 10%
Mechanical Data: No. of Columns (Display): 4, Type Area: 315 x 220mm, Col Length: 315mm, Page Width: 220mm, Trim Size: 335 x 240mm, Bleed Size: 341 x 246mm
Copy instructions: Copy Date: 20th of the month prior to publication date

First entry (top right column continuation):
Agency Commission: 10%
Mechanical Data: Type Area: 255 x 190mm, Bleed Size: 281 x 216mm, Trim Size: 275 x 210mm, Col Length: 275mm, Page Width: 190mm, Film: Digital
Copy instructions: Copy Date: 4 weeks prior to publication date
Average advertising content per issue: 50%
BUSINESS: ENVIRONMENT & POLLUTION

Average advertising content per issue: 35%
BUSINESS: FOOD: Fish Trade

SEAFOOD PROCESSOR
1743627U22C-504

Editorial Address: 6th Floor, Eldon House, 2 Eldon Street, LONDON, EC2M 7LS **Tel:** 020 7017 4522
Email: velo.mitrovich@intrafish.com
Advertising Address: As above. **Tel:** 020 7650 1037
Fax: 020 7017 4536
Email: daniel.rich@intrafish.com
Web site: http://www.seafoodprocessor.com
Publisher: IntraFish Media AS
Frequency: Monthly - Published around the 28th of the month prior to cover month
Annual Sub.: £85.00
Circulation: 6,500 (Publisher's Statement)
Editor: Velo Mitrovich
Summary of Content: Publication focusing on the seafood processing industry with features on equipment developments, packaging, cold storage, logistics, research and development and company news.
Readership/Target Audience: Aimed at seafood processing companies, factory managers and equipment manufacturers.
ADVERTISING RATES:
Full Page Mono £1665.00
Full Page Colour £2680.00
Agency Commission: 10%
Mechanical Data: Type Area: 315 x 220mm, Bleed Size: 341 x 246mm, Trim Size: 335 x 240mm, Col Length: 315mm, Page Width: 220mm, Film: Digital, No. of Columns (Display): 4, Print Process: Litho
Copy instructions: Copy Date: 20th of the month prior to publication date
Average advertising content per issue: 35%
BUSINESS: FOOD: Food Processing & Packaging

SEALING TECHNOLOGY NEWSLETTER
37636U19D-590

Editorial Address: The Boulevard, Langford Lane, KIDLINGTON, OX5 1GB **Tel:** 01865 843239
Fax: 01865 843933
Email: s.barrett@elsevier.com
Web site: http://www.sealingtechnology.info
ISSN: 1350-4789
Publisher: Elsevier Ltd
Date Established: 1994
Frequency: Monthly
Annual Sub.: EUR1112.00
Circulation: 4,000 (Publisher's Statement)
Usual Pagination: 16
Editor: Steve Barrett
Summary of Content: Newsletter covering all aspects of fluid sealing technology and materials, including applications.
Readership/Target Audience: Aimed at seal designers and manufacturers, consultants, designers, engineers and seal end-users.
ADVERTISING: No Advertising taken
BUSINESS: ENGINEERING & MACHINERY: Hydraulic Power

SEATRADE
39400U45C-130

Editorial Address: Seatrade House, 42 North Station Road, COLCHESTER, CO1 1RB **Tel:** 01206 545121
Fax: 01206 545190
Email: nnadkarni@seatrade-global.com
Advertising Address: As above.
Email: sales@seatrade-global.com
Web site: http://www.seatrade-global.com
ISSN: 0964-8895
Publisher: Seatrade Communications Ltd
Date Established: 1970
Frequency: 6 issues yearly - Published in the 2nd week of the 1st cover month
Annual Sub.: £85.00
Circulation: 6,426 (ABC 01/01/2008 to 31/12/2008)
Usual Pagination: 80
Editor: Bob Jaques; **Managing Director:** Christopher Hayman; **Publisher:** Christopher Hayman
Summary of Content: Magazine containing analysis of the latest worldwide maritime news and information, with surveys of various geographic areas and maritime-related subjects.
Readership/Target Audience: Read by directors and management in shipping and related industries.
ADVERTISING RATES:
Full Page Colour £3100.00
Agency Commission: 10%
Mechanical Data: Trim Size: 297 x 210mm, Bleed Size: 303 x 216mm
Copy instructions: Copy Date: 4 weeks prior to publication date
BUSINESS: MARINE & SHIPPING: Maritime Freight

SEATRADE CRUISE REVIEW
39399U45C-140

Editorial Address: Seatrade House, 42 North Station Road, COLCHESTER, CO1 1RB **Tel:** 01206 545121
Fax: 01206 545190
Email: editorial@seatrade-global.com
Advertising Address: As above.
Email: ivernau@seatrade-global.com
Web site: http://www.seatrade-global.com
ISSN: 1367-1774
Publisher: Seatrade Communications Ltd
Date Established: 1996
Frequency: Quarterly - Published in the 1st week of the cover month
Annual Sub.: £72.00
Circulation: 6,286 (ABC 01/01/2008 to 31/12/2008)
Editor: Mary Bond
Summary of Content: Journal covering the global cruise industry.
Readership/Target Audience: Aimed at directors, managers, executives and other named contacts in the cruise, ferry and related industries.
ADVERTISING RATES:
Full Page Colour £3420.00
Agency Commission: 10%
Mechanical Data: Page Width: 178mm, Type Area: 254 x 178mm, Col Length: 254mm, Film: Digital, Trim Size: 297 x 210mm, Bleed Size: 303 x 216mm
Copy instructions: Copy Date: 4 weeks prior to publication date
Average advertising content per issue: 40%
BUSINESS: MARINE & SHIPPING: Maritime Freight

SEAWAYS
39350U45A-155

Editorial Address: 202 Lambeth Road, LONDON, SE1 7LQ **Tel:** 020 7928 1351 **Fax:** 020 7401 2817
Email: clairew@nildram.co.uk
Advertising Address: Tony Stein and Associates, 12 Braehead, BO'NESS, EH51 0BZ **Tel:** 01506 828800
Email: tony.r.stein@btinternet.com
Web site: http://www.nautinst.org
ISSN: 0144-1019
Publisher: The Nautical Institute
Frequency: Monthly
Annual Sub.: £65.00
Circulation: 7,500 (Publisher's Statement)
Usual Pagination: 36
Editor: Claire Walsh; **Advertising Manager:** Tony Stein
Summary of Content: The Journal of the Nautical Institute; covering maritime subjects, marine equipment and professional issues.
Readership/Target Audience: Read by members of the Nautical Institute and others in control of seagoing vessels.
ADVERTISING RATES:
Full Page Mono £1378.00
Full Page Colour £1678.00
Agency Commission: 10%
Mechanical Data: Trim Size: 297 x 210mm, Film: Digital, Bleed Size: 303 x 216 mm, Type Area: 267 x 180mm, Col Length: 267mm, Page Width: 180mm
BUSINESS: MARINE & SHIPPING

SECED
1615357U62B-1404

Editorial Address: St. Jude's Church, Dulwich Road, LONDON, SE24 0PB **Tel:** 020 7501 6771
Fax: 020 7326 8319
Email: pete.h@markallengroup.com
Advertising Address: As above. **Tel:** 020 7501 6735
Fax: 020 7326 4835
Email: jonb@markallengroup.com
Web site: http://www.sec-ed.com
ISSN: 1479-7704
Publisher: MA Education Ltd
Date Established: 2003
Frequency: 38 issues yearly
Cover Price: £1.00
Free to qualifying individuals
Circulation: 15,000 (Publisher's Statement)
Usual Pagination: 20
Editor: Pete Henshaw
Summary of Content: Newspaper covering news stories and features relating to secondary education and recruitment section.
Readership/Target Audience: Aimed at secondary school teachers.
ADVERTISING RATES:
Full Page Colour £4950.00
SCC £19.99
Agency Commission: 10%
Mechanical Data: Film: Digital, Type Area: 380 x 277mm, Col Length: 380mm, Page Width: 277mm, Bleed Size: 426 x 303mm, Trim Size: 420 x 297mm
Copy instructions: Copy Date: Friday 4pm prior to publication date
Average advertising content per issue: 50%
BUSINESS: CHURCH & SCHOOL EQUIPMENT & EDUCATION: Education Teachers

SECURE TIMES
39920U54C-101

Editorial Address: 50 Queens Road, BUCKHURST HILL, IG9 5DD **Tel:** 020 8504 1661 **Fax:** 020 8505 4336
Email: secure@sheenpublishing.co.uk
Advertising Address: As above.
Email: tina@sheenpublishing.co.uk
Web site: http://www.sheenpublishing.co.uk
ISSN: 1471-3063
Publisher: Sheen Publishing Ltd
Frequency: 3 issues yearly - Published in February, June and October
Circulation: 9,002 (Publisher's Statement)
Editor: Tony Prior; **Advertising Manager:** Tina Oberman; **Publisher:** Carole Titmuss
Summary of Content: Journal providing news and information on all fire, safety and security matters.
Readership/Target Audience: Aimed at fire, safety and security professionals, specifiers and builders.
ADVERTISING RATES:
Full Page Mono £675.00
Full Page Colour £750.00
Agency Commission: 10%
Mechanical Data: Type Area: 260 x 184mm, Bleed Size: 300 x 218mm, Trim Size: 296 x 210mm, Film: Digital, Col Length: 260mm, Page Width: 184mm
Copy instructions: Copy Date: 2 weeks prior to publication date
Average advertising content per issue: 20%
Supplement to: reFURB
BUSINESS: SAFETY & SECURITY: Security

SECURITIES & INVESTMENT REVIEW
35300U1F-404

Editorial Address: 8 Eastcheap, LONDON, EC3M 1AE **Tel:** 020 7645 0749 **Fax:** 020 7645 0601
Email: richard.mitchell@wardour.co.uk
Advertising Address: Walmar House, 296 Regent Street, LONDON, W1B 3AW **Tel:** 020 7645 0735
Fax: 020 7636 2040
Email: bruce@wardour.co.uk
Web site: http://www.sii.org.uk
ISSN: 1357-7069
Publisher: Wardour Publishing and Design
Date Established: 1992
Frequency: 10 issues yearly
Free to qualifying individuals
Annual Sub.: £120.00
Circulation: 19,394 (ABC 01/07/2008 to 30/06/2009)
Usual Pagination: 40
Editor: Richard Mitchell; **Advertising Manager:** Bruce Settle; **Publisher:** Ciaran Jennings
Summary of Content: Magazine covering news, technology, strategies and members profiles.
Readership/Target Audience: Read by members of the Securities & Investment Institute.
ADVERTISING RATES:
Full Page Colour £4345.00
Agency Commission: 10%
Mechanical Data: Type Area: 287 x 200mm, Bleed Size: 303 x 216mm, Trim Size: 297 x 210mm, Col Length: 287mm, Page Width: 200mm, Film: Digital
Copy instructions: Copy Date: 3 weeks prior to publication date
Average advertising content per issue: 30%
BUSINESS: FINANCE & ECONOMICS: Investment

SECURITY EUROPE
1698539U54C-323

Editorial Address: 8 The Old Yarn Mills, SHERBORNE, DT9 3RQ **Tel:** 01935 816030 **Fax:** 01935 817200
Email: s.elder@hisdorset.com
Advertising Address: As above.
Email: m.coward@hisdorset.com
Web site: http://www.securitydirectory.net
Publisher: Hemming Group Ltd
Date Established: 2000
Frequency: Annual
Cover Price: £75.00
(Publisher's Statement)
Editor: Sylke Elder; **Advertising Manager:** Mike Coward
Summary of Content: Directory of equipment and suppliers for the European and Middle East security market.
Readership/Target Audience: Aimed at manufacturers, specifiers, installers, consultants and end users.
ADVERTISING RATES:
Full Page Colour £2237.00
Mechanical Data: Type Area: 275 x 185mm, Bleed Size: 303 x 216mm, Trim Size: 297 x 210mm, Col Length: 275mm, Page Width: 185mm, Film: Digital
BUSINESS: SAFETY & SECURITY: Security

SECURITY INSTALLER
39923U54C-115

Editorial Address: 7th Floor, Ludgate House, 245 Blackfriars Road, LONDON, SE1 9UY **Tel:** 020 7921 8288
Fax: 020 7921 8060
Email: alan.hyder@ubm.com

Advertising Address: Ludgate House, 245 Blackfriars Road, LONDON, SE1 9UY **Tel:** 020 7921 5000
Fax: 020 7921 8059
Email: samuel.mitcham@ubm.com
Web site: http://www.info4security.com
ISSN: 0950-7329
Publisher: UBM Information Ltd
Date Established: 1986
Frequency: Monthly - Published in the middle of the month prior to cover date
Cover Price: £4.00
Free to qualifying individuals
Annual Sub.: £51.00
Circulation: 8,013 (ABC 01/07/2008 to 30/06/2009)
Usual Pagination: 76
Editor: Alan Hyder
Summary of Content: Magazine containing news and equipment tests for domestic, commercial and industrial security equipment.
Readership/Target Audience: Read by those involved with security installation.
ADVERTISING RATES:
Full Page Colour £1880.00
Agency Commission: 10%
Mechanical Data: Type Area: 254 x 178mm, Col Length: 254mm, Trim Size: 297 x 210mm, Bleed Size: 305 x 216mm, Film: Digital, Page Width: 178mm
Copy instructions: Copy Date: 3 weeks prior to publication date
Supplement(s): Access Solutions - 1xY, CCTV Solutions - 1xY, The IFSEC Magazine - 1xY, Network Solutions - 1xY
BUSINESS: SAFETY & SECURITY: Security

SECURITY MIDDLE EAST
1695104U54C-315

Editorial Address: PO Box 10, UPMINSTER, RM14 1LQ
Tel: 01708 229354
Email: sme@dovetailcomms.co.uk
Advertising Address: 166 Front Lane, UPMINSTER, RM14 1LN **Tel:** 01708 229354 **Fax:** 01708 220017
Email: barry@pubint.co.uk
Web site: http://www.securitymiddleeastmagazine.com
Publisher: Publications International Ltd
Date Established: 1998
Frequency: 6 issues yearly - Published on the 30th of the cover month
Free to qualifying individuals
Circulation: 13,693 (ABC 01/07/2006 to 30/06/2007)
Usual Pagination: 52
Editor: Claire Mahoney; **Advertising Manager:** Barry Bebbington
Summary of Content: Magazine designed to provide information and contacts for buyers and suppliers of security products.
Readership/Target Audience: Aimed at end users of security products and installers in the Middle East.
ADVERTISING RATES:
Full Page Colour $3000.00
Agency Commission: 15%
Mechanical Data: Type Area: 277 x 190mm, Bleed Size: 303 x 196mm, Trim Size: 297 x 210mm, Col Length: 277mm, Page Width: 190mm, Film: Digital
Copy instructions: Copy Date: 15th of the month prior to cover month
Average advertising content per issue: 40%
BUSINESS: SAFETY & SECURITY: Security

SECURITY SPECIFIER
39926U54C-118

Editorial Address: 32 Portland Street, CHELTENHAM, GL52 2PE **Tel:** 01242 583222 **Fax:** 01242 222331
Email: specifier@btconnect.com
Advertising Address: As above.
Email: specifier@btconnect.com
Publisher: Specifier Publishing
Date Established: 1982
Frequency: 6 issues yearly - Published in the last week of the 2nd cover month
Cover Price: £5.00
Annual Sub.: £30.00
Circulation: 9,000 (Publisher's Statement)
Usual Pagination: 24
Editor: Christopher Musk; **Features Editor:** Linda Brindley; **Advertising Manager:** David Constantine; **Publisher:** David Constantine
Summary of Content: Magazine covering security products for commercial and residential premises.
Readership/Target Audience: Read by security installers, building contractors, retail and commercial distributors, company directors and commercial managers and buyers.
ADVERTISING RATES:
Full Page Colour £950.00
SCC £36.00
Agency Commission: 10%
Mechanical Data: Trim Size: 297 x 210mm
Copy instructions: Copy Date: 3 weeks prior to publication date
Average advertising content per issue: 60%
BUSINESS: SAFETY & SECURITY: Security

SEED ABSTRACTS
40074U55-160

Editorial Address: Nosworthy Way, WALLINGFORD, OX10 8DE **Tel:** 01491 832111 **Fax:** 01491 829292
Email: d.simpson@cabi.org
Web site: http://www.cabi.org
ISSN: 0960-2585
Publisher: CABI
Date Established: 1991
Frequency: Monthly
Annual Sub.: £590.00
Circulation: 200 (Publisher's Statement)
Editor: David Simpson
Summary of Content: Journal containing scientific research on seeds.
Readership/Target Audience: Aimed at seed scientists in academic and government institutions and seed and agrochemical companies.
ADVERTISING: No Advertising taken
BUSINESS: APPLIED SCIENCE & LABORATORIES

SELF STORAGE FOCUS
1692789U10-214

Formerly: Focus
Editorial Address: Priestley House, The Gullet, NANTWICH, CW5 5SZ **Tel:** 01270 623150 **Fax:** 01270 623471
Email: suebrash@ssauk.com
Advertising Address: As above.
Email: admin@ssauk.com
Publisher: Johnson Matthey plc
Date Established: 2002
Frequency: Quarterly
Free to qualifying individuals
Circulation: 2,000 (Publisher's Statement)
Usual Pagination: 48
Editor: Sue Brash; **Advertising Manager:** Jane Massey
Summary of Content: Magazine focusing on the self storage industry including news, equipment and service news, company profiles and meeting reports.
Readership/Target Audience: Aimed at all staff working in the self storage industry in Europe.
ADVERTISING RATES:
Full Page Mono £460.00
Full Page Colour £718.00
Agency Commission: 10%
Mechanical Data: Bleed Size: 303 x 216mm, Trim Size: 297 x 210mm, Film: Digital
Copy instructions: Copy Date: 4 weeks prior to publication date
Average advertising content per issue: 45%
BUSINESS: MATERIALS HANDLING

SELF-ADHESIVE MATERIALS AND MARKETS BULLETIN
38833U39-80

Editorial Address: PO Box 14, DORKING, RH5 4YN
Tel: 01306 884473 **Fax:** 01306 884473
Email: info@datatranscripts.com
Web site: http://www.flexpackworld.com
ISSN: 1361-1631
Publisher: Data Transcripts
Date Established: 1975
Frequency: 10 issues yearly
Annual Sub.: £255.00
Circulation: 2,500 (Publisher's Statement)
Usual Pagination: 6
Editor: Robert Higham; **Advertising Manager:** Denise Martin; **Publisher:** Robert Higham; **Circulation Manager:** Stella Roscoe
Summary of Content: Newsletter covering technical process systems, markets and products, company finances and acquisitions specifically for each particular market.
Readership/Target Audience: Read by product managers, technical and marketing directors and chief executives worldwide.
ADVERTISING: No Advertising taken
BUSINESS: PLASTICS & RUBBER

SELFBUILDER
1789978U4D-422

Formerly: Selfbuild Update
Editorial Address: National House, 121-123 High Street, EPPING, CM16 4BD **Tel:** 01992 570030 **Fax:** 01992 570031
Email: info@media-ten.com
Advertising Address: As above. **Fax:** 01992 563403
Email: info@selfbuildupdate.com
Web site: http://www.theselfbuilder.com
Publisher: Media 10
Date Established: 2006
Frequency: Monthly
Free to qualifying individuals
Circulation: 20,000 (Publisher's Statement)
Editor: Paul O'Neal; **Advertising Manager:** Craig Liebman
Summary of Content: Magazine featuring products and services and suppliers for the selfbuild industry.
Readership/Target Audience: Aimed at selfbuilders and those renovating their homes.
ADVERTISING: Rates on application

Agency Commission: 10%
BUSINESS: ARCHITECTURE & BUILDING: Planning & Housing

SELLING LONG HAUL
39734U50-24

Editorial Address: Suffolk House, George Street, CROYDON, CR9 1SR **Tel:** 020 8649 7233
Fax: 020 8649 7234
Email: editorial@bmipublications.com
Advertising Address: As above.
Email: steven.thompson@bmipublications.com
Web site: http://www.bmipublications.com
ISSN: 0253-8324
Publisher: BMI Publications Ltd
Date Established: 1990
Frequency: 11 issues yearly - Double issue in July/August. Published at the end of the 1st week of the cover month
Cover Price: Free
Circulation: 16,500 (Publisher's Statement)
Usual Pagination: 72
Editor: Steve Hartridge; **Managing Director:** Martin Steady; **Advertising Manager:** Steven Thompson; **Managing Editor:** Alan Orbell; **Group Editor:** Jo Austin; **Publisher:** Sally Parker
Summary of Content: Journal covering information for travel agents selling long-haul travel and tourism. Also includes a training guide.
Readership/Target Audience: Read by managers and senior counter clerks of all ABTA travel agencies and most independents.
ADVERTISING RATES:
Full Page Colour £3750.00
Agency Commission: 10%
Mechanical Data: Type Area: 265 x 187mm, Bleed Size: 303 x 216mm, Trim Size: 297 x 210mm, Col Length: 265mm, Page Width: 187mm, Film: Digital
Copy instructions: Copy Date: 2 weeks prior to publication date
Average advertising content per issue: 40%
BUSINESS: TRAVEL & TOURISM

SEMICONDUCTOR FABTECH
37385U18A-411

Editorial Address: Trans-World House, 100 City Road, LONDON, EC1Y 2BP **Tel:** 020 7871 0123
Fax: 020 7871 0101
Email: mosborne@fabtech.org
Advertising Address: As above.
Email: amorrison@fabtech.org
Web site: http://www.fabtech.org
ISSN: 1355-8633
Publisher: Semiconductor Media Ltd
Date Established: 1995
Frequency: Quarterly
Free to qualifying individuals
Annual Sub.: £195.00
Circulation: 13,000 (Publisher's Statement)
Usual Pagination: 190
Editor: Mark Osborne; **Editor-in-Chief:** Mark Osborne; **Advertising Manager:** Adam Morrison
Summary of Content: Journal covering technological developments in semiconductor manufacturing.
Readership/Target Audience: Aimed at key decision makers in semiconductor fabrication plants.
ADVERTISING RATES:
Full Page Colour £5950.00
Agency Commission: 15%
Mechanical Data: Trim Size: 297 x 210mm, Film: Digital
Copy instructions: Copy Date: 4 weeks prior to publication date
Average advertising content per issue: 30%
BUSINESS: ELECTRONICS

SEN SPECIAL EDUCATION NEEDS
1616582U62G-421

Editorial Address: 5 Shaw Bridge Street, CLITHEROE, BB7 1LY **Tel:** 01200 453000 **Fax:** 01200 453009
Email: editor@senmagazine.co.uk
Advertising Address: As above.
Email: denise@senmagazine.co.uk
Web site: http://www.senmagazine.co.uk
Publisher: Sen Magazine Ltd
Date Established: 2002
Frequency: 6 issues yearly
Free to qualifying individuals
Annual Sub.: £32.00
Circulation: 12,000 (Publisher's Statement)
Usual Pagination: 100
Editor: Peter Sutcliffe; **Publisher:** Jeremy Nicholls
Summary of Content: Magazine containing features written by practitioners and researchers providing an overview on topics such as inclusion, autism, dyslexia, hearing impairment, gifted children, resources, exhibition previews and reviews, school management and training.
Readership/Target Audience: Read by education professionals and carers, headteachers, school governors, heads of learning support, LEA's heads of learning support,

SENCOs, educational psychologists, learning support assistants, teachers and resource centres.
ADVERTISING RATES:
Full Page Colour £1295.00
Mechanical Data: Bleed Size: 303 x 216mm, Trim Size: 297 x 210mm, No. of Columns (Display): 3, Film: Digital, Print Process: Sheet-fed litho
Supplement(s): Jobs - 6xY
BUSINESS: CHURCH & SCHOOL EQUIPMENT & EDUCATION: Special Needs Education

SENSOR REVIEW
35998U5A-230
Editorial Address: 17 Old Lane, Low Mill Village, Addingham, ILKLEY, LS29 0SA **Tel:** 01943 830399
Fax: 01943 831876
Email: news@engineeringfirst.com
Web site: http://www.emeraldinsight.com/sr.htm
ISSN: 2260-2288
Publisher: Emerald Group Publishing Ltd
Frequency: Quarterly
Usual Pagination: 90
Editor: Clive Loughlin; **Publisher:** Harry Colson
Summary of Content: Publication featuring articles and reviews of sensor technology in manufacturing processes.
Readership/Target Audience: Aimed at industrial management development, design and production engineers in a wide range of user industries such as domestic appliance, food and pharmaceuticals and mechanical, electrical and electronic engineering.
ADVERTISING: No Advertising taken
BUSINESS: COMPUTERS & AUTOMATION: Automation & Instrumentation

SEQUAL NEWS
40435U56L-123
Editorial Address: 3 Ploughmans Corner, Wharf Road, ELLESMERE, SY12 0EJ **Tel:** 01691 624222
Fax: 01691 624222
Email: liz@thesequaltrust.co.uk
Advertising Address: As above.
Email: thesequaltrust@freeuk.com
Web site: http://www.thesequaltrust.org.uk
Publisher: The Sequal Trust
Date Established: 1970
Frequency: Annual
Cover Price: Free
Circulation: 2,000 (Publisher's Statement)
Usual Pagination: 12
Editor: Liz Downes; **Advertising Manager:** Liz Downes
Summary of Content: Magazine focusing on disability issues including information on communication aids.
Readership/Target Audience: Read by people with disabilities, carers and professionals in the field of disability as well as other companies and trusts.
ADVERTISING: Rates on application
Average advertising content per issue: 25%
BUSINESS: HEALTH & MEDICAL: Disability & Rehabilitation

SERVICE DEALER
38111U26B-63
Editorial Address: 25A New Street, SALISBURY, SP1 2PH
Tel: 01722 414245 **Fax:** 01722 414561
Email: chris@nelsonpublishing.co.uk
Advertising Address: As above.
Email: nicky@nelsonpublishing.co.uk
Web site: http://www.nelsonpublishing.co.uk
Publisher: Nelson Publishing Ltd
Date Established: 1988
Frequency: Monthly - Published in the 2nd week of the cover month
Annual Sub.: £60.00
Circulation: 4,000 (Publisher's Statement)
Editor: Chris Biddle; **Managing Director:** Chris Biddle; **Publisher:** Chris Biddle
Summary of Content: Magazine containing news, views and comment on the agricultural, garden and turf care machinery and equipment market.
Readership/Target Audience: Aimed at the garden, agricultural and turf care machinery trade, dealers, suppliers, importers and distributors.
ADVERTISING RATES:
Full Page Colour £1250.00
SCC £20.00
Agency Commission: 10%
Mechanical Data: Page Width: 190mm, Film: Digital, Type Area: 272 x 190mm, Print Process: Litho, Bleed Size: 305 x 218mm, Trim Size: 297 x 210mm, No. of Columns (Display): 2, Col Length: 272mm, Col Widths (Display): 92mm
Copy instructions: Copy Date: 2 weeks prior to publication date
Average advertising content per issue: 35%
BUSINESS: GARDEN TRADE: Garden Trade Supplies

SERVICE MANAGEMENT
37386U18A-412
Editorial Address: Ludgate House, 245 Blackfriars Road, LONDON, SE1 9UY **Tel:** 020 7921 5000 **Fax:** 020 7921 8549
Email: dennis.flower@ubm.com

Advertising Address: As above.
Email: rebecca.soni@ubm.com
Web site: http://www.servicemanagementmagazine.co.uk
ISSN: 0953-9212
Publisher: UBM Live
Date Established: 1986
Frequency: 9 issues yearly - Published at the beginning of the 2nd cover month. Single issues: Middle of the cover month
Free to qualifying individuals
Annual Sub.: £99.00
Circulation: 8,000 (Publisher's Statement)
Usual Pagination: 52
Editor: Dennis Flower
Summary of Content: Magazine containing management solutions and ideas for organisations running teams of engineers and operatives. Including news, product information, case studies, features for mobile resource managers, fixing and maintaining equipment and offering an on-site service.
Readership/Target Audience: Read by senior service professionals interested in high-tech and IT solutions.
ADVERTISING RATES:
Full Page Colour £1995.00
Agency Commission: 10%
Mechanical Data: Type Area: 254 x 178mm, Col Length: 254mm, Bleed Size: 292 x 216mm, Trim Size: 286 x 210mm, Film: Digital, Page Width: 178mm
Copy instructions: Copy Date: 3 weeks prior to publication date
Average advertising content per issue: 40%
BUSINESS: ELECTRONICS

SERVICE POINT
40912U60B-145
Editorial Address: 3 Spring Garden, Hensall, GOOLE, DN14 0QL **Tel:** 01977 663143
Email: ian_bmlg@hotmail.com
Advertising Address: As above.
Email: ianmstringer@googlemail.com
Web site: http://www.cilip.org.uk/bmlg
ISSN: 0306-0942
Publisher: Branch & Mobile Libraries Group
Date Established: 1972
Frequency: 3 issues yearly - Published in spring, autumn and winter
Annual Sub.: £20.00
Circulation: 1,500 (Publisher's Statement)
Usual Pagination: 40
Editor: Ian Stringer; **Advertising Manager:** Ian Stringer
Summary of Content: Publication containing articles on branch and mobile libraries in Great Britain and overseas, advance notices and reports on branch and mobile library group meetings and other relevant library events.
Readership/Target Audience: Aimed at members of the branch and mobile libraries group, Chartered Institute of Library and Information Professionals and affiliated members of the group.
ADVERTISING RATES:
Full Page Mono £100.00
Full Page Colour £150.00
Agency Commission: 10%
Mechanical Data: Type Area: 177 x 110mm, Col Length: 177mm, Page Width: 110mm
Average advertising content per issue: 25%
BUSINESS: PUBLISHING: Libraries

SERVICETALK THE JOURNAL
36094U5B-167
Formerly: ITSMF News
Editorial Address: 150 Wharfedale Road, Winnersh Triangle, WOKINGHAM, RG41 5RB **Tel:** 0118 918 6500
Fax: 0870 706 1531
Email: marketing@itsmf.co.uk
Advertising Address: As above. **Fax:** 0118 969 9749
Email: marketing@itsmf.co.uk
Web site: http://www.itsmf.co.uk
Publisher: ITSMF
Date Established: 1992
Frequency: Quarterly
Cover Price: £3.00
Free to qualifying individuals
Annual Sub.: £12.00
Circulation: 15,000 (Publisher's Statement)
Usual Pagination: 30
Editor: Alexandra Isaac; **Advertising Manager:** Alexandra Isaac
Summary of Content: Newsletter of the ITSMF reporting on the management and use of IT in business.
Readership/Target Audience: Read by members of the ITSMF who are IT managers in major corporations.
ADVERTISING: Rates on application
Copy instructions: Copy Date: 4 weeks prior to publication date
Average advertising content per issue: 40%
BUSINESS: COMPUTERS & AUTOMATION: Data Processing

SEXUAL & RELATIONSHIP THERAPY
40077U55-9004
Editorial Address: 4 Park Square, Milton Park, ABINGDON, OX14 4RN **Tel:** 020 7017 6000 **Fax:** 020 7017 6336
Email: samantha.cragg@tandf.co.uk
Web site: http://www.informaworld.com/csmt
ISSN: 1468-1994
Publisher: Routledge, Taylor & Francis
Date Established: 1986
Frequency: Quarterly
Free to qualifying individuals
Annual Sub.: £82.00
Circulation: 1,100 (Publisher's Statement)
Usual Pagination: 128
Editor: Samantha Cragg
Summary of Content: Journal containing papers examining the different aspects of sexual and relationship difficulties and their alleviation.
Readership/Target Audience: Aimed at medics, psychologists, psychotherapists, counsellors, nurses and social workers.
ADVERTISING: Rates on application
BUSINESS: APPLIED SCIENCE & LABORATORIES

SEXUALITIES
40078U55-165
Editorial Address: Sociology Department, University of Essex, Wivenhoe Park, COLCHESTER, CO4 3SQ
Tel: 020 7324 8500 **Fax:** 020 7324 8600
Email: jrnsexu@essex.ac.uk
Advertising Address: 1 Oliver's Yard, 55 City Road, LONDON, EC1Y 1SP **Tel:** 020 7324 8500
Fax: 020 7324 8600
Email: sheena.karim@sagepub.co.uk
Web site: http://www.sagepub.co.uk
ISSN: 1363-4607
Publisher: Sage Publications
Date Established: 1998
Frequency: Quarterly
Annual Sub.: £52.00
Circulation: 450 (Publisher's Statement)
Usual Pagination: 128
Editor: Ken Plummer; **Advertising Manager:** Sheena Karim
Summary of Content: Publication providing a forum for debate on the shifting nature of human sexuality.
Readership/Target Audience: Aimed at those involved in social sciences, cultural history, cultural anthropology, social geography, feminism, gender studies, cultural studies and lesbian and gay studies.
ADVERTISING RATES:
Full Page Mono £400.00
Agency Commission: 5%
Mechanical Data: Col Length: 205mm, Page Width: 130mm, Film: Digital, Type Area: 205 x 130mm
BUSINESS: APPLIED SCIENCE & LABORATORIES

SGB GOLF
766702U48B-75
Editorial Address: 15A London Road, MAIDSTONE, ME16 8LY **Tel:** 01622 687031 **Fax:** 01622 757646
Email: sgbgolf@datateam.co.uk
Advertising Address: As above.
Email: pryder@datateam.co.uk
Web site: http://www.sgb-sports.com
ISSN: 1475-8636
Publisher: Datateam Publishing Ltd
Date Established: 2001
Frequency: 10 issues yearly - Published in the 1st week of the cover month
Cover Price: Free
Circulation: 7,832 (Publisher's Statement)
Usual Pagination: 36
Editor: Robin Barwick; **Advertising Manager:** Paul Ryder; **Group Editor:** Jon Bruford; **Publisher:** Paul Ryder
Summary of Content: Magazine covering the latest golf industry news, product information and market intelligence including golfing equipment reviews, interviews, clothing and accessories, buying groups, PGA of Europe and directory of manufacturers.
Readership/Target Audience: Aimed at pro shop owners and managers.
ADVERTISING RATES:
Full Page Colour £1575.00
Agency Commission: 10%
Mechanical Data: Col Length: 275mm, No. of Columns (Display): 2, Page Width: 195mm, Print Process: Sheet-fed offset litho, Trim Size: 306 x 229mm, Bleed Size: 312 x 235mm, Type Area: 275 x 195mm, Film: Positive, right reading, emulsion side down. Digital
Copy instructions: Copy Date: 4 weeks prior to publication date
Average advertising content per issue: 40%
BUSINESS: TOY TRADE & SPORTS GOODS: Sports Goods

SGB SPORTS & OUTDOOR
39554U48B-60
Formerly: SGB Outdoor
Editorial Address: 15A London Road, MAIDSTONE, ME16 8LY **Tel:** 01622 687031

Email: dawn@datateam.co.uk
Advertising Address: As above. **Tel:** 01622 699160
Fax: 01622 757646
Email: sgboutdoor@datateam.co.uk
Web site: http://www.sgbmagazines.co.uk
ISSN: 1475-8628
Publisher: Datateam Publishing Ltd
Date Established: 1998
Frequency: Monthly - Published in the 1st week of the cover month
Free to qualifying individuals
Annual Sub.: £66.00
Circulation: 4,886 (Publisher's Statement)
Usual Pagination: 32
Editor: Jon Bruford
Summary of Content: Magazine covering the outdoor and snowsport retail sector. Contains industry updates, company profiles, exhibitions, equipment, footwear, clothing and product reviews.
Readership/Target Audience: Aimed at outdoor retailers and mail order houses.
ADVERTISING RATES:
Full Page Colour £1575.00
Agency Commission: 10%
Mechanical Data: Type Area: 275 x 210mm, Bleed Size: 312 x 235mm, Trim Size: 306 x 229mm, Film: Digital, Print Process: Sheet-fed offset litho, Col Length: 275mm, Page Width: 210mm
Copy instructions: Copy Date: 4 weeks prior to publication date
Average advertising content per issue: 40%
BUSINESS: TOY TRADE & SPORTS GOODS: Sports Goods

SHANG YE XIAN FENG (BUSINESS TO BUSINESS MAGAZINE FOR CHINA)

36979U14C-180

Editorial Address: 26 Ives Street, LONDON, SW3 2ND
Tel: 020 7581 6300 **Fax:** 020 7581 6400
Email: info@shangmagazine.com
Advertising Address: As above.
Email: info@shangmagazine.com
Web site: http://www.shangmagazine.com
Publisher: Regions Publishing Ltd
Date Established: 1989
Frequency: Quarterly
Cover Price: Free
Circulation: 16,000 (Publisher's Statement)
Usual Pagination: 32
Editor: Emile Bekheit; **Advertising Manager:** Emile Bekheit; **Publisher:** Emile Bekheit
Summary of Content: Business to business magazine covering developments in China.
Readership/Target Audience: Read by decision makers in China.
ADVERTISING RATES:
Full Page Mono £1900.00
Full Page Colour £2500.00
Agency Commission: 10%
Mechanical Data: Type Area: 254 x 178mm, Bleed Size: 286 x 213mm, Trim Size: 280 x 210mm, Col Length: 254mm, Page Width: 178mm, Film: Digital
Copy instructions: Copy Date: 10th of the month prior to publication date
Average advertising content per issue: 50%
BUSINESS: COMMERCE, INDUSTRY & MANAGEMENT: International Commerce

---

SHARES

26083U1F-589

Editorial Address: Thames House, 18 Park Street, LONDON, SE1 9ER **Tel:** 020 7378 7131 **Fax:** 020 7378 6605
Email: editorial@shares.msm.co.uk
Advertising Address: As above. **Tel:** 020 7378 4582
Fax: 0870 770 9300
Email: rcollins@msm.co.uk
Web site: http://www.sharesmagazine.co.uk
ISSN: 1468-1102
Publisher: MSM International Ltd
Date Established: 1999
Frequency: Weekly
Cover Price: £3.75
Annual Sub.: £139.00
Circulation: 13,561 (ABC 01/07/2007 to 30/06/2008)
Usual Pagination: 56
Editor: Russ Mould; **Managing Director:** Niall Sweeney;
Advertising Manager: Marcus Riley; **Publisher:** Mark van de Weyer
Summary of Content: Magazine containing share market tables, company reviews and features on share market sectors, managed funds as well as commodities, foreign exchange and derivative equity instruments.
Readership/Target Audience: Aimed at all share market investors, professional and private.
ADVERTISING RATES:
Full Page Mono £3190.00
Full Page Colour £4180.00
Agency Commission: 10%
Mechanical Data: Type Area: 240 x 181mm, Film: Digital, Col Length: 240mm, Page Width: 181mm

---

Copy instructions: Copy Date: Thursday prior to publication date
Average advertising content per issue: 20%
BUSINESS: FINANCE & ECONOMICS: Investment

SHAW'S DIRECTORY OF COURTS IN THE UNITED KINGDOM

39302U44-1786

Editorial Address: Shaway House, 21 Bourne Park, Bourne Road, CRAYFORD, DA1 4BZ **Tel:** 01322 621100 *
Fax: 01322 550991
Advertising Address: As above.
Email: publications@shaws.co.uk
Web site: http://www.shaws.co.uk
ISSN: 0264-312X
Publisher: Shaw & Sons Ltd
Frequency: Annual - Published in September
Cover Price: £48.50
Circulation: 2,900 (Publisher's Statement)
Usual Pagination: 448
Editor: Crispin Williams; **Advertising Manager:** Sarah Bruty
Summary of Content: Directory containing names, addresses, telephone numbers and where appropriate, DX numbers of courts of summary jurisdiction, county, high and crown courts, crown prosecution service, coroners and penal establishments.
Readership/Target Audience: Aimed at lawyers, courts, criminal justice sectors and licensed trade.
ADVERTISING: Rates on application
BUSINESS: LEGAL

SHAW'S LOCAL GOVERNMENT DIRECTORY

38399U32A-220

Editorial Address: Shaway House, 21 Bourne Park, Bourne Road, CRAYFORD, DA1 4BZ **Tel:** 01322 621100
Fax: 01322 550991
Email: publications@shaws.co.uk
Advertising Address: As above.
Web site: http://www.shaws.co.uk
ISSN: 1462-821X
Publisher: Shaw & Sons Ltd
Frequency: Annual - Published in May
Annual Sub.: £39.50
Circulation: 400 (Publisher's Statement)
Usual Pagination: 452
Editor: Sarah Bruty; **Advertising Manager:** Crispin Williams;
Managing Editor: Kelly Young; **Publisher:** Crispin Williams
Summary of Content: Directory containing Officers' names, departmental addresses, telephone and fax numbers and email addresses of local authorities. Also lists functions relevant to conveyances, as well as authority-specific information of conveyance fees and charges.
Readership/Target Audience: Read by members of local authorities, the legal profession and suppliers to local government.
ADVERTISING: Rates on application
BUSINESS: LOCAL GOVERNMENT, LEISURE & RECREATION: Local Government

---

SHEEP FARMER

37847U21D-850

Editorial Address: The Sheep Centre, MALVERN, WR13 6PH **Tel:** 01684 565533 **Fax:** 01684 565577
Email: info@shepherdpublishing.co.uk
Advertising Address: As above.
Email: info@shepherdpublishing.co.uk
Web site: http://www.nationalsheep.org.uk
ISSN: 0141-2434
Publisher: Shepherd Publishing Ltd
Date Established: 1975
Frequency: 6 issues yearly
Free to qualifying individuals
Annual Sub.: £45.00
Circulation: 10,000 (Publisher's Statement)
Usual Pagination: 40
Editor: Sheila Spence; **Managing Director:** Howard Venters; **Advertising Manager:** Howard Venters; **Publisher:** Howard Venters
Summary of Content: Journal covering disease, nutrition, flock management, welfare and breeding. Includes research, marketing and politics.
Readership/Target Audience: Aimed at sheep farmers and allied industries.
ADVERTISING RATES:
Full Page Colour £1470.00
SCC £10.95
Agency Commission: 10%
Mechanical Data: Trim Size: 210 x 297mm, Film: Digital
Copy instructions: Copy Date: 4 weeks prior to publication date
Average advertising content per issue: 40%
Supplement(s): Breeding Focus - 1xY, Forage Matters - 1xY, Lambing Focus - 1xY, NSA Summer Focus - 1xY, NSA Winter Focus - 1xY
BUSINESS: AGRICULTURE & FARMING: Livestock

SHIP & BOAT INTERNATIONAL

39351U45A-160

Editorial Address: 10 Upper Belgrave Street, LONDON, SW1X 8BQ **Tel:** 020 7235 4622 **Fax:** 020 7245 6959
Email: sfisk@rina.org.uk
Advertising Address: As above.
Email: advertising@rina.org.uk
Web site: http://www.rina.org.uk
ISSN: 0037-3834
Publisher: The Royal Institution of Naval Architects
Date Established: 1947
Frequency: 6 issues yearly - Published in the 1st week of the cover month
Free to qualifying individuals
Annual Sub.: £84.00
Circulation: 6,656 (ABC 01/01/2008 to 31/12/2008)
Usual Pagination: 68
Editor: Samantha Fisk; **Publisher:** Mark Staunton-Lambert
Summary of Content: Publication containing news on the latest technical developments and technical descriptions of new vessels, building techniques and equipment.
Language(s): Chinese; English
Readership/Target Audience: Read by naval architects, designers, consultants, equipment manufacturers, ship owners and operators.
ADVERTISING RATES:
Full Page Colour £1710.00
Agency Commission: 10%
Mechanical Data: Film: Negative, right reading, emulsion side down. Digital, Bleed Size: 303 x 216mm, Trim Size: 297 x 210mm, Print Process: Offset litho
Copy instructions: Copy Date: 4 weeks prior to publication date
Average advertising content per issue: 40%
BUSINESS: MARINE & SHIPPING

SHIPPING & TRANSPORT INTERNATIONAL

39237U44-1790

Formerly: Shipping & Transport Lawyer International
Editorial Address: Guthrum House, 145 Angel Street, Hadleigh, IPSWICH, IP7 5BY **Tel:** 01473 822061
Fax: 01473 822839
Advertising Address: As above.
Email: kathryn@guthrumhouse.co.uk
Web site: http://www.stl-mag.co.uk
ISSN: 1751-9896
Publisher: Guthrum House Ltd
Date Established: 1998
Frequency: Quarterly
Annual Sub.: £225.00
Usual Pagination: 44
Editor: Roger White; **Advertising Manager:** Kathryn Grandon
Summary of Content: Magazine covering transport law, maritime law, the legal aspects of road, rail and air transport and technical features.
Readership/Target Audience: Aimed at transport lawyers, law firms and those interested in shipping law and insurance.
ADVERTISING RATES:
Full Page Mono £1500.00
Full Page Colour £1782.00
Agency Commission: 10% *
Mechanical Data: Film: Digital, Bleed Size: 303 x 216mm, Type Area: 237 x 178mm, Col Length: 237mm, Page Width: 178mm, No. of Columns (Display): 2, Trim Size: 297 x 210mm
Copy instructions: Copy Date: 4 weeks prior to publication date
BUSINESS: LEGAL

SHIPPING WORLD & SHIPBUILDER

39354U45A-200

Editorial Address: 22 Highfield Road, Berrylands, SURBITON, KT5 9LP **Tel:** 020 8399 3073
Email: patrik.wheater@btinternet.com
Advertising Address: 80 Coleman Street, LONDON, EC2R 5BJ **Tel:** 020 7382 2627 **Fax:** 020 7382 2669
Email: alwyn.topliss@imarest.org
Web site: http://www.shippingworld.org
ISSN: 0037-3931
Publisher: IMarEST
Date Established: 1883
Frequency: 10 issues yearly - Published around the 20th of the cover month
Free to qualifying individuals
Annual Sub.: £65.00
Circulation: 5,982 (ABC 01/01/2008 to 31/12/2008)
Editor: Patrik Wheater; **Advertising Manager:** Alwyn Topliss
Summary of Content: Magazine reporting on the major developments in the marine world.
Readership/Target Audience: Read by shipowners, operators, managers, builders and repairers, shipbrokers, legal and financial service providers and government and trade bodies.
ADVERTISING RATES:
Full Page Colour £2840.00
Agency Commission: 10%

Business Magazines

Mechanical Data: Type Area: 280 x 190mm, Col Length: 280mm, Page Width: 190mm, Film: Digital, Trim Size: 210 x 207mm, Bleed Size: 220 x 217mm
Copy instructions: Copy Date: 4 weeks prior to publication date
Average advertising content per issue: 40%
Supplement(s): Maritime IT & Electronics - 5xY, Safety Of Shipping - 1xY
BUSINESS: MARINE & SHIPPING

SHIPREPAIR AND CONVERSION TECHNOLOGY 39414U45D-250
Editorial Address: 10 Upper Belgrave Street, LONDON, SW1X 8BQ **Tel:** 020 7235 4622 **Fax:** 020 7245 6959
Email: editorial@rina.org.uk
Advertising Address: As above. **Tel:** 020 7234 4622
Email: rlittle@rina.org.uk
Web site: http://www.rina.org.uk
ISSN: 0306-0209
Publisher: The Royal Institution of Naval Architects
Date Established: 1971
Frequency: Quarterly - Published in the 1st week of the cover month
Annual Sub.: £39.00
Circulation: 6,096 (ABC 01/01/2008 to 31/12/2008)
Usual Pagination: 50
Editor: Hugh O'Mahony; **Managing Editor:** Hugh O'Mahony
Summary of Content: Journal containing reports, reviews and technical papers covering every aspect of the repair and conversion market worldwide.
Readership/Target Audience: Read by shipowners, operators, repairers and consultants.
ADVERTISING RATES:
Full Page Mono £1420.00
Full Page Colour £1870.00
Agency Commission: 10%
Mechanical Data: Type Area: 254 x 178mm, Bleed Size: 303 x 216mm, Trim Size: 297 x 210mm, Print Process: Offset litho, Col Length: 254mm, Film: Digital, Page Width: 178mm
Copy instructions: Copy Date: 4 weeks prior to publication date
Average advertising content per issue: 40%
BUSINESS: MARINE & SHIPPING: Marine Engineering Equipment

SHIPS MONTHLY 48391U45A-517
Editorial Address: 222 Branston Road, BURTON-ON-TRENT, DE14 3BT **Tel:** 01283 542721 **Fax:** 01283 546436
Email: shipsmonthly@ipcmedia.com
Advertising Address: As above.
Email: ships_advertising@ipcmedia.com
Web site: http://www.shipsmonthly.com
ISSN: 0037-394X
Publisher: IPC Media Ltd
Date Established: 1966
Frequency: Monthly
Cover Price: £3.60
Annual Sub.: £43.20
Circulation: 21,000 (Publisher's Statement)
Usual Pagination: 68
Editor: Iain Wakefield; **Advertising Manager:** Susan Philo
Summary of Content: Magazine containing news and articles on all types of deep sea shipping including new cruise ships, ferries, naval vessels and cargo ships. Includes articles on tugs, new ships and preserved vessels as well as personal recollections and voyages reports plus interviews with ship's captains, chief engineers, department heads and a historical look back at shipping companies and their ships.
Readership/Target Audience: Aimed at ship enthusiasts, maritime professionals and historians.
ADVERTISING RATES:
Full Page Mono £410.00
Full Page Colour £620.00
SCC £15.00
Agency Commission: 10%
Mechanical Data: Type Area: 267 x 188mm, Bleed Size: 303 x 216mm, Trim Size: 297 x 210mm, Print Process: Web-fed offset litho, Film: Positive, right reading, emulsion side down, No. of Columns (Display): 2, Col Length: 267mm, Screen: Mono 48 lpc Colour 70 lpc, Page Width: 188mm
Copy instructions: Copy Date: 6 weeks prior to publication date
Average advertising content per issue: 10%
BUSINESS: MARINE & SHIPPING

SHOE SERVICE 38225U29-100
Formerly: Shoe Service Journal
Editorial Address: PO Box 9378, NEWARK, NG24 9FE
Tel: 01400 281298 **Fax:** 01400 282326
Email: editor@msauk.biz
Advertising Address: As above.
Email: info@msauk.biz
Web site: http://www.msauk.biz
Publisher: MultiService Association Ltd
Date Established: 1963
Frequency: Quarterly

Cover Price: Free
Circulation: 5,000 (Publisher's Statement)
Usual Pagination: 32
Editor: Martyn Harvey; **Advertising Manager:** Martyn Harvey
Summary of Content: Journal covering news, information, views and profiles of shoe repairing outlets and companies.
Readership/Target Audience: Aimed at members of the Multiservice Association and those involved in the shoe repair, engraving, key cutting and watch repair trade, and other small service industry businesses.
ADVERTISING RATES:
Full Page Mono £35.00
Full Page Colour £50.00
Mechanical Data: Bleed Size: 216 x 154mm, Trim Size: 210 x 148mm, Film: Digital
Average advertising content per issue: 25%
BUSINESS: FOOTWEAR

SHOP, BAR & OFFICE FITTER 719354U64S-350
Editorial Address: 29 High Street, RYE, TN31 7JG
Tel: 01797 224816
Email: bill@willowe.demon.co.uk
Advertising Address: As above.
Email: bill@willowe.demon.co.uk
Publisher: Willowe Magazines Limited
Date Established: 2001
Frequency: Quarterly - Published at the beginning of the cover month
Free to qualifying individuals
Annual Sub.: EUR10.00
Circulation: 4,500 (Publisher's Statement)
Usual Pagination: 28
Editor: Bill Lowe; **Managing Director:** Bill Lowe;
Advertising Manager: Bill Lowe
Summary of Content: Magazine covering articles on shop fittings and accessories. Includes latest machinery developments, tools and products.
Readership/Target Audience: Read by decision makers within shop and bar fitting companies and specialist craftsmen within the industry.
ADVERTISING RATES:
Full Page Mono £700.00
Full Page Colour £900.00
Agency Commission: 10%
Mechanical Data: Type Area: 275 x 205mm, Col Length: 275mm, Page Width: 205mm, Bleed Size: 304 x 228mm, Col Widths (Display): 100mm, No. of Columns (Display): 2, Trim Size: 295 x 225mm
Average advertising content per issue: 30%
BUSINESS: OTHER CLASSIFICATIONS: Shop Equipment

SHOP SPEC 1812712U4B-185
Editorial Address: 2nd Floor, 207-215 High Street, ORPINGTON, BR6 0PF **Tel:** 01689 899170
Fax: 01689 899171
Email: chris.horsenell@purplems.com
Advertising Address: As above.
Email: gordon.green@purplems.com
Publisher: Purple Media Solutions Ltd
Date Established: 1984
Frequency: Annual - Published in July
Editor: Chris Horsenell; **Advertising Manager:** Gordon Green
Summary of Content: Publication covering shop interior design and fitting.
Readership/Target Audience: Aimed at senior retail managers, interior designers for retail clients and shop fitters.
ADVERTISING RATES:
Full Page Colour £1869.00
Agency Commission: 10%
Mechanical Data: Film: Digital, Trim Size: 297 x 210mm
Copy instructions: Copy Date: June 1st
Average advertising content per issue: 30%
BUSINESS: ARCHITECTURE & BUILDING: Interior Design & Flooring

SHOPPING CENTRE 35209U1E-353
Editorial Address: 34 Porchester Road, LONDON, W2 6ES
Tel: 020 7563 5662
Email: graham.parker@jldmedia.com
Advertising Address: As above. **Tel:** 01293 613400
Fax: 01293 610330
Email: graham.harvey@jldmedia.com
Web site: http://www.william-reed.co.uk
ISSN: 0964-1793
Publisher: JLD Media
Date Established: 1991
Frequency: Monthly - Published in the 2nd week of the cover month
Cover Price: £6.20
Free to qualifying individuals
Annual Sub.: £50.00
Circulation: 12,241 (ABC 01/07/2008 to 30/06/2009)
Editor: Graham Parker

Summary of Content: Business magazine covering news, regional property and features on shopping centre ownership and management.
Readership/Target Audience: Readership includes centre management, estate and store operations departments, developers, architects, surveyors, facilities and project managers, sponsors, local authority planners and chief executives.
ADVERTISING RATES:
Full Page Mono £2269.00
Full Page Colour £2998.00
Agency Commission: 10%
Mechanical Data: Type Area: 317 x 221mm, Col Length: 317mm, Page Width: 221mm, Trim Size: 340 x 245mm, Bleed Size: 346 x 251mm, Film: Digital
Copy instructions: Copy Date: 3 weeks prior to publication date
Average advertising content per issue: 50%
BUSINESS: FINANCE & ECONOMICS: Property

SHOPPING CENTRE IRELAND 1748243U1E-392
Editorial Address: Broadfield Park, CRAWLEY, RH11 9RT
Tel: 01293 610294 **Fax:** 01293 610330
Email: graham.parker@jldmedia.com
Advertising Address: As above. **Tel:** 01293 613400
Email: graham.harvey@jldmedia.com
Web site: http://www.shopping-centre.co.uk
Publisher: William Reed Business Media
Frequency: Quarterly
Cover Price: £6.20
Annual Sub.: £20.00
Circulation: 8,485 (Publisher's Statement)
Editor: Graham Parker
Summary of Content: Business magazine covering news, regional property and features on shopping centre development, management and planning.
Readership/Target Audience: Readership includes centre management, estate and store operations departments, developers, architects, surveyors, facilities and project managers, sponsors, local authority planners, chief executives and constructors.
ADVERTISING RATES:
Full Page Mono £1500.00
Full Page Colour £2000.00
Agency Commission: 10%
Mechanical Data: Type Area: 267 x 185mm, Bleed Size: 303 x 216mm, Trim Size: 297 x 210mm, Col Length: 267mm, Page Width: 185mm, Film: Digital
Average advertising content per issue: 50%
BUSINESS: FINANCE & ECONOMICS: Property

SHORT BREAKS & HOLIDAYS 39735U50-24_5
Formerly: Short Breaks Worldwide
Editorial Address: Suffolk House, George Street, CROYDON, CR9 1SR **Tel:** 020 8649 7233
Fax: 020 8649 7234
Email: editorial@bmipublications.com
Advertising Address: As above.
Email: steven.thompson@bmipublications.com
Web site: http://www.bmipublications.com
Publisher: BMI Publications Ltd
Date Established: 1994
Frequency: Quarterly - Published around the 1st of the cover month
Cover Price: Free
Circulation: 16,500 (Publisher's Statement)
Usual Pagination: 52
Editor: Steve Hartridge; **Managing Director:** Martin Steady; **Advertising Manager:** Steven Thompson; **Managing Editor:** Alan Orbell; **Group Editor:** Jo Austin; **Publisher:** Sally Parker
Summary of Content: Magazine covering the latest news and information on short breaks for the travel trade.
Readership/Target Audience: Aimed at retail travel agencies and tour operators in the UK and Ireland.
ADVERTISING RATES:
Full Page Mono £2750.00
Full Page Colour £2750.00
Agency Commission: 10%
Mechanical Data: Film: Digital, Print Process: Sheet fed, Type Area: 200 x 150mm, Bleed Size: 231 x 170mm, Trim Size: 225 x 170mm, Col Length: 200mm, Page Width: 150mm
Copy instructions: Copy Date: 2 weeks prior to publication date
Average advertising content per issue: 40%
BUSINESS: TRAVEL & TOURISM

SHORTHORN JOURNAL 37848U21D-860
Editorial Address: 4th Street, NAC, Stoneleigh Park, KENILWORTH, CV8 2LG **Tel:** 024 7669 6549
Fax: 024 7669 6729
Email: shorthorn@shorthorn.co.uk
Advertising Address: As above.
Email: shorthorn@shorthorn.co.uk
Web site: http://www.shorthorn.co.uk
Publisher: Shorthorn Cattle Society

Section 4 (b) Business Magazines

Date Established: 1876
Frequency: Annual - Published in December
Cover Price: £5.00
Free to qualifying individuals
Circulation: 2,000 (Publisher's Statement)
Usual Pagination: 92
Editor: Frank Milnes; **Advertising Manager:** Sue Walters
Summary of Content: Journal of the Shorthorn Society of the United Kingdom of Great Britain and Ireland. Includes news for members, show results and agricultural news.
Readership/Target Audience: Aimed at the farming community and all agricultural readers.
ADVERTISING: Rates on application
Average advertising content per issue: 30%
BUSINESS: AGRICULTURE & FARMING: Livestock

SHOTS
25961U2A-168_70
Editorial Address: Greater London House, Hampstead Road, LONDON, NW1 7EJ **Tel:** 020 7728 5000
Fax: 020 7728 4800
Email: news@shots.net
Advertising Address: As above.
Email: maxine@shots.net
Web site: http://www.shots.net
Publisher: EMAP Communications
Frequency: 6 issues yearly
Annual Sub.: £595.00
Usual Pagination: 100
Editor: Laura Swinton
Summary of Content: Magazine covering the latest news on international advertising and creativity. Features include comprehensive reviews of television commercials, promos, film effects and press and poster campaigns.
Readership/Target Audience: Aimed at advertising and production professionals worldwide.
ADVERTISING RATES:
Full Page Colour £2940.00
Agency Commission: 10%
Mechanical Data: Type Area: 277 x 215mm, Trim Size: 297 x 235mm, Film: Digital, Col Length: 277mm, Page Width: 215mm
Copy instructions: Copy Date: 2 weeks prior to publication date
Average advertising content per issue: 35%
BUSINESS: COMMUNICATIONS, ADVERTISING & MARKETING

THE SHOW GUIDE
1809963U38-191
Editorial Address: 6 Bath Street, RHYL, LL18 3EB
Tel: 01745 356935
Email: colin@swpp.co.uk
Advertising Address: As above.
Email: cliveinsley@btinternet.com
Web site: http://www.swwp.co.uk
Publisher: SWPP & BPPA
Frequency: Annual - Published in December
Cover Price: Free
Circulation: 10,000 (Publisher's Statement)
Usual Pagination: 140
Editor: Colin Jones; **Advertising Manager:** Clive Insley
Summary of Content: Publication providing a preview of the Society of Wedding and Portrait Photographers convention, an overview of what is happening and articles by speakers.
Readership/Target Audience: Aimed at professional photographers.
ADVERTISING RATES:
Full Page Mono £900.00
Full Page Colour £900.00
Agency Commission: 10%
Mechanical Data: Bleed Size: 303 x 216mm, Trim Size: 297 x 210mm, Film: Digital
Copy instructions: Copy Date: 3 weeks prior to publication date
Average advertising content per issue: 40%
Supplement to: Professional Imagemaker Photographic Magazine
BUSINESS: PHOTOGRAPHIC TRADE

SHOW HOUSE
35210U1E-354
Editorial Address: 1st Floor, 1 East Poultry Avenue, LONDON, EC1A 9PT **Tel:** 020 7002 8300
Fax: 020 7002 8310
Email: kh@globespanmedia.com
Advertising Address: As above.
Email: sph@globespanmedia.com
Web site: http://www.showhouse.co.uk
ISSN: 1468-747X
Publisher: Globespan Media Ltd
Frequency: Monthly - Published in the 1st week of the cover month
Free to qualifying individuals
Annual Sub.: £90.00
Circulation: 11,954 (ABC 01/09/2008 to 30/11/2008)
Usual Pagination: 124

Editor: Kate Hamilton
Summary of Content: Magazine covering every aspect of new homes property. Provides information on products and services and contains news and opinions from within the new homes property industry.
Readership/Target Audience: Aimed at sales and marketing directors, architects, surveyors and buyers.
ADVERTISING RATES:
Full Page Colour £3550.00
Agency Commission: 10%
Mechanical Data: Film: Digital, Type Area: 322 x 217mm, Bleed Size: 352 x 251mm, Trim Size: 346 x 245mm, Col Length: 322mm, Page Width: 217mm
Copy instructions: Copy Date: 4 weeks prior to publication date
Average advertising content per issue: 40%
BUSINESS: FINANCE & ECONOMICS: Property

SIGHTLINE
1698507U64K-650
Editorial Address: 55 Farringdon Road, LONDON, EC1M 3JB **Tel:** 020 7242 9200
Email: office@abtt.org.uk
Advertising Address: The Studio, High Green, Great Shelford, CAMBRIDGE, CB2 5EG **Tel:** 01223 550805
Fax: 01223 550806
Email: editor@etnow.com
Web site: http://www.etnow.com/sightline
Publisher: Entertainment Technology Press Ltd
Frequency: Quarterly
Free to qualifying individuals
Annual Sub.: £30.00
Circulation: 2,000 (Publisher's Statement)
Usual Pagination: 40
Editor: A. Bennett-Hunter; **Advertising Manager:** John Offord
Summary of Content: Magazine providing technical information on matters of theatrical technology.
Readership/Target Audience: Aimed at theatre technicians, designers and architects.
ADVERTISING RATES:
Full Page Colour £695.00
Mechanical Data: Type Area: 277 x 190mm, Col Length: 277mm, Page Width: 190mm, Film: Digital
BUSINESS: OTHER CLASSIFICATIONS: Cinema Entertainment

SIGN DIRECTIONS
35744U64S-355
Formerly: Sign Directions with SDG
Editorial Address: Unit 1B Melrose Nurseries, Longland Lane, Farnsfield, NEWARK, NG22 8HD **Tel:** 01623 882398
Advertising Address: As above.
Email: maurice.hoare@btconnect.com
Web site: http://www.signdirections.net
Publisher: Visage Communications
Date Established: 1996
Frequency: 8 issues yearly
Free to qualifying individuals
Annual Sub.: £50.00
Circulation: 6,845 (ABC 01/01/2008 to 31/12/2008)
Usual Pagination: 60
Editor: Val Hirst; **Advertising Manager:** Maurice Hoare; **Managing Editor:** Val Hirst; **Publisher:** Maurice Hoare
Summary of Content: Magazine covering news and features on the sign industry.
Readership/Target Audience: Read by producers within the sign industry and end-users of signs.
ADVERTISING RATES:
Full Page Colour £890.00
Agency Commission: 10%
Mechanical Data: Page Width: 190mm, Film: Digital, Trim Size: 297 x 210mm, Type Area: 277 x 190mm, Bleed Size: 303 x 216mm, Col Length: 277mm
Copy instructions: Copy Date: 1 week prior to publication date
Average advertising content per issue: 40%
BUSINESS: OTHER CLASSIFICATIONS: Shop Equipment

SIGN UPDATE
35746U64S-360
Editorial Address: Allens Orchard, Chipping Warden, BANBURY, OX17 1LX **Tel:** 01295 660666
Fax: 0560 112 0149
Email: heather.rutter1@btinternet.com
Advertising Address: As above.
Email: roger@sign-update-magazine.co.uk
Web site: http://www.sign-update-magazine.co.uk
Publisher: Sign Update Ltd
Date Established: 1990
Frequency: 6 issues yearly
Cover Price: £2.50
Free to qualifying individuals
Annual Sub.: £14.00
Circulation: 8,309 (Publisher's Statement)
Usual Pagination: 116

Editor: Heather Rutter; **Managing Director:** Roger Hinchcliffe; **Advertising Manager:** Roger Hinchcliffe; **Publisher:** Roger Hinchcliffe
Summary of Content: Magazine that covers all aspects of sign, engraving, POS, digital and screen printing as well as the shopfitting industry.
Readership/Target Audience: Aimed at sign makers, engravers, screen printers and digital printers, POS, designers and shopfitters.
ADVERTISING RATES:
Full Page Mono £510.00
Full Page Colour £880.00
SCC £20.00
Agency Commission: 10%
Mechanical Data: No. of Columns (Display): 2, Type Area: 275 x 190mm, Bleed Size: 303 x 213mm, Trim Size: 297 x 207mm, Col Length: 275mm, Page Width: 190mm
Average advertising content per issue: 50%
BUSINESS: OTHER CLASSIFICATIONS: Shop Equipment

SIGN WORLD
35747U64S-370
Editorial Address: 8A High Street, EPSOM, KT19 8AD
Tel: 01372 741411 **Fax:** 01372 744493
Email: valerie@aemorgan.co.uk
Advertising Address: As above.
Email: derek@aemorgan.co.uk
Publisher: A.E. Morgan Publications Ltd
Date Established: 1967
Frequency: 10 issues yearly
Free to qualifying individuals
Annual Sub.: £19.55
Circulation: 6,340 (Publisher's Statement)
Usual Pagination: 40
Editor: Valerie Atkins; **Advertising Manager:** Derek Pearson; **Publisher:** Terence Morgan
Summary of Content: Magazine covering profiles, news and information on sign manufacturing and the graphics industry.
Readership/Target Audience: Aimed at sign and screen print manufacturers, trade suppliers and end-users.
ADVERTISING RATES:
Full Page Colour £615.00
Agency Commission: 10%
Mechanical Data: Type Area: 310 x 228mm, Film: Digital, Col Length: 310mm, No. of Columns (Display): 4, Bleed Size: 346 x 251mm, Trim Size: 340 x 245mm, Col Widths (Display): 54mm, Page Width: 228mm
Average advertising content per issue: 50%
BUSINESS: OTHER CLASSIFICATIONS: Shop Equipment

SIGN-LINK
1694371U41A-332
Editorial Address: 1st Floor Offices, 27-31 Church Road, Lawrence Hill, BRISTOL, BS5 9JJ **Fax:** 0117 954 1476
Email: editor@signlink.co.uk
Advertising Address: As above. **Tel:** 0117 954 7371
Email: chris@sign-link.com
Publisher: Link Publishing
Date Established: 2003
Frequency: Monthly - Published on the 3rd Friday of the cover month
Free to qualifying individuals
Annual Sub.: £35.00
Circulation: 14,500 (Publisher's Statement)
Usual Pagination: 84
Editor: James Matthews-Paul
Summary of Content: News and features covering the sign, screen and digital print market. Includes large-format and graphic arts sectors.
Readership/Target Audience: Aimed at industry professionals.
ADVERTISING RATES:
Full Page Colour £1395.00
Agency Commission: 10%
Mechanical Data: Type Area: 267 x 180mm, Bleed Size: 303 x 216mm, Trim Size: 297 x 210mm, Col Length: 267mm, Page Width: 180mm, Film: Digital
Copy instructions: Copy Date: 1 week prior to publication date
Average advertising content per issue: 30%
BUSINESS: PRINTING & STATIONERY: Printing

THE SIMMENTAL REVIEW
37849U21D-880
Editorial Address: National Agricultural Centre, Stoneleigh Park, KENILWORTH, CV8 2LG **Tel:** 024 7669 6513
Fax: 024 7669 6724
Email: information@britishsimmental.co.uk
Advertising Address: As above.
Email: information@britishsimmental.co.uk
Web site: http://www.britishsimmental.co.uk
Publisher: The British Simmental Cattle Society Ltd
Frequency: Annual - Published in January
Free to qualifying individuals
Circulation: 4,000 (Publisher's Statement)
Usual Pagination: 98
Editor: Claire Rowbotham; **Advertising Manager:** Claire Rowbotham

Business Magazines

Summary of Content: Magazine for members of the British Simmental Cattle Society and those interested in breed, shows and news.
Readership/Target Audience: Aimed at members of the British Simmental Cattle Society.
ADVERTISING RATES:
Full Page Mono £288.75
Full Page Colour £462.00
Mechanical Data: Type Area: 255 x 177mm, Col Length: 255mm, Page Width: 177mm, Bleed Size: 303 x 216mm, Trim Size: 297 x 210mm, Film: Digital
Copy instructions: Copy Date: November 30th
Average advertising content per issue: 33%
BUSINESS: AGRICULTURE & FARMING: Livestock

SIMON'S WEEKLY TAX INTELLIGENCE
35408U1M-40
Editorial Address: Halsbury House, 35 Chancery Lane, LONDON, WC2A 1EL **Tel:** 020 7400 2500
Fax: 020 7400 2842
Email: tanya.stewart@lexisnexis.co.uk
Web site: http://www.lexisnexis.co.uk
ISSN: 1357-7905
Publisher: LexisNexis
Frequency: Weekly
Annual Sub.: £249.00
Circulation: 3,000 (Publisher's Statement)
Editor: Tanya Stewart
Summary of Content: Magazine covering news and information on taxation matters.
Readership/Target Audience: Read by lawyers, accountants and those whose work involves taxes or the Budget.
ADVERTISING: No Advertising taken
BUSINESS: FINANCE & ECONOMICS: Taxation

THE SINGER
40958U61-300
Editorial Address: 241 Shaftesbury Avenue, LONDON, WC2H 8TF **Tel:** 020 7333 1746 **Fax:** 020 7333 1769
Email: the.singer@rhinegold.co.uk
Advertising Address: As above. **Tel:** 020 7333 1733
Fax: 020 7333 1736
Email: ad.sales@rhinegold.co.uk
Web site: http://www.rhinegold.co.uk
Publisher: Rhinegold Publishing Ltd
Date Established: 1992
Frequency: 6 issues yearly
Annual Sub.: £18.25
Circulation: 15,600 (Publisher's Statement)
Usual Pagination: 44
Editor: Antonia Couling
Summary of Content: Magazine covering all aspects of singing including classical, jazz, cabaret, choral and musicals.
Readership/Target Audience: Aimed at singers of all types of music.
ADVERTISING RATES:
Full Page Mono £990.00
Full Page Colour £1600.00
Agency Commission: 10%
Mechanical Data: Type Area: 278 x 190mm, Col Length: 278mm, No. of Columns (Display): 4, Print Process: Web-fed offset litho, Film: Positive, right reading, emulsion side down. Digital, Trim Size: 297 x 210mm, Bleed Size: 306 x 216mm, Page Width: 190mm
Copy instructions: Copy Date: 3 weeks prior to publication date
Average advertising content per issue: 30%
BUSINESS: MUSIC TRADE

SITE RECORDER
35903U4E-160
Formerly: On Site
Editorial Address: Equinox, 28 Commerce Road, Peterborough Business Park, Lynchwood, PETERBOROUGH, PE2 6LR **Tel:** 01733 405160
Fax: 01733 405161
Email: r.morris@icwgb.co.uk
Advertising Address: 28 Burghley Road, BRISTOL, BS6 5BN **Tel:** 01899 221012 **Fax:** 01899 220500
Email: rob@gildenburgh.co.uk
Web site: http://www.icwgb.org
ISSN: 1741-3761
Publisher: Gildenburgh Ltd
Date Established: 1968
Frequency: Monthly
Free to qualifying individuals*
Annual Sub.: £35.00
Circulation: 4,500 (Publisher's Statement)
Usual Pagination: 20
Editor: Rachel Morris; **Advertising Manager:** Rob Gutteridge
Summary of Content: Magazine containing construction news and information relevant to those working in site inspection related roles. Covers sustainability, health and safety, technical, product testing, product directory, recruitment, learning and CPD.

Readership/Target Audience: Aimed at all those involved in site inspection.
ADVERTISING RATES:
Full Page Colour £1045.00
SCC £15.00
Agency Commission: 10%
Mechanical Data: Trim Size: 297 x 210mm, Film: Digital
Copy instructions: Copy Date: 2 weeks prior to publication date
Average advertising content per issue: 20%
BUSINESS: ARCHITECTURE & BUILDING: Building

SITELINES
35866U4D-225
Editorial Address: Trelawney House, Chestergate, MACCLESFIELD, SK11 6DW **Tel:** 01625 667541
Fax: 01625 435078
Email: anthony.woodburn@tenalpspublishing.com
Advertising Address: As above. **Tel:** 01625 613000
Fax: 01625 667521
Email: alan.charnock@tenalpspublishing.com
Web site: http://www.sitelines.co.uk
Publisher: Ten Alps Publishing
Date Established: 1997
Frequency: Quarterly
Cover Price: Free
Circulation: 20,000 (Publisher's Statement)
Usual Pagination: 100
Editor: Anthony Woodburn
Summary of Content: Journal of the Local Authority Building Control Services. Contains general construction news, government initiatives and building regulations.
Readership/Target Audience: Aimed at local and central government, building industry federations and professional institutes, construction companies, property developers, housing associations, architects and construction engineers.
ADVERTISING RATES:
Full Page Mono £1400.00
Full Page Colour £1600.00
Agency Commission: 10%
Mechanical Data: Type Area: 360 x 267mm, Bleed Size: 395 x 287mm, Trim Size: 282 x 390mm, Col Widths (Display): 31mm, No. of Columns (Display): 8, Print Process: Litho, Film: Digital, Col Length: 360mm, Page Width: 267mm
Copy instructions: Copy Date: 6 weeks prior to publication date
BUSINESS: ARCHITECTURE & BUILDING: Planning & Housing

SKILLS 4 NURSES
1833922U56B-297
Editorial Address: Gibbs Yard, Auchincruive, AYR, KA6 5HN **Tel:** 01292 525970 **Fax:** 01292 525979
Email: evolution1200@btopenworld.com
Advertising Address: As above.
Email: strathayr@btclick.com
Web site: http://www.scottishhealthcare.com
Publisher: Global Media Ltd
Frequency: Monthly - Published at the beginning of the cover month
Cover Price: Free
Circulation: 60,000 (Publisher's Statement)
Editor: Shona McMahon; **Managing Director:** Jim Brown; **Advertising Manager:** Jim Brown
Summary of Content: Magazine featuring job vacancies and product news from both the NHS trusts and private health care providers in the UK, Ireland and overseas.
Readership/Target Audience: Aimed at nursing professionals of all grades and disciplines.
ADVERTISING RATES:
Full Page Mono £1455.00
Full Page Colour £1855.00
Mechanical Data: Type Area: 267 x 190mm, Bleed Size: 303 x 216mm, Trim Size: 297 x 210mm, Col Length: 267mm, Page Width: 190mm, Film: Digital
Copy instructions: Copy Date: 2 weeks prior to publication date
BUSINESS: HEALTH & MEDICAL: Nursing

SKYPORT HEATHROW
36384U6B-251
Editorial Address: 93 Staines Road, HOUNSLOW, TW3 3JB
Tel: 020 8538 2235 **Fax:** 020 8741 1973
Email: editor@skyportuk.co.uk
Advertising Address: 89 Eastworth Road, CHERTSEY, KT16 8DX **Tel:** 01932 573247 **Fax:** 01932 573222
Email: gaynorwhite@trinitysouth.co.uk
Publisher: Trinity Mirror
Date Established: 1976
Frequency: Weekly
Free to qualifying individuals
Annual Sub.: £60.00
Circulation: 31,000 (Publisher's Statement)
Usual Pagination: 32
Editor: Ailsa Dixon; **Advertising Manager:** Gaynor White
Summary of Content: Newspaper covering airport-related current affairs, local and company news and lifestyle issues.
Readership/Target Audience: Read by staff at Heathrow, Gatwick and Stansted airports.
ADVERTISING: Rates on application

Agency Commission: 10%
Copy instructions: Copy Date: Wednesday 4pm prior to publication date
Average advertising content per issue: 50%
Editions:
Skyport Gatwick
Skyport Stansted
BUSINESS: AVIATION & AERONAUTICS: Airports

SLEEPER
601206U4B-170
Editorial Address: Waterloo Place, Watson Square, STOCKPORT, SK1 3AZ **Tel:** 0161 476 8390
Fax: 0161 476 7214
Email: c.martin@mondiale.co.uk
Advertising Address: As above. **Fax:** 0161 429 7214
Email: s.quiligotti@mondiale.co.uk
Web site: http://www.sleepermagazine.co.uk
Publisher: Sleeper Media Ltd
Date Established: 1999
Frequency: 6 issues yearly - Published on the 1st of the cover month
Circulation: 10,500 (Publisher's Statement)
Usual Pagination: 68
Editor: Matthew Turner; **Advertising Manager:** Stephen Quiligotti
Summary of Content: Magazine covering all aspects of the design of contemporary hotels. Contains features and profiles on hotels, product reviews and industry news.
Readership/Target Audience: Aimed at hotel owners, architects, designers and suppliers.
ADVERTISING RATES:
Full Page Colour £2450.00
Agency Commission: 10%
Mechanical Data: Col Length: 245mm, Type Area: 245 x 206mm, Trim Size: 275 x 236mm, Bleed Size: 281 x 242mm, Film: Digital, Page Width: 206mm
Average advertising content per issue: 40%
BUSINESS: ARCHITECTURE & BUILDING: Interior Design & Flooring

SMALL CAP SHARES
601007U1F-408_70
Formerly: Small Cap Shares Newsletter
Editorial Address: 3rd Floor, Henry Thomas House, 5-11 Worship Street, LONDON, EC2A 2BH **Tel:** 020 7562 3370
Fax: 020 7628 3815
Email: richard@t1ps.com
Advertising Address: As above.
Email: robert.tyson@t1ps.com
Web site: http://www.smallcapshares.co.uk
ISSN: 1466-9307
Publisher: T1ps.com Limited
Date Established: 1999
Frequency: Monthly
Annual Sub.: £99.00
Circulation: 600 (Publisher's Statement)
Usual Pagination: 24
Editor: Richard Gill; **Advertising Manager:** Robert Tyson; **Managing Editor:** Richard Gill
Summary of Content: Newsletter dedicated to small cap stock picks quoted on the LSE's Official List and AIM. Offers readers investment tips, covers relevant news updates on all the stocks in the portfolio as well as editorial content.
Readership/Target Audience: Aimed at private investors, stockbrokers and investment managers.
ADVERTISING: Rates on application
BUSINESS: FINANCE & ECONOMICS: Investment

THE SMALL COMPANY SHAREWATCH
35305U1F-409
Editorial Address: 84 Addiscombe Road, CROYDON, CR0 5PP **Tel:** 020 8656 4648 **Fax:** 020 8656 0111
Email: smit.berry@scsw.co.uk
ISSN: 1358-183X
Publisher: Equitylink Ltd
Date Established: 1994
Frequency: Monthly
Annual Sub.: £119.50
Usual Pagination: 8
Editor: Smit Berry
Summary of Content: Newsletter providing news and market comment, plus updates on stocks and shares in small UK companies.
Readership/Target Audience: Aimed at private and professional investors.
ADVERTISING: No Advertising taken
BUSINESS: FINANCE & ECONOMICS: Investment

SMALLHOLDER
37850U21R-1507
Editorial Address: Hook House, Hook Road, Wimblington, MARCH, PE15 0QL **Tel:** 01354 741538 **Fax:** 01354 741182
Email: liz.wright1@btconnect.com
Advertising Address: 3 Falmouth Business Park, Bickland Water Road, FALMOUTH, TR11 4SZ **Tel:** 01326 213303
Fax: 01326 212084

Email: wendy.symons@packetseries.co.uk
Web site: http://www.smallholder.co.uk
Publisher: Newsquest PLC
Frequency: 13 issues yearly - Published the 1st week of the cover month
Cover Price: £3.25
Annual Sub.: £35.95
Circulation: 20,000 (Publisher's Statement)
Usual Pagination: 116
Editor: Liz Wright; **Advertising Manager:** Wendy Symons; **Group Editor:** Stephen Ivall
Summary of Content: Journal covering a range of topics relating to the country and producing food in an ecological and welfare-orientated way. Includes crop growing, animal husbandry, bee-keeping and financial issues.
Readership/Target Audience: Aimed at farmers, allotment gardeners, first time landowners and country lovers. Also all those with poultry and small country businesses.
ADVERTISING RATES:
Full Page Mono £388.00
Full Page Colour £494.00
Agency Commission: 10%
Mechanical Data: Print Process: Heatset web-offset litho, Type Area: 250 x 185mm, Col Length: 250mm, No. of Columns (Display): 6, Page Width: 185mm
Copy instructions: Copy Date: 2 weeks prior to publication date
Average advertising content per issue: 40%
BUSINESS: AGRICULTURE & FARMING: Agriculture & Farming Related

SMART BUSINESS TRAVEL 1848134U50-242

Editorial Address: Western House, St.James Place, High Street, CRANLEIGH, GU6 8RL **Tel:** 01483 276788
Fax: 01483 277646
Email: contact@smartbusinesstravel.co.uk
Web site: http://www.smartbusinesstravel.co.uk
Publisher: Smart Group
Date Established: 1998
Frequency: 6 issues yearly
Cover Price: £4.95
Circulation: 100,000 (Publisher's Statement)
Usual Pagination: 40
Editor: Tony Williams; **Managing Editor:** Tony Williams
Summary of Content: Magazine covering air travel, airlines, airports, airport lounges, car rental, chauffeur drive, coach travel, conference and meeting venues, expense management and hotels.
Readership/Target Audience: Aimed at corporate travel buyers.
BUSINESS: TRAVEL & TOURISM

SMART CARD AND IDENTITY NEWS 35348U1G-100

Formerly: Smart Card News
Editorial Address: 3 Anchor Springs, Duke Street, LITTLEHAMPTON, BN17 6BP **Tel:** 01903 734677
Fax: 01903 734318
Email: lesley.dann@smartcard.co.uk
Advertising Address: As above. **Tel:** 01903 691779
Email: lesley.dann@smartcardgroup.co.uk
Web site: http://www.smartcard.co.uk
ISSN: 1755-1021
Publisher: Smart Card News Ltd
Date Established: 1992
Frequency: Monthly
Annual Sub.: £475.00
Usual Pagination: 22
Editor: Lesley Dann; **Managing Director:** Patsy Everett; **Advertising Manager:** Lesley Dann
Summary of Content: Newsletter covering news, developments and applications from the Smart Card industry worldwide.
Readership/Target Audience: Aimed at decision makers and managers.
ADVERTISING RATES:
Full Page Colour £1500.00
Mechanical Data: Film: Positive, right reading, emulsion side down. Digital
Copy instructions: Copy Date: 10th of the month prior to publication date
Average advertising content per issue: 5%
BUSINESS: FINANCE & ECONOMICS: Credit Trading

SMART TEXTILES AND NANOTECHNOLOGY 1793872U47A-585

Editorial Address: 9A Victoria Square, DROITWICH, WR9 8DE **Tel:** 0870 165 7211 **Fax:** 0870 165 7212
Email: stan@intnews.com
Web site: http://www.technical-textiles.net
ISSN: 1752-2668
Publisher: International Newsletters
Date Established: 2006
Frequency: Monthly
Annual Sub.: £295.00
Usual Pagination: 16

Editor: Nick Butler; **Publisher:** Guy Kitteringham
Summary of Content: Newsletter and online news service covering the new products, material and applications relating to functional textiles in the clothing industry and others. Also covers the nanotechnology involved in the finishing and coating processes used in the textile field.
Readership/Target Audience: Aimed at marketing and technical directors of textile, manufacturing and engineering companies.
ADVERTISING: No Advertising taken
BUSINESS: CLOTHING & TEXTILES

SMILE 40391U56D-79

Formerly: The Hygienist
Editorial Address: 2nd Floor, 207-215 High Street, ORPINGTON, BR6 0PF **Tel:** 01689 899170
Fax: 01689 899171
Email: georgina.smith@purplems.com
Advertising Address: As above. **Tel:** 01689 899177
Email: ed.hunt@purpleems.com
Web site: http://www.purplems.com
Publisher: Purple Media Solutions Ltd
Frequency: 8 issues yearly
Cover Price: Free
Circulation: 4,300 (Publisher's Statement)
Usual Pagination: 30
Editor: Georgina Smith
Summary of Content: Magazine promoting dental hygiene as a growing sector of the dental profession, offering advice on training, marketing, communications and financial features and news.
Readership/Target Audience: Aimed at dental hygienists.
ADVERTISING RATES:
Full Page Colour £1785.00
SCC £35.00
Agency Commission: 10%
Mechanical Data: Film: Digital, Page Width: 185mm, Bleed Size: 303 x 216mm, Trim Size: 297 x 210mm, Type Area: 278 x 185mm, Col Length: 278mm
Copy instructions: Copy Date: 2 weeks prior to publication date
Average advertising content per issue: 50%
BUSINESS: HEALTH & MEDICAL: Dental

THE SNACKS MAGAZINE 37983U22A-340

Editorial Address: Kepplegate, The Avenue, Comberbach, NORTHWICH, CW9 6HT **Tel:** 01606 892439
Email: snacksmagazine@clevercopy.co.uk
Advertising Address: Rock House, Rudyard, LEEK, ST13 8RL **Tel:** 01538 757308 **Fax:** 01538 757308
Email: production@snacksmagazine.co.uk
Web site: http://www.esa.org.uk
ISSN: 1351-3133
Publisher: Mill Design & Print
Date Established: 1985
Frequency: Quarterly - Published in the 1st week of the cover month
Annual Sub.: £30.00
Circulation: 2,600 (Publisher's Statement)
Usual Pagination: 52
Editor: Lynda Searby; **Advertising Manager:** Pauline Keeling
Summary of Content: Journal covering the savoury snack food industry in Europe and its suppliers. Covers new products, ingredients and equipment, market trends, production techniques and industry issues.
Readership/Target Audience: Aimed at senior management and key decision makers.
ADVERTISING RATES:
Full Page Mono £1090.00
Full Page Colour £1370.00
Agency Commission: 10%
Mechanical Data: Print Process: Sheet-fed litho, Bleed Size: 303 x 216mm, Trim Size: 297 x 210mm, Page Width: 185mm, Type Area: 280 x 185mm, Col Length: 280mm, Film: Digital
Average advertising content per issue: 50%
BUSINESS: FOOD

SNS EUROPE 601564U5B-84_25

Formerly: Fibre Channel Focus
Editorial Address: Hannay House, 39 Clarendon Road, WATFORD, WD17 1JA **Tel:** 01923 690200
Fax: 01923 690201
Email: phil@martinspikemedia.com
Advertising Address: As above. **Tel:** 01923 690206
Email: hm@angelbcl.co.uk
Web site: http://www.snseurope.com
Publisher: Angel Business Communications Ltd
Frequency: 8 issues yearly - Published on the 1st of the cover month
Cover Price: Free
Circulation: 12,000 (Publisher's Statement)
Editor: Philip Alsop

Summary of Content: Magazine covering news, features on storage area networking, new products, case studies and technical articles.
Readership/Target Audience: Aimed at European IT managers.
ADVERTISING RATES:
Full Page Mono £3400.00
Full Page Colour £3800.00
Agency Commission: 10%
Mechanical Data: Bleed Size: 261 x 189mm, Page Width: 163mm, Type Area: 235 x 163mm, Col Length: 235mm, Film: Digital, Trim Size: 255 x 183mm
Copy instructions: Copy Date: 2 weeks prior to publication date
Average advertising content per issue: 40%
BUSINESS: COMPUTERS & AUTOMATION: Data Processing

SOCIAL & LEGAL STUDIES 40107U55-168

Editorial Address: 1 Oliver's Yard, 55 City Road, LONDON, EC1Y 1SP **Tel:** 020 7324 8500 **Fax:** 020 7324 8600
Advertising Address: As above.
Email: advertising@sagepub.co.uk
Web site: http://www.sagepub.co.uk
ISSN: 0964-6639
Publisher: Sage Publications
Frequency: Quarterly
Cover Price: £15.00
Annual Sub.: £49.00
Circulation: 400 (Publisher's Statement)
Usual Pagination: 150
Editor: Linda Mulcahy; **Advertising Manager:** Sheena Karim
Summary of Content: An international forum for the latest research in critical legal studies from a variety of perspectives within social theory.
Readership/Target Audience: Aimed at those involved in socio-legal research.
ADVERTISING RATES:
Full Page Mono £400.00
Copy instructions: Copy Date: 12 weeks prior to publication date
BUSINESS: APPLIED SCIENCE & LABORATORIES

SOCIAL COMPASS 40104U55-169

Editorial Address: 1 Oliver's Yard, 55 City Road, LONDON, EC1Y 1SP **Tel:** 020 7324 8500 **Fax:** 020 7324 8600
Advertising Address: As above.
Email: sheena.karim@sagepub.co.uk
Web site: http://www.sagepub.co.uk
ISSN: 0037-7686
Publisher: Sage Publications
Date Established: 1970
Frequency: Quarterly
Cover Price: £14.00
Annual Sub.: £44.00
Circulation: 750 (Publisher's Statement)
Editor: Celine Polain
Summary of Content: Journal of the International Federation of Institutes for Social and Socio-Religious Research (FERES), covering current social scientific research on religion in society.
Readership/Target Audience: Aimed at all scholars in sociology, anthropology, religious studies and theology concerned with the sociology of religion.
ADVERTISING RATES:
Full Page Mono £400.00
Agency Commission: 5%
Mechanical Data: Col Length: 205mm, Type Area: 205 x 130mm, Page Width: 130mm, Film: Digital
BUSINESS: APPLIED SCIENCE & LABORATORIES

SOCIAL ENTERPRISE 761161U14R-390

Editorial Address: Unit 4, 25A Vyner Street, LONDON, E2 9DG **Tel:** 020 8983 1987
Email: news@socialenterprisemag.co.uk
Advertising Address: As above.
Email: ad@socialenterprisemag.co.uk
Web site: http://www.socialenterprisemag.co.uk
ISSN: 1476-3931
Publisher: London Fields Publishing Ltd
Date Established: 2002
Frequency: 10 issues yearly
Annual Sub.: £90.00
Circulation: 3,000 (Publisher's Statement)
Usual Pagination: 36
Editor: Chrisanthi Giotis; **Advertising Manager:** Deniz Hassan
Summary of Content: Magazine covering news and advice on business and innovation for social aims. Includes events, analysis, good practice, debate and ideas.
Readership/Target Audience: Aimed at social entrepreneurs, voluntary groups who aim to become more entrepreneurial and business professionals with social aims.
ADVERTISING RATES:
Full Page Colour £1498.00
Agency Commission: 10%

Mechanical Data: Film: Digital, Type Area: 270 x 192mm, Col Length: 270mm, Page Width: 192mm, Bleed Size: +3mm, Trim Size: 300 x 230mm
Copy instructions: Copy Date: Middle of the month prior to publication date
Average advertising content per issue: 10%
BUSINESS: COMMERCE, INDUSTRY & MANAGEMENT: Commerce Related

SOCIAL HOUSING
35871U4D-230
Editorial Address: Fifth Floor, 57a Great Suffolk Street, LONDON, SE1 0BB **Tel:** 020 7934 0166 **Fax:** 020 7934 0179
Email: editor@socialhousing.co.uk
Advertising Address: As above. **Tel:** 020 7378 3041
Fax: 020 7378 3040
Email: editor@socialhousing.co.uk
Web site: http://www.socialhousing.co.uk
ISSN: 1351-4288
Publisher: The Financial Information Company Ltd
Date Established: 1988
Frequency: Monthly - Published in the 1st week of the cover month
Annual Sub.: £150.00
Circulation: 2,000 (Publisher's Statement)
Usual Pagination: 28
Editor: Kate Allen; **Advertising Manager:** Cassandra Karanjia
Summary of Content: Journal focusing on finance, business and governance in housing.
Readership/Target Audience: Aimed at decision makers in the affordable housing sector, RSLs, ALMOs, social housing lenders, lawyers, surveyors builders, developers and government departments.
ADVERTISING RATES:
Full Page Mono £1350.00
Full Page Colour £1750.00
Agency Commission: 10%
Mechanical Data: Film: Digital, Type Area: 276 x 186mm, Col Length: 276mm, Page Width: 186mm, Bleed Size: +3mm, Trim Size: 298 x 216mm
Copy instructions: Copy Date: 2 weeks prior to publication date
Average advertising content per issue: 20%
BUSINESS: ARCHITECTURE & BUILDING: Planning & Housing

SOCIAL IDENTITIES
40106U55-169_50
Editorial Address: 4 Park Square, Milton Park, ABINGDON, OX14 4RN **Tel:** 020 7017 6000 **Fax:** 020 7017 6336
Email: matthew.cannon@tandf.co.uk
Advertising Address: LH Marketing Solutions, 60 Upper Broadmoor Road, CROWTHORNE, RG45 7DE
Tel: 01344 779945 **Fax:** 01344 775713
Email: lhann@lhms.fsnet.co.uk
Web site: http://www.informaworld.com/csid
ISSN: 1350-4630
Publisher: Routledge, Taylor & Francis
Date Established: 1995
Frequency: 6 issues yearly
Circulation: 300 (Publisher's Statement)
Usual Pagination: 144
Editor: Matthew Cannon; **Managing Editor:** Jane Oakley
Summary of Content: Journal covering the study of race, nation and culture.
Readership/Target Audience: Aimed at academics and researchers.
BUSINESS: APPLIED SCIENCE & LABORATORIES

SOCIAL SCIENCE INFORMATION
40108U55-169_60
Editorial Address: 1 Oliver's Yard, 55 City Road, LONDON, EC1Y 1SP **Tel:** 020 7324 8500 **Fax:** 020 7324 8600
Advertising Address: As above.
Email: advertising@sagepub.co.uk
Web site: http://www.sagepub.co.uk
ISSN: 0539-0184
Publisher: Sage Publications
Date Established: 1978
Frequency: Quarterly
Annual Sub.: £60.00
Editor: Nora Scott; **Editor-in-Chief:** Anne Rocha Perazzo; **Advertising Manager:** Sheena Karim
Summary of Content: Journal covering research in social anthropology, sociology of science and sociological theory.
Language(s): English; French
Readership/Target Audience: Aimed at those involved in anthropology, sociology, psychology, philosophy, political science and economics.
ADVERTISING RATES:
Full Page Mono £400.00
Mechanical Data: Type Area: 205 x 130mm, Col Length: 205mm, Film: Digital, Page Width: 130mm
Copy instructions: Copy Date: 12 weeks prior to publication date
BUSINESS: APPLIED SCIENCE & LABORATORIES

SOCIAL STUDIES OF SCIENCE
40109U55-169_70
Editorial Address: 1 Oliver's Yard, 55 City Road, LONDON, EC1Y 1SP **Tel:** 020 7374 8500 **Fax:** 020 7374 8600
Advertising Address: As above. **Tel:** 020 7324 8500
Fax: 020 7324 8600
Email: sheena.karim@sagepub.co.uk
Web site: http://www.sagepub.co.uk
ISSN: 0306-3127
Publisher: Sage Publications
Frequency: 6 issues yearly
Annual Sub.: £62.00
Editor: Michael Lynch; **Advertising Manager:** Sheena Karim
Summary of Content: Journal covering the study of science in its social dimension.
Readership/Target Audience: Aimed at historians, philosophers, sociologists, political scientists and economists who are contributing research on the study of social science in its social dimension.
ADVERTISING RATES:
Full Page Mono £450.00
Agency Commission: 5%
Mechanical Data: Film: Digital, Col Length: 190mm, Page Width: 110mm, Type Area: 190 x 110mm
BUSINESS: APPLIED SCIENCE & LABORATORIES

SOFHT FOCUS
38051U22R-345
Editorial Address: The Granary, Middleton House Farm, Tamworth Rd, STAFFORDSHIRE, B78 2BD
Tel: 01827 872500 **Fax:** 01827 875800
Email: admin@sofht.co.uk
Advertising Address: As above.
Email: amberstaynings@sofht.co.uk
Web site: http://www.sofht.co.uk
ISSN: 1477-7401
Publisher: The Society of Food, Hygiene and Technology
Date Established: 1988
Frequency: Quarterly
Cover Price: Free
Circulation: 8,000 (Publisher's Statement)
Usual Pagination: 20
Editor: Amber Staynings; **Advertising Manager:** Amber Staynings
Summary of Content: Publication of The Society of Food Hygiene Technology. Covering food hygiene and safety throughout the commercial food chain.
Readership/Target Audience: Read by members and selected technical directors, quality assurance managers, consultants, trainers and environmental health officers.
ADVERTISING: Rates on application
BUSINESS: FOOD: Food Related

SOFT DRINKS INTERNATIONAL
38053U22R-350
Editorial Address: PO Box 4173, WIMBORNE, BH21 1YX
Tel: 01202 842222 **Fax:** 01202 848494
Email: editorial@softdrinksinternational.com
Advertising Address: As above.
Email: advertising@softdrinksinternational.com
Web site: http://www.softdrinksjournal.com
ISSN: 1367-8302
Publisher: ASAP Publishing Ltd
Date Established: 1888
Frequency: Monthly - Published in the 1st week of the cover month
Cover Price: £10.00
Annual Sub.: £90.00
Circulation: 3,500 (Publisher's Statement)
Usual Pagination: 60
Editor: Philip Tappenden; **News Editor:** Annette Farr; **Advertising Manager:** Philip Tappenden
Summary of Content: Journal of the soft drinks industry.
Readership/Target Audience: Aimed at soft drinks manufacturers and suppliers worldwide.
ADVERTISING RATES:
Full Page Colour £2495.00
Agency Commission: 15%
Mechanical Data: Film: Digital, Type Area: 266 x 182mm, Bleed Size: 303 x 216mm, Trim Size: 297 x 210mm, Col Length: 266mm, No. of Columns (Display): 3, Page Width: 182mm
Copy instructions: Copy Date: 15th of the month prior to publication date
Average advertising content per issue: 37%
BUSINESS: FOOD: Food Related

SOFTWARE WORLD
36131U5B-220
Editorial Address: 58 Ryecroft Way, LUTON, LU2 7TU
Tel: 01582 722219
Email: smpluton@ntlworld.com
Web site: http://www.softwareworldpublication.com
ISSN: 0038-0652
Publisher: AP Publications Ltd
Date Established: 1969
Frequency: 6 issues yearly - Published 15th of the month

Cover Price: £24.00
Annual Sub.: £135.00
Circulation: 1,000 (Publisher's Statement)
Usual Pagination: 28
Editor: Steven Patterson
Summary of Content: Publication containing coverage of the software market, security issues, including sections on languages, software writing techniques, business and contract news and book reviews.
Readership/Target Audience: Aimed at librarians, university staff and professionals involved in IT.
ADVERTISING: No Advertising taken
BUSINESS: COMPUTERS & AUTOMATION: Data Processing

SOILS & FERTILIZERS
37820U21B-38
Editorial Address: Nosworthy Way, WALLINGFORD, OX10 8DE **Tel:** 01491 832111 **Fax:** 01491 829198
Email: cabi@cabi.org
Web site: http://www.cabi-publishing.org
ISSN: 0038-0792
Publisher: CABI
Frequency: Monthly
Annual Sub.: £1900.00
Circulation: 350 (Publisher's Statement)
Editor: Halina Dawson
Summary of Content: Journal features articles on soils, fertilizers, irrigation, drainage and land management.
Readership/Target Audience: Academic and government research institutes, general agricultural/natural resources organisations, fertilizer manufacturers and environmental organisations.
ADVERTISING: No Advertising taken
BUSINESS: AGRICULTURE & FARMING: Agriculture - Supplies & Services

---

SOLDERING & SURFACE MOUNT TECHNOLOGY
1615246U18A-9005
Editorial Address: Howard House, Wagon Lane, BINGLEY, BD16 1WA **Tel:** 01274 777700 **Fax:** 01274 785200
Email: hcolson@emeraldinsight.com
Web site: http://www.emeraldinsight.com
ISSN: 0954-0911
Publisher: Emerald Group Publishing Ltd
Frequency: Quarterly
Annual Sub.: £919.00
Usual Pagination: 76
Editor: Harry Colson; **Publisher:** Harry Colson
Summary of Content: Journal covering research and development, applications, processes and current practices relating to all areas of soldering and surface mount technology.
Readership/Target Audience: Aimed at academics, researchers, engineers, practitioners and managers within the industry.
ADVERTISING: No Advertising taken
BUSINESS: ELECTRONICS

SOLDIER
38884U40-270
Editorial Address: Parsons House, Ordnance Road, ALDERSHOT, GU11 2DU **Tel:** 01252 347353
Fax: 01252 347358
Email: dcadwallader@soldiermagazine.co.uk
Advertising Address: As above. **Tel:** 01252 347352
Fax: 01252 340463
Email: advertising@soldiermagazine.co.uk
Web site: http://www.soldiermagazine.co.uk
ISSN: 0038-1004
Publisher: Ministry of Defence
Date Established: 1945
Frequency: Monthly
Cover Price: £2.50
Circulation: 98,000 (Publisher's Statement)
Usual Pagination: 92
Editor: Stephen Tyler
Summary of Content: Magazine containing news and features relating to the British Army.
Readership/Target Audience: Read by all ranks and age groups of the British regular and territorial Armies and their families, ex-servicemen and women and interested civilians.
ADVERTISING RATES:
Full Page Mono £1060.00
Full Page Colour £1325.00
Agency Commission: 10%
Mechanical Data: Type Area: 270 x 186mm, Print Process: Offset litho, Bleed Size: 303 x 213mm, Trim Size: 297 x 210mm, No. of Columns (Display): 4, Col Widths (Display): 45mm, Col Length: 270mm, Page Width: 186mm, Film: Digital
Copy instructions: Copy Date: 4 weeks prior to publication date
Average advertising content per issue: 33%
BUSINESS: DEFENCE

SOLICITORS' JOURNAL
39238U44-1800

Editorial Address: 3rd Floor, 6-14 Underwood Street, LONDON, N1 7JQ **Tel:** 020 7490 0049 **Fax:** 020 7324 2366
Email: editorial@solicitorsjournal.com
Advertising Address: As above. **Fax:** 020 7324 2341
Email: chanley@waterlow.com
Web site: http://www.solicitorsjournal.com
ISSN: 0038-1047
Publisher: Waterlow Professional Publishing
Date Established: 1856
Frequency: Weekly
Annual Sub.: £219.00
Circulation: 5,000 (Publisher's Statement)
Usual Pagination: 36
Editor: Jean-Yves Gilg; **News Editor:** Nick Hilborne;
Features Editor: Jenny Ramage; **Advertising Director:** Chris Hanley
Summary of Content: Weekly magazine and online resource providing news and features on legal developments and practice for medium sized solicitors firms.
Readership/Target Audience: Aimed at solicitors in private practice, in government departments and employed in-house.
ADVERTISING RATES:
Full Page Colour £1215.00
Agency Commission: 10%
Mechanical Data: Film: Digital, Trim Size: 297 x 210mm, Bleed Size: 303 x 216mm
Copy instructions: Copy Date: 1 week prior to publication date
Average advertising content per issue: 33%
BUSINESS: LEGAL

SOLIDS AND BULK HANDLING
36522U10-12

Formerly: Bulk Handling International
Editorial Address: Armstrong House, 38 Market Square, UXBRIDGE, UB8 1LN **Tel:** 01895 454600 **Fax:** 01895 454643
Email: kellyrose@quartzltd.com
Advertising Address: As above. **Tel:** 01895 454474
Fax: 01895 454647
Email: nevillefreedman@quartz.uk.net
Web site: http://www.solidsandbulk.com
Publisher: Quartz Publishing
Date Established: 1974
Frequency: 8 issues yearly - Published on the 7th of the cover month
Free to qualifying individuals
Annual Sub.: £110.00
Circulation: 8,521 (ABC 01/01/2008 to 31/12/2008)
Usual Pagination: 64
Editor: Kelly Rose; **Advertising Manager:** Neville Freedman
Summary of Content: Magazine containing information regarding all aspects of bulk solids handling, processing, storage, transport, health and safety.
Readership/Target Audience: Read by managing directors and senior management level decision makers within all types of processing industries.
ADVERTISING RATES:
Full Page Colour £1900.00
Agency Commission: 10%
Mechanical Data: Trim Size: 297 x 210mm, Type Area: 254 x 178mm, Col Length: 254mm, Page Width: 178mm, Bleed Size: 303 x 216mm
Copy instructions: Copy Date: 8 weeks prior to publication date
Average advertising content per issue: 55%
BUSINESS: MATERIALS HANDLING

THE SOLIHULL JOURNAL
713916U63B-1950

Editorial Address: 33 Middle Meadow Avenue, BIRMINGHAM, B32 1NU **Tel:** 0121 687 1054
Fax: 0121 687 1051
Email: lee@freshmedia-uk.co.uk
Advertising Address: As above.
Email: bestpracticeuk@aol.com
Publisher: Fresh Media UK Ltd
Date Established: 1990
Frequency: 26 issues yearly
Cover Price: £1.00
Annual Sub.: £52.00
Circulation: 5,000 (Publisher's Statement)
Editor: Andre Laurent; **Advertising Manager:** Andre Laurent
Summary of Content: Magazine covering local business news, recruitment, what's on guide and events listings.
Readership/Target Audience: Aimed at home and business owners in Solihull and the surrounding area.
ADVERTISING: Rates on application
Supplement to: The City of Birmingham Journal
BUSINESS: REGIONAL BUSINESS: Regional Business English Counties

SOLUTIONS FOR INDUSTRY
1698555U14A-557

Editorial Address: 5th Floor, Scala House, Holloway Circus, BIRMINGHAM, B1 1EQ **Tel:** 0121 687 1041
Fax: 0121 687 1051
Email: freshmediacopy@aol.com

Advertising Address: As above. **Tel:** 0121 687 1044
Email: freshmediacopy@aol.com
Web site: http://www.freshmedia-uk.co.uk
Publisher: Fresh Media UK Ltd
Date Established: 2005
Frequency: Weekly
Free to qualifying individuals
Annual Sub.: £95.00
Circulation: 5,000 (Publisher's Statement)
Usual Pagination: 20
Editor: Ian Bird; **Advertising Manager:** Tony Jacques
Summary of Content: Magazine focusing on industrial sectors across the UK. Articles covered include engineering, manufacturing, materials handling and construction.
Readership/Target Audience: Aimed at decision makers within UK industry.
ADVERTISING RATES:
Full Page Colour £2217.60
Agency Commission: 10%
Mechanical Data: Type Area: 360 x 262mm, Col Length: 360mm, Page Width: 262mm, Film: Digital, Bleed Size: +5mm
Copy instructions: Copy Date: 1 day prior to publication date
Average advertising content per issue: 20%
BUSINESS: COMMERCE, INDUSTRY & MANAGEMENT

THE SOROPTIMIST
37238U14R-400

Editorial Address: Willow Lodge Office, Fowley Lane, High Hurstwood, UCKFIELD, TN22 4BG **Tel:** 01825 733843
Email: soroptimist@written-image.com
Advertising Address: PO Box 234, UCKFIELD, TN22 9AH **Tel:** 01825 733843
Email: soroptimist@written-image.com
Publisher: Pisces Media Ltd
Date Established: 1930
Frequency: 6 issues yearly
Cover Price: £7.50
Free to qualifying individuals
Circulation: 12,500 (Publisher's Statement)
Usual Pagination: 16
Editor: Sheila Manchester; **Advertising Manager:** Sheila Manchester
Summary of Content: Magazine of the worldwide women's service organisation, Soroptimist International.
Readership/Target Audience: Aimed at business and professional women holding senior management positions and above.
ADVERTISING: Rates on application
BUSINESS: COMMERCE, INDUSTRY & MANAGEMENT: Commerce Related

SOUNDING BOARD
40960U61-340

Editorial Address: Riverside House, Rattlesden, BURY ST EDMUNDS, IP30 0SF
Email: info@soundsense.org
Advertising Address: As above.
Email: info@soundsense.org
Web site: http://www.soundsense.org
ISSN: 1464-6730
Publisher: Sound Sense
Date Established: 1990
Frequency: Quarterly
Free to qualifying individuals
Circulation: 750 (Publisher's Statement)
Usual Pagination: 16
Editor: Kathryn Deane; **Advertising Manager:** Kathryn Deane
Summary of Content: Magazine containing news, discussion, features and opinions on all aspects of participatory music-making.
Readership/Target Audience: Read by musicians, arts administrators, local government officers, youth and community workers and music teachers.
ADVERTISING RATES:
Full Page Mono £250.00
Full Page Colour £400.00
Mechanical Data: Film: Digital
Average advertising content per issue: 20%
BUSINESS: MUSIC TRADE

SOURCES
35565U2A-107_3

Formerly: The Journalist's Handbook
Editorial Address: 66 John Finnie Street, KILMARNOCK, KA1 1BS **Tel:** 01563 530830 **Fax:** 01563 549503
Email: enquiries@journalistshandbook.co.uk
Advertising Address: As above.
Email: editor@journalistshandbook.co.uk
Web site: http://www.journalistshandbook.co.uk
Publisher: Standfirst
Date Established: 1985
Frequency: Annual - Published in the summer
Cover Price: Free
Circulation: 2,600 (Publisher's Statement)
Usual Pagination: 120

Editor: Fiona MacDonald; **Advertising Manager:** Fiona MacDonald
Summary of Content: Journal featuring articles on journalism and contacts section.
Readership/Target Audience: Aimed at senior UK journalists.
ADVERTISING: Rates on application
BUSINESS: COMMUNICATIONS, ADVERTISING & MARKETING

SOUTH EAST BUSINESS
41315U63B-933

Editorial Address: PR br email only
Email: newsdesk@southeastbusiness.net
Advertising Address: Evegate Publishing Ltd, Spicer House, Lympne Business Park, Lympne, HYTHE, CT21 4LR **Tel:** 01303 233880 **Fax:** 01303 239517
Email: tim.davies@southeastbusiness.net
Web site: http://www.southeastbusiness.net
ISSN: 0262-8597
Publisher: Evegate Publishing Ltd
Date Established: 1982
Frequency: Monthly
Free to qualifying individuals
Annual Sub.: £80.00
Circulation: 13,341 (ABC 01/07/2008 to 30/06/2009)
Usual Pagination: 52
Editor: Newsdesk
Summary of Content: Magazine covering business news, legal issues, finance, marketing, IT, training and executive motoring.
Readership/Target Audience: Read by directors and senior management in the South East of England.
ADVERTISING RATES:
Full Page Mono £1259.00
Full Page Colour £1469.00
Agency Commission: 10%
Mechanical Data: No. of Columns (Display): 4, Trim Size: 297 x 210mm, Type Area: 293 x 206mm, Bleed Size: 303 x 216mm, Col Length: 293mm, Page Width: 206mm, Film: Digital
Average advertising content per issue: 40%
BUSINESS: REGIONAL BUSINESS: Regional Business English Counties

SOUTH EAST FARMER
37919U21J-305

Editorial Address: PR by email only **Tel:** 01303 233880
Email: newsdesk@southeastfarmer.net
Advertising Address: Spicer House, Lympne Business Park, Lympne, HYTHE, CT21 4LR **Tel:** 01303 233880
Fax: 01303 263785
Email: jamie@southeastfarmer.net
Web site: http://www.southeastfarmer.net
ISSN: 0953-7546
Publisher: Evegate Publishing Ltd
Date Established: 1979
Frequency: Monthly - Published on the 2nd Monday of the month
Annual Sub.: £50.00
Circulation: 13,324 (ABC 01/01/2008 to 31/12/2008)
Usual Pagination: 62
Editor: Newsdesk; **Advertising Manager:** Jamie McGrorty
Summary of Content: Magazine covering news affecting all aspects of farming in the South East of England.
Readership/Target Audience: Read by farmers and growers.
ADVERTISING RATES:
Full Page Colour £1199.00
Mechanical Data: Type Area: 293 x 206mm, Col Length: 293mm, Page Width: 206mm, Trim Size: 297 x 210mm, Bleed Size: 303 x 216mm, Film: Digital
Copy instructions: Copy Date: 4th Friday of the month prior to publication date
Average advertising content per issue: 40%
Supplement(s): South East Farm Machinery - 12xY
BUSINESS: AGRICULTURE & FARMING: Agriculture & Farming - Regional

SOUTH LONDON BUSINESS
1800746U63B-2577

Editorial Address: Portland Buildings, 127-129 Portland Street, MANCHESTER, M1 4PZ **Tel:** 0161 236 2782
Fax: 0161 236 2783
Email: laurie.prescott@excelpublishing.co.uk
Publisher: Excel Publishing Company Ltd
Date Established: 2007
Frequency: 6 issues yearly
Free to qualifying individuals
Editor: Laurie Prescott
Summary of Content: Official publication of South London Business featuring business and company news, workplace issues and workforce development. Aims to promote the economic development of the area.
Readership/Target Audience: Aimed at members of the business community in South London.
ADVERTISING: Rates on application
BUSINESS: REGIONAL BUSINESS: Regional Business English Counties

SOUTH WEST BUILDING AND CONSTRUCTION
35930U4E-325

Editorial Address: PR by e-mail only **Tel:** 0844 232 7513
Email: whitepaul@orange.fr
Advertising Address: 10 Pound Park, OKEHAMPTON, EX20 1SX **Tel:** 01837 658941 **Fax:** 01837 55196
Email: judithjewel@btinternet.com
Publisher: Tavistock Newspapers Ltd
Date Established: 1997
Frequency: Monthly
Cover Price: Free
Circulation: 10,000 (Publisher's Statement)
Usual Pagination: 56
Editor: Paul White; **Advertising Manager:** Judith Jewel
Summary of Content: Magazine covering contracts, products, projects, services and equipment including vehicles in the building industry in the South West.
Readership/Target Audience: Aimed at architects, surveyors, civil engineers, quantity surveyors, structural engineers, construction companies and members of all building trades throughout Cornwall, Devon and Somerset.
ADVERTISING: Rates on application
BUSINESS: ARCHITECTURE & BUILDING: Building

SOUTH WEST FARMER
37921U21J-315

Editorial Address: 3 Falmouth Business Park, Bickland Water Road, FALMOUTH, TR11 4SZ **Tel:** 01326 213333
Fax: 01326 318749
Email: editorial@southwestfarmer.co.uk
Advertising Address: As above. **Fax:** 01326 212084
Email: wendy.symons@packetseries.co.uk
Web site: http://www.southwestfarmer.co.uk
Publisher: Newsquest (Media Group) Ltd
Frequency: Monthly - Published in the 3rd week of the cover month
Free to qualifying individuals
Annual Sub.: £12.00
Circulation: 21,000 (Publisher's Statement)
Editor: Stephen Ivall
Summary of Content: Magazine containing news and information on farming in the South West.
Readership/Target Audience: Read by the farming community and associated industries.
ADVERTISING RATES:
SCC £8.15
Agency Commission: 10%
Mechanical Data: Col Length: 350mm, Type Area: 350 x 264mm, No. of Columns (Display): 9, Trim Size: 420 x 297mm, Film: Digital, Page Width: 264mm
Copy instructions: Copy Date: 1 week prior to publication date
Average advertising content per issue: 60%
BUSINESS: AGRICULTURE & FARMING: Agriculture & Farming - Regional

SOUTH YORKSHIRE BUSINESS
1858386U63B-2591

Editorial Address: Brookfields Way, Manvers, Wath Upon Dearne, ROTHERHAM, S63 5DL **Tel:** 01709 768155
Fax: 01709 768053
Email: david.lawson@garnett-dickinson.co.uk
Web site: http://www.southyorkshirebusinessmagazine.co.uk
Publisher: Garnett Dickinson Group Ltd
Frequency: 6 issues yearly
Cover Price: £4.50
Free to qualifying individuals
Circulation: 9,000 (Publisher's Statement)
Editor: David Lawson
Summary of Content: Business to business magazine covering businesses, sectors and news in South Yorkshire.
Readership/Target Audience: Aimed at Managing Directors, local government and businesses in South Yorkshire.
BUSINESS: REGIONAL BUSINESS: Regional Business English Counties

SOUTHERN AFRICA MONITOR
1641987U14C-355

Editorial Address: Mermaid House, 2 Puddle Dock, LONDON, EC4V 3DS **Tel:** 020 7248 0468
Fax: 020 7248 0467
Email: emartins@businessmonitor.com
Web site: http://www.businessmonitor.com
Publisher: Business Monitor International Ltd
Frequency: Monthly
Annual Sub.: £325.00
Circulation: 550 (Publisher's Statement)
Editor: Elizabeth Martins
Summary of Content: Publication covering economic and political developments in Southern Africa including government, economy, finance and the business environment.
Readership/Target Audience: Aimed at investors who have invested or are looking to invest in Africa.

ADVERTISING: No Advertising taken
BUSINESS: COMMERCE, INDUSTRY & MANAGEMENT: International Commerce

SOUTHERN AFRICAN WIRELESS COMMUNICATIONS
37389U18A-440

Editorial Address: 3rd Floor, Brassey House, New Zealand Avenue, WALTON-ON-THAMES, KT12 1QD
Tel: 01932 886537 **Fax:** 01932 886539
Email: rahieln@kadiumpublishing.com
Advertising Address: As above.
Email: richardl@kadiumpublishing.com
Web site: http://www.wirelesscomms.org
ISSN: 1364-4394
Publisher: Kadium Ltd
Date Established: 1996
Frequency: 6 issues yearly - Published in the middle of the 2nd cover month
Free to qualifying individuals
Circulation: 7,000 (Publisher's Statement)
Usual Pagination: 36
Editor: Rahiel Nasir
Summary of Content: Magazine dedicated to all aspects of wireless and mobile communications in southern equatorial Africa.
Readership/Target Audience: Aimed at companies and organisations that use mobile and wireless communications as part of their business.
ADVERTISING RATES:
Full Page Colour £3695.00
Agency Commission: 10%
Mechanical Data: Page Width: 190mm, Type Area: 280 x 190mm, Bleed Size: 307 x 220mm, Trim Size: 297 x 210mm, Col Length: 280mm, Film: Digital
Copy instructions: Copy Date: 1 week prior to publication date
Average advertising content per issue: 40%
BUSINESS: ELECTRONICS

SOUTHERN GAZETTE
601385U63B-2270

Formerly: Southern Business Times
Editorial Address: 39-41 St. Nicholas Street, BRISTOL, BS1 1TP **Tel:** 0117 929 1176
Email: southerngazette@aol.com
Advertising Address: As above.
Email: southerngazette@aol.com
Publisher: JPC Ltd
Date Established: 1999
Frequency: Weekly
Cover Price: Free
Circulation: 10,000 (Publisher's Statement)
Usual Pagination: 26
Editor: Sonia Waters; **Managing Director:** Martin Sanders;
Advertising Manager: Sonia Waters
Summary of Content: Newspaper covering recruitment in and around Southampton.
Readership/Target Audience: Aimed at small businesses.
ADVERTISING RATES:
SCC £10.00
Copy instructions: Copy Date: Monday 3pm prior to publication date
BUSINESS: REGIONAL BUSINESS: Regional Business English Counties

SP2
765115U13-191

Editorial Address: Global House, 13 Market Square, HORSHAM, RH12 1EU **Tel:** 01403 220760
Fax: 01403 220761
Email: tom@avakado.eu
Advertising Address: As above. **Tel:** 01403 220754
Email: jaymin@sp2.uk.com
Web site: http://www.sp2.uk.com
ISSN: 1476-184X
Publisher: avakado Ltd
Date Established: 2002
Frequency: 10 issues yearly - Published on the 1st Friday of the cover month
Free to qualifying individuals
Annual Sub.: £95.00
Circulation: 8,507 (Publisher's Statement)
Usual Pagination: 48
Editor: Tom Mulligan; **Publisher:** Mark Harrington
Summary of Content: Magazine covering the integration of small-molecule chemistry with biotechnology to provide solutions for the pharmaceutical, biotechnology, biopharmaceutical and agrochemical industries.
Readership/Target Audience: Aimed at research chemists, academics, development chemists, molecular biologists, senior research managers, technology managers and senior executives.
ADVERTISING RATES:
Full Page Colour £3038.00
Agency Commission: 10%
Mechanical Data: Type Area: 265 x 185mm, Bleed Size: +3mm, Trim Size: 297x 210mm, Col Length: 265mm, Page Width: 185mm, Film: Digital

Average advertising content per issue: 40%
Supplement(s): Purple Book - 1xY
BUSINESS: CHEMICALS

SPA BUSINESS
1642444U32H-461

Editorial Address: Portmill House, Portmill Lane, HITCHIN, SG5 1DJ **Tel:** 01462 431385 **Fax:** 01462 433909
Email: theteam@spabusiness.com
Advertising Address: As above.
Email: nuzhathayat@leisuremedia.com
Web site: http://www.spabusiness.com
Publisher: The Leisure Media Company Ltd
Date Established: 2004
Frequency: Quarterly
Annual Sub.: £27.50
Usual Pagination: 140
Editor: Rhianon Howells; **Advertising Manager:** Nuzht Hayat; **Publisher:** Nuzht Hayat
Summary of Content: Magazine featuring news, interviews, features and profiles of projects, people, facilities and events in the international spa industry.
Readership/Target Audience: Aimed at owners and operators of all types of spa facilities, including day spas, health club spas, hotel spas, destination and medical spas.
ADVERTISING RATES:
Full Page Colour £1550.00
Agency Commission: 10%
Mechanical Data: Type Area: 260 x 172mm, Bleed Size: 303 x 213mm, Trim Size: 297 x 210mm, Col Length: 260mm, Page Width: 172mm, Film: Digital
Average advertising content per issue: 40%
BUSINESS: LOCAL GOVERNMENT, LEISURE & RECREATION: Leisure, Recreation & Entertainment

SPA OPPORTUNITIES
1799136U32H-473

Editorial Address: Portmill House, Portmill Lane, HITCHIN, SG5 1DJ **Tel:** 01462 431385 **Fax:** 01462 433909
Email: sarahtodd@leisuremedia.com
Advertising Address: As above.
Email: emmamatthews@leisuremedia.com
Web site: http://www.spaopportunities.com
ISSN: 1753-3430
Publisher: The Leisure Media Company Ltd
Date Established: 2007
Frequency: 26 issues yearly
Circulation: 12,000 (Publisher's Statement)
Usual Pagination: 20
Editor: Sarah Todd; **Advertising Manager:** Emma Matthews
Summary of Content: Magazine containing news about the international spa industry. Carries latest jobs in spas and resorts worldwide plus details of training courses and institutions as well as featuring up-to-the minute news about the spa industry.
Readership/Target Audience: Aimed at people looking for jobs in the spa industry, from students to experienced professionals looking for a career change.
ADVERTISING RATES:
Full Page Colour £1550.00
Agency Commission: 10%
Mechanical Data: Type Area: 260 x 172mm, Col Length: 260mm, Page Width: 172mm, Film: Digital
Copy instructions: Copy Date: 1 week prior to publication date
Average advertising content per issue: 50%
BUSINESS: LOCAL GOVERNMENT, LEISURE & RECREATION: Leisure, Recreation & Entertainment

SPACEFLIGHT
36394U6C-200

Editorial Address: Springfields House, Camel Gate, SPALDING, PE12 6ES **Tel:** 01775 711558
Fax: 01775 711558
Email: spaceflight@simcomm.co.uk
Advertising Address: As above. **Fax:** 01775 711552
Email: spaceflight@simcomm.co.uk
Web site: http://www.simcomm-europe.com
ISSN: 0038-6340
Publisher: British Interplanetary Society
Date Established: 1956
Frequency: Monthly
Cover Price: £2.75
Annual Sub.: £48.00
Circulation: 10,000 (Publisher's Statement)
Usual Pagination: 44
Editor: Clive Simpson; **Advertising Manager:** Clive Simpson
Summary of Content: Magazine covering space exploration, technology and research, manned and unmanned, planetary exploration, commercial space technology development, space tourism.
Readership/Target Audience: Aimed at major aerospace companies and spacecraft manufacturers, astronauts, NASA, ESA, space agencies, engineers, scientists, academics and anyone with a general interest in space.
ADVERTISING RATES:
Full Page Mono £750.00
Full Page Colour £1000.00

Agency Commission: 10%
Mechanical Data: Film: Digital, Type Area: 280 x 186mm, Bleed Size: 303 x 216mm, Col Length: 280mm, Trim Size: 293 x 206mm, Page Width: 186mm
BUSINESS: AVIATION & AERONAUTICS: Space Research

SPACES&PLACES
1665553U32D-146

Editorial Address: Caversham Court, Church Road, Caversham, READING, RG4 7AD **Tel:** 0118 946 9066
Fax: 0118 946 9061
Email: news@green-space.org.uk
Advertising Address: As above. **Tel:** 0118 946 9068
Email: emmad@green-space.org.uk
Web site: http://www.green-space.org.uk
Publisher: GreenSpace
Date Established: 2001
Frequency: 6 issues yearly - Published on the 1st day of the cover month
Annual Sub.: £25.00
Circulation: 1,000 (Publisher's Statement)
Usual Pagination: 32
Editor: Emma Donaldson; **Advertising Manager:** Emma Donaldson
Summary of Content: Magazine focusing on parks and public spaces including design, management, planning, horticulture and community involvement.
Readership/Target Audience: Aimed at local authority park managers, planners, landscape designers, architects and park-based community groups.
ADVERTISING RATES:
Full Page Mono £325.00
Full Page Colour £375.00
Agency Commission: 10%
Mechanical Data: Type Area: 267 x 185mm, Col Length: 267mm, Page Width: 185mm, Film: Digital
Copy instructions: Copy Date: 9th of the month prior to publication date
Average advertising content per issue: 10%
BUSINESS: LOCAL GOVERNMENT, LEISURE & RECREATION: Parks

SPAR INTOUCH
37984U22A-363

Formerly: Spar Network
Editorial Address: Tansor PR, 1 Holywell Hill, ST. ALBANS, AL1 1ER **Tel:** 01727 800166 **Fax:** 01727 800144
Email: pr@tansor.co.uk
Advertising Address: As above.
Email: pr@tansor.co.uk
Publisher: Spar UK Ltd
Frequency: Monthly
Circulation: 2,500 (Publisher's Statement)
Usual Pagination: 12
Editor: Tina Carey; **Advertising Manager:** Tina Carey
Summary of Content: Magazine containing news about the Spar organisation and general retail developments.
Readership/Target Audience: Read by all Spar retailers, personnel and advertisers.
ADVERTISING RATES:
Full Page Mono £500.00
Full Page Colour £1000.00
Agency Commission: 10%
Mechanical Data: Bleed Size: 303 x 216mm, Trim Size: 297 x 210mm, Film: Digital
Copy instructions: Copy Date: 1 week prior to publication date
Average advertising content per issue: 10%
BUSINESS: FOOD

SPARKS MAGAZINE
1851937U17-270

Editorial Address: Unit 22, Midsomer Enterprise Park, Radstock Road, Midsomer Norton, RADSTOCK, BA3 2BB
Tel: 0870 774 3049 **Fax:** 0870 758 5906
Email: celia@sng-publishing.co.uk
Web site: http://www.sng-publishing.co.uk/publications/sparks-magazine.html
Publisher: SNG Publishing Ltd
Date Established: 2008
Frequency: Half-yearly - Published in February and May
Free to qualifying individuals
Circulation: 14,000 (Publisher's Statement)
Usual Pagination: 80
Editor: Celia Matthews; **Publisher:** Celia Matthews
Summary of Content: Magazine covering the latest products on the market, useful tips from lecturers, student focus groups and upcoming events.
Readership/Target Audience: Aimed at final year electrical students and apprentices.
BUSINESS: ELECTRICAL

SPC (SOAP, PERFUMERY & COSMETICS)
37256U15A-90

Formerly: SPC Soap, Perfumery & Cosmetics
Editorial Address: Paulton House, 8 Shepherdess Walk, LONDON, N1 7LB **Tel:** 020 7549 2580 **Fax:** 020 7549 8622

Email: spc@hpcimedia.com
Advertising Address: As above. **Tel:** 020 7549 8635
Email: smurphy@wilmington.co.uk
Web site: http://www.cosmeticsbusiness.com
ISSN: 0037-749X
Publisher: HPCi Media Ltd
Date Established: 1928
Frequency: Monthly - Published in the 2nd week of the cover month
Free to qualifying individuals
Annual Sub.: £126.00
Circulation: 5,000 (Publisher's Statement)
Usual Pagination: 80
Editor: Clare Henderson
Summary of Content: International cosmetics and toiletries business magazine covering industry news, new products, technology, regulations and marketing.
Readership/Target Audience: Aimed at technical and marketing personnel within companies manufacturing cosmetics and toiletries.
ADVERTISING RATES:
Full Page Colour £2275.00
Agency Commission: 10%
Mechanical Data: Film: Digital, Type Area: 254 x 178mm, Bleed Size: 303 x 216mm, Trim Size: 297 x 210mm, Col Length: 254mm, Page Width: 178mm
Copy instructions: Copy Date: 2 weeks prior to publication date
Average advertising content per issue: 50%
BUSINESS: COSMETICS & HAIRDRESSING: Cosmetics

SPC SOAP, PERFUMERY & COSMETICS ASIA
37257U15A-100

Editorial Address: 6-14 Underwood Street, LONDON, N1 7JQ **Tel:** 020 7549 8621 **Fax:** 020 7549 8622
Email: spc@wilmington.co.uk
Advertising Address: As above. **Tel:** 020 7490 0049
Email: smurphy@wilmington.co.uk
Web site: http://www.spcasia-magazine.com
ISSN: 0037-749X
Publisher: Wilmington Business Information
Date Established: 1996
Frequency: Quarterly
Annual Sub.: £75.00
Circulation: 3,500 (Publisher's Statement)
Usual Pagination: 68
Editor: Clare Henderson
Summary of Content: Magazine covering the manufacture of cosmetics, toiletries and fragrances in Asia Pacific.
Language(s): Chinese; English
Readership/Target Audience: Aimed at marketing and technical personnel in Asia Pacific.
ADVERTISING RATES:
Full Page Colour £2275.00
Agency Commission: 10%
Mechanical Data: Type Area: 254 x 178mm, Bleed Size: 303 x 216mm, Trim Size: 297 x 210mm, Film: Digital, Page Width: 178mm, Col Length: 254mm
Average advertising content per issue: 50%
BUSINESS: COSMETICS & HAIRDRESSING: Cosmetics

SPE REVIEW
38633U33-55_50

Editorial Address: Crown Reach, 147A Grosvenor Road, LONDON, SW1V 3JY **Tel:** 020 7798 2000
Email: nicki.shearer@loewygroup.com
Advertising Address: As above. **Fax:** 020 7798 2020
Email: nicki.shearer@loewygroup.com
Web site: http://www.spe-uk.org
Publisher: Loewy Group
Frequency: 11 issues yearly
Annual Sub.: £24.00
Circulation: 4,000 (Publisher's Statement)
Usual Pagination: 16
Editor: Nicki Shearer; **Advertising Manager:** Nicki Shearer
Summary of Content: Published on behalf of the Society of Petroleum Engineers, including news, features and interviews relevant to the UK petroleum industry.
Readership/Target Audience: Read by UK petroleum engineers.
ADVERTISING RATES:
Full Page Mono £1143.00
Full Page Colour £1643.00
Agency Commission: 10%
Mechanical Data: Type Area: 266 x 184mm, Col Length: 266mm, Trim Size: 297 x 210mm, Film: Digital, Page Width: 184mm, Bleed Size: 303 x 216mm
Copy instructions: Copy Date: 3 weeks prior to publication date
BUSINESS: OIL & PETROLEUM

SPEAKING ENGLISH
25373U62B-970

Editorial Address: 26A Princes Street, SOUTHPORT, PR8 1EQ **Tel:** 01704 501730 **Fax:** 01704 539637
Email: admin@esbuk.org
Advertising Address: As above.
Email: admin@esbuk.org

Web site: http://www.esbuk.org
ISSN: 1465-153X
Publisher: English Speaking Board Ltd
Frequency: Half-yearly - Published in April and October
Annual Sub.: £21.00
Circulation: 450 (Publisher's Statement)
Editor: Rosemary Ham; **Advertising Manager:** Rosemary Ham
Summary of Content: Publication featuring articles on spoken communication, ventures and projects in training, industry, the arts and all other branches of education.
Readership/Target Audience: Aimed at English teachers, voice coaches, broadcasters, voice-over artists and actors.
ADVERTISING RATES:
Full Page Mono £100.00
Mechanical Data: Film: Digital, No. of Columns (Display): 2
BUSINESS: CHURCH & SCHOOL EQUIPMENT & EDUCATION: Education Teachers

SPECIAL
1773212U62G-425

Formerly: Special!
Editorial Address: Nasen House, 4-5 Amber Business Village, Amber Close, Amington, TAMWORTH, B77 4RP
Tel: 01827 311500 **Fax:** 01422 375205
Email: seans@nasen.org.uk
Advertising Address: 2 Oak Lane, Fishponds Trading Estate, BRISTOL, BS5 7UY **Tel:** 0117 958 4572
Fax: 0117 958 4694
Email: april@edsol.co.uk
Web site: http://www.nasen.org.uk
Publisher: nasen
Frequency: 6 issues yearly
Cover Price: £5.00
Free to qualifying individuals
Circulation: 8,000 (Print Run)
Editor: Sean Stockdale
Summary of Content: Publication covering additional and special educational needs.
Readership/Target Audience: Aimed at those involved in the education of children and young adults with special educational needs.
ADVERTISING RATES:
Full Page Colour £1195.00
Agency Commission: 10%
Copy instructions: Copy Date: 4 weeks prior to publication date
Average advertising content per issue: 40%
BUSINESS: CHURCH & SCHOOL EQUIPMENT & EDUCATION: Special Needs Education

SPECIAL CHILDREN
41123U62G-250

Editorial Address: 51 Philip Victor Road, BIRMINGHAM, B20 2QB **Tel:** 0121 554 0882
Email: mickarcher@mac.com
Advertising Address: 33-41 Dallington Street, LONDON, EC1V 0BB **Tel:** 020 7954 3400 **Fax:** 020 7954 3511
Email: jon.pyser@electricwordplc.com
Web site: http://www.teachingexpertise.com
ISSN: 0951-6875
Publisher: Optimus Education
Date Established: 1986
Frequency: 6 issues yearly
Annual Sub.: £60.00
Circulation: 5,057 (ABC 01/07/2008 to 30/06/2009)
Usual Pagination: 64
Editor: Mick Archer
Summary of Content: Magazine covering special educational needs issues, good practice, current debates and practical guidance.
Readership/Target Audience: Aimed at teachers, parents and other professionals working with children with special needs.
ADVERTISING RATES:
Full Page Colour £1100.00
Copy instructions: Copy Date: 2 weeks prior to publication date
BUSINESS: CHURCH & SCHOOL EQUIPMENT & EDUCATION: Special Needs Education

SPECIALIST BUILDING FINISHES
1732401U4R-622

Editorial Address: 128 Warwick Street, LEAMINGTON SPA, CV32 4QY **Tel:** 01926 420660 **Fax:** 01926 420990
Email: ajmarsh@campbellmarsh.com
Advertising Address: As above.
Email: marketing@fpdc.org
Web site: http://www.fpdc.org
Publisher: Campbell Marsh Communications
Date Established: 2005
Frequency: 6 issues yearly
Free to qualifying individuals
Circulation: 6,000 (Publisher's Statement)
Usual Pagination: 28
Editor: Adrian Marsh; **Advertising Manager:** Kelly White

Business Magazines

Summary of Content: Magazine covering news about interior finishing, wall, floor, ceiling and cladding design and construction, legal, employment, contracts, technical, products, health and safety, environmental and projects associated with the building finishes, insulation, facades, plastering and drywall sector.
Readership/Target Audience: Aimed at architects, drywall contractors, surveyors, building contractors, ceiling, flooring, specialist interior contractors, partitioning and plastering contractors.
ADVERTISING RATES:
Full Page Colour £1750.00
Agency Commission: 10%
Mechanical Data: Type Area: 385 x 277mm, Bleed Size: 430 x 307mm, Trim Size: 420 x 297mm, Col Length: 385mm, Page Width: 277mm, Film: Digital
Copy instructions: Copy Date: 4 weeks prior to publication date
Average advertising content per issue: 40%
BUSINESS: ARCHITECTURE & BUILDING: Building Related

SPECIALIST PRINTING
1840851U41A-340
Editorial Address: 1 Cantelupe Mews, Cantelupe Road, EAST GRINSTEAD, RH19 3BG **Tel:** 01342 322133
Fax: 01342 322664
Email: editor@specialistprinting.com
Web site: http://www.specialistprinting.com
ISSN: 1754-6230
Publisher: Chameleon Business Media Ltd
Frequency: Quarterly
Cover Price: Free
Editor: Dave Fordham
Summary of Content: Magazine covering all types of printing including printing on glass and fabric.
Readership/Target Audience: Aimed at screen, digital and wide format printers.
BUSINESS: PRINTING & STATIONERY: Printing

SPECIALITY CHEMICALS MAGAZINE
36685U13-128
Editorial Address: Westgate House, 120-130 Station Road, REDHILL, RH1 1ET **Tel:** 01737 855000 **Fax:** 01737 855418
Email: andrewwarmington@dmgworldmedia.com
Advertising Address: As above.
Email: peterdavis@dmgworldmedia.com
Web site: http://www.specchemonline.com
ISSN: 0262-2262
Publisher: DMG Business Media
Date Established: 1981
Frequency: 10 issues yearly - Published in the middle of the cover month
Annual Sub.: £184.00
Circulation: 8,500 (BPA Worldwide 01/01/2008 to 30/06/2008)
Usual Pagination: 36
Editor: Andrew Warmington; **News Editor:** Nikki Weller
Summary of Content: Journal covering manufacture and end-use applications of performance chemicals, including high value and low volume chemicals, fine chemicals and custom manufacture.
Readership/Target Audience: Read by chemical manufacturers and industrial users of chemicals.
ADVERTISING RATES:
Full Page Colour £3486.00
Agency Commission: 10%
Mechanical Data: Type Area: 265 x 185mm, Bleed Size: 305 x 213mm, Trim Size: 297 x 210mm, Col Length: 265mm, Film: Digital, Page Width: 185mm
Copy instructions: Copy Date: 4 weeks prior to publication date
Average advertising content per issue: 40%
Supplement(s): Chiral Technologies - 1xY, Outsourcing - 1xY
BUSINESS: CHEMICALS

SPECIALITY FOOD
1614126U22A-380
Editorial Address: 25 Phoenix Court, Hawkins Road, COLCHESTER, CO2 8JY **Tel:** 01206 505981
Fax: 01206 505945
Email: nicola.mallett@aceville.co.uk
Advertising Address: 21-23 Phoenix Court, Hawkins Road, COLCHESTER, CO2 8JY **Tel:** 01206 505936
Fax: 01206 505935
Email: sam.reubin@aceville.co.uk
Web site: http://www.specialityfoodmagazine.co.uk
Publisher: Aceville Publications Ltd
Date Established: 2002
Frequency: 9 issues yearly
Cover Price: £3.25
Free to qualifying individuals
Circulation: 8,699 (ABC 01/07/2007 to 30/06/2008)
Usual Pagination: 40
Editor: Nicola Mallett; **News Editor:** Raphael Giacardi; **Group Editor:** Nicola Mallett
Summary of Content: Magazine covering speciality and fine foods, organic products and deli ranges.

Readership/Target Audience: Aimed at buyers, independent shop owners and those within the specialty food business.
ADVERTISING RATES:
Full Page Colour £1950.00
Agency Commission: 10%
Mechanical Data: Type Area: 359 x 254mm, Trim Size: 380 x 280mm, Bleed Size: 390 x 290mm, Col Length: 359mm, Page Width: 254mm
Average advertising content per issue: 40%
BUSINESS: FOOD

SPECIFICATION MAGAZINE
1638246U4E-414
Formerly: Specification Product Update
Editorial Address: Grosvenor House, Central Park, TELFORD, TF2 9TW **Tel:** 01952 234000 **Fax:** 01952 234003
Email: katie@tspltd.co.uk
Advertising Address: As above.
Email: jim@tspltd.co.uk
Web site: http://www.tspltd.co.uk
Publisher: Tanner Stiles Publishing Ltd
Date Established: 1994
Frequency: 10 issues yearly - Published in the 3rd week of the cover month
Cover Price: Free
Circulation: 18,350 (ABC 01/01/2007 to 30/06/2008)
Usual Pagination: 68
Editor: Katie Wilcox; **Advertising Manager:** Jim Hastings
Summary of Content: Magazine promoting building product services and new ideas.
Readership/Target Audience: Aimed at those involved in the building and architecture sector.
ADVERTISING RATES:
Full Page Colour £2600.00
Agency Commission: 10%
Mechanical Data: Trim Size: 300 x 230mm, Film: Digital, Bleed Size: 306 x 216mm, Print Process: Sheet-fed offset litho
Copy instructions: Copy Date: 5 weeks prior to publication date
Average advertising content per issue: 40%
BUSINESS: ARCHITECTURE & BUILDING: Building

SPECIFIER REVIEW
1637486U4R-612
Editorial Address: 28A Jubilee Trade Centre, Jubilee Road, LETCHWORTH GARDEN CITY, SG6 1SP
Tel: 020 8241 1766 **Fax:** 020 8942 3477
Email: kirsty@specifierreview.info
Advertising Address: As above.
Email: sales@specifierreview.info
Web site: http://www.specifierinfo.com
Publisher: First City Media
Date Established: 1980
Frequency: Monthly - Published at the end of the cover month
Cover Price: Free
Circulation: 19,302 (ABC 01/07/2007 to 30/06/2008)
Editor: Kirsty Hammond; **Advertising Manager:** Simon Clark-Taylor
Summary of Content: Magazine covering building products and services.
Readership/Target Audience: Aimed at architects and specifiers in the building industry.
ADVERTISING RATES:
Full Page Colour £2400.00
Agency Commission: 10%
Mechanical Data: Trim Size: 297 x 210mm, Bleed Size: 303 x 216mm, Film: Digital, Print Process: Litho, Type Area: 278 x 182mm, Col Length: 278mm, Page Width: 182mm
Copy instructions: Copy Date: 4 weeks prior to publication date
Average advertising content per issue: 100%
Supplement(s): ESP Environmentally Sustainable Products - 4xY
BUSINESS: ARCHITECTURE & BUILDING: Building Related

THE SPECIFIER'S GUIDE
35752U3A-200
Formerly: The Specifier's Guide to Heating, Ventilating, Air Conditioning & Refrigeration Directory
Editorial Address: Greater London House, Hampstead Road, LONDON, NW1 7EJ **Tel:** 020 7728 5000
Fax: 020 7728 4400
Email: simon.duddy@emap.com
Advertising Address: As above.
Email: mark.palmer@emap.com
Web site: http://www.specguide.co.uk
Publisher: EMAP Inform
Frequency: Annual - Published in February
Editor: Simon Duddy; **Advertising Manager:** Mark Palmer
Summary of Content: Provides a directory of heating, ventilation, refrigeration and air conditioning. Published on behalf of the Heating and Ventilating Contractors Association.
Readership/Target Audience: Aimed at specifiers of heating, ventilation, refrigeration, air conditioning products and services.

ADVERTISING RATES:
Full Page Colour £1405.00
Mechanical Data: Type Area: 362 x 260mm, Bleed Size: 394 x 284mm, Trim Size: 387 x 278mm, Film: Positive, right reading, emulsion side down. Digital, Col Length: 362mm, Page Width: 260mm
BUSINESS: HEATING & VENTILATION: Domestic Heating & Ventilation

SPECIFY
35931U4E-330
Editorial Address: 5B Edgewater Business Park, Belfast Harbour Estate, BELFAST, BT3 9JQ **Tel:** 028 9078 3200
Fax: 028 9078 3210
Email: emma.cowan@btinternet.com
Advertising Address: As above.
Email: carolinemcclean@greerpublications.com
Web site: http://www.greerpublications.com
Publisher: Greer Publications Ltd
Date Established: 1980
Frequency: 6 issues yearly - Published on the 1st working day of the 2nd cover month
Cover Price: £3.00
Free to qualifying individuals
Annual Sub.: £18.00
Circulation: 3,096 (ABC 01/07/2007 to 30/06/2008)
Usual Pagination: 84
Editor: Emma Cowan; **Publisher:** James Greer
Summary of Content: Magazine covering architectural design and building and construction news.
Readership/Target Audience: Aimed at architects, suppliers, manufacturers, contractors, professionals and associations in Northern Ireland.
ADVERTISING RATES:
Full Page Colour £1350.00
Agency Commission: 15%
Mechanical Data: Bleed Size: 340 x 250mm, Trim Size: 330 x 240mm, Col Length: 299mm, Page Width: 206mm, Film: Digital, Type Area: 299 x 206mm
Average advertising content per issue: 40%
BUSINESS: ARCHITECTURE & BUILDING: Building

SPECTATOR BUSINESS
1859012U1R-385
Editorial Address: 22 Old Queen Street, LONDON, SW1H 9HP **Tel:** 020 7961 0200
Email: editor@spectator.co.uk
Web site: http://www.spectator.co.uk/business
Publisher: Pressholdings
Date Established: 2008
Frequency: Quarterly
Cover Price: £4.50
Editor: Martin vander Weyer
Summary of Content: Magazine covering global business, investment, economic issues and wealth management.
Readership/Target Audience: Aimed at CEOs, senior management and senior executives.
ADVERTISING: Rates on application
BUSINESS: FINANCE & ECONOMICS: Financial Related

SPECTROSCOPY EUROPE
40006U55-170
Editorial Address: 6 Charlton Mill, Charlton, CHICHESTER, PO18 0HY **Tel:** 01243 811334 **Fax:** 01243 811711
Email: info@spectroscopyeurope.com
Advertising Address: As above.
Email: gill.stockford@spectroscopyeurope.com
Web site: http://www.spectroscopyeurope.com
ISSN: 0966-0941
Publisher: John Wiley & Sons Ltd
Date Established: 1992
Frequency: 7 issues yearly
Free to qualifying individuals
Circulation: 21,000 (Publisher's Statement)
Usual Pagination: 40
Editor: Gill Stockford; **Managing Director:** Ian Michael; **Advertising Manager:** Gill Stockford; **Publisher:** Ian Michael
Summary of Content: The Journal of the Association of British Spectroscopists, covering industry news and new applications in process monitoring and quality control.
Readership/Target Audience: Read by spectroscopists within the industry and academics engaged in research and development.
ADVERTISING RATES:
Full Page Mono £3840.00
Full Page Colour £5030.00
Agency Commission: 15%
Mechanical Data: Type Area: 237 x 175mm, Bleed Size: 303 x 216mm, Film: Digital, Trim Size: 297 x 210mm, Col Length: 237mm, Page Width: 175mm
Copy instructions: Copy Date: 3 weeks prior to publication date
Average advertising content per issue: 30%
BUSINESS: APPLIED SCIENCE & LABORATORIES

SPECTRUM
38479U32G-74

Formerly: Keeping You Posted
Editorial Address: Stirling Enterprise Park, STIRLING, FK7 7RP **Tel:** 01786 479593 **Fax:** 01786 449285
Email: shirley.bwye@vds.org.uk
Web site: http://www.vds.org.uk
ISSN: 1479-7518
Publisher: Volunteer Development Scotland
Date Established: 2003
Frequency: Quarterly
Free to qualifying individuals
Annual Sub.: £15.00
Circulation: 700 (Publisher's Statement)
Usual Pagination: 8
Editor: Shirley Bwye; **Advertising Manager:** Shirley Bwye
Summary of Content: Magazine for members of Volunteer Development Scotland. Covers policy, good practice issues, special insights, legal matters, training courses, events and the role of volunteer centres in Scotland.
Readership/Target Audience: Aimed at volunteer-involving organisations interested in voluntary and community involvement in public, private and voluntary sector.
ADVERTISING: No Advertising taken
BUSINESS: LOCAL GOVERNMENT, LEISURE & RECREATION: Community Care & Social Services

SPEECH & LANGUAGE THERAPY IN PRACTICE
40552U56R-200

Editorial Address: 33 Kinnear Square, LAURENCEKIRK, AB30 1UL **Tel:** 01561 377415 **Fax:** 01561 377415
Email: avrilnicoll@speechmag.com
Advertising Address: As above.
Email: avrilnicoll@speechmag.com
Web site: http://www.speechmag.com
ISSN: 1368-2105
Publisher: Avril Nicoll Business
Date Established: 1997
Frequency: Quarterly
Annual Sub.: £28.00
Circulation: 1,500 (Publisher's Statement)
Usual Pagination: 32
Editor: Avril Nicoll; **Advertising Manager:** Avril Nicoll; **Publisher:** Avril Nicoll
Summary of Content: Publication containing practical information and advice on speech and language therapy.
Readership/Target Audience: Aimed at speech and language therapists and associated professionals.
ADVERTISING RATES:
Full Page Colour £470.00
Agency Commission: 10%
Mechanical Data: Type Area: 267 x 200mm, Bleed Size: 303 x 228mm, Film: Digital, Col Length: 267mm, Page Width: 200mm, Trim Size: 297 x 225mm
Copy instructions: Copy Date: 4 weeks prior to publication
BUSINESS: HEALTH & MEDICAL: Health Medical Related

SPEED
1779106U1C-358

Editorial Address: Incisive Media, Haymarket House, 28-29 Haymarket, LONDON, SW1Y 4RX **Tel:** 020 7484 9700
Fax: 020 7484 9758
Email: info@centralbanking.co.uk
Advertising Address: As above.
Email: info@centralbanking.co.uk
Web site: http://www.centralbanking.co.uk
Publisher: Central Banking Publications
Frequency: Quarterly
Annual Sub.: £160.00
Editor: Nick Carver; **Executive Editor:** Nick Carver; **Advertising Manager:** Philip Ansley
Summary of Content: Publication covering settlements, payments, E-money and E-trading development and focusing on policy developments affecting financial infrastructures at national and international level.
Readership/Target Audience: Aimed at people who run and use exchanges, payment processors, banks, regulators and payment service providers.
ADVERTISING: Rates on application
BUSINESS: FINANCE & ECONOMICS: Banking

SPICE BUSINESS MAGAZINE
624024U11A-189

Editorial Address: 211 Firtree Road, Driftbridge, EPSOM DOWNS, KT17 3LB **Tel:** 01737 210022 **Fax:** 01737 211903
Email: info@spicebusiness.co.uk
Advertising Address: As above.
Email: info@spicebusiness.co.uk
Web site: http://www.spicebusiness.co.uk
Publisher: Spice Business Magazine
Date Established: 1999
Cover Price: £2.00
Free to qualifying individuals
Annual Sub.: £12.00
Circulation: 14,000 (Publisher's Statement)
Usual Pagination: 58

Editor: Enam Ali; **News Editor:** Shafiqul Islam; **Advertising Manager:** Mohammad Raheem; **Publisher:** Enam Ali
Summary of Content: Magazine containing news, articles, entertainment and information on the Bangladeshi and Indian restaurant trade.
Language(s): Bengali; English
Readership/Target Audience: Aimed at Bangladeshi and Indian restaurateurs, suppliers, wholesalers, surgeries, solicitors, media people and other businesses within the Asian community.
ADVERTISING RATES:
Full Page Mono £1000.00
Full Page Colour £1850.00
Agency Commission: 10%
Mechanical Data: Film: Positive, right reading, emulsion side down. Digital, Type Area: 278 x 230mm, Col Length: 278mm, Page Width: 230mm
Copy instructions: Copy Date: 4 weeks prior to publication date
Average advertising content per issue: 28%
BUSINESS: CATERING: Catering, Hotels & Restaurants

THE SPIRITS BUSINESS
1923220U9A-271

Editorial Address: Unit 222-223, 30 Great Guildford Street, LONDON, SE1 0HS **Tel:** 020 7803 2420 **Fax:** 020 7803 2421
Email: info@thespiritsbusiness.com
Web site: http://www.thespiritsbusiness.com
Publisher: Union Press Ltd
Frequency: 7 issues yearly
Annual Sub.: £99.00
Circulation: 13,000 (Controlled Circulation)
Editor: Patience Gould
Summary of Content: Magazine dedicated to what is going on globally in the world of spirits including vodka, whisky, gin, cognac, brandy, liqueurs and cocktails.
Readership/Target Audience: Aimed at buyers in the spirits industry.
ADVERTISING: Rates on application
BUSINESS: DRINKS & LICENSED TRADE: Drinks, Licensed Trade, Wines & Spirits

SPONSORSHIP NEWS
35748U2R-170

Editorial Address: PO Box 66, WOKINGHAM, RG41 5FS
Tel: 0870 241 4466
Email: info@sponsorshipnews.com
Advertising Address: As above.
Email: info@sponsorshipnews.com
Web site: http://www.sponsorshipnews.com
ISSN: 0263-3809
Publisher: Charterhouse Business Publications
Date Established: 1982
Frequency: Monthly
Annual Sub.: £199.00
Usual Pagination: 32
Editor: Jonathan Gee; **Advertising Manager:** Jonathan Gee
Summary of Content: Announcements of new sponsorships in sport, arts, charities, conservation and media.
Readership/Target Audience: Aimed at sponsorship professionals.
ADVERTISING RATES:
Full Page Mono £650.00
Full Page Colour £900.00
Agency Commission: 10%
Mechanical Data: Type Area: 276 x 192mm, Bleed Size: +5m, Film: Digital, Col Length: 276mm, Page Width: 192mm
Copy instructions: Copy Date: 10th of the month prior to publication date
Average advertising content per issue: 25%
BUSINESS: COMMUNICATIONS, ADVERTISING & MARKETING: Communications Related

SPORT BUSINESS INTERNATIONAL
38541U32H-267

Editorial Address: 33-41 Dallington Street, LONDON, EC1V 0BB **Tel:** 020 7954 3515 **Fax:** 020 7954 3511
Email: miriam@sportbusiness.com
Advertising Address: As above.
Email: adam.colthorpe@sportbusiness.com
Web site: http://www.sportbusiness.com
ISSN: 1363-4453
Publisher: SPG Companys Ltd
Frequency: Monthly - Published on the 1st of the cover month
Free to qualifying individuals
Circulation: 10,000 (Publisher's Statement)
Usual Pagination: 70
Editor: Miriam Sherlock
Summary of Content: Magazine covering news and analysis of the sports industry. Includes events and profiles of sports industry leaders.
Readership/Target Audience: Read by key decision makers within the sport industry.
ADVERTISING RATES:
Full Page Colour £3995.00
Agency Commission: 10%

Mechanical Data: Type Area: 263 x 199mm, Col Length: 263mm, Trim Size: 297 x 230mm, Bleed Size: 303 x 236mm, Film: Digital, Page Width: 199mm
Copy instructions: Copy Date: 10th of the month prior to publication date
Average advertising content per issue: 40%
BUSINESS: LOCAL GOVERNMENT, LEISURE & RECREATION: Leisure, Recreation & Entertainment

SPORTEX HEALTH
1696198U56A-202

Formerly: healthEX Specialist
Editorial Address: 86-88 Nelson Road, Wimbledon, LONDON, SW19 1HX **Tel:** 020 8287 3312
Email: tor@sportex.net
Advertising Address: As above.
Email: paul@sportex.net
Web site: http://www.sportex.net
Publisher: Centor Publishing Ltd
Date Established: 2004
Frequency: Quarterly
Annual Sub.: £50.00
Circulation: 1,000 (Publisher's Statement)
Usual Pagination: 24
Editor: Tor Davies; **Advertising Manager:** Paul Harris; **Publisher:** Tor Davies
Summary of Content: Magazine covering behaviour change, physical activity, medical conditions, health promotion resources and tools plus additional articles on physical activity promotion.
Readership/Target Audience: Aimed at physical activity health promotion specialists, medical professionals and clinical exercise specialists working with special groups.
ADVERTISING RATES:
Full Page Mono £850.00
Agency Commission: 10%
Mechanical Data: Bleed Size: 303 x 216mm, Trim Size: 297 x 210mm, Film: Digital
Copy instructions: Copy Date: 4 weeks prior to publication date
BUSINESS: HEALTH & MEDICAL

SPORTEX MEDICINE
634388U56A-178

Editorial Address: 86-88 Nelson Road, Wimbledon, LONDON, SW19 1HX **Tel:** 020 8287 3312
Fax: 0845 652 1907
Email: tor@sportex.net
Advertising Address: As above. **Fax:** 020 8404 8261
Email: paul@sportex.net
Web site: http://www.sportex.net
ISSN: 1471-8138
Publisher: Centor Publishing Ltd
Date Established: 1999
Frequency: Quarterly
Annual Sub.: £39.00
Circulation: 4,500 (Publisher's Statement)
Usual Pagination: 32
Editor: Tor Davies; **Advertising Manager:** Paul Harris
Summary of Content: Magazine containing joint examination, injury diagnosis, treatment and rehabilitation as well as information about new educational products, courses and books.
Readership/Target Audience: Aimed at medical professionals specialising in musculoskeletal medicine including sports physicians, physiotherapists, osteopaths, chiropractors, podiatrists and advanced sports therapists and sports massage practitioners.
ADVERTISING: Rates on application
BUSINESS: HEALTH & MEDICAL

SPORTS INSIGHT
1636540U48B-76

Editorial Address: 49 Old Steine, BRIGHTON, BN1 1NH
Tel: 01273 748675
Email: jeff@partridgeltd.co.uk
Advertising Address: 21-23 Phoenix Court, Hawkins Road, COLCHESTER, CO2 8JY **Tel:** 01206 505947
Fax: 01206 500243
Email: keith@sports-insight.co.uk
Web site: http://www.sports-insight.co.uk
Publisher: Partridge Publications
Date Established: 2004
Frequency: 10 issues yearly
Cover Price: Free
Circulation: 5,488 (ABC 01/07/2007 to 30/06/2008)
Usual Pagination: 68
Editor: Jeff James; **Advertising Manager:** Keith Marshall
Summary of Content: Magazine covering new products and industry news.
Readership/Target Audience: Aimed at UK sports retailers, manufacturers and distributors.
ADVERTISING RATES:
Full Page Colour £1500.00
Agency Commission: 10%
Mechanical Data: Type Area: 270 x 190mm, Bleed Size: +5mm, Trim Size: 297 x 210mm, Film: Digital, Col Length: 270mm, Page Width: 190mm

Business Magazines

Copy instructions: Copy Date: 7 days prior to publication date
Average advertising content per issue: 60%
BUSINESS: TOY TRADE & SPORTS GOODS: Sports Goods

SPORTS LAW ADMINISTRATION AND PRACTICE
39239U44-1820

Editorial Address: Ivy Dene, East End, Hook Norton, BANBURY, OX15 5LG Tel: 01608 730595
Fax: 01608 730623
Email: info@ivyhousepublications.co.uk
ISSN: 0968-6037
Publisher: Ivy House Sport Law Publications Ltd
Frequency: 6 issues yearly
Annual Sub.: £385.00
Circulation: 150 (Publisher's Statement)
Usual Pagination: 16
Editor: Darren Bailey
Summary of Content: Newsletter focusing on law, tax and finance with respect to sporting issues.
Readership/Target Audience: Aimed at sports bodies, sportsmen, broadcasters and sponsors.
ADVERTISING: No Advertising taken
BUSINESS: LEGAL

SPORTS MANAGEMENT
38543U32H-283

Editorial Address: Portmill House, Portmill Lane, HITCHIN, SG5 1DJ Tel: 01462 471920 Fax: 01462 433909
Email: karenmaxwell@leisuremedia.com
Advertising Address: As above. Tel: 01462 431385
Email: nadeemshaikh@leisuremedia.com
Web site: http://www.sportsmanagement.com
ISSN: 0952-8210
Publisher: The Leisure Media Company Ltd
Date Established: 1997
Frequency: Quarterly - Published in the 1st week of the 1st cover month
Annual Sub.: £30.00
Circulation: 5,500 (Publisher's Statement)
Usual Pagination: 80
Editor: Karen Maxwell; Advertising Manager: Nadeem Shaikh; Managing Editor: Karen Maxwell; Publisher: Nadeem Shaikh
Summary of Content: Contains news, interviews. profiles and projects about the sports industry. The official Magazine of the Sports and Play contractors association (SAPCA).
Readership/Target Audience: Read by members of SAPCA as well as managers of sports clubs, stadia and sports governing bodies.
ADVERTISING RATES:
Full Page Colour £1013.00
Agency Commission: 10%
Mechanical Data: Page Width: 172mm, Film: Digital, Type Area: 260 x 172mm, Col Length: 260mm, Trim Size: 297 x 210mm, Bleed Size: 303 x 216mm
Average advertising content per issue: 40%
BUSINESS: LOCAL GOVERNMENT, LEISURE & RECREATION: Leisure, Recreation & Entertainment

SPORTSMEDIA
38544U32H-287

Formerly: SporTVision
Editorial Address: 292 Vauxhall Bridge Road, LONDON, SW1V 1AE Tel: 020 7963 7893 Fax: 020 7963 7894
Email: rory.squires@pa-sport.com
Advertising Address: PO Box 48, Old Hall Street, LIVERPOOL, L69 3EB Tel: 0151 472 2705
Email: neil.johnson@liverpool.com
Web site: http://www.thesportbriefing.com
Publisher: Press Association Sport Services
Date Established: 1996
Frequency: Half-yearly - Published in October and April
Annual Sub.: £175.00
Circulation: 5,000 (Publisher's Statement)
Usual Pagination: 32
Editor: Rob Ridley; Advertising Manager: Neil Johnson; Managing Editor: Rory Squires
Summary of Content: Magazine containing international sports media, management and federation news and analysis.
Readership/Target Audience: Aimed at people working within federations and sports businesses.
ADVERTISING RATES:
Full Page Colour £1950.00
Agency Commission: 10%
Mechanical Data: Trim Size: 268 x 180mm, Bleed Size: 306 x 216mm, Film: Digital
Average advertising content per issue: 40%
BUSINESS: LOCAL GOVERNMENT, LEISURE & RECREATION: Leisure, Recreation & Entertainment

SPORTSPRO
1745224U14A-568

Formerly: BusinessF1
Editorial Address: Kemp House, 152 - 160 City Road, LONDON, EC1V 2NX Tel: 020 7837 6240
Fax: 020 7837 6243
Email: editor@sportspromedia.com
Advertising Address: As above. Fax: 020 7608 1160
Email: svarma@sportspromedia.com
Web site: http://www.sportspro.com
ISSN: 1740-1224
Publisher: SportsPro Media
Frequency: Monthly - Published at the end of the month prior to publication date
Cover Price: £25.00
Circulation: 7,061 (Publisher's Statement)
Editor: Tom Rubython
Summary of Content: Magazine covering the finance and management of the Formula One industry with statistics, analysis and features.
Readership/Target Audience: Aimed at people in the Formula One business community.
ADVERTISING RATES:
Full Page Colour £6000.00
Agency Commission: 15%
Mechanical Data: Bleed Size: 292 x 220mm, Trim Size: 282 x 210mm, Film: Digital
Copy instructions: Copy Date: Last friday of the month prior to publication
Average advertising content per issue: 30%
BUSINESS: COMMERCE, INDUSTRY & MANAGEMENT

STADIA
623441U32H-292

Editorial Address: Abinger House, Church Street, DORKING, RH4 1DF Tel: 01306 743744 Fax: 01306 742525
Email: stadia@ukintpress.com
Advertising Address: Parsonage Square, DORKING, RH4 1UP Tel: 020 8133 7678 Fax: 01306 743928
Email: damien@ukintpress.com
ISSN: 1468-3067
Publisher: UKIP Media & Events Ltd
Date Established: 1999
Frequency: Quarterly
Annual Sub.: £105.00
Circulation: 14,500 (Publisher's Statement)
Usual Pagination: 80
Editor: Anthony James; Managing Director: Graham Johnson
Summary of Content: Magazine reviewing sports venue design, operations and technology. Contains news stories, interviews with key industry figures, new facility profiles, operator perspectives, technology surveys, market studies and expert viewpoints.
Readership/Target Audience: Aimed at owners and operators of sports venues, stadiums and arenas at professional, collegiate and municipal level.
ADVERTISING RATES:
Full Page Colour £3650.00
Agency Commission: 10%
Mechanical Data: Film: Digital
Copy instructions: Copy Date: 2 weeks prior to publication date
Average advertising content per issue: 30%
BUSINESS: LOCAL GOVERNMENT, LEISURE & RECREATION: Leisure, Recreation & Entertainment

STADIUM & ARENA MANAGEMENT
41481U64C-200

Editorial Address: 4 North Street, Rothersthorpe, NORTHAMPTON, NN7 3JB Tel: 01604 832149
Email: mark.webb@tesco.net
Advertising Address: Bat and Ball Studio, 168 St. Johns Hill, SEVENOAKS, TN13 3PF Tel: 01732 459683
Fax: 01732 455837
Email: alan@aladltd.co.uk
Web site: http://www.sam.uk.com
Publisher: Alad Ltd
Date Established: 1996
Frequency: 6 issues yearly - Published in the 1st week of the cover month
Free to qualifying individuals
Annual Sub.: £46.00
Circulation: 5,096 (Publisher's Statement)
Usual Pagination: 44
Editor: Mark Webb; Advertising Manager: Alan Levett
Summary of Content: Magazine covering all aspects of large sports facility management and construction.
Readership/Target Audience: Aimed at facilities managers, owners, architects and engineers of stadiums and arenas.
ADVERTISING RATES:
Full Page Mono £1150.00
Full Page Colour £1700.00
Agency Commission: 10%
Mechanical Data: Type Area: 264 x 181mm, Bleed Size: 303 x 216mm, Trim Size: 297 x 210mm, Film: Digital, Page Width: 181mm, Col Length: 264mm
Copy instructions: Copy Date: 3rd Friday of the month prior to publication date

Average advertising content per issue: 30%
BUSINESS: OTHER CLASSIFICATIONS: Clubs

STAGE SCREEN & RADIO
37204U14L-645

Editorial Address: 373-377 Clapham Road, LONDON, SW9 9BT Tel: 020 7346 0900 Fax: 020 7346 0901
Email: janice@stagescreenandradio.org.uk
Advertising Address: Mainline Media, The Barn, Oakley Hay Lodge Business Park, Great Oakley, NORTHANTS, NN18 9AS Tel: 01536 747333 Fax: 01536 746565
Email: lynn.newman@mainlinemedia.co.uk
Web site: http://www.bectu.org.uk
ISSN: 0969-6652
Publisher: BECTU
Date Established: 1935
Frequency: 8 issues yearly
Cover Price: £2.00
Annual Sub.: £20.00
Circulation: 30,000 (Publisher's Statement)
Usual Pagination: 28
Editor: Janice Turner; Advertising Manager: Lynn Newman
Summary of Content: Journal of the Broadcasting Entertainment Cinematograph and Theatre Union (BECTU). Covers industrial issues, technical and industry news.
Readership/Target Audience: Aimed at members of the BECTU, and people working in film, television and theatre.
ADVERTISING RATES:
Full Page Colour £1850.00
SCC £25.00
Agency Commission: 10%
Mechanical Data: Bleed Size: 303 x 216mm, Trim Size: 297 x 210mm, Type Area: 280 x 184mm, Col Length: 280mm, Page Width: 184mm, Film: Digital, Col Widths (Display): 44mm, No. of Columns (Display): 4
Copy instructions: Copy Date: 10 days prior to publication date
Average advertising content per issue: 40%
BUSINESS: COMMERCE, INDUSTRY & MANAGEMENT: Trade Unions

STAINLESS STEEL FOCUS
38169U27-135

Editorial Address: Morgan House, Gilbert Drive, Wyberton Fen, BOSTON, PE21 7TR Tel: 01205 319093
Fax: 01205 319095
Email: r.clark@stainless-steel-focus.co.uk
Advertising Address: As above.
Email: mike@liaisoncommunications.com
Web site: http://www.stainless-steel-focus.com
ISSN: 1478-1824
Publisher: Stainless Steel Focus Limited
Date Established: 1990
Frequency: Monthly - Published in the 1st week of the cover month
Annual Sub.: £248.00
Usual Pagination: 68
Editor: Richard Clark; Managing Director: Richard Clark; Advertising Manager: Mike Mikunda; Managing Editor: Richard Clark
Summary of Content: Magazine covering news and analysis of the markets for stainless steel. Includes articles on its raw materials including nickel, chrome and stainless steel scrap.
Language(s): English; German
Readership/Target Audience: Read by senior management and producers in the stainless steel, stockholding and fabricating industries. Also aimed at those who trade in stainless steel scrap, nickel and chrome.
ADVERTISING RATES:
Full Page Mono £1620.00
Full Page Colour £1940.00
Agency Commission: 10%
Mechanical Data: Type Area: 274 x 170mm, Col Length: 274mm, Page Width: 170mm, Film: Digital
Copy instructions: Copy Date: 2 weeks prior to publication date
BUSINESS: METAL, IRON & STEEL

STAINLESS STEEL INDUSTRY
38170U27-140

Editorial Address: PO Box 1187, GERRARDS CROSS, SL9 7YP Tel: 01753 885968 Fax: 01753 882980
Email: frankrussell@stainless-steel-ind.com
Advertising Address: As above.
Email: advertising@stainless-steel-ind.com
Web site: http://www.stainless-steel-ind.com
ISSN: 0306-2988
Publisher: Modern Metals Publications Ltd
Date Established: 1973
Frequency: 6 issues yearly - Published on the 15th of the cover month
Free to qualifying individuals
Annual Sub.: £105.00
Circulation: 6,000 (Publisher's Statement)
Usual Pagination: 28
Editor: Frank Russell; Managing Director: Frank Russell; Advertising Manager: Frank Russell; Publisher: Frank Russell

Summary of Content: Official magazine of the British Stainless Steel Association. Covers technical and commercial information relating to the production, processing, distribution, fabrication and end use of stainless steel.
Readership/Target Audience: Aimed at stainless steel manufacturers, stockholders, fabricators and end users.
ADVERTISING RATES:
Full Page Colour £1500.00
Agency Commission: 10%
Mechanical Data: Page Width: 174mm, Trim Size: 297 x 210mm, Col Widths (Display): 84mm, Type Area: 262 x 174mm, Col Length: 262mm, Film: Positive, right reading emulsion side down. Digital, Print Process: Offset litho
Copy instructions: Copy Date: 15th of the month prior to publication date
Average advertising content per issue: 50%
BUSINESS: METAL, IRON & STEEL

STAN SCOTTISH TRAVEL AGENTS NEWS
39733U50-24_30
Editorial Address: 71 Henderson Street, Bridge of Allan, STIRLING, FK9 4HG **Tel:** 01786 834238 **Fax:** 01786 834295
Email: susan@stannews.co.uk
Advertising Address: As above.
Email: susan@stannews.co.uk
Web site: http://www.scottishtravelagentsnews.co.uk
Publisher: S&G Publishing (Scotland) Ltd
Date Established: 1990
Frequency: Weekly - Published every Monday
Free to qualifying individuals
Annual Sub.: £79.00
Circulation: 1,300 (Publisher's Statement)
Usual Pagination: 24
Editor: Susan Harris; **Advertising Manager:** Susan Harris
Summary of Content: Magazine containing news items relating to the travel trade in Scotland.
Readership/Target Audience: Read by those involved in the Scottish travel trade.
ADVERTISING RATES:
Full Page Colour £1950.00
SCC £20.00
Agency Commission: 10%
Mechanical Data: Col Length: 275mm, No. of Columns (Display): 4, Type Area: 275 x 200mm, Trim Size: 299 x 211mm, Page Width: 200mm, Bleed Size: 309 x 221mm, Film: Digital
Copy instructions: Copy Date: 5 days prior to publication date
Average advertising content per issue: 50%
BUSINESS: TRAVEL & TOURISM

STAND OUT
1683485U2C-509
Formerly: stand
Editorial Address: Barham Court, Teston, MAIDSTONE, ME18 5BZ **Tel:** 01622 618798 **Fax:** 01622 618793
Email: neil@cimltd.co.uk
Advertising Address: As above.
Email: jo@cimltd.co.uk
Web site: http://www.standoutmagazine.co.uk
Publisher: CIM LLP
Date Established: 2005
Frequency: 11 issues yearly - Published in the 4th week of the month prior to the cover date
Circulation: 9,800 (Publisher's Statement)
Usual Pagination: 56
Editor: Caroline Clift; **Advertising Manager:** Jo Sapsford
Summary of Content: Magazine providing advice on planning corporate events and exhibitions.
Readership/Target Audience: Aimed at marketing directors, events and exhibition organisers, party, wedding and themed event organisers.
ADVERTISING RATES:
Full Page Colour £2002.00
Agency Commission: 10%
Mechanical Data: Trim Size: 300 x 215mm, Bleed Size: 306 x 221mm, Film: Digital
Copy instructions: Copy Date: 4 weeks prior to publication date
Average advertising content per issue: 60%
BUSINESS: COMMUNICATIONS, ADVERTISING & MARKETING: Conferences & Exhibitions

STATIONERY & OFFICE UPDATE
38951U41B-270
Editorial Address: 15A London Road, MAIDSTONE, ME16 8LY **Tel:** 01622 687031 **Fax:** 01622 757646
Email: stationery@datateam.co.uk
Advertising Address: As above.
Email: stationery@datateam.co.uk
Web site: http://www.stationeryandofficeupdate.com
ISSN: 1475-8644
Publisher: Datateam Publishing Ltd
Date Established: 1989
Frequency: Monthly - Published at the end of the 1st week of the cover month

Free to qualifying individuals
Annual Sub.: £28.00
Circulation: 5,595 (Publisher's Statement)
Usual Pagination: 40
Editor: Kelly Byne; **Advertising Manager:** Kelly Byne
Summary of Content: Magazine containing product-based information on stationery and office equipment.
Readership/Target Audience: Read by stationery and office equipment dealers, suppliers, retailers and wholesalers.
ADVERTISING RATES:
Full Page Colour £1782.00
Agency Commission: 10%
Mechanical Data: Type Area: 275 x 195mm, Col Length: 275mm, Print Process: Sheet-fed offset litho, Bleed Size: 312 x 235mm, Trim Size: 306 x 229mm, Film: Positive, right reading, emulsion side down. Digital, Page Width: 195mm
Copy instructions: Copy Date: 3 weeks prior to publication date
Average advertising content per issue: 40%
BUSINESS: PRINTING & STATIONERY: Stationery

STATISTICAL METHODS IN MEDICAL RESEARCH
22795U56R-220
Editorial Address: 1 Oliver's Yard, 55 City Road, LONDON, EC1Y 1SP **Tel:** 020 7324 8500 **Fax:** 020 7324 8600
Email: market@sagepub.co.uk
Advertising Address: As above.
Email: sheena.karim@sagepub.co.uk
Web site: http://www.sagepub.co.uk
ISSN: 0962-2802
Publisher: Sage Publications
Date Established: 1992
Frequency: 6 issues yearly
Annual Sub.: £410.00
Editor: Brian Everitt
Summary of Content: Publication focusing on the statistical techniques available to the medical profession.
Readership/Target Audience: Read by professors of statistics and academics in the field.
ADVERTISING RATES:
Full Page Mono £450.00
Agency Commission: 5%
Mechanical Data: Type Area: 215 x 160mm, Col Length: 215mm, Trim Size: 246 x 189mm, Page Width: 160mm, Film: Positive, right reading, emulsion side down. Digital, Print Process: Sheet-fed litho, Screen: Mono 52 lpc Colour 60 lpc, Bleed Size: 254 x 195mm
BUSINESS: HEALTH & MEDICAL: Health Medical Related

STATUTE LAW REVIEW
39312U44-1835
Editorial Address: 24 Mona Street, Douglas, ISLE OF MAN **Tel:** 01624 611522
Email: bates@manx.net
Advertising Address: Great Clarendon Street, OXFORD, OX2 6DP **Tel:** 01865 353329
Email: jnlsadvertising@oxfordjournals.org
Web site: http://www3.oup.co.uk/stalaw
ISSN: 0144-3593
Publisher: OUP
Date Established: 1980
Frequency: 3 issues yearly - Published in February, June and October
Cover Price: £28.00
Annual Sub.: £67.00
Usual Pagination: 92
Editor: T. St John Bates
Summary of Content: Journal focusing on the legislative process. Contains discussion on the use of legislation as an instrument of public policy and covers the drafting and interpretation of new legislation in the UK and overseas.
Readership/Target Audience: Aimed at lawyers, academics and political scientists.
ADVERTISING RATES:
Full Page Mono £270.00
Agency Commission: 10%
Mechanical Data: Type Area: 210 x 115mm, Film: Digital, Col Length: 210mm, Page Width: 115mm
Copy instructions: Copy Date: 13th of the month prior to publication date
BUSINESS: LEGAL

STAYING ALIVE
39887U54B-97_60
Editorial Address: Edgbaston Park, 353 Bristol Road, Edgbaston, BIRMINGHAM, B5 7ST **Tel:** 0121 248 2000 **Fax:** 0121 248 2001
Email: jcave@rospa.com
Advertising Address: Orchard Barn, The Green, Uffington, OXON, SN7 7SB **Tel:** 01367 820367 **Fax:** 01367 820367
Email: susanphilo@talktalk.net
Web site: http://www.rospa.co.uk
Publisher: Royal Society for the Prevention of Accidents
Frequency: Quarterly - Published on the 18th of each cover month
Annual Sub.: £18.00
Circulation: 600 (Publisher's Statement)

Usual Pagination: 12
Editor: Janice Cave; **Managing Editor:** Janice Cave
Summary of Content: Magazine reviewing accident trends, legislation, new safety products and services in home, leisure and water safety.
Readership/Target Audience: Aimed at local authority officers and health service staff in education, housing and public safety and company employees.
ADVERTISING RATES:
Full Page Mono £840.00
Full Page Colour £1040.00
Agency Commission: 10%
Mechanical Data: Type Area: 275 x 190mm, Bleed Size: 303 x 216mm, Trim Size: 297 x 210mm, Col Length: 275mm, Page Width: 190mm, Film: Digital
Copy instructions: Copy Date: 24th of the month prior to publication date
BUSINESS: SAFETY & SECURITY: Safety

STEEL TIMES INTERNATIONAL INCORPORATING STEEL TIMES
38175U27-150_50
Editorial Address: Westgate House, 120-130 Station Road, REDHILL, RH1 1ET **Tel:** 01737 855154 **Fax:** 01737 855474
Email: timsmith@dmgworldmedia.com
Advertising Address: As above. **Tel:** 01737 855133
Email: tammybreese@dmgworldmedia.com
Web site: http://www.steeltimesint.com
ISSN: 0143-7798
Publisher: DMG Business Media
Date Established: 1976
Frequency: 8 issues yearly - Published in the 2nd week of the cover month
Cover Price: £32.00
Free to qualifying individuals
Annual Sub.: £145.00
Circulation: 8,000 (Publisher's Statement)
Usual Pagination: 30
Editor: Tim Smith
Summary of Content: Journal focusing on technical developments within the iron and steel making industry.
Language(s): Arabic; Chinese; English; Russian; Spanish
Readership/Target Audience: Read by steel production managers.
ADVERTISING RATES:
Full Page Mono £2800.00
Full Page Colour £3460.00
Agency Commission: 15%
Mechanical Data: Type Area: 265 x 185mm, Col Length: 265mm, Trim Size: 297 x 210mm, Bleed Size: 303 x 213mm, Film: Digital, Page Width: 185mm
Copy instructions: Copy Date: 3 weeks prior to publication date
Average advertising content per issue: 40%
BUSINESS: METAL, IRON & STEEL

STEERING WHEEL
41521U64G-490
Editorial Address: PO Box 3472, BARNET, EN5 9HF **Tel:** 020 8440 3333
Email: cabdriver@btconnect.com
Advertising Address: As above.
Web site: http://www.thecabdriver.co.uk
Publisher: DJA Design
Date Established: 1921
Frequency: Monthly
Free to qualifying individuals
Annual Sub.: £20.00
Circulation: 16,500 (Publisher's Statement)
Editor: Philip Warren; **Managing Director:** Dave Allen; **Advertising Manager:** Dave Allen
Summary of Content: Magazine covering the taxi trade, with articles on tourism, travel, vehicles, holidays, night-life, restaurants, sport and theatre.
Readership/Target Audience: Aimed at cab drivers and private hire drivers in the UK.
ADVERTISING RATES:
Full Page Colour £1200.00
Agency Commission: 15%
Mechanical Data: Type Area: 384 x 257mm, Col Length: 384mm, Col Widths (Display): 38mm, No. of Columns (Display): 6, Page Width: 257mm, Film: Digital
Copy instructions: Copy Date: 7 days prior to publication date
Average advertising content per issue: 50%
BUSINESS: OTHER CLASSIFICATIONS: Taxi Trade

STEP JOURNAL
718046U1F-277_25
Formerly: The Journal
Editorial Address: Artillery House (South) 11-19, Artillery Row, LONDON, SW1P 1RT **Tel:** 020 7340 0500
Fax: 020 7340 0501
Email: editor@step.org
Advertising Address: Barker Brooks House, 4 Greengate, Cardale Park, HARROGATE, HG3 1GY **Tel:** 01423 851150
Fax: 01423 851151
Email: patrick@barkerbrooks.co.uk

Web site: http://www.step.org
Publisher: Barker Brooks Media
Date Established: 1992
Frequency: 10 issues yearly
Free to qualifying individuals
Annual Sub.: £345.00
Circulation: 14,500 (Publisher's Statement)
Usual Pagination: 84
Editor: Louise Polcaro; **Advertising Manager:** Patrick
Procter; **Managing Editor:** Louise Polcaro; **Publisher:** Lucy
Barker
Summary of Content: Journal of the Society of Trust and
Estate Practitioners covering the latest developments in UK
and International trust, tax and estates.
Readership/Target Audience: Aimed at Private client
lawyers, accountants, IFAs, bankers, barristers and trustees.
ADVERTISING RATES:
Full Page Colour £3250.00
Agency Commission: 10%
Mechanical Data: Film: Digital, Type Area: 275 x 190mm,
Col Length: 275mm, Page Width: 190mm, Trim Size: 297 x
210mm, Bleed Size: 303 x 216mm
Copy instructions: Copy Date: 4 weeks prior to publication
date
Average advertising content per issue: 60%
BUSINESS: FINANCE & ECONOMICS: Investment

THE STOCKLISTS WITH FLOORING NEWS
38071U23B-500
Formerly: The Stocklists with Carpet & Rug News
Editorial Address: 219 West Ella Road, West Ella, HULL,
HU10 7SD **Tel:** 01482 659396 **Fax:** 01482 659397
Email: diane@mayvillepublishing.co.uk
Advertising Address: As above.
Email: diane@mayvillepublishing.co.uk
Web site: http://www.thestocklists.com
Publisher: Mayville Publishing Co Ltd
Date Established: 1973
Frequency: Monthly
Cover Price: Free
Circulation: 8,000 (Publisher's Statement)
Usual Pagination: 56
Editor: Diane Martin; **Managing Director:** Diane Martin;
Advertising Manager: Diane Martin; **Publisher:** Diane
Martin
Summary of Content: Publication covering news and
information on floor covering and carpet qualities, displays
and manufacturers.
Readership/Target Audience: Aimed at the retail and
contract market.
ADVERTISING RATES:
Full Page Mono £436.00
Full Page Colour £960.00
SCC £38.00
Agency Commission: 10%
Mechanical Data: Type Area: 266 x 185mm, Col Length:
266mm, Film: Digital, Trim Size: 297 x 210mm, Print
Process: Sheet-fed litho, Bleed Size: 303 x 216mm, Page
Width: 185mm
Copy instructions: Copy Date: 2 weeks prior to publication
date
Average advertising content per issue: 75%
BUSINESS: FURNISHINGS & FURNITURE: Furnishings,
Carpets & Flooring

STOCKPOT
623547U11A-184
Editorial Address: Progressive House, 2 Maidstone Road,
SIDCUP, DA14 5HZ **Tel:** 020 8269 7939
Email: sheilae@dewberryredpoint.co.uk
Advertising Address: As above. **Tel:** 0845 000 2500
Email: janj@dewred.co.uk
Web site: http://www.craftguildofchefs.org
ISSN: 1744-1080
Publisher: Dewberry Redpoint Ltd
Frequency: Quarterly
Cover Price: £3.50
Free to qualifying individuals
Circulation: 5,000 (Publisher's Statement)
Usual Pagination: 68
Editor: Sheila Eggleston
Summary of Content: Official Publication of The Craft Guild
of Chefs. Covers Guild news, industry news, recipes, menus
and chef profiles.
Readership/Target Audience: Read by members of the
Craft Guild of Chefs and its business partners who are
leading suppliers and manufacturers within the food
industry.
ADVERTISING RATES:
Full Page Colour £2500.00
Agency Commission: 10%
Mechanical Data: Col Length: 270mm, Page Width:
186mm, Trim Size: 297 x 210mm, Bleed Size: 303 x 216mm,
Film: Digital, Type Area: 270 x 186mm
Copy instructions: Copy Date: 3 weeks prior to publication
date
Average advertising content per issue: 30%
BUSINESS: CATERING: Catering, Hotels & Restaurants

STORAGE HANDLING DISTRIBUTION
36544U10-130
Editorial Address: Armstrong House, 38 Market Square,
UXBRIDGE, UB8 1LH **Tel:** 01895 454600 **Fax:** 01895 454647
Email: petermacleod@quartzltd.com
Advertising Address: As above. **Fax:** 01895 454643
Email: robfisher@quartz.uk.net
Web site: http://www.pressonshd.com
ISSN: 0039-1832
Publisher: Quartz Publishing
Date Established: 1957
Frequency: Monthly - Published on the 4th of the cover
month
Free to qualifying individuals
Circulation: 14,024 (ABC 01/01/2008 to 31/12/2008)
Usual Pagination: 90
Editor: Peter MacLeod; **Publisher:** Rob Fisher
Summary of Content: Magazine containing the latest
equipment developments, news reports and in-depth
features on the fast developing world of logistics, including
warehousing and distribution management.
Readership/Target Audience: Aimed at warehouse and
logistics managers.
ADVERTISING RATES:
Full Page Colour £2350.00
Agency Commission: 10%
Mechanical Data: Type Area: 254 x 178mm, Bleed Size:
303 x 216mm, Trim Size: 297 x 210mm, Col Length: 254mm,
Page Width: 178mm, Film: Digital
Copy instructions: Copy Date: 14th of the month prior to
publication date
Average advertising content per issue: 60%
BUSINESS: MATERIALS HANDLING

STORAGE TODAY
1697245U5C-914
Editorial Address: Commerce House, 6 Grove Road,
HITCHIN, SG5 1SE **Tel:** 01462 620222 **Fax:** 01462 642464
Email: editorial@showtimemedia.com
Advertising Address: As above.
Email: sarah@showtimemedia.com
Web site: http://www.showtimemedia.com
Publisher: SMS Ltd
Date Established: 2003
Frequency: Quarterly
Free to qualifying individuals
Circulation: 7,500 (Publisher's Statement)
Editor: Luke Murphy; **Advertising Manager:** Sarah LeLarge;
Publisher: David Benson
Summary of Content: Magazine focusing on all aspects of
data storage.
Readership/Target Audience: Aimed at industry
professionals.
ADVERTISING: Rates on application
BUSINESS: COMPUTERS & AUTOMATION: Professional
Personal Computers

STRAIGHT TALK
622733U56R-230
Editorial Address: 64 Leman Street, LONDON, E1 8EU
Tel: 020 7264 0510 **Fax:** 020 7488 9213
Email: contact@alcoholconcern.org.uk
Advertising Address: As above. **Tel:** 020 264 0510
Email: lleonard@alcoholconcern.org.uk
Web site: http://www.alcoholconcern.org.uk
ISSN: 0267-3282
Publisher: Alcohol Concern
Frequency: Quarterly
Annual Sub.: £25.00
Circulation: 1,000 (Publisher's Statement)
Usual Pagination: 24
Editor: Lisa Leonard
Summary of Content: Magazine containing news and
articles on alcohol abuse and related illnesses.
Readership/Target Audience: Read by Alcohol Concern
members, local alcohol services, health promotion, social
services and policy makers.
ADVERTISING RATES:
Full Page Mono £160.00
BUSINESS: HEALTH & MEDICAL: Health Medical Related

STRATEGIC COMMUNICATION MANAGEMENT
36805U14A-313
Editorial Address: 322B King Street, LONDON, W6 0AX
Tel: 020 8600 4670 **Fax:** 020 8741 9975
Email: kelly.dyer@melcrum.com
Web site: http://www.melcrum.com
ISSN: 1363-9064
Publisher: Melcrum Publishing Ltd
Date Established: 1996
Frequency: 6 issues yearly - Published on the 8th of the 1st
cover month
Annual Sub.: £225.00
Circulation: 5,000 (Publisher's Statement)
Usual Pagination: 40
Editor: Kelly Dyer

Summary of Content: Magazine covering communication
strategy, including conference reviews, a diary of events,
Internet resources, reports, ideas and trends in the
communication field.
Readership/Target Audience: Read by communication
professionals working at policy-level in large organisations
throughout North America, Europe and Australasia.
ADVERTISING: No Advertising taken
BUSINESS: COMMERCE, INDUSTRY & MANAGEMENT

STRATEGIC DIRECTION
36806U14A-315
Editorial Address: Howard House, Wagon Lane, BINGLEY,
BD16 1WA **Tel:** 01274 777700 **Fax:** 01274 785200
Email: rbrown@emeraldinsight.com
Web site: http://www.emeraldinsight.com
ISSN: 0258-0543
Publisher: Emerald Group Publishing Ltd
Frequency: 11 issues yearly
Annual Sub.: £4999.00
Usual Pagination: 40
Editor: Martin Fojt; **Publisher:** Rebecca Foster
Summary of Content: Journal providing an executive
briefing of the world's best business strategies.
Readership/Target Audience: Aimed at top management
within large organisations.
ADVERTISING: No Advertising taken
BUSINESS: COMMERCE, INDUSTRY & MANAGEMENT

STRATEGIC HR REVIEW
758558U14F-75
Editorial Address: Howard House, Wagon Lane, BINGLEY,
BD16 1WA **Tel:** 01274 777700 **Fax:** 01274 785200
Email: shr@emeraldinsight.com
Web site: http://www.emeraldinsight.com
ISSN: 1475-4398
Publisher: Emerald Group Publishing Ltd
Date Established: 2001
Frequency: 6 issues yearly - Published at the beginning of
the 1st cover month
Usual Pagination: 60
Editor: Sara Nolan; **Publisher:** Nancy Rolph
Summary of Content: Journal covering trends, techniques
and ideas in human resource strategy through case study
features and best practice guides.
Readership/Target Audience: Aimed at senior HR
professionals, also professionals working in training,
organisational development, organisational effectiveness
and personnel.
ADVERTISING: No Advertising taken
BUSINESS: COMMERCE, INDUSTRY & MANAGEMENT:
Training & Recruitment

STRATEGIC MARKETING
35548U2A-180
Editorial Address: Regency House, Westminster Place,
York Business Park, YORK, YO26 6RW **Tel:** 01904 520820
Email: jamie.austin@marketing-guild.com
Web site: http://www.marketing-guild.com
Publisher: The Marketing Guild
Frequency: 11 issues yearly
Free to qualifying individuals
Circulation: 420 (Publisher's Statement)
Usual Pagination: 12
Editor: Jamie Austin; **Managing Director:** Jamie Austin
Summary of Content: Magazine covering marketing ideas
and techniques.
Readership/Target Audience: Aimed at business-to-
business companies.
ADVERTISING: No Advertising taken
BUSINESS: COMMUNICATIONS, ADVERTISING &
MARKETING

STRATEGIC RISK
624623U1C-36
Editorial Address: 30 Cannon Street, LONDON, EC4M 6YJ
Tel: 020 7618 3403
Email: sue.copeman@strategicrisk.co.uk
Advertising Address: As above. **Tel:** 020 7618 3456
Fax: 020 7618 3400
Email: claire.lavery@strategicrisk.co.uk
Web site: http://www.strategicrisk.co.uk
Publisher: Newsquest Specialist Media Ltd
Date Established: 2000
Frequency: 6 issues yearly
Free to qualifying individuals
Annual Sub.: £190.00
Circulation: 11,051 (BPA Worldwide)
Usual Pagination: 60
Editor: Sue Copeman
Summary of Content: Magazine covering corporate
governance and risk related issues for business as well as
information on strategic, environmental and ethical issues.
Readership/Target Audience: Aimed at CEOs, chief
financial officers, chief risk officers, internal auditors,
treasurers, main board directors and risk professionals. Also
those who deal with risk at strategic level with a
responsibility for corporate governance.

ADVERTISING RATES:
Full Page Colour £5461.00
Agency Commission: 10%
Mechanical Data: Film: Digital, Col Length: 285mm, Page Width: 215mm, Type Area: 285 x 215mm, Trim Size: 309 x 239mm, Bleed Size: 313 x 243mm
Average advertising content per issue: 40%
BUSINESS: FINANCE & ECONOMICS: Banking

STRATEGIC SURVEY
601518U1A-276_52
Formerly: Strategic Studies
Editorial Address: Arundel House, 13-15 Arundel Street, LONDON, WC2R 3DX **Tel:** 020 7379 7676
Fax: 020 7836 3108
Web site: http://www.iiss.org/publications/strategic-survey
ISSN: 0459-7230
Publisher: Routledge, Taylor & Francis
Date Established: 1967
Frequency: Annual
Annual Sub.: £50.00
Circulation: 5,800 (Publisher's Statement)
Usual Pagination: 400
Editor: Alex Nicoll; **Managing Editor:** Ayse Abdullah
Summary of Content: Journal features the year's significant events and their importance for international security and relations.
Readership/Target Audience: Read by politicians and diplomats, economists and analysts, defence professionals, military personnel, students of international affairs, researchers, journalists and librarians.
ADVERTISING: No Advertising taken
BUSINESS: FINANCE & ECONOMICS

STRATEGY
36807U14A-501
Editorial Address: Grist, 21 Noel Street, LONDON, W1F 8GP **Tel:** 020 7434 1447
Email: markwellings@gristonline.com
Advertising Address: Buxton House, 7 Highbury Hill, LONDON, N5 1SU **Tel:** 020 7434 1447 **Fax:** 020 7434 1545
Email: markwellings@gristonline.com
Web site: http://www.sps.org.uk
Publisher: The Strategic Planning Society
Frequency: Quarterly
Circulation: 1,500 (Publisher's Statement)
Usual Pagination: 24
Editor: Mark Wellings; **Advertising Manager:** Mark Wellings
Summary of Content: Magazine covering new management techniques, business and management analysis, book reviews and case studies on strategic management.
Readership/Target Audience: Aimed at members of the Strategic Planning Society.
ADVERTISING: Rates on application
BUSINESS: COMMERCE, INDUSTRY & MANAGEMENT

STRONGER TOGETHER
37189U14L-315
Formerly: ISTC Today
Editorial Address: Swinton House, 324 Gray's Inn Road, LONDON, WC1X 8DD **Tel:** 020 7239 1200
Fax: 020 7278 8378
Email: editor@community-tu.org
Advertising Address: As above.
Email: nhill@community-tu.org
Web site: http://www.community-tu.org
Publisher: Community
Date Established: 2004
Frequency: Half-yearly - Published in June and December
Cover Price: Free
Circulation: 35,000 (Publisher's Statement)
Usual Pagination: 32
Editor: Duncan Harrod; **Advertising Manager:** Nada Hill
Summary of Content: Newspaper containing features on Community Union and related industries.
Readership/Target Audience: Read by members of Community Union and other trade unions.
ADVERTISING: Rates on application
BUSINESS: COMMERCE, INDUSTRY & MANAGEMENT: Trade Unions

THE STRUCTURAL ENGINEER
39028U42A-179
Editorial Address: 11 Upper Belgrave Street, LONDON, SW1X 8BH **Tel:** 020 7201 9120 **Fax:** 020 7201 9109
Email: kathy.stansfield@istructe.org
Advertising Address: Structural Promotions Ltd, Lawrance Way, Thurlby, BOURNE, PE10 0HU **Tel:** 01778 420857
Fax: 01778 424771
Email: steve@structuralpromotions.co.uk
Web site: http://www.istructe.org
ISSN: 1466-5123
Publisher: Institution of Structural Engineers
Date Established: 1922
Frequency: 23 issues yearly - Published fortnightly
Cover Price: £11.00
Free to qualifying individuals
Annual Sub.: £195.00

Circulation: 20,739 (Publisher's Statement)
Usual Pagination: 44
Editor: Kathy Stansfield; **Managing Editor:** Kathy Stansfield
Summary of Content: Publication containing technical and project based articles and papers on the design and construction of buildings, bridges and similar structures worldwide. Also includes news and a products and services section.
Readership/Target Audience: Read by members of the Institution of Structural Engineers and construction professionals.
ADVERTISING RATES:
Full Page Mono £1400.00
Full Page Colour £2020.00
Agency Commission: 10%
Mechanical Data: Col Length: 275mm, Type Area: 275 x 190mm, Bleed Size: 303 x 216mm, Trim Size: 297 x 210mm, Film: Digital, Page Width: 190mm
Copy instructions: Copy Date: 5 days prior to publication date
Average advertising content per issue: 35%
BUSINESS: CONSTRUCTION

STRUCTURAL SURVEY
35842U4C-235
Editorial Address: Nottingham Trent University, School of Architecture, Design & Built Environment, Burton Street, NOTTINGHAM, NG1 4BU **Tel:** 0115 848 4690
Email: mike.hoxley@ntu.ac.uk
Web site: http://www.emeraldinsight.com
ISSN: 0263-080X
Publisher: Emerald Group Publishing Ltd
Frequency: 5 issues yearly
Annual Sub.: £1569.00
Usual Pagination: 64
Editor: Mike Hoxley; **Publisher:** Valerie Robillard
Summary of Content: Academic journal examining structural surveying within the building industry.
Readership/Target Audience: Aimed at building surveyors, architects, structural and building services engineers.
ADVERTISING: No Advertising taken
BUSINESS: ARCHITECTURE & BUILDING: Surveying

STRUCTURED PRODUCTS
1685727U1F-601
Editorial Address: Haymarket House, 28-29 Haymarket, LONDON, SW1Y 4RX **Tel:** 020 7484 9802
Email: richard.jory@incisivemedia.com
Advertising Address: As above. **Tel:** 020 7484 9700
Email: peter.petkov@incisivemedia.com
Web site: http://www.structuredproducts.com
Publisher: Incisive Media Investments
Date Established: 2004
Frequency: 11 issues yearly
Annual Sub.: £649.00
Usual Pagination: 60
Editor: Richard Jory; **Advertising Manager:** Peter Petkov; **Publisher:** Joanna Russell
Summary of Content: Magazine dedicated to the wholesale market for derivatives-based investment products. Topics covered include news, regulatory data, commentary and profiles.
Readership/Target Audience: Aimed at IFAs, private bankers, retail distributors, insurance companies, stock brokers, index providers, regulators, accountants and lawyers.
ADVERTISING RATES:
Full Page Colour £8000.00
Agency Commission: 10%
Mechanical Data: Type Area: 239 x 175mm, Col Length: 239mm, Page Width: 175mm, Bleed Size: 286 x 221mm, Trim Size: 280 x 216mm, Film: Digital, No. of Columns (Display): 2
Copy instructions: Copy Date: 1 week prior to publication date
Average advertising content per issue: 30%
BUSINESS: FINANCE & ECONOMICS: Investment

STUDENT ACCOUNTANT
35025U1B-314
Formerly: ACCA Students' Newsletter
Editorial Address: 29 Lincoln's Inn Fields, LONDON, WC2A 3EE **Tel:** 020 7059 5981 **Fax:** 020 7059 5982
Email: victoria.morgan@accaglobal.com
Advertising Address: As above. **Tel:** 020 7059 5918
Email: richard.gooding@accaglobal.com
Web site: http://www.accaglobal.com
ISSN: 1473-0979
Publisher: Certified Accountants Educational Trust
Frequency: 10 issues yearly - Combined issues in June/July and November/ December
Free to qualifying individuals
Annual Sub.: £24.00
Circulation: 325,000 (Publisher's Statement)
Usual Pagination: 88
Editor: Victoria Morgan; **Advertising Manager:** Richard Gooding
Summary of Content: Magazine published in co-operation with the Association of Chartered Certified Accountants.

Readership/Target Audience: Read by students of accountancy, finance and business.
ADVERTISING RATES:
Full Page Mono £2366.00
Full Page Colour £2957.00
Agency Commission: 10%
Mechanical Data: Bleed Size: 281 x 221mm, Trim Size: 275 x 215mm, Type Area: 243.5 x 183.5mm, Print Process: Web-fed offset litho, Col Length: 243.5mm, Page Width: 183.5mm, Film: Digital
Copy instructions: Copy Date: 10th of the month prior to publication date
Average advertising content per issue: 20%
BUSINESS: FINANCE & ECONOMICS: Accountancy

STUDENT BMA NEWS
1682049U56A-187
Editorial Address: BMA House, Tavistock Square, LONDON, WC1H 9JP **Tel:** 020 7383 6122
Fax: 020 7383 6566
Email: studentbmanews@bma.org.uk
Advertising Address: As above. **Tel:** 020 7387 4499
Fax: 020 7383 6556
Email: nickgray@bmj.com
Web site: http://www.bma.org.uk
Publisher: British Medical Association
Date Established: 2003
Frequency: 11 issues yearly
Free to qualifying individuals
Circulation: 20,000 (Publisher's Statement)
Usual Pagination: 8
Editor: Lisa Pritchard
Summary of Content: Magazine containing medical student news, medical politics, features and analysis.
Readership/Target Audience: Read by medical students of the British Medical Association.
ADVERTISING RATES:
Full Page Mono £1520.00
Full Page Colour £2430.00
Agency Commission: 10%
Mechanical Data: Bleed Size: 393 x 296mm, Trim Size: 387 x 290mm, Film: Digital, Print Process: Web-fed offset litho
Copy instructions: Copy Date: 10 days prior to publication date
BUSINESS: HEALTH & MEDICAL

STUDENT BMJ
40228U56A-141
Editorial Address: BMA House, Tavistock Square, LONDON, WC1H 9JR **Tel:** 020 7387 4499
Fax: 020 7383 6418
Email: studenteditor@bmj.com
Advertising Address: As above. **Tel:** 020 7383 6386
Fax: 020 7383 6556
Email: sjohnson@bmjgroup.com
Web site: http://www.student.bmj.com
ISSN: 0966-6494
Publisher: BMJ Publishing Group
Date Established: 1992
Frequency: 11 issues yearly
Annual Sub.: £37.00
Circulation: 20,000 (Publisher's Statement)
Usual Pagination: 48
Editor: Jessie Colquhoun
Summary of Content: Magazine covering medical education and student life, with socio-political and medical news.
Readership/Target Audience: Aimed at international medical students.
ADVERTISING RATES:
Full Page Mono £685.00
Full Page Colour £1390.00
Mechanical Data: Bleed Size: 303 x 216mm, Trim Size: 297 x 210mm, Type Area: 264 x 186mm, Col Length: 264mm, Page Width: 186mm, Film: Digital
Average advertising content per issue: 20%
BUSINESS: HEALTH & MEDICAL

STUDENT LAW REVIEW
39241U44-1840
Editorial Address: Building 2, Floor 2, Social Sciences, 2 Park Square, Milton Park, ABINGDON, OX14 4RN
Tel: 020 7017 6000 **Fax:** 020 7278 8080
Email: fiona.kinnear@informa.com
Advertising Address: As above. **Fax:** 01536 424854
Email: sophie.dickson@mainlinemedia.co.uk
Web site: http://www.routledgecavendish.com
ISSN: 0961-0391
Publisher: Routledge Cavendish Publishing Ltd
Date Established: 1990
Frequency: 3 issues yearly - Published in January, April and October
Free to qualifying individuals
Annual Sub.: £16.00
Circulation: 20,000 (Publisher's Statement)
Usual Pagination: 64
Editor: Fiona Kinnear; **Advertising Manager:** Sophie Dickson
Summary of Content: Magazine containing comprehensive updates on case law and legislation.

Business Magazines

Readership/Target Audience: Aimed at university students, academics and libraries.
ADVERTISING RATES:
Full Page Mono £2100.00
Full Page Colour £2100.00
Agency Commission: 10%
Mechanical Data: Col Length: 275mm, Film: Digital, Type Area: 275 x 185mm, Trim Size: 297 x 210mm, Bleed Size: 303 x 216mm, Page Width: 185mm, No. of Columns (Display): 2, Col Widths (Display): 89mm
Copy instructions: Copy Date: 2 months prior to publication date
Average advertising content per issue: 25%
BUSINESS: LEGAL

STUDIES IN CONSERVATION
24293U64F-93

Editorial Address: 6 Buckingham Street, LONDON, WC2N 6BA **Tel:** 020 7839 5975
Email: iic@iiconservation.org
Web site: http://www.iiconservation.org
Publisher: IIC
Frequency: Quarterly
Free to qualifying individuals
Circulation: 3,000 (Publisher's Statement)
Editor: Graham Voce
Summary of Content: Journal covering advances in conservation including both practical and scientific aspects. Includes the latest research on historic materials and methods of conservation. Also includes reviews of the latest publications in the field.
Readership/Target Audience: Aimed at conservation professionals.
ADVERTISING: No Advertising taken
BUSINESS: OTHER CLASSIFICATIONS: Museums

STUDIES IN EUROPEAN CINEMA
1696523U62R-495

Editorial Address: Department of Media and Communication Studies, Digital Technium Building, University of Wales, Singleton Park, SWANSEA, SA2 8PP
Tel: 01792 513375 **Fax:** 01792 513453
Email: owen@ecrf.org.uk
Web site: http://www.intellectbooks.co.uk
ISSN: 1476-4504
Publisher: Intellect Ltd
Date Established: 2002
Frequency: 3 issues yearly - Published in April, August and December
Annual Sub.: £180.00
Circulation: 300 (Publisher's Statement)
Usual Pagination: 80
Editor: Owen Evans
Summary of Content: Journal covering historical and cultural dimensions in European film culture.
Readership/Target Audience: Aimed at all readers interested in European cinema and European film cultures.
ADVERTISING: No Advertising taken
BUSINESS: CHURCH & SCHOOL EQUIPMENT & EDUCATION: Education Related

STUDIES IN FRENCH CINEMA
1696524U62R-494

Editorial Address: Film Studies Department, The Queens Drive, University of Exeter, EXETER, EX4 4QH
Tel: 01392 264342 **Fax:** 01392 264222
Email: s.hayward@ex.ac.uk
Web site: http://www.intellectbooks.co.uk
ISSN: 1471-5880
Publisher: Intellect Ltd
Date Established: 2001
Frequency: 3 issues yearly - Published in April, August and December
Annual Sub.: £180.00
Circulation: 400 (Publisher's Statement)
Editor: Susan Hayward
Summary of Content: Journal covering French cinema.
Readership/Target Audience: Aimed at academics and students of French cinema.
ADVERTISING: No Advertising taken
BUSINESS: CHURCH & SCHOOL EQUIPMENT & EDUCATION: Education Related

STUDIES IN HISPANIC CINEMA
1696525U62R-491

Editorial Address: Department of Media and Cultural Production, Clepham Building, De Montfort University, The Gateway, LEICESTER, LE1 9BH **Tel:** 0116 257 7267
Fax: 0116 257 7199
Email: bjordan@dmu.ac.uk
Web site: http://www.intellectbooks.co.uk
ISSN: 1478-0488
Publisher: Intellect Ltd
Date Established: 2004
Frequency: 3 issues yearly - Published in April, August and December

Annual Sub.: £180.00
Circulation: 300 (Publisher's Statement)
Usual Pagination: 80
Editor: Barry Jordan
Summary of Content: Journal covering all aspects of Hispanic cinema.
Readership/Target Audience: Aimed at students, teachers and scholars in Hispanic Studies and Hispanic Cultural Studies.
ADVERTISING: No Advertising taken
BUSINESS: CHURCH & SCHOOL EQUIPMENT & EDUCATION: Education Related

STUDIES IN THE EDUCATION OF ADULTS
41119U62F-700

Editorial Address: 21 De Montfort Street, LEICESTER, LE1 7GE **Tel:** 0116 204 4200 **Fax:** 0116 204 4262
Email: enquiries@niace.org.uk
Advertising Address: As above.
Email: virman@niace.org.uk
Web site: http://www.niace.org.uk/publications/periodicals
ISSN: 0266-0830
Publisher: National Institute of Adult Continuing Education
Frequency: Half-yearly - Published in April and October
Annual Sub.: £33.00
Circulation: 650 (Publisher's Statement)
Usual Pagination: 120
Editor: Miriam Zukas; **Advertising Manager:** Virman Man; **Publisher:** Virman Man
Summary of Content: Journal containing articles on adult education research.
Readership/Target Audience: Aimed at adult educators, researchers and academics.
ADVERTISING RATES:
Full Page Mono £220.00
Mechanical Data: Type Area: 203 x 128mm, Col Length: 203mm, Bleed Size: +3mm, Trim Size: 240 x 170mm, Film: Digital, Page Width: 128mm
BUSINESS: CHURCH & SCHOOL EQUIPMENT & EDUCATION: Adult Education

STUDIES IN THEATRE AND PERFORMANCE
633843U62B-985

Editorial Address: Dept. of Drama, University of Exeter, Thornlea, New North Road, EXETER, EX4 4LA
Tel: 01392 264580 **Fax:** 01392 264594
Email: p.w.thomson@exeter.ac.uk
ISSN: 1468-2761
Publisher: Intellect Ltd
Date Established: 2000
Frequency: 3 issues yearly - Published in March, July and October
Cover Price: £30.00
Circulation: 800 (Publisher's Statement)
Usual Pagination: 64
Editor: Peter Thomson
Summary of Content: Journal covering the methods and results of practical research, discussion of issues related to theatre practice and examination of experiments in teaching and performance. Articles report on research undertaken in the studio, rehearsal room and performance.
Readership/Target Audience: Read by scholars, teachers and practitioners in drama departments.
ADVERTISING: No Advertising taken
BUSINESS: CHURCH & SCHOOL EQUIPMENT & EDUCATION: Education Teachers

STYLING LARD
1698518U2A-677

Editorial Address: 41-42 Eastcastle Street, LONDON, W1W 8DU **Tel:** 020 7631 1649
Email: mark@coy-com.com
Advertising Address: 3rd Floor, 41-42 Eastcastle Street, LONDON, W1W 8DU **Tel:** 020 7436 5191
Fax: 020 7637 1707
Email: mark@mddesign.com
Date Established: 2005
Frequency: Half-yearly - Published in April and October
Cover Price: £10.00
Editor: Mark Denton; **Advertising Manager:** Mark Denton
Summary of Content: Magazine focusing on the advertising industry.
Readership/Target Audience: Aimed at creative personnel working in design and advertising.
ADVERTISING: Rates on application
BUSINESS: COMMUNICATIONS, ADVERTISING & MARKETING

THE SUBPOSTMASTER
37239U14R-450

Editorial Address: Evelyn House, 22 Windlesham Gardens, SHOREHAM-BY-SEA, BN43 5AZ **Tel:** 01273 452324
Fax: 01273 465403
Email: thesubpostmaster@nfsp.org.uk
Web site: http://www.nfsp.org.uk
Publisher: National Federation of Subpostmasters

Date Established: 1897
Frequency: Monthly
Free to qualifying individuals
Circulation: 8,321 (ABC 01/07/2008 to 30/06/2009)
Usual Pagination: 16
Editor: Clare Allan
Summary of Content: Official journal of the National Federation of Sub-Postmasters.
Readership/Target Audience: Read by Sub-Postmasters.
BUSINESS: COMMERCE, INDUSTRY & MANAGEMENT: Commerce Related

SUBSEA ENGINEERING NEWS
38635U33-56

Editorial Address: PO Box 27, CHELTENHAM, GL53 0YH
Tel: 01242 574027 **Fax:** 01242 574102
Email: sen@btinternet.com
Advertising Address: As above.
Email: sen@btinternet.com
Web site: http://www.subsea-news.co.uk
ISSN: 0266-2205
Publisher: Knighton Enterprises Ltd
Date Established: 1984
Frequency: 24 issues yearly
Annual Sub.: £375.00
Circulation: 600 (Publisher's Statement)
Usual Pagination: 10
Editor: Steven Sasanow; **Managing Director:** Steven Sasanow; **Advertising Manager:** Steven Sasanow
Summary of Content: Magazine focusing on the subject of sub sea and underwater engineering, floating production systems and pipelines.
Readership/Target Audience: Aimed at oil companies, engineering and design consultancies, manufacturers and contractors worldwide.
ADVERTISING: Rates on application
BUSINESS: OIL & PETROLEUM

SUCCESS
1749167U63D-720

Editorial Address: 200 Renfield Street, GLASGOW, G2 3QB
Tel: 0141 302 7000 **Fax:** 0141 302 7798
Email: editorial@successmag.org.uk
Advertising Address: As above.
Email: sophie.watsonsmyth@heraldtimesgroupmagazines. co.uk
Publisher: Newsquest (Herald and Times) Ltd
Date Established: 2006
Frequency: Quarterly
Cover Price: Free
Circulation: 66,000 (Publisher's Statement)
Usual Pagination: 68
Editor: Roland Main
Summary of Content: Magazine covering issues that affect Scottish businesses and the local economy with management profiles, case studies and analysis of ideas for enterprise.
Readership/Target Audience: Aimed at businesses who have been operating for a year or more and have five or more employees.
ADVERTISING RATES:
Full Page Colour £1750.00
Agency Commission: 15%
Mechanical Data: Type Area: 267 x 188mm, Bleed Size: 305 x 215mm, Trim Size: 297 x 210mm, Col Length: 267mm, Page Width: 188mm, Print Process: Web-fed offset litho, Film: Digital
Copy instructions: Copy Date: 4 weeks prior to publication date
Average advertising content per issue: 20%
BUSINESS: REGIONAL BUSINESS: Regional Business Scotland

THE SUCCESSFUL OWNER MANAGER
37139U14H-100

Editorial Address: PO Box 5753, MILTON KEYNES, MK10 1AE **Tel:** 01525 211145 **Fax:** 01525 211145
Email: clare@entrepreneursuk.com
Web site: http://www.sfedi.co.uk
Publisher: SFEDI Ltd
Date Established: 1996
Frequency: 3 issues yearly - Published approximately February, June and October
Cover Price: Free
Circulation: 16,000 (Publisher's Statement)
Editor: Tony Robinson; **Circulation Manager:** Clare Francis
Summary of Content: Newsletter providing case studies, testimonials, information and advice in order to serve the needs of the small firms sector. Includes case studies and news on appropriate standards and qualifications.
Readership/Target Audience: Aimed at intermediaries working with small businesses and self employed owner managers.
ADVERTISING: No Advertising taken
BUSINESS: COMMERCE, INDUSTRY & MANAGEMENT: Small Business

SUGAR CANE INTERNATIONAL
1665158U21R-1504

Editorial Address: 80 Calverley Road, TUNBRIDGE WELLS, TN1 2UN **Tel:** 020 7017 7500 **Fax:** 020 7017 7599
Email: marketing@agra-net.com
Web site: http://www.agra-net.com
ISSN: 0265-7406
Publisher: Agra Informa Ltd
Frequency: 6 issues yearly
Annual Sub.: £405.00
Summary of Content: Publication containing the latest developments in sugar cane genetics agronomy, crop protection and harvesting. Features research papers, trends in science and technology and abstracts on sugar cane.
Readership/Target Audience: Aimed at professionals in cane production, research and consultancy.
ADVERTISING: No Advertising taken
BUSINESS: AGRICULTURE & FARMING: Agriculture & Farming Related

SUGAR EXTRACTS
37936U21R-1500

Formerly: News 4 U
Editorial Address: 25 Church Drive, Orton Waterville, PETERBOROUGH, PE2 5AF **Tel:** 01733 238267
Fax: 01733 238267
Email: billhollowell@biwell.freeserve.co.uk
Publisher: British Sugar plc
Date Established: 1974
Frequency: Half-yearly
Cover Price: Free
Circulation: 800 (Publisher's Statement)
Usual Pagination: 16
Editor: Bill Hollowell
Summary of Content: In-house newspaper covering company developments and employee activities.
Readership/Target Audience: Aimed at company employees of British Sugar.
ADVERTISING: No Advertising taken
BUSINESS: AGRICULTURE & FARMING: Agriculture & Farming Related

SUGAR INDUSTRY ABSTRACTS
38054U22R-400

Editorial Address: Nosworthy Way, WALLINGFORD, OX10 8DE **Tel:** 01491 832111 **Fax:** 01491 833508
Email: m.palmer@cabi.org
Web site: http://www.cabi.org/sia
ISSN: 0957-5022
Publisher: CABI
Date Established: 1938
Frequency: 6 issues yearly
Annual Sub.: £805.00
Circulation: 100 (Publisher's Statement)
Usual Pagination: 50
Editor: Mark Palmer
Summary of Content: Journal containing scientific information on all aspects of sugar processing technology and related subjects.
Readership/Target Audience: Aimed at those involved in the worldwide sugar industry.
ADVERTISING: No Advertising taken
BUSINESS: FOOD: Food Related

SULPHUR
36686U13-130

Editorial Address: Southbank House, Black Prince Road, LONDON, SE1 7SJ **Tel:** 020 7793 2567 **Fax:** 020 7793 2577
Email: richard.hands@bcinsight.com
Advertising Address: As above.
Email: tina.firman@bcinsight.com
Web site: http://www.bcinsight.com
Publisher: BC Insight
Date Established: 1953
Frequency: 6 issues yearly - Published at the beginning of the 1st cover month
Annual Sub.: £440.00
Editor: Des Owen; **Advertising Manager:** Tina Firman
Summary of Content: Journal of the sulphur, sulphuric acid and related industries, with emphasis on the marketing and technology of sulphur recovery from oil, gas and coal.
Readership/Target Audience: Aimed at people within oil refining and gas processing management, sulphur handling and distribution and sulphuric acid industry.
ADVERTISING RATES:
Full Page Mono £1250.00
Full Page Colour £2000.00
Mechanical Data: Film: Digital, Col Length: 254mm, Page Width: 178mm, Trim Size: 297 x 210mm, Type Area: 254 x 178mm, Bleed Size: 304 x 216mm
Copy instructions: Copy Date: 1 week prior to publication date
BUSINESS: CHEMICALS

THE SUPERINTENDENT
1667562U32F-704

Editorial Address: 67A Reading Road, Pangbourne, READING, RG8 7JD **Tel:** 0118 984 4005
Email: sarah.gibbons@policesupers.com
Advertising Address: As above. **Fax:** 0118 984 5642
Email: policesupers@tiscali.co.uk
Web site: http://www.policesupers.com
Publisher: National Executive Committee of the Police Superintendents' Association of England and Wales
Frequency: Quarterly
Cover Price: Free
Circulation: 2,500 (Publisher's Statement)
Editor: Sarah Gibbons; **Advertising Manager:** Peter Williams
Summary of Content: Official journal of the Police Superintendents Association including articles on pay, conferences, interviews and issues affecting its members.
Readership/Target Audience: Aimed at members of the Police Superintendents' Association.
ADVERTISING RATES:
Full Page Colour £600.00
Mechanical Data: Film: Digital, Trim Size: 297 x 210mm, Type Area: 260 x 165mm, Col Length: 260mm, Page Width: 165mm, Col Widths (Display): 55mm, No. of Columns (Display): 3
Copy instructions: Copy Date: 3 weeks prior to publication date
Average advertising content per issue: 10%
BUSINESS: LOCAL GOVERNMENT, LEISURE & RECREATION: Police

SUPERYACHT BUSINESS
1834304U45E-372

Editorial Address: Leon House, 233 High Street, CROYDON, CR9 1HZ **Tel:** 020 8726 8138
Email: dennis_o'neill@ipcmedia.com
Advertising Address: As above. **Tel:** 020 8726 8000
Fax: 020 8726 8199
Email: philip_pereira@ipcmedia.com
Web site: http://www.superyachtbusiness.net
Publisher: IPC Inspire
Frequency: 6 issues yearly
Free to qualifying individuals
Circulation: 6,000 (Publisher's Statement)
Editor: Dennis O'Neill; **Managing Editor:** Ed Slack
Summary of Content: Magazine covering news and developments from designers, stylists, boat builders, project managers, surveyors, equipment manufactures and service providers. Also featuring analysis on what's going on in the yacht broker, yacht charter and yacht management areas, new product reviews, applications and techniques.
Readership/Target Audience: Aimed at the yachting industry including those involved with the design, building, maintenance and operation of professional crewed yachts.
ADVERTISING RATES:
Full Page Colour £2565.00
Agency Commission: 10%
Mechanical Data: Type Area: 260 x 179mm, Col Length: 260mm, Page Width: 179mm, Film: Digital
Copy instructions: Copy Date: 3 weeks prior to publication date
Average advertising content per issue: 30%
BUSINESS: MARINE & SHIPPING: Boat Trade

SUPPLY CHAIN EUROPE
35981U5A-100

Formerly: Frontline Solutions Europe
Editorial Address: Oak House Mews, 43 The Parade, Claygate, ESHER, KT10 0PD **Tel:** 01392 202591
Email: kevin@via-mediatld.com
Advertising Address: As above. **Tel:** 01372 471541
Email: simon@via-mediatld.com
Web site: http://www.scemagazine.com
ISSN: 1363-9765
Publisher: Via Media Ltd
Date Established: 1993
Frequency: 6 issues yearly - Published in the 4th week of the 1st cover month
Free to qualifying individuals
Circulation: 15,000 (Publisher's Statement)
Usual Pagination: 52
Editor: Samuel Tulip; **Features Editor:** Sam Tulip;
Advertising Manager: Simon Jones
Summary of Content: Magazine covering supply chain solutions for manufacturing, warehousing and logistics.
Readership/Target Audience: Aimed at users and potential users of supply chain hardware, technology and services.
ADVERTISING RATES:
Full Page Colour £3020.00
Agency Commission: 15%
Mechanical Data: Col Length: 250mm, Page Width: 180mm, Film: Digital, Trim Size: 280 x 210mm, Type Area: 250 x 180mm, Bleed Size: 286 x 216mm
Copy instructions: Copy Date: 4 weeks prior to publication date
Average advertising content per issue: 40%
BUSINESS: COMPUTERS & AUTOMATION: Automation & Instrumentation

SUPPLY CHAIN MANAGEMENT: AN INTERNATIONAL JOURNAL
36545U10-150

Formerly: Supply Chain Management
Editorial Address: Howard House, Wagon Lane, BINGLEY, BD16 1WA **Tel:** 01274 777700 **Fax:** 01274 785200
Email: lsootheran@emeraldinsight.com
Web site: http://www.emeraldinsight.com
ISSN: 1359-8546
Publisher: Emerald Group Publishing Ltd
Date Established: 1996
Frequency: 5 issues yearly
Usual Pagination: 80
Editor: Lucy Sootheran; **Publisher:** Lucy Sootheran
Summary of Content: Journal about goods distribution, from sourcing raw materials and manufacturing products, to delivering the finished product.
Readership/Target Audience: Aimed at supply chain managers in industry.
ADVERTISING: No Advertising taken
BUSINESS: MATERIALS HANDLING

SUPPLY MANAGEMENT
37021U14D-400

Editorial Address: 17 Britton Street, LONDON, EC1M 5TP **Tel:** 020 7324 2746 **Fax:** 020 7324 2791
Email: editorial@supplymanagement.com
Advertising Address: As above. **Tel:** 020 7880 6232
Fax: 020 7880 7553
Email: lindsay@supplymanagement.com
Web site: http://www.supplymanagement.com
ISSN: 1362-2021
Publisher: Redactive Media Group
Date Established: 1996
Frequency: 25 issues yearly
Free to qualifying individuals
Annual Sub.: £80.00
Circulation: 40,559 (ABC 01/01/2008 to 31/12/2008)
Usual Pagination: 60
Editor: Paul Snell; **Features Editor:** Paul Snell; **Editor-in-Chief:** Geraint John
Summary of Content: Magazine covering news, advice and in-depth features on purchasing, supply chain and logistics, from defining supply strategies to managing day-to-day procurement. Features articles dealing with e-commerce and related issues.
Readership/Target Audience: Aimed at chief executives and those involved in procurement, purchasing, operations and logistics. Also read by supply chain directors, managers and buyers at all levels.
ADVERTISING RATES:
Full Page Mono £3500.00
Full Page Colour £4440.00
Agency Commission: 10%
Mechanical Data: Type Area: 240 x 185mm, Bleed Size: 282 x 221mm, Trim Size: 276 x 215mm, Col Length: 240mm, Page Width: 185mm
Copy instructions: Copy Date: 2 weeks prior to publication date
Average advertising content per issue: 40%
BUSINESS: COMMERCE, INDUSTRY & MANAGEMENT: Purchasing

SUPPORT FOR LEARNING
41125U62G-420

Formerly: Support for Learning - British Journal of Learning Support
Editorial Address: School of Education, University of Northampton, Park Campus, Boughton Green Road, NORTHAMPTON, NN2 7AL **Tel:** 01604 892418
Email: philip.garner@northampton.ac.uk
Advertising Address: Nasen House, 4-5 Amber Business Village, Amber Close, Amington, TAMWORTH, B77 4RP **Tel:** 01827 311500 **Fax:** 01827 313005
Email: welcome@nasen.org.uk
Web site: http://www.nasen.org.uk
ISSN: 0268-2141
Publisher: Wiley-Blackwell Publishing
Date Established: 1985
Frequency: Quarterly
Annual Sub.: £235.00
Editor: Philip Garner; **Advertising Manager:** Sean Stockdale
Summary of Content: The articles in Support for Learning examine the practical and theoretical issues surrounding the education of pupils with special educational needs in mainstream schools. Support for Learning aims to act as a bridge between academics and practitioners. All aspects of curriculum delivery, classroom management and the use of support services are covered. Strategies to eliminate underachievement and promote best practice are especially featured. Most, but not all, issues of Support for Learning, focus on a topical theme.
Readership/Target Audience: Aimed at all who work with or support children and young people with special educational needs.
ADVERTISING RATES:
Full Page Mono £520.00
Mechanical Data: Type Area: 250 x 170mm, Col Length: 250mm, Page Width: 170mm

Copy instructions: Copy Date: 8 weeks prior to publication date
BUSINESS: CHURCH & SCHOOL EQUIPMENT & EDUCATION: Special Needs Education

SUPPORTWORLD
1644117U5R-682
Formerly: Support World
Editorial Address: 21 High Street, Green Street Green, ORPINGTON, BR6 6BG Tel: 01689 889100
Fax: 01689 889227
Email: brianw@supportworld.co.uk
Advertising Address: As above.
Email: robertb@hdi-europe.com
Web site: http://www.supportworld.co.uk
Publisher: SDI
Date Established: 2004
Frequency: 6 issues yearly
Free to qualifying individuals
Circulation: 8,000 (Publisher's Statement)
Usual Pagination: 36
Editor: Brian Wall; Advertising Manager: Robert Beswick
Summary of Content: Magazine focusing specifically on the issues that affect the helpdesk and IT support industry.
Readership/Target Audience: Aimed at helpdesk and IT support professionals.
ADVERTISING RATES:
Full Page Colour £800.00
Agency Commission: 20%
Mechanical Data: Bleed Size: 297 x 210mm, Trim Size: 282 x 192mm, Film: Digital
Average advertising content per issue: 20%
BUSINESS: COMPUTERS & AUTOMATION: Computers Related

SURFACE COATINGS INTERNATIONAL
37284U16B-200
Editorial Address: Priory House, 967 Harrow Road, WEMBLEY, HA0 2SF Tel: 020 8908 1086
Fax: 020 8908 1219
Email: publications@occa.org.uk
Advertising Address: PO Box 28, SEVENOAKS, TN13 1WD Tel: 01732 460452 Fax: 01732 456561
Email: maxharlow@btinternet.com
Web site: http://www.occa.org.uk/publications
ISSN: 1356-0751
Publisher: Oil & Colour Chemists' Association
Date Established: 1915
Frequency: 8 issues yearly
Free to qualifying individuals
Annual Sub.: £100.00
Circulation: 2,550 (Publisher's Statement)
Usual Pagination: 44
Editor: Chris Pacey-Day; Managing Editor: Chris Pacey-Day
Summary of Content: Technological magazine covering news and articles on the paint, printing ink and allied industries.
Readership/Target Audience: Read by senior executives in the surface coatings industry.
ADVERTISING RATES:
Full Page Mono £1300.00
Full Page Colour £2000.00
Agency Commission: 15%
Mechanical Data: Type Area: 254 x 178mm, Bleed Size: 305 x 218mm, Trim Size: 297 x 210mm, Film: Digital, Col Length: 254mm, Page Width: 178mm
Copy instructions: Copy Date: 2 weeks prior to publication date
Average advertising content per issue: 35%
BUSINESS: DECORATING & PAINT: Paint - Technical Manufacture

SURFACE ENGINEERING
37629U19C-625
Editorial Address: 1 Carlton House Terrace, LONDON, SW1Y 5DB Tel: 020 7451 7300 Fax: 020 7451 7307
Email: mark_hull@materials.org.uk
Advertising Address: Suite 1C, Josephs Well, Hanover Walk, LEEDS, LS3 1AB Tel: 01527 404295
Fax: 01527 540503
Email: n.taylor@maney.co.uk
Web site: http://www.maney.co.uk
ISSN: 0267-0844
Publisher: Maney Publishing
Date Established: 1985
Frequency: 6 issues yearly
Annual Sub.: £614.00
Circulation: 700 (Publisher's Statement)
Usual Pagination: 88
Editor: Mark Hull; Advertising Manager: Natalie Taylor
Summary of Content: Journal covering the surface treatment and modification of engineering and functional materials, with particular emphasis on scientific and technological developments and functional applications.
Readership/Target Audience: Aimed at professionals in the surface engineering and heat treatment industry. Also academic and industrial based researchers in this area.

ADVERTISING RATES:
Full Page Mono £500.00
Full Page Colour £1100.00
Agency Commission: 10%
Mechanical Data: Type Area: 266 x 188mm, Bleed Size: 305 x 215mm, Trim Size: 297 x 210mm, Film: Digital, Col Length: 266mm, Page Width: 188mm
Copy instructions: Copy Date: 15th of the month prior to publication date
BUSINESS: ENGINEERING & MACHINERY: Finishing

SURFACE WORLD
37630U19C-635
Editorial Address: 3 Maple Close, Chudleigh Knighton, NEWTON ABBOT, TQ13 0RA Tel: 01626 854505
Fax: 01626 854505
Email: sworlded@aol.com
Advertising Address: Marash House, 2-5 Brook Street, TRING, HP23 5ED Tel: 01442 826826 Fax: 01442 823400
Email: hilmedia@aol.com
Web site: http://www.surfaceworldshow.com
ISSN: 1351-0525
Publisher: Hill Media Ltd
Date Established: 1994
Frequency: 11 issues yearly - Published around the 20th of the cover month (combined issue: 20th of the 1st cover month)
Free to qualifying individuals
Annual Sub.: £90.00
Circulation: 10,000 (Publisher's Statement)
Usual Pagination: 64
Editor: Tony Dolphin; Advertising Manager: Nigel Bean; Publisher: Nigel Bean
Summary of Content: Journal covering all forms of surface engineering, surface treatment, surface coating and product finishing technology and associated products, processes and equipment.
Readership/Target Audience: Aimed at specifiers and users of surface treatment/ finishing products, processes and equipment.
ADVERTISING RATES:
Full Page Mono £950.00
Full Page Colour £1400.00
Agency Commission: 10%
Mechanical Data: Col Length: 254mm, Page Width: 178mm, Film: Digital, Type Area: 297 x 210mm, Type Area: 254 x 178mm, Bleed Size: 303 x 216mm
Copy instructions: Copy Date: 4 weeks prior to publication date
Average advertising content per issue: 60%
BUSINESS: ENGINEERING & MACHINERY: Finishing

SURGERY
40368U56C-380
Editorial Address: The Boulevard, Langford Lane, KIDLINGTON, OX5 1GB Tel: 01865 843463
Email: surgery@medicinepublishing.com
Advertising Address: 32 Jamestown Road, LONDON, NW1 7BY Tel: 020 7424 4300 Fax: 020 7424 4433
Email: b.kill@elsevier.com
Web site: http://www.medicinepublishing.co.uk
ISSN: 0263-9319
Publisher: The Medicine Publishing Company
Date Established: 1983
Frequency: Monthly - Published in the 1st week of the cover month
Annual Sub.: £94.80
Circulation: 5,200 (Publisher's Statement)
Usual Pagination: 40
Editor: Roger Wayman
Summary of Content: Journal forming a continuously updated postgraduate textbook of surgery.
Readership/Target Audience: Aimed at senior house officers in all specialities preparing for MRCS, but also relevant to consultants who are involved in surgical training.
ADVERTISING RATES:
Full Page Mono EUR1134.00
Full Page Colour EUR1872.00
Agency Commission: 10%
Mechanical Data: Type Area: 256 x 181mm, Print Process: Offset litho, Bleed Size: 286 x 213mm, Trim Size: 280 x 210mm, Film: Positive right reading emulsion side down. Digital, Col Length: 256mm, Page Width: 181mm
Copy instructions: Copy Date: 4 weeks prior to publication date
BUSINESS: HEALTH & MEDICAL: Hospitals

SURREY DIRECTOR
41358U63B-1670
Formerly: West Surrey Director
Editorial Address: 14 Middletons Road, Yaxley, PETERBOROUGH, PE7 3LR Tel: 01733 242312
Fax: 01733 244035
Email: carol@pridepublications.co.uk
Advertising Address: As above.
Email: maxine@pridepublications.co.uk
Web site: http://www.pridepublications.co.uk
Publisher: Pride Publications Ltd
Frequency: 8 issues yearly
Cover Price: Free

Circulation: 3,600 (Publisher's Statement)
Editor: Carol Lawless; Managing Director: Carol Lawless; Advertisement Director: Maxine Coward; Publisher: Carol Lawless
Summary of Content: Journal covering business articles, business advice and regional business news.
Readership/Target Audience: Aimed at chief executive officers, senior partners and prime decision makers.
ADVERTISING RATES:
Full Page Mono £675.00
Full Page Colour £675.00
Agency Commission: 10%
Mechanical Data: Type Area: 272 x 187mm, Bleed Size: 309 x 218mm, Trim Size: 303 x 210mm, Col Length: 272mm, Page Width: 187mm, Col Widths (Display): 60mm, No. of Columns (Display): 3, Film: Digital
Copy instructions: Copy Date: 1 week prior to publication date
Average advertising content per issue: 50%
BUSINESS: REGIONAL BUSINESS: Regional Business English Counties

THE SURREY LAWYER
1851572U44-3057
Editorial Address: 4th Floor, Orleans House, Edmund Street, LIVERPOOL, L3 9NG Tel: 0151 236 4141
Fax: 0151 236 0440
Email: phillightfoot@benhampublishing.com
Web site: http://www.benhampublishing.com/magazines.htm
Publisher: Benham Publishing Limited
Frequency: Quarterly
Free to qualifying individuals
Editor: Phil Lightfoot
Summary of Content: Official magazine of the Surrey Law Society featuring society news, members events and awards.
Readership/Target Audience: Aimed at members of the Surrey Law Society.
BUSINESS: LEGAL

SURVEYOR
39030U42A-180
Editorial Address: 32 Vauxhall Bridge Road, LONDON, SW1V 2SS Tel: 020 7973 6400 Fax: 020 7973 6677
Email: editorial.surveyor@hgluk.com
Advertising Address: As above. Fax: 020 7233 5053
Email: a.suttle@hgluk.com
Web site: http://www.surveyormagazine.com
ISSN: 0039-3606
Publisher: Hemming Group Ltd
Date Established: 1892
Frequency: Weekly - Published every Thursday
Annual Sub.: £93.00
Circulation: 5,311 (ABC 01/07/2008 to 30/06/2009)
Usual Pagination: 36
Editor: Adrian Tatum; News Editor: Robin Mannering; Features Editor: Belinda Totton; Managing Director: Graham Bond
Summary of Content: Magazine covering all aspects of local authority technical services including highway maintenance, parking, traffic control and transport policy and articles on waste management, contaminated land, coastal protection and drainage.
Readership/Target Audience: Read by professionals in the areas of highways and transportation, waste management and environmental protection within local government technical services and their contractors.
ADVERTISING RATES:
Full Page Colour £1827.00
Agency Commission: 10%
Mechanical Data: Type Area: 270 x 190mm, Bleed Size: 303 x 216mm, Trim Size: 297 x 210mm, Col Length: 270mm, Film: Digital, Page Width: 190mm
Copy instructions: Copy Date: Tuesday 5pm prior to publication date
Average advertising content per issue: 20%
BUSINESS: CONSTRUCTION

SUSTAIN
601279U4E-345
Editorial Address: Deansgate Mews, 253 Deansgate, MANCHESTER, M3 4EN Tel: 0161 950 4500
Fax: 0161 834 3344
Email: editorial@sustainmagazine.com
Advertising Address: As above.
Email: j.holt@sustainmagazine.com
Web site: http://www.sustainmagazine.com
ISSN: 1476-1572
Publisher: McClelland Publishing
Date Established: 1999
Frequency: 6 issues yearly - Published in the 1st week of the cover month
Free to qualifying individuals
Annual Sub.: £57.00
Circulation: 30,000 (Publisher's Statement)
Usual Pagination: 83
Features Editor: Gary Ramsay; Publisher: Jim McClelland
Summary of Content: Magazine covering built environment matters, contaminated land, regeneration, waste

management, climate change, renewable energy issues and sustainable development. Also contains industry news, overseas section, case studies and appointments.
Readership/Target Audience: Aimed at developers, private and public, designers and those working within the construction industry.
ADVERTISING RATES:
Full Page Mono £1895.00
Full Page Colour £1895.00
SCC £21.50
Agency Commission: 10%
Mechanical Data: Bleed Size: 300 x 213mm, Trim Size: 297 x 210mm, Film: Digital, Type Area: 287 x 200mm, Col Length: 287mm, Page Width: 200mm, Col Widths (Display): 90mm, No. of Columns (Display): 2
Copy instructions: Copy Date: 3 weeks prior to publication date
Average advertising content per issue: 35%
Supplement(s): C-Minus - 2xY, CSR - 3xY, OSC - 2xY
BUSINESS: ARCHITECTURE & BUILDING: Building

SUSTAINABLE BUILDING
1824342U4D-426

Editorial Address: The Chapel, Wellington Road, LONDON, NW10 5LJ **Tel:** 020 8969 1008 **Fax:** 020 8969 1334
Email: editorial@sustainable-build.com
Advertising Address: As above.
Email: editorial@sustainable-build.com
Web site: http://www.sustainable-build.com
Publisher: Newzeye Ltd
Date Established: 2007
Frequency: Monthly - Also one monthly e-bulletin
Annual Sub.: £350.00
Circulation: 4,000 (Publisher's Statement)
Usual Pagination: 20
Editor: Ian Grant; **Managing Editor:** Ian Grant
Summary of Content: Newsletter covering energy efficiency and green building. Featuring news, features on using renewable energy and analysis of energy policy.
Readership/Target Audience: Aimed at architects, building service engineers, environmental consultants, quantity surveyors, local authorities, town planners, housing associations, construction companies, facilities managers and property developers.
ADVERTISING: Rates on application
BUSINESS: ARCHITECTURE & BUILDING: Planning & Housing

SUSTAINABLE BUSINESS
40644U57-21_70

Formerly: Environment Business
Editorial Address: Faversham House, 232A Addington Road, SOUTH CROYDON, CR2 8LE **Tel:** 020 8651 7100
Fax: 020 8651 7117
Email: tom.idle@fav-house.com
Advertising Address: As above. **Tel:** 020 8651 7132
Email: jane.martin@fav-house.com
Web site: http://www.sustainablebusinessnetwork.net
ISSN: 1352-8882
Publisher: Faversham House Group Ltd
Date Established: 1994
Frequency: Monthly - Published at the beginning of the cover month
Free to qualifying individuals
Annual Sub.: £97.00
Circulation: 9,135 (ABC 01/07/2006 to 30/06/2007)
Usual Pagination: 44
Editor: Tom Idle; **Publisher:** Angela Himus
Summary of Content: Magazine for those responsible for the sustainability and environmental performance of their business or organisation.
Readership/Target Audience: Read by senior managers, consultants and those who work in the public sector.
ADVERTISING RATES:
Full Page Colour £2500.00
Agency Commission: 10%
Mechanical Data: Type Area: 270 x 180mm, Col Length: 270mm, Page Width: 180mm, Bleed Size: 303 x 216mm, Trim Size: 297 x 210mm, Film: Digital
Copy instructions: Copy Date: 3 weeks prior to publication date
Supplement(s): Consultancy Survey - 1xY, FutureProof - 10xY, Training - 2xY
BUSINESS: ENVIRONMENT & POLLUTION

SUSTAINABLE COMMUNITIES MAGAZINE
1843462U57-164

Editorial Address: 8th Floor, Bridgewater House, Whitworth Street, MANCHESTER, M1 6LT **Tel:** 0161 832 6000
Fax: 0161 832 4176
Email: ian.clappison@tenalpspublishing.com
Advertising Address: As above.
Email: ian.clappison@tenalpspublishing.com
Publisher: Ten Alps Publishing
Date Established: 2008
Frequency: Quarterly - Published around the end of the cover month
Cover Price: Free

Editor: Ian Clappison
Summary of Content: Magazine addressing the roles that central and local government, housing associations and developers can play in not only developing built sustainability in homes but also sustainable communities for the future. Featuring news, features and case studies from local authorities and housing associations.
Readership/Target Audience: Aimed at key decision makers within house builders and developers, planning departments, housing associations, social landlords, central and local government departments, master planners, regional development agencies, architects, regeneration companies, universities and key trade associations.
ADVERTISING: Rates on application
Copy instructions: Copy Date: 4 weeks prior to publication date
BUSINESS: ENVIRONMENT & POLLUTION

SUSTAINABLE DEVELOPMENT
40686U57-55

Editorial Address: The Atrium, Southern Gate, CHICHESTER, PO19 8SQ **Tel:** 01243 779777
Advertising Address: As above. **Tel:** 01243 770254
Fax: 01243 770432
Email: adsales@wiley.co.uk
Web site: http://www.interscience.wiley.com/journal/sd
ISSN: 0968-0802
Publisher: Wiley-Blackwell
Frequency: 6 issues yearly
Annual Sub.: £140.00
Circulation: 2,400 (Publisher's Statement)
Usual Pagination: 80
Editor-in-Chief: Richard Welford
Summary of Content: Journal focusing on environmental management and sustainability, including global, national and regional development issues.
Readership/Target Audience: Aimed at policy makers in local and central government, decision makers in business, engineers, researchers and academics.
ADVERTISING RATES:
Full Page Mono £2000.00
Full Page Colour £4375.00
Agency Commission: 10%
Mechanical Data: Print Process: Sheet-fed offset litho, Film: Digital, Type Area: 230 x 170mm, Col Length: 230mm, Page Width: 170mm, Trim Size: 260 x 200mm
BUSINESS: ENVIRONMENT & POLLUTION

SUSTAINABLE FM
1819377U4R-626

Editorial Address: Apex House, 28 Ruskin Avenue, WALTHAM ABBEY, EN9 3BP **Tel:** 0845 652 1012
Fax: 01992 767672
Email: duane@abbeypublishing.co.uk
Advertising Address: As above. **Tel:** 01920 870055
Fax: 01920 877265
Email: ralph@abbeypublishing.co.uk
Web site: http://www.abbeypublishing.co.uk
Publisher: Abbey Publishing
Date Established: 2007
Frequency: 6 issues yearly
Circulation: 11,500 (Print Run)
Editor: Duane Daviner; **Managing Director:** Ralph Scrivens;
Advertising Manager: Ralph Scrivens; **Publisher:** Ralph Scrivens
Summary of Content: Magazine looking at issues from an environmental sustainable standpoint. Features include news stories, product related features, opinions, interviews and case studies.
Readership/Target Audience: Aimed at facilities and estate managers, energy managers, building service managers, LA21 officers, environment managers and purchasing managers throughout the public sector and the top 3000 multinational private sector companies.
ADVERTISING RATES:
Full Page Mono £1000.00
Full Page Colour £1500.00
Mechanical Data: Type Area: 270 x 180mm, Bleed Size: 307 x 220mm, Trim Size: 297 x 210mm, Col Length: 270mm, Page Width: 180mm, Film: Digital
BUSINESS: ARCHITECTURE & BUILDING: Building Related

SUSTAINABLE IRELAND
1648848U57-129

Editorial Address: 3 Tudor Grange, Waringstown, CRAIGAVON, BT66 7PX **Tel:** 028 3882 0211
Fax: 028 3882 0211
Email: jkeditorial@aol.com
Advertising Address: The Old Coach House, 12 Main Street, HILLSBOROUGH, BT26 6AE **Tel:** 028 9268 8888
Fax: 028 9268 8866
Email: paul@4squaremedia.net
Publisher: 4 Square Media
Date Established: 2004
Frequency: Quarterly
Cover Price: £2.00
Free to qualifying individuals
Circulation: 4,274 (Publisher's Statement)
Usual Pagination: 68

Editor: David Stokes; **Advertising Manager:** Paul Beattie;
Managing Editor: Helen Beggs; **Group Editor:** David Stokes
Summary of Content: Magazine covering all aspects of sustainable development, including articles on energy efficiency and waste management.
Readership/Target Audience: Aimed at local authorities, waste recycling operators, landfill site owners, environmental agencies and consultancies and manufacturers.
ADVERTISING RATES:
Full Page Colour £1100.00
Mechanical Data: Type Area: 267 x 180mm, Bleed Size: 303 x 216mm, Trim Size: 297 x 210mm, Col Length: 267mm, Col Widths (Display): 42mm, Page Width: 180mm, Film: Digital
Copy instructions: Copy Date: 3 weeks prior to publication date
BUSINESS: ENVIRONMENT & POLLUTION

SVI MAGAZINE
1616060U43B-81

Formerly: What's New: Sound Vision Install
Editorial Address: 25 Phoenix Court, Hawkins Road, COLCHESTER, CO2 8JY **Tel:** 01206 505959
Fax: 01206 505929
Email: jacob.stow@aceville.co.uk
Advertising Address: 2nd Floor, Ewer House, 44-46 Crouch Street, COLCHESTER, CO3 3HH **Tel:** 01206 505900
Fax: 01206 500180
Email: svimag@mspublications.co.uk
Web site: http://www.svimag.com
ISSN: 1478-1123
Publisher: Partridge Publications (2000) Ltd
Date Established: 2003
Frequency: 10 issues yearly
Free to qualifying individuals
Annual Sub.: £29.95
Circulation: 4,320 (ABC 01/07/2006 to 30/06/2007)
Usual Pagination: 52
Editor: Jacob Stow; **Editor-in-Chief:** Stuart Pritchard;
Advertising Manager: Bonnie Howard
Summary of Content: Product led publication covering hi-fi, home cinema, custom install, accessories, show reports, industry comments, product news and industry news within the hi-fi and audio visual world from industry gossip to show venues.
Readership/Target Audience: Aimed at AV retailers, custom installers, home cinema distributors, electronics manufacturers, specifiers and architects.
ADVERTISING RATES:
Full Page Colour £950.00
Agency Commission: 10%
Mechanical Data: Type Area: 270 x 183mm, Trim Size: 297 x 210mm, Bleed Size: 303 x 216mm, Col Length: 270mm, Page Width: 183mm, Film: Digital
Average advertising content per issue: 40%
BUSINESS: ELECTRICAL RETAIL TRADE: Radio & Hi-Fi

SWIM & SAVE
1609465U62B-1403

Editorial Address: 10 Innage Lane, BRIDGNORTH, WV16 4HL **Tel:** 01746 763576
Email: staeditor@imagine-comms.co.uk
Web site: http://www.sta.co.uk
Publisher: The Swimming Teachers' Association
Frequency: 6 issues yearly
Free to qualifying individuals
Annual Sub.: £18.00
Circulation: 6,000 (Publisher's Statement)
Usual Pagination: 24
Editor: Samantha Stewart
Summary of Content: Journal of the Swimming Teachers' Association, covering teaching, water safety, life guarding, aquacise and first aid.
Readership/Target Audience: Read by members of the association worldwide.
ADVERTISING: No Advertising taken
BUSINESS: CHURCH & SCHOOL EQUIPMENT & EDUCATION: Education Teachers

SWIMMING POOL NEWS
1750276U32E-266

Editorial Address: 3rd Floor, 104 Great Portland Street, LONDON, W1W 6PE **Tel:** 07976 725837
Email: alan@lewisbusiness.fsnet.co.uk
Advertising Address: Redactive Media, 17 Britton Street, LONDON, EC1M 5TP **Tel:** 020 7880 6222
Email: terry.arnold@redactive.co.uk
Publisher: Go Publishing Ltd
Date Established: 1960
Frequency: 6 issues yearly
Cover Price: Free
Circulation: 8,400 (Publisher's Statement)
Usual Pagination: 84
Editor: Alan Lewis; **Publisher:** Alan Lewis
Summary of Content: Magazine covering all aspects of swimming pool maintenance and installation including up-keep, investment, cleaning, site planning and technology.

Business Magazines

Readership/Target Audience: Aimed at trade and domestic swimming pool owners.
ADVERTISING RATES:
Full Page Colour £1250.00
Mechanical Data: Bleed Size: 426 x 303mm, Trim Size: 420 x 297mm, Film: Digital
Copy instructions: Copy Date: 2 weeks prior to publication date
Average advertising content per issue: 40%
BUSINESS: LOCAL GOVERNMENT, LEISURE & RECREATION: Swimming Pools

SWINDON BUSINESS NEWS
41393U63B-2000
Editorial Address: 26 Wood Street, SWINDON, SN1 4AB
Tel: 01793 615393 **Fax:** 01793 488517
Email: info@swindon-business.net
Advertising Address: As above.
Email: ann@swindon-business.net
Web site: http://www.swindon-business.com
Publisher: County Business Publishing Ltd
Date Established: 1981
Frequency: 11 issues yearly
Annual Sub.: £25.00
Circulation: 10,000 (Publisher's Statement)
Usual Pagination: 24
Editor: Lorne Barling; **Managing Director:** Lorne Barling; **Advertising Manager:** Ann Freegard
Summary of Content: Business publication covering the expansion and growth of companies in Swindon and the South West.
Readership/Target Audience: Read by directors and sales managers.
ADVERTISING RATES:
Full Page Mono £1524.00
Full Page Colour £1828.80
Mechanical Data: Trim Size: 395 x 297mm, Col Widths (Display): 50mm, No. of Columns (Display): 5, Film: Digital
BUSINESS: REGIONAL BUSINESS: Regional Business English Counties

SYNERGY - IMAGING AND THERAPY PRACTICE
40444U56J-100
Formerly: Synergy
Editorial Address: Ewell House, Graveney Road, FAVERSHAM, ME13 8UP **Tel:** 01795 542437
Fax: 01795 535469
Email: racheld@synergymagazine.co.uk
Advertising Address: As above. **Tel:** 01795 542405
Email: stevenr@synergymagazine.co.uk
Web site: http://www.synergymagazine.co.uk
ISSN: 1360-5518
Publisher: GTC
Date Established: 1995
Frequency: Monthly
Cover Price: £5.00
Free to qualifying individuals
Circulation: 23,900 (Publisher's Statement)
Usual Pagination: 32
Editor: Rachel Deeson; **Advertising Manager:** Steven Riley; **Publisher:** Dominic Deeson
Summary of Content: Magazine containing practice based and technical articles on imaging and therapy radiography.
Readership/Target Audience: Read by members of the Society of Radiographers.
ADVERTISING RATES:
Full Page Mono £920.00
Full Page Colour £1675.00
Agency Commission: 10%
Mechanical Data: Col Length: 275mm, No. of Columns (Display): 4, Type Area: 275 x 188mm, Print Process: Web-fed offset litho, Bleed Size: 303 x 216mm, Trim Size: 297 x 210mm, Page Width: 188mm
Copy instructions: Copy Date: 19th of the month prior to publication date
Average advertising content per issue: 30%
BUSINESS: HEALTH & MEDICAL: Radiography

T & G RECORD
37205U14L-660
Editorial Address: 128 Theobalds Road, LONDON, WC1X 8TN **Tel:** 020 7611 2500 **Fax:** 020 7611 2555
Email: andrew.d.murray@unitetheunion.org
Web site: http://www.tgwu.org.uk
Publisher: Transport & General Workers' Union
Date Established: 1921
Frequency: 6 issues yearly
Cover Price: Free
Circulation: 140,000 (Publisher's Statement)
Usual Pagination: 32
Editor: Andrew Murray; **Advertising Manager:** Pat Farragher; **Circulation Manager:** Andrew Ionton
Summary of Content: Magazine containing industrial news, sports diary, stories and cartoons.
Readership/Target Audience: For members of the Transport & General Workers Union.

ADVERTISING: No Advertising taken
BUSINESS: COMMERCE, INDUSTRY & MANAGEMENT: Trade Unions

TABLER
48721U32G-164
Editorial Address: Marchesi House, 4 Embassy Drive, Calthorpe Road, Edgbaston, BIRMINGHAM, B15 1TP
Tel: 0121 456 4402 **Fax:** 0121 456 4185
Email: hq@roundtable.org.uk
Advertising Address: Jam Media Ltd, Amherst House, 22 London Road, Riverhead, SEVENOAKS, TN13 2BT
Tel: 0844 499 1562 **Fax:** 0844 499 1561
Email: tm@jam-media.com
Web site: http://www.roundtable.org.uk
Publisher: National Association of Round Tables
Date Established: 1929
Frequency: Quarterly
Cover Price: £3.50
Free to qualifying individuals
Circulation: 14,000 (Publisher's Statement)
Usual Pagination: 60
Editor: Ron Shea
Summary of Content: Magazine for Round Table members covering social activities, sports, international visits and community service.
Readership/Target Audience: Read by members and prospective members of the Round Table.
ADVERTISING RATES:
Full Page Colour £1376.00
Agency Commission: 10%
Mechanical Data: Bleed Size: 303 x 216mm, Trim Size: 297 x 210mm, Film: Digital
Copy instructions: Copy Date: 3 weeks prior to publication date
Average advertising content per issue: 40%
BUSINESS: LOCAL GOVERNMENT, LEISURE & RECREATION: Community Care & Social Services

TABLEWARE INTERNATIONAL
36616U12A-70
Editorial Address: 1 Churchgates, The Wilderness, BERKHAMSTED, HP4 2UB **Tel:** 01442 289930
Fax: 01422 289950
Email: jo@lemapublishing.co.uk
Advertising Address: As above. **Fax:** 01442 289950
Email: robert@lemapublishing.co.uk
Web site: http://www.tablewareinternational.com
ISSN: 0143-7755
Publisher: Lema Publishing
Date Established: 1970
Frequency: 6 issues yearly
Free to qualifying individuals
Annual Sub.: £45.00
Circulation: 10,600 (Publisher's Statement)
Usual Pagination: 92
Editor: Jo Cooper; **Advertising Manager:** Robert Thomas; **Publisher:** Mark Naish
Summary of Content: Journal containing information on all aspects of the tableware, homeware and gifts business, including trade fairs.
Readership/Target Audience: Aimed at trade buyers, interior designers and retailers of tableware, homeware and giftware.
ADVERTISING RATES:
Full Page Colour £3250.00
Agency Commission: 10%
Mechanical Data: Page Width: 185mm, Bleed Size: 303 x 213mm, Type Area: 265 x 185mm, Col Length: 265mm, Trim Size: 297 x 210mm, Film: Digital
Average advertising content per issue: 40%
BUSINESS: CERAMICS, POTTERY & GLASS: Ceramics & Pottery

TACKLE & GUNS
39560U48B-73
Editorial Address: 2 Stephenson Close, Drayton Fields Industrial Estate, DAVENTRY, NN11 8RF **Tel:** 01327 311999
Fax: 01327 315430
Email: john@dhpub.co.uk
Advertising Address: As above.
Email: lee.m@dhpub.co.uk
Web site: http://www.davidhallpublishing.com
Publisher: David Hall Publishing Ltd
Frequency: Monthly
Free to qualifying individuals
Circulation: 6,000 (Publisher's Statement)
Usual Pagination: 100
Editor: John Hunter; **Advertising Manager:** Lee Mandaracas; **Publisher:** Sean O'Driscoll
Summary of Content: Magazine containing news, product reviews and business to business information.
Readership/Target Audience: Aimed at all those involved in the retail shooting and fishing trade.
ADVERTISING RATES:
Full Page Mono £950.00
Full Page Colour £950.00
Agency Commission: 10%

Mechanical Data: Type Area: 273 x 185mm, Bleed Size: 303 x 216mm, Col Length: 273mm, Page Width: 185mm, Trim Size: 297 x 210mm, Film: Digital
Copy instructions: Copy Date: 4 weeks prior to publication date
Average advertising content per issue: 40%
BUSINESS: TOY TRADE & SPORTS GOODS: Sports Goods

TACKLE TRADE WORLD
718529U45B-220
Editorial Address: 2 Stephenson Close, Drayton Fields Industrial Estate, DAVENTRY, NN11 8RF **Tel:** 01327 315429
Fax: 01327 315430
Email: nick@dhpub.co.uk
Advertising Address: As above. **Tel:** 01327 311999
Email: sue@dhpub.co.uk
Publisher: David Hall Publishing Ltd
Date Established: 2000
Frequency: Monthly
Free to qualifying individuals
Circulation: 13,300 (Publisher's Statement)
Usual Pagination: 116
Editor: Nick Marlow
Summary of Content: Magazine covering business to business for the global fishing tackle trade.
Readership/Target Audience: Aimed at fishing tackle manufacturers, wholesalers, retailers and trade associations worldwide.
ADVERTISING RATES:
Full Page Colour £1150.00
Agency Commission: 10%
Mechanical Data: Bleed Size: 303 x 216mm, Trim Size: 297 x 210mm, Page Width: 185mm, Col Length: 273mm, Type Area: 273 x 185mm
Average advertising content per issue: 45%
BUSINESS: MARINE & SHIPPING: Commercial Fishing

TALKBACK
40516U56Q-40
Editorial Address: 16 Elmtree Road, TEDDINGTON, TW11 8ST **Tel:** 020 8977 5474 **Fax:** 020 8943 5318
Email: info@backcare.org.uk
Advertising Address: As above.
Email: talkback@backcare.org.uk
Web site: http://www.backcare.org.uk
ISSN: 1750-1016
Publisher: Backcare - The Charity for Healthier Backs
Frequency: Quarterly
Cover Price: £2.95
Free to qualifying individuals
Circulation: 3,500 (Publisher's Statement)
Usual Pagination: 32
Editor: Diana Gordon; **Advertising Manager:** Margaret Floate
Summary of Content: Magazine of Backcare - the Charity for Healthier Backs. Educates and informs readers on active recovery as well as developments in research, treatment and equipment.
Readership/Target Audience: Aimed at members and those concerned with treating back pain.
ADVERTISING RATES:
Full Page Colour £800.00
Agency Commission: 10%
Mechanical Data: Type Area: 273 x 186mm, Bleed Size: 303 x 216mm, Col Length: 273mm, Page Width: 186mm, Trim Size: 297 x 210mm, Film: Digital
Average advertising content per issue: 20%
BUSINESS: HEALTH & MEDICAL: Chiropractic

TAN*BIZ
1629423U32H-456
Formerly: Tanning Business
Editorial Address: Laurel Cottage, Botley Road, Shedfield, SOUTHAMPTON, SO32 2JG **Tel:** 01582 431273
Fax: 01329 832290
Email: femke.vaniperen@health-and-beauty.com
Advertising Address: Karl-Friedrich-Strasse 14-18, KARLSRUHE, 76133 **Tel:** 721 165 136 **Fax:** 721 165 150
Email: stephan.drescher@health-and-beauty.com
Web site: http://www.tan-biz.co.uk
Publisher: Health and Beauty Business Media GmbH
Date Established: 1996
Frequency: 6 issues yearly
Annual Sub.: £24.00
Circulation: 10,375 (Publisher's Statement)
Usual Pagination: 68
Editor: Femke van Iperen; **Advertising Manager:** Stephan Drescher
Summary of Content: Magazine covering all aspects of running a modern tanning salon or outlet within a large business.
Language(s): Dutch; English; French; German; Italian; Polish; Russian; Spanish
Readership/Target Audience: Aimed at owners and managers of all tanning salons and outlets, beauty salons, nail and/or hair salons, health clubs, hotels, spas and leisure centres.
ADVERTISING RATES:
Full Page Colour £1780.00

Mechanical Data: Type Area: 280 x 200mm, Col Length: 280mm, Page Width: 200mm, Trim Size: 310 x 297mm, Bleed Size: 316 x 303mm, Film: Digital
BUSINESS: LOCAL GOVERNMENT, LEISURE & RECREATION: Leisure, Recreation & Entertainment

TANDOORI MAGAZINE
36599U11A-185

Editorial Address: Alexander House, 14-16 Peterborough Road, LONDON, SW6 3BN Tel: 020 7348 7997
Fax: 020 7348 7996
Email: humayun@subcontinent.co.uk
Advertising Address: As above.
Email: suman@subcontinent.co.uk
Web site: http://www.tandoorimagazine.com
Publisher: Subcontinent Publishing
Date Established: 1994
Frequency: 6 issues yearly
Cover Price: £4.00
Free to qualifying individuals
Annual Sub.: £16.00
Circulation: 10,575 (Publisher's Statement)
Usual Pagination: 84
Editor: Humayun Hussain; Advertising Manager: Suman Sinha; Publisher: Ajay Patel
Summary of Content: Magazine reporting on upcoming trends in the Indian food and drink industry. Features new products, book and website reviews, recipe ideas, restaurant interiors, hotels, travel, drinks, information on basic hygiene, equipment and kitchen design issues.
Readership/Target Audience: Aimed at the Indian restaurant market and consumers interested in Indian food and drink.
ADVERTISING RATES:
Full Page Colour £2500.00
Agency Commission: 10%
Mechanical Data: Trim Size: 274 x 206mm, Film: Digital, Bleed Size: +3mm
Copy instructions: Copy Date: 4 weeks prior to publication date
Average advertising content per issue: 40%
BUSINESS: CATERING: Catering, Hotels & Restaurants

TANK STORAGE MAGAZINE
1804493U58-184

Editorial Address: Marshall House, 124 Middleton Road, MORDEN, SM4 6RW Tel: 020 8687 4126
Fax: 020 8687 4130
Email: margaret@tankstoragemag.com
Advertising Address: As above. Tel: 020 8687 4139
Email: joseph@tankstoragemag.com
Web site: http://www.tankstoragemag.com
ISSN: 1750-841X
Publisher: Horseshoe Media Ltd
Date Established: 2005
Frequency: 5 issues yearly
Annual Sub.: £120.00
Circulation: 3,000 (Publisher's Statement)
Usual Pagination: 104
Editor: Margaret Garn; Managing Director: Peter Patterson; Advertising Manager: Joseph Quinn
Summary of Content: Magazine containing industry news or the tank terminal sector. Each issue contains interviews with a leading terminal operator, technical articles, updates on regulations and new products.
Readership/Target Audience: Aimed at managers in companies involved in the storage of oils, chemicals and gases.
ADVERTISING: Rates on application
Agency Commission: 15%
Copy instructions: Copy Date: 3 weeks prior to publication date
Average advertising content per issue: 45%
BUSINESS: ENERGY, FUEL & NUCLEAR

TANKER OPERATOR
1664634U45C-802

Editorial Address: 213 Marsh Wall, LONDON, E14 9FJ
Tel: 020 7510 4933 Fax: 020 7510 2344
Email: cochran@tankeroperator.com
Advertising Address: As above.
Email: djeffries@tankeroperator.com
Web site: http://www.tankeroperator.com
Publisher: Tanker Operator Ltd
Date Established: 2002
Frequency: 8 issues yearly
Annual Sub.: £75.00
Circulation: 2,000 (ABC 01/01/2008 to 31/12/2008)
Usual Pagination: 56
Editor: Ian Cochran; Advertising Manager: David Jeffries
Summary of Content: Magazine covering news and technical issues affecting the tanker industry.
Readership/Target Audience: Aimed at tanker operators, owners, managers, charterers, brokers and equipment manufacturers with an interest in the tanker sector.
ADVERTISING RATES:
Full Page Mono £1980.00
Full Page Colour £1980.00
Mechanical Data: Type Area: 297 x 210mm, Col Length: 297mm, Page Width: 210mm, Print Process: Offset litho,

Film: Positive, right reading, emulsion side down. Digital, Screen: Mono 54 lpc Colour 60 lpc
BUSINESS: MARINE & SHIPPING: Maritime Freight

TANKER SHIPPING & TRADE
1795331U45C-807

Editorial Address: Mitre House, 66 Abbey Road, ENFIELD, EN1 2QN Tel: 020 8364 1551
Email: tony.wilson@rivieramm.com
Advertising Address: As above.
Email: paul.dowling@rivieramm.com
Web site: http://www.tankershipping.com
Publisher: Riviera Maritime Media
Frequency: 6 issues yearly - Published around the 2nd week of the 2nd cover month
Annual Sub.: £129.00
Circulation: 5,256 (ABC 01/01/2008 to 31/12/2008)
Editor: Edwin Lampert
Summary of Content: Publication looking at the elements that contribute to successful tanker management both commercial and technical covering all types and sizes of oil and chemical tankers. Topics covered include news from around the world, safety, operational and technical issues, design, propulsion and developments.
Readership/Target Audience: Aimed at those involved with the design, construction, outfitting, operation and maintenance of oil and chemical tankers.
ADVERTISING RATES:
Full Page Colour £2365.00
Agency Commission: 10%
Mechanical Data: Type Area: 277 x 190mm, Bleed Size: 303 x 216mm, Trim Size: 297 x 210mm, Col Length: 277mm, Page Width: 190mm, Film: Digital
Copy instructions: Copy Date: 3 weeks prior to publication date
Average advertising content per issue: 40%
BUSINESS: MARINE & SHIPPING: Maritime Freight

TANNING WORLD
1626307U15A-192

Editorial Address: 3 Charnwood Street, DERBY, DE1 2GT
Tel: 01332 227683 Fax: 01332 227688
Email: melissa@beautyserve.net
Advertising Address: As above. Tel: 01332 227680
Email: ruth@beautyserve.net
Web site: http://www.beautyserve.com
Publisher: Guild Press Ltd
Date Established: 2003
Frequency: Quarterly
Free to qualifying individuals
Annual Sub.: £15.00
Circulation: 4,755 (Publisher's Statement)
Usual Pagination: 64
Editor: Melissa Dennis; Group Editor: Melissa Dennis
Summary of Content: Magazine covering the UK indoor tanning industry, including news, product launches, equipment reviews, training, business advice, marketing and business profiles.
Readership/Target Audience: Aimed at tanning salon owners and managers, beauty salons, hairdressing salons, health and fitness centres, leisure centres and spas.
ADVERTISING RATES:
Full Page Colour £1495.00
Agency Commission: 10%
Mechanical Data: Type Area: 270 x 186mm, Trim Size: 297 x 210mm, Bleed Size: 300 x 213mm, Col Length: 270mm, Page Width: 186mm, Film: Digital
Average advertising content per issue: 45%
BUSINESS: COSMETICS & HAIRDRESSING: Cosmetics

TARGET MD
40466U56L-100

Editorial Address: 61 Southwark Street, LONDON, SE1 0HL
Tel: 020 7803 4800 Fax: 020 7401 3495
Email: targetmd@muscular-dystrophy.org
Web site: http://www.muscular-dystrophy.org
ISSN: 1463-4538
Publisher: Muscular Dystrophy Campaign
Date Established: 1982
Frequency: Quarterly
Cover Price: Free
Circulation: 10,000 (Publisher's Statement)
Usual Pagination: 36
Editor: Ingrid Ambrose
Summary of Content: Publication containing articles on muscular dystrophy and related disorders, medical research news, medical management issues and disability issues.
Readership/Target Audience: Read by people with, or affected by muscular dystrophy, medical professionals and researchers.
ADVERTISING: No Advertising taken
BUSINESS: HEALTH & MEDICAL: Disability & Rehabilitation

TAX ADVISER
35413U1M-43

Formerly: Taxation Practitioner
Editorial Address: 145 London Road, KINGSTON UPON THAMES, KT2 6SR Tel: 0870 240 4388
Email: lesley.bolton@cch.co.uk

Advertising Address: As above. Tel: 020 8247 1350
Fax: 020 8247 1388
Email: mark.cleeve@cch.co.uk
Web site: http://www.cch.co.uk
ISSN: 1367-3246
Publisher: Wolters Kluwer (UK) Ltd
Frequency: Monthly
Free to qualifying individuals
Annual Sub.: £64.00
Circulation: 20,915 (ABC 01/07/2008 to 30/06/2009)
Usual Pagination: 60
Editor: Lesley Bolton; Editor-in-Chief: David Milne
Summary of Content: Magazine covering news of recent tax legislation's and topical tax issues.
Readership/Target Audience: Aimed at members of the Chartered Institute of Taxation and the Association of Taxation Technicians.
ADVERTISING RATES:
Full Page Mono £3070.00
Full Page Colour £3070.00
Agency Commission: 10%
Mechanical Data: Type Area: 270 x 185mm, Col Length: 270mm, Page Width: 185mm, Trim Size: 297 x 210mm, Film: Digital, Bleed Size: 303 x 216mm
Copy instructions: Copy Date: Last Friday of the month prior to publication date
Average advertising content per issue: 40%
Supplement(s): Tax Adviser Education - 2xY
BUSINESS: FINANCE & ECONOMICS: Taxation

THE TAX JOURNAL
35409U1M-45

Editorial Address: 2 Addiscombe Road, CROYDON, CR9 5AF Tel: 020 8212 1912 Fax: 020 8212 1988
Email: alison.lovejoy@lexisnexis.co.uk
Advertising Address: As above. Tel: 020 8212 1997
Fax: 020 8212 1970
Email: stuart.cousins@lexisnexis.co.uk
Web site: http://www.lexisnexis.co.uk
ISSN: 0954-7274
Publisher: LexisNexis UK
Date Established: 1989
Frequency: Weekly
Cover Price: £7.00
Annual Sub.: £307.00
Circulation: 1,800 (Publisher's Statement)
Usual Pagination: 24
Editor: Alison Lovejoy
Summary of Content: Journal containing information and news concerning taxation and in depth coverage of tax cases.
Readership/Target Audience: Aimed at tax experts in legal and accountancy firms, tax managers in public companies and finance directors in private companies.
ADVERTISING RATES:
Full Page Mono £1240.00
Full Page Colour £1715.00
Agency Commission: 10%
Mechanical Data: Type Area: 260 x 185mm, Bleed Size: 303 x 216mm, Trim Size: 297 x 210mm, Col Length: 260mm, Film: Digital, Page Width: 185mm
Copy instructions: Copy Date: 1 week prior to publication date
Average advertising content per issue: 30%
BUSINESS: FINANCE & ECONOMICS: Taxation

TAX PLANNING INTERNATIONAL EUROPEAN TAX SERVICE
601009U1M-47_70

Formerly: Tax Planning International European Union Focus
Editorial Address: Millbank Tower, 21-24 Millbank, LONDON, SW1P 4QP Tel: 020 7559 4807
Fax: 020 7559 4880
Email: amclaurin@bna.com
Web site: http://www.bnai.com
ISSN: 1464-8911
Publisher: BNA International
Date Established: 1999
Frequency: Monthly
Annual Sub.: £965.00
Usual Pagination: 32
Editor: Amelia McLaurin; Managing Editor: Stephen Mullaly
Summary of Content: Magazine with news and analysis of European tax issues and their application in Member States.
Readership/Target Audience: Aimed at International tax specialists.
ADVERTISING: No Advertising taken
BUSINESS: FINANCE & ECONOMICS: Taxation

TAX PLANNING INTERNATIONAL INDIRECT TAXES
601011U1M-47_50

Formerly: Tax Planning International E Commerce
Editorial Address: Millbank Tower, 21-24 Millbank, LONDON, SW1P 4QP Tel: 020 7559 4800
Fax: 020 7559 4880
Email: bspicer@bna.com
Web site: http://www.bnai.com
ISSN: 1464-8903

Business Magazines

Publisher: BNA International
Date Established: 1999
Frequency: Monthly
Annual Sub.: £650.00
Usual Pagination: 28
Editor: Bronwyn Spicer
Summary of Content: Journal covering indirect taxation developments worldwide.
Readership/Target Audience: Aimed at those dealing with indirect taxation.
ADVERTISING: No Advertising taken
BUSINESS: FINANCE & ECONOMICS: Taxation

TAX PLANNING INTERNATIONAL TRANSFER PRICING
634199U1M-49
Editorial Address: Millbank Tower, 21-24 Millbank, LONDON, SW1P 4QP **Tel:** 020 7559 4800
Fax: 020 7559 4880
Email: lillianadams@bna.com
Web site: http://www.bnai.com
ISSN: 1472-0841
Publisher: BNA International
Date Established: 2000
Frequency: Monthly
Annual Sub.: £865.00
Usual Pagination: 36
Editor: Lillian Adams
Summary of Content: Journal covering economic news and analysis of pricing issues for traditional and electronic business.
Readership/Target Audience: Aimed at those dealing with inter-company pricing issues.
ADVERTISING: No Advertising taken
BUSINESS: FINANCE & ECONOMICS: Taxation

THE TAX SHELTER REPORT
35311U1F-450
Editorial Address: 17 Hill Street, Mayfair, LONDON, W1J 5NZ **Tel:** 020 7409 1111 **Fax:** 020 7629 7026
Email: priti.patel@allenbridge.co.uk
Web site: http://www.tax-shelter-report.co.uk
Publisher: Allenbridge Group plc
Date Established: 1985
Frequency: Monthly
Annual Sub.: £395.00
Circulation: 2,000 (Publisher's Statement)
Usual Pagination: 12
Editor: Priti Patel
Summary of Content: Magazine covering all aspects of tax shelter investments.
Readership/Target Audience: Read by advisers on tax shelter products.
ADVERTISING: No Advertising taken
BUSINESS: FINANCE & ECONOMICS: Investment

TAXATION
35412U1M-50
Editorial Address: 2 Addiscombe Road, CROYDON, CR9 5AF **Tel:** 020 8686 9141 **Fax:** 020 8212 1988
Email: taxation@lexisnexis.co.uk
Advertising Address: As above. **Tel:** 020 8212 1989
Fax: 020 8212 1970
Email: laura.thompson@lexisnexis.co.uk
Web site: http://www.taxation.co.uk
ISSN: 0040-0149
Publisher: LexisNexis
Date Established: 1927
Frequency: Weekly
Annual Sub.: £210.00
Circulation: 8,358 (ABC 01/07/2007 to 30/06/2008)
Usual Pagination: 24
Editor: Allison Plager; **Advertising Manager:** Laura Thompson
Summary of Content: Journal written by tax practitioners for tax practitioners containing practical solutions to problems, lively debate, commentary, announcements, news and book reviews. Covers changes in legislation affecting tax practice, tax software and technical issues.
Readership/Target Audience: Primarily aimed at United Kingdom tax practitioners.
ADVERTISING RATES:
Full Page Colour £2785.00
Agency Commission: 10%
Mechanical Data: Type Area: 247 x 184mm, Bleed Size: 286 x 222mm, Trim Size: 280 x 216mm, Col Length: 247mm, Film: Digital, Page Width: 184mm
Copy instructions: Copy Date: 1 week prior to publication date
Average advertising content per issue: 40%
BUSINESS: FINANCE & ECONOMICS: Taxation

TAXI GLOBE
41523U64G-520
Editorial Address: 12 Firs Close, HATFIELD, AL10 8NP
Tel: 01707 885439 **Fax:** 01707 696034
Email: sandiegoodwin@hotmail.com

Advertising Address: The Maltings, West Street, BOURNE, PE10 9PH **Tel:** 01778 392048 **Fax:** 01778 392079
Email: sarahh@warnersgroup.co.uk
Web site: http://www.taxiglobeinfo.co.uk
Publisher: Warners Group Publications plc
Date Established: 1980
Frequency: 26 issues yearly
Cover Price: Free
Circulation: 18,500 (Publisher's Statement)
Usual Pagination: 40
Editor: Sandie Goodwin; **Advertising Manager:** Sarah Hubbard
Summary of Content: Newspaper covering taxi trade developments and news.
Readership/Target Audience: Aimed at taxi drivers, garage owners, radio circuit owners and those connected with the licensed taxi trade.
ADVERTISING RATES:
Full Page Colour £550.00
SCC £12.00
Agency Commission: 10%
Mechanical Data: Type Area: 342 x 264mm, No. of Columns (Display): 4, Col Length: 342mm, Page Width: 264mm, Film: Digital
Copy instructions: Copy Date: 6 days prior to publication date
BUSINESS: OTHER CLASSIFICATIONS: Taxi Trade

TAXI NEWSPAPER
41522U64G-530
Editorial Address: Taxi House, 11 Woodfield Road, LONDON, W9 2BA **Tel:** 020 7286 1046 **Fax:** 020 7286 2494
Email: taxinewspaper@ltda.co.uk
Advertising Address: As above. **Tel:** 020 8971 8450
Fax: 020 8971 8480
Email: anu@cabbell.co.uk
Web site: http://www.taxinewspaper.co.uk
Publisher: Licensed Taxi Drivers' Association
Date Established: 1970
Frequency: 26 issues yearly
Free to qualifying individuals
Annual Sub.: £23.00
Circulation: 14,000 (Publisher's Statement)
Usual Pagination: 48
Editor: Stuart Pessok; **News Editor:** Stuart Pessok
Summary of Content: Publication of the Licensed Taxi Drivers' Association. Contains news and articles on the taxi industry, law, finance, leisure, motoring and taxation.
Readership/Target Audience: Aimed at cab drivers, local government, trade and central government.
ADVERTISING RATES:
Full Page Mono £931.00
Full Page Colour £1269.00
Agency Commission: 10%
Mechanical Data: Type Area: 316 x 259mm, Col Length: 316mm, Film: Digital, Page Width: 259mm
Copy instructions: Copy Date: 2 weeks prior to publication date
Average advertising content per issue: 50%
BUSINESS: OTHER CLASSIFICATIONS: Taxi Trade

TAXI-TODAY
1805073U64G-533
Editorial Address: Cubic Business Centre, 533 Stanningley Road, LEEDS, LS13 4EN **Tel:** 0113 218 0117
Email: tony@parklanepublishing.co.uk
Advertising Address: As above. **Tel:** 01274 420029
Fax: 01274 420021
Email: tony@taxi-today.com
Web site: http://www.taxi-today.com
Publisher: Park Lane Publishing Ltd
Frequency: Monthly
Annual Sub.: £18.00
Circulation: 30,000 (Publisher's Statement)
Usual Pagination: 80
Editor: Tony Mite; **Advertising Manager:** Tony Mite
Summary of Content: Magazine featuring news and views, taxi licence legislation, classified ads and a forum for drivers.
Readership/Target Audience: Aimed at drivers of private hire vehicles, minicabs, taxis and stretch limousines, chauffeurs and couriers.
ADVERTISING RATES:
Full Page Colour £1350.00
Agency Commission: 10%
Mechanical Data: Bleed Size: 303 x 216mm, Trim Size: 297 x 210mm, Film: Digital
Copy instructions: Copy Date: 18th of the cover month
Average advertising content per issue: 40%
BUSINESS: OTHER CLASSIFICATIONS: Taxi Trade

TBI TELEVISION BUSINESS INTERNATIONAL
35691U2D-85
Editorial Address: Mortimer House, 37-41 Mortimer Street, LONDON, W1T 3JH **Tel:** 020 7017 5000
Email: stewart.clarke@informa.com
Advertising Address: As above. **Fax:** 020 7017 4953
Email: tbi@informa.com
Web site: http://www.tbivision.com

ISSN: 0953-6841
Publisher: T&F Informa Group PLC
Date Established: 1988
Frequency: 10 issues yearly
Free to qualifying individuals
Circulation: 8,000 (Publisher's Statement)
Editor: Stewart Clarke; **Publisher:** Lydia Blackwood
Summary of Content: Journal covering television programme production and distribution.
Readership/Target Audience: Read by senior international television executives.
ADVERTISING RATES:
Full Page Colour £2000.00
Agency Commission: 10%
Mechanical Data: Type Area: 255 x 196mm, Bleed Size: +10mm, Trim Size: 275 x 216mm, Col Length: 255mm, Film: Digital, Page Width: .196mm
Average advertising content per issue: 40%
BUSINESS: COMMUNICATIONS, ADVERTISING & MARKETING: Broadcasting

TCE
36648U13-180
Editorial Address: Davis Building, 165-189 Railway Terrace, RUGBY, CV21 3HQ **Tel:** 01788 578214 **Fax:** 01788 560833
Email: tce@icheme.org
Advertising Address: The Barn, Oakley Hay Lodge Industrial Park, Great Folds Road, GREAT OAKLEY, NN18 9AS **Tel:** 01536 747333 **Fax:** 01536 746565
Email: nigel.stephens@mainlinemedia.co.uk
Web site: http://www.tcetoday.com
ISSN: 0302-0797
Publisher: Institution of Chemical Engineers
Date Established: 1956
Frequency: 11 issues yearly - Published around the 28th of the month prior to cover date
Cover Price: £15.00
Annual Sub.: £150.00
Circulation: 24,754 (ABC 01/01/2008 to 31/12/2008)
Usual Pagination: 76
Editor: Adam Duckett; **Advertising Manager:** Nigel Stephens; **Managing Editor:** Delyth Forsdyke
Summary of Content: Journal containing news, features and product information about chemical and process engineering worldwide.
Readership/Target Audience: Read by chemical and process engineers, including all members of The Institution of Chemical Engineers.
ADVERTISING RATES:
Full Page Colour £2595.00
Agency Commission: 10%
Mechanical Data: Bleed Size: 303 x 216mm, Trim Size: 297 x 210mm, Col Length: 265mm, No. of Columns (Display): 4, Film: Digital, Page Width: 185mm, Type Area: 265 x 185mm
Copy instructions: Copy Date: 7 working days prior to publication date
Average advertising content per issue: 20%
BUSINESS: CHEMICALS

TCS&D
35769U3C-200
Editorial Address: PO Box 88, EDENBRIDGE, TN8 6ZW
Tel: 01732 868288 **Fax:** 01732 865874
Email: publisher@tcsandd.com
Advertising Address: As above.
Email: sales@tcsandd.com
Web site: http://www.tcsandd.com
ISSN: 1469-1752
Publisher: Sherwin Publications Ltd
Date Established: 1977
Frequency: 6 issues yearly
Annual Sub.: £85.00
Circulation: 5,500 (Publisher's Statement)
Usual Pagination: 32
Editor: Richard Cogan; **Advertising Manager:** Martyn Cogan; **Publisher:** Richard Cogan
Summary of Content: International magazine about temperature controlled storage, distribution equipment and services.
Readership/Target Audience: Aimed at end-users and suppliers.
ADVERTISING RATES:
Full Page Colour £1605.00
Agency Commission: 10%
Mechanical Data: Print Process: Litho, Type Area: 265 x 185mm, Col Length: 265mm, Bleed Size: 304 x 213mm, Trim Size: 297 x 210mm, Page Width: 185mm
Copy instructions: Copy Date: 2 weeks prior to publication date
Average advertising content per issue: 60%
Supplement(s): Annual Buyer's Guide - 1xY
BUSINESS: HEATING & VENTILATION: Refrigeration & Ventilation

TCT MAGAZINE
601249U19A-531
Formerly: Time-Compression Technologies Europe
Editorial Address: Unit 2, Chowley Court, Chowley Oak Lane, Tattenhall, CHESTER, CH3 9GA **Tel:** 01829 770037
Fax: 01829 770047

Email: tct@rapidnews.com
Advertising Address: As above.
Email: carol@rapidnews.com
Web site: http://www.tctmagazine.com
Publisher: Rapid News Publications
Date Established: 1992
Frequency: 6 issues yearly - Published around the 1st of the 2nd cover month
Cover Price: Free
Circulation: 11,103 (ABC 01/01/2008 to 31/12/2008)
Usual Pagination: 64
Editor: Duncan Wood; **Advertising Manager:** Carol Hardy; **Publisher:** Mark Blezard
Summary of Content: Journal covering time compression engineering, design engineering and rapid product development. Technologies include 3D CAD/CAM/CAE, software analysis (FEA/CFD, virtual prototyping), rapid prototyping and rapid tooling, production tooling, reverse engineering metrology, inspection and materials.
Readership/Target Audience: Read by design engineers and senior management involved with the implementation of new technologies to reduce product development time and cost.
ADVERTISING RATES:
Full Page Mono £2000.00
Full Page Colour £2000.00
Agency Commission: 15%
Mechanical Data: No. of Columns (Display): 3, Type Area: 278 x 192mm, Col Length: 278mm, Page Width: 192mm, Trim Size: 297 x 210mm, Bleed Size: 305 x 214mm, Film: Digital
Average advertising content per issue: 50%
BUSINESS: ENGINEERING & MACHINERY

TEACH PRIMARY!
1813665U62C-740

Formerly: Primary Choice
Editorial Address: 25 Phoenix Court, Hawkins Road, COLCHESTER, CO2 8JY **Tel:** 01206 505925
Fax: 01206 505935
Email: joe@teachprimary.com
Advertising Address: 21-23 Phoenix Court, Hawkins Road, COLCHESTER, CO2 8JY **Tel:** 01206 505900
Fax: 01206 505935
Email: richard@teachprimary.com
Web site: http://www.teachprimary.com
Publisher: Maze Media (2000) Ltd
Date Established: 2007
Frequency: 8 issues yearly
Circulation: 22,000 (Publisher's Statement)
Usual Pagination: 84
Editor: Joe Carter; **Advertising Manager:** Richard Stebbing
Summary of Content: Magazine focusing on Key Stage 1 and 2 resources for all areas of the curriculum. Features product tests and reviews and advice on how to use them in the classroom.
Readership/Target Audience: Aimed at teachers of children aged 5 to 11 years old.
ADVERTISING RATES:
Full Page Mono £1200.00
Full Page Colour £1200.00
Agency Commission: 10%
Mechanical Data: Type Area: 270 x 190mm, Bleed Size: 307 x 220mm, Trim Size: 297 x 210mm, Col Length: 270mm, Page Width: 190mm, Film: Digital
Copy instructions: Copy Date: 3 weeks prior to publication date
Average advertising content per issue: 25%
BUSINESS: CHURCH & SCHOOL EQUIPMENT & EDUCATION: Junior Education

THE TEACHER
37207U14L-690

Editorial Address: Hamilton House, Mabledon Place, LONDON, WC1H 9BD **Tel:** 020 7380 4708
Fax: 020 7387 8458
Email: teacher@nut.org.uk
Advertising Address: Century One Publishing, Arguen House, 4-6 Spicer Street, ST. ALBANS, AL3 4PQ
Tel: 01727 893894 **Fax:** 01727 893895
Email: ollie@centuryonepublishing.ltd.uk
Web site: http://www.teachers.org.uk
Publisher: National Union of Teachers
Frequency: 8 issues yearly
Cover Price: Free
Circulation: 320,000 (Publisher's Statement)
Usual Pagination: 52
Editor: Ellie Campbell-Barr; **Advertising Manager:** Oliver Kirkman
Summary of Content: Magazine of the National Union of Teachers. Contains news and features on education in England and Wales. Also includes information about NUT policy.
Readership/Target Audience: Aimed at NUT members, student members and education departments of colleges and universities.
ADVERTISING RATES:
Full Page Colour £6285.00
Agency Commission: 10%

Mechanical Data: Page Width: 181mm, Type Area: 275 x 181mm, Bleed Size: 303 x 216mm, Trim Size: 297 x 210mm, Film: Digital, Col Length: 275mm
Copy instructions: Copy Date: 4 weeks prior to publication date
Average advertising content per issue: 31%
BUSINESS: COMMERCE, INDUSTRY & MANAGEMENT: Trade Unions

THE TEACHER'S GUIDE
41163U62J-1100

Formerly: The Teacher's Guide - Places to Visit
Editorial Address: 1A Melbourn Street, ROYSTON, SG8 7BP **Tel:** 01763 243760 **Fax:** 01763 249396
Email: info@teachers-guide.co.uk
Advertising Address: As above.
Email: info@teachers-guide.co.uk
Web site: http://www.teachers-guide.co.uk
Publisher: Fourways Sales & Marketing
Date Established: 1994
Frequency: Annual - Published in January
Cover Price: Free
Circulation: 26,000 (Publisher's Statement)
Usual Pagination: 68
Editor: Carole Leatherland; **Managing Director:** Rupert Matthews; **Advertising Manager:** Carole Leatherland
Summary of Content: Guide listing educational and recreational venues of interest for school day and residential trips, what's on, education jobs and education suppliers.
Readership/Target Audience: Aimed at teachers.
ADVERTISING RATES:
Full Page Mono £450.00
Full Page Colour £450.00
Agency Commission: 10%
Mechanical Data: Film: Digital, Col Length: 194mm, No. of Columns (Display): 2, Type Area: 194 x 130mm, Bleed Size: 220 x 155mm, Trim Size: 210 x 145mm, Page Width: 130mm
Copy instructions: Copy Date: 31st December prior to publication date
Average advertising content per issue: 85%
BUSINESS: CHURCH & SCHOOL EQUIPMENT & EDUCATION: Teachers & Education Management

TEACHERS MAGAZINE
622716U62B-990

Editorial Address: 136-142 Bramley Road, LONDON, W10 6SR **Tel:** 020 7565 3000 **Fax:** 020 7565 3050
Email: sara.grossman@johnbrowngroup.co.uk
Web site: http://www.johnbrowngroup.co.uk
Publisher: John Brown Group
Frequency: 6 issues yearly - Combined circulation includes the Primary and Secondary editions
Cover Price: Free
Circulation: 333,000 (Publisher's Statement)
Usual Pagination: 36
Editor: Melissa Crowther; **Managing Editor:** Melissa Crowther; **Publisher:** Christine Cavaleros
Summary of Content: Magazine offering helpful advice and tips for the classroom, covering government information on policies and aims for education. Includes interviews, articles on new technology and advice on problem solving.
Readership/Target Audience: Aimed at primary and secondary school classroom teachers, heads of department, senior teachers and headteachers.
ADVERTISING: No Advertising taken
BUSINESS: CHURCH & SCHOOL EQUIPMENT & EDUCATION: Education Teachers

TEACHING AND LEARNING
1615911U62C-727

Editorial Address: 33-41 Dallington Street, LONDON, EC1V 0BB **Tel:** 0845 450 6404 **Fax:** 0845 450 6410
Email: juliet.smith@optimuseducation.com
Advertising Address: As above. **Tel:** 020 7954 3400
Fax: 020 7954 3511
Email: jon.pyser@electricwordplc.com
Web site: http://www.teachingexpertise.com
Publisher: Optimus Education
Date Established: 2003
Frequency: 6 issues yearly
Circulation: 3,020 (Publisher's Statement)
Usual Pagination: 64
Editor: Juliet Smith
Summary of Content: Magazine covering educational resources and information from reception to Key Stage 3.
Readership/Target Audience: Aimed at educational professionals.
ADVERTISING RATES:
Full Page Colour £1000.00
Copy instructions: Copy Date: 2 weeks prior to publication date
BUSINESS: CHURCH & SCHOOL EQUIPMENT & EDUCATION: Junior Education

TEACHING BUSINESS AND ECONOMICS
41046U62B-1070

Editorial Address: The Forum, 277 London Road, BURGESS HILL, RH15 9QU **Tel:** 01444 240150
Fax: 01444 240101
Email: office@ebea.org.uk
Advertising Address: As above.
Email: office@ebea.org.uk
Web site: http://www.ebea.org.uk
ISSN: 1367-3289
Publisher: EBEA
Date Established: 1997
Frequency: 3 issues yearly - Published in February, May and October
Annual Sub.: £50.00
Circulation: 2,500 (Publisher's Statement)
Usual Pagination: 46
Editor: Nancy Wall; **Advertising Manager:** Claire Annels
Summary of Content: Journal covering current issues in economics and business studies teaching.
Readership/Target Audience: Read by teachers of business studies and economics.
ADVERTISING RATES:
Full Page Mono £350.00
Full Page Colour £500.00
Mechanical Data: Bleed Size: +4mm, Trim Size: 275 x 190mm, Digital: Digital
Copy instructions: Copy Date: 4 weeks prior to publication date
Average advertising content per issue: 5%
BUSINESS: CHURCH & SCHOOL EQUIPMENT & EDUCATION: Education Teachers

TEACHING DRAMA
1695161U62B-1407

Editorial Address: 239 Shaftesbury Avenue, LONDON, WC2H 8TF **Tel:** 020 7333 1745 **Fax:** 020 7333 1765
Email: teaching.drama@rhinegold.co.uk
Advertising Address: As above. **Tel:** 020 7333 1733
Fax: 020 7333 1736
Email: mathew.cheadle@rhinegold.co.uk
Web site: http://www.rhinegold.co.uk
Publisher: Rhinegold Publishing Ltd
Date Established: 2005
Frequency: 6 issues yearly
Annual Sub.: £60.00
Circulation: 1,500 (Publisher's Statement)
Usual Pagination: 68
Editor: Claudine Nightingale; **Advertising Manager:** Matthew Cheadle
Summary of Content: Magazine providing product reviews, new ideas and lesson plans.
Readership/Target Audience: Aimed at drama and non-specialist teachers.
ADVERTISING RATES:
Full Page Mono £1220.00
Full Page Colour £1480.00
Agency Commission: 10%
Mechanical Data: Type Area: 272 x 184mm, Bleed Size: 303 x 216mm, Trim Size: 297 x 210mm, Col Length: 272mm, Page Width: 184mm, Film: Digital
Copy instructions: Copy Date: 2 weeks prior to publication date
Average advertising content per issue: 15%
BUSINESS: CHURCH & SCHOOL EQUIPMENT & EDUCATION: Education Teachers

TEACHING MATHEMATICS AND ITS APPLICATIONS
29996U62J-1101

Editorial Address: The Mathematics Centre, University College Chichester, Upper Bognor Road, BOGNOR REGIS, PO21 1HR **Tel:** 01865 353907 **Fax:** 01865 353485
Email: h.williams@ucc.ac.uk
Advertising Address: Great Clarendon Street, OXFORD, OX2 6DP **Tel:** 01865 353907
Email: jnlsadvertising@oxfordjournals.org
Web site: http://www3.oup.co.uk/teamat
ISSN: 0268-3679
Publisher: OUP
Date Established: 1982
Frequency: Quarterly
Cover Price: £25.00
Annual Sub.: £80.00
Editor: Honor Williams
Summary of Content: Publication providing teaching aids for mathematics.
Readership/Target Audience: Aimed at mathematics teachers in secondary and tertiary education.
ADVERTISING RATES:
Full Page Mono £646.00
Agency Commission: 10%
Mechanical Data: Col Length: 210mm, Type Area: 210 x 125mm, Print Process: Litho, Bleed Size: 254 x 182mm, Trim Size: 249 x 176mm, Film: Digital, Page Width: 125mm
BUSINESS: CHURCH & SCHOOL EQUIPMENT & EDUCATION: Teachers & Education Management

TEACHING TODAY
37208U14L-705

Editorial Address: Hillscourt Education Centre, Rose Hill, Rednal, BIRMINGHAM, B45 8RS **Tel:** 0121 453 6150
Email: michelle.graham@mail.nasuwt.org.uk
Advertising Address: As above. **Fax:** 0121 457 6251
Email: paul.maclachlan@mail.nasuwt.org.uk
Web site: http://www.teachersunion.org.uk
Publisher: NASUWT
Frequency: 5 issues yearly - Published once each school holiday
Cover Price: £2.95
Free to qualifying individuals
Circulation: 245,000 (Publisher's Statement)
Usual Pagination: 32
Editor: Michelle Graham; **Advertising Manager:** Paul McLachlan
Summary of Content: Magazine providing information, news, updates and features on issues relevant to education and trade union sectors.
Readership/Target Audience: Read by members of NASUWT in primary, secondary and further education and student members, also anybody with an interest or involvement in education and schools. Distributed to the homes of NASUWT members.
ADVERTISING: Rates on application
Agency Commission: 10%
Copy instructions: Copy Date: 24 days prior to publication date
BUSINESS: COMMERCE, INDUSTRY & MANAGEMENT: Trade Unions

TEC TRAFFIC ENGINEERING & CONTROL
39050U42B-190

Editorial Address: 32 Vauxhall Bridge Road, LONDON, SW1V 2SS **Tel:** 01935 816030 **Fax:** 01935 817200
Email: c.debell@hgluk.com
Advertising Address: 8 Old Yarn Mills, SHERBORNE, DT9 3RQ **Tel:** 01935 816030 **Fax:** 01935 817200
Email: a.mitchell@hgluk.com
Web site: http://www.tecmagazine.com
ISSN: 0041-0683
Publisher: Hemming Group Ltd
Date Established: 1960
Frequency: 11 issues yearly
Annual Sub.: £105.00
Circulation: 4,500 (Publisher's Statement)
Usual Pagination: 52
Editor: Carol Debell; **News Editor:** Charlotte Watson; **Managing Director:** Graham Bond; **Advertising Manager:** Andrew Mitchell
Summary of Content: Magazine focusing on traffic management and road safety, including street lighting, parking and signs.
Readership/Target Audience: Aimed at transport academics, central and local government, public and development corporations, road researchers, civil engineers and universities.
ADVERTISING RATES:
Full Page Mono £1025.00
Full Page Colour £1575.00
Agency Commission: 10%
Mechanical Data: Col Length: 273mm, No. of Columns (Display): 4, Type Area: 273 x 190mm, Bleed Size: 303 x 213mm, Trim Size: 297 x 210mm, Film: Digital, Page Width: 190mm
Copy instructions: Copy Date: 15th of the month prior to publication date
Average advertising content per issue: 25%
BUSINESS: CONSTRUCTION: Roads

THE TECHNICAL ANALYST
1697438U1F-613

Editorial Address: Jeffries House, 1-5 Jeffries Passage, GUILDFORD, GU1 4AP **Tel:** 01483 573150
Email: editor@technicalanalyst.co.uk
Advertising Address: As above.
Email: advertising@technicalanalyst.co.uk
Web site: http://www.technicalanalyst.co.uk
Publisher: Global Markets Media Ltd
Date Established: 2004
Frequency: 6 issues yearly
Annual Sub.: £150.00
Circulation: 5,000 (Publisher's Statement)
Editor: Matthew Clements; **Advertising Manager:** Jim Biss; **Managing Editor:** Jim Biss
Summary of Content: Magazine covering trading strategies for the financial markets.
Readership/Target Audience: Aimed at fund managers, traders and information and software providers.
ADVERTISING RATES:
Full Page Colour £1900.00
Agency Commission: 10%
Mechanical Data: Type Area: 280 x 190mm, Bleed Size: 303 x 216mm, Trim Size: 297 x 210mm, Col Length: 280mm, Page Width: 190mm, Film: Digital
Copy instructions: Copy Date: 5th of the month prior to publication date
BUSINESS: FINANCE & ECONOMICS: Investment

TECHNICAL REVIEW MIDDLE EAST
36984U14C-245

Editorial Address: University House, 11-13 Lower Grosvenor Place, LONDON, SW1W 0EX **Tel:** 020 7834 7676
Fax: 020 7973 0076
Email: trme@alaincharles.com
Advertising Address: As above.
Email: graham.brown@alaincharles.com
Web site: http://www.alaincharles.com
ISSN: 0267-5307
Publisher: Alain Charles Publishing Ltd
Date Established: 1984
Frequency: 6 issues yearly - Published at the beginning of the cover month
Cover Price: £13.00
Annual Sub.: £78.00
Circulation: 12,017 (ABC 01/07/2008 to 30/06/2009)
Usual Pagination: 124
Editor: David Clancy; **Managing Director:** Derek Fordham; **Managing Editor:** David Clancy; **Publisher:** Derek Fordham
Summary of Content: Magazine covering trade, information technology, water, aviation, travel, manufacturing, industry, telecommunications, transport, logistics, power, oil and gas in the Middle East and North Africa.
Language(s): Arabic; English
Readership/Target Audience: Read by senior executives in Middle Eastern businesses and government departments throughout the Middle East and North Africa.
ADVERTISING RATES:
Full Page Mono £2950.00
Full Page Colour £4350.00
Agency Commission: 15%
Mechanical Data: Type Area: 255 x 180mm, Bleed Size: 286 x 216mm, Trim Size: 276 x 210mm, Print Process: Sheet-fed litho, Col Length: 255mm, Page Width: 180mm, Film: Digital
Copy instructions: Copy Date: 3 weeks prior to publication date
BUSINESS: COMMERCE, INDUSTRY & MANAGEMENT: International Commerce

TECHNICAL TEXTILE MARKETS
23891U47A-280

Editorial Address: Suite 6, 1st Floor, Alderley House, Alderley Road, WILMSLOW, SK9 1AT **Tel:** 01625 536136
Fax: 01625 536137
Email: editorial@textilesintelligence.com
Web site: http://www.textilesintelligence.com
ISSN: 0959-9185
Publisher: Textiles Intelligence Ltd
Date Established: 1990
Frequency: Quarterly
Annual Sub.: £805.00
Usual Pagination: 130
Editor: Belinda Carp
Summary of Content: Publication containing information on the availability of products, their applications and growth prospect, including medical textiles, geotextiles, automotive and aerospace, communications including fibre optics, agriculture, sportswear, performance apparel, construction, protection, safety and packaging.
Readership/Target Audience: Aimed at senior management in the textile industry.
ADVERTISING: No Advertising taken
BUSINESS: CLOTHING & TEXTILES

TECHNICAL TEXTILES INTERNATIONAL
39508U47A-300

Editorial Address: 9A Victoria Square, DROITWICH, WR9 8DE **Tel:** 0870 165 7211 **Fax:** 0870 165 7212
Email: editorial@intnews.com
Advertising Address: As above. **Tel:** 0870 165 7210
Email: sales@intnews.com
Web site: http://www.technical-textiles.net
ISSN: 0964-5993
Publisher: International Newsletters
Date Established: 1992
Frequency: 8 issues yearly
Annual Sub.: £199.00
Circulation: 2,000 (Publisher's Statement)
Usual Pagination: 48
Editor: Nick Butler; **Advertising Manager:** David Kay; **Publisher:** Nick Butler
Summary of Content: Magazine covering advanced textiles and fibres used in technical applications.
Readership/Target Audience: Read by senior management and senior technical managers.
ADVERTISING RATES:
Full Page Mono £1291.00
Full Page Colour £1998.00
Agency Commission: 10%
Mechanical Data: Film: Digital, Type Area: 270 x 192mm, Col Length: 270mm, Print Process: Sheet-fed litho, Bleed Size: 305 x 214mm, Trim Size: 297 x 210mm, Page Width: 192mm
Average advertising content per issue: 15%
BUSINESS: CLOTHING & TEXTILES

TECHNOLOGY IN EDUCATION
41048U62B-1300

Editorial Address: 3 Crescent Terrace, CHELTENHAM, GL50 3PE **Tel:** 01242 510760 **Fax:** 01242 226626
Email: bernardhubbard@prb-marketing.com
Advertising Address: As above.
Email: bernardhubbard@prb-marketing.com
Web site: http://www.technology-in-education.co.uk
Publisher: B & S Publications
Frequency: 8 issues yearly
Free to qualifying individuals
Annual Sub.: £20.00
Circulation: 6,200 (Publisher's Statement)
Usual Pagination: 32
Editor: Bernard Hubbard; **Advertising Manager:** Bernard Hubbard
Summary of Content: Magazine covering the teaching of design and technology, science and ICT in secondary and tertiary education.
Readership/Target Audience: Aimed at teachers of design and technology, science and ICT, department heads and headteachers.
ADVERTISING RATES:
Full Page Mono £1051.75
Full Page Colour £1382.04
Agency Commission: 10%
Mechanical Data: No. of Columns (Display): 4, Type Area: 265 x 180mm, Col Length: 265mm, Page Width: 180mm, Bleed Size: 303 x 213mm, Trim Size: 297 x 210mm, Film: Digital
Average advertising content per issue: 60%
BUSINESS: CHURCH & SCHOOL EQUIPMENT & EDUCATION: Education Teachers

TELECOM FINANCE
35312U1F-470

Editorial Address: 292 Vauxhall Bridge Road, LONDON, SW1V 1AE **Tel:** 020 7963 7680 **Fax:** 020 7963 7682
Email: claire.landon@telecomfinance.com
Web site: http://www.telecomfinance.com
ISSN: 1352-6456
Publisher: PA Business
Date Established: 1994
Frequency: 11 issues yearly
Annual Sub.: £1095.00
Circulation: 2,000 (Publisher's Statement)
Usual Pagination: 44
Editor: Claire Landon
Summary of Content: Newsletter reporting on the public and private financing activity of the European telecom sector coverings terms and conditions of funding and strategy.
Readership/Target Audience: Aimed at those working in the telecommunications industry, investment banks and law firms.
ADVERTISING: No Advertising taken
BUSINESS: FINANCE & ECONOMICS: Investment

TELECOM MARKETS
37505U18B-1380

Formerly: New Network Operator
Editorial Address: Mortimer House, 37-41 Mortimer Street, LONDON, W1T 3JH **Tel:** 020 7017 5000
Email: rob.gallagher@informa.com
Web site: http://www.informatm.com/telemmarkets
ISSN: 0267-1484
Publisher: T&F Informa Group PLC
Date Established: 1986
Frequency: 23 issues yearly
Annual Sub.: £1095.00
Usual Pagination: 12
Editor: Rob Gallagher
Summary of Content: Publication covering news and analysis of major telecommunications events in the UK. Europe and worldwide.
Readership/Target Audience: Aimed at fixed network operators and equipment manufactures.
ADVERTISING: No Advertising taken
BUSINESS: ELECTRONICS: Telecommunications

TELECOMS INSIGHT
37468U18B-940

Formerly: International Telecommunications Intelligence
Editorial Address: Mermaid House, 2 Puddle Dock, LONDON, EC4V 3DS **Tel:** 020 7248 0468
Fax: 020 7248 0467
Email: gthethy@businessmonitor.com
Web site: http://www.telecomsinsight.com
ISSN: 0268-9960
Publisher: Business Monitor International Ltd
Date Established: 1985
Frequency: Monthly - Plus a daily online news service
Editor: Gunita Thethy
Summary of Content: Magazine and daily online news service providing analysis on the main trends affecting the global telecommunications industry.
Readership/Target Audience: Aimed at the telecommunications industry.
ADVERTISING: No Advertising taken
BUSINESS: ELECTRONICS: Telecommunications

TELEMATICS UPDATE MAGAZINE

762342U31R-51

Editorial Address: 7-9 Fashion Street, LONDON, E1 6PX
Tel: 020 7375 7185 **Fax:** 020 7375 7511
Email: thomas@telematicsupdate.com
Advertising Address: As above.
Email: thomas@telematicsupdate.com
Web site: http://www.telematicsupdate.com
Publisher: First Conferences
Frequency: 6 issues yearly
Cover Price: Free
Circulation: 8,000 (Publisher's Statement)
Usual Pagination: 32
Editor: Thomas Hallauer; **Advertising Manager:** Thomas Hallauer
Summary of Content: Magazine covering wireless intelligence for the auto industry.
Readership/Target Audience: Aimed at professionals involved in auto manufacturing and servicing.
ADVERTISING RATES:
Full Page Colour $2500.00
Agency Commission: 10%
Mechanical Data: Film: Digital
BUSINESS: MOTOR TRADE: Motor Trade Related

TELEMEDIA MAGAZINE

22326U18B-1939

Formerly: WORLD telemedia
Editorial Address: 44 High St, Cheddington, BUCKS, LU7 0RQ **Tel:** 01296 660251
Email: paulskeldon@paulskeldon.com
Advertising Address: Virginia Cottage, Nash Lane, Scaynes Hill, HAYWARDS HEATH, RH17 7NJ **Tel:** 0870 732 7327
Fax: 0870 732 7326
Email: jarvis@worldtelemedia.co.uk
Web site: http://www.wtmag.co.uk
Publisher: World Telemedia Ltd
Date Established: 2001
Frequency: 6 issues yearly
Cover Price: Free
Circulation: 10,000 (Publisher's Statement)
Usual Pagination: 74
Editor: Paul Skeldon; **Advertising Manager:** Jarvis Todd
Summary of Content: Magazine for anyone looking to maximise the potential of their online, mobile, TV and fixed telecoms premium rate entertainment content.
Readership/Target Audience: Aimed at those working in IT and telecommunications who want to make money from value added content.
ADVERTISING RATES:
Full Page Colour £3500.00
Mechanical Data: Type Area: 277 x 190mm, Trim Size: 297 x 210mm, Bleed Size: 303 x 216mm, Col Length: 277mm, Page Width: 190mm, Film: Digital
Copy instructions: Copy Date: 6 weeks prior to publication date
BUSINESS: ELECTRONICS: Telecommunications

TELEVISION

39106U43C-90

Editorial Address: Kildare House, 3 Dorsett Rise, LONDON, EC4Y 8EH **Tel:** 020 7822 2810
Email: publications@rts.org.uk
Advertising Address: As above.
Email: publications@rts.org.uk
Web site: http://www.rts.org.uk
ISSN: 0308-454X
Publisher: RTS
Frequency: 10 issues yearly - Published on the 3rd Monday of the cover month
Cover Price: £8.00
Annual Sub.: £82.00
Circulation: 3,500 (Publisher's Statement)
Usual Pagination: 32
Editor: Steve Clarke; **Advertising Manager:** Steve Clark
Summary of Content: Journal of The Royal Television Society. Contains details of RTS events and television news.
Readership/Target Audience: Read by members of the society.
ADVERTISING: Rates on application
BUSINESS: ELECTRICAL RETAIL TRADE: TV

TELEVISUAL

39115U43D-20

Editorial Address: 48 Charlotte Street, LONDON, W1T 2NS
Tel: 020 3008 5750 **Fax:** 020 3008 5784
Email: jon@televisual.com
Advertising Address: As above. **Tel:** 020 3008 5781
Email: kate@televisual.com
Web site: http://www.televisual.com
ISSN: 0264-9845
Publisher: Televisual Media UK Ltd
Date Established: 1982
Frequency: Monthly - Published at the beginning of the cover month
Cover Price: £3.85
Free to qualifying individuals
Annual Sub.: £38.50

Circulation: 4,787 (ABC 01/07/2008 to 30/06/2009)
Editor: Jon Creamer; **Managing Director:** James Bennett;
Advertising Manager: Kate Dinwoodie
Summary of Content: Magazine containing news from the broadcasting, production, corporate communication and facilities services sectors.
Readership/Target Audience: Aimed at independent producers, broadcasters, commissioners, editors and directors in the TV industry.
ADVERTISING RATES:
Full Page Colour £2195.00
Agency Commission: 10%
Mechanical Data: Film: Positive, right reading, emulsion side down, Print Process: Sheet-fed offset litho, Screen: Mono 48 lpc Colour 60 lpc, Bleed Size: 295 x 245mm, Trim Size: 285 x 235mm, Page Width: 207mm, Type Area: 260 x 207mm, Col Length: 260mm
Copy instructions: Copy Date: 2 weeks prior to publication date
Average advertising content per issue: 50%
BUSINESS: ELECTRICAL RETAIL TRADE: Video

TEST MAGAZINE

1659894U18A-9017

Formerly: Electronic Production
Editorial Address: Kentons House, 24 Blendon Road, BEXLEY, DA5 1BW **Tel:** 0870 701 3536
Email: testmagazine@ntlworld.com
Advertising Address: As above. **Fax:** 0870 701 3537
Email: testmagazine@ntlworld.com
Web site: http://www.directpublishing.webeden.co.uk
Publisher: Direct Publishing Ltd
Date Established: 1977
Frequency: Quarterly
Free to qualifying individuals
Annual Sub.: £45.00
Circulation: 4,100 (Publisher's Statement)
Editor: Phil Brown; **Advertising Manager:** Phil Brown;
Publisher: Phil Brown
Summary of Content: Magazine covering all aspects of electronic product testing.
Readership/Target Audience: Aimed at electronic testing engineers.
ADVERTISING RATES:
Full Page Colour £1395.00
Agency Commission: 10%
Mechanical Data: Bleed Size: 303 x 216mm, Trim Size: 297 x 210mm, Film: Digital, Type Area: 263 x 186mm, Col Length: 263mm, Page Width: 186mm
Copy instructions: Copy Date: 4 weeks prior to publication date
Average advertising content per issue: 40%
BUSINESS: ELECTRONICS

TEXTILE HORIZONS

39509U47A-333

Editorial Address: Perkin House, 1 Longlands Street, BRADFORD, BD1 2TP **Tel:** 01274 378800
Fax: 01274 378811
Email: mcurtis@world-textile.net
Advertising Address: As above.
Email: jwilson@world-textile.net
Web site: http://www.inteletex.com
ISSN: 1353-6184
Publisher: World Textile Publications Ltd
Frequency: 6 issues yearly
Annual Sub.: £65.00
Circulation: 1,000 (Publisher's Statement)
Usual Pagination: 24
Editor: Marianne Curtis
Summary of Content: Magazine covering textile developments including fibres, knitted, woven and non-woven fabrics and apparel. Also carries features on education and training.
Readership/Target Audience: Aimed at decision-makers within the textile industry.
ADVERTISING: Rates on application
Agency Commission: 10%
BUSINESS: CLOTHING & TEXTILES

TEXTILE MONTH

39510U47A-355

Editorial Address: Perkin House, 1 Longlands Street, BRADFORD, BD1 2TP **Tel:** 01274 378800
Fax: 01274 378811
Email: adawilson@gmail.com
Advertising Address: As above. **Tel:** 01274 378825
Email: jwilson@world-textile.net
Web site: http://www.world-textile.net
ISSN: 0040-5116
Publisher: World Textile Publications Ltd
Frequency: 6 issues yearly
Annual Sub.: £190.00
Circulation: 9,000 (Publisher's Statement)
Usual Pagination: 64
Editor: Andrew Thornton; **Managing Director:** Mark Jarvis;
Managing Editor: Adrian Wilson

Summary of Content: Journal covering the machinery and processes involved in the manufacture of textiles, from fibre through to finished product.
Readership/Target Audience: Aimed at management-level textile industrialists.
ADVERTISING RATES:
Full Page Mono £1504.00
Full Page Colour £2417.00
Agency Commission: 10%
Mechanical Data: Type Area: 257 x 175mm, Bleed Size: 303 x 216mm, Trim Size: 297 x 210mm, Film: Digital, Col Length: 257mm, Page Width: 175mm
BUSINESS: CLOTHING & TEXTILES

TEXTILE OUTLOOK INTERNATIONAL

23892U47A-563

Editorial Address: Suite 6, 1st Floor, Alderley House, Alderley Road, WILMSLOW, SK9 1AT **Tel:** 01625 536136
Fax: 01625 536137
Email: editorial@textilesintelligence.com
Web site: http://www.textilesintelligence.com
ISSN: 0268-4764
Publisher: Textiles Intelligence Ltd
Date Established: 1985
Frequency: 6 issues yearly
Annual Sub.: £795.00
Usual Pagination: 120
Editor: Belinda Carp; **Managing Director:** Robin Anson
Summary of Content: Journal containing news of recent global developments and detailed forecasts of future trends. Coverage includes company profiles, country comparisons and reviews, updates of world trade and production trends and studies of specialist fibre and textile areas.
Readership/Target Audience: Aimed at chief executive officers, managing directors, export directors and financial analysts within the global fibre textile and apparel industries.
ADVERTISING: No Advertising taken
BUSINESS: CLOTHING & TEXTILES

TEXTILE PROGRESS

39525U47A-356

Editorial Address: 1st Floor, St. James's Building, Oxford Street, MANCHESTER, M1 6FQ **Tel:** 0161 237 1188
Fax: 0161 236 1991
Email: tiihq@textileinst.org.uk
Web site: http://www.textileinst.org
ISSN: 0040-5167
Publisher: The Textile Institute
Frequency: Quarterly
Annual Sub.: £89.00
Circulation: 600 (Publisher's Statement)
Usual Pagination: 80
Editor: David Buchanan
Summary of Content: Magazine which examines the origination and application of developments in the international fibre, textile and apparel industry.
Readership/Target Audience: Aimed at professionals within the textile, fibre and apparel industry.
ADVERTISING: No Advertising taken
BUSINESS: CLOTHING & TEXTILES

TEXTILE: THE JOURNAL OF CLOTH AND CULTURE

767403U47A-565

Editorial Address: 1st Floor, Angel Court, 81 St. Clements Street, OXFORD, OX4 1AW **Tel:** 01865 245104
Fax: 01865 791165
Email: enquiry@bergpublishers.com
Advertising Address: As above.
Email: enquiry@bergpublishers.com
Web site: http://www.bergpublishers.com
ISSN: 1475-9756
Publisher: Berg Publishers
Date Established: 2003
Frequency: 3 issues yearly - Published in March, July and November on the 1st of the cover month
Annual Sub.: £46.00
Circulation: 600 (Publisher's Statement)
Usual Pagination: 130
Editor: Corina Kapinos; **Advertising Manager:** Corina Kapinos
Summary of Content: Journal covering all aspects of textiles in relation to visual culture including art and craft, gender and identity, cloth, body and architecture, labour and technology, techno-design and practice, with exhibition and book reviews.
Readership/Target Audience: Aimed at academics and students of art and textile history and technology, architecture, anthropology, political economy, media studies, psychoanalysis, philosophy, history and cultural theory.
ADVERTISING RATES:
Full Page Colour £325.00
Mechanical Data: Trim Size: 230 x 150mm
BUSINESS: CLOTHING & TEXTILES

Business Magazines

TEXTILES
39513U47A-370

Editorial Address: PO Box 78, MANCHESTER, M29 7QY
Tel: 01942 886402 **Fax:** 01942 886402
Email: vanessa@pebbleinternational.com
Advertising Address: 1st Floor, St. James's Building,
Oxford Street, MANCHESTER, M1 6FQ **Tel:** 0161 237 1188
Fax: 0161 236 1991
Email: runsworth@textileinst.org.uk
Web site: http://www.textileinstitute.org
ISSN: 1367-1308
Publisher: The Textile Institute
Date Established: 1970
Frequency: Quarterly
Free to qualifying individuals
Annual Sub.: £50.00
Circulation: 4,000 (Publisher's Statement)
Usual Pagination: 32
Editor: Vanessa Knowles; **Advertising Manager:** Chris
Shaw; **Managing Editor:** Vanessa Knowles
Summary of Content: textiles is the international
membership publication of The Textile Institute providing
informative articles on all aspects of the textile chain from
fibre production to retailing, including clothing and footwear.
Readership/Target Audience: Aimed at all members of The
Textile Institute. Written with an easy understanding for all
those involved in the textile sector.
ADVERTISING RATES:
Full Page Mono $2200.00
Full Page Colour $3500.00
Mechanical Data: Type Area: 275 x 187mm, Col Length:
275mm, Page Width: 187mm, Film: Digital, Bleed Size: 3mm
Copy instructions: Copy Date: 8 weeks prior to publication
date
Average advertising content per issue: 5%
BUSINESS: CLOTHING & TEXTILES

TEXTILES EASTERN EUROPE
39512U47A-361

Editorial Address: 2A Bridge Street, Silsden, KEIGHLEY,
BD20 9NB **Tel:** 01535 656489 **Fax:** 0870 094 0863
Email: gfisher@textilemedia.com
Advertising Address: As above. **Fax:** 0870 094 0868
Email: jholland@textilemedia.com
Web site: http://www.textilemedia.com
ISSN: 1354-5981
Publisher: Textile Media Services Ltd
Date Established: 1994
Frequency: Monthly
Annual Sub.: £345.00
Circulation: 1,000 (Publisher's Statement)
Usual Pagination: 16
Editor: Geoff Fisher; **Advertising Manager:** Judy Holland;
Publisher: Judy Holland
Summary of Content: Newsletter containing commercial
news and information of the textile and clothing industries in
the emerging markets of Central and Eastern Europe and the
former Soviet Union.
Readership/Target Audience: Aimed at owners, managers,
investors and buyers in the textile and clothing industry.
ADVERTISING: Rates on application
Agency Commission: 10%
Copy instructions: Copy Date: 3 weeks prior to publication
date
Average advertising content per issue: 5%
BUSINESS: CLOTHING & TEXTILES

TEXTILES SOUTH EAST ASIA
1645524U47A-569

Editorial Address: 2A Bridge Street, Silsden, KEIGHLEY,
BD20 9NB **Tel:** 01535 656489 **Fax:** 0870 094 0863
Email: gfisher@textilemedia.com
Advertising Address: As above.
Email: jholland@textilemedia.com
Web site: http://www.textilemedia.com
ISSN: 1354-5981
Publisher: Textile Media Services Ltd
Date Established: 2004
Frequency: Monthly
Annual Sub.: £345.00
Circulation: 1,000 (Publisher's Statement)
Usual Pagination: 16
Editor: Geoff Fisher; **News Editor:** Judy Holland;
Advertising Manager: Judy Holland; **Publisher:** Judy
Holland
Summary of Content: Newsletter containing commercial
news and information on the textile and clothing industries in
South East Asia.
Readership/Target Audience: Aimed at owners, managers,
investors and buyers in the textile and clothing industry.
ADVERTISING: Rates on application
BUSINESS: CLOTHING & TEXTILES

THAMES VALLEY NEWS
37141U14H-110

Formerly: The Voice
Editorial Address: PO Box 109, CHIPPING NORTON, OX7
6GL **Tel:** 01993 832357 **Fax:** 01993 832366
Advertising Address: As above.
Web site: http://www.fsb.org.uk/103

ISSN: 1365-1463
Publisher: Federation of Small Businesses
Date Established: 1998
Frequency: 6 issues yearly - Published on the 1st of the
cover month
Cover Price: £3.00
Free to qualifying individuals
Circulation: 7,500 (Publisher's Statement)
Usual Pagination: 16
Editor: Jan Harvey; **Advertising Manager:** Jan Harvey
Summary of Content: Business magazine with a focus on
small businesses. Published on behalf of the regional
Federation of Small Businesses.
Readership/Target Audience: Aimed at owners of small
businesses.
ADVERTISING: Rates on application
BUSINESS: COMMERCE, INDUSTRY & MANAGEMENT:
Small Business

THEHRDIRECTOR
1644027U14F-241

Formerly: HRDIRECTOR
Editorial Address: Brook Farm, Heathend, Cromhall,
GLOUCESTER, GL12 8AT **Tel:** 01454 292060
Fax: 01454 294787
Email: editor@thehrdirector.com
Advertising Address: As above.
Email: lee@thehrdirector.com
Web site: http://www.thehrdirector.com
ISSN: 1754-0224
Publisher: The HR Director
Date Established: 2004
Frequency: 11 issues yearly - Published in the 1st week of
the cover month
Annual Sub.: £125.00
Circulation: 10,998 (Publisher's Statement)
Usual Pagination: 56
Editor: Charlie Duff
Summary of Content: Providing in-depth analysis and
proven strategies, case studies from key companies and
industry professionals, from an editorial panel of experts.
Readership/Target Audience: Aimed at HR directors and
other senior HR practitioners in companies of 100
employees plus.
ADVERTISING RATES:
Full Page Colour £3995.00
Agency Commission: 10%
Mechanical Data: Bleed Size: 303 x 216mm, Trim Size: 297
x 210mm, Film: Digital
Copy instructions: Copy Date: 10th of the month prior to
publication date
Average advertising content per issue: 25%
BUSINESS: COMMERCE, INDUSTRY & MANAGEMENT:
Training & Recruitment

THEME MAGAZINE
36499U9A-185

Editorial Address: Ludgate House, 245 Blackfriars Road,
LONDON, SE1 9UY **Tel:** 020 7921 5000
Email: ian.cameron@ubm.com
Advertising Address: As above. **Tel:** 020 7955 3720
Fax: 020 7955 3755
Email: nadia.barnes@ubm.com
Web site: http://www.thememagazine.co.uk
ISSN: 1476-4083
Publisher: UBM Information Ltd
Date Established: 1995
Frequency: Monthly - Published in the middle of the cover
month
Cover Price: £4.00
Free to qualifying individuals
Circulation: 9,367 (ABC 01/07/2008 to 30/06/2009)
Usual Pagination: 120
Editor: Ian Cameron; **Publisher:** Andy Bishop
Summary of Content: Magazine providing the latest news,
opinions, bar and restaurant reviews, legal articles, overseas
design, food, drink and product information.
Readership/Target Audience: Aimed at owners, managers
and key personnel within the modern generation bars, clubs,
diners and restaurants.
ADVERTISING RATES:
Full Page Colour £2415.00
Agency Commission: 10%
Mechanical Data: Bleed Size: 303 x 236mm, Page Width:
208mm, Trim Size: 297 x 230mm, Type Area: 270 x 208mm,
Col Length: 270mm, Film: Digital
Copy instructions: Copy Date: 2 weeks prior to publication
date
Average advertising content per issue: 50%
Supplement(s): Cocktails - 3xY, Coffee - 4xY, Furniture -
2xY
BUSINESS: DRINKS & LICENSED TRADE: Drinks, Licensed
Trade, Wines & Spirits

THEORY & PSYCHOLOGY
40611U56R-240

Editorial Address: 1 Oliver's Yard, 55 City Road, LONDON,
EC1Y 1SP **Tel:** 020 7324 8500 **Fax:** 020 7324 8600
Email: thpsyc@ucalgary.ca

Advertising Address: As above.
Email: sheena.karim@sagepub.co.uk
Web site: http://www.sagepub.co.uk
ISSN: 0959-3543
Publisher: Sage Publications
Date Established: 1991
Frequency: 6 issues yearly
Cover Price: £11.00
Annual Sub.: £50.00
Usual Pagination: 144
Editor: Henderikus Stam; **Advertising Manager:** Sheena
Karim
Summary of Content: Journal focusing on the emergent
themes at the centre of contemporary psychological debate.
Readership/Target Audience: Aimed at academics and
professionals in the field.
ADVERTISING RATES:
Full Page Mono £400.00
Agency Commission: 5%
Mechanical Data: Col Length: 205mm, Page Width:
130mm, Film: Digital, Type Area: 205 x 130mm
BUSINESS: HEALTH & MEDICAL: Health Medical Related

THEORY, CULTURE & SOCIETY
48825U62R-469

Editorial Address: Faculty of Humanities, Nottingham Trent
University, Clifton Lane, NOTTINGHAM, NG11 8NS
Tel: 0115 848 6330 **Fax:** 0115 848 6331
Email: tcs@ntu.ac.uk
Advertising Address: 6 Bonhill Street, LONDON, EC2A 4PU
Tel: 020 7330 1277 **Fax:** 020 7374 8741
Web site: http://www.sagepub.co.uk
ISSN: 0263-2764
Publisher: Sage Publications
Date Established: 1982
Frequency: 8 issues yearly
Annual Sub.: £55.00
Circulation: 1,100 (Publisher's Statement)
Usual Pagination: 176
Editor: Mike Featherstone; **Advertising Manager:** Sheena
Karim
Summary of Content: Journal catering for the resurgence of
interest in culture within contemporary social science.
Readership/Target Audience: Aimed at individuals with
interests in social and cultural issues.
ADVERTISING RATES:
Full Page Mono £450.00
Agency Commission: 5%
Mechanical Data: Col Length: 205mm, Film: Digital, Page
Width: 130mm, Type Area: 205 x 130mm
Copy instructions: Copy Date: 12 weeks prior to
publication date
BUSINESS: CHURCH & SCHOOL EQUIPMENT &
EDUCATION: Education Related

THERAPY TODAY
38467U32G-26

Formerly: CPJ (Counselling & Psychotherapy Journal)
Editorial Address: BACP House, Unit 15, St. John's
Business Park, LUTTERWORTH, LE17 4HB
Tel: 01455 883300 **Fax:** 01455 550243
Email: therapytoday@bacp.co.uk
Advertising Address: As above.
Email: kate.morris@bacp.co.uk
Web site: http://www.therapytoday.net
ISSN: 1474-5372
Publisher: British Association for Counselling &
Psychotherapy
Date Established: 1981
Frequency: 10 issues yearly
Cover Price: £8.50
Free to qualifying individuals
Annual Sub.: £69.00
Circulation: 31,634 (ABC 01/01/2008 to 31/12/2008)
Usual Pagination: 90
Editor: Sarah Browne; **Advertising Manager:** Kate Morris
Summary of Content: Journal of the British Association for
Counselling and Psychotherapy covering news, features,
theory, developments, book reviews, practice management
and world perspectives.
Readership/Target Audience: Read by counsellors,
psychotherapists, members of the association and those
interested in counselling in general.
ADVERTISING RATES:
Full Page Mono £830.00
Full Page Colour £1400.00
Agency Commission: 10%
Mechanical Data: Film: Digital, Type Area: 254 x 165mm,
Col Length: 254mm, Page Width: 165mm
Average advertising content per issue: 40%
BUSINESS: LOCAL GOVERNMENT, LEISURE &
RECREATION: Community Care & Social Services

THIIS THE HOMECARE INDUSTRY
INFORMATION SERVICE
38495U32G-127

Editorial Address: The Stables, 16C High Street,
RUSHTON, NN14 1RQ **Tel:** 01536 710050
Fax: 01536 418280

Email: info@thiis.co.uk
Advertising Address: As above.
Email: info@thiis.co.uk
Web site: http://www.thiis.co.uk
Publisher: Homecare Publishing Limited
Date Established: 1998
Frequency: Monthly
Annual Sub.: £95.00
Circulation: 1,250 (Publisher's Statement)
Usual Pagination: 48
Editor: David Russell; **Advertising Manager:** David Russell;
Publisher: David Russell
Summary of Content: Bulletin containing general news and
news on products, dealers, companies, publications,
exhibitions and people in the homecare and disability
marketplace.
Readership/Target Audience: Aimed at dealers,
distributors, suppliers and manufacturers.
ADVERTISING RATES:
Full Page Mono £250.00
Agency Commission: 10%
Mechanical Data: Type Area: 275 x 190mm, Col Length:
275mm, Page Width: 190mm
Copy instructions: Copy Date: 15th of the month prior to
publication date
Average advertising content per issue: 30%
BUSINESS: LOCAL GOVERNMENT, LEISURE &
RECREATION: Community Care & Social Services

THE THIN RED LINE
38914U40-305

Editorial Address: Sutherland Press House, Main Street,
GOLSPIE, KW10 6RA **Tel:** 01408 633871 **Fax:** 01408 633876
Email: magazinesales@methodpublishing.co.uk
Advertising Address: As above.
Email: magazinesales@methodpublishing.co.uk
Web site: http://www.methodpublishing.co.uk
Publisher: Method Publishing
Frequency: Half-yearly - Published in April and October
Circulation: 1,600 (Publisher's Statement)
Editor: Linda Bennett
Summary of Content: The regimental magazine of The
Argyll and Sutherland Highlanders.
Readership/Target Audience: Aimed at all elements of the
regiment - regular and territorial army, affiliated cadet forces,
allied regiments in Canada and Australia, members of
regimental associations throughout the country and ex-
members of the regiment worldwide.
ADVERTISING RATES:
Full Page Mono £290.00
Full Page Colour £490.00
Agency Commission: 10%
Mechanical Data: Type Area: 266 x 186mm, Bleed Size:
303 x 216mm, Trim Size: 297 x 210mm, Col Length: 266mm,
Print Process: Sheet-fed Offset, Film: Digital, Page Width:
186mm
Average advertising content per issue: 10%
BUSINESS: DEFENCE

THINKING HIGHWAYS EUROPE/REST OF THE WORLD EDITION
1881498U42B-255

Editorial Address: 15 Onslow Gardens, WALLINGTON,
SM6 9QL **Tel:** 020 8254 9406 **Fax:** 020 8647 0045
Email: kevin@h3bmedia.com
Web site: http://www.thinkinghihgways.com
ISSN: 1753-433X
Publisher: H3B Media Ltd
Date Established: 2006
Frequency: Quarterly
Free to qualifying individuals
Annual Sub.: £30.00
Usual Pagination: 88
Editor: Kevin Borras; **News Editor:** Lucy Cone
Summary of Content: Magazine for the advanced
transportation management and intelligent transportation
systems market. Covering homeland security, cross border
mobility, public transport and rapid response.
Readership/Target Audience: Aimed at advanced
transportation management, intelligent transportation
systems, homeland security, cross border mobility, public
transit and transport security.
BUSINESS: CONSTRUCTION: Roads

THINKING HIGHWAYS NORTH AMERICAN EDITION
1881500U42B-254

Editorial Address: 15 Onslow Gardens, WALLINGTON,
SM6 9QL **Tel:** 020 8254 9406 **Fax:** 020 8647 0045
Email: kevin@h3bmedia.com
Web site: http://www.thinkinghihgways.com
Publisher: H3B Media Ltd
Frequency: Quarterly
Free to qualifying individuals
Annual Sub.: £30.00
Usual Pagination: 88
Editor: Kevin Borras; **News Editor:** Lucy Cone
Summary of Content: Magazine addressing the issues that
directly affect the following markets in the USA, Canada and

Mexico - advanced transportation management, intelligent
transportation systems, homeland security, cross-border
mobility, public transit, transport security.
Readership/Target Audience: Aimed at advanced
transportation management, intelligent transportation
systems, homeland security, cross border mobility, public
transit and transport security.
BUSINESS: CONSTRUCTION: Roads

THIRD FORCE NEWS
38498U32G-128

Editorial Address: Mansfield Traquair Centre, 15 Mansfield
Place, EDINBURGH, EH3 6BB **Tel:** 0131 556 3882
Fax: 0131 556 0279
Email: tfn@scvo.org.uk
Advertising Address: As above.
Email: katrionawilliamson@yahoo.co.uk
Web site: http://www.scvo.org.uk/tfn/
ISSN: 0969-9406
Publisher: Scottish Council for Voluntary Organisations
Date Established: 1990
Frequency: Weekly
Annual Sub.: £110.00
Circulation: 5,500 (Publisher's Statement)
Usual Pagination: 16
Editor: Robert Armour; **Advertising Manager:** Katriona
Williamson
Summary of Content: Newspaper of the Scottish Council
for Voluntary Organisations. Covers Scottish voluntary
sector news, features, comment and debate.
Readership/Target Audience: Aimed at major voluntary
organisations in Scotland, plus central and local
government, charitable trusts, trade unions, businesses and
universities.
ADVERTISING RATES:
Full Page Mono £1200.00
Full Page Colour £1500.00
Agency Commission: 10%
Mechanical Data: Type Area: 375 x 270mm, Col Length:
375mm, Page Width: 270mm, Film: Digital
Copy instructions: Copy Date: Friday 3.30pm prior to
publication date
Average advertising content per issue: 35%
BUSINESS: LOCAL GOVERNMENT, LEISURE &
RECREATION: Community Care & Social Services

THIRD SECTOR
35446U1P-200

Formerly: ThirdSector
Editorial Address: 174 Hammersmith Road, LONDON, W6
7JP **Tel:** 020 8267 5000 **Fax:** 020 8267 4806
Email: thirdsector@haymarket.com
Advertising Address: As above. **Tel:** 020 8267 4813
Email: natasha.lumsden@haymarket.com
Web site: http://www.thirdsector.co.uk
ISSN: 1355-6371
Publisher: Haymarket Business Media Ltd
Date Established: 1992
Frequency: Weekly
Annual Sub.: £70.00
Circulation: 12,345 (ABC 01/07/2008 to 30/06/2009)
Usual Pagination: 52
Features Editor: Helen Barrett; **Advertising Manager:**
Natasha Lumsden
Summary of Content: Magazine covering news, fundraising
features, analysis and issues.
Readership/Target Audience: Read by those involved in
charities, fundraising and voluntary organisations.
ADVERTISING RATES:
Full Page Colour £3280.00
Agency Commission: 10%
Mechanical Data: Type Area: 274 x 226mm, Bleed Size:
300 x 253mm, Trim Size: 294 x 250mm, Col Length: 274mm,
Film: Digital, Page Width: 226mm
Copy instructions: Copy Date: Friday 10am prior to
publication date
BUSINESS: FINANCE & ECONOMICS: Fundraising

THIS IS THE BUSINESS
41327U63B-1100

Formerly: Business Echo
Editorial Address: Brayford Wharf East, LINCOLN, LN5 7AT
Tel: 01522 820000 **Fax:** 01522 804493
Email: mel.west@lincolnshiremedia.co.uk
Advertising Address: As above. **Tel:** 01522 804491
Email: stacey.murphy@lincolnshiremedia.co.uk
Web site: http://www.thisislincolnshire.co.uk
Publisher: Lincolnshire Media Ltd
Frequency: Monthly
Cover Price: Free
Circulation: 31,000 (Publisher's Statement)
Editor: Mel West
Summary of Content: Regional newspaper containing
business information and news.
Readership/Target Audience: Read by local business
people.
ADVERTISING RATES:
Full Page Mono £2246.40
Full Page Colour £2808.00

SCC £7.80
Mechanical Data: Col Length: 360mm, Film: Digital, Print
Process: Web-fed offset litho, Page Width: 270mm, Type
Area: 360 x 270mm, No. of Columns (Display): 8
Copy instructions: Copy Date: 1 week prior to publication
date
Average advertising content per issue: 50%
Supplement to: Lincolnshire Echo
BUSINESS: REGIONAL BUSINESS: Regional Business
English Counties

THOMAS COOK EUROPEAN RAIL TIMETABLE
39760U50-24_77

Formerly: Thomas Cook European Timetable
Editorial Address: PO Box 227, Coningsby Road, Thomas
Cook Business Park, PETERBOROUGH, PE3 8SB
Tel: 01733 416477 **Fax:** 01733 416688
Email: timetables@thomascook.com
Advertising Address: As above.
Email: timetables@thomascook.com
Web site: http://www.thomascookpublishing.com
ISSN: 0952-620X
Publisher: Thomas Cook Tour Operations Ltd
Date Established: 1873
Frequency: Monthly
Cover Price: £11.50
Usual Pagination: 544
Editor: Brendan Fox; **Advertising Manager:** Brendan Fox
Summary of Content: Publication containing timetables of
European rail systems, shipping services, airport rail links
and maps.
Readership/Target Audience: Aimed at the travel trade,
business travellers, InterRail/Eurail travellers, independent
travellers, rail enthusiasts and libraries.
ADVERTISING: Rates on application
Agency Commission: 10%
BUSINESS: TRAVEL & TOURISM

TILE & STONE JOURNAL
1645671U23C-93

Editorial Address: The Old Corn Store, Heartenoak Lane,
Hawkhurst, CRANBROOK, TN18 4DZ **Tel:** 01580 752400
Fax: 01580 752604
Email: tandsjournal@aol.com
Advertising Address: The Oast, Great Danegate, Eridge,
TUNBRIDGE WELLS, TN3 9HU **Tel:** 01892 752400
Fax: 01892 752404
Email: john.passmore@kick-startpublishing.co.uk
ISSN: 1744-4276
Publisher: Kick-Start Publishing Ltd
Date Established: 2004
Frequency: 10 issues yearly
Free to qualifying individuals
Annual Sub.: £28.00
Circulation: 9,300 (Publisher's Statement)
Usual Pagination: 80
Editor: Joe Simpson; **Advertising Manager:** Andy Turner
Summary of Content: Official journal of the Tile Association.
Covers local and international news, market statistics and
analysis, company profiles, technical articles, site reports
and new products.
Readership/Target Audience: Aimed at tiling contractors,
retailers, builder's merchants, garden centres and kitchen
and bathroom specialists.
ADVERTISING RATES:
Full Page Mono £940.00
Full Page Colour £1390.00
Agency Commission: 10%
Mechanical Data: Type Area: 268 x 185mm, Trim Size: 297
x 210mm, Bleed Size: 303 x 213mm, Col Length: 268mm,
Film: Digital, Page Width: 185mm
Copy instructions: Copy Date: 2 weeks prior to publication
date
Average advertising content per issue: 40%
BUSINESS: FURNISHINGS & FURNITURE: Furnishings &
Furniture - Kitchens & Bathrooms

TILE UK
36617U12A-151

Editorial Address: 4 Red Barn Mews, High Street, BATTLE,
TN33 0AG **Tel:** 01424 774982
Email: jobeth@gearingmediagroup.com
Advertising Address: As above. **Fax:** 01424 775077
Email: roger@gearingmediagroup.com
Web site: http://www.tileuk-magazine.com
ISSN: 1363-948X
Publisher: Gearing Media Group
Date Established: 1996
Frequency: Monthly - Published on the 1st of the cover
month
Annual Sub.: £49.00
Circulation: 5,711 (Publisher's Statement)
Usual Pagination: 64
Editor: JoBeth Phillips; **Advertising Manager:** Roger Howis
Summary of Content: Magazine covering material analysis,
new products and information.
Readership/Target Audience: Aimed at tile fixers, retailers,
manufacturers, distributors and professional specifiers.

Business Magazines

ADVERTISING RATES:
Full Page Colour £1675.00
Mechanical Data: Bleed Size: 303 x 222mm, Trim Size: 297 x 216mm, Film: Digital
Copy instructions: Copy Date: 3 weeks prior to publication date
BUSINESS: CERAMICS, POTTERY & GLASS: Ceramics & Pottery

TIMBER BUILDING
1744655U42A-236

Editorial Address: Progressive House, 2 Maidstone Road, Foots Cray, SIDCUP, DA14 5HZ **Tel:** 020 8269 7809
Fax: 020 8269 7844
Email: mjeffree@ttjonline.com
Advertising Address: As above. **Tel:** 020 8269 7700
Email: mricker@ttjonline.com
Web site: http://www.timber-building.com
ISSN: 1748-9741
Publisher: Progressive Media Publications
Date Established: 2005
Frequency: Quarterly
Annual Sub.: £40.00
Circulation: 20,000 (Publisher's Statement)
Editor: Mike Jeffree; **News Editor:** Stephen Powney; **Managing Editor:** Sally Spencer
Summary of Content: Magazine covering the market for timber in the construction industry including structural and other applications of timber use.
Readership/Target Audience: Aimed at architects, structural engineers, local authorities, housing associations, contractors, builders, timber frame suppliers, timber importers and distributors.
ADVERTISING RATES:
Full Page Colour £2130.00
Agency Commission: 10%
Mechanical Data: Type Area: 280 x 195mm, Bleed Size: 306 x 236mm, Trim Size: 300 x 230mm, Col Length: 280mm, Page Width: 195mm, Film: Digital
Copy instructions: Copy Date: 3 weeks prior to publication date
Average advertising content per issue: 40%
BUSINESS: CONSTRUCTION

TIMBER IN CONSTRUCTION
1809519U42A-240

Editorial Address: Portland Buildings, 127-129 Portland Street, MANCHESTER, M1 4PZ **Tel:** 0161 236 2782
Fax: 0161 236 2783
Email: info@excelpublishing.co.uk
Advertising Address: As above.
Email: info@excelpublishing.co.uk
Web site: http://www.timberinconstruction.co.uk
Publisher: Excel Publishing Company Ltd
Frequency: Quarterly - Published in the middle of the cover month
Cover Price: £4.00
Annual Sub.: £20.00
Circulation: 10,080 (Publisher's Statement)
Usual Pagination: 54
Editor: Chris Newbould
Summary of Content: Magazine covering timber and wood-based products in modern building and architecture. Features news, industry developments and articles about timber frame construction, engineered wood and associated products.
Readership/Target Audience: Aimed at architects, structural engineers, consultants and house builders.
ADVERTISING RATES:
Full Page Colour £1595.00
Mechanical Data: Type Area: 266 x 185mm, Bleed Size: 303 x 216mm, Trim Size: 297 x 210mm, Col Length: 266mm, Page Width: 185mm, Film: Digital
Copy instructions: Copy Date: 2 weeks prior to publication date
BUSINESS: CONSTRUCTION

TIME & SOCIETY
40612U56R-251

Editorial Address: 1 Oliver's Yard, 55 City Road, LONDON, EC1Y 1SP **Tel:** 020 7324 8500 **Fax:** 020 7324 8600
Advertising Address: As above.
Email: advertising@sagepub.co.uk
Web site: http://www.sagepub.co.uk
ISSN: 0961-463X
Publisher: Sage Publications
Date Established: 1992
Frequency: 3 issues yearly - Published in March, June and September
Cover Price: £17.00
Annual Sub.: £39.00
Usual Pagination: 150
Editor: Robert Hassan; **Advertising Manager:** Matthew Schlag
Summary of Content: Journal containing analyses on temporality, relating it to society and culture and to theories of individual and social behaviour and action.
Readership/Target Audience: Read by academics working in the field.

ADVERTISING RATES:
Full Page Mono £400.00
Agency Commission: 5%
Mechanical Data: Col Length: 185mm, Type Area: 185 x 105mm, Page Width: 105mm, Film: Digital
Copy instructions: Copy Date: 12 weeks prior to publication date
BUSINESS: HEALTH & MEDICAL: Health Medical Related

THE TIMES LAW REPORTS
39311U44-1855

Editorial Address: Halsbury House, 35 Chancery Lane, LONDON, WC2A 1EL **Tel:** 020 7520 5349
Email: craig.rose@lexisnexis.co.uk
Publisher: LexisNexis Butterworths
Date Established: 1990
Frequency: 22 issues yearly
Annual Sub.: £244.00
Editor: Craig Rose; **Publisher:** Craig Rose
Summary of Content: Journal containing law reports as published daily in The Times newspaper, with comprehensive indexes.
Readership/Target Audience: Aimed at solicitors and barristers.
ADVERTISING: No Advertising taken
BUSINESS: LEGAL

TIO2 WORLDWIDE UPDATE
36687U13-190

Editorial Address: 39 Cromwell Road, BECKENHAM, BR3 4LL **Tel:** 020 8658 2621 **Fax:** 020 8402 1544
Email: regadams@artikol.com
Web site: http://www.artikol.com
ISSN: 1350-908X
Publisher: Artikol
Date Established: 1993
Frequency: 6 issues yearly
Annual Sub.: $3000.00
Circulation: 452 (Publisher's Statement 01/01/2008 to 31/12/2008)
Usual Pagination: 52
Editor: Reg Adams
Summary of Content: Independent newsletter covering news and developments affecting national and international TiO2 pigments, raw materials and end-user industries.
Readership/Target Audience: Aimed at major chemical, paint, paper and plastics companies, mining companies and investment analysts.
ADVERTISING: No Advertising taken
BUSINESS: CHEMICALS

TIPS & ADVICE COMPANY DIRECTOR
623001U14H-120

Formerly: Tips & Advice Business Matters
Editorial Address: Calgarth House, 39-41 Bank Street, ASHFORD, TN23 1DQ **Tel:** 01233 653500
Fax: 01233 647100
Email: editorial@indicator.co.uk
Web site: http://www.indicator.co.uk
Publisher: Indicator Limited
Date Established: 1999
Frequency: 22 issues yearly
Annual Sub.: £101.00
Circulation: 10,000 (Publisher's Statement)
Usual Pagination: 8
Editor: Duncan Callow; **Managing Editor:** Duncan Callow
Summary of Content: Newsletter covering personnel and employment issues, with legal, financial and tax advice.
Readership/Target Audience: Aimed at small business outlets and directors of limited companies.
ADVERTISING: No Advertising taken
BUSINESS: COMMERCE, INDUSTRY & MANAGEMENT: Small Business

TIPS & ADVICE PERSONNEL
37084U14F-82

Editorial Address: Calgarth House, 39-41 Bank Street, ASHFORD, TN23 1DQ **Tel:** 01233 653500
Fax: 01233 647100
Email: editorial@indicator.co.uk
Web site: http://www.indicator.co.uk
Publisher: Indicator Limited
Date Established: 1998
Frequency: 22 issues yearly
Annual Sub.: £124.00
Circulation: 15,000 (Publisher's Statement)
Usual Pagination: 8
Editor: Duncan Callow; **Managing Editor:** Duncan Callow
Summary of Content: Newsletter containing practical advice and tips on personnel and employment law issues.
Readership/Target Audience: Aimed at employers in smaller businesses.
ADVERTISING: No Advertising taken
BUSINESS: COMMERCE, INDUSTRY & MANAGEMENT: Training & Recruitment

TIPS & ADVICE TAX
763267U1M-81

Editorial Address: Calgarth House, 39-41 Bank Street, ASHFORD, TN23 1DQ **Tel:** 01233 653500
Fax: 01233 647200
Email: tony.court@indicator.co.uk
Web site: http://www.indicator.co.uk
Publisher: Indicator Limited
Frequency: 22 issues yearly
Annual Sub.: £117.00
Circulation: 20,000 (Publisher's Statement)
Usual Pagination: 8
Editor: Tony Court
Summary of Content: Newsletter covering practical and feasible tips for deducting business expenses, recovering VAT, capital allowances, cutting costs, extracting profit from a business and recent legislation.
Readership/Target Audience: Aimed at small business owners.
ADVERTISING: No Advertising taken
BUSINESS: FINANCE & ECONOMICS: Taxation

TIRE TECHNOLOGY INTERNATIONAL
38322U31A-152_50

Editorial Address: Abinger House, Church Street, DORKING, RH4 1DF **Tel:** 01306 743744 **Fax:** 01306 887546
Email: a.gavine@ukintpress.com
Advertising Address: As above. **Fax:** 01306 742525
Email: colinscott@ukintpress.com
Web site: http://www.ukintpress.com
ISSN: 1462-4729
Publisher: UKIP Media & Events Ltd
Date Established: 1993
Frequency: 5 issues yearly
Free to qualifying individuals
Annual Sub.: £125.00
Circulation: 6,009 (ABC 01/01/2008 to 31/12/2008)
Usual Pagination: 80
Editor: Adam Gavine
Summary of Content: Magazine covering the technology and systems used in the production, research and future development of tyres, including articles on the chemistry, testing, inspection and basic engineering of tyres.
Readership/Target Audience: Aimed at tyre manufacturers and supplier companies.
ADVERTISING RATES:
Full Page Mono EUR5500.00
Full Page Colour EUR5500.00
Mechanical Data: Film: Digital, Trim Size: 297 x 210mm
Copy instructions: Copy Date: 1st of the month prior to publication date
BUSINESS: MOTOR TRADE: Motor Trade Accessories

TIZARD LEARNING DISABILITY REVIEW
601103U56L-120

Formerly: The Learning Disability Review
Editorial Address: Richmond House, Richmond Road, BRIGHTON, BN2 3RL **Tel:** 01273 666725
Fax: 01273 625526
Email: joannas@pavpub.com
Advertising Address: As above. **Tel:** 0870 890 1080
Fax: 0870 890 1081
Email: pauls@pavpub.com
Web site: http://pavilionjournals.metapress.com/home/main.mpx
ISSN: 1359-5474
Publisher: Pavilion Journals (Brighton) Ltd
Date Established: 1996
Frequency: Quarterly
Annual Sub.: £45.00
Circulation: 800 (Publisher's Statement)
Usual Pagination: 44
Editor: Jim Mansell; **Advertising Manager:** Paul Somerville
Summary of Content: Journal covering research, development and every day practices within the learning disability field.
Readership/Target Audience: Aimed at practitioners and managers in learning disability services.
ADVERTISING RATES:
Full Page Mono £350.00
Agency Commission: 10%
Mechanical Data: Film: Digital, Type Area: 225 x 160mm, Col Length: 225mm, Page Width: 160mm
Average advertising content per issue: 4.5%
BUSINESS: HEALTH & MEDICAL: Disability & Rehabilitation

TJ
37090U14F-9

Formerly: Training Journal
Editorial Address: 28 St. Thomas Place, Cambridgeshire Business Park, ELY, CB7 4EX **Tel:** 01353 654877
Fax: 01353 663644
Email: debbie.carter@trainingjournal.com
Advertising Address: 4 Grosvenor Place, LONDON, SW1X 7DL **Tel:** 020 7096 2937 **Fax:** 020 7091 7605
Email: stephen.pyner@trainingjournal.com
Web site: http://www.trainingjournal.com

ISSN: 1465-6523
Publisher: Fenman Ltd
Date Established: 1965
Frequency: Monthly - Published in the 1st week of the cover month
Annual Sub.: £155.00
Circulation: 6,000 (Publisher's Statement)
Usual Pagination: 78
Editor: Elizabeth Eyre; **Managing Editor:** Elizabeth Eyre;
Publisher: Guy Cleaver
Summary of Content: Magazine focusing on training and recruitment, including extensive news analysis and reviews section covering books, videos, CD-Rom, training materials and websites.
Readership/Target Audience: Aimed at workplace learning professionals in industry, commerce, education, training associations, employment service agencies, government departments and libraries.
ADVERTISING RATES:
Full Page £1415.00
Agency Commission: 10%
Mechanical Data: Page Width: 186mm, Type Area: 272 x 186mm, Col Length: 272mm, Bleed Size: 307 x 220mm, Trim Size: 297 x 210mm
Copy instructions: Copy Date: 4 weeks prior to publication date
Average advertising content per issue: 20%
BUSINESS: COMMERCE, INDUSTRY & MANAGEMENT: Training & Recruitment

TM TRAINING MATTERS
38773U37-200
Editorial Address: 207 Linen Hall, 162-168 Regent Street, LONDON, W1B 5TB **Tel:** 020 7434 1530 **Fax:** 020 7437 0915
Email: tm@1530.com
Advertising Address: As above.
Email: martin.caldersmith@1530.com
Publisher: Communications International Group
Frequency: Monthly - Published around the 15th of the cover month
Annual Sub.: £67.50
Circulation: 19,000 (Publisher's Statement)
Usual Pagination: 40
Editor: Rosanne Please; **Advertising Manager:** Martin Calder-Smith
Summary of Content: Magazine focusing on training in OTC treatment areas, people and product news, a health update, and sections on customer skills, the NHS and the human body.
Readership/Target Audience: Aimed at pharmacy assistants.
ADVERTISING RATES:
Full Page Colour £4565.00
Agency Commission: 10%
Mechanical Data: Type Area: 306 x 225mm, Bleed Size: 341 x 248mm, Trim Size: 335 x 245mm, Col Length: 306mm, Film: Digital, Page Width: 225mm, No. of Columns (Display): 5, Col Widths (Display): 44mm
Copy instructions: Copy Date: 3rd week of the month prior to publication date
Average advertising content per issue: 40%
Supplement to: Pharmacy Magazine
BUSINESS: PHARMACEUTICAL & CHEMISTS

TMB WEEKLY: THE MAGAZINE BUSINESS WEEKLY
35622U2B-200
Formerly: TMB Weekly Magazine Intelligence for Professionals
Editorial Address: 98 Hillfield Avenue, Hornsey, LONDON, N8 7DN **Tel:** 020 8292 0822
Email: tmbweekly@btinternet.com
Publisher: Duvan Ltd
Date Established: 1982
Frequency: Weekly
Annual Sub.: £520.00
Circulation: 2,500 (Publisher's Statement)
Usual Pagination: 8
Editor: Alan MacFarlane; **Managing Director:** Alan MacFarlane; **Managing Editor:** Alan MacFarlane
Summary of Content: Newsletter covering magazine launches, closures, circulation analysis, acquisitions and financial news.
Readership/Target Audience: Aimed at senior decision makers in the magazine publishing industry.
ADVERTISING: No Advertising taken
BUSINESS: COMMUNICATIONS, ADVERTISING & MARKETING: Press

TODAY'S ANAESTHETIST
40229U56A-143
Editorial Address: Media House, 48 High Street, SWANLEY, BR8 8BQ **Tel:** 01322 660434 **Fax:** 01322 666539
Email: mediajournals@aol.com
Advertising Address: As above.
Email: mediajournals@aol.com
Web site: http://www.mediapublishingcompany.com
Publisher: Media Publishing
Date Established: 1985

Frequency: Quarterly
Annual Sub.: £20.00
Circulation: 4,500 (Publisher's Statement)
Usual Pagination: 28
Editor: Quentin Smith; **Managing Director:** Terry Gardner;
Advertising Manager: Terry Gardner
Summary of Content: Journal containing clinical papers, conference news, case reports, product news and features.
Readership/Target Audience: Aimed at all UK consultant anaesthetists and major departments of anaesthesia.
ADVERTISING RATES:
Full Page Mono £800.00
Full Page Colour £1200.00
Agency Commission: 10%
Mechanical Data: Type Area: 270 x 185mm, Trim Size: 297 x 210mm, Bleed Size: 303 x 216mm, Film: Digital, Col Length: 270mm, Page Width: 185mm
BUSINESS: HEALTH & MEDICAL

TODAY'S TECHNICIAN
38409U32B-180
Editorial Address: NPTA House, Hall Lane, Kinoulton, NOTTINGHAM, NG12 3EF **Tel:** 01949 81133
Fax: 01949 823905
Email: officenpta@aol.com
Advertising Address: As above.
Email: officenpta@aol.com
Web site: http://www.npta.org.uk
Publisher: National Pest Technicians' Association
Frequency: Quarterly
Cover Price: Free
Circulation: 2,000 (Publisher's Statement)
Usual Pagination: 36
Editor: Julie Gillies
Summary of Content: Journal of the NPTA. Aims to improve communications within the public health pest control industry.
Readership/Target Audience: Read by pest controllers, food industry personnel, environmental health officers, local authorities and dog wardens.
ADVERTISING RATES:
Full Page Mono £377.00
Full Page Colour £577.00
Mechanical Data: Bleed Size: 303 x 216mm, Page Width: 185mm, Trim Size: 297 x 210mm, Type Area: 268 x 185mm, Col Length: 268mm, Film: Digital
Copy instructions: Copy Date: Last Friday of February, May, August and November
Average advertising content per issue: 20%
BUSINESS: LOCAL GOVERNMENT, LEISURE & RECREATION: Public Health & Cleaning

TODAY'S THERAPIST
623180U56A-145
Editorial Address: 1 Granville Walk, Chadderton, OLDHAM, OL9 6SR **Tel:** 0161 284 6602 **Fax:** 0161 284 3790
Email: angela@todaystherapist.com
Advertising Address: As above.
Email: angela@todaystherapist.com
Web site: http://www.todaystherapist.com
Publisher: Topaz Publications
Date Established: 1999
Frequency: 6 issues yearly
Annual Sub.: £27.00
Circulation: 6,000 (Publisher's Statement)
Usual Pagination: 58
Editor: Angela Mahandru; **Managing Director:** Angela Mahandru; **Advertising Manager:** Angela Mahandru
Summary of Content: Journal covering aromatherapy, complementary therapies, health and nutrition, sports and fitness, natural beauty, medical matters, world news and education.
Readership/Target Audience: Aimed at complementary and conventional therapists, aromatherapists, beauticians, fitness consultants and people working in health clubs, hospitals and sports injury clinics.
ADVERTISING RATES:
Full Page Mono £500.00
Full Page Colour £700.00
Agency Commission: 10%
Mechanical Data: Type Area: 277 x 190mm, Bleed Size: 300 x 213mm, Trim Size: 297 x 210mm, Col Length: 277mm, Page Width: 190mm, Film: Digital
Average advertising content per issue: 35%
BUSINESS: HEALTH & MEDICAL

TOGETHER
37210U14L-765
Editorial Address: 128 Theobalds Road, LONDON, WC1X 8TN **Tel:** 020 7611 2500 **Fax:** 020 7611 2555
Email: andrew.d.murray@unitetheunion.com
Advertising Address: As above. **Tel:** 020 7611 2552
Fax: 020 7611 2500
Web site: http://www.tgwu.org.uk
ISSN: 0967-3857
Publisher: Transport & General Workers' Union
Date Established: 1992
Frequency: Half-yearly
Cover Price: Free

Circulation: 26,800 (Publisher's Statement)
Usual Pagination: 16
Editor: Andrew Murray; **Advertising Manager:** Martha Campbell
Summary of Content: Magazine of the Transport and General Workers' Union.
Readership/Target Audience: Aimed at women members of TGWU.
ADVERTISING RATES:
Full Page Colour £2000.00
Mechanical Data: Type Area: 285 x 210mm, Col Length: 285mm, Page Width: 210mm, Bleed Size: 303 x 216mm, Trim Size: 297 x 210mm, Film: Digital
BUSINESS: COMMERCE, INDUSTRY & MANAGEMENT: Trade Unions

TOLLEY'S COMPANY SECRETARY'S REVIEW
37113U14G-30
Formerly: Company Secretary's Review
Editorial Address: Halsbury House, 35 Chancery Lane, LONDON, WC2A 1EL **Tel:** 020 7400 2500
Fax: 020 7400 2988
Email: jennie.dunn@lexisnexis.co.uk
Web site: http://www.lexisnexis.co.uk
ISSN: 0309-703X
Publisher: LexisNexis
Date Established: 1977
Frequency: 26 issues yearly
Circulation: 1,500 (Publisher's Statement)
Usual Pagination: 8
Editor: Jennie Dunn; **Managing Editor:** Andrew Trinder
Summary of Content: Newsletter covering topics affecting company administration, developments in company law, employment law, health and safety, accounting, taxation, pensions, corporate governance, competition and finance.
Readership/Target Audience: Aimed at company secretaries,and senior company administrators and officers.
ADVERTISING: No Advertising taken
BUSINESS: COMMERCE, INDUSTRY & MANAGEMENT: Company Secretaries

TOLLEY'S EMPLOYMENT LAW NEWSLETTER
39244U44-1870
Formerly: Tolley's Employment Law-Line
Editorial Address: Halsbury House, 35 Chancery Lane, LONDON, WC2A 1EL **Tel:** 020 7400 2500
Fax: 020 7400 2583
Email: rebecca.smith@lexisnexis.co.uk
Web site: http://www.lexisnexis.co.uk
ISSN: 1747-6070
Publisher: LexisNexis Butterworths
Date Established: 1995
Frequency: Monthly
Annual Sub.: £162.00
Usual Pagination: 8
Editor: Rebecca Smith; **Publisher:** Delia Cook
Summary of Content: Newsletter dealing with all aspects of employment law and human resource issues in a concise format.
Readership/Target Audience: Aimed at legal professionals.
ADVERTISING: No Advertising taken
BUSINESS: LEGAL

TOLLEY'S PRACTICAL AUDIT & ACCOUNTING
35048U1B-315
Editorial Address: Halsbury House, 35 Chancery Lane, LONDON, WC2A 1EL **Tel:** 020 7400 2500
Fax: 020 7400 2791
Email: sylvia.courtnage@lexisnexis.co.uk
ISSN: 1367-1871
Publisher: LexisNexis
Date Established: 1990
Frequency: Monthly
Annual Sub.: £150.00
Usual Pagination: 12
Editor: Sylvia Courtnage; **Circulation Manager:** Ann Beard
Summary of Content: Publication providing news and comprehensive updates on the latest regulatory, ethical and legislative changes and developments in auditing and accounting.
Readership/Target Audience: Aimed at auditors and accountants.
ADVERTISING: No Advertising taken
BUSINESS: FINANCE & ECONOMICS: Accountancy

TOLLEY'S PRACTICAL NIC SERVICE
35414U1M-57
Formerly: Tolley's National Insurance Brief
Editorial Address: Halsbury House, 35 Chancery Lane, LONDON, WC2A 1EL **Tel:** 020 7400 2500
Fax: 020 7400 2791
Email: stuart.egan@lexisnexis.co.uk
Web site: http://www.lexisnexis.co.uk
ISSN: 1461-3360

Business Magazines

Publisher: LexisNexis
Frequency: Monthly
Annual Sub.: £195.00
Circulation: 1,500 (Publisher's Statement)
Usual Pagination: 8
Editor: Stuart Egan; **Managing Editor:** Alan Blanchard
Summary of Content: Newsletter covering all aspects of National Insurance, concentrating on contributions.
Readership/Target Audience: Read by those involved in small to medium sized accounts businesses.
ADVERTISING: No Advertising taken
BUSINESS: FINANCE & ECONOMICS: Taxation

TOLLEY'S PRACTICAL TAX NEWSLETTER
35415U1M-60
Editorial Address: Halsbury House, 35 Chancery Lane, LONDON, WC2A 1EL **Tel:** 020 7400 2500
Email: andrew.goodall@lexisnexis.co.uk
Web site: http://www.lexisnexis.co.uk
ISSN: 1475-2352
Publisher: LexisNexis
Date Established: 1980
Frequency: 26 issues yearly
Circulation: 2,000 (Publisher's Statement)
Usual Pagination: 8
Editor: Andrew Goodall
Summary of Content: Newsletter covering the latest tax developments.
Readership/Target Audience: Read by tax advisers, lawyers and accountants in private practice and commerce.
ADVERTISING: No Advertising taken
Supplement(s): Tax - 12xY
BUSINESS: FINANCE & ECONOMICS: Taxation

TOMORROW'S CLEANING
1913809U4F-112
Editorial Address: Bollinbrook House, Beech Lane, MACCLESFIELD, SK10 2XZ **Tel:** 01625 426054
Email: charlotte@opusbusinessmedia.co.uk
Web site: http://www.tomorrowscleaning.com
Publisher: Opus Business Media
Frequency: Monthly
Cover Price: Free
Editor: Charlotte Taylor
Summary of Content: Magazine featuring all aspects of cleaning.
Readership/Target Audience: Aimed at those interested in cleaning and cleaning products.
BUSINESS: ARCHITECTURE & BUILDING: Cleaning & Maintenance

TOOL BUSINESS + HIRE
38098U25-500
Editorial Address: 59-61 The Broadway, HAYWARDS HEATH, RH16 3AS **Tel:** 01444 440188 **Fax:** 01444 414813
Email: info@airstream.co.uk
Advertising Address: As above.
Email: christine@airstream.co.uk
Web site: http://www.toolbusiness.co.uk
Publisher: Airstream Communications Ltd
Frequency: 10 issues yearly - Published in the 1st week of the cover month
Free to qualifying individuals
Annual Sub.: £30.00
Circulation: 6,000 (Publisher's Statement)
Usual Pagination: 32
Editor: Belinda May; **Features Editor:** Brian Hall;
Advertising Manager: Christine Williams; **Publisher:** Brian Hall
Summary of Content: Magazine covering news, products and features on portable tools.
Readership/Target Audience: Aimed at buying directors in independent tool shops, large retail outlets, hire shops, builders' merchants and distributors.
ADVERTISING RATES:
Full Page Colour £1200.00
Agency Commission: 10%
Mechanical Data: Film: Digital, Trim Size: 297 x 210mm, Bleed Size: +3mm
Copy instructions: Copy Date: 16th of the month prior to publication date
BUSINESS: HARDWARE

TOTAL HOSPITALITY
1645791U14J-554
Formerly: Front Desk
Editorial Address: Suite 4, Goldlay House, Parkway, CHELMSFORD, CM2 7PR **Tel:** 01245 292841
Fax: 01245 292858
Advertising Address: As above. **Tel:** 01245 292840
Fax: 01245 292841
Email: jason.holland@tell-itmediauk.co.uk
Web site: http://www.totalhospitalitymagazine.com
Publisher: Tell-it Media Promotions
Date Established: 2004
Frequency: Monthly
Free to qualifying individuals

Annual Sub.: £54.00
Circulation: 10,500 (Publisher's Statement)
Usual Pagination: 68
Editor: Gill Anderson
Summary of Content: Magazine covering design in the hospitality industry, including hotels, restaurants, cafes and leisure complexes.
Readership/Target Audience: Aimed at architects, designers, buyers and specifiers.
ADVERTISING RATES:
Full Page Colour £2000.00
Mechanical Data: Bleed Size: 303 x 216mm, Trim Size: 297 x 210mm, Film: Digital
BUSINESS: COMMERCE, INDUSTRY & MANAGEMENT: Commercial Design

TOTAL LICENSING
1622769U53-677
Editorial Address: 4 Wadhurst Business Park, Faircrouch Lane, WADHURST, TN5 6PT **Tel:** 01892 782220
Fax: 01892 782226
Email: francesca@totallicensing.com
Advertising Address: As above.
Email: jerry@totallicensing.com
Web site: http://www.totallicensing.com
Publisher: Total Licensing Ltd
Date Established: 2003
Frequency: Quarterly
Free to qualifying individuals
Annual Sub.: £35.00
Circulation: 30,000 (Publisher's Statement)
Usual Pagination: 126
Editor: Francesca Ash; **Advertising Director:** Jerry Wooldridge
Summary of Content: Magazine covering worldwide news and developments in brand and character licensing within the entertainment, brand, sports and film industries.
Readership/Target Audience: Aimed at retailers and manufacturers.
ADVERTISING RATES:
Full Page Mono £1175.00
Full Page Colour £1700.00
Mechanical Data: Bleed Size: 286 x 222mm, Trim Size: 280 x 216mm, Film: Digital
BUSINESS: RETAILING & WHOLESALING

TOTAL LIGHTING
1639802U17-271
Formerly: Lighting Design
Editorial Address: Suite 4, Goldlay House, Parkway, CHELMSFORD, CM2 7PR **Tel:** 01245 292840
Fax: 01245 292841
Email: lyndsey@timpuk.com
Advertising Address: As above.
Email: mark.norman@tell-itmediauk.co.uk
Web site: http://www.totallightingmagazine.com
Publisher: Tell-it Media Promotions
Date Established: 2004
Frequency: Monthly - Published in the 1st week of the cover month
Cover Price: £4.50
Free to qualifying individuals
Annual Sub.: £54.00
Circulation: 16,000 (Publisher's Statement)
Usual Pagination: 68
Editor: Lyndsey Hubbard
Summary of Content: Magazine covering all aspects of the lighting industry, including decorative and commercial lighting.
Readership/Target Audience: Aimed at lighting design manufacturers and retailers.
ADVERTISING RATES:
Full Page Colour £2000.00
Agency Commission: 10%
Mechanical Data: Bleed Size: 303 x 216mm, Trim Size: 297 x 210mm, Film: Digital
Copy instructions: Copy Date: 6 weeks prior to publication date
Average advertising content per issue: 40%
BUSINESS: ELECTRICAL

TOTAL RETAIL
1640254U53-718
Formerly: Retail Design
Editorial Address: Suite 4, Goldlay House, Parkway, CHELMSFORD, CM2 7PR **Tel:** 01245 292840
Fax: 01245 292841
Email: lyndsey@timpuk.com
Advertising Address: As above.
Email: lee.cullumbine@tell-itmediauk.co.uk
Web site: http://www.totalretailmagazine.com
Publisher: Tell-it Media Promotions
Date Established: 2004
Frequency: Monthly - Published in the 1st week of the cover month
Cover Price: £4.50
Free to qualifying individuals
Annual Sub.: £54.00
Circulation: 16,000 (Publisher's Statement)

Usual Pagination: 68
News Editor: Gill Anderson; **Features Editor:** Lyndsey Hubbard
Summary of Content: Magazine covering all aspects of the retail design industry.
Readership/Target Audience: Aimed at architects, designers, specifiers, shop fitters and manufacturers.
ADVERTISING RATES:
Full Page Mono £2000.00
Full Page Colour £2000.00
Agency Commission: 10%
Mechanical Data: Bleed Size: 303 x 216mm, Trim Size: 297 x 210mm, Film: Digital
Copy instructions: Copy Date: 15th of the month prior to publication date
Average advertising content per issue: 40%
BUSINESS: RETAILING & WHOLESALING

TOTAL SECURITIZATION
35308U1F-416
Formerly: Structured Finance International
Editorial Address: Nestor House, Playhouse Yard, LONDON, EC4V 5EX **Tel:** 020 7303 1735
Fax: 020 7779 8585
Email: cpittelli@euromoneyplc.com
Advertising Address: 225 Park Avenue South, New York, NY10003 **Tel:** 212 224 3300
Web site: http://www.totalsecuritization.com
Publisher: Euromoney Institutional Investor plc
Date Established: 1999
Frequency: Weekly
Annual Sub.: £1225.00
Usual Pagination: 64
Editor: Cristina Pittelli; **Advertising Manager:** Patricia Bertucci; **Managing Editor:** Olivia Thetgyi; **Publisher:** Elayne Glick
Summary of Content: Magazine dedicated to the business of securitization. Contains international features, profiles, news, market moves, comment and upcoming deals. Includes new technology and data on international asset backed issues.
Readership/Target Audience: Aimed at people within the securitization market.
ADVERTISING RATES:
Full Page Mono $3800.00
Full Page Colour $5000.00
Supplement(s): Asset Backed Commercial Paper Handbook - 1xY
BUSINESS: FINANCE & ECONOMICS: Investment

TOTAL TELECOM MAGAZINE
1613863U18B-1943
Editorial Address: Wren House, 43 Hatton Garden, LONDON, EC1N 8EL **Tel:** 020 7242 1548
Fax: 020 7242 4303
Email: info@totaltele.com
Advertising Address: As above.
Email: richard.silver@totaltele.com
Web site: http://www.totaltele.com
ISSN: 1740-1267
Publisher: Terrapinn Holdings Ltd.
Date Established: 2003
Frequency: 11 issues yearly - Published on the last Monday of the cover month
Free to qualifying individuals
Annual Sub.: £300.00
Circulation: 18,954 (BPA Worldwide 01/07/2007 to 31/12/2007)
Usual Pagination: 36
Editor: Anne Morris; **Advertising Manager:** Richard Silver
Summary of Content: Magazine covering telecoms business including network services and infrastructure, business and financial news, data applications, voice applications and building networks.
Readership/Target Audience: Aimed at those within the global telecoms business.
ADVERTISING RATES:
Full Page Colour £6335.00
Agency Commission: 15%
Mechanical Data: Film: Digital, Type Area: 297 x 230mm, Col Length: 297mm, Page Width: 230mm
Copy instructions: Copy Date: 4 weeks prior to publication date
Average advertising content per issue: 40%
BUSINESS: ELECTRONICS: Telecommunications

TOUCHBASE
1809419U3D-104
Editorial Address: Unit 6, Crown Yard, Bedgebury Estate, Bedgebury Road, Goudhurst, CRANBROOK, TN17 2QZ
Tel: 01580 213500 **Fax:** 01580 213600
Email: touchbase@octoberbuildingmedia.co.uk
Advertising Address: As above.
Email: touchbase@octoberbuildingmedia.co.uk
Web site: http://www.octoberbuildingmedia.co.uk
Publisher: October Building Media Ltd
Date Established: 2007

Section 4 (b) Business Magazines

Frequency: 6 issues yearly - Published on the 1st Monday of the 1st cover month
Cover Price: Free
Circulation: 27,800 (Publisher's Statement)
Usual Pagination: 64
Editor: Brett Pearson; **Advertising Manager:** Brett Pearson; **Publisher:** Brett Pearson
Summary of Content: Magazine featuring new products for heating, plumbing and bathrooms, plumbing regulations, training and business advice.
Readership/Target Audience: Aimed at plumbers and heating installers using Plumbase and Plumline plumbers' merchants.
ADVERTISING RATES:
Full Page Colour £1750.00
Agency Commission: 10%
Mechanical Data: Type Area: 277 x 190mm, Bleed Size: 303 x 216mm, Trim Size: 297 x 210mm, Col Length: 277mm, Page Width: 190mm, Film: Digital
Copy instructions: Copy Date: 2 weeks prior to publication date
BUSINESS: HEATING & VENTILATION: Heating & Plumbing

TOUCHING LIVES
40465U56L-21_50

Formerly: Research in Action
Editorial Address: Vincent House, HORSHAM, RH12 2DP
Tel: 01403 210406 **Fax:** 01403 210541
Email: editor@action.org.uk
Web site: http://www.action.org.uk
Publisher: Action Medical Research
Date Established: 1952
Frequency: 3 issues yearly - Published in March, June and November
Cover Price: Free
Circulation: 25,000 (Publisher's Statement)
Usual Pagination: 24
Editor: Karen Walker
Summary of Content: Magazine containing informative news and articles about the charity from the medical research projects it funds.
Readership/Target Audience: Circulated to the charity's supporters and researchers.
ADVERTISING: No Advertising taken
BUSINESS: HEALTH & MEDICAL: Disability & Rehabilitation

TOURISM
39738U50-24_80

Editorial Address: Trinity Court, 34 West Street, SUTTON, SM1 1SH **Tel:** 020 8661 4636 **Fax:** 020 8661 4637
Email: flo@tourismsociety.org
Advertising Address: As above.
Email: admin@tourismsociety.org
Web site: http://www.tourismsociety.org
ISSN: 0261-3700
Publisher: Tourism Society
Date Established: 1978
Frequency: Quarterly
Annual Sub.: £78.00
Circulation: 3,000 (Publisher's Statement)
Usual Pagination: 32
Editor: Flo Powell; **Advertising Manager:** Flo Powell
Summary of Content: Journal of the Tourism Society carrying news, articles and book reviews concerning the tourism industry.
Readership/Target Audience: Read by national and regional tourist boards, local government, travel agencies, visitor attractions and tourism consultants.
ADVERTISING RATES:
Full Page Colour £610.00
Mechanical Data: Film: Digital, Type Area: 277 x 188mm, Trim Size: 297 x 210, No. of Columns (Display): 2
Copy instructions: Copy Date: 3 weeks prior to publication date
Average advertising content per issue: 5%
BUSINESS: TRAVEL & TOURISM

TOURISM, TRAVEL & HOTELS
1705978U50-227

Editorial Address: Kentons House, 24 Blendon Road, BEXLEY, DA5 1BW **Tel:** 0870 701 3536
Email: tthmagazine@ntlworld.com
Advertising Address: As above.
Email: tthmagazine@ntlworld.com
Web site: http://www.directpublishing.org.uk
Publisher: Direct Publishing Ltd
Date Established: 2006
Frequency: Quarterly
Free to qualifying individuals
Circulation: 4,100 (Publisher's Statement)
Editor: Phil Brown; **Advertising Manager:** Phil Brown; **Publisher:** Phil Brown
Summary of Content: Magazine featuring products and services for the travel and tourism industry.
Readership/Target Audience: Aimed at industry professionals.
ADVERTISING RATES:
Full Page Colour £980.00
Agency Commission: 10%

Mechanical Data: Type Area: 190 x 128mm, Trim Size: 210 x 148mm, Bleed Size: 216 x 154mm, Col Length: 190mm, Page Width: 128mm, Film: Digital
BUSINESS: TRAVEL & TOURISM

TOURIST STUDIES
622669U50-25

Editorial Address: 1 Oliver's Yard, 55 City Road, LONDON, EC1Y 1SP **Tel:** 020 7324 8500 **Fax:** 020 7324 8600
Advertising Address: As above.
Email: advertising@sagepub.co.uk
Web site: http://www.sagepub.co.uk/journalsProdDesc.nav?prodId=Journal201263
ISSN: 1468-7976
Publisher: Sage Publications
Date Established: 2001
Frequency: 3 issues yearly - Published in April, August and December
Annual Sub.: £42.00
Editor: Mike Crang; **Advertising Manager:** Sheena Karim
Summary of Content: Journal providing a platform for the development of critical perspectives on the nature of tourism as a social phenomenon. The journal evaluates, compares and integrates approaches to tourism from sociology, socio-psychology, leisure studies, cultural studies, geography and anthropology.
Readership/Target Audience: Aimed at those working in the tourism industry.
ADVERTISING RATES:
Full Page Mono £350.00
Agency Commission: 5%
Mechanical Data: Type Area: 205 x 130mm, Col Length: 205mm, Page Width: 130mm, Film: Digital
Copy instructions: Copy Date: 12 weeks prior to publication date
BUSINESS: TRAVEL & TOURISM

TOWN & COUNTRY PLANNING
35872U4D-260

Formerly: T&CP Town & Country Planning
Editorial Address: 17 Carlton House Terrace, LONDON, SW1Y 5AS **Tel:** 020 7930 8903 **Fax:** 020 7930 3280
Email: editor@tcpa.org.uk
Advertising Address: As above.
Email: michael.mclean@tcpa.org.uk
Web site: http://www.tcpa.org.uk
ISSN: 0040-9960
Publisher: Town & Country Planning Association
Date Established: 1904
Frequency: 11 issues yearly
Free to qualifying individuals
Annual Sub.: £94.00
Circulation: 4,000 (Publisher's Statement)
Usual Pagination: 36
Editor: Kate Henderson; **Advertising Manager:** Michael McLean
Summary of Content: Magazine containing land use planning, regional planning, housing and town development, transport and environmental issues.
Readership/Target Audience: Read by local authorities, developers and land holders, planning consultancies and environmental charities.
ADVERTISING RATES:
Full Page Mono £325.00
Full Page Colour £425.00
Agency Commission: 10%
Mechanical Data: Col Length: 235mm, Page Width: 156mm, Trim Size: 254 x 174mm, Film: Digital, Type Area: 235 x 156mm
Average advertising content per issue: 5%
BUSINESS: ARCHITECTURE & BUILDING: Planning & Housing

TOWN HALL
38394U32A-250

Editorial Address: PO Box 2087, SHOREHAM-BY-SEA, BN43 5ZF **Tel:** 01273 273941
Email: tim@infopub.co.uk
Web site: http://www.ukauthority.com
ISSN: 1365-7186
Publisher: Informed Publications Ltd
Date Established: 1993
Frequency: 23 issues yearly
Annual Sub.: £285.00
Usual Pagination: 8
Editor: Tim Hampson; **Managing Editor:** Helen Olsen; **Publisher:** Helen Olsen
Summary of Content: Journal containing market information on technology within local government and development of e-government.
Readership/Target Audience: Aimed at senior managers in local government and consultants providing IT and communications services to local government.
ADVERTISING: No Advertising taken
BUSINESS: LOCAL GOVERNMENT, LEISURE & RECREATION: Local Government

---

TOYNEWS
39545U48A-80

Editorial Address: Saxon House, 6A St. Andrews Street, HERTFORD, SG14 1JA **Tel:** 01992 535646
Fax: 01992 535648
Email: ronnie.dungan@intentmedia.co.uk
Advertising Address: As above.
Email: adrian.miles@intentmedia.co.uk
Web site: http://www.toynewsmag.com
ISSN: 0969-0107
Publisher: Intent Media
Date Established: 2001
Frequency: Monthly - Published at the beginning of the cover month
Cover Price: £3.95
Annual Sub.: £50.00
Circulation: 6,011 (ABC 01/07/2008 to 30/06/2009)
Usual Pagination: 72
Editor: Ronnie Dungan; **Managing Director:** Stuart Dinsey; **Advertising Manager:** Adrian Miles; **Managing Editor:** Lisa Foster; **Publisher:** Stuart Dinsey
Summary of Content: Journal covering all aspects of the toy trade.
Readership/Target Audience: Read by members of the British Association of Toy Retailers, other independent toy retailers, wholesalers, multiple retailers and chains.
ADVERTISING RATES:
Full Page Colour £1155.00
Agency Commission: 10%
Mechanical Data: Type Area: 291 x 206mm, Bleed Size: 321 x 236mm, Trim Size: 315 x 230mm, Col Length: 291mm, Page Width: 206mm, Film: Digital
Average advertising content per issue: 60%
BUSINESS: TOY TRADE & SPORTS GOODS: Toy Trade

TOYS 'N' PLAYTHINGS
39544U48A-85

Editorial Address: 1 Churchgates, The Wilderness, BERKHAMSTED, HP4 2UB **Tel:** 01442 289930
Fax: 01442 289950
Email: andy@lemapublishing.co.uk
Advertising Address: As above.
Email: rob@lemapublishing.co.uk
Web site: http://www.toysnplaythings.co.uk
Publisher: Lema Publishing
Date Established: 1981
Frequency: Monthly
Free to qualifying individuals
Annual Sub.: £60.00
Circulation: 5,125 (ABC 01/07/2008 to 30/06/2009)
Usual Pagination: 100
Editor: Andy Myall; **Publisher:** Malcolm Naish
Summary of Content: Journal containing news and information on the toy trade.
Readership/Target Audience: Read by manufacturers, buyers, designers and retailers within the toy trade.
ADVERTISING RATES:
Full Page Colour £1695.00
Agency Commission: 10%
Mechanical Data: Type Area: 300 x 225mm, Col Length: 300mm, Trim Size: 315 x 240mm, Bleed Size: 321 x 246mm, Page Width: 225mm, Film: Digital
Average advertising content per issue: 45%
BUSINESS: TOY TRADE & SPORTS GOODS: Toy Trade

TPR TOWN PLANNING REVIEW
35873U4D-264

Editorial Address: 74 Bedford Street South, Dept. Of Civic Design, University of Liverpool, LIVERPOOL, L69 7ZQ
Tel: 0151 794 3118 **Fax:** 0151 794 3125
Email: sandrob@liverpool.ac.uk
Advertising Address: 4 Cambridge Street, LIVERPOOL, L69 7ZU **Tel:** 0151 794 2233 **Fax:** 0151 794 2235
Email: sbell@liv.ac.uk
Web site: http://www.liverpool-unipress.co.uk/town
ISSN: 0041-0020
Publisher: Liverpool University Press
Date Established: 1910
Frequency: 6 issues yearly
Annual Sub.: £98.00
Circulation: 900 (Publisher's Statement)
Usual Pagination: 120
Editor: Sandra Robinson; **Publisher:** Anthony Cord
Summary of Content: Academic journal that covers all aspects of town and regional planning and development. Provides a forum for communication between planners, teachers and students.
Readership/Target Audience: Read by academics, planning practitioners, policy-makers and students.
ADVERTISING RATES:
Full Page Mono £250.00
Agency Commission: 5%
BUSINESS: ARCHITECTURE & BUILDING: Planning & Housing

TRACTOR & FARM TRADER
1810688U21E-875

Editorial Address: 5 New Smithy Avenue, Thurlstone, SHEFFIELD, S36 9QZ **Tel:** 07773 785525
Email: peterffa@dsl.pipex.com

Business Magazines

Advertising Address: Cudham Tithe Barn, Berrys Hill, Berrys Green, Cudham, WESTERHAM, TN16 3AG
Tel: 01959 541444 **Fax:** 01959 543585
Email: nickbond@kelsey.co.uk
ISSN: 1746-0034
Publisher: Kelsey Publishing Ltd
Date Established: 2006
Frequency: 26 issues yearly
Cover Price: £2.10
Circulation: 12,980 (Publisher's Statement)
Usual Pagination: 132
Editor: Peter Simpson; **Managing Editor:** Peter Simpson
Summary of Content: Magazine featuring agricultural technical articles, mechanical reviews, workshop news and information about biofuel developments; focuses on tractors and farm machinery less than 10 years old.
Readership/Target Audience: Aimed at farmers, contractors and dealers.
ADVERTISING RATES:
Full Page Colour £900.00
Mechanical Data: Type Area: 272 x 188mm, Bleed Size: 303 x 216mm, Trim Size: 297 x 210mm, Col Length: 272mm, Page Width: 188mm, Film: Digital
Average advertising content per issue: 75%
BUSINESS: AGRICULTURE & FARMING: Agriculture - Machinery & Plant

TRADE FINANCE
34969U1A-276_65

Editorial Address: Nestor House, Playhouse Yard, LONDON, EC4V 5EX **Tel:** 020 7779 8348
Fax: 020 7779 7977
Email: dharris@euromoneyplc.com
Advertising Address: As above. **Tel:** 020 7779 8099
Fax: 020 7779 8846
Email: dkloiber@euromoneyplc.com
Web site: http://www.tradefinancemagazine.com
ISSN: 1464-8873
Publisher: Euromoney Institutional Investor plc
Date Established: 1998
Frequency: 10 issues yearly - Combined issues December/January and July/August
Annual Sub.: £495.00
Circulation: 5,000 (Publisher's Statement)
Usual Pagination: 48
Editor: Oliver O'Connell; **Managing Editor:** Jonathan Bell; **Publisher:** Gary Parker
Summary of Content: Magazine reporting on international trade, commodity financing, trade services and supply chain, emerging and export finance markets. Covers new financial services and products, major deals and changes in market conditions.
Readership/Target Audience: Aimed at corporate exporters, heads of trade and commodity, finance, supply chain finance, trade services and logistics providers, finance workers in banks, export credit agencies, as well as other service providers such as lawyers, insurers, risk managers and trade officials.
ADVERTISING RATES:
Full Page Mono £7000.00
Full Page Colour £8200.00
Agency Commission: 15%
Mechanical Data: Type Area: 271 x 184mm, Trim Size: 297 x 210mm, Film: Digital, Col Length: 271mm, Page Width: 184mm, Bleed Size: 307 x 220mm, Print Process: Litho
Copy instructions: Copy Date: 1st week of the month prior to publication date
Average advertising content per issue: 25%
Supplement(s): Central and Eastern European Trade Finance - 1xY, Commodities - 1xY, Latin American Trade Finance - 1xY, North American Trade Finance - 1xY, Russian and CIS Trade Finance - 1xY, Structured Commodity Finance - 1xY, Trade Finance Handbook - 1xY, Trade Services - 1xY, World Export Credit Guide - 1xY
BUSINESS: FINANCE & ECONOMICS

TRADE SUPPLIERS DIRECTORY
755897U48B-20

Formerly: British Trade Suppliers Directory
Editorial Address: Stockeld Park, WETHERBY, LS22 4AW
Tel: 01937 582111 **Fax:** 01937 582778
Email: clairet@beta-int.com
Advertising Address: As above.
Email: sales@equestriantradenews.com
Publisher: Equestrian Management Consultants Ltd
Frequency: Annual
Annual Sub.: £16.00
Circulation: 4,000 (Publisher's Statement)
Usual Pagination: 90
Editor: Claire Thomas; **Advertising Manager:** Jennifer Dalton
Summary of Content: Directory containing an A-Z of equestrian suppliers, equipment and facilities including abbatoirs, livery and consumer goods.
Readership/Target Audience: Aimed at companies who supply the retail trade.
ADVERTISING RATES:
Full Page Mono £995.00
Full Page Colour £1360.00

Mechanical Data: Type Area: 272 x 186mm, Col Length: 272mm, Page Height: 186mm, Bleed Size: 303 x 216mm, Trim Size: 297 x 210mm, Film: Digital
Copy instructions: Copy Date: May
BUSINESS: TOY TRADE & SPORTS GOODS: Sports Goods

THE TRADER
23884U47A-379

Editorial Address: 6th Floor, Davis House, 2 Robert Street, CROYDON, CR0 1QQ **Tel:** 0870 253 4600
Email: info@thetrader.co.uk
Advertising Address: As above. **Tel:** 020 8253 8600
Fax: 020 8253 8380
Email: wayne.boys@metropolis.co.uk
Web site: http://www.thetrader.co.uk
Publisher: Metropolis International (UK) Limited
Date Established: 1935
Frequency: Monthly
Cover Price: £3.30
Annual Sub.: £30.00
Circulation: 50,469 (VFD 01/01/2007 to 01/07/2007)
Usual Pagination: 300
Summary of Content: Publication containing advertising of stock items for sale.
Readership/Target Audience: Aimed at shopkeepers, market traders, party planners and wholesalers.
ADVERTISING RATES:
Full Page Mono £645.00
Full Page Colour £1119.00
Agency Commission: 10%
Mechanical Data: Trim Size: 275 x 180mm, Bleed Size: 281 x 186mm, Film: Digital
Copy instructions: Copy Date: 2 weeks prior to publication date
Average advertising content per issue: 100%
BUSINESS: CLOTHING & TEXTILES

TRADER MONTHLY MAGAZINE
1694982U1G-103

Formerly: Trader Monthly
Editorial Address: 90 Long Acre, LONDON, WC2E 9PR
Tel: 020 7842 9600
Email: rlane@tradermonthly.com
Advertising Address: As above. **Fax:** 020 7842 9642
Email: christian.price@dowjones.com
Web site: http://www.traderdaily.co.uk
Publisher: Dow Jones International, Ltd.
Date Established: 2005
Frequency: 6 issues yearly
Cover Price: £6.00
Free to qualifying individuals
Circulation: 52,000 (Publisher's Statement)
Usual Pagination: 96
Editor: Randall Lane; **Advertising Director:** Christian Price
Summary of Content: Magazine focusing on the trading lifestyle including news, strategies and profiles of successful traders from around the globe.
Readership/Target Audience: Aimed at the stock trading and hedge fund community.
ADVERTISING RATES:
Full Page Colour £9500.00
Agency Commission: 15%
Copy instructions: Copy Date: 3 weeks prior to publication date
Average advertising content per issue: 30%
BUSINESS: FINANCE & ECONOMICS: Credit Trading

TRADEWINDS
39357U45A-240

Editorial Address: International Press Centre, 4th Floor, 76 Shoe Lane, LONDON, EC4A 3JB **Tel:** 020 7842 2720
Fax: 020 7842 2725
Email: letters@tradewinds.no
Advertising Address: As above. **Tel:** 020 7842 2700
Fax: 020 7842 2705
Email: sales@tradewinds.no
Web site: http://www.tradewinds.no
Publisher: TradeWinds A/S
Date Established: 1990
Frequency: Weekly
Annual Sub.: £725.00
Circulation: 8,484 (ABC 01/01/2008 to 31/12/2008)
Usual Pagination: 40
Editor: John Landells; **News Editor:** John Landells; **Executive Editor:** Julian Bray
Summary of Content: Newspaper covering shipping industry news and reports.
Readership/Target Audience: Read by people working in all areas of the shipping industry.
ADVERTISING RATES:
Full Page Mono £5625.00
Full Page Colour £9075.00
SCC £34.00
Agency Commission: 15%
Mechanical Data: Film: Positive, right reading, emulsion side down, Col Length: 365mm, Col Widths (Single): 46mm, Print Process: Offset, Screen: 34 lpc, Type Area: 365 x 246mm, No. of Columns (Display): 5, Page Width: 246mm

Copy instructions: Copy Date: 1 week prior to publication date
Average advertising content per issue: 15%
BUSINESS: MARINE & SHIPPING

TRADEX NEWS
1898644U63-3

Editorial Address: Suite 4.4b, 4th Floor, Maybrook House, HALESOWEN, B63 4AH **Tel:** 0121 550 5445
Fax: 0121 550 4612
Email: tradexnews@btconnect.com
Web site: http://www.tradexnews.co.uk
Publisher: Business and Industry Today Ltd
Date Established: 2009
Frequency: Monthly
Free to qualifying individuals
Annual Sub.: £100
Circulation: 5,000 (Publisher's Statement)
Usual Pagination: 32
Editor: Chris Hackett
Summary of Content: Magazine targeting industrial sectors of UK manufacturing and engineering. Key focus includes new products, contract news, product development and exhibition reviews and previews. Other features include selected interview style case studies.
Readership/Target Audience: Aimed at company directors, senior managers and facilities managers within industrial companies.
BUSINESS: REGIONAL BUSINESS

TRADING PLACES
1706841U1R-374

Editorial Address: 2A Raffin Park, Datchworth, KNEBWORTH, SG3 6RR **Tel:** 01438 817018
Fax: 01438 817656
Email: herbie.skeete@exchange-handbook.co.uk
Advertising Address: 3rd Floor, Kinetic House, 44 Hatton Garden, LONDON, EC1N 8ER **Tel:** 020 7404 1940
Fax: 020 7404 1942
Email: michael.bulmer@exchange-handbook.co.uk
Web site: http://www.exchange-handbook.co.uk
ISSN: 1748-5339
Publisher: Mondo Visione Ltd
Date Established: 2005
Frequency: 11 issues yearly - Not published in December
Annual Sub.: £250.00
Circulation: 1,100 (Publisher's Statement)
Editor: Herbie Skeete
Summary of Content: Magazine covering news and comment about exchanges and trading venues worldwide.
Readership/Target Audience: Aimed at exchanges, investment banks, private equity houses, law firms, financial PR companies, information vendors, consultancies, central banks and regulators.
ADVERTISING: Rates on application
BUSINESS: FINANCE & ECONOMICS: Financial Related

TRAFFIC TECHNOLOGY INTERNATIONAL
39586U49A-196

Editorial Address: Abinger House, Church Street, DORKING, RH4 1DF **Tel:** 01306 743744 **Fax:** 01306 887546
Email: traffic@ukipme.com
Advertising Address: As above. **Fax:** 01306 742525
Email: m.robinson@ukintpress.com
Web site: http://www.ukipme.com
ISSN: 1356-9252
Publisher: UKIP Media & Events Ltd
Date Established: 1994
Frequency: 6 issues yearly - Published in the 1st week of the 1st cover month
Free to qualifying individuals
Annual Sub.: £200.00
Circulation: 18,018 (ABC 01/01/2008 to 31/12/2008)
Usual Pagination: 104
Editor: Nick Bradley; **Managing Director:** Graham Johnson; **Advertising Manager:** Mike Robinson
Summary of Content: Magazine focusing on advanced traffic management and control, ITS and traffic technologies around the world.
Readership/Target Audience: Aimed at traffic control managers and decision makers.
ADVERTISING RATES:
Full Page Colour £4250.00
Agency Commission: 10%
Mechanical Data: Film: Digital, Trim Size: 297 x 210mm, Type Area: 270 x 180mm, Col Length: 270mm, No. of Columns (Display): 4, Page Width: 180mm
Copy instructions: Copy Date: 4 weeks prior to publication date
Average advertising content per issue: 35%
Supplement(s): Tolltrans - 1xY, Traffic Technology International Annual Review - 1xY
BUSINESS: TRANSPORT

TRAINING & COACHING TODAY

1739390U14F-256

Editorial Address: Quadrant House, The Quadrant, SUTTON, SM2 5AS **Tel:** 020 8652 3500 **Fax:** 020 8652 8805
Email: training.editor@rbi.co.uk
Advertising Address: As above. **Fax:** 020 8652 8923
Email: mark.pickup@rbi.co.uk
Publisher: Reed Business Information
Date Established: 2006
Frequency: 10 issues yearly - Published in the 3rd week of the cover month. Combined issues 3rd week of the 1st cover month
Free to qualifying individuals
Circulation: 13,500 (Publisher's Statement)
Editor: John Charlton; **Advertising Manager:** Mark Pickup
Summary of Content: Magazine covering news and features for in-company training departments.
Readership/Target Audience: Aimed at HR and training managers.
ADVERTISING RATES:
Full Page Mono £2137.00
Full Page Colour £2786.00
Agency Commission: 10%
Mechanical Data: Type Area: 245 x 179mm, Bleed Size: 303 x 273mm, Trim Size: 267 x 197mm, Col Length: 245mm, Page Width: 179mm, Film: Digital
Copy instructions: Copy Date: 2 weeks prior to publication date
Average advertising content per issue: 40%
BUSINESS: COMMERCE, INDUSTRY & MANAGEMENT: Training & Recruitment

TRAINING & MANAGEMENT DEVELOPMENT METHODS

37087U14F-91

Editorial Address: European Briefing Unit, University of Bradford, BRADFORD, BD7 1DP **Tel:** 01274 777700
Fax: 01274 785200
Email: david.pollitt@talktalk.net
Web site: http://www.emeraldinsight.com
ISSN: 0951-3507
Publisher: Emerald Group Publishing Ltd
Frequency: 5 issues yearly
Annual Sub.: £5969.00
Usual Pagination: 64
Editor: David Pollitt; **Publisher:** Nancy Rolph
Summary of Content: Magazine giving practical guidelines on key training and development methods in management.
Readership/Target Audience: Read by training and management development personnel.
ADVERTISING: No Advertising taken
BUSINESS: COMMERCE, INDUSTRY & MANAGEMENT: Training & Recruitment

TRAMWAYS & URBAN TRANSIT

39692U49E-250

Editorial Address: Elm House, 14 Green End Road, Sawtry, HUNTINGDON, PE28 5UX **Tel:** 01487 834000
Fax: 01487 832001
Email: hj@howardjohnston.co.uk
Advertising Address: PO Box 26, Sawtry, HUNTINGDON, PE28 5WY **Tel:** 01487 830001 **Fax:** 01487 832001
Email: sue.graves@lrtap.com
Web site: http://www.tramnews.net
ISSN: 0964-9255
Publisher: LRTA Publishing
Date Established: 1938
Frequency: Monthly - Published on the last Friday of the month prior to publication date
Cover Price: £2.95
Circulation: 7,500 (Publisher's Statement)
Usual Pagination: 40
Editor: Howard Johnston; **News Editor:** John Symons; **Editor-in-Chief:** Howard Johnston; **Managing Director:** Howard Johnston; **Advertising Manager:** Vicki Binley
Summary of Content: Journal of the Light Rail Transit Association, containing news and information about urban rail transport worldwide.
Readership/Target Audience: Aimed at urban transit manufacturers and decision makers in transport planning offices and supply industries. Also read by transport enthusiasts.
ADVERTISING RATES:
Full Page Mono £815.00
Full Page Colour £1210.00
Agency Commission: 10%
Mechanical Data: Type Area: 272 x 186mm, Col Length: 272mm, Trim Size: 297 x 210mm, Bleed Size: 303 x 216mm, Page Width: 186mm, Film: Digital
BUSINESS: TRANSPORT: Railways

TRANSACTIONS OF THE INSTITUTE OF METAL FINISHING

37631U19C-700

Editorial Address: Exeter House, 48 Holloway Head, BIRMINGHAM, B1 1NQ **Tel:** 0121 622 7387
Fax: 0121 666 6316
Email: exeterhouse@instituteofmetalfinishing.org

Advertising Address: As above.
Email: exeterhouse@instituteofmetalfinishing.org
Web site: http://www.maney.co.uk/journals/imf
ISSN: 0020-2967
Publisher: Maney Publishing
Frequency: 6 issues yearly
Cover Price: £54.00
Annual Sub.: £283.00
Circulation: 1,500 (Publisher's Statement)
Usual Pagination: 64
Editor: Gavin Larson; **Executive Editor:** Gavin Larson; **Advertising Manager:** Ken Hoare
Summary of Content: Official journal of the Institute of Metal Finishing, focusing on all aspects of surface finishing and surface engineering, covering the science and technology, properties of treated components, test methods, quality control and environmental issues relating to surface treatment.
Readership/Target Audience: Read by members of the Institute, corporate libraries and companies involved in metal finishing.
ADVERTISING: Rates on application
BUSINESS: ENGINEERING & MACHINERY: Finishing

TRANSCULTURAL PSYCHIATRY

40597U56R-255

Editorial Address: 1 Oliver's Yard, 55 City Road, LONDON, EC1Y 1SP **Tel:** 020 7324 8500 **Fax:** 020 7324 8600
Email: transcultural.psychiatry@mcgill.ca
Advertising Address: As above.
Email: advertising@sagepub.co.uk
Web site: http://www.sagepub.co.uk
ISSN: 1363-4615
Publisher: Sage Publications
Date Established: 1997
Frequency: Quarterly
Cover Price: £16.00
Annual Sub.: £48.00
Editor: Laurence Kirmayer; **Editor-in-Chief:** Laurence Kirmayer; **Advertising Manager:** Sheena Karim
Summary of Content: Journal containing research about the social and cultural determinants of psychopathology and psychosocial treatments of mental and behavioural problems in individuals, families and human groups.
Readership/Target Audience: Aimed at psychiatrists, mental health professionals and social scientists.
ADVERTISING RATES:
Full Page Mono £400.00
Agency Commission: 5%
Mechanical Data: Col Length: 205mm, Type Area: 205 x 130mm, Page Width: 130mm, Film: Digital
BUSINESS: HEALTH & MEDICAL: Health Medical Related

TRANSMIT

36385U6B-350

Editorial Address: 4 St. Marys Road, Bingham, NOTTINGHAM, NG13 8DW **Tel:** 01425 674516
Email: transmit@gatco.org
Web site: http://www.gatco.org
Publisher: Guild of Air Traffic Control Officers
Date Established: 1954
Frequency: Half-yearly - Published in December and June
Free to qualifying individuals
Annual Sub.: £20.00
Circulation: 2,500 (Publisher's Statement)
Usual Pagination: 36
Editor: John Freeman
Summary of Content: Magazine of the Guild of Air Traffic Control Officers. Covers industry news, regional airfield news and updates in the satellite and aviation industry.
Readership/Target Audience: Read by members, company personnel, government departments and aviation authorities. Also training establishments and airlines dealing with air traffic control and managers within the field.
ADVERTISING: No Advertising taken
BUSINESS: AVIATION & AERONAUTICS: Airports

TRANSPORT BUSINESS INTERNATIONAL

1837338U10-224

Formerly: Transport Business
Editorial Address: 226 High Road, LOUGHTON, IG10 1ET
Tel: 020 8532 0055 **Fax:** 020 8532 0066
Email: editor@psp-media.co.uk
Web site: http://www.transportbusiness.net
Publisher: Public Sector Publishing Ltd
Date Established: 2008
Frequency: 6 issues yearly
Cover Price: Free
Circulation: 5,700 (Publisher's Statement)
Editor: Sofie Lidefjard; **Publisher:** Martin Freedman
Summary of Content: Magazine featuring comment, analysis and views of the experts in the transport and logistics industry.
Readership/Target Audience: Aimed at senior transport managers working in both the private and public sectors.

Supplement to: GreenFleet
BUSINESS: MATERIALS HANDLING

TRANSPORT DISTRIBUTION EUROPE

1866750U49A-424

Editorial Address: The Anderson Centre, Unit D (A), Spitfire Close, Ermine Business Park, HUNTINGDON, PE29 6XY
Tel: 01480 455660 **Fax:** 01480 455661
Email: david@transportmag.org
Advertising Address: As above.
Email: mike@logisticsbusiness.com
Web site: http://www.transportmag.org
Publisher: Logistics Business Publishing Ltd
Date Established: 2008
Frequency: Quarterly
Cover Price: Free
Circulation: 10,000 (Print Run)
Editor: David Priestman
Summary of Content: Magazine covering finished products and components. Featuring products and services, technology and applications.
Readership/Target Audience: Aimed at the European road transport market including fleet managers, road hauliers and transport managers.
ADVERTISING RATES:
Full Page Mono £2600.00
Full Page Colour £3275.00
Mechanical Data: Bleed Size: 430 x 302mm, Trim Size: 420 x 297mm, Film: Digital
BUSINESS: TRANSPORT

TRANSPORT ENGINEER

39588U49A-240

Editorial Address: 1 Bankside, Churt Road, HINDHEAD, GU26 6NR **Tel:** 01428 605605 **Fax:** 01428 714278
Email: transeng@aztecxpress.com
Advertising Address: As above.
Email: ads@aztecxpress.com
Web site: http://www.aztec-media.co.uk
ISSN: 0020-3122
Publisher: Aztec Media Services Ltd
Date Established: 1944
Frequency: Monthly - Published in the 1st full week of the cover month
Cover Price: £5.00
Free to qualifying individuals
Annual Sub.: £60.00
Circulation: 11,212 (ABC 01/01/2008 to 31/12/2008)
Usual Pagination: 40
Editor: Tim Blakemore; **Advertising Manager:** Debbie Trout
Summary of Content: Magazine covering all aspects of news relevant to transport engineering, including products, training and technology.
Readership/Target Audience: Aimed at those who specify and maintain fleets of trucks, buses, vans and cars.
ADVERTISING RATES:
Full Page Mono £1258.00
Full Page Colour £2310.00
SCC £25.00
Agency Commission: 10%
Mechanical Data: Type Area: 263 x 186mm, Col Length: 263mm, Film: Digital, Bleed Size: 305 x 218mm, Trim Size: 297 x 210mm, Page Width: 186mm
Copy instructions: Copy Date: 1 week prior to publication date
Average advertising content per issue: 40%
BUSINESS: TRANSPORT

TRANSPORT JOURNAL

39589U49A-245

Editorial Address: Unit 64, 14-20 George Street, BIRMINGHAM, B12 9RG **Tel:** 0121 440 3003
Fax: 0121 440 4644
Email: editorial@itmworld.com
Advertising Address: As above.
Email: info@itmworld.com
Web site: http://www.itmworld.com
Publisher: Transport Journal
Date Established: 1942
Frequency: Quarterly
Free to qualifying individuals
Annual Sub.: £100.00
Circulation: 17,500 (Publisher's Statement)
Usual Pagination: 68
Editor: Catriona Gavin; **Advertising Manager:** Patrick Sheedy
Summary of Content: Journal of the Institute of Transport Management, containing news and information on transport management and government legislation.
Readership/Target Audience: Aimed at transport managers, fleet owners, communications specialists, transport associations and equipment manufacturers.
ADVERTISING RATES:
Full Page Colour £5000.00
Agency Commission: 10%
Mechanical Data: Type Area: 275 x 182mm, Col Length: 275mm, Trim Size: 297 x 210mm, Bleed Size: 303 x 216mm, Page Width: 182mm, Film: Digital

Copy instructions: Copy Date: 2 weeks prior to publication date
Average advertising content per issue: 40%
BUSINESS: TRANSPORT

TRANSPORT MANAGEMENT   39590U49A-250

Editorial Address: The Old Studio, 25 Greenfield Road, Westoning, BEDFORD, MK45 5JD **Tel:** 01525 634940
Fax: 01525 750016
Email: director@iota.org.uk
Advertising Address: As above.
Email: director@iota.org.uk
Web site: http://www.iota.org.uk
Publisher: Institute of Transport Administration
Date Established: 1944
Frequency: Quarterly
Free to qualifying individuals
Annual Sub.: £30.00
Circulation: 2,700 (Publisher's Statement)
Usual Pagination: 32
Editor: David Dalglish; **Advertising Manager:** David Dalglish
Summary of Content: Official newsletter of the Institute of Transport Administration. Contains information on activities within the institute and features on general transport issues.
Readership/Target Audience: Aimed at professional managers and supervisors within the transport and distribution industry.
ADVERTISING RATES:
Full Page Mono £250.00
Full Page Colour £290.00
Official Journal of: The Institute of Transport Administration
BUSINESS: TRANSPORT

TRANSPORT MANAGER'S & OPERATOR'S HANDBOOK   39602U49A-260

Editorial Address: 120 Pentonville Road, LONDON, N1 9JN
Tel: 020 7278 0433 **Fax:** 020 7837 6348
Email: hberry@koganpage.com
Advertising Address: Petersham Publishing, Petersham House, 57A Hatton Garden, LONDON, EC1N 8JD
Tel: 020 7831 1131 **Fax:** 020 7242 0832
Email: simon@petershampublishing.co.uk
Web site: http://www.koganpage.com
Publisher: Kogan Page Ltd
Date Established: 1969
Frequency: Annual - Published in December
Cover Price: £52.00
Usual Pagination: 760
Editor: Martha Fumagalli
Summary of Content: Guide to legislation, European Union law, vehicle exhaust emission standards and operational advice to road transport.
Readership/Target Audience: Aimed at road transport hauliers and transport managers.
ADVERTISING RATES:
Full Page Mono £3250.00
Full Page Colour £4950.00
Agency Commission: 10%
Mechanical Data: Trim Size: 240 x 170mm, Film: Digital
Copy instructions: Copy Date: 2 months prior to publication
Average advertising content per issue: 10%
BUSINESS: TRANSPORT

TRANSPORT NEWS   39664U49D-130

Editorial Address: Wheatsheaf House, Montgomery Street, The Village, East Kilbride, GLASGOW, G74 4JS
Tel: 01355 279077 **Fax:** 01355 279088
Email: info@transportnews.co.uk
Advertising Address: As above.
Email: info@transportnews.co.uk
Web site: http://www.transportnews.co.uk
ISSN: 0969-1022
Publisher: KAV Publicity Ltd
Date Established: 1978
Frequency: Monthly
Cover Price: £1.80
Annual Sub.: £18.00
Circulation: 9,500 (Publisher's Statement)
Usual Pagination: 64
Editor: Alistair Vallance; **Features Editor:** John Henderson;
Advertising Manager: Alistair Vallance; **Publisher:** Alistair Vallance
Summary of Content: Magazine covering all aspects of the road haulage industry and commercial vehicles.
Readership/Target Audience: Read by owner operators, drivers and commercial vehicle buyers in road haulage firms and the major Scottish and North of England companies.
ADVERTISING RATES:
Full Page Mono £675.00
Full Page Colour £990.00
SCC £8.00
Agency Commission: 10%
Mechanical Data: Type Area: 275 x 183mm, Bleed Size: 305 x 215mm, Trim Size: 297 x 210mm, Print Process: Web-fed offset litho, Film: Digital, Col Length: 275mm, Col Widths

(Display): 42mm, Page Width: 183mm, No. of Columns (Display): 4
Average advertising content per issue: 40%
BUSINESS: TRANSPORT: Commercial Vehicles

TRANSPORT NEWS DIGEST   39591U49A-280

Editorial Address: 38 Portobello Road, LONDON, W11 3DH
Tel: 020 7727 0253 **Fax:** 020 7229 5909
Email: jds@transportpressservices.com
ISSN: 0306-2252
Publisher: Transport Press Services
Date Established: 1968
Frequency: Monthly
Annual Sub.: £28.00
Circulation: 300 (Publisher's Statement)
Usual Pagination: 4
Editor: John Dickson-Simpson; **Publisher:** John Dickson-Simpson
Summary of Content: Digest covering the latest news in the road freight transport industry.
Readership/Target Audience: Read by top executives.
ADVERTISING: No Advertising taken
BUSINESS: TRANSPORT

TRANSPORT TIMES   1694990U49A-409

Editorial Address: Suite 21, Grosvenor Gardens House, 35-37 Grosvenor Gardens, LONDON, SW1W 0BS
Tel: 020 7828 3804 **Fax:** 020 7828 3803
Email: editorial@transporttimes.co.uk
Advertising Address: Cabbell Publishing, Woodman Works, 204 Durnsford Road, LONDON, SW19 8DR
Tel: 020 8971 8450 **Fax:** 020 8971 8480
Email: michael@cabbell.co.uk
Web site: http://www.transporttimes.co.uk
Publisher: Transport Times Ltd
Date Established: 2005
Frequency: Monthly
Free to qualifying individuals
Annual Sub.: £75.00
Circulation: 1,000 (Publisher's Statement)
Usual Pagination: 48
Editor: David Fowler; **Advertising Manager:** Michael Delaney; **Publisher:** David Begg
Summary of Content: Magazine covering surface public transport, focusing on policy, strategy and sustainable transport.
Readership/Target Audience: Aimed at industry professionals, politicians, academics and civil servants in the public transport world.
ADVERTISING RATES:
Full Page Colour £3500.00
Agency Commission: 10%
Mechanical Data: Type Area: 284 x 216mm, Bleed Size: 306 x 236mm, Trim Size: 300 x 230mm, Col Length: 284mm, Page Width: 216mm
BUSINESS: TRANSPORT

TRANSPORTATION PROFESSIONAL   39047U42B-10

Formerly: H & T
Editorial Address: Linden House, Linden Close, TUNBRIDGE WELLS, TN4 8HH **Tel:** 01892 524468
Fax: 01892 524456
Email: mike@transportation-mag.com
Advertising Address: As above.
Email: sally@transportation-mag.com
Web site: http://www.iht.org
ISSN: 1478-4467
Publisher: Barrett, Byrd Associates
Date Established: 2002
Frequency: 10 issues yearly
Free to qualifying individuals
Annual Sub.: £64.00
Circulation: 10,906 (ABC 01/07/2008 to 30/06/2009)
Usual Pagination: 36
Editor: Mike Walter; **News Editor:** Mike Walter; **Features Editor:** Jon Masters
Summary of Content: Journal of the Institution of Highways and Transportation containing features, news, product and services update and a classified section.
Readership/Target Audience: Aimed at highway engineers and planners, railway engineers, public transport planners, consultants, county surveyors, central government, safety officers, local authorities and maintenance contractors.
ADVERTISING RATES:
Full Page Mono £1600.00
Full Page Colour £1600.00
Agency Commission: 10%
Mechanical Data: Type Area: 260 x 177mm, Film: Digital, Col Length: 260mm, Trim Size: 297 x 210mm, Page Width: 177mm
Copy instructions: Copy Date: 2 weeks prior to publication date
Average advertising content per issue: 30%
Supplement(s): Transportation Consultants Directory - 1xY
BUSINESS: CONSTRUCTION: Roads

TRAUMA   40231U56A-147

Editorial Address: 1 Oliver's Yard, 55 City Road, LONDON, EC1Y 1SP **Tel:** 020 7324 8500 **Fax:** 020 7324 8600
Email: market@sagepub.co.uk
Advertising Address: As above.
Email: sheena.karim@sagepub.co.uk
Web site: http://www.sagepub.co.uk
ISSN: 1460-4086
Publisher: Sage Publications
Date Established: 1999
Frequency: Quarterly
Annual Sub.: £260.00
Usual Pagination: 96
Editor: Ian Greaves
Summary of Content: Journal reviewing all aspects of trauma care, from prevention through to rehabilitation.
Readership/Target Audience: Aimed at those involved in the management of trauma patients.
ADVERTISING RATES:
Full Page Mono £450.00
Agency Commission: 10%
Mechanical Data: Bleed Size: +4mm, Film: Digital, Screen:, Print Process: Sheet-fed litho, Type Area: 215 x 160mm, Trim Size: 246 x 189mm, Page Width: 160mm, Col Length: 215mm
Copy instructions: Copy Date: 12 weeks prior to publication date
Average advertising content per issue: 2%
BUSINESS: HEALTH & MEDICAL

TRAVEL AGENTS NEWS   758685U50-27_50

Editorial Address: 14 Chapel Lane, WILMSLOW, SK9 5HX
Tel: 01625 530580 **Fax:** 01625 535225
Email: editorial@travelagentsnews.co.uk
Web site: http://www.travelagentsnews.co.uk
Publisher: Travel Agents News
Date Established: 2001
Frequency: Monthly
Cover Price: Free
Circulation: 6,000 (Publisher's Statement)
Usual Pagination: 16
Editor: Mike Kiddey
Summary of Content: Magazine covering travel related news in the UK and abroad including industry profiles, new airlines, destinations, airports, shipping, cruising and rail.
Readership/Target Audience: Aimed at travel agents and those who sell holidays including call centres, travel hypermarkets and home workers.
ADVERTISING: No Advertising taken
BUSINESS: TRAVEL & TOURISM

TRAVEL BULLETIN   39741U50-33

Editorial Address: University House, 11-13 Lower Grosvenor Place, LONDON, SW1W 0EX **Tel:** 020 7834 6661
Fax: 020 7834 7519
Email: jill.sayles@travelbulletin.co.uk
Advertising Address: As above. **Tel:** 020 7834 7676
Email: tim@travelbulletin.co.uk
Web site: http://www.travelbulletin.co.uk
ISSN: 0956-2419
Publisher: Alain Charles Publishing (Travel) Ltd
Date Established: 1975
Frequency: Weekly
Free to qualifying individuals
Annual Sub.: £75.00
Circulation: 8,291 (ABC 01/07/2008 to 30/06/2009)
Usual Pagination: 32
Editor: Lauretta Wright; **Managing Director:** Derek Fordham; **Publisher:** Jeanette Ratcliffe
Summary of Content: Magazine focusing on travel and product news and information including late availability.
Readership/Target Audience: Aimed at travel agents.
ADVERTISING RATES:
Full Page Mono £2080.00
Full Page Colour £2900.00
Agency Commission: 10%
Mechanical Data: Film: Digital, Type Area: 275 x 180mm, Col Length: 275mm, Page Width: 180mm, Bleed Size: 303 x 216mm, Print Process: Web-fed offset litho, Col Widths (Display): 44mm, No. of Columns (Display): 4
Copy instructions: Copy Date: 1 week prior to publication date
Average advertising content per issue: 40%
BUSINESS: TRAVEL & TOURISM

TRAVEL DAILY   1793969U50-231

Editorial Address: PR by email only **Tel:** 0845 686 1220
Fax: 0845 686 1221
Email: info@traveldaily.co.uk
Advertising Address: Travel Daily (Australia), PO Box 428, WEST RYDE, NSW 1685 **Tel:** 1300 799 220
Fax: 1300 799 221
Email: advertising@traveldaily.com.au
Web site: http://www.traveldaily.co.uk
Publisher: Travel Daily
Date Established: 2006

Frequency: Daily
Cover Price: Free
Circulation: 28,000 (Publisher's Statement)
Usual Pagination: 6
Editor: Bruce Piper; **Advertising Manager:** Lisa Maroun
Summary of Content: Electronic newsletter covering news, views, special offers and appointments within the travel industry.
Readership/Target Audience: Aimed at the UK travel industry including travel agents, airlines, wholesalers, tour operators, hotels and government departments.
ADVERTISING RATES:
Full Page Colour $480.00
Mechanical Data: Trim Size: 297 x 210mm, Film: Digital
BUSINESS: TRAVEL & TOURISM

TRAVEL GBI
39745U50-34
Editorial Address: 3rd Floor, Foundation House, Perseverance Works, 38 Kingsland Road, LONDON, E2 8DD
Tel: 020 7729 4337 **Fax:** 020 7729 1716
Email: travelgbi@talk21.com
Advertising Address: As above.
Email: travelgbi@talk21.com
Web site: http://www.travelgbi.com
ISSN: 1355-462X
Publisher: Travelscope Publications
Date Established: 1979
Frequency: Monthly - Published at the beginning of the cover month
Free to qualifying individuals
Annual Sub.: £37.00
Circulation: 10,836 (ABC 01/07/2008 to 30/06/2009)
Usual Pagination: 24
Editor: Mike Swindell; **Executive Editor:** Richard Cawthorne; **Editor-in-Chief:** Bob Macbeth-Seath; **Advertising Manager:** Gary Kaye; **Publisher:** Bob Macbeth-Seath
Summary of Content: Newspaper focusing on tourism in the UK and Ireland, transport services and business travel.
Language(s): Chinese; English
Readership/Target Audience: Aimed at group travel organisers, travel wholesalers, coach tour operators, retail travel agents, accommodation providers, conference organisers, incentive buyers and transport organisations - ferries, railways, coaches and domestic airlines in the UK and Ireland.
ADVERTISING RATES:
Full Page Colour £3000.00
SCC £25.00
Agency Commission: 10%
Mechanical Data: Col Length: 371mm, Col Widths (Display): 40mm, Film: Digital, No. of Columns (Display): 6, Type Area: 371 x 262mm, Bleed Size: 400 x 290mm, Trim Size: 390 x 280mm, Page Width: 262mm
Copy instructions: Copy Date: 24th of the month prior to cover month
Average advertising content per issue: 40%
BUSINESS: TRAVEL & TOURISM

TRAVEL RETAILER INTERNATIONAL INC.TAX FREE TRADER
39831U53-650
Editorial Address: 6th Floor, Davis House, 2 Robert Street, CROYDON, CR0 1QQ **Tel:** 020 8253 8604
Fax: 020 8253 4603
Email: mematters@btconnect.com
Advertising Address: As above.
Email: amanda.felix@dfnionline
Web site: http://www.ravenfox.com
ISSN: 1357-3489
Publisher: Metropolis International Group Ltd
Date Established: 1991
Frequency: Quarterly - Published in the 1st week of the cover month
Annual Sub.: £425.00
Circulation: 4,040 (Publisher's Statement)
Usual Pagination: 60
Editor: Michael Eaton; **Managing Director:** Kevin Crook; **Advertising Manager:** Amanda Felix; **Publisher:** Amanda Felix
Summary of Content: Magazine covering all aspects of the travel-retail trade across the luxury goods business.
Readership/Target Audience: Aimed at duty-paid and duty-free retailers operating in airports, aircraft, ships, airlines, hotels and others selling to the traveller.
ADVERTISING RATES:
Full Page Colour £3190.00
Agency Commission: 10%
Mechanical Data: Type Area: 272 x 185mm, Bleed Size: 305 x 216mm, Trim Size: 298 x 210mm, Print Process: Offset litho, Film: Digital, Col Length: 272mm, No. of Columns (Display): 2, Page Width: 185mm
Copy instructions: Copy Date: 4 weeks prior to publication date
Average advertising content per issue: 40%
BUSINESS: RETAILING & WHOLESALING

TRAVEL TRADE GAZETTE
39737U50-24_75
Formerly: TTG-UK & Ireland
Editorial Address: Ludgate House, 245 Blackfriars Road, LONDON, SE1 9UY **Tel:** 020 7921 8029 **Fax:** 020 7921 8034
Email: lhayhurst@ttglive.com
Advertising Address: As above. **Tel:** 020 7921 5000
Email: smakin@ttglive.com
Web site: http://www.ttglive.com
ISSN: 0262-4397
Publisher: UBM Information Ltd
Date Established: 1954
Frequency: Weekly
Cover Price: £2.42
Circulation: 21,912 (ABC 01/07/2008 to 30/06/2009)
Editor: Lee Hayhurst; **News Editor:** Lee Hayhurst; **Features Editor:** Robin Searle; **Advertising Manager:** Sheryl Makin; **Publisher:** Paula Martin
Summary of Content: Magazine containing news, destination reviews and market reports.
Readership/Target Audience: Read by retail travel agents, tour operators, hotels, airlines, cruise lines, car hire companies, travel technology companies, travel insurance companies, airports, ferry lines and rail companies.
ADVERTISING RATES:
Full Page Colour £5880.00
Agency Commission: 10%
Mechanical Data: Film: Digital, Type Area: 270 x 200mm, Print Process: Web-fed offset litho, Bleed Size: 306 x 236mm, Trim Size: 300 x 230mm, Col Length: 270mm, Page Width: 200mm
Copy instructions: Copy Date: 2 weeks prior to publication date
Average advertising content per issue: 55%
BUSINESS: TRAVEL & TOURISM

TRAVEL WEEKLY
39749U50-160
Editorial Address: Quadrant House, The Quadrant, SUTTON, SM2 5AS **Tel:** 020 8652 3799 **Fax:** 020 8652 3956
Email: travel.weekly@travelweekly.co.uk
Advertising Address: As above. **Tel:** 020 8652 8295
Fax: 020 8652 3873
Email: twsales@travelweekly.co.uk
Web site: http://www.travelweekly.co.uk
ISSN: 0049-4577
Publisher: Reed Business Information
Frequency: Weekly
Annual Sub.: £105.00
Circulation: 16,137 (ABC 01/07/2008 to 30/06/2009)
Editor: Michelle Perrett; **News Editor:** Michelle Perrett; **Features Editor:** Karl Cushing; **Managing Editor:** Martin Couzins; **Group Editor:** Karen Dempsey; **Publisher:** Roger Williams
Summary of Content: Newspaper containing the latest travel news and information, with features on destinations and regular columns from industry experts.
Readership/Target Audience: Aimed at UK travel agents, tour operators and key personnel within the travel sector including airlines, cruise lines, hotels and tourist offices.
ADVERTISING RATES:
Full Page Colour £4860.00
Agency Commission: 10%
Mechanical Data: Type Area: 278 x 206mm, Trim Size: 300 x 226mm, Bleed Size: 310 x 236mm, Film: Positive, right reading, emulsion side down. Digital, Col Length: 278mm, Page Width: 206mm
Copy instructions: Copy Date: 1 week prior to publication date
BUSINESS: TRAVEL & TOURISM

TRAVELPLUS MAGAZINE
765058U50-202
Editorial Address: PO Box 1121, Yalding, MAIDSTONE, ME18 6WU **Tel:** 01892 730678
Email: simon.ward@travelplus.co.uk
Advertising Address: As above.
Email: charles.avenel@travelplus.co.uk
Web site: http://www.travelplus.co.uk
ISSN: 1477-2132
Publisher: TravelPlus Media Limited
Date Established: 1995
Frequency: Monthly
Cover Price: £3.10
Free to qualifying individuals
Circulation: 150,000 (Publisher's Statement)
Usual Pagination: 20
Editor: Simon Ward; **Editor-in-Chief:** Simon Ward; **Publisher:** Simon Ward
Summary of Content: Magazine covering travel, tourism and the world it inhabits.
Readership/Target Audience: The business and frequent travellers.
ADVERTISING RATES:
Full Page Colour £4100.00
Agency Commission: 15%
Mechanical Data: Film: Digital, Type Area: 199 x 143mm, Trim Size: 233 x 168mm, Bleed Size: 229 x 174mm, Col Length: 199mm, Page Width: 143mm
Copy instructions: Copy Date: 25th of the month prior to publication date

Average advertising content per issue: 40%
BUSINESS: TRAVEL & TOURISM

TRAVOLUTION
1700662U50-226
Editorial Address: Quadrant House, The Quadrant, SUTTON, SM2 5AS **Tel:** 020 8652 3500 **Fax:** 020 8652 3873
Email: lea.fox@virgin.net
Advertising Address: As above.
Email: charlotte.davies@rbi.co.uk
Web site: http://www.travolution.co.uk
ISSN: 1750-256X
Publisher: Reed Business Information
Date Established: 2005
Frequency: 6 issues yearly
Cover Price: Free
Circulation: 8,500 (Publisher's Statement)
Usual Pagination: 76
Editor: Linda Fox; **Group Editor:** Karen Dempsey
Summary of Content: Magazine covering all aspects of the online travel industry.
Readership/Target Audience: Aimed at mid to senior management in the travel industry.
ADVERTISING RATES:
Full Page Colour £1600.00
Agency Commission: 10%
Mechanical Data: Type Area: 238 x 200mm, Bleed Size: 278 x 231mm, Trim Size: 272 x 225mm, Col Length: 238mm, Page Width: 200mm, Film: Digital
BUSINESS: TRAVEL & TOURISM

TRAX
1799746U32H-471
Editorial Address: The Sail Loft, 3-11 Dod Street, LONDON, E14 7EQ **Tel:** 0870 608 0001 **Fax:** 0870 042 0102
Email: steven.turner@multitraxgroup.com
Advertising Address: As above.
Email: greg.jenkins@multitraxgroup.com
Web site: http://www.multitraxuk.com
Publisher: Multitrax UK Ltd
Frequency: Quarterly
Annual Sub.: £15.00
Circulation: 10,000 (Publisher's Statement)
Editor: Steven Turner
Summary of Content: Magazine covering all aspects of the health and fitness industry including health, fitness, gadgets and equipment.
Readership/Target Audience: Aimed at those working in the health and fitness sector.
ADVERTISING RATES:
Full Page Colour £1300.00
Mechanical Data: Bleed Size: 303 x 226mm, Trim Size: 297 x 220mm, Film: Digital
BUSINESS: LOCAL GOVERNMENT, LEISURE & RECREATION: Leisure, Recreation & Entertainment

THE TREASURER
34972U1A-278
Editorial Address: 51 Moorgate, LONDON, EC2R 6BH
Tel: 020 7847 2540 **Fax:** 020 7374 8744
Email: enquiries@treasurers.org
Advertising Address: As above.
Email: nbaruwa@treasurers.org
Web site: http://www.treasurers.org
ISSN: 0264-0937
Publisher: The Association of Corporate Treasurers
Date Established: 1980
Frequency: 10 issues yearly - Published in the 1st week of the cover month
Annual Sub.: £190.00
Circulation: 7,750 (Publisher's Statement 2008)
Usual Pagination: 52
Editor: Peter Williams
Summary of Content: Official journal of the Association of Corporate Treasurers.
Readership/Target Audience: Aimed at finance, corporate treasury and risk professionals.
ADVERTISING RATES:
Full Page Mono £3660.00
Full Page Colour £6330.00
Agency Commission: 10%
Mechanical Data: Page Width: 190mm, Film: Digital, Type Area: 280 x 190mm, Print Process: Litho, Bleed Size: 303 x 216mm, Trim Size: 297 x 210mm, Col Length: 280mm
Copy instructions: Copy Date: 3 weeks prior to publication date
Average advertising content per issue: 20%
BUSINESS: FINANCE & ECONOMICS

TREASURY MANAGEMENT INTERNATIONAL
34973U1A-279
Editorial Address: Temple House, 20 Holywell Row, LONDON, EC2A 4XH **Tel:** 0118 947 8057
Fax: 0118 947 8062
Email: hsanders@treasury-management.com
Advertising Address: As above.
Email: rpage@treasury-management.com

Web site: http://www.treasury-management.com
ISSN: 0967-523X
Publisher: P4 Publishing Ltd
Date Established: 1992
Frequency: 10 issues yearly - Published in the 1st week of the cover month
Annual Sub.: £235.00
Circulation: 8,000 (Publisher's Statement)
Usual Pagination: 56
Editor: Helen Sanders; **Advertising Manager:** Robin Page
Summary of Content: Magazine providing information on international corporate treasury issues.
Readership/Target Audience: Read by corporate treasurers, finance directors and advisers.
ADVERTISING RATES:
Full Page Colour £7300.00
Agency Commission: 10%
Mechanical Data: Type Area: 273 x 186mm, Bleed Size: 307 x 220mm, Trim Size: 297 x 210mm, Col Length: 273mm, Film: Digital, Page Width: 186mm
Copy instructions: Copy Date: End of the 3rd week of the month prior to publication date
Average advertising content per issue: 20%
BUSINESS: FINANCE & ECONOMICS

TREE NEWS
40688U57-65
Editorial Address: The Tree Council, 71 Newcomen Street, LONDON, SE1 1YT **Tel:** 020 7407 9992 **Fax:** 020 7407 9908
Email: editor@treecouncil.org.uk
Advertising Address: 20-23 Woodisde Place, GLASGOW, G3 7QF **Tel:** 0141 582 1280
Email: mediap@aol.com
Web site: http://www.treenews.org.uk
Publisher: Think Publishing
Frequency: Half-yearly - Published in April and September
Cover Price: £3.50
Circulation: 15,000 (Publisher's Statement)
Usual Pagination: 52
Editor: Malcolm Tait; **Advertising Manager:** John Innes
Summary of Content: Magazine covering investment in real estate overseas, tourism and holidays.
Readership/Target Audience: Aimed at property investors.
ADVERTISING RATES:
Full Page Colour £975.00
Mechanical Data: Type Area: 280 x 180mm, Col Length: 280mm, Bleed Size: 310 x 215mm, No. of Columns (Display): 3, Film: Digital, Page Width: 180mm
BUSINESS: ENVIRONMENT & POLLUTION

TRENDS IN BIOCHEMICAL SCIENCES
1657649U62R-488
Editorial Address: 32 Jamestown Road, LONDON, NW1 7BY **Tel:** 020 7424 4200
Email: tibs@elsevier.com
Advertising Address: As above. **Tel:** 020 7424 4400
Fax: 01865 853136
Email: j.kenney@elsevier.com
Web site: http://www.elsevier.com
ISSN: 0968-0004
Publisher: Elsevier London Ltd
Date Established: 1976
Frequency: Monthly
Annual Sub.: EUR174.00
Usual Pagination: 58
Editor: Jonathan Tyzack
Summary of Content: Journal covering recent developments in the fields of biophysics, microbiology, plant sciences and medical science.
Readership/Target Audience: Aimed at research scientists, lecturers and students of biochemistry, molecular and cell biology.
ADVERTISING RATES:
Full Page Mono ....:.......... $2055.00
Full Page Colour $3450.00
Mechanical Data: Film: Digital
BUSINESS: CHURCH & SCHOOL EQUIPMENT & EDUCATION: Education Related

TRENDS IN BIOTECHNOLOGY
1657650U62R-487
Editorial Address: 32 Jamestown Road, LONDON, NW1 7BY **Tel:** 020 7424 4200
Email: ttec@elsevier.com
Advertising Address: As above. **Tel:** 020 7424 4400
Fax: 01865 853136
Email: j.kenney@elsevier.com
Web site: http://www.elsevier.com
ISSN: 0167-7799
Publisher: Elsevier London Ltd
Date Established: 1983
Frequency: Monthly
Annual Sub.: EUR196.00
Usual Pagination: 54
Editor: Petra Gross

Summary of Content: Journal covering all aspects of biotechnology, from molecular genetics to biochemical engineering.
Readership/Target Audience: Aimed at biotechnologists who take an integrated, multidisciplinary approach to the applied biosciences.
ADVERTISING RATES:
Full Page Mono $2055.00
Full Page Colour $3450.00
Mechanical Data: Film: Digital
BUSINESS: CHURCH & SCHOOL EQUIPMENT & EDUCATION: Education Related

TRENDS IN CELL BIOLOGY
1657653U62R-481
Editorial Address: 32 Jamestown Road, LONDON, NW1 7BY **Tel:** 020 7424 4200
Email: etj.tcb@elsevier.com
Advertising Address: As above. **Tel:** 020 7424 4400
Fax: 01865 853136
Email: j.kenney@elsevier.com
Web site: http://www.elsevier.com
ISSN: 0962-8924
Publisher: Elsevier London Ltd
Date Established: 1991
Frequency: Monthly
Annual Sub.: EUR174.00
Usual Pagination: 58
Editor: C. Rose Hoskin
Summary of Content: Journal covering current research in cell biology, reporting on new developments as they happen and integrating methods, disciplines and principles.
Readership/Target Audience: Aimed at research scientists, students and teachers.
ADVERTISING RATES:
Full Page Mono $2055.00
Full Page Colour $3450.00
Mechanical Data: Film: Digital
BUSINESS: CHURCH & SCHOOL EQUIPMENT & EDUCATION: Education Related

TRENDS IN COGNITIVE SCIENCES
40007U55-174
Editorial Address: 32 Jamestown Road, LONDON, NW1 7BY **Tel:** 020 7611 4400 **Fax:** 020 7611 4470
Email: tics@elsevier.com
Advertising Address: As above. **Fax:** 01865 853136
Email: j.kenney@elsevier.com
Web site: http://www.trends.com
ISSN: 1366-2562
Publisher: Elsevier London Ltd
Date Established: 1997
Frequency: Monthly
Cover Price: EUR160.00
Usual Pagination: 46
Editor: Stavroula Kousta
Summary of Content: Journal containing reviews, comment and opinion articles on a wide range of areas within the cognitive sciences. Covers artificial intelligence, cognitive neuroscience, computational modelling and consciousness, linguistics and psychology.
Readership/Target Audience: Aimed at students and professionals within the cognitive science industry.
ADVERTISING RATES:
Full Page Mono £1465.00
Full Page Colour £2380.00
Agency Commission: 15%
Mechanical Data: Bleed Size: 286 x 222mm, Trim Size: 297 x 210mm, Film: Digital
Copy instructions: Copy Date: 4 weeks prior to publication date
Average advertising content per issue: 10%
BUSINESS: APPLIED SCIENCE & LABORATORIES

TRENDS IN ECOLOGY & EVOLUTION
1657654U62R-480
Editorial Address: 32 Jamestown Road, LONDON, NW1 7BY **Tel:** 020 7424 4200
Email: tree@elsevier.com
Advertising Address: As above. **Tel:** 020 7424 4400
Fax: 01865 853136
Email: j.kenney@elsevier.com
Web site: http://www.elsevier.com
ISSN: 0169-5347
Publisher: Elsevier London Ltd
Frequency: Monthly
Annual Sub.: EUR174.00
Usual Pagination: 54
Editor: Katrina Lythgoe
Summary of Content: Journal covering reviews, opinions and letters in all areas of ecology and evolutionary science.
Readership/Target Audience: Aimed at research workers, university teachers and students concerned with ecology, behaviour and evolution.
ADVERTISING RATES:
Full Page Mono $2055.00
Full Page Colour $3450.00

Mechanical Data: Film: Digital
BUSINESS: CHURCH & SCHOOL EQUIPMENT & EDUCATION: Education Related

TRENDS IN FOOD SCIENCE & TECHNOLOGY
40008U55-178
Editorial Address: The Boulevard, Langford Lane, KIDLINGTON, OX5 1GB **Tel:** 01865 843610
Fax: 01865 843960
Email: w.hurp@elsevier.com
Advertising Address: 32 Jamestown Road, LONDON, NW1 7BY **Tel:** 020 7424 4400 **Fax:** 01865 853136
Email: j.kenney@elsevier.com
Web site: http://www.elsevier.com/locate/tifs
ISSN: 0924-2244
Publisher: Elsevier Ltd
Date Established: 1990
Frequency: Monthly
Usual Pagination: 50
Editor: Wendy Hurp
Summary of Content: Journal covering news and developments in all areas of food science with a focus on new research directions and applications.
Readership/Target Audience: Read by food biotechnologists, food chemists, nutritionists, government scientists, quality control managers, food analysts and product development researchers.
ADVERTISING RATES:
Full Page Mono £1465.00
Full Page Colour ....:.............. £2380.00
Agency Commission: 15%
Mechanical Data: Type Area: 250 x 180mm, Trim Size: 280 x 210mm, Col Length: 250mm, Bleed Size: 286 x 216mm, Print Process: Sheet-fed offset, Film: Digital, Page Width: 180mm
BUSINESS: APPLIED SCIENCE & LABORATORIES

TRENDS IN IMMUNOLOGY
40529U56R-258
Editorial Address: 32 Jamestown Road, LONDON, NW1 7BY **Tel:** 020 7424 4200
Email: immunology@elsevier.com
Advertising Address: As above. **Tel:** 020 7611 4400
Fax: 01865 853136
Email: j.kenney@elsevier.com
Web site: http://www.sciencedirect.com
ISSN: 0167-5699
Publisher: Elsevier London Ltd
Date Established: 1980
Frequency: Monthly
Annual Sub.: $190.00
Circulation: 10,800 (Publisher's Statement)
Usual Pagination: 56
Editor: Zoltan Fehervari
Summary of Content: Journal about the latest developments in basic and applied immunology.
Readership/Target Audience: Aimed at immunologists, cell biologists, molecular biologists, microbiologists, virologists and haematologists.
ADVERTISING RATES:
Full Page Mono £1465.00
Full Page Colour £2380.00
Mechanical Data: Type Area: 230 x 160mm, Col Length: 230mm, Page Width: 160mm, Film: Digital, Trim Size: 262 x 192mm
Copy instructions: Copy Date: 5 weeks prior to publication date
BUSINESS: HEALTH & MEDICAL: Health Medical Related

TRENDS IN MICROBIOLOGY
1657657U62R-483
Editorial Address: 32 Jamestown Road, LONDON, NW1 7BY **Tel:** 020 7424 4200
Email: etj.tim@elsevier.com
Advertising Address: As above. **Tel:** 020 7424 4400
Fax: 01865 853136
Email: j.kenney@elsevier.com
Web site: http://www.elsevier.com
ISSN: 0966-842X
Publisher: Elsevier London Ltd
Date Established: 1993
Frequency: Monthly
Annual Sub.: £174.00
Usual Pagination: 52
Editor: Sam Morris
Summary of Content: Journal covering all aspects of microbiology, from cell biology and immunology to genetics and evolution and ranges across virology, bacteriology, protozoology and mycology.
Readership/Target Audience: Aimed at microbiologists, virologists, bacteriologists, mycologists, biotechnologists, molecular biologists and geneticists, cell biologists, parasitologists, protozoologists and immunologists.
ADVERTISING RATES:
Full Page Mono $2055.00
Full Page Colour $3450.00

Mechanical Data: Film: Digital
BUSINESS: CHURCH & SCHOOL EQUIPMENT & EDUCATION: Education Related

TRENDS IN MOLECULAR MEDICINE

1657658U62R-485

Editorial Address: 32 Jamestown Road, LONDON, NW1 8RR **Tel:** 020 7611 4400
Email: tmm@elsevier.com
Advertising Address: As above. **Tel:** 020 7424 4400
Fax: 01865 853136
Email: j.kenney@elsevier.com
Web site: http://www.elsevier.com
ISSN: 1471-4914
Publisher: Elsevier London Ltd
Date Established: 1995
Frequency: Monthly
Annual Sub.: EUR174.00
Usual Pagination: 52
Editor: Romina Emilianus
Summary of Content: Journal covering all aspects of molecular medicine.
Readership/Target Audience: Aimed at medical students, graduate students in the biomedical sciences, scientists and clinicians with an interest in understanding the molecular basis of disease and molecular biology to prevent, diagnose and treat disease.
ADVERTISING RATES:
Full Page Mono $2055.00
Full Page Colour $3450.00
Mechanical Data: Film: Digital
BUSINESS: CHURCH & SCHOOL EQUIPMENT & EDUCATION: Education Related

TRENDS IN NEUROSCIENCES

40009U55-180

Editorial Address: 84 Theobalds Road, LONDON, WC1X 8RR **Tel:** 020 7611 4000 **Fax:** 020 7611 4470
Email: tins@elsevier.com
Web site: http://www.elsevier.com
ISSN: 0166-2236
Publisher: Elsevier Ltd
Date Established: 1978
Frequency: Monthly
Annual Sub.: EUR92.00
Usual Pagination: 56
Editor: Sian Lewis
Summary of Content: Journal covering all aspects of neuroscience, including the brain, nervous system, psychiatry, neurology, behaviour, physiology and basic cell biology.
Readership/Target Audience: Read by neuroscientists, physiologists, pharmacologists, neurogeneticists, molecular biologists and neurologists.
ADVERTISING: No Advertising taken
BUSINESS: APPLIED SCIENCE & LABORATORIES

TRENDS IN PARASITOLOGY

1657659U62R-486

Editorial Address: 32 Jamestown Road, LONDON, NW1 7BY **Tel:** 020 7424 4200
Email: parasites@elsevier.com
Advertising Address: As above. **Tel:** 020 7424 4200
Fax: 01865 853136
Email: j.kenney@elsevier.com
Web site: http://www.elsevier.com
ISSN: 1471-4922
Publisher: Elsevier London Ltd
Date Established: 1985
Frequency: Monthly
Annual Sub.: EUR174.00
Usual Pagination: 54
Editor: Sally Hirst
Summary of Content: Journal focusing on medical and veterinary parasites.
Readership/Target Audience: Aimed at clinicians, veterinarians, lecturers, students and research workers in all fields of medicinal and veterinary parasitology.
ADVERTISING RATES:
Full Page Mono £1465.00
Full Page Colour £2380.00
Mechanical Data: Type Area: 258 x 186mm, Bleed Size: 303 x 216mm, Trim Size: 280 x 216mm, Col Length: 258mm, Page Width: 186mm, Film: Digital
BUSINESS: CHURCH & SCHOOL EQUIPMENT & EDUCATION: Education Related

TRENDS IN PHARMACOLOGICAL SCIENCES

1657661U62R-484

Editorial Address: 32 Jamestown Road, LONDON, NW1 7BY **Tel:** 020 7424 4200
Email: etj.tips@elsevier.com
Advertising Address: As above. **Tel:** 020 7424 4200
Fax: 01865 853136
Email: j.kenney@elsevier.com
Web site: http://www.elsevier.com
ISSN: 0165-6147

Publisher: Elsevier London Ltd
Date Established: 1979
Frequency: Monthly
Annual Sub.: EUR174.00
Usual Pagination: 54
Editor: Lekshmy Balakrishnan
Summary of Content: Journal covering recent developments in pharmacology and toxicology research.
Readership/Target Audience: Aimed at pharmacologists, toxicologists, clinical pharmacologists and medicinal chemists.
ADVERTISING RATES:
Full Page Mono $2055.00
Full Page Colour $3450.00
Mechanical Data: Film: Digital
BUSINESS: CHURCH & SCHOOL EQUIPMENT & EDUCATION: Education Related

TRENDS IN PLANT SCIENCE

41497U64F-500

Editorial Address: 32 Jamestown Road, LONDON, NW1 7BY **Tel:** 020 7424 4200 **Fax:** 01865 853067
Email: plants@elsevier.com
Advertising Address: As above. **Tel:** 020 7611 4400
Fax: 01865 853136
Email: j.kenney@elsevier.com
Web site: http://www.trends.com/plants
ISSN: 1360-1385
Publisher: Elsevier London Ltd
Date Established: 1996
Frequency: Monthly
Free to qualifying individuals
Annual Sub.: EUR188.00
Circulation: 2,600 (Publisher's Statement)
Usual Pagination: 52
Editor: Susanne Brink
Summary of Content: Journal covering plant sciences from molecular biology to ecology. Contains articles on plant development, growth regulation, molecular cell biology and genetics, signal transduction, pathogen defence, secondary metabolism and ecology.
Readership/Target Audience: Read by academics, industrial and applied scientists, students and researchers with an interest in plant science.
ADVERTISING RATES:
Full Page Mono $2055.00
Full Page Colour $3450.00
Mechanical Data: Film: Digital, Trim Size: 280 x 217mm
BUSINESS: OTHER CLASSIFICATIONS: Biology

TRENDS IN UROLOGY, GYNAECOLOGY & SEXUAL HEALTH

40233U56A-149

Editorial Address: The Atrium, Southern Gate, CHICHESTER, PO19 8SQ **Tel:** 01243 770237
Fax: 01243 770144
Email: trends@wiley.co.uk
Advertising Address: As above. **Tel:** 01243 779777
Email: sripsher@wiley.co.uk
Web site: http://www.escriber.com
ISSN: 1362-5306
Publisher: John Wiley & Sons Ltd
Date Established: 1996
Frequency: 6 issues yearly
Free to qualifying individuals
Annual Sub.: £50.00
Circulation: 17,000 (Publisher's Statement)
Usual Pagination: 32
Editor: Alison Burn
Summary of Content: Journal containing articles on current opinion and practice in urology, gynaecology and sexual health.
Readership/Target Audience: Read mainly by GPs and hospital doctors.
ADVERTISING: Rates on application
Copy instructions: Copy Date: 6 weeks prior to publication date
BUSINESS: HEALTH & MEDICAL

TROPHY & ENGRAVING NEWS INC. INDUSTRIAL & INCENTIVE MARKING

38956U27-204

Editorial Address: Marash House, 2-5 Brook Street, TRING, HP23 5ED **Tel:** 01442 826826 **Fax:** 01442 823400
Email: kyliegould1@aol.com
Advertising Address: As above.
Email: tencoling@aol.com
Web site: http://www.trophex.com
ISSN: 0266-3295
Publisher: Hill Media Ltd
Frequency: Monthly - Published on the 10th of the cover month
Annual Sub.: £32.00
Circulation: 14,000 (Publisher's Statement)
Usual Pagination: 44

Editor: Kylie Gould; **Managing Director:** Nigel Bean; **Advertising Manager:** Colin Gallimore; **Publisher:** Colin Gallimore
Summary of Content: Magazine covering trophies, components, awards, engraving, sublimation etching, enamelling, personalization, signage and allied businesses.
Readership/Target Audience: Aimed at trophy retailers and people involved in the awards and engraving industry.
ADVERTISING RATES:
Full Page Mono £756.00
Full Page Colour £1129.00
Mechanical Data: Page Width: 178mm, Film: Digital, Type Area: 254 x 178mm, Col Length: 254mm, Trim Size: 297 x 210mm, Bleed Size: 303 x 216mm
Copy instructions: Copy Date: 28th of the month prior to publication date
BUSINESS: METAL, IRON & STEEL

TROPICAL MEDICINE & INTERNATIONAL HEALTH

40599U56R-265

Editorial Address: LSHTM, Keppel Street, LONDON, WC1E 7HT **Tel:** 020 7927 2433 **Fax:** 020 7637 4314
Email: susanne.groener@lshtm.ac.uk
Advertising Address: 9600 Garsington Road, Cowley, OXFORD, OX4 2DQ **Tel:** 01865 776868
Email: mia.scott-ruddock@oxon.blackwellpublishing.com
Web site: http://www.blackwellpublishing.com/tmi
ISSN: 1360-2276
Publisher: Wiley-Blackwell Publishing
Date Established: 1996
Frequency: Monthly
Annual Sub.: £75.00
Circulation: 2,500 (Publisher's Statement)
Usual Pagination: 144
Editor: Susanne Groener; **Advertising Manager:** Mia Scott-Ruddock; **Managing Editor:** Susanne Groener
Summary of Content: Journal containing information on the field of tropical medicine and international health, including infectious and non-infectious diseases, parasitology, clinical sciences, tropical medicine, epidemiological theory and fieldwork, tropical medical microbiology, medical entomology and community medicine.
Language(s): English; French; Spanish
Readership/Target Audience: Aimed at physicians and scientists working, teaching and researching tropical medicine.
ADVERTISING RATES:
Full Page Mono £582.00
Full Page Colour £1461.00
Agency Commission: 10%
Mechanical Data: Type Area: 245 x 180mm, Col Length: 245mm, Trim Size: 276 x 210mm, Bleed Size: 282 x 216mm, Film: Digital, Page Width: 180mm
Copy instructions: Copy Date: 5 weeks prior to publication date
BUSINESS: HEALTH & MEDICAL: Health Medical Related

TRUCK & BUS BUILDER

39666U49D-150

Editorial Address: PO Box 15, Williton, TAUNTON, TA4 4YP **Tel:** 01984 618707 **Fax:** 01984 618708
Email: info@truckandbusbuilder.com
Web site: http://www.truckandbusbuilder.com
ISSN: 0263-6263
Publisher: Truck and Bus Builder Publishing Ltd
Date Established: 1978
Frequency: Monthly
Annual Sub.: £174.00
Usual Pagination: 12
Editor: Jim Gibbins; **Circulation Manager:** Lee Gibbins
Summary of Content: Newsletter containing news and information on commercial vehicle manufacturing developments.
Readership/Target Audience: Aimed at truck, bus and coach manufacturers, trailer and vehicle body makers as well as associated component manufacturers.
ADVERTISING: No Advertising taken
BUSINESS: TRANSPORT: Commercial Vehicles

THE TRUCK & CV DIRECTORY

39674U49D-60

Formerly: The Commercial Vehicle Directory
Editorial Address: The Firs, High Street, Whitchurch, AYLESBURY, HP22 4JU **Tel:** 01296 642800
Fax: 01296 640044
Email: info@truckandcv.com
Advertising Address: As above.
Email: amy@bodyshopmag.com
Web site: http://www.truckandcv.com
Publisher: Plenham Ltd
Date Established: 1982
Frequency: Annual - Published in April
Cover Price: £40.00
Free to qualifying individuals
Circulation: 11,000 (Publisher's Statement)
Editor: Christopher Mann; **Advertising Manager:** Amy Manson; **Publisher:** Christopher Mann

Business Magazines

Summary of Content: Directory of vehicle bodybuilders and repairers, and suppliers of ancillary and refinish equipment. Also includes chassis manufacturers and their vehicle specifications.
Readership/Target Audience: Aimed at key personnel of commercial vehicle users including local and district councils, fleet managers and commercial vehicle management.
ADVERTISING RATES:
Full Page Mono £1130.00
Full Page Colour £1840.00
Agency Commission: 10%
Mechanical Data: No. of Columns (Display): 4, Bleed Size: 303 x 216, Trim Size: 297 x 210mm, Film: Digital
Average advertising content per issue: 100%
BUSINESS: TRANSPORT: Commercial Vehicles

TRUCK AND DRIVER
39668U49D-180

Editorial Address: Quadrant House, The Quadrant, SUTTON, SM2 5AS **Tel:** 020 8652 3251 **Fax:** 020 8652 8988
Email: will.shiers@rbi.co.uk
Advertising Address: As above. **Fax:** 020 8652 8960
Email: trevor.hayes@rbi.co.uk
Web site: http://www.roadtransport.com
ISSN: 0966-3533
Publisher: Reed Business Information
Date Established: 1984
Frequency: Monthly - Published in the 1st week of the cover month
Cover Price: £2.70
Circulation: 26,599 (ABC 01/01/2008 to 31/12/2008)
Usual Pagination: 100
Advertising Manager: Trevor Hayes
Summary of Content: Magazine focusing on the lives of truck drivers, with a mixture of news, information and entertainment.
Readership/Target Audience: Read by enthusiasts and professional truck drivers, both employed and owner drivers.
ADVERTISING RATES:
Full Page Colour £2500.00
Agency Commission: 10%
Mechanical Data: Film: Digital, Trim Size: 297 x 210mm, Type Area: 275 x 190mm, Col Length: 275mm, Page Width: 190mm, Bleed Size: 303 x 216mm
Copy instructions: Copy Date: 3 weeks prior to publication date
Average advertising content per issue: 30%
BUSINESS: TRANSPORT: Commercial Vehicles

TRUCK AND PLANT TRADER
1898986U49D-367

Editorial Address: 3rd Floor, 41-47 Hartfield Road, Wimbledon, LONDON, SW19 3RQ **Tel:** 020 8544 7000
Fax: 020 8879 1879
Email: stuart.milne@autotrader.co.uk
Web site: http://www.autotrader.co.uk/trucks
Publisher: TNT Publishing
Date Established: 1996
Annual Sub.: £130.00
Circulation: 19,758 (Publisher's Statement)
Editor: Stuart Milne
Summary of Content: Magazine looking at commercial vehicles and plant machinery in the marketplace.
Readership/Target Audience: Aimed at truck and plant machinery buyers.
BUSINESS: TRANSPORT: Commercial Vehicles

TRUCKING
39670U49D-200

Editorial Address: 30 Monmouth Street, BATH, BA1 2BW
Tel: 01225 442244
Email: steev.hayes@futurenet.co.uk
Advertising Address: As above.
Email: sarah.cassidy@futurenet.co.uk
Web site: http://www.truckingmag.co.uk
ISSN: 1740-066X
Publisher: Future Publishing Ltd
Date Established: 1983
Frequency: Monthly
Cover Price: £2.60
Annual Sub.: £28.00
Circulation: 20,284 (ABC 01/01/2008 to 31/12/2008)
Usual Pagination: 140
Editor: Steev Hayes
Summary of Content: Magazine featuring operators profiles, road tests, legal advice and exclusive news on the trucking industry.
Readership/Target Audience: Read by road transport professionals, including drivers, transport managers and proprietors of small haulage businesses.
ADVERTISING RATES:
Full Page Colour £1453.00
Agency Commission: 10%
Mechanical Data: Type Area: 277 x 190mm, Bleed Size: 303 x 216mm, Trim Size: 297 x 210mm, Col Length: 277mm, Page Width: 190mm, Film: Digital
BUSINESS: TRANSPORT: Commercial Vehicles

TRUCKSTOP NEWS
39671U49D-230

Editorial Address: 30 Monmouth Street, BATH, BA1 2BW
Tel: 01225 442244
Email: steev.hayes@futurenet.co.uk
Advertising Address: As above. **Fax:** 01225 732206
Email: sarah.cassidy@futurenet.co.uk
Web site: http://www.truckstopnews.co.uk
Publisher: Future Publishing Ltd
Date Established: 1987
Frequency: Monthly
Cover Price: Free
Circulation: 43,000 (Publisher's Statement)
Usual Pagination: 24
Editor: Steev Hayes
Summary of Content: Newspaper covering truck manufacturing, components, ancillary equipment, truck racing and general information on the haulage business.
Readership/Target Audience: Aimed at those involved in the truck industry.
ADVERTISING RATES:
Full Page Colour £3424.00
Agency Commission: 10%
Mechanical Data: Type Area: 360 x 262mm, Col Length: 360mm, Page Width: 262mm, Film: Digital
Copy instructions: Copy Date: 2 weeks prior to publication date
Average advertising content per issue: 55%
BUSINESS: TRANSPORT: Commercial Vehicles

TRUST LAW INTERNATIONAL
39248U44-2000

Editorial Address: Maxwelton House, 41-43 Boltro Road, HAYWARDS HEATH, RH16 1BJ **Tel:** 01444 416119
Fax: 01444 440426
Web site: http://www.tottelpublishing.com
ISSN: 0962-2624
Publisher: Tottel Publishing
Date Established: 1991
Frequency: Quarterly
Usual Pagination: 64
Editor: Linda Whittle
Summary of Content: Journal covering the law affecting trusts worldwide, pension funds, commercial trusts and charities.
Readership/Target Audience: Aimed at trust lawyers, practitioners and academics.
ADVERTISING: No Advertising taken
BUSINESS: LEGAL

TRUSTS & ESTATES
39249U44-2020

Editorial Address: Telephone House, 69-77 Paul Street, LONDON, EC2A 4LQ **Tel:** 020 7017 4600
Fax: 020 7017 4135
Email: frida.fischer@informa.com
Web site: http://www.informafinance.com
ISSN: 0269-9087
Publisher: Informa PLC
Date Established: 1986
Frequency: 10 issues yearly
Usual Pagination: 8
Editor: Frida Fischer
Summary of Content: Newsletter containing key issues, analysis and practical advice on tax planning and new legislation affecting the law relating to trusts and estates.
Readership/Target Audience: Aimed at solicitors, businessmen and associated professionals.
ADVERTISING: No Advertising taken
BUSINESS: LEGAL

TRUSTS & TRUSTEES
39250U44-2040

Editorial Address: The Mill Office, Royston Road, Wendens Ambo, SAFFRON WALDEN, CB11 4JX **Tel:** 01799 541152
Fax: 01799 541972
Email: trusts@dial.pipex.com
Advertising Address: 44 Leeway Avenue, Great Shelford, CAMBRIDGE, CB2 5AU **Tel:** 01799 542292
Fax: 01799 541972
Email: rea@hemscott.net
Web site: http://www.oup.com
ISSN: 1363-1780
Publisher: OUP
Date Established: 1994
Frequency: 10 issues yearly
Annual Sub.: £360.00
Circulation: 5,000 (Publisher's Statement)
Usual Pagination: 36
Editor: John Goldsworth
Summary of Content: Magazine containing articles and reports on the law and practice of international trusts and foundations particularly in the UK, USA and offshore countries.
Readership/Target Audience: Aimed at trustees and bankers, trust and estate lawyers, accountants and tax advisors and international investment advisors.
ADVERTISING RATES:
Full Page Mono £1200.00
Full Page Colour £1500.00

Agency Commission: 10%
Copy instructions: Copy Date: 15th of the month prior to publication date
Average advertising content per issue: 20%
BUSINESS: LEGAL

TS TODAY
36811U14A-317_50

Formerly: Trading Standards Review
Editorial Address: 275 Newmarket Road, CAMBRIDGE, CB5 8JE **Tel:** 0870 777 3468 **Fax:** 01223 327356
Email: tstoday@tsi.org.uk
Advertising Address: 1 Sylvan Court, Sylvan Way, Southfields Business Park, BASILDON, SS15 6TH
Tel: 0870 872 9000 **Fax:** 0845 608 9425
Email: juditht@tsi.org.uk
Web site: http://www.tsi.org.uk
ISSN: 1475-1464
Publisher: Trading Standards Institute
Frequency: Monthly
Annual Sub.: £6.50
Circulation: 3,000 (Publisher's Statement)
Usual Pagination: 40
Editor: Lucy Meakin
Summary of Content: Magazine containing items dealing with trading standards and consumer protection.
Readership/Target Audience: Read by members of the Institute and outside subscribers with an interest in trading standards.
ADVERTISING RATES:
Full Page Colour £668.00
Agency Commission: 10%
Mechanical Data: Trim Size: 297 x 210mm, Film: Digital, Type Area: 270 x 190mm, Bleed Size: 303 x 216mm, Col Length: 270mm, Page Width: 190mm
BUSINESS: COMMERCE, INDUSTRY & MANAGEMENT

TSSA JOURNAL
37206U14L-775

Formerly: TSS Journal
Editorial Address: Walkden House, 10 Melton Street, LONDON, NW1 2EJ **Tel:** 020 7387 2101 **Fax:** 020 7383 0656
Email: journal@tssa.org.uk
Advertising Address: As above.
Email: wardf@tssa.org.uk
Web site: http://www.tssa.org.uk
Publisher: Transport Salaried Staffs' Association
Frequency: 6 issues yearly
Cover Price: Free
Circulation: 30,000 (Publisher's Statement)
Usual Pagination: 24
Editor: Tom Condon; **Advertising Manager:** Frank Ward
Summary of Content: Magazine of the Transport Salaried Staffs' Association containing industry news, members' features and employment issues.
Readership/Target Audience: Read by members of the TSSA.
ADVERTISING: Rates on application
BUSINESS: COMMERCE, INDUSTRY & MANAGEMENT: Trade Unions

TTG LUXURY
1829673U50-240

Editorial Address: 1st Floor, Ludgate House, 245 Blackfriars Road, LONDON, SE1 9UY **Tel:** 07866 691899
Email: alhutchinson@ttgluxury.com
Advertising Address: As above. **Tel:** 020 7921 5000
Email: ebarnes@ttglive.com
Web site: http://www.ttgluxury.com
Publisher: UBM Information Ltd
Date Established: 2007
Frequency: Quarterly
Cover Price: £7.50
Free to qualifying individuals
Circulation: 12,000 (Publisher's Statement)
Editor: April Hutchinson
Summary of Content: Magazine covering the luxury travel market with destination focused features and tips on how to sell destination products more effectively. Featuring reviews of products and services available in the market, luxury leisure travel, business travel and meetings and events products.
Readership/Target Audience: Aimed at premium travel professionals, agents and suppliers working within the luxury travel industry.
ADVERTISING RATES:
Full Page Colour £4800.00
Mechanical Data: Bleed Size: 376 x 286mm, Trim Size: 370 x 280mm, Type Area: 340 x 250mm, Col Length: 340mm, Page Width: 250mm
Copy instructions: Copy Date: 2 weeks prior to publication date
BUSINESS: TRAVEL & TOURISM

TTJ
39468U46-60

Formerly: Timber & Wood Products
Editorial Address: Progressive House, 2 Maidstone Road, Foots Cray, SIDCUP, DA14 5HZ **Tel:** 020 8269 7809
Fax: 020 8269 7844
Email: mjeffree@ttjonline.com
Advertising Address: As above. **Tel:** 020 8269 7700
Email: mricker@ttjonline.com
Web site: http://www.ttjonline.com
ISSN: 1740-701X
Publisher: Progressive Media Publications
Date Established: 1873
Frequency: 26 issues yearly
Annual Sub.: £141.00
Circulation: 3,220 (Publisher's Statement)
Usual Pagination: 35
Editor: Mike Jeffree; **News Editor:** Stephen Powney; **Managing Editor:** Sally Spencer; **Publisher:** David Wildman
Summary of Content: Magazine covering process wood working, machinery and finishing techniques, timber and wood based sheet materials, trading, importing and shipping.
Readership/Target Audience: Aimed at timber producers, merchants, exporters, importers and agents, forestry managers and joinery and furniture manufacturers.
ADVERTISING RATES:
Full Page Colour £2195.00
Agency Commission: 10%
Mechanical Data: Type Area: 280 x 192mm, Bleed Size: 303 x 213mm, Trim Size: 297 x 210mm, Film: Digital, Print Process: Sheet-fed offset litho, Col Length: 280mm, Page Width: 192mm
Copy instructions: Copy Date: 3 weeks prior to publication date
Average advertising content per issue: 40%
BUSINESS: TIMBER, WOOD & FORESTRY

TTJ ADDRESS BOOK & BUYERS GUIDE
23850U46-42

Formerly: Timber Trades Address Book
Editorial Address: Priory Park, Beech Green Lane, Withyham, HARTFIELD, TN7 4DB **Tel:** 01892 771047
Fax: 01892 771048
Email: ttjbg@boundaryimedia.co.uk
Web site: http://www.ttjonline.com
Publisher: Progressive Media Publications
Date Established: 1973
Frequency: Annual
Cover Price: £85.00
Editor: Peter Morris
Summary of Content: Directory of all major companies in the timber business, including a buyers' guide yellow pages, and who's who in the industry.
Readership/Target Audience: Used by company executives buying and selling timber and wood products.
ADVERTISING: No Advertising taken
BUSINESS: TIMBER, WOOD & FORESTRY

TTN TRAVEL & TOURISM NEWS MIDDLE EAST
39740U50-29

Formerly: Travel & Tourism Middle East
Editorial Address: Crescent Court, 102 Victor Road, TEDDINGTON, TW11 8SS **Tel:** 020 8943 3630
Fax: 020 8943 3701
Email: nhorne@hilal.co.uk
Advertising Address: As above.
Email: nhorne@hilal.co.uk
Publisher: Hilal International (UK) Ltd
Frequency: Monthly - Published on the 1st of the cover month
Cover Price: Free
Circulation: 7,313 (Publisher's Statement)
Usual Pagination: 32
Editor: Nick Horne; **Advertising Manager:** Nick Horne
Summary of Content: Magazine providing coverage of international and regional news relating to the travel industry in the Middle East.
Readership/Target Audience: Aimed at airline and airport personnel working in the travel industry from and within the Middle East including flight caterers, handling agencies, travel agents and tour operators.
ADVERTISING RATES:
Full Page Mono $4410.00
Full Page Colour $6174.00
SCC $15.75
Agency Commission: 15%
Mechanical Data: Bleed Size: + 5mm, Film: Positive, right reading, emulsion side down. Digital, No. of Columns (Display): 7, Type Area: 400 x 275mm, Print Process: Sheet-fed offset litho, Col Length: 400mm, Trim Size: 420 x 290mm, Col Widths (Display): 35mm, Page Width: 275mm
Copy instructions: Copy Date: 3 weeks prior to publication date
BUSINESS: TRAVEL & TOURISM

TUBE & PIPE TECHNOLOGY
37677U19G-190

Editorial Address: 46 Holly Walk, LEAMINGTON SPA, CV32 4HY **Tel:** 01926 334137 **Fax:** 01926 314755
Email: richard@intras.co.uk
Advertising Address: As above.
Email: intras@intras.co.uk
Web site: http://www.read-tpt.com
ISSN: 0953-2366
Publisher: Intras Ltd
Date Established: 1988
Frequency: 6 issues yearly - Published on the 1st of the cover month
Free to qualifying individuals
Annual Sub.: £85.00
Circulation: 12,500 (Publisher's Statement)
Editor: Richard Sears; **Publisher:** Caroline Sullens
Summary of Content: International journal covering all aspects of the production and utilisation of tubes, pipes and hollows worldwide.
Readership/Target Audience: Aimed at industry managers, engineers, buyers and specifiers.
ADVERTISING RATES:
Full Page Mono £835.00
Full Page Colour £1235.00
Agency Commission: 15%
Mechanical Data: Col Length: 260mm, Film: Digital, No. of Columns (Display): 3, Type Area: 260 x 180mm, Print Process: Offset litho, Bleed Size: 303 x 214mm, Trim Size: 297 x 210mm, Page Width: 180mm
Copy instructions: Copy Date: 6 weeks prior to publication date
BUSINESS: ENGINEERING & MACHINERY: Pipelines

TUNNELS & TUNNELLING INTERNATIONAL
39031U42A-183

Editorial Address: Progressive House, 2 Maidstone Road, Foots Cray, SIDCUP, DA14 5HZ **Tel:** 020 8269 7893
Fax: 020 8629 7850
Email: tthomas@tunnelsonline.info
Advertising Address: As above. **Tel:** 020 8269 7700
Fax: 020 8269 7840
Email: gtween@progressivemediagroup.com
Web site: http://www.tunnelsonline.info
ISSN: 0041-414X
Publisher: Progressive Media Publications
Date Established: 1969
Frequency: Monthly - Published on the 15th of the cover month
Annual Sub.: £90.00
Circulation: 5,314 (ABC 01/07/2008 to 30/06/2009)
Usual Pagination: 60
Editor: Tristan Thomas; **News Editor:** Patrick Reynolds
Summary of Content: The official magazine of the British Tunnelling Society, covering all areas of underground construction from large bore tunnels to micro tunnelling. Includes international news, developments, contracts, project coverage, technology and techniques.
Language(s): Chinese; English
Readership/Target Audience: Aimed at engineers working in all sectors of the world tunnelling market.
ADVERTISING RATES:
Full Page Mono £2395.00
Full Page Colour £2930.00
Agency Commission: 10%
Mechanical Data: Type Area: 280 x 192mm, Bleed Size: 303 x 213mm, Trim Size: 297 x 210mm, Print Process: Litho, Col Length: 280mm, Page Width: 192mm, Film: Digital
Copy instructions: Copy Date: 6 weeks prior to publication date
Average advertising content per issue: 40%
Supplement(s): China - 1xY, North America - 4xY
BUSINESS: CONSTRUCTION

TURF BUSINESS
1683776U64D-92

Editorial Address: Green Hedges, Melfort Road, CROWBOROUGH, TN6 1QT **Tel:** 01892 664555
Fax: 01560 1256390
Email: neville@smartemedia.co.uk
Advertising Address: As above. **Fax:** 05601 125390
Email: martin@dpspublishing.co.uk
Web site: http://www.smartemedia.co.uk
Publisher: DPS Publishing Limited
Date Established: 2005
Frequency: 10 issues yearly
Free to qualifying individuals
Circulation: 5,300 (Publisher's Statement)
Usual Pagination: 36
Editor: Martin Smart; **Advertising Manager:** Martin Smart; **Publisher:** Martin Smart
Summary of Content: Magazine covering all aspects of professional turf care.
Readership/Target Audience: Aimed at groundsmen, green keepers and local authority personnel.
ADVERTISING RATES:
Full Page Colour £1200.00
SCC £25.00
Agency Commission: 10%

Mechanical Data: Type Area: 270 x 180mm, Bleed Size: 306 x 216mm, Trim Size: 297 x 210mm, Col Length: 270mm, Page Width: 180mm, Film: Digital
Copy instructions: Copy Date: 4 weeks prior to publication date
Average advertising content per issue: 30%
BUSINESS: OTHER CLASSIFICATIONS: Course Maintenance

TURF PROFESSIONAL
38420U64D-90

Editorial Address: 25A New Street, SALISBURY, SP1 2PH **Tel:** 01722 414245 **Fax:** 01722 414561
Email: chris@nelsonpublishing.co.uk
Advertising Address: As above.
Email: nicky@nelsonpublishing.co.uk
Web site: http://www.turfpro.co.uk
Publisher: Nelson Publishing Ltd
Date Established: 1998
Frequency: 6 issues yearly - Published in the 1st week of the 2nd cover month
Free to qualifying individuals
Annual Sub.: £60.00
Circulation: 7,100 (Publisher's Statement)
Usual Pagination: 60
Editor: Steve Gibbs; **Managing Director:** Chris Biddle
Summary of Content: Magazine containing news and information on the professional turf-care industry.
Readership/Target Audience: Aimed at UK and Irish golf course managers, sports turf groundsmen, local authorities, educational establishments, contractors, dealers and manufacturers.
ADVERTISING RATES:
Full Page Colour £1250.00
Agency Commission: 10%
Mechanical Data: Film: Digital, Col Length: 272mm, Print Process: Litho, Bleed Size: 305 x 218mm, Trim Size: 297 x 210mm, Page Width: 190mm, Col Widths (Display): 92mm, No. of Columns (Display): 2, Type Area: 272 x 190mm
Average advertising content per issue: 35%
BUSINESS: OTHER CLASSIFICATIONS: Course Maintenance

TV INTERNATIONAL
35694U2D-95

Editorial Address: Mortimer House, 37-41 Mortimer Street, LONDON, W1T 3JH **Tel:** 020 7017 4244 **Fax:** 020 7017 4289
Email: stewart.clarke@informa.com
Web site: http://www.informamedia.com
ISSN: 1071-9261
Publisher: T&F Informa Group PLC
Frequency: 23 issues yearly
Annual Sub.: £528.00
Usual Pagination: 12
Editor: Stewart Clarke
Summary of Content: Newsletter covering programming, ratings, distribution, finance, cable, satellite co-production, regulation and technology as well as company and country profiles.
Readership/Target Audience: Aimed at those in the television, cable and satellite industries.
ADVERTISING: No Advertising taken
BUSINESS: COMMUNICATIONS, ADVERTISING & MARKETING: Broadcasting

TV INTERNATIONAL DAILY
35695U2D-96

Editorial Address: Mortimer House, 37-41 Mortimer Street, LONDON, W1T 3JH **Tel:** 020 7017 4244 **Fax:** 020 7017 4289
Email: stewart.clarke@informa.com
Web site: http://www.informamedia.com
ISSN: 1086-5675
Publisher: T&F Informa Group PLC
Frequency: 260 issues yearly
Annual Sub.: £999.00
Editor: Stewart Clarke
Summary of Content: Newsletter covering all aspects of the TV, cable and satellite broadcasting industry. Includes news, analysis, developments and mergers.
Readership/Target Audience: Aimed at TV international executives and senior personnel within the industry.
ADVERTISING: No Advertising taken
BUSINESS: COMMUNICATIONS, ADVERTISING & MARKETING: Broadcasting

TV SPORTS MARKETS
26072U2D-98

Editorial Address: 3rd Floor, 33-41 Dallington Street, LONDON, EC1V 0BB **Tel:** 020 7954 3500
Fax: 020 7954 3511
Email: sportsdesk@tvsportsmarkets.com
Web site: http://www.tvsportsmarkets.com
Publisher: Electric Word
Date Established: 1997
Frequency: 23 issues yearly
Annual Sub.: £1195.00
Usual Pagination: 24
Editor: James Pickles

Summary of Content: Industry newsletter covering the business of television sport.
Readership/Target Audience: Read by people in the TV sports industry including broadcasters, sport agencies and sport organisations.
ADVERTISING: No Advertising taken
BUSINESS: COMMUNICATIONS, ADVERTISING & MARKETING: Broadcasting

TV TECHNOLOGY EUROPE
20623U2D-132

Formerly: TV Technology and Production
Editorial Address: 1st Floor, 1 Cabot House, Compass Point Business Park, Stocks Bridge Way, ST. IVES, PE27 5JL **Tel:** 01480 461555 **Fax:** 01480 461550
Email: a.brown@audiomedia.com
Advertising Address: As above.
Email: bkennedy@imaspub.com
Web site: http://www.tvtechnology.com
Publisher: IMAS Publishing (UK) Ltd
Date Established: 1997
Frequency: 7 issues yearly
Cover Price: Free
Circulation: 5,000 (BPA Worldwide)
Usual Pagination: 68
Editor: Angela Brown; **Managing Director:** Angela Brown; **Advertisement Director:** Bob Kennedy
Summary of Content: Magazine covering the technical side of broadcasting.
Readership/Target Audience: Aimed at professional TV engineers, producers and creative people in the broadcast and production industry.
ADVERTISING: Rates on application
BUSINESS: COMMUNICATIONS, ADVERTISING & MARKETING: Broadcasting

TWENTIETH CENTURY BRITISH HISTORY
30836U62R-464

Editorial Address: Department of Politics, University of York, Heslington, YORK, YO1 5DD **Tel:** 01865 353907
Fax: 01865 790819
Email: sjbrooke@yorku.ca
Advertising Address: Great Clarendon Street, OXFORD, OX2 6DP **Tel:** 01865 353329
Email: jnlsadvertising@oxfordjournals.org
Web site: http://tcbh.oupjournals.org
ISSN: 0955-2359
Publisher: OUP
Date Established: 1990
Frequency: Quarterly
Cover Price: £15.00
Annual Sub.: £48.00
Circulation: 700 (Publisher's Statement)
Usual Pagination: 140
Editor: Duncan Tanner
Summary of Content: Journal covering the variety of British history in the 20th century in all its aspects. Links the many different and specialised branches of historical scholarship with work in political science and related disciplines.
Readership/Target Audience: Aimed at academics and people with a general interest in twentieth century history in Britain.
ADVERTISING RATES:
Full Page Mono £270.00
Agency Commission: 10%
Mechanical Data: Film: Digital, Page Width: 130mm, Type Area: 200 x 130mm, Col Length: 200mm
Copy instructions: Copy Date: 20th of the month prior to publication date
BUSINESS: CHURCH & SCHOOL EQUIPMENT & EDUCATION: Education Related

TWIST - THE NEW WOOL RECORD
39516U47A-400

Formerly: Wool Record
Editorial Address: Perkin House, 1 Longlands Street, BRADFORD, BD1 2TP **Tel:** 01274 378800
Fax: 01274 378811
Email: jdyson@world-textile.net
Advertising Address: As above.
Email: lpollard@world-textile.net
Web site: http://www.twist-international.com
ISSN: 0263-6131
Publisher: World Textile Publications Ltd
Date Established: 1909
Frequency: Monthly
Annual Sub.: £235.00
Usual Pagination: 60
Editor: Jonathan Dyson; **Managing Director:** Mark Jarvis
Summary of Content: Journal containing information on all aspects of the world wool-textile industry including all stages of all sectors from fleece to fashion and carpets, plus rare and speciality fibres.
Readership/Target Audience: Read by chief executives, sales and marketing directors, senior managers, clothiers, fabric buyers, designers and stylists in the international wool-textile industry.

ADVERTISING RATES:
Full Page Mono £1448.00
Full Page Colour £1930.00
Agency Commission: 10%
Mechanical Data: Type Area: 251 x 179mm, Film: Digital, Bleed Size: 303 x 216mm, Trim Size: 297 x 210mm, Col Length: 251mm, Page Width: 179mm
BUSINESS: CLOTHING & TEXTILES

TYRE TRADE NEWS
38325U31A-200

Editorial Address: 6B Acorn Farm Business Centre, Cublington Road, WING, LU7 0LB **Tel:** 01296 681424
Fax: 01296 682628
Email: tyres@tyretradenews.co.uk
Advertising Address: As above.
Email: tyres@tyretradenews.co.uk
Web site: http://www.tyretradenews.co.uk
ISSN: 1476-6744
Publisher: Technique Publishing Co Ltd
Date Established: 1991
Frequency: Monthly - Published in the 1st week of the cover month
Cover Price: £4.50
Free to qualifying individuals
Annual Sub.: £40.00
Circulation: 6,200 (Publisher's Statement)
Usual Pagination: 80
Editor: Mike Scanlon; **Managing Editor:** Mike Scanlon
Summary of Content: Magazine covering news, products and information.
Readership/Target Audience: Aimed at people working in the tyre and after-market industry.
ADVERTISING RATES:
Full Page Colour £1190.00
Agency Commission: 10%
Mechanical Data: No. of Columns (Display): 2, Bleed Size: 305 x 213mm, Trim Size: 297 x 210mm, Film: Digital, Type Area: 275 x 188mm, Col Length: 275mm, Page Width: 188mm
Average advertising content per issue: 54%
BUSINESS: MOTOR TRADE: Motor Trade Accessories

TYRES & ACCESSORIES
38326U31A-160

Editorial Address: 6A Salem Street, STOKE-ON-TRENT, ST1 5PR **Tel:** 01782 214224 **Fax:** 01255 222234
Email: chris.anthony@tyrepress.com
Advertising Address: Unit 1, Magnolia Centre, Telford Road, CLACTON-ON-SEA, CO15 4LP **Tel:** 01255 222233
Fax: 01255 222234
Email: alan@tyrepress.com
Web site: http://www.tyrepress.com
ISSN: 0041-4859
Publisher: Tyre Industry Publications Ltd
Date Established: 1946
Frequency: Monthly - Published in the 3rd week of cover month
Annual Sub.: £60.00
Circulation: 7,064 (ABC 01/07/2008 to 30/06/2009)
Usual Pagination: 116
Editor: Chris Anthony; **Publisher:** Klaus Haddenbrock
Summary of Content: Journal covering retail, fitting, repair, manufacture and re-treading of tyres and vehicle accessories.
Readership/Target Audience: Aimed at all those involved in the tyre, wheel and automotive trade.
ADVERTISING RATES:
Full Page Mono £897.00
Full Page Colour £1237.00
SCC £15.00
Agency Commission: 15%
Mechanical Data: Type Area: 273 x 190mm, Bleed Size: 303 x 216mm, Trim Size: 297 x 210mm, Film: Digital, No. of Columns (Display): 4, Col Length: 273mm, Page Width: 190mm
Average advertising content per issue: 50%
BUSINESS: MOTOR TRADE: Motor Trade Accessories

UC
1745297U14L-933

Editorial Address: 27 Britannia Street, LONDON, WC1X 9JP **Tel:** 020 7670 9700 **Fax:** 020 7670 9749
Email: editors@ucu.org.uk
Advertising Address: Redactive Media, 17 Britton Street, LONDON, EC1M 5TP **Tel:** 020 7880 6200
Fax: 020 7880 7553
Email: terry.arnold@redactive.co.uk
Web site: http://www.ucu.org.uk
Publisher: UCU
Date Established: 2006
Frequency: Quarterly
Cover Price: Free
Circulation: 128,000 (Publisher's Statement)
Editor: Matt Waddup
Summary of Content: Official publication of the University and College Union. Covers work related news and features relating to people working in post-school education including campaigns, law, professional issues and development.

Readership/Target Audience: Aimed at lecturers, teachers in colleges, academic and academic related staff.
ADVERTISING RATES:
Full Page Colour £4630.00
Agency Commission: 10%
Mechanical Data: Type Area: 271 x 210mm, Bleed Size: 306 x 236mm, Trim Size: 300 x 230mm, Col Length: 271mm, Page Width: 210mm, Film: Digital
Copy instructions: Copy Date: 4 weeks prior to publication date
BUSINESS: COMMERCE, INDUSTRY & MANAGEMENT: Trade Unions

UCATT BUILDING WORKER
37212U14L-780

Editorial Address: UCATT House, 177 Abbeville Road, LONDON, SW4 9RL **Tel:** 020 7228 6504 **Fax:** 020 7720 4081
Email: buildingworker@ucatt.org.uk
Advertising Address: 17 Britton Street, LONDON, EC1M 5TP **Tel:** 020 7880 6222
Email: john.nahar@redactive.co.uk
Web site: http://www.ucatt.org.uk
Publisher: UCATT
Frequency: Quarterly
Cover Price: Free
Circulation: 85,000 (Publisher's Statement)
Usual Pagination: 20
Editor: Jim Jump
Summary of Content: Newspaper of the Union of Construction, Allied Trades and Technicians, focusing on industry and trade union news.
Readership/Target Audience: Read by construction workers.
ADVERTISING RATES:
Full Page Colour £2095.00
Mechanical Data: Type Area: 279 x 195mm, Col Length: 279mm, Page Width: 195mm, Film: Digital, Bleed Size: 303 x 213mm, Trim Size: 297 x 210mm
Copy instructions: Copy Date: 4 weeks prior to publication date
Average advertising content per issue: 25%
BUSINESS: COMMERCE, INDUSTRY & MANAGEMENT: Trade Unions

UK COAL NEWSCENE
38274U30-132

Formerly: RJB Newscene
Editorial Address: Harworth Park, Blyth Road, Harworth, DONCASTER, DN11 8DB **Tel:** 01302 751751
Fax: 01302 751707
Email: stuartoliverpr@aol.com
Advertising Address: As above. **Tel:** 01525 381759
Fax: 01525 852092
Email: stuartoliverpr@aol.com
Publisher: UK Coal Plc
Date Established: 1995
Frequency: 7 issues yearly
Annual Sub.: £15.00
Circulation: 4,000 (Publisher's Statement)
Usual Pagination: 16
Editor: Stuart Oliver; **Advertising Manager:** Stuart Oliver; **Managing Editor:** Stuart Oliver
Summary of Content: Journal providing information on coal and smokeless fuel production as well as sales.
Readership/Target Audience: Read by those in Britain's coal industry including management, mineworkers, engineers, scientists, accountants office staff, suppliers, officials, members of trade unions and professional organisations and distributed to MPs, local authorities and international subscribers.
ADVERTISING RATES:
Full Page Mono £1000.00
Full Page Colour £1250.00
Agency Commission: 10%
Mechanical Data: Trim Size: 297 x 210mm, Film: Digital, No. of Columns (Display): 4, Print Process: Web-fed offset litho
Average advertising content per issue: 10%
BUSINESS: MINING & QUARRYING

UK CONSTRUCTION MAGAZINE
39033U42A-190

Editorial Address: Unit N4, Chorley Business & Technology Centre, Euxton Lane, Euxton, CHORLEY, PR7 6TE
Tel: 01204 386363 **Fax:** 01204 387727
Email: edit@esengroup.co.uk
Advertising Address: As above. **Fax:** 01204 386365
Email: john.chapman@esengroup.co.uk
Web site: http://www.esengroup.co.uk
ISSN: 1461-2720
Publisher: ESEN Group
Date Established: 1997
Frequency: Monthly
Annual Sub.: £57.50
Circulation: 5,002 (ABC 01/07/2007 to 30/06/2008)
Usual Pagination: 200
Editor: Victoria Lee; **Managing Director:** David Edge

Summary of Content: Magazine covering nationwide construction projects, legislation changes, EU edicts and new products and services.
Readership/Target Audience: Aimed at quantity surveyors, architects, contractors, construction companies, suppliers, local authorities and housing associations.
ADVERTISING RATES:
Full Page Colour £1695.00
Agency Commission: 10%
Mechanical Data: Type Area: 266 x 185mm, Col Widths (Display): 185mm, Col Length: 266mm, Bleed Size: 307 x 216mm, Film: Digital
Copy instructions: Copy Date: 3 weeks prior to publication date
Average advertising content per issue: 45%
BUSINESS: CONSTRUCTION

UK DIRECTORY OF TALENT MANAGEMENT
601144U14R-500

Formerly: Directory of Executive Recruitment - UK Edition
Editorial Address: New Barnes Mill, Cottonmill Lane, ST. ALBANS, AL1 2HA **Tel:** 01727 844335 **Fax:** 01727 844779
Email: editorial@executive-grapevine.co.uk
Advertising Address: As above.
Email: dene.souster@executive-grapevine.co.uk
Web site: http://www.askgrapevine.com
Publisher: Executive Grapevine International Ltd
Date Established: 1980
Frequency: Annual - Published in August
Cover Price: £249.00
Usual Pagination: 600
Editor: Christine Lawler; **Advertising Manager:** Dene Souster
Summary of Content: Directory containing authoritative source of information on executive recruitment with an 8 part index to enable the user to target consultants with the appropriate experience. Details on over 900 consultancies may include company statistics, function and industry specialisation, method of recruitment, location of assignments and salary levels.
Readership/Target Audience: Aimed at human resource professionals and senior managers.
ADVERTISING RATES:
Full Page Colour £2500.00
Agency Commission: 10%
Mechanical Data: Type Area: 253 x 177mm, Bleed Size: 307 x 220mm, Trim Size: 297 x 210mm, Film: Digital, Col Length: 253mm, Page Width: 177mm
Copy instructions: Copy Date: 1 week prior to publication date
Average advertising content per issue: 10%
BUSINESS: COMMERCE, INDUSTRY & MANAGEMENT: Commerce Related

UK ENVIRONMENT NEWS
40690U57-72

Editorial Address: 35 Hollywood Road, LONDON, SW10 9HT **Tel:** 020 7351 3954
Email: pressroom@ukenvironment.com
Web site: http://www.ukendata.com
ISSN: 1368-924X
Publisher: UKEN Ltd
Date Established: 1997
Frequency: 6 issues yearly
Annual Sub.: £265.00
Usual Pagination: 16
Editor: Nicholas Paget-Brown
Summary of Content: Newsletter providing early warning of forthcoming UK and EU environmental regulation and legislation. Also contains a policy checklist.
Readership/Target Audience: Aimed at senior managers with responsibility for environmental compliance, corporate strategy and financial good practice. Distributed to leading companies and local authorities.
ADVERTISING: No Advertising taken
BUSINESS: ENVIRONMENT & POLLUTION

UK IRON AND STEEL INDUSTRY: ANNUAL STATISTICS
38194U27-165

Editorial Address: 1 Carlton House Terrace, LONDON, SW1Y 5DB **Tel:** 020 7343 3916 **Fax:** 020 7343 3903
Email: p.hunt@issb.co.uk
Web site: http://www.issb.co.uk
ISSN: 0952-5505
Publisher: ISSB Ltd (Iron and Steel Statistics Bureau)
Date Established: 1920
Frequency: Annual
Annual Sub.: £195.00
Circulation: 120 (Publisher's Statement)
Usual Pagination: 46
Editor: Phil Hunt
Summary of Content: Contains 47 detailed statistical tables relating to the UK Iron and Steel Industry, with historical comparisons and detailed trade information.
Readership/Target Audience: Aimed at the steel industry, consultants, traders and producers.

ADVERTISING: No Advertising taken
BUSINESS: METAL, IRON & STEEL

UK LANDLORD
35863U4D-227

Formerly: NLA Newsletter
Editorial Address: 22-26 Albert Embankment, LONDON, SE1 7TJ **Tel:** 020 7722 4334
Email: editorial@uklandlord.org.uk
Advertising Address: As above. **Tel:** 020 7840 8900
Fax: 0871 247 7535
Email: info@landlords.org.uk
Web site: http://www.landlords.org.uk
Publisher: National Landlords Association
Date Established: 1973
Frequency: 6 issues yearly
Free to qualifying individuals
Circulation: 15,668 (ABC 01/07/2008 to 30/06/2009)
Usual Pagination: 40
Editor: Simon Gordon; **Advertising Manager:** Steve Pearce; **Managing Editor:** Louise Gale
Summary of Content: Newsletter of the National Landlords' Association containing recent news and announcements relating to the private rented sector of housing, as well as features on various aspects of being a landlord and making buy-to-let investments.
Readership/Target Audience: Aimed at private residential landlords.
ADVERTISING RATES:
Full Page Colour £1330.00
Mechanical Data: Film: Digital, Type Area: 255 x 170mm, Print Process: Offset litho, Col Length: 255mm, Page Width: 170mm, Trim Size: 297 x 210mm, Bleed Size: 303 x 216mm
BUSINESS: ARCHITECTURE & BUILDING: Planning & Housing

UK LANDSCAPE TODAY
1824271U26B-75

Editorial Address: Publishing House, 3 Bridgebank Industrial Estate, Taylor Street, Horwich, BOLTON, BL6 7PD **Tel:** 0161 909 0909 **Fax:** 0161 909 0919
Email: feedback@uklandscapetoday.co.uk
Advertising Address: As above.
Email: lance@bigspark.co.uk
Publisher: The Big Spark
Frequency: Monthly
Cover Price: Free
Circulation: 9,000 (Publisher's Statement)
Usual Pagination: 40
Editor: Dave Beevers
Summary of Content: Tabloid newspaper featuring landscape news, new initiatives, plantings, structure and layout, plant and equipment, education, domestic garden design and landscaping, grounds and estate management, interior landscaping, arboriculture, awards, new appointments, initiatives, tenders, jobs and equipment.
Readership/Target Audience: Aimed at landscape specialists including producers, service users and constructors, those working in the landscape industry and potential users.
ADVERTISING RATES:
Full Page Mono £1495.00
Full Page Colour £1995.00
Agency Commission: 10%
Copy instructions: Copy Date: 10 days prior to publication date
Average advertising content per issue: 40%
BUSINESS: GARDEN TRADE: Garden Trade Supplies

UK LEISURE NEWS
1664896U32H-462

Formerly: UK Leisure Centre & Health Clubs Direct
Editorial Address: 3rd Floor, 104 Great Portland Street, LONDON, W1W 6PE **Tel:** 07976 725837
Email: alan.lewis@lewisbusiness.fsnet.co.uk
Web site: http://www.gopublishing.co.uk
Publisher: Go Publishing Ltd
Date Established: 2004
Frequency: 6 issues yearly
Free to qualifying individuals
Circulation: 8,912 (Publisher's Statement)
Usual Pagination: 60
Editor: Alan Lewis; **Publisher:** Alan Lewis
Summary of Content: Magazine covering news, products and services for the UK leisure industry.
Readership/Target Audience: Aimed at specifiers and budget holders within the leisure industry.
ADVERTISING: No Advertising taken
BUSINESS: LOCAL GOVERNMENT, LEISURE & RECREATION: Leisure, Recreation & Entertainment

UK POWER AND PROCESS ENGINEERING
40784U58-75

Formerly: UK Power
Editorial Address: Floor 8, Bridgewater House, Whitworth Street, MANCHESTER, M1 6LT **Tel:** 0161 832 6000
Email: rachel.bridgewater@tenalpspublishing.com

Advertising Address: 8th Floor, Bridgewater House, Whitworth Street, MANCHESTER, M1 6LT
Tel: 0161 832 6000 **Fax:** 0161 832 4176
Email: mandy.diamond@tenalpspublishing.com
Web site: http://tenalpspublishing.com/
Publisher: Ten Alps Publishing
Date Established: 1995
Frequency: Quarterly - Published at the end of the cover month
Cover Price: £6.20
Annual Sub.: £20.00
Circulation: 10,000 (Publisher's Statement)
Usual Pagination: 70
Editor: Rachel Bridgewater; **Managing Director:** Scott Masheder; **Publisher:** Stuart Fleming
Summary of Content: Journal containing topical features and case studies concerning power generation.
Readership/Target Audience: Aimed at those in industry requiring information on energy technology.
ADVERTISING RATES:
Full Page Colour £2195.00
Agency Commission: 10%
Mechanical Data: Film: Digital, Bleed Size: 308 x 215mm, Trim Size: 297 x 210mm, Type Area: 260 x 178mm, Col Length: 260mm, Page Width: 178mm
Copy instructions: Copy Date: 6 weeks prior to publication date
Average advertising content per issue: 50%
BUSINESS: ENERGY, FUEL & NUCLEAR

UK QUARRIES & MINES
38275U30-138

Editorial Address: Trelawney House, Chestergate, MACCLESFIELD, SK11 6DW **Tel:** 01625 613000
Fax: 01625 500286
Email: marie.roberts@tenalpspublishing.com
Advertising Address: 8th Floor, Bridgewater House, Whitworth Street, MANCHESTER, M1 6LT
Tel: 0161 832 6000 **Fax:** 0161 832 4176
Email: trade3@tenalpspublishing.com
Web site: http://www.tenalpspublishing.com
Publisher: Ten Alps Publishing
Date Established: 1993
Frequency: Annual - Published in September
Cover Price: £25.00
Free to qualifying individuals
Circulation: 4,000 (Publisher's Statement)
Usual Pagination: 160
Editor: Marie Roberts; **Advertising Manager:** James Ndhlovu
Summary of Content: Journal containing topical articles and news items on the quarrying and mining industry. Also contains an information directory covering operators, suppliers, mineral planning authorities, government and trade organisations.
Readership/Target Audience: Aimed at people involved in quarries, mines and associated processing plants, purchasers of raw materials and manufactured mineral extractive products.
ADVERTISING RATES:
Full Page Mono £1590.00
Full Page Colour £2200.00
Agency Commission: 10%
Mechanical Data: Bleed Size: +3mm, Page Width: 178mm, Type Area: 260 x 178mm, Trim Size: 297 x 210mm, Col Length: 260mm, Print Process: Offset litho, Film: Digital, Screen: 60 lpc
Copy instructions: Copy Date: End of October prior to publication date
BUSINESS: MINING & QUARRYING

THE UK REGISTER OF EXPERT WITNESSES
39314U44-2050

Editorial Address: PO Box 505, NEWMARKET, CB8 7TF
Tel: 01638 561590 **Fax:** 01638 560924
Email: ukrew@jspubs.com
Advertising Address: As above.
Email: ukrew@jspubs.com
Web site: http://www.jspubs.com
ISSN: 0968-3119
Publisher: JS Publications
Date Established: 1988
Frequency: Annual - Published in April
Annual Sub.: £95.00
Circulation: 4,000 (Publisher's Statement)
Usual Pagination: 500
Editor: Chris Pamplin
Summary of Content: Directory of individuals qualified to give expert evidence in court and experienced in the requirements of litigation.
Readership/Target Audience: Aimed at litigation lawyers, the media and PR.
ADVERTISING: No Advertising taken
BUSINESS: LEGAL

Business Magazines

UK VET COMPANION ANIMAL   41533U64H-160
Formerly: UK Vet Animal Companion
Editorial Address: Kennet Building, Trade Street, Woolton Hill, NEWBURY, RG20 9UJ **Tel:** 01635 255511
Fax: 01635 255445
Email: ukvet@ukvet.co.uk
Advertising Address: As above. **Tel:** 01635 254961
Email: ukvet@ukvet.co.uk
Web site: http://www.ukvet.co.uk
ISSN: 1464-4630
Publisher: Wiley-Blackwell Publishing
Date Established: 1995
Frequency: 9 issues yearly
Free to qualifying individuals
Annual Sub.: £55.00
Circulation: 6,348 (ABC 01/07/2007 to 30/06/2008)
Usual Pagination: 92
Editor: Janet Woodhart; **Editor-in-Chief:** Mike Howe
Summary of Content: Journal featuring different aspects of veterinary medicine and surgery.
Readership/Target Audience: Aimed at veterinary surgeons in small animal and equine practices, veterinary nurses and other professionals.
ADVERTISING RATES:
Full Page Colour £1280.00
Agency Commission: 10%
Mechanical Data: Type Area: 277 x 190mm, Trim Size: 297 x 210mm, Bleed Size: 307 x 220mm, Col Length: 277mm, Col Widths (Display): 78mm, No. of Columns (Display): 2, Film: Digital, Page Width: 190mm
Copy instructions: Copy Date: 5th of the month prior to publication date
Average advertising content per issue: 35%
BUSINESS: OTHER CLASSIFICATIONS: Veterinary

UK VET LIVESTOCK   749474U64H-161
Editorial Address: Kennet Building, Trade Street, Woolton Hill, NEWBURY, RG20 9UJ **Tel:** 01635 255511
Fax: 01635 255445
Email: ukvet@ukvet.co.uk
Advertising Address: As above.
Email: ukvet@ukvet.co.uk
Web site: http://www.ukvet.co.uk
ISSN: 1464-262X
Publisher: Wiley-Blackwell Publishing
Date Established: 1997
Frequency: 7 issues yearly
Free to qualifying individuals
Annual Sub.: £65.00
Circulation: 3,200 (Publisher's Statement)
Usual Pagination: 64
Editor: Janet Woodhart
Summary of Content: Journal covering livestock veterinary issues including farm practice.
Readership/Target Audience: Aimed at veterinary surgeons in farm practice.
ADVERTISING RATES:
Full Page Colour £1220.00
Agency Commission: 10%
Mechanical Data: Col Length: 277mm, Page Width: 190mm, Type Area: 277 x 190mm, No. of Columns (Display): 2, Bleed Size: 307 x 220mm, Film: Digital, Trim Size: 297 x 210mm, Col Widths (Display): 78mm
Copy instructions: Copy Date: 6th of the month prior to publication date
Average advertising content per issue: 35%
BUSINESS: OTHER CLASSIFICATIONS: Veterinary

THE UK'S REGIONAL CHARITY FINDER   35448U1P-250
Formerly: Charities by Counties & Regions
Editorial Address: 8 Hamble House, Meadrow, GODALMING, GU7 3HJ **Tel:** 01483 429800
Fax: 01483 429500
Email: liz_barber@btconnect.com
Advertising Address: As above.
Email: willtocharity@btconnect.com
Web site: http://www.willtocharity.co.uk
Publisher: Will to Charity Ltd
Date Established: 1978
Frequency: Annual - Published in December
Free to qualifying individuals
Circulation: 13,000 (Publisher's Statement)
Usual Pagination: 500
Editor: Elizabeth Barber
Summary of Content: Magazine containing a geographical charity fundraising directory.
Readership/Target Audience: Read by solicitors, UK funeral directors, public libraries, bank trust offices, universities and colleges.
ADVERTISING RATES:
Full Page Mono £800.00
Full Page Colour £900.00
Agency Commission: 10%
Mechanical Data: Col Length: 180mm, Type Area: 180 x 115mm, Film: Positive, right reading, emulsion side down. Digital, Page Width: 115mm

Average advertising content per issue: 90%
BUSINESS: FINANCE & ECONOMICS: Fundraising

ULSTER BUSINESS   41456U63E-500
Editorial Address: 5B Edgewater Business Park, Belfast Harbour Estate, BELFAST, BT3 9JQ **Tel:** 028 9078 3200
Fax: 028 9078 3210
Email: davidelliott@greerpublications.com
Advertising Address: As above. **Tel:** 028 9078 3212
Email: louisehunter@greerpublications.com
Web site: http://www.ulsterbusiness.com
Publisher: Greer Publications Ltd
Date Established: 1983
Frequency: 11 issues yearly
Free to qualifying individuals
Annual Sub.: £27.50
Circulation: 6,852 (ABC 01/07/2007 to 30/06/2008)
Usual Pagination: 100
Editor: David Elliott; **Publisher:** James Greer
Summary of Content: Business magazine for Northern Ireland, including news, profiles, appointments and views.
Readership/Target Audience: Aimed at senior managers and directors in Northern Ireland.
ADVERTISING RATES:
Full Page Mono £1350.00
Full Page Colour £1995.00
Agency Commission: 10%
Mechanical Data: Type Area: 270 x 183mm, Print Process: Litho, Screen: 54 lpc, Bleed Size: 305 x 215mm, Trim Size: 297 x 210mm, Film: Right reading, emulsion side down. Digital, Col Length: 270mm, Page Width: 183mm
Copy instructions: Copy Date: 2 weeks prior to publication date
Average advertising content per issue: 30%
BUSINESS: REGIONAL BUSINESS: Regional Business Northern Ireland

ULSTER CHEMIST REVIEW   38774U37-400
Editorial Address: 10 Dargan Crescent, Duncrue Road, BELFAST, BT3 9JP **Tel:** 028 9080 9091 **Fax:** 028 9077 6909
Email: frances.privilege@nimedical.info
Advertising Address: As above. **Tel:** 028 9080 9090
Fax: 028 9077 6906
Email: julie.patterson@nimedical.info
Publisher: Medical Communications Ltd
Date Established: 1996
Frequency: 11 issues yearly - Published in the 3rd week of the cover month. Combined issues are published around the 1st of the cover month
Annual Sub.: £47.00
Circulation: 2,600 (Publisher's Statement)
Usual Pagination: 60
Editor: Frances Privilege; **Advertising Manager:** Julie Patterson
Summary of Content: Journal for the pharmaceutical and healthcare industry in Northern Ireland.
Readership/Target Audience: Read by pharmacists in Northern Ireland, health care decision makers in the Department of Health, Social Services and Public Safety, and members of the industry in both Northern and Southern Ireland and Britain.
ADVERTISING RATES:
Full Page Colour £1565.00
Agency Commission: 10%
Mechanical Data: Bleed Size: 307 x 220mm, Trim Size: 297 x 210mm, Film: Digital, Type Area: 267 x 180mm, Col Length: 267mm, Page Width: 180mm
Copy instructions: Copy Date: 2 weeks prior to publication date
Average advertising content per issue: 40%
BUSINESS: PHARMACEUTICAL & CHEMISTS

ULSTER FARMER   37922U21J-340
Editorial Address: Ann Street, DUNGANNON, BT70 1ET
Tel: 028 8772 2557 **Fax:** 028 8772 7334
Email: editor@observernewspapersni.com
Advertising Address: As above.
Email: editor@observernewspapersni.com
Publisher: Observer Newspapers Northern Ireland Ltd
Frequency: Weekly
Cover Price: Free
Usual Pagination: 4
Editor: Desmond Mallon; **Advertising Manager:** Desmond Mallon
Summary of Content: Journal covering agriculture and farming in Northern Ireland.
Readership/Target Audience: Read by farmers, producers and those involved in the agricultural industry.
ADVERTISING RATES:
Full Page Mono £3712.50
SCC £7.50
Agency Commission: 15%
Mechanical Data: Col Length: 550mm, No. of Columns (Display): 9, Type Area: 550 x 368mm, Col Widths (Display): 37.75mm, Print Process: Web-fed offset litho, Page Width: 368mm, Film: Digital

Copy instructions: Copy Date: Monday prior to publication date
BUSINESS: AGRICULTURE & FARMING: Agriculture & Farming - Regional

ULSTER GROCER   37986U22A-368
Editorial Address: 5B Edgewater Business Park, Belfast Harbour Estate, BELFAST, BT3 9JQ **Tel:** 028 9078 3200
Fax: 028 9078 3210
Email: kathyj@writenow.prestel.co.uk
Advertising Address: As above.
Email: michellekearney@greerpublications.com
Web site: http://www.ulstergrocer.com
Publisher: Greer Publications Ltd
Date Established: 1972
Frequency: 11 issues yearly - Published in the 1st week of the cover month
Free to qualifying individuals
Annual Sub.: £27.50
Circulation: 4,153 (ABC 01/07/2008 to 30/06/2009)
Usual Pagination: 76
Editor: Kathy Jensen; **News Editor:** Kathy Jensen; **Features Editor:** Kathy Jensen; **Advertising Manager:** Michelle Kearney
Summary of Content: Magazine covering news and views of the independent grocery trade including product news, category features, personnel, company profiles, industry issues and business advice.
Readership/Target Audience: Read by retailers, wholesalers, agents and distributors, food manufacturers and associated businesses in the grocer, convenience and CTN market in Northern Ireland.
ADVERTISING RATES:
Full Page Colour £1785.00
Agency Commission: 10%
Mechanical Data: Type Area: 270 x 183mm, Bleed Size: 307 x 220mm, Trim Size: 297 x 210mm, Col Length: 270mm, Page Width: 183mm, Film: Digital
Average advertising content per issue: 40%
BUSINESS: FOOD

ULTRASOUND   40442U56J-5
Formerly: BMUS Bulletin
Editorial Address: Dept of Cardiovascular Sciences, University of Leicester, LEICESTER
Email: emlc@le.ac.uk
Advertising Address: As above. **Tel:** 020 7306 0300
Email: lhitra@mongoosemedia.com
Web site: http://www.maney.co.uk/journals/ultrasound
ISSN: 1742-271X
Publisher: Maney Publishing
Date Established: 1983
Frequency: Quarterly
Annual Sub.: £64.00
Circulation: 3,050 (Publisher's Statement)
Usual Pagination: 56
Editor: Emma Chung; **Advertising Manager:** Louise Hitra
Summary of Content: Publication carrying authoritative review articles relating to the latest developments in medical ultrasound techniques and technology, book reviews and news on the professional activities of BMUS members.
Readership/Target Audience: Aimed at radiologists, radiographers, medical physicists, obstetricians, cardiologists and midwives.
ADVERTISING RATES:
Full Page Mono £950.00
Full Page Colour £1260.00
Agency Commission: 10%
Mechanical Data: Col Length: 270mm, Page Width: 180mm, Bleed Size: 303 x 216mm, Film: Digital, Type Area: 270 x 180mm, Trim Size: 297 x 210mm, No. of Columns (Display): 4
Copy instructions: Copy Date: 6 weeks prior to publication date
Average advertising content per issue: 25%
BUSINESS: HEALTH & MEDICAL: Radiography

UNDERLINES   39538U47B-300
Editorial Address: Room 102, Curtain House, 134-146 Curtain Road, LONDON, EC2A 3AR **Tel:** 020 7729 3664
Fax: 020 7729 3701
Email: pamunderlines@aol.com
Advertising Address: As above.
Email: sueunderlines@aol.com
Web site: http://www.networkdessous.com
ISSN: 0957-8633
Publisher: Underlines Ltd
Date Established: 1989
Frequency: 5 issues yearly
Cover Price: £12.00
Free to qualifying individuals
Annual Sub.: £55.00
Circulation: 5,202 (Publisher's Statement)
Usual Pagination: 68
Editor: Pamela Scott; **Advertising Director:** Sue Hall

Summary of Content: Magazine containing articles about the lingerie, hosiery and swimwear industry.
Readership/Target Audience: Read by manufacturers, retailers and buyers within the clothing industry.
ADVERTISING RATES:
Full Page Mono £1900.00
Full Page Colour £2750.00
Agency Commission: 15%
Mechanical Data: Page Width: 186mm, Type Area: 270 x 186mm, Print Process: Sheet-fed litho, Bleed Size: 303 x 216mm, Trim Size: 297 x 210mm, Film: Positive, right reading, emulsion side down. Digital, Col Length: 270mm
Average advertising content per issue: 40%
BUSINESS: CLOTHING & TEXTILES: Lingerie, Hosiery/Swimwear

UNDERWATER CONTRACTOR INTERNATIONAL
39448U45R-310
Editorial Address: 55 High Street, TEDDINGTON, TW11 8HA **Tel:** 020 8943 4288 **Fax:** 020 8943 4312
Email: enquiries@divermag.co.uk
Advertising Address: As above.
Email: jenny@divermag.co.uk
Web site: http://www.under-water.co.uk
ISSN: 1362-0487
Publisher: Underwater World Publications Ltd
Date Established: 1987
Frequency: 6 issues yearly
Free to qualifying individuals
Annual Sub.: £39.00
Circulation: 4,000 (Publisher's Statement)
Usual Pagination: 36
Editor: John Bevan; **Managing Editor:** Daniel Johnson; **Advertising Director:** Jenny Webb; **Publisher:** Bernard Eaton
Summary of Content: Magazine covering all aspects of commercial diving and offshore, onshore and underwater technology including remote-controlled operated vehicles.
Readership/Target Audience: Aimed at professionals in the underwater industry.
ADVERTISING RATES:
Full Page Mono £975.00
Full Page Colour £1460.00
Agency Commission: 10%
Mechanical Data: Page Width: 185mm, Digital: Digital, Type Area: 270 x 185mm, Col Length: 270mm
Copy instructions: Copy Date: 3 weeks prior to publication date
Average advertising content per issue: 45%
BUSINESS: MARINE & SHIPPING: Marine Related

UNDERWATER TECHNOLOGY
39449U45R-350
Editorial Address: 80 Coleman Street, LONDON, EC2R 5BJ
Tel: 020 7382 2601 **Fax:** 020 7382 2684
Email: mariam@sut.org.uk
Web site: http://www.sut.org.uk/journal
ISSN: 0141-0814
Publisher: Society for Underwater Technology
Date Established: 1965
Frequency: Quarterly
Cover Price: £20.00
Free to qualifying individuals
Circulation: 1,800 (Publisher's Statement)
Usual Pagination: 54
Editor: Mariam Pourshoushtari
Summary of Content: Journal carrying articles on underwater technology.
Readership/Target Audience: Read by professional engineers, academics in the oil and gas industries and marine scientists.
ADVERTISING: No Advertising taken
BUSINESS: MARINE & SHIPPING: Marine Related

UNIMER NEWS
35932U4E-365
Editorial Address: Brecon House, Mamhilad Park Estate, PONTYPOOL, NP4 0HZ **Tel:** 01495 740050
Fax: 01495 740050
Email: unimernews@constructivemedia.co.uk
Advertising Address: As above.
Email: sales@constructivemedia.co.uk
Web site: http://www.constructivemedia.co.uk
Publisher: Constructive Media
Frequency: 6 issues yearly
Cover Price: £2.00
Annual Sub.: £15.00
Circulation: 5,000 (Publisher's Statement)
Usual Pagination: 20
Editor: Glenn Ingle; **Managing Director:** Glenn Ingle;
Advertising Manager: Glenn Ingle
Summary of Content: Magazine of the Unimer trade association. Includes news, products and information.
Readership/Target Audience: Aimed at builders merchants and suppliers.
ADVERTISING RATES:
Full Page Colour £750.00
Agency Commission: 10%

Mechanical Data: Film: Digital, Print Process: Sheet-fed litho, Trim Size: 405 x 295mm
Copy instructions: Copy Date: 3 weeks prior to publication date
Average advertising content per issue: 20%
BUSINESS: ARCHITECTURE & BUILDING: Building

UNITED MAGAZINE
37214U14L-825
Formerly: Unite the Magazine
Editorial Address: 35 King Street, LONDON, WC2E 8JB
Tel: 020 7420 8947
Email: amanda.campbell@unitetheunion.com
Advertising Address: As above. **Tel:** 020 8462 7755
Fax: 020 8315 8201
Email: beverley.jenisis@unitetheunion.com
Web site: http://www.amicustheunion.org
Publisher: Unite the Union
Date Established: 2004
Frequency: Quarterly
Cover Price: Free
Circulation: 1,800,000 (Publisher's Statement)
Usual Pagination: 48
Editor: Amanda Campbell; **Advertising Manager:** Beverley Jenisis; **Managing Editor:** Amanda Campbell; **Publisher:** Derek Simpson
Summary of Content: Newsletter of Amicus AEEU Trade Union. Covers industrial and political manufacturing issues.
Readership/Target Audience: Read by members of Amicus AEEU Trade Union.
ADVERTISING: Rates on application
BUSINESS: COMMERCE, INDUSTRY & MANAGEMENT: Trade Unions

UNITED NEWS
37881U21J-348
Editorial Address: Dale Farm House, 15 Dargan Road, BELFAST, BT3 9LS **Tel:** 028 9037 2237 **Fax:** 028 9037 2206
Email: euel.agnew@utdni.co.uk
Advertising Address: 10 The Craig Lane, DOWNPATRICK, BT30 9FE **Tel:** 028 4483 1862 **Fax:** 028 4483 2956
Email: grace@g2-m.com
Web site: http://www.utdni.co.uk
Publisher: G2 Media
Date Established: 1995
Frequency: Monthly - Published in the 3rd week of the cover month
Free to qualifying individuals
Annual Sub.: £15.00
Circulation: 3,000 (Publisher's Statement)
Usual Pagination: 32
Editor: Euel Agnew; **Advertising Manager:** Grace McGauley
Summary of Content: Journal of the United Dairy Farmers. Includes articles related to dairying and also general agriculture topics, relating to farming, finances, dairy product news and farm profiles.
Readership/Target Audience: Read by dairy farmers within Northern Ireland and staff of United Dairy Farmers group.
ADVERTISING RATES:
Full Page Colour £830.00
Agency Commission: 10%
Mechanical Data: Print Process: Sheet-fed litho, Bleed Size: 310 x 223mm, Trim Size: 297 x 210mm, Film: Digital
Copy instructions: Copy Date: 2 weeks prior to publication date
BUSINESS: AGRICULTURE & FARMING: Agriculture & Farming - Regional

UNITY NEWS
37199U14L-560
Formerly: CATU News
Editorial Address: 11 Noblefield Heights, Great North Road, LONDON, N2 0NX **Tel:** 020 8341 6660 **Fax:** 0870 135 7143
Email: stephenbarry@clara.co.uk
Publisher: Stephen Barry Publicity
Frequency: Quarterly
Cover Price: Free
Circulation: 10,000 (Publisher's Statement)
Usual Pagination: 8
Editor: Stephen Barry
Summary of Content: Journal of the Unity Trade Union containing union news, views and articles of interest.
Readership/Target Audience: Aimed at members of Unity Trades Union.
ADVERTISING: No Advertising taken
BUSINESS: COMMERCE, INDUSTRY & MANAGEMENT: Trade Unions

UNIVERSITY CATERER
1739882U11A-214
Editorial Address: Unit 2.4, Paintworks, Bath Road, BRISTOL, BS4 3EH **Tel:** 0117 902 9977 **Fax:** 0117 902 9978
Email: matt@wildfirecomms.co.uk
Advertising Address: As above.
Email: beth@wildfirecomms.co.uk
Web site: http://www.tuco.org
Publisher: Wildfire Communications

Frequency: Monthly
Cover Price: Free
Circulation: 7,000 (Publisher's Statement)
Usual Pagination: 58
Editor: Matthew Robinson
Summary of Content: Magazine covering news, recipes, celebrity interviews and equipment reviews.
Readership/Target Audience: Aimed at catering managers, operational managers, chefs and front of house staff working in universities and colleges across the UK.
ADVERTISING RATES:
Full Page Colour £1250.00
Mechanical Data: Trim Size: 297 x 210mm
Copy instructions: Copy Date: 25th 8 weeks prior to publication date
BUSINESS: CATERING: Catering, Hotels & Restaurants

UNLIMITED MAGAZINE
45665U14A-514
Editorial Address: Creative Media Centre, 45 Robertson Street, HASTINGS, TN34 1NL **Tel:** 01424 439683
Fax: 01424 205401
Email: admin@tomorrowsbusinessgroup.com
Advertising Address: The Creative Media Centre, 45 Robertson Street, HASTINGS, TN34 1HL **Tel:** 01424 439683
Fax: 01424 205401
Email: admin@tomorrowsbusinessgroup.com
Web site: http://www.tomorrowsbusinessgroup.com
Publisher: Tomorrow's Business Ltd
Date Established: 1999
Frequency: Quarterly
Cover Price: £2.95
Circulation: 47,599 (Publisher's Statement)
Usual Pagination: 64
Editor: Debi Arnold; **Managing Director:** Debi Arnold; **Advertising Manager:** Debi Arnold; **Publisher:** Debi Arnold
Summary of Content: Magazine includes features on business interests, corporate issues, professional development and lifestyle.
Readership/Target Audience: Aimed at managers and their teams in purchasing, marketing, training, IT and customer service. Also office workers interested in improving their lives in and out of the office.
ADVERTISING RATES:
Full Page Colour £3600.00
Agency Commission: 10%
Mechanical Data: Page Width: 183mm, Film: Digital, Type Area: 265 x 183mm, Bleed Size: 307 x 220mm, Trim Size: 297 x 210mm, Col Length: 265mm
Average advertising content per issue: 40%
Supplement(s): Audience - 4xY, Knock off at 5ish - 4xY, Office Management Monthly - 8xY, What's Nu for Technology - 4xY, Working Smarter - 4xY
BUSINESS: COMMERCE, INDUSTRY & MANAGEMENT

UNMANNED VEHICLES
39709U49R-400
Editorial Address: 268 Bath Road, SLOUGH, SL1 4DX
Tel: 01753 727001 **Fax:** 01753 727002
Email: dl@shephard.co.uk
Advertising Address: As above.
Email: mw@shephard.co.uk
Web site: http://www.uvonline.com
ISSN: 1351-3478
Publisher: The Shephard Group
Date Established: 1995
Frequency: 6 issues yearly
Annual Sub.: £74.00
Circulation: 5,200 (Publisher's Statement)
Usual Pagination: 44
Editor: Darren Lake; **Publisher:** Mike Wild
Summary of Content: B2B publication covering all aspects of the unmanned systems industry.
Readership/Target Audience: Aimed at ministries of defence, armies, navies, governments, air forces and military/civil sectors including manufacturers and associated organisations.
ADVERTISING RATES:
Full Page Colour $7980.00
Agency Commission: 15%
Mechanical Data: Type Area: 254 x 182mm, Col Length: 254mm, Trim Size: 273 x 205mm, Bleed Size: 279 x 211mm, Page Width: 182mm, No. of Columns (Display): 3, Print Process: Offset litho, Film: Digital
Average advertising content per issue: 40%
BUSINESS: TRANSPORT: Transport Related

UNMANNED VEHICLES HANDBOOK
36364U6A-167
Formerly: Shephard's Unmanned Vehicles Handbook
Editorial Address: 268 Bath Road, SLOUGH, SL1 4DX
Tel: 01753 727001 **Fax:** 01753 727002
Email: dl@shephard.co.uk
Advertising Address: As above.
Email: gb@shephard.co.uk
Web site: http://www.uvonline.com
ISSN: 1365-6546
Publisher: The Shephard Group

Frequency: Annual - Published in December
Cover Price: £60.00
Circulation: 5,200 (Publisher's Statement)
Editor: Darren Lake
Summary of Content: Directory containing key industry contact details.
Readership/Target Audience: Aimed at all civil and military procurement agencies and users of land, sea and air UVs.
ADVERTISING RATES:
Full Page Colour £3595.00
Agency Commission: 15%
Mechanical Data: No. of Columns (Display): 3, Bleed Size: 216 x 156mm, Trim Size: 210 x 150mm, Film: Digital
Average advertising content per issue: 40%
BUSINESS: AVIATION & AERONAUTICS

UNQUOTE
35431U1N-55

Editorial Address: 4th Floor, Haymarket House, 28-29 Haymarket, LONDON, SW1Y 4RX **Tel:** 020 7484 9700
Fax: 020 7004 7548
Email: kimberly.romaine@incisivemedia.com
Advertising Address: Haymarket House, 28-29 Haymarket, LONDON, SW1Y 4RX **Tel:** 020 7484 9823
Fax: 020 7004 7548
Email: stephen.osullivan@incisivemedia.com
Web site: http://www.unquote.com
ISSN: 1467-0062
Publisher: Incisive Media Investments
Date Established: 1992
Frequency: 22 issues yearly
Annual Sub.: £1495.00
Usual Pagination: 40
Editor: Kimberly Romaine
Summary of Content: Newsletter providing the latest news on UK private equity and the venture capital industry.
Readership/Target Audience: Read by lawyers, debt providers and those involved in the UK venture capital industry.
ADVERTISING RATES:
Full Page Mono £1650.00
Full Page Colour £3300.00
Agency Commission: 10%
Mechanical Data: Film: Digital, Bleed Size: 218.9 x 285.4mm, Trim Size: 215.9 x 279.4mm
Copy instructions: Copy Date: 1 week prior to publication date
Average advertising content per issue: 10%
BUSINESS: FINANCE & ECONOMICS: Venture Capital

UPBEAT
38444U32F-700

Formerly: The Wire
Editorial Address: 173 Pitt Street, GLASGOW, G2 4JS
Tel: 0141 532 2659 **Fax:** 0141 532 2409
Email: forcepublications@strathclyde.pnn.police.uk
Advertising Address: Contact Publicity, 15 Newton Terrace, GLASGOW, G3 7PJ **Tel:** 0141 204 2042 **Fax:** 0141 204 2043
Email: info@contactpublicity.co.uk
Web site: http://www.strathclyde.police.uk
Publisher: Strathclyde Police HQ
Date Established: 2003
Frequency: Monthly
Cover Price: Free
Circulation: 11,000 (Publisher's Statement)
Usual Pagination: 24
Editor: Caroline McLafferty; **Advertising Manager:** Stewart Horn
Summary of Content: Newspaper containing topical policing issues and news from around the force as well as sport and leisure, entertainment, health and lifestyle issues.
Readership/Target Audience: Circulated to Strathclyde's police and civilian employees, retired officers, local authority leaders, libraries, the media and other forces.
ADVERTISING RATES:
Full Page Mono £1000.00
Full Page Colour £1500.00
SCC £10.00
Agency Commission: 10%
Mechanical Data: Trim Size: 420 x 297mm, Film: Digital
Copy instructions: Copy Date: 7 days prior to publication date
Average advertising content per issue: 15%
BUSINESS: LOCAL GOVERNMENT, LEISURE & RECREATION: Police

UPDATE
48655U56A-150

Formerly: Update (The Newsletter of Prostate Research Campaign UK)
Editorial Address: 10 Northfields Prospect, Putney Bridge Road, LONDON, SW18 1PE **Tel:** 020 8877 5840
Fax: 020 8877 2609
Email: info@prostate-research.org.uk
Web site: http://www.prostate-research.org.uk
Publisher: Prostate Research Campaign UK
Date Established: 1998
Frequency: Quarterly
Cover Price: Free

Circulation: 11,500 (Publisher's Statement)
Usual Pagination: 8
Editor: John Anderson
Summary of Content: Newsletter of the Prostate Research Campaign UK, containing the latest information on both benign and malignant prostate research, and fundraising for that research.
Readership/Target Audience: Aimed at men with prostate problems, their wives and families, as well as charity supporters and doctors (particularly urologists).
ADVERTISING: No Advertising taken
BUSINESS: HEALTH & MEDICAL

UPLOAD
36724U14A-18

Formerly: BT Talking Business
Editorial Address: 7 St. Martin's Place, LONDON, WC2N 4HA **Tel:** 020 7747 0700 **Fax:** 020 7747 0701
Email: sarah.bale@redwoodgroup.net
Publisher: Redwood
Date Established: 2007
Frequency: Quarterly
Cover Price: Free
Circulation: 85,000 (Publisher's Statement)
Usual Pagination: 52
Editor: Sarah Bale
Summary of Content: Magazine covering management, general business communications issues including features, case studies and practical advice.
Readership/Target Audience: Read by BT business customers in medium sized businesses.
ADVERTISING: No Advertising taken
BUSINESS: COMMERCE, INDUSTRY & MANAGEMENT

UPSTREAM
628863U33-57

Editorial Address: The International Press Centre, 4th Floor, 76 Shoe Lane, LONDON, EC4A 3JB **Tel:** 020 7842 2730
Fax: 020 7842 2735
Email: editorial@upstreamonline.com
Advertising Address: Grev Wedels plass 5, Sentrum, N-0107 OSLO **Tel:** 22 00 13 00 **Fax:** 22 00 13 10
Email: advertise@upstreamonline.com
Web site: http://www.upstreamonline.com
ISSN: 0807-6472
Publisher: NHST Media Group
Date Established: 1996
Frequency: Weekly
Annual Sub.: EUR850.00
Circulation: 7,078 (ABC 01/01/2008 to 31/12/2008)
Usual Pagination: 52
Editor: Mark Hillier; **News Editor:** Mark Hillier; **Features Editor:** Amanda Battersby; **Editor-in-Chief:** Erik Means; **Advertising Manager:** Sidsel Norvik
Summary of Content: Newspaper covering politics, topical features, opinion, personal profiles and market information on the oil and gas industry worldwide.
Readership/Target Audience: Aimed at oil and gas professionals.
ADVERTISING RATES:
Full Page Mono EUR8550.00
Full Page Colour EUR13050.00
Agency Commission: 15%
Mechanical Data: Trim Size: 365 x 246mm, Print Process: Offset litho, Film: Digital, Col Widths (Display): 49mm, Bleed Size: 395 x 386mm, No. of Columns (Display): 5, Type Area: 265 x 246mm, Col Length: 265mm, Page Width: 246mm
Copy instructions: Copy Date: 2pm Monday prior to publication date
Average advertising content per issue: 25%
Supplement(s): LNG Inside - 12xY
BUSINESS: OIL & PETROLEUM

URBAN STUDIES
35876U4D-285

Editorial Address: Adam Smith Building, University of Glasgow, 40 Bute Gardens, GLASGOW, G12 8RT
Tel: 0141 330 6631 **Fax:** 0141 330 3651
Email: jurbs@gla.ac.uk
Web site: http://www.gla.ac.uk/urbanstudiesjournal
ISSN: 0042-0980
Publisher: Sage Publications
Date Established: 1964
Frequency: Monthly
Annual Sub.: £227.00
Circulation: 1,800 (Publisher's Statement)
Usual Pagination: 200
Editor: Andrew Cumbers; **Managing Editor:** Andrew Cumbers
Summary of Content: Journal containing articles and book reviews on the subject of urban and regional planning, politics and economics.
Readership/Target Audience: Aimed at academics and professionals in planning and housing.
ADVERTISING: No Advertising taken
BUSINESS: ARCHITECTURE & BUILDING: Planning & Housing

URBAN WATER JOURNAL
637990U42C-500

Formerly: Urban Water
Editorial Address: School of Engineering, Computer Science & Mathematics, University of Exeter, North Park Road, EXETER, EX4 4QF **Tel:** 01392 264064
Fax: 020 7225 2716
Email: urbanwater@exeter.ac.uk
Web site: http://www.urbanwater.net
ISSN: 1426-0758
Publisher: Routledge, Taylor & Francis
Date Established: 1999
Frequency: Quarterly
Annual Sub.: EUR53.00
Usual Pagination: 90
Editor: David Butler; **Managing Editor:** Christos Macropoulos
Summary of Content: Journal covering all aspects of urban water engineering.
Readership/Target Audience: Aimed at professionals working in universities, research organisations, software houses, consulting companies, water utilities and governmental bodies.
ADVERTISING: No Advertising taken
BUSINESS: CONSTRUCTION: Water Engineering

URETHANES TECHNOLOGY INTERNATIONAL
38835U39-100

Formerly: Urethanes Technology
Editorial Address: 3rd Floor, 21 St. Thomas Street, LONDON, SE1 9RY **Tel:** 020 7457 1400 **Fax:** 020 7457 1440
Email: lwhite@crain.co.uk
Advertising Address: As above.
Email: pmitchell@crain.com
Web site: http://www.urethanes-technology-international.com
ISSN: 0265-637X
Publisher: Crain Communications Ltd
Date Established: 1984
Frequency: 6 issues yearly
Cover Price: £13.50
Annual Sub.: £73.00
Circulation: 6,274 (ABC 01/01/2007 to 31/12/2007)
Usual Pagination: 48
Editor: Liz White; **Managing Director:** Paul Mitchell; **Advertising Manager:** Paul Mitchell; **Publisher:** Paul Mitchell
Summary of Content: Magazine covering commercial and technical developments within the global polyurethanes industry.
Language(s): Chinese; English
Readership/Target Audience: Aimed at polyurethane based product manufacturers and the suppliers of raw materials, additives and processing equipment.
ADVERTISING RATES:
Full Page Mono EUR2266.00
Full Page Colour EUR3706.00
Agency Commission: 10%
Mechanical Data: Type Area: 254 x 184mm, Bleed Size: 292 x 215mm, Trim Size: 284 x 208mm, Col Length: 254mm, Page Width: 184mm, Film: Digital
Copy instructions: Copy Date: 6 weeks prior to publication date
Average advertising content per issue: 48%
BUSINESS: PLASTICS & RUBBER

UROLOGY NEWS
1665766U56A-183

Editorial Address: 9 Gayfield Square, EDINBURGH, EH1 3NT **Tel:** 0131 557 4184 **Fax:** 0131 557 4701
Email: jennifer@pinpoint-scotland.com
Advertising Address: As above.
Email: urologynews@pinpoint-scotland.com
Web site: http://www.pinpointmedical.com/urologynews
ISSN: 1368-8960
Publisher: Pinpoint Scotland Ltd
Date Established: 1996
Frequency: 6 issues yearly
Annual Sub.: £17.00
Circulation: 4,000 (Publisher's Statement)
Usual Pagination: 48
Editor: Alasdair Grierson; **Advertising Manager:** Ian Murphy
Summary of Content: Magazine with features of relevance to urology, journal, book and web reviews, reports on international urology conferences, events calendar and information on new products.
Readership/Target Audience: Aimed at urologists and related professionals.
ADVERTISING RATES:
Full Page Mono £992.00
Full Page Colour £1307.00
BUSINESS: HEALTH & MEDICAL

USDAW NETWORK
600973U14L-870

Editorial Address: 188 Wilmslow Road, MANCHESTER, M14 6LJ **Tel:** 0161 224 2804 **Fax:** 0161 249 2490
Email: network@usdaw.org.uk

Advertising Address: Century One Publishing, Arquen House, 4 -6 Spicer Street, ST. ALBANS, AL3 4PQ
Tel: 01727 739184 **Fax:** 01727 893895
Email: ollie@centuryonepublishing.ltd.uk
Web site: http://www.usdaw.org.uk
Publisher: USDAW
Date Established: 1999
Frequency: 6 issues yearly
Free to qualifying individuals
Circulation: 12,500 (Publisher's Statement)
Usual Pagination: 32
Editor: Peter Rees-Farrell; **Advertising Manager:** Oliver Kirkman
Summary of Content: Magazine of the Union of Shop, Distributive and Allied Workers containing political, legislative and industrial information and news.
Readership/Target Audience: Aimed at union activists.
ADVERTISING RATES:
Full Page Mono £995.00
Full Page Colour £995.00
Agency Commission: 10%
Mechanical Data: Type Area: 284 x 190mm, Col Length: 284mm, Page Width: 190mm, Trim Size: 298 x 210mm, Bleed Size: 302 x 216mm, Film: Digital
BUSINESS: COMMERCE, INDUSTRY & MANAGEMENT: Trade Unions

THE USE OF ENGLISH
41076U62B-1400

Editorial Address: University of Leicester, University Road, LEICESTER, LE1 7RH **Tel:** 0116 252 3982
Fax: 0116 252 2301
Email: engassoc@le.ac.uk
Advertising Address: As above.
Email: engassoc@le.ac.uk
Web site: http://www.le.ac.uk/engassoc
ISSN: 0013-8215
Publisher: The English Association
Date Established: 1948
Frequency: 3 issues yearly - Published in April, July and October
Annual Sub.: £42.00
Circulation: 600 (Publisher's Statement)
Usual Pagination: 96
Editor: Helen Lucas; **Advertising Manager:** Helen Lucas
Summary of Content: Magazine featuring English language, literature and education.
Readership/Target Audience: Aimed at academics and those with general interest in this field.
ADVERTISING RATES:
Full Page Mono £400.00
Mechanical Data: Film: Digital
Copy instructions: Copy Date: 4 weeks prior to publication date
Average advertising content per issue: 5%
BUSINESS: CHURCH & SCHOOL EQUIPMENT & EDUCATION: Education Teachers

USP MAGAZINE
707909U34-84

Formerly: Product Talk
Editorial Address: Suite 223, Business Design Centre, 52 Upper Street, LONDON, N1 0QH **Tel:** 020 7288 6833
Fax: 020 7288 6834
Email: julia.dennison@intelligentmedia.co.uk
Advertising Address: As above.
Email: matthew.moore@intelligentmedia.co.uk
Web site: http://www.uspmagazine.co.uk
Publisher: Intelligent Media Solutions
Frequency: Monthly - Published 3rd of the cover month
Free to qualifying individuals
Circulation: 8,300 (Publisher's Statement)
Usual Pagination: 32
Editor: Julia Dennison; **Advertising Manager:** Matthew Moore
Summary of Content: Journal covering news, practical advice and information on new office products.
Readership/Target Audience: Aimed at sales, marketing and purchasing staff within dealerships.
ADVERTISING RATES:
Full Page Colour £1675.00
Agency Commission: 10%
Mechanical Data: Type Area: 265 x 185mm, Col Length: 265mm, Trim Size: 297 x 210mm, Bleed Size: 307 x 220mm, Film: Digital, Print Process: Offset litho, Page Width: 185mm
Copy instructions: Copy Date: 20th of the month prior to publication date
Average advertising content per issue: 40%
BUSINESS: OFFICE EQUIPMENT

UT2
1826989U33-91

Editorial Address: 7 Allens Orchard, Brampton, HUNTINGDON, PE28 4NW **Tel:** 01480 370007
Email: john.howes@ntlworld.com
Advertising Address: As above.
Email: john.howes@ntlworld.com
Web site: http://www.ut-2.com
ISSN: 1752-0592

Publisher: UT2 Publishing
Date Established: 2006
Frequency: Quarterly
Cover Price: £10.00
Free to qualifying individuals
Annual Sub.: £30.00
Circulation: 4,500 (Print Run)
Usual Pagination: 52
Editor: John Howes; **Advertising Manager:** John Howes
Summary of Content: Magazine covering sub-sea sectors including offshore, survey and sub-sea engineering.
Readership/Target Audience: Aimed at members of the SUT - Society For Underwater Technology and qualified non-members and available at SUT training courses and trade exhibitions.
ADVERTISING: Rates on application
BUSINESS: OIL & PETROLEUM

UTILITIES LAW REVIEW
25986U44-2060

Editorial Address: Office G18, Spinners Court, 55 West End, WITNEY, OX28 1NH **Tel:** 01993 706183
Fax: 01993 709410
Email: ltp@lawtext.com
Web site: http://www.lawtext.com
ISSN: 0960-2356
Publisher: Lawtext Publishing Ltd
Frequency: 6 issues yearly
Annual Sub.: £405.00
Usual Pagination: 33
Editor: Nick Gingell; **Editor-in-Chief:** Cosmo Graham; **Publisher:** Nick Gingell
Summary of Content: Journal containing information on international utilities law, including legal cases, legislative and policy changes, recent surveys and analytical articles.
Readership/Target Audience: Aimed at people working in utility companies, lawyers, consumer groups and legal academics.
ADVERTISING: No Advertising taken
BUSINESS: LEGAL

UTILITY ENGINEERING
1786083U58-181

Editorial Address: For all contact details see main record, Utility Week
Frequency: Quarterly
ADVERTISING: Rates on application
Supplement to: Utility Week
BUSINESS: ENERGY, FUEL & NUCLEAR

UTILITY WEEK
40786U58-80

Editorial Address: Quadrant House, The Quadrant, SUTTON, SM2 5AS **Tel:** 020 8652 3878 **Fax:** 020 8652 8906
Email: janet.wood@rbi.co.uk
Advertising Address: As above. **Tel:** 020 8652 3875
Fax: 020 8652 3062
Email: richard.bennett@rbi.co.uk
Web site: http://www.utilityweek.co.uk
ISSN: 1356-5532
Publisher: Reed Business Information
Date Established: 1994
Frequency: Weekly
Free to qualifying individuals
Annual Sub.: £395.00
Circulation: 3,539 (ABC 01/01/2008 to 31/12/2008)
Usual Pagination: 40
Editor: Janet Wood; **Features Editor:** Karma Ockenden
Summary of Content: Magazine covering utilities - gas, water and electricity.
Readership/Target Audience: Aimed at senior managers in utility companies and major business users in the United Kingdom and Europe.
ADVERTISING RATES:
Full Page Mono £2546.00
Full Page Colour £3571.00
Agency Commission: 10%
Mechanical Data: Film: Digital, Type Area: 270 x 187mm, Bleed Size: 296 x 213mm, Trim Size: 290 x 210mm, Col Length: 270mm, Page Width: 187mm
Copy instructions: Copy Date: 1 week prior to publication date
Average advertising content per issue: 20%
Supplement(s): Utility Engineering - 4xY
BUSINESS: ENERGY, FUEL & NUCLEAR

VACATION INDUSTRY REVIEW
39730U50-180

Formerly: Network
Editorial Address: Coombe Hill House, Beverley Way, LONDON, SW20 0AR **Tel:** 020 8336 9573
Fax: 020 8336 9110
Email: adrian.bascombe@intervalintl.com
Advertising Address: As above. **Tel:** 020 8336 9299
Fax: 020 8336 9112
Email: tania.burnstock@intervalintl.com
Web site: http://www.intervalworld.com
Publisher: Interval International Ltd

Frequency: Quarterly
Cover Price: Free
Circulation: 30,000 (Publisher's Statement)
Usual Pagination: 52
Editor: Adrian Bascombe; **Advertising Manager:** Tania Burnstocks
Summary of Content: Magazine covering news on the timeshare industry worldwide plus company news from holiday exchange organisation Interval International.
Language(s): English; French; German; Italian; Spanish
Readership/Target Audience: Aimed at senior professionals in the timeshare, hospitality, travel and tourism industries.
ADVERTISING RATES:
Full Page Mono £1301.00
Full Page Colour £1794.00
Agency Commission: 10%
Mechanical Data: Film: Digital, Print Process: Offset litho
Copy instructions: Copy Date: 1st of the month prior to publication date
BUSINESS: TRAVEL & TOURISM

VAN FLEET WORLD
1605052U49D-358

Formerly: Commercial Fleet World
Editorial Address: 18 Alban Park, Hatfield Road, ST. ALBANS, AL4 0JJ **Tel:** 01727 739160 **Fax:** 01727 739169
Email: john@fleetworldgroup.co.uk
Advertising Address: As above.
Email: anne@fleetworldgroup.co.uk
Web site: http://www.fleetworldgroup.co.uk
Publisher: Stag Publications Ltd
Frequency: 10 issues yearly
Cover Price: Free
Circulation: 12,934 (Publisher's Statement)
Editor: John Kendall; **Managing Editor:** Ross Durkin
Summary of Content: Magazine covering road tests on vans and light commercial vehicles, with features on equipment and other allied services.
Readership/Target Audience: Aimed at company van operators.
ADVERTISING RATES:
Full Page Colour £3190.00
SCC £30.00
Mechanical Data: Type Area: 265 x 190mm, Bleed Size: 303 x 213mm, Trim Size: 297 x 210mm, Col Length: 265mm, Page Width: 190mm, Film: Digital
BUSINESS: TRANSPORT: Commercial Vehicles

VAN USER
39672U49D-300

Editorial Address: 27 Norwich Road, HALESWORTH, IP19 8BX **Tel:** 01986 834286 **Fax:** 01986 834255
Email: dangilkes1@mac.com
Advertising Address: As above. **Tel:** 01986 834216
Email: vanuser@micropress.co.uk
Web site: http://www.vanuser.co.uk
Publisher: Countrywide Publications
Date Established: 1985
Frequency: Monthly
Free to qualifying individuals
Annual Sub.: £22.50
Circulation: 10,000 (Publisher's Statement)
Usual Pagination: 32
Editor: Dan Gilkes
Summary of Content: Journal providing articles on new light commercial vehicles and products, including leasing, major manufacturers and users.
Readership/Target Audience: Aimed at operators of light commercial vehicles.
ADVERTISING RATES:
Full Page Colour £1500.00
Agency Commission: 10%
Mechanical Data: Film: Positive, right reading, emulsion side down. Digital, Type Area: 273 x 185mm, Bleed Size: 307 x 215mm, Trim Size: 297 x 210mm, Col Widths (Display): 42mm, No. of Columns (Display): 4, Page Width: 185mm, Col Length: 273mm
Average advertising content per issue: 40%
BUSINESS: TRANSPORT: Commercial Vehicles

VANILLAPLUS MAGAZINE
625553U18B-1762

Formerly: VanillaPlus incorporating Network Intelligence
Editorial Address: Suite 117, 70 Churchill Square, Kings Hill, WEST MALLING, ME19 4YU **Tel:** 01420 588638
Email: editorial@vanillaplus.com
Advertising Address: As above. **Tel:** 01732 844017
Fax: 01732 523509
Email: katherine@vanillaplus.com
Web site: http://www.vanillaplus.com
Publisher: Prestige Media Ltd
Date Established: 1999
Frequency: 6 issues yearly
Free to qualifying individuals
Annual Sub.: £99.00
Circulation: 5,604 (Publisher's Statement)
Usual Pagination: 52
Editor: Jeremy Cowan; **Publisher:** Jeremy Cowan

Business Magazines

Summary of Content: Magazine covering billing, CRM, OSS, fraud control, revenue and service assurance systems for voice and data communication service providers across Europe.
Readership/Target Audience: Aimed at named directors and senior managers involved in the procurement, integration, management and operations of voice and data communications networks.
ADVERTISING RATES:
Full Page Colour £2950.00
Agency Commission: 10%
Mechanical Data: Col Length: 273mm, Page Width: 186mm, Film: Digital, Type Area: 273 x 186mm, Bleed Size: 300 x 213mm, Trim Size: 297 x 210mm
Average advertising content per issue: 40%
Supplement(s): Management World CEO Guide - 1xY, VanillaPlus Directory - 1xY
BUSINESS: ELECTRONICS: Telecommunications

VARIETY
41571U64K-620

Editorial Address: 3rd Floor, Procter House, 1 Procter Street, LONDON, WC1V 6EU **Tel:** 020 7911 1924
Email: ali.jaafar@variety.com
Advertising Address: As above. **Tel:** 020 7911 1701
Fax: 020 7911 1921
Email: alberto.lopez@variety.com
Web site: http://www.variety.com
ISSN: 0042-2738
Publisher: Reed Business Information
Date Established: 1905
Frequency: Weekly
Cover Price: £5.00
Circulation: 35,000 (Publisher's Statement)
Editor: Ali Jaafar; **Advertising Manager:** Alberto Lopez
Summary of Content: Magazine containing news of the latest show business developments.
Readership/Target Audience: Aimed at people in the entertainment industry.
ADVERTISING RATES:
Full Page Mono $6971.00
Full Page Colour $11509.00
Agency Commission: 15%
Mechanical Data: Col Length: 349mm, Film: Digital, No. of Columns (Display): 5, Print Process: Web-fed offset litho, Type Area: 349 x 273mm, Page Width: 273mm
Copy instructions: Copy Date: 7 days prior to publication date
Average advertising content per issue: 50%
BUSINESS: OTHER CLASSIFICATIONS: Cinema Entertainment

VASCULAR MEDICINE
24685U56A-152

Editorial Address: 1 Oliver's Yard, 55 City Road, LONDON, EC1Y 1SP **Tel:** 020 7324 8500 **Fax:** 020 7324 8600
Email: market@sagepub.co.uk
Advertising Address: As above.
Email: advertising@sagepub.co.uk
Web site: http://www.sagepub.co.uk
ISSN: 1358-863X
Publisher: Sage Publications
Date Established: 1996
Frequency: Quarterly
Annual Sub.: £404.00
Usual Pagination: 96
Editor: Mark Creager; **Editor-in-Chief:** Mark Creager; **Advertising Manager:** Sheena Karim
Summary of Content: Publication focusing on research and developments in the field of vascular medicine.
Readership/Target Audience: Aimed at professionals in the field of vascular medicine.
ADVERTISING RATES:
Full Page Mono £900.00
Full Page Colour £2095.0
Agency Commission: 10%
Mechanical Data: Type Area: 280 x 21️0mm, Col Length: 280mm, Page Width: 210mm, Trim Size: 420 x 280mm, Film: Digital
Copy instructions: Copy Date: 8 weeks prior to publication date
Average advertising content per issue: 5%
BUSINESS: HEALTH & MEDICAL

THE VEGETABLE FARMER
37784U21A-1075

Editorial Address: Lion House, Church Street, MAIDSTONE, ME14 1EN **Tel:** 01622 695656
Fax: 01622 663733
Email: jc@actpub.co.uk
Advertising Address: As above.
Email: veg@actpub.co.uk
Web site: http://www.actpub.co.uk
ISSN: 0960-863X
Publisher: ACT Publishing
Date Established: 1989
Frequency: Monthly - Published at the beginning of the cover month
Cover Price: £2.70
Free to qualifying individuals

Annual Sub.: £30.00
Circulation: 3,000 (Publisher's Statement)
Usual Pagination: 36
Editor: Joseph Champneys; **Advertising Manager:** Joseph Champneys; **Managing Editor:** Joseph Champneys;
Publisher: John Jarrett
Summary of Content: Magazine covering all aspects of vegetable, potato and outdoor salad growing.
Readership/Target Audience: Aimed at commercial vegetable and potato growers and others involved in the industry.
ADVERTISING RATES:
Full Page Mono £1030.00
Full Page Colour £1600.00
Agency Commission: 10%
Mechanical Data: Type Area: 267 x 190mm, Trim Size: 297 x 210mm, Bleed Size: 303 x 216mm, Print Process: Sheet-fed litho, Film: Digital, Col Length: 267mm, Page Width: 190mm
Copy instructions: Copy Date: 2 weeks prior to publication date
BUSINESS: AGRICULTURE & FARMING

VEHICLE DYNAMICS INTERNATIONAL
1616242U31A-378

Editorial Address: Abinger House, Church Street, DORKING, RH4 1DF **Tel:** 01306 743744 **Fax:** 01306 887546
Email: vehicledynamics@ukintpress.com
Advertising Address: As above. **Tel:** 01306 741200
Fax: 01306 742525
Email: jason.sullivan@ukintpress.com
Web site: http://www.ukintpress.com
Publisher: UKIP Media & Events Ltd
Date Established: 2003
Frequency: Quarterly - Published in the middle of the cover month
Annual Sub.: £140.00
Circulation: 10,196 (ABC 01/01/2008 to 31/12/2008)
Editor: Graham Heeps; **Advertising Manager:** Jason Sullivan
Summary of Content: Magazine covering news, technologies and developments relating to suspension, chassis, engineering, stability and traction controls, steering, braking, ride, handling and corner module engineering.
Readership/Target Audience: Aimed at car manufacturers and vehicle dynamics experts.
ADVERTISING RATES:
Full Page Colour £3600.00
Agency Commission: 15%
Mechanical Data: Type Area: 270 x 180mm, Bleed Size: 307 x 220mm, Trim Size: 297 x 210mm, Col Length: 270mm, Film: Digital, Page Width: 180mm
Copy instructions: Copy Date: Beginning of the month prior to publication date
Average advertising content per issue: 35%
BUSINESS: MOTOR TRADE: Motor Trade Accessories

VEHICLE ELECTRICS & ELECTRONICS DIAGNOSTIC & EMISSIONS (INCORPORATING FUEL INJECTION NEWS)
38329U31A-250

Formerly: Vehicle Electrics & Electronics
Editorial Address: Oakapple Cottage, Furnace Lane, Broad Oak Brede, RYE, TN31 6ES **Tel:** 01424 882702
Fax: 01424 882702
Advertising Address: As above.
Email: info@rgoltd.co.uk
Web site: http://www.rgoltd.co.uk
Publisher: RGO Exhibitions & Publications Ltd
Frequency: Quarterly
Annual Sub.: £20.00
Circulation: 5,000 (Publisher's Statement)
Usual Pagination: 44
Editor: Chris Hancock; **Advertising Manager:** Pam Bourne
Summary of Content: Magazine about all aspects of electrical and electronic technology that is currently installed in all forms of motor vehicles.
Readership/Target Audience: Read by vehicle electricians, fuel injection specialists and fleet operators.
ADVERTISING RATES:
Full Page Mono £425.00
Full Page Colour £680.00
Agency Commission: 10%
Mechanical Data: Trim Size: 212 x 150mm, Type Area: 184 x 126mm, Col Length: 184mm, Page Width: 126mm, Bleed Size: 218 x 156mm
Copy instructions: Copy Date: 3 weeks prior to publication date
Average advertising content per issue: 40%
BUSINESS: MOTOR TRADE: Motor Trade Accessories

VEHICLE SALVAGE PROFESSIONAL
752837U31R-50

Formerly: Vehicle Salvage
Editorial Address: Suite 1, Cornerstone House, Stafford Park 13, TELFORD, TF3 3AZ **Tel:** 01952 204920
Fax: 01952 204929
Email: steve.rooney@busandcoach.com
Advertising Address: As above.
Email: jo.taylor@busandcoach.com
Publisher: Plum Publishing Limited
Date Established: 2001
Frequency: Quarterly
Free to qualifying individuals
Annual Sub.: £25.00
Circulation: 2,500 (Publisher's Statement)
Usual Pagination: 32
Editor: Steve Rooney; **Advertising Manager:** Jo Taylor; **Managing Editor:** Steve Rooney
Summary of Content: Magazine covering all aspects of the vehicle salvage industry.
Readership/Target Audience: Aimed at those working in the industry and for members of the British Vehicle Salvage Federation.
ADVERTISING RATES:
Full Page Colour £1240.00
Agency Commission: 10%
Mechanical Data: Bleed Size: +3mm, Trim Size: 297 x 210mm, Page Width: 186mm, Type Area: 273 x 186mm, Col Length: 273mm, Film: Digital, No. of Columns (Display): 4, Col Widths (Display): 43mm
Copy instructions: Copy Date: 1 week prior to publication date
Average advertising content per issue: 50%
BUSINESS: MOTOR TRADE: Motor Trade Related

VENDING INTERNATIONAL
36605U11B-190

Editorial Address: 15A London Road, MAIDSTONE, ME16 8LY **Tel:** 01622 687031 **Fax:** 01622 757646
Email: jsewell@datateam.co.uk
Advertising Address: As above.
Email: vending@datateam.co.uk
Web site: http://www.datateam.co.uk
Publisher: Datateam Publishing Ltd
Date Established: 1967
Frequency: Monthly - Published in the 1st week of the cover month
Free to qualifying individuals
Annual Sub.: £60.00
Circulation: 17,000 (Publisher's Statement)
Usual Pagination: 40
Editor: John Sewell; **Managing Director:** Parvez Kayani; **Advertising Manager:** Jenny Thompson
Summary of Content: Publication containing news and information concerning the automatic merchandising business.
Readership/Target Audience: Aimed at end-users, operators, manufacturers and suppliers within the industry.
ADVERTISING RATES:
Full Page Colour £1575.00
Agency Commission: 10%
Mechanical Data: Type Area: 275 x 210mm, Col Length: 275mm, Film: Digital, No. of Columns (Display): 2, Page Width: 210mm, Trim Size: 306 x 229mm, Bleed Size: 312 x 235mm
Copy instructions: Copy Date: 14th of the month prior to publication date
Average advertising content per issue: 40%
BUSINESS: CATERING: Vending Machines

VENTURE
652218U14A-98

Editorial Address: Unit 10, Cringleford Business Centre, Intwood Road, Cringleford, NORWICH, NR4 6AU
Tel: 01603 274130 **Fax:** 01603 274136
Email: libbie@schofieldpublishing.co.uk
Advertising Address: As above. **Fax:** 01603 274131
Email: dg@schofieldpublishing.co.uk
Web site: http://www.schofield-media.com
ISSN: 1474-1075
Publisher: Schofield Publishing Ltd
Date Established: 1999
Frequency: 6 issues yearly - Published at the end of the 1st cover month
Cover Price: £3.50
Free to qualifying individuals
Circulation: 10,000 (Publisher's Statement)
Usual Pagination: 140
Editor: Libbie Hammond; **Advertising Director:** David Garner; **Publisher:** Mike Tulloch
Summary of Content: Magazine covering current business and management issues, including corporate news, business profiles, new technologies, interviews with business and political figures, appointments and work and lifestyle features.
Readership/Target Audience: Aimed at senior directors and CEOs.
ADVERTISING RATES:
Full Page Mono £1995.00
Full Page Colour £2595.00

Section 4 (b) Business Magazines

Mechanical Data: Bleed Size: 303 x 216mm, Trim Size: 297 x 210mm
Copy instructions: Copy Date: 2 weeks prior to publication date
Average advertising content per issue: 30%
BUSINESS: COMMERCE, INDUSTRY & MANAGEMENT

THE VENTURER
41284U63B-438
Editorial Address: 24A Market Square, Potton, SANDY, SG19 2NP **Tel:** 01767 261620 **Fax:** 01767 262120
Email: editor@venturer.co.uk
Advertising Address: As above.
Email: liz@venturer.co.uk
Web site: http://www.venturer.co.uk
Publisher: Clickworks Ltd
Date Established: 1992
Frequency: 10 issues yearly - Published in the 1st week of the cover month
Cover Price: £3.00
Free to qualifying individuals
Circulation: 5,000 (Publisher's Statement)
Usual Pagination: 28
Editor: Tom Fleming; **Advertising Manager:** Liz Norman; **Publisher:** Tom Fleming
Summary of Content: Magazine covering local business news and features on motoring, commercial property, training, marketing, technology, money and legal issues.
Readership/Target Audience: Aimed at SME owners throughout East Anglia, Milton Keynes and London.
ADVERTISING RATES:
Full Page Colour £950.00
Agency Commission: 10%
Mechanical Data: Col Length: 268mm, Col Widths (Display): 44.5mm, No. of Columns (Display): 4, Type Area: 268 x 190mm, Page Width: 190mm, Bleed Size: 303 x 216mm, Trim Size: 297 x 210mm, Film: Digital
Copy instructions: Copy Date: 3 weeks prior to publication date
Average advertising content per issue: 50%
BUSINESS: REGIONAL BUSINESS: Regional Business English Counties

THE VETERINARY BUSINESS JOURNAL
624924U64H-241
Editorial Address: Olympus House, Werrington Centre, PETERBOROUGH, PE4 6NA **Tel:** 01733 325522
Fax: 01733 325512
Email: paulimrie@vbd.uk.com
Advertising Address: As above.
Email: lancehoppe@vetsonline.com
Web site: http://www.vbd.co.uk
ISSN: 1474-1652
Publisher: Veterinary Business Development Ltd
Date Established: 1994
Frequency: 6 issues yearly
Free to qualifying individuals
Annual Sub.: £77.00
Circulation: 16,000 (Publisher's Statement)
Usual Pagination: 40
Editor: Paul Imrie
Summary of Content: Magazine covering management and financial issues, services and equipment for veterinary practices.
Readership/Target Audience: Aimed at veterinary surgeons, nurses, practice managers, suppliers and academics.
ADVERTISING RATES:
Full Page Colour £1545.00
Agency Commission: 10%
Mechanical Data: Film: Digital, Bleed Size: 303 x 216mm, Trim Size: 297 x 210mm
Average advertising content per issue: 40%
BUSINESS: OTHER CLASSIFICATIONS: Veterinary

VETERINARY MANAGEMENT FOR TODAY
1654978U64H-242
Editorial Address: Elmtree Business Park, Elmswell, BURY ST. EDMUNDS, IP30 9HR **Tel:** 01359 243400
Fax: 01359 242921
Email: editor@visionline.co.uk
Advertising Address: As above.
Email: melvyn@vetsystems.com
ISSN: 1467-5196
Publisher: Vision Online
Frequency: Quarterly
Free to qualifying individuals
Annual Sub.: £35.00
Circulation: 5,000 (Publisher's Statement)
Usual Pagination: 44
Editor: Amanda Smith; **Advertising Manager:** Melvyn Wilkins
Summary of Content: Magazine covering all aspects of veterinary practice management, including articles on finance, personnel, IT, marketing and health and safety.
Readership/Target Audience: Aimed at vets and practice managers.

ADVERTISING RATES:
Full Page Colour £1200.00
Agency Commission: 10%
Mechanical Data: Bleed Size: +3mm, Trim Size: 297 x 210mm, Film: Digital
Copy instructions: Copy Date: 4 weeks prior to publication date
Average advertising content per issue: 25%
BUSINESS: OTHER CLASSIFICATIONS: Veterinary

VETERINARY PRACTICE
1836937U64H-248
Editorial Address: 30 Diamond Ridge, CAMBERLEY, GU15 4LD **Tel:** 01276 686654 **Fax:** 01276 63307
Email: teamwork@ukonline.co.uk
Advertising Address: As above.
Email: john@jcagroup.com
Web site: http://www.veterinary-practice.com
Publisher: V P Publishing Limited
Date Established: 1968
Frequency: Monthly - Published on the 1st of the cover month
Free to qualifying individuals
Annual Sub.: £36.00
Circulation: 12,600 (Publisher's Statement)
Usual Pagination: 36
Editor: David Ritchie
Summary of Content: Magazine covering the issues facing veterinary practices in the 21st century.
Readership/Target Audience: Aimed at the veterinary profession.
ADVERTISING RATES:
Full Page Colour £1200.00
Mechanical Data: Type Area: 320 x 228mm, Bleed Size: 346 x 251mm, Trim Size: 340 x 245mm, Col Length: 320mm, Page Width: 228mm, Film: Digital
Copy instructions: Copy Date: 15th of the month prior to publication date
BUSINESS: OTHER CLASSIFICATIONS: Veterinary

THE VETERINARY RECORD
41538U64H-170
Editorial Address: 7 Mansfield Street, LONDON, W1G 9NQ
Tel: 020 7636 6541 **Fax:** 020 7908 6329
Email: editorial@bva-edit.co.uk
Web site: http://www.bvapublications.com
ISSN: 0042-4900
Publisher: British Veterinary Association
Date Established: 1888
Frequency: Weekly
Annual Sub.: £210.00
Circulation: 9,957 (ABC 01/01/2008 to 31/12/2008)
Usual Pagination: 28
Editor: Kathryn Clark
Summary of Content: Journal of the British Veterinary Association. Contains professional news, comment, letters and clinical research papers.
Readership/Target Audience: Read by veterinarians.
ADVERTISING: No Advertising taken
BUSINESS: OTHER CLASSIFICATIONS: Veterinary

VETERINARY TIMES
41540U64H-180
Editorial Address: Olympus House, Werrington Centre, PETERBOROUGH, PE4 6NA **Tel:** 01733 325522
Fax: 01733 325512
Email: jackiemorrison@vbd.uk.com
Advertising Address: As above.
Email: joharley@vetsonline.com
Web site: http://www.vetsonline.com
ISSN: 1352-9374
Publisher: Veterinary Business Development Ltd
Date Established: 1973
Frequency: Weekly
Cover Price: £6.95
Free to qualifying individuals
Annual Sub.: £175.00
Circulation: 18,264 (ABC 01/01/2008 to 31/12/2008)
Usual Pagination: 32
Editor: Paul Imrie; **Features Editor:** Robin Fearon; **Advertising Manager:** Jo Harley
Summary of Content: Magazine covering veterinary medical topics, products, equipment, referral practice, industry news and meeting reports.
Readership/Target Audience: Aimed at veterinary surgeons in practice.
ADVERTISING RATES:
Full Page Colour £2000.00
SCC £17.50
Agency Commission: 10%
Mechanical Data: Bleed Size: 406 x 290mm, Trim Size: 400 x 284mm, Col Widths (Display): 40mm, No. of Columns (Display): 6, Type Area: 370 x 260mm, Col Length: 370mm, Film: Digital, Page Width: 260mm
Copy instructions: Copy Date: 2 weeks prior to publication date
Average advertising content per issue: 45%
BUSINESS: OTHER CLASSIFICATIONS: Veterinary

VETSTREAM
622727U64H-240
Editorial Address: Three Hills Farm, Bartlow, CAMBRIDGE, CB21 4EN **Tel:** 01223 895818 **Fax:** 01223 895820
Email: editorial@vetstream.com
Advertising Address: As above.
Web site: http://www.vetstream.com
Publisher: Vetstream Ltd
Date Established: 1997
Frequency: Quarterly
Circulation: 4,500 (Publisher's Statement)
Editor: Katie Dunn
Summary of Content: CD-ROM containing information on diagnosis, treatment and client communication in the field of veterinary practice.
Readership/Target Audience: Aimed at veterinary surgeons.
ADVERTISING: No Advertising taken
BUSINESS: OTHER CLASSIFICATIONS: Veterinary

VIA INMARSAT
37518U18B-1770
Formerly: Via Inmarsat Incorporating Ocean Voice
Editorial Address: 99 City Road, LONDON, EC1Y 1AX
Tel: 020 7728 1291 **Fax:** 020 7728 1179
Email: safina_hussein@inmarsat.com
Advertising Address: 23 Howland Street, LONDON, W1A 1AQ **Tel:** 020 7462 7946 **Fax:** 020 7462 7931
Email: peter.honeywell@publicis-blueprint.co.uk
Web site: http://www.inmarsat.com
Publisher: Publicis Blueprint Ltd
Date Established: 1997
Frequency: Quarterly
Annual Sub.: £20.00
Circulation: 26,000 (Publisher's Statement)
Usual Pagination: 60
Editor: Safina Hussein
Summary of Content: International magazine covering mobile satellite communication via Inmarsat.
Readership/Target Audience: Aimed at users of Inmarsat satellite systems and those who distribute Inmarsat based products and services.
ADVERTISING RATES:
Full Page Colour £3750.00
Agency Commission: 10%
Mechanical Data: Trim Size: 270 x 210mm, Film: Digital
Copy instructions: Copy Date: 1 month prior to publication date
Average advertising content per issue: 25%
BUSINESS: ELECTRONICS: Telecommunications

VIEWFINDER
41115U62F-950
Editorial Address: 77 Wells Street, LONDON, W1T 3QJ
Tel: 020 7393 1500 **Fax:** 020 7393 1555
Email: viewfinder@bufvc.ac.uk
Advertising Address: As above.
Email: viewfinder@bufvc.ac.uk
Web site: http://www.bufvc.ac.uk
ISSN: 0952-4444
Publisher: BUFVC
Frequency: Quarterly
Free to qualifying individuals
Circulation: 4,500 (Publisher's Statement)
Usual Pagination: 32
Editor: Sergio Angelini; **Managing Director:** Murray Weston; **Advertising Manager:** Sergio Angelini
Summary of Content: Magazine of the British Universities Film and Video Council, containing articles on the production, study and use of film, television and related media for higher education and research.
Readership/Target Audience: Aimed at AV librarians, subject librarians, technicians, academics with an interest in using moving images within teaching, students and anyone in higher and further education and research.
ADVERTISING RATES:
Full Page Colour £350.00
Mechanical Data: Page Width: 186mm, Film: Digital, Type Area: 256 x 186mm, Col Length: 256mm, Trim Size: 297 x 210mm
Average advertising content per issue: 10%
Supplement(s): Media Online Focus - 4xY
BUSINESS: CHURCH & SCHOOL EQUIPMENT & EDUCATION: Adult Education

VIEWPOINT
40495U56N-202
Editorial Address: 123 Golden Lane, LONDON, EC1Y 0RT
Tel: 020 7696 5599 **Fax:** 020 7454 9193
Email: viewpoint@mencap.org.uk
Advertising Address: As above. **Tel:** 020 7696 5509
Email: viewpoint@mencap.org.uk
Web site: http://www.mencap.org.uk/viewpoint
ISSN: 1358-6076
Publisher: MENCAP
Date Established: 1995
Frequency: 6 issues yearly
Free to qualifying individuals
Annual Sub.: £18.00

Business Magazines

Circulation: 6,000 (Publisher's Statement)
Usual Pagination: 40
Editor: Claire Hall; **Advertising Manager:** Helen Burger
Summary of Content: Campaigning magazine covering news, stories and opinions on learning disabilities.
Readership/Target Audience: Aimed at professionals, carers and people with a learning disability.
ADVERTISING RATES:
Full Page Colour £700.00
Mechanical Data: Trim Size: 261 x 180mm, Bleed Size: 303 x 216mm, Film: Digital
Average advertising content per issue: 5%
BUSINESS: HEALTH & MEDICAL: Mental Health

VIEWPOINT MAGAZINE
712519U2A-370

Editorial Address: Studio 2, 181 Cannon Street Road, LONDON, E1 2LX **Tel:** 020 7791 2020 **Fax:** 020 7791 2021
Email: wordsmith@thefuturelaboratory.com
Web site: http://www.thefuturelaboratory.com
Publisher: Metropolitan Publishing BV
Date Established: 1996
Frequency: Half-yearly - Published in October and April
Cover Price: £45.00
Annual Sub.: £90.00
Circulation: 20,000 (Publisher's Statement)
Usual Pagination: 180
Editor: Max Reyner; **Editor-in-Chief:** Martin Raymond
Summary of Content: Journal of trends, brands and futures that looks at how changing cultural attitudes are set to impact on brands, design, architecture, interiors, graphics and consumer buying patterns.
Readership/Target Audience: Aimed at company CEOs, creatives, opinion leaders and formers.
ADVERTISING: No Advertising taken
BUSINESS: COMMUNICATIONS, ADVERTISING & MARKETING

VINE: THE JOURNAL OF INFORMATION AND KNOWLEDGE MANAGEMENT SYSTEMS
40880U60B-300

Formerly: VINE
Editorial Address: Howard House, Wagon Lane, BINGLEY, BD16 1WA **Tel:** 01274 777700 **Fax:** 01274 785200
Email: mstanko@gwu.edu
Web site: http://www.emeraldinsight.com/vine.htm
ISSN: 0305-5728
Publisher: Emerald Group Publishing Ltd
Frequency: Quarterly
Annual Sub.: £259.00
Usual Pagination: 60
Editor: Michael Stankosky
Summary of Content: Journal covering library automation products and developments.
Readership/Target Audience: Aimed at professional librarians.
ADVERTISING: No Advertising taken
BUSINESS: PUBLISHING: Libraries

VINYL CHLORIDE REPORT
38836U39-150

Editorial Address: 24-25 Scala Street, LONDON, W1T 2HP
Tel: 020 7462 1860 **Fax:** 020 7462 1861
Email: info@harriman.co.uk
Advertising Address: As above.
Web site: http://www.harriman.co.uk
Publisher: Harriman Chemsult Ltd
Frequency: Monthly
Annual Sub.: £3500.00
Usual Pagination: 28
Editor: Henry Warren; **Managing Director:** Stephen Harriman
Summary of Content: Publication reviewing the current production and applications of vinyl chloride.
Readership/Target Audience: Aimed at those working in the vinyl chloride industry.
ADVERTISING: No Advertising taken
BUSINESS: PLASTICS & RUBBER

VIRTUAL REALITY
36011U5R-590

Editorial Address: Ashbourne House, The Guildway, Old Portsmouth Road, Artington, GUILDFORD, GU3 1LP
Tel: 01483 734635
Email: rhonda.lane@springer.com
Advertising Address: As above. **Tel:** 01483 734437
Email: rhonda.lane@springer.com
Web site: http://www.springer.com
ISSN: 1359-4338
Publisher: Springer
Frequency: Quarterly
Annual Sub.: £73.00
Editor: Rhonda Lane; **Advertising Manager:** Rhonda Lane
Summary of Content: Journal covering virtual reality technology and software systems, human factors, virtual reality applications, philosophical and ethical issues and advances made in the field of virtual reality.

Readership/Target Audience: Read by academics in that field.
ADVERTISING RATES:
Full Page Mono £440.00
Full Page Colour £1175.00
Agency Commission: 10%
Mechanical Data: Trim Size: 277 x 210mm, Type Area: 237 x 172mm, Bleed Size: 283 x 216mm, Col Length: 237mm, Page Width: 172mm, No. of Columns (Display): 2, Film: Digital
Copy instructions: Copy Date: 4 weeks prior to publication date
BUSINESS: COMPUTERS & AUTOMATION: Computers Related

VISTA
1639213U26D-201

Editorial Address: Walmar House, 296 Regent Street, LONDON, W1B 3AW **Tel:** 020 7016 2571
Fax: 020 7907 4820
Email: ben@wardour.co.uk
Web site: http://www.wardour.co.uk
Publisher: Wardour Publishing and Design
Date Established: 2004
Frequency: Monthly
Cover Price: Free
Circulation: 5,000 (Publisher's Statement)
Usual Pagination: 8
Editor: Ben Stevens
Summary of Content: Newspaper covering industry news for the landscape architecture professions.
Readership/Target Audience: Aimed at landscape architects and other professionals working within the industry.
ADVERTISING: No Advertising taken
BUSINESS: GARDEN TRADE: Garden Trade Horticulture

VISUAL SYSTEMS JOURNAL
36139U5B-231_65

Editorial Address: Oak Tree House, LEYBURN, DL8 5SE
Tel: 020 7336 0666 **Fax:** 01969 624375
Email: mike.james@infomaxgroup.co.uk
Advertising Address: 63 Gee Street, LONDON, EC1V 3RS
Tel: 020 7336 0666 **Fax:** 020 7336 0866
Email: john.sunter@bearpark.co.uk
Web site: http://www.vsj.co.uk
Publisher: Bearpark Publishing
Date Established: 1997
Frequency: 10 issues yearly
Cover Price: £5.00
Free to qualifying individuals
Circulation: 13,900 (BPA Worldwide 01/01/2008 to 30/06/2008)
Usual Pagination: 52
Editor: Mike James; **Advertising Manager:** John Sunter; **Publisher:** Nick Payne
Summary of Content: Magazine featuring in-depth technical articles on all computer software.
Readership/Target Audience: Aimed at software developers, team leaders, software architects and programming managers.
ADVERTISING RATES:
Full Page Colour £2895.00
Agency Commission: 10%
Mechanical Data: Type Area: 267 x 180mm, Col Length: 267mm, Page Width: 180mm, Film: Digital, Trim Size: 297 x 210mm
Copy instructions: Copy Date: 10th of the month prior to publication date
Average advertising content per issue: 40%
BUSINESS: COMPUTERS & AUTOMATION: Data Processing

VITALITY
624028U15A-150

Formerly: In Touch
Editorial Address: Ambrose House, Meteor Court, Barnett Way, Barnwood, GLOUCESTER, GL4 3GG
Tel: 0845 065 9000 **Fax:** 0845 065 9001
Email: davidc@babtac.com
Advertising Address: As above.
Email: charlottew@babtac.com
Web site: http://www.babtac.com
Publisher: BABTAC Ltd
Date Established: 1977
Frequency: 6 issues yearly - Published around the beginning of the 1st cover month
Free to qualifying individuals
Circulation: 13,344 (ABC 01/07/2008 to 30/06/2009)
Usual Pagination: 80
Editor: David Clifford
Summary of Content: Journal of BABTAC. Includes news and information on the beauty industry both in the UK and overseas.
Readership/Target Audience: Aimed at qualified beauticians, holistic and beauty therapists, electrolysists and students.
ADVERTISING RATES:
Full Page Colour £1245.00
Agency Commission: 10%

Mechanical Data: Bleed Size: 303 x 216mm, Type Area: 277 x 190mm, Col Length: 277mm, Trim Size: 297 x 210mm, Page Width: 190mm, Film: Digital
Copy instructions: Copy Date: 2 weeks prior to publication date
Average advertising content per issue: 40%
BUSINESS: COSMETICS & HAIRDRESSING: Cosmetics

VLV BULLETIN
760195U2D-131

Editorial Address: PO Box 401, GRAVESEND, DA12 9FY
Tel: 01474 352835 **Fax:** 01474 351112
Email: bulletin@vlv.org.uk
Web site: http://www.vlv.org.uk
ISSN: 1475-2948
Publisher: Voice of the Listener & Viewer
Date Established: 1984
Frequency: Quarterly
Annual Sub.: £30.00
Circulation: 3,000 (Publisher's Statement)
Usual Pagination: 8
Editor: Robert Beverigde
Summary of Content: Newsletter containing reports and briefings on broadcasting developments, including funding and regulations of the British broadcasting system and the future of public service broadcasting.
Readership/Target Audience: Aimed at opinion formers, broadcasters, regulators, academics, consumer and civic groups.
ADVERTISING: No Advertising taken
BUSINESS: COMMUNICATIONS, ADVERTISING & MARKETING: Broadcasting

---

THE VN TIMES
624925U64H-164

Formerly: Veterinary Nursing Times
Editorial Address: Olympus House, Werrington Centre, PETERBOROUGH, PE4 6NA **Tel:** 01733 325522
Fax: 01733 325512
Email: emmadahm@vbd.uk.com
Advertising Address: As above.
Email: jennyfrost@vetsonline.com
Web site: http://www.vetsonline.com
Publisher: Veterinary Business Development Ltd
Date Established: 2000
Frequency: Monthly - Published in the 1st week of the cover month
Cover Price: £6.95
Free to qualifying individuals
Annual Sub.: £175.00
Circulation: 9,315 (ABC 01/01/2008 to 31/12/2008)
Usual Pagination: 24
Editor: Joel Dudley
Summary of Content: Magazine covering all aspects of veterinary nursing, including information on products and developments and articles from nurses about veterinary experiences.
Readership/Target Audience: Aimed at qualified, final year and second year student veterinary nurses.
ADVERTISING RATES:
Full Page Colour £1400.00
Agency Commission: 10%
Mechanical Data: Bleed Size: 348 x 251mm, Trim Size: 342 x 245mm, Col Widths (Display): 34mm, No. of Columns (Display): 6, Film: Digital
Copy instructions: Copy Date: 13th of the month prior to publication date
Average advertising content per issue: 40%
BUSINESS: OTHER CLASSIFICATIONS: Veterinary

VNJ VETERINARY NURSING JOURNAL
41535U64H-163

Formerly: Veterinary Nursing
Editorial Address: 9600 Garsington Road, Cowley, OXFORD, OX4 2DQ **Tel:** 01865 776868
Email: s.f.badger@bristol.ac.uk
Advertising Address: Diss Business Centre, Dark Lane, Scole, DISS, IP21 4HD **Tel:** 01379 651607
Fax: 01379 643204
Email: jennie@jcagroup.com
Web site: http://www.blackwellpublishing.com/vnj
Publisher: Wiley-Blackwell Publishing
Date Established: 1985
Frequency: Monthly - Published on the 1st of the cover month
Free to qualifying individuals
Annual Sub.: £52.00
Circulation: 5,300 (Publisher's Statement)
Usual Pagination: 40
Editor: Sue Badger
Summary of Content: Official journal of The British Veterinary Nursing Association. Includes information on the care and nursing of animals and developments in the veterinary nursing profession.
Readership/Target Audience: Aimed at veterinary nurses in training and practice.
ADVERTISING RATES:
Full Page Colour £1325.00

Mechanical Data: Col Length: 287mm, Page Width: 200mm, Type Area: 287 x 200mm, Bleed Size: 303 x 216mm, Trim Size: 297 x 210mm
Copy instructions: Copy Date: 1st of the month prior to publication date
Official Journal of: The British Veterinary Nursing Association
BUSINESS: OTHER CLASSIFICATIONS: Veterinary

THE VOICE
761755U31A-371
Formerly: Vauxhall Standard
Editorial Address: Griffin House, Osborne Road, LUTON, LU1 3YT **Tel:** 01582 427190 **Fax:** 01582 426926
Email: nick.cash@gm.com
Publisher: Vauxhall Motors Ltd
Date Established: 2003
Frequency: Quarterly
Cover Price: Free
Circulation: 15,000 (Publisher's Statement)
Usual Pagination: 16
Editor: Nick Cash
Summary of Content: Newspaper covering all aspects of the motor trade including sales, staff, servicing, after-sales and parts.
Readership/Target Audience: Aimed at those working in the motor trade.
ADVERTISING: No Advertising taken
BUSINESS: MOTOR TRADE: Motor Trade Accessories

THE VOLUNTEER
1843184U40-443
Editorial Address: Publishing House, 3 Bridgebank Industrial Estate, Taylor Street, Horwich, BOLTON, BL6 7PD
Tel: 0161 909 0909 **Fax:** 0161 909 0919
Email: andy.forster@bigspark.co.uk
Advertising Address: As above.
Email: lance@bigspark.co.uk
Web site: http://www.bigspark.co.uk
Publisher: The Big Spark
Date Established: 2000
Frequency: Quarterly
Cover Price: Free
Circulation: 8,000 (Publisher's Statement)
Usual Pagination: 68
Editor: Katie Beckham
Summary of Content: Official magazine of the North West reserve forces and cadets association.
Readership/Target Audience: Aimed at the reserve and cadet forces in the North West of England.
ADVERTISING RATES:
Full Page Mono £425.00
Full Page Colour £500.00
Mechanical Data: Type Area: 270 x 190mm, Bleed Size: 303 x 216mm, Trim Size: 297 x 210mm, Col Length: 270mm, Page Width: 190mm, Film: Digital
Copy instructions: Copy Date: 2 weeks prior to publication date
Average advertising content per issue: 25%
BUSINESS: DEFENCE

VRL VEHICLE RECOVERY LINK
1842731U31R-64
Editorial Address: 1 New Cross Road, Headington, OXFORD, OX3 8LP **Tel:** 07884 137282
Email: jonathan@tlrcomms.co.uk
Advertising Address: 6 Harforde Court, John Tate Road, HERTFORD, SG13 7NW **Tel:** 0871 226 6690
Fax: 0871 226 6691
Email: michael@leadmedia.co.uk
Web site: http://www.vrlmagazine.co.uk
Publisher: Lead Media Ltd
Frequency: 6 issues yearly
Circulation: 7,500 (Publisher's Statement)
Usual Pagination: 60
Editor: Jonathan Ives; **Advertising Manager:** Michael Linegar
Summary of Content: Magazine covering the rescue and recovery industry as well as body-shops, garages, vehicle movement and salvage.
Readership/Target Audience: Aimed at the Vehicle recovery industry both commercial and cars.
ADVERTISING: Rates on application
Agency Commission: 10%
BUSINESS: MOTOR TRADE: Motor Trade Related

WALES BUSINESS INSIDER
1746709U63C-37
Editorial Address: Eastgate House, 35-43 Newport Road, CARDIFF, CF24 0AB **Tel:** 029 2043 4500
Email: douglas.friedli@newsco.com
Advertising Address: As above. **Tel:** 029 2043 4511
Email: lynn.gregory@newsco.com
Publisher: Newsco Insider Ltd
Frequency: 10 issues yearly
Free to qualifying individuals
Annual Sub.: £60.00

Circulation: 8,010 (ABC 01/07/2008 to 30/06/2009)
Editor: Douglas Friedli
Summary of Content: Business magazine containing coverage of the major issues affecting Welsh companies.
Readership/Target Audience: Aimed at CEOs and the top management of medium to large sized companies.
ADVERTISING RATES:
Full Page Colour £2090.00
Agency Commission: 10%
Mechanical Data: Type Area: 267 x 174mm, Bleed Size: 303 x 216mm, Trim Size: 297 x 210mm, Col Length: 267mm, Page Width: 174mm, Film: Digital
Copy instructions: Copy Date: 10th of month prior to publication date
Average advertising content per issue: 35%
BUSINESS: REGIONAL BUSINESS: Regional Business Wales

WAREHOUSE & LOGISTICS NEWS
36546U10-200
Editorial Address: Flame House, 12 Kings Park, Primrose Hill, KINGS LANGLEY, WD4 8ST **Tel:** 01923 272960
Fax: 01923 270760
Email: warehouse@flame1.com
Advertising Address: As above.
Email: warehouse@flame1.com
Web site: http://www.warehousenews.co.uk
ISSN: 1368-5147
Publisher: Grandflame Ltd
Date Established: 1994
Frequency: 21 issues yearly
Free to qualifying individuals
Annual Sub.: £50.00
Circulation: 7,300 (Publisher's Statement)
Usual Pagination: 36
Editor: James Surridge; **Advertising Manager:** James Surridge
Summary of Content: Newspaper focusing on the warehouse equipment and services sector, including property news and logistics.
Readership/Target Audience: Aimed at warehouse operatives, managers, e-commerce, logistics and IT managers.
ADVERTISING RATES:
Full Page Colour £1690.00
Mechanical Data: Trim Size: 420 x 297mm, Film: Digital
Average advertising content per issue: 33%
BUSINESS: MATERIALS HANDLING

WARFARE
38915U40-379
Editorial Address: 157 Vicarage Road, Leyton, LONDON, E10 5DU **Tel:** 020 8539 3876 **Fax:** 020 8539 3876
Email: keys@fsmail.net
ISSN: 0308-0676
Publisher: Delane Press
Date Established: 1974
Frequency: Quarterly
Free to qualifying individuals
Usual Pagination: 20
Editor: Ronald King
Summary of Content: Journal featuring defence studies, military history, civil defence and subversion.
Readership/Target Audience: Aimed at anyone with a personal, academic or professional interest in defence matters.
ADVERTISING: No Advertising taken
BUSINESS: DEFENCE

WARMER BULLETIN
40787U58-90
Editorial Address: Yellow Cottatge, Draughton, SKIPTON, BD23 6EA **Tel:** 01756 711362 **Fax:** 01756 711360
Email: bulletin@residua.com
Advertising Address: As above.
Email: info@residua.com
Web site: http://www.resourcesnotwaste.org
ISSN: 1362-654X
Publisher: Residua Ltd
Date Established: 1984
Cover Price: £20.00
Annual Sub.: £120.00
Circulation: 2,000 (Publisher's Statement)
Usual Pagination: 24
Editor: Kit Strange; **Managing Director:** Kit Strange;
Advertising Manager: Kit Strange
Summary of Content: Magazine covering worldwide information service on the sustainable management and recovery of resources from post-consumer wastes.
Language(s): English; Spanish
Readership/Target Audience: Aimed at waste management professionals, environmentalists, politicians and educational institutions.
ADVERTISING RATES:
Full Page Colour £1200.00
Agency Commission: 30%
BUSINESS: ENERGY, FUEL & NUCLEAR

WARSHIP TECHNOLOGY
39415U45D-380
Editorial Address: 1 Morley Road, FARNHAM, GU9 8LX
Tel: 01252 717898 **Fax:** 01252 717898
Email: foxwelld@aol.com
Advertising Address: 10 Upper Belgrave Street, LONDON, SW1X 8BQ **Tel:** 020 7235 4622 **Fax:** 020 7245 6959
Email: dmcgrath@rina.org.uk
Web site: http://www.rina.org.uk
Publisher: The Royal Institution of Naval Architects
Frequency: 5 issues yearly
Circulation: 9,000 (Publisher's Statement)
Usual Pagination: 24
Editor: David Foxwell
Summary of Content: Journal covering the latest advances in the construction, design and outfitting of naval vessels. Includes news and reports on ship technology.
Readership/Target Audience: Read by naval personnel and naval shipbuilders.
ADVERTISING RATES:
Full Page Colour £2495.00
Agency Commission: 10%
Mechanical Data: Film: Digital, Trim Size: 297 x 210mm, Bleed Size: 303 x 216mm, Type Area: 269 x 175mm, Col Length: 269mm, Page Width: 175mm
Copy instructions: Copy Date: 7th of the month prior to publication date
Average advertising content per issue: 40%
Supplement to: The Naval Architect
BUSINESS: MARINE & SHIPPING: Marine Engineering Equipment

WARSHIPS INTERNATIONAL FLEET REVIEW
38888U40-400
Editorial Address: Drury Lane, ST. LEONARDS-ON-SEA, TN38 9BJ **Tel:** 01424 720477 **Fax:** 01424 443693
Email: editor@warshipsifr.com
Advertising Address: As above. **Tel:** 01424 205530
Email: admin@hpcpublishing.com
Web site: http://www.warshipsifr.com
Publisher: HPC Publishing
Date Established: 1998
Frequency: Monthly
Free to qualifying individuals
Annual Sub.: £44.00
Circulation: 14,000 (Publisher's Statement)
Usual Pagination: 56
Editor: Iain Ballantyne; **Advertising Manager:** Edina Worthington; **Publisher:** Derek Knoll
Summary of Content: Magazine containing information on the latest developments in the world's navies, topics include news, news analysis, fleet profiles, type/class profiles of warships, commentaries on geo-political events involving navies, naval heritage/history and books covered, Amphibious forces and their missions, maritime aviation and defence industry news topics relating to naval forces.
Readership/Target Audience: Aimed at those interested in naval/military affairs and geo-politics including serving and retired officers, as well as those in defence industry and members of the public.
ADVERTISING RATES:
Full Page Colour £500.00
Agency Commission: 10%
Mechanical Data: Page Width: 180mm, Type Area: 267 x 180mm, Col Length: 267mm, Trim Size: 297 x 210mm, Bleed Size: 307 x 215mm, Film: Digital
Copy instructions: Copy Date: 4 weeks prior to publication date
Supplement(s): WARSHIPS IFR "Guide to the Royal Navy" - 2xY
BUSINESS: DEFENCE

WASTE MANAGEMENT WORLD
1640256U32B-241
Editorial Address: Warlies Park House, Horseshoe Hill, Upshire, WALTHAM ABBEY, EN9 3SR **Tel:** 01992 656600
Fax: 01992 656700
Email: wmw@pennwell.com
Advertising Address: As above.
Email: wmwadsales@pennwell.com
Web site: http://www.waste-management-world.com
Publisher: PennWell Publications International Ltd
Date Established: 1998
Frequency: 6 issues yearly
Free to qualifying individuals
Circulation: 12,000 (BPA Worldwide 01/07/2007 to 31/12/2007)
Editor: Claudine Capel
Summary of Content: Magazine focusing on sustainable waste management including news, articles and forthcoming events.
Readership/Target Audience: Aimed at decision makers within the waste management industry.
ADVERTISING RATES:
Full Page Mono £2400.00
Full Page Colour £3180.00
Agency Commission: 10%

Mechanical Data: Type Area: 277 x 190mm, Bleed Size: 307 x 220mm, Trim Size: 297 x 210mm, Col Length: 277mm, Page Width: 190mm; Film: Digital
Copy instructions: Copy Date: 2 weeks prior to publication date
BUSINESS: LOCAL GOVERNMENT, LEISURE & RECREATION: Public Health & Cleaning

WASTE MANAGEMENT YEARBOOK
40694U57-87_70

Editorial Address: Trelawney House, Chestergate, MACCLESFIELD, SK11 6DW **Tel:** 01625 613000
Fax: 01625 435078
Email: marie.roberts@tenalpspublishing.com
Advertising Address: 8th Floor, Bridgewater House, Whitworth Street, MANCHESTER, M1 6LT
Tel: 0161 832 6000 **Fax:** 0161 832 4176
Email: trade3@tenalpspublishing.com
Web site: http://www.tenalpspublishing.com
Publisher: Ten Alps Publishing
Date Established: 1995
Frequency: Annual - Published in February
Cover Price: £25.00
Free to qualifying individuals
Circulation: 7,000 (Publisher's Statement)
Usual Pagination: 124
Editor: Marie Roberts
Summary of Content: Yearbook containing industry news, updates on new technology, projects and general features on waste management, recycling and environmental topics.
Readership/Target Audience: Aimed at environmental officers working in local and central government, contractors, suppliers, lawyers and engineers.
ADVERTISING RATES:
Full Page Mono £1280.00
Full Page Colour £1875.00
Agency Commission: 10%
Mechanical Data: Trim Size: 297 x 210mm
Average advertising content per issue: 60%
BUSINESS: ENVIRONMENT & POLLUTION

WASTE PLANNING
38410U32B-200

Editorial Address: Suite 1, Fullers Court, Lower Quay Street, GLOUCESTER, GL1 2LW **Tel:** 01452 835820
Fax: 01452 835822
Email: dcs@haymarket.com
Advertising Address: 11-17 Wolverton Gardens, LONDON, W6 7BY **Tel:** 020 8267 5000 **Fax:** 020 8267 4702
Email: paul.stone@haymarket.com
Web site: http://www.planningresource.co.uk/dcs
ISSN: 0965-3147
Publisher: Development Control Sevices Ltd
Date Established: 1992
Frequency: 6 issues yearly
Annual Sub.: £90.00
Circulation: 600 (Publisher's Statement)
Usual Pagination: 56
Editor: Martin Shingler
Summary of Content: Publication focusing on the environmental and practical planning aspects of waste, particularly in the fields of legislation and policy, in theory and practice.
Readership/Target Audience: Aimed at local authorities, government departments, environmental pressure groups, the waste industry, educational institutions, environmental consultants and lawyers.
ADVERTISING RATES:
Full Page Mono £278.00
Mechanical Data: Type Area: 265 x 183mm, Col Length: 265mm, Trim Size: 297 x 210mm, Page Width: 183mm
Copy instructions: Copy Date: 1st of the month prior to publication date
Average advertising content per issue: 7%
BUSINESS: LOCAL GOVERNMENT, LEISURE & RECREATION: Public Health & Cleaning

WATER21
39070U42C-635

Editorial Address: Alliance House, 12 Caxton Street, LONDON, SW1H 0QS **Tel:** 020 7654 5500
Fax: 020 7654 5555
Email: khayward@iwap.co.uk
Advertising Address: 1 Birdcage Walk, LONDON, SW1H 9JJ **Tel:** 020 7222 3337 **Fax:** 020 7799 2479
Email: johnh@pepublishing.com
Web site: http://www.water21.co.uk
ISSN: 1561-9508
Publisher: IWA Publishing
Date Established: 1999
Frequency: 6 issues yearly
Free to qualifying individuals
Circulation: 13,000 (Publisher's Statement)
Usual Pagination: 80
Editor: Keith Hayward
Summary of Content: Magazine of the International Water Association, covering business, technology and environmental issues affecting the global water sector.

Readership/Target Audience: Read by IWA members and professionals in the water industry.
ADVERTISING RATES:
Full Page Mono £3670.00
Full Page Colour £1100.00
Agency Commission: 10%
Mechanical Data: Type Area: 267 x 180mm, Bleed Size: 303 x 216mm, Trim Size: 297 x 210mm, Col Length: 267mm, Page Width: 180mm
Copy instructions: Copy Date: 2 weeks prior to publication date
Average advertising content per issue: 40%
BUSINESS: CONSTRUCTION: Water Engineering

WATER ACTIVE
1704061U42C-761

Editorial Address: Unit 2, 57 Bushey Grove Road, BUSHEY, WD23 2JW **Tel:** 01923 235050 **Fax:** 01923 252220
Email: phil@wateractive.co.uk
Advertising Address: As above.
Email: dan@wateractive.co.uk
Web site: http://www.wateractive.co.uk
Publisher: Water Active Ltd.
Date Established: 2005
Frequency: Monthly
Free to qualifying individuals
Circulation: 7,000 (Publisher's Statement)
Usual Pagination: 28
Editor: Philip Alsop; **Advertising Manager:** Daniel Ware
Summary of Content: Magazine covering water treatment, distribution, sewage and effluent treatment, instrumentation, papers, pumps, valves, tanks, filtration, trench less technology and pollution control.
Readership/Target Audience: Aimed at management and engineering professionals within the water industry.
ADVERTISING RATES:
Full Page Colour £2000.00
Agency Commission: 10%
Mechanical Data: Type Area: 380 x 265mm, Bleed Size: 426 x 303mm, Trim Size: 420 x 297mm, Col Length: 380mm, Page Width: 265mm; Film: Digital
Average advertising content per issue: 50%
BUSINESS: CONSTRUCTION: Water Engineering

WATER AND ENVIRONMENT JOURNAL
762401U57-0

Formerly: The Journal
Editorial Address: CIWEM, 15 John Street, LONDON, WC1N 2EB **Tel:** 020 7831 3110 **Fax:** 020 7405 4967
Email: jcooper@ciwem.org
Advertising Address: Lead Media Ltd, 6 Harforde Court, John Tate Road, HERTFORD, SG13 7NW
Tel: 0870 300 0690 **Fax:** 0870 300 0691
Email: michael@leadmedia.co.uk
Web site: http://www.ciwem.org
ISSN: 1747-6585
Publisher: Wiley-Blackwell Publishing
Frequency: Quarterly
Annual Sub.: £173.00
Circulation: 12,000 (Publisher's Statement)
Usual Pagination: 80
Editor: Joanna Cooper; **Advertising Manager:** Michael Linegar
Summary of Content: Journal covering a wide range of issues within the environment sector.
Readership/Target Audience: Read by engineers, scientists and professionally qualified personnel engaged in water and environmental management.
ADVERTISING RATES:
Full Page Mono £1175.00
Full Page Colour £1795.00
Mechanical Data: Type Area: 271 x 186mm, Col Length: 271mm, Bleed Size: 301 x 214mm, Trim Size: 297 x 210mm, Film: Digital, Page Width: 186mm
BUSINESS: ENVIRONMENT & POLLUTION

WATER & SEWERAGE JOURNAL
39065U42C-655

Editorial Address: Trelawney House, Chestergate, MACCLESFIELD, SK11 6DW **Tel:** 01625 667611
Fax: 01625 455078
Email: michael.parry@tenalpspublishing.com
Advertising Address: 8th Floor, Bridgewater House, Whitworth Street, MANCHESTER, M1 6LT
Tel: 0161 832 6000 **Fax:** 0161 832 4176
Email: mandy.diamond@tenalpspublishing.com
Web site: http://www.waterjournal.co.uk
Publisher: Ten Alps Publishing
Frequency: Quarterly
Cover Price: Free
Circulation: 5,000 (Publisher's Statement)
Usual Pagination: 56
Editor: Michael Parry; **Managing Director:** Scott Masheder
Summary of Content: Journal covering all aspects of water engineering and sewage treatment.

Readership/Target Audience: Aimed at privatised water utilities and all those who work in and service the water and service utilities.
ADVERTISING RATES:
Full Page Mono £1560.00
Full Page Colour £1950.00
Agency Commission: 10%
Mechanical Data: Trim Size: 297 x 210mm, Type Area: 260 x 178mm, Col Length: 260mm, Page Width: 178mm; Film: Digital, Bleed Size: 308 x 215mm
Copy instructions: Copy Date: 6 weeks prior to publication date
Average advertising content per issue: 50%
BUSINESS: CONSTRUCTION: Water Engineering

WATER & WASTEWATER INTERNATIONAL
39066U42C-663

Editorial Address: Warlies Park House, Horseshoe Hill, Upshire, WALTHAM ABBEY, EN9 3SR **Tel:** 01992 656600
Email: davidm@pennwell.com
Advertising Address: As above. **Fax:** 01992 656700
Email: stephenj@pennwell.com
Web site: http://www.wwinternational.com
Publisher: PennWell Publishing Ltd
Date Established: 1986
Frequency: 6 issues yearly - Published in the middle of the 1st cover month
Free to qualifying individuals
Annual Sub.: $217.00
Circulation: 12,000 (Publisher's Statement)
Usual Pagination: 52
Editor: David Mogollon; **Managing Editor:** David Mogollon
Summary of Content: Magazine focusing on international water and wastewater management and treatment, irrigation and groundwater development.
Readership/Target Audience: Aimed at managers and engineers in the water and wastewater industries.
ADVERTISING RATES:
Full Page Colour $5630.00
Agency Commission: 15%
Mechanical Data: Type Area: 270 x 184mm, Col Length: 270mm, Page Width: 184mm; Film: Digital, Trim Size: 297 x 210mm, Bleed Size: 303 x 216mm
Average advertising content per issue: 50%
BUSINESS: CONSTRUCTION: Water Engineering

WATER & WASTEWATER TREATMENT
39061U42C-750

Formerly: Water & Waste Treatment
Editorial Address: Faversham House, 232A Addington Road, SOUTH CROYDON, CR2 8LE **Tel:** 020 8651 7100
Fax: 020 8651 7117
Email: natasha.wiseman@ntlworld.com
Advertising Address: As above.
Email: adamj@fav-house.com
Web site: http://www.wwt-magazine.info
ISSN: 0950-6651
Publisher: Faversham House Group Ltd
Date Established: 1950
Frequency: Monthly - Published on the 15th of the cover month
Free to qualifying individuals
Annual Sub.: £77.00
Circulation: 8,680 (ABC 01/01/2008 to 31/12/2008)
Usual Pagination: 52
Editor: Natasha Wiseman; **Advertising Manager:** Adam Jeffery
Summary of Content: Magazine covering all aspects of the treatment and supply of potable water, the treatment and supply of waste water, and the treatment of industrial effluent.
Readership/Target Audience: Aimed at managers, engineers and scientists in the water and waste water industry.
ADVERTISING RATES:
Full Page Mono £1620.00
Full Page Colour £1920.00
Agency Commission: 10%
Mechanical Data: Page Width: 180mm, Type Area: 270 x 180mm, Col Length: 270mm; Film: Digital, Trim Size: 297 x 210mm, Bleed Size: 303 x 215mm
Copy instructions: Copy Date: 15th of the month prior to publication date
Supplement(s): Ireland - 2xY, Pipes FactFinder - 1xY, Round Table - 1xY, Tank FactFinder - 1xY
BUSINESS: CONSTRUCTION: Water Engineering

WATER ASSET MANAGEMENT INTERNATIONAL
1698267U42C-759

Editorial Address: Alliance House, 12 Caxton Street, LONDON, SW1H 0QS **Tel:** 020 7654 5500
Fax: 020 7654 5555
Email: cfitzpatrick@iwap.co.uk
Web site: http://www.iwapublishing.com
ISSN: 1814-5434
Publisher: IWA Publishing

Date Established: 2005
Frequency: Quarterly
Annual Sub.: £187.00
Usual Pagination: 24
Editor: Catherine Fitzpatrick
Summary of Content: Newsletter focusing on asset management in water and wastewater utilities.
Readership/Target Audience: Aimed at asset managers working in the water industry.
ADVERTISING: No Advertising taken
BUSINESS: CONSTRUCTION: Water Engineering

WATER, ENERGY & ENVIRONMENT JOURNAL
39067U42C-665
Editorial Address: 33-35 Cantelupe Road, EAST GRINSTEAD, RH19 3BE **Tel:** 01342 316390
Fax: 01342 333701
Email: tmcsmith@western-bp.co.uk
Advertising Address: As above. **Tel:** 01342 333725
Email: scoles@progressive-media.co.uk
Web site: http://www.energy-online.net
ISSN: 0964-8321
Publisher: Progressive Media
Date Established: 1999
Frequency: 6 issues yearly - Published at the end of the first cover month
Free to qualifying individuals
Circulation: 15,048 (ABC 01/01/2008 to 31/12/2008)
Usual Pagination: 92
Editor: Tim McManan-Smith; **Managing Editor:** Tim McManan-Smith; **Publisher:** Eamonn Brennan
Summary of Content: Journal covering new products, technologies and trends in energy efficiency, environmental compliance and water use. Provides solutions to the problems of running an industrial location or commercial building.
Readership/Target Audience: Aimed at those looking for advice on energy efficiency, good environmental practice and water and waste management.
ADVERTISING RATES:
Full Page Mono £2585.00
Full Page Colour £2985.00
Agency Commission: 10%
Mechanical Data: Type Area: 287 x 200mm, Col Length: 287mm, Page Width: 200mm, Trim Size: 297 x 210mm, Bleed Size: 303 x 216mm, Film: Digital
Copy instructions: Copy Date: 2 weeks prior to publication date
Average advertising content per issue: 50%
Supplement(s): Energy Efficient Solutions - 1xY, Water Efficient Solutions - 1xY
BUSINESS: CONSTRUCTION: Water Engineering

WATER INNOVATION
627327U35-8
Formerly: bottledwaterworld
Editorial Address: 7 Kingsmead Square, BATH, BA1 2AB
Tel: 01225 327890 **Fax:** 01225 327891
Email: nd@zipublishing.com
Advertising Address: As above.
Email: sales@zipublishing.com
Web site: http://www.foodbev.com/water
Publisher: Zenith International
Date Established: 2000
Frequency: 6 issues yearly
Free to qualifying individuals
Annual Sub.: £95.00
Circulation: 5,005 (Publisher's Statement)
Usual Pagination: 42
Editor: Nayl D'Souza
Summary of Content: Publication containing news, innovation, views, interviews, company profiles and expert opinion of the global packaged water industry.
Readership/Target Audience: Aimed at brand and process managers, retail specifiers, suppliers and analysts.
ADVERTISING RATES:
Full Page Colour £2435.00
Agency Commission: 15%
Mechanical Data: Trim Size: 297 x 210mm, Bleed Size: 303 x 213mm, Film: Digital
Copy instructions: Copy Date: 2 weeks prior to publication date
Average advertising content per issue: 28%
BUSINESS: PACKAGING & BOTTLING

WATERBORNE & HIGH SOLIDS COATINGS
37288U16B-230
Editorial Address: 14 Castle Mews, High Street, HAMPTON, TW12 2NP **Tel:** 020 8487 0800
Fax: 020 8487 0801
Email: coatings@pra-world.com
Web site: http://www.pra-world.com
ISSN: 0140-8798
Publisher: PRA
Frequency: Monthly
Annual Sub.: £390.00
Circulation: 80 (Publisher's Statement)

Usual Pagination: 28
Editor: Richard Kennedy; **Advertising Manager:** Andrew Doroszkowski
Summary of Content: Journal covering colloid and surface science, polymers and resins, environment coatings, and water borne and high solids technology. Also covers patents and news items.
Readership/Target Audience: Aimed at technical staff, product development managers of coatings manufacturers and raw materials suppliers.
ADVERTISING: No Advertising taken
BUSINESS: DECORATING & PAINT: Paint - Technical Manufacture

WATERLINES
39073U42C-666
Editorial Address: Bourton Hall, Bourton, RUGBY, CV23 9QZ **Tel:** 01926 634501 **Fax:** 01926 634502
Email: journals.edit@itpubs.org.uk
Advertising Address: As above.
Email: marketing@itpubs.org.uk
Web site: http://www.practicalactionpublishing.org.uk/waterlines.htm
ISSN: 0262-8104
Publisher: Practical Action Publishing
Date Established: 1979
Frequency: Quarterly
Annual Sub.: £50.00
Circulation: 1,200 (Publisher's Statement)
Usual Pagination: 80
Managing Director: Toby Milner
Summary of Content: Journal covering all aspects of water supply and sanitation in developing countries.
Readership/Target Audience: Aimed at water and sanitation engineers within international development agencies.
ADVERTISING RATES:
Full Page Mono £500.00
Full Page Colour £900.00
Agency Commission: 5%
Mechanical Data: Film: Digital, Type Area: 267 x 180mm, Col Length: 267mm, Page Width: 180mm
Copy instructions: Copy Date: 6 weeks prior to publication date
BUSINESS: CONSTRUCTION: Water Engineering

WATSONIA
38139U26D-170
Editorial Address: SBRC, The Museum, High Street, IPSWICH, IP1 3QH **Tel:** 01473 433547 **Fax:** 01473 433558
Email: sbrc@globalnet.co.uk
Web site: http://www.bsbi.org.uk/publications
ISSN: 0043-1532
Publisher: Botanical Society of the British Isles
Date Established: 1957
Frequency: Half-yearly - Published in February and August
Annual Sub.: £22.00
Circulation: 3,200 (Publisher's Statement)
Usual Pagination: 140
Editor: Martin Sanford
Summary of Content: Journal containing articles on botany, taxonomy, biosystematics, ecology, conservation and distribution of British and Irish vascular plants, book reviews, plant records and obituaries.
Readership/Target Audience: Aimed at botanical taxonomists, ecologists and conservationists.
ADVERTISING: No Advertising taken
BUSINESS: GARDEN TRADE: Garden Trade Horticulture

WAYMARK
40696U57-95
Editorial Address: PO Box 78, SKIPTON, BD23 4UP
Tel: 07000 782316
Email: editor@iprow.co.uk
Advertising Address: As above. **Tel:** 07000 782318
Email: iprow@iprow.co.uk
Web site: http://www.iprow.co.uk
ISSN: 1363-7649
Publisher: Waymark
Date Established: 1986
Frequency: Quarterly
Cover Price: £7.50
Free to qualifying individuals
Circulation: 600 (Publisher's Statement)
Usual Pagination: 20
Editor: Mike Furness; **Advertising Manager:** Mike Furness
Summary of Content: Journal of the Institute of Public Rights of Way and Access Management. Covers issues relating predominantly to public access to open spaces and the legislation and practice behind rights of way.
Readership/Target Audience: Read by countryside access managers in the public, private and charitable sectors, plus lobbyists and private enthusiasts.
ADVERTISING: Rates on application
Agency Commission: 10%
Copy instructions: Copy Date: 6 weeks prior to publication date
Average advertising content per issue: 40%
BUSINESS: ENVIRONMENT & POLLUTION

WEALTH MANAGEMENT
35317U1F-560
Editorial Address: 22 Buckingham Gate, LONDON, SW1E 6LB **Tel:** 020 7674 0400 **Fax:** 020 7674 0404
Email: iorton@tru-est.com
Web site: http://www.tru-est.com
ISSN: 1462-2807
Publisher: Tru-Est Group
Date Established: 1997
Frequency: Quarterly
Annual Sub.: £890.00
Circulation: 7,500 (Publisher's Statement)
Usual Pagination: 44
Editor: Ian Orton
Summary of Content: Magazine providing analysis of key topics such as new investment products and services, risk adjusted performance analysis, professional fees, real estate, tax and estate planning, hedge funds, sector analysis and profiles of leading firms.
Readership/Target Audience: Aimed at anyone involved with private wealth management, family offices, tax specialists, lawyers, private bankers, real estate advisers, asset managers and technology suppliers.
ADVERTISING: No Advertising taken
BUSINESS: FINANCE & ECONOMICS: Investment

WEATHER
41586U64N-80
Editorial Address: The Atrium, Southern Gate, CHICHESTER, PO19 8SQ **Tel:** 01243 779777
Email: weather@wiley.com
Advertising Address: As above.
Email: tturner@wiley.co.uk
Web site: http://www.rmets.org
ISSN: 0043-1656
Publisher: John Wiley & Sons Ltd
Date Established: 1946
Frequency: Monthly - Published on the 1st of the month
Free to qualifying individuals
Annual Sub.: £40.00
Circulation: 4,200 (Publisher's Statement)
Usual Pagination: 32
Editor: Laura Sampson
Summary of Content: Magazine containing articles on new developments, climatic variations and their impact, climate and meteorological events.
Readership/Target Audience: Aimed at those interested in meteorology.
ADVERTISING: Rates on application
Copy instructions: Copy Date: 6 weeks prior to publication date
Average advertising content per issue: 5%
BUSINESS: OTHER CLASSIFICATIONS: Weather

WEDDING PROFESSIONAL
1779362U52C-162
Editorial Address: 47 Church Street, BARNSLEY, S70 2AS
Tel: 01226 734712
Email: mf@whpl.net
Advertising Address: As above. **Tel:** 01226 734333
Fax: 01226 734477
Email: dlh@whpl.net
Web site: http://www.weddingprofessional.co.uk
Publisher: Wharncliffe Publishing Ltd
Frequency: 6 issues yearly - Published in the last week of the 1st cover month
Free to qualifying individuals
Circulation: 8,000 (Publisher's Statement)
Usual Pagination: 32
Editor: Mary Ferguson; **Advertising Manager:** Danielle Hornby; **Group Editor:** Andrew Harrod
Summary of Content: Publication covering all aspects of wedding planning including catering, photography, floristry, venues, overseas weddings, legal issues and insurance.
Readership/Target Audience: Aimed at the professional wedding planning market including wedding planners, organisers and specialist wedding intermediaries.
ADVERTISING RATES:
Full Page Colour £1295.00
Agency Commission: 10%
Mechanical Data: Type Area: 320 x 220mm, Bleed Size: 346 x 246mm, Trim Size: 340 x 240mm, Col Length: 320mm, Page Width: 220mm, Film: Digital
Copy instructions: Copy Date: 2 weeks prior to publication date
BUSINESS: GIFT TRADE: Fancy Goods

WEED ABSTRACTS
38140U26D-172
Editorial Address: Nosworthy Way, WALLINGFORD, OX10 8DE **Tel:** 01491 832111 **Fax:** 01491 829198
Web site: http://www.cabi.org
ISSN: 0043-1729
Publisher: CABI
Frequency: Monthly
Circulation: 265 (Publisher's Statement)
Editor: Debbie Cousins
Summary of Content: An abstract journal covering the ecology of weeds, including parasitic, aquatic and poisonous species. Weed control using biological, chemical,

environmental and non-target effects, residues and legislation.
Readership/Target Audience: Aimed at weed scientists, researchers and extension workers.
ADVERTISING: No Advertising taken
BUSINESS: GARDEN TRADE: Garden Trade Horticulture

WEEKLY CAPITAL EVENT DIARY
760838U1R-350

Editorial Address: Fitzroy House, 13-17 Epworth Street, LONDON, EC2A 4DL **Tel:** 020 7825 8100
Fax: 020 7608 2032
Email: steve.crisp@interactivedata.com
Advertising Address: As above.
Email: david.gilbert@interactivedata.com
Web site: http://www.interactivedataclients.com
Publisher: Interactive Data (Europe) Limited
Frequency: Weekly
Annual Sub.: £1450.00
Editor: Steve Crisp
Summary of Content: Journal featuring capital events and in-depth corporate actions. Includes adjustment and apportionment articles.
Readership/Target Audience: Aimed at those involved in financial settlements.
ADVERTISING: Rates on application
BUSINESS: FINANCE & ECONOMICS: Financial Related

WEEKLY PETROLEUM ARGUS
38637U33-58

Editorial Address: 175 St. John Street, LONDON, EC1V 4LW **Tel:** 020 7780 4200 **Fax:** 020 7780 4201
Email: wpa@argusmediagroup.com
Web site: http://www.argusmediagroup.com
Publisher: Argus Media Ltd
Frequency: Weekly
Annual Sub.: $1200.00
Usual Pagination: 16
Editor: Richard Child; **Editor-in-Chief:** Ian Bourne
Summary of Content: Newsletter containing news and reports on oil and gas investment.
Readership/Target Audience: Aimed at Chief Executives and Senior Executives of oil and gas companies.
ADVERTISING: No Advertising taken
BUSINESS: OIL & PETROLEUM

WEEKLY TRIBUNE
759533U21D-950

Editorial Address: Flaxfield, Wittons Lane, Hoxne, EYE, IP21 5AE **Tel:** 01379 669157 **Fax:** 01379 669157
Email: wt@bcnewslink.com
Advertising Address: As above.
Email: wt@bcnewslink.com
Publisher: Newslink
Date Established: 1994
Frequency: Weekly
Annual Sub.: £70.00
Usual Pagination: 5
Editor: Brian Chester; **Advertising Manager:** Brian Chester
Summary of Content: Newsletter of the British and European pig markets covering up-to-date news from home and abroad, on the state of the pig industry, as well as market prices and trends.
Readership/Target Audience: Read by pig farmers, suppliers, meat processors and retailers in the UK and Europe.
ADVERTISING RATES:
SCC £50.00
Agency Commission: 10%
Mechanical Data: No. of Columns (Display): 3, Digital: Pdf
Copy instructions: Copy Date: Tuesday, 4pm prior to publication date
Average advertising content per issue: 20%
BUSINESS: AGRICULTURE & FARMING: Livestock

WEIR BULLETIN
37600U19A-537

Editorial Address: 20 Waterloo Street, GLASGOW, G2 6DB
Tel: 0141 637 7111 **Fax:** 0141 221 9789
Email: helen.walker@weir.co.uk
Web site: http://www.weir.co.uk
Publisher: The Weir Group PLC
Date Established: 1920
Frequency: Half-yearly
Cover Price: Free
Circulation: 8,000 (Publisher's Statement)
Usual Pagination: 16
Editor: Helen Walker
Summary of Content: Magazine covering engineering developments in the Weir Group and its subsidiary companies.
Readership/Target Audience: Aimed at investors, customers, suppliers and employees.
ADVERTISING: No Advertising taken
BUSINESS: ENGINEERING & MACHINERY

WELSH FARMER (Y TIR)
37923U21J-345

Editorial Address: Llys Amaeth, Plas Gogerddan, ABERYSTWYTH, SY23 3BT **Tel:** 01970 820820
Fax: 01970 820823
Email: ytir@fuw.org.uk
Advertising Address: South West Wales Media Ltd, 18 King Street, CARMARTHEN, SA31 1BN **Tel:** 01267 227275
Email: rhian.jones@swwmedia.co.uk
Web site: http://www.fuw.org.uk
Publisher: Farmers' Union of Wales
Date Established: 1956
Frequency: Monthly - Published in the 1st week of the cover month
Cover Price: £0.35
Free to qualifying individuals
Annual Sub.: £10.00
Circulation: 13,549 (Publisher's Statement)
Usual Pagination: 24
Editor: Peter Roberts; **Advertising Manager:** Rhian Jones
Summary of Content: Journal focusing on Welsh livestock farming, including news items and information on farm vehicles and livestock rearing.
Language(s): English; Welsh
Readership/Target Audience: Aimed at commercial farmers and rural dwellers.
ADVERTISING RATES:
Full Page Mono £2217.60
Full Page Colour £2661.12
SCC £7.70
Agency Commission: 10%
Mechanical Data: Type Area: 360 x 270mm, Col Length: 360mm, Trim Size: 393 x 300mm, Print Process: Web-fed offset litho, Film: Digital, Page Width: 270mm, No. of Columns (Display): 8, Col Widths (Display): 32mm
Copy instructions: Copy Date: 2 weeks prior to publication date
Average advertising content per issue: 40%
BUSINESS: AGRICULTURE & FARMING: Agriculture & Farming - Regional

WEM (WATER AND ENVIRONMENT MAGAZINE)
39064U42C-650

Formerly: Water & Environment Manager
Editorial Address: 29 Reades Lane, Sonning Common, READING, RG4 9LL **Tel:** 0118 972 2810 **Fax:** 0118 972 1177
Email: wememeditor@ciwem.org
Advertising Address: 6 Harforde Court, John Tate Road, HERTFORD, SG14 1DW **Tel:** 0871 622 6690
Fax: 0871 310 0348
Email: wem@leadmedia.co.uk
Web site: http://www.ciwem.org
ISSN: 1362-9360
Publisher: Lead Media Ltd
Frequency: 10 issues yearly - Published on the 29th of the month prior to publication date
Annual Sub.: £95.00
Circulation: 12,500 (Publisher's Statement)
Usual Pagination: 48
Editor: Erika Yarrow
Summary of Content: Magazine covering a wide range of environmental stories.
Readership/Target Audience: Read mainly by environmental professionals and those interested in the environment.
ADVERTISING RATES:
Full Page Mono £1175.00
Full Page Colour £1795.00
Agency Commission: 10%
Mechanical Data: Col Length: 271mm, Type Area: 271 x 186mm, Bleed Size: 301 x 214mm, Trim Size: 297 x 210mm, Page Width: 186mm, Film: Digital
Copy instructions: Copy Date: 16th of the month prior to publication date
Average advertising content per issue: 40%
BUSINESS: CONSTRUCTION: Water Engineering

WEST & CENTRAL AFRICA MONITOR
1641988U14C-356

Editorial Address: Mermaid House, 2 Puddle Dock, LONDON, EC4V 3DS **Tel:** 020 7248 0468
Fax: 020 7248 0467
Email: emartins@businessmonitor.com
Web site: http://www.businessmonitor.com
Publisher: Business Monitor International Ltd
Frequency: Monthly
Annual Sub.: £325.00
Circulation: 300 (Publisher's Statement)
Editor: Elizabeth Martins
Summary of Content: Publication covering economic and political developments in West and Central Africa including government, economy, finance and the business environment.
Readership/Target Audience: Aimed at investors who have invested or are looking to invest in Africa.
ADVERTISING: No Advertising taken
BUSINESS: COMMERCE, INDUSTRY & MANAGEMENT: International Commerce

WEST MIDLANDS HERALD
41387U63B-1975_30

Editorial Address: Building D, Templar Buisness Park, off Torrington Avenue, COVENTRY, CV4 9AP
Tel: 024 7647 4310 **Fax:** 024 7646 2694
Email: stevenprice@bizworldonline.com
Advertising Address: As above. **Tel:** 024 7646 5000
Email: wmh@bizworldonline.com
Web site: http://www.bizworldonline.com
Publisher: Artfeks Publishing
Frequency: 11 issues yearly
Annual Sub.: £38.00
Circulation: 79,000 (Publisher's Statement)
Usual Pagination: 44
Editor: Peter Marshall; **Advertising Manager:** Andrew Laing; **Group Editor:** Vince Clarke
Summary of Content: Publication covering local news in the West Midlands area.
Readership/Target Audience: Read by businesses in the area.
ADVERTISING RATES:
Full Page Mono £1560.00
Full Page Colour £1872.00
BUSINESS: REGIONAL BUSINESS: Regional Business English Counties

WESTERN & SOUTH WALES AUTO TRADER
38349U31A-320

Editorial Address: 1 Buckingham Court, Beaufort Business Park, Bradley, Stoke North, BRISTOL, BS32 4NF
Tel: 01454 616161 **Fax:** 01454 616716
Email: james.cole@autotrader.co.uk
Advertising Address: As above.
Email: westerntrade@autotrader.co.uk
Publisher: Western Regional Publishing
Frequency: Weekly
Circulation: 11,500 (Publisher's Statement)
Editor: James Cole; **Advertising Manager:** James Cole
Summary of Content: Magazine listing cars and vehicles for sale, both private and trade.
Readership/Target Audience: Read by prospective buyers and sellers.
ADVERTISING: Rates on application
Agency Commission: 10%
Copy instructions: Copy Date: Monday prior to publication date
Average advertising content per issue: 97%
BUSINESS: MOTOR TRADE: Motor Trade Accessories

WESTERN COUNTIES BUSINESS NEWS
1800703U63B-2575

Editorial Address: The Tindle Suite, Webbs House, The Parade, LISKEARD, PL14 6AH **Tel:** 01579 342174
Email: businessnews@internet-today.co.uk
Publisher: Cornish Times Group
Frequency: 8 issues yearly
Free to qualifying individuals
Editor: Brian Doel; **Managing Director:** Brian Doel
Summary of Content: Newspaper focusing on local business issues.
Readership/Target Audience: Aimed at members of the business community in Cornwall, Devon and Somerset.
ADVERTISING: Rates on application
BUSINESS: REGIONAL BUSINESS: Regional Business English Counties

WESTMINSTER PLANNING
35877U4D-400

Editorial Address: 8 Crane Grove, LONDON, N7 8LE
Tel: 020 7267 5224
Email: leemallett@btinternet.com
Web site: http://www.greaterlondonpublishing.com
Publisher: Greater London Publishing
Date Established: 1984
Frequency: Monthly
Annual Sub.: £200.00
Circulation: 400 (Publisher's Statement)
Usual Pagination: 20
Editor: Lee Mallett
Summary of Content: Newsletter reporting on the activities of Westminster Planning Committee.
Readership/Target Audience: Aimed at city planners.
ADVERTISING: No Advertising taken
BUSINESS: ARCHITECTURE & BUILDING: Planning & Housing

WET NEWS
39060U42C-697

Editorial Address: Faversham House, 232A Addington Road, SOUTH CROYDON, CR2 8LE **Tel:** 020 8651 7100
Fax: 020 8651 7117
Email: newsdesk@edie.net
Advertising Address: As above.
Email: deborah.lilley@fav-house.com
Web site: http://www.wetnews.co.uk
ISSN: 1364-4513

Publisher: Faversham House Group Ltd
Date Established: 1995
Frequency: Monthly
Free to qualifying individuals
Annual Sub.: £75.00
Circulation: 6,110 (ABC 01/01/2008 to 31/12/2008)
Usual Pagination: 32
Editor: Sam Bond
Summary of Content: Newspaper for the water and effluent treatment industries.
Readership/Target Audience: Aimed at water industry contractors.
ADVERTISING RATES:
Full Page Mono £1750.00
Full Page Colour £2150.00
Agency Commission: 10%
Mechanical Data: Type Area: 254 x 178mm, Col Length: 254mm, Page Width: 178mm, Film: Digital
Copy instructions: Copy Date: 2 weeks prior to publication date
Average advertising content per issue: 50%
BUSINESS: CONSTRUCTION: Water Engineering

WHAT FRANCHISE
1665919U14A-540
Editorial Address: 49 Old Steine, BRIGHTON, BN1 1NH
Tel: 01273 748675
Email: jeff@partridgeltd.co.uk
Advertising Address: Gloucester House, 9 Gloucester Mews, South Street, EASTBOURNE, BN21 4XH
Tel: 01323 636000 **Fax:** 01323 646144
Email: richard@partridgeltd.co.uk
Web site: http://www.whatfranchisemagazine.co.uk
Publisher: Partridge Publications
Date Established: 2005
Frequency: Quarterly
Cover Price: £3.75
Free to qualifying individuals
Circulation: 11,883 (ABC 01/01/2008 to 31/12/2008)
Editor: Jeff James
Summary of Content: Magazine focusing on all elements of franchising in the UK.
Readership/Target Audience: Aimed at those wishing to invest in a franchise.
ADVERTISING RATES:
Full Page Colour £2995.00
Agency Commission: 10%
Mechanical Data: Type Area: 270 x 183mm, Bleed Size: 306 x 220mm, Trim Size: 297 x 210mm, Col Length: 270mm, Page Width: 183mm, Film: Digital
Average advertising content per issue: 40%
BUSINESS: COMMERCE, INDUSTRY & MANAGEMENT

WHEAT, BARLEY & TRITICALE ABSTRACTS
37821U21B-980
Editorial Address: Nosworthy Way, WALLINGFORD, OX10 8DE **Tel:** 01491 832111 **Fax:** 01491 829292
Email: cabi@cabi.org
Web site: http://www.cabi.org
ISSN: 0265-7880
Publisher: CABI
Date Established: 1984
Frequency: 6 issues yearly
Annual Sub.: £1120.00
Circulation: 35 (Publisher's Statement)
Editor: Halina Dawson
Summary of Content: International journal covering plant breeding and genetics, plant physiology, soil science, pests and diseases, agricultural engineering, crop science, seeds and grains, weeds and weed control, agricultural economics, human and animal nutrition and agronomy.
Readership/Target Audience: Aimed at academic and government research institutes, seed companies and plant breeding centres.
ADVERTISING: No Advertising taken
BUSINESS: AGRICULTURE & FARMING: Agriculture - Supplies & Services

WHEELS
37219U14L-900
Editorial Address: Almond House, Oak Green, Stanley Green Business Park, CHEADLE HULME, SK8 6QL
Tel: 0161 486 2103 **Fax:** 0161 485 3109
Email: info@urtu.com
Advertising Address: As above.
Email: info@urtu.com
Web site: http://www.urtu.com
Publisher: URTU
Frequency: 6 issues yearly
Free to qualifying individuals
Circulation: 15,500 (Publisher's Statement)
Usual Pagination: 24
Editor: James Bower; **Advertising Manager:** James Bower
Summary of Content: Journal of the United Road Transport Union.
Readership/Target Audience: Aimed at the road transport industry, especially drivers.

ADVERTISING RATES:
Full Page Colour £500.00
Mechanical Data: Trim Size: 297 x 210mm, Bleed Size: 303 x 216mm, Film: Digital
BUSINESS: COMMERCE, INDUSTRY & MANAGEMENT: Trade Unions

THE WHEELS OF BUSINESS
1852607U49D-364
Editorial Address: The Courtyard, Ladycross Farm, Hollow Lane, Dormansland, LINGFIELD, RH7 6PB
Tel: 01342 872020
Email: vicky.stewart@streampublishing.net
Publisher: Stream Publishing Ltd
Date Established: 2008
Frequency: 3 issues yearly - Published in spring, summer and winter
Cover Price: Free
Circulation: 30,000 (Publisher's Statement)
Usual Pagination: 20
Editor: Vicky Stewart; **Managing Director:** Darren Styles
Summary of Content: Customer magazine for Vauxhall commercial vehicles. Featuring case studies, tips and advice on running a small business plus road tests featuring Vauxhalls commercial vehicles line up.
Readership/Target Audience: Aimed at customers and prospects of Vauxhall commercial vehicles.
ADVERTISING: No Advertising taken
BUSINESS: TRANSPORT: Commercial Vehicles

WHO CARES?
38503U32G-137
Editorial Address: Kemp House, 152-160 City Road, LONDON, EC1V 2NP **Tel:** 020 7251 3117
Fax: 020 7251 3123
Email: mark.tobin@thewhocarestrust.org.uk
Web site: http://www.thewhocarestrust.org.uk
ISSN: 0951-8444
Publisher: The Who Cares? Trust
Date Established: 1987
Frequency: Quarterly
Circulation: 31,500 (Publisher's Statement)
Usual Pagination: 24
Editor: Mark Tobin
Summary of Content: Magazine containing photostories, interviews, letters, poems and reviews of films, games and music.
Readership/Target Audience: Read by 10 to 18 year olds in public care throughout the UK.
ADVERTISING: No Advertising taken
BUSINESS: LOCAL GOVERNMENT, LEISURE & RECREATION: Community Care & Social Services

WHO MINDS?
38504U32G-138
Editorial Address: Royal Court, 81 Tweedy Road, BROMLEY, BR1 1TG **Tel:** 020 8290 2512
Fax: 0845 880 0043
Email: whominds@ncma.org.uk
Advertising Address: As above. **Tel:** 020 8290 2515
Email: promotions@ncma.org.uk
Web site: http://www.ncma.org.uk
ISSN: 0141-7126
Publisher: National Childminding Association
Date Established: 1977
Frequency: 6 issues yearly
Free to qualifying individuals
Circulation: 45,000 (Publisher's Statement)
Usual Pagination: 52
Editor: Hannah McEwen; **Advertising Manager:** Julie Fennelly
Summary of Content: Magazine of the National Childminding Association. Contains news, views and issues relating to childminding and childcare. Including health and safety matters, legal changes, new product development, nutrition, child psychology, education, play ideas and competitions for childminders and children.
Language(s): English; Welsh
Readership/Target Audience: Aimed at registered childminders throughout England and Wales.
ADVERTISING RATES:
Full Page Colour £1460.00
Agency Commission: 10%
Mechanical Data: Film: Digital, Trim Size: 297 x 210mm, Bleed Size: 303 x 216mm, Type Area: 277 x 190mm, Col Length: 277mm, Page Width: 190mm
Average advertising content per issue: 15%
BUSINESS: LOCAL GOVERNMENT, LEISURE & RECREATION: Community Care & Social Services

WILTSHIRE BUSINESS
41389U63B-1980
Formerly: The Business (Swindon Chamber of Commerce & Industry)
Editorial Address: 100 Victoria Road, SWINDON, SN1 3BE
Tel: 01793 528144 **Fax:** 01793 501888
Email: lrobinson@newswilts.co.uk
Advertising Address: As above. **Fax:** 01793 501746
Email: jgreer@newswilts.co.uk

Web site: http://www.thisiswiltshire.co.uk
Publisher: Newsquest (Wiltshire) Ltd
Frequency: 11 issues yearly
Cover Price: Free
Circulation: 7,000 (Publisher's Statement)
Usual Pagination: 40
Editor: Leigh Robinson; **Managing Director:** Shamus Donald; **Advertising Manager:** Jane Greer
Summary of Content: Regional business and financial news magazine.
Readership/Target Audience: Aimed at the local business community.
ADVERTISING RATES:
Full Page Colour £1529.00
SCC £5.15
Agency Commission: 10%
Mechanical Data: Col Length: 330mm, Col Widths (Display): 25mm, No. of Columns (Display): 9, Type Area: 330 x 250mm, Film: Digital, Page Width: 250mm
Copy instructions: Copy Date: 1 week prior to publication date
Average advertising content per issue: 50%
Supplement to: Swindon Advertiser
BUSINESS: REGIONAL BUSINESS: Regional Business English Counties

WIND DIRECTIONS
713846U58-140
Editorial Address: Hockpitt Farm, Hockpitt Lane, Over Stowey, BRIDGWATER, TA5 1EX **Tel:** 01278 732921
Email: crispin@aubrey.fslife.co.uk
Advertising Address: Rue d'Arlon 63-65, B-1040 BRUSSELS **Tel:** 2 400 1056 **Fax:** 2 546 1944
Email: jc@ewea.org
Web site: http://www.ewea.org
Publisher: European Wind Energy Association
Date Established: 1978
Frequency: 5 issues yearly
Annual Sub.: EUR60.00
Circulation: 4,000 (Publisher's Statement)
Usual Pagination: 48
Editor: Crispin Aubrey; **Advertising Manager:** Jonathan Collings
Summary of Content: Journal of the European Wind Energy Association containing key policy issues, industry activities, new technologies, technical developments, project, company and country profiles and interviews with those involved in the wind and renewable energy industry.
Readership/Target Audience: Read by officials of European institutions and national governments, politicians, journalists, researchers, industry representatives, university lecturers, members of the EWEA and its member associations at national level and members of the public with an interest in wind power.
ADVERTISING RATES:
Full Page Colour EUR2400.00
Mechanical Data: Trim Size: 297 x 210mm, Bleed Size: 307 x 220mm, Film: Digital, Type Area: 287 x 200mm, Col Length: 287mm, Page Width: 200mm
Copy instructions: Copy Date: 2 weeks prior to publication date
BUSINESS: ENERGY, FUEL & NUCLEAR

WIND ENERGY
40788U58-150
Editorial Address: The Atrium, Southern Gate, CHICHESTER, PO19 8SQ **Tel:** 01243 779777
Fax: 01243 775878
Advertising Address: As above. **Tel:** 01243 770254
Fax: 01243 770432
Email: fpidduck@wiley.co.uk
Web site: http://www.interscience.wiley.com
ISSN: 1095-4244
Publisher: John Wiley & Sons Ltd
Date Established: 1998
Frequency: 8 issues yearly
Cover Price: £710.00
Usual Pagination: 104
Editor: Peter Mitchell; **Executive Editor:** Peter Mitchell
Summary of Content: Journal reporting on the advances and technology available for harnessing clean energy from the wind.
Readership/Target Audience: Aimed at design and consulting engineers, the wind energy industry, wind farm development planners and academics.
ADVERTISING RATES:
Full Page Mono £1175.00
Full Page Colour £2575.00
Agency Commission: 10%
Mechanical Data: Trim Size: 260 x 200mm, Type Area: 230 x 170mm, Col Length: 230mm, Page Width: 170mm, Print Process: Sheet-fed litho, Film: Digital
BUSINESS: ENERGY, FUEL & NUCLEAR

WINDOW FABRICATOR AND INSTALLER
35934U12B-77
Editorial Address: Regal House, Regal Way, WATFORD, WD24 4YF **Tel:** 01923 237799 **Fax:** 01923 246901
Email: wfi@hamerville.co.uk

Business Magazines

Advertising Address: As above.
Email: wfi@hamerville.co.uk
Web site: http://www.hamerville.co.uk
Publisher: Hamerville Magazines Ltd
Frequency: 11 issues yearly - Published in the 1st week of the cover month
Annual Sub.: £30.00
Circulation: 9,625 (ABC 01/01/2008 to 31/12/2008)
Usual Pagination: 72
Editor: Keely Portway; **Managing Editor:** Terry Smith;
Publisher: Bryan Shannon
Summary of Content: Magazine covering news and features on the manufacturing and installation of windows, conservatories and doors.
Readership/Target Audience: Read by glaziers and those involved in window fabrication and installation.
ADVERTISING RATES:
Full Page Mono £1470.00
Full Page Colour £1470.00
Agency Commission: 10%
Mechanical Data: Type Area: 260 x 180mm, Bleed Size: 303 x 216mm, Trim Size: 297 x 210mm, Page Width: 180mm, Film: Digital, Col Length: 260mm
Copy instructions: Copy Date: Middle of the month prior to publication date
Average advertising content per issue: 50%
BUSINESS: CERAMICS, POTTERY & GLASS: Glass

WINDOW INDUSTRIES
36635U12B-75

Editorial Address: 173 High Street, RICKMANSWORTH, WD3 1AY **Tel:** 01923 692670 **Fax:** 01923 692679
Email: j.hatcher@turretgroup.com
Advertising Address: As above. **Tel:** 01923 692660
Email: m.haroon@turretgroup.com
Web site: http://www.turretgroup.com
Publisher: Turret Group Ltd.
Frequency: Monthly - Published in the 1st week of the cover month
Free to qualifying individuals
Annual Sub.: £73.00
Circulation: 7,418 (ABC 01/01/2008 to 31/12/2008)
Editor: John Hatcher; **Managing Director:** Richard Hease
Summary of Content: Journal containing new product information and features of interest to anyone in the windows, doors and conservatories business.
Readership/Target Audience: Read by manufacturers and installers of windows and doors.
ADVERTISING RATES:
Full Page Colour £1465.00
SCC £25.00
Agency Commission: 10%
Mechanical Data: Page Width: 178mm, Type Area: 254 x 178mm, Trim Size: 297 x 210mm, Bleed Size: 303 x 216mm, Col Length: 254mm, Film: Digital
Copy instructions: Copy Date: 2 weeks prior to publication date
Average advertising content per issue: 50%
BUSINESS: CERAMICS, POTTERY & GLASS: Glass

WINDOWS ACTIVE
1665755U12B-84

Editorial Address: PO Box 627, RICKMANSWORTH, WD3 0BQ **Tel:** 0870 766 1653 **Fax:** 0870 766 8529
Email: edit@windowsactive.co.uk
Advertising Address: As above. **Tel:** 0870 766 8419
Email: sales@windowsactive.co.uk
Web site: http://www.windowsactive.co.uk
Publisher: Active Magazines Ltd
Date Established: 2005
Frequency: 10 issues yearly
Cover Price: Free
Circulation: 10,000 (Publisher's Statement)
Usual Pagination: 96
Editor: John Cowie; **Advertising Manager:** Steve Gravestock
Summary of Content: Magazine covering specification, fabrication and installation of windows, doors and conservatories.
Readership/Target Audience: Aimed at the window, door and conservatory industry.
ADVERTISING RATES:
Full Page Colour £1170.00
SCC £25.00
Agency Commission: 10%
Mechanical Data: Type Area: 277 x 190mm, Bleed Size: 303 x 216mm, Trim Size: 297 x 210mm, Col Length: 277mm, Page Width: 190mm, Film: Digital
Copy instructions: Copy Date: 3rd of the cover month
Average advertising content per issue: 50%
BUSINESS: CERAMICS, POTTERY & GLASS: Glass

WINGBEAT
40724U57-120

Editorial Address: The Lodge, SANDY, SG19 2DL
Tel: 01767 680551 **Fax:** 01767 683262
Email: derek.niemann@rspb.org.uk
Advertising Address: As above.
Email: lynda.whytock@rspb.org.uk

Publisher: The Royal Society for the Protection of Birds
Frequency: Quarterly
Circulation: 40,000 (Publisher's Statement)
Usual Pagination: 12
Editor: Derek Niemann
Summary of Content: Magazine covering teenage involvement in conservation issues.
Readership/Target Audience: Aimed at environmentally aware youth and organisations associated with conservation issues.
ADVERTISING: Rates on application
BUSINESS: ENVIRONMENT & POLLUTION

WIN.MAC.LINUX
36141U5B-270

Formerly: Win.Mac.Web
Editorial Address: 6 Querrin Street, LONDON, SW6 2SJ
Tel: 07050 600420
Advertising Address: As above.
Email: davidbp@msn.com
ISSN: 0966-9191
Publisher: Business Connexion$
Date Established: 1984
Frequency: Monthly
Annual Sub.: £48.00
Circulation: 16,510 (Publisher's Statement)
Usual Pagination: 72
Editor: David Bach-Price; **Advertising Manager:** David Bach-Price; **Publisher:** David Bach-Price
Summary of Content: Journal covering software, hardware and communications issues within the European and International business community.
Language(s): Arabic; English
Readership/Target Audience: Aimed at business and marketing managers of international companies.
ADVERTISING: Rates on application
BUSINESS: COMPUTERS & AUTOMATION: Data Processing

WINNING EDGE
35731U2F-50

Formerly: Sales & Marketing Professional
Editorial Address: Harrier Court, Woodside Road, Lower Woodside, LUTON, LU1 4DQ **Tel:** 01582 840001
Fax: 01582 849142
Email: magazine@ismm.co.uk
Advertising Address: As above. **Tel:** 01582 843261
Email: magazine@ismm.co.uk
Web site: http://www.ismm.co.uk
ISSN: 1470-3009
Publisher: The Institute of Sales & Marketing Management
Date Established: 1966
Frequency: 6 issues yearly
Free to qualifying individuals
Circulation: 7,500 (Publisher's Statement)
Usual Pagination: 52
Editor: Tom Nash; **Advertising Manager:** Stuart Morgan
Summary of Content: Official magazine of the Institute of Sales and Marketing Management. Covers market intelligence, sales techniques and marketing strategy.
Readership/Target Audience: Read by members of the Institute.
ADVERTISING RATES:
Full Page Colour £1540.00
Agency Commission: 10%
Mechanical Data: Type Area: 272 x 174mm, Col Length: 272mm, Trim Size: 297 x 210mm, Bleed Size: 303 x 216mm, Page Width: 174mm, Film: Digital
Copy instructions: Copy Date: 2 weeks prior to publication date
BUSINESS: COMMUNICATIONS, ADVERTISING & MARKETING: Selling

WIRE & CABLE ASIA
38181U27-175

Editorial Address: 46 Holly Walk, LEAMINGTON SPA, CV32 4HY **Tel:** 01926 334137 **Fax:** 01926 314755
Email: gill@intras.co.uk
Advertising Address: As above.
Email: paul.b@intras.co.uk
Web site: http://www.read-wca.com
ISSN: 0218-3277
Publisher: Intras Ltd
Date Established: 1992
Frequency: 6 issues yearly - Published on the 1st of the cover month
Annual Sub.: £85.00
Circulation: 9,200 (Publisher's Statement)
Usual Pagination: 80
Editor: Gill Watson; **Publisher:** Caroline Sullens
Summary of Content: Journal covering the latest developments in production. Includes articles on supply and processing machinery plus, cable and wire industry news.
Language(s): Chinese; English
Readership/Target Audience: Read by industry managers, engineers and technicians in Asia.
ADVERTISING RATES:
Full Page Mono $1655.00
Full Page Colour $2205.00

Agency Commission: 15%
Mechanical Data: Col Length: 260mm, No. of Columns (Display): 3, Type Area: 260 x 180mm, Bleed Size: 303 x 214mm, Trim Size: 297 x 210mm, Film: Digital, Page Width: 180mm
Copy instructions: Copy Date: 4 weeks prior to publication date
Average advertising content per issue: 40%
BUSINESS: METAL, IRON & STEEL

WIRED
1873236U5B-9026

Editorial Address: 6-8 Old Bond Street, LONDON, W1S 4PH
Email: wired.pr@condenast.co.uk
Web site: http://www.wired.co.uk
Publisher: Conde Nast Publications Ltd
Date Established: 2009
Frequency: Monthly
Cover Price: £3.80
Summary of Content: Magazine featuring new ideas, innovations and trends in technology, science, social science and culture.
Readership/Target Audience: Aimed at those interested in new ideas, innovations and trends.
ADVERTISING: Rates on application
BUSINESS: COMPUTERS & AUTOMATION: Data Processing

WIREIN
1660518U17-255

Formerly: Wired-IN
Editorial Address: 29 Main Street, Bothwell, GLASGOW, G71 8RD **Tel:** 01698 330015 **Fax:** 01698 854208
Email: wirein@straightlinepublishing.com
Advertising Address: As above. **Tel:** 01698 853000
Email: alex@straightlinepublishing.com
Web site: http://www.wirein.co.uk
Publisher: Straight Line Publishing Ltd
Date Established: 2005
Frequency: 6 issues yearly
Cover Price: £4.00
Free to qualifying individuals
Circulation: 10,604 (ABC 01/01/2007 to 31/12/2007)
Usual Pagination: 76
Editor: Alexander Duncan; **Advertising Manager:** Alexander Duncan
Summary of Content: Magazine focusing on the electrical industry in Scotland and Ireland. Includes the latest leads, tenders, opportunities, unbiased industry news, technical features, new products, all legislation and developments affecting the industry.
Readership/Target Audience: Aimed at electrical contractors, installers, builders, councils, specifiers, wholesalers and end users.
ADVERTISING RATES:
Full Page Colour £2750.00
Agency Commission: 10%
Mechanical Data: Type Area: 270 x 190mm, Bleed Size: 303 x 216mm, Trim Size: 297 x 210mm, Col Length: 270mm, Page Width: 190mm, Film: Digital
Average advertising content per issue: 40%
BUSINESS: ELECTRICAL

WIRELESS BUSINESS REVIEW
1790454U18B-1973

Editorial Address: PR by email only
Email: editorial@morianmediagroup.com
Advertising Address: 2 Granger Row, CHELMSFORD, CM1 4WF **Tel:** 020 7871 2958
Email: t.roll@morianamediagroup.com
Web site: http://www.telecomredux.net
Publisher: Moriana Media Group
Frequency: Quarterly
Cover Price: Free
Circulation: 15,000 (Publisher's Statement)
Usual Pagination: 52
Editor: Priscilla Awde; **Advertising Manager:** Terry Roll
Summary of Content: Publication focused on wireless practitioners with features and reports on current trends and developments within the global wireless community.
Readership/Target Audience: Aimed at higher management within the global wireless community including operators, vendors and service providers.
ADVERTISING RATES:
Full Page Colour £5500.00
Agency Commission: 10%
Mechanical Data: Trim Size: 297 x 210mm, Bleed Size: 303 x 216mm, Type Area: 277 x 190mm, Col Length: 277mm, Page Width: 190mm, Film: Digital
Copy instructions: Copy Date: 1 month prior to publication date
Average advertising content per issue: 40%
BUSINESS: ELECTRONICS: Telecommunications

WIRELESS WATCH
1642084U5B-9009

Editorial Address: 4 Metro Central Heights, 119 Newington Causeway, LONDON, SE1 6BA **Tel:** 020 7403 3292
Fax: 0870 420 5172
Email: caroline@rethinkresearch.biz
Web site: http://www.rethinkresearch.biz
Publisher: Rethink Research Associates
Date Established: 2003
Frequency: Weekly
Annual Sub.: £1000.00
Usual Pagination: 30
Editor: Caroline Gabriel
Summary of Content: Research service covering wireless broadband, ultra wideband, mobile telephony, enterprise wireless, mobility, PDAs, smart antenna and smartphones.
Readership/Target Audience: Aimed at operators, enterprise software houses, wireless equipment and software suppliers, investors and enterprise wireless teams.
ADVERTISING: No Advertising taken
BUSINESS: COMPUTERS & AUTOMATION: Data Processing

WIRING MATTERS
37330U17-250

Editorial Address: Michael Faraday House, Six Hills Way, STEVENAGE, SG1 2AY **Tel:** 01438 313311
Fax: 01438 318361
Email: gcronshaw@theiet.org
Advertising Address: As above. **Tel:** 01438 767351
Fax: 01438 765515
Email: advert@theiet.org
Web site: http://www.theiet.org
ISSN: 1749-978X
Publisher: The Institution of Engineering and Technology
Date Established: 1991
Frequency: Quarterly - Published in the middle of the cover months, March, June, September and November
Cover Price: Free
Circulation: 42,500 (Publisher's Statement)
Usual Pagination: 24
Editor: Geoff Cronshaw
Summary of Content: Magazine covering electrical installation contracting and associated standards, regulations and products.
Readership/Target Audience: Aimed at electrical contractors, architects, specifiers, designers and people working in the electrical industry.
ADVERTISING RATES:
Full Page Mono £1817.00
Full Page Colour £2076.00
Agency Commission: 15%
Mechanical Data: Bleed Size: 303 x 216mm, Col Length: 270mm, Page Width: 178mm, Type Area: 270 x 178mm, Trim Size: 297 x 210mm, Film: Digital
Copy instructions: Copy Date: 2 weeks prior to publication date
BUSINESS: ELECTRICAL

THE WOMAN ENGINEER
37564U19A-540

Editorial Address: Michael Faraday House, Six Hills Way, Stevenage, HERTFORDSHIRE, SG1 2AY **Tel:** 01483 569248
Email: editor@wes.org.uk
Advertising Address: As above. **Tel:** 01438 765506
Email: info@wes.org.uk
Web site: http://www.wes.org.uk
ISSN: 0043-7298
Publisher: Women's Engineering Society
Date Established: 1920
Frequency: Quarterly
Annual Sub.: £25.00
Circulation: 1,300 (Publisher's Statement)
Usual Pagination: 12
Editor: Patricia Battams; **Advertising Manager:** Patricia Battams
Summary of Content: Journal of the Women's Engineering Society. Covering society news, technical articles, international profiles, engineering events and issues concerning a family friendly workplace.
Readership/Target Audience: Aimed at women in engineering industries and female students.
ADVERTISING RATES:
Full Page Mono £300.00
Full Page Colour £350.00
SCC £0.80
Mechanical Data: Type Area: 270 x 190mm, Col Length: 270mm, Page Width: 190mm, Bleed Size: 303 x 216mm, Trim Size: 297 x 210mm, No. of Columns (Display): 3, Col Widths (Display): 58mm
Copy instructions: Copy Date: 7th of the month prior to publication date
BUSINESS: ENGINEERING & MACHINERY

WOMEN'S FARM & GARDEN ASSOCIATION
38141U26D-200

Editorial Address: 175 Gloucester Street, CIRENCESTER, GL7 2DP **Tel:** 01285 658339
Email: admin@wfga.org.uk

Advertising Address: As above.
Email: admin@wfga.org.uk
Web site: http://www.wfga.org.uk
Publisher: WFGA
Frequency: 6 issues yearly
Free to qualifying individuals
Annual Sub.: £20.00
Circulation: 1,000 (Publisher's Statement)
Usual Pagination: 12
Editor: Jane Adams; **Advertising Manager:** Jane Adams
Summary of Content: Newsletter containing association news and items of interest, including details of tours, workshops and conferences.
Readership/Target Audience: Aimed at professional women and men working in horticulture and agriculture.
ADVERTISING: Rates on application
Copy instructions: Copy Date: 3 weeks prior to publication date
Average advertising content per issue: 5%
BUSINESS: GARDEN TRADE: Garden Trade Horticulture

WOMEN'S WEAR DAILY
39515U47A-385

Editorial Address: 20 Shorts Gardens, LONDON, WC2H 9AU **Tel:** 020 7240 0420 **Fax:** 020 7240 0290
Email: samantha.conti@fairchildpub.com
Advertising Address: 9 rue Royale, 75008 PARIS
Tel: 1 44 51 13 03 **Fax:** 1 42 68 12 33
Email: elizabeth.haynes@fairchildpub.com
Web site: http://www.wwd.com
Publisher: Fairchild Publications
Frequency: 250 issues yearly
Annual Sub.: £410.00
Circulation: 43,000 (Publisher's Statement)
Editor: Nina Jones; **Advertising Director:** Elizabeth Haynes
Summary of Content: Magazine covering trends, ready-to-wear, sports wear, accessories and leg wear for women and children and menswear.
Readership/Target Audience: Aimed at retailers, designers and those with an interest in fashion and beauty.
ADVERTISING RATES:
Full Page Mono $26420.00
Full Page Colour $33025.00
Agency Commission: 15%
Mechanical Data: Trim Size: 325 x 264mm, Film: Digital
Copy instructions: Copy Date: 10 days prior to publication date
Average advertising content per issue: 50%
BUSINESS: CLOTHING & TEXTILES

WOOD BASED PANELS INTERNATIONAL
39471U46-73

Editorial Address: Progressive House, 2 Maidstone Road, Foots Cray, SIDCUP, DA14 5HZ **Tel:** 01371 856072
Fax: 01371 856072
Email: mbotting@wbpionline.com
Advertising Address: As above. **Tel:** 01234 713008
Fax: 01234 714248
Email: kporter@wbpionline.com
Web site: http://www.wbpionline.com
ISSN: 0144-7238
Publisher: Progressive Media Publications
Date Established: 1980
Frequency: 6 issues yearly - Published in the 1st week of the 1st cover month
Annual Sub.: £289.00
Circulation: 4,782 (ABC 01/01/2008 to 31/12/2008)
Usual Pagination: 60
Editor: Michael Botting; **News Editor:** Derek Steel
Summary of Content: Journal covering all aspects of wood based panels and agricultural fibre based panels.
Readership/Target Audience: Aimed at panel manufacturers worldwide, using wood, urban wood waste or agricultural residues to make panels.
ADVERTISING RATES:
Full Page Colour EUR6435.00
Agency Commission: 10%
Mechanical Data: Type Area: 265 x 180mm, Film: Digital, Bleed Size: 303 x 216mm, Trim Size: 297 x 210mm, Print Process: Sheet-fed offset litho, Col Length: 265mm, Page Width: 180mm
Copy instructions: Copy Date: 6 weeks prior to publication date
Average advertising content per issue: 50%
BUSINESS: TIMBER, WOOD & FORESTRY

WOODLAND HERITAGE JOURNAL
39473U46-105

Editorial Address: PO Box 168, HASLEMERE, GU27 1XQ
Tel: 01428 652159
Email: enquiries@woodlandheritage.org.uk
Advertising Address: As above. **Fax:** 01428 652159
Email: enquiries@woodlandheritage.org.uk
Web site: http://www.woodlandheritage.org.uk
Publisher: Alphaprint Colchester Ltd
Date Established: 1994
Frequency: Annual - Published in March

Cover Price: £1.00
Free to qualifying individuals
Circulation: 3,000 (Publisher's Statement)
Usual Pagination: 80
Editor: Lewis Scott; **Advertising Manager:** Lewis Scott
Summary of Content: Official Journal of Woodland Heritage, containing information on the management of trees and woodlands, publication of reports of study tours and projects funded by Woodland Heritage.
Readership/Target Audience: Read by members of Woodland Heritage, other like-minded initiatives and groups.
ADVERTISING: Rates on application
Copy instructions: Copy Date: End of November prior to publication date
BUSINESS: TIMBER, WOOD & FORESTRY

WOODTURNING
39474U46-120

Editorial Address: 86 High Street, LEWES, BN7 1XN
Tel: 01273 477374 **Fax:** 01273 478676
Email: markb@thegmcgroup.com
Advertising Address: As above. **Tel:** 01273 402897
Fax: 01273 487692
Email: rhonab@thegmcgroup.com
Web site: http://www.thegmcgroup.com
ISSN: 0958-9457
Publisher: GMC Publications Ltd
Frequency: 13 issues yearly
Cover Price: £3.45
Annual Sub.: £37.25
Usual Pagination: 100
Editor: Mark Baker; **Advertising Manager:** Rhona Bolger; **Publisher:** Simon McKeown
Summary of Content: Journal of The Guild of Master Craftsmen. Covers new tools, specialist equipment and machinery, with articles on technique and project ideas.
Readership/Target Audience: Aimed at woodturners.
ADVERTISING RATES:
Full Page Mono £825.00
Full Page Colour £825.00
Agency Commission: 10%
Mechanical Data: Type Area: 268 x 186mm, Bleed Size: 305 x 218mm, Trim Size: 297 x 210mm, Col Length: 268mm, Film: Digital, Page Width: 186mm
Copy instructions: Copy Date: 7 weeks prior to publication date
Average advertising content per issue: 30%
BUSINESS: TIMBER, WOOD & FORESTRY

WOODWORKING INTERNATIONAL
1667497U46-143

Editorial Address: 2 Kilvinton Drive, ENFIELD, EN2 0BD
Tel: 020 8363 3052
Email: ademby@fmtwin.fsnet.co.uk
Advertising Address: As above.
Email: ademby@fmtwin.fsnet.co.uk
Web site: http://www.harnisch.com/win
Publisher: Dr Harnisch Verlagsges Mbh
Date Established: 1911
Frequency: Quarterly
Annual Sub.: £82.00
Circulation: 12,000 (Publisher's Statement)
Usual Pagination: 50
Editor: Alexander Demby; **Advertising Manager:** Alexander Demby
Summary of Content: Magazine focusing on all aspects of woodworking including wood treatment, tools, timber engineering, supplies and technology.
Language(s): English; Finnish; German; Russian
Readership/Target Audience: Aimed at factory managers and production engineers.
ADVERTISING RATES:
Full Page Mono EUR3420.00
Full Page Colour EUR4770.00
Mechanical Data: Type Area: 270 x 190mm, Bleed Size: 303 x 216mm, Col Length: 270mm, Page Width: 190mm, Trim Size: 297 X 210mm, Film: Digital
BUSINESS: TIMBER, WOOD & FORESTRY

WOODWORKING NEWS
39475U46-140

Editorial Address: The Old Sun, Crete Hall Road, GRAVESEND, DA11 9AA **Tel:** 01474 536535
Fax: 01474 536552
Email: wwn@nelton.co.uk
Advertising Address: As above.
Email: publications@nelton.co.uk
Web site: http://www.nelton.co.uk
ISSN: 0959-1622
Publisher: Nelton Publications
Date Established: 1986
Frequency: 10 issues yearly
Cover Price: £5.00
Free to qualifying individuals
Annual Sub.: £33.00
Circulation: 5,300 (Publisher's Statement)
Usual Pagination: 24

Business Magazines

Editor: Neil Herbert-Smith; **Advertising Manager:** Donna Ludbrook
Summary of Content: Newspaper combining a mixture of industry news, new products and technical articles.
Readership/Target Audience: Aimed at manufacturers and craftsmen in the professional wood trade.
ADVERTISING RATES:
Full Page Colour £2139.00
Agency Commission: 10%
Mechanical Data: Trim Size: 420 x 297mm, Film: Digital, Type Area: 390 x 274mm, Col Length: 390mm, Page Width: 274mm, Bleed Size: 426 x 303mm
BUSINESS: TIMBER, WOOD & FORESTRY

WOODWORKING PRODUCTS
1692179U23A-312

Editorial Address: The Old Sun, Crete Hall Road, GRAVESEND, DA11 9AA **Tel:** 01474 536535
Fax: 01474 536552
Advertising Address: As above.
Email: donna@nelton.co.uk
Web site: http://www.nelton.co.uk
Publisher: Nelton Publications
Frequency: Quarterly
Annual Sub.: £10.00
Circulation: 9,972 (Publisher's Statement)
Editor: Donna Ludbrook; **Advertising Manager:** Donna Ludbrook
Summary of Content: Magazine covering all aspects of woodworking products.
Readership/Target Audience: Aimed at carpenters, joiners, shop fitters and other related trades.
ADVERTISING RATES:
Full Page Colour £350.00
Agency Commission: 10%
Mechanical Data: Type Area: 190 x 128mm, Col Length: 190mm, Page Width: 128mm, Film: Digital, Bleed Size: +3mm
Copy instructions: Copy Date: 1 week prior to publication date
BUSINESS: FURNISHINGS & FURNITURE

WOOL RECORD'S WEEKLY MARKET REPORT
35397U1L-80

Editorial Address: Perkin House, 1 Longlands Street, BRADFORD, BD1 2TP **Tel:** 01274 378800
Fax: 01274 378811
Email: bchyzy@world-textile.net
Advertising Address: As above.
Email: info@world-textile.net
Web site: http://www.world-textile.net
Publisher: World Textile Publications Ltd
Date Established: 1909
Frequency: Weekly
Annual Sub.: £255.00
Usual Pagination: 4
Editor: Bernard Chyzy; **Managing Director:** Mark Jarvis
Summary of Content: Newsletter providing wool and noble-fibre prices from around the world, market news and market analysis.
Readership/Target Audience: Aimed at senior managers.
ADVERTISING RATES:
Full Page Mono £925.00
Full Page Colour £1700.00
Mechanical Data: Type Area: 251 x 179mm, Col Length: 251mm, Page Width: 179mm, Bleed Size: 303 x 216mm, Film: Digital
Copy instructions: Copy Date: 3 weeks prior to publication date
BUSINESS: FINANCE & ECONOMICS: Commodities

WORK OUT
38547U32H-300

Editorial Address: 47 Church Street, BARNSLEY, S70 2AS
Tel: 01226 734333
Email: nl@whpl.net
Advertising Address: As above. **Tel:** 01226 734699
Fax: 01226 734477
Email: tb@whpl.net
Web site: http://www.workout-uk.co.uk
Publisher: Wharncliffe Publishing Ltd
Frequency: Monthly - Published around the 22nd of the cover month
Free to qualifying individuals
Annual Sub.: £28.00
Circulation: 8,591 (ABC 01/07/2008 to 30/06/2009)
Usual Pagination: 44
Editor: Mary Ferguson; **News Editor:** Mary Ferguson; **Group Editor:** Andrew Harrod
Summary of Content: Magazine covering all aspects of the UK fitness industry.
Readership/Target Audience: Read by proprietors of fitness clubs and fitness managers.
ADVERTISING: Rates on application
Copy instructions: Copy Date: 2 weeks prior to publication date
BUSINESS: LOCAL GOVERNMENT, LEISURE & RECREATION: Leisure, Recreation & Entertainment

WORKING WITH OLDER PEOPLE
601554U32G-160

Editorial Address: Richmond House, Richmond Road, BRIGHTON, BN2 3RL **Tel:** 01273 623222
Fax: 01273 625526
Email: joannas@pavpub.com
Advertising Address: As above. **Tel:** 0870 890 1080
Fax: 0870 890 1081
Email: pauls@pavpub.com
Web site: http://www.pavpub.com
ISSN: 1366-3666
Publisher: Pavilion Journals (Brighton) Ltd
Date Established: 1997
Frequency: Quarterly
Annual Sub.: £75.00
Circulation: 550 (Publisher's Statement)
Usual Pagination: 40
Editor: Joanna Sharrocks; **Advertising Manager:** Paul Somerville
Summary of Content: Journal covering policy and practice developments related to the elderly care sector.
Readership/Target Audience: Aimed at managers, social workers, residential care staff, day centre staff, community nurses, families and carers.
ADVERTISING RATES:
Full Page Mono £350.00
Agency Commission: 10%
Mechanical Data: Type Area: 240 x 170mm, Col Length: 240mm, Page Width: 170mm
BUSINESS: LOCAL GOVERNMENT, LEISURE & RECREATION: Community Care & Social Services

WORKPLACE REPORT
36901U14B-45

Formerly: Bargaining Report
Editorial Address: 78 Blackfriars Road, LONDON, SE1 8HF
Tel: 020 7902 9813 **Fax:** 020 7928 0621
Email: rjohnson@lrd.org.uk
Web site: http://www.lrd.org.uk
Publisher: LRD Publications Ltd
Date Established: 1979
Frequency: 11 issues yearly - Not published in August
Cover Price: £4.40
Annual Sub.: £60.00
Circulation: 2,000 (Publisher's Statement)
Usual Pagination: 20
Editor: Rebecca Johnson
Summary of Content: Magazine providing information on wages, conditions, equality, training, health and safety, union recruitment and collective bargaining issues. Includes regular review of legal cases in key areas of employment law.
Readership/Target Audience: Aimed at trade union workplace representatives.
ADVERTISING: No Advertising taken
BUSINESS: COMMERCE, INDUSTRY & MANAGEMENT: Industry & Factories

WORKS MANAGEMENT
36817U14A-430

Editorial Address: Hawley Mill, Hawley Road, DARTFORD, DA2 7TJ **Tel:** 01322 221144 **Fax:** 01322 221188
Email: khurst@findlay.co.uk
Advertising Address: As above. **Fax:** 01322 421546
Email: rhenley@findlay.co.uk
Web site: http://www.worksmanagement.co.uk
ISSN: 0374-4795
Publisher: Findlay Media Ltd
Date Established: 1947
Frequency: Monthly - Published in the 3rd week of the cover month
Free to qualifying individuals
Annual Sub.: £79.00
Circulation: 17,939 (ABC 01/01/2008 to 31/12/2008)
Editor: Ken Hurst; **Managing Editor:** Laura Cork
Summary of Content: Journal covering all aspects of manufacturing management.
Readership/Target Audience: Aimed at decision makers in manufacturing establishments with over 50 employees.
ADVERTISING RATES:
Full Page Colour £2700.00
Agency Commission: 10%
Mechanical Data: Bleed Size: 292 x 216mm, Trim Size: 286 x 210mm, Type Area: 254 x 178mm, Col Length: 254mm, Page Width: 178mm, Film: Digital
Copy instructions: Copy Date: Middle of the month prior to publication date
Supplement(s): Energy - 1xY, Manufacturing IT Shortlist - 1xY, Manufacturing IT Strategy - 1xY, Materials Handling - 1xY
BUSINESS: COMMERCE, INDUSTRY & MANAGEMENT

WORLD AGRICULTURAL ECONOMICS & RURAL SOCIOLOGY ABSTRACTS
37799U21A-1100

Editorial Address: Nosworthy Way, WALLINGFORD, OX10 8DE **Tel:** 01491 832111 **Fax:** 01491 829198

Email: publishing@cabi.org
Web site: http://www.cabi-publishing.org
ISSN: 0043-8219
Publisher: CABI
Date Established: 1958
Frequency: Monthly
Annual Sub.: £1205.00
Editor: Janice Osborn
Summary of Content: International journal containing information on agricultural and environmental economics and rural sociology.
Readership/Target Audience: Aimed at university and college departmental libraries, rural and resource management studies, development studies, governments and international agencies.
ADVERTISING: No Advertising taken
BUSINESS: AGRICULTURE & FARMING

WORLD AIRCRAFT SALES MAGAZINE
601077U6A-190

Editorial Address: Cowleaze House, 39 Cowleaze Road, KINGSTON UPON THAMES, KT2 6DZ **Tel:** 020 8255 4000
Fax: 020 8255 4300
Email: editorial@avbuyer.com
Advertising Address: As above.
Email: john@avbuyer.com
Web site: http://www.avbuyer.com
Publisher: World Aviation Communications Ltd
Date Established: 1996
Frequency: Monthly
Free to qualifying individuals
Annual Sub.: £40.00
Circulation: 32,000 (Publisher's Statement)
Usual Pagination: 160
Editor: John Brennan; **Advertising Manager:** John Brennan; **Publisher:** John Brennan
Summary of Content: Magazine covering articles and features on business configured aircraft and other material related to all aspects of avionics, engines, refurbishment, modifications and maintenance of business aircraft.
Readership/Target Audience: Aimed at all owners and operators of business aircraft, including presidents, CEOs, chief pilots, heads of maintenance, aircraft dealers, brokers and providers of services.
ADVERTISING RATES:
Full Page Colour £1825.00
Agency Commission: 15%
Mechanical Data: Col Length: 246mm, Col Widths (Display): 89mm, Film: Negative, right reading, emulsion side down. Digital, No. of Columns (Display): 2, Type Area: 246 x 185mm, Print Process: Web offset, Screen: 60 lpc, Trim Size: 270 x 205mm, Page Width: 185mm, Bleed Size: 270 x 211mm, Trim Size: 270 x 205mm
Copy instructions: Copy Date: Middle of month prior to publication date
Average advertising content per issue: 75%
BUSINESS: AVIATION & AERONAUTICS

WORLD ARCHITECTURE
35808U4A-300

Editorial Address: 3rd Floor, Ludgate House, 245 Blackfriars Road, LONDON, SE1 9UY **Tel:** 020 7921 8600
Email: katherine.hayes@ubm.com
Advertising Address: 7th Floor, Ludgate House, 245 Blackfriars Road, LONDON, SE1 9UY **Tel:** 020 7560 4000
Fax: 020 7560 4008
Email: peter.menzies@ubm.com
Web site: http://www.world-architecture.com
ISSN: 0956-9758
Publisher: UBM Information Ltd
Frequency: Annual - Published in January
Circulation: 14,000 (Publisher's Statement)
Editor: Katherine Hayes
Summary of Content: Directory containing profiles of leading architects, news of current international projects and comment.
Readership/Target Audience: Read by architects and project manager specifiers.
ADVERTISING RATES:
Full Page Mono £2249.00
Full Page Colour £3117.00
Agency Commission: 10%
Mechanical Data: Page Width: 218mm, Print Process: Digital, Type Area: 288 x 218mm, Col Length: 288mm, Trim Size: 300 x 230mm, Bleed Size: 306 x 236mm
Copy instructions: Copy Date: 6 weeks prior to publication date
Average advertising content per issue: 40%
BUSINESS: ARCHITECTURE & BUILDING: Architecture

WORLD BUNKERING
39402U45C-800

Editorial Address: The Diary House, Rickett Street, LONDON, SW6 1RU **Tel:** 020 7386 6100
Email: lucy.budd@mar-media.com
Advertising Address: As above. **Fax:** 020 7381 8890
Email: inbox@mar-media.com
Web site: http://www.worldbunkering.com

ISSN: 1367-5018
Publisher: Maritime Media Ltd
Date Established: 1995
Frequency: Quarterly - Published in the 1st week of the cover month
Free to qualifying individuals
Circulation: 4,000 (Publisher's Statement)
Usual Pagination: 60
Editor: Lucy Budd; **Advertising Manager:** Alex Corboude
Summary of Content: Magazine covering all aspects of the supply and purchase of fuel for world shipping.
Readership/Target Audience: Read by members of the International Bunker Industry Association.
ADVERTISING RATES:
Full Page Colour £3950.00
Copy instructions: Copy Date: 2 weeks prior to publication date
BUSINESS: MARINE & SHIPPING: Maritime Freight

THE WORLD BUS AND COACH MANUFACTURING INDUSTRY   714031U49D-355
Editorial Address: PO Box 15, Williton, TAUNTON, TA4 4YP
Tel: 01984 618707 **Fax:** 01984 618708
Email: info@truckandbusbuilder.com
Advertising Address: As above. **Tel:** 01984 639300
Fax: 01984 639301
Email: advertising@truckandbusbuilder.com
ISSN: 0958-1408
Publisher: Truck and Bus Builder Publishing Ltd
Date Established: 2001
Frequency: Published every 2 years in June
Annual Sub.: £995.00
Usual Pagination: 300
Editor: Jim Gibbins; **Advertising Manager:** Jim Gibbins; **Publisher:** Jim Gibbins
Summary of Content: Report giving an overview of the global bus industry with market reviews and forecasts for markets from all regions.
Readership/Target Audience: Read by senior executives in the bus and coach manufacturing and operating industries worldwide.
ADVERTISING RATES:
Full Page Colour £2250.00
Agency Commission: 10%
Mechanical Data: Type Area: 275 x 180mm, Col Length: 275mm, Page Width: 180mm
Average advertising content per issue: 10%
BUSINESS: TRANSPORT: Commercial Vehicles

WORLD CEMENT   39034U42A-195
Editorial Address: 15 South Street, FARNHAM, GU9 7QU
Tel: 01252 718999 **Fax:** 01252 718992
Email: editorial@worldcement.com
Advertising Address: As above.
Email: ian.lewis@worldcement.com
Web site: http://www.worldcement.com
ISSN: 0263-6050
Publisher: Palladian Publications Ltd
Date Established: 1928
Frequency: Monthly - Published in the 1st week of the cover month
Cover Price: £20.00
Annual Sub.: £140.00
Circulation: 5,760 (ABC 01/07/2008 to 30/06/2009)
Usual Pagination: 120
Editor: Paul Maxwell-Cook; **Managing Editor:** Paul Maxwell-Cook; **Publisher:** Nigel Hardy
Summary of Content: Periodical covering all business and technical aspects of cement and lime manufacture from quarrying of raw materials to the distribution of the finished product.
Readership/Target Audience: Read by executives within the cement and lime industries, cement and lime plant managers and associated personnel.
ADVERTISING RATES:
Full Page Colour £2400.00
Agency Commission: 10%
Mechanical Data: Print Process: Offset litho, Film: Digital, Type Area: 268 x 178mm, Col Length: 268mm, Page Width: 178mm, Bleed Size: 303 x 216mm, Trim Size: 297 x 210mm
Average advertising content per issue: 50%
Supplement(s): Bulk Materials Handling Review - 1xY, Emerging Markets Report - 1xY
BUSINESS: CONSTRUCTION

WORLD CERAMICS & REFRACTORIES   36618U12A-150
Editorial Address: PO Box 1187, GERRARDS CROSS, SL9 7YP **Tel:** 01753 885968 **Fax:** 01753 882980
Email: info@ceramrefractories.co.uk
Advertising Address: As above.
Email: info@ceramrefractories.co.uk
Web site: http://www.ceramrefractories.co.uk
ISSN: 0959-6127
Publisher: Modern Metals Publications Ltd
Date Established: 1927

Frequency: 6 issues yearly
Annual Sub.: £210.00
Circulation: 3,200 (Publisher's Statement)
Usual Pagination: 12
Editor: Frank Russell; **Advertising Manager:** Frank Russell
Summary of Content: Magazine covering all aspects of the heavy clay, refractories and technical ceramics market.
Readership/Target Audience: Read by senior and middle management worldwide.
ADVERTISING RATES:
Full Page Mono £600.00
Full Page Colour £900.00
Agency Commission: 10%
Mechanical Data: Page Width: 174mm, Type Area: 260 x 174mm, Col Length: 260mm
Copy instructions: Copy Date: 4 weeks prior to publication date
Average advertising content per issue: 20%
BUSINESS: CERAMICS, POTTERY & GLASS: Ceramics & Pottery

WORLD COAL   38252U30-148
Editorial Address: 15 South Street, FARNHAM, GU9 7QU
Tel: 01252 718999 **Fax:** 01252 718992
Email: rachael.johnson@worldcoal.com
Advertising Address: As above.
Email: mail@worldcoal.com
Web site: http://www.worldcoal.com
ISSN: 0968-3224
Publisher: Palladian Publications Ltd
Date Established: 1992
Frequency: Monthly
Free to qualifying individuals
Annual Sub.: £110.00
Circulation: 4,641 (ABC 01/01/2008 to 31/12/2008)
Usual Pagination: 64
Editor: Jonathan Rowland; **Managing Editor:** James Little
Summary of Content: Magazine covering the international coal industry, from mining to end-use. Includes coal news, monthly international reports, trade forecasts, technical case-studies, mine reports and product news.
Readership/Target Audience: Read by personnel involved in all sectors of the global coal industry.
ADVERTISING RATES:
Full Page Colour £2250.00
Agency Commission: 10%
Mechanical Data: Bleed Size: 303 x 216mm, Film: Positive, right reading, emulsion side down. Digital, Type Area: 268 x 178mm, Page Width: 178mm, Print Process: Offset litho, Col Length: 268mm, Trim Size: 297 x 210mm
Copy instructions: Copy Date: 4 weeks prior to publication date
Average advertising content per issue: 40%
BUSINESS: MINING & QUARRYING

WORLD CRUISE INDUSTRY REVIEW   39751U50-200
Editorial Address: Brunel House, 55-57 North Wharf Road, LONDON, W2 1LA **Tel:** 020 7915 9600 **Fax:** 020 7915 9737
Email: christopherkanal@spgmedia.com
Advertising Address: As above.
Web site: http://www.worldcruise-network.com
Publisher: SPG Media Ltd
Frequency: Half-yearly - Published in March and September
Annual Sub.: £19.95
Circulation: 5,200 (ABC 01/07/2008 to 30/06/2009)
Editor: Christopher Kanal; **Advertising Manager:** Tanvir Choudhury
Summary of Content: Magazine covering all aspects of the world cruise industry.
Readership/Target Audience: Aimed at presidents, CEOs, vice-presidents, operations directors, cruise directors, chief concessionaires, naval architects, itinerary planners, ship superintendents, port and harbour authorities, shipping agencies and travel agencies throughout the world.
BUSINESS: TRAVEL & TOURISM

WORLD DREDGING, MINING & CONSTRUCTION   39416U45D-400
Editorial Address: South Place, Derby Road, HASLEMERE, GU27 1BP **Tel:** 01428 642208 **Fax:** 01428 642208
Email: mcworlddredging@aol.com
Advertising Address: As above.
Email: mcworlddredging@aol.com
Web site: http://www.worlddredging.com
Publisher: WODCON Association
Frequency: 6 issues yearly - Published in the last week of the cover month
Annual Sub.: $40.00
Circulation: 3,000 (Publisher's Statement)
Usual Pagination: 30
Editor: Mark Carter; **Advertising Manager:** Mark Carter; **Publisher:** Mort Richardson
Summary of Content: Magazine covering news, techniques and features on dredging operations.

Readership/Target Audience: Read mainly by engineers and managers in the dredging and dredge mining industry.
ADVERTISING RATES:
Full Page Mono $1100.00
Full Page Colour $1950.00
Agency Commission: 15%
Mechanical Data: Type Area: 254 x 178mm, Col Length: 254mm, Film: Digital, Page Width: 178mm
Copy instructions: Copy Date: 2 weeks prior to publication date
BUSINESS: MARINE & SHIPPING: Marine Engineering Equipment

WORLD DRINKS REPORT   22789U9A-250
Editorial Address: 80 Calverley Road, TUNBRIDGE WELLS, TN1 2UN **Tel:** 020 7017 7500 **Fax:** 020 7017 7599
Email: marketing@agra-net.com
Web site: http://www.agra-net.com
ISSN: 1360-7995
Publisher: Agra Informa Ltd
Date Established: 1995
Frequency: 25 issues yearly
Annual Sub.: £473.00
Usual Pagination: 24
Summary of Content: Newsletter on the global drinks industry containing information on mergers, acquisitions, joint ventures, global market trends and International legislation.
Readership/Target Audience: Aimed at the global drinks industry.
ADVERTISING: No Advertising taken
BUSINESS: DRINKS & LICENSED TRADE: Drinks, Licensed Trade, Wines & Spirits

WORLD ENERGY REVIEW   1639151U58-169
Editorial Address: PO Box 881, WOKING, GU22 7ZN
Tel: 01483 715539 **Fax:** 01483 755447
Email: editorial@worldenergyreview.com
Advertising Address: As above.
Email: advertising@worldenergyreview.com
Web site: http://www.worldenergyreview.com
Publisher: Marketing Communications Media Ltd
Date Established: 2002
Frequency: 6 issues yearly - Published in the 2nd week of the cover month
Annual Sub.: £350.00
Circulation: 5,000 (Publisher's Statement)
Editor: Trevor Leek; **Advertising Manager:** Trevor Leek; **Publisher:** Trevor Leek
Summary of Content: Magazine covering analysis of the key issues impacting on the global energy industry. Includes articles on technology, energy economics, international trade, politics, environmental, social and regulatory issues.
Readership/Target Audience: Aimed at energy ministers, government departments, senior executives, shareholders and environmental groups.
ADVERTISING RATES:
Full Page Mono £3187.00
Full Page Colour £3750.00
Mechanical Data: Type Area: 274 x 184mm, Bleed Size: 303 x 216mm, Trim Size: 297 x 210mm, Col Length: 274mm, Page Width: 184mm, Print Process: Offset litho, Film: Digital
BUSINESS: ENERGY, FUEL & NUCLEAR

THE WORLD FACTORING YEARBOOK   37673U19F-670
Editorial Address: 3 Cobden Court, Wimpole Close, BROMLEY, BR2 9JF **Tel:** 020 8466 6987
Fax: 020 8466 0654
Email: info@bcrpub.co.uk
Advertising Address: As above.
Web site: http://www.bcrpub.co.uk
Publisher: BCR Publishing Ltd
Date Established: 1994
Frequency: Annual - Published in December
Cover Price: £140.00
Circulation: 3,000 (Publisher's Statement)
Usual Pagination: 300
Editor: Michael Bickers; **Advertising Manager:** Michael Bickers
Summary of Content: Yearbook containing analysis of the global receivable finance industry.
Readership/Target Audience: Read by senior decision-making executives in receivables finance companies, banks, financial institutions, lawyers, accounting firms, brokers, consultants, business libraries and bookshops.
ADVERTISING RATES:
Full Page Mono £1495.00
Full Page Colour £2295.00
Mechanical Data: Trim Size: 297 x 210mm, Bleed Size: 307 x 220mm, Type Area: 277 x 190mm, Print Process: Litho, Film: Digital, Page Width: 190mm, Col Length: 277mm
Copy instructions: Copy Date: July 30th
Average advertising content per issue: 10%
BUSINESS: ENGINEERING & MACHINERY: Production & Mechanical Engineering

Business Magazines

WORLD FINANCE
1683783U1A-313

Editorial Address: 37-42 Compton Street, LONDON, EC1V 0AP **Tel:** 020 7014 0330 **Fax:** 020 7014 0302
Email: michael@worldfinance.com
Advertising Address: As above. **Fax:** 020 7014 0301
Email: martins@wnmedia.com
Web site: http://www.worldfinance.com
Publisher: World News Media
Date Established: 2004
Frequency: 6 issues yearly
Free to qualifying individuals
Circulation: 120,000 (Publisher's Statement)
Editor: Michael McCaw; **Features Editor:** Stephen Poole;
Advertising Manager: Jack Darcy
Summary of Content: Magazine covering current news and features on the financial markets.
Readership/Target Audience: Aimed at directors and senior decision makers.
ADVERTISING RATES:
Full Page Mono £14900.00
Full Page Colour £15200.00
Mechanical Data: Bleed Size: 288 x 218mm, Trim Size: 280 x 210mm, Film: Digital
BUSINESS: FINANCE & ECONOMICS

WORLD FISHING MAGAZINE
39388U45B-240

Formerly: World Fishing
Editorial Address: The Old Mill, Lower Quay, FAREHAM, PO16 0RA **Tel:** 01329 825335
Email: cwills@mercatormedia.com
Advertising Address: As above. **Fax:** 01329 825330
Email: thills@worldfishing.net
Web site: http://www.worldfishing.net
ISSN: 0043-8480
Publisher: Mercator Media Ltd
Date Established: 1951
Frequency: 11 issues yearly - Published in the 1st week of the cover month
Annual Sub.: £95.00
Circulation: 3,325 (ABC 01/07/2007 to 30/06/2008)
Usual Pagination: 32
Editor: Carly Wills
Summary of Content: Magazine containing news on commercial fishing, processing, gear and equipment, vessels and shipyards worldwide.
Language(s): English; Spanish
Readership/Target Audience: Aimed at vessel owners, seafood and fishing companies, fishermen, processors, research institution personnel and government officials.
ADVERTISING RATES:
Full Page Colour £2085.00
Agency Commission: 15%
Mechanical Data: Page Width: 186mm, Film: Digital, Type Area: 274 x 186mm, Col Length: 274mm, Trim Size: 297 x 210mm, Bleed Size: 303 x 216mm, Col Widths (Display): 45mm, No. of Columns (Display): 4
Copy instructions: Copy Date: 18th of the month prior to publication date
Average advertising content per issue: 60%
BUSINESS: MARINE & SHIPPING: Commercial Fishing

WORLD FOOD LAW
39253U22R-760

Editorial Address: 80 Calverley Road, TUNBRIDGE WELLS, TN1 2UN **Tel:** 020 7017 7500 **Fax:** 020 7017 7599
Email: marketing@agra-net.com
Web site: http://www.agra-net.com
ISSN: 1462-6489
Publisher: Agra Informa Ltd
Frequency: 11 issues yearly
Annual Sub.: £399.00
Summary of Content: Newsletter reporting on the regulation of food and food products.
Readership/Target Audience: Aimed at food industry executives who need to keep in touch with current and pending changes to food legislation.
ADVERTISING: No Advertising taken
BUSINESS: FOOD: Food Related

WORLD FOOD REGULATION REVIEW
25957U22R-650

Editorial Address: Grenville Court, Britwell Road, Burnham, SLOUGH, SL1 8DF **Tel:** 01628 600499 **Fax:** 01628 600488
Email: info@researchinformation.co.uk
Web site: http://www.researchinformation.co.uk
ISSN: 0963-4894
Publisher: Research Information Ltd
Date Established: 1991
Frequency: Monthly
Annual Sub.: £545.00
Circulation: 375 (Publisher's Statement)
Usual Pagination: 32
Editor: Ras Patel
Summary of Content: Magazine focusing on new laws, regulations, codes of practice and government actions affecting the food industry in the EU and around the world.

Covers food safety, agriculture, nutrition labelling, food additives and pesticides residues. Also reports on genetically modified organisms in foods and industry activities.
Readership/Target Audience: Read by people within quality assurance and regulatory affairs organisations as well as those involved in the food industry.
ADVERTISING: No Advertising taken
BUSINESS: FOOD: Food Related

WORLD FOOTWEAR
1654895U29-106

Editorial Address: 36 Crosby Road North, LIVERPOOL, L22 0QN **Tel:** 0151 928 8288 **Fax:** 0151 928 4190
Email: stierney@worldtrades.co.uk
Advertising Address: As above.
Email: wl@worldtrades.co.uk
Web site: http://www.footwearbiz.com
Publisher: World Trades Publishing Ltd
Date Established: 1986
Frequency: 6 issues yearly
Annual Sub.: £55.00
Circulation: 7,255 (Publisher's Statement)
Editor: Stephen Tierney; **Advertising Manager:** Simon Yarwood
Summary of Content: Magazine covering all aspects of the footwear industry, including business management, technology, materials, design and news.
Readership/Target Audience: Aimed at manufacturers.
ADVERTISING RATES:
Full Page Mono EUR3276.00
Full Page Colour EUR5040.00
Mechanical Data: Type Area: 275 x 177mm, Bleed Size: 303 x 216mm, Trim Size: 297 x 210mm, Col Length: 275mm, Page Width: 177mm, Film: Digital
BUSINESS: FOOTWEAR

WORLD GOLD
38253U30-149

Editorial Address: 153-155 Hedges House, Regent Street, LONDON, W1B 4JE **Tel:** 020 7478 1750 **Fax:** 020 7478 1779
Email: paul.burton@gfmsworldgold.com
Advertising Address: 45 Victoria Road, South Woodford, LONDON, E18 1LJ **Tel:** 020 8530 1775 **Fax:** 020 8530 1772
Email: paul.burton@gfmsworldgold.com
Web site: http://www.gfmsworldgold.com
ISSN: 1463-9319
Publisher: GFMS World Gold
Frequency: Quarterly
Annual Sub.: £365.00
Usual Pagination: 20
Editor: Paul Burton; **Advertising Manager:** Paul Burton;
Publisher: Paul Burton
Summary of Content: Newsletter containing reports on gold, silver and platinum mining companies, as well as news of mining activities in all of the world's main and emerging regions.
Readership/Target Audience: Aimed at investors, financiers, analysts and mining executives.
ADVERTISING: Rates on application
Copy instructions: Copy Date: 28th of the cover month
BUSINESS: MINING & QUARRYING

WORLD HIGHWAYS/ROUTES DU MONDE
39051U42B-250

Editorial Address: Horizon House, Azalea Drive, SWANLEY, BR8 8JR **Tel:** 01322 612055 **Fax:** 0161 603 0891
Email: mwoof@ropl.com
Advertising Address: As above. **Fax:** 0870 751 8327
Email: mbattista@ropl.com
Web site: http://www.worldhighways.com
ISSN: 0964-4598
Publisher: Route One Publishing Ltd
Date Established: 1991
Frequency: 9 issues yearly - Published in the middle of the cover month
Cover Price: £15.00
Annual Sub.: £100.00
Circulation: 15,406 (BPA Worldwide 01/07/2008 to 31/12/2008)
Usual Pagination: 82
Editor: Mike Woof; **Managing Editor:** Patrick Smith;
Publisher: Roger Adshead
Summary of Content: Journal of the International Road Federation. Covers all aspects of road infrastructure worldwide, including finance, planning, construction and highway maintenance. Includes articles on vehicle technology and traffic management systems.
Readership/Target Audience: Aimed at highway infrastructure professionals.
ADVERTISING RATES:
Full Page Colour £4425.00
Agency Commission: 10%
Mechanical Data: Bleed Size: 305 x 218mm, Trim Size: 297 x 210mm, Type Area: 256 x 184mm, Film: Digital, Page Width: 184mm, Col Length: 256mm
Copy instructions: Copy Date: 3 weeks prior to publication date

Average advertising content per issue: 40%
BUSINESS: CONSTRUCTION: Roads

WORLD INSURANCE REPORT
35166U1D-400

Editorial Address: Telephone House, 69-77 Paul Street, LONDON, EC2A 4LQ **Tel:** 020 7017 4103
Fax: 020 7017 7912
Email: rasaad.jamie@informa.com
Web site: http://www.evanvale.co.uk
ISSN: 0306-3445
Publisher: Informa PLC
Date Established: 1976
Frequency: 24 issues yearly
Annual Sub.: £1200.00
Usual Pagination: 20
Editor: Rasaad Jamie
Summary of Content: Magazine covering news and data on worldwide developments in insurance and reinsurance.
Readership/Target Audience: Aimed at executives of insurance and reinsurance companies, service companies to the insurance industry, lawyers and accountants.
ADVERTISING: No Advertising taken
BUSINESS: FINANCE & ECONOMICS: Insurance

WORLD LEASING YEARBOOK
38662U34-200

Editorial Address: 11 North Hill, COLCHESTER, CO1 1DZ **Tel:** 01206 579591 **Fax:** 01206 765309
Email: lisa@euromoney-yearbooks.co.uk
Advertising Address: As above.
Email: lisa@euromoney-yearbooks.co.uk
Web site: http://www.euromoney-yearbooks.com
Publisher: Euromoney Institutional Investor plc
Date Established: 1979
Frequency: Annual
Cover Price: £170.00
Circulation: 10,192 (Publisher's Statement)
Usual Pagination: 470
Editor: Lisa Paul; **Advertising Manager:** Faye Parker;
Managing Editor: Lisa Paul; **Publisher:** Adrian Hornbrook
Summary of Content: Yearbook containing articles on global leasing and a database of companies active in the sector.
Readership/Target Audience: Aimed at corporate leasing managers and lessees, corporate financial officers, municipal financial officers, accountants, company secretaries and legal specialists, international bankers, leading companies and brokers.
ADVERTISING RATES:
Full Page Mono £2600.00
Full Page Colour £4390.00
Agency Commission: 10%
Mechanical Data: Type Area: 273 x 190mm, Print Process: Offset litho, Bleed Size: 303 x 216mm, Trim Size: 297 x 210mm, Col Length: 273mm, Page Width: 190mm
Copy instructions: Copy Date: 4 weeks prior to publication date
Average advertising content per issue: 12%
BUSINESS: OFFICE EQUIPMENT

WORLD LEATHER
39792U52D-51

Editorial Address: 36 Crosby Road North, LIVERPOOL, L22 0QN **Tel:** 0151 928 8288 **Fax:** 0151 928 4190
Email: stierney@worldtrades.co.uk
Advertising Address: As above.
Email: wl@worldtrades.co.uk
Web site: http://www.leatherbiz.com
Publisher: World Trades Publishing Ltd
Date Established: 1985
Frequency: 8 issues yearly
Annual Sub.: £55.00
Circulation: 15,000 (Publisher's Statement)
Editor: Stephen Tierney; **Advertising Manager:** Simon Yarwood
Summary of Content: Magazine covering news, features and new product information for the leather industry worldwide.
Readership/Target Audience: Read mainly by tanners, leather producers and manufacturers of leather products.
ADVERTISING RATES:
Full Page Mono EUR3276.00
Full Page Colour EUR5040.00
Mechanical Data: Type Area: 275 x 177mm, Bleed Size: 303 x 216mm, Trim Size: 297 x 210mm, Col Length: 275mm, Page Width: 177mm, Film: Digital
BUSINESS: GIFT TRADE: Leather

WORLD ONLINE GAMBLING LAW REPORT
762617U44-3004

Editorial Address: 17 The Timber Yard, Drysdale Street, LONDON, N1 6ND **Tel:** 020 7012 1380 **Fax:** 020 7729 6093
Email: lindsey.greig@e-comlaw.com
Web site: http://www.e-comlaw.com
ISSN: 1477-2922
Publisher: Cecile Park Publishing Ltd

Date Established: 2002
Frequency: Monthly
Annual Sub.: £485.00
Circulation: 3,000 (Publisher's Statement)
Usual Pagination: 16
Editor: Lindsey Greig; **Managing Editor:** Lindsey Greig
Summary of Content: Magazine covering regulatory and jurisdictional matters, data protection, online payments, software licensing, interactive television, security and money laundering.
Readership/Target Audience: Aimed at those working in the online gambling industry.
ADVERTISING: No Advertising taken
BUSINESS: LEGAL

WORLD PETROLEUM
1666017U33-74

Editorial Address: 56 Haymarket, LONDON, SW1Y 4RN
Tel: 020 7389 9650 **Fax:** 020 7389 9644
Email: e.daly@world-petroleum.net
Advertising Address: As above.
Email: e.daly@world-petroleum.net
Web site: http://www.world-petroleum.net
Publisher: First Magazine Limited
Date Established: 2001
Frequency: Quarterly
Annual Sub.: £140.00
Editor: Eamonn Daly; **Advertising Manager:** Eamonn Daly
Summary of Content: Magazine focusing on the key issues affecting the oil and gas industries worldwide.
Readership/Target Audience: Aimed at key decision makers in the petroleum industry, financial sector, government and the academic community.
ADVERTISING RATES:
Full Page Mono EUR12500.00
Full Page Colour EUR15200.00
Mechanical Data: Film: Digital, Type Area: 265 x 177mm, Bleed Size: 303 x 226mm, Trim Size: 297 x 220mm, Col Length: 265mm, Page Width: 177mm, Print Process: Sheet-fed litho
BUSINESS: OIL & PETROLEUM

WORLD PHARMACEUTICAL FRONTIERS
1665944U37-409

Editorial Address: Brunel House, 55-57 North Wharf Road, LONDON, W2 1LA **Tel:** 020 7915 9789 **Fax:** 020 7915 9776
Email: andrewtunnicliffe@spgmedia.com
Advertising Address: As above. **Tel:** 020 7753 4260
Email: nathanpark@spgmedia.com
Web site: http://www.worldpharmaceuticals.net
ISSN: 1742-3791
Publisher: SPG Media Ltd
Frequency: Half-yearly - Published in March and September
Circulation: 10,200 (ABC 01/01/2008 to 31/12/2008)
Editor: Andrew Tunnicliffe; **Advertising Manager:** Nathan Park
Summary of Content: Magazine focusing on the pharmaceutical and biotech industries.
Readership/Target Audience: Aimed at CEOs, CFOs, CIOs and COOs of major pharmaceutical companies.
ADVERTISING RATES:
Full Page Mono £5100.00
Full Page Colour £5900.00
BUSINESS: PHARMACEUTICAL & CHEMISTS

WORLD PIPELINES
713886U33-70

Editorial Address: 15 South Street, FARNHAM, GU9 7QU
Tel: 01252 718999 **Fax:** 01252 718992
Email: mail@palladian-publications.com
Advertising Address: As above.
Email: chris.lethbridge@worldpipelines.com
Web site: http://www.worldpipelines.com
ISSN: 1472-7390
Publisher: Palladian Publications Ltd
Date Established: 2001
Frequency: Monthly - Published in the 2nd week of the cover month
Free to qualifying individuals
Annual Sub.: £54.00
Circulation: 10,066 (ABC 01/01/2008 to 31/12/2008)
Usual Pagination: 80
Editor: Elizabeth Corner; **Advertising Manager:** Chris Lethbridge; **Managing Editor:** James Little
Summary of Content: Magazine addressing all aspects of the international oil and gas pipeline industry, including global industry news, reports and developments with information on new contracts and tenders, regional overviews and economic and technical features.
Readership/Target Audience: Aimed at pipeline owners and operators, as well as engineers and contractors, purchasing officers, technical directors, plant managers, environmental specialists, process engineers, equipment suppliers and sales managers.
ADVERTISING RATES:
Full Page Colour £3090.00
Agency Commission: 10%

Mechanical Data: No. of Columns (Display): 3, Page Width: 178mm, Film: Digital, Type Area: 268 x 178mm, Col Length: 268mm, Trim Size: 297 x 210mm, Bleed Size: 303 x 216mm
Copy instructions: Copy Date: 4 weeks prior to publication date
Average advertising content per issue: 40%
BUSINESS: OIL & PETROLEUM

WORLD POULTRYMEAT
1665236U21F-881

Editorial Address: 80 Calverley Road, TUNBRIDGE WELLS, TN1 2UN **Tel:** 020 7017 7500 **Fax:** 020 7017 7599
Email: marketing@agra-net.com
Web site: http://www.agra-net.com
ISSN: 1740-049X
Publisher: Agra Informa Ltd
Frequency: 24 issues yearly
Annual Sub.: £834.00
Summary of Content: Publication covering news, comment, analysis and statistics on poultry meat markets including political and regulatory developments affecting the global industry.
Readership/Target Audience: Aimed at poultry producers, traders and food companies worldwide.
ADVERTISING: No Advertising taken
BUSINESS: AGRICULTURE & FARMING: Poultry

WORLD PUMPS
37637U19D-620

Editorial Address: The Boulevard, Langford Lane, KIDLINGTON, OX5 1GB **Tel:** 01865 843686
Fax: 01865 843971
Email: a.burrows@elsevier.com
Advertising Address: As above. **Tel:** 01865 843000
Fax: 01865 843973
Email: peter.morgan@elsevier.com
Web site: http://www.worldpumps.com
ISSN: 0262-1762
Publisher: Elsevier Ltd
Date Established: 1959
Frequency: Monthly - Published on the 1st of the cover month
Free to qualifying individuals
Annual Sub.: EUR341.00
Circulation: 16,951 (BPA Worldwide 01/07/2007 to 31/12/2007)
Usual Pagination: 48
Editor: Alan Burrows; **News Editor:** Mark Holmes
Summary of Content: Magazine focusing on pumps and pumping system technology worldwide.
Readership/Target Audience: Aimed at plant production managers, managing directors and engineering staff of companies who use pumping equipment.
ADVERTISING RATES:
Full Page Colour $5655.00
Agency Commission: 10%
Mechanical Data: Col Length: 258mm, Type Area: 258 x 185mm, Bleed Size: 303 x 216mm, Trim Size: 297 x 210mm, Film: Digital, Page Width: 185mm
Average advertising content per issue: 50%
BUSINESS: ENGINEERING & MACHINERY: Hydraulic Power

WORLD SHIP REVIEW
624103U45R-370

Editorial Address: No 3 The Green, Ketton, STAMFORD, PE9 3RA **Tel:** 01780 721628 **Fax:** 01780 721980
Email: pridgway@globalnet.co.uk
Advertising Address: As above.
Email: pridgway@globalnet.co.uk
Web site: http://www.worldshiptrust.org
Publisher: The World Ship Trust
Date Established: 1982
Frequency: Quarterly
Annual Sub.: £15.00
Circulation: 800 (Publisher's Statement)
Usual Pagination: 16
Editor: Paul Ridgway; **Advertising Manager:** Paul Ridgway
Summary of Content: Magazine focusing on the Maritime Museum's historic ships and their preservation, maritime artefacts and naval history.
Readership/Target Audience: Aimed at enthusiasts and museum professionals.
ADVERTISING: Rates on application
Copy instructions: Copy Date: 4 weeks prior to publication date
Average advertising content per issue: 25%
BUSINESS: MARINE & SHIPPING: Marine Related

WORLD SHIPPING DIRECTORY
39360U45A-42

Formerly: Fairplay World Shipping Directory
Editorial Address: 3rd Floor, Lombard House, 3 Princess Way, REDHILL, RH1 1UP **Tel:** 01737 379000
Fax: 01737 379001
Email: editorial@lrfairplay.com
Advertising Address: As above.
Email: sales@lrfairplay.com
Web site: http://www.lrfairplay.com

ISSN: 1477-3236
Publisher: Lloyd's Register-Fairplay Ltd
Date Established: 1990
Frequency: Annual - Published in May
Annual Sub.: £325.00
Circulation: 6,000 (Publisher's Statement)
Usual Pagination: 3300
Editor: Barbara Matthews; **Managing Director:** Richard Silk; **Advertising Manager:** Adam Foster
Summary of Content: Directory of international shipping companies.
Readership/Target Audience: Aimed at all those involved in the maritime industry.
ADVERTISING RATES:
Full Page Mono £2226.00
Full Page Colour £2740.00
Mechanical Data: Type Area: 252 x 194mm, Bleed Size: 281 x 216mm, Film: Digital, Col Length: 252mm, Page Width: 194mm
BUSINESS: MARINE & SHIPPING

WORLD STEEL EXPORTS - ALL QUALITIES
37741U20-300

Editorial Address: 1 Carlton House Terrace, LONDON, SW1Y 5DB **Tel:** 020 7343 3916 **Fax:** 020 7343 3902
Email: p.hunt@issb.co.uk
Web site: http://www.issb.co.uk
ISSN: 1361-8954
Publisher: ISSB Ltd (Iron and Steel Statistics Bureau)
Date Established: 2000
Frequency: Quarterly
Annual Sub.: £660.00
Circulation: 16 (Publisher's Statement)
Usual Pagination: 45
Editor: Phil Hunt
Summary of Content: Journal detailing export trade of 34 major steel producing countries accounting for over 90% of world exports.
Readership/Target Audience: Aimed at steel analysts.
ADVERTISING: No Advertising taken
BUSINESS: IMPORT & EXPORT

WORLD STEEL STATISTICS MONTHLY
38213U27-200

Editorial Address: 1 Carlton House Terrace, LONDON, SW1Y 5DB **Tel:** 020 7343 3916 **Fax:** 020 7343 3903
Email: p.hunt@issb.co.uk
Web site: http://www.issb.co.uk
ISSN: 1359-4249
Publisher: ISSB Ltd (Iron and Steel Statistics Bureau)
Date Established: 1995
Frequency: Monthly
Annual Sub.: £950.00
Circulation: 20 (Publisher's Statement)
Usual Pagination: 144
Editor: Phil Hunt
Summary of Content: Journal containing regularly updated trade information for 42 countries plus summary production figures. Published in partnership with the International Iron and Steel Institute.
Readership/Target Audience: Read by steel traders, steel companies, investment houses and consultancies.
ADVERTISING: No Advertising taken
BUSINESS: METAL, IRON & STEEL

WORLD SUGAR YEARBOOK
600862U22R-750

Formerly: World Sugar and Sweetener Yearbook
Editorial Address: 80 Calverley Road, TUNBRIDGE WELLS, TN1 2UN **Tel:** 020 7017 7500 **Fax:** 020 7017 7599
Email: marketing@agra-net.com
Advertising Address: As above. **Tel:** 020 7017 7493
Fax: 020 7017 7593
Email: advertising@fo-licht.com
Web site: http://www.agra-net.com
Publisher: Agra Informa Ltd
Date Established: 1938
Frequency: Annual - Published in January
Annual Sub.: £220.00
Usual Pagination: 472
Editor: Suzy Eade; **Advertising Manager:** Helen Spencer
Summary of Content: Directory providing contact details for over 4000 sugar companies, organisations, factories, refineries, traders and distilleries. Contains world sugar statistics, buyer's guide and product reports.
Language(s): English; German
Readership/Target Audience: Read by senior executives in the sugar industry.
ADVERTISING RATES:
Full Page Mono £1200.00
Full Page Colour £2400.00
Agency Commission: 15%
Mechanical Data: No. of Columns (Display): 4, Bleed Size: 303 x 216mm, Trim Size: 297 x 210mm, Film: Digital
Copy instructions: Copy Date: October 1st prior to publication date
Average advertising content per issue: 20%

Supplement(s): World Sugar Statistics - 1xY
BUSINESS: FOOD: Food Related

WORLD TUNNELLING/TRENCHLESS WORLD
1697630U42A-233

Formerly: Tunnelling & Trenchless Construction
Editorial Address: Albert House, 1 Singer Street, LONDON, EC2A 4BQ **Tel:** 020 7216 6060 **Fax:** 020 7216 6050
Email: george.demetri@aspermontuk.com
Advertising Address: As above.
Email: jim.moore@mining-journal.com
Web site: http://www.world-tunnelling.com
ISSN: 1743-9469
Publisher: Aspermont
Date Established: 2004
Frequency: 10 issues yearly
Free to qualifying individuals
Annual Sub.: £95.00
Circulation: 8,000 (Publisher's Statement)
Usual Pagination: 52
Editor: George Demetri
Summary of Content: Magazine covering large and small bore underground construction projects.
Readership/Target Audience: Aimed at engineers, managers and owners involved in all kinds of large and small bore underground construction work world-wide.
ADVERTISING RATES:
Full Page Colour £2604.00
Mechanical Data: Bleed Size: 279 x 204mm, Trim Size: 275 x 200mm, Film: Digital
Copy instructions: Copy Date: 10 days prior to publication date
BUSINESS: CONSTRUCTION

WORLD WATER & ENVIRONMENTAL ENGINEERING
39075U42C-700

Editorial Address: 6 Brewery Square, LONDON, EC1V 4LE **Tel:** 020 7251 8778 **Fax:** 020 7336 0377
Email: pwolfe@wefpublishinguk.com
Advertising Address: As above.
Email: nchristy@wefpublishinguk.com
Web site: http://www.wef.org
ISSN: 1354-313X
Publisher: WEF Publishing UK Ltd
Date Established: 1977
Frequency: 6 issues yearly - Published at the end of the 1st cover month
Free to qualifying individuals
Annual Sub.: £97.00
Circulation: 12,000 (Publisher's Statement)
Usual Pagination: 60
Editor: Pamela Wolfe; **Advertising Manager:** Nic Christy;
Publisher: Nic Christy
Summary of Content: Journal covering all aspects of the water and sewerage industry, from developing nations to industrialised areas.
Readership/Target Audience: Read by professionals working in the water and wastewater industry, including contractors, consultants, funding agencies and public and privately owned utilities.
ADVERTISING RATES:
Full Page Mono £2610.00
Full Page Colour £2810.00
Agency Commission: 15%
Mechanical Data: Page Width: 180mm, Type Area: 270 x 180mm, Col Length: 270mm, Trim Size: 297 x 210mm, Bleed Size: 303 x 215mm, Film: Digital
BUSINESS: CONSTRUCTION: Water Engineering

WORLDCARGO NEWS
39646U49C-500

Editorial Address: Northbank House, 5 Bridge Street, LEATHERHEAD, KT22 8BL **Tel:** 01372 375511
Fax: 01372 370111
Email: vchampion@wcnpublishing.com
Advertising Address: As above.
Email: gtilbury@wcnpublishing.com
Web site: http://www.worldcargonews.com
ISSN: 1355-0551
Publisher: WCN Publishing
Date Established: 1994
Frequency: Monthly
Free to qualifying individuals
Annual Sub.: £295.00
Circulation: 7,901 (BPA Worldwide 01/01/2007 to 30/06/2007)
Editor: Vincent Champion; **Advertising Manager:** Gilly Tilbury
Summary of Content: Magazine covering most kinds of cargo handling, containerisation, intermodalism and port development.
Readership/Target Audience: Aimed at cargo handling and transportation professionals worldwide.
ADVERTISING RATES:
Full Page Mono £4065.00
Full Page Colour £5285.00
Agency Commission: 10%

Mechanical Data: Page Width: 268mm, Type Area: 390 x 268mm, Col Length: 390mm, Trim Size: 420 x 297mm, Bleed Size: 426 x 303mm, Film: Digital
Copy instructions: Copy Date: 3 weeks prior to publication date
Average advertising content per issue: 50%
BUSINESS: TRANSPORT: Freight

WORLDFISH REPORT
39389U45B-300

Editorial Address: 80 Calverley Road, TUNBRIDGE WELLS, TN1 2UN **Tel:** 020 7017 7500 **Fax:** 020 7017 7599
Email: marketing@agra-net.com
Web site: http://www.agra-net.com
ISSN: 1360-7391
Publisher: Agra Informa Ltd
Date Established: 1977
Frequency: 25 issues yearly
Annual Sub.: £1344.00
Summary of Content: Bulletin covering the European and world fisheries, policy and trade. Includes Brussels briefing, world fishing scene, supplies and prices, policy and legislation.
Readership/Target Audience: Read by industry executives in the International fishing industry.
ADVERTISING: No Advertising taken
BUSINESS: MARINE & SHIPPING: Commercial Fishing

WORLD'S FAIR
41470U64A-170

Editorial Address: 3rd Floor, Hollinwood Business Centre, Albert Street, OLDHAM, OL8 3QL **Tel:** 0161 683 8000
Fax: 0161 683 8001
Email: wfair@worldsfair.co.uk
Advertising Address: As above.
Email: info@worldsfair.co.uk
Web site: http://www.worldsfair.co.uk
Publisher: The World's Fair Ltd
Date Established: 1904
Frequency: Weekly
Cover Price: £1.00
Circulation: 17,000 (Publisher's Statement)
Usual Pagination: 32
Editor: Paul Whatmore
Summary of Content: Newspaper containing articles on fairgrounds, steam preservation, circuses, market traders and amusement caterers.
Readership/Target Audience: Aimed at those working in the leisure and retail industries.
ADVERTISING RATES:
Full Page Mono £965.00
Full Page Colour £1100.00
SCC £6.00
Agency Commission: 10%
Mechanical Data: Col Length: 370mm, Film: Digital, Type Area: 370 x 262mm, No. of Columns (Display): 6, Page Width: 262mm
Copy instructions: Copy Date: Friday prior to publication date
Average advertising content per issue: 50%
Supplement(s): Market Trader and Independent Retailer - 52xY
BUSINESS: OTHER CLASSIFICATIONS: Amusement Trade

WORLDWIDE COMPUTER PRODUCTS NEWS
36146U5B-450

Editorial Address: PR by email only **Tel:** 020 7047 0200
Email: m2pw@m2.com
Web site: http://www.m2.com
Publisher: M2 Communications Ltd
Frequency: 104 issues yearly
Annual Sub.: £200.00
Editor: Jamie Ayres
Summary of Content: Magazine covering information on new computer products and services around the world.
Readership/Target Audience: Read by corporate, consumer and consultancy companies involved in IT.
ADVERTISING: No Advertising taken
BUSINESS: COMPUTERS & AUTOMATION: Data Processing

WORLDWIDE CONVENTION CENTRES DIRECTORY
35660U2C-500

Editorial Address: Woodley House, Oak Road, Rivenhall End, WITHAM, CM8 3HE **Tel:** 01376 512073
Fax: 01376 502691
Email: robspalding@btinternet.com
Advertising Address: Kings House, Cantelupe Road, EAST GRINSTEAD, RH19 3BE **Tel:** 01342 306700
Fax: 01342 302547
Email: cat@cat-publications.com
Web site: http://www.meetpie.com
Publisher: Conference & Travel Publications Ltd
Frequency: Annual - Published in January
Cover Price: Free
Circulation: 10,200 (Publisher's Statement)

Usual Pagination: 164
Editor: Rob Spalding; **Managing Editor:** Martin Lewis;
Publisher: Steve Lewis
Summary of Content: Directory of international conference facilities.
Readership/Target Audience: Read by worldwide event organisers.
ADVERTISING RATES:
Full Page Colour EUR4995.00
Mechanical Data: Film: Digital
BUSINESS: COMMUNICATIONS, ADVERTISING & MARKETING: Conferences & Exhibitions

WORLDWIDE COST OF LIVING SURVEY
36886U14A-462

Editorial Address: 26 Red Lion Square, LONDON, WC1R 4HQ **Tel:** 020 7576 1000 **Fax:** 020 7576 8485
Email: london@eiu.com
Advertising Address: As above.
Web site: http://www.wcol.eiu.com
Publisher: Economist Intelligence Unit
Date Established: 1975
Frequency: Half-yearly - Published in June and December
Annual Sub.: £540.00
Editor: Jon Copestake
Summary of Content: Journal providing an up-to-date survey of the cost of living in and around 140 cities spanning more than 90 countries.
Readership/Target Audience: Aimed at companies transferring executives abroad.
ADVERTISING: No Advertising taken
BUSINESS: COMMERCE, INDUSTRY & MANAGEMENT

WORLDWIDE INDEPENDENT POWER
622717U58-160

Editorial Address: Global House, 13 Market Square, HORSHAM, RH12 1EU **Tel:** 01403 220750
Fax: 01403 220751
Email: powereditorial@gmp.uk.com
Advertising Address: As above.
Email: power@gmp.uk.com
Web site: http://www.gmp.uk.com
ISSN: 1468-7100
Publisher: Global Media Publishing Ltd
Date Established: 2000
Frequency: 11 issues yearly - Published in the 4th week of the cover month. Double issue in January/February is published 4th week of 2nd month
Free to qualifying individuals
Annual Sub.: £120.00
Circulation: 8,000 (Publisher's Statement)
Usual Pagination: 44
Editor: Aidan Turnbull; **Advertising Manager:** Neb Saric;
Managing Editor: Aidan Turnbull
Summary of Content: Publication containing company profiles, regular coverage on Gen-Sets, CHP, engines and applications, renewables, turbines, fuels and in-depth news analysis. Includes updates and association news, Internet reviews, market analysis and utilities.
Readership/Target Audience: Aimed at consultants, engineers, construction firms, contract management companies, IPPs and end-users.
ADVERTISING RATES:
Full Page Mono £2840.00
Full Page Colour £3512.00
Agency Commission: 10%
Mechanical Data: Col Length: 265mm, Film: Digital, Type Area: 265 x 185mm, Bleed Size: 303 x 216mm, Trim Size: 297 x 210mm, Page Width: 185mm
Copy instructions: Copy Date: 2nd week of the cover month
Average advertising content per issue: 45%
Supplement(s): American Independent Power - 3xY, Independent Power Asia - 2xY
BUSINESS: ENERGY, FUEL & NUCLEAR

WRIGHTS FARMING REGISTER
1667453U21A-1114

Editorial Address: Media Centre, Morton Way, HORNCASTLE, LN9 6JR **Tel:** 01507 529466
Fax: 01507 528980
Email: spalmer@mortons.co.uk
Advertising Address: As above. **Tel:** 01507 524004
Email: sneedham@mortons.co.uk
Web site: http://www.wrightsregister.com
ISSN: 1477-5379
Publisher: Mortons Heritage Media
Frequency: Monthly
Cover Price: Free
Cover Price: £1.40
Annual Sub.: £9.50
Circulation: 30,000 (Publisher's Statement)
Usual Pagination: 40
Editor: Sarah Palmer
Summary of Content: Magazine focusing on all aspects of arable farming.

Readership/Target Audience: Aimed at farmers and those involved within the agricultural industry.
ADVERTISING RATES:
Full Page Colour £1202.00
Agency Commission: 10%
Mechanical Data: Type Area: 370 x 260mm, Col Length: 370mm, Page Width: 260mm, Col Widths (Display): 40mm, No. of Columns (Display): 6, Film: Digital
Average advertising content per issue: 80%
BUSINESS: AGRICULTURE & FARMING

THE WRIT
39254U44-3000
Editorial Address: 40 Linenhall Street, BELFAST, BT2 8BA
Tel: 028 9023 1614 **Fax:** 028 9023 2606
Email: alan.hunter@lawsoc-ni.org
Advertising Address: As above. **Tel:** 028 9040 2296
Fax: 028 9040 2291
Email: karen.irwin@dcppr.co.uk
Web site: http://www.lawsoc-ni.org
Publisher: The Law Society of Northern Ireland
Frequency: 10 issues yearly
Cover Price: Free
Circulation: 3,200 (Publisher's Statement)
Usual Pagination: 52
Editor: Paul O'Connor; **Advertising Manager:** Karen Irwin
Summary of Content: Journal providing information relevant to the legal business in Northern Ireland covering new legislation and regulations, court calendars and a section on interest groups.
Readership/Target Audience: Aimed at solicitors in Northern Ireland.
ADVERTISING RATES:
Full Page Colour £400.00
Mechanical Data: Page Width: 189mm, Trim Size: 297 x 210mm, No. of Columns (Display): 3, Type Area: 246 x 189mm, Col Length: 246mm, Print Process: Litho, Film: Digital, Col Widths (Display): 55mm
Copy instructions: Copy Date: 3 weeks prior to publication date
Average advertising content per issue: 25%
BUSINESS: LEGAL

WRITERS' FORUM
40928U60R-60
Editorial Address: PO Box 6337, BOURNEMOUTH, BH1 9EH **Tel:** 01202 586848
Email: features@writers-forum.com
Advertising Address: 4 Endsleigh Crescent, Clyst Honiton, EXETER, EX5 2AW **Tel:** 01392 367962 **Fax:** 01392 360701
Email: wendy.obrien3@virgin.net
Web site: http://www.writers-forum.com
ISSN: 1467-2529
Publisher: Select Publisher Services
Date Established: 1995
Frequency: 11 issues yearly - Double issue in July/August
Cover Price: £3.50
Annual Sub.: £33.00
Circulation: 25,000 (Publisher's Statement)
Usual Pagination: 68
Editor: Carl Styants; **Advertising Manager:** Wendy O'Brien
Summary of Content: Magazine covering all aspects of the craft and business of writing including short fiction, novels, non-fiction books, freelance journalism and poetry. Contains market news, reviews, advice on writing techniques and features on writers, editors and publishers.
Readership/Target Audience: Aimed at new and improving writers in the UK, Ireland and abroad.
ADVERTISING RATES:
Full Page Colour £1350.00
Agency Commission: 10%
Mechanical Data: Type Area: 298 x 210mm, Page Width: 210mm, Col Length: 298mm, Film: Positive, right reading, emulsion side down. Digital, Screen: 60 lpc, Trim Size: 297 x 210mm, Bleed Size: +5mm
Copy instructions: Copy Date: 5th of the month prior to publication date
Average advertising content per issue: 20%
BUSINESS: PUBLISHING: Publishing Related

WRITERS' NEWS
40930U60R-90
Editorial Address: 31-32 Park Row, LEEDS, LS1 5JD
Tel: 0113 200 2929 **Fax:** 0113 200 2928
Email: jtelfer@writersnews.co.uk
Advertising Address: As above.
Email: brendas@writersnews.co.uk
Web site: http://www.writersnews.co.uk
ISSN: 0957-3577
Publisher: Warners Group Publications plc
Date Established: 1989
Frequency: Monthly
Annual Sub.: £44.90
Usual Pagination: 40
Editor: Jonathan Telfer; **Managing Director:** Stephen Warner
Summary of Content: Magazine containing news and articles on writing and techniques.
Readership/Target Audience: Aimed at professional and aspiring writers.

ADVERTISING RATES:
Full Page Mono £550.00
Full Page Colour £670.00
SCC £10.50
Agency Commission: 10%
Mechanical Data: Page Width: 190mm, Trim Size: 297 x 210mm, Type Area: 274 x 190mm, Bleed Size: 303 x 216mm, Col Length: 274mm, Film: Digital
Copy instructions: Copy Date: 4 weeks prior to publication date
Average advertising content per issue: 35%
BUSINESS: PUBLISHING: Publishing Related

WRITING MAGAZINE
40931U60R-100
Editorial Address: 31-32 Park Row, LEEDS, LS1 5JD
Tel: 0113 200 2929 **Fax:** 0113 200 2928
Email: writersnews@writersnews.co.uk
Advertising Address: As above.
Email: brendas@writersnews.co.uk
Web site: http://www.writersnews.co.uk
ISSN: 0964-9166
Publisher: Warners Group Publications plc
Date Established: 1992
Frequency: Monthly
Cover Price: £3.60
Usual Pagination: 72
Editor: Jonathan Telfer; **Managing Director:** Stephen Warner; **Publisher:** Janet Davison
Summary of Content: Magazine containing news and articles on writing and techniques.
Readership/Target Audience: Aimed at professional and aspiring writers.
ADVERTISING RATES:
Full Page Mono £1100.00
Full Page Colour £1320.00
Agency Commission: 10%
Mechanical Data: Page Width: 190mm, Type Area: 274 x 190mm, Bleed Size: 303 x 216mm, Trim Size: 297 x 210mm, Col Length: 274mm, Film: Digital
BUSINESS: PUBLISHING: Publishing Related

WSA
39518U47A-500
Editorial Address: 36 Crosby Road North, LIVERPOOL, L22 0QN **Tel:** 0151 928 9288 **Fax:** 0151 928 4190
Email: stierney@worldtrades.co.uk
Advertising Address: As above.
Email: wsa@worldtrades.co.uk
Web site: http://www.sportstextiles.com
ISSN: 1356-644X
Publisher: World Trades Publishing Ltd
Date Established: 1995
Frequency: 6 issues yearly
Annual Sub.: £65.00
Circulation: 5,146 (Publisher's Statement)
Usual Pagination: 68
Editor: Stephen Tierney; **Advertising Manager:** Simon Yarwood; **Publisher:** Simon Yarwood
Summary of Content: Magazine that covers the performance and technology of fibres, textiles and components.
Readership/Target Audience: Aimed at design and development managers, manufacturers and retailers of sports active wear, outdoor wear, work wear, military, street ware and associated footwear and equipment.
ADVERTISING RATES:
Full Page Mono EUR4400.00
Full Page Colour EUR5500.00
Agency Commission: 15%
Mechanical Data: Film: Positive, right reading, emulsion side down, Type Area: 275 x 177mm, Bleed Size: 303 x 216mm, Trim Size: 297 x 210mm, Col Width: 275mm, Page Width: 177mm
BUSINESS: CLOTHING & TEXTILES

WWB WOMENSWEAR BUYER
39514U47A-560
Editorial Address: The Old Town Hall, Lewisham Road, Slaithwaite, HUDDERSFIELD, HD7 5AL **Tel:** 01484 846069
Fax: 01484 846232
Email: isabella@ras-publishing.com
Advertising Address: As above.
Email: mina@ras-publishing.com
Web site: http://www.ras-publishing.com
Publisher: RAS Publishing Ltd
Frequency: 11 issues yearly
Cover Price: £4.00
Circulation: 7,300 (Publisher's Statement)
Editor: Isabella Galuschka; **Managing Director:** Colette Tebbutt; **Managing Editor:** Martin Wanless
Summary of Content: Magazine covering news and trends in womenswear.
Readership/Target Audience: Aimed at womenswear buyers within the fashion industry.
ADVERTISING RATES:
Full Page Colour £3235.00
Agency Commission: 10%
Mechanical Data: Page Width: 219mm, Type Area: 312 x 219mm, Col Length: 312mm, Trim Size: 336 x 243mm, Bleed

---

Size: 342 x 249mm, Col Widths (Display): 40mm, No. of Columns (Display): 3, Film: Positive, right reading, emulsion side down
Average advertising content per issue: 40%
BUSINESS: CLOTHING & TEXTILES

WWD BEAUTY BIZ
37258U15A-190
Formerly: WWD Beauty Report International
Editorial Address: 20 Shorts Gardens, LONDON, WC2H 9AU **Tel:** 020 7240 0420 **Fax:** 020 7240 0290
Email: brid.costello@fairchildpub.com
Advertising Address: 9 Rue Royale, 75008 PARIS
Tel: 14 45 11 300 **Fax:** 14 26 81 233
Email: amelie.barsi@fairchildpub.com
Web site: http://www.wwd.com
Publisher: Fairchild Publications
Frequency: Monthly
Annual Sub.: £60.00
Circulation: 48,000 (Publisher's Statement)
Editor: Brid Costello; **Advertising Director:** Amélie Barsi
Summary of Content: Magazine providing news and updates on the international beauty products industry.
Readership/Target Audience: Aimed at professionals within the beauty industry.
ADVERTISING RATES:
Full Page Mono $7850.00
Full Page Colour $7850.00
Agency Commission: 15%
Mechanical Data: Bleed Size: 307 x 237mm, Film: Digital, Trim Size: 297 x 227mm
BUSINESS: COSMETICS & HAIRDRESSING: Cosmetics

WWW.VEHICLETECHNOLOGY.ORG
38332U31A-280
Formerly: Vehicle Technology Update
Editorial Address: PO Box 13312, BIRMINGHAM, B28 1BG
Tel: 0121 270 6592 **Fax:** 0121 270 6596
Email: anthony@sae-uk.org
Advertising Address: As above. **Tel:** 0121 444 0841
Email: info@sae-uk.org
Web site: http://www.sae-uk.org
ISSN: 1478-3584
Publisher: Society of Automotive Engineers Inc.
Date Established: 2002
Frequency: Quarterly
Cover Price: £2.50
Free to qualifying individuals
Circulation: 26,000 (Publisher's Statement)
Usual Pagination: 64
Editor: Anthony McDonagh-Smith; **Advertising Manager:** Jonathan Masding
Summary of Content: Magazine covering news of the motor industry, as well as providing information on new products and developments and education and training.
Readership/Target Audience: Aimed at automotive industries, student automotive engineers and vehicle component suppliers.
ADVERTISING RATES:
Full Page Colour £1000.00
Mechanical Data: Trim Size: 297 x 210mm, Type Area: 270 x 190mm, Col Length: 270mm, Page Width: 190mm, Film: Digital, Bleed Size: 303 x 216mm
BUSINESS: MOTOR TRADE: Motor Trade Accessories

X2
1861538U4A-321
Editorial Address: 91 Charterhouse Street, LONDON, EC1M 6HR **Tel:** 020 7336 5200
Email: tdowling@fxmagazine.co.uk
Publisher: Progressive Media Publications
Frequency: Quarterly
Free to qualifying individuals
Circulation: 8,000 (Publisher's Statement)
Editor: Theresa Dowling
Summary of Content: Publication covering the design of hotels from boutique to International.
Readership/Target Audience: Aimed at key decision makers within the luxury hotel industry including architects, interior designers, consultants and contractors.
BUSINESS: ARCHITECTURE & BUILDING: Architecture

THE YACHT REPORT GROUP
39428U45E-370
Formerly: The Yacht Report
Editorial Address: Lansdowne House, 3-7 Northcote Road, LONDON, SW11 1NG **Tel:** 020 7924 4004
Fax: 020 7924 1004
Email: newsdesk@theyachtreport.com
Advertising Address: As above.
Email: thea@theyachtreport.com
Web site: http://www.synfo.com
ISSN: 1897-8780
Publisher: TRP Magazines
Frequency: 10 issues yearly
Free to qualifying individuals
Annual Sub.: £65.00

Section 4 (b) Business Magazines

Business Magazines

Circulation: 14,060 (Publisher's Statement)
Usual Pagination: 220
Editor: Rachel Redhead; **Editor-in-Chief:** Martin Redmayne; **Advertising Manager:** Thea Cheney; **Managing Editor:** Rachel Redhead; **Publisher:** Martin Redmayne
Summary of Content: Magazine providing news and advice on the construction, management and operation of large yachts.
Readership/Target Audience: Aimed at personnel and owners directly involved in the construction, operation and running of luxury yachts.
ADVERTISING RATES:
Full Page Colour £2700.00
Agency Commission: 10%
Mechanical Data: Trim Size: 297 x 210mm, Bleed Size: 303 x 216mm, Film: Positive, right reading, emulsion side down. Digital, Page Width: 180mm, Type Area: 275 x 180mm, Col Length: 275mm
Average advertising content per issue: 40%
BUSINESS: MARINE & SHIPPING: Boat Trade

YEM - YOUR ENTREPRENEUR MAGAZINE (NORTH WEST)
1777335U63B-2567
Editorial Address: For all contact details see main edition, YE Magazine
Frequency: 6 issues yearly
Annual Sub.: £36.00
Circulation: 10,000 (Publisher's Statement)
Usual Pagination: 52
BUSINESS: REGIONAL BUSINESS: Regional Business English Counties

YEM - YOUR ENTREPRENEUR MAGAZINE (YORKSHIRE & HUMBER)
1777334U63B-2566
Editorial Address: For all contact details see main edition, YE Magazine
Frequency: 6 issues yearly
Annual Sub.: £36.00
Circulation: 10,000 (Print Run)
BUSINESS: REGIONAL BUSINESS: Regional Business English Counties

YES CHEF! MAGAZINE
1809293U11A-224
Editorial Address: 28 Ballmoor, Celtic Court, BUCKINGHAM, MK18 1RQ **Tel:** 01280 829300
Fax: 01280 829350
Email: info@yeschefmagazine.com
Advertising Address: As above.
Email: sue.prain@yeschefmagazine.com
Web site: http://www.yeschefmagazine.com
Publisher: Yes Chef! Magazine Ltd
Date Established: 2007
Frequency: Quarterly
Cover Price: £5.00
Annual Sub.: £25.00
Circulation: 7,000 (Publisher's Statement)
Usual Pagination: 84
Editor: John Radford; **Advertising Manager:** Sue Prain; **Managing Editor:** Shirley Embleton; **Publisher:** Peter Marshall
Summary of Content: Magazine focusing on industry trends, ingredients, techniques, product launches, fine wines, cookbook, cookery school and restaurant reviews.
Readership/Target Audience: Aimed at professional chefs and front-of-house staff as well as enthusiastic amateur cooks.
ADVERTISING RATES:
Full Page Colour £3000.00
Mechanical Data: Type Area: 285 x 200mm, Bleed Size: 326 x 231mm, Trim Size: 320 x 225mm, Col Length: 285mm, Page Width: 200mm, Film: Digital
Copy instructions: Copy Date: 2 weeks prior to publication date
BUSINESS: CATERING: Catering, Hotels & Restaurants

YORKSHIRE BUSINESS INSIDER
41408U63B-2380
Editorial Address: D5 Josephs Well, Hanover Walk, LEEDS, LS3 1AB **Tel:** 0113 220 4415 **Fax:** 0113 220 4419
Email: julie.hayes@newsco.com
Advertising Address: As above. **Tel:** 0113 220 4410
Email: mark.webb@newsco.com
Web site: http://www.insidermedia.com
Publisher: Newsco Insider Ltd
Date Established: 1998
Frequency: Monthly - Published around the 20th of the cover month
Annual Sub.: £48.00
Circulation: 9,968 (ABC 01/07/2008 to 30/06/2009)
Usual Pagination: 72
Editor: Julie Hayes
Summary of Content: Magazine containing business news, analysis and features.

Readership/Target Audience: Aimed at top corporate managers, chairmen, financial directors and professional advisors.
ADVERTISING RATES:
Full Page Colour £2400.00
Agency Commission: 10%
Mechanical Data: Page Width: 174mm, Film: Digital, Type Area: 267 x 174mm, Bleed Size: 303 x 216mm, Trim Size: 297 x 210mm, Col Length: 267mm
Copy instructions: Copy Date: 3 weeks prior to publication date
Average advertising content per issue: 40%
BUSINESS: REGIONAL BUSINESS: Regional Business English Counties

YOUNG COMPANY FINANCE
1657870U1A-300
Editorial Address: 8 Oxford Terrace, EDINBURGH, EH4 1PX **Tel:** 0131 315 4443 **Fax:** 0131 315 4443
Email: jonathan@ycf.co.uk
Web site: http://www.ycf.co.uk
Publisher: Edinburgh House Publishing
Date Established: 1998
Frequency: Monthly
Annual Sub.: £160.00
Usual Pagination: 12
Editor: Jonathan Harris
Summary of Content: Newsletter providing a source of information about early stage high growth ventures and the commercialisation environment in which they operate, with special reference to how they are financed.
Readership/Target Audience: Aimed at investors and business support organisations.
ADVERTISING: No Advertising taken
Editions:
Young Company Finance North of England
Young Company Finance Scotland
BUSINESS: FINANCE & ECONOMICS

YOUNG CONSUMERS
35468U2A-107_10
Formerly: International Journal of Advertising & Marketing to Children
Editorial Address: University of Exeter, School of Psychology, Washington Singer Laboratori, Perry Road, EXETER, EX4 4QG **Tel:** 01392 263789
Email: b.m.young@exeter.ac.uk
Web site: http://info.emeraldinsight.com/products/journals/journals.htm?id=YC
ISSN: 1464-6676
Publisher: Emerald Group Publishing Ltd
Date Established: 1999
Frequency: Quarterly
Annual Sub.: £195.00
Circulation: 800 (Publisher's Statement)
Usual Pagination: 76
Editor: Brian Young
Summary of Content: Journal delivers academic papers on all aspects of consumer practices of young people and consumer insights relevant for practitioners involved in child-related marketing.
Readership/Target Audience: Aimed at academics, advertising agencies and marketing directors.
ADVERTISING: No Advertising taken
BUSINESS: COMMUNICATIONS, ADVERTISING & MARKETING

YOUNGMINDSMAGAZINE
1813187U32G-177
Editorial Address: 48-50 St. John Street, LONDON, EC1M 4DG **Tel:** 020 7336 8445 **Fax:** 020 7336 8446
Email: susan.delgado@youngminds.org.uk
Advertising Address: As above.
Email: susan.delgado@youngminds.org.uk
Web site: http://www.youngminds.org.uk
Publisher: YoungMinds
Frequency: 6 issues yearly
Annual Sub.: £26.00
Circulation: 6,000 (Publisher's Statement)
Editor: Susan Delgado; **Advertising Manager:** Susan Delgado
Summary of Content: Independent magazine focusing on child and adolescent mental health. Includes news, analysis, parliamentary coverage, opinion, features, reviews, conferences and appointments.
Readership/Target Audience: Aimed at members of YoungMinds, including mental health professionals, teachers, Connexions personal advisors and social workers.
ADVERTISING: Rates on application
BUSINESS: LOCAL GOVERNMENT, LEISURE & RECREATION: Community Care & Social Services

YOUR CONSORTIUM
39795U53-40
Formerly: The Consortium
Editorial Address: PO Box 30, CROWBOROUGH, TN6 3ZY
Tel: 01892 661166 **Fax:** 01892 661122
Email: news@consortiumpublishing.co.uk
Advertising Address: As above.

Email: christian@consortiumpublishing.co.uk
Web site: http://www.consortiumpublishing.co.uk
Publisher: Consortium Publishing Ltd
Date Established: 1992
Frequency: 11 issues yearly
Cover Price: £3.00
Free to qualifying individuals
Annual Sub.: £36.00
Circulation: 13,250 (Publisher's Statement)
Usual Pagination: 60
Editor: Kate Barker; **Features Editor:** Kate Barker; **Advertising Manager:** Christian Britten; **Publisher:** Mike Horton
Summary of Content: Magazine covering news, foods, licensed drinks, drinks, frozen and chilled foods and chemists.
Readership/Target Audience: Aimed at retailers and wholesalers in the independent food sector.
ADVERTISING RATES:
Full Page Colour £2550.00
Agency Commission: 10%
Mechanical Data: Film: Digital, Type Area: 305 x 212mm, Bleed Size: 331 x 238mm, Trim Size: 325 x 232mm, Col Length: 305mm, No. of Columns (Display): 4, Page Width: 212mm
Average advertising content per issue: 40%
BUSINESS: RETAILING & WHOLESALING

YOUR SHOW HOME
1833062U4E-452
Editorial Address: 60 Churchill Square, Kings Hill, WEST MALLING, ME19 4YU **Tel:** 01732 525800
Fax: 01732 525801
Email: steve@yourshow-home.co.uk
Advertising Address: As above.
Email: steve@yourshow-home.co.uk
Web site: http://www.yourshow-home.co.uk
Publisher: NCG Media
Frequency: 6 issues yearly
Cover Price: Free
Circulation: 8,082 (Publisher's Statement)
Editor: Steve Grossmith
Summary of Content: Magazine for the homebuilding industry covering environment, construction and community issues, architectural specifying, marketing and sales, interior design, finance and land planning. Also features a listings directory.
Readership/Target Audience: Aimed at architects and construction directors and UK house builders.
ADVERTISING RATES:
Full Page Colour £3300.00
Mechanical Data: Trim Size: 297 x 210mm, Type Area: 270 x 190mm, Bleed Size: 303 x 216mm, Col Length: 270mm, Page Width: 190mm, Film: Digital
BUSINESS: ARCHITECTURE & BUILDING: Building

YOUR VOICE
41161U62J-910
Formerly: Professionalism in Practice: The PAT Journal
Editorial Address: 2 St. James' Court, Friar Gate, DERBY, DE1 1BT **Tel:** 01332 372337 **Fax:** 01332 292431
Email: pressoffice@voicetheunion.org.uk
Web site: http://www.voicetheunion.org.uk/yourvoice
ISSN: 1756-8528
Publisher: Voice: the union for education professional
Date Established: 2008
Frequency: Quarterly
Cover Price: £2.00
Free to qualifying individuals
Annual Sub.: £9.20
Circulation: 30,000 (Publisher's Statement)
Usual Pagination: 24
Editor: Richard Fraser
Summary of Content: Magazine containing news, views and advice on issues of concern to teachers, head teachers, lecturers, education support staff and child carers.
Readership/Target Audience: Aimed at members of Voice: the union for education professionals, chief education officers, the national press and libraries.
ADVERTISING: No Advertising taken
BUSINESS: CHURCH & SCHOOL EQUIPMENT & EDUCATION: Teachers & Education Management

YOUR WITNESS
1744948U44-3042
Editorial Address: 14 Booth Street, SALFORD, M3 5DG
Tel: 0161 839 1420 **Fax:** 0161 830 4559
Email: chris.wilson@networkmediagroup.co.uk
Advertising Address: As above. **Tel:** 0161 830 4560
Email: chris.wilson@networkmediagroup.co.uk
Web site: http://www.your-witness.com
Publisher: Destination Maps & Media Ltd
Date Established: 2006
Frequency: Quarterly
Cover Price: Free
Circulation: 5,000 (Publisher's Statement)
Editor: Chris Wilson

Summary of Content: Magazine promoting the services of expert witnesses with news stories, features, court reports and case studies.
Readership/Target Audience: Aimed at solicitors, lawyers, courts, major insurance companies and media companies.
ADVERTISING RATES:
Full Page Colour £1495.00
Agency Commission: 10%
Mechanical Data: Bleed Size: 295 x 215mm, Trim Size: 290 x 210mm, Film: Digital
Copy instructions: Copy Date: Last working day of the month prior to publication date
Average advertising content per issue: 40%
BUSINESS: LEGAL

YOUTH & POLICY
25426U62R-450

Editorial Address: Durham University, Community and Youth Work Studies Unit, Elvet Riverside 2, New Elvet, DURHAM, DH1 3JT **Tel:** 0116 242 7350 **Fax:** 0116 242 7444
Email: andyh@nya.org.uk
Advertising Address: Eastgate House, 19-23 Humberstone Road, LEICESTER, LE5 3GJ **Tel:** 0116 242 7483
Fax: 0116 242 7444
Email: timb@nya.org.uk
Web site: http://www.nya.org.uk
ISSN: 0262-9798
Publisher: The National Youth Agency
Date Established: 1982
Frequency: Quarterly
Annual Sub.: £28.00
Circulation: 700 (Publisher's Statement)
Usual Pagination: 112
Editor: Andy Hopkinson; **Advertising Manager:** Tim Burke; **Publisher:** Andy Hopkinson
Summary of Content: Journal containing analytical articles on theory, practice and policy issues around young people in society.
Readership/Target Audience: Aimed at academics and professionals involved in youth study and youth work.
ADVERTISING RATES:
Full Page Mono £225.00
Agency Commission: 10%
Mechanical Data: Col Length: 195mm, Type Area: 195 x 125mm, Page Width: 125mm
Copy instructions: Copy Date: 4 weeks prior to publication
Average advertising content per issue: 5%
BUSINESS: CHURCH & SCHOOL EQUIPMENT & EDUCATION: Education Related

ZERB
35701U2D-130

Editorial Address: Sunnyside, Church Street, Charlbury, CHIPPING NORTON, OX7 3PR **Tel:** 01608 810954
Email: alichap@mac.com
Advertising Address: 3 Alexander Avenue, Droitwich Spa, DROITWICH, WR9 8NH **Tel:** 01905 796910
Email: jkfrench@mac.com
Web site: http://www.gtc.org.uk
Publisher: GTC
Frequency: Half-yearly - Published in February and August
Cover Price: £5.50
Circulation: 3,000 (Publisher's Statement)
Usual Pagination: 76
Editor: Alison Chapman; **Advertising Manager:** James French; **Publisher:** Alison Chapman
Summary of Content: Magazine covering features on all TV broadcasting subjects, with emphasis on camerawork, cameras equipment. Also includes human interest articles and production reports.
Readership/Target Audience: Aimed at members of the Guild of Television Cameramen, cameramen around the world, managers in the BBC and ITV companies and advertising agents.
ADVERTISING RATES:
Full Page Colour £1425.00
Agency Commission: 10%
Mechanical Data: Type Area: 270 x 185mm, Bleed Size: 303 x 216mm, Trim Size: 297 x 210mm, Col Length: 270mm, No. of Columns (Display): 4, Page Width: 185mm
Average advertising content per issue: 30%
BUSINESS: COMMUNICATIONS, ADVERTISING & MARKETING: Broadcasting

Consumer Magazines

#5
1896801U86C-751

Editorial Address: 9 Arundel Mews, 13-18 Arundel Place, BRIGHTON, BN2 1GD **Tel:** 01273 574020
Advertising Address: As above.

Web site: http://www.rioferdinand.com
Publisher: Made Up Media
Frequency: 6 issues yearly
Cover Price: Free
Editor: Danny Crouch; **Managing Director:** Danny Crouch
Summary of Content: Digital lifestyle magazine featuring film, music, gadgets and fashion.
CONSUMER: ADULT & GAY MAGAZINES: Men's Lifestyle Magazines

.NET
36246U78E-8

Editorial Address: 30 Monmouth Street, BATH, BA1 2BW
Tel: 01225 442244
Email: dan.oliver@futurenet.co.uk
Advertising Address: As above. **Fax:** 01225 732206
Email: george.lucas@futurenet.com
Web site: http://www.netmag.co.uk
Publisher: Future Publishing Ltd
Date Established: 1994
Frequency: 13 issues yearly - Published 2 weeks prior to cover date
Cover Price: £5.99
Circulation: 18,343 (ABC 01/01/2008 to 31/12/2008)
Usual Pagination: 140
Editor: Dan Oliver; **Managing Director:** Robert Price; **Publisher:** Matt Pierce
Summary of Content: Magazine covering all aspects of the Internet. Includes news, technical tips, software and features on how to build websites.
Readership/Target Audience: Aimed at expert internet users and website designers and developers.
ADVERTISING RATES:
Full Page Colour £2850.00
Agency Commission: 10%
Mechanical Data: Film: Digital, Type Area: 280 x 213mm, Bleed Size: 306 x 238mm, Trim Size: 300 x 232mm, Col Length: 280mm, Page Width: 213mm
Copy instructions: Copy Date: 4 weeks prior to publication date
Average advertising content per issue: 30%
CONSUMER: CONSUMER ELECTRONICS: Home Computing

0161 MAGAZINE
1657690U80C-5142

Editorial Address: Crown House, Trafford Park Road, Trafford Park, MANCHESTER, M17 1HG **Tel:** 0161 848 9222
Fax: 0161 848 9444
Email: connect@0161magazine.com
Web site: http://www.0161magazine.com
Publisher: Manchester Media Limited
Date Established: 2004
Frequency: Monthly
Cover Price: £1.00
Free to qualifying individuals
Circulation: 20,000 (Publisher's Statement)
Usual Pagination: 100
Editor: Rory McNamara
Summary of Content: Magazine covering the thoughts, opinions and views of those living in Manchester as well as features on fashion, the homeless community, club nights, reviews of bands and musicians, music and gadget reviews, lifestyle and creativity.
Readership/Target Audience: Aimed at the general public and students in Manchester aged between 18 and 35 years old.
ADVERTISING: No Advertising taken
CONSUMER: RURAL & REGIONAL INTEREST: Regional Interest English Counties

100% BIKER
601360U77B-50

Editorial Address: The Old School, Higher Kinnerton, CHESTER, CH4 9AJ **Tel:** 01244 660044 **Fax:** 01244 660611
Email: editor@100-biker.co.uk
Advertising Address: As above. **Tel:** 01244 663400
Email: ads@100-biker.co.uk
Web site: http://www.100-biker.co.uk
ISSN: 1468-0890
Publisher: Jazz Publishing
Date Established: 1999
Frequency: 13 issues yearly
Cover Price: £3.40
Circulation: 30,000 (Publisher's Statement)
Usual Pagination: 90
Editor: Nick Samson; **Managing Director:** Stuart Mears; **Advertising Manager:** Natalie Beamish; **Publisher:** Stuart Mears
Summary of Content: Magazine dedicated to customised bikes and trikes. Contains news, technical articles, rally coverage and information on legislative changes.
Readership/Target Audience: Aimed at owners and those with an interest in custom motorcycling and motorcycling in general.
ADVERTISING RATES:
Full Page Colour £467.00
Mechanical Data: Bleed Size: 303 x 216mm, Trim Size: 297 x 210mm, Film: Digital

Copy instructions: Copy Date: 4 weeks prior to publication date
CONSUMER: MOTORING & CYCLING: Motorcycling

100 CROSSWORDS
46671U79F-2

Editorial Address: Stonecroft, 69 Station Road, REDHILL, RH1 1EY **Tel:** 01737 378700 **Fax:** 01737 767248
Email: reception@puzzlermedia.com
Advertising Address: As above.
Email: brian.aimes@puzzlermedia.com
Publisher: Puzzler Media Ltd
Frequency: 13 issues yearly
Cover Price: £1.60
Editor: Deborah Hardy
Summary of Content: Publication containing a compilation of straight crosswords.
Readership/Target Audience: Aimed at crossword enthusiasts.
ADVERTISING: Rates on application
Agency Commission: 10%
CONSUMER: HOBBIES & DIY: Games & Puzzles

10 MAGAZINE
749503U74B-707

Editorial Address: 3 Lower John Street, LONDON, W1F 9DX **Tel:** 020 7434 0042
Email: info@10magazine.com
Web site: http://www.10magazine.com
Publisher: Zac Publishing
Date Established: 2001
Frequency: Quarterly
Cover Price: £10.00
Circulation: 10,000 (Publisher's Statement)
Usual Pagination: 300
Editor: Sophia Neophitou-Apostolou; **Editor-in-Chief:** Sophia Neophitou-Apostolou
Summary of Content: Magazine focusing on fashion, contemporary art and beauty and offering an environment for photographers and stylists to showcase their work.
Readership/Target Audience: Aimed at fashion focused men and women.
ADVERTISING: Rates on application
CONSUMER: WOMEN'S INTEREST CONSUMER MAGAZINES: Women's Interest - Fashion

125 MAGAZINE
1749515U85A-206

Editorial Address: 3 Calvert Avenue, LONDON, E2 7JP
Tel: 020 7613 2015
Email: info@125magazine.com
Advertising Address: TK Media, 3rd Floor, 1 Munro Terrace, LONDON, SW10 0DL **Tel:** 020 7751 4792
Email: tolga@tkmedia.co.uk
Web site: http://www.125magazine.com
Publisher: 125 World
Date Established: 2002
Frequency: Half-yearly - Published in March and September
Cover Price: £6.99
Circulation: 55,000 (Publisher's Statement)
Usual Pagination: 300
Editor: Bella Haigh; **Editor-in-Chief:** Perry Curties; **Advertising Manager:** Tolga Kadioglu
Summary of Content: Magazine featuring the work of 25 photographers each issue covering all aspects of photography including fashion, beauty and landscape.
Readership/Target Audience: Aimed at those interested in art and design.
ADVERTISING RATES:
Full Page Colour £4450.00
Agency Commission: 10%
Mechanical Data: Type Area: 250 x 210mm, Bleed Size: 276 x 236mm, Trim Size: 270 x 230mm, Col Length: 250mm, Page Width: 210mm, Film: Digital
Copy instructions: Copy Date: 4 weeks prior to publication date
Average advertising content per issue: 10%
CONSUMER: PHOTOGRAPHY & FILM MAKING: Photography

1940
1840314U94X-300

Editorial Address: 26 Sandown Road, Hazel Grove, STOCKPORT, SK7 4SH **Tel:** 0161 483 1790
Email: geoffsimpsonemail@gmail.com
Web site: http://www.battleofbritainmemorial.org
Date Established: 2001
Frequency: Annual - Published in spring
Cover Price: Free
Circulation: 1,000 (Publisher's Statement)
Usual Pagination: 16
Editor: Geoff Simpson
Summary of Content: Magazine with historical material relating to 1940, particularly the contribution of the RAF as well as book reviews.
Readership/Target Audience: Aimed at members of the Friends of the Few and others with an interest in 1940.

ADVERTISING: No Advertising taken
CONSUMER: OTHER CLASSIFICATIONS: Miscellaneous

2000 AD
45401U79L-15

Editorial Address: Riverside House, Osney Mead, OXFORD, OX2 0ES **Tel:** 01865 792201 **Fax:** 01865 792254
Email: matt.smith@rebellion.co.uk
Advertising Address: As above. **Fax:** 01865 200610
Email: keith.richardson@rebellion.co.uk
Web site: http://www.2000adonline.com
ISSN: 0262-284X
Publisher: Rebellion
Date Established: 1977
Frequency: Weekly
Cover Price: £1.90
Circulation: 28,000 (Publisher's Statement)
Usual Pagination: 32
Editor: Matt Smith; **Advertising Manager:** Keith Richardson
Summary of Content: Award winning cult weekly anthology comic, featuring SF, fantasy and horror strips, including the UK's most popular comic character, Judge Dredd.
Readership/Target Audience: Aimed at comic enthusiasts and fans of science-fiction and horror aged between 15 and 45.
ADVERTISING RATES:
Full Page Colour £1200.00
Agency Commission: 10%
Mechanical Data: Film: Digital, Bleed Size: 282 x 216mm, Trim Size: 276 x 210mm
Copy instructions: Copy Date: 4 weeks prior to publication date
CONSUMER: HOBBIES & DIY: Fantasy Games & Science Fiction

---

220 TRIATHLON
45895U75J-601

Editorial Address: 9th Floor, Tower House, Fairfax Street, BRISTOL, BS1 3BN **Tel:** 0117 927 9009 **Fax:** 0117 934 9008
Email: jameswitts@originpublishing.co.uk
Advertising Address: As above. **Tel:** 0117 314 8364
Email: eleanorgodwin@originpublishing.co.uk
Web site: http://www.220magazine.com
Publisher: Origin Publishing Ltd
Date Established: 1989
Frequency: 13 issues yearly
Cover Price: £3.99
Circulation: 20,000 (Publisher's Statement)
Usual Pagination: 90
Editor: James Witts; **Publisher:** Andrew Davies
Summary of Content: Magazine covering swimming, running and cycling training programmes. Also includes information on nutrition, international and national events, product reviews and injury prevention and cure.
Readership/Target Audience: Aimed at all triathlon, adventure sports and run-bike enthusiasts.
ADVERTISING RATES:
Full Page Colour £1390.00
Agency Commission: 10%
Mechanical Data: Trim Size: 297 x 210mm, Bleed Size: 303 x 216mm, Film: Digital, Type Area: 281 x 195mm, Col Length: 281mm, Page Width: 195mm
CONSUMER: SPORT: Athletics

247
714573U80C-3734

Formerly: twenty4-seven magazine
Editorial Address: Grosvenor House, Belgrave Lane, PLYMOUTH, PL4 7DA **Tel:** 01752 294130
Email: 247@outofhand.co.uk
Advertising Address: As above. **Fax:** 01752 601199
Email: nigel@outofhand.co.uk
Web site: http://www.247mag.co.uk
Publisher: Out of Hand Ltd
Date Established: 2000
Frequency: 11 issues yearly
Cover Price: Free
Circulation: 35,000 (Publisher's Statement)
Usual Pagination: 84
Editor: Lauren Brown; **Advertising Manager:** Nigel Muntz
Summary of Content: Music and lifestyle magazine for the South-West/West Country. Including lifestyle features, news, interviews and reviews on clubs, bands, comedy, music, graffiti, films, arts and theatre.
Readership/Target Audience: Aimed at 18 to 35 year olds living in or visiting the South-West of England.
ADVERTISING RATES:
Full Page Colour £495.00
Agency Commission: 10%
Mechanical Data: Film: Digital, Trim Size: 210 x 148mm, Bleed Size: 216 x 154mm
Copy instructions: Copy Date: 12th of the month prior to publication date
Average advertising content per issue: 40%
CONSUMER: RURAL & REGIONAL INTEREST: Regional Interest English Counties

---

247 MAGAZINE - WEST AND WALES
47388U83-8_5

Formerly: 247 Magazine - West Wales
Editorial Address: Grosvenor House, Belgrave Lane, PLYMOUTH, PL4 7DA **Tel:** 01752 294130
Fax: 01752 564010
Email: 247@outofhand.co.uk
Advertising Address: Nebron House, Sion Road, BRISTOL, BS3 3BD **Tel:** 0117 953 6363 **Fax:** 0117 953 6364
Email: nigel@outofhand.co.uk
Web site: http://www.247magazine.co.uk
Publisher: Out of Hand Ltd
Date Established: 2000
Frequency: Quarterly
Cover Price: Free
Circulation: 25,000 (Publisher's Statement)
Usual Pagination: 68
Editor: Lauren Taverna-Brown; **Advertising Manager:** Nigel Muntz
Summary of Content: Entertainment magazine featuring regional and national entertainment news, interviews, film and album reviews, competitions, club, gig and comedy previews and listings.
Readership/Target Audience: Aimed at people aged between 18 and 35 years old.
ADVERTISING RATES:
Full Page Colour £495.00
Agency Commission: 10%
Mechanical Data: Trim Size: 210 x 148mm, Bleed Size: 216 x 154mm, Film: Digital
Copy instructions: Copy Date: 12th of the month prior to publication date
Average advertising content per issue: 40%
CONSUMER: STUDENT PUBLICATIONS

---

24 THE OFFICIAL MAGAZINE
1745733U76C-838

Editorial Address: Titan House, 144 Southwark Street, LONDON, SE1 0UP **Tel:** 020 7620 0200 **Fax:** 020 7620 0032
Advertising Address: As above. **Fax:** 020 7803 1803
Email: james.willmott@titanemail.com
Web site: http://www.titanmagazines.com
Publisher: Titan Magazines
Date Established: 2006
Frequency: 6 issues yearly
Cover Price: £3.75
Editor: Martin Eden; **Advertising Manager:** James Willmott
Summary of Content: Magazine with cast and crew interviews, highlights from the show, behind-the-scene features, posters, competitions and news from the show.
Readership/Target Audience: Aimed at fans of the TV series 24.
ADVERTISING RATES:
Full Page Colour £2500.00
Mechanical Data: Trim Size: 276 x 200mm, Film: Digital
CONSUMER: MUSIC & PERFORMING ARTS: TV & Radio

---

25 BEAUTIFUL HOMES
45240U74C-10

Editorial Address: 6th Floor, Blue Fin Building, 110 Southwark Street, LONDON, SE1 0SU **Tel:** 020 3148 5000
Fax: 020 3148 8117
Email: 25_beautiful_homes@ipcmedia.com
Advertising Address: Blue Fin Building, 110 Southwark Street, LONDON, SE1 0SU **Tel:** 020 3148 5000
Email: james_zaman@ipcmedia.com
Web site: http://www.ipcmedia.com
ISSN: 1369-5290
Publisher: IPC Southbank
Date Established: 1997
Frequency: Monthly
Cover Price: £3.50
Circulation: 102,868 (ABC 01/01/2009 to 30/06/2009)
Usual Pagination: 148
Editor: Penny Botting; **Advertising Manager:** James Zaman
Summary of Content: Magazine featuring the style, colour schemes, and furnishings of 25 different homes.
Readership/Target Audience: Aimed at people with an interest in home decorating.
ADVERTISING RATES:
Full Page Colour £5280.00
Mechanical Data: Type Area: 258 x 194mm, Col Length: 258mm, Trim Size: 284 x 220mm, Bleed Size: 290 x 226mm, Film: Digital, Page Width: 194mm
CONSUMER: WOMEN'S INTEREST CONSUMER MAGAZINES: Home & Family

2CVGB NEWS
46441U77E-5

Editorial Address: The Byre, RUGBY, CV23 0RA **Tel:** 07502 134633
Email: editor@2cvgb.com
Advertising Address: 130 Allport Street, CANNOCK, WS11 1JZ **Tel:** 07860 711286
Email: small.ads@2cvgb.uk
Web site: http://www.2cvgb.co.uk
Publisher: The Deux Chevaux Club of Great Britain
Date Established: 1978

Frequency: Monthly
Cover Price: £2.50
Free to qualifying individuals
Annual Sub.: £25.00
Circulation: 3,600 (Publisher's Statement)
Usual Pagination: 68
Editor: John Barnes; **Advertising Manager:** Laurence Broadhurst
Summary of Content: Magazine of the 2CVGB Club of Great Britain. Includes historical, technical and general articles, events, activities, reports and information. Also local group news, details of DIY servicing and repairs.
Readership/Target Audience: Read by Citroen A series owners and enthusiasts.
ADVERTISING: Rates on application
Copy instructions: Copy Date: 10th of the month prior to publication date
CONSUMER: MOTORING & CYCLING: Club Cars

---

360 GAMER
1702739U78D-322

Editorial Address: B10 Arena Business Centre, Holyrood Close, POOLE, BH17 7BA **Tel:** 01202 606385
Fax: 01202 606386
Email: simon@360-gamer.com
Advertising Address: As above.
Email: tarik@uncookedmedia.com
Web site: http://www.360-gamer.com
Publisher: Uncooked Media Ltd
Date Established: 2005
Frequency: 17 issues yearly
Cover Price: £2.99
Circulation: 13,968 (ABC 01/07/2007 to 31/12/2007)
Usual Pagination: 132
Editor: Simon Phillips; **Advertising Manager:** Rob Cox
Summary of Content: Magazine covering the latest gaming news, reviews and previews.
Readership/Target Audience: Aimed at gamers aged 13 to 25 years old.
ADVERTISING RATES:
Full Page Colour £2895.00
Agency Commission: 10%
Mechanical Data: Type Area: 297 x 230mm, Bleed Size: 303 x 236mm, Trim Size: 287 x 220mm, Col Length: 297mm, Page Width: 230mm, Film: Digital
Copy instructions: Copy Date: 3 weeks prior to publication date
CONSUMER: CONSUMER ELECTRONICS: Games

3D ARTIST
1895585U84A-471

Editorial Address: Richmond House, 33 Richmond Hill, BOURNEMOUTH, BH2 6EZ **Tel:** 01202 586200
Email: duncan.evans@imagine-publishing.co.uk
Advertising Address: As above. **Tel:** 01202 856441
Email: michaela.cotty@imagine-publishing.co.uk
Web site: http://www.3dartistonline.com
Publisher: Imagine Publishing
Date Established: 2009
Frequency: 13 issues yearly
Cover Price: £6.00
Annual Sub.: £62.40
Circulation: 35,000 (Print Run)
Usual Pagination: 116
Editor: Duncan Evans; **Advertising Manager:** Michaela Cotty
Summary of Content: Magazine showcasing 3D images and features interviews with people in the 3D industry and looks at development and technologies that shape what is seen on TV and in film, in advertising and architecture and in art.
Readership/Target Audience: Anyone with an interest in 3D art.
CONSUMER: THE ARTS & LITERARY: Arts

3D WORLD
623147U78E-5

Editorial Address: 30 Monmouth Street, BATH, BA1 2BW **Tel:** 01225 442244
Email: 3dworldmag@futurenet.com
Advertising Address: As above. **Fax:** 01225 782885
Email: george.lucas@futurenet.co.uk
Web site: http://www.3dworldmag.com
ISSN: 1470-4380
Publisher: Future Publishing Ltd
Date Established: 2000
Frequency: 13 issues yearly
Cover Price: £6.00
Circulation: 14,558 (ABC 01/01/2008 to 31/12/2008)
Usual Pagination: 116
Editor: Jim Thacker; **Advertising Manager:** Georgina Lucas
Summary of Content: Design magazine focusing on the creation of 3D graphics for use in TV and film, computer games, advertising and product design and visualisation.
Readership/Target Audience: Aimed at 3D studios, programmers, animators, designers, artists and post-production film houses.
ADVERTISING RATES:
Full Page Colour £2289.00

Agency Commission: 10%
Mechanical Data: Type Area: 255 x 203mm, Col Length: 255mm, Film: Digital, Page Width: 203mm, Trim Size: 270 x 222mm
Copy instructions: Copy Date: 4 weeks prior to publication date
CONSUMER: CONSUMER ELECTRONICS: Home Computing

3SIXTY
1775096U86B-176

Editorial Address: 4 Steine Street, BRIGHTON, BN2 1TE
Tel: 0870 620 1360 **Fax:** 01273 676201
Email: info@3sixtymag.co.uk
Advertising Address: As above.
Email: advertising@3sixtymag.co.uk
Web site: http://www.3sixtymag.co.uk
Publisher: Marble Media Publishing Ltd
Date Established: 2002
Frequency: Monthly
Cover Price: Free
Circulation: 25,000 (Publisher's Statement)
Usual Pagination: 100
Editor: Torsten Højer
Summary of Content: Magazine covering gay lifestyle, news, community services, entertainment, travel and show business.
Readership/Target Audience: Aimed at LGBT communities in the South of England and South Wales.
ADVERTISING RATES:
Full Page Colour £1725.00
Agency Commission: 10%
Mechanical Data: Trim Size: 297 x 210mm, Bleed Size: 303 x 216mm
Average advertising content per issue: 50%
CONSUMER: ADULT & GAY MAGAZINES: Gay & Lesbian Magazines

3TOUCH VOLLEYBALL
629056U75X-920

Editorial Address: Suite B, Loughborough Technology Centre, Epinal Way, LOUGHBOROUGH, LE11 3GE
Tel: 01509 631699 **Fax:** 01509 631689
Email: m.pritchard@volleyballengland.org
Advertising Address: As above.
Email: r.lee@volleyballengland.org
Web site: http://www.3touchvolleyball.co.uk
ISSN: 1479-0785
Publisher: The English Volleyball Association
Date Established: 1998
Frequency: 6 issues yearly
Cover Price: £2.50
Free to qualifying individuals
Circulation: 3,000 (Publisher's Statement)
Usual Pagination: 16
Editor: Mark Pritchard; **Advertising Manager:** Rebecca Lee
Summary of Content: Magazine covering all aspects and types of volleyball, both professional and amateur, including news, sport politics, coverage of national and international events and profiles of players, coaches and referees.
Readership/Target Audience: Aimed at all those with an interest in volleyball.
ADVERTISING RATES:
Full Page Colour £295.00
CONSUMER: SPORT: Other Sport

360
1695157U78D-318

Editorial Address: Richmond House, 33 Richmond Hill, BOURNEMOUTH, BH2 6EZ **Tel:** 01202 586200
Email: 360@imagine-publishing.co.uk
Advertising Address: As above. **Tel:** 01202 586422
Email: james.haley@imagine-publishing.co.uk
Web site: http://www.imagine-publishing.co.uk
Publisher: Imagine Publishing
Date Established: 2005
Frequency: 13 issues yearly
Cover Price: £2.95
Circulation: 11,518 (ABC 01/01/2009 to 30/06/2009)
Usual Pagination: 132
Editor: Nick Jones; **Editor-in-Chief:** Nick Jones
Summary of Content: Magazine covering all aspects of the Xbox 360 games console.
Readership/Target Audience: Aimed at males aged between 24 and 35 years old.
ADVERTISING RATES:
Full Page Colour £3200.00
Mechanical Data: Type Area: 277 x 210mm, Bleed Size: 307 x 240mm, Trim Size: 297 x 230mm, Col Length: 277mm, Page Width: 210mm, Film: Digital
CONSUMER: CONSUMER ELECTRONICS: Games

---

4 CORNERS
47826U87-2

Editorial Address: 145 Faringdon Road, SWINDON, SN1 5DL **Tel:** 01793 610515
Email: ufm@ufm.org.uk
Web site: http://www.ufm.org.uk
Publisher: UFM Worldwide

Frequency: 3 issues yearly - Published in January, May and September
Cover Price: Free
Circulation: 9,500 (Publisher's Statement)
Usual Pagination: 12
Editor: Richard Myerscough
Summary of Content: Magazine containing information about church and missionary enterprises abroad.
Readership/Target Audience: Aimed at those interested in missions and supporters of the missionary society.
ADVERTISING: No Advertising taken
CONSUMER: RELIGIOUS

4X4
46324U77A-355

Formerly: Off Road & 4 Wheel Drive
Editorial Address: Cudham Tithe Barn, Berrys Hill, Berrys Green, Cudham, WESTERHAM, TN16 3AG
Tel: 01959 541444
Email: 4x4.ed@kelsey.co.uk
Advertising Address: As above. **Tel:** 01733 353353
Email: james.gunns@kelseypb.co.uk
Web site: http://www.4x4i.co.uk
Publisher: Kelsey Publishing Ltd
Frequency: Monthly - Published on the third Friday of each month
Cover Price: £3.90
Annual Sub.: £31.92
Circulation: 32,000 (Publisher's Statement)
Usual Pagination: 132
Editor: Hils Everitt; **Advertising Manager:** James Gunns
Summary of Content: Magazine containing articles on 4-wheel drive motors, road tests, foreign travel, technical aspects, accessories and competitions.
Readership/Target Audience: Read by 4-wheel drive owners and enthusiasts.
ADVERTISING: Rates on application
Copy instructions: Copy Date: 3 weeks prior to publication date
CONSUMER: MOTORING & CYCLING: Motoring

4X4 MART
46296U77A-511

Formerly: 4x4 & Off Road Mart
Editorial Address: Alliance House, 49 Sidney Street, CAMBRIDGE, CB2 3JF **Tel:** 01223 460490
Fax: 01223 315960
Email: editor4x4mart@4x4mart.co.uk
Advertising Address: As above.
Email: claire@4x4mart.co.uk
Publisher: CSL Publishing Ltd
Date Established: 1996
Frequency: Monthly
Cover Price: £2.00
Circulation: 14,000 (Publisher's Statement)
Usual Pagination: 132
Editor: Paul Guinness; **Advertising Manager:** Claire Broadmore
Summary of Content: Magazine covering all aspects of both new and secondhand 4x4 vehicles.
Readership/Target Audience: Aimed at owners and enthusiasts.
ADVERTISING RATES:
Full Page Colour £800.00
Agency Commission: 10%
Mechanical Data: Type Area: 270 x 190mm, Bleed Size: 303 x 216mm, Trim Size: 297 x 210mm, Col Length: 270mm, Page Width: 190mm, Film: Digital, No. of Columns (Display): 4
Copy instructions: Copy Date: 3 weeks prior to publication date
Average advertising content per issue: 50%
CONSUMER: MOTORING & CYCLING: Motoring

---

69 MAGAZINE MIDLANDS
622653U89C-20

Formerly: 69 Magazine
Editorial Address: 15 Leatherline House, 71 Narrow Lane, Aylestone, LEICESTER, LE2 8NA **Tel:** 0871 426 9696
Email: info@69-247.com
Advertising Address: As above.
Email: info@69-247.com
Web site: http://www.69-247.com
Publisher: 69 Magazine LTD
Date Established: 1999
Frequency: 5 issues yearly
Cover Price: Free
Circulation: 29,428 (ABC 01/01/2007 to 30/06/2007)
Usual Pagination: 132
Editor: Kevin Urquhart; **Managing Director:** Jon Fraser;
Advertising Manager: Jon Fraser
Summary of Content: Lifestyle magazine covering fashion, grooming and beauty, bars and clubs, events, films, arts, music, books, shopping, travel and technology.
Readership/Target Audience: Aimed at urban professionals between 20 and 40 across the Midlands with a high disposable income and an interest in fashion, entertainment and technology.

ADVERTISING RATES:
Full Page Colour £1389.00
Agency Commission: 10%
Mechanical Data: Print Process: Web-fed offset litho, Bleed Size: 307 x 220mm, Trim Size: 297 x 210mm, Type Area: 277 x 190mm, Col Length: 277mm, Page Width: 190mm
Copy instructions: Copy Date: 4 weeks prior to publication date
Average advertising content per issue: 30%
CONSUMER: HOLIDAYS & TRAVEL: Entertainment Guides

---

69 MAGAZINE NORTH
1743309U89C-1076

Editorial Address: 15 Leatherline House, 71 Narrow Lane, Aylestone, LEICESTER, LE2 8NA **Tel:** 0871 426 9696
Email: kevin@69-247.com
Advertising Address: As above. **Fax:** 0116 251 4891
Email: sales@69-247.com
Web site: http://www.69-247.com
Publisher: 69 Magazine LTD
Date Established: 2006
Frequency: 5 issues yearly
Cover Price: Free
Circulation: 30,000 (Publisher's Statement)
Usual Pagination: 100
Editor: Kevin Urquhart; **Managing Director:** Jon Fraser
Summary of Content: Lifestyle magazine covering fashion, grooming and beauty, bars, clubs, events, films, arts, music, books, shopping, travel and technology.
Readership/Target Audience: Aimed at urban professionals with a high disposable income and aged between 20 and 30 something across the North West including Manchester, Liverpool, Leeds and Sheffield.
ADVERTISING RATES:
Full Page Colour £1389.00
Agency Commission: 10%
Mechanical Data: Type Area: 277 x 190mm, Bleed Size: 303 x 216mm, Trim Size: 297 x 210mm, Col Length: 277mm, Page Width: 190mm, Film: Digital
Copy instructions: Copy Date: 4 weeks prior to publication date
Average advertising content per issue: 40%
CONSUMER: HOLIDAYS & TRAVEL: Entertainment Guides

---

911 & PORSCHE WORLD
46297U77E-18

Editorial Address: Nimax House, 20 Ullswater Crescent, Ullswater Business Park, COULSDON, CR5 2HR
Tel: 020 8655 6400
Email: porscheworld@chpltd.com
Advertising Address: As above. **Fax:** 020 8763 1001
Email: james.stainer@chpltd.com
Web site: http://www.chpltd.com
ISSN: 0959-8782
Publisher: CH Publications Ltd
Date Established: 1990
Frequency: Monthly
Cover Price: £4.35
Annual Sub.: £43.00
Usual Pagination: 140
Editor: Steve Bennett; **Features Editor:** Keith Seume;
Managing Director: Clive Househam; **Publisher:** Nigel Fryatt
Summary of Content: Independent magazine focusing on all models of Porsche past and present.
Readership/Target Audience: Aimed at Porsche owners and enthusiasts.
ADVERTISING RATES:
Full Page Mono £1150.00
Full Page Colour £1420.00
Agency Commission: 10%
Mechanical Data: Film: Digital, Trim Size: 297 x 210mm, Bleed Size: 306 x 216mm
Average advertising content per issue: 45%
CONSUMER: MOTORING & CYCLING: Club Cars

@HOME
1640099U74K-674

Formerly: Town & Country Properties
Editorial Address: Zetland House, Scrutton Street, LONDON, EC2A 4HJ **Tel:** 020 7749 3300
Fax: 020 7749 3325
Email: sarah.heavens@augustmedia.net
Advertising Address: As above.
Publisher: August Media
Frequency: Half-yearly - Published in May and September
Cover Price: £3.50
Free to qualifying individuals
Circulation: 50,000 (Publisher's Statement)
Editor: Sarah Heavens; **Managing Director:** Mark Lonergan; **Advertising Manager:** Mark Lonergan
Summary of Content: Magazine covering property news and a regional breakdown of property for sale as well as lifestyle features and news. Published on behalf of Strutt & Parker Estate Agents.
Readership/Target Audience: Aimed at affluent people with an interest in property.
ADVERTISING RATES:
Full Page Colour £2600.00
Agency Commission: 15%

Mechanical Data: Type Area: 260 x 195mm, Bleed Size: 297 x 226mm, Trim Size: 293 x 222mm, Col Length: 260mm, Page Width: 195mm; Film: Digital
Copy instructions: Copy Date: 4 weeks prior to publication date
Average advertising content per issue: 15%
CONSUMER: WOMEN'S INTEREST CONSUMER MAGAZINES: Home Purchase

A470 - WHAT'S ON IN LITERARY WALES
762288U84B-120

Formerly: A470
Editorial Address: 3ydd Llawr, Ty Mount Stuart, Sgwar Mount Stuart, CARDIFF, CF10 5FQ **Tel:** 029 2047 2266
Fax: 029 2049 2930
Email: post@academi.org
Web site: http://www.academi.org
Publisher: Yr Academi Gymreig
Date Established: 1998
Frequency: Quarterly
Free to qualifying individuals
Circulation: 5,000 (Publisher's Statement)
Usual Pagination: 24
Editor: Petra Bennett
Summary of Content: Magazine covering literary events in Wales and the borders, the magazine is bilingual.
Language(s): English; Welsh
Readership/Target Audience: Aimed at writers and readers.
ADVERTISING: No Advertising taken
CONSUMER: THE ARTS & LITERARY: Literary

THE A & B NEWS
1841173U87-2051

Editorial Address: PO Box 8455, NEWARK, NG23 5WX
Tel: 01636 525607
Email: johnclawson@xln.co.uk
Advertising Address: As above.
Email: johnclawson@xln.co.uk
Publisher: Bellcourt Limited
Frequency: Monthly
Cover Price: Free
Circulation: 13,000 (Publisher's Statement)
Editor: John Clawson; **Managing Director:** John Clawson;
Advertising Manager: John Clawson
Summary of Content: Newspaper covering religious topics, events, news and opinion.
Readership/Target Audience: Aimed at Roman Catholic churchgoers in the Diocese of Arundel and Brighton.
ADVERTISING: Rates on application
CONSUMER: RELIGIOUS

A PLACE IN THE SUN
1641011U74K-676

Editorial Address: 2nd Floor, Rear West Office, 16 Winchester Walk, LONDON, SE1 9AQ **Tel:** 020 3207 2920
Fax: 020 7357 9292
Email: richardw@apitsltd.com
Advertising Address: As above.
Email: keithg@apitsltd.com
Web site: http://www.aplaceinthesun.com
Publisher: APITS Ltd
Date Established: 2004
Frequency: 13 issues yearly
Cover Price: £3.50
Free to qualifying individuals
Circulation: 22,914 (Publisher's Statement)
Usual Pagination: 228
Editor: Richard Way; **Publisher:** Sarah Norman
Summary of Content: Magazine covering international property news and features, inspirational homes and case studies as well as property related advice.
Readership/Target Audience: Aimed at aspirational property buyers.
ADVERTISING RATES:
Full Page Colour £3995.00
Agency Commission: 10%
Mechanical Data: Bleed Size: 286 x 221mm, Trim Size: 278 x 213mm, Film: Digital
Average advertising content per issue: 40%
CONSUMER: WOMEN'S INTEREST CONSUMER MAGAZINES: Home Purchase

A U MAGAZINE
1692775U76D-802

Formerly: Alternative Ulster
Editorial Address: 56 Bradbury Place, BELFAST, BT7 1RU
Tel: 028 9032 4455
Email: jonny@iheartau.com
Advertising Address: As above.
Email: joanne@iheartau.com
Web site: http://www.alternativeulster.com
Publisher: Alternative Ulster
Date Established: 2002
Frequency: 10 issues yearly
Cover Price: £3.30
Circulation: 20,000 (Publisher's Statement)

Usual Pagination: 84
Editor: Francis Jones
Summary of Content: Magazine covering local and international bands as well as lifestyle, culture, movies and artistic Ulster.
Readership/Target Audience: Aimed at 18 to 35 year olds in Northern Ireland.
ADVERTISING RATES:
Full Page Colour £795.00
Mechanical Data: Bleed Size: 307 x 220mm, Trim Size: 297 x 210mm, Film: Digital
CONSUMER: MUSIC & PERFORMING ARTS: Music

THE AA MEMBERS CLUB MAGAZINE
1695584U77A-596

Formerly: Roadside
Editorial Address: Fanum House, Basing View, BASINGSTOKE, RG21 4EA **Tel:** 01256 492926
Email: aamembersclub@theaa.co.uk
Advertising Address: As above. **Tel:** 0117 925 1696
Fax: 0117 925 1808
Email: aaeditor@specialistuk.com
Publisher: The AA
Date Established: 2005
Frequency: 3 issues yearly
Cover Price: Free
Circulation: 3,800,000 (Publisher's Statement)
Usual Pagination: 32
Editor: Jo Grimer; **Advertising Manager:** Emily Day
Summary of Content: Magazine informing readers of members benefits as well as motoring advice.
Readership/Target Audience: Aimed at members of the AA.
ADVERTISING: Rates on application
CONSUMER: MOTORING & CYCLING: Motoring

ABC MAGAZINE BERKSHIRE
1772525U74D-642

Editorial Address: PO Box 2780, BRIGHTON, BN1 5QR
Tel: 01273 552842 **Fax:** 01273 542257
Email: berkshire@abcmag.co.uk
Advertising Address: As above. **Tel:** 01344 483783
Fax: 0870 458 1773
Email: berkshire@abcmag.co.uk
Web site: http://www.abcmag.co.uk
Publisher: ABC Magazine Berkshire
Date Established: 2006
Frequency: 3 issues yearly - Published in March, July and November
Cover Price: Free
Circulation: 20,000 (Publisher's Statement)
Editor: Rachel Boyle; **Advertising Manager:** Rachel Boyle
Summary of Content: Magazine featuring local information, health, lifestyle, out and about, early education, employment, training and homes and gardens.
Readership/Target Audience: Aimed at parents-to-be and parents of babies and children up to 11 years old living in Berkshire.
ADVERTISING: Rates on application
CONSUMER: WOMEN'S INTEREST CONSUMER MAGAZINES: Child Care

ABC MAGAZINE ESSEX
1772527U74D-643

Editorial Address: PO Box 9308, DUNMOW, CM6 2WP
Tel: 01371 832116 **Fax:** 01371 832116
Email: essex@abcmag.co.uk
Advertising Address: As above.
Email: essex@abcmag.co.uk
Web site: http://www.abcmag.co.uk
Publisher: Parent Publishing Ltd
Date Established: 2006
Frequency: 3 issues yearly - Published in March, July and November
Cover Price: Free
Circulation: 22,000 (Publisher's Statement)
Usual Pagination: 64
Editor: Simon Payne; **Advertising Manager:** Simon Payne
Summary of Content: Magazine covering local information, services, facilities, activities, advice and support for mums to be and young families.
Readership/Target Audience: Aimed at parents of pre-school and primary school children in Essex.
ADVERTISING RATES:
Full Page Mono £670.00
Full Page Colour £790.00
Agency Commission: 10%
Mechanical Data: Type Area: 278 x 190mm, Col Length: 278mm, Page Width: 190mm; Film: Digital, Trim Size: 297 x 210mm
Copy instructions: Copy Date: 6 weeks prior to publication date
Average advertising content per issue: 35%
CONSUMER: WOMEN'S INTEREST CONSUMER MAGAZINES: Child Care

ABC MAGAZINE HAMPSHIRE
1813966U74D-658

Editorial Address: 38 Lynford Avenue, WINCHESTER, SO22 6BN **Tel:** 01962 620331 **Fax:** 01962 620331
Email: hampshire@abcmag.co.uk
Advertising Address: As above.
Email: hampshire@abcmag.co.uk
Web site: http://www.abcmag.co.uk
Publisher: Hampshire Family Publications Ltd
Date Established: 2007
Frequency: 3 issues yearly - Published in March, July and November
Cover Price: Free
Circulation: 17,000 (Print Run)
Usual Pagination: 48
Editor: Rachel Boyle; **Advertising Manager:** Rachel Boyle
Summary of Content: Magazine covering child related issues including health, childcare, education, pregnancy, back to work information, days out and entertainment.
Readership/Target Audience: Aimed at pregnant women and parents of children up to the age of 11 years old.
ADVERTISING RATES:
Full Page Mono £670.00
Full Page Colour £790.00
Mechanical Data: Type Area: 278 x 190mm, Col Length: 278mm, Page Width: 190mm; Film: Digital
CONSUMER: WOMEN'S INTEREST CONSUMER MAGAZINES: Child Care

ABC MAGAZINE HERTFORDSHIRE
1813190U74D-657

Editorial Address: PO Box 255, LETCHWORTH, SG6 9AZ
Tel: 01462 679992
Email: hertfordshire@abcmag.co.uk
Advertising Address: As above. **Fax:** 01462 675933
Email: hertfordshire@abcmag.co.uk
Web site: http://www.abcmag.co.uk
Publisher: Kids Life Ltd
Date Established: 2007
Frequency: 3 issues yearly - Published in March, November and July
Cover Price: Free
Circulation: 20,000 (Publisher's Statement)
Usual Pagination: 48
Editor: Roz Ringe; **Advertising Manager:** Rebecca Ward
Summary of Content: Magazine covering all aspects of life with children including education, activities, diary of events, information, health updates, ideas and competitions.
Readership/Target Audience: Aimed at parents of children aged 0 to 11 years old in Hertfordshire.
ADVERTISING RATES:
Full Page Mono £670.00
Full Page Colour £790.00
Agency Commission: 10%
Mechanical Data: Type Area: 278 x 190mm, Col Length: 278mm, Page Width: 190mm; Film: Digital
Copy instructions: Copy Date: 6 weeks prior to publication date
Average advertising content per issue: 40%
CONSUMER: WOMEN'S INTEREST CONSUMER MAGAZINES: Child Care

ABC MAGAZINE KENT
1702949U74D-617

Editorial Address: PO Box 2780, BRIGHTON, BN1 5QR
Tel: 01273 552842 **Fax:** 01273 542257
Email: kent@abcmag.co.uk
Advertising Address: As above.
Email: kent@abcmag.co.uk
Web site: http://www.abcmag.co.uk
Publisher: Oast Publishing Ltd
Date Established: 2006
Frequency: 3 issues yearly - Published in March, July and November
Cover Price: Free
Circulation: 17,000 (Publisher's Statement)
Usual Pagination: 48
Editor: Rachel Boyle; **Advertising Manager:** Rachel Boyle
Summary of Content: Magazine covering local information, services, facilities, activities, advice and support which is relevant to all local parents.
Readership/Target Audience: Aimed at parents-to-be and parents of babies and children up to 11 years old, living in Kent.
ADVERTISING RATES:
Full Page Mono £670.00
Full Page Colour £790.00
Agency Commission: 10%
Mechanical Data: Bleed Size: 303 x 216mm, Trim Size: 297 x 210mm, Film: Digital, Type Area: 278 x 190mm, Col Length: 278mm, Page Width: 190mm
Copy instructions: Copy Date: 6 weeks prior to publication date
Average advertising content per issue: 40%
CONSUMER: WOMEN'S INTEREST CONSUMER MAGAZINES: Child Care

ABC MAGAZINE SURREY
1643632U74D-563

Editorial Address: PO Box 941A, SURBITON, KT1 9RQ
Tel: 020 8661 5353 **Fax:** 020 3163 0287
Email: surrey@abcmag.co.uk
Advertising Address: As above. **Fax:** 020 8642 9688
Email: surrey@abcmag.co.uk
Web site: http://www.abcmag.co.uk
Publisher: Langley & Allen Ltd
Date Established: 2003
Frequency: 3 issues yearly - Published in March, July and November
Free to qualifying individuals
Annual Sub.: £10.00
Circulation: 105,000 (Publisher's Statement)
Usual Pagination: 128
Editor: Louise de Kock; **Advertising Manager:** Louise de Kock
Summary of Content: Magazine covering all aspects of life with children. Includes education, activities, diary of events, information, health updates, ideas and competitions, homes and interiors, fashion, holidays and travel, return to work and childcare.
Readership/Target Audience: Aimed at pregnant mums and parents of children under 11 living in Surrey.
ADVERTISING RATES:
Full Page Mono £670.00
Full Page Colour £790.00
Agency Commission: 10%
Mechanical Data: Type Area: 278 x 190mm, Col Length: 278mm, Page Width: 190mm, Film: Digital, Bleed Size: 281 x 193mm
Copy instructions: Copy Date: 6 weeks prior to publication date
Average advertising content per issue: 40%
CONSUMER: WOMEN'S INTEREST CONSUMER MAGAZINES: Child Care

ABC MAGAZINE SUSSEX
45310U74D-10

Formerly: ABC Magazine
Editorial Address: PO Box 2780, BRIGHTON, BN1 5QR
Tel: 01273 542257 **Fax:** 01273 542257
Email: sussex@abcmag.co.uk
Advertising Address: As above.
Email: sussex@abcmag.co.uk
Web site: http://www.abcmag.co.uk
Publisher: Alphabet Publishing Ltd
Date Established: 1996
Frequency: 3 issues yearly - Published in March, July and November
Free to qualifying individuals
Annual Sub.: £12.00
Circulation: 35,000 (Publisher's Statement)
Usual Pagination: 240
Editor: Rachel Boyle; **Advertising Manager:** Rachel Boyle
Summary of Content: Magazine covering all aspects of life with children under 11 years old. Includes education, activities, diary of events, information, health updates, ideas and competitions.
Readership/Target Audience: Aimed at parents of children under 11 years old living in Sussex.
ADVERTISING RATES:
Full Page Mono £670.00
Full Page Colour £790.00
Agency Commission: 10%
Mechanical Data: Page Width: 190mm, Type Area: 278 x 190mm, Col Length: 278mm, Film: Digital
Copy instructions: Copy Date: 6 weeks prior to publication date
Average advertising content per issue: 40%
CONSUMER: WOMEN'S INTEREST CONSUMER MAGAZINES: Child Care

ABILITY
48620U94F-1004

Editorial Address: Pellingbrook House, Lewes Road, Scaynes Hill, HAYWARDS HEATH, RH17 7NG
Tel: 01444 831226
Email: john.lamb@abilitymagazine.org.uk
Advertising Address: As above.
Email: advertise@abilitymagazine.org.uk
Web site: http://www.abilitymagazine.org.uk
ISSN: 1352-7665
Publisher: John Lamb Media Ltd
Date Established: 1991
Frequency: Quarterly
Free to qualifying individuals
Annual Sub.: £150.00
Circulation: 5,000 (Publisher's Statement)
Usual Pagination: 40
Editor: John Lamb; **Advertising Manager:** John Lamb
Summary of Content: Magazine providing insight into the products, techniques and skills required to deliver systems for users who find it difficult to use IT.
Readership/Target Audience: Aimed at those who make decisions about IT for disabled people.
ADVERTISING RATES:
Full Page Mono £850.00
Full Page Colour £850.00
Agency Commission: 10%

Mechanical Data: Trim Size: 297 x 210mm, Bleed Size: 306 x 215mm, Film: Digital
Copy instructions: Copy Date: 3 weeks prior to publication date
Average advertising content per issue: 30%
CONSUMER: OTHER CLASSIFICATIONS: Disability

ABILITY NEEDS MAGAZINE
1698878U94F-1007

Editorial Address: 62 Castlepark Drive, Fairlie, LARGS, KA29 0DG **Tel:** 01475 560177 **Fax:** 01475 568117
Email: info@abilityneeds.com
Advertising Address: As above. **Tel:** 01475 560134
Email: info@abilityneeds.com
Web site: http://www.abilityneeds.com
ISSN: 1477-1225
Publisher: KCM Media
Date Established: 2002
Frequency: Quarterly
Cover Price: £2.00
Annual Sub.: £10.00
Circulation: 148,000 (Publisher's Statement)
Editor: Karen McNaught; **Advertising Manager:** Colin McNaught
Summary of Content: Magazine covering products and services for people with disabilities.
Readership/Target Audience: Aimed at those with disabilities and their carers.
ADVERTISING RATES:
Full Page Colour £1995.00
Agency Commission: 10%
Mechanical Data: Type Area: 270 x 188mm, Bleed Size: 303 x 213mm, Trim Size: 297 x 210mm, Col Length: 270mm, Page Width: 188mm, Film: Digital
Copy instructions: Copy Date: 3 weeks prior to publication date
Average advertising content per issue: 50%
CONSUMER: OTHER CLASSIFICATIONS: Disability

ABILITY NORTHERN IRELAND
1779665U94F-1016

Editorial Address: 7B Lower Ballinderry Road, Upper Ballinderry, LISBURN, BT28 2JB **Tel:** 028 9265 2773
Email: beryl@bebmedia.com
Publisher: BeB Media Ltd
Frequency: Quarterly
Cover Price: £2.20
Circulation: 7,000 (Publisher's Statement)
Usual Pagination: 56
Editor: Laura Dunlop; **Publisher:** Beryl Bickerstaff
Summary of Content: Magazine covering lifestyle features and information on equipment and accessories .
Readership/Target Audience: Aimed at people with disabilities.
CONSUMER: OTHER CLASSIFICATIONS: Disability

ABLE
48628U94F-330

Formerly: Disability View
Editorial Address: 15-39 Durham Street, Kinning Park, GLASGOW, G41 1BS **Tel:** 0141 419 0044
Fax: 0141 419 0077
Email: edit@cravenpublishing.co.uk
Advertising Address: As above.
Email: bobby@cravenpublishing.co.uk
Web site: http://www.ablemagazine.co.uk
ISSN: 1358-5401
Publisher: Craven Publishing Ltd
Date Established: 1994
Frequency: 6 issues yearly
Cover Price: £2.00
Annual Sub.: £12.00
Circulation: 31,055 (ABC 01/01/2008 to 31/12/2008)
Usual Pagination: 100
Editor: Paul Cockburn; **Managing Director:** Steve Craven; **Advertising Manager:** Bobby McNicol
Summary of Content: Magazine covering issues, events and personalities that affect the lives of people with disabilities. Also features art, politics, health, leisure and travel.
Readership/Target Audience: Aimed at disabled people of all ages, their families, carers and enablers and professionals within this field.
ADVERTISING RATES:
Full Page Colour £3495.00
Agency Commission: 10%
Mechanical Data: Bleed Size: 303 x 216mm, Trim Size: 297 x 210mm, Film: Digital
Average advertising content per issue: 50%
CONSUMER: OTHER CLASSIFICATIONS: Disability

ABOUT THE HOUSE
46279U76F-40

Formerly: Opera House Magazine
Editorial Address: 14th Floor, Tower House, Fairfax Street, BRISTOL, BS1 3BN **Tel:** 0117 927 9009

Advertising Address: 9th Floor, Tower House, Fairfax Street, BRISTOL, BS1 3BN **Tel:** 0117 927 9009
Fax: 0117 933 8088
Email: duncanreid@bbcmagazinesbristol.com
Web site: http://www.royaloperahouse.org
Publisher: BBC Magazines Bristol
Date Established: 2003
Frequency: 5 issues yearly
Cover Price: £2.50
Circulation: 31,000 (Publisher's Statement)
Usual Pagination: 64
Editor: Amanda Holloway
Summary of Content: Magazine containing details of Royal Opera House performances by The Royal Ballet and The Royal Opera.
Readership/Target Audience: Read by Trust members and Friends of the Royal Opera House .
ADVERTISING RATES:
Full Page Colour £3750.00
Agency Commission: 10%
Mechanical Data: Type Area: 256 x 180mm, Col Length: 256mm, Page Width: 180mm, Film: Digital, Bleed Size: 292 x 226mm, Trim Size: 286 x 220mm
Average advertising content per issue: 20%
CONSUMER: MUSIC & PERFORMING ARTS: Opera

ABSOLUTE BRIGHTON
1665507U80C-5212

Editorial Address: 42 Wilbury Villas, HOVE, BN3 6GD
Tel: 0845 389 0662 **Fax:** 0845 389 0663
Email: verity@absolutemagazine.co.uk
Advertising Address: As above.
Email: sales@absolutebrighton.com
Web site: http://www.absolutebrighton.co.uk
Publisher: Absolute Media Ltd
Date Established: 2005
Frequency: Monthly
Cover Price: Free
Circulation: 15,000 (Publisher's Statement)
Usual Pagination: 120
Editor: Verity Smart; **Advertising Manager:** Kate Cowling
Summary of Content: Lifestyle magazine covering fashion, beauty, property, travel, society, celebrity interviews and motoring.
Readership/Target Audience: Aimed at aspirational residents and visitors to Brighton.
ADVERTISING RATES:
Full Page Mono £1200.00
Full Page Colour £1200.00
Agency Commission: 10%
Mechanical Data: Type Area: 267 x 188mm, Col Length: 267mm, Page Width: 188mm, No. of Columns (Display): 2, Col Widths (Display): 91.5mm, Bleed Size: 303 x 216mm, Trim Size: 297 x 210mm, Film: Digital
Copy instructions: Copy Date: 12th of the month prior to publication date
Average advertising content per issue: 40%
CONSUMER: RURAL & REGIONAL INTEREST: Regional Interest English Counties

ABSOLUTE HORSE
47118U81D-10

Editorial Address: Home Barn, Grove Hill, Belstead, IPSWICH, IP8 3LS **Tel:** 01473 731220 **Fax:** 01473 731227
Email: info.ahmagazine@btconnect.com
Advertising Address: As above.
Email: info.ahmagazine@btconnect.com
Web site: http://www.ahmagazine.com
Publisher: PCD Media (East Anglia) Ltd
Frequency: Monthly - Published on the 1st of the cover month
Cover Price: £2.50
Annual Sub.: £24.99
Circulation: 8,000 (Publisher's Statement)
Usual Pagination: 96
Editor: Emma Tilley; **Managing Director:** Peter Dodd; **Advertising Manager:** Emma Tilley; **Publisher:** Peter Dodd
Summary of Content: Magazine covering equestrian disciplines with informative articles, local news, results and full show dates listings.
Readership/Target Audience: Aimed at horse owners and riders aged between 6 and 60 years old.
ADVERTISING RATES:
Full Page Colour £645.00
SCC £6.00
Agency Commission: 10%
Mechanical Data: Type Area: 277 x 190.5mm, Bleed Size: 306 x 221mm, Trim Size: 300 x 215mm, Col Length: 277mm, Film: Digital, Page Width: 190.5mm
Copy instructions: Copy Date: 1st of the month prior to publication date
Average advertising content per issue: 35%
CONSUMER: ANIMALS & PETS: Horses & Ponies

ABSOLUTE LONDON
1775856U80B-422

Editorial Address: 42 Wilbury Villas, HOVE, BN3 6GD
Tel: 0845 389 0662 **Fax:** 0845 389 0663
Email: verity@absolutemagazine.co.uk
Advertising Address: As above.

Email: kate@absolutemagazine.co.uk
Web site: http://www.absolutemagazine.co.uk
Publisher: Absolute Media Ltd
Date Established: 2006
Frequency: Monthly
Cover Price: Free
Circulation: 45,000 (Publisher's Statement)
Editor: Verity Smart; **Advertising Manager:** Kate Cowling
Summary of Content: Magazine covering fashion, beauty, property, travel, society, celebrity interviews and motoring.
Readership/Target Audience: Aimed at aspirational residents and visitors to London.
ADVERTISING RATES:
Full Page Colour £1440.00
Agency Commission: 10%
Mechanical Data: Bleed Size: 303 x 216mm, Trim Size: 297 x 210mm, Film: Digital
Copy instructions: Copy Date: 14th of the month prior to publication date
Average advertising content per issue: 50%
CONSUMER: RURAL & REGIONAL INTEREST: Regional Interest Greater London

ABSOLUTELEEDS
601191U80C-3593
Editorial Address: PO Box 168, Wellington Street, LEEDS, LS1 1RF **Tel:** 0113 243 2701 **Fax:** 0113 238 8521
Email: jill.armstrong@ypn.co.uk
Advertising Address: As above. **Tel:** 0113 238 8082
Fax: 0113 383 1438
Email: annah.thompson@ypn.co.uk
Web site: http://www.absoluteleeds.co.uk
Publisher: Johnston Press plc
Date Established: 1999
Frequency: Monthly
Cover Price: £1.50
Circulation: 15,000 (Publisher's Statement)
Usual Pagination: 80
Editor: Jill Armstrong; **Advertising Manager:** Annah Thompson
Summary of Content: Lifestyle magazine for Leeds featuring celebrity interviews, cafe, bar and club listings, cooking and interiors.
Readership/Target Audience: Aimed at 20 to 35 year old professionals who live and work in Leeds.
ADVERTISING RATES:
Full Page Colour £824.00
Agency Commission: 10%
Mechanical Data: Type Area: 264 x 186mm, Bleed Size: +3mm, Trim Size: 297 x 210mm, Film: Digital, Col Length: 264mm, Page Width: 186mm
Copy instructions: Copy Date: 3rd week of the month prior to publication date
Average advertising content per issue: 40%
CONSUMER: RURAL & REGIONAL INTEREST: Regional Interest English Counties

ACCENT
634524U80C-5055
Editorial Address: 5-11 Causey Street, Gosforth, NEWCASTLE UPON TYNE, NE3 4DJ **Tel:** 0191 284 9994
Fax: 0191 284 9995
Email: kevin.wright@accentmagazines.co.uk
Advertising Address: 93-105 St. James Boulevard, NEWCASTLE UPON TYNE, NE1 4BW **Tel:** 0191 255 8888
Email: mike.grahamslaw@accentmagazines.co.uk
Web site: http://www.accent-magazines.co.uk
ISSN: 1468-3016
Publisher: Accent Magazines Ltd
Date Established: 1999
Frequency: 11 issues yearly
Cover Price: £1.95
Free to qualifying individuals
Circulation: 15,000 (Publisher's Statement)
Usual Pagination: 148
Editor: Kevin Wright; **Advertising Manager:** Michael Grahamslaw; **Group Editor:** Richard Holmes; **Publisher:** Mick O'Hare
Summary of Content: Magazine featuring fashion, food and drink, business news, motoring, social events and The Arts.
Readership/Target Audience: Aimed at those living in the North East of England.
ADVERTISING RATES:
Full Page Colour £950.00
Agency Commission: 10%
Mechanical Data: Type Area: 267 x 203mm, Bleed Size: 303 x 233mm, Col Length: 267mm, Page Width: 203mm, Film: Digital, Trim Size: 297 x 230mm
Average advertising content per issue: 60%
CONSUMER: RURAL & REGIONAL INTEREST: Regional Interest English Counties

ACCEO MATTERS
1786325U91B-312
Editorial Address: 6 Harford Court, John Tate Road, HERTFORD, SG13 7NW **Tel:** 0871 622 6690
Fax: 0871 310 0346
Email: ameditor@acceo.org.uk
Advertising Address: As above. **Tel:** 0870 300 0690
Fax: 0870 300 0691

Email: acceo@leadmedia.co.uk
Web site: http://www.acceo.co.uk
Publisher: Lead Media Ltd
Date Established: 2006
Frequency: Quarterly
Cover Price: £2.50
Circulation: 3,355 (Publisher's Statement)
Usual Pagination: 20
Editor: Elaine Nicholls; **Advertising Manager:** Michael Linegar; **Publisher:** Jonathan Hankin
Summary of Content: Magazine covering current events, news and caravan and product reviews.
Readership/Target Audience: Aimed at members of caravan clubs.
ADVERTISING RATES:
Full Page Colour £995.00
Mechanical Data: Type Area: 271 x 186mm, Bleed Size: 301 x 214mm, Trim Size: 297 x 210mm, Col Length: 271mm, Page Width: 186mm, Film: Digital
CONSUMER: RECREATION & LEISURE: Camping & Caravanning

ACE TENNIS MAGAZINE
45883U75H-10
Formerly: ACE Tennis
Editorial Address: Sea Containers House, 20 Upper Ground, LONDON, SE1 9PD **Tel:** 020 7775 5777
Email: alexandra.willis@sevensquared.co.uk
Advertising Address: As above. **Tel:** 020 8947 0100
Email: chris.brown@acemag.co.uk
ISSN: 1363-4674
Publisher: Seven Squared
Date Established: 1996
Frequency: 6 issues yearly
Cover Price: £3.50
Free to qualifying individuals
Annual Sub.: £35.00
Circulation: 47,145 (ABC 01/07/2007 to 31/12/2007)
Usual Pagination: 100
Editor: Scott Manson; **Advertising Manager:** Chris Brown
Summary of Content: Magazine containing tennis news, features, tournaments, interviews and coaching.
Readership/Target Audience: Aimed at those with an interest in tennis.
ADVERTISING RATES:
Full Page Colour £3500.00
Agency Commission: 10%
Mechanical Data: Col Length: 265mm, Page Width: 204mm, Type Area: 265 x 204mm, Trim Size: 285 x 224mm, Film: Digital
Copy instructions: Copy Date: 2 weeks prior to publication date
CONSUMER: SPORT: Racquet Sports

ACT NOW
47673U87-3
Editorial Address: 94A London Road, ST. ALBANS, AL1 1NX **Tel:** 01727 840298 **Fax:** 01727 848966
Email: act@christians-in-education.org.uk
Advertising Address: As above.
Email: act@christians-in-education.org.uk
Web site: http://www.christians-in-education.org.uk
ISSN: 0265-0549
Publisher: Association of Christian Teachers
Frequency: 3 issues yearly - Published in January, May and September
Cover Price: £3.50
Circulation: 3,000 (Publisher's Statement)
Editor: Robert Hall; **Advertising Manager:** Jan Hodgkinson
Summary of Content: Magazine containing articles of general interest to Christian teachers.
Readership/Target Audience: Aimed at Christian teachers in nursery, primary, secondary, further and higher education.
ADVERTISING RATES:
Full Page Mono £495.00
Full Page Colour £510.00
Agency Commission: 10%
Mechanical Data: Type Area: 254 x 176mm, Trim Size: 297 x 210mm, Bleed Size: 303 x 213mm, Film: Digital, Col Length: 254mm, Page Width: 176mm
Copy instructions: Copy Date: 8 weeks prior to publication date
CONSUMER: RELIGIOUS

ACTIVE
749410U80A-20
Formerly: Volunteer Link
Editorial Address: PO Box 220, AMERSHAM, HP6 5XD **Tel:** 01494 794961
Email: trevor.lawson@redfoxmedia.com
Web site: http://www.nationaltrust.org.uk/volunteering
Publisher: The National Trust
Date Established: 2002
Frequency: Quarterly
Cover Price: Free
Circulation: 49,000 (Publisher's Statement)
Usual Pagination: 16
Editor: Trevor Lawson

Summary of Content: Magazine covering wildlife, environment, historic buildings, history, art, culture and gardening.
Readership/Target Audience: Aimed at volunteers of the National Trust.
ADVERTISING: No Advertising taken
CONSUMER: RURAL & REGIONAL INTEREST: Rural Interest

ACTIVE
1655557U89E-225
Formerly: Go Active
Editorial Address: 1 Victoria Villas, RICHMOND, TW9 2GW
Tel: 020 8332 8440 **Fax:** 020 8332 9307
Email: graeme@circlepublishing.net
Advertising Address: As above.
Email: graeme.spratley@circlepublishing.net
Web site: http://www.goactivemag.co.uk
Publisher: Circle Publishing
Date Established: 2004
Frequency: 10 issues yearly
Cover Price: Free
Circulation: 40,000 (Publisher's Statement)
Usual Pagination: 68
Editor: Graeme Gourlay
Summary of Content: Magazine containing active lifestyle features including activities in the UK, active holidays abroad and adventure travel as well as news, gear reviews and destination recommendations. Sports featured are dinghy sailing, windsurfing, kite surfing, hiking, adventure racing, mountain biking and new sport focus.
Readership/Target Audience: Aimed at 25 to 52 year olds who have or would like to have an active lifestyle.
ADVERTISING RATES:
Full Page Colour £2200.00
Agency Commission: 10%
Mechanical Data: Type Area: 280 x 210mm, Bleed Size: 310 x 240mm, Trim Size: 300 x 230mm, Col Length: 280mm, Page Width: 210mm, Film: Digital
Copy instructions: Copy Date: 10 days prior to publication date
Average advertising content per issue: 30%
CONSUMER: HOLIDAYS & TRAVEL: Holidays

ACTSA NEWS
47291U82-1_20
Editorial Address: 231 Vauxhall Bridge Road, LONDON, SW1 1EH **Tel:** 020 3263 2001 **Fax:** 020 7931 9398
Email: kathryn.llewellyn@actsa.org
Web site: http://www.actsa.org
ISSN: 0003-5580
Publisher: Action for South Africa (ACTSA)
Frequency: Quarterly
Cover Price: £1.00
Free to qualifying individuals
Circulation: 4,000 (Publisher's Statement)
Usual Pagination: 12
Editor: Kathryn Llewellyn
Summary of Content: Magazine containing news and analysis from Southern Africa. News of ACTSA campaigns and events.
Readership/Target Audience: Aimed at members and those interested in Southern African issues.
ADVERTISING: No Advertising taken
CONSUMER: CURRENT AFFAIRS & POLITICS

ACUMEN
1820682U84B-369
Editorial Address: 6 The Mount, Higher Furzeham Road, BRIXHAM, TQ5 8QY **Tel:** 01803 851098
Email: pwoxley@aol.com
Advertising Address: As above.
Email: pwoxley@aol.com
Web site: http://www.acumen-poetry.co.uk
Publisher: Acumen Publications
Frequency: 3 issues yearly - Published in January, May and September
Cover Price: £4.50
Annual Sub.: £12.50
Circulation: 800 (Publisher's Statement)
Usual Pagination: 120
Editor: Patricia Oxley; **Advertising Manager:** Patricia Oxley
Summary of Content: Magazine covering all aspects of poetry with poetry related articles, interviews and reviews.
Readership/Target Audience: Aimed at poetry lovers and those with an interest in the arts.
ADVERTISING: Rates on application
CONSUMER: THE ARTS & LITERARY: Literary

AD FAMILIARES
1865308U94X-305
Editorial Address: 51 Achilles Road, LONDON, NW6 1DZ
Tel: 020 7431 5088
Email: classics@friends-classics.demon.co.uk
Web site: http://www.friends-classics.demon.co.uk
Publisher: Friends of Classics
Frequency: Half-yearly
Circulation: 5,000 (Publisher's Statement)

Editor: Peter Jones.
Summary of Content: Magazine covering information on ancient Greeks and Romans.
Readership/Target Audience: Aimed at people with an interest in ancient Greeks and Romans.
ADVERTISING: No Advertising taken
CONSUMER: OTHER CLASSIFICATIONS: Miscellaneous

AD GUIDE
1666813U94X-292

Editorial Address: Shine, Harehills Road, LEEDS, LS8 5HS
Tel: 0870 360 8606 **Fax:** 0870 360 8605
Email: editor@asianexpress.co.uk
Advertising Address: As above.
Email: patrick@asianexpress.co.uk
Publisher: Open Media Publications Ltd
Frequency: Monthly
Cover Price: Free
Circulation: 30,000 (Publisher's Statement)
Usual Pagination: 56
Editor: Andleeb Hanif
Summary of Content: A-Z listing of advertisements.
Readership/Target Audience: Aimed at the general public.
ADVERTISING RATES:
Full Page Colour £1135.00
Mechanical Data: Type Area: 338 x 264mm, Col Length: 338mm, Page Width: 264mm, Film: Digital
Copy instructions: Copy Date: 3 days prior to publication date
Average advertising content per issue: 100%
CONSUMER: OTHER CLASSIFICATIONS: Miscellaneous

ADD LIB
1657295U74Q-1198

Editorial Address: 35-37 William Road, LONDON, NW1 3ER
Tel: 020 7255 4224
Email: emma@addlib.co.uk
Advertising Address: As above.
Email: emma@addlib.co.uk
Web site: http://www.addlib.co.uk
Publisher: Addison Lee Plc
Date Established: 2003
Frequency: Quarterly
Cover Price: Free
Circulation: 36,000 (Publisher's Statement)
Usual Pagination: 38
Editor: Emma Keyne; **Advertising Manager:** Emma Keyne
Summary of Content: Lifestyle magazine covering London bars, restaurants, clubs, art, architecture, fashion, health and beauty.
Readership/Target Audience: Aimed at customers of Addison Lee.
ADVERTISING RATES:
Full Page Mono £2250.00
Full Page Colour £2250.00
Mechanical Data: Type Area: 220 x 150mm, Bleed Size: 246 x 176mm, Trim Size: 240 x 170mm, Col Length: 220mm, Page Width: 150mm
CONSUMER: WOMEN'S INTEREST CONSUMER MAGAZINES: Lifestyle

THE ADELPHI PAPERS (IISS)
29516U82-2_4

Editorial Address: 4 Park Square, Milton Park, ABINGDON, OX14 4RN **Tel:** 020 7017 6000 **Fax:** 020 7017 6336
Web site: http://www.tandf.co.uk/journals
Publisher: Routledge, Taylor & Francis
Date Established: 1964
Frequency: 8 issues yearly
Annual Sub.: £359.00
Circulation: 4,200 (Publisher's Statement)
Usual Pagination: 144
Editor: Richard Delahunty; **Publisher:** Richard Delahunty
Summary of Content: Publication featuring current and future problems of international relations and security.
Readership/Target Audience: Aimed at embassies, universities, students and analysts.
ADVERTISING: No Advertising taken
CONSUMER: CURRENT AFFAIRS & POLITICS

ADULT LEARNING YEARBOOK
47906U88B-120

Formerly: Year Book of Adult Continuing Education
Editorial Address: 21 De Montfort Street, LEICESTER, LE1 7GE **Tel:** 0116 204 4200 **Fax:** 0116 285 4514
Email: publications@niace.org.uk
Advertising Address: As above. **Fax:** 0116 204 4262
Email: enquiries@niace.org.uk
Web site: http://www.niace.org.uk
ISSN: 0265-1726
Publisher: National Institute of Adult Continuing Education
Frequency: Annual - Published in January
Cover Price: £21.95
Usual Pagination: 330
Editor: Virman Man; **Advertising Manager:** Alec Mcaulay; **Publisher:** Virman Man
Summary of Content: Annually up-dated directory covering adult, community and continuing education.

Readership/Target Audience: Aimed at contacts in the field of adult education.
ADVERTISING RATES:
Full Page Mono £220.00
Mechanical Data: Trim Size: 210 x 140mm, Film: Digital
CONSUMER: EDUCATION: Adult Education

ADULT SPORT
749649U86A-20

Editorial Address: 19 Great Ancoats Street, MANCHESTER, M60 4BT **Tel:** 0161 236 4466 **Fax:** 0161 236 4535
Email: mark.harris@sportnewspapers.co.uk
Advertising Address: As above. **Tel:** 0870 211 0101
Fax: 0161 237 4612
Email: advertising@sportnewspapers.co.uk
Web site: http://www.adultsport.co.uk
Publisher: More Sport Ltd
Date Established: 2001
Frequency: 26 issues yearly
Cover Price: £1.20
Circulation: 40,000 (Publisher's Statement)
Usual Pagination: 68
Editor: Mark Harris; **Advertising Manager:** Arun Parmar
Summary of Content: Magazine publishing uncensored photographs of naked show business stars as well as show-biz news and views and in-depth features.
Readership/Target Audience: Aimed at men and women between 18 and 40 years old.
ADVERTISING RATES:
Full Page Colour £800.00
Agency Commission: 10%
Mechanical Data: Film: Digital, Col Widths (Display): 33mm, No. of Columns (Display): 6
Copy instructions: Copy Date: 1 week prior to publication date
Average advertising content per issue: 40%
CONSUMER: ADULT & GAY MAGAZINES: Adult Magazines

ADVANCED CARP FISHING
48517U92-5

Editorial Address: 2 Stephenson Close, Drayton Fields Industrial Estate, DAVENTRY, NN11 8RF **Tel:** 01327 311999
Fax: 01327 311190
Email: marccoulson@dhpub.co.uk
Advertising Address: As above.
Email: john.watson@dhpub.co.uk
Web site: http://www.total-fishing.com
ISSN: 1360-3086
Publisher: David Hall Publishing Ltd
Date Established: 1995
Frequency: Monthly
Cover Price: £3.50
Annual Sub.: £35.80
Circulation: 16,912 (Publisher's Statement)
Usual Pagination: 116
Editor: Marc Coulson; **Advertising Manager:** Garth Ethelston; **Group Editor:** Marc Coulson
Summary of Content: Magazine focusing on tactical carp angling. Includes articles on equipment, tactics, tips and techniques.
Readership/Target Audience: Aimed at the more advanced carp angler.
ADVERTISING: Rates on application
CONSUMER: ANGLING & FISHING

ADVANCED DRIVING
46498U77R-7

Editorial Address: 510 Chiswick High Road, LONDON, W4 5RJ **Tel:** 020 8996 9600
Email: editor@iam.org.uk
Advertising Address: Mongoose Media Ltd, 2 Lonsdale Road, LONDON, NW6 6RD **Tel:** 020 7306 0300
Fax: 020 7306 0301
Email: iam@mongoosemedia.com
Web site: http://www.iam.org.uk
Publisher: IAM Group Services Ltd
Date Established: 1956
Frequency: 3 issues yearly - Published in March, July and October
Free to qualifying individuals
Circulation: 120,000 (Publisher's Statement)
Usual Pagination: 80
Editor: Vince Yearley; **Editor-in-Chief:** Vince Yearley
Summary of Content: Magazine covering driving, traffic and road safety matters, plus reports on new cars and foreign touring.
Readership/Target Audience: Read by members of the Institute of Advanced Motorists.
ADVERTISING RATES:
Full Page Colour £1991.00
Agency Commission: 10%
Mechanical Data: Bleed Size: 303 x 216mm, Type Area: 270 x 185mm, Col Length: 270mm, Page Width: 185mm, Trim Size: 297 x 210mm
Copy instructions: Copy Date: 4 weeks prior to publication date
Average advertising content per issue: 20%
CONSUMER: MOTORING & CYCLING: Motoring & Cycling Related

ADVANCED PHOTOSHOP
1708410U85A-205

Editorial Address: Richmond House, 33 Richmond Hill, BOURNEMOUTH, BH2 6EZ **Tel:** 01202 586200
Email: advancedpshop@imagine-publishing.co.uk
Advertising Address: As above.
Email: hang.deretz@imagine-publishing.co.uk
Web site: http://www.advancedphotoshop.co.uk
Publisher: Imagine Publishing
Date Established: 2005
Frequency: 13 issues yearly
Cover Price: £5.99
Usual Pagination: 100
Editor: Julie Easton; **Advertising Manager:** Hang Deretz
Summary of Content: Magazine with tutorials, interviews, product reviews and artist portfolios.
Readership/Target Audience: Aimed at Photoshop professionals and advanced amateurs.
ADVERTISING RATES:
Full Page Colour £2000.00
Mechanical Data: Type Area: 277 x 210mm, Bleed Size: 307 x 240mm, Trim Size: 297 x 230mm, Col Length: 277mm, Page Width: 210mm, Film: Digital
CONSUMER: PHOTOGRAPHY & FILM MAKING: Photography

ADVANCED POLE FISHING
48527U92-8

Editorial Address: 2 Stephenson Close, Drayton Fields Industrial Estate, DAVENTRY, NN11 8RF **Tel:** 01327 311999
Fax: 01327 311190
Email: patrick@dhpub.co.uk
Advertising Address: As above.
Email: graham.muddeman@dhpub.co.uk
Web site: http://www.advancedpolefishing.com
ISSN: 1356-6350
Publisher: David Hall Publishing Ltd
Frequency: Monthly
Cover Price: £2.85
Circulation: 16,000 (Publisher's Statement)
Usual Pagination: 100
Editor: Patrick MacInnes
Summary of Content: Magazine covering all aspects of equipment and techniques relating to pole fishing.
Readership/Target Audience: Read by pleasure anglers, newcomers to fishing and some professionals.
ADVERTISING: Rates on application
CONSUMER: ANGLING & FISHING

ADVENTURE TRAVEL
48224U89E-15

Editorial Address: 5 Alscott Workshop, Alscot Park, Atherstone On Stour, STRATFORD-UPON-AVON, CV37 8BL
Tel: 01789 450000 **Fax:** 01789 459046
Email: lara@atmagazine.co.uk
Advertising Address: As above. **Tel:** 01789 450050
Email: lucy@atmagazine.co.uk
Web site: http://www.atmagazine.co.uk
ISSN: 1368-0773
Publisher: Independent & Specialist Travel
Date Established: 1995
Frequency: 6 issues yearly
Cover Price: £3.50
Annual Sub.: £15.00
Circulation: 20,000 (Publisher's Statement)
Usual Pagination: 128
Editor: Lara Dunn; **Publisher:** Alun Davies
Summary of Content: Magazine covering worldwide and UK adventure and outdoor travel, specialising in trekking and mountaineering with destination features and information.
Readership/Target Audience: Aimed at experienced and novice outdoor travellers aged between 25 to 45 years old.
ADVERTISING RATES:
Full Page Colour £2400.00
Agency Commission: 10%
Mechanical Data: Type Area: 275 x 185mm, Bleed Size: 303 x 216mm, Trim Size: 297 x 210mm, Col Length: 275mm, Col Widths (Display): 87mm, No. of Columns (Display): 2, Page Width: 185mm, Film: Digital
Copy instructions: Copy Date: 3rd week of the month prior to publication date
Average advertising content per issue: 30%
CONSUMER: HOLIDAYS & TRAVEL: Holidays

AEROPLANE MONTHLY
36319U75N-40

Editorial Address: Blue Fin Building, 110 Southwark Street, LONDON, SE1 0SU **Tel:** 020 3148 5000
Email: editor_aero@ipcmedia.com
Advertising Address: As above.
Email: ashlyn_english@ipcmedia.com
Web site: http://www.aeroplanemonthly.com
ISSN: 0143-7240
Publisher: IPC Inspire
Date Established: 1973
Frequency: Monthly
Cover Price: £3.95
Annual Sub.: £47.40
Circulation: 35,169 (ABC 01/01/2008 to 31/12/2008)

Consumer Magazines

Usual Pagination: 108
Editor: Michael Oakey; **Features Editor:** Nick Stroud;
Managing Director: Paul Williams
Summary of Content: Magazine featuring aviation history, preservation, nostalgia and personal recollections from pilots and ground crew.
Readership/Target Audience: Aimed at enthusiasts of all ages.
ADVERTISING RATES:
Full Page Colour £1081.00
Agency Commission: 10%
Mechanical Data: Col Length: 279mm, Film: Digital, Type Area: 279 x 185mm, Bleed Size: 303 x 216mm, Trim Size: 297 x 210mm, Page Width: 185mm
Copy instructions: Copy Date: 6 weeks prior to publication date
Average advertising content per issue: 15%
CONSUMER: SPORT: Flight

AEROSTAT
45965U75N-50
Editorial Address: 1 Home Farm Cottages, Lenham Heath Road, Sandway, MAIDSTONE, ME17 2HX
Tel: 01622 858956 **Fax:** 01622 853817
Email: aerostat@bbac.org
Advertising Address: Associa, Agricultural House, North Gate, Uppingham, OAKHAM, LE15 9PL **Tel:** 01572 824700
Fax: 01572 824731
Email: mandy.frisby@associa.co.uk
Web site: http://www.bbac.org
Publisher: British Balloon & Airship Club
Frequency: 6 issues yearly
Free to qualifying individuals
Annual Sub.: £30.00
Circulation: 2,500 (Publisher's Statement)
Usual Pagination: 52
Editor: Liz Meek
Summary of Content: Official journal of the British Balloon and Airship Club containing news and updates from around the world.
Readership/Target Audience: Read by balloonists.
ADVERTISING RATES:
Full Page Colour £640.00
Agency Commission: 10%
Mechanical Data: Page Width: 185mm, Trim Size: 297 x 210mm, Bleed Size: 303 x 216mm, Film: Digital, Type Area: 264 x 185mm, Col Length: 264mm, Col Widths (Display): 44mm, No. of Columns (Display): 4
Copy instructions: Copy Date: 1 month prior to publication date
Average advertising content per issue: 35%
CONSUMER: SPORT: Flight

AESTHETICA
1837251U84A-466
Editorial Address: PO Box 371, YORK, YO23 1WL
Tel: 01904 479168 **Fax:** 01904 479749
Email: info@aestheticamagazine.com
Advertising Address: As above. **Tel:** 01904 527560
Fax: 01904 527451
Email: rachel@aestheticamagazine.com
Web site: http://www.aestheticamagazine.com
ISSN: 1743-2715
Publisher: Aesthetica Magazine Ltd
Date Established: 2002
Frequency: 6 issues yearly
Cover Price: £3.90
Circulation: 15,000 (Publisher's Statement)
Usual Pagination: 68
Editor: Cherie Federico; **Advertising Manager:** Rachel Nardiello
Summary of Content: Magazine with current and up-to-date information on British arts and culture including literature, visual arts, music, film and theatre.
Readership/Target Audience: Aimed at those with an interest in arts as well as buyers, critics and enthusiasts.
ADVERTISING RATES:
Full Page Colour £875.00
CONSUMER: THE ARTS & LITERARY: Arts

AFF JOURNAL
45678U74R-30
Formerly: AFF Families Journal
Editorial Address: Trenchard Lines, Upavon, PEWSEY, SN9 6BE **Tel:** 01980 615518 **Fax:** 01980 615526
Email: editor@afj.org.uk
Advertising Address: New Century House, Stadium Road, INVERNESS, IV1 1FG **Tel:** 01463 732255 **Fax:** 01463 732289
Email: sales@methodpublishing.co.uk
Web site: http://www.aff.org.uk
Publisher: Method Publishing
Date Established: 1990
Frequency: Quarterly - Published at the beginning of the first week of the cover month
Free to qualifying individuals
Annual Sub.: £10.00
Circulation: 64,000 (Publisher's Statement)
Usual Pagination: 64
Editor: Charlotte Eadie; **Advertising Manager:** Jeanne Alker

Summary of Content: Magazine containing news, advice and general interest features for army families.
Readership/Target Audience: Aimed at Army families in the UK and overseas.
ADVERTISING RATES:
Full Page Colour £2700.00
Agency Commission: 10%
Mechanical Data: Trim Size: 297 x 210mm, Type Area: 266 x 186mm, Col Length: 266mm, Page Width: 186mm, Film: Digital, Bleed Size: 303 x 216mm
Copy instructions: Copy Date: 5 weeks prior to publication date
Average advertising content per issue: 45%
CONSUMER: WOMEN'S INTEREST CONSUMER MAGAZINES: Women's Interest Related

THE AFRICA REVIEW
47298U82-2_8
Editorial Address: 11 Clarendon Street, CAMBRIDGE, CB1 1JU **Tel:** 01223 351584 **Fax:** 01223 351584
Email: sue@worldinformation.com
Advertising Address: As above.
Email: sue@worldinformation.com
Web site: http://www.worldinformation.com
ISSN: 0296-3844
Publisher: World of Information
Date Established: 1977
Frequency: Annual - Published in spring
Annual Sub.: £55.00
Circulation: 4,000 (Publisher's Statement)
Usual Pagination: 350
Editor: Anthony Axon; **Managing Director:** Sue Hewitt;
Advertising Manager: Sue Hewitt; **Publisher:** Anthony Axon
Summary of Content: Publication containing economic, political and practical information, analysis and interpretation on all African countries.
Readership/Target Audience: Aimed at those interested in the political and economic growth of Africa, including Government, businesses, universities and NGOs.
ADVERTISING RATES:
Full Page Colour £4950.00
Agency Commission: 15%
Mechanical Data: Type Area: 235.5 x 172mm, Bleed Size: 276 x 216mm, Trim Size: 270 x 210mm, Col Length: 235.5mm, Page Width: 172mm, Print Process: Offset litho, Film: Digital
Copy instructions: Copy Date: End of September
Average advertising content per issue: 10%
CONSUMER: CURRENT AFFAIRS & POLITICS

AFRICAN AFFAIRS
47199U82-2_6
Editorial Address: Politics, University of Newcastle, 40-42 Great North Road, NEWCASTLE UPON TYNE, NE1 7RU
Tel: 0191 222 8824 **Fax:** 0191 222 5069
Email: african.affairs@ncl.ac.uk
Advertising Address: 60 Upper Broadmoor Road, CROWTHORNE, RG45 7DE **Tel:** 01344 779945
Fax: 01344 779945
Email: lhann@lhms.fsnet.co.uk
Web site: http://www.afraf.oupjournals.org
ISSN: 0001-9909
Publisher: OUP
Date Established: 1901
Frequency: Quarterly
Annual Sub.: £47.00
Circulation: 2,100 (Publisher's Statement)
Usual Pagination: 160
Editor: Rita Abrahamsen
Summary of Content: Journal covering social, economic and political developments in Africa.
Readership/Target Audience: Read by those interested in African culture and politics.
ADVERTISING RATES:
Full Page Mono £360.00
Agency Commission: 10%
Mechanical Data: Film: Digital, Type Area: 200 x 130mm, Col Length: 200mm, Page Width: 130mm
Copy instructions: Copy Date: 1 month prior to publication date
CONSUMER: CURRENT AFFAIRS & POLITICS

AFRICAN ECHO
1790455U90-1000
Editorial Address: Suite C, Queensway House, 275-285 High Street, Stratford, LONDON, E15 2TF
Tel: 020 8534 2255 **Fax:** 020 8519 5564
Email: editor@africanecho.co.uk
Advertising Address: As above.
Email: sales@africanecho.co.uk
Web site: http://www.africanecho.co.uk
Publisher: The Ethnic Minority Information & Advisory Centre
Date Established: 2004
Frequency: 26 issues yearly
Cover Price: Free
Circulation: 25,000 (Publisher's Statement)
Usual Pagination: 24
Editor: Eric Orjie

Summary of Content: Newspaper with objective analysis, news, views and topical events taking place in Africa including economic, social, religious, educational, political and health features as well as highlighting community events in the UK.
Readership/Target Audience: Aimed at African men and women in the UK.
ADVERTISING RATES:
Full Page Mono £1620.00
Full Page Colour £2268.00
SCC £7.50
Agency Commission: 10%
Mechanical Data: Type Area: 365 x 275mm, Col Length: 365mm, Page Width: 275mm, Col Widths (Display): 36mm, No. of Columns (Display): 6, Film: Digital
Copy instructions: Copy Date: 1 week prior to publication date
Average advertising content per issue: 20%
CONSUMER: ETHNIC

AFTER HOURS
1666402U86C-721
Editorial Address: 116 Pall Mall, LONDON, SW1Y 5ED
Tel: 020 7766 8950 **Fax:** 020 7766 8840
Email: afterhours@iod.com
Advertising Address: As above. **Tel:** 020 7766 8900
Email: claire.henderson@iod.com
Web site: http://www.afterhoursmagazine.co.uk
Publisher: Director Publications Ltd
Date Established: 2005
Frequency: Quarterly
Cover Price: Free
Circulation: 58,370 (Publisher's Statement)
Editor: Richard Cree; **Advertising Manager:** Claire Henderson
Summary of Content: Lifestyle magazine covering cars, cigars, wine, food and drink, travel, holidays and sport.
Readership/Target Audience: Aimed at company directors of small to medium businesses and goes out free of charge with Directors Magazine.
ADVERTISING RATES:
Full Page Colour £7450.00
Agency Commission: 15%
Mechanical Data: Bleed Size: 261 x 231mm, Trim Size: 255 x 225mm, Film: Digital
Copy instructions: Copy Date: 4 weeks prior to publication date
Average advertising content per issue: 40%
CONSUMER: ADULT & GAY MAGAZINES: Men's Lifestyle Magazines

AFTER THE BATTLE
48733U94X-4_50
Editorial Address: The Mews, Hobbs Cross House, OLD HARLOW, CM17 0NN **Tel:** 01279 418833
Fax: 01279 419386
Email: hq@afterthebattle.com
Web site: http://www.afterthebattle.com
ISSN: 0306-154X
Publisher: Battle of Britain International Ltd
Date Established: 1973
Frequency: Quarterly
Cover Price: £4.25
Circulation: 11,000 (Publisher's Statement)
Usual Pagination: 56
Editor: Karel Margry; **Managing Editor:** Winston Ramsey
Summary of Content: Magazine providing coverage of World War II battlefields through the use of then and now comparison photographs. Includes regular features on wreck recoveries, personalities, preservation, war crimes and war films.
Readership/Target Audience: Aimed at military enthusiasts and historians.
ADVERTISING: No Advertising taken
CONSUMER: OTHER CLASSIFICATIONS: Miscellaneous

AFTERDARK MAGAZINE
1795104U89C-1098
Editorial Address: Studio 257, 20 Winchcombe Street, CHELTENHAM, GL52 2LY **Tel:** 07796 670273
Email: justin@afterdarkmagazine.co.uk
Advertising Address: As above.
Email: sales@afterdarkmagazine.co.uk
Web site: http://www.afterdarkmagazine.co.uk
Publisher: AfterDark Magazine LTD
Date Established: 2005
Frequency: Monthly
Cover Price: Free
Circulation: 7,000 (Publisher's Statement)
Usual Pagination: 64
Editor: Justin Box; **Advertising Manager:** Justin Box
Summary of Content: Magazine covering reviews of events, restaurants and venues, artists, albums, games and films, community work, environmental issues, AfterDark discount card scheme, policing issues and films press releases, theatre and performances, as well as a what's on guide for the local area. New sections include hair products and fashion, as well as new products reviews (electrical) and competitions.

Readership/Target Audience: Aimed at 18 to 40 year olds interested in what's on in the Southwest, Oxfordshire and Worcestershire.
ADVERTISING RATES:
Full Page Colour £250.00
Agency Commission: 10%
Mechanical Data: Type Area: 174 x 126mm, Col Length: 174mm, Page Width: 126mm
Copy instructions: Copy Date: 19th of the month prior to cover date
Average advertising content per issue: 30%
CONSUMER: HOLIDAYS & TRAVEL: Entertainment Guides

AFV MODELLER
1745231U79B-202
Editorial Address: 176 New Bridge Street, NEWCASTLE UPON TYNE, NE1 2TE **Tel:** 0191 209 1107
Fax: 0191 209 2002
Email: david@afvmodeller.com
Advertising Address: As above.
Email: keith@afvmodeller.com
Web site: http://www.afvmodeller.com
Publisher: AFV Modeller Ltd
Frequency: 6 issues yearly
Cover Price: £6.00
Circulation: 8,000 (Publisher's Statement)
Editor: David Parker
Summary of Content: Magazine covering armoured fighting vehicle modelling with step by step guides, history, latest release news and details and photographs of vehicles.
Readership/Target Audience: Aimed at AFV modelling enthusiasts.
ADVERTISING RATES:
Full Page Mono £410.00
Full Page Colour £595.00
Mechanical Data: Type Area: 277 x 190mm, Bleed Size: 303 x 216mm, Trim Size: 297 x 210mm, Col Length: 277mm, Page Width: 190mm, Film: Digital
Copy instructions: Copy Date: 3 weeks prior to publication date
CONSUMER: HOBBIES & DIY: Models & Modelling

AG
1639144U85A-200
Editorial Address: Dulwich Lodge, 62 Pemberton Road, EAST MOLESEY, KT8 9LH **Tel:** 020 8941 0249
Fax: 020 8941 1088
Email: info@ag-photo.co.uk
Web site: http://www.ag-photo.co.uk
ISSN: 1475-116X
Publisher: Picture-Box Media Ltd
Date Established: 1991
Frequency: Quarterly
Cover Price: £12.50
Annual Sub.: £37.50
Circulation: 2,000 (Publisher's Statement)
Usual Pagination: 100
Editor: Chris Dickie; **Publisher:** Chris Dickie
Summary of Content: Magazine covering the art and practice of photography.
Readership/Target Audience: Aimed at professional and enthusiast photographers.
ADVERTISING: No Advertising taken
CONSUMER: PHOTOGRAPHY & FILM MAKING: Photography

AGA LIVING
45642U74Q-2
Formerly: AGA Magazine
Editorial Address: The Round House, Butters Bank, Croxton, STAFFORD, ST21 6NN **Tel:** 01630 620340
Email: sallyannbloomer@btinternet.com
Advertising Address: Unit 28B Harris Business Park, Hanbury Road, Stoke Prior, BROMSGROVE, B60 4DJ
Tel: 01527 871747 **Fax:** 01527 882501
Email: sharonb@bee3.biz
Web site: http://www.agaliving.co.uk
Publisher: Bee3 Ltd
Date Established: 1996
Frequency: 6 issues yearly
Free to qualifying individuals
Annual Sub.: £15.95
Circulation: 68,000 (Publisher's Statement)
Usual Pagination: 120
Editor: Sally-Ann Bloomer; **Advertising Manager:** Sharon Blick
Summary of Content: Magazine containing lifestyle features including articles on interior design, holidays, cooking, wine and antiques.
Readership/Target Audience: Aimed at Aga owners with a high disposable income.
ADVERTISING RATES:
Full Page Colour £1495.00
Mechanical Data: Page Width: 180mm, Film: Digital, Type Area: 273 x 180mm, Col Length: 273mm, Trim Size: 297 x 210mm, Bleed Size: +3mm
CONSUMER: WOMEN'S INTEREST CONSUMER MAGAZINES: Lifestyle

AGILITY VOICE
47094U81B-5
Editorial Address: 6 Fane Way, MAIDENHEAD, SL6 2TL
Tel: 01628 680823
Email: editor@agilityclub.co.uk
Advertising Address: As above.
Email: editor@agilityclub.co.uk
Web site: http://www.agilityclub.co.uk
Publisher: The Agility Club
Frequency: Monthly
Annual Sub.: £23.00 (single)
Circulation: 3,000 (Publisher's Statement)
Usual Pagination: 64
Editor: Virginia Harry; **Advertising Manager:** Virginia Harry
Summary of Content: Magazine of the Agility Club covering shows and events in the agility calendar.
Readership/Target Audience: Aimed at people competing in dog agility trials.
ADVERTISING RATES:
Full Page Colour £150.00
Agency Commission: 15%
Copy instructions: Copy Date: 15th of the month prior to publication date
CONSUMER: ANIMALS & PETS: Dogs

AI
711922U84A-15
Editorial Address: 27 Norwich Road, HALESWORTH, IP19 8BX **Tel:** 01986 834250
Email: editors@artsindustry.co.uk
Advertising Address: As above. **Fax:** 01986 834255
Email: jo@micropress.co.uk
Web site: http://www.artsindustry.co.uk
Publisher: BC Publications
Date Established: 2001
Frequency: 24 issues yearly
Annual Sub.: £36.00
Circulation: 6,500 (Publisher's Statement)
Usual Pagination: 32
Editor: Patrick Kelly; **Advertising Manager:** Jo Leverett; **Publisher:** Simon Tooth
Summary of Content: Magazine covering UK culture industry news, features, diary and recruitment.
Readership/Target Audience: Read by management level professionals throughout the UK culture industry, encompassing the arts heritage and culture business.
ADVERTISING RATES:
Full Page Colour £900.00
SCC £21.50
Agency Commission: 10%
Mechanical Data: Bleed Size: 246 x 171mm, No. of Columns (Display): 4, Trim Size: 240 x 165mm, Col Widths (Display): 33mm, Film: Digital
Copy instructions: Copy Date: Monday 5pm prior to publication date
Average advertising content per issue: 30%
CONSUMER: THE ARTS & LITERARY: Arts

AIN ALMUSAFER MAGAZINE
1842562U90-1029
Editorial Address: 2nd Floor, 145-157 St. John Street, LONDON, EC1V 4PY **Tel:** 020 7608 5137
Fax: 0870 428 5885
Email: ka@ainalmusafer.com
Web site: http://www.ainalmusafer.com
Publisher: G&T Media Ltd
Date Established: 2007
Frequency: 6 issues yearly
Cover Price: AED30
Annual Sub.: AED170
Circulation: 70,000 (Publisher's Statement)
Usual Pagination: 132
Editor: Kahled Algaay
Summary of Content: Luxury lifestyle and travel magazine which explores the places, ideas and trends that define modern global culture.
Language(s): Arabic
Readership/Target Audience: Aimed at affluent Arabs interested in travel.
CONSUMER: ETHNIC

AIR GUNNER
45855U75F-10
Editorial Address: 3 The Courtyard, Denmark Street, WOKINGHAM, RG40 2AZ **Tel:** 0118 977 1677
Fax: 0118 977 2903
Email: terry.doe@archant.co.uk
Advertising Address: As above.
Email: neil.dyson@archant.co.uk
Web site: http://www.airgunshooting.org
Publisher: Archant Specialist (Wokingham)
Frequency: Monthly
Cover Price: £3.40
Circulation: 10,000 (Publisher's Statement)
Usual Pagination: 96
Editor: Terry Doe; **Editor-in-Chief:** Terry Doe
Summary of Content: Magazine containing gun and kit reviews, features on target shooting, airgun hunting and technical aspects.

Readership/Target Audience: Aimed at airgun enthusiasts of all ages.
ADVERTISING RATES:
Full Page Colour £900.00
Agency Commission: 10%
Mechanical Data: Type Area: 270 x 189mm, Col Length: 270mm, Trim Size: 297 x 210mm, Bleed Size: 305 x 218mm, Film: Digital, Page Width: 189mm
Copy instructions: Copy Date: 4 weeks prior to publication date
Average advertising content per issue: 55%
CONSUMER: SPORT: Shooting

AIR MODELLER
1745228U79B-201
Editorial Address: 176 New Bridge Street, NEWCASTLE UPON TYNE, NE1 2TE **Tel:** 0191 209 1107
Fax: 0191 209 2002
Email: david@afvmodeller.com
Advertising Address: As above.
Email: keith@afvmodeller.com
Web site: http://www.airmodeller.com
Publisher: AFV Modeller Ltd
Frequency: 6 issues yearly
Cover Price: £6.00
Free to qualifying individuals
Circulation: 8,000 (Publisher's Statement)
Editor: David Parker; **Advertising Manager:** Keith Smith
Summary of Content: Magazine covering precision aircraft modelling with step to step guides, latest release information, details and photographs of aircraft.
Readership/Target Audience: Aimed at aircraft modelling enthusiasts.
ADVERTISING RATES:
Full Page Mono £410.00
Full Page Colour £595.00
Mechanical Data: Type Area: 276 x 190mm, Bleed Size: 303 x 216mm, Trim Size: 297 x 210mm, Col Length: 276mm, Page Width: 190mm, Film: Digital
CONSUMER: HOBBIES & DIY: Models & Modelling

AIRGUN WORLD
45856U75F-20
Editorial Address: 3 The Courtyard, Denmark Street, WOKINGHAM, RG40 2AZ **Tel:** 0118 977 1677
Fax: 0118 977 2903
Email: agw@archant.co.uk
Advertising Address: As above. **Tel:** 0118 989 7264
Email: neil.dyson@archant.co.uk
Web site: http://www.airgunmags.co.uk
Publisher: Archant Specialist (Wokingham)
Frequency: Monthly
Cover Price: £3.25
Circulation: 15,000 (Publisher's Statement)
Usual Pagination: 96
Editor: Terry Doe; **Publisher:** Derek Barnes
Summary of Content: Magazine covering authoritative tests on new rifles, pistols, scopes and accessories. Includes hunting, field target, match and fun shooting.
Readership/Target Audience: Aimed at airgun enthusiasts.
ADVERTISING RATES:
Full Page Colour £900.00
Agency Commission: 10%
Mechanical Data: Page Width: 189mm, Trim Size: 297 x 210mm, Film: Digital, Type Area: 270 x 189mm, Col Length: 270mm, Bleed Size: 305 x 218mm
Copy instructions: Copy Date: 4 weeks prior to publication date
CONSUMER: SPORT: Shooting

AIRLINER WORLD
46775U79R-6
Editorial Address: PO Box 100, STAMFORD, PE9 1XQ
Tel: 01780 755131 **Fax:** 01780 757261
Email: tony.dixon@keypublishing.com
Advertising Address: As above.
Email: andrew.mason@keypublishing.com
Web site: http://www.airlinerworld.com
Publisher: Key Publishing Ltd
Date Established: 1999
Frequency: Monthly
Cover Price: £3.95
Circulation: 33,842 (ABC 01/01/2008 to 31/12/2008)
Usual Pagination: 100
Editor: Tony Dixon; **Advertising Manager:** Andy Mason
Summary of Content: Magazine providing an insight into all aspects of commercial aviation. Contains news, reviews, interviews and features on airliners, airlines and airports.
Readership/Target Audience: Aimed at aircraft enthusiasts as well as industry professionals, airline and airport staff.
ADVERTISING RATES:
Full Page Colour £1680.00
SCC £15.00
Agency Commission: 10%
Mechanical Data: Page Width: 180mm, No. of Columns (Display): 2, Col Widths (Display): 87mm, Film: Digital, Trim Size: 297 x 210mm, Bleed Size: 307 x 220mm, Type Area: 267 x 190mm, Col Length: 267mm
Copy instructions: Copy Date: 3 weeks prior to publication date

Consumer Magazines

Average advertising content per issue: 25%
CONSUMER: HOBBIES & DIY: Hobbies & DIY Related

AIRSOFT INTERNATIONAL
1753139U79F-100

Editorial Address: 2 Shaw Close, Peneden Heath, MAIDSTONE, ME14 5DN **Tel:** 01622 692885
Fax: 01622 683093
Email: paul@ai-mag.com
Advertising Address: As above.
Email: paul@ai-mag.com
Web site: http://www.ai-mag.com
Publisher: Ebcon Publishing
Date Established: 2006
Frequency: 13 issues yearly
Cover Price: £4.00
Circulation: 30,000 (Publisher's Statement)
Usual Pagination: 76
Editor: Paul Monaf; **Advertising Manager:** Paul Monaf
Summary of Content: Magazine covering war games with reviews, previews, commentary and discussion of the global world of Airsoft.
Readership/Target Audience: Aimed at players and collectors of Airsoft and related products.
ADVERTISING RATES:
Full Page Colour £750.00
Agency Commission: 10%
Mechanical Data: Bleed Size: 303 x 216mm, Trim Size: 297 x 210mm, Film: Digital
Copy instructions: Copy Date: 10 days prior to publication date
Average advertising content per issue: 40%
CONSUMER: HOBBIES & DIY: Games & Puzzles

AL-ARAB
1804127U90-1008

Editorial Address: Office W123, Westminster Business Square, 1-45 Durham Street, LONDON, SE11 5JH
Tel: 020 7735 9977 **Fax:** 020 7735 9976
Email: ghassan.ibrahim@yahoo.co.uk
Advertising Address: As above.
Email: yasin@alarab.co.uk
Web site: http://www.alarabonline.info
ISSN: 0140-010X
Publisher: Al-Arab Publishing House
Date Established: 1977
Frequency: 312 issues yearly - Not published on Sunday
Cover Price: £0.75
Usual Pagination: 16
Editor: Ghassán Ibrahim; **Advertising Manager:** Yasin El-Huni; **Managing Editor:** Ghassan Ibrahim
Summary of Content: Newspaper covering political, social, economic and cultural issues as well as education and business.
Language(s): Arabic; English
Readership/Target Audience: Aimed at Arab communities in the UK, Europe, North Africa and parts of the Middle East.
ADVERTISING RATES:
Full Page Mono £1920.00
Full Page Colour £3840.00
Mechanical Data: Type Area: 535 x 380mm, Col Length: 535mm, Page Width: 380mm, Col Widths (Display): 45mm, No. of Columns (Display): 8, Film: Digital
Copy instructions: Copy Date: 3 days prior to publication date
CONSUMER: ETHNIC

ALDERNEY JOURNAL
47068U80G-13

Editorial Address: 2A Olivier Court, Ollivier Street, Alderney, GUERNSEY, GY9 3TD **Tel:** 01481 823243
Fax: 01481 823824
Email: editor@alderneyjournal.com
Advertising Address: As above.
Email: advertising@alderneyjournal.com
Web site: http://www.alderneyjournal.com
Publisher: Alderney Journal Ltd
Date Established: 1971
Frequency: 24 issues yearly
Cover Price: £0.85
Annual Sub.: £27.36
Circulation: 1,500 (Publisher's Statement)
Usual Pagination: 36
Editor: James Adair; **Advertising Manager:** Stephen Godfrey
Summary of Content: Magazine covering community news, what's on and the local history of Alderney.
Readership/Target Audience: Read by the residents of Alderney Island.
ADVERTISING RATES:
Full Page Mono £160.00
Mechanical Data: Type Area: 194 x 127mm, Col Length: 194mm, Page Width: 127mm, No. of Columns (Display): 2, Film: Digital
Copy instructions: Copy Date: 1 week prior to publication date
CONSUMER: RURAL & REGIONAL INTEREST: Regional Interest Channel Islands

ALEF
1842301U74B-736

Editorial Address: Milk Studios, 34 Southern Row, LONDON, W10 5AN **Tel:** 020 8962 2006 **Fax:** 020 8962 2006
Email: melsayed@alefmag.com
Web site: http://www.alefmag.com
ISSN: 1991-4601
Publisher: Modern Middle East Publishing Ltd
Date Established: 2006
Frequency: Quarterly
Circulation: 40,000 (Publisher's Statement)
Usual Pagination: 184
Editor: Paul de Zwart; **Publisher:** Paul de Zwart
Summary of Content: Magazine covering fashion, jewellery luxury goods, art, culture and lifestyle.
Readership/Target Audience: Aimed at those interested in the culture of the Middle East.
CONSUMER: WOMEN'S INTEREST CONSUMER MAGAZINES: Women's Interest - Fashion

THE ALFRED DUNHILL LINKS CHAMPIONSHIP
1824297U75D-560

Editorial Address: 134 Liverpool Road, LONDON, N1 1LA
Tel: 020 7665 1111 **Fax:** 020 7609 5837
Email: editorial@cwcomms.com
Advertising Address: As above.
Email: andy.roberts@cwcomms.com
Publisher: CW Publishing Group
Frequency: Annual - Published in September
Cover Price: £3.50
Circulation: 10,000 (Publisher's Statement)
Editor: Trisha Doyle; **Advertising Manager:** Sema Demir
Summary of Content: Official souvenir programme of the Dunhill Golf Championship with player profiles, golf travel and interviews.
Readership/Target Audience: Aimed at golf fans.
ADVERTISING: Rates on application
CONSUMER: SPORT: Golf

ALL ABOUT ANIMALS
1818700U91D-968

Editorial Address: Media Centre, 201 Wood Lane, LONDON, W12 7TQ **Tel:** 020 8433 2000
Email: bea.appleby@bbc.com
Advertising Address: The Garden House, 201 Wood Lane, LONDON, W12 7TQ **Tel:** 020 8433 2000
Email: sophie.hunt@bbc.com
Publisher: BBC Children's Magazines
Date Established: 2007
Frequency: Monthly
Cover Price: £1.99
Circulation: 35,469 (ABC 01/01/2009 to 30/06/2009)
Editor: Bea Appleby; **Advertising Manager:** Claire Stidwell
Summary of Content: Children's magazine all about animals with photo stories, cartoons, puzzles and cover mounts.
Readership/Target Audience: Aimed at girls aged 7 to 12 years old.
ADVERTISING RATES:
Full Page Colour £1500.00
Agency Commission: 10%
Mechanical Data: Type Area: 280 x 200mm, Bleed Size: 308 x 228mm, Trim Size: 300 x 220mm, Col Length: 280mm, Page Width: 200mm, Film: Digital
Copy instructions: Copy Date: 3 weeks prior to publication date
Average advertising content per issue: 11%
CONSUMER: RECREATION & LEISURE: Children & Youth

ALL ABOUT SOAP
601234U76C-60

Editorial Address: 64 North Row, LONDON, W1K 7LL
Tel: 020 7150 7000 **Fax:** 020 7150 7681
Email: allaboutsoap@hf-uk.com
Advertising Address: As above.
Email: awetton@hf-uk.com
Web site: http://www.allaboutsoap.co.uk
Publisher: Hachette Filipacchi (UK) Ltd
Date Established: 1999
Frequency: 26 issues yearly
Cover Price: £1.45
Circulation: 107,162 (ABC 01/01/2009 to 30/06/2009)
Usual Pagination: 68
Editor: Johnathon Hughes; **Features Editor:** Kerry Barrett; **Advertising Director:** Annabel Wetton; **Publisher:** Grace Stewart
Summary of Content: Television soap opera magazine covering news, features, celebrity interviews and gossip.
Readership/Target Audience: Aimed at women in their early 20s.
ADVERTISING RATES:
Full Page Colour £2700.00
Agency Commission: 15%
Mechanical Data: Type Area: 265 x 195mm, Col Length: 265mm, Trim Size: 275 x 205mm, Bleed Size: 285 x 215mm, Page Width: 195mm, Film: Digital

Copy instructions: Copy Date: 10 days prior to publication date
CONSUMER: MUSIC & PERFORMING ARTS: TV & Radio

ALL AT SEA
766857U91A-282

Editorial Address: Alliance House, 49 Sidney Street, CAMBRIDGE, CB2 3JF **Tel:** 01223 460490
Fax: 01223 315960
Email: bsatchwell@aol.com
Advertising Address: As above. **Tel:** 01223 444084
Email: jodyb@allatsea.co.uk
Web site: http://www.allatsea.co.uk
ISSN: 1475-8237
Publisher: CSL Publishing Ltd
Date Established: 2001
Frequency: Monthly
Free to qualifying individuals
Annual Sub.: £22.00
Circulation: 55,000 (Publisher's Statement)
Usual Pagination: 40
Editor: Robert Satchwell; **Managing Director:** Sue Baggaley; **Advertising Manager:** Katie Hawksworth
Summary of Content: Newspaper covering news from, and about, the waterfront as well as product information, trading news and advice from the waterfront and boating communities around the coast and estuaries.
Readership/Target Audience: Aimed at cruising and racing yachtsmen, windsurfers, power boaters, dinghy sailors and those with an interest in marine leisure activities.
ADVERTISING RATES:
Full Page Colour £1800.00
Agency Commission: 10%
Mechanical Data: Film: Digital
Copy instructions: Copy Date: 24th of the month prior to publication date
CONSUMER: RECREATION & LEISURE: Boating & Yachting

ALL HORSE
1698925U81D-367

Editorial Address: Unit 2, Devizes Trade Centre, Hopton Park, DEVIZES, SN10 2EH **Tel:** 01380 730888
Fax: 01380 730899
Email: sales@redpin.co.uk
Advertising Address: As above. **Tel:** 0845 644 2236
Email: lisadure@redpin.co.uk
Web site: http://www.all-horse.co.uk
Publisher: Redpin Publishing Ltd
Frequency: Monthly
Cover Price: Free
Circulation: 13,250 (Publisher's Statement)
Editor: Sara Haines
Summary of Content: Magazine covering all-round equestrian interests and disciplines, features articles, product reviews and events.
Readership/Target Audience: Aimed at riders in the West Midlands.
ADVERTISING: Rates on application
CONSUMER: ANIMALS & PETS: Horses & Ponies

THE ALL IRELAND KITCHEN GUIDE
45280U74C-18

Editorial Address: PO Box 42, BANGOR, BT19 7AD
Tel: 028 9147 3979 **Fax:** 028 9145 7226
Email: editorial@ihil.net
Advertising Address: Unit 65 Dunlop Commercial Park, 4 Balloo Drive, BANGOR, BT19 7QY **Tel:** 028 9147 3979
Fax: 028 9145 4223
Email: advertising@ihil.net
Web site: http://www.irelandshomesinteriorsandliving.com
Publisher: Ireland's Homes Interiors and Living
Date Established: 2001
Frequency: Half-yearly - Published in April and September
Cover Price: £8.00
Circulation: 7,816 (ABC 01/01/2008 to 31/12/2008)
Usual Pagination: 230
Editor: Samantha Blair; **Publisher:** Mike Keenan
Summary of Content: Specialist kitchen magazine featuring readers kitchens as well as the latest in kitchen design, appliances and accessories.
Readership/Target Audience: Aimed at women interested in new ideas for the kitchen.
ADVERTISING RATES:
Full Page Colour £1600.00
Agency Commission: 10%
Mechanical Data: Col Length: 277mm, Page Width: 210mm, Film: Digital, Type Area: 277 x 210mm, Bleed Size: 303 x 236mm, Trim Size: 297 x 230mm
Copy instructions: Copy Date: 4 weeks prior to publication date
Average advertising content per issue: 30%
CONSUMER: WOMEN'S INTEREST CONSUMER MAGAZINES: Home & Family

ALL OUT CRICKET
1643588U75K-851

Editorial Address: c/o Trinorth Ltd, The Brit Oval, Kennington, LONDON, SE11 5SS **Tel:** 020 7820 4190
Fax: 020 7953 8329
Email: comments@alloutcricket.co.uk
Advertising Address: The Oval, Kennington, LONDON, SE11 5SS **Tel:** 020 7820 4190
Email: ian@trinorth.co.uk
Web site: http://www.alloutcricket.co.uk
Publisher: Cricnet Magazines Ltd
Date Established: 2004
Frequency: Monthly
Cover Price: £3.75
Circulation: 30,000 (Print Run)
Usual Pagination: 100
Editor: Andy Afford; **Advertising Manager:** Ian Sykes
Summary of Content: Magazine with a young and lively approach to presenting cricket with features on cricketing lifestyle and interviews with the stars.
Readership/Target Audience: Aimed at followers of cricket aged from 15 years old.
ADVERTISING RATES:
Full Page Colour £1595.00
Agency Commission: 10%
Mechanical Data: Type Area: 227 x 190mm, Bleed Size: 303 x 216mm, Trim Size: 297 x 210mm, Col Length: 227mm, Page Width: 190mm, Film: Digital
Average advertising content per issue: 20%
CONSUMER: SPORT: Cricket

ALL TOGETHER NOW!
48635U94F-430

Formerly: I Can Do That!
Editorial Address: The Bradbury Centre, Youens Way, LIVERPOOL, L14 2EP **Tel:** 0151 230 0307
Fax: 0151 220 4446
Email: news@alltogethernow.org.uk
Advertising Address: As above.
Email: sales@alltogethernow.org.uk
Web site: http://www.alltogethernow.org.uk
Publisher: All Together Now! Ltd
Date Established: 2005
Frequency: 6 issues yearly
Free to qualifying individuals
Annual Sub.: £10.00
Circulation: 60,000 (Publisher's Statement)
Usual Pagination: 32
Editor: Tom Dowling
Summary of Content: Magazine with a focus on issues affecting families affected by disability, those with wide ranging health problems the elderly and their carers. Sections cover the arts, sport, education, employment, computers, health, holidays, motoring, research and technological developments.
Readership/Target Audience: Aimed at disabled people, the elderly, their families, carers and professionals.
ADVERTISING RATES:
Full Page Mono £1800.00
Full Page Colour £3000.00
SCC £13.95
Agency Commission: 10%
Mechanical Data: Trim Size: 385 x 300mm, Film: Digital, Col Widths (Display): 31mm, No. of Columns (Display): 8, Col Length: 360mm, Page Width: 272mm, Type Area: 360 x 272mm
Average advertising content per issue: 25%
CONSUMER: OTHER CLASSIFICATIONS: Disability

ALL TORQUE
1665811U77E-514

Editorial Address: 1 Blomfield Dale, BINFIELD, RG42 1FY
Tel: 07802 696540 **Fax:** 01344 641626
Email: chris.kenward@tipec.net
Advertising Address: 10 Whitecroft Gardens, Woodford Halse, DAVENTRY, NN11 3PY **Tel:** 0845 602 0052
Email: cluboffice@tipec.net
Web site: http://www.tipec.net
Publisher: The Independent Porsche Enthusiasts Club
Date Established: 1994
Frequency: 6 issues yearly
Cover Price: Free
Circulation: 1,200 (Publisher's Statement)
Usual Pagination: 48
Editor: Trig Ellis; **Advertising Manager:** Shaun smallman
Summary of Content: Magazine covering general interest Porsche stories, product reviews and readers articles.
Readership/Target Audience: Aimed at Porsche enthusiasts.
ADVERTISING: Rates on application
Agency Commission: 10%
CONSUMER: MOTORING & CYCLING: Club Cars

ALLOTMENT & LEISURE GARDENER
48550U93-7

Editorial Address: O'Dell House, Hunters Road, Weldon North Industrial Estate, CORBY, NN17 5JE
Tel: 01536 266576 **Fax:** 01536 264509
Email: natsoc@nsalg.org.uk

Advertising Address: 20 Moulton Business Park, Scirocco Close, NORTHAMPTON, NN3 6AP **Tel:** 01604 495495
Fax: 01604 495465
Email: kelly@crestpublications.com
Web site: http://www.nsalg.org.uk
Publisher: Crest Publications
Frequency: Quarterly
Free to qualifying individuals
Annual Sub.: £6.00
Circulation: 5,000 (Publisher's Statement)
Usual Pagination: 30
Editor: Geoff Stokes
Summary of Content: Magazine of the National Society for Allotment and Leisure Gardeners containing news, letters and topical articles.
Readership/Target Audience: Read by leisure and allotment gardeners.
ADVERTISING RATES:
Full Page Mono £550.00
Full Page Colour £700.00
Agency Commission: 10%
Mechanical Data: Film: Digital, Trim Size: 297 x 210mm, Bleed Size: +4mm
Copy instructions: Copy Date: 6 weeks prior to publication date
CONSUMER: GARDENING

ALLSCOT NEWS LETTER
47062U80E-15

Formerly: Allscot News
Editorial Address: PO Box 6, HADDINGTON, EH41 3NQ
Tel: 01620 822578 **Fax:** 01620 822578
Email: allscotnews@btinternet.com
Advertising Address: As above.
Publisher: Allscot
Date Established: 1999
Frequency: 10 issues yearly
Annual Sub.: £20.00
Circulation: 2,500 (Publisher's Statement)
Editor: Richard Brown; **Advertising Manager:** Richard Brown
Summary of Content: Magazine featuring current affairs and news on Scotland.
Readership/Target Audience: Aimed at those interested in current affairs in Scotland.
ADVERTISING: Rates on application
Average advertising content per issue: 10%
CONSUMER: RURAL & REGIONAL INTEREST: Regional Interest Scotland

THE ALMANACH DE GOTHA REVIEW OF ROYAL BOOKS
47532U84B-5

Editorial Address: 328 Linen Hall, 162-168 Regent Street, LONDON, W1B 5TD **Tel:** 020 8404 2489 **Fax:** 020 8404 2629
Email: admin@almanachdegotha.com
Advertising Address: As above.
Email: gotha1763@aol.com
Publisher: Almanach de Gotha Ltd
Date Established: 1763
Frequency: Monthly
Annual Sub.: £60.00
Circulation: 18,000 (Publisher's Statement)
Usual Pagination: 1000
Editor: John Kennedy; **Advertising Manager:** John Kennedy; **Managing Editor:** John Kennedy; **Publisher:** John Kennedy
Summary of Content: Publication dedicated to reviewing royal biographies and other royalty related topics.
Readership/Target Audience: Aimed at libraries, media and diplomatic missions.
ADVERTISING: Rates on application
CONSUMER: THE ARTS & LITERARY: Literary

THE ALTERNATIVE GUIDE
31129U74G-5

Editorial Address: PO Box 16, ST. LEONARDS-ON-SEA, TN37 6YE **Tel:** 01424 465543
Email: david@altguide.com
Advertising Address: As above.
Email: david@altguide.com
Web site: http://www.altguide.com
Publisher: Power Publishing
Date Established: 1994
Frequency: Quarterly
Cover Price: Free
Circulation: 260,000 (Publisher's Statement)
Editor: David Baird; **Advertising Manager:** David Baird;
Publisher: David Baird
Summary of Content: Guide to alternative and complementary medicine, spirituality and self development. Contains a comprehensive listing of local events, plus information on a variety of therapies and details of the therapists who provide them.
Readership/Target Audience: Aimed at health store consumers and those with an interest in complementary medicine and self development. Distributed throughout natural health and whole food stores, hospitals and libraries.

ADVERTISING: Rates on application
Agency Commission: 10%
Copy instructions: Copy Date: 1st of the month prior to publication date
Average advertising content per issue: 50%
Editions:
The Alternative Guide to East Sussex
The Alternative Guide to Greater London
The Alternative Guide to Kent
The Alternative Guide to The New Forest
CONSUMER: WOMEN'S INTEREST CONSUMER MAGAZINES: Slimming & Health

THE ALUMNI NEWSLETTER
601569U84A-260

Formerly: In Touch
Editorial Address: Embassy Theatre, 64 Eton Avenue, LONDON, NW3 3HY **Tel:** 020 7559 3904
Fax: 020 7586 6781
Email: c.clark@cssd.ac.uk
Web site: http://www.cssd.ac.uk
Publisher: Central School of Speech & Drama
Date Established: 1998
Frequency: Half-yearly - Published in Spring and Autumn
Cover Price: Free
Circulation: 4,000 (Publisher's Statement)
Usual Pagination: 12
Editor: Caroline Clark
Summary of Content: Alumni magazine containing articles related to former students and courses offered by the school. Covers acting, voice, foundation art and design, puppetry, musical theatre, circus, drama therapy, prop making, production lighting, lighting design, production sound, production design and drama and education.
Readership/Target Audience: Aimed at former students of the Central School of Speech and Drama.
ADVERTISING: No Advertising taken
CONSUMER: THE ARTS & LITERARY: Arts

AM QUARTERLY
46443U77E-35

Formerly: AM Magazine
Editorial Address: Drayton St. Leonard, WALLINGFORD, OX10 7BG **Tel:** 01865 400400 **Fax:** 01865 400200
Email: am@amoc.org
Advertising Address: As above.
Email: marcella.brown@amoc.org
Web site: http://www.amoc.org
Publisher: AMOC Ltd
Date Established: 1948
Frequency: Quarterly
Free to qualifying individuals
Circulation: 5,500 (Publisher's Statement)
Usual Pagination: 56
Editor: David Lewington
Summary of Content: Official journal of the Aston Martin Owners Club.
Readership/Target Audience: Read by members of the AMOC worldwide.
ADVERTISING RATES:
Full Page Colour £910.00
Mechanical Data: Type Area: 260 x 185mm, Bleed Size: 270 x 195mm, Col Length: 260mm, Page Width: 185mm, Trim Size: 285 x 210mm, Film: Digital
Copy instructions: Copy Date: 2 months prior to publication date
Average advertising content per issue: 12%
CONSUMER: MOTORING & CYCLING: Club Cars

AMATEUR GARDENING
48551U93-10

Editorial Address: Westover House, West Quay Road, POOLE, BH15 1JG **Tel:** 01202 440840 **Fax:** 01202 440860
Email: amateurgardening@ipcmedia.com
Advertising Address: Blue Fin Building, 110 Southwark Street, LONDON, SE1 0SU **Tel:** 020 3148 5000
Fax: 020 3148 8155
Email: mark_read@ipcmedia.com
Web site: http://www.amateurgardening.com
ISSN: 0954-8513
Publisher: IPC Inspire
Date Established: 1884
Frequency: Weekly
Cover Price: £1.80
Circulation: 42,691 (ABC 01/01/2009 to 30/06/2009)
Usual Pagination: 50
Editor: Marc Rosenberg; **News Editor:** Marc Rosenberg;
Managing Director: Paul Williams; **Publisher:** Hazel Eccles
Summary of Content: Magazine containing practical gardening tips, celebrity garden experts, news, letters, and advice on gardening problems.
Readership/Target Audience: Read by those interested in plants and gardening.
ADVERTISING RATES:
Full Page Mono £2160.00
Full Page Colour £2825.00
Agency Commission: 15%

Consumer Magazines

Mechanical Data: Trim Size: 297 x 210mm, Bleed Size: 303 x 216mm, Film: Digital, Type Area: 251 x 190mm, Col Length: 251mm, Page Width: 190mm
CONSUMER: GARDENING

AMATEUR PHOTOGRAPHER
47588U85A-10

Editorial Address: Blue Fin Building, 110 Southwark Street, LONDON, SE1 0SU **Tel:** 020 3148 5000 **Fax:** 020 3148 8130
Email: amateurphotographer@ipcmedia.com
Advertising Address: As above.
Email: dave_stone@ipcmedia.com
Web site: http://www.amateurphotographer.com
ISSN: 0002-6840
Publisher: IPC Inspire
Date Established: 1884
Frequency: Weekly
Cover Price: £2.40
Annual Sub.: £119.60
Circulation: 22,242 (ABC 01/01/2008 to 31/12/2008)
Usual Pagination: 100
Editor: Chris Cheesman; **News Editor:** Chris Cheesman; **Features Editor:** Gemma Padley; **Advertising Manager:** Dave Stone
Summary of Content: Magazine containing news and product tests, plus interviews and articles about photographic techniques.
Readership/Target Audience: Aimed at amateur photographers, semi-professionals and professionals.
ADVERTISING RATES:
Full Page Mono £925.00
Full Page Colour £1500.00
Agency Commission: 10%
Mechanical Data: Type Area: 282 x 188mm, Col Length: 282mm, Page Width: 188mm, Film: Digital, Bleed Size: 303 x 216mm, Trim Size: 297 x 210mm
Copy instructions: Copy Date: 2 weeks prior to publication date
Average advertising content per issue: 50%
CONSUMER: PHOTOGRAPHY & FILM MAKING: Photography

AMATEUR STAGE
46072U76B-100

Editorial Address: Hampden House, 2 Weymouth Street, LONDON, W1W 5BT **Tel:** 020 7636 4343
Fax: 020 7636 2323
Email: editor@asmagazine.co.uk
Advertising Address: As above.
Email: editor@asmagazine.co.uk
Web site: http://www.amateurstagemagazine.co.uk
Publisher: Mixed Phase Media Ltd
Date Established: 1946
Frequency: Monthly - Published on the 1st of every month
Cover Price: £2.40
Annual Sub.: £24.00
Circulation: 6,000 (Publisher's Statement)
Usual Pagination: 36
Editor: Doug Mayo
Summary of Content: Magazine covering the amateur theatre world. Contains reviews of the latest productions and practical techniques.
Readership/Target Audience: Read by anyone involved in amateur or community theatre.
ADVERTISING RATES:
Full Page Colour £400.00
Agency Commission: 10%
Mechanical Data: Col Length: 273mm, Page Width: 190mm, Trim Size: 297 x 210mm, Bleed Size: 303 x 216mm, Type Area: 273 x 190mm, Film: Digital
Copy instructions: Copy Date: 1st of the month prior to publication date
Average advertising content per issue: 33%
CONSUMER: MUSIC & PERFORMING ARTS: Theatre

AMATEUR SWIMMING ASSOCIATION HANDBOOK
45963U75M-10

Editorial Address: Harold Fern House, Derby Square, LOUGHBOROUGH, LE11 5AL **Tel:** 01509 618700
Fax: 01509 618701
Email: reception@swimming.org
Advertising Address: 41 Granby Street, LOUGHBOROUGH, LE11 3DU **Tel:** 01509 632231
Fax: 01509 632233
Email: advertising@swimming.org
Web site: http://www.britishswimming.org
Publisher: Amateur Swimming Association
Frequency: Annual - Published the beginning of January
Cover Price: £7.00
Circulation: 3,500 (Publisher's Statement)
Usual Pagination: 250
Editor: David Richards
Summary of Content: Handbook containing ASA laws, championship conditions and results, records, award schemes, teaching certificates, reviews, ASA/GB past and present champions in all disciplines.
Readership/Target Audience: Aimed at affiliated ASA swimming club members.

ADVERTISING RATES:
Full Page Mono £645.00
Full Page Colour £755.00
Agency Commission: 10%
Mechanical Data: Col Widths (Display): 87mm, No. of Columns (Display): 3, Film: Digital
Copy instructions: Copy Date: 10 days prior to publication date
Average advertising content per issue: 50%
CONSUMER: SPORT: Water Sports

AMBIT
47533U84B-10

Editorial Address: 17 Priory Gardens, LONDON, N6 5QY
Tel: 020 8340 3566
Advertising Address: As above.
Web site: http://www.ambitmagazine.co.uk
ISSN: 0002-6772
Publisher: Ambit
Date Established: 1959
Frequency: Quarterly
Cover Price: £7.00
Annual Sub.: £28.00
Circulation: 1,250 (Publisher's Statement)
Usual Pagination: 96
Editor: Martin Bax; **Advertising Manager:** Pamela Courtney; **Circulation Manager:** Kate Pemberton
Summary of Content: Magazine with poems, short stories, reviews and art.
Readership/Target Audience: Read by art and literature enthusiasts.
CONSUMER: THE ARTS & LITERARY: Literary

THE AMBRIDGE VOICE
713854U76C-85

Formerly: The Archers Ambridge Voice
Editorial Address: The Village Voice Company, The Mansley Centre, Timothys Bridge Road, STRATFORD-UPON-AVON, CV37 9NQ **Tel:** 0870 874 4400
Fax: 01789 207481
Email: dum.di.dum@archers-addicts.com
Advertising Address: As above.
Email: dum.di.dum@archers-addicts.com
Web site: http://www.archers-addicts.com
Publisher: Archers Addicts
Date Established: 2001
Frequency: Quarterly
Annual Sub.: £21.00
Circulation: 20,000 (Publisher's Statement)
Usual Pagination: 16
Editor: Kate Tanner; **Advertising Manager:** Hedli Tanner
Summary of Content: Magazine covering issues related to storylines in 'The Archers' radio programme including food, wine, health, beauty, home, recipes, gardening, travel, lifestyle, competitions and giveaways. Includes 'Village Shop' brochure selling Archers memorabilia.
Readership/Target Audience: Read by members of Archers Addicts official fan club for BBC Radio 4's The Archers.
ADVERTISING: Rates on application
CONSUMER: MUSIC & PERFORMING ARTS: TV & Radio

THE AMERICAN
48278U90-20

Editorial Address: Old Byre House, East Knoyle, SALISBURY, SP3 6AW **Tel:** 01747 830520
Fax: 01747 830691
Email: theamerican@blueedge.co.uk
Advertising Address: As above.
Email: theamerican@blueedge.co.uk
Web site: http://www.theamerican.co.uk
Publisher: Blue Edge Publishing
Date Established: 1976
Frequency: Monthly - Published at the end of the month prior to cover date
Cover Price: £2.00
Free to qualifying individuals
Circulation: 10,600 (Publisher's Statement)
Usual Pagination: 68
Editor: Michael Burland; **Advertising Manager:** Sabrina Sully; **Publisher:** Sabrina Sully
Summary of Content: Magazine featuring important information about living in the UK and entertainment sources for Americans living in and visiting the UK.
Readership/Target Audience: Aimed at Americans and their families living in the UK and American tourists visiting Britain. Distributed at The American Embassy, major international businesses, American clubs and associations, schools and colleges, church and faith groups, military bases, hotels, airport lounges and private hospitals.
ADVERTISING RATES:
Full Page Colour £950.00
Agency Commission: 15%
Mechanical Data: Trim Size: 380 x 270mm, Film: Digital, Col Widths (Display): 41mm, No. of Columns (Display): 6
Copy instructions: Copy Date: 12th of the month prior to publication date
CONSUMER: ETHNIC

AMERICAN CAR WORLD
46507U77R-400

Formerly: Street Machine
Editorial Address: Nimax House, 20 Ullswater Crescent, Ullswater Business Park, COULSDON, CH5 2HR
Tel: 020 8655 6400
Email: acw@chpltd.com
Advertising Address: As above.
Email: ads@chpltd.com
Web site: http://www.chpltd.com
ISSN: 0969-3726
Publisher: CH Publications Ltd
Date Established: 1993
Frequency: Monthly
Cover Price: £3.60
Annual Sub.: £32.00
Circulation: 20,219 (Publisher's Statement)
Usual Pagination: 84
Editor: Richard Nicholls; **Managing Director:** Clive Househam; **Advertising Manager:** Frank Archer; **Publisher:** Nigel Fryatt
Summary of Content: Magazine covering trends in the performance American car scene.
Readership/Target Audience: Read by those with an interest in American cars, modifying and new products for American cars.
ADVERTISING RATES:
Full Page Mono £880.00
Full Page Colour £980.00
Agency Commission: 10%
Mechanical Data: Page Width: 190mm, Type Area: 267 x 190mm, Col Length: 267mm, Trim Size: 297 x 210mm, Bleed Size: 306 x 216mm, Film: Digital
Copy instructions: Copy Date: 2 weeks prior to publication date
CONSUMER: MOTORING & CYCLING: Motoring & Cycling Related

AMERICAN IN BRITAIN
48279U90-21

Editorial Address: PO Box 921, SUTTON, SM1 2WB
Tel: 020 8661 0186 **Fax:** 020 8652 3564
Email: helen@theamericanhour.com
Advertising Address: As above.
Publisher: American in Britain
Date Established: 1983
Frequency: Quarterly
Cover Price: £5.00
Annual Sub.: £20.00
Circulation: 20,000 (Publisher's Statement)
Usual Pagination: 40
Editor: Helen Elliott; **Managing Director:** Helen Elliott; **Advertising Manager:** Helen Elliott; **Publisher:** Helen Elliott
Summary of Content: Magazine featuring news, features and places to visit in the UK. Includes articles on finance, education, property, theatre and women's clubs news.
Readership/Target Audience: Aimed at Americans living in Britain.
ADVERTISING RATES:
Full Page Mono £2200.00
Full Page Colour £2800.00
Agency Commission: 10%
Mechanical Data: Type Area: 264 x 180mm, Col Length: 264mm, Page Width: 180mm, Trim Size: 297 x 210mm, Bleed Size: 304 x 216mm, No. of Columns (Display): 3, Film: Digital
Average advertising content per issue: 30%
CONSUMER: ETHNIC

THE AMERICAS REVIEW
47304U82-2_11

Editorial Address: 11 Clarendon Street, CAMBRIDGE, CB1 1JU **Tel:** 01223 351584 **Fax:** 01224 351584
Email: suehewitt11@hotmail.com
Advertising Address: As above. **Fax:** 01223 351584
Email: suehewitt11@hotmail.com
Web site: http://www.worldinformation.com
ISSN: 1351-4571
Publisher: World of Information
Date Established: 1979
Frequency: Annual - Published in the spring
Cover Price: £50.00
Circulation: 5,000 (Publisher's Statement)
Usual Pagination: 280
Editor: Anthony Axon; **Advertising Manager:** Sue Hewitt; **Publisher:** Anthony Axon
Summary of Content: Magazine containing country economic and political profiles.
Readership/Target Audience: Aimed at those interested in the economic and political growth in the Americas, including Government, businesses, universities and NGOs.
ADVERTISING RATES:
Full Page Colour £4950.00
Agency Commission: 15%
Mechanical Data: Trim Size: 270 x 210mm, Bleed Size: 276 x 216mm, Type Area: 235.5 x 172mm, Col Length: 235.5mm, Page Width: 172mm, Print Process: Offset litho, Film: Digital
Copy instructions: Copy Date: End of September prior to publication date

Average advertising content per issue: 10%
CONSUMER: CURRENT AFFAIRS & POLITICS

AMERSHAM EXCLUSIVE
1892643U80C-5490

Editorial Address: For all contact details see main edition, Exclusive (Chilterns)
Frequency: Quarterly
Cover Price: Free
Circulation: 5,000 (Publisher's Statement)
ADVERTISING: Rates on application
Edition of: Exclusive (Chilterns)
CONSUMER: RURAL & REGIONAL INTEREST: Regional Interest English Counties

AMNESTY
47200U82-2_10

Editorial Address: 17-25 New Inn Yard, LONDON, EC2A 3EY **Tel:** 020 7033 1500 **Fax:** 020 7033 1503
Email: sct@amnesty.org.uk
Advertising Address: Terry Lock Media Sales, 3 Forest Way, ASHTEAD, KT21 1JN **Tel:** 01372 276233
Fax: 0870 705 1901
Email: tslock@terrylockmediasales.co.uk
Web site: http://www.amnesty.org.uk
ISSN: 0264-3278
Publisher: Amnesty International UK
Frequency: 6 issues yearly
Cover Price: £2.00
Free to qualifying individuals
Annual Sub.: £12.00
Circulation: 200,000 (Publisher's Statement)
Usual Pagination: 32
Editor: Maggie Paterson; **Advertising Manager:** Terry Lock
Summary of Content: Magazine with news and features on human rights issues around the world. Also carries key campaign news and occasional book, music and theatre reviews.
Readership/Target Audience: Aimed at Amnesty International members.
ADVERTISING RATES:
Full Page Colour £3500.00
Agency Commission: 10%
Mechanical Data: Type Area: 250 x 184mm, Col Length: 250mm, Trim Size: 280 x 210mm, Bleed Size: 286 x 216mm, Film: Digital, Page Width: 184mm
CONSUMER: CURRENT AFFAIRS & POLITICS

THE AMPLEFORTH JOURNAL
47674U87-7

Editorial Address: Ampleforth College, YORK, YO62 4EY **Tel:** 01439 766867 **Fax:** 01439 788182
Email: lfk@ampleforth.org.uk
Advertising Address: As above. **Tel:** 01439 766000
Fax: 01439 788770
Publisher: Ampleforth Abbey Trustees
Date Established: 1895
Frequency: Annual - Published in December
Cover Price: £12.95
Circulation: 5,000 (Publisher's Statement)
Usual Pagination: 350
Editor: Liam Kelly
Summary of Content: Magazine containing articles on theology, current affairs and spirituality.
Readership/Target Audience: Read by Roman Catholics aged between 18 and 80 years old and those interested in spirituality.
ADVERTISING: Rates on application
CONSUMER: RELIGIOUS

AN ESSEX WEDDING
1790465U74L-256

Editorial Address: Broseley House, Newland Drive, WITHAM, CM8 2UL **Tel:** 01376 514000 **Fax:** 01376 514555
Email: editor@anessexwedding.com
Advertising Address: As above. **Tel:** 0870 609 1628
Email: markw@countymediamagazines.com
Web site: http://www.anessexwedding.com
ISSN: 1745-6541
Publisher: Kline Davis Ltd
Date Established: 2005
Frequency: 6 issues yearly
Cover Price: £2.95
Circulation: 5,000 (Publisher's Statement)
Usual Pagination: 108
Editor: Lisa Morgan; **Features Editor:** Lisa Morgan; **Group Editor:** Emma Cant
Summary of Content: Magazine covering all aspects of weddings including venues, fashion, real weddings, honeymoons, grooms, cakes, catering, news, events, give-aways, letters, questions and answer.
Readership/Target Audience: Aimed at brides and grooms in the Essex area and surrounds.
ADVERTISING RATES:
Full Page Colour £900.00
Agency Commission: 10%
Mechanical Data: Bleed Size: 303 x 216mm, Trim Size: 297 x 210mm, Film: Digital

Copy instructions: Copy Date: 2 weeks prior to publication date
Average advertising content per issue: 40%
CONSUMER: WOMEN'S INTEREST CONSUMER MAGAZINES: Brides

AN MAGAZINE
47482U84A-25

Editorial Address: 1st Floor, 7-15 Pink Lane, NEWCASTLE UPON TYNE, NE1 5DW **Tel:** 0191 241 8000
Fax: 0191 241 8001
Email: edit@a-n.co.uk
Advertising Address: Unit 16, 28 Commercial Street, LONDON, E1 6AB **Tel:** 020 7655 0390 **Fax:** 020 7655 0396
Email: ads@a-n.co.uk
Web site: http://www.a-n.co.uk
Publisher: AN: The Artists Information Company
Frequency: 10 issues yearly
Cover Price: £5.95
Annual Sub.: £60.00
Circulation: 16,000 (Publisher's Statement)
Usual Pagination: 60
Editor: Stephen Palmer; **Advertising Manager:** Maggie Tran
Summary of Content: Magazine containing features on visual arts practice, reviews of artist-led events, jobs and opportunities for artists, directory of art services suppliers, and extensive exhibition listings.
Readership/Target Audience: Aimed at visual and applied artists, photographers and arts professionals.
ADVERTISING RATES:
Full Page Colour £1555.00
Agency Commission: 10%
Mechanical Data: Trim Size: 297 x 210mm, Bleed Size: 303 x 216mm, No. of Columns (Display): 4, Col Length: 262mm, Film: Digital, Col Widths (Display): 44mm, Type Area: 262 x 191mm, Page Width: 191mm
Copy instructions: Copy Date: 8th of the month prior to publication date
Average advertising content per issue: 45%
CONSUMER: THE ARTS & LITERARY: Arts

ANCESTORS
754891U94X-4_75

Editorial Address: Ruskin Avenue, RICHMOND, TW9 4DU **Tel:** 020 8392 5370 **Fax:** 020 8392 5266
Email: ancestors@nationalarchives.gov.uk
Advertising Address: The Drill Hall, Eastgate, BARNSLEY, S70 2EU **Tel:** 01226 734704 **Fax:** 01226 734703
Email: carolynm@whmagazines.co.uk
Web site: http://www.ancestorsmagazine.co.uk
ISSN: 1474-2470
Publisher: The National Archives
Date Established: 2001
Frequency: 13 issues yearly
Cover Price: £3.99
Circulation: 10,000 (Publisher's Statement)
Usual Pagination: 74
Editor: Simon Fowler; **Advertising Manager:** Carolyn Mills
Summary of Content: Official family history magazine of the National Archives covering genealogy, family, military, social and local history, news from the National Archives and the Family Records centre and other archives. Also includes articles on related internet and computer technology issues.
Readership/Target Audience: Aimed at family historians, local historians and military historians.
ADVERTISING RATES:
Full Page Mono £500.00
Full Page Colour £700.00
SCC £13.50
Agency Commission: 10%
Average advertising content per issue: 20%
CONSUMER: OTHER CLASSIFICATIONS: Miscellaneous

ANCIENT EGYPT
626273U94X-256

Editorial Address: 6 Branden Drive, KNUTSFORD, WA16 8EJ **Tel:** 01565 633106
Email: ancientegyptmag@aol.com
Advertising Address: 1 Newton Street, MANCHESTER, M1 1HW **Tel:** 0161 872 3319 **Fax:** 0161 872 4721
Email: adverts@ancientegyptmagazine.com
Web site: http://www.ancientegyptmagazine.com
ISSN: 1470-9990
Publisher: Ancient Egypt Magazine Ltd
Date Established: 2000
Frequency: 6 issues yearly
Cover Price: £4.40
Annual Sub.: £24.00
Usual Pagination: 68
Editor: Robert Partridge; **Advertising Manager:** Mike Massey; **Publisher:** Peter Ireland
Summary of Content: Magazine on the history, people and culture of ancient Egypt, with articles on the latest discoveries and research written by Egyptologists or experts in their specialist field. Also includes reviews of international exhibitions, educational material and books and full listing of the many Egyptology Societies in the UK and some in Europe and details of their meetings.

Readership/Target Audience: Aimed at experts, enthusiasts, students and anyone with an interest in Ancient Egypt.
ADVERTISING RATES:
Full Page Mono £450.00
Full Page Colour £700.00
Agency Commission: 10%
Mechanical Data: Col Length: 265mm, Film: Positive, right reading, emulsion side down. Digital, No. of Columns (Display): 4, Type Area: 265 x 190mm, Screen: 60 lpc, Bleed Size: 301 x 216mm, Page Width: 190mm
Copy instructions: Copy Date: 3 weeks prior to publication date
CONSUMER: OTHER CLASSIFICATIONS: Miscellaneous

ANGEL & NORTH
46817U80B-10

Formerly: Angel Magazine
Editorial Address: Avon House 5th Floor, Kensington Village, Avonmore Road, LONDON, W14 8TS **Tel:** 020 7605 2270 **Fax:** 020 7359 6001
Email: mark.kebble@archant.co.uk
Advertising Address: Unit 2, Whitehorse Yard, 78 Liverpool Road, LONDON, N1 0QD **Tel:** 020 7359 5500
Fax: 020 7359 6001
Email: karen.brodie@archant.co.uk
Web site: http://www.angelmagazine.co.uk
Publisher: Archant Life
Frequency: Monthly
Cover Price: Free
Circulation: 52,635 (Publisher's Statement)
Editor: Mark Kebble; **Publisher:** Jeremy Moreton
Summary of Content: Magazine containing local news, entertainment, events and views.
Readership/Target Audience: Read by residents and local businesses in London.
ADVERTISING RATES:
Full Page Colour £1804.00
Agency Commission: 10%
Mechanical Data: Type Area: 273 x 200mm, Bleed Size: 306 x 236mm, Trim Size: 300 x 230mm, Film: Digital, Col Length: 273mm, Page Width: 200mm
Copy instructions: Copy Date: 3 weeks prior to publication date
Average advertising content per issue: 40%
CONSUMER: RURAL & REGIONAL INTEREST: Regional Interest Greater London

ANGELS & URCHINS
1637772U80B-396

Editorial Address: PO Box 32654, LONDON, W14 0EW **Tel:** 020 7603 1366 **Fax:** 020 7602 7208
Email: annie@angelsandurchins.co.uk
Advertising Address: 11 Dewhurst Road, LONDON, W14 0ET **Tel:** 020 8749 2470 **Fax:** 020 7602 7208
Email: advertising@angelsandurchins.co.uk
Web site: http://www.angelsandurchins.co.uk
Publisher: Angels & Urchins Ltd
Date Established: 2001
Frequency: Quarterly
Free to qualifying individuals
Annual Sub.: £12.00
Circulation: 50,000 (Publisher's Statement)
Usual Pagination: 100
Editor: Annie Reid
Summary of Content: Magazine covering day trips, shopping, restaurant reviews, nannies, children's party ideas, parenting resources and pregnancy advice as well as travel ideas with and without children, homeopathic remedies, book and film and an extensive kids' London section including drama, sports, music and movement classes.
Readership/Target Audience: Aimed at parents of children aged under 10 years old in London.
ADVERTISING RATES:
Full Page Colour £1400.00
Agency Commission: 10%
Mechanical Data: Type Area: 271 x 184mm, Col Length: 271mm, Page Width: 184mm, Film: Digital, Trim Size: 297 x 210mm, Bleed Size: +3mm, Col Widths (Display): 44mm, No. of Columns (Display): 4
Copy instructions: Copy Date: 4 weeks prior to publication date
Average advertising content per issue: 40%
CONSUMER: RURAL & REGIONAL INTEREST: Regional Interest Greater London

ANGLER'S MAIL
48518U92-10

Editorial Address: Blue Fin Building, 110 Southwark Street, LONDON, SE1 0SU **Tel:** 020 3148 5000 **Fax:** 020 3148 8129
Email: anglersmail@ipcmedia.com
Advertising Address: As above. **Tel:** 020 3148 2517
Email: lee_morris@ipcmedia.com
Web site: http://www.anglersmail.com
ISSN: 0003-3423
Publisher: IPC Inspire
Frequency: Weekly
Cover Price: £1.70
Circulation: 34,668 (ABC 01/01/2008 to 31/12/2008)

Consumer Magazines

Usual Pagination: 72
Editor: Tim Knight; **Features Editor:** Richard Howard;
Advertising Manager: Lee Morris
Summary of Content: Magazine focusing on coarse and
sea fishing events, performances and tackle.
Readership/Target Audience: Read by coarse anglers and
some sea anglers.
ADVERTISING RATES:
Full Page Colour £1500.00
Agency Commission: 15%
Mechanical Data: Film: Digital, Type Area: 258 x 189mm,
Bleed Size: 303 x 216mm, Trim Size: 297 x 210mm, Col
Length: 258mm, Page Width: 189mm
Copy instructions: Copy Date: Tuesday midday prior to
publication date
Average advertising content per issue: 25%
CONSUMER: ANGLING & FISHING

ANGLIA AFLOAT
1659231U91A-286
Formerly: Norfolk Afloat
Editorial Address: Prospect House, Rouen Road,
NORWICH, NR1 1RE **Tel:** 07768 392800
Email: angliaafloat@archant.co.uk
Advertising Address: As above. **Tel:** 01603 772184
Fax: 01603 615343
Email: wendy.wright@archant.co.uk
Web site: http://www.angliaafloat.co.uk
Publisher: Archant Norfolk
Date Established: 2003
Frequency: 6 issues yearly
Cover Price: £3.95
Circulation: 5,500 (Publisher's Statement)
Usual Pagination: 132
Editor: Sophie Duncan
Summary of Content: Magazine covering tests on the latest
yachts, dinghies, cruisers and engines, news from classic
sailing regattas and environmental issues as well as eating
out, natural history, nostalgia, angling, walks, competitions,
news, safety, offers and giveaways.
Readership/Target Audience: Aimed at those who love
boating and water activities either sail or power.
ADVERTISING RATES:
Full Page Mono £700.00
Full Page Colour £700.00
Agency Commission: 15%
Mechanical Data: Type Area: 271 x 199mm, Col Length:
271mm, Page Width: 199mm, Film: Digital, Bleed Size: 306 x
226mm, Trim Size: 300 x 220mm, No. of Columns (Display):
4, Col Widths (Display): 46mm
Average advertising content per issue: 30%
CONSUMER: RECREATION & LEISURE: Boating & Yachting

ANGLING TIMES
48519U92-30
Editorial Address: Bushfield House, Orton Centre,
PETERBOROUGH, PE2 5UW **Tel:** 01733 232600
Fax: 01733 465658
Email: stephen.stones@bauermedia.co.uk
Advertising Address: As above. **Tel:** 01733 468000
Fax: 01733 288025
Email: kaylea.frost@bauerconsumer.co.uk
Publisher: Bauer Media Ltd (Orton)
Date Established: 1953
Frequency: Weekly - Double issue week before Christmas
Cover Price: £1.60
Annual Sub.: £60.00
Circulation: 51,114 (ABC 01/01/2008 to 31/12/2008)
Usual Pagination: 56
Editor: Steven Partner; **News Editor:** Stephen Stones
Summary of Content: Publication covering angling news
and features on coarse and sea fishing. Includes the latest
match results and product reviews.
Readership/Target Audience: Aimed at those with a
general interest in fishing.
ADVERTISING RATES:
Full Page Colour £2500.00
Agency Commission: 10%
Mechanical Data: Film: Digital, Trim Size: 326 x 270mm
Copy instructions: Copy Date: Tuesday prior to publication
date
Average advertising content per issue: 30%
CONSUMER: ANGLING & FISHING

THE ANGLO-HELLENIC REVIEW
626453U90-21_50
Editorial Address: 23 Jeffreys Street, LONDON, NW1 9PS
Tel: 020 7267 3877
Email: paul.watkins@virgin.net
Advertising Address: As above.
Email: paul.watkins@virgin.net
Web site: http://www.hellenicbookservice.com/ahr.htm
ISSN: 1351-9107
Publisher: Anglo-Hellenic League
Date Established: 1990
Frequency: Half-yearly - Published in April and September
Cover Price: £2.00
Annual Sub.: £6.00

Circulation: 1,500 (Publisher's Statement)
Usual Pagination: 32
Editor: Paul Watkins; **Advertising Manager:** Paul Watkins
Summary of Content: Magazine covering Greek cultural
affairs and academic reviews.
Readership/Target Audience: Aimed at academics and
Philhellenes.
ADVERTISING RATES:
Full Page Mono £150.00
Mechanical Data: Page Width: 180mm, Type Area: 260 x
180mm, Col Length: 260mm, Print Process: Litho, Trim Size:
297 x 210mm, Bleed Size: 303 x 216mm
Average advertising content per issue: 10%
CONSUMER: ETHNIC

ANIMAL ACTION
47074U81A-18
Editorial Address: Wilberforce Way, Southwater,
HORSHAM, RH13 9RS **Tel:** 0300 123 0100
Fax: 0300 123 0048
Email: publications@rspca.org.uk
Advertising Address: Orange 20, 20 Orange Street,
LONDON, WC2H 7EF **Tel:** 01372 802802
Fax: 01372 723322
Email: sales@o20.co.uk
Web site: http://www.rspca.org.uk
Publisher: RSPCA
Date Established: 1994
Frequency: 7 issues yearly
Cover Price: £1.99
Free to qualifying individuals
Annual Sub.: £10.00
Circulation: 23,950 (ABC 01/01/2008 to 31/12/2008)
Usual Pagination: 44
Editor: Sarah Evans; **Advertising Manager:** Robin Johnson
Summary of Content: Official magazine of the RSPCA.
Contains news stories relating to animal welfare,
environmental issues and topical campaigns. Also includes
celebrity interviews, competitions and a creature feature
page.
Readership/Target Audience: Aimed at younger members
of the RSPCA aged 8 to 13 years old.
ADVERTISING RATES:
Full Page Colour £1850.00
Agency Commission: 10%
Mechanical Data: Bleed Size: 305 x 215mm, Trim Size: 297
x 210mm, Type Area: 272 x 186mm, Film: Digital, Col
Length: 272mm, Page Width: 186mm
Copy instructions: Copy Date: 6 weeks prior to publication
date
CONSUMER: ANIMALS & PETS: Animals & Pets Protection

ANIMAL DEFENDER AND THE CAMPAIGNER
47083U81A-40
Formerly: The Campaigner and Animal Defender
Editorial Address: Millbank Tower, Millbank, LONDON,
SW1P 4QP **Tel:** 020 7630 3340 **Fax:** 020 7828 2179
Email: pr@ad-international.org
Advertising Address: As above.
Email: sarahdickinson@ad-international.org.uk
Web site: http://www.ad-international.org
Publisher: Animal Defenders International
Date Established: 1881
Frequency: Half-yearly - Published in July and November
Cover Price: £2.50
Free to qualifying individuals
Circulation: 150,000
Usual Pagination: 30
Editor: Jan Creamer; **Advertising Manager:** Sarah
Dickinson
Summary of Content: Journal of the Animal Defenders,
Animal Welfare and Conservation group. Covers news,
campaigns, reports, promotions and features on undercover
investigations as well as reports on the campaign against
live animal experiments and reviews of the activities of the
National Anti-Vivisection Society.
Readership/Target Audience: Read by members and those
with an interest in animal welfare.
ADVERTISING: Rates on application
CONSUMER: ANIMALS & PETS: Animals & Pets Protection

ANIMAL LIFE
47075U81A-20
Editorial Address: Wilberforce Way, Southwater,
HORSHAM, RH13 9RS **Tel:** 0870 010 1181
Fax: 0870 753 0048
Email: publications@rspca.org.uk
Advertising Address: Terry Lock Media Sales Ltd, 3 Forest
Way, ASHTEAD, KT21 1JN **Tel:** 01372 276233
Fax: 0870 705 1901
Email: tslock@terrylockmediasales.co.uk
Web site: http://www.rspca.org.uk
ISSN: 0964-4628
Publisher: RSPCA
Frequency: Quarterly
Cover Price: £3.50
Free to qualifying individuals
Annual Sub.: £10.00

Circulation: 50,000 (Publisher's Statement)
Usual Pagination: 36
Editor: Elayne DeLaurian; **Advertising Manager:** Terry Lock
Summary of Content: Official journal of the RSPCA with
news and reports on all aspects of animal welfare.
Readership/Target Audience: Read by members of the
RSPCA.
ADVERTISING RATES:
Full Page Colour £4000.00
Agency Commission: 10%
Mechanical Data: Type Area: 272 x 186mm, Trim Size: 297
x 210mm, Bleed Size: 303 x 216mm, Col Length: 272mm,
Film: Digital, Page Width: 186mm
Copy instructions: Copy Date: 4 weeks prior to publication
date
Average advertising content per issue: 25%
CONSUMER: ANIMALS & PETS: Animals & Pets Protection

ANIMALS AND YOU
48445U91D-9
Formerly: Animals and You Monthly
Editorial Address: 2 Albert Square, DUNDEE, DD1 9QJ
Tel: 01382 223131 **Fax:** 01382 322214
Email: mmonaghan@dcthomson.co.uk
Advertising Address: Orange 20 Ltd, 20 Orange Street,
LONDON, WC2H 7EF **Tel:** 01372 802802
Fax: 01372 723322
Email: sales@o20.co.uk
Publisher: D.C. Thomson & Co Ltd
Date Established: 1998
Frequency: 17 issues yearly
Cover Price: £1.99
Circulation: 23,045 (ABC 01/01/2009 to 30/06/2009)
Usual Pagination: 44
Editor: Margaret Monaghan; **Features Editor:** Jackie Guild;
Advertising Manager: Michelle Fairlamb
Summary of Content: Children's magazine containing
features on animals and pets. Includes stories, pet charities,
puzzles, new products and activities.
Readership/Target Audience: Aimed at 7 to 11 year old
girls who care about animals.
ADVERTISING RATES:
Full Page Colour £2500.00
Agency Commission: 15%
Mechanical Data: Film: Digital, Type Area: 276 x 200mm,
Bleed Size: 311 x 231mm, Trim Size: 305 x 225mm, Page
Width: 200mm, Col Length: 276mm
Copy instructions: Copy Date: 5 weeks prior to publication
date
Average advertising content per issue: 10%
CONSUMER: RECREATION & LEISURE: Children & Youth

ANIMALS INTERNATIONAL
47077U81A-30
Editorial Address: 89 Albert Embankment, LONDON, SE1
7TP **Tel:** 020 7587 5000 **Fax:** 020 7793 0208
Email: press@wspa.org.uk
Web site: http://www.wspa-international.org
ISSN: 0254-3923
Publisher: World Society for the Protection of Animals
Frequency: Half-yearly
Cover Price: Free
Circulation: 55,000 (Publisher's Statement)
Usual Pagination: 36
Editor: Sarah Pickering
Summary of Content: Magazine concerned with the
promotion of animal protection, the prevention of cruelty and
the relief of suffering to animals.
Readership/Target Audience: Read by members and
supporters of the World Society for the Protection of
Animals.
ADVERTISING: No Advertising taken
CONSUMER: ANIMALS & PETS: Animals & Pets Protection

ANIMALS MATTER
47078U81A-33
Editorial Address: King's Bush Farm, London Road,
Godmanchester, HUNTINGDON, PE29 2NH
Tel: 0870 190 4090 **Fax:** 01480 832379
Email: nicola.bacon@woodgreen.org.uk
Advertising Address: As above.
Email: nicola.bacon@woodgreen.org.uk
Web site: http://www.woodgreen.org.uk
Publisher: Wood Green Animal Shelters
Date Established: 1987
Frequency: 3 issues yearly - Published in March, July and
October
Cover Price: Free
Circulation: 30,000 (Publisher's Statement)
Usual Pagination: 24
Editor: Nicola Bacon; **Advertising Manager:** Nicola Bacon
Summary of Content: Magazine about the work of the
Wood Green Animal Shelters and issues concerned with
animal welfare.
Readership/Target Audience: Aimed at supporters and
animal lovers.
ADVERTISING RATES:
Full Page Colour £1200.00

Mechanical Data: Film: Digital, Type Area: 267 x 190mm, Bleed Size: 303 x 216mm, Trim Size: 297 x 210mm, Col Length: 267mm, Page Width: 190mm
Copy instructions: Copy Date: 30 days prior to publication date
Average advertising content per issue: 10%
CONSUMER: ANIMALS & PETS: Animals & Pets Protection

ANNUAL BULLETIN OF HISTORICAL LITERATURE
31008U84B-12
Editorial Address: 76 South Parade, PUDSEY, LS28 8NX
Tel: 01484 422288
Email: enquiry@history.org.uk
Advertising Address: 9600 Garsington Road, Cowley, OXFORD, OX4 2DQ **Tel:** 01865 476261 **Fax:** 01359 242880
Email: craig.pickett@wiley.com
Web site: http://www.blackwellpub.com
ISSN: 0066-3832
Publisher: Wiley-Blackwell Publishing
Date Established: 1916
Frequency: Annual - Published in November
Annual Sub.: £88.00
Circulation: 1,000 (Publisher's Statement)
Usual Pagination: 280
Editor: Keith Laybourn
Summary of Content: A critical analysis of publications in historical literature produced two years before.
Readership/Target Audience: Read by historians, academics, librarians and those interested in historical literature.
ADVERTISING RATES:
Full Page Mono £420.00
Agency Commission: 10%
Mechanical Data: Type Area: 190 x 112mm, Col Length: 190mm, Page Width: 112mm, Film: Digital, Trim Size: 229 x 152mm
Copy instructions: Copy Date: 6 weeks prior to publication date
CONSUMER: THE ARTS & LITERARY: Literary

ANORAK
1779196U91D-967
Editorial Address: 57 Connaught Works, 251 Old Ford Road, LONDON, E3 5PS **Tel:** 07967 174954
Email: cathy@anorak-magazine.co.uk
Advertising Address: As above.
Email: cathy@anorak-magazine.co.uk
Web site: http://www.anorak-magazine.co.uk
Publisher: Oksar Ltd
Date Established: 2006
Frequency: Quarterly
Cover Price: £3.50
Circulation: 5,000 (Publisher's Statement)
Usual Pagination: 80
Editor: Cathy Olmedillas; **Advertising Manager:** Cathy Olmedillas
Summary of Content: Children's magazine covering all aspects of a child's world from fashion to stories, culture to science and sport to food.
Readership/Target Audience: Aimed at boys and girls aged 5 to 10 years old.
ADVERTISING RATES:
Full Page Mono £1000.00
Full Page Colour £1000.00
Agency Commission: 10%
Mechanical Data: Type Area: 260 x 220mm, Col Length: 260mm, Page Width: 220mm, Film: Digital
CONSUMER: RECREATION & LEISURE: Children & Youth

ANOTHER MAGAZINE
712147U74Q-4
Editorial Address: 112-116 Old Street, LONDON, EC1V 9BG **Tel:** 020 7336 0766 **Fax:** 020 7336 0966
Email: nancy@dazedgroup.com
Advertising Address: As above.
Email: advertising@dazedgroup.com
Web site: http://www.anothermag.com
Publisher: The Dazed Magazine Group
Date Established: 2001
Frequency: Half-yearly - Published in February and September
Cover Price: £6.95
Circulation: 137,266 (Publisher's Statement)
Usual Pagination: 410
Editor: Nancy Waters; **Editor-in-Chief:** Jefferson Hack; **Advertising Director:** Stephen White
Summary of Content: Luxury lifestyle magazine covering fashion and culture.
Readership/Target Audience: Aimed at men and women between 22 and 45 years old.
ADVERTISING RATES:
Full Page Mono £14220.00
Full Page Colour £14220.00
Agency Commission: 10%
Mechanical Data: Col Length: 292mm, Page Width: 222mm, Film: Digital, Type Area: 292 x 222mm
Copy instructions: Copy Date: 12 weeks prior to publication date

Average advertising content per issue: 40%
CONSUMER: WOMEN'S INTEREST CONSUMER MAGAZINES: Lifestyle

ANOTHER MAN
1695434U86C-724
Editorial Address: 112-116 Old Street, LONDON, EC1V 9BG **Tel:** 020 7336 0766
Email: caroline@dazedgroup.com
Advertising Address: As above. **Fax:** 020 7549 6860
Email: sam@dazedgroup.com
Publisher: The Dazed Magazine Group
Date Established: 2005
Frequency: Half-yearly - Published in March and October
Circulation: 155,000 (Print Run)
Editor: Caroline Lever; **Features Editor:** Hannah Lack; **Editor-in-Chief:** Jefferson Hack; **Advertising Manager:** Sam O'Shaughnessy
Summary of Content: Magazine covering men's fashion and culture.
Readership/Target Audience: Aimed at modern thinking, culture savvy and stylish men.
ADVERTISING RATES:
Full Page Mono £13006.00
Full Page Colour £13006.00
Agency Commission: 10%
Mechanical Data: Type Area: 292 x 222mm, Col Length: 292mm, Page Width: 222mm, Film: Digital, Trim Size: 302 x 232mm, Bleed Size: 308 240mm
Copy instructions: Copy Date: 8 weeks prior to publication date
Average advertising content per issue: 30%
CONSUMER: ADULT & GAY MAGAZINES: Men's Lifestyle Magazines

ANSTEY SCENE
1626732U80C-5066
Editorial Address: PO Box 8454, LEICESTER, LE9 2WU
Tel: 0116 239 4284
Email: glenfieldgazette@aol.com
Advertising Address: As above.
Email: ansteyscene@aol.com
Publisher: Gazette Publications (Leicester) Limited
Frequency: 6 issues yearly
Cover Price: Free
Circulation: 3,000 (Publisher's Statement)
Usual Pagination: 20
Editor: Ken Russell; **Advertising Manager:** Krys Lakin
Summary of Content: Local newspaper for the Anstey area covering civic, social and industrial matters.
Readership/Target Audience: Aimed at those living in the Anstey area.
ADVERTISING: Rates on application
CONSUMER: RURAL & REGIONAL INTEREST: Regional Interest English Counties

ANTHROPOLOGY TODAY
48667U94X-5
Editorial Address: 50 Fitzroy Street, LONDON, W1T 5BT
Email: anthropologytodaynews@gmail.com
Advertising Address: As above. **Tel:** 020 7387 0455
Fax: 020 7383 4235
Email: atadverts@gmail.com
Web site: http://www.therai.org.uk
ISSN: 0268-540X
Publisher: Wiley-Blackwell Publishing
Date Established: 1985
Frequency: 6 issues yearly
Annual Sub.: £20.00
Circulation: 2,000 (Publisher's Statement)
Usual Pagination: 32
Editor: Gustaaf Houtman; **Advertising Manager:** Dominique Remars
Summary of Content: Journal covering contemporary anthropology with a special focus on public and topical issues.
Readership/Target Audience: Read by anthropologists, ethnographers, Third World development experts, aid and relief specialists.
ADVERTISING RATES:
Full Page Mono £532.90
Mechanical Data: No. of Columns (Display): 3, Trim Size: 297 x 210mm, Type Area: 273 x 187mm, Page Width: 187mm, Film: Digital, Col Length: 273mm, Col Widths (Display): 60mm
Copy instructions: Copy Date: 7th of the month prior to publication date
Average advertising content per issue: 20%
CONSUMER: OTHER CLASSIFICATIONS: Miscellaneous

ANTIQUARIES JOURNAL
48748U94X-6
Editorial Address: Burlington House, Piccadilly, LONDON, W1J 0BE **Tel:** 020 7479 7080 **Fax:** 020 7287 6967
Email: admin@sal.org.uk
Web site: http://www.sal.org.uk
ISSN: 0003-5815
Publisher: The Society of Antiquaries of London

Date Established: 1920
Frequency: Annual - Published in December
Free to qualifying individuals
Annual Sub.: £87.50
Circulation: 3,000 (Publisher's Statement)
Usual Pagination: 440
Editor: Kate Owen
Summary of Content: Journal reporting on excavations in Britain and abroad, descriptions of finds, surveys of archaeological history in special fields and studies in ancient and medieval art, crafts, heraldry, social and economic life; all aspects of material culture, in Britain and the rest of the world.
Readership/Target Audience: Aimed at archaeologists, general historians, art and architectural historians and heraldists.
ADVERTISING: No Advertising taken
CONSUMER: OTHER CLASSIFICATIONS: Miscellaneous

ANTIQUE COLLECTING
46725U79K-60
Editorial Address: Sandy Lane, Old Martlesham, WOODBRIDGE, IP12 4SD **Tel:** 01394 389950
Fax: 01394 389999
Email: magazine@antique-acc.com
Advertising Address: As above. **Tel:** 01394 389970
Fax: 01394 385615
Email: paul.cawthorn@antique-acc.com
Web site: http://www.antique-collecting.co.uk
ISSN: 0003-584X
Publisher: Antique Collectors' Club Ltd
Date Established: 1966
Frequency: 10 issues yearly - Published on the 1st of the month of cover date
Annual Sub.: £35.00
Circulation: 5,000 (Publisher's Statement)
Usual Pagination: 64
Editor: Susan Wilson; **Managing Director:** Diana Steel; **Managing Editor:** John Andrews; **Publisher:** Diana Steel
Summary of Content: Magazine containing articles and features on antiques with an emphasis on practical information.
Readership/Target Audience: Aimed at those with a serious interest in antiques.
ADVERTISING RATES:
Full Page Mono £400.00
Full Page Colour £650.00
Agency Commission: 10%
Mechanical Data: Type Area: 254 x 178mm, Bleed Size: 303 x 216mm, Print Process: Offset litho, Col Length: 254mm, Page Width: 178mm, Film: Digital, Trim Size: 297 x 210mm
Copy instructions: Copy Date: 6 weeks prior to publication date
Average advertising content per issue: 20%
CONSUMER: HOBBIES & DIY: Collectors Magazines

ANTIQUES INFO
46729U79K-120
Formerly: Antiques Info Market & Price Guide
Editorial Address: Wallsend House, PO Box 93, BROADSTAIRS, CT10 3YR **Tel:** 01843 862069
Fax: 01843 862014
Email: john.ainsley@antiques-info.co.uk
Advertising Address: As above.
Web site: http://www.antiques-info.co.uk
ISSN: 1365-585X
Publisher: Antiques Information Services Ltd
Frequency: 6 issues yearly
Cover Price: £3.50
Annual Sub.: £21.00
Circulation: 25,000 (Publisher's Statement)
Usual Pagination: 100
Editor: John Ainsley; **Advertising Manager:** John Ainsley
Summary of Content: Magazine containing information on all aspects of the collecting scene including fairs, auctions, valuations, price guides, advice, support services and features on a variety of collecting related topics.
Readership/Target Audience: Aimed at those with an interest in antiques and collecting.
ADVERTISING RATES:
Full Page Mono £1000.00
Full Page Colour £1250.00
Mechanical Data: Type Area: 261 x 186mm, Col Length: 261mm, Trim Size: 288 x 213mm, Bleed Size: 294 x 219mm, Film: Digital, Page Width: 186mm
Copy instructions: Copy Date: 15th of the month prior to publication date
Average advertising content per issue: 23%
CONSUMER: HOBBIES & DIY: Collectors Magazines

ANTIQUITY
48668U94X-7
Editorial Address: King's Manor, YORK, YO1 7EP
Tel: 01904 433994 **Fax:** 01904 433994
Email: editor@antiquity.ac.uk
Advertising Address: As above.
Email: webmaster@antiquity.ac.uk
Web site: http://antiquity.ac.uk
ISSN: 0003-598X

Publisher: Antiquity Publications Ltd
Date Established: 1927
Frequency: Quarterly
Annual Sub.: £53.00
Circulation: 2,000 (Publisher's Statement)
Usual Pagination: 288
Editor: Martin Carver; **Advertising Manager:** Jo Tozer
Summary of Content: International archaeological journal containing in-depth reports, news, projects, book reviews and heritage issues. Includes articles on new methods and technologies, new research and archaeological debate.
Readership/Target Audience: Aimed at students, academics, researchers, amateurs and those involved or interested in archaeology.
ADVERTISING RATES:
Full Page Mono £365.00
Mechanical Data: Type Area: 200 x 135mm, Col Length: 200mm, Page Width: 135mm
Copy instructions: Copy Date: 10 weeks prior to publication date
CONSUMER: OTHER CLASSIFICATIONS: Miscellaneous

ANTRIM BOROUGH COUNCIL GUIDE
1686813U89C-1040

Editorial Address: Media House, 5 Broadway Court, High Street, CHESHAM, HP5 1EG **Tel:** 01494 771144
Fax: 01494 771277
Email: info@bpcmagazines.com
Advertising Address: As above.
Email: copy@bpcmagazines.com
Web site: http://www.bpcmagazines.com
Publisher: BPC Magazines
Frequency: Annual - Published in August
Cover Price: Free
Circulation: 10,000 (Publisher's Statement)
Editor: Stella Adams; **Advertising Manager:** Clare George;
Publisher: Robert Adams
Summary of Content: Town guide covering what to do, where to go, entertainment, accommodation and places to eat.
Readership/Target Audience: Aimed at residents and visitors to Co. Antrim.
ADVERTISING: Rates on application
Copy instructions: Copy Date: February 2008
CONSUMER: HOLIDAYS & TRAVEL: Entertainment Guides

THE APEX
47365U83-1_5

Editorial Address: Room 125, Helmore Building, East Road, CAMBRIDGE, CB1 1PT **Tel:** 01223 460008
Fax: 01223 417718
Email: l.pool@angliastudent.com
Advertising Address: As above.
Email: p.brizio@angliastudent.com
Web site: http://www.apusu.com/main/apex
Publisher: Anglia Ruskin Students Union
Date Established: 1992
Frequency: 8 issues yearly - Published during term time
Cover Price: Free
Circulation: 2,500 (Publisher's Statement)
Usual Pagination: 16
Editor: Lisa Pool; **Advertising Manager:** Peter Brizio
Summary of Content: Newspaper covering student issues, entertainment listings, travel, arts, music and sports.
Readership/Target Audience: Aimed at students of APU.
ADVERTISING RATES:
Full Page Colour £300.00
Agency Commission: 10%
Mechanical Data: Film: Digital, Type Area: 335 x 265 mm, Col Length: 335mm, Page Width: 265mm
CONSUMER: STUDENT PUBLICATIONS

APHRA
767533U74Q-1124

Editorial Address: PO Box 173, PETERBOROUGH, PE2 6WS **Tel:** 0845 702 3153 **Fax:** 01733 375001
Email: editorial@rnib.org.uk
Advertising Address: As above.
Email: joanna.franks@rnib.org.uk
Web site: http://www.rnib.org.uk
Publisher: Royal National Institute of Blind People
Frequency: Monthly
Cover Price: £1.90
Circulation: 200 (Publisher's Statement)
Usual Pagination: 60
Editor: Joanna Franks; **Advertising Manager:** Joanna Franks
Summary of Content: Magazine covering lifestyle, sex, fashion and politics.
Readership/Target Audience: Aimed at visually impaired women of all ages.
ADVERTISING: Rates on application
CONSUMER: WOMEN'S INTEREST CONSUMER MAGAZINES: Lifestyle

APOLLO
47483U84A-50

Editorial Address: 22 Old Queen Street, LONDON, SW1H 9HP **Tel:** 020 7961 0150
Email: editorial@apollomag.com
Advertising Address: As above. **Tel:** 020 7961 0104
Fax: 020 7961 0110
Email: advertising@apollomag.com
Web site: http://www.apollo-magazine.com
ISSN: 0003-6356
Publisher: Pressholdings
Date Established: 1925
Frequency: 11 issues yearly - Published on the 1st of each month
Cover Price: £5.50
Circulation: 10,000 (Publisher's Statement)
Usual Pagination: 100
Editor: Michael Hall; **Publisher:** Celia Baily
Summary of Content: Magazine containing articles on fine art, design and antiques.
Readership/Target Audience: Aimed at those interested in art and antiques, art galleries and museums.
ADVERTISING RATES:
Full Page Colour £1840.00
Agency Commission: 10%
Mechanical Data: No. of Columns (Display): 2, Type Area: 255 x 185mm, Col Length: 255mm, Page Width: 185mm, Col Widths (Display): 90mm, Film: Digital, Bleed Size: 291 x 226mm, Trim Size: 285 x 220mm
Copy instructions: Copy Date: 3 weeks prior to publication date
Average advertising content per issue: 35%
CONSUMER: THE ARTS & LITERARY: Arts

AQUILA MAGAZINE
48486U91D-9_20

Editorial Address: Studio 2 Willowfield Studios, 67A Willowfield Road, EASTBOURNE, BN22 8AP
Tel: 01323 431313 **Fax:** 01323 731136
Email: info@aquila.co.uk
Web site: http://www.aquila.co.uk
ISSN: 0965-4003
Publisher: New Leaf Publishing
Date Established: 1993
Frequency: Monthly
Annual Sub.: £40.00
Circulation: 8,000 (Publisher's Statement)
Usual Pagination: 24
Editor: Jackie Berry; **Publisher:** Ron Bryant-Funnell
Summary of Content: Children's magazine featuring a compilation of stories, puzzles, word games and features.
Readership/Target Audience: Aimed at lively minded children between 8 and 13 years old.
ADVERTISING: No Advertising taken
CONSUMER: RECREATION & LEISURE: Children & Youth

THE ARDS VISITOR GUIDE
1686816U80F-203

Editorial Address: Media House, 5 Broadway Court, High Street, CHESHAM, HP5 1EG **Tel:** 01494 771144
Fax: 01494 771277
Email: info@bpcmagazines.com
Advertising Address: As above.
Email: copy@bpcmagazines.com
Web site: http://www.bpcmagazines.com
Publisher: BPC Magazines
Frequency: Annual - Published in March
Cover Price: Free
Editor: Stella Adams
Summary of Content: Magazine published for Newtownards Council with local information, attractions for visitors, places to eat, accommodation and entertainment.
Readership/Target Audience: Aimed at visitors to Northern Ireland, especially the Ards region and Belfast.
ADVERTISING: Rates on application
CONSUMER: RURAL & REGIONAL INTEREST: Regional Interest Northern Ireland

---

AREA MAGAZINE
1796302U80C-5392

Editorial Address: 4B Kellaway Avenue, BRISTOL, BS6 7XR
Tel: 0845 050 4534
Email: aw@areamagazine.co.uk
Advertising Address: As above.
Email: aw@areamagazine.co.uk
Web site: http://www.areamagazine.co.uk
Publisher: Pointblank Publishing
Date Established: 2006
Frequency: Monthly
Free to qualifying individuals
Annual Sub.: £20.00
Circulation: 10,000 (Print Run)
Usual Pagination: 70
Editor: Anette Wildar; **Advertising Manager:** Anette Wildar
Summary of Content: Magazine covering entertainment, health and beauty, fashion, home and garden, travel, motoring, food and drink.
Readership/Target Audience: Aimed at affluent residents and businesses in Bristol.

ADVERTISING RATES:
Full Page Colour £800.00
Agency Commission: 10%
Mechanical Data: Bleed Size: 303 x 216mm, Trim Size: 297 x 210mm, Film: Digital
Copy instructions: Copy Date: 11th of the month prior to publication date
Average advertising content per issue: 30%
CONSUMER: RURAL & REGIONAL INTEREST: Regional Interest English Counties

---

ARENA HOMME PLUS
47639U86C-55

Editorial Address: Mappin House, 4 Winsley Street, LONDON, W1W 8HF **Tel:** 020 7182 8000
Fax: 020 7520 6560
Advertising Address: Endeavour House, 189 Shaftesbury Avenue, LONDON, WC2H 8JG **Tel:** 020 7295 5000
Fax: 020 7295 5444
Email: miles.dunbar@bauerconsumer.co.uk
ISSN: 1353-1972
Publisher: Bauer Consumer Media Ltd (Mappin House)
Date Established: 1994
Frequency: Half-yearly - Published in March and September
Cover Price: £5.00
Usual Pagination: 340
Editor: Joel Bough; **Advertising Director:** Miles Dunbar
Summary of Content: Magazine covering all aspects of fashion.
Readership/Target Audience: Aimed at fashion conscious men.
ADVERTISING RATES:
Full Page Mono £8452.50
Full Page Colour £8452.50
Agency Commission: 15%
Mechanical Data: Type Area: 280 x 210mm, Film: Digital, Col Length: 280mm, Page Width: 210mm, Bleed Size: 306 x 236mm, Trim Size: 300 x 230mm
Copy instructions: Copy Date: 1 month prior to publication date
Average advertising content per issue: 35%
CONSUMER: ADULT & GAY MAGAZINES: Men's Lifestyle Magazines

THE ARMOURER
46694U79H-10

Editorial Address: PO Box 161, CONGLETON, CW12 3WJ
Tel: 01260 278044 **Fax:** 01260 278044
Email: editor@armourer.co.uk
Advertising Address: As above.
Email: editor@armourer.co.uk
Web site: http://www.armourer.co.uk
ISSN: 1363-1004
Publisher: Beaumont Publishing Ltd
Date Established: 1994
Frequency: 6 issues yearly
Cover Price: £3.50
Annual Sub.: £22.00
Circulation: 12,500 (Publisher's Statement)
Usual Pagination: 100
Editor: Irene Moore; **Advertising Manager:** Irene Moore
Summary of Content: Magazine covering all aspects of arms and militaria with an emphasis on twentieth-century warfare.
Readership/Target Audience: Aimed at militaria and medal collectors and military history enthusiasts.
ADVERTISING RATES:
Full Page Mono £220.00
Full Page Colour £395.00
Agency Commission: 10%
Mechanical Data: Type Area: 275 x 188mm, Bleed Size: 303 x 216mm, Trim Size: 297 x 210mm, Film: Digital, Screen: 60 lpc, Col Length: 275mm, Page Width: 188mm
Copy instructions: Copy Date: 10th of the month prior to publication date
Average advertising content per issue: 40%
CONSUMER: HOBBIES & DIY: Military History

AROUND THE GLOBE
622770U76B-105

Editorial Address: 21 New Globe Walk, Bankside, LONDON, SE1 9DT **Tel:** 020 7902 1400 **Fax:** 020 7902 1401
Email: robins_nick@hotmail.com
Advertising Address: OnlyMedia, 73A New Park Road, LONDON, SW2 4EN **Tel:** 020 8674 9444 **Fax:** 020 8674 2743
Email: djeffries@onlymedia.co.uk
Web site: http://www.shakespeares-globe.org
ISSN: 1366-2317
Publisher: The Shakespeare Globe Trust
Date Established: 1996
Frequency: 3 issues yearly - Published in January, May and September
Cover Price: £2.95
Annual Sub.: £18.00
Circulation: 10,000 (Publisher's Statement)
Usual Pagination: 48
Editor: Nick Robins; **Advertising Manager:** David Jeffries
Summary of Content: Magazine covering historical and modern Shakespeare in performance, and Globe Theatre news and reviews.

Readership/Target Audience: Aimed at arts lovers, theatre goers, teachers and academics.
ADVERTISING RATES:
Full Page Mono £800.00
Full Page Colour £1000.00
Mechanical Data: Trim Size: 297 x 210mm, Film: Digital
Copy instructions: Copy Date: 1 week prior to publication date
Average advertising content per issue: 10%
CONSUMER: MUSIC & PERFORMING ARTS: Theatre

ARSENAL
45738U75B-32
Editorial Address: Highbury House, 75 Drayton Park, LONDON, N5 1BU **Tel:** 020 7704 4000 **Fax:** 020 7704 4011
Email: magazine@arsenal.co.uk
Advertising Address: Sports Revolution, 11-12 Tottenham Mews, LONDON, W1T 4AG **Tel:** 0845 226 7566
Email: sales@sportsrevolution.co.uk
Web site: http://www.arsenal.com
Publisher: CRE8
Frequency: Monthly
Cover Price: £3.25
Circulation: 30,000 (Publisher's Statement)
Usual Pagination: 84
Editor: Andy Exley
Summary of Content: Magazine of Arsenal Football Club.
Readership/Target Audience: Aimed at fans of Arsenal Football Club.
ADVERTISING RATES:
Full Page Colour £3000.00
SCC £40.00
Agency Commission: 10%
Mechanical Data: Page Width: 190mm, Type Area: 277 x 190mm, Col Length: 277mm, Trim Size: 297 x 210mm, Bleed Size: 303 x 216mm, Film: Digital
Copy instructions: Copy Date: 10 days prior to publication date
Average advertising content per issue: 8%
CONSUMER: SPORT: Football

ART ATTACK
48446U91D-10
Editorial Address: Brockbourne House, Mount Ephraim, TUNBRIDGE WELLS, TN4 8BS **Tel:** 01892 500100
Fax: 01892 545666
Email: sfrith@panini.co.uk
Advertising Address: Orange20 Ltd, Station House, Bunbury Way, EPSOM, KT17 4JP **Tel:** 01372 802800
Fax: 01372 723332
Email: panini.adsales@o20.co.uk
ISSN: 1364-0763
Publisher: Panini UK Ltd
Date Established: 1996
Frequency: 13 issues yearly
Cover Price: £2.25
Circulation: 102,000 (Publisher's Statement)
Usual Pagination: 36
Editor: Simon Frith; **Managing Director:** Mike Riddell; **Advertising Manager:** Michelle Fairlamb; **Managing Editor:** Alan O'Keefe
Summary of Content: Children's magazine and comic, featuring things to make, draw and cut-out.
Readership/Target Audience: Aimed at 7 to 12 year olds.
ADVERTISING RATES:
Full Page Colour £2500.00
Mechanical Data: Type Area: 280 x 200mm, Trim Size: 300 x 220mm, Bleed Size: 310 x 230mm, Col Length: 280mm, Page Width: 200mm, Film: Digital
CONSUMER: RECREATION & LEISURE: Children & Youth

THE ART BOOK
47534U84B-15
Editorial Address: Laughton Cottage, Brickhurst Lane, Laughton, LEWES, BN8 6DD **Tel:** 01323 811759
Email: ed-exec-theartbook@aah.org.uk
Advertising Address: 9600 Garsington Road, Cowley, OXFORD, OX4 2DQ **Tel:** 01865 776868 **Fax:** 01865 471271
Email: craig.pickett@oxon.blackwellpublishing.com
Web site: http://www.blackwellpublishing.com/journals/artbook
ISSN: 1368-6267
Publisher: Wiley-Blackwell Publishing
Date Established: 1993
Frequency: Quarterly
Cover Price: £7.00
Annual Sub.: £32.00
Circulation: 9,000 (Publisher's Statement)
Usual Pagination: 64
Editor: Sue Ward; **Executive Editor:** Sue Ward; **Advertising Manager:** Craig Pickett
Summary of Content: Magazine devoted to the critical review of newly published books on decorative, fine and applied art, art history, photography, architecture and design and screen studies. Published on behalf of the Association of Art Historians.
Readership/Target Audience: Read by librarians, professional book buyers and people interested in art, photography, architecture and design, including students and teachers of art and art history.

ADVERTISING RATES:
Full Page Mono £505.00
Full Page Colour £680.00
Mechanical Data: Trim Size: 297 x 210mm, Type Area: 265 x 175mm, Col Length: 265mm, Film: Digital, Page Width: 175mm
CONSUMER: THE ARTS & LITERARY: Literary

ART MONTHLY
47485U84A-80
Editorial Address: 4th Floor, 28 Charing Cross Road, LONDON, WC2H 0DB **Tel:** 020 7240 0389
Fax: 020 7497 0726
Email: info@artmonthly.co.uk
Advertising Address: As above. **Tel:** 020 7240 0418
Email: ads@artmonthly.co.uk
Web site: http://www.artmonthly.co.uk
ISSN: 0142-6702
Publisher: Britannia Art Publications
Date Established: 1976
Frequency: 10 issues yearly
Cover Price: £4.20
Annual Sub.: £38.00
Circulation: 6,000 (Publisher's Statement)
Usual Pagination: 58
Editor: Patricia Bickers; **Advertising Manager:** Matt Hale; **Publisher:** Jack Wendler
Summary of Content: Magazine covering modern and contemporary visual arts, interviews with leading artists, profiles, art law, news, reports from salesrooms and book reviews.
Readership/Target Audience: Read by artists, critics, curators, art historians, students, dealers, art administrators and those interested in the arts.
ADVERTISING RATES:
Full Page Mono £1330.00
Agency Commission: 10%
Mechanical Data: Page Width: 180mm, Type Area: 267 x 180mm, Bleed Size: 303 x 216mm, Trim Size: 297 x 210mm, Col Length: 267mm, Film: Digital
Copy instructions: Copy Date: 5th of the month prior to publication date
Average advertising content per issue: 20%
CONSUMER: THE ARTS & LITERARY: Arts

THE ART NEWSPAPER
47486U84A-85
Editorial Address: 70 South Lambeth Road, LONDON, SW8 1RL **Tel:** 020 7735 3331 **Fax:** 020 7735 3332
Email: listings@theartnewspaper.com
Advertising Address: As above.
Email: l.hamlin@theartnewspaper.com
Web site: http://www.theartnewspaper.com
ISSN: 0960-6556
Publisher: Umberto Allemandi & Co. Publishing, Turin
Date Established: 1990
Frequency: 11 issues yearly - Published every month except August
Cover Price: £6.95
Annual Sub.: £69.00
Circulation: 22,000 (Publisher's Statement)
Usual Pagination: 72
Editor: William Oliver; **Managing Director:** James Knox; **Publisher:** Umberto Allemandi
Summary of Content: Newspaper covering art news and visual culture worldwide. Reviews and previews of exhibitions, books, archaeology and conservation, plus in-depth discussion of the art market, dealers and galleries from around the world.
Language(s): English; French; Greek; Italian
Readership/Target Audience: Read by art dealers, collectors, museum directors, auctioneers and art professionals.
ADVERTISING RATES:
Full Page Mono £3285.00
Full Page Colour £4700.00
Agency Commission: 15%
Mechanical Data: Film: Digital, Type Area: 372 x 268mm, Col Length: 372mm, Page Width: 268mm
Copy instructions: Copy Date: 4th of month prior to publication date
Average advertising content per issue: 40%
CONSUMER: THE ARTS & LITERARY: Arts

ART OF ENGLAND
1703204U84A-449
Editorial Address: Airedale Lodge, Stafford Road, Eccleshall, STAFFORD, ST21 6JP **Tel:** 01785 851660
Fax: 01785 850173
Email: info@artofengland.uk.com
Advertising Address: As above.
Email: info@artofengland.uk.com
Web site: http://www.artofengland.com
ISSN: 1744-1930
Publisher: PMB Media
Date Established: 2003
Frequency: Monthly
Cover Price: £3.30
Annual Sub.: £25.00
Circulation: 12,000 (Publisher's Statement)

Usual Pagination: 84
Editor: Pamela Bates; **Advertising Manager:** Pamela Bates
Summary of Content: Magazine featuring galleries, exhibitions, artists' section, step by step guides on how artists produce their work, gallery reviews and a guide to what's on throughout the country.
Readership/Target Audience: Aimed at those who work within or simply enjoy the world of art.
ADVERTISING RATES:
Full Page Colour £995.00
Mechanical Data: Trim Size: 300 x 230mm, Bleed Size: 310 x 240mm, Film: Digital
CONSUMER: THE ARTS & LITERARY: Arts

ART QUARTERLY
47487U84A-90
Editorial Address: Millais House, 7 Cromwell Place, LONDON, SW7 2JN **Tel:** 020 7225 4800 **Fax:** 020 7225 4807
Email: cbugler@artfund.org
Advertising Address: As above. **Tel:** 020 7225 4835
Email: rwelbourn@artfund.org
Web site: http://www.artfund.org
Publisher: The Art Fund
Date Established: 1990
Frequency: Quarterly
Cover Price: Free
Circulation: 50,649 (ABC 01/01/2008 to 31/12/2008)
Usual Pagination: 80
Editor: Caroline Bugler; **Advertising Manager:** Rosie Welbourn
Summary of Content: General interest visual arts magazine covering art, design, sculpture and photography.
Readership/Target Audience: Read by members of the National Art Collections Fund, interested public and art world institutions and research students.
ADVERTISING RATES:
Full Page Mono £1500.00
Full Page Colour £2300.00
Mechanical Data: Film: Digital, Trim Size: 297 x 232mm, Bleed Size: +3mm, Type Area: 266 x 200mm, Col Length: 266mm, Page Width: 200mm
Copy instructions: Copy Date: 6 weeks prior to publication date
CONSUMER: THE ARTS & LITERARY: Arts

ART WORLD
1832939U84A-465
Editorial Address: 502 Clerkenwell Workshops, 27-31 Clerkenwell Close, LONDON, EC1R 0AU **Tel:** 020 7014 3438
Fax: 020 7014 3435
Email: carlayarish@artworldmagazine.com
Advertising Address: As above.
Email: kathboon@artworldmagazine.com
Web site: http://www.artworldmagazine.com
Publisher: B5 Media
Date Established: 2007
Frequency: 6 issues yearly
Cover Price: £5.95
Circulation: 16,000 (Publisher's Statement)
Usual Pagination: 144
Editor: Carla Yarish; **Advertising Director:** Kath Boon; **Publisher:** Lisa Goldstein
Summary of Content: Magazine covering wide range of emerging and established contemporary artists practicing across all disciplines with news, previews and inside information.
Readership/Target Audience: Aimed at highly educated men and women aged 25 to 54 years old who are frequent travellers with an interest in art and design.
ADVERTISING: Rates on application
CONSUMER: THE ARTS & LITERARY: Arts

ARTHRITIS NEWS
40451U94F-996
Editorial Address: 18 Stephenson Way, LONDON, NW1 2HD **Tel:** 020 7380 6521 **Fax:** 020 7380 6504
Email: editor@arthritiscare.org.uk
Web site: http://www.arthritiscare.org.uk
ISSN: 0144-6339
Publisher: Arthritis Care
Date Established: 1980
Frequency: 6 issues yearly - Published in the 3rd week of the month prior to cover month
Cover Price: £2.00
Annual Sub.: £12.00
Circulation: 50,000 (Print Run)
Usual Pagination: 48
Editor: Minal Chande; **Advertising Manager:** Steve Forsdick
Summary of Content: Lifestyle magazine featuring material designed to encourage self-help for people with arthritis.
Readership/Target Audience: Aimed at people with arthritis and those who care for them, both personally and professionally.
CONSUMER: OTHER CLASSIFICATIONS: Disability

Consumer Magazines

ARTHRITIS TODAY
1639945U94F-993

Editorial Address: Copeman House, St. Mary's Court, St. Mary's Gate, CHESTERFIELD, S41 7TD **Tel:** 01246 541107
Fax: 01246 558007
Email: j.tadman@arc.org.uk
Advertising Address: 17 Britton Street, LONDON, EC1M 5TP **Tel:** 020 7880 7668 **Fax:** 020 7880 7553
Email: claire.barber@redactive.co.uk
Web site: http://www.arc.org.uk
Publisher: Arthritis Today
Date Established: 1965
Frequency: Quarterly
Free to qualifying individuals
Annual Sub.: £15.00
Circulation: 85,000 (Publisher's Statement)
Usual Pagination: 36
Editor: Jane Tadman
Summary of Content: Magazine covering news and latest research on arthritis and musculoskeletal conditions with human interest stories.
Readership/Target Audience: Aimed at people with arthritis and their carers.
ADVERTISING RATES:
Full Page Colour £3195.00
Mechanical Data: Type Area: 279 x 195mm, Bleed Size: 303 x 216mm, Trim Size: 297 x 210mm, Film: Digital, Col Length: 279mm, Page Width: 195mm
CONSUMER: OTHER CLASSIFICATIONS: Disability

THE ARTIST (INC. ART & ARTISTS)
47489U84A-70

Editorial Address: Caxton House, 63-65 High Street, TENTERDEN, TN30 6BD **Tel:** 01580 763673
Fax: 01580 765411
Advertising Address: As above. **Tel:** 01580 763315
Email: linde@tapc.co.uk
Web site: http://www.painters-online.co.uk
ISSN: 0004-3877
Publisher: The Artists' Publishing Company Ltd
Date Established: 1931
Frequency: Monthly - Published on the 12th of the month prior to cover date
Cover Price: £3.25
Annual Sub.: £29.50
Circulation: 22,000 (Publisher's Statement)
Usual Pagination: 68
Editor: Deborah Wanstall; **Managing Director:** Sally Bulgin; **Advertising Manager:** Linde Ovington-Lee; **Publisher:** Sally Bulgin
Summary of Content: Magazine covering practical art tuition, news and profiles.
Readership/Target Audience: Read by art tutors, art students and amateur painters and exhibition visitors.
ADVERTISING RATES:
Full Page Colour £1170.00
Agency Commission: 10%
Mechanical Data: Col Widths (Display): 45mm, Col Length: 265mm, Film: Digital, No. of Columns (Display): 4, Type Area: 265 x 190mm, Print Process: Web-fed offset, Bleed Size: 305 x 215mm, Trim Size: 297 x 210mm, Page Width: 190mm
Copy instructions: Copy Date: 10th of the month prior to publication date
Average advertising content per issue: 30%
CONSUMER: THE ARTS & LITERARY: Arts

ARTISTS AND AGENTS
1616584U89C-955

Editorial Address: 70-76 Bell Street, LONDON, NW1 6SP
Tel: 020 7224 9666 **Fax:** 020 7224 9688
Email: sales@rhpco.co.uk
Advertising Address: As above.
Email: sales@rhpco.co.uk
Web site: http://www.rhpco.co.uk
Publisher: Richmond House Publishing Co Ltd
Date Established: 1981
Frequency: Annual - Published in January
Cover Price: £44.95
Circulation: 2,500 (Publisher's Statement)
Editor: Spencer Block; **Managing Director:** Spencer Block; **Advertising Manager:** Spencer Block
Summary of Content: Annual directory listing all the agents and personal managers in the United Kingdom along with the artists they represent. Also incorporating a corporate event organiser.
Readership/Target Audience: Aimed at the entertainment industry, charities and corporate event organisers.
ADVERTISING RATES:
Full Page Mono £630.00
Full Page Colour £1030.00
Mechanical Data: Trim Size: 420 x 297mm, Bleed Size: 426 x 300mm, Film: Digital
CONSUMER: HOLIDAYS & TRAVEL: Entertainment Guides

ARTISTS & ILLUSTRATORS MAGAZINE
47490U84A-75

Editorial Address: 26-30 Old Church Street, LONDON, SW3 5BY **Tel:** 020 7349 3150 **Fax:** 020 7349 3160
Email: info@artistsandillustrators.co.uk
Advertising Address: As above.
Email: steve.ross@artistsandillustrators.co.uk
Web site: http://www.artistsandillustrators.co.uk
ISSN: 0269-4697
Publisher: The Chelsea Magazine Company
Date Established: 1986
Frequency: 13 issues yearly
Cover Price: £3.50
Circulation: 49,000 (Publisher's Statement)
Usual Pagination: 100
Editor: Lynn Parr; **Advertisement Director:** Steve Ross
Summary of Content: Magazine covering techniques of practical art, profiles on artists, new products and business features.
Readership/Target Audience: Read by amateur and professional artists and commercial illustrators.
ADVERTISING RATES:
Full Page Mono £2200.00
Full Page Colour £2200.00
Agency Commission: 10%
Mechanical Data: Type Area: 280 x 202mm, Col Length: 280mm, Page Width: 202mm, Bleed Size: 306 x 236mm, Trim Size: 300 x 230mm, Film: Digital
Copy instructions: Copy Date: 6 weeks prior to publication date
CONSUMER: THE ARTS & LITERARY: Arts

ARTREVIEW
47488U84A-95

Editorial Address: 1 Sekforde Street, LONDON, EC1R 0BE
Tel: 020 7107 2760 **Fax:** 020 7107 2761
Email: editorial@artreview.com
Advertising Address: As above.
Email: michaelgill@artreview.com
Web site: http://www.art-review.com
ISSN: 0004-4091
Publisher: ArtReview Ltd
Date Established: 1949
Frequency: 10 issues yearly - Jan/Feb and Jul/Aug are double issues
Cover Price: £5.50
Annual Sub.: £70.00
Circulation: 35,000 (Publisher's Statement)
Usual Pagination: 182
Editor: Mark Rappolt; **Executive Editor:** David Terrien; **Advertising Manager:** Michael Gill; **Publisher:** Charlotte Robinson
Summary of Content: Magazine covering all aspects of the British and international, modern and contemporary, visual art scene.
Readership/Target Audience: Read by those interested in art for business and pleasure.
ADVERTISING RATES:
Full Page Colour £2500.00
Agency Commission: 10%
Mechanical Data: Type Area: 264 x 198mm, Bleed Size: 310 x 235mm, Trim Size: 300 x 230mm, Col Length: 264mm, Film: Digital, Page Width: 198mm
Copy instructions: Copy Date: 4 weeks prior to publication date
Average advertising content per issue: 30%
CONSUMER: THE ARTS & LITERARY: Arts

ARTROCKER MAGAZINE
1739996U76D-829

Formerly: Artrocker
Editorial Address: 43 Chute House, LONDON, SW9 0DW
Tel: 07709 365247
Email: marc@artrockermagazine.com
Advertising Address: As above. **Tel:** 07855 968189
Email: chris@artrockermagazine.com
Web site: http://www.artrocker.tv
Publisher: Artrocker Magazine Ltd
Date Established: 2005
Frequency: Monthly
Cover Price: £2.95
Circulation: 25,000 (Publisher's Statement)
Usual Pagination: 100
Editor: Marc Sallis; **Advertising Manager:** Chris Hornby
Summary of Content: Magazine covering guitar and electro music with reviews and interviews with new, emerging bands.
Readership/Target Audience: Aimed at teenagers, students and those from their early twenties to late thirties who are fans of new guitar and electro music.
ADVERTISING RATES:
Full Page Colour £1000.00
Mechanical Data: Bleed Size: 320 x 240mm, Trim Size: 292 x 220mm, Film: Digital
Copy instructions: Copy Date: 2 weeks prior to publication date
CONSUMER: MUSIC & PERFORMING ARTS: Music

ARTWORK
48065U89C-65

Editorial Address: PO Box 3, ELLON, AB41 9EA
Tel: 01651 842429 **Fax:** 01651 842180
Advertising Address: As above.
Web site: http://www.artwork.co.uk
Publisher: Famedram Publishers Ltd.
Frequency: Quarterly
Cover Price: Free
Circulation: 25,000 (Publisher's Statement)
Usual Pagination: 18
Editor: Bill Williams; **Advertising Manager:** Sandra Moore; **Managing Editor:** Bill Williams
Summary of Content: Publication providing a guide to the arts including interviews, reviews and opinions plus a comprehensive listing of arts event throughout the North of Britain.
Readership/Target Audience: Read by those interested in arts policy exhibitions and events in Scotland and the North of England.
ADVERTISING: Rates on application
CONSUMER: HOLIDAYS & TRAVEL: Entertainment Guides

ASHARQ AL-AWSAT
48281U90-24

Editorial Address: Arab Press House, 184 High Holborn, LONDON, WC1V 7AP **Tel:** 020 7831 8181
Fax: 020 7831 2310
Email: editorial@asharqalawsat.com
Advertising Address: As above. **Fax:** 020 7404 6963
Email: moira@alkhaleejiah.com
Web site: http://www.aawsat.com
Publisher: H.H Saudi Research & Marketing UK Ltd
Date Established: 1977
Frequency: Daily
Cover Price: £1.20
Circulation: 250,000 (Publisher's Statement)
Usual Pagination: 24
Editor: Mowasaq Alnowarsir; **Editor-in-Chief:** Tariq Al-Homayed; **Managing Director:** Tariq Algain
Summary of Content: National newspaper covering national and international news, politics, business, finance, sport and entertainment.
Language(s): Arabic; English
Readership/Target Audience: Aimed at an international Arab readership.
ADVERTISING RATES:
Full Page Mono SAR60000.00
Full Page Colour SAR90000.00
SCC SAR150.00
Agency Commission: 15%
Mechanical Data: Type Area: 500 x 324mm, Col Length: 500mm, Page Width: 324mm, Col Widths (Display): 37mm, No. of Columns (Display): 8, Film: Digital
Copy instructions: Copy Date: 4 days prior to publication date
Average advertising content per issue: 60%
CONSUMER: ETHNIC

ASHFORD VOICE
1685512U80C-5237

Editorial Address: Civic Centre, Tannery Lane, ASHFORD, TN23 1PL **Tel:** 01233 330209 **Fax:** 01233 330610
Email: caroline.owen@ashford.gov.uk
Web site: http://www.ashford.gov.uk
Publisher: Ashford Borough Council
Date Established: 2005
Frequency: Quarterly
Cover Price: Free
Circulation: 50,000 (Publisher's Statement)
Usual Pagination: 24
Editor: Caroline Owen
Summary of Content: Magazine containing features, stories, topical news items and photographs as well as competitions, restaurant and leisure reviews, reader's offers and advertisements.
Readership/Target Audience: Aimed at residents in the Ashford Borough Council area.
ADVERTISING: No Advertising taken
CONSUMER: RURAL & REGIONAL INTEREST: Regional Interest English Counties

THE ASIA & PACIFIC REVIEW
47312U82-2_34

Editorial Address: 11 Clarendon Street, CAMBRIDGE, CB1 1JU **Tel:** 01223 351584 **Fax:** 01223 351584
Email: suehewitt11@hotmail.com
Advertising Address: As above.
Email: suehewitt11@hotmail.com
Web site: http://www.worldinformation.com
Publisher: World of Information
Date Established: 1980
Frequency: Annual - Published in spring
Annual Sub.: £55.00
Circulation: 6,000 (Publisher's Statement)
Editor: Anthony Axon; **Advertising Manager:** Sue Hewitt; **Publisher:** Anthony Axon
Summary of Content: International publication containing economic and political country profiles.

Readership/Target Audience: Aimed at those working in business, banking, industry, professional services and government.
ADVERTISING RATES:
Full Page Colour £4950.00
Agency Commission: 15%
Mechanical Data: Type Area: 235.5 x 172mm, Bleed Size: 276 x 216mm, Trim Size: 270 x 210mm, Col Length: 235.5mm, Page Width: 172mm, Film: Digital, Print Process: Offset litho
Copy instructions: Copy Date: End of September prior to publication date
Average advertising content per issue: 10%
CONSUMER: CURRENT AFFAIRS & POLITICS

ASIAN ART NEWSPAPER
625711U84A-155

Editorial Address: PO Box 22521, LONDON, W8 4GT
Tel: 020 7229 6040 Fax: 020 7565 2913
Email: sarah.asianart@btinternet.com
Advertising Address: As above.
Email: info@asianartnewspaper.com
Web site: http://www.asianartnewspaper.com
ISSN: 1460-8537
Publisher: The Asian Art Ltd
Date Established: 1997
Frequency: 10 issues yearly - Not published in July and August
Cover Price: £5.00
Annual Sub.: £45.00
Circulation: 8,000 (Publisher's Statement)
Usual Pagination: 24
Editor: Sarah Callaghan; Publisher: Sarah Callaghan
Summary of Content: Magazine covering Asian arts and culture worldwide.
Readership/Target Audience: Aimed at galleries, museums, collectors and dealers worldwide as well as libraries and universities with Asian departments.
ADVERTISING RATES:
Full Page Mono £1145.00
Full Page Colour £2195.00
Agency Commission: 10%
Mechanical Data: Type Area: 380 x 260mm, Col Length: 380mm, Film: Digital, Page Width: 260mm
Copy instructions: Copy Date: 4 weeks prior to publication date
Average advertising content per issue: 40%
Supplement(s): Asian Art Newspaper Best Books of the Year - 1xY, Asian Art Newspaper Guide to London - 1xY, Asian Art Newspaper Guide to New York - 2xY, Asian Art Newspaper Guide to Paris - 1xY, Asian Art Newspaper Guide to Southeast Asian Museums - 1xY, Asian Art Newspaper Guide to West Coast America - 1xY
CONSUMER: THE ARTS & LITERARY: Arts

ASIAN BRIDE
1620612U74L-217

Editorial Address: The Accessory House, Cox Lane, CHESSINGTON, KT9 1SD Tel: 0870 755 5502
Fax: 0870 755 5503
Email: editorial2@asianwomanmag.com
Advertising Address: As above. Tel: 0870 755 5501
Email: sales@asianwomanmag.com
Web site: http://www.asianwomanmag.com
Publisher: Asian Interactive Media
Date Established: 2001
Frequency: 6 issues yearly
Cover Price: £4.50
Annual Sub.: £23.95
Circulation: 86,274 (Publisher's Statement)
Editor: Brianna Ragel
Summary of Content: Magazine featuring bridal and wedding ideas including a directory of services and products for planning your ideal wedding.
Readership/Target Audience: Aimed at women in the Asian community.
ADVERTISING RATES:
Full Page Colour £3600.00
Agency Commission: 10%
Mechanical Data: Film: Digital, Type Area: 269 x 192mm, Bleed Size: 303 x 226mm, Trim Size: 297 x 220mm, Col Length: 269mm, Page Width: 192mm
Copy instructions: Copy Date: 1 month prior to publication date
Average advertising content per issue: 60%
CONSUMER: WOMEN'S INTEREST CONSUMER MAGAZINES: Brides

ASIAN CHOICE MAGAZINE
1666810U90-961

Editorial Address: Shine, Harehills Road, LEEDS, LS8 5HS
Tel: 0870 360 8606 Fax: 0870 360 8605
Email: editor@asianexpress.co.uk
Advertising Address: As above.
Email: sales@asianexpress.co.uk
Publisher: Open Media Publications Ltd
Date Established: 2000
Frequency: Quarterly
Cover Price: Free
Circulation: 36,000 (Publisher's Statement)

Usual Pagination: 64
Editor: Nadim Hanif; Managing Director: Nadim Hanif;
Advertising Manager: Nadim Hanif
Summary of Content: Magazine covering Asian lifestyle, Asian music scene, Bollywood, celeb gossip, humour features, profiles and star interviews.
Readership/Target Audience: Aimed at second and third generation Asians in Yorkshire and Lancashire.
ADVERTISING: Rates on application
CONSUMER: ETHNIC

THE ASIAN EXPRESS NEWSPAPER
48283U90-8

Formerly: The AEN Newspaper
Editorial Address: 211 Piccadilly, LONDON, W1J 9HF
Tel: 020 7917 2744 Fax: 020 7537 2141
Email: info@asianexpressnewspaper.com
Advertising Address: As above.
Email: vallabh.kaviraj@asianexpressnewspaper.com
Web site: http://www.asianexpressnewspaper.com
ISSN: 0268-8484
Publisher: The Asian Express Newspaper
Date Established: 1974
Frequency: Daily
Editor: Vallabh Kaviraj; Advertising Manager: Vallabh Kaviraj; Publisher: Vallabh Kaviraj
Summary of Content: Newspaper containing international news and issues. Includes articles on technology, environment, arts literature, culture and sport.
Readership/Target Audience: Aimed at Asian-Indians worldwide.
ADVERTISING: Rates on application
Editions:
AEN News Diary
Global Business Focus
CONSUMER: ETHNIC

ASIAN EXPRESS NEWSPAPER
1666802U90-960

Editorial Address: Shine, Harehills Road, LEEDS, LS8 5HS
Tel: 0870 360 8606 Fax: 0870 360 8605
Email: editor@asianexpress.co.uk
Advertising Address: As above.
Email: nadim@asianexpress.co.uk
Web site: http://www.asianexpress.co.uk
Publisher: Open Media Publications Ltd
Date Established: 2001
Frequency: 24 issues yearly
Cover Price: Free
Circulation: 42,000 (Publisher's Statement)
Usual Pagination: 48
Editor: Tanya Shah; Editor-in-Chief: Andleeb Hanif;
Advertising Manager: Tanya Shah
Summary of Content: Newspaper covering local news of South Asian interest, lifestyle, South Asian sports people and organisations, health and beauty, entertainment, Bollywood exclusive interviews, music, Bollywood listings, Hollywood listings, Bollygossip, features, competitions, recruitment, motors, travel, property, romance and business.
Readership/Target Audience: Aimed at the South Asian communities and businesses in Yorkshire and Lancashire aiming at the second and third generation.
ADVERTISING RATES:
Full Page Colour £1249.00
Agency Commission: 10%
Mechanical Data: Film: Digital, Trim Size: 363 x 265mm, No. of Columns (Display): 7
Editions:
Asian Express Newspaper Lancashire & Greater Manchester
Asian Express Newspaper Yorkshire
CONSUMER: ETHNIC

ASIAN EXPRESS NEWSPAPER LANCASHIRE & GREATER MANCHESTER
1893871U90-1031

Editorial Address: For all contact details see main edition, Asian Express Newspaper
Frequency: Monthly
Cover Price: Free
Edition of: Asian Express Newspaper
CONSUMER: ETHNIC

ASIAN EXPRESS NEWSPAPER YORKSHIRE
1893870U90-1032

Editorial Address: For all contact details see main edition, Asian Express Newspaper
Frequency: 26 issues yearly
Cover Price: Free
Edition of: Asian Express Newspaper
CONSUMER: ETHNIC

ASIAN EYE
600866U90-30_50

Editorial Address: Hall Ings, BRADFORD, BD1 1JR
Tel: 01274 705215 Fax: 01274 723634
Advertising Address: As above. Fax: 01274 724907
Email: marc.kenny@bradford.newsquest.co.uk
Web site: http://www.asian-eye.co.uk
Publisher: Newsquest Yorkshire and North East (Bradford)
Date Established: 1998
Frequency: Monthly
Cover Price: £0.38
Usual Pagination: 40
Editor: Perry Austin-Clarke; Advertising Manager: Marc Kenny
Summary of Content: Publication containing local news, sports coverage and general interest features.
Readership/Target Audience: Aimed at the Asian community in Bradford.
ADVERTISING RATES:
Full Page Mono £950.00
Full Page Colour £1187.50
SCC £5.00
Agency Commission: 10%
Mechanical Data: Print Process: Web-fed offset litho, Film: Digital, Type Area: 340 x 259mm, No. of Columns (Display): 9, Col Length: 340mm, Page Width: 259mm
Copy instructions: Copy Date: Wednesday prior to publication date
CONSUMER: ETHNIC

ASIAN IMAGE
48284U90-31

Formerly: Asian Image Lancashire
Editorial Address: Newspaper House, High Street, BLACKBURN, BB1 1HT Tel: 01254 678678
Fax: 01254 680429
Email: skhan@lancashire.newsquest.co.uk
Advertising Address: As above. Fax: 01254 682185
Email: hkajee@lancashire.newsquest.co.uk
Web site: http://www.asianimage.co.uk
Publisher: Newsquest (Blackburn) Ltd
Date Established: 1997
Frequency: Monthly
Free to qualifying individuals
Annual Sub.: £10.00
Circulation: 30,000 (Publisher's Statement)
Usual Pagination: 48
Editor: Shuiab Khan; Advertising Manager: Hussein Kajee
Summary of Content: Publication containing sport, sub-continent news, ethnic entertainment, recruitment, competitions and local issues.
Language(s): English; Gujarati; Urdu
Readership/Target Audience: Aimed at the Asian community.
ADVERTISING RATES:
SCC £3.65
Agency Commission: 10%
Mechanical Data: Type Area: 350 x 273mm, Col Length: 350mm, Film: Digital, No. of Columns (Display): 9, Page Width: 273mm
Copy instructions: Copy Date: 25th of the month prior to publication date
Average advertising content per issue: 75%
CONSUMER: ETHNIC

ASIAN LEADER (NORTHWEST AND YORKSHIRE EDITION)
1622704U90-910

Formerly: Asian Leader
Editorial Address: 187 Drake Street, ROCHDALE, OL11 1EF Tel: 01706 670119 Fax: 01706 649908
Email: newsdesk@asianleader.co.uk
Advertising Address: As above.
Email: parwez@asianleader.co.uk
Web site: http://www.lookasia.co.uk
Publisher: Best Asian Media
Date Established: 2001
Frequency: 26 issues yearly
Cover Price: Free
Circulation: 30,000 (Publisher's Statement)
Usual Pagination: 32
Editor: Shmoun Maqsood
Summary of Content: Newspaper covering issues relevant to Asian communities including national and local news with an Asian angle, community news, entertainment, health awareness, legal advice, sport, news from India, Pakistan and Bangladesh, children's section, Urdu pages and recruitment pages.
Language(s): English; Urdu
Readership/Target Audience: Aimed at Asian communities in particular second and third generation Asians.
ADVERTISING RATES:
Full Page Mono £2448.00
Full Page Colour £3182.40
SCC £8.00
Agency Commission: 10%
Mechanical Data: Col Length: 340mm, No. of Columns (Display): 9, Type Area: 340 x 274mm, Print Process: Web-fed litho, Page Width: 274mm, Col Widths (Display): 27mm, Film: Digital

Consumer Magazines

Copy instructions: Copy Date: 3 days prior to publication date
Average advertising content per issue: 40%
Supplement(s): Asian Life Eid Magazine - 1xY
CONSUMER: ETHNIC

ASIAN LITE
1851528U90-1030

Editorial Address: EMF House, 12 Charlotte Street, MANCHESTER, M1 4FL **Tel:** 0161 245 3257
Fax: 0161 245 3333
Email: editor@asianlite.co.uk
Web site: http://www.asianlite.com
Publisher: New Asian Media Ltd
Date Established: 2007
Frequency: Monthly
Cover Price: Free
Circulation: 40,000 (Publisher's Statement)
Usual Pagination: 56
News Editor: Ahmed Shariq Khan
Summary of Content: Newspaper covering news, social stories, entrepreneurs, immigration, parenting, campus, travel, food, Asian community related events, brown pound, Bollywood, sport, fashion and lifestyle.
Readership/Target Audience: Aimed at British Asian professionals and the business community.
CONSUMER: ETHNIC

ASIAN POST
1778644U90-998

Editorial Address: 779 High Road, Leytonstone, LONDON, E11 4QS **Tel:** 020 8558 9127
Email: hazratpk@hotmail.com
Advertising Address: As above. **Fax:** 020 8558 2247
Email: kash@theasianpost.co.uk
Publisher: Hussain Media
Frequency: Weekly
Cover Price: £0.70
Circulation: 45,000 (Publisher's Statement)
Editor: Murtaza Ali; **Advertising Manager:** Kash Hussain
Summary of Content: Newspaper covering news on British Asians of South Asian origins with a focus on entertainment followed by British Asian News.
Readership/Target Audience: Aimed at Asian communities in the UK.
ADVERTISING RATES:
Full Page Mono £2800.00
Full Page Colour £3600.00
Agency Commission: 10%
Mechanical Data: Type Area: 370 x 260mm, Col Length: 370mm, Page Width: 260mm, Film: Digital
Copy instructions: Copy Date: 1 week prior to publication date
CONSUMER: ETHNIC

THE ASIAN TODAY
1641592U90-926

Formerly: Asian Leader (Birmingham)
Editorial Address: 1162 Coventry Road, Yardley, BIRMINGHAM, B25 8DA **Tel:** 0871 990 2305
Fax: 0871 990 2306
Email: zakia@urbanmedialtd.com
Advertising Address: As above.
Email: ajmal@urbanmedialtd.com
Web site: http://www.theasiantoday.com
Publisher: Urban Media Ltd
Date Established: 2003
Frequency: Monthly
Free to qualifying individuals
Annual Sub.: £48.00
Circulation: 100,000 (Publisher's Statement)
Usual Pagination: 48
Editor: Zakia Yousaf; **Advertising Manager:** Ajmal Hanif
Summary of Content: Newspaper covering news, lifestyle, fashion, entertainment and sport.
Readership/Target Audience: Aimed at the South Asian communities in the UK.
ADVERTISING RATES:
Full Page Mono £1296.00
Full Page Colour £1684.80
SCC £6.00
Agency Commission: 10%
Mechanical Data: Film: Digital, Trim Size: 420 x 297mm, Type Area: 380 x 271mm, Col Length: 380mm, Page Width: 271mm, No. of Columns (Display): 6, Col Widths (Display): 42mm, Bleed Size: +3mm
Copy instructions: Copy Date: 1 week prior to publication date
Average advertising content per issue: 45%
CONSUMER: ETHNIC

ASIAN VOICE
1604990U90-911

Editorial Address: Unit 2, Karma Yoga House, 12 Hoxton Market, LONDON, N1 6HW **Tel:** 020 7749 4080
Fax: 020 7749 4081
Email: aveditorial@abplgroup.com
Advertising Address: As above.
Email: alka@abplgroup.com

Web site: http://www.asian-voice.com
Publisher: Asian Business Publications Ltd
Date Established: 2000
Frequency: Weekly
Cover Price: £0.80
Annual Sub.: £25.00
Circulation: 27,000 (Publisher's Statement)
Usual Pagination: 40
Advertising Manager: Alka Shah
Summary of Content: Publication covering news from Britain and India for members of the Gujarat community. Includes features on cooking, beauty, health, finance and property.
Readership/Target Audience: Read by students, teachers, professionals and those who are involved in charitable and community organisations.
ADVERTISING RATES:
Full Page Mono £3132.00
Full Page Colour £4104.00
Agency Commission: 10%
Mechanical Data: Type Area: 360 x 253mm, Col Length: 360mm, Page Width: 253mm, No. of Columns (Display): 6, Col Widths (Display): 38mm, Film: Digital
Copy instructions: Copy Date: Friday prior to publication date
Average advertising content per issue: 60%
CONSUMER: ETHNIC

ASIAN WOMAN
755643U74Q-5_50

Editorial Address: The Accessory House, Cox Lane, CHESSINGTON, KT9 1SD **Tel:** 0870 755 5502
Fax: 0870 755 5503
Email: editorial@asianwomanmag.com
Advertising Address: As above. **Tel:** 0870 755 5501
Email: sales@asianwomanmag.com
Web site: http://www.asianwomanmag.com
Publisher: Asian Interactive Media
Frequency: Monthly
Cover Price: £4.50
Annual Sub.: £33.00
Circulation: 98,773 (Publisher's Statement)
Usual Pagination: 300
Editor: Jay Rimal; **Advertising Manager:** Peter Davies
Summary of Content: Magazine covering style, fashion, interiors, lifestyle, beauty and food.
Readership/Target Audience: Aimed at Asian women aged between 18 and 45 years old.
ADVERTISING RATES:
Full Page Colour £3600.00
Agency Commission: 10%
Mechanical Data: Bleed Size: 303 x 226mm, Trim Size: 297 x 220mm, Type Area: 269 x 192mm, Col Length: 269mm, Page Width: 192mm
CONSUMER: WOMEN'S INTEREST CONSUMER MAGAZINES: Lifestyle

ASIANA
1645619U90-933

Editorial Address: Tower Bridge Business Centre, 46-48 East Smithfield, LONDON, E1W 1AW **Tel:** 020 7709 2010
Fax: 020 7709 2012
Email: info@asianamag.com
Advertising Address: As above.
Email: riyaz@asianamag.com
Web site: http://www.asianamag.com
ISSN: 1742-2361
Publisher: i and i media Ltd
Date Established: 2003
Frequency: Quarterly
Cover Price: £4.50
Circulation: 38,655 (Publisher's Statement)
Usual Pagination: 324
Editor: Shihab Salim; **Features Editor:** Sonia Ahmed;
Editor-in-Chief: Shihab Salim; **Advertising Manager:** Riyaz Manwa
Summary of Content: Lifestyle magazine covering fashion, beauty, health and celebrity interviews as well as real life stories from modern Asian women.
Readership/Target Audience: Aimed at modern Asian women aged between 16 and 34 years old.
ADVERTISING RATES:
Full Page Colour £5150.00
Agency Commission: 10%
Mechanical Data: Type Area: 269 x 192mm, Bleed Size: 303 x 226mm, Trim Size: 297 x 220mm, Col Length: 269mm, Page Width: 192mm, Film: Digital
Copy instructions: Copy Date: 4 weeks prior to publication date
Average advertising content per issue: 30%
CONSUMER: ETHNIC

ASOS
1775345U74B-722

Editorial Address: Greater London House, Hampstead Road, LONDON, NW1 7SB **Tel:** 020 7756 1000
Email: asosmagazine@asos.com
Advertising Address: As above.
Email: jasmin.woodcock@sevensquared.co.uk
Web site: http://www.asos.com

Publisher: ASOS
Date Established: 2006
Frequency: Monthly
Cover Price: Free
Circulation: 400,000 (Print Run)
Usual Pagination: 100
Editor: Marina Crook; **Advertising Manager:** Jasmin Woodcock
Summary of Content: Magazine covering fashion, beauty and celebrity interviews.
Readership/Target Audience: Aimed at customers of ASOS.com (As Seen on Screen) both men and women.
ADVERTISING RATES:
Full Page Colour £7000.00
Agency Commission: 15%
Mechanical Data: Type Area: 202 x 148mm, Bleed Size: 228 x 174mm, Trim Size: 222 x 168mm, Col Length: 202mm, Page Width: 148mm, Film: Digital
Copy instructions: Copy Date: 2 weeks prior to publication date
Average advertising content per issue: 30%
CONSUMER: WOMEN'S INTEREST CONSUMER MAGAZINES: Women's Interest - Fashion

ASPECT COUNTY
46985U80C-3180

Editorial Address: 6 Old Ladies Court, High Street, BATTLE, TN33 9AH **Tel:** 01424 777444
Email: mail@aspect-county.co.uk
Advertising Address: As above.
Email: mail@aspect-county.co.uk
Web site: http://www.aspect-county.co.uk
Publisher: Media South
Date Established: 1989
Frequency: Monthly
Cover Price: Free
Circulation: 22,000 (Publisher's Statement)
Usual Pagination: 32
Editor: Nigel Lelew; **Advertising Manager:** Neil McGuigan; **Publisher:** Neil McGuigan
Summary of Content: Magazine covering motoring and travel, music, fashion & beauty, wining & dining, antiques, homes & gardens, history and rural issues.
Readership/Target Audience: Aimed at 28 to 60 year olds in West Kent and East Sussex.
ADVERTISING RATES:
Full Page Colour £650.00
Agency Commission: 10%
Mechanical Data: Type Area: 270 x 190mm, Film: Digital, Page Width: 190mm, Col Length: 270mm, Bleed Size: +3mm
Copy instructions: Copy Date: Middle of the month prior to publication date
Average advertising content per issue: 40%
Supplement(s): Aspect County Golf - 1xY, Aspect County Leisure Time - 1xY
CONSUMER: RURAL & REGIONAL INTEREST: Regional Interest English Counties

ASPECTS
47366U83-1_15

Editorial Address: Alumni Office, Anglia Ruskin University, Rivermead Gate, Bishop Hall Lane, CHELMSFORD, CM1 1SQ **Tel:** 0845 196 4714 **Fax:** 0845 196 4718
Email: alumni@anglia.ac.uk
Web site: http://www.anglia.ac.uk/alumni
Publisher: Anglia Ruskin University
Date Established: 1994
Frequency: Half-yearly - Published in January and August
Cover Price: Free
Circulation: 38,000 (Publisher's Statement)
Usual Pagination: 24
Editor: Sue Jacobs
Summary of Content: Alumni magazine of Anglia Polytechnic University. Covers news about APU; graduates and work-related issues.
Readership/Target Audience: Aimed at graduates and post-graduate students of Anglia Polytechnic University.
ADVERTISING: No Advertising taken
CONSUMER: STUDENT PUBLICATIONS

ASPINALL'S MAGAZINE
1748198U74Q-1315

Editorial Address: 5 Jubilee Place, LONDON, SW3 3TD
Tel: 020 7985 0002 **Fax:** 020 7792 9244
Email: penelope.bennett@luxurypublishing.com
Advertising Address: As above. **Tel:** 020 7591 2900
Fax: 020 7591 2929
Email: wendy@luxurypublshing.com
Web site: http://www.spearmedia.co.uk
Publisher: Spear Media
Date Established: 2006
Frequency: Half-yearly - Published in the summer and winter
Usual Pagination: 80
Editor: Penelope Bennett
Summary of Content: Magazine covering gambling, lifestyle, fashion, wildlife, wine, food, social, travel and nightlife.

Readership/Target Audience: Aimed at Aspinall's members plus selected high net worth individuals.
ADVERTISING RATES:
Full Page Colour £3995.00
Mechanical Data: Type Area: 260 x 210mm, Bleed Size: 266 x 216mm, Trim Size: 260 x 210mm, Col Length: 260mm, Page Width: 210mm, Film: Digital, Print Process: Sheet-fed litho
Average advertising content per issue: 40%
CONSUMER: WOMEN'S INTEREST CONSUMER MAGAZINES: Lifestyle

ASTON TIMES
47371U83-11_50

Formerly: Helios
Editorial Address: Aston Students Guild, Aston Triangle, BIRMINGHAM, B4 7ES **Tel:** 0121 359 6531
Fax: 0121 333 4218
Email: guild.editor@astonguild.org.uk
Advertising Address: As above. **Tel:** 0121 204 4855
Fax: 0121 204 4910
Email: sales@astonguild.org.uk
Web site: http://www.astonguild.org.uk
Publisher: Aston Students Guild
Date Established: 1947
Frequency: 9 issues yearly - 3 issues per term in autumn, spring and summer terms
Cover Price: Free
Circulation: 5,000 (Publisher's Statement)
Usual Pagination: 24
Editor: Gemma Baker
Summary of Content: Magazine covering entertainment listings, travel, arts, music and sports.
Readership/Target Audience: Read by students and staff at Aston University and Aston Science Park.
ADVERTISING RATES:
Full Page Colour £550.00
Agency Commission: 10%
Mechanical Data: Trim Size: 350 x 264mm, Film: Digital
Copy instructions: Copy Date: 7 days prior to publication date
Average advertising content per issue: 20%
CONSUMER: STUDENT PUBLICATIONS

ASTRONOMY NOW
48670U94X-10

Editorial Address: PO Box 175, TONBRIDGE, TN10 4ZY
Tel: 01732 367542 **Fax:** 01732 300148
Email: editorial2008@astronomynow.com
Advertising Address: 55 Quarry Hill Road, TONBRIDGE, TN9 2SA **Tel:** 01732 446112
Email: wendy@astronomynow.com
Web site: http://www.astronomynow.com
ISSN: 0951-9726
Publisher: Pole Star Publications
Frequency: Monthly
Cover Price: £3.25
Annual Sub.: £31.00
Circulation: 35,000 (Publisher's Statement)
Usual Pagination: 98
Editor: Steven Young; **Advertising Manager:** Wendy Collins; **Managing Editor:** Steven Young
Summary of Content: Magazine containing news section, book reviews, beginners' guide and features on observing, cosmology, the history of astronomy and space science. Also includes 'Focus' section and an eight page pull-out on the night sky.
Readership/Target Audience: Read by professional and amateur astronomers, students and star gazers.
ADVERTISING RATES:
Full Page Colour £950.00
Agency Commission: 10%
Mechanical Data: Trim Size: 297 x 210mm, Bleed Size: 303 x 216mm, Film: Digital, Type Area: 277 x 190mm, Col Length: 277mm, Page Width: 190mm
CONSUMER: OTHER CLASSIFICATIONS: Miscellaneous

AT EASE
1657338U74N-171

Editorial Address: Unit 8, Woodcock Hill Industrial Estate, Harefield Road, RICKMANSWORTH, WD3 1PQ
Tel: 01923 774111 **Fax:** 01923 721818
Email: richard.g@evolve-print.com
Web site: http://www.evolve-print.com
Publisher: Evolve
Date Established: 2000
Frequency: Half-yearly - Published in February and August
Cover Price: Free
Circulation: 105,000 (Publisher's Statement)
Usual Pagination: 6
Editor: Richard Gregory
Summary of Content: Magazine covering lifestyle, health and personal finance.
Readership/Target Audience: Aimed at pensioners.
ADVERTISING: No Advertising taken
CONSUMER: WOMEN'S INTEREST CONSUMER MAGAZINES: Retirement

AT HOME
1793371U74C-866

Editorial Address: 1379 High Road, LONDON, N20 9LP
Tel: 020 8492 3830 **Fax:** 020 8446 5642
Email: carly@emp.plc.uk
Web site: http://www.athomemagazine.co.uk
Publisher: EMP Media
Date Established: 2000
Frequency: Monthly
Cover Price: £3.50
Usual Pagination: 250
Editor: Carly Rigley
Summary of Content: Magazine covering travel, interiors, property at home and abroad, cookery, gardening, DIY, parenting and relationships as well as advice each month, from a leading celebrity on their field of expertise.
Readership/Target Audience: Aimed at women aged 25 to 55 years old.
CONSUMER: WOMEN'S INTEREST CONSUMER MAGAZINES: Home & Family

AT HOME IN WALES
767709U80D-501

Formerly: At Home On The Waterfront
Editorial Address: Enterprise House, 127 Bute Street, CARDIFF, CF10 5LE **Tel:** 029 2045 0532 **Fax:** 029 2045 0533
Email: info@citypublications.org
Advertising Address: As above.
Email: info@citypublications.org
Web site: http://www.athomeinwales.com
Publisher: City Publications
Date Established: 1988
Frequency: Monthly
Cover Price: Free
Circulation: 31,500 (Publisher's Statement)
Usual Pagination: 28
Editor: Alison Tucker; **Features Editor:** Sarah Caple; **Advertising Manager:** Adrian Stone
Summary of Content: Magazine covering property, interior design, restaurants, shopping and lifestyle in Cardiff Bay.
Readership/Target Audience: Aimed at those living in and visiting Cardiff.
ADVERTISING RATES:
Full Page Colour £850.00
Agency Commission: 10%
Mechanical Data: Film: Digital, Trim Size: 297 x 210mm, Bleed Size: 303 x 216mm
Copy instructions: Copy Date: 3 weeks prior to publication date
Average advertising content per issue: 40%
CONSUMER: RURAL & REGIONAL INTEREST: Regional Interest Wales

ATHLETICS WEEKLY
45896U75J-100

Editorial Address: 83 Park Road, PETERBOROUGH, PE1 2TN **Tel:** 01733 808550 **Fax:** 01733 898441
Email: jason.henderson@athletics-weekly.com
Advertising Address: As above. **Fax:** 01733 898443
Email: advertising@athletics-weekly.co.uk
Web site: http://www.athletics-weekly.com/
Publisher: Descartes Publishing Ltd
Date Established: 1945
Frequency: Weekly
Cover Price: £2.60
Circulation: 14,000 (Publisher's Statement)
Usual Pagination: 52
Editor: Jason Henderson; **Managing Director:** Matthew Fraser Moat; **Advertising Manager:** Elizabeth Cammell
Summary of Content: Magazine covering track and field events, fell racing, race walking, road, cross-country and Olympic news.
Readership/Target Audience: Aimed at athletes, coaches, fans and administrators.
ADVERTISING RATES:
Full Page Colour £1500.00
Agency Commission: 10%
Mechanical Data: No. of Columns (Display): 4, Type Area: 276 x 192mm, Col Length: 276mm, Trim Size: 297 x 210mm, Bleed Size: 216 x 303mm, Page Width: 192mm, Film: Digital
Copy instructions: Copy Date: 9 days prior to publication date
Average advertising content per issue: 20%
CONSUMER: SPORT: Athletics

ATLANTA UK MAGAZINE
27574U73-9003

Formerly: Atlanta
Editorial Address: Unit 3A, 13 North Bank Street, EDINBURGH, EH1 2LP **Tel:** 0131 225 8730
Email: nicky@atlanta.uk.com
Web site: http://www.atlanta.uk.com
Publisher: Innovative Writing Ltd
Date Established: 2000
Frequency: 3 issues yearly - Published April, August and December
Annual Sub.: £950.00
Circulation: 7,000 (Publisher's Statement)
Usual Pagination: 100

Editor: Sarit Freed; **Managing Director:** Nicolette Du Preez; **Publisher:** Nicolette Du Preez
Summary of Content: Business magazine with lifestyle content and original photography.
Readership/Target Audience: Aimed at CEO's in major corporate entities and PLCs, entrepreneurs, government agencies, private limited companies and senior lawyers.
ADVERTISING: No Advertising taken
CONSUMER: NATIONAL & INTERNATIONAL PERIODICALS

ATLAS MAGAZINE
45378U84A-160

Editorial Address: 16 Talfourd Road, LONDON, SE15 5NY
Tel: 020 7701 7245
Web site: http://www.areaatlas.com
ISSN: 0267-484X
Publisher: Atlas Magazine
Editor: Jake Tilson
Summary of Content: Magazine focusing on artists work containing prints and drawings.
Readership/Target Audience: Aimed at those interested in art.
ADVERTISING: No Advertising taken
CONSUMER: THE ARTS & LITERARY: Arts

ATM MAGAZINE
1626270U76D-809

Editorial Address: G1 Unit 121, The Old Truman Brewery, 91 Brick Lane, LONDON, E1 6QL **Tel:** 020 7375 2297
Fax: 020 7375 2296
Email: editor@atm-mag.com
Advertising Address: As above.
Email: ray@atm-mag.com
Web site: http://www.atm-mag.com
Publisher: Planet Media Publishing
Frequency: 6 issues yearly
Cover Price: £3.49
Circulation: 30,000 (Print Run)
Usual Pagination: 94
Editor: Mark Od
Summary of Content: Music magazine specialising in drum and base also touching on hip-hop, breaks and hard core.
Readership/Target Audience: Aimed at keen music enthusiasts and clubbers aged between 18 and 35 years old.
ADVERTISING: Rates on application
CONSUMER: MUSIC & PERFORMING ARTS: Music

ATTITUDE
47621U86B-10

Editorial Address: Ground Floor, 211 Old Street, LONDON, EC1V 9NR **Tel:** 020 7608 6500 **Fax:** 020 7608 6320
Email: attitude@attitude.co.uk
Advertising Address: As above.
Email: andy.goddard@attitude.co.uk
Web site: http://www.myspace.com/attitude_magazine
Publisher: Trojan Publishing
Date Established: 1994
Frequency: Monthly
Cover Price: £3.25
Annual Sub.: £29.25
Circulation: 80,000 (Publisher's Statement)
Usual Pagination: 148
Editor: Matthew Todd; **Advertising Manager:** Andy Goddard
Summary of Content: Lifestyle magazine covering movies, fashion, music and book reviews.
Readership/Target Audience: Aimed primarily but not exclusively at gay men.
ADVERTISING RATES:
Full Page Mono £3200.00
Full Page Colour £3500.00
Agency Commission: 10%
Mechanical Data: Type Area: 275 x 210mm, Col Length: 275mm, Page Width: 210mm, Bleed Size: 281 x 216mm, Trim Size: 275 x 210mm, Film: Digital
Copy instructions: Copy Date: 5 weeks prior to publication date
Average advertising content per issue: 35%
CONSUMER: ADULT & GAY MAGAZINES: Gay & Lesbian Magazines

AUDI DRIVER
46444U77E-65

Editorial Address: Campion House, 1 Greenfield Road, Westoning, BEDFORD, MK45 5JD **Tel:** 01525 750500
Fax: 01525 750700
Email: paul.harris@autometrix.co.uk
Advertising Address: As above.
Email: sales@autometrix.co.uk
Web site: http://www.autometrix.co.uk
ISSN: 1369-4340
Publisher: AutoMetrix Publications
Date Established: 1997
Frequency: Monthly
Cover Price: £3.95
Circulation: 20,000 (Publisher's Statement)
Usual Pagination: 84

Consumer Magazines

Editor: Paul Harris; **Managing Director:** Paul Harris; **Advertising Manager:** Debbie Forbes; **Publisher:** Paul Harris
Summary of Content: Magazine containing road tests, technical, touring and travel articles.
Readership/Target Audience: Aimed predominantly at males aged 25 and upwards who are owners of new and company Audi cars.
ADVERTISING RATES:
Full Page Colour £650.00
Agency Commission: 10%
Mechanical Data: Type Area: 260 x 182mm, Bleed Size: 303 x 213mm, Film: Digital, Page Width: 182mm, Trim Size: 297 x 210mm, Col Length: 260mm
Copy instructions: Copy Date: 3 weeks prior to publication date
Average advertising content per issue: 40%
CONSUMER: MOTORING & CYCLING: Club Cars

THE AUDI MAGAZINE
46445U77E-529
Editorial Address: Yeomans Drive, Blakelands, MILTON KEYNES, MK14 5AN **Tel:** 020 7833 7415
Fax: 020 7833 7411
Web site: http://www.northstarpublishing.com
Publisher: Northstar Publishing Ltd
Date Established: 1987
Frequency: 3 issues yearly - Published in March, July and October
Cover Price: £4.50
Free to qualifying individuals
Circulation: 300,000 (Publisher's Statement)
Usual Pagination: 92
Editor: Mark Walton
Summary of Content: Magazine containing a mix of Audi lifestyle features, news and in-depth stories, stories about people and products in the world of Audi.
Readership/Target Audience: Read by owners and prospective owners of Audi cars and those interested in the marque.
ADVERTISING: No Advertising taken
CONSUMER: MOTORING & CYCLING: Club Cars

AUSTRALIA & NEW ZEALAND
1697072U89E-268
Formerly: Escape to Australia & New Zealand
Editorial Address: Unit 3, The Old Estate Yard, North Stoke lane, Upton Cheyney, BRISTOL, BA2 3DZ
Tel: 01179 323586
Web site: http://www.australiamagazine.co.uk
Publisher: Evolve Digital Publishing
Date Established: 2005
Frequency: 13 issues yearly
Cover Price: £3.99
Circulation: 25,000 (Publisher's Statement)
Usual Pagination: 130
Editor: John Weir
Summary of Content: Magazine covering travel, holidays, things to do, culture, food, wine, lifestyle, interiors, real life stories and all things antipodean.
Readership/Target Audience: Aimed at those looking to migrate to Australia or New Zealand as well as those planning a holiday.
ADVERTISING RATES:
Full Page Colour £1950.00
Agency Commission: 10%
Mechanical Data: Bleed Size: 306 x 226mm, Trim Size: 300 x 220mm, Film: Digital
Copy instructions: Copy Date: 3 weeks prior to publication date
Average advertising content per issue: 20%
CONSUMER: HOLIDAYS & TRAVEL: Holidays

AUSTRALIAN OUTLOOK
48226U89E-28
Editorial Address: 13 London Road, BEXHILL-ON-SEA, TN39 3JR **Tel:** 01424 223111 **Fax:** 01424 224992
Email: consylpublishing@btconnect.com
Advertising Address: As above.
Email: consylpublishing@btconnect.com
Web site: http://www.consylpublishing.co.uk
Publisher: Consyl Publishing & Publicity Ltd
Date Established: 1970
Frequency: Monthly
Cover Price: £0.95
Annual Sub.: £18.00
Circulation: 5,000 (Publisher's Statement)
Usual Pagination: 36
Editor: Shirley Gilbertson; **Advertising Manager:** Shirley Gilbertson
Summary of Content: Newspaper covering employment, government policy, visas, housing, shopping and holidays.
Readership/Target Audience: Read mainly by potential migrants and visitors to Australia.
ADVERTISING RATES:
Full Page Mono £850.00
Full Page Colour £1100.00
SCC £7.00
Agency Commission: 10%

Mechanical Data: Type Area: 390 x 263mm, Col Length: 390mm, Page Width: 263mm, No. of Columns (Display): 7, Col Widths (Display): 36mm, Film: Digital
Copy instructions: Copy Date: 10th of the month prior to publication date
Average advertising content per issue: 30%
CONSUMER: HOLIDAYS & TRAVEL: Holidays

AUSTRALIAN TIMES
1666675U90-958
Editorial Address: Unit 7, Commodore House, Juniper Drive, LONDON, SW18 1TW **Tel:** 0845 456 4910
Fax: 0845 456 4912
Email: editor@australiantimes.co.uk
Advertising Address: As above.
Email: wernerh@blueskygroup.co.uk
Web site: http://www.australiantimes.co.uk
Publisher: Blue Sky Publications Ltd
Date Established: 2004
Frequency: Weekly
Free to qualifying individuals
Annual Sub.: £42.00
Circulation: 18,000 (Print Run)
Usual Pagination: 20
Editor: Frances Paddick
Summary of Content: Newspaper covering Australian news as well as London life, events, travel, finance and property, recruitment and sport.
Readership/Target Audience: Aimed at Australians living in London.
ADVERTISING RATES:
Full Page Colour £500.00
Agency Commission: 10%
Mechanical Data: Film: Digital, Type Area: 350 x 266mm, Col Length: 350mm, Page Width: 266mm
Copy instructions: Copy Date: 1 week prior to publication date
CONSUMER: ETHNIC

AUTHOR
47536U84B-20
Editorial Address: 84 Drayton Gardens, LONDON, SW10 9SB **Tel:** 020 7373 6642 **Fax:** 020 7373 5768
Email: info@societyofauthors.org
Advertising Address: As above.
Email: kpool@societyofauthors.org
Web site: http://www.societyofauthors.org
ISSN: 0005-0628
Publisher: Society of Authors
Date Established: 1890
Frequency: Quarterly
Cover Price: £12.00
Free to qualifying individuals
Annual Sub.: £30.00
Circulation: 8,500 (Publisher's Statement)
Usual Pagination: 44
Editor: Andrew Rosenheim; **Advertising Manager:** Kate Pool
Summary of Content: Magazine providing information on all aspects of the business of writing for media.
Readership/Target Audience: Read by members of the Society of Authors, publishers, agents and librarians.
ADVERTISING RATES:
Full Page Mono £450.00
Agency Commission: 10%
Copy instructions: Copy Date: 6 weeks prior to publication date
Average advertising content per issue: 15%
CONSUMER: THE ARTS & LITERARY: Literary

AUTO EXCHANGE
28700U77A-19
Editorial Address: Robert Rogers House, New Orchard, POOLE, BH15 1LU **Tel:** 01202 207750 **Fax:** 01202 207765
Email: hnewman@exchangeandmart.co.uk
Advertising Address: As above. **Tel:** 01202 207810
Fax: 01202 227765
Email: npointer@exchangeandmart.co.uk
Web site: http://www.exchangeandmart.co.uk
Publisher: Exchange Enterprises Ltd
Date Established: 1996
Frequency: Weekly
Cover Price: Free
Circulation: 257,796 (Publisher's Statement)
Usual Pagination: 70
Editor: Heiki Newman; **Advertising Manager:** Nicci Pointer
Summary of Content: Local motor classified available in 21 local titles in England and Wales.
Readership/Target Audience: Aimed primarily at men between 25 and 54 years old interested in buying and selling cars.
ADVERTISING RATES:
Full Page Colour £500.00
Agency Commission: 15%
Mechanical Data: Type Area: 230 x 185mm, Col Length: 230mm, Page Width: 185mm, Film: Digital
Copy instructions: Copy Date: 3 days prior to publication date
Average advertising content per issue: 80%

Editions:
Auto Exchange Beds, Bucks, North Herts & Cambridge
Auto Exchange Essex & East Anglia
Auto Exchange Greater Manchester
Auto Exchange Lancashire & Cumbria
Auto Exchange Leicestershire & Northants
Auto Exchange Merseyside & Cheshire
Auto Exchange North East
Auto Exchange North East London & West Essex
Auto Exchange North West Midlands
Auto Exchange Nottingham, Derby & Mansfield
Auto Exchange South & West Wales
Auto Exchange South London & Kent
Auto Exchange South West Midlands
Auto Exchange South Yorkshire
Auto Exchange Southern
Auto Exchange Staffordshire, Cheshire & Shropshire
Auto Exchange Thames Valley
Auto Exchange West & North Yorkshire
Auto Exchange West London
Auto Exchange Western
CONSUMER: MOTORING & CYCLING: Motoring

AUTO EXPRESS
46298U77A-20
Editorial Address: 30 Cleveland Street, LONDON, W1T 4JD
Tel: 020 7907 6200 **Fax:** 020 7907 6234
Email: julie_sinclair@dennis.co.uk
Advertising Address: As above. **Tel:** 020 7907 6745
Fax: 020 7907 6601
Email: ads@autoexpress.co.uk
Web site: http://www.autoexpress.co.uk
Publisher: Dennis Publishing Ltd
Date Established: 1989
Frequency: Weekly
Cover Price: £1.95
Circulation: 68,757 (ABC 01/01/2009 to 30/06/2009)
Usual Pagination: 100
Editor: Julie Sinclair; **Editor-in-Chief:** David Johns; **Managing Director:** Peter Wootton
Summary of Content: Motoring magazine with features on car tests, road reports and motoring news.
Twitter: http://twitter.com/AutoExpress.
Readership/Target Audience: Aimed at men aged between 25 and 54 years old.
ADVERTISING RATES:
Full Page Colour £7150.00
Agency Commission: 15%
Mechanical Data: Page Width: 206mm, Film: Digital, Type Area: 285 x 206mm, Bleed Size: 306 x 232mm, Trim Size: 300 x 226mm, Col Length: 285mm
Copy instructions: Copy Date: 3 weeks prior to publication date
Average advertising content per issue: 25%
CONSUMER: MOTORING & CYCLING: Motoring

AUTO ITALIA
46299U77E-528
Editorial Address: PO Box 7, LETCHWORTH, SG6 3XG
Tel: 01462 678205 **Fax:** 01462 678205
Email: phil.ward@chpltd.com
Advertising Address: Nimax House, 20 Ullswater Crescent, Ullswater Business Park, COULSDON, CR5 2HR
Tel: 020 8655 6400
Email: frank.archer@chpltd.com
Web site: http://www.auto-italia.co.uk
ISSN: 1357-4515
Publisher: CH Publications Ltd
Date Established: 1995
Frequency: 13 issues yearly
Cover Price: £3.95
Annual Sub.: £47.40
Circulation: 20,000 (Publisher's Statement)
Usual Pagination: 96
Summary of Content: Magazine covering new, classic and historic cars and motorcycles. Also contains international motorsport news involving Italian cars.
Readership/Target Audience: Aimed at owners, collectors and enthusiasts of Italian cars and motorcycles.
ADVERTISING RATES:
Full Page Colour £2000.00
Agency Commission: 10%
Mechanical Data: Film: Digital, Print Process: Web-fed offset litho, Type Area: 270 x 186mm, Bleed Size: 303 x 216mm, Trim Size: 297 x 210mm, Col Length: 270mm, Page Width: 186mm
CONSUMER: MOTORING & CYCLING: Club Cars

AUTO TRADER
1656085U77A-515
Editorial Address: 3rd Floor, 41-47 Hartfield Road, Wimbledon, LONDON, SW19 3RQ **Tel:** 020 8544 7000
Fax: 020 8879 1879
Email: stuart.milne@autotrader.co.uk
Advertising Address: As above.
Email: andy.smith@tradermedia.co.uk
Web site: http://www.autotrader.co.uk
Publisher: TNT Publishing
Frequency: Weekly
Circulation: 239,205 (ABC 01/01/2008 to 31/12/2008)

News Editor: Adrian Hearn
Summary of Content: Magazine with automotive classifieds in your region.
Twitter: http://twitter.com/autotrader_uk.
Readership/Target Audience: Aimed at those looking to buy a new or used car.
ADVERTISING RATES:
Full Page Colour £12980.00
Agency Commission: 10%
Mechanical Data: Type Area: 274 x 204mm, Col Length: 274mm, Page Width: 204mm, No. of Columns (Display): 6
Copy instructions: Copy Date: Thursday 1pm prior to publication date
Average advertising content per issue: 99%
Editions:
Auto Trader Anglia
Auto Trader Midland
Auto Trader North East
Auto Trader North London, Herts & Beds and East London/ Essex
Auto Trader North West
Auto Trader Northern Ireland
Auto Trader Republic of Ireland
Auto Trader Scottish
Auto Trader South London/Kent/Sussex, E Surrey, S East
Auto Trader South West
Auto Trader Southern
Auto Trader Thames Valley
Auto Trader Western and South Wales
Auto Trader Yorkshire
CONSUMER: MOTORING & CYCLING: Motoring

AUTOCAR
46301U77A-30
Editorial Address: Teddington Studios, Broom Road, TEDDINGTON, TW11 9BE **Tel:** 020 8267 5630
Fax: 020 8267 5759
Email: autocar@haymarket.com
Advertising Address: As above. **Tel:** 020 8267 5000
Email: walton.musgrave@haymarket.com
Web site: http://www.autocar.co.uk
ISSN: 1355-8293
Publisher: Haymarket Business Media Ltd
Frequency: Weekly
Cover Price: £2.50
Circulation: 50,007 (ABC 01/01/2009 to 30/06/2009)
Usual Pagination: 130
Editor: Daniel Stevens; **News Editor:** Daniel Stevens;
Features Editor: Matt Saunders; **Editor-in-Chief:** Steve Cropley
Summary of Content: Magazine containing new model, industry, consumer and used car news. Includes road tests, profiles, Grand Prix coverage and a variety of automotive features.
Readership/Target Audience: Aimed at new car buyers seeking advice.
ADVERTISING RATES:
Full Page Colour £10240.00
Agency Commission: 10%
Mechanical Data: Page Width: 206mm, Type Area: 280 x 206mm, Bleed Size: 306 x 236mm, Trim Size: 300 x 230mm, Film: Digital, Col Length: 280mm, No. of Columns (Display): 4
Copy instructions: Copy Date: 1 week prior to publication date
Average advertising content per issue: 20%
CONSUMER: MOTORING & CYCLING: Motoring

THE AUTOMOBILE
46487U77F-30
Editorial Address: PO Box 153, CRANLEIGH, GU6 8ZL
Tel: 01483 268818 **Fax:** 01483 268993
Email: jonathanrishton@hotmail.com
Advertising Address: 9 Old Coach Road, TRURO, TR3 6ER
Tel: 01872 870700 **Fax:** 01872 870706
Email: peterbromley@btconnect.com
Web site: http://www.the-automobile.co.uk
ISSN: 0955-1328
Publisher: Enthusiast Publishing Ltd
Date Established: 1983
Frequency: Monthly - Published on 3rd Monday of the month before cover date
Cover Price: £3.95
Annual Sub.: £38.50
Circulation: 39,000 (Publisher's Statement)
Usual Pagination: 100
Editor: Jonathan Rishton; **Managing Director:** Brenda Hart;
Advertising Manager: Peter Bromley; **Managing Editor:** Lionel Burrell
Summary of Content: International magazine devoted exclusively to pre-1960 cars and commercial vehicles.
Readership/Target Audience: Read by those interested in buying, selling and restoring old vehicles.
ADVERTISING RATES:
Full Page Colour £800.00
Agency Commission: 10%
Mechanical Data: Type Area: 270 x 186mm, Trim Size: 295 x 210mm, Bleed Size: +3mm, Col Length: 270mm, Page Width: 186mm, Film: Digital
Copy instructions: Copy Date: 4th Friday of the month prior to publication date

Average advertising content per issue: 40%
CONSUMER: MOTORING & CYCLING: Veteran Cars

AUTOSPORT
46412U77D-90
Editorial Address: Teddington Studios, Broom Road, TEDDINGTON, TW11 9BE **Tel:** 020 8267 5998
Fax: 020 8267 5922
Email: autosport.editorial@haynet.com
Advertising Address: As above. **Tel:** 020 8267 5000
Fax: 020 8267 5850
Email: pierre.clements@haymarket.com
Web site: http://www.autosport.com
ISSN: 0269-946X
Publisher: Haymarket Media Group Ltd
Date Established: 1950
Frequency: Weekly
Cover Price: £3.00
Circulation: 34,442 (ABC 01/01/2008 to 31/12/2008)
Usual Pagination: 112
Editor: Andrew Van De Burgt; **Managing Editor:** Peter Hodges
Summary of Content: Magazine providing comprehensive coverage of the motorsports world from Formula 1 and championship cars to touring cars. Includes news, analysis and race reports.
Readership/Target Audience: Read by motor sport enthusiasts and those working in the industry.
ADVERTISING RATES:
Full Page Colour £3832.00
Agency Commission: 10%
Mechanical Data: Film: Digital, Type Area: 278 x 216mm, Bleed Size: 308 x 236mm, Trim Size: 302 x 230mm, Col Length: 278mm, Page Width: 216mm
Copy instructions: Copy Date: Monday 12 noon prior to publication date
CONSUMER: MOTORING & CYCLING: Motor Sports

THE AVENGERS UNITED
1663408U91D-905
Editorial Address: Brockbourne House, Mount Ephraim, TUNBRIDGE WELLS, TN4 8BS **Tel:** 01892 500100
Fax: 01892 545666
Email: collectorsed@panini.co.uk
Advertising Address: Orange 20 Ltd, Station House, Bunbury Way, EPSOM, KT17 4JP **Tel:** 01372 802800
Fax: 01372 723322
Email: robin@o20.co.uk
Web site: http://www.paninicomics.co.uk
ISSN: 1474-1571
Publisher: Panini UK Ltd
Frequency: 13 issues yearly
Cover Price: £2.50
Annual Sub.: £28.80
Usual Pagination: 76
Editor: Scott Gray; **Advertising Manager:** Robin Johnson
Summary of Content: Magazine with action from The Hulk, Captain America, Iron Man, Hawkeye and Scarlet, covering four decades of comic history.
Readership/Target Audience: Aimed at comic enthusiasts aged from 12 years old.
ADVERTISING RATES:
Full Page Colour £1500.00
Agency Commission: 10%
Copy instructions: Copy Date: 4 weeks prior to publication date
CONSUMER: RECREATION & LEISURE: Children & Youth

AVIATION MODELLER INTERNATIONAL
31188U79B-191
Editorial Address: Unit 5, Chiltern Business Centre, 63-65 Woodside Road, AMERSHAM, HP6 6AA **Tel:** 01494 433453
Fax: 01494 433456
Email: enginetorque@aol.com
Advertising Address: As above. **Tel:** 01684 311514
Fax: 01684 311514
Email: adverts@modelactivitypress.com
Web site: http://www.modelactivitypress.com
Publisher: Model Activity Press Ltd
Frequency: Monthly - Published on the 4th Thursday of each month
Cover Price: £3.25
Annual Sub.: £36.00
Circulation: 22,000 (Publisher's Statement)
Usual Pagination: 108
Editor: Steve Dowling
Summary of Content: Magazine covering all types of flying model aeroplanes from indoor to free flight, control line and radio control.
Readership/Target Audience: Aimed at those with an interest in aviation modelling.
ADVERTISING RATES:
Full Page Mono £510.00
Full Page Colour £610.00
Agency Commission: 10%
Mechanical Data: Col Length: 270mm, Trim Size: 297 x 210mm, Type Area: 270 x 185mm, Page Width: 185mm, Film: Digital

Copy instructions: Copy Date: 4 weeks prior to publication date
Average advertising content per issue: 30%
CONSUMER: HOBBIES & DIY: Models & Modelling

AVIATION WORLD
1655116U79R-152
Formerly: Air-Britain Aviation World
Editorial Address: Whitmore, Rockshaw Road, MERSTHAM, RH1 3BZ **Tel:** 01737 642527
Fax: 01737 644442
Email: rod.simpson@air-britain.co.uk
Web site: http://www.air-britain.com
ISSN: 1742-996X
Publisher: Air-Britain (Historians) Ltd
Frequency: Quarterly
Cover Price: £2.50
Annual Sub.: £15.00
Circulation: 4,500 (Publisher's Statement)
Usual Pagination: 48
Editor: Roderick Simpson
Summary of Content: Magazine covering contemporary and historical aviation subjects.
Readership/Target Audience: Aimed at aircraft historians and spotters.
ADVERTISING: No Advertising taken
CONSUMER: HOBBIES & DIY: Hobbies & DIY Related

AVRUPA NEWSPAPER
1666596U90-955
Editorial Address: 118 Green Lanes, Newington Green, LONDON, N16 9EH **Tel:** 020 7275 7610 **Fax:** 020 7241 1908
Email: editor@avrupagazete.com
Advertising Address: As above.
Email: avrupa@btopenworld.com
Web site: http://www.avrupagazete.com
Publisher: Azilla Ltd
Date Established: 2002
Frequency: Weekly
Cover Price: £1.00
Circulation: 20,000 (Publisher's Statement)
Usual Pagination: 32
Editor: Vatan Oz; **Advertising Manager:** Vatan Oz
Summary of Content: Newspaper written in Turkish and covering world news, articles and events.
Language(s): Turkish
Readership/Target Audience: Aimed at Turkish communities in the UK particularly those that are non-English speakers.
ADVERTISING RATES:
Full Page Mono £400.00
Full Page Colour £600.00
Agency Commission: 10%
Mechanical Data: Type Area: 515 x 355mm, Col Length: 515mm, Page Width: 355mm, Film: Digital
Copy instructions: Copy Date: Tuesday 4pm prior to publication date
CONSUMER: ETHNIC

AWAAZ
1614092U90-908
Editorial Address: PO Box 15, BATLEY, WF17 7YY
Tel: 01924 510512 **Fax:** 01924 510513
Email: info@awaaznews.com
Advertising Address: As above.
Email: info@awaaznews.com
Web site: http://www.awaaznews.com
Publisher: Asian Voice Group
Date Established: 1983
Frequency: Monthly
Cover Price: Free
Circulation: 25,000 (Publisher's Statement)
Editor: Shaista Mohyudin; **Advertising Manager:** Shaista Mohyudin
Summary of Content: Multi-lingual newspaper featuring campaign stories, sport, competitions and special sections on legal matters.
Readership/Target Audience: Aimed at the Asian community living in and around Yorkshire.
ADVERTISING RATES:
Full Page Colour £655.00
Agency Commission: 10%
Mechanical Data: Type Area: 337 x 258mm, Col Length: 337mm, Page Width: 258mm, Film: Digital
Copy instructions: Copy Date: 20th of the month prior to publication date
CONSUMER: ETHNIC

AWARD JOURNAL
48447U91D-12
Editorial Address: Gulliver House, Madeira Walk, WINDSOR, SL4 1EU **Tel:** 01753 727470 **Fax:** 01753 810666
Email: journal@theaward.org/awardjournal
Advertising Address: Fellows Media Ltd., The Gallery, Manor Farm, Southam, CHELTENHAM, GL52 3PB
Tel: 01242 259240 **Fax:** 01242 259248
Email: mark@fellowsmedia.com
Web site: http://www.theaward.org
ISSN: 1367-188X

Publisher: The Award Scheme Ltd
Date Established: 1956
Frequency: 3 issues yearly - Published in January, April and September
Cover Price: Free
Circulation: 50,000 (Print Run)
Usual Pagination: 48
Editor: Dave Wood
Summary of Content: The magazine of The Duke of Edinburgh's Award scheme. Includes articles covering sport and leisure.
Readership/Target Audience: Aimed at young adults concerned with running or participating in The Duke of Edinburgh's Award scheme.
ADVERTISING RATES:
Full Page Colour £1500.00
Agency Commission: 10%
Mechanical Data: Type Area: 270 x 184mm, Col Length: 270mm, Page Width: 184mm, Trim Size: 297 x 210mm, Film: Digital
Copy instructions: Copy Date: 9 weeks prior to publication date
CONSUMER: RECREATION & LEISURE: Children & Youth

AXIS MAGAZINE
1640197U80C-5135
Editorial Address: Harlow Enterprise Hub, Kao Hockham Building, Edinburgh Way, HARLOW, CM20 2NQ
Tel: 01279 311447 **Fax:** 01279 311443
Email: news@axispublications.co.uk
Advertising Address: As above. **Tel:** 01920 885162
Fax: 01920 885172
Email: info@axispublications.co.uk
Web site: http://www.axismagazine.co.uk
Publisher: Axis Publications Ltd
Date Established: 2003
Frequency: Monthly
Cover Price: Free
Circulation: 40,000 (Publisher's Statement)
Usual Pagination: 32
Editor: Aaron Gransby; **Advertising Manager:** Justine Woods; **Publisher:** Justine Woods
Summary of Content: Magazine covering useful, informative, relevant local news, features, what's on and dining out information, shopping news, gardening news, health, beauty and well-being pages, education, business, finance, legal and property news and features along with motoring and advertising.
Readership/Target Audience: Aimed at residents and visitors to North London and East Hertfordshire aged 21 and over.
ADVERTISING RATES:
Full Page Colour £500.00
Agency Commission: 10%
Mechanical Data: Trim Size: 275 x 210mm, Film: Digital, Type Area: 255 x 190mm, Col Length: 255mm, Page Width: 190mm, Bleed Size: +3mm
Copy instructions: Copy Date: 2 weeks prior to publication date
Average advertising content per issue: 60%
CONSUMER: RURAL & REGIONAL INTEREST: Regional Interest English Counties

B2L
1685740U74K-732
Editorial Address: Walmar House, 288-300 Regent Street, LONDON, W1B 3AL **Tel:** 020 7016 2555 **Fax:** 020 7636 2040
Email: andrew.strange@wardour.co.uk
Advertising Address: As above.
Web site: http://www.wardour.co.uk
Publisher: Wardour Publishing and Design
Date Established: 2005
Frequency: Quarterly
Cover Price: Free
Circulation: 140,000 (Publisher's Statement)
Usual Pagination: 16
Editor: Andrew Strange
Summary of Content: Magazine containing news and features of practical interest about the buy to let market.
Readership/Target Audience: Aimed at Mortgage Express buy to let customers.
ADVERTISING: Rates on application
CONSUMER: WOMEN'S INTEREST CONSUMER MAGAZINES: Home Purchase

B & G (BRIDES & GROOMS)
45533U74L-51
Editorial Address: Media House, 539 High Road, ILFORD, IG1 1UD **Tel:** 020 8477 3771 **Fax:** 020 8477 3710
Email: jackie.ross@archant.co.uk
Advertising Address: As above. **Fax:** 020 8478 6606
Email: jackie.ross@archant.co.uk
Publisher: Recorder Newspapers
Date Established: 1995
Frequency: Half-yearly – Published in February and July
Cover Price: £2.00
Free to qualifying individuals
Circulation: 25,000 (Publisher's Statement)
Usual Pagination: 100

Editor: Jackie Ross; **Publisher:** Jackie Ross
Summary of Content: Magazine containing ideas on all aspects of weddings.
Readership/Target Audience: Read by brides-to-be, grooms, bridesmaids and mothers of the bride.
ADVERTISING RATES:
Full Page Colour £600.00
SCC £6.00
Agency Commission: 10%
Mechanical Data: Page Width: 190mm, Type Area: 260 x 190mm, Col Length: 260mm, Trim Size: 297 x 210mm, Bleed Size: 303 x 216mm, Film: Digital
Copy instructions: Copy Date: 1st of the month prior to publication date
CONSUMER: WOMEN'S INTEREST CONSUMER MAGAZINES: Brides

BACK STREET HEROES
46348U77B-480
Editorial Address: 1 Canada Square, 19th Floor, Canary Wharf, LONDON, E14 5AP **Tel:** 020 7772 8300
Fax: 020 7772 8585
Email: bsh_magazine@yahoo.co.uk
Advertising Address: As above. **Tel:** 020 7293 3000
Email: phil_gibbs@oceanmedia.co.uk
Web site: http://www.backstreetheroes.com
ISSN: 0267-9841
Publisher: Ocean Media Group Ltd
Date Established: 1983
Frequency: Monthly
Cover Price: £3.99
Circulation: 30,000 (Publisher's Statement)
Usual Pagination: 132
Editor: Stu Garland; **Managing Director:** Trevor Barrett; **Advertising Manager:** Phil Gibbs; **Managing Editor:** Stu Garland
Summary of Content: Magazine focusing on customised bikes and the ethos and lifestyle behind the machinery.
Readership/Target Audience: Read by biker enthusiasts.
ADVERTISING RATES:
Full Page Colour £1260.00
Agency Commission: 10%
Mechanical Data: Type Area: 287 x 200mm, Bleed Size: 303 x 216mm, Page Width: 200mm, Film: Digital, Col Length: 287mm, Trim Size: 297 x 210mm
Copy instructions: Copy Date: 3 weeks prior to publication date
Average advertising content per issue: 36%
CONSUMER: MOTORING & CYCLING: Motorcycling

BACKPASS
1851569U75B-296
Editorial Address: Greystones, Beechgrove, KINGTON, HR5 3RH **Tel:** 01544 230317
Email: backpassmail@aol.com
Web site: http://www.backpassmagazine.co.uk
Publisher: Backpass Ltd
Date Established: 2007
Frequency: 6 issues yearly
Cover Price: £3.00
Circulation: 20,000 (Print Run)
Editor: Mike Berry
Summary of Content: Magazine covering football from the 60s, 70s and 80s.
Readership/Target Audience: Aimed at men over 30 years old.
CONSUMER: SPORT: Football

BACKTRACK
46700U79J-5
Editorial Address: PO Box 3, Easingwold, YORK, YO61 3YS **Tel:** 01347 824397 **Fax:** 01347 824397
Email: pendragonpublishing@btinternet.com
Advertising Address: As above.
Email: pendragonpublishing@btinternet.com
Web site: http://www.pendragonpublishing.co.uk
ISSN: 0955-5382
Publisher: Pendragon Publishing
Date Established: 1986
Frequency: Monthly - Published on the 3rd Thursday of the month preceding
Cover Price: £3.70
Annual Sub.: £42.00
Circulation: 10,000 (Publisher's Statement)
Usual Pagination: 64
Editor: Mike Blakemore; **Advertising Manager:** Mike Blakemore; **Publisher:** Mike Blakemore
Summary of Content: Magazine covering the whole spectrum of railway history from the earliest times to the present day.
Readership/Target Audience: Read by railway enthusiasts and historians worldwide.
ADVERTISING RATES:
Full Page Mono £240.00
Full Page Colour £290.00
Agency Commission: 10%
Mechanical Data: Col Length: 269mm, Film: Digital, Trim Size: 297 x 210mm, Type Area: 269 x 185mm, Page Width: 185mm

Copy instructions: Copy Date: 5 weeks prior to publication date
Average advertising content per issue: 10%
CONSUMER: HOBBIES & DIY: Rail Enthusiasts

THE BADGER
47368U83-2_1
Editorial Address: Falmer House, Falmer, BRIGHTON, BN1 9QF **Tel:** 01273 678875
Email: badger@ussu.sussex.ac.uk
Advertising Address: BAM UK, 2nd Floor Offices, 8 Castle Square, SWANSEA, SA1 1DW **Tel:** 0845 130 0667
Fax: 0845 130 0668
Email: gc@bamuk.com
Web site: http://www.badger.ussu.info
Publisher: University of Sussex Students Union
Frequency: 30 issues yearly - Published weekly during term time
Cover Price: Free
Circulation: 3,000 (Publisher's Statement)
Usual Pagination: 28
Summary of Content: Publication containing student-related features including music, film, arts, TV, radio and games reviews and sports. Also includes university and local news, plus local entertainment listings and a spoof section.
Readership/Target Audience: Aimed at students of the University of Sussex.
ADVERTISING RATES:
Full Page Mono £450.00
Full Page Colour £595.00
CONSUMER: STUDENT PUBLICATIONS

BADMINTON
45884U75H-163
Formerly: badminton magazine
Editorial Address: 4 The Spinney, Chester Road, Poynton, STOCKPORT, SK12 1HB **Tel:** 07766 576834
Email: rachel.pullen@isportgroup.com
Advertising Address: As above. **Tel:** 07973 544719
Email: rachel.pullan@isportgroup.com
Web site: http://www.badmintonengland.co.uk
Publisher: internationalSPORTgroup
Date Established: 1989
Frequency: Quarterly
Cover Price: £3.00
Free to qualifying individuals
Circulation: 40,000 (Publisher's Statement)
Usual Pagination: 48
Editor: Paul Walters
Summary of Content: Magazine featuring club players information, national and international event reports, features on players, general badminton news and sports product news. News from the governing body and how it affects the club player.
Readership/Target Audience: Aimed at enthusiasts, club players and those with a keen interest in badminton.
ADVERTISING RATES:
Full Page Colour £2000.00
Mechanical Data: Type Area: 267 x 185mm, Trim Size: 297 x 210mm, Bleed Size: 301 x 214mm, Col Length: 267mm, Film: Digital, Page Width: 185mm
Copy instructions: Copy Date: 4 weeks prior to publication date
Average advertising content per issue: 50%
CONSUMER: SPORT: Racquet Sports

BAG-O-FUN
1665923U91D-923
Editorial Address: Suite 2, Prospect House, Belle Vue Road, SHREWSBURY, SY3 7NR **Tel:** 01743 364433
Fax: 01743 271528
Email: info@redan.com
Advertising Address: As above.
Email: emily@redan.com
Publisher: Redan Publishing
Date Established: 2005
Frequency: 10 issues yearly
Cover Price: £3.99
Circulation: 80,000 (Publisher's Statement)
Usual Pagination: 44
Editor: Emily Bell; **Advertising Manager:** Emily Bell
Summary of Content: Children's magazine featuring fun and educational activities, stories based on popular licensed characters such as Mr Men, Brum and Spot as well as extra gifts.
Readership/Target Audience: Aimed at boys and girls aged between 3 and 7 years old.
ADVERTISING: Rates on application
CONSUMER: RECREATION & LEISURE: Children & Youth

BALANCELIFE
1668416U74Q-1255
Editorial Address: Howletts, Chignal St. James, CHELMSFORD, CM1 4TP **Tel:** 01245 441994
Fax: 01245 442012
Email: cheryl@balancelifemagazine.com
Advertising Address: As above.
Email: sales@balancelifemagazine.com
Web site: http://www.balancelifemagazine.com

Publisher: Balance Life Ltd
Date Established: 2000
Frequency: Monthly
Annual Sub.: £24.00
Circulation: 30,000 (Publisher's Statement)
Usual Pagination: 64
Editor: Cheryl Rees; **Advertising Manager:** Cheryl Rees
Summary of Content: Magazine covering lifestyle features including fashion, beauty, health, nutrition, home interiors, property, food & drink, gardening, travel, recipes, restaurants, weddings, fitness, motoring, gadgets, celebrity news and profiles, leisure and entertainment.
Readership/Target Audience: Aimed at affluent residents of Essex.
ADVERTISING: Rates on application
CONSUMER: WOMEN'S INTEREST CONSUMER MAGAZINES: Lifestyle

BANGLA MIRROR
1706719U90-978

Editorial Address: Unit 1, 10-14 Hollybush Gardens, LONDON, E2 9QP **Tel:** 020 7739 8290 **Fax:** 020 7729 0653
Email: info@banglamirrornews.com
Advertising Address: As above. **Tel:** 020 7247 4614
Fax: 020 7377 5326
Email: info@banglamirrornews.com
Web site: http://www.banglamirrornews.com
Publisher: Langutec Media Ltd
Date Established: 2002
Frequency: Weekly
Cover Price: £0.50
Circulation: 13,000 (Publisher's Statement)
Usual Pagination: 32
Editor: Abdul Karim; **Advertising Manager:** Abdul Karim
Summary of Content: Newspaper covering fashion, music, business, health, religion, legal advice, sports and culture.
Readership/Target Audience: Aimed at British born Bangladeshis.
ADVERTISING RATES:
Full Page Colour £1976.00
Agency Commission: 10%
Mechanical Data: Type Area: 360 x 260mm, Col Length: 360mm, Page Width: 260mm, Film: Digital
Copy instructions: Copy Date: 1 week prior to publication date
Average advertising content per issue: 40%
CONSUMER: ETHNIC

BANGLA POST
1698830U90-973

Editorial Address: Unit 4G, Room 5, BJ House, 10-14 Holly Bush Gardens, LONDON, E2 9QP **Tel:** 020 7729 5295
Fax: 020 8983 4959
Email: info@banglapost.co.uk
Advertising Address: As above. **Fax:** 05601 140651
Email: info@banglapost.co.uk
Web site: http://www.banglapost.co.uk
Publisher: Bangla Post Media Services Ltd
Frequency: Weekly - Published on Friday
Cover Price: £0.50
Circulation: 17,500 (Publisher's Statement)
Editor: Taz Choudhury; **Advertising Manager:** Mofizur Rehman
Summary of Content: Newspaper with profiles of successful Bengalis in various professions, health, business, community focus covering issues relevant to British Bengalis and news from the sub-continent, events including films, theatre, meals, political events, shows and educations.
Readership/Target Audience: Aimed at Bengali communities in the UK.
ADVERTISING RATES:
Full Page Mono £1700.00
Full Page Colour £2210.00
Agency Commission: 10%
Mechanical Data: Type Area: 350 x 260mm, Trim Size: 380 x 290mm, Col Length: 350mm, Page Width: 260mm, Col Widths (Display): 40mm, No. of Columns (Display): 6, Film: Positive, right reading, emulsion side down. Digital
Copy instructions: Copy Date: Tuesday 3pm prior to publication date
CONSUMER: ETHNIC

THE BANTER
47364U83-1_3

Formerly: A.M.
Editorial Address: University of the West of Scotland, Storie Street, PAISLEY, PA1 2HB **Tel:** 0141 849 4166
Fax: 0141 849 4158
Email: president@upsa.org.uk
Advertising Address: As above. **Tel:** 0141 849 4155
Email: news@upsa.org.uk
Web site: http://www.upsa.org.uk
Publisher: University of the West of Scotland Association
Frequency: Monthly
Cover Price: Free
Circulation: 3,000 (Publisher's Statement)
Usual Pagination: 40
Advertising Manager: John Frew

Summary of Content: Student paper from the University of Paisley Students' Association featuring news, events, music, films and entertainment listings.
Readership/Target Audience: Read mainly by students and staff.
ADVERTISING: Rates on application
Agency Commission: 10%
Copy instructions: Copy Date: 1 week prior to publication date
Average advertising content per issue: 20%
CONSUMER: STUDENT PUBLICATIONS

BANZAI MAGAZINE
714921U77A-46

Editorial Address: Becket House, Vestry Road, SEVENOAKS, TN14 5EJ **Tel:** 01732 748000
Fax: 01732 748001
Email: banzai@unity-media.com
Advertising Address: As above. **Tel:** 01732 748055
Email: clacey@unity-media.com
Web site: http://www.banzaimagazine.com
ISSN: 1468-456X
Publisher: Unity Media plc
Frequency: Monthly
Cover Price: £4.40
Annual Sub.: £43.20
Circulation: 60,000 (Publisher's Statement)
Usual Pagination: 164
Editor: Joe Clifford; **Advertising Manager:** Cinnamon Lacey; **Publisher:** Colin Wilkinson
Summary of Content: Magazine covering all aspects of Japanese performance cars including tuning, styling and markets.
Readership/Target Audience: Aimed at Japanese car enthusiasts between 20 and 65 years old.
ADVERTISING RATES:
Full Page Mono £1050.00
Agency Commission: 10%
Mechanical Data: Type Area: 266 x 190mm, Trim Size: 297 x 210mm, Bleed Size: 303 x 216mm, Film: Digital, Col Length: 266mm, Page Width: 190mm
Copy instructions: Copy Date: 5 weeks prior to publication date
Average advertising content per issue: 40%
CONSUMER: MOTORING & CYCLING: Motoring

BAPTIST QUARTERLY
47800U87-9_50

Editorial Address: Regents Park College, Pusey Street, OXFORD, OX1 2LB **Tel:** 01865 288120 **Fax:** 01865 288121
Email: john.briggs@regents.ox.ac.uk
Web site: http://www.baptisthistory.org.uk
ISSN: 0005-576X
Publisher: Baptist Historical Society
Date Established: 1908
Frequency: Quarterly
Cover Price: £7.25
Free to qualifying individuals
Circulation: 600 (Publisher's Statement per year)
Usual Pagination: 62
Editor: John Briggs
Summary of Content: Journal focusing on Baptist history and theology.
Readership/Target Audience: Aimed at Baptist historians, librarians and amateur historians.
ADVERTISING: No Advertising taken
CONSUMER: RELIGIOUS

BAPTIST TIMES
47676U87-10

Editorial Address: Baptist House, PO Box 54, 129 Broadway, DIDCOT, OX11 8XB **Tel:** 01235 517672
Fax: 01235 517678
Email: editor@baptisttimes.co.uk
Advertising Address: The Defining Way, Unit 144A, Culham No 1 Site, Station Road, ABINGDON, OX14 3DA
Tel: 01865 407991 **Fax:** 01865 407993
Email: tim.woods@thedefiningway.co.uk
Web site: http://www.baptisttimes.co.uk
Publisher: Baptist Times Ltd.
Date Established: 1855
Frequency: Weekly
Cover Price: £0.85
Circulation: 7,000 (Publisher's Statement)
Usual Pagination: 20
Editor: Mark Woods; **News Editor:** Paul Hobson; **Advertising Manager:** Tim Woods
Summary of Content: Publication containing news and views regarding the Baptist denomination and coverage of wider Christian issues including Christian reflection on world and national news.
Readership/Target Audience: Read by members of Baptist churches.
ADVERTISING RATES:
Full Page Mono £1000.00
Full Page Colour £1200.00
SCC £10.00
Agency Commission: 10%

Mechanical Data: Col Length: 355mm, No. of Columns (Display): 6, Type Area: 355 x 266mm, Col Widths (Display): 42mm, Page Width: 266mm, Film: Digital
Copy instructions: Copy Date: Friday prior to publication date
CONSUMER: RELIGIOUS

BARBIE
48507U91D-14

Editorial Address: 239 Kensington High Street, LONDON, W8 6SA **Tel:** 020 7761 3500 **Fax:** 020 7761 3510
Email: rjamieson@euk.egmont.com
Advertising Address: As above.
Email: aallen@euk.egmont.com
Web site: http://www.egmontmagazines.co.uk
ISSN: 0963-8911
Publisher: Egmont Magazines UK
Frequency: 26 issues yearly
Cover Price: £1.80
Circulation: 51,504 (ABC 01/01/2009 to 30/06/2009)
Usual Pagination: 32
Editor: Rebecca Jamieson; **Advertising Manager:** Annett Allen
Summary of Content: Children's magazine featuring fashion and beauty tips, fantasy stories, photo drama and the latest gossip about Barbie, her friends and her family.
Readership/Target Audience: Aimed at girls between 3 to 7 years old.
ADVERTISING RATES:
Full Page Colour £2500.00
Agency Commission: 10%
Mechanical Data: Film: Digital, Col Length: 282mm, Page Width: 202mm, Type Area: 282 x 202mm, Bleed Size: 306 x 226mm, Trim Size: 300 x 220mm
Copy instructions: Copy Date: 4 weeks prior to publication date
Average advertising content per issue: 10%
CONSUMER: RECREATION & LEISURE: Children & Youth

THE BARKER
45679U74R-50

Editorial Address: Variety Club House, 93 Bayham Street, LONDON, NW1 0AG **Tel:** 020 7428 8100
Fax: 020 7428 8123
Email: editor@varietyclub.org.uk
Advertising Address: As above.
Web site: http://www.varietyclub.org.uk
Publisher: Variety Club of Great Britain
Date Established: 1957
Frequency: 3 issues yearly - Published in March, July and November
Cover Price: £2.50
Free to qualifying individuals
Circulation: 4,000 (Publisher's Statement)
Usual Pagination: 52
Editor: James Gadspy-Peet; **Publisher:** Pip Burley
Summary of Content: Journal containing reports and pictures of events of the Variety Club of Great Britain.
Readership/Target Audience: Read by Variety Club members throughout Britain, the media and senior executives of large companies.
ADVERTISING RATES:
Full Page Mono £800.00
Full Page Colour £1000.00
Mechanical Data: Trim Size: 297 x 210mm, Bleed Size: 303 x 216mm, Type Area: 275 x 190mm, Col Length: 275mm, Film: Digital, Page Width: 190mm
CONSUMER: WOMEN'S INTEREST CONSUMER MAGAZINES: Women's Interest Related

THE BARNSLEY EYE
1639993U80C-5081

Formerly: The Barnsleye
Editorial Address: F1-F3 Holme Suite, Oaks Lane, Oaks Business Park, BARNSLEY, S71 1HT **Tel:** 0114 288 5988
Fax: 01226 240202
Email: sheilah@zmpl.co.uk
Advertising Address: As above. **Tel:** 01226 321450
Email: sheilah@zmpl.co.uk
Publisher: ClearView Publishing
Date Established: 2003
Frequency: Monthly
Cover Price: Free
Circulation: 18,000 (Publisher's Statement)
Usual Pagination: 68
Editor: Sheilah Reed; **Advertising Manager:** Sheilah Reed
Summary of Content: Lifestyle magazine for Barnsley covering local news, pubs, clubs, restaurants, cinema, theatre, fashion, what's on, gadgets and property as well as a clothing directory, business directory and company profiles.
Readership/Target Audience: Aimed at residents and visitors to Barnsley.
ADVERTISING RATES:
Full Page Colour £650.00
Mechanical Data: Film: Digital
Copy instructions: Copy Date: 1 week prior to publication date

Consumer Magazines

Average advertising content per issue: 50%
CONSUMER: RURAL & REGIONAL INTEREST: Regional Interest English Counties

BARRHEAD PRESS
1809921U80E-370

Editorial Address: Unit 3, 47 Back Sneddon Street, PAISLEY, PA3 2DD **Tel:** 0141 842 1010 **Fax:** 0141 887 7122
Email: david@newvisionpublishing.co.uk
Advertising Address: Unit 7, 42 Back Sneddon Street, PAISLEY, PA3 2DD **Tel:** 0141 842 1010 **Fax:** 0141 887 7122
Email: enquiries@newvisionpublishiong.co.uk
Web site: http://www.newvisionpublishing.co.uk
Publisher: New Vision Print & Publishing Ltd
Date Established: 2007
Frequency: 10 issues yearly
Cover Price: Free
Circulation: 10,000 (Publisher's Statement)
Usual Pagination: 32
Editor: David Wilson
Summary of Content: Magazine with local stories and lifestyle features including business, personal, sport, health, beauty, recipes, gardening, housing, finance, legal and books.
Readership/Target Audience: Aimed at residents of Barrhead.
ADVERTISING RATES:
Full Page Colour £400.00
Mechanical Data: Type Area: 267 x 190mm, Trim Size: 297 x 210mm, Col Length: 267mm, Page Width: 190mm, Film: Digital
Copy instructions: Copy Date: 10 days prior to publication date
CONSUMER: RURAL & REGIONAL INTEREST: Regional Interest Scotland

BART SIMPSON
1664054U91D-910

Editorial Address: Titan House, 144 Southwark Street, LONDON, SE1 0UP **Tel:** 020 7620 0200 **Fax:** 020 7620 0032
Email: ned.hartley@titanemail.com
Advertising Address: As above. **Tel:** 020 7803 1922
Fax: 020 7803 1803
Email: james.willmott@titanemail.com
Web site: http://www.titanmagazines.com
Publisher: Titan Magazines
Frequency: Quarterly
Cover Price: £2.99
Circulation: 90,005 (Publisher's Statement)
Usual Pagination: 68
Editor: Ned Hartley; **Advertising Manager:** James Willmott
Summary of Content: Magazine made up of material from Bongo Bart Simpson comics.
Readership/Target Audience: Aimed at fans of The Simpsons.
ADVERTISING RATES:
Full Page Colour £4000.00
Agency Commission: 10%
Mechanical Data: Type Area: 277 x 210mm, Bleed Size: 303 x 236mm, Trim Size: 297 x 230mm, Col Length: 277mm, Page Width: 210mm, Film: Digital
Copy instructions: Copy Date: 6 weeks prior to publication date
Average advertising content per issue: 10%
CONSUMER: RECREATION & LEISURE: Children & Youth

BASS GUITAR MAGAZINE
1620690U76D-765

Editorial Address: Oyster House, Hunter's Lodge, KENTISBEARE, EX15 2DY **Tel:** 01884 266100
Fax: 01884 266101
Email: editor@bassguitarmagazine.com
Advertising Address: As above.
Email: advertising@bassguitarmagazine.com
Web site: http://www.bassguitarmagazine.com
ISSN: 1476-5217
Publisher: Bass Media Ltd
Date Established: 2001
Frequency: 6 issues yearly
Cover Price: £3.95
Free to qualifying individuals
Annual Sub.: £20.00
Circulation: 19,000 (Publisher's Statement)
Usual Pagination: 84
Editor: Nick Wells
Summary of Content: Magazine covering all aspects of bass playing, including gear and equipment reviews, interviews, transcriptions and tutorials.
Readership/Target Audience: Aimed at anyone interested or involved in bass guitars.
ADVERTISING RATES:
Full Page Colour £795.00
Agency Commission: 10%
Mechanical Data: Type Area: 262 x 184mm, Bleed Size: 307 x 220mm, Trim Size: 297 x 210mm, Page Width: 184mm, Col Length: 262mm, Col Widths (Display): 90mm, Film: Digital
Copy instructions: Copy Date: 4 weeks prior to publication date

---

Average advertising content per issue: 40%
CONSUMER: MUSIC & PERFORMING ARTS: Music

BATH & WELLS DIOCESAN DIRECTORY
47801U87-12

Editorial Address: The Old Deanery, WELLS, BA5 2UG
Tel: 01749 670777 **Fax:** 01749 674240
Email: general@bathwells.anglican.org
Web site: http://www.bathandwells.org.uk
Publisher: Bath & Wells Diocesan Board of Finance
Frequency: Annual - Published in August
Cover Price: £6.00
Circulation: 1,200 (Publisher's Statement)
Usual Pagination: 200
Editor: John Andrews
Summary of Content: Journal about diocesan and parochial organisations.
Readership/Target Audience: Aimed at those interested in the organisational affairs of the Church of England.
ADVERTISING: No Advertising taken
CONSUMER: RELIGIOUS

BATH LIFE
1622705U80C-5060

Editorial Address: Circus Mews House, Circus Mews, BATH, BA1 2PW **Tel:** 01225 475800 **Fax:** 01225 475802
Email: info@mediaclash.co.uk
Advertising Address: As above.
Email: pat.white@mediaclash.co.uk
Web site: http://www.mediaclash.co.uk
Publisher: Media Clash
Date Established: 2002
Frequency: 26 issues yearly
Cover Price: Free
Circulation: 10,000 (Publisher's Statement)
Usual Pagination: 116
Editor: Catherine Authers; **Managing Director:** Jane Ingham; **Advertising Manager:** Pat White; **Managing Editor:** Deri Robins
Summary of Content: Property and lifestyle magazine for Bath with features on wine, food, arts and out and about.
Readership/Target Audience: Aimed at affluent home owners in Bath.
ADVERTISING RATES:
Full Page Colour £750.00
Agency Commission: 10%
Mechanical Data: Type Area: 265 x 195mm, Bleed Size: 291 x 226mm, Trim Size: 285 x 220mm, Col Length: 265mm, Film: Digital, Page Width: 195mm
Copy instructions: Copy Date: 2 weeks prior to publication date
Average advertising content per issue: 40%
CONSUMER: RURAL & REGIONAL INTEREST: Regional Interest English Counties

THE BATH MAGAZINE
1605877U80C-5049

Editorial Address: 25 Milsom Street, BATH, BA1 1DG
Tel: 01225 424499 **Fax:** 01225 426677
Email: editor@thebathmagazine.co.uk
Advertising Address: As above.
Email: sales@thebathmagazine.co.uk
Web site: http://www.thebathmagazine.co.uk
Publisher: MC Publishing Ltd
Date Established: 2002
Frequency: Monthly
Cover Price: Free
Circulation: 30,000 (Publisher's Statement)
Usual Pagination: 100
Editor: Lindsey Harrad; **Advertising Manager:** Steve Miklos
Summary of Content: Magazine covering lifestyle, leisure, local issues, arts, events, culture, property, antiques, gardening, food, commercial activities, architecture and regional news.
Readership/Target Audience: Aimed at owners of properties in Bath and the surrounding areas that are valued higher than £250,000.
ADVERTISING RATES:
Full Page Colour £1075.00
Agency Commission: 15%
Mechanical Data: Type Area: 270 x 190mm, Col Length: 270mm, Page Width: 190mm, Film: Digital
Copy instructions: Copy Date: 15th of the month prior to publication date
Average advertising content per issue: 70%
CONSUMER: RURAL & REGIONAL INTEREST: Regional Interest English Counties

THE BATH PARENT
1852863U74D-675

Editorial Address: 70 Warminster Road, BATH, BA2 6RU
Tel: 01225 421984
Email: editor@thebathparent.co.uk
Web site: http://www.thebathparent.co.uk
Publisher: The Bath Parent
Date Established: 2008
Frequency: 6 issues yearly

Cover Price: Free
Circulation: 11,000 (Publisher's Statement)
Usual Pagination: 36
Editor: Sam Walker
Summary of Content: Magazine covering parenting, education, news, features, what's on, books and competitions.
Readership/Target Audience: Aimed at families with children aged 0 to 11 years old in Bath and the surrounding area.
CONSUMER: WOMEN'S INTEREST CONSUMER MAGAZINES: Child Care

BATMAN LEGENDS
1800451U91D-958

Editorial Address: Titan House, 144 Southwark Street, LONDON, SE1 0UP **Tel:** 020 7620 0200 **Fax:** 020 7620 0032
Email: ned.hartley@titanemail.com
Advertising Address: As above. **Fax:** 020 7803 1803
Email: james.willmott@titanemail.com
Web site: http://www.tots.titanmagazines.co.uk
Publisher: Titan Magazines
Date Established: 2006
Frequency: 6 issues yearly
Cover Price: £2.60
Circulation: 20,000 (Publisher's Statement)
Usual Pagination: 84
Editor: Ned Hartley; **Advertising Manager:** James Willmott
Summary of Content: Children's magazine with re-prints of DC Comics comic strips.
Readership/Target Audience: Aimed at boys and girls aged 8 to 12 years old.
ADVERTISING RATES:
Full Page Colour £1500.00
Agency Commission: 10%
Mechanical Data: Bleed Size: 264 x 176mm, Trim Size: 258 x 170mm, Film: Digital
Copy instructions: Copy Date: 6 weeks prior to publication date
CONSUMER: RECREATION & LEISURE: Children & Youth

BATTERSEA EXCLUSIVE
1892650U80C-5496

Editorial Address: For all contact details see main edition, Exclusive (London)
Frequency: 10 issues yearly
Cover Price: Free
Circulation: 7,500 (Publisher's Statement)
ADVERTISING: Rates on application
Edition of: Exclusive (London)
CONSUMER: RURAL & REGIONAL INTEREST: Regional Interest English Counties

BBC EASY COOK
1643862U74P-913

Formerly: BBC Easy Food
Editorial Address: Media Centre, 201 Wood Lane, LONDON, W12 7TQ **Tel:** 020 8433 3153 **Fax:** 020 8433 3931
Email: marie-louise.stevens@bbc.com
Publisher: BBC Worldwide Publishing
Date Established: 2004
Frequency: 7 issues yearly
Cover Price: £2.60
Circulation: 73,050 (ABC 01/01/2009 to 30/06/2009)
Usual Pagination: 100
Editor: Marie-Louise Stevens; **Advertising Manager:** Gemma Pitts
Summary of Content: Magazine covering family cooking, simple recipes with not too many ingredients and time saving products as well as a small entertainment section.
Readership/Target Audience: Aimed at busy people and mums who are looking to eat quickly and healthily.
ADVERTISING: Rates on application
CONSUMER: WOMEN'S INTEREST CONSUMER MAGAZINES: Food & Cookery

BBC FOCUS
45149U73-140

Formerly: Focus
Editorial Address: 8th Floor, Tower House, Fairfax Street, BRISTOL, BS1 3BN **Tel:** 0117 927 9009 **Fax:** 0117 933 8032
Email: focus@bbcmagazinesbristol.com
Advertising Address: 5th Floor, Tower House, Fairfax Street, BRISTOL, BS1 3BN **Tel:** 0117 927 9009
Fax: 0117 933 8008
Email: james.tawton@bbcmagazinesbristol.com
Web site: http://www.bbcfocusmagazine.com
ISSN: 0966-4270
Publisher: BBC Magazines Bristol
Date Established: 1992
Frequency: 13 issues yearly
Cover Price: £3.40
Annual Sub.: £46.80
Circulation: 68,144 (ABC 01/01/2009 to 30/06/2009)
Usual Pagination: 108
Editor: Jheni Osman; **News Editor:** Andy Ridgway;
Features Editor: Andy Ridgway; **Managing Director:** Andy

Marshall; **Advertising Manager:** Amie Price-Bates;
Publisher: Andrew Davies
Summary of Content: Science magazine covering new developments in technology and scientific discovery, including space exploration, health and the environment, culture and conservation.
Readership/Target Audience: Aimed at men and women aged 15 years old and over.
ADVERTISING RATES:
Full Page Colour £3750.00
Agency Commission: 10%
Copy instructions: Copy Date: 4 weeks prior to publication date
Average advertising content per issue: 30%
CONSUMER: NATIONAL & INTERNATIONAL PERIODICALS

BBC FOCUS ON AFRICA MAGAZINE

47202U82-2_40

Editorial Address: Room 345, Centre Block, Bush House, The Strand, LONDON, WC2B 4PH **Tel:** 020 7557 2906
Fax: 020 7379 0519
Email: focus.magazine@bbc.co.uk
Advertising Address: As above. **Tel:** 020 7557 2792
Email: focus.magazine@bbc.co.uk
Web site: http://www.bbcworldservice.com/focus
ISSN: 0959-9576
Publisher: BBC World Service
Date Established: 1989
Frequency: Quarterly
Cover Price: £3.25
Annual Sub: £14.00
Circulation: 65,000 (Publisher's Statement)
Usual Pagination: 78
Editor: Alison Kingsley-Hall; **Editor-in-Chief:** Joseph Warungu; **Advertising Manager:** Alison Kingsley-Hall; **Managing Editor:** Alison Kingsley-Hall
Summary of Content: Magazine with feature articles and news reports covering the latest political, economic, sporting and cultural events on the African sub-continent.
Readership/Target Audience: Aimed at professionals with an interest in African affairs.
ADVERTISING RATES:
Full Page Colour £3600.00
Agency Commission: 15%
Mechanical Data: Bleed Size: +3mm, Film: Digital, Trim Size: 297 x 210mm, Type Area: 270 x 185mm, Col Length: 270mm, Page Width: 185mm
Copy instructions: Copy Date: 6 weeks prior to publication date
CONSUMER: CURRENT AFFAIRS & POLITICS

BBC GARDENERS' WORLD MAGAZINE

48552U93-11

Editorial Address: Media Centre, 201 Wood Lane, LONDON, W12 7TQ **Tel:** 020 8433 3959 **Fax:** 020 8433 3986
Email: adam.pasco@bbc.com
Advertising Address: Floor 2, Garden House, Media Centre, Wood Lane, LONDON, W12 7TQ **Tel:** 020 8433 2000
Fax: 020 8433 3824
Email: tim.robinson.01@bbc.com
Web site: http://www.gardenersworld.com
Publisher: BBC Magazines
Date Established: 1991
Frequency: Monthly
Cover Price: £3.50
Annual Sub: £42.00
Circulation: 266,179 (ABC 01/01/2009 to 30/06/2009)
Usual Pagination: 172
Editor: Adam Pasco; **Managing Director:** Peter Phippen; **Managing Editor:** Anne Millman; **Publisher:** Dominic Murray
Summary of Content: Magazine providing practical advice and ideas with features contributed by gardening experts and top writers.
Twitter: http://twitter.com/BBC_GW_Live.
Readership/Target Audience: Read by those with an interest in gardening.
ADVERTISING RATES:
Full Page Colour £7850.00
Agency Commission: 10%
Mechanical Data: Film: Digital, Type Area: 272 x 207mm, Col Length: 272mm, Page Width: 207mm, Bleed Size: 308 x 236mm, Trim Size: 300 x 228mm
Copy instructions: Copy Date: 4 weeks prior to publication date
Average advertising content per issue: 40%
CONSUMER: GARDENING

BBC GOOD FOOD

45597U74P-30

Editorial Address: Media Centre, 201 Wood Lane, LONDON, W12 7TQ **Tel:** 020 8433 2000 **Fax:** 020 8433 3931
Email: goodfood@bbc.co.uk
Advertising Address: Garden House, 201 Wood Lane, LONDON, W12 7TQ **Tel:** 020 8433 2000 **Fax:** 020 8433 3824
Email: gemma.baldwin@bbc.com
Web site: http://www.bbcgoodfood.com
ISSN: 0957-588X

Publisher: BBC Worldwide Publishing
Date Established: 1989
Frequency: Monthly
Cover Price: £3.10
Annual Sub.: £35.00
Circulation: 323,171 (ABC 01/01/2009 to 30/06/2009)
Usual Pagination: 146
Editor: Sarah Sysum; **Features Editor:** Sharon Brown; **Managing Director:** Peter Phippen; **Advertising Manager:** Gemma Baldwin
Summary of Content: Magazine providing recipe ideas on home cooking. Includes simple supper ideas, full dinner party menus, advice on food related health problems and kitchenware and appliance reviews.
Twitter: http://twitter.com/bbcgoodfood.
Readership/Target Audience: Aimed at cookery enthusiasts.
ADVERTISING RATES:
Full Page Colour £11000.00
Agency Commission: 15%
Mechanical Data: Film: Digital, Trim Size: 300 x 228mm, Bleed Size: 308 x 236mm
Copy instructions: Copy Date: 7 weeks prior to publication date
Average advertising content per issue: 35%
CONSUMER: WOMEN'S INTEREST CONSUMER MAGAZINES: Food & Cookery

BBC HISTORY MAGAZINE

622736U94X-12_75

Formerly: BBC History Magazine incorporating Living History
Editorial Address: 9th Floor, Tower House, Fairfax Street, BRISTOL, BS1 3BN **Tel:** 0117 933 8048 **Fax:** 0117 934 9008
Email: robertattar@bbcmagazinesbristol.com
Advertising Address: As above. **Tel:** 0117 933 8073
Email: jamestawton@bbcmagazinesbristol.com
Web site: http://www.bbchistorymagazine.com
ISSN: 1469-8552
Publisher: BBC Magazines Bristol
Date Established: 2000
Frequency: Monthly
Cover Price: £3.60
Circulation: 63,888 (ABC 01/01/2009 to 30/06/2009)
Usual Pagination: 100
Editor: David Musgrove; **Features Editor:** Robert Attar; **Publisher:** Andy Healy
Summary of Content: Magazine covering general history topics. Includes articles from historians focusing on a particular period in history.
Readership/Target Audience: Aimed at those with a keen interest in history.
ADVERTISING RATES:
Full Page Colour £3575.00
Agency Commission: 10%
Mechanical Data: Type Area: 264 x 196mm, Col Length: 264mm, Page Width: 196mm, Trim Size: 286 x 216mm, Bleed Size: 292 x 222mm, Film: Digital
Copy instructions: Copy Date: 3rd week of the month prior to publication date
Average advertising content per issue: 10%
CONSUMER: OTHER CLASSIFICATIONS: Miscellaneous

BBC HOMES & ANTIQUES

45239U74C-45

Editorial Address: 9th Floor, Tower House, Fairfax Street, BRISTOL, BS1 3BN **Tel:** 0117 927 9009 **Fax:** 0117 934 9008
Advertising Address: Woodlands, 80 Wood Lane, LONDON, W12 0TT **Tel:** 020 8433 2000 **Fax:** 020 8433 3752
Email: jamie.bolton@bbc.co.uk
Web site: http://www.homesandantiques.com
ISSN: 0968-1485
Publisher: BBC Magazines Bristol
Date Established: 1993
Frequency: Monthly
Cover Price: £3.40
Annual Sub.: £30.60
Circulation: 54,083 (ABC 01/01/2009 to 30/06/2009)
Usual Pagination: 180
Editor: Angela Linforth; **Managing Director:** Andy Marshall; **Advertising Manager:** Jamie Bolton; **Publisher:** Andy Healy
Summary of Content: Magazine combining a blend of home, antiques and heritage related features.
Readership/Target Audience: Aimed at antiques enthusiasts.
ADVERTISING RATES:
Full Page Colour £6870.00
SCC £65.00
Agency Commission: 10%
Mechanical Data: Type Area: 258 x 187mm, Bleed Size: 292 x 221mm, Trim Size: 286 x 215mm, Film: Digital, Col Length: 258mm, Page Width: 187mm
Copy instructions: Copy Date: 2nd week of the month prior to publication date
Average advertising content per issue: 30%
CONSUMER: WOMEN'S INTEREST CONSUMER MAGAZINES: Home & Family

BBC KNOWLEDGE MAGAZINE

1872627U94X-2427

Editorial Address: 8th Floor, Tower House, Fairfax Street, BRISTOL, BS1 3BN **Tel:** 0117 927 9009
Email: editor@bbcknowledge.com
Web site: http://www.bbcknowledgemagazine.com
Publisher: BBC Magazines Bristol
Date Established: 2008
Frequency: 6 issues yearly
Cover Price: $5.99
Circulation: 100,000 (Print Run)
Editor: Sally Palmer; **Managing Editor:** Paul McGuinness
Summary of Content: Magazine featuring informative, entertaining and inspirational features on science, history and nature.
Readership/Target Audience: Aimed at readers interested in history, science and the natural world.
CONSUMER: OTHER CLASSIFICATIONS: Miscellaneous

BBC MUSIC MAGAZINE

46126U76D-200

Editorial Address: 14th Floor, Tower House, Fairfax Street, BRISTOL, BS1 3BN **Tel:** 0117 927 9009 **Fax:** 0117 933 8032
Email: music@bbcmagazinesbristol.com
Advertising Address: 9th Floor, Tower House, Fairfax Street, BRISTOL, BS1 3BN **Tel:** 0117 927 9009
Email: mattstanley@bbcmagazinesbristol.com
Web site: http://www.bbcmusicmagazine.com
ISSN: 0966-7180
Publisher: BBC Magazines Bristol
Date Established: 1992
Frequency: 13 issues yearly
Cover Price: £4.25
Circulation: 45,144 (ABC 01/01/2008 to 31/12/2008)
Usual Pagination: 122
Editor: Tabitha Morton; **Advertising Manager:** Tom Drew; **Publisher:** Andrew Davies
Summary of Content: Music magazine covering all aspects of classical music.
Readership/Target Audience: Aimed at all music lovers and musicians.
ADVERTISING RATES:
Full Page Colour £4060.00
Agency Commission: 10%
Mechanical Data: Film: Digital, Type Area: 251 x 196mm, Col Length: 251mm, Trim Size: 277 x 216mm, Bleed Size: 283 x 222mm, Page Width: 196mm
Average advertising content per issue: 30%
CONSUMER: MUSIC & PERFORMING ARTS: Music

BBC SKY AT NIGHT MAGAZINE

1667073U94X-279

Formerly: BBC Sky at Night
Editorial Address: 9th Floor, Tower House, Fairfax Street, BRISTOL, BS1 3BN **Tel:** 0117 934 9009 **Fax:** 0117 927 9008
Email: inbox@skyatnightmagazine.com
Advertising Address: As above. **Tel:** 0117 927 9009
Fax: 0117 934 9008
Email: graemekirk@bbcmagazinesbristol.com
Web site: http://www.skyatnightmagazine.com
ISSN: 1745-9869
Publisher: BBC Magazines Bristol
Date Established: 2005
Frequency: Monthly
Cover Price: £4.25
Usual Pagination: 108
Editor: Graham Southorn; **Advertising Manager:** Graeme Kirk; **Publisher:** Andrew Davies
Summary of Content: Magazine covering space and astronomy.
Readership/Target Audience: Aimed at armchair and active observers.
ADVERTISING RATES:
Full Page Mono £2275.00
Full Page Colour £2275.00
Agency Commission: 10%
Mechanical Data: Type Area: 251 x 196mm, Bleed Size: 289 x 228mm, Trim Size: 277 x 216mm, Col Length: 251mm, Page Width: 196mm, Film: Digital
Copy instructions: Copy Date: Middle of the month prior to publication date
Average advertising content per issue: 30%
CONSUMER: OTHER CLASSIFICATIONS: Miscellaneous

BBC TOP GEAR MAGAZINE

46303U77A-50

Editorial Address: 2nd FloorA, Energy Centre, Media Village, 201 Wood Lane, LONDON, W12 7TN
Tel: 020 8433 2313 **Fax:** 020 8433 3754
Email: lizzie.bryce@bbc.com
Advertising Address: Garden House, 201 Wood Lane, LONDON, W12 7TQ **Tel:** 020 8433 2000
Email: andy.cowan@bbc.com
Web site: http://www.topgear.com
ISSN: 1350-9624
Publisher: BBC Worldwide Publishing
Frequency: 13 issues yearly

Consumer Magazines

Cover Price: £3.95
Annual Sub.: £39.75
Circulation: 200,761 (ABC 01/01/2009 to 30/06/2009)
Usual Pagination: 306
Editor: Lizzie Bryce; **Managing Director:** Adam Waddell;
Advertising Manager: Andrew Cowan
Summary of Content: Magazine covering information designed to complement the BBC programme of the same name. Offering a comprehensive car buyer's guide and a broad range of features.
Twitter: http://twitter.com/tg_news.
Language(s): Arabic; English
Readership/Target Audience: Aimed at all motoring enthusiasts and those with an interest in the BBC programme.
ADVERTISING RATES:
Full Page Colour £11332.00
Agency Commission: 10%
Mechanical Data: Type Area: 260 x 196mm, Trim Size: 285 x 222mm, Bleed Size: 291 x 228mm, Film: Digital, Col Length: 260mm, Page Width: 196mm
Copy instructions: Copy Date: 3 weeks prior to publication date
Average advertising content per issue: 40%
CONSUMER: MOTORING & CYCLING: Motoring

BBC WHO DO YOU THINK YOU ARE? MAGAZINE
1824046U94X-295
Formerly: BBC Who Do You Think You Are Magazine
Editorial Address: 9th Floor, Tower House, Fairfax Street, BRISTOL, BS1 3BN **Tel:** 0117 927 9009
Email: danielcossins@bbcmagazinesbristol.com
Advertising Address: As above. **Fax:** 0117 934 9008
Email: tomdrew@bbcmagazinesbristol.com
Web site: http://www.bbcwhodoyouthinkyouare.com
Publisher: BBC Magazines Bristol
Date Established: 2007
Frequency: 13 issues yearly
Cover Price: £4.25
Circulation: 45,000 (Print Run)
Usual Pagination: 100
Editor: Dan Cossins; **Publisher:** Andy Benham
Summary of Content: Magazine featuring family and social history with practical advice, celebrity extras from the TV series and a regular section on local history.
Readership/Target Audience: Aimed at those with an interest in family and social history.
ADVERTISING RATES:
Full Page Mono £1800.00
Full Page Colour £1800.00
Agency Commission: 10%
Mechanical Data: Type Area: 264 x 196mm, Bleed Size: 292 x 222mm, Trim Size: 286 x 216mm, Col Length: 264mm, Page Width: 196mm, Film: Digital
Copy instructions: Copy Date: 6 weeks prior to publication date
Average advertising content per issue: 8%
CONSUMER: OTHER CLASSIFICATIONS: Miscellaneous

BBC WILDLIFE MAGAZINE
47184U81X-50
Editorial Address: 14th Floor, Tower House, Fairfax Street, BRISTOL, BS1 3BN **Tel:** 0117 927 9009 **Fax:** 0117 934 9008
Email: wildlifemagazine@bbcmagazinesbristol.com
Advertising Address: 9th Floor, Tower House, Fairfax Street, BRISTOL, BS1 3BN **Tel:** 0117 927 9009
Email: jamiebolton@bbcmagazinebristol.com
Web site: http://www.bbcwildlifemagazine.com
ISSN: 0265-3656
Publisher: BBC Magazines Bristol
Date Established: 1963
Frequency: 13 issues yearly
Cover Price: £3.45
Annual Sub.: £31.20
Circulation: 44,101 (ABC 01/01/2009 to 30/06/2009)
Usual Pagination: 100
Editor: James Fair; **Features Editor:** Fergus Collins;
Advertising Manager: Jamie Bolton; **Publisher:** Jemima Ransome
Summary of Content: Magazine focusing on wildlife, conservation and the environment worldwide, plus TV and radio links.
Readership/Target Audience: Aimed at those wishing to understand more about natural history, conservation and the environment.
ADVERTISING RATES:
Full Page Colour £3558.00
Agency Commission: 10%
Mechanical Data: Type Area: 264 x 196mm, Bleed Size: 292 x 222mm, Trim Size: 286 x 216mm, Film: Digital, Col Length: 264mm, Page Width: 196mm
Average advertising content per issue: 15%
CONSUMER: ANIMALS & PETS

BBC WORLD AGENDA
46091U76C-100
Formerly: BBC On Air Magazine
Editorial Address: Room 500 NE, Bush House, The Strand, LONDON, WC2B 4PH **Tel:** 020 7557 2956
Fax: 020 7240 4899
Email: world.agenda@bbc.co.uk
Web site: http://www.bbcworldservice.com/worldagenda
Publisher: BBC World Service
Frequency: 6 issues yearly
Cover Price: Free
Circulation: 15,000 (Publisher's Statement)
Usual Pagination: 36
Editor: Jo McLeod
Summary of Content: International Journal for the BBC World Service.
Readership/Target Audience: Distributed to those working in Government, Diplomatic services, Media, Cultural Organisations, Development Agencies, NGOs, Research and Educational Institutions and business and trade.
ADVERTISING: No Advertising taken
CONSUMER: MUSIC & PERFORMING ARTS: TV & Radio

BC BIG CARP MAGAZINE
1810840U92-112
Editorial Address: 44 Herbs End, Cove, FARNBOROUGH, GU14 9YD **Tel:** 01252 373658 **Fax:** 01252 373658
Email: bigcarpstudio@hotmail.co.uk
Advertising Address: As above.
Email: bigcarpstudio@hotmail.co.uk
Web site: http://www.bigcarpmagazine.co.uk
Publisher: Bounty Hunter Publications
Date Established: 1991
Frequency: Monthly
Cover Price: £4.25
Annual Sub.: £60.00
Circulation: 11,000 (Publisher's Statement)
Usual Pagination: 100
Editor: Rob Maylin
Summary of Content: Magazine concentrating on the latest method of carp fishing as well as interviews with fishermen from around the world.
Readership/Target Audience: Aimed at carp fishermen.
ADVERTISING RATES:
Full Page Colour £500.00
Mechanical Data: Bleed Size: 303 x 216mm, Trim Size: 297 x 210mm, Film: Digital
CONSUMER: ANGLING & FISHING

BE
1829775U74G-290
Editorial Address: 94 Chandos Avenue, Whetstone, LONDON, N20 9DZ
Email: michelesimmons@btinternet.com
Advertising Address: Marketing Department, Phillips House, Crescent Road, TUNBRIDGE WELLS, TN1 2PL **Tel:** 01892 512345
Email: jo.murphy@axa-ppp.co.uk
Publisher: AXA PPP Healthcare
Frequency: 3 issues yearly - Published in spring, summer and autumn
Cover Price: Free
Circulation: 100,000 (Publisher's Statement)
Usual Pagination: 36
Editor: Michele Simmons; **Advertising Manager:** Jo McCarthy
Summary of Content: Magazine covering all aspects of health and well-being.
Readership/Target Audience: Aimed at AXA PPP customers.
ADVERTISING RATES:
Full Page Colour £2000.00
Mechanical Data: Type Area: 245 x 185mm, Bleed Size: 275 x 215mm, Trim Size: 265 x 205mm, Col Length: 245mm, Page Width: 185mm, Film: Digital
Copy instructions: Copy Date: 2 weeks prior to publication date
CONSUMER: WOMEN'S INTEREST CONSUMER MAGAZINES: Slimming & Health

THE BEACON
46943U80C-3763
Editorial Address: 101 Thunder Lane, NORWICH, NR7 0JG **Tel:** 01603 433972
Email: profilepublishing@hotmail.co.uk
Advertising Address: As above.
Email: profilepublishing@hotmail.co.uk
Publisher: Profile Publishing & Design
Date Established: 1992
Frequency: Quarterly
Cover Price: £2.00
Free to qualifying individuals
Annual Sub.: £5.00
Circulation: 7,000 (Publisher's Statement)
Usual Pagination: 12
Editor: Steven Ford
Summary of Content: Magazine covering local news, events and information.

Readership/Target Audience: Aimed at residents of Thorpe St. Andrew, Norwich and the surrounding areas.
ADVERTISING RATES:
Full Page Mono £260.00
Full Page Colour £310.00
SCC £3.44
Agency Commission: 10%
Mechanical Data: Type Area: 360 x 350mm, Col Length: 360mm, Page Width: 350mm, No. of Columns (Display): 4, Col Widths (Display): 65mm, Print Process: Web-fed offset litho
Average advertising content per issue: 50%
CONSUMER: RURAL & REGIONAL INTEREST: Regional Interest English Counties

BEACONSFIELD EXCLUSIVE
1892645U80C-5492
Editorial Address: For all contact details see main edition, Exclusive (Chilterns)
Frequency: 10 issues yearly
Cover Price: Free
Circulation: 5,000 (Publisher's Statement)
ADVERTISING: Rates on application
Edition of: Exclusive (Chilterns)
CONSUMER: RURAL & REGIONAL INTEREST: Regional Interest English Counties

BEAD
1775348U74E-700
Formerly: Creative Beading Designs
Editorial Address: Ancient Lights, 19 River Road, ARUNDEL, BN18 9EY **Tel:** 01903 884988
Fax: 01903 885514
Email: jean@ashdown.co.uk
Advertising Address: As above.
Email: maria@ashdown.co.uk
Web site: http://www.beadmagazine.co.uk
Publisher: Ashdown.co.uk Ltd
Date Established: 2006
Frequency: 6 issues yearly
Cover Price: £3.95
Editor: Jean Power; **Advertising Manager:** Maria Fitzgerald;
Publisher: Richard Jennings
Summary of Content: Magazine covering all aspects of bead making and jewellery making.
Readership/Target Audience: Aimed at those interested in bead and jewellery making.
ADVERTISING RATES:
Full Page Mono £635.00
Full Page Colour £895.00
Mechanical Data: Type Area: 263 x 185mm, Bleed Size: 303 x 216mm, Trim Size: 297 x 210mm, Col Length: 263mm, Page Width: 185mm
CONSUMER: WOMEN'S INTEREST CONSUMER MAGAZINES: Crafts

BEADS & BEYOND
1824374U74E-706
Editorial Address: Traplet House, Pendragon Close, MALVERN, WR14 1GA **Tel:** 01684 588500
Fax: 01684 578558
Email: rebecca.hughes@traplet.com
Advertising Address: As above.
Web site: http://www.beadsandbeyondmagazine.com
Publisher: Traplet Publications Ltd
Date Established: 2007
Frequency: Monthly
Cover Price: £3.95
Circulation: 105,000 (Publisher's Statement)
Editor: Rebecca Hughes
Summary of Content: Magazine featuring technical, studio-based projects focused on flame and glass kiln work, woodturning and precious metals and easy to follow step by step guides.
Readership/Target Audience: Aimed at women who are interested in high street fashion, accessories and home decor. Men will enjoy reading the technical projects.
CONSUMER: WOMEN'S INTEREST CONSUMER MAGAZINES: Crafts

THE BEANO
48508U91D-19
Editorial Address: 2 Albert Square, DUNDEE, DD1 9QJ **Tel:** 01382 223131 **Fax:** 01382 322214
Email: adigby@dcthomson.co.uk
Advertising Address: 20 Orange Street, LONDON, WC2H 7EF **Tel:** 01372 802800 **Fax:** 01372 723322
Email: robin@o20.co.uk
Web site: http://www.beanotown.com
Publisher: D.C. Thomson & Co Ltd
Date Established: 1938
Frequency: Weekly
Cover Price: £0.65
Circulation: 53,964 (ABC 01/01/2009 to 30/06/2009)
Usual Pagination: 32
Editor: Alan Digby; **Advertising Manager:** Robin Johnson
Summary of Content: Children's magazine featuring cartoons and comic strips.

Readership/Target Audience: Aimed primarily at children between 6 and 12 years old.
ADVERTISING RATES:
Full Page Colour £3935.00
Agency Commission: 15%
Mechanical Data: Page Width: 200mm, Type Area: 276 x 200mm, Bleed Size: 300 x 231mm, Trim Size: 295 x 225mm, Col Length: 276mm, Film: Digital
Copy instructions: Copy Date: 19 working days prior to publication date
Average advertising content per issue: 20%
CONSUMER: RECREATION & LEISURE: Children & Youth

BEANOMAX
1800452U91D-959
Editorial Address: 2 Albert Square, DUNDEE, DD1 9QJ **Tel:** 01382 223131 **Fax:** 01382 322214
Email: joanderson@dcthomson.co.uk
Advertising Address: Orange 20, Station House, Bunbury Way, EPSOM, KT17 4JP **Tel:** 01372 802800
Fax: 01372 723322
Email: robin@o20.co.uk
Publisher: D.C. Thomson & Co Ltd
Date Established: 2007
Frequency: Monthly
Cover Price: £2.50
Circulation: 42,565 (ABC 01/01/2009 to 30/06/2009)
Usual Pagination: 44
Editor: John Anderson; **Features Editor:** John Anderson
Summary of Content: Children's magazine with comic stories, lifestyle features, games reviews, celebrities, puzzles and competitions.
Readership/Target Audience: Aimed at boys aged 8 to 12 years old.
ADVERTISING RATES:
Full Page Colour £2500.00
Agency Commission: 15%
Mechanical Data: Type Area: 276 x 200mm, Bleed Size: 300 x 231mm, Trim Size: 295 x 225mm, Col Length: 276mm, Page Width: 200mm, Film: Digital
Copy instructions: Copy Date: 5 weeks prior to publication date
Average advertising content per issue: 20%
CONSUMER: RECREATION & LEISURE: Children & Youth

THE BEAT
766688U76D-755
Formerly: And the Beat Still Goes On
Editorial Address: Home Close, Teffont, SALISBURY, SP3 5QY **Tel:** 01722 716268 **Fax:** 01722 716781
Email: davidparker@aol.com
Advertising Address: As above.
Email: davidparker@aol.com
Web site: http://www.thebeatmagazine.co.uk
Publisher: Kingsley House (Publishing)
Date Established: 2002
Frequency: Monthly
Cover Price: £2.95
Free to qualifying individuals
Annual Sub.: £36.00
Circulation: 2,500 (Publisher's Statement)
Usual Pagination: 28
Editor: David Parker; **Advertising Manager:** Karl Plaskett
Summary of Content: Magazine covering 60s rock and roll, jazz, rhythm and blues, news, views, gig guides, reviews of shows and news from behind the scenes.
Readership/Target Audience: Aimed primarily at followers of 60s music between 20 and 65 years old.
ADVERTISING RATES:
Full Page Colour £220.00
Mechanical Data: Trim Size: 297 x 210mm, Film: Digital, No. of Columns (Display): 4, Bleed Size: + 5mm, Col Widths (Display): 45mm
Copy instructions: Copy Date: 20th of the month prior to publication date
Average advertising content per issue: 30%
CONSUMER: MUSIC & PERFORMING ARTS: Music

BEAUTIFUL BRITAIN
1785452U80A-175
Editorial Address: PO Box 52, CHELTENHAM, GL50 1YQ **Tel:** 01242 537900
Email: editor@beautifulbritain.net
Advertising Address: As above. **Fax:** 01242 537901
Email: palmer@beautifulbritain.net
Web site: http://www.beautifulbritain.net
Publisher: Beautiful Britain Ltd
Date Established: 2006
Frequency: Quarterly
Cover Price: £3.95
Annual Sub.: £16.00
Circulation: 70,000 (Print Run)
Usual Pagination: 80
Editor: Robert Yarham; **Advertising Manager:** Mark Palmer; **Publisher:** Simon O'Brien
Summary of Content: Magazine covering Britain's countryside, towns, villages, people and wildlife.
Readership/Target Audience: Aimed at residents and visitors to the UK, and those with family roots in Britain.

ADVERTISING RATES:
Full Page Mono £2450.00
Full Page Colour £2450.00
Agency Commission: 10%
Mechanical Data: Type Area: 275 x 206mm, Col Length: 275mm, Page Width: 206mm, Film: Digital
Copy instructions: Copy Date: 7 weeks prior to publication date
Average advertising content per issue: 10%
CONSUMER: RURAL & REGIONAL INTEREST: Rural Interest

BEAUTIFUL CARDS
1696576U74E-697
Editorial Address: 14th Floor, Tower House, Fairfax Street, BRISTOL, BS1 3BN **Tel:** 0117 927 9009 **Fax:** 0117 934 9008
Email: annadavenport@originpublishing.co.uk
Advertising Address: 9th Floor, Tower House, Fairfax Street, BRISTOL, BS1 3BN **Tel:** 0117 927 9009
Fax: 0117 927 9008
Email: alisonzak-collins@originpublishing.co.uk
Web site: http://www.cardmakingandpapercraft.com
Publisher: Origin Publishing Ltd
Date Established: 2005
Frequency: 9 issues yearly
Cover Price: £4.99
Circulation: 35,000 (Print Run)
Usual Pagination: 100
Editor: Anna Davenport; **Advertising Manager:** David Manson; **Publisher:** Anna Davenport
Summary of Content: Magazine covering cardmaking ideas, products and tips including card designs to mark every occasion throughout the calendar year.
Readership/Target Audience: Aimed at enthusiastic card makers.
ADVERTISING RATES:
Full Page Colour £1050.00
Agency Commission: 10%
Mechanical Data: Type Area: 281 x 195mm, Bleed Size: 303 x 216mm, Trim Size: 297 x 210mm, Col Length: 281mm, Page Width: 195mm
Copy instructions: Copy Date: 6 weeks prior to publication date
Average advertising content per issue: 10%
CONSUMER: WOMEN'S INTEREST CONSUMER MAGAZINES: Crafts

BEAUTIFUL KITCHENS
623199U74C-12
Formerly: 25 Beautiful Kitchens
Editorial Address: 7th Floor, Blue Fin Building, 110 Southwark Street, LONDON, SE1 0SU **Tel:** 020 3148 5000
Fax: 020 3148 8121
Email: ysanne_brooks@ipcmedia.com
Advertising Address: Blue Fin Building, 110 Southwark Street, LONDON, SE1 0SU **Tel:** 020 3148 5000
Email: james_zaman@ipcmedia.com
Web site: http://www.ipcmedia.com
Publisher: IPC Southbank
Frequency: 10 issues yearly
Cover Price: £3.99
Circulation: 29,677 (ABC 01/01/2008 to 31/12/2008)
Usual Pagination: 130
Editor: Ysanne Brooks; **Advertising Manager:** James Zaman; **Advertising Director:** Joanne O'Hara; **Publisher:** Belinda Cooper
Summary of Content: Magazine profiling real kitchens. Also contains product features on items such as utensils, kettles and sinks.
Readership/Target Audience: Aimed at people with an interest in home decorating.
ADVERTISING RATES:
Full Page Colour £5600.00
Mechanical Data: Page Width: 194mm, Type Area: 258 x 194mm, Bleed Size: 290 x 224mm, Trim Size: 284 x 220mm, Col Length: 258mm, Film: Digital, Print Process: Web-fed offset litho
CONSUMER: WOMEN'S INTEREST CONSUMER MAGAZINES: Home & Family

THE BEAVER
47370U83-2_3
Editorial Address: East Building, Houghton Street, LONDON, WC2A 2AE **Tel:** 020 7955 6705
Fax: 020 7955 6789
Email: thebeaver.editor@lse.ac.uk
Advertising Address: As above.
Email: thebeaver.business@lse.ac.uk
Web site: http://www.thebeaveronline.co.uk
Publisher: London School of Economics Students' Union (LSE SU)
Date Established: 1949
Frequency: Weekly
Free to qualifying individuals
Circulation: 4,000 (Publisher's Statement)
Usual Pagination: 56
Editor: Joseph Cotterill; **Advertising Manager:** Anmol Tiwari

Summary of Content: Magazine covering student issues, politics, the arts, what's on and events.
Readership/Target Audience: Read by undergraduate and graduate students of the London School of Economics.
ADVERTISING RATES:
Full Page Mono £949.00
Full Page Colour £1249.00
Agency Commission: 10%
Mechanical Data: Film: Digital, No. of Columns (Display): 5, Trim Size: 369 x 272mm
Copy instructions: Copy Date: Friday 12pm prior to publication date
Average advertising content per issue: 10%
CONSUMER: STUDENT PUBLICATIONS

BEDFORDSHIRE COUNTY LIFE MAGAZINE
46855U80C-190
Editorial Address: PO Box 32, BIGGLESWADE, SG18 8TE **Tel:** 01462 819496 **Fax:** 01462 819496
Email: editor@bedfordshiremagazine.co.uk
Advertising Address: As above.
Email: sales@bedfordshiremagazine.co.uk
Web site: http://www.bedfordshiremagazine.co.uk
ISSN: 1463-2055
Publisher: Select Publishing
Date Established: 1998
Frequency: Quarterly
Cover Price: £2.99
Annual Sub.: £16.00
Circulation: 15,000 (Publisher's Statement)
Usual Pagination: 64
Editor: Alan Humphreys; **Advertising Manager:** Alan Humphreys
Summary of Content: Magazine containing historical profiles on local villages and towns. Covers gardening, homes, eating out, recipes, motoring, industrial heritage, local history and events.
Readership/Target Audience: Read by residents, ex-residents and visitors to Bedfordshire.
ADVERTISING RATES:
Full Page Mono £820.00
Full Page Colour £1050.00
Mechanical Data: Type Area: 266 x 190mm, Bleed Size: 305 x 215mm, Trim Size: 295 x 210mm
Average advertising content per issue: 30%
CONSUMER: RURAL & REGIONAL INTEREST: Regional Interest English Counties

BEE CRAFT
47177U81G-40
Editorial Address: Stoneycroft, Back Lane, Little Addington, KETTERING, NN14 4AX **Tel:** 01933 650297
Fax: 01933 650297
Email: editor@bee-craft.com
Advertising Address: 34 Cambridge Road, Wimpole, ROYSTON, SG8 5QE **Tel:** 01223 208552 **Fax:** 01223 208552
Email: display.ads@bee-craft.com
Web site: http://www.bee-craft.com
ISSN: 0005-7703
Publisher: Bee Craft Ltd
Date Established: 1919
Frequency: Monthly - Published on the 1st of the month
Cover Price: £3.00
Annual Sub.: £22.00
Circulation: 5,300 (Publisher's Statement)
Usual Pagination: 32
Editor: Claire Waring; **Advertising Manager:** Pauline Aslin
Summary of Content: Official journal of the British Beekeepers' Association, with news and articles on bees, beekeeping techniques and related subjects, also includes the 'B' Kids.
Readership/Target Audience: Read by those interested in the countryside and in keeping bees.
ADVERTISING RATES:
Full Page Mono £261.00
Full Page Colour £382.00
Mechanical Data: Col Length: 277mm, No. of Columns (Display): 2, Type Area: 277 x 190mm, Bleed Size: 303 x 216mm, Page Width: 190mm, Film: Digital
Copy instructions: Copy Date: 1st of the month prior to publication date
Average advertising content per issue: 30%
CONSUMER: ANIMALS & PETS: Bees

THE BEEF
752873U75P-70
Editorial Address: 10 Alpha Court, Denton, MANCHESTER, M34 3RB **Tel:** 0161 320 5123 **Fax:** 0161 320 5123
Email: muscleco@aol.com
Advertising Address: 5 Windmill Trading Estate, Denton, MANCHESTER, M34 3JN **Tel:** 0161 320 5123
Fax: 0161 320 5123
Email: muscleco@aol.com
Web site: http://www.thebeef.info
ISSN: 1476-0215
Publisher: Muscle News
Date Established: 2001
Frequency: 8 issues yearly
Cover Price: £2.95

Consumer Magazines

Circulation: 20,000 (Publisher's Statement)
Usual Pagination: 80
Editor: Alex McKenna; **Advertising Manager:** Alex McKenna
Summary of Content: Magazine covering bodybuilding, fitness and nutrition.
Readership/Target Audience: Aimed at bodybuilding enthusiasts and gym owners.
ADVERTISING: Rates on application
CONSUMER: SPORT: Fitness/Bodybuilding

THE BEEKEEPERS QUARTERLY
47179U81G-121

Editorial Address: Scout Bottom Farm, Mytholmroyd, HEBDEN BRIDGE, HX7 5JS **Tel:** 01422 882751
Fax: 01422 886157
Email: bkg@recordermail.demon.co.uk
Advertising Address: As above.
Email: ian@recordermail.demon.co.uk
Web site: http://www.beedata.com
ISSN: 0268-4780
Publisher: Northern Bee Books
Frequency: Quarterly
Annual Sub.: £24.00
Circulation: 3,000 (Publisher's Statement)
Usual Pagination: 56
Editor: Jeremy Burbidge; **Advertising Manager:** Ian Davies; **Publisher:** Jeremy Burbidge
Summary of Content: Magazine covering national and international news on beekeeping, countryside issues and the environment, with advice and book reviews.
Readership/Target Audience: Read by apiarists.
ADVERTISING: Rates on application
CONSUMER: ANIMALS & PETS: Bees

BEEKEEPING
47180U81G-80

Editorial Address: Landscore, Eastern Road, Ashburton, NEWTON ABBOT, TQ13 7AR **Tel:** 01364 652640
Email: landscore@eclipse.co.uk
Advertising Address: As above. **Fax:** 01363 866687
Email: landscore@eclipse.co.uk
Publisher: Devon Beekeepers Association
Date Established: 1935
Frequency: 10 issues yearly - Combined issues published in May/June and October/November
Cover Price: £1.50
Annual Sub.: £11.50
Circulation: 900 (Publisher's Statement)
Usual Pagination: 28
Editor: Glyn Davies; **Advertising Manager:** Glyn Davies; **Publisher:** John ladler
Summary of Content: Publication containing reports and news on all aspects of bees and beekeeping including disease reports, research, history, beekeeping archaeology, book reviews, honey cookery and beekeeping memorabilia.
Readership/Target Audience: Read by members of the Devon Beekeepers Association and other beekeepers.
ADVERTISING RATES:
Full Page Mono £32.00
Mechanical Data: Trim Size: 210 x 148mm, Type Area: 170 x 118mm, Col Length: 170mm, Page Width: 118mm, Film: Digital
Copy instructions: Copy Date: 5th of the month prior to publication date
Average advertising content per issue: 20%
CONSUMER: ANIMALS & PETS: Bees

BEERS OF THE WORLD
1692334U74P-930

Editorial Address: St. Faiths House, Mountergate, NORWICH, NR1 1PY **Tel:** 01603 633808 **Fax:** 01603 632808
Email: sally@paragraphpublishing.com
Advertising Address: As above.
Email: joanne@paragraphpublishing.com
Web site: http://www.beers-of-the-world.com
Publisher: Paragraph Publishing
Date Established: 2005
Frequency: 6 issues yearly
Cover Price: £3.50
Circulation: 20,000 (Publisher's Statement)
Usual Pagination: 84
Editor: Sally Toms; **Publisher:** Damian Riley Smith
Summary of Content: Magazine covering all aspects of beer, its history and heritage, regional focuses, individual breweries and its production processes and flavours.
Readership/Target Audience: Aimed at anyone who enjoys beer.
ADVERTISING RATES:
Full Page Colour £3125.00
Agency Commission: 10%
Mechanical Data: Type Area: 258 x 185mm, Bleed Size: 286 x 221mm, Trim Size: 280 x 215mm, Col Length: 258mm, Page Width: 185mm, Film: Digital
Copy instructions: Copy Date: 4 weeks prior to publication date

Average advertising content per issue: 40%
CONSUMER: WOMEN'S INTEREST CONSUMER MAGAZINES: Food & Cookery

BEES FOR DEVELOPMENT JOURNAL
47181U81G-90

Formerly: Beekeeping & Development
Editorial Address: PO Box 105, MONMOUTH, NP25 9AA
Tel: 01600 713648 **Fax:** 01600 716167
Email: info@beesfordevelopment.org
Advertising Address: As above.
Email: info@beesfordevelopment.org
Web site: http://www.beesfordevelopment.org
ISSN: 1447-6568
Publisher: Bees for Development
Date Established: 1986
Frequency: Quarterly - Published on the 1st of the month Free to qualifying individuals
Annual Sub.: £20.00
Circulation: 5,000 (Publisher's Statement)
Usual Pagination: 16
Editor: Nicola Bradbear; **Advertising Manager:** Helen Jackson
Summary of Content: Journal which projects beekeeping as a worthwhile and interesting form of agriculture.
Language(s): English; French
Readership/Target Audience: Aimed at beekeepers worldwide and academics, also development and aid agency professionals.
ADVERTISING RATES:
Full Page Colour £250.00
Copy instructions: Copy Date: 1st of 2 months prior to publication date
CONSUMER: ANIMALS & PETS: Bees

BEIGE MAGAZINE
1840812U86B-184

Editorial Address: Suite 404 Albany House, 324-326 Regent Street, LONDON, W1B 3HH **Tel:** 020 7636 4343
Fax: 020 7636 2323
Email: douglas@beigeuk.com
Advertising Address: As above.
Email: sales@beigeuk.com
Web site: http://www.beigeuk.com
ISSN: 1756-7211
Publisher: Mixed Phase Media Ltd
Date Established: 2007
Frequency: Monthly
Cover Price: Free
Circulation: 30,000 (Publisher's Statement)
Usual Pagination: 84
Editor: Doug Mayo
Summary of Content: Magazine focusing on lifestyle, shopping, the arts, property, fashion and current affairs.
Readership/Target Audience: Aimed at gay, urban, professional men across the UK.
ADVERTISING RATES:
Full Page Colour £1200.00
Mechanical Data: Trim Size: 297 x 210mm
Average advertising content per issue: 40%
CONSUMER: ADULT & GAY MAGAZINES: Gay & Lesbian Magazines

THE BELFAST BEAT
1693728U80F-206

Editorial Address: 5 University Street, BELFAST, BT7 1FY
Tel: 028 9024 6624 **Fax:** 028 9024 6936
Email: info@admanpublishing.com
Advertising Address: As above.
Email: thebelfastbeat@admanpublishing.com
Web site: http://www.admanpublishing.com
Publisher: Adman Publishing Ltd
Frequency: Monthly
Cover Price: Free
Circulation: 20,000 (Publisher's Statement)
Usual Pagination: 32
Editor: Henry Davidson
Summary of Content: Magazine covering travel, arts, out and about, health, fashion. shopping, restaurants, pubs and clubs, films, hair and competitions.
Readership/Target Audience: Aimed at residents, businesses and visitors to Belfast.
ADVERTISING RATES:
Full Page Mono £1095.00
Full Page Colour £1095.00
Agency Commission: 15%
Mechanical Data: Bleed Size: +5mm, Type Area: 320 x 220mm, Col Length: 320mm, Page Width: 220mm, Film: Digital
Copy instructions: Copy Date: 20th of the month prior to publication date
Average advertising content per issue: 40%
CONSUMER: RURAL & REGIONAL INTEREST: Regional Interest Northern Ireland

BELFAST MAGAZINE
1691327U80F-205

Editorial Address: Ashton Centre, 5 Churchill Street, BELFAST, BT15 2BP **Tel:** 028 9020 2100
Fax: 028 9020 2227
Email: glenravel@ashtoncentre.com
Advertising Address: As above.
Email: joe@ashtoncentre.com
Web site: http://www.glenravel.com
Publisher: Glenravel Publications
Date Established: 1995
Frequency: 6 issues yearly
Cover Price: £2.50
Circulation: 45,000 (Publisher's Statement)
Usual Pagination: 88
Editor: Joe Baker; **Advertising Manager:** Joe Baker
Summary of Content: Magazine covering local interest stories and local historical topics ranging from true murder cases through to major events.
Language(s): English; Gaelic
Readership/Target Audience: Aimed at a general readership.
ADVERTISING RATES:
Full Page Mono £600.00
Full Page Colour £800.00
Agency Commission: 10%
Mechanical Data: Trim Size: 190 x 130mm, Bleed Size: 208 x 145mm, Film: Digital
Average advertising content per issue: 60%
CONSUMER: RURAL & REGIONAL INTEREST: Regional Interest Northern Ireland

BELGRAVIA
46818U80B-30

Editorial Address: Blandel Bridge House, 56 Sloane Square, LONDON, SW1W 8AX **Tel:** 020 7259 1050
Fax: 020 7901 9042
Email: kate@pubbiz.com
Advertising Address: As above.
Email: sam@pubbiz.com
Web site: http://www.pubbiz.com
Publisher: Publishing Business
Date Established: 1989
Frequency: 6 issues yearly
Cover Price: Free
Circulation: 8,000 (Publisher's Statement)
Usual Pagination: 24
Editor: Kate White; **News Editor:** Kate White; **Executive Editor:** Sophie Brewitt; **Advertising Manager:** Katie Thomas; **Publisher:** Adrian Day
Summary of Content: Magazine containing news and features on life and work in the Belgravia area of London.
Readership/Target Audience: Aimed at residents and businesses within the area of Belgravia.
ADVERTISING RATES:
Full Page Mono £2029.00
Full Page Colour £2329.00
SCC £12.50
Agency Commission: 10%
Mechanical Data: Bleed Size: 426 x 306mm, Trim Size: 420 x 300mm, No. of Columns (Display): 6, Print Process: Litho, Film: Digital, Col Widths (Display): 39mm
Copy instructions: Copy Date: 4 weeks prior to publication date
Average advertising content per issue: 40%
CONSUMER: RURAL & REGIONAL INTEREST: Regional Interest Greater London

BELLA
45167U74A-12

Editorial Address: Academic House, 24-28 Oval Road, LONDON, NW1 7DT **Tel:** 020 7241 8000 **Fax:** 020 7241 8056
Advertising Address: As above.
Email: harriet.edery@bauer.co.uk
Web site: http://www.bauer.co.uk/our-magazines/bella
Publisher: H. Bauer Publishing
Date Established: 1987
Frequency: Weekly
Cover Price: £0.85
Circulation: 243,991 (ABC 01/01/2009 to 30/06/2009)
Usual Pagination: 62
Editor: Eileen Shears; **Features Editor:** Unity Rowe; **Managing Director:** David Goodchild; **Advertising Manager:** Harriet Edery
Summary of Content: Women's magazine, combining practicals and real life.
Twitter: http://twitter.com/Bellamag.
Readership/Target Audience: Aimed at female consumers between 25 and 44 years old.
ADVERTISING RATES:
Full Page Colour £18150.00
Agency Commission: 15%
Mechanical Data: Type Area: 266 x 207mm, Bleed Size: 298 x 238mm, Trim Size: 290 x 230mm, Film: Digital, Col Length: 266mm, Page Width: 207mm
Copy instructions: Copy Date: 3 weeks prior to publication date
Average advertising content per issue: 30%
CONSUMER: WOMEN'S INTEREST CONSUMER MAGAZINES: Women's Interest

Section 4 (c) Consumer Magazines

BENT
47629U86B-60

Formerly: NOW UK

Editorial Address: APN House, Temple Crescent, LEEDS, LS11 8BP **Tel:** 0871 224 6511 **Fax:** 0870 122 2666

Email: editor@bent.com

Advertising Address: As above. **Tel:** 0871 220 1675

Email: darrell@bent.com

Web site: http://www.mag.bent.com

ISSN: 1742-3031

Publisher: Bent Ltd

Date Established: 1998

Frequency: Monthly - Published on the 1st Tuesday of every month
Free to qualifying individuals

Annual Sub.: £36.00

Circulation: 60,000 (Publisher's Statement)

Usual Pagination: 80

Editor: Gordon Hopps; **Features Editor:** Adam Lowe;

Advertising Manager: Darrell Hirst; **Publisher:** Terry George

Summary of Content: Magazine containing news, celebrity interviews, events coverage, what's on section, music, games, book reviews and competitions.

Readership/Target Audience: Aimed primarily at the gay market.

ADVERTISING RATES:

Full Page Colour £1740.00

Agency Commission: 10%

Mechanical Data: Type Area: 277 x 185mm, Col Length: 277mm, Bleed Size: 313 x 216mm, Trim Size: 297 x 210mm, Film: Digital, Page Width: 185mm

Copy instructions: Copy Date: 15th of the month prior to publication date

Average advertising content per issue: 55%

CONSUMER: ADULT & GAY MAGAZINES: Gay & Lesbian Magazines

BENTLEY MAGAZINE
1601497U77A-503

Editorial Address: New Barn, Fanhams Grange, Fanhams Hall Road, WARE, SG12 7QA **Tel:** 01920 467492

Fax: 01920 460149

Advertising Address: As above. **Tel:** 01920 444892

Email: louise@fms.co.uk

Web site: http://www.bentleymagazine.com

Publisher: FMS Publishing

Date Established: 2002

Frequency: Quarterly
Free to qualifying individuals

Circulation: 65,000 (Publisher's Statement)

Usual Pagination: 80

Editor: Irene Mateides

Summary of Content: Magazine covering lifestyle & motoring issues and articles on new and old Bentleys and forthcoming Bentley products, travel, leisure, homes, luxury goods and owner profiles.

Readership/Target Audience: Aimed at Bentley owners.

ADVERTISING RATES:

Full Page Colour £7950.00

Agency Commission: 10%

Mechanical Data: Trim Size: 327 x 239mm, Film: Digital

Copy instructions: Copy Date: 1 month prior to publication date

CONSUMER: MOTORING & CYCLING: Motoring

BERKHAMSTED EXCLUSIVE
1892639U80C-5487

Editorial Address: For all contact details see main edition, Exclusive (Chilterns)

Frequency: 10 issues yearly

Cover Price: Free

Circulation: 5,000 (Publisher's Statement)

ADVERTISING: Rates on application

Edition of: Exclusive (Chilterns)

CONSUMER: RURAL & REGIONAL INTEREST: Regional Interest English Counties

BERKSHIRE LIVING
749658U80C-260

Formerly: Berkshire Style

Editorial Address: 48 Bell Street, MAIDENHEAD, SL6 1HX **Tel:** 01628 678229 **Fax:** 01628 678245

Email: rosellam@baylismedia.co.uk

Advertising Address: As above. **Tel:** 01628 678215

Fax: 01628 682700

Email: janed@maidenads.co.uk

Web site: http://www.maidenads.co.uk

Publisher: Baylis & Co.

Date Established: 2001

Frequency: Quarterly - Published on the 1st Thursday of the month of publication

Cover Price: Free

Circulation: 25,000 (Publisher's Statement)

Usual Pagination: 68

Editor: Rosella Masters; **Features Editor:** Rosella Masters;

Advertising Manager: Jane Donovan

Summary of Content: Magazine covering entertainment, food, fashion, motoring, golf, travel and property.

Readership/Target Audience: Aimed at affluent and aspirational households in the Berkshire area.

ADVERTISING RATES:

Full Page Colour £500.00

Agency Commission: 10%

Mechanical Data: Type Area: 270 x 190mm, Bleed Size: 303 x 216mm, Trim Size: 297 x 210mm, Col Length: 270mm, Film: Digital, Page Width: 190mm

Copy instructions: Copy Date: 2 weeks prior to publication date

Average advertising content per issue: 50%

Supplement to: Maidenhead Advertiser Series

CONSUMER: RURAL & REGIONAL INTEREST: Regional Interest English Counties

BEST
45168U74A-15

Editorial Address: National Magazine House, 33 Broadwick Street, LONDON, W1F 0DQ **Tel:** 020 7339 4500

Fax: 020 7339 4580

Email: best@natmags.co.uk

Advertising Address: As above. **Tel:** 020 7339 4567

Fax: 020 7339 4527

Email: james.graham@natmags.co.uk

Web site: http://www.bestmagazine.co.uk

ISSN: 0954-8955

Publisher: National Magazine Company Ltd

Date Established: 1987

Frequency: Weekly

Cover Price: £0.87

Circulation: 296,971 (ABC 01/01/2009 to 30/06/2009)

Usual Pagination: 68

Editor: Jane Ennis; **Features Editor:** Charlotte Seligman

Summary of Content: Magazine covering fashion, beauty, food, health and celebrity interviews.
Twitter: http://twitter.com/NatMags.

Readership/Target Audience: Aimed at women.

ADVERTISING RATES:

Full Page Colour £20555.00

Agency Commission: 10%

Mechanical Data: Film: Digital, Type Area: 267 x 207mm, Trim Size: 284 x 225mm, Bleed Size: 290 x 231mm, Col Length: 267mm, Page Width: 207mm

Copy instructions: Copy Date: 7 days prior to publication date

Average advertising content per issue: 15%

Supplement(s): Celebrity Insider - 52xY

CONSUMER: WOMEN'S INTEREST CONSUMER MAGAZINES: Women's Interest

BEST OF BRITISH
46793U80A-30

Editorial Address: The Clock Tower, 6 Market Gate, Market Deeping, PETERBOROUGH, PE6 8DL **Tel:** 01778 342814

Fax: 01778 342814

Email: info@bestofbritishmag.co.uk

Advertising Address: As above.

Email: info@bestofbritishmag.co.uk

Web site: http://www.bestofbritishmag.co.uk

ISSN: 1355-6681

Publisher: Church Lane Publishing Ltd

Date Established: 1994

Frequency: Monthly

Cover Price: £3.60

Annual Sub.: £38.00

Circulation: 27,500 (Publisher's Statement)

Usual Pagination: 80

Editor: Linne Matthews; **Editor-in-Chief:** Ian Beacham;

Publisher: Ian Beacham

Summary of Content: Magazine focusing on nostalgia from the 1940s, 1950s and 1960s together with the best of British life today.

Readership/Target Audience: Aimed at people aged 45 years old and over and all those interested in history, heritage and nostalgia.

ADVERTISING RATES:

Full Page Colour £900.00

Agency Commission: 10%

Mechanical Data: Type Area: 280 x 188mm, Col Length: 280mm, No. of Columns (Display): 4, Bleed Size: 303 x 216mm, Trim Size: 297 x 210mm, Page Width: 188mm, Film: Digital

Copy instructions: Copy Date: 4 weeks prior to publication date

CONSUMER: RURAL & REGIONAL INTEREST: Rural Interest

BEST OF FORUM
1799713U86A-188

Editorial Address: 211 Old Street, Ground Floor, LONDON, EC1V 9NR **Tel:** 020 7608 6500

Email: liz.coldwell@trojanpublishing.co.uk

Advertising Address: As above. **Tel:** 020 7608 6300

Email: louise.mcmahon@trojanpublishing.co.uk

Web site: http://www.ukforum.co.uk

Publisher: Trojan Publishing

Date Established: 1986

Frequency: 9 issues yearly

Cover Price: £4.99

Annual Sub.: £31.00

Circulation: 20,000 (Publisher's Statement)

Usual Pagination: 196

Editor: Elizabeth Coldwell

Summary of Content: Magazine containing re-printed material from the UK and US editions of Forum including all aspects of human sexuality and relationships.

Readership/Target Audience: Aimed at men and women aged over 18 years old.

ADVERTISING RATES:

Full Page Colour £500.00

Agency Commission: 10%

Mechanical Data: Type Area: 185 x 123mm, Col Length: 185mm, Page Width: 123mm, Film: Digital, Bleed Size: 216 x 154mm, Trim Size: 210 x 148mm

Copy instructions: Copy Date: 3 weeks prior to publication date

Average advertising content per issue: 25%

CONSUMER: ADULT & GAY MAGAZINES: Adult Magazines

THE BEST SCOTTISH WEDDINGS
754719U74L-55

Editorial Address: Suite 4, Sovereign House, 58 Elliot Street, GLASGOW, G3 8DZ **Tel:** 0141 567 6000

Fax: 0141 221 3337

Email: gillian.welsh@peeblesmedia.com

Advertising Address: As above. **Tel:** 0141 221 5559

Email: susan.white@peeblesmedia.com

Web site: http://www.thebestscottishweddings.co.uk

Publisher: Peebles Media Group Ltd

Frequency: Half-yearly - Published in January and July

Cover Price: £2.95

Circulation: 20,000 (Publisher's Statement)

Editor: Gillian Welsh; **Managing Editor:** Iain McEwan;

Advertising Director: Susan White

Summary of Content: Magazine covering all aspects of weddings including fashion, gifts, receptions, honeymoons and setting up home.

Readership/Target Audience: Aimed at brides, grooms and those with high disposable income planning a wedding.

ADVERTISING RATES:

Full Page Colour £1495.00

Agency Commission: 10%

Mechanical Data: Page Width: 180mm, Type Area: 245 x 180mm, Col Length: 245mm, Trim Size: 285 x 220mm, Bleed Size: 291 x 226mm, Film: Digital

Copy instructions: Copy Date: 6 weeks prior to publication date

Average advertising content per issue: 40%

CONSUMER: WOMEN'S INTEREST CONSUMER MAGAZINES: Brides

BETTING MONTHLY
1828595U75A-1033

Formerly: Antepost

Editorial Address: Chelwood House, Chelwood Drive, LEEDS, LS8 2AT **Tel:** 0845 833 0909 **Fax:** 0845 833 0910

Email: info@bettingmonthly.com

Advertising Address: As above.

Email: david@antepostmag.com

Web site: http://www.bettingmonthly.com

ISSN: 1758-2709

Publisher: Betrescue Ltd

Date Established: 2006

Frequency: Monthly

Cover Price: £2.95

Circulation: 30,000 (Publisher's Statement)

Usual Pagination: 68

Editor: Jonathan Shepherd; **Advertising Manager:** David Russell

Summary of Content: Magazine covering sports betting including horse racing, football and all major sporting events. Poker and Casino/gaming sections.

Readership/Target Audience: Aimed at both recreational and serious punters.

ADVERTISING RATES:

Full Page Colour £750.00

Agency Commission: 10%

Mechanical Data: Trim Size: 210 x 148.5mm, Film: Digital

Copy instructions: Copy Date: 1 week prior to publication date

Average advertising content per issue: 25%

CONSUMER: SPORT

BH EXCLUSIVE
1894030U74Q-1430

Formerly: Lloyd's Living The Dream

Editorial Address: Old Rectory Cottage, Park Lane, ABBOTS WORTHY, SO21 1DT **Tel:** 01202 765988

Email: lizfreelance@hotmail.com

Web site: http://www.bh-publications.co.uk

Publisher: BH Publications

Frequency: Half-yearly - Published in April and November

Cover Price: Free

Circulation: 30,000 (Publisher's Statement)

Usual Pagination: 116

Editor: Liz Kavanagh

Consumer Magazines

Summary of Content: Luxury lifestyle magazine covering property, fine food, travel, designer fashion, celebrities, motoring and interiors.
Readership/Target Audience: Aimed at an AB1 audience in the Bournemouth area.
CONSUMER: WOMEN'S INTEREST CONSUMER MAGAZINES: Lifestyle

BH THE MAGAZINE
1656918U74A-972

Editorial Address: The Gatehouse, Gatehouse Way, AYLESBURY, HP19 8DB **Tel:** 01296 619770
Fax: 01296 399069
Email: carly.lewthwaite@ccnltd.com
Advertising Address: Ground Floor, The Gatehouse, Gatehouse Way, AYLESBURY, HP19 8DB
Tel: 01296 619770 **Fax:** 01296 393451
Email: angela.macdonald@ccnltd.com
Web site: http://www.aylesburytoday.co.uk
Publisher: Central Counties Newspapers South Ltd
Date Established: 2002
Frequency: Monthly
Cover Price: Free
Circulation: 19,640 (Publisher's Statement)
Usual Pagination: 52
Editor: Carly Lewthwaite; **Advertising Manager:** Angela Macdonald
Summary of Content: Magazine covering women's issues, real life stories, beauty, fashion, alternative therapies, babies and children, homes and gardens, health and fitness, travel, competitions and reviews.
Readership/Target Audience: Aimed at female readers of The Bucks Herald.
ADVERTISING RATES:
Full Page Colour £575.00
Agency Commission: 10%
Mechanical Data: Film: Digital
Copy instructions: Copy Date: 1 week prior to publication date
Average advertising content per issue: 60%
Supplement to: The Bucks Herald Series
CONSUMER: WOMEN'S INTEREST CONSUMER MAGAZINES: Women's Interest

BICESTER COMMUNITY TIMES
1915222U80C-5509

Editorial Address: 39 Jay Close, BICESTER, OX26 6XN
Tel: 01869 660082
Email: ian@ctbicester.co.uk
Advertising Address: As above.
Email: ian@ctbicester.co.uk
Web site: http://www.ctbicester.co.uk
Publisher: Community Times UK Ltd
Date Established: 2009
Frequency: Monthly
Cover Price: Free
Circulation: 6,000 (Publisher's Statement)
Editor: Ian Payne
Summary of Content: Magazine enabling local businesses to advertise their products or services to the local community and increase their community profile.
Readership/Target Audience: Aimed at householders and communals throughout Bicester.
ADVERTISING: Rates on application
CONSUMER: RURAL & REGIONAL INTEREST: Regional Interest English Counties

THE BICYCLE BUYER
1849711U77C-954

Editorial Address: 1 West Smithfield, LONDON, EC1A 9JU
Tel: 020 7332 9703 **Fax:** 020 7332 9799
Email: james.carter@factorymedia.com
Web site: http://www.thebicyclebuyer.com
Publisher: Factory Media
Date Established: 2008
Frequency: 6 issues yearly
Cover Price: £3.95
Circulation: 35,000 (Publisher's Statement)
Usual Pagination: 164
Editor: James Carter
Summary of Content: Magazine with a mixture of reviews, guidance on riding on trails and advice on family cycling as well as articles from industry professional, designers and riders.
Readership/Target Audience: Aimed at anyone about to buy a bicycle.
CONSUMER: MOTORING & CYCLING: Cycling

THE BIG BUZZ
48069U89C-75

Editorial Address: 6 Glenview Terrace, CRUMLIN, BT29 4XX **Tel:** 028 9447 0784
Email: barry@bigbuzzireland.com
Advertising Address: As above. **Fax:** 028 9445 9758
Email: jenny@bigbuzzireland.com
Web site: http://www.bigbuzzireland.com
Publisher: Buzz Magazine

Frequency: 11 issues yearly
Cover Price: £0.95
Annual Sub.: £26.00
Circulation: 25,000 (Publisher's Statement)
Usual Pagination: 80
Editor: Barry O'Kane; **Features Editor:** Barry O'Kane;
Advertising Manager: Jennifer O'Kane
Summary of Content: Magazine covering entertainment in Ireland.
Readership/Target Audience: Aimed at 18 to 35 year olds living in Northern Ireland, Dublin and Donegal.
ADVERTISING RATES:
Full Page Colour £650.00
Agency Commission: 10%
Copy instructions: Copy Date: 20th of the month prior to publication date
Average advertising content per issue: 80%
CONSUMER: HOLIDAYS & TRAVEL: Entertainment Guides

BIG CHEESE
45382U74F-350

Editorial Address: Unit 7, Clarendon Buildings, 25 Horsell Road, LONDON, N5 1XL **Tel:** 020 7607 0303
Fax: 020 7607 0303
Email: info@bigcheesemagazine.com
Advertising Address: As above.
Email: info@bigcheesemagazine.com
Web site: http://www.bigcheesemagazine.com
ISSN: 1365-358X
Publisher: Big Cheese Publishing Ltd
Date Established: 1996
Frequency: Monthly
Cover Price: £3.55
Annual Sub.: £29.99
Circulation: 18,000 (Publisher's Statement)
Usual Pagination: 120
Editor: Eugene Butcher; **Features Editor:** Jim Sharples;
Advertising Manager: Eugene Butcher; **Publisher:** Eugene Butcher
Summary of Content: Magazine providing articles on rock, punk and metal music, with a monthly free CD.
Readership/Target Audience: Aimed at men and women between 15 and 30 years old.
ADVERTISING RATES:
Full Page Mono £1320.00
Full Page Colour £1320.00
Agency Commission: 10%
Mechanical Data: Page Width: 200mm, Type Area: 287 x 200mm, Trim Size: 297 x 210mm, Bleed Size: 303 x 216mm, Col Length: 287mm
Average advertising content per issue: 20%
CONSUMER: WOMEN'S INTEREST CONSUMER MAGAZINES: Teenage

THE BIG ISSUE
47203U82-2_50

Editorial Address: 1-5 Wandsworth Road, LONDON, SW8 2LN **Tel:** 020 7526 3200 **Fax:** 020 7526 3201
Email: editorialinfo@bigissue.com
Advertising Address: As above. **Tel:** 020 7526 3240
Fax: 020 7526 3241
Email: steve.nicolaou@bigissue.com
Web site: http://www.bigissue.com
Publisher: The Big Issue Ltd
Date Established: 1991
Frequency: Weekly
Cover Price: £1.50
Circulation: 75,027 (ABC 01/07/2008 to 31/12/2008)
Usual Pagination: 56
Editor: Charles Howgego; **Advertising Manager:** Steve Nicolaou; **Publisher:** Lisa Woodman
Summary of Content: Current affairs magazine containing features on news, society and social justice as well as interviews with key political figures and celebrities. Contains an extensive section covering the world of arts and entertainment. Also campaigns for the homeless and socially excluded people.
Readership/Target Audience: Aimed at socially aware people of all ages with an interest in current affairs.
ADVERTISING RATES:
Full Page Mono £2200.00
Full Page Colour £3300.00
Agency Commission: 10%
Mechanical Data: Film: Digital, Bleed Size: 307 x 220mm, Trim Size: 297 x 210mm, Type Area: 280 x 195mm, Col Length: 280mm, Page Width: 195mm
Copy instructions: Copy Date: 7 days prior to publication date
Average advertising content per issue: 40%
CONSUMER: CURRENT AFFAIRS & POLITICS

THE BIG ISSUE CYMRU
625015U82-2_51

Editorial Address: 55 Charles Street, CARDIFF, CF10 2GD
Tel: 029 2025 5670 **Fax:** 029 2025 5673
Email: editorial@bigissuecymru.co.uk
Advertising Address: As above.
Email: jane@bigissuecymru.co.uk
Web site: http://www.bigissuecymru.co.uk
Publisher: The Big Issue Ltd

Date Established: 1994
Frequency: Weekly
Cover Price: £1.50
Circulation: 9,250 (ABC 01/07/2008 to 31/12/2008)
Usual Pagination: 48
Editor: Rachel Howells; **Advertising Manager:** Jane Thomas
Summary of Content: Current affairs magazine containing features on news, society and social justice as well as interviews with key political figures and celebrities. Contains extensive section covering the world of arts and entertainment. Also campaigns for the homeless and socially excluded people.
Language(s): English; Welsh
Readership/Target Audience: Aimed at socially aware people of all ages.
ADVERTISING RATES:
Full Page Colour £420.00
Agency Commission: 10%
Mechanical Data: Bleed Size: 303 x 216mm, Trim Size: 297 x 210mm, Film: Digital
Copy instructions: Copy Date: Thursday 2pm prior to publication
CONSUMER: CURRENT AFFAIRS & POLITICS

THE BIG ISSUE IN SCOTLAND
47206U82-2_55

Editorial Address: 2nd floor, 43 Bath Street, GLASGOW, G2 1HW **Tel:** 0141 352 7260 **Fax:** 0141 333 9049
Email: editorial@bigissuescotland.com
Advertising Address: As above. **Tel:** 0141 352 7270
Email: susan.reid@bigissue.com
Web site: http://www.bigissuescotland.com
Publisher: The Big Issue in Scotland Ltd
Date Established: 1993
Frequency: Weekly
Cover Price: £1.50
Circulation: 21,846 (ABC 01/07/2008 to 31/12/2008)
Usual Pagination: 48
Editor: Paul McNamee; **Advertising Manager:** Susan Reid
Summary of Content: Magazine containing social issues, with a special focus on homelessness as well as arts coverage and news analysis.
Readership/Target Audience: Aimed at socially aware and socially responsible young professionals.
ADVERTISING RATES:
Full Page Mono £960.00
Full Page Colour £1400.00
Agency Commission: 10%
Mechanical Data: Film: Digital, No. of Columns (Display): 4, Type Area: 287 x 200mm, Trim Size: 297 x 210mm, Col Length: 287mm, Bleed Size: 300 x 215mm, Page Width: 200mm
Copy instructions: Copy Date: 1 week prior to publication date
Average advertising content per issue: 33%
CONSUMER: CURRENT AFFAIRS & POLITICS

THE BIG ISSUE IN THE NORTH
47205U82-2_53

Editorial Address: 10 Swan Street, MANCHESTER, M4 5JN
Tel: 0161 831 5550
Email: kevin.gopal@bigissuenorth.co.uk
Advertising Address: As above. **Fax:** 0161 831 5577
Email: claire.lawton@bigissueinthenorth.com
Web site: http://www.bigissueinthenorth.com
Publisher: The Big Life Company
Date Established: 1993
Frequency: Weekly
Cover Price: £2.00
Annual Sub.: £98.00
Circulation: 25,589 (ABC 01/07/2008 to 31/12/2008)
Usual Pagination: 48
Editor: Kevin Gopal
Summary of Content: Magazine covering news, politics, arts, environmental and lifestyle features, international issues and social comment. Also included are arts and entertainment listings, film, music, theatre reviews, campaigns and celebrity interviews.
Readership/Target Audience: Read by those aged 16 years and over.
ADVERTISING RATES:
Full Page Mono £1068.00
Full Page Colour £1401.00
Agency Commission: 10%
Mechanical Data: Col Length: 280mm, Film: Digital, Type Area: 280 x 195mm, Trim Size: 297 x 210mm, Page Width: 195mm, Bleed Size: 307 x 220mm
Copy instructions: Copy Date: 4 days prior to publication date
Average advertising content per issue: 40%
CONSUMER: CURRENT AFFAIRS & POLITICS

THE BIG ISSUE SOUTH WEST
47204U82-2_57

Editorial Address: 5 Brunswick Court, Brunswick Square, BRISTOL, BS2 8PE **Tel:** 0117 916 6593 **Fax:** 0117 916 6599
Email: charles.howgego@bigissue.com
Advertising Address: As above.
Email: rich@bigissuesouthwest.co.uk

Consumer Magazines

Web site: http://www.bigissuesouthwest.co.uk
Publisher: The Big Issue (South West) Ltd
Date Established: 1993
Frequency: Weekly
Cover Price: £1.50
Circulation: 15,011 (ABC 01/07/2008 to 31/12/2008)
Usual Pagination: 48
Editor: Charles Howgego; **Advertising Manager:** Rich Kelly
Summary of Content: Magazine covering news and features on celebrities, arts and culture, plus in-depth investigations into social issues. Includes training and recruitment information and advice.
Readership/Target Audience: Aimed at socially aware young people.
ADVERTISING RATES:
Full Page Mono £550.00
Full Page Colour £650.00
Agency Commission: 10%
Mechanical Data: Type Area: 280 x 195mm, Trim Size: 297 x 210mm, Bleed Size: 307 x 220mm, Col Length: 280mm, Page Width: 195mm, Film: Digital
Copy instructions: Copy Date: Thursday prior to publication date
Average advertising content per issue: 40%
CONSUMER: CURRENT AFFAIRS & POLITICS

THE BIG LIST
628751U89C-75_50
Editorial Address: 48-50 York Street, BELFAST, BT15 1AS
Tel: 028 9031 9008 **Fax:** 028 9072 7800
Email: listnewscopy@flagshipmedia.co.uk
Advertising Address: As above.
Email: apaul@thebiglist.co.uk
Web site: http://www.thebiglist.co.uk
Publisher: Flagship Media Group Ltd
Date Established: 1999
Frequency: Monthly
Cover Price: Free
Circulation: 16,853 (Publisher's Statement)
Usual Pagination: 24
Editor: Damien Whinnery.
Summary of Content: Entertainment guide for Northern Ireland, containing classified listings plus previews and reviews of the local music and club scene.
Readership/Target Audience: Aimed at the general public.
ADVERTISING RATES:
Full Page Colour £1450.00
Agency Commission: 15%
Mechanical Data: Col Length: 366mm, No. of Columns (Display): 4, Col Widths (Display): 62.75mm, Page Width: 266mm, Film: Digital, Type Area: 366 x 266mm
Copy instructions: Copy Date: 1 week prior to publication date
Average advertising content per issue: 40%
CONSUMER: HOLIDAYS & TRAVEL: Entertainment Guides

BIG PRINT
47207U94F-992
Editorial Address: PO Box 173, PETERBOROUGH, PE2 6WS **Tel:** 0303 123 9999 **Fax:** 01733 375383
Email: editorial@rnib.org.uk
Advertising Address: As above. **Tel:** 0800 124007
Fax: 01733 375001
Email: editorial@rnib.org.uk
Web site: http://www.rnib.org.uk
Publisher: Royal National Institute of Blind People
Date Established: 1993
Frequency: Weekly
Annual Sub.: £61.36
Circulation: 3,900 (Publisher's Statement)
Usual Pagination: 16
Editor: Joan Longstaff
Summary of Content: National newspaper containing conventional news and reviews of national and international events.
Readership/Target Audience: Aimed at those with failing eyesight.
ADVERTISING RATES:
Full Page Mono £200.00
Mechanical Data: Type Area: 420 x 297mm, Col Length: 420mm, Page Width: 297mm, Film: Digital
Copy instructions: Copy Date: 1 week prior to publication date
CONSUMER: OTHER CLASSIFICATIONS: Disability

BIG SMOKE MAGAZINE
765804U76D-754
Editorial Address: PO Box 38799, LONDON, E10 5UV
Tel: 07966 472051
Email: dirtyharry@bigsmokelive.com
Advertising Address: As above.
Email: editorial@bigsmokelive.com
Web site: http://www.bigsmokelive.com
ISSN: 1474-3604
Publisher: BIG SMOKE PROJECTS LTD
Date Established: 1999
Frequency: Quarterly
Cover Price: £3.50
Circulation: 6,000 (Publisher's Statement)

Usual Pagination: 84
Editor: Harry Adams; **Advertising Manager:** Charlee Gyamfi; **Publisher:** Harry Adams
Summary of Content: Magazine covering all aspects of hip-hop lifestyle and music.
Readership/Target Audience: Aimed at hip-hop music enthusiasts between 15 and 35 years old.
ADVERTISING RATES:
Full Page Colour £800.00
Mechanical Data: Film: Digital, Bleed Size: +3mm, Type Area: 275 x 230mm, Col Length: 275mm, Page Width: 230mm
Copy instructions: Copy Date: 3 weeks prior to publication date
Average advertising content per issue: 30%
CONSUMER: MUSIC & PERFORMING ARTS: Music

BIGSCREEN
1810686U76A-208
Editorial Address: Office 14, Newport Market, Dock Street, NEWPORT, NP20 1DD **Tel:** 01633 251800
Email: richard@firewaterpublishing.com
Advertising Address: As above.
Email: richard@firewaterpublishing.com
Web site: http://www.devonbigscreen.co.uk
Publisher: Firewater Publishing
Frequency: 6 issues yearly
Cover Price: Free
Usual Pagination: 32
Editor: Richard Stevens; **Advertising Manager:** Richard Stevens; **Publisher:** Richard Stevens
Summary of Content: Magazine covering new film releases, DVD releases, computer games, interviews with stars and competitions.
Readership/Target Audience: Aimed at families.
ADVERTISING: Rates on application
CONSUMER: MUSIC & PERFORMING ARTS: Cinema

BIKE
46349U77B-485
Editorial Address: Media House, Lynchwood, Peterborough Business Park, PETERBOROUGH, PE2 6EA
Tel: 01733 468181 **Fax:** 01733 468196
Email: bike@bauermedia.co.uk
Advertising Address: As above. **Tel:** 01733 468000
Fax: 01733 468007
Email: anna.skuse@bauerconsumer.co.uk
Web site: http://www.bikemagazine.co.uk
ISSN: 0140-4547
Publisher: Bauer Consumer Media Ltd (Media House)
Date Established: 1971
Frequency: Monthly
Cover Price: £3.99
Free to qualifying individuals
Annual Sub.: £45.60
Circulation: 74,339 (ABC 01/01/2008 to 31/12/2008)
Usual Pagination: 192
Editor: Khal Harris
Summary of Content: Magazine covering all aspects of motorcycling. Includes a section on buying and running bikes.
Readership/Target Audience: Read by motorcyclists of all ages.
ADVERTISING RATES:
Full Page Colour £3820.00
Agency Commission: 10%
Mechanical Data: Col Length: 270mm, Film: Digital, Type Area: 270 x 200mm, Trim Size: 300 x 220mm, Bleed Size: 306 x 226mm, Page Width: 200mm
Copy instructions: Copy Date: 4 weeks prior to publication date
Average advertising content per issue: 30%
CONSUMER: MOTORING & CYCLING: Motorcycling

BIKE SPORT NEWS
1744896U77B-718
Editorial Address: Paddock 2, Donington Park, Castle Donington, DERBY, DE74 2RP **Tel:** 01332 818800
Email: bikesportnews@googlemail.com
Advertising Address: As above.
Email: carterbsn@googlemail.com
Web site: http://www.bikesportnews.com
Publisher: Bike Sport News Ltd
Date Established: 1999
Frequency: 25 issues yearly
Cover Price: £1.99
Annual Sub.: £42.50
Circulation: 45,000 (Publisher's Statement)
Usual Pagination: 44
Advertising Manager: Chris Carter
Summary of Content: Magazine covering motorcycle racing with in-depth race reports, results, photos, news, gossip, features, competitions and what's on.
Readership/Target Audience: Aimed at road-racing fans.
ADVERTISING: Rates on application
CONSUMER: MOTORING & CYCLING: Motorcycling

BIKERESS
1752599U77B-719
Editorial Address: PO Box 801, TAUNTON, TA1 9DS
Tel: 0845 094 2034
Email: editor@bikeress.co.uk
Advertising Address: As above.
Email: adverts@bikeress.co.uk
Web site: http://www.bikeress.co.uk
Publisher: uandi design
Date Established: 2006
Frequency: Quarterly
Cover Price: £3.50
Annual Sub.: £12.25
Circulation: 5,000 (Print Run)
Editor: Tracy Kearley; **Advertising Manager:** Tracy Kearley
Summary of Content: Magazine covering product reviews and suggestions, features, events and clubs, profiles on women riders, tips on riding, places to go and bike reviews.
Readership/Target Audience: Aimed at female motor cyclists and pillions.
ADVERTISING: Rates on application
CONSUMER: MOTORING & CYCLING: Motorcycling

BILLBOARD
40935U76D-781
Editorial Address: 5th Floor, Endeavour House, 189 Shaftesbury Avenue, LONDON, WC2H 8TJ
Tel: 020 7420 6003 **Fax:** 020 7420 6014
Email: msutherland@eu.billboard.com
Advertising Address: As above.
Email: f.fenucci@eu.billboard.com
Web site: http://www.billboard.biz
Publisher: Nielsen Business Media
Date Established: 1894
Frequency: Weekly
Cover Price: £5.50
Circulation: 30,000 (Publisher's Statement)
Editor: Mark Sutherland; **Advertising Manager:** Frederic Fenucci
Summary of Content: International news magazine covering music, home entertainment, reviews and events.
Readership/Target Audience: Aimed at those interested in music and home entertainment.
ADVERTISING: Rates on application
CONSUMER: MUSIC & PERFORMING ARTS: Music

BIRD LIFE
47161U81F-50
Editorial Address: The Lodge, SANDY, SG19 2DL
Tel: 01767 680551 **Fax:** 01767 683262
Email: derek.niemann@rspb.org.uk
Advertising Address: As above.
Email: lynda.whytock@rspb.org.uk
Publisher: The Royal Society for the Protection of Birds
Date Established: 1965
Frequency: 6 issues yearly
Free to qualifying individuals
Annual Sub.: £12.00
Circulation: 83,000 (Publisher's Statement)
Usual Pagination: 32
Editor: Derek Niemann
Summary of Content: Magazine containing news on birds, natural history, the environment, conservation and projects. Also contains competitions and puzzles.
Readership/Target Audience: Aimed at children between 8 and 13 years old.
ADVERTISING RATES:
Full Page Colour £2000.00
Agency Commission: 10%
Mechanical Data: Bleed Size: 303 x 216mm, Trim Size: 297 x 210mm, Type Area: 277 x 190mm, Print Process: Web-fed litho, Col Length: 277mm, Page Width: 190mm
Copy instructions: Copy Date: 12 weeks prior to publication date
CONSUMER: ANIMALS & PETS: Birds

BIRD WATCHING
47162U81F-80
Editorial Address: Media House, Lynchwood, Peterborough Business Park, PETERBOROUGH, PE2 6EA
Tel: 01733 468000 **Fax:** 01733 468387
Email: sheena.harvey@bauermedia.co.uk
Advertising Address: As above.
Email: kimbereley.robertson@bauermedia.co.uk
Web site: http://www.birdwatching.co.uk
Publisher: Bauer Consumer Media Ltd (Media House)
Date Established: 1986
Frequency: 13 issues yearly
Cover Price: £3.95
Circulation: 18,732 (ABC 01/01/2008 to 31/12/2008)
Usual Pagination: 116
Editor: Sheena Harvey; **Features Editor:** Matt Merritt
Summary of Content: Magazine seeking to enhance the enjoyment of watching wild birds for general enthusiasts by providing a wide range of articles on birds, their characteristics and behaviour, news items, fieldcraft, bird photography, optical and outdoor product reviews, walks and information on UK bird sightings.

Section 4 (c) Consumer Magazines

Readership/Target Audience: Aimed at all birdwatchers - novice, improving and experienced.
ADVERTISING RATES:
Full Page Colour £2166.00
Agency Commission: 10%
Mechanical Data: Type Area: 275 x 184mm, Col Length: 275mm, Page Width: 184mm, Bleed Size: 303 x 216mm, Trim Size: 297 x 210mm, Col Widths (Display): 33mm, No. of Columns (Display): 5, Film: Digital
Copy instructions: Copy Date: 3rd of the month prior to publication date
Average advertising content per issue: 28%
CONSUMER: ANIMALS & PETS: Birds

BIRDING WORLD
47163U81F-30

Editorial Address: Sea Lawn, Coast Road, Cley-next-the-Sea, HOLT, NR25 7RZ **Tel:** 01263 740913
Fax: 01263 741173
Email: steve@birdingworld.co.uk
Advertising Address: As above.
Email: sue@birdingworld.co.uk
Web site: http://www.birdingworld.co.uk
ISSN: 0969-6024
Publisher: Birding World
Date Established: 1987
Frequency: Monthly
Annual Sub.: £47.00
Circulation: 6,000 (Publisher's Statement)
Usual Pagination: 60
Editor: Steve Gantlett; **Advertising Manager:** Sue Gantlett
Summary of Content: Magazine containing news, information and features about birdwatching in Britain and overseas.
Readership/Target Audience: Aimed at keen, knowledgeable, high-spending birdwatchers who travel widely in pursuit of their hobby.
ADVERTISING RATES:
Full Page Mono £210.00
Full Page Colour £396.00
Agency Commission: 10%
Mechanical Data: Col Length: 203mm, Film: Positive, right reading, emulsion side down, Type Area: 203 x 142mm, Print Process: Litho, Bleed Size: 253 x 178mm, Trim Size: 245 x 168mm, Page Width: 142mm, Col Widths (Display): 71mm, No. of Columns (Display): 2
Copy instructions: Copy Date: 15th of the month prior to publication date
CONSUMER: ANIMALS & PETS: Birds

BIRDS - THE MAGAZINE OF THE RSPB
47165U81F-55

Editorial Address: The Lodge, SANDY, SG19 2DL
Tel: 01767 680551 **Fax:** 01767 683262
Email: sarah.brennan@rspb.org.uk
Advertising Address: As above.
Email: lynda.whytock@rspb.org.uk
Web site: http://www.rspb.org.uk
Publisher: The Royal Society for the Protection of Birds
Date Established: 1966
Frequency: Quarterly
Free to qualifying individuals
Circulation: 625,553 (ABC 01/01/2009 to 30/06/2009)
Usual Pagination: 104
Editor: Sarah Brennan
Summary of Content: Magazine of The Royal Society for the Protection of Birds. Includes features on wild birds, the work of the RSPB worldwide and developments on the conservation and the environmental front.
Readership/Target Audience: Read by members of The Royal Society for the Protection of Birds.
ADVERTISING RATES:
Full Page Colour £9340.00
SCC £135.00
Agency Commission: 10%
Mechanical Data: Col Length: 272mm, Type Area: 272 x 202mm, Print Process: Web-fed offset litho, Bleed Size: 308 x 238mm, Trim Size: 300 x 230mm, Film: Digital, Page Width: 202mm
Copy instructions: Copy Date: 12 weeks prior to publication date
Average advertising content per issue: 45%
CONSUMER: ANIMALS & PETS: Birds

BIRDWATCH
47164U81F-65

Editorial Address: B403A The Chocolate Factory, 5 Clarendon Road, LONDON, N22 6XJ **Tel:** 020 8881 0550
Fax: 020 8881 0990
Email: editorial@birdwatch.co.uk
Advertising Address: As above.
Email: advertising@birdwatch.co.uk
Web site: http://www.birdwatch.co.uk
ISSN: 0967-1870
Publisher: Solo Publishing Ltd
Date Established: 1992
Frequency: Monthly
Cover Price: £3.80
Circulation: 14,000 (Print Run)

Usual Pagination: 76
Editor: Dominic Mitchell; **Managing Director:** Dominic Mitchell; **Advertising Manager:** Ian Lycett
Summary of Content: Magazine covering news and features relating to birds throughout the world.
Readership/Target Audience: Read by active and keen birdwatchers of all ages and experience.
ADVERTISING RATES:
Full Page Mono £1075.00
Full Page Colour £1700.00
Agency Commission: 10%
Mechanical Data: Type Area: 270 x 192mm, Bleed Size: 305 x 218mm, Trim Size: 297 x 210mm, Col Length: 270mm, Page Width: 192mm
Copy instructions: Copy Date: 1 week prior to publication date
Average advertising content per issue: 26%
CONSUMER: ANIMALS & PETS: Birds

THE BIRMINGHAM JEWISH RECORDER
47677U87-15

Editorial Address: PO Box 13512, BIRMINGHAM, B32 9BX
Tel: 0121 428 3347
Email: editors@recorder.org.uk
Advertising Address: As above.
Email: advertising@recorder.org.uk
Publisher: Birmingham Jewish Cultural Society
Date Established: 1936
Frequency: Monthly
Annual Sub.: £22.00
Circulation: 700 (Publisher's Statement)
Usual Pagination: 28
Editor: Keith Drapkin; **Advertising Manager:** Keith Drapkin
Summary of Content: Magazine covering news and information on Jewish culture and events.
Readership/Target Audience: Read by members of Birmingham's Jewish Community.
ADVERTISING RATES:
Full Page Mono £150.00
Mechanical Data: Print Process: Litho, Col Length: 262mm, No. of Columns (Display): 4, Film: Digital, Trim Size: 297 x 210mm, Page Width: 177mm, Type Area: 262 x 177mm, Col Widths (Display): 41mm
Copy instructions: Copy Date: 18th of the month prior to publication date
Average advertising content per issue: 30%
CONSUMER: RELIGIOUS

BIZARRE
47640U86C-70

Editorial Address: 30 Cleveland Street, LONDON, W1T 4JD
Tel: 020 7907 6000 **Fax:** 020 7907 7620
Email: bizarre@dennis.co.uk
Advertising Address: As above. **Fax:** 020 7907 6601
Email: max_wright@dennis.co.uk
Web site: http://www.bizarremag.com
Publisher: Dennis Publishing Ltd
Frequency: 13 issues yearly
Cover Price: £3.50
Annual Sub.: £29.97
Circulation: 40,936 (ABC 01/01/2008 to 31/12/2008)
Usual Pagination: 140
Editor: David McComb; **Publisher:** Simon Clark
Summary of Content: Magazine covering strange and unusual stories from around the world. Includes features on crime, war and sex.
Readership/Target Audience: Aimed at men between 18 and 35 years old.
ADVERTISING RATES:
Full Page Colour £4500.00
Agency Commission: 10%
Mechanical Data: Type Area: 269 x 182mm, Col Length: 269mm, Film: Digital, Bleed Size: 303 x 216mm, Trim Size: 297 x 210mm, Page Width: 182mm
Copy instructions: Copy Date: 4 weeks prior to publication date
Average advertising content per issue: 15%
CONSUMER: ADULT & GAY MAGAZINES: Men's Lifestyle Magazines

BLACK & WHITE PHOTOGRAPHY
762770U85A-191

Editorial Address: 86 High Street, LEWES, BN7 1XN
Tel: 01273 477374 **Fax:** 01273 402849
Email: lizr@thegmcgroup.com
Advertising Address: As above. **Tel:** 01273 402825
Fax: 01273 487692
Email: melanieb@thegmcgroup.com
Web site: http://www.thegmcgroup.com
ISSN: 1473-2467
Publisher: GMC Publications Ltd
Date Established: 2001
Frequency: 13 issues yearly
Cover Price: £3.99
Annual Sub.: £41.40
Circulation: 20,000 (Publisher's Statement)
Usual Pagination: 98

Editor: Elizabeth Roberts; **Publisher:** Simon McKeown
Summary of Content: Magazine covering all aspects of black and white photography including photographic techniques, a reader's gallery and test reports.
Readership/Target Audience: Aimed at amateur and professional photographers.
ADVERTISING RATES:
Full Page Mono £1045.00
Full Page Colour £1045.00
SCC £22.50
Agency Commission: 10%
Mechanical Data: Type Area: 268 x 195mm, Col Length: 268mm, Page Width: 195mm, Film: Digital, Bleed Size: 303 x 236mm, Trim Size: 297 x 210mm
Copy instructions: Copy Date: 4 weeks prior to publication date
Average advertising content per issue: 30%
CONSUMER: PHOTOGRAPHY & FILM MAKING: Photography

BLACK BEAUTY & HAIR
45460U74H-10

Editorial Address: 2nd Floor, Culvert House, Culvert Road, Battersea, LONDON, SW11 5DH **Tel:** 020 7720 2108
Fax: 020 7498 3023
Email: info@blackbeautyandhair.com
Advertising Address: As above.
Email: petker@hawkpublications.com
Web site: http://www.blackbeautyandhair.com
Publisher: Hawker Consumer Publications Ltd
Date Established: 1982
Frequency: 6 issues yearly
Cover Price: £2.75
Annual Sub.: £15.00
Circulation: 19,600 (Publisher's Statement)
Usual Pagination: 132
Editor: Irene Shelley; **Advertising Director:** Pat Petker; **Publisher:** Pat Petker
Summary of Content: Magazine containing hairstyles, beauty, fashion features, makeovers, lifestyles, celebrity profiles and product updates.
Readership/Target Audience: Read by young, fashion-conscious, black women between 16 and 35 years old.
ADVERTISING RATES:
Full Page Mono £1250.00
Full Page Colour £1650.00
Agency Commission: 10%
Mechanical Data: Col Length: 272mm, Film: Digital, Type Area: 272 x 185mm, Print Process: Web-fed offset litho, Bleed Size: 304 x 219mm, Trim Size: 298 x 213mm, No. of Columns (Display): 4, Page Width: 185mm
Copy instructions: Copy Date: 1 month prior to publication date
Average advertising content per issue: 40%
CONSUMER: WOMEN'S INTEREST CONSUMER MAGAZINES: Hair & Beauty

BLACK HERITAGE
1644309U90-931

Editorial Address: 102 Mallinson Road, Battersea, LONDON, SW11 1BN **Tel:** 020 7207 2734
Fax: 020 7207 6503
Email: livelistings@aol.com
Advertising Address: As above.
Email: all3mags@yahoo.co.uk
Web site: http://www.livelistingsmag.com
Publisher: Barb Wire Enterprises Ltd
Date Established: 2000
Frequency: Annual - Published in October
Free to qualifying individuals
Annual Sub.: £5.00
Circulation: 70,000 (Publisher's Statement)
Usual Pagination: 116
Editor: Barbara Campbell; **Advertising Manager:** Barbara Campbell
Summary of Content: Black history month events with features, entertainment, news and profiles of achievers and people who are making a difference to the community.
Readership/Target Audience: Aimed at men and women aged between 18 and 40 years old and distributed to schools, colleges, universities and corporate organisations.
ADVERTISING RATES:
Full Page Colour £2900.00
Mechanical Data: Type Area: 262 x 185mm, Bleed Size: 297 x 210mm, Col Length: 262mm, Page Width: 185mm
CONSUMER: ETHNIC

THE BLACK STATIC
1646063U79L-381

Formerly: The 3rd Alternative
Editorial Address: 5 Martins Lane, Witcham, ELY, CB6 2LB
Tel: 01353 777931
Email: andy@ttapress.demon.co.uk
Advertising Address: As above.
Email: andy@ttapress.demon.co.uk
ISSN: 1352-3783
Publisher: TTA Press
Frequency: 6 issues yearly
Cover Price: £3.75
Annual Sub.: £21.00

Consumer Magazines

Circulation: 10,000 (Publisher's Statement)
Usual Pagination: 68
Editor: Andy Cox; **Advertising Manager:** Andy Cox
Summary of Content: Magazine covering horror and thriller stories as well as reviews of videos, books, films and interviews of the genre.
Readership/Target Audience: Aimed at horror enthusiasts aged 18 years and over.
ADVERTISING RATES:
Full Page Mono £300.00
Agency Commission: 10%
Mechanical Data: Bleed Size: 282 x 206mm, Trim Size: 276 x 200mm, Film: Digital
Copy instructions: Copy Date: 1 month prior to publication date
CONSUMER: HOBBIES & DIY: Fantasy Games & Science Fiction

BLACKBIRD PIE
1641846U74D-560

Editorial Address: 3 Basset Place, FALMOUTH, TR11 2SS
Tel: 01326 314242
Email: post@blackbirdpie.co.uk
Advertising Address: As above.
Email: post@blackbirdpie.co.uk
Web site: http://www.blackbirdpie.co.uk
Publisher: Flying Pig Publishing
Date Established: 2003
Frequency: 6 issues yearly
Cover Price: Free
Circulation: 25,500 (Publisher's Statement)
Usual Pagination: 32
Editor: Vanessa Roebuck; **Advertising Manager:** Vanessa Roebuck
Summary of Content: Magazine covering lifestyle and what's on for families with reviews and competitions.
Readership/Target Audience: Aimed at families within the Cornwall area distributed via pre-schools, nurseries, primary schools, health visitors and libraries.
ADVERTISING RATES:
Full Page Colour £750.00
Agency Commission: 10%
Mechanical Data: Bleed Size: 300 x 213mm, Trim Size: 297 x 210mm, Film: Digital
Copy instructions: Copy Date: 3 weeks prior to publication date
Average advertising content per issue: 35%
CONSUMER: WOMEN'S INTEREST CONSUMER MAGAZINES: Child Care

BLACKHAIR
45461U74H-20

Editorial Address: Freebournes House, Freebournes Road, WITHAM, CM8 3US **Tel:** 01376 534531 **Fax:** 01376 534500
Email: afua.acheampong@hairmags.co.uk
Advertising Address: As above. **Tel:** 01376 534500
Email: holly.balser@freebournes.com
ISSN: 1460-8146
Publisher: Haversham Publications Ltd
Date Established: 1997
Frequency: 6 issues yearly
Cover Price: £2.95
Annual Sub.: £15.95
Circulation: 40,000 (Publisher's Statement)
Usual Pagination: 164
Editor: Afua Acheampong; **Managing Director:** Simon Fox
Summary of Content: Magazine covering all aspects of hair and beauty.
Readership/Target Audience: Aimed at young black women between 18 and 35 years old.
ADVERTISING RATES:
Full Page Mono £1600.00
Full Page Colour £1800.00
Agency Commission: 10%
Mechanical Data: Film: Positive, right reading, emulsion side down, Bleed Size: 305 x 218mm, Type Area: 277 x 190mm, No. of Columns (Display): 4, Trim Size: 297 x 210mm, Col Widths (Display): 51.2mm, Col Length: 277mm, Page Width: 190mm
Copy instructions: Copy Date: 9 weeks prior to publication date
CONSUMER: WOMEN'S INTEREST CONSUMER MAGAZINES: Hair & Beauty

BLACKMORE VALE MAGAZINE
46889U80C-1170

Editorial Address: High Street, Stalbridge, STURMINSTER NEWTON, DT10 2LH **Tel:** 01963 365117 **Fax:** 01963 364029
Email: rholmes@bvmedia.co.uk
Advertising Address: As above. **Tel:** 01963 365100
Fax: 01963 363236
Email: cpengilly@bvmedia.co.uk
Web site: http://www.icwessex.co.uk
Publisher: Blackmore Vale Media
Date Established: 1978
Frequency: Weekly - Published on Fridays
Cover Price: Free
Circulation: 54,000 (Publisher's Statement)

Usual Pagination: 152
Editor: Fanny Charles; **Features Editor:** Jackie Spiteri;
Managing Director: Sven Thomas
Summary of Content: Magazine covering local news, the arts, food and drink and travel. Includes articles on motoring, sport, education, health and the environment.
Readership/Target Audience: Read by residents of Blackmore Vale, South Somerset and South West Wiltshire.
ADVERTISING RATES:
Full Page Mono £749.00
Full Page Colour £973.00
SCC £5.75
Agency Commission: 10%
Mechanical Data: Col Length: 280mm, No. of Columns (Display): 5, Type Area: 280 x 195mm, Trim Size: 297 x 210mm, Film: Digital, Page Width: 195mm, Col Widths (Display): 37mm
Copy instructions: Copy Date: Monday prior to publication date
Average advertising content per issue: 70%
CONSUMER: RURAL & REGIONAL INTEREST: Regional Interest English Counties

---

BLADES
752727U80C-2620

Formerly: The Regatta Magazine Ltd
Editorial Address: 56 Brook Street, WATLINGTON, OX49 5EH **Tel:** 07766 810385
Email: info@regattamagazine.co.uk
Advertising Address: As above.
Email: info@regattamagazine.co.uk
Web site: http://www.regattamagazine.co.uk
Publisher: The Regatta Magazine Ltd
Date Established: 2007
Frequency: Annual - Published in May
Cover Price: £3.00
Free to qualifying individuals
Circulation: 20,000 (Publisher's Statement)
Usual Pagination: 68
Editor: Helen Pattinson; **Advertising Manager:** Helen Pattinson
Summary of Content: Magazine focusing on the Henley regatta with features on fashion, cookery, drinks, eating out and homes.
Readership/Target Audience: Aimed at those living in Henley on Thames and visitors to the Henley regatta.
ADVERTISING RATES:
Full Page Colour £1395.00
Agency Commission: 10%
Mechanical Data: Bleed Size: 303 x 216mm, Film: Digital, Trim Size: 297 x 210mm
Copy instructions: Copy Date: 8 weeks prior to publication date
CONSUMER: RURAL & REGIONAL INTEREST: Regional Interest English Counties

---

BLAG
31140U76D-833

Editorial Address: PR by email only **Tel:** 0870 138 9430
Fax: 0870 138 9430
Email: blag@blagmagazine.com
Web site: http://www.blagmagazine.com
ISSN: 1366-4522
Publisher: Blag UK Ltd
Date Established: 2004
Frequency: Quarterly
Cover Price: £4.95
Free to qualifying individuals
Annual Sub.: £18.00
Usual Pagination: 100
Editor: Sally Edwards
Summary of Content: Magazine covering music, films, art and fashion.
Readership/Target Audience: Aimed at men and women aged 18 to 40 years old.
ADVERTISING: No Advertising taken
CONSUMER: MUSIC & PERFORMING ARTS: Music

BLAH BLAH
48070U89C-78

Editorial Address: PO Box 2622, READING, RG1 9DJ
Tel: 0118 962 4112
Email: editorial@blahblah.co.uk
Advertising Address: As above.
Email: advertising@blahblah.co.uk
Web site: http://www.blahblah.co.uk
ISSN: 1471-1494
Publisher: Blah Blah Magazine
Date Established: 1993
Frequency: Monthly
Cover Price: Free
Annual Sub.: £15.00
Circulation: 40,000 (Publisher's Statement)
Usual Pagination: 48
Editor: Marc Wiles; **Advertising Manager:** Marc Wiles
Summary of Content: Entertainment guide covering listings for live music, comedy, film, theatre and the arts, Internet columns and tourist information.

Readership/Target Audience: Aimed at young professionals living in and visitors to the Home Counties and Thames Valley area.
ADVERTISING RATES:
Full Page Mono £500.00
Full Page Colour £600.00
Agency Commission: 10%
Mechanical Data: Print Process: Web-fed litho, Film: Digital
Copy instructions: Copy Date: 17th of the month prior to publication date
Average advertising content per issue: 40%
CONSUMER: HOLIDAYS & TRAVEL: Entertainment Guides

BLISS
45383U74F-352

Editorial Address: Brockbourne House, 77 Mount Ephraim, TUNBRIDGE WELLS, TN4 8BS **Tel:** 01892 500100
Fax: 01892 545666
Email: bliss@panini.co.uk
Advertising Address: Orange20 Ltd, 20 Orange Street, LONDON, WC2H 7EF **Tel:** 020 7321 0701
Email: sales@o20.co.uk
Web site: http://www.mybliss.co.uk
Publisher: Panini UK Ltd
Date Established: 1995
Frequency: 13 issues yearly
Cover Price: £2.50
Annual Sub.: £22.80
Circulation: 86,054 (ABC 01/01/2009 to 30/06/2009)
Usual Pagination: 126
Editor: Zoe Shenton; **News Editor:** Angeli Milburn;
Features Editor: Angeli Milburn; **Managing Director:** Mike Riddell; **Advertising Manager:** Christel Davidson;
Managing Editor: Alan O'Keefe
Summary of Content: Magazine containing articles on fashion, health and beauty, celebrity interviews and gossip.
Readership/Target Audience: Aimed at females between 13 and 18 years old.
ADVERTISING RATES:
Full Page Colour £7800.00
Agency Commission: 15%
Mechanical Data: Type Area: 197 x 137mm, Trim Size: 207 x 147mm, Bleed Size: 213 x 153mm, Col Length: 197mm, Page Width: 137mm, Film: Digital
Copy instructions: Copy Date: 4 weeks prior to publication date
Average advertising content per issue: 35%
CONSUMER: WOMEN'S INTEREST CONSUMER MAGAZINES: Teenage

BLONDE HAIR
1813202U74H-306

Editorial Address: 9th Floor, Tower House, Fairfax Street, BRISTOL, BS1 3BN **Tel:** 0117 927 9009 **Fax:** 0117 314 8310
Email: michelletiernan@originpublishing.co.uk
Advertising Address: As above. **Fax:** 0117 934 9008
Email: tyronejones@originpublishing.co.uk
Web site: http://www.blondehairmagazine.co.uk
Publisher: Origin Publishing Ltd
Frequency: 6 issues yearly
Cover Price: £2.99
Circulation: 11,264 (ABC 01/01/2009 to 30/06/2009)
Usual Pagination: 196
Editor: Michelle Tiernan
Summary of Content: Magazine covering style ideas cuts and colours, the latest catwalk trends and product tests as well as handy hints and a questions and answers section.
Readership/Target Audience: Aimed at blondes of all ages.
ADVERTISING RATES:
Full Page Colour £2011.00
Agency Commission: 10%
Mechanical Data: Type Area: 184 x 128mm, Bleed Size: 216 x 154mm, Trim Size: 210 x 148mm, Col Length: 184mm, Page Width: 128mm, Film: Digital
Copy instructions: Copy Date: 6 weeks prior to publication date
Average advertising content per issue: 20%
CONSUMER: WOMEN'S INTEREST CONSUMER MAGAZINES: Hair & Beauty

BLUEBELL NEWS
46701U79J-10

Editorial Address: Station House, 1 Horncastle Road, Wragby, MARKET RASEN, LN8 5RB **Tel:** 01507 529306
Fax: 01507 529495
Email: ctyson@mortons.co.uk
Advertising Address: As above.
Email: ctyson@mortons.co.uk
Web site: http://www.bluebell-railway.co.uk
Publisher: Mortons Heritage Media
Date Established: 1959
Frequency: Quarterly
Annual Sub.: £16.00
Circulation: 10,200 (Publisher's Statement)
Usual Pagination: 64
Editor: Colin Tyson; **Advertising Manager:** Colin Tyson
Summary of Content: Magazine covering regular news on Britain's first full-sized preserved steam railway.

Section 4 (c) Consumer Magazines

Consumer Magazines

Readership/Target Audience: Read by 9,500 Bluebell Railway Preservation Society members. Also on sale in souvenir shop at Bluebell Railway.
ADVERTISING RATES:
Full Page Mono £75.00
Full Page Colour £100.00
Mechanical Data: Trim Size: 210 x 148mm, Film: Digital
CONSUMER: HOBBIES & DIY: Rail Enthusiasts

BLUES & SOUL
46129U76D-265

Editorial Address: 153 Praed Street, LONDON, W2 1RL
Tel: 020 8656 5651
Email: editorial@bluesandsoul.com
Advertising Address: As above. **Fax:** 020 8656 5651
Email: info@bluesandsoul.com
Web site: http://www.bluesandsoul.com
Publisher: Blues & Soul Ltd
Date Established: 1967
Frequency: Monthly
Cover Price: £2.95
Circulation: 28,700 (Publisher's Statement)
Usual Pagination: 62
Editor: Lee Tyler; **Advertising Manager:** Claire Daniell
Summary of Content: Comprehensive review of urban music, Hip-Hop, Soul, Jazz, Dance and R&B. Focuses on clubs, charts, record reviews, and includes reports from the USA and celebrity interviews.
Readership/Target Audience: Read by males between 16 and 50 years and females between 16 and 38 years.
ADVERTISING: Rates on application
Agency Commission: 10%
Copy instructions: Copy Date: 7 days prior to publication date
Average advertising content per issue: 33%
CONSUMER: MUSIC & PERFORMING ARTS: Music

BLUES IN BRITAIN
46128U76D-257

Formerly: Blueprint - The Magazine of the British Blues Connection
Editorial Address: 10 Messaline Avenue, LONDON, W3 6JX
Tel: 020 8723 7376 **Fax:** 020 8723 7380
Email: fran@bluesinbritain.org
Web site: http://www.bluesinbritain.org
ISSN: 1475-9721
Publisher: Abacabe Publishing
Date Established: 2002
Frequency: Monthly
Cover Price: £4.25
Annual Sub.: £43.00
Circulation: 4,500 (Publisher's Statement)
Usual Pagination: 42
Editor: Fran Leslie; **News Editor:** Tina Goldstone;
Managing Director: Fran Leslie; **Publisher:** Fran Leslie
Summary of Content: Magazine covering the contemporary British blues scene with news, interviews and profiles, live, events, CD and DVD reviews and a national Gig Guide to blues events.
Readership/Target Audience: Aimed at those interested in the live British blues scene and blues music in general.
ADVERTISING: No Advertising taken
CONSUMER: MUSIC & PERFORMING ARTS: Music

BLUESCI
1667012U83-267

Editorial Address: Old Examination Hall, Free School Lane, CAMBRIDGE, CB2 3RF **Tel:** 01223 337575
Fax: 01223 760949
Email: info@bluesci.org
Advertising Address: As above.
Email: business@varsity.co.uk
Web site: http://www.bluesci.org
Publisher: Varsity Publications Ltd
Frequency: 3 issues yearly - Published in January, April and October
Cover Price: Free
Circulation: 10,000 (Publisher's Statement)
Usual Pagination: 32
Editor: Jonathan Zwart; **Advertising Manager:** Michael Derringer
Summary of Content: Magazine offering a forum for students from all disciplines interested in topical science debate.
Readership/Target Audience: Aimed at graduates and undergraduates of Cambridge University.
ADVERTISING RATES:
Full Page Colour £1200.00
Agency Commission: 10%
Mechanical Data: Bleed Size: 285 x 220mm, Film: Digital, Trim Size: 275 x 210mm
Copy instructions: Copy Date: 2 weeks prior to publication date
Average advertising content per issue: 6%
CONSUMER: STUDENT PUBLICATIONS

BLUEWATER
1655836U74Q-1197

Editorial Address: 15B St. Georges Mews, Primrose Hill, LONDON, NW1 8XE **Tel:** 020 7449 1500 **Fax:** 020 7722 1851
Email: editor@bluewater.co.uk
Advertising Address: As above.
Email: phillip.every@storyworldwide.co.uk
Publisher: Story Worldwide
Frequency: Quarterly
Cover Price: Free
Circulation: 250,000 (Print Run)
Usual Pagination: 52
Editor: Gaynor Wetherall
Summary of Content: Magazine covering fashion and lifestyle.
Readership/Target Audience: Aimed at stylish and discerning shoppers at Bluewater Shopping Centre.
ADVERTISING RATES:
Full Page Colour £5250.00
Agency Commission: 10%
Mechanical Data: Type Area: 227 x 200mm, Bleed Size: 251 x 226mm, Trim Size: 245 x 220mm, Col Length: 227mm, Page Width: 200mm, Film: Digital
Copy instructions: Copy Date: 6 weeks prior to publication date
Average advertising content per issue: 30%
CONSUMER: WOMEN'S INTEREST CONSUMER MAGAZINES: Lifestyle

BM
1654915U74A-969

Formerly: Bonmarche Magazine
Editorial Address: 1 Neal Street, Covent Garden, LONDON, WC2H 9QL **Tel:** 020 7306 0304 **Fax:** 020 7306 0314
Email: stouquet@riverltd.co.uk
Advertising Address: As above. **Tel:** 020 7413 9377
Email: hfriend@riverltd.co.uk
Publisher: River Publishing Ltd
Date Established: 2003
Frequency: Quarterly
Cover Price: £0.75
Circulation: 127,206 (ABC 01/01/2007 to 31/12/2007)
Usual Pagination: 52
Editor: Sarah Touquet
Summary of Content: Lifestyle magazine with real-life features, fashion, beauty, cookery, travel and puzzles.
Readership/Target Audience: Aimed at customers of Bonmarche stores predominantly women aged 40 years old plus.
ADVERTISING RATES:
Full Page Colour £5450.00
Agency Commission: 10%
Mechanical Data: Type Area: 258 x 196mm, Bleed Size: 284 x 222mm, Trim Size: 278 x 216mm, Col Length: 258mm, Page Width: 196mm, Film: Digital
CONSUMER: WOMEN'S INTEREST CONSUMER MAGAZINES: Women's Interest

---

BMFA NEWS
46591U79B-11

Editorial Address: Chacksfield House, 31 St. Andrews Road, LEICESTER, LE2 8RE **Tel:** 0116 244 0028
Fax: 0116 244 0645
Email: admin@bmfa.org
Advertising Address: JI Media Sales, 9 New Road, Elsenham, BISHOP'S STORTFORD, CM22 6HA
Tel: 01279 812082
Email: jimediasales@supanet.com
Web site: http://www.bmfa.org
Publisher: British Model Flying Association
Date Established: 1992
Frequency: 6 issues yearly
Cover Price: £1.25
Free to qualifying individuals
Annual Sub.: £7.00
Circulation: 40,000 (Publisher's Statement)
Usual Pagination: 24
Editor: Eric Clark; **Advertising Manager:** John Irish
Summary of Content: Newspaper covering all aspects of model flying and building.
Readership/Target Audience: Aimed at enthusiasts and members of the association.
ADVERTISING RATES:
Full Page Colour £840.00
SCC £10.80
Agency Commission: 10%
Mechanical Data: Bleed Size: 277 x 203mm, No. of Columns (Display): 4, Col Widths (Display): 42mm, Type Area: 250 x 180mm, Col Length: 250mm, Page Width: 180mm, Film: Digital, Trim Size: 270 x 200mm
Copy instructions: Copy Date: 4 weeks prior to publication date
CONSUMER: HOBBIES & DIY: Models & Modelling

BMW CAR
46446U77E-100

Editorial Address: Becket House, Vestry Road, SEVENOAKS, TN14 5EJ **Tel:** 01732 748000
Fax: 01732 748001
Email: bmwcar@unity-media.com

Advertising Address: As above.
Email: moneill@unity-media.com
Web site: http://www.bmwcarmagazine.com
ISSN: 1353-7954
Publisher: Unity Media plc
Frequency: Monthly
Cover Price: £4.50
Annual Sub.: £43.00
Circulation: 55,000 (Publisher's Statement)
Usual Pagination: 132
Editor: Bob Harper; **Advertising Manager:** Melanie O'Neill;
Publisher: Colin Wilkinson
Summary of Content: Magazine containing news and information on the BMW car. Includes products and articles on BMW tuned vehicles.
Readership/Target Audience: Read by BMW drivers, owners and enthusiasts around the world.
ADVERTISING RATES:
Full Page Colour £1650.00
Agency Commission: 10%
Mechanical Data: Page Width: 200mm, Trim Size: 285 x 220mm, Bleed Size: 291 x 226mm, Type Area: 255 x 200mm, Col Length: 255mm, Film: Digital
Copy instructions: Copy Date: 4 weeks prior to publication date
Average advertising content per issue: 30%
CONSUMER: MOTORING & CYCLING: Club Cars

BMW MAGAZINE
46447U77E-105

Editorial Address: Ellesfield Avenue, BRACKNELL, RG12 8TA **Tel:** 01344 480364 **Fax:** 01344 359364
Email: bmwmagazine@bmw.co.uk
Advertising Address: Power Turner Group, Gordon House, 10 Greencoat Place, LONDON, SW1P 1PH
Tel: 020 7592 8300 **Fax:** 020 7592 8301
Email: smustafa@publicitas.com
Web site: http://www.bmw.co.uk/bmwmagazine
Publisher: Hoffman and Campe
Date Established: 1996
Frequency: 3 issues yearly - Published in April, August and November
Free to qualifying individuals
Circulation: 300,000 (Publisher's Statement)
Usual Pagination: 100
Editor: Camilla Ellis
Summary of Content: Magazine containing news and features on BMW cars, food, drink, travel, business, sport and lifestyle.
Language(s): Arabic; Chinese; Czech; Danish; English; French; German; Greek; Hungarian; Indonesian; Italian; Japanese; Portuguese; Russian; Spanish; Thai
Readership/Target Audience: Read by BMW customers or those interested in the car.
ADVERTISING RATES:
Full Page Colour EUR9900.00
Agency Commission: 10%
Mechanical Data: Page Width: 190mm, Film: Digital, Type Area: 260 x 190mm, Bleed Size: 286 x 221mm, Trim Size: 280 x 215mm, Col Length: 260mm
Copy instructions: Copy Date: 6 weeks prior to publication date
Average advertising content per issue: 20%
CONSUMER: MOTORING & CYCLING: Club Cars

BOARDS
45937U75M-20

Editorial Address: 196 Eastern Esplanade, SOUTHEND-ON-SEA, SS1 3AB **Tel:** 01702 582245 **Fax:** 01702 588434
Email: news@boards.co.uk
Advertising Address: As above.
Email: advertising@boards.co.uk
Web site: http://www.boards.co.uk
Publisher: Yachting Press Ltd
Date Established: 1984
Frequency: 10 issues yearly
Cover Price: £4.10
Annual Sub.: £30.00
Circulation: 22,000 (Publisher's Statement)
Usual Pagination: 128
Editor: Gary Crossley; **Managing Director:** John Heyes
Summary of Content: Windsurfing magazine covering new products, equipment and techniques for all levels of ability.
Readership/Target Audience: Aimed at all levels of windsurfers from beginners to experts.
ADVERTISING RATES:
Full Page Colour £1920.00
SCC £38.00
Agency Commission: 10%
Mechanical Data: Col Widths (Display): 57mm, Type Area: 270 x 190mm, Bleed Size: 306 x 236mm, Trim Size: 300 x 230mm, Col Length: 270mm, No. of Columns (Display): 3, Film: Digital, Page Width: 190mm
Copy instructions: Copy Date: 2 weeks prior to publication date
Average advertising content per issue: 40%
CONSUMER: SPORT: Water Sports

BOAT FISHING MONTHLY
1752660U92-108

Editorial Address: The Maltings, West Street, BOURNE, PE10 9PH **Tel:** 01778 391000 **Fax:** 01778 394748
Email: davebarham@warnersgroup.co.uk
Advertising Address: As above. **Fax:** 01778 392079
Email: jaynen@warnersgroup.co.uk
Web site: http://www.boatfishing-monthly.co.uk
Publisher: Warners Group Publications plc
Date Established: 2002
Frequency: Monthly
Cover Price: £3.20
Annual Sub.: £38.88
Usual Pagination: 100
Editor: Dave Barham; **Publisher:** Jackie Green
Summary of Content: Magazine covering sport fishing from a boat.
Readership/Target Audience: Aimed at charter boat, private boat and dinghy anglers.
ADVERTISING RATES:
Full Page Colour £640.00
Agency Commission: 10%
Mechanical Data: Type Area: 275 x 190mm, Bleed Size: 303 x 216mm, Trim Size: 297 x 210mm, Col Length: 275mm, Page Width: 190mm, Film: Digital
Copy instructions: Copy Date: 1 month prior to publication date
Average advertising content per issue: 30%
CONSUMER: ANGLING & FISHING

BOAT INTERNATIONAL
48365U91A-9

Editorial Address: Hartfield House, 41-42 Hartfield Road, LONDON, SW19 3RQ **Tel:** 020 8545 9330
Fax: 020 8545 9333
Email: amanda.mccracken@boatinternationalmedia.com
Advertising Address: As above.
Email: info@boatinternational.co.uk
Web site: http://www.boatinternational.com
ISSN: 0264-9136
Publisher: Edisea Ltd
Date Established: 1983
Frequency: Monthly
Cover Price: £4.80
Circulation: 35,000 (Publisher's Statement)
Usual Pagination: 320
Editor: Amanda McCracken
Summary of Content: Magazine covering all aspects of luxury yachting. Contains news, legal column, technology, international show previews, design focus, review and on board features of yachts from around the world, charter and brokerage, charter features and Market Intelligence.
Readership/Target Audience: Read by affluent boat owners and industry professionals.
ADVERTISING RATES:
Full Page Colour £4600.00
Agency Commission: 10%
Mechanical Data: Type Area: 275 x 195mm, Col Length: 275mm, Page Width: 195mm, Bleed Size: 306 x 229mm, Trim Size: 300 x 223mm, Film: Digital
Copy instructions: Copy Date: 1 month prior to publication date
Supplement(s): America's Cup - 1xY, Boat International Interiors - 1xY, Palma Superyacht Regatta - 1xY, The SuperPorts - 1xY, The Superyacht Owner's Guide to Valencia - 1xY, Les Voiles de Saint Tropez & Antigua Classic Week - 1xY
CONSUMER: RECREATION & LEISURE: Boating & Yachting

BOAT MART
48366U91A-9_25

Editorial Address: PO Box 9633, COLCHESTER, CO1 9DS
Tel: 01223 460490
Email: editorboatmart@boatmart.co.uk
Advertising Address: Alliance House, 49 Sidney Street, CAMBRIDGE, CB2 3JS **Tel:** 01223 460490
Fax: 01223 315960
Email: jody@sportsboat.co.uk
Web site: http://www.boatmart.co.uk
Publisher: CSL Publishing Ltd
Frequency: 13 issues yearly
Cover Price: £3.35
Usual Pagination: 176
Editor: Jane Rickard
Summary of Content: Magazine containing information on buying and selling boats. Also covers new and used boat tests, marine news, equipment round-ups, diary dates, sailing and owners' club listings and practical projects.
Readership/Target Audience: Aimed at new and experienced boating enthusiasts.
ADVERTISING: Rates on application
Agency Commission: 10%
Mechanical Data: Type Area: 270 x 190mm, Film: Digital, Col Length: 270mm, Page Width: 190mm
CONSUMER: RECREATION & LEISURE: Boating & Yachting

BOAT TRADER
48408U91A-9_70

Formerly: Buy a Boat (for under £20000)
Editorial Address: 44A North Street, CHICHESTER, PO19 1NF **Tel:** 01243 533394 **Fax:** 01243 532025
Email: sales@boatshop24.co.uk
Advertising Address: As above.
Email: sales@boatshop24.co.uk
Web site: http://www.boatshop24.co.uk
Publisher: Boat Shop 24 Ltd
Date Established: 1994
Frequency: Monthly
Cover Price: £2.99
Circulation: 14,551 (Publisher's Statement)
Usual Pagination: 104
Editor: Sandra Mackenzie
Summary of Content: Publication listing boats for sale for under £20000.
Readership/Target Audience: Aimed at those looking to purchase a boat.
ADVERTISING RATES:
Full Page Colour £465.00
Agency Commission: 10%
Mechanical Data: Bleed Size: 310 x 240mm, Trim Size: 300 x 230mm, Film: Digital
Copy instructions: Copy Date: 10 days prior to publication date
Average advertising content per issue: 98%
CONSUMER: RECREATION & LEISURE: Boating & Yachting

BOATS & YACHTS FOR SALE
48406U91A-9_50

Editorial Address: 44A North Street, CHICHESTER, PO19 1NF **Tel:** 01243 533394 **Fax:** 01243 532025
Email: sales@boatshop24.co.uk
Advertising Address: As above.
Email: sales@boatshop24.co.uk
Web site: http://www.boatshop24.co.uk
Publisher: Boat Shop 24 Ltd
Date Established: 1985
Frequency: Monthly
Cover Price: £3.60
Circulation: 9,413 (Publisher's Statement)
Usual Pagination: 170
Editor: Sandra Mackenzie; **Advertising Manager:** Julie Reed
Summary of Content: Magazine containing second-hand and new boats for sale.
Readership/Target Audience: Aimed at those interested in purchasing boats.
ADVERTISING RATES:
Full Page Colour £970.00
Agency Commission: 10%
Mechanical Data: Film: Digital
Copy instructions: Copy Date: 2 weeks prior to publication date
Average advertising content per issue: 100%
CONSUMER: RECREATION & LEISURE: Boating & Yachting

BODY & SOUL
1614806U74G-231

Editorial Address: 371 Bury Old Road, Prestwich, MANCHESTER, M25 1QA **Tel:** 0161 798 7662
Fax: 0161 798 7662
Email: body.soul@virgin.net
Advertising Address: As above.
Email: body.soul@virgin.net
Web site: http://www.mybodyandsoul.org
ISSN: 1476-5101
Publisher: Temple Design Publishing Solutions
Date Established: 2002
Frequency: 6 issues yearly
Cover Price: Free
Circulation: 10,000 (Publisher's Statement)
Usual Pagination: 36
Editor: Jane Bowler; **Advertising Manager:** Jane Bowler
Summary of Content: Magazine covering the activities of alternative and complementary therapists in Manchester and the north west as well as features on alternative therapies and eco-friendly lifestyles, diary dates and listings of therapists.
Readership/Target Audience: Aimed at those interested in complementary therapies, green living and ethical alternatives.
ADVERTISING RATES:
Full Page Mono £205.00
Full Page Colour £250.00
Copy instructions: Copy Date: End of month prior to publication date
Average advertising content per issue: 30%
CONSUMER: WOMEN'S INTEREST CONSUMER MAGAZINES: Slimming & Health

BODYCONFIDENTIAL.COM
1895424U74Q-1374

Editorial Address: 2nd Floor North Square, 11-13 Spear Street, MANCHESTER, M1 1JU **Tel:** 161 228 0044
Email: lyndam@planetconfidential.com
Web site: http://www.bodyconfidential.com
Publisher: 2m Media

Frequency: Daily
Cover Price: Free
Circulation: 23,174 (Publisher's Statement)
Editor: Lynda Moyo
Summary of Content: Website covering all areas of health and beauty.
Readership/Target Audience: Aimed at men and women with an interest in beauty and fitness.
CONSUMER: WOMEN'S INTEREST CONSUMER MAGAZINES: Lifestyle

BOOK AND MAGAZINE COLLECTOR
46731U79K-300

Editorial Address: 5th Floor, 31-32 Park Row, LEEDS, LS1 5JD **Tel:** 0113 200 2929 **Fax:** 0113 200 2928
Email: editor@bookandmagazinecollector.com
Advertising Address: As above.
Email: brendas@writersnews.co.uk
Publisher: Warners Group Publications plc
Date Established: 1985
Frequency: 13 issues yearly
Cover Price: £3.50
Annual Sub.: £40.75
Circulation: 20,000 (Publisher's Statement)
Usual Pagination: 132
Editor: Christopher Peachment; **Advertising Manager:** Brenda Shillito; **Publisher:** Janet Davison
Summary of Content: Magazine containing feature articles about rare and collectable publications. Focusing on modern firsts, comics and auctions.
Readership/Target Audience: Read by collectors of books and magazines.
ADVERTISING RATES:
Full Page Mono £205.00
Full Page Colour £265.00
Agency Commission: 15%
Mechanical Data: Bleed Size: +3mm, Col Length: 190mm, Page Width: 132mm, Type Area: 190 x 132mm, Film: Digital
Copy instructions: Copy Date: 3 weeks prior to publication date
CONSUMER: HOBBIES & DIY: Collectors Magazines

BOOKS FOR KEEPS
41172U84B-359

Editorial Address: 1 Effingham Road, LONDON, SE12 8NZ
Tel: 020 8852 4953 **Fax:** 020 8318 7580
Email: richard@booksforkeeps.co.uk
Advertising Address: As above.
Email: enquiries@booksforkeeps.co.uk
Web site: http://www.booksforkeeps.co.uk
ISSN: 0143-909X
Publisher: School Bookshop Association Ltd
Date Established: 1980
Frequency: 6 issues yearly
Cover Price: £4.45
Annual Sub.: £26.50
Circulation: 8,500 (Publisher's Statement)
Usual Pagination: 28
Editor: Richard Hill; **Managing Director:** Richard Hill; **Advertising Manager:** Richard Hill
Summary of Content: Magazine with an overview of children's book publishing.
Readership/Target Audience: Aimed at teachers, professionals and parents interested in children's books.
ADVERTISING RATES:
Full Page Mono £700.00
Full Page Colour £700.00
Mechanical Data: Type Area: 270 x 188mm, Col Length: 270mm, Page Width: 188mm, Trim Size: 297 x 210mm, Bleed Size: 303 x 216mm, Film: Digital
Copy instructions: Copy Date: 4 weeks prior to publication date
CONSUMER: THE ARTS & LITERARY: Literary

BOOKTALK
626107U84B-32

Editorial Address: 115 Anglesea Road, IPSWICH, IP1 3PJ
Tel: 01473 250949
Email: sblbooktalk@btinternet.com
Web site: http://www.sbl.org.uk
Publisher: The Suffolk Book League
Date Established: 1982
Frequency: Quarterly
Free to qualifying individuals
Circulation: 200 (Publisher's Statement)
Usual Pagination: 16
Editor: Kay McElhinney
Summary of Content: Newsletter containing book news, details of forthcoming events and local and national features.
Readership/Target Audience: Read by members of the Suffolk Book League.
ADVERTISING: No Advertising taken
CONSUMER: THE ARTS & LITERARY: Literary

Consumer Magazines

BOOST YOUR WEIGHT LOSS! 760953U74G-8_50

Editorial Address: 47 St Mary's Court, Huntly Street, ABERDEEN, AB10 1TH **Tel:** 01224 211868
Fax: 01224 256118
Email: editorial@scottishslimmers.com
Web site: http://www.scottishslimmers.com
ISSN: 1743-8446
Publisher: Weight Management UK Ltd
Date Established: 2001
Frequency: 3 issues yearly - Published in January, April and August
Cover Price: £2.00
Circulation: 50,000 (Publisher's Statement)
Usual Pagination: 100
Editor: Yvette Rayner
Summary of Content: Magazine covering weight loss success stories, makeovers, healthy eating recipes, fashion and beauty advice.
Readership/Target Audience: Aimed at those committed to weight-loss and living a healthier life and members of Scottish Slimmers and Your Dietline.
ADVERTISING: No Advertising taken
CONSUMER: WOMEN'S INTEREST CONSUMER MAGAZINES: Slimming & Health

BOOTS HEALTH & BEAUTY 31250U74G-9

Editorial Address: 7 St. Martin's Place, LONDON, WC2N 4HA **Tel:** 020 7747 0700 **Fax:** 020 7747 0649
Email: kerry.foster@redwoodgroup.net
Advertising Address: As above. **Fax:** 020 7747 7299
Email: adrian.odds@redwoodgroup.net
Web site: http://www.redwoodgroup.net/clients/boots.html
Publisher: Redwood
Date Established: 1999
Frequency: 6 issues yearly
Cover Price: £1.00
Free to qualifying individuals
Circulation: 1,800,000 (Publisher's Statement)
Usual Pagination: 100
Advertising Director: Adrian Odds
Summary of Content: Magazine focusing on health and beauty issues. Contains articles on hair, skincare and medical problems.
Readership/Target Audience: Aimed at Boots' Advantage Card holders, primarily women between 25 and 45 years old.
ADVERTISING RATES:
Full Page Colour £24150.00
Agency Commission: 15%
Mechanical Data: Trim Size: 275 x 210mm, Type Area: 224 x 175mm, Bleed Size: 281 x 216mm, Col Length: 224mm, Page Width: 175mm, Film: Digital
Copy instructions: Copy Date: 8 weeks prior to publication date
Average advertising content per issue: 40%
CONSUMER: WOMEN'S INTEREST CONSUMER MAGAZINES: Slimming & Health

BORDER LIFE 47041U80E-20

Editorial Address: The Hermitage, High Street, SELKIRK, TD7 4DA **Tel:** 01750 721581 **Fax:** 01750 721239
Email: bobburgess@tweeddalepress.co.uk
Advertising Address: 90 Marygate, BERWICK-UPON-TWEED, TD15 1BW **Tel:** 01289 306677 **Fax:** 01289 334454
Email: jobell@tweeddalepress.co.uk
Web site: http://www.borderstoday.com
ISSN: 1367-2851
Publisher: Tweeddale Press Group
Frequency: Quarterly
Cover Price: £1.95
Circulation: 5,000 (Publisher's Statement)
Usual Pagination: 40
Editor: Bob Burgess; **Advertising Manager:** Jo Bell
Summary of Content: Magazine covering country life, local history and heritage, art, sport, business, music and people.
Readership/Target Audience: Aimed at residents of Northumberland and the Scottish Borders.
ADVERTISING: Rates on application
Agency Commission: 10%
Copy instructions: Copy Date: 3 weeks prior to publication date
Average advertising content per issue: 30%
CONSUMER: RURAL & REGIONAL INTEREST: Regional Interest Scotland

BOREREVENTS 1706771U89C-1071

Editorial Address: 2 Heatherlie Park, SELKIRK, TD7 5AL
Tel: 01750 725480 **Fax:** 0870 286 9320
Email: info@borderevents.com
Advertising Address: As above.
Email: info@borderevents.com
Web site: http://www.borderevents.com
Publisher: Border Events.com Ltd
Date Established: 2002
Frequency: 6 issues yearly
Cover Price: Free
Circulation: 20,000 (Publisher's Statement)

Usual Pagination: 72
Editor: Lesley Wilkinson; **Advertising Manager:** Andrew Lang
Summary of Content: Local What's On magazine covering attractions, sport, restaurants, accommodation, events, exhibitions and business services.
Readership/Target Audience: Aimed at residents and visitors to the Scottish Borders and North Northumberland.
ADVERTISING RATES:
Full Page Mono £595.00
Full Page Colour £695.00
Agency Commission: 10%
Mechanical Data: Type Area: 195 x 130mm, Col Length: 195mm, Page Width: 130mm, Film: Digital
Copy instructions: Copy Date: 3 weeks prior to publication date
CONSUMER: HOLIDAYS & TRAVEL: Entertainment Guides

BORE DA 47942U88E-5

Editorial Address: Swyddfa'r Urdd, Llanbadarn Road, ABERYSTWYTH, SY23 1EY **Tel:** 01970 613118
Fax: 01970 626120
Email: boreda@urdd.org
Advertising Address: As above.
Email: boreda@urdd.org
Web site: http://www.urdd.org
ISSN: 0006-7709
Publisher: Urdd Gobaith Cymru
Date Established: 1955
Frequency: 10 issues yearly
Annual Sub.: £9.00
Circulation: 4,200 (Publisher's Statement)
Usual Pagination: 16
Editor: Sian Eleri Davies; **Advertising Manager:** Sian Eleri Davies
Summary of Content: Magazine containing language teaching material, exercises and games.
Language(s): English; Welsh
Readership/Target Audience: Aimed at children under the age of 11 learning the Welsh language.
ADVERTISING RATES:
Full Page Mono £130.00
Full Page Colour £200.00
Mechanical Data: Trim Size: 297 x 210mm
Average advertising content per issue: 10%
CONSUMER: EDUCATION: Preparatory & Junior Education

BOWLERS WORLD 45994U75X-100

Editorial Address: 2 Braunton Road, WALLASEY, CH45 5HL **Tel:** 07984 348341
Email: bowlersworld05@aol.com
Advertising Address: As above.
Email: bowlersworld05@aol.com
Publisher: Bowlers' World
Date Established: 1977
Frequency: Monthly
Cover Price: £1.30
Annual Sub.: £15.00
Circulation: 13,000 (Publisher's Statement)
Usual Pagination: 12
Editor: Brian Hampson; **Advertising Manager:** Brian Hampson
Summary of Content: Magazine covering Crown Green Bowls.
Readership/Target Audience: Read by bowls enthusiasts.
ADVERTISING RATES:
Full Page Mono £600.00
Agency Commission: 15%
Mechanical Data: Film: Digital
Copy instructions: Copy Date: Beginning of the month prior to publication date
CONSUMER: SPORT: Other Sport

BOWLS INTERNATIONAL INCORPORATING WORLD BOWLS
45995U75X-120

Editorial Address: PO Box 100, STAMFORD, PE9 1XQ
Tel: 01780 755131 **Fax:** 01780 757261
Email: bowls@keypublishing.com
Advertising Address: As above.
Email: dave.thorpe@keypublishing.com
Web site: http://www.bowlsinternational.com
ISSN: 0262-6942
Publisher: Key Publishing Ltd
Date Established: 1981
Frequency: Monthly
Cover Price: £3.20
Annual Sub.: £31.90
Circulation: 14,000 (Publisher's Statement)
Usual Pagination: 64
Editor: Melvyn Beck; **Managing Director:** Adrian Cox;
Advertising Manager: David Thorpe; **Publisher:** Adrian Cox
Summary of Content: Magazine containing news and coaching tips.
Readership/Target Audience: Read by bowls players and enthusiasts.

ADVERTISING RATES:
Full Page Mono £1136.00
Full Page Colour £1340.00
SCC £13.40
Agency Commission: 10%
Mechanical Data: Film: Digital, Col Length: 267mm, Page Width: 180mm, Type Area: 267 x 180mm, Trim Size: 297 x 210mm, Bleed Size: 307 x 215mm
Copy instructions: Copy Date: 4 weeks prior to publication date
CONSUMER: SPORT: Other Sport

BOXING MONTHLY 45986U75Q-150

Editorial Address: 40 Morpeth Road, LONDON, E9 7LD
Tel: 020 8986 4141 **Fax:** 020 8986 4145
Email: glyn@boxing-monthly.co.uk
Advertising Address: As above.
Email: nigel@boxing-monthly.demon.co.uk
Web site: http://www.boxingmonthly.com
Publisher: Topwave Ltd
Date Established: 1989
Frequency: Monthly
Cover Price: £3.60
Annual Sub.: £40.00
Circulation: 30,000 (Publisher's Statement)
Usual Pagination: 64
Editor: Glyn Leach; **Advertising Manager:** Nigel Baker
Summary of Content: Magazine covering all aspects of boxing. Features fight previews, ringside reports, book and video reviews and interviews.
Readership/Target Audience: Aimed predominantly at men under the age of 45 as well as boxers, promoters, trainers and others involved at every level of the sport.
ADVERTISING RATES:
Full Page Mono £800.00
Full Page Colour £900.00
SCC £10.00
Agency Commission: 10%
Mechanical Data: Col Length: 265mm, Film: Digital, Type Area: 265 x 187mm, Trim Size: 297 x 210mm, Bleed Size: 304 x 216mm, Page Width: 187mm
Copy instructions: Copy Date: 2 weeks prior to publication date
Average advertising content per issue: 20%
CONSUMER: SPORT: Combat Sports

BOXING NEWS 45987U75Q-170

Editorial Address: 30 Cannon Street, LONDON, EC4M 6YJ
Tel: 020 7618 3456 **Fax:** 020 7618 3467
Email: claude.abrams@newsquestmagazines.com
Advertising Address: As above. **Tel:** 020 7618 3428
Fax: 020 7618 3400
Email: david.hennessey@newsquestspecialistmedia.com
Web site: http://www.boxingnewsonline.net
Publisher: Newsquest Specialist Media Ltd
Date Established: 1909
Frequency: Weekly
Cover Price: £2.15
Circulation: 11,749 (ABC 01/01/2008 to 31/12/2008)
Usual Pagination: 24
Editor: Claude Abrams; **Managing Director:** Tim Whitehouse; **Advertising Manager:** David Hennessey
Summary of Content: Magazine covering the latest previews, reviews and boxing information from around the world.
Readership/Target Audience: Aimed at 18 to 45 year old men with an interest in boxing.
ADVERTISING RATES:
Full Page Colour £1315.00
SCC £17.00
Agency Commission: 10%
Mechanical Data: Page Width: 210mm, Trim Size: 390 x 295mm, Bleed Size: 303 x 216mm, Type Area: 297 x 210mm, Col Length: 297mm, Film: Digital
Copy instructions: Copy Date: Tuesday prior to publication date
Average advertising content per issue: 13%
CONSUMER: SPORT: Combat Sports

BOYZ 47624U86B-15

Editorial Address: 18 Brewer Street, LONDON, W1F 0SH
Tel: 020 7025 6110 **Fax:** 020 7025 6109
Email: editor@boyz.co.uk
Advertising Address: As above. **Tel:** 020 7025 6103
Email: chris@boyz.co.uk
Web site: http://www.boyz.co.uk
Publisher: Greens Court Advertising Ltd.
Date Established: 1991
Frequency: Weekly
Cover Price: £1.80
Free to qualifying individuals
Annual Sub.: £85.00
Circulation: 40,000 (Publisher's Statement)
Usual Pagination: 100
Editor: Stuart Brumfitt; **Editor-in-Chief:** David Bridle
Summary of Content: Magazine containing features, celebrity interviews, club scene news and arts reviews.

Readership/Target Audience: Aimed at gay men.
ADVERTISING RATES:
Full Page Colour £850.00
Agency Commission: 10%
Mechanical Data: Type Area: 278 x 200mm, Bleed Size: +5mm, Col Length: 278mm, Page Width: 200mm, Col Widths (Display): 40mm, No. of Columns (Display): 4, Film: Digital
Copy instructions: Copy Date: 1 week prior to publication date
Average advertising content per issue: 60%
CONSUMER: ADULT & GAY MAGAZINES: Gay & Lesbian Magazines

BRADFORD MELA
1799447U90-1007
Editorial Address: Shine, Harehills Road, LEEDS, LS8 5HS
Tel: 0870 360 8606 **Fax:** 0870 360 8605
Email: nadim@asianexpress.co.uk
Advertising Address: As above.
Email: patrick@asianexpress.co.uk
Publisher: Open Media Publications Ltd
Frequency: Annual - Published in July
Cover Price: Free
Circulation: 200,000 (Publisher's Statement)
Editor: Nadim Hanif
Summary of Content: Magazine published in conjunction with Bradford City Council promoting the Asian Festival of Mela.
Readership/Target Audience: Aimed at those interested in the event.
ADVERTISING RATES:
Full Page Colour £1135.00
Mechanical Data: Type Area: 345 x 265mm, Col Length: 345mm, Page Width: 265mm, Film: Digital
Copy instructions: Copy Date: 1 week prior to publication date
CONSUMER: ETHNIC

THE BRAILLE SPORTING RECORD
45689U75A-510
Editorial Address: Craigmillar Park, EDINBURGH, EH16 5NB **Tel:** 0131 662 4445 **Fax:** 0131 662 1968
Email: enquiries@scottish-braille-press.org
Web site: http://www.scottish-braille-press.org
Publisher: Scottish Braille Press
Frequency: Weekly - Published each Wednesday
Annual Sub.: £10.50
Circulation: 250 (Publisher's Statement)
Usual Pagination: 36
Editor: Allan Balfour
Summary of Content: Magazine covering news of current sporting events focusing mainly on racing and football.
Readership/Target Audience: Aimed at those who are visually impaired with an interest in sport.
ADVERTISING: No Advertising taken
CONSUMER: SPORT

BRASS BAND WORLD
46131U76D-267
Editorial Address: 2nd Floor, Century House, 11 St. Peters Square, MANCHESTER, M2 3DN **Tel:** 0161 236 9526
Fax: 0161 247 7978
Email: info@brassbandworld.com
Advertising Address: As above. **Tel:** 0161 236 9886
Email: jhall@impromptupublishing.com
Web site: http://www.brassbandworld.com
Publisher: Impromptu Publishing Ltd
Date Established: 1991
Frequency: 10 issues yearly - Combined issues July/August and December/January
Cover Price: £3.85
Annual Sub.: £38.50
Circulation: 1,500 (Publisher's Statement)
Usual Pagination: 45
Editor: Carol Jarvis; **Advertising Manager:** Jeremy Hall
Summary of Content: Magazine containing independent international information on brass band playing and concert news.
Readership/Target Audience: Aimed at those who enjoy listening to, or playing in brass bands in Britain and overseas.
ADVERTISING RATES:
Full Page Colour £650.00
Agency Commission: 10%
Mechanical Data: Page Width: 185mm, Film: Digital, Type Area: 270 x 185mm, Bleed Size: 303 x 216mm, Trim Size: 297 x 210mm, Col Length: 270mm
CONSUMER: MUSIC & PERFORMING ARTS: Music

THE BRASS HERALD
1743618U76D-810
Editorial Address: 2 The Coppice, Impington, CAMBRIDGE, CB24 9PP **Tel:** 01223 234090 **Fax:** 01223 234090
Email: editor@thebrassherald.com
Advertising Address: As above.
Email: editor@thebrassherald.com

Web site: http://www.thebrassherald.com
ISSN: 1746-1472
Publisher: The Brass Herald
Date Established: 2003
Frequency: 5 issues yearly - Published in February, May, August, October and December
Cover Price: £5.00
Circulation: 7,000 (Publisher's Statement)
Usual Pagination: 92
Editor: Philip Biggs; **Advertising Manager:** Philip Biggs
Summary of Content: Magazine covering the full range of brass music from brass bands to orchestral brass, Salvation Army bands to big bands and Military bands to jazz.
Readership/Target Audience: Aimed at players of all types of brass instrument.
ADVERTISING: Rates on application
CONSUMER: MUSIC & PERFORMING ARTS: Music

BRATZ
1648409U91D-892
Editorial Address: Albert Square, DUNDEE, DD1 9QJ
Tel: 01382 223131 **Fax:** 01382 322214
Email: bratzmag@dcthomson.co.uk
Advertising Address: Orange20 Limited, 20 Orange Street, LONDON, WC2H 7EF **Tel:** 020 7321 0701
Fax: 020 7839 6933
Email: robin@o20.co.uk
Web site: http://www.dcthomson.co.uk
ISSN: 1742-9951
Publisher: D.C. Thomson & Co Ltd
Date Established: 2004
Frequency: 13 issues yearly
Cover Price: £2.50
Annual Sub.: £30.00
Circulation: 34,642 (ABC 01/01/2009 to 30/06/2009)
Usual Pagination: 44
Editor: Gillian Henney
Summary of Content: Children's magazine according to the Bratz lifestyle covering hair, make-up, celebrity interviews, gossip and competitions.
Readership/Target Audience: Aimed at girls aged between 7 and 10 years old.
ADVERTISING: Rates on application
CONSUMER: RECREATION & LEISURE: Children & Youth

BREAKOUT (ABINGDON)
48451U91D-25
Editorial Address: 9-11 Cholswell Court, Cholswell Road, Shippon, ABINGDON, OX13 6HX **Tel:** 01235 553444
Fax: 01235 547819
Email: news@youroxfordshire.co.uk
Advertising Address: As above. **Tel:** 01235 554465
Email: fatima@youroxfordshire.co.uk
Web site: http://www.youroxfordshire.co.uk
Publisher: Tri Media Group
Frequency: 3 issues yearly - Published at the end of each school term
Cover Price: Free
Circulation: 10,000 (Publisher's Statement)
Editor: Ric Sumner; **News Editor:** Ric Sumner; **Advertising Manager:** Fatima Mansoor
Summary of Content: Children's magazine featuring competitions to win the latest games and toys, plus film reviews, fun news and stories.
Readership/Target Audience: Aimed at 7 to 11 year olds.
ADVERTISING RATES:
Full Page Mono £500.00
Full Page Colour £550.00
Agency Commission: 10%
Mechanical Data: Page Width: 178mm, Film: Digital, Col Length: 250mm, Type Area: 250 x 178mm, No. of Columns (Display): 6
Average advertising content per issue: 66%
CONSUMER: RECREATION & LEISURE: Children & Youth

BREATHING SPACE
1668034U94F-1000
Editorial Address: 73-75 Goswell Road, LONDON, EC1V 7ER **Tel:** 020 7688 5555 **Fax:** 020 7688 5556
Email: breathing.space@blf-uk.org
Advertising Address: As above.
Email: amy.smock@blf-uk.org
Web site: http://www.lunguk.org
Publisher: British Lung Foundation
Date Established: 2005
Frequency: Quarterly
Cover Price: Free
Circulation: 5,000 (Publisher's Statement)
Usual Pagination: 36
Editor: Sharon Woolston
Summary of Content: Magazine with an underlying theme of respiratory health but with features on holidays, cookery and general lifestyle.
Readership/Target Audience: Distributed to members of the British Lung Foundation.
ADVERTISING RATES:
Full Page Colour £1500.00

Mechanical Data: Type Area: 241 x 181mm, Bleed Size: 271 x 211mm, Trim Size: 265 x 205mm, Col Length: 241mm, Page Width: 181mm, Film: Digital
CONSUMER: OTHER CLASSIFICATIONS: Disability

BREEZE MAGAZINE
1774816U90-993
Editorial Address: Coopers Yard (Amani Training), Westow Hill, LONDON, SE19 1TQ **Tel:** 020 8670 8200
Email: info@ebonyonline.net
Advertising Address: As above.
Email: info@ebonyonline.net
Publisher: Ebonyonline Communications Ltd
Date Established: 2006
Frequency: 6 issues yearly
Cover Price: Free
Circulation: 30,000 (Publisher's Statement)
Editor: Ade Idowu; **Advertising Manager:** Tayo Idowu
Summary of Content: Magazine covering clubs, restaurants, celebrity interviews, music, concerts, fashion, lifestyle, family, education, the arts and events.
Readership/Target Audience: Aimed at minority ethnic communities in London, Bedfordshire and Buckinghamshire.
ADVERTISING: Rates on application
CONSUMER: ETHNIC

BRIDGE
46653U79F-5
Editorial Address: 369 Euston Road, LONDON, NW1 3AR
Tel: 020 7388 2404 **Fax:** 020 7388 2407
Email: info@bridgeshop.com
Advertising Address: As above.
Email: info@chess.co.uk
Web site: http://www.bridgemagazine.co.uk
Publisher: Chess & Bridge Ltd
Date Established: 1926
Frequency: Monthly
Cover Price: £3.95
Annual Sub.: £34.95
Circulation: 5,000 (Publisher's Statement)
Usual Pagination: 52
Editor: Mark Horton; **Managing Director:** Malcolm Pein; **Advertising Manager:** Matthew Reid
Summary of Content: Magazine containing articles on bidding and play, instruction, competitions, tournament reports and humour with contributions from some of the world's respected bridge players and writers.
Readership/Target Audience: Read by regular bridge players and club players.
ADVERTISING RATES:
Full Page Colour £450.00
Mechanical Data: Trim Size: 297 x 210mm, Film: Digital
Copy instructions: Copy Date: 2 weeks prior to publication date
CONSUMER: HOBBIES & DIY: Games & Puzzles

THE BRIDGE
1762815U83-278
Editorial Address: Bakehouse Unit J108, 100 Clements Road, LONDON, SE16 4DG **Tel:** 020 7064 8400
Fax: 020 7231 1231
Email: tim@aspectmediauk.com
Web site: http://www.aspectmediauk.com
Publisher: Aspect Media
Frequency: Annual - Published in June
Cover Price: Free
Circulation: 50,000 (Publisher's Statement)
Usual Pagination: 28
Editor: Tim Lloyd; **Publisher:** Tim Lloyd
Summary of Content: Magazine covering stories from in and around the university, research being undertaken by the university and stories of successful Alumni.
Readership/Target Audience: Aimed at Alumni of the University of Sunderland.
ADVERTISING: No Advertising taken
CONSUMER: STUDENT PUBLICATIONS

THE BRIDGE
623615U87-17
Editorial Address: 57 Neal Road, West Kingsdown, SEVENOAKS, TN15 6DG **Tel:** 01474 852474
Email: bridge@church-media.co.uk
Advertising Address: As above.
Email: bridge@church-media.co.uk
Web site: http://www.church-media.co.uk
Publisher: Kent Christian Press
Date Established: 1994
Frequency: 10 issues yearly - Published on the last week of the month except January and August
Cover Price: Free
Circulation: 20,000 (Publisher's Statement)
Usual Pagination: 12
Editor: Bryan Harris; **Advertising Manager:** Bryan Harris; **Publisher:** Bryan Harris
Summary of Content: Church of England newspaper covering news, listings and book reviews relevant to churchgoers. Also contains articles featuring community issues of relevance.

Readership/Target Audience: Aimed at churchgoers within the Diocese of Southwark.
ADVERTISING RATES:
SCC £6.60
Agency Commission: 10%
Mechanical Data: Type Area: 375 x 279mm, Col Widths (Display): 41.3mm, Print Process: Offset Litho, Col Length: 375mm, Page Width: 279mm
Average advertising content per issue: 25%
CONSUMER: RELIGIOUS

BRIDGEND & DISTRICT PROPERTY NEWS 45480U74K-20

Editorial Address: Banner House, Briar Close, EVESHAM, WR11 4XA **Tel:** 01386 765832 **Fax:** 01386 40650
Email: sara@ppsprint.co.uk
Advertising Address: As above.
Email: info@ppsprint.co.uk
Web site: http://www.propertyprintservices.com
Publisher: PPS
Date Established: 1984
Frequency: 26 issues yearly
Free to qualifying individuals
Circulation: 15,000 (Publisher's Statement)
Usual Pagination: 32
Editor: Vernon Pethard; **Advertising Manager:** Sara Cresswell
Summary of Content: Newspaper covering local and national articles of interest.
Readership/Target Audience: Aimed at homebuyers and sellers in Bridgend, Maesteg, Porthcawl and surrounding areas.
Agency Commission: 10%
Average advertising content per issue: 80%
CONSUMER: WOMEN'S INTEREST CONSUMER MAGAZINES: Home Purchase

BRIG 47372U83-2_80

Editorial Address: The Robbins Centre, The University of Stirling, STIRLING, FK9 4LA **Tel:** 01786 467166
Fax: 01786 467176
Email: editor@brigonline.co.uk
Advertising Address: As above. **Tel:** 01786 467176
Fax: 01786 467190
Email: editor@brigonline.co.uk
Web site: http://brig.susaonline.org.uk
Publisher: Stirling University Students Association
Frequency: 5 issues yearly - Published monthly during term time
Cover Price: Free
Circulation: 9,000 (Publisher's Statement)
Usual Pagination: 28
Editor: Mark Cullen; **Advertising Manager:** Advertising Manager
Summary of Content: Student publication covering news, politics and sport with a features and entertainment supplement.
Readership/Target Audience: Aimed at students at the University of Stirling.
ADVERTISING: Rates on application
Copy instructions: Copy Date: 2 weeks prior to publication date
CONSUMER: STUDENT PUBLICATIONS

THE BRIGHTON SOURCE 31258U89C-79

Editorial Address: PO Box 3313, BRIGHTON, BN1 4BJ
Tel: 01273 609955
Email: info@brightonsource.co.uk
Advertising Address: Argus House, Crowhurst Road, Hollingbury, BRIGHTON, BN1 8AR **Tel:** 01273 609090
Email: sam@brightonsource.co.uk
Web site: http://www.brightonsource.co.uk
Publisher: Brighton Source Ltd
Date Established: 1998
Frequency: Monthly
Cover Price: Free
Circulation: 15,000 (Publisher's Statement)
Usual Pagination: 64
Editor: James Kendall; **Advertising Manager:** Sam Watts
Summary of Content: Guide to what's on in Brighton including clubbing, eating out, theatre and shopping.
Readership/Target Audience: Aimed at 18 to 35 year olds.
ADVERTISING RATES:
Full Page Colour £570.00
Agency Commission: 10%
Mechanical Data: Trim Size: 245 x 170mm, Bleed Size: +5mm, Film: Digital
Copy instructions: Copy Date: 15th of the month prior to publication date
Average advertising content per issue: 40%
CONSUMER: HOLIDAYS & TRAVEL: Entertainment Guides

THE BRISTOL MAGAZINE 1648458U80C-5130

Editorial Address: 25 Milsom Street, BATH, BA1 1DG
Tel: 01225 424499 **Fax:** 01225 426677
Email: editor@thebristolmagazine.co.uk
Advertising Address: As above.
Email: steve@thebristolmagazine.co.uk
Web site: http://www.thebristolmagazine.co.uk
Publisher: MC Publishing Ltd
Date Established: 2004
Frequency: Monthly
Cover Price: Free
Circulation: 28,000 (Print Run)
Usual Pagination: 84
Editor: Lindsey Harrad; **Advertising Manager:** Steve Miklos
Summary of Content: Magazine covering lifestyle, leisure, local issues, events, culture, property, antiques, gardening, food, commercial activities, architecture and regional news.
Readership/Target Audience: Aimed at owners of property in Bristol and the surrounding areas that have a value in excess of £200,000.
ADVERTISING RATES:
Full Page Colour £1075.00
Agency Commission: 15%
Mechanical Data: Type Area: 270 x 190mm, Bleed Size: 303 x 216mm, Trim Size: 297 x 210mm, Col Length: 270mm, Page Width: 190mm, Film: Digital, No. of Columns (Display): 2, Col Widths (Display): 92mm, Print Process: Web-offset
Copy instructions: Copy Date: 2 weeks prior to publication date
CONSUMER: RURAL & REGIONAL INTEREST: Regional Interest English Counties

BRISTOL SECRETARY 45471U74J-30

Editorial Address: 10-12 Queens Road, Portishead, BRISTOL, BS20 8HT **Tel:** 01275 818383 **Fax:** 01275 818490
Email: info@mediawest.co.uk
Advertising Address: As above. **Tel:** 01275 845846
Fax: 01275 817585
Email: steve@mediawest.co.uk
Web site: http://www.mediawest.co.uk
Publisher: Media West 2001 Ltd
Date Established: 1987
Frequency: Monthly
Cover Price: Free
Circulation: 6,000 (Publisher's Statement)
Usual Pagination: 40
Editor: Dan Lawton; **Managing Director:** James Crombleholme; **Advertising Manager:** Steve Davis
Summary of Content: Magazine containing features on fashion, beauty, restaurants, training, office equipment, conference facilities, hotels and job vacancies.
Readership/Target Audience: Aimed at senior secretaries, PAs and office managers.
ADVERTISING RATES:
Full Page Colour £950.00
Agency Commission: 10%
Mechanical Data: Trim Size: 297 x 210mm, Type Area: 272 x 186mm, Col Length: 272mm, Page Width: 186mm, Film: Digital
CONSUMER: WOMEN'S INTEREST CONSUMER MAGAZINES: Secretary & PA

BRITAIN 47963U89A-360

Formerly: In Britain
Editorial Address: 26-30 Old Church Street, Chelsea, LONDON, SW3 5BY **Tel:** 020 7349 3150 **Fax:** 020 73493160
Email: andrea.spain@chelseamagazines.com
Advertising Address: As above.
Email: erica.stuart@chelseamagazines.com
Web site: http://www.britain-magazine.com
ISSN: 0019-3143
Publisher: The Chelsea Magazine Company
Date Established: 1932
Frequency: 6 issues yearly
Annual Sub.: £23.70
Circulation: 27,882 (ABC 01/01/2007 to 31/12/2007)
Usual Pagination: 100
Editor: Andrea Spain; **Advertising Manager:** Erica Stuart
Summary of Content: Magazine published on behalf of Visit Britain. Includes features on all aspects of travel in Britain.
Readership/Target Audience: Aimed at visitors to Britain.
ADVERTISING RATES:
Full Page Colour £3200.00
Agency Commission: 10%
Mechanical Data: Type Area: 262 x 180mm, Col Length: 262mm, Page Width: 180mm, Bleed Size: 302 x 220mm, Trim Size: 297 x 210mm, Film: Digital
Copy instructions: Copy Date: 3 weeks prior to publication date
Average advertising content per issue: 30%
CONSUMER: HOLIDAYS & TRAVEL: Travel

BRITAIN AT WAR MAGAZINE 1813188U79H-165

Editorial Address: Green Arbor, Rectory Road, Storrington, PULBOROUGH, RH20 4EF **Tel:** 020 8971 8452
Fax: 020 8971 8480

Email: contact@britain-at-war-magazine.com
Advertising Address: Cabbell Ltd, Woodman Works, 204 Durnsford Road, LONDON, SW19 8DR **Tel:** 020 8971 8450
Fax: 020 8971 8480
Email: adam@cabbell.co.uk
Web site: http://www.britain-at-war-magazine.com
Publisher: Green Arbor Publishing Ltd
Date Established: 2007
Frequency: Monthly
Cover Price: £3.75
Circulation: 23,000 (Publisher's Statement)
Usual Pagination: 96
Editor: Martin Mace; **Advertising Director:** Adam Lister
Summary of Content: Magazine covering subjects on naval, military, aviation and home front themes and covering the entire spectrum of British involvement from the beginning of the twentieth century until now.
Readership/Target Audience: Aimed at enthusiasts who are interested in British and military history.
ADVERTISING RATES:
Full Page Colour £1250.00
Agency Commission: 10%
Mechanical Data: Type Area: 271 x 185mm, Bleed Size: 303 x 216mm, Trim Size: 297 x 210mm, Col Length: 271mm, Page Width: 185mm, Film: Digital
Copy instructions: Copy Date: 6 weeks prior to publication date
Average advertising content per issue: 30%
CONSUMER: HOBBIES & DIY: Military History

BRITAIN'S BEST LEISURE AND RELAXATION GUIDE 47985U89A-62

Formerly: Britain's Best Holidays
Editorial Address: Abbey Mill Business Centre, Seedhill, PAISLEY, PA1 1TJ **Tel:** 0141 887 0428 **Fax:** 0141 889 7204
Email: editorial@fhguides.co.uk
Advertising Address: As above.
Email: dorothy@fhguides.co.uk
Web site: http://www.holidayguides.com
ISSN: 9781-8505
Publisher: FHG Guides
Date Established: 1973
Frequency: Annual - Published in January
Cover Price: £5.99
Circulation: 12,000 (Publisher's Statement)
Editor: Anne Cuthbertson
Summary of Content: Guide to all kinds of holiday accommodation throughout Britain.
Readership/Target Audience: Read by holidaymakers in the UK.
ADVERTISING RATES:
Full Page Mono £489.00
Full Page Colour £779.00
Agency Commission: 10%
Mechanical Data: Page Width: 118mm, Bleed Size: 216 x 151mm, Trim Size: 210 x 154mm, Type Area: 190 x 118mm, Col Length: 190mm, Film: Digital
Copy instructions: Copy Date: October 2008
CONSUMER: HOLIDAYS & TRAVEL: Travel

THE BRITISH AND INTERNATIONAL FEDERATION OF FESTIVALS FOR MUSIC, DANCE & SPEECH 46195U76D-274

Editorial Address: Festival House, 198 Park Lane, MACCLESFIELD, SK11 6UD **Tel:** 01625 428297
Fax: 01625 503229
Email: info@federationoffestivals.org.uk
Web site: http://www.federationoffestivals.org.uk
Publisher: The British Federation of Festivals
Date Established: 1921
Frequency: Annual - Published in January
Cover Price: £8.00
Circulation: 3,500 (Publisher's Statement)
Usual Pagination: 56
Editor: Julia Crow
Summary of Content: Members' handbook of amateur festivals, music, dance and speech.
Readership/Target Audience: Aimed at members, major libraries, universities, colleges and conservatoires.
ADVERTISING: No Advertising taken
CONSUMER: MUSIC & PERFORMING ARTS: Music

THE BRITISH ART JOURNAL 601288U84A-170

Editorial Address: 46 Grove Lane, LONDON, SE5 8ST
Tel: 020 7787 6944 **Fax:** 020 7701 3299
Email: editor@britishartjournal.co.uk
Advertising Address: As above.
Email: editor@britishartjournal.co.uk
Web site: http://www.britishartjournal.co.uk
ISSN: 1467-2006
Publisher: British Art Journal
Date Established: 1999
Frequency: 3 issues yearly - Published in May, September and December
Cover Price: £10.50

Annual Sub.: £30.00
Circulation: 3,500 (Publisher's Statement)
Usual Pagination: 120
Editor: Robin Simon; **Advertising Manager:** Robin Simon; **Publisher:** Robin Simon
Summary of Content: Journal covering all periods of the history of British art including painting, sculpture, architecture, photography and decorative arts.
Readership/Target Audience: Read by art historians and those interested in British art.
ADVERTISING RATES:
Full Page Mono £1500.00
Full Page Colour £2500.00
Mechanical Data: Type Area: 277 x 190mm, Trim Size: 297 x 210mm, Film: Digital, Col Length: 277mm, Page Width: 190mm
CONSUMER: THE ARTS & LITERARY: Arts

THE BRITISH BANDSMAN
46132U76D-270
Editorial Address: 66-78 Denington Road, Denington Industrial Estate, WELLINGBOROUGH, NN8 2QH
Tel: 01933 445442 **Fax:** 01933 445435
Email: info@britishbandsman.com
Advertising Address: As above.
Email: info@britishbandsman.com
Web site: http://www.britishbandsman.com
Publisher: British Bandsman Ltd
Date Established: 1887
Frequency: Weekly - Published each Saturday
Cover Price: £1.25
Annual Sub.: £52.00
Circulation: 8,000 (Publisher's Statement)
Usual Pagination: 12
Editor: Kenneth Crookston; **Features Editor:** Rodney Newton; **Managing Director:** Trevor Caffull; **Advertising Manager:** John Ward
Summary of Content: Magazine containing contest results, news items, concerts and technical articles on brass playing and music.
Readership/Target Audience: Aimed at those interested in brass bands and their music.
ADVERTISING RATES:
Full Page Mono £419.00
Full Page Colour £625.00
Agency Commission: 10%
Mechanical Data: Page Width: 190mm, Type Area: 266 x 190mm, Col Length: 266mm, Trim Size: 297 x 210mm, Film: Digital, No. of Columns (Display): 4
Copy instructions: Copy Date: 10 days prior to publication date
Average advertising content per issue: 33%
CONSUMER: MUSIC & PERFORMING ARTS: Music

BRITISH BIRDS
47166U81F-110
Editorial Address: 4 Harlequin Gardens, ST. LEONARDS-ON-SEA, TN37 7PF **Tel:** 01424 755155 **Fax:** 01424 755155
Email: editor@britishbirds.co.uk
Advertising Address: As above.
Email: ian.lycett@birdwatch.co.uk
Web site: http://www.britishbirds.co.uk
ISSN: 0007-0335
Publisher: British Birds
Date Established: 1903
Frequency: Monthly - Published 1st day of the cover month
Annual Sub.: £49.00
Circulation: 5,000 (Publisher's Statement)
Usual Pagination: 64
Editor: Hazel Jenner
Summary of Content: Magazine containing observations on the birds of Britain and Europe. Covers migration, identification, behaviour, rarities and breeding.
Readership/Target Audience: Read by professional ornithologists and amateur birdwatchers.
ADVERTISING: Rates on application
Agency Commission: 10%
Copy instructions: Copy Date: 10th of the month prior to publication date
CONSUMER: ANIMALS & PETS: Birds

BRITISH BOTTLE REVIEW INCORPORATING COLLECTORS MART
706987U79K-320
Editorial Address: Elsecar Heritage Centre, Wath Road, Elsecar, BARNSLEY, S74 8HJ **Tel:** 01226 745156
Fax: 01226 361561
Email: sales@onlinebbr.com
Advertising Address: As above.
Email: sales@onlinebbr.com
Web site: http://www.onlinebbr.com
ISSN: 0963-7443
Publisher: BBR
Date Established: 1979
Frequency: Quarterly
Cover Price: £6.00
Annual Sub.: £24.00
Circulation: 10,000 (Publisher's Statement)

Usual Pagination: 48
Editor: Alan Blakeman; **Advertising Manager:** Alan Blakeman
Summary of Content: Publication containing information on antique bottles, pot lids and antique advertising as well as recent finds, sale news, club news, books and news on fakes.
Readership/Target Audience: Aimed at collectors and dealers.
ADVERTISING RATES:
Full Page Colour £200.00
Agency Commission: 10%
Mechanical Data: Bleed Size: 307 x 220mm, Trim Size: 297 x 210mm, Film: Digital
Copy instructions: Copy Date: 6 weeks prior to publication date
Average advertising content per issue: 25%
CONSUMER: HOBBIES & DIY: Collectors Magazines

BRITISH CHESS MAGAZINE
46654U79F-7
Editorial Address: 44 Baker Street, LONDON, W1U 7RT
Tel: 020 7486 8222 **Fax:** 020 7486 3355
Email: editor@bcmchess.co.uk
Advertising Address: As above.
Email: johnsaunders@bcmchess.co.uk
Web site: http://www.bcmchess.co.uk
ISSN: 0007-0440
Publisher: British Chess Magazine Limited
Date Established: 1881
Frequency: Monthly
Cover Price: £3.70
Annual Sub.: £38.00
Circulation: 2,500 (Publisher's Statement)
Usual Pagination: 56
Editor: John Saunders; **Advertising Manager:** John Saunders
Summary of Content: Worldwide coverage of chess, practical play, literature, book reviews, history, player profiles and computer chess.
Readership/Target Audience: Read by UK and overseas chess enthusiasts.
ADVERTISING RATES:
Full Page Mono £250.00
Full Page Colour £362.50
Mechanical Data: Page Width: 124mm, Type Area: 180 x 124mm, Print Process: Litho, Film: Digital, Col Length: 180mm
Copy instructions: Copy Date: 12th of the month prior to publication date
Average advertising content per issue: 6%
CONSUMER: HOBBIES & DIY: Games & Puzzles

BRITISH COINS MARKET VALUES
46651U79E-75
Formerly: Coins Market Values
Editorial Address: Leon House, 233 High Street, CROYDON, CR9 1HZ **Tel:** 020 8726 8242
Fax: 020 8726 8299
Email: julia_lee@ipcmedia.com
Advertising Address: As above. **Tel:** 020 8726 8000
Email: jay_jones@ipcmedia.com
Publisher: IPC Inspire
Frequency: Annual - Published in October
Cover Price: £8.99
Editor: Julia Lee
Summary of Content: Journal about numismatics, all British coinage, both medieval and modern.
Readership/Target Audience: Read by coin collectors.
ADVERTISING: Rates on application
CONSUMER: HOBBIES & DIY: Numismatics

BRITISH DEAF NEWS
48621U94F-100
Formerly: SIGNMatters
Editorial Address: 10th Floor, Coventry Point, Market Way, COVENTRY, CV1 1EA **Tel:** 024 7655 0936
Fax: 024 7622 1541
Email: bdn@bda.org.uk
Advertising Address: Mainline Media Ltd, The Barn, Oakley Hay Lodge Business Park, Great Folds Road, Great Oakley, CORBY, NN18 9AS **Tel:** 01536 747333 **Fax:** 01536 746565
Email: tricia.mcdougal@mainlinemedia.co.uk
Web site: http://www.bda.org.uk
Publisher: British Deaf Association
Frequency: Monthly
Cover Price: £2.00
Annual Sub.: £20.00
Circulation: 5,000 (Publisher's Statement)
Usual Pagination: 44
Editor: Alison Gudgeon
Summary of Content: Magazine containing news, events, reviews, topical articles, personal opinions and features on every subject that affects deaf people and their families.
Readership/Target Audience: Read by deaf and hard of hearing people and their families, British Sign Language students, teachers for the deaf, librarians, educationalists,

interpreters, international social activists, social services and the charity sector in the UK and overseas.
ADVERTISING RATES:
Full Page Mono £1000.00
Full Page Colour £1100.00
Mechanical Data: Type Area: 274 x 190mm, Bleed Size: 303 x 216mm, Trim Size: 297 x 210mm, Col Length: 274mm, Page Width: 190mm, Film: Digital
CONSUMER: OTHER CLASSIFICATIONS: Disability

BRITISH DRESSAGE
45997U81D-12
Editorial Address: Barn House, ALDSWORTH, GL54 3RE
Tel: 01451 844748
Advertising Address: 160-164 Barkby Road, LEICESTER, LE4 9LF **Tel:** 0116 202 2600 **Fax:** 0116 202 2730
Email: victoria.simmonds@greenshirespublishing.com
Web site: http://www.britishdressage.co.uk
Publisher: Greenshires Publishing Ltd
Frequency: 6 issues yearly
Cover Price: £3.00
Free to qualifying individuals
Circulation: 15,000 (Publisher's Statement)
Usual Pagination: 120
Editor: Jane Kidd
Summary of Content: Official magazine of British Dressage. Includes complete listings of scheduled events throughout the country, reports on training, dressage, international events, junior level reports and committee news.
Readership/Target Audience: Aimed at members of British Dressage.
ADVERTISING RATES:
Full Page Colour £1600.00
SCC £25.00
Agency Commission: 10%
Mechanical Data: Type Area: 273 x 190mm, Print Process: Sheet-fed litho, Bleed Size: 303 x 216mm, Trim Size: 297 x 210mm, Film: Digital, Col Length: 273mm, Page Width: 190mm
Copy instructions: Copy Date: End of the 1st week of the month prior to publication date
Average advertising content per issue: 40%
CONSUMER: ANIMALS & PETS: Horses & Ponies

BRITISH EQUESTRIAN DIRECTORY
47145U81D-15
Editorial Address: Stockeld Park, WETHERBY, LS22 4AW
Tel: 01937 582111
Email: clairet@beta-int.com
Advertising Address: As above. **Fax:** 01937 582778
Email: jenniferd@beta-int.com
Web site: http://www.beta-int.com
ISSN: 0144-7203
Publisher: Equestrian Management Consultants Ltd
Frequency: Half-yearly - Published in December
Cover Price: £16.00
Circulation: 25,000 (Publisher's Statement)
Usual Pagination: 500
Editor: Claire Thomas; **Advertising Manager:** Jennifer Dalton
Summary of Content: Directory containing 18000 addresses, indexed and cross-referenced of equestrian supplies, facilities, livery and consumer goods.
Readership/Target Audience: Aimed at equestrian businesses and consumers.
ADVERTISING: Rates on application
CONSUMER: ANIMALS & PETS: Horses & Ponies

BRITISH HOMING WORLD
45998U75X-250
Editorial Address: Severn Farm Enterprise Park, Severn Road, WELSHPOOL, SY21 7DF **Tel:** 01938 552360
Fax: 01938 553969
Email: editor@britishhomingworld.co.uk
Advertising Address: As above.
Email: editor@britishhomingworld.co.uk
Web site: http://www.rpra.org
Publisher: Royal Pigeon Racing Association
Frequency: Weekly
Cover Price: £0.65
Annual Sub.: £49.00
Circulation: 25,000 (Publisher's Statement)
Usual Pagination: 120
Editor: Stephen Richards; **Advertising Manager:** Tracy Jones
Summary of Content: Pigeon racing and showing magazine. Includes race and show results, features on winning birds and performances and articles on the management and conditioning of pigeons for racing.
Readership/Target Audience: Read by pigeon racers and breeders.
ADVERTISING RATES:
Full Page Mono £164.85
Full Page Colour £216.32
SCC £8.40
Agency Commission: 15%

Consumer Magazines

Mechanical Data: Page Width: 180mm, No. of Columns (Display): 3, Type Area: 245 x 180mm, Col Length: 245mm, Film: Digital, Bleed Size: 280 x 210mm
Copy instructions: Copy Date: Thursday prior to publication date
CONSUMER: SPORT: Other Sport

BRITISH HORSE
47119U81D-20

Editorial Address: Stoneleigh Deer Park, KENILWORTH, CV8 2XZ **Tel:** 01926 707700 **Fax:** 01926 707746
Email: communications@bhs.org.uk
Advertising Address: The Gallery, Manor Farm, Southam, CHELTENHAM, GL52 3PB **Tel:** 01242 259249
Fax: 01242 259248
Email: mark@fellowsmedia.com
Web site: http://www.bhs.org.uk
Publisher: The Hardy Group
Date Established: 1985
Frequency: 6 issues yearly - Published at the beginning of the 1st cover month
Cover Price: £2.50
Free to qualifying individuals
Circulation: 62,162 (ABC 01/01/2008 to 31/12/2008)
Usual Pagination: 76
Editor: Suzanne Goldby; **Advertising Manager:** Mark Brown
Summary of Content: Magazine covering the involvement of The British Horse Society in equestrian welfare, safety, education and access to the countryside.
Readership/Target Audience: Aimed at members of the British Horse Society.
ADVERTISING RATES:
Full Page Mono £2475.00
Full Page Colour £2750.00
Agency Commission: 10%
Mechanical Data: Type Area: 267 x 185mm, Col Length: 267mm, Page Width: 185mm, Col Widths (Display): 42.5mm, No. of Columns (Display): 4, Trim Size: 297 x 210mm, Film: Digital, Bleed Size: 303 x 216mm
Copy instructions: Copy Date: 10th of the month prior to publication date
Average advertising content per issue: 40%
CONSUMER: ANIMALS & PETS: Horses & Ponies

THE BRITISH JOURNAL OF AESTHETICS
47493U84A-180

Editorial Address: University of York, YORK, YO10 5DD **Tel:** 01904 433251 **Fax:** 01904 433251
Email: p.v.lamarque@york.ac.uk
Advertising Address: 60 Upper Broadmoor Road, CROWTHORNE, RG45 7DE **Tel:** 01344 779945
Fax: 01344 779945
Email: lhann@lhms.fsnet.co.uk
Web site: http://www.oup.co.uk/jnls
ISSN: 0007-0904
Publisher: OUP
Date Established: 1960
Frequency: Quarterly
Annual Sub.: £39.00
Circulation: 1,700 (Publisher's Statement)
Usual Pagination: 116
Editor: John Hyman
Summary of Content: Journal focusing on the study of the philosophy of art and the principles of aesthetic appreciation in the context of the arts.
Readership/Target Audience: Aimed at critics and academics in philosophy and the arts.
ADVERTISING RATES:
Full Page Mono £340.00
Agency Commission: 10%
Mechanical Data: Type Area: 200 x 130mm, Col Length: 200mm, Page Width: 130mm, Film: Digital
Copy instructions: Copy Date: 20th of 2 months prior to publication date
CONSUMER: THE ARTS & LITERARY: Arts

BRITISH JOURNAL OF RELIGIOUS EDUCATION
1895919U87-2056

Editorial Address: 4 Park Square, Milton Park, ABINGDON, OX14 4RN **Tel:** 020 7017 6000
Email: r.jackson@warwick.ac.uk
Web site: http://www.tandf.co.uk/journals/titles/01416200.asp
ISSN: 0141-6200
Publisher: Routledge, Taylor & Francis
Date Established: 1934
Frequency: 3 issues yearly
Annual Sub.: £195.00
Editor: Robert Jackson
Summary of Content: Journal aiming to promote and report research and scholarship in religious education and related fields such as values education, spiritual education and intercultural education in so far as they relate to the discussion of religion or religious traditions and movements.

Readership/Target Audience: Aimed at religious education students.
CONSUMER: RELIGIOUS

BRITISH MUSEUM MAGAZINE
47494U84A-190

Editorial Address: British Museum, Great Russell Street, LONDON, WC1B 3DG **Tel:** 020 7323 8195
Fax: 020 7323 8985
Email: mhudson@thebritishmuseum.ac.uk
Advertising Address: Royal Academy of Arts, Burlington House, Piccadilly, LONDON, W1J 0BD **Tel:** 020 7300 5661
Email: kim.jenner@royalacademy.org.uk
Web site: http://www.thebritishmuseum.ac.uk
ISSN: 0965-8297
Publisher: British Museum Friends
Frequency: 3 issues yearly - Published in April, August and December
Cover Price: £3.50
Free to qualifying individuals
Circulation: 15,000 (Publisher's Statement)
Usual Pagination: 64
Editor: Mira Hudson; **Advertising Manager:** Jane Grylls
Summary of Content: Magazine containing articles on news, exhibitions, research and new acquisitions at British Museum; also archaeological work and outside research.
Readership/Target Audience: Read by members of the British Museum Friends and those with an interest in the British Museum.
ADVERTISING RATES:
Full Page Mono £1200.00
Full Page Colour £1800.00
Agency Commission: 10%
Mechanical Data: Bleed Size: 303 x 236mm, Film: Digital, Trim Size: 297 x 230mm
Copy instructions: Copy Date: 2 months prior to publication date
CONSUMER: THE ARTS & LITERARY: Arts

BRITISH NATURISM
48671U94X-14

Editorial Address: 30-32 Wycliffe Road, NORTHAMPTON, NN1 5JF **Tel:** 01604 620361 **Fax:** 01604 230176
Advertising Address: As above.
Email: general.secretary@british-naturism.org.uk
Email: headoffice@british-naturism.org.uk
Web site: http://www.british-naturism.org.uk
ISSN: 0264-0406
Publisher: CCBN
Date Established: 1964
Frequency: Quarterly
Cover Price: £3.50
Circulation: 12,500 (Publisher's Statement)
Usual Pagination: 64
Editor: Tracey Major; **Advertising Manager:** Tracey Major
Summary of Content: Magazine of the Central Council for British Naturism. Contains information and features on naturist clubs and holidays, health and other issues.
Readership/Target Audience: Read by naturists.
ADVERTISING RATES:
Full Page Colour £750.00
Agency Commission: 10%
Mechanical Data: Film: Digital, Type Area: 274 x 190mm, Col Length: 274mm, Page Width: 190mm
Copy instructions: Copy Date: 6 weeks prior to publication date
Average advertising content per issue: 40%
CONSUMER: OTHER CLASSIFICATIONS: Miscellaneous

BRITISH PHILATELIC BULLETIN
46636U79C-10

Editorial Address: 35-50 RathbonePlace, LONDON, W1T 1HQ **Tel:** 020 7441 4744
Email: john.r.holman@royalmail.co.uk
Web site: http://www.royalmail.com/stamps
ISSN: 0953-8119
Publisher: Royal Mail Group Ltd
Date Established: 1963
Frequency: Monthly
Cover Price: £1.20
Annual Sub.: £12.95
Circulation: 20,000 (Publisher's Statement)
Usual Pagination: 36
Editor: John Holman
Summary of Content: Journal covering news and features on British stamps and stamp collecting.
Readership/Target Audience: Aimed at philatelists and postal historians.
ADVERTISING: No Advertising taken
Supplement(s): Commemorative Cover Review - 12xY
CONSUMER: HOBBIES & DIY: Philately

BRITISH POSTMARK BULLETIN
46637U79C-13

Editorial Address: 35-50 Rathbone Place, LONDON, W1T 1HQ **Tel:** 020 7441 4744
Email: john.r.holman@royalmail.co.uk
Web site: http://www.royalmail.com/stamps

ISSN: 0955-923X
Publisher: Royal Mail Group Ltd
Date Established: 1971
Frequency: 26 issues yearly
Annual Sub.: £12.25
Circulation: 1,200 (Publisher's Statement)
Usual Pagination: 16
Editor: John Holman
Summary of Content: Journal contains advance information on forthcoming British special postmarks.
Readership/Target Audience: Aimed at postmark and first day cover collectors.
ADVERTISING: No Advertising taken
CONSUMER: HOBBIES & DIY: Philately

BRITISH RAILWAY JOURNAL
46720U79J-334

Editorial Address: 1-3 Hagbourne Road, DIDCOT, OX11 8DP **Tel:** 01235 816478
ISSN: 0265-4105
Publisher: Wild Swan Publications Ltd
Date Established: 1983
Frequency: Half-yearly
Cover Price: £9.95
Usual Pagination: 80
Editor: Paul Karau
Summary of Content: Journal covering the history of the railways, stations, locomotives and branch lines.
Readership/Target Audience: Aimed at discerning railway enthusiasts.
ADVERTISING: No Advertising taken
CONSUMER: HOBBIES & DIY: Rail Enthusiasts

BRITISH RAILWAY MODELLING
46592U79B-15

Editorial Address: The Maltings, West Street, BOURNE, PE10 9PH **Tel:** 01778 391027 **Fax:** 01778 425437
Email: johne@warnersgroup.co.uk
Advertising Address: As above. **Tel:** 01778 391000
Email: patsisko@warnersgroup.co.uk
Web site: http://www.brmodelling.co.uk
ISSN: 0968-0764
Publisher: Warners Group Publications plc
Date Established: 1993
Frequency: Monthly - There is an Annual published in November
Cover Price: £3.40
Circulation: 28,500 (Publisher's Statement)
Usual Pagination: 96
Editor: John Emerson; **Managing Director:** Stephen Warner; **Managing Editor:** David Brown; **Publisher:** John Greenwood
Summary of Content: Magazine reflecting the various aspects of railway modelling as a creative hobby.
Readership/Target Audience: Aimed at those who enjoy railway modelling as a hobby.
ADVERTISING RATES:
Full Page Mono £380.00
Full Page Colour £609.00
Agency Commission: 10%
Mechanical Data: Type Area: 275 x 190mm, Col Length: 275mm, Trim Size: 297 x 210mm, Bleed Size: 313 x 216mm, Print Process: Web-fed offset, Film: Digital, Page Width: 190mm
Copy instructions: Copy Date: 4 weeks prior to publication date
Average advertising content per issue: 45%
Supplement(s): Steam Pictorial - 4xY
CONSUMER: HOBBIES & DIY: Models & Modelling

BRITISH TENNIS
1641022U75H-912

Editorial Address: 1st Floor, Barry House, 20-22 Worple Road, LONDON, SW19 4DH **Tel:** 020 8947 0100
Fax: 020 8947 0117
Email: alexandra.willis@acemag.co.uk
Web site: http://www.lta.org.uk
Publisher: Advantage Publishing (UK) Ltd
Date Established: 1996
Frequency: 11 issues yearly
Free to qualifying individuals
Circulation: 45,000 (Publisher's Statement)
Usual Pagination: 32
Editor: Alexandra Willis
Summary of Content: Magazine about British tennis grassroots activities. Containing interviews with British players, news, features and reports on British tennis and associated events.
Readership/Target Audience: Aimed at members of the Lawn Tennis Association (LTA).
ADVERTISING: No Advertising taken
CONSUMER: SPORT: Racquet Sports

BRITISH VETERANS NEWS
1775347U94A-121

Editorial Address: Little Troys, Faulkbourne, WITHAM, CM8 1SL **Tel:** 01376 513215
Email: info@britishveterans.co.uk

Advertising Address: As above.
Email: simonlamb@britishveterans.co.uk
Web site: http://www.britishveterans.co.uk
Publisher: Trilogy Services Ltd
Frequency: Quarterly
Cover Price: £1.00
Free to qualifying individuals
Circulation: 5,000 (Publisher's Statement)
Usual Pagination: 6
Editor: Simon Lamb; **Advertising Manager:** Simon Lamb
Summary of Content: Newsletter covering British veterans' issues, lifestyle and news.
Readership/Target Audience: Aimed at all ex-servicemen and women, regular or reserve, who have served in the British Armed Forces; particularly the younger veteran.
ADVERTISING: Rates on application
CONSUMER: OTHER CLASSIFICATIONS: War Veterans

BRITISH WATER SKI & WAKEBOARD

45938U75M-40
Formerly: British Waterskier
Editorial Address: The Tower, Thorpe Road, CHERTSEY, KT16 8PH **Tel:** 01932 570885 **Fax:** 01932 566719
Email: editor@bwsf.co.uk
Advertising Address: Mongoose Media, Mongoose House, 2 Lonsdale Road, LONDON, NW6 6RD **Tel:** 020 7306 0300
Fax: 020 7306 0301
Email: waterski@mongoosemedia.com
Web site: http://www.britishwaterski.org.uk
Publisher: British Water Ski Federation Limited
Date Established: 1994
Frequency: 5 issues yearly
Cover Price: £3.00
Free to qualifying individuals
Circulation: 11,000 (Publisher's Statement)
Usual Pagination: 48
Editor: Patrick Donovan
Summary of Content: Magazine aimed at promoting water skiing, wakeboarding, kneeboarding and barefooters as a safe, healthy and fun family sport. Includes news, features and events.
Readership/Target Audience: Read by members of British Water Ski from the UK and other countries.
ADVERTISING RATES:
Full Page Colour £1310.00
Agency Commission: 10%
Mechanical Data: Page Width: 179mm, Film: Digital, Bleed Size: 303 x 216mm, Trim Size: 297 x 210mm, Type Area: 264 x 179mm, Col Length: 264mm
Average advertising content per issue: 20%
CONSUMER: SPORT: Water Sports

BRITISH WOODWORKING MAGAZINE

46583U79A-165
Formerly: Traditional Woodworking
Editorial Address: Ampney St. Peter, CIRENCESTER, GL7 5SH **Tel:** 01285 850481
Email: nick.gibbs@britishwoodworking.com
Advertising Address: As above.
Email: nick.gibbs@britishwoodworking.com
Publisher: Freshwood Publishing
Frequency: 6 issues yearly
Cover Price: £3.50
Annual Sub.: £18.50
Circulation: 8,100 (Publisher's Statement)
Usual Pagination: 86
Editor: Nick Gibbs; **Advertising Manager:** Nick Gibbs
Summary of Content: Magazine focusing on woodworking, particularly cabinet and furniture making. Covers woodworking projects, techniques and product testing of power tools, hand tools and machinery. Also articles on woodworking and wood, including personalities, history, events, design and forestry.
Readership/Target Audience: Aimed at hobbyist woodworkers typically aged over 50 years, predominantly male.
ADVERTISING: Rates on application
Agency Commission: 10%
Copy instructions: Copy Date: 4 weeks prior to publication date
Average advertising content per issue: 40%
Supplement(s): Power Tool Guide - 1xY
CONSUMER: HOBBIES & DIY

THE BROOKLANDS SOCIETY GAZETTE

46416U77D-150
Editorial Address: 94 Connaught Road, Brookwood, WOKING, GU24 0HJ **Tel:** 01483 481836
Email: chris@chrisbass.co.uk
Advertising Address: As above.
Email: chris@chrisbass.co.uk
Web site: http://www.brooklands.org.uk
ISSN: 1472-4286
Publisher: The Brooklands Society Ltd
Date Established: 1976

Frequency: Quarterly
Annual Sub.: £25.00
Circulation: 1,100 (Publisher's Statement)
Usual Pagination: 36
Editor: Chris Bass; **Advertising Manager:** Chris Bass
Summary of Content: Publication reporting on the activities of the Society, its track, drivers, aviation and history.
Readership/Target Audience: Aimed at those who are interested in or collectors of pre-1939 cars, motorcycles, aircraft and memorabilia.
ADVERTISING RATES:
Full Page Mono £200.00
Full Page Colour £350.00
Average advertising content per issue: 10%
CONSUMER: MOTORING & CYCLING: Motor Sports

BRSCC RACING NEWS

1866237U77D-469
Editorial Address: The Old Bakery, 55A Belmont Road, WALLINGTON, SM6 8TE **Tel:** 020 8773 3404
Fax: 020 8773 3704
Email: racingnews@xenogamy-plc.co.uk
Web site: http://www.brscc.co.uk
Publisher: Xenogamy Limited
Frequency: Monthly
Circulation: 3,000 (Publisher's Statement)
Usual Pagination: 10
Editor: Martin Sharp
Summary of Content: Electronically delivered newsletter published on behalf of the British Racing & Sports Car Club Limited covering club news and a racing diary.
Readership/Target Audience: Aimed at competitors, club members and motor sport enthusiasts.
CONSUMER: MOTORING & CYCLING: Motor Sports

BRUMMELL

1739535U74Q-1313
Editorial Address: 2nd Floor, Stapleton House, 29-33 Scrutton Street, LONDON, EC2A 4HU **Tel:** 020 7426 3333
Email: bwright@efinancialnews.com
Advertising Address: As above. **Fax:** 020 7426 3329
Email: dmcrae@efinancialnews.com
Web site: http://www.efinancialnews.com/brummell
Publisher: Efinancialnews.com
Date Established: 2006
Frequency: 6 issues yearly
Cover Price: £5.00
Free to qualifying individuals
Circulation: 20,000 (Publisher's Statement)
Editor: Ben Wright; **Advertisement Director:** Duncan McRae
Summary of Content: Lifestyle magazine covering information on elegant living including interiors, travel, property, style, art and motoring.
Readership/Target Audience: Aimed at people working in the financial services.
ADVERTISING RATES:
Full Page Colour £6000.00
Agency Commission: 10%
Mechanical Data: Trim Size: 275 x 210mm, Film: Digital
Copy instructions: Copy Date: 3 weeks prior to publication date
Average advertising content per issue: 40%
Supplement to: Financial News
CONSUMER: WOMEN'S INTEREST CONSUMER MAGAZINES: Lifestyle

B.SPIRIT!

1698523U89D-520
Formerly: Spirit of SN
Editorial Address: 141-143 Shoreditch High Street, LONDON, E1 6JE **Tel:** 020 7613 6948 **Fax:** 020 7613 8776
Email: chloe.greenbank@ink-publishing.com
Advertising Address: As above.
Email: stephanie.cregut@ink-publishing.com
Web site: http://www.ink-publishing.com
Publisher: Ink Publishing
Date Established: 2006
Frequency: 6 issues yearly
Cover Price: Free
Circulation: 25,000 (Publisher's Statement)
Usual Pagination: 100
Editor: Chloë Greenbank; **Advertising Manager:** Stephanie Cregut
Summary of Content: Magazine covering all the destinations on the Brussels Airlines network across East and West Africa, as well as Russia, Israel and Belgium.
Language(s): English; Flemish; French
Readership/Target Audience: Aimed at passengers on SN Brussels Airlines.
ADVERTISING RATES:
Full Page Mono EUR6650.00
Full Page Colour EUR6650.00
Agency Commission: 10%
Mechanical Data: Trim Size: 275 x 230mm
Average advertising content per issue: 30%
CONSUMER: HOLIDAYS & TRAVEL: In-Flight Magazines

B.THERE!

48221U89D-455
Formerly: Virgin Express Red Hot
Editorial Address: 141-143 Shoreditch High Street, LONDON, E1 6JE **Tel:** 020 7613 8777 **Fax:** 020 7613 8776
Email: chloe.greenbank@ink-publishing.com
Advertising Address: As above. **Fax:** 020 7613 8778
Email: anna.szpunar@ink-publishing.com
Web site: http://www.btheremag.com
Publisher: Ink Publishing
Date Established: 2006
Frequency: Quarterly
Cover Price: Free
Circulation: 100,000 (Publisher's Statement)
Usual Pagination: 152
Editor: Richard Bence; **Advertising Manager:** Anna Szpunar
Summary of Content: In-flight magazine of Brussels Airline. Covers news and trends from around Europe, business, sport, arts and events listings as well as city guides for Brussels Airline destinations.
Language(s): English; Flemish; French
Readership/Target Audience: Read by customers of Virgin Express.
ADVERTISING RATES:
Full Page Colour £6926.00
Agency Commission: 10%
Mechanical Data: Bleed Size: 271 x 216mm, Trim Size: 265 x 210mm, Film: Digital
Average advertising content per issue: 27%
CONSUMER: HOLIDAYS & TRAVEL: In-Flight Magazines

BTO NEWS

47159U81F-20
Editorial Address: The Nunnery, THETFORD, IP24 2PU
Tel: 01842 750050
Email: jeff.baker@bto.org
Advertising Address: As above.
Email: info@bto.org
Web site: http://www.bto.org
ISSN: 0005-3392
Publisher: British Trust for Ornithology
Date Established: 1964
Frequency: 6 issues yearly
Free to qualifying individuals
Circulation: 13,000 (Publisher's Statement)
Usual Pagination: 24
Editor: Jeff Baker; **Advertising Manager:** Su Gough
Summary of Content: Magazine of the British Trust for Ornithology. Details results of bird survey work and related articles.
Readership/Target Audience: Aimed at birdwatchers.
ADVERTISING: Rates on application
CONSUMER: ANIMALS & PETS: Birds

BUCKINGHAMSHIRE COUNTRYSIDE

46861U80C-380
Editorial Address: PO Box 5, HITCHIN, SG5 1GJ
Tel: 01462 431237 **Fax:** 01462 422015
Email: martin_small@btconnect.com
Advertising Address: As above. **Tel:** 01462 422014
Email: martin_small@btconnect.com
ISSN: 1360-3450
Publisher: Beaumonde Publications Ltd
Date Established: 1995
Frequency: 6 issues yearly
Cover Price: £1.25
Annual Sub.: £9.00
Circulation: 8,000 (Publisher's Statement)
Usual Pagination: 36
Editor: Sandra Small; **Advertising Manager:** Martin Small
Summary of Content: Regional interest magazine covering the county of Buckinghamshire.
Readership/Target Audience: Aimed at readers with a high disposable income.
ADVERTISING RATES:
Full Page Mono £375.00
Full Page Colour £450.00
Agency Commission: 10%
Mechanical Data: Col Length: 270mm, Page Width: 190mm, Trim Size: 297 x 210mm, Type Area: 270 x 190mm, Bleed Size: 303 x 216mm, Film: Digital
Copy instructions: Copy Date: 2 weeks prior to publication date
Average advertising content per issue: 25%
CONSUMER: RURAL & REGIONAL INTEREST: Regional Interest English Counties

BUCKINGHAMSHIRE LIFE

1849783U80C-5467
Editorial Address: 28 Teville Road, Worthing, WEST SUSSEX, BN11 1UG **Tel:** 07918 721644
Email: tessa.harris@archant.co.uk
Advertising Address: As above.
Web site: http://www.buckinghamshirelife.co.uk
Publisher: Archant Life Cambridgeshire, Hertfordshire and Essex
Frequency: 6 issues yearly

Cover Price: £1.95
Circulation: 12,000 (Print Run)
Usual Pagination: 100
Editor: Tessa Harris; **Publisher:** Guy Hanson
Summary of Content: Buckinghamshire county magazine containing features on interiors, events, people, places, sights and sounds, restaurants, food and wine. Also includes homes and gardens, antiques, competitions and a county events guide.
Readership/Target Audience: Aimed at residents and visitors to Buckinghamshire.
CONSUMER: RURAL & REGIONAL INTEREST: Regional Interest English Counties

THE BUDGERIGAR
47167U81F-130
Editorial Address: Spring Gardens, NORTHAMPTON, NN1 1DR **Tel:** 01604 624549 **Fax:** 01604 627108
Advertising Address: As above.
Web site: http://www.budgerigarsociety.com
Publisher: Budgerigar Society
Frequency: 6 issues yearly
Free to qualifying individuals
Annual Sub.: £22.00
Circulation: 3,500 (Publisher's Statement)
Usual Pagination: 28
Editor: David Whittaker; **Advertising Manager:** David Whittaker
Summary of Content: Magazine about keeping, breeding and exhibiting budgerigars.
Readership/Target Audience: Aimed at breeders and owners.
ADVERTISING: Rates on application
Copy instructions: Copy Date: 6 weeks prior to publication date
CONSUMER: ANIMALS & PETS: Birds

BUDGERIGAR WORLD
47168U81F-140
Editorial Address: The County Press Buildings, Station Road, BALA, LL23 7PG **Tel:** 01678 520262
Fax: 01678 521251
Email: budgerigarworld@msn.com
Advertising Address: As above.
Web site: http://www.budgerigarworld.com
Publisher: The County Press
Date Established: 1982
Frequency: Monthly
Cover Price: £3.00
Annual Sub.: £36.00
Circulation: 6,800 (Publisher's Statement)
Usual Pagination: 48
Editor: Gwyn Evans; **Executive Editor:** Gwyn Evans; **Advertising Manager:** Gwyn Evans
Summary of Content: Magazine covering all aspects of the care and breeding of budgerigars.
Readership/Target Audience: Read by budgerigar breeders and owners.
ADVERTISING RATES:
Full Page Mono £230.00
Full Page Colour £430.00
Mechanical Data: Film: Digital
Copy instructions: Copy Date: 1 month prior to publication date
Average advertising content per issue: 25%
CONSUMER: ANIMALS & PETS: Birds

BUILD IT
46571U79A-5
Editorial Address: 1 Canada Square, 19th Floor, Canary Wharf, LONDON, E14 5AP **Tel:** 020 7772 8300
Fax: 020 7772 8584
Email: annamarie.desouza@oceanmedia.co.uk
Advertising Address: As above.
Email: andy.pitois@oceanmedia.co.uk
Web site: http://www.buildit-online.co.uk
Publisher: Ocean Media Group Ltd
Date Established: 1990
Frequency: Monthly - Published on the 1st of the month
Cover Price: £3.99
Circulation: 12,927 (ABC 01/01/2008 to 31/12/2008)
Usual Pagination: 180
Editor: Sarah Herbert; **Advertising Manager:** Andy Pitois
Summary of Content: Magazine with case studies and product information on house building.
Readership/Target Audience: Aimed at people organising the building and conversion of their own home.
ADVERTISING RATES:
Full Page Colour £1935.00
Agency Commission: 10%
Mechanical Data: Film: Digital, Trim Size: 300 x 230mm, Bleed Size: +6mm
Copy instructions: Copy Date: 6 weeks prior to publication date
Average advertising content per issue: 40%
CONSUMER: HOBBIES & DIY

BULLETIN OF THE VINTAGE SPORTS CAR CLUB
46488U77F-40
Editorial Address: Woodforde Villa, Hongham Road, Weston Longville, NORWICH, NR9 5JU **Tel:** 01603 881112
Email: johnstaveley@ic24.net
Advertising Address: The Old Post Office, West Street, CHIPPING NORTON, OX7 5EL **Tel:** 01608 644777
Fax: 01608 644888
Email: gillian.carr@vscc.co.uk
ISSN: 1355-543X
Publisher: VSCC Ltd
Date Established: 1935
Frequency: Quarterly
Free to qualifying individuals
Circulation: 7,200 (Publisher's Statement)
Usual Pagination: 100
Editor: John Staveley; **Advertising Manager:** Gillian Carr
Summary of Content: Magazine devoted to vintage and historic motor sport competitions, club news and articles on vintage motoring, humour, reviews and related topics.
Readership/Target Audience: Aimed at members of the Vintage Sports Car Club and people interested in pre-war sporting motor cars.
ADVERTISING RATES:
Full Page Mono £715.00
Full Page Colour £1075.00
Mechanical Data: Page Width: 158mm, Type Area: 210 x 158mm, Col Length: 210mm, Trim Size: 245 x 183mm, Bleed Size: 251 x 189mm, Film: Digital
Copy instructions: Copy Date: 4 weeks prior to publication date
Average advertising content per issue: 20%
CONSUMER: MOTORING & CYCLING: Veteran Cars

BUMPS & BABIES
760594U74D-125
Editorial Address: Alexandra House, Oldham Terrace, LONDON, W3 6NH **Tel:** 0844 243 6000 **Fax:** 0844 243 6001
Email: bumpsandbabies@nct.org.uk
Advertising Address: Mongoose Media, 2 Lonsdale Road, LONDON, NW6 6RD **Tel:** 020 7306 0300
Fax: 020 7306 0301
Email: nct@mongoosemedia.com
Web site: http://www.nct.org.uk
ISSN: 1474-8894
Publisher: The NCT
Date Established: 2001
Frequency: Quarterly
Cover Price: Free
Circulation: 150,000 (Publisher's Statement)
Usual Pagination: 64
Editor: Kay Doragh; **Advertising Manager:** Heather Bird
Summary of Content: Magazine covering pregnancy, birth, labour and the early stages of parenthood.
Readership/Target Audience: Read by prospective parents.
ADVERTISING RATES:
Full Page Colour £6250.00
Agency Commission: 10%
Mechanical Data: Type Area: 269 x 182mm, Col Length: 269mm, Page Width: 182mm, Bleed Size: 303 x 213mm, Trim Size: 297 x 210mm
Copy instructions: Copy Date: 4 weeks prior to publication date
Average advertising content per issue: 20%
CONSUMER: WOMEN'S INTEREST CONSUMER MAGAZINES: Child Care

BUNKERED
28254U75D-35
Editorial Address: 50 High Craighall Road, GLASGOW, G4 9UD **Tel:** 0141 353 2222 **Fax:** 0141 332 3811
Email: mdempster@bunkered.co.uk
Advertising Address: As above. **Fax:** 0141 332 3839
Email: stephen.mccann@psp.uk.net
Web site: http://www.bunkered.co.uk
Publisher: PSP Publishing Ltd
Date Established: 1996
Frequency: 8 issues yearly
Cover Price: £3.70
Annual Sub.: £24.95
Circulation: 22,714 (ABC 01/01/2008 to 31/12/2008)
Usual Pagination: 174
Editor: Martin Dempster; **Publisher:** Paul Grant
Summary of Content: Magazine covering all aspects of golf. Includes interviews, player profiles, product reviews and golf instruction as well as competitions and offers.
Readership/Target Audience: Aimed at all levels of golfers, club secretaries and greenkeepers.
ADVERTISING RATES:
Full Page Colour £1795.00
Agency Commission: 10%
Mechanical Data: Col Length: 273mm, Page Width: 183mm, Type Area: 273 x 183mm, Trim Size: 297 x 210mm, Bleed Size: 303 x 216mm, Film: Digital
Copy instructions: Copy Date: 15 days prior to publication date
Average advertising content per issue: 39%
CONSUMER: SPORT: Golf

BURDA MODEMAGAZIN
45225U74B-50
Formerly: Burda Media Magazin
Editorial Address: 32-34 Great Marlborough Street, LONDON, W1F 7JB **Tel:** 020 7439 2444 **Fax:** 020 7439 2555
Email: cdurrant@burdamedia.co.uk
Publisher: Burda Media
Frequency: Monthly
Cover Price: EUR4.50
Circulation: 360,000 (Publisher's Statement)
Editor: Carmen Durrant
Summary of Content: Magazine focusing on women's fashion. Also contains features on sewing, handicrafts, home decorating, recipes, hair and beauty.
Language(s): German
Readership/Target Audience: Aimed at women interested in fashion, lifestyle and crafts.
ADVERTISING: No Advertising taken
CONSUMER: WOMEN'S INTEREST CONSUMER MAGAZINES: Women's Interest - Fashion

THE BURLINGTON MAGAZINE
47495U84A-200
Editorial Address: 14-16 Duke's Road, LONDON, WC1H 9SZ **Tel:** 020 7388 1228 **Fax:** 020 7388 1229
Email: editorial@burlington.org.uk
Advertising Address: As above.
Email: burlington@burlington.org.uk
Web site: http://www.burlington.org.uk
ISSN: 0007-6287
Publisher: The Burlington Magazine Publications Ltd
Frequency: Monthly
Cover Price: £13.20
Annual Sub.: £183.00
Usual Pagination: 64
Editor: Anne Blood; **Managing Director:** Kate Trevelyan; **Advertising Director:** Mark Scott; **Publisher:** Kate Trevelyan
Summary of Content: Magazine covering fine and decorative arts with articles on exhibitions, reviews and books and a world wide calendar of events.
Readership/Target Audience: Read by art collectors and fine art enthusiasts.
ADVERTISING RATES:
Full Page Mono £1065.00
Full Page Colour £1535.00
Agency Commission: 15%
Mechanical Data: Type Area: 273 x 194mm, Col Length: 273mm, Bleed Size: 314 x 239mm, Trim Size: 308 x 235mm, Film: Positive, right reading, emulsion side down, Print Process: Offset litho, Page Width: 194mm
Average advertising content per issue: 20%
CONSUMER: THE ARTS & LITERARY: Arts

BURNHAM TOWN GUIDE
1686827U80C-5245
Editorial Address: Media House, 5 Broadway Court, High Street, CHESHAM, HP5 1EG **Tel:** 01494 771144
Fax: 01494 771277
Email: info@bpcmagazines.com
Advertising Address: As above. **Tel:** 01494 771177
Email: copy@bpcmagazines.com
Web site: http://www.bpcmagazines.com
Publisher: BPC Magazines
Frequency: Annual - Published in August
Cover Price: Free
Circulation: 8,000 (Publisher's Statement)
Editor: Stella Adams; **Advertising Manager:** Clare George; **Publisher:** Robert Adams
Summary of Content: Magazine published for the local authority covering council news and local businesses.
Readership/Target Audience: Aimed primarily at residents in the Burnham-on-Crouch area.
ADVERTISING: Rates on application
CONSUMER: RURAL & REGIONAL INTEREST: Regional Interest English Counties

THE BURNS CHRONICLE
47539U84B-35
Editorial Address: 1 Cairnsmore Road, CASTLE DOUGLAS, DG7 1BN **Tel:** 01556 504448 **Fax:** 01556 504448
Email: admin@worldburnsclub.com
Web site: http://www.worldburnsclub.com
Publisher: The Robert Burns World Federation Ltd
Date Established: 1892
Frequency: 3 issues yearly - Published in March, September and December
Annual Sub.: £8.00
Circulation: 1,200 (Publisher's Statement)
Editor: Peter Westwood
Summary of Content: Publication looking at the life and work of Robert Burns and Scottish literature.
Readership/Target Audience: Aimed at members of the Robert Burns World Federation and related clubs and societies.
ADVERTISING: No Advertising taken
CONSUMER: THE ARTS & LITERARY: Literary

BUSINESS LIFE
48195U89D-53

Editorial Address: 85 Strand, LONDON, WC2R 0DW
Tel: 020 7550 8000 **Fax:** 020 7550 8250
Email: businesslife@cedarcom.co.uk
Advertising Address: As above.
Email: marc.milford@bamedia.co.uk
Web site: http://www.babusinesslife.com
Publisher: Cedar Communications
Date Established: 1986
Frequency: Monthly
Cover Price: Free
Circulation: 95,855 (ABC 01/01/2009 to 30/06/2009)
Usual Pagination: 98
Editor: Derek Harbinson; **Managing Director:** Clare Broadbent; **Advertising Manager:** Marc Milford
Summary of Content: Magazine distributed on British Airways European and UK routes.
Readership/Target Audience: Aimed at business class passengers on British Airways short-haul flights.
ADVERTISING RATES:
Full Page Colour £7300.00
Mechanical Data: Type Area: 265 x 195mm, Col Length: 265mm, Page Width: 195mm, Trim Size: 289 x 210mm, Bleed Size: 295 x 216mm, Film: Digital
Copy instructions: Copy Date: 5 weeks prior to publication date
Average advertising content per issue: 40%
CONSUMER: HOLIDAYS & TRAVEL: In-Flight Magazines

BUSINESS TRAVELLER
48229U89A-62_50

Editorial Address: 2nd Floor, Cardinal House, 39-40 Albemarle Street, LONDON, W1S 4TE **Tel:** 020 7647 6330
Email: editorial@businesstraveller.com
Advertising Address: As above. **Fax:** 020 7647 6331
Email: advertising@businesstraveller.com
Web site: http://www.businesstraveller.com
ISSN: 0309-9334
Publisher: Perry Publications Ltd
Date Established: 1976
Frequency: 10 issues yearly - Published on the 1st of the month
Cover Price: £3.95
Annual Sub.: £42.95
Circulation: 54,969 (ABC 01/01/2008 to 31/12/2008)
Usual Pagination: 90
Editor: Tom Otley; **Features Editor:** Felicity Cousins; **Managing Director:** Julian Gregory; **Advertising Manager:** Rania Apthorpe; **Publisher:** Rania Apthorpe; **Circulation Manager:** Jamie Halling
Summary of Content: Magazine containing news and features on international business travel.
Language(s): Chinese; English; Hungarian; Spanish
Readership/Target Audience: Aimed at business and frequent travellers.
ADVERTISING RATES:
Full Page Colour £5950.00
Agency Commission: 10%
Mechanical Data: Bleed Size: 281 x 214mm, Trim Size: 275 x 208mm, Film: Digital
Copy instructions: Copy Date: 4 weeks prior to publication date
CONSUMER: HOLIDAYS & TRAVEL: Travel

BUTTERFLY
47185U81X-80

Formerly: Butterfly Conservation News
Editorial Address: Manor Yard, East Lulworth, WAREHAM, BH20 5QP **Tel:** 0870 774 4309
Email: lcowling@butterfly-conservation.org
Advertising Address: The Gallery, Manor Farm, Southam, CHELTENHAM, GL52 3PB **Tel:** 01242 259249
Email: mark@fellowsmedia.com
Web site: http://www.butterfly-conservation.org
Publisher: Fellows Media
Frequency: 3 issues yearly - Published in February, June and October
Free to qualifying individuals
Circulation: 11,500 (Publisher's Statement)
Usual Pagination: 40
Editor: Lester Cowling; **Advertising Manager:** Mark Brown
Summary of Content: Magazine containing conservation and society activity, articles and features on butterflies and moths, identification guidelines and butterfly travel hotspots. Includes gardening advice, reviews of books and equipment and interviews with key conservationists.
Readership/Target Audience: Aimed at those interested in butterflies and moths, the environment, wildlife and wildlife gardening and conversation issues as well as members of the Butterfly Conservation.
ADVERTISING RATES:
Full Page Colour £750.00
Mechanical Data: Film: Digital, Type Area: 267 x 185mm, Bleed Size: 303 x 216mm, Trim Size: 297 x 210mm, Col Length: 267mm, Page Width: 185mm
Copy instructions: Copy Date: 2 weeks prior to publication date
Average advertising content per issue: 30%
CONSUMER: ANIMALS & PETS

BUY SELL (FLINTSHIRE EDITION)
45516U74K-25

Editorial Address: Tudor House, 64 High Street, Tarvin, CHESTER, CH3 8JB **Tel:** 01829 742500 **Fax:** 01829 742509
Email: marketing@chronicle.v-net.com
Advertising Address: Office 2, Daniel Owen Precinct, MOLD, C87 1AP **Tel:** 01352 707190 **Fax:** 01352 707199
Email: trade.ads@buysell.co.uk
Publisher: Buy-Sell
Date Established: 1987
Frequency: Weekly
Cover Price: Free
Circulation: 31,000 (Publisher's Statement)
Usual Pagination: 48
Advertising Manager: Pat Darke
ADVERTISING RATES:
Full Page Mono £510.00
Full Page Colour £620.00
Agency Commission: 10%
Mechanical Data: Type Area: 260 x 169mm, Col Length: 260mm, Page Width: 169mm, Film: Digital
Copy instructions: Copy Date: Monday 1.30pm prior to publication date
Average advertising content per issue: 100%
CONSUMER: WOMEN'S INTEREST CONSUMER MAGAZINES: Home Purchase

BUY SELL (MID CHESHIRE & CHESTER EDITION)
45517U74K-27

Editorial Address: 123 Main Street, FRODSHAM, WA6 7AF **Tel:** 01928 736220 **Fax:** 01928 736208
Advertising Address: As above.
Email: trade.ads@buysell.co.uk
Publisher: Buy-Sell
Date Established: 1984
Frequency: Weekly
Cover Price: Free
Circulation: 37,000 (Publisher's Statement)
Usual Pagination: 56
ADVERTISING RATES:
Full Page Mono £522.75
Full Page Colour £706.60
Agency Commission: 10%
Mechanical Data: Page Width: 169mm, No. of Columns (Display): 5, Col Widths (Display): 31mm, Film: Digital, Type Area: 260 x 169mm, Col Length: 260mm
Copy instructions: Copy Date: 1 day prior to publication date
Average advertising content per issue: 100%
CONSUMER: WOMEN'S INTEREST CONSUMER MAGAZINES: Home Purchase

BUY-SELL (SOUTH CHESHIRE & NORTH SHROPSHIRE)
45518U74K-28

Editorial Address: 1st Floor, 234 Nantwich Road, CREWE, CW2 6BP **Tel:** 01270 250970 **Fax:** 01270 250971
Advertising Address: 32-34 Victoria Street, CREWE, CW1 2JE **Tel:** 01270 502449
Email: crewe.tradeads@buysell.co.uk
Publisher: Buy-Sell
Date Established: 1979
Frequency: Weekly
Cover Price: Free
Circulation: 37,000 (Publisher's Statement)
Advertising Manager: Steve Creer
ADVERTISING RATES:
SCC £6.15
Agency Commission: 10%
Mechanical Data: Page Width: 169mm, Film: Digital, Type Area: 260 x 169mm, Col Length: 260mm
Average advertising content per issue: 100%
CONSUMER: WOMEN'S INTEREST CONSUMER MAGAZINES: Home Purchase

BUZZ
48071U89C-80

Editorial Address: Suite 3, 2nd Floor, 1-7 Castle Street, CARDIFF, CF10 2BS **Tel:** 029 2022 7677
Email: editorial@buzzmag.co.uk
Advertising Address: As above. **Tel:** 029 2023 6888
Email: editorial@buzzmag.co.uk
Publisher: EAC Publishing
Date Established: 1996
Frequency: Monthly
Cover Price: Free
Circulation: 30,000 (Publisher's Statement)
Usual Pagination: 64
Editor: Rachel England; **Managing Director:** Emma Clark; **Advertising Manager:** Emma Clark; **Publisher:** Emma Clark
Summary of Content: Magazine featuring a what's on guide to Cardiff and South Wales including cinema, culture, theatre, nightlife, visual arts, food, gigs, fashion, beauty, music, sport and lifestyle as well as local events and current affairs.
Language(s): English; Welsh

Readership/Target Audience: Aimed at those visiting and residing in South Wales.
ADVERTISING RATES:
Full Page Mono £720.00
Full Page Colour £900.00
Agency Commission: 10%
Mechanical Data: Type Area: 275 x 190mm, Page Width: 190mm, Trim Size: 297 x 210mm, Bleed Size: 303 x 216mm, Col Length: 275mm, Film: Digital
Copy instructions: Copy Date: 12 days prior to publication date
Average advertising content per issue: 35%
CONSUMER: HOLIDAYS & TRAVEL: Entertainment Guides

CACTUSWORLD JOURNAL OF THE BRITISH CACTUS AND SUCCULENT SOCIETY
48553U93-12

Formerly: British Cactus and Succulent Journal
Editorial Address: Whitestone Gardens, Sutton-under-Whitestonecliffe, THIRSK, YO7 2PZ **Tel:** 01845 597467
Fax: 01845 597035
Email: editor@cactus-mall.com
Advertising Address: Old Oak Farm, Moor Edge Low Side, Harden, BINGLEY, BD16 1LD **Tel:** 01535 273615
Email: de.quail@virgin.net
Web site: http://www.bcss.org.uk
ISSN: 1751-1429
Publisher: British Cactus & Succulent Society
Date Established: 2006
Frequency: Quarterly
Annual Sub.: £15.00
Circulation: 3,700 (Publisher's Statement)
Usual Pagination: 56
Editor: Roy Mottram; **Advertising Manager:** David Quail
Summary of Content: Magazine containing original articles on cacti and succulent plants including plant profiles and advice on cultivation, propagation and conservation. Includes news of the society at national and local levels.
Readership/Target Audience: Read by cacti and succulent enthusiasts.
ADVERTISING RATES:
Full Page Mono £175.00
Full Page Colour £210.00
Mechanical Data: Film: Digital
Copy instructions: Copy Date: 9 weeks prior to publication date
Average advertising content per issue: 15%
CONSUMER: GARDENING

CADUCEUS
45412U74G-10

Editorial Address: 9 Nine Acres, MIDHURST, GU29 9EP
Tel: 01730 816799
Email: simon@caduceus.info
Advertising Address: As above.
Email: simon@cybersite3000.com
Web site: http://www.caduceus.info
ISSN: 0952-4584
Publisher: Caduceus Journal Ltd
Date Established: 1987
Frequency: Quarterly
Cover Price: £3.95
Annual Sub.: £16.00
Circulation: 12,000 (Publisher's Statement)
Usual Pagination: 48
Editor: Simon Best; **Advertising Manager:** Simon Best; **Publisher:** Simon Best
Summary of Content: Journal focusing on healing, health and holistic therapies and spiritual, personal, psychological and emotional development, as well as ecological/environmental healing.
Readership/Target Audience: Read by those with an interest in holistic medicine, ecology, spirituality, science and psychology.
ADVERTISING RATES:
Full Page Mono £790.00
Full Page Colour £1160.00
Agency Commission: 10%
Mechanical Data: Print Process: Litho, Film: Digital, Trim Size: 297 x 210mm
Average advertising content per issue: 23%
CONSUMER: WOMEN'S INTEREST CONSUMER MAGAZINES: Slimming & Health

CAGE & AVIARY BIRDS
47169U81F-150

Editorial Address: Blue Fin Building, 110 Southwark Street, LONDON, SE1 0SU **Tel:** 020 3148 4171
Email: birds@ipcmedia.com
Advertising Address: As above. **Tel:** 020 3148 5000
Fax: 020 3148 8155
Email: lee_morris@ipcmedia.com
Web site: http://www.cageandaviarybirds.com
ISSN: 0007-9561
Publisher: IPC Inspire
Date Established: 1902
Frequency: Weekly
Cover Price: £1.50

Consumer Magazines

Annual Sub.: £76.40
Circulation: 15,185 (ABC 01/01/2008 to 31/12/2008)
Usual Pagination: 28
Editor: Kim Forrester; **News Editor:** Duncan MacRae;
Advertising Manager: Lee Morris
Summary of Content: Newspaper containing information about keeping, breeding and showing birds of all kinds.
Twitter: http://twitter.com/CageAviaryBirds.
Readership/Target Audience: Aimed at birdkeepers and those interested in birds.
ADVERTISING RATES:
Full Page Mono £1285.00
Full Page Colour £1928.00
Agency Commission: 10%
Mechanical Data: Page Width: 270mm, Type Area: 345 x 270mm, Col Length: 345mm, Film: Digital
Copy instructions: Copy Date: Monday 11am prior to publication date
Average advertising content per issue: 20%
CONSUMER: ANIMALS & PETS: Birds

CAKE CRAFT AND DECORATION
45600U74P-190

Editorial Address: PO Box 3693, NUNEATON, CV10 8YQ
Tel: 024 7673 8846 **Fax:** 024 7673 8846
Email: editor@cake-craft.com
Advertising Address: 58 The Terrace, TORQUAY, TQ1 1DE
Tel: 01745 823140
Email: melanie@cake-craft.com
Web site: http://www.cake-craft.com
ISSN: 1473-0383
Publisher: Anglo American Media Ltd
Date Established: 1994
Frequency: Monthly - Published the 2nd Thursday of each month
Cover Price: £3.50
Annual Sub.: £32.00
Circulation: 27,000 (Publisher's Statement)
Usual Pagination: 84
Editor: Julie Askew; **Advertising Manager:** Melanie Dixon;
Publisher: Judy Reed
Summary of Content: Magazine covering all aspects of cake decoration, baking and sugarcraft.
Readership/Target Audience: Aimed at sugar crafters, cake decorators and cake making enthusiasts.
ADVERTISING RATES:
Full Page Mono £960.00
Full Page Colour £1371.00
Agency Commission: 10%
Mechanical Data: Type Area: 280 x 203mm, Col Length: 280mm, Page Width: 203mm, Trim Size: 300 x 222mm, Bleed Size: 306 x 228mm, Film: Digital
Copy instructions: Copy Date: End of the month prior to publication date
Average advertising content per issue: 40%
CONSUMER: WOMEN'S INTEREST CONSUMER MAGAZINES: Food & Cookery

CAKE CRAFT & DECORATION MAGAZINE MONTHLY
1698979U74P-934

Formerly: Cake Craft Guide
Editorial Address: PO Box 3693, NUNEATON, CV10 8YQ
Tel: 024 7673 8846 **Fax:** 024 7673 8846
Email: editor@cake-craft.com
Advertising Address: 58 The Terrace, TORQUAY, TQ1 1DE
Tel: 01745 823140
Email: melanie@cake-craft.com
Web site: http://www.cake-craft.com
ISSN: 1473-0383
Publisher: Anglo American Media Ltd
Date Established: 1994
Frequency: Monthly
Cover Price: £3.50
Circulation: 25,000 (Print Run)
Usual Pagination: 82
Editor: Julie Askew
Summary of Content: Magazine with cake making and decorating tips, step by step projects, cake decorating and sugar flower projects, photographs of readers' cakes, events guide, new products, letters or problems cake related in over to you, a directory of suppliers, baking selection, food facts, book reviews and show reports.
Readership/Target Audience: Aimed at aspiring cake makers, home chefs and professional bakers.
ADVERTISING RATES:
Full Page Mono £960.00
Full Page Colour £1371.00
Agency Commission: 10%
Mechanical Data: Type Area: 280 x 203mm, Bleed Size: 304 x 226mm, Trim Size: 298 x 220mm, Col Length: 280mm, Page Width: 203mm, Film: Digital
CONSUMER: WOMEN'S INTEREST CONSUMER MAGAZINES: Food & Cookery

CAKES & SUGARCRAFT
45601U74P-220

Editorial Address: Alfred House, Hones Business Park, FARNHAM, GU9 8BB **Tel:** 0845 225 5671
Fax: 0845 225 5673
Email: editorial@squires-group.co.uk
Advertising Address: As above.
Email: advertising@squires-group.co.uk
Web site: http://www.cakesandsugarcraft.co.uk
ISSN: 1464-9039
Publisher: Squires Kitchen Magazine Publishing
Date Established: 1993
Frequency: Quarterly
Cover Price: £4.99
Circulation: 10,000 (Publisher's Statement)
Usual Pagination: 128
Editor: Beverley Dutton; **Advertising Manager:** Natalie Chivers
Summary of Content: Magazine covering tips and information on cake decorating and sugarcraft.
Readership/Target Audience: Aimed at cake decorators and home cake bakers.
ADVERTISING RATES:
Full Page Mono £900.00
Full Page Colour £1500.00
Agency Commission: 10%
Mechanical Data: Trim Size: 290 x 210mm
Copy instructions: Copy Date: 3 months prior to publication date
CONSUMER: WOMEN'S INTEREST CONSUMER MAGAZINES: Food & Cookery

CALCIO ITALIA
45753U75B-115

Formerly: Football Italia
Editorial Address: 249 Main Road, Walters Ash, HIGH WYCOMBE, HP14 4TH **Tel:** 01494 564564
Fax: 01494 564564
Email: editorial@calcioitalia.co.uk
Advertising Address: Suite 6, Piccadilly House, London Road, BATH, BA1 6PL **Tel:** 01225 489984
Fax: 01225 489980
Email: simon.lewis@anthem-publishing.com
Web site: http://www.calcioitalia.co.uk
Publisher: Anthem Publishing Ltd
Date Established: 1992
Frequency: Monthly
Cover Price: £3.50
Annual Sub.: £34.99
Circulation: 50,000 (Publisher's Statement)
Usual Pagination: 100
Editor: John Taylor; **Advertising Manager:** Simon Lewis;
Publisher: Jon Bickley
Summary of Content: Magazine containing interviews, stories and pictures of Italian football.
Readership/Target Audience: Aimed at those with an interest in the Italian football league.
ADVERTISING RATES:
Full Page Colour £950.00
Mechanical Data: Type Area: 255 x 180mm, Bleed Size: 303 x 216mm, Trim Size: 297 x 210mm, Col Length: 255mm, Page Width: 180mm, Film: Digital
Copy instructions: Copy Date: 2nd Friday of the month prior to publication date
Average advertising content per issue: 30%
CONSUMER: SPORT: Football

CAM CAMBRIDGE ALUMNI MAGAZINE
47373U83-3

Editorial Address: 1 Quayside, Bridge Street, CAMBRIDGE, CB5 8AB **Tel:** 01223 332288 **Fax:** 01223 764476
Email: alumni@foundation.cam.ac.uk
Advertising Address: Landmark Publishing Services, 2 Windmill Street, LONDON, W1T 2HX **Tel:** 020 7692 9292
Email: amf@lps.co.uk
Web site: http://www.alumni.cam.ac.uk
Publisher: University of Cambridge Development Office
Date Established: 1990
Frequency: 3 issues yearly - Published in March, June and November
Free to qualifying individuals
Annual Sub.: £8.00
Circulation: 182,000 (Publisher's Statement)
Usual Pagination: 52
Advertising Manager: Anne Marie Fox
Summary of Content: Magazine containing university news and articles on and about Cambridge.
Readership/Target Audience: Aimed at Cambridge University graduates and not current students.
ADVERTISING RATES:
Full Page Colour £5082.00
CONSUMER: STUDENT PUBLICATIONS

CAMBRIA THE NATIONAL MAGAZINE OF WALES
47031U80D-55

Editorial Address: PO Box 22, CARMARTHEN, SA32 7YH
Tel: 01267 290188

Email: editor@cambriamagazine.com
Advertising Address: As above.
Email: sales@cambriamagazine.com
Web site: http://www.cambriamagazine.com
ISSN: 1366-0675
Publisher: Cyhoeddwyr Cymrica Cyfyngedig
Date Established: 1997
Frequency: 6 issues yearly
Cover Price: £3.50
Annual Sub.: £18.00
Circulation: 10,000 (Publisher's Statement per year)
Usual Pagination: 76
Editor: Frances Davies; **Advertising Manager:** Alison Mostyn; **Publisher:** Henry Jones-Davies
Summary of Content: Magazine featuring articles on the arts, culture, history, literature, travel, social news, hotels, restaurants, wine, environment and motoring.
Language(s): English; Welsh
Readership/Target Audience: Aimed at Welsh residents, expatriates and all those interested in Wales worldwide.
ADVERTISING RATES:
Full Page Colour £850.00
Agency Commission: 10%
Mechanical Data: Bleed Size: 284 x 211mm, Trim Size: 276 x 203mm, Film: Digital
Copy instructions: Copy Date: 2 weeks prior to publication date
Average advertising content per issue: 20%
CONSUMER: RURAL & REGIONAL INTEREST: Regional Interest Wales

CAMBRIDGE AGENDA
1601238U80C-5044

Editorial Address: Suite 3, Alexander House, 1 Milton Road, CAMBRIDGE, CB4 1UY **Tel:** 01223 365733
Email: olivia.abbott@archant.co.uk
Advertising Address: Alexander House, 1 Milton Road, CAMBRIDGE, CB4 1UY **Tel:** 01223 309227
Fax: 01223 309226
Email: sarah.lahassan@archant.co.uk
Web site: http://www.cambridgeshireagenda.co.uk
Publisher: Archant Herts & Cambs
Date Established: 2002
Frequency: Monthly
Cover Price: Free
Circulation: 30,000 (Publisher's Statement)
Usual Pagination: 100
Editor: Olivia Abbott; **Advertising Manager:** Alison Haynes
Summary of Content: Magazine covering local news, culture, business and people with entertainment listings.
Twitter: http://www.twitter.com/CambridgeAgenda.
Readership/Target Audience: Aimed at professionals aged 28 years and over living and working in Cambridge.
ADVERTISING RATES:
Full Page Colour £995.00
Agency Commission: 10%
Mechanical Data: Bleed Size: 303 x 216mm, Trim Size: 297 x 210mm, Film: Digital
Copy instructions: Copy Date: 15th of the month prior to publication date
CONSUMER: RURAL & REGIONAL INTEREST: Regional Interest English Counties

CAMBRIDGE MATTERS
1694983U94X-284

Editorial Address: Environmental Services, Mandela House, 4 Regent Street, CAMBRIDGE, CB2 1BY **Tel:** 01223 457651
Fax: 01223 457909
Email: cambridgematters@cambridge.gov.uk
Advertising Address: The Irwin Centre, Scotland Road, Dry Drayton, CAMBRIDGE, CB3 8AR **Tel:** 01954 212906
Fax: 01954 212105
Email: chris@manpublishing.co.uk
Web site: http://www.cambridge.gov.uk/recycling
Publisher: Bright Publishing Ltd
Date Established: 2004
Frequency: Quarterly
Cover Price: Free
Circulation: 43,000 (Publisher's Statement)
Usual Pagination: 24
Editor: Vicky Kelso
Summary of Content: Magazine covering local and global environmental issues.
Readership/Target Audience: Aimed at households in Cambridge.
ADVERTISING RATES:
Full Page Colour £1595.00
Agency Commission: 10%
Mechanical Data: Type Area: 277 x 190mm, Col Length: 277mm, Page Width: 190mm, Bleed Size: 305 x 218mm, Trim Size: 297 x 210mm, Film: Digital
Copy instructions: Copy Date: 3 weeks prior to publication date
Average advertising content per issue: 35%
CONSUMER: OTHER CLASSIFICATIONS: Miscellaneous

CAMBRIDGESHIRE COUNTY LIFE MAGAZINE
1810394U80C-5423

Editorial Address: PO Box 32, BIGGLESWADE, SG18 8TE
Tel: 01462 819496 **Fax:** 01462 819496
Email: editor@cambridgeshiremagazine.co.uk
Advertising Address: As above.
Email: lesley@cambridgeshiremagazine.co.uk
Web site: http://www.cambridgeshiremagazine.co.uk
ISSN: 1753-4909
Publisher: Select Publishing
Date Established: 2007
Frequency: Quarterly
Cover Price: £2.50
Annual Sub.: £14.00
Circulation: 12,000 (Publisher's Statement)
Usual Pagination: 60
Editor: Alan Humphreys; **Advertising Manager:** Lesley Humphreys
Summary of Content: Magazine containing historical profiles on local villages and towns. Covers gardening, homes, eating out, recipes, motoring, industrial heritage, local history and events.
Readership/Target Audience: Read by residents, ex-residents and visitors to Cambridgeshire.
ADVERTISING RATES:
Full Page Mono £820.00
Full Page Colour £1050.00
Agency Commission: 10%
Mechanical Data: Type Area: 266 x 190mm, Bleed Size: 305 x 215mm, Trim Size: 295 x 210mm, Col Length: 266mm, Page Width: 190mm, Film: Digital
Copy instructions: Copy Date: 3 weeks prior to publication date
Average advertising content per issue: 40%
CONSUMER: RURAL & REGIONAL INTEREST: Regional Interest English Counties

CAMBRIDGESHIRE JOURNAL
1658643U80C-5164

Formerly: Cambridgeshire Journal and East Anglian Life
Editorial Address: Winship Road, Milton, CAMBRIDGE, CB24 6PP **Tel:** 01223 434434 **Fax:** 01223 434415
Email: debbie.tweedie@cambridge-news.co.uk
Advertising Address: As above.
Email: sue.walden@cambridge-news.co.uk
Publisher: Cambridge Newspapers Ltd
Frequency: Monthly
Cover Price: £1.95
Circulation: 10,000 (Publisher's Statement)
Usual Pagination: 108
Editor: Debbie Tweedie; **Advertising Manager:** Sue Walden
Summary of Content: Lifestyle magazine covering fashion, beauty, food, motoring, home, gardens, antiques and listings for local events.
Readership/Target Audience: Aimed at readers in Cambridgeshire with a high disposable income.
ADVERTISING: Rates on application
CONSUMER: RURAL & REGIONAL INTEREST: Regional Interest English Counties

CAMBRIDGESHIRE PRIDE MAGAZINE
46867U80C-520

Editorial Address: 14 Middletons Road, Yaxley, PETERBOROUGH, PE7 3LR **Tel:** 01733 242312
Fax: 01733 244035
Email: carol@pridepublications.co.uk
Advertising Address: As above.
Email: carol@pridepublications.co.uk
Web site: http://www.pridepublications.co.uk
Publisher: Pride Publications Ltd
Date Established: 1982
Frequency: Monthly
Free to qualifying individuals
Annual Sub.: £18.00
Circulation: 15,000 (Publisher's Statement)
Usual Pagination: 32
Editor: David Ruckwood; **Managing Director:** Carol Lawless; **Publisher:** Carol Lawless
Summary of Content: Magazine covering motoring, finance, music, books, gardening, fashion, travel, restaurants and features on schools.
Readership/Target Audience: Aimed at residents of Cambridgeshire and Stamford with a high disposable income.
ADVERTISING RATES:
Full Page Colour £675.00
Agency Commission: 10%
Mechanical Data: Type Area: 272 x 187mm, Col Length: 272mm, Trim Size: 297 x 210mm, Bleed Size: 303 x 213mm, Film: Digital, Page Width: 187mm
Copy instructions: Copy Date: 1 week prior to publication date
Average advertising content per issue: 50%
CONSUMER: RURAL & REGIONAL INTEREST: Regional Interest English Counties

CAMPAIGN UPDATE
47089U81A-180

Formerly: Wildlife Guardian
Editorial Address: 83-87 Union Street, LONDON, SE1 1SG
Tel: 020 7403 6155 **Fax:** 020 7357 6749
Email: lousierobertson@league.org.uk
Advertising Address: As above. **Tel:** 020 7089 5228
Fax: 020 7378 6940
Email: jamesrobinson@league.org.uk
Web site: http://www.league.org.uk
Publisher: League Against Cruel Sports
Frequency: Quarterly
Cover Price: £2.50
Free to qualifying individuals
Circulation: 25,000 (Publisher's Statement)
Usual Pagination: 24
Editor: Louise Robertson; **Advertising Manager:** James Robinson
Summary of Content: Magazine covering news and information on the struggle for the protection of wildlife against cruelty.
Readership/Target Audience: Read by members and supporters of the League Against Cruel Sports, also journalists, MPs, conservation and animal welfare bodies.
ADVERTISING: Rates on application
Copy instructions: Copy Date: 1 month prior to publication date
Average advertising content per issue: 10%
CONSUMER: ANIMALS & PETS: Animals & Pets Protection

CAMPING & CARAVANNING
48417U91B-10

Editorial Address: Greenfields House, Westwood Way, COVENTRY, CV4 8JH **Tel:** 024 7647 5300
Fax: 024 7647 5413
Email: magazine@thefriendlyclub.co.uk
Advertising Address: Mongoose Media Ltd, 2 Lonsdale Road, LONDON, NW6 6RD **Tel:** 020 7306 0300
Fax: 020 7306 0301
Email: mstyrka@mongoosemedia.com
Web site: http://www.campingandcaravanningclub.co.uk
Publisher: The Camping and Caravanning Club
Date Established: 1905
Frequency: Monthly
Cover Price: £3.20
Free to qualifying individuals
Circulation: 219,381 (ABC 01/01/2008 to 31/12/2008)
Usual Pagination: 100
Editor: Sue Taylor; **Features Editor:** Sue Taylor; **Advertising Manager:** Matt Styrka
Summary of Content: Magazine containing articles on touring, road tests, holiday ideas, tips and equipment information.
Readership/Target Audience: Read by members of The Camping and Caravanning Club.
ADVERTISING RATES:
Full Page Colour £3402.00
SCC £45.00
Agency Commission: 10%
Mechanical Data: Page Width: 190mm, Trim Size: 297 x 210mm, Film: Digital, Type Area: 270 x 190mm, Col Length: 270mm, Bleed Size: 303 x 216mm
Supplement(s): Out & About - 4xY
CONSUMER: RECREATION & LEISURE: Camping & Caravanning

CAMPING MAGAZINE
48418U91B-20

Editorial Address: The Maltings, West Street, BOURNE, PE10 9PH
Email: cliveg@warnersgroup.co.uk
Advertising Address: As above. **Tel:** 01778 391119
Fax: 01778 392422
Email: darrenw@warnersgroup.co.uk
Web site: http://www.campingmagazine.co.uk
Publisher: Warners Group Publications plc
Frequency: Monthly
Cover Price: £3.20
Annual Sub.: £29.99
Circulation: 25,000 (Publisher's Statement)
Usual Pagination: 60
Editor: Clive Garrett; **Advertising Manager:** Darren Webb; **Publisher:** Rob McDonnell
Summary of Content: Magazine covering product news gear tests and reviews, camp site reports, walks, soft outdoor pursuits, travel features, entertainment and advice.
Readership/Target Audience: Aimed at outdoor enthusiasts, holiday and lightweight campers.
ADVERTISING RATES:
Full Page Colour £1575.00
Agency Commission: 10%
Mechanical Data: Page Width: 190mm, Type Area: 275 x 190mm, Bleed Size: 303 x 216mm, Trim Size: 297 x 210mm, Col Length: 275mm, Film: Digital
Average advertising content per issue: 30%
CONSUMER: RECREATION & LEISURE: Camping & Caravanning

THE CANADA POST
48291U90-43

Editorial Address: PO Box 46249, LONDON, W5 2YN
Tel: 020 8840 9765
Email: info@canadapost.co.uk
Advertising Address: As above. **Fax:** 020 8840 9765
Email: info@canadapost.co.uk
Web site: http://www.canadapost.co.uk
ISSN: 1367-2479
Publisher: RoseMaple Media Ltd
Date Established: 1997
Frequency: Monthly
Free to qualifying individuals
Annual Sub.: £25.00
Circulation: 20,000 (Publisher's Statement)
Usual Pagination: 24
Editor: Paula Adamick; **Advertising Manager:** Denis Adamick; **Managing Editor:** Paula Adamick
Summary of Content: Publication covering news from Canada and Canadian news in the UK. Includes articles of Canadian and expatriate interest on general news, finance, travel, arts, books, entertainment, Canadian food and wine, employment and sports.
Readership/Target Audience: Aimed at Canadian expatriates living in the UK and Britons with a interest in Canada.
ADVERTISING RATES:
Full Page Mono £1200.00
Full Page Colour £1500.00
Agency Commission: 10%
Mechanical Data: Trim Size: 420 x 297mm, Film: Digital, No. of Columns (Display): 4, Type Area: 390 x 245mm, Col Length: 390mm, Page Width: 245mm
Copy instructions: Copy Date: Penultimate Friday of the month prior to publication date
Average advertising content per issue: 50%
CONSUMER: ETHNIC

CANAL BOAT
48368U91A-13

Formerly: Canal Boat and Inland Waterways
Editorial Address: 3 The Courtyard, Denmark Street, WOKINGHAM, RG40 2AZ **Tel:** 0118 989 7215
Fax: 0118 977 2903
Email: editor@canalboat.co.uk
Advertising Address: As above. **Tel:** 0118 977 1677
Email: ads@canalboat.co.uk
Web site: http://www.canalboat.co.uk
Publisher: Archant Specialist Ltd (Saffron Walden)
Date Established: 1996
Frequency: Monthly
Cover Price: £3.25
Annual Sub.: £34.10
Circulation: 12,639 (ABC 01/01/2008 to 31/12/2008)
Usual Pagination: 148
Editor: Nick Wall
Summary of Content: Magazine containing technical features and cruise articles on all aspects of boating on rivers, canals and lakes.
Readership/Target Audience: Read by boat-owners, hirers and waterway enthusiasts.
ADVERTISING RATES:
Full Page Mono £700.00
Full Page Colour £755.00
Agency Commission: 10%
Mechanical Data: Film: Digital, Trim Size: 460 x 300mm, Bleed Size: +5mm
Copy instructions: Copy Date: 6 weeks prior to publication date
Average advertising content per issue: 60%
CONSUMER: RECREATION & LEISURE: Boating & Yachting

CANALS & RIVERS
48367U91A-10

Formerly: Canal & Riverboat
Editorial Address: PO Box 618, NORWICH, NR7 OQT
Tel: 01603 708930
Email: chris@themag.fsnet.co.uk
Advertising Address: 8A High Street, EPSOM, KT19 8AD
Tel: 01280 847038 **Fax:** 01372 847158
Email: sue@aemorgan.co.uk
Web site: http://www.canalsandrivers.co.uk
ISSN: 0263-6379
Publisher: A.E. Morgan Publications Ltd
Date Established: 1978
Frequency: Monthly - Published on the 2nd Thursday of the month prior to cover date
Cover Price: £3.30
Annual Sub.: £36.95
Circulation: 12,500 (Publisher's Statement)
Usual Pagination: 104
Editor: Chris Cattrall; **Advertising Manager:** Doreen Reed; **Publisher:** Terence Morgan
Summary of Content: Magazine covering all aspects of canals and river. Includes cruise reports, boat reviews, advice, restoration news and articles on the history of canals and rivers.
Readership/Target Audience: Aimed at enthusiasts with real waterways experience, new boaters and holiday makers looking for boats to hire.

Consumer Magazines

ADVERTISING RATES:
Full Page Colour £745.00
SCC £13.65
Agency Commission: 10%
Mechanical Data: Trim Size: 297 x 210mm, Page Width: 182mm, Type Area: 267 x 182mm, Col Length: 267mm, Bleed Size: 303 x 216mm, Film: Digital, Col Widths (Display): 43mm, No. of Columns (Display): 4
Copy instructions: Copy Date: 5 weeks prior to publication date
CONSUMER: RECREATION & LEISURE: Boating & Yachting

CANARY WHARF CITY LIFE MAGAZINE
1773015U74Q-1322
Formerly: Canary Wharf E14 Magazine
Editorial Address: 16 Heron Quay, Canary Wharf, LONDON, E14 4JB **Tel:** 020 7005 0044
Email: le@runwildmedia.com
Advertising Address: As above.
Email: zt@runwildmedia.com
Web site: http://www.runwildmedia.com
Publisher: Run Wild Media - London
Date Established: 2005
Frequency: Monthly
Cover Price: Free
Circulation: 62,500 (Publisher's Statement)
Editor: Lesley Ellwood; **Advertising Director:** Zainab Talati
Summary of Content: Magazine covering fashion, beauty, art, entertainment, motoring, lifestyle, property, food and drink and shopping.
Readership/Target Audience: Aimed at high earners in London E14.
ADVERTISING RATES:
Full Page Colour £3995.00
Mechanical Data: Bleed Size: 303 x 216mm, Trim Size: 297 x 210mm, Film: Digital
CONSUMER: WOMEN'S INTEREST CONSUMER MAGAZINES: Lifestyle

CANDIS
45241U74C-65
Editorial Address: Newhall Lane, Hoylake, WIRRAL, CH47 4BQ **Tel:** 0844 545 8100 **Fax:** 0844 545 8103
Email: sally@candis.co.uk
Advertising Address: Publicom Ltd, 80 Silverthorne Road, LONDON, SW8 3XA **Tel:** 0870 803 4271
Email: jpeskett@publicom-uk.com
Web site: http://www.candis.co.uk
Publisher: Newhall Publications Ltd
Date Established: 1962
Frequency: Monthly
Annual Sub.: £30.00
Circulation: 272,145 (ABC 01/01/2009 to 30/06/2009)
Usual Pagination: 164
Editor: Debbie Attewell; **Features Editor:** Helen Etheridge; **Managing Director:** Andrew Douglas
Summary of Content: Magazine featuring general features, health and relationship advice. Includes recipes, knitting, gardening, competitions and reports on charities.
Readership/Target Audience: Aimed at women with families.
ADVERTISING RATES:
Full Page Mono £4995.00
Full Page Colour £6995.00
Agency Commission: 10%
Mechanical Data: Film: Digital, Bleed Size: 201 x 151mm, Trim Size: 195 x 145mm, Type Area: 185 x 135mm, Col Length: 185mm, Page Width: 135mm
Copy instructions: Copy Date: 4 weeks prior to publication date
Average advertising content per issue: 16%
CONSUMER: WOMEN'S INTEREST CONSUMER MAGAZINES: Home & Family

CANOE AND KAYAK MAGAZINE UK
706934U91A-15
Editorial Address: The Maltings, West Street, BOURNE, PE10 9PH **Tel:** 01778 391000 **Fax:** 01778 421706
Email: jasons@warnersgroup.co.uk
Advertising Address: As above. **Fax:** 01778 392079
Email: andyf@warnersgroup.co.uk
Web site: http://www.canoekayak.co.uk
ISSN: 1473-303X
Publisher: Warners Group Publications plc
Date Established: 2001
Frequency: Monthly
Cover Price: £3.20
Annual Sub.: £35.20
Circulation: 18,000 (Publisher's Statement)
Usual Pagination: 76
Editor: Jason Smith; **Advertising Manager:** Andy Fraser
Summary of Content: Magazine containing all aspects of canoes and kayaks. Includes news, product reviews, beginners' guides and articles on techniques.
Readership/Target Audience: Aimed at canoeists of all levels.

ADVERTISING RATES:
Full Page Colour £724.00
Agency Commission: 10%
Mechanical Data: Trim Size: 297 x 210mm, Bleed Size: 300 x 213mm, Film: Digital
Copy instructions: Copy Date: 8th of the month prior to publication date
Average advertising content per issue: 55%
CONSUMER: RECREATION & LEISURE: Boating & Yachting

CANOE FOCUS
48369U91A-16
Editorial Address: 2B Graphic Design, 49 Greenfields, ST. IVES, PE27 5HB **Tel:** 01480 465081 **Fax:** 01480 465081
Email: peter@canoefocus.co.uk
Advertising Address: As above.
Email: advertising@canoefocus.co.uk
Web site: http://www.canoefocus.co.uk
Publisher: British Canoe Union
Date Established: 1976
Frequency: 6 issues yearly
Cover Price: £3.50
Annual Sub.: £21.00
Circulation: 30,000 (Publisher's Statement)
Usual Pagination: 68
Editor: Peter Tranter; **Advertising Manager:** Anne Egan
Summary of Content: Magazine of the British Canoe Union. Covers news, events, features and competitions.
Readership/Target Audience: Read by members and those interested in canoeing.
ADVERTISING RATES:
Fulf Page Colour £695.00
SCC £13.50
Agency Commission: 10%
Mechanical Data: Col Length: 270mm, No. of Columns (Display): 4, Type Area: 270 x 190mm, Print Process: Web-fed litho, Bleed Size: 303 x 216mm, Trim Size: 297 x 210mm, Film: Digital, Page Width: 190mm, Col Widths (Display): 42mm
Copy instructions: Copy Date: 10th of the month prior to publication date
Average advertising content per issue: 35%
CONSUMER: RECREATION & LEISURE: Boating & Yachting

CANTERBURY OUTLOOK
601137U87-18
Editorial Address: 57 Neal Road, West Kingsdown, SEVENOAKS, TN15 6DG **Tel:** 01474 852474
Fax: 01474 854755
Email: outlook@church-media.co.uk
Advertising Address: As above. **Fax:** 01474 855601
Email: kcpress@church-media.co.uk
Web site: http://www.church-media.co.uk
Publisher: Kent Christian Press
Date Established: 1994
Frequency: 10 issues yearly - Published monthly on the last week of the month except for January and August
Cover Price: Free
Circulation: 20,000 (Publisher's Statement)
Usual Pagination: 12
Editor: Bryan Harris; **Advertising Manager:** Bryan Harris
Summary of Content: Church of England newspaper covering news, listings and book reviews relevant to churchgoers. Also contains articles featuring community issues of relevance.
Readership/Target Audience: Aimed at churchgoers within the Diocese of Canterbury.
ADVERTISING RATES:
SCC £6.00
Agency Commission: 10%
Mechanical Data: Col Length: 340mm, Film: Digital, No. of Columns (Display): 6, Type Area: 340 x 288mm, Print Process: Offset litho, Col Widths (Display): 42mm, Page Width: 288mm
Copy instructions: Copy Date: Friday prior to publication date
Average advertising content per issue: 25%
CONSUMER: RELIGIOUS

CAPITAL
1708231U89D-523
Formerly: Capital Letter
Editorial Address: Publishing House, 3 Bridgebank Industrial Estate, Taylor Street, Horwich, BOLTON, BL6 7PD **Tel:** 0161 909 0909 **Fax:** 0161 909 0919
Email: jonathan.richards@bigspark.co.uk
Advertising Address: As above.
Email: stuart.parker@bigspark.co.uk
Publisher: The Big Spark
Frequency: Quarterly
Cover Price: Free
Circulation: 20,000 (Publisher's Statement)
Usual Pagination: 52
Editor: Jonathan Richards; **Advertising Manager:** Stuart Parker
Summary of Content: Lifestyle magazine covering celebrity interviews, car tests, financial pages and destinations.
Readership/Target Audience: Aimed at in-coming and out-going passengers at Edinburgh Airport.

ADVERTISING RATES:
Full Page Colour £1250.00
Agency Commission: 10%
Mechanical Data: Type Area: 280 x 190mm, Bleed Size: 303 x 216mm, Trim Size: 297 x 210mm, Col Length: 280mm, Page Width: 190mm, Film: Digital
CONSUMER: HOLIDAYS & TRAVEL: In-Flight Magazines

CAPTURE
1745299U85A-215
Editorial Address: Park View House, 19 The Avenue, EASTBOURNE, BN21 3YD **Tel:** 01323 411601
Fax: 01323 411654
Email: lknight@parkviewmedia.co.uk
Web site: http://www.parkview-publishing.co.uk/capture/
Publisher: Park View Publishing Ltd
Date Established: 2006
Frequency: Quarterly
Cover Price: £1.50
Free to qualifying individuals
Circulation: 20,000 (Publisher's Statement)
Editor: Laura Knight; **Advertising Manager:** Simon Dunning; **Managing Editor:** James Mansfield
Summary of Content: Magazine covering photographic accessories.
Readership/Target Audience: Aimed at those with an interest in photography.
CONSUMER: PHOTOGRAPHY & FILM MAKING: Photography

CAR
46305U77A-100
Editorial Address: Media House, Lynchwood, Peterborough Business Park, PETERBOROUGH, PE2 6EA
Tel: 01733 468379 **Fax:** 01733 468660
Email: car@bauermedia.co.uk
Advertising Address: Endeavour House, 189 Shaftesbury House, LONDON, WC2H 8JG **Tel:** 020 7437 9011
Fax: 020 7095 5444
Email: nima.shahraz@baueradvertising.co.uk
Web site: http://www.carmagazine.co.uk/
ISSN: 0008-5987
Publisher: Bauer Consumer Media Ltd (Media House)
Date Established: 1962
Frequency: Monthly
Cover Price: £4.20
Annual Sub.: £45.60
Circulation: 62,041 (ABC 01/01/2009 to 30/06/2009)
Usual Pagination: 226
Editor: Phil McNamara; **Advertising Manager:** Nima Shahraz; **Managing Editor:** Greg Fountain; **Publisher:** Ed Kenyon
Summary of Content: Magazine containing news, features and reviews of cars.
Readership/Target Audience: Read by motoring enthusiasts and people involved in the motoring industry.
ADVERTISING RATES:
Full Page Colour £6741.00
Agency Commission: 10%
Mechanical Data: Page Width: 178mm, Bleed Size: 303 x 216mm, Trim Size: 297 x 210mm, Type Area: 262 x 178mm, Film: Digital, Col Length: 262mm
Copy instructions: Copy Date: 4 weeks prior to publication date
Average advertising content per issue: 40%
CONSUMER: MOTORING & CYCLING: Motoring

CAR PARTS AND ACCESSORIES MART
622504U77A-125
Editorial Address: 2nd Floor, Ewer House, 44-46 Crouch Street, COLCHESTER, CO3 3HH **Tel:** 01206 506236
Fax: 01206 500227
Email: helenb@mspublications.co.uk
Advertising Address: As above. **Tel:** 01206 506250
Email: carpartsmart@mspublications.co.uk
Publisher: MS Publications (2001) Ltd
Date Established: 1999
Frequency: Monthly
Cover Price: £0.99
Usual Pagination: 172
Editor: Belinda Buckle
Summary of Content: Magazine featuring new, second hand and reconditioned car parts and accessories for sale.
Readership/Target Audience: Aimed at car enthusiasts with a keen interest in restoration, modification and tuning.
ADVERTISING RATES:
Full Page Mono £380.00
Full Page Colour £64.00
SCC £10.00
Agency Commission: 10%
Mechanical Data: Type Area: 246 x 152mm, Bleed Size: 285 x 190mm, Trim Size: 275 x 180mm, Col Length: 246mm, No. of Columns (Display): 4, Page Width: 152mm, Film: Digital
Average advertising content per issue: 100%
CONSUMER: MOTORING & CYCLING: Motoring

CARAVAN BUYER

1663925U91B-306

Formerly: The Buyer's Guide
Editorial Address: Leon House, 233 High Street, CROYDON, CR9 1HZ **Tel:** 020 8726 8244
Fax: 020 8726 8299
Email: caravan@ipcmedia.com
Advertising Address: As above. **Fax:** 020 8726 8298
Email: beverley_meliniotis@ipcmedia.com
Web site: http://www.caravanmagazine.co.uk
Publisher: IPC Inspire
Date Established: 2002
Frequency: Annual - Published in January
Cover Price: £4.99
Circulation: 20,000 (Publisher's Statement)
Editor: Victoria Bentley
Summary of Content: Magazine covering all aspects of caravanning with a beginner's guide and buyer's guide.
Readership/Target Audience: Aimed at newcomers to caravanning and those looking to change their van.
ADVERTISING RATES:
Full Page Mono £1157.00
Full Page Colour £1514.00
Agency Commission: 10%
Mechanical Data: Type Area: 278 x 190mm, Bleed Size: 304 x 216mm, Trim Size: 298 x 210mm, Col Length: 278mm, Page Width: 190mm, Film: Digital
Copy instructions: Copy Date: 6 weeks prior to publication date
Average advertising content per issue: 35%
CONSUMER: RECREATION & LEISURE: Camping & Caravanning

THE CARAVAN CLUB MAGAZINE

48419U91B-27

Editorial Address: East Grinstead House, Wood Street, EAST GRINSTEAD, RH19 1UA **Tel:** 01342 336804
Fax: 01342 410258
Email: magazine@caravanclub.co.uk
Web site: http://www.caravanclub.co.uk
Publisher: The Caravan Club
Date Established: 1964
Frequency: Monthly
Free to qualifying individuals
Annual Sub.: £36.00
Circulation: 374,390 (ABC 01/01/2008 to 31/12/2008)
Usual Pagination: 124
Editor: Gary Martin
Summary of Content: Magazine containing caravan, motor caravan and car reviews with information on touring in the UK and Europe, book reviews, CD-ROMs and products of interest, as well as technical matters and legislation affecting the touring caravanner in the UK and abroad.
Readership/Target Audience: Aimed at those who own a caravan, motor caravan or trailer tent and stay on Club sites and those thinking of purchasing a caravan.
ADVERTISING: No Advertising taken
CONSUMER: RECREATION & LEISURE: Camping & Caravanning

CARAVAN MAGAZINE

48421U91B-40

Editorial Address: Leon House, 233 High Street, CROYDON, CR9 1HZ **Tel:** 020 8726 8000
Fax: 020 8726 8299
Email: caravan@ipcmedia.com
Advertising Address: As above. **Tel:** 020 8726 8233
Fax: 020 8726 8298
Email: kathleen_retourne@ipcmedia.com
Web site: http://www.caravanmagazine.co.uk
ISSN: 0268-0440
Publisher: IPC Inspire
Date Established: 1933
Frequency: Monthly
Cover Price: £3.55
Annual Sub.: £38.40
Circulation: 15,844 (ABC 01/01/2008 to 31/12/2008)
Usual Pagination: 132
Editor: Victoria Bentley; **Advertising Manager:** Beverley Meliniotis; **Group Editor:** Victoria Bentley
Summary of Content: Magazine featuring touring caravans and car testing as well as park reports and reviews of a full range of accessories.
Readership/Target Audience: Read by caravan enthusiasts.
ADVERTISING RATES:
Full Page Mono £1191.00
Full Page Colour £2028.00
SCC £18.00
Agency Commission: 10%
Mechanical Data: Type Area: 278 x 190mm, Col Length: 278mm, Page Width: 190mm, Trim Size: 297 x 210mm, Bleed Size: 303 x 216mm, Col Widths (Display): 42mm, No. of Columns (Display): 4, Print Process: Web-fed offset litho, Film: Digital
Copy instructions: Copy Date: 4 weeks prior to publication date
Average advertising content per issue: 40%
CONSUMER: RECREATION & LEISURE: Camping & Caravanning

CARAVAN MOTORHOME & CAMPING MART

48422U91B-301

Formerly: CARAVAN MOTORCARAVAN AND CAMPING MART
Editorial Address: The Maltings, West Street, BOURNE, PE10 9PH **Tel:** 01778 392059 **Fax:** 01778 425437
Email: peters@warnersgroup.co.uk
Advertising Address: As above. **Tel:** 01778 392071
Email: saml@warnersgroup.co.uk
Web site: http://www.outandaboutlive.co.uk
Publisher: Warners Group Publications plc
Frequency: Monthly
Cover Price: £2.10
Circulation: 10,000 (Publisher's Statement)
Usual Pagination: 120
Editor: Peter Sharpe; **Publisher:** Fleur Bonsels
Summary of Content: Magazine covering dealers, second-hand and accessories.
Readership/Target Audience: Aimed at caravanners, motorhomers and campers.
ADVERTISING RATES:
Full Page Colour £500.00
Agency Commission: 10%
Mechanical Data: Type Area: 275 x 190mm, Bleed Size: 303 x 216mm, Trim Size: 297 x 210mm, Col Length: 275mm, Page Width: 190mm, Film: Positive, right reading, emulsion side down. Digital
CONSUMER: RECREATION & LEISURE: Camping & Caravanning

CARD TIMES

46732U79K-350

Editorial Address: 70 Winifred Lane, Aughton, ORMSKIRK, L39 5DL **Tel:** 01695 423470 **Fax:** 01695 420185
Email: david@cardtimes.co.uk
Advertising Address: As above.
Email: joan@cardtimes.co.uk
Web site: http://www.cardtimes.co.uk
ISSN: 0956-5124
Publisher: Magpie Publications
Date Established: 1988
Frequency: 11 issues yearly
Cover Price: £2.10
Annual Sub.: £21.00
Circulation: 2,000 (Publisher's Statement)
Usual Pagination: 32
Editor: David Stuckey; **Advertising Manager:** Joan Stuckey
Summary of Content: Magazine focusing on cigarette, gum and tea card collecting, news, features, an auction list and a diary of events which includes card collectors' fairs, clubs' meetings and conventions.
Readership/Target Audience: Aimed at collectors of cigarette cards, trade cards, gum cards and related ephemera.
ADVERTISING RATES:
Full Page Mono £180.00
Full Page Colour £270.00
Mechanical Data: Trim Size: 297 x 210mm, Type Area: 260 x 180mm, Film: Digital, Col Length: 260mm, Page Width: 180mm
Copy instructions: Copy Date: 10 days prior to publication date
Average advertising content per issue: 50%
CONSUMER: HOBBIES & DIY: Collectors Magazines

CARDIFF LIFE

1827085U80D-515

Editorial Address: Circus Mews House, Circus Mews, BATH, BA1 2PW **Tel:** 01225 475800 **Fax:** 01225 475801
Email: info@mediaclash.co.uk
Advertising Address: As above.
Email: debbie.blackman@mediaclash.co.uk
Web site: http://www.cardifflifemag.co.uk
Publisher: Media Clash
Date Established: 2007
Frequency: 17 issues yearly
Cover Price: £2.50
Free to qualifying individuals
Circulation: 10,000 (Print Run)
Usual Pagination: 116
Editor: Laura Rowe; **Advertising Manager:** Debbie Blackman; **Managing Editor:** Deri Robins
Summary of Content: Magazine covering life and living in Cardiff, Cowbridge and Penarth including property, interiors, food, arts and out and about.
Readership/Target Audience: Aimed at affluent households in Cardiff and surrounding areas.
ADVERTISING RATES:
Full Page Colour £715.00
Agency Commission: 10%
Mechanical Data: Bleed Size: 291 x 226mm, Trim Size: 285 x 220mm, Film: Digital
Copy instructions: Copy Date: 2 weeks prior to publication date
Average advertising content per issue: 40%
CONSUMER: RURAL & REGIONAL INTEREST: Regional Interest Wales

CARDMAKING & PAPERCRAFT

1657884U74E-687

Formerly: Card Making & Papercraft
Editorial Address: 9th Floor, Tower House, Fairfax Street, BRISTOL, BS1 3BN **Tel:** 0117 927 9009
Email: writetous@cardmakingandpapercraft.com
Advertising Address: As above. **Fax:** 0117 927 9008
Email: davidmanson@originpublishing.co.uk
Web site: http://www.cardmakingandpapercraft.com
Publisher: Origin Publishing Ltd
Date Established: 2004
Frequency: 13 issues yearly
Cover Price: £3.99
Annual Sub.: £44.00
Circulation: 31,015 (ABC 01/01/2008 to 31/12/2008)
Usual Pagination: 100
Editor: Kirstie Sleight
Summary of Content: Magazine covering card and papercraft designs with clear step by step instructions, expert advice, free gifts, best buys, give aways, competitions and events listings.
Readership/Target Audience: Aimed at all levels of card maker.
ADVERTISING RATES:
Full Page Colour £1050.00
Agency Commission: 10%
Mechanical Data: Type Area: 281 x 195mm, Bleed Size: 303 x 216mm, Trim Size: 297 x 210mm, Col Length: 281mm, Page Width: 195mm
Copy instructions: Copy Date: 6 weeks prior to publication date
Average advertising content per issue: 25%
CONSUMER: WOMEN'S INTEREST CONSUMER MAGAZINES: Crafts

CAREER GUIDANCE TODAY

47909U88C-15

Editorial Address: Ground Floor, 1 Copthall House, New Road, STOURBRIDGE, DY8 1PH **Tel:** 01384 376464
Fax: 01384 440830
Email: linda.hills@icg-uk.org
Advertising Address: Independent House, 191 Marsh Wall, LONDON, E14 9RS **Tel:** 020 7005 2100 **Fax:** 020 7005 2999
Email: j.baldwin-webb@independent.co.uk
Web site: http://www.icg-uk.org
Publisher: Independent Educational Publishing Ltd
Frequency: Quarterly
Free to qualifying individuals
Circulation: 5,000 (Publisher's Statement)
Usual Pagination: 44
Editor: Linda Hills; **Advertising Manager:** James Baldwin-Webb
Summary of Content: Journal featuring news, information, research and discussion concerning careers guidance issues.
Readership/Target Audience: Aimed at career guidance professionals.
ADVERTISING RATES:
Full Page Colour £2320.00
Agency Commission: 10%
Mechanical Data: Type Area: 260 x 190mm, Trim Size: 280 x 210mm, Bleed Size: 286 x 216mm, Col Length: 260mm, Page Width: 190mm, Film: Digital
Copy instructions: Copy Date: 3 weeks prior to publication date
Average advertising content per issue: 40%
CONSUMER: EDUCATION: Careers

CAREER TRACK

1667552U88C-170

Editorial Address: Thomson House, Havelock Street, CARDIFF, CF10 1XR **Tel:** 029 2058 3592
Email: simon.farrington@mediawales.co.uk
Advertising Address: 6 Park Street, CARDIFF, CF10 1XR **Tel:** 029 2022 3333
Email: deborah.steer@mediawales.co.uk
Publisher: Media Wales Ltd
Web site: http://www.icwales.com
Frequency: Annual - Published in March
Cover Price: Free
Circulation: 23,000 (Publisher's Statement)
Usual Pagination: 100
Editor: Simon Farrington
Summary of Content: Careers Guide covering 70 to 80 jobs with advice on what qualifications are necessary, courses available and salary to expect.
Readership/Target Audience: Aimed at 15 to 18 year olds in schools throughout Wales.
ADVERTISING RATES:
Full Page Colour £577.50
Mechanical Data: Bleed Size: 307 x 220mm, Trim Size: 297 x 210mm, Film: Digital
CONSUMER: EDUCATION: Careers

CAREERMAKEOVER

1800036U88C-179

Editorial Address: 93 Blackamoor Lane, MAIDENHEAD, SL6 8RJ **Tel:** 07092 276160 **Fax:** 07092 276160
Email: daniell@careermakeover.co.uk

Consumer Magazines

Advertising Address: As above.
Email: daniell@careermakeover.co.uk
Web site: http://www.careermakeover.co.uk
Publisher: Careermakeover Ltd
Date Established: 2006
Frequency: Monthly
Cover Price: Free
Editor: Daniell Morrisey; **Advertising Manager:** Daniell Morrisey
Summary of Content: Magazine covering practical, down-to-earth career knowledge including CV and interview tips and career planning.
Readership/Target Audience: Aimed at job seekers, people looking to develop their career, managers and career advisors.
ADVERTISING: Rates on application
CONSUMER: EDUCATION: Careers

CARIBBEAN WORLD
48231U89E-70
Editorial Address: PO Box 4386, West Kensington, LONDON, W14 0YE **Tel:** 020 7751 1689
Email: publisher@caribbeanworld-magazine.com
Advertising Address: 55 Kensington West, Blythe Road, LONDON, W14 0JQ **Tel:** 020 7751 1689 **Fax:** 020 7371 2096
Email: publisher@caribbeanworld-magazine.com
Web site: http://www.caribbeanworld-magazine.com
Publisher: World Travel Media Ltd
Date Established: 1991
Frequency: Quarterly
Cover Price: £3.50
Annual Sub.: £14.00
Circulation: 136,163 (Publisher's Statement)
Usual Pagination: 116
Editor: Polly Evans; **Advertising Manager:** Ray Carmen; **Publisher:** Ray Carmen
Summary of Content: Magazine containing island profiles with features on food, music, fashion, business, homes and interiors. Includes articles on sport, sailing, yachting, cruising, celebrity profiles, diving, hotels and resorts.
Readership/Target Audience: Aimed at those aged between 25 and 54 years old with an interest in the Caribbean.
ADVERTISING: Rates on application
Supplement(s): Caribbean World of Real Estate and Interiors - 4xY
CONSUMER: HOLIDAYS & TRAVEL: Holidays

CARIS
1850114U74F-776
Editorial Address: 13-17 Long Lane, LONDON, EC1A 9PN **Tel:** 020 7776 1010 **Fax:** 020 7776 1017
Email: features@carismag.co.uk
Advertising Address: As above.
Email: stephen@churchtimes.co.uk
Web site: http://www.carismag.co.uk
Publisher: Hymns ancient & modern
Date Established: 2007
Frequency: Quarterly - Published in December, March, June and September
Cover Price: £3.00
Annual Sub.: £10.00
Usual Pagination: 48
Editor: Christine Miles
Summary of Content: Magazine covering real-life stories, competitions, quizzes, fashion, beauty, music, interviews, DVD and book reviews, problem pages, eco tips and global features on the lives of young people overseas.
Readership/Target Audience: Aimed at girls aged between 12 to 16 years old.
ADVERTISING RATES:
Full Page Colour EUR510.00
Agency Commission: 10%
Mechanical Data: Trim Size: 208 x 147mm, Bleed Size: 214 x 153mm, Film: Digital
Copy instructions: Copy Date: 6 weeks prior to publication date
Average advertising content per issue: 12%
CONSUMER: WOMEN'S INTEREST CONSUMER MAGAZINES: Teenage

CARLISLE LIVING
1847138U80C-5466
Editorial Address: Media House, Barras Lane, Dalston, CARLISLE, CA5 7LX **Tel:** 01228 713000 **Fax:** 01228 713001
Email: jane.loughran@cngroup.co.uk
Web site: http://www.carlisleliving.co.uk
Publisher: Cumbrian Newspapers Ltd
Date Established: 2008
Frequency: Monthly
Cover Price: £2.00
Usual Pagination: 100
Editor: Jane Loughran
Summary of Content: Lifestyle magazine covering local news and celebrities with profiles and interviews, interiors, fashion, beauty, motoring, property, arts and Q&As.

Readership/Target Audience: Aimed at residents in Carlisle and the surrounding area predominantly aged 30 to 45 years old.
CONSUMER: RURAL & REGIONAL INTEREST: Regional Interest English Counties

CAROUSEL THE GUIDE TO CHILDREN'S BOOKS
47540U84B-36
Editorial Address: The Saturn Centre, 54-76 Bissell Street, BIRMINGHAM, B5 7HX **Tel:** 0121 622 7458
Fax: 0121 666 7526
Email: carousel.guide@virgin.net
Advertising Address: As above.
Email: carousel.guide@virgin.net
Web site: http://www.carouselguide.co.uk
ISSN: 1368-6361
Publisher: Carousel
Date Established: 1995
Frequency: 3 issues yearly - Published in March, June and October
Cover Price: £3.50
Annual Sub.: £10.50
Circulation: 10,000 (Publisher's Statement)
Usual Pagination: 44
Editor: Jenny Blanch; **Managing Director:** David Blanch; **Advertising Manager:** David Blanch
Summary of Content: Magazine featuring book reviews, news, articles and profiles.
Readership/Target Audience: Aimed at parents with young children and people with an interest in children's books.
ADVERTISING: Rates on application
Copy instructions: Copy Date: 6 weeks prior to publication date
Average advertising content per issue: 15%
CONSUMER: THE ARTS & LITERARY: Literary

CARP TALK
48521U92-39
Editorial Address: Sandholme Grange, NEWPORT, HU15 2QG **Tel:** 01430 440624 **Fax:** 01430 441319
Email: carper@btconnect.com
Advertising Address: 5 Pilley Hill, Pilley, LYMINGTON, S041 5QF **Tel:** 01590 678400 **Fax:** 01590 678400
Email: chrisball2@virgin.net
Web site: http://www.carptalk-online.co.uk
Publisher: Carp Fishing News Ltd
Date Established: 1994
Frequency: Weekly
Cover Price: £1.65
Annual Sub.: £90.00
Circulation: 13,500 (Publisher's Statement)
Usual Pagination: 66
Editor: Kevin Clifford; **Advertising Director:** Chris Ball
Summary of Content: Magazine covering all aspects of carp fishing.
Readership/Target Audience: Aimed at carp and specialist anglers.
ADVERTISING RATES:
Full Page Mono £280.00
Full Page Colour £399.00
Agency Commission: 10%
Mechanical Data: Film: Digital, Type Area: 262 x 185mm, Print Process: Web-fed offset, Col Length: 262mm, Page Width: 185mm, Trim Size: 297 x 210mm, No. of Columns (Display): 4, Bleed Size: +5mm
Copy instructions: Copy Date: 7 days prior to publication date
Average advertising content per issue: 38%
CONSUMER: ANGLING & FISHING

CARPOLOGY
1643861U92-103
Editorial Address: PO Box 28, HARLESTON, IP20 0WT **Tel:** 01986 788899 **Fax:** 01986 788655
Email: editorial@carpology.net
Advertising Address: As above. **Tel:** 01986 788854
Email: sales@carpology.net
Web site: http://www.carpology.net
Publisher: Toffee Publications Ltd
Date Established: 2004
Frequency: Monthly
Cover Price: £3.70
Circulation: 10,000 (Publisher's Statement)
Usual Pagination: 132
Editor: Joe Wright; **Advertising Manager:** Robert Bell
Summary of Content: Magazine covering carp fishing with features, product reviews and interviews as well as CD and DVD reviews, gadgets and toys.
Readership/Target Audience: Aimed at men aged between 16 and 40 years old.
ADVERTISING RATES:
Full Page Colour £360.00
Mechanical Data: Trim Size: 297 x 210mm, Bleed Size: 303 x 216mm, Print Process: Web-fed litho, Film: Digital
Average advertising content per issue: 50%
CONSUMER: ANGLING & FISHING

CARPWORLD
48522U92-40
Editorial Address: Regent House, 101 Broadfield Road, SHEFFIELD, S8 0XH **Tel:** 0114 258 0812
Fax: 0114 258 2728
Email: info@anglingpublications.co.uk
Advertising Address: As above.
Email: info@anglingpublications.co.uk
Web site: http://www.anglingpublications.co.uk/carpworld
Publisher: Angling Publications Ltd
Date Established: 1988
Frequency: Monthly
Cover Price: £4.40
Circulation: 18,000 (Publisher's Statement)
Usual Pagination: 214
Editor: Martin Ford; **Advertising Manager:** Scott Day
Summary of Content: Magazine covering articles and advice on all aspects of carp fishing, including bait and tactics.
Readership/Target Audience: Aimed at carp anglers and fishermen.
ADVERTISING RATES:
Full Page Colour £500.00
Agency Commission: 10%
Mechanical Data: Bleed Size: 303 x 216mm, Trim Size: 297 x 210mm, Film: Digital
Copy instructions: Copy Date: 3 weeks prior to publication date
Average advertising content per issue: 40%
CONSUMER: ANGLING & FISHING

CARRIAGE DRIVING
46000U81D-25
Editorial Address: Jesses Farm, Snow Hill, Dinton, SALISBURY, SP3 5HN **Tel:** 01722 716997
Fax: 01722 716926
Email: edit@carriage-driving.com
Advertising Address: As above. **Tel:** 01722 716996
Fax: 01722 716887
Email: advert@carriage-driving.com
Web site: http://www.carriage-driving.com
Publisher: A & D Media Ltd
Date Established: 1982
Frequency: Monthly
Cover Price: £3.99
Annual Sub.: £49.99
Circulation: 9,000 (Publisher's Statement)
Usual Pagination: 64
Editor: Stephanie Kill; **Advertising Manager:** Claire Burden; **Publisher:** Fiona Richards
Summary of Content: Magazine dedicated to all forms of carriage driving.
Readership/Target Audience: Read by carriage driving enthusiasts.
ADVERTISING RATES:
Full Page Colour £900.00
SCC £10.00
Agency Commission: 10%
Mechanical Data: Film: Digital, Type Area: 255 x 186mm, Bleed Size: 303 x 216mm, Col Length: 255mm, Page Width: 186mm, Trim Size: 297 x 210mm
Copy instructions: Copy Date: 10th of the month prior to publication date
Average advertising content per issue: 60%
CONSUMER: ANIMALS & PETS: Horses & Ponies

CARS FOR THE CONNOISSEUR
1685565U77E-517
Editorial Address: Prospect House, Shaftesbury Road, East Knoyle, SALISBURY, SP3 6AR **Tel:** 01747 830977
Email: charles@carsfortheconnoisseur.com
Advertising Address: As above.
Email: charles@carsfortheconnoisseur.com
Web site: http://www.carsfortheconnoisseur.com
Publisher: Cars for the Connoisseur
Date Established: 2001
Frequency: Monthly
Annual Sub.: £48.00
Circulation: 1,500 (Publisher's Statement)
Usual Pagination: 30
Editor: Charles Harbord; **Advertising Manager:** Charles Harbord; **Publisher:** Charles Harbord
Summary of Content: Magazine covering nostalgia from behind the wheel, racing reminiscences and cars I have owned.
Readership/Target Audience: Aimed at connoisseurs of cars, collectors and enthusiasts.
ADVERTISING RATES:
Full Page Mono £300.00
Mechanical Data: Type Area: 270 x 190mm, Trim Size: 297 x 210mm, Col Length: 270mm, Page Width: 190mm, Film: Digital
Copy instructions: Copy Date: 15th of month prior to publication date
Average advertising content per issue: 30%
CONSUMER: MOTORING & CYCLING: Club Cars

CARSPORT
46418U77D-160

Editorial Address: 5B Edgewater Business Park, Belfast Harbour Estate, BELFAST, BT3 9JQ **Tel:** 028 9078 3200
Fax: 028 9078 3210
Email: patburns@greerpublications.com
Advertising Address: As above.
Email: jasoncurran@greerpublications.com
Web site: http://www.greerpublications.com/carsport.htm
ISSN: 1363-2493
Publisher: Greer Publications Ltd
Date Established: 1982
Frequency: Monthly
Cover Price: £2.75
Circulation: 12,000 (Publisher's Statement)
Usual Pagination: 100
Editor: Pat Burns; **Publisher:** James Greer
Summary of Content: Magazine with an emphasis on motor sport, but also covering the new car market, including new car design, technology and test drives.
Readership/Target Audience: Aimed at motoring and motor sports enthusiasts.
ADVERTISING: Rates on application
Copy instructions: Copy Date: 3 weeks prior to publication date
CONSUMER: MOTORING & CYCLING: Motor Sports

CARVE SURFING MAGAZINE
45939U75M-100

Editorial Address: Berry Road Studios, Berry Road, NEWQUAY, TR7 1AT **Tel:** 01637 878074 **Fax:** 01637 850226
Email: steve@carvemag.com
Advertising Address: As above.
Email: steve@carvemag.com
Web site: http://www.orcasurf.co.uk
Publisher: Orca Publications
Date Established: 1994
Frequency: 9 issues yearly
Cover Price: £3.50
Annual Sub.: £21.95
Circulation: 36,000 (Publisher's Statement)
Usual Pagination: 148
Editor: Steve England; **Advertising Manager:** Steve England; **Publisher:** Steve England
Summary of Content: Special interest surfing magazine concentrating on British and European photo stories, plus product news and reviews and contest results.
Readership/Target Audience: Read by active surfers across the country plus members of the British Surfing Association.
ADVERTISING RATES:
Full Page Colour £1680.00
Agency Commission: 10%
Mechanical Data: Film: Digital, Page Width: 202mm, Bleed Size: 306 x 236mm, Trim Size: 297 x 230mm, Type Area: 264 x 202mm, Col Length: 264mm
Copy instructions: Copy Date: 6 weeks prior to publication date
CONSUMER: SPORT: Water Sports

Y CASGLWR (THE COLLECTOR)
46755U79K-990

Editorial Address: Tan-Y-Castell, Llanuwchllyn, Y BALA, LL23 7TA **Tel:** 01678 540652
Email: tanycastell@yahoo.com
Advertising Address: As above.
Email: tanycastell@yahoo.com
Publisher: Cymdeithas Bob Owen
Frequency: 3 issues yearly - Published in March, June and November
Annual Sub.: £7.50
Circulation: 1,500 (Publisher's Statement)
Usual Pagination: 24
Editor: Melfyn Williams; **Advertising Manager:** Melfyn Williams
Summary of Content: Journal of the Bob Owen Society. Covers book, map and picture collecting and associated matters.
Language(s): Welsh
Readership/Target Audience: Read by older collectors of Welsh souvenirs.
ADVERTISING RATES:
Full Page Mono £200.00
Full Page Colour £280.00
Agency Commission: 10%
Mechanical Data: Film: Digital, Trim Size: 297 x 210mm
Copy instructions: Copy Date: 6 weeks prior to publication date
Average advertising content per issue: 25%
CONSUMER: HOBBIES & DIY: Collectors Magazines

THE CAT
47114U81C-50

Editorial Address: PO Box 617, HAYWARDS HEATH, RH17 9WU **Tel:** 0870 770 8649 **Fax:** 0870 770 8265
Email: editorial@cats.org.uk
Advertising Address: Terry Lock Media Sales, 3 Forest Way, ASHTEAD, KT21 1JN **Tel:** 01372 276233
Fax: 0870 705 1901
Email: tslock@terrylockmedia.co.uk
Web site: http://www.thecat.org.uk
Publisher: Cats Protection
Date Established: 1934
Frequency: Quarterly - Published at the end of the month prior to cover date
Annual Sub.: £15.00
Circulation: 25,000 (Publisher's Statement)
Usual Pagination: 64
Editor: Francesca Watson; **Advertisement Director:** Terry Lock
Summary of Content: Magazine including news, views and information about cats and cat ownership. It includes reviews of the latest products, interviews with celebrities, competitions, letters and features.
Readership/Target Audience: Readership is primarily professional, affluent and mature females, people involved in animal welfare, veterinary surgeons and supporters of Cats Protection.
ADVERTISING RATES:
Full Page Colour £1500.00
Agency Commission: 10%
Mechanical Data: Trim Size: 297 x 210mm, Type Area: 272 x 190mm, Bleed Size: 310 x 220mm, Page Width: 190mm, Film: Digital, Col Length: 272mm
Average advertising content per issue: 30%
CONSUMER: ANIMALS & PETS: Cats

CAT WORLD
47116U81C-190

Editorial Address: Ancient Lights, 19 River Road, ARUNDEL, BN18 9EY **Tel:** 01903 884988
Fax: 01903 885514
Email: laura@ashdown.co.uk
Advertising Address: As above.
Email: maria@ashdown.co.uk
Web site: http://www.catworld.co.uk
Publisher: Ashdown.co.uk Ltd
Date Established: 1981
Frequency: Monthly
Cover Price: £2.95
Circulation: 20,000 (Publisher's Statement)
Usual Pagination: 92
Editor: Laura Quiggan; **Managing Director:** David King
Summary of Content: Magazine containing articles and features on all aspects of cats and cat ownership, including where to buy a kitten, advice on veterinary matters and breed profiles.
Readership/Target Audience: Aimed at owners of pedigree and non-pedigree cats.
ADVERTISING RATES:
Full Page Mono £684.00
Full Page Colour £1029.00
Agency Commission: 10%
Mechanical Data: Type Area: 263 x 185mm, No. of Columns (Display): 3, Bleed Size: 303 x 216mm, Trim Size: 297 x 210mm, Col Length: 263mm, Page Width: 185mm, Film: Digital
Copy instructions: Copy Date: 6 weeks prior to publication date
CONSUMER: ANIMALS & PETS: Cats

THE CATHOLIC HERALD
47680U87-30

Editorial Address: Herald House, 15 Lamb's Passage, Bunhill Row, LONDON, EC1Y 8TQ **Tel:** 020 7448 3600
Fax: 020 7256 9728
Email: editorial@catholicherald.co.uk
Advertising Address: As above. **Tel:** 020 7448 3614
Email: advertising@catholicherald.co.uk
Web site: http://www.catholicherald.co.uk
Publisher: Catholic Herald Ltd
Date Established: 1888
Frequency: Weekly
Cover Price: £1.20
Circulation: 22,500 (Publisher's Statement)
Usual Pagination: 20
Editor: Luke Coppen; **News Editor:** Simon Caldwell;
Features Editor: Ed West; **Editor-in-Chief:** Damian Thompson; **Advertising Manager:** James Quantrill
Summary of Content: Newspaper includes news from home and abroad. Includes analysis of secular stories from a church viewpoint.
Readership/Target Audience: Read by people concerned with religious issues, particularly Catholics.
ADVERTISING RATES:
Full Page Mono £2550.00
Full Page Colour £2670.00
SCC £7.40
Agency Commission: 10%
Mechanical Data: Type Area: 540 x 341mm, Col Length: 540mm, Col Widths (Display): 39mm, No. of Columns (Display): 8, Page Width: 341mm, Film: Digital
Copy instructions: Copy Date: Tuesday midday prior to publication date
Average advertising content per issue: 35%
CONSUMER: RELIGIOUS

CATHOLIC HERALD (& STANDARD)
29907U87-2015

Formerly: Catholic Herald & Standard
Editorial Address: Herald House, 15 Lamb's Passage, Bunhill Row, LONDON, EC1Y 8TQ **Tel:** 020 7448 3603
Fax: 020 7256 9728
Email: editorial@catholicherald.co.uk
Advertising Address: As above. **Tel:** 020 7488 3101
Email: advertising@catholicherald.co.uk
Web site: http://www.catholicherald.co.uk
Publisher: Catholic Herald Ltd
Date Established: 1888
Frequency: Weekly
Cover Price: £1.20
Circulation: 20,000 (Publisher's Statement)
Editor: Simon Caldwell; **News Editor:** Simon Caldwell;
Features Editor: Ed West; **Advertising Manager:** James Quantrill
Summary of Content: Newspaper covering religious news, comment and current affairs.
Readership/Target Audience: Read by Catholics.
ADVERTISING RATES:
Full Page Mono £2550.00
Full Page Colour £2550.00
Agency Commission: 10%
Mechanical Data: Type Area: 540 x 341mm, Trim Size: 578 x 375mm, Col Length: 540mm, Col Widths (Display): 39mm, No. of Columns (Display): 8, Page Width: 341mm
Copy instructions: Copy Date: Tuesday midday prior to publication date
Average advertising content per issue: 35%
CONSUMER: RELIGIOUS

CATHOLIC LIFE
47681U87-32

Editorial Address: 4th Floor, Landmark House, Station Road, Cheadle Hulme, CHEADLE, SK8 7JH
Tel: 0161 488 1700 **Fax:** 0161 488 1701
Email: lynda.walker@totalcatholic.com
Advertising Address: As above. **Fax:** 0161 488 1782
Email: advertising@totalcatholic.net
Web site: http://www.totalcatholic.com
Publisher: Gabriel Communications Ltd
Frequency: Monthly
Cover Price: £3.00
Circulation: 12,000 (Publisher's Statement)
Usual Pagination: 64
Editor: Lynda Walker; **Advertising Manager:** Chris Morley
Summary of Content: Magazine covering the history and culture of the Catholic Church.
Readership/Target Audience: Read predominantly by Catholic families.
ADVERTISING RATES:
Full Page Colour £1001.00
Agency Commission: 10%
Mechanical Data: Col Length: 277mm, Film: Positive, right reading, emulsion side down, Type Area: 277 x 190mm, Print Process: Litho, Page Width: 190mm, Bleed Size: 303 x 216mm
Copy instructions: Copy Date: 3 weeks prior to publication date
Average advertising content per issue: 20%
CONSUMER: RELIGIOUS

THE CATHOLIC NEWS
624743U87-31

Editorial Address: PO Box 8455, NEWARK, NG23 5WX
Tel: 01636 525607
Email: johnclawson@xln.co.uk
Advertising Address: As above. **Tel:** 01636 505607
Email: johnclawson@xln.co.uk
Publisher: Bellcourt Limited
Date Established: 1996
Frequency: Monthly
Cover Price: Free
Circulation: 8,000 (Publisher's Statement)
Usual Pagination: 12
Editor: John Clawson; **Managing Director:** John Clawson;
Advertising Manager: John Clawson
Summary of Content: Magazine covering news and information of interest to Roman Catholic churchgoers.
Readership/Target Audience: Read by Roman Catholic churchgoers in the diocese of Nottingham.
ADVERTISING RATES:
Full Page Mono £400.00
Agency Commission: 10%
Copy instructions: Copy Date: 5th of the month prior to publication date
CONSUMER: RELIGIOUS

CATHOLIC PICTORIAL
47682U87-33

Editorial Address: Archdiocese of Liverpool, Croxteth Drive, Sefton Park, LIVERPOOL, L17 1AA **Tel:** 0151 709 7567
Fax: 0151 522 1008
Email: catholicpictorial@rcaol.co.uk
Advertising Address: 36 Henry Street, LIVERPOOL, L1 5BS
Tel: 0151 709 7567 **Fax:** 0151 707 1678
Email: andy@merseymirror.com

Consumer Magazines

Publisher: Mersey Mirror
Date Established: 1962
Frequency: Monthly
Cover Price: £1.00
Circulation: 6,000 (Publisher's Statement)
Usual Pagination: 36
Editor: Peter Heneghan; **Advertising Manager:** Andrew Rogers
Summary of Content: Newspaper of the Roman Catholic Archdiocese of Liverpool, covering religious issues.
Readership/Target Audience: Read by those concerned with religious issues, predominantly Catholics.
ADVERTISING RATES:
Full Page Colour £915.00
Agency Commission: 10%
Mechanical Data: Trim Size: 297 x 210mm, Film: Digital, Bleed Size: 303 x 216mm
Copy instructions: Copy Date: 5 days prior to publication date
Average advertising content per issue: 40%
CONSUMER: RELIGIOUS

CATHOLIC TIMES
47683U87-33_30
Editorial Address: 4th Floor, Landmark House, Station Road, Cheadle Hulme, CHEADLE, SK8 7JH
Tel: 0161 488 1700 **Fax:** 0161 488 1701
Email: kevin.flaherty@totalcatholic.com
Advertising Address: As above. **Fax:** 0161 488 1782
Email: advertising@totalcatholic.net
Web site: http://www.totalcatholic.com
Publisher: Gabriel Communications Ltd
Frequency: Weekly
Cover Price: £1.00
Annual Sub.: £52.00
Circulation: 13,320 (Publisher's Statement)
Editor: Kevin Flaherty
Summary of Content: Newspaper covering issues of relevance to Catholicism.
Readership/Target Audience: Aimed at Catholics in the UK and Ireland.
ADVERTISING RATES:
Full Page Mono £3280.00
Full Page Colour £4100.00
Agency Commission: 10%
Mechanical Data: Col Length: 540mm, No. of Columns (Display): 9, Type Area: 540 x 345mm, Print Process: Web offset, Page Width: 345mm, Film: Digital
Copy instructions: Copy Date: 11 days prior to publication date
Average advertising content per issue: 50%
CONSUMER: RELIGIOUS

CATHOLIC VOICE (MIDDLESBROUGH)
47685U87-35
Editorial Address: The Curial Offices, 50A The Avenue, Linthorpe, MIDDLESBROUGH, TS5 6QT **Tel:** 01642 850505
Fax: 01642 851404
Email: catholicvoice@dioceseofmiddlesbrough.co.uk
Advertising Address: Boltons Court, PRESTON, PR1 3TY
Tel: 01772 254553 **Fax:** 01772 204697
Email: tsnape.printers@virgin.net
Web site: http://www.middlesbrough-diocese.org.uk
Publisher: T Snape & Co Ltd
Date Established: 1980
Frequency: Monthly
Cover Price: Free
Circulation: 15,000 (Publisher's Statement)
Usual Pagination: 8
Editor: James Whiston
Summary of Content: Publication of the Diocese of Middlesbrough.
Readership/Target Audience: Aimed at Catholics living in Middlesbrough, York, Hull and the surrounding areas.
ADVERTISING RATES:
SCC £5.00
Agency Commission: 10%
Mechanical Data: Film: Digital, Type Area: 360 x 261mm, Col Length: 360mm, Page Width: 261mm, No. of Columns (Display): 8
Copy instructions: Copy Date: 2 weeks prior to publication date
CONSUMER: RELIGIOUS

THE CATHOLIC VOICE OF LANCASTER
47684U87-33_50
Formerly: The Voice
Editorial Address: 99 Commonside, LYTHAM ST. ANNES, FY8 4DJ **Tel:** 01253 736630
Email: voicenews@hotmail.co.uk
Advertising Address: T Snape & Co Ltd, Boltons Court, PRESTON, PR1 3TY **Tel:** 01772 254553 **Fax:** 01772 204697
Email: tsnape.printers@virgin.net
Publisher: Roman Catholic Diocese Lancaster
Frequency: Monthly
Cover Price: Free
Circulation: 13,000 (Publisher's Statement)

Usual Pagination: 8
Editor: Edwina Gillett; **Advertising Manager:** Lance Aldwinckle
Summary of Content: Publication of the Diocese of Lancaster.
Readership/Target Audience: Aimed at Catholics living in Lancaster.
ADVERTISING RATES:
Full Page Mono £1250.00
Full Page Colour £1250.00
SCC £6.00
Agency Commission: 10%
Mechanical Data: Type Area: 360 x 261mm, Bleed Size: +3mm, Col Length: 360mm, Col Widths (Display): 30mm, No. of Columns (Display): 8, Page Width: 261mm, Film: Digital
Copy instructions: Copy Date: 2nd week of the month prior to publication date
Average advertising content per issue: 40%
CONSUMER: RELIGIOUS

CBEEBIES ANIMALS
1836941U91D-976
Editorial Address: Media Centre, 201 Wood Lane, LONDON, W12 7TQ **Tel:** 020 8433 2000
Email: cbeebiesanimals@bbc.com
Web site: http://www.cbeebies.com
Publisher: BBC Children's Magazines
Date Established: 2008
Frequency: 13 issues yearly
Cover Price: £2.25
Circulation: 37,696 (ABC 01/01/2009 to 30/06/2009)
Usual Pagination: 28
Editor: Stephanie Cooper
Summary of Content: Magazine covering things to make and do, stories, facts and stickers.
Readership/Target Audience: Aimed at boys and girls aged 3 to 6 years old who love animals and Cbeebies.
CONSUMER: RECREATION & LEISURE: Children & Youth

CBEEBIES ART
1852286U91D-980
Editorial Address: Media Centre, 201 Wood Lane, LONDON, W12 7TQ **Tel:** 020 8422 2000
Email: cebeebiesart@bbc.com
Publisher: BBC Magazines
Date Established: 2008
Frequency: 13 issues yearly
Cover Price: £2.50
Circulation: 41,970 (ABC 01/01/2009 to 30/06/2009)
Editor: Stephanie Cooper; **Advertising Manager:** Duncan Carr
Summary of Content: Magazine covering pre-school art.
Readership/Target Audience: Aimed at children aged 4 to 6 years old.
CONSUMER: RECREATION & LEISURE: Children & Youth

THE CELEBRITY ANGELS SERIES
1841177U74A-1051
Formerly: The Angel Series
Editorial Address: 21-24 Bruges Place, Baynes Street, LONDON, NW1 0TF **Tel:** 020 7870 9000
Email: fionas@oxygen10.com
Web site: http://www.celebrityangels.co.uk
ISSN: 1757-3963
Publisher: Oxygen 10
Frequency: 6 issues yearly
Cover Price: £3.95
Editor: Fiona Shield
Summary of Content: Magazine series covering food & drink, travel, home & interiors, Christmas, health & fitness, beauty & fashion.
Readership/Target Audience: Aimed at men and women aged between 24 to 59 years old.
Editions:
Beauty Angels
Celebrity Angels
Home Angels
Kitchen Angels
CONSUMER: WOMEN'S INTEREST CONSUMER MAGAZINES: Women's Interest

THE CELEBRITY BULLETIN
47294U94X-20
Editorial Address: 10 Wiseton Road, LONDON, SW17 7EE
Tel: 020 8672 3191 **Fax:** 020 8672 2282
Email: terry.bodfish@celebrity-bulletin.co.uk
Web site: http://www.celebrity-bulletin.co.uk
ISSN: 0045-6020
Publisher: FENS
Date Established: 1952
Frequency: 104 issues yearly - Published Mondays and Thursdays
Usual Pagination: 4
Editor: Terry Bodfish; **Managing Director:** Neal Goddard
Summary of Content: Magazine detailing London arrivals and activities of celebrities. Includes a diary, profiles and

international page as well as details of their press and media contacts.
Readership/Target Audience: Aimed at those interested in the whereabouts of celebrities including journalists, foreign press, TV journalists, tabloids, broadsheets, magazines, advertising agencies, casting agencies and production companies.
ADVERTISING: No Advertising taken
CONSUMER: OTHER CLASSIFICATIONS: Miscellaneous

CELEBRITY DIET NOW
713818U74G-40_25
Formerly: Now Star Diet and Fitness
Editorial Address: Blue Fin Building, 110 Southwark Street, LONDON, SE1 0AU **Tel:** 020 3148 5000 **Fax:** 020 3148 8173
Email: jennifer_dunkerley@ipcmedia.com
Advertising Address: As above.
Email: yasmine_connor@ipcmedia.com
Web site: http://www.nowmagazine.co.uk
Publisher: IPC Connect Ltd
Date Established: 2000
Frequency: Half-yearly - Published in January and June
Cover Price: £2.50
Circulation: 200,000 (Publisher's Statement)
Usual Pagination: 100
Editor: Jennifer Dunkerley
Summary of Content: Magazine featuring celebrity diets, menus, fitness regimes and celebrity interviews.
Readership/Target Audience: Aimed at health conscious women between 18 and 44 years old.
ADVERTISING RATES:
Full Page Mono £9000.00
Full Page Colour £9000.00
Mechanical Data: Film: Digital
Copy instructions: Copy Date: 3 weeks prior to publication date
Average advertising content per issue: 8%
CONSUMER: WOMEN'S INTEREST CONSUMER MAGAZINES: Slimming & Health

CELEBRITY HAIR NOW
45466U74H-150
Formerly: Hair Now
Editorial Address: 211 Old Street, LONDON, EC1V 9NR
Tel: 020 7608 6300
Email: kirsten.kearney@scissorhandsmedia.com
Advertising Address: As above. **Tel:** 020 7436 9766
Fax: 020 7436 9957
Email: robert.hough@scissorhandsmedia.com
Publisher: Scissorhands Media
Frequency: 6 issues yearly
Cover Price: £2.60
Annual Sub.: £23.40
Circulation: 76,221 (ABC 01/01/2009 to 30/06/2009)
Usual Pagination: 112
Editor: Kirsten Kearney; **Advertising Manager:** Robert Hough; **Publisher:** Damian Hockney
Summary of Content: Magazine covering hair and styling ideas.
Readership/Target Audience: Aimed at women between 16 and 35 years old.
ADVERTISING RATES:
Full Page Mono £1400.00
Full Page Colour £1750.00
Agency Commission: 10%
Mechanical Data: Film: Digital
CONSUMER: WOMEN'S INTEREST CONSUMER MAGAZINES: Hair & Beauty

CELTIC VIEW
45741U75B-80
Editorial Address: The Celtic Football Club, Celtic Park, GLASGOW, G40 3RE **Tel:** 0141 551 4218
Fax: 0141 551 8106
Email: celticview@celticfc.co.uk
Advertising Address: The Old Brewery, Priory Lane, BURFORD, OX18 4SG **Tel:** 01993 822811
Fax: 01993 825928
Email: pgeddes@cre8ing.com
Web site: http://www.celticfc.net
Publisher: CRE8
Frequency: 45 issues yearly
Circulation: 35,000 (Publisher's Statement)
Editor: Paul Cuddihy
Summary of Content: Newspaper containing articles and features on Celtic Football Club.
Readership/Target Audience: Read by Celtic FC fans.
ADVERTISING RATES:
Full Page Colour £900.00
Agency Commission: 10%
Mechanical Data: Trim Size: 297 x 210mm, Film: Digital
Copy instructions: Copy Date: Friday prior to publication date
Average advertising content per issue: 40%
CONSUMER: SPORT: Football

CENT
1665779U74Q-1261

Editorial Address: 9 Albany Mews, Albany Road, LONDON, SE5 0DQ **Tel:** 020 7701 7601 **Fax:** 020 7701 7601
Email: editorial@centmagazine.co.uk
Advertising Address: As above.
Email: editorial@centmagazine.co.uk
Web site: http://www.centmagazine.co.uk
ISSN: 1750-8444
Publisher: Onehundredpercent Publishing Ltd
Date Established: 2004
Frequency: Half-yearly
Cover Price: £9.95
Annual Sub.: £26.00
Circulation: 7,000 (Publisher's Statement)
Usual Pagination: 130
Advertising Manager: Jo Phillips
Summary of Content: Magazine featuring a well known guest Editor for each edition and covering fashion, music, art, design, illustration, photography, literature and poetry.
Readership/Target Audience: Aimed at those with an interest in fashion and creativity.
ADVERTISING: Rates on application
CONSUMER: WOMEN'S INTEREST CONSUMER MAGAZINES: Lifestyle

CENTRAL HORSE NEWS
623010U81D-30

Editorial Address: Blenheim Cottage, Millers Lane, Hornton, BANBURY, OX15 6BS **Tel:** 01295 670639
Fax: 01295 670043
Email: b.gadd@centralhorsenews.co.uk
Advertising Address: As above.
Email: mary.baker@centralhorsenews.co.uk
Web site: http://www.centralhorsenews.co.uk
ISSN: 0968-6932
Publisher: B Gadd Communications
Date Established: 1992
Frequency: 6 issues yearly
Cover Price: £2.40
Annual Sub.: £15.00
Circulation: 6,500 (Publisher's Statement)
Usual Pagination: 84
Editor: Barbara Gadd; **Advertising Manager:** Mary Baker
Summary of Content: Magazine covering news, events and issues relating to riders and owners. Includes show results, reports and diary.
Readership/Target Audience: Aimed at horse owners and riders living in central counties of England, including Oxfordshire, Buckinghamshire, Northamptonshire, Warwickshire, West Midlands, Herefordshire, Worcestershire, Gloucestershire, Berkshire and Wiltshire.
ADVERTISING RATES:
Full Page Mono £290.40
Full Page Colour £546.00
Agency Commission: 10%
Mechanical Data: Type Area: 275 x 185mm, Page Width: 185mm, Bleed Size: 307 x 220mm, Col Length: 275mm, Trim Size: 297 x 210mm, No. of Columns (Display): 3, Col Widths (Display): 60mm, Film: Digital
Copy instructions: Copy Date: 1st of the month prior to publication date
Average advertising content per issue: 50%
CONSUMER: ANIMALS & PETS: Horses & Ponies

CENTRAL LONDON INDEPENDENT
48074U89C-84_40

Editorial Address: Orchardton Hall, Auchencairn, CASTLE DOUGLAS, DG7 1QL **Tel:** 0845 658 8329
Email: edit@bnw.demon.co.uk
Advertising Address: As above. **Tel:** 0845 130 6249
Email: advert@bnw.demon.co.uk
Web site: http://www.londonmag.net
Publisher: Brave New World International Ltd
Date Established: 1992
Frequency: Quarterly
Cover Price: £0.90
Circulation: 30,000 (Publisher's Statement)
Usual Pagination: 32
Editor: Dave Burbidge; **Advertising Manager:** Lee Darcy; **Publisher:** Susan Foster
Summary of Content: Entertainment magazine covering Central London with features on travel, lifestyles, entertainment, film, video, personal computer games and motoring.
Readership/Target Audience: Aimed at 18 to 30 year olds interested in going out in Central London.
ADVERTISING: Rates on application
Supplement(s): Movie Club News - 6xY
CONSUMER: HOLIDAYS & TRAVEL: Entertainment Guides

CENTREPOINT
47776U82-2_87

Editorial Address: 157 Vicarage Road, Leyton, LONDON, E10 5DU **Tel:** 020 8539 3876 **Fax:** 020 8539 3876
Email: keys@fsmail.net
ISSN: 0577-1935
Publisher: Delane Press
Date Established: 1974

Frequency: Quarterly
Cover Price: Free
Usual Pagination: 20
Editor: Ronald King
Summary of Content: Magazine focusing on reviews of political and international affairs.
Language(s): Afrikaans; Dutch; English; French
Readership/Target Audience: Aimed at the general public.
ADVERTISING: No Advertising taken
CONSUMER: CURRENT AFFAIRS & POLITICS

CHALLENGE NEWSLINE INCORPORATING THE GOOD NEWSPAPER
47688U87-2029

Formerly: Challenge
Editorial Address: 8 St John's Parade, Alinora Crescent, Goring-by-Sea, WORTHING, BN12 4HJ **Tel:** 0845 166 8463
Fax: 0845 166 8459
Email: challenge@veritecm.com
Web site: http://www.challengenewsline.com
Publisher: Verite CM Ltd
Date Established: 1958
Frequency: Monthly
Cover Price: £0.30
Free to qualifying individuals
Circulation: 50,000 (Publisher's Statement)
Usual Pagination: 8
Editor: Debbie Bunn; **Publisher:** Chris Powell
Summary of Content: Evangelistic newspaper promoting the Christian Gospel.
Readership/Target Audience: Aimed at those with an interest in exploring the Christian faith.
ADVERTISING: No Advertising taken
Mechanical Data: Col Length: 370mm, Type Area: 370 x 264mm, No. of Columns (Display): 7, Page Width: 264mm
CONSUMER: RELIGIOUS

CHAMPIONS
1633160U75B-270

Editorial Address: Teddington Studios, Broom Road, TEDDINGTON, TW11 9BE **Tel:** 020 8267 5876
Fax: 020 8267 5194
Email: champion@haymarket.com
Publisher: Haymarket Network
Date Established: 2003
Frequency: 6 issues yearly
Cover Price: £3.95
Annual Sub.: £17.76
Circulation: 21,810 (ABC 01/01/2008 to 31/12/2008)
Usual Pagination: 116
Editor: Paul Simpson; **Managing Editor:** Martin Rosser
Summary of Content: Official magazine of the UEFA Champions League. Covers matches, clubs and players.
Language(s): Chinese; English; Japanese; Russian
Readership/Target Audience: Aimed at football fans.
ADVERTISING: No Advertising taken
CONSUMER: SPORT: Football

CHANGING LONDON - LONDON CITY MISSION MAGAZINE
47860U87-213

Formerly: Span London City Mission Magazine
Editorial Address: 175 Tower Bridge Road, LONDON, SE1 2AH **Tel:** 020 7407 7585
Email: editor@lcm.org.uk
Web site: http://www.lcm.org.uk
Publisher: London City Mission
Date Established: 1835
Frequency: Quarterly
Cover Price: Free
Circulation: 31,000 (Publisher's Statement)
Usual Pagination: 24
Editor: Iain Macdonald
Summary of Content: Magazine featuring articles on Evangelism and social concern in London, primarily organisation's own work.
Readership/Target Audience: Aimed at supporters of London City Mission.
ADVERTISING: No Advertising taken
CONSUMER: RELIGIOUS

THE CHAP
1851418U86C-746

Editorial Address: 17 Ardmere Road, LONDON, SE13 6EL
Tel: 020 8305 0244
Email: post@thechap.net
Web site: http://www.thechap.net
Publisher: The Chap Ltd
Date Established: 1999
Frequency: 6 issues yearly
Cover Price: £2.95
Annual Sub.: £17.00
Circulation: 16,500 (Publisher's Statement)
Usual Pagination: 64
Editor: Gustav Temple

Summary of Content: Journal covering culture, sartorial, men's fashion, style, etiquette and grooming.
Readership/Target Audience: Aimed at gentlemen aged 25 to 55 years old.
CONSUMER: ADULT & GAY MAGAZINES: Men's Lifestyle Magazines

THE CHAPELFIELD MAGAZINE
1841176U74Q-1365

Editorial Address: Plain Speaking PR Limited, 24 North Walsham Road, NORWICH, NR6 7QB **Tel:** 01603 301287
Email: amber@plainspeakingpr.co.uk
Web site: http://www.chapelfield.co.uk
Publisher: Chapelfield Shopping Centre
Frequency: 3 issues yearly - Published in February, June and October
Cover Price: Free
Circulation: 100,000 (Publisher's Statement)
Usual Pagination: 36
Editor: Amber Davis
Summary of Content: Magazine covering lifestyle and shopping, featuring brands, products and retailers that are represented in the Chapelfield Shopping Centre in Norwich.
Readership/Target Audience: Aimed at people of all ages in the East of England.
ADVERTISING: No Advertising taken
CONSUMER: WOMEN'S INTEREST CONSUMER MAGAZINES: Lifestyle

CHAPMAN
47541U84B-40

Editorial Address: 4 Broughton Place, EDINBURGH, EH1 3RX **Tel:** 0131 557 2207
Email: chapman-pub@blueyonder.co.uk
Advertising Address: As above.
Email: chapman-pub@blueyonder.co.uk
Web site: http://www.chapman-pub.co.uk
ISSN: 0308-2695
Publisher: Chapman Publishing
Date Established: 1970
Frequency: 3 issues yearly - Published in April, August and December
Cover Price: £6.95
Annual Sub.: £24.00
Circulation: 2,000 (Publisher's Statement)
Usual Pagination: 144
Editor: Joy Hendry; **Managing Director:** Joy Hendry; **Advertising Manager:** Joy Hendry
Summary of Content: Magazine focusing predominantly on new creative writing, Scottish culture, debate, articles and book reviews.
Language(s): English; Gaelic
Readership/Target Audience: Aimed at people engaged in debate about culture in Scotland and lovers of good literature everywhere.
ADVERTISING: Rates on application
CONSUMER: THE ARTS & LITERARY: Literary

CHARTIST MAGAZINE
47211U82-4

Editorial Address: PO Box 52751, LONDON, EC2P 2XF
Tel: 0845 456 4977
Email: editor@chartist.org.uk
Advertising Address: As above.
Email: admin@chartist.org.uk
Web site: http://www.chartist.org.uk
ISSN: 0968-7866
Publisher: Chartist Editorial Collective
Date Established: 1970
Frequency: 6 issues yearly
Cover Price: £2.00
Annual Sub.: £15.00
Circulation: 1,500 (Publisher's Statement)
Usual Pagination: 32
Editor: Mike Davis; **Advertising Manager:** Peter Kenyon
Summary of Content: Magazine promoting debate across the spectrum of politics, economics, science, philosophy, art and inter-personal relations. Also covers democratic alternatives to the oppression, exploitation and injustices of capitalism and class society.
Readership/Target Audience: Aimed mainly at people active in the Labour Party and the trade union movement.
ADVERTISING: Rates on application
Average advertising content per issue: 5%
CONSUMER: CURRENT AFFAIRS & POLITICS

CHAT
45169U74A-20

Editorial Address: Blue Fin Building, 110 Southwark Street, LONDON, SE1 0SU **Tel:** 020 3148 5000 **Fax:** 020 3148 8111
Email: chat_magazine@ipcmedia.com
Advertising Address: As above.
Email: richard_smith@ipcmedia.com
Web site: http://www.ipcmedia.com
ISSN: 0269-9891
Publisher: IPC Connect Ltd
Date Established: 1985

Frequency: Weekly
Cover Price: £0.78
Circulation: 434,929 (ABC 01/01/2009 to 30/06/2009)
Usual Pagination: 68
Editor: Gilly Sinclair; **Features Editor:** Devinder Bains;
Advertising Manager: Richard Smith
Summary of Content: Magazine covering fashion, beauty,
cookery, stories, puzzles, gossip and features on the home.
Twitter: http://twitter.com/goodtoknow.
Readership/Target Audience: Aimed at women between
20 and 50 years old.
ADVERTISING RATES:
Full Page Colour £10774.00
Mechanical Data: Type Area: 267 x 207mm, Bleed Size:
290 x 228mm, Trim Size: 284 x 225mm, Col Length: 267mm,
Film: Digital, Page Width: 207mm
CONSUMER: WOMEN'S INTEREST CONSUMER
MAGAZINES: Women's Interest

CHAT IT'S FATE
1637738U94E-355
Formerly: It's Fate
Editorial Address: Blue Fin Building, 110 Southwark Street,
LONDON, SE1 0SU **Tel:** 020 3148 5000
Email: mary_bryce@ipcmedia.com
Advertising Address: As above. **Fax:** 020 3148 8160
Email: howard_jones@ipcmedia.com
Publisher: IPC Connect Ltd
Date Established: 2001
Frequency: Monthly
Cover Price: £1.90
Circulation: 75,000 (Publisher's Statement)
Usual Pagination: 76
Editor: Mary Bryce; **Features Editor:** Amanda Vlietstra;
Advertising Manager: Howard Jones
Summary of Content: Magazine covering the supernatural,
psychic, alternative healing and alternative spiritual beliefs.
Readership/Target Audience: Aimed at women aged 25 to
50 years old.
ADVERTISING RATES:
Full Page Mono £2000.00
Full Page Colour £2000.00
Mechanical Data: Film: Digital, Type Area: 267 x 207mm,
Page Width: 207mm, Col Length: 267mm
Copy instructions: Copy Date: 5 weeks prior to publication
date
CONSUMER: OTHER CLASSIFICATIONS: Paranormal

CHEERING WORDS
47771U87-40_50
Editorial Address: 22 Victoria Road, STAMFORD, PE9 1HB
Tel: 01780 763780
ISSN: 0009-2126
Publisher: Cheering Words
Date Established: 1851
Frequency: Monthly
Free to qualifying individuals
Annual Sub.: £6.65
Circulation: 4,250 (Publisher's Statement)
Usual Pagination: 16
Editor: David Oldham
Summary of Content: Evangelical Protestant magazine
covering news, views and events.
Readership/Target Audience: Aimed at Evangelical
Protestants.
ADVERTISING: No Advertising taken
CONSUMER: RELIGIOUS

CHELSEA MAGAZINE
1664051U75B-277
Editorial Address: 3rd Floor, Stamford Bridge, Fulham
Road, LONDON, SW6 1HS **Tel:** 020 7958 2168
Fax: 020 7352 2001
Email: chelsea@programmemaster.co.uk
Advertising Address: 1st Floor, Mermaid House, 2 Puddle
Dock, LONDON, EC4V 3DS **Tel:** 020 7332 2000
Fax: 020 7332 2001
Email: kevin@programmemaster.com
Web site: http://www.profilesportsmedia.com
ISSN: 1362-8364
Publisher: Programme Master Ltd
Date Established: 2004
Frequency: Monthly
Cover Price: £3.25
Free to qualifying individuals
Circulation: 64,939 (ABC 01/01/2008 to 31/12/2008)
Usual Pagination: 70
Editor: David Antill; **Advertising Manager:** Grant Levy
Summary of Content: Magazine covering fixtures, match
reports, previews, player interviews and football news.
Readership/Target Audience: Aimed at Chelsea Football
Club season ticket holders and general fans.
ADVERTISING RATES:
Full Page Colour £4950.00
Mechanical Data: Film: Digital, Type Area: 287 x 200mm,
Col Length: 287mm, Page Width: 200mm, Trim Size: 297 x
210mm, Bleed Size: 307 x 220mm
Average advertising content per issue: 30%
CONSUMER: SPORT: Football

CHERWELL
47375U83-4
Editorial Address: 7 St. Aldates, OXFORD, OX1 1BS
Tel: 01865 200322 **Fax:** 01865 200341
Email: editor@cherwell.org
Advertising Address: As above. **Tel:** 01865 246461
Email: chairman@ospl.org
Web site: http://www.cherwell.org
Publisher: Mortons Media Group Ltd
Date Established: 1920
Frequency: 24 issues yearly - Published weekly during term
time
Cover Price: Free
Circulation: 5,000 (Publisher's Statement)
Usual Pagination: 32
Editor: Theo Brainin; **Advertising Manager:** Jacob Rawel
Summary of Content: Newspaper covering news, sport, the
arts, features, opinion and debate.
Readership/Target Audience: Read by students at Oxford
University.
ADVERTISING RATES:
Full Page Colour £1080.00
Mechanical Data: Film: Digital
Copy instructions: Copy Date: 3 days prior to publication
date
Average advertising content per issue: 10%
CONSUMER: STUDENT PUBLICATIONS

CHESHAM TOWN TALK
46864U80C-398
Editorial Address: c/o The White Hill Centre, White Hill,
CHESHAM, HP5 1AG **Tel:** 01494 775190
Email: cheshamtt@aol.com
Advertising Address: As above. **Tel:** 01494 793000
Email: cheshamtt@aol.com
Web site: http://www.cheshamtowntalk.org.uk
ISSN: 1465-0991
Publisher: Town Talk Team
Date Established: 1994
Frequency: Half-yearly - Published in May and November
Cover Price: Free
Circulation: 5,000 (Publisher's Statement)
Usual Pagination: 32
Editor: Peter Hawkes; **Advertising Manager:** Sue
Hutcheson
Summary of Content: Magazine containing articles on local
interest, the environment, heritage, festivities, arts, youth,
community initiatives, health and exercise.
Readership/Target Audience: Read by people living and
working in Chesham.
ADVERTISING RATES:
Full Page Mono £300.00
Full Page Colour £500.00
Mechanical Data: Col Length: 265mm, No. of Columns
(Display): 4, Type Area: 265 x 190mm, Bleed Size: 303 x
213mm, Print Process: Litho, Trim Size: 297 x 210mm, Page
Width: 190mm, Film: Digital
Average advertising content per issue: 40%
CONSUMER: RURAL & REGIONAL INTEREST: Regional
Interest English Counties

CHESHIRE LIFE
46869U80C-600
Editorial Address: 3 Tustin Court, Port Way, PRESTON,
PR2 2YQ **Tel:** 01772 722022 **Fax:** 01772 760905
Email: enquiries@cheshirelife.co.uk
Advertising Address: As above. **Fax:** 01772 736496
Email: jackie.allen@cheshirelife.co.uk
Web site: http://www.cheshirelife.co.uk
Publisher: Archant Norfolk
Date Established: 1934
Frequency: Monthly
Cover Price: £3.20
Annual Sub.: £36.00
Circulation: 17,973 (ABC 01/01/2008 to 31/12/2008)
Usual Pagination: 240
Editor: Louise Taylor; **Advertising Manager:** Jackie Allen
Summary of Content: Magazine covering food, cookery,
dining out, fashion, gardening and property. Also features
motoring, antiques, socialising, weddings and the heritage
and agricultural interest in Cheshire.
Readership/Target Audience: Read by residents, visitors
and those with an interest in Cheshire.
ADVERTISING RATES:
Full Page Colour £2090.00
Agency Commission: 10%
Mechanical Data: Page Width: 198mm, Type Area: 275 x
198mm, Bleed Size: 306 x 226mm, Trim Size: 300 x 220mm,
Col Length: 275mm, Print Process: Sheet-fed litho, Film:
Digital
Copy instructions: Copy Date: 19th of 2 months prior to
publication date
Average advertising content per issue: 42%
CONSUMER: RURAL & REGIONAL INTEREST: Regional
Interest English Counties

CHESHIRE STYLE MAGAZINE
1827087U80C-5434
Editorial Address: 11A Ravenoak Road, Cheadle Hulme,
CHESHIRE, SK8 5LL **Tel:** 0161 486 1100
Email: cheshirestylemag@aol.com
Advertising Address: 4A Ravenoak Road, Cheadle Hulme,
CHESHIRE, SK8 7BL **Tel:** 0161 486 1100
Email: cheshirestylemag@aol.com
Web site: http://www.stylemag.co.uk
Publisher: Citizen Newspapers Ltd
Date Established: 2006
Frequency: Monthly
Cover Price: Free
Circulation: 10,000 (Publisher's Statement)
Editor: Mike Sheils
Summary of Content: Lifestyle magazine featuring travel,
what's on and interviews with personalities.
Readership/Target Audience: Aimed at readers aged 25 to
55 years old living in Cheshire.
ADVERTISING RATES:
Full Page Colour £799.00
Agency Commission: 10%
Mechanical Data: Bleed Size: 291 x 191mm, Trim Size: 285
x 185mm, Film: Digital
Copy instructions: Copy Date: 1 week prior to publication
date
Average advertising content per issue: 40%
CONSUMER: RURAL & REGIONAL INTEREST: Regional
Interest English Counties

CHESS MONTHLY
46656U79F-10
Editorial Address: 369 Euston Road, LONDON, NW1 3AR
Tel: 020 7388 2404 **Fax:** 020 7388 2407
Email: info@chess.co.uk
Advertising Address: As above.
Email: info@chess.co.uk
Web site: http://www.chess.co.uk
ISSN: 0994-6221
Publisher: Chess & Bridge Ltd
Date Established: 1927
Frequency: Monthly
Cover Price: £3.95
Annual Sub.: £39.95
Circulation: 5,500 (Publisher's Statement)
Usual Pagination: 70
Editor: Jimmy Adams; **Managing Director:** Malcolm Pein;
Advertising Manager: Matthew Read
Summary of Content: Review of the British and
international chess scene in an entertaining, illustrated style.
Covers all levels up to Grandmaster standard with full
analysis of games.
Readership/Target Audience: Aimed at club and
tournament chess players.
ADVERTISING RATES:
Full Page Colour £650.00
Agency Commission: 10%
Mechanical Data: Trim Size: 297 x 210mm, Film: Digital,
Bleed Size: 303 x 216mm
Copy instructions: Copy Date: 5th of the month prior to
publication date
Average advertising content per issue: 10%
CONSUMER: HOBBIES & DIY: Games & Puzzles

CHESSMOVES
46673U79F-11
Editorial Address: The Watch Oak, Chain Lane, BATTLE,
TN33 0YD **Tel:** 01424 775222 **Fax:** 01424 775904
Email: office@englishchess.org.uk
Advertising Address: As above. **Fax:** 01424 755904
Email: office@englishchess.org.uk
Web site: http://www.bcf.org.uk
Publisher: English Chess Federation
Frequency: 6 issues yearly
Free to qualifying individuals
Annual Sub.: £15.00
Circulation: 1,600 (Publisher's Statement)
Usual Pagination: 12
Editor: Cynthia Gurney; **Advertising Manager:** Cynthia
Gurney
Summary of Content: Magazine containing national and
international chess news for members and subscribers.
Readership/Target Audience: Aimed at chess players.
ADVERTISING RATES:
Full Page Mono £130.00
Mechanical Data: No. of Columns (Display): 3, Film: Digital
Copy instructions: Copy Date: 10th of the month prior to
publication date
CONSUMER: HOBBIES & DIY: Games & Puzzles

CHIC CHAT
1696196U80C-5280
Editorial Address: 1 Warwick Road, BEACONSFIELD, HP9
2PE **Tel:** 01494 677362 **Fax:** 01494 675385
Email: editorial@chicchat.co.uk
Advertising Address: As above.
Email: editorial@chicchat.co.uk
Web site: http://www.chicchat.co.uk
Publisher: Pison Publishing

Date Established: 2005
Frequency: Quarterly
Cover Price: £3.00
Free to qualifying individuals
Circulation: 26,000 (Publisher's Statement)
Usual Pagination: 80
Editor: Jean Dean; **Advertising Manager:** Jean Dean
Summary of Content: Lifestyle magazine covering health and beauty, travel, gardening, restaurant reviews, sport, antiques, cars and local events.
Readership/Target Audience: Aimed at affluent households in South Buckinghamshire and Chiltern area.
ADVERTISING RATES:
Full Page Colour £950.00
Agency Commission: 15%
Mechanical Data: Film: Digital, Type Area: 277 x 207mm, Bleed Size: 303 x 233mm, Trim Size: 297 x 227mm, Col Length: 277mm, Page Width: 207mm
Average advertising content per issue: 50%
CONSUMER: RURAL & REGIONAL INTEREST: Regional Interest English Counties

---

THE CHICHESTER MAGAZINE   47689U87-40_80

Editorial Address: Diocesan Church House, 211 New Church Road, HOVE, BN3 4ED **Tel:** 01273 421021
Fax: 01273 421041
Email: media@diochi.org.uk
Advertising Address: As above.
Email: lisa.williamson@diochi.org.uk
Web site: http://www.chichester.anglican.org
Publisher: Chichester Diocesan Fund and Board of Finance Inc.
Date Established: 1988
Frequency: Quarterly
Cover Price: £1.00
Annual Sub.: £6.00
Circulation: 6,000 (Publisher's Statement)
Usual Pagination: 40
Editor: David Guest; **Advertising Manager:** Lisa Williamson
Summary of Content: Magazine providing news and information for members of the Church of England, especially in East and West Sussex.
Readership/Target Audience: Aimed at Church of England families.
ADVERTISING RATES:
Full Page Mono £350.00
Full Page Colour £500.00
Agency Commission: 10%
Mechanical Data: Bleed Size: +4mm, Trim Size: 295 x 210mm, Film: Digital
Copy instructions: Copy Date: 1 month prior to publication date
Average advertising content per issue: 15%
CONSUMER: RELIGIOUS

CHILD LANGUAGE TEACHING AND THERAPY   30081U88R-15

Editorial Address: 1 Oliver's Yard, 55 City Road, LONDON, EC1Y 1SP **Tel:** 020 7324 8500 **Fax:** 020 7324 8600
Email: market@sagepub.co.uk
Advertising Address: As above.
Email: sheena.karim@sagepub.co.uk
Web site: http://clt.sagepub.com
ISSN: 0265-6590
Publisher: Sage Publications
Date Established: 1985
Frequency: 3 issues yearly - Published in February, June and October
Annual Sub.: £244.00
Editor: Judy Clegg; **Advertising Manager:** Sheena Karim
Summary of Content: Academic journal focusing on the teaching of children handicapped by an inadequate command of the spoken or written language.
Readership/Target Audience: Aimed at teachers and therapists of children with special language need or learning disabilities.
ADVERTISING RATES:
Full Page Mono £400.00
Agency Commission: 10%
Mechanical Data: Trim Size: 244 x 172mm, Screen: Mono 2 lpc Colour 60 lpc, Print Process: Sheet-fed litho, Page Width: 120mm, Film: Positive, right reading, emulsion side down. Digital, Type Area: 200 x 120mm, Col Length: 200mm
CONSUMER: EDUCATION: Education Related

CHILL OUT   48452U91D-40

Editorial Address: Napier House, 2 Auckland Park, Bond Avenue, Bletchley, MILTON KEYNES, MK1 1BU
Tel: 01908 651244 **Fax:** 01908 632214
Email: sam.giltrow@mkcitizen.co.uk
Advertising Address: As above. **Tel:** 01908 371133
Fax: 01908 371112
Email: advertising@mkcitizen.co.uk
Web site: http://www.miltonkeynes.co.uk
Publisher: Premier Newspapers
Date Established: 1992

Frequency: 3 issues yearly - Published in March, July and October
Cover Price: Free
Circulation: 25,000 (Publisher's Statement)
Usual Pagination: 28
Editor: Sue Thomas
Summary of Content: Children's magazine covering a guide to events and activities in the school holidays as well as new products, books, films, toys, environmental features, fashion, and interviews.
Readership/Target Audience: Delivered to every 8 to 12 year old in the Borough of Milton Keynes and Leighton Buzzard area.
ADVERTISING RATES:
Full Page Colour £560.00
Agency Commission: 10%
Mechanical Data: Type Area: 270 x 195mm, Col Length: 270mm, Page Width: 195mm
Copy instructions: Copy Date: 10 days prior to publication date
CONSUMER: RECREATION & LEISURE: Children & Youth

CHILTERN & THAMES RIDER   767418U81D-365

Editorial Address: Suite 108, Crystal House, New Bedford Road, LUTON, LU1 1HS **Tel:** 0870 224 1262
Email: info@chilternrider.co.uk
Advertising Address: As above.
Email: info@chilternrider.co.uk
Web site: http://www.chilternrider.co.uk
Publisher: Chiltern & Thames Rider
Date Established: 1993
Frequency: 13 issues yearly
Cover Price: £2.85
Circulation: 8,500 (Publisher's Statement)
Usual Pagination: 108
Editor: Sue Mitchell; **Advertising Manager:** Julia Beardsworth
Summary of Content: Magazine covering the latest equestrian news as well as events, equipment, clothing, vehicles, feedstuffs, grooming, medical products, training, what's on, celebrity interviews and topical features.
Readership/Target Audience: Aimed at competitive horse and pony owners and riders throughout the Thames and Chiltern areas.
ADVERTISING: Rates on application
CONSUMER: ANIMALS & PETS: Horses & Ponies

CHILTERN DISTRICT COUNCILLORS GUIDE   1686824U80C-5244

Formerly: Chiltern District Council Guide
Editorial Address: Media House, 5 Broadway Court, High Street, CHESHAM, HP5 1EG **Tel:** 01494 771144
Fax: 01494 771277
Email: info@bpcmagazines.com
Advertising Address: As above. **Tel:** 01494 771177
Email: info@bpcmagazines.com
Web site: http://www.bpcmagazines.com
Publisher: BPC Magazines
Frequency: Published every 2 years
Cover Price: Free
Circulation: 45,000 (Publisher's Statement)
Usual Pagination: 10
Editor: Stella Adams
Summary of Content: Magazine published on behalf of Chiltern District Council with information about services and council laws.
Readership/Target Audience: Aimed at the general public and businesses within the Chiltern District Council area.
ADVERTISING RATES:
Full Page Colour £850.00
Agency Commission: 10%
Mechanical Data: Type Area: 190 x 128mm, Bleed Size: 213 x 151mm, Trim Size: 210 x 148mm, Col Length: 190mm, Page Width: 128mm, Film: Digital
Copy instructions: Copy Date: 6 weeks prior to publication date
Average advertising content per issue: 20%
CONSUMER: RURAL & REGIONAL INTEREST: Regional Interest English Counties

---

CHOICE   45570U74N-40

Editorial Address: 1st Floor, 2 King Street, PETERBOROUGH, PE1 1LT **Tel:** 01733 555123
Fax: 01733 427500
Email: editorial@choicemag.co.uk
Advertising Address: Medialine, 23-25 Hockliffe Street, LEIGHTON BUZZARD, LU7 1EZ **Tel:** 0870 250 8701
Fax: 0870 250 9697
Email: anniel@medialine.eu.com
Web site: http://www.choicemag.co.uk
ISSN: 0262-2201
Publisher: Choice Publishing Ltd
Date Established: 1972
Frequency: Monthly
Cover Price: £2.70
Annual Sub.: £43.60

Circulation: 85,000 (Publisher's Statement)
Usual Pagination: 130
Editor: Norman Wright; **Advertising Manager:** Annie Lynch;
Advertisement Director: Nicky Lane; **Publisher:** Clive Nicholls
Summary of Content: Magazine providing information on new technology, computers, health, travel, hobbies, gardening, motoring, food and drink, finance and pensions.
Readership/Target Audience: Aimed at retired people and those approaching retirement. Also working men and women aged 50 and over.
ADVERTISING RATES:
Full Page Colour £4955.00
SCC £29.00
Agency Commission: 10%
Mechanical Data: Type Area: 250 X 186mm, Bleed Size: 281 X 213mm, Trim Size: 275 x 210mm, Col Length: 250mm, Page Width: 186mm
Copy instructions: Copy Date: 8 weeks prior to publication date
Average advertising content per issue: 40%
CONSUMER: WOMEN'S INTEREST CONSUMER MAGAZINES: Retirement

CHOICE DAYS OUT & ATTRACTIONS
1656960U89C-959

Formerly: Choice Museums & Attractions
Editorial Address: First Floor, 114 Cranbrook Road, ILFORD, IG1 4LZ **Tel:** 020 8554 4456 **Fax:** 020 8554 4443
Email: keeleyg@tlmags.com
Advertising Address: As above.
Email: info@tlmags.com
Web site: http://www.tlmags.com
Publisher: Travel & Leisure Magazines Ltd
Frequency: Half-yearly - Published in March and July
Cover Price: Free
Circulation: 60,000 (Publisher's Statement)
Usual Pagination: 32
Editor: Keeley Gordon; **Publisher:** Peter Lewsey
Summary of Content: Magazine covering museums, stately homes, country parks, theme parks and other attractions.
Readership/Target Audience: Aimed at residents planning days out, visitors and tourists.
ADVERTISING RATES:
Full Page Colour £1460.00
Agency Commission: 15%
Mechanical Data: Type Area: 273 x 186mm, Col Length: 273mm, Page Width: 186mm, Film: Digital, Trim Size: 297 x 210mm
Copy instructions: Copy Date: 8 weeks prior to publication date
Editions:
Choice Days Out & Attractions (Central England)
Choice Days Out & Attractions (Southern England)
CONSUMER: HOLIDAYS & TRAVEL: Entertainment Guides

CHOICE HOLIDAY PARKS & COTTAGES
1656962U89A-714

Formerly: Choice Holiday & Leisure Parks
Editorial Address: First Floor, 114 Cranbrook Road, ILFORD, IG1 4LZ **Tel:** 020 8554 4456 **Fax:** 020 8554 4443
Email: keeleyg@tlmags.com
Advertising Address: As above.
Email: jeannettec@tlmags.com
Web site: http://www.tlmags.com
Publisher: Travel & Leisure Magazines Ltd
Frequency: 3 issues yearly - Published in January, March and June
Cover Price: Free
Circulation: 60,000 (Publisher's Statement)
Usual Pagination: 32
Editor: Keeley Gordon; **Advertising Manager:** Jeannette Cumbers; **Publisher:** Peter Lewsey
Summary of Content: Magazine covering caravans and holiday homes to buy or rent throughout the UK and Europe plus local information, useful contact details, features and competitions.
Readership/Target Audience: Aimed at those planning their main holidays or a short break.
ADVERTISING RATES:
Full Page Colour £1460.00
Agency Commission: 15%
Mechanical Data: Film: Digital
Copy instructions: Copy Date: 8 weeks prior to publication date
Average advertising content per issue: 90%
CONSUMER: HOLIDAYS & TRAVEL: Travel

CHOICE VILLAS & APARTMENTS
47951U89A-90

Editorial Address: First Floor, 114 Cranbrook Road, ILFORD, IG1 4LZ **Tel:** 020 8554 4456 **Fax:** 020 8554 4443
Email: choice@tlmags.com
Advertising Address: As above.
Email: bevs@tlmags.com
Web site: http://www.tlmags.com

Consumer Magazines

Publisher: Travel & Leisure Magazines Ltd
Frequency: Quarterly
Cover Price: Free
Circulation: 50,000 (Publisher's Statement per quarter)
Usual Pagination: 56
Editor: Keeley Gordon; **Advertising Manager:** Beverley Sennett
Summary of Content: Magazine containing details of villas and apartments available for rental or buying worldwide.
Readership/Target Audience: Aimed at customers of Tesco and Sainsburys looking to book their holiday or to purchase a villa or apartment.
ADVERTISING RATES:
Full Page Colour £1460.00
Agency Commission: 10%
Mechanical Data: Type Area: 273 x 186mm, Film: Digital, Trim Size: 297 x 210mm, Bleed Size: 303 x 216mm, Col Length: 273mm, Page Width: 186mm
Copy instructions: Copy Date: 4 weeks prior to publication date
Average advertising content per issue: 60%
CONSUMER: HOLIDAYS & TRAVEL: Travel

CHOIR & ORGAN
46133U76D-285
Editorial Address: 239-241 Shaftesbury Avenue, LONDON, WC2H 8TF **Tel:** 020 7333 1745
Email: choirandorgan@rhinegold.co.uk
Advertising Address: 2nd Floor, 30 Cannon Street, LONDON, EC4M 6YJ **Tel:** 020 7618 3456
Fax: 020 7618 3483
Email: lawrence.orourke@orpheuspublications.com
Web site: http://www.choirandorgan.com
ISSN: 0968-7262
Publisher: Rhinegold Publishing Ltd
Date Established: 1993
Frequency: 6 issues yearly
Cover Price: £3.99
Circulation: 9,300 (Publisher's Statement)
Usual Pagination: 80
Editor: Maggie Hamilton; **Advertising Manager:** Lawrence O'Rourke
Summary of Content: Magazine covers all aspects of secular and sacred choral music, organs and organ music.
Readership/Target Audience: Aimed at organists, singers, conductors, composers, organ builders, professional and amateur musicians.
ADVERTISING RATES:
Full Page Colour £1150.00
Mechanical Data: Page Width: 180mm, Bleed Size: 282 x 216mm, Trim Size: 276 x 210mm, Film: Digital, Type Area: 240 x 180mm, Col Length: 240mm
CONSUMER: MUSIC & PERFORMING ARTS: Music

CHRISTIAN AID NEWS
47690U87-41
Editorial Address: PO Box 100, LONDON, SE1 7RT
Tel: 020 7620 4444 **Fax:** 020 7620 0712
Email: canews@christian-aid.org
Web site: http://www.christian-aid.org.uk
Publisher: Christian Aid
Frequency: Quarterly
Cover Price: Free
Circulation: 350,000 (Publisher's Statement)
Usual Pagination: 24
Editor: Melanie Marks; **News Editor:** Andrew Hogg
Summary of Content: Magazine containing news and features about overseas projects supported by Christian Aid, plus fundraising and campaigning activities in the UK.
Readership/Target Audience: Read by individuals, church group supporters of Christian Aid and those who are not necessarily church-going or Christian.
ADVERTISING: No Advertising taken
CONSUMER: RELIGIOUS

CHRISTIAN MARKETPLACE
765671U87-2018
Editorial Address: Broadway House, The Broadway, CROWBOROUGH, TN6 1HQ **Tel:** 01892 652658
Fax: 01892 663329
Email: christianmarketplace@premier.org.uk
Advertising Address: As above.
Email: kevin.campbell@premier.org.uk
Web site: http://www.christianmarketplace.org.uk
ISSN: 1475-5289
Publisher: CCP Ltd
Date Established: 2001
Frequency: Monthly
Cover Price: £2.50
Free to qualifying individuals
Annual Sub.: £25.00
Circulation: 2,500 (Publisher's Statement)
Usual Pagination: 56
Editor: Clem Jackson
Summary of Content: Magazine covering all aspects of Christian business including news and reviews of Christian books, music and videos.

Readership/Target Audience: Aimed at Christian retailers and booksellers, church bookstall agents, publishers and church leaders.
ADVERTISING RATES:
Full Page Colour £750.00
Agency Commission: 10%
Mechanical Data: Type Area: 270 x 186mm, Bleed Size: 303 x 216mm, Trim Size: 297 x 210mm, Col Length: 270mm, Film: Digital, Page Width: 186mm
Copy instructions: Copy Date: 12th of the month prior to publication date
Average advertising content per issue: 30%
CONSUMER: RELIGIOUS

CHRISTIANITY
47692U87-46
Formerly: Christianity + Renewal
Editorial Address: PO Box 17911, LONDON, SW1P 4YX
Tel: 020 7316 1450 **Fax:** 020 7233 6706
Email: ccp@premier.org.uk
Advertising Address: Broadway House, The Broadway, CROWBOROUGH, TN6 1HQ **Tel:** 020 7316 1456
Fax: 01892 663329
Email: candy.odonovan@premier.org.uk
Web site: http://www.christianitymagazine.co.uk
ISSN: 1365-3695
Publisher: CCP Ltd
Date Established: 2001
Frequency: Monthly
Cover Price: £3.20
Annual Sub.: £28.80
Circulation: 16,000 (Publisher's Statement)
Usual Pagination: 80
Editor: Ruth Dickinson
Summary of Content: Magazine covering Christian faith, news, features, analysis, culture, book reviews and church growth trends.
Readership/Target Audience: Read by those interested in all aspects of Christianity.
ADVERTISING RATES:
Full Page Mono £990.00
Full Page Colour £990.00
SCC £9.17
Agency Commission: 10%
Mechanical Data: Type Area: 270 x 186mm, Col Length: 270mm, Bleed Size: 303 x 216mm, Trim Size: 297 x 210mm, Page Width: 186mm, Film: Digital
Copy instructions: Copy Date: 23rd of 2 months prior to publication date
Average advertising content per issue: 30%
Supplement(s): Enough - 4xY
CONSUMER: RELIGIOUS

CHRISTIE'S MAGAZINE
47496U84A-203
Editorial Address: 8 King Street, St. James's, LONDON, SW1Y 6QT **Tel:** 020 7839 9060
Email: info@christies.com
Advertising Address: As above. **Fax:** 020 7389 2387
Email: dariel@mac.com
Web site: http://www.christies.com
ISSN: 0266-1217
Publisher: Christie's International plc
Frequency: 8 issues yearly
Cover Price: £40.00
Circulation: 25,748 (Publisher's Statement)
Usual Pagination: 218
Editor: Mandy O'Flynn; **Editor-in-Chief:** Meredith Etherington-Smith; **Advertising Manager:** Dariel Garnett; **Publisher:** Dariel Garnett
Summary of Content: Magazine covering art related subjects. Also contains information on forthcoming auctions and special events.
Readership/Target Audience: Read by affluent people aged between 35 and 64 years old.
ADVERTISING RATES:
Full Page Mono £3800.00
Full Page Colour £5500.00
Mechanical Data: Type Area: 270 x 208mm, Col Length: 270mm, Page Width: 208mm, Film: Digital, Bleed Size: 290 x 228mm, Trim Size: 280 x 218mm
Copy instructions: Copy Date: 2 months prior to publication dates
CONSUMER: THE ARTS & LITERARY: Arts

CHROMA
1655751U74Q-1196
Editorial Address: 7 Corsham Street, LONDON, N1 6DP
Tel: 020 7608 3770 **Fax:** 020 7608 3736
Email: editorial@chromagazine.co.uk
Advertising Address: As above.
Email: adsales@chromagazine.co.uk
Web site: http://www.chromagazine.co.uk
ISSN: 1740-1763
Publisher: Jealous Nosh Media Ltd
Date Established: 2004
Frequency: Half-yearly
Cover Price: £4.95
Free to qualifying individuals
Annual Sub.: £9.50

Circulation: 10,000 (Publisher's Statement)
Usual Pagination: 128
Editor: Elise Jones; **Advertising Manager:** Paul Coker
Summary of Content: Lifestyle magazine with inspirational content covering avant garde fashion, art, architecture, design, beauty, holiday destination, cars, hotels.
Readership/Target Audience: Read by affluent well-travelled people who know what they want and are prepared to pay for it.
ADVERTISING: Rates on application
CONSUMER: WOMEN'S INTEREST CONSUMER MAGAZINES: Lifestyle

THE CHRONICLE
47042U80E-35
Formerly: Craigmillar Chronicle
Editorial Address: Unit 9A, Castlebrae Business Centre, Peffer Place, EDINBURGH, EH16 4BB **Tel:** 0131 661 0791
Email: craigmillar@chronicle.org.uk
Advertising Address: As above.
Email: craigmillar@chronicle.org.uk
Publisher: Craigmillar Community Newspaper Ltd
Date Established: 2000
Frequency: Monthly
Cover Price: Free
Circulation: 7,000 (Publisher's Statement)
Usual Pagination: 12
Editor: Sally Fraser; **Advertising Manager:** Sally Fraser
Summary of Content: Publication containing local news and an events guide.
Readership/Target Audience: Aimed at the community of Craigmillar and surrounding areas.
ADVERTISING RATES:
Full Page Mono £400.00
Full Page Colour £400.00
Agency Commission: 10%
Copy instructions: Copy Date: 12th of month prior to publication date
Average advertising content per issue: 30%
CONSUMER: RURAL & REGIONAL INTEREST: Regional Interest Scotland

CHUGGINGTON
1895887U91D-982
Editorial Address: 2 Albert Square, DUNDEE, DD1 9QJ
Tel: 01382 575735
Email: aanderson@dcthomson.co.uk
Publisher: D.C. Thomson & Co Ltd
Date Established: 2009
Frequency: 17 issues yearly
Cover Price: £1.99
Editor: Alison Anderson
Summary of Content: Children's magazine based on the CBeebies tv programme Chuggington containing stories, activities, puzzles, colouring and facts and fun.
Readership/Target Audience: Aimed at pre-school children.
CONSUMER: RECREATION & LEISURE: Children & Youth

CHURCH MONUMENTS
47481U87-46_50
Editorial Address: Department of History of Art and Film, Leicester University, University Road, LEICESTER, LE1 7RH
Tel: 0116 252 2866 **Fax:** 0116 252 5128
Email: so4@leicester.ac.uk
Web site: http://www.churchmonumentssociety.org
ISSN: 0268-7511
Publisher: The Church Monuments Society
Date Established: 1985
Frequency: Annual - Published in February
Cover Price: £15.00
Free to qualifying individuals
Circulation: 600 (Publisher's Statement)
Usual Pagination: 160
Editor: John Bromilow
Summary of Content: Publication containing scholarly articles on all aspects of church monuments of all periods.
Readership/Target Audience: Aimed at those with an interest in church monuments commemoration, sculpture, history and family history.
ADVERTISING: No Advertising taken
CONSUMER: RELIGIOUS

CHURCH MUSIC QUARTERLY
46134U76D-295
Editorial Address: 19 The Close, SALIBURY, SP1 2EB
Tel: 01722 424848 **Fax:** 01722 424849
Email: cmq@rscm.com
Advertising Address: 13-17 Long Lane, LONDON, EC1A 9PN **Tel:** 020 7776 1010 **Fax:** 020 7776 1017
Email: stephen@churchtimes.co.uk
Web site: http://www.rscm.com
ISSN: 0307-6334
Publisher: The Royal School of Church Music
Date Established: 1977
Frequency: Quarterly
Free to qualifying individuals
Circulation: 15,500 (Publisher's Statement)

Usual Pagination: 56
Editor: Cathy Markall; **Advertising Manager:** Stephen Dutton
Summary of Content: Publication containing articles on church music and related topics. Includes news of courses and other activities, also carries book, music and record reviews.
Readership/Target Audience: Aimed at those who attend church or are interested in church music.
ADVERTISING RATES:
Full Page Mono £775.00
Full Page Colour £1125.00
Mechanical Data: Col Length: 262mm, Type Area: 262 x 185mm, Film: Digital, Page Width: 185mm
CONSUMER: MUSIC & PERFORMING ARTS: Music

THE CHURCH OF ENGLAND NEWSPAPER
47694U87-47
Editorial Address: 14 Great College Street, LONDON, SW1P 3RX **Tel:** 020 7878 1001 **Fax:** 020 7878 1031
Email: cen@churchnewspaper.com
Advertising Address: As above. **Tel:** 020 7417 5801
Fax: 020 7216 6410
Email: ads@churchnewspaper.com
Web site: http://www.churchnewspaper.com
ISSN: 0964-816X
Publisher: Religious Intelligence Ltd
Date Established: 1828
Frequency: Weekly
Cover Price: £1.00
Annual Sub.: £55.00
Circulation: 9,000 (Publisher's Statement)
Usual Pagination: 32
Editor: Colin Blakely; **News Editor:** Toby Cohen;
Advertising Manager: Chris Turner; **Publisher:** Keith Young
Summary of Content: Publication containing news and features on the Church nationally and internationally, plus articles on how faith affects the everyday life of Christians.
Readership/Target Audience: Read by clergy and informed laity of The Church of England.
ADVERTISING RATES:
Full Page Mono £825.00
Full Page Colour £925.00
SCC £8.00
Agency Commission: 10%
Mechanical Data: Col Length: 365mm, Type Area: 365 x 265mm, Page Width: 265mm, Film: Digital
Copy instructions: Copy Date: Monday 2pm prior to publication date
CONSUMER: RELIGIOUS

CHURCH OF ENGLAND YEAR BOOK
47787U87-48
Editorial Address: Church House, Great Smith Street, LONDON, SW1P 3AZ **Tel:** 020 7898 1451
Fax: 020 7898 1449
Advertising Address: As above.
Email: publishing@c-of-e.org.uk
Web site: http://www.chpublishing.co.uk
ISSN: 0069-3987
Publisher: Church House Publishing
Frequency: Annual - Published in December
Cover Price: £30.00
Circulation: 5,000 (Publisher's Statement)
Usual Pagination: 500
Editor: Penny Phillips; **Advertising Manager:** Tracy Somorjay
Summary of Content: Year book of the Church of England.
Readership/Target Audience: Aimed at clergy, church councils, diocesan bodies and religious organisations.
ADVERTISING: Rates on application
Copy instructions: Copy Date: September prior to publication date
CONSUMER: RELIGIOUS

CHURCH OF IRELAND GAZETTE
47695U87-50
Editorial Address: 3 Wallace Avenue, LISBURN, BT27 4AA
Tel: 028 9267 5743 **Fax:** 028 9266 7580
Email: gazette@ireland.anglican.org
Advertising Address: As above.
Email: gazette@ireland.anglican.org
Web site: http://www.gazette.ireland.anglican.org
Publisher: The Church of Ireland Press
Date Established: 1856
Frequency: Weekly
Cover Price: £0.60
Circulation: 4,500 (Publisher's Statement)
Usual Pagination: 16
Editor: Ian Ellis; **Advertising Manager:** Ella Mcloughlin
Summary of Content: Periodical covering religion and theology.
Readership/Target Audience: Aimed at the clergy and laity of The Church of Ireland.
ADVERTISING RATES:
Full Page Mono £480.00
Full Page Colour £480.00

SCC £4.80
Agency Commission: 15%
Mechanical Data: No. of Columns (Display): 4, Type Area: 250 x175mm, Col Length: 250mm, Page Width: 175mm
Copy instructions: Copy Date: Friday prior to publication date
Average advertising content per issue: 15%
CONSUMER: RELIGIOUS

CHURCH TIMES
47696U87-63
Editorial Address: 13-17 Long Lane, LONDON, EC1A 9PN
Tel: 020 7776 1060
Email: news@churchtimes.co.uk
Advertising Address: As above.
Email: stephen@churchtimes.co.uk
Web site: http://www.churchtimes.co.uk
ISSN: 0009-658X
Publisher: Hymns ancient & modern
Date Established: 1863
Frequency: Weekly
Cover Price: £1.10
Annual Sub.: £65.00
Circulation: 28,000 (Publisher's Statement)
Usual Pagination: 40
Editor: Helen Saxbee; **News Editor:** Helen Saxbee;
Features Editor: Christine Miles
Summary of Content: Magazine covering news and comments about current affairs and church events.
Readership/Target Audience: Aimed at interested churchgoers and clergy.
ADVERTISING RATES:
Full Page Mono £2335.00
Full Page Colour £2455.00
Agency Commission: 10%
Mechanical Data: Col Length: 362mm, Film: Digital, No. of Columns (Display): 5, Type Area: 362 x 262mm, Print Process: Web-fed offset litho, Page Width: 262mm, Col Widths (Display): 49mm
Copy instructions: Copy Date: 7 days prior to publication date
Average advertising content per issue: 30%
CONSUMER: RELIGIOUS

CHURCHMAN
47697U87-64
Editorial Address: Dean Wace House, 16 Rosslyn Road, WATFORD, WD18 0NY **Tel:** 01923 235111
Fax: 01923 800362
Email: churchman@churchsociety.org
Web site: http://www.churchsociety.org
ISSN: 0009-661X
Publisher: Church Society
Date Established: 1878
Frequency: Quarterly
Annual Sub.: £24.00
Circulation: 1,000 (Publisher's Statement)
Usual Pagination: 100
Editor: Gerald Bray
Summary of Content: Magazine containing articles with Anglican and conservative evangelical bias and extensive book reviews.
Readership/Target Audience: Aimed at theological libraries and students and those interested in Christian theology.
ADVERTISING: No Advertising taken
CONSUMER: RELIGIOUS

CINEWORLD UNLIMITED
1646019U76A-173
Editorial Address: BBC Customer Publishing, Tower House, Fairfax Street, BRISTOL, BS1 3BN
Tel: 0117 314 8333 **Fax:** 0117 934 9008
Email: patreid@bbccustomerpublishing.com
Advertising Address: As above. **Tel:** 0117 927 9009
Email: tomhazleton@bbccustomerpublishing.com
Web site: http://www.bbccustomerpublishing.com
Publisher: BBC Magazines Bristol
Date Established: 2003
Frequency: 10 issues yearly
Cover Price: Free
Circulation: 453,833 (Publisher's Statement)
Usual Pagination: 36
Editor: Pat Reid; **Managing Director:** Andy Marshall
Summary of Content: Magazine featuring reviews of the latest films, star interviews and director profiles.
Readership/Target Audience: Aimed at customers of Cineworld cinemas.
ADVERTISING RATES:
Full Page Colour £6000.00
Agency Commission: 10%
Mechanical Data: Type Area: 265 x 190mm, Bleed Size: 286 x 211mm, Trim Size: 280 x 205mm, Col Length: 265mm, Page Width: 190mm, Film: Digital
Average advertising content per issue: 35%
CONSUMER: MUSIC & PERFORMING ARTS: Cinema

CIP
47943U88E-12
Editorial Address: Swyddfa'r Urdd, Llanbadarn Road, ABERYSTWYTH, SY23 1EY **Tel:** 01970 613118
Fax: 01970 626120
Email: cip@urdd.org
Advertising Address: As above.
Email: cip@urdd.org
Web site: http://www.urdd.org
ISSN: 1350-8547
Publisher: Urdd Gobaith Cymru
Date Established: 1892
Frequency: 10 issues yearly - Published from September to June
Cover Price: £1.00
Annual Sub.: £10.00
Circulation: 3,000 (Publisher's Statement)
Usual Pagination: 20
Editor: Sian Eleri Davies; **Advertising Manager:** Sian Eleri Davies
Summary of Content: Magazine covering news, gossip, features and competitions.
Language(s): Welsh
Readership/Target Audience: Aimed at Welsh speaking children between the ages of 7 and 11.
ADVERTISING RATES:
Full Page Mono £200.00
Full Page Colour £260.00
Copy instructions: Copy Date: 3 weeks prior to publication date
Average advertising content per issue: 10%
CONSUMER: EDUCATION: Preparatory & Junior Education

CITY
1696119U80C-5390
Editorial Address: Municipal Buildings, Dale Street, LIVERPOOL, L69 2DH **Tel:** 0151 233 3000
Email: damian.richards-clarke@liverpool.gov.uk
Advertising Address: Brodie Publishing Ltd, 2 Century Building, Tower Street, Brunswick Business Park, LIVERPOOL, L3 4BJ **Tel:** 0151 707 2323
Fax: 0151 707 2424
Email: jonathan.bedford@brodiepublishing.com
Web site: http://www.liverpool.gov.uk
Publisher: Liverpool City Council
Frequency: 6 issues yearly
Cover Price: Free
Circulation: 228,000 (Publisher's Statement)
Usual Pagination: 40
Editor: Damian Richards-Clarke
Summary of Content: Magazine covering community news, what's on.
Readership/Target Audience: Aimed at households and businesses in Liverpool.
ADVERTISING RATES:
Full Page Colour £2495.00
Agency Commission: 10%
Mechanical Data: Type Area: 274 x 183mm, Bleed Size: + 3mm, Trim Size: 297 x 210mm, Col Length: 274mm, Page Width: 183mm, Print Process: Web-fed litho, Film: Positive, right reading, emulsion side down. Digital
Average advertising content per issue: 25%
CONSUMER: RURAL & REGIONAL INTEREST: Regional Interest English Counties

CITY CENTRE NEWS
1824607U80E-378
Editorial Address: For all contact details see main edition, Southside News
Frequency: Monthly
Cover Price: Free
Circulation: 20,000 (Publisher's Statement)
Edition of: Southside News
CONSUMER: RURAL & REGIONAL INTEREST: Regional Interest Scotland

CITY LIFE
1666203U89D-514
Editorial Address: Publishing House, 3 Bridgebank Industrial Estate, Taylor Street, Horwich, BOLTON, BL6 7PD
Tel: 0161 909 0909 **Fax:** 0161 909 0919
Email: jonathan.richards@bigspark.co.uk
Advertising Address: As above.
Email: tony@bigsparkpublishing.co.uk
Publisher: The Big Spark
Date Established: 2001
Frequency: Quarterly
Cover Price: Free
Circulation: 8,000 (Publisher's Statement)
Usual Pagination: 52
Editor: Jonathan Richards; **Managing Director:** Stuart Parker
Summary of Content: Lifestyle magazine covering celebrity interviews, car tests, financial pages and destinations.
Readership/Target Audience: Aimed at in-coming and out-going passengers using Belfast City Airport.
ADVERTISING RATES:
Full Page Colour £950.00
Agency Commission: 10%

Mechanical Data: Type Area: 275 x 190mm, Bleed Size: 307 x 220mm, Trim Size: 297 x 210mm, Col Length: 275mm, Page Width: 190mm, Film: Digital
Copy instructions: Copy Date: 11 days prior to publication date
CONSUMER: HOLIDAYS & TRAVEL: In-Flight Magazines

CITY LIFE & COUNTY LIVING MAGAZINE (EAST MIDLANDS)
1663455U80C-5200
Formerly: City Life Magazine (East Midlands)
Editorial Address: Halifax House, Halifax Place, NOTTINGHAM, NG1 1QN Tel: 0115 924 2433
Fax: 0115 924 3433
Email: editorial@citylifemedia.com
Advertising Address: As above.
Email: rb@citylifemedia.com
Web site: http://www.citylifemedia.com
Publisher: City Life Media Ltd
Date Established: 2003
Frequency: Quarterly
Cover Price: Free
Circulation: 125,000 (Publisher's Statement)
Usual Pagination: 132
Editor: Nick Smith; Advertising Manager: Richard Bushell
Summary of Content: Magazine covering fashion, what's on, property, motoring, bars, restaurants, home, furnishings, shopping, lifestyle and much more.
Readership/Target Audience: Aimed at residents and visitors to the East Midlands.
ADVERTISING: Rates on application
Agency Commission: 15%
Mechanical Data: Trim Size: 297 x 210mm, Bleed Size: 303 x 216mm, Film: Digital
Copy instructions: Copy Date: 2 weeks prior to publication date
Average advertising content per issue: 50%
Editions:
City Life & County Living Magazine (Northamptonshire)
City Life & County Living Magazine (Derbyshire)
City Life & County Living Magazine (Leicestershire)
City Life & County Living Magazine (Lincolnshire)
City Life & County Living Magazine (Nottinghamshire)
CONSUMER: RURAL & REGIONAL INTEREST: Regional Interest English Counties

THE CITY MAGAZINE
1773018U74Q-1324
Formerly: E1 City Life
Editorial Address: 16 Heron Quay, Canary Wharf, LONDON, E14 4JB Tel: 020 7987 4320 Fax: 020 7005 0045
Email: le@runwildmedia.com
Advertising Address: As above. Tel: 020 7005 0044
Email: zt@runwildmedia.com
Web site: http://www.runwildmedia.com
Publisher: Run Wild Media - London
Date Established: 2007
Frequency: Monthly
Cover Price: Free
Circulation: 75,000 (Publisher's Statement)
Usual Pagination: 140
Editor: Lesley Ellwood; Advertising Director: Zainab Talati
Summary of Content: Lifestyle magazine covering topics such as fashion, beauty, entertainment, motoring, lifestyle, property, food, drink, shopping and events.
Readership/Target Audience: Aimed at high earners in The City, N1, E1 and WC1 areas of London.
ADVERTISING RATES:
Full Page Colour £2950.00
Mechanical Data: Bleed Size: 303 x 216mm, Trim Size: 297 x 210mm, Film: Digital
Copy instructions: Copy Date: 2 weeks prior to publication date
CONSUMER: WOMEN'S INTEREST CONSUMER MAGAZINES: Lifestyle

CITY MATCHDAY MAGAZINE
45745U75B-82
Editorial Address: Walkers Stadium, Filbert Way, LEICESTER, LE2 7FL Tel: 0116 229 4923
Fax: 0116 229 4549
Email: scott.renshaw@lcfc.co.uk
Advertising Address: As above. Tel: 0116 229 4536
Fax: 0116 291 1254
Email: lcfccorporatesales@lcfc.co.uk
Web site: http://www.lcfc.com
Publisher: Leicester City Football Club
Frequency: 24 issues yearly - During football season
Cover Price: £3.00
Annual Sub.: £70.00
Circulation: 11,000 (Publisher's Statement)
Usual Pagination: 80
Editor: Scott Renshaw
Summary of Content: Magazine relating to Leicester City Football Club home matches.
Readership/Target Audience: Aimed at Leicester City fans.
ADVERTISING RATES:
Full Page Mono £350.00
Full Page Colour £350.00

Mechanical Data: Page Width: 170mm, Type Area: 240 x 170mm, Col Length: 240mm, Film: Digital
CONSUMER: SPORT: Football

CITY MATTERS
1834013U80F-209
Editorial Address: 3 Wellington Park, Malone Road, BELFAST, BT9 6DJ Tel: 028 9092 3347 Fax: 028 9092 3348
Email: copy@bpcmagazines.com
Advertising Address: As above.
Email: info@bpcmagazines.com
Web site: http://www.belfastcity.gov.uk/citymatters/index.asp
Publisher: Business Publication Company (NI) Ltd
Frequency: Quarterly
Cover Price: Free
Circulation: 64,081 (Publisher's Statement)
Usual Pagination: 40
Editor: Alex Wright; Advertising Manager: Sarah Logue
Summary of Content: Magazine covering useful telephone numbers for contacting council departments, an events section, competition and features on current and future improvements happening in Belfast.
Readership/Target Audience: Aimed primarily at residents of Belfast City as well as visitors to the Belfast area.
ADVERTISING RATES:
Full Page Colour £5500.00
Agency Commission: 10%
Mechanical Data: Type Area: 267 x 188mm, Bleed Size: 303 x 216mm, Trim Size: 297 x 210mm, Col Length: 188mm, Col Widths (Display): 58, No. of Columns (Display): 3, Page Width: 188mm, Film: Digital
Copy instructions: Copy Date: 4 weeks prior to publication date
Average advertising content per issue: 25%
CONSUMER: RURAL & REGIONAL INTEREST: Regional Interest Northern Ireland

CITYLIFE
623191U80C-2450
Editorial Address: Room 161, Civic Centre, Barras Bridge, NEWCASTLE UPON TYNE, NE99 2BN Tel: 0191 211 5093
Fax: 0191 211 4888
Email: citylife@newcastle.gov.uk
Advertising Address: As above. Tel: 0191 232 8520
Email: julie.knox@newcastle.gov.uk
Web site: http://www.newcastle.gov.uk/citylife
Publisher: Newcastle City Council
Date Established: 1999
Frequency: 6 issues yearly
Cover Price: Free
Circulation: 145,000 (Publisher's Statement)
Usual Pagination: 44
Editor: Nadine Aston; Advertising Manager: Julie Knox
Summary of Content: Magazine covering news and information from Newcastle City Council.
Readership/Target Audience: Aimed at Newcastle residents and people who work in or visit the city.
ADVERTISING RATES:
Full Page Colour £2000.00
Agency Commission: 10%
CONSUMER: RURAL & REGIONAL INTEREST: Regional Interest English Counties

THE CIVIL SERVICE PENSIONER
45571U74N-60
Editorial Address: 9 North Holmes Close, HORSHAM, RH12 4HB Tel: 01403 250251
Email: editor@cspa.co.uk
Advertising Address: 1st Floor, 102-104 Park Lane, CROYDON, CR0 1JB Tel: 020 8688 8418
Fax: 020 8760 9806
Email: advertising@cspa.co.uk
Web site: http://www.cspa.co.uk
ISSN: 1360-3132
Publisher: Civil Service Pensioners' Alliance
Date Established: 1953
Frequency: Quarterly
Cover Price: Free
Circulation: 53,000 (Publisher's Statement)
Usual Pagination: 80
Editor: Ralph Groves; Advertising Manager: Darlene Vendryes
Summary of Content: Guide covering all aspects to successful living on an index-linked pension.
Readership/Target Audience: Read by civil servants and others in similar pension schemes.
ADVERTISING RATES:
Full Page Mono £585.00
Full Page Colour £760.00
Agency Commission: 10%
Mechanical Data: Page Width: 130mm, Film: Digital, Trim Size: 206 x 149mm, Bleed Size: 212 x 152mm, Print Process: Offset, Type Area: 190 x 130mm, Col Length: 190mm

Copy instructions: Copy Date: 8 weeks prior to publication date
CONSUMER: WOMEN'S INTEREST CONSUMER MAGAZINES: Retirement

CIVIL SERVICE WORLD
1696779U82-269
Formerly: Whitehall & Westminster World
Editorial Address: Westminster Tower, 3rd Floor, 3 Albert Embankment, LONDON, SE1 7SP Tel: 020 7091 7500
Fax: 020 7091 7525
Email: editorial@civilserviceworld.com
Advertising Address: As above. Tel: 020 7091 7600
Email: leo.caporali@dods.co.uk
Web site: http://www.civilservicenetwork.com
Publisher: Dods
Date Established: 2005
Frequency: 26 issues yearly
Free to qualifying individuals
Circulation: 7,510 (ABC 01/07/2007 to 30/06/2008)
Usual Pagination: 48
Editor: Matt Ross
Summary of Content: Magazine published for the upper ranks of the civil service, covering policy and management issues.
Readership/Target Audience: Aimed at senior civil servants and MPs.
ADVERTISING RATES:
Full Page Colour £6320.00
Agency Commission: 10%
Mechanical Data: Type Area: 365 x 265mm, Col Length: 365mm, Page Width: 265mm, Film: Digital
Copy instructions: Copy Date: 5 days prior to publication date
Average advertising content per issue: 30%
CONSUMER: CURRENT AFFAIRS & POLITICS

CIVVY STREET
1841579U88C-185
Editorial Address: 15-39 Durham Street, Kinning Park, GLASGOW, G41 1BS Tel: 0141 419 0044
Fax: 0141 419 0077
Email: paul@cravenpublishing.co.uk
Advertising Address: As above.
Web site: http://www.civvystreetmagazine.co.uk
ISSN: 1746-8426
Publisher: Craven Publishing Ltd
Frequency: 6 issues yearly
Cover Price: Free
Circulation: 25,000 (Publisher's Statement)
Usual Pagination: 68
Editor: Paul Cockburn
Summary of Content: Magazine covering resettlement and careers.
Readership/Target Audience: Aimed at members of British Armed Forces personnel returning to civilian life.
CONSUMER: EDUCATION: Careers

CLARINET & SAXOPHONE
46135U76D-300
Editorial Address: Y Fron, Llansadwrn, MENAI BRIDGE, LL59 5SL Tel: 01248 811285
Email: editor@cassgb.org
Advertising Address: As above. Fax: 01248 811285
Email: advertising@cassgb.org
Web site: http://www.cassgb.co.uk
ISSN: 0260-390X
Publisher: Clarinet & Saxophone Society (CASS)
Date Established: 1980
Frequency: Quarterly
Free to qualifying individuals
Annual Sub.: £24.00
Circulation: 2,100 (Publisher's Statement)
Usual Pagination: 68
Editor: Richard Edwards; Advertising Manager: Richard Edwards
Summary of Content: Magazine featuring new music, records, concerts and new instruments. Also includes general articles on players.
Readership/Target Audience: Aimed at clarinet and saxophone players, professionals and teachers.
ADVERTISING RATES:
Full Page Mono £320.00
Full Page Colour £390.00
Mechanical Data: Type Area: 265 x 182mm, Bleed Size: 303 x 216mm, Trim Size: 297 x 210mm, Film: Digital, Col Length: 265mm, Page Width: 182mm
Average advertising content per issue: 33%
CONSUMER: MUSIC & PERFORMING ARTS: Music

CLASH
1641679U76D-77
Editorial Address: 143C Nethergate, DUNDEE, DD1 4DP
Tel: 01382 870870
Email: info@clashmusic.com
Advertising Address: As above. Tel: 01382 808808
Fax: 01382 909909
Email: john@clashmagazine.com

Web site: http://www.clashmagazine.com
ISSN: 1743-0801
Publisher: Clash Magazine Ltd.
Date Established: 2004
Frequency: Monthly
Cover Price: £3.80
Circulation: 30,000 (Publisher's Statement)
Usual Pagination: 142
Editor: Simon Harper; **Advertising Manager:** John O'Rourke; **Publisher:** John O'Rourke
Summary of Content: Magazine covering music, fashion and lifestyle, DVDs and live reviews.
Readership/Target Audience: Aimed at 18 to 35 year old music savvy, culture conscious people.
ADVERTISING RATES:
Full Page Colour £1750.00
Agency Commission: 10%
Mechanical Data: Bleed Size: 286 x 251mm, Trim Size: 280 x 245mm
Copy instructions: Copy Date: 16th of the month prior to publication date
Average advertising content per issue: 20%
CONSUMER: MUSIC & PERFORMING ARTS: Music

CLASSIC AMERICAN
46499U77R-18

Editorial Address: Optimum House, Clippers Quay, Salford Quays, SALFORD, M50 3XP **Tel:** 0161 877 9977
Fax: 0161 872 6238
Email: email@classic-american.com
Advertising Address: As above.
Email: nick.noone@classic-american.com
Web site: http://www.classic-american.com
ISSN: 0957-2406
Publisher: Trader Media Publishing
Date Established: 1988
Frequency: Monthly
Cover Price: £3.95
Annual Sub.: £30.00
Circulation: 25,000 (Publisher's Statement)
Usual Pagination: 156
Editor: Ben Klemenzson
Summary of Content: Magazine dedicated to the pleasure of owning and driving an American automobile, from pre-war classics to current hi-tech models.
Readership/Target Audience: Aimed at American car enthusiasts.
ADVERTISING RATES:
Full Page Colour £670.00
Agency Commission: 10%
Mechanical Data: Page Width: 190mm, Bleed Size: 303 x 216mm, Trim Size: 297 x 210mm, Film: Digital, Type Area: 277 x 190mm, Col Length: 277mm
Copy instructions: Copy Date: 2 weeks prior to publication date
Average advertising content per issue: 50%
CONSUMER: MOTORING & CYCLING: Motoring & Cycling Related

CLASSIC & SPORTS CAR
46493U77F-45

Editorial Address: Teddington Studios, Broom Road, TEDDINGTON, TW11 9BE **Tel:** 020 8267 5000
Fax: 020 8267 5318
Email: letters.classicandsportscar@haynet.com
Advertising Address: As above. **Tel:** 020 8267 5377
Fax: 020 8267 5312
Email: ben.guynan@haymarket.com
Web site: http://www.classicandsportscar.com
ISSN: 0263-3183
Publisher: Haymarket Media Group Ltd
Date Established: 1982
Frequency: Monthly
Cover Price: £4.20
Annual Sub.: £43.20
Circulation: 73,079 (ABC 01/01/2009 to 30/06/2009)
Usual Pagination: 245
Editor: James Elliott; **Editor-in-Chief:** Mick Walsh; **Managing Director:** Kevin Costello; **Advertising Director:** Ben Guynan
Summary of Content: Magazine containing features on buying, maintaining and restoring cars.
Readership/Target Audience: Aimed at classic and sportscar enthusiasts.
ADVERTISING RATES:
Full Page Colour £4064.00
Agency Commission: 10%
Mechanical Data: Bleed Size: 301 x 226mm, Trim Size: 295 x 220mm, Film: Digital, Type Area: 275 x 200mm, Col Length: 275mm, Page Width: 200mm
Copy instructions: Copy Date: 4 weeks prior to publication date
Average advertising content per issue: 50%
CONSUMER: MOTORING & CYCLING: Veteran Cars

CLASSIC AND VINTAGE COMMERCIALS
46494U77F-48

Editorial Address: Cudham Tithe Barn, Berrys Hill, Berrys Green, Cudham, WESTERHAM, TN16 3AG
Tel: 01733 347776 **Fax:** 01959 541400
Email: cvc.ed@kelsey.co.uk
Advertising Address: 1st Floor, South Wing, Broadway Court, Broadway, PETERBOROUGH, PE1 1RP
Tel: 01959 541444 **Fax:** 01959 541400
Email: matt.carson@kelseypb.co.uk
Web site: http://www.kelsey.co.uk
Publisher: Kelsey Publishing Ltd
Date Established: 1996
Frequency: Monthly
Cover Price: £3.60
Annual Sub.: £38.40
Circulation: 20,108 (ABC 01/01/2008 to 31/12/2008)
Editor: Ted Connolly; **Managing Director:** Stephen Wright;
Publisher: Matt Carson
Summary of Content: Magazine containing features on restoration projects, as well as auction reports and events related to classic and vintage commercials.
Readership/Target Audience: Read by owners of classic and vintage commercial vehicles.
ADVERTISING RATES:
Full Page Mono £500.00
Full Page Colour £800.00
Agency Commission: 10%
Mechanical Data: Type Area: 272 x 188mm, Col Length: 272mm, Page Width: 188mm, Bleed Size: 303 x 216mm, Film: Digital, Trim Size: 297 x 210mm
Copy instructions: Copy Date: 4 weeks prior to publication date
CONSUMER: MOTORING & CYCLING: Veteran Cars

CLASSIC ANGLING
628983U92-45

Editorial Address: PMA House, Free Church Passage, ST. IVES, PE27 5AY **Tel:** 01480 463565 **Fax:** 01480 496022
Email: angling@classictitles.com
Advertising Address: As above.
Email: hayley@classictitles.com
Web site: http://www.classictitles.com
Publisher: Classic Titles
Date Established: 1999
Frequency: 6 issues yearly
Cover Price: £6.00
Annual Sub.: £30.00
Circulation: 2,900 (Publisher's Statement)
Usual Pagination: 56
Editor: Keith Elliott; **Advertising Manager:** Hayley Coulter
Summary of Content: International magazine covering vintage and collectable fishing tackle, art, books and the history of angling.
Readership/Target Audience: Aimed at Worldwide collectors of vintage fishing tackle and those interested in fishing history, books and art.
ADVERTISING RATES:
Full Page Colour £800.00
Agency Commission: 15%
Mechanical Data: Page Width: 185mm, No. of Columns (Display): 4, Type Area: 250 x 185mm, Col Length: 250mm, Trim Size: 297 x 210mm, Film: Digital
Copy instructions: Copy Date: 15th of the month prior to publication date
Average advertising content per issue: 20%
CONSUMER: ANGLING & FISHING

CLASSIC BIKE
46353U77B-490

Editorial Address: Media House, Lynchwood, Peterborough Business Park, PETERBOROUGH, PE2 6EA
Tel: 01733 468188 **Fax:** 01733 468466
Email: classic.bike@bauermedia.co.uk
Advertising Address: As above. **Tel:** 01733 468067
Fax: 01733 468867
Email: sarah.nunn@bauerconsumer.co.uk
ISSN: 0959-7123
Publisher: Bauer Consumer Media Ltd (Media House)
Date Established: 1978
Frequency: Monthly
Cover Price: £3.50
Circulation: 40,647 (ABC 01/01/2008 to 31/12/2008)
Usual Pagination: 116
Summary of Content: Magazine covering classic and thoroughbred motorcycles from the 1950s to the 1980s, including Japanese machines.
Readership/Target Audience: Aimed at classic motorcycle enthusiasts.
ADVERTISING RATES:
Full Page Colour £1919.00
Agency Commission: 10%
Mechanical Data: Page Width: 184mm, Trim Size: 297 x 210mm, Bleed Size: 303 x 214mm, Type Area: 267 x 184mm, Film: Digital, Col Length: 267mm
Copy instructions: Copy Date: 4 weeks prior to publication date
CONSUMER: MOTORING & CYCLING: Motorcycling

THE CLASSIC BIKE GUIDE
46354U77B-491

Editorial Address: PO Box 99, HORNCASTLE, LN9 6LZ
Tel: 01507 529300 **Fax:** 01507 529495
Email: nclark@mortons.co.uk
Advertising Address: Media Centre, Morton Way, HORNCASTLE, LN9 6JR **Tel:** 01507 524004
Fax: 01507 529499
Email: sfisher@mortons.co.uk
Web site: http://www.classicbikeguide.com
ISSN: 0959-7123
Publisher: Mortons Media Group Ltd
Frequency: Monthly
Cover Price: £3.50
Circulation: 42,000 (Publisher's Statement)
Usual Pagination: 132
Editor: Nigel Clark; **Advertising Manager:** Sandra Fisher
Summary of Content: Guide to owning and riding mainly British, with some European, American and an occasional Japanese classic motorcycle. Includes specification guides and articles on restoration, servicing and maintenance.
Readership/Target Audience: Read by classic motorcycle enthusiasts.
ADVERTISING RATES:
Full Page Colour £1250.00
Agency Commission: 10%
Mechanical Data: Col Length: 270mm, Type Area: 270 x 188mm, Bleed Size: 307.5 x 220mm, Trim Size: 297.5 x 210mm, Page Width: 188mm, No. of Columns (Display): 4, Col Widths (Display): 42mm, Film: Digital
Average advertising content per issue: 30%
CONSUMER: MOTORING & CYCLING: Motorcycling

CLASSIC BOAT MAGAZINE
48371U91A-28

Editorial Address: Leon House, 233 High Street, CROYDON, CR9 1HZ **Tel:** 020 8726 8000
Fax: 020 8726 8195
Email: cb@ipcmedia.com
Advertising Address: As above.
Email: jenny_evanson@ipcmedia.com
Web site: http://www.classicboat.co.uk
ISSN: 0950-3315
Publisher: IPC Inspire
Date Established: 1987
Frequency: Monthly
Cover Price: £4.40
Circulation: 12,658 (ABC 01/01/2008 to 31/12/2008)
Usual Pagination: 116
Editor: Dan Houston; **Advertising Manager:** Jenny Evanson
Summary of Content: Magazine covering vintage craft and traditionally styled new boats, power and sail, large and small. Also contains technical articles, boat tests and product reviews.
Readership/Target Audience: Aimed at the classic boat enthusiast.
ADVERTISING RATES:
Full Page Colour £2285.00
Agency Commission: 10%
Mechanical Data: Type Area: 271 x 186mm, Bleed Size: 303 x 216mm, Trim Size: 297 x 210mm, Col Length: 271mm, Page Width: 186mm, Film: Digital
Copy instructions: Copy Date: 2nd Friday of the month prior to publication date
Average advertising content per issue: 30%
CONSUMER: RECREATION & LEISURE: Boating & Yachting

CLASSIC BUS
46777U79R-13

Editorial Address: 15 Starfield Road, LONDON, W12 9SN
Email: ed@classicbusmag.co.uk
Advertising Address: As above.
Email: ed@classicbusmag.co.uk
ISSN: 0966-8438
Publisher: Classic Bus Ltd
Date Established: 1992
Frequency: 6 issues yearly
Cover Price: £3.70
Circulation: 12,000 (Publisher's Statement)
Usual Pagination: 56
Editor: Ray Stenning; **Advertising Manager:** Ray Stenning
Summary of Content: Magazine containing nostalgic articles on older motorbuses and trolleybuses.
Readership/Target Audience: Aimed at bus enthusiasts and transport students.
ADVERTISING: Rates on application
Copy instructions: Copy Date: 6 weeks prior to publication date
CONSUMER: HOBBIES & DIY: Hobbies & DIY Related

CLASSIC CAR MART
46489U77F-51

Editorial Address: Alliance House, 49 Sidney Street, CAMBRIDGE, CB2 3HX **Tel:** 01223 460490
Fax: 01223 315960
Email: keith@classic-car-mart.co.uk
Advertising Address: As above.
Email: jody@sportsboat.co.uk
Web site: http://www.classic-car-mart.co.uk
Publisher: CSL Publishing Ltd

Consumer Magazines

Date Established: 1993
Frequency: 13 issues yearly
Cover Price: £3.50
Annual Sub.: £34.00
Circulation: 11,733 (ABC 01/01/2008 to 31/12/2008)
Usual Pagination: 242
Editor: Keith Moody; **Managing Director:** Sue Baggaley
Summary of Content: Magazine with features on classic cars. Includes information on spare parts and servicing.
Readership/Target Audience: Aimed at classic and specialist car enthusiasts.
ADVERTISING: Rates on application
Agency Commission: 10%
Copy instructions: Copy Date: 2 weeks prior to publication date
CONSUMER: MOTORING & CYCLING: Veteran Cars

CLASSIC CAR WEEKLY   46490U77F-55
Editorial Address: PO Box 978, PETERBOROUGH, PE1 9FL **Tel:** 01733 347559 **Fax:** 01733 557235
Email: ccw.ed@kelseypb.co.uk
Advertising Address: 1st Floor, South Wing, Broadway Court, Broadway, PETERBOROUGH, PE1 1RP
Tel: 01733 347559 **Fax:** 01733 891342
Email: sarah.garrod@kelseypb.co.uk
Web site: http://www.classic-car-weekly.co.uk
Publisher: Kelsey Publishing Ltd
Date Established: 1990
Frequency: Weekly
Cover Price: £2.20
Circulation: 24,468 (ABC 01/01/2008 to 31/12/2008)
Usual Pagination: 60
Editor: Peter Simpson; **Advertising Manager:** Sarah Garrod
Summary of Content: Newspaper containing news and features on the buying and selling of classic cars, plus other features of interest to classic car owners.
Readership/Target Audience: Aimed at classic car enthusiasts.
ADVERTISING RATES:
Full Page Colour £900.00
SCC £4.00
Agency Commission: 10%
Mechanical Data: Type Area: 340 x 260mm, Col Length: 340mm, Page Width: 260mm, Film: Digital
Copy instructions: Copy Date: 1 week prior to publication date
Average advertising content per issue: 55%
CONSUMER: MOTORING & CYCLING: Veteran Cars

CLASSIC CARS   46491U77F-400
Formerly: Thoroughbred & Classic Cars
Editorial Address: Media House, Lynchwood, Peterborough Business Park, PETERBOROUGH, PE2 6EA
Tel: 01733 468000 **Fax:** 01733 468888
Email: classic.cars@bauerconsumer.co.uk
Advertising Address: As above. **Fax:** 01733 468228
Email: louise.rizzo@bauermedia.co.uk
Web site: http://www.classiccarsmagazine.co.uk
ISSN: 0143-7267
Publisher: Bauer Consumer Media Ltd (Media House)
Date Established: 1973
Frequency: Monthly
Cover Price: £4.20
Circulation: 35,564 (ABC 01/01/2009 to 30/06/2009)
Usual Pagination: 220
Editor: Mike Goodbun; **Advertising Manager:** Louise Rizzo
Summary of Content: Magazine containing news, practical, historical and driving features, also details of classic car runs and events.
Readership/Target Audience: Aimed at classic car enthusiasts between 15 and 55 years old.
ADVERTISING RATES:
Full Page Colour £3578.00
Agency Commission: 10%
Mechanical Data: Type Area: 252 x 184mm, Bleed Size: +3mm, Trim Size: 297 x 210mm, Col Length: 252mm, Page Width: 184mm, Film: Digital
Average advertising content per issue: 50%
CONSUMER: MOTORING & CYCLING: Veteran Cars

CLASSIC CARS FOR SALE   624636U77F-53
Editorial Address: 2nd Floor, Ewer House, 44-46 Crouch Street, COLCHESTER, CO3 3HH **Tel:** 01206 506250
Fax: 01206 500180
Email: bradcamanderson@aol.com
Advertising Address: As above.
Email: jo.kelshaw@mspublications.co.uk
Web site: http://www.classiccars4sale.net/
Publisher: MS Publications (2001) Ltd
Date Established: 2000
Frequency: Monthly
Cover Price: £3.10
Annual Sub.: £29.16
Circulation: 32,000 (Publisher's Statement)
Editor: Alan Anderson; **Advertising Manager:** Jo Kelshaw

Summary of Content: Magazine containing articles on classic cars. Includes features on auctions, events, museums and information on buying and selling classic cars, their components and accessories.
Readership/Target Audience: Aimed at those with an interest in classic cars.
ADVERTISING RATES:
Full Page Colour £510.00
Agency Commission: 10%
Mechanical Data: Page Width: 190mm, Type Area: 270 x 190mm, Col Length: 270mm, Trim Size: 297 x 210mm, Bleed Size: 307 x 220mm, Film: Digital
Copy instructions: Copy Date: 2 weeks prior to publication date
Average advertising content per issue: 75%
CONSUMER: MOTORING & CYCLING: Veteran Cars

CLASSIC DIRTBIKE MAGAZINE
1825297U77B-723
Editorial Address: Media Centre, Morton Way, HORNCASTLE, LN9 6JR **Tel:** 01507 529529
Fax: 01507 529495
Email: tbritton@mortons.co.uk
Advertising Address: As above. **Fax:** 01507 529499
Email: jkane@mortons.co.uk
Web site: http://www.classicdirtbike.co.uk
Publisher: Mortons Media Group Ltd
Date Established: 2006
Frequency: Quarterly
Cover Price: £4.99
Circulation: 10,000 (Publisher's Statement)
Usual Pagination: 84
Editor: Tim Britton
Summary of Content: Magazine covering trials, motocross and enduros from pre-65 to twin shock eras with events, features, historical profiles, interviews and bike tests.
Readership/Target Audience: Aimed at fans of classic and twin shock trails, motocross and enduros.
ADVERTISING RATES:
Full Page Colour £824.00
Agency Commission: 15%
Mechanical Data: Type Area: 270 x 188mm, Bleed Size: 307 x 220mm, Trim Size: 297 x 210mm, Col Length: 270mm, Page Width: 188mm, Film: Digital
Average advertising content per issue: 8.4%
CONSUMER: MOTORING & CYCLING: Motorcycling

CLASSIC FM MAGAZINE   45630U74Q-110
Editorial Address: Teddington Studios, Broom Road, TEDDINGTON, TW11 9BE **Tel:** 020 8267 5180
Fax: 020 8267 5150
Email: classicfm@haymarket.com
Advertising Address: As above. **Tel:** 020 8267 5000
Fax: 020 8267 5850
Email: sandra.spencer@haymarket.com
Web site: http://www.classicfm.com
ISSN: 1356-2592
Publisher: Haymarket Consumer Media
Date Established: 1995
Frequency: Monthly
Cover Price: £4.50
Annual Sub.: £45.99
Circulation: 35,751 (ABC 01/01/2008 to 31/12/2008)
Usual Pagination: 100
Editor: Sarah Kirkup; **Managing Director:** Kevin Costello
Summary of Content: Music magazine with a lifestyle slant including listings for Classic FM and presenter reviews.
Readership/Target Audience: Aimed at Classic FM listeners and classical music lovers.
ADVERTISING RATES:
Full Page Colour £4433.00
Agency Commission: 10%
Mechanical Data: Type Area: 254 x 190mm, Trim Size: 278 x 215mm, Bleed Size: 284 x 221mm, Col Length: 254mm, Film: Digital, Page Width: 190mm
Copy instructions: Copy Date: 4 weeks prior to publication date
CONSUMER: WOMEN'S INTEREST CONSUMER MAGAZINES: Lifestyle

CLASSIC FORD   46449U77E-125
Editorial Address: 30 Monmouth Street, BATH, BA1 2BW
Tel: 01225 442244 **Fax:** 01225 446019
Email: gareth.charlton@futurenet.co.uk
Advertising Address: As above. **Fax:** 01225 732206
Email: ehare@futurenet.co.uk
Web site: http://www.classicfordmag.co.uk
ISSN: 0958-0522
Publisher: Future Publishing Ltd
Date Established: 1997
Frequency: 13 issues yearly
Cover Price: £3.99
Circulation: 33,000 (Publisher's Statement)
Usual Pagination: 162

Editor: Gareth Charlton; **Features Editor:** Gareth Charlton; **Advertising Manager:** Lara Bakshi; **Publisher:** Helen Richmond
Summary of Content: Magazine covering Ford cars dating from the 1960s to the early 1980s including modified and standard cars.
Readership/Target Audience: Read mainly by 18 to 65 year old men.
ADVERTISING RATES:
Full Page Colour £650.00
Agency Commission: 10%
Mechanical Data: Page Width: 190mm, Print Process: Web-fed offset litho, Type Area: 277 x 190mm, Bleed Size: 309 x 222mm, Trim Size: 297 x 210mm, Col Length: 277mm, Film: Digital
Copy instructions: Copy Date: 23 days prior to publication date
CONSUMER: MOTORING & CYCLING: Club Cars

CLASSIC MILITARY VEHICLE   765119U79H-161
Editorial Address: Cudham Tithe Barn, Berrys Hill, Berrys Green, Cudham, WESTERHAM, TN16 3AG
Tel: 01959 541444 **Fax:** 01959 541400
Email: cmv.ed@kelsey.co.uk
Advertising Address: Broadway Court, Broadway, PETERBOROUGH, PE1 1RP **Tel:** 01733 353359
Fax: 01733 891342
Email: julia.johnston@kelseypb.co.uk
Web site: http://www.kelsey.co.uk
Publisher: Kelsey Publishing Ltd
Date Established: 2001
Frequency: Monthly
Cover Price: £3.95
Annual Sub.: £43.44
Circulation: 16,500 (Publisher's Statement)
Usual Pagination: 84
Editor: John Blackman; **Managing Director:** Stephen Wright; **Publisher:** Pat Ware
Summary of Content: Magazine covering all aspects of the military vehicle scene. Includes news, events, vehicle and manufacturer profiles.
Readership/Target Audience: Aimed at military vehicle enthusiasts, historians, modellers and re-enactors.
ADVERTISING RATES:
Full Page Mono £485.00
Full Page Colour £485.00
Agency Commission: 10%
Mechanical Data: Type Area: 277 x 190mm, Col Length: 277mm, Trim Size: 297 x 210mm, Bleed Size: 303 x 216mm, Film: Digital, Page Width: 190mm
Copy instructions: Copy Date: 4 weeks prior to publication date
Average advertising content per issue: 25%
CONSUMER: HOBBIES & DIY: Military History

CLASSIC MOTOR MONTHLY   46492U77F-65
Editorial Address: PO Box 129, BOLTON, BL3 4YQ
Tel: 01204 657212 **Fax:** 01204 652764
Email: editor@classicmotor.co.uk
Advertising Address: As above.
Email: postmaster@classicmotor.co.uk
Web site: http://www.classicmotor.co.uk
Publisher: CMM Publications
Date Established: 1989
Frequency: Monthly
Cover Price: £1.50
Annual Sub.: £12.00
Circulation: 33,000 (Publisher's Statement)
Usual Pagination: 32
Editor: John Hodson; **Advertising Manager:** Garry Rollinson; **Publisher:** John Hodson
Summary of Content: Magazine covering the general classic car scene. Includes shows, runs, auctions, club meetings, autojumbles and hints and tips.
Readership/Target Audience: Aimed at classic car enthusiasts.
ADVERTISING RATES:
Full Page Mono £880.00
Full Page Colour £1700.00
Agency Commission: 10%
Mechanical Data: Page Width: 260mm, Film: Digital, Trim Size: 420 x 297mm, Type Area: 378 x 260mm, Col Length: 378mm, Print Process: Web-fed offset litho
Copy instructions: Copy Date: 20th of the month prior to publication date
Average advertising content per issue: 60%
CONSUMER: MOTORING & CYCLING: Veteran Cars

THE CLASSIC MOTORCYCLE   46355U77B-493
Editorial Address: PO Box 99, HORNCASTLE, LN9 6LZ
Tel: 01507 529300 **Fax:** 01507 529495
Email: jrobinson@mortons.co.uk
Advertising Address: As above. **Fax:** 01507 529499
Email: dengland@mortons.co.uk
Web site: http://www.classicmotorcycle.co.uk
Publisher: Mortons Media Group Ltd
Date Established: 1981

Frequency: Monthly
Cover Price: £3.70
Annual Sub.: £32.00
Circulation: 30,000 (Publisher's Statement)
Usual Pagination: 116
Editor: James Robinson; **Managing Director:** Brian Hill;
Advertising Manager: David England
Summary of Content: Magazine covering vintage and classic motorcycles and their riders, with special emphasis on historical research.
Readership/Target Audience: Aimed at enthusiasts of the golden era of motorcycling.
ADVERTISING RATES:
Full Page Mono £1250.00
Full Page Colour £1250.00
Agency Commission: 10%
Mechanical Data: Col Length: 270mm, No. of Columns (Display): 4, Type Area: 270 x 188mm, Bleed Size: 307.5 x 220mm, Trim Size: 297.5 x 210mm, Film: Digital, Page Width: 188mm
Copy instructions: Copy Date: 3 weeks prior to publication date
Average advertising content per issue: 25%
CONSUMER: MOTORING & CYCLING: Motorcycling

CLASSIC MOTORCYCLE MECHANICS

46352U77B-489

Formerly: Classic & Motorcycle Mechanics
Editorial Address: Media Centre, Morton Way, HORNCASTLE, LN9 6JR **Tel:** 01507 525771
Fax: 01507 529495
Email: rgibson@mortons.co.uk
Advertising Address: As above. **Tel:** 01507 524004
Fax: 01507 529499
Email: acatton@mortons.co.uk
Web site: http://www.classicmechanics.com
Publisher: Mortons Media Group Ltd
Frequency: Monthly
Cover Price: £3.30
Annual Sub.: £32.00
Circulation: 35,000 (Publisher's Statement)
Usual Pagination: 100
Editor: John Carroll; **Managing Director:** Brian Hill;
Advertising Manager: Andy Catton
Summary of Content: Magazine containing information on motorcycle restoration projects and tests. Also includes practical advice.
Readership/Target Audience: Aimed at restorers and collectors of pre-1990 motorcycles.
ADVERTISING RATES:
Full Page Colour £765.00
Agency Commission: 10%
Mechanical Data: Type Area: 270 x 188mm, Bleed Size: +5mm, Col Length: 270mm, No. of Columns (Display): 4, Page Width: 188mm, Film: Digital, Trim Size: 297 x 210mm, Col Widths (Display): 42mm
Copy instructions: Copy Date: Last Thursday of each month prior to publication date
Average advertising content per issue: 25%
CONSUMER: MOTORING & CYCLING: Motorcycling

CLASSIC PLANT & MACHINERY

766721U79K-993

Editorial Address: Cudham Tithe Barn, Berrys Hill, Berrys Green, Cudham, WESTERHAM, TN16 3AG
Tel: 01959 541444 **Fax:** 01959 541400
Email: cpm.ed@kelsey.co.uk
Advertising Address: As above. **Tel:** 01959 543500
Email: graham@kelsey.co.uk
Web site: http://www.kelsey.co.uk
Publisher: Kelsey Publishing Ltd
Date Established: 2002
Frequency: Monthly
Cover Price: £3.00
Annual Sub.: £33.00
Circulation: 11,012 (Publisher's Statement)
Usual Pagination: 68
Editor: Peter Simpson; **Managing Editor:** Peter Simpson;
Publisher: Stephen Curtis
Summary of Content: Magazine covering dump trucks, excavators, compressors, forklifts, mining machinery and road rollers. Includes news, restorations, auction reports, manufacturers' histories, finds and discoveries and events listings.
Readership/Target Audience: Read by collectors, restorers and person within the trade.
ADVERTISING RATES:
Full Page Colour £485.00
Agency Commission: 10%
Mechanical Data: Page Width: 188mm, Trim Size: 297 x 210mm, Bleed Size: 303 x 216mm, Type Area: 270 x 188mm, Col Length: 270mm, Film: Digital
Copy instructions: Copy Date: 3 weeks prior to publication date
Average advertising content per issue: 30%
CONSUMER: HOBBIES & DIY: Collectors Magazines

CLASSIC RACER

46356U77B-493_5

Editorial Address: Media Centre, Morton Way, HORNCASTLE, LN9 6JR **Tel:** 01507 523456
Fax: 01507 525002
Email: mwheeler@mortons.co.uk
Advertising Address: As above. **Tel:** 01507 524004
Fax: 01507 529499
Email: sfisher@mortons.co.uk
Web site: http://www.classicracer.co.uk
Publisher: Mortons Media Group Ltd
Date Established: 1982
Frequency: 6 issues yearly
Cover Price: £3.60
Annual Sub.: £19.00
Circulation: 30,000 (Publisher's Statement)
Usual Pagination: 100
Editor: Malcolm Wheeler; **Advertising Manager:** Sandra Fisher
Summary of Content: Magazine covering road racing from the turn of the century to present day with a focus on the current classic scene.
Readership/Target Audience: Aimed at classic racing enthusiasts.
ADVERTISING RATES:
Full Page Colour £742.00
Agency Commission: 10%
Mechanical Data: Type Area: 270 x 188mm, Col Length: 270mm, No. of Columns (Display): 4, Bleed Size: 307.5 x 220mm, Trim Size: 297.5 x 210mm, Film: Digital, Page Width: 188mm
Copy instructions: Copy Date: 20 days prior to publication date
Average advertising content per issue: 25%
CONSUMER: MOTORING & CYCLING: Motorcycling

CLASSIC ROCK

31113U76E-57

Editorial Address: 2 Balcombe Street, LONDON, NW1 6NW
Tel: 020 7042 4000
Email: sian.llewellyn@futurenet.com
Advertising Address: As above. **Fax:** 020 7042 4419
Email: classicrockads@futurenet.co.uk
Web site: http://www.classicrockmagazine.co.uk
Publisher: Future Publishing Limited
Date Established: 1998
Frequency: 13 issues yearly
Cover Price: £4.50
Circulation: 70,301 (ABC 01/01/2009 to 30/06/2009)
Usual Pagination: 132
Editor: Sian Llewellyn; **Editor-in-Chief:** Scott Rowley
Summary of Content: Magazine containing in-depth profiles and features from the hard rock and heavy metal music scene. Includes interviews, tour dates, retrospective articles and a reviews section.
Readership/Target Audience: Read by rock lovers of all ages.
ADVERTISING RATES:
Full Page Colour £2992.00
Agency Commission: 10%
Mechanical Data: Type Area: 280 x 203mm, Bleed Size: 306 x 228mm, Trim Size: 300 x 222mm, Col Length: 280mm, Page Width: 203mm
Copy instructions: Copy Date: 4 weeks prior to publication date
Average advertising content per issue: 30%
CONSUMER: MUSIC & PERFORMING ARTS: Pop Music

CLASSIC SCOOTERIST SCENE MAGAZINE

1695533U77B-716

Formerly: Classic & Modern Scooterist Scene Magazine
Editorial Address: Media Centre, Morton Way, HORNCASTLE, LN9 6JR **Tel:** 01507 529300
Fax: 01507 529495
Email: mauspencer@scooteristscene.com
Advertising Address: As above. **Fax:** 01507 529499
Email: mpercival@mortons.co.uk
Web site: http://www.scooteristscene.com
Publisher: Mortons Media Group Ltd
Date Established: 1997
Frequency: 6 issues yearly
Cover Price: £2.75
Circulation: 25,000 (Publisher's Statement)
Usual Pagination: 76
Editor: Mau Spencer
Summary of Content: Magazine dedicated to the classic and modern scooterist and the lifestyle surrounding it, scootering events and classic and modern features.
Readership/Target Audience: Aimed at classic scooter enthusiasts.
ADVERTISING RATES:
Full Page Colour £499.00
Agency Commission: 10%
Mechanical Data: Type Area: 270 x 188mm, Col Length: 270mm, Page Width: 188mm, Bleed Size: 307 x 220mm, Trim Size: 297 x 210mm, Film: Digital
Copy instructions: Copy Date: 3 weeks prior to publication date

---

Average advertising content per issue: 32%
CONSUMER: MOTORING & CYCLING: Motorcycling

CLASSIC SPEEDWAY

1841377U77B-724

Editorial Address: 103 Douglas Road, HORNCHURCH, RM11 1AW **Tel:** 01708 734502
Email: editorial@retro-speedway.com
Web site: http://www.retro-speedway.com
Publisher: Retro Speedway
Date Established: 2008
Frequency: Quarterly
Cover Price: £3.00
Circulation: 3,000 (Publisher's Statement)
Usual Pagination: 48
Editor: Tony McDonald; **Advertising Manager:** Susie Muir;
Publisher: Tony McDonald
Summary of Content: Magazine covering speedway predominantly from to 1950s and 60s.
Readership/Target Audience: Magazine aimed at past riders, officials and fans of speedway.
CONSUMER: MOTORING & CYCLING: Motorcycling

CLASSIC STITCHES

45353U74E-29

Editorial Address: 80 Kingsway East, DUNDEE, DD4 8SL
Tel: 01382 223131 **Fax:** 01382 452491
Email: editorial@classicstitches.com
Advertising Address: As above. **Fax:** 01382 575538
Email: chorn@dcthomson.co.uk
Web site: http://www.classicstitches.com
Publisher: D.C. Thomson & Co Ltd
Date Established: 1994
Frequency: 6 issues yearly
Cover Price: £4.20
Annual Sub.: £21.00
Circulation: 10,790 (Publisher's Statement)
Usual Pagination: 76
Editor: Bea Neilson; **Advertising Manager:** Arthur McEwan;
Managing Editor: Irene Duncan
Summary of Content: Magazine containing needlework projects, interviews and advice.
Readership/Target Audience: Aimed at needlework enthusiasts.
ADVERTISING RATES:
Full Page Mono £1390.00
Full Page Colour £1970.00
Agency Commission: 15%
Mechanical Data: Col Length: 276mm, Col Widths (Display): 48mm, Film: Digital, Type Area: 276 x 200mm, Bleed Size: 311 x 232mm, Trim Size: 305 x 225mm, Page Width: 200mm
Copy instructions: Copy Date: 8 weeks prior to publication date
CONSUMER: WOMEN'S INTEREST CONSUMER MAGAZINES: Crafts

CLASSIC TRACTOR

1659016U77F-454

Editorial Address: Sundial House, 17 Wickham Road, BECKENHAM, BR3 5JS **Tel:** 020 8639 4400
Fax: 01507 606158
Email: classictractor@btinternet.com
Advertising Address: As above. **Tel:** 020 8639 4411
Email: ads@sundialmagazines.co.uk
Web site: http://www.classictractormagazine.co.uk
Publisher: Sundial Magazines Ltd
Date Established: 2001
Frequency: Monthly
Cover Price: £3.40
Annual Sub.: £35.80
Circulation: 60,000 (Publisher's Statement)
Editor: Rory Day
Summary of Content: Magazine covering all makes of tractors and farm machinery built over the last 40 years.
Readership/Target Audience: Aimed at small and medium family farms and collectors.
ADVERTISING RATES:
Full Page Mono £495.00
Full Page Colour £750.00
Agency Commission: 10%
Mechanical Data: Type Area: 272 x 188mm, Bleed Size: 303 x 213mm, Trim Size: 297 x 210mm, Col Length: 272mm, Page Width: 188mm, Film: Digital
Copy instructions: Copy Date: 8 weeks prior to publication date
Average advertising content per issue: 25%
CONSUMER: MOTORING & CYCLING: Veteran Cars

CLASSIC VAN AND PICK-UP

766724U79K-994

Editorial Address: PO Box 978, PETERBOROUGH, PE1 9FL **Tel:** 01733 347559 **Fax:** 01733 557235
Email: van.ed@kelseypb.co.uk
Advertising Address: 1st Floor, Southwing, Broadway Court, Broadway, PETERBOROUGH, PE1 1RP
Tel: 01733 353543 **Fax:** 01733 891342
Email: matt.carson@kelseypb.co.uk
Web site: http://www.kelsey.co.uk/magazines/van
Publisher: Kelsey Publishing Ltd

Consumer Magazines

Date Established: 2000
Frequency: Monthly
Cover Price: £3.30
Annual Sub.: £36.00
Usual Pagination: 48
Editor: Ted Connolly; **Advertising Manager:** Graham Mazey
Summary of Content: Magazine with coverage of pre-1980 small vans, trucks, pick-ups, motor caravans and ambulances with news, reviews and events listings.
Readership/Target Audience: Aimed at enthusiasts and owners of classic light commercial vehicles.
ADVERTISING RATES:
Full Page Mono £300.00
Full Page Colour £550.00
Agency Commission: 10%
Mechanical Data: Page Width: 190mm, Film: Digital, Type Area: 270 x 190mm, Col Length: 270mm, Bleed Size: 303 x 216mm, Trim Size: 297 x 210mm
Copy instructions: Copy Date: 4 weeks prior to publication date
CONSUMER: HOBBIES & DIY: Collectors Magazines

CLASSICAL GUITAR
46137U76D-302
Editorial Address: 1-2 Vance Court, Trans Britannia Enterprise Park, BLAYDON ON TYNE, NE21 5NH
Tel: 0191 414 9000 **Fax:** 0191 414 9001
Email: classicalguitar@ashleymark.co.uk
Advertising Address: As above.
Email: david@ashleymark.co.uk
Web site: http://www.classicalguitarmagazine.com
ISSN: 0950-429X
Publisher: Ashley Mark Publishing Co.
Frequency: Monthly
Cover Price: £3.95
Annual Sub.: £54.00
Circulation: 8,000 (Publisher's Statement)
Usual Pagination: 52
Editor: Guy Traviss; **News Editor:** Therese Saba; **Features Editor:** Guy Traviss; **Advertising Manager:** David English; **Managing Editor:** Maurice Summerfield
Summary of Content: Magazine covering classical guitar music featuring interviews, news and events. Contains reviews of records, music, concerts and books. Also includes some flamenco and flute coverage.
Readership/Target Audience: Aimed at classical guitarists.
ADVERTISING RATES:
Full Page Mono £495.00
Full Page Colour £885.00
Agency Commission: 15%
Mechanical Data: Col Length: 264mm, Film: Positive, right reading, emulsion side down. Digital, Print Process: Offset litho, Type Area: 264 x 176mm, Trim Size: 297 x 210mm, Page Width: 176mm, Bleed Size: 303 x 213mm
Copy instructions: Copy Date: 1st of the month prior to publication date
CONSUMER: MUSIC & PERFORMING ARTS: Music

CLASSICAL MUSIC
46138U76D-303
Editorial Address: 241 Shaftesbury Avenue, LONDON, WC2H 8TF **Tel:** 020 7333 1742 **Fax:** 020 7333 1769
Email: classical.music@rhinegold.co.uk
Advertising Address: As above. **Tel:** 020 7333 1733
Fax: 020 7333 1736
Email: ad.sales@rhinegold.co.uk
Web site: http://www.rhinegold.co.uk
ISSN: 0961-2696
Publisher: Rhinegold Publishing Ltd
Date Established: 1976
Frequency: 26 issues yearly
Cover Price: £3.95
Annual Sub.: £80.00
Usual Pagination: 52
Editor: Keith Clarke; **Advertising Manager:** Matthew Cheadle
Summary of Content: News magazine covering all aspects of the classical music industry in Britain.
Readership/Target Audience: Aimed at anyone involved in the performance, promotion and management of classical music in Britain.
ADVERTISING RATES:
Full Page Mono £1220.00
Full Page Colour £1600.00
SCC £35.00
Agency Commission: 10%
Mechanical Data: Type Area: 272 x 184mm, Col Length: 272mm, Trim Size: 297 x 210mm, Bleed Size: 303 x 216mm, Film: Digital, Page Width: 184mm
Copy instructions: Copy Date: 10 days prior to publication date
Supplement(s): Classical Music Competitions - 1xY, Classical Music Festivals - 1xY, Classical Music Summer Schools - 1xY, Music Scholarships - 1xY
CONSUMER: MUSIC & PERFORMING ARTS: Music

CLASSICS MONTHLY
46500U77F-70
Formerly: Classics
Editorial Address: 30 Monmouth Street, BATH, BA1 2BW
Tel: 01225 442244
Email: classicsmonthly@futurenet.com
Advertising Address: As above. **Fax:** 01225 732206
Email: lara.bakshi@futurenet.co.uk
Web site: http://www.futurenet.co.uk
ISSN: 1369-1007
Publisher: Future Publishing Ltd
Date Established: 1997
Frequency: 13 issues yearly
Cover Price: £3.99
Annual Sub.: £50.05
Circulation: 55,000 (Publisher's Statement)
Usual Pagination: 164
Editor: Gary Stretton; **Advertising Manager:** Lara Bakshi
Summary of Content: Magazine featuring classic cars including comparisons, driving features, practical hints and tips and a directory of classic car specialists.
Readership/Target Audience: Aimed at enthusiasts and owners of classic cars.
ADVERTISING RATES:
Full Page Colour £1023.00
Mechanical Data: No. of Columns (Display): 4, Type Area: 270 x 202mm, Film: Digital, Trim Size: 290 x 222mm, Bleed Size: 363.5 x 204mm, Col Length: 270mm, Page Width: 202mm
Copy instructions: Copy Date: 4 weeks prior to publication date
CONSUMER: MOTORING & CYCLING: Veteran Cars

CLAY SHOOTING
45857U75F-30
Editorial Address: Lawrence House, Morrell Street, LEAMINGTON SPA, CV32 5SZ **Tel:** 0870 046 8778
Fax: 01926 470400
Advertising Address: As above.
Email: mark@blazepublishing.co.uk
Web site: http://www.clay-shooting.com
Publisher: Blaze Publishing Limited
Frequency: Monthly
Cover Price: £3.30
Circulation: 17,000 (Publisher's Statement)
Usual Pagination: 104
Editor: Theone Wilson; **Publisher:** Wesley Stanton
Summary of Content: Magazine focusing on the sport of clay target shooting. Features coming events, results, championship reports, shooting tips, advice from the world's best shooters and a weekly bulletin providing the latest shooting information.
Readership/Target Audience: Read by clay pigeon shooting enthusiasts.
ADVERTISING RATES:
Full Page Mono £600.00
Full Page Colour £600.00
Agency Commission: 10%
Mechanical Data: Page Width: 186mm, Col Length: 265mm, No. of Columns (Display): 2, Type Area: 265 x 186mm, Print Process: Digital, Bleed Size: 303 x 216mm, Trim Size: 297 x 210mm
Copy instructions: Copy Date: 3 weeks prior to publication date
Average advertising content per issue: 45%
CONSUMER: SPORT: Shooting

CLIFTON LIFE
1665744U80C-5214
Editorial Address: Circus Mews House, Circus Mews, BATH, BA1 2PW **Tel:** 01225 475800
Email: victoria.green@mediaclash.co.uk
Advertising Address: As above. **Fax:** 01225 475801
Email: debbie.blackman@mediaclash.co.uk
Web site: http://www.mediaclash.co.uk
Publisher: Media Clash
Date Established: 2004
Frequency: 17 issues yearly
Cover Price: £3.00
Free to qualifying individuals
Circulation: 10,000 (Publisher's Statement)
Usual Pagination: 100
Editor: Victoria Green; **Advertising Manager:** Debbie Blackman
Summary of Content: Property and lifestyle magazine covering food, arts, out and about, travel, dining, shopping, gardening, health, beauty, eco and Q&A.
Readership/Target Audience: Aimed at affluent home owners in Clifton and surrounding areas.
ADVERTISING RATES:
Full Page Mono £715.00
Full Page Colour £715.00
Agency Commission: 10%
Mechanical Data: Type Area: 260 x 195mm, Col Length: 260mm, Page Width: 195mm, Bleed Size: 291 x 226mm, Trim Size: 285 x 220mm, Film: Digital
Copy instructions: Copy Date: 3 weeks prior to publication date

Average advertising content per issue: 50%
CONSUMER: RURAL & REGIONAL INTEREST: Regional Interest English Counties

CLIMB
1665480U75L-810
Editorial Address: PO Box 21, BUXTON, SK17 9BR
Tel: 01298 72801
Email: neilp@climbmagazine.com
Advertising Address: Telford Way, Telford Way Industrial Estate, KETTERING, NN16 8UN **Tel:** 01536 382500
Fax: 01536 382501
Email: gill.wootton@greenshirespublishing.com
Web site: http://www.climbmagazine.com
Publisher: Greenshires Publishing Ltd
Date Established: 2005
Frequency: Monthly - Published on the 2nd Thursday of the month preceding the cover date
Cover Price: £3.50
Circulation: 15,000 (Print Run)
Usual Pagination: 100
Editor: Neil Pearsons; **Executive Editor:** Gill Kent; **Advertising Manager:** Gill Wootton
Summary of Content: Magazine covering rock climbing, bouldering and mountaineering.
Readership/Target Audience: Aimed at active rock climbers and mountaineers.
ADVERTISING RATES:
Full Page Colour £1450.00
Mechanical Data: Type Area: 276 x 206mm, Bleed Size: 306 x 236mm, Col Length: 276mm, Page Width: 206mm, Film: Digital, Trim Size: 300 x 230mm, No. of Columns (Display): 4
Copy instructions: Copy Date: 4 weeks prior to publication date
CONSUMER: SPORT: Outdoor

CLIMBER
45919U75L-130
Editorial Address: The Maltings, West Street, BOURNE, PE10 9PH **Tel:** 01778 391000 **Fax:** 01778 394748
Email: climbercomments@warnersgroup.co.uk
Advertising Address: As above. **Fax:** 01778 392079
Email: jot@warnersgroup.co.uk
Web site: http://www.climber.co.uk
ISSN: 0955-3045
Publisher: Warners Group Publications plc
Date Established: 1964
Frequency: Monthly
Cover Price: £3.50
Circulation: 18,000 (Publisher's Statement)
Usual Pagination: 76
Editor: Andy McCue; **News Editor:** Bernard Newman
Summary of Content: Magazine covering rock climbing.
Readership/Target Audience: Read by climbing and mountaineering enthusiasts.
ADVERTISING RATES:
Full Page Colour £1530.00
Agency Commission: 10%
Mechanical Data: Col Length: 275mm, Film: Digital, Bleed Size: 303 x 216mm, Trim Size: 297 x 210mm, Page Width: 190mm, Type Area: 275 x 190mm, Print Process: Web-fed offset litho
Average advertising content per issue: 25%
CONSUMER: SPORT: Outdoor

CLOCKS
46733U79K-380
Editorial Address: 141B Lower Granton Road, EDINBURGH, EH5 1EX **Tel:** 0131 331 3200
Email: enquiries@clocksmagazine.com
Advertising Address: As above.
Email: advertising@clocksmagazine.com
Web site: http://www.clocksmagazine.com
ISSN: 0968-2380
Publisher: Splat Publishing Ltd
Date Established: 1977
Frequency: Monthly
Cover Price: £3.95
Circulation: 4,000 (Publisher's Statement)
Usual Pagination: 52
Editor: John Hunter; **Advertising Manager:** Claire Loughran
Summary of Content: Magazine covering collecting, restoring and repairing of clocks from around the world.
Readership/Target Audience: Aimed at enthusiasts, dealers, collectors and material suppliers.
ADVERTISING RATES:
Full Page Mono £275.00
Full Page Colour £400.00
Agency Commission: 10%
Mechanical Data: Trim Size: 297 x 210mm, Bleed Size: +12mm, Type Area: 267 x 184mm, Col Length: 267mm, Page Width: 184mm, Film: Digital
Copy instructions: Copy Date: 4 weeks prior to publication date
Average advertising content per issue: 10%
CONSUMER: HOBBIES & DIY: Collectors Magazines

CLOSE UP
1762520U79F-101

Editorial Address: Bakehouse Unit J108, 100 Clements Road, LONDON, SE16 4DG **Tel:** 020 7064 8400
Fax: 020 7231 1232
Email: andreu@aspectmediauk.com
Advertising Address: As above.
Email: lesley@aspectmediauk.com
Web site: http://www.aspectmediauk.com
ISSN: 1753-5026
Publisher: Aspect Media
Date Established: 2006
Frequency: Quarterly
Cover Price: Free
Circulation: 40,000 (Publisher's Statement)
Usual Pagination: 60
Editor: Andreu Machancoses; **Managing Editor:** Andreu Machancoses; **Publisher:** Tim Lloyd
Summary of Content: Magazine covering sports and betting. Major sporting events throughout the year as well as niche areas such as darts, ice hockey, American sports and greyhound racing. Also covers poker, casino games and other forms of betting.
Readership/Target Audience: Aimed at top spending customers of Ladbrokes.
ADVERTISING: Rates on application
CONSUMER: HOBBIES & DIY: Games & Puzzles

CLOSER
766859U74Q-1125

Editorial Address: Endeavour House, 189 Shaftesbury Avenue, LONDON, WC2H 8JG **Tel:** 020 7437 9011
Fax: 020 7859 8600
Email: closer@closermag.com
Advertising Address: As above. **Tel:** 020 7295 5000
Email: marie.morrison@baueradvertising.co.uk
Web site: http://www.closeronline.co.uk
ISSN: 1478-078X
Publisher: Bauer Media
Date Established: 2002
Frequency: Weekly
Cover Price: £1.30
Annual Sub: £48.00
Circulation: 530,371 (ABC 01/01/2009 to 30/06/2009)
Usual Pagination: 98
Editor: Kirsty Lee; **Features Editor:** Helen Morgan;
Managing Director: David Davies; **Managing Editor:** Anita Pyne
Summary of Content: Magazine containing celebrity news and gossip plus TV listings, puzzles and horoscopes. Twitter: https://twitter.com/CloserOnline.
Readership/Target Audience: Aimed at women aged between 25 and 35 years old.
ADVERTISING RATES:
Full Page Colour £18618.00
Agency Commission: 15%
Mechanical Data: Type Area: 274 x 194mm, Bleed Size: 306 x 226mm, Trim Size: 300 x 220mm, Col Length: 274mm, Page Width: 194mm, Film: Digital
Copy instructions: Copy Date: 2 weeks prior to publication date
Average advertising content per issue: 20%
CONSUMER: WOMEN'S INTEREST CONSUMER MAGAZINES: Lifestyle

CLOUD NINE
1833109U89E-257

Editorial Address: 1st Floor, 43 Market Place, WETHERBY, LS22 6LN **Tel:** 01937 589777 **Fax:** 01937 587788
Email: james.odonnell@divinemarketing.co.uk
Advertising Address: Garnett Dickinson Ltd, Brookfields Way, Manvers, Wath-upon-Dearne, ROTHERHAM, S63 5DL **Tel:** 01709 768000
Email: steven.cox@garnett-dickinson.co.uk
Web site: http://www.cloudninemagazine.co.uk
Publisher: Divine Marketing Ltd
Date Established: 2000
Frequency: Quarterly
Cover Price: Free
Circulation: 125,000 (Publisher's Statement)
Usual Pagination: 84
Editor: James O'Donnell
Summary of Content: Magazine covering flights, destinations and holidays as well as UK leisure and lifestyle.
Readership/Target Audience: Aimed at Flight Club members who are frequent fliers.
ADVERTISING RATES:
Full Page Colour £4500.00
Agency Commission: 10%
Mechanical Data: Trim Size: 297 x 210mm, Bleed Size: 303 x 216mm, Film: Digital
Copy instructions: Copy Date: 2 weeks prior to publication date
Average advertising content per issue: 40%
CONSUMER: HOLIDAYS & TRAVEL: Holidays

CLUB CRICKET CONFERENCE YEARBOOK
45913U75K-10

Editorial Address: 22 Dene Avenue, HOUNSLOW, TW3 3AH **Tel:** 020 8570 5434
Email: charlie.puckett54@gmail.com
Advertising Address: Top Floor, High Street, Hampton Hill, HAMPTON, TW12 1PD **Tel:** 020 8973 1612
Fax: 0870 143 2824
Email: ccc@club-cricket.co.uk
Web site: http://www.club-cricket.com
Publisher: The Club Cricket Conference
Frequency: Annual - Published in March
Cover Price: £7.50
Circulation: 10,000 (Publisher's Statement)
Editor: Charlie Puckett; **Advertising Manager:** Stan Nicholson
Summary of Content: Yearbook covering details on cricket clubs. Featuring the grounds, courses and umpires.
Readership/Target Audience: Aimed at all cricket clubs and registered Midland League Conference members.
ADVERTISING RATES:
Full Page Mono £510.00
Full Page Colour £582.00
Mechanical Data: Type Area: 190 x126mm, Col Length: 190mm, Page Width: 126mm
Average advertising content per issue: 10%
CONSUMER: SPORT: Cricket

CLUB INTERNATIONAL
47604U86A-50

Editorial Address: 2 Archer Street, LONDON, W1D 7AW **Tel:** 020 7292 8000 **Fax:** 020 7734 5030
Email: clubint@paulraymond.com
Advertising Address: As above. **Fax:** 020 7292 8009
Email: nickys@paulraymond.com
Web site: http://www.sexclub.co.uk
Publisher: Paul Raymond Publications Ltd
Frequency: 13 issues yearly
Cover Price: £3.50
Circulation: 80,000 (Publisher's Statement)
Usual Pagination: 100
Editor: Matt Wheeler; **Managing Director:** Mark Quinn;
Advertising Manager: Nicola Swift
Summary of Content: Magazine covering photographs, humour, reviews, interviews and new products.
Readership/Target Audience: Aimed primarily at men 18 years and over, also read by women and couples.
ADVERTISING RATES:
Full Page Colour £3000.00
Mechanical Data: Type Area: 290 x 212mm, Col Length: 290mm, Film: Digital, Page Width: 212mm, Trim Size: 300 x 222mm
Average advertising content per issue: 20%
CONSUMER: ADULT & GAY MAGAZINES: Adult Magazines

CNN TRAVELLER
1646136U89A-710

Editorial Address: The Old Truman Brewery, Unit 23-24, 91 Brick Lane, LONDON, E1 6QL **Tel:** 020 3355 8262
Fax: 020 3355 8268
Email: dhayes@emphasis.net
Advertising Address: As above.
Email: slehnert@emphasis.net
Web site: http://www.cnntraveller.com
ISSN: 1740-441X
Publisher: Emphasis Media UK Ltd
Frequency: 6 issues yearly
Cover Price: £2.95
Free to qualifying individuals
Circulation: 106,000 (Publisher's Statement)
Usual Pagination: 132
Editor: Daniel Hayes
Summary of Content: Magazine covering travel and current affairs in conjunction with CNN.
Readership/Target Audience: Aimed at business travellers and high end leisure travellers aged 35 to 50 years old.
ADVERTISING RATES:
Full Page Colour £7690.00
Agency Commission: 10%
Mechanical Data: Bleed Size: 281 x 216mm, Trim Size: 275 x 210mm, Film: Digital
Copy instructions: Copy Date: 3 weeks prior to publication date
CONSUMER: HOLIDAYS & TRAVEL: Travel

CNN TRAVELLER ASIA PACIFIC
1698519U89A-728

Editorial Address: 141-143 Shoreditch High Street, LONDON, E1 6JE **Tel:** 020 7613 8777 **Fax:** 020 7613 6985
Email: dan.hayes@ink-publishing.com
Advertising Address: As above. **Tel:** 020 7613 6959
Fax: 020 7613 8778
Email: silvia.lehnert@ink-publishing.com
Web site: http://www.cnntraveller.com
Publisher: Ink Publishing
Date Established: 2005
Frequency: 6 issues yearly

Cover Price: £2.95
Usual Pagination: 100
Editor: Daniel Hayes
Summary of Content: Magazine covering travel news, current affairs and sport.
Readership/Target Audience: Aimed at Asian travellers and readers.
ADVERTISING RATES:
Full Page Colour £7690.00
Agency Commission: 15%
Mechanical Data: Type Area: 255 x 190mm, Bleed Size: 281 x 216mm, Trim Size: 275 x 210mm, Col Length: 255mm, Page Width: 190mm, Film: Digital
CONSUMER: HOLIDAYS & TRAVEL: Travel

COARSE ANGLING TODAY
717796U92-48

Editorial Address: 18 Haverbreaks Place, LANCASTER, LA1 5BH **Tel:** 01524 60713 **Fax:** 01524 60713
Email: pikeandpredators@btopenworld.com
Advertising Address: 5 Pilley Hill, Pilley, Lymington, HAMPSHIRE, SO41 5QF **Tel:** 01590 678400
Fax: 01590 678400
Email: chris.ball2@virgin.net
Web site: http://www.totalcoarsefishing.com
Publisher: Predator Publications Ltd
Date Established: 2001
Frequency: Monthly
Cover Price: £2.50
Annual Sub: £36.00
Circulation: 12,000 (Publisher's Statement)
Usual Pagination: 90
Editor: Neville Fickling; **Advertising Manager:** Chris Ball;
Publisher: Kevin Clifford
Summary of Content: Magazine focusing on coarse angling includes news, top fishing tips, interviews and previews & reviews on all the latest fishing tackle.
Readership/Target Audience: Aimed at specialist coarse anglers.
ADVERTISING RATES:
Full Page Mono £235.00
Full Page Colour £300.00
Agency Commission: 10%
Mechanical Data: Trim Size: 297 x 210mm, Film: Digital, Type Area: 265 x 185mm, Col Length: 265mm, Bleed Size: 303 x 216mm, Page Width: 185mm, Print Process: Sheet-fed litho
Copy instructions: Copy Date: 10th of month prior to publication date
Average advertising content per issue: 22%
CONSUMER: ANGLING & FISHING

COARSE FISHERMAN
48524U92-50

Editorial Address: 2 Harcourt Way, Meridian Business Park, Braunstone Town, LEICESTER, LE19 1WP
Tel: 0116 289 4567 **Fax:** 0116 289 4889
Email: info@conceptdesignltd.co.uk
Advertising Address: West Street, BOURNE, PE10 9WB
Tel: 01778 391000 **Fax:** 0116 289 4889
Email: info@conceptdesignltd.co.uk
Web site: http://www.coarsefisherman.co.uk/
ISSN: 0309-8281
Publisher: Metrocrest Ltd
Frequency: Monthly
Cover Price: £2.95
Circulation: 20,000 (Publisher's Statement)
Usual Pagination: 100
Editor: Stuart Dexter; **Managing Director:** Simon Roff;
Advertising Manager: Jayne Notley
Summary of Content: Magazine containing news and equipment reviews and articles on conservation.
Readership/Target Audience: Read by serious male fishermen between 18 and 50 years old who care about the sport and the countryside environment.
ADVERTISING: Rates on application
Agency Commission: 15%
Copy instructions: Copy Date: 3 weeks prior to publication date
Average advertising content per issue: 20%
CONSUMER: ANGLING & FISHING

COAST
1693921U74A-1010

Editorial Address: National Magazine House, 72 Broadwick Street, LONDON, W1F 9EP **Tel:** 020 7439 5000
Fax: 020 7439 5077
Email: enquiries.coast@natmags.co.uk
Advertising Address: As above. **Fax:** 020 7439 5052
Email: alana.jones@natmags.co.uk
Web site: http://www.coastmagazine.co.uk
Publisher: National Magazine Company Ltd
Date Established: 2004
Frequency: 10 issues yearly
Cover Price: £3.99
Circulation: 41,724 (ABC 01/01/2009 to 30/06/2009)
Editor: Clare Gogerty; **Editor-in-Chief:** Susy Smith;
Advertising Manager: Simon Catley

Consumer Magazines

Summary of Content: Magazine covering life by the sea including houses, hotels, restaurants, B&Bs, decorating and design ideas, cooking seasonal food, complementary health and beauty, fashion, profiles of people who live or work by the sea and photographs of seascapes and coastal landscapes.
Readership/Target Audience: Aimed at active, discerning women aged 35 to 50 years old with a high household income who like to visit or live on the coast and are health, fitness, fashion and beauty conscious.
ADVERTISING RATES:
Full Page Colour £3333.00
Agency Commission: 10%
Mechanical Data: Type Area: 270 x 192mm, Bleed Size: 296 x 221mm, Trim Size: 290 x 215mm, Col Length: 270mm, Page Width: 192mm, Film: Digital
Copy instructions: Copy Date: 1 month prior to publication date
Average advertising content per issue: 20%
CONSUMER: WOMEN'S INTEREST CONSUMER MAGAZINES: Women's Interest

COIN NEWS INC. BANKNOTE NEWS
46648U79E-50

Editorial Address: Orchard House, Duchy Road, Heathpark, HONITON, EX14 1YD **Tel:** 01404 46972 **Fax:** 01404 44788
Email: info@tokenpublishing.com
Advertising Address: As above.
Email: carol@tokenpublishing.com
Web site: http://www.tokenpublishing.com
ISSN: 0958-1391
Publisher: Token Publishing Ltd
Frequency: Monthly
Cover Price: £3.35
Annual Sub.: £34.00
Circulation: 10,000 (Publisher's Statement)
Usual Pagination: 88
Editor: Philip Mussell; **Advertising Director:** Carol Hartman
Summary of Content: Magazine containing news, book reviews, international market movements and features on coins, minting and banknotes.
Readership/Target Audience: Aimed at collectors of coins, medals and banknotes.
ADVERTISING RATES:
Full Page Mono £310.00
Full Page Colour £630.00
Agency Commission: 10%
Mechanical Data: Bleed Size: 307 x 215mm, Trim Size: 297 x 210mm, Col Length: 267mm, Type Area: 267 x 180mm, Film: Digital, Page Width: 180mm
Copy instructions: Copy Date: 4 weeks prior to publication date
Average advertising content per issue: 60%
CONSUMER: HOBBIES & DIY: Numismatics

COIN YEARBOOK
46650U79E-100

Editorial Address: Orchard House, Duchy Road, Heathpark, HONITON, EX14 1YD **Tel:** 01404 46972 **Fax:** 01404 44788
Email: info@tokenpublishing.com
Advertising Address: As above.
Email: info@tokenpublishing.com
Web site: http://www.tokenpublishing.com
Publisher: Token Publishing Ltd
Date Established: 1993
Frequency: Annual - Published in November
Cover Price: £9.95
Circulation: 10,000 (Publisher's Statement)
Usual Pagination: 352
Editor: Philip Mussell
Summary of Content: Yearbook covering all aspects of coin collecting and price-guide to coins, bank notes and medallions.
Readership/Target Audience: Read by coin collectors and those with an interest in numismatics.
ADVERTISING RATES:
Full Page Mono £415.00
Full Page Colour £550.00
Agency Commission: 10%
Mechanical Data: Film: Digital, Trim Size: 210 x 148mm
Copy instructions: Copy Date: July 18th
CONSUMER: HOBBIES & DIY: Numismatics

COLLECT IT!
46735U79K-390

Editorial Address: The Maltings, West Street, BOURNE, PE10 9PH **Tel:** 01778 392400 **Fax:** 01778 394748
Email: jeanhodge@warnersgroup.co.uk
Advertising Address: As above. **Tel:** 01778 392055
Fax: 01778 423663
Email: bevf@warnersgroup.co.uk
Web site: http://www.collectit.info
Publisher: Warners Group Publications plc
Date Established: 1997
Frequency: Monthly
Cover Price: £3.25
Annual Sub.: £32.45
Circulation: 28,000 (Publisher's Statement)
Usual Pagination: 80

Editor: Jean Hodge; **Advertising Manager:** Bev Francis
Summary of Content: Magazine containing collecting features and market news as well as price guides and auction news.
Readership/Target Audience: Aimed at general collectors.
ADVERTISING RATES:
Full Page Colour £1200.00
Agency Commission: 10%
Mechanical Data: Page Width: 194mm, Film: Digital, Type Area: 273 x 194mm, Col Length: 273mm, Trim Size: 297 x 220mm, Bleed Size: 303 x 226mm
Copy instructions: Copy Date: 3 weeks prior to publication date
Average advertising content per issue: 15%
CONSUMER: HOBBIES & DIY: Collectors Magazines

COLLECTIONS
600930U84A-203_50

Editorial Address: 21-24 Bruges Place, Randolph Street, LONDON, NW1 0TF **Tel:** 020 7870 9000 **Fax:** 020 7870 9095
Email: managingeditor@bostonhannah.com
Advertising Address: As above.
Email: collections@bostonhannah.com
Web site: http://www.contractpublishing.com
Publisher: Boston Hannah International
Date Established: 1997
Frequency: 3 issues yearly - Published in March, July and October
Free to qualifying individuals
Circulation: 29,000 (Publisher's Statement)
Usual Pagination: 84
Editor: Charles Ford; **Advertising Manager:** David Amos; **Managing Editor:** Charles Ford
Summary of Content: Fine art magazine containing articles on international collections, collector profiles and features on art from classic to contemporary times. Also contains market news and analysis, book reviews and an events calendar.
Readership/Target Audience: Aimed at patrons of the arts, collectors and connoisseurs of the arts.
ADVERTISING RATES:
Full Page Colour £9750.00
Agency Commission: 10%
Mechanical Data: Type Area: 265 x 200mm, Col Length: 265mm, Page Width: 200mm, Bleed Size: 291 x 236mm, Trim Size: 285 x 230mm, Film: Digital
Copy instructions: Copy Date: 6 weeks prior to publication date
Average advertising content per issue: 33%
CONSUMER: THE ARTS & LITERARY: Arts

COLLECTIVE MAGAZINE
1645234U80C-5124

Editorial Address: Eagle Building, Wylam Wharf, Low Street, SUNDERLAND, SR1 2AX **Tel:** 0191 514 3598
Fax: 0191 565 7672
Email: info@collectivemagazine.com
Advertising Address: As above.
Email: phillip@collectivemagazine.com
Web site: http://www.collectivemagazine.com
Publisher: Watershed Media
Date Established: 2003
Frequency: 6 issues yearly
Cover Price: £2.00
Free to qualifying individuals
Circulation: 14,000 (Publisher's Statement)
Usual Pagination: 104
Editor: Sally Anderson; **Managing Director:** Karen Bell
Summary of Content: Magazine covering lifestyle, art galleries, entertainment, restaurants, fashion, health and beauty, interiors, business, technology as well as celebrity interviews.
Readership/Target Audience: Aimed at residents and visitors to the North East.
ADVERTISING RATES:
Full Page Colour £1750.00
Mechanical Data: Trim Size: 300 x 230mm, Film: Digital, Bleed Size: + 3mm
Copy instructions: Copy Date: 2 weeks prior to publication date
Average advertising content per issue: 40%
CONSUMER: RURAL & REGIONAL INTEREST: Regional Interest English Counties

COLLECTORS GAZETTE
46738U79K-450

Editorial Address: The Maltings, West Street, BOURNE, PE10 9PH **Tel:** 01778 391000 **Fax:** 01778 423063
Email: deniseburrows@warnersgroup.co.uk
Advertising Address: As above.
Email: matthewt@warnersgroup.co.uk
Web site: http://www.collectorsgazette.com
ISSN: 0957-6304
Publisher: Warners Group Publications plc
Date Established: 1978
Frequency: Monthly
Cover Price: £2.50
Annual Sub.: £27.00
Circulation: 12,000 (Publisher's Statement)
Usual Pagination: 44

Editor: Denise Burrows; **Advertising Manager:** Geoff Butler; **Publisher:** John Greenwood
Summary of Content: Magazine containing articles on old toys, trains and toy soldiers, dolls and teddies, Meccano, tinplate, TV and film- related models, toy fairs and auction news.
Readership/Target Audience: Aimed at toy collectors and dealers.
ADVERTISING RATES:
Full Page Colour £750.00
Agency Commission: 10%
Mechanical Data: Col Length: 340mm, Type Area: 340 x 267mm, Page Width: 267mm, Film: Digital
Copy instructions: Copy Date: 3 weeks prior to publication date
Average advertising content per issue: 45%
CONSUMER: HOBBIES & DIY: Collectors Magazines

COMBAT AIRCRAFT
1645143U79H-162

Editorial Address: Riverdene Business Park, Molesey Road, HERSHAM, KT12 4RG **Tel:** 01932 266600
Fax: 01932 266633
Email: jamie.hunter@ianallanpublishing.co.uk
Advertising Address: Foundry Road, STAMFORD, PE9 2PP **Tel:** 01780 484634 **Fax:** 01780 763388
Email: kirsty.flatt@ianallanpublishing.co.uk
Web site: http://www.ianallanpublishing.com
ISSN: 1367-8418
Publisher: Ian Allan Publishing Ltd
Frequency: 6 issues yearly - Published on the 4th Friday of every other month
Cover Price: £3.80
Annual Sub.: £18.00
Circulation: 55,000 (Publisher's Statement)
Usual Pagination: 92
Editor: Jamie Hunter; **News Editor:** Tom Kaminski
Summary of Content: Military aviation magazine dealing with air arms and aircraft around the world.
Readership/Target Audience: Aimed at enthusiasts, professionals and service personnel.
ADVERTISING RATES:
Full Page Colour £800.00
SCC £10.00
Agency Commission: 10%
Mechanical Data: Film: Digital, Trim Size: 276 x 209mm, Bleed Size: 282 x 216mm, Type Area: 246 x 185mm, Col Length: 246mm, Page Width: 185mm
Copy instructions: Copy Date: 3 weeks prior to publication date
Average advertising content per issue: 20%
CONSUMER: HOBBIES & DIY: Military History

COMBAT MARTIAL ARTS MAGAZINE
45988U75Q-250

Formerly: Combat Marshall Arts Magazine
Editorial Address: Regent House, 135 Aldridge Road, Perry Barr, BIRMINGHAM, B42 2ET **Tel:** 0121 344 3737
Fax: 0121 356 7300
Email: combat@martialartsinprint.com
Advertising Address: As above.
Email: paul@martialartsinprint.com
Web site: http://www.combatmag.co.uk
Publisher: Martial Arts Publications Ltd
Date Established: 1974
Frequency: Monthly
Cover Price: £3.50
Annual Sub.: £38.95
Circulation: 89,000 (Publisher's Statement)
Usual Pagination: 166
Editor: Barbera Haig; **Managing Director:** Paul Clifton; **Advertising Manager:** Paul Clifton; **Publisher:** Paul Clifton
Summary of Content: Magazine covering the full range of martial arts practised around the world including techniques, advice, profiles, interviews and associations.
Readership/Target Audience: Read by martial arts enthusiasts, instructors and club owners.
ADVERTISING RATES:
Full Page Mono £550.00
Full Page Colour £795.00
Agency Commission: 20%
Mechanical Data: Page Width: 190mm, Col Length: 270mm, No. of Columns (Display): 3, Trim Size: 297 x 210mm, Type Area: 270 x 190mm, Bleed Size: +5mm, Col Widths (Display): 65mm, Film: Digital
Copy instructions: Copy Date: 2nd Thursday of 2 months prior to publication date
Average advertising content per issue: 38%
CONSUMER: SPORT: Combat Sports

COMICS INTERNATIONAL
1616251U79K-99

Editorial Address: PO Box 9844, COLCHESTER, CO1 9EE **Tel:** 01322 340207
Email: editorial@comics-international.co.uk
Advertising Address: As above.
Email: editorial@comics-international.co.uk
Web site: http://www.comicsinternational.co.uk
Publisher: Cosmic Publications Ltd

Date Established: 1990
Frequency: 13 issues yearly
Cover Price: £2.99
Circulation: 18,000 (Publisher's Statement)
Usual Pagination: 100
Editor: Mike Conroy; **Advertising Manager:** Mike Conroy
Summary of Content: Magazine with news, reviews features, interviews and listings of everything UK and US in the comic industry from Batman to Beano, Judge Dredd to X-Men.
Readership/Target Audience: Read by fans, creators, publishers and licensing companies to enable them to keep up on latest trends.
ADVERTISING: Rates on application
CONSUMER: HOBBIES & DIY: Collectors Magazines

COMMON CAUSE
47213U82-5_70

Editorial Address: Hamlyn House, Macdonald Road, LONDON, N19 5PG **Tel:** 020 7561 7561 **Fax:** 020 7281 5146
Email: commoncause@actionaid.org.uk
Web site: http://www.actionaid.org.uk
ISSN: 0967-0130
Publisher: ActionAid
Date Established: 1989
Frequency: 3 issues yearly - Published in February, June and October
Cover Price: Free -
Circulation: 157,000 (Publisher's Statement)
Usual Pagination: 20
Editor: Stephanie Ross
Summary of Content: Magazine describing ActionAid's work with poor communities throughout Africa, Asia, Latin America and the Caribbean to improve access to food, water, education, healthcare and shelter. Also covers ActionAid's campaigning work in the UK on HIV and Aids and food rights and policy.
Readership/Target Audience: Read by ActionAid supporters.
ADVERTISING: No Advertising taken
CONSUMER: CURRENT AFFAIRS & POLITICS

COMMON GROUND
47698U87-75

Editorial Address: 1st Floor, Camelford House, 87-89 Albert Embankment, LONDON, SE1 7TP **Tel:** 020 7820 0090
Fax: 020 7820 0504
Email: cjrelations@ccj.org.uk
Advertising Address: As above.
Email: cjrelations@ccj.org.uk
Web site: http://www.ccj.org.uk
Publisher: The Council of Christians and Jews
Date Established: 1944
Frequency: Half-yearly
Cover Price: Free
Circulation: 15,000 (Publisher's Statement)
Usual Pagination: 38
Editor: David Gifford; **Advertising Manager:** David Gifford
Summary of Content: Journal concerned with issues of mutual interest to Christians and Jews, from theology to current affairs and daily life.
Readership/Target Audience: Aimed at Christians and Jews.
ADVERTISING: Rates on application
CONSUMER: RELIGIOUS

COMMUNICATION
48622U94F-160

Editorial Address: 393 City Road, LONDON, EC1V 1NG
Tel: 01273 475257
Email: communication@nas.org.uk
Web site: http://www.autism.org.uk
ISSN: 0045-7663
Publisher: The National Autistic Society
Frequency: Quarterly
Free to qualifying individuals
Annual Sub.: £16.00
Circulation: 15,500 (Publisher's Statement)
Usual Pagination: 40
Editor: Miranda Kemp
Summary of Content: Magazine for the National Autistic Society, focusing on autism and Asperger Syndrome. Includes advice, support, news, features and information.
Readership/Target Audience: Aimed at members of the NAS, mainly parents and carers of children with autism, professionals who work with autism and those with autistic spectrum disorders.
ADVERTISING: No Advertising taken
CONSUMER: OTHER CLASSIFICATIONS: Disability

COMMUNITY CONNECTING
1666332U94F-1006

Editorial Address: 2nd Floor, Culvert House, Culvert Road, Battersea, LONDON, SW11 5DH **Tel:** 020 7720 2108
Fax: 020 7498 3023
Email: kate@hawkerpublications.com
Advertising Address: As above.
Email: lisa@hawkerpublications.com

Web site: http://www.careinfo.com
ISSN: 1746-7985
Publisher: Hawker Publications
Date Established: 2005
Frequency: 6 issues yearly
Cover Price: £10.00
Free to qualifying individuals
Annual Sub.: £50.00
Circulation: 3,000 (Publisher's Statement)
Usual Pagination: 36
Editor: Steven Rose; **Advertising Manager:** Lisa Thompson
Summary of Content: Magazine covering all aspects of the personalisation agenda in social care particularly using the experience of people with learning disabilities and their support networks.
Readership/Target Audience: Aimed at social health professionals with an interest in personalisation, direct support and social care.
ADVERTISING: Rates on application
Mechanical Data: Trim Size: 297 x 210mm, Film: Digital
CONSUMER: OTHER CLASSIFICATIONS: Disability

COMPANIONS
755544U81A-42_50

Editorial Address: Whitechapel Way, Priorslee, TELFORD, TF2 9PQ **Tel:** 01952 290999 **Fax:** 01952 291035
Email: pr@pdsa.org.uk
Advertising Address: Landmark Publishing Services, 2 Windmill Street, LONDON, W1T 2HX **Tel:** 020 7692 9292
Fax: 020 7692 9393
Email: sharon@lps.co.uk
Web site: http://www.pdsa.org.uk
Publisher: PDSA
Frequency: Quarterly
Free to qualifying individuals
Circulation: 63,807 (ABC 01/01/2008 to 31/12/2008)
Usual Pagination: 64
Editor: Melanie Graham
Summary of Content: Magazine containing articles and features on favourite pets as well as hints and tips on animal care. Also includes updates on how donations are being used to help pets.
Readership/Target Audience: Read by members of the PDSA.
ADVERTISING RATES:
Full Page £3200.00
Agency Commission: 10%
Mechanical Data: Trim Size: 297 x 210mm, Film: Digital
CONSUMER: ANIMALS & PETS: Animals & Pets Protection

COMPANY MAGAZINE
45171U74A-60

Editorial Address: National Magazine House, 72 Broadwick Street, LONDON, W1F 9EP **Tel:** 020 7439 5000
Fax: 020 7312 3797
Email: company.mail@natmags.co.uk
Advertising Address: As above.
Email: katherine.eills@natmags.co.uk
Web site: http://www.company.co.uk
ISSN: 1011-1144
Publisher: National Magazine Company Ltd
Frequency: Monthly
Cover Price: £2.00
Annual Sub.: £21.60
Circulation: 230,214 (ABC 01/01/2009 to 30/06/2009)
Usual Pagination: 212
Editor: Samantha Flowers; **Managing Director:** Jessica Burley; **Advertisement Director:** Antonia Wigan
Summary of Content: Magazine covering reviews on cinema, books and music. Includes features on beauty, fashion, health and fitness, finance, careers, horoscopes and travel.
Twitter: https://twitter.com/COMPANYMAGAZINE.
Readership/Target Audience: Aimed at young working women.
ADVERTISING RATES:
Full Page Mono £15060.00
Full Page Colour £15060.00
Agency Commission: 15%
Copy instructions: Copy Date: 5 weeks prior to publication date
Average advertising content per issue: 40%
CONSUMER: WOMEN'S INTEREST CONSUMER MAGAZINES: Women's Interest

COMPASS MAGAZINE
46890U80C-1215

Formerly: Compass South
Editorial Address: Homelife House, 26-32 Oxford Road, BOURNEMOUTH, BH8 8EZ **Tel:** 01202 310011
Fax: 01202 298577
Email: peter.cranham@archant.co.uk
Advertising Address: As above.
Email: penny.davage@archant.co.uk
Publisher: Southern Publications Ltd
Date Established: 1998
Frequency: Monthly
Free to qualifying individuals
Annual Sub.: £30.00

Circulation: 100,000 (Publisher's Statement)
Usual Pagination: 100
Editor: Peter Cranham; **Advertising Manager:** Penny Davage; **Managing Editor:** Peter Cranham
Summary of Content: Lifestyle magazine with national editorial content. Features include motoring, travel, fashion, celebrities, beauty, fitness, home, shopping, dining out, wine and property.
Readership/Target Audience: Aimed at residents of Dorset, Hampshire and Surrey.
ADVERTISING RATES:
Full Page Mono £950.00
Full Page Colour £950.00
Agency Commission: 10%
Mechanical Data: Page Width: 186mm, Film: Digital, Type Area: 273 x 186mm, Bleed Size: 303 x 216mm, Trim Size: 297 x 210mm, Col Length: 273mm
Copy instructions: Copy Date: 15th of the month prior to publication date
Average advertising content per issue: 50%
Editions:
Compass South
Compass Surrey
Compass Wessex
Supplement(s): Compass Fine Dining - 2xY, Compass Health and Beauty - 2xY, Compass Homes & Interiors - 2xY, Compass Travel - 2xY
CONSUMER: RURAL & REGIONAL INTEREST: Regional Interest English Counties

COMPASS SPORT
45920U75L-150

Formerly: Compass Sport (Orienteer)
Editorial Address: 6 Glenmore Park, TUNBRIDGE WELLS, TN2 5NZ
Email: nick@compasssport.co.uk
Advertising Address: As above. **Tel:** 07720 952241
Email: advertising@compasssport.co.uk
Web site: http://www.compasssport.co.uk
ISSN: 0263-6697
Publisher: CompassSport
Date Established: 1979
Frequency: 6 issues yearly
Annual Sub.: £24.00
Circulation: 1,650 (Publisher's Statement)
Usual Pagination: 52
Editor: Nick Barrable; **Advertising Manager:** Nick Barrable
Summary of Content: Magazine covering mountain marathons and all forms of orienteering, including mountain bike orienteering, ski-orienteering and trail orienteering.
Readership/Target Audience: Read by active orienteers.
ADVERTISING RATES:
Full Page Colour £395.00
Agency Commission: 10%
Mechanical Data: Type Area: 270 x 186mm, Trim Size: 297 x 210mm, Col Length: 270mm, Bleed Size: 306 x 219mm, Page Width: 186mm
Copy instructions: Copy Date: 4 weeks prior to publication date
CONSUMER: SPORT: Outdoor

COMPETITIONS GALORE
1696956U79F-94

Editorial Address: 2nd Floor, Barclay House, 242-254 Banbury Road, OXFORD, OX2 7BY **Tel:** 01865 515840
Fax: 01865 556588
Email: alastair@prizemags.co.uk
Web site: http://www.prizemagazines.co.uk
Publisher: Prize Magazines
Frequency: 6 issues yearly
Circulation: 40,000 (Publisher's Statement)
Usual Pagination: 52
Editor: Alastair Fry
Summary of Content: Magazine with puzzles and competitions.
Readership/Target Audience: Aimed at women aged 35 years old plus.
ADVERTISING: No Advertising taken
CONSUMER: HOBBIES & DIY: Games & Puzzles

COMPETITORS COMPANION
48672U94X-25

Editorial Address: Zetland House, 5-25 Scrutton Street, LONDON, EC2A 4HJ **Tel:** 020 7613 7477
Fax: 020 7168 7956
Email: nigel@accoladepublishing.co.uk
Web site: http://www.accoladepublishing.co.uk
Publisher: Accolade Publishing
Frequency: Monthly
Annual Sub.: £59.40
Circulation: 25,000 (Publisher's Statement)
Usual Pagination: 24
Editor: Kathy Walker
Summary of Content: Magazine covering competitions available nationwide.
Readership/Target Audience: Aimed at those who enjoy entering competitions.
ADVERTISING: No Advertising taken
CONSUMER: OTHER CLASSIFICATIONS: Miscellaneous

Consumer Magazines

COMPLETE CARD MAKING
1804165U74E-702

Editorial Address: Unit 1 Adlington Court, Adlington Industrial Estate, Adlington, MACCLESFIELD, SK10 4NL
Tel: 0870 242 7038
Email: diane.grimshaw@practicalpublishing.co.uk
Advertising Address: As above.
Email: nouna.sarkissian@practicalpublishing.co.uk
Web site: http://www.practicalpublishing.co.uk
Publisher: Practical Publishing International Ltd
Date Established: 2006
Frequency: 6 issues yearly
Cover Price: £5.99
Usual Pagination: 164
Editor: Diane Grimshaw
Summary of Content: Magazine covering all aspects of card-making with instructions on all types of cards.
Readership/Target Audience: Aimed at all car-makers from beginners to advanced.
ADVERTISING: Rates on application
CONSUMER: WOMEN'S INTEREST CONSUMER MAGAZINES: Crafts

COMPLETE KIT CAR?
46509U77R-750

Formerly: Which Kit Car?
Editorial Address: 30 Henley Road, TAUNTON, TA1 5BJ
Tel: 01823 335443
Email: ian@performancepublishing.co.uk
Advertising Address: County House, 3 Shelley Road, WORTHING, BN11 1TT **Tel:** 01903 236268
Email: dan@performancepublishing.co.uk
Web site: http://www.completekitcar.co.uk
Publisher: Performance Publishing Ltd
Frequency: Monthly - 3rd Friday of cover month
Cover Price: £3.95
Annual Sub.: £40.00
Circulation: 16,000 (Publisher's Statement)
Usual Pagination: 100
Editor: Ian Stent; **Features Editor:** Adam Wilkins;
Advertising Manager: Daniel Large
Summary of Content: Magazine covering the latest news on the British kitcar industry, road tests and exhibitions.
Readership/Target Audience: Aimed at those with an interest in kitcars.
ADVERTISING RATES:
Full Page Mono £550.00
Full Page Colour £550.00
Agency Commission: 10%
Mechanical Data: Page Width: 190mm, Bleed Size: +3mm, Col Length: 260mm, Type Area: 260 x 190mm, Print Process: Web-fed offset, Trim Size: 297 x 230mm, Film: Digital
Copy instructions: Copy Date: 4 weeks prior to publication date
Average advertising content per issue: 40%
CONSUMER: MOTORING & CYCLING: Motoring & Cycling Related

COMPUTER ARTS
36193U78E-9

Editorial Address: 30 Monmouth Street, BATH, BA1 2BW
Tel: 01225 442244
Email: ca.mail@futurenet.co.uk
Advertising Address: As above. **Fax:** 01225 732282
Email: matt.king@futurenet.co.uk
Web site: http://www.computerarts.co.uk
Publisher: Future Publishing Ltd
Date Established: 1995
Frequency: 13 issues yearly
Cover Price: £6.00
Annual Sub.: £54.00
Circulation: 21,209 (ABC 01/01/2008 to 31/12/2008)
Usual Pagination: 124
Editor: Rob Carney; **Advertising Manager:** Matt King
Summary of Content: Magazine covering reviews of hardware and software, computer generated graphics and multimedia, profiles of designers and in-depth tutorials.
Readership/Target Audience: Aimed at graphic and web designers, illustrators, 3D artists and animators.
ADVERTISING RATES:
Full Page Colour £2470.00
Agency Commission: 10%
Mechanical Data: Bleed Size: 286 x 238mm, Page Width: 215mm, Film: Digital, Trim Size: 280 x 232mm, Type Area: 265 X 215mm, Col Length: 265mm
Copy instructions: Copy Date: 3 weeks prior to publication date
Average advertising content per issue: 40%
CONSUMER: CONSUMER ELECTRONICS: Home Computing

COMPUTER ARTS PROJECTS
601475U78E-6

Formerly: Computer Arts Special
Editorial Address: 30 Monmouth Street, BATH, BA1 2BW
Tel: 01225 442244 **Fax:** 01225 732295
Email: ca.mail@futurenet.co.uk
Advertising Address: As above. **Fax:** 01225 822885
Email: helen.crossman@futurenet.co.uk

Web site: http://www.computerarts.co.uk
Publisher: Future Publishing Ltd
Date Established: 1999
Frequency: 13 issues yearly
Cover Price: £7.50
Annual Sub.: £59.50
Circulation: 10,472 (ABC 01/01/2008 to 31/12/2008)
Usual Pagination: 100
Editor: Kate Evans; **Managing Director:** Robert Price; **Publisher:** Liz Taylor
Summary of Content: Magazine focusing on a different aspect of computer creativity per issue. Covering design, illustration, 3D and digital video. Including tutorials, features and tips on software and hardware.
Readership/Target Audience: Aimed at those with an interest in computer arts, from beginners to design professionals.
ADVERTISING RATES:
Full Page Colour £2068.00
SCC £20.00
Agency Commission: 10%
Mechanical Data: Type Area: 215 x 215mm, Bleed Size: 238 x 238mm, Trim Size: 232 x 232mm, Col Length: 215mm, Page Width: 215mm, Film: Digital
Average advertising content per issue: 20%
CONSUMER: CONSUMER ELECTRONICS: Home Computing

COMPUTER MUSIC
36194U76D-798

Editorial Address: 30 Monmouth Street, BATH, BA1 2BW
Tel: 01225 442244 **Fax:** 01225 822793
Email: ronan.macdonald@futurenet.co.uk
Advertising Address: As above.
Email: adrian.major@futurenet.co.uk
Web site: http://www.computermusic.co.uk
Publisher: Future Publishing Ltd
Date Established: 1998
Frequency: 13 issues yearly
Cover Price: £5.99
Circulation: 18,261 (ABC 01/01/2008 to 31/12/2008)
Usual Pagination: 132
Editor: Ronan MacDonald; **Advertising Director:** Adrian Major
Summary of Content: Magazine covering all aspects of how to make music with a computer. Covers news, reviews and tutorials.
Readership/Target Audience: Aimed at computer musicians and those with an interest.
ADVERTISING RATES:
Full Page Colour £1430.00
Agency Commission: 10%
Mechanical Data: Page Width: 203mm, Film: Digital, Trim Size: 300 x 222mm, Type Area: 280 x 203mm, Col Length: 280mm, Bleed Size: 306 x 228mm
Copy instructions: Copy Date: 2 weeks prior to publication date
CONSUMER: MUSIC & PERFORMING ARTS: Music

COMPUTER SHOPPER
36165U78E-22

Editorial Address: 30 Cleveland Street, LONDON, W1T 4JD
Tel: 020 7907 6000 **Fax:** 020 7907 6304
Email: news@computershopper.co.uk
Advertising Address: As above. **Tel:** 020 7907 6640
Fax: 020 7907 6600
Email: richard_bennett@dennis.co.uk
Web site: http://www.computershopper.co.uk
ISSN: 0955-8578
Publisher: Dennis Publishing Ltd
Frequency: Monthly - Published on the 3rd Thursday of each month
Cover Price: £3.99
Circulation: 53,114 (ABC 01/01/2008 to 31/12/2008)
Usual Pagination: 200
Editor: David Ludlow; **Features Editor:** Simon Edwards;
Managing Director: James Tye; **Advertising Manager:** Richard Bennett; **Managing Editor:** Jane Goulding;
Advertising Director: Jonathan Kitchen; **Publisher:** John Garewal
Summary of Content: Magazine covering the latest news and reviews on personal computers. Includes features on the Internet, new equipment and advice for successful buying.
Readership/Target Audience: Read by consumers looking to purchase a computer.
ADVERTISING RATES:
Full Page Colour £3889.00
Agency Commission: 10%
Mechanical Data: Type Area: 275 x 185mm, Col Length: 275mm, Trim Size: 297 x 210mm, Film: Digital, Bleed Size: 303 x 216mm, Page Width: 185mm
Copy instructions: Copy Date: 3 weeks prior to publication date
Average advertising content per issue: 40%
CONSUMER: CONSUMER ELECTRONICS: Home Computing

COMPUTERACTIVE
36192U78E-25

Editorial Address: 32-34 Broadwick Street, LONDON, W1A 2HG **Tel:** 020 7316 9000 **Fax:** 020 7316 9520
Email: news@computeractive.co.uk
Advertising Address: As above. **Tel:** 020 7316 9420
Fax: 020 7316 9257
Email: paul.harvey@incisivemedia.com
Web site: http://www.computeractive.co.uk
ISSN: 1461-6211
Publisher: Incisive Media
Date Established: 1998
Frequency: 24 issues yearly
Cover Price: £1.59
Annual Sub.: £24.95
Circulation: 177,330 (ABC 01/01/2008 to 31/12/2008)
Usual Pagination: 100
Editor: Dinah Greek; **News Editor:** Dinah Greek; **Publisher:** Dylan Armbrust
Summary of Content: Magazine featuring news, advice and practical tips on personal computing at home and at work.
Readership/Target Audience: Aimed at people who want to know how to work their personal computer without the jargon.
ADVERTISING RATES:
Full Page Mono £6384.00
Full Page Colour £6384.00
Agency Commission: 10%
Mechanical Data: Film: Digital, Trim Size: 327 x 236mm
CONSUMER: CONSUMER ELECTRONICS: Home Computing

CONCEPT FOR LIVING
714738U74C-810

Editorial Address: The Old School, Higher Kinnerton, CHESTER, CH4 9AJ **Tel:** 01244 663400
Email: paula.woods@conceptforliving.co.uk
Advertising Address: As above. **Fax:** 01244 660611
Email: vicky.martin@conceptforliving.co.uk
Web site: http://www.conceptforliving.co.uk
Publisher: Concept for Living Ltd
Frequency: Monthly - Published in the first week of the month prior to cover date
Cover Price: £3.00
Annual Sub.: £30.00
Circulation: 35,000 (Publisher's Statement)
Usual Pagination: 162
Publisher: Stuart Mears
Summary of Content: Magazine covering homes and gardens of the north of England. Includes articles on design, interiors, architecture, gardens and new products as well as features on cuisine and art reviews.
Readership/Target Audience: Aimed at those looking for ideas to improve their homes and gardens, living in the north of England.
ADVERTISING RATES:
Full Page Mono £2000.00
Full Page Colour £2000.00
Agency Commission: 10%
Mechanical Data: Type Area: 277 x 210mm, Bleed Size: 303 x 236mm, Trim Size: 297 x 230mm, Col Length: 277mm, Page Width: 210mm, Film: Digital
Copy instructions: Copy Date: 6 weeks prior to publication date
Average advertising content per issue: 40%
CONSUMER: WOMEN'S INTEREST CONSUMER MAGAZINES: Home & Family

CONCOURSE
47450U83-20_70

Formerly: Kinetic
Editorial Address: KUSU, Keele University, NEWCASTLE, ST5 5BJ **Tel:** 01782 583702 **Fax:** 01782 712671
Email: vp.comms@kusu.keele.ac.uk
Advertising Address: As above.
Email: sta65@kusu.keele.ac.uk
Web site: http://www.kusu.net
Publisher: Keele Students' Union
Frequency: 26 issues yearly - Published fortnightly in term time only
Cover Price: Free
Circulation: 10,000 (Publisher's Statement)
Usual Pagination: 12
Advertising Manager: Emma Walker
Summary of Content: Magazine featuring news, events, music, films and art.
Readership/Target Audience: Aimed at students and staff of Keele University and North Staffordshire Nursing & Midwifery College.
ADVERTISING RATES:
Full Page Mono £200.00
Full Page Colour £280.00
Agency Commission: 10%
Mechanical Data: Bleed Size: +5mm, Type Area: 264 x 250mm, Film: Digital, Col Length: 264mm, Page Width: 250mm
Copy instructions: Copy Date: 11 days prior to publication date
Average advertising content per issue: 20%
CONSUMER: STUDENT PUBLICATIONS

CONCRETE
47376U83-5_3

Editorial Address: PO Box 410, NORWICH, NR4 7TB
Tel: 01603 250558 **Fax:** 01603 506822
Email: concrete.editor@uea.ac.uk
Advertising Address: Advertising and Marketing
Department, Union House, UEA, NORWICH, NR4 7TG
Tel: 01603 592507 **Fax:** 01603 250144
Email: jean.wills@ueastudent.com
Web site: http://www.concrete-online.co.uk
ISSN: 1351-2773
Publisher: Union of UEA Students
Date Established: 1992
Frequency: 13 issues yearly - Published fortnightly during
term time
Cover Price: Free
Circulation: 5,000 (Publisher's Statement)
Usual Pagination: 48
Editor: Fiona Billings; **Advertising Manager:** Jean Wills
Summary of Content: Student newspaper of the University
of East Anglia and Norwich containing news, features, sport
and listings of local music, films, arts, TV and games.
Readership/Target Audience: Read by students at UEA
and members of staff.
ADVERTISING RATES:
Full Page Colour £750.00
Mechanical Data: Film: Digital, Col Length: 360mm, Type
Area: 360 x 270mm, Page Width: 270mm
CONSUMER: STUDENT PUBLICATIONS

CONDE NAST BRIDES
45527U74L-63

Editorial Address: Vogue House, 1 Hanover Square,
LONDON, W1S 1JU **Tel:** 020 7499 9080 **Fax:** 020 7152 3369
Email: fiona.kerr@condenast.co.uk
Advertising Address: As above. **Tel:** 020 7152 3364
Fax: 020 7491 9281
Email: cnewman@condenast.co.uk
Web site: http://www.bridesmagazine.co.uk
Publisher: Conde Nast Publications Ltd
Date Established: 1955
Frequency: 6 issues yearly
Cover Price: £4.70
Circulation: 68,349 (ABC 01/01/2008 to 31/12/2008)
Usual Pagination: 330
Editor: Fiona Kerr; **Managing Director:** Nicholas Coleridge;
Advertisement Director: Camilla Newman; **Publisher:**
Simon Leadsford
Summary of Content: Magazine containing features on
bridal wear, wedding receptions, beauty, travel, home
furnishings and decor.
Readership/Target Audience: Aimed at women intending
to marry in the near future.
ADVERTISING RATES:
Full Page Colour £8400.00
Agency Commission: 15%
Mechanical Data: Type Area: 265 x 200mm, Bleed Size:
291 x 226mm, Trim Size: 285 x 220mm, Col Length: 265mm,
Print Process: Web-fed offset litho, Film: Digital, Page Width:
200mm
Average advertising content per issue: 50%
Supplement(s): Wedding Planner - 1xY
CONSUMER: WOMEN'S INTEREST CONSUMER
MAGAZINES: Brides

CONDE NAST TRAVELLER
48233U89E-76

Editorial Address: Vogue House, 1 Hanover Square,
LONDON, W1S 1JU **Tel:** 020 7499 9080 **Fax:** 020 7493 3758
Email: cntraveller@condenast.co.uk
Advertising Address: As above. **Tel:** 020 7491 3602
Email: sarah.brookes@condenast.co.uk
Web site: http://www.cntraveller.com
Publisher: Conde Nast Publications Ltd
Date Established: 1997
Frequency: Monthly
Cover Price: £3.70
Annual Sub.: £38.40
Circulation: 81,514 (ABC 01/01/2009 to 30/06/2009)
Usual Pagination: 112
Editor: Sarah Miller; **Executive Editor:** Stephen Wood;
Managing Director: Nicholas Coleridge; **Advertising
Manager:** Polly Warrick; **Managing Editor:** Paula Maynard;
Publisher: Simon Leadsford
Summary of Content: Magazine containing travel articles,
new ideas, culture and features on architecture and design.
Readership/Target Audience: Aimed at the independent
traveller.
ADVERTISING RATES:
Full Page Colour £7803.00
Agency Commission: 15%
Mechanical Data: Type Area: 265 x 200mm, Bleed Size:
291 x 226mm, Trim Size: 285 x 220mm, Col Length: 265mm,
Page Width: 200mm
Copy instructions: Copy Date: 4 weeks prior to publication
date
Average advertising content per issue: 40%
CONSUMER: HOLIDAYS & TRAVEL: Holidays

CONNECTED
1849785U89D-534

Editorial Address: Publishing House, 3 Bridgebank
Industrial Estate, Taylor Street, Horwich, BOLTON, BL6 7PD
Tel: 0161 909 0909 **Fax:** 0161 909 0919
Email: jonathan.richards@bigspark.co.uk
Advertising Address: As above.
Web site: http://www.connectedmagazine.co.uk
Publisher: The Big Spark
Date Established: 2008
Frequency: Quarterly
Cover Price: Free
Circulation: 24,000 (Publisher's Statement)
Usual Pagination: 48
Editor: Jonathan Richards
Summary of Content: Magazine covering celebrity
interviews, car tests, financial pages and destinations.
Readership/Target Audience: Aimed at incoming and
outgoing passengers at Stansted airport.
CONSUMER: HOLIDAYS & TRAVEL: In-Flight Magazines

CONSCIENCE UPDATE
47215U82-6

Editorial Address: Archway Resource Centre, 1B Waterlow
Road, LONDON, N19 5NJ **Tel:** 020 7561 1061
Fax: 020 7281 6508
Email: info@conscienceonline.org.uk
Advertising Address: As above.
Email: outreach@conscienceonline.org.uk
Web site: http://www.conscienceonline.org.uk
ISSN: 1474-8789
Publisher: Conscience - The Peace Tax Campaign
Date Established: 1979
Frequency: Quarterly
Free to qualifying individuals
Circulation: 2,500 (Publisher's Statement)
Usual Pagination: 8
Editor: Nick Wilson; **Advertising Manager:** Nick Wilson
Summary of Content: Magazine of campaign working for
the legal rights of those who have a conscientious objection
to war.
Readership/Target Audience: Aimed at those who have a
conscientious objection to paying tax in order to fund war
around the world.
ADVERTISING: Rates on application
CONSUMER: CURRENT AFFAIRS & POLITICS

THE CONSERVATOR
29705U84A-424

Editorial Address: The Institute of Conservation, 3rd Floor,
Downstream Building, 1 London Bridge, LONDON, SE1 9BG
Tel: 020 7785 3805 **Fax:** 020 7721 8722
Web site: http://www.ukic.org.uk
ISSN: 0140-0096
Publisher: York Publishing Services Ltd
Frequency: Annual
Free to qualifying individuals
Circulation: 3,000 (Publisher's Statement)
Editor: Irit Narkiss
Summary of Content: Contains case studies, research and
papers on conservation.
Readership/Target Audience: Aimed at all members of
UKIC.
ADVERTISING: No Advertising taken
CONSUMER: THE ARTS & LITERARY: Arts

THE CONSORT, EARLY MUSIC JOURNAL
46191U76D-304

Formerly: The Consort, European Journal of Early Music
Editorial Address: 2 Parkfields, High Street, Butleigh,
GLASTONBURY, BA6 8SZ **Tel:** 01458 851561
Email: elizabethrees_ocv@hotmail.com
Advertising Address: As above.
Email: elizabethrees_ocv@hotmail.com
Web site: http://www.dolmetsch.com
ISSN: 0268-9111
Publisher: The Dolmetsch Foundation
Date Established: 1929
Frequency: Annual - Published in July
Annual Sub.: £17.50
Circulation: 400 (Publisher's Statement)
Usual Pagination: 100
Editor: Elizabeth Rees; **Advertising Manager:** Elizabeth
Rees
Summary of Content: Journal focusing the early music,
covering composers, performance and musical instruments
up to 1800.
Readership/Target Audience: Aimed at early music
enthusiasts, musicians and members of schools, universities
and other academic institutions worldwide.
ADVERTISING RATES:
Full Page Mono £100.00
Mechanical Data: Film: Digital, Type Area: A5
Copy instructions: Copy Date: 3 months prior to publication
date
Average advertising content per issue: 3%
CONSUMER: MUSIC & PERFORMING ARTS: Music

CONTACT
47699U87-75_40

Editorial Address: Church House, 123 Queen Street,
SHEFFIELD, S1 2DU **Tel:** 0114 272 1938
Fax: 0114 272 1938
Email: gen.sec@thewru.co.uk
Advertising Address: As above.
Email: gen.sec@thewru.co.uk
Web site: http://www.thewru.com
Publisher: Wesleyan Reform Union
Frequency: Monthly
Cover Price: £0.50
Circulation: 1,250 (Publisher's Statement)
Usual Pagination: 12
Editor: Colin Braithwaite; **Advertising Manager:** Colin
Braithwaite
Summary of Content: Magazine of the Wesleyan Reform
Union covering news and items of interest.
Readership/Target Audience: Aimed at members of the
Wesleyan Reform Union.
ADVERTISING: Rates on application
CONSUMER: RELIGIOUS

CONTACT
48746U94X-30

Formerly: Fisons Contact
Editorial Address: 27 Norwich Road, HALESWORTH, IP19
8BX **Tel:** 01986 834216 **Fax:** 01986 834270
Email: barry.spouge@micropress.co.uk
Publisher: Countrywide Publications
Date Established: 1986
Frequency: Half-yearly - Published in March and September
Cover Price: Free
Circulation: 5,500 (Publisher's Statement)
Usual Pagination: 8
Editor: Barry Spouge; **Publisher:** Barry Spouge
Summary of Content: A news magazine for pensioners of
Fisons plc.
Readership/Target Audience: Aimed at all former Fisons
group pensioners.
ADVERTISING: No Advertising taken
CONSUMER: OTHER CLASSIFICATIONS: Miscellaneous

CONTACT ILLUSTRATORS & CONTACT PHOTOGRAPHERS (2 VOLUMES)
47600U85A-50

Formerly: Contact Illustrators & Photographers (2 Volumes)
Editorial Address: Surrey House, 31 Church Street,
LEATHERHEAD, KT22 8EF **Tel:** 01372 220330
Fax: 01372 220340
Email: mail@contact-uk.com
Web site: http://www.contact-uk.com
Publisher: Elfande Ltd
Frequency: Annual - Published in April
Cover Price: £35.00
Free to qualifying individuals
Circulation: 20,000 (Publisher's Statement)
Usual Pagination: 400
Publisher: Nick Gould; **Circulation Manager:** Annabelle
Gardener
Summary of Content: Visual source book used by art
buyers all over the UK and Europe.
Readership/Target Audience: Aimed at art buyers, art
directors, editors and designers.
ADVERTISING: No Advertising taken
CONSUMER: PHOTOGRAPHY & FILM MAKING:
Photography

CONTEMPORARY
47497U84A-208

Editorial Address: Studio 56, 4 Montpelier Street,
LONDON, SW7 1EE **Tel:** 020 7019 6205
Email: info@contemporary-magazine.com
Advertising Address: As above. **Fax:** 020 7100 5998
Email: nick@contemporary-magazine.com
Web site: http://www.contemporary-magazine.com
ISSN: 1028-5040
Publisher: Art 21 Ltd
Date Established: 1992
Frequency: Monthly
Cover Price: £5.95
Annual Sub.: £49.00
Circulation: 30,000 (Publisher's Statement)
Usual Pagination: 96
Editor: Emiliano Valdes; **News Editor:** Richard Dyer;
Managing Editor: Emiliano Valdes; **Publisher:** Brian Muller
Summary of Content: Magazine containing features and
reviews. Also includes articles on the relationship between
visual arts and the worlds of architecture, film and fashion,
as well as international news and regular interviews.
Readership/Target Audience: Read by people interested in
contemporary visual arts.
ADVERTISING RATES:
Full Page Colour £4000.00
Agency Commission: 10%
Mechanical Data: Film: Digital, Bleed Size: 305 x 235mm,
Trim Size: 300 x 230mm

Copy instructions: Copy Date: 6 weeks prior to publication date
Average advertising content per issue: 20%
CONSUMER: THE ARTS & LITERARY: Arts

CONTEMPORARY ZONE   1705245U74C-853

Editorial Address: 6 Beechfield Road, Boxmoor, HEMEL HEMPSTEAD, HP1 1PP
Publisher: Dutch Publishing
Frequency: 6 issues yearly
Cover Price: £5.00
Circulation: 12,000 (Publisher's Statement)
Editor: Maria Vida
Summary of Content: Magazine focusing on contemporary interior design.
Readership/Target Audience: Aimed at all those interested in contemporary art and interior design.
ADVERTISING: Rates on application
CONSUMER: WOMEN'S INTEREST CONSUMER MAGAZINES: Home & Family

CONTEXT   48588U94B-10

Editorial Address: Jubilee House, High Street, TISBURY, SP3 6HA Tel: 01747 873133
Email: editor@ihbc.org.uk
Advertising Address: As above. Tel: 01747 871717
Fax: 01747 871718
Email: gordon@cathcomm.demon.co.uk
Web site: http://www.ihbc.org.uk
ISSN: 0958-2746
Publisher: Cathedral Communications
Date Established: 1987
Frequency: 5 issues yearly
Free to qualifying individuals
Annual Sub.: £50.00
Circulation: 2,500 (Publisher's Statement)
Usual Pagination: 50
Editor: Rob Cowan; Advertising Manager: Gordon Sorensen
Summary of Content: Journal of the Institute of Historic Building Conservation. Covers all aspects of conservation and repair of historic and listed buildings and gardens, new developments, urban design and architecture. Includes news, products, views and craft techniques.
Readership/Target Audience: Aimed at conservation professionals both members and those with an interest in historic buildings, conservation, education and urban and landscape design.
ADVERTISING RATES:
Full Page Colour £700.00
Agency Commission: 10%
Mechanical Data: Film: Digital, Print Process: Offset litho, Type Area: 254 x 178mm, Col Length: 254mm, Page Width: 178mm, Bleed Size: 305 x 213mm, Trim Size: 297 x 210mm, No. of Columns (Display): 2
Copy instructions: Copy Date: End of the month prior to publication date
Average advertising content per issue: 20%
CONSUMER: OTHER CLASSIFICATIONS: Historic Buildings

CONTINENTAL MODELLER   28955U79B-193

Editorial Address: Underleys, Beer, SEATON, EX12 3NA
Tel: 01297 20580 Fax: 01297 20229
Email: cm-editor@btconnect.com
Advertising Address: As above.
Email: pecopubs@btconnect.com
Web site: http://www.peco-uk.com
Publisher: Peco Publications & Publicity Ltd.
Date Established: 1979
Frequency: Monthly
Cover Price: £3.25
Annual Sub.: £39.00
Circulation: 12,000 (Publisher's Statement)
Usual Pagination: 86
Editor: Andrew Burnham; Advertising Manager: John King
Summary of Content: Magazine covering information on model railways from all over the world.
Readership/Target Audience: Read by anyone interested in model railways from around the world.
ADVERTISING RATES:
Full Page Colour £255.00
Mechanical Data: Type Area: 268 x 204mm, Col Length: 268mm, Page Width: 204mm, Film: Digital
Copy instructions: Copy Date: 5 weeks prior to publication date
CONSUMER: HOBBIES & DIY: Models & Modelling

COOK VEGETARIAN!   1849936U74P-960

Editorial Address: 25 Phoenix Court, Hawkins Road, COLCHESTER, CO2 8JY Tel: 01206 505491
Email: rachel@cookveg.co.uk
Advertising Address: 21-23 Phoenix Court, Hawkins Road, COLCHESTER, CO2 8JY Tel: 01206 505900
Fax: 01206 505915
Email: jay.hurley@aceville.co.uk

Publisher: Aceville Publications Ltd
Date Established: 2008
Frequency: Monthly
Circulation: 45,000 (Publisher's Statement)
Editor: Rachel Callen
Summary of Content: A vegetarian cookery magazine covering vegetarian ingredients and foods, restaurants, cookery courses, electricals, cookware and tableware.
Readership/Target Audience: Aimed at people who like to cook vegetarian food.
ADVERTISING RATES:
Full Page Colour £1345.00
Agency Commission: 10%
Mechanical Data: Type Area: 276 x 210mm, Bleed Size: 310 x 240mm, Trim Size: 300 x 230mm, Col Length: 276mm, Page Width: 210mm, Film: Digital
Average advertising content per issue: 31%
CONSUMER: WOMEN'S INTEREST CONSUMER MAGAZINES: Food & Cookery

COOLER   1687360U75G-655

Editorial Address: 1 West Smithfield, LONDON, EC1A 9JU
Tel: 020 7332 9700 Fax: 020 7332 9799
Email: sam@coolermag.com
Advertising Address: As above.
Email: craig.scrivener@factorymedia.com
Web site: http://www.coolermag.com
Publisher: Factory Media
Date Established: 2005
Frequency: 6 issues yearly
Cover Price: £2.95
Circulation: 47,000 (Publisher's Statement)
Usual Pagination: 132
Editor: Sam Haddad; Advertising Manager: Craig Scrivener
Summary of Content: Magazine covering women's action sports in Europe including snowboarding, skiing, surfing, skating, mountain biking, fixed gear cycling and with features on lifestyle, travel, culture and fashion.
Readership/Target Audience: Aimed at 16 to 25 year old women who live, or aspire to, the board and free sports culture.
ADVERTISING RATES:
Full Page Colour £4700.00
Agency Commission: 10%
Mechanical Data: Bleed Size: 275 x 215mm, Trim Size: 265 x 205mm, Film: Digital
CONSUMER: SPORT: Winter Sports

COOLTURA   1749967U90-989

Editorial Address: Unit 6, King Street Cloisters, Clifton Walk, LONDON, W6 0GY Tel: 0870 041 4677
Fax: 020 7386 3771
Email: info@cooltura.co.uk
Advertising Address: As above. Tel: 020 8846 3615
Fax: 020 8741 9490
Email: joanna@cooltura.co.uk
Web site: http://www.cooltura.co.uk
ISSN: 1743-8489
Publisher: Sara-Int Ltd
Date Established: 2004
Frequency: Weekly - Published on Friday
Cover Price: Free
Circulation: 45,000 (Publisher's Statement)
Usual Pagination: 116
Editor: Dariusz Zeller; Advertising Manager: Joanna Rozek
Summary of Content: Magazine covering news, fashion, culture, technology, sport, jobs and national and local events.
Language(s): Polish
Readership/Target Audience: Aimed at Polish communities in the UK.
ADVERTISING RATES:
Full Page Colour £1450.00
Agency Commission: 10%
Mechanical Data: Trim Size: 297 x 210mm, Film: Digital, Type Area: 262 x 185mm, Bleed Size: 5mm, Col Length: 262mm, Page Width: 185mm
Copy instructions: Copy Date: Monday 3.00pm prior to publication date
Average advertising content per issue: 30%
CONSUMER: ETHNIC

CO-OP TRAVELLER   1665815U89E-237

Editorial Address: 1 Neal Street, Covent Garden, LONDON, WC2H 9QL Tel: 020 7306 0304 Fax: 020 7306 0314
Email: cooptraveller@riverltd.co.uk
Advertising Address: As above.
Email: kmurdoch@riverltd.co.uk
Publisher: River Publishing Ltd
Frequency: 3 issues yearly - Published in May, July and December
Cover Price: Free
Circulation: 360,000 (Publisher's Statement)
Editor: Heather Farmbrough; Advertising Manager: Kate Murdoch

Summary of Content: Magazine with travel features, tips and news.
Readership/Target Audience: Aimed at customers of the Co-op travel group.
ADVERTISING RATES:
Full Page Colour £7500.00
Agency Commission: 10%
Copy instructions: Copy Date: 4 weeks prior to publication date
CONSUMER: HOLIDAYS & TRAVEL: Holidays

COREL PAINTER OFFICIAL MAGAZINE   1799703U78E-55

Editorial Address: Richmond House, 33 Richmond Hill, BOURNEMOUTH, BH2 6EZ Tel: 01202 586200
Email: jo.cole@imagine-publishing.co.uk
Advertising Address: As above. Fax: 01202 294032
Email: andy.wooldridge@imagine-publishing.co.uk
Web site: http://www.paintermagazine.co.uk
ISSN: 1753-3155
Publisher: Imagine Publishing
Date Established: 2007
Frequency: 13 issues yearly
Cover Price: £6.00
Circulation: 30,000 (Publisher's Statement)
Usual Pagination: 100
Editor: Jo Cole
Summary of Content: Magazine with tutorials and tips on Corel Painter as well as traditional art theory.
Readership/Target Audience: Aimed at new and existing Corel Painter users, predominantly men aged 20 to 45 years old who are creative professional or enthusiastic home users as well as design and art students.
ADVERTISING RATES:
Full Page Colour £2000.00
Agency Commission: 10%
Mechanical Data: Type Area: 277 x 210mm, Bleed Size: 307 x 240mm, Trim Size: 297 x 230mm, Col Length: 277mm, Page Width: 210mm, Film: Digital
Copy instructions: Copy Date: 4 weeks prior to publication date
Average advertising content per issue: 10%
CONSUMER: CONSUMER ELECTRONICS: Home Computing

CORNERSTONE   48591U94B-90

Formerly: SPAB News
Editorial Address: 37 Spital Square, LONDON, E1 6DY
Tel: 020 7377 1644 Fax: 020 7247 5296
Email: info@spab.org.uk
Advertising Address: PO Box 21, BALDOCK, SG7 5SH
Tel: 01462 896688 Fax: 01462 896677
Email: geoff@hall-mccartney.co.uk
Web site: http://www.spab.org.uk
ISSN: 0969-4250
Publisher: SPAB
Date Established: 1979
Frequency: Quarterly
Free to qualifying individuals
Annual Sub.: £36.00
Circulation: 8,700 (Publisher's Statement)
Usual Pagination: 95
Editor: Robin Stummer; Editor-in-Chief: Philip Venning; Advertising Manager: Geoff Connelly
Summary of Content: Journal of the Society for the Protection of Ancient Buildings. Features information on historic architecture and its conservation.
Readership/Target Audience: Read by architects, surveyors and owners of listed buildings.
ADVERTISING RATES:
Full Page Mono £739.00
Full Page Colour £883.00
Agency Commission: 10%
Mechanical Data: Type Area: 265 x 220mm, Bleed Size: 304 x 246mm, Trim Size: 298 x 240mm, Col Length: 265mm, Col Widths (Display): 65mm, No. of Columns (Display): 3, Page Width: 220mm, Print Process: Offset litho, Film: Digital
Copy instructions: Copy Date: 4 weeks prior to publication date
Average advertising content per issue: 25%
CONSUMER: OTHER CLASSIFICATIONS: Historic Buildings

CORNISH BRIDES   1614513U74L-216

Editorial Address: Seton Business Centre, Scorrier, REDRUTH, TR16 5AW Tel: 01209 315646
Email: info@cornishbrides.co.uk
Advertising Address: As above.
Email: info@cornishbrides.co.uk
Web site: http://www.cornishbrides.co.uk
Publisher: Purple Media
Date Established: 2003
Frequency: Half-yearly - Published in March and September
Cover Price: Free
Circulation: 20,000 (Publisher's Statement)
Usual Pagination: 64

Editor: Janice Matthews; **Advertising Manager:** Colin Robinson; **Publisher:** Colin Robinson
Summary of Content: Directory covering all aspects of wedding planning including information on florists, jewellers, weddings gowns and how to get married.
Readership/Target Audience: Aimed at brides to be.
ADVERTISING RATES:
Full Page Colour £700.00
Agency Commission: 15%
Mechanical Data: Type Area: 210 x 148.5mm, Col Length: 210mm, Page Width: 148.5mm, Col Widths (Display): 60mm, No. of Columns (Display): 2, Film: Digital
Average advertising content per issue: 30%
CONSUMER: WOMEN'S INTEREST CONSUMER MAGAZINES: Brides

CORNISH WORLD
46875U80C-750

Editorial Address: Jennings House, Jennings Street, PENZANCE, TR18 2LU **Tel:** 01736 365896
Fax: 01736 330538
Email: editor@cornish-world.fsnet.co.uk
Advertising Address: As above.
Email: editor@cornish-world.fsnet.co.uk
Web site: http://www.cornishworldmagazine.co.uk
ISSN: 1355-672X
Publisher: Pentreath Industries
Date Established: 1994
Frequency: 6 issues yearly
Cover Price: £2.95
Free to qualifying individuals
Annual Sub.: £24.00
Circulation: 14,000 (Publisher's Statement)
Usual Pagination: 120
Editor: Nigel Pengelly; **Advertising Manager:** Chris Hanby
Summary of Content: Magazine covering Cornish heritage, history and news.
Readership/Target Audience: Aimed at those originating from, or interested in Cornwall.
ADVERTISING RATES:
Full Page Colour £450.00
Agency Commission: 30%
Mechanical Data: Type Area: 287 x 200mm, Trim Size: 297 x 210mm, Bleed Size: 303 x 215mm, Col Length: 287mm, Page Width: 200mm, Film: Digital
Copy instructions: Copy Date: 1 week prior to publication date
Average advertising content per issue: 20%
CONSUMER: RURAL & REGIONAL INTEREST: Regional Interest English Counties

---

CORNWALL FAMILY HISTORY SOCIETY JOURNAL
48675U94X-32

Editorial Address: 5 Victoria Square, TRURO, TR1 2RS
Tel: 01872 264044
Email: secretary@cornwallfhs.com
Advertising Address: As above.
Email: editor@cornwallfhs.com
Web site: http://www.cornwallfhs.com
ISSN: 0141-7614
Publisher: Cornwall Family History Society
Date Established: 1976
Frequency: Quarterly
Annual Sub.: £12.00
Circulation: 5,500 (Publisher's Statement)
Usual Pagination: 36
Editor: Pat Fawcett; **Advertising Manager:** Lawrence Smith
Summary of Content: Magazine containing articles of genealogical, social and cultural interest to those of Cornish ancestry.
Readership/Target Audience: Aimed at those interested in tracing their family history.
ADVERTISING: Rates on application
Copy instructions: Copy Date: 2 months prior to publication date
Average advertising content per issue: 10%
CONSUMER: OTHER CLASSIFICATIONS: Miscellaneous

CORNWALL LIFE
1658897U80C-5174

Editorial Address: Archant House, Babbage Road, TOTNES, TQ9 5JA **Tel:** 01803 860910 **Fax:** 01803 860922
Email: jennie.wilkinson@archant.co.uk
Web site: http://www.cornwalllife.co.uk
Publisher: Archant Life
Frequency: Monthly
Cover Price: £2.75
Circulation: 12,000 (Publisher's Statement)
Editor: Jennie Wilkinson
Summary of Content: Magazine containing features on the Cornwall area.
Readership/Target Audience: Aimed at residents and visitors to Cornwall.
ADVERTISING: Rates on application
Edition of: Devon Life
CONSUMER: RURAL & REGIONAL INTEREST: Regional Interest English Counties

---

CORNWALL TODAY
1638850U80C-5077

Editorial Address: Harmsworth House, City Wharf, Malpas Road, TRURO, TR1 1QH **Tel:** 01872 247458
Email: knewton@cornwalltoday.co.uk
Advertising Address: As above. **Tel:** 01872 247548
Fax: 01872 247434
Email: elaine@cornwalltoday.co.uk
Publisher: Cornwall & Devon Media Limited
Date Established: 1995
Frequency: Monthly
Cover Price: £2.95
Circulation: 15,000 (Publisher's Statement)
Usual Pagination: 152
Editor: Kirstie Newton
Summary of Content: Lifestyle magazine focusing on issues of interest to those living in and around Cornwall.
Readership/Target Audience: Aimed at those 35 and over living in and around Cornwall.
ADVERTISING RATES:
Full Page Colour £625.00
Mechanical Data: Trim Size: 297 x 210mm.
Copy instructions: Copy Date: 4 weeks prior to publication date
CONSUMER: RURAL & REGIONAL INTEREST: Regional Interest English Counties

---

COSMOPOLITAN
45172U74A-70

Editorial Address: National Magazine House, 72 Broadwick Street, LONDON, W1F 9EP **Tel:** 020 7439 5000
Fax: 020 7439 5016
Email: cosmo.mail@natmags.co.uk
Advertising Address: As above. **Fax:** 020 7439 5232
Email: nicola.spooner@natmags.co.uk
Web site: http://www.cosmopolitan.co.uk
Publisher: National Magazine Company Ltd
Date Established: 1972
Frequency: Monthly
Cover Price: £3.20
Circulation: 441,663 (ABC 01/01/2009 to 30/06/2009)
Usual Pagination: 370
Editor: Lisa Kirkby; **Features Editor:** Fiona Cowood;
Advertising Manager: Nicola Spooner
Summary of Content: Magazine covering fashion, beauty, relationships, travel and work.
Twitter: https://twitter.com/CosmopolitanUK.
Readership/Target Audience: Aimed at young professional women.
ADVERTISING RATES:
Full Page Colour £21945.00
Agency Commission: 15%
Mechanical Data: Type Area: 270 x 192mm, Col Length: 270mm, Page Width: 192mm, Film: Digital
Copy instructions: Copy Date: 2nd of the month prior to publication date
Average advertising content per issue: 45%
CONSUMER: WOMEN'S INTEREST CONSUMER MAGAZINES: Women's Interest

---

COSMOPOLITAN BRIDE
707850U74L-75

Editorial Address: National Magazine House, 72 Broadwick Street, LONDON, W1F 9EP **Tel:** 020 7439 5000
Fax: 020 7734 5383
Email: cosmobride.mail@natmags.co.uk
Advertising Address: As above. **Fax:** 020 7312 3717
Email: katie.rose@natmags.co.uk
Web site: http://www.youandyourwedding.co.uk
Publisher: National Magazine Company Ltd
Date Established: 2001
Frequency: 6 issues yearly
Cover Price: £3.99
Annual Sub.: £23.94
Circulation: 37,148 (ABC 01/01/2008 to 31/12/2008)
Usual Pagination: 288
Editor: Gemma Askham
Summary of Content: Magazine covering all aspects of planning a wedding, including fashion, beauty, travel and venues.
Readership/Target Audience: Aimed at brides to be.
ADVERTISING RATES:
Full Page Colour £7540.00
Agency Commission: 15%
Mechanical Data: Type Area: 252 x 180mm, Bleed Size: 278 x 206mm, Col Length: 252mm, Page Width: 180mm, Film: Digital, Print Process: Web-fed offset litho, Trim Size: 272 x 200mm
Copy instructions: Copy Date: 4 weeks prior to publication date
Average advertising content per issue: 50%
CONSUMER: WOMEN'S INTEREST CONSUMER MAGAZINES: Brides

COTSWOLD LIFE
761855U80C-250

Editorial Address: Archant House, Oriel Road, CHELTENHAM, GL50 1BB **Tel:** 01242 216050
Fax: 01242 255116
Email: editorial@cotswoldlife.co.uk

Advertising Address: As above. **Tel:** 01242 216058
Email: mary.holtham@cotswoldlife.co.uk
Web site: http://www.cotswoldlife.co.uk
Publisher: Archant Life
Date Established: 1967
Frequency: Monthly
Cover Price: £3.25
Circulation: 15,136 (ABC 01/01/2008 to 31/12/2008)
Usual Pagination: 266
Editor: Candia McKormack; **Editor-in-Chief:** Mike Lowe;
Advertising Manager: Mary Holtham
Summary of Content: Lifestyle magazine covering property, fashion, dining, interiors, beauty, celebrity interviews, town features, rural issues, heritage, arts, antiques, business, gardens and events.
Readership/Target Audience: Aimed at affluent residents of Berkshire.
ADVERTISING RATES:
Full Page Colour £1452.00
Agency Commission: 10%
Mechanical Data: Film: Digital, Type Area: 271 x 199mm, Col Length: 271mm, Trim Size: 300 x 220mm, Bleed Size: 306 x 226mm, Page Width: 199mm
Copy instructions: Copy Date: Beginning of the month prior to publication date
Average advertising content per issue: 50%
Editions:
Berkshire and Chiltern Life
Oxfordshire Life
Supplement(s): Cotswold Weddings - 2xY
CONSUMER: RURAL & REGIONAL INTEREST: Regional Interest English Counties

---

COTSWOLD WATER PARK LIFE
1832316U80A-177

Editorial Address: The Marketing House, Meadow Road, CIRENCESTER, GL7 1YA **Tel:** 01285 715776
Email: editor@waterparklife.co.uk
Advertising Address: As above. **Tel:** 01285 650661
Email: sales@waterparklife.co.uk
Web site: http://www.waterparklife.co.uk
Publisher: Cotswold Water Park Media Ltd
Date Established: 2008
Frequency: 6 issues yearly
Cover Price: £1.50
Free to qualifying individuals
Circulation: 10,000 (Publisher's Statement)
Usual Pagination: 32
Editor: Paul Fisher; **Advertising Manager:** Barbara Eadon
Summary of Content: Magazine covering leisure and lifestyle, business to business, biodiversity and the environment as well as residential property.
Readership/Target Audience: Aimed at residents, day visitors, tourists and businesses in the Cotswolds.
ADVERTISING RATES:
Full Page Colour £435.00
Mechanical Data: Trim Size: 265.5 x 185mm, Film: Digital
Copy instructions: Copy Date: 2 weeks prior to publication date
CONSUMER: RURAL & REGIONAL INTEREST: Rural Interest

COTSWOLD WEDDINGS
1786176U74L-251

Editorial Address: Archant House, Oriel Road, CHELTENHAM, GL50 1BB **Tel:** 01242 216050
Fax: 01242 255116
Email: editorial@cotswoldlife.co.uk
Advertising Address: As above.
Email: mary.holtham@cotswoldlife.com
Publisher: Archant Life
Frequency: Half-yearly - Published in April and January
Cover Price: Free
Circulation: 20,000 (Print Run)
Editor: Sandra Fraser; **Advertising Manager:** Mary Holtham
Summary of Content: Magazine covering all aspects of weddings in the Cotswolds including planning, fashion, venues, legal advice, flowers, photograph, feature weddings, receptions, cakes, hair and grooming.
Readership/Target Audience: Aimed at brides-to-be in the Cotswolds.
ADVERTISING RATES:
Full Page Colour £1530.00
Agency Commission: 10%
Mechanical Data: Type Area: 271 x 199mm, Bleed Size: 306 x 226mm, Trim Size: 300 x 220mm, Col Length: 271mm, Page Width: 199mm, Film: Digital
Copy instructions: Copy Date: Beginning of the month prior to publication date
Average advertising content per issue: 50%
Supplement to: Cotswold Life
CONSUMER: WOMEN'S INTEREST CONSUMER MAGAZINES: Brides

Consumer Magazines

COUNTIES TODAY
1895209U80C-5502

Editorial Address: 4 Copthall House, Station Square, COVENTRY, CV1 2FY **Tel:** 0845 128 0163
Fax: 0845 128 0164
Email: editorials@counties-today.co.uk
Advertising Address: As above.
Email: advertising@counties-today.co.uk
Web site: http://www.counties-today.co.uk
Publisher: Counties Newspapers Ltd
Frequency: 6 issues yearly
Cover Price: Free
Circulation: 60,000 (Publisher's Statement)
Editor: Seema Bhalsod; **Advertising Manager:** Seema Bhalsod
Summary of Content: Magazine focusing on local business, travel, health and beauty, motors, fashion, gadgets, technology, education, training, celebrity news, men's interest, women's interest, children, entertainment and what's on.
Readership/Target Audience: Aimed at businessmen and women and anybody with an interest in modern business and lifestyle.
ADVERTISING RATES:
Full Page Colour £1400.00
CONSUMER: RURAL & REGIONAL INTEREST: Regional Interest English Counties

COUNTRY & BORDER LIFE MAGAZINE
1667978U80D-513

Formerly: Country & Border Life
Editorial Address: Salop House, Salop Road, OSWESTRY, SY11 2NS **Tel:** 01691 662709
Email: editorial@borderpublishing.com
Advertising Address: As above. **Fax:** 01691 679889
Email: hellen@borderpublishing.com
Web site: http://www.cbl.org.uk
ISSN: 1741-1734
Publisher: Border Publishing Ltd
Date Established: 2003
Frequency: Monthly
Cover Price: £1.95
Circulation: 12,000 (Publisher's Statement)
Usual Pagination: 164
Editor: Howard Gudgeon; **Advertising Manager:** Hellen Wolstenholme
Summary of Content: Magazine covering property, homes, interiors, art, crafts, product page, literature, poetry, walking, hostels, wildlife, history, education, food and drink, fashion, gardening, motoring, finance and what's on.
Readership/Target Audience: Aimed at residents and visitors to Wales and the English Border Counties.
ADVERTISING RATES:
Full Page Colour £895.00
Agency Commission: 10%
Mechanical Data: Trim Size: 297 x 220mm, Col Length: 267mm, Page Width: 192.5mm, Type Area: 267 x 192.5mm, Bleed Size: 303 x 226mm, Film: Digital
Copy instructions: Copy Date: 2 weeks prior to publication date
Average advertising content per issue: 40%
CONSUMER: RURAL & REGIONAL INTEREST: Regional Interest Wales

COUNTRY AND TOWN HOUSE
1804158U74Q-1352

Formerly: Country and Town House magazine
Editorial Address: The Studio, 1 Linver Road, LONDON, SW6 3RA **Tel:** 020 7731 9470
Email: editorial@countryandtownhouse.co.uk
Advertising Address: As above. **Fax:** 020 7731 9488
Email: jeremy@countryhousemagazine.co.uk
Web site: http://www.countryandtownhouse.co.uk
Publisher: Country and Town House Ltd
Date Established: 2007
Frequency: Monthly
Cover Price: £3.00
Free to qualifying individuals
Annual Sub.: £34.95
Circulation: 7,000 (Publisher's Statement)
Usual Pagination: 138
Editor: Lucy Cleland; **Advertising Manager:** Jeremy Isaac
Summary of Content: Lifestyle magazine covering fashion, style, interiors, gardens, travel, food and property.
Readership/Target Audience: Aimed at Londoners wanting to invest in rural property.
ADVERTISING RATES:
Full Page Colour £1500.00
Agency Commission: 10%
Mechanical Data: Type Area: 263 x 195mm, Bleed Size: 304 x 231mm, Trim Size: 298 x 225mm, Col Length: 263mm, Page Width: 195mm, Film: Digital
Copy instructions: Copy Date: 10 days prior to publication date
Average advertising content per issue: 30%
CONSUMER: WOMEN'S INTEREST CONSUMER MAGAZINES: Lifestyle

COUNTRY GARDENER
622808U93-12_75

Editorial Address: Sherborne Road, YEOVIL, BA21 4YA
Tel: 01935 700500 **Fax:** 01935 432266
Email: editorial@countrygardener.co.uk
Advertising Address: Threshing Barn, Woodhayes, Luppitt, HONITON, EX14 4TP **Fax:** 01404 548355
Email: sales@countrygardener.co.uk
Web site: http://www.countrygardener.co.uk
Publisher: Cornwall & Devon Media Ltd
Date Established: 1997
Frequency: 7 issues yearly
Cover Price: Free
Circulation: 140,000 (Publisher's Statement)
Usual Pagination: 40
Editor: Ann Goff; **Advertising Manager:** Ann Goff
Summary of Content: Magazine covering news, event listings, gardens to visit, seasonal advice and information for gardeners.
Readership/Target Audience: Aimed at gardening enthusiasts, farmers and landowners.
ADVERTISING RATES:
Full Page Mono £415.00
Mechanical Data: Trim Size: 262 x 170mm, Film: Digital
Editions:
Cornish Country Gardener
Cotswold Country Gardener
Devon Country Gardener
Dorset Country Gardener
Norfolk Country Gardener
Somerset Country Gardener
Suffolk Country Gardener
Wiltshire Country Gardener
CONSUMER: GARDENING

COUNTRY HOMES & INTERIORS
45246U74C-72

Editorial Address: Blue Fin Building, 110 Southwark Street, LONDON, SE1 0SU **Tel:** 020 3148 5000 **Fax:** 020 7261 6895
Email: countryhomes@ipcmedia.com
Advertising Address: As above.
Email: james_zaman@ipcmedia.com
Web site: http://www.countryhomesandinteriors.co.uk
ISSN: 0951-3019
Publisher: IPC Southbank
Frequency: Monthly
Cover Price: £3.50
Circulation: 84,453 (ABC 01/01/2009 to 30/06/2009)
Usual Pagination: 156
Editor: Claire Dorey; **Advertising Manager:** James Zaman; **Publisher:** Belinda Cooper; **Circulation Manager:** Jenny Pillay
Summary of Content: Magazine covering all aspects of country homes and interior design including accessories, fabrics and furnishings. Also carries features on food, travel and lifestyle ideas.
Readership/Target Audience: Aimed predominantly at women between 35 and 55 years old.
ADVERTISING RATES:
Full Page Colour £5400.00
Agency Commission: 10%
Mechanical Data: Film: Digital, Type Area: 255 x 194mm, Col Length: 255mm, Page Width: 194mm, Trim Size: 284 x 220mm, Bleed Size: 290 x 226mm, Print Process: Web-fed offset litho
Copy instructions: Copy Date: 6 weeks prior to publication date
Editions:
Turkey
CONSUMER: WOMEN'S INTEREST CONSUMER MAGAZINES: Home & Family

COUNTRY ILLUSTRATED
46797U80A-74

Editorial Address: 93-95 Wigmore Street, LONDON, W1U 1HH **Tel:** 020 7935 0888 **Fax:** 020 7935 0898
Email: info@countryclubuk.com
Advertising Address: As above.
Email: charlotte.rodger@countryclubuk.com
Web site: http://www.countryclubuk.com
Publisher: St. Martin's Magazines plc
Date Established: 1992
Frequency: 6 issues yearly
Cover Price: £3.40
Annual Sub.: £40.80
Circulation: 36,000 (Publisher's Statement)
Usual Pagination: 164
Editor: Julie Spencer; **Managing Director:** Julie Spencer
Summary of Content: Magazine covering all aspects of life in the country, including environmental matters, hunting, fishing, shooting and conservation.
Readership/Target Audience: Aimed at those who live in or are interested in the countryside.
ADVERTISING RATES:
Full Page Mono £2275.00
Full Page Colour £3075.00
SCC £30.00
Agency Commission: 10%
Mechanical Data: Type Area: 264 x 194mm, Col Length: 264mm, Film: Digital, Trim Size: 300 x 230mm, Bleed Size:

306 x 236mm, Page Width: 194mm, Col Widths (Display): 40mm
Copy instructions: Copy Date: 10 days prior to publication date
Average advertising content per issue: 40%
CONSUMER: RURAL & REGIONAL INTEREST: Rural Interest

COUNTRY KITCHEN
1697076U74P-940

Editorial Address: Cudham Tithe Barn, Berrys Hill, Berrys Green, Cudham, WESTERHAM, TN16 3AG
Tel: 01959 541444 **Fax:** 01959 541400
Email: ck.info@kelsey.co.uk
Advertising Address: As above.
Email: ck.adsales@kelsey.co.uk
Web site: http://www.countrykitchenmag.com
Publisher: Kelsey Publishing Ltd
Date Established: 2005
Frequency: Monthly
Cover Price: £2.95
Circulation: 19,825 (Publisher's Statement)
Usual Pagination: 80
Editor: Rachel Graham; **Advertisement Director:** David Lerpiniere
Summary of Content: Magazine covering seasonal, traditional and healthy food and filled with seasonal recipes each month.
Readership/Target Audience: Aimed at those who either grow their own food, buy from farmers' markets or want to buy the best quality food from supermarkets.
ADVERTISING RATES:
Full Page Colour £1200.00
Agency Commission: 10%
Mechanical Data: Type Area: 262 x 186mm, Bleed Size: 304 x 217mm, Trim Size: 297 x 210mm, Col Length: 262mm, Page Width: 186mm, Film: Digital, Col Widths (Display): 62mm, No. of Columns (Display): 3
Copy instructions: Copy Date: 2nd week of 2 months prior to publication date
Average advertising content per issue: 10%
CONSUMER: WOMEN'S INTEREST CONSUMER MAGAZINES: Food & Cookery

COUNTRY LANDOWNER
46798U80A-75

Editorial Address: 16 Belgrave Square, LONDON, SW1X 8PQ **Tel:** 020 7235 0511
Email: tom.quinn@cla.org.uk
Advertising Address: Fair Oak Close, Exeter Airport Business Park, Clyst Honiton, EXETER, EX5 2UL
Tel: 01392 888555 **Fax:** 01392 888470
Email: nicky.webber@archant.co.uk
Web site: http://www.cla.org.uk
Publisher: Archant South West
Frequency: Monthly
Free to qualifying individuals
Circulation: 36,341 (ABC 01/01/2007 to 31/12/2007)
Usual Pagination: 76
Editor: Tom Quinn
Summary of Content: Official journal of the Country Land and Business Association (CLA). Contains advice on how members can seek their land's full potential for food, timber production, public access and recreation.
Readership/Target Audience: Read by members of the Country Land and Business Association (CLA).
ADVERTISING RATES:
Full Page Colour £2789.00
Agency Commission: 10%
Mechanical Data: Type Area: 278 x 190mm, Bleed Size: 306 x 226mm, Trim Size: 300 x 220mm, Film: Digital, Col Length: 278mm, Page Width: 190mm
Copy instructions: Copy Date: 1st of the month prior to publication date
Average advertising content per issue: 50%
CONSUMER: RURAL & REGIONAL INTEREST: Rural Interest

COUNTRY LIFE
46799U80A-80

Editorial Address: Blue Fin Building, 110 Southwark Street, LONDON, SE1 0SU **Tel:** 020 3148 5000
Email: flora_birtles@ipcmedia.com
Advertising Address: As above.
Email: rosemary_archer@ipcmedia.com
Web site: http://www.countrylife.co.uk
Publisher: IPC Inspire
Date Established: 1897
Frequency: Weekly
Cover Price: £3.00
Annual Sub.: £133.10
Circulation: 39,674 (ABC 01/01/2008 to 31/12/2008)
Editor: Mark Hedges; **News Editor:** Kate Green; **Features Editor:** Rebecca Pearson; **Managing Director:** Paul Williams; **Advertising Manager:** Rosemary Archer;
Publisher: Joanna Pieters
Summary of Content: Magazine concerned with British country life, social history, fine arts, architecture, sport, agriculture and gardening.
Twitter: https://twitter.com/Countrylifeprop.

Readership/Target Audience: Aimed at those who live in, or are interested in the countryside.
ADVERTISING RATES:
Full Page Colour £5445.00
Agency Commission: 15%
Mechanical Data: Type Area: 267 x 203mm, Bleed Size: 306 x 236mm, Trim Size: 300 x 230mm, Film: Digital, Page Width: 203mm, Col Length: 267mm
Copy instructions: Copy Date: 15 days prior to publication date
Supplement(s): Country Life International - 3xY
CONSUMER: RURAL & REGIONAL INTEREST: Rural Interest

COUNTRY LIFE INTERNATIONAL

1791199U74K-774

Editorial Address: Blue Fin Building, 110 Southwark Street, LONDON, SE1 0SU **Tel:** 020 3148 5000
Email: arabella_youens@ipcmedia.com
Advertising Address: As above. **Fax:** 020 3148 8130
Email: gayle_stevenson@ipcmedia.com
Publisher: IPC Inspire
Date Established: 2006
Frequency: 3 issues yearly - Published in March, May and October. See main record for circulation figure
Editor: Arabella Youens; **Advertising Manager:** Gayle Stevenson
Summary of Content: Magazine covering International property priced at around €1million as well as travel destinations.
Readership/Target Audience: Aimed at readers of Country Life.
ADVERTISING RATES:
Full Page Colour £2350.00
Agency Commission: 10%
Mechanical Data: Type Area: 268 x 203mm, Bleed Size: 306 x 236mm, Trim Size: 300 x 230mm, Col Length: 268mm, Page Width: 203mm, Film: Digital
Copy instructions: Copy Date: 4 weeks prior to publication date
Average advertising content per issue: 60%
Supplement to: Country Life
CONSUMER: WOMEN'S INTEREST CONSUMER MAGAZINES: Home Purchase

COUNTRY LIVING

46800U74C-74

Editorial Address: National Magazine House, 72 Broadwick Street, LONDON, W1F 9EP **Tel:** 020 7439 5000
Fax: 020 7439 5093
Email: kitty.corrigan@natmags.co.uk
Advertising Address: As above.
Email: david.parker@natmags.co.uk
Web site: http://www.allaboutyou.com
ISSN: 0951-0281
Publisher: National Magazine Company Ltd
Date Established: 1985
Frequency: Monthly
Cover Price: £3.50
Annual Sub.: £33.84
Circulation: 192,475 (ABC 01/01/2009 to 30/06/2009)
Editor: Susy Smith; **Features Editor:** Lisa Sykes; **Managing Director:** Jessica Burley; **Advertising Manager:** David Parker
Summary of Content: Magazine providing coverage of country style homes and gardens, with creative ideas, profiles, wildlife stories, green and rural issues. Also contains features on contemporary arts and crafts, health, fashion, beauty, UK travel and leisure.
Twitter: https://twitter.com/CountryLiving
Readership/Target Audience: Aimed at homeowners aged 35 years old and over who either live or aspire to living in the country.
ADVERTISING RATES:
Full Page Colour £7670.00
CONSUMER: WOMEN'S INTEREST CONSUMER MAGAZINES: Home & Family

COUNTRY MUSIC PEOPLE

46141U76D-305

Editorial Address: PO Box 75, ATTLEBOROUGH, NR17 1WL **Tel:** 01953 853068
Email: info@countrymusicpeople.co.uk
Advertising Address: As above. **Tel:** 020 8854 7217
Fax: 020 8855 6370
Email: info@countrymusicpeople.com
Web site: http://www.countrymusicpeople.com
Publisher: Kickin' Cuts Ltd
Date Established: 1970
Frequency: Monthly
Cover Price: £3.10
Annual Sub.: £35.00
Circulation: 19,000 (Publisher's Statement)
Usual Pagination: 68
Editor: Duncan Warwick; **Advertising Manager:** Julie Flaskett
Summary of Content: Country music magazine carrying UK and import record reviews, charts, star features and news.

Readership/Target Audience: Read by country music fans, radio station personnel, dealers, musicians and record buyers.
ADVERTISING RATES:
Full Page Mono £695.00
Full Page Colour £895.00
Agency Commission: 10%
Mechanical Data: Page Width: 185mm, Type Area: 270 x 185mm, Col Length: 270mm, Print Process: Sheet-fed litho, Trim Size: 297 x 210mm, Bleed Size: 303 x 216mm, Film: Digital
CONSUMER: MUSIC & PERFORMING ARTS: Music

COUNTRY SMALLHOLDING

46804U80A-97

Editorial Address: Fair Oak Close, Exeter Airport Business Park, Clyst Honiton, EXETER, EX5 2UL **Tel:** 01392 888481
Fax: 01392 888550
Email: editorial.csh@archant.co.uk
Advertising Address: As above. **Tel:** 01392 888555
Fax: 01392 888470
Email: nicky.webber@archant.co.uk
Web site: http://www.countrysmallholding.com
ISSN: 1358-216X
Publisher: Archant South West
Date Established: 1975
Frequency: 13 issues yearly
Cover Price: £3.25
Annual Sub.: £33.00
Circulation: 18,302 (ABC 01/01/2008 to 31/12/2008)
Usual Pagination: 108
Editor: Simon McEwan
Summary of Content: Magazine containing information on smallholding, hobby farming, poultry, smallholding animals, organic gardening, alternative lifestyle and organic living.
Readership/Target Audience: Read by smallholders, poultry keepers and organic gardeners.
ADVERTISING RATES:
Full Page Mono £615.00
Full Page Colour £615.00
SCC £9.35
Agency Commission: 10%
Mechanical Data: Type Area: 271 x 190mm, Bleed Size: 303 x 216mm, Trim Size: 297 x 210mm, Col Length: 271mm, Page Width: 190mm, Film: Digital, Page Widths (Display): 90mm, No. of Columns (Display): 2
Copy instructions: Copy Date: 1st Friday of the month prior to publication date
Average advertising content per issue: 40%
CONSUMER: RURAL & REGIONAL INTEREST: Rural Interest

COUNTRY THE MAGAZINE OF THE CGA

1645734U80A-164

Editorial Address: Chalke House, Station Road, Codford, WARMINSTER, BA12 0JX **Tel:** 01985 850706
Fax: 01985 850378
Email: rorysd@thecga.co.uk
Advertising Address: As above. **Tel:** 01963 824116
Fax: 0870 486 0495
Email: enquiries@thecga.co.uk
Web site: http://www.thecga.co.uk
Publisher: The CGA
Frequency: 8 issues yearly
Cover Price: Free
Circulation: 11,000 (Publisher's Statement)
Usual Pagination: 100
Editor: Rory Stormonth Darling; **Advertising Manager:** Rory Stormonth Darling
Summary of Content: Magazine covering country news and features as well as travel, restaurants, sport, finance and fashion.
Readership/Target Audience: Aimed at members of The Country Gentleman's Association.
ADVERTISING RATES:
Full Page Colour £900.00
Agency Commission: 10%
Mechanical Data: Type Area: 267 x 180mm, Bleed Size: 303 x 216mm, Col Length: 267mm, Film: Digital, Trim Size: 297 x 210mm, No. of Columns (Display): 4, Page Width: 180mm, Print Process: Sheet-fed litho
Copy instructions: Copy Date: 2 weeks prior to publication date
Average advertising content per issue: 20%
CONSUMER: RURAL & REGIONAL INTEREST: Rural Interest

COUNTRY WALKING

45922U75L-180

Editorial Address: Media House, Lynchwood, Peterborough Business Park, PETERBOROUGH, PE2 6EA
Tel: 01733 468000 **Fax:** 01733 468387
Email: jonathan.manning@bauermedia.co.uk
Advertising Address: As above. **Fax:** 01733 468048
Email: justin.gould@bauermedia.com
Web site: http://www.countrywalking.co.uk
Publisher: Bauer Consumer Media Ltd (Media House)
Date Established: 1987

Frequency: 13 issues yearly - Published 20th of previous month
Cover Price: £3.90
Annual Sub.: £42.00
Circulation: 44,044 (ABC 01/01/2008 to 31/12/2008)
Usual Pagination: 140
Editor: Jonathan Manning; **Editor-in-Chief:** Guy Procter;
Publisher: Rob Croxall
Summary of Content: Magazine offering advice and information on places, routes and equipment for walking.
Readership/Target Audience: Aimed at 30 to 65 year olds interested in walking and the countryside.
ADVERTISING RATES:
Full Page Colour £3150.00
Agency Commission: 10%
Mechanical Data: Page Width: 184mm, Type Area: 275 x 184mm, Bleed Size: 307 x 220mm, Trim Size: 297 x 210mm, Col Length: 275mm, Film: Digital
Average advertising content per issue: 22%
CONSUMER: SPORT: Outdoor

COUNTRY WAY

47700U87-76

Editorial Address: Arthur Rank Centre, National Agricultural Centre, STONELEIGH PARK, CV8 2LG **Tel:** 024 7685 3060
Fax: 024 7669 6460
Email: jillh@rase.org.uk
Advertising Address: As above.
Email: jillh@rase.org.uk
Web site: http://www.arthurrankcentre.org.uk
ISSN: 0969-6172
Publisher: Country Way
Date Established: 1992
Frequency: 3 issues yearly - Published in January, May and September
Annual Sub.: £9.00
Circulation: 4,000 (Publisher's Statement)
Usual Pagination: 32
Editor: Jill Hopkinson
Summary of Content: Magazine containing news, features, reviews and letters covering a wide range of rural issues of interest linking the local church leaders to the general public.
Readership/Target Audience: Aimed at the general public concerned with rural issues.
ADVERTISING RATES:
Full Page Mono £400.00
Full Page Colour £500.00
Agency Commission: 10%
Mechanical Data: Type Area: 270 x 182mm, Col Length: 270mm, No. of Columns (Display): 2, Print Process: Offset litho, Trim Size: 297 x 210mm, Page Width: 182mm
Average advertising content per issue: 5%
CONSUMER: RELIGIOUS

COUNTRYCLUBUK

1657700U80A-167

Editorial Address: 93-95 Wigmore Street, LONDON, W1U 1HH **Tel:** 020 7935 0888
Email: editorial@countryclubuk.com
Advertising Address: As above. **Fax:** 020 7935 0898
Email: charlotte.rodger@countryclubuk.com
Web site: http://www.countryclubuk.com
Publisher: St. Martin's Magazines plc
Date Established: 2000
Frequency: Quarterly
Annual Sub.: £69.00
Circulation: 40,000 (Publisher's Statement)
Usual Pagination: 116
Editor: Rosanne Klatzko
Summary of Content: Magazine covering country pursuits, rural politics, farming, conservation, events and country sports including hunting, shooting and fishing.
Readership/Target Audience: Aimed at those interested in country living.
ADVERTISING RATES:
Full Page Mono £2500.00
Full Page Colour £3300.00
SCC £30.00
Agency Commission: 10%
Mechanical Data: Type Area: 264 x 194mm, Bleed Size: 306 x 236mm, Trim Size: 300 x 230mm, Col Length: 264mm, Page Width: 194mm, Film: Digital
Copy instructions: Copy Date: 10 days prior to publication date
Average advertising content per issue: 50%
CONSUMER: RURAL & REGIONAL INTEREST: Rural Interest

COUNTRYFILE

1805817U80A-176

Formerly: BBC Countryfile
Editorial Address: 9th Floor, Tower House, Fairfax Street, BRISTOL, BS1 3BN **Tel:** 0117 927 9009 **Fax:** 0117 933 8032
Email: cavanscott@bbcmagazinesbristol.com
Advertising Address: 5th Floor, Tower House, Fairfax Street, BRISTOL, BS1 3BN **Tel:** 0117 927 9009
Fax: 0117 934 9008
Email: jamestawton@bbcmagazinesbristol.com
Web site: http://www.bbccountryfile.com
Publisher: BBC Magazines Bristol

Consumer Magazines

Date Established: 2007
Frequency: 13 issues yearly
Cover Price: £3.40
Circulation: 35,000 (Publisher's Statement)
Usual Pagination: 132
Editor: Cavan Scott; **Publisher:** Andy Benham
Summary of Content: Magazine celebrating the British countryside and encouraging people to get involved in country life including walking, local food, environmental matters and people profiles.
Readership/Target Audience: Aimed at men and women aged 35 to 55 years old who have an interest in the countryside.
ADVERTISING RATES:
Full Page Colour £3750.00
SCC £14.00
Agency Commission: 10%
Mechanical Data: Type Area: 264 x 196mm, Bleed Size: 292 x 222mm, Trim Size: 286 x 216mm, Col Length: 264mm, Page Width: 196mm, Film: Digital
Copy instructions: Copy Date: 4 weeks prior to publication date
Average advertising content per issue: 8%
CONSUMER: RURAL & REGIONAL INTEREST: Rural Interest

THE COUNTRYMAN
46801U80A-90

Editorial Address: The Water Mill, Broughton Hall, SKIPTON, BD23 3AG **Tel:** 01756 701381 **Fax:** 01756 701326
Email: editorial@thecountryman.co.uk
Advertising Address: As above.
Email: tracy@dalesman.co.uk
Web site: http://www.thecountryman.co.uk
ISSN: 0011-0272
Publisher: Country Publications Ltd
Date Established: 1927
Frequency: Monthly
Cover Price: £3.25
Circulation: 18,240 (ABC 01/01/2008 to 31/12/2008)
Usual Pagination: 116
Editor: Paul Jackson
Summary of Content: Magazine containing countryside, wildlife, country people, traditions, crafts and rural issues.
Readership/Target Audience: Aimed at those interested in the past, present and future of the British countryside.
ADVERTISING RATES:
Full Page Colour £1500.00
Agency Commission: 10%
Mechanical Data: Type Area: 180 x 123mm, Col Length: 180mm, Page Width: 123mm, Bleed Size: 220 x 158mm, Trim Size: 210 x 148mm, Film: Digital
Copy instructions: Copy Date: 4 weeks prior to publication date
Average advertising content per issue: 20%
CONSUMER: RURAL & REGIONAL INTEREST: Rural Interest

THE COUNTRYMAN'S WEEKLY
45858U75F-35

Editorial Address: Unit 2, Lynher House, 3 Bush Park, Estover, PLYMOUTH, PL6 7RG **Tel:** 01752 762990
Fax: 01752 771751
Email: dave.venner@metropolis.co.uk
Advertising Address: As above.
Email: advertising@countrymansweekly.com
Web site: http://www.countrymansweekly.com
ISSN: 1350-9683
Publisher: Diamond Publishing Ltd
Frequency: Weekly
Cover Price: £1.90
Circulation: 22,000 (Publisher's Statement)
Usual Pagination: 40
Editor: David Venner; **Advertising Manager:** Tracey Allen
Summary of Content: Newspaper containing editorial opinion, information on political trends, legal advice, products and services.
Readership/Target Audience: Aimed at those interested in angling, clay shooting, game shooting, gun dogs, terriers, lurchers, stalking and trapping.
ADVERTISING RATES:
Full Page Mono £400.00
Full Page Colour £560.00
SCC £3.00
Agency Commission: 10%
Mechanical Data: Bleed Size: +3mm, Trim Size: 420 x 297mm, Film: Digital, Type Area: 360 x 260mm, Col Length: 360mm, Page Width: 260mm, No. of Columns (Display): 6, Col Widths (Display): 40mm
Copy instructions: Copy Date: 2 weeks prior to publication date
Average advertising content per issue: 45%
CONSUMER: SPORT: Shooting

COUNTRYSIDE LA VIE
1620681U74Q-1153

Editorial Address: Arlington Mews, Overton Road, LEICESTER, LE5 0JB **Tel:** 0116 212 2555
Fax: 0116 246 0352
Email: sue@countryside-lavie.com

Advertising Address: As above.
Email: mike@countryside-lavie.com
Web site: http://www.countryside-lavie.com
Publisher: Ryans Holdings Ltd
Date Established: 1993
Frequency: 6 issues yearly
Cover Price: £2.75
Free to qualifying individuals
Annual Sub.: £23.00
Circulation: 10,000 (Publisher's Statement)
Usual Pagination: 152
Editor: Sue Brindley; **Advertising Director:** Mike Stevens
Summary of Content: Lifestyle magazine covering prestige country homes, homes and gardens, interiors, motoring, fashions, health, beauty and eating out.
Readership/Target Audience: Aimed at anyone aged 25 years old and over.
ADVERTISING RATES:
Full Page Colour £1000.00
Agency Commission: 10%
Mechanical Data: Bleed Size: 303 x 216mm, Type Area: 270 x 180mm, Col Length: 270mm, Page Width: 180mm, Film: Digital, Trim Size: 297 x 210mm
Average advertising content per issue: 40%
CONSUMER: WOMEN'S INTEREST CONSUMER MAGAZINES: Lifestyle

COUNTRYSIDE MAGAZINE
37772U80A-94

Editorial Address: Agriculture House, North Gate, Uppingham, OAKHAM, LE15 9PL **Tel:** 0870 264 0202
Fax: 01572 824646
Email: lorna.maybery@associa.co.uk
Advertising Address: As above. **Tel:** 01572 824600
Fax: 01572 824731
Email: david.leach@associa.co.uk
Web site: http://www.countrysideonline.co.uk
ISSN: 1462-0839
Publisher: Associa Ltd
Date Established: 1992
Frequency: Monthly
Annual Sub.: £41.50
Circulation: 53,330 (ABC 01/01/2007 to 31/12/2007)
Usual Pagination: 116
Editor: Lesley Bayley; **Advertising Manager:** David Leach-Davies
Summary of Content: Magazine covering countryside issues and lifestyle, with practical advice on land management, smallholding, animal husbandry, veterinary matters, horses, dogs, gardening, environment, wildlife, conservation, travel, rural skills, campaigns and product reviews.
Readership/Target Audience: Aimed at those living and working in the country excluding commercial farmers.
ADVERTISING RATES:
Full Page Colour £3500.00
SCC £30.00
Agency Commission: 10%
Mechanical Data: Trim Size: 297 x 210mm, Bleed Size: 305 x 218mm, Col Widths (Display): 43.5mm
Copy instructions: Copy Date: 5th of the month prior to publication date
Average advertising content per issue: 45%
Supplement(s): Clothing - 1xY, Equine - 1xY, Gardening - 1xY
CONSUMER: RURAL & REGIONAL INTEREST: Rural Interest

COUNTRYSIDE RECREATION
46803U80A-95

Editorial Address: Unit 1, Sheffield Science Park, Howard Street, SHEFFIELD, S1 2LX **Tel:** 0114 225 4494
Fax: 0114 225 2197
Email: k.haigh@shu.ac.uk
Web site: http://www.countrysiderecreation.org.uk
ISSN: 0968-459X
Publisher: Countryside Recreation Network
Frequency: 3 issues yearly - Published in February/March, June/July and October/November
Cover Price: Free
Circulation: 2,922 (Publisher's Statement)
Usual Pagination: 40
Editor: Kim Haigh
Summary of Content: Newsletter of the Countryside Recreation Network covering policy within the countryside, environmental impact, countryside recreation, tourism and leisure.
Readership/Target Audience: Read by those with an interest in countryside recreation and its environmental impact.
ADVERTISING: No Advertising taken
CONSUMER: RURAL & REGIONAL INTEREST: Rural Interest

COUNTRYSIDE VOICE
1638222U80A-163

Editorial Address: The Pall Mall Deposit, 124-128 Barlby Road, LONDON, W10 6BL **Tel:** 020 8962 3020
Fax: 020 8962 8689
Email: sarah.notton@thinkpublishing.co.uk

Advertising Address: As above.
Email: tamzin@thinkpublishing.co.uk
Web site: http://www.thinkpublishing.co.uk
ISSN: 1742-8777
Publisher: Think Publishing Ltd
Frequency: Half-yearly - Published in February and October
Cover Price: Free
Circulation: 35,000 (Publisher's Statement)
Usual Pagination: 60
Editor: Jenny Darwent; **Advertising Manager:** Tamzin Freeman; **Publisher:** Emma Jones
Summary of Content: Magazine of the Campaign to Protect Rural England, covers recent stories and campaign updates, landscape protection, energy conservation and book reviews.
Readership/Target Audience: Aimed at members of the CPRE.
ADVERTISING RATES:
Full Page Colour £1200.00
Agency Commission: 10%
Mechanical Data: Type Area: 229 x 152mm, Bleed Size: 251 x 174mm, Trim Size: 245 x 168mm, Col Length: 229mm, Page Width: 152mm, Film: Digital
Copy instructions: Copy Date: 6 weeks prior to publication date
Average advertising content per issue: 35%
CONSUMER: RURAL & REGIONAL INTEREST: Rural Interest

THE COUNTY MAGAZINE
1692980U80C-5272

Formerly: London Bromley County Magazine
Editorial Address: 2 Bexley Cottages, The Street, Horton Kirby, DARTFORD, DA4 9BU **Tel:** 01322 860100
Fax: 01322 860200
Email: editorial@countymag.co.uk
Advertising Address: As above.
Email: sales@countymag.co.uk
Web site: http://www.thecountymagazine.co.uk
Publisher: County Magazine Publications Ltd
Date Established: 2005
Frequency: Monthly
Cover Price: Free
Circulation: 60,000 (Print Run)
Usual Pagination: 60
Editor: Sharon Sperling; **Managing Editor:** Maggie Garside
Summary of Content: Magazine covering home style, health, beauty, eating and drinking, business, gardening, motoring and competitions.
Readership/Target Audience: Aimed at those living in Bromley and the surrounding area.
ADVERTISING RATES:
Full Page Colour £950.00
Mechanical Data: Film: Digital, Trim Size: 297 x 210mm, Bleed Size: 303 x 216mm
Editions:
Kent County Magazine
London Bromley County Magazine
CONSUMER: RURAL & REGIONAL INTEREST: Regional Interest English Counties

---

THE COURIER
47378U83-6

Formerly: Courier Newcastle
Editorial Address: University of Newcastle-Upon-Tyne, Kings Walk, NEWCASTLE UPON TYNE, NE1 8QB
Tel: 0191 239 3940
Email: editor.union@ncl.ac.uk
Advertising Address: As above.
Email: marketingsales.union@ncl.ac.uk
Web site: http://www.unionsociety.co.uk/courier
Publisher: The Union Society
Date Established: 1948
Frequency: 18 issues yearly - Published weekly during term time
Cover Price: Free
Circulation: 12,000 (Publisher's Statement)
Usual Pagination: 36
Editor: Sam Parker; **Advertising Manager:** Abby Goode
Summary of Content: Newspaper of the Union Society of the University of Newcastle containing news, sport and local entertainment listings.
Readership/Target Audience: Read mainly by students and staff.
ADVERTISING RATES:
Full Page Mono £470.00
Full Page Colour £700.00
Agency Commission: 10%
Mechanical Data: Bleed Size: +5mm, Page Width: 277mm, Type Area: 350 x 277mm, Col Length: 350mm, Film: Digital
Copy instructions: Copy Date: 1 week prior to publication date
Average advertising content per issue: 10%
CONSUMER: STUDENT PUBLICATIONS

THE COURIER (ABERYSTWYTH) 47377U83-5_5

Editorial Address: Students' Union, Penglais, UWA, ABERYSTWYTH, SY23 3DX **Tel:** 01970 621738
Fax: 01970 621701
Email: courier@aber.ac.uk
Advertising Address: As above.
Email: coustaff@aber.ac.uk
Web site: http://www.thecourier.org.uk
Publisher: Caric Press
Date Established: 1948
Frequency: 6 issues yearly - Published monthly during term time
Cover Price: Free
Circulation: 1,200 (Publisher's Statement)
Usual Pagination: 32
Editor: Ben Hallett; **News Editor:** Will Gant; **Features Editor:** Laura Sutcliffe; **Advertising Manager:** Matthew Thwaite; **Managing Editor:** Ben Hallett
Summary of Content: Magazine of the Students' Union for the University of Wales, Aberystwyth, containing news, reviews, features and local entertainment listings.
Language(s): English; Welsh
Readership/Target Audience: Primarily read by students, but also anyone who picks up a copy.
ADVERTISING RATES:
Full Page Mono £150.00
Full Page Colour £200.00
Mechanical Data: Type Area: 210 x 148mm, No. of Columns (Display): 2, Film: Digital
Average advertising content per issue: 10%
CONSUMER: STUDENT PUBLICATIONS

THE CRACK 48080U89C-128

Editorial Address: 1 Pink Lane, NEWCASTLE UPON TYNE, NE1 5DW **Tel:** 0191 230 3038 **Fax:** 0191 230 4484
Email: editorial@thecrackmagazine.com
Advertising Address: As above.
Email: advertising@thecrackmagazine.com
Web site: http://www.thecrackmagazine.com
Publisher: Crack Ltd
Date Established: 1985
Frequency: Monthly
Cover Price: £1.80
Free to qualifying individuals
Annual Sub.: £18.00
Circulation: 21,202 (ABC 01/01/2008 to 31/12/2008)
Usual Pagination: 64
Editor: Robert Meddes; **Managing Director:** Mandy Baxter;
Advertising Manager: Graham Tuttiett; **Publisher:** Mandy Baxter
Summary of Content: Magazine covering what's happening in and around the North East.
Readership/Target Audience: Aimed at those both living and visiting the area.
ADVERTISING RATES:
Full Page Colour £1850.00
Agency Commission: 10%
Mechanical Data: Bleed Size: 307 x 230mm, Trim Size: 297 x 220mm, Col Length: 277mm, Film: Digital, Type Area: 277 x 200mm, Page Width: 200mm
Copy instructions: Copy Date: 10 days prior to publication date
Average advertising content per issue: 25%
CONSUMER: HOLIDAYS & TRAVEL: Entertainment Guides

THE CRACK GUIDE TO THE NORTH EAST 48081U89C-129

Editorial Address: 1 Pink Lane, NEWCASTLE UPON TYNE, NE1 5DW **Tel:** 0191 230 3038 **Fax:** 0191 230 4484
Email: rob@thecrackmagazine.com
Advertising Address: As above.
Email: advertising@thecrackmagazine.com
Web site: http://www.thecrackmagazine.com
Publisher: Crack Ltd
Date Established: 1993
Frequency: Annual - Published in September
Cover Price: £4.50
Free to qualifying individuals
Circulation: 22,000 (Publisher's Statement)
Usual Pagination: 124
Editor: Robert Meddes; **Advertising Manager:** Graham Tuttiett
Summary of Content: Guide book containing accommodation information and entertainment including pubs, clubs, galleries and places of interest in the North East.
Readership/Target Audience: Aimed at those visiting or moving to the North East of England.
ADVERTISING RATES:
Full Page Colour £1500.00
Agency Commission: 10%
Mechanical Data: Film: Digital, Bleed Size: 307 x 230mm, Trim Size: 297 x 220mm
Average advertising content per issue: 30%
CONSUMER: HOLIDAYS & TRAVEL: Entertainment Guides

CRAFT STAMPER 718017U88D-27

Editorial Address: Traplet House, Pendragon Close, MALVERN, WR14 1GA **Tel:** 01684 588500
Fax: 01684 578558
Email: katy.fox@traplet.com
Advertising Address: As above.
Email: advertising@traplet.com
Web site: http://www.thestampbug.co.uk
Publisher: Traplet Publications Ltd
Date Established: 2000
Frequency: Monthly
Cover Price: £3.95
Usual Pagination: 84
Editor: Katy Fox
Summary of Content: Magazine covering all aspects of stamping. Includes techniques, inspirational projects, best buys, ideas, embossing, ink sponging, braying and paper-making. Also quilling, tea bag folding, parchment craft and step by step projects from cards to entire rooms.
Readership/Target Audience: Aimed at both beginners and experienced stamping enthusiasts of all ages.
ADVERTISING RATES:
Full Page Colour £695.00
SCC £7.00
Agency Commission: 10%
Mechanical Data: Film: Digital
Copy instructions: Copy Date: 6 weeks prior to publication date
CONSUMER: EDUCATION: Crafts

CRAFTS 47933U88D-23

Editorial Address: 44A Pentonville Road, Islington, LONDON, N1 9BY **Tel:** 020 7806 2538 **Fax:** 020 7837 0858
Email: crafts@craftscouncil.org.uk
Advertising Address: As above. **Tel:** 020 7806 2541
Email: emilypalmer@cultureshockmedia.co.uk
Web site: http://www.craftscouncil.org.uk
ISSN: 0306-610X
Publisher: Crafts Council
Date Established: 1973
Frequency: 6 issues yearly
Cover Price: £6.20
Annual Sub.: £34.00
Circulation: 16,000 (Publisher's Statement)
Usual Pagination: 116
Editor: Teleri Lloyd-Jones; **News Editor:** Diana Woolf;
Advertising Manager: Emily Palmer; **Publisher:** Keith Grosvenor
Summary of Content: Journal of the applied and decorative arts. Features expert coverage of all crafts media including studio work, modern experimental work and traditional and historic designs.
Readership/Target Audience: Read by craftspeople, collectors and enthusiasts of art and craft.
ADVERTISING RATES:
Full Page Colour £1320.00
Agency Commission: 10%
Mechanical Data: Trim Size: 297 x 237mm, Film: Digital, Bleed Size: 303 x 243mm, Type Area: 259 x 199mm, Col Length: 259mm, Page Width: 199mm
Copy instructions: Copy Date: 5 weeks prior to publication date
Average advertising content per issue: 33%
CONSUMER: EDUCATION: Crafts

CRAFTS BEAUTIFUL 47934U88D-24

Editorial Address: 1 Phoenix Court, Hawkins Road, COLCHESTER, CO2 8JY **Tel:** 01206 505975
Fax: 01206 505945
Email: sarah@aceville.co.uk
Advertising Address: 21-23 Phoenix Court, Hawkins Road, COLCHESTER, CO2 8JY **Tel:** 01206 505940
Fax: 01206 505945
Email: martin.lack@aceville.co.uk
Web site: http://www.craftsbeautiful.com
Publisher: Aceville Publications Ltd
Date Established: 1993
Frequency: 13 issues yearly
Cover Price: £3.65
Free to qualifying individuals
Circulation: 150,000 (Publisher's Statement)
Usual Pagination: 132
Editor: Sarah Crosland; **Advertising Manager:** Vanessa Witchlow; **Publisher:** Matthew Tudor
Summary of Content: Magazine covering traditional and modern crafts and celebrity interviews, as well as simple projects, step-by-step instructions and photographs of the finished products.
Readership/Target Audience: Read mainly by women over 30 years old with an interest in crafts.
ADVERTISING RATES:
Full Page Mono £726.00
Full Page Colour £935.00
SCC £12.00
Agency Commission: 10%
Mechanical Data: Col Length: 270mm, Film: Digital, No. of Columns (Display): 4, Print Process: Web-fed offset litho,

Trim Size: 297 x 210mm, Bleed Size: 309 x 222mm, Type Area: 270 x 190mm, Page Width: 190mm
Copy instructions: Copy Date: 4 weeks prior to publication date
Average advertising content per issue: 40%
CONSUMER: EDUCATION: Crafts

CRAFTSMAN CRAFT&DESIGN MAGAZINE 47935U88D-25

Editorial Address: PO Box 5, DRIFFIELD, YO25 8JD
Tel: 01377 255213
Email: editor@craftanddesign.net
Advertising Address: As above. **Fax:** 01377 255730
Email: sales@craftanddesign.net
Web site: http://www.craftanddesign.net
ISSN: 0953-9190
Publisher: PSB Design & Print Consultants Ltd
Date Established: 1983
Frequency: 6 issues yearly
Cover Price: £5.95
Annual Sub.: £35.00
Circulation: 6,000 (Publisher's Statement)
Usual Pagination: 100
Editor: Angie Boyer; **Managing Director:** Paul Boyer;
Advertising Manager: Wendy Watkins; **Publisher:** Paul Boyer
Summary of Content: Magazine for professional designer makers, with information on craft galleries & fairs, event and exhibition dates and organisers, suppliers of materials, guilds, makers, workshops, courses, and business advice.
Readership/Target Audience: Aimed at the UK craft industry in particular design makers who wish to sell their work, and people who buy British crafts.
ADVERTISING RATES:
Full Page Mono £1400.00
Full Page Colour £1400.00
SCC £19.00
Agency Commission: 10%
Mechanical Data: Film: Digital, Col Length: 272mm, Type Area: 272 x 190mm, No. of Columns (Display): 3, Page Width: 190mm, Trim Size: 297 x 210mm, Col Widths (Display): 60mm, Print Process: Web-fed offset litho, Bleed Size: +3mm
Copy instructions: Copy Date: 6 weeks prior to publication date
Average advertising content per issue: 25%
CONSUMER: EDUCATION: Crafts

CRAFTY CARPER 48525U92-52

Editorial Address: Regent House, 101 Broadfield Road, SHEFFIELD, S8 0XH **Tel:** 0114 258 0812
Fax: 0114 258 2728
Email: info@craftycarper.uk.com
Advertising Address: As above.
Email: info@anglingpublications.co.uk
Web site: http://www.anglingpublications.co.uk
Publisher: Angling Publications Ltd
Date Established: 1997
Frequency: Monthly
Cover Price: £3.30
Annual Sub.: £39.00
Circulation: 22,000 (Publisher's Statement)
Usual Pagination: 160
Editor: Lewis Porter; **Advertising Director:** Philippa Dean;
Publisher: Tim Paisley
Summary of Content: Magazine containing information, articles and advice on all aspects of carp fishing, including bait, tackle and tactics.
Readership/Target Audience: Aimed at carp anglers and fishermen.
ADVERTISING RATES:
Full Page Colour £600.00
Agency Commission: 10%
Mechanical Data: Bleed Size: 303 x 216mm, Trim Size: 297 x 210mm, Film: Digital, Type Area: 297 x 210mm, Col Length: 297mm, Page Width: 210mm
Copy instructions: Copy Date: 1st Monday of the month prior to publication date
Average advertising content per issue: 60%
CONSUMER: ANGLING & FISHING

CRESCENDO & JAZZ MUSIC 46143U76D-310

Editorial Address: 13 Buckfast House, Priory Close, Southgate, LONDON, N14 4AZ **Tel:** 020 8440 5526
Fax: 020 8440 5526
Advertising Address: As above.
ISSN: 0962-7472
Publisher: Crescendo
Date Established: 1962
Frequency: Quarterly
Cover Price: £6.25
Circulation: 10,000 (Publisher's Statement)
Usual Pagination: 40
Editor: Dennis Matthews; **Advertising Manager:** Dennis Matthews; **Managing Editor:** Dennis Matthews

Consumer Magazines

Summary of Content: Magazine focusing on jazz and the big band scene. Also covers film music and includes technical articles on musical instruments and music production.
Readership/Target Audience: Aimed at professional musicians, musicians generally and jazz fans.
ADVERTISING RATES:
Full Page Mono £120.00
Full Page Colour £220.00
Mechanical Data: Trim Size: 297 x 210mm
CONSUMER: MUSIC & PERFORMING ARTS: Music

CRICKET WORLD
45907U75K-50

Formerly: Cricket World Monthly
Editorial Address: 24-26 London Road, GRANTHAM, NG31 6EJ **Tel:** 01476 565569 **Fax:** 01476 572901
Email: info@cricketworld.com
Advertising Address: As above.
Email: jt@cricketworld.com
Web site: http://www.cricketworld.com
ISSN: 1361-8547
Publisher: Cricket World Media Ltd
Date Established: 1987
Frequency: Quarterly
Cover Price: £3.95
Circulation: 25,000 (Publisher's Statement)
Usual Pagination: 80
Editor: John Pennington; **Publisher:** Alastair Symondson
Summary of Content: Magazine covering test and international cricket, recreational cricket, player profiles, school, youth and women's league, club news and features.
Readership/Target Audience: Read by males aged between 10 and 55 years old.
ADVERTISING RATES:
Full Page Colour £3750.00
Agency Commission: 10%
Mechanical Data: Film: Digital, Page Width: 190mm, Type Area: 265 x 190mm, Col Length: 265mm, Trim Size: 297 x 210mm, Bleed Size: 303 x 216mm
CONSUMER: SPORT: Cricket

CRIME TIME
47542U84B-47

Editorial Address: 7A King Henry's Walk, Islington, LONDON, N1 4NX **Tel:** 020 7249 5940
Email: crimetime@ntlworld.com
Advertising Address: As above.
Email: crimetime@ntlworld.com
Web site: http://www.crimetime.co.uk
Publisher: Crime Time Publishing Ltd
Frequency: 6 issues yearly
Cover Price: £4.99
Circulation: 40,000 (Publisher's Statement)
Usual Pagination: 100
Editor: Barry Forshaw; **Advertising Manager:** Jeremy Cook; **Publisher:** Ion Mills
Summary of Content: Magazine covering all aspects of fictional crime including books and the cinema. Also contains features and advice from crime writers.
Readership/Target Audience: Aimed at lovers of crime fiction and films.
ADVERTISING RATES:
Full Page Mono £100.00
Mechanical Data: Film: Digital
CONSUMER: THE ARTS & LITERARY: Literary

CRIMEWAVE
1646064U79L-382

Editorial Address: 5 Martins Lane, Witcham, ELY, CB6 2LB **Tel:** 01353 777931
Email: andy@ttapress.com
Advertising Address: As above.
Email: andy@ttapress.demon.co.uk
Web site: http://www.ttapress.com
ISSN: 1463-1350
Publisher: TTA Press
Frequency: Half-yearly - Publishes as summer and winter issue
Cover Price: £3.85
Annual Sub.: £21.00
Circulation: 10,000 (Publisher's Statement)
Usual Pagination: 68
Editor: Andy Cox; **Advertising Manager:** Andy Cox
Summary of Content: Magazine covering crime and mystery stories as well as reviews of videos, books, films and interviews of the genre.
Readership/Target Audience: Aimed at crime and mystery enthusiasts aged 18 years and over.
ADVERTISING: Rates on application
Agency Commission: 10%
Copy instructions: Copy Date: 4 weeks prior to publication date
CONSUMER: HOBBIES & DIY: Fantasy Games & Science Fiction

CRISS CROSS
46657U79F-13

Formerly: Criss Crosses
Editorial Address: Academic House, 24-28 Oval Road, LONDON, NW1 7DT **Tel:** 020 7241 8399 **Fax:** 020 7241 8009
Email: criss.cross@bauer.co.uk
Advertising Address: 8 Upper St. Martin's Lane, LONDON, WC2H 9DW **Tel:** 020 7240 9400 **Fax:** 020 7240 9040
Email: heleng@tpc-manchester.com
ISSN: 1461-4901
Publisher: H. Bauer Publishing
Frequency: Monthly
Cover Price: £1.80
Circulation: 62,000 (Publisher's Statement)
Usual Pagination: 96
Editor: Ben Howard; **Advertising Manager:** Helen Greenwood
Summary of Content: Puzzle magazine featuring fill ins, criss crosses and word fits.
Readership/Target Audience: Aimed at those aged 45 years old and over who enjoy doing puzzles.
ADVERTISING RATES:
Full Page Colour £2600.00
Agency Commission: 15%
Mechanical Data: Page Width: 165mm, Film: Digital, Type Area: 235 x 165mm, Bleed Size: 265 x 195mm, Trim Size: 255 x 185mm, Col Length: 235mm
Copy instructions: Copy Date: 3 weeks prior to publication date
Average advertising content per issue: 5%
CONSUMER: HOBBIES & DIY: Games & Puzzles

CRITICAL SOCIAL POLICY
47361U82-8

Editorial Address: 1 Oliver's Yard, 55 City Road, LONDON, EC1Y 1SP **Tel:** 020 7324 8500 **Fax:** 020 7324 8600
Email: francisca.perez@sagepub.co.uk
Advertising Address: As above.
Email: advertising@sagepub.co.uk
Web site: http://www.sagepub.co.uk
ISSN: 0261-0183
Publisher: Sage Publications
Frequency: Quarterly
Annual Sub.: £38.00
Circulation: 625 (Publisher's Statement)
Editor: Francisca Perez; **Advertising Manager:** Sheena Karim
Summary of Content: Journal providing an international forum to develop an understanding of welfare from socialist, feminist, antiracist and radical perspectives.
Readership/Target Audience: Aimed at those who are actively involved in welfare issues through pressure groups, consumer groups and community action.
ADVERTISING RATES:
Full Page Mono £400.00
Agency Commission: 5%
Mechanical Data: Type Area: 205 x 130mm, Col Length: 205mm, Page Width: 130mm, Film: Digital
Copy instructions: Copy Date: 12 weeks prior to publication date
CONSUMER: CURRENT AFFAIRS & POLITICS

THE CROQUET GAZETTE
46001U75X-340

Editorial Address: 22 Cranbourne Terrace, STOCKTON-ON-TEES, TS18 3PX **Tel:** 07752 356880
Email: gail.curry@croquet.org.uk
Advertising Address: As above.
Email: gailecurry@hotmail.com
Web site: http://www.croquet.org.uk
Publisher: Croquet Association
Date Established: 1900
Frequency: 6 issues yearly
Cover Price: £3.00
Circulation: 5,000 (Publisher's Statement)
Usual Pagination: 24
Editor: Gail Curry; **Advertising Manager:** Gail Curry
Summary of Content: Magazine covering news on croquet tournaments from home and overseas.
Readership/Target Audience: Aimed at those who play croquet.
ADVERTISING: Rates on application
Copy instructions: Copy Date: 1st of the month prior to publication date
CONSUMER: SPORT: Other Sport

CROSS STITCH COLLECTION
45356U74E-29_97

Formerly: Needlecraft's Cross Stitch Collection
Editorial Address: 30 Monmouth Street, BATH, BA1 2BW **Tel:** 01225 442244 **Fax:** 01225 822793
Email: csc@futurenet.co.uk
Advertising Address: As above. **Fax:** 01225 732282
Email: amanda.haughey@futurenet.co.uk
Web site: http://www.futurenet.co.uk
Publisher: Future Publishing Ltd
Frequency: 13 issues yearly
Cover Price: £3.99
Usual Pagination: 74

Editor: Bob Wade
Summary of Content: Magazine containing designs, projects, news, kit reviews, technique advice and letters.
Readership/Target Audience: Read mainly by women between 35 and 44 years old who are at an intermediate or advanced level.
ADVERTISING RATES:
Full Page Colour £688.00
Agency Commission: 10%
Mechanical Data: Page Width: 190mm, Film: Digital, Type Area: 270 x 190mm, Bleed Size: 303 x 216mm, Trim Size: 297 x 210mm, Col Length: 270mm
Copy instructions: Copy Date: 4 weeks prior to publication date
Average advertising content per issue: 7%
CONSUMER: WOMEN'S INTEREST CONSUMER MAGAZINES: Crafts

CROSS STITCH CRAZY
622946U74E-29_98

Editorial Address: 9th Floor, Tower House, Fairfax Street, BRISTOL, BS1 3BN **Tel:** 0117 927 9009 **Fax:** 0117 934 9008
Email: sianadekavanagh@originpublishing.co.uk
Advertising Address: 5th Floor, Tower House, Fairfax Street, BRISTOL, BS1 3BN **Tel:** 0117 927 9009
Email: melanieharris@originpublishing.co.uk
Web site: http://www.cross-stitching.com
Publisher: Origin Publishing Ltd
Date Established: 1999
Frequency: 13 issues yearly
Cover Price: £3.75
Circulation: 19,225 (ABC 01/01/2008 to 31/12/2008)
Usual Pagination: 84
Editor: Emma Roberts
Summary of Content: Magazine containing cross stitch designs and technical information, including stories, puzzles and news.
Readership/Target Audience: Aimed at women of any age who love to stitch and are young at heart.
ADVERTISING RATES:
Full Page Colour £1050.00
Mechanical Data: Type Area: 281 x 195mm, Bleed Size: 303 x 216mm, Trim Size: 297 x 210mm, Col Length: 280mm, Page Width: 195mm, Film: Digital
Copy instructions: Copy Date: 5 weeks prior to publication date
CONSUMER: WOMEN'S INTEREST CONSUMER MAGAZINES: Crafts

CROSS STITCH GOLD
1659047U74E-688

Editorial Address: 9th Floor, Tower House, Fairfax Street, BRISTOL, BS1 3BN **Tel:** 0117 927 9009 **Fax:** 0117 934 9008
Email: charlottelyon@originpublishing.co.uk
Advertising Address: 14th Floor, Tower House, Fairfax Street, BRISTOL, BS1 3BN **Tel:** 0117 927 9009 **Fax:** 0117 934 9008
Email: melanieharris@originpublishing.co.uk
Web site: http://www.cross-stitching.com
Publisher: Origin Publishing Ltd
Frequency: 9 issues yearly
Cover Price: £3.99
Circulation: 35,000 (Publisher's Statement)
Usual Pagination: 64
Editor: Charlotte Lyon; **Publisher:** Catherine Parnham
Summary of Content: Magazine covering large cross stitch designs from around the world.
Readership/Target Audience: Aimed at experienced stitchers.
ADVERTISING RATES:
Full Page Colour £1030.00
CONSUMER: WOMEN'S INTEREST CONSUMER MAGAZINES: Crafts

CROSS STITCHER
45357U74E-29_99

Editorial Address: 30 Monmouth Street, BATH, BA1 2BW **Tel:** 01225 442244 **Fax:** 01225 822793
Email: cathy.lewis@futurenet.co.uk
Advertising Address: As above. **Fax:** 01225 732206
Email: amanda.haughey@futurenet.com
Web site: http://www.futurenet.co.uk
Publisher: Future Publishing Ltd
Frequency: 13 issues yearly
Cover Price: £3.75
Circulation: 62,229 (ABC 01/01/2008 to 31/12/2008)
Usual Pagination: 98
Editor: Cathy Lewis
Summary of Content: Magazine for every cross stitcher. Contains a mix of large and small projects, free gifts and design information.
Readership/Target Audience: Aimed at cross stitch enthusiasts and beginners.
ADVERTISING RATES:
Full Page Colour £1875.00
Agency Commission: 10%
Mechanical Data: Col Length: 280mm, Page Width: 213mm, Film: Digital, Type Area: 280 x 213mm, Bleed Size:

306 x 238mm, Trim Size: 300 x 232mm, No. of Columns (Display): 4, Col Widths (Display): 68mm
Copy instructions: Copy Date: 4 weeks prior to publication date
Average advertising content per issue: 20%
CONSUMER: WOMEN'S INTEREST CONSUMER MAGAZINES: Crafts

CROSS WAY
47701U87-78

Editorial Address: Dean Wace House, 16 Rosslyn Road, WATFORD, WD18 0NY **Tel:** 01923 235111
Fax: 01923 800362
Email: crossway@churchsociety.org
Web site: http://www.churchsociety.org
ISSN: 0261-8915
Publisher: Church Society
Date Established: 1980
Frequency: Quarterly
Cover Price: £1.50
Annual Sub.: £6.00
Circulation: 1,000 (Publisher's Statement)
Usual Pagination: 16
Editor: David Phillips
Summary of Content: Anglican magazine with articles on current issues facing the Church of England, written from a conservative point of view and seeking to uphold evangelical doctrine.
Readership/Target Audience: Aimed primarily at members of Church Society.
ADVERTISING: No Advertising taken
CONSUMER: RELIGIOUS

CROSSBOW
47218U82-10

Editorial Address: Can Mezzanine Building, 32-36 Loman Street, LONDON, SE1 0EH **Tel:** 020 7922 7718
Email: office@bowgroup.org
Advertising Address: As above.
Email: office@bowgroup.org
Web site: http://www.bowgroup.org
ISSN: 0011-1988
Publisher: The Bow Group
Date Established: 1957
Frequency: 3 issues yearly - Published in winter, spring and summer
Cover Price: £5.00
Circulation: 2,000 (Publisher's Statement)
Usual Pagination: 30
Editor: Irene Harris; **Advertising Manager:** Irene Harris
Summary of Content: Magazine covering Conservative views on current affairs and policy.
Readership/Target Audience: Read by members of The Bow Group, MPs, MEPs and media organisations.
ADVERTISING RATES:
Full Page Mono £300.00
Full Page Colour £750.00
CONSUMER: CURRENT AFFAIRS & POLITICS

CROSSED GRAIN
1638723U74G-239

Editorial Address: Suite A-D, Octagon Court, HIGH WYCOMBE, HP11 2HS **Tel:** 01494 437278
Fax: 01494 474349
Email: crossedgrain@coeliac.org.uk
Advertising Address: Mountain View, Ffordd Penrhwylfa, PRESTATYN, LL19 8HW **Tel:** 01745 888086
Fax: 01745 888086
Email: ckettmc@aol.com
Web site: http://www.coeliac.org.uk
Publisher: Coeliac UK
Frequency: 3 issues yearly - Published in February, May and October
Cover Price: £4.25
Free to qualifying individuals
Circulation: 70,000 (Publisher's Statement)
Usual Pagination: 48
Editor: Holly Ellicott
Summary of Content: Magazine covering everything about gluten free living, lifestyle, keeping fit, general health, travel, holidays, research on coeliac disease and new products.
Readership/Target Audience: Aimed at a wide readership of both men and women including those who have a gluten intolerance.
ADVERTISING RATES:
Full Page Colour £3750.00
Mechanical Data: Trim Size: 297 x 210mm, Film: Digital
Copy instructions: Copy Date: 6 weeks prior to publication date
CONSUMER: WOMEN'S INTEREST CONSUMER MAGAZINES: Slimming & Health

CRUCIBLE
47702U87-80

Editorial Address: Manchester Cathedral, Victoria Street, MANCHESTER, M3 1SX **Tel:** 0161 833 2220
Email: office@manchestercathedral.com
Advertising Address: 13-17 Long Lane, LONDON, EC1A 9PN **Tel:** 020 7776 1060

Email: stephen@churchtimes.co.uk
ISSN: 0011-2100
Publisher: Hymns ancient & modern
Date Established: 1961
Frequency: Quarterly
Cover Price: £4.00
Annual Sub.: £14.00
Circulation: 500 (Publisher's Statement)
Usual Pagination: 64
Editor: Peter Sedgwick
Summary of Content: Magazine containing Christian analysis and reflection on contemporary issues.
Readership/Target Audience: Read by people with interests in Christian social ethics.
ADVERTISING: Rates on application
CONSUMER: RELIGIOUS

CRUISE INTERNATIONAL
1895157U89E-262

Editorial Address: 26-30 Old Church Street, LONDON, SW3 5BY **Tel:** 020 7349 3150
Email: info@cruise-international.com
Web site: http://www.cruise-international.com
Publisher: The Chelsea Magazine Company
Date Established: 2009
Frequency: 6 issues yearly
Cover Price: £3.75
Circulation: 50,000 (Print Run)
Editor: Gillian Bendall
Summary of Content: Magazine containing features and photographs of exotic destinations, romantic ports and secret hideaways. Includes information about life on board and advice on which ship to choose and the best time to travel.
Readership/Target Audience: Aimed at anyone who has ever dreamed of a holiday at sea.
CONSUMER: HOLIDAYS & TRAVEL: Holidays

CRUISE MAGAZINE FOR GROUPS
1638225U89E-209

Formerly: Cruise Magazine
Editorial Address: PO Box 5122, Tongwell, MILTON KEYNES, MK15 8ZP **Tel:** 01908 613323 **Fax:** 01908 210656
Email: editorial@yandellmedia.com
Advertising Address: As above.
Email: sales@cruisemagazine.co.uk
Web site: http://www.cruisemagazine.co.uk
ISSN: 1741-2110
Publisher: Yandell Publishing Limited
Date Established: 2003
Frequency: Half-yearly - Published in March and August
Free to qualifying individuals
Circulation: 11,000 (Publisher's Statement)
Usual Pagination: 40
Editor: Rob Yandell; **Managing Editor:** Rob Yandell
Summary of Content: Magazine covering ships, destinations, fashion and general news about the cruising industry.
Readership/Target Audience: Aimed at Group travel organisers, organising holidays for leisure groups.
ADVERTISING RATES:
Full Page Colour £1800.00
Agency Commission: 10%
Mechanical Data: Film: Digital, Bleed Size: 303 x 216mm, Trim Size: 297 x 210mm
Copy instructions: Copy Date: 1st of the month prior to publication date
Average advertising content per issue: 25%
CONSUMER: HOLIDAYS & TRAVEL: Holidays

CRUISING - JOURNAL OF THE CRUISING ASSOCIATION
48372U91A-30

Editorial Address: CA House, 1 Northey Street, Limehouse Basin, LONDON, E14 8BT **Tel:** 020 7537 2828
Fax: 020 7537 2266
Email: office@cruising.org.uk
Advertising Address: Mongoose Media, 2 Lonsdale Road, LONDON, NW6 6RD **Tel:** 020 7306 0300
Fax: 020 7306 0301
Email: cruising@mongoosemedia.com
Web site: http://www.cruising.org.uk
Publisher: Cruising Association
Frequency: Quarterly
Cover Price: Free
Circulation: 5,000 (Publisher's Statement)
Editor: Frederick Barter
Summary of Content: Journal containing information on all facets of cruising in sail and motor boats.
Readership/Target Audience: Aimed at the members of the Cruising Association.
ADVERTISING RATES:
Full Page Colour £625.00
Agency Commission: 10%
Mechanical Data: Trim Size: 297 x 210mm, Bleed Size: +3mm, Type Area: 272 x 186mm, Film: Digital, Col Length: 272mm, Page Width: 186mm

Copy instructions: Copy Date: 4 weeks prior to publication date
CONSUMER: RECREATION & LEISURE: Boating & Yachting

CRYSTAL PALACE FOUNDATION NEWS
46791U80B-60

Editorial Address: 58 Laurier Road, CROYDON, CR0 6JQ
Tel: 07889 338812
Email: crystalpalacefoundation@hotmail.com
Advertising Address: As above.
Email: crystalpalacefoundation@hotmail.com
Web site: http://www.crystalpalacefoundation.org.uk
ISSN: 0964-802X
Publisher: The Crystal Palace Foundation
Date Established: 2001
Frequency: Quarterly
Free to qualifying individuals
Annual Sub.: £8.00
Circulation: 500 (Publisher's Statement)
Usual Pagination: 4
Editor: Melvyn Harrison; **Advertising Manager:** Melvyn Harrison
Summary of Content: Magazine containing up to date information relating to the Great Exhibition of 1851, The Crystal Palace at Sydenham and the Crystal Palace area.
Readership/Target Audience: Aimed at members of the Crystal Palace Foundation.
ADVERTISING: Rates on application
CONSUMER: RURAL & REGIONAL INTEREST: Regional Interest Greater London

CRYSTAL PALACE MATTERS
46849U80B-165

Formerly: New Crystal Palace Matters
Editorial Address: 58 Laurier Road, CROYDON, CR0 6JQ
Tel: 07889 338812
Email: crystalpalacefoundation@hotmail.com
Advertising Address: As above. **Fax:** 0870 133 7920
Email: crystalpalacefoundation@hotmail.com
Web site: http://www.crystalpalacefoundation.org.uk
ISSN: 0964-8011
Publisher: The Crystal Palace Foundation
Date Established: 1980
Frequency: Quarterly
Cover Price: £1.00
Free to qualifying individuals
Circulation: 500 (Publisher's Statement)
Usual Pagination: 20
Editor: John Brown; **Advertising Manager:** Bernard Winchester
Summary of Content: Publication containing historical information relating to the Great Exhibition of 1851, the Crystal Palace at Sydenham and the Crystal Palace area.
Readership/Target Audience: Aimed at members of the Crystal Palace Foundation and those interested in the history of the Crystal Palace.
ADVERTISING: Rates on application
CONSUMER: RURAL & REGIONAL INTEREST: Regional Interest Greater London

CSI: CRIME SCENE INVESTIGATION
1827910U76C-835

Editorial Address: Titan House, 144 Southwark Street, LONDON, SE1 0UP **Tel:** 020 7620 0200 **Fax:** 020 7620 0032
Email: csimagazine@titanmail.com
Advertising Address: As above. **Fax:** 020 7803 1803
Email: james.willmott@titanemail.com
Web site: http://www.titanmagazines.co.uk
Publisher: Titan Magazines
Date Established: 2007
Frequency: 6 issues yearly
Cover Price: £3.99
Editor: Kate Lloyd; **Advertising Manager:** James Willmott
Summary of Content: Magazine covering the hit TV programmes CSI with cast interviews, behind the scenes stories and competitions.
Readership/Target Audience: Aimed at fans of the TV shows.
ADVERTISING RATES:
Full Page Colour £2500.00
Mechanical Data: Trim Size: 276 x 200mm, Film: Digital
CONSUMER: MUSIC & PERFORMING ARTS: TV & Radio

CSMA CLUB MAGAZINE
46471U77E-200

Formerly: Motoring & Leisure
Editorial Address: Britannia House, 21 Station Street, BRIGHTON, BN1 4DE **Tel:** 01273 744744
Email: sean.mcgreevy@csmaclub.co.uk
Advertising Address: National Magazine Company Ltd, 21 Station Street, BRIGHTON, BN1 4DE **Tel:** 020 7312 3986
Fax: 020 7312 4180
Email: sean.mcgreevy@csmaclub.co.uk
Web site: http://www.csma.uk.com
Publisher: csma Ltd
Date Established: 1985

Consumer Magazines

Frequency: 10 issues yearly - Published on the 1st of the cover month
Annual Sub.: £15.00
Circulation: 294,107 (ABC 01/01/2007 to 31/12/2007)
Usual Pagination: 128
Editor: Sean McGreevy
Summary of Content: Magazine of the Civil Service Motoring Association. Includes new car news, entertainment, celebrity interviews, features on travel, travel offers and promotions, nostalgia, motor sport, leisure activities and outdoors, home, gardens and finance.
Readership/Target Audience: Read by members, private car owners and serving and retired civil servants.
ADVERTISING RATES:
Full Page Colour £5300.00
Agency Commission: 10%
Mechanical Data: Type Area: 270 x 190mm, Bleed Size: 303 x 216mm, Trim Size: 297 x 210mm, Col Length: 270mm, Page Width: 190mm, Film: Digital
Copy instructions: Copy Date: 4 weeks prior to publication date
CONSUMER: MOTORING & CYCLING: Club Cars

CTC CYCLE DIGEST
46388U77C-520
Editorial Address: Parklands, GUILDFORD, GU2 9JX
Tel: 0870 873 0063 **Fax:** 0870 873 0064
Email: cherry.allan@ctc.org.uk
Web site: http://www.ctc.org.uk/cycledigest
Publisher: Cyclists' Touring Club
Frequency: Quarterly
Cover Price: Free
Circulation: 4,000 (Publisher's Statement)
Usual Pagination: 8
Editor: Cherry Allan
Summary of Content: Newsletter containing cycle planning and policy news, information and comment.
Readership/Target Audience: Aimed at cyclists, transport professionals and health authorities.
ADVERTISING: No Advertising taken
CONSUMER: MOTORING & CYCLING: Cycling

CTRL+ALT+SHIFT
1846238U82-281
Editorial Address: 35 Lower Marsh, LONDON, SE1 7RL
Tel: 020 7620 4444 **Fax:** 020 7620 0712
Email: NBoorman@christian-aid.org
Web site: http://www.ctrlaltshift.co.uk
Publisher: Christian Aid
Date Established: 2008
Frequency: Quarterly
Cover Price: Free
Circulation: 40,000 (Print Run)
Usual Pagination: 36
Editor: Neil Boorman; **Managing Editor:** Neil Boorman
Summary of Content: Magazine covering ethical and political activities including world development and environmental issues.
Readership/Target Audience: Aimed at 16 to 25 year olds.
CONSUMER: CURRENT AFFAIRS & POLITICS

CUB
47379U83-6_5
Editorial Address: Queen Mary College Students Union, 432 Bancroft Road, LONDON, E1 4DH **Tel:** 020 7882 8041
Fax: 020 8981 0802
Email: vpmedia@qmsu.org
Advertising Address: Fielden House, Westfield Way, LONDON, E1 4NP **Tel:** 020 7882 8041 **Fax:** 020 8981 0802
Email: advertising@cubmagazine.co.uk
Web site: http://www.cubmagazine.co.uk
Publisher: QMSU
Date Established: 1947
Frequency: 8 issues yearly - Published every four weeks during term time
Cover Price: Free
Circulation: 13,000 (Publisher's Statement)
Usual Pagination: 36
Editor: Claire Rutter; **Advertising Manager:** Claire Rutter
Summary of Content: Newspaper of Queen Mary College Students' Union. Includes college news, national student news, arts and music reviews.
Readership/Target Audience: Aimed at London students.
ADVERTISING RATES:
Full Page Colour £450.00
Agency Commission: 10%
Mechanical Data: Type Area: 287 x 200mm, Bleed Size: 3mm, Trim Size: 297 x 210mm, Print Process: Litho
Copy instructions: Copy Date: 10 days prior to publication date
Average advertising content per issue: 10%
CONSUMER: STUDENT PUBLICATIONS

CUBASI
47219U82-12
Editorial Address: c/o Unite - Woodberry, 218 Green Lanes, LONDON, N4 2HB **Tel:** 020 8800 0155 **Fax:** 020 8800 9844
Email: office@cuba-solidarity.org.uk

Advertising Address: As above. **Tel:** 020 7263 6452
Fax: 020 7561 0191
Email: office@cuba-solidarity.org.uk
Web site: http://www.cuba-solidarity.org.uk
Publisher: Cuba Solidarity Campaign
Frequency: Quarterly
Cover Price: £2.00
Free to qualifying individuals
Circulation: 7,000 (Publisher's Statement)
Usual Pagination: 32
Editor: Natasha Hickman; **Advertising Manager:** Rob Miller
Summary of Content: Official magazine of the Cuba Solidarity Campaign. Contains features on Cuban music, politics and holidays.
Readership/Target Audience: Read by those with an interest in Cuban affairs.
ADVERTISING: Rates on application
CONSUMER: CURRENT AFFAIRS & POLITICS

CUE SPORT
753655U75X-50
Editorial Address: 8 Sam Road, Diggle, OLDHAM, OL3 5PU
Tel: 01457 829845 **Fax:** 0121 505 1130
Email: editor@cuesport.net
Advertising Address: As above. **Fax:** 01457 829845
Email: trevor@redandwhitesport.co.uk
Web site: http://www.cuesport.net
ISSN: 1471-7662
Publisher: Deebax International
Date Established: 2000
Frequency: 9 issues yearly - Published on the 1st Friday of the cover month
Cover Price: £2.20
Annual Sub.: £20.00
Circulation: 7,000 (Publisher's Statement)
Usual Pagination: 44
Editor: Trevor Baxter; **Advertising Manager:** Trevor Baxter
Summary of Content: Magazine focusing on snooker and pool featuring news and stories, player profiles, tournaments, results, coaching and tips.
Readership/Target Audience: Aimed at fans and players of snooker and pool.
ADVERTISING RATES:
Full Page Colour £625.00
Agency Commission: 10%
Mechanical Data: Type Area: 274 x 190mm, Bleed Size: 307 x 215mm, Trim Size: 297 x 210mm, Col Length: 274mm, Film: Positive, right reading, emulsion side down. Digital, Page Width: 190mm
CONSUMER: SPORT: Other Sport

CULT TIMES
46759U79L-50
Editorial Address: 9-10 Blades Court, Deodar Road, LONDON, SW15 2NU **Tel:** 020 8875 1520
Fax: 020 8875 1588
Email: culttimes@visimag.com
Advertising Address: As above. **Tel:** 020 8875 7400
Email: mclarke@visimag.com
Web site: http://www.visimag.com
ISSN: 1360-6530
Publisher: Visual Imagination Ltd
Date Established: 1995
Frequency: Monthly
Cover Price: £3.99
Annual Sub.: £36.00
Circulation: 25,000 (Publisher's Statement)
Usual Pagination: 72
Editor: Stuart Weightman; **Managing Director:** Stephen Payne; **Advertising Manager:** Martin Clarke
Summary of Content: Magazine covering cult, science fiction and adventure television. Includes news, reviews, interviews and TV listings for terrestrial, cable and satellite channels.
Readership/Target Audience: Aimed at those interested in science fiction, cult and adventure television.
ADVERTISING RATES:
Full Page Colour £950.00
Agency Commission: 10%
Mechanical Data: Film: Digital, Bleed Size: 310 x 232mm, Trim Size: 300 x 222mm, Type Area: 270 x 192mm, Col Length: 270mm, Page Width: 192mm
Copy instructions: Copy Date: 3 weeks prior to publication date
Average advertising content per issue: 30%
CONSUMER: HOBBIES & DIY: Fantasy Games & Science Fiction

CULT TV - THE OFFICIAL MAGAZINE
46096U76C-190
Editorial Address: PO Box 1701, PETERBOROUGH, PE7 1ER **Tel:** 070 0428 5888 **Fax:** 01733 205009
Email: editor@cult.tv
Advertising Address: As above.
Email: alex@cult.tv
Web site: http://www.cult.tv
ISSN: 1368-5384
Publisher: Cult TV Publishing

Date Established: 1985
Frequency: Annual - Published in October
Cover Price: £4.00
Free to qualifying individuals
Circulation: 700 (Publisher's Statement)
Usual Pagination: 40
Editor: Alex Geairns; **Advertising Manager:** Alex Geairns
Summary of Content: Magazine covering fictional television that is a little extraordinary. Includes comedy, science fiction, drama, action adventure, animation, children's series, detectives shows and westerns with a "cult" following.
Readership/Target Audience: Aimed at those with an interest in Cult TV programmes.
ADVERTISING RATES:
Full Page Mono £350.00
Full Page Colour £700.00
Agency Commission: 15%
Mechanical Data: Trim Size: 297 x 210mm, Film: Digital
Copy instructions: Copy Date: 3 weeks prior to publication date
Average advertising content per issue: 15%
CONSUMER: MUSIC & PERFORMING ARTS: TV & Radio

CUMBRIA
46876U80C-900
Formerly: Cumbria and Lake District Magazine
Editorial Address: The Water Mill, Broughton Hall, SKIPTON, BD23 3AG **Tel:** 01756 701381 **Fax:** 01756 701326
Email: editorial@dalesman.co.uk
Advertising Address: As above.
Email: ads@dalesman.co.uk
Web site: http://www.dalesman.co.uk
Publisher: Country Publications Ltd
Date Established: 1951
Frequency: Monthly
Cover Price: £2.25
Annual Sub.: £22.20
Circulation: 12,183 (ABC 01/01/2008 to 31/12/2008)
Usual Pagination: 100
Editor: Paul Jackson
Summary of Content: Regional interest magazine about people and places in the Lake District. Strong outdoor emphasis.
Readership/Target Audience: Aimed at visitors to the Lake District and residents of the area.
ADVERTISING RATES:
Full Page Mono £650.00
Full Page Colour £650.00
Agency Commission: 10%
Mechanical Data: Bleed Size: 220 x 158mm, Col Length: 180mm, No. of Columns (Display): 2, Page Width: 123mm, Col Widths (Display): 60mm, Type Area: 180 x 123mm, Film: Digital, Trim Size: 210 x 148mm
Copy instructions: Copy Date: 1 month prior to publication date
Average advertising content per issue: 40%
CONSUMER: RURAL & REGIONAL INTEREST: Regional Interest English Counties

---

CUMBRIA LIFE
46877U80C-919
Editorial Address: Media House, Barras Lane, Dalston, CARLISLE, CA5 7LX **Tel:** 01228 713000 **Fax:** 01228 713001
Email: editor@cumbrialife.co.uk
Advertising Address: As above.
Email: cliff.abbott@cumbrialife.co.uk
Web site: http://www.cumbrialife.co.uk
Publisher: Cumbrian Newspapers Ltd
Frequency: Monthly
Cover Price: £3.40
Circulation: 17,500 (Publisher's Statement)
Usual Pagination: 196
Editor: Richard Eccles; **Advertising Manager:** Cliff Abbott
Summary of Content: Magazine containing features and information on Cumbria.
Readership/Target Audience: Read by residents and visitors to Cumbria predominantly aged 35 to 65 years old.
ADVERTISING RATES:
Full Page Colour £1450.00
Agency Commission: 10%
Mechanical Data: Page Width: 196mm, No. of Columns (Display): 4, Type Area: 273 x 196mm, Col Length: 273mm, Print Process: Sheet-fed litho, Bleed Size: 303 x 226mm, Trim Size: 297 x 220mm, Film: Digital
Average advertising content per issue: 40%
CONSUMER: RURAL & REGIONAL INTEREST: Regional Interest English Counties

---

CURRENT ARCHAEOLOGY
31004U94X-32_75
Editorial Address: 9 Nassington Road, LONDON, NW3 2TX
Tel: 020 7435 7517 **Fax:** 020 7916 2405
Email: editor@archaeology.co.uk
Web site: http://www.archaeology.co.uk
ISSN: 0011-3212
Publisher: Current Archaeology
Date Established: 1967
Frequency: Monthly
Cover Price: £4.00
Annual Sub.: £38.00

Circulation: 18,000 (Publisher's Statement)
Usual Pagination: 40
Editor: Andrew Selkirk; **Managing Editor:** Lisa Westcott;
Publisher: Robert Selkirk
Summary of Content: Magazine containing the latest archaeological news in Britain.
Readership/Target Audience: Aimed at all those interested in archaeology, including academics and professionals as well as amateur archaeologists.
ADVERTISING: No Advertising taken
Supplement(s): Archaeology Handbook - 1xY
CONSUMER: OTHER CLASSIFICATIONS: Miscellaneous

CURRENT WORLD ARCHAEOLOGY
1629420U94X-262
Editorial Address: Lamb House, Church Street, LONDON, W4 2PD **Tel:** 0845 644 7707 **Fax:** 0845 644 7708
Email: cwa@archaeology.co.uk
Advertising Address: As above.
Email: advertising@archaeology.co.uk
Web site: http://www.archaeology.co.uk
Publisher: Current Publishing
Date Established: 2003
Frequency: 6 issues yearly
Cover Price: £4.00
Annual Sub.: £20.00
Circulation: 10,000 (Publisher's Statement)
Usual Pagination: 68
Editor: Nadia Durrani; **Editor-in-Chief:** Andrew Selkirk;
Advertising Manager: Libby Selkirk; **Publisher:** Robert Selkirk
Summary of Content: Magazine covering the latest discoveries worldwide and the latest excavations, bridging the gap between the layman and professional archaeologists.
Readership/Target Audience: Aimed at amateur and professional archaeologists.
ADVERTISING RATES:
Full Page Colour £1250.00
Mechanical Data: Bleed Size: 288 x 220mm, Film: Digital, Type Area: 262 x 190mm, Col Length: 262mm, Page Width: 190mm, Trim Size: 282 x 210mm
CONSUMER: OTHER CLASSIFICATIONS: Miscellaneous

CUSTOM CAR
46501U77R-25
Editorial Address: Cudham Tithe Barn, Berrys Hill, Berrys Green, Cudham, WESTERHAM, TN16 3AG
Tel: 01959 541444 **Fax:** 01959 541400
Email: cc.info@kelsey.co.uk
Advertising Address: As above. **Fax:** 01959 543585
Email: graham@kelsey.co.uk
Web site: http://www.customcarmag.uk
Publisher: Kelsey Publishing Ltd
Date Established: 1971
Frequency: Monthly
Cover Price: £3.60
Annual Sub.: £39.60
Circulation: 20,000 (Publisher's Statement)
Usual Pagination: 80
Editor: Dave Biggadyke; **Features Editor:** Mike Pye;
Advertising Manager: Graham Mazey; **Publisher:** Phil Weeden
Summary of Content: Magazine covering news and features on custom cars, hot rods, drag racing and products.
Readership/Target Audience: Aimed at custom car and hot rod enthusiasts.
ADVERTISING RATES:
Full Page Colour £900.00
Agency Commission: 10%
Mechanical Data: Page Width: 188mm, Film: Digital, Type Area: 272 x 188mm, Bleed Size: 303 x 216mm, Trim Size: 297 x 210mm, Col Length: 272mm, No. of Columns (Display): 2
Copy instructions: Copy Date: 4 weeks prior to publication date
Average advertising content per issue: 30%
CONSUMER: MOTORING & CYCLING: Motoring & Cycling Related

CUSTOM PC
1623145U78R-484
Editorial Address: 30 Cleveland Street, LONDON, W1T 4JD
Tel: 020 7907 6000 **Fax:** 020 7907 6020
Email: alex_watson@dennis.co.uk
Advertising Address: As above. **Fax:** 020 7907 6620
Email: jonathan_kitchen@dennis.co.uk
Web site: http://www.custompc.co.uk
Publisher: Dennis Publishing Ltd
Date Established: 2003
Frequency: Monthly
Cover Price: £3.75
Free to qualifying individuals
Annual Sub.: £30.00
Circulation: 23,667 (ABC 01/01/2008 to 31/12/2008)
Usual Pagination: 132

Editor: Alex Watson; **News Editor:** Ben Hardwidge;
Advertising Director: Jonathan Kitchen
Summary of Content: Magazine covering performance hardware and customisation. Includes features on highend IT and articles on the latest technology.
Readership/Target Audience: Aimed predominantly at male hardware fanatics between 18 and 35 years old.
ADVERTISING RATES:
Full Page Colour £2084.00
Agency Commission: 10%
Mechanical Data: Trim Size: 300 x 230mm, Film: Digital, Type Area: 287 x 218mm, Bleed Size: 306 x 236mm, Col Length: 287mm, Page Width: 218mm
CONSUMER: CONSUMER ELECTRONICS: Consumer Electronics Related

CYCLE
46387U77C-724
Formerly: Cycle Touring & Campaigning
Editorial Address: PO Box 313, SCARBOROUGH, YO12 6WZ **Tel:** 01723 377521 **Fax:** 01723 377521
Email: editor@ctc.org.uk
Advertising Address: Mongoose Media, Mongoose House, 2 Lonsdale Road, LONDON, NW6 6ED **Tel:** 020 7306 0300
Fax: 020 7306 0301
Email: ctc@mongoosemedia.com
Web site: http://www.ctc.org.uk
ISSN: 0965-0776
Publisher: Cyclists' Touring Club
Date Established: 1878
Frequency: 6 issues yearly
Cover Price: £3.00
Free to qualifying individuals
Circulation: 40,000 (Publisher's Statement)
Usual Pagination: 84
Editor: Dan Joyce; **Advertising Manager:** Robert Forisky
Summary of Content: Magazine of the Cyclists' Touring Club which campaigns for the rights and safety of all cyclists and promotes leisure and utility cycling and cycling travel.
Readership/Target Audience: Read by cycling enthusiasts of all ages and abilities.
ADVERTISING RATES:
Full Page Mono £1390.00
Full Page Colour £1740.00
Agency Commission: 10%
Mechanical Data: Film: Digital, Type Area: 260 x 190mm, Col Length: 260mm, Page Width: 190mm, Bleed Size: +3mm
CONSUMER: MOTORING & CYCLING: Cycling

CYCLE SPORT
46390U77C-700
Editorial Address: Leon House, 233 High Street, CROYDON, CR9 1HZ **Tel:** 020 8726 8462
Fax: 020 8726 8499
Email: cyclesport@ipcmedia.com
Advertising Address: As above. **Tel:** 020 8726 8414
Fax: 020 8726 8294
Email: jason_dilworth@ipcmedia.com
Web site: http://www.cyclesport.co.uk
Publisher: IPC Inspire
Frequency: Monthly
Cover Price: £4.00
Circulation: 17,073 (ABC 01/01/2008 to 31/12/2008)
Usual Pagination: 164
Editor: Edward Pickering; **Advertising Manager:** Jason Dilworth; **Publisher:** Keith Foster
Summary of Content: Magazine dedicated to professional cycle racing.
Readership/Target Audience: Aimed at people interested in continental racing and famous cyclists.
ADVERTISING RATES:
Full Page Colour £1200.00
SCC £30.00
Agency Commission: 10%
Mechanical Data: Page Width: 178mm, Type Area: 230 x 178mm, Col Length: 230mm, Trim Size: 268 x 204mm, Bleed Size: 274 x 210mm, Film: Digital
Copy instructions: Copy Date: 3 weeks prior to publication date
CONSUMER: MOTORING & CYCLING: Cycling

CYCLING PLUS
46391U77C-723
Editorial Address: 30 Monmouth Street, BATH, BA1 2BW
Tel: 01225 442244 **Fax:** 01225 822793
Email: cyclingplus@futurenet.com
Advertising Address: As above. **Fax:** 01225 732206
Email: steve.hulbert@futurenet.co.uk
Web site: http://www.cyclingplus.co.uk
ISSN: 0964-6868
Publisher: Future Publishing Ltd
Date Established: 1992
Frequency: 13 issues yearly
Cover Price: £3.99
Annual Sub.: £38.00
Circulation: 35,223 (ABC 01/01/2008 to 31/12/2008)
Usual Pagination: 100
Editor: Paul Vincent; **Advertising Manager:** Steve Hulbert

Summary of Content: Magazine covering all forms of performance, leisure and utility cycling. Includes equipment tests, fitness and touring advice.
Readership/Target Audience: Read by experienced cyclists, cycling enthusiasts and complete beginners aged between 25 and 40 years old.
ADVERTISING RATES:
Full Page Mono £1300.00
Mechanical Data: Film: Digital, Type Area: 270 x 190mm, Col Length: 270mm, Page Width: 190mm, Bleed Size: 303 x 216mm, Trim Size: 297 x 210mm
CONSUMER: MOTORING & CYCLING: Cycling

CYCLING WEEKLY
46393U77C-725
Editorial Address: Leon House, 233 High Street, CROYDON, CR9 1HZ **Tel:** 020 8726 8462
Fax: 020 8726 8499
Email: cycling@ipcmedia.com
Advertising Address: As above. **Tel:** 020 8726 8484
Fax: 020 8726 8294
Email: kevin_attridge@ipcmedia.com
Web site: http://www.cyclingweekly.co.uk
ISSN: 0011-4316
Publisher: IPC Inspire
Date Established: 1891
Frequency: Weekly
Cover Price: £2.50
Circulation: 27,212 (ABC 01/01/2008 to 31/12/2008)
Usual Pagination: 88
Editor: Simon Richardson; **Managing Editor:** Robert Garbutt; **Publisher:** Keith Foster
Summary of Content: Magazine containing a comprehensive guide to the cycling scene covering all aspects of cycling including road racing, time trialling and touring.
Readership/Target Audience: Read by cyclists, triathletes, road racers and mountain bikers.
ADVERTISING RATES:
Full Page Colour £1485.00
Agency Commission: 10%
Mechanical Data: Page Width: 179mm, Col Length: 254mm, Trim Size: 280 x 200mm, Bleed Size: 286 x 206mm, Film: Digital, Type Area: 254 x 179mm
CONSUMER: MOTORING & CYCLING: Cycling

CYCLING WORLD
46394U77C-730
Editorial Address: Unit 7 Drywall, Castle Road, Eurolink Industrial Estate, SITTINGBOURNE, ME10 3RX
Tel: 01795 599191 **Fax:** 01795 599282
Email: cw.editor@yahoo.co.uk
Advertising Address: As above.
Email: jo@cplmedia.co.uk
Web site: http://www.cyclingworldmagazine.co.uk
ISSN: 0143-0238
Publisher: CPL Media Ltd
Date Established: 1979
Frequency: Monthly
Cover Price: £2.80
Circulation: 18,000 (Publisher's Statement)
Usual Pagination: 40
Editor: Steven Dyster; **Advertising Manager:** Jo Atara;
Publisher: Colin Woolley
Summary of Content: Magazine covering touring and recreational cycling.
Readership/Target Audience: Read by cyclists.
ADVERTISING RATES:
Full Page Mono £895.00
Full Page Colour £895.00
Agency Commission: 10%
Mechanical Data: Type Area: 274 x 184mm, Trim Size: 297 x 210mm, Bleed Size: 303 x 216mm, Col Length: 274mm, Film: Digital, Page Width: 184mm
Copy instructions: Copy Date: 3 weeks prior to publication date
Average advertising content per issue: 40%
CONSUMER: MOTORING & CYCLING: Cycling

DAILY BREAD
47792U87-82
Editorial Address: 207-209 Queensway, Bletchley, MILTON KEYNES, MK2 2EB **Tel:** 01908 856000 **Fax:** 01908 856111
Email: triciaw@scriptureunion.org.uk
Web site: http://www.dailybread.org.uk
ISSN: 0963-4797
Publisher: Scripture Union
Date Established: 1937
Frequency: Quarterly
Cover Price: £3.50
Circulation: 36,000 (Publisher's Statement)
Usual Pagination: 112
Editor: Terry Clutterham
Summary of Content: Magazine containing daily Bible reading notes.
Readership/Target Audience: Aimed at adult Bible readers.
ADVERTISING: No Advertising taken
CONSUMER: RELIGIOUS

Consumer Magazines

THE DAILY JANG LONDON
48295U90-47

Editorial Address: 1 Sanctuary Street, LONDON, SE1 1ED
Tel: 020 7403 5833 **Fax:** 020 7378 1653
Email: newsdesk@janglondon.co.uk
Advertising Address: As above. **Fax:** 020 7403 3612
Email: thenewsse1@yahoo.com
Web site: http://www.jang.com.pk
ISSN: 1352-7541
Publisher: Jang Publications Ltd
Date Established: 1971
Frequency: 360 issues yearly
Cover Price: £0.50
Circulation: 10,000 (Publisher's Statement)
Usual Pagination: 12
Editor: Zahoor Niazi; **Editor-in-Chief:** Shakilur Rahman;
Advertising Manager: Shabna Maqsord
Summary of Content: Newspaper covering national and international events, plus news of the Asian community in the UK and Europe.
Language(s): English; Urdu
Readership/Target Audience: Aimed at the Asian community.
ADVERTISING RATES:
Full Page Mono £7776.00
Full Page Colour £19440.00
Agency Commission: 15%
Mechanical Data: Film: Digital, Type Area: 610 x 457mm, Col Length: 610mm, Page Width: 457mm
CONSUMER: ETHNIC

DAILY MAIL SKI & SNOWBOARD MAGAZINE
45869U75G-100

Editorial Address: Equitable House, Lyon Road, HARROW, HA1 2EW **Tel:** 020 8515 2000 **Fax:** 020 8515 2080
Email: henrydruce@dmgworldmedia.com
Advertising Address: As above. **Fax:** 020 8515 2089
Email: sarahsepahi@dmgworldmedia.com
Web site: http://www.skiandsnowboardmag.com
Publisher: DMG World Media
Date Established: 1988
Frequency: 6 issues yearly - Published monthly from September to February
Cover Price: £3.70
Annual Sub.: £42.00
Circulation: 14,236 (ABC 01/01/2008 to 31/12/2008)
Usual Pagination: 132
Editor: Henry Druce; **Editor-in-Chief:** Dave Watts;
Advertising Manager: Sarah Sepahi
Summary of Content: Magazine offering essential information on all aspects of skiing and snowboarding.
Readership/Target Audience: Aimed at winter sports enthusiasts.
ADVERTISING RATES:
Full Page Colour £3000.00
Agency Commission: 10%
Mechanical Data: Col Length: 275mm, Page Width: 208mm, Trim Size: 302 x 232mm, Bleed Size: 310 x 240mm, Film: Digital, Type Area: 275 x 208mm
Average advertising content per issue: 35%
CONSUMER: SPORT: Winter Sports

DALES LIFE
47005U80C-3598

Editorial Address: Suite 2 Market Chambers, 14 Market Place, BEDALE, DL8 1EQ **Tel:** 01677 425217
Fax: 01677 425251
Email: sue@daleslife.demon.co.uk
Advertising Address: As above. **Fax:** 01429 425251
Email: sue@daleslife.demon.co.uk
Publisher: Dales Life
Frequency: 6 issues yearly
Cover Price: Free
Circulation: 30,000 (Publisher's Statement)
Usual Pagination: 132
Editor: Sue Gillman; **Advertising Manager:** Sue Gillman
Summary of Content: Local interest magazine delivered to homes and businesses throughout North Yorkshire.
Readership/Target Audience: Aimed at those living and working in North Yorkshire.
ADVERTISING RATES:
Full Page Colour £550.00
Agency Commission: 15%
Mechanical Data: Bleed Size: 216 x 154mm, Trim Size: 210 x 148mm, Film: Digital
Copy instructions: Copy Date: 4 weeks prior to publication date
Average advertising content per issue: 55%
CONSUMER: RURAL & REGIONAL INTEREST: Regional Interest English Counties

DALESMAN
47006U80C-3600

Editorial Address: The Water Mill, Broughton Hall, SKIPTON, BD23 3AG **Tel:** 01756 701381 **Fax:** 01756 701326
Email: editorial@dalesman.co.uk
Advertising Address: As above.
Email: ads@dalesman.co.uk
Web site: http://www.dalesman.co.uk

Publisher: Country Publications Ltd
Date Established: 1939
Frequency: Monthly
Cover Price: £1.99
Annual Sub.: £23.88
Circulation: 37,463 (ABC 01/01/2008 to 31/12/2008)
Usual Pagination: 116
Editor: Paul Jackson
Summary of Content: Magazine covering articles specifically on the Yorkshire countryside, people, customs and traditions.
Readership/Target Audience: Read by residents and visitors to Yorkshire and expats.
ADVERTISING RATES:
Full Page Colour £1600.00
Agency Commission: 10%
Mechanical Data: Type Area: 180 x 123mm, Col Length: 180mm, Page Width: 123mm, Bleed Size: 220 x 158mm, Trim Size: 210 x 148mm, Film: Digital
Copy instructions: Copy Date: 5 weeks prior to publication date
Average advertising content per issue: 40%
CONSUMER: RURAL & REGIONAL INTEREST: Regional Interest English Counties

DALTONS WEEKLY
45672U74K-42

Editorial Address: 11th Floor, CI Tower, St. Georges Square, NEW MALDEN, KY3 4TE **Tel:** 020 7955 3760
Fax: 020 7955 3761
Email: tony.arnold@ubm.com
Advertising Address: As above.
Email: tony.arnold@ubm.com
Web site: http://www.daltonsbusiness.com
Publisher: UBM Information Ltd
Date Established: 1870
Frequency: Weekly - Published every Thursday
Cover Price: £1.95
Circulation: 13,128 (Publisher's Statement)
Usual Pagination: 56
Editor: Tony Arnold; **Advertising Manager:** Tony Arnold;
Publisher: Tony Arnold
Summary of Content: Publication for buying and selling property, businesses and holiday accommodation both UK and overseas.
Readership/Target Audience: Aimed at people looking for holiday accommodation, property purchasers and business buyers.
ADVERTISING: Rates on application
Agency Commission: 10%
Copy instructions: Copy Date: Monday prior to publication date
Average advertising content per issue: 100%
Supplement(s): Business Start Up - 2xY, Franchise Supplement - 3xY, Ideal Holidays - 1xY
CONSUMER: WOMEN'S INTEREST CONSUMER MAGAZINES: Home Purchase

DANCE EUROPE
46281U76G-106

Editorial Address: PO Box 12661, LONDON, E5 9TZ
Tel: 020 8985 7767 **Fax:** 020 8525 0462
Email: edit@danceeurope.net
Advertising Address: As above. **Tel:** 020 7682 1733
Email: ads@danceeurope.net
Web site: http://www.danceeurope.net
ISSN: 1359-9798
Publisher: Dance Europe
Date Established: 1995
Frequency: 11 issues yearly - Combined issue August/September
Cover Price: £2.95
Circulation: 18,000 (Publisher's Statement)
Usual Pagination: 68
Editor: Emma Manning; **Advertising Manager:** Naresh Kaul
Summary of Content: Publication reviews dance companies across Europe. Features leading figures in the dance world and includes a comprehensive performance diary.
Language(s): English; Japanese
Readership/Target Audience: Aimed at professional students and dancers and their audiences.
ADVERTISING RATES:
Full Page Mono £595.00
Full Page Colour £845.00
Mechanical Data: Film: Digital, Bleed Size: 304 x 214mm
CONSUMER: MUSIC & PERFORMING ARTS: Dance

DANCE EXPRESSION
46282U76G-108

Formerly: Dance Express
Editorial Address: 38 Ambleside Drive, SPALDING, PE11 1JU **Tel:** 01775 712856 **Fax:** 01775 712856
Email: catalina@globalnet.co.uk
Advertising Address: 51 Earl's Court Square, LONDON, SW5 9DG **Tel:** 020 7370 7324 **Fax:** 020 7370 5456
Email: dance-ads@hotmail.co.uk
Web site: http://www.danceexpression.co.uk
ISSN: 1468-5809

Publisher: A.E. Morgan Publications Ltd
Date Established: 1996
Frequency: Monthly
Cover Price: £2.75
Annual Sub.: £24.30
Circulation: 10,000 (Publisher's Statement)
Usual Pagination: 48
Editor: Chris Cattrall; **Managing Director:** Terence Morgan;
Advertising Manager: Gavin Roebuck; **Publisher:** Terence Morgan
Summary of Content: Magazine containing news, advice and reviews on all aspects of dance, including schools, shows and competitions, previews of dance events nationwide and three month in advance dance diary.
Readership/Target Audience: Aimed at performers, instructors and enthusiasts of all ages.
ADVERTISING RATES:
Full Page Mono £690.00
Full Page Colour £820.00
Agency Commission: 10%
Mechanical Data: Col Length: 340mm, No. of Columns (Display): 4, Type Area: 340 x 245mm, Bleed Size: 346 x 251mm, Trim Size: 340 x 245mm, Page Width: 245mm, Col Widths (Display): 40mm
Copy instructions: Copy Date: 1st of month prior to publication date
Average advertising content per issue: 35%
CONSUMER: MUSIC & PERFORMING ARTS: Dance

DANCE GAZETTE
46283U76G-110

Editorial Address: 36 Battersea Square, LONDON, SW11 3RA **Tel:** 020 7326 8091 **Fax:** 020 7924 3129
Email: gazette@rad.org.uk
Advertising Address: As above. **Tel:** 020 7326 8038
Email: vspyropoulou@rad.org.uk
Web site: http://www.rad.org.uk
Publisher: Royal Academy of Dance
Frequency: 3 issues yearly - Published in February, June and October
Cover Price: £2.20
Circulation: 17,000 (Publisher's Statement)
Editor: David Jays; **Advertising Manager:** Vassiliki Spyropoulou
Summary of Content: Magazine covering articles on dancers, dance companies, training and teaching, choreography, ballet and features relating to the Royal Academy of Dance.
Readership/Target Audience: Read by dance teachers, students, examiners and those interested in dance.
ADVERTISING RATES:
Full Page Mono £550.00
Full Page Colour £750.00
Agency Commission: 10%
Mechanical Data: Trim Size: 297 x 210mm, Film: Digital, Col Length: 272mm, Type Area: 272 x 185mm, Bleed Size: 303 x 216mm, Page Width: 185mm
Copy instructions: Copy Date: 8 weeks prior to publication date
Average advertising content per issue: 40%
CONSUMER: MUSIC & PERFORMING ARTS: Dance

DANCE NEWS
46284U76G-120

Editorial Address: Hamble House, Meadrow, GODALMING, GU7 3HJ **Tel:** 01483 428679 **Fax:** 01483 417650
Email: editor@dance-news.co.uk
Advertising Address: As above.
Email: editor@dance-news.co.uk
Web site: http://www.dance-news.co.uk
ISSN: 0956-2613
Publisher: Dance News Ltd.
Date Established: 1938
Frequency: Weekly
Cover Price: £1.50
Annual Sub.: £70.00
Usual Pagination: 16
Editor: John Leach; **Managing Director:** Linda Short;
Advertising Manager: John Leach; **Managing Editor:** John Leach
Summary of Content: International reviews of the ballroom dancing scene with junior sections and competition previews and results and a diary of forthcoming events.
Readership/Target Audience: Read by professional and amateur ballroom dancers.
ADVERTISING: Rates on application
CONSUMER: MUSIC & PERFORMING ARTS: Dance

DANCE RESEARCH
28608U76G-125

Editorial Address: 22 George Square, EDINBURGH, EH8 9LF **Tel:** 0131 650 4220 **Fax:** 0131 662 0053
Email: journals@eup.ed.ac.uk
Web site: http://www.eup.ed.ac.uk
ISSN: 0264-2875
Publisher: Edinburgh University Press Ltd
Frequency: Half-yearly - Published Spring and Autumn
Cover Price: £27.50
Annual Sub.: £41.00
Circulation: 400 (Publisher's Statement)

Usual Pagination: 150
Editor: Richard Ralph
Summary of Content: Academic journal covering the history of dance.
Readership/Target Audience: Aimed at dance researchers and practitioners.
ADVERTISING: No Advertising taken
CONSUMER: MUSIC & PERFORMING ARTS: Dance

DANCE THEATRE JOURNAL
46286U76G-130
Editorial Address: Laban, Creekside, LONDON, SE8 3DZ
Tel: 020 8691 8600 **Fax:** 020 8691 8400
Email: dtj@laban.org
Advertising Address: As above.
Email: d.smith@laban.org
Web site: http://www.laban.org
ISSN: 0264-9160
Publisher: Laban
Date Established: 1983
Frequency: Quarterly
Cover Price: £4.00
Annual Sub.: £15.00
Circulation: 2,000 (Publisher's Statement)
Usual Pagination: 48
Editor: Martin Hargreaves; **Advertising Manager:** David Smith
Summary of Content: Magazine covering contemporary dance, ballet and non-western dance forms. Includes interviews with choreographers and performers.
Readership/Target Audience: Aimed at those who take an informed interest in dance.
ADVERTISING RATES:
Full Page Mono £890.00
Full Page Colour £1180.00
Mechanical Data: Col Length: 272mm, Type Area: 272 x 185mm, Film: Digital, Page Width: 185mm
Copy instructions: Copy Date: 4 weeks prior to publication date
Average advertising content per issue: 5%
CONSUMER: MUSIC & PERFORMING ARTS: Dance

DANCE TODAY
46280U76G-144
Editorial Address: 45-47 Clerkenwell Green, LONDON, EC1R 0EB **Tel:** 020 7250 3006 **Fax:** 020 7253 6679
Email: dancetoday@dancing-times.co.uk
Advertising Address: As above.
Email: ann@dancing-times.co.uk
Web site: http://www.dancing-times.co.uk
ISSN: 0005-4380
Publisher: The Dancing Times Ltd
Date Established: 1956
Frequency: Monthly - Published on the second week of each month
Cover Price: £1.75
Annual Sub.: £19.25
Circulation: 3,500 (Publisher's Statement)
Usual Pagination: 68
Editor: Katie Gregory; **Advertising Manager:** Ann Mottram
Summary of Content: Magazine focusing on ballroom and Latin dance as well as other social dance forms, containing news, features, advice on technique, health and nutrition articles, interviews and competition reports.
Readership/Target Audience: Aimed at amateur and professional dancers as well as social dancers of all ages.
ADVERTISING RATES:
Full Page Mono £146.00
Full Page Colour £268.00
Agency Commission: 10%
Mechanical Data: Film: Digital, Type Area: 190 x 143mm, Print Process: Web-fed offset litho, Col Length: 190mm, Trim Size: 220 x 168mm, Page Width: 143mm
Copy instructions: Copy Date: 10th of the month prior to publication date
CONSUMER: MUSIC & PERFORMING ARTS: Dance

DANCING TIMES
46287U76G-140
Editorial Address: 45-47 Clerkenwell Green, LONDON, EC1R 0EB **Tel:** 020 7250 3006 **Fax:** 020 7253 6679
Email: editorial@dancing-times.co.uk
Advertising Address: As above.
Email: ann@dancing-times.co.uk
Web site: http://www.dancing-times.co.uk
ISSN: 0011-605X
Publisher: The Dancing Times Ltd
Date Established: 1910
Frequency: Monthly
Cover Price: £2.95
Annual Sub.: £32.45
Circulation: 9,000 (Publisher's Statement)
Usual Pagination: 108
Editor: Jonathan Gray; **Advertising Manager:** Ann Mottram
Summary of Content: Magazine covering all types of stage dancing but mainly focusing on ballet, contemporary dance and musical theatre.
Readership/Target Audience: Aimed at performers, instructors and enthusiasts of all ages.

ADVERTISING RATES:
Full Page Mono £612.00
Full Page Colour £855.00
Agency Commission: 10%
Mechanical Data: Film: Digital, Bleed Size: 303 x 216mm, Trim Size: 297 x 210mm, Type Area: 267 x 180mm, Col Length: 267mm, Page Width: 180mm
Copy instructions: Copy Date: 1st of the month prior to publication date
CONSUMER: MUSIC & PERFORMING ARTS: Dance

THE DANDY XTREME
30998U91D-865
Formerly: The Dandy
Editorial Address: PO Box 305, LONDON, NW1 1TX
Tel: 01382 223131 **Fax:** 01382 322214
Email: dandy@dcthomson.co.uk
Advertising Address: Orange 20 Limited, 20 Orange Street, LONDON, WC2H 7EF **Tel:** 01372 802800
Fax: 01372 723322
Email: robin@o20.co.uk
Publisher: D.C. Thomson & Co Ltd
Frequency: 26 issues yearly
Cover Price: £1.99
Circulation: 20,403 (ABC 01/01/2009 to 30/06/2009)
Editor: Craig Graham
Summary of Content: Children's comic featuring cartoon stories.
Readership/Target Audience: Aimed at children.
ADVERTISING RATES:
Full Page Colour £3935.00
Agency Commission: 15%
Mechanical Data: Col Length: 276mm, Page Width: 200mm, Type Area: 276 x 200mm, Bleed Size: 300 x 231mm, Trim Size: 295 x 225mm, Film: Digital
Copy instructions: Copy Date: 5 weeks prior to publication date
Average advertising content per issue: 20%
CONSUMER: RECREATION & LEISURE: Children & Youth

DARE
623476U74A-545
Formerly: Spirit
Editorial Address: 1 Neal Street, Covent Garden, LONDON, WC2H 9QL **Tel:** 020 7306 0304 **Fax:** 020 7306 0303
Email: ngibbins@riverltd.co.uk
Advertising Address: As above. **Fax:** 020 7534 3310
Email: vreis@riverltd.co.uk
Web site: http://www.dare-magazine.co.uk
Publisher: River Publishing Ltd
Date Established: 2000
Frequency: 7 issues yearly
Cover Price: Free
Circulation: 750,000 (Publisher's Statement)
Usual Pagination: 52
Editor: Nathalie Gibbins; **Advertising Manager:** Victor Reis;
Publisher: Joanna Crawley
Summary of Content: Magazine covering beauty, fashion, celebrity, health, travel, entertainment and advice.
Readership/Target Audience: Aimed at women between 25 and 34 years old.
ADVERTISING RATES:
Full Page Colour £15000.00
Agency Commission: 10%
Mechanical Data: Film: Digital, Type Area: 260 x 190mm, Bleed Size: 286 x 216mm, Trim Size: 280 x 210mm, Col Length: 260mm, Page Width: 190mm
Copy instructions: Copy Date: 6 weeks prior to publication date
Average advertising content per issue: 40%
CONSUMER: WOMEN'S INTEREST CONSUMER MAGAZINES: Women's Interest

THE DARK SIDE
46760U79L-70
Editorial Address: PO Box 36, LISKEARD, PL14 4YT
Tel: 01579 340400 **Fax:** 01579 340400
Email: darkside@darksidemagazine.com
Advertising Address: As above.
Email: paul@darksidemagazine.com
Web site: http://www.darksidemagazine.com
ISSN: 0960-6653
Publisher: Darkside Publishing Ltd
Date Established: 1990
Frequency: 6 issues yearly
Cover Price: £3.95
Annual Sub.: £38.40
Circulation: 35,000 (Publisher's Statement)
Usual Pagination: 64
Editor: Allan Bryce; **Managing Director:** Michelle Mills;
Advertising Manager: Paul Elkin
Summary of Content: Magazine focusing on horror and fantasy. Covers books, videos, memorabilia, computer games and comics.
Readership/Target Audience: Aimed at people between 15 and 45 who are interested in horror and fantasy.
ADVERTISING RATES:
Full Page Mono £550.00
Full Page Colour £830.00

SCC £5.00
Agency Commission: 10%
Mechanical Data: Film: Digital, Type Area: 276 x 182mm, Bleed Size: 303 x 216mm, Trim Size: 297 x 210mm, Col Length: 276mm, Page Width: 182mm
Copy instructions: Copy Date: 6 weeks prior to publication date
CONSUMER: HOBBIES & DIY: Fantasy Games & Science Fiction

DARK SUMMER
1687720U75G-657
Editorial Address: 143 Walkley Crescent Road, SHEFFIELD, S6 5BA **Tel:** 07815 888157 **Fax:** 0870 705 2143
Email: zack@darksummer.co.uk
Advertising Address: As above. **Tel:** 07968 479503
Email: andrea@darksummer.co.uk
Web site: http://www.darksummer.co.uk
Publisher: Dark Summer Ltd
Date Established: 2003
Frequency: Half-yearly - Published in October and December
Cover Price: Free
Circulation: 22,000 (Publisher's Statement)
Usual Pagination: 132
Editor: Zack Wragg; **Advertising Manager:** Andrea Conneely
Summary of Content: Magazine covering free skiing including articles, product reviews, book reviews, interviews, resort reviews and events.
Readership/Target Audience: Aimed at skiers in the freesports market, primarily freeskiers.
ADVERTISING RATES:
Full Page Colour £1700.00
Agency Commission: 10%
Mechanical Data: Film: Digital, Trim Size: 297 x 210mm, Bleed Size: 303 x 216mm
Average advertising content per issue: 25%
CONSUMER: SPORT: Winter Sports

DARLINGTON TODAY
1693924U80C-5335
Editorial Address: 45 Atkinson Gardens, Aycliffe, NEWTON AYCLIFFE, DL5 6LH **Tel:** 01325 304360 **Fax:** 01325 314283
Email: sue@cherrington.onyxnet.co.uk
Advertising Address: As above.
Email: sue@cherrington.onyxnet.co.uk
ISSN: 1745-4654
Publisher: Cherrington Advertising Ltd
Date Established: 2005
Frequency: Quarterly
Cover Price: Free
Circulation: 45,000 (Publisher's Statement)
Usual Pagination: 36
Editor: Sue Riney-Smith; **Advertising Manager:** Sue Riney-Smith
Summary of Content: Lifestyle magazine covering fashion, health, food, eating out and celebrity profiles as well as local news and events.
Readership/Target Audience: Aimed at affluent households in Darlington and the surrounding area.
ADVERTISING RATES:
Full Page Colour £850.00
Agency Commission: 10%
Mechanical Data: Bleed Size: 276 x 216mm, Trim Size: 270 x 210mm, Film: Digital
Copy instructions: Copy Date: 3 weeks prior to publication date
Average advertising content per issue: 50%
CONSUMER: RURAL & REGIONAL INTEREST: Regional Interest English Counties

DARTMOOR MAGAZINE
46808U80A-98
Editorial Address: 2 Steward Cottages, Moretonhampstead, NEWTON ABBOT, TQ13 8SD
Tel: 01647 441174
Email: enquiries@dartmoormagazine.co.uk
Advertising Address: Zara Media & Design, 14 Kingfisher Court, Vennybridge, EXETER, EX4 8JN **Tel:** 01392 201227
Fax: 01392 201228
Email: grant@zaramedia.co.uk
Web site: http://www.dartmoormagazine.co.uk
ISSN: 0268-5027
Publisher: Edgemoor Publishing Ltd
Date Established: 1985
Frequency: Quarterly
Cover Price: £2.50
Annual Sub.: £12.00
Circulation: 4,000 (Publisher's Statement)
Usual Pagination: 68
Editor: Sue Viccars; **Advertising Manager:** Grant Harrison;
Publisher: Simon Lloyd
Summary of Content: Magazine containing local information, national park news, towns and villages, walks, personalities, local history, outdoor equipment, book reviews, events, wine and dine.
Readership/Target Audience: Aimed at residents throughout Devon and the UK.

Consumer Magazines

ADVERTISING RATES:
Full Page Mono £375.00
Full Page Colour £425.00
SCC £10.00
Agency Commission: 10%
Mechanical Data: Type Area: 265 x 180mm, Col Length: 265mm, Page Width: 180mm, Film: Digital, Trim Size: 297 x 210mm
Copy instructions: Copy Date: 1st day of the month prior to publication date
Average advertising content per issue: 35%
CONSUMER: RURAL & REGIONAL INTEREST: Rural Interest

DARTS PLAYER
46003U75X-360
Editorial Address: 81 Selwood Road, CROYDON, CR0 7JW **Tel:** 020 8650 6580 **Fax:** 020 8654 4343
Email: dartsworld@blueyonder.co.uk
Advertising Address: 28 Arrol Road, BECKENHAM, BR3 4PA **Tel:** 020 8650 6580 **Fax:** 020 8654 4343
Email: dartsworld@blueyonder.co.uk
Web site: http://www.dartsworld.com
Publisher: World Magazines Ltd
Date Established: 1987
Frequency: Annual - Published at the beginning of December
Cover Price: £2.95
Circulation: 8,000 (Publisher's Statement)
Usual Pagination: 68
Editor: Tony Wood; **Advertising Manager:** Maureen Vansittart
Summary of Content: Magazine with features on all aspects of darts.
Readership/Target Audience: Read by darts enthusiasts.
ADVERTISING: Rates on application
Agency Commission: 10%
Copy instructions: Copy Date: 3 weeks prior to publication date
Average advertising content per issue: 25%
CONSUMER: SPORT: Other Sport

DARTS WORLD
46004U75X-370
Editorial Address: 81 Selwood Road, CROYDON, CR0 7JW **Tel:** 020 8650 6580 **Fax:** 020 8654 4343
Email: dartsworld@blueyonder.co.uk
Advertising Address: 28 Arrol Road, BECKENHAM, BR3 4PA **Tel:** 020 8650 6580 **Fax:** 020 8654 4343
Email: dartsworld@blueyonder.co.uk
Web site: http://www.dartsworld.com
ISSN: 0140-6000
Publisher: World Magazines Ltd
Date Established: 1972
Frequency: Monthly - Published on the 1st of the cover month
Annual Sub.: £35.75
Circulation: 10,320 (Publisher's Statement)
Usual Pagination: 68
Editor: Tony Wood; **Advertising Manager:** Maureen Vansittart
Summary of Content: Magazine covering all aspects of marketing at all levels within the darts world.
Readership/Target Audience: Read by darts enthusiasts and sport officials.
ADVERTISING RATES:
Full Page Mono £538.00
Full Page Colour £735.00
SCC £16.00
Agency Commission: 10%
Mechanical Data: Col Length: 270mm, Col Widths (Display): 31mm, No. of Columns (Display): 5, Print Process: Litho, Type Area: 270 x 180mm, Page Width: 180mm, Film: Digital
Copy instructions: Copy Date: 3 weeks prior to publication date
Average advertising content per issue: 30%
CONSUMER: SPORT: Other Sport

DAYS OUT
1639116U89C-957
Editorial Address: 41 Parkland Avenue, UPMINSTER, RM14 2EX **Tel:** 01708 222394 **Fax:** 01708 228339
Email: david@daysout.co.uk
Advertising Address: Days Out Publishing Ltd, 6 Greatford Gardens, Greatford, STAMFORD, PE9 4PX
Tel: 01778 560801
Email: elisabeth@daysout.co.uk
Web site: http://www.daysout.co.uk
ISSN: 1476-153X
Publisher: Days Out Publishing Ltd
Date Established: 1991
Frequency: Annual - Published in February
Cover Price: £3.95
Circulation: 60,000 (Publisher's Statement)
Usual Pagination: 84
Editor: David Darkins; **Advertising Director:** Elisabeth Beckett; **Publisher:** David Darkins
Summary of Content: Magazine covering a whole range of family attractions throughout Great Britain.

Readership/Target Audience: Aimed at families planning days out.
ADVERTISING RATES:
Full Page Colour £3850.00
Agency Commission: 10%
Mechanical Data: Bleed Size: 303 x 216mm, Type Area: 260 x 180mm, Trim Size: 297 x 210mm, Col Length: 260mm, Page Width: 180mm, Film: Digital
Copy instructions: Copy Date: November 30th
Average advertising content per issue: 95%
CONSUMER: HOLIDAYS & TRAVEL: Entertainment Guides

DAZED & CONFUSED
46223U76E-70
Editorial Address: 112-116 Old Street, LONDON, EC1V 9BG **Tel:** 020 7336 0766 **Fax:** 020 7336 0966
Email: dazed@dazedgroup.com
Advertising Address: As above. **Tel:** 020 7549 6833
Fax: 020 7549 6860
Email: sam@dazedgroup.com
Web site: http://www.dazeddigital.com
ISSN: 1355-5901
Publisher: Waddell Ltd
Frequency: Monthly
Cover Price: £3.95
Circulation: 84,437 (Publisher's Statement)
Editor: Rod Stanley; **Advertising Manager:** Sam O'Shaughnessy
Summary of Content: Magazine covering lifestyle and music.
Language(s): English; Japanese
Readership/Target Audience: Aimed at club going, fashion conscious young people.
ADVERTISING RATES:
Full Page Mono £5251.00
Full Page Colour £5251.00
Agency Commission: 10%
Mechanical Data: Type Area: 280 x 210mm, Bleed Size: 310 x 240mm, Trim Size: 300 x 230mm, Film: Digital, Col Length: 280mm, Page Width: 210mm
Copy instructions: Copy Date: 2 weeks prior to publication date
Average advertising content per issue: 40%
CONSUMER: MUSIC & PERFORMING ARTS: Pop Music

Y DDRAENEN
47472U83-250
Editorial Address: University of Wales, Deiniol Road, BANGOR, LL57 2TH **Tel:** 01248 388006 **Fax:** 01248 388020
Advertising Address: As above.
Email: golygydd@undeb.bangor.ac.uk
Publisher: Students Union Bangor
Frequency: Quarterly - Published twice during each term
Cover Price: Free
Circulation: 1,000 (Publisher's Statement)
Summary of Content: Magazine of the University of Wales, Bangor Students' Union.
Language(s): Welsh
Readership/Target Audience: Read by Welsh speaking students and lecturers.
ADVERTISING: Rates on application
CONSUMER: STUDENT PUBLICATIONS

DEATH RAY
1804615U79L-388
Editorial Address: 20 Monmouth Place, BATH, BA1 2AY **Tel:** 01225 338828 **Fax:** 01225 338890
Email: mail@blackfishpublishing.com
Advertising Address: As above.
Email: allie@allulla.co.uk
Web site: http://www.blackfishpublishing.com
Publisher: Blackfish Publishing Ltd
Date Established: 2007
Frequency: 6 issues yearly
Cover Price: £4.99
Circulation: 40,000 (Print Run)
Usual Pagination: 132
Editor: Guy Haley; **Editor-in-Chief:** Matt Bielby; **Advertising Manager:** Allie Gill
Summary of Content: Magazine covering science fiction and fantasy in films, TV, books and all other mediums.
Readership/Target Audience: Aimed at fans of the genre predominantly men between 16 and 30 years of age.
ADVERTISING RATES:
Full Page Colour £1300.00
Mechanical Data: Type Area: 287 x 200mm, Bleed Size: 303 x 216mm, Trim Size: 297 x 210mm, Col Length: 287mm, Page Width: 200mm
CONSUMER: HOBBIES & DIY: Fantasy Games & Science Fiction

DEBENHAM'S DESIRE
1647477U74Q-1189
Advertising Address: Debenhams, 6th Floor, 33 Wigmore Street, LONDON, W1U 1QX **Tel:** 020 7408 3477
Email: toby.elford@debenhams.com
Publisher: Velo Agency
Date Established: 2004
Frequency: Quarterly

Cover Price: £1.00
Free to qualifying individuals
Circulation: 747,251 (Publisher's Statement)
Usual Pagination: 116
Summary of Content: Magazine covering the 'Designers at Debenhams' ranges, fashion, beauty and homes.
Readership/Target Audience: Aimed at customers of Debenhams stores, particularly women who have a high disposable income between 25 to 54 years old.
ADVERTISING RATES:
Full Page Mono £12500.00
Full Page Colour £12500.00
Agency Commission: 10%
Mechanical Data: Trim Size: 254 x 210mm, Film: Digital
Average advertising content per issue: 30%
CONSUMER: WOMEN'S INTEREST CONSUMER MAGAZINES: Lifestyle

DEKHO!
48586U94A-30
Editorial Address: 4 Lower Belgrave Street, LONDON, SW1W 0LA **Tel:** 020 7823 4273 **Fax:** 020 7730 7882
Email: pecbsa@btconnect.com
Advertising Address: As above.
Email: pecbsa@btconnect.com
Publisher: Burma Star Association
Date Established: 1951
Frequency: 3 issues yearly - Published in May, August and December
Free to qualifying individuals
Annual Sub.: £20.00
Circulation: 7,200 (Publisher's Statement)
Usual Pagination: 32
Editor: Phil Crawley; **Advertising Manager:** Phil Crawley
Summary of Content: Journal focusing on military history, mainly the Burma campaign 1942-45 and contains information concerning members and branch and association activities.
Readership/Target Audience: Aimed at members of the Burma Star Association.
ADVERTISING: Rates on application
Average advertising content per issue: 1%
CONSUMER: OTHER CLASSIFICATIONS: War Veterans

DELICIOUS
1637491U74P-911
Editorial Address: Sea Containers House, 20 Upper Ground, LONDON, SE1 9PD **Tel:** 020 7775 7775
Email: info@deliciousmagazine.co.uk
Advertising Address: As above.
Web site: http://www.deliciousmagazine.co.uk
Publisher: Seven Publishing
Date Established: 2003
Frequency: Monthly
Cover Price: £3.20
Circulation: 101,039 (ABC 01/01/2009 to 30/06/2009)
Editor: Tanya Grossman; **Advertising Manager:** Ruth White
Summary of Content: Magazine with features on the food industry, the people behind food business and chefs as well as topical food issues.
Readership/Target Audience: Aimed at all food lovers but predominantly those aged between 25 and 45 years old.
ADVERTISING RATES:
Full Page Colour £5500.00
Agency Commission: 15%
Mechanical Data: Type Area: 260 x 204mm, Col Length: 260mm, Page Width: 204mm, Film: Digital
CONSUMER: WOMEN'S INTEREST CONSUMER MAGAZINES: Food & Cookery

---

THE DEMOCRAT
47316U82-13_50
Editorial Address: PO Box 46295, LONDON, W5 2UG
Tel: 0845 345 8902
Email: caef@caef.org.uk
Web site: http://www.caef.org.uk
ISSN: 0967-3806
Publisher: Campaign Against Euro-Federalism
Date Established: 1991
Frequency: Monthly
Cover Price: £0.40
Free to qualifying individuals
Annual Sub.: £6.00
Circulation: 3,000 (Publisher's Statement)
Usual Pagination: 12
Editor: John Boyd
Summary of Content: Publication containing comment on the politics of the European Community and Britain's membership. Includes discussion, features, reviews, local, national and international campaign news and letters.
Readership/Target Audience: Aimed at general readers and in particular trades councils, trade unions and their members, socialists, students, pensioners and the unemployed.
ADVERTISING: No advertising taken
CONSUMER: CURRENT AFFAIRS & POLITICS

DERBYSHIRE LIFE & COUNTRYSIDE

46882U80C-1000

Editorial Address: 61 Friar Gate, DERBY, DE1 1DJ
Tel: 01332 227850 **Fax:** 01332 227860
Email: joy.hales@derbyshirelife.co.uk
Advertising Address: As above.
Email: rachael.morley@archant.co.uk
Web site: http://www.derbyshirelife.co.uk
ISSN: 0011-8990
Publisher: Archant Life (North) PLC
Date Established: 1931
Frequency: Monthly
Cover Price: £2.50
Circulation: 16,106 (ABC 01/01/2008 to 31/12/2008)
Usual Pagination: 166
Editor: Joy Hales; **Advertising Manager:** Rachael Morley
Summary of Content: Publication containing pictorial articles on Derbyshire people, places, natural history, antiques and collecting, wining and dining, theatre and coming events.
Readership/Target Audience: Aimed at the more affluent and influential members of the community living within the county or in bordering areas.
ADVERTISING RATES:
Full Page Mono £674.00
Full Page Colour £787.00
Agency Commission: 10%
Mechanical Data: Type Area: 271 x 199mm, Bleed Size: 306 x 226mm, Trim Size: 300 x 220mm, Film: Digital, Col Length: 271mm, Page Width: 199mm
Copy instructions: Copy Date: 26th of the month prior to publication date
Average advertising content per issue: 45%
CONSUMER: RURAL & REGIONAL INTEREST: Regional Interest English Counties

THE DERBYSHIRE MAGAZINE

46883U80C-1010

Formerly: Derbyshire Today
Editorial Address: Northcliffe House, Meadow Road, DERBY, DE1 2BH **Tel:** 01332 291111 **Fax:** 01332 253027
Email: jgallone@derbytelegraph.co.uk
Advertising Address: As above. **Fax:** 01332 253011
Email: mgutteridge@derbytelegraph.co.uk
Web site: http://www.thisisderbyshire.co.uk/index.jsp
Publisher: Derby Daily Telegraph Ltd
Date Established: 2000
Frequency: Monthly
Cover Price: £1.75
Circulation: 10,000 (Publisher's Statement)
Usual Pagination: 108
Editor: Jill Gallone; **Advertising Manager:** Mandy Gutteridge
Summary of Content: Magazine covering interiors, fashion, beauty, travel, property, motoring, eating out and entertainment.
Readership/Target Audience: Aimed at those between 25 to 45 years old within Derby and the surrounding areas.
ADVERTISING RATES:
Full Page Colour £1000.00
Mechanical Data: Type Area: 270 x 190mm, Col Length: 270mm, Col Length: 190mm
CONSUMER: RURAL & REGIONAL INTEREST: Regional Interest English Counties

DESCENT - THE MAGAZINE OF UNDERGROUND EXPLORATION

45923U75L-200

Editorial Address: PO Box 100, ABERGAVENNY, NP7 9WY
Tel: 070 0428 5888
Email: descent@wildplaces.co.uk
Advertising Address: 40 Colchester Avenue, Penylan, CARDIFF, CF23 9BP **Tel:** 029 2021 8091
Email: jonesaj@ntlworld.com
Web site: http://www.caving.uk.com
ISSN: 0046-0036
Publisher: Wild Places Publishing
Date Established: 1969
Frequency: 6 issues yearly
Cover Price: £4.00
Annual Sub.: £24.00
Usual Pagination: 40
Editor: Chris Howes; **Advertising Manager:** Alan Jones
Summary of Content: Magazine covering the sport of cave and mine exploration. Includes equipment and book reviews, news, competitions and articles on underground structures.
Readership/Target Audience: Read by cavers and mine enthusiasts plus academics and institutions.
ADVERTISING RATES:
Full Page Mono £695.00
Full Page Colour £1045.00
Mechanical Data: Trim Size: 297 x 210mm, Film: Digital, Bleed Size: 303 x 216mm
Copy instructions: Copy Date: 4 weeks prior to publication date
CONSUMER: SPORT: Outdoor

DESIGN ET AL

1789528U74C-861

Editorial Address: Watergate House, Watergate Street, CHESTER, CH1 2LF **Tel:** 01244 346347 **Fax:** 01244 344833
Email: kate.greenhalgh@design-et-al.co.uk
Advertising Address: As above.
Email: advertising@design-et-al.co.uk
Web site: http://www.design-et-al.co.uk
Publisher: The Event Partnership
Frequency: Monthly
Cover Price: £3.80
Circulation: 20,000 (Publisher's Statement)
Editor: Kate Greenhalgh; **Advertising Manager:** Richard Stockton; **Publisher:** William Beedles
Summary of Content: Magazine covering all aspects of interior design including the latest looks, trends and forecasts from around the world.
Readership/Target Audience: Aimed at interior designers, architects and high end, discerning consumers who want to gain real inspiration and direction.
ADVERTISING RATES:
Full Page Colour £2300.00
Agency Commission: 10%
Mechanical Data: Type Area: 277 x 210mm, Bleed Size: 303 x 236mm, Trim Size: 297 x 230mm, Col Length: 277mm, Page Width: 210mm, Film: Digital
Copy instructions: Copy Date: 2 weeks prior to publication date
CONSUMER: WOMEN'S INTEREST CONSUMER MAGAZINES: Home & Family

DESIRE

634547U86A-55

Editorial Address: Ground Floor, 211 Old Street, LONDON, EC1V 9NR **Tel:** 020 7608 6383 **Fax:** 020 7608 6320
Email: editorial@desire.co.uk
Advertising Address: As above. **Tel:** 020 7608 6300
Fax: 020 7608 6382
Email: sara.alexander@trojanpublishing.co.uk
Web site: http://www.desire.co.uk
ISSN: 1366-9311
Publisher: Trojan Publishing
Date Established: 1996
Frequency: 6 issues yearly
Cover Price: £4.99
Annual Sub.: £15.00
Circulation: 60,000 (Publisher's Statement)
Usual Pagination: 148
Editor: Ian Jackson
Summary of Content: Adult magazine covering all aspects of erotica and sexual relationships.
Readership/Target Audience: Read by men and women with an interest in erotica.
ADVERTISING RATES:
Full Page Colour £900.00
Mechanical Data: Type Area: 185 x 123mm, Col Length: 185mm, Page Width: 123mm, Bleed Size: 260 x 154mm, Film: Digital
Copy instructions: Copy Date: 3 weeks prior to publication date
CONSUMER: ADULT & GAY MAGAZINES: Adult Magazines

DESTINATION FRANCE

1660450U91B-305

Formerly: Camping in France
Editorial Address: 151 Station Street, BURTON-ON-TRENT, DE14 1BG **Tel:** 01283 742950 **Fax:** 01283 742957
Email: carmen.konopka@wwonline.co.uk
Advertising Address: Cabbell Ltd, Woodman Works, 204 Durnsford Road, LONDON, SW19 8DR **Tel:** 020 8971 8450
Fax: 020 8971 8480
Email: george.miller@cabbell.co.uk
Web site: http://www.destinationfrancemagazine.co.uk
ISSN: 1744-3423
Publisher: WW Magazines
Date Established: 2004
Frequency: Quarterly
Cover Price: £3.95
Annual Sub.: £14.20
Circulation: 15,000 (Publisher's Statement)
Usual Pagination: 148
Editor: Carmen Konopka; **Advertising Manager:** George Miller
Summary of Content: Magazine covering outdoor France and French culture. As well as travel features, coverage includes food and wine, art and architecture, personalities, books, history and lifestyle.
Readership/Target Audience: Aimed at UK families and individuals predominantly those with school aged children and the retired.
ADVERTISING RATES:
Full Page Colour £2000.00
Agency Commission: 10%
Mechanical Data: Type Area: 272 x 186mm, Bleed Size: 305 x 218mm, Trim Size: 297 x 210mm, Col Length: 272mm, Page Width: 186mm, Film: Digital, Print Process: Web-fed offset litho
Copy instructions: Copy Date: 2 weeks prior to publication date

Average advertising content per issue: 25%
CONSUMER: RECREATION & LEISURE: Camping & Caravanning

DEVELOPMENTS

47220U82-15

Editorial Address: 1 Palace Street, LONDON, SW1E 5HE
Tel: 020 7023 0504 **Fax:** 020 7023 0223
Email: malcomdoney@blueyonder.co.uk
Advertising Address: Landmark Publishing Services, 2 Windmill Street, LONDON, W1T 2HX **Tel:** 020 7692 9292
Fax: 020 7692 9393
Email: landmark@lps.co.uk
Web site: http://www.developments.org.uk
ISSN: 1461-474X
Publisher: Department for International Development
Date Established: 1998
Frequency: Quarterly
Cover Price: Free
Circulation: 70,000 (Publisher's Statement)
Usual Pagination: 40
Editor: Matthew Bell
Summary of Content: Magazine providing an overview of international development and the latest news on how British aid works in partnership with developing countries to get rid of poverty.
Readership/Target Audience: Read by those interested in international development.
ADVERTISING RATES:
Full Page Colour £2000.00
Agency Commission: 10%
Mechanical Data: Type Area: 290 x 220mm, Col Length: 290mm, Trim Size: 300 x 230mm, Bleed Size: 303 x 233mm, Film: Digital, Page Width: 220mm
CONSUMER: CURRENT AFFAIRS & POLITICS

DEVON DIARY

1706706U80C-5336

Editorial Address: Old Manor House, 63 Wolborough Street, NEWTON ABBOT, TQ12 1NE **Tel:** 01626 353555
Fax: 01626 333589
Email: devon.diary@tindlenews.co.uk
Advertising Address: As above. **Tel:** 01626 204766
Email: mda.sales@internet-today.co.uk
Publisher: Devon & Cornwall Newspapers Ltd
Frequency: Monthly
Cover Price: Free
Circulation: 5,000 (Print Run)
Usual Pagination: 56
Editor: Ruth Davey
Summary of Content: Magazine covering interesting facts about the area, listings and events as well as lifestyle features including fashion and beauty, interiors, cars, travel and property.
Readership/Target Audience: Aimed at affluent households in South Devon.
ADVERTISING RATES:
Full Page Colour £230.00
Agency Commission: 10%
Mechanical Data: Type Area: 194 x 132mm, Bleed Size: 214 x 152mm, Trim Size: 210 x 148mm, Col Length: 194mm, Page Width: 132mm, Film: Digital
Copy instructions: Copy Date: 2 weeks prior to publication date
Average advertising content per issue: 50%
CONSUMER: RURAL & REGIONAL INTEREST: Regional Interest English Counties

DEVON LIFE

46885U80C-1100

Editorial Address: Archant House, Babbage Road, TOTNES, TQ9 5JA **Tel:** 01803 860910 **Fax:** 01803 860922
Email: devonlife@archant.co.uk
Advertising Address: As above.
Email: devonlifesales@archant.co.uk
Web site: http://www.devonlife.co.uk
ISSN: 1362-8682
Publisher: Archant Life
Date Established: 1996
Frequency: Monthly
Cover Price: £3.25
Annual Sub.: £39.50
Circulation: 15,625 (ABC 01/01/2008 to 31/12/2008)
Usual Pagination: 340
Editor: Jane Fitzgerald; **Publisher:** Tim Randell
Summary of Content: Magazine containing features on the Devon area.
Readership/Target Audience: Aimed at those living in and visiting Devon.
ADVERTISING RATES:
Full Page Colour £1368.00
Agency Commission: 10%
Mechanical Data: Type Area: 271 x 199mm, Col Length: 271mm, Trim Size: 300 x 220mm, Bleed Size: 306 x 226mm, Page Width: 199mm, Film: Digital
Copy instructions: Copy Date: 2nd week of the month prior to publication date
Average advertising content per issue: 45%
Editions:
Cornwall Life

Dorset Magazine
Somerset Life
Supplement(s): Devon Life Bridal - 2xY
CONSUMER: RURAL & REGIONAL INTEREST: Regional
Interest English Counties

DEVON LINK
48624U94F-220

Editorial Address: Adult & Community Services Directorate,
County Hall, Topsham Road, EXETER, EX2 4QR
Tel: 01392 382332 **Fax:** 01392 382363
Email: devonlink@devon.gov.uk
Advertising Address: Zara Media and Design, 14 Kingfisher
Court, Vennybridge, EXETER, EX4 8JN **Tel:** 01392 201227
Fax: 01392 201228
Email: info@zaramedia.co.uk
Web site: http://www.devon.gov.uk/devonlink
ISSN: 0266-5964
Publisher: Devon County Council and Torbay Council
Date Established: 1984
Frequency: 3 issues yearly - Published in April, July and
November
Cover Price: Free
Circulation: 7,500 (Publisher's Statement)
Usual Pagination: 32
Editor: Sarah Avery; **Advertising Manager:** Grant Harrison
Summary of Content: Magazine covering physical sensory
and disability issues, transportation, advice and healthcare
articles.
Readership/Target Audience: Aimed at those with physical
and sensory disabilities and their carers.
ADVERTISING RATES:
Full Page Mono £500.00
Full Page Colour £595.00
Mechanical Data: Film: Digital
CONSUMER: OTHER CLASSIFICATIONS: Disability

DEVON WEDDINGS
45529U74L-85

Editorial Address: 17 Brest Road, Derriford, PLYMOUTH,
PL6 5AA **Tel:** 01392 207122 **Fax:** 01392 442473
Email: kmanning@expressandecho.com
Advertising Address: As above. **Tel:** 01752 765500
Fax: 01752 765666
Email: sslater@swmg.co.uk
Web site: http://www.devonweddings.co.uk
Publisher: South West Media Group Ltd
Date Established: 1999
Frequency: Quarterly
Cover Price: £2.50
Circulation: 10,000 (Publisher's Statement)
Usual Pagination: 100
Editor: Katy Manning; **Advertising Manager:** Sarah Slater
Summary of Content: Magazine covering all aspects of
weddings in Devon including photographers, videos,
dresses, rings, cars and honeymoons.
Readership/Target Audience: Aimed at everybody involved
in organising a wedding.
ADVERTISING RATES:
Full Page Colour £590.00
Agency Commission: 10%
Mechanical Data: Bleed Size: 305 x 220mm, Trim Size: 296
x 209mm, Screen: 60 lpc, Film: Digital, Type Area: 272 x
187mm, Col Length: 272mm, Page Width: 187mm
Copy instructions: Copy Date: 1st of the month prior to
publication date
Average advertising content per issue: 30%
CONSUMER: WOMEN'S INTEREST CONSUMER
MAGAZINES: Brides

DIDSBURY MAGAZINE
1799195U80C-5393

Editorial Address: St. James House, 676 Wilmslow Road,
MANCHESTER, M20 2DM **Tel:** 0161 445 2883
Fax: 0161 445 2281
Email: beverley@didsburymagazine.com
Advertising Address: As above. **Fax:** 0161 445 2881
Email: claire@didsburymagazine.com
Web site: http://www.didsburymagazine.com
Publisher: Salutions Ltd
Date Established: 2002
Frequency: 10 issues yearly
Cover Price: Free
Circulation: 12,500 (Publisher's Statement)
Usual Pagination: 68
Editor: Beverley Uddin-Khandakar
Summary of Content: Magazine covering local news and
events as well as lifestyle, fashion, motors, health, property,
gardening, food and drink, travel, family and education.
Readership/Target Audience: Aimed at residents and
businesses in Didsbury.
ADVERTISING RATES:
Full Page Colour £995.00
Agency Commission: 10%
Mechanical Data: Bleed Size: 281 x 216mm, Trim Size: 275
x 210mm, Film: Digital
Copy instructions: Copy Date: 2 weeks prior to publication
date

Average advertising content per issue: 45%
CONSUMER: RURAL & REGIONAL INTEREST: Regional
Interest English Counties

THE DIECAST COLLECTOR
46740U79K-464

Editorial Address: The Maltings, West Street, BOURNE,
PE10 9PH **Tel:** 01778 391175 **Fax:** 01778 423063
Email: mikef@warnersgroup.co.uk
Advertising Address: As above. **Tel:** 01778 391000
Email: matthewt@warnersgroup.co.uk
Web site: http://www.diecast-collector.com
Publisher: Warners Group Publications plc
Frequency: Monthly
Cover Price: £3.30
Circulation: 19,500 (Publisher's Statement)
Usual Pagination: 96
Editor: Mike Forbes; **Advertising Manager:** Matthew
Tipton; **Publisher:** Simon Epton
Summary of Content: Magazine featuring collectors and
their diecast models and vehicle collections.
Readership/Target Audience: Aimed at diecast collectors.
ADVERTISING RATES:
Full Page Mono £380.00
Full Page Colour £580.00
Agency Commission: 10%
Mechanical Data: Trim Size: 297 x 210mm, Bleed Size: 306
x 216mm, Film: Digital, Type Area: 275 x 190mm, Col
Length: 275mm, Page Width: 190mm
Copy instructions: Copy Date: 4 weeks prior to publication
date
Average advertising content per issue: 36%
CONSUMER: HOBBIES & DIY: Collectors Magazines

DIG BMX MAGAZINE
31260U77C-735

Editorial Address: Studio 153, 355 Byres Road,
GLASGOW, G12 8QZ **Tel:** 0141 945 5019
Email: info@digbmx.com
Advertising Address: 1 West Smithfield, LONDON, EC1A
9JU **Tel:** 020 7332 9700 **Fax:** 020 7332 9799
Email: ian.gunner@factorymedia.com
Web site: http://www.digbmx.com
Publisher: Factory Media
Date Established: 1993
Frequency: 6 issues yearly
Cover Price: £3.20
Annual Sub.: £17.25
Circulation: 30,000 (Publisher's Statement)
Usual Pagination: 148
Editor: Will Smyth; **Advertising Manager:** Ian Gunner
Summary of Content: Magazine featuring new products,
interviews with BMX riders, BMX lifestyle and coverage of
events worldwide.
Readership/Target Audience: Aimed at BMX riders
between 14 and 30 years old.
ADVERTISING: Rates on application
Copy instructions: Copy Date: 4 weeks prior to publication
date
Average advertising content per issue: 35%
CONSUMER: MOTORING & CYCLING: Cycling

DIGITAL CAMERA ESSENTIALS
752665U85A-70

Formerly: Digital Camera Buyer
Editorial Address: Richmond House, 33 Richmond Hill,
BOURNEMOUTH, BH2 6EZ **Tel:** 01202 586200
Email: dcb@imagine-publishing.co.uk
Advertising Address: As above. **Fax:** 01202 294032
Email: jennifer.farrell@imagine-publishing.co.uk
Web site: http://www.digicambuyer.co.uk
ISSN: 1475-0538
Publisher: Imagine Publishing
Date Established: 2002
Frequency: 13 issues yearly
Cover Price: £3.99
Circulation: 12,040 (Publisher's Statement)
Usual Pagination: 132
Editor: Matt Tuffin
Summary of Content: Magazine containing information and
advice on buying digital cameras, from entry-level models to
the latest power snappers. Includes guides to the best
software for editing and improving digital photos and regular
round-ups of camera accessories.
Readership/Target Audience: Aimed at potential buyers of
digital cameras and accessories.
ADVERTISING RATES:
Full Page Colour £2094.00
Agency Commission: 10%
Mechanical Data: Type Area: 277 x 210mm, Col Length:
277mm, Page Width: 210mm, Trim Size: 297 x 230mm,
Bleed Size: 307 x 240mm, Film: Digital
CONSUMER: PHOTOGRAPHY & FILM MAKING:
Photography

DIGITAL CAMERA MAGAZINE
1601490U85A-193

Editorial Address: 30 Monmouth Street, BATH, BA1 2BW
Tel: 01225 442244 **Fax:** 01225 446019
Email: editor.dcm@futurenet.com
Advertising Address: As above.
Email: keith.jepson@futurenet.co.uk
Web site: http://www.digitalcameramagazine.co.uk
Publisher: Future Publishing Ltd
Date Established: 2002
Frequency: 13 issues yearly
Cover Price: £3.99
Circulation: 52,039 (ABC 01/07/2008 to 31/12/2008)
Usual Pagination: 156
Editor: Marcus Hawkins
Summary of Content: Magazine covering all aspects of
digital photography, including equipment reviews, buyers'
guide, photography locations, tips and tutorials.
Readership/Target Audience: Aimed at amateur digital
photographers.
ADVERTISING RATES:
Full Page Colour £2250.00
Agency Commission: 10%
Mechanical Data: Film: Digital, Trim Size: 297 x 210mm
Copy instructions: Copy Date: 4 weeks prior to publication
date
CONSUMER: PHOTOGRAPHY & FILM MAKING:
Photography

DIGITAL PHOTO
47591U85A-83_50

Editorial Address: Media House, Lynchwood, Peterborough
Business Park, PETERBOROUGH, PE2 6EA
Tel: 01733 468000 **Fax:** 01733 468397
Email: dp@bauermedia.co.uk
Advertising Address: As above. **Fax:** 01733 465246
Email: iain.grundy@bauerconsumer.co.uk
Web site: http://www.dpmag.co.uk
ISSN: 1460-6801
Publisher: Bauer Consumer Media Ltd (Media House)
Date Established: 1997
Frequency: 13 issues yearly
Cover Price: £4.99
Annual Sub.: £56.00
Circulation: 68,687 (ABC 01/01/2008 to 31/12/2008)
Usual Pagination: 108
Editor: Kingsley Singleton
Summary of Content: Guide to buying and using digital
cameras and equipment and downloading images onto
computer. Features image manipulation software and how to
use them and advice on equipment required and movie
tutorials on CD.
Readership/Target Audience: Aimed at the digital image
maker.
ADVERTISING RATES:
Full Page Colour £2730.00
Agency Commission: 10%
Mechanical Data: Page Width: 181mm, Film: Digital, Type
Area: 268 x 181mm, Col Length: 268mm, Trim Size: 297 x
210mm, Bleed Size: 303 x 216mm
Copy instructions: Copy Date: 4 weeks prior to publication
date
Average advertising content per issue: 40%
CONSUMER: PHOTOGRAPHY & FILM MAKING:
Photography

DIGITAL PHOTOGRAPHER
1616412U85A-198

Editorial Address: Richmond House, 33 Richmond Hill,
BOURNEMOUTH, BH2 6EZ **Tel:** 01202 586200
Email: dphotographer@imagine-publishing.co.uk
Advertising Address: As above. **Fax:** 01202 294032
Email: jennifer.farrell@imagine-publishing.co.uk
Web site: http://www.dphotographer.co.uk
ISSN: 1477-6650
Publisher: Imagine Publishing
Date Established: 2001
Frequency: 13 issues yearly
Cover Price: £5.00
Annual Sub.: £52.00
Circulation: 25,004 (ABC 01/01/2008 to 31/12/2008)
Usual Pagination: 148
Editor: Debbi Allen
Summary of Content: Magazine containing information on
contemporary photography, buyers guide, tips and advice
on digital imaging techniques.
Language(s): English; French; Italian; Spanish; Ukrainian
Readership/Target Audience: Aimed at digital enthusiasts
and professional photographers.
ADVERTISING RATES:
Full Page Colour £2094.00
Agency Commission: 10%
Mechanical Data: Type Area: 277 x 210mm, Col Length:
277mm, Page Width: 210mm, Trim Size: 297 x 230mm,
Bleed Size: 307 x 240mm, Film: Digital
CONSUMER: PHOTOGRAPHY & FILM MAKING:
Photography

DIGITAL SLR PHOTOGRAPHY 1791020U85A-210

Editorial Address: 6 Swan Court, Cygnet Park, Hampton, PETERBOROUGH, PE7 8FD **Tel:** 01733 567401
Fax: 01733 352650
Email: enquiries@digitalslrphoto.com
Advertising Address: As above.
Email: natasha.blatcher@halo-publishing.com
Web site: http://www.digitalslrphoto.com
Publisher: Dennis Publishing Ltd
Date Established: 2006
Frequency: Monthly
Cover Price: £3.80
Circulation: 23,000 (ABC 01/01/2008 to 31/12/2008)
Usual Pagination: 156
Editor: Daniel Lezano; **Advertising Director:** Natasha Blatcher
Summary of Content: Magazine with tests and reviews of digital SLR equipment, technique guides, expert advice and interviews with top-end, professional photographers.
Readership/Target Audience: Aimed at high end enthusiast, semi-pro and professional photographers.
ADVERTISING RATES:
Full Page Mono £2500.00
Full Page Colour £2500.00
Agency Commission: 10%
Mechanical Data: Type Area: 277 x 190mm, Bleed Size: 303 x 216mm, Trim Size: 297 x 210mm, Col Length: 277mm, Page Width: 190mm, Film: Digital
Copy instructions: Copy Date: 2 weeks prior to publication date
Average advertising content per issue: 25%
CONSUMER: PHOTOGRAPHY & FILM MAKING: Photography

DIGITAL SLR USER 1789975U85A-209

Editorial Address: Bright house, 82 High Street, Sawston, CAMBRIDGE, CB22 3HJ **Tel:** 01223 499450
Email: terryhope@bright-publishing.com
Advertising Address: Bright House, 82 High Street, Sawston, CAMBRIDGE, CB22 3HJ **Tel:** 01223 499450
Fax: 01223 839953
Email: mattsnow@bright-publishing.com
Web site: http://www.dslruser.co.uk
Publisher: Bright Publishing Ltd
Date Established: 2006
Frequency: Monthly
Cover Price: £3.60
Circulation: 30,000 (Publisher's Statement)
Usual Pagination: 162
Editor: Terry Hope; **News Editor:** Charlotte Griffiths; **Features Editor:** Charlotte Griffiths; **Advertising Manager:** Matt Snow
Summary of Content: Magazine containing straightforward advice and step-by-step techniques on how to get the most from SLR photography.
Readership/Target Audience: Aimed at existing users of DSLRs and those buying into the marker for the first time.
ADVERTISING RATES:
Full Page Colour £2200.00
Mechanical Data: Bleed Size: 303 x 216mm, Trim Size: 297 x 210mm, Film: Digital
CONSUMER: PHOTOGRAPHY & FILM MAKING: Photography

DINGHY SAILING MAGAZINE 1685365U91A-312

Editorial Address: 28 Ballmoor, Celtic Court, BUCKINGHAM, MK18 1RQ **Tel:** 01280 829300
Fax: 01280 829350
Email: georgie@seascapemedia.co.uk
Advertising Address: As above. **Tel:** 01329 834545
Fax: 023 9238 8010
Email: dale@seascapemedia.co.uk
Web site: http://www.dinghysailingmagazine.co.uk
Publisher: Seascape Media Ltd
Frequency: Monthly
Cover Price: £3.50
Circulation: 33,000 (Publisher's Statement)
Usual Pagination: 96
Editor: Georgie Corlett
Summary of Content: Magazine covering all aspects of the dinghy sailor's world including boat reviews, gear tests and practical projects.
Readership/Target Audience: Aimed at active sailors and their families.
ADVERTISING: Rates on application
Agency Commission: 10%
Copy instructions: Copy Date: 2nd Friday of the month prior to publication date
Average advertising content per issue: 40%
Supplement(s): Holiday - 12xY, Practical - 12xY
CONSUMER: RECREATION & LEISURE: Boating & Yachting

DINOMITE 1824269U91D-969

Editorial Address: Headley House, Headley Road, Grayshott, HINDHEAD, GU26 6TU **Tel:** 01428 601020
Fax: 01428 601030

Email: dinomite@signaturepl.co.uk
Advertising Address: As above.
Email: abi.cannon@signaturepl.co.uk
Web site: http://www.dinomitemag.com
Publisher: Signature Publishing Ltd
Date Established: 2007
Frequency: Monthly
Cover Price: £2.99
Circulation: 40,500 (Print Run)
Usual Pagination: 32
Editor: Amanda Clifford; **Advertising Manager:** Abigail Cannon
Summary of Content: Children's magazine about dinosaurs with puzzles, posters, facts, information and competitions.
Readership/Target Audience: Aimed at children aged 4 to 10 years old.
ADVERTISING: Rates on application
CONSUMER: RECREATION & LEISURE: Children & Youth

DIPLOMAT 47221U82-17

Editorial Address: 11 Grosvenor Crescent, LONDON, SW1X 7EE **Tel:** 020 7245 6794 **Fax:** 020 7823 2679
Email: vvk@diplomatmagazine.com
Advertising Address: As above.
Email: hugo@diplomatmagazine.com
Web site: http://www.diplomatmagazine.com
ISSN: 0951-032X
Publisher: Envoy Media Ltd
Date Established: 1947
Frequency: 10 issues yearly - Published monthly excluding January and August
Cover Price: £10.00
Free to qualifying individuals
Annual Sub.: £100.00
Circulation: 10,000 (Publisher's Statement)
Usual Pagination: 60
Editor: Venetia de Blocq Van Kufferler; **Advertising Manager:** Hugo de Blocq Van Kuffeler
Summary of Content: Magazine covering international current affairs, consumer issues, property, motoring, education, books, eating out, art, retail and other social activities.
Readership/Target Audience: Aimed at the foreign diplomatic community in London including nationals, leading companies and foreign companies.
ADVERTISING RATES:
Full Page Colour £2000.00
Agency Commission: 10%
Copy instructions: Copy Date: 15th of the month prior to publication date
Supplement(s): Diplomat Education Guide - 1xY, Diplomat Hotel and Hospitality Guide - 1xY, Diplomat Yearbook - 1xY
CONSUMER: CURRENT AFFAIRS & POLITICS

DIRECTION 47704U87-88_30

Editorial Address: PO Box 777, NOTTINGHAM, NG11 6ZZ **Tel:** 0115 921 7285 **Fax:** 0115 984 5251
Email: editor@newlife.co.uk
Advertising Address: As above. **Tel:** 0115 921 7280
Email: sales@newlifepublishing.co.uk
Web site: http://www.newlifepublishing.co.uk/direction
ISSN: 0957-9397
Publisher: New Life Publishing Company
Date Established: 1989
Frequency: Monthly
Cover Price: £1.70
Annual Sub.: £22.00
Circulation: 9,000 (Print Run)
Usual Pagination: 52
Editor: Peter Wreford; **Editor-in-Chief:** John Glass; **Advertising Manager:** Barry Wilson
Summary of Content: Magazine covering issues of interest to Christians.
Readership/Target Audience: Read mainly by Christians, particularly families.
ADVERTISING RATES:
Full Page Colour £775.00
SCC £10.00
Agency Commission: 10%
Mechanical Data: Col Length: 233mm, Film: Digital, No. of Columns (Display): 4, Type Area: 233 x 188mm, Trim Size: 297 x 210mm, Page Width: 188mm, Col Widths (Display): 44mm
Copy instructions: Copy Date: 30th of the month prior to publication date
Average advertising content per issue: 33%
Supplement(s): Christian Holidays Guide - 1xY, Christian Learning Guide - 1xY
CONSUMER: RELIGIOUS

DIRECTORY OF BRITISH ASSOCIATIONS 48803U94X-33_60

Editorial Address: Chancery House, 15 Wickham Road, BECKENHAM, BR3 5JS **Tel:** 020 8650 7745
Fax: 020 8650 0768
Email: cbd@cbdresearch.com

Web site: http://www.cbdresearch.com
ISSN: 0309-5487
Publisher: CBD Research Ltd
Date Established: 1965
Frequency: Published every two years
Cover Price: £215.00
Circulation: 7,000 (Publisher's Statement)
Usual Pagination: 830
Editor: Antony Henderson
Summary of Content: Directory listing over 7250 national organisations in the UK and Eire in all fields of activity.
Readership/Target Audience: Aimed at reference libraries both public and corporate, all media categories and all other businesses.
ADVERTISING: No Advertising taken
CONSUMER: OTHER CLASSIFICATIONS: Miscellaneous

DIRECTORY OF VOCATIONAL AND FURTHER EDUCATION 47929U88C-20

Editorial Address: Edinburgh Gate, HARLOW, CM20 2JE. **Tel:** 01279 623623 **Fax:** 01279 621287
Email: directories@pearson.com
Web site: http://www.pearson-books.com/yearbook
Publisher: Pearson Education Ltd
Date Established: 1962
Frequency: Annual - Published in April
Cover Price: £95.00
Circulation: 800 (Publisher's Statement)
Usual Pagination: 450
Editor: Shamini Sriskandarajah
Summary of Content: Directory of vocational and further education colleges.
Readership/Target Audience: Aimed at those interested in further or vocational education.
ADVERTISING: No Advertising taken
CONSUMER: EDUCATION: Careers

DIRT 46395U77C-740

Formerly: Dirt M T B Magazine
Editorial Address: 1 West Smithfield, LONDON, EC1A 9JU **Tel:** 020 7332 9700 **Fax:** 020 7332 9799
Email: dirt@dirtmag.co.uk
Advertising Address: As above.
Email: jonathan.vincent@factorymedia.com
Web site: http://www.dirtmag.co.uk
ISSN: 1364-8764
Publisher: Factory Media
Date Established: 1996
Frequency: Monthly
Cover Price: £3.20
Annual Sub.: £18.95
Circulation: 56,250 (Publisher's Statement)
Usual Pagination: 164
Editor: Michael Rose
Summary of Content: Magazine covering downhill mountain bike racing, BSX, trails, free riding and off road biking. Covers bike tests, accessories, news and reports of the sport.
Readership/Target Audience: Aimed at those interested in mountain biking, dual slalom racing, trials riding, dirt bike riding, motocross and BMX.
ADVERTISING RATES:
Full Page Colour £1385.00
Agency Commission: 10%
Mechanical Data: Film: Digital, Trim Size: 300 x 230mm, Bleed Size: 306 x 236mm
Average advertising content per issue: 40%
CONSUMER: MOTORING & CYCLING: Cycling

DIRT BIKE RIDER 46358U77B-494

Editorial Address: 12 Victoria Street, MORECAMBE, LA4 4AG **Tel:** 01524 833111 **Fax:** 01524 425469
Email: sean.lawless@dirtbikerider.co.uk
Advertising Address: As above. **Tel:** 01524 834030
Fax: 01524 834045
Email: sarah.greenwood@tmxnews.co.uk
Web site: http://www.dirtbikerider.com
Publisher: Johnston Press plc
Date Established: 1981
Frequency: Monthly
Cover Price: £3.40
Annual Sub.: £30.00
Circulation: 17,000 (Publisher's Statement)
Usual Pagination: 140
Editor: Sean Lawless; **Managing Director:** Mike Harper
Summary of Content: Magazine giving an overview of the off-road bike scene.
Readership/Target Audience: Aimed at motorcyclists and fans of off-road motorcycling.
ADVERTISING RATES:
Full Page Colour £1030.00
Agency Commission: 10%
Mechanical Data: Film: Digital, Bleed Size: 303 x 216mm, Trim Size: 297 x 210mm
Copy instructions: Copy Date: 2 weeks prior to publication date

Average advertising content per issue: 33%
CONSUMER: MOTORING & CYCLING: Motorcycling

DISABILITY NOW
48625U94F-280

Editorial Address: 6 Market Road, LONDON, N7 9PW
Tel: 020 7619 7323 **Fax:** 020 7619 7331
Email: editor@disabilitynow.org.uk
Advertising Address: As above.
Email: patrick.durhammatthews@disabilitynow.org.uk
Web site: http://www.disabilitynow.org.uk
Publisher: Scope
Date Established: 1984
Frequency: Monthly - Published on the last week of cover date
Cover Price: £1.80
Free to qualifying individuals
Circulation: 18,514 (ABC 01/01/2008 to 31/12/2008)
Usual Pagination: 40
Editor: Kelly Mullan; **News Editor:** Katharine Quarmby
Summary of Content: Newspaper providing information and comment on disability.
Readership/Target Audience: Aimed at disabled people and their families, carers and professionals.
ADVERTISING RATES:
Full Page Colour £2985.00
SCC £35.00
Agency Commission: 10%
Mechanical Data: Col Length: 275mm, Film: Digital, Type Area: 275 x 215mm, Page Width: 215mm, Bleed Size: +5mm, No. of Columns (Display): 4, Page Width: 44mm
Average advertising content per issue: 50%
CONSUMER: OTHER CLASSIFICATIONS: Disability

DISABILITY PRODUCT NEWS
1665921U94F-997

Editorial Address: 25 Phoenix Court, Hawkins Road, COLCHESTER, CO2 8JY **Tel:** 01206 505115
Fax: 01206 505945
Email: raphael@disabilityproductnews.co.uk
Advertising Address: 2nd Floor, Ewer House, 44-46 Crouch Street, COLCHESTER, CO3 3HH **Tel:** 01206 506237
Fax: 01206 500227
Email: belinda@disabilityproductnews.co.uk
Web site: http://www.disabilityproductnews.co.uk
Publisher: Maze Media (2000) Ltd
Date Established: 2005
Frequency: 8 issues yearly
Cover Price: £3.50
Free to qualifying individuals
Circulation: 14,609 (Publisher's Statement)
Usual Pagination: 100
Editor: Raphael Giacardi
Summary of Content: Buyer's guide for disability products looking at a wide range of items in sections such as mobility, home, living aids and holidays.
Readership/Target Audience: Aimed at people who are registered disabled and car owners as well as owners and managers of NHS care homes.
ADVERTISING RATES:
Full Page Colour £1565.00
Agency Commission: 10%
Mechanical Data: Type Area: 270 x 190mm, Bleed Size: 307 x 220mm, Trim Size: 297 x 210mm, Col Length: 270mm, Page Width: 190mm, Film: Digital
CONSUMER: OTHER CLASSIFICATIONS: Disability

DISABLED & SUPPORTIVE CARER INCORPORATING CHALLENGE
48629U94F-340

Editorial Address: Unit 8, Chorley West Business Park, Ackhurst Road, CHORLEY, PR7 1NL **Tel:** 0870 444 8955
Fax: 0870 444 8956
Email: editorial@euromedia-al.com
Advertising Address: As above.
Email: ads@euromedia-al.co.uk
Publisher: Euromedia Associates Ltd
Frequency: 6 issues yearly
Cover Price: £1.50
Circulation: 10,000 (Publisher's Statement)
Usual Pagination: 116
Editor: Richard Cheesbrough; **Advertising Manager:** Susan Wheeler
Summary of Content: Magazine with features on mobility, holidays, hobbies and car reports.
Readership/Target Audience: Aimed at disabled people and their carers.
ADVERTISING RATES:
Full Page Colour £1700.00
Agency Commission: 10%
Mechanical Data: Film: Digital, Type Area: 280 x 190mm, Bleed Size: 303 x 216mm, Trim Size: 297 x 210mm, Page Width: 190mm, Col Length: 280mm
Copy instructions: Copy Date: 3 weeks prior to publication date
Average advertising content per issue: 40%
Supplement(s): Disability Motoring News - 6xY
CONSUMER: OTHER CLASSIFICATIONS: Disability

DISCOVER
48119U89C-277

Formerly: Birmingham Visitor Guide
Editorial Address: Marketing Birmingham, Millennium Point, Level L2, Curzon Street, BIRMINGHAM, B4 7XG
Tel: 0121 202 5115 **Fax:** 0121 202 5116
Email: info@marketingbirmingham.com
Advertising Address: Brilliiant Media, Innovation Centre, 1 Devon Way, BIRMINGHAM, B31 2TS **Tel:** 0121 222 5522
Fax: 0121 222 5523
Email: bramwell@brilliantmedia.co.uk
Web site: http://www.visitbirmingham.com
Publisher: Trinity Mirror
Frequency: Annual - Published in March or April depending when Easter falls
Cover Price: Free
Circulation: 70,000 (Publisher's Statement)
Usual Pagination: 100
Editor: Emma Ward; **Advertising Manager:** Paul Bramwell
Summary of Content: Visitors guide to Birmingham and the central England region.
Readership/Target Audience: Aimed at visitors to Birmingham.
ADVERTISING RATES:
Full Page Colour £3360.00
Mechanical Data: Type Area: 270 x 180mm, Col Length: 270mm, Page Width: 180mm, Trim Size: 297 x 210mm, Bleed Size: 303 x 216mm, Film: Digital
CONSUMER: HOLIDAYS & TRAVEL: Entertainment Guides

DISCOVER BEDFORDSHIRE
1659892U80C-5210

Formerly: Discover Bedfordshire & Luton
Editorial Address: The Treacle Factory, 2A Reginald Street, LUTON, LU2 7QZ **Tel:** 01582 416171 **Fax:** 01582 416328
Email: jeremy@discoverbedfordshire.co.uk
Advertising Address: As above.
Email: ian@discoverbedfordshire.co.uk
Web site: http://www.discoverbedfordshire.co.uk
Publisher: JNB Publishing
Date Established: 2004
Frequency: Quarterly
Free to qualifying individuals
Circulation: 30,000 (Publisher's Statement)
Usual Pagination: 52
Editor: Jeremy Brown; **Advertising Manager:** Ian Abrahams; **Publisher:** Ian Abrahams
Summary of Content: Magazine covering activities, places of interest, attractions, places to eat, homes and gardens.
Readership/Target Audience: Aimed at residents and visitors to Bedfordshire.
ADVERTISING RATES:
Full Page Colour £995.00
Agency Commission: 10%
Mechanical Data: Type Area: 291 x 204mm, Bleed Size: 301 x 214mm, Trim Size: 297 x 210mm, Col Length: 291mm, Page Width: 204mm, Film: Digital
Copy instructions: Copy Date: 4 weeks prior to publication date
Average advertising content per issue: 40%
CONSUMER: RURAL & REGIONAL INTEREST: Regional Interest English Counties

DISNEY & ME
48498U91D-44_50

Editorial Address: 239 Kensington High Street, LONDON, W8 6SA **Tel:** 020 7761 3500 **Fax:** 020 7761 3510
Email: disneyreaderpost@euk.egmont.com
Advertising Address: As above.
Email: aallen@euk.egmont.com
Web site: http://www.egmontmagazines.co.uk
ISSN: 0961-477X
Publisher: Egmont Magazines UK
Frequency: 20 issues yearly
Cover Price: £1.99
Circulation: 50,050 (ABC 01/01/2009 to 30/06/2009)
Usual Pagination: 40
Editor: Lynne Harwood; **Advertising Manager:** Annett Allen
Summary of Content: Children's magazine containing stories, puzzles, posters and things to make and do featuring Disney characters.
Readership/Target Audience: Aimed at 4 to 8 year olds.
ADVERTISING RATES:
Full Page Colour £1800.00
Agency Commission: 10%
Mechanical Data: Film: Digital, Col Length: 282mm, Page Width: 202mm, Type Area: 282 x 202mm, Bleed Size: 306 x 226mm, Trim Size: 300 x 220mm
Copy instructions: Copy Date: 4 weeks prior to publication date
Average advertising content per issue: 10%
CONSUMER: RECREATION & LEISURE: Children & Youth

DISNEY GIRL
1849422U91D-978

Editorial Address: Brockbourne House, 77 Mount Ephraim, TUNBRIDGE WELLS, TN4 8BS **Tel:** 01892 500100
Email: kvrhead@gmail.com
Publisher: Panini UK Ltd
Date Established: 2008

Frequency: 13 issues yearly
Cover Price: £1.99
Usual Pagination: 36
Editor: Kate Rhead
Summary of Content: Magazine featuring all the classic and current Disney properties including HSM, Hannah Montana and Camp Rock as well as fashion, lifestyle, hobbies, gossip, blushes, quizzes, craft projects, puzzles, posters, shopping, friendship and competitions.
Readership/Target Audience: Aimed at girls aged 7 to 12 years old.
CONSUMER: RECREATION & LEISURE: Children & Youth

DISNEY'S PRINCESS
718024U91D-48

Editorial Address: 239 Kensington High Street, LONDON, W8 6SA **Tel:** 020 7761 3500 **Fax:** 020 7761 3510
Email: princesspostbag@euk.egmont.com
Advertising Address: As above.
Email: svernon@euk.egmont.com
Web site: http://www.egmontmagazines.co.uk
ISSN: 1462-7345
Publisher: Egmont Magazines UK
Date Established: 1998
Frequency: 26 issues yearly
Cover Price: £1.80
Circulation: 62,541 (ABC 01/01/2009 to 30/06/2009)
Usual Pagination: 32
Editor: Lynne Harwood
Summary of Content: Children's magazine featuring stories, puzzles, posters and things to make and do.
Readership/Target Audience: Aimed at girls between 4 and 8 years old.
ADVERTISING RATES:
Full Page Colour £1800.00
Agency Commission: 10%
Mechanical Data: Film: Digital, Type Area: 282 x 202mm, Col Length: 282mm, Trim Size: 300 x 220mm, Bleed Size: 306 x 226mm, Page Width: 202mm
Copy instructions: Copy Date: 4 weeks prior to publication date
Average advertising content per issue: 12%
CONSUMER: RECREATION & LEISURE: Children & Youth

DISORDER MAGAZINE
1692636U74Q-1266

Editorial Address: Unit 4-5, Universal House, 88-94 Wentworth Street, LONDON, E1 7SA **Tel:** 020 7247 6504
Email: taylor@disordermagazine.com
Advertising Address: As above.
Email: gary@alive-advertising.com
Web site: http://www.disordermagazine.com
Publisher: Eat Me Media
Frequency: Monthly
Cover Price: £2.95
Annual Sub.: £48.00
Circulation: 35,000 (Publisher's Statement)
Usual Pagination: 116
Editor: Taylor Glasby; **Executive Editor:** Davide Ferminger; **Advertising Manager:** Gary Pitt
Summary of Content: Lifestyle magazine covering culture, street style and fashion and rock and indie music.
Readership/Target Audience: Aimed at 16 to 28 year olds interested in street culture.
ADVERTISING: Rates on application
CONSUMER: WOMEN'S INTEREST CONSUMER MAGAZINES: Lifestyle

DIVA
47626U86B-25

Editorial Address: Unit M, Spectrum House, 32-34 Gordon House Road, LONDON, NW5 1LP **Tel:** 020 7424 7400
Fax: 020 7424 7401
Email: edit@divamag.co.uk
Advertising Address: As above.
Email: maggie@divamag.co.uk
Web site: http://www.divamag.co.uk
ISSN: 1353-4912
Publisher: Millivres-Prowler Ltd
Date Established: 1994
Frequency: Monthly
Cover Price: £3.25
Annual Sub.: £28.50
Circulation: 50,000 (Publisher's Statement)
Usual Pagination: 116
Editor: Jane Czyzyselska; **News Editor:** Peter Lloyd; **Features Editor:** Darren Scott; **Advertising Manager:** Maggie Travers; **Publisher:** Kim Watson
Summary of Content: Magazine containing features on lifestyle, fashion, current affairs, entertainment, travel, music, cinema, video, books, club culture, health, fitness, beauty, activism, home and motoring.
Readership/Target Audience: Aimed at lesbians and bisexual women.
ADVERTISING RATES:
Full Page Colour £1250.00
Agency Commission: 10%
Mechanical Data: Film: Digital, No. of Columns (Display): 5, Type Area: 270 x 200mm, Bleed Size: 306 x 236mm, Trim

Size: 300 x 230mm, Col Length: 270mm, Col Widths (Display): 36mm, Page Width: 200mm
Copy instructions: Copy Date: 13 days prior to publication date
Average advertising content per issue: 20%
CONSUMER: ADULT & GAY MAGAZINES: Gay & Lesbian Magazines

DIVE MAGAZINE
45940U75M-150

Editorial Address: 1 Victoria Villas, RICHMOND, TW9 2GW
Tel: 020 8332 9995 **Fax:** 020 8332 9307
Email: simon@dive.uk.com
Advertising Address: As above. **Tel:** 020 8332 2713
Email: jim@dive.uk.com
Web site: http://www.divemagazine.co.uk
ISSN: 1360-6913
Publisher: Circle Publishing
Date Established: 1999
Frequency: Monthly
Cover Price: £3.90
Annual Sub.: £33.00
Circulation: 38,624 (ABC 01/01/2008 to 31/12/2008)
Usual Pagination: 116
Editor: Simon Rogerson; **Publisher:** Paul Critcher
Summary of Content: Magazine covering all aspects of scuba diving.
Readership/Target Audience: Aimed at scuba divers and people interested in the underwater world.
ADVERTISING RATES:
Full Page Colour £1995.00
Mechanical Data: Type Area: 271 x 187mm, Bleed Size: 300 x 213mm, Trim Size: 297 x 210mm, Col Length: 271mm, Film: Digital, Page Width: 187mm
Copy instructions: Copy Date: 5 weeks prior to publication date
CONSUMER: SPORT: Water Sports

DIVER
45941U75M-200

Editorial Address: 55 High Street, TEDDINGTON, TW11 8HA **Tel:** 020 8943 4288 **Fax:** 020 8943 4312
Email: enquiries@divermag.co.uk
Advertising Address: As above.
Email: jenny@divermag.co.uk
Web site: http://www.divernet.com
ISSN: 0141-3465
Publisher: Eaton Publications
Date Established: 1963
Frequency: Monthly
Cover Price: £3.99
Annual Sub.: £47.88
Circulation: 30,000 (Publisher's Statement)
Usual Pagination: 124
Editor: Steve Weinman; **News Editor:** Paul Fenner; **Editor-in-Chief:** Nigel Eaton
Summary of Content: Magazine covering all aspects of diving for pleasure. Includes destinations, reefs and wrecks, equipment reviews, marine biology, archaeology, boats, technical diving, conservation, training and safety.
Readership/Target Audience: Read by sport diving enthusiasts and professionals, marine biologists, underwater archaeologists, conservationists and holiday divers.
ADVERTISING RATES:
Full Page Mono £1265.00
Full Page Colour £1860.00
SCC £20.00
Agency Commission: 10%
Mechanical Data: Type Area: 271 x 187mm, Col Length: 271mm, Trim Size: 297 x 210mm, Bleed Size: 304 x 216mm, Film: Digital, Page Width: 187mm
Copy instructions: Copy Date: 4 weeks prior to publication date
Average advertising content per issue: 45%
CONSUMER: SPORT: Water Sports

DIWALI UK
1627069U90-912

Editorial Address: Eton House, 66 Eton Avenue, WEMBLEY, HA0 3AU **Tel:** 0845 013 8401
Fax: 0845 013 8402
Email: neena.kent@memediagroup.com
Advertising Address: As above.
Email: info@memediagroup.com
Web site: http://www.clickwalla.com
Publisher: ME Media Ltd
Frequency: Annual - Published in October
Cover Price: Free
Circulation: 50,000 (Publisher's Statement)
Usual Pagination: 60
Editor: Neena Kent; **Advertising Manager:** Neena Kent
Summary of Content: Magazine with information on religious resources, Bollywood, festival guides and profiles of prominent Hindus/Sikhs that are of interest to the community.
Readership/Target Audience: Aimed at Hindu, Sikh and Jain communities in the UK.
ADVERTISING RATES:
Full Page Mono £3000.00
Full Page Colour £3000.00

Mechanical Data: Trim Size: 297 x 210mm
Copy instructions: Copy Date: October 22nd
CONSUMER: ETHNIC

DJ
40937U76D-774

Editorial Address: The Old Truman Brewery, 91 Brick Lane, LONDON, E1 6QL **Tel:** 020 7247 8855 **Fax:** 020 7247 5874
Email: editors@djmag.com
Advertising Address: As above.
Email: heath@djmag.com
Web site: http://www.djmag.com
Publisher: DJ Magazine Ltd
Date Established: 1991
Frequency: Monthly
Cover Price: £3.95
Circulation: 15,000 (Publisher's Statement)
Usual Pagination: 180
Editor: Lesley Wright; **Advertising Manager:** Heath Holmes; **Publisher:** James Robertson
Summary of Content: Dance music journal which includes club and album reviews, interviews and information about music equipment.
Readership/Target Audience: Read by radio and club DJs, club-goers, mobile DJs, record shop owners, retailers and equipment manufacturers.
ADVERTISING RATES:
Full Page Colour £2500.00
Agency Commission: 10%
Mechanical Data: Type Area: 276 x 212mm, Col Length: 276mm, Bleed Size: 308 x 236mm, Trim Size: 300 x 230mm, Page Width: 212mm, Film: Digital
Copy instructions: Copy Date: 2 weeks prior to publication date
Average advertising content per issue: 40%
Supplement(s): EQ - 2xY, Ibiza Guide - 2xY
CONSUMER: MUSIC & PERFORMING ARTS: Music

DN
629694U83-7_3

Formerly: Degrees North
Editorial Address: USSU, 1st Floor, Edinburgh Building, Chester Road, SUNDERLAND, SR1 3SD **Tel:** 0191 515 2957
Fax: 0191 515 2441
Email: dnmagazine@sunderland.ac.uk
Advertising Address: As above.
Email: allen.humes@sunderland.ac.uk
Web site: http://www.dnmagazine.co.uk
Publisher: Potts Printers Ltd
Frequency: Quarterly
Cover Price: Free
Circulation: 5,000 (Print Run)
Usual Pagination: 42
Editor: Josh Halliday; **Advertising Manager:** Allen Humes
Summary of Content: Student lifestyle magazine containing fashion, film, competitions celebrity interviews, features, reviews, music, clubs, sport and student union news.
Readership/Target Audience: Aimed at students of the University of Sunderland and residents of the local area.
ADVERTISING RATES:
Full Page Colour £295.00
Agency Commission: 10%
Mechanical Data: Film: Digital, Trim Size: 248 x 170mm, Bleed Size: 254 x 176mm
CONSUMER: STUDENT PUBLICATIONS

DOCTOR WHO ADVENTURES
1739884U91D-942

Formerly: Dr Who Adventures
Editorial Address: Media Centre, 201 Wood Lane, LONDON, W12 7TQ **Tel:** 020 8433 2000
Email: moray.laing@bbc.com
Advertising Address: Garden News, 201 Wood Lane, LONDON, W12 7TQ **Tel:** 020 8433 2000 **Fax:** 020 8433 2427
Email: sophie.hunt@bbc.com
Publisher: BBC Magazines
Date Established: 2006
Frequency: Weekly
Cover Price: £2.10
Circulation: 56,986 (ABC 01/01/2009 to 30/06/2009)
Usual Pagination: 36
Editor: Moray Laing
Summary of Content: Children's magazine covering the Dr Who television programme with features, comic strips, interviews, competitions, posters, makes, humour and puzzles.
Readership/Target Audience: Aimed at 6 to 12 year old fans of Dr Who.
ADVERTISING: Rates on application
Agency Commission: 10%
Copy instructions: Copy Date: 4 weeks prior to publication date
CONSUMER: RECREATION & LEISURE: Children & Youth

DOCUMENT SNOWBOARD
760368U75G-110

Editorial Address: South Wing, Broadway Court, Broadway, PETERBOROUGH, PE1 1RP **Tel:** 01733 293250
Fax: 01733 293269
Email: rachel@fall-line.co.uk
Advertising Address: As above.
Email: luke@fall-line.co.uk
Web site: http://www.documentsnowboard.co.uk
Publisher: Fall Line Media Limited
Date Established: 2000
Frequency: 7 issues yearly - Published over the winter months March to Sepetember
Cover Price: £3.80
Annual Sub.: £21.80
Circulation: 20,000 (Publisher's Statement)
Usual Pagination: 148
Editor: Rachel Devlin; **Publisher:** Richard Fincher
Summary of Content: Magazine focusing on all aspects of snowboarding including clothing, equipment, destination information, coming events and resort and product reviews.
Readership/Target Audience: Aimed at snowboard enthusiasts and frequent travellers between 15 and 35 years old.
ADVERTISING RATES:
Full Page Colour £1300.00
Agency Commission: 10%
Mechanical Data: Type Area: 280 x 204mm, Bleed Size: 306 x 228mm, Trim Size: 300 x 222mm, Film: Digital, Col Length: 280mm, Print Process: Heatset web offset, Page Width: 204mm
Copy instructions: Copy Date: 4 weeks prior to publication date
Average advertising content per issue: 40%
CONSUMER: SPORT: Winter Sports

DOG TRAINING WEEKLY
47098U81B-40

Editorial Address: 6 High Street, FISHGUARD, SA65 9AR
Tel: 01348 875011
Email: dtwpress@aol.com
Advertising Address: As above.
Email: dtwpress@aol.com
Web site: http://www.dogtrainingweekly.com
Publisher: Pembrokeshire & Canine Press
Date Established: 1962
Frequency: Weekly
Annual Sub.: £81.00
Circulation: 2,000 (Publisher's Statement)
Usual Pagination: 44
Editor: Angela Barrah; **Advertising Manager:** Angela Barrah
Summary of Content: Specialist magazine containing information on training dogs for obedience, flyball, heelwork to music, canine freestyle and pet ownership.
Readership/Target Audience: Aimed at all dog owners training their dogs and those whose dogs compete in classes.
ADVERTISING: Rates on application
CONSUMER: ANIMALS & PETS: Dogs

DOG WORLD
47099U81B-50

Editorial Address: Somerfield House, Wotton Road, ASHFORD, TN23 6LW **Tel:** 01233 621877
Fax: 01233 645669
Email: editor@dogworld.co.uk
Advertising Address: As above.
Email: advertising@dogworld.co.uk
Web site: http://www.dogworld.co.uk
ISSN: 0012-4885
Publisher: Dog World Ltd
Frequency: Weekly
Cover Price: £2.00
Annual Sub.: £90.00
Circulation: 16,846 (ABC 01/01/2008 to 31/12/2008)
Usual Pagination: 72
Editor: Christine Smith; **News Editor:** Christine Smith; **Managing Director:** Kerry Williamson; **Advertising Manager:** Lee Hutton
Summary of Content: Newspaper providing news and results from dog shows and articles on the individual breeds.
Readership/Target Audience: Aimed at the pedigree dog owner.
ADVERTISING RATES:
Full Page Mono £800.00
Full Page Colour £1100.00
Agency Commission: 10%
Mechanical Data: Col Length: 366mm, Type Area: 366 x 262mm, No. of Columns (Display): 6, Page Width: 262mm, Film: Digital, Col Widths (Display): 41mm
Copy instructions: Copy Date: Tuesday prior to publication date
Average advertising content per issue: 40%
CONSUMER: ANIMALS & PETS: Dogs

DOGS MONTHLY
47100U81B-60

Editorial Address: 61 Great Whyte, Ramsey, HUNTINGDON, PE26 1HJ **Tel:** 0845 094 8958
Fax: 0870 766 2273

Consumer Magazines

Email: info@dogsmonthly.co.uk
Advertising Address: As above. **Tel:** 01778 392445
Email: paulat@warnersgroup.co.uk
Web site: http://www.dogsmonthly.co.uk
Publisher: ABM Publishing Ltd
Date Established: 1983
Frequency: Monthly
Cover Price: £3.50
Usual Pagination: 116
Editor: Hannah Roche; **Advertising Manager:** Paula Turner
Summary of Content: Magazine directed at all dog owners, featuring articles on physical and mental canine health care, training, equipment, products, ownership, training, lifestyles, general care, activities, breeding and feeding. Also a complementary medicine and therapy section and a new junior section.
Readership/Target Audience: Aimed at all dog owners.
ADVERTISING RATES:
Full Page Colour £1000.00
Mechanical Data: Col Length: 262mm, Type Area: 262 x 188mm, Page Width: 188mm, Bleed Size: 303 x 216mm, Trim Size: 297 x 210mm, Film: Digital
Copy instructions: Copy Date: 4 weeks prior to publication date
CONSUMER: ANIMALS & PETS: Dogs

DOGS TODAY
47101U81B-80
Editorial Address: Town Mill, Bagshot Road, Chobham, WOKING, GU24 8BZ **Tel:** 01276 858880 **Fax:** 01276 858860
Email: editorial@dogstodaymagazine.co.uk
Advertising Address: As above.
Email: melanie@dogstodaymagazine.co.uk
Web site: http://www.dogstodaymagazine.co.uk
ISSN: 0959-8910
Publisher: Pet Subjects Ltd
Date Established: 1990
Frequency: Monthly
Cover Price: £3.50
Circulation: 41,382 (Publisher's Statement)
Usual Pagination: 132
Editor: Karen Redpath; **Managing Director:** Beverley Cuddy; **Advertising Manager:** Melanie Hosegood; **Managing Editor:** Beverley Cuddy; **Publisher:** Beverley Cuddy
Summary of Content: Magazine containing information, news, features and advice on choosing the correct breed of dog.
Readership/Target Audience: Aimed at those who love their dog as part of the family.
ADVERTISING RATES:
Full Page Mono £1000.00
Full Page Colour £1200.00
SCC £20.00
Agency Commission: 10%
Mechanical Data: Type Area: 273 x 204mm, No. of Columns (Display): 4, Trim Size: 300 x 232mm, Bleed Size: 308 x 236mm, Film: Digital
Average advertising content per issue: 40%
CONSUMER: ANIMALS & PETS: Dogs

LA DOLCE VITA
1825901U89D-531
Editorial Address: Hillgarth, 2A Pump Hill, LOUGHTON, IG10 1RT **Tel:** 020 8502 0801
Email: info@the-luxury-directory.com
Advertising Address: As above. **Fax:** 020 8502 0801
Email: advertising@the-luxury-directory.com
Web site: http://www.ladolcevita-magazine.com
Publisher: The Luxury Directory Ltd
Date Established: 2007
Frequency: 7 issues yearly
Cover Price: £12.95
Annual Sub.: £70.00
Circulation: 184,000 (Publisher's Statement)
Usual Pagination: 148
Editor: Adam Blake; **Advertising Director:** Andrew Pearson
Summary of Content: Luxury travel and lifestyle magazine covering the finest destinations, travel experiences, luxury hotels, spa resorts, company profiles and luxury products.
Readership/Target Audience: Aimed at first and private class travellers.
ADVERTISING RATES:
Full Page Mono £5400.00
Full Page Colour £5400.00
Agency Commission: 15%
Mechanical Data: Type Area: 270 x 210mm, Bleed Size: 296 x 236mm, Trim Size: 290 x 230mm, Col Length: 270mm, Page Width: 210mm, Film: Digital
Copy instructions: Copy Date: 10 days prior to publication date
Average advertising content per issue: 33%
CONSUMER: HOLIDAYS & TRAVEL: In-Flight Magazines

DOLLS HOUSE AND MINIATURE SCENE
46745U79K-466_50
Editorial Address: The Maltings, West Street, BOURNE, PE10 9PH **Tel:** 01778 391107 **Fax:** 01778 392079

Email: janet@kirkwoodwgp.freeserve.co.uk
Advertising Address: As above. **Tel:** 01778 391158
Email: sarahh@warnersgroup.co.uk
Web site: http://www.dollshousemag.co.uk
ISSN: 0967-4918
Publisher: Warners Group Publications plc
Frequency: Monthly
Cover Price: £3.95
Annual Sub.: £35.00
Usual Pagination: 88
Editor: Janet Kirkwood; **Advertising Manager:** Sarah Hubbard; **Publisher:** Lucie Roper
Summary of Content: Magazine covering news, products, readers' views, book reviews, doll's house items to make, features, fairs and competitions.
Readership/Target Audience: Aimed at doll's house enthusiasts and those that collect miniatures.
ADVERTISING RATES:
Full Page Mono £440.00
Full Page Colour £750.00
Agency Commission: 10%
Mechanical Data: Type Area: 275 x 190mm, Col Length: 275mm, Page Width: 190mm, Bleed Size: 303 x 216mm, Film: Digital
Copy instructions: Copy Date: 6 weeks prior to publication date
Average advertising content per issue: 20%
CONSUMER: HOBBIES & DIY: Collectors Magazines

THE DOLLS HOUSE MAGAZINE
46742U79K-467
Editorial Address: 86 High Street, LEWES, BN7 1XN
Tel: 01273 477374 **Fax:** 01273 402849
Email: christianeb@thegmcgroup.com
Advertising Address: As above. **Fax:** 01273 487692
Email: sallyj@thegmcgroup.com
Web site: http://www.gmcpubs.com
ISSN: 1461-569X
Publisher: GMC Publications Ltd
Frequency: Monthly
Cover Price: £3.99
Circulation: 12,000 (Publisher's Statement)
Usual Pagination: 96
Editor: Christiane Berridge
Summary of Content: Magazine containing articles on collections, DIY projects, kit reviews, lighting, decorating and profiles of makers.
Readership/Target Audience: Aimed at adult miniature and dolls house enthusiasts and collectors.
ADVERTISING: Rates on application
Copy instructions: Copy Date: 7 weeks prior to publication date
CONSUMER: HOBBIES & DIY: Collectors Magazines

DOLLS HOUSE WORLD
46744U79K-468
Editorial Address: Ancient Lights, 19 River Road, ARUNDEL, BN18 9EY **Tel:** 01903 884988
Fax: 01903 885514
Email: joyce@ashdown.co.uk
Advertising Address: As above.
Email: krystyna@ashdown.co.uk
Web site: http://www.dollshouseworld.com
ISSN: 0961-0928
Publisher: Ashdown.co.uk Ltd
Date Established: 1989
Frequency: Monthly
Cover Price: £3.95
Annual Sub.: £46.00
Circulation: 26,000 (Publisher's Statement)
Usual Pagination: 100
Editor: Joyce Dean; **Publisher:** Richard Jennings
Summary of Content: Magazine covering all aspects of doll's houses and miniatures.
Readership/Target Audience: Aimed at adult collectors and craftspeople.
ADVERTISING RATES:
Full Page Mono £550.00
Full Page Colour £850.00
Agency Commission: 10%
Mechanical Data: Type Area: 263 x 185mm, Bleed Size: 307 x 220mm, Film: Digital, Trim Size: 297 x 210mm, Col Length: 263mm, Page Width: 185mm
Copy instructions: Copy Date: 6 weeks prior to publication date
Average advertising content per issue: 30%
CONSUMER: HOBBIES & DIY: Collectors Magazines

THE DOOR
47705U87-89
Editorial Address: Diocesan Church House, North Hinksey Lane, Botley, OXFORD, OX2 0NB **Tel:** 01865 208227
Fax: 01865 790470
Email: door@oxford.anglican.org
Advertising Address: Cornerstone Vision, Cornerstone House, 28 Old Park Road, PLYMOUTH, PL3 4PY
Tel: 01752 225623 **Fax:** 01752 673441
Email: diocesan@cornerstonevision.com
Web site: http://www.oxford.anglican.org

Publisher: Oxford Diocesan Publications Ltd
Date Established: 1989
Frequency: 10 issues yearly
Cover Price: Free
Circulation: 38,000 (Publisher's Statement)
Usual Pagination: 20
Editor: Jo Duckles
Summary of Content: Newspaper of The Diocese of Oxford covering all issues on Christianity. Includes reports and comments on Christian news, views and articles of interest.
Readership/Target Audience: Aimed predominantly at Church of England members in Berks, Bucks and Oxon. Also those that attend churches of other denominations.
ADVERTISING RATES:
SCC £6.50
Agency Commission: 10%
Mechanical Data: Film: Digital, No. of Columns (Display): 8
Copy instructions: Copy Date: 3 weeks prior to publication date
CONSUMER: RELIGIOUS

DORA THE EXPLORER
1698513U91D-937
Editorial Address: 239 Kensington High Street, LONDON, W8 6SA **Tel:** 020 7761 3500 **Fax:** 020 7761 3510
Email: rjamieson@euk.egmont.com
Advertising Address: As above. **Tel:** 020 7761 3745
Email: lcrichlow@euk.egmont.com
Publisher: Egmont Magazines UK
Date Established: 2005
Frequency: 18 issues yearly
Cover Price: £1.85
Circulation: 49,520 (ABC 01/01/2009 to 30/06/2009)
Usual Pagination: 24
Editor: Rebecca Jamieson
Summary of Content: Children's magazine based on the popular Nick Jr character, content includes puzzles, stories, posters, basic educational elements and simple Spanish.
Language(s): English; Spanish
Readership/Target Audience: Aimed at boys and girls aged between 3 and 6 years old.
ADVERTISING RATES:
Full Page Colour £1800.00
Agency Commission: 10%
Mechanical Data: Type Area: 282 x 202mm, Bleed Size: 306 x 226mm, Trim Size: 300 x 220mm, Col Length: 282mm, Page Width: 202mm, Film: Digital
Copy instructions: Copy Date: 4 weeks prior to publication date
CONSUMER: RECREATION & LEISURE: Children & Youth

DORSET
46892U80C-1240
Editorial Address: Higher Hogleaze Farm, Compton Valence, DORCHESTER, DT2 9ET **Tel:** 01305 889033
Email: enquiries@dorsetmagazine.co.uk
Advertising Address: 3A Poundbury Business Centre, Poundbury, DORCHESTER, DT1 3RS **Tel:** 01305 211840
Fax: 01305 211841
Email: tina.richards@archant.co.uk
Web site: http://www.archantlife.co.uk
Publisher: Archant Life
Date Established: 1994
Frequency: Monthly
Cover Price: £2.75
Annual Sub.: £36.00
Circulation: 11,000 (Publisher's Statement)
Usual Pagination: 180
Editor: Bridget Swann
Summary of Content: County magazine covering natural history, landscape and village features. Also contains interviews with local people and events listings.
Readership/Target Audience: Aimed at those aged 35 years old and above living and working in Dorset.
ADVERTISING RATES:
Full Page Colour £1140.00
Agency Commission: 10%
Mechanical Data: Type Area: 271 x 199mm, Bleed Size: 306 x 226mm, Trim Size: 300 x 220mm, Col Length: 271mm, Page Width: 199mm, Film: Digital
Copy instructions: Copy Date: 3 weeks prior to publication date
Average advertising content per issue: 50%
CONSUMER: RURAL & REGIONAL INTEREST: Regional Interest English Counties

DORSET LIFE THE DORSET MAGAZINE
46893U80C-1245
Editorial Address: 7 The Leanne, Sandford Lane, WAREHAM, BH20 4DY **Tel:** 01929 551264
Fax: 01929 552099
Email: editor@dorsetlife.co.uk
Advertising Address: As above.
Email: office@dorsetlife.co.uk
Web site: http://www.dorsetlife.co.uk
ISSN: 0959-1079
Publisher: The Dorset Magazine Ltd
Frequency: Monthly

Cover Price: £2.30
Annual Sub.: £32.00
Circulation: 10,000 (Publisher's Statement)
Editor: John Newth
Summary of Content: Publication containing articles on all aspects of Dorset's history and current activities.
Readership/Target Audience: Read by residents and visitors to Dorset.
ADVERTISING RATES:
Full Page Colour £985.00
Agency Commission: 10%
Mechanical Data: Bleed Size: 303 x 216mm, Type Area: 268 x 183mm, Col Length: 268mm, Page Width: 183mm, Trim Size: 297 x 210mm, Film: Digital
Copy instructions: Copy Date: 4 weeks prior to publication date
Average advertising content per issue: 50%
CONSUMER: RURAL & REGIONAL INTEREST: Regional Interest English Counties

DORSET SOCIETY
652117U80C-3714
Formerly: Society
Editorial Address: Richmond Hill, BOURNEMOUTH, BH2 6HH **Tel:** 01202 411227 **Fax:** 01202 551246
Email: lorraine.gibson@bournemouthecho.co.uk
Advertising Address: As above. **Tel:** 01202 411252
Email: angela.boyer@bournemouthecho.co.uk
Web site: http://www.dorsetsociety.co.uk
Publisher: Newsquest (Media Group) Ltd
Date Established: 2000
Frequency: Monthly
Cover Price: £2.00
Free to qualifying individuals
Annual Sub.: £20.00
Circulation: 40,000 (Publisher's Statement)
Usual Pagination: 132
Editor: Lorraine Gibson; **Advertising Manager:** Angela Boyer
Summary of Content: Lifestyle magazine covering luxury property, food and drink, beauty, fashion, interiors, gardens, celebrity interviews and a society events diary.
Readership/Target Audience: Aimed at affluent 30 to 55 year olds living in Dorset.
ADVERTISING RATES:
Full Page Colour £769.00
Mechanical Data: Trim Size: 297 x 210mm, Page Width: 190mm, Type Area: 267 x 190mm, Col Length: 267mm, Bleed Size: 303 x 216mm, Film: Digital
Copy instructions: Copy Date: 1st of the cover month
Supplement(s): Dorset Society Brides - 1xY, Dorset Society Fashion - 6xY
CONSUMER: RURAL & REGIONAL INTEREST: Regional Interest English Counties

DOWN YOUR WAY
47007U80C-3620
Editorial Address: The Water Mill, Broughton Hall, Skipton, LEEDS, BD23 3AG **Tel:** 0113 260 9020
Email: averil.thornton@btconnect.com
Advertising Address: As above. **Tel:** 01756 701381
Fax: 01754 701326
Email: tracy@dalesman.co.uk
ISSN: 1365-8506
Publisher: Country Publications Ltd
Date Established: 2000
Frequency: Monthly
Cover Price: £1.99
Annual Sub.: £19.00
Circulation: 20,000 (Publisher's Statement)
Usual Pagination: 64
Editor: Averil Thornton
Summary of Content: Magazine covering all aspects of Yorkshire heritage including local and family history, artists, recipes and readers' letters. Also includes features on restoration and preservation.
Readership/Target Audience: Aimed at residents of and visitors to Yorkshire and the surrounding areas.
ADVERTISING RATES:
Full Page Mono £475.00
Full Page Colour £475.00
Agency Commission: 10%
Mechanical Data: Type Area: 222 x 156mm, Film: Digital, Col Length: 222mm, Page Width: 156mm, No. of Columns (Display): 2
Copy instructions: Copy Date: 4 weeks prior to publication date
Average advertising content per issue: 40%
CONSUMER: RURAL & REGIONAL INTEREST: Regional Interest English Counties

DOWSING TODAY
48802U94X-34_20
Editorial Address: 2 St. Anns Road, MALVERN, WR14 4RG
Tel: 01684 576969 **Fax:** 01684 576969
Email: info@britishdowsers.org
Advertising Address: As above.
Email: info@britishdowsers.org
Web site: http://www.britishdowsers.org
ISSN: 1472-023X

Publisher: British Society of Dowsers
Date Established: 2000
Frequency: Quarterly
Annual Sub.: £39.00
Circulation: 1,440 (Publisher's Statement)
Usual Pagination: 24
Editor: John Moss; **Advertising Manager:** Helen Lamb
Summary of Content: Publication covering all aspects of dowsing. Includes events, equipment, water divining and articles on dowsers.
Readership/Target Audience: Aimed at members of The British Society of Dowsers and those interested in dowsing.
ADVERTISING: Rates on application
CONSUMER: OTHER CLASSIFICATIONS: Miscellaneous

DR WHO MAGAZINE
1663451U91D-921
Editorial Address: Brockbourne House, Mount Ephraim, TUNBRIDGE WELLS, TN4 8BS **Tel:** 01892 500100
Fax: 01892 545666
Email: dwm@panini.co.uk
Advertising Address: Orange20 Ltd, Station House, Bunbury Way, EPSOM, KT17 4JP **Tel:** 01372 802800
Fax: 01372 723322
Email: michelle@o20.co.uk
Web site: http://www.panini.co.uk
ISSN: 0957-9818
Publisher: Panini UK Ltd
Date Established: 1975
Frequency: 13 issues yearly
Cover Price: £3.99
Circulation: 35,000 (Publisher's Statement)
Usual Pagination: 68
Editor: Tom Spilsbury; **Advertising Manager:** Michelle Fairlamb; **Managing Editor:** Alan O'Keefe
Summary of Content: Magazine with strip cartoons, articles and features about the adventures of Dr Who.
Readership/Target Audience: Aimed at Dr Who fans aged 14 years old plus.
ADVERTISING RATES:
Full Page Colour £1500.00
CONSUMER: RECREATION & LEISURE: Children & Youth

DREAM
1667564U77E-518
Editorial Address: 1 Neal Street, Covent Garden, LONDON, WC2H 9QL **Tel:** 020 7306 0304
Email: dream_editor@riverltd.co.uk
Advertising Address: As above. **Tel:** 020 306 0304
Fax: 020 7413 9409
Email: kmurdoch@riverltd.co.uk
Web site: http://www.honda.co.uk/dreamonline
Publisher: River Publishing Ltd
Date Established: 2004
Frequency: Quarterly
Free to qualifying individuals
Circulation: 220,000 (Publisher's Statement)
Usual Pagination: 52
Editor: Chris Hatherill; **Advertising Manager:** Kate Murdoch
Summary of Content: Magazine covering Honda news and product information with thought pieces, travel, architecture, design, technology, people profiles and environmental issues. Includes two-three promotions per issue.
Readership/Target Audience: Aimed at owners of Honda cars and motorbikes as well as new customers at motor shows and other Honda events.
ADVERTISING RATES:
Full Page Colour £6000.00
Agency Commission: 10%
Average advertising content per issue: 15%
CONSUMER: MOTORING & CYCLING: Club Cars

DREAMWORKS TALES
1813093U91D-966
Editorial Address: Titan House, 144 Southwark Street, LONDON, SE1 0UP **Tel:** 020 7620 0200 **Fax:** 020 7620 0032
Email: andrew.james@titanemail.com
Advertising Address: As above. **Tel:** 020 7803 1803
Email: james.willmott@titanemail.com
Web site: http://www.titanmagazines.co.uk
Publisher: Titan Magazines
Date Established: 2007
Frequency: 13 issues yearly
Cover Price: £2.60
Usual Pagination: 52
Editor: Andrew James; **Advertising Manager:** James Willmott
Summary of Content: Children's magazine with comic strips and features running across the DreamWorks films as well as activities and competitions.
Readership/Target Audience: Children aged 8 to 14 years old.
ADVERTISING RATES:
Full Page Colour £4200.00
Agency Commission: 10%
Mechanical Data: Type Area: 272 x 200mm, Bleed Size: 305 x 238mm, Trim Size: 297 x 230mm, Col Length: 272mm, Page Width: 200mm, Film: Digital

Copy instructions: Copy Date: 6 weeks prior to publication date
Average advertising content per issue: 10%
CONSUMER: RECREATION & LEISURE: Children & Youth

DRIFT
1753007U75M-1001
Editorial Address: 22 Church Lane, Clifton, BRISTOL, BS8 4TR **Tel:** 0117 929 1390
Email: enquiries@driftmagazine.co.uk
Web site: http://www.driftmagazine.co.uk
Publisher: Drift Magazine
Date Established: 2006
Frequency: 6 issues yearly
Cover Price: £4.95
Annual Sub.: £19.95
Usual Pagination: 104
Editor: Howard Swanwick; **Advertising Manager:** Nick Charles
Summary of Content: Magazine covering most aspects of amateur surfing including product reviews, interviews with surfers, travel, photos and environmental issues.
Readership/Target Audience: Aimed at surfers.
ADVERTISING: Rates on application
CONSUMER: SPORT: Water Sports

DRUMMER
1753138U76D-828
Editorial Address: Alexander House, Forehill, ELY, CB7 4ZA **Tel:** 01353 665577 **Fax:** 01353 662489
Email: samantha@mbmediagroup.co.uk
Advertising Address: As above.
Email: helen@mbmediagroup.co.uk
Web site: http://www.drummer-mag.com
Publisher: MB Media Ltd
Frequency: Monthly
Cover Price: £3.50
Circulation: 15,000 (Print Run)
Usual Pagination: 122
Editor: Samantha Slater
Summary of Content: Magazine covering drums and percussion featuring interviews with international players, product reviews and news.
Readership/Target Audience: Aimed at the young aspiring drummer.
ADVERTISING RATES:
Full Page Colour £800.00
Agency Commission: 10%
Mechanical Data: Type Area: 277 x 190mm, Bleed Size: 303 x 216mm, Trim Size: 297 x 210mm, Col Length: 277mm, Page Width: 190mm, Film: Digital
Copy instructions: Copy Date: 2 weeks prior to publication date
Average advertising content per issue: 40%
CONSUMER: MUSIC & PERFORMING ARTS: Music

DURHAM NEWSLINK
1657038U87-2040
Formerly: Durham Network
Editorial Address: St. Luke's Vicarage, 5 Tunstall Avenue, HARTLEPOOL, TS26 8NF **Tel:** 01429 293111
Fax: 01429 293111
Email: durham.newslink@durham.anglican.org
Web site: http://www.durhamnewslink.org.uk
Publisher: The Diocese of Durham
Date Established: 1993
Frequency: 6 issues yearly
Cover Price: Free
Circulation: 24,000 (Publisher's Statement)
Usual Pagination: 12
Editor: Paul Judson
Summary of Content: Newspaper covering the news and views of the Diocese of Durham, the north-east region of the Church of England.
Readership/Target Audience: Aimed at church-goers and local communities.
CONSUMER: RELIGIOUS

DUSTED
47381U83-7_4
Formerly: Eclipse
Editorial Address: Students Union, University of Derby, Kedleston Road, DERBY, DE22 1GB **Tel:** 01332 591515
Fax: 01332 591501
Email: dusted@udsu.co.uk
Advertising Address: As above. **Tel:** 01332 591507
Email: alex.young@udsu.co.uk
Web site: http://www.udsu.co.uk
Publisher: UDSU
Date Established: 2001
Frequency: 9 issues yearly - Published during term time
Cover Price: Free
Circulation: 4,000 (Publisher's Statement)
Usual Pagination: 40
Advertising Manager: Alex Young
Summary of Content: Publication including features on music, film, art, literature, theatre, news and current affairs

as well as reports from clubs and societies and sports results.
Readership/Target Audience: Read by students of the University of Derby.
ADVERTISING RATES:
Full Page Colour £300.00
Agency Commission: 10%
Mechanical Data: Bleed Size: +5mm, Type Area: 245 x 170mm, Col Length: 245mm, Page Width: 170mm
Copy instructions: Copy Date: 10 days prior to publication date
Average advertising content per issue: 10%
CONSUMER: STUDENT PUBLICATIONS

DV8 MAGAZINE BOURNEMOUTH

48082U89C-129_50

Formerly: DV8 Magazine
Editorial Address: 28 Poole Hill, BOURNEMOUTH, BH2 5PS **Tel:** 01202 388388 **Fax:** 01202 250869
Email: vicki@dv8online.co.uk
Advertising Address: As above.
Email: sales@dv8online.co.uk
Web site: http://www.dv8online.co.uk
Publisher: DV8 Publications Ltd
Date Established: 1996
Frequency: Monthly
Cover Price: Free
Circulation: 15,000 (Publisher's Statement)
Usual Pagination: 48
Editor: Victoria Vinton; **Managing Director:** Matthew Churcher; **Advertising Manager:** Carla Summers
Summary of Content: Cultural lifestyle magazine covering events, cinema, celebrity interviews, pubs, clubs and music.
Readership/Target Audience: Aimed at 18 to 35 year olds.
ADVERTISING RATES:
Full Page Colour £600.00
Agency Commission: 10%
Mechanical Data: Bleed Size: 303 x 216mm, Trim Size: 297 x 210mm, Film: Digital
Copy instructions: Copy Date: 23rd of the month prior to publication date
Average advertising content per issue: 40%
Editions:
DV8 Guide Portsmouth
DV8 Guides Bath
DV8 Guides Bristol
DV8 Guides Exeter
DV8 Guides Guildford
DV8 Guides London
DV8 Guides Manchester
DV8 Guides Oxford
DV8 Guides Reading
DV8 Guides Winchester
DV8 Magazine Southampton
CONSUMER: HOLIDAYS & TRAVEL: Entertainment Guides

DVD & BLU-RAY REVIEW

601415U78B-64

Formerly: DVD Review
Editorial Address: 2 Balcombe Street, LONDON, NW1 6NW **Tel:** 020 7042 4000 **Fax:** 020 7042 4389
Email: alastair.upham@futurenet.com
Advertising Address: As above. **Fax:** 020 7042 4471
Email: rob.dean@futurenet.com
Publisher: Future Publishing Limited
Frequency: 13 issues yearly
Cover Price: £3.99
Annual Sub.: £34.99
Circulation: 21,378 (ABC 01/01/2007 to 31/12/2007)
Usual Pagination: 156
Editor: Alastair Upham; **Advertising Manager:** Rob Dean
Summary of Content: Magazine covering news, reviews and features on the latest film, TV and music DVDs in the UK & US and the latest hardware.
Readership/Target Audience: Aimed at DVD and film enthusiasts.
ADVERTISING RATES:
Full Page Colour £3910.00
Agency Commission: 10%
Mechanical Data: Type Area: 280 x 203mm, Bleed Size: 306 x 228mm, Trim Size: 300 x 222mm, Col Length: 280mm, Page Width: 203mm, Film: Digital
Average advertising content per issue: 30%
CONSUMER: CONSUMER ELECTRONICS: Video & DVD

DVD MAKER

1785446U78B-661

Editorial Address: 3 East Avenue, BOURNEMOUTH, BH3 7BW **Tel:** 01202 317557
Email: johntaylor01@aol.com
Advertising Address: Uncooked Media Ltd, B10 Arena Business Centre, Holyrood Close, POOLE, BH17 7BA **Tel:** 01202 606385 **Fax:** 01202 606386
Email: ella@uncookedmedia.com
Publisher: Taylor Made Publishing
Date Established: 2006
Frequency: Quarterly
Cover Price: £4.99

Circulation: 12,000 (Publisher's Statement)
Usual Pagination: 116
Editor: John Taylor
Summary of Content: Magazine with tips and advice on how to use, produce and copy DVDs.
Readership/Target Audience: Aimed at those interested in DVDs, videos and PVRs.
ADVERTISING RATES:
Full Page Colour £2940.00
Agency Commission: 10%
CONSUMER: CONSUMER ELECTRONICS: Video & DVD

DVD MONTHLY

624125U78B-62

Editorial Address: Suite 1, 47 Marsh Green Road West, Marsh Barton Trading Estate, EXETER, EX2 8PN **Tel:** 01392 253755 **Fax:** 01392 434477
Email: timissac@dvd-monthly.co.uk
Advertising Address: The Old School, Higher Kinnerton, CHESTER, CH4 9AJ **Tel:** 01244 663400
Email: advertising@dvd-monthly.co.uk
Web site: http://www.dvd-monthly.co.uk
ISSN: 1469-6916
Publisher: Jazz Publishing
Date Established: 2000
Frequency: 13 issues yearly
Cover Price: £3.85
Annual Sub.: £25.00
Circulation: 30,000 (Publisher's Statement)
Usual Pagination: 132
Editor: Tim Isaac
Summary of Content: Magazine covering news, reviews, gossip, movie listings and previews of the latest home cinema and DVD releases and hardware.
Readership/Target Audience: Aimed at 22 to 40 year old enthusiasts of new technology and home cinema.
ADVERTISING RATES:
Full Page Colour £2295.00
Agency Commission: 10%
Mechanical Data: Type Area: 287 x 200mm, Trim Size: 297 x 210mm, Bleed Size: 303 x 216mm, Film: Digital, Col Length: 287mm, Page Width: 200mm
Copy instructions: Copy Date: 2 weeks prior to publication date
Average advertising content per issue: 10%
CONSUMER: CONSUMER ELECTRONICS: Video & DVD

DVD WORLD

1743100U76A-194

Editorial Address: UKD House, Norstead Place, LONDON, SW15 3SA **Tel:** 020 8246 5900 **Fax:** 020 8246 5920
Email: dvdworld@flipmediauk.com
Advertising Address: As above. **Tel:** 020 7689 3916
Publisher: Fire Publishing
Frequency: Monthly
Cover Price: £4.99
Circulation: 20,000 (Publisher's Statement)
Usual Pagination: 100
Editor: Allan Bryce; **Managing Director:** John Wreaves; **Advertising Manager:** Neville King
Summary of Content: Magazine with news, reviews and features on DVDs and new and cult films covering sex and horror.
Readership/Target Audience: Aimed at fans of the genre generally aged between 20 and 40 years old.
ADVERTISING RATES:
Full Page Colour £1905.00
Agency Commission: 10%
Mechanical Data: Type Area: 266 x 181mm, Bleed Size: 307 x 215mm, Trim Size: 297 x 210mm, Col Length: 266mm, Page Width: 181mm, Film: Digital
Copy instructions: Copy Date: 3 weeks prior to publication date
Average advertising content per issue: 33%
CONSUMER: MUSIC & PERFORMING ARTS: Cinema

DZIENNIK POLSKI

48298U90-48_50

Editorial Address: 63 Jeddo Road, LONDON, W12 9ED **Tel:** 020 8740 1991 **Fax:** 020 8746 1661
Email: dziennik@dziennikpolski.co.uk
Advertising Address: As above.
Email: ads@dziennikpolski.co.uk
Web site: http://www.dziennikpolski.co.uk
ISSN: 1359-2718
Publisher: The Polish Daily (Publishers) Ltd
Date Established: 1940
Frequency: 260 issues yearly
Cover Price: £0.70
Circulation: 6,000 (Publisher's Statement)
Usual Pagination: 12
Editor: Jaroslaw Kozminski; **Advertising Manager:** Karola Chanerley
Summary of Content: Newspaper covering news and events in Poland and the rest of the world as well as Polish ex-servicemen issues and Polish presence in British social and cultural life.
Language(s): English; Polish

Readership/Target Audience: Aimed at the Polish community in the UK.
ADVERTISING RATES:
Full Page Mono £720.00
Full Page Colour £864.00
Agency Commission: 10%
Mechanical Data: Type Area: 340 x 255mm, Col Length: 340mm, Trim Size: 356 x 290mm, No. of Columns (Display): 5, Col Width (Display): 255mm, Col Widths (Display): 50mm, Film: Digital
Copy instructions: Copy Date: Tuesday prior to publication date
CONSUMER: ETHNIC

EARLY MUSIC

46145U76D-316

Editorial Address: Faculty of Music, University of Cambridge, 11 West Road, CAMBRIDGE, CB3 9DP **Tel:** 01223 335178 **Fax:** 01223 335178
Email: earlymusic@oxfordjournals.org
Advertising Address: Rose Cottage, Brigg Road, South Kelsey, MARKET RASEN, LN7 6PQ **Tel:** 01652 678230 **Fax:** 01652 678230
Email: em.adverts@btopenworld.com
Web site: http://www.oup.co.uk/jnls
ISSN: 0306-1078
Publisher: OUP
Date Established: 1973
Frequency: Quarterly
Annual Sub.: £47.00
Circulation: 3,500 (Publisher's Statement)
Usual Pagination: 180
Editor: Tess Knighton; **Advertising Manager:** Jane Beeson
Summary of Content: Journal about medieval, renaissance, baroque and pre-classical music.
Readership/Target Audience: Read by amateurs, students and performers.
ADVERTISING RATES:
Full Page Mono £460.00
Full Page Colour £875.00
Agency Commission: 10%
Mechanical Data: Bleed Size: 252 x 195mm, No. of Columns (Display): 3, Type Area: 200 x 152mm, Col Length: 200mm, Trim Size: 246 x 189mm, Film: Digital, Col Widths (Display): 47mm, Page Width: 152mm
Copy instructions: Copy Date: 1st of the month prior to publication month
CONSUMER: MUSIC & PERFORMING ARTS: Music

EARLY MUSIC PERFORMER

767407U76D-756

Editorial Address: Scout Bottom Farm, Mytholmroyd, HEBDEN BRIDGE, HX7 5JS **Tel:** 01422 882751 **Fax:** 01422 886157
Email: earlymusicperformer@recordermail.demon.co.uk
Advertising Address: As above.
Email: ian@recordermail.demon.co.uk
ISSN: 0967-6619
Publisher: Ruxbury Publications
Frequency: Half-yearly - Published in January and August
Annual Sub.: £14.00
Circulation: 700 (Publisher's Statement)
Usual Pagination: 40
Editor: Jeremy Burbidge; **Advertising Manager:** Ian Davies; **Publisher:** Jeremy Burbidge
Summary of Content: Magazine covering news and features on medieval, baroque, renaissance and pre-classical music.
Readership/Target Audience: Aimed at amateurs, students and performers and members of the National Early Music Association.
ADVERTISING RATES:
Full Page Mono £125.00
Agency Commission: 10%
Mechanical Data: Type Area: 264 x 177mm, Col Length: 264mm, Trim Size: 297 x 210mm, Page Width: 177mm
CONSUMER: MUSIC & PERFORMING ARTS: Music

EARLY MUSIC TODAY

46147U76D-316_50

Editorial Address: 241 Shaftesbury Avenue, LONDON, WC2H 8TF **Tel:** 020 7333 1744 **Fax:** 020 7333 1769
Email: emt@rhinegold.co.uk
Advertising Address: As above. **Fax:** 020 7333 1736
Email: elinor.morgan@rhinegold.co.uk
Web site: http://www.rhinegold.co.uk
Publisher: Rhinegold Publishing Ltd
Date Established: 1993
Frequency: 6 issues yearly
Cover Price: £3.75
Circulation: 9,000 (Publisher's Statement)
Usual Pagination: 36
Editor: Jonathan Wikeley; **Advertising Manager:** Elinor Morgan
Summary of Content: Magazine containing news and features on the early music scene.
Readership/Target Audience: Aimed at all those involved in the performance, promotion, study and enjoyment of early music.

ADVERTISING RATES:
Full Page Mono £975.00
Full Page Colour £1575.00
Agency Commission: 10%
Mechanical Data: Film: Digital
CONSUMER: MUSIC & PERFORMING ARTS: Music

EARLY TIMES LANCASHIRE   1789976U74D-648
Editorial Address: 12 Roche Gardens, Cheadle Hulme, CHEADLE, SK8 7QT **Tel:** 0161 439 4694
Fax: 0161 439 4694
Email: belinda.etl@ntlworld.com
Advertising Address: As above.
Email: belinda.etl@ntlworld.com
Publisher: It's Manchester Ltd
Date Established: 2006
Frequency: 3 issues yearly - Published in February, June and October
Cover Price: Free
Circulation: 15,000 (Publisher's Statement)
Usual Pagination: 24
Editor: Belinda Harman-Craddock; **Advertising Manager:** Belinda Harman-Craddock
Summary of Content: Magazine covering health issues and family matters with a what's on and where to go guide.
Readership/Target Audience: Aimed at parents of children aged 0 to 4 years old.
ADVERTISING RATES:
Full Page Colour £800.00
Agency Commission: 10%
Mechanical Data: Type Area: 273 x 184mm, Col Length: 273mm, Page Width: 184mm, Film: Digital
Copy instructions: Copy Date: 3 weeks prior to publication date
Average advertising content per issue: 40%
CONSUMER: WOMEN'S INTEREST CONSUMER MAGAZINES: Child Care

EAST ANGLIAN DAILY TIMES SUFFOLK
                                        1639599U80C-5078
Editorial Address: Press House, 30 Lower Brook Street, IPSWICH, IP4 1AN **Tel:** 01473 324763 **Fax:** 01473 324628
Email: suffolkmagazine@archant.co.uk
Advertising Address: As above. **Tel:** 01473 230023
Email: alison.lynch@archant.co.uk
Web site: http://www.suffolkmagazine.co.uk
Publisher: Archant Suffolk
Date Established: 2000
Frequency: Monthly
Cover Price: £2.95
Annual Sub.: £34.00
Circulation: 13,000 (Print Run)
Usual Pagination: 188
Editor: Richard Bryson; **Advertising Manager:** Alison Lynch; **Publisher:** Richard Bryson
Summary of Content: Magazine covering fashion, interiors, food, gardening, health and beauty, travel, motoring, antiques, education, books, local events, hotels, restaurants and property.
Readership/Target Audience: Aimed at those living and working in Suffolk.
ADVERTISING RATES:
Full Page Colour £1300.00
Agency Commission: 10%
Mechanical Data: Bleed Size: 306 x 226mm, Type Area: 271 x 199mm, Film: Digital, Col Length: 271mm, Page Width: 199mm
Copy instructions: Copy Date: 3 weeks prior to publication date
CONSUMER: RURAL & REGIONAL INTEREST: Regional Interest English Counties

EAST CAMBRIDGESHIRE MAGAZINE
                                        1696589U80C-5328
Formerly: ECDC
Editorial Address: The Grange, Nutholt Lane, ELY, CB7 4PL
Tel: 01353 665555 **Fax:** 01353 665240
Email: tony.taylorson@cambridgeshire.gov.uk
Advertising Address: 275 Newmarket Road, CAMBRIDGE, CB5 8JE **Tel:** 01223 477411 **Fax:** 01223 327356
Email: marc@cpl.biz
Web site: http://www.eastcambs.gov.uk
Publisher: CPL Ltd
Date Established: 2007
Frequency: Quarterly
Cover Price: Free
Circulation: 33,500 (Publisher's Statement)
Editor: Tony Taylorson
Summary of Content: Magazine covering community information from environmental health and planning issues to local development schemes.
Readership/Target Audience: Aimed at households in East Cambridgeshire as well as public libraries, press, radio and local authority offices.
ADVERTISING RATES:
Full Page Colour £1500.00

Agency Commission: 10%
Mechanical Data: Type Area: 277 x 190mm, Bleed Size: 305 x 218mm, Trim Size: 297 x 210mm, Col Length: 277mm, Page Width: 190mm, Film: Digital
Copy instructions: Copy Date: 2 weeks prior to publication date
Average advertising content per issue: 30%
CONSUMER: RURAL & REGIONAL INTEREST: Regional Interest English Counties

EAST EIGHT   1834302U80B-430
Editorial Address: 39 Bocking Street, LONDON, E8 3GL
Tel: 020 8144 8588
Email: andrew@easteight.com
Advertising Address: As above.
Web site: http://www.easteight.com
Publisher: Creative Juices Ltd
Date Established: 2006
Frequency: Monthly
Cover Price: Free
Circulation: 15,000 (Publisher's Statement)
Usual Pagination: 24
Editor: Andrew Boff
Summary of Content: Magazine covering local news, events, listings, arts, culture, politics, clubs, pubs and restaurants.
Language(s): English; Turkish
Readership/Target Audience: Aimed at households in Hackney.
CONSUMER: RURAL & REGIONAL INTEREST: Regional Interest Greater London

EAST END NEWS   1824606U80E-377
Editorial Address: For all contact details see main edition, Southside News
Frequency: Monthly
Cover Price: Free
Circulation: 20,000 (Publisher's Statement)
Edition of: Southside News
CONSUMER: RURAL & REGIONAL INTEREST: Regional Interest Scotland

EAST LOTHIAN LIFE   47043U80E-40
Editorial Address: 1 Beveridge Row, Belhaven, DUNBAR, EH42 1TP **Tel:** 01368 863593 **Fax:** 01368 863593
Email: info@eastlothianlife.co.uk
Advertising Address: As above.
Email: info@eastlothianlife.co.uk
Web site: http://www.eastlothianlife.co.uk
Publisher: PJ Design
Date Established: 1989
Frequency: Quarterly
Cover Price: £2.50
Annual Sub.: £12.00
Circulation: 3,500 (Publisher's Statement)
Usual Pagination: 60
Editor: Pauline Jaffray; **Advertising Manager:** Pauline Jaffray
Summary of Content: County magazine containing features on property, fashion, books, food, sports, health and beauty, gardening and the arts.
Readership/Target Audience: Read by residents and those who have a connection with East Lothian.
ADVERTISING RATES:
Full Page Mono £550.00
Full Page Colour £795.00
SCC £10.00
Agency Commission: 10%
Mechanical Data: Col Length: 267mm, Type Area: 267 x 184mm, No. of Columns (Display): 3, Page Width: 184mm
Copy instructions: Copy Date: 6 weeks prior to publication date
Average advertising content per issue: 35%
CONSUMER: RURAL & REGIONAL INTEREST: Regional Interest Scotland

EAST WEEK   48345U90-156_20
Formerly: Sing Tao Weekly
Editorial Address: 1st Floor, Unit 3, Technology Park, Colindeep Lane, LONDON, NW9 6BX **Tel:** 020 8732 7601
Fax: 020 8732 7600
Email: editor@singtao.co.uk
Advertising Address: As above. **Tel:** 020 8732 7628
Fax: 020 8732 7630
Email: sales@singtao.co.uk
Web site: http://www.singtaoeu.com
Publisher: Sing Tao (UK) Ltd
Date Established: 1993
Frequency: Weekly
Cover Price: £1.50
Circulation: 50,000 (Publisher's Statement)
Usual Pagination: 90
Editor: Alego Poon

Summary of Content: Newspaper covering health and food, entertainment, law and finance with feature stories relating to Chinese communities in Europe.
Language(s): Chinese
Readership/Target Audience: Read by the Chinese community.
ADVERTISING RATES:
Full Page Colour £660.00
Agency Commission: 10%
Mechanical Data: Type Area: 260 x 205mm, Trim Size: 270 x 215mm, Page Width: 205mm, Col Length: 260mm, Bleed Size: 280 x 225mm, Film: Digital
Copy instructions: Copy Date: Monday prior to publication date
Average advertising content per issue: 30%
Supplement to: Sing Tao Daily (European Edition)
CONSUMER: ETHNIC

EASTERN ART REPORT   47498U84A-220
Editorial Address: PO Box 13666, LONDON, SW14 8WF
Tel: 020 8392 1122 **Fax:** 020 8392 1422
Email: ear@eapgroup.com
Advertising Address: As above.
Email: sales@eapgroup.com
Web site: http://www.eapgroup.com
ISSN: 0269-8404
Publisher: EAPGroup International Media
Date Established: 1989
Frequency: Quarterly
Cover Price: £6.00
Free to qualifying individuals
Annual Sub.: £30.00
Circulation: 14,600 (Publisher's Statement)
Usual Pagination: 64
Editor: Sajid Rizvi; **Advertising Manager:** Sajid Rizvi;
Publisher: Sajid Rizvi
Summary of Content: Magazine covering the traditional and contemporary arts of Asia, Africa, Oceania and the multi-cultural scene in Europe and North America.
Language(s): Chinese; English; Japanese; Korean
Readership/Target Audience: Aimed at private and institutional collectors, dealers, auction houses, museums, art schools and galleries.
ADVERTISING RATES:
Full Page Mono £1450.00
Full Page Colour £2450.00
Agency Commission: 10%
Mechanical Data: Col Length: 267mm, Page Width: 175mm, Type Area: 267 x 175mm, Bleed Size: 303 x 216mm, Trim Size: 297 x 210mm, Film: Digital, Print Process: Offset litho
Copy instructions: Copy Date: 1 month prior to publication date
CONSUMER: THE ARTS & LITERARY: Arts

EASTERN DAILY PRESS NORFOLK MAGAZINE   46944U80C-2300
Editorial Address: Prospect House, Rouen Road, NORWICH, NR1 1RE **Tel:** 01603 772321 **Fax:** 01603 615343
Email: nancy.wedge@archant.co.uk
Advertising Address: As above. **Tel:** 01603 628311
Email: enquiry@archant.co.uk
Web site: http://www.edp24.co.uk/edpnorfolk
Publisher: Archant Norfolk
Date Established: 1998
Frequency: Monthly - Published the last Thursday of the month prior to cover date
Cover Price: £2.95
Circulation: 11,035 (ABC 01/01/2008 to 31/12/2008)
Usual Pagination: 144
Editor: Nancy Wedge; **Advertising Manager:** Mel Secker
Summary of Content: Lifestyle magazine covering specifically Norfolk food, fashion, interiors, property, gardening, the countryside, places to visit, eating out and topical issues.
Readership/Target Audience: Aimed at those who live, work and holiday in Norfolk.
ADVERTISING RATES:
Full Page Mono £1586.00
Full Page Colour £1586.00
Agency Commission: 10%
Mechanical Data: Trim Size: 300 x 220mm, Film: Digital, Bleed Size: 306 x 226mm
Copy instructions: Copy Date: 4 weeks prior to publication date
Average advertising content per issue: 40%
Supplement(s): Eastern Daily Press Norfolk Magazine Men's - 2xY
CONSUMER: RURAL & REGIONAL INTEREST: Regional Interest English Counties

EASTERN EYE   48299U90-49_5
Editorial Address: Unit 2, Whitechapel Technology Centre, 65 Whitechapel Road, LONDON, E1 1DU
Tel: 020 7650 2000 **Fax:** 020 7650 2001
Email: editor@easterneyeuk.co.uk
Advertising Address: As above. **Fax:** 020 7650 2002

Consumer Magazines

Email: dean@ethnicmedia.co.uk
Web site: http://www.easterneyeonline.co.uk
ISSN: 0965-464X
Publisher: Ethnic Media Group
Date Established: 1989
Frequency: Weekly
Cover Price: £0.70
Circulation: 20,844 (Publisher's Statement)
Usual Pagination: 52
Editor: Hamant Verma; **Publisher:** Wayne Bower
Summary of Content: Newspaper covering general news and features including Bollywood, entertainment listings, TV listings, fashion and music.
Readership/Target Audience: Aimed at second and third generation Asians living in the UK aged between 16 and 40 years old.
ADVERTISING RATES:
Full Page Mono £4556.00
Full Page Colour £5467.20
Agency Commission: 10%
Mechanical Data: Type Area: 340 x 260mm, Film: Digital, Col Length: 340mm, Page Width: 260mm
Average advertising content per issue: 40%
Editions:
Eastern Eye Scotland
Supplement(s): e-guide - 52xY
CONSUMER: ETHNIC

EASY LIVING
1647088U74A-968

Editorial Address: 6-8 Old Bond Street, LONDON, W1S 4PH **Tel:** 020 7499 9080 **Fax:** 020 7399 2625
Email: easylivingeditorial@condenast.co.uk
Advertising Address: As above. **Tel:** 020 7399 2659
Fax: 020 7399 2651
Email: jane.white@condenast.co.uk
Web site: http://www.easylivingmagazine.com
Publisher: Conde Nast Publications Ltd
Date Established: 2005
Frequency: Monthly
Cover Price: £2.80
Circulation: 180,034 (ABC 01/01/2009 to 30/06/2009)
Editor: Susie Forbes; **Advertising Manager:** Charlotte Joly;
Managing Editor: Cameron Alexander; **Publisher:** Chris Hughes
Summary of Content: Magazine covering fashion, food, relationships, home, film, arts, health and beauty. Twitter: https://twitter.com/condenast.
Readership/Target Audience: Aimed at women aged between 30 and 59 years old.
ADVERTISING RATES:
Full Page Colour £13320.00
Agency Commission: 15%
Mechanical Data: Type Area: 256 x 193mm, Bleed Size: 283 x 219mm, Trim Size: 276 x 213mm, Col Length: 256mm, Page Width: 193mm, Print Process: Web offset, Film: Digital
Copy instructions: Copy Date: 2 months prior to publication date
Average advertising content per issue: 40%
CONSUMER: WOMEN'S INTEREST CONSUMER MAGAZINES: Women's Interest

---

EASY PEAZY
1832651U91D-975

Editorial Address: Headley House, Headley Road, Grayshott, HINDHEAD, GU26 6TU **Tel:** 01428 601020
Fax: 01428 601027
Email: easypeazy@signaturepl.co.uk
Advertising Address: As above.
Email: abi@djmurphy.co.uk
Publisher: Signature Publishing Ltd
Frequency: Monthly
Cover Price: £2.99
Circulation: 50,000 (Print Run)
Editor: Amanda Clifford; **Advertising Manager:** Abigail Cannon
Summary of Content: Craft magazine with projects to make or cook as well as stories, colouring. activities and cover-mounts.
Readership/Target Audience: Aimed at girls aged 5 to 9 years old.
ADVERTISING RATES:
Full Page Colour £1650.00
CONSUMER: RECREATION & LEISURE: Children & Youth

EASYJET INFLIGHT
48201U89D-67

Editorial Address: 141-143 Shoreditch High Street, LONDON, E1 6JE **Tel:** 020 7613 6947 **Fax:** 020 7613 8776
Email: editorial@easyflight.com
Advertising Address: As above. **Tel:** 020 7613 8777
Fax: 0845 280 9898
Email: tara.brady@ink-publishing.com
Web site: http://www.ink-publishing.com
Publisher: Ink Publishing
Date Established: 1997
Frequency: Monthly
Cover Price: Free
Circulation: 280,000 (Publisher's Statement)

Usual Pagination: 196
Editor: Piers Townley; **Editor-in-Chief:** Michael Keating
Summary of Content: In-flight magazine containing celebrity interviews, music, fashion, humour, lifestyle, health and beauty, property and business.
Readership/Target Audience: Read by easyJet passengers.
ADVERTISING RATES:
Full Page Colour £12046.00
Agency Commission: 10%
Mechanical Data: Trim Size: 297 x 210mm, Film: Digital
Copy instructions: Copy Date: 7th of the month prior to publication date
CONSUMER: HOLIDAYS & TRAVEL: In-Flight Magazines

EAT IN
1894796U74P-966

Editorial Address: 24-28 Oval Road, Camden, LONDON, NW1 7DT **Tel:** 020 7241 8000
Email: cookeryed@eatinmagazine.co.uk
Web site: http://www.eatinmagazine.co.uk
Publisher: H. Bauer Publishing
Date Established: 2009
Frequency: Monthly
Cover Price: £2.50
Circulation: 120,000 (Print Run)
Editor: Keith Kendrick; **Advertising Manager:** Jenny Murray
Summary of Content: Magazine offering food lovers inspiration on creating dishes, using quality, affordable and easily accessible ingredients.
Readership/Target Audience: Aimed at anyone and everyone who loves to cook.
CONSUMER: WOMEN'S INTEREST CONSUMER MAGAZINES: Food & Cookery

---

EATING OUT WEST
45674U74Q-200

Editorial Address: 2nd Floor, Bristol News & Media, Temple Way, BRISTOL, BS99 7HD **Tel:** 0117 942 8491
Fax: 0117 942 0369
Email: editor@venue.co.uk
Advertising Address: As above. **Fax:** 0117 934 3566
Email: sales@venue.co.uk
Web site: http://www.venue.co.uk
Publisher: Venue Publishing
Date Established: 1982
Frequency: Annual - Published in April
Cover Price: £4.95
Free to qualifying individuals
Circulation: 25,000 (Publisher's Statement)
Usual Pagination: 350
Editor: David Higgitt; **Group Editor:** David Higgitt
Summary of Content: Guide to the region's restaurants, bars and cafes, plus top takeaways, best delicatessens and specialist food shops.
Readership/Target Audience: Aimed at those interested in food and dining out.
ADVERTISING RATES:
Full Page Colour £1200.00
Agency Commission: 10%
Mechanical Data: Film: Digital, Page Width: 184mm, Type Area: 273 x 184mm, Bleed Size: 301 x 214mm, Trim Size: 297 x 210mm, Col Length: 273mm
Copy instructions: Copy Date: April 3rd
Supplement to: Venue
CONSUMER: WOMEN'S INTEREST CONSUMER MAGAZINES: Lifestyle

THE ECHO
1732058U80C-5316

Editorial Address: 351 Lichfield Road, Aston, BIRMINGHAM, B6 7ST **Tel:** 0121 326 7755
Fax: 0121 328 3806
Email: excelprinting@btconnect.com
Advertising Address: As above. **Fax:** 0121 326 3489
Email: excelprinting@btconnect.com
Publisher: Excel Printing Ltd
Frequency: Monthly
Cover Price: Free
Circulation: 58,500 (Publisher's Statement)
Editor: Rebecca Weston
Summary of Content: Community magazine covering local news, information and events as well as health, beauty, sport and motoring.
Readership/Target Audience: Aimed at households in the Birmingham area.
ADVERTISING: Rates on application
Mechanical Data: Type Area: 230 x 155mm, Col Length: 230mm, Page Width: 155mm, Film: Digital
Editions:
The Echo
The Echo Castle Bromwich
The Echo Coleshill
The Echo Mergreen
The Echo Warmley
CONSUMER: RURAL & REGIONAL INTEREST: Regional Interest English Counties

---

ECHOES
46226U76E-90

Editorial Address: 100 Dunstans Road, LONDON, SE22 0HE **Tel:** 020 8299 8846
Email: echoesmag@btconnect.com
Advertising Address: 68 King James Way, ROYSTON, SG8 7EF **Tel:** 01763 244366 **Fax:** 01763 244366
Email: advertising@echoesmagazine.co.uk
Web site: http://www.echoesmagazine.co.uk
Publisher: NBM Ltd
Date Established: 1976
Frequency: Monthly
Cover Price: £2.95
Circulation: 25,000 (Publisher's Statement)
Usual Pagination: 64
Editor: Chris Wells; **Advertisement Director:** Paul Phillips
Summary of Content: Magazine focusing on soul, r'n'b, jazz, reggae and hip hop music. Contains album reviews and interviews.
Readership/Target Audience: Read by 17 to 55 year olds.
ADVERTISING RATES:
Full Page Mono £850.00
Full Page Colour £1500.00
Agency Commission: 10%
Mechanical Data: Bleed Size: 303 x 216mm, Type Area: 273 x 185mm, Col Length: 273mm, Page Width: 185mm, Film: Digital, Trim Size: 297 x 210mm
Copy instructions: Copy Date: 10 days prior to publication date
Average advertising content per issue: 35%
CONSUMER: MUSIC & PERFORMING ARTS: Pop Music

ECOIDEAS
1865035U74A-1058

Editorial Address: 20 Portland Square, BRISTOL, BS2 8SJ **Tel:** 0117 230 8844
Email: jen@figure8media.com
Web site: http://www.ecoideasmagazine.com
Publisher: Figure 8 Media
Frequency: Quarterly
Cover Price: £2.80
Free to qualifying individuals
Annual Sub.: £10.00
Circulation: 10,000 (Publisher's Statement)
Editor: Jen Dallison
Summary of Content: Magazine covering health and beauty, travel, house and garden, fairtrade issues, ecoliving with a green and ethical twist.
Readership/Target Audience: Aimed at women aged between 25 and 45.
CONSUMER: WOMEN'S INTEREST CONSUMER MAGAZINES: Women's Interest

---

THE ECONOMIST
45147U73-90

Editorial Address: 25 St. James's Street, LONDON, SW1A 1HG **Tel:** 020 7830 7000 **Fax:** 020 7839 2968
Email: pressreleases@economist.com
Advertising Address: As above. **Fax:** 020 7839 4104
Email: davidweeks@economist.com
Web site: http://www.economist.com
ISSN: 0013-0613
Publisher: The Economist Newspaper Ltd
Date Established: 1843
Frequency: Weekly
Cover Price: £3.90
Annual Sub.: £86.00
Circulation: 187,341 (ABC 01/01/2009 to 30/06/2009)
Usual Pagination: 140
Executive Editor: Daniel Franklin; **Editor-in-Chief:** John Micklethwait; **Managing Editor:** Adrian Wooldridge;
Advertisement Director: David Weeks
Summary of Content: News and business magazine covering timely reporting, concise commentary and comprehensive analysis of global news. With objective authority, clarity and wit, presenting the world's political, business scientific, technological and cultural affairs and the connections between them.
Twitter: https://twitter.com/TheEconomist.
Readership/Target Audience: Readership includes senior figures in the world of politics and business.
ADVERTISING RATES:
Full Page Mono £10400.00
Full Page Colour £18850.00
Agency Commission: 15%
Mechanical Data: Page Width: 180mm, Type Area: 240 x 180mm, Bleed Size: 273 x 209mm, Trim Size: 267 x 203mm, Col Length: 240mm, Film: Negative, wrong reading, emulsion side up. Digital, Print Process: Litho
Copy instructions: Copy Date: Monday prior to publication date
Average advertising content per issue: 40%
Supplement(s): Technology Quarterly - 4xY
CONSUMER: NATIONAL & INTERNATIONAL PERIODICALS

THE EDGE
761519U78B-80

Editorial Address: 65 Guinness Buildings, Hammersmith, LONDON, W6 8BD **Tel:** 0845 456 9337
Email: davec@theedge.abelgratis.co.uk

Advertising Address: As above.
Email: davec@theedge.abelgratis.co.uk
Web site: http://www.theedge.abelgratis.co.uk
ISSN: 0955-2316
Publisher: The Edge
Frequency: Quarterly
Cover Price: £4.00
Annual Sub.: £12.00
Circulation: 20,000 (Publisher's Statement)
Usual Pagination: 70
Editor: Dave Clark; **Advertising Manager:** Dave Clark
Summary of Content: Magazine covering book, film, video and DVD reviews and competitions. Includes interviews with writers and film makers and also features original fiction.
Readership/Target Audience: Aimed at men and women between 20 and 40 years old.
ADVERTISING RATES:
Full Page Mono £250.00
Mechanical Data: Trim Size: 297 x 210mm, Film: Digital
Copy instructions: Copy Date: 2 weeks prior to publication date
CONSUMER: CONSUMER ELECTRONICS: Video & DVD

EDGE
46530U78D-145

Editorial Address: 30 Monmouth Street, BATH, BA1 2BW
Tel: 01225 442244 **Fax:** 01225 732275
Advertising Address: As above. **Fax:** 01225 822885
Email: julian.house@futurenet.co.uk
Web site: http://www.edge-online.com
Publisher: Future Publishing Ltd
Date Established: 1993
Frequency: 13 issues yearly
Cover Price: £4.50
Circulation: 28,898 (ABC 01/07/2008 to 31/12/2008)
Usual Pagination: 132
Editor: Tony Mott; **Editor-in-Chief:** Tony Mott; **Publisher:** James Binns
Summary of Content: Magazine with previews and reviews on a limited number of games across all video gaming formats. Includes news on the latest technology and interviews with the creators of games.
Readership/Target Audience: Aimed at males over 25 years old.
ADVERTISING RATES:
Full Page Colour £3500.00
Agency Commission: 10%
Mechanical Data: Type Area: 255 x 215mm, Col Length: 255mm, Trim Size: 270 x 233mm, Bleed Size: 276 x 238mm, Film: Digital, Page Width: 215mm
Average advertising content per issue: 10%
CONSUMER: CONSUMER ELECTRONICS: Games

THE EDGE
625434U88D-31

Editorial Address: 54 Boileau Road, LONDON, SW13 9BL
Tel: 020 8741 7886
Email: sue@clas.co.uk
Web site: http://www.clas.co.uk
ISSN: 1358-6688
Publisher: The Calligraphy & Lettering Arts Society
Date Established: 1995
Frequency: 5 issues yearly
Annual Sub.: £25.00
Circulation: 2,000 (Publisher's Statement)
Usual Pagination: 24
Editor: Sue Cavendish
Summary of Content: Magazine covering all aspects of calligraphy and lettering from historical and medieval manuscripts to cutting edge, contemporary calligraphy and typography.
Readership/Target Audience: Aimed at artists, calligraphy and lettering enthusiasts.
ADVERTISING: No Advertising taken
CONSUMER: EDUCATION: Crafts

EDGES
47223U82-21

Editorial Address: St. Anne's House, France Street, BLACKBURN, BB2 1LX **Tel:** 01254 59240 **Fax:** 01254 56884
Email: edges@globalnet.co.uk
Web site: http://www.users.globalnet.co.uk/~edges/online/index.htm
Publisher: THOMAS Publication
Frequency: Quarterly
Cover Price: Free
Circulation: 15,000 (Publisher's Statement)
Usual Pagination: 20
Editor: James McCartney
Summary of Content: Magazine focusing on all forms of marginalization. Contains articles and interviews with those who feel isolated from society.
Language(s): English; French; German; Italian; Portuguese; Spanish
Readership/Target Audience: Aimed at organisations who deal with problems around exclusion.
ADVERTISING: No Advertising taken
CONSUMER: CURRENT AFFAIRS & POLITICS

EDINBURGH STUDENT
47383U83-257

Editorial Address: 5-2 Bristo Square, EDINBURGH, EH8 9AL **Tel:** 0131 650 2363 **Fax:** 0131 684177
Email: editors@studentnewspaper.org
Advertising Address: As above. **Tel:** 0131 650 9189
Fax: 0131 668 4177
Email: tony.foster@eusa.ed.ac.uk
Web site: http://www.eusa.ed.ac.uk/advertising
Publisher: Edinburgh University Student Newspaper Society
Date Established: 1887
Frequency: 21 issues yearly - Published weekly during term time
Cover Price: Free
Circulation: 8,000 (Publisher's Statement)
Usual Pagination: 24
Editor: Tony Foster; **Advertising Manager:** Tony Foster
Summary of Content: Magazine containing news, interviews, reviews of films, music, books and the arts, plus a seven day TV guide and listing guide. Also covers fashion, sport and recruitment.
Readership/Target Audience: Aimed at all Edinburgh students.
ADVERTISING RATES:
Full Page Colour £1350.00
Agency Commission: 10%
Mechanical Data: Trim Size: 360 x 260mm, Film: Digital
Copy instructions: Copy Date: 1 week prior to publication date
Average advertising content per issue: 25%
CONSUMER: STUDENT PUBLICATIONS

EDITION
1789331U74Q-1341

Formerly: Editon
Editorial Address: 136-142 Bramley Road, LONDON, W10 6SR **Tel:** 020 7565 3000 **Fax:** 020 7565 3050
Advertising Address: As above.
Email: source@johnbrowngroup.co.uk
Publisher: John Brown Group
Date Established: 2006
Frequency: 5 issues yearly
Cover Price: Free
Circulation: 650,000 (Print Run)
Usual Pagination: 100
Editor: Kim Reeder; **Advertising Director:** Paul Laugeé
Summary of Content: Magazine covering theatre, arts, culture, celebrity features and interviews, topical debates, life and style including home, food, beauty, fashion and health, money property, travel, free time and shopping.
Readership/Target Audience: Aimed at customers of John Lewis and Waitrose stores.
ADVERTISING RATES:
Full Page Colour £15000.00
Agency Commission: 15%
Mechanical Data: Type Area: 258 x 202mm, Bleed Size: 284 x 228mm, Trim Size: 278 x 222mm, Col Length: 258mm, Page Width: 202mm, Film: Digital
Average advertising content per issue: 25%
CONSUMER: WOMEN'S INTEREST CONSUMER MAGAZINES: Lifestyle

EDITION MAGAZINE
1643462U74Q-1199

Editorial Address: PO Box 500, Happisburgh, NORWICH, NR12 0WX **Tel:** 01692 650847 **Fax:** 01692 651158
Email: office@edition-mag.co.uk
Advertising Address: As above.
Email: office@editionmagazine.co.uk
Web site: http://www.edition-mag.co.uk
Publisher: Edition Magazine Ltd
Frequency: Monthly
Cover Price: Free
Circulation: 120,000 (Publisher's Statement)
Usual Pagination: 36
Editor: Jo Stewart; **Features Editor:** Jo Stewart; **Advertising Manager:** Phil Stewart
Summary of Content: Lifestyle and entertainment magazine featuring competitions, interviews, features, music, TV, books, DVDs, theatre, computer games, home improvements and history.
Readership/Target Audience: Aimed at residents and visitors to Norfolk.
ADVERTISING RATES:
Full Page Colour £525.00
Mechanical Data: Type Area: 282 x 197mm, Col Length: 282mm, Page Width: 197mm, Film: Digital
Copy instructions: Copy Date: 3 weeks prior to publication date
CONSUMER: WOMEN'S INTEREST CONSUMER MAGAZINES: Lifestyle

EDUC8 MAGAZINE
1775928U74F-767

Editorial Address: Suite 3, Newspaper House, Brook Street, LEEK, ST13 5JE **Tel:** 01538 384400 **Fax:** 01538 384777
Email: news@m-storm.co.uk
Advertising Address: 2nd Floor, Newspaper House, Brook Street, LEEK, ST13 5JE **Tel:** 01538 384400
Fax: 01538 384777

Email: comms@m-storm.co.uk
Web site: http://www.m-storm.co.uk
Publisher: MediaStorm Publishing
Date Established: 2006
Frequency: 6 issues yearly - Published in first week of each school half term
Cover Price: Free
Circulation: 58,000 (Publisher's Statement)
Usual Pagination: 32
Editor: Joanne Hine; **Advertising Manager:** Fiona Hawkins
Summary of Content: Magazine covering schools news, careers advice, health and fitness, entertainment, fashion, what's on, new cinema and music releases, computer games, new technology and finance advice for kids as well as a parents section.
Readership/Target Audience: Aimed at 14 to 17 year olds in Staffordshire, Birmingham and West Midlands and distributed through schools.
ADVERTISING RATES:
Full Page Colour £1200.00
Agency Commission: 10%
Mechanical Data: Trim Size: 285 x 200mm, Film: Digital, Bleed Size: +3mm
Average advertising content per issue: 50%
Editions:
Educ8 Birmingham/West Midlands
Educ8 Staffordshire
CONSUMER: WOMEN'S INTEREST CONSUMER MAGAZINES: Teenage

EDUCATION NEWS
1923234U88A-237

Editorial Address: The Old School Room, 358 Old Birmingham Road, BIRMINGHAM, B45 8ES
Tel: 0121 445 0668 **Fax:** 0121 445 0654
Email: editor@mytvonline.com
Web site: http://www.educ8tv.co.uk
Publisher: My TV Online
Frequency: 8 issues yearly
Cover Price: Free
Editor: Gail Owen
Summary of Content: Magazine containing features and news stories about education.
Readership/Target Audience: Aimed at households in Birmingham.
CONSUMER: EDUCATION

EID UK
1628220U90-915

Editorial Address: Eton House, 66 Eton Avenue, WEMBLEY, HA0 3AU **Tel:** 0845 013 8401
Fax: 0845 013 8402
Email: amit@memediagroup.com
Advertising Address: As above.
Email: neena.kent@memediagroup.com
Web site: http://www.memediagroup.com
Publisher: ME Media Ltd
Frequency: Annual - Published in November
Cover Price: Free
Circulation: 50,000 (Publisher's Statement)
Editor: Amit Daryanani; **Advertising Manager:** Neena Kent
Summary of Content: Magazine with features on charities, events, Hajj, mosques, Islamic art and culture as well as interviews with prominent Muslims.
Readership/Target Audience: Aimed at Muslim communities in the UK.
ADVERTISING: Rates on application
CONSUMER: ETHNIC

ELECTRIC!
1827155U76C-839

Editorial Address: 7 St. Martin's Place, LONDON, WC2N 4HA **Tel:** 020 7747 0700 **Fax:** 020 7747 0700
Email: georgie.williams@redwoodgroup.net
Advertising Address: As above.
Email: michael.grace@redwoodgroup.net
Publisher: Redwood
Date Established: 2007
Frequency: Quarterly
Cover Price: Free
Circulation: 1,000,000 (Publisher's Statement)
Usual Pagination: 84
Editor: Mark Hooper; **Advertising Manager:** Michael Grace
Summary of Content: Magazine with features on the latest films, TV shows and music as well as information on Virgin Media services.
Readership/Target Audience: Aimed at Virgin Media customers.
ADVERTISING: Rates on application
Agency Commission: 10%
CONSUMER: MUSIC & PERFORMING ARTS: TV & Radio

ELECTRIC SHEEP
1831345U76A-213

Editorial Address: 6 Market Place, LONDON, W1W 8AF
Tel: 020 7436 9494
Email: thepuppetmaster@electricsheep.com
Advertising Address: As above.

Consumer Magazines

Email: saraifg@aol.com
Web site: http://www.electricsheepmagazine.com
Publisher: Wallflower Press
Date Established: 2007
Frequency: Quarterly
Cover Price: £3.25
Circulation: 10,000 (Publisher's Statement)
Usual Pagination: 68
Editor: Virginie Sélavy; **Advertising Manager:** Sara Tyler; **Publisher:** Yoram Allon
Summary of Content: Magazine covering cult cinema with reviews, news and features.
Readership/Target Audience: Aimed at those interested in cult films.
ADVERTISING RATES:
Full Page Colour £500.00
Agency Commission: 15%
Mechanical Data: Type Area: 220 x 170mm, Bleed Size: 246 x 196mm, Trim Size: 240 x 190mm, Col Length: 220mm, Page Width: 170mm, Film: Digital
CONSUMER: MUSIC & PERFORMING ARTS: Cinema

ELEGANCE MAGAZINE 1704768U80C-5391
Editorial Address: 1 Cardale Park, Beckwith Head Road, HARROGATE, HG3 1RZ **Tel:** 01423 564321
Fax: 01423 564228
Email: ackrill.news@ypn.co.uk
Advertising Address: As above. **Fax:** 01423 531431
Email: sarah.mcmillan@ypn.co.uk
Publisher: Ackrill Group Ltd
Date Established: 2005
Frequency: 8 issues yearly
Cover Price: Free
Circulation: 22,500 (Publisher's Statement)
Editor: Jean MacQuarrie
Summary of Content: Lifestyle magazine covering homes, gardens, women's and men's fashion, beauty and dining as well as local events, arts and entertainment.
Readership/Target Audience: Aimed at men and women with a high disposable income in Harrogate, Rippon, Knaresborough and surrounding areas.
ADVERTISING RATES:
Full Page Colour £750.00
SCC £5.25
Agency Commission: 10%
Mechanical Data: Type Area: 295 x 205mm, Col Length: 295mm, Page Width: 205mm, Film: Digital
CONSUMER: RURAL & REGIONAL INTEREST: Regional Interest English Counties

ELITE MAGAZINE 45173U74A-78
Editorial Address: Trehwbwb, St. Lythan's, CARDIFF, CF5 6BQ **Tel:** 029 2059 3310 **Fax:** 029 2059 3310
Advertising Address: As above.
Publisher: Elite Media Marketing
Date Established: 1993
Frequency: Quarterly
Cover Price: Free
Circulation: 25,000 (Publisher's Statement)
Usual Pagination: 56
Editor: Elizabeth Williams; **Managing Director:** Elizabeth Williams; **Advertising Manager:** Ian Goldsworthy
Summary of Content: Magazine containing fashion, beauty, home improvement and lifestyle features.
Readership/Target Audience: Aimed at women in South and West Wales.
ADVERTISING RATES:
Full Page Colour £1800.00
CONSUMER: WOMEN'S INTEREST CONSUMER MAGAZINES: Women's Interest

ELIXIR 1785628U74G-275
Editorial Address: 7 Munroe House, Lorne Close, LONDON, NW8 7JN **Tel:** 020 7569 8676
Email: editor@elixirnews.com
Advertising Address: Suite D211, Macmillan House, Paddington Station, LONDON, W2 1FT **Tel:** 020 7993 3300
Fax: 020 7706 2438
Email: ok@elixirpress.co.uk
Web site: http://www.elixirnews.com
ISSN: 1753-3864
Publisher: Elixir Magazine Ltd
Date Established: 2007
Frequency: Quarterly
Cover Price: £3.80
Circulation: 100,000 (Print Run)
Usual Pagination: 200
Editor: Avril O'Connor; **Advertising Manager:** Oskar Keysell
Summary of Content: Magazine covering everything anti-aging including aesthetics, cosmetics, cosmetic surgery, cosmetic dentistry, lifestyle, nutrition, exercise, complimentary medicine, spas, holidays, leisure, gadgets and pets.
Readership/Target Audience: Aimed at men and women aged over 30 years old with the ability to spend on anti-ageing products and services and lifestyle.

ADVERTISING RATES:
Full Page Colour £9950.00
Agency Commission: 10%
Mechanical Data: Type Area: 217 x 147mm, Bleed Size: 247 x 177mm, Trim Size: 237 x 167mm, Col Length: 217mm, Page Width: 147mm, Film: Digital
Copy instructions: Copy Date: 3 weeks prior to publication date
Average advertising content per issue: 35%
CONSUMER: WOMEN'S INTEREST CONSUMER MAGAZINES: Slimming & Health

ELLE 45174U74A-80
Editorial Address: 64 North Row, LONDON, W1K 7LL
Tel: 020 7150 7000 **Fax:** 020 7150 7670
Advertising Address: As above.
Email: jayne.ellis@hf-uk.com
Web site: http://www.elleuk.com
Publisher: Hachette Filipacchi (UK) Ltd
Date Established: 1985
Frequency: Monthly
Cover Price: £3.30
Circulation: 195,192 (ABC 01/01/2009 to 30/06/2009)
Usual Pagination: 300
Editor: Hannah Swerling; **Executive Editor:** Tom Macklin; **Editor-in-Chief:** Lorraine Candy; **Advertising Manager:** Jayne Ellis; **Managing Editor:** Andrew Falconer
Summary of Content: Magazine covering fashion, beauty, celebrities and health with articles on women's issues.
Twitter: https://twitter.com/elle_com.
Readership/Target Audience: Aimed at women between 18 and 26 years of age with high disposable incomes and a passion for shopping.
ADVERTISING RATES:
Full Page Colour £13125.00
Agency Commission: 15%
Mechanical Data: Type Area: 265 x 200mm, Bleed Size: 295 x 230mm, Trim Size: 285 x 220mm, Col Length: 265mm, Film: Digital, Page Width: 200mm
Copy instructions: Copy Date: 2 months prior to publication date
Average advertising content per issue: 45%
CONSUMER: WOMEN'S INTEREST CONSUMER MAGAZINES: Women's Interest

ELLE DECORATION 45250U74C-100
Editorial Address: 64 North Row, LONDON, W1K 7LL
Tel: 020 7150 7000 **Fax:** 020 7150 7671
Email: suzie.lockwood@hf-uk.com
Advertising Address: As above. **Fax:** 020 7150 7001
Email: chrisdaunt@hf-uk.com
Publisher: Hachette Filipacchi (UK) Ltd
Date Established: 1989
Frequency: Monthly
Annual Sub.: £38.40
Circulation: 58,020 (ABC 01/01/2009 to 30/06/2009)
Usual Pagination: 160
Editor: Suzie Lockwood; **Features Editor:** Amy Bradford; **Managing Editor:** Andrew Falconer; **Advertising Director:** Chris Daunt
Summary of Content: Magazine containing contemporary interior design and decorating ideas.
Twitter: https://twitter.com/elle_com.
Readership/Target Audience: Aimed at the discerning homemaker.
ADVERTISING RATES:
Full Page Colour £8020.00
Agency Commission: 10%
Mechanical Data: Col Length: 270mm, Page Width: 190mm, Trim Size: 297 x 210mm, Film: Digital, Type Area: 270 x 190mm
Average advertising content per issue: 40%
CONSUMER: WOMEN'S INTEREST CONSUMER MAGAZINES: Home & Family

THE ELMBRIDGE LIFESTYLE MAGAZINE
624201U80C-2950
Editorial Address: Unit A4, Kingsway Business Park, Oldfield Road, HAMPTON, TW12 2HD **Tel:** 020 8939 5600
Fax: 020 8939 5610
Email: editorial@sheengate.co.uk
Advertising Address: As above.
Email: elmbridge@sheengate.co.uk
Web site: http://www.elmbridgemagazine.co.uk
Publisher: Sheengate Publishing Ltd
Date Established: 2000
Frequency: Monthly
Cover Price: Free
Circulation: 40,000 (Publisher's Statement)
Usual Pagination: 64
Editor: Richard Nye; **Advertising Manager:** Cathy Woods
Summary of Content: Magazine containing mainly lifestyle and local interest articles and interviews, including features on history, fashion, theatre, art, health, education, shopping and property.

Readership/Target Audience: Aimed at households and businesses in the borough of Elmbridge.
ADVERTISING RATES:
Full Page Colour £1155.00
Agency Commission: 10%
Mechanical Data: Film: Digital, Type Area: 270 x 180mm, Bleed Size: 303 x 216mm, Trim Size: 297 x 210mm, Col Length: 270mm, Page Width: 180mm
Copy instructions: Copy Date: 2 weeks prior to publication date
Average advertising content per issue: 65%
CONSUMER: RURAL & REGIONAL INTEREST: Regional Interest English Counties

THE ELMBRIDGE REVIEW 46976U80C-3000
Editorial Address: Civic Centre, High Street, ESHER, KT10 9SD **Tel:** 01372 474391 **Fax:** 01372 474932
Email: communications@elmbridge.gov.uk
Web site: http://www.elmbridge.gov.uk
Publisher: Elmbridge Borough Council
Date Established: 1992
Frequency: Quarterly
Cover Price: Free
Circulation: 53,000 (Publisher's Statement)
Usual Pagination: 16
Editor: Michael Monk
Summary of Content: Magazine covering the services, activities and news of the Elmbridge Borough Council.
Readership/Target Audience: Read by borough residents.
ADVERTISING: No Advertising taken
CONSUMER: RURAL & REGIONAL INTEREST: Regional Interest English Counties

EMBODY 1924561U74G-308
Editorial Address: Richardson House, 21-24 New Street, WORCESTER, WR1 2DP **Tel:** 01905 723011
Fax: 01905 780103
Email: sharon@pw-media.co.uk
Advertising Address: As above. **Tel:** 01905 727900
Email: rachel@pw-media.co.uk
Web site: http://www.pw-media.co.uk/embody.html
Publisher: PW Media & Publishing Ltd
Frequency: Quarterly
Cover Price: £3.50
Circulation: 11,500 (Publisher's Statement)
Editor: Sharon Martin; **Advertising Manager:** Rachel Seabright
Summary of Content: Magazine of the Complementary Therapists Association.
Readership/Target Audience: Aimed at those involved in the complementary therapy industry including CThA members, students, academics, training schools, colleges and complementary therapists.
ADVERTISING RATES:
Full Page Colour £900.00
Mechanical Data: Trim Size: 297 x210mm
CONSUMER: WOMEN'S INTEREST CONSUMER MAGAZINES: Slimming & Health

EMBRACE 1645456U74Q-1185
Editorial Address: Mercury House, 7 Sheep Market, STAMFORD, PE9 2QZ **Tel:** 01780 762255
Fax: 01780 751371
Email: lisa.bruen@stamfordmercury.co.uk
Advertising Address: As above.
Email: sonja.allen@jpress.co.uk
Web site: http://www.embracemagazine.co.uk
ISSN: 1744-5914
Publisher: Johnston Press plc
Date Established: 2004
Frequency: Monthly
Cover Price: Free
Circulation: 6,000 (Publisher's Statement)
Usual Pagination: 44
Editor: Lisa Bruen; **News Editor:** Lisa Bruen
Summary of Content: Magazine covering arts, fashion, homes and gardens, people, lifestyle, books, cars and women's interests.
Readership/Target Audience: Aimed at men and women aged from 18 years old to retirement and beyond.
ADVERTISING RATES:
Full Page Colour £650.00
Mechanical Data: Trim Size: 297 x 210mm, Bleed Size: 307 x 220mm, Film: Digital
Supplement to: Rutland Times
CONSUMER: WOMEN'S INTEREST CONSUMER MAGAZINES: Lifestyle

EMBROIDERY 45376U74E-80
Editorial Address: Apartment 41, Hampton Court Palace, EAST MOLESEY, KT8 9AU **Tel:** 01260 373891
Email: jo.editor@btinternet.com
Advertising Address: Mongoose Media, 2 Lonsdale Road, LONDON, NW6 6RD **Tel:** 020 7306 0300
Fax: 020 8399 3060

Email: embroidersguild@mongoosemedia.com
Web site: http://www.embroiderersguild.com
ISSN: 1351-9603
Publisher: E.G. Enterprises Ltd
Date Established: 1932
Frequency: 6 issues yearly
Cover Price: £4.90
Annual Sub.: £29.40
Circulation: 6,500 (Publisher's Statement)
Usual Pagination: 64
Editor: Joanne Hall; **Advertising Manager:** Carly Brown
Summary of Content: Magazine covering articles on contemporary and world embroidery, textile art, plus information on history and techniques of embroidery.
Readership/Target Audience: Aimed at those interested in all aspects of creative stitched textile art, including tutors, students, artists, curators, professionals and amateurs.
ADVERTISING RATES:
Full Page Mono £545.00
Full Page Colour £990.00
SCC £6.50
Agency Commission: 10%
Mechanical Data: Col Length: 262mm, No. of Columns (Display): 2, Page Width: 180mm, Film: Digital, Type Area: 262 x 180mm, Print Process: Offset litho, Bleed Size: 303 x 216mm, Trim Size: 297 x 210mm
Copy instructions: Copy Date: 5 weeks prior to publication date
Average advertising content per issue: 40%
CONSUMER: WOMEN'S INTEREST CONSUMER MAGAZINES: Crafts

EMEL
1698861U90-975

Editorial Address: Barakat House, 116 Finchley Road, LONDON, NW3 5HT **Tel:** 020 7431 5300 **Fax:** 020 7431 5324
Email: info@emelmagazine.com
Advertising Address: As above.
Email: info@emelmagazine.com
Web site: http://www.emel.com
ISSN: 1741-542X
Publisher: Emel Media Ltd
Date Established: 2003
Frequency: Monthly
Cover Price: £3.50
Circulation: 20,000 (Publisher's Statement)
Usual Pagination: 132
Editor: Remona Aly; **Advertising Manager:** Mohsin Aboobakr
Summary of Content: Muslim lifestyle magazine covering culture, art, fashion, travel, interior design, gardens, travel, music, health, finance, sport and food.
Readership/Target Audience: Aimed at Muslim communities in the UK between 25 and 40 years old.
ADVERTISING RATES:
Full Page Colour £3500.00
Agency Commission: 10%
Mechanical Data: Type Area: 251 x 185mm, Bleed Size: 281 x 211mm, Trim Size: 275 x 205mm, Col Length: 251mm, Page Width: 185mm, Print Process: Web-fed offset litho, Film: Digital
Copy instructions: Copy Date: 1st Monday of the month prior to publication date
Average advertising content per issue: 20%
CONSUMER: ETHNIC

EMERALD RUGBY
1687242U75C-472

Editorial Address: 32 The Slopes, Portadown, Ballydougan, CRAIGAVON, BT63 5NT **Tel:** 028 3834 4333
Email: editor@emeraldrugby.com
Advertising Address: As above. **Fax:** 028 3834 3454
Email: emma@emeraldrugby.com
Web site: http://www.emeraldrugby.com
Publisher: EML Publishing
Date Established: 2003
Frequency: 10 issues yearly - Combined issue December/January
Cover Price: £2.60
Circulation: 14,000 (Publisher's Statement)
Usual Pagination: 64
Editor: Manus Lappin; **Advertising Manager:** Emma Lappin
Summary of Content: Magazine covering all aspects of Irish rugby. Featuring news, reviews and interviews with leading rugby figures from Ireland and abroad and a training and coaching section with training tips and techniques.
Readership/Target Audience: Aimed at fans, players and administrators of Irish rugby.
ADVERTISING RATES:
Full Page Mono £1200.00
Full Page Colour £1560.00
Agency Commission: 10%
Mechanical Data: Bleed Size: 303 x 213mm, Trim Size: 297 x 210mm, Film: Digital
Average advertising content per issue: 25%
CONSUMER: SPORT: Rugby

EMIGRANT
1895660U90-1033

Editorial Address: 28 John Finnie Street, KILMARNOCK, KA1 1DD **Tel:** 01563 539611 **Fax:** 01563 543956
Email: marketing@magazynemigrant.pl
Web site: http://www.magazynemigrant.pl
Publisher: GoodPoint Press LLP
Date Established: 2009
Frequency: Monthly
Cover Price: Free
Circulation: 15,000 (Print Run)
Usual Pagination: 40
Editor: Ola Korytnicka
Summary of Content: Magazine featuring news from Scotland, England and Poland, guides, interviews, culture, sport and entertainment.
Language(s): Polish
Readership/Target Audience: Aimed at Poles living in Scotland and the North East as well as people living in Poland thinking about emigrating to the UK.
CONSUMER: ETHNIC

EMIGRATE
48771U94X-34_48

Editorial Address: 1 Commercial Road, EASTBOURNE, BN1 3XQ **Tel:** 01323 726040 **Fax:** 01323 649240
Email: info@outboundmedia.co.uk
Advertising Address: As above. **Fax:** 01323 735002
Email: brenda.ticehurst@emigrate2.co.uk
Web site: http://www.emigrate2.co.uk
ISSN: 1362-3273
Publisher: Outbound Media and Exhibitions
Date Established: 1995
Frequency: Annual - Published in February
Cover Price: Free
Circulation: 100,000 (Publisher's Statement)
Usual Pagination: 128
Editor: Paul Beasley; **Managing Director:** Mike Schwarz
Summary of Content: Magazine containing practical advice and information as well as inspiring personal accounts of emigrating to Australia, New Zealand, Canada and USA.
Readership/Target Audience: Read by intending migrants and their families.
ADVERTISING RATES:
Full Page Colour £1585.00
Agency Commission: 10%
Mechanical Data: Type Area: 270 x 185mm, Bleed Size: 303 x 216mm, Film: Digital, Col Length: 270mm, Page Width: 185mm, Trim Size: 297 x 210mm
Copy instructions: Copy Date: 2 months prior to publication date
CONSUMER: OTHER CLASSIFICATIONS: Miscellaneous

EMIGRATE AMERICA
48247U89E-120

Formerly: Emigrate USA
Editorial Address: 1 Commercial Road, EASTBOURNE, BN21 3XQ **Tel:** 01323 726040 **Fax:** 01323 649240
Email: news@outboundmedia.co.uk
Advertising Address: As above. **Fax:** 01323 735002
Email: brenda.ticehurst@emigrate2.co.uk
Web site: http://www.emigrate2.co.uk
ISSN: 0965-3732
Publisher: Outbound Media and Exhibitions
Frequency: Monthly
Annual Sub.: £21.00
Circulation: 18,000 (Publisher's Statement)
Usual Pagination: 20
Editor: Paul Beasley; **Managing Director:** Mike Schwarz
Summary of Content: Publication covering all aspects of migrating to the United States of America.
Readership/Target Audience: Aimed at those planning to emigrate to the USA.
ADVERTISING RATES:
Full Page Mono £1046.00
Full Page Colour £1570.00
Agency Commission: 10%
Mechanical Data: Col Length: 340mm, Type Area: 340 x 277mm, Page Width: 277mm, Film: Digital
Copy instructions: Copy Date: 1st of the month prior to publication date
CONSUMER: HOLIDAYS & TRAVEL: Holidays

EMIGRATE AUSTRALIA
48225U89E-26

Formerly: Australian News
Editorial Address: 1 Commercial Road, EASTBOURNE, BN21 3XQ **Tel:** 01323 726040 **Fax:** 01323 649240
Email: news@outboundmedia.co.uk
Advertising Address: As above.
Email: brenda.ticehurst@emigrate2.co.uk
Web site: http://www.emigrate2.co.uk
ISSN: 0965-3740
Publisher: Outbound Media and Exhibitions
Frequency: Monthly
Annual Sub.: £19.50
Circulation: 25,000 (Publisher's Statement)
Usual Pagination: 40
Editor: Paul Beasley; **Managing Director:** Mike Schwarz

Summary of Content: Newspaper covering news and articles of interest.
Readership/Target Audience: Read by those planning to emigrate to Australia.
ADVERTISING RATES:
Full Page Mono £1085.00
Full Page Colour £1626.00
Agency Commission: 10%
Mechanical Data: Col Length: 340mm, Type Area: 340 x 277mm, Page Width: 277mm, Film: Digital
Copy instructions: Copy Date: 1st of the month prior to publication date
CONSUMER: HOLIDAYS & TRAVEL: Holidays

EMIGRATE CANADA
48230U89E-60

Formerly: Canada News
Editorial Address: 1 Commercial Road, EASTBOURNE, BN21 3XQ **Tel:** 01323 726040 **Fax:** 01323 649249
Email: news@outboundmedia.co.uk
Advertising Address: As above. **Fax:** 01323 735002
Email: marie.harmer@outboundmedia.co.uk
Web site: http://www.emigrate2.co.uk
ISSN: 0951-5297
Publisher: Outbound Media and Exhibitions
Frequency: Monthly
Cover Price: £3.25
Circulation: 50,000 (Publisher's Statement)
Usual Pagination: 108
Editor: Paul Beasley; **Managing Director:** Mike Schwarz; **Advertising Manager:** Marie Harmer
Summary of Content: Newspaper covering emigration information, residential tips and employment and travel advice.
Readership/Target Audience: Aimed at potential migrants and visitors to Canada.
ADVERTISING RATES:
Full Page Mono £1182.00
Full Page Colour £1773.00
Agency Commission: 10%
Copy instructions: Copy Date: 1st of the month prior to publication date
CONSUMER: HOLIDAYS & TRAVEL: Holidays

EMIGRATE NEW ZEALAND
48234U89E-80

Formerly: Destination New Zealand
Editorial Address: 1 Commercial Road, EASTBOURNE, BN21 3XQ **Tel:** 01323 726040 **Fax:** 01323 649249
Email: news@outboundmedia.co.uk
Advertising Address: As above. **Fax:** 01323 735002
Email: brenda.ticehurst@outboundmedia.co.uk
Web site: http://www.emigrate2.co.uk
ISSN: 1352-4771
Publisher: Outbound Media and Exhibitions
Frequency: Monthly
Annual Sub.: £19.50
Circulation: 18,000 (Publisher's Statement)
Usual Pagination: 28
Editor: Paul Beasley; **Managing Director:** Mike Schwarz
Summary of Content: Newspaper carrying information and advice about migration or travel to New Zealand.
Readership/Target Audience: Aimed at potential migrants and visitors to New Zealand.
ADVERTISING RATES:
Full Page Mono £910.00
Full Page Colour £1362.00
Agency Commission: 10%
Mechanical Data: Col Length: 340mm, Type Area: 340 x 277mm, Film: Digital, Page Width: 277mm
Copy instructions: Copy Date: 1st of the month prior to publication date
CONSUMER: HOLIDAYS & TRAVEL: Holidays

EMMA'S DIARY PREGNANCY GUIDE
45316U74D-190

Formerly: Emma's Diary Pregnancy
Editorial Address: 1 Globeside Business Park, Field House Lane, MARLOW, SL7 1HY **Tel:** 01628 891644
Fax: 01628 816883
Email: enquiries@emmasdiary.co.uk
Advertising Address: As above.
Email: ranjit.mudher@tntpost.co.uk
Web site: http://www.emmasdiary.co.uk
Publisher: Lifecycle Marketing Limited
Frequency: Half-yearly - Published April and October
Cover Price: Free
Circulation: 407,191 (ABC 01/01/2009 to 30/06/2009)
Usual Pagination: 128
Editor: Lorraine Rowe; **Editor-in-Chief:** Alison Mackonochie; **Advertising Manager:** Ranjit Mudher
Summary of Content: Pregnancy guide published on behalf of the RCGP, given out to women on confirmation of their pregnancy.
Readership/Target Audience: Read by expectant mothers.
ADVERTISING RATES:
Full Page Colour £13566.00
Agency Commission: 15%

Mechanical Data: Film: Digital, Bleed Size: 221 x 166mm, Trim Size: 215 x 160mm
Copy instructions: Copy Date: 2 months prior to publication date
Average advertising content per issue: 25%
CONSUMER: WOMEN'S INTEREST CONSUMER MAGAZINES: Child Care

EMPIRE
46044U76A-10

Editorial Address: Mappin House, 4 Winsley Street, LONDON, W1W 8HF **Tel:** 020 7182 8000
Fax: 020 7182 8703
Email: empire@bauermedia.co.uk
Advertising Address: Endeavour House, 189 Shaftesbury Avenue, LONDON, WC2H 8JG **Tel:** 020 7437 9011
Fax: 020 7295 5400
Email: andrew.turner@bauceradvertising.co.uk
Web site: http://www.empireonline.com
Publisher: Bauer Consumer Media Ltd (Mappin House)
Date Established: 1989
Frequency: Monthly
Cover Price: £3.70
Annual Sub.: £36.00
Circulation: 194,016 (ABC 01/01/2009 to 30/06/2009)
Usual Pagination: 200
Editor: Debi Berry; **News Editor:** Nick Desemlyen;
Executive Editor: Ian Nathan; **Features Editor:** Dan Jolin;
Editor-in-Chief: Mark Dinning; **Publisher:** Mark Dinning
Summary of Content: Magazine focusing on news and features on cinema, DVDs and video films.
Twitter: https://twitter.com/empiremagazine.
Readership/Target Audience: Aimed at movie fans.
ADVERTISING RATES:
Full Page Colour £7705.00
Agency Commission: 15%
Mechanical Data: Col Length: 265mm, Page Width: 200mm, Film: Digital, Type Area: 265 x 200mm, Bleed Size: 291 x 226mm, Trim Size: 285 x 220mm
CONSUMER: MUSIC & PERFORMING ARTS: Cinema

EMPORIUM
45668U74Q-1241

Formerly: WorldPoints Magazine
Editorial Address: Ground Floor, 1-2 Ravey Street, LONDON, EC2A 4QP **Tel:** 020 3222 0101
Fax: 020 7739 1369
Email: lucy@showmedia.net
Advertising Address: As above.
Email: juliap@nbmp.net
Web site: http://www.showmedia.net
Publisher: Show Media Ltd
Frequency: 3 issues yearly - Published in March, June and November
Cover Price: Free
Circulation: 230,000 (Publisher's Statement)
Usual Pagination: 72
Editor: Lucy Teasdale; **Advertising Director:** Julia Pasaron
Summary of Content: Magazine containing articles on fashion, beauty, retail technology and gifts sold at BAA airports and includes a directory of airports. Also travel stories and celebrity interviews.
Readership/Target Audience: Aimed at BAA's WorldPoints card holders.
ADVERTISING RATES:
Full Page Colour £5300.00
Agency Commission: 15%
Mechanical Data: Bleed Size: 292 x 221mm, Trim Size: 286 x 215mm, Type Area: 266 x 192mm, Col Length: 266mm, Page Width: 192mm, Film: Digital
Copy instructions: Copy Date: 4 weeks prior to publication date
Average advertising content per issue: 30%
CONSUMER: WOMEN'S INTEREST CONSUMER MAGAZINES: Lifestyle

END OF TERM
47910U88C-25

Editorial Address: 15-39 Durham Street, Kinning Park, GLASGOW, G41 1BS **Tel:** 0141 419 0044
Fax: 0141 419 0077
Email: james@cravenpublishing.co.uk
Advertising Address: As above.
Email: rachel@cravenpublishing.co.uk
Web site: http://www.end-of-term.co.uk
ISSN: 1366-8188
Publisher: Craven Publishing Ltd
Date Established: 1985
Frequency: Quarterly
Cover Price: Free
Circulation: 25,000 (Publisher's Statement)
Usual Pagination: 68
Editor: James Glasgow; **Advertising Manager:** Rachel Smith
Summary of Content: Magazine covering careers, further training, education opportunities and job search skills.
Readership/Target Audience: Aimed at final year pupils in Scotland, aged between 15 and 18 years old.

ADVERTISING RATES:
Full Page Colour £3495.00
Agency Commission: 10%
Mechanical Data: Type Area: 270 x 188mm, Bleed Size: 303 x 216mm, Trim Size: 297 x 210mm, Col Length: 270mm, Page Width: 188mm
Average advertising content per issue: 40%
CONSUMER: EDUCATION: Careers

ENGINEERING IN MINIATURE
46594U79B-29

Editorial Address: The Fosse, Fosse Way, LEAMINGTON SPA, CV31 1XN **Tel:** 01926 614101 **Fax:** 01926 614293
Email: info@engineeringinminiature.co.uk
Advertising Address: As above.
Email: info@engineeringinminiature.co.uk
Web site: http://www.engineeringinminiature.co.uk
ISSN: 0955-7644
Publisher: TEE Publishing Ltd
Date Established: 1978
Frequency: Monthly - Published on the 20th of the month prior to the dated issue
Cover Price: £2.70
Annual Sub.: £29.16
Circulation: 10,000 (Publisher's Statement)
Usual Pagination: 52
Editor: C L Deith; **Advertising Manager:** Avril Spence;
Managing Editor: C L Deith
Summary of Content: Magazine containing information on how to build steam locomotives and stationary engines on a miniature scale. Also features club and association rally reports, new product reviews and historical articles.
Readership/Target Audience: Aimed at model engineering enthusiasts of any age.
ADVERTISING RATES:
Full Page Mono £360.00
Full Page Colour £500.00
Agency Commission: 10%
Mechanical Data: Col Length: 260mm, Type Area: 260 x 184mm, Print Process: Offset litho, Page Width: 184mm
Copy instructions: Copy Date: Last day of 2 months prior to publication date
CONSUMER: HOBBIES & DIY: Models & Modelling

ENGLAND RUGBY
754900U75C-30

Editorial Address: Winchester Court, 1 Forum Place, Fiddlebridge Lane, HATFIELD, AL10 0RN **Tel:** 01707 273999
Fax: 01707 276555
Email: paula@trmg.co.uk
Advertising Address: As above. **Fax:** 01707 269333
Email: katherine.chapman@trmg.co.uk
Web site: http://www.trmg.co.uk
Publisher: TRMG Ltd
Date Established: 2002
Frequency: Quarterly
Cover Price: £3.95
Free to qualifying individuals
Circulation: 50,000 (Publisher's Statement)
Usual Pagination: 140
Editor: Howard Johnson; **Advertising Manager:** Katherine Chapman; **Publisher:** Paula Skinner
Summary of Content: Official magazine of the England RFU and England Rugby Supporters Club. Covering all levels of rugby featuring player's interviews, tactics and fitness advice.
Readership/Target Audience: Aimed at rugby enthusiasts.
ADVERTISING RATES:
Full Page Colour £5500.00
Agency Commission: 10%
Mechanical Data: Page Width: 186mm, Film: Digital, Type Area: 270 x 186mm, Bleed Size: 303 x 216mm, Trim Size: 297 x 210mm, Col Length: 270mm
Average advertising content per issue: 35%
CONSUMER: SPORT: Rugby

ENGLISH CHURCHMAN
47706U87-90

Editorial Address: PR by email only **Tel:** 07946 465156
Email: englishchurchman@aol.com
Advertising Address: 64 Ripley Road, WORTHING, BN11 5NH **Tel:** 01903 505555
Web site: http://www.englishchurchman.com
Publisher: English Churchman Trust
Date Established: 1761
Frequency: 26 issues yearly
Cover Price: £0.40
Annual Sub.: £17.50
Usual Pagination: 10
Editor: P. Ratcliffe; **Advertising Manager:** Theo Evans
Summary of Content: Newspaper containing articles from a Protestant Reformed Evangelical viewpoint from worldwide sources.
Readership/Target Audience: Read by Church of England members and other protestants, clerics and laity.
ADVERTISING RATES:
Full Page Mono £140.00
Mechanical Data: Col Widths (Display): 60mm, No. of Columns (Display): 4

Copy instructions: Copy Date: 2 weeks prior to publication date
CONSUMER: RELIGIOUS

ENGLISH CLUB GOLFER
1665557U75D-540

Editorial Address: 50 High Craighall Road, GLASGOW, G4 9UD **Tel:** 0141 353 2222 **Fax:** 0141 332 3811
Email: martin.dempster@psp.uk.net
Advertising Address: As above. **Fax:** 0141 332 3831
Email: ann.liddle@psp.uk.net
Web site: http://www.englishclubgolfer.com
Publisher: PSP Publishing Ltd
Date Established: 2004
Frequency: 6 issues yearly
Cover Price: Free
Circulation: 50,000 (Publisher's Statement)
Editor: Martin Dempster
Summary of Content: Magazine covering amateur golf in England including fixtures, results, player profiles and interviews and equipment reviews.
Readership/Target Audience: Aimed at amateur golfers in England.
ADVERTISING RATES:
Full Page Colour £1795.00
Agency Commission: 10%
Mechanical Data: Bleed Size: 366 x 286mm, Trim Size: 360 x 280mm, Film: Digital
Average advertising content per issue: 35%
CONSUMER: SPORT: Golf

THE ENGLISH GARDEN
48554U93-13

Editorial Address: Archant House, Oriel Road, CHELTENHAM, GL50 1BB **Tel:** 01242 211080
Fax: 01242 211081
Email: theenglishgarden@archant.co.uk
Advertising Address: 5th Floor, Avon House, Kensington Village, Avonmore Road, LONDON, W14 8TS
Tel: 020 7605 2200
Email: dan.robinson@archant.co.uk
Web site: http://www.theenglishgarden.co.uk
ISSN: 1361-2840
Publisher: Archant Life
Date Established: 1997
Frequency: Monthly
Cover Price: £3.60
Annual Sub.: £40.00
Circulation: 34,180 (ABC 01/01/2008 to 31/12/2008)
Usual Pagination: 116
Editor: Vicky Kingsbury
Summary of Content: Magazine covering all aspects of the British garden particularly features on design and planting.
Readership/Target Audience: Aimed at men and women aged over 35 years.
ADVERTISING RATES:
Full Page Colour £3600.00
Agency Commission: 10%
Mechanical Data: Film: Digital, Bleed Size: 306 x 236mm, Trim Size: 300 x 230mm, Type Area: 254 x 189mm, Col Length: 254mm, Page Width: 189mm
Copy instructions: Copy Date: 4 weeks prior to publication date
Average advertising content per issue: 30%
CONSUMER: GARDENING

THE ENGLISH HOME
601262U74C-101

Editorial Address: Archant House, Oriel Road, CHELTENHAM, GL50 1BB **Tel:** 01242 216050
Fax: 01242 211081
Email: theenglishhome@archant.co.uk
Advertising Address: 5th Floor, Avon House, Kensington Village, Avonmore Road, LONDON, W14 8TS
Tel: 020 7605 2200
Email: dan.robinson@archant.co.uk
Web site: http://www.theenglishhome.co.uk
ISSN: 1468-0238
Publisher: Archant Life
Date Established: 2000
Frequency: 6 issues yearly
Cover Price: £3.20
Annual Sub.: £24.50
Circulation: 32,850 (ABC 01/07/2007 to 31/12/2007)
Usual Pagination: 130
Editor: Sarah Kent
Summary of Content: Magazine covering the exploration of beautiful properties, encouraging readers to select furnishings that will become treasured heirlooms.
Readership/Target Audience: Aimed at female readers aged 35 years old and above.
ADVERTISING RATES:
Full Page Colour £3750.00
SCC £36.91
Agency Commission: 10%
Mechanical Data: Type Area: 254 x 189mm, Col Length: 254mm, Trim Size: 300 x 230mm, Film: Digital, Page Width: 189mm, Bleed Size: 306 x 236mm
Copy instructions: Copy Date: 4 weeks prior to publication date

Average advertising content per issue: 30%
CONSUMER: WOMEN'S INTEREST CONSUMER MAGAZINES: Home & Family

ENJOY DORSET & HAMPSHIRE MAGAZINE
48084U89C-134_50

Editorial Address: 15 Whitecliff Road, POOLE, BH14 8DU
Tel: 01202 737678 **Fax:** 01202 710544
Email: info@enjoydorset.co.uk
Advertising Address: As above.
Email: zoe@enjoydorset.co.uk
Web site: http://www.enjoydorset.co.uk
Publisher: Eastwick Publishing Ltd
Date Established: 1993
Frequency: Annual - Published in April
Cover Price: Free
Circulation: 30,000 (Publisher's Statement)
Usual Pagination: 60
Editor: Zoe Wilson
Summary of Content: Magazine providing information on leisure, shopping, sightseeing and dining out.
Readership/Target Audience: Aimed at tourists and locals in Hampshire and Dorset.
ADVERTISING RATES:
Full Page Colour £2700.00
Agency Commission: 10%
Mechanical Data: Film: Digital, Type Area: 277 x 190mm, Col Length: 277mm, Page Width: 190mm, Trim Size: 297 x 210mm, Bleed Size: 303 x 216mm
Copy instructions: Copy Date: End of February
Average advertising content per issue: 60%
CONSUMER: HOLIDAYS & TRAVEL: Entertainment Guides

ENJOY JERSEY MAGAZINE
48085U89C-134_75

Editorial Address: PO Box 243, ST HELIER, JE4 5PL
Tel: 01534 510824
Email: jersey@1530.com
Advertising Address: First Floor, 15-17 New Street, St. Helier, JERSEY, JE2 3RA **Tel:** 01534 504800
Fax: 01534 504900
Email: sara@marketingbureaujersey.com
Publisher: Contact 94 Sales Ltd
Date Established: 1986
Frequency: Annual - Published in May
Cover Price: Free
Circulation: 25,000 (Publisher's Statement)
Usual Pagination: 68
Editor: Aileen Scoular; **Advertising Manager:** Sara Kempster-Smyth
Summary of Content: Glossy magazine with top hotel distribution around Jersey, available in hotel rooms/suites. Editorial sections include sightseeing, retail attractions, diary of events, shopping, weddings, business, travel around the Island and to neighbouring islands, leisure and sport, eating out, night life - plus special features which vary each year.
Readership/Target Audience: Aimed at business and holiday visitors.
ADVERTISING RATES:
Full Page Colour £2195.00
Agency Commission: 10%
Mechanical Data: Trim Size: 297 x 210mm, Bleed Size: 303 x 216mm, Film: Positive, right reading, emulsion side down, Type Area: 277 x 190mm, Col Length: 277mm, Page Width: 190mm
CONSUMER: HOLIDAYS & TRAVEL: Entertainment Guides

ENJOYING MG
46420U77E-152

Editorial Address: Octagon House, Swavesey, CAMBRIDGE, CB24 4QZ **Tel:** 01954 231125
Fax: 01954 232106
Email: mgmagazine@mgownersclub.co.uk
Advertising Address: As above.
Email: mariannes@mgownersclub.co.uk
Web site: http://www.mgownersclub.co.uk
Publisher: MG Owners Club
Date Established: 1973
Frequency: Monthly
Annual Sub.: £33.00
Circulation: 34,000 (Publisher's Statement)
Usual Pagination: 96
Editor: Richard Ladds; **Advertising Manager:** Marianne Howard
Summary of Content: Magazine containing articles relating to modern MG Rover and classic MG sports cars. In the context of historical, mechanical, technical, as well as motorsport, rally and travel information.
Readership/Target Audience: Aimed at MG Owners Club members.
ADVERTISING RATES:
Full Page Mono £1020.00
Full Page Colour £1492.00
Mechanical Data: Type Area: 275 x 190mm, Film: Digital, Col Length: 275mm, Trim Size: 297 x 210mm, Page Width: 190mm

Copy instructions: Copy Date: 25th of the month prior to publication date
CONSUMER: MOTORING & CYCLING: Club Cars

ENNISKILLEN AIRSHOW PROGRAMME
1686815U75N-753

Editorial Address: Media House, 5 Broadway Court, High Street, CHESHAM, HP5 1EG **Tel:** 01494 771144
Fax: 01494 771277
Email: info@bpcmagazines.com
Advertising Address: As above. **Tel:** 01494 771177
Email: copy@bpcmagazines.com
Web site: http://www.bpcmagazines.com
Publisher: BPC Magazines
Frequency: Annual - Published in May
Circulation: 3,000 (Publisher's Statement)
Editor: Stella Adams; **Advertising Manager:** Clare George; **Publisher:** Robert Adams
Summary of Content: Programme providing a showcase for companies associated with the Air Show.
Readership/Target Audience: Aimed at those attending the Air Show.
ADVERTISING: Rates on application
CONSUMER: SPORT: Flight

ENOUGH
765678U87-2017

Editorial Address: For all contact details see main record, Christianity
Frequency: Quarterly
Supplement to: Christianity
CONSUMER: RELIGIOUS

ENSIGN
48236U89E-87

Editorial Address: Wootton Grange, Wootton Mount, BOURNEMOUTH, BH1 1PJ **Tel:** 01202 414200
Fax: 01202 414244
Email: ideas@thewalkeragency.co.uk
Advertising Address: As above.
Email: ideas@thewalkeragency.co.uk
Publisher: Walker Agency
Date Established: 1999
Frequency: Half-yearly - Published in March and September
Cover Price: Free
Circulation: 50,000 (Publisher's Statement)
Usual Pagination: 56
Editor: Karen Portnall
Summary of Content: On-board magazine of Condor Ferries. Contains information on accommodation, sightseeing, shopping and dining.
Readership/Target Audience: Read by passengers of Condor Ferries.
ADVERTISING RATES:
Full Page Colour £2000.00
Agency Commission: 10%
Mechanical Data: Type Area: 240 x 190mm, Bleed Size: 270 x 215mm, Trim Size: 265 x 210mm, Col Length: 240mm, Page Width: 190mm, Film: Digital
CONSUMER: HOLIDAYS & TRAVEL: Holidays

THE ENTERTAINER
48086U89C-135

Formerly: The Entertainer (Doncaster)
Editorial Address: 10 Sunny Bar, DONCASTER, DN1 1NB
Tel: 01302 347299 **Fax:** 01302 348521
Email: entertainer@doncastertoday.co.uk
Advertising Address: As above. **Tel:** 01302 347281
Fax: 01302 348525
Email: acairns@doncastertoday.co.uk
Publisher: Johnston Press plc
Date Established: 1990
Frequency: Weekly
Cover Price: Free
Circulation: 10,500 (Publisher's Statement)
Usual Pagination: 32
Editor: Barry Crabtree; **Managing Director:** Paul Bentham; **Advertising Manager:** Amanda Cairns
Summary of Content: Magazine covering what's on, in and around Doncaster.
Readership/Target Audience: Aimed at people living in the Doncaster and Dearne Valley area.
ADVERTISING RATES:
Full Page Colour £120.00
SCC £1.15
Agency Commission: 10%
Mechanical Data: Film: Digital, Trim Size: 260 x 176mm
Copy instructions: Copy Date: Monday 4pm prior to publication date
Average advertising content per issue: 70%
CONSUMER: HOLIDAYS & TRAVEL: Entertainment Guides

ENVOI
47561U84B-57

Editorial Address: Ty Meirion, Glan yr afon, Tanygrisiau, BLAENAU FFESTINIOG, LL41 3SU **Tel:** 01766 832112

Email: jan@envoipoetry.com
Advertising Address: As above.
Email: mike@cinnamonpress.com
Web site: http://www.envoipoetry.com
ISSN: 0897-4888
Publisher: Cinnamon Press
Date Established: 1957
Frequency: 3 issues yearly - Published in February, June and October
Annual Sub.: £15.00
Circulation: 1,200 (Publisher's Statement)
Usual Pagination: 96
Editor: Jan Fortune-Wood; **Advertising Manager:** Jan Fortune Wood
Summary of Content: Publication featuring poetry, reviews and competitions. Includes articles on modern poets, poetic creativity and poetry in translation.
Readership/Target Audience: Aimed at poets and poetry readers.
ADVERTISING: Rates on application
CONSUMER: THE ARTS & LITERARY: Literary

EOS MAGAZINE
47595U85A-90

Editorial Address: The Old Barn, Ball Lane, Tackley, KIDLINGTON, OX5 3AG **Tel:** 01869 331741
Fax: 01869 331641
Email: editorial@eos-magazine.com
Advertising Address: As above.
Email: adverts@eos-magazine.com
Web site: http://www.eos-magazine.com
ISSN: 1748-5568
Publisher: Robert Scott Publishing Limited
Date Established: 1993
Frequency: Quarterly
Annual Sub.: £21.95
Circulation: 22,000 (Publisher's Statement)
Usual Pagination: 84
Editor: Angela August; **Advertising Manager:** Brian Hall; **Publisher:** Robert Scott
Summary of Content: Magazine about Canon EOS cameras and photographic techniques.
Readership/Target Audience: Aimed at people using EOS cameras.
ADVERTISING RATES:
Full Page Colour £1100.00
Agency Commission: 10%
Mechanical Data: Bleed Size: 303 x 216mm, Trim Size: 297 x 210mm, Film: Digital, Print Process: Web-fed offset
Copy instructions: Copy Date: 4 weeks prior to publication date
Average advertising content per issue: 15%
CONSUMER: PHOTOGRAPHY & FILM MAKING: Photography

EP MAGAZINE
46225U76E-100

Editorial Address: Alliance House, 37 Holybrook Road, READING, RG1 6DG **Tel:** 0845 644 5513
Email: epmagazine@vigilante.co.uk
Advertising Address: As above. **Fax:** 0870 705 8562
Email: epmagazine@vigilante.co.uk
Web site: http://www.vigilante.co.uk
Publisher: Vigilante Publications
Date Established: 1991
Frequency: 10 issues yearly - Not published in the Summer
Cover Price: Free
Circulation: 15,000 (Publisher's Statement)
Usual Pagination: 40
Editor: Jon Ewing; **Features Editor:** Emma Coop; **Advertising Manager:** Jon Ewing
Summary of Content: Music and film magazine that covers entertainment, celebrity interviews and popular fiction.
Readership/Target Audience: Aimed at young people, students and musicians in East Anglia.
ADVERTISING RATES:
Full Page Mono £575.00
Agency Commission: 10%
Mechanical Data: Bleed Size: 309 x 220mm, Trim Size: 297 x 210mm, Type Area: 275 x 195mm, Page Width: 195mm, Col Length: 275mm, Film: Digital
Copy instructions: Copy Date: 10 days prior to publication date
Average advertising content per issue: 50%
CONSUMER: MUSIC & PERFORMING ARTS: Pop Music

EPICUREAN LIFE
1826649U74Q-1356

Editorial Address: Suite 114, 2 Old Brompton Road, LONDON, SW7 3DQ **Tel:** 020 7731 0942
Email: info@epicureanlife.co.uk
Advertising Address: As above.
Email: alexandra@epicureanlife.co.uk
Web site: http://www.epicureanlife.co.uk
Publisher: Portfolio Publishing Ltd
Date Established: 1994
Frequency: Quarterly
Cover Price: £5.00
Circulation: 37,000 (Publisher's Statement)

Consumer Magazines

Usual Pagination: 132
Editor: Azzy Asghar; **Advertising Manager:** Alexandra Jacobs
Summary of Content: Luxury lifestyle magazine covering restaurants, travel, fashion, motoring, lifestyle and society.
Readership/Target Audience: Aimed at those aged 25 to 55 years old with a high disposable income.
ADVERTISING: Rates on application
CONSUMER: WOMEN'S INTEREST CONSUMER MAGAZINES: Lifestyle

EPIGRAM
47384U83-7_12

Editorial Address: Queens Road, Clifton, BRISTOL, BS8 1LN **Tel:** 0117 954 5857 **Fax:** 0117 954 5817
Email: editor@epigram.org.uk
Advertising Address: As above. **Tel:** 0117 954 5815
Fax: 0117 954 5883
Email: advertising-ubu@bris.ac.uk
Web site: http://www.epigram.org.uk
Publisher: University of Bristol Union
Date Established: 1989
Frequency: Monthly - Fortnightly during term time
Cover Price: Free
Circulation: 6,000 (Publisher's Statement)
Usual Pagination: 48
Editor: Will Miles; **Advertising Manager:** Amy Lewis
Summary of Content: Bristol University's independent student newspaper covering Bristol and student news, music, the arts, travel and sport.
Readership/Target Audience: Aimed at students in Bristol.
ADVERTISING RATES:
Full Page Mono £840.00
Full Page Colour £840.00
Agency Commission: 10%
Mechanical Data: Trim Size: 350 x 272mm, Film: Digital
Copy instructions: Copy Date: 7 days prior to publication date
Average advertising content per issue: 70%
CONSUMER: STUDENT PUBLICATIONS

EPILEPSY REVIEW
1704178U94F-1002

Editorial Address: Chesham Lane, CHALFONT ST PETER, SL9 0RJ **Tel:** 01494 601300 **Fax:** 01494 871927
Email: amanda.cleaver@epilepsynse.org.uk
Web site: http://www.epilepsynse.org.uk
Publisher: National Society for Epilepsy
Frequency: 3 issues yearly - Published in February, June and October
Free to qualifying individuals
Annual Sub.: £17.50
Circulation: 2,500 (Publisher's Statement)
Usual Pagination: 24
Editor: Amanda Cleaver
Summary of Content: Magazine of the National Society for Epilepsy covering news, research, book reviews, letters to the Editor and fundraising.
Readership/Target Audience: Aimed at people with epilepsy, their families and carers.
ADVERTISING: No Advertising taken
CONSUMER: OTHER CLASSIFICATIONS: Disability

EPILEPSY TODAY
48631U94F-370

Editorial Address: New Anstey House, Gate Way Drive, Yeadon, LEEDS, LS19 7XY **Tel:** 0113 210 8800
Fax: 0113 391 0300
Email: pfox@epilepsy.org.uk
Web site: http://www.epilepsy.org.uk
ISSN: 0958-496X
Publisher: Epilepsy Action
Date Established: 1992
Frequency: 6 issues yearly
Free to qualifying individuals
Annual Sub.: £15.00
Circulation: 15,000 (Publisher's Statement)
Usual Pagination: 24
Editor: Peter Fox
Summary of Content: Magazine containing articles, real-life stories, news and letters on epilepsy.
Readership/Target Audience: Aimed at health professionals, people with epilepsy and their families.
ADVERTISING: No Advertising taken
CONSUMER: OTHER CLASSIFICATIONS: Disability

THE EPOCH TIMES
1819384U82-282

Editorial Address: Unit LG 1, 88-94 Wentworth Street, LONDON, E1 7SA **Tel:** 020 7247 2719
Email: newsdesk@epochtimes.co.uk
Advertising Address: As above.
Email: advertising@epochtimes.co.uk
Web site: http://www.theepochtimes.com
ISSN: 1749-5997
Publisher: The Epoch Times
Date Established: 2005

Frequency: Weekly - Published on Wednesday
Cover Price: Free
Circulation: 10,000 (Publisher's Statement)
Editor: News Desk
Summary of Content: Newspaper featuring current affairs, news and politics with an emphasis on news from China.
Readership/Target Audience: Aimed predominantly at readers aged between 18 and 35 years.
ADVERTISING RATES:
Full Page Mono £950.00
Full Page Colour £1474.00
SCC £2.16
Mechanical Data: Type Area: 550 x 350mm, Col Length: 550mm, Page Width: 350mm, Col Widths (Display): 41mm, No. of Columns (Display): 8, Film: Digital
Copy instructions: Copy Date: Friday 12 noon prior to publication date
CONSUMER: CURRENT AFFAIRS & POLITICS

EQUALITY BRITAIN
1749981U90-990

Formerly: Ethnic Britain
Editorial Address: 2nd Floor, 42 Whitechapel, LIVERPOOL, L1 6DZ **Tel:** 0151 707 6688 **Fax:** 0151 707 6665
Email: admin@pearsonpresslimited.co.uk
Advertising Address: As above.
Email: caroline@pearsonpresslimited.co.uk
Web site: http://www.equalitybritain.co.uk
Publisher: Pearson Press Limited
Frequency: Annual - Published in October
Cover Price: Free
Circulation: 14,000 (Publisher's Statement)
Editor: Caroline Tyler
Summary of Content: Directory promoting equal opportunities in employment, education and housing.
Readership/Target Audience: Aimed at those looking for employment, education or housing.
ADVERTISING RATES:
Full Page Colour £1995.00
Agency Commission: 10%
Mechanical Data: Type Area: 272 x 115mm, Col Length: 272mm, Page Width: 115mm, Film: Digital
Copy instructions: Copy Date: 30 days prior to publication date
Average advertising content per issue: 50%
CONSUMER: ETHNIC

THE EQUESTRIAN LIFESTYLE MAGAZINE
1685483U81D-363

Formerly: England's Equestrian
Editorial Address: 16 Leas Road, Mansfield Woodhouse, MANSFIELD, NG19 8JH **Tel:** 01623 474227
Email: sue@theequestrianmag.co.uk
Advertising Address: 106 Oak Tree Lane, MANSFIELD, NG18 3HL **Tel:** 01623 621149 **Fax:** 01623 621149
Email: philip.equestmagazine@btinternet.com
Web site: http://www.theequestrianmag.co.uk
Publisher: MAI Publications
Date Established: 2004
Frequency: 6 issues yearly
Cover Price: £3.25
Circulation: 55,000 (Publisher's Statement)
Usual Pagination: 148
Editor: Sue Porter
Summary of Content: Magazine focusing on the equestrian scene in England. Includes features on holidays, veterinary, equestrian fashion, tack, health, breeding and rider profiles. Also articles on horse care, stable management, feeding and products.
Readership/Target Audience: Aimed at lovers of all things equestrian.
ADVERTISING RATES:
Full Page Colour £1320.00
Agency Commission: 10%
Mechanical Data: Type Area: 267 x 180mm, Bleed Size: 307 x 220mm, Trim Size: 297 x 210mm, Col Length: 267mm, Page Width: 180mm, Film: Digital
Copy instructions: Copy Date: 3 weeks prior to publication date
Average advertising content per issue: 30%
CONSUMER: ANIMALS & PETS: Horses & Ponies

EQUESTRIAN PLUS
1698966U81D-368

Editorial Address: Unit 2, Devizes Trade Centre, Hopton Park, DEVIZES, SN10 2EH **Tel:** 0845 644 2236
Fax: 01380 730899
Email: sales@redpin.co.uk
Advertising Address: As above.
Email: lisadure@redpin.co.uk
Web site: http://www.redpin.co.uk
Publisher: Redpin Publishing Ltd
Frequency: Monthly
Cover Price: Free
Circulation: 13,500 (Publisher's Statement)
Editor: Sara Haines

Summary of Content: Magazine covering all-round equestrian interests and disciplines, feature articles, product reviews and events.
Readership/Target Audience: Aimed at riders in the North of England.
ADVERTISING: Rates on application
CONSUMER: ANIMALS & PETS: Horses & Ponies

EQUINE CANINE AND COUNTRY LIFE
1828210U81D-373

Editorial Address: Westside, Bow Farm, Badgworth, AXBRIDGE, BS26 2QA **Tel:** 01934 751171
Email: celia@equinecanineandcountrylife.co.uk
Advertising Address: As above.
Email: celia@equinecanineandcountrylife.co.uk
Web site: http://www.equinecanineandcountrylife.co.uk
Publisher: Equine Canine and Country Life
Date Established: 2007
Frequency: Monthly
Cover Price: Free
Circulation: 20,000 (Publisher's Statement)
Usual Pagination: 80
Editor: Celia Gadd; **Advertising Manager:** Celia Gadd
Summary of Content: Country lifestyle magazine covering equestrianism and dogs with product reviews, show reports and features.
Readership/Target Audience: Aimed at those interested in life in the country.
ADVERTISING RATES:
Full Page Colour £600.00
Agency Commission: 10%
Mechanical Data: No. of Columns (Display): 4, Film: Digital
Copy instructions: Copy Date: 10th of the month prior to publication date
Average advertising content per issue: 50%
CONSUMER: ANIMALS & PETS: Horses & Ponies

EROTIC REVIEW
47605U86A-57

Editorial Address: Lower Ria, 31 Sinclair Road, LONDON, W14 0NS **Tel:** 020 7371 1532 **Fax:** 020 7603 8378
Email: jmaclean@eroticprints.org
Advertising Address: As above. **Tel:** 0870 383 1114
Email: timon@eroticreviewmagazine.org
Web site: http://www.eroticreviewmagazine.com
ISSN: 1477-1594
Publisher: The Erotic Print Society
Date Established: 1995
Frequency: 10 issues yearly
Cover Price: £3.50
Annual Sub.: £25.00
Circulation: 15,000 (Publisher's Statement)
Usual Pagination: 72
Editor: Jamie Maclean; **Advertising Manager:** Eddie Timon
Summary of Content: Magazine covering all aspects of erotica and sexual behaviour including the historical, medical, scientific, psychological and socio-political aspects.
Readership/Target Audience: Aimed at discerning, literate readers aged 30 years old plus.
ADVERTISING RATES:
Full Page Colour £600.00
CONSUMER: ADULT & GAY MAGAZINES: Adult Magazines

ESCAPE
1866422U76A-215

Editorial Address: 23-25 Waterloo Place, Warwick Street, LEAMINGTON SPA, CV32 5LA **Tel:** 01926 339949
Fax: 01926 313713
Email: daniel.bowles@summersault.co.uk
Web site: http://www.summersault.co.uk
Publisher: Summersault Communications
Frequency: 6 issues yearly
Cover Price: Free
Circulation: 100,000 (Print Run)
Usual Pagination: 36
Editor: Danny Bowles; **Managing Editor:** Samantha Tame
Summary of Content: Magazine covering forthcoming films, reviews, behind the scene news, features and competitions.
Readership/Target Audience: Aimed at customers of Empire cinemas.
CONSUMER: MUSIC & PERFORMING ARTS: Cinema

ESCAPE
1837072U89A-748

Editorial Address: Unit 1, Windsor Business Park, 16-18 Lower Windsor Avenue, BELFAST, BT9 7DW
Tel: 028 9066 6151 **Fax:** 028 9068 3819
Email: paul@nitravelnews.com
Publisher: Northern Ireland Travel and Leisure News
Date Established: 2008
Frequency: Quarterly
Cover Price: £1.90
Circulation: 25,000 (Print Run)
Usual Pagination: 120
Editor: Paul Wilson

Summary of Content: Magazine covering global destinations including hotels, travel and lifestyle.
Readership/Target Audience: Aimed at woman aged 35 years old and over with a high disposable income.
CONSUMER: HOLIDAYS & TRAVEL: Travel

ESCAPISM TRAVEL MAGAZINE

1882025U89A-753

Editorial Address: 127 Birchanger Road, LONDON, SE25 5BH **Tel:** 020 8407 0107
Email: editor@escapism-magazine.com
Web site: http://www.escapism-magazine.com
Publisher: Revolution Publishing
Date Established: 2009
Frequency: Quarterly
Cover Price: £4.99
Free to qualifying individuals
Circulation: 110,000 (Publisher's Statement per month)
Usual Pagination: 140
Editor: Nic Havers; **News Editor:** Oivind Karlsen; **Publisher:** Nigel Browning
Summary of Content: Magazine featuring barefoot luxury, designer hotels, island and jungle escapes, unforgettable trips, rich cultural heritage and adventure, off the beaten track destinations, eco-tourism and wildlife, gastronomy, motoring and fashion.
Readership/Target Audience: Aimed at affluent travellers.
CONSUMER: HOLIDAYS & TRAVEL: Travel

ESCORT

47606U86A-60

Editorial Address: 2 Archer Street, LONDON, W1D 7AW
Tel: 020 7292 8000 **Fax:** 020 7734 5030
Email: escort@paulraymond.com
Advertising Address: As above. **Fax:** 020 7292 8009
Email: nickys@paulraymond.com
Web site: http://www.sexclub.co.uk
ISSN: 0952-6706
Publisher: Paul Raymond Publications Ltd
Date Established: 1980
Frequency: 13 issues yearly
Cover Price: £2.99
Annual Sub.: £32.00
Usual Pagination: 86
Editor: Natalie Longman; **Managing Director:** Mark Quinn;
Advertising Manager: Nicola Swift
Summary of Content: Adult magazine containing glamour photography and features.
Readership/Target Audience: Aimed at men and couples with an interest in glamour.
ADVERTISING RATES:
Full Page Colour £3500.00
Mechanical Data: Type Area: 300 x 210mm, Col Length: 300mm, Page Width: 210mm, Bleed Size: +3mm, No. of Columns (Display): 5, Col Widths (Display): 30mm, Film: Digital
Average advertising content per issue: 20%
CONSUMER: ADULT & GAY MAGAZINES: Adult Magazines

ESP MAGAZINE

48129U89C-135_50

Formerly: Peterborough's ESP Magazine
Editorial Address: PO Box 431, PETERBOROUGH, PE6 7FG **Tel:** 01733 579707 **Fax:** 01733 579708
Email: editorial@espmag.co.uk
Advertising Address: As above.
Email: sean.mcallister@espmag.co.uk
Web site: http://www.espmag.co.uk
Publisher: ESP Magazine Ltd
Date Established: 1998
Frequency: Monthly
Cover Price: Free
Circulation: 21,000 (Publisher's Statement)
Usual Pagination: 64
Editor: Sharon McAllister; **Advertising Manager:** Sean McAllister
Summary of Content: Entertainment and lifestyle guide for the Greater Peterborough area. Covers live music, sport, cinema, theatre, arts, events, pubs, clubs, eating out, news, fitness, travel, motoring, reviews, competitions and features on celebrities and health and beauty.
Readership/Target Audience: Read predominantly by 18 to 40 year olds in the Greater Peterborough area.
ADVERTISING RATES:
Full Page Mono £580.00
Full Page Colour £580.00
Agency Commission: 10%
Mechanical Data: Trim Size: 297 x 210mm, Bleed Size: 303 x 216mm, Film: Digital, Type Area: 277 x 190mm, Col Length: 277mm, Page Width: 190mm
Copy instructions: Copy Date: 14th of the month prior to publication date
Average advertising content per issue: 50%
CONSUMER: HOLIDAYS & TRAVEL: Entertainment Guides

ESPCHOMEPAGES

45482U74K-70

Editorial Address: 90A George Street, EDINBURGH, EH2 3DF **Tel:** 0131 624 8000 **Fax:** 0131 624 8570
Email: marketing@espc.com
Advertising Address: As above. **Fax:** 0131 624 8874
Email: erin.dearden@espc.com
Web site: http://www.espc.com
Publisher: ESPC (UK) Limited
Date Established: 1982
Frequency: Weekly
Cover Price: Free
Circulation: 42,000 (Publisher's Statement)
Usual Pagination: 88
Editor: Amy Flavell; **Advertising Manager:** Erin Dearden
Summary of Content: Journal containing information of interest on residential properties. Also has features on letting and commercial property.
Readership/Target Audience: Read by homebuyers and sellers.
ADVERTISING RATES:
Full Page Mono £2415.00
Full Page Colour £3220.00
SCC £24.50
Mechanical Data: Page Width: 265mm, Type Area: 346 x 265mm, Col Length: 346mm, No. of Columns (Display): 5, Film: Digital
Copy instructions: Copy Date: Friday 5pm prior to publication date
CONSUMER: WOMEN'S INTEREST CONSUMER MAGAZINES: Home Purchase

ESQUIRE

47644U86C-150

Editorial Address: National Magazine House, 72 Broadwick Street, LONDON, W1F 9EP **Tel:** 020 7439 5000
Fax: 020 7439 5675
Email: iona.willis@esquire.co.uk
Advertising Address: As above. **Fax:** 020 7439 5696
Web site: http://www.esquire.co.uk
Publisher: National Magazine Company Ltd
Date Established: 1991
Frequency: Monthly
Cover Price: £3.99
Annual Sub.: £20.00
Circulation: 52,705 (ABC 01/01/2009 to 30/06/2009)
Usual Pagination: 260
Editor: Iona Willis; **Advertising Director:** Darren Singh
Summary of Content: Magazine covering fashion, arts, music and lifestyle.
Readership/Target Audience: Read by men between 20 and 40 years old.
ADVERTISING RATES:
Full Page Colour £8685.00
Agency Commission: 15%
Mechanical Data: Film: Digital, Print Process: Web-fed offset litho, Type Area: 255 x 182mm, Col Length: 255mm, Page Width: 182mm, Trim Size: 275 x 205mm, Bleed Size: 281 x 211mm
Copy instructions: Copy Date: 8 weeks prior to publication date
Average advertising content per issue: 40%
CONSUMER: ADULT & GAY MAGAZINES: Men's Lifestyle Magazines

THE ESSENTIAL KITCHEN, BATHROOM, BEDROOM MAGAZINE

45251U74C-102

Editorial Address: The Tower, Phoenix Square, Wyncolls Road, Severalls Industrial Park, COLCHESTER, CO4 9HU
Tel: 01206 851117 **Fax:** 01206 849078
Email: anna.wignall@burdamagazines.co.uk
Advertising Address: As above. **Fax:** 01206 849079
Email: nikki@essentialpublishing.co.uk
Web site: http://www.ekbb.co.uk
Publisher: Hubert Burda Media UK
Frequency: Monthly - Published 5th of month prior to cover date
Cover Price: £4.25
Annual Sub.: £39.50
Circulation: 30,000 (Publisher's Statement)
Usual Pagination: 128
Editor: Anna Wignall; **Managing Director:** Luke Patten
Summary of Content: Magazine that focuses on quality kitchen, bathroom and bedroom design, plus a buyer's guide, interior design advice, latest trends and newest products and ideas for these three key rooms.
Readership/Target Audience: Aimed at readers with a high disposable income and actively looking to purchase products and services.
ADVERTISING RATES:
Full Page Colour £2995.00
Agency Commission: 10%
Mechanical Data: Type Area: 276 x 206mm, Bleed Size: 336 x 306mm, Trim Size: 300 x 230mm, Col Length: 276mm, Film: Positive, right reading, emulsion side down. Digital, Page Width: 206mm
Average advertising content per issue: 30%
CONSUMER: WOMEN'S INTEREST CONSUMER MAGAZINES: Home & Family

ESSENTIAL LIVING

1703857U89C-1056

Editorial Address: PO Box 208, STAMFORD, PE9 9FY
Tel: 01780 765571 **Fax:** 01780 765571
Email: localliving@btopenworld.com
Advertising Address: As above.
Email: localliving@btopenworld.com
Web site: http://www.locallivingltd.co.uk
Publisher: Local Living Ltd
Date Established: 2003
Frequency: Annual
Cover Price: Free
Circulation: 8,000 (Publisher's Statement)
Usual Pagination: 148
Editor: Nicholas Rudd-Jones; **Advertising Manager:** Nicholas Rudd-Jones; **Advertising Director:** Helen Walton
Summary of Content: Magazine covering what's on, eating out and where to shop.
Readership/Target Audience: Aimed at residents and visitors to Stamford, Peterborough, Oundle, Rutland and Market Harborough.
ADVERTISING RATES:
Full Page Colour £750.00
Mechanical Data: Type Area: 277 x 190mm, Col Length: 277mm, Page Width: 190mm, Bleed Size: 298 x 210mm, Film: Digital
Copy instructions: Copy Date: 2 weeks prior to publication date
CONSUMER: HOLIDAYS & TRAVEL: Entertainment Guides

ESSENTIAL LOCAL

1849075U80B-435

Editorial Address: 149 Ramsden Road, LONDON, SW12 8RF **Tel:** 020 8675 7697
Email: editorial@essentiallocal.com
Advertising Address: As above.
Web site: http://www.essentiallocal.com
Publisher: Essential Local Marketing
Date Established: 2006
Frequency: 6 issues yearly
Cover Price: Free
Circulation: 15,000 (Publisher's Statement)
Usual Pagination: 54
Editor: Richard Chumbley; **Managing Editor:** Richard Chumbley
Summary of Content: Magazine with local reviews, restaurant reviews, celebrity interviews, lifestyle articles, events previews, fashion, local organisations, charities and markets, recipes, local news, events listing and business directories.
Readership/Target Audience: Aimed at residents with a high disposable income in Clapham, Battersea, Balham and in soon-to-launch publications in the surrounding area.
CONSUMER: RURAL & REGIONAL INTEREST: Regional Interest Greater London

---

ESSENTIAL X-MEN

48499U91D-50

Editorial Address: Brockbourne House, Mount Ephraim, TUNBRIDGE WELLS, TN4 8BS **Tel:** 01892 500100
Fax: 01892 545666
Email: collectorsed@panini.co.uk
Advertising Address: Orange20 Ltd, Station House, Bunbury Way, EPSOM, KT17 4JP **Tel:** 01732 802800
Fax: 01372 723322
Email: robin@o20.co.uk
Web site: http://www.paninicomics.co.uk
Publisher: Panini UK Ltd
Frequency: 13 issues yearly
Cover Price: £2.50
Usual Pagination: 76
Editor: Scott Gray; **Advertising Manager:** Robin Johnson
Summary of Content: Magazine featuring stories of the Essential X-Men.
Readership/Target Audience: Aimed at children 12 years old and over.
ADVERTISING RATES:
Full Page Colour £1500.00
CONSUMER: RECREATION & LEISURE: Children & Youth

ESSENTIALLY AMERICA

48238U89E-90

Editorial Address: 55 Hereford Road, LONDON, W2 5BB
Tel: 020 7243 6954 **Fax:** 020 7243 2047
Email: marymooremason@phoenixip.com
Advertising Address: Northeast Media, Inc, 140 Sherman Street, FAIRFIELD, CT 06824 **Tel:** 203 255 8800
Fax: 203 255 8804
Email: larrycohen@northeast-media.com
Web site: http://www.essentiallyamerica.com
ISSN: 1352-2825
Publisher: Phoenix International Publishing
Date Established: 1994
Frequency: 3 issues yearly - Published in the 3rd week of the month prior to publication date
Cover Price: £2.95
Circulation: 50,000 (Publisher's Statement)
Usual Pagination: 132
Editor: Mary Moore Mason

Consumer Magazines

Summary of Content: Magazine covering travel and lifestyle to and within the USA, Canada and Mexico.
Readership/Target Audience: Aimed at frequent leisure travellers with medium to high disposable incomes.
ADVERTISING RATES:
Full Page Colour $7794.00
Mechanical Data: Type Area: 277 x 190mm, Bleed Size: 303 x 216mm, Trim Size: 297 x 210mm, Col Length: 277mm, Page Width: 190mm, Film: Digital
Copy instructions: Copy Date: 5 weeks prior to publication date
CONSUMER: HOLIDAYS & TRAVEL: Holidays

ESSENTIALLY WORTHING
45591U80C-5140

Formerly: Worthing Plus
Editorial Address: 7 Phrosso Road, WORTHING, BN11 5SJ
Tel: 01903 240517
Email: edit@essentiallyworthing.co.uk
Advertising Address: As above. **Tel:** 01903 244700
Fax: 01903 244700
Email: ads@essentiallyworthing.co.uk
Web site: http://www.essentiallyworthing.co.uk
Publisher: Ganda Publishing
Date Established: 2006
Frequency: Monthly
Cover Price: Free
Circulation: 20,000 (Publisher's Statement)
Usual Pagination: 28
Editor: Gill Etter; **Advertising Manager:** Denise Tayler
Summary of Content: Magazine containing information on local features and events, food, health, home, gardening, holidays, food and drink and personal finance.
Readership/Target Audience: Aimed at people over 25 years old and living in Worthing and the surrounding area.
ADVERTISING RATES:
Full Page Mono £700.00
Full Page Colour £875.00
Agency Commission: 10%
Mechanical Data: Type Area: 273 x 185mm, Col Length: 273mm, Print Process: Web-fed offset litho, Page Width: 185mm
Copy instructions: Copy Date: 2nd week of the month prior to publication date
Average advertising content per issue: 40%
CONSUMER: RURAL & REGIONAL INTEREST: Regional Interest English Counties

---

ESSENTIALS
45175U74A-90

Editorial Address: 6th Floor, Blue Fin Building, 110 Southwark Street, LONDON, SE1 0SU **Tel:** 020 3148 5000
Advertising Address: 7th Floor, Blue Fin Building, 110 Southwark Street, LONDON, SE1 0SU **Tel:** 020 3148 5000
Fax: 020 3148 7595
Email: vanessa_schofield_pope@ipcmedia.com
Web site: http://www.ipcmedia.com
ISSN: 0953-6337
Publisher: IPC Media Ltd
Date Established: 1988
Frequency: Monthly
Cover Price: £2.50
Annual Sub.: £26.50
Circulation: 102,260 (ABC 01/01/2009 to 30/06/2009)
Usual Pagination: 190
Editor: Julie Barton-Breck; **Features Editor:** Angela Cooke; **Publisher:** Ilka Schmitt
Summary of Content: General interest magazine with cookery, shopping, fashion, beauty and health features as well as a focus on celebrities.
Readership/Target Audience: Aimed at modern practical women between 25 and 35 years old.
ADVERTISING RATES:
Full Page Colour £7700.00
Agency Commission: 10%
Mechanical Data: Type Area: 239 x 183mm, Bleed Size: 275 x 219mm, Trim Size: 269 x 213mm, Col Length: 239mm, Page Width: 183mm, Film: Digital
Average advertising content per issue: 25%
CONSUMER: WOMEN'S INTEREST CONSUMER MAGAZINES: Women's Interest

---

ESSEX JEWISH NEWS
47707U87-90_50

Editorial Address: Suite 314, Premier House, 112-114 Station Road, EDGWARE, HA8 7AQ **Tel:** 020 8952 9526
Email: manny@robinson73.fsnet.co.uk
Advertising Address: As above.
Email: barbejn@aol.com
Publisher: Essex Jewish News Ltd
Date Established: 1989
Frequency: 3 issues yearly - Published in April, September and December
Cover Price: Free
Circulation: 14,000 (Publisher's Statement)
Usual Pagination: 32
Editor: Manny Robinson; **Advertising Manager:** Barbara Newman

Summary of Content: Community newspaper containing local news, real-life stories, profiles and travel.
Readership/Target Audience: Read predominantly by the Jewish community in Essex.
ADVERTISING RATES:
Full Page Mono £495.00
Mechanical Data: Film: Digital
Copy instructions: Copy Date: 6 weeks prior to publication date
Average advertising content per issue: 50%
CONSUMER: RELIGIOUS

ESSEX JOURNAL
48677U94X-35

Editorial Address: 30 Main Road, Broomfield, CHELMSFORD, CM1 7EF **Tel:** 01245 440271
Email: neilwissen@hotmail.com
Publisher: Intercity Print Plc
Date Established: 1960
Frequency: Half-yearly - Published in April/May and October/November
Cover Price: £5.00
Annual Sub.: £10.00
Circulation: 500 (Publisher's Statement)
Usual Pagination: 36
Editor: Neil Wissen
Summary of Content: Journal reviews local history and archaeology within the county of Essex.
Readership/Target Audience: Aimed at historians and archaeologists interested in Essex.
ADVERTISING: No Advertising taken
CONSUMER: OTHER CLASSIFICATIONS: Miscellaneous

ESSEX LIFE
767632U80C-5040

Formerly: Essex Life & Countryside
Editorial Address: 427 High Road, WOODFORD GREEN, IG8 0XE
Email: editorialenquiries@essexlife.net
Advertising Address: 28 Teville Road, WORTHING, BN11 1UG **Tel:** 01903 703749 **Fax:** 01903 703770
Email: denise.evers@archant.co.uk
Web site: http://www.essexlifemag.co.uk
Publisher: Archant Life Cambridgeshire, Hertfordshire and Essex
Date Established: 1952
Frequency: Monthly
Cover Price: £2.95
Annual Sub.: £24.99
(Publisher's Statement)
Usual Pagination: 196
Editor: Julian Read; **Publisher:** Robyn Bechelet; **Circulation Manager:** Phil Elcome
Summary of Content: Magazine focusing on Essex featuring places, people, antiques, gardening, food and drink, property and coming events.
Readership/Target Audience: Aimed at those living in Essex.
ADVERTISING RATES:
Full Page Colour £1800.00
Agency Commission: 10%
Mechanical Data: Trim Size: 300 x 220mm, Bleed Size: 306 x 226mm, Col Length: 300mm, Film: Digital, Page Width: 220mm, No. of Columns (Display): 4, Type Area: 300 x 220mm
CONSUMER: RURAL & REGIONAL INTEREST: Regional Interest English Counties

---

THE ESSEX RIDER
767794U81D-351

Editorial Address: 175 Waldegrave, BASILDON, SS16 5EL
Tel: 01268 288088 **Fax:** 01268 288088
Advertising Address: As above.
Email: alec.wynn@tiscali.co.uk
Publisher: The Essex Rider
Date Established: 1983
Frequency: Monthly
Cover Price: £1.70
Annual Sub.: £28.80
Editor: Alec Wynn; **Advertising Manager:** Alec Wynn
Summary of Content: Magazine covering all aspects of equestrianism, including news, reports and advice, training and horsecare.
Readership/Target Audience: Aimed at horse owners and riders.
ADVERTISING RATES:
Full Page Mono £320.00
Full Page Colour £420.00
Mechanical Data: Trim Size: 297 x 210mm, Film: Digital
Copy instructions: Copy Date: 15th of the month prior to publication date
CONSUMER: ANIMALS & PETS: Horses & Ponies

ETC
1613587U74Q-1134

Editorial Address: Barker Brooks House, 4 Greengate, Cardale Park, HARROGATE, HG3 1GY **Tel:** 01423 851150
Fax: 01423 851151
Email: emma.stratton@barkerbrooks.co.uk

Advertising Address: As above.
Email: simon.bell@barkerbrooks.co.uk
Web site: http://www.etcmag.co.uk
ISSN: 1478-8365
Publisher: Barker Brooks Media
Date Established: 2003
Frequency: Quarterly
Free to qualifying individuals
Annual Sub.: £12.00
Circulation: 50,000 (Publisher's Statement)
Usual Pagination: 100
Editor: Emma Stratton; **Editor-in-Chief:** Evan Jeffries; **Publisher:** Lucy Barker
Summary of Content: Magazine containing practical advice on making the leap from school into the world of work, travel or further education. Includes features on career options, travel, finance, health, leaving home, music, fashion and gap years.
Readership/Target Audience: Aimed at 16 to 18 year old students still in full time education.
ADVERTISING RATES:
Full Page Colour £3000.00
Agency Commission: 10%
Mechanical Data: Type Area: 275 x 190mm, Bleed Size: + 3mm, Col Length: 275mm, Page Width: 190mm
CONSUMER: WOMEN'S INTEREST CONSUMER MAGAZINES: Lifestyle

THE ETHICAL CONSUMER
27631U94X-35_50

Editorial Address: Unit 21, 41 Old Birley Street, MANCHESTER, M15 5RF **Tel:** 0161 226 2929
Fax: 0161 226 6277
Email: news@ethicalconsumer.org
Advertising Address: As above.
Email: birch@ethicalconsumer.org
Web site: http://www.ethicalconsumer.org
Publisher: ECRA Publishing Ltd
Date Established: 1989
Frequency: 6 issues yearly
Cover Price: £3.50
Annual Sub.: £19.00
Circulation: 8,000 (Publisher's Statement)
Usual Pagination: 36
Editor: Jane Turner; **News Editor:** Jane Turner; **Advertising Manager:** Simon Birch
Summary of Content: Magazine which considers the social, ethical and environmental policies of the companies behind the brand name.
Readership/Target Audience: Aimed at those with a social and environmental awareness.
ADVERTISING RATES:
Full Page Colour £875.00
Agency Commission: 10%
Mechanical Data: Type Area: 277 x 185mm, Film: Digital, Col Length: 277mm, Page Width: 185mm, Trim Size: 297 x 210mm, Bleed Size: 307 x 220mm
Copy instructions: Copy Date: 3 weeks prior to publication date
Average advertising content per issue: 15%
CONSUMER: OTHER CLASSIFICATIONS: Miscellaneous

ETHICAL LIVING
1828594U94X-298

Editorial Address: PO Box 282, STAMFORD, PE9 9BW
Tel: 0845 643 2499 **Fax:** 0845 643 2499
Email: editor@ethical-living.org
Advertising Address: As above.
Email: mwilkinson@ethicalpublishing.co.uk
Web site: http://www.ethical-living.org
ISSN: 1754-047X
Publisher: Ethical Publishing
Date Established: 2007
Frequency: 6 issues yearly
Cover Price: £3.00
Annual Sub.: £15.00
Circulation: 10,000 (Publisher's Statement)
Usual Pagination: 64
Editor: Kim Marks
Summary of Content: Lifestyle magazine with features on recycling, carbon emissions and climate change as well as fashion, health, beauty, homes and gardens, food and drink, travel, work, finance and family life.
Readership/Target Audience: Aimed at those interested in an ethical lifestyle.
ADVERTISING RATES:
Full Page Colour £1000.00
Agency Commission: 10%
Mechanical Data: Type Area: 265 x 185mm, Bleed Size: 303 x 213mm, Trim Size: 297 x 210mm, Col Length: 265mm, Page Width: 185mm, Film: Digital
Copy instructions: Copy Date: 4 weeks prior to publication date
Average advertising content per issue: 20%
CONSUMER: OTHER CLASSIFICATIONS: Miscellaneous

EUMAGAZINE
1692644U74Q-1267

Editorial Address: Belvedere, Basing View, BASINGSTOKE, RG21 4HG **Tel:** 01256 857156

Email: sunita.sharma@euphony.com
Advertising Address: As above. **Tel:** 01256 857100
Email: marketingenquiries.uk@euphony.com
Web site: http://www.euphony.com
Publisher: Euphony Communications Ltd
Date Established: 1998
Frequency: Quarterly
Cover Price: £1.00
Free to qualifying individuals
Circulation: 50,000 (Publisher's Statement)
Usual Pagination: 24
Editor: Sunita Sharma; **Advertising Manager:** Julian Pertwee
Summary of Content: Lifestyle magazine covering food, clothing, health, gadgets, films, DVD, TV, music, furnishings, events and electrical goods.
Readership/Target Audience: Aimed at staff and customers of Euphony Communications.
ADVERTISING: Rates on application
Copy instructions: Copy Date: 6 weeks prior to publication date
CONSUMER: WOMEN'S INTEREST CONSUMER MAGAZINES: Lifestyle

EUREKA
1664180U77E-519

Editorial Address: 3rd Floor, 21-22 Great Sutton Street, Farringdon Barbican, LONDON, EC1V 0DY
Tel: 020 7566 9910
Email: info@psprarepublishing.co.uk
Web site: http://www.pspcom.com
Publisher: PSPRare Publishing
Date Established: 2005
Frequency: 3 issues yearly - Published in February, July and October
Cover Price: Free
Editor: Paul Winslow
Summary of Content: Magazine covering innovative ideas, good value, product reviews and lifestyle features.
Readership/Target Audience: Aimed at owners of Kia cars.
ADVERTISING: No Advertising taken
CONSUMER: MOTORING & CYCLING: Club Cars

THE EUROPE REVIEW
47322U82-22

Editorial Address: 11 Clarendon Street, CAMBRIDGE, CB1 1JU **Tel:** 01223 351584 **Fax:** 01223 351584
Email: sue@worldinformation.com
Advertising Address: As above.
Email: sue@worldinformation.com
Web site: http://www.worldinformation.com
ISSN: 0269-3852
Publisher: World of Information
Date Established: 1985
Frequency: Annual - Published in the spring
Cover Price: £55.00
Circulation: 4,000 (Publisher's Statement)
Usual Pagination: 300
Editor: Anthony Axon; **Managing Editor:** Sue Hewitt;
Advertising Director: Sue Hewitt; **Publisher:** Anthony Axon
Summary of Content: Journal containing country economic and political profiles.
Readership/Target Audience: Aimed at business, banking, industry, professional services and government, including European politics and economics, government, businesses, universities and NGOs.
ADVERTISING RATES:
Full Page Colour £4950.00
Agency Commission: 15%
Mechanical Data: Type Area: 235.5 x 172mm, Bleed Size: 276 x 216mm, Trim Size: 270 x 210mm, Col Length: 235.5mm, Page Width: 172mm, Print Process: Offset litho, Film: Digital
Copy instructions: Copy Date: End of September prior to publication date
Average advertising content per issue: 10%
CONSUMER: CURRENT AFFAIRS & POLITICS

EUROPEAN JOURNAL OF INTERNATIONAL RELATIONS
47300U82-21_85

Editorial Address: 1 Oliver's Yard, 55 City Road, LONDON, EC1Y 1SP **Tel:** 020 7324 8500 **Fax:** 020 7324 8600
Email: market@sagepub.co.uk
Advertising Address: As above.
Email: advertising@sagepub.co.uk
Web site: http://www.sagepub.co.uk
ISSN: 1354-0661
Publisher: Sage Publications
Date Established: 1995
Frequency: Quarterly
Annual Sub: £49.00
Circulation: 500 (Publisher's Statement)
Editor: Tim Dunne; **Advertising Manager:** Sheena Karim
Summary of Content: Journal aiming to stimulate and disseminate the latest research in international relations.
Readership/Target Audience: Aimed at academics and professionals in the International Relations field.

ADVERTISING RATES:
Full Page Mono £500.00
Agency Commission: 5%
Mechanical Data: Col Length: 205mm, Page Width: 130mm, Type Area: 205 x 130mm
Copy instructions: Copy Date: 12 weeks prior to publication date
CONSUMER: CURRENT AFFAIRS & POLITICS

EUROPEAN UNION POLITICS
601445U82-21_95

Editorial Address: 1 Oliver's Yard, 55 City Road, LONDON, EC1Y 1SP **Tel:** 020 7324 8500 **Fax:** 020 7324 8600
Email: eup@uni-konstanz.de
Advertising Address: As above.
Email: sheena.karim@sagepub.co.uk
Web site: http://www.uni-konstanz.de/eup
ISSN: 1465-1165
Publisher: Sage Publications
Date Established: 2000
Frequency: Quarterly
Annual Sub.: £41.00
Circulation: 420 (Publisher's Statement)
Usual Pagination: 128
Editor: Simon Hix; **Executive Editor:** Gerald Schneider; **Advertising Manager:** Sheena Karim
Summary of Content: Journal containing research on the political processes and institutions of the European Union.
Readership/Target Audience: Aimed at academics, civil servants and decision makers.
ADVERTISING RATES:
Full Page Mono £400.00
Agency Commission: 5%
Mechanical Data: Col Length: 205mm, Page Width: 130mm, Type Area: 205 x 130mm
Copy instructions: Copy Date: 3 months prior to publication date
CONSUMER: CURRENT AFFAIRS & POLITICS

THE EVANGELICAL MAGAZINE
47708U87-91

Formerly: The Evangelical Magazine of Wales
Editorial Address: Bryntirion, BRIDGEND, CF31 4DX
Tel: 01656 655886 **Fax:** 01656 665919
Email: huw@emw.org.uk
Advertising Address: As above. **Fax:** 01656 656095
Email: huw@emw.org.uk
Web site: http://www.emw.org.uk
ISSN: 0421-8094
Publisher: Evangelical Movement of Wales
Date Established: 1958
Frequency: 6 issues yearly
Cover Price: £2.00
Circulation: 1,600 (Publisher's Statement)
Usual Pagination: 32
Editor: Huw Kinsey; **Advertising Manager:** Huw Kinsey
Summary of Content: Magazine of the Evangelical Movement of Wales. Includes information and articles on the historic evangelical faith of the Christian Church.
Readership/Target Audience: Read by Evangelical Christians in Wales and beyond.
ADVERTISING RATES:
Full Page Mono £220.00
Full Page Colour £295.00
Agency Commission: 10%
Mechanical Data: Trim Size: 297 x 210mm, Col Widths (Display): 90mm, No. of Columns (Display): 2
Copy instructions: Copy Date: 1 month prior to publication date
Average advertising content per issue: 15%
CONSUMER: RELIGIOUS

EVANGELICAL TIMES
1656516U87-2028

Editorial Address: Faverdale North, DARLINGTON, DL3 0PH **Tel:** 01325 380232 **Fax:** 01325 466153
Email: office@evangelicaltimes.org
Advertising Address: As above.
Email: office@evangelicaltimes.org
Web site: http://www.evangelicaltimes.org
Publisher: Evangelical Times
Frequency: Monthly
Cover Price: £0.95
Circulation: 8,500 (Publisher's Statement)
Usual Pagination: 32
Editor: Roger Fay
Summary of Content: Newspaper providing news and articles for today's Christian church.
Readership/Target Audience: Aimed at Christians.
ADVERTISING RATES:
Full Page Mono £895.00
SCC £11.50
Agency Commission: 10%
Mechanical Data: Film: Digital, No. of Columns (Display): 4, Col Widths (Display): 62mm, Type Area: 360 x 254mm, Col Length: 360mm, Page Width: 254mm
Copy instructions: Copy Date: 1st of month prior to publication date

Average advertising content per issue: 30%
CONSUMER: RELIGIOUS

EVENING GAZETTE SPORTS (MIDDLESBROUGH)
45718U75A-530

Formerly: Sports Gazette
Editorial Address: Gazette Buildings, 105-111 Borough Road, MIDDLESBROUGH, TS1 3AZ **Tel:** 01642 245401
Fax: 01642 232014
Email: sport@eveninggazette.co.uk
Advertising Address: As above. **Fax:** 01642 234619
Email: fieldsales@gazettemedia.co.uk
Web site: http://www.gazettelive.co.uk
Publisher: Gazette Media Company Ltd
Date Established: 1997
Frequency: 260 issues yearly
Cover Price: £0.42
Circulation: 55,000 (Publisher's Statement)
Usual Pagination: 28
Editor: Phillip Tallentire
Summary of Content: Saturday sports paper.
Readership/Target Audience: Aimed at football supporters.
ADVERTISING RATES:
Full Page Mono £3776.30
Full Page Colour £4389.00
SCC £14.05
Agency Commission: 10%
Copy instructions: Copy Date: 2 days prior to publication date
Supplement to: Evening Gazette (Middlesbrough)
CONSUMER: SPORT

EVENING TIMES WEE RED BOOK
45787U75B-91

Editorial Address: 200 Renfield Street, GLASGOW, G2 3QB
Tel: 0141 302 6614 **Fax:** 0141 333 1897
Email: sport@eveningtimes.co.uk
Advertising Address: As above. **Tel:** 0141 302 6131
Fax: 0141 302 6363
Email: pauline.cairns@glasgow.newsquest.co.uk
Web site: http://www.eveningtimes.co.uk
Publisher: Newsquest Herald & Times Ltd
Date Established: 1928
Frequency: Annual - Published in July
Cover Price: £3.00
Usual Pagination: 244
Editor: Fraser Gibson; **Advertising Manager:** Pauline Cairns
Summary of Content: Publication covering all aspects of football.
Readership/Target Audience: Aimed at football enthusiasts.
ADVERTISING RATES:
Full Page Mono £250.00
Full Page Colour £365.00
Agency Commission: 10%
Mechanical Data: Type Area: 120 x 68mm, Col Length: 120mm, Page Width: 68mm, Film: Digital
Copy instructions: Copy Date: 6 weeks prior to publication date
CONSUMER: SPORT: Football

EVENTING
47126U81D-53

Editorial Address: Blue Fin Building, 110 Southwark Street, LONDON, SE1 0SU **Tel:** 020 3148 5000 **Fax:** 020 3148 8127
Email: julie_harding@ipcmedia.com
Advertising Address: As above. **Fax:** 020 3148 8130
Email: emma_sharp@ipcmedia.com
Web site: http://www.ipcmedia.com
Publisher: IPC Inspire
Date Established: 1985
Frequency: 11 issues yearly - Published on the 15th of the month prior to cover date
Cover Price: £3.80
Circulation: 12,000 (Publisher's Statement)
Usual Pagination: 68
Editor: Julie Harding; **Advertising Manager:** Emma Sharp
Summary of Content: Magazine containing information on affiliated horse trials in the UK and overseas, plus related features.
Readership/Target Audience: Aimed at horse trial enthusiasts and professionals.
ADVERTISING RATES:
Full Page Mono £813.00
Full Page Colour £1183.00
Agency Commission: 15%
Mechanical Data: Type Area: 271 x 188mm, Col Length: 271mm, Page Width: 188mm, Bleed Size: 304 x 216mm, Film: Digital, Trim Size: 297 x 210mm, No. of Columns (Display): 4
Copy instructions: Copy Date: 6 weeks prior to publication date
CONSUMER: ANIMALS & PETS: Horses & Ponies

Consumer Magazines

THE EVERTONIAN
45748U75B-93

Editorial Address: PO Box 48, Old Hall Street, LIVERPOOL, L69 3EB **Tel:** 0151 285 8442 **Fax:** 0151 285 8466
Email: evertonian@sportmedia-tm.com
Advertising Address: As above. **Tel:** 0151 227 2000
Email: neil.johnson@liverpool.com
Web site: http://www.icliverpool.com
ISSN: 1357-3500
Publisher: Liverpool Daily Post & Echo Ltd
Frequency: Monthly
Cover Price: £2.95
Circulation: 9,500 (Publisher's Statement)
Usual Pagination: 72
Editor: Paul Dove
Summary of Content: Official club magazine for Everton FC featuring exclusive player interviews, news and features.
Readership/Target Audience: Aimed at supporters of Everton football club.
ADVERTISING RATES:
Full Page Colour £1000.00
Agency Commission: 10%
Mechanical Data: Trim Size: 297 x 210mm, Bleed Size: +5mm, Film: Digital
Copy instructions: Copy Date: 2 weeks prior to publication date
Average advertising content per issue: 10%
CONSUMER: SPORT: Football

EVERY MAN
1796309U86C-735

Editorial Address: PO Box 158, BROMLEY, BR1 4YH
Tel: 020 8289 3410 **Fax:** 020 8523 8352
Email: katechubb@xcessmedia.co.uk
Advertising Address: As above. **Fax:** 020 8325 8352
Email: lisaa@xcessmedia.co.uk
Publisher: Xcess Media Ltd
Date Established: 2006
Frequency: Annual - Published in June
Cover Price: £3.50
Circulation: 50,000 (Publisher's Statement)
Usual Pagination: 148
Editor: Kate Chubb; **Advertising Director:** Lisa Allen; **Publisher:** Kate Chubb
Summary of Content: Men's lifestyle magazine covering fashion, cars, grooming, music, travel, gadgets and celebrities as well as male cancer issues.
Readership/Target Audience: Aimed at men aged 20 to 40 years old.
ADVERTISING RATES:
Full Page Mono £7200.00
Full Page Colour £8000.00
Agency Commission: 10%
Mechanical Data: Type Area: 260 x 185mm, Bleed Size: 296 x 216mm, Trim Size: 290 x 210mm, Col Length: 260mm, Page Width: 185mm, Film: Digital
Copy instructions: Copy Date: May 12th
CONSUMER: ADULT & GAY MAGAZINES: Men's Lifestyle Magazines

EVERYDAY PRACTICAL ELECTRONICS
46641U79D-15

Formerly: Everyday Practical Electronics with ETI
Editorial Address: Sequoia House, 398A Ringwood Road, FERNDOWN, BH22 9AU **Tel:** 01202 873872
Fax: 01202 874562
Email: editorial@wimborne.co.uk
Advertising Address: As above.
Email: stewart.kearn@wimborne.co.uk
Web site: http://www.epemag.com
ISSN: 0262-3617
Publisher: Wimborne Publishing Limited
Date Established: 1971
Frequency: Monthly
Cover Price: £3.95
Annual Sub.: £37.90
Circulation: 19,000 (Publisher's Statement)
Usual Pagination: 80
Editor: Matthew Pulzer; **Managing Director:** Mike Kenward; **Advertising Manager:** Stewart Kearn
Summary of Content: Magazine featuring projects and news on electronics. Also including information on building techniques, circuits and components.
Readership/Target Audience: Aimed at students, trainers and those interested in electronics.
ADVERTISING RATES:
Full Page Colour £500.00
Agency Commission: 10%
Mechanical Data: Page Width: 177mm, No. of Columns (Display): 3, Film: Digital, Type Area: 265 x 177mm, Col Length: 265mm, Bleed Size: 303 x 216mm, Trim Size: 297 x 210mm, Print Process: Web-fed offset litho
Average advertising content per issue: 20%
CONSUMER: HOBBIES & DIY: Radio Electronics

EVERYTHING AEROSPACE
1741079U88C-175

Editorial Address: Northcliffe House, 2 Derry Street, LONDON, W8 5TT **Tel:** 020 7005 2187 **Fax:** 020 7005 2292

Email: d.poole@independent.co.uk
Advertising Address: As above. **Tel:** 020 7005 2000
Email: j.baldwin.webb@independent.co.uk
Web site: http://www.independent.co.uk
Publisher: Independent News and Media (UK) Ltd
Frequency: Half-yearly - Published in May and October
Cover Price: Free
Circulation: 30,000 (Publisher's Statement)
Usual Pagination: 44
Editor: Anne Giacomantonio; **Advertising Manager:** James Baldwin-Webb
Summary of Content: Magazine covering careers in aerospace including courses, events, jobs and recruitment with company profiles, interviews with industry figures and case studies.
Readership/Target Audience: Aimed at 18 to 24 year old students.
ADVERTISING RATES:
Full Page Colour £2450.00
Agency Commission: 10%
Mechanical Data: Type Area: 253 x 190mm, Bleed Size: 286 x 216mm, Trim Size: 280 x 210mm, Col Length: 253mm, Page Width: 190mm, Film: Digital
Copy instructions: Copy Date: 2 weeks prior to publication date
Average advertising content per issue: 50%
CONSUMER: EDUCATION: Careers

EVO
46314U77A-153

Editorial Address: 5 Tower Court, Irchester Road, Wollaston, WELLINGBOROUGH, NN29 7PJ
Tel: 020 7907 6310 **Fax:** 01933 663367
Email: eds@evo.co.uk
Advertising Address: 30 Cleveland Street, LONDON, W1P 5FF **Tel:** 020 7907 6000 **Fax:** 020 7907 6601
Email: ads.evo@dennis.co.uk
Web site: http://www.evo.co.uk
ISSN: 1464-2786
Publisher: Dennis Publishing Ltd
Date Established: 1998
Frequency: 13 issues yearly
Cover Price: £4.20
Annual Sub.: £32.95
Circulation: 62,682 (ABC 01/01/2009 to 30/06/2009)
Usual Pagination: 180
Editor: Stephen Dobie; **Managing Editor:** Peter Tomalin
Summary of Content: Magazine focusing on the latest performance cars. Contains road test articles, car reviews and news on motor sport and the motor industry.
Language(s): English; Greek; Italian
Readership/Target Audience: Aimed at car enthusiasts between 25 and 50 years old.
ADVERTISING RATES:
Full Page Colour £4563.00
Agency Commission: 10%
Mechanical Data: Col Length: 256mm, Type Area: 256 x 196mm, Bleed Size: 295 x 232mm, Trim Size: 285 x 222mm, Page Width: 196mm, Film: Digital
Copy instructions: Copy Date: 2 weeks prior to publication date
Average advertising content per issue: 33%
CONSUMER: MOTORING & CYCLING: Motoring

EXAM RESULTS
753115U88A-48

Editorial Address: Northcliffe House, 2 Derry Street, LONDON, W8 5TT **Tel:** 020 7005 2000 **Fax:** 020 7005 2273
Email: d.poole@independent.co.uk
Advertising Address: As above. **Fax:** 020 7005 2488
Email: s.chard@independent.co.uk
Web site: http://www.independent.co.uk
Publisher: Independent News and Media (UK) Ltd
Date Established: 2001
Frequency: Annual - Published in August
Cover Price: Free
Circulation: 29,171 (Publisher's Statement)
Usual Pagination: 30
Editor: Dan Poole; **Advertising Manager:** Steven Chard
Summary of Content: Magazine published in the clearing period providing careers advice and course option choices.
Readership/Target Audience: Read by A-level students after their exam results.
ADVERTISING RATES:
Full Page Colour £3480.00
Agency Commission: 10%
Mechanical Data: Trim Size: 280 x 210mm, Bleed Size: 286 x 216mm, Film: Digital, Type Area: 260 x 190mm, Col Length: 260mm, Page Width: 190mm
Copy instructions: Copy Date: 2 weeks prior to publication date
Average advertising content per issue: 50%
CONSUMER: EDUCATION

EXCELLE MAGAZINE
1750008U74Q-1316

Editorial Address: Flockton House, Audby Lane, WETHERBY, LS22 7FD **Tel:** 01937 581400
Fax: 01937 581444
Email: news@excellemagazine.co.uk

Advertising Address: As above.
Email: jane@excellemagazine.co.uk
Web site: http://www.excellemagazine.co.uk
Publisher: Red Leaf Media Ltd
Date Established: 2001
Frequency: Monthly
Cover Price: Free
Circulation: 23,000 (Publisher's Statement)
Usual Pagination: 68
Editor: Jane Pratt; **Advertising Manager:** Jane Pratt
Summary of Content: Magazine with features on dining out, leisure activities, health and beauty, property, cars, fashion, interiors, culture and local life and events.
Readership/Target Audience: Aimed at selected households in Yorkshire.
ADVERTISING: Rates on application
Agency Commission: 10%
Mechanical Data: Type Area: 270 x 190mm, Bleed Size: 303 x 216mm, Trim Size: 297 x 210mm, Col Length: 270mm, Page Width: 190mm, Film: Digital
Copy instructions: Copy Date: 3 weeks prior to publication date
Average advertising content per issue: 50%
Editions:
Excelle Magazine Wakefield, Halifax & Huddersfield
Excelle Magazine York, Leeds, Wetherby & Harrogate
CONSUMER: WOMEN'S INTEREST CONSUMER MAGAZINES: Lifestyle

EXCHANGE & MART
45302U74C-105

Editorial Address: Robert Rogers House, New Orchard, POOLE, BH15 1LU **Tel:** 01202 207750 **Fax:** 01202 207755
Advertising Address: As above.
Email: schapman@exchangeandmart.co.uk
Web site: http://www.exchangeandmart.co.uk
ISSN: 0014-4460
Publisher: Exchange Enterprises Ltd
Date Established: 1868
Frequency: Weekly
Cover Price: £1.50
Annual Sub.: £78.00
Circulation: 280,560 (Publisher's Statement)
Usual Pagination: 200
Editor: Michael Tang; **Advertising Manager:** Sally Chapman
Summary of Content: Magazine focusing on buying and selling all kinds of goods. Includes motor, home, leisure and business sections.
Readership/Target Audience: Aimed at motor dealers, the general public and small businesses.
ADVERTISING: Rates on application
Agency Commission: 10%
Copy instructions: Copy Date: Friday 5pm prior to publication date
Average advertising content per issue: 95%
CONSUMER: WOMEN'S INTEREST CONSUMER MAGAZINES: Home & Family

EXCLUSIVE (CHILTERNS)
1686823U80C-5243

Formerly: Dacorum Life
Editorial Address: Media House, 5 Broadway Court, High Street, CHESHAM, HP5 1EG **Tel:** 01494 771144
Fax: 01494 771277
Email: info@bpcmagazines.com
Advertising Address: As above.
Email: ifranklin@bpcmagazines.com
Web site: http://www.bpcmagazines.com
Publisher: BPC Magazines
Frequency: 10 issues yearly - Double editions published in July/August and December/January
Cover Price: Free
Circulation: 30,000 (Combined Circulation)
Usual Pagination: 40
Editor: Clare George; **Managing Director:** Stella Adams; **Publisher:** Steven Adams
Summary of Content: Magazine covering local issues and news as well as lifestyle, food and drink, education, health and fitness, homes, property, hotels, restaurants, weddings, motoring, theatres, sports facilities and local businesses.
Readership/Target Audience: Aimed at residents and businesses in Hertfordshire and Buckinghamshire.
ADVERTISING RATES:
Full Page Colour £1200.00
Agency Commission: 10%
Mechanical Data: Trim Size: 297 x 210mm, Film: Digital, Type Area: 257mm x 186mm, Bleed Size: 300mm x 213mm, Col Length: 257mm, Page Width: 186mm, No. of Columns (Display): 2
Copy instructions: Copy Date: 4 weeks prior to publication date
Average advertising content per issue: 40%
Editions:
Amersham Exclusive
Beaconsfield Exclusive
Berkhamsted Exclusive
Gerrards Cross Exclusive
Rickmansworth Exclusive

St Albans Exclusive
CONSUMER: RURAL & REGIONAL INTEREST: Regional Interest English Counties

EXCLUSIVE (LONDON)
1686819U80B-419

Formerly: Westone Magazine
Editorial Address: Media House, 5 Broadway Court, High Street, CHESHAM, HP5 1EG **Tel:** 01494 771144
Fax: 01494 771277
Email: info@bpcmagazines.com
Advertising Address: As above.
Email: kcyrus@bpcmagazines.com
Web site: http://www.bpcmagazines.com
Publisher: BPC Magazines
Frequency: 10 issues yearly - Double issues published in July/August and December/January
Cover Price: Free
Circulation: 30,000 (Combined Circulation)
Usual Pagination: 48
Editor: Clare George; **Advertising Manager:** Keygan Cyrus;
Publisher: Stella Adams
Summary of Content: Magazine covering events and news, restaurants and bars hotels, weddings, motoring, arts and culture, buying, renting and selling property in Kensington and Chelsea, Fulham, Battersea and the W1 area of London. Also includes health and beauty, fashion and lifestyle articles.
Readership/Target Audience: Aimed at residents and businesses in Kensington and Chelsea, Fulham, Battersea and London W1.
ADVERTISING RATES:
Full Page Colour £1200.00
Mechanical Data: Type Area: 257 x 186mm, Bleed Size: 301 x 214mm, Trim Size: 297 x 210mm, Col Length: 257mm, Page Width: 186mm, Film: Digital
Copy instructions: Copy Date: 4 weeks prior to publication date
Editions:
Battersea Exclusive
Fulham Exclusive
Kensington & Chelsea Exclusive westOne Exclusive
CONSUMER: RURAL & REGIONAL INTEREST: Regional Interest Greater London

EXCLUSIVE LONDON
1826781U90-1017

Editorial Address: 12 Devereux Court, 215 Strand, LONDON, WC2R 1AP **Tel:** 020 7353 5370
Fax: 020 7353 5375
Email: tatiana@russianmedia.co.uk
Publisher: Russian Media House
Frequency: Half-yearly - Published in April and November
Cover Price: Free
Circulation: 10,000 (Publisher's Statement)
Editor: Tatiana Rodionova
Summary of Content: Shopping guide also covering dining out, bars, clubs and restaurants.
Language(s): Russian
Readership/Target Audience: Aimed at Russian speakers in London through hotels, airlines and tour operators.
CONSUMER: ETHNIC

EXECITE!
46887U80C-1130

Editorial Address: 62 Exe Vale Road, Countess Wear, EXETER, EX2 6LF **Tel:** 01392 427576
Email: geminipublishing@blueyonder.co.uk
Advertising Address: As above. **Fax:** 01392 427576
Email: geminipublishing@blueyonder.co.uk
Web site: http://www.geminipublishing.net
Publisher: Gemini Publishing & Design
Date Established: 1998
Frequency: 6 issues yearly
Cover Price: Free
Circulation: 32,300 (Publisher's Statement)
Usual Pagination: 24
Editor: Gill Tippins; **Advertising Manager:** Gill Tippins
Summary of Content: Magazine containing features of local interest, what's on and gardening.
Readership/Target Audience: Aimed at residents in rural areas within 7 miles of Exeter and professionals in Exeter.
ADVERTISING RATES:
Full Page Mono £500.00
Full Page Colour £698.00
Agency Commission: 10%
Mechanical Data: Col Length: 254mm, Bleed Size: 274 x 170mm, Type Area: 254 x 160mm, Page Width: 160mm, Film: Digital
Copy instructions: Copy Date: 6 weeks prior to publication date
Average advertising content per issue: 40%
CONSUMER: RURAL & REGIONAL INTEREST: Regional Interest English Counties

EXECUTARY NEWS
45473U74J-50

Editorial Address: Groves Business Centre, Milton-under-Wychwood, CHIPPING NORTON, OX7 6JF
Tel: 01993 832555 **Fax:** 01993 832999
Email: john@executary.co.uk
Advertising Address: As above.
Email: john@executary.co.uk
Web site: http://www.executary.co.uk
Publisher: Executary International Magazine Ltd
Date Established: 1999
Frequency: 6 issues yearly
Free to qualifying individuals
Annual Sub.: £24.00
Circulation: 16,500 (Publisher's Statement)
Usual Pagination: 32
Editor: John Whittle; **News Editor:** Rachel Spence;
Advertising Manager: John Whittle; **Publisher:** John Whittle
Summary of Content: Magazine covering all aspects of administrative support and business to business issues providing help in decision making and the purchasing processes.
Readership/Target Audience: Aimed at executive secretaries, PAs, senior administrators primarily at board-level.
ADVERTISING RATES:
Full Page Colour £2590.00
SCC £30.00
Agency Commission: 10%
Mechanical Data: Page Width: 230mm, Film: Digital, Bleed Size: 356 x 254mm, Trim Size: 350 x 248mm, Type Area: 325 x 230mm, Col Length: 325mm
Copy instructions: Copy Date: 2 weeks prior to publication date
Average advertising content per issue: 30%
CONSUMER: WOMEN'S INTEREST CONSUMER MAGAZINES: Secretary & PA

EXECUTIVE GOLF
1683489U75D-539

Editorial Address: 68 Lombard Street, LONDON, EC3V 9LJ
Tel: 020 3145 1240
Email: martin@martingillingham.co.uk
Advertising Address: As above.
Email: david.james@ibm-group.com
Publisher: International Business Media Group Ltd.
Date Established: 2005
Frequency: Quarterly
Cover Price: Free
Circulation: 70,000 (Print Run)
Usual Pagination: 98
Editor: Martin Gillingham; **Advertising Manager:** David James
Summary of Content: Lifestyle magazine for golfers covering interviews, profile features, regular columnists, travel, consumer features, specialist collecting, luxury goods, personal finance, property and motoring.
Readership/Target Audience: Aimed at members of up-market golf clubs.
ADVERTISING RATES:
Full Page Colour £4950.00
Agency Commission: 10%
Mechanical Data: Trim Size: 297 x 210mm, Film: Digital
Copy instructions: Copy Date: 2 weeks prior to publication date
Average advertising content per issue: 40%
CONSUMER: SPORT: Golf

EXECUTIVE PA
45474U74J-60

Editorial Address: 15-17 Black Friars Lane, LONDON, EC4V 6ER **Tel:** 020 7236 1118 **Fax:** 020 7489 5809
Email: andrew.organ@solutionspublish.co.uk
Advertising Address: As above.
Email: michael@solutionspublish.co.uk
Web site: http://www.executivepa.net
Publisher: Solutions Publish Ltd
Date Established: 1991
Frequency: 6 issues yearly
Annual Sub.: £21.00
Circulation: 15,000 (Publisher's Statement)
Usual Pagination: 64
Editor: Andrew Organ; **Advertising Manager:** Mike Dingle;
Publisher: Russell Peacock
Summary of Content: Magazine covering personnel, career development, training, business venues, technology, hospitality, travel, law and a broad spectrum of activities relevant to an office environment.
Readership/Target Audience: Read by senior personal assistants.
ADVERTISING RATES:
Full Page Colour £3100.00
Agency Commission: 10%
Mechanical Data: No. of Columns (Display): 4, Trim Size: 297 x 210mm, Bleed Size: 303 x 216mm, Film: Digital
Copy instructions: Copy Date: 3 weeks prior to publication date
Average advertising content per issue: 40%
CONSUMER: WOMEN'S INTEREST CONSUMER MAGAZINES: Secretary & PA

EXEPOSÉ
47385U83-7_17

Editorial Address: University of Exeter, Cornwall House, St. Germans Road, EXETER, EX4 6TG **Tel:** 01392 263513
Fax: 01392 263560
Email: editors@exepose.com
Advertising Address: As above. **Tel:** 01392 263546
Email: a.hunt@ex.ac.uk
Web site: http://www.exepose.com
Publisher: Exeter University Guild of Students
Date Established: 1987
Frequency: 14 issues yearly - Published fortnightly during term time
Cover Price: Free
Circulation: 5,000 (Publisher's Statement)
Usual Pagination: 40
Editor: Gemma Dye; **Advertising Manager:** Adam Hunt
Summary of Content: Publication of Exeter University Guild of Students containing news, sport, entertainment listings and a culture section.
Readership/Target Audience: Aimed at students.
ADVERTISING RATES:
Full Page Colour £600.00
Agency Commission: 10%
Mechanical Data: Film: Digital, Type Area: 360 x 270mm, Col Length: 360mm, Page Width: 270mm
Copy instructions: Copy Date: 1 week prior to publication date
CONSUMER: STUDENT PUBLICATIONS

EXETER LIVING
1694489U80C-5275

Editorial Address: Circus Mews House, Circus Mews, BATH, BA1 2PW **Tel:** 01225 475800 **Fax:** 01225 475801
Email: joseph.woodward@mediaclash.co.uk
Advertising Address: As above.
Email: kathy.williams@mediaclash.co.uk
Web site: http://www.exeterlivingmagazine.co.uk
Publisher: Media Clash
Date Established: 2005
Frequency: 17 issues yearly
Cover Price: £2.50
Free to qualifying individuals
Annual Sub.: £37.50
Circulation: 10,000 (Publisher's Statement)
Usual Pagination: 108
Advertising Manager: Kathy Williams
Summary of Content: Property and lifestyle magazine covering food, arts, out and about and gardening.
Readership/Target Audience: Aimed at affluent home owners in Exeter and the surrounding villages.
ADVERTISING RATES:
Full Page Colour £650.00
Agency Commission: 10%
Mechanical Data: Type Area: 260 x 195mm, Bleed Size: 291 x 226mm, Trim Size: 285 x 220mm, Col Length: 260mm, Page Width: 195mm, Film: Digital
Copy instructions: Copy Date: 2 weeks prior to publication date
CONSUMER: RURAL & REGIONAL INTEREST: Regional Interest English Counties

EXIT
711947U74Q-225

Editorial Address: 205 Regent Street, LONDON, W1B 4HB
Tel: 020 7734 5299 **Fax:** 020 7734 5392
Email: steve@exitmagazine.co.uk
Advertising Address: As above.
Email: steve@exitmagazine.co.uk
Web site: http://www.exitmagazine.co.uk
ISSN: 1472-0035
Publisher: Exit Ltd
Date Established: 2000
Frequency: Half-yearly
Cover Price: £12.00
Annual Sub.: £24.00
Circulation: 42,000 (Publisher's Statement)
Usual Pagination: 304
Editor: Stephen Toner; **Editor-in-Chief:** Stephen Toner;
Advertising Manager: Stephen Toner
Summary of Content: Magazine containing features on fashion, photography, new culture, art, music and architecture.
Readership/Target Audience: Aimed at men and women between 20 and 35 years old with a high disposable income.
ADVERTISING RATES:
Full Page Mono £4500.00
Full Page Colour £4500.00
Agency Commission: 10%
Mechanical Data: Page Width: 220mm, Type Area: 300 x 220mm, Bleed Size: 326 x 251mm, Trim Size: 320 x 245mm, Col Length: 300mm, Film: Digital
Average advertising content per issue: 20%
CONSUMER: WOMEN'S INTEREST CONSUMER MAGAZINES: Lifestyle

EXMOOR REVIEW
1685513U80C-5238

Editorial Address: The Parish Rooms, Rosemary Lane, DULVERTON, TA22 9DP **Tel:** 01598 763393

Email: hoaroak.publishing@googlemail.com
Advertising Address: Halsgrove House, Ryelands Farm Industrial Estate, Bagley Green, Wellington, SOMERSET, TA21 9PZ **Tel:** 01823 653772 **Fax:** 01823 665294
Email: magazines@halsgrove.com
Publisher: The Exmoor Society
Date Established: 1959
Frequency: Annual - Published in October
Cover Price: £4.99
Free to qualifying individuals
Circulation: 8,000 (Publisher's Statement)
Usual Pagination: 100
Editor: Brian Pearce; **Advertising Manager:** Steven Pugsley
Summary of Content: Magazine of the Exmoor Society covering issues concerning Exmoor, features on news, local interest, local history, poetry, photographs and short stories.
Readership/Target Audience: Aimed at Society members and those with an interest in the area.
ADVERTISING RATES:
Full Page Mono £160.00
Agency Commission: 10%
Mechanical Data: Type Area: 180 x 139mm, Col Length: 180mm, Page Width: 139mm
Copy instructions: Copy Date: 8th August
Average advertising content per issue: 25%
CONSUMER: RURAL & REGIONAL INTEREST: Regional Interest English Counties

EXMOOR - THE COUNTRY MAGAZINE

718820U80C-1135

Editorial Address: Martinhoe Cleave, Martinhoe, Parracombe, BARNSTAPLE, EX31 4PZ **Tel:** 0845 224 1203
Email: hilary.binding@btinternet.com
Advertising Address: As above.
Email: hoaroak.publishing@googlemail.com
Web site: http://www.theexmoormagazine.co.uk
Publisher: Hoar Oak Publishing
Date Established: 1997
Frequency: Quarterly
Cover Price: £2.75
Circulation: 6,000 (Publisher's Statement)
Usual Pagination: 80
Editor: Hilary Binding; **Advertising Manager:** Brian Pearce
Summary of Content: Magazine covering local towns and places of interest in Exmoor with lifestyle features including celebrity profiles, news and views, local produce, book reviews, the environment and local events.
Readership/Target Audience: Aimed at those aged 30 years and over living or working in Exmoor or who have links with Exmoor.
ADVERTISING RATES:
Full Page Mono £600.00
Full Page Colour £600.00
Agency Commission: 10%
Mechanical Data: Col Length: 262mm, Page Width: 180mm, Trim Size: 297 x 210mm, Film: Digital, Type Area: 262 x 180mm, Bleed Size: 303 x 213mm
CONSUMER: RURAL & REGIONAL INTEREST: Regional Interest English Counties

EXPAT INVESTOR

45545U74M-60

Editorial Address: PO Box 2205, HOVE, BN3 6RJ
Tel: 01273 777463
Email: hannahbeecham@fastnet.co.uk
Advertising Address: 27 John Street, LONDON, WC1N 2BX
Tel: 020 7269 8900 **Fax:** 020 7269 8909
Email: rosemary.nolte@ipgonline.cc
Web site: http://www.expatinvestor.com
Publisher: International Publishing Group
Date Established: 1988
Frequency: 11 issues yearly
Cover Price: Free
Circulation: 25,000 (Publisher's Statement)
Usual Pagination: 24
Editor: Hannah Beecham; **Advertising Manager:** Rosemary Nolte; **Publisher:** Simon Lambert
Summary of Content: Magazine covering information on taxation and all aspects of personal finance. Includes savings, investment, assurance, pensions, buying foreign and UK property.
Readership/Target Audience: Read by British investors who live abroad.
ADVERTISING RATES:
Full Page Colour £5750.00
Agency Commission: 10%
Mechanical Data: Bleed Size: 389 x 278mm, Trim Size: 383 x 272mm
Copy instructions: Copy Date: 3 weeks prior to publication date
Average advertising content per issue: 50%
CONSUMER: WOMEN'S INTEREST CONSUMER MAGAZINES: Personal Finance

EXPATRIATE MAGAZINE

1836393U94D-292

Editorial Address: Suite 46, 24-28 St. Leonards Road, WINDSOR, SL4 3BB **Tel:** 0845 056 9611 **Fax:** 01784 242051

Email: info@expatriateliving.com
Advertising Address: As above.
Email: info@expatriateliving.com
Web site: http://www.expatriateliving.com
Publisher: Expatriate Living Ltd
Date Established: 2004
Frequency: Quarterly
Cover Price: £3.95
Circulation: 10,000 (Publisher's Statement)
Usual Pagination: 60
Editor: Delaina Stone; **Advertising Manager:** Delaina Stone
Summary of Content: Magazine covering international lifestyle, travel, food, wine, shopping, fashion, and expat issues including healthcare, taxes, housing, cars and cost of living.
Readership/Target Audience: Aimed at professional expatriates in the UK.
ADVERTISING: Rates on application
CONSUMER: OTHER CLASSIFICATIONS: Expatriates

EXPOSED

1639600U80C-5079

Editorial Address: Unit 1 Beehive Works, Milton Street, SHEFFIELD, S3 7WL **Tel:** 0114 275 7709
Fax: 0114 275 7750
Email: editor@exposedmagazine.co.uk
Advertising Address: As above.
Email: steve@exposedmagazine.co.uk
Web site: http://www.exposedmagazine.co.uk
Publisher: Blind Mice Media Ltd
Date Established: 2003
Frequency: Monthly
Cover Price: Free
Circulation: 35,000 (Publisher's Statement)
Usual Pagination: 96
Editor: Carl Reid; **Advertising Manager:** Simon McLean
Summary of Content: Magazine covering entertainment, lifestyle and listings.
Readership/Target Audience: Aimed at those aged 18 to 40 years old living or working in Sheffield, South Yorkshire, Nottingham and Nottinghamshire.
ADVERTISING RATES:
Full Page Mono £936.00
Full Page Colour £1040.00
Agency Commission: 10%
Mechanical Data: Type Area: 265 x 190mm, Bleed Size: 303 x 216mm, Trim Size: 297 x 210mm, Film: Digital, Page Width: 190mm, Col Length: 265mm
Copy instructions: Copy Date: 1 week prior to publication date
Average advertising content per issue: 40%
CONSUMER: RURAL & REGIONAL INTEREST: Regional Interest English Counties

EXPOSITORY TIMES

47710U87-93

Editorial Address: New College, Mound Place, EDINBURGH, EH1 2LX **Tel:** 0131 650 8944
Fax: 0131 650 7952
Email: extim@div.ed.ac.uk
Web site: http://www.ext.sagepub.com
ISSN: 0014-5246
Publisher: Sage Publications
Date Established: 1889
Frequency: Monthly
Annual Sub.: £28.00
Circulation: 4,000 (Publisher's Statement)
Usual Pagination: 44
Editor: Karen Wenell
Summary of Content: Journal containing practical and academic articles on biblical and theological topics.
Readership/Target Audience: Aimed at members of the clergy, ministers, university and college lecturers.
ADVERTISING: No Advertising taken
CONSUMER: RELIGIOUS

EXPOSURE

45385U74F-355

Editorial Address: The Bigger Shoe Box, Muswell Hill Centre, Hillfield Park, LONDON, N10 3QJ
Tel: 020 8883 0260 **Fax:** 020 8883 2906
Email: editor@exposure.org.uk
Advertising Address: As above.
Email: editor@exposure.org.uk
Web site: http://www.exposure.org.uk
ISSN: 1362-8585
Publisher: Exposure Organisation Ltd
Date Established: 1996
Frequency: 6 issues yearly
Cover Price: Free
Circulation: 4,250 (Publisher's Statement)
Usual Pagination: 32
Editor: David Warrington; **Advertising Manager:** Andy Koumi
Summary of Content: Magazine containing news and views from a youth perspective.
Readership/Target Audience: Aimed at young people between 14 and 25 in secondary schools, colleges and youth groups in central and North London.

ADVERTISING RATES:
Full Page Colour £400.00
Mechanical Data: Trim Size: 210 x 148mm
Copy instructions: Copy Date: 15th of the month prior to publication date
CONSUMER: WOMEN'S INTEREST CONSUMER MAGAZINES: Teenage

EXTRA COVER

45910U75K-300

Editorial Address: 22 Dene Avenue, HOUNSLOW, TW3 3AH **Tel:** 020 8570 5434
Email: charlie.puckett54@gmail.com
Advertising Address: As above.
Email: puckett@middxlge.fsnet.co.uk
Web site: http://www.club-cricket.com
Publisher: The Club Cricket Conference
Date Established: 1999
Frequency: Quarterly
Free to qualifying individuals
Annual Sub.: £10.00
Circulation: 5,000 (Publisher's Statement)
Usual Pagination: 24
Editor: Charlie Puckett; **Advertising Manager:** Charlie Puckett
Summary of Content: Magazine of the Club Cricket Conference, containing cricket news and information concerning club and league cricket.
Readership/Target Audience: Read by players, officials and supporters.
ADVERTISING: Rates on application
CONSUMER: SPORT: Cricket

EYE SPY INTELLIGENCE MAGAZINE

711615U79H-50

Formerly: Eye Spy!
Editorial Address: PO Box 10, SKIPTON, BD23 5US
Tel: 01756 770199
Email: editor@eyespymag.com
Advertising Address: As above. **Fax:** 01756 770199
Email: editor@eyespymag.com
Web site: http://www.eyespymag.com
ISSN: 1364-8446
Publisher: Eye Spy Publishing Ltd
Date Established: 2001
Frequency: 8 issues yearly
Cover Price: £3.75
Annual Sub.: £27.50
Circulation: 10,000 (Publisher's Statement)
Usual Pagination: 84
Editor: Mark Birdsall; **Advertising Manager:** Debbie McDonald
Summary of Content: Magazine covering UK/USA and global aspects of intelligence, espionage, security, special forces, terrorism, counter-intelligence, specialist equipment for the intelligence trade, analysis and comment.
Readership/Target Audience: Aimed at those with an interest in intelligence, security and espionage.
ADVERTISING RATES:
Full Page Colour £600.00
Agency Commission: 25%
Mechanical Data: Trim Size: 297 x 210mm, Film: Digital, Type Area: 270 x 185mm, Bleed Size: 308 x 220mm, Col Length: 270mm, Page Width: 185mm
Copy instructions: Copy Date: 14 days prior to publication date
Average advertising content per issue: 5%
CONSUMER: HOBBIES & DIY: Military History

F1 RACING

46422U77D-172

Editorial Address: Teddington Studios, Broom Road, TEDDINGTON, TW11 9BE **Tel:** 020 8267 5026
Fax: 020 8267 5022
Email: hans.seeberg@haymarket.com
Advertising Address: As above. **Fax:** 020 8267 5079
Email: f1racingads@haymarket.com
Web site: http://www.f1racing.co.uk
ISSN: 1361-4487
Publisher: Haymarket Media Group Ltd
Date Established: 1996
Frequency: Monthly
Cover Price: £4.20
Free to qualifying individuals
Circulation: 58,806 (ABC 01/01/2008 to 31/12/2008)
Usual Pagination: 148
Editor: Helen Spinney; **News Editor:** Jimmy Roberts
Summary of Content: Magazine covering all aspects of Formula 1 motor racing including news, updates, driver profiles, track profiles and race analysis.
Language(s): Czech; Dutch; English; French; German; Greek; Indonesian; Italian; Polish; Spanish; Swedish; Turkish
Readership/Target Audience: Read by Formula 1 enthusiasts.
ADVERTISING RATES:
Full Page Colour £5490.00
Agency Commission: 10%

Mechanical Data: Type Area: 257 x 187mm, Col Length: 257mm, Page Width: 187mm, Film: Digital
CONSUMER: MOTORING & CYCLING: Motor Sports

FABIAN REVIEW
47301U82-22_30

Editorial Address: 11 Dartmouth Street, LONDON, SW1H 9BN **Tel:** 020 7227 4900 **Fax:** 020 7976 7153
Email: review@fabian-society.org.uk
Advertising Address: As above.
Email: review@fabian-society.org.uk
Web site: http://www.fabian-society.org.uk
ISSN: 1356-1812
Publisher: Fabian Society
Date Established: 1884
Frequency: Quarterly
Cover Price: £4.95
Free to qualifying individuals
Annual Sub.: £33.00
Circulation: 6,000 (Publisher's Statement)
Usual Pagination: 32
Editor: Tom Hampson; **Advertising Manager:** Hannah Jameson
Summary of Content: Magazine containing detailed information on political issues.
Readership/Target Audience: Read by Fabian members, policy makers, MPs, journalists and academics.
ADVERTISING RATES:
Full Page Colour £500.00
Copy instructions: Copy Date: 3 weeks prior to publication date
CONSUMER: CURRENT AFFAIRS & POLITICS

FACT
1626205U76D-768

Editorial Address: Basement Studio, 45 Foubert's Place, LONDON, W1F 7QH **Tel:** 020 7025 1385 **Fax:** 020 7287 4912
Email: info@factmagazine.co.uk
Advertising Address: As above.
Email: antony.hill@vinylfactory.co.uk
Web site: http://www.factmagazine.co.uk
Publisher: Vinyl Factory Publishing Ltd
Date Established: 2003
Frequency: 6 issues yearly
Free to qualifying individuals
Annual Sub.: £24.00
Circulation: 25,000 (Publisher's Statement)
Usual Pagination: 76
Editor: Sean Bidder; **Advertising Manager:** Antony Hill
Summary of Content: Music and vinyl-lovers magazine including features, reviews, interviews, profiles and opinion pieces on music.
Readership/Target Audience: Aimed predominantly at vinyl record enthusiasts and music lovers of all ages.
ADVERTISING RATES:
Full Page Mono £750.00
Full Page Colour £750.00
Agency Commission: 10%
Mechanical Data: Type Area: 248 x 248mm, Trim Size: 173 x 173mm, Bleed Size: 179 x 179mm, Col Length: 248mm, Page Width: 248mm, Print Process: Digital
Average advertising content per issue: 35%
CONSUMER: MUSIC & PERFORMING ARTS: Music

FAIRGAME
1665012U75B-279

Editorial Address: Baltic Business Centre, Saltmeadows Road, GATESHEAD, NE8 3DA **Tel:** 0191 442 4001
Fax: 0191 442 4002
Email: jen@fgmag.com
Advertising Address: As above. **Tel:** 0191 442 4006
Email: anthony@fgmag.com
Web site: http://www.fgmag.com
ISSN: 1749-1062
Publisher: Fairgame Publishing
Date Established: 2003
Frequency: 6 issues yearly
Cover Price: £2.25
Circulation: 15,000 (Publisher's Statement)
Usual Pagination: 52
Editor: Jen O'Neill; **News Editor:** Wilf Frith
Summary of Content: Magazine covering player profiles, match reports, fixtures, training advice, fun features and product.
Readership/Target Audience: Aimed at players and fans of women's football.
ADVERTISING RATES:
Full Page Colour £1995.00
Mechanical Data: Trim Size: 297 x 210mm, Film: Digital
Copy instructions: Copy Date: 2 weeks prior to publication date
CONSUMER: SPORT: Football

THE FAIRWAY GOLFING NEWS
45806U75D-60

Editorial Address: 216 Christchurch Road, NEWPORT, NP19 8BJ **Tel:** 01633 666700 **Fax:** 01633 277766
Email: enquiries@fairway.org.uk
Advertising Address: As above.

Email: enquiries@fairway.org.uk
Web site: http://www.fairway.org.uk
Publisher: The Fairway
Date Established: 1995
Frequency: Monthly
Cover Price: Free
Circulation: 50,000 (Publisher's Statement)
Usual Pagination: 16
Editor: John Doherty; **Advertising Manager:** Jacqui Strickland
Summary of Content: Newspaper covering events and items of interest from the world of golf.
Readership/Target Audience: Aimed at golfers of all ages both amateur and professional.
ADVERTISING RATES:
Full Page Mono £1000.00
Full Page Colour £1700.00
SCC £8.00
Agency Commission: 10%
Mechanical Data: Col Length: 340mm, Type Area: 340 x 285mm, Print Process: Web-fed offset litho, No. of Columns (Display): 8, Col Widths (Display): 34mm, Page Width: 285mm, Film: Digital
Copy instructions: Copy Date: 2 weeks prior to publication date
Average advertising content per issue: 50%
CONSUMER: SPORT: Golf

FAIRWAY TO GREEN
1615781U75D-502

Editorial Address: Upper Cowgrove, Heath Farm, Heath Road East, PETERSFIELD, GU31 4HT **Tel:** 01730 711922
Email: news@fairwaytogreen.com
Advertising Address: Floor 1, Room 113, Brook Drive, READING, RG2 6UB **Tel:** 01865 291950 **Fax:** 01865 847033
Email: denise.huss@fairwaytogreen.com
Web site: http://www.fairwaytogreen.com
Publisher: Fairway To Green Ltd
Date Established: 1999
Frequency: 10 issues yearly
Cover Price: Free
Circulation: 45,000 (Publisher's Statement)
Usual Pagination: 140
Editor: Dave Bowers; **News Editor:** David Connor
Summary of Content: Magazine covering both amateur and professional golf including seniors, ladies and juniors.
Readership/Target Audience: Aimed at local club golfers and golf clubs.
ADVERTISING RATES:
Full Page Colour £1695.00
Agency Commission: 10%
Mechanical Data: Type Area: 257 x 191mm, Col Length: 257mm, Page Width: 191mm, Film: Digital, Bleed Size: 301 x 221mm, Trim Size: 295 x 215mm
Average advertising content per issue: 50%
Editions:
Fairway to Green in Berkshire
Fairway to Green in Buckinghamshire
Fairway to Green in Essex
Fairway to Green in Hampshire
Fairway to Green in Hertfordshire
Fairway to Green in Kent
Fairway to Green in Surrey
Fairway to Green in Wiltshire
Fairway to Green Middlesex
Fairway to Green Oxfordshire
Fairway to Green Sussex
CONSUMER: SPORT: Golf

THE FALCONERS & RAPTOR CONSERVATION MAGAZINE
47170U81F-160

Editorial Address: Arrowsmith Court, Station Approach, BROADSTONE, BH18 8PW **Tel:** 01202 659920
Fax: 01202 659950
Email: peter@pwpublishing.ltd.uk
Advertising Address: As above.
Web site: http://www.pwpublishing.ltd.uk
ISSN: 0967-2206
Publisher: PW Publishing Ltd
Frequency: Quarterly
Cover Price: £3.50
Annual Sub.: £16.50
Circulation: 5,000 (Publisher's Statement)
Usual Pagination: 50
Editor: Peter Eldrett; **Advertising Manager:** Roger Hall; **Publisher:** Stephen Hunt
Summary of Content: Magazine featuring articles and news on falcons and falconry both in the UK and abroad.
Readership/Target Audience: Aimed at falconers and conservationists.
ADVERTISING RATES:
Full Page Mono £300.00
Full Page Colour £490.00
Agency Commission: 10%
Mechanical Data: Trim Size: 297 x 210mm, Bleed Size: 303 x 216mm, Film: Digital
Copy instructions: Copy Date: 4 weeks prior to publication date
CONSUMER: ANIMALS & PETS: Birds

FALL LINE SKIING
45870U75G-150

Formerly: Fall Line
Editorial Address: South Wing, Broadway Court, Broadway, PETERBOROUGH, PE1 1RS **Tel:** 01733 293250
Fax: 01733 293269
Email: hannah@fall-line.co.uk
Advertising Address: As above.
Email: georgie@fall-line.co.uk
Web site: http://www.fall-lineskiing.co.uk
ISSN: 9770-9675
Publisher: Fall Line Media Limited
Date Established: 1991
Frequency: 6 issues yearly
Cover Price: £3.80
Annual Sub.: £21.00
Circulation: 30,000 (Publisher's Statement)
Usual Pagination: 132
Editor: Hannah Engelkamp; **Editor-in-Chief:** Hannah Engelkamp; **Advertising Manager:** Georgie Horgan; **Publisher:** Richard Fincher
Summary of Content: Magazine covering all aspects of alpine sports including destination information, tips on what to do before you go and when you get there, products, reviews and news.
Readership/Target Audience: Aimed at enthusiasts, including skiers, snowboarders and climbers.
ADVERTISING RATES:
Full Page Colour £1800.00
Agency Commission: 10%
Mechanical Data: Film: Digital, Type Area: 280 x 204mm, Col Length: 280mm, Page Width: 204mm, Trim Size: 300 x 230mm, Bleed Size: 306 x 230mm
Copy instructions: Copy Date: 4 weeks prior to publication date
Average advertising content per issue: 33%
CONSUMER: SPORT: Winter Sports

FAMILIES BRISTOL
1896964U74D-687

Editorial Address: PO Box 2736, BRISTOL, BS6 9DY
Tel: 0117 377 0856
Email: editor@familiesbristol.co.uk
Web site: http://www.familiesonline.co.uk
Publisher: Families Magazines Ltd
Frequency: 10 issues yearly
Cover Price: Free
Circulation: 12,000 (Print Run)
Editor: Janet Raeburn
Summary of Content: Magazine covering activities, news, education, book reviews, health and information.
Readership/Target Audience: Aimed at parents and nannies with young children living in Bristol.
CONSUMER: WOMEN'S INTEREST CONSUMER MAGAZINES: Child Care

FAMILIES CHILTERN
1664930U74D-589

Editorial Address: PO Box 1037, BEACONSFIELD, HP9 1ZF **Tel:** 01494 673427 **Fax:** 01494 673427
Email: editor@familieschiltern.co.uk
Advertising Address: As above.
Email: editor@familieschiltern.co.uk
Web site: http://www.familieschiltern.co.uk
Publisher: Families Magazines Ltd
Date Established: 2003
Frequency: 6 issues yearly
Cover Price: Free
Circulation: 17,500 (Publisher's Statement)
Usual Pagination: 24
Editor: Allison Thomas; **Advertising Manager:** Allison Thomas
Summary of Content: Magazine with local news and information as well as articles on child care, health, education, travel and events.
Readership/Target Audience: Aimed at families with children under 11 years old.
ADVERTISING RATES:
Full Page Mono £890.00
Full Page Colour £1157.00
Mechanical Data: Film: Digital, Trim Size: 297 x 210mm
Copy instructions: Copy Date: 7th of month prior to publication date
Average advertising content per issue: 33%
CONSUMER: WOMEN'S INTEREST CONSUMER MAGAZINES: Child Care

FAMILIES EAST LONDON
1896970U74D-690

Editorial Address: po bOX 60479, LONDON, E9 9AJ
Tel: 07976 313279
Email: editor@familieseast.co.uk
Web site: http://www.familiesonline.co.uk
Publisher: Families Magazines Ltd
Frequency: 10 issues yearly
Cover Price: Free
Circulation: 15,000 (Print Run)
Editor: Dinah Robertshaw

Consumer Magazines

Summary of Content: Magazine covering activities, news, education, book reviews, health and information.
Readership/Target Audience: Aimed at parents and nannies with young children living in East London, Docklands and out to the M25.
CONSUMER: WOMEN'S INTEREST CONSUMER MAGAZINES: Child Care

FAMILIES EDINBURGH
630184U74D-198

Editorial Address: PO Box 23802, EDINBURGH, EH7 4XL
Tel: 0131 622 0405
Email: editor@familiesedinburgh.co.uk
Advertising Address: As above.
Email: editor@familiesedinburgh.co.uk
Web site: http://www.familiesedinburgh.co.uk
Publisher: Families Magazines Ltd
Date Established: 1990
Frequency: 6 issues yearly
Annual Sub: £18.00
Circulation: 17,000 (Publisher's Statement)
Usual Pagination: 24
Editor: Sarah Adair
Summary of Content: Magazine providing information on local clubs, classes, shows, events and local features on parenting.
Readership/Target Audience: Aimed at parents and carers of children up to the age of 15 years old.
ADVERTISING: Rates on application
CONSUMER: WOMEN'S INTEREST CONSUMER MAGAZINES: Child Care

FAMILIES EPSOM, SUTTON & CROYDON
1896975U74D-691

Editorial Address: PO Box 3176, SOUTH CROYDON, CR2 6XD **Tel:** 020 8405 8482
Email: familiesesc@familiesmagazine.co.uk
Web site: http://www.familiesonline.co.uk
Publisher: Families Magazines Ltd
Frequency: 10 issues yearly
Cover Price: Free
Circulation: 14,000 (Print Run)
Editor: Vikki Pilbeam
Summary of Content: Magazine covering activities, news, education, book reviews, health and information.
Readership/Target Audience: Aimed at parents and nannies with young children living in Epsom, Sutton and Croydon.
CONSUMER: WOMEN'S INTEREST CONSUMER MAGAZINES: Child Care

FAMILIES FIRST
1641479U74C-884

Formerly: Home and Family
Editorial Address: The Mary Summer House, 24 Tufton Street, LONDON, SW1P 3RB **Tel:** 020 7222 5533
Email: publications@themothersunion.org
Web site: http://www.familiesfirstmagazine.com
Publisher: MU Enterprises Ltd
Frequency: 6 issues yearly
Cover Price: £2.50
Circulation: 46,798 (ABC 01/01/2007 to 31/12/2007)
Editor: Catherine Butcher
Summary of Content: Lifestyle magazine containing practical features about making marriages loving and lasting, good parenting, plus Christian faith in action.
Readership/Target Audience: Aimed at members of the Mothers' Union.
ADVERTISING: Rates on application
CONSUMER: WOMEN'S INTEREST CONSUMER MAGAZINES: Home & Family

FAMILIES GLASGOW
1896977U74D-692

Editorial Address: PO Box 26327, GLASGOW, G76 6AT
Tel: 0141 632 6579 **Fax:** 0141 626 1567
Email: editor@familiesglasgow.co.uk
Web site: http://www.familiesonline.co.uk
Frequency: 10 issues yearly
Cover Price: Free
Circulation: 15,000 (Print Run)
Editor: Anna Wignall
Summary of Content: Magazine covering activities, news, education, book reviews, health and information.
Readership/Target Audience: Aimed at parents and nannies with young children living in Glasgow.
CONSUMER: WOMEN'S INTEREST CONSUMER MAGAZINES: Child Care

FAMILIES HERTS
1896979U74D-693

Editorial Address: PO Box 434, PINNER, HA5 9AH
Tel: 020 8428 6384
Email: editor@familiesherts.co.uk
Web site: http://www.familiesonline.co.uk
Publisher: Families Magazines Ltd

Frequency: 10 issues yearly
Cover Price: Free
Circulation: 17,500 (Print Run)
Editor: Shelley Cooper
Summary of Content: Magazine covering activities, news, education, book reviews, health and information.
Readership/Target Audience: Aimed at parents and nannies with young children living in Chorleywood, Hemel Hempstead, St Albans, Harpenden, Welwyn Garden City, Stevenage, Hitchin and surrounding areas.
CONSUMER: WOMEN'S INTEREST CONSUMER MAGAZINES: Child Care

FAMILIES IN THE VALE OF YORK
1896959U74D-680

Editorial Address: PO Box 201, GOOLE, DN14 9ZW
Tel: 01405 860831
Email: editor@familiesvoy.co.uk
Web site: http://www.familiesonline.co.uk
Publisher: Families Magazines Ltd
Frequency: 10 issues yearly
Cover Price: Free
Circulation: 13,000 (Print Run)
Editor: Belinda Maunsell
Summary of Content: Magazine covering activities, news, education, book reviews, health and information.
Readership/Target Audience: Aimed at parents and nannies with young children living in the Vale of York.
CONSUMER: WOMEN'S INTEREST CONSUMER MAGAZINES: Child Care

FAMILIES LEEDS
1896980U74D-694

Editorial Address: PO Box 403, LEEDS, LS17 1EP
Tel: 01937 579065
Email: editor@familiesleeds.co.uk
Web site: http://www.familiesonline.co.uk
Publisher: Families Magazines Ltd
Frequency: 10 issues yearly
Cover Price: Free
Circulation: 12,000 (Print Run)
Editor: Sarah Butters
Summary of Content: Magazine covering activities, news, education, book reviews, health and information.
Readership/Target Audience: Aimed at parents and nannies with young children living in Leeds.
CONSUMER: WOMEN'S INTEREST CONSUMER MAGAZINES: Child Care

FAMILIES LIVERPOOL
1664928U74D-600

Editorial Address: PO Box 4302, LONDON, SW16 1ZS
Tel: 020 8696 9680 **Fax:** 020 8696 9679
Email: editor@familiesmagazine.co.uk
Advertising Address: Little Orchard, Old Mill Road, TORQUAY, TQ2 6HW **Tel:** 01803 390606
Email: ciaris@blueyonder.co.uk
Web site: http://www.familiesliverpool.com
Publisher: Families Magazines Ltd
Date Established: 2001
Frequency: 6 issues yearly
Cover Price: Free
Circulation: 17,000 (Publisher's Statement)
Usual Pagination: 16
Editor: Pascale Gravell; **Advertising Manager:** Ciaris Perry-Bowden
Summary of Content: Magazine covering local news and listings as well as features on childcare, education, health, parenting, children's parties, travel and family related events.
Readership/Target Audience: Aimed at families and carers of children aged between 0 and 15 years old in Liverpool.
ADVERTISING RATES:
Full Page Mono £940.00
Full Page Colour £1220.00
Mechanical Data: Type Area: 267 x 180mm, Trim Size: 303 x 216mm, Trim Size: 297 x 210mm, Col Widths (Display): 55mm, Col Length: 267mm, Page Width: 180mm
Average advertising content per issue: 40%
CONSUMER: WOMEN'S INTEREST CONSUMER MAGAZINES: Child Care

FAMILIES LONDON
1896961U74D-682

Editorial Address: PO Box 56943, LONDON, N10 9AE
Tel: 020 8815 1351
Email: editor@familiesnorth.co.uk
Web site: http://familiesonline.co.uk
Publisher: Families Magazines Ltd
Frequency: 10 issues yearly
Cover Price: Free
Circulation: 20,000 (Publisher's Statement)
Editor: Harriet Taylor
Summary of Content: Magazine covering activities, news, education, book reviews, health and information.

Readership/Target Audience: Aimed at parents and nannies with young children living in North London.
CONSUMER: WOMEN'S INTEREST CONSUMER MAGAZINES: Child Care

FAMILIES MANCHESTER
1896955U74D-678

Editorial Address: PO Box 614, STOCKPORT, SW4 4WE
Tel: 0161 215 0596
Email: editor@familiesmanchester.co.uk
Web site: http://www.familiesonline.co.uk
Publisher: Families Magazines Ltd
Date Established: 2007
Frequency: 6 issues yearly
Cover Price: Free
Circulation: 20,000 (Publisher's Statement)
Usual Pagination: 16
Editor: Helen Ash
Summary of Content: Magazine covering activities, news, education, book reviews, health and information.
Readership/Target Audience: Aimed at parents and nannies with young children living in Greater Manchester.
CONSUMER: WOMEN'S INTEREST CONSUMER MAGAZINES: Child Care

FAMILIES NORTH WEST
1664931U74D-591

Editorial Address: PO Box 22358, LONDON, W13 8GQ
Tel: 020 8810 5388 **Fax:** 020 8997 3415
Email: editor@familiesnw.co.uk
Advertising Address: As above.
Email: editor@familiesnw.co.uk
Web site: http://www.familiesonline.co.uk
Publisher: Families North West Magazine
Frequency: 6 issues yearly - Published around the 1st of the 1st cover month
Circulation: 22,000 (Publisher's Statement)
Usual Pagination: 30
Editor: Vivienne Kaler; **Advertising Manager:** Vivienne Kaler
Summary of Content: Magazine with local news and information as well as articles on education, childcare, health, travel and events.
Readership/Target Audience: Aimed at families with young children in north west London within the A5, M1, A/M4 and M25.
ADVERTISING RATES:
Full Page Colour £1222.00
Mechanical Data: Trim Size: 297 x 210mm, Bleed Size: +3mm, Type Area: 270 x 180mm, Col Length: 270mm, Page Width: 180mm, Film: Digital
Copy instructions: Copy Date: 4 weeks prior to publication date
Average advertising content per issue: 30%
CONSUMER: WOMEN'S INTEREST CONSUMER MAGAZINES: Child Care

FAMILIES SOLENT EAST
1896962U74D-684

Editorial Address: PO Box 731, SOUTHSEA, PO1 9AR
Tel: 02392 782726
Email: editor@familiessolenteast.co.uk
Web site: http://www.familiesonline.co.uk
Publisher: Families Magazines Ltd
Frequency: 6 issues yearly
Cover Price: Free
Circulation: 23,000 (Publisher's Statement)
Editor: Liz Bourne
Summary of Content: Magazine covering activities, news, education, book reviews, health and information.
Readership/Target Audience: Aimed at parents and nannies with young children living in Portsmouth, PO postcodes, South East Hampshire and the Isle of Wight.
ADVERTISING: No Advertising taken
CONSUMER: WOMEN'S INTEREST CONSUMER MAGAZINES: Child Care

FAMILIES SOLENT WEST
1896965U74D-685

Editorial Address: PO Box 1584, SOUTHAMPTON, SO17 1WJ **Tel:** 02380 671664
Email: editor@familiessolentwest.co.uk
Web site: http://www.familiesonline.co.uk
Publisher: Families Magazines Ltd
Frequency: 10 issues yearly
Cover Price: Free
Circulation: 13,000 (Publisher's Statement)
Summary of Content: Magazine covering activities, news, education, book reviews, health and information.
Readership/Target Audience: Aimed at parents and nannies with young children living in Eastleigh, Southampton, Romsey and New Forest East.
ADVERTISING: No Advertising taken
CONSUMER: WOMEN'S INTEREST CONSUMER MAGAZINES: Child Care

FAMILIES SOUTH EAST
623418U74D-225

Editorial Address: PO Box 11591, LONDON, SE26 6WB
Tel: 020 8699 7240
Email: editor@familiesse.co.uk
Advertising Address: As above.
Email: info@familiesse.co.uk
Web site: http://www.familiesse.co.uk
Publisher: Families Magazines Ltd
Date Established: 1996
Frequency: 10 issues yearly
Free to qualifying individuals
Annual Sub.: £18.00
Circulation: 16,250 (Publisher's Statement)
Usual Pagination: 20
Editor: Robina Cowan; **Advertising Manager:** Robina
Cowan; **Publisher:** Robina Cowan
Summary of Content: Magazine covering parenting,
education, health and childcare issues with product reviews.
Readership/Target Audience: Aimed at parents with
children between 0 and early teens.
ADVERTISING RATES:
Full Page Mono £940.00
Full Page Colour £1222.00
SCC £15.00
Mechanical Data: Col Length: 260mm, Page Width:
180mm, Type Area: 260 x 180mm, Film: Digital
Copy instructions: Copy Date: 1st week of the month prior
to publication date
Average advertising content per issue: 40%
CONSUMER: WOMEN'S INTEREST CONSUMER
MAGAZINES: Child Care

FAMILIES SURREY EAST
1896968U74D-689

Editorial Address: PO Box 816, RICHMOND, TW10 6TA
Tel: 020 8948 6895
Email: editor@familiessurreyeast.co.uk
Web site: http://www.familiesonline.co.uk
Publisher: Families Magazines Ltd
Frequency: 10 issues yearly
Cover Price: Free
Circulation: 20,000 (Print Run)
Editor: Eleanor Lines
Summary of Content: Magazine covering activities, news,
education, book reviews, health and information.
Readership/Target Audience: Aimed at parents and
nannies with young children living in East Surrey.
CONSUMER: WOMEN'S INTEREST CONSUMER
MAGAZINES: Child Care

FAMILIES SURREY WEST
1896967U74D-688

Editorial Address: PO Box 2910, COULSDON, CR5 3WP
Tel: 01737 558898
Email: editor@familiessurreywest.co.uk
Web site: http://www.familiesonline.co.uk
Publisher: Families Magazines Ltd
Frequency: 10 issues yearly
Cover Price: Free
Circulation: 12,000 (Print Run)
Editor: Sarah Hatch
Summary of Content: Magazine covering activities, news,
education, book reviews, health and information.
Readership/Target Audience: Aimed at parents and
nannies with young children living in West Surrey.
CONSUMER: WOMEN'S INTEREST CONSUMER
MAGAZINES: Child Care

FAMILIES SUSSEX COAST
1896963U74D-686

Editorial Address: PO Box 5189, BRIGHTON, BN50 9WN
Tel: 01273 231155
Email: editor@familiessussexcoast.co.uk
Web site: http://www.familiesonline.co.uk
Publisher: Families Magazines Ltd
Frequency: 10 issues yearly
Cover Price: Free
Circulation: 12,000 (Print Run)
Editor: Susan Lightfoot
Summary of Content: Magazine covering activities, news,
education, book reviews, health and information.
Readership/Target Audience: Aimed at parents and
nannies with young children living in Sussex.
CONSUMER: WOMEN'S INTEREST CONSUMER
MAGAZINES: Child Care

FAMILIES SW LONDON
45318U74D-220

Formerly: Families Magazine
Editorial Address: PO Box 4302, LONDON, SW16 1ZS
Tel: 020 8696 9680 **Fax:** 020 8696 9679
Advertising Address: As above.
Email: adverts@familiesmagazine.co.uk
Web site: http://www.familiesmagazine.co.uk
ISSN: 1354-9553
Publisher: Families Magazines Ltd

Date Established: 1990
Frequency: 10 issues yearly - Published in the 1st week of
each cover month
Cover Price: Free
Circulation: 26,000 (Publisher's Statement)
Usual Pagination: 36
Editor: Pascale Gravell; **Advertising Manager:** Pascale
Gravell; **Publisher:** J. D. Gravell
Summary of Content: Magazine covering activities, news,
education, book reviews, health and information.
Language(s): English; French
Readership/Target Audience: Aimed at parents and
nannies with young children living in South West London.
ADVERTISING RATES:
Full Page Mono £940.00
Full Page Colour £1220.00
Copy instructions: Copy Date: 1st of the month prior to
publication date
Average advertising content per issue: 40%
CONSUMER: WOMEN'S INTEREST CONSUMER
MAGAZINES: Child Care

FAMILIES THAMES VALLEY EAST
1664911U74D-601

Editorial Address: PO Box 3902, MAIDENHEAD, SL60 1AD
Tel: 01628 627586 **Fax:** 0871 7146305
Email: editor@familiestveast.co.uk
Advertising Address: As above.
Email: editor@familiestveast.co.uk
Web site: http://www.familiestveast.co.uk
Publisher: Families Magazines Ltd
Date Established: 2002
Frequency: 6 issues yearly - Published in the last week of
the month prior to 1st cover month
Cover Price: Free
Annual Sub.: £15.50
Circulation: 18,000 (Publisher's Statement)
Usual Pagination: 28
Editor: Claire Winter; **Advertising Manager:** Claire Winter
Summary of Content: Magazine with local news and
information, competitions, features on education, child care,
health, leisure, travel, school holiday activities and an in-
depth What's On section.
Readership/Target Audience: Aimed at professional
families with children under 10 years old.
ADVERTISING RATES:
Full Page Mono £940.00
Full Page Colour £1220.00
Mechanical Data: Type Area: 260 x 180mm, Col Length:
260mm, Page Width: 180mm, Col Widths (Display): 55mm,
No. of Columns (Display): 3, Film: Digital
Copy instructions: Copy Date: 3 weeks prior to publication
date
Average advertising content per issue: 40%
CONSUMER: WOMEN'S INTEREST CONSUMER
MAGAZINES: Child Care

FAMILIES THAMES VALLEY WEST
1664905U74D-592

Editorial Address: PO Box 2955, CAVERSHAM, RG1 9PH
Tel: 0118 954 6893 **Fax:** 954 6893
Email: editor@familiestvw.co.uk
Advertising Address: As above.
Email: adverts@familiestvw.co.uk
Web site: http://www.familiestvw.co.uk
Publisher: Families Magazines Ltd
Date Established: 2002
Frequency: 6 issues yearly
Cover Price: Free
Circulation: 19,000 (Publisher's Statement)
Usual Pagination: 32
Editor: Karen Roberts; **Advertising Manager:** Jane
Brianboys
Summary of Content: Magazine with local news and listings
as well as features on child care, education, health,
parenting, children's parties, travel and family-related
events.
Readership/Target Audience: Aimed at families with
children aged 0 to 12 years old.
ADVERTISING RATES:
Full Page Mono £940.00
Full Page Colour £1222.00
Mechanical Data: Type Area: 280 x 180mm, Col Length:
280mm, Page Width: 180mm, Film: Digital
CONSUMER: WOMEN'S INTEREST CONSUMER
MAGAZINES: Child Care

FAMILIES UPON AVON
1896960U74D-683

Editorial Address: PO Box 3296, CORSHAM, SN13 9QY
Tel: 01249 714652
Email: editor@familiesuponavon.co.uk
Web site: http://www.familiesonline.co.uk
Publisher: Families Magazines Ltd
Frequency: 10 issues yearly
Cover Price: Free
Circulation: 13,000 (Print Run)

Editor: Emma Allen
Summary of Content: Magazine covering activities, news,
education, book reviews, health and information.
Readership/Target Audience: Aimed at parents and
nannies with young children living in Bath, Northeast
Somerset, North Wiltshire and Bradford-on-Avon.
CONSUMER: WOMEN'S INTEREST CONSUMER
MAGAZINES: Child Care

FAMILIES UPON THAMES
1664720U74D-590

Editorial Address: PO Box 425, WALTON-ON-THAMES,
KT12 5AG **Tel:** 01932 254584
Email: editor@familiesuponthames.co.uk
Advertising Address: As above.
Email: editor@familiesuponthames.co.uk
Web site: http://www.familiesonline.co.uk
Publisher: Families Magazines Ltd
Frequency: 6 issues yearly
Cover Price: Free
Circulation: 19,000 (Publisher's Statement)
Usual Pagination: 24
Editor: Frances Loates; **Advertising Manager:** Frances
Loates
Summary of Content: Magazine with local news and
information including education, childcare, health, travel and
events.
Readership/Target Audience: Aimed at families with young
children.
ADVERTISING RATES:
Full Page Mono £890.00
Full Page Colour £1157.00
Mechanical Data: Trim Size: 297 x 210mm, Film: Digital
Copy instructions: Copy Date: 1st of the month prior to
publication date
Average advertising content per issue: 40%
CONSUMER: WOMEN'S INTEREST CONSUMER
MAGAZINES: Child Care

FAMILIES WEST
1664907U74D-588

Editorial Address: PO Box 32231, LONDON, W5 1JR
Tel: 020 8930 4707 **Fax:** 020 8930 7704
Email: familieswest@yahoo.co.uk
Advertising Address: As above.
Email: familieswest@yahoo.co.uk
Web site: http://www.familiesonline.co.uk
Publisher: Families Magazines Ltd
Frequency: 6 issues yearly
Cover Price: Free
Annual Sub.: £15.50
Circulation: 17,000 (Publisher's Statement)
Usual Pagination: 24
Editor: Roma Reeves; **Advertising Manager:** Advertising
Manager
Summary of Content: Magazine with local news and
information as well as education, child care, health, travel
and events.
Readership/Target Audience: Aimed at families with young
children.
ADVERTISING: Rates on application
CONSUMER: WOMEN'S INTEREST CONSUMER
MAGAZINES: Child Care

FAMILY
1698255U74C-875

Editorial Address: Kings Place, 90 York Way, LONDON,
N19GU **Tel:** 020 3353 2000
Email: family@guardian.co.uk
Advertising Address: As above.
Email: louise.hemming@guardian.co.uk
Publisher: Guardian Media Group plc
Frequency: Weekly - Published on Saturday within The
Guardian. See main record for circulation figure
Editor: Sally Weale; **Advertising Manager:** Louise
Hemming
Summary of Content: Supplement covering all aspects of
family life including parenting, retirement, family finance,
wellbeing, activities and going out.
ADVERTISING RATES:
Full Page Mono £11400.00
Full Page Colour £18000.00
Mechanical Data: Col Widths (Display): 44mm, No. of
Columns (Display): 10, Film: Digital, Type Area: 440 X
286mm
Supplement to: The Guardian
CONSUMER: WOMEN'S INTEREST CONSUMER
MAGAZINES: Home & Family

FAMILY BREAKS IN BRITAIN
47978U89A-80

Formerly: Children Welcome! Family Holiday & Attractions
Guide
Editorial Address: Abbey Mill Business Centre, Seedhill,
PAISLEY, PA1 1TJ **Tel:** 0141 887 0428 **Fax:** 0141 889 7204
Email: editorial@fhguides.co.uk
Advertising Address: As above. **Fax:** 0141 889 1491
Email: dorothy@fhguides.co.uk
Web site: http://www.holidayguides.com

Consumer Magazines

ISSN: 9781-8505
Publisher: FHG Guides
Date Established: 1970
Frequency: Annual - Published in December
Cover Price: £7.99
Circulation: 15,000 (Publisher's Statement)
Usual Pagination: 180
Editor: Anne Cuthbertson
Summary of Content: Guide containing information on where to go, places to visit, places to stay where families are welcome. Britain's best beaches, tidy beaches, a good beach guide and family-friendly pubs.
Readership/Target Audience: Aimed at parents and families, especially those with babies and young children.
ADVERTISING: Rates on application
CONSUMER: HOLIDAYS & TRAVEL: Travel

THE FAMILY GRAPEVINE   1750244U80C-5350
Editorial Address: Hawthorns, 11 Bell Close, Westbury Sub Mendip, WELLS, BA5 1ET **Tel:** 01793 849928
Email: info@thegrapevine.co.uk
Advertising Address: 11 Bell Close, Westbury Sub Mendip, WELLS, BA5 1ET **Tel:** 01749 870471
Email: info@thegrapevine.co.uk
Web site: http://www.thefamilygrapevine.co.uk
Publisher: Gone to Press Ltd
Date Established: 1996
Frequency: 3 issues yearly - Published in March, July and November
Cover Price: Free
Circulation: 600,000 (Publisher's Statement)
Usual Pagination: 48
Editor: Sheridan Hudson; **Advertising Manager:** Sheridan Hudson
Summary of Content: Free local telephone directory for families covering places to go, things to do, education, helplines, support services and leisure.
Readership/Target Audience: Aimed at families with children of all ages.
ADVERTISING: Rates on application
Editions:
The Family Garapevine North West Leicestershire
The Family Grapevine Ashford and Maidstone
The Family Grapevine Aylesbury & High Wycombe
The Family Grapevine Bath and Wells
The Family Grapevine Bexley
The Family Grapevine Bracknell, Windsor & Camberley
The Family Grapevine Brighton & Hove
The Family Grapevine Bromley Area
The Family Grapevine Cambridge Area
The Family Grapevine Chichester Area
The Family Grapevine Crawley and Horsham
The Family Grapevine Croydon and Sutton
The Family Grapevine East Surrey
The Family Grapevine Eastbourne and Wealden
The Family Grapevine Eastleigh
The Family Grapevine Exeter
The Family Grapevine Fareham & Gosport
The Family Grapevine Great Yarmouth and Broadland
The Family Grapevine Guildford and Farnham
The Family Grapevine Hastings, Rother and Weald of Kent
The Family Grapevine Kingston, Richmond and Wimbledon
The Family Grapevine Lewes & Uckfield
The Family Grapevine Mid Surrey
The Family Grapevine Mid Sussex
The Family Grapevine Midhurst
The Family Grapevine Milton Keynes
Family Grapevine North Somerset
The Family Grapevine North Yorkshire and South Durham
The Family Grapevine Norwich & North Norfolk
Family Grapevine Oadby, Wigston & Harborough District
The Family Grapevine Peterborough and Fenland
Family Grapevine Reading
Family Grapevine Rushmoor & Mid Hart
The Family Grapevine Salisbury
Family Grapevine Sedgemoor
The Family Grapevine Shrewsbury and Telford
The Family Grapevine South Bucks, Chilterns and Slough
The Family Grapevine South Somerset
Family Grapevine South West Leicestershire
Family Grapevine South West Nottinghamshire
The Family Grapevine South West Thames
The Family Grapevine Stockport
The Family Grapevine West Kent
Family Grapevine Winshester
The Family Grapevine Woking, Bagshot and Spelthorne
The Family Grapevine Worthing
CONSUMER: RURAL & REGIONAL INTEREST: Regional Interest English Counties

FAMILY HISTORY MONTHLY   48679U94X-257
Editorial Address: Unit 101, 140 Wales Farm Road, Acton, LONDON, W3 6UG **Tel:** 020 8752 8181 **Fax:** 020 8752 8185
Email: fhm@metropolis.co.uk
Advertising Address: As above. **Tel:** 0870 732 8080
Fax: 0870 732 6060
Email: fhads@metropolis.co.uk
Web site: http://www.familyhistorymonthly.com
Publisher: Diamond Publishing Ltd

Date Established: 1995
Frequency: 13 issues yearly
Cover Price: £3.75
Circulation: 20,000 (Publisher's Statement)
Usual Pagination: 100
Editor: Penny Law; **Publisher:** Andy McDuff
Summary of Content: Magazine covering popular genealogy and British social and military history.
Readership/Target Audience: Aimed at family historians and others interested in social history.
ADVERTISING RATES:
Full Page Mono £530.00
Full Page Colour £550.00
Agency Commission: 15%
Mechanical Data: Type Area: 265 x 182mm, Film: Digital, Col Length: 265mm, Page Width: 182mm, Trim Size: 297 x 210mm
Copy instructions: Copy Date: 4 weeks prior to publication date
CONSUMER: OTHER CLASSIFICATIONS: Miscellaneous

FAMILY INTEREST MAGAZINE
                                                1833006U74D-667
Editorial Address: PO Box 395, SEVENOAKS, TN13 3YG
Tel: 01732 227898 **Fax:** 01732 227881
Email: info@familyinterest.co.uk
Advertising Address: Space Marketing, 10 Clayfield Mews, Newcomen Road, TUNBRIDGE WELLS, TN4 9PA
Tel: 01892 677740
Email: carolyns@spacemarketing.co.uk
Web site: http://www.familyinterest.co.uk
Publisher: Family Interest Magazine
Date Established: 2002
Frequency: 6 issues yearly
Cover Price: Free
Circulation: 20,000 (Publisher's Statement)
Usual Pagination: 32
Editor: Julie McCarthy
Summary of Content: Magazine covering education, health and safety, childcare, pregnancy, women's well-being, lifestyle, green living and parenting as well as events, places to go, local activities, shops and services.
Readership/Target Audience: Aimed at parents of children aged 0 to 12 years old and parents-to-be in East Kent.
ADVERTISING RATES:
Full Page Colour £552.00
Agency Commission: 10%
Mechanical Data: Type Area: 275 x 190mm, Bleed Size: 303 x 216mm, Trim Size: 297 x 210mm, Col Length: 275mm, Page Width: 190mm, Film: Digital
Copy instructions: Copy Date: 4 weeks prior to publication date
CONSUMER: WOMEN'S INTEREST CONSUMER MAGAZINES: Child Care

FAMILY MAGAZINE   707994U74D-245
Editorial Address: 5 Shaw Bridge Street, CLITHEROE, BB7 1LY **Tel:** 01200 453000 **Fax:** 01200 453009
Email: editor@familymagazine.co.uk
Advertising Address: As above.
Email: emma@familymagazine.co.uk
Web site: http://www.familymagazine.co.uk
Publisher: Family Magazine Ltd
Date Established: 1998
Frequency: Quarterly
Cover Price: Free
Circulation: 210,000 (Publisher's Statement)
Usual Pagination: 48
Editor: Liz Burns
Summary of Content: Magazine covering education, recreation and home life for the parents of primary school children.
Readership/Target Audience: Aimed at parents of primary school children.
ADVERTISING RATES:
Full Page Colour £1295.00
Agency Commission: 10%
Mechanical Data: Type Area: 277 x 190mm, Bleed Size: 303 x 216mm, Col Length: 277mm, Film: Digital, Trim Size: 297 x 210mm, Page Width: 190mm
Copy instructions: Copy Date: 3 weeks prior to publication date
Average advertising content per issue: 45%
Editions:
Family Magazine Greater Manchester
Family Magazine Isle of Man
Family Magazine Lancashire
Family Magazine Mersey-Cheshire
Family Magazine Shropshire
Family Magazine Staffordshire
Family Magazine Yorkshire
CONSUMER: WOMEN'S INTEREST CONSUMER MAGAZINES: Child Care

FAMILY TREE MAGAZINE   48680U94X-50
Editorial Address: 61 Great Whyte, Ramsey, HUNTINGDON, PE26 1HJ **Tel:** 01487 814050
Fax: 01487 711361
Email: helen.t@family-tree.co.uk
Advertising Address: As above. **Tel:** 0870 766 2272
Fax: 0870 766 2273
Email: bridgett.b@abmpublishing.co.uk
Web site: http://www.family-tree.co.uk
ISSN: 0267-1131
Publisher: ABM Publishing Ltd
Date Established: 1984
Frequency: 13 issues yearly
Cover Price: £3.75
Annual Sub.: £44.00
Circulation: 42,000 (Publisher's Statement)
Usual Pagination: 100
Editor: Helen Tovey; **Advertising Manager:** Bridgett Baker
Summary of Content: Magazine focusing on family history and genealogy, including a computer section, news, views and name lists.
Readership/Target Audience: Aimed at those with an interest in family history and genealogy.
ADVERTISING RATES:
Full Page Mono £450.00
Full Page Colour £550.00
Agency Commission: 10%
Mechanical Data: Trim Size: 297 x 210mm, Bleed Size: 303 x 216mm, Film: Digital
Copy instructions: Copy Date: 1st of 3 months prior to publication date
CONSUMER: OTHER CLASSIFICATIONS: Miscellaneous

FAMILY WEEKENDER   714072U74D-491_35
Formerly: Family Matters
Editorial Address: Brayford Wharf East, LINCOLN, LN5 7AT
Tel: 01522 820000
Email: karen.parsons@lincolnshireecho.co.uk
Advertising Address: Lincolnshire Echo, Brayford Wharf East, LINCOLN, LN5 7AT **Tel:** 01522 804421
Fax: 01522 804491
Email: ceri@primary-times.co.uk
Web site: http://www.thisislincolnshire.co.uk
Publisher: Lincolnshire Media Ltd
Frequency: 7 issues yearly
Cover Price: Free
Circulation: 20,000 (Publisher's Statement)
Usual Pagination: 40
Editor: Karen Parsons; **Features Editor:** Sarah Overton; **Advertising Manager:** Sarah Eddy
Summary of Content: Magazine covering current educational issues and forthcoming events.
Readership/Target Audience: Read by teachers, parents and children in Lincolnshire.
ADVERTISING: Rates on application
Copy instructions: Copy Date: 2 weeks prior to publication date
CONSUMER: WOMEN'S INTEREST CONSUMER MAGAZINES: Child Care

FAMILY WORDSEARCH   29027U79F-17_75
Editorial Address: Sea Containers House, 20 Upper Ground, LONDON, SE1 9PD **Tel:** 0200 7779 7799
Fax: 020 7928 8157
Email: enquiries@lucky7puzzles.co.uk
Advertising Address: As above. **Tel:** 020 7775 7767
Email: guy.haslam@7publishing.co.uk
Publisher: Seven Publishing
Frequency: 13 issues yearly
Cover Price: £1.99
Usual Pagination: 132
Editor: Guy Haslam; **Advertising Manager:** Guy Haslam; **Managing Editor:** Guy Haslam
Summary of Content: Wordsearch magazine for all of the family.
Readership/Target Audience: Aimed at those who enjoy wordsearch puzzles.
ADVERTISING RATES:
Full Page Colour £1500.00
Agency Commission: 15%
Mechanical Data: Type Area: 245 x 155mm, Col Length: 245mm, Page Width: 155mm, Bleed Size: 275 x 185mm, Trim Size: 265 x 175mm, Film: Digital
Copy instructions: Copy Date: 4 weeks prior to publication date
Average advertising content per issue: 2%
CONSUMER: HOBBIES & DIY: Games & Puzzles

FAMITSU PLAYSTATION+
Formerly: Famitsu PS2!
Editorial Address: 16 Weare Gifford, Shoeburyness, SOUTHEND-ON-SEA, SS3 8AB **Tel:** 01702 589169
Email: rik@modified.demon.co.uk   1638086U78D-302
Advertising Address: As above.
Publisher: Enterbrain Inc.
Date Established: 2000

Frequency: Monthly
Cover Price: £5.49
Circulation: 250,000 (Publisher's Statement)
Editor: Rik Haynes; **Advertising Manager:** Rik Haynes
Summary of Content: Magazine dedicated to Sony's PlayStation 3, PlayStation 2 and PSP videogame consoles with in-depth looks into play strategies as well as features on new gadgets, DVDs, films, TV, music, websites, toys and books.
Readership/Target Audience: Aimed at those who play PlayStation 3, PlayStation 2 or PSP, watch DVDs and buy gadgets.
ADVERTISING: Rates on application
CONSUMER: CONSUMER ELECTRONICS: Games

FARM ANIMAL VOICE
47073U81A-55

Editorial Address: 2nd Floor, River Court, Mill Lane, GODALMING, GU7 1EZ **Tel:** 01483 521950
Fax: 01483 861639
Email: richard@ciwf.co.uk
Web site: http://www.ciwf.org
ISSN: 1473-1800
Publisher: Compassion in World Farming
Frequency: Quarterly
Cover Price: £3.50
Free to qualifying individuals
Annual Sub.: £24.00
Circulation: 26,000 (Publisher's Statement)
Usual Pagination: 24
Editor: Valentina Moressa; **Editor-in-Chief:** Philip Lymbery
Summary of Content: Newsletter of Compassion in World Farming containing campaigns to end the factory farming of animals and long distance transport through hard-hitting political lobbying, investigations and legal battles.
Readership/Target Audience: Aimed at CIWF supporters.
ADVERTISING: No Advertising taken
CONSUMER: ANIMALS & PETS: Animals & Pets Protection

FAST BIKES
46359U77B-494_20

Editorial Address: 30 Monmouth Street, BATH, BA1 2BW
Tel: 01225 442244 **Fax:** 01225 446019
Email: fastbikes@futurenet.com
Advertising Address: As above.
Email: giles.butcher@futurenet.co.uk
Web site: http://www.fastbikesmag.com
Publisher: Future Publishing
Frequency: 13 issues yearly
Cover Price: £3.99
Circulation: 31,418 (ABC 01/01/2008 to 31/12/2008)
Editor: Richard Newland; **Publisher:** Richard Schofield
Summary of Content: Magazine covering all aspects of sports bike riding. Includes news, equipment, road tests and personality profiles.
Readership/Target Audience: Read predominantly by men aged 35 and over with high disposable incomes.
ADVERTISING RATES:
Full Page Colour £1978.00
Agency Commission: 10%
Mechanical Data: Trim Size: 297 x 210mm, Type Area: 277 x 190mm, Col Length: 277mm, Page Width: 190mm, Film: Digital
Copy instructions: Copy Date: 4 weeks prior to publication date
Average advertising content per issue: 30%
CONSUMER: MOTORING & CYCLING: Motorcycling

FAST CAR MAGAZINE
46316U77A-160

Editorial Address: 30 Monmouth Street, BATH, BA1 2BW
Tel: 01225 442244 **Fax:** 01225 446019
Email: steve.chalmers@futurenet.com
Advertising Address: As above.
Email: phil.jones@futurenet.co.uk
Web site: http://www.fastcar.co.uk
ISSN: 0951-7499
Publisher: Future Publishing Ltd
Frequency: 13 issues yearly
Cover Price: £4.35
Circulation: 36,009 (ABC 01/01/2008 to 31/12/2008)
Usual Pagination: 280
Editor: Glenn Rowswell; **Features Editor:** Jamie Burr; **Publisher:** Gez Jones
Summary of Content: Magazine covering performance tuning. Includes the latest street styles and music, people and their cars, product information and tests.
Readership/Target Audience: Read by men between 18 and 35 years old.
ADVERTISING RATES:
Full Page Colour £1897.00
Agency Commission: 10%
Copy instructions: Copy Date: 4 weeks prior to publication date
Average advertising content per issue: 45%
CONSUMER: MOTORING & CYCLING: Motoring

FAST FORD
46317U77A-170

Editorial Address: 30 Monmouth Street, BATH, BA1 2BW
Tel: 01225 442244 **Fax:** 01225 446019
Email: fastford@futurenet.co.uk
Web site: http://www.fastfordmag.co.uk
ISSN: 0958-0522
Publisher: Future Publishing Ltd
Frequency: 13 issues yearly
Cover Price: £4.25
Annual Sub.: £39.00
Circulation: 15,000 (Publisher's Statement)
Usual Pagination: 172
Editor: Dan White; **Features Editor:** Neil Davies;
Advertising Manager: Marc Graham; **Circulation Manager:** Marianne Wulkan
Summary of Content: Magazine covering independent advice on tuning and modifying all Ford models, plus road tests on new launches. Includes features on reader's cars and informed industry and sport comments.
Readership/Target Audience: Read by Ford enthusiasts between 17 and 35 years old.
ADVERTISING: No Advertising taken
CONSUMER: MOTORING & CYCLING: Motoring

FATE & FORTUNE
1637732U94E-354

Editorial Address: Academic House, 24-28 Oval Road, LONDON, NW1 7DT **Tel:** 020 7241 8000 **Fax:** 020 7241 8056
Email: fate.fortune@bauer.co.uk
Advertising Address: As above.
Email: lisa.carver@bauer.co.uk
Publisher: H. Bauer Publishing
Date Established: 2001
Frequency: Monthly
Cover Price: £1.70
Circulation: 90,000 (Publisher's Statement)
Usual Pagination: 60
Editor: Sue Ricketts; **Features Editor:** Clair Stretton; **Advertising Manager:** Lisa Carver
Summary of Content: Magazine covering aspects of astrology, psychic interest and the paranormal in the style of real life experience.
Readership/Target Audience: Aimed at readers of Take a Break and all women aged between 25 and 55 years old.
ADVERTISING RATES:
Full Page Colour £3500.00
Agency Commission: 15%
Mechanical Data: Film: Digital, Type Area: 260 x 190mm, Bleed Size: 288 x 218mm, Trim Size: 280 x 210mm, Col Length: 260mm, Page Width: 190mm
Copy instructions: Copy Date: 4 weeks prior to publication date
Average advertising content per issue: 10%
CONSUMER: OTHER CLASSIFICATIONS: Paranormal

FEATHERED WORLD
47171U81F-170

Editorial Address: 5 Winckley Street, PRESTON, PR1 2AA
Tel: 0870 417 8910 **Fax:** 0870 417 8910
Email: feathered.world@winckley.co.uk
Advertising Address: As above.
Email: bob@winckley.co.uk
Web site: http://www.pigeonmagazine.co.uk
ISSN: 0264-9063
Publisher: Winckley Press
Date Established: 1984
Frequency: Monthly - Published on the 15th of the month
Annual Sub.: £24.00
Circulation: 1,200 (Publisher's Statement)
Usual Pagination: 28
Editor: Robert Batty; **Advertising Manager:** Dorothy Silver; **Managing Editor:** Robert Batty
Summary of Content: Publication featuring fancy pigeon and poultry news.
Readership/Target Audience: Read by breeders and exhibitors.
ADVERTISING RATES:
Full Page Mono £181.00
Full Page Colour £290.00
SCC £3.40
Agency Commission: 10%
Mechanical Data: Col Length: 270mm, Col Widths (Display): 90mm, Film: Positive, right reading, emulsion side down, Print Process: Offset litho, No. of Columns (Display): 2, Trim Size: 297 x 210mm, Bleed Size: 310 x 210mm, Page Width: 180mm, Type Area: 270 x 180mm
Copy instructions: Copy Date: Last day of month prior to publication date
Average advertising content per issue: 5%
CONSUMER: ANIMALS & PETS: Birds

FEEL ALIVE
1862580U80C-5476

Editorial Address: 1 Castle Yard, Off Hay Lane, COVENTRY, CV1 5RF **Tel:** 024 7660 7015
Fax: 024 7660 7001
Email: feelalive@cvone.co.uk
Advertising Address: As above.
Web site: http://www.feelalivemagazine.co.uk

Publisher: Trinity Mirror
Date Established: 2005
Frequency: 3 issues yearly - Published in April, July and November
Cover Price: Free
Circulation: 150,000 (Publisher's Statement)
Editor: Mick McLaughlin
Summary of Content: Magazine covering lifestyle, city centre business, news, fashion, features and competitions.
Readership/Target Audience: Aimed at residents living in Coventry and the surrounding areas.
CONSUMER: RURAL & REGIONAL INTEREST: Regional Interest English Counties

FELIX
47387U83-8

Editorial Address: Beit Quad, Prince Consort Road, LONDON, SW7 2BB **Tel:** 020 7594 8072 **Fax:** 020 7594 8065
Email: felix@imperial.ac.uk
Advertising Address: As above.
Email: felix@imperial.ac.uk
Web site: http://www.felixonline.co.uk
ISSN: 1040-0711
Publisher: Imperial College Union Media Group
Date Established: 1949
Frequency: 29 issues yearly - Published every Friday during academic terms
Cover Price: Free
Circulation: 11,000 (Publisher's Statement)
Usual Pagination: 28
Advertising Manager: Advertising Contact
Summary of Content: Newspaper covering news and reviews, sport, competitions, topical and scientific features.
Readership/Target Audience: Read by students and staff.
ADVERTISING RATES:
Full Page Colour £1650.00
Agency Commission: 5%
Mechanical Data: Trim Size: 369 x 272mm, Film: Digital
Copy instructions: Copy Date: 7 days prior to publication date
CONSUMER: STUDENT PUBLICATIONS

FELIXSTOWE TOWN CRIER
46973U80C-2933

Editorial Address: Unit 1, Mannings Amusement Park, Mackle Gate Road, FELIXSTOWE, IP11 2DN
Tel: 01394 270811
Email: chris@felixstowetowncrierltd.com
Advertising Address: As above.
Email: ads@felixstowetowncrierltd.co.uk
Web site: http://www.felixstowetowncrierltd.co.uk
Publisher: Felixstowe Town Crier Ltd
Date Established: 1978
Frequency: Monthly - Published on the 1st of each month
Cover Price: Free
Circulation: 14,600 (Publisher's Statement)
Usual Pagination: 16
Editor: Chris Taylor; **Advertising Manager:** Chris Taylor
Summary of Content: Publication covering local news, business, society and club news, events and information.
Readership/Target Audience: Aimed at residents and businesses in the Felixstowe area.
ADVERTISING RATES:
Full Page Colour £350.00
Agency Commission: 10%
Mechanical Data: Type Area: 468 x 316mm, Col Length: 468mm, Page Width: 316mm, Bleed Size: +5mm, Film: Digital
Copy instructions: Copy Date: Middle of the month prior to publication date
Average advertising content per issue: 40%
CONSUMER: RURAL & REGIONAL INTEREST: Regional Interest English Counties

FEMINISM & PSYCHOLOGY
45671U74Q-230

Editorial Address: 1 Oliver's Yard, 55 City Road, LONDON, EC1Y 1SP **Tel:** 020 7324 8500 **Fax:** 020 7324 8600
Email: Sue_Wilkinson_2000@yahoo.com
Advertising Address: As above.
Email: advertising@sagepub.co.uk
Web site: http://www.sagepub.co.uk
ISSN: 0959-3535
Publisher: Sage Publications
Date Established: 1992
Frequency: Quarterly
Annual Sub.: £49.00
Circulation: 500 (Publisher's Statement)
Editor: Sue Wilkinson; **Advertising Manager:** Sheena Karim
Summary of Content: Magazine focusing on the development of feminist theory and practice.
Readership/Target Audience: Read by psychologists, feminists and students.
ADVERTISING RATES:
Full Page Mono £500.00
Agency Commission: 5%
Mechanical Data: Col Length: 205mm, Page Width: 130mm, Film: Digital, Type Area: 205 x 130mm

Copy instructions: Copy Date: 12 weeks prior to publication date
CONSUMER: WOMEN'S INTEREST CONSUMER MAGAZINES: Lifestyle

FEMINIST THEORY
601447U82-22_80

Editorial Address: 1 Oliver's Yard, 55 City Road, LONDON, EC1Y 1SP **Tel:** 020 7324 8500 **Fax:** 020 7324 8600
Advertising Address: As above.
Email: advertising@sagepub.co.uk
Web site: http://www.sagepub.co.uk
ISSN: 1464-7001
Publisher: Sage Publications
Date Established: 2000
Frequency: 3 issues yearly - Published in April, August and December
Annual Sub.: £41.00
Circulation: 475 (Publisher's Statement)
Usual Pagination: 128
Editor: Sasha Roseneil
Summary of Content: International, interdisciplinary journal providing a forum for critical analysis and debate within feminist theory.
Readership/Target Audience: Aimed at academics with an interest in the Feminist Theory.
ADVERTISING RATES:
Full Page Mono £450.00
Agency Commission: 5%
Mechanical Data: Type Area: 210 x 140mm, Col Length: 210mm, Page Width: 140mm, Film: Digital
Copy instructions: Copy Date: 3 months prior to publication date
CONSUMER: CURRENT AFFAIRS & POLITICS

FERRARI MAGAZINE
46452U77E-153

Editorial Address: 14 Lynn Road, Snettisham, KING'S LYNN, PE317PT **Tel:** 01485 544500 **Fax:** 01485 544515
Email: ever.focuk@btinternet.com
Advertising Address: 360 Advertising, 13 Victoria Road, STAMFORD, PE9 1HB **Tel:** 01780 767080
Email: mark@360advertising.co.uk
Web site: http://www.ferrariownersclub.co.uk
Publisher: The Ferrari Owners Club Ltd
Date Established: 1967
Frequency: Quarterly
Annual Sub.: £20.00
Circulation: 3,200 (Publisher's Statement)
Usual Pagination: 64
Editor: Peter Everingham; **Advertising Manager:** Mark Wibberley
Summary of Content: Magazine of the Ferrari Owners Club, containing articles relating to Ferrari cars, historical information, current activity, Ferrari events worldwide, competition and Formula 1.
Readership/Target Audience: Read by Ferrari owners and enthusiasts.
ADVERTISING RATES:
Full Page Mono £480.00
Full Page Colour £805.00
Mechanical Data: Trim Size: 297 x 210mm, Col Length: 275mm, Page Width: 188mm, Type Area: 275 x 188mm, Bleed Size: +3mm, Film: Digital
Copy instructions: Copy Date: 3 weeks prior to publication date
Average advertising content per issue: 30%
CONSUMER: MOTORING & CYCLING: Club Cars

FERRARI NEWS
46453U77E-154

Editorial Address: 14 Lynn Road, Snettisham, KING'S LYNN, PE31 7PT **Tel:** 01485 544500 **Fax:** 01485 544515
Email: ever.focuk@btinternet.com
Advertising Address: 13 Victoria Road, STAMFORD, PE9 1HB **Tel:** 01780 767080 **Fax:** 01780 753993
Email: mark@wibbs.co.uk
Web site: http://www.ferrariownersclub.co.uk
Publisher: The Ferrari Owners Club Ltd
Date Established: 1967
Frequency: 6 issues yearly
Free to qualifying individuals
Circulation: 3,000 (Publisher's Statement)
Usual Pagination: 64
Editor: Peter Everingham; **Advertising Manager:** Mark Wibberley
Summary of Content: Newsletter of the Ferrari Owners Club. Covers news, events, personalities, club activities, events and Formula One.
Readership/Target Audience: Read by club members and Ferrari enthusiasts.
ADVERTISING: Rates on application
Copy instructions: Copy Date: 4 weeks prior to publication date
Average advertising content per issue: 30%
CONSUMER: MOTORING & CYCLING: Club Cars

FFESTINIOG RAILWAY MAGAZINE
46702U79J-17

Editorial Address: Harbour Station, PORTHMADOG, LL49 9NF **Tel:** 01766 530670
Email: editor@ffestiniograilway.org.uk
Advertising Address: 3 Glebe Road, WALLASEY, CH45 6UL **Tel:** 0151 639 8693 **Fax:** 0151 639 8693
Email: advertising@ffestiniograilway.org.uk
Web site: http://www.festrail.co.uk
ISSN: 0015-0355
Publisher: Ffestiniog Railway Society
Date Established: 1958
Frequency: Quarterly - Published on 1st January, April, July and October
Cover Price: £3.00
Free to qualifying individuals
Annual Sub.: £22.00
Circulation: 4,600 (Publisher's Statement)
Usual Pagination: 48
Editor: John Dobson; **Advertising Manager:** Tom Bowen
Summary of Content: The Journal of the Ffestiniog Railway Society, containing news and articles relating to Ffestiniog Railway and narrow-gauge railways worldwide.
Language(s): English; Welsh
Readership/Target Audience: Read by staff and supporters of Ffestiniog Railway.
ADVERTISING RATES:
Full Page Mono £150.00
Full Page Colour £225.00
Mechanical Data: Page Width: 130mm, Film: Digital, Type Area: 190 x 130mm, Col Length: 190mm
Copy instructions: Copy Date: 10th of the month prior to publication date
Average advertising content per issue: 10%
CONSUMER: HOBBIES & DIY: Rail Enthusiasts

FHG COAST & COUNTRY HOLIDAYS
47980U89A-160

Formerly: Farm Holiday Guide to Coast & Country Holidays
Editorial Address: Abbey Mill Business Centre, Seedhill, PAISLEY, PA1 1TJ **Tel:** 0141 887 0428 **Fax:** 0141 889 7204
Email: editorial@fhguides.co.uk
Advertising Address: As above.
Email: sales@fhguides.co.uk
Web site: http://www.holidayguides.com
Publisher: FHG Guides
Date Established: 1948
Frequency: Annual - Published in November
Cover Price: £6.99
Circulation: 25,000 (Publisher's Statement)
Usual Pagination: 320
Editor: Anne Cuthbertson; **Advertising Manager:** Dorothy Clements
Summary of Content: Guide to coast and country holidays throughout England, Wales, Ireland and the Channel Islands, including boarding, self catering accommodation, caravan and camping sites and activity holidays.
Readership/Target Audience: Read by holidaymakers in the UK.
ADVERTISING: Rates on application
CONSUMER: HOLIDAYS & TRAVEL: Travel

FHM
47645U86C-180

Editorial Address: Mappin House, 4 Winsley Street, LONDON, W1W 8HF **Tel:** 020 7182 8000
Fax: 020 7182 8021
Email: general@fhm.com
Advertising Address: Endeavour House, 189 Shaftesbury Avenue, LONDON, WC2H 8JG **Tel:** 020 7295 5000
Fax: 020 7295 5400
Email: liz.jazayeri@baueradvertising.co.uk
Web site: http://www.fhm.com
ISSN: 0966-0933
Publisher: Bauer Consumer Media Ltd (Mappin House)
Frequency: Monthly
Cover Price: £3.80
Circulation: 235,027 (ABC 01/01/2009 to 30/06/2009)
Usual Pagination: 300
Editor: Sarah Ketterer; **Advertising Manager:** Liz Jazayeri
Summary of Content: Men's lifestyle magazine covering celebrity gossip, fashion, music and film reviews.
Twitter: https://twitter.com/FHM_UK.
Readership/Target Audience: Aimed at men aged 20 years old and over.
ADVERTISING RATES:
Full Page Colour £21000.00
Agency Commission: 15%
Mechanical Data: Type Area: 274 x 188mm, Bleed Size: 306 x 226mm, Trim Size: 300 x 220mm, Film: Digital, Col Length: 274mm, Page Width: 188mm
Copy instructions: Copy Date: 1 month prior to publication date
CONSUMER: ADULT & GAY MAGAZINES: Men's Lifestyle Magazines

FHP MAGAZINE
1626076U80C-5064

Editorial Address: Unit 2A Stoney House, 26-30 Stoney Street, The Lacemarket, NOTTINGHAM, NG1 1LL
Tel: 0115 924 2681 **Fax:** 0115 950 6075
Email: enquiries@fhpmagazine.co.uk
Advertising Address: As above.
Email: enquiries@fhpmagazine.co.uk
Web site: http://www.fhpmagazine.co.uk
Publisher: Trident Media
Date Established: 2002
Frequency: 6 issues yearly
Cover Price: £2.95
Free to qualifying individuals
Circulation: 20,000 (Publisher's Statement)
Usual Pagination: 140
Editor: Kathryn Clifford
Summary of Content: Lifestyle magazine covering city development, property, social events, entertainment, places to eat and drink, theatre and a who's who.
Readership/Target Audience: Aimed at those living and working in Nottingham.
ADVERTISING RATES:
Full Page Colour £1450.00
Agency Commission: 10%
Mechanical Data: Trim Size: 270 x 190mm, Bleed Size: 280 x 200mm
Average advertising content per issue: 50%
CONSUMER: RURAL & REGIONAL INTEREST: Regional Interest English Counties

FICTION
1705246U76A-191

Editorial Address: 7 Alicia Gardens, HARROW, HA3 8JB
Tel: 020 8837 3025
Email: fiction_red@yahoo.com
Advertising Address: As above.
Publisher: La Cantina
Frequency: Monthly
Cover Price: £2.00
Annual Sub.: £24.00
Circulation: 20,000 (Publisher's Statement)
Editor: Margarita Pardo
Summary of Content: Magazine providing news and reviews of cinematic releases.
Language(s): English; Spanish
Readership/Target Audience: Aimed at cinema enthusiasts.
ADVERTISING: Rates on application
CONSUMER: MUSIC & PERFORMING ARTS: Cinema

THE FIELD
46805U80A-100

Editorial Address: Blue Fin Building, 110 Southwark Street, LONDON, SE1 0SU **Tel:** 020 3148 5000 **Fax:** 020 3148 8179
Email: field_secretary@ipcmedia.com
Advertising Address: As above.
Email: rosemary_archer@ipcmedia.com
Web site: http://www.thefield.co.uk
ISSN: 0015-0649
Publisher: IPC Inspire
Date Established: 1853
Frequency: Monthly - Published the 1st of the month
Cover Price: £3.80
Annual Sub.: £42.00
Circulation: 31,292 (ABC 01/01/2008 to 31/12/2008)
Editor: Sarah Fitzpatrick; **Features Editor:** Sarah Fitzpatrick; **Advertising Manager:** Rosemary Archer;
Publisher: Fiona Mercer
Summary of Content: Magazine covering hunting, shooting, fishing, cars, property, gardening, food, fine arts and antiques.
Readership/Target Audience: Read by residents in the country and those who enjoy country pursuits.
ADVERTISING RATES:
Full Page Colour £3318.00
Agency Commission: 10%
Mechanical Data: Type Area: 267 x 203mm, Bleed Size: 306 x 236mm, Trim Size: 300 x 230mm, Col Length: 267mm, Page Width: 203mm, Film: Digital
Copy instructions: Copy Date: 1st of month prior to publication date
Average advertising content per issue: 42%
CONSUMER: RURAL & REGIONAL INTEREST: Rural Interest

FIELDSPORTS
1794223U75F-213

Editorial Address: Roebuck House, 33 Broad Street, STAMFORD, PE9 1RB **Tel:** 01780 766199
Fax: 01780 766416
Email: info@fieldsportsmagazine.co.uk
Advertising Address: As above. **Tel:** 01780 754900
Fax: 01780 754774
Email: a.desborough@bournepublishinggroup.co.uk
Web site: http://www.fieldsportsmag.co.uk
Publisher: BPG (Stamford) Ltd
Date Established: 2006
Frequency: Quarterly
Cover Price: £5.00

Annual Sub.: £22.50
Circulation: 20,000 (Publisher's Statement)
Usual Pagination: 164
Editor: Mike Barnes
Summary of Content: Magazine covering field sports including shooting and fishing.
Readership/Target Audience: Aimed at men and women who are passionate about field sports.
ADVERTISING RATES:
Full Page Colour £2880.00
Agency Commission: 10%
Mechanical Data: Type Area: 240 x 200mm, Bleed Size: 284 x 238mm, Trim Size: 275 x 228mm, Col Length: 240mm, Page Width: 200mm, Film: Digital
Copy instructions: Copy Date: 4 weeks prior to publication date
Average advertising content per issue: 15%
CONSUMER: SPORT: Shooting

FIESTA
47607U86A-70

Editorial Address: PO Box 312, WITHAM, CM8 3SZ
Tel: 01376 534538 **Fax:** 01376 534546
Email: editor@fiesta.co.uk
Advertising Address: As above.
Email: sales@galaxy.co.uk
Web site: http://www.fiesta.co.uk
Publisher: Galaxy Publications
Date Established: 1966
Frequency: 13 issues yearly
Cover Price: £3.25
Circulation: 70,000 (Publisher's Statement)
Usual Pagination: 132
Editor: Matthew Elliott; **Advertising Manager:** Anne Hanley
Summary of Content: Glamour magazine including film and occasional video, book, game and music reviews.
Readership/Target Audience: Aimed at men but has women enthusiasts.
ADVERTISING: Rates on application
Agency Commission: 15%
Copy instructions: Copy Date: 6 weeks prior to publication date
CONSUMER: ADULT & GAY MAGAZINES: Adult Magazines

FIGHTERS & KICK BOXING NEWS
45989U75Q-300

Formerly: Fighters - The Martial Arts Magazine
Editorial Address: Unit 20, Maybrook Business Park, Maybrook Road, SUTTON COLDFIELD, B76 1BE
Tel: 0121 351 6930
Email: fighters@martialartsinprint.com
Advertising Address: Regent House, 135 Aldridge Road, Perry Barr, BIRMINGHAM, B42 2ET **Tel:** 0121 344 3737
Fax: 0121 356 7300
Email: paul@martialartsinprint.com
Web site: http://www.martialartsinprint.com
ISSN: 0260-4965
Publisher: Martial Arts Publications Ltd
Date Established: 1976
Frequency: Monthly
Cover Price: £3.50
Annual Sub.: £38.95
Usual Pagination: 100
Advertising Manager: Paul Clifton; **Publisher:** Paul Clifton
Summary of Content: Magazine covering all aspects of competitive martial arts, in particular kick boxing, Thai boxing, mixed martial arts, K1 and all sporting martial arts.
Readership/Target Audience: Aimed at all martial arts enthusiasts and competitors.
ADVERTISING RATES:
Full Page Colour £795.50
Agency Commission: 10%
Mechanical Data: Trim Size: 297 x 210mm, Print Process: Web-fed offset litho, Film: Digital
Copy instructions: Copy Date: 5 weeks prior to publication date
Average advertising content per issue: 20%
CONSUMER: SPORT: Combat Sports

FIGHTERS ONLY
1912403U75Q-858

Editorial Address: i2 Media ltd, 200 Portland Road, Shieldfield, NEWCASTLE UPON TYNE, NE2 1DJ
Tel: 0191 233 2225
Email: fighters.only@googlemail.com
Web site: http://www.fightersonlymagazine.co.uk
Editor: Hywel Teague
Summary of Content: magazine aimed at fans of mixed martial arts.
Readership/Target Audience: Aimed at anyone with an interest in martial arts.
CONSUMER: SPORT: Combat Sports

FIGHTING FIT
1896487U75Q-854

Editorial Address: 30 Cannon Street, LONDON, EC4M 6YJ
Tel: 020 7618 3456
Email: tris.dixon@fightingfitmagazine.co.uk

Web site: http://www.fightingfitmagazine.co.uk
Publisher: Newsquest Specialist Media Ltd
Date Established: 2009
Frequency: 6 issues yearly
Cover Price: £4.35
Circulation: 20,000 (Print Run)
Usual Pagination: 100
Editor: Tris Dixon
Summary of Content: Magazine covering boxing, mixed martial arts, judo, taekwondo, karate and thai boxing with advice from experts concerning strength, power, nutrition, fitness and psychology and interviews from some of the leading fighters in the world. Also features a lifestyle section covering gyms, product reviews and articles on trends in the industry.
Readership/Target Audience: Aimed at combat athletes of all levels.
CONSUMER: SPORT: Combat Sports

FIGHTING SPIRIT
1745354U75Q-852

Editorial Address: B10 Arena Business Centre, Holyrood Close, POOLE, BH17 7BA **Tel:** 01202 606385
Fax: 01202 606386
Email: customerservice@uncookedmedia.com
Advertising Address: As above.
Email: rob@uncookedmedia.com
Web site: http://www.fightingspiritmagazine.co.uk
Publisher: Uncooked Media Ltd
Date Established: 2006
Frequency: Monthly
Cover Price: £2.99
Circulation: 35,000 (Print Run)
Usual Pagination: 82
Editor: Martin Mathers; **Advertising Manager:** Rob Cox
Summary of Content: Magazine covering pro-wrestling, mixed martial arts, features, interviews and events.
Readership/Target Audience: Aimed at fight fans.
ADVERTISING RATES:
Full Page Colour £2350.00
Agency Commission: 10%
Mechanical Data: Type Area: 287 x 200mm, Bleed Size: 303 x 216mm, Trim Size: 297 x 210mm, Col Length: 287mm, Page Width: 200mm, Film: Digital
Average advertising content per issue: 25%
CONSUMER: SPORT: Combat Sports

FIGHTSPORT
1854667U75Q-853

Editorial Address: UKD House, Norstead Place, LONDON, SW15 3SA **Tel:** 020 8246 5900 **Fax:** 020 8246 5920
Email: info@fightsportmagazine.co.uk
Web site: http://www.fightsportmagazine.co.uk
Publisher: UK Distribution Services Ltd
Frequency: Monthly
Cover Price: £3.75
Circulation: 120,000 (Publisher's Statement)
Usual Pagination: 100
Editor: Sheena Findlay
Summary of Content: Magazine covering all aspects of mixed martial arts.
Readership/Target Audience: Aimed predominately at males aged between 12 and 45 years old.
CONSUMER: SPORT: Combat Sports

FILM & FESTIVALS
1794072U76A-205

Formerly: The FILMFESTIVAL Magazine
Editorial Address: The Hat Factory, 65-67 Bute Street, LUTON, LU1 2EY **Tel:** 01582 727330 **Fax:** 01582 726910
Email: rose@filmandfestivals.com
Advertising Address: 6 Market Place, LONDON, W1W 8AF
Tel: 020 7436 9494
Email: saratyleruk@aol.com
Web site: http://www.filmandfestivals.com
ISSN: 1755-5485
Publisher: Wallflower Press
Date Established: 2006
Frequency: Quarterly
Cover Price: £3.75
Free to qualifying individuals
Annual Sub.: £15.00
Circulation: 5,000 (Publisher's Statement)
Usual Pagination: 60
Editor: Vicki Psarias; **Editor-in-Chief:** Rose Chamberlain; **Advertising Manager:** Sara Tyler
Summary of Content: Magazine covering film festivals in the UK and Europe. Show-cases non specialised films.
Readership/Target Audience: Aimed at cinema lovers and film professionals.
ADVERTISING RATES:
Full Page Colour £800.00
Mechanical Data: Trim Size: 335 x 245mm
CONSUMER: MUSIC & PERFORMING ARTS: Cinema

FILM AND VIDEO MAKER
47603U85B-50

Editorial Address: 40 Runnymeade, Swinton, MANCHESTER, M27 5WA **Tel:** 0161 794 6743
Fax: 0161 794 6743
Email: garth.hope@ntlworld.com
Advertising Address: 37 Canberra, STONEHOUSE, GL10 .2PR **Tel:** 01453 823802
Email: leepres@anglovideogxy.demon.co.uk
Web site: http://www.theaic.org.uk
Publisher: Film Maker Publications Ltd
Frequency: 6 issues yearly
Annual Sub.: £36.50
Circulation: 2,000 (Publisher's Statement)
Usual Pagination: 36
Editor: Garth Hope; **Advertising Manager:** Lee Prescott
Summary of Content: Magazine promoting video, film and audio-visual.
Readership/Target Audience: Read by members of video and cine clubs and people interested in film & video.
ADVERTISING RATES:
Full Page Mono £195.00
Full Page Colour £250.00
SCC £4.95
Agency Commission: 10%
Mechanical Data: Col Length: 270mm, Col Widths (Display): 57mm, No. of Columns (Display): 3, Bleed Size: +3mm, Page Width: 185mm, Film: Digital, Type Area: 270 x 185mm, Trim Size: 297 x 210mm
Copy instructions: Copy Date: 25th of the month prior to publication date
CONSUMER: PHOTOGRAPHY & FILM MAKING: Film Making

FILM REVIEW
46046U76A-25

Editorial Address: 9-10 Blades Court, Deodar Road, LONDON, SW15 2NU **Tel:** 020 8875 7417
Fax: 020 8875 1588
Email: filmreview@visimag.com
Advertising Address: As above. **Tel:** 020 8875 1520
Email: mclarke@visimag.com
Web site: http://www.visimag.com/filmreview
ISSN: 0957-1809
Publisher: Visual Imagination Ltd
Date Established: 1955
Frequency: Monthly
Cover Price: £3.99
Annual Sub.: £35.00
Circulation: 44,000 (Publisher's Statement)
Usual Pagination: 132
Editor: Nikki Baughan; **Managing Director:** Stephen Payne
Summary of Content: Film magazine covering the latest releases in the British and international scene. Includes news, interviews and film, DVD, book and CD reviews.
Readership/Target Audience: Aimed at movie enthusiasts aged between 15 and 80 years old.
ADVERTISING RATES:
Full Page Colour £1150.00
Agency Commission: 10%
Mechanical Data: Type Area: 270 x 192mm, Bleed Size: 307 x 230mm, Trim Size: 297 x 220mm, Col Length: 270mm, Film: Digital, Page Width: 192mm
Copy instructions: Copy Date: 2 weeks prior to publication date
CONSUMER: MUSIC & PERFORMING ARTS: Cinema

FILMSTAR
1900531U76A-232

Editorial Address: 20 Monmouth Place, BATH, BA1 2AY
Tel: 01225 338828 **Fax:** 01225 338890
Email: mail@blackfishpublishing.com
Web site: http://blackfishpublishing.com
Publisher: Blackfish Publishing Ltd
Date Established: 2009
Frequency: Monthly
Cover Price: £3.99
Circulation: 55,000 (Publisher's Statement)
Editor: Matt Bielby
Summary of Content: Magazine covering in-depth interviews with major actors, directors and other key film makers.
Readership/Target Audience: Aimed at film-goers and DVD purchasers aged 25 and older.
CONSUMER: MUSIC & PERFORMING ARTS: Cinema

FINE & COUNTRY
1645902U74K-681

Formerly: Prestige Properties
Editorial Address: 3 Signet Court, Swann Road, CAMBRIDGE, CB5 8LA **Tel:** 01223 443904
Email: admin@fineandcountry.com
Web site: http://www.fineandcountry.com
Publisher: Fine & Country Ltd
Date Established: 1993
Frequency: 10 issues yearly
Cover Price: £3.95
Free to qualifying individuals
Circulation: 15,000 (Publisher's Statement)
Usual Pagination: 164

Editor: Becky Bing
Summary of Content: Magazine covering property, lifestyle, interiors, interior design, kitchens and bathrooms.
Readership/Target Audience: Aimed at prospective house purchasers.
ADVERTISING: No Advertising taken
CONSUMER: WOMEN'S INTEREST CONSUMER MAGAZINES: Home Purchase

FIREMAN SAM
1777371U91D-947

Editorial Address: 239 Kensington High Street, LONDON, W8 6SA **Tel:** 020 7761 3500 **Fax:** 020 7761 3510
Email: jtarrant@euk.egmont.com
Advertising Address: As above.
Email: aallen@euk.egmont.com
Publisher: Egmont Magazines UK
Date Established: 2006
Frequency: 13 issues yearly
Cover Price: £1.85
Circulation: 29,532 (ABC 01/01/2009 to 30/06/2009)
Usual Pagination: 32
Editor: Jane Tarrant; **Advertising Manager:** Annett Allen
Summary of Content: Children's magazine with stories, puzzles and posters based on the TV character Fireman Sam.
Readership/Target Audience: Aimed at boys aged between 3 and 6 years old.
ADVERTISING RATES:
Full Page Colour £1800.00
Agency Commission: 10%
Mechanical Data: Type Area: 282 x 202mm, Bleed Size: 306 x 226mm, Trim Size: 300 x 220mm, Col Length: 282mm, Page Width: 202mm, Film: Digital
Copy instructions: Copy Date: 4 weeks prior to publication date
Average advertising content per issue: 40%
CONSUMER: RECREATION & LEISURE: Children & Youth

THE FIRESIDE BOOK OF DAVID HOPE
47558U84B-59

Editorial Address: 185 Fleet Street, LONDON, EC4A 2HS
Tel: 01382 223131 **Fax:** 01382 322214
Email: mail@scotsmagazine.com
Publisher: D.C. Thomson & Co Ltd
Date Established: 1968
Frequency: Annual - Published in September
Circulation: 30,000 (Publisher's Statement)
Editor: John Methven
Summary of Content: Anthology of old and new poems.
Readership/Target Audience: Aimed at all people interested in poetry.
ADVERTISING: No Advertising taken
CONSUMER: THE ARTS & LITERARY: Literary

FIRST LIFE
1703375U89D-521

Editorial Address: 85 Strand, LONDON, WC2R 0DW
Tel: 020 7550 8000 **Fax:** 020 7550 8250
Email: harriet.cooper@cedarcom.co.uk
Advertising Address: As above. **Fax:** 020 7550 8252
Email: jennie.edwards@bamedia.co.uk
Publisher: Cedar Communications
Frequency: 6 issues yearly
Cover Price: Free
Usual Pagination: 46
Editor: Harriet Cooper; **Advertising Manager:** Jennie Edwards
Summary of Content: Magazine covering luxury travel, gadgets, fashion, restaurants, hotels and spas worldwide.
Readership/Target Audience: Aimed at passengers in first class cabins on British Airways flights.
ADVERTISING RATES:
Full Page Colour £4218.00
Mechanical Data: Type Area: 265 x 195mm, Bleed Size: 295 x 216mm, Trim Size: 289 x 210mm, Col Length: 265mm, Page Width: 195mm, Film: Digital
Copy instructions: Copy Date: 5 weeks prior to publication date
Average advertising content per issue: 40%
CONSUMER: HOLIDAYS & TRAVEL: In-Flight Magazines

FIRST NEWS
1744889U74F-764

Editorial Address: First News House, 95 The Street, West Horsley, LEATHERHEAD, KT24 6DD **Tel:** 01483 281005
Email: newsdesk@firstnews.co.uk
Advertising Address: As above.
Email: lindsaye.fox@firstnews.co.uk
Web site: http://www.firstnews.co.uk
Publisher: Newsbridge Ltd
Date Established: 2006
Frequency: Weekly
Cover Price: £1.10
Circulation: 37,038 (ABC 01/07/2008 to 31/12/2008)
Usual Pagination: 24

Editor: Gabrielle Utton; **Advertisement Director:** Lindsaye Fox
Summary of Content: Newspaper with hard-hitting news as well as show-biz, movies, travel, computer games, sport, puzzles, health and competitions.
Readership/Target Audience: Aimed at 7 to 15 year olds.
ADVERTISING RATES:
Full Page Mono £1620.00
Full Page Colour £1780.00
Agency Commission: 10%
Mechanical Data: Type Area: 365 x 285mm, Col Length: 365mm, Page Width: 285mm, Film: Digital
Copy instructions: Copy Date: 1 week prior to publication date
Average advertising content per issue: 25%
CONSUMER: WOMEN'S INTEREST CONSUMER MAGAZINES: Teenage

FISHING IN BRITAIN & EUROPE
1646098U92-104

Editorial Address: PO Box 5135, Strand-on-the-Green, Chiswick, LONDON, W4 3WN **Tel:** 020 8560 0897
Fax: 020 8560 0897
Email: peerage@aol.com
Advertising Address: As above.
Email: thepeeragegroup@yahoo.co.uk
Publisher: The Peerage Group Ltd
Frequency: Annual - Published in December
Cover Price: £9.95
Circulation: 15,000 (Publisher's Statement)
Usual Pagination: 250
Editor: Sara Marden-King; **Advertising Manager:** Bruce Duncan
Summary of Content: Guide covering angling and accommodation throughout the UK and Europe.
Readership/Target Audience: Aimed at anglers.
ADVERTISING RATES:
Full Page Mono £460.00
Full Page Colour £830.00
Agency Commission: 10%
Mechanical Data: Type Area: 272 x 145mm, Col Length: 272mm, Page Width: 145mm, Film: Positive, right reading, emulsion side down. Digital, Trim Size: 234 x 165mm, Bleed Size: 240 x 168mm
Copy instructions: Copy Date: 30 days prior to publication date
Average advertising content per issue: 20%
CONSUMER: ANGLING & FISHING

THE FLAG
47307U82-22_90

Editorial Address: BCM The Flag, LONDON, WC1N 3XX
Tel: 020 8592 3021 **Fax:** 020 8592 3021
Advertising Address: As above.
Email: ian.anderson@netmatters.co.uk
Web site: http://www.the-flag.co.uk
ISSN: 0952-2912
Publisher: Flag Newspapers
Date Established: 1987
Frequency: Monthly
Cover Price: £0.60
Annual Sub.: £20.00
Circulation: 10,000 (Publisher's Statement)
Usual Pagination: 8
Editor: Ian Anderson; **Advertising Manager:** Ian Anderson
Summary of Content: Journal of the new right, covering current affairs, politics and the activities of democratic centre right parties.
Readership/Target Audience: Aimed at the general public.
ADVERTISING RATES:
Full Page Mono £200.00
CONSUMER: CURRENT AFFAIRS & POLITICS

FLAVOUR
1753422U74P-947

Editorial Address: The Old Library, Church Green West, REDDITCH, B97 4DU **Tel:** 01527 453726 **Fax:** 01527 453724
Email: vanessa@osdesign.net
Advertising Address: As above.
Email: vanessa@osdesign.net
Web site: http://www.osdesign.net
Publisher: Observer Standard Newspapers Magazine Division
Frequency: Annual - Published in May
Cover Price: Free
Circulation: 20,000 (Publisher's Statement)
Usual Pagination: 108
Editor: Vanessa Bradford
Summary of Content: Magazine covering places to go and places to eat, wine, recipes, interviews with chefs and money off vouchers in Warwickshire, Worcestershire and South Birmingham.
Readership/Target Audience: Aimed at those in Worcestershire, Warwickshire and South Birmingham, who enjoy food and drinks.
ADVERTISING RATES:
Full Page Colour £450.00
Agency Commission: 10%

Mechanical Data: Bleed Size: 216 x 153mm, Trim Size: 210 x 147mm, Film: Digital
Copy instructions: Copy Date: 1 week prior to publication date
Average advertising content per issue: 60%
CONSUMER: WOMEN'S INTEREST CONSUMER MAGAZINES: Food & Cookery

FLAVOUR MAGAZINE
1799030U74Q-1347

Editorial Address: PO Box 55748, LONDON, E16 3XY
Tel: 07958 205413
Email: editor@flavourmag.co.uk
Advertising Address: As above. **Tel:** 07949 310050
Email: info@flavourmag.co.uk
Web site: http://www.flavourmag.co.uk
Publisher: Flavour Magazine Ltd
Date Established: 2006
Frequency: 6 issues yearly
Cover Price: Free
Circulation: 12,500 (Publisher's Statement)
Usual Pagination: 40
Editor: Annika Allen; **Advertising Manager:** Leonard Foster;
Publisher: Leonard Foster
Summary of Content: Urban lifestyle magazine covering new talent in the world of music, sport, entertainment, art and fashion as well as technology, events and book reviews.
Readership/Target Audience: Aimed at multicultural men and women aged 18 to 30 years old in London and within the M25.
ADVERTISING RATES:
Full Page Colour £900.00
Mechanical Data: Bleed Size: 213 x 151mm, Trim Size: 210 x 148mm, Film: Digital
Copy instructions: Copy Date: 3 weeks prior to publication date
Average advertising content per issue: 35%
CONSUMER: WOMEN'S INTEREST CONSUMER MAGAZINES: Lifestyle

FLEX
45975U75P-250

Editorial Address: 10 Windsor Court, Clarence Drive, HARROGATE, HG1 2PE **Tel:** 01423 504516
Fax: 01423 561494
Email: ukpub@weideruk.com
Advertising Address: As above.
Email: slund@weideruk.com
Web site: http://www.flexonline.co.uk
Publisher: Weider Publishing Ltd
Date Established: 1985
Frequency: Monthly
Cover Price: £3.60
Annual Sub.: £29.97
Circulation: 37,800 (Publisher's Statement)
Usual Pagination: 196
Editor: Chris Lund; **Editor-in-Chief:** Geoff Evans;
Advertising Director: Samantha Lund
Summary of Content: Magazine covering weight training and bodybuilding.
Language(s): Dutch; English; French; German; Italian
Readership/Target Audience: Aimed at hardcore bodybuilding enthusiasts.
ADVERTISING RATES:
Full Page Mono £1189.00
Full Page Colour £1393.00
Agency Commission: 15%
Mechanical Data: Trim Size: 267 x 200mm, Bleed Size: 273 x 206mm, Print Process: Web-fed offset litho, Film: Digital, Type Area: 237 x 170mm, Col Length: 237mm, Page Width: 170mm
Copy instructions: Copy Date: 5 weeks prior to publication date
CONSUMER: SPORT: Fitness/Bodybuilding

FLIGHT
1843080U89D-533

Editorial Address: Publishing House, 3 Bridgebank Industrial Estate, Taylor Street, Horwich, BOLTON, BL6 7PD
Tel: 0161 909 0909 **Fax:** 0161 909 0919
Email: dave.beevers@bigspark.co.uk
Advertising Address: As above.
Email: tony@bigspark.co.uk
Web site: http://www.flightmagazine.co.uk
Publisher: The Big Spark
Date Established: 2008
Frequency: Quarterly
Cover Price: Free
Circulation: 12,000 (Publisher's Statement)
Usual Pagination: 48
Editor: Dave Beevers
Summary of Content: Lifestyle magazine covering celebrity interviews, car tests, financial pages and destinations.
Readership/Target Audience: Aimed at passenger using Glasgow Prestwick Airport and also distributed through local hotels and tourist information centres.
ADVERTISING RATES:
Full Page Colour £950.00
Agency Commission: 10%

Mechanical Data: Type Area: 275 x 190mm, Bleed Size: 307 x 220mm, Trim Size: 297 x 210mm, Col Length: 275mm, Page Width: 190mm
CONSUMER: HOLIDAYS & TRAVEL: In-Flight Magazines

FLIPSIDE
1665300U74F-761

Editorial Address: Michael Faraday House, Six Hills Way, STEVENAGE, SG1 2AY **Tel:** 01438 767676
Fax: 01438 767397
Email: flipside@flipside.org.uk
Advertising Address: As above. **Tel:** 01438 313311
Fax: 01438 313465
Email: lhall@theiet.org
Web site: http://www.flipside.org.uk
ISSN: 1746-0409
Publisher: The Institution of Engineering and Technology
Date Established: 2005
Frequency: 8 issues yearly
Cover Price: £2.50
Annual Sub.: £24.00
Circulation: 15,500 (Publisher's Statement)
Usual Pagination: 84
Editor: Sean Blair; **Advertising Manager:** Louise Hall
Summary of Content: Magazine covering film, music, sport, adventure and gadgets.
Readership/Target Audience: Aimed at young teenagers.
ADVERTISING RATES:
Full Page Colour £1625.00
Mechanical Data: Type Area: 270 x 210mm, Bleed Size: 303 x 236mm, Trim Size: 297 x 230mm, Col Length: 270mm, Page Width: 210mm, Film: Digital
Copy instructions: Copy Date: 2 weeks prior to publication date
CONSUMER: WOMEN'S INTEREST CONSUMER MAGAZINES: Teenage

FLOODLIGHT
1779194U88B-153

Editorial Address: 150-152 King Street, LONDON, W6 0QU
Tel: 020 8600 5307
Email: jessie-may.murphy@hotcourses.com
Advertising Address: As above. **Tel:** 020 8600 5314
Fax: 020 8741 7716
Email: danica.hill@hotcourses.com
Web site: http://www.floodlight.co.uk
Publisher: Hotcourses
Frequency: Half-yearly - Published in January and July
Cover Price: £2.95
Free to qualifying individuals
Usual Pagination: 500
Editor: Jessie-May Murphy; **Advertising Manager:** Danica Hill
Summary of Content: Magazine covering adult learning in London.
Readership/Target Audience: Aimed at those looking for courses.
ADVERTISING RATES:
Full Page Colour £1970.00
Agency Commission: 10%
Mechanical Data: Type Area: 277 x 190mm, Bleed Size: 303 x 216mm, Trim Size: 297 x 210mm, Col Length: 277mm, Page Width: 190mm, Film: Digital
CONSUMER: EDUCATION: Adult Education

FLORA INTERNATIONAL
46779U79R-14

Editorial Address: 77 Bulbridge Road, Wilton, SALISBURY, SP2 0LE **Tel:** 01722 743207 **Fax:** 01722 743207
Email: floramag@aol.com
Advertising Address: KM Media & Marketing, County House, Checkpoint Court, Sadler Road, LINCOLN, LN6 3PW
Tel: 01522 513515 **Fax:** 01522 842000
Email: info@km-media.co.uk
ISSN: 0306-882X
Publisher: The Fishing Lodge Studio
Date Established: 1974
Frequency: 6 issues yearly
Cover Price: £3.15
Annual Sub.: £21.40
Circulation: 18,000 (Publisher's Statement)
Usual Pagination: 64
Editor: Maureen Foster
Summary of Content: Magazine covering flower arranging and floristry with floral crafts, new plants and flower arrangers' gardens.
Readership/Target Audience: Aimed at flower arrangers and florists.
ADVERTISING RATES:
Full Page Mono £650.00
Full Page Colour £650.00
Agency Commission: 10%
Mechanical Data: Bleed Size: 297 x 210mm, Col Length: 270mm, Type Area: 270 x 175mm, Page Width: 175mm, Film: Digital
CONSUMER: HOBBIES & DIY: Hobbies & DIY Related

FLOURISH
46148U76D-317

Editorial Address: Trinity College London, 89 Albert Embankment, LONDON, SE1 7TP **Tel:** 020 7820 6100
Fax: 020 7820 6161
Email: flourish@trinitycollege.co.uk
Web site: http://www.trinitycollege.co.uk
ISSN: 1463-4244
Publisher: Trinity College London
Frequency: Half-yearly - Varies
Cover Price: Free
Circulation: 20,000 (Publisher's Statement)
Usual Pagination: 16
Editor: Claire Webb
Summary of Content: Magazine covering all aspects of music in both performance and education. Includes scholarly articles, profiles and practical teacher support.
Readership/Target Audience: Aimed at music teachers in all sectors.
ADVERTISING: No Advertising taken
CONSUMER: MUSIC & PERFORMING ARTS: Music

FLOURISH
47714U87-96_7

Editorial Address: 196 Clyde Street, GLASGOW, G1 4JY
Tel: 0141 226 5898 **Fax:** 0141 225 2600
Email: flourish@rcag.org.uk
Advertising Address: IPM Ltd, 426 Drumoyne Road, GLASGOW, G51 4DX **Tel:** 0141 810 9001
Fax: 0141 810 9010
Email: ann@inpositionmedia.co.uk
Web site: http://www.rcag.org.uk
Publisher: Flourish Publications (Scotland) Ltd
Date Established: 1976
Frequency: Monthly
Cover Price: £0.60
Annual Sub.: £14.00
Circulation: 12,000 (Publisher's Statement)
Usual Pagination: 24
Editor: Vincent Toal
Summary of Content: Official journal of the Archdiocese of Glasgow (RC) containing news and comment.
Readership/Target Audience: Aimed at members of the community within the Archdiocese of Glasgow.
ADVERTISING RATES:
Full Page Mono £650.00
Full Page Colour £800.00
SCC £3.25
Agency Commission: 10%
Mechanical Data: Col Length: 350mm, No. of Columns (Display): 6, Type Area: 350 x 275mm, Page Width: 275mm, Col Widths (Display): 42.5mm, Film: Digital
Copy instructions: Copy Date: 10 days prior to publication date
CONSUMER: RELIGIOUS

THE FLOWER ARRANGER
46780U79R-15

Editorial Address: 52 Suffolk Road, LONDON, SW13 9NR
Tel: 0207 235 6235
Email: editor@judithblacklock.com
Advertising Address: Warners Group Publications plc, The Maltings, West Street, BOURNE, PE10 9PH
Tel: 01778 391000 **Fax:** 01778 392079
Email: jaynen@warnersgroup.co.uk
Web site: http://www.nafas.org.uk
ISSN: 0046-421X
Publisher: NAFAS Enterprises Limited
Date Established: 1961
Frequency: Quarterly
Cover Price: £3.20
Circulation: 51,000 (Publisher's Statement)
Usual Pagination: 64
Editor: Judith Blacklock
Summary of Content: Journal of the National Association of Flower Arrangement Societies. Includes news, events, tips and trends in flower arrangements.
Readership/Target Audience: Read by flower arrangers, florists and interior designers.
ADVERTISING RATES:
Full Page Colour £1600.00
SCC £35.00
Agency Commission: 10%
Mechanical Data: Page Width: 175mm, Col Widths (Display): 41mm, Bleed Size: 303 x 216mm, Trim Size: 297 x 210mm, Type Area: 255 x 175mm, Col Length: 255mm, Film: Digital
Copy instructions: Copy Date: 8 weeks prior to publication date
CONSUMER: HOBBIES & DIY: Hobbies & DIY Related

FLUSH
1753000U79F-104

Editorial Address: 211 Old Street, Ground Floor, LONDON, EC1V 9NR **Tel:** 020 7608 6400
Email: dave.bland@trojanpublishing.co.uk
Advertising Address: As above.
Email: simon.la-thangue@trojanpublishing.co.uk
Web site: http://www.flushmag.co.uk
Publisher: Trojan Publishing

Date Established: 2005
Frequency: Monthly
Cover Price: £3.00
Circulation: 85,000 (Publisher's Statement)
Usual Pagination: 100
Editor: Dave Bland; **Advertising Manager:** Simon La Thangue
Summary of Content: Magazine covering all facets of online and mobile gaming and gambling from poker to sports betting.
Readership/Target Audience: Aimed at 25 to 55 year old men and women gaming enthusiasts.
ADVERTISING RATES:
Full Page Colour £6800.00
Agency Commission: 10%
Mechanical Data: Bleed Size: 307 x 220mm, Trim Size: 297 x 210mm, Film: Digital
Copy instructions: Copy Date: 10 days prior to publication date
Average advertising content per issue: 30%
CONSUMER: HOBBIES & DIY: Games & Puzzles

FLUX
600871U74Q-260

Editorial Address: 42 Edge Street, MANCHESTER, M4 1HN
Tel: 0161 832 0300 **Fax:** 0161 819 1196
Email: editorial@fluxmagazine.com
Advertising Address: As above.
Email: lee@fluxmagazine.com
Web site: http://www.fluxmagazine.com
Publisher: Flux Publications
Date Established: 1996
Frequency: Quarterly
Cover Price: £3.80
Circulation: 57,000 (Publisher's Statement)
Usual Pagination: 118
Editor: Lee Taylor; **Advertising Manager:** Lee Taylor
Summary of Content: Culture and fashion magazine containing profiles on international arts and fashion figures and influential individuals shaping the future, plus features on music, fashion, films, art and clubs.
Readership/Target Audience: Aimed at 18 to 30 year olds.
ADVERTISING: Rates on application
CONSUMER: WOMEN'S INTEREST CONSUMER MAGAZINES: Lifestyle

THE FLY
601107U76E-120

Editorial Address: 59-61 Worship Street, LONDON, EC2A 2DU **Tel:** 020 7688 9000
Email: niall.doherty@channelfly.com
Advertising Address: As above. **Fax:** 020 7688 8999
Email: richard.mehta@channelfly.com
Web site: http://www.the-fly.co.uk
Publisher: Channelfly plc
Date Established: 1999
Frequency: 11 issues yearly
Cover Price: Free
Circulation: 107,771 (ABC 01/01/2009 to 30/06/2009)
Usual Pagination: 96
Editor: Niall Doherty
Summary of Content: Magazine includes music reviews, interviews and news.
Readership/Target Audience: Aimed at 16 to 24 year olds.
ADVERTISING RATES:
Full Page Colour £3000.00
Agency Commission: 10%
Mechanical Data: Film: Digital, Bleed Size: 216 x 149.5mm, Trim Size: 210 x 143.5mm, Type Area: 204 x 137.5mm, Col Length: 204mm, Page Width: 137.5mm
Copy instructions: Copy Date: 15th of the month prior to publication date
Average advertising content per issue: 25%
CONSUMER: MUSIC & PERFORMING ARTS: Pop Music

FLY
1914463U86C-761

Editorial Address: 1 Chartwell Lodge, 9 Brackley Road, BECKENHAM, BR3 1SW **Tel:** 020 8650 3645
Publisher: Vineyard Publishing
Cover Price: Free
Circulation: 250,000 (Publisher's Statement)
Editor: Richard Allen
Summary of Content: Fashion magazine covering men's formal and casual wear.
Readership/Target Audience: Aimed at men with an interest in fashion.
CONSUMER: ADULT & GAY MAGAZINES: Men's Lifestyle Magazines

FLYBE UNCOVERED
48211U89D-44

Formerly: Flybe. Flying Colours
Editorial Address: The Courtyard, Ladycross Farm, Hollow Lane, Dormansland, LINGFIELD, RH7 6PB
Tel: 01342 870409
Email: vicky.stewart@streampublishing.net
Advertising Address: As above.

Email: vicky.stewart@streampublishing.net
Publisher: Stream Publishing Ltd
Date Established: 1994
Frequency: 6 issues yearly
Cover Price: Free
Circulation: 36,000 (Publisher's Statement)
Usual Pagination: 180
Editor: Vicky Stewart; **Managing Director:** Darren Styles
Summary of Content: In-flight magazine for Flybe covering destination information and general interest features.
Readership/Target Audience: Read by passengers.
ADVERTISING RATES:
Full Page Mono £5000.00
Full Page Colour £5000.00
Agency Commission: 10%
Mechanical Data: Page Width: 193mm, Col Length: 258mm, Film: Digital, Type Area: 258 x 193mm, Bleed Size: 286 x 221mm, Trim Size: 278 x 213mm
Average advertising content per issue: 46%
CONSUMER: HOLIDAYS & TRAVEL: In-Flight Magazines

FLYER
46782U79R-25

Editorial Address: 9 Riverside Court, Lower Bristol Road, BATH, BA2 3DZ **Tel:** 01225 481440 **Fax:** 01225 481262
Email: ianw@flyermag.co.uk
Advertising Address: As above.
Email: darran@flyermag.co.uk
Web site: http://www.flyer.co.uk
Publisher: Seager Publishing Ltd
Date Established: 1990
Frequency: 13 issues yearly
Cover Price: £3.60
Annual Sub.: £35.80
Circulation: 25,000 (Publisher's Statement)
Usual Pagination: 116
Editor: Ian Waller; **Managing Director:** Ian Seager;
Advertising Manager: Darran Ward; **Publisher:** Ian Seager
Summary of Content: Magazine covering light aviation, aircraft reviews, destination reports and product news.
Readership/Target Audience: Read by private pilot licence holders, student pilots, commercial pilots and those interested in flying.
ADVERTISING: Rates on application
Agency Commission: 10%
Average advertising content per issue: 50%
CONSUMER: HOBBIES & DIY: Hobbies & DIY Related

FLYFISHERS' JOURNAL
48532U92-60

Editorial Address: 27 Lillian Avenue, LONDON, W3 9AN
Publisher: Flyfishers Club
Date Established: 1911
Frequency: Half-yearly - Published in June and December
Free to qualifying individuals
Annual Sub.: £18.00
Circulation: 700 (Publisher's Statement)
Usual Pagination: 72
Editor: Peter Lapsley
Summary of Content: Magazine covering all aspects of fly fishing.
Readership/Target Audience: Aimed at fly fishermen.
ADVERTISING: No Advertising taken
CONSUMER: ANGLING & FISHING

FLY-FISHING AND FLY-TYING
48531U92-58

Editorial Address: The Locus Centre, The Square, ABERFELDY, PH15 2DD **Tel:** 01887 829868
Fax: 01887 829856
Email: markb.ffft@btinternet.com
Advertising Address: As above. **Tel:** 01368 829868
Email: adsales.ffft@btopenworld.com
Web site: http://www.flyfishing-and-flytying.co.uk
ISSN: 0959-8383
Publisher: Rolling River Publications Ltd
Date Established: 1990
Frequency: Monthly
Cover Price: £3.10
Annual Sub.: £36.00
Circulation: 14,192 (ABC 01/01/2008 to 31/12/2008)
Usual Pagination: 100
Editor: Mark Bowler
Summary of Content: Magazine with features on flies, patterns, venues, tackle, travel and news for trout, salmon, grayling, coarse fish, sea trout and saltwater fly fishermen.
Readership/Target Audience: Aimed at river and stillwater fly-fishers.
ADVERTISING RATES:
Full Page Colour £1055.00
SCC £13.20
Agency Commission: 10%
Mechanical Data: Col Length: 267mm, Page Width: 186mm, Film: Digital, Type Area: 267 x 186mm, Bleed Size: 303 x 216mm, Trim Size: 297 x 210mm
Average advertising content per issue: 25%
CONSUMER: ANGLING & FISHING

FLYING SCALE MODELS
46595U79B-29_50

Editorial Address: Unit 5, Chiltern Business Centre, 63-65 Woodside Road, AMERSHAM, HP6 6AA **Tel:** 01494 433453
Fax: 01494 433456
Email: tony@modelactivitypress.com
Advertising Address: As above.
Email: adverts@modelactivitypress.com
Web site: http://www.modelactivitypress.com
ISSN: 1368-9002
Publisher: Model Activity Press Ltd
Frequency: Daily
Cover Price: £3.50
Annual Sub.: £39.00
Circulation: 12,000 (Publisher's Statement)
Editor: Tony Dowdeswell; **Managing Director:** Tony Dowdeswell
Summary of Content: Magazine covering all aspects of flying and building scale-model aircraft.
Readership/Target Audience: Aimed at modelling enthusiasts.
ADVERTISING RATES:
Full Page Mono £400.00
Full Page Colour £425.00
Mechanical Data: Col Length: 270mm, Trim Size: 297 x 210mm, Film: Digital, Type Area: 270 x 185mm, Page Width: 185mm
Copy instructions: Copy Date: 4 weeks prior to publication date
CONSUMER: HOBBIES & DIY: Models & Modelling

FLYING START PARENTING MAGAZINE
1629334U74D-557

Formerly: Flying Start
Editorial Address: 45 Centurion House, Centurion Way, Leyland Business Park, Farington, LEYLAND, PR25 3GR
Tel: 01772 459418
Email: judith@flyingstartmagazine.co.uk
Advertising Address: As above.
Email: judith@flyingstartmagazine.co.uk
Web site: http://www.flyingstartmagazine.co.uk
ISSN: 1745-2015
Publisher: Magenta Press Ltd
Date Established: 2003
Frequency: Quarterly
Cover Price: £3.60
Free to qualifying individuals
Circulation: 20,000 (Publisher's Statement)
Usual Pagination: 84
Editor: Judith McKay; **Advertising Manager:** Judith McKay
Summary of Content: Magazine covering pregnancy, birth, early years learning and child development.
Readership/Target Audience: Aimed at parents to be, parents, carers, nursery staff and teachers of children aged 0 to 10 years old.
ADVERTISING RATES:
Full Page Colour £1100.00
Agency Commission: 10%
Mechanical Data: Trim Size: 297 x 210mm, Bleed Size: 305 x 218mm
Average advertising content per issue: 33%
CONSUMER: WOMEN'S INTEREST CONSUMER MAGAZINES: Child Care

FLYPAST
46781U79R-20

Editorial Address: PO Box 100, STAMFORD, PE9 1XQ
Tel: 01780 755131 **Fax:** 01780 757261
Email: flypast@keypublishing.com
Advertising Address: As above. **Fax:** 01780 751323
Email: geoff.butler@keypublishing.com
Web site: http://www.flypast.com
ISSN: 0262-6950
Publisher: Key Publishing Ltd
Date Established: 1981
Frequency: Monthly
Cover Price: £3.95
Annual Sub.: £39.00
Circulation: 41,118 (ABC 01/01/2008 to 31/12/2008)
Usual Pagination: 100
Editor: Ken Ellis
Summary of Content: Magazine covering news and articles on preserved and vintage aircraft and modern airshows.
Readership/Target Audience: Aimed at those with an interest in historic aviation.
ADVERTISING RATES:
Full Page Colour £1815.00
Agency Commission: 10%
Mechanical Data: Page Width: 180mm, Type Area: 267 x 180mm, Col Length: 267mm, Trim Size: 297 x 210mm, Bleed Size: 307 x 215mm, Film: Digital
Copy instructions: Copy Date: 3 weeks prior to publication date
CONSUMER: HOBBIES & DIY: Hobbies & DIY Related

FOCUS
1819915U76A-210

Editorial Address: 22 Golden Square, LONDON, W1F 9JW
Tel: 07710 471401

Email: anwar@netcomuk.co.uk
Advertising Address: As above. **Tel:** 020 7437 4383
Fax: 020 7734 0912
Email: arowley@fda.uk.net
Web site: http://www.focusonmovies.co.uk
Publisher: FDA
Date Established: 2007
Frequency: Quarterly
Cover Price: Free
Circulation: 800,000 (Publisher's Statement)
Usual Pagination: 20
Editor: Anwar Brett; **Advertising Manager:** Alex Rowley
Summary of Content: Guide to films released in local cinemas by the UK's distribution companies, designed to raise awareness of cinema and increase cinema going frequency.
Readership/Target Audience: Aimed at potential cinema goers, both frequent and infrequent, targeted in particular cinema catchment areas.
ADVERTISING: Rates on application
CONSUMER: MUSIC & PERFORMING ARTS: Cinema

FOCUS
46978U80C-3020

Editorial Address: 59 Carlton Hill, St. John's Wood, LONDON, NW8 0EN **Tel:** 020 7624 3433 **Fax:** 020 7604 4433
Email: info@focusonline.co.uk
Advertising Address: As above.
Email: info@focusonline.co.uk
Web site: http://www.focusonline.co.uk
Publisher: Focus Worldwide Publications Ltd
Date Established: 1996
Frequency: Quarterly
Cover Price: Free
Circulation: 21,247 (Publisher's Statement)
Usual Pagination: 68
Editor: Nora McDonagh; **Advertising Manager:** Nora McDonagh; **Publisher:** Nora McDonagh
Summary of Content: Lifestyle magazine containing articles on property, interiors, home entertainment, gardening, education, fashion, health and fitness, arts and antiques, food and wine.
Readership/Target Audience: Aimed at those living in high net worth homes and in Private and Crown Estates in Surrey, Berkshire and South West London.
ADVERTISING RATES:
Full Page Colour £1625.00
Agency Commission: 10%
Mechanical Data: Col Length: 260mm, Page Width: 170mm, Film: Digital, Type Area: 260 x 170mm, Bleed Size: 289 x 206mm, Trim Size: 283 x 200mm
Copy instructions: Copy Date: 3 weeks prior to publication date
Average advertising content per issue: 60%
CONSUMER: RURAL & REGIONAL INTEREST: Regional Interest English Counties

---

FOCUS
749480U80C-3677

Editorial Address: Ginsbury House, Sir Thomas Longley Road, Medway City Estate, ROCHESTER, ME2 4DU
Tel: 01634 227800
Email: whatsoneditor@thekmgroup.co.uk
Advertising Address: 6-7 Middle Row, MAIDSTONE, ME14 1TG **Tel:** 01622 697777 **Fax:** 01622 664988
Email: maidstoneads@thekmgroup.co.uk
Web site: http://www.kentonline.co.uk
Publisher: Kent Messenger Group
Date Established: 2001
Frequency: Monthly
Cover Price: Free
Circulation: 120,000 (Publisher's Statement)
Usual Pagination: 48
Editor: Digby Kennard
Summary of Content: Lifestyle magazine with real life stories, social diary, shopping, competitions and features on fashion, health, beauty, entertainment, home, gardening, antiques, gadgets, food and drink and motoring.
Readership/Target Audience: Aimed at high income householders and readers of KM Group paid for newspapers.
ADVERTISING RATES:
Full Page Colour £769.00
Mechanical Data: Page Width: 184mm, Trim Size: 297 x 210mm, Bleed Size: 303 x 216mm, Film: Digital, Type Area: 260 x 184mm, Col Length: 260mm
CONSUMER: RURAL & REGIONAL INTEREST: Regional Interest English Counties

---

FOCUS MAGAZINE
47793U87-96_80

Editorial Address: Alma Park, GRANTHAM, NG31 9SL
Tel: 01476 591700 **Fax:** 01476 577144
Email: editordnm@mac.com
ISSN: 1403-7925
Publisher: Stanborough Press Ltd
Date Established: 1979
Frequency: Quarterly
Cover Price: £0.25

Circulation: 20,000 (Publisher's Statement)
Usual Pagination: 16
Editor: David Marshall
Summary of Content: Christian magazine covering news, views and articles of interest.
Readership/Target Audience: Aimed at Christians and those looking for an answer to life's problems in Christian terms.
ADVERTISING: No Advertising taken
CONSUMER: RELIGIOUS

FOCUS MAGAZINE SOUTH WARWICKSHIRE AND THE COTSWOLDS

762124U80C-3764

Editorial Address: York House, 17 Rother Street, STRATFORD-UPON-AVON, CV37 6NB Tel: 01789 266261
Fax: 01789 269519
Email: shiggins@stratford-herald.co.uk
Advertising Address: As above.
Email: sbeard@stratford-herald.co.uk
Web site: http://www.stratford-herald.co.uk
Publisher: Herald Publishing
Frequency: Monthly
Cover Price: Free
Circulation: 20,000 (Publisher's Statement)
Editor: Sharon Higgins; Advertising Manager: Sandie Beard
Summary of Content: Magazine containing articles on property, interiors, gardening, independent education, travel, art, antiques, health and fitness and eating out.
Readership/Target Audience: Aimed at those living in exclusive estates in South Warwickshire and the Cotswolds as well as customers of health farms, hotels and restaurants and golf and tennis club members in the area.
ADVERTISING RATES:
Full Page Colour £1213.00
Agency Commission: 10%
Mechanical Data: Bleed Size: 315 x 220mm, Trim Size: 297 x 210mm, Film: Digital
Copy instructions: Copy Date: Middle of the month prior to publication date
CONSUMER: RURAL & REGIONAL INTEREST: Regional Interest English Counties

FOLIO

46859U80C-340

Editorial Address: 2nd Floor, Bristol News & Media, Temple Way, BRISTOL, BS99 7HD Tel: 0117 942 8491
Fax: 0117 934 3566
Email: editor@foliomagazine.co.uk
Advertising Address: As above.
Email: ads@venue.co.uk
Web site: http://www.foliomagazine.co.uk
Publisher: Venue Publishing
Date Established: 1993
Frequency: Monthly
Cover Price: Free
Circulation: 42,000 (Publisher's Statement)
Usual Pagination: 116
Editor: Laura Dixon; Group Editor: David Higgitt
Summary of Content: Magazine covering leisure, lifestyle, interiors and entertainment listings.
Readership/Target Audience: Aimed at men and women aged between 30 and 55 years old, living in the Bristol and Bath area.
ADVERTISING RATES:
Full Page Colour £1075.00
Agency Commission: 10%
Mechanical Data: Type Area: 273 x 184mm, Bleed Size: 301 x 214mm, Trim Size: 297 x 210mm, Col Length: 273mm, Page Width: 184mm, Film: Digital
Copy instructions: Copy Date: 2 weeks prior to publication date
Average advertising content per issue: 40%
CONSUMER: RURAL & REGIONAL INTEREST: Regional Interest English Counties

FOLK MUSIC JOURNAL

46295U76G-160

Editorial Address: Cecil Sharp House, 2 Regent's Park Road, LONDON, NW1 7AY Tel: 020 7485 2206
Fax: 020 7284 0534
Email: fmj@efdss.org
Web site: http://www.efdss.org/fmj/fmj.htm
ISSN: 0531-9684
Publisher: English Folk Dance and Song Society
Date Established: 1899
Frequency: Annual - Published in December
Cover Price: £7.50
Circulation: 4,000 (Publisher's Statement)
Usual Pagination: 144
Editor: David Atkinson
Summary of Content: Academic journal of folk music, song and dance studies. The reviews section provides information on the latest studies and collections that have been published. Recent audio and video materials which document music and dance traditions also receive informed reviews.

Readership/Target Audience: Read by music, song and dance scholars and students, and others with an interest in folk music, song and dance.
ADVERTISING: No Advertising taken
CONSUMER: MUSIC & PERFORMING ARTS: Dance

FOLK NORTH WEST

46149U76D-317_50

Editorial Address: 36 The Oaks, Eaves Green, CHORLEY, PR7 3QU Tel: 01257 263678
Email: four.fools@virgin.net
Advertising Address: 7 Sunleigh Road, Hindley, WIGAN, WN2 2RE Tel: 01942 258459
Email: holdenpaul@tiscali.co.uk
Web site: http://www.folknorthwest.co.uk
ISSN: 0135-8083
Publisher: North West Federation of Folk Clubs
Date Established: 1976
Frequency: Quarterly
Cover Price: £2.00
Circulation: 1,000 (Publisher's Statement)
Usual Pagination: 52
Editor: Ken Bladen; Advertising Manager: Paul Holden
Summary of Content: Magazine covering traditional and contemporary folk music in the North West. Contains club dates, features, CD articles, interviews and live reviews.
Readership/Target Audience: Aimed at folk music enthusiasts.
ADVERTISING RATES:
Full Page Mono £90.00
Full Page Colour £110.00
Mechanical Data: Type Area: 275 x 185mm, Col Length: 275mm, Page Width: 185mm, Trim Size: 297 x 210mm, Col Widths (Display): 2, No. of Columns (Display): 2
CONSUMER: MUSIC & PERFORMING ARTS: Music

FOOD

1660045U74P-920

Editorial Address: 1st Floor, 5 Cross Street, BARNSTAPLE, EX31 1BA Tel: 01271 859299 Fax: 01271 859292
Email: info@food-mag.co.uk
Advertising Address: As above. Tel: 01271 859160
Email: info@food-mag.co.uk
Web site: http://www.food-mag.co.uk
ISSN: 1748-0566
Publisher: Salt Media Ltd
Date Established: 2004
Frequency: 6 issues yearly
Cover Price: Free
Circulation: 55,000 (Publisher's Statement)
Usual Pagination: 40
Editor: Jo Rees; Advertising Manager: Nick Cooper; Publisher: Nick Cooper
Summary of Content: Magazine promoting the best local eating, shopping, accommodation and activities. Features celebrity chefs, local producers, recipes, products, accommodation and restaurant guide and details on when, where and how to buy the best food.
Readership/Target Audience: Aimed predominantly at affluent, 30 to 65 year old women.
ADVERTISING RATES:
Full Page Colour £930.00
Agency Commission: 10%
Mechanical Data: Bleed Size: 266 x 204mm, Trim Size: 260 x 198mm, Film: Digital
Copy instructions: Copy Date: 9th of the month prior to publication date
Average advertising content per issue: 35%
Editions:
Food (Bristol, Bath & Somerset)
Food (Cornwall)
Food (Devon)
CONSUMER: WOMEN'S INTEREST CONSUMER MAGAZINES: Food & Cookery

FOOD & DRINK

1665239U74P-925

Editorial Address: 292 Vauxhall Bridge Road, LONDON, SW1V 1AE Tel: 020 7963 7256 Fax: 020 7963 7295
Email: claire.spreadbury@pa-entertainment.co.uk
Advertising Address: Mediaforce Ltd, 1 Gunpowder Square, Fleet Street, LONDON, EC4A 3EP
Tel: 020 7583 2100 Fax: 020 7583 2111
Email: sgill@mediaforce.com
Publisher: Johnston Press plc
Date Established: 2005
Frequency: Annual - Published in December
Cover Price: Free
Circulation: 1,200,000 (Publisher's Statement)
Usual Pagination: 16
Editor: Claire Spreadbury; Advertising Manager: Scott Gill
Summary of Content: Magazine with interviews, restaurant reviews, wine guides and recipe ideas as well as covering health and nutrition.
Readership/Target Audience: Aimed at readers of Johnston Press local newspapers.
ADVERTISING: Rates on application
CONSUMER: WOMEN'S INTEREST CONSUMER MAGAZINES: Food & Cookery

FOOD AND TRAVEL

45606U74P-918

Editorial Address: Suite 51, The Business Centre, Ingate Place, LONDON, SW8 3NS Tel: 020 7501 0511
Fax: 020 7501 0510
Email: info@foodandtravel.com
Advertising Address: As above.
Email: gregor.rankin@foodandtravel.com
Web site: http://www.foodandtravel.com
ISSN: 1366-6967
Publisher: Green Pea Publishing
Date Established: 1997
Frequency: 10 issues yearly - Double issue for February/March and August/September
Cover Price: £3.80
Annual Sub.: £45.60
Circulation: 26,000 (Publisher's Statement)
Usual Pagination: 130
Editor: Charlotte Swift; Features Editor: Rachel Truman; Advertising Manager: Louise Fanthorpe; Publisher: Gregor Rankin
Summary of Content: Magazine featuring short and long haul travel, weekend breaks, food and drink ideas, restaurant reviews and entertaining.
Readership/Target Audience: Aimed at people who are passionate about the best in food, wine and travel.
ADVERTISING RATES:
Full Page Mono £3600.00
Full Page Colour £3600.00
SCC £45.00
Agency Commission: 15%
Mechanical Data: Print Process: Web-fed offset litho, No. of Columns (Display): 4, Col Widths (Display): 46.5mm, Col Length: 265mm, Bleed Size: 291 x 226mm, Trim Size: 285 x 220mm, Type Area: 265 x 200mm, Film: Digital, Page Width: 200mm
Copy instructions: Copy Date: 3 weeks prior to publication date
Average advertising content per issue: 30%
CONSUMER: WOMEN'S INTEREST CONSUMER MAGAZINES: Food & Cookery

THE FOOD MAGAZINE

1748510U74P-945

Editorial Address: 94 White Lion Street, LONDON, N1 9PF
Tel: 020 7837 2250
Email: enquires@foodcomm.org.uk
Web site: http://www.foodcomm.org.uk
ISSN: 0953-5047
Publisher: The Food Commission
Date Established: 1988
Frequency: Quarterly
Annual Sub.: £25.00
Circulation: 10,000 (Publisher's Statement)
Usual Pagination: 24
Editor: Jessica Mitchell
Summary of Content: Magazine covering food facts, food product investigations, the latest news on diet and health and ideas on safer food campaigns.
Readership/Target Audience: Aimed at the general public, health professionals and the food industry.
ADVERTISING: No Advertising taken
CONSUMER: WOMEN'S INTEREST CONSUMER MAGAZINES: Food & Cookery

FOODS MATTER

45434U74G-37

Formerly: Foods Matter at the Inside Story
Editorial Address: 5 Lawn Road, LONDON, NW3 2XS
Tel: 020 7722 2866 Fax: 020 7722 7685
Email: michelle@foodsmatter.com
Advertising Address: As above.
Email: marketing@foodsmatter.com
Web site: http://www.foodsmatter.com
ISSN: 1369-8664
Publisher: Berrydales Publishing
Date Established: 1997
Frequency: Monthly
Free to qualifying individuals
Annual Sub.: £39.95
Circulation: 2,000 (Publisher's Statement)
Usual Pagination: 32
Editor: Michelle Berriedale-Johnson; Managing Director: Michelle Berriedale-Johnson; Advertising Manager: Laura Lebetkin
Summary of Content: Magazine covering all aspects of allergy, food allergies and restricted diets.
Readership/Target Audience: Read by health professionals and people with dietary problems or living on special diets.
ADVERTISING RATES:
Full Page Colour £635.00
Mechanical Data: Col Length: 267mm, Film: Digital, No. of Columns (Display): 2, Type Area: 267 x 180mm, Print Process: Heatset web-offset, Bleed Size: 303 x 216mm, Trim Size: 298 x 209mm, Page Width: 180mm
Copy instructions: Copy Date: 5 weeks prior to publication date
Average advertising content per issue: 30%
CONSUMER: WOMEN'S INTEREST CONSUMER MAGAZINES: Slimming & Health

Consumer Magazines

FOOTBALL ECHO (LIVERPOOL) 45693U75A-550
Editorial Address: For all contact details see main record, Liverpool Echo
Frequency: Weekly - Published every Saturday
ADVERTISING: Rates on application
Supplement to: Liverpool Echo
CONSUMER: SPORT

FOOTBALL ECHO (SUNDERLAND)
45751U75B-108
Editorial Address: Echo House, Pennywell, SUNDERLAND, SR4 9ER **Tel:** 0191 501 5800 **Fax:** 0191 534 5975
Email: echo.sport@northeast-press.co.uk
Advertising Address: As above. **Fax:** 0191 534 6687
Email: lynn.wilde@northeast-press.co.uk
Web site: http://www.sunderlandtoday.co.uk
Publisher: Northeast Press Ltd
Date Established: 1873
Frequency: 40 issues yearly - Published on Saturday evenings
Cover Price: £0.50
Circulation: 15,000 (Publisher's Statement)
Usual Pagination: 28
Editor: Neil Watson; **Advertising Manager:** Sharon Ewart
Summary of Content: Sports newspaper for the Sunderland area, with an emphasis on football.
Readership/Target Audience: Aimed mainly at Sunderland FC supporters.
ADVERTISING RATES:
Full Page Mono £3090.00
Full Page Colour £4017.00
SCC £15.37
Agency Commission: 10%
Mechanical Data: Type Area: 340 x 276mm, Col Length: 340mm, Page Width: 276mm, Col Widths (Display): 28mm, No. of Columns (Display): 9, Film: Digital
Copy instructions: Copy Date: 2 days prior to publication date
CONSUMER: SPORT: Football

FOOTBALL POST (NOTTINGHAM)
45755U75B-121
Editorial Address: Castle Wharf House, NOTTINGHAM, NG1 7EU **Tel:** 0115 948 2000 **Fax:** 0115 964 4032
Email: footballpost@nottinghameveningpost.co.uk
Advertising Address: As above. **Fax:** 0115 964 4097
Email: robert.carter@nottinghameveningpost.co.uk
Publisher: Nottingham Post Media Group Ltd
Date Established: 1903
Frequency: Weekly
Cover Price: £0.60
Circulation: 6,500 (Publisher's Statement)
Usual Pagination: 36
Editor: Mick Holland; **Advertising Manager:** Robert Carter
Summary of Content: Football newspaper with an emphasis on the East Midlands. Also some coverage of other sports such as rugby union and ice hockey.
Readership/Target Audience: Aimed at sports enthusiasts.
ADVERTISING RATES:
Full Page Mono £949.24
Full Page Colour £1186.56
Agency Commission: 10%
Mechanical Data: Type Area: 360 x 270mm, Col Length: 360mm, Page Width: 270mm, Col Widths (Display): 31mm, No. of Columns (Display): 8, Film: Digital
Copy instructions: Copy Date: 4 days prior to publication date
CONSUMER: SPORT: Football

FOOTBALL PUNK 1852120U75B-297
Editorial Address: Unit 3, The Sussex Innovation Centre, Science Square, BRIGHTON, BN1 9SD **Tel:** 01273 704400
Fax: 01273 704499
Email: jonathan.richards@jf-media.co.uk
Publisher: J.F. Media Ltd
Date Established: 2008
Frequency: Monthly
Cover Price: £2.00
Circulation: 16,444 (Publisher's Statement)
Editor: Richard Lenton
Summary of Content: Magazine covering football with interviews led by footballers, lifestyle features on players, romantic history pieces on past legends, travel features on the global game, views from the terraces and pieces from those who follow the game.
Readership/Target Audience: Aimed at football fans.
CONSUMER: SPORT: Football

FORGE PRESS 1692418U83-273
Formerly: Sheffield Steel Press
Editorial Address: Western Bank, SHEFFIELD, S10 2TG
Tel: 0114 222 8646
Email: forgepress@forgetoday.com

Advertising Address: As above. **Tel:** 0114 222 8500
Fax: 0114 222 8542
Email: thestudentconnection@sheffield.ac.uk
Publisher: University of Sheffield Student Union
Frequency: Monthly
Cover Price: Free
Circulation: 5,000 (Publisher's Statement)
Usual Pagination: 44
Summary of Content: Newspaper and magazine covering student issues, local Sheffield news, sport, entertainment, music, clubs and bars, food and drink, film and arts.
Readership/Target Audience: Aimed at students at Sheffield University.
ADVERTISING RATES:
Full Page Mono £840.00
Full Page Colour £995.00
Mechanical Data: Type Area: 352 x 265mm, Col Length: 352mm, Page Width: 265mm, Film: Digital
Copy instructions: Copy Date: 10 days prior to publication date
CONSUMER: STUDENT PUBLICATIONS

FORTEAN TIMES 48612U94E-30
Editorial Address: 30 Cleveland Street, LONDON, W1T 4JD
Tel: 020 7907 6235 **Fax:** 020 7907 6406
Email: david_sutton@dennis.co.uk
Advertising Address: As above. **Tel:** 020 7907 6000
Fax: 020 7907 6601
Email: max_wright@dennis.co.uk
Web site: http://www.forteantimes.com
ISSN: 0308-5899
Publisher: Dennis Publishing Ltd
Date Established: 1973
Frequency: 13 issues yearly
Cover Price: £4.25
Annual Sub.: £35.10
Circulation: 20,941 (ABC 01/01/2008 to 31/12/2008)
Usual Pagination: 84
Editor: David Sutton; **Publisher:** Simon Davies
Summary of Content: Magazine which documents strange phenomena from around the world.
Readership/Target Audience: Read by those with an interest in strange phenomena.
ADVERTISING RATES:
Full Page Colour £2500.00
Agency Commission: 10%
Mechanical Data: Film: Digital, Type Area: 269 x 182mm, Col Length: 269mm, Page Width: 182mm, Bleed Size: 303 x 216mm, Trim Size: 297 x 210mm
Copy instructions: Copy Date: 3 weeks prior to publication date
CONSUMER: OTHER CLASSIFICATIONS: Paranormal

THE FORTH NATURALIST & HISTORIAN
48749U94X-58
Editorial Address: Department of Biology, University of Stirling, STIRLING, FK9 4LA **Tel:** 01786 833409
Email: fnh@stir.ac.uk
Web site: http://www.fnh.stir.ac.uk
ISSN: 0309-7560
Publisher: Forth Naturalist and Historian
Date Established: 1975
Frequency: Annual - Published in November
Cover Price: £8.00
Circulation: 300 (Publisher's Statement)
Usual Pagination: 130
Summary of Content: Magazine that contains refereed studies of central Scotland's heritage and environment, as well as book reviews and general news.
Readership/Target Audience: Aimed at naturalists and historians.
ADVERTISING: No Advertising taken
CONSUMER: OTHER CLASSIFICATIONS: Miscellaneous

FORUM 48682U86A-186
Editorial Address: Ground Floor, 211 Old Street, LONDON, EC1V 9NR **Tel:** 020 7608 6500
Email: editor@ukforum.co.uk
Advertising Address: As above. **Tel:** 020 7608 6360
Fax: 020 7608 6320
Email: louise.mcmahon@trojanpublishing.co.uk
Web site: http://www.ukforum.co.uk
Publisher: Trojan Publishing
Date Established: 1967
Frequency: 13 issues yearly
Cover Price: £4.50
Annual Sub.: £36.00
Circulation: 40,000 (Publisher's Statement)
Usual Pagination: 196
Editor: Elizabeth Coldwell
Summary of Content: UK's readers' letters magazine dealing with sexuality, erotica and human relations as well as articles, features, fiction and advice.
Readership/Target Audience: Aimed at those with an open mind and an interest in sexual behaviour, couples looking for

titillation and those seeking advice from the board of consultants.
ADVERTISING RATES:
Full Page Colour £2400.00
Agency Commission: 10%
Mechanical Data: Type Area: 185 x 123mm, Col Length: 185mm, Page Width: 123mm, Film: Digital, Bleed Size: 216 x 154mm, Trim Size: 210 x 148mm
Copy instructions: Copy Date: 6 weeks prior to publication date
CONSUMER: ADULT & GAY MAGAZINES: Adult Magazines

FORWARD 1664721U80C-5438
Editorial Address: Council House, Victoria Square, BIRMINGHAM, B1 1BB **Tel:** 0121 303 4110
Fax: 0121 303 1365
Email: forward@birmingham.gov.uk
Web site: http://www.birmingham.gov.uk
Publisher: Birmingham City Council
Frequency: 24 issues yearly
Cover Price: Free
Circulation: 392,152 (Publisher's Statement)
Editor: Karen Pagett
Summary of Content: Magazine profiling Birmingham City Council policies, initiatives and events.
Readership/Target Audience: Aimed at residents of Birmingham.
ADVERTISING: No Advertising taken
CONSUMER: RURAL & REGIONAL INTEREST: Regional Interest English Counties

FOSSE WAY MAGAZINE 46964U80C-2780
Editorial Address: High Street, Stalbridge, STURMINSTER NEWTON, DT10 2LH **Tel:** 01963 365117 **Fax:** 01963 364029
Email: rholmes@bvmedia.co.uk
Web site: http://www.icwessex.co.uk
Publisher: Blackmore Vale Media
Date Established: 1994
Frequency: Weekly - Published on Friday
Cover Price: Free
Circulation: 32,000 (Publisher's Statement)
Usual Pagination: 64
Editor: Fanny Charles; **Features Editor:** Jackie Spiteri; **Managing Director:** Sven Thomas
Summary of Content: Current affairs magazine with particular interest in arts, environment, planning, health, education and agricultural issues.
Readership/Target Audience: Aimed at those living in the Somerset area.
ADVERTISING: No Advertising taken
CONSUMER: RURAL & REGIONAL INTEREST: Regional Interest English Counties

FOUR FOUR TWO 45757U75B-124
Editorial Address: Teddington Studios, Broom Road, TEDDINGTON, TW11 9BE **Tel:** 020 8267 5848
Fax: 020 8267 5061
Email: louis.massarella@haymarket.com
Advertising Address: As above. **Tel:** 020 8267 5000
Fax: 020 8267 5815
Email: stuart.staves@haymarket.com
Web site: http://www.fourfourtwo.com
ISSN: 1355-0276
Publisher: Haymarket Consumer Media
Date Established: 1994
Frequency: Monthly
Cover Price: £3.60
Circulation: 94,084 (ABC 01/01/2009 to 30/06/2009)
Usual Pagination: 150
Editor: Louis Massarella; **Features Editor:** Louis Massarella; **Managing Director:** Kevin Costello
Summary of Content: Magazine featuring player profiles, interviews, features and readers letters.
Readership/Target Audience: Aimed at football fans aged 16 years old and over.
ADVERTISING RATES:
Full Page Colour £5875.00
Agency Commission: 10%
Mechanical Data: Type Area: 280 x 200mm, Trim Size: 300 x 220mm, Bleed Size: 306 x 226mm, Col Length: 280mm, Film: Digital, Page Width: 200mm
Copy instructions: Copy Date: 3 weeks prior to publication date
Average advertising content per issue: 40%
CONSUMER: SPORT: Football

FOUR SHIRES MAGAZINE 46792U80A-120
Editorial Address: Borough House, Marlborough Road, BANBURY, OX16 5TH **Tel:** 01295 273138
Fax: 01295 273139
Email: copy@fourshires.co.uk
Advertising Address: 7 Borough House, Marlborough Road, BANBURY, OX16 5TH **Tel:** 01295 709999
Fax: 01295 709999
Email: elle@fourshires.co.uk

Web site: http://www.fourshires.co.uk
Publisher: Four Shires Publishing
Date Established: 1997
Frequency: Monthly
Cover Price: £2.20
Annual Sub.: £36.00
Circulation: 5,000 (Publisher's Statement)
Usual Pagination: 88
Editor: Jeremy Wilton; **Publisher:** Jeremy Wilton
Summary of Content: Magazine covering all aspects of life in the four shires - countryside, wining and dining, going out and about, food fairs, property, social pages, health, pictures from the past - all that celebrates the area and all that's good about the area.
Readership/Target Audience: Read mainly by 25 year olds and over.
ADVERTISING RATES:
Full Page Colour £650.00
Agency Commission: 10%
Mechanical Data: Film: Digital, Bleed Size: 303 x 213mm, Type Area: 270 x 190mm, Col Length: 270mm, Page Width: 190mm
Copy instructions: Copy Date: 3 weeks prior to publication date
Average advertising content per issue: 40%
CONSUMER: RURAL & REGIONAL INTEREST: Rural Interest

FOURTH WORLD REVIEW
47226U82-24_25

Editorial Address: The Close, 26 High Street, Purton, SWINDON, SN5 4AE **Tel:** 01793 772214
Web site: http://www.cesc.net
Publisher: The Leopold Kohr
Date Established: 1984
Frequency: 6 issues yearly
Cover Price: £2.00
Free to qualifying individuals
Circulation: 800 (Publisher's Statement)
Usual Pagination: 32
Editor: John Papworth
Summary of Content: Newsletter campaigning for the restoration of the human scale in institutions and communities around the world. Concerns are to counter giantism and promote the small scale in all political and economic spheres.
Readership/Target Audience: Aimed at those concerned about international conflict, social decay and environmental destruction.
ADVERTISING: No Advertising taken
CONSUMER: CURRENT AFFAIRS & POLITICS

FQ MAGAZINE
1620694U86C-709

Formerly: FQ The Essential Dad Mag
Editorial Address: Touchline, 3-5 Spafield Street, LONDON, EC1R 4QB **Tel:** 020 7841 0344 **Fax:** 020 7278 7100
Email: michael@touchline.com
Advertising Address: Seymour House, South Street, BROMLEY, BR1 1RH **Tel:** 020 8460 6060
Fax: 020 8460 6050
Email: john@3dmediaworld.com
Web site: http://www.fqmagazine.co.uk
Publisher: 3-D Media Ltd
Date Established: 2003
Frequency: 6 issues yearly
Cover Price: £3.25
Annual Sub.: £15.99
Circulation: 87,000 (Publisher's Statement)
Usual Pagination: 116
Editor: Michael Stoneman; **Advertising Manager:** John Donovan
Summary of Content: Magazine entirely for the generation of family-oriented men, who've grown up and subsequently grown out of the available men's magazines. Featuring articles on health, fitness, fashion, shopping, finance, investment, food and drink.
Readership/Target Audience: Aimed at men between 25 and 42 years old.
ADVERTISING RATES:
Full Page Colour £4900.00
Agency Commission: 10%
Mechanical Data: Trim Size: 297 x 210mm, Film: Digital
Copy instructions: Copy Date: 4 weeks prior to publication date
CONSUMER: ADULT & GAY MAGAZINES: Men's Lifestyle Magazines

FRANCE MAGAZINE
48243U89E-95

Editorial Address: Archant House, Oriel Road, CHELTENHAM, GL50 1BB **Tel:** 01242 216050
Fax: 01242 216094
Email: editorial@francemag.com
Advertising Address: As above. **Tel:** 01242 216087
Email: advertising@francemag.com
Web site: http://www.francemag.com
ISSN: 0958-8213
Publisher: Archant Life

Date Established: 1990
Frequency: Monthly
Cover Price: £3.99
Annual Sub.: £38.00
Circulation: 34,815 (Publisher's Statement)
Usual Pagination: 124
Editor: Anna McKittrick; **Managing Director:** Miller Hogg
Summary of Content: Magazine on all things French. Includes articles on the countryside, cities, culture, people, customs, food and wine.
Language(s): English; French
Readership/Target Audience: Aimed at the discerning Francophile.
ADVERTISING RATES:
Full Page Colour £1750.00
Agency Commission: 10%
Mechanical Data: Film: Digital, Col Length: 273mm, Type Area: 273 x 188mm, Bleed Size: 303 x 216mm, Trim Size: 297 x 210mm, Page Width: 188mm
Copy instructions: Copy Date: 3 weeks prior to publication date
Average advertising content per issue: 25%
CONSUMER: HOLIDAYS & TRAVEL: Holidays

FREE LIFE
47228U82-25_25

Editorial Address: Suite 35, 2 Lansdowne Row, LONDON, W1J 6HL **Tel:** 0870 242 1712
Email: sean@libertarian.co.uk
Advertising Address: As above. **Tel:** 07956 472199
Email: sean@libertarian.co.uk
Web site: http://www.libertarian.co.uk
ISSN: 0260-5112
Publisher: The Libertarian Alliance
Frequency: Monthly
Annual Sub.: £20.00
Circulation: 1,800 (Publisher's Statement)
Usual Pagination: 20
Editor: Sean Gabb; **Advertising Manager:** Sean Gabb
Summary of Content: Journal of the Libertarian Alliance. Includes articles on classical liberal and libertarian views, politics, economics, law and philosophy.
Readership/Target Audience: Aimed at journalists, students and politicians.
ADVERTISING RATES:
Full Page Mono £100.00
Mechanical Data: Film: Digital
CONSUMER: CURRENT AFFAIRS & POLITICS

FREEDOM TODAY
47227U82-25

Editorial Address: PO Box 3394, FARINGDON, SN7 7FN
Tel: 0845 833 9626
Email: freedomtoday@blueyonder.co.uk
Advertising Address: As above.
Email: mail@tfa.net
Web site: http://www.tfa.net
Publisher: Far and Wide Publishers Ltd
Date Established: 1975
Frequency: 6 issues yearly
Cover Price: £3.50
Free to qualifying individuals
Circulation: 4,100 (Publisher's Statement)
Usual Pagination: 28
Editor: Simon Richards; **Advertising Manager:** Vicki Stevens
Summary of Content: Magazine containing educational and campaigning political ideas, includes economic, political and moral principles.
Readership/Target Audience: Read by members of The Freedom Association, MPs, MEPs, political journalists and opinion formers.
ADVERTISING RATES:
Full Page Colour £500.00
Mechanical Data: Trim Size: 297 x 210mm
Copy instructions: Copy Date: 1st of the month prior to publication date
Average advertising content per issue: 10%
CONSUMER: CURRENT AFFAIRS & POLITICS

FREEHAND
48633U94F-390

Editorial Address: 21A Vincent Square, LONDON, SW1P 2NA **Tel:** 020 7834 1066 **Fax:** 020 7828 1828
Email: info@abucon.co.uk
Publisher: Abucon
Frequency: Quarterly
Free to qualifying individuals
Circulation: 4,500 (Publisher's Statement)
Usual Pagination: 40
Editor: Liza Jones
Summary of Content: Magazine promoting wider interests among disabled and elderly people. Also includes information on products and services available to them.
Readership/Target Audience: Aimed at the disabled and elderly, many of whom are house-bound.
ADVERTISING: No Advertising taken
CONSUMER: OTHER CLASSIFICATIONS: Disability

FREEMASONRY TODAY
48684U94X-66

Editorial Address: Freemasons Hall, 60 Great Queen Street, LONDON, WC2B 5AZ **Tel:** 020 7831 9811
Fax: 020 7395 9307
Email: fmt@ugle.org.uk
Advertising Address: Holly Mount House, Southend Road, BILLERICAY, CM12 9QH **Tel:** 01277 625504
Email: alan.goodes@btinternet.com
Web site: http://www.freemasonrytoday.co.uk
ISSN: 1369-040X
Publisher: Grand Lodge Publications Ltd
Date Established: 1997
Frequency: Quarterly
Annual Sub.: £13.45
Circulation: 224,185 (ABC 01/01/2008 to 31/12/2008)
Usual Pagination: 64
Editor: Michael Baigent; **News Editor:** John Jackson; **Managing Director:** Bill Hanbury-Bateman; **Advertising Manager:** Alan Goodes; **Publisher:** Geoffrey Baber
Summary of Content: Magazine covering the history, present and future of freemasonry. Contains news, entertainment pages and articles of interest.
Readership/Target Audience: Read by members of the United Grand Lodge of England, freemasons worldwide and individuals interested in freemasonry.
ADVERTISING RATES:
Full Page Mono £2820.00
Full Page Colour £3760.00
Agency Commission: 10%
Mechanical Data: Film: Digital, Type Area: 272 x 190mm, Bleed Size: 303 x 216mm, Trim Size: 297 x 210mm, Page Width: 190mm, Col Length: 272mm
Copy instructions: Copy Date: 1st of month prior to publication date
CONSUMER: OTHER CLASSIFICATIONS: Miscellaneous

FRENCH MAGAZINE
713061U89E-110

Editorial Address: Unit 3, The Old Estate Yard, North Stoke Lane, Upton Cheyney, BRISTOL, BS30 6ND
Tel: 01225 329381
Email: justin.postlethwaite@edpltd.co.uk
Advertising Address: As above. **Tel:** 0117 932 3586
Web site: http://www.frenchmagazine.co.uk
Publisher: Evolve Digital Publishing
Date Established: 2001
Frequency: 6 issues yearly
Cover Price: £3.99
Circulation: 20,000 (Publisher's Statement)
Usual Pagination: 150
Editor: Justin Postlethwaite
Summary of Content: Magazine covering travel, holidays, city breaks, wine, food, health and beauty, stylish French homes, renovating property and general lifestyle. Also contains a section featuring homes in France to buy or rent.
Language(s): English; French
Readership/Target Audience: Aimed at UK residents and those interested in travelling to France or buying a home there.
ADVERTISING RATES:
Full Page Colour £2000.00
Agency Commission: 10%
Mechanical Data: Bleed Size: 306 x 226mm, Film: Digital, Type Area: 300 x 220mm, Col Length: 300mm, Page Width: 220mm, No. of Columns (Display): 4
Copy instructions: Copy Date: 3 weeks prior to publication date
Average advertising content per issue: 29%
CONSUMER: HOLIDAYS & TRAVEL: Holidays

FRENCH PROPERTY NEWS
45483U74K-90

Editorial Address: Battersey Studios, Unit F3, 80 Silverthorne Road, LONDON, SW8 3HE **Tel:** 020 7978 3493
Email: karen.tait@archant.co.uk
Advertising Address: Archant House, Oriel Road, CHELTENHAM, GL50 1BB **Tel:** 01242 265896
Fax: 01242 216094
Email: advertising.fpn@virgin.net
Web site: http://www.french-property-news.com
Publisher: Archant Life
Date Established: 1989
Frequency: Monthly
Free to qualifying individuals
Annual Sub.: £22.00
Circulation: 50,000 (Publisher's Statement)
Usual Pagination: 132
Editor: Karen Tait; **Publisher:** Miller Hogg
Summary of Content: Magazine covering the issues involved in buying property and living in France.
Readership/Target Audience: Aimed at those interested in purchasing French property.
ADVERTISING RATES:
Full Page Mono £1275.00
Full Page Colour £1750.00
Agency Commission: 10%
Mechanical Data: Col Length: 273mm, Bleed Size: 307 x 220mm, Trim Size: 297 x 210mm, Film: Digital, Type Area: 273 x 188mm, Page Width: 188mm

Consumer Magazines

Copy instructions: Copy Date: 20th of the month prior to publication date
Average advertising content per issue: 60%
CONSUMER: WOMEN'S INTEREST CONSUMER MAGAZINES: Home Purchase

FRESH
1665237U74F-760

Editorial Address: 9-10 St. Andrews Square, EDINBURGH, EH2 2AF **Tel:** 07973 198230
Email: stephen.penman@sundayherald.com
Publisher: Newsquest Sunday Herald Ltd
Date Established: 2004
Frequency: 10 issues yearly - Not published in July and August
Cover Price: Free
Circulation: 130,000 (Publisher's Statement)
Usual Pagination: 20
Editor: Stephen Penman
Summary of Content: Magazine covering social issues including homelessness and bullying as well as international news items, entertainment, reviews, celebrity interviews and profiles.
Readership/Target Audience: Aimed at girls and boys ages 11 to 15 years old.
ADVERTISING: No Advertising taken
Supplement to: Sunday Herald
CONSUMER: WOMEN'S INTEREST CONSUMER MAGAZINES: Teenage

FRESH DIRECTION
47389U83-8_7

Formerly: FD
Editorial Address: Building D, Berkeley Works, Berkley Grove, LONDON, NW1 8XY **Tel:** 020 7449 0900
Fax: 020 7449 0901
Email: editor@freshdirection.co.uk
Advertising Address: As above.
Email: nasar.niaz@fd-media.co.uk
Web site: http://www.freshdirection.co.uk
Publisher: Antonville Ltd
Date Established: 1990
Frequency: 3 issues yearly - Published in January, May and September
Cover Price: Free
Circulation: 400,000 (Publisher's Statement)
Usual Pagination: 144
Editor: Paul Russell; **Advertising Manager:** Nasar Niaz; **Publisher:** Paul Russell
Summary of Content: Magazine covering entertainment listings for cities around the UK. Includes lifestyle features on student issues, music, cinema, beauty, fashion, health, computers, money, careers, relationships and celebrity interviews.
Readership/Target Audience: Read by fun loving university students and those between 18 and 24 years old.
ADVERTISING RATES:
Full Page Colour £8250.00
Agency Commission: 10%
Mechanical Data: Film: Digital, Type Area: 188 x 126mm, Bleed Size: 216 x 154mm, Trim Size: 210 x 148mm, Col Length: 188mm, Page Width: 126mm, Print Process: Web-fed offset
Copy instructions: Copy Date: 4 weeks prior to publication date
Average advertising content per issue: 25%
CONSUMER: STUDENT PUBLICATIONS

FRESHWATER INFORMER
1814268U92-113

Editorial Address: Cowden Close, Horns Road, Hawkhurst, CRANBROOK, TN18 4QT **Tel:** 01580 753322
Fax: 01580 754104
Email: fwi@wealdenad.co.uk
Advertising Address: As above.
Email: fwi@wealdenad.co.uk
Web site: http://www.freshwaterinformer.com
Publisher: The Wealden Advertiser
Frequency: Monthly
Cover Price: Free
Circulation: 7,500 (Publisher's Statement)
Usual Pagination: 36
Editor: Nick Norton; **Managing Editor:** Graham Thorn
Summary of Content: Magazine covering all aspects of fresh water fishing.
Readership/Target Audience: Aimed at fresh water anglers.
ADVERTISING RATES:
Full Page Mono £255.00
Full Page Colour £325.00
SCC £4.25
Agency Commission: 10%
Mechanical Data: Type Area: 290 x 207mm, Col Length: 290mm, Page Width: 207mm, Bleed Size: 296 x 213mm, Trim Size: 297 x 210mm, Col Widths (Display): 47mm, No. of Columns (Display): 4, Film: Digital
Copy instructions: Copy Date: 21st of the cover month
Average advertising content per issue: 40%
CONSUMER: ANGLING & FISHING

THE FRIEND
47716U87-100

Editorial Address: Friends House, 173 Euston Road, LONDON, NW1 2BJ **Tel:** 020 7663 1010 **Fax:** 020 7663 1182
Email: news@thefriend.org
Advertising Address: 54A Main Street, Cononley, KEIGHLEY, BD20 8LL **Tel:** 01535 630230
Fax: 01535 630230
Email: ads@thefriend.org
Web site: http://www.thefriend.org
Publisher: The Friend Publications Ltd
Date Established: 1843
Frequency: Weekly - Published on Friday
Cover Price: £1.70
Annual Sub.: £72.00
Circulation: 3,200 (Publisher's Statement)
Usual Pagination: 20
Editor: Judy Kirby
Summary of Content: Quaker magazine covering news, views and articles on spirituality, peace, social issues and Quaker beliefs, plus letters.
Readership/Target Audience: Read by those attending Quaker meetings and others interested in justice, peace, religious and theological issues.
ADVERTISING RATES:
Full Page Mono £575.00
Agency Commission: 10%
Mechanical Data: Col Length: 225mm, Type Area: 225 x 165mm, Trim Size: 270 x 195mm, Page Width: 165mm
Copy instructions: Copy Date: Wednesday prior to publication date
Average advertising content per issue: 20%
CONSUMER: RELIGIOUS

FRIEND
1665922U94X-277

Editorial Address: 26-28 Underwood Street, LONDON, N1 7JQ **Tel:** 020 7490 1555 **Fax:** 020 7490 0881
Email: info@foe.co.uk
Web site: http://www.foe.co.uk
Publisher: Friends of the Earth
Date Established: 2005
Frequency: 3 issues yearly - Published in February, May and September
Free to qualifying individuals
Circulation: 15,000 (Publisher's Statement)
Usual Pagination: 16
Editor: James Dickson
Summary of Content: Magazine featuring interviews with celebrities who support green issues as well as fashion, art, sport and politics.
Readership/Target Audience: Aimed at a cosmopolitan audience aged between 25 and 35 years old.
ADVERTISING: No Advertising taken
CONSUMER: OTHER CLASSIFICATIONS: Miscellaneous

FRIENDS
47634U86B-160

Formerly: Stonewall
Editorial Address: Tower Building, York Road, LONDON, SE1 7NX **Tel:** 020 7593 1850 **Fax:** 020 7593 1877
Email: gary.nunn@stonewall.org.uk
Advertising Address: As above.
Email: thomas.woodward@stonewall.org.uk
Web site: http://www.stonewall.org.uk
Publisher: Stonewall
Frequency: 3 issues yearly - Published in April, August and November
Free to qualifying individuals
Circulation: 4,000 (Publisher's Statement)
Usual Pagination: 12
Editor: Gary Nunn
Summary of Content: Magazine of the lobby group Stonewall. Covers legal equality and social justice for lesbian, gay and bisexual people.
Readership/Target Audience: Read by supporters of the lobby group.
ADVERTISING: Rates on application
Mechanical Data: Film: Digital
Copy instructions: Copy Date: 3 weeks prior to publication date
Average advertising content per issue: 15%
CONSUMER: ADULT & GAY MAGAZINES: Gay & Lesbian Magazines

FRIEZE
47499U84A-230

Editorial Address: 81 Rivington Street, LONDON, EC2A 3AY **Tel:** 020 3372 6111 **Fax:** 020 3178 7042
Email: editors@frieze.com
Advertising Address: As above.
Email: marisa@frieze.com
Web site: http://www.frieze.com
ISSN: 0962-0672
Publisher: Durian Publications Ltd
Date Established: 1991
Frequency: 8 issues yearly
Cover Price: £5.95
Annual Sub.: £33.50
Circulation: 25,000 (Publisher's Statement)

Usual Pagination: 116
Editor: Jonathan Griffin; **Managing Director:** Matthew Slotover; **Advertising Manager:** Marisa Futernick; **Publisher:** Amanda Sharp
Summary of Content: Magazine about contemporary art and culture.
Language(s): English; German
Readership/Target Audience: Read by higher income earners between 18 and 34 years old with an interest in visual arts and contemporary culture.
ADVERTISING RATES:
Full Page Mono £2850.00
Full Page Colour £3350.00
Agency Commission: 10%
Mechanical Data: Film: Digital, Bleed Size: 308 x 238mm, Trim Size: 300 x 230mm, Type Area: 254 x 196mm, Col Length: 254mm, Page Width: 196mm
Average advertising content per issue: 40%
CONSUMER: THE ARTS & LITERARY: Arts

FRONT
47649U86C-240

Editorial Address: 2-4 Noel Street, LONDON, W1F 8GB
Tel: 020 3358 3305
Email: front@frontarmy.co.uk
Advertising Address: As above. **Tel:** 020 7689 3919
Email: neville@frontarmy.co.uk
Web site: www.frontarmy.co.uk
Publisher: Kane
Date Established: 1998
Frequency: 13 issues yearly
Cover Price: £3.50
Annual Sub.: £30.00
Circulation: 63,910 (Publisher's Statement)
Usual Pagination: 164
Editor: Mike Rampton; **News Editor:** Mike Rampton; **Features Editor:** Sam Coare; **Managing Director:** Richard Olsen; **Advertising Manager:** Neville King; **Advertising Director:** Ben Crudgington
Summary of Content: Lifestyle magazine covering fashion, music, sport, sex, film and television with features on the weird and bizarre.
Readership/Target Audience: Read by men between 18 and 30 years old.
ADVERTISING: Rates on application
Agency Commission: 10%
Average advertising content per issue: 30%
CONSUMER: ADULT & GAY MAGAZINES: Men's Lifestyle Magazines

FROOTS
46150U76D-318

Editorial Address: PO Box 337, LONDON, N4 1TW
Tel: 020 8340 9651 **Fax:** 020 8348 5626
Email: froots@frootsmag.com
Advertising Address: As above.
Email: ads@frootsmag.com
Web site: http://www.frootsmag.com
ISSN: 0951-1326
Publisher: Southern Rag Ltd
Date Established: 1979
Frequency: 10 issues yearly
Cover Price: £4.20
Annual Sub.: £46.00
Circulation: 14,000 (Publisher's Statement)
Usual Pagination: 90
Editor: Sarah Coxson; **News Editor:** Sarah Coxson; **Managing Director:** Ian Anderson; **Advertising Manager:** Gina Jennings
Summary of Content: Magazine about folk, roots and world music with news, reviews, interviews and features on the UK and international scene.
Readership/Target Audience: Aimed at roots music lovers.
ADVERTISING RATES:
Full Page Mono £725.00
Full Page Colour £930.00
Agency Commission: 10%
Mechanical Data: Page Width: 190mm, Bleed Size: 303 x 216mm, Type Area: 275 x 190mm, Col Length: 275mm, Trim Size: 297 x 210mm, Film: Digital
Copy instructions: Copy Date: 12th of the month prior to publication date
CONSUMER: MUSIC & PERFORMING ARTS: Music

FULHAM EXCLUSIVE
1892648U80C-5494

Editorial Address: For all contact details see main edition, Exclusive (London)
Frequency: 10 issues yearly
Cover Price: Free
Circulation: 7,500 (Publisher's Statement)
ADVERTISING: Rates on application
Edition of: Exclusive (London)
CONSUMER: RURAL & REGIONAL INTEREST: Regional Interest English Counties

FULL HOUSE
1666508U74A-987

Editorial Address: The Tower, Phoenix Square, Wyncolls Road, Severalls Industrial Park, COLCHESTER, CO4 9HU
Tel: 01206 851117 **Fax:** 01206 849078
Email: features@fullhousemagazine.co.uk
Advertising Address: Hubert Burda Media UK, Swan House, 37-39 High Holborn, LONDON, WC1V 6AA
Tel: 020 7242 0553 **Fax:** 01206 849079
Email: harriet.edery@burdamagazines.co.uk
Web site: http://www.fullhousemagazine.co.uk
ISSN: 1746-6725
Publisher: Hubert Burda Media UK
Frequency: Weekly
Cover Price: £0.50
Circulation: 135,592 (ABC 01/01/2009 to 30/06/2009)
Usual Pagination: 56
Editor: Johanna Burrows; **Features Editor:** Charlotte Potter;
Advertising Manager: Harriet Edery
Summary of Content: Magazine with a mixture of real-life stories, entertainment, puzzles and competitions.
Readership/Target Audience: Aimed at women aged 25 years old and over.
ADVERTISING RATES:
Full Page Colour £4500.00
Agency Commission: 10%
Mechanical Data: Type Area: 245 x 196mm, Bleed Size: 271 x 221mm, Trim Size: 265 x 215mm, Col Length: 245mm, Page Width: 196mm
Copy instructions: Copy Date: 2 weeks prior to publication date
Average advertising content per issue: 15%
CONSUMER: WOMEN'S INTEREST CONSUMER MAGAZINES: Women's Interest

FULL ON!
1601517U74Q-1128

Editorial Address: The Busworks, United House, North Road, LONDON, N7 9DP **Tel:** 020 7609 4254
Fax: 020 7609 4424
Advertising Address: As above.
Email: nosheen@fullonmag.co.uk
Web site: http://www.fullonmag.co.uk
Publisher: Full On Publications Ltd
Date Established: 2002
Frequency: 5 issues yearly
Cover Price: Free
Circulation: 80,000 (Publisher's Statement)
Usual Pagination: 28
Editor: Jude Schofield; **Advertising Manager:** Nosheen Riaz
Summary of Content: Magazine covering general teen interest, music, games, fashion, celebrities blended with educational information.
Readership/Target Audience: Aimed at 14 to 16 year old students at secondary schools across England.
ADVERTISING: Rates on application
Agency Commission: 10%
Copy instructions: Copy Date: 18 days prior to publication date
Average advertising content per issue: 40%
CONSUMER: WOMEN'S INTEREST CONSUMER MAGAZINES: Lifestyle

THE FULL PINT MAGAZINE
1685821U74P-927

Editorial Address: Flat 4-22, Northwood Hall, 81 Hornsey Lane, LONDON, N6 5PJ **Tel:** 07910 151494
Email: steve.ducker@yahoo.co.uk
Advertising Address: 37 Rivulet Road, LONDON, N17 7JT
Tel: 07775 936216 **Fax:** 0870 280 0533
Email: gary@gw1.demon.co.uk
Web site: http://www.camranorthlondon.co.uk
Publisher: Campaign for Real Ale Ltd
Date Established: 1999
Frequency: 5 issues yearly
Cover Price: Free
Circulation: 3,500 (Publisher's Statement)
Usual Pagination: 8
Editor: Steve Ducker; **Advertising Manager:** Gary White
Summary of Content: Newsletter covering real ale and beer, pub architecture and preservation and general issues for licensees. Distributed through pubs that sell real ale.
Readership/Target Audience: Aimed at real ale drinkers and publicans.
ADVERTISING: Rates on application
Average advertising content per issue: 25%
CONSUMER: WOMEN'S INTEREST CONSUMER MAGAZINES: Food & Cookery

FUN TO LEARN PEPPA PIG
1794767U91D-953

Editorial Address: Suite 2, Prospect House, Belle Vue Road, SHREWSBURY, SY3 7NR **Tel:** 01743 364433
Fax: 01743 271528
Email: info@redan.com
Advertising Address: As above.
Email: emily@redan.com
Publisher: Redan Publishing

Date Established: 2007
Frequency: 18 issues yearly
Cover Price: £1.99
Circulation: 83,896 (ABC 01/01/2009 to 30/06/2009)
Usual Pagination: 32
Editor: Emily Bell; **Advertising Manager:** Emily Bell
Summary of Content: Children's magazine with stories and activities based on the television programme Peppa Pig.
Readership/Target Audience: Aimed at boys and girls aged 3 to 7 years old.
ADVERTISING RATES:
Full Page Colour £1800.00
Agency Commission: 10%
Mechanical Data: Type Area: 300 x 220mm, Col Length: 300mm, Page Width: 220mm, Film: Digital
Copy instructions: Copy Date: 5 weeks prior to publication date
Average advertising content per issue: 2%
CONSUMER: RECREATION & LEISURE: Children & Youth

FUNDOKU
1695166U79F-90

Editorial Address: Stonecroft, 69 Station Road, REDHILL, RH1 1EY **Tel:** 01737 378700 **Fax:** 01737 781800
Email: enquiries@puzzlermedia.com
Publisher: Puzzler Media Ltd
Date Established: 2005
Frequency: Monthly
Cover Price: £1.80
Circulation: 85,000 (Publisher's Statement)
Usual Pagination: 48
Editor: Ariane Blok
Summary of Content: Magazine of Sudoku puzzles for beginners with prizes in each issue.
Readership/Target Audience: Aimed at beginners and older children.
ADVERTISING: No Advertising taken
CONSUMER: HOBBIES & DIY: Games & Puzzles

FUNTASTIC
1832650U91D-974

Editorial Address: Headley House, Headley Road, Grayshott, HINDHEAD, GU26 6TU **Tel:** 01428 601020
Fax: 01428 601027
Email: funtastic@signaturepl.co.uk
Advertising Address: As above.
Email: abi@djmurphy.co.uk
Publisher: Signature Publishing Ltd
Date Established: 2008
Frequency: Monthly
Cover Price: £2.99
Circulation: 50,000 (Print Run)
Usual Pagination: 32
Editor: Amanda Clifford; **Advertising Manager:** Abigail Cannon
Summary of Content: Magazine covering all areas of pre-school learning and a range of licensed and unlicensed characters and book characters with activities, colouring, stories and cover-mounts as well as advice to parents.
Readership/Target Audience: Aimed at girls and boys aged 3 to 5 years old.
ADVERTISING RATES:
Full Page Colour £1650.00
CONSUMER: RECREATION & LEISURE: Children & Youth

FUR AND FEATHER INCORPORATING RABBITS
47186U81X-130

Editorial Address: Elder House, The Street, Chattisham, IPSWICH, IP8 3QE **Tel:** 01473 652789 **Fax:** 01473 652788
Email: pat@furandfeather.co.uk
Advertising Address: As above.
Email: pat@furandfeather.co.uk
Web site: http://www.furandfeather.co.uk
ISSN: 0262-6849
Publisher: Printing for Pleasure Ltd
Date Established: 1882
Frequency: Monthly - Published the 3rd week of the month prior to cover date
Cover Price: £3.75
Annual Sub.: £38.00
Circulation: 2,500 (Publisher's Statement)
Usual Pagination: 80
Editor: Patricia Gaskin; **Advertising Manager:** Patricia Gaskin
Summary of Content: Specialist magazine and official journal of the British Rabbit Council covering all aspects of keeping and exhibiting exhibition rabbits, companion rabbits, gerbils, mice, rats and hamsters.
Readership/Target Audience: Aimed at breeders, exhibitors and keepers of these animals.
ADVERTISING RATES:
Full Page Mono £175.00
Full Page Colour £250.00
Agency Commission: 10%
Mechanical Data: Trim Size: 297 x 210mm
Copy instructions: Copy Date: 1st of the month prior to publication date

Average advertising content per issue: 10%
CONSUMER: ANIMALS & PETS

FUSED MAGAZINE
717534U76D-318_20

Editorial Address: 315 The Greenhouse, Gibb Square, Gibb Street, BIRMINGHAM, B9 4AA **Tel:** 0121 246 1946
Email: dave@fusedmagazine.com
Advertising Address: As above.
Email: kerry@fusedmagazine.com
Web site: http://www.fusedmagazine.com
Publisher: FUSED
Date Established: 2000
Frequency: Quarterly
Cover Price: £2.95
Circulation: 25,000 (Publisher's Statement)
Usual Pagination: 64
Editor: David O'Coy; **Advertising Manager:** Kerry Thomas;
Publisher: David O'Coy
Summary of Content: Cutting-edge youth culture magazine covering music, art and fashion.
Readership/Target Audience: Aimed at men and women between 18 and 35 years old.
ADVERTISING RATES:
Full Page Colour £800.00
Agency Commission: 10%
Average advertising content per issue: 10%
CONSUMER: MUSIC & PERFORMING ARTS: Music

FUTURE MUSIC
46512U78A-150

Editorial Address: 30 Monmouth Street, BATH, BA1 2BW
Tel: 01225 442244 **Fax:** 01225 446019
Email: futuremusic@futurenet.com
Advertising Address: As above. **Tel:** 01225 732282
Email: daniel.fitzhenry@futurenet.co.uk
Web site: http://www.futuremusic.co.uk
ISSN: 0967-0378
Publisher: Future Publishing Ltd
Date Established: 1992
Frequency: 13 issues yearly
Cover Price: £5.99
Circulation: 10,860 (ABC 01/01/2008 to 31/12/2008)
Usual Pagination: 188
Editor: Daniel Griffiths; **Features Editor:** Chris Barker;
Publisher: Rob Last
Summary of Content: Magazine containing a guide to the equipment required to create, play and record music using the latest technology.
Language(s): English; Spanish
Readership/Target Audience: Aimed at musicians using modern technology.
ADVERTISING RATES:
Full Page Colour £1600.00
Agency Commission: 10%
Mechanical Data: Page Width: 190mm, Type Area: 270 x 190mm, Col Length: 270mm, Trim Size: 297 x 210mm, Bleed Size: 303 x 216mm, Film: Digital
Average advertising content per issue: 25%
CONSUMER: CONSUMER ELECTRONICS: Hi-Fi & Recording

FYNE TIMES
1616091U86B-167

Editorial Address: Linde Buildings, 7 Nuffield Way, ABINGDON, OX14 1RJ **Tel:** 01235 468428
Fax: 01235 468427
Email: jill@fyne.co.uk
Advertising Address: As above.
Email: jill@fyne.co.uk
Web site: http://www.fyne.co.uk
Publisher: Fyne Associates Ltd
Date Established: 2001
Frequency: Monthly
Cover Price: Free
Circulation: 50,000 (Publisher's Statement)
Usual Pagination: 64
Editor: Jill Rayner; **Advertising Manager:** Jill Rayner
Summary of Content: Lifestyle magazine containing features on local news, travel, motors, health, general articles, gossip, chat, property and recruitment.
Readership/Target Audience: Aimed at the gay and lesbian community.
ADVERTISING: Rates on application
CONSUMER: ADULT & GAY MAGAZINES: Gay & Lesbian Magazines

G3 MAGAZINE
767658U86B-165

Editorial Address: 37 Ivor Place, LONDON, NW1 6EA
Tel: 020 7258 1777 **Fax:** 020 7258 1787
Email: sarah@g3magazine.co.uk
Advertising Address: As above.
Email: dan@g3magazine.co.uk
Web site: http://www.g3mag.co.uk
Publisher: Square Peg Media
Date Established: 2001
Frequency: Monthly

Consumer Magazines

Cover Price: Free
Circulation: 40,000 (Publisher's Statement)
Editor: Sarah Garrett; **Managing Editor:** Sarah Garrett
Summary of Content: Magazine covering arts and culture, community, sports, Internet, music, bars and clubs.
Readership/Target Audience: Aimed at gay, urban women.
ADVERTISING RATES:
Full Page Colour £2500.00
Agency Commission: 10%
Mechanical Data: Bleed Size: 307 x 220mm, Film: Digital, Trim Size: 297 x 210mm
Copy instructions: Copy Date: 2 weeks prior to publication date
Average advertising content per issue: 50%
CONSUMER: ADULT & GAY MAGAZINES: Gay & Lesbian Magazines

G MAG
633840U76D-753

Formerly: Gargamel Magazine
Editorial Address: PO Box 18542, LONDON, E17 5UY
Tel: 020 8527 2720 **Fax:** 020 8531 6050
Email: mel@campro.freeserve.co.uk
Advertising Address: As above.
Email: mel@campro.freeserve.co.uk
Publisher: Campro Entertainment
Date Established: 1999
Frequency: 6 issues yearly - Published in the first week of the month
Cover Price: Free
Circulation: 30,000 (Publisher's Statement)
Usual Pagination: 64
Editor: Melissa Sinclair; **Advertising Manager:** Melissa Sinclair; **Publisher:** Melissa Sinclair
Summary of Content: Magazine covering different styles of reggae and black music including African, dancehall, bashment, gospel, hip-hop, R&B, reggaeton, roots reggae, soca and salsa. features include lifestyle and culture, the arts, fashion, food, drink, ideology and sport.
Readership/Target Audience: Aimed at Reggae and Urban music enthusiasts.
ADVERTISING RATES:
Full Page Colour £950.00
Agency Commission: 10%
Mechanical Data: Film: Digital, Trim Size: 270 x 190mm
Copy instructions: Copy Date: 15 days prior to publication date
Average advertising content per issue: 33%
CONSUMER: MUSIC & PERFORMING ARTS: Music

GAEL SPORTS
1693633U75X-1708

Editorial Address: 5 University Street, BELFAST, BT7 1FY
Tel: 028 9024 6624 **Fax:** 028 9024 6936
Email: info@admanpublishing.com
Advertising Address: As above.
Email: info@admanpublishing.com
Web site: http://www.admanpublishing.com
ISSN: 1478-5536
Publisher: Adman Publishing Ltd
Frequency: Monthly
Cover Price: £2.50
Circulation: 10,000 (Publisher's Statement)
Usual Pagination: 48
Editor: Henry Davidson; **Managing Director:** Henry Davidson; **Advertising Manager:** Henry Davidson
Summary of Content: Magazine covering Gaelic games particularly in Ulster including Gaelic football, hurling, handball, ladies' football and camogie.
Language(s): English; Gaelic
Readership/Target Audience: Aimed at GAA fans of all ages.
ADVERTISING RATES:
Full Page Colour £895.00
Mechanical Data: Type Area: 270 x 190mm, Trim Size: 297 x 210mm, Col Length: 270mm, Page Width: 190mm
CONSUMER: SPORT: Other Sport

GAIR RHYDD
47392U83-9

Editorial Address: Cardiff University, Students Union, Park Place, CARDIFF, CF10 3QN **Tel:** 029 2078 1436
Fax: 029 2078 1407
Email: enquiries@gairrhydd.com
Advertising Address: As above. **Tel:** 029 20 781 400
Fax: 029 20 781 407
Email: suadvertising@cardiff.ac.uk
Web site: http://www.gairrhydd.com
Publisher: Cardiff Union Services Ltd
Date Established: 1975
Frequency: 30 issues yearly - Published weekly during term time
Cover Price: Free
Circulation: 25,000 (Publisher's Statement)
Usual Pagination: 52
Editor: Amy Harrison; **Advertising Manager:** Huw Selwyn
Summary of Content: Newspaper containing news and comment, letters, interviews, television and sport.
Language(s): English; Welsh

Readership/Target Audience: Distributed to students of the University of Wales, College of Cardiff and College of Medicine, University of Wales Institute (Cardiff), Welsh College of Music and Drama and some local outlets.
ADVERTISING RATES:
Full Page Colour £995.00
Agency Commission: 10%
Mechanical Data: Type Area: 342 x 264mm, Col Length: 342mm, Trim Size: 420 x 297mm, Film: Digital, Page Width: 264mm
Copy instructions: Copy Date: Thursday, 12pm prior to publication date
CONSUMER: STUDENT PUBLICATIONS

GALA BUZZ
1660737U79F-85

Editorial Address: Sea Containers House, 20 Upper Ground, LONDON, SE1 9PD **Tel:** 020 7775 5777
Email: tj.barber@ntlworld.com
Advertising Address: As above.
Email: christian@sevensquared.co.uk
Publisher: Seven Squared
Date Established: 2001
Frequency: 3 issues yearly - Published in February, May and September
Cover Price: Free
Circulation: 140,000 (Publisher's Statement)
Usual Pagination: 48
Editor: Terry Barber; **Advertising Manager:** Christian Harris
Summary of Content: Magazine covering Gala winners' news, celebrity interviews, real life stories, crosswords, puzzles and give-aways as well as openings and refurbishments.
Readership/Target Audience: Aimed at customers of Gala bingo.
ADVERTISING RATES:
Full Page Colour £4500.00
Agency Commission: 10%
Mechanical Data: Type Area: 251 x 186mm, Bleed Size: 295 x 220mm, Trim Size: 275 x 210mm, Col Length: 251mm, Page Width: 186mm, Film: Digital
Average advertising content per issue: 30%
CONSUMER: HOBBIES & DIY: Games & Puzzles

GAME & WILDLIFE CONSERVATION TRUST ANNUAL REVIEW
46811U80A-126

Formerly: Game Conservancy Trust Annual Review
Editorial Address: Burgate Manor, FORDINGBRIDGE, SP6 1EF **Tel:** 01425 652381 **Fax:** 01425 655848
Email: lshervington@gct.org.uk
Web site: http://www.gct.org.uk
Publisher: Game & Wildlife Conservation Trust
Frequency: Annual - Published in June
Free to qualifying individuals
Circulation: 25,000 (Publisher's Statement)
Usual Pagination: 112
Editor: Louise Shervington
Summary of Content: Magazine containing information on game, wildlife, habitat and farmland conservation.
Readership/Target Audience: Aimed at members of the Game Conservancy Trust.
ADVERTISING: No Advertising taken
CONSUMER: RURAL & REGIONAL INTEREST: Rural Interest

GAME & WILDLIFE CONSERVATION TRUST MAGAZINE: GAMEWISE
46813U80A-125

Editorial Address: Burgate Manor, FORDINGBRIDGE, SP6 1EF **Tel:** 01425 652381 **Fax:** 01425 655848
Email: lshervington@gct.org.uk
Advertising Address: Fellows Media Ltd, The Gallery, Manor Farm, Southam, CHELTENHAM, GL52 3PB
Tel: 01242 259249 **Fax:** 01242 259248
Email: mark@fellowsmedia.com
Web site: http://www.gct.org.uk
Publisher: Game & Wildlife Conservation Trust
Date Established: 1996
Frequency: 3 issues yearly - Published in March, June and October
Cover Price: Free
Circulation: 24,000 (Publisher's Statement)
Usual Pagination: 48
Editor: Louise Shervington; **Advertising Manager:** Mark Brown
Summary of Content: Magazine about game, habitat, farmland and wildlife conservation.
Readership/Target Audience: Aimed at members of The Game and Wildlife Conservation Trust.
ADVERTISING RATES:
Full Page Colour £1300.00
Agency Commission: 10%
Mechanical Data: Film: Digital, Type Area: 272 x 190mm, Bleed Size: 303 x 216mm, Trim Size: 297 x 210mm, Col Length: 272mm, Page Width: 190mm
Copy instructions: Copy Date: 1st of the month prior to publication date

Average advertising content per issue: 40%
CONSUMER: RURAL & REGIONAL INTEREST: Rural Interest

GAMES MASTER
46536U78D-160

Editorial Address: 30 Monmouth Street, BATH, BA1 2BW
Tel: 01225 442244 **Fax:** 01225 446019
Email: gamesmaster@futurenet.com
Advertising Address: 2 Balcombe Street, LONDON, NW1 6NW **Tel:** 020 7042 4000
Email: ecull@futurenet.co.uk
Web site: http://www.futurenet.co.uk
Publisher: Future Publishing Ltd
Date Established: 1993
Frequency: 13 issues yearly
Cover Price: £3.99
Circulation: 40,940 (ABC 01/07/2008 to 31/12/2008)
Usual Pagination: 114
Editor: Robin Alway; **Advertising Manager:** Emma Cull
Summary of Content: Official magazine of the 'GamesMaster' TV show. Reviews and previews the latest video games to rent or buy on every gaming format.
Readership/Target Audience: Read by owners of electronic games machines.
ADVERTISING RATES:
Full Page Colour £3500.00
Agency Commission: 10%
Mechanical Data: Film: Digital, Type Area: 280 x 203mm, Bleed Size: 306 x 228mm, Trim Size: 300 x 222mm, Col Length: 280mm, Page Width: 203mm
Copy instructions: Copy Date: 4 weeks prior to publication date
Average advertising content per issue: 20%
CONSUMER: CONSUMER ELECTRONICS: Games

GAMES TM
1639573U78D-304

Formerly: games?
Editorial Address: Richmond House, 33 Richmond Hill, BOURNEMOUTH, BH2 6EZ **Tel:** 01202 586200
Email: rick.porter@imagine-publishing.co.uk
Advertising Address: As above.
Email: james.haley@imagine-publishing.co.uk
Web site: http://www.gamestm.co.uk
Publisher: Imagine Publishing
Date Established: 2003
Frequency: 13 issues yearly
Cover Price: £4.50
Annual Sub.: £41.60
Circulation: 21,677 (ABC 01/01/2008 to 31/12/2008)
Usual Pagination: 180
Editor: Rick Porter; **Features Editor:** Matthew Handrahan
Summary of Content: Magazine covering past, present and future videogames.
Readership/Target Audience: Aimed at aspirational videogamers aged 25 years old plus.
ADVERTISING RATES:
Full Page Colour £3200.00
Mechanical Data: Film: Digital, Type Area: 255 x 190mm, Col Length: 255mm, Page Width: 190mm, Bleed Size: 285 x 220mm, Trim Size: 275 x 210mm
CONSUMER: CONSUMER ELECTRONICS: Games

GARAGELAND
1749823U84A-456

Editorial Address: Unit 25A, Regent Studios, 8 Andrews Road, LONDON, E8 4QN **Tel:** 020 7254 4202
Email: info@transitiongallery.co.uk
Advertising Address: As above.
Web site: http://www.transitiongallery.co.uk/garageland
ISSN: 1749-9267
Publisher: Transition Editions
Date Established: 2005
Frequency: Half-yearly - Published in May and November
Cover Price: £3.95
Annual Sub.: £12.00
Circulation: 3,000 (Publisher's Statement)
Usual Pagination: 64
Editor: Cathy Lomax; **Advertising Manager:** Cathy Lomax
Summary of Content: Magazine covering art, ideas and culture with features about emerging art, artists and art movements.
Readership/Target Audience: Aimed at artists, art collectors and those with an interest in art.
CONSUMER: THE ARTS & LITERARY: Arts

GARAVI GUJARAT
48302U90-50

Editorial Address: Garavi Gujarat House, 1 Silex Street, LONDON, SE1 0DW **Tel:** 020 7928 1234 **Fax:** 020 7261 0055
Email: garavi@gujarat.co.uk
Advertising Address: As above. **Tel:** 020 7654 7767
Email: prif@gg2.net
Web site: http://www.gg2.net
Publisher: Garavi Gujarat Publications Ltd
Date Established: 1968
Frequency: Weekly

Cover Price: £0.70
Annual Sub.: £28.00
Circulation: 43,000 (Publisher's Statement)
Usual Pagination: 52
Editor: Ramniklal Solanki; Executive Editor: Shailesh Solanki; Editor-in-Chief: Ramniklal Solanki; Advertising Manager: Prif Viswandan; Managing Editor: Kalpesh Solanki
Summary of Content: Journal containing Asian news from the British Asian viewpoint.
Language(s): English; Gujarati
Readership/Target Audience: Aimed at all Asians but particularly those speaking Gujarati and English.
ADVERTISING RATES:
Full Page Colour £3201.00
Agency Commission: 10%
Mechanical Data: Film: Digital, Type Area: 280 x 195mm, Bleed Size: 303 x 216mm, Trim Size: 297 x 210mm, Col Length: 280mm, Page Width: 195mm
Supplement(s): GG2 - 52xY
CONSUMER: ETHNIC

THE GARDEN
48556U93-15
Editorial Address: 4th Floor, Churchgate, New Road, PETERBOROUGH, PE1 1TT Tel: 0845 260 0909
Fax: 01733 341633
Email: thegarden@rhs.org.uk
Advertising Address: As above. Fax: 01733 775900
Email: advertising@rhspublications.co.uk
Web site: http://www.rhs.org.uk
Publisher: RHS Media
Date Established: 1866
Frequency: Monthly
Cover Price: £4.25
Free to qualifying individuals
Circulation: 342,858 (ABC 01/01/2009 to 30/06/2009)
Usual Pagination: 124
Editor: Anisa Gress; News Editor: Anisa Gress; Features Editor: Philip Clayton; Advertising Manager: Daren Davis
Summary of Content: Journal of the Royal Horticultural Society, containing news and information with a focus on practical gardening.
Readership/Target Audience: Aimed at keen horticulturists.
ADVERTISING RATES:
Full Page Colour £10000.00
Agency Commission: 10%
Mechanical Data: Type Area: 240 x 172mm, Trim Size: 275 x 212mm, Bleed Size: 282 x 218mm, Col Length: 240mm, Film: Digital, Page Width: 172mm
Copy instructions: Copy Date: 5 weeks prior to publication date
Average advertising content per issue: 34%
CONSUMER: GARDENING

GARDEN ANSWERS
48557U93-16
Editorial Address: Bushfield House, Orton Centre, PETERBOROUGH, PE2 5UW Tel: 01733 237111
Fax: 01733 465779
Email: gardenanswers@bauermedia.co.uk
Advertising Address: As above. Fax: 01733 465897
Email: helen.bavister@bauermedia.co.uk
Web site: http://www.gardeningmags.co.uk
Publisher: Bauer Media Ltd (Orton)
Date Established: 1986
Frequency: Monthly
Cover Price: £3.10
Annual Sub.: £34.80
Circulation: 23,360 (ABC 01/01/2009 to 30/06/2009)
Usual Pagination: 116
Editor: Geoff Stebbings; Managing Editor: Neil Pope
Summary of Content: Magazine covering practical advice and inspirational gardening ideas.
Readership/Target Audience: Read by those with a passion for gardening.
ADVERTISING: Rates on application
Agency Commission: 10%
Average advertising content per issue: 40%
CONSUMER: GARDENING

GARDEN NEWS
48560U93-20
Editorial Address: Bushfield House, Orton Centre, PETERBOROUGH, PE2 5UW Tel: 01733 237111
Email: carol.warters@bauermedia.co.uk
Advertising Address: As above. Fax: 01733 465897
Email: rachel.thorne@bauerconsumer.co.uk
Web site: http://www.gardennews-mag.com
Publisher: Bauer Media Ltd (Orton)
Date Established: 1958
Frequency: Weekly - Published on Wednesday
Cover Price: £1.70
Circulation: 35,538 (ABC 01/01/2009 to 30/06/2009)
Usual Pagination: 48
Editor: Carol Warters; News Editor: Carol Warters
Summary of Content: Magazine containing helpful gardening hints and tips, including articles on creative ideas,

people and their gardens, product information and regular news from gardening experts.
Readership/Target Audience: Read by keen gardening enthusiasts and hobby gardeners.
ADVERTISING RATES:
Full Page Colour £1900.00
Agency Commission: 10%
Mechanical Data: No. of Columns (Display): 6, Film: Digital
Copy instructions: Copy Date: 1 week prior to publication date
CONSUMER: GARDENING

GARDEN RAIL
46596U79B-29_75
Editorial Address: 58 Beatrice Avenue, SALTASH, PL12 4NG Tel: 01752 845938
Email: 0tag@atlanticpublishers.com
Advertising Address: 83 Parkanaur Avenue, SOUTHEND-ON-SEA, SS1 3JA Tel: 01702 580409 Fax: 01702 588970
Email: ja@atlanticpublishers.com
Web site: http://www.atlanticpublishers.com
ISSN: 0969-952X
Publisher: Atlantic Publishers
Date Established: 1990
Frequency: Monthly
Cover Price: £3.85
Annual Sub.: £46.20
Circulation: 5,500 (Publisher's Statement)
Usual Pagination: 56
Editor: Tag Gorton; Advertising Manager: Juliet Arthur
Summary of Content: Magazine covering all aspects of outdoor railway modelling.
Readership/Target Audience: Aimed at outdoor railway modelling enthusiasts.
ADVERTISING RATES:
Full Page Mono £250.00
Full Page Colour £279.00
Agency Commission: 10%
Mechanical Data: Film: Digital, Bleed Size: 307 x 220mm, Page Width: 192mm, Type Area: 266 x 192mm, Col Length: 266mm, Trim Size: 297 x 210mm
Copy instructions: Copy Date: 5 weeks prior to publication date
Average advertising content per issue: 30%
CONSUMER: HOBBIES & DIY: Models & Modelling

GARDEN WILDLIFE
1837350U81A-257
Editorial Address: 25 Phoenix Court, Hawkins Road, COLCHESTER, CO2 8JY Tel: 01206 505900
Email: jeannine@aceville.co.uk
Advertising Address: As above.
Email: teresa.tudge@aceville.co.uk
Publisher: Aceville Publications Ltd
Date Established: 2008
Frequency: Annual - Published in May
Cover Price: £7.99
Editor: Jeannine McAndrew; Advertising Manager: Teresa Tudge
Summary of Content: Magazine covering British garden wildlife and how to attract native species to your garden.
Readership/Target Audience: Aimed at those who enjoy wildlife.
ADVERTISING: Rates on application
CONSUMER: ANIMALS & PETS: Animals & Pets Protection

GARDENING WHICH?
48561U93-25
Editorial Address: 2 Marylebone Road, LONDON, NW1 4DF
Tel: 020 7770 7000 Fax: 020 7770 7676
Email: gardening@which.co.uk
Web site: http://www.which.co.uk
ISSN: 0264-1917
Publisher: Which? Ltd
Date Established: 1982
Frequency: 10 issues yearly - Combined issues July/August and January/February
Annual Sub.: £55.00
Circulation: 80,000 (Publisher's Statement)
Usual Pagination: 70
Editor: Ceri Thomas; Features Editor: Veronica Peerless
Summary of Content: Magazine providing advice and new product information for gardeners.
Readership/Target Audience: Aimed at gardeners of all ages.
ADVERTISING: No Advertising taken
CONSUMER: GARDENING

GARDENS ILLUSTRATED
48562U93-30
Editorial Address: 14th Floor, Tower House, Fairfax Street, BRISTOL, BS1 3BN Tel: 0117 314 8774
Email: gardens@bbcmagazinesbristol.com
Advertising Address: 9th Floor, Tower House, Fairfax Street, BRISTOL, BS1 3BN Tel: 0117 314 8768
Fax: 0117 934 9008
Email: jenniferhendry@bbcmagazinesbristol.com
Web site: http://www.gardensillustrated.com
ISSN: 0968-8927

Publisher: BBC Magazines Bristol
Date Established: 1993
Frequency: Monthly
Cover Price: £3.85
Annual Sub.: £34.65
Circulation: 29,323 (ABC 01/10/2008 to 31/12/2008)
Usual Pagination: 132
Editor: Janine Kay; Publisher: Andy Healy
Summary of Content: Magazine about plants, gardens and gardeners. Includes articles on travel and landscape design.
Readership/Target Audience: Aimed at discerning gardeners between 30 and 54 years old.
ADVERTISING RATES:
Full Page Mono £2970.00
Full Page Colour £2970.00
SCC £50.00
Agency Commission: 10%
Mechanical Data: Col Length: 264mm, Film: Digital, No. of Columns (Display): 2, Type Area: 264 x 186mm, Bleed Size: 306 x 228mm, Trim Size: 300 x 222mm, Page Width: 186mm
Average advertising content per issue: 40%
CONSUMER: GARDENING

GATEWAY
1664649U89D-518
Editorial Address: Publishing House, 3 Bridgebank Industrial Estate, Taylor Street, Horwich, BOLTON, BL6 7PD
Tel: 0161 909 0909 Fax: 0161 909 0919
Email: jonathan.richards@theretheremedia.com
Advertising Address: As above.
Email: tony.holder@bigsparkpublishing.co.uk
Web site: http://www.gatewaymagazine.co.uk
Publisher: The Big Spark
Date Established: 2005
Frequency: Quarterly
Cover Price: Free
Circulation: 15,000 (Print Run)
Usual Pagination: 48
Editor: Jonathan Richards
Summary of Content: Lifestyle magazine covering celebrity interviews, car tests, financial pages and destinations.
Readership/Target Audience: Aimed at in-coming and out-going passengers using Glasgow Airport.
ADVERTISING RATES:
Full Page Colour £1250.00
Agency Commission: 10%
Mechanical Data: Type Area: 275 x 190mm, Bleed Size: 307 x 220mm, Trim Size: 297 x 210mm, Col Length: 275mm, Page Width: 190mm, Film: Digital
CONSUMER: HOLIDAYS & TRAVEL: In-Flight Magazines

GAUDIE
47393U83-10
Editorial Address: University of Aberdeen, The Hub, ABERDEEN, AB24 3TU Tel: 01224 272980
Fax: 01224 272977
Email: gaudie.editor@abdn.ac.uk
Advertising Address: The Hub, Elphinstone Road, OLD ABERDEEN, AB24 3TU Tel: 01224 272965
Fax: 01224 272977
Email: s.tubby@abdn.ac.uk
Web site: http://www.ausa.org.uk/
Publisher: Aberdeen University Students' Association
Date Established: 1934
Frequency: 28 issues yearly - Published weekly during term time
Cover Price: Free
Circulation: 20,000 (Publisher's Statement)
Usual Pagination: 12
Editor: Christopher Regan; Advertising Manager: Shannon Tubby
Summary of Content: University of Aberdeen Student newspaper containing all aspects of student life including staff information.
Readership/Target Audience: Read by University of Aberdeen students, staff and local residents.
ADVERTISING RATES:
Full Page Mono £430.00
Full Page Colour £660.00
Agency Commission: 10%
Mechanical Data: Trim Size: 297 x 210mm, Bleed Size: 303 x 216mm, Film: Digital
Copy instructions: Copy Date: Wednesday morning prior to publication date
Average advertising content per issue: 10%
CONSUMER: STUDENT PUBLICATIONS

GAZETA NIEDZIELNA
1746605U90-986
Editorial Address: 63 Jeddo Road, LONDON, W12 9EE
Tel: 020 8749 4957 Fax: 020 8749 4965
Email: veritas@polish.co.uk
Advertising Address: As above.
Email: redakcja@gazetaniedzielna.co.uk
Web site: http://www.veritas-london.co.uk
Publisher: Veritas Foundation Publications Centre
Date Established: 1949
Frequency: Weekly
Cover Price: £0.60

Free to qualifying individuals
Circulation: 3,000 (Publisher's Statement)
Usual Pagination: 8
Editor: Szymon Gurbin; **Advertising Manager:** Anna Zabihi
Summary of Content: Newspaper covering Catholic, religious news and views.
Language(s): Polish
Readership/Target Audience: Aimed at the Polish population in the UK.
ADVERTISING RATES:
SCC £10.00
CONSUMER: ETHNIC

THE GAZETTE SERIES
1732102U80C-5322
Editorial Address: 113 Fazeley Street, Digbeth, BIRMINGHAM, B5 5RX **Tel:** 0121 202 1595
Fax: 0121 202 1598
Email: editorialgazette@aol.com
Advertising Address: As above. **Tel:** 0121 202 1581
Fax: 0121 685 1110
Email: lyn@westpointmarketing.co.uk
Publisher: Westpoint Publishing
Frequency: Monthly
Cover Price: Free
Circulation: 43,500 (Combined Circulation)
Editor: Peter Millington
Summary of Content: Magazine covering local news and interests, entertainment, events, days out, travel, motoring, gardening, cookery and local sport.
Readership/Target Audience: Aimed at households in Birmingham, Solihull and North Warwickshire.
ADVERTISING RATES:
Full Page Mono £175.00
Full Page Colour £230.00
Agency Commission: 10%
Mechanical Data: Bleed Size: 303 x 216mm, Trim Size: 280 x 190mm, Film: Digital
Copy instructions: Copy Date: 3 weeks prior to publication date
Editions:
The Castle Bromwich Gazette
The Coleshill, Water Orton Gazette
The Harbourne Edgbaston Gazette
The Hodge Hill Gazette
The Marston Green Gazette
CONSUMER: RURAL & REGIONAL INTEREST: Regional Interest English Counties

THE GAZETTE - SERVING THE ISLE OF PURBECK & THE FROME VALLEY
1639677U80C-5080
Editorial Address: 17B Commercial Road, SWANAGE, BH19 1DF **Tel:** 01929 424239 **Fax:** 01929 424239
Email: ed@purbeck-gazette.co.uk
Advertising Address: As above.
Email: ed@purbeck-gazette.co.uk
Web site: http://www.purbeck-gazette.co.uk
Publisher: Tindle Newspapers Ltd
Date Established: 1996
Frequency: Monthly
Cover Price: Free
Circulation: 19,000 (Publisher's Statement)
Usual Pagination: 40
Editor: Nico Campbell-Allen
Summary of Content: Regional magazine covering local news and views, events, theatre, sports and leisure.
Readership/Target Audience: Aimed at those living and working in the Frome Valley and Isle of Purbeck as well as tourists, walkers and other visitors to the World Heritage Site and Areas of Outstanding Natural Beauty.
ADVERTISING RATES:
Full Page Mono £352.00
Full Page Colour £420.00
SCC £31.50
Agency Commission: 10%
Mechanical Data: Type Area: 252 x 165mm, Col Length: 252mm, Page Width: 165mm, Film: Digital, No. of Columns (Display): 2, Col Widths (Display): 80mm
Copy instructions: Copy Date: 10th of the month prior to publication date
Average advertising content per issue: 35%
CONSUMER: RURAL & REGIONAL INTEREST: Regional Interest English Counties

GEAR
1613664U76D-766
Editorial Address: Salem House, Parkinson Approach, Garforth, LEEDS, LS25 2HR **Tel:** 0113 286 5381
Fax: 0113 286 8515
Email: publicity@jhs.co.uk
Advertising Address: As above.
Web site: http://www.jhs.co.uk
Publisher: John Hornby Skewes & Co. Ltd
Date Established: 1997
Frequency: Half-yearly - Published in April and October
Cover Price: Free
Circulation: 190,000 (Publisher's Statement)

Editor: Gibson Keddie; **Advertising Manager:** Simon Turnbull; **Publisher:** Simon Turnbull
Summary of Content: Free musical magazine containing interviews, reviews and competitions.
Readership/Target Audience: Aimed at musicians.
ADVERTISING RATES:
Full Page Colour £1500.00
Mechanical Data: Trim Size: 297 x 210mm
CONSUMER: MUSIC & PERFORMING ARTS: Music

GENEALOGISTS' MAGAZINE
48686U94X-67
Editorial Address: 14 Charterhouse Buildings, Goswell Road, LONDON, EC1M 7BA **Tel:** 020 7251 8799
Fax: 020 7250 1800
Email: publishing@sog.org.uk
Advertising Address: As above. **Tel:** 020 7553 3294
Email: publishing@sog.org.uk
Web site: http://www.sog.org.uk
ISSN: 0016-6391
Publisher: Society of Genealogists Enterprises Ltd
Date Established: 1925
Frequency: Quarterly
Cover Price: £1.85
Free to qualifying individuals
Annual Sub.: £12.00
Circulation: 15,000 (Publisher's Statement)
Usual Pagination: 44
Editor: Michael Gandy; **Advertising Manager:** Graham Collett
Summary of Content: Magazine covering all aspects of genealogy and the history behind it.
Readership/Target Audience: Read by genealogists and local historians.
ADVERTISING RATES:
Full Page Mono £305.00
Full Page Colour £385.00
Mechanical Data: Type Area: 215 x 146mm, Col Length: 215mm, Page Width: 146mm, Bleed Size: +3mm, Trim Size: 215 x 146mm, Col Widths (Display): 69mm, No. of Columns (Display): 2
Copy instructions: Copy Date: 20th of 2 months prior to publication date
Average advertising content per issue: 15%
CONSUMER: OTHER CLASSIFICATIONS: Miscellaneous

GEOGRAPHICAL
47230U82-25_50
Editorial Address: One Victoria Villas, RICHMOND, TW9 2GW **Tel:** 020 8332 8400 **Fax:** 020 8332 9307
Email: magazine@geographical.co.uk
Advertising Address: As above. **Tel:** 020 8332 8440
Email: sophie@geographical.co.uk
Web site: http://www.geographical.co.uk
Publisher: Circle Publishing
Date Established: 1935
Frequency: Monthly
Cover Price: £3.90
Circulation: 21,217 (Publisher's Statement)
Usual Pagination: 116
Editor: Natalie Hoare; **Features Editor:** Natalie Hoare; **Advertising Manager:** Sophie Sweatman; **Publisher:** Graeme Gourlay
Summary of Content: Magazine of the Royal Geographical Society focusing on current geopolitical, cultural and environmental issues. Also covers expeditions, exploration and scientific developments and adventure travel.
Readership/Target Audience: Aimed at society members, professional geographers, frequent holidaymakers, alternative travellers of all ages and those interested in the world around them.
ADVERTISING RATES:
Full Page Colour £1750.00
Agency Commission: 10%
Mechanical Data: Type Area: 273 x 187mm, No. of Columns (Display): 4, Bleed Size: 303 x 216mm, Trim Size: 297 x 210mm, Film: Digital, Col Length: 273mm, Page Width: 187mm, Col Widths (Display): 43mm
Copy instructions: Copy Date: 15th of the month prior to publication date
Average advertising content per issue: 20%
CONSUMER: CURRENT AFFAIRS & POLITICS

GERMAN HISTORY
30809U94X-67_50
Editorial Address: 1 Oliver's Yard, 55 City Road, LONDON, EC1Y 1SP **Tel:** 020 7324 8500 **Fax:** 020 7324 8600
Email: market@sagepub.co.uk
Advertising Address: As above.
Email: sheena.karim@sagepub.co.uk
Web site: http://www.sagepub.co.uk
ISSN: 0266-3554
Publisher: Sage Publications
Date Established: 1983
Frequency: Quarterly
Annual Sub.: £160.00
Usual Pagination: 140
Editor: Paul Betts

Summary of Content: Journal of the German History Society. Covers all periods of German history and German-speaking areas.
Readership/Target Audience: Read by German historians and scholars in related disciplines.
ADVERTISING RATES:
Full Page Mono £400.00
Agency Commission: 5%
Mechanical Data: Type Area: 205 x 130mm, Col Length: 205mm, Page Width: 130mm, Trim Size: 234 x 156mm
Copy instructions: Copy Date: 12 weeks prior to publication date
CONSUMER: OTHER CLASSIFICATIONS: Miscellaneous

GERRARDS CROSS EXCLUSIVE
1892640U80C-5488
Editorial Address: For all contact details see main edition, Exclusive (Chilterns)
Frequency: 10 issues yearly
Cover Price: Free
Circulation: 5,000 (Publisher's Statement)
ADVERTISING: Rates on application
Edition of: Exclusive (Chilterns)
CONSUMER: RURAL & REGIONAL INTEREST: Regional Interest English Counties

GET FRESH
1748870U74P-946
Editorial Address: Unit 4, Aylsham Business Park, Shepheards Close, NORWICH, NR11 6SZ
Tel: 0845 833 7017 **Fax:** 08700 940077
Email: sarah@fresh-network.com
Advertising Address: As above.
Email: info@fresh-network.com
Web site: http://www.fresh-network.com
Publisher: The Fresh Network Limited
Date Established: 1992
Frequency: Quarterly
Cover Price: £3.95
Annual Sub.: £14.25
Circulation: 8,000 (Publisher's Statement)
Usual Pagination: 60
Editor: Sarah Best; **Advertising Manager:** Kate Cuckow
Summary of Content: Magazine covering healthy eating, juicing, detoxing, raw foods, super-foods.
Readership/Target Audience: Aimed at healthy eaters.
ADVERTISING RATES:
Full Page Colour £1000.00
Mechanical Data: Type Area: 277 x 190mm, Bleed Size: 303 x 216mm, Trim Size: 297 x 210mm, Col Length: 277mm, Page Width: 190mm, Film: Digital
Copy instructions: Copy Date: 21st of 2 months prior to publication date
CONSUMER: WOMEN'S INTEREST CONSUMER MAGAZINES: Food & Cookery

GETTING MARRIED IN NORTHERN IRELAND
623509U74L-110
Editorial Address: T9 Dungannon Business Park, Coalisland Road, DUNGANNON, BT71 6JT
Tel: 028 8772 2788 **Fax:** 028 8772 9495
Email: info@reddotpublications.co.uk
Advertising Address: As above. **Fax:** 028 877 9495
Email: info@gettingmarried-ni.co.uk
Web site: http://www.gettingmarried-ni.co.uk
Publisher: Red Dot Publications
Date Established: 1985
Frequency: Quarterly
Cover Price: £2.95
Circulation: 9,000 (Publisher's Statement per quarter)
Usual Pagination: 210
Editor: Dawn Hamilton; **Advertising Manager:** Claire Leonard; **Publisher:** Dawn Hamilton
Summary of Content: Magazine covering all aspects of getting married and setting-up home in Northern Ireland.
Readership/Target Audience: Aimed at those who need help and information on how to plan for the big day.
ADVERTISING RATES:
Full Page Colour £950.00
Agency Commission: 10%
Mechanical Data: Film: Digital, Type Area: 277 x 185mm, Col Length: 277mm, Trim Size: 297 x 210mm, Bleed Size: 303 x 216mm, Page Width: 185mm
Copy instructions: Copy Date: 3 weeks prior to publication date
Average advertising content per issue: 40%
CONSUMER: WOMEN'S INTEREST CONSUMER MAGAZINES: Brides

GIBBONS STAMP MONTHLY
46628U79C-20
Editorial Address: 7 Parkside, Christchurch Road, RINGWOOD, BH24 3SH **Tel:** 01425 472363
Fax: 01425 470247
Email: gsm@stanleygibbons.co.uk
Advertising Address: As above. **Tel:** 01425 481054

Email: advertising@stanleygibbons.co.uk
Web site: http://www.gibbonsstampmonthly.com
ISSN: 0954-8084
Publisher: Stanley Gibbons Ltd
Date Established: 1890
Frequency: Monthly
Cover Price: £3.25
Annual Sub.: £39.00
Circulation: 22,000 (Publisher's Statement)
Usual Pagination: 156
Editor: John Moody; **News Editor:** John Moody
Summary of Content: Journal providing articles on philatelic topics. Includes news, tips, book reviews and new stamp issues.
Readership/Target Audience: Aimed at general and specialised stamp collectors.
ADVERTISING RATES:
Full Page Mono £950.00
Full Page Colour £950.00
SCC £37.50
Agency Commission: 10%
Mechanical Data: Type Area: 260 x 175mm, Col Length: 260mm, Bleed Size: 303 x 216mm, Trim Size: 297 x 210mm, Page Width: 175mm, Film: Digital
Copy instructions: Copy Date: 6 weeks prior to publication date
Average advertising content per issue: 60%
CONSUMER: HOBBIES & DIY: Philately

GIRL
626608U91D-59_50
Editorial Address: Suite 2.1, Level 2, Renslade House, Bonhay Road, EXETER, EX4 3AY **Tel:** 01392 664141
Fax: 01392 221794
Email: jo@lcdpublishing.co.uk
Advertising Address: As above.
Email: jo@lcdpublishing.co.uk
Publisher: LCD Publishing
Date Established: 1998
Frequency: 13 issues yearly
Cover Price: £1.99
Circulation: 80,000 (Publisher's Statement)
Usual Pagination: 32
Editor: Joanne Trump; **Advertising Manager:** Joanne Trump
Summary of Content: Magazine covering young fashion and pop music, with quizzes and stories.
Readership/Target Audience: Read by girls between 10 and 12 years.
ADVERTISING: Rates on application
Agency Commission: 10%
Copy instructions: Copy Date: 1 month prior to publication date
CONSUMER: RECREATION & LEISURE: Children & Youth

GIRL TALK
48459U91D-60
Editorial Address: Media Centre, 201 Wood Lane, LONDON, W12 7TQ **Tel:** 020 8433 1010 **Fax:** 020 8433 2941
Email: rebecca.davison@bbc.com
Advertising Address: Garden House, 201 Wood Lane, LONDON, W12 7TQ **Tel:** 020 8433 2000 **Fax:** 020 8433 2407
Web site: http://www.bbcgirltalk.com
Publisher: BBC Worldwide Publishing
Date Established: 1995
Frequency: 26 issues yearly
Cover Price: £1.75
Circulation: 60,443 (ABC 01/01/2009 to 30/06/2009)
Usual Pagination: 34
Editor: Rebecca Davison; **Managing Director:** Toni Round; **Group Editor:** Samantha Robinson
Summary of Content: Children's magazine containing comic strips, interactive games and quizzes, as well as features on pop bands, fashion, craft and pets.
Readership/Target Audience: Aimed at girls between 8 and 12 years old.
ADVERTISING: Rates on application
Agency Commission: 10%
Copy instructions: Copy Date: 4 weeks prior to publication date
CONSUMER: RECREATION & LEISURE: Children & Youth

GIRL TALK EXTRA
1860048U91D-981
Editorial Address: Media Centre, 201 Wood Lane, LONDON, W12 7TQ **Tel:** 020 8433 1010 **Fax:** 020 8433 2941
Email: rebecca.davison@bbc.com
Advertising Address: As above.
Web site: http://www.bbcgirltalk/extra
Publisher: BBC Worldwide Publishing
Frequency: Monthly
Cover Price: £2.25
Circulation: 21,232 (ABC 01/01/2009 to 30/06/2009)
Usual Pagination: 68
Editor: Rebecca Davison; **Managing Director:** Peter Phippen; **Group Editor:** Samantha Robinson
Summary of Content: Children's magazine containing comic strips, interactive games and quizzes, as well as features on pop bands, fashion, crafts and pets.

Readership/Target Audience: Aimed at girls between 8 and 12 years old.
ADVERTISING: Rates on application
CONSUMER: RECREATION & LEISURE: Children & Youth

THE GIRLS' GUIDE TO PROPERTY
1833919U74K-785
Editorial Address: Publishing House, 3 Bridgebank Industrial Estate, Taylor Street, Horwich, BOLTON, BL6 7PD
Tel: 0161 909 0909 **Fax:** 0161 909 0919
Email: nikkimurphitt@aol.com
Advertising Address: As above.
Web site: http://www.girlsguidetoproperty.co.uk
Publisher: The Big Spark
Date Established: 2008
Frequency: Quarterly
Cover Price: Free
Circulation: 90,000 (Print Run)
Usual Pagination: 52
Editor: Nikki Murfitt
Summary of Content: Magazine covering all aspects of buying property from a girl's point of view with help and advice on buying and selling, interiors and exteriors and dealing with tradesmen and estate agents.
Readership/Target Audience: Aimed at women looking to buy or sell property and distributed through Tescos and Sainsburys supermarkets.
CONSUMER: WOMEN'S INTEREST CONSUMER MAGAZINES: Home Purchase

THE GLADE
46009U75X-430
Editorial Address: Withnell Farm, Bury Lane, Withnell, CHORLEY, PR6 8SD **Tel:** 01254 832849
Email: geoff@theglade.co.uk
Advertising Address: As above.
Email: paul@theglade.co.uk
Web site: http://www.theglade.co.uk
Publisher: The Glade
Date Established: 1973
Frequency: Quarterly
Cover Price: £3.95
Annual Sub.: £19.00
Usual Pagination: 68
Editor: Geoff Tittensor; **Advertising Manager:** Paul Tittensor
Summary of Content: Magazine covering all aspects of archery. Includes news, equipment, reviews and history and coaching articles.
Readership/Target Audience: Read by novice, national and international archers and those with an interest.
ADVERTISING RATES:
Full Page Colour £660.00
Mechanical Data: Type Area: 270 x 185mm, Trim Size: 297 x 210mm, Col Length: 270mm, Page Width: 185mm
CONSUMER: SPORT: Other Sport

THE GLADES MAGAZINE
759725U74Q-455
Formerly: Into the Green - The Glades Magazine
Editorial Address: 56 Burbage Road, LONDON, SE24 9HE
Tel: 07836 702812
Email: yvonnewilcox@btconnect.com
Web site: http://www.theglades.uk.com
Publisher: Blackfox Creative Ltd
Date Established: 1999
Frequency: Quarterly
Cover Price: Free
Circulation: 110,000 (Publisher's Statement)
Usual Pagination: 24
Editor: Yvonne Wilcox
Summary of Content: Magazine for The Glades shopping centre. Includes fashion, cosmetics, housewares, children's products, events, offers, competitions and promotions within The Glades shopping centre in Bromley.
Readership/Target Audience: Read mainly by women aged between 25 and 50 years old.
ADVERTISING: No Advertising taken
CONSUMER: WOMEN'S INTEREST CONSUMER MAGAZINES: Lifestyle

GLAMOUR
628837U74B-705
Editorial Address: 6-8 Old Bond Street, LONDON, W1S 4PH **Tel:** 020 7499 9080 **Fax:** 020 7491 2551
Email: letters@glamourmagazine.co.uk
Advertising Address: As above. **Fax:** 020 7491 2561
Email: rebecca.vafiadis@condenast.co.uk
Web site: http://www.glamourmagazine.co.uk
Publisher: Conde Nast Publications Ltd
Date Established: 2001
Frequency: Monthly
Cover Price: £2.00
Annual Sub.: £14.00
Circulation: 526,145 (ABC 01/01/2009 to 30/06/2009)
Usual Pagination: 350

Editor: Jo Elvin; **Features Editor:** Corrie Jackson;
Advertising Manager: Sallie Berkerey; **Managing Editor:** Helen Placito; **Publisher:** Simon Kippin
Summary of Content: Magazine covering beauty, fashion and celebrity features.
Twitter: https://twitter.com/DailyGlamour.
Readership/Target Audience: Aimed at beauty and fashion conscious women between 18 and 34 years old.
ADVERTISING RATES:
Full Page Colour £20674.00
Mechanical Data: Type Area: 203 x 148mm, Col Length: 203mm, Page Width: 148mm, Bleed Size: 233 x 178mm, Trim Size: 223 x 168mm, Film: Digital
Copy instructions: Copy Date: 5 weeks prior to publication date
CONSUMER: WOMEN'S INTEREST CONSUMER MAGAZINES: Women's Interest - Fashion

GLASGOW UNIVERSITY GUARDIAN
47394U83-10_5
Editorial Address: John McIntyre Building, University Avenue, GLASGOW, G12 8QQ **Tel:** 0141 341 6215
Email: guardian@src.gla.ac.uk
Advertising Address: As above.
Email: guardian@src.gla.ac.uk
Web site: http://www.glasgowguardian.co.uk
ISSN: 0017-0917
Publisher: Glasgow University S R C
Frequency: 20 issues yearly - Published every two weeks during term time
Cover Price: Free
Circulation: 15,000 (Publisher's Statement)
Usual Pagination: 28
Editor: David Crow; **Advertising Manager:** Lucy Smith
Summary of Content: Newspaper covering local, national and international issues. Includes articles on media, local businesses, the arts, sport and education issues.
Readership/Target Audience: Aimed at students and staff of the university.
ADVERTISING RATES:
Full Page Colour £895.00
Mechanical Data: Trim Size: 400 x 282mm
Copy instructions: Copy Date: 1 week prior to publication date
Average advertising content per issue: 25%
CONSUMER: STUDENT PUBLICATIONS

GLENFIELD GAZETTE
46938U80C-2090
Editorial Address: PO Box 8454, LEICESTER, LE9 2WU
Tel: 0116 239 4284
Email: glenfieldgazette@aol.com
Advertising Address: As above. **Tel:** 0116 231 2811
Web site: http://www.thisisglenfield.com
Publisher: Gazette Publications (Leicester) Limited
Date Established: 1985
Frequency: Monthly
Cover Price: £2.00
Free to qualifying individuals
Circulation: 5,000 (Publisher's Statement)
Usual Pagination: 24
Editor: Ken Russell; **Advertising Manager:** Krys Lakin
Summary of Content: Local newspaper for the Glenfield area covering civic, social and industrial matters, women, health and beauty, radio and TV, children, toys, books, puzzles, entertainment, CDs, videos, travel and recreational activities.
Readership/Target Audience: Aimed at Glenfield residents and visitors.
ADVERTISING: Rates on application
Agency Commission: 10%
Mechanical Data: Trim Size: 297 x 210mm, Film: Digital
Copy instructions: Copy Date: 1st of the month prior to publication date
Average advertising content per issue: 50%
CONSUMER: RURAL & REGIONAL INTEREST: Regional Interest English Counties

GLOUCESTER RUGBY FOOTBALL CLUB MATCHDAY MAGAZINE
1638720U75C-455
Formerly: Gloucester Rugby Football Club Magazine
Editorial Address: Kingsholm Stadium, Kingsholm Road, GLOUCESTER, GL1 3AX **Tel:** 01452 300951
Fax: 01452 416300
Email: alastairdowney@gloucesterrugby.co.uk
Advertising Address: As above.
Email: alastairdowney@gloucesterrugby.co.uk
Web site: http://www.gloucesterrugby.co.uk
Publisher: Dunwoody Marketing Communications
Date Established: 1995
Frequency: Quarterly
Cover Price: £2.50
Circulation: 10,000 (Publisher's Statement)
Usual Pagination: 64
Editor: Alastair Downey; **Advertising Manager:** Alastair Downey

Consumer Magazines

Summary of Content: Magazine of Gloucester Rugby Football Club covering on the field interviews and off the field news. Features include player interviews, car reviews, lifestyle articles and on-line focus.
Readership/Target Audience: Aimed at supporters of Gloucester Rugby Football Club.
ADVERTISING: Rates on application
CONSUMER: SPORT: Rugby

GO BELFAST
1785491U89C-1090

Editorial Address: Penton House, 38 Heron Road, Sydenham Business Park, BELFAST, BT3 9LE
Tel: 028 9045 7457 **Fax:** 028 90456 622
Email: sinead.doyle@pentonpublications.co.uk
Advertising Address: As above. **Fax:** 028 9045 6611
Email: leia.kelly@pentonpublications.co.uk
Web site: http://www.gobelfastawards.com
Publisher: Penton Publications Ltd
Date Established: 2006
Frequency: 6 issues yearly
Cover Price: Free
Circulation: 25,300 (ABC 01/01/2008 to 31/12/2008)
Usual Pagination: 184
Editor: Sinead Doyle
Summary of Content: Magazine covering fashion, music, culture, interviews, profiles, what's on, shopping, homes, sport, health, eating out and hotels.
Readership/Target Audience: Aimed at residents and visitors to Belfast.
ADVERTISING RATES:
Full Page Mono £950.00
Full Page Colour £1200.00
Agency Commission: 10%
Mechanical Data: Bleed Size: 216 x 154mm, Trim Size: 210 x 148mm, Film: Digital
CONSUMER: HOLIDAYS & TRAVEL: Entertainment Guides

GO CARAVAN
1861229U91B-313

Editorial Address: The Maltings, West Street, BOURNE, PE10 9PH **Tel:** 01778 391000 **Fax:** 01778 425437
Email: go-caravan@warnersgroup.co.uk
Web site: http://www.go-caravan.co.uk
Publisher: Warners Group Publications plc
Date Established: 2008
Frequency: Quarterly
Cover Price: £3.25
Circulation: 12,000 (Print Run)
Usual Pagination: 145
Editor: Sally Pepper; **Managing Editor:** Val Chapman
Summary of Content: Magazine focusing on where to stay, places to go, product testing, site reports and previews.
Readership/Target Audience: Aimed at younger caravanners and families.
ADVERTISING: Rates on application
CONSUMER: RECREATION & LEISURE: Camping & Caravanning

GO GIRL
624196U74F-358

Editorial Address: 239 Kensington High Street, LONDON, W8 6SA **Tel:** 020 7761 3500 **Fax:** 020 7761 3510
Email: eprosser@euk.egmont.com
Advertising Address: As above.
Email: svernon@euk.egmont.com
Web site: http://www.gogirlmag.co.uk
ISSN: 1470-272X
Publisher: Egmont Magazines UK
Date Established: 2000
Frequency: 17 issues yearly
Cover Price: £1.95
Circulation: 48,004 (ABC 01/01/2009 to 30/06/2009)
Usual Pagination: 36
Editor: Joanna Tubbs; **Group Editor:** Sarah Delmege
Summary of Content: Lifestyle magazine containing articles on fashion, beauty, reader stories, celebrities, song words, dance moves, pop, gossip, puzzles, quizzes and posters.
Readership/Target Audience: Aimed at girls between 7 and 11 years old.
ADVERTISING RATES:
Full Page Colour £2400.00
Agency Commission: 10%
Mechanical Data: Type Area: 282 x 202mm, Bleed Size: 306 x 226mm, Trim Size: 300 x 220mm, Page Width: 202mm, Film: Digital, Col Length: 282mm
Copy instructions: Copy Date: 4 weeks prior to publication date
Average advertising content per issue: 10%
CONSUMER: WOMEN'S INTEREST CONSUMER MAGAZINES: Teenage

GO OUT
1655126U80C-5133

Formerly: Move Out
Editorial Address: 36 Henry Street, LIVERPOOL, L1 5BS
Tel: 0151 709 3871 **Fax:** 0151 707 1678
Email: post@movepublishing.co.uk
Advertising Address: As above.

Email: jo@movepublishing.co.uk
Publisher: Move Publishing
Date Established: 2002
Frequency: Quarterly
Cover Price: Free
Circulation: 60,000 (Publisher's Statement)
Usual Pagination: 50
Editor: Jonathan Kearney; **Advertising Manager:** Jeff Porter
Summary of Content: Listings magazine covering hotels, restaurants, music, theatre, days out and events.
Readership/Target Audience: Aimed at residents and visitors to Liverpool.
ADVERTISING RATES:
Full Page Colour £795.00
Agency Commission: 10%
Mechanical Data: Type Area: 196 x 181mm, Trim Size: 210 x 195mm, Col Length: 196mm, Page Width: 181mm, Film: Digital, Bleed Size: 216 x 201mm
Copy instructions: Copy Date: 2 weeks prior to publication date
Average advertising content per issue: 40%
CONSUMER: RURAL & REGIONAL INTEREST: Regional Interest English Counties

GO TENPIN
46010U75X-440

Editorial Address: 11 Cliff Road, SHERINGHAM, NR26 8BJ
Tel: 01263 821463
Email: editor@gotenpin.clara.net
Advertising Address: 44 Friars Walk, Southgate, LONDON, N14 5LP **Tel:** 020 8361 1188 **Fax:** 020 8361 1188
Email: a.rileyontheball@btconnect.com
Publisher: On the Ball Publications
Frequency: Monthly
Cover Price: £2.50
Annual Sub.: £30.00
Circulation: 25,000 (Publisher's Statement)
Usual Pagination: 40
Editor: Eric Hayton; **Advertising Director:** Tony Riley
Summary of Content: Magazine covering all aspects of tenpin bowling. Includes news and stories, player profiles, tournaments, results, coaching and tips.
Readership/Target Audience: Aimed at those with an interest in tenpin bowling.
ADVERTISING RATES:
Full Page Mono £625.00
Full Page Colour £825.00
Agency Commission: 10%
Mechanical Data: Page Width: 190mm, Type Area: 274 x 190mm, Bleed Size: 307 x 215mm, Trim Size: 297 x 210mm, Col Length: 274mm, Film: Digital, Print Process: Web-fed litho
Copy instructions: Copy Date: 2nd Friday of the month prior to publication date
Average advertising content per issue: 30%
CONSUMER: SPORT: Other Sport

GO TO...
1655558U89E-223

Formerly: Reach
Editorial Address: Sea Containers House, 20 Upper Ground, LONDON, SE1 9PD **Tel:** 020 7775 5777
Email: alex.mead@sevensquared.co.uk
Advertising Address: As above. **Tel:** 01782 320036
Fax: 01603 627823
Email: julie.lin@ntlworld.com
Web site: http://www.firstgreatwestern.co.uk/goto
Publisher: Seven Squared
Date Established: 2004
Frequency: Quarterly
Cover Price: Free
Circulation: 125,000 (Publisher's Statement)
Usual Pagination: 60
Editor: Alex Mead
Summary of Content: Magazine with local lifestyle features, celebrity interviews, travel ideas and events.
Readership/Target Audience: Aimed at travellers on First Great Western and First Great Western Link rail networks.
ADVERTISING RATES:
Full Page Colour £3120.00
Mechanical Data: Bleed Size: 303 x 216mm, Trim Size: 297 x 210mm, Type Area: 277 x 190mm, Col Length: 277mm, Page Width: 190mm, Film: Digital
CONSUMER: HOLIDAYS & TRAVEL: Holidays

GOING FOR GOLF MAGAZINE
31127U75D-65

Editorial Address: 71 St Stephen's Road, CANTERBURY, CT2 7JW **Tel:** 01227 457948 **Fax:** 01227 763384
Email: kentmedia@tesco.net
Advertising Address: 134 Sandon Road, Pitsea, BASILDON, SS14 1TS **Tel:** 01268 554100
Fax: 01268 552000
Email: admin@goingforgolf.com
Web site: http://www.goingforgolf.com
Publisher: Going For Golf
Date Established: 1994
Frequency: Quarterly

Cover Price: £2.50
Free to qualifying individuals
Circulation: 27,836 (Publisher's Statement)
Usual Pagination: 68
Editor: Neil Webber
Summary of Content: Magazine containing a guide to golf holiday destinations throughout the world.
Readership/Target Audience: Aimed at golfers across a range of budgets who are interested in golf playing opportunities throughout the world.
ADVERTISING RATES:
Full Page Mono £1250.00
Full Page Colour £1500.00
Agency Commission: 10%
Mechanical Data: Film: Digital, Type Area: 277 x 190mm, Col Length: 277mm, Trim Size: 297 x 210mm, Page Width: 190mm
Copy instructions: Copy Date: 1 month prior to publication date
Average advertising content per issue: 50%
CONSUMER: SPORT: Golf

GOLDEN WING
46360U77B-494_26

Editorial Address: Unit 1B & 5B, Kemps Quay Industrial Park, Quayside Road, SOUTHAMPTON, SO18 1BZ
Email: editor@hoc.org.uk
Advertising Address: As above. **Tel:** 07799 492235
Email: erica.gassor@googlemail.com
Web site: http://www.hoc.org.uk
Publisher: Honda Owners Club (GB)
Date Established: 1963
Frequency: Quarterly
Free to qualifying individuals
Annual Sub.: £18.00
Circulation: 3,000 (Publisher's Statement)
Usual Pagination: 80
Editor: Tim Lee
Summary of Content: Magazine covering old and new Honda motorcycles, club events, shows and rallies.
Readership/Target Audience: Read by members of the Honda Owners Club of Great Britain.
ADVERTISING RATES:
Full Page Colour £120.00
Mechanical Data: Type Area: 190 x 130mm, Print Process: Sheet-fed litho, Trim Size: 210 x 148mm, Col Length: 190mm, Page Width: 130mm, Film: Digital, Bleed Size: 214 x 152mm
Copy instructions: Copy Date: 4 weeks prior to publication date
CONSUMER: MOTORING & CYCLING: Motorcycling

GOLF & TRAVEL
1639895U75D-505

Editorial Address: PO Box 324, FLEET, GU51 3ZH
Tel: 01252 621513
Email: info@golf-and-travel.com
Advertising Address: As above.
Email: advertising@golf-and-travel.com
Web site: http://www.golf-and-travel.com
Publisher: VRA Media
Date Established: 2003
Frequency: 6 issues yearly
Cover Price: £2.95
Circulation: 15,000 (Publisher's Statement)
Usual Pagination: 68
Editor: Vic Robbie; **Advertising Manager:** Vic Robbie; **Publisher:** Vic Robbie
Summary of Content: Magazine for adventurous golfer's covering domestic and international golf travel, advice on where to invest in golfing property overseas, reviews of the world's best courses, interviews with stars, where to play competitive golf on holiday and where to watch top players in action.
Readership/Target Audience: Aimed at adventurous golfers.
ADVERTISING RATES:
Full Page Colour £2950.00
SCC £75.00
Agency Commission: 10%
Mechanical Data: Bleed Size: 303 x 216mm, Trim Size: 297 x 210mm, Film: Digital
Copy instructions: Copy Date: 2 weeks prior to publication date
Average advertising content per issue: 30%
CONSUMER: SPORT: Golf

THE GOLF GUIDE: WHERE TO PLAY/ WHERE TO STAY
45835U75D-100

Editorial Address: Abbey Mill Business Centre, Seedhill, PAISLEY, PA1 1TJ **Tel:** 0141 887 0428 **Fax:** 0141 889 7204
Email: anne@fhguides.co.uk
Advertising Address: As above. **Fax:** 0141 889 1491
Email: sales@fhguides.co.uk
Web site: http://www.holidayguides.com
Publisher: FHG Guides
Date Established: 1970
Frequency: Annual - Published in October

Cover Price: £9.99
Circulation: 15,000 (Publisher's Statement)
Usual Pagination: 624
Editor: Anne Cuthbertson
Summary of Content: Journal featuring information on golf clubs and courses throughout Britain and Ireland. Includes details on accommodation and articles on holiday golf in France, Spain, Portugal and USA.
Readership/Target Audience: Aimed at golf enthusiasts.
ADVERTISING RATES:
Full Page Mono £817.00
Full Page Colour £1109.00
Agency Commission: 10%
Mechanical Data: Trim Size: 190 x 118mm, Page Width: 118mm, Type Area: 210 x 145mm, Col Length: 190mm, Film: Digital
CONSUMER: SPORT: Golf

GOLF INTERNATIONAL
31208U75D-102

Editorial Address: 10 Buckingham Place, LONDON, SW1E 6HX Tel: 020 7828 3003
Email: info@golfinternationalmag.com
Advertising Address: As above.
Email: peter@golfinternationalmag.com
Web site: http://www.golfinternationalmag.com
Publisher: Golf International Services
Date Established: 1997
Frequency: 6 issues yearly
Cover Price: £4.25
Annual Sub.: £19.99
Circulation: 19,245 (ABC 01/01/2009 to 30/06/2009)
Usual Pagination: 148
Editor: Richard Simmons; Editor-in-Chief: Robert Green;
Advertising Manager: Peter Simmons
Summary of Content: Magazine covering instruction and articles from the top names in golf.
Readership/Target Audience: Aimed at affluent male golfers aged 30 years and over.
ADVERTISING RATES:
Full Page Mono £1900.00
Full Page Colour £2640.00
Agency Commission: 10%
Mechanical Data: Film: Digital, Trim Size: 297 x 210mm, Bleed Size: +3mm
Copy instructions: Copy Date: 3 weeks prior to publication date
Average advertising content per issue: 25%
CONSUMER: SPORT: Golf

GOLF LINKS
1659875U75D-524

Editorial Address: PO Box 29407, Cupar, FIFE, KY14 7WW
Tel: 0845 680 0049 Fax: 0845 458 0370
Email: editor@howardpublicity.co.uk
Advertising Address: As above.
Email: brians@howardpublicity.co.uk
Publisher: Howard Publicity Services Ltd
Date Established: 1999
Frequency: 6 issues yearly
Cover Price: Free
Usual Pagination: 100
Editor: Bill Robertson; Advertising Manager: Brian Stewart;
Publisher: Brian Stewart
Summary of Content: Magazine covering golf instruction and equipment news and reviews. Golf Links is an IAGTO approved publication and features extensive travel content looking at golfing destinations both at home and abroad. News on overseas and UK golf properties as well as advice on finding and purchasing property. Other areas include luxury golf resort reviews; car tests and player profiles.
Readership/Target Audience: Aimed at committed club golfers with an average age of about 45 and average handicap of 14.
ADVERTISING RATES:
Full Page Colour £2750.00
Agency Commission: 10%
Mechanical Data: Type Area: 277 x 190mm, Col Length: 277mm, Page Width: 190mm, Bleed Size: 303 x 216mm, Trim Size: 297 x 210mm, Film: Digital
Copy instructions: Copy Date: Beginning of the month prior to publication date
Average advertising content per issue: 40%
CONSUMER: SPORT: Golf

GOLF MONTHLY
45810U75D-110

Editorial Address: Blue Fin Building, 110 Southwark Street, LONDON, SE1 0SU Tel: 020 3148 5000
Email: golfmonthly@ipcmedia.com
Advertising Address: As above. Fax: 020 3148 8130
Email: andrew_boxer@ipcmedia.com
Web site: http://www.golf-monthly.co.uk
ISSN: 0017-1816
Publisher: IPC Inspire
Date Established: 1911
Frequency: Monthly - Published on the first week of each month
Cover Price: £3.70
Annual Sub.: £43.20

Circulation: 67,314 (ABC 01/01/2009 to 30/06/2009)
Usual Pagination: 180
Editor: Michael Harris; Managing Director: Paul Williams;
Group Editor: Garry Coward-Williams; Publisher: Adrian Booker
Summary of Content: Magazine covering tournament news, tips and advice on golf. Includes equipment listings and features on golf courses and instruction.
Readership/Target Audience: Read by the serious golfer.
ADVERTISING RATES:
Full Page Colour £4835.00
Agency Commission: 10%
Mechanical Data: Page Width: 188mm, Bleed Size: 304 x 216mm, Trim Size: 297 x 210mm, Type Area: 271 x 188mm, Col Length: 271mm, No. of Columns (Display): 4, Film: Digital
Copy instructions: Copy Date: 3 weeks prior to publication date
CONSUMER: SPORT: Golf

GOLF NEWS
45811U75D-117

Editorial Address: 14 Deanway, HOVE, BN3 6DG
Tel: 01273 556377
Email: editor@golfnews.co.uk
Advertising Address: As above. Tel: 01273 715810
Fax: 01273 730334
Email: info@golfnews.co.uk
Web site: http://www.golfnews.co.uk
Publisher: Blue Green Media Ltd
Frequency: Monthly
Cover Price: Free
Circulation: 42,000 (Publisher's Statement)
Usual Pagination: 64
Editor: Nick Bayly; Publisher: Matt Nicholson
Summary of Content: Magazine covering features on golf and news concerning local, national and international clubs.
Readership/Target Audience: Read by members of golf clubs and those with an interest in golf.
ADVERTISING: Rates on application
CONSUMER: SPORT: Golf

GOLF NEWS NORTH
45805U75D-50

Formerly: Club Golf
Editorial Address: 14 Deanway, HOVE, BN3 6DG
Tel: 01273 556377
Email: info@golfnews.co.uk
Advertising Address: As above. Tel: 01273 715810
Email: info@golfnews.co.uk
Web site: http://www.golfnews.co.uk
Publisher: Blue Green Media Ltd
Date Established: 1990
Frequency: 5 issues yearly
Cover Price: Free
Circulation: 25,000 (Publisher's Statement)
Usual Pagination: 32
Editor: Nick Bayly; Advertising Manager: Lorraine Heath;
Publisher: Matthew Nicholson
Summary of Content: Newspaper includes golfing information and news.
Readership/Target Audience: Read by members of golf clubs in the north of England and North Wales.
ADVERTISING RATES:
Full Page Colour £1814.00
Agency Commission: 10%
Mechanical Data: Film: Digital, Trim Size: 360 x 262mm, Bleed Size: 366 x 268mm, No. of Columns (Display): 6
Copy instructions: Copy Date: 2 weeks prior to publication date
Average advertising content per issue: 60%
CONSUMER: SPORT: Golf

GOLF NORTH EAST
713572U75D-115

Editorial Address: Groat Market, NEWCASTLE UPON TYNE, NE1 1ED Tel: 07758 386518
Email: allan.boughey@mac.com
Advertising Address: As above. Tel: 0191 232 7500
Fax: 0191 204 3375
Email: gillian.corney@ncjmedia.co.uk
Web site: http://www.golfnortheast.co.uk
Publisher: NCJ Media Ltd
Date Established: 2001
Frequency: 11 issues yearly
Cover Price: £1.20
Free to qualifying individuals
Circulation: 15,000 (Publisher's Statement)
Usual Pagination: 48
Editor: Allan Boughey
Summary of Content: Magazine covering local golfing news, golf travel news and features.
Readership/Target Audience: Read by members of golf clubs throughout the North East.
ADVERTISING RATES:
Full Page Colour £1325.56
Agency Commission: 10%
Mechanical Data: Bleed Size: 374 x 274mm, Trim Size: 316 x 246mm, Film: Digital

Copy instructions: Copy Date: 3rd week of the month prior to publication date
Average advertising content per issue: 65%
CONSUMER: SPORT: Golf

GOLF NOW
45815U75D-135

Editorial Address: The Old Chapel, The Mead, Farmborough, BATH, BA2 0AF Tel: 01761 472468
Fax: 01761 472851
Email: news@regionalgolf.co.uk
Advertising Address: As above.
Email: info@regionalgolf.co.uk
Web site: http://www.regionalgolf.net
Publisher: Regional Golf Ltd
Date Established: 2007
Frequency: 6 issues yearly
Free to qualifying individuals
Annual Sub.: £28.00
Circulation: 80,000 (Publisher's Statement)
Usual Pagination: 132
Editor: Grenville Jones; Advertising Manager: Eva Graham
Summary of Content: Publication covering golfing features, events and club news across the PGA regions of the UK.
Readership/Target Audience: Read by members of private and public golf clubs.
ADVERTISING: Rates on application
Supplement(s): Golf en France - 1xY, Golf Society Directory - 1xY, Golf West Holidays First - 1xY
CONSUMER: SPORT: Golf

GOLF PUNK
1642260U75D-507

Editorial Address: Unit 3, The Sussex Innovation Centre, Science Square, BRIGHTON, BN1 9SD Tel: 01273 704400
Fax: 01273 704499
Email: shaun.mcguckian@jf-media.co.uk
Advertising Address: As above.
Email: lynne.jarrett@jf-media.co.uk
Web site: http://www.golfpunkonline.com
ISSN: 1743-0968
Publisher: J.F. Media Ltd
Date Established: 2004
Frequency: 11 issues yearly
Cover Price: £3.75
Circulation: 14,928 (ABC 01/01/2008 to 31/12/2008)
Usual Pagination: 152
Editor: Shaun McGuckian
Summary of Content: Magazine covering everything great about golf including the greatest and the worst shots ever played, golf fashion, great film moments, iconic celebrity golfers past and present and equipment.
Readership/Target Audience: Aimed at the new breed of golfers, men aged between 18 and 34 years old.
ADVERTISING RATES:
Full Page Colour £6250.00
Agency Commission: 10%
Mechanical Data: Bleed Size: 306 x 231mm, Trim Size: 300 x 225mm, Film: Digital
Copy instructions: Copy Date: 3 weeks prior to publication date
Average advertising content per issue: 35%
CONSUMER: SPORT: Golf

GOLF WORLD
45816U75D-140

Editorial Address: Media House, Lynch Wood, Peterborough Business Park, PETERBOROUGH, PE2 6EA
Tel: 01733 468000
Email: golf.world@bauermedia.co.uk
Advertising Address: As above. Fax: 01733 468671
Email: dave.allen@bauermedia.co.uk
Publisher: Bauer Media Ltd (Orton)
Frequency: Monthly
Cover Price: £3.90
Circulation: 36,852 (ABC 01/01/2009 to 30/06/2009)
Usual Pagination: 164
Editor: Jock Howard
Summary of Content: Magazine containing coverage of tour events, plus tour pro, interviews, tips and equipment reviews as well as readers comments, fashion up-dates, competitions and regular features.
Readership/Target Audience: Aimed at club golfers and more experienced golfers.
ADVERTISING RATES:
Full Page Colour £4220.00
Agency Commission: 10%
Mechanical Data: Page Width: 178mm, Type Area: 267 x 178mm, Bleed Size: 303 x 216mm, Trim Size: 297 x 210mm, Col Length: 267mm, Film: Digital
Copy instructions: Copy Date: 6 weeks prior to publication date
Average advertising content per issue: 30%
CONSUMER: SPORT: Golf

Consumer Magazines

GOLFING AROUND THE M25 1826725U75D-561
Editorial Address: PO Box 5135, Strand-on-the-Green, Chiswick, LONDON, W4 3WN **Tel:** 020 8560 0897
Fax: 020 8560 0897
Email: peerage@aol.com
Advertising Address: As above.
Email: peerage@aol.com
Publisher: The Peerage Group Ltd
Date Established: 2007
Frequency: Annual - Published in December
Cover Price: £9.95
Circulation: 18,000 (Publisher's Statement)
Editor: Sara Marden-King; **Advertising Manager:** Bruce Duncan
Summary of Content: Golf Guide covering all aspects of golf courses around the UK.
Readership/Target Audience: Aimed at golf enthusiasts.
ADVERTISING RATES:
Full Page Colour £830.00
CONSUMER: SPORT: Golf

GOLFING IN BRITAIN & EUROPE
45817U75D-155
Editorial Address: PO Box 5135, Strand-on-the-Green, Chiswick, LONDON, W4 3WN **Tel:** 020 8560 0897
Fax: 020 8560 0897
Email: peerage@aol.com
Advertising Address: As above.
Email: thepeeragegroup@yahoo.co.uk
Publisher: The Peerage Group Ltd
Frequency: Annual - Published in December
Cover Price: £9.95
Circulation: 19,000 (Publisher's Statement)
Usual Pagination: 188
Editor: Sara Marden-King; **Advertising Manager:** Bruce Duncan
Summary of Content: Guide covering all aspects of golfing in the UK, Republic of Ireland and Europe. Includes details on accommodation, golf courses, clubs, fees, schools, restrictions and driving ranges.
Readership/Target Audience: Aimed at golfers on holiday, business or looking for somewhere different to play.
ADVERTISING RATES:
Full Page Mono £460.00
Full Page Colour £830.00
Agency Commission: 10%
Mechanical Data: Page Width: 185mm, Print Process: Litho, Bleed Size: 303 x 215mm, Type Area: 274 x 185mm, Col Length: 274mm, Film: Positive, right reading, emulsion side down. Digital
Copy instructions: Copy Date: 30 days prior to publication date
Average advertising content per issue: 20%
CONSUMER: SPORT: Golf

GOLWG 47231U82-25_90
Editorial Address: PO Box 4, LAMPETER, SA48 7LX
Tel: 01570 423529 **Fax:** 01570 423538
Email: golygyddol@golwg.com
Advertising Address: As above.
Email: hysbysebion@golwg.com
Web site: http://www.golwg.com
Publisher: Golwg CYF
Date Established: 1988
Frequency: Weekly
Cover Price: £1.50
Annual Sub.: £75.00
Circulation: 4,500 (Publisher's Statement)
Usual Pagination: 32
Editor: Sian Sutton; **Managing Editor:** Dylan Iorwerth
Summary of Content: Magazine containing current affairs, media, arts, sports and fashion.
Language(s): Welsh
Readership/Target Audience: Aimed at those with an interest in Wales and Welsh affairs.
ADVERTISING RATES:
Full Page Mono £620.00
Full Page Colour £805.00
Agency Commission: 10%
Mechanical Data: Col Length: 320mm, Type Area: 320mm x 220mm, Bleed Size: 346 x 246mm, Trim Size: 340mm x 240mm, Page Width: 220mm, Film: Digital, Col Widths (Display): 32mm, No. of Columns (Display): 6
Copy instructions: Copy Date: 1 week prior to publication date
Average advertising content per issue: 18%
CONSUMER: CURRENT AFFAIRS & POLITICS

GONIEC POLSKI 1745541U90-985
Editorial Address: 48 Haven Green, LONDON, W5 2NX
Tel: 020 3067 1020 **Fax:** 020 3067 1010
Email: marketing@goniec.com
Advertising Address: As above.
Email: marketing@goniec.com
Web site: http://www.goniec.com
Publisher: Goniec Ltd

Frequency: Weekly
Cover Price: Free
Circulation: 30,000 (Publisher's Statement)
Usual Pagination: 72
Editor: Ceaser Olszewska; **Advertising Manager:** Sylvia Bohatyrewycz
Summary of Content: Magazine covering news from Poland and the UK, advice on problems of Poles in the UK, careers, economy, properties and Polish culture as well as lifestyle articles, events and Polish sport in the UK.
Readership/Target Audience: Aimed at Polish communities within the UK.
ADVERTISING RATES:
Full Page Colour £1690.00
Mechanical Data: Bleed Size: 301 x 214mm, Trim Size: 297 x 210mm, Film: Digital, Type Area: 270 x 194mm, Col Length: 270mm, Page Width: 194mm
Copy instructions: Copy Date: Friday 7 days prior to publication date
CONSUMER: ETHNIC

GOOD HOLIDAY MAGAZINE 47956U89A-205
Editorial Address: Parman House, 30-36 Fife Road, KINGSTON UPON THAMES, KT1 1SY **Tel:** 020 8547 9822
Fax: 020 8546 0984
Email: edit@goodholidayideas.com
Advertising Address: As above.
Email: info@goodholidayideas.com
Web site: http://www.goodskiguide.com
Publisher: Mountain Leisure Ltd
Date Established: 1983
Frequency: Quarterly
Cover Price: £3.60
Circulation: 50,000 (Publisher's Statement)
Usual Pagination: 92
Editor: Karen Willmer; **Managing Director:** John Hill; **Advertising Manager:** Gideon Reeves
Summary of Content: Magazine covering holidays in the world's best locations.
Readership/Target Audience: Aimed at families with a high disposable income. Distributed by British Airways.
ADVERTISING RATES:
Full Page Colour £4950.00
Agency Commission: 10%
Mechanical Data: Type Area: 255 x 190mm, Bleed Size: 295 x 230mm, Film: Digital, Col Length: 255mm, Page Width: 190mm
Copy instructions: Copy Date: 1st of the month prior to publication date
Average advertising content per issue: 40%
CONSUMER: HOLIDAYS & TRAVEL: Travel

GOOD HOMES 45238U74C-30
Formerly: BBC Good Homes Magazine
Editorial Address: Cudham Tithe Barn, Berrys Hill, Berrys Green, Cudham, WESTERHAM, TN16 3AG
Tel: 01959 541444 **Fax:** 01959 541400
Email: good.homes@kelsey.co.uk
Advertising Address: As above.
Email: gh.adsales@kelsey.co.uk
ISSN: 1461-5231
Publisher: Kelsey Publishing Ltd
Date Established: 1998
Frequency: Monthly
Cover Price: £2.99
Circulation: 90,429 (ABC 01/01/2009 to 30/06/2009)
Usual Pagination: 160
Editor: Emma Bartlett; **Publisher:** Stephen Curtis
Summary of Content: Magazine featuring real-life homes, home style, shopping pages, make-overs, project and outdoor pages.
Readership/Target Audience: Aimed at home owners between 20 and 50 years old.
ADVERTISING: Rates on application
CONSUMER: WOMEN'S INTEREST CONSUMER MAGAZINES: Home & Family

GOOD HOUSEKEEPING 45256U74C-170
Editorial Address: National Magazine House, 72 Broadwick Street, LONDON, W1F 9EP **Tel:** 020 7439 5000
Fax: 020 7439 5616
Email: laura.mannering@natmags.co.uk
Advertising Address: As above.
Email: clare.james@natmags.co.uk
Web site: http://www.goodhousekeeping.co.uk
Publisher: National Magazine Company Ltd
Frequency: Monthly
Cover Price: £3.20
Circulation: 410,011 (ABC 01/01/2009 to 30/06/2009)
Usual Pagination: 248
Features Editor: Lucy Moore; **Managing Director:** Jessica Burley; **Advertising Manager:** Clare James
Summary of Content: General interest magazine containing features on family, health and beauty, relationships, food,

fashion and working mothers. Includes readers' experiences as well as articles on home and design, travel and fiction.
Twitter: https://twitter.com/goodhousemag
Readership/Target Audience: Aimed at mature women with partners and families, living comfortable lifestyles aged 40 years old and above.
ADVERTISING RATES:
Full Page Colour £20060.00
Agency Commission: 15%
Mechanical Data: Film: Digital, Type Area: 270 x 192mm, Trim Size: 290 x 215mm, Bleed Size: 296 x 221mm, Col Length: 270mm, Page Width: 192mm
Copy instructions: Copy Date: 12 weeks prior to publication date
Average advertising content per issue: 35%
CONSUMER: WOMEN'S,INTEREST CONSUMER MAGAZINES: Home & Family

GOOD MOTORING 46318U77A-190
Editorial Address: Station Road, FOREST ROW, RH18 5EN
Tel: 01342 825676 **Fax:** 01342 824847
Email: james@jamesluckhurst.co.uk
Advertising Address: The Maltings, West Street, BOURNE, PE10 9PH **Tel:** 01778 391000 **Fax:** 01778 392079
Email: rosso@warnersgroup.co.uk
Web site: http://www.motoringassist.com
Publisher: Warners Group Publications plc
Date Established: 1935
Frequency: Quarterly
Free to qualifying individuals
Circulation: 50,000 (Publisher's Statement)
Usual Pagination: 84
Editor: James Luckhurst; **Advertising Manager:** Ross O'Loughlin; **Managing Editor:** David Williams; **Publisher:** Simon Moody
Summary of Content: Magazine of GEM Motoring Assist. Covers information, services, road tests, insurance and tips.
Readership/Target Audience: Aimed at GEM Motoring Assist members, road safety officers, government departments and motoring writers.
ADVERTISING RATES:
Full Page Colour £900.00
Agency Commission: 10%
Mechanical Data: Type Area: 277 x 192mm, Trim Size: 297 x 210mm, Bleed Size: 303 x 216mm, Film: Digital, Col Length: 277mm, Page Width: 192mm
Copy instructions: Copy Date: 3 weeks prior to publication date
Average advertising content per issue: 25%
CONSUMER: MOTORING & CYCLING: Motoring

GOOD NEIGHBOURS NEWS 48687U94X-68
Editorial Address: Unit 7, Avonside Industrial Park, Avonside Road, BRISTOL, BS2 0UQ **Tel:** 0117 300 5766
Fax: 0117 300 5776
Email: gnnmag@aol.com
Publisher: The Tudor Press
Date Established: 1986
Frequency: 13 issues yearly
Cover Price: £2.50
Circulation: 15,000 (Publisher's Statement)
Usual Pagination: 32
Editor: Judy Pritchard
Summary of Content: Magazine containing charity issues, travel, cooking, book reviews, disability issues, competitions, the environment and DVD reviews.
Readership/Target Audience: Aimed at those involved in or interested in registered charitable organisations.
ADVERTISING: No Advertising taken
CONSUMER: OTHER CLASSIFICATIONS: Miscellaneous

GOOD NEWS 29867U87-101
Editorial Address: 9 Spinney Close, West Bridgford, NOTTINGHAM, NG2 6HH **Tel:** 0115 9233 424
Email: goodnewseditor@ntlworld.com
Advertising Address: As above. **Tel:** 0115 923 3424
Email: goodnewseditor@ntlworld.com
Web site: http://www.goodnews-paper.org.uk
Publisher: Good News Fellowship
Date Established: 2001
Frequency: Monthly
Cover Price: £0.12
Circulation: 60,000 (Publisher's Statement)
Usual Pagination: 8
Editor: Andrew Halloway; **Advertising Manager:** Andrew Halloway
Summary of Content: Newspaper containing stories of people whose lives have been changed by God. Used by churches in their outreach.
Readership/Target Audience: Aimed at general readership.
ADVERTISING: Rates on application
Copy instructions: Copy Date: 6 weeks prior to publication date
CONSUMER: RELIGIOUS

GOOD SKI GUIDE
47957U89A-206

Editorial Address: Parman House, 30-36 Fife Road, KINGSTON UPON THAMES, KT1 1SY **Tel:** 020 8547 9822
Email: edit@goodholidayideas.com
Advertising Address: As above. **Fax:** 020 8546 0984
Email: info@goodholidayideas.com
Web site: http://www.goodskiguide.com
Publisher: Mountain Leisure Ltd
Date Established: 1976
Frequency: 6 issues yearly - Published monthly between September and February
Cover Price: £3.60
Circulation: 250,000 (Publisher's Statement)
Usual Pagination: 132
Editor: John Hill; **Advertising Manager:** Gideon Reeves
Summary of Content: Classic ski magazine covering skiing and everything associated with winter lifestyle in ski resorts around the world.
Language(s): English; German
Readership/Target Audience: Aimed at affluent skiers and snowboarders of all levels.
ADVERTISING RATES:
Full Page Colour £4500.00
Agency Commission: 10%
Mechanical Data: Type Area: 255 x 190mm, Bleed Size: 280 x 220mm, Trim Size: 270 x 210mm, Film: Digital, Col Length: 255mm, Page Width: 190mm
Copy instructions: Copy Date: 2 weeks prior to publication date
Average advertising content per issue: 40%
CONSUMER: HOLIDAYS & TRAVEL: Travel

GOOD SKI GUIDE A-Z
47970U89A-450

Formerly: Ski Guide A-Z
Editorial Address: Parman House, 30-36 Fife Road, KINGSTON UPON THAMES, KT1 1SY **Tel:** 020 8547 9822
Email: info@goodholidayideas.com
Advertising Address: As above. **Fax:** 020 8546 0984
Email: info@goodholidayideas.com
Web site: http://www.goodskiguide.com
Publisher: Mountain Leisure Ltd
Date Established: 1975
Frequency: Quarterly
Cover Price: £3.95
Circulation: 150,000 (Publisher's Statement)
Usual Pagination: 148
Editor: John Hill; **Advertising Manager:** Gideon Reeves
Summary of Content: A guide to ski resorts around the world.
Readership/Target Audience: Aimed at those interested in a skiing holiday.
ADVERTISING RATES:
Full Page Colour £4950.00
Mechanical Data: Type Area: 255 x 190mm, Bleed Size: 280 x 220mm, Trim Size: 270 x 210mm, Col Length: 255mm, Page Width: 190mm, Film: Digital
CONSUMER: HOLIDAYS & TRAVEL: Travel

GOOD WOODWORKING
46572U79A-12

Editorial Address: Berwick House, 8-10 Knoll Rise, ORPINGTON, BR6 0EL **Tel:** 01689 899256
Fax: 01689 899266
Email: andrew.king@magicalia.com
Advertising Address: As above. **Tel:** 01689 899200
Email: clare.hiscock@magicalia.com
Web site: http://www.goodwoodworking.com
Publisher: My Hobby Store Media
Date Established: 1992
Frequency: 13 issues yearly
Cover Price: £3.30
Circulation: 14,824 (ABC 01/01/2005 to 31/12/2005)
Usual Pagination: 100
Editor: Dave Roberts
Summary of Content: Magazine covering all aspects of woodworking. Includes news, events, product tests, advice and tips.
Readership/Target Audience: Aimed at people interested in woodwork, from beginners through to professionals.
ADVERTISING RATES:
Full Page Colour £1153.00
Agency Commission: 10%
Mechanical Data: Type Area: 270 x 190mm, Bleed Size: 303 x 216mm, Trim Size: 297 x 210mm, Col Length: 270mm, Page Width: 190mm, Film: Digital
Copy instructions: Copy Date: 4 weeks prior to publication date
CONSUMER: HOBBIES & DIY

GOODIE BAG MAGAZINE
1639115U91D-875

Editorial Address: Albert Square, DUNDEE, DD1 9QJ
Tel: 01382 575885 **Fax:** 01382 575750
Email: smanthorp@dcthomson.co.uk
Advertising Address: Orange 20 Ltd, 20 Orange Street, LONDON, WC2H 7EF **Tel:** 020 7321 0701
Fax: 01372 723322
Email: sales@o20.co.uk

Web site: http://www.goodiebagmag.co.uk
Publisher: D.C. Thomson & Co Ltd
Date Established: 2003
Frequency: Monthly
Cover Price: £2.99
Circulation: 31,903 (ABC)
Usual Pagination: 32
Editor: Stephanie Manthorp
Summary of Content: Children's magazine covering celebrity features, interviews, fashion posters, puzzles, quizzes, flow charts and competitions.
Readership/Target Audience: Aimed at girls aged between 7 and 11 years old.
ADVERTISING RATES:
Full Page Colour £2000.00
Agency Commission: 15%
Mechanical Data: Film: Digital, Type Area: 276 x 200mm, Bleed Size: 301 x 231mm, Trim Size: 295 x 225mm, Col Length: 276mm, Page Width: 200mm
CONSUMER: RECREATION & LEISURE: Children & Youth

GOODLIFE MAGAZINE
45632U74Q-380

Editorial Address: Suite 58, 235 Earls Court Road, LONDON, SW5 9FE **Tel:** 020 7373 7282 **Fax:** 020 7373 3215
Email: editorgoodlife@bethere.co.uk
Advertising Address: As above.
Email: info.goodllifemedia@virgin.net
Web site: http://www.london-hotelmagazine.co.uk
Publisher: Goodlife Media PR and Promotions Ltd
Date Established: 1987
Frequency: 5 issues yearly
Cover Price: £2.00
Annual Sub.: £16.00
Circulation: 42,000 (Publisher's Statement)
Usual Pagination: 68
Editor: Eileen Spence; **Advertising Manager:** Ursula Fisher
Summary of Content: Magazine covering fashion, health and beauty, interiors, real estate, social events and entertainment. Also includes travel and other lifestyle issues.
Readership/Target Audience: Aimed at people living and working in London.
ADVERTISING RATES:
Full Page Colour £2750.00
Agency Commission: 10%
Mechanical Data: Type Area: 273 x 186mm, Trim Size: 297 x 210mm, Bleed Size: 303 x 216mm, Col Length: 273mm, Page Width: 186mm
Copy instructions: Copy Date: 6 weeks prior to publication date
Average advertising content per issue: 60%
CONSUMER: WOMEN'S INTEREST CONSUMER MAGAZINES: Lifestyle

GOODWOOD MAGAZINE
45850U75E-50

Editorial Address: Goodwood House, CHICHESTER, PO18 0PX **Tel:** 01243 755000 **Fax:** 01243 755005
Email: pr@goodwood.co.uk
Advertising Address: 20A The Coda Centre, 189 Munster Road, LONDON, SW6 6AW **Tel:** 020 7381 1200
Email: oliver@redgiantprojects.com
Web site: http://www.goodwood.co.uk
Publisher: Goodwood Estate
Date Established: 1980
Frequency: Annual - Published in April
Cover Price: Free
Circulation: 17,000 (Publisher's Statement)
Usual Pagination: 48
Editor: Chiara Guardascione; **Advertising Director:** Oliver Skelding
Summary of Content: Magazine of the Goodwood Estate. Includes news and features on horse racing, cricket, farming and motor sport.
Readership/Target Audience: Read by members, top business personnel and high profile decision makers.
ADVERTISING RATES:
Full Page Colour £5750.00
Agency Commission: 10%
Mechanical Data: Bleed Size: 326 x 246mm, Trim Size: 320 x 240mm, Film: Digital
Copy instructions: Copy Date: March 17th
Average advertising content per issue: 30%
CONSUMER: SPORT: Horse Racing

GOREZONE
1810481U76A-207

Editorial Address: PO Box 487, WOOTTON, NN4 6XY
Tel: 0844 800 2885 **Fax:** 01604 708515
Email: gorezone_05@yahoo.co.uk
Advertising Address: As above.
Email: bryn.hammond@gorezone.co.uk
Web site: http://www.gorezone.co.uk
Publisher: Lucky3 Publishers
Date Established: 2005
Frequency: Monthly
Cover Price: £3.50
Annual Sub.: £40.00
Circulation: 50,046 (Publisher's Statement)

Usual Pagination: 60
Editor: Bryn Hammond; **Advertising Manager:** Bryn Hammond
Summary of Content: Magazine covering the horror entertainment industry including DVD, films and music with reviews of the UK and the US horror movie scene plus TV shows and direct to video or DVD movies.
Readership/Target Audience: Aimed at fans of the genre.
ADVERTISING RATES:
Full Page Colour £900.00
Mechanical Data: Type Area: 266 x 171mm, Bleed Size: 307 x 205mm, Trim Size: 297 x 200mm, Col Length: 266mm, Page Width: 171mm, Film: Digital
Copy instructions: Copy Date: 24th of the publication month
CONSUMER: MUSIC & PERFORMING ARTS: Cinema

GQ
47650U86C-250

Editorial Address: Vogue House, 1 Hanover Square, LONDON, W1S 1JU **Tel:** 020 7499 9080 **Fax:** 020 7495 1679
Email: andy.morris@condenast.co.uk
Advertising Address: As above. **Fax:** 020 7491 3889
Email: agnes.stamp@condenast.co.uk
Web site: http://www.gq.com
Publisher: Conde Nast Publications Ltd
Date Established: 1988
Frequency: Monthly
Cover Price: £3.80
Annual Sub.: £33.00
Circulation: 120,019 (ABC 01/01/2009 to 30/06/2009)
Editor: Andy Morris; **Managing Director:** Nicholas Coleridge; **Advertising Manager:** Agnes Stamp; **Managing Editor:** Charlotte Zamani
Summary of Content: Magazine covering style, politics, culture, sport, health, music, fashion and lifestyle.
Readership/Target Audience: Aimed at men between 20 and 45 years old.
ADVERTISING RATES:
Full Page Mono £10750.00
Full Page Colour £10750.00
Agency Commission: 15%
Mechanical Data: Page Width: 200mm, Bleed Size: 291 x 226mm, Trim Size: 285 x 220mm, Type Area: 265 x 200mm, Col Length: 265mm, Film: Digital
Average advertising content per issue: 40%
Supplement(s): GQ Sport - 2xY
CONSUMER: ADULT & GAY MAGAZINES: Men's Lifestyle Magazines

GQ STYLE
1666425U86C-722

Editorial Address: Vogue House, 1 Hanover Square, LONDON, W1S 1JU **Tel:** 020 7499 9080 **Fax:** 020 7495 1679
Email: gqstyleassistant@condenast.co.uk
Advertising Address: As above. **Fax:** 020 7491 3889
Email: lewis.tucker@condenast.co.uk
Web site: http://www.gqstyle.com
Publisher: Conde Nast Publications Ltd
Date Established: 2005
Frequency: Half-yearly - Published in March and September
Editor: Jamal Rahman; **Editor-in-Chief:** Dylan Jones; **Advertising Director:** Lewis Tucker
Summary of Content: Magazine covering men's fashion and style.
Readership/Target Audience: Aimed at men aged between 20 and 45 years old.
ADVERTISING RATES:
Full Page Colour £6950.00
Agency Commission: 15%
Mechanical Data: Trim Size: 298 x 230mm, Film: Digital
Copy instructions: Copy Date: 6 weeks prior to publication date
Average advertising content per issue: 30%
CONSUMER: ADULT & GAY MAGAZINES: Men's Lifestyle Magazines

THE GRAMOPHONE
46151U76D-320

Editorial Address: Teddington Studios, Broom Road, TEDDINGTON, TW11 9BE **Tel:** 020 8267 5000
Fax: 020 8267 5844
Email: gramophone@haymarket.com
Advertising Address: As above. **Tel:** 020 8267 5853
Fax: 020 8267 5866
Email: ashley.murison@haymarket.com
Web site: http://www.gramophone.co.uk
ISSN: 0017-310X
Publisher: Haymarket Consumer Media
Date Established: 1923
Frequency: 13 issues yearly
Cover Price: £4.50
Annual Sub.: £53.30
Circulation: 34,628 (ABC 01/01/2008 to 31/12/2008)
Usual Pagination: 172
Editor: Charlotte Smith; **Editor-in-Chief:** James Jolly; **Publisher:** Simon Temlett
Summary of Content: Magazine covering reviews of classical CDs, videos and audio equipment.

Consumer Magazines

Readership/Target Audience: Aimed at those interested in classical music between 40 and 50 years old.
ADVERTISING RATES:
Full Page Mono £2063.00
Full Page Colour £3806.00
Agency Commission: 10%
Mechanical Data: Page Width: 190mm, Bleed Size: 284 x 221mm, Trim Size: 278 x 215mm, Type Area: 254 x 190mm, Col Length: 254mm, Film: Digital
Copy instructions: Copy Date: 8 weeks prior to publication date
Average advertising content per issue: 40%
CONSUMER: MUSIC & PERFORMING ARTS: Music

GRAND DESIGNS
1638151U74K-672

Editorial Address: National House, 121-123 High Street, EPPING, CM16 4BD **Tel:** 01992 570030
Email: info@granddesignsmagazine.com
Advertising Address: As above. **Fax:** 01992 570031
Web site: http://www.granddesignsmagazine.com
Publisher: Media 10
Date Established: 2004
Frequency: Monthly
Cover Price: £3.40
Circulation: 26,603 (ABC 01/01/2009 to 30/06/2009)
Usual Pagination: 130
Editor: Claire Barrett; **Features Editor:** Luke Tebbutt; **Advertising Manager:** Justin Levett
Summary of Content: Magazine covering self build homes, interiors, design, gardens, kitchens, bathrooms and home products.
Readership/Target Audience: Aimed at those looking to build their own homes.
ADVERTISING RATES:
Full Page Colour £6000.00
Supplement(s): Eco, Grand Designs Bathrooms - 1xY, Grand Designs Home Technology - 1xY, Grand Designs Kitchens - 1xY
CONSUMER: WOMEN'S INTEREST CONSUMER MAGAZINES: Home Purchase

GRANGE NOW
46879U80C-927

Editorial Address: Palace Studio, Main Street, GRANGE-OVER-SANDS, LA11 6AB **Tel:** 01539 535453
Fax: 01539 535454
Email: mab@grange-now.co.uk
Advertising Address: As above.
Email: mab@grange-now.co.uk
Web site: http://www.grange-now.co.uk
Publisher: Grange Now
Date Established: 1991
Frequency: Monthly
Cover Price: Free
Circulation: 7,000 (Publisher's Statement)
Usual Pagination: 28
Editor: Mary-Ann Best; **Advertising Manager:** Mary-Ann Best; **Publisher:** Mary-Ann Best
Summary of Content: Magazine covering local news, issues, clubs and societies, schools, churches and local organisations.
Readership/Target Audience: Aimed at residents and visitors in the Grange-over-Sands, Cartmel Peninsula/South Cumbria area.
ADVERTISING RATES:
Full Page Mono £372.75
Agency Commission: 10%
Mechanical Data: Film: Digital, Type Area: 277 x 190mm, Col Length: 277mm, Page Width: 190mm
Copy instructions: Copy Date: 1 week prior to publication date
Average advertising content per issue: 50%
CONSUMER: RURAL & REGIONAL INTEREST: Regional Interest English Counties

---

GRANTA
47544U84B-60

Editorial Address: 12 Addison Avenue, LONDON, W11 4QR
Tel: 020 7605 1360 **Fax:** 020 7605 1361
Email: editorial@granta.com
Advertising Address: As above.
Email: krochester@granta.com
Web site: http://www.granta.com
Publisher: Granta Publications
Date Established: 1979
Frequency: Quarterly
Cover Price: £9.99
Annual Sub.: £27.95
Circulation: 80,000 (Publisher's Statement)
Usual Pagination: 256
Managing Director: David Graham; **Advertising Manager:** Kate Rochester; **Publisher:** Sigrid Rausing
Summary of Content: Magazine of new writing, including fiction, photography and reportage.
Readership/Target Audience: Read by avid book buyers.
ADVERTISING RATES:
Full Page Mono £990.00
Full Page Colour £2000.00
Agency Commission: 10%

Mechanical Data: Type Area: 195 x 130mm, Trim Size: 210 x 145mm, Bleed Size: 225 x 160mm, Film: Digital, Col Length: 195mm, Page Width: 130mm
Copy instructions: Copy Date: 2 months prior to publication date
CONSUMER: THE ARTS & LITERARY: Literary

THE GRAPEVINE
47717U87-102

Editorial Address: Cherry Tree House, Ham Lane, Kingston Seymour, CLEVEDON, BS21 6XE **Tel:** 01934 830208
Fax: 01934 830577
Email: john.andrews@bathwells.anglican.org
Advertising Address: 28 Old Park Road, PLYMOUTH, PL3 4PY **Tel:** 01752 225623 **Fax:** 01752 673441
Email: diocesan@cornerstonevision.com
Web site: http://www.bathwells.anglican.org
Publisher: Diocese of Bath & Wells
Date Established: 1991
Frequency: Monthly
Cover Price: Free
Circulation: 30,000 (Publisher's Statement)
Usual Pagination: 16
Editor: Celia Andrews
Summary of Content: Official publication of the Diocese of Bath and Wells with religious news and information.
Readership/Target Audience: Aimed at churchgoers.
ADVERTISING RATES:
SCC £5.75
Agency Commission: 10%
Mechanical Data: Film: Digital, Type Area: 390 x 262mm, No. of Columns (Display): 8, Col Widths (Display): 30mm, Page Width: 262mm, Col Length: 390mm
Copy instructions: Copy Date: 14 days prior to publication date
Average advertising content per issue: 35%
CONSUMER: RELIGIOUS

GRAZIA
1659646U74B-712

Editorial Address: Endeavour House, 189 Shaftesbury Avenue, LONDON, WC2H 8JG **Tel:** 020 7437 9011
Fax: 020 7520 6599
Email: graziadaily@graziamagazine.co.uk
Advertising Address: As above.
Email: alison.reeves@bauermedia.co.uk
Web site: http://www.graziadaily.co.uk
Publisher: Bauer Media
Date Established: 2005
Frequency: Weekly
Cover Price: £1.90
Circulation: 228,694 (ABC 01/01/2009 to 30/06/2009)
Editor: Siam Goorwich; **News Editor:** Claire Newbon;
Advertising Manager: Carlise George; **Managing Editor:** Lucinda Greasley
Summary of Content: Magazine covering fashion and style. Twitter: https://twitter.com/Grazia_Live.
Readership/Target Audience: Aimed at affluent women aged between 25 and 45 years old.
ADVERTISING RATES:
Full Page Colour £12420.00
Agency Commission: 15%
Copy instructions: Copy Date: 2 weeks prior to publication date
CONSUMER: WOMEN'S INTEREST CONSUMER MAGAZINES: Women's Interest - Fashion

---

GREAT BRITISH FOOD
1895466U74P-967

Editorial Address: 21-23 Phoenix Court, Hawkins Road, COLCHESTER, CO2 8JY **Tel:** 01206 505900
Fax: 01206 505915
Email: nicola.mallett@aceville.co.uk
Web site: http://www.greatbritishfoodmagazine.com
Publisher: Aceville Publications Ltd
Frequency: Quarterly - Frequency is seasonal
Circulation: 45,000 (Publisher's Statement)
Editor: Nicola Mallett
Summary of Content: Magazine covering British food. Includes features on food producers, recipes, interviews with top chefs, showcases of the latest food in the shops.
Readership/Target Audience: Aimed at those who love eating, drinking and shopping for British food.
CONSUMER: WOMEN'S INTEREST CONSUMER MAGAZINES: Food & Cookery

---

THE GREEN
46822U80B-117

Editorial Address: Avon House, 5th Floor, Kensington Village, Avonmore Road, LONDON, W14 8TS
Tel: 020 7605 2200
Email: editor@thegreenmag.co.uk
Advertising Address: As above. **Tel:** 020 7792 2626
Fax: 020 7792 2020
Email: nial.phillimore@archant.co.uk
Web site: http://www.thegreenmag.co.uk
Publisher: Archant Life
Date Established: 1991

Frequency: Monthly
Cover Price: Free
Circulation: 50,500 (Publisher's Statement)
Usual Pagination: 84
Editor: ShelleyJo Harper; **Managing Director:** Jeremy Moreton; **Advertising Manager:** Nial Phillimore
Summary of Content: Magazine focusing on news, local issues, property and food in Chiswick and Richmond.
Readership/Target Audience: Aimed at West London residents and businesses.
ADVERTISING RATES:
Full Page Colour £1625.00
Agency Commission: 10%
Mechanical Data: Type Area: 270 x 190mm, Col Length: 270mm, Page Width: 190mm, Bleed Size: 303 x 216mm, Trim Size: 297 x 210mm, Film: Digital
Copy instructions: Copy Date: 10 days prior to publication date
Average advertising content per issue: 40%
CONSUMER: RURAL & REGIONAL INTEREST: Regional Interest Greater London

---

GREEN EVENTS
47232U80B-118

Editorial Address: 48 Clifftown Gardens, HERNE BAY, CT6 8DE **Tel:** 01227 749991
Email: greenevents@btconnect.com
Advertising Address: As above.
Email: greenevents@btconnect.com
Web site: http://www.greenevents.co.uk/london
Publisher: Green Events
Date Established: 1991
Frequency: 6 issues yearly
Cover Price: Free
Circulation: 12,000 (Publisher's Statement)
Usual Pagination: 16
Editor: Peter McCaig; **Advertising Manager:** Peter McCaig
Summary of Content: Newsletter covering holistic and environmental interests and activities in the London area.
Readership/Target Audience: Aimed at those sympathetic with green and holistic concerns.
ADVERTISING RATES:
Full Page Mono £650.00
Full Page Colour £850.00
Agency Commission: 10%
CONSUMER: RURAL & REGIONAL INTEREST: Regional Interest Greater London

---

THE GREEN PARENT
1659526U74D-662

Editorial Address: PO Box 104, East Hoathly, LEWES, BN7 9AX **Tel:** 01825 872858
Email: info@thegreenparent.co.uk
Advertising Address: Space Marketing, 10 Clayfield Mews, Newcomen Road, TUNBRIDGE WELLS, TN4 9PA
Tel: 01892 677740 **Fax:** 01892 677743
Email: sales@spacemarketing.co.uk
Web site: http://www.thegreenparent.co.uk
Publisher: Green Parent Publications
Frequency: 6 issues yearly
Cover Price: £3.50
Circulation: 25,000 (Publisher's Statement)
Usual Pagination: 100
Editor: Melissa Corkhill
Summary of Content: Magazine covering parenting and green issues including house and garden, pregnancy and birth, nutrition, education, health and beauty.
Readership/Target Audience: Aimed at parents with children up to the age of 12 years old.
ADVERTISING RATES:
Full Page Colour £1990.00
Agency Commission: 10%
Mechanical Data: Type Area: 245 x 190mm, Bleed Size: 281 x 226mm, Trim Size: 275 x 220mm, Col Length: 245mm, Page Width: 190mm, Film: Digital
Copy instructions: Copy Date: 6 weeks prior to publication date
Average advertising content per issue: 30%
CONSUMER: WOMEN'S INTEREST CONSUMER MAGAZINES: Child Care

GREEN TOURISM AND HERITAGE GUIDE
713785U89A-208

Editorial Address: 150 Burnley Road, ACCRINGTON, BB5 6DW **Tel:** 01254 390066 **Fax:** 01254 390077
Email: editorial@euromedia-al.com
Advertising Address: Unit 8, Chorley West Business Park, Ackhurst Road, CHORLEY, PR7 1NL **Tel:** 0870 444 8955
Fax: 0870 444 8956
Email: ads@euromedia-al.co.uk
Web site: http://www.euromediaal.com
ISSN: 1369-5096
Publisher: Euromedia Associates Ltd
Date Established: 1998
Frequency: Annual - Published in May
Cover Price: £3.50
Free to qualifying individuals
Circulation: 10,000 (Publisher's Statement)

Usual Pagination: 200
Editor: Richard Cheesbrough
Summary of Content: Magazine covering all aspects of sustainable tourism and heritage. Includes articles on cycling and walking activities, castles, industrial heritage and steam railways.
Readership/Target Audience: Aimed at groups and individuals with an interest in heritage attractions and green activities.
ADVERTISING RATES:
Full Page Colour £1500.00
Agency Commission: 10%
Mechanical Data: Col Widths (Display): 30mm, Film: Digital, Trim Size: 297 x 210mm, Type Area: 270 x 190mm, Col Length: 270mm, Page Width: 190mm, No. of Columns (Display): 6, Bleed Size: 303 x 216mm
Copy instructions: Copy Date: 1 month prior to publication date
CONSUMER: HOLIDAYS & TRAVEL: Travel

GREEN 'UN (IPSWICH)   45762U75B-127_50
Editorial Address: Press House, 30 Lower Brook Street, IPSWICH, IP4 1AN **Tel:** 01473 324835 **Fax:** 01473 324850
Email: mike.bacon@archant.co.uk
Advertising Address: As above. **Tel:** 01473 324753
Fax: 01473 324830
Email: lesley.rawlinson@archant.co.uk
Publisher: Archant Suffolk
Frequency: 40 issues yearly - Published weekly during the football season
Cover Price: £1.00
Circulation: 7,000 (Publisher's Statement)
Usual Pagination: 48
Editor: Michael Bacon; **Advertising Manager:** Lesley Rawlinson
Summary of Content: Football edition of the Evening Star.
Readership/Target Audience: Aimed at football fans of Ipswich, Colchester, Cambridge and many non-league and local football teams across Suffolk, Essex, east Cambridgeshire and south Norfolk.
ADVERTISING RATES:
Full Page Mono £299.00
Full Page Colour £399.00
SCC £3.00
Agency Commission: 10%
Mechanical Data: Type Area: 360 x 270mm, Col Length: 360mm, No. of Columns (Display): 8, Page Width: 270mm, Film: Digital, Col Widths (Display): 32mm
Copy instructions: Copy Date: 1 week prior to publication date
Average advertising content per issue: 15%
CONSUMER: SPORT: Football

GREEN WORLD   47233U82-28
Editorial Address: 62 Ashbourne Road, DERBY, DE22 3AF
Tel: 01332 298599 **Fax:** 01332 202422
Email: editor@greenworld.org.uk
Advertising Address: 2 Dolphin Close, LONDON, SE16 6DX
Tel: 020 7231 6427
Email: adverts@green-world.org.uk
Web site: http://www.greenworld.org.uk
ISSN: 1359-110X
Publisher: Green Party
Date Established: 1992
Frequency: Quarterly
Cover Price: £2.00
Free to qualifying individuals
Annual Sub.: £10.00
Circulation: 10,000 (Publisher's Statement)
Usual Pagination: 32
Editor: Philip Sainty; **Advertising Manager:** Jacob Sanders
Summary of Content: Magazine covering Green Party news, UK green politics, environmental and social issues.
Language(s): English; Welsh
Readership/Target Audience: Aimed at members and supporters of the Green Party and those interested or involved in green issues and politics.
ADVERTISING RATES:
Full Page Mono £400.00
Full Page Colour £400.00
Mechanical Data: No. of Columns (Display): 4, Type Area: 277 x 190mm, Col Length: 277mm, Film: Digital, Trim Size: 297 x 210mm, Page Width: 190mm, Bleed Size: 303 x 216mm
Copy instructions: Copy Date: 4 weeks prior to publication date
Average advertising content per issue: 20%
CONSUMER: CURRENT AFFAIRS & POLITICS

GREENBITS   47084U81A-60
Editorial Address: Margrove Heritage Centre, Margrove Park, Boosbeck, SALTBURN-BY-THE-SEA, TS12 3BZ
Tel: 01287 636382 **Fax:** 01642 636383
Email: info@teeswildlife.org
Advertising Address: Gazette Buildings, Borough Road, MIDDLESBOROUGH, TS1 3AZ **Tel:** 01642 234344
Fax: 01642 254764

Email: maureen.brady@gazettemedia.co.uk
Web site: http://www.teeswildlife.org/greenbits.htm
Publisher: Tees Valley Wildlife Trust
Date Established: 1989
Frequency: Quarterly
Cover Price: Free
Circulation: 70,000 (Publisher's Statement)
Usual Pagination: 20
Editor: Jeremy Garside
Summary of Content: Community wildlife magazine of the Tees Valley Wildlife Trust. Contains articles on environment, wildlife and green issues.
Readership/Target Audience: Read by Wildlife Trust members and those interested in environmental issues.
ADVERTISING RATES:
Full Page Colour £2000.00
Agency Commission: 10%
Mechanical Data: Bleed Size: 348 x 276mm, Film: Digital, Trim Size: 316 x 246mm
Copy instructions: Copy Date: 2 weeks prior to publication date
Average advertising content per issue: 40%
Supplement to: Evening Gazette (Middlesbrough)
CONSUMER: ANIMALS & PETS: Animals & Pets Protection

GREENSIDE   754818U75D-160
Editorial Address: Teddington Studios, Broom Road, TEDDINGTON, TW11 9BE **Tel:** 020 8267 5000
Fax: 020 8267 5194
Email: david.cottrell@haymarket.com
Advertising Address: As above. **Fax:** 020 8267 5815
Email: kavita.brown@haymarket.com
Web site: http://www.foremostonline.com
Publisher: Haymarket Network
Date Established: 1998
Frequency: 3 issues yearly - Published in March, June and September
Free to qualifying individuals
Circulation: 115,000 (Publisher's Statement)
Usual Pagination: 52
Editor: David Cottrell
Summary of Content: Magazine covering all aspects of golf and golfing.
Readership/Target Audience: Aimed at members of private golf clubs within the Foremost group.
ADVERTISING RATES:
Full Page Colour £2500.00
Mechanical Data: Bleed Size: 303 x 216mm, Film: Digital, Trim Size: 297 x 210mm
Average advertising content per issue: 30%
CONSUMER: SPORT: Golf

GREYHOUND STAR   47103U75X-1704
Editorial Address: PO Box 49, LETCHWORTH, SG6 2XB
Tel: 01462 679439 **Fax:** 01462 485512
Email: admin@greyhoundstar.fsnet.co.uk
Advertising Address: As above.
Email: admin@greyhoundstar.fsnet.co.uk
Web site: http://www.greyhoundstar.net
Publisher: Orchestrate Ltd
Frequency: Monthly
Cover Price: £2.00
Circulation: 10,500 (Publisher's Statement)
Usual Pagination: 48
Editor: Floyd Amphlett; **Advertising Manager:** Floyd Amphlett
Summary of Content: Magazine providing coverage of every major greyhound race. Includes articles on breeding and veterinary advice.
Readership/Target Audience: Read by owners, trainers, track operators and breeders.
ADVERTISING RATES:
Full Page Mono £675.00
Full Page Colour £775.00
Mechanical Data: Type Area: 383 x 264mm, Col Length: 383mm, Page Width: 264mm, Film: Digital
CONSUMER: SPORT: Other Sport

GROBY & FIELD HEAD SPOTLIGHT
1776309U80C-5358
Editorial Address: PO Box 8, MARKFIELD, LE67 9ZT
Tel: 01530 244069 **Fax:** 01530 249557
Email: info@grobyspotlight.co.uk
Advertising Address: As above.
Email: info@grobyspotlight.co.uk
Web site: http://www.grobyspotlight.co.uk
Publisher: Builder Magazines
Date Established: 2004
Frequency: 11 issues yearly
Cover Price: Free
Circulation: 3,500 (Publisher's Statement)
Usual Pagination: 32
Editor: Mike Wilkinson; **Features Editor:** Susan Hatton;
Advertising Manager: Mike Wilkinson
Summary of Content: Magazine covering local news articles for the Groby & Field Head area of Leicestershire,

events, book and DVD reviews, profiles of local clubs and societies, competitions, jokes and quotes.
Readership/Target Audience: Aimed at households in the Leicestershire villages of Groby and Field Head.
ADVERTISING RATES:
Full Page Mono £140.00
Full Page Colour £190.00
Agency Commission: 10%
Mechanical Data: Type Area: 268 x 194mm, Col Length: 268mm, Page Width: 194mm, Film: Digital
Copy instructions: Copy Date: 28th of the month prior to publication date
Average advertising content per issue: 50%
CONSUMER: RURAL & REGIONAL INTEREST: Regional Interest English Counties

GROW IT   1799740U93-195
Editorial Address: Cudham Tithe Barn, Berrys Hill, Berrys Green, Cudham, WESTERHAM, TN16 3AG
Tel: 01959 541444 **Fax:** 01959 541400
Email: gi.ed@kelsey.co.uk
Advertising Address: As above. **Fax:** 01959 543585
Email: david@kelsey.co.uk
Web site: http://www.growitmag.com
Publisher: Kelsey Publishing Ltd
Date Established: 2007
Frequency: Monthly
Cover Price: £3.20
Circulation: 50,000 (Print Run)
Usual Pagination: 84
Editor: Ben Vanheems; **Advertising Director:** David Lerpiniere; **Publisher:** Stephen Curtis
Summary of Content: Magazine covering all aspects of vegetable and fruit growing. Also regular column on poultry.
Readership/Target Audience: Aimed at those who love to grow their own vegetables.
ADVERTISING RATES:
Full Page Colour £900.00
Agency Commission: 10%
Mechanical Data: Type Area: 262 x 185mm, Col Length: 262mm, Page Width: 185mm, Film: Digital
Copy instructions: Copy Date: 3 weeks prior to publication date
Average advertising content per issue: 30%
CONSUMER: GARDENING

GROW YOUR OWN   1666789U93-191
Editorial Address: 25 Phoenix Court, Hawkins Road, COLCHESTER, CO2 8JY **Tel:** 01206 505979
Email: lucy.halsall@aceville.co.uk
Advertising Address: 21-23 Phoenix Court, Hawkins Road, COLCHESTER, CO2 8JY **Tel:** 01206 505940
Fax: 01206 505945
Email: teresa@aceville.co.uk
Web site: http://www.growfruitandveg.co.uk
Publisher: Aceville Publications Ltd
Date Established: 2005
Frequency: Monthly
Cover Price: £3.45
Circulation: 60,000 (Print Run)
Usual Pagination: 100
Editor: Lucy Halsall; **Advertising Manager:** Teresa Tudge;
Group Editor: Jeannine McAndrew
Summary of Content: Magazine with tips on how to live the good life including how to grow your own fruit and vegetables and recipes using garden fresh produce as well as keeping your own bees and chickens.
Readership/Target Audience: Aimed at those in their 30s and 40s whether they have a small back garden, a substantial plot or an allotment.
ADVERTISING RATES:
Full Page Mono £835.00
Full Page Colour £1075.00
Agency Commission: 10%
Mechanical Data: Type Area: 276 x 211mm, Bleed Size: 308 x 238mm, Trim Size: 300 x 230mm, Col Length: 276mm, Page Width: 211mm, Film: Digital
Copy instructions: Copy Date: 4 weeks prior to publication date
Average advertising content per issue: 40%
CONSUMER: GARDENING

THE GROWER NEWSLETTER   1861490U93-201
Editorial Address: 11 Lynton Road, CHESHAM, HP5 2BU
Email: thegrowernewsletter@googlemail.com
Web site: http://www.tgn2.co.uk
Web site: http://twitter.com/tgn2
Web site: http://www.flickr.com/photos/tgn2
Web site: Skype: tg.newsletter
Frequency: Quarterly
Cover Price: Free
Circulation: 200 (Publisher's Statement)
Usual Pagination: 4
Summary of Content: Newsletter covering the cultivation of fruit, vegetables and flowers on allotment gardens, both organic and traditional, seasonal advice, news and local topical articles.

Consumer Magazines

Readership/Target Audience: Aimed at allotment holders in the Chesham area, Chesham residents and those growing their own food for their own consumption.
CONSUMER: GARDENING

GSCENE
1796312U86B-180

Editorial Address: 111 Western Road, HOVE, BN3 1DD
Tel: 01273 722457
Email: info@gscene.com
Advertising Address: As above.
Email: info@gscene.com
Web site: http://www.gscene.com
Publisher: Gscene Ltd
Date Established: 1995
Frequency: Monthly
Cover Price: Free
Circulation: 30,000 (Print Run)
Usual Pagination: 96
Editor: James Ledward
Summary of Content: Community news and listings magazine.
Readership/Target Audience: Aimed at lesbian, gay, bi-sexual and trans-sexual men and women of all ages in Brighton and the surrounding area.
ADVERTISING RATES:
Full Page Colour £500.00
Mechanical Data: Type Area: 277 x 190mm, Bleed Size: 303 x 216mm, Trim Size: 297 x 210mm, Col Length: 277mm, Page Width: 190mm, Film: Digital
Copy instructions: Copy Date: Middle of the month prior to publication date
Average advertising content per issue: 40%
CONSUMER: ADULT & GAY MAGAZINES: Gay & Lesbian Magazines

GT
47628U86B-30

Formerly: Gay Times inc. Gay News
Editorial Address: Unit M, Spectrum House, 32-34 Gordon House Road, LONDON, NW5 1LP **Tel:** 020 7424 7400
Fax: 020 7424 7401
Email: edit@gaytimes.co.uk
Advertising Address: As above.
Email: advertising@millivres.co.uk
Web site: http://www.gaytimes.co.uk
ISSN: 0950-6101
Publisher: Millivres-Prowler Ltd
Date Established: 1984
Frequency: Monthly
Cover Price: £3.50
Annual Sub.: £30.00
Circulation: 68,000 (Publisher's Statement)
Usual Pagination: 240
Editor: Tris Reid-Smith; **News Editor:** Peter Lloyd; **Features Editor:** Darren Scott; **Managing Director:** Simon Topham; **Publisher:** Kim Watson
Summary of Content: Magazine covering news and reviews, arts, politics, travel, health, film and theatre.
Readership/Target Audience: Read by gay men between 18 and 70 years old.
ADVERTISING RATES:
Full Page Colour £2136.00
Agency Commission: 10%
Mechanical Data: Col Length: 270mm, Film: Digital, No. of Columns (Display): 4, Bleed Size: 306 x 236mm, Trim Size: 300 x 230mm, Type Area: 270 x 200mm, Page Width: 200mm
Copy instructions: Copy Date: 3 weeks prior to publication date
Average advertising content per issue: 50%
CONSUMER: ADULT & GAY MAGAZINES: Gay & Lesbian Magazines

GT PURELY PORSCHE
754186U77E-157

Editorial Address: Becket House, Vestry Road, SEVENOAKS, TN14 5EJ **Tel:** 01732 748000
Fax: 01732 748001
Email: gtpurelyporsche@unity-media.com
Advertising Address: As above.
Email: hrush@unity-media.com
Web site: http://www.gtpurelyporsche.com
ISSN: 1474-654X
Publisher: Unity Media plc
Date Established: 2001
Frequency: Monthly
Cover Price: £4.35
Annual Sub.: £52.20
Circulation: 60,000 (Publisher's Statement)
Usual Pagination: 148
Editor: Stuart Gallagher; **Advertising Manager:** Helen Rush; **Publisher:** Colin Wilkinson
Summary of Content: Magazine covering Porsche related articles, news, features and a guide to buying a Porsche.
Readership/Target Audience: Aimed at Porsche owners and enthusiasts.
ADVERTISING RATES:
Full Page Mono £1050.00

Full Page Colour £1850.00
Agency Commission: 10%
Mechanical Data: Col Length: 255mm, Film: Digital, Trim Size: 285 x 220mm, Bleed Size: 291 x 226mm, Type Area: 255 x 200mm, Page Width: 200mm
Copy instructions: Copy Date: 3 weeks prior to publication date
Average advertising content per issue: 25%
CONSUMER: MOTORING & CYCLING: Club Cars

THE GUARDIAN WEEKLY
47234U82-30

Editorial Address: Kings Place, 90 York Way, LONDON, N1 9GU **Tel:** 020 3353 2000
Email: weekly@guardian.co.uk
Advertising Address: 4th Floor Display Sales, 119 Farringdon Road, LONDON, EC1R 3ER **Tel:** 020 7713 4039
Fax: 020 7278 1449
Email: sarah.adams@guardian.co.uk
Web site: http://www.guardianweekly.co.uk
Publisher: Guardian Media Group plc
Date Established: 1919
Frequency: Weekly
Cover Price: £1.75
Annual Sub.: £77.00
Circulation: 70,733 (ABC 01/01/2008 to 31/12/2008)
Usual Pagination: 36
Editor: Natalie Bennett; **Advertising Manager:** Sarah Adams
Summary of Content: Newspaper containing compilation of Guardian and Observer reviews and features, including extracts from Le Monde and The Washington Post; includes a section for ex-patriate readers.
Readership/Target Audience: Aimed at executives, academics, students, professionals and those involved in institutes and embassies, as well as anyone with an interest in news and current affairs.
ADVERTISING RATES:
Full Page Mono £5000.00
Full Page Colour £600.00
Agency Commission: 15%
Mechanical Data: Col Length: 290mm, Print Process: Web-fed offset litho, Page Width: 209mm, Type Area: 290 x 209mm, Film: Digital, No. of Columns (Display): 4
Copy instructions: Copy Date: Friday 7 days prior to publication date
Average advertising content per issue: 25%
Supplement(s): Learning English - 12xY.
CONSUMER: CURRENT AFFAIRS & POLITICS

THE GUERNSEY LIFE
1804470U80G-506

Editorial Address: Chamber House, 25 Pier Road, St. Helier, JERSEY, JE1 4HF **Tel:** 01534 619882
Fax: 01534 728724
Email: theguernseylife@fishmedia.biz
Advertising Address: As above.
Email: sarah@fishmedia.biz
Web site: http://www.lifemagazines.biz
Publisher: Fish Media Ltd
Frequency: Monthly
Cover Price: £2.60
Circulation: 30,000 (Publisher's Statement)
Usual Pagination: 80
Editor: Jamie Fisher
Summary of Content: Magazine covering beauty, celebrity, entertainment, fashion, travel, property and shopping.
Readership/Target Audience: Aimed at residents, visitors and businesses in Guernsey.
ADVERTISING RATES:
Full Page Colour £1995.00
Mechanical Data: Type Area: 255 x 185mm, Bleed Size: 286 x 216mm, Trim Size: 280 x 210mm, Col Length: 255mm, Page Width: 185mm, Film: Digital
CONSUMER: RURAL & REGIONAL INTEREST: Regional Interest Channel Islands

GUERNSEY NOW
1663211U80G-504

Editorial Address: PO Box 57, Braye Road, Vale, GUERNSEY, GY1 3BW **Tel:** 01481 240240
Fax: 01481 240235
Email: newsroom@guernsey-press.com
Advertising Address: As above. **Fax:** 01481 240275
Email: jtodd@guernsey-press.com
Web site: http://www.thisisguernsey.com
ISSN: 1470-3513
Publisher: Guernsey Press Co Ltd
Date Established: 2003
Frequency: Quarterly
Cover Price: £2.50
Free to qualifying individuals
Circulation: 16,000 (Publisher's Statement)
Usual Pagination: 76
Editor: Louise Cole; **Advertising Manager:** Julie Todd
Summary of Content: Magazine covering lifestyle, property, food, fashion, health and business.
Readership/Target Audience: Aimed at residents and visitors to Guernsey.

ADVERTISING RATES:
Full Page Colour £1400.00
Agency Commission: 10%
Mechanical Data: Type Area: 265 x 182mm, Bleed Size: 303 x 216mm, Trim Size: 297 x 210mm, Col Length: 265mm, Page Width: 182mm, Film: Digital
Copy instructions: Copy Date: 6 weeks prior to publication date
CONSUMER: RURAL & REGIONAL INTEREST: Regional Interest Channel Islands

THE GUIDE
1615987U80C-5056

Formerly: This is Brighton
Editorial Address: Argus House, Crowhurst Road, Hollingbury, BRIGHTON, BN1 8AR **Tel:** 01273 544569
Fax: 01273 544594
Email: theguide@theargus.co.uk
Advertising Address: As above. **Tel:** 01273 544544
Fax: 01273 889500
Email: andrea.smith@theargus.co.uk
Web site: http://www.theargus.co.uk
Publisher: Newsquest (Sussex) Ltd
Date Established: 2002
Frequency: Weekly
Cover Price: £0.38
Circulation: 37,000 (Publisher's Statement)
Usual Pagination: 40
Editor: Kim Protheroe; **Advertising Manager:** Andrea Smith
Summary of Content: Lifestyle and entertainment listings magazine containing theatre, comedy, music, books, films, digital culture, food, drinks and consumer fashion.
Readership/Target Audience: Aimed at residents of and visitors to Brighton and Hove aged between 25 and 45 years old.
ADVERTISING RATES:
Full Page Mono £1373.00
Full Page Colour £1633.00
Agency Commission: 10%
Mechanical Data: Type Area: 340 x 225mm, Col Length: 340mm, Page Width: 225mm, Film: Digital, No. of Columns (Display): 8, Col Widths (Display): 28mm
Copy instructions: Copy Date: Friday 2pm prior to publication date
CONSUMER: RURAL & REGIONAL INTEREST: Regional Interest English Counties

GUIDE FOR THE BRIDE
45542U74L-120

Editorial Address: 62 Exe Vale Road, Countess Wear, EXETER, EX2 6LF **Tel:** 01392 427576 **Fax:** 01392 426264
Email: geminipublishing@blueyonder.co.uk
Advertising Address: As above. **Fax:** 01392 427576
Email: geminipublishing@blueyonder.co.uk
Web site: http://www.geminipublishing.net
Publisher: Gemini Publishing & Design
Date Established: 1993
Frequency: 3 issues yearly - Published in spring, autumn and winter
Cover Price: Free
Circulation: 15,000 (Publisher's Statement)
Usual Pagination: 48
Editor: Gill Tippins; **Advertising Manager:** Gill Tippins
Summary of Content: Magazine covering all aspects of weddings, including information and advice of interest.
Readership/Target Audience: Aimed at those involved in organising a wedding.
ADVERTISING RATES:
Full Page Mono £399.00
Full Page Colour £514.00
Agency Commission: 10%
Mechanical Data: Type Area: 210 x 145mm, Page Width: 145mm, Col Length: 210mm, Film: Digital
Average advertising content per issue: 40%
Editions:
Guide for the Bride (Exeter)
Guide for the Bride (Plymouth)
Guide for the Bride (Torbay)
CONSUMER: WOMEN'S INTEREST CONSUMER MAGAZINES: Brides

THE GUIDE (GUARDIAN)
48093U89C-144_50

Editorial Address: Kings Place, 90 York Way, LONDON, N1 9GU **Tel:** 020 7278 2332 **Fax:** 020 7963 7805
Email: art@pa-entertainment.co.uk
Advertising Address: As above. **Tel:** 020 7239 9531
Web site: http://www.guardian.co.uk/theguide
Publisher: Guardian Media Group plc
Date Established: 1993
Frequency: Weekly - Published on Saturday. See main record for circulation figure
Cover Price: Free
Usual Pagination: 100
Editor: Malik Meer
Summary of Content: Television and entertainment guide including film, theatre and music listings and previews.
Readership/Target Audience: Aimed at those interested in the arts and entertainment.

ADVERTISING RATES:
Full Page Mono £9000.00
SCC £150.00
Mechanical Data: Bleed Size: 240 x 155mm, Type Area: 205 x 130mm, Col Length: 205mm, Page Width: 130mm, Film: Digital
Copy instructions: Copy Date: Monday 5 days prior to publication date
Supplement to: The Guardian
CONSUMER: HOLIDAYS & TRAVEL: Entertainment Guides

THE GUIDE MAGAZINE
46824U80B-122

Formerly: The Guide Magazine Blackheath and Greenwich
Editorial Address: Unit F3, Battersea Studios, 80 Silverthorne Road, LONDON, SW8 3XA **Tel:** 020 7978 3485
Fax: 020 7978 3485
Email: victoria.purcell@archant.co.uk
Advertising Address: As above. **Tel:** 020 7978 3480
Email: heather.jones-hughes@archant.co.uk
Web site: http://www.theguidemag.co.uk
Publisher: Archant Life
Date Established: 1889
Frequency: Monthly
Cover Price: Free
Circulation: 48,000 (Publisher's Statement)
Usual Pagination: 72
Editor: Victoria Purcell; **Advertising Manager:** Heather Jones-Hughes
Summary of Content: Magazine covering news, what's on, food, health and beauty, history, travel, family, interiors, celebrity profiles, competitions, property, fashion, restaurants and theatre.
Readership/Target Audience: Aimed at residents living in Greenwich, Blackheath, Lee Green, Eltham, Docklands, Bromley, Chislehurst and Lewisham.
ADVERTISING RATES:
Full Page Colour £1202.00
Agency Commission: 10%
Mechanical Data: Type Area: 270 x 190mm, Col Length: 270mm, Page Width: 190mm, Trim Size: 297 x 210mm, Bleed Size: 303 x 216mm, Film: Digital
Copy instructions: Copy Date: 2 weeks prior to publication date
Average advertising content per issue: 35%
CONSUMER: RURAL & REGIONAL INTEREST: Regional Interest Greater London

GUIDE TO CARAVAN & CAMPING HOLIDAYS
48432U91B-80

Editorial Address: Abbey Mill Business Centre, Seedhill, PAISLEY, PA1 1TJ **Tel:** 0141 887 0428 **Fax:** 0141 889 7204
Email: anne@fhguides.co.uk
Advertising Address: As above.
Email: dorothy@fhguides.co.uk
Web site: http://www.holidayguides.com
Publisher: FHG Guides
Frequency: Annual - Published in January
Cover Price: £6.99
Circulation: 20,000 (Publisher's Statement)
Usual Pagination: 176
Editor: Anne Cuthbertson
Summary of Content: Publication containing details of caravans for hire, caravan and camping sites and holiday centres.
Readership/Target Audience: Aimed at caravanning and camping enthusiasts.
ADVERTISING RATES:
Full Page Mono £464.00
Full Page Colour £779.00
Agency Commission: 10%
Mechanical Data: Page Width: 118mm, Type Area: 190 x 118mm, Col Length: 190mm, Film: Digital, Bleed Size: +3mm
Copy instructions: Copy Date: October 31st
Average advertising content per issue: 90%
CONSUMER: RECREATION & LEISURE: Camping & Caravanning

GUIDE TO CUMBRIA MAGAZINE
1622905U80C-5063

Editorial Address: 3 Chatsworth Square, CARLISLE, CA1 1HB **Tel:** 0228 547144
Email: editor@cumbriapress.co.uk
Advertising Address: As above.
Email: alan@cumbriapress.com
Publisher: Cumbrian Press Group
Frequency: Half-yearly
Cover Price: Free
Circulation: 5,000 (Publisher's Statement)
Usual Pagination: 72
Editor: Tony Thornton; **Advertising Manager:** Alan Taylor;
Publisher: Alan Taylor
Summary of Content: Magazine covering lifestyle and industry issues in Cumbria. Also includes local book reviews.
Readership/Target Audience: Aimed at the Cumbrians.

ADVERTISING RATES:
Full Page Colour £795.00
Agency Commission: 10%
Mechanical Data: Type Area: 195 x 135mm, Col Length: 195mm, Film: Digital, Trim Size: 210 x 148mm, Page Width: 135mm, Bleed Size: +5mm
Copy instructions: Copy Date: 2 weeks prior to publication date
Average advertising content per issue: 50%
CONSUMER: RURAL & REGIONAL INTEREST: Regional Interest English Counties

GUIDING MAGAZINE
48460U91D-70

Editorial Address: 17-19 Buckingham Palace Road, LONDON, SW1W 0PT **Tel:** 020 7834 6242
Fax: 020 7828 5791
Email: guiding@girlguiding.org.uk
Advertising Address: Think Publishing, The Pall Mall Deposit, 124-128 Barlby Road, LONDON, W10 6BL
Tel: 020 8962 3020 **Fax:** 020 8962 8689
Email: tom@thinkpublishing.co.uk
Web site: http://www.girlguiding.org.uk
Publisher: Girl Guiding UK
Frequency: Monthly
Cover Price: £2.00
Free to qualifying individuals
Circulation: 80,000 (Publisher's Statement)
Usual Pagination: 48
Editor: Tracy Tran
Summary of Content: Magazine covering news, features and activity ideas.
Readership/Target Audience: Read by adult members of Girlguiding UK.
ADVERTISING RATES:
Full Page Colour £2500.00
Agency Commission: 10%
Mechanical Data: Page Width: 190mm, Type Area: 259 x 190mm, Bleed Size: 303 x 213mm, Trim Size: 297 x 210mm, Col Length: 259mm, Film: Digital
CONSUMER: RECREATION & LEISURE: Children & Youth

THE GUILDFORD MAGAZINE
1638122U80C-5071

Editorial Address: Unit A4, Kingsway Business Park, Oldfield Road, HAMPTON, TW12 2HD **Tel:** 020 8939 5600
Fax: 020 8939 5610
Email: maggie@sheengate.co.uk
Advertising Address: As above.
Email: sarah@sheengate.co.uk
Web site: http://www.guildfordmagazine.co.uk
Publisher: Sheengate Publishing Ltd
Frequency: Monthly
Cover Price: Free
Circulation: 43,000 (Publisher's Statement)
Usual Pagination: 64
Editor: Maggie Walsh; **Advertising Manager:** Leon Cook
Summary of Content: Lifestyle magazine containing local interest articles and interviews as well as features on fashion, theatre, health, education, shopping and property.
Readership/Target Audience: Aimed at households in Guildford and surrounding areas.
ADVERTISING RATES:
Full Page Colour £1155.00
Agency Commission: 10%
Mechanical Data: Type Area: 270 x 180mm, Bleed Size: 307 x 220mm, Trim Size: 297 x 210mm, Col Length: 270mm, Page Width: 180mm, Film: Digital
Copy instructions: Copy Date: 1 week prior to publication date
CONSUMER: RURAL & REGIONAL INTEREST: Regional Interest English Counties

GUITAR & BASS
46152U76D-325

Formerly: The Guitar Magazine
Editorial Address: Leon House, 233 High Street, CROYDON, CR9 1HZ **Tel:** 020 8726 8000
Fax: 020 8726 8397
Email: guitar@ipcmedia.com
Advertising Address: As above. **Fax:** 020 8726 8399
Email: gemma_bown@ipcmedia.com
Publisher: IPC Inspire
Frequency: 13 issues yearly
Cover Price: £3.95
Annual Sub.: £39.78
Circulation: 11,994 (ABC 01/01/2008 to 31/12/2008)
Usual Pagination: 132
Editor: John Callaghan; **Publisher:** Richard Marcroft
Summary of Content: Magazine featuring equipment reviews, personality interviews, printed music and technical articles.
Readership/Target Audience: Read by practising guitarists.
ADVERTISING RATES:
Full Page Colour £895.00
Agency Commission: 10%

Mechanical Data: Type Area: 266 x 196mm, Col Length: 266mm, Page Width: 196mm, Film: Digital, Bleed Size: 303 x 216mm, Trim Size: 297 x 210mm
Copy instructions: Copy Date: 4 weeks prior to publication date
Average advertising content per issue: 65%
CONSUMER: MUSIC & PERFORMING ARTS: Music

GUITAR BUYER
718205U76D-322

Editorial Address: Alexander House, Forehill, ELY, CB7 4ZA
Tel: 01353 665577 **Fax:** 01353 662489
Email: info@mbmediagroup.co.uk
Advertising Address: As above.
Email: helen@mbmediagroup.co.uk
ISSN: 1474-1636
Publisher: MB Media Ltd
Date Established: 2001
Frequency: Monthly
Cover Price: £3.20
Circulation: 22,000 (Publisher's Statement)
Usual Pagination: 140
Editor: David Greeves; **Advertising Manager:** Helen Bavester
Summary of Content: Magazine focussing on equipment reviews, interviews and news.
Readership/Target Audience: Aimed at guitar players of all ages.
ADVERTISING RATES:
Full Page Mono £600.00
Full Page Colour £800.00
Agency Commission: 10%
Mechanical Data: Page Width: 190mm, Trim Size: 297 x 210mm, Type Area: 277 x 190mm, Col Length: 277mm, Bleed Size: 303 x 216mm, Film: Digital
Copy instructions: Copy Date: 3 weeks prior to publication date
Average advertising content per issue: 40%
CONSUMER: MUSIC & PERFORMING ARTS: Music

GUITAR TECHNIQUES
46233U76E-133

Editorial Address: 30 Monmouth Street, BATH, BA1 2BW
Tel: 01225 442244 **Fax:** 01225 732275
Email: guitar.tech@futurenet.com
Advertising Address: As above. **Fax:** 01225 732396
Email: adrian.major@futurenet.co.uk
Web site: http://www.guitartechniques.com
Publisher: Future Publishing Ltd
Date Established: 1994
Frequency: 13 issues yearly
Cover Price: £4.99
Annual Sub.: £46.97
Circulation: 22,387 (ABC 01/01/2008 to 31/12/2008)
Usual Pagination: 100
Editor: Neville Marten; **Advertising Director:** Adrian Major
Summary of Content: Magazine focusing on guitar learning techniques, featuring master classes from expert tutors and step-by-step guides. Includes CD and album reviews and long transcriptions.
Readership/Target Audience: Aimed at guitarists who want to improve their technique.
ADVERTISING RATES:
Full Page Colour £1095.00
Agency Commission: 10%
Mechanical Data: Page Width: 190mm, Film: Digital, Type Area: 270 x 190mm, Trim Size: 297 x 210mm, Bleed Size: 303 x 216mm, Col Length: 270mm
CONSUMER: MUSIC & PERFORMING ARTS: Pop Music

GUITARIST
46153U76D-24

Editorial Address: 30 Monmouth Street, BATH, BA1 2BW
Tel: 01225 442244
Email: guitarist@futurenet.com
Advertising Address: As above. **Fax:** 01225 822793
Email: adrian.major@futurenet.co.uk
Web site: http://www.guitarist.co.uk
Publisher: Future Publishing Ltd
Date Established: 1984
Frequency: 13 issues yearly
Cover Price: £5.25
Circulation: 31,917 (ABC 01/01/2008 to 31/12/2008)
Usual Pagination: 196
Editor: Owen Bailey; **Advertising Director:** Adrian Major
Summary of Content: Magazine covering all aspects of acoustic, bass and electric guitars. Includes product news, reviews, interviews and techniques.
Readership/Target Audience: Read by guitarists and bass players.
ADVERTISING RATES:
Full Page Colour £1690.00
Agency Commission: 10%
Mechanical Data: Page Width: 190mm, Film: Digital, Type Area: 270 x 190mm, Trim Size: 297 x 210mm, Bleed Size: 303 x 216mm, Col Length: 270mm
CONSUMER: MUSIC & PERFORMING ARTS: Music

GUJARAT SAMACHAR
48303U90-57

Editorial Address: Unit 2, Karma Yoga House, 12 Hoxton Market, LONDON, N1 6HW **Tel:** 020 7749 4082
Fax: 020 7749 4081
Email: gseditorial@abplgroup.com
Advertising Address: 12 Hoxton Market, LONDON, N1 6HG
Tel: 020 7749 4082 **Fax:** 020 7749 4081
Email: urja@abplgroup.com
Web site: http://www.abplgroup.com
Publisher: Asian Business Publications Ltd
Date Established: 1972
Frequency: Weekly
Cover Price: £0.80
Annual Sub.: £25.00
Circulation: 27,000 (Publisher's Statement)
Usual Pagination: 32
Editor: Jyotsana Shah; **Executive Editor:** Kokila Patel; **Managing Director:** Chandrakant Patel; **Managing Editor:** Jyotsana Shah; **Publisher:** Chandrakant Patel
Summary of Content: Publication covering news from India for members of the Gujarat community. Includes features on cooking, beauty, health, finance and property.
Language(s): Gujarati
Readership/Target Audience: Read by students, teachers, professionals and those who are involved in charitable and community organisations.
ADVERTISING RATES:
SCC £14.50
Agency Commission: 10%
Mechanical Data: Type Area: 360 x 253mm, Col Length: 360mm, Film: Digital, Page Width: 253mm
Copy instructions: Copy Date: Friday 6pm prior to publication date
Average advertising content per issue: 60%
CONSUMER: ETHNIC

GULF LIFE
1810843U89D-529

Editorial Address: 141-143 Shoreditch High Street, LONDON, E1 6JE **Tel:** 020 7613 8777 **Fax:** 020 7613 6985
Email: andrew.humphreys@ink-publishing.com
Advertising Address: As above. **Fax:** 020 7613 8778
Email: anthony.azoury@ink-publishing.com
Web site: http://www.gulf-life.com
Publisher: Ink Publishing
Date Established: 2007
Frequency: Monthly
Cover Price: Free
Circulation: 600,000 (Publisher's Statement)
Usual Pagination: 120
Editor: Andrew Humphreys; **Advertising Manager:** Anthony Azoury
Summary of Content: Lifestyle and destinations magazine focusing on the Gulf, the Middle East and India.
Language(s): Arabic; English
Readership/Target Audience: Aimed at passengers on Gulf Air flights.
ADVERTISING RATES:
Full Page Colour $9999.00
Agency Commission: 10%
Mechanical Data: Type Area: 245 x 178mm, Bleed Size: 276 x 211mm, Trim Size: 270 x 205mm, Col Length: 245mm, Page Width: 178mm, Film: Digital
CONSUMER: HOLIDAYS & TRAVEL: In-Flight Magazines

GUN MART
45859U75F-40

Editorial Address: 21-23 Phoenix Court, Hawkins Road, COLCHESTER, CO2 8JY **Tel:** 01702 479884
Fax: 01702 479884
Email: pat_farey@tiscali.co.uk
Advertising Address: 2nd Floor, Ewer House, 44-46 Crouch Street, COLCHESTER, CO3 3HH **Tel:** 01206 506247
Fax: 01206 500226
Email: vanessa@mspublications.co.uk
Publisher: Aceville Publications Ltd
Frequency: Monthly
Cover Price: £3.30
Circulation: 40,000 (Publisher's Statement)
Usual Pagination: 350
Editor: Pat Farey; **Advertising Manager:** Vanessa Green; **Publisher:** Anthony Phelps
Summary of Content: Magazine covering all areas of guns, shooting and accessories.
Readership/Target Audience: Read by those looking to purchase a gun or with an interest in guns.
ADVERTISING RATES:
Full Page Mono £400.00
Full Page Colour £550.00
Agency Commission: 10%
Mechanical Data: Col Length: 270mm, No. of Columns (Display): 4, Type Area: 270 x 190mm, Bleed Size: 313 x 220mm, Trim Size: 303 x 210mm, Film: Digital, Page Width: 190mm
Copy instructions: Copy Date: 3 weeks prior to publication date
Average advertising content per issue: 75%
CONSUMER: SPORT: Shooting

THE GUY FOX FAMILY NEWSLETTER
1860047U80B-440

Editorial Address: Unit LF.B4, The Leathermarket, Weston Street, LONDON, SE1 3HN **Tel:** 020 7407 4785
Fax: 020 7407 4785
Email: media@guyfox.org.uk
Web site: http://www.guyfox.org.uk
Publisher: Guy Fox History Project Limited
Date Established: 2007
Frequency: 3 issues yearly - Published in March, July and October
Cover Price: Free
Circulation: 10,000 (Publisher's Statement)
Usual Pagination: 8
Summary of Content: Newsletter featuring family friendly events and activities in London. Includes information from museums, galleries and organisations detailing activities, events and workshops for children and families.
Readership/Target Audience: Aimed at families across London.
CONSUMER: RURAL & REGIONAL INTEREST: Regional Interest Greater London

GVZ
1892610U74F-777

Editorial Address: Starting Points, 16 Pickering Road, BARKING, IG11 8PG **Tel:** 020 3288 2269
Email: info@gvzmag.com
Web site: http://www.gvzmag.com
Publisher: GVZ Ltd
Frequency: Monthly
Cover Price: Free
Circulation: 5,000 (Publisher's Statement)
Editor: Ryan Downes
Summary of Content: Magazine covering lifestyle and inspirational messages.
Readership/Target Audience: Aimed at readers aged between 16 and 21 years old.
CONSUMER: WOMEN'S INTEREST CONSUMER MAGAZINES: Teenage

GYBE
45944U75M-350

Editorial Address: Sheridan, Rutland Gardens, Bursledon, SOUTHAMPTON, SO31 8FZ **Tel:** 023 8040 2194
Email: eddie@eddiemays.com
Advertising Address: As above.
Email: eddie@eddiemays.com
Web site: http://www.laser.org.uk
Publisher: Eddie Mays
Date Established: 1993
Frequency: Quarterly
Free to qualifying individuals
Circulation: 2,500 (Publisher's Statement)
Usual Pagination: 24
Editor: Eddie Mays; **Managing Director:** Eddie Mays; **Advertising Manager:** Eddie Mays; **Publisher:** Eddie Mays
Summary of Content: Official journal of the UK Laser Association. Covers technical and practical features, sailing tips, reports, news and members' information.
Readership/Target Audience: Read by all active Laser sailors who are members of the UK Laser Association.
ADVERTISING RATES:
Full Page Colour £200.00
Agency Commission: 10%
Mechanical Data: Trim Size: 297 x 210mm, Film: Digital, No. of Columns (Display): 4
Copy instructions: Copy Date: 4 weeks prior to publication date
Average advertising content per issue: 25%
CONSUMER: SPORT: Water Sports

THE GYMNAST
45899U75J-320

Editorial Address: Ford Hall, Lilleshall National Sports Centre, NEWPORT, TF10 9NB **Tel:** 0845 129 7129
Fax: 0845 124 9089
Email: mark.young@british-gymnastics.org
Advertising Address: Cabbell Ltd, Woodman Works, 204 Durnsford Road, LONDON, SW19 8DR **Tel:** 020 8971 8450
Fax: 020 8971 8480
Email: george.miller@cabbell.co.uk
Web site: http://www.british-gymnastics.org
Publisher: British Amateur Gymnastics Association
Date Established: 1906
Frequency: 10 issues yearly
Annual Sub.: £30.00
Circulation: 20,949 (Publisher's Statement)
Usual Pagination: 40
Editor: Mark Young; **Advertising Manager:** George Miller
Summary of Content: Magazine covering major international, national and regional events and championships.
Readership/Target Audience: Read by judges, coaches, parents and participants.
ADVERTISING RATES:
Full Page Colour £1850.00
Agency Commission: 10%

Mechanical Data: Page Width: 205mm, Film: Digital, Trim Size: 300 x 230mm, Type Area: 280 x 205mm, Bleed Size: 306 x 236mm, Col Length: 280mm
CONSUMER: SPORT: Athletics

H2B JOURNAL
1820089U80C-5431

Editorial Address: 1 Cottage Road, LEEDS, LS6 4DD
Tel: 0113 274 1308
Email: info@h2bjournal.co.uk
Advertising Address: As above.
Email: joanne@h2bjournal.co.uk
Web site: http://www.h2bjournal.co.uk
Publisher: H2B Journal Ltd
Frequency: 5 issues yearly
Cover Price: Free
Circulation: 35,000 (Publisher's Statement)
Usual Pagination: 164
Editor: Joanne Brook-Smith; **Advertising Manager:** Joanne Brook-Smith
Summary of Content: Magazine covering local business, fashion, hair, beauty, homes, motors, property, restaurants, sport, travel and weddings.
Readership/Target Audience: Aimed at those 25 to 55 years old with a high disposable income.
ADVERTISING RATES:
Full Page Mono £1095.00
Full Page Colour £1095.00
Agency Commission: 10%
Mechanical Data: Bleed Size: 303 x 216mm, Trim Size: 297 x 210mm, Film: Digital
Copy instructions: Copy Date: 3 weeks prior to publication date
Average advertising content per issue: 40%
CONSUMER: RURAL & REGIONAL INTEREST: Regional Interest English Counties

H & E NATURISM
1660040U74Q-1235

Editorial Address: Burlington Court, Carlisle Street, GOOLE, DN14 5EG **Tel:** 01405 760298 **Fax:** 01405 763815
Email: editor@henaturist.net
Advertising Address: As above.
Email: sylvia-smith@btconnect.com
Web site: http://www.henaturist.net
Publisher: New Freedom Publications Ltd
Date Established: 1899
Frequency: Monthly
Cover Price: £3.95
Annual Sub.: £41.00
Circulation: 20,000 (Publisher's Statement)
Usual Pagination: 84
Editor: Sam Hawcroft; **Advertising Manager:** Sylvia Smith
Summary of Content: Magazine covering naturist travel, arts, naturist resorts, news, clubs and swims.
Readership/Target Audience: Aimed at naturists.
ADVERTISING RATES:
Full Page Colour £500.00
SCC £32.00
Agency Commission: 10%
Mechanical Data: Type Area: 262 x 180mm, Col Length: 262mm, Page Width: 180mm, Film: Digital
Copy instructions: Copy Date: 4 weeks prior to publication date
CONSUMER: WOMEN'S INTEREST CONSUMER MAGAZINES: Lifestyle

H & F NEWS
1641951U80B-405

Formerly: hfm Hammersmith & Fulham Magazine
Editorial Address: Room 6, Hammersmith Town Hall, King Street, LONDON, W6 9JU **Tel:** 020 8753 6597
Fax: 020 8741 2685
Email: handfnews@lbhf.gov.uk
Advertising Address: As above.
Email: handfnews@lbhf.gov.uk
Web site: http://www.lbhf.gov.uk
Publisher: Archant London
Date Established: 2006
Frequency: 26 issues yearly
Cover Price: Free
Circulation: 90,000 (Print Run)
Usual Pagination: 24
Editor: Geoff Cowart
Summary of Content: Magazine covering local issues in the context of London-wide and local news, schools, local police issues, NHS, local jobs, events and a what's on section.
Readership/Target Audience: Aimed at local residents, businesses and visitors to the London Borough of Hammersmith and Fulham.
ADVERTISING RATES:
Full Page Mono £2000.00
Full Page Colour £2000.00
Agency Commission: 10%
Mechanical Data: Trim Size: 365 x 270mm
CONSUMER: RURAL & REGIONAL INTEREST: Regional Interest Greater London

H&K
1914465U91D-993
Editorial Address: 1 Chartwell Lodge, 9 Brackley Road, BECKENHAM, BR3 1SW **Tel:** 020 8650 3645
Publisher: Lighthouse Publishing
Date Established: 2009
Cover Price: Free
Circulation: 250,000 (Publisher's Statement)
Editor: Richard Allen
Summary of Content: Magazine covering children's fashion.
Readership/Target Audience: Aimed at parents with an interest in Children's fashion.
CONSUMER: RECREATION & LEISURE: Children & Youth

HACKNEY TODAY
1637596U80B-394
Editorial Address: Communications, 2 Hillman Street, LONDON, E8 1FB **Tel:** 020 8356 3275 **Fax:** 020 8356 3118
Email: htnews@hackney.gov.uk
Advertising Address: Annexe, 3rd Floor, 2 Hillman Street, LONDON, E8 1EA **Tel:** 020 8356 3445 **Fax:** 020 8356 3209
Email: david.roberts@hackney.gov.uk
Web site: http://www.hackney.gov.uk/hackneytoday
Publisher: London Borough of Hackney
Frequency: 24 issues yearly
Cover Price: Free
Circulation: 108,000 (Publisher's Statement)
Usual Pagination: 32
Editor: Jane Young; **Advertising Manager:** David Roberts
Summary of Content: Newspaper covering council and community news with a pull out listings guide.
Readership/Target Audience: Aimed at those living and working in the London Borough of Hackney.
ADVERTISING RATES:
Full Page Colour £1980.00
SCC £12.00
Agency Commission: 10%
Mechanical Data: Film: Digital, Trim Size: 297 x 210mm, Type Area: 337 x 271mm, Col Length: 337mm, Page Width: 271mm
Copy instructions: Copy Date: 1 week prior to publication date
Average advertising content per issue: 25%
CONSUMER: RURAL & REGIONAL INTEREST: Regional Interest Greater London

HAIR
45462U74H-90
Editorial Address: Blue Fin Building, 110 Southwark Street, LONDON, SE1 0SU **Tel:** 020 3148 7274
Email: jane_moscardini@ipcmedia.com
Advertising Address: As above. **Tel:** 020 3148 5000
Email: laura_makin@ipcmedia.com
Web site: http://www.ipcmedia.com
ISSN: 0143-7968
Publisher: IPC Media Ltd
Frequency: Monthly
Cover Price: £2.99
Annual Sub.: £24.80
Circulation: 69,266 (ABC 01/01/2008 to 31/12/2008)
Usual Pagination: 132
Editor: Jane Moscardini
Summary of Content: Magazine covering hair and beauty advice.
Readership/Target Audience: Aimed at women between 18 and 30 years old.
ADVERTISING RATES:
Full Page Colour £4350.00
Mechanical Data: Film: Digital
CONSUMER: WOMEN'S INTEREST CONSUMER MAGAZINES: Hair & Beauty

HAIR & BEAUTY INSPIRATIONS
1655078U74H-305
Editorial Address: 211 Old Street, LONDON, EC1V 9NR
Tel: 020 7608 6300
Email: laura@style-media.net
Advertising Address: As above. **Tel:** 020 7436 9766
Fax: 020 7436 9957
Web site: http://www.scissorhandsmedia.com/Hair_inspirations.aspx
Publisher: Scissorhands Media
Frequency: 6 issues yearly
Cover Price: £1.95
Circulation: 22,482 (ABC 01/01/2009 to 30/06/2009)
Usual Pagination: 200
Editor: Laura Curtis; **Editor-in-Chief:** Tim Frisby;
Advertising Manager: Robert Hough
Summary of Content: Magazine covering hair and beauty trends.
Readership/Target Audience: Aimed at women aged 16 to 40 years old.
ADVERTISING RATES:
Full Page Mono £1400.00
Full Page Colour £1750.00

Mechanical Data: Bleed Size: 231 x 176mm, Trim Size: 225 x 170mm, Film: Digital
CONSUMER: WOMEN'S INTEREST CONSUMER MAGAZINES: Hair & Beauty

HAIR IDEAS
1616516U74H-302
Editorial Address: 9th Floor, Tower House, Fairfax Street, BRISTOL, BS1 3BN **Tel:** 0117 927 9009 **Fax:** 0117 934 9008
Email: michelletiernan@originpublishing.co.uk
Advertising Address: As above.
Email: tyronejones@originpublishing.co.uk
Web site: http://www.hairideasmagazine.co.uk
Publisher: Origin Publishing Ltd
Date Established: 2003
Frequency: Monthly
Cover Price: £1.99
Circulation: 71,864 (ABC 01/01/2009 to 30/06/2009)
Usual Pagination: 196
Editor: Michelle Tiernan; **Publisher:** Alison Worthington
Summary of Content: Magazine featuring hairstyles, hair advice, product tests and make-overs.
Readership/Target Audience: Aimed at women between 18 and 40 years old.
ADVERTISING RATES:
Full Page Colour £2011.00
Agency Commission: 10%
Mechanical Data: Type Area: 195 x 133mm, Bleed Size: 216 x 154mm, Trim Size: 210 x 148mm, Col Length: 195mm, Page Width: 133mm, Film: Digital
CONSUMER: WOMEN'S INTEREST CONSUMER MAGAZINES: Hair & Beauty

HAIRFLAIR & BEAUTY
45464U74H-120
Formerly: Hairflair
Editorial Address: Freebournes House, Freebournes Road, WITHAM, CM8 3US **Tel:** 01376 534504 **Fax:** 01376 534546
Email: claire.muffett-reece@hairmags.co.uk
Advertising Address: As above. **Tel:** 01376 534527
Fax: 01376 534531
Email: hollie.bennett@freebournes.com
ISSN: 0954-2787
Publisher: Haversham Publications Ltd
Date Established: 1983
Frequency: 6 issues yearly
Cover Price: £2.50
Annual Sub.: £23.95
Circulation: 9,770 (Publisher's Statement)
Usual Pagination: 135
Editor: Ruth Page
Summary of Content: Magazine with articles on hairstyles and beauty, with competitions, make-overs and new products also featured.
Readership/Target Audience: Aimed at women between 15 and 40 years old.
ADVERTISING RATES:
Full Page Colour £1300.00
Agency Commission: 10%
Mechanical Data: Type Area: 220 x 150mm, Bleed Size: 248 x 178mm, Trim Size: 240x 170mm, Page Width: 150mm, Film: Digital, Col Length: 220mm
CONSUMER: WOMEN'S INTEREST CONSUMER MAGAZINES: Hair & Beauty

HAIRSTYLES ONLY
45467U74H-180
Editorial Address: Freebournes House, Freebournes Road, WITHAM, CM8 3US **Tel:** 01376 534504 **Fax:** 01376 534546
Email: claire.muffett-reece@hairmags.co.uk
Advertising Address: As above. **Tel:** 01376 534519
Fax: 01376 534531
Email: holly.bennett@freebournes.co.uk
ISSN: 1461-4901
Publisher: Haversham Publications Ltd
Date Established: 1998
Frequency: 8 issues yearly
Cover Price: £2.00
Annual Sub.: £15.95
Circulation: 111,993 (ABC 01/01/2009 to 30/06/2009)
Usual Pagination: 131
Editor: Claire Muffett-Reece; **Group Editor:** Ruth Page
Summary of Content: Magazine containing articles and photographs of modern hairstyles.
Language(s): Dutch; English; German; Spanish
Readership/Target Audience: Aimed at women between 15 and 38 years old.
ADVERTISING RATES:
Full Page Colour £1500.00
Agency Commission: 10%
Mechanical Data: Trim Size: 180 x 128mm, Film: Digital
CONSUMER: WOMEN'S INTEREST CONSUMER MAGAZINES: Hair & Beauty

HALE & BOWDON MAGAZINE
1799197U80C-5395
Editorial Address: St. James House, 676 Wilmslow Road, MANCHESTER, M20 2DM **Tel:** 0161 445 2883
Fax: 0161 445 2881
Email: beverley@haleandbowdonmagazine.co.uk
Advertising Address: As above.
Email: claire@didsburymagazine.com
Web site: http://www.haleandbowdonmagazine.co.uk
Publisher: Salutions Ltd
Date Established: 2005
Frequency: 10 issues yearly
Cover Price: Free
Circulation: 18,000 (Publisher's Statement)
Usual Pagination: 80
Editor: Beverley Uddin-Khandakar
Summary of Content: Magazine covering local news and events as well as lifestyle, fashion, health and beauty, men's and women's fashion, property, education, business, motors and food and drink.
Readership/Target Audience: Aimed at residents and businesses in Hale and Bowdon.
ADVERTISING RATES:
Full Page Colour £995.00
Agency Commission: 10%
Mechanical Data: Bleed Size: 281 x 216mm, Trim Size: 275 x 210mm, Film: Digital
Copy instructions: Copy Date: 2 weeks prior to publication date
Average advertising content per issue: 45%
CONSUMER: RURAL & REGIONAL INTEREST: Regional Interest English Counties

HALESWORTH & SOUTHWOLD COMMUNITY NEWS
44339U80C-5498
Formerly: Halesworth Community News
Editorial Address: 27 Norwich Road, HALESWORTH, IP19 8BX **Tel:** 01986 834212 **Fax:** 01986 834225
Email: hcn@micropress.co.uk
Advertising Address: As above.
Email: hcn@micropress.co.uk
Publisher: Micropress
Date Established: 1970
Frequency: Monthly - Published on the 1st Friday of the month
Cover Price: Free
Circulation: 5,500 (Publisher's Statement)
Usual Pagination: 28
Editor: Carolyn Clarke; **Advertising Manager:** Carolyn Clarke
ADVERTISING RATES:
Full Page Mono £275.00
SCC £1.80
Mechanical Data: No. of Columns (Display): 7, Page Width: 267mm, Col Length: 400mm, Col Widths (Display): 35mm, Type Area: 400 x 267mm, Film: Digital
Copy instructions: Copy Date: 10 days prior to publication date
Average advertising content per issue: 70%
CONSUMER: RURAL & REGIONAL INTEREST: Regional Interest English Counties

HALLAM NEWS
47718U87-2050
Editorial Address: PO Box 8455, NEWARK, NG23 5WX
Tel: 01636 525607
Email: johnclawson@xln.co.uk
Advertising Address: As above.
Email: johnclawson@xln.co.uk
Publisher: Bellcourt Limited
Frequency: Monthly
Cover Price: Free
Circulation: 11,000 (Publisher's Statement)
Editor: John Clawson; **Managing Director:** John Clawson;
Advertising Manager: John Clawson
Summary of Content: Newspaper covering religious topics, events, news and opinion.
Readership/Target Audience: Aimed at Roman Catholics churchgoers within the Roman Catholic Diocese of Hallam.
ADVERTISING: Rates on application
CONSUMER: RELIGIOUS

HAMODIA
47719U87-104
Editorial Address: 113 Fairview Road, LONDON, N15 6TS
Tel: 020 8442 7777 **Fax:** 020 8442 7778
Email: editor@hamodia.co.uk
Advertising Address: As above.
Email: advertising@hamodia.co.uk
Web site: http://www.hamodia.co.uk
Publisher: Hamodia
Frequency: Weekly
Cover Price: £1.00
Circulation: 10,000 (Publisher's Statement)
Editor: Y. Cymerman; **Advertising Manager:** David Khan
Summary of Content: Jewish orthodox newspaper covering news from Britain, America and Israel.

Consumer Magazines

Readership/Target Audience: Aimed at the Jewish orthodox community.
ADVERTISING RATES:
Full Page Mono £800.00
Full Page Colour £1200.00
Agency Commission: 10%
Mechanical Data: Type Area: 350 x 250mm, Trim Size: 420 x 297mm, No. of Columns (Display): 5, Col Widths (Display): 46mm, Film: Digital, Col Length: 350mm, Page Width: 250mm
Copy instructions: Copy Date: Monday prior to publication date
CONSUMER: RELIGIOUS

HAMPSHIRE LIFE
1657865U80C-5153
Editorial Address: 28 Teville Road, WORTHING, BN11 1UG **Tel:** 01903 703730
Advertising Address: As above.
Web site: http://www.hampshire-life.co.uk
Publisher: Archant South East
Frequency: Monthly
Cover Price: £2.75
Editor: Claire Pitcher
Summary of Content: Magazine covering lifestyle, food, fashion, local issues, property, interiors, entertainment and events.
Readership/Target Audience: Aimed at residents and visitors to Hampshire.
CONSUMER: RURAL & REGIONAL INTEREST: Regional Interest English Counties

HAMPSHIRE SOCIETY MAGAZINE & WINCHESTER SOCIETY
626550U80C-5036
Editorial Address: Newspaper House, Test Lane, Redbridge, SOUTHAMPTON, SO16 9JX **Tel:** 023 8042 4488
Fax: 023 8042 4762
Email: hampshire.society@dailyecho.co.uk
Advertising Address: As above. **Tel:** 023 8042 4777
Fax: 023 8042 4928
Email: linda.markham@dailyecho.co.uk
Web site: http://www.hampshiresociety.co.uk
Publisher: Newsquest (Media Group) Ltd
Date Established: 1999
Frequency: Monthly
Cover Price: £1.95
Free to qualifying individuals
Circulation: 29,000 (Publisher's Statement)
Usual Pagination: 116
Editor: Sara Mills
Summary of Content: Lifestyle magazine covering travel, fashion, home and garden, eating out, property and local events.
Readership/Target Audience: Aimed at affluent people aged between 35 and 60 years old living in Hampshire.
ADVERTISING RATES:
Full Page Colour £540.00
Agency Commission: 10%
Mechanical Data: Type Area: 267 x 190mm, Bleed Size: 307 x 220mm, Col Length: 267mm, Page Width: 190mm, Film: Digital, Trim Size: 297 x 210mm
Copy instructions: Copy Date: 12th of the month prior to publication date
Average advertising content per issue: 40%
CONSUMER: RURAL & REGIONAL INTEREST: Regional Interest English Counties

HAMPSHIRE THE COUNTY MAGAZINE
46913U80C-1660
Formerly: Hampshire County Magazine
Editorial Address: Jesses Farm, Snow Hill, Dinton, SALISBURY, SP3 5HN **Tel:** 01722 716996
Email: geoffrey.w@markallengroup.co.uk
Advertising Address: As above. **Fax:** 01722 716926
Email: adam.c@markallengroup.co.uk
Publisher: A & D Media Ltd
Date Established: 1960
Frequency: Monthly
Cover Price: £2.50
Annual Sub.: £38.00
Circulation: 9,000 (Publisher's Statement)
Usual Pagination: 76
Editor: Geoffrey Williams; **Advertising Manager:** Adam Costigan; **Publisher:** Mark Allen
Summary of Content: Magazine containing current and historical county articles. Series include Made in Hampshire, Past in the Present, Hampshire Heroes, Hampshire Interview, Island Scene.
Readership/Target Audience: Aimed at those interested in the history and current interests of Hampshire and the surrounding areas.
ADVERTISING RATES:
Full Page Mono £500.00
Full Page Colour £895.00
Agency Commission: 10%
Mechanical Data: Bleed Size: 303 x 216mm, Film: Digital

Copy instructions: Copy Date: 10th of the month prior to publication date
Average advertising content per issue: 30%
CONSUMER: RURAL & REGIONAL INTEREST: Regional Interest English Counties

HAPPY FAMILIES
1793920U74C-863
Editorial Address: Orchardton Hall, Auchencairn, CASTLE DOUGLAS, DG7 1QL **Tel:** 0845 658 8329
Email: daveb@happyfam.co.uk
Advertising Address: As above. **Tel:** 0845 130 6249
Email: susan@happyfamiliesonline.com
Web site: http://www.happyfamiliesonline.com
Publisher: Brave New World International Ltd
Date Established: 2006
Frequency: Quarterly
Cover Price: £0.50
Free to qualifying individuals
Circulation: 30,000 (Publisher's Statement)
Usual Pagination: 32
Editor: Dave Burbidge; **Advertising Manager:** Susan Foster
Summary of Content: Magazine with general family features as well as books, motoring, films, games, computer games and animals.
Readership/Target Audience: Aimed at all the family and available through health clubs, doctors' surgeries, waiting rooms and selected news agents.
ADVERTISING RATES:
Full Page Colour £1500.00
Agency Commission: 15%
Mechanical Data: Trim Size: 297 x 210mm, Film: Digital
Copy instructions: Copy Date: 3 weeks prior to publication date
Average advertising content per issue: 10%
CONSUMER: WOMEN'S INTEREST CONSUMER MAGAZINES: Home & Family

THE HARDY PLANT
48563U93-40
Editorial Address: 7 Guyzance Village, Guyzance, MORPETH, NE65 9AQ **Tel:** 01386 710317
Fax: 01386 710117
Email: editor@hardy-plant.org.uk
Advertising Address: Media Projects, Hazlebury, Horsted Lane, ISFIELD, TN22 5TX **Tel:** 01825 750784
Fax: 01825 750551
Email: mediap@aol.com
Web site: http://www.hardy-plant.org.uk
ISSN: 0969-1901
Publisher: The Hardy Plant Society
Date Established: 1957
Frequency: Half-yearly - Published in April and October
Free to qualifying individuals
Annual Sub.: £13.00
Circulation: 10,000 (Publisher's Statement)
Usual Pagination: 84
Editor: Pam Ratcliffe; **Advertising Manager:** Patrick Wade
Summary of Content: Journal containing articles relating to hardy perennial plants. Includes gardening techniques, cultivated plant conservation, identification, garden design and theory and book reviews.
Readership/Target Audience: Aimed at active, knowledgeable and enthusiastic gardeners.
ADVERTISING RATES:
Full Page Mono £330.00
Full Page Colour £445.00
Agency Commission: 10%
Mechanical Data: Col Length: 180mm, Type Area: 180 x 125mm, Trim Size: 210 x 148mm, Page Width: 125mm, Film: Digital, Bleed Size: +10mm
Average advertising content per issue: 15%
CONSUMER: GARDENING

HARINGEY PEOPLE
46825U80B-123
Editorial Address: 8th Floor, Riverpark House, 225 High Road, LONDON, N22 8HQ **Tel:** 020 8489 2674
Fax: 020 8888 5484
Email: john.seekings@haringey.gov.uk
Advertising Address: As above. **Tel:** 020 8489 2996
Email: laura.mitchell@haringey.gov.uk
Web site: http://www.haringey.gov.uk
Publisher: Haringey Council Communications and Consultations Unit
Date Established: 1992
Frequency: 10 issues yearly
Cover Price: Free
Circulation: 106,000 (Publisher's Statement)
Usual Pagination: 32
Editor: John Seekings; **Advertising Manager:** Laura Mitchell
Summary of Content: Magazine covering features on major issues affecting the Borough. Also includes articles on entertainment, events and lifestyle.
Readership/Target Audience: Aimed at residents of the London Borough of Haringey.
ADVERTISING RATES:
Full Page Colour £2000.00

Mechanical Data: Bleed Size: 303 x 216mm, Trim Size: 297 x 210mm, Film: Digital, Type Area: 267 x 190mm, Col Length: 267mm, Page Width: 190mm
Copy instructions: Copy Date: 4 weeks prior to publication date
CONSUMER: RURAL & REGIONAL INTEREST: Regional Interest Greater London

HARPENDEN LIFE
1804620U80C-5405
Editorial Address: 6 Albany Chambers, 26 Bridge Road East, WELWYN GARDEN CITY, AL7 1HL **Tel:** 0844 800 8439
Email: rory@fishmediagroup.co.uk
Advertising Address: As above.
Email: rory@fishmediagroup.co.uk
Web site: http://www.life-mags.com
Publisher: Fish Media Group Ltd
Frequency: Monthly
Cover Price: Free
Circulation: 11,000 (Publisher's Statement)
Usual Pagination: 96
Editor: Rory Smith; **Managing Director:** Rory Smith; **Advertising Manager:** Rory Smith; **Publisher:** Patrick Smith
Summary of Content: Magazine covering local news and luxury lifestyle including fashion, health, beauty, home interest, food and drink, property and motors.
Readership/Target Audience: Aimed at affluent households in Harpenden, St. Albans, Radlett, Hadley Wood, Berkhamsted, Amersham, Beaconsfield and Gerrards Cross.
ADVERTISING: Rates on application
Agency Commission: 10%
Mechanical Data: Type Area: 255 x 185mm, Bleed Size: 286 x 216mm, Trim Size: 280 x 210mm, Col Length: 255mm, Page Width: 185mm, Film: Digital
Copy instructions: Copy Date: 1 week prior to publication date
Average advertising content per issue: 50%
Editions:
Amersham Life
Beaconsfield Life
Berkhamsted Life
Gerrards Cross Life
Hadley Wood Life
Radlett Life
St. Albans Life
CONSUMER: RURAL & REGIONAL INTEREST: Regional Interest English Counties

HARPERS 4 LIFE
1667574U74G-258
Editorial Address: Low Lane, Horsforth, LEEDS, LS18 4ER **Tel:** 0117 330 9024
Email: sam@blueskiesfitness.co.uk
Web site: http://www.leisureconnection.co.uk
Publisher: Leisure Connection
Frequency: Monthly
Cover Price: Free
Circulation: 60,000 (Print Run)
Usual Pagination: 4
Editor: Sam Jones
Summary of Content: Magazine covering health, fitness, lifestyle and well-being.
Readership/Target Audience: Aimed at Harpers Gym & Fitness members.
ADVERTISING: No Advertising taken
CONSUMER: WOMEN'S INTEREST CONSUMER MAGAZINES: Slimming & Health

HARPER'S BAZAAR
45228U74B-175
Formerly: Harpers & Queen
Editorial Address: National Magazine House, 72 Broadwick Street, LONDON, W1F 9EP **Tel:** 020 7439 5000
Fax: 020 7439 5506
Email: features@harpersbazaar.co.uk
Advertising Address: As above. **Fax:** 020 7439 5696
Email: antonia.wigan@natmags.co.uk
Web site: http://www.harpersbazaar.co.uk
Publisher: National Magazine Company Ltd
Date Established: 1970
Frequency: Monthly
Cover Price: £3.80
Circulation: 109,646 (ABC 01/01/2009 to 30/06/2009)
Editor: Lucy Yeomans; **Features Editor:** Sara Buys; **Managing Director:** Jessica Burley; **Advertising Director:** Antonia Wigan
Summary of Content: Magazine containing features on health, beauty, fashion, arts, interiors, gardening, food and current issues.
Twitter: https://twitter.com/BazaarUK.
Readership/Target Audience: Aimed at upmarket, discerning adults.
ADVERTISING RATES:
Full Page Colour £11339.00
Agency Commission: 15%
Mechanical Data: Type Area: 270 x 192mm, Trim Size: 290 x 215mm, Bleed Size: 296 x 218mm, Col Length: 270mm, Page Width: 192mm, Film: Digital

Copy instructions: Copy Date: 4 weeks prior to publication date
Average advertising content per issue: 50%
Supplement(s): Bags & Shoes - 1xY, Best Dressed - 1xY, Harpers Abroad - 2xY, Harpers Business - 2xY, Restaurant Supplement - 1xY
CONSUMER: WOMEN'S INTEREST CONSUMER MAGAZINES: Women's Interest - Fashion

---

HARPSICHORD & FORTEPIANO

46154U76D-332

Editorial Address: Scout Bottom Farm, Mytholmroyd, HEBDEN BRIDGE, HX7 5JS **Tel:** 01422 882751
Fax: 01422 886157
Email: hfp@recordermail.demon.co.uk
Advertising Address: As above.
Email: julie.dower@btopenworld.com
Web site: http://www.beedata.com/harp
ISSN: 1463-0036
Publisher: Ruxbury Publications
Date Established: 1973
Frequency: Half-yearly - Published in December and June
Annual Sub.: £18.00
Circulation: 1,200 (Publisher's Statement)
Usual Pagination: 40
Editor: Micaela Schmitz; **Advertising Manager:** Jeremy Burbidge; **Publisher:** Jeremy Burbidge
Summary of Content: Magazine featuring scholarly and informal articles on early keyboard instruments.
Readership/Target Audience: Read by students, historians and those with an interest in early keyboard instruments.
ADVERTISING RATES:
Full Page Mono £250.00
Agency Commission: 10%
Mechanical Data: Page Width: 180mm, Type Area: 264 x 180mm, Col Length: 264mm
CONSUMER: MUSIC & PERFORMING ARTS: Music

THE HARRODS MAGAZINE

754610U74Q-395

Editorial Address: Victory House, 14 Leicester Place, Leicester Square, LONDON, WC2H 7BZ **Tel:** 020 7306 0304
Fax: 020 7306 0314
Email: ffruzza@riverltd.co.uk
Advertising Address: Marketing Department, 7th Floor, Harrods, Knightsbridge, LONDON, SW1X 7XL
Tel: 020 7893 5996 **Fax:** 020 7893 8945
Email: roanne.randell@harrods.com
Publisher: River Publishing Ltd
Date Established: 2002
Frequency: 10 issues yearly
Cover Price: £3.00
Free to qualifying individuals
Circulation: 100,000 (Publisher's Statement)
Editor: Fleur Fruzza; **Managing Editor:** Fleur Fruzza; **Publisher:** Beth Hodder
Summary of Content: Magazine containing features on lifestyle including interiors, food, fashion and beauty.
Readership/Target Audience: Read by Harrods account customers and those shopping in the store.
ADVERTISING RATES:
Full Page Colour £6500.00
Mechanical Data: Film: Digital, Type Area: 277 x 210mm, Col Length: 277mm, Page Width: 210mm, Bleed Size: 303 x 236mm, Trim Size: 297 x 230mm
Copy instructions: Copy Date: 6 weeks prior to publication date
Average advertising content per issue: 40%
CONSUMER: WOMEN'S INTEREST CONSUMER MAGAZINES: Lifestyle

HARROW PEOPLE

46826U80B-123_50

Editorial Address: Communications Unit, M12, London Borough of Harrow, Civic Centre, Station Road, HARROW, HA1 2XF **Tel:** 020 8424 1290 **Fax:** 020 8424 1966
Email: angela.hart@harrow.gov.uk
Advertising Address: As above. **Tel:** 020 8863 5611
Email: angela.hart@harrow.gov.uk
Web site: http://www.harrow.gov.uk
Publisher: Harrow Borough
Frequency: 6 issues yearly
Cover Price: Free
Circulation: 100,000 (Publisher's Statement)
Usual Pagination: 28
Editor: Angela Hart; **Advertising Manager:** Angela Hart
Summary of Content: Magazine covering news, events and local issues.
Readership/Target Audience: Read by residents and visitors in the London Borough of Harrow.
ADVERTISING: Rates on application
CONSUMER: RURAL & REGIONAL INTEREST: Regional Interest Greater London

---

HARVEY NICHOLS EDIT

1743246U74B-719

Editorial Address: 67 Brompton Road, LONDON, SW3 1DB
Tel: 020 7201 8717 **Fax:** 020 7235 9507
Email: neil.holbrook@harveynichols.com
Advertising Address: As above. **Tel:** 020 7201 8552
Email: neil.holbrook@harveynichols.com
Web site: http://www.harveynichols.com
Publisher: Harvey Nichols
Date Established: 2006
Frequency: Half-yearly - Published in February and September
Cover Price: Free
Circulation: 30,000 (Print Run)
Editor: Neil Holbrook; **Advertising Manager:** Neil Holbrook
Summary of Content: Magazine covering women's and men's fashion and accessories.
Readership/Target Audience: Aimed at customers of Harvey Nichols department stores.
ADVERTISING: Rates on application
CONSUMER: WOMEN'S INTEREST CONSUMER MAGAZINES: Women's Interest - Fashion

---

AL HAYAT

42852U90-940

Editorial Address: Kensington Centre, 66 Hammersmith Road, LONDON, W14 8YT **Tel:** 020 7602 9988
Fax: 020 7371 4215
Email: nawal@alhayat.com
Advertising Address: As above. **Fax:** 020 7371 1125
Email: maria@alhayat.com
Web site: http://www.alhayat.com
Publisher: Al Hayat Publishing
Frequency: Daily
Circulation: 88,000 (Publisher's Statement)
Editor: Ghassan Charbel; **Editor-in-Chief:** Ghassan Charbel; **Advertising Manager:** Maria Chrysostomou; **Managing Editor:** Adballah Iskandar
Summary of Content: National newspaper covering national and international news, current affairs, business, culture, the arts and sport.
Language(s): Arabic
ADVERTISING RATES:
Full Page Mono $14560.00
Full Page Colour $17056.00
SCC $41.00
Agency Commission: 35%
Mechanical Data: Film: Digital, No. of Columns (Display): 8, Col Widths (Display): 40mm, Type Area: 520 x 355mm, Col Length: 520mm, Page Width: 355mm
Copy instructions: Copy Date: 3 working days prior to publication date
Average advertising content per issue: 35%
CONSUMER: ETHNIC

HEADLINES

1666110U80E-365

Editorial Address: Council Headquarters, London Road, KILMARNOCK, KA3 7BU **Tel:** 01563 576177
Fax: 01563 576068
Email: caroline.gordon@east-ayrshire.gov.uk
Advertising Address: As above. **Tel:** 01563 576258
Fax: 01563 576500
Email: stephanie.wilson@east-ayrshire.gov.uk
Web site: http://www.east-ayrshire.gov.uk
Publisher: East Ayrshire Council
Date Established: 1997
Frequency: Annual - Published in November
Cover Price: Free
Circulation: 57,000 (Publisher's Statement)
Usual Pagination: 32
Editor: Caroline Gordon; **Advertising Manager:** Stephanie Wilson
Summary of Content: Magazine covering council news, information and services.
Readership/Target Audience: Aimed at residents and businesses in East Ayrshire.
ADVERTISING: Rates on application
CONSUMER: RURAL & REGIONAL INTEREST: Regional Interest Scotland

---

HEALTH & FITNESS FOR CYCLISTS

1895118U77C-955

Editorial Address: Leon House, 233 High Street, CROYDON, CR9 1HZ **Tel:** 020 8726 8462
Email: hannah_reynolds@ipcmedia.com
Web site: http://www.cyclingweekly.co.uk
Publisher: IPC Inspire
Date Established: 2007
Frequency: Quarterly
Cover Price: £5.95
Editor: Hannah Reynolds
Summary of Content: Magazine featuring advice to help cyclists progress at all levels. Includes training tips, equipment and technique advice.
Readership/Target Audience: Aimed at cyclists looking to get fit.
CONSUMER: MOTORING & CYCLING: Cycling

HEALTH & FITNESS MAGAZINE

45977U74G-242

Editorial Address: Swan House, 37-39 High Holborn, LONDON, WC1V 6AA **Tel:** 0845 481 0661
Fax: 0845 481 0662
Email: margaret.bartlett@burdamagazines.co.uk
Advertising Address: As above.
Email: robert.biddiss@burdamagazines.co.uk
Web site: http://www.healthandfitnessonline.co.uk
Publisher: Hubert Burda Media UK
Date Established: 1981
Frequency: Monthly
Cover Price: £2.99
Annual Sub.: £28.60
Circulation: 80,000 (Publisher's Statement)
Usual Pagination: 138
Editor: Mary Comber; **Advertising Manager:** James Warren
Summary of Content: Magazine covering exercise, beauty, nutrition, health and fitness news and competitions.
Readership/Target Audience: Read by health conscious women.
ADVERTISING RATES:
Full Page Colour £3300.00
Agency Commission: 10%
Mechanical Data: Film: Digital, Bleed Size: 308 x 234mm, Trim Size: 300 x 230mm
Copy instructions: Copy Date: 3 weeks prior to publication date
Average advertising content per issue: 40%
CONSUMER: WOMEN'S INTEREST CONSUMER MAGAZINES: Slimming & Health

---

HEALTH & HOMEOPATHY

45419U74G-16

Editorial Address: Hahnemann House, 29 Park Street West, LUTON, LU1 3BE **Tel:** 0870 444 3950 **Fax:** 0870 444 3960
Email: sbuckingham@trusthomeopathy.org
Advertising Address: As above.
Email: sbuckingham@trusthomeopathy.org
Web site: http://www.trusthomeopathy.org
ISSN: 0261-2828
Publisher: British Homeopathic Association
Date Established: 1980
Frequency: Quarterly
Annual Sub.: £25.00
Circulation: 3,500 (Publisher's Statement)
Usual Pagination: 36
Editor: Sarah Buckingham; **Advertising Manager:** Sarah Buckingham
Summary of Content: Magazine of the British Homeopathic Association. Includes news and developments in homeopathy, listings and events.
Readership/Target Audience: Read by the general public and health care professionals in the medical and veterinary fields.
ADVERTISING RATES:
Full Page Colour £290.00
Mechanical Data: Type Area: 266 x 181mm, Film: Digital, Bleed Size: +3mm, Col Length: 266mm, Page Width: 181mm
Copy instructions: Copy Date: 6 weeks prior to publication date
Average advertising content per issue: 25%
CONSUMER: WOMEN'S INTEREST CONSUMER MAGAZINES: Slimming & Health

---

THE HEALTH STORE MAGAZINE

45420U74G-20

Editorial Address: 9 Eustace Road, LONDON, SW6 1JB
Tel: 020 7385 0074 **Fax:** 020 7385 0074
Email: jane@janegarton.com
Advertising Address: Unit 10, Blenheim Park Road, NOTTINGHAM, NG6 8YP. **Tel:** 0115 976 7200
Fax: 0115 976 7290
Email: stuartc@thehealthstore.co.uk
Web site: http://www.thehealthstore.co.uk
Publisher: The Health Store
Date Established: 1990
Frequency: 6 issues yearly
Cover Price: Free
Circulation: 150,000 (Publisher's Statement)
Usual Pagination: 40
Editor: Jane Garton; **Advertising Manager:** Stuart Cook
Summary of Content: Consumer magazine distributed to members of the National Association of Health Stores. Covers diet, nutritional information and natural remedies.
Readership/Target Audience: Aimed at the health-conscious adult.
ADVERTISING RATES:
Full Page Colour £2350.00
Mechanical Data: Type Area: 256 x 180mm, Col Length: 256mm, Page Width: 180mm, Bleed Size: 303 x 216mm, Trim Size: 297 x 210mm, Film: Digital
Copy instructions: Copy Date: 6 weeks prior to publication date
Average advertising content per issue: 30%
CONSUMER: WOMEN'S INTEREST CONSUMER MAGAZINES: Slimming & Health

Consumer Magazines

HEALTHY
45427U74G-25_85

Editorial Address: Victory House, 14 Leicester Place, Leicester Square, LONDON, WC2H 7BZ **Tel:** 020 7306 0304
Fax: 020 7306 0314
Email: hfox@riverltd.co.uk
Advertising Address: As above. **Fax:** 020 7306 0303
Email: acline@riverltd.co.uk
Web site: http://www.healthy-magazine.co.uk
Publisher: River Publishing Ltd
Date Established: 1999
Frequency: 8 issues yearly
Cover Price: £1.50
Circulation: 163,329 (ABC 01/01/2009 to 30/06/2009)
Usual Pagination: 154
Editor: Hannah Fox; **Advertising Manager:** Vicki Scaife
Summary of Content: Magazine focusing on maintaining a healthy lifestyle. Includes articles on vegetarianism, new products and information on alternative therapies and supplements.
Readership/Target Audience: Aimed at men and women interested in health, fitness and natural lifestyle.
ADVERTISING RATES:
Full Page Colour £6500.00
Agency Commission: 10%
Mechanical Data: Film: Digital, Type Area: 255 x 192mm, Trim Size: 275 x 210mm, Bleed Size: 281 x 216mm, Print Process: Web-fed offset litho, Col Length: 255mm, Page Width: 192mm
Copy instructions: Copy Date: 6 weeks prior to publication date
Average advertising content per issue: 40%
CONSUMER: WOMEN'S INTEREST CONSUMER MAGAZINES: Slimming & Health

HEALTHY FOR MEN
639446U86C-727

Formerly: Real Health & Fitness
Editorial Address: Victory House, 14 Leicester Place, Leicester Square, LONDON, WC2H 7BZ **Tel:** 020 7306 0304
Fax: 020 7306 0314
Email: andydarling@ntlworld.com
Advertising Address: As above.
Email: vreis@riverltd.co.uk
Web site: http://www.therivergroup.co.uk
ISSN: 1743-0240
Publisher: River Publishing Ltd
Date Established: 1999
Frequency: 6 issues yearly
Cover Price: £0.75
Circulation: 66,753 (ABC 01/01/2009 to 30/06/2009)
Usual Pagination: 64
Editor: Andy Darling; **Advertising Manager:** Victor Reis
Summary of Content: Health and fitness magazine covering sports nutrition, celebrity sports interviews and work out plans.
Readership/Target Audience: Aimed at those with a serious interest in fitness.
ADVERTISING RATES:
Full Page Colour £2950.00
Agency Commission: 10%
Mechanical Data: Type Area: 255 x 185mm, Col Length: 255mm, Page Width: 185mm, Bleed Size: 281 x 211mm, Trim Size: 275 x 205mm, Film: Digital
Copy instructions: Copy Date: 6 weeks prior to publication date
Average advertising content per issue: 40%
CONSUMER: ADULT & GAY MAGAZINES: Men's Lifestyle Magazines

HEARING CONCERN
48634U94F-400

Editorial Address: 19 Hartfield Road, EASTBOURNE, BN21 2AR **Tel:** 01323 739998
Email: alisa.maykin@fanfarehc.co.uk
Advertising Address: As above. **Tel:** 020 7440 9871
Fax: 020 7440 9872
Email: info@hearingconcern.org.uk
Web site: http://www.hearingconcern.org.uk
ISSN: 1470-238X
Publisher: Hearing Concern
Frequency: Quarterly
Cover Price: £2.75
Free to qualifying individuals
Circulation: 5,000 (Publisher's Statement)
Usual Pagination: 36
Editor: Alicia Makin
Summary of Content: Magazine of the charity Hearing Concern covering information about deaf and hard of hearing issues.
Readership/Target Audience: Read by healthcare professionals, hearing impaired adults, welfare providers and the general public.
ADVERTISING RATES:
Full Page Mono £850.00
Full Page Colour £1050.00
Agency Commission: 10%
Mechanical Data: Type Area: 277 x 190mm, Film: Digital, Col Length: 277mm, Page Width: 190mm
CONSUMER: OTHER CLASSIFICATIONS: Disability

HEART HEALTH
1704266U74G-265

Editorial Address: 14 Fitzhardinge Street, LONDON, W1H 6DH **Tel:** 020 7487 7142
Email: hearthealthmag@bhf.org.uk
Web site: http://www.bhf.org.uk/hearthealthmag
ISSN: 1745-9753
Publisher: PSPRare Publishing
Date Established: 2004
Frequency: 6 issues yearly
Cover Price: Free
Circulation: 125,000 (Publisher's Statement)
Usual Pagination: 24
Editor: Olena Baker
Summary of Content: British Heart Foundation magazine covering all issues surrounding heart care including the latest treatment and medication, insurance and patient services as well as healthy living tips, recipes and readers offers.
Readership/Target Audience: Aimed at those with heart conditions and their carers.
ADVERTISING: No Advertising taken
CONSUMER: WOMEN'S INTEREST CONSUMER MAGAZINES: Slimming & Health

HEAT
46099U76C-205

Editorial Address: Endeavour House, 189 Shaftesbury Avenue, LONDON, WC2H 8JG **Tel:** 020 7437 9011
Fax: 020 7859 8670
Email: heat@bauerconsumer.co.uk
Advertising Address: As above. **Tel:** 020 7295 5000
Fax: 020 7295 5480
Email: marie.morrison@bauermedia.co.uk
Web site: http://www.heatworld.com
ISSN: 1465-6264
Publisher: Bauer Media
Date Established: 1999
Frequency: Weekly - Published on Tuesday
Cover Price: £1.65
Annual Sub.: £79.05
Circulation: 445,192 (ABC 01/01/2009 to 30/06/2009)
Usual Pagination: 130
Editor: Sam Delaney; **Executive Editor:** Lucie Cave;
Managing Director: David Davies; **Managing Editor:** Anita Pyne; **Publisher:** Liz Settle
Summary of Content: Magazine covering celebrity news, TV, radio, films and music.
Twitter: https://twitter.com/heatworld.
Readership/Target Audience: Aimed at those between 18 and 40 years old.
ADVERTISING RATES:
Full Page Colour £21735.00
Agency Commission: 15%
Mechanical Data: Page Width: 194mm, Type Area: 274 x 194mm, Bleed Size: 306 x 226mm, Trim Size: 300 x 220mm, Film: Digital, Col Length: 274mm
Copy instructions: Copy Date: Tuesday prior to publication date
CONSUMER: MUSIC & PERFORMING ARTS: TV & Radio

HEAVY HORSE WORLD
47127U81D-60

Editorial Address: Lindford Cottage, Church Lane, Cocking, MIDHURST, GU29 0HW **Tel:** 01730 812419
Fax: 01730 812419
Email: editor@heavyhorseworld.co.uk
Advertising Address: As above.
Email: editor@heavyhorseworld.co.uk
Web site: http://www.heavyhorseworld.co.uk
ISSN: 0951-2640
Publisher: Diana Zeuna
Date Established: 1987
Frequency: Quarterly
Annual Sub.: £20.00
Circulation: 3,200 (Publisher's Statement)
Usual Pagination: 68
Editor: Diana Zeuner; **Advertising Manager:** Diana Zeuner;
Publisher: Diana Zeuner
Summary of Content: Magazine devoted to news, features and events involving heavy horse breeds.
Readership/Target Audience: Aimed at draught horse owners and heavy horse enthusiasts.
ADVERTISING RATES:
Full Page Mono £230.00
Full Page Colour £300.00
Agency Commission: 10%
Mechanical Data: Page Width: 190mm, Type Area: 250 x 190mm, Bleed Size: 303 x 213mm, Col Length: 250mm, Film: Positive, right reading, emulsion side down. Digital
Copy instructions: Copy Date: 16th of the month prior to publication date
Average advertising content per issue: 35%
CONSUMER: ANIMALS & PETS: Horses & Ponies

HEDGE MAGAZINE
1840355U80B-434

Editorial Address: 4 Tun Yard, Peardon Street, LONDON, SW8 3HT **Tel:** 020 7819 9999 **Fax:** 020 7819 9840
Email: editorial@squaremilemagazine.co.uk
Advertising Address: As above.
Email: editorial@squaremilemagazine.co.uk
Web site: http://www.hedgefundclub.co.uk
Publisher: Square Up Media Ltd
Date Established: 2008
Frequency: 6 issues yearly
Free to qualifying individuals
Circulation: 5,900 (ABC 01/01/2009 to 30/06/2009)
Editor: Christian Smith
Summary of Content: Magazine covering art, lifestyle, property, events and charity.
Readership/Target Audience: Aimed at hedge fund managers in London.
ADVERTISING: Rates on application
CONSUMER: RURAL & REGIONAL INTEREST: Regional Interest Greater London

HELLO!
45634U74Q-407

Editorial Address: Wellington House, 69-71 Upper Ground, LONDON, SE1 9PQ **Tel:** 020 7667 8700 **Fax:** 020 7667 8716
Email: mconway@hellomagazine.com
Advertising Address: As above. **Fax:** 020 7667 8742
Email: advertising@hellomagazine.com
Web site: http://www.hellomagazine.com
Publisher: HELLO! Ltd
Date Established: 1988
Frequency: Weekly
Cover Price: £1.90
Annual Sub.: £94.00
Circulation: 397,634 (ABC 01/01/2009 to 30/06/2009)
Usual Pagination: 124
Editor: Megan Conway; **News Editor:** Thomas Whitaker;
Features Editor: Rosie Nixon; **Managing Director:** Eduardo Sanchez-Junco; **Advertising Manager:** Sara Salarkia;
Advertisement Director: Jacqueline O'Donnell
Summary of Content: Celebrity and news magazine with interviews and photo sessions of famous people, world events and geographic features.
Twitter: https://twitter.com/hellomag.
Readership/Target Audience: Read by ABC1 women aged 25 to 44 years old.
ADVERTISING RATES:
Full Page Colour £18650.00
Mechanical Data: Bleed Size: 336 x 246mm, Trim Size: 330 x 240mm, Film: Digital, Type Area: 298 x 220mm, Col Length: 298mm, Page Width: 220mm
Copy instructions: Copy Date: 3 weeks prior to publication date
CONSUMER: WOMEN'S INTEREST CONSUMER MAGAZINES: Lifestyle

THE HERALD
29259U80C-5054

Formerly: Waterside Herald
Editorial Address: 6 High Street, Hythe, SOUTHAMPTON, SO45 6AH **Tel:** 023 8084 5700 **Fax:** 023 8084 6999
Email: editor@herald-publishing.co.uk
Advertising Address: As above.
Email: editor@herald-publishing.co.uk
Publisher: Herald Publishing
Date Established: 1994
Frequency: 17 issues yearly
Cover Price: Free
Circulation: 10,000 (Publisher's Statement)
Usual Pagination: 80
Editor: Janice Taylor; **Advertising Manager:** Tracy Cole
Summary of Content: Magazine containing local news, community events and local advertising in the Totton, Waterside, Romsey and New Forest East area of Hampshire.
Readership/Target Audience: Aimed at residents and small businesses in the circulation area.
ADVERTISING RATES:
Full Page Mono £170.00
SCC £1.50
Mechanical Data: Trim Size: 297mm x 210mm, Type Area: 270 x 190mm, No. of Columns (Display): 6, Print Process: Offset litho, Col Length: 270mm, Page Width: 190mm, Col Widths (Display): 28mm
Copy instructions: Copy Date: 14 days prior to publication date
Average advertising content per issue: 60%
CONSUMER: RURAL & REGIONAL INTEREST: Regional Interest English Counties

THE HERALD
1832729U80C-5439

Formerly: Markfield & Stanton Herald
Editorial Address: PO Box 8, MARKFIELD, LE67 9ZT
Tel: 01530 244069 **Fax:** 01530 249557
Email: info@markfieldherald.co.uk
Advertising Address: As above.
Email: info@markfieldherald.co.uk
Web site: http://www.markfieldherald.co.uk
Publisher: Builder Magazines
Frequency: 11 issues yearly
Cover Price: Free
Circulation: 4,000 (Publisher's Statement)
Usual Pagination: 36

Editor: Mike Wilkinson; **Features Editor:** Susan Hatton
Summary of Content: Magazine with local community news, parish council minutes, county/borough councillor's reports, forthcoming events, news from local clubs and societies, short story, competitions and jokes.
Readership/Target Audience: Delivered to every home and business in Markfield, Field Head and Stanton-under-Bardon.
ADVERTISING RATES:
Full Page Mono £105.00
Full Page Colour £170.00
Agency Commission: 10%
Mechanical Data: Type Area: 268 x 194mm, Col Length: 268mm, Page Width: 194mm, Film: Digital
Copy instructions: Copy Date: 2 weeks prior to publication date
Average advertising content per issue: 50%
CONSUMER: RURAL & REGIONAL INTEREST: Regional Interest English Counties

HERBS
48564U93-45
Editorial Address: Sulgrave Manor, Sulgrave, BANBURY, OX17 2SD **Tel:** 01295 768899
Email: info@herbsociety.co.uk
Advertising Address: As above.
Email: info@herbsociety.org.uk
Web site: http://www.herbsociety.org.uk
ISSN: 0961-5871
Publisher: The Herb Society
Date Established: 1990
Frequency: Quarterly
Cover Price: £2.50
Circulation: 1,200 (Publisher's Statement)
Usual Pagination: 32
Editor: Barbara Segall; **Advertising Manager:** Felicity Kingston
Summary of Content: Journal of The Herb Society. Covers all aspects of the cultivation and uses of herbs.
Readership/Target Audience: Aimed at members of The Herb Society and those interested in herbs.
ADVERTISING RATES:
Full Page Mono £110.00
Full Page Colour £220.00
Mechanical Data: Film: Digital, Type Area: 257 x 184mm, Col Length: 257mm, Page Width: 184mm
Copy instructions: Copy Date: 6 weeks prior to publication date
Average advertising content per issue: 10%
CONSUMER: GARDENING

HERE & NOW
1820085U80C-5427
Editorial Address: Suites 1-7 Albion Mills, Greengates, BRADFORD, BD10 9TQ **Tel:** 01274 420091
Fax: 01274 347291
Email: editor@hereandnowmagazine.co.uk
Advertising Address: As above.
Email: editor@madpublications.co.uk
Web site: http://www.hereandnowmagazine.co.uk
Publisher: Mad Publications Ltd
Date Established: 2006
Frequency: 6 issues yearly
Free to qualifying individuals
Annual Sub.: £15.00
Circulation: 40,000 (Publisher's Statement)
Usual Pagination: 60
Editor: Angela Riches; **Advertising Manager:** Angela Riches
Summary of Content: Magazine covering local news and events, opinions and people stories as well as health and well being, homes and gardens, style, mums and kids, sport, what's on and local businesses.
Readership/Target Audience: Aimed at affluent homes and businesses in the Leeds, Bradford and Aire Valley regions.
ADVERTISING: Rates on application
Editions:
Here & Now Aire Valley
Here & Now Leeds and Bradford
CONSUMER: RURAL & REGIONAL INTEREST: Regional Interest English Counties

HEREFORD SOCIETY
1806117U80C-5418
Editorial Address: Holmer Road, HEREFORD, HR4 9UJ
Tel: 01432 274413
Email: hsociety@midlands.newsquest.co.uk
Advertising Address: As above. **Fax:** 01432 845898
Email: jenny.powell@midlands.newsquest.co.uk
Web site: http://www.societymagazine.co.uk
Publisher: Newsquest Media Group
Frequency: 6 issues yearly
Cover Price: Free
Circulation: 12,000 (Publisher's Statement)
Usual Pagination: 108
Editor: Juliette Kemp; **Advertising Manager:** Jenny Powell
Summary of Content: Lifestyle Magazine covering profiles of county personalities, events, fashion, beauty, society pages and food all with a Hereford slant.

Readership/Target Audience: Aimed at households in Herefordshire with a high disposable income.
ADVERTISING RATES:
Full Page Mono £515.00
Full Page Colour £515.00
Agency Commission: 10%
Mechanical Data: Trim Size: 270 x 192mm, Film: Digital
Copy instructions: Copy Date: 2 weeks prior to publication date
Average advertising content per issue: 60%
CONSUMER: RURAL & REGIONAL INTEREST: Regional Interest English Counties

HEREFORDSHIRE LIFE
1658622U80C-5168
Formerly: Hereford & Worcestershire County Magazine
Editorial Address: Archant House, Oriel Road, CHELTENHAM, GL50 1BB **Tel:** 01242 216050
Fax: 01242 255446
Email: editorial@herefordshirelife.co.uk
Advertising Address: 17 The Courtyard, Buntsford Gate, BROMSGROVE, B60 3DJ **Tel:** 01527 558470
Fax: 01527 558477
Email: fiona.ambler@archant.co.uk
Publisher: Archant Life
Frequency: Monthly
Cover Price: £2.50
Circulation: 12,000 (Publisher's Statement)
Usual Pagination: 110
Editor: Hilary Engel; **Advertising Manager:** Fiona Ambler
Summary of Content: Magazine covering art, entertainment, celebrity interviews, food and drink, interiors, health and beauty, travel, social events, motoring and local interest stories.
Readership/Target Audience: Aimed at residents of Herefordshire, Monmouthshire and Powys.
ADVERTISING RATES:
Full Page Colour £1200.00
Agency Commission: 10%
Mechanical Data: Type Area: 271 x 199mm, Bleed Size: 306 x 226mm, Trim Size: 300 x 220mm, Col Length: 271mm, Page Width: 199mm, Film: Digital
Copy instructions: Copy Date: 10th of the publication month
Average advertising content per issue: 40%
CONSUMER: RURAL & REGIONAL INTEREST: Regional Interest English Counties

HERITAGE
47958U89A-250
Editorial Address: Archant House, Oriel Road, CHELTENHAM, GL50 1BB **Tel:** 01242 211080
Fax: 01242 211081
Email: editorial@heritagemagazine.co.uk
Advertising Address: 5th Floor, Avon House, Kensington Village, Avonmore Road, LONDON, W14 8TS
Tel: 020 7605 2200
Email: dan.robinson@archant.co.uk
Web site: http://www.heritagemagazine.co.uk
ISSN: 0950-5245
Publisher: Archant Life
Date Established: 1984
Frequency: 6 issues yearly
Annual Sub.: £27.50
Circulation: 44,446 (ABC 01/01/2008 to 31/12/2008)
Usual Pagination: 100
Editor: Matt Havercroft
Summary of Content: Magazine containing illustrated features about British life, history, places to visit and the countryside.
Readership/Target Audience: Aimed at those over 30 years old.
ADVERTISING RATES:
Full Page Colour £2800.00
Agency Commission: 10%
Mechanical Data: Type Area: 265.5 x 189mm, Bleed Size: 306 x 236mm, Trim Size: 300 x 230mm, Col Length: 265.5mm, Page Width: 189mm, Film: Digital, No. of Columns (Display): 4, Col Widths (Display): 42mm
Copy instructions: Copy Date: 5 weeks prior to publication date
Average advertising content per issue: 30%
CONSUMER: HOLIDAYS & TRAVEL: Travel

HERITAGE COMMERCIALS
46789U79R-35
Formerly: Vintage Commercial Vehicles Magazine
Editorial Address: Media Centre, Morton Way, HORNCASTLE, LN9 6JR **Tel:** 01507 529300
Fax: 01507 529301
Email: info@heritagecommercials.com
Advertising Address: As above. **Tel:** 01507 524004
Fax: 01507 529499
Email: tglover-brown@mortons.co.uk
Web site: http://www.heritagecommercials.com
ISSN: 1476-2110
Publisher: Mortons Heritage Media
Date Established: 1984

Frequency: Monthly - Published on the first Thursday of every month
Cover Price: £3.50
Annual Sub.: £33.00
Circulation: 25,000 (Print Run)
Usual Pagination: 100
Editor: David Craggs; **Managing Director:** Brian Hill;
Advertising Manager: Tracy Glover-Brown; **Publisher:** Dan Savage
Summary of Content: Magazine featuring commercial vehicles, both vintage and classic. Includes news, features, events, archives, restoration projects and a classified section.
Readership/Target Audience: Aimed at vintage commercial vehicle owners and enthusiasts as well as modern truck drivers and haulage companies.
ADVERTISING RATES:
Full Page Colour £766.00
Agency Commission: 10%
Mechanical Data: Bleed Size: 303 x 216mm, Trim Size: 297.5 x 210mm, Page Width: 188mm, Type Area: 270 x 188mm, Col Length: 270mm, Film: Digital
Copy instructions: Copy Date: 20 days prior to publication date
CONSUMER: HOBBIES & DIY: Hobbies & DIY Related

HERITAGE HOMES
765135U94B-201
Formerly: Listed Heritage
Editorial Address: Unit 5, The Oast House, 62 Bell Road, SITTINGBOURNE, ME10 4HE **Tel:** 01795 599191
Fax: 01795 599282
Email: editorial@cplmedia.co.uk
Advertising Address: As above.
Email: jo@cplmedia.co.uk
Web site: http://www.listedheritage.co.uk
Publisher: CPL Media Ltd
Date Established: 1999
Frequency: Monthly
Cover Price: £2.85
Annual Sub.: £23.00
Circulation: 48,000 (Publisher's Statement)
Usual Pagination: 78
Editor: Vicki Watson; **Advertising Manager:** Jo Atara
Summary of Content: Magazine offering tailored advice, services and benefits of a club network.
Readership/Target Audience: Aimed at owners of listed properties.
ADVERTISING RATES:
Full Page Mono £1500.00
Full Page Colour £1500.00
Agency Commission: 10%
Copy instructions: Copy Date: 2 weeks prior to publication date
CONSUMER: OTHER CLASSIFICATIONS: Historic Buildings

HERITAGE RAILWAY
46703U79J-25
Editorial Address: Media Centre, Morton Way, HORNCASTLE, LN9 6JR **Tel:** 01507 529300
Fax: 01507 529495
Email: rjones@mortons.co.uk
Advertising Address: As above. **Fax:** 01507 529499
Email: tgloverbrown@mortons.co.uk
Web site: http://www.heritagerailway.co.uk
ISSN: 1466-3562
Publisher: Mortons Heritage Media
Date Established: 1999
Frequency: 13 issues yearly - Published on the second Thursday of every month
Cover Price: £3.50
Annual Sub.: £34.00
Circulation: 17,000 (Publisher's Statement)
Usual Pagination: 92
Editor: Robin Jones; **Managing Director:** Terry Clark;
Advertising Manager: Tracey Glover-Brown
Summary of Content: Magazine dedicated to preserving heritage railways including steam, diesel and electric locomotive engines.
Readership/Target Audience: Aimed at railway enthusiasts.
ADVERTISING RATES:
Full Page Colour £710.00
Agency Commission: 10%
Mechanical Data: Col Length: 270mm, Type Area: 270 x 188mm, Page Width: 188mm, Trim Size: 297 x 210mm, Bleed Size: 307 x 220mm, Film: Digital
Copy instructions: Copy Date: 20 days prior to publication date
Average advertising content per issue: 20%
CONSUMER: HOBBIES & DIY: Rail Enthusiasts

HERITAGE TODAY
48589U94B-25
Editorial Address: Sea Containers House, 20 Upper Ground, LONDON, SE1 9PD **Tel:** 020 7775 5777
Email: heritagetoday@sevensquared.co.uk
Advertising Address: As above.
Email: jessica.mclaughlin@sevensquared.co.uk
Web site: http://www.english-heritage.org.uk

Consumer Magazines

Publisher: Seven Squared
Frequency: Quarterly
Free to qualifying individuals
Circulation: 275,761 (ABC 01/07/2008 to 31/12/2008)
Usual Pagination: 66
Editor: Justine Ragány; **Advertising Manager:** Jessica Mclaughlin
Summary of Content: Magazine containing news and features relating to historic English buildings, architecture and monuments of national importance.
Readership/Target Audience: Read by members of English Heritage.
ADVERTISING RATES:
Full Page Colour £6000.00
Agency Commission: 10%
Mechanical Data: Trim Size: 297 x 210mm, Bleed Size: 303 x 216mm, Type Area: 255 x 190mm, Page Width: 190mm, Col Length: 255mm, Film: Digital
Copy instructions: Copy Date: 6 weeks prior to publication date
Average advertising content per issue: 30%
CONSUMER: OTHER CLASSIFICATIONS: Historic Buildings

HEROES
1827914U76C-837

Editorial Address: Titan House, 144 Southwark Street, LONDON, SE1 0UP **Tel:** 020 7620 0200 **Fax:** 020 7620 0032
Advertising Address: As above. **Fax:** 020 7803 1803
Email: alejandra.velez@titanemail.com
Web site: http://www.titanmagazines.com
Publisher: Titan Magazines
Frequency: 6 issues yearly
Cover Price: £3.75
Editor: Zoe Hedges; **Advertising Manager:** James Willmott
Summary of Content: Magazine covering the television programme Heroes with interviews, behind the scene stories, posters, competitions and news.
Readership/Target Audience: Aimed at fans of the TV programme.
ADVERTISING RATES:
Full Page Colour £2500.00
Mechanical Data: Trim Size: 276 x 200mm, Film: Digital
CONSUMER: MUSIC & PERFORMING ARTS: TV & Radio

HERTFORDSHIRE COUNTRYSIDE
46921U80C-1790

Editorial Address: PO Box 5, HITCHIN, SG5 1GJ
Tel: 01462 422014 **Fax:** 01462 422015
Email: martin_small@btconnect.com
Advertising Address: As above. **Tel:** 01462 431237
Email: martin_small@btconnect.com
ISSN: 0306-672X
Publisher: Beaumonde Publications Ltd
Date Established: 1946
Frequency: Monthly
Cover Price: £2.25
Free to qualifying individuals
Annual Sub.: £25.00
Circulation: 9,000 (Publisher's Statement)
Usual Pagination: 60
Editor: Sandra Small; **Advertising Manager:** Martin Small
Summary of Content: Publication covering historical and topical news of the county. Features the arts, gardening, fashion, property, home interests, food and drink, cars and antiques.
Readership/Target Audience: Aimed at those living in Hertfordshire and the surrounding areas.
ADVERTISING RATES:
Full Page Mono £475.00
Full Page Colour £550.00
Agency Commission: 10%
Mechanical Data: Page Width: 190mm, No. of Columns (Display): 4, Col Widths (Display): 46mm, Col Length: 270mm, Type Area: 270 x 190mm, Bleed Size: 303 x 216mm, Trim Size: 297 x 210mm, Film: Digital
Copy instructions: Copy Date: 14th of the month prior to publication date
Average advertising content per issue: 40%
CONSUMER: RURAL & REGIONAL INTEREST: Regional Interest English Counties

HERTFORDSHIRE LIFE
712182U80C-1787

Editorial Address: PO Box 1322, Widmer End, HIGH WYCOMBE, HP15 6YW **Tel:** 07918 721644
Email: clare.bourke@archant.co.uk
Advertising Address: Baskerville Place, Teville Road, WORTHING, BN11 1UG **Tel:** 01962 712936
Email: jenny.mcdougall@archant.co.uk
Web site: http://www.hertfordshirelife.co.uk
Publisher: Archant Life Cambridgeshire, Hertfordshire and Essex
Date Established: 1999
Frequency: Monthly
Cover Price: £2.75
Circulation: 7,000 (Publisher's Statement)
Usual Pagination: 164

Editor: Clare Bourke; **Advertising Manager:** Jenny McDougall; **Publisher:** Robyn Bechelet
Summary of Content: County magazine containing features on interiors, events, people, places, sights and sounds, restaurants, food and wine. Also includes homes and gardens, antiques, competitions and a county events guide.
Readership/Target Audience: Read by residents and visitors to Hertfordshire.
ADVERTISING RATES:
Full Page Colour £1600.00
Agency Commission: 10%
Mechanical Data: Trim Size: 300 x 220mm, Bleed Size: 306 x 223mm, Page Width: 199mm, Type Area: 271 x 199mm, Col Length: 271mm, Film: Digital, No. of Columns (Display): 4
Copy instructions: Copy Date: 4 weeks prior to publication date
Average advertising content per issue: 40%
CONSUMER: RURAL & REGIONAL INTEREST: Regional Interest English Counties

HI-FI CHOICE
46513U78A-170

Editorial Address: 2 Balcombe Street, LONDON, NW1 6NW
Tel: 020 7042 4000
Email: dan.george@futurenet.com
Advertising Address: As above. **Fax:** 020 7042 4471
Email: brad.francis@futurenet.co.uk
Web site: http://www.hifichoice.co.uk
ISSN: 0955-1115
Publisher: Future Publishing Limited
Date Established: 1975
Frequency: 13 issues yearly
Cover Price: £3.99
Annual Sub.: £44.96
Circulation: 8,479 (ABC 01/01/2008 to 31/12/2008)
Usual Pagination: 140
Editor: Dan George; **Publisher:** Andy Ford
Summary of Content: Magazine containing information on buying a hi-fi. Includes product tests, news and general articles.
Readership/Target Audience: Aimed at hi-fi enthusiasts and prospective purchasers of home audio equipment.
ADVERTISING RATES:
Full Page Colour £1600.00
Agency Commission: 10%
Mechanical Data: Bleed Size: 303 x 216mm, Trim Size: 297 x 210mm, Type Area: 270 x 190mm, Col Length: 270mm, Page Width: 190mm, Film: Digital
Copy instructions: Copy Date: 4 weeks prior to publication date
Average advertising content per issue: 40%
CONSUMER: CONSUMER ELECTRONICS: Hi-Fi & Recording

HI-FI NEWS
46514U78A-193

Formerly: Hi-Fi News & Record Review
Editorial Address: 10th Floor, Leon House, 233 High Street, CROYDON, CR9 1HZ **Tel:** 020 8726 8311
Fax: 020 8726 8397
Email: hifinews@ipcmedia.co.uk
Advertising Address: 9th Floor, Leon House, 233 High Street, CROYDON, CR9 1HZ **Tel:** 020 8726 8312
Fax: 020 8726 8399
Email: susan_bann@ipcmedia.com
Web site: http://www.hifinews.co.uk
ISSN: 0142-6230
Publisher: IPC Inspire
Date Established: 1956
Frequency: 13 issues yearly
Cover Price: £4.00
Annual Sub.: £37.44
Circulation: 10,013 (ABC 01/01/2008 to 31/12/2008)
Usual Pagination: 140
Editor: Paul Miller; **Publisher:** Richard Marcroft
Summary of Content: Magazine covering high-end stereo and multi channel audio equipment features, AV, technology advances in hi-fi and musical listening equipment, music reviews and discussion.
Readership/Target Audience: Read by music enthusiasts who own a hi-fi system and are interested in AV and new technologies.
ADVERTISING RATES:
Full Page Colour £1800.00
Agency Commission: 10%
Mechanical Data: Film: Digital
CONSUMER: CONSUMER ELECTRONICS: Hi-Fi & Recording

HI-FI WORLD
46515U78A-199

Editorial Address: Unit G4, Argo House, Kilburn Park Road, LONDON, NW6 5LF **Tel:** 020 7625 3134 **Fax:** 020 7328 1844
Email: editorial@hi-fiworld.co.uk
Advertising Address: As above.
Email: advertising@hi-fiworld.co.uk
Web site: http://www.hi-fiworld.co.uk
Publisher: Audio Publishing Ltd
Frequency: Monthly

Cover Price: £3.40
Annual Sub.: £36.00
Circulation: 18,000 (Publisher's Statement)
Usual Pagination: 130
Editor: David Price; **Managing Director:** Noel Keywood; **Advertising Manager:** Marina Nik; **Publisher:** Noel Keywood
Summary of Content: Magazine covering hi-fi, audio visual equipment, computers and music, both classical and popular.
Readership/Target Audience: Aimed at music enthusiasts.
ADVERTISING RATES:
Full Page Colour £1800.00
Agency Commission: 10%
Mechanical Data: Type Area: 272 x 182mm, Col Length: 272mm, Trim Size: 297 x 210mm, Bleed Size: 303 x 213mm, Film: Digital, Page Width: 182mm
Copy instructions: Copy Date: 3 weeks prior to publication date
Average advertising content per issue: 40%
CONSUMER: CONSUMER ELECTRONICS: Hi-Fi & Recording

HIFICRITIC
1831352U78A-605

Editorial Address: PO Box 59214, LONDON, NW3 9EZ
Fax: 020 7433 3220
Email: info@hificritic.com
Web site: http://www.hificritic.com
ISSN: 1759-7919
Publisher: HIFICRITIC Ltd
Frequency: 6 issues yearly
Cover Price: £9.00
Annual Sub.: £55.00
Circulation: 2,000 (Publisher's Statement)
Usual Pagination: 52
Editor: Martin Colloms; **Publisher:** Martin Colloms
Summary of Content: Magazine covering high quality stereo audio including equipment reviews, serious technical features and classical and pop music reviews.
Readership/Target Audience: Aimed at stereo enthusiasts, audio designers and the audio trade.
ADVERTISING: No Advertising taken
CONSUMER: CONSUMER ELECTRONICS: Hi-Fi & Recording

HIGH LIFE
48205U89D-140

Editorial Address: 85 Strand, LONDON, WC2R 0DW
Tel: 020 7550 8000 **Fax:** 020 7550 8250
Email: high.life@cedarcom.co.uk
Advertising Address: As above. **Fax:** 020 7550 8252
Email: tim.barber@bamedia.co.uk
Web site: http://www.cedarcom.co.uk
Publisher: Cedar Communications
Frequency: Monthly
Free to qualifying individuals
Annual Sub.: £37.00
Circulation: 190,257 (ABC 01/01/2009 to 30/06/2009)
Editor: Emma Parfitt; **Managing Director:** Clare Broadbent; **Managing Editor:** Kate Chambers
Summary of Content: In flight magazine of British Airways featuring celebrity profiles, fashion and beauty features and travel articles.
Readership/Target Audience: Aimed at passengers on British Airways scheduled flights.
ADVERTISING RATES:
Full Page Colour £13670.00
Agency Commission: 15%
Mechanical Data: Type Area: 265 x 195mm, Col Length: 265mm, Page Width: 195mm, Trim Size: 289 x 210mm, Bleed Size: 295 x 216mm, Film: Digital
Copy instructions: Copy Date: 5 weeks prior to publication date
Average advertising content per issue: 40%
CONSUMER: HOLIDAYS & TRAVEL: In-Flight Magazines

HIGH LIFE SHOP!
1693039U89D-517

Editorial Address: 85 Strand, LONDON, WC2R 0DW
Tel: 020 7550 8000 **Fax:** 020 7550 8250
Email: nikki.dodds@cedarcom.co.uk
Web site: http://www.highlifeshop.com
Publisher: Cedar Communications
Date Established: 2005
Frequency: 6 issues yearly
Cover Price: Free
Circulation: 250,000 (Print Run)
Editor: Nikki Dodds
Summary of Content: Magazine with product reviews, expert endorsements and informative lifestyle articles.
Readership/Target Audience: Aimed at British Airways passengers both long and short haul.
ADVERTISING: No Advertising taken
CONSUMER: HOLIDAYS & TRAVEL: In-Flight Magazines

HIGH SCHOOL MUSICAL
1826724U91D-970

Editorial Address: Brockbourne House, Mount Ephraim, TUNBRIDGE WELLS, TN4 8BS **Tel:** 01892 500100
Fax: 01892 545666
Email: acooper@panini.co.uk
Web site: http://www.paninicomics.co.uk
Publisher: Panini UK Ltd
Date Established: 2007
Frequency: Monthly
Cover Price: £1.99
Circulation: 150,000 (Publisher's Statement)
Editor: Alex Cooper
Summary of Content: Children's magazine covering all aspects of the High School Musical films including features on the film, fun facts and character profiles.
Readership/Target Audience: Aimed at girls aged between 10 and 13 years old.
ADVERTISING: No Advertising taken
CONSUMER: RECREATION & LEISURE: Children & Youth

HIGHEND MAGAZINE
1843684U74Q-1367

Editorial Address: 10 Knowle Cottages, Wadhurst Road, Frant, TUNBRIDGE WELLS, TN3 9EJ **Tel:** 01892 750851
Email: shaw.geo@googlemail.com
Web site: http://www.highendmagazine.co.uk
Publisher: Highend Ltd
Date Established: 2008
Frequency: 10 issues yearly
Cover Price: Free
Circulation: 100,000 (Print Run)
Usual Pagination: 36
Editor: George Shaw
Summary of Content: Lifestyle magazine covering food and drink, property, travel, homes and interiors, fashion, cars and high end jobs in the City of London and Canary Wharf.
Readership/Target Audience: Aimed at professionals in the financial services sector.
CONSUMER: WOMEN'S INTEREST CONSUMER MAGAZINES: Lifestyle

HIGHLAND LIFE MAGAZINE
1665011U74Q-1245

Formerly: Life & Style Magazine
Editorial Address: New Century House, Stadium Road, INVERNESS, IV1 1FG **Tel:** 01463 732222 **Fax:** 01463 732220
Email: editor@highland-life.co.uk
Advertising Address: As above. **Fax:** 01463 732289
Email: l.shaw@executive-magazine.co.uk
Web site: http://www.highland-life.co.uk
Publisher: New Century Publishing Group
Date Established: 2004
Frequency: Monthly
Cover Price: Free
Circulation: 15,000 (Publisher's Statement)
Usual Pagination: 52
Editor: Katrina Ashford; **Advertising Manager:** Steve Barron
Summary of Content: Magazine covering food and drink, travel, crafts, golf, weddings, fashion, shopping, health and beauty, personal finance, homes and gardens.
Readership/Target Audience: Aimed at professionals in the North of Scotland.
ADVERTISING RATES:
Full Page Colour £980.00
Agency Commission: 10%
Mechanical Data: Trim Size: 297 x 210mm, Type Area: 262 x 182mm, Col Length: 262mm, Page Width: 182mm, Bleed Size: 303 x 213mm, Film: Digital
CONSUMER: WOMEN'S INTEREST CONSUMER MAGAZINES: Lifestyle

THE HILL
46827U80B-124

Editorial Address: Avon House, Kensington Village, Avonmore Road, LONDON, W14 8TS **Tel:** 020 7792 2626
Fax: 020 7792 2020
Email: nina.cuthbert@archant.co.uk
Advertising Address: As above.
Email: richard.wise@archant.co.uk
Web site: http://www.thehillmag.co.uk
Publisher: Archant Life
Date Established: 1984
Frequency: Monthly
Cover Price: Free
Circulation: 74,000 (Publisher's Statement)
Usual Pagination: 100
Editor: Nina Cuthbert; **Managing Director:** Jeremy Moreton; **Advertising Manager:** Richard Wise
Summary of Content: General interest magazine covering local lifestyle issues.
Readership/Target Audience: Aimed at residents of Notting Hill, Kensington, South Kensington, Holland Park, Bayswater, North Kensington, Paddington and Chelsea.
ADVERTISING RATES:
Full Page Colour £1875.00
Agency Commission: 10%

Mechanical Data: Type Area: 270 x 190mm, Col Length: 270mm, Page Width: 190mm, Trim Size: 297 x 210mm, Film: Digital, Bleed Size: 303 x 216mm
Copy instructions: Copy Date: 3 weeks prior to publication date
Average advertising content per issue: 65%
CONSUMER: RURAL & REGIONAL INTEREST: Regional Interest Greater London

HILLINGDON PEOPLE
46828U80B-124_3

Editorial Address: Corporate Communications, 3 East/07, Civic Centre, High Street, UXBRIDGE, UB8 1UW
Tel: 01895 250530 **Fax:** 01895 277233
Email: hillingdonpeople@hillingdon.gov.uk
Advertising Address: As above. **Tel:** 01895 250282
Email: hpadvert@hillingdon.gov.uk
Web site: http://www.hillingdon.gov.uk
Publisher: London Borough of Hillingdon
Date Established: 1994
Frequency: 6 issues yearly
Cover Price: Free
Circulation: 112,000 (Publisher's Statement)
Usual Pagination: 32
Editor: Hannah Collins; **Advertising Manager:** Hannah Collins
Summary of Content: Council magazine covering news and information on council services, events and local issues.
Readership/Target Audience: Aimed at residents and those working in the London Borough of Hillingdon.
ADVERTISING RATES:
Full Page Colour £1400.00
Mechanical Data: Type Area: 272 x 190mm, Col Length: 272mm, Trim Size: 297 x 210mm, Bleed Size: 303 x 216mm, Page Width: 190mm, Film: Digital
Copy instructions: Copy Date: 6 weeks prior to publication date
Average advertising content per issue: 33%
CONSUMER: RURAL & REGIONAL INTEREST: Regional Interest Greater London

HILLSTREET MAGAZINE
1655355U74Q-1195

Editorial Address: 199 St. Vincent Street, GLASGOW, G2 5QD **Tel:** 0131 225 4367
Email: jon.walton@dtz.com
Advertising Address: 17 North Street, MIDDLESBROUGH, TS2 1JP **Tel:** 01642 252023 **Fax:** 01642 230657
Email: quoinpublishing@yahoo.co.uk
Publisher: DTZ
Date Established: 2005
Frequency: Annual - Published in November
Cover Price: Free
Circulation: 80,000 (Publisher's Statement)
Usual Pagination: 16
Editor: Jon Walton; **Advertising Manager:** Lesley Palmer
Summary of Content: Magazine covering gifts, fashion, beauty, travel, competitions and celebrity interviews.
Readership/Target Audience: Aimed at customers of the Hillstreet Shopping Centre in Middlesborough.
ADVERTISING RATES:
Full Page Colour £800.00
CONSUMER: WOMEN'S INTEREST CONSUMER MAGAZINES: Lifestyle

HISTORIC GARDENS REVIEW
749458U93-50

Formerly: European Gardens
Editorial Address: 34 River Court, Upper Ground, LONDON, SE1 9PE **Tel:** 020 7633 9165 **Fax:** 020 7401 7072
Email: office@historicgardens.org
Web site: http://www.historicgardens.org
ISSN: 1461-0191
Publisher: The Historic Gardens Foundation
Date Established: 1995
Frequency: Half-yearly
Free to qualifying individuals
Circulation: 1,000 (Publisher's Statement)
Usual Pagination: 48
Editor: Gillian Mawrey
Summary of Content: Magazine promoting interest in and containing articles on historic gardens worldwide and their conservation.
Readership/Target Audience: Read by amateurs and professionals concerned with the preservation, restoration and management of historic gardens.
ADVERTISING: No Advertising taken
CONSUMER: GARDENING

HISTORIC GRAND PRIX CARS ASSOCIATION MAGAZINE
1748202U77F-457

Editorial Address: Network House, 28 Ballmoor, Celtic Court, Buckingham Industrial Estate, BUCKINGHAM, MK18 1RQ **Tel:** 01280 829300 **Fax:** 01280 829350
Email: samj@networklifestyle.com
Advertising Address: As above.
Email: helen.james-ellett@networkinglifestyle.com

Web site: http://www.networkpublishingltd.com
Publisher: Network Publishing Ltd
Date Established: 2006
Frequency: Annual - Published in the March
Cover Price: Free
Usual Pagination: 48
Editor: Sam Jones; **Managing Editor:** Shirley Embleton
Summary of Content: Magazine covering historic grand prix car racing and historic cars, travel and lifestyle features.
Readership/Target Audience: Aimed at members of the HGPCA.
ADVERTISING: Rates on application
Agency Commission: 10%
Copy instructions: Copy Date: 4 weeks prior to publication date
Average advertising content per issue: 25%
CONSUMER: MOTORING & CYCLING: Veteran Cars

HISTORIC HOUSE
48590U94B-30

Editorial Address: 2 Chester Street, LONDON, SW1X 7BB
Tel: 020 7259 5688 **Fax:** 020 7259 5590
Email: info@hha.org.uk
Advertising Address: PO Box 21, Heritage House, BALDOCK, SG7 5SH **Tel:** 01462 896688 **Fax:** 01462 896677
Email: bernadette@hall-mccartney.co.uk
Web site: http://www.hha.org.uk
ISSN: 0260-8707
Publisher: Hall-McCartney Limited
Frequency: Quarterly
Free to qualifying individuals
Annual Sub.: £36.00
Circulation: 20,000 (Publisher's Statement)
Usual Pagination: 50
Editor: Peter Sinclair; **Advertising Manager:** Bernadette Dyson; **Publisher:** David Lewis
Summary of Content: Journal of the Historic Houses Association, covering country houses, gardens and parks, conservation, tourism, technical problems, taxation and fine arts.
Readership/Target Audience: Aimed at members of the Historic Houses Association.
ADVERTISING RATES:
Full Page Mono £624.00
Full Page Colour £753.00
Agency Commission: 10%
Mechanical Data: Col Length: 270mm, No. of Columns (Display): 4, Type Area: 270 x 180mm, Bleed Size: 303 x 210mm, Trim Size: 297 x 210mm, Page Width: 180mm, Film: Digital
Copy instructions: Copy Date: 5 weeks prior to publication date
CONSUMER: OTHER CLASSIFICATIONS: Historic Buildings

HISTORIC MOTOR RACING NEWS
46423U77D-190

Editorial Address: Unit 38, Chelsea Wharf, 15 Lots Road, LONDON, SW10 0QJ **Tel:** 020 7349 8484
Email: contact@historicmotorracingnews.com
Advertising Address: As above.
Email: steve.ross@historicmotorracingnews.com
Web site: http://www.historicmotorracingnews.com
ISSN: 1472-2135
Publisher: Historic Motor Racing News Ltd
Date Established: 1994
Frequency: 11 issues yearly - Published on the 1st of the cover month
Annual Sub.: £50.00
Circulation: 1,000 (Publisher's Statement)
Usual Pagination: 40
Editor: Carol Spagg; **Managing Director:** Carol Spagg; **Advertisement Director:** Steve Ross
Summary of Content: Magazine covering all aspects of historic motor sport, racing and rallying.
Readership/Target Audience: Read by European historic racers.
ADVERTISING RATES:
Full Page Mono £600.00
Full Page Colour £600.00
Agency Commission: 10%
Mechanical Data: Type Area: 270 x 190mm, Col Length: 270mm, Page Width: 190mm, Bleed Size: 303 x 216mm, Trim Size: 297 x 210mm
Copy instructions: Copy Date: 13th of the month prior to publication date
Average advertising content per issue: 40%
CONSUMER: MOTORING & CYCLING: Motor Sports

HISTORY OF PHOTOGRAPHY
47596U85A-100

Editorial Address: 4 Park Square, Milton Park, ABINGDON, OX14 4RN **Tel:** 020 7017 6000 **Fax:** 020 7017 6336
Web site: http://www.tandf.co.uk
ISSN: 0308-7298
Publisher: Routledge, Taylor & Francis
Date Established: 1997
Frequency: Quarterly
Annual Sub.: £203.00

Consumer Magazines

Usual Pagination: 100
Editor: Graham Smith; **Managing Editor:** Stacey Gubb;
Publisher: Christine Appel
Summary of Content: Journal covering all aspects of the
history of photography.
Readership/Target Audience: Aimed at those with an
interest in photography.
ADVERTISING: Rates on application
CONSUMER: PHOTOGRAPHY & FILM MAKING:
Photography

HISTORY SCOTLAND 1638158U94X-264
Editorial Address: 18 (1F2) Gladstone Terrace,
EDINBURGH, EH9 1LS **Tel:** 0131 668 4864
Fax: 0131 668 4864
Email: editorial@historyscotland.com
Advertising Address: Hall Marketing, Unit 3, Craighall
House, 58A High Craighall Road, GLASGOW, G4 9UD
Tel: 0141 332 3500 **Fax:** 0870 132 5003
Email: hall.mark@tiscali.co.uk
Web site: http://www.historyscotland.com
Publisher: Knowledge Media Ltd
Frequency: 6 issues yearly
Cover Price: £3.95
Annual Sub.: £21.00
Circulation: 7,500 (Publisher's Statement)
Usual Pagination: 56
Editor: Joy Arden; **News Editor:** Joy Arden; **Advertising
Manager:** Julie Hall
Summary of Content: Magazine covering archaeology and
history of Scotland and the Scots.
Readership/Target Audience: Aimed at those interested in
Scotland and Scottish history.
ADVERTISING RATES:
Full Page Mono £800.00
Full Page Colour £1000.00
Agency Commission: 10%
Mechanical Data: Type Area: 268 x 179mm, Trim Size: 300
x 213mm, Bleed Size: 306 x 216mm, Col Length: 268mm,
Page Width: 179mm, Film: Digital
Copy instructions: Copy Date: 4 weeks prior to publication
date
CONSUMER: OTHER CLASSIFICATIONS: Miscellaneous

HISTORY TODAY 47235U82-40
Editorial Address: 20 Old Compton Street, LONDON, W1D
4TW **Tel:** 020 7534 8000
Email: admin@historytoday.com
Advertising Address: Cabbell Publishing Ltd, 204 Durnsford
Road, LONDON, SW19 8DR **Tel:** 020 8971 8000
Fax: 020 8971 8480
Email: adam.lister@historytoday.com
Web site: http://www.historytoday.com
ISSN: 0018-2753
Publisher: History Today Ltd
Date Established: 1951
Frequency: Monthly
Cover Price: £4.20
Annual Sub.: £39.00
Circulation: 23,313 (ABC 01/01/2008 to 31/12/2008)
Usual Pagination: 72
Editor: Paul Lay; **Advertising Manager:** Adam Lister;
Publisher: Andy Patterson
Summary of Content: Magazine focusing on current issues
from a historical perspective. Includes news items of
relevance to international research.
Readership/Target Audience: Aimed at those who have a
specialist or general interest in history, heritage and current
affairs.
ADVERTISING RATES:
Full Page Colour £1850.00
Agency Commission: 15%
Mechanical Data: Type Area: 267 x 182mm, Bleed Size:
303 x 213mm, Trim Size: 297 x 210mm, Film: Digital, Print
Process: Web-fed litho, Col Length: 267mm, Page Width:
182mm
Copy instructions: Copy Date: 4 weeks prior to publication
date
Average advertising content per issue: 10%
CONSUMER: CURRENT AFFAIRS & POLITICS

HMV CHOICE 601073U76D-331
Editorial Address: Film House, 142 Wardour Street,
LONDON, W1F 8LN **Tel:** 020 7432 2000 **Fax:** 020 7534 8112
Email: paula.taylor@hmv.co.uk
Advertising Address: 9th Floor, Tower House, Fairfax
Street, BRISTOL, BS1 3BN **Tel:** 0117 927 9009
Fax: 0117 933 8008
Email: graemekirk@bbcmagazinesbristol.com
Web site: http://www.hmv.co.uk
ISSN: 1467-6923
Publisher: BBC Magazines Bristol
Date Established: 1999
Frequency: Quarterly
Cover Price: Free
Circulation: 100,000 (Publisher's Statement)
Usual Pagination: 52

Editor: Paula Taylor; **Advertising Manager:** Graeme Kirk;
Managing Editor: Rob Williams
Summary of Content: Magazine dedicated to new
specialist music with interviews, news and features. Includes
music reviews on classical, jazz, country, easy listening,
original soundtracks, folk and blues and world music.
Readership/Target Audience: Read by customers of HMV
stores.
ADVERTISING RATES:
Full Page Mono £3250.00
Full Page Colour £3250.00
Agency Commission: 10%
Average advertising content per issue: 15%
CONSUMER: MUSIC & PERFORMING ARTS: Music

HMV GAMES 1786090U78D-333
Editorial Address: 30 Monmouth Street, BATH, BA1 2BW
Tel: 01225 442244 **Fax:** 01225 446019
Email: hmvgamesmag@futurenet.com
Publisher: Future Publishing Ltd
Date Established: 2006
Frequency: Quarterly
Cover Price: Free
Circulation: 150,000 (Print Run)
Usual Pagination: 40
Editor: Paula Taylor
Summary of Content: Magazine reviewing the latest games
and consoles as well as games news.
Readership/Target Audience: Aimed at customers of HMV
stores.
ADVERTISING: No Advertising taken
CONSUMER: CONSUMER ELECTRONICS: Games

HOBBIES HANDBOOK 46625U79B-29_95
Editorial Address: Units 8-11, The Raveningham Centre,
NORWICH, NR14 6NU **Tel:** 01508 549330
Fax: 01508 549331
Email: enquires@alwayshobbies.com
Web site: http://www.alwayshobbies.com
Publisher: Hobbies (Dereham) 1985 Ltd
Date Established: 1980
Frequency: Annual - Published in August
Cover Price: £2.95
Circulation: 350,000 (Publisher's Statement)
Usual Pagination: 120
Editor: Andrew Meeks; **Circulation Manager:** John
Strouler
Summary of Content: International publication containing
plans and fittings for toys and model making.
Readership/Target Audience: Aimed at home crafts-folk
and hobbyists.
ADVERTISING: No Advertising taken
CONSUMER: HOBBIES & DIY: Models & Modelling

HOBBY'S ANNUAL 46626U79B-29_96
Editorial Address: Knights Hill Square, LONDON, SE27
0HH **Tel:** 020 8761 4244 **Fax:** 020 8761 8796
Email: mail@hobby.uk.com
Web site: http://www.hobby.uk.com
ISSN: 0144-5464
Publisher: W. Hobby Ltd
Date Established: 1970
Frequency: Annual - Published in September
Cover Price: £3.15
Circulation: 80,000 (Publisher's Statement)
Usual Pagination: 304
Editor: Mike Crossland
Summary of Content: Publication containing plans and
model making material.
Readership/Target Audience: Aimed at home model
makers.
ADVERTISING: No Advertising taken
Copy instructions: Copy Date: June 15th
CONSUMER: HOBBIES & DIY: Models & Modelling

HOCKEY SCOTLAND 1839676U75X-1720
Editorial Address: 17A South Street, LANCING, BN15 8AE
Tel: 0870 803 4891
Email: editor@pushhockey.co.uk
Advertising Address: As above.
Email: editor@pushhockey.co.uk
Publisher: Push Hockey Ltd
Frequency: Half-yearly - Publsihed in March and August
Cover Price: £3.50
Free to qualifying individuals
Circulation: 10,000 (Publisher's Statement)
Usual Pagination: 32
Editor: Chris Henry; **Advertising Manager:** Jeremy
Subedar; **Publisher:** Jeremy Subedar
Summary of Content: Magazine covering field hockey in
Scotland with interviews, international and local news,
coaching, lifestyle and product reviews.
Readership/Target Audience: Aimed at hockey players,
coaches and volunteers affiliated to hockey in Scotland.

ADVERTISING: Rates on application
Agency Commission: 10%
CONSUMER: SPORT: Other Sport

HOG TALES 46363U77B-494_35
Formerly: HOG News
Editorial Address: Harley-Davidson Europe, Oxford
Business Park, 6000 Garsington Road, Cowley, OXFORD,
OX4 2DQ **Tel:** 0870 850 1903 **Fax:** 0870 850 2003
Email: hogtaleseurope@harley-davidson.com
Web site: http://www.harley-davidson.com
Publisher: Harley-Davidson Europe
Date Established: 1983
Frequency: Quarterly
Annual Sub.: £46.00
Circulation: 90,000 (Publisher's Statement)
Usual Pagination: 72
Editor: Jeremy Pick
Summary of Content: Magazine of the Harley Owners
Group (HOG). Includes news, reports and reviews of interest.
Language(s): Dutch; English; French; German; Italian;
Spanish
Readership/Target Audience: Read by Harley-Davidson
owners and riders.
ADVERTISING: No Advertising taken
CONSUMER: MOTORING & CYCLING: Motorcycling

HOG TALES 1791017U77B-720
Editorial Address: Prospect House, Rouen Road,
NORWICH, NR1 1RE **Tel:** 01603 664242
Email: zoe.francis@archantdialogue.co.uk
Publisher: Archant Dialogue
Date Established: 2006
Frequency: Quarterly
Cover Price: Free
Circulation: 103,000 (Publisher's Statement)
Usual Pagination: 84
Editor: Zoe Francis; **Features Editor:** Amy Nicholson
Summary of Content: Magazine featuring news, stories
about people and their bikes and reader contributions.
Readership/Target Audience: Aimed at owners of Harley-
Davidson motorbikes.
ADVERTISING: No Advertising taken
CONSUMER: MOTORING & CYCLING: Motorcycling

HOLIDAY COTTAGES MAGAZINE 1641359U89A-707
Editorial Address: Wessex Buildings, Somerton Business
Park, Bancombe Road, SOMERTON, TA11 6SB
Tel: 01458 274447
Email: john@merrickspublishing.com
Advertising Address: As above. **Tel:** 01458 271817
Fax: 01458 274059
Email: advertising@merrickspublishing.com
Web site: http://www.holidaycottages.cc
Publisher: Merricks Publishing Ltd
Date Established: 2003
Frequency: 6 issues yearly
Cover Price: £2.95
Circulation: 20,000 (Print Run)
Usual Pagination: 212
Editor: John Kerswill
Summary of Content: Magazine covering general travel and
holiday information about the UK and Ireland including
destination reports.
Readership/Target Audience: Aimed at those looking to
rent self-catering holiday cottages and apartments in rural
areas in the UK and Ireland.
ADVERTISING RATES:
Full Page Colour £800.00
Agency Commission: 10%
Mechanical Data: Type Area: 280 x 204mm, Col Length:
280mm, Bleed Size: 306 x 226mm, Trim Size: 300 x 220mm,
Film: Digital, Page Width: 204mm
Copy instructions: Copy Date: 4 weeks prior to publication
date
Average advertising content per issue: 30%
CONSUMER: HOLIDAYS & TRAVEL: Travel

HOLIDAY THE RCI MAGAZINE 48248U89E-130
Editorial Address: Kettering Parkway, KETTERING, NN15
6EY **Tel:** 01536 310101 **Fax:** 01536 314682
Email: holiday@europe.rci.com
Advertising Address: Media Line, 23-25 Hockcliffe Street,
LEIGHTON BUZZARD, LE7 1EZ **Tel:** 0870 250 8704
Fax: 0870 250 9697
Email: nickyl@medialine.eu.com
Web site: http://www.rci.com
Publisher: Story Worldwide
Frequency: 3 issues yearly - Published in January, May and
September
Free to qualifying individuals
Circulation: 168,928 (ABC 01/01/2008 to 31/12/2008)
Usual Pagination: 68

Editor: Kathi Hall; **Advertising Director:** Nicky Lane
Summary of Content: Magazine covering travel destinations, advice and information on new holiday resorts.
Language(s): Danish; Dutch; English; Finnish; French; German; Greek; Hungarian; Italian; Portuguese; Russian; Spanish; Swedish; Turkish
Readership/Target Audience: Read by RCI members who are timeshare owners.
ADVERTISING RATES:
Full Page Colour £7700.00
Agency Commission: 10%
Mechanical Data: Film: Digital
CONSUMER: HOLIDAYS & TRAVEL: Holidays

HOLIDAY VILLAS MAGAZINE
623223U89A-344_50

Editorial Address: Wessex Buildings, Somerton Business Park, Bancombe Road, SOMERTON, TA11 6SB
Tel: 01458 274447
Email: john@merrickspublishing.com
Advertising Address: 39 Gay Street, BATH, BA1 2NT
Tel: 01225 808792 **Fax:** 01225 429558
Email: sales@merrickspublishing.com
Web site: http://www.villaseek.com
ISSN: 1461-4170
Publisher: Merricks Publishing Ltd
Date Established: 1998
Frequency: 6 issues yearly
Cover Price: £2.95
Annual Sub.: £18.00
Circulation: 20,000 (Publisher's Statement)
Usual Pagination: 406
Editor: John Kerswill; **Advertising Manager:** John Kerswill;
Publisher: John Kerswill
Summary of Content: Magazine containing resort and location features, focusing on the USA, especially Florida, southern and eastern Europe and Turkey. Covering self-catering villa and apartment holidays, food and restaurants, motoring and new products and sport.
Readership/Target Audience: Aimed at the independent, self-catering traveller.
ADVERTISING: Rates on application
Agency Commission: 10%
Copy instructions: Copy Date: 4 weeks prior to publication date
Average advertising content per issue: 90%
CONSUMER: HOLIDAYS & TRAVEL: Travel

HOLYROOD MAGAZINE
47236U82-45

Formerly: Holyrood - The Magazine for Scotland's Parliament
Editorial Address: 14-16 Holyrood Road, EDINBURGH, EH8 8AF **Tel:** 0131 272 2114 **Fax:** 0131 272 2116
Email: editor@holyrood.com
Advertising Address: As above. **Tel:** 0131 272 2113
Fax: 0131 272 2115
Email: sales@holyrood.com
Web site: http://www.holyrood.com
ISSN: 1466-741X
Publisher: Holyrood Communications Ltd
Date Established: 1999
Frequency: 22 issues yearly
Annual Sub.: £195.00
Circulation: 2,200 (Publisher's Statement)
Usual Pagination: 64
Editor: Mandy Rhodes; **Publisher:** Hamish Miller
Summary of Content: Magazine providing impartial and incisive commentary on Scottish politics as they happen. Covers news and profiles on leading MSPs.
Readership/Target Audience: Read by business people, MSPs, MPs, Government Ministers, policy experts, civil society and academics.
ADVERTISING RATES:
Full Page Colour £2310.00
Mechanical Data: Trim Size: 272 x 210mm, Bleed Size: 278 x 216mm, Film: Digital
Copy instructions: Copy Date: 1 week prior to publication date
Average advertising content per issue: 25%
CONSUMER: CURRENT AFFAIRS & POLITICS

HOME & GARDEN
1663951U74C-837

Formerly: House & Home
Editorial Address: PO Box 29, 76-86 Walmgate, YORK, YO1 9YN **Tel:** 01904 653051 **Fax:** 01904 612853
Email: lynne.martin@thepress.co.uk
Advertising Address: As above. **Fax:** 01904 611488
Email: charlotte.baker@ycp.co.uk
Web site: http://www.thepress.co.uk
Publisher: Newsquest Yorkshire and North East (York)
Frequency: 3 issues yearly - Published in March, May and September
Cover Price: Free
Circulation: 30,000 (Publisher's Statement)
Usual Pagination: 36
Editor: Lynne Martin

Summary of Content: Magazine covering homes and gardens.
Readership/Target Audience: Aimed at those looking to renovate their homes or gardens.
ADVERTISING RATES:
Full Page Colour £800.00
Agency Commission: 10%
Mechanical Data: Trim Size: 328 x 233mm, Film: Digital, No. of Columns (Display): 8
Copy instructions: Copy Date: 2 weeks prior to publication date
Average advertising content per issue: 60%
Supplement to: The Press (York)
CONSUMER: WOMEN'S INTEREST CONSUMER MAGAZINES: Home & Family

HOME CINEMA CHOICE
46519U78B-120

Editorial Address: 2 Balcombe Street, LONDON, NW1 6NW
Tel: 020 7042 4000 **Fax:** 020 7042 4539
Email: rik.henderson@futurenet.co.uk
Advertising Address: As above. **Fax:** 020 7042 4471
Email: mo.elmoudden@futurenet.co.uk
Web site: http://www.homecinemachoice.com
Publisher: Future Publishing Limited
Date Established: 1995
Frequency: 13 issues yearly
Cover Price: £3.99
Circulation: 11,779 (ABC 01/01/2008 to 31/12/2008)
Usual Pagination: 148
Editor: Rik Henderson; **News Editor:** Anton Van Beek;
Managing Director: Robert Price
Summary of Content: Magazine focusing on home cinema and home entertainment equipment. Covers large screen televisions, amplifiers, speakers, projectors, plus video and audio-related gadgetry.
Readership/Target Audience: Aimed at those interested in home cinema technology and home entertainment technology.
ADVERTISING RATES:
Full Page Colour £2380.00
Agency Commission: 10%
Mechanical Data: Page Width: 212mm, Type Area: 266 x 212mm, Bleed Size: 306 x 238mm, Trim Size: 300 x 232mm, Film: Digital, Col Length: 266mm
Copy instructions: Copy Date: 4 weeks prior to publication date
Average advertising content per issue: 50%
CONSUMER: CONSUMER ELECTRONICS: Video & DVD

HOME FARMER
1835416U93-199

Editorial Address: PO Box 536, PRESTON, PR2 9ZY
Tel: 01772 720671
Email: editor@homefarmer.co.uk
Advertising Address: EF Media Management Ltd, South Fens Business Centre, Fenton Way, CHATTERIS, PE16 6TT
Tel: 0845 226 0477 **Fax:** 0845 226 0377
Email: bob@homefarmer.co.uk
Web site: http://www.homefarmer.co.uk
Publisher: The Good Life Press Ltd
Date Established: 2008
Frequency: Monthly
Cover Price: £3.25
Circulation: 20,000 (Print Run)
Usual Pagination: 100
Editor: Paul Peacock
Summary of Content: Magazine covering all aspects of self sufficiency, small holdings, food production, renewable energy, recycling, composting and the environment.
Readership/Target Audience: Aimed at those interested in the good life whether in the country or in towns.
ADVERTISING RATES:
Full Page Colour £500.00
Agency Commission: 10%
Mechanical Data: Bleed Size: 303 x 216mm, Trim Size: 297 x 210mm, Film: Digital
Copy instructions: Copy Date: 15th of the month prior to publication date
Average advertising content per issue: 30%
CONSUMER: GARDENING

THE HOME MAGAZINE
1865965U54C-882

Editorial Address: Headley House, Headley Road, Grayshott, HINDHEAD, GU26 6TU **Tel:** 01428 601020
Fax: 01428 601027
Email: info@signaturepl.co.uk
Publisher: Signature Publishing Ltd
Frequency: Annual
Circulation: 22,653 (Publisher's Statement)
Editor: Louise Beale
Summary of Content: Magazine focusing on affordable contemporary style. Provides ideas and tips for furnishing the home.
Readership/Target Audience: Aimed at homeowners.
ADVERTISING: Rates on application
CONSUMER: WOMEN'S INTEREST CONSUMER MAGAZINES: Home & Family

HOME PLUS SCOTLAND
766968U74C-809

Editorial Address: 6 Freskyn Place, East Mains Industrial Estate, BROXBURN, EH52 5NF **Tel:** 01506 508001
Fax: 01506 508002
Email: leah@homeplusscotland.com
Advertising Address: As above.
Email: adverts@homeplusscotland.com
Web site: http://www.capitalgroupuk.com
Publisher: Capital Publishing
Date Established: 2001
Frequency: 6 issues yearly
Cover Price: £2.95
Annual Sub.: £17.70
Circulation: 20,000 (Publisher's Statement)
Usual Pagination: 144
Editor: Leah Parker; **Advertising Manager:** Ewan Connolly;
Publisher: Lawrence Service
Summary of Content: Magazine featuring homes interiors and lifestyle features. Includes articles on gardens, homes, interiors, DIY, food and drink, travel and Scottish crafts.
Readership/Target Audience: Aimed at home owners in Scotland.
ADVERTISING RATES:
Full Page Colour £1470.00
Agency Commission: 10%
Mechanical Data: Film: Digital, Trim Size: 297 x 210mm, Type Area: 268 x 188mm, Col Length: 268mm, Page Width: 188mm
Copy instructions: Copy Date: 3 weeks prior to publication date
CONSUMER: WOMEN'S INTEREST CONSUMER MAGAZINES: Home & Family

HOME WORDS
47722U87-113

Editorial Address: 77 Verulam Road, ST. ALBANS, AL3 4DJ
Tel: 01727 833400
Email: terence@harrowweald.org
Advertising Address: 13-17 Long Lane, LONDON, EC1A 9PN **Tel:** 020 7776 1060
Email: stephen@churchtimes.co.uk
ISSN: 0018-4144
Publisher: Hymns ancient & modern
Date Established: 1870
Frequency: Monthly
Circulation: 44,000 (Publisher's Statement)
Usual Pagination: 16
Editor: Terence Handley-MacMath; **Advertising Manager:** Stephen Dutton; **Managing Editor:** Paul Handley
Summary of Content: Insert for parish magazines covering all aspects of Christian life. Includes features on the church, arts, family issues and Christian literature.
Readership/Target Audience: Aimed at readers of Anglican parish magazines.
ADVERTISING RATES:
SCC £25.00
Agency Commission: 10%
Mechanical Data: Type Area: 190 x 125mm, Col Length: 190mm, Col Widths (Display): 40mm, No. of Columns (Display): 3, Page Width: 125mm, Print Process: Web offset, Film: Digital
Copy instructions: Copy Date: 8 weeks prior to publication date
Average advertising content per issue: 20%
CONSUMER: RELIGIOUS

HOMEBASE GARDEN LIVING
1872531U93-202

Editorial Address: 7 St. Martin's Place, LONDON, WC2N 4HA **Tel:** 020 7747 0700 **Fax:** 020 7747 0701
Email: sarah.miles@redwoodgroup.net
Publisher: Redwood
Frequency: Quarterly
Cover Price: Free
Circulation: 220,000 (Publisher's Statement)
Usual Pagination: 16
Editor: Sarah Miles
Summary of Content: Magazine featuring hints and tips on gardening, practical ideas about planting and garden design, inspiration, offers, discounts and information about products sold at Homebase.
Readership/Target Audience: Aimed at seasoned gardeners and novices who are members of Garden Living Club.
CONSUMER: GARDENING

HOMEBUILDING & RENOVATING
45259U74C-197

Editorial Address: 2 Sugar Brook Court, Aston Road, BROMSGROVE, B60 3EX **Tel:** 01527 834400
Fax: 01527 834486
Email: homebuilding@centaur.co.uk
Advertising Address: As above. **Fax:** 01527 574759
Email: gill.grimshaw@centaur.co.uk
Web site: http://www.homebuilding.co.uk
ISSN: 1471-5791
Publisher: Centaur Special Interest Media
Date Established: 1990

Consumer Magazines

Frequency: Monthly - Published 1st of month prior to cover month
Cover Price: £3.99
Annual Sub.: £38.75
Circulation: 33,100 (ABC 01/01/2008 to 31/12/2008)
Usual Pagination: 196
Editor: Melanie Griffiths; **Editor-in-Chief:** Michael Holmes;
Managing Director: Peter Harris; **Publisher:** Peter Harris
Summary of Content: Magazine covering advice and features on building, renovating, converting and extensions.
Readership/Target Audience: Aimed at active self-builders, architects, designers and home owners.
ADVERTISING RATES:
Full Page Colour £2277.00
Agency Commission: 10%
Mechanical Data: Page Width: 210mm, Type Area: 277 x 210mm, Bleed Size: 303 x 236mm, Trim Size: 297 x 230mm, Col Length: 277mm, Film: Digital
Copy instructions: Copy Date: 6 weeks prior to publication date
Average advertising content per issue: 40%
CONSUMER: WOMEN'S INTEREST CONSUMER MAGAZINES: Home & Family

HOME-LIFE MAGAZINE
48778U74Q-410

Editorial Address: CIDO Business Complex, Charles Street, Lurgan, CRAIGAVON, BT66 6HG **Tel:** 028 3832 4006
Fax: 028 3832 5213
Email: sales@homelifemagazines.co.uk
Advertising Address: As above.
Email: sales@homelifemagazines.co.uk
Publisher: Motoring and Home Life Magazines Ltd
Date Established: 1988
Frequency: Monthly
Cover Price: Free
Circulation: 25,000 (Publisher's Statement)
Usual Pagination: 32
Editor: Margaret Kinsella; **Features Editor:** Martine Mason;
Advertising Manager: Martine Mason
Summary of Content: Magazine covering all aspects of home-life, gardening, travel, fashion, DIY and motoring. Contains a children's corner, book reviews, recipes, new homes, toys, eating out, entertainment, competitions and general interest features.
Readership/Target Audience: Read by those in Northern Ireland who are interested in general lifestyle news.
ADVERTISING RATES:
Full Page Mono £494.00
Full Page Colour £741.00
Mechanical Data: Type Area: 268 x 185mm, Page Width: 185mm, Film: Digital, Col Length: 268mm
Copy instructions: Copy Date: Tuesday 3pm prior to publication date
CONSUMER: WOMEN'S INTEREST CONSUMER MAGAZINES: Lifestyle

HOMES
1658011U74K-684

Editorial Address: London Road, Sayers Common, HASSOCKS, BN6 9HS **Tel:** 01273 837733
Fax: 01273 837734
Email: editorial@homesweekly.co.uk
Advertising Address: As above. **Tel:** 0844 871 0042
Fax: 0844 871 0043
Email: sales@homesweekly.co.uk
Web site: http://www.homesweekly.co.uk
Publisher: Friday Holdings Ltd
Date Established: 2003
Frequency: Weekly
Cover Price: Free
Circulation: 46,000 (Publisher's Statement)
Usual Pagination: 48
Editor: David Somerville; **Advertising Manager:** Jo Chubb
Summary of Content: Magazine covering properties for sale or let as well as homes, gardens and moving house.
Readership/Target Audience: Aimed at active homebuyers and home owners in Sussex.
ADVERTISING RATES:
Full Page Colour £275.00
SCC £3.75
Agency Commission: 10%
Mechanical Data: Type Area: 290 x 219mm, Col Length: 290mm, Page Width: 219mm, Film: Digital
Copy instructions: Copy Date: Friday 5pm prior to publication
Average advertising content per issue: 90%
Editions:
Homes Eastbourne & Seaford
Homes Hastings
Homes Heart of Sussex
CONSUMER: WOMEN'S INTEREST CONSUMER MAGAZINES: Home Purchase

HOMES & GARDENS
45263U74C-203

Editorial Address: Blue Fin Building, 110 Southwark Street, LONDON, SE1 0SU **Tel:** 020 3148 7311
Advertising Address: As above. **Tel:** 020 3148 5000
Email: sharon_goode@ipcmedia.com

Web site: http://www.ipcmedia.com
Publisher: IPC Southbank
Date Established: 1919
Frequency: Monthly
Cover Price: £3.40
Circulation: 135,004 (ABC 01/01/2009 to 30/06/2009)
Editor: Deborah Barker; **Features Editor:** Helen Stone;
Advertising Manager: Sharon Goode; **Managing Editor:** Jane Akers; **Publisher:** Yvonne Ramsden
Summary of Content: Magazine covering homes, furnishing, cookery, gardening and travel.
Readership/Target Audience: Aimed at those aged 30 years old and over who are interested in creating a beautiful home.
ADVERTISING RATES:
Full Page Colour £10120.00
Mechanical Data: Type Area: 270 x 198mm, Col Length: 270mm, Page Width: 198mm, Film: Digital, Bleed Size: 306 x 236mm, Trim Size: 300 x 230mm
Supplement(s): Homes & Gardens Fabric - 1xY, Homes & Gardens Outdoor Living - 1xY, Kitchen & Bathroom - 1xY
CONSUMER: WOMEN'S INTEREST CONSUMER MAGAZINES: Home & Family

HOMES & INTERIORS SCOTLAND
45265U74C-203_60

Editorial Address: Bergius House, 20 Clifton Street, GLASGOW, G3 7LA **Tel:** 0141 567 6000 **Fax:** 0141 332 2153
Email: sandra.colamartino@peeblesmedia.com
Advertising Address: Suite 4, Sovereign House, 58 Elliot Street, GLASGOW, G3 8DZ **Tel:** 0141 567 6000
Email: tracey@intermags.co.uk
Web site: http://www.homesandinteriorsscotland.com
ISSN: 1361-6056
Publisher: Peebles Media Group Ltd
Frequency: 6 issues yearly
Cover Price: £2.95
Free to qualifying individuals
Annual Sub.: £15.00
Circulation: 9,802 (ABC 01/01/2009 to 30/06/2009)
Usual Pagination: 230
Editor: Sandra Colamartino; **Features Editor:** Catherine Coyle; **Managing Director:** Yvonne Bremner
Summary of Content: Magazine offering advice and ideas on home improvement and decorating.
Readership/Target Audience: Aimed at adults aged 25 years old and over seeking to invest in the quality of their living environment.
ADVERTISING RATES:
Full Page Mono £1400.00
Full Page Colour £1500.00
Agency Commission: 10%
Mechanical Data: Page Width: 180mm, Type Area: 262 x 180mm, Bleed Size: 303 x 216mm, Trim Size: 297 x 210mm, Col Length: 262mm, Film: Digital
Copy instructions: Copy Date: 3 weeks prior to publication date
CONSUMER: WOMEN'S INTEREST CONSUMER MAGAZINES: Home & Family

HOMES OVERSEAS
45487U74K-150

Editorial Address: 1st Floor, 1 East Poultry Avenue, LONDON, EC1A 9PT **Tel:** 020 7002 8300
Fax: 020 7002 8310
Email: kh@globespanmedia.com
Advertising Address: As above.
Email: ag@globespanmedia.com
Web site: http://www.homesoverseas.co.uk
ISSN: 0018-4241
Publisher: Globespan Media Ltd
Date Established: 1997
Frequency: 10 issues yearly
Cover Price: £3.25
Annual Sub.: £34.00
Circulation: 51,255 (Publisher's Statement)
Usual Pagination: 196
Editor: Kate Hamilton; **Features Editor:** Marc Da Silva;
Publisher: Derek Smith
Summary of Content: Magazine containing information on the legal, financial and lifestyle aspects of living abroad.
Readership/Target Audience: Aimed at those looking to purchase a second, retirement or investment home abroad.
ADVERTISING RATES:
Full Page Colour £2986.00
Agency Commission: 10%
Mechanical Data: Type Area: 270 x 195mm, Bleed Size: 306 x 231mm, Trim Size: 300 x 225mm, Film: Digital, Col Length: 270mm, Page Width: 195mm
Average advertising content per issue: 64%
CONSUMER: WOMEN'S INTEREST CONSUMER MAGAZINES: Home Purchase

HOMESEEKER
45521U74K-177

Editorial Address: 17 Brest Road, Derriford Business Park, PLYMOUTH, PL6 5AA **Tel:** 01752 765500
Fax: 01752 765527

Email: homeseeker@swmg.co.uk
Advertising Address: As above. **Fax:** 01752 765666
Email: slyndon@smg.co.uk
Web site: http://www.thisisplymouth.co.uk
Publisher: Western Morning News & Media Ltd
Date Established: 1989
Frequency: Weekly
Circulation: 44,379 (Publisher's Statement)
Usual Pagination: 108
Editor: Linda Haston
Summary of Content: Magazine listing property advertising and editorial in Plymouth and surrounding areas.
Readership/Target Audience: Read by those looking for a new property.
ADVERTISING RATES:
Full Page Colour £580.00
Copy instructions: Copy Date: Friday prior to publication date
CONSUMER: WOMEN'S INTEREST CONSUMER MAGAZINES: Home Purchase

HOMESFORSALEANDTOLET.COM
35217U74K-668

Formerly: Oldham & District Property News
Editorial Address: Banner House, Briar Close, EVESHAM, WR11 4XA **Tel:** 01386 765832 **Fax:** 01386 40650
Email: info@ppsprint.co.uk
Advertising Address: As above.
Email: sara@homesforsalesandtolet.com
Web site: http://www.propertyprintservices.com
Publisher: PPS
Date Established: 1994
Frequency: 26 issues yearly
Cover Price: Free
Circulation: 15,000 (Publisher's Statement)
Usual Pagination: 40
Editor: Vernon Pethard; **Advertising Manager:** Sara Cresswell
Summary of Content: Newspaper covering local and national articles of interest.
Readership/Target Audience: Aimed at home buyers and sellers in Oldham and the surrounding areas.
ADVERTISING: Rates on application
Copy instructions: Copy Date: Monday 10.30am prior to publication date
CONSUMER: WOMEN'S INTEREST CONSUMER MAGAZINES: Home Purchase

HOOFPRINT
47128U81D-80

Editorial Address: PO Box 7, KNUTSFORD, WA16 7PP
Tel: 01565 872107 **Fax:** 01565 873943
Advertising Address: As above.
Publisher: Penn House Publishing Ltd
Date Established: 1969
Frequency: Monthly
Cover Price: £1.00
Circulation: 10,347 (Publisher's Statement)
Usual Pagination: 40
Editor: Barry Hook; **Advertising Manager:** Tom England
Summary of Content: Magazine covering amateur riding club news and competitions.
Readership/Target Audience: Aimed at riding club members and amateur competitors in the North West.
ADVERTISING RATES:
Full Page Mono £490.00
Full Page Colour £695.00
Agency Commission: 15%
Mechanical Data: Type Area: 270 x 190mm, Trim Size: 297 x 210mm, Col Length: 270mm, Page Width: 190mm, Bleed Size: 307 x 220mm, Film: Digital
Copy instructions: Copy Date: 10th of the month prior to publication date
Average advertising content per issue: 50%
CONSUMER: ANIMALS & PETS: Horses & Ponies

HOOKER RUGBY
1687730U75C-473

Formerly: Hooker
Editorial Address: BT3 Business Centre, 10 Dargan Crescent, BELFAST, BT3 9JP **Tel:** 028 9077 5577
Email: info@hookerrugby.com
Advertising Address: As above. **Fax:** 028 9077 1805
Email: info@hookerrugby.com
Web site: http://www.hookerrugby.com
Publisher: CRM Publishing Ltd
Date Established: 2005
Frequency: 6 issues yearly
Cover Price: £2.50
Circulation: 2,955 (Publisher's Statement)
Usual Pagination: 94
Editor: Laura Dunlop; **Advertising Manager:** Caroline Harvey; **Managing Editor:** Caroline Harvey; **Publisher:** Caroline Harvey
Summary of Content: Rugby lifestyle magazine for men covering male grooming, fashion and accessories as well as

rugby, food, motoring, travel, finance, leisure and big boy's toys.
Readership/Target Audience: Aimed at men aged between 18 and 65 years old.
ADVERTISING RATES:
Full Page Colour £1495.00
Agency Commission: 15%
Mechanical Data: Bleed Size: +3mm, Trim Size: 297 x 210mm, Film: Digital
Copy instructions: Copy Date: 3 weeks prior to publication date
Average advertising content per issue: 40%
CONSUMER: SPORT: Rugby

HORIZON
47398U83-11_70
Editorial Address: Graduate Relations, Staffordshire University, College Road, STOKE-ON-TRENT, ST4 2DE
Tel: 01782 294942 **Fax:** 01782 294950
Email: graduate.relations@staffs.ac.uk
Advertising Address: As above.
Email: graduate.relations@staffs.ac.uk
Web site: http://www.staffs.ac.uk
Publisher: Staffordshire University
Date Established: 1992
Frequency: Half-yearly - Months published vary each year
Cover Price: Free
Circulation: 10,000 (Publisher's Statement)
Editor: Laura Perrins; **Advertising Manager:** Laura Perrins
Summary of Content: Graduate magazine covering news, sport, art and reviews of music and films.
Readership/Target Audience: Aimed at graduates of Staffordshire University.
ADVERTISING: Rates on application
CONSUMER: STUDENT PUBLICATIONS

HORIZONS
622623U74G-35_80
Editorial Address: Unit 5, Hortonwood 32, TELFORD, TF1 7YL **Tel:** 01952 671600 **Fax:** 01952 671601
Email: ruthr@natr.com
Web site: http://www.naturessunshine.co.uk
Publisher: Nature's Sunshine
Frequency: Half-yearly - Publication date varies Free to qualifying individuals
Annual Sub.: £6.00
Circulation: 7,500 (Publisher's Statement)
Usual Pagination: 20
Editor: Ruth Reeves
Summary of Content: Magazine covering alternative and complementary health products, including health supplements and homeopathic remedies, health news, research, diet, weight loss, children's health, skin care and aromatherapy.
Readership/Target Audience: Aimed at those with an interest in alternative and complementary medicine.
ADVERTISING: No Advertising taken
CONSUMER: WOMEN'S INTEREST CONSUMER MAGAZINES: Slimming & Health

HORIZONS
1882352U89E-261
Editorial Address: 85 Strand, LONDON, WC2R 0DW
Tel: 020 7550 8000 **Fax:** 020 7550 8250
Email: alison.crampin@cedarcom.co.uk
Publisher: Cedar Communications
Date Established: 2009
Frequency: Quarterly
Cover Price: Free
Editor: Alison Crampin
Summary of Content: Travel magazine covering Thomson cruises and destinations around the world.
Readership/Target Audience: Aimed at customers of Thomson cruises.
ADVERTISING: Rates on application
CONSUMER: HOLIDAYS & TRAVEL: Holidays

HORNBY MAGAZINE
1800092U79J-333
Editorial Address: PO Box 945, PETERBOROUGH, PE1 9ER **Tel:** 01733 271152
Email: hornby.magazine@wildcomms.com
Advertising Address: Foundry Road, STAMFORD, PE9 2PP
Tel: 01780 484630 **Fax:** 01780 763388
Email: linda.freeman@ianallanpublishing.co.uk
Publisher: Ian Allan Publishing Ltd
Date Established: 2007
Frequency: Monthly
Cover Price: £3.35
Usual Pagination: 116
Editor: Mike Wild
Summary of Content: Magazine covering 1950s and 1960s railways in model form with features to assist readers starting to build their own model railways.
Readership/Target Audience: Aimed at model railway enthusiasts.
ADVERTISING: Rates on application
CONSUMER: HOBBIES & DIY: Rail Enthusiasts

THE HORNSEY MAGAZINE
1638126U80B-397
Formerly: N8
Editorial Address: 64 Uplands Road, LONDON, N8 9NJ
Tel: 020 8292 5509
Email: winskill@blueyonder.co.uk
Advertising Address: As above.
Publisher: Wingale Publishing
Frequency: Quarterly
Cover Price: Free
Circulation: 8,000 (Publisher's Statement)
Usual Pagination: 40
Editor: David Winskill; **Advertising Manager:** David Winskill
Summary of Content: Magazine covering items of local interest, history, planning, property, arts, entertainment, celebrity, restaurants and clubs.
Readership/Target Audience: Aimed at those living and working in London N8.
ADVERTISING RATES:
Full Page Mono £500.00
Full Page Colour £650.00
Mechanical Data: Type Area: 262 x 186mm, Bleed Size: 303 x 216mm, Trim Size: 297 x 210mm, Col Length: 262mm, Page Width: 186mm, Film: Digital
Copy instructions: Copy Date: 10 days prior to publication date
CONSUMER: RURAL & REGIONAL INTEREST: Regional Interest Greater London

HOROSCOPE
1637734U94E-353
Editorial Address: Sequoia House, 398A Ringwood Road, FERNDOWN, BH22 9AU **Tel:** 01202 873872
Fax: 01202 874562
Email: horoscope@wimborne.co.uk
Advertising Address: As above.
Email: stewart.kearn@wimborne.co.uk
Web site: http://www.horoscope.co.uk
ISSN: 0954-9587
Publisher: Wimborne Publishing Limited
Frequency: Monthly
Cover Price: £2.95
Annual Sub.: £31.00
Circulation: 17,000 (Publisher's Statement)
Usual Pagination: 80
Editor: Mike Kenward; **Managing Director:** Mike Kenward;
Advertising Manager: Stewart Kearn
Summary of Content: Magazine covering astrology in all its forms including handwriting, dreams, dream interpretation, tarot and palmistry.
Readership/Target Audience: Aimed at those interested in astrology.
ADVERTISING RATES:
Full Page Colour £550.00
Agency Commission: 10%
Mechanical Data: Type Area: 265 x 177mm, Col Length: 265mm, Page Width: 177mm, Bleed Size: 303 x 216mm, Trim Size: 297 x 210mm, Film: Digital
Copy instructions: Copy Date: 6 weeks prior to publication date
CONSUMER: OTHER CLASSIFICATIONS: Paranormal

HORSE
47133U81D-165
Formerly: Horse Magazine
Editorial Address: Blue Fin Building, 110 Southwark Street, LONDON, SE1 0SU **Tel:** 020 3148 5000 **Fax:** 020 3148 8128
Email: joanna_browne@ipcmedia.com
Advertising Address: As above. **Tel:** 020 3148 4224
Fax: 020 3148 8130
Email: emma_sharp@ipcmedia.com
Web site: http://www.horsemagazine.co.uk
Publisher: IPC Inspire
Date Established: 1997
Frequency: 13 issues yearly - Published in the middle of the month prior to cover date
Cover Price: £3.50
Circulation: 18,268 (ABC 01/01/2008 to 31/12/2008)
Usual Pagination: 140
Editor: Jo Browne; **Advertising Manager:** Emma Sharp;
Publisher: Simon Hare
Summary of Content: Magazine focusing on some of the best riders and biggest names in the equestrian world. Featuring real rider's experiences and all things equestrian with features, news, gossip, vet articles, behind-the-scenes content, training tips and shopping pages.
Readership/Target Audience: Aimed at riders of all levels, especially those competing in both affiliated and unaffiliated events, leisure riders and those looking to improve their veterinary and horse care knowledge.
ADVERTISING RATES:
Full Page Mono £1800.00
Full Page Colour £2400.00
Agency Commission: 15%
Mechanical Data: Type Area: 271 x 188mm, Col Length: 271mm, Page Width: 188mm, Bleed Size: 303 x 216mm, Trim Size: 297 x 210mm, Film: Digital, No. of Columns (Display): 4, Col Widths (Display): 65mm
Copy instructions: Copy Date: 6 weeks prior to publication date

Average advertising content per issue: 40%
CONSUMER: ANIMALS & PETS: Horses & Ponies

HORSE AND HOUND
47129U81D-120
Editorial Address: Blue Fin Building, 110 Southwark Street, LONDON, SE1 0SU **Tel:** 020 3148 5000 **Fax:** 020 3148 8128
Email: jenny_sims@ipcmedia.com
Advertising Address: As above. **Tel:** 020 3148 4224
Fax: 020 3148 8130
Email: emma_sharp@ipcmedia.com
Web site: http://www.horseandhound.co.uk
Publisher: IPC Inspire
Date Established: 1884
Frequency: Weekly
Cover Price: £2.30
Annual Sub.: £125.00
Circulation: 61,445 (ABC 01/01/2008 to 31/12/2008)
Usual Pagination: 150
Editor: Abi Butcher; **News Editor:** Abi Butcher; **Editor-in-Chief:** Mark Hedges; **Advertising Manager:** Emma Sharp;
Managing Editor: Karen Spinner; **Publisher:** Joanna Pieters
Summary of Content: Magazine covering all aspects of equestrianism. Includes news, reports, training and advice on horse care.
Readership/Target Audience: Aimed at horse enthusiasts.
ADVERTISING RATES:
Full Page Mono £2286.00
Full Page Colour £4085.00
Agency Commission: 15%
Mechanical Data: Page Width: 188mm, Film: Digital, Type Area: 271 x 188mm, Bleed Size: 304 x 216mm, Trim Size: 297 x 210mm, Col Length: 271mm, Col Widths (Display): 46mm, No. of Columns (Display): 4
Copy instructions: Copy Date: 2 weeks prior to publication date
CONSUMER: ANIMALS & PETS: Horses & Ponies

HORSE + PONY
1692412U81D-364
Editorial Address: Roebuck House, 33 Broad Street, STAMFORD, PE9 1RB **Tel:** 01780 754900
Fax: 01780 754744
Email: s.whittington@bournepublishinggroup.co.uk
Advertising Address: As above. **Fax:** 01780 754774
Email: j.cousins@bournepublishinggroup.co.uk
Web site: http://www.horseandpony.com
ISSN: 1471-4019
Publisher: BPG (Stamford) Ltd
Date Established: 2005
Frequency: Monthly
Cover Price: £2.30
Free to qualifying individuals
Annual Sub.: £27.60
Circulation: 20,000 (Publisher's Statement)
Usual Pagination: 68
Editor: Sarah Whittington
Summary of Content: Magazine covering everything to do with horses and ponies including care, riding and general equestrian lifestyle.
Readership/Target Audience: Aimed at girls aged between 8 and 16 years old.
ADVERTISING RATES:
Full Page Mono £1950.00
Full Page Colour £1950.00
SCC £25.00
Mechanical Data: Type Area: 276 x 185mm, Bleed Size: 307 x 215mm, Trim Size: 297 x 210mm, Col Length: 276mm, Page Width: 185mm, Film: Digital
CONSUMER: ANIMALS & PETS: Horses & Ponies

HORSE & RIDER
47131U81D-145
Editorial Address: Headley House, Headley Road, Grayshott, HINDHEAD, GU26 6TU **Tel:** 01428 601020
Fax: 01428 601027
Email: djm@djmurphy.co.uk
Advertising Address: As above. **Tel:** 01428 601039
Fax: 01428 601030
Email: andrea@djmurphy.co.uk
Web site: http://www.horseandrideruk.com
Publisher: D.J. Murphy (Publishers) Ltd
Date Established: 1950
Frequency: 13 issues yearly
Cover Price: £3.70
Annual Sub.: £48.10
Circulation: 45,037 (Publisher's Statement per year)
Usual Pagination: 164
Editor: Mel Rutherford; **News Editor:** Mel Rutherford;
Advertisement Director: Andrea Moffatt
Summary of Content: Magazine covering in-depth instructional features on riding, stable management, behaviour and advice from veterinary experts.
Readership/Target Audience: Read by teenage and adult horse riders and owners.
ADVERTISING RATES:
Full Page Colour £2730.00
Agency Commission: 10%
Mechanical Data: Type Area: 273 x 186mm, Bleed Size: 307 x 220mm, Trim Size: 297 x 210mm, Col Length: 273mm,

Page Width: 186mm, Film: Digital, No. of Columns (Display): 4
Copy instructions: Copy Date: 4 weeks prior to publication date
Average advertising content per issue: 30%
CONSUMER: ANIMALS & PETS: Horses & Ponies

HORTUS: A GARDENING JOURNAL

1687728U93-193

Formerly: Hortus
Editorial Address: Bryans Ground, Stapleton, PRESTEIGNE, LD8 2LP **Tel:** 01544 260001
Fax: 01544 260015
Email: all@hortus.co.uk
Advertising Address: As above.
Email: all@hortus.co.uk
Web site: http://www.hortus.co.uk
ISSN: 0950-1657
Publisher: The Bryansground Press
Date Established: 1987
Frequency: Quarterly
Annual Sub.: £38.00
Circulation: 2,500 (Publisher's Statement)
Usual Pagination: 128
Editor: David Wheeler; **Advertising Manager:** David Wheeler
Summary of Content: Magazine with articles on gardens, plants, people, books, history, design and ornament.
Readership/Target Audience: Aimed at private gardeners, botanic gardens, horticultural colleges and libraries.
ADVERTISING RATES:
Full Page Mono £175.00
Agency Commission: 10%
Mechanical Data: Type Area: 165 x 102mm, Film: Digital, Col Length: 165mm, Page Width: 102mm
Copy instructions: Copy Date: 4 weeks prior to publication date
Average advertising content per issue: 5%
CONSUMER: GARDENING

HOT STARS

1626223U74Q-1156

Editorial Address: 10 Lower Thames Street, LONDON, EC3R 6EN **Tel:** 0871 434 1010 **Fax:** 0871 434 7505
Email: hotstars@express.co.uk
Advertising Address: As above.
Email: sam.how@express.co.uk
Publisher: Northern & Shell plc
Frequency: Weekly
Cover Price: Free
Circulation: 600,000 (Publisher's Statement)
Usual Pagination: 88
Editor: Elizabeth Gardiner; **Advertising Manager:** Sam How
Summary of Content: Magazine covering celebrity news and gossip.
Readership/Target Audience: Aimed at readers of OK! magazine.
ADVERTISING RATES:
Full Page Colour £16170.00
Agency Commission: 15%
Mechanical Data: Film: Digital
Copy instructions: Copy Date: 10 days prior to publication date
Supplement to: OK!
CONSUMER: WOMEN'S INTEREST CONSUMER MAGAZINES: Lifestyle

HOTCOURSES

1779190U88A-232

Editorial Address: 150-152 King Street, LONDON, W6 0QU **Tel:** 020 8600 5307
Email: ed.colley@hotcourses.com
Advertising Address: As above. **Tel:** 020 8600 5300
Email: danica.hillh@hotcourses.com
Web site: http://www.hotcourses.com
Publisher: Hotcourses
Date Established: 1996
Frequency: 6 issues yearly
Cover Price: £2.95
Free to qualifying individuals
Circulation: 651,720 (ABC/Electronic 01/01/2009 to 31/01/2009)
Editor: Ed Colley
Summary of Content: Directory of course listings.
Readership/Target Audience: Aimed at men and women aged 18 to 35 years old.
ADVERTISING: Rates on application
CONSUMER: EDUCATION

HOTLINE

48249U89E-132

Editorial Address: 141-143 Shoreditch High Street, LONDON, E1 6JE **Tel:** 020 8749 2329
Email: andrew.humphreys@ink-publishing.com
Advertising Address: As above. **Tel:** 020 7613 8777
Fax: 020 7613 8776
Email: stuart.wass@ink-publishing.com

ISSN: 1460-3306
Publisher: Ink Publishing
Date Established: 1998
Frequency: Monthly
Cover Price: Free
Circulation: 100,000 (Publisher's Statement)
Usual Pagination: 84
Editor: Andrew Humphreys; **Advertising Manager:** Stuart Wass
Summary of Content: Magazine covering all aspects of style, political and social issues, celebrity profiles, sports, music, movies and theatre with extracts from forthcoming books and films. Also contains a listings and destination guide.
Readership/Target Audience: Aimed at Virgin Trains passengers.
ADVERTISING RATES:
Full Page Colour £5995.00
Agency Commission: 10%
Mechanical Data: Bleed Size: 286 x 219mm, Trim Size: 280 x 213mm, Film: Digital
CONSUMER: HOLIDAYS & TRAVEL: Holidays

HOTSPUR

1750349U75B-284

Editorial Address: Bill Nicholson Way, 748 High Road, LONDON, N17 0AP **Tel:** 0844 499 5000
Email: editor@hotspurmagazine.com
Publisher: Tottenham Hotspur Football Club
Date Established: 2006
Frequency: Monthly
Cover Price: £3.45
Circulation: 33,000 (Publisher's Statement)
Usual Pagination: 68
Editor: Chris Hunt
Summary of Content: Magazine written by Spurs fans for Spurs fans with fixtures, results, player interviews and club news as well as gadgets, new products and sportswear.
Readership/Target Audience: Aimed at fans of Tottenham Hotspur football club.
ADVERTISING: No Advertising taken
CONSUMER: SPORT: Football

HOTTV

633803U89C-367

Formerly: Star TV Mag
Editorial Address: The Northern & Shell Building, 10 Lower Thames Street, LONDON, EC3R 6EN **Tel:** 0871 434 1010
Fax: 0871 520 7766
Email: belinda.wanis@dailystar.co.uk
Advertising Address: As above. **Tel:** 0871 520 1000
Fax: 0871 434 2753
Email: steve.molloy@express.co.uk
Publisher: Express Newspapers Ltd
Frequency: Weekly - Published every Saturday. See main record for circulation figure
Cover Price: Free
Usual Pagination: 64
Editor: Belinda Wanis; **Advertising Manager:** Steve Molloy
Summary of Content: TV guide with TV personality-led features.
Readership/Target Audience: Aimed at readers of the Daily Star.
ADVERTISING RATES:
Full Page Colour £15000.00
Agency Commission: 15%
Mechanical Data: No. of Columns (Display): 7, Film: Digital, Type Area: 260 x 185mm, Col Length: 260mm, Page Width: 185mm, Bleed Size: 290 x 215mm, Trim Size: 280 x 205mm
Copy instructions: Copy Date: Tuesday 12pm two weeks prior to publication date
Supplement to: Daily Star
CONSUMER: HOLIDAYS & TRAVEL: Entertainment Guides

HOUNDS

47104U81B-120

Editorial Address: Rose Cottage, Hughley, SHREWSBURY, SY5 6NX **Tel:** 01746 785637
Email: linda.sagar@yahoo.co.uk
Advertising Address: As above.
Email: linda.sagar@yahoo.co.uk
Publisher: Ravensworld Ltd
Date Established: 1984
Frequency: 8 issues yearly
Annual Sub.: £30.00
Circulation: 10,000 (Publisher's Statement)
Usual Pagination: 60
Editor: Michael Sagar; **Advertising Manager:** John Gittens; **Publisher:** Michael Sagar
Summary of Content: Magazine containing information on keeping and breeding hounds and articles on hunting.
Readership/Target Audience: Aimed at hunt masters, hound owners and those interested in field sports.
ADVERTISING RATES:
Full Page Mono £400.00
Full Page Colour £400.00
Agency Commission: 10%
Mechanical Data: Type Area: 253 x 181mm, Trim Size: 297 x 210mm, Bleed Size: 301 x 214mm, Print Process: Offset

Litho, Col Length: 253mm, No. of Columns (Display): 2, Page Width: 181mm
Copy instructions: Copy Date: 1st of the month prior to publication date
Average advertising content per issue: 40%
CONSUMER: ANIMALS & PETS: Dogs

HOUNSLOW MATTERS

1641729U80B-404

Formerly: hm (Hounslow Magazine)
Editorial Address: Civic Centre, Lampton Road, HOUNSLOW, TW3 4DN **Tel:** 020 8583 2183
Fax: 020 8583 2187
Email: hm@hounslow.gov.uk
Advertising Address: As above. **Fax:** 020 7383 0357
Email: adsales@big-agency.com
Web site: http://www.hounslow.gov.uk
Publisher: The Big Agency
Date Established: 2004
Frequency: 11 issues yearly
Cover Price: Free
Circulation: 102,000 (Publisher's Statement)
Usual Pagination: 24
Editor: Alexandra Platt; **Advertising Manager:** Alexandra Platt
Summary of Content: Magazine produced by the London Borough of Hounslow covering community and council news. Includes a what's on events and activities guide.
Readership/Target Audience: Aimed at residents of the London Borough of Hounslow and visitors to the area.
ADVERTISING RATES:
Full Page Colour £2150.00
Mechanical Data: Type Area: 270 x 185mm, Bleed Size: 303 x 216mm, Trim Size: 297 x 210mm, Col Length: 270mm, Page Width: 185mm, Film: Digital
Copy instructions: Copy Date: 2 weeks prior to publication date
Average advertising content per issue: 25%
CONSUMER: RURAL & REGIONAL INTEREST: Regional Interest Greater London

HOUSE & GARDEN

45267U74C-223

Editorial Address: Vogue House, 1 Hanover Square, LONDON, W1S 1JU **Tel:** 020 7499 9080 **Fax:** 020 7629 2907
Advertising Address: As above. **Fax:** 020 7152 3875
Email: julia.griffithjones@condenast.co.uk
Web site: http://www.houseandgarden.co.uk
Publisher: Conde Nast Publications Ltd
Frequency: Monthly
Cover Price: £3.70
Circulation: 130,692 (ABC 01/01/2009 to 30/06/2009)
Editor: Susan Crewe; **Executive Editor:** Petra Kenyon; **Features Editor:** Hatta Byng; **Managing Director:** Nicholas Coleridge; **Managing Editor:** Teresa Marlow; **Advertising Director:** Liz Jeans
Summary of Content: Magazine focusing on home decor, gardening and entertaining.
Twitter: https://twitter.com/houseandgarden
Readership/Target Audience: Aimed predominantly at women between 25 and 54 years old.
ADVERTISING RATES:
Full Page Colour £15855.00
Agency Commission: 15%
Mechanical Data: Col Length: 265mm, Page Width: 200mm, Trim Size: 285 x 220mm, Bleed Size: 291 x 226mm, Type Area: 265 x 200mm, Film: Digital
CONSUMER: WOMEN'S INTEREST CONSUMER MAGAZINES: Home & Family

HOUSE BEAUTIFUL

45268U74C-235

Editorial Address: National Magazine House, 72 Broadwick Street, LONDON, W1F 9EP **Tel:** 020 7439 5000
Fax: 020 7439 5141
Email: houseb.mail@natmags.co.uk
Advertising Address: As above.
Email: chris.tarafa@natmags.co.uk
Web site: http://www.housebeautiful.co.uk
Publisher: National Magazine Company Ltd
Date Established: 1989
Frequency: Monthly
Cover Price: £3.20
Circulation: 150,076 (ABC 01/01/2009 to 30/06/2009)
Editor: Keri Field; **Managing Director:** Jessica Burley; **Advertising Manager:** Chris Tarafa; **Publisher:** Liz Kershaw
Summary of Content: Magazine offering ideas and inspiration on home improvements, decor and lifestyle features.
Readership/Target Audience: Read mainly by homeowners between 25 and 44 years old.
ADVERTISING RATES:
Full Page Colour £10360.00
Agency Commission: 15%
Mechanical Data: Type Area: 270 x 205mm, Bleed Size: 296 x 235mm, Trim Size: 290 x 228, Col Length: 270mm, Page Width: 205mm

Copy instructions: Copy Date: 25th of month prior to publication date
CONSUMER: WOMEN'S INTEREST CONSUMER MAGAZINES: Home & Family

THE HOUSE MAGAZINE
47237U82-50

Editorial Address: Westminster Tower, 3rd Floor, 3 Albert Embankment, LONDON, SE1 7SP **Tel:** 020 7091 7500
Fax: 020 7091 7525
Email: editorial.housemag@dods.co.uk
Advertising Address: As above. **Fax:** 020 7091 7655
Email: adam.rowe@dods.co.uk
Web site: http://www.epolitix.com/house
ISSN: 0309-0426
Publisher: Dods
Date Established: 1976
Frequency: Weekly - Published weekly while Parliament sits
Annual Sub.: £195.00
Circulation: 2,603 (ABC 01/07/2007 to 30/06/2008)
Usual Pagination: 44
Editor: Richard Hall; **Managing Editor:** Richard Hall
Summary of Content: Parliamentary journal containing Westminster news, features and comments.
Readership/Target Audience: Readership includes local, national and European politicians and their staff. Also read by public affairs professionals and political journalists.
ADVERTISING RATES:
Full Page Mono £3310.85
Full Page Colour £4417.15
Agency Commission: 10%
Mechanical Data: Type Area: 225 x 180mm, Col Length: 225mm, Page Width: 150mm, Film: Digital
Copy instructions: Copy Date: Thursday prior to publication date
Average advertising content per issue: 35%
CONSUMER: CURRENT AFFAIRS & POLITICS

HOW TO SPEND IT
45636U74Q-418

Editorial Address: 1 Southwark Bridge, LONDON, SE1 9HL
Tel: 020 7873 3203
Email: rochelle.reef@ft.com
Advertising Address: As above. **Fax:** 020 7873 4336
Email: andrea.frias-andrade@ft.com
Web site: http://www.ft.com
Publisher: Financial Times
Date Established: 1994
Frequency: 26 issues yearly - See main record for circulation figure
Cover Price: Free
Usual Pagination: 72
Editor: Gillian de Bono
Summary of Content: Magazine containing features on fashion, beauty, the home, art, motoring, food and drink, health and consumer issues.
Readership/Target Audience: Read by readers of the Financial Times.
ADVERTISING RATES:
Full Page Mono £20500.00
Full Page Colour £20500.00
Agency Commission: 15%
Mechanical Data: Page Width: 245mm, Type Area: 310 x 245mm, Col Length: 310mm, Bleed Size: 356 x 283mm, Trim Size: 350 x 280mm, Film: Digital
Copy instructions: Copy Date: 3 weeks prior to publication date
Average advertising content per issue: 50%
Supplement to: Financial Times
Supplement(s): A Passion For Fashion - 2xY, Boats That Rock - 1xY, Bonus Issue - 4xY, Christmas Unwrapped - 1xY, Fine Times - 1xY, Superior Interiors - 2xY, Travel Unravelled - 1xY
CONSUMER: WOMEN'S INTEREST CONSUMER MAGAZINES: Lifestyle

HPM
46458U77E-160

Formerly: High Performer
Editorial Address: Vauxhall Sports Car Club, PO Box 976, LUTON, LU1 3WE **Tel:** 0870 240 3112 **Fax:** 01303 892984
Email: info@vxlscc.co.uk
Web site: http://www.vauxhallsportscarclub.co.uk
Publisher: Vauxhall Motors Ltd
Date Established: 2001
Frequency: 6 issues yearly
Cover Price: £2.50
Circulation: 3,000 (Publisher's Statement)
Usual Pagination: 36
Editor: Nick Reed
Summary of Content: Magazine includes news and information relating to Vauxhall cars and club events.
Readership/Target Audience: Aimed at members of Vauxhall Sports Car Club.
ADVERTISING: No Advertising taken
CONSUMER: MOTORING & CYCLING: Club Cars

HUCK
1772450U75X-1713

Editorial Address: Studio 209, Curtain House, 134-146 Curtain Road, LONDON, EC2A 3AR **Tel:** 020 7729 3675
Email: editorial@huckmagazine.com
Advertising Address: As above.
Email: dean@huckmagazine.com
Web site: http://www.huckmagazine.com
Publisher: Story Publishing Ltd
Date Established: 2006
Frequency: 6 issues yearly
Cover Price: £3.75
Circulation: 60,000 (Print Run)
Usual Pagination: 140
Editor: Vince Medeiros; **Editor-in-Chief:** Vince Medeiros; **Managing Director:** Danny Miller; **Advertising Manager:** Dean Faulkner
Summary of Content: Magazine covering surfing, skating, snowboarding and lifestyle.
Language(s): English; French; German; Italian
Readership/Target Audience: Aimed at sports enthusiasts aged between 18 and 35 years old.
ADVERTISING: Rates on application
CONSUMER: SPORT: Other Sport

THE HUDDERSFIELD EYE
1692646U80C-5270

Editorial Address: F1-F3 Holme Suite, Oaks Lane, Oaks Business Park, BARNSLEY, S71 1HT **Tel:** 0114 288 5988
Fax: 01226 240202
Email: sheilah@zmpl.co.uk
Advertising Address: As above. **Tel:** 01226 321450
Email: sheilah@zmpl.co.uk
Publisher: ClearView Publishing
Date Established: 2005
Frequency: Monthly
Circulation: 45,000 (Publisher's Statement)
Usual Pagination: 68
Editor: Sheilah Reed; **Advertising Manager:** Sheilah Reed
Summary of Content: Magazine covering local news, pubs, clubs, restaurants, theatre, fashion, what's on, gadgets and property as well as a business directory and company profiles.
Readership/Target Audience: Aimed at residents and visitors to Huddersfield.
ADVERTISING: Rates on application
Mechanical Data: Film: Digital
CONSUMER: RURAL & REGIONAL INTEREST: Regional Interest English Counties

HULL IN PRINT
44644U80C-1383

Editorial Address: Guildhall, Alfred Gelder Street, HULL, HU1 2AA **Tel:** 01482 300300 **Fax:** 01482 613845
Email: hullinprint@hullcc.gov.uk
Advertising Address: As above. **Tel:** 01782 300300
Fax: 01782 634233
Email: lynn@onestopmedia.co.uk
Web site: http://www.hullcc.gov.uk
Publisher: Hull City Council
Date Established: 2000
Frequency: Monthly
Cover Price: Free
Circulation: 135,000 (Publisher's Statement)
Usual Pagination: 44
Editor: David Speck; **Advertising Manager:** Lynn Benton
Summary of Content: Magazine containing articles, local news stories, sport and lifestyle features with an events listing and local council news.
Readership/Target Audience: Aimed at local residents and businesses.
ADVERTISING RATES:
Full Page Mono £1300.00
Full Page Colour £1300.00
Mechanical Data: Type Area: 264 x 180mm, Col Length: 264mm, Page Width: 180mm, Bleed Size: 303 x 216mm, Trim Size: 297 x 210mm, Film: Digital
Copy instructions: Copy Date: 3 weeks prior to publication date
Average advertising content per issue: 16%
CONSUMER: RURAL & REGIONAL INTEREST: Regional Interest English Counties

HUMANISM IRELAND
1687291U82-266

Formerly: Humani
Editorial Address: 25 Riverside Drive, LISBURN, BT27 4HE
Tel: 028 9267 7264
Email: brianmcclinton@btinternet.com
Advertising Address: As above.
Email: brianmcclinton@btinternet.com
Web site: http://www.nireland.humanists.net
ISSN: 1466-0555
Date Established: 1989
Frequency: 6 issues yearly
Cover Price: £2.00
Free to qualifying individuals
Circulation: 400 (Publisher's Statement)
Usual Pagination: 28

Editor: Brian McClinton; **Advertising Manager:** Brian McClinton
Summary of Content: Magazine containing articles on topics of social, political, religious, philosophical and scientific interest.
Readership/Target Audience: Aimed at humanists, freethinkers and liberals.
ADVERTISING: Rates on application
CONSUMER: CURRENT AFFAIRS & POLITICS

HURLINGHAM
1687132U75X-1707

Editorial Address: 47-49 Chelsea Manor Street, LONDON, SW3 5RZ **Tel:** 020 3239 9347
Email: hurlingham@hpa-polo.co.uk
Advertising Address: As above. **Tel:** 020 7870 3170
Email: hurlingham@hpa-polo.co.uk
Web site: http://www.hpa-polo.co.uk
ISSN: 1750-0486
Publisher: Hurlingham Media
Date Established: 2005
Frequency: 3 issues yearly - Published in February, June and October
Cover Price: £12.50
Free to qualifying individuals
Circulation: 10,000 (Publisher's Statement)
Usual Pagination: 68
Editor: Ed Barrett; **Advertising Manager:** Roderick Vere Nicoll; **Publisher:** Roderick Vere Nicoll
Summary of Content: Magazine of the Hurlingham Polo Association covering the latest news and information about polo in the UK and around the world. Also has profiles of players as well as features on lifestyle, travel, food, drink and adventure.
Readership/Target Audience: Aimed at polo players, riders and fans.
ADVERTISING RATES:
Full Page Colour £4000.00
Agency Commission: 10%
Mechanical Data: Type Area: 271 x 184mm, Bleed Size: +5mm, Trim Size: 297 x 210mm, Col Length: 271mm, Page Width: 184mm, Film: Digital
Average advertising content per issue: 25%
CONSUMER: SPORT: Other Sport

HUSTLER
1813030U86A-189

Editorial Address: UKD House, Norstead Place, LONDON, SW15 3SA **Tel:** 020 8246 5900 **Fax:** 020 8246 5920
Email: kevin@ukdltd.com
Advertising Address: As above. **Tel:** 020 7228 6366
Fax: 020 7228 6330
Email: john@ukdltd.com
Web site: http://www.adultmagstore.com
Publisher: Fire Publishing
Frequency: 13 issues yearly
Cover Price: £4.99
Circulation: 40,000 (Publisher's Statement)
Usual Pagination: 152
Editor: Kevin Maloney; **Advertising Manager:** John Reaves
Summary of Content: Magazine featuring the latest UK and American top models as well as book reviews and DVDs.
Readership/Target Audience: Aimed at men aged 18 to 40 years old.
ADVERTISING: Rates on application
CONSUMER: ADULT & GAY MAGAZINES: Adult Magazines

HYPE
634419U83-13

Editorial Address: The Potterrow, 5/2 Bristo Square, EDINBURGH, EH8 9AL **Tel:** 0131 650 2656
Fax: 0131 668 4177
Email: vpsa@eusa.ed.ac.uk
Advertising Address: As above.
Email: tony.foster@eusa.ed.ac.uk
Web site: http://www.eusa.ed.ac.uk
Publisher: EUSA
Date Established: 1998
Frequency: 26 issues yearly
Cover Price: Free
Circulation: 4,000 (Publisher's Statement)
Usual Pagination: 20
Editor: Tony Foster; **Advertising Manager:** Tony Foster
Summary of Content: Magazine of Edinburgh University Students' Association containing information on societies, entertainment, training and jobs as well as advice on a variety of issues.
Readership/Target Audience: Aimed at students of the University.
ADVERTISING RATES:
Full Page Mono £650.00
Full Page Colour £850.00
Agency Commission: 10%
Mechanical Data: Bleed Size: +3mm, Trim Size: 303 x 216mm, Film: Digital
Copy instructions: Copy Date: 1 week prior to publication date
Average advertising content per issue: 25%
CONSUMER: STUDENT PUBLICATIONS

Consumer Magazines

IAW!
47946U88R-28

Editorial Address: Swyddfa'r Urdd, Llanbadarn Road, ABERYSTWYTH, SY23 1EY **Tel:** 01970 613118
Fax: 01970 626120
Email: iaw@urdd.org
Advertising Address: As above.
Web site: http://www.urdd.org
ISSN: 1359-7396
Publisher: Urdd Gobaith Cymru
Date Established: 1995
Frequency: 10 issues yearly
Annual Sub.: £10.00
Circulation: 3,000 (Publisher's Statement)
Usual Pagination: 16
Editor: Sian Eleri Davies; **Advertising Manager:** Sian Eleri Davies
Summary of Content: Magazine for secondary school children with Welsh as a second language.
Language(s): English; Welsh
Readership/Target Audience: Aimed at 11 to 18 year olds.
ADVERTISING RATES:
Full Page Colour £200.00
Mechanical Data: Trim Size: 297 x 210mm
CONSUMER: EDUCATION: Education Related

IBIS
47172U81F-200

Editorial Address: Department of Zoology, Downing Street, CAMBRIDGE, CB2 3EJ **Tel:** 01223 336610
Fax: 01223 336676
Email: m.brooke@zoo.cam.ac.uk
Advertising Address: 9600 Garsington Road, Cowley, OXFORD, OX4 2DQ **Tel:** 01865 776868 **Fax:** 01865 714591
Email: craig.pickett@wiley.com
Web site: http://www.bou.org.uk
ISSN: 0019-1019
Publisher: Wiley-Blackwell Publishing
Date Established: 1859
Frequency: Quarterly
Free to qualifying individuals
Annual Sub.: £27.50
Circulation: 2,500 (Publisher's Statement)
Usual Pagination: 200
Editor: Steve Dudley; **Managing Director:** Steve Dudley
Summary of Content: Scientific ornithology publication covering worldwide interests.
Readership/Target Audience: Aimed at ornithologists and biologists interested in birds.
ADVERTISING RATES:
Full Page Mono £450.00
Full Page Colour £850.00
Agency Commission: 10%
Mechanical Data: Trim Size: 276 x 210mm, Film: Digital, Bleed Size: + 3mm
Copy instructions: Copy Date: 6 weeks prior to publication date
CONSUMER: ANIMALS & PETS: Birds

ICON (INTEGRATED CANCER AND ONCOLOGY NEWS)
1615875U74G-233

Editorial Address: The Elms, Radclive Road, Gawcott, BUCKINGHAM, MK18 4JB **Tel:** 01280 821211
Email: enquiries@iconmag.co.uk
Web site: http://www.iconmag.co.uk
Publisher: Health Issues Limited
Date Established: 2002
Frequency: Quarterly
Free to qualifying individuals
Annual Sub.: £30.00
Circulation: 35,000 (Print Run)
Usual Pagination: 52
Editor: Chris Woollams
Summary of Content: Magazine covering the latest knowledge on medical and complementary treatments, from surgery to supplements and radiotherapy to reiki.
Readership/Target Audience: Aimed at those touched by cancer.
ADVERTISING: No Advertising taken
CONSUMER: WOMEN'S INTEREST CONSUMER MAGAZINES: Slimming & Health

ICREATE
1667010U78E-51

Editorial Address: Richmond House, 33 Richmond Hill, BOURNEMOUTH, BH2 6EZ **Tel:** 01202 586200
Email: icreate@imagine-publishing.co.uk
Advertising Address: As above. **Fax:** 01202 294032
Email: cassandra.gilbert@imagine-publishing.co.uk
Web site: http://www.icreatemagazine.com
ISSN: 1740-2786
Publisher: Imagine Publishing
Frequency: 13 issues yearly
Cover Price: £6.00
Annual Sub.: £41.99
Circulation: 14,787 (ABC 01/07/2004 to 31/12/2004)
Usual Pagination: 132
Editor: Ben Harvell; **News Editor:** Jimmy Hayes

Summary of Content: Magazine with reviews and tutorials for software for Macs also has a cover mounted CD.
Readership/Target Audience: Aimed at users of Macs.
ADVERTISING RATES:
Full Page Colour £2000.00
Agency Commission: 10%
Mechanical Data: Type Area: 260 x 210mm, Bleed Size: 290 x 240mm, Trim Size: 280 x 230mm, Col Length: 260mm, Page Width: 210mm, Film: Digital
Copy instructions: Copy Date: 4 weeks prior to publication date
Average advertising content per issue: 30%
CONSUMER: CONSUMER ELECTRONICS: Home Computing

I-D MAGAZINE
45387U74F-360

Editorial Address: 124 Tabernacle Street, LONDON, EC2A 4SA **Tel:** 020 7490 9710 **Fax:** 020 7490 9737
Email: ben.reardon@i-dmagazine.co.uk
Advertising Address: As above. **Fax:** 020 7490 9737
Email: nicki.lemasurier@i-dmagazine.co.uk
Web site: http://www.i-dmagazine.com
ISSN: 0262-3579
Publisher: Levelprint Ltd
Date Established: 1980
Frequency: 6 issues yearly - Published in September, October, November, February, March and April
Cover Price: £4.00
Annual Sub.: £38.00
Circulation: 68,304 (Publisher's Statement)
Usual Pagination: 330
Editor: Ben Reardon; **Editor-in-Chief:** Terry Jones; **Managing Editor:** Karen Hodkinson; **Advertising Director:** Nicki Le Masurier
Summary of Content: Magazine containing articles on fashion, youth culture and music.
Readership/Target Audience: Aimed at men and women between 16 and 30 years old.
ADVERTISING RATES:
Full Page Colour £4160.00
Agency Commission: 10%
Mechanical Data: Type Area: 290 x 221mm, Film: Digital, Col Length: 290mm, Page Width: 221mm, Bleed Size: 306 x 237mm, Trim Size: 300 x 231mm
Copy instructions: Copy Date: 4 weeks prior to publication date
Average advertising content per issue: 40%
CONSUMER: WOMEN'S INTEREST CONSUMER MAGAZINES: Teenage

IDEA MAGAZINE
47723U87-114

Editorial Address: Whitefield House, 186 Kennington Park Road, LONDON, SE11 4BT **Tel:** 020 7207 2118
Fax: 020 7207 2150
Email: idea@eauk.org
Advertising Address: As above. **Tel:** 020 7207 2146
Email: j.merrifield@eauk.org
Web site: http://www.eauk.org/idea
Publisher: The Evangelical Alliance
Frequency: 6 issues yearly
Free to qualifying individuals
Circulation: 45,000 (Publisher's Statement)
Usual Pagination: 36
Editor: Rich Cline
Summary of Content: Magazine of the Evangelical Alliance UK, covering political issues, social responsibilities and theological debates.
Readership/Target Audience: Read by members of the Evangelical Alliance UK from 30 Christian denominations.
ADVERTISING RATES:
Full Page Colour £1100.00
Agency Commission: 10%
Mechanical Data: Bleed Size: 303 x 216mm, Trim Size: 297 x 210mm, No. of Columns (Display): 2
Copy instructions: Copy Date: End of month prior to publication date
Average advertising content per issue: 32%
CONSUMER: RELIGIOUS

IDEAL HOME
45270U74C-240

Editorial Address: 7th Floor, Blue Fin Building, 110 Southwark Street, LONDON, SE1 0SU **Tel:** 020 3148 5000
Fax: 020 3148 8121
Email: ideal_home@ipcmedia.com
Advertising Address: Blue Fin Building, 110 Southwark Street, LONDON, SE1 0SU **Tel:** 020 3148 5000
Email: james_zaman@ipcmedia.com
Web site: http://www.ipcmedia.com
Publisher: IPC Southbank
Date Established: 1920
Frequency: Monthly
Cover Price: £3.10
Circulation: 194,633 (ABC 01/01/2009 to 30/06/2009)
Usual Pagination: 200
Editor: Carol Pott; **Advertising Manager:** James Zaman

Summary of Content: Magazine covering home improvements, finance, travel, cookery, consumer issues, new products and shopping.
Readership/Target Audience: Aimed predominantly at women between 25 and 45 years old.
ADVERTISING RATES:
Full Page Colour £11495.00
Agency Commission: 10%
Mechanical Data: Type Area: 270 x 196mm, Trim Size: 300 x 225mm, Bleed Size: 306 x 231mm, Col Length: 270mm, Page Width: 196mm, Film: Digital
Copy instructions: Copy Date: 6 weeks prior to publication date
CONSUMER: WOMEN'S INTEREST CONSUMER MAGAZINES: Home & Family

IDJ
762694U76E-771

Editorial Address: 15-16 Lower Park Row, BRISTOL, BS1 5BN **Tel:** 0117 929 7462 **Fax:** 0117 927 6535
Email: idj@i-dj.co.uk
Advertising Address: As above.
Email: aaron@i-dj.co.uk
Web site: http://www.i-dj.co.uk
Publisher: Create Publishing
Frequency: 13 issues yearly
Cover Price: £3.60
Annual Sub.: £39.00
Circulation: 20,000 (Publisher's Statement)
Usual Pagination: 116
Editor: David Jenkins; **Advertising Manager:** Aaron Slater; **Publisher:** Chris Kempster
Summary of Content: Magazine covering DJing of all types of music including beatmatching, scratching skills and CD mixing techniques, as well as reviews of DJ gear, interviews with top DJs and record and CD reviews.
Readership/Target Audience: Aimed at DJs from beginners to advanced level.
ADVERTISING RATES:
Full Page Colour £1250.00
Agency Commission: 10%
Mechanical Data: Trim Size: 300 x 220mm, Bleed Size: +5mm, Film: Digital, Type Area: 273 x 200mm, Col Length: 273mm, Page Width: 200mm
Copy instructions: Copy Date: 4 weeks prior to publication date
Average advertising content per issue: 35%
CONSUMER: MUSIC & PERFORMING ARTS: Pop Music

THE IDLER
45637U74Q-450

Editorial Address: 13 Little London, CHICHESTER, PO19 1NZ
Email: dan@idler.co.uk
Advertising Address: As above.
Email: dan@idler.co.uk
Web site: http://www.idler.co.uk
Publisher: Ebury Press
Date Established: 1993
Frequency: Half-yearly - Published in May and October
Cover Price: £10.99
Circulation: 20,000 (Publisher's Statement)
Usual Pagination: 250
Editor: Tom Hodgkinson; **Managing Director:** Tom Hodgkinson; **Advertising Manager:** Dan Kieran; **Publisher:** Dan Kieran
Summary of Content: Magazine offering alternative views on life and society.
Readership/Target Audience: Aimed at professional males and females who predominantly work in the media.
ADVERTISING: Rates on application
CONSUMER: WOMEN'S INTEREST CONSUMER MAGAZINES: Lifestyle

IKEA FAMILY LIVE
1774774U74C-873

Editorial Address: Zetland House, Scrutton Street, LONDON, EC2A 4HJ **Tel:** 020 7749 3300
Fax: 020 7749 3325
Email: info@augustmedia.com
Advertising Address: Mongoose Media, 2 Lonsdale Road, LONDON, NW6 6RD **Tel:** 020 7306 0300
Fax: 020 7306 0301
Email: ikea@mongoosemedia.com
Web site: http://ikeaeu.ecweb.is/09/flsugb
Publisher: August Media
Frequency: Quarterly
Cover Price: Free
Circulation: 150,000 (ABC 01/01/2009 to 30/06/2009)
Usual Pagination: 100
Editor: Helen Bazuaye; **Managing Director:** Mark Lonergan; **Advertising Manager:** Heather Bird; **Managing Editor:** Carl Davidson
Summary of Content: Magazine covering real homes, lifestyle and family.
Readership/Target Audience: Aimed at members of the IKEA FAMILY loyalty scheme.
ADVERTISING RATES:
Full Page Colour £4950.00
Agency Commission: 10%

Mechanical Data: Bleed Size: 290 x 225mm, Trim Size: 280 x 215mm, Film: Digital
Copy instructions: Copy Date: 8 weeks prior to publication date
Average advertising content per issue: 9%
CONSUMER: WOMEN'S INTEREST CONSUMER MAGAZINES: Home & Family

ILLUSTRATION
1745690U84B-364

Editorial Address: 39 Elmsleigh Road, TWICKENHAM, TW2 5EF **Tel:** 07766 280221
Email: ruth.prickett@illustration-mag.com
Advertising Address: As above. **Tel:** 07900 698142
Email: sean@blainandgriermedia.com
Web site: http://www.illustration-mag.co.uk
Publisher: Illustration Magazine
Date Established: 2004
Frequency: Quarterly
Cover Price: £6.00
Circulation: 2,000 (Print Run)
Usual Pagination: 48
Editor: Ruth Prickett; **Advertisement Director:** Sean Murphy
Summary of Content: Magazine covering all aspects of historical and contemporary illustration from the artists, the collectors, the collections, the exhibitions, the history, the philosophy and the key events relating to this subject.
Readership/Target Audience: Aimed at book collectors and dealers, lecturers, professional illustrators, book publishers, fine press printers, bookbinders and current illustration students.
ADVERTISING RATES:
Full Page Colour £980.00
Mechanical Data: Col Length: 270mm, Page Width: 186mm, Type Area: 270 x 186mm, Bleed Size: 303 x 213mm, Trim Size: 297 x 210mm, Film: Digital
CONSUMER: THE ARTS & LITERARY: Literary

I'M PREGNANT!
761612U74D-265

Editorial Address: 80 Kingsway East, DUNDEE, DD4 8SL **Tel:** 01382 575130 **Fax:** 01382 452491
Email: vsmith@dcthomson.co.uk
Advertising Address: 185 Fleet Street, LONDON, EC4A 2HS **Tel:** 020 7400 1050 **Fax:** 020 7400 1090
Email: alwilson@dcthomson.co.uk
Web site: http://www.impregnantmagazine.co.uk
Publisher: D.C. Thomson & Co Ltd
Date Established: 2002
Frequency: Quarterly
Cover Price: £4.99
Circulation: 16,032 (Publisher's Statement)
Usual Pagination: 316
Editor: Valerie Smith; **Advertising Manager:** Alistair Wilson
Summary of Content: Magazine containing a complete guide from conception to birth including information on medical developments, latest products and prices, ante-natal care and maternity rights.
Readership/Target Audience: Aimed at expectant mothers.
ADVERTISING RATES:
Full Page Colour £4500.00
Agency Commission: 15%
Mechanical Data: Type Area: 276 x 200mm, Col Length: 276mm, Page Width: 200mm, Bleed Size: 311 x 231mm, Trim Size: 305 x 225mm, No. of Columns (Display): 4, Film: Digital
CONSUMER: WOMEN'S INTEREST CONSUMER MAGAZINES: Child Care

IMAGE
46948U80C-2390

Editorial Address: Upper Mounts, NORTHAMPTON, NN1 3HR **Tel:** 01604 467000 **Fax:** 01604 467190
Email: image@northantsnews.co.uk
Advertising Address: As above. **Fax:** 01604 467270
Email: claire.dalton@northantsnews.co.uk
Web site: http://www.northantsnews.com
Publisher: Northamptonshire Newspapers Ltd
Date Established: 1905
Frequency: 16 issues yearly
Cover Price: Free
Circulation: 15,000 (Publisher's Statement)
Usual Pagination: 60
Editor: Ruth Supple; **Managing Director:** Nick Mills
Summary of Content: County magazine with emphasis on local people and events. Covers fashion, homes, food and wine, travel, motoring, sport, antiques, entertainment, health and beauty.
Readership/Target Audience: Aimed at affluent residents of Northamptonshire.
ADVERTISING RATES:
Full Page Colour £754.00
Agency Commission: 10%
Mechanical Data: Trim Size: 297 x 210mm
Copy instructions: Copy Date: 2nd Friday of the month prior to publication date

Average advertising content per issue: 50%
CONSUMER: RURAL & REGIONAL INTEREST: Regional Interest English Counties

IMAGE MAGAZINE
1637926U80C-5069

Editorial Address: RMC House, Broadfield Court, Broadfield Business Park, SHEFFIELD, S8 0XF
Tel: 0114 250 6300 **Fax:** 0114 255 5881
Email: chris.wilson@regionalmagazine.co.uk
Advertising Address: As above. **Fax:** 0114 250 6320
Email: paul.wood@regionalmagazine.co.uk
Web site: http://www.northernlifestyle.com
Publisher: Regional Magazine Company
Frequency: Monthly
Cover Price: Free
Circulation: 18,600 (Publisher's Statement)
Usual Pagination: 30
Editor: Chris Wilson; **Advertising Manager:** Paul Wood
Summary of Content: Lifestyle magazine covering fashion, beauty, travel, motoring, restaurants, food and drink.
Readership/Target Audience: Aimed at households in Sheffield, Eckington, Killamarsh, Mosborough and Beighton.
ADVERTISING RATES:
Full Page Colour £944.00
Agency Commission: 10%
Mechanical Data: Type Area: 260 x 185mm, Bleed Size: 303 x 216mm, Trim Size: 297 x 210mm, Film: Digital, Col Length: 260mm, Page Width: 185mm
Copy instructions: Copy Date: 18th of the month prior to publication date
CONSUMER: RURAL & REGIONAL INTEREST: Regional Interest English Counties

IMAGINEFX
1739541U79L-386

Editorial Address: 30 Monmouth Street, BATH, BA1 2BW
Tel: 01225 442244 **Fax:** 01225 732295
Email: claire@imaginefx.com
Advertising Address: As above. **Fax:** 01225 822885
Email: helen.crossman@futurenet.co.uk
Web site: http://www.imaginefx.com
Publisher: Future Publishing Ltd
Date Established: 2006
Frequency: 13 issues yearly
Cover Price: £5.99
Circulation: 16,809 (ABC 01/01/2008 to 31/12/2008)
Usual Pagination: 116
Editor: Claire Howlett
Summary of Content: Magazine with community news, reviews, interviews, workshops and tips.
Readership/Target Audience: Aimed at fantasy and sci-fi enthusiasts.
ADVERTISING RATES:
Full Page Colour £2068.00
Agency Commission: 10%
Mechanical Data: Type Area: 265 x 215mm, Bleed Size: 286 x 238mm, Trim Size: 280 x 232mm, Col Length: 265mm, Page Width: 215mm, Film: Digital
Copy instructions: Copy Date: 3 weeks prior to publication date
CONSUMER: HOBBIES & DIY: Fantasy Games & Science Fiction

IMPACT
46050U76A-35

Editorial Address: Revenue Chambers, St. Peters Street, HUDDERSFIELD, HD1 1DL **Tel:** 01484 435011
Fax: 01484 422177
Email: martialartsltd@btconnect.com
Advertising Address: As above.
Email: martialartsltd@btconnect.com
Web site: http://www.impactmoviemagazine.co.uk
ISSN: 0964-6957
Publisher: MAI Publications
Date Established: 1991
Frequency: Monthly
Cover Price: £3.95
Circulation: 25,000 (Publisher's Statement)
Usual Pagination: 84
Editor: John Mosby; **Managing Director:** Roy Jessop
Summary of Content: Film magazine covering action, science fiction, thrillers, anime, horror, TV and film.
Readership/Target Audience: Aimed at enthusiasts of adventure and science fiction films.
ADVERTISING RATES:
Full Page Colour £1150.00
SCC £8.00
Agency Commission: 10%
Mechanical Data: Page Width: 186mm, Type Area: 271 x 186mm, Bleed Size: 303 x 216mm, Trim Size: 297 x 210mm, Col Length: 271mm, No. of Columns (Display): 3, Film: Digital
Copy instructions: Copy Date: 3rd Thursday prior to publication date
Average advertising content per issue: 20%
CONSUMER: MUSIC & PERFORMING ARTS: Cinema

IMPACT INTERNATIONAL
47238U82-65

Editorial Address: Suite B, 233 Seven Sisters Road, LONDON, N4 2DA **Tel:** 020 7263 1417 **Fax:** 020 7272 8934
Email: info@impact-magazine.com
Advertising Address: As above.
Email: info@impact-magazine.com
Web site: http://www.impact-magazine.com
ISSN: 0046-8703
Publisher: News & Media Ltd
Date Established: 1971
Frequency: Monthly
Cover Price: £3.50
Annual Sub.: £35.00
Circulation: 22,000 (Publisher's Statement)
Usual Pagination: 52
Editor: Ahmed Irfan; **Managing Director:** Mohammad Faruqi; **Advertising Manager:** Shoib Niam
Summary of Content: Magazine covering international Muslim news and political analysis.
Readership/Target Audience: Read by political analysts.
ADVERTISING RATES:
Full Page Mono £2800.00
Full Page Colour £2800.00
Agency Commission: 15%
Mechanical Data: Col Length: 270mm, Type Area: 270 x 205mm, Bleed Size: +3mm, Page Width: 205mm, Film: Digital
Copy instructions: Copy Date: 2 weeks prior to publication date
CONSUMER: CURRENT AFFAIRS & POLITICS

IMPACT (NOTTINGHAM)
47400U83-17

Editorial Address: Portland Building, University Park, NOTTINGHAM, NG7 2RD **Tel:** 0115 846 8716
Fax: 0115 935 1101
Email: magazine@impactnottingham.com
Advertising Address: As above. **Tel:** 0115 846 8742
Email: gary.cully@nottingham.ac.uk
Web site: http://www.impactnottingham.com
Publisher: University of Nottingham Student Union
Frequency: 8 issues yearly - Published monthly during term time
Cover Price: Free
Circulation: 40,000 (Publisher's Statement)
Usual Pagination: 48
Advertising Manager: Gary Cully
Summary of Content: Student magazine covering local, national and international issues. Includes articles on music, clubs, arts, sport, travel and news.
Readership/Target Audience: Aimed at students at Nottingham University and post graduates.
ADVERTISING RATES:
Full Page Colour £700.00
Agency Commission: 10%
Mechanical Data: Trim Size: 280 x 210mm, Film: Digital
Copy instructions: Copy Date: 2 weeks prior to publication date
CONSUMER: STUDENT PUBLICATIONS

IMPROVE YOUR COARSE FISHING
48533U92-72

Editorial Address: Bushfield House, Orton Centre, PETERBOROUGH, PE2 5UW **Tel:** 01733 237111
Fax: 01733 465810
Email: kevin.green@bauermedia.co.uk
Advertising Address: As above. **Fax:** 01733 288025
Email: donna.harris@bauerconsumer.co.uk
Web site: http://www.improveyourcoarsefishing.com
Publisher: Bauer Media Ltd (Orton)
Date Established: 1991
Frequency: 13 issues yearly
Cover Price: £3.10
Annual Sub.: £39.00
Circulation: 48,883 (ABC 01/01/2008 to 31/12/2008)
Usual Pagination: 140
Editor: Kevin Green; **Managing Director:** Steve Prentice
Summary of Content: Coarse fishing magazine covering advice and features on tackle. Also includes information on where to fish.
Readership/Target Audience: Aimed at anglers who want to improve their skills.
ADVERTISING RATES:
Full Page Colour £2500.00
Agency Commission: 10%
Mechanical Data: Type Area: 281 x 194mm, Col Length: 281mm, Page Width: 194mm, Trim Size: 297 x 210mm, Bleed Size: 303 x 216mm, Film: Digital
Copy instructions: Copy Date: 4 weeks prior to publication date
Average advertising content per issue: 35%
CONSUMER: ANGLING & FISHING

IMPURE MAGAZINE
48174U89C-355

Formerly: Pure Magazine
Editorial Address: 4 Kemp House, Sewardstone Road, LONDON, E2 9JL **Tel:** 020 8980 8635

Consumer Magazines

Email: tim@iampure.co.uk
Advertising Address: As above.
Email: tim@iampure.co.uk
Publisher: Create UK
Date Established: 2001
Frequency: 6 issues yearly
Cover Price: Free
Circulation: 30,000 (Publisher's Statement)
Usual Pagination: 48
Editor: Tim Hirschmann; **Advertising Manager:** Tim Hirschmann
Summary of Content: Cutting edge style magazine covering fashion, art, beauty, music and popular culture in Brighton and London.
Readership/Target Audience: Aimed at 18 and 35 years olds.
ADVERTISING RATES:
Full Page Colour £595.00
Mechanical Data: Col Length: 200mm, Page Width: 149mm, Type Area: 200 x 149mm, Bleed Size: +3mm, Film: Digital
CONSUMER: HOLIDAYS & TRAVEL: Entertainment Guides

IN
1668028U74Q-1254
Editorial Address: 2nd Floor, 9 The Broadway, WOODFORD GREEN, IG8 0HL **Tel:** 0871 226 2690
Fax: 020 8505 8252
Email: info@in-magazine.com
Advertising Address: As above. **Tel:** 020 8505 5544
Email: kelly@in-magazine.com
Web site: http://www.in-magazine.com
Publisher: In Publications Ltd
Date Established: 2005
Frequency: Monthly
Cover Price: Free
Circulation: 33,000 (Publisher's Statement)
Usual Pagination: 68
Editor: Zoe Bowditch; **Publisher:** Zoe Bowditch
Summary of Content: Lifestyle magazine covering fashion, food, interiors, travel and beauty.
Readership/Target Audience: Aimed at women and men aged 20 to 40 years old.
ADVERTISING RATES:
Full Page Colour £1000.00
Mechanical Data: Bleed Size: 303 x 216mm, Trim Size: 297 x 210mm, Film: Digital
CONSUMER: WOMEN'S INTEREST CONSUMER MAGAZINES: Lifestyle

IN AND AROUND COVENT GARDEN
1664486U89C-1029
Editorial Address: 19 Shorts Gardens, LONDON, WC2H 9AW **Tel:** 020 7240 9731 **Fax:** 020 7836 3137
Email: info@coventgarden.uk.com
Advertising Address: As above.
Email: frederic@coventgarden.uk.com
Web site: http://www.coventgarden.uk.com
Publisher: In and Around Ltd
Date Established: 1992
Frequency: Monthly
Cover Price: Free
Circulation: 52,000 (Publisher's Statement)
Usual Pagination: 40
Editor: Lorie Church; **Advertising Manager:** Frederic Galligani; **Publisher:** Kim Church
Summary of Content: Magazine covering entertainment, theatre, shopping, wining and dining, history and reviews as well as issues in and around Covent Garden.
Readership/Target Audience: Aimed at households, businesses and visitors to London WC2, Covent Garden, Central London and the West End.
ADVERTISING RATES:
Full Page Colour £2575.00
Agency Commission: 10%
Mechanical Data: Type Area: 253 x 183mm, Bleed Size: 303 x 213mm, Trim Size: 297 x 210mm, Col Length: 253mm, Page Width: 183mm, Film: Digital
Copy instructions: Copy Date: 10th of month prior to publication date
Average advertising content per issue: 25%
CONSUMER: HOLIDAYS & TRAVEL: Entertainment Guides

IN LONDON
48060U89B-185
Formerly: Londinium
Editorial Address: 233 High Holborn, LONDON, WC1V 7DN
Tel: 020 7242 5222 **Fax:** 020 7242 4184
Email: johnson@morriseurope.com
Advertising Address: As above. **Fax:** 020 7611 4666
Email: lionel.richard@morriseurope.com
Web site: http://www.morriseurope.com
ISSN: 1358-0329
Publisher: MVP Europe
Frequency: Quarterly
Free to qualifying individuals
Circulation: 75,000 (Publisher's Statement)
Usual Pagination: 82

Editor: Chris Johnson; **Publisher:** Chris Manning
Summary of Content: Magazine containing news and reviews on London. Includes features on art, theatre, fairs, business, property, shopping and restaurants. Only available for purchase in Harrods' Bookshop and Selfridges.
Readership/Target Audience: Aimed at the affluent business and leisure visitor to London.
ADVERTISING RATES:
Full Page Colour £4000.00
Agency Commission: 10%
Mechanical Data: Col Length: 248mm, Bleed Size: +5mm, Film: Digital, Type Area: 248 x 184mm, Trim Size: 300 x 225mm, Page Width: 184mm
Copy instructions: Copy Date: 30 days prior to publication date
Average advertising content per issue: 48%
CONSUMER: HOLIDAYS & TRAVEL: Hotel Magazines

IN SE 1
1772600U89C-1085
Editorial Address: 27 Blackfriars Road, LONDON, SE1 8NY
Tel: 020 7633 0766 **Fax:** 020 7401 2521
Advertising Address: As above.
Email: sales@inse1.co.uk
Web site: http://www.inse1.co.uk
ISSN: 1750-1334
Publisher: Bankside Press
Date Established: 1998
Frequency: Monthly
Cover Price: Free
Circulation: 5,000 (Publisher's Statement per month)
Usual Pagination: 8
Editor: Leigh Hatts; **Advertising Manager:** Leigh Hatts
Summary of Content: Listings magazine with features on restaurants, books and local history.
Readership/Target Audience: Aimed at those who live, work or are visiting the South Bank and Bankside areas of London.
ADVERTISING RATES:
Full Page Mono £450.00
Mechanical Data: No. of Columns (Display): 4, Type Area: 265 x 190mm, Col Length: 265mm, Page Width: 190mm, Film: Digital
Copy instructions: Copy Date: 10 days prior to publication date
CONSUMER: HOLIDAYS & TRAVEL: Entertainment Guides

IN STYLE
628899U74A-200
Editorial Address: Blue Fin Building, 110 Southwark Street, LONDON, SE1 0SU **Tel:** 020 3148 5000 **Fax:** 020 3148 8166
Advertising Address: As above.
Email: olivia_smith@ipcmedia.com
Web site: http://www.instylemagazine.co.uk
Publisher: IPC Southbank
Date Established: 2001
Frequency: Monthly
Cover Price: £3.10
Annual Sub.: £30.00
Circulation: 182,989 (ABC 01/01/2009 to 30/06/2009)
Usual Pagination: 220
Editor: Lucy Pavia; **Advertising Manager:** Olivia Smith; **Managing Editor:** Jeanette Arnold; **Advertising Director:** Lewis Tucker; **Publisher:** Kirsten Price
Summary of Content: Magazine covering fashion, beauty and celebrity lifestyle features.
Twitter: https://twitter.com/instyle_co_uk.
Readership/Target Audience: Aimed at women between 25 and 35 years old.
ADVERTISING RATES:
Full Page Colour £18321.00
Agency Commission: 10%
Mechanical Data: Page Width: 196mm, Film: Digital, Trim Size: 300 x 225mm, Bleed Size: 306 x 231mm, Type Area: 270 x 196mm, Col Length: 270mm
Copy instructions: Copy Date: 6 weeks prior to publication date
Average advertising content per issue: 40%
CONSUMER: WOMEN'S INTEREST CONSUMER MAGAZINES: Women's Interest

IN THE NIGHT GARDEN
1795324U91D-962
Editorial Address: Media Centre, 201 Wood Lane, LONDON, W12 7TQ **Tel:** 020 8433 2000
Email: stephanie.cooper@bbc.com
Advertising Address: As above. **Tel:** 020 8433 2497
Email: sophie.dennis@bbc.com
Publisher: BBC Magazines
Date Established: 2007
Frequency: 24 issues yearly
Cover Price: £1.99
Circulation: 80,334 (ABC 01/01/2009 to 30/06/2009)
Usual Pagination: 24
Editor: Stephanie Cooper
Summary of Content: Children's magazine based on the BBC children's TV show and covering the adventures of Iggle Piggle and his friends on the way to bed each evening.

Readership/Target Audience: Aimed at boys and girls aged 18 months to 3 years old.
ADVERTISING RATES:
Full Page Mono £3000.00
Full Page Colour £3000.00
Agency Commission: 10%
Mechanical Data: Type Area: 280 x 200mm, Bleed Size: 308 x 228m, Trim Size: 300 x 220mm, Col Length: 280mm, Page Width: 200mm, Film: Digital
CONSUMER: RECREATION & LEISURE: Children & Youth

INCHESHIRE
1925340U80C-5523
Editorial Address: PO Box 7, KNUTSFORD, WA16 7PP
Tel: 01565 872107 **Fax:** 01565 873943
Email: barry.hook@fsmail.net
Web site: http://www.incheshiremagazine.co.uk
Publisher: Junction 19 Media Limited
Date Established: 2001
Frequency: Monthly - 10th of the preceeding month
Cover Price: Free
Circulation: 14,500 (Publisher's Statement)
Usual Pagination: 48
Editor: Barry Hook; **Group Editor:** Barry Hook
Summary of Content: Magazine featuring articles relating to Cheshire and its personalities, news stories, light gossip and motoring.
Readership/Target Audience: Aimed at inhabitants of selected owner-occupied homes and businesses in Knutsford, Wilmslow, Alderly Edge and Prestbury and surrounding villages.
CONSUMER: RURAL & REGIONAL INTEREST: Regional Interest English Counties

THE INDEX MAGAZINE
48098U80C-3655
Formerly: The Index
Editorial Address: 39 Little Mount Sion, TUNBRIDGE WELLS, TN1 1YS **Tel:** 01892 517320 **Fax:** 01892 547370
Email: editorial@indexmagazine.co.uk
Advertising Address: As above.
Email: advertising@indexmagazine.co.uk
Web site: http://www.indexmagazine.co.uk
Publisher: S.G. Media Publications Ltd
Date Established: 1993
Frequency: Monthly
Free to qualifying individuals
Annual Sub.: £12.00
Circulation: 70,000 (Publisher's Statement)
Usual Pagination: 96
Editor: Jennie Buist-Brown; **Advertising Manager:** Stephen Gurney
Summary of Content: Lifestyle magazine covering health, fitness, travel, education, fashion, motoring, interviews, property, gardens and entertainment.
Readership/Target Audience: Aimed at residents and visitors of West Kent, East and Mid Sussex and East Surrey.
ADVERTISING RATES:
Full Page Colour £890.00
SCC £7.44
Agency Commission: 10%
Mechanical Data: Type Area: 297 x 225mm, Film: Digital, Col Length: 297mm, No. of Columns (Display): 4, Page Width: 225mm, Print Process: Web-fed offset litho
Copy instructions: Copy Date: 10th of the month prior to publication date
Average advertising content per issue: 54%
Editions:
Mid Sussex and East Surrey
West Kent and East Sussex
CONSUMER: RURAL & REGIONAL INTEREST: Regional Interest English Counties

INDEX ON CENSORSHIP
47239U82-70
Editorial Address: Free Word Centre, 60 Farringdon Road, LONDON, EC1R 3GA **Tel:** 020 7324 2522
Email: jo@indexoncensorship.org
Web site: http://www.indexonline.org
ISSN: 0306-4220
Publisher: Routledge, Taylor & Francis
Date Established: 1972
Frequency: Quarterly
Cover Price: £9.50
Annual Sub.: £32.00
Circulation: 12,000 (Publisher's Statement)
Usual Pagination: 224
Editor: Jo Glanville
Summary of Content: Publication covering all aspects of free expression.
Language(s): English; Russian; Spanish
Readership/Target Audience: Aimed at journalists, human rights groups, university teachers, lawyers, writers and the general public.
ADVERTISING: No Advertising taken
CONSUMER: CURRENT AFFAIRS & POLITICS

INDIA LINK INTERNATIONAL
1698862U90-974

Editorial Address: 42 Farm Avenue, HARROW, HA2 7LR
Tel: 020 8866 8421 **Fax:** 020 8868 7462
Email: indialink@hotmail.com
Advertising Address: As above. **Fax:** 020 8248 8417
Email: indialink@hotmail.com
Web site: http://www.indialink-online.com
ISSN: 1354-0963
Publisher: Indialink (UK) Ltd
Date Established: 1993
Frequency: 6 issues yearly
Cover Price: £3.00
Circulation: 10,000 (Publisher's Statement)
Usual Pagination: 72
Editor: Krishan Ralleigh; **Advertising Manager:** Krishan Ralleigh
Summary of Content: Magazine covering politics, business and international news as well as lifestyle, travel, health and sport.
Readership/Target Audience: Aimed at Indians living in the UK, USA and South Africa.
ADVERTISING RATES:
Full Page Colour £600.00
Mechanical Data: Bleed Size: 316 x 303mm, Trim Size: 297 x 210mm, Film: Digital
Copy instructions: Copy Date: 10th of the month prior to publication date
CONSUMER: ETHNIC

INDIANA JONES THE OFFICIAL MAGAZINE
1841983U74F-775

Editorial Address: Titan House, 144 Southwark Street, LONDON, SE1 0UP **Tel:** 020 7620 0200 **Fax:** 020 7620 0032
Email: jonathan.wilkins@titanemail.com
Advertising Address: As above.
Email: david.baluchi@titanemail.com
Publisher: Titan Magazines
Date Established: 2008
Frequency: 6 issues yearly
Cover Price: £3.75
Editor: Jonathan Wilkins
Summary of Content: Magazine covering the Indiana Jones movies with interviews, features on the making of the films, stunts and costumes.
Readership/Target Audience: Aimed at Indiana Jones fans and the public in general.
ADVERTISING RATES:
Full Page Colour $5000.00
Mechanical Data: Type Area: 256 x 180mm, Col Length: 256mm, Page Width: 180mm, Bleed Size: 282 x 206mm, Trim Size: 276 x 200mm
CONSUMER: WOMEN'S INTEREST CONSUMER MAGAZINES: Teenage

INDUBAI
1792881U74Q-1345

Editorial Address: 14-16 Peterborough Road, Fulham, LONDON, SW6 3BN **Tel:** 020 7348 7997 **Fax:** 020 7348 7996
Email: ajay@subcontinent.co.uk
Advertising Address: As above.
Email: praf@subcontinent.co.uk
Web site: http://www.indubaimag.com
Publisher: Subcontinent Publishing Ltd
Date Established: 2006
Frequency: Quarterly
Annual Sub.: £16.00
Circulation: 20,000 (Publisher's Statement)
Usual Pagination: 100
Editor: Ajay Patel
Summary of Content: Magazine covering lifestyle, travel, property and business in Dubai.
Readership/Target Audience: Aimed at those with an interest in Dubai through property, lifestyle, travel and trade shows, Emirates Airlines airport lounges, in-flight on Etihad Airways and Barclays Bank premium account holders.
ADVERTISING RATES:
Full Page Colour £2500.00
Agency Commission: 10%
Mechanical Data: Type Area: 285 x 220mm, Bleed Size: +3mm, Film: Digital
Copy instructions: Copy Date: 3 weeks prior to publication date
Average advertising content per issue: 40%
CONSUMER: WOMEN'S INTEREST CONSUMER MAGAZINES: Lifestyle

THE INFORMATION
48099U89C-147

Editorial Address: Northcliffe House, 2 Derry Street, LONDON, W8 5TT **Tel:** 020 7005 2000 **Fax:** 020 7005 2182
Advertising Address: As above. **Fax:** 020 7005 2581
Email: p.ellwood@independent.co.uk
Web site: http://www.independent.co.uk
Publisher: Independent News and Media (UK) Ltd
Frequency: Weekly - Published with Saturday's Independent. Please see main title for circulation figure
Usual Pagination: 68

Editor: Stuart Price; **Advertising Manager:** Paula Ellwood
Summary of Content: Magazine covering listings for TV, theatre and clubs and includes features on classical, jazz and dance music, comedy, Internet, events, radio, art, books and children.
Readership/Target Audience: Aimed at those who enjoy the arts.
ADVERTISING RATES:
Full Page Colour £10000.00
Mechanical Data: Page Width: 189mm, Type Area: 231 x 189mm, Col Length: 231mm, Trim Size: 256 x 213mm, Bleed Size: 262 x 219mm, Film: Digital
Copy instructions: Copy Date: 11 days prior to publication date
Editions:
North of England
South of England
Supplement to: The Independent
CONSUMER: HOLIDAYS & TRAVEL: Entertainment Guides

THE INFORMER
1817518U89C-1105

Editorial Address: PO Box 72, HEXHAM, NE47 9YY
Tel: 0191 286 5020
Email: informermag@btinternet.com
Advertising Address: As above.
Email: informermag@btinternet.com
Publisher: Informer Magazine Ltd
Frequency: Monthly
Cover Price: Free
Circulation: 20,000 (Publisher's Statement)
Editor: Peter Dixon
Summary of Content: Magazine containing arts and entertainment listings and information about upcoming live performances and festivals.
Readership/Target Audience: Aimed at men and women aged 15 to 60 years old who want to find out about local events in their area.
ADVERTISING RATES:
Full Page Mono £900.00
Full Page Colour £900.00
CONSUMER: HOLIDAYS & TRAVEL: Entertainment Guides

INNERPLACE
1913333U74Q-1437

Editorial Address: International House, 1-6 Yarmouth Place, Mayfair, LONDON, W1J 7BU
Email: newsletter@innerplace.co.uk
Web site: http://www.innerplace.co.uk
Publisher: Innerplace
Date Established: 2003
Frequency: Monthly
Cover Price: Free
Circulation: 18,000 (Publisher's Statement)
Editor: Florence Hill
Summary of Content: Newsletter covering Members clubs, restaurants, parties, film premieres, awards shows, concerts, sports, theatre, and VIP entertainment.
Readership/Target Audience: Aimed at young professionals with a high disposable income and with an interest in the best restaurants, bars and members clubs in London.
CONSUMER: WOMEN'S INTEREST CONSUMER MAGAZINES: Lifestyle

INQUIRE
47403U83-22

Formerly: Kred
Editorial Address: Mandela Building, University Of Kent, CANTERBURY, CT2 7NZ **Tel:** 01227 824257
Fax: 01227 824219
Email: chairman@inquiremedia.co.uk
Advertising Address: As above. **Tel:** 01227 824200
Fax: 01227 824204
Email: v.todd@kent.ac.uk
Publisher: University of Kent Students' Union
Date Established: 1985
Frequency: 9 issues yearly - Published monthly during university term time
Cover Price: Free
Circulation: 14,000 (Publisher's Statement)
Usual Pagination: 28
Editor: Sam Edgar; **Advertising Manager:** Vicky Todd
Summary of Content: Magazine covering campus news, sport, art and music reviews.
Readership/Target Audience: Read by students of the University of Kent.
ADVERTISING RATES:
Full Page Colour £400.00
Average advertising content per issue: 10%
CONSUMER: STUDENT PUBLICATIONS

THE INQUIRER
47724U87-115

Editorial Address: 46A Newmarket Road, Cringleford, NORWICH, NR4 6UF **Tel:** 01603 505281
Email: inquirer@btinternet.com
Advertising Address: As above.

Email: inquirer@btinternet.com
Publisher: Inquirer Publishing Co. Ltd.
Date Established: 1842
Frequency: 24 issues yearly
Cover Price: £0.65
Annual Sub.: £24.00
Circulation: 2,000 (Publisher's Statement)
Editor: M. Colleen Burns; **Advertising Manager:** M. Colleen Burns
Summary of Content: Magazine covering aspects of Unitarianism, including book reviews, letters, meditations and international religious news.
Readership/Target Audience: Aimed at people interested in liberal religion and Unitarians.
ADVERTISING RATES:
SCC £5.50
Mechanical Data: Bleed Size: 3mm, Trim Size: 297 x 210mm, Film: Digital
Copy instructions: Copy Date: 4 weeks prior to publication date
Average advertising content per issue: 5%
CONSUMER: RELIGIOUS

INSIDE72
1775583U80C-5365

Editorial Address: 46 Collingwood Road, Long Eaton, NOTTINGHAM, NG10 1DR **Tel:** 0115 919 5231
Email: info@inside72.com
Advertising Address: As above.
Email: info@inside72.com
Web site: http://www.inside72.com
Publisher: Inside72
Date Established: 2006
Frequency: Monthly
Cover Price: Free
Circulation: 4,000 (Publisher's Statement)
Usual Pagination: 36
Editor: Michelle Rowe; **Advertising Manager:** Michelle Rowe
Summary of Content: Magazine covering community information, events, local and national charities, clubs and a local business directory.
Readership/Target Audience: Aimed at households and businesses in the DE72 postcode area including Breaston, Draycott, Borrowash and Shardlow.
ADVERTISING RATES:
Full Page Mono £95.00
Full Page Colour £95.00
Copy instructions: Copy Date: 9th of the cover month
CONSUMER: RURAL & REGIONAL INTEREST: Regional Interest English Counties

INSIDE CORNWALL
48100U89C-149

Formerly: Inside Cornwall Arts Gardens Food and Top Events
Editorial Address: 2-4 The Fradgan, Newlyn, PENZANCE, TR18 5BE **Tel:** 01736 334800 **Fax:** 01736 334808
Email: mail@insidecornwall.co.uk
Advertising Address: As above.
Email: mail@insidecornwall.co.uk
Web site: http://www.insidecornwall.co.uk
ISSN: 1362-5845
Publisher: Creative Copy Ltd
Date Established: 1991
Frequency: Monthly
Cover Price: £2.80
Annual Sub.: £25.00
Circulation: 10,000 (Print Run)
Usual Pagination: 68
Editor: Kathy Hill; **Advertising Director:** Alison Waghorn; **Publisher:** Ian Waghorn
Summary of Content: Magazine featuring arts, music, theatre, gardens, events, food and drink and interiors.
Readership/Target Audience: Aimed at residents and visitors to Cornwall.
ADVERTISING RATES:
Full Page Colour £725.00
Mechanical Data: Bleed Size: +4mm, Col Widths (Display): 45.4mm, No. of Columns (Display): 4
Copy instructions: Copy Date: 2nd of the month prior to publication date
CONSUMER: HOLIDAYS & TRAVEL: Entertainment Guides

INSIDE LIVING MILTON KEYNES
1623178U80C-5083

Editorial Address: 151 Silbury Boulevard, MILTON KEYNES, MK9 1LH **Tel:** 01908 545380 **Fax:** 01908 545389
Email: sales@insidebusiness.co.uk
Advertising Address: As above.
Email: sales@insidebusiness.co.uk
Web site: http://www.insidebusiness.co.uk
Publisher: Inside Business
Frequency: 6 issues yearly
Cover Price: Free
Circulation: 18,000 (Publisher's Statement)
Editor: Alan Price; **Advertising Manager:** Paul Price

Consumer Magazines

Summary of Content: Lifestyle magazine containing news and information for Milton Keynes and featuring fashion, entertainment, food, travel, interior design, motoring and finance.
Readership/Target Audience: Aimed at those living in Milton Keynes with a high disposable income primarily 30 years old plus.
ADVERTISING RATES:
Full Page Colour £600.00
Agency Commission: 10%
Mechanical Data: Type Area: 270 x 190mm, Col Length: 270mm, Bleed Size: 303 x 216mm, Trim Size: 297 x 210mm, Page Width: 190mm
Copy instructions: Copy Date: 4 weeks prior to publication date
Average advertising content per issue: 70%
CONSUMER: RURAL & REGIONAL INTEREST: Regional Interest English Counties

INSIDE OUT
1753419U80C-5352
Editorial Address: The Old Library, Church Green West, REDDITCH, B97 4DU **Tel:** 01527 453726 **Fax:** 01527 453724
Email: maria.clift@bullivantmedia.com
Advertising Address: As above.
Email: vanessa.bradford@bullivantmedia.com
Web site: http://www.osdesign.net
Publisher: Observer Standard Newspapers Magazine Division
Frequency: 6 issues yearly
Cover Price: Free
Circulation: 30,000 (Publisher's Statement)
Usual Pagination: 68
Editor: Maria Clift
Summary of Content: Magazine covering beauty, health, fashion, interviews with celebrities and local people, cars, holidays and lifestyle.
Readership/Target Audience: Aimed at affluent home owner in Worcestershire, Warwickshire and South Birmingham.
ADVERTISING RATES:
Full Page Colour £1000.00
Agency Commission: 10%
Mechanical Data: Bleed Size: 303 x 216mm, Trim Size: 297 x 210mm, Film: Digital
Copy instructions: Copy Date: 1 week prior to publication date
Average advertising content per issue: 60%
CONSUMER: RURAL & REGIONAL INTEREST: Regional Interest English Counties

INSIDE SOAP
46100U76C-207
Editorial Address: 64 North Row, LONDON, W1K 7LL **Tel:** 020 7150 7000 **Fax:** 020 7150 7683
Email: laurajayne.tyler@insidesoap.co.uk
Advertising Address: As above. **Fax:** 020 7150 7674
Email: annabel.wetton@hf-uk.com
Web site: http://www.insidesoap.co.uk
Publisher: Hachette Filipacchi (UK) Ltd
Date Established: 1992
Frequency: Weekly
Cover Price: £1.40
Circulation: 181,883 (ABC 01/01/2009 to 30/06/2009)
Usual Pagination: 90
Editor: Steven Murphy; **News Editor:** Kate Woodward; **Features Editor:** Allison Maund; **Advertising Director:** Annabel Wetton; **Publisher:** Grace Stewart
Summary of Content: Magazine covering news and stories on television soap operas and those who star in them.
Readership/Target Audience: Aimed at soap opera enthusiasts.
ADVERTISING RATES:
Full Page Colour £4500.00
Agency Commission: 15%
Mechanical Data: Film: Digital, No. of Columns (Display): 4, Bleed Size: 285 x 215mm, Trim Size: 275 x 205mm, Type Area: 265 x 195mm, Col Length: 265mm, Page Width: 195mm
Copy instructions: Copy Date: 2 weeks prior to publication date
Average advertising content per issue: 15%
CONSUMER: MUSIC & PERFORMING ARTS: TV & Radio

INSIDE TIME
48689U94X-69_75
Editorial Address: PO Box 251, Hedge End, SOUTHAMPTON, SO30 4XJ **Tel:** 01489 795945
Fax: 01489 786495
Email: johnpbowers@tiscali.co.uk
Advertising Address: As above.
Email: jr@insidetime.co.uk
Web site: http://www.insidetime.org
ISSN: 1743-7342
Publisher: The New Bridge
Date Established: 1990
Frequency: Monthly
Annual Sub.: £25.00
Circulation: 42,000 (Publisher's Statement)
Usual Pagination: 24

Editor: John Bowers; **Advertising Manager:** John Roberts; **Managing Editor:** Eric McGraw
Summary of Content: Publication of the charity New Bridge. Contains news, letters, legal advice and features on social issues and prisons.
Readership/Target Audience: Aimed at prisoners nationwide.
ADVERTISING RATES:
Full Page Mono £2500.00
Full Page Colour £2875.00
Mechanical Data: Trim Size: 420 x 297mm, Film: Digital
Copy instructions: Copy Date: 20th of the month prior to publication date
Average advertising content per issue: 27%
CONSUMER: OTHER CLASSIFICATIONS: Miscellaneous

INSIDE UNITED
1832468U75B-293
Editorial Address: Teddington Studios, Broom Road, TEDDINGTON, TW11 9BE **Tel:** 020 8267 5000
Fax: 020 8267 5194
Email: insideunited@haymarket.com
Advertising Address: As above. **Fax:** 020 8267 5815
Email: kavita.brown@haymarket.com
Web site: http://www.haymarket.com
Publisher: Haymarket Network
Frequency: Monthly
Cover Price: £3.50
Circulation: 38,608 (ABC 01/01/2008 to 31/12/2008)
Usual Pagination: 100
Editor: Ian McLeish; **Editor-in-Chief:** Ian McLeish
Summary of Content: Magazine covering all aspects of Manchester United Football Club.
Readership/Target Audience: Aimed at United fans of all ages.
ADVERTISING RATES:
Full Page Colour £3133.00
CONSUMER: SPORT: Football

INSIDEPOKER
1640861U79F-78
Formerly: InsideEdge
Editorial Address: 30 Cleveland Street, LONDON, W1T 4JD **Tel:** 020 7907 6000
Email: editor@insidepokermag.co.uk
Advertising Address: As above. **Tel:** 020 7907 6666
Fax: 020 7907 6600
Email: russell_blackman@dennis.co.uk
Web site: http://www.insidepokermag.co.uk
Publisher: Dennis Publishing Ltd
Date Established: 2004
Frequency: Monthly
Cover Price: £2.75
Circulation: 18,319 (Publisher's Statement)
Usual Pagination: 124
Editor: Alun Bowden; **Features Editor:** Paul Cheung; **Advertising Manager:** Russell Blackman
Summary of Content: Magazine covering strategy, how to bet effectively and maximise chances of winning, improving your skills, sports betting and casino games section as well as features on professional gamblers. Specialises and mainly focuses on poker.
Readership/Target Audience: Aimed at 25 to 45 year old men with a high disposable income.
ADVERTISING RATES:
Full Page Colour £5950.00
Agency Commission: 10%
Mechanical Data: Type Area: 287 x 218mm, Bleed Size: 306 x 236mm, Trim Size: 300 x 230mm, Col Length: 287mm, Page Width: 218mm, Film: Digital
Copy instructions: Copy Date: 3 weeks prior to publication date
Average advertising content per issue: 20%
CONSUMER: HOBBIES & DIY: Games & Puzzles

INSIDER
47045U80E-46
Formerly: Glasgow City Insider
Editorial Address: City Chambers, George Square, GLASGOW, G2 1DU **Tel:** 0141 287 5740
Fax: 0141 287 0925
Email: colette.keaveny@ced.glasgow.gov.uk
Advertising Address: As above. **Tel:** 0141 287 3799
Fax: 0141 287 0940
Email: tom.cassidy@ced.glasgow.gov.uk
Web site: http://www.glasgow.gov.uk
Publisher: Glasgow City Council
Date Established: 1997
Frequency: Monthly
Cover Price: Free
Circulation: 34,500 (Publisher's Statement)
Usual Pagination: 24
Editor: Colette Keaveny; **Advertising Manager:** Tom Cassidy
Summary of Content: Magazine with articles covering features and news stories about Glasgow City Council policies, strategies, council news, staff profiles, job vacancies, competitions, offers and charity events.

Readership/Target Audience: Read by Glasgow City Council staff.
ADVERTISING RATES:
Full Page Mono £1650.00
Full Page Colour £1995.00
Agency Commission: 15%
Mechanical Data: Type Area: 270 x 185mm, Col Length: 270mm, Trim Size: 300 x 220mm, Film: Digital, Page Width: 185mm
Average advertising content per issue: 15%
CONSUMER: RURAL & REGIONAL INTEREST: Regional Interest Scotland

INSIGHT
1704771U94F-1003
Editorial Address: 105 Judd Street, LONDON, WC1H 9NE
Tel: 020 7391 2018
Email: martyn.harris@rnib.org.uk
Web site: http://www.rnib.org.uk/insightmagazine
ISSN: 1749-8902
Publisher: Royal National Institute of Blind People
Date Established: 2006
Frequency: 6 issues yearly
Annual Sub.: £21.00
Usual Pagination: 48
Editor: Martyn Harris
Summary of Content: Magazine detailing the latest in developments for children and young people with sight problems and children with additional or complex disabilities. It covers practical ideas, personal stories and help and advice from teachers, parents and learning experts to inspire at home and in the classroom.
Readership/Target Audience: Aimed at those with an interest in the education, health and well-being of children and young people with sight problems including children with complex needs.
ADVERTISING: No Advertising taken
Supplement(s): Insight Curriculum Bites - 3xY
CONSUMER: OTHER CLASSIFICATIONS: Disability

INSPIRE
1744942U87-2041
Editorial Address: CPO, Garcia Estate, Canterbury Road, WORTHING, BN13 1BW **Tel:** 01903 264556
Email: russbravo@cpo.org.uk
Advertising Address: As above.
Email: paulataylor@cpo.org.uk
Web site: http://www.inspiremagazine.org.uk
Publisher: Christian Publishing & Outreach Ltd
Date Established: 2006
Frequency: Monthly
Cover Price: Free
Circulation: 80,000 (Publisher's Statement)
Usual Pagination: 32
Editor: Russ Bravo; **Advertising Manager:** Paula Taylor
Summary of Content: Magazine covering good news stories from the UK and world church, practical advice for churches on serving their communities, interviews with well known Christians, stories of how faith has changed people's lives. Plus puzzles, news, competitions, humour and giveaways.
Readership/Target Audience: Aimed at UK Christians and others involved with their local church.
ADVERTISING RATES:
Full Page Colour £1200.00
Agency Commission: 10%
Mechanical Data: Bleed Size: 246 x 171mm, Type Area: 215 x 145mm, Col Length: 215mm, Page Width: 145mm, Digital: Digital, Trim Size: 240 x 165mm
Copy instructions: Copy Date: 5th of the month prior to publication date
Average advertising content per issue: 40%
CONSUMER: RELIGIOUS

INSPIRE
1808698U88C-180
Editorial Address: Sea Containers House, 20 Upper Ground, LONDON, SE1 9PD **Tel:** 020 7775 5777
Fax: 020 7775 5711
Email: steve.mcgrath@sevensquared.co.uk
Publisher: Seven Squared
Frequency: Quarterly
Cover Price: Free
Usual Pagination: 24
Editor: Steve McGrath; **Publisher:** Sian Dudley
Summary of Content: Magazine published on behalf of Jobcentre Plus to encourage job seekers back into work and covering employment issues, work/life balance and training and employment opportunities.
Readership/Target Audience: Aimed at job seekers.
ADVERTISING: No Advertising taken
CONSUMER: EDUCATION: Careers

INSPIRES
47754U87-208
Formerly: The Scottish Episcopalian
Editorial Address: 21 Grosvenor Crescent, EDINBURGH, EH12 5EE **Tel:** 0131 225 6357 **Fax:** 0131 346 7247
Email: inspires@scotland.anglican.org

Advertising Address: As above.
Email: press@scotland.anglican.org
Web site: http://www.scotland.anglican.org
Publisher: Newscan Ltd.
Frequency: 10 issues yearly
Annual Sub.: £10.00
Circulation: 3,000 (Publisher's Statement)
Usual Pagination: 16
Editor: Cliff Piper; **Advertising Manager:** Mary Wilkinson
Summary of Content: Magazine covering news and issues relating to the church and society.
Readership/Target Audience: Read by clergy, congregation members and other interested parties.
ADVERTISING RATES:
Full Page Mono £586.00
Full Page Colour £938.00
Agency Commission: 10%
Mechanical Data: Type Area: 287 x 200mm, Page Width: 200mm, Col Length: 287mm, Film: Digital
Copy instructions: Copy Date: 6 weeks prior to publication date
CONSUMER: RELIGIOUS

INSTANT
1827406U80E-381
Editorial Address: Whittinghame House, HADDINGTON, EH41 4QA **Tel:** 07968 198032
Email: editor@instantmagazine.co.uk
Web site: http://www.instantmagazine.co.uk
Publisher: Instant Publications
Date Established: 1999
Frequency: 6 issues yearly
Cover Price: Free
Circulation: 25,000 (Publisher's Statement)
Usual Pagination: 64
Editor: Ian Sclater; **Publisher:** Christie Dessy
Summary of Content: Magazine dedicated to cafe culture with cafe new and events as well as features on travel, food and drink, fiction, poetry, fashion, health, photography, arts, lifestyle, environment, psychology, sport and business.
Readership/Target Audience: Aimed at cafe customers in Edinburgh and East Lothian.
CONSUMER: RURAL & REGIONAL INTEREST: Regional Interest Scotland

INTELLIGENT LIFE
1643659U73-9010
Editorial Address: 25 St. James Street, LONDON, SW1A 1HG **Tel:** 020 7830 7000 **Fax:** 020 7839 4092
Email: intelligentlife@economist.com
Advertising Address: As above. **Fax:** 020 7839 4104
Email: emmawinchurch-beale@economist.com
Web site: http://www.moreintelligentlife.com
Publisher: The Economist Newspaper Ltd
Frequency: Quarterly
Cover Price: £4.95
Editor: Caroline Carter
Summary of Content: Lifestyle and luxury magazine covering fashion, beauty, travel, cars, science and general interest features.
Readership/Target Audience: Aimed at affluent and successful men and women.
ADVERTISING RATES:
Full Page Mono £5975.00
Full Page Colour £9950.00
Mechanical Data: Type Area: 270 x 210mm, Bleed Size: 296 x 236mm, Trim Size: 290 x 230mm, Col Length: 270mm, Page Width: 210mm, Film: Digital
CONSUMER: NATIONAL & INTERNATIONAL PERIODICALS

INTERACT
47210U87-2036
Formerly: CIIR News
Editorial Address: Unit 3, Canonbury Yard, 190A New North Road, LONDON, N1 7BJ **Tel:** 020 7288 8600
Fax: 020 7359 0017
Email: comms@ciir.org
Web site: http://www.progressio.org.uk
ISSN: 1816-045X
Publisher: Progressio
Date Established: 2003
Frequency: Quarterly
Cover Price: Free
Circulation: 3,000 (Publisher's Statement)
Usual Pagination: 20
Editor: Alastair Whitson
Summary of Content: Journal of Progressio includes news, analysis and features on international development issues.
Language(s): English; Spanish
Readership/Target Audience: Aimed at members of Progressio, partner organisations, media, decision makers, opinion formers and those interested in international development.
ADVERTISING: No Advertising taken
CONSUMER: RELIGIOUS

INTERFACE NEWSLETTER
761791U87-261
Formerly: Link Church Newsletter
Editorial Address: Coombswood Way, HALESOWEN, B62 8BH **Tel:** 0121 502 9620 **Fax:** 0121 561 4035
Email: merisa.macinnes@yfc.co.uk
Web site: http://www.yfc.co.uk
Publisher: Youth for Christ
Date Established: 2000
Frequency: 3 issues yearly - Published at the beginning of the school term at Christmas, in spring and summer
Cover Price: Free
Circulation: 2,000 (Print Run)
Usual Pagination: 6
Editor: Merisa MacInnes
Summary of Content: Newsletter of Youth for Christ containing church and youth work news and information on forthcoming events.
Readership/Target Audience: Read by church youth workers.
ADVERTISING: No Advertising taken
CONSUMER: RELIGIOUS

INTERNATIONAL CONNECTION
46067U76A-35_30
Editorial Address: Orchardton Hall, Auchencairn, CASTLE DOUGLAS, DG7 1QL **Tel:** 0845 130 6249
Email: edit@bnw.demon.co.uk
Advertising Address: As above.
Email: advert@bnw.demon.co.uk
Web site: http://www.britishfilm.tv
Publisher: Brave New World International Ltd
Frequency: Quarterly
Circulation: 50,000 (Publisher's Statement)
Usual Pagination: 64
Editor: Susan Foster; **Advertising Manager:** Susan Foster
Summary of Content: Publication containing British film and TV industry news and features.
Readership/Target Audience: Aimed at those involved in the TV industry.
ADVERTISING RATES:
Full Page Colour £1225.00
Mechanical Data: Trim Size: 210 x 148mm, Film: Digital
CONSUMER: MUSIC & PERFORMING ARTS: Cinema

THE INTERNATIONAL FILM GUIDE
46068U76A-214
Formerly: The TCM International Film Guide
Editorial Address: 6 Market Place, LONDON, W1W 8AF
Tel: 020 7436 9494
Email: editor.ifg@wallflowerpress.co.uk
Advertising Address: As above.
Email: saraifg@aol.com
Web site: http://www.wallflowerpress.co.uk
Publisher: Wallflower Press
Date Established: 1963
Frequency: Annual - Published in January
Cover Price: £19.99
Circulation: 10,000 (Publisher's Statement)
Usual Pagination: 450
Editor: Ian Haydn Smith; **Advertising Manager:** Sara Tyler
Summary of Content: International publication containing articles on filmmaking and the film industry in more than 120 countries plus global film festivals directory.
Readership/Target Audience: Aimed at the industry, scholars and those with an interest in the world of cinema.
ADVERTISING RATES:
Full Page Mono £2350.00
Full Page Colour £2690.00
Mechanical Data: Type Area: 204 x 138mm, Bleed Size: 246 x 174mm, Trim Size: 240 x 168mm, Col Length: 204mm, Page Width: 138mm, Film: Digital
Copy instructions: Copy Date: November 1st
CONSUMER: MUSIC & PERFORMING ARTS: Cinema

INTERNATIONAL HOMES LUXURY COLLECTION
45491U74K-792
Formerly: International Homes Investor
Editorial Address: 3 St. Johns Court, Moulsham Street, CHELMSFORD, CM2 0JD **Tel:** 01245 358877
Fax: 01245 357767
Email: jill@international-homes.com
Advertising Address: As above.
Email: gerard@international-homes.com
Web site: http://www.international-homes.com
ISSN: 1351-0746
Publisher: PPASS Ltd
Date Established: 1990
Frequency: 10 issues yearly
Cover Price: £4.50
Circulation: 28,340 (Publisher's Statement)
Usual Pagination: 212
Editor: Jill Keene; **Editor-in-Chief:** Helen Shield; **Publisher:** Stuart Shield

Summary of Content: Lifestyle and property magazine covering property sales and related services.
Readership/Target Audience: Aimed at international travellers, home buyers and sellers.
ADVERTISING RATES:
Full Page Colour £2500.00
Mechanical Data: Page Width: 180mm, Trim Size: 297 x 210mm, Bleed Size: 307 x 220mm, Film: Digital, Type Area: 260 x 180mm, Col Length: 260mm
Copy instructions: Copy Date: 2 weeks prior to publication date
Average advertising content per issue: 60%
CONSUMER: WOMEN'S INTEREST CONSUMER MAGAZINES: Home Purchase

INTERNATIONAL JOURNAL OF HERITAGE STUDIES
48844U94X-70_25
Editorial Address: Heritage Futures, The Glasgow Caledonian University, Cowcaddens Road, GLASGOW, G4 0BA **Tel:** 0141 331 8027
Email: david.boyd@tandf.co.uk
Web site: http://www.tandf.co.uk/journals
ISSN: 1352-7258
Publisher: Routledge, Taylor & Francis
Date Established: 1994
Frequency: 6 issues yearly
Annual Sub.: £126.00
Circulation: 350 (Print Run)
Usual Pagination: 96
Editor: David Boyd
Summary of Content: Journal covering heritage theory, management and history, museum studies, and tourism studies.
Readership/Target Audience: Aimed at academics and practitioners in heritage.
ADVERTISING: Rates on application
CONSUMER: OTHER CLASSIFICATIONS: Miscellaneous

INTERNATIONAL PIANO
46157U76D-340_50
Formerly: International Piano Quarterly
Editorial Address: 2nd Floor, 30 Cannon Street, LONDON, EC4M 6YJ **Tel:** 020 7618 3456 **Fax:** 020 7618 3483
Email: internationalpiano@orpheuspublications.com
Advertising Address: As above. **Tel:** 020 7618 3452
Email: lawrence.orourke@orpheuspublications.com
Web site: http://www.international-piano.com
ISSN: 1368-9770
Publisher: Orpheus Portfolio at Newsquest Specialist Media Ltd
Date Established: 1998
Frequency: 6 issues yearly
Cover Price: £5.50
Circulation: 6,934 (Publisher's Statement)
Usual Pagination: 80
Editor: Chloe Cutts
Summary of Content: Magazine covering the piano world including reviews, interviews with pianists, articles on historical pianists, concerts, CD, DVD and sheet music reviews and articles on technique and repertoire.
Readership/Target Audience: Aimed at piano enthusiasts, record collectors and pianists.
ADVERTISING RATES:
Full Page Colour £1270.00
Agency Commission: 10%
Mechanical Data: Type Area: 248 x 188mm, Col Length: 248mm, Page Width: 188mm, Bleed Size: 286 x 221mm, Trim Size: 280 x 215mm, Film: Digital
CONSUMER: MUSIC & PERFORMING ARTS: Music

INTERNATIONAL POLITICAL SCIENCE REVIEW
47324U82-78
Editorial Address: 1 Oliver's Yard, 55 City Road, LONDON, EC1Y 1SP **Tel:** 020 7324 8500 **Fax:** 020 7324 8600
Email: info@sagepub.co.uk
Advertising Address: As above.
Email: tamara.haq@sagepub.co.uk
Web site: http://www.sagepub.co.uk
ISSN: 0192-5121
Publisher: Sage Publications
Date Established: 1996
Frequency: Quarterly
Annual Sub.: £56.00
Circulation: 1,400 (Publisher's Statement)
Usual Pagination: 110
Summary of Content: Journal covering international politics. Includes articles on political analysis and methodologies.
Language(s): English; French
Readership/Target Audience: Aimed at those interested in political science.
ADVERTISING RATES:
Full Page Mono £350.00
Agency Commission: 5%
Mechanical Data: Trim Size: 190 x 125mm
CONSUMER: CURRENT AFFAIRS & POLITICS

INTERNATIONAL RECORD REVIEW

1663828U76F-216

Editorial Address: 9 Spring Bridge Mews, LONDON, W5 2AB **Tel:** 020 8567 9244 **Fax:** 020 8840 5447
Email: info@recordreview.co.uk
Advertising Address: As above.
Email: info@recordreview.co.uk
Web site: http://www.recordreview.co.uk
ISSN: 1468-5027
Date Established: 2000
Frequency: Monthly
Cover Price: £4.00
Annual Sub.: £40.00
Circulation: 10,000 (Publisher's Statement)
Usual Pagination: 96
Editor: Maire Taylor; **Advertising Manager:** Barry Irving
Summary of Content: Magazine with reviews of classical music including orchestral, chamber, instrumental, choral, vocal and opera as well as DVDs and books. Also contains news pages and letters to the Editor.
Readership/Target Audience: Aimed at classical CD and DVD collectors who know their music. Who want up-to-date comment on new and historical classical recordings being released worldwide.
ADVERTISING RATES:
Full Page Mono £750.00
Full Page Colour £1650.00
Agency Commission: 10%
Mechanical Data: Type Area: 250 x 190mm, Bleed Size: 285 x 222mm, Trim Size: 279 x 216mm, Col Length: 250mm, Page Width: 190mm, Print Process: Web-fed offset litho, Film: Digital
Copy instructions: Copy Date: 3 weeks prior to publication date
Average advertising content per issue: 20%
CONSUMER: MUSIC & PERFORMING ARTS: Opera

INTERNATIONAL RUGBY NEWS

45798U75C-310

Formerly: Rugby News
Editorial Address: Independent House, 191 Marsh Wall, LONDON, E14 9RS **Tel:** 020 7005 5077
Email: intrugbynews@indmags.co.uk
Advertising Address: As above. **Tel:** 020 7005 5031
Fax: 020 7005 5444
Email: clare.hughes@indmags.co.uk
Publisher: Independent News & Media Group
Frequency: Monthly
Cover Price: £3.20
Circulation: 44,000 (Publisher's Statement)
Usual Pagination: 116
Editor: Jon Edwards; **Advertising Manager:** Clare Hughes
Summary of Content: Magazine with news and features from the world of rugby union.
Readership/Target Audience: Read by players, fans and coaches.
ADVERTISING RATES:
Full Page Colour £2500.00
Agency Commission: 10%
Mechanical Data: Col Length: 280mm, Page Width: 195mm, Trim Size: 300 x 215mm, Type Area: 280 x 195mm, Bleed Size: 306 x 221mm, Film: Digital
Average advertising content per issue: 25%
CONSUMER: SPORT: Rugby

INTERNATIONAL SOROPTIMIST

48782U94X-70_65

Editorial Address: 87 Glisson Road, CAMBRIDGE, CB1 2HG **Tel:** 01223 311833 **Fax:** 01223 467951
Email: hq@soroptimistinternational.org
Web site: http://www.soroptimistinternational.org
Publisher: Soroptimist International
Frequency: Quarterly
Free to qualifying individuals
Annual Sub.: £2.50
Circulation: 17,000 (Publisher's Statement)
Usual Pagination: 16
Editor: Rosie Coutts
Summary of Content: Magazine containing news of Soroptimist International activities throughout the world. Includes reports of representatives to the United Nations in 5 centres, New York, Geneva, Paris, Rome and Vienna.
Language(s): English; French
Readership/Target Audience: Aimed at members of the Soroptimist Clubs.
ADVERTISING: No Advertising taken
CONSUMER: OTHER CLASSIFICATIONS: Miscellaneous

INTERNATIONAL SQUASH MAGAZINE

1695649U75H-915

Editorial Address: 4 The Spinney, Chester Road, Poynton, STOCKPORT, SK12 1HB **Tel:** 07766 576834
Email: paul.walters@isportgroup.com
Advertising Address: As above. **Tel:** 07973 544719
Email: rachelpullan@isportgroup.com

Web site: http://www.isportgroup.com
Publisher: internationalSPORTgroup
Date Established: 2005
Frequency: Quarterly
Cover Price: £3.00
Free to qualifying individuals
Circulation: 40,000 (Publisher's Statement)
Usual Pagination: 16
Editor: Paul Walters; **Advertising Manager:** Rachel Pullan
Summary of Content: Magazine reviews of the squash world tour events within each quarter as well as player profiles.
Readership/Target Audience: Aimed at squash players of all levels.
ADVERTISING RATES:
Full Page Colour £1500.00
Mechanical Data: Type Area: 277 x 190mm, Bleed Size: 307 x 220mm, Trim Size: 297 x 210mm, Col Length: 277mm, Page Width: 190mm, Film: Digital
Copy instructions: Copy Date: 30 days prior to publication date
CONSUMER: SPORT: Racquet Sports

INTERNATIONAL ZOO YEARBOOK

47091U81A-80

Editorial Address: Regents Park, LONDON, NW1 4RY
Tel: 020 7449 6282 **Fax:** 020 7449 6411
Email: yearbook@zsl.org
Advertising Address: As above.
Email: yearbook@zsl.org
Web site: http://www.zsl.org
ISSN: 0074-9664
Publisher: The Zoological Society of London
Date Established: 1960
Frequency: Annual - Published in April
Annual Sub.: £96.00
Circulation: 1,300 (Publisher's Statement)
Usual Pagination: 468
Editor: Fiona Fisken; **Advertising Manager:** Fiona Fisken;
Managing Editor: Fiona Fisken
Summary of Content: Yearbook about animals and zoology.
Readership/Target Audience: Aimed at zoologists, veterinarians, educationalists and those concerned with the care, conservation, biology and behaviour of wild animals.
ADVERTISING: Rates on application
CONSUMER: ANIMALS & PETS: Animals & Pets Protection

INTERZONE

46762U79L-120

Editorial Address: 5 Martins Lane, Witcham, ELY, CB6 2LB
Tel: 01353 777931
Email: andy@ttapress.demon.co.uk
Advertising Address: As above.
Email: andy@ttapress.demon.co.uk
Web site: http://www.ttapress.com
ISSN: 0264-3596
Publisher: TTA Press
Frequency: 6 issues yearly
Cover Price: £3.75
Annual Sub.: £21.00
Circulation: 15,000 (Publisher's Statement)
Usual Pagination: 68
Editor: Andy Cox; **Advertising Manager:** Andy Cox
Summary of Content: Magazine with science fiction and fantasy short stories and as well as reviews of video games, books and films of the genre and interviews.
Readership/Target Audience: Aimed at science fiction enthusiasts aged 18 and over.
ADVERTISING RATES:
Full Page Colour £550.00
Agency Commission: 10%
Mechanical Data: Bleed Size: 303 x 221mm, Trim Size: 297 x 215mm, Film: Digital
Copy instructions: Copy Date: 4 weeks prior to publication date
Average advertising content per issue: 15%
CONSUMER: HOBBIES & DIY: Fantasy Games & Science Fiction

INTHEPINK

1796308U74G-280

Editorial Address: PO Box 158, BROMLEY, BR1 4YH
Tel: 020 8289 3386 **Fax:** 020 8325 8352
Email: katechubb@xcessmedia.co.uk
Advertising Address: As above. **Tel:** 020 8289 3410
Email: lisaa@xcessmedia.co.uk
Publisher: Xcess Media Ltd
Date Established: 2004
Frequency: Annual - Published in October
Cover Price: £3.50
Circulation: 75,000 (Publisher's Statement)
Usual Pagination: 148
Editor: Kate Chubb; **Advertising Director:** Lisa Allen;
Publisher: Kate Chubb
Summary of Content: Lifestyle magazine covering women's fashion, travel, health, beauty and celebrities as well as covering breast cancer issues.

Readership/Target Audience: Aimed at women aged 18 to 38 years old.
ADVERTISING RATES:
Full Page Colour £8000.00
Agency Commission: 10%
Mechanical Data: Type Area: 260 x 185mm, Bleed Size: 296 x 216mm, Trim Size: 290 x 210mm, Col Length: 260mm, Page Width: 185mm, Film: Digital
Copy instructions: Copy Date: September 8th
Average advertising content per issue: 30%
CONSUMER: WOMEN'S INTEREST CONSUMER MAGAZINES: Slimming & Health

IN-THE-STICKS

45522U74K-40

Formerly: Country Homes
Editorial Address: Market House, Market Place, ALSTON, CA9 3HS **Tel:** 01434 382680 **Fax:** 01434 382264
Email: info@inthesticks.com
Advertising Address: As above.
Email: info@inthesticks.com
Web site: http://www.inthesticks.com
ISSN: 0966-6680
Publisher: Market House Publishing
Date Established: 1989
Frequency: Quarterly
Annual Sub.: £20.00
Circulation: 2,500 (Publisher's Statement)
Usual Pagination: 36
Editor: Fiona McBain; **Advertising Manager:** Jeremy Higgs
Summary of Content: Publication featuring property for sale in rural areas, villages and small country towns.
Readership/Target Audience: Aimed at those interested in buying property in rural areas.
ADVERTISING RATES:
Full Page Colour £350.00
Mechanical Data: No. of Columns (Display): 2, Trim Size: 297 x 210mm, Film: Digital
Copy instructions: Copy Date: 2 weeks prior to publication date
CONSUMER: WOMEN'S INTEREST CONSUMER MAGAZINES: Home Purchase

INTO VIEW

47725U87-120

Editorial Address: Coombswood Way, HALESOWEN, B62 8BH **Tel:** 0121 502 9620 **Fax:** 0121 561 4035
Email: tim.adams@yfc.co.uk
Web site: http://www.yfc.co.uk
Publisher: Youth for Christ
Frequency: 3 issues yearly - Published in March, July and October
Free to qualifying individuals
Circulation: 6,000 (Publisher's Statement)
Usual Pagination: 16
Editor: Tim Adams
Summary of Content: Magazine of Youth for Christ. Includes articles on news, support and events.
Readership/Target Audience: Aimed at partners of Youth for Christ, primarily those who offer financial support.
ADVERTISING: No Advertising taken
CONSUMER: RELIGIOUS

INVERCLYDER

1809918U80E-367

Editorial Address: 43A Esplanade, GREENOCK, PA16 7RY
Tel: 01475 783000 **Fax:** 01475 728145
Email: inverclyder@btinternet.com
Advertising Address: As above.
Email: inverclyder@btinternet.com
Web site: http://www.newvisionpublishing.co.uk
Publisher: New Vision Print & Publishing Ltd
Date Established: 2000
Frequency: 6 issues yearly
Cover Price: Free
Circulation: 10,000 (Publisher's Statement)
Usual Pagination: 32
Editor: Chris Jewell; **Advertising Manager:** Chris Jewell
Summary of Content: Magazine with local stories and lifestyle features including business, personal, sport, health, beauty, recipes, gardening, housing, finance and books.
Readership/Target Audience: Aimed at residents of Inverclyde.
ADVERTISING RATES:
Full Page Colour £400.00
Agency Commission: 10%
Mechanical Data: Type Area: 277 x 190mm, Col Length: 277mm, Page Width: 190mm, Film: Digital
Copy instructions: Copy Date: 2 weeks prior to publication date
Average advertising content per issue: 30%
CONSUMER: RURAL & REGIONAL INTEREST: Regional Interest Scotland

INVEST TODAY

1847140U74M-434

Editorial Address: 4 The Willows, Mill Farm Courtyard, Beachampton, MILTON KEYNES, MK19 6DS
Tel: 01908 566800 **Fax:** 01908 566802

Email: publishing@chancerypalladium.co.uk
Web site: http://www.investtoday.co.uk
ISSN: 1757-0697
Publisher: Chancery Palladium LLP
Date Established: 2007
Frequency: Quarterly
Cover Price: £3.50
Free to qualifying individuals
Circulation: 273,242 (ABC 01/01/2007 to 31/12/2007)
Usual Pagination: 132
Editor: Stephen Aaron
Summary of Content: Lifestyle orientated personal finance magazine focusing on investment and tax planning opportunities and includes in-depth features as well as general strategic articles.
Readership/Target Audience: Aimed at those wanting to make more of their money.
CONSUMER: WOMEN'S INTEREST CONSUMER MAGAZINES: Personal Finance

INVESTMENT TRUSTS
45550U74M-111

Editorial Address: 5 Malvern Drive, WOODFORD GREEN, IG8 0JR **Tel:** 020 8504 6862
Advertising Address: PO Box 49, Waldron, HEATHFIELD, TN21 0ZG **Tel:** 01435 813481 **Fax:** 01435 813075
Email: rupertsimmons@supanet.com
Web site: http://www.investment-trusts-magazine.co.uk
ISSN: 0959-9568
Publisher: Flaxdale Printers
Date Established: 1986
Frequency: Quarterly
Cover Price: £4.50
Annual Sub.: £16.00
Circulation: 20,000 (Publisher's Statement)
Usual Pagination: 100
Editor: John Davis; **Advertising Director:** Rupert Simmons; **Publisher:** John Davis
Summary of Content: The only magazine covering investment trust news and information not available from any other single source.
Readership/Target Audience: Aimed at people seeking advice on investments trusts.
ADVERTISING RATES:
Full Page Mono £1450.00
Full Page Colour £1750.00
Agency Commission: 15%
Mechanical Data: Type Area: 264 x 182mm, Col Length: 264mm, Page Width: 182mm, Film: Digital
Copy instructions: Copy Date: 3 weeks prior to publication date
Average advertising content per issue: 20%
CONSUMER: WOMEN'S INTEREST CONSUMER MAGAZINES: Personal Finance

I-ON EDINBURGH
1813516U80E-372

Editorial Address: Suite 9, 2 Commercial Street, EDINBURGH, EH6 6JA **Tel:** 0131 555 4126
Fax: 0131 554 9303
Email: info@ionmagazine.co.uk
Advertising Address: As above.
Email: info@ionmagazine.co.uk
Web site: http://www.ionmagazine.co.uk
Publisher: Treacle Productions Ltd
Date Established: 2005
Frequency: Monthly
Cover Price: Free
Circulation: 20,000 (Publisher's Statement)
Usual Pagination: 100
Editor: Laura Wood; **Advertising Manager:** Jo Morris
Summary of Content: Lifestyle magazine covering fashion, health, beauty, property, food and drink. culture news and events.
Readership/Target Audience: Aimed at men and women in Edinburgh aged 25 to 49.
ADVERTISING RATES:
Full Page Colour £1200.00
Agency Commission: 10%
Mechanical Data: Type Area: 200 x 155mm, Col Length: 200mm, Page Width: 155mm, Trim Size: 210 x 165mm
Copy instructions: Copy Date: 19th of the month prior to publication date
CONSUMER: RURAL & REGIONAL INTEREST: Regional Interest Scotland

I-ON GLASGOW
1813517U80E-373

Editorial Address: The Art House, 752-756 Argyle Street, GLASGOW, G3 8UJ **Tel:** 0141 221 6948
Email: info@ionmagazine.co.uk
Advertising Address: As above.
Email: info@ionmagazine.co.uk
Web site: http://www.ionmagazine.co.uk
Publisher: Treacle Productions Ltd
Date Established: 2007
Frequency: Monthly
Cover Price: Free
Circulation: 20,000 (Publisher's Statement)

Usual Pagination: 100
Editor: Susie Cormack
Summary of Content: Lifestyle magazine covering fashion, health, beauty, property. food and drink, culture, news and events.
Readership/Target Audience: Aimed at men and women in Glasgow aged 25 to 49 years old.
ADVERTISING RATES:
Full Page Colour £1200.00
Agency Commission: 10%
Mechanical Data: Type Area: 200 x 155mm, Col Length: 200mm, Page Width: 155mm, Trim Size: 210 x 165mm
Copy instructions: Copy Date: 14th of the month prior to publication date
CONSUMER: RURAL & REGIONAL INTEREST: Regional Interest Scotland

IPOD USER
1664989U78E-46

Formerly: Macworld Plus
Editorial Address: 4th Floor, 101 Euston Road, LONDON, NW1 2RA **Tel:** 020 7756 2880
Email: andy_penfold@idg.co.uk
Advertising Address: As above. **Tel:** 020 7756 2800
Fax: 020 7756 2838
Email: jamesp@idg.co.uk
Web site: http://www.ipoduser.co.uk
ISSN: 0957-2341
Publisher: IDG (International Data Group)
Frequency: 6 issues yearly
Cover Price: £5.99
Circulation: 20,000 (Publisher's Statement)
Usual Pagination: 100
Editor: Andy Penfold; **Advertising Manager:** James Poulson
Summary of Content: Magazine covering the range of iPods and iPhones, reviews new iPod peripherals and offers advice and tips and tricks.
Readership/Target Audience: Aimed at iPod and music fans and people who have just purchased an iPod.
ADVERTISING RATES:
Full Page Colour £2151.00
Agency Commission: 10%
Mechanical Data: Type Area: 275 x 185mm, Bleed Size: 303 x 216mm, Col Length: 275mm, Page Width: 185mm, Trim Size: 297 x 210mm, Film: Digital
Copy instructions: Copy Date: 10 days prior to publication date
Average advertising content per issue: 35%
CONSUMER: CONSUMER ELECTRONICS: Home Computing

IRELAND'S EQUESTRIAN
47134U81D-182

Editorial Address: 16 Leas Road, Mansfield Woodhouse, MANSFIELD, NG19 8JH **Tel:** 01623 474227
Email: editor.irelandsequest@ntlworld.com
Advertising Address: 106 Oak Tree Lane, MANSFIELD, NG18 3HL **Tel:** 01623 621149 **Fax:** 01484 422177
Email: martialartsltd@btconnect.com
Web site: http://www.irelandsequestrian.co.uk
ISSN: 1369-121X
Publisher: MAI Publications
Date Established: 1999
Frequency: 6 issues yearly
Cover Price: £2.50
Circulation: 20,000 (Publisher's Statement)
Usual Pagination: 100
Editor: Sue Porter; **Advertising Manager:** Philip Hardy
Summary of Content: Magazine focusing on the equestrian scene in Ireland. Includes features on holidays, veterinary, farriery, equestrian fashion, tack, health, breeding and rider profiles. Also covers articles on horse care, stable management, feeding and products.
Readership/Target Audience: Aimed at horse owners, riders and general enthusiasts.
ADVERTISING RATES:
Full Page Colour £1200.00
Agency Commission: 10%
Mechanical Data: Bleed Size: 426 x 303mm, Trim Size: 420 x 297mm, Type Area: 390 x 260mm, Col Length: 390mm, Page Width: 260mm, Film: Digital
Average advertising content per issue: 30%
CONSUMER: ANIMALS & PETS: Horses & Ponies

IRELAND'S HOMES, INTERIORS & LIVING
628769U74Q-460

Editorial Address: PO Box 42, BANGOR, BT19 7AD
Tel: 028 9147 3979 **Fax:** 028 9145 7226
Email: editorial@ihil.net
Advertising Address: As above. **Fax:** 028 9147 4223
Email: lhagerty@ihil.net
Web site: http://www.ihil.net
ISSN: 1470-7209
Publisher: Ireland's Homes Interiors and Living
Frequency: Monthly
Cover Price: £3.50
Circulation: 14,624 (ABC 01/01/2009 to 30/06/2009)

Usual Pagination: 230
Editor: Andrea Hobson; **Advertising Manager:** Louise Hagerty; **Publisher:** Mike Keenan
Summary of Content: Home and lifestyle magazine containing features on local celebrity homes, local arts and crafts, what's on, beauty, home products, cookery and gardening.
Readership/Target Audience: Aimed predominantly at women 25 years of age and over.
ADVERTISING RATES:
Full Page Colour £1600.00
Agency Commission: 10%
Mechanical Data: Page Width: 210mm, Type Area: 277 x 210mm, Bleed Size: 303 x 236mm, Col Length: 277mm, Film: Digital, Trim Size: 297 x 230mm
Copy instructions: Copy Date: 4 weeks prior to publication date
Average advertising content per issue: 30%
CONSUMER: WOMEN'S INTEREST CONSUMER MAGAZINES: Lifestyle

IRELAND'S WEDDING JOURNAL
45539U74L-195

Formerly: Wedding Journal
Editorial Address: Penton House, 38 Heron Road, Sydenham Business Park, BELFAST, BT3 9LE
Tel: 028 9045 7457 **Fax:** 028 9045 6622
Email: tara.craig@pentonpublications.co.uk
Advertising Address: As above. **Fax:** 028 9045 6611
Email: julie.boyde@pentonpublications.co.uk
Web site: http://www.weddingjournalonline.com
Publisher: Penton Publications Ltd
Date Established: 1995
Frequency: Quarterly
Cover Price: £3.95
Circulation: 15,128 (ABC 01/01/2009 to 30/06/2009)
Usual Pagination: 266
Editor: Sarah Coburn; **Advertising Manager:** Julie Boyde; **Publisher:** Bill Penton
Summary of Content: Magazine covering all aspects of weddings. Articles include choosing the dress, organising the wedding list, booking the reception, honeymoon features and setting up home.
Readership/Target Audience: Aimed at brides-to-be, grooms, mothers of future brides and bridesmaids.
ADVERTISING RATES:
Full Page Mono £1100.00
Full Page Colour £1450.00
Agency Commission: 10%
Mechanical Data: Film: Digital, Trim Size: 297 x 225mm, Bleed Size: 303 x 231mm
Copy instructions: Copy Date: 10th of the month prior to publication date
CONSUMER: WOMEN'S INTEREST CONSUMER MAGAZINES: Brides

IRISH BATHROOMS
1847717U74C-878

Editorial Address: 57A-59 Prospect Road, BANGOR, BT20 5DF **Tel:** 028 9147 8703 **Fax:** 020 9147 2045
Email: editorial@bayviewpublishing.net
Publisher: Bayview Publishing Ltd
Date Established: 2008
Frequency: Half-yearly - Published in June and December
Cover Price: £3.25
Circulation: 15,000 (Publisher's Statement)
Editor: Judith Robinson
Summary of Content: Magazine covering high end bathrooms including baths, taps, showers, Editor's choice, readers' homes and designer profiles.
Readership/Target Audience: Aimed at those looking to renew their bathrooms.
CONSUMER: WOMEN'S INTEREST CONSUMER MAGAZINES: Home & Family

IRISH BIKE
46364U77B-494_55

Editorial Address: 77 Urbal Road, Coagh, COOKSTOWN, BT80 0DR **Tel:** 028 8673 7170 **Fax:** 028 8673 7170
Email: irishbike69@btinternet.com
Advertising Address: As above.
Email: irishbike69@btinternet.com
Publisher: Mark 1 Promotions
Frequency: Monthly
Cover Price: £2.50
Annual Sub.: £24.00
Circulation: 12,000 (Publisher's Statement)
Usual Pagination: 28
Editor: Mark Hamilton; **Advertising Manager:** Mark Hamilton
Summary of Content: Newspaper covering the Irish motorcycling racing scene.
Readership/Target Audience: Read by men aged between 25 and 55 years old.
ADVERTISING: Rates on application
Agency Commission: 10%
Copy instructions: Copy Date: 5 days prior to publication date

Consumer Magazines

Average advertising content per issue: 20%
CONSUMER: MOTORING & CYCLING: Motorcycling

IRISH COUNTRY SPORTS & COUNTRY LIFE
1667556U80A-169

Editorial Address: Cranley Hill, Woodgrange Road, Hollymount, DOWNPATRICK, BT30 8JE **Tel:** 028 4483 9167
Email: countrysportsandcountrylife@btinternet.com
Advertising Address: As above.
Email: countrysportsandcountrylife@btinternet.com
Web site: http://www.countrysportsandcountrylife.com
ISSN: 1476-8240
Publisher: IMTC
Date Established: 1987
Frequency: Quarterly
Cover Price: £3.00
Circulation: 15,000 (Publisher's Statement)
Usual Pagination: 142
Editor: Albert Titterington; **Advertising Manager:** Albert Titterington
Summary of Content: Magazine covering all aspects of field and country sports in Ireland, as well as a range of features on country living, visiting the great estates of Ireland, looking at wildlife, homes and gardens, food and drink, and country art and crafts.
Readership/Target Audience: Aimed at those with an interest in country sports and country living in Ireland.
ADVERTISING RATES:
Full Page Colour £700.00
Agency Commission: 15%
Mechanical Data: Trim Size: 297 x 210mm, Type Area: 270 x 190mm, Col Length: 270mm, Print Process: 190mm
Copy instructions: Copy Date: 1 month prior to publication date
Average advertising content per issue: 30%
CONSUMER: RURAL & REGIONAL INTEREST: Rural Interest

IRISH DANCING AND CULTURE MAGAZINE
46288U76G-200

Formerly: International Irish Dancing Magazine
Editorial Address: Unit 2.4, Paintworks, Bath Road, BRISTOL, BS4 3EH **Tel:** 0117 902 9977 **Fax:** 0117 902 9978
Email: lucy.reeves@wildfirecomms.co.uk
Advertising Address: As above. **Tel:** 117 902 9977
Fax: 117 902 9978
Email: nicola@irishdancing.com
Web site: http://www.irishdancing.com
Publisher: Wildfire Communications
Date Established: 1998
Frequency: Monthly
Cover Price: £2.99
Annual Sub.: £27.50
Circulation: 30,000 (Publisher's Statement)
Usual Pagination: 80
Editor: Lucy Reeves
Summary of Content: Magazine covering Irish dancing news from around the world. Includes articles on personalities, championship results and schools and teachers information.
Readership/Target Audience: Aimed at dancers, teachers and Irish dance enthusiasts around the world.
ADVERTISING RATES:
Full Page Colour £1155.00
Mechanical Data: Trim Size: 285 x 210mm, Film: Digital, Bleed Size: 291 x 216mm
Copy instructions: Copy Date: 3 weeks prior to publication date
CONSUMER: MUSIC & PERFORMING ARTS: Dance

IRISH DEMOCRAT
47328U82-80

Editorial Address: 244 Gray's Inn Road, LONDON, WC1X 8JR **Tel:** 020 7833 3022
Email: editor@irishdemocrat.co.uk
Web site: http://www.irishdemocrat.co.uk
ISSN: 0021-1125
Publisher: Connolly Publications Ltd
Date Established: 1939
Frequency: 6 issues yearly
Cover Price: £1.00
Annual Sub.: £7.00
Circulation: 2,500 (Publisher's Statement)
Usual Pagination: 12
Editor: Michael Hall
Summary of Content: Publication containing news and analysis of Irish politics, book reviews and political commentary on the UK's role in Ireland.
Language(s): English; Gaelic
Readership/Target Audience: Aimed at the Irish in Britain, British Trade Unions and the Labour Movement.
ADVERTISING: No Advertising taken
CONSUMER: CURRENT AFFAIRS & POLITICS

IRISH KITCHENS
1847718U74C-879

Editorial Address: 57A-59 Prospect Road, BANGOR, BT20 5DF **Tel:** 028 9147 8703 **Fax:** 028 9147 2045
Email: editorial@bayviewpublishing.net
Publisher: Bayview Publishing Ltd
Frequency: Quarterly
Cover Price: £3.75
Circulation: 7,985 (ABC 01/07/2008 to 31/12/2008)
Editor: Judith Robinson
Summary of Content: Magazine covering high end kitchens including appliances, furniture, editor's choice and designer reviews.
Readership/Target Audience: Aimed at those looking to renew their kitchens.
CONSUMER: WOMEN'S INTEREST CONSUMER MAGAZINES: Home & Family

THE IRISH POST
48310U90-64

Editorial Address: 1st Floor, West Wing, 26-28 Hammersmith Grove, LONDON, W6 7HA **Tel:** 020 8741 0649
Fax: 020 8741 3382
Email: siobhanbreatnach@irishpost.co.uk
Advertising Address: As above.
Email: niamhkelly@irishpost.co.uk
Web site: http://www.irishpost.co.uk
Publisher: Thomas Crosbie Holdings Ltd
Date Established: 1970
Frequency: Weekly
Cover Price: £1.20
Annual Sub.: £55.00
Circulation: 21,794 (ABC 01/01/2008 to 31/12/2008)
Usual Pagination: 52
Editor: Jon Myles; **News Editor:** Siobhan Breatnach;
Advertising Manager: Niamh Kelly
Summary of Content: Newspaper providing a digest of the week's news from Ireland and a round-up of Irish community news from across Britain. Includes entertainment, Irish dancing news, travel, health and property.
Readership/Target Audience: Aimed at the Irish community living in Britain.
ADVERTISING RATES:
Full Page Mono £3800.00
Full Page Colour £3800.00
Agency Commission: 15%
Mechanical Data: No. of Columns (Display): 6, Type Area: 360 x 260mm, Col Length: 360mm, Page Width: 260mm, Film: Digital
Copy instructions: Copy Date: Monday prior to publication date
Average advertising content per issue: 25%
CONSUMER: ETHNIC

THE IRISH WORLD
48311U90-68

Editorial Address: 934 North Circular Road, LONDON, NW2 7JR **Tel:** 020 8453 7800 **Fax:** 020 8208 1103
Email: admin@theirishworld.com
Advertising Address: As above.
Email: sales@theirishworld.com
Web site: http://www.theirishworld.com
ISSN: 0958-0395
Publisher: I.W. Publications Ltd
Date Established: 1987
Frequency: Weekly - Published on Saturdays
Cover Price: £1.20
Circulation: 25,000 (Publisher's Statement)
Usual Pagination: 48
Editor: Maura Clancy; **News Editor:** Angela Salmon;
Managing Director: Paddy Cowan; **Publisher:** Paddy Cowan
Summary of Content: News magazine with sports and entertainment coverage.
Readership/Target Audience: Aimed at the Irish community living in Britain.
ADVERTISING RATES:
Full Page Mono £2040.00
Full Page Colour £2448.00
Agency Commission: 15%
Mechanical Data: Type Area: 340 x 257mm, Trim Size: 420 x 297mm, Col Widths (Display): 40mm, No. of Columns (Display): 6, Film: Digital, Col Length: 340mm, Page Width: 257mm
Copy instructions: Copy Date: Friday prior to publication date
Average advertising content per issue: 30%
CONSUMER: ETHNIC

ISKATE
1789452U75A-1028

Editorial Address: Albion House, 11 The Chase, CROWTHORNE, RG45 6HT **Tel:** 01344 774839
Fax: 01344 774340
Email: news@iskatemagazine.com
Advertising Address: As above. **Fax:** 01344 774839
Email: advertising@iskatemagazine.com
Web site: http://www.iskatemagazine.com
Publisher: iSkate Publications llp
Date Established: 2006
Frequency: Monthly
Cover Price: £3.50
Annual Sub.: £39.90
Circulation: 5,000 (Print Run)
Usual Pagination: 60
Editor: Scott Waller; **Advertising Manager:** Julia Greenhough
Summary of Content: Magazine covering British ice skating with news and views and profiles of skaters and clubs as well as information on learning to skate, tips and advice on topics such as fitness and nutrition and how to improve skating techniques.
Readership/Target Audience: Aimed at ice skaters and those with an interest in ice skating.
ADVERTISING RATES:
Full Page Colour £650.00
Mechanical Data: Trim Size: 303 x 216mm, Film: Digital
Copy instructions: Copy Date: 2 weeks prior to publication date
CONSUMER: SPORT

ISLAMIC TOURISM MAGAZINE
1695103U89E-244

Editorial Address: Unit 2C, 2nd Floor, 289 Cricklewood Broadway, LONDON, NW2 6NX **Tel:** 020 8452 5244
Fax: 020 8452 5388
Email: post@islamictourism.com
Advertising Address: As above.
Email: post@islamictourism.com
Web site: http://www.islamictourism.com
Publisher: TCPH Ltd
Frequency: 6 issues yearly
Cover Price: £3.00
Annual Sub.: EUR35.00
Circulation: 6,000 (Publisher's Statement)
Usual Pagination: 80
Editor: A.R. Hassan; **Editor-in-Chief:** A.R. Hassan;
Advertising Manager: Motaz Othman
Summary of Content: Magazine covering Islamic civilisation and heritage as well as tourism in Muslim countries and worldwide.
Language(s): Arabic; English; French; German; Spanish
Readership/Target Audience: Aimed at those planning holidays in Muslim countries.
ADVERTISING RATES:
Full Page Colour £2350.00
CONSUMER: HOLIDAYS & TRAVEL: Holidays

ISLAND CONNECTIONS
1666207U89E-239

Editorial Address: 87 Loopland Drive, Castlereagh Road, BELFAST, BT6 9DW **Tel:** 028 9073 8008 **Fax:** 028 9045 5684
Email: editorial@imagine8withus.com
Advertising Address: As above.
Email: jim@imagine8withus.com
Web site: http://www.imagine8withus.com
Publisher: Imagine 8 International Ltd
Date Established: 2004
Frequency: Half-yearly - Published in March and August
Cover Price: Free
Circulation: 30,000 (Publisher's Statement)
Usual Pagination: 68
Editor: Sharon Gillespie
Summary of Content: Magazine covering travel destinations, hotels and holiday attractions.
Readership/Target Audience: Aimed at passengers on the Isle of Man Steam Packet Company ferries.
ADVERTISING RATES:
Full Page Colour £1500.00
Agency Commission: 15%
Mechanical Data: Trim Size: 297 x 210mm, Film: Digital, Bleed Size: +4mm, Print Process: Litho
Average advertising content per issue: 40%
CONSUMER: HOLIDAYS & TRAVEL: Holidays

ISLAND RACER
1667150U77B-709

Editorial Address: Media Centre, Morton Way, HORNCASTLE, LN9 6JR **Tel:** 01507 529300
Fax: 01507 529499
Advertising Address: As above. **Tel:** 01507 524004
Email: swoodhouse@mortons.co.uk
Web site: http://www.islandracer.co.uk
ISSN: 1743-5838
Publisher: Mortons Media Group Ltd
Date Established: 2002
Frequency: Annual - Published in May
Cover Price: £4.45
Circulation: 22,000 (Publisher's Statement)
Usual Pagination: 148
Editor: Gerard Kane; **Advertising Manager:** Steff Woodhouse; **Publisher:** Gerard Kane
Summary of Content: Magazine covering the Isle of Man TT races.
Readership/Target Audience: Aimed at fans of the TT races as well as riders and teams.
ADVERTISING RATES:
Full Page Colour £1595.00

Agency Commission: 10%
Mechanical Data: Col Widths (Display): 44mm, Type Area: 270 x 188mm, Bleed Size: 307.5 x 220mm, Trim Size: 297.5 x 210mm, Col Length: 270mm, Page Width: 188mm, No. of Columns (Display): 4, Film: Digital
CONSUMER: MOTORING & CYCLING: Motorcycling

ISM
47391U83-8_20

Formerly: Student Metro
Editorial Address: 2 Goulston Street, LONDON, E1 7TP
Tel: 020 7320 2223 **Fax:** 020 7320 2244
Email: communications.su@londonmet.ac.uk
Advertising Address: As above.
Email: e.rowley@londonmet.ac.uk
Web site: http://www.londonmetsu.org.uk
Publisher: London Metropolitan University Students' Union
Date Established: 1974
Frequency: 6 issues yearly
Cover Price: Free
Circulation: 4,000 (Publisher's Statement)
Usual Pagination: 24
Editor: Sharif Hyder; **Advertising Manager:** Eddie Rowley
Summary of Content: Publication covering politics, cultural and educational issues. Includes news, sports, fashion, music, theatre, societies and competitions.
Readership/Target Audience: Aimed at the students of London Metropolitan University.
ADVERTISING: Rates on application
CONSUMER: STUDENT PUBLICATIONS

ITALIA!
1654972U89E-222

Editorial Address: Suite 6, Piccadilly House, London Road, BATH, BA1 6PL **Tel:** 01225 489984 **Fax:** 01225 489980
Email: paul.pettengale@anthem-publishing.com
Advertising Address: As above.
Email: sarah.hartley@anthem-publishing.com
Web site: http://www.italia-magazine.com
ISSN: 1744-7968
Publisher: Anthem Publishing Ltd
Date Established: 2004
Frequency: Monthly
Cover Price: £3.95
Circulation: 30,000 (Publisher's Statement)
Usual Pagination: 100
Editor: Amanda Robinson; **Managing Director:** Jon Bickley; **Advertising Manager:** Sarah Hartley
Summary of Content: Magazine covering Italian culture, food and wine, holidays and property.
Readership/Target Audience: Aimed at people who holiday or are interested in buying a property in Italy.
ADVERTISING RATES:
Full Page Colour £950.00
Agency Commission: 10%
Mechanical Data: Type Area: 265 x 200mm, Bleed Size: 291 x 226mm, Trim Size: 285 x 220mm, Col Length: 265mm, Page Width: 200mm, Film: Digital
Copy instructions: Copy Date: 10th of the month prior to publication date
Average advertising content per issue: 30%
CONSUMER: HOLIDAYS & TRAVEL: Holidays

ITALIAN STUDIES
47902U88A-52_80

Editorial Address: c/o Robert Gordon, Gonville and Caius College, CAMBRIDGE, CB5 8AL **Tel:** 01223 335038
Fax: 01223 335062
Email: rscg1@cam.ac.uk
Advertising Address: Suite 1C, Joseph's Well, Hanover Walk, LEEDS, LS3 1AB **Tel:** 0113 243 2800
Fax: 0113 386 8178
Email: a.holgate@maney.co.uk
Web site: http://www.sis.ac.uk
ISSN: 0075-1634
Publisher: W.S. Maney and Son Ltd
Date Established: 1937
Frequency: Half-yearly - Published in May and November
Cover Price: £28.00
Circulation: 600 (Publisher's Statement)
Usual Pagination: 200
Editor: Robert Gordon; **Advertising Manager:** Lynne Medhurst
Summary of Content: Publication covering all aspects of Italian studies.
Language(s): English; Italian
Readership/Target Audience: Aimed at academics, graduate and undergraduate students and others with an informed interest in Italian scholarly studies.
ADVERTISING: Rates on application
Average advertising content per issue: 5%
CONSUMER: EDUCATION

ITALY
754720U89E-245

Editorial Address: Middle Farm, Middle Farm Way, Poundbury, DORCHESTER, DT1 3RS **Tel:** 01305 266360
Email: editor@italymag.co.uk

Advertising Address: 2nd Floor, Bedford Chambers, The Piazza, Covent Garden, LONDON, WC2E 8HA
Tel: 020 7240 3519
Email: advertising@italymag.co.uk
Web site: http://www.italymag.co.uk
Publisher: Poundbury Publishing Ltd
Date Established: 2002
Frequency: Monthly
Cover Price: £3.75
Annual Sub.: £55.00
Circulation: 20,000 (Publisher's Statement)
Usual Pagination: 92
Editor: Peter Shaw
Summary of Content: Magazine covering places, events, fashion, holidays, property, clothes, history, food, wine, sports, celebrities and gardens in Italy.
Readership/Target Audience: Aimed at those with an interest in Italy or Italian culture.
ADVERTISING RATES:
Full Page Colour £999.00
Agency Commission: 10%
Mechanical Data: Type Area: 265 x 198mm, Bleed Size: 306 x 236mm, Trim Size: 300 x 230mm, Col Length: 265mm, Page Width: 198mm, Film: Digital
Copy instructions: Copy Date: 3 weeks prior to publication date
Average advertising content per issue: 40%
CONSUMER: HOLIDAYS & TRAVEL: Holidays

J LIFE
1810041U87-2046

Editorial Address: Host Media Centre, Savile Mount, LEEDS, LS7 3HZ **Tel:** 0845 052 2911 **Fax:** 0845 052 2912
Email: jlife@media-mad.co.uk
Advertising Address: As above.
Email: elliot@media-mad.co.uk
Web site: http://www.media-mad.co.uk
Publisher: Media Mad
Date Established: 2006
Frequency: Monthly
Cover Price: Free
Circulation: 10,000 (Publisher's Statement)
Usual Pagination: 48
Editor: Elliot Landy; **Advertising Manager:** Elliot Landy
Summary of Content: Magazine covering community information and lifestyle topics including fashion, beauty, motor reviews, home, body, health and entertainment.
Readership/Target Audience: Aimed at the Jewish community in Leeds.
ADVERTISING RATES:
Full Page Mono £800.00
Agency Commission: 10%
Mechanical Data: Type Area: 297 x 210mm, Col Length: 297mm, Page Width: 210mm, Bleed Size: +3mm, Film: Digital
Average advertising content per issue: 50%
CONSUMER: RELIGIOUS

THE JACKDAW
1626021U84A-426

Editorial Address: 93 Clissold Crescent, LONDON, N16 9AS **Tel:** 020 7254 4027 **Fax:** 020 7254 4027
Email: dg.lee@virgin.net
Advertising Address: As above.
Email: dg.lee@virgin.net
Web site: http://www.thejackdaw.co.uk
Publisher: Jackdaw Newsletters Ltd
Date Established: 2000
Frequency: 6 issues yearly
Cover Price: £4.00
Annual Sub.: £35.00
Circulation: 1,500 (Publisher's Statement)
Usual Pagination: 32
Editor: David Lee; **Advertising Manager:** David Lee
Summary of Content: Magazine taking an alternative look at visual arts and visual arts news.
Readership/Target Audience: Aimed at those interested in visual arts who do not like the existing glossy magazines.
ADVERTISING RATES:
Full Page Mono £100.00
Mechanical Data: Type Area: 269 x 200mm, Bleed Size: 270 x 210mm, Film: Digital, Col Length: 269mm, Page Width: 200mm
Copy instructions: Copy Date: 4 weeks prior to publication date
Average advertising content per issue: 14%
CONSUMER: THE ARTS & LITERARY: Arts

THE JAGUAR DRIVER
46460U77E-180

Editorial Address: Jaguar House, 18 Stuart Street, LUTON, LU1 2SL **Tel:** 01582 419332 **Fax:** 01582 455412
Email: jaguar_drivers_club@lineone.net
Advertising Address: As above.
Email: jaguar_drivers_club@lineone.net
Web site: http://www.jaguardriver.co.uk
Publisher: The Jaguar Drivers Club
Frequency: Monthly - Published on the 1st of the month
Annual Sub.: £33.00

Circulation: 13,000 (Publisher's Statement)
Editor: Steve Fermor; **Advertising Manager:** Margaret Shephard
Summary of Content: Official journal of the Jaguar Drivers Club. Includes developments of new models, technical innovations and the competition scene.
Readership/Target Audience: Read by Jaguar owners and enthusiasts.
ADVERTISING RATES:
Full Page Mono £330.00
Full Page Colour £600.00
Agency Commission: 10%
Mechanical Data: Type Area: 265 x 185mm, Trim Size: 297 x 210mm, Bleed Size: 303 x 216mm, Film: Digital, Col Length: 265mm, Page Width: 185mm
Copy instructions: Copy Date: 14th of month prior to publication date
Average advertising content per issue: 25%
CONSUMER: MOTORING & CYCLING: Club Cars

JAGUAR ENTHUSIAST
46461U77E-182

Editorial Address: 3 The Hollows, School Lane, Auckley, DONCASTER, DN9 3LB **Tel:** 01302 771818
Fax: 01302 770911
Email: nigel.thorley@btinternet.com
Advertising Address: Cudham Tithe Barn, Berrys Hill, Berrys Green, Cudham, WESTERHAM, TN16 3AG
Tel: 01959 543500 **Fax:** 01959 543585
Email: alex@kelsey.co.uk
Web site: http://www.jec.org.uk
Publisher: Kelsey Publishing Ltd
Date Established: 1985
Frequency: Monthly
Annual Sub.: £32.00
Circulation: 21,000 (Publisher's Statement)
Usual Pagination: 124
Editor: Nigel Thorley; **Advertising Manager:** Malcolm Geggus; **Publisher:** Gordon Wright
Summary of Content: Magazine featuring new and classic Jaguars, information, spares and tools.
Readership/Target Audience: Read by members of the Jaguar Enthusiasts Club, franchised dealers and traders.
ADVERTISING RATES:
Full Page Colour £1000.00
SCC £12.00
Agency Commission: 10%
Mechanical Data: Col Length: 270mm, Film: Digital, Type Area: 270 x 188mm, Print Process: Web-fed litho, Bleed Size: 303 x 216mm, Trim Size: 297 x 210mm, Page Width: 188mm
Copy instructions: Copy Date: 2nd Monday of the month prior to publication date
Average advertising content per issue: 30%
CONSUMER: MOTORING & CYCLING: Club Cars

JAGUAR HERITAGE ARCHIVE
1639205U77F-452

Editorial Address: Browns Lane, Allesley, COVENTRY, CV5 9DR **Tel:** 024 7640 1288
Email: editor@jdhtsales.co.uk
Advertising Address: As above.
Email: ads@jdhtsales.co.uk
Web site: http://www.jdht.com
ISSN: 1742-2302
Publisher: Jaguar Daimler Heritage Trust
Date Established: 2004
Frequency: Quarterly
Cover Price: £4.95
Circulation: 15,000 (Publisher's Statement)
Usual Pagination: 132
Editor: François Prins; **Advertising Manager:** François Prins
Summary of Content: Magazine produced in collaboration with the Jaguar Daimler Heritage Trust (Jaguar cars) covering the story of these uniquely British marques from 1897.
Readership/Target Audience: Aimed at fans of Jaguar cars aged 35 years plus.
ADVERTISING: Rates on application
CONSUMER: MOTORING & CYCLING: Veteran Cars

JAGUAR MAGAZINE
623138U77D-195

Formerly: Jaguar Racing Magazine
Editorial Address: Teddington Studios, Broom Road, TEDDINGTON, TW11 9BE **Tel:** 020 8267 5000
Fax: 020 8267 5872
Email: jaguar-magazine@haymarket.com
Advertising Address: As above. **Tel:** 020 8267 8601
Fax: 020 8267 5852
Email: jaguar-magazine@haymarket.com
Publisher: Haymarket Media Group Ltd
Date Established: 2000
Frequency: Half-yearly - Published in March and September
Cover Price: Free
Circulation: 200,000 (Publisher's Statement)
Usual Pagination: 84
Editor: Richard Robinson; **Advertising Manager:** Steph Allister; **Publisher:** Steph Allister

Consumer Magazines

Summary of Content: Magazine focusing on Jaguar cars and the lifestyle surrounding the cars' ownership.
Language(s): Dutch; English; French; German; Japanese; Spanish
Readership/Target Audience: Read by owners of new Jaguar cars.
ADVERTISING RATES:
Full Page Colour £8800.00
Agency Commission: 10%
Mechanical Data: Bleed Size: +3mm, Trim Size: 275 x 215mm, Film: Digital
Copy instructions: Copy Date: 4 weeks prior to publication date
Average advertising content per issue: 16%
CONSUMER: MOTORING & CYCLING: Motor Sports

JAGUAR WORLD MONTHLY   46463U77E-132

Formerly: Classic Jaguar World
Editorial Address: PO Box 13, WESTERHAM, TN16 3WT
Tel: 01959 541444 **Fax:** 01959 541400
Email: jwm.ed@kelsey.co.uk
Advertising Address: Cudham Tithe Barn, Berrys Hill, Berrys Green, Cudham, WESTERHAM, TN16 3AG
Tel: 01959 543509 **Fax:** 01959 541400
Email: matt.carson@kelseypb.co.uk
Web site: http://www.jaguar-world.com
Publisher: Kelsey Publishing Ltd
Date Established: 1988
Frequency: Monthly - Published every second Friday of the month
Cover Price: £4.25
Annual Sub.: £46.70
Circulation: 25,000 (Publisher's Statement)
Usual Pagination: 132
Editor: Matt Skelton; **Executive Editor:** Jim Patten; **Managing Editor:** Paul Skilleter; **Publisher:** Phil Weeden
Summary of Content: Magazine covering in-depth news and comment on Jaguars old and new. Includes articles on racing and restoration.
Readership/Target Audience: Aimed at Jaguar owners and drivers.
ADVERTISING RATES:
Full Page Mono £900.00
Full Page Colour £1200.00
SCC £12.00
Agency Commission: 10%
Mechanical Data: Col Length: 270mm, Film: Digital, Type Area: 270 x 188mm, Bleed Size: 303 x 216mm, Trim Size: 297 x 210mm, Print Process: Web-fed, Page Width: 188mm
Copy instructions: Copy Date: 5 weeks prior to publication date
Average advertising content per issue: 30%
CONSUMER: MOTORING & CYCLING: Club Cars

JANOMOT BENGALI NEWSWEEKLY
48312U90-82

Editorial Address: Unit 2, 20B Spelman Street, LONDON, E1 5LQ **Tel:** 020 7377 6032 **Fax:** 020 7247 0141
Email: janomot@btconnect.com
Advertising Address: As above.
Email: janomot@btconnect.com
Web site: http://www.janomotnews.com
Publisher: Publication 1969 Ltd
Date Established: 1969
Frequency: Weekly
Cover Price: £0.50
Annual Sub.: £55.00
Circulation: 20,000 (Publisher's Statement)
Usual Pagination: 72
Editor: Nobab Uddin; **Managing Director:** Amriul Choudhury; **Advertising Manager:** Syed Pasha
Summary of Content: Newspaper containing news from Bangladesh and from Bangladeshi emigrants living around the world.
Language(s): Bengali
Readership/Target Audience: Aimed at the older generation of Bangladeshi immigrants.
ADVERTISING RATES:
Full Page Mono £1800.00
Full Page Colour £2000.00
Agency Commission: 10%
Mechanical Data: Col Length: 380mm, Page Width: 260mm, Film: Digital, Type Area: 380 x 260mm, No. of Columns (Display): 6
Copy instructions: Copy Date: 1 week prior to publication date
Average advertising content per issue: 35%
CONSUMER: ETHNIC

JAPANESE PERFORMANCE   601074U77E-520

Editorial Address: Nimax House, 20 Ullswater Crescent, Ullswater Business Park, COULSDON, CR5 2HR
Tel: 01344 648532 **Fax:** 020 8763 1001
Email: jap@chpltd.com
Advertising Address: As above. **Tel:** 020 8655 6400
Email: ads@chpltd.com
Web site: http://www.chpltd.com

Publisher: CH Publications Ltd
Frequency: Monthly
Cover Price: £4.25
Circulation: 40,000 (Publisher's Statement)
Usual Pagination: 132
Editor: Christopher Rees
Summary of Content: Magazine covering all aspects of the Japanese performance car scene. Includes advice on buying, owning, running and modifying a Japanese car. Also contains tuning and customising guides and features on some of the best modified cars.
Readership/Target Audience: Aimed at Japanese car owners and enthusiasts.
ADVERTISING RATES:
Full Page Mono £1150.00
Full Page Colour £1420.00
Agency Commission: 10%
Mechanical Data: Type Area: 267 x 190mm, Col Length: 267mm, Page Width: 190mm, Trim Size: 297 x 210mm, Film: Positive, right reading, emulsion side down. Digital, Bleed Size: 309 x 222mm
Copy instructions: Copy Date: 4 weeks prior to publication date
Average advertising content per issue: 45%
CONSUMER: MOTORING & CYCLING: Club Cars

JAZZ GUIDE   46203U76D-344

Editorial Address: 44 Rawlins Road, Bradwell, MILTON KEYNES, MK13 9DL **Tel:** 01908 312392 **Fax:** 01908 312392
Advertising Address: As above.
Publisher: Jazz Music Society
Date Established: 1976
Frequency: Monthly
Free to qualifying individuals
Circulation: 12,000 (Publisher's Statement)
Usual Pagination: 76
Editor: Bernard Tyrrell; **Advertising Manager:** Bernard Tyrrell
Summary of Content: Guide covering details of traditional and mainstream jazz bands and venues throughout the country.
Readership/Target Audience: Aimed at those with an interest in jazz music.
ADVERTISING RATES:
Full Page Mono £130.00
Mechanical Data: Type Area: 196 x 136mm, Col Widths (Display): 65mm, No. of Columns (Display): 2, Film: Digital, Col Length: 196mm, Page Width: 136mm
Copy instructions: Copy Date: 10th of the month prior to publication date
Average advertising content per issue: 100%
CONSUMER: MUSIC & PERFORMING ARTS: Music

JAZZ JOURNAL INTERNATIONAL
46159U76D-345

Editorial Address: 3 Forest Road, LOUGHTON, IG10 1DR
Tel: 020 8532 0456 **Fax:** 020 8532 0440
Advertising Address: As above.
ISSN: 0140-2285
Publisher: Jazz Journal Ltd
Date Established: 1948
Frequency: Monthly
Cover Price: £3.75
Annual Sub.: £40.00
Circulation: 8,000 (Publisher's Statement)
Usual Pagination: 52
Editor: Janet Cook; **Managing Director:** Eddie Cook; **Advertising Manager:** Janet Cook
Summary of Content: Magazine covering record, book, cinema and video reviews. Includes features on jazz history and interviews with musicians.
Readership/Target Audience: Aimed primarily at jazz record collectors.
ADVERTISING RATES:
Full Page Mono £850.00
Full Page Colour £1200.00
SCC £12.00
Agency Commission: 10%
Mechanical Data: Type Area: 270 x 190mm, Print Process: Sheet-fed offset litho, Film: Positive, right reading, emulsion side down. Digital, Col Length: 270mm, Trim Size: 297 x 210mm, Page Width: 190mm, No. of Columns (Display): 3, Col Widths (Display): 59mm, Bleed Size: 305 x 214mm
Copy instructions: Copy Date: 4 weeks prior to publication date
Average advertising content per issue: 20%
CONSUMER: MUSIC & PERFORMING ARTS: Music

THE JAZZ RAG   46160U76D-347

Editorial Address: PO Box 944, BIRMINGHAM, B16 8UT
Tel: 0121 454 7020 **Fax:** 0121 454 9996
Email: jazzrag@bigbearmusic.com
Advertising Address: As above.
Email: jazzrag@bigbearmusic.com
Web site: http://www.thejazzrag.com
ISSN: 1365-7410
Publisher: Big Bear Music Group

Date Established: 1988
Frequency: 6 issues yearly
Cover Price: £2.75
Annual Sub.: £15.50
Circulation: 4,250 (Publisher's Statement)
Usual Pagination: 36
Editor: Jim Simpson; **News Editor:** Ron Simpson; **Features Editor:** Ron Simpson; **Managing Director:** Jim Simpson; **Publisher:** Jim Simpson
Summary of Content: Magazine covering all aspects of the British and international jazz scene.
Readership/Target Audience: Aimed at jazz enthusiasts between 25 and 75 years old.
ADVERTISING RATES:
Full Page Mono £510.00
Full Page Colour £995.00
Agency Commission: 10%
Mechanical Data: Col Length: 275mm, Type Area: 275 x 195mm, Page Width: 195mm, Bleed Size: 275 x 195mm
Copy instructions: Copy Date: 2 weeks prior to publication date
CONSUMER: MUSIC & PERFORMING ARTS: Music

JAZZ UK   46161U76D-347_50

Editorial Address: 26 The Balcony, Castle Arcade, CARDIFF, CF10 1BY **Tel:** 029 2066 5161
Fax: 029 2066 5160
Email: jazzuk.cardiff@virgin.net
Advertising Address: As above.
Email: jazzuk.production@virgin.net
Web site: http://www.jazzservices.org.uk
ISSN: 1472-0728
Publisher: Jazz Newspapers Ltd
Date Established: 1995
Frequency: 6 issues yearly
Free to qualifying individuals
Annual Sub.: £15.00
Circulation: 30,000 (Publisher's Statement)
Usual Pagination: 64
Editor: Nick Brown; **Advertising Manager:** Nick Brown
Summary of Content: Magazine containing jazz news, previews and musician interviews. Also covers workshop activities and education.
Readership/Target Audience: Aimed at all jazz enthusiasts.
ADVERTISING RATES:
Full Page Colour £500.00
Agency Commission: 10%
Mechanical Data: Bleed Size: 220 x 168mm, Trim Size: 210 x 148mm, Film: Digital
Average advertising content per issue: 20%
CONSUMER: MUSIC & PERFORMING ARTS: Music

JAZZWISE   600820U76D-347_75

Editorial Address: 2B Gleneagle Mews, Ambleside Avenue, LONDON, SW16 6AE **Tel:** 020 8677 0012
Fax: 020 8677 7128
Email: stephen@jazzwise.com
Advertising Address: 18 Hyndland Road, GLASGOW, G12 9UP **Tel:** 0141 334 1735 **Fax:** 0141 339 1029
Email: ros.mcrae@btopenworld.com
Web site: http://www.jazzwise.com
ISSN: 1368-0021
Publisher: Jazzwise Publications Ltd
Date Established: 1997
Frequency: 11 issues yearly
Cover Price: £4.10
Annual Sub.: £41.00
Usual Pagination: 76
Editor: Stephen Graham; **Managing Director:** Charles Alexander; **Advertising Manager:** Ros McRae; **Publisher:** Jon Newey
Summary of Content: Magazine covering contemporary jazz, jazz-dance and world jazz with news features and reviews.
Readership/Target Audience: Aimed at record collectors, musicians and jazz fans.
ADVERTISING RATES:
Full Page Mono £1250.00
Full Page Colour £1500.00
Mechanical Data: Page Width: 185mm, Type Area: 280 x 185mm, Bleed Size: 300 x 215mm, Trim Size: 297 x 210mm, Col Length: 280mm, Film: Digital
Copy instructions: Copy Date: 12th of month prior to publication date
CONSUMER: MUSIC & PERFORMING ARTS: Music

THE JERSEY LIFE   1804469U80G-505

Editorial Address: Chamber House, 25 Pier Road, St. Helier, JERSEY, JE1 4HF **Tel:** 01534 619882
Fax: 01534 728724
Advertising Address: As above.
Email: nadine@fishmedia.biz
Web site: http://www.life-mags.com
Publisher: Fish Media Ltd
Frequency: Monthly
Cover Price: £2.60
Circulation: 30,000 (Publisher's Statement)

Usual Pagination: 80
Editor: Jamie Fisher
Summary of Content: Magazine covering beauty, celebrity, entertainment, fashion, travel, property and shopping.
Readership/Target Audience: Aimed at residents, visitors and businesses in Jersey.
ADVERTISING RATES:
Full Page Colour £1995.00
Mechanical Data: Type Area: 255 x 185mm, Bleed Size: 286 x 216mm, Trim Size: 280 x 210mm, Col Length: 255mm, Page Width: 185mm, Film: Digital
CONSUMER: RURAL & REGIONAL INTEREST: Regional Interest Channel Islands

---

JERSEY NOW
47069U80G-500

Editorial Address: PO Box 582, JERSEY, JE4 8XQ
Tel: 01534 611743 **Fax:** 01534 611610
Email: eperchard@msppublishing.com
Advertising Address: As above. **Tel:** 01534 611611
Fax: 01534 611737
Email: peloury@jerseyeveningpost.com
Web site: http://www.thisisjersey.com
Publisher: MSP Publishing
Date Established: 1987
Frequency: Quarterly
Cover Price: Free
Circulation: 26,000 (Publisher's Statement)
Usual Pagination: 64
Editor: Elisabeth Perchard; **Managing Director:** Jerry Ramsden; **Advertising Manager:** Philippa Eloury
Summary of Content: Lifestyle magazine focusing on Jersey.
Readership/Target Audience: Aimed at residents of Jersey.
ADVERTISING RATES:
Full Page Colour £2331.00
Agency Commission: 10%
Mechanical Data: Film: Digital, Type Area: 265 x 182mm, Trim Size: 297 x 210mm, Col Length: 265mm, Page Width: 182mm
Copy instructions: Copy Date: 5 weeks prior to publication date
Average advertising content per issue: 40%
CONSUMER: RURAL & REGIONAL INTEREST: Regional Interest Channel Islands

---

JESUITS & FRIENDS
47823U87-130

Editorial Address: 11 Edge Hill, LONDON, SW19 4LR
Tel: 020 8946 0466 **Fax:** 020 8946 2292
Email: director@jesuitmissions.org.uk
Web site: http://www.jesuitmissions.org.uk
Publisher: Jesuits & Friends
Date Established: 1985
Frequency: 3 issues yearly - Published in March, July and November
Cover Price: Free
Circulation: 30,000 (Print Run)
Usual Pagination: 24
Editor: Ged Clapson; **Circulation Manager:** A. Montfort
Summary of Content: Magazine containing news of Jesuit work at home & abroad.
Readership/Target Audience: Aimed at Jesuits of the British province at home & overseas, friends and supporters.
ADVERTISING: No Advertising taken
CONSUMER: RELIGIOUS

JET SKIER & PERSONAL WATERCRAFT MAGAZINE
48376U91A-65

Editorial Address: Alliance House, 49 Sidney Street, CAMBRIDGE, CB2 3HX **Tel:** 01223 460490
Fax: 01223 315960
Email: spicer@jetskier.co.uk
Advertising Address: As above.
Email: michelle@jetskier.co.uk
Web site: http://www.jetskier.co.uk
Publisher: CSL Publishing Ltd
Date Established: 1990
Frequency: Monthly
Cover Price: £3.20
Annual Sub.: £38.20
Circulation: 8,500 (Publisher's Statement)
Usual Pagination: 100
Editor: Tim Spicer; **Advertising Manager:** Michelle Simpson; **Publisher:** Sue Baggaley
Summary of Content: Personal watercraft magazine covering machines, sport, accessories and tips for the dedicated user.
Readership/Target Audience: Aimed at those who own or are interested in watercraft.
ADVERTISING RATES:
Full Page Colour £1540.00
Agency Commission: 10%
Mechanical Data: Film: Digital, Trim Size: 297 x 210mm, Bleed Size: 305 x 218mm, Type Area: 253 x 176mm, Col Length: 253mm, Page Width: 176mm
CONSUMER: RECREATION & LEISURE: Boating & Yachting

JETAWAY
48220U89D-350

Formerly: Taking Off
Editorial Address: 141-143 Shoreditch High Street, LONDON, E1 6JE **Tel:** 020 7613 8777 **Fax:** 020 7613 8776
Email: lucille.howe@ink-publishing.com
Advertising Address: As above. **Fax:** 020 7613 8778
Email: stuart.wass@ink-publishing.com
Web site: http://jet2mag.com
Publisher: Ink Publishing
Date Established: 2002
Frequency: 6 issues yearly
Cover Price: Free
Circulation: 750,000 (Publisher's Statement)
Editor: Lucille Howe; **Advertising Manager:** Stuart Wass
Summary of Content: Magazine containing a mixture of travel information including sun, ski and city breaks, sport, entertainment, health and beauty, and property news.
Readership/Target Audience: Aimed at passengers of Jet2 aircraft, going to European destinations from Leeds-Bradford Airport and Manchester Airport.
ADVERTISING RATES:
Full Page Colour £5940.00
Agency Commission: 10%
Mechanical Data: Bleed Size: 281 x 216mm, Trim Size: 275 x 210mm, Film: Digital
Copy instructions: Copy Date: 3 weeks prior to publication date
Average advertising content per issue: 35%
CONSUMER: HOLIDAYS & TRAVEL: In-Flight Magazines

JEWISH CHRONICLE
47726U87-140

Editorial Address: 25 Furnival Street, LONDON, EC4A 1JT
Tel: 020 7415 1500 **Fax:** 020 7405 9040
Email: editorial@thejc.com
Advertising Address: As above. **Fax:** 020 7831 5188
Email: advertising@thejc.com
Web site: http://www.thejc.com
Publisher: Jewish Chronicle Newspaper Ltd
Date Established: 1841
Frequency: Weekly
Cover Price: £0.90
Annual Sub.: £40.00
Circulation: 30,436 (ABC 01/01/2009 to 30/06/2009)
Usual Pagination: 60
Editor: Stephen Pollard; **News Editor:** Jenni Frazer;
Managing Editor: Richard Burton
Summary of Content: Magazine containing news and features of Jewish interest. Including news from Israel, fashion, motoring, food and wine, property and finance.
Readership/Target Audience: Aimed at the Jewish community in the UK and throughout the world.
ADVERTISING RATES:
Full Page Mono £5040.00
Full Page Colour £6300.00
Agency Commission: 10%
Mechanical Data: Col Length: 400mm, No. of Columns (Display): 5, Type Area: 400 x 270mm, Page Width: 270mm, Film: Digital, Col Widths (Display): 50mm
Copy instructions: Copy Date: Tuesday prior to publication date
Average advertising content per issue: 40%
CONSUMER: RELIGIOUS

THE JEWISH NEWS
47731U87-155_50

Formerly: London Jewish News
Editorial Address: PO Box 34296, LONDON, NW5 1YW
Tel: 020 7692 6929 **Fax:** 020 7692 6689
Email: newsdesk@thejngroup.com
Advertising Address: Unit 611 Highgate Studios, 53-79 Highgate Road, LONDON, NW5 1TL **Tel:** 020 7692 6929
Fax: 020 7692 6689
Email: russellb@thejngroup.com
Web site: http://www.totallyjewish.com
Publisher: Jewish News and Media Group
Date Established: 1997
Frequency: Weekly
Cover Price: Free
Circulation: 20,146 (ABC 01/01/2009 to 30/06/2009)
Usual Pagination: 52
Editor: Zeddy Lawrence; **News Editor:** Justin Cohen;
Features Editor: Lauren Krotosky; **Advertising Manager:** Russell Bahar
Summary of Content: Newspaper covering restaurants, travel, films, fashion, books, property and motoring.
Readership/Target Audience: Aimed at the Jewish community.
ADVERTISING RATES:
Full Page Mono £3712.00
Full Page Colour £4498.00
Mechanical Data: Film: Digital
Copy instructions: Copy Date: 1 week prior to publication date
CONSUMER: RELIGIOUS

THE JEWISH QUARTERLY
47545U84B-70

Editorial Address: 6 Park End, LONDON, NW3 2SE
Tel: 020 7443 5155 **Fax:** 020 7443 5159
Email: editor@jewishquarterly.org
Advertising Address: Haskell House, 152 West End Lane, LONDON, NW6 1SD **Tel:** 020 8343 4675
Fax: 020 8343 4675
Email: admin@jewishquarterly.org
Web site: http://www.jewishquarterly.org
ISSN: 0449-010X
Publisher: Jewish Literary Trust
Date Established: 1953
Frequency: Quarterly
Cover Price: £4.95
Annual Sub.: £25.00
Circulation: 2,000 (Publisher's Statement)
Usual Pagination: 88
Editor: Rachel Lasserson; **Advertising Manager:** Pam Lewis
Summary of Content: Magazine of contemporary writing with articles of political interest, history, philosophy, arts and music, Judaism, film, poetry and literary reviews.
Readership/Target Audience: Read by those with an interest in Jewish art and culture.
ADVERTISING RATES:
Full Page Mono £400.00
Full Page Colour £500.00
Mechanical Data: Type Area: 240 x 180mm, Film: Digital, Trim Size: 274 x 210mm, Bleed Size: 284 x 220mm, Col Length: 240mm, Page Width: 180mm
Copy instructions: Copy Date: 3 weeks prior to publication date
Average advertising content per issue: 10%
CONSUMER: THE ARTS & LITERARY: Literary

JEWISH RENAISSANCE
749425U87-44

Editorial Address: PO Box 28849, LONDON, SW13 0WA
Tel: 020 8876 1891 **Fax:** 020 8392 1339
Email: editor@jewishrenaissance.org.uk
Advertising Address: As above.
Email: ads@jewishrenaissance.org.uk
Web site: http://www.jewishrenaissance.org.uk
ISSN: 1476-1769
Publisher: Renaissance Publishing Ltd
Date Established: 2001
Frequency: Quarterly
Cover Price: £4.50
Annual Sub.: £18.00
Circulation: 4,000 (Publisher's Statement)
Usual Pagination: 48
Editor: Janet Levin; **Advertising Manager:** Julie Reichman;
Publisher: Janet Levin
Summary of Content: Magazine covering arts, music, literature, history, community, ideas and events.
Readership/Target Audience: Aimed at the Jewish community and individuals of all religions interested in Jewish culture.
ADVERTISING: Rates on application
Agency Commission: 10%
Copy instructions: Copy Date: 3rd week of month prior to publication date
Average advertising content per issue: 10%
CONSUMER: RELIGIOUS

JEWISH TELEGRAPH
47727U87-148

Editorial Address: Telegraph House, 11 Park Hill, Bury Old Road, Prestwich, MANCHESTER, M25 0HH
Tel: 0161 740 9321 **Fax:** 0161 740 9325
Email: newsdesk@jewishtelegraph.com
Advertising Address: As above. **Tel:** 0161 741 2630
Fax: 0161 740 0444
Email: artwork@jewishtelegraph.com
Web site: http://www.jewishtelegraph.com
ISSN: 0021-6750
Publisher: Jewish Telegraph Ltd
Date Established: 1950
Frequency: Weekly
Cover Price: £0.60
Circulation: 16,000 (Publisher's Statement)
Usual Pagination: 40
Editor: Paul Harris; **Managing Director:** Paul Harris;
Advertising Manager: Leslie Holt; **Publisher:** Paul Harris
Summary of Content: Newspaper covering local, national and international news and features on the Jewish community.
Readership/Target Audience: Aimed at the Jewish community in the UK and expatriates abroad.
ADVERTISING RATES:
Full Page Mono £1100.00
SCC £5.00
Agency Commission: 10%
Mechanical Data: Col Length: 380mm, No. of Columns (Display): 7, Type Area: 380 x 265mm, Page Width: 265mm
Copy instructions: Copy Date: Tuesday 5pm prior to publication date
Average advertising content per issue: 40%
CONSUMER: RELIGIOUS

JEWISH TRIBUNE
47728U87-150

Editorial Address: 8 Grosvenor Way, LONDON, E5 9ND
Tel: 020 8806 1778 **Fax:** 020 8806 5556
Email: editor@jewishtribune.com
Advertising Address: As above. **Tel:** 020 8806 1978
Fax: 020 8806 5550
Email: display@jewishtribune.com
Publisher: AGUDAS Yisroel of Great Britain
Date Established: 1962
Frequency: Weekly
Cover Price: £0.75
Circulation: 8,500 (Publisher's Statement)
Usual Pagination: 36
Editor: Dan Levy; **Advertising Manager:** Rachel Salzman
Summary of Content: Publication covering news and current affairs.
Readership/Target Audience: Aimed at the orthodox Jewish community.
ADVERTISING RATES:
Full Page Mono £700.00
Full Page Colour £875.00
Agency Commission: 10%
Mechanical Data: Type Area: 388 x 263mm, Film: Digital, Col Length: 388mm, Page Width: 263mm
Copy instructions: Copy Date: Monday prior to publication date
CONSUMER: RELIGIOUS

THE JEWISH VEGETARIAN
45611U74P-460

Editorial Address: 853-855 Finchley Road, LONDON, NW11 8LX **Tel:** 020 8455 0692 **Fax:** 020 8455 1465
Email: jewishvegetarian@onetel.com
Advertising Address: As above.
Email: jewishvegetarian@onetel.com
Publisher: International Jewish Vegetarian Society
Date Established: 1966
Frequency: Quarterly
Cover Price: £1.50
Free to qualifying individuals
Annual Sub.: £12.00
Circulation: 5,000 (Publisher's Statement)
Usual Pagination: 54
Editor: Shirley Labelda; **Advertising Manager:** Shirley Labelda
Summary of Content: Official journal of the Jewish Vegetarian and Natural Health Society. Contains features on ethics, health, diet, alternative medicine, recipes, beauty, travel, books and animal rights.
Readership/Target Audience: Aimed at practising vegetarians and others in sympathy with the movement.
ADVERTISING RATES:
Full Page Mono £150.00
Full Page Colour £225.00
Mechanical Data: Film: Digital
Copy instructions: Copy Date: 6 weeks prior to publication date
Average advertising content per issue: 20%
CONSUMER: WOMEN'S INTEREST CONSUMER MAGAZINES: Food & Cookery

JLIFESTYLE
1826688U74Q-1361

Editorial Address: PO Box 585, EDGWARE, HA8 4DU
Tel: 020 7993 0092 **Fax:** 020 7657 4420
Email: editorial@jlifestyle.co.uk
Advertising Address: As above.
Email: advertising@jlifestyle.co.uk
Web site: http://www.jlifestyle.co.uk
ISSN: 1756-1612
Publisher: JLifestyle Ltd
Date Established: 2007
Frequency: 6 issues yearly
Cover Price: Free
Circulation: 20,000 (Publisher's Statement)
Usual Pagination: 52
Editor: Leslie Bunder
Summary of Content: Jewish lifestyle magazine covering celebrity features, travel, property, gadgets, interviews, shopping, fashion, entertainment and the arts.
Readership/Target Audience: Aimed at men and women aged 20 to 40 years old.
ADVERTISING RATES:
Full Page Colour £1000.00
Agency Commission: 10%
Mechanical Data: Type Area: 268 x 190mm, Trim Size: 297 x 210mm, Col Length: 268mm, Page Width: 190mm, Film: Digital
CONSUMER: WOMEN'S INTEREST CONSUMER MAGAZINES: Lifestyle

JOBS NORTH WEST
47930U88C-56_50

Editorial Address: 1 Scott Place, Hardman Street, MANCHESTER, M3 3RN **Tel:** 0845 050 8040
Fax: 0161 829 3344
Email: jnw@menmediasales.co.uk
Advertising Address: As above. **Fax:** 0161 829 3310
Email: jnw@menmediasales.co.uk

Web site: http://www.manchestereveningnews.co.uk
Publisher: Manchester Evening News Ltd
Frequency: Weekly
Cover Price: £2.00
Circulation: 60,000 (Publisher's Statement)
Usual Pagination: 80
Editor: Jonathan Perkins; **Advertising Manager:** James Patterson
Summary of Content: Publication containing classified advertising for jobs.
Readership/Target Audience: Aimed at those seeking new employment, transport, domestic and commercial jobs.
ADVERTISING RATES:
Full Page Mono £3901.50
Full Page Colour £5426.00
Mechanical Data: Page Width: 267mm, Film: Digital, Col Length: 340mm, Type Area: 340 x 267mm, No. of Columns (Display): 9
Copy instructions: Copy Date: Tuesday 5pm prior to publication date
Average advertising content per issue: 100%
CONSUMER: EDUCATION: Careers

THE JOURNAL (HULL)
46902U80C-1385

Editorial Address: Blundell's Corner, Beverley Road, HULL, HU3 1XS **Tel:** 01482 315272 **Fax:** 01482 315474
Email: journal@mailnewsmedia.co.uk
Advertising Address: As above. **Tel:** 01482 327111
Fax: 01482 599485
Email: k.matthews@mailnewsmedia.co.uk
Publisher: Mail News & Media Ltd
Date Established: 1989
Frequency: Monthly
Cover Price: £3.00
Free to qualifying individuals
Circulation: 17,024 (Publisher's Statement)
Usual Pagination: 100
Editor: Roy Woodcock; **Advertising Manager:** Kim Matthews
Summary of Content: Magazine covering all aspects of news and events in East Yorkshire.
Readership/Target Audience: Aimed at residents in Hull, York and the East Riding of Yorkshire.
ADVERTISING RATES:
Full Page Colour £1700.00
SCC £12.30
Agency Commission: 10%
Mechanical Data: Type Area: 390 x 270mm, Film: Digital, Col Length: 390mm, Page Width: 270mm
Copy instructions: Copy Date: 2 weeks prior to publication date
Average advertising content per issue: 60%
CONSUMER: RURAL & REGIONAL INTEREST: Regional Interest English Counties

THE JOURNAL (LINCOLN)
762068U80C-3761

Editorial Address: Blundell's Corner, Beverly Road, HULL, HU3 1XS **Tel:** 01482 315272
Email: r.woodcock@mailnewsmedia.co.uk
Advertising Address: Brayford Wharf East, LINCOLN, LN5 7AT **Tel:** 01472 372065 **Fax:** 01472 372235
Email: michaela.sams-rylatt@gsmg.co.uk
Publisher: Mail News & Media Ltd
Date Established: 2000
Frequency: Monthly
Cover Price: £2.50
Free to qualifying individuals
Annual Sub.: £12.00
Circulation: 22,500 (Publisher's Statement)
Usual Pagination: 40
Editor: Roy Woodcock; **Advertising Manager:** Michaela Sams-Rylatt
Summary of Content: Regional magazine containing features on lifestyle in Lincolnshire including the arts, music, opera, antiques, polo, watersports and top end cars. Includes articles on interesting characters from within the Lincoln area.
Readership/Target Audience: Aimed at high income residents in Lincolnshire.
ADVERTISING RATES:
Full Page Colour £970.00
Agency Commission: 10%
Mechanical Data: Film: Digital, Type Area: 390 x 270mm, Col Length: 390mm, Page Width: 270mm
Copy instructions: Copy Date: 2 weeks prior to publication date
CONSUMER: RURAL & REGIONAL INTEREST: Regional Interest English Counties

THE JOURNAL MAGAZINE
47002U80C-2870

Editorial Address: Sentinel House, Etruria, STOKE-ON-TRENT, ST1 5SS **Tel:** 01827 848586 **Fax:** 01827 848640
Email: jacqui.gray@cintamworth.co.uk
Advertising Address: Ventura Park Road, Bitterscote, TAMWORTH, B78 3LZ **Tel:** 0845 600 2567
Fax: 0845 600 8385
Email: the.journal@cintamworth.co.uk

Web site: http://www.tamworthherald.co.uk
ISSN: 1472-264X
Publisher: Central Independent News & Media Ltd
Frequency: Monthly
Cover Price: £2.00
Free to qualifying individuals
Circulation: 50,000 (Publisher's Statement)
Usual Pagination: 72
Editor: Jenny Amphlett; **Advertising Manager:** Debi Jones
Summary of Content: Magazine with features on people, lifestyle, fashion, food and wine, travel, the arts, property, interiors, motoring, gardening, antiques, days out and celebrity profiles.
Readership/Target Audience: Read predominantly by local householders with a high disposable income in South Staffordshire, North Birmingham and Solihull.
ADVERTISING RATES:
Full Page Colour £1647.00
Agency Commission: 10%
Mechanical Data: Col Length: 380mm, Film: Digital, No. of Columns (Display): 6, Type Area: 380 x 270mm, Trim Size: 407 x 290mm, Page Width: 270mm
Copy instructions: Copy Date: 2 weeks prior to publication date
Average advertising content per issue: 60%
CONSUMER: RURAL & REGIONAL INTEREST: Regional Interest English Counties

JOURNAL OF APICULTURAL RESEARCH
47182U81G-120

Editorial Address: 16 North Road, CARDIFF, CF10 3DY
Tel: 029 2037 2409 **Fax:** 05601 135640
Email: mail@ibra.org.uk
Advertising Address: As above.
Email: mail@ibra.org.uk
Web site: http://www.ibra.org.uk
ISSN: 0021-8839
Publisher: International Bee Research Association
Frequency: Quarterly
Annual Sub.: £160.00
Circulation: 500 (Publisher's Statement)
Editor: Richard Jones; **Advertising Manager:** Richard Jones
Summary of Content: Journal of peer reviewed scientific research papers covering international bee science and apiculture.
Readership/Target Audience: Read by scientists and researchers.
ADVERTISING RATES:
Full Page Colour £200.00
Agency Commission: 10%
Mechanical Data: Type Area: 260 x 170mm, No. of Columns (Display): 2, Col Length: 260mm, Page Width: 170mm, Film: Digital
CONSUMER: ANIMALS & PETS: Bees

JOURNAL OF THE BRITISH ASTRONOMICAL ASSOCIATION
48692U94X-71_60

Editorial Address: Starfield, Dedswell Drive, West Clandon, GUILDFORD, GU4 7TQ **Tel:** 01483 222791
Email: hazelmcgee@btinternet.com
Advertising Address: Burlington House, Piccadilly, LONDON, W1J 0DU **Tel:** 01635 30598
Email: anndavies@dsl.pipex.com
Web site: http://www.britastro.org/journal
ISSN: 0007-0297
Publisher: The British Astronomical Association
Date Established: 1890
Frequency: 6 issues yearly
Free to qualifying individuals
Annual Sub.: £44.00
Circulation: 3,500 (Publisher's Statement)
Usual Pagination: 54
Editor: Hazel McGee; **Advertising Manager:** Ann Davies
Summary of Content: Amateur astronomy journal containing news, book reviews, letters, articles and members' research papers.
Readership/Target Audience: Aimed at members of the British Astronomical Association, amateur and professional astronomers.
ADVERTISING: Rates on application
CONSUMER: OTHER CLASSIFICATIONS: Miscellaneous

JOURNAL OF CONTEMPORARY AFRICAN STUDIES
47331U82-85

Editorial Address: 4 Park Square, Milton Park, ABINGDON, OX14 4RN **Tel:** 020 7017 6000 **Fax:** 020 7017 6336
Email: editorjcas@ru.ac.za
Advertising Address: As above. **Fax:** 020 7017 6713
Email: jenna.johnston@tandf.co.uk
Web site: http://www.tandf.co.uk
ISSN: 0258-9001
Publisher: Routledge, Taylor & Francis

Frequency: 3 issues yearly - Published in January, May and September
Annual Sub.: £83.00
Editor: Nora de Villiers; **Advertising Manager:** Jenna Johnston
Summary of Content: Interdisciplinary journal of research and writing in the human sciences including economics, political science, international affairs, military strategy, modern history, law and sociology. Also education, industrial relations, urban studies, demography, social anthropology, literature, development studies and related fields.
Readership/Target Audience: Aimed at those interested in contemporary African affairs.
ADVERTISING RATES:
Full Page Mono £300.00
Agency Commission: 10%
Mechanical Data: Type Area: 210 x 130mm, Trim Size: 240 x 165mm, Col Length: 210mm, Page Width: 130mm, Film: Digital
CONSUMER: CURRENT AFFAIRS & POLITICS

JOURNAL OF EUROPEAN SOCIAL POLICY
47362U82-86
Editorial Address: 1 Oliver's Yard, 55 City Road, LONDON, EC1Y 1SP **Tel:** 020 7324 8500 **Fax:** 020 7324 8600
Email: hssirg@bath.ac.uk
Advertising Address: As above.
Email: advertising@sagepub.co.uk
Web site: http://www.sagepub.co.uk
ISSN: 0958-9287
Publisher: Sage Publications
Date Established: 1990
Frequency: Quarterly
Annual Sub.: £56.00
Circulation: 650 (Publisher's Statement)
Usual Pagination: 96
Editor: Emma Carmel; **Advertising Manager:** Sheena Karim
Summary of Content: Publication providing coverage of key European social policy issues. Includes articles on the latest European legislation and research, European briefing papers, research notes, occasional debates and book reviews.
Readership/Target Audience: Aimed at those interested in European politics.
ADVERTISING RATES:
Full Page Mono £400.00
Agency Commission: 5%
Mechanical Data: Type Area: 210 x 140mm, Col Length: 210mm, Page Width: 140mm, Film: Digital
Copy instructions: Copy Date: 12 weeks prior to publication date
CONSUMER: CURRENT AFFAIRS & POLITICS

JOURNAL OF HELLENIC STUDIES
47565U84B-77
Editorial Address: Senate House, Malet Street, LONDON, WC1E 7HU **Tel:** 020 7862 8730 **Fax:** 020 7862 8731
Email: office@hellenicsociety.org.uk
Advertising Address: As above.
Email: office@hellenicsociety.org.uk
Web site: http://www.hellenicsociety.org.uk
ISSN: 0075-4269
Publisher: Society for the Promotion of Hellenic Studies
Date Established: 1880
Frequency: Annual - Published in November
Annual Sub.: £41.00
Circulation: 3,200 (Publisher's Statement)
Usual Pagination: 276
Editor: Richella Doyle; **Advertising Manager:** Richella Doyle
Summary of Content: Journal covering Greek language, literature, history, art and archaeology.
Readership/Target Audience: Aimed at those interested in Hellenic studies.
ADVERTISING: Rates on application
Supplement(s): Archaeological Reports - 1xY
CONSUMER: THE ARTS & LITERARY: Literary

JOURNAL OF LONDON SOCIETY
48793U94X-71_55
Editorial Address: Mortimer Wheeler House, 46 Eagle Wharf Road, LONDON, N1 7ED **Tel:** 020 7253 9400
Email: info@londonsociety.org.uk
Web site: http://www.londonsociety.org.uk
ISSN: 0954-6685
Publisher: The London Society
Date Established: 1913
Frequency: Half-yearly - Published in May and November
Cover Price: £5.00
Free to qualifying individuals
Annual Sub.: £10.00
Circulation: 800 (Publisher's Statement)
Usual Pagination: 32
Editor: Lizzie Wells
Summary of Content: Publication containing articles on the history, development and planning of London.

Readership/Target Audience: Aimed at members of the London Society and allied organisations.
ADVERTISING: No Advertising taken
CONSUMER: OTHER CLASSIFICATIONS: Miscellaneous

JOURNAL OF PSYCHOPHARMACOLOGY
48851U94X-71_58
Editorial Address: The Psychopharmacology Unit, University of Bristol, Dorothy Hodgkin Building, Whitson Street, BRISTOL, BS1 3NY **Tel:** 0117 331 3178
Fax: 0117 331 3180
Email: jaci.hopkins@bristol.ac.uk
Advertising Address: 1 Oliver's Yard, 55 City Road, LONDON, EC1Y 1SJ **Tel:** 020 7324 8500
Fax: 020 7324 8600
Email: ross.hildrew@sagepub.co.uk
Web site: http://www.sagepub.co.uk
ISSN: 0269-8811
Publisher: Sage Publications
Date Established: 1990
Frequency: 8 issues yearly
Circulation: 1,400 (Publisher's Statement)
Usual Pagination: 112
Editor: Jaci Hopkins
Summary of Content: International journal covering research and review articles on both preclinical and clinical aspects of psychopharmacology.
Readership/Target Audience: Aimed at psychiatrists, psychopharmacologists, psychologists and behavioural pharmacologists.
ADVERTISING RATES:
Full Page Mono £500.00
Full Page Colour £900.00
Agency Commission: 10%
Mechanical Data: Type Area: 240 x 177mm, Bleed Size: 286 x 221mm, Col Length: 240mm, Page Width: 177mm, Trim Size: 280 x 215mm, Film: Digital
Copy instructions: Copy Date: 5 weeks prior to publication date
CONSUMER: OTHER CLASSIFICATIONS: Miscellaneous

JOURNAL OF THE ROYAL MUSICAL ASSOCIATION
28533U76D-348_5
Editorial Address: Department of Music, Royal Holloway, University of London, EGHAM, TW20 0EX
Tel: 01865 353907
Email: r.cowgill@rhul.ac.uk
Advertising Address: Great Clarendon Street, OXFORD, OX2 6DP **Tel:** 01865 353329
Email: jnlsadvertising@oxfordjournals.com
Web site: http://www3.oup.co.uk/roymus/
ISSN: 0269-0403
Publisher: OUP
Date Established: 1874
Frequency: Half-yearly - Published in May and November
Annual Sub.: £88.00
Circulation: 1,225 (Publisher's Statement)
Usual Pagination: 168
Editor: Rachel Cowgill
Summary of Content: Journal which addresses new research in all branches of musical scholarship - historical musicology and ethnomusicology, theory and analysis, textual criticism, archival research, organology and performing practice.
Readership/Target Audience: Aimed at academics, teachers, students and librarians.
ADVERTISING RATES:
Full Page Mono £310.00
Agency Commission: 10%
Mechanical Data: Type Area: 200 x 130mm, Film: Digital, Col Length: 200mm, Page Width: 130mm
CONSUMER: MUSIC & PERFORMING ARTS: Music

JOURNAL OF SOUTHERN AFRICAN STUDIES
47333U82-89
Editorial Address: 4 Park Square, Milton Park, ABINGDON, OX14 4RN **Tel:** 01235 828600 **Fax:** 01235 829000
Advertising Address: As above. **Tel:** 020 7017 6000
Fax: 020 7017 6713
Email: enquiry@tandf.co.uk
Web site: http://www.tandf.co.uk
ISSN: 0305-7070
Publisher: Routledge, Taylor & Francis
Frequency: Quarterly
Circulation: 800 (Publisher's Statement)
Editor: Joost Fontein; **Advertising Manager:** Jenna Johnston
Summary of Content: A scholarly inquiry and exposition in the fields of economics, sociology, geography, demography, social anthropology and administration.
Readership/Target Audience: Aimed at social scientists, anthropologists, demographers, historians and geographers.
ADVERTISING RATES:
Full Page Mono £400.00

Mechanical Data: Type Area: 218 x 154mm, Col Length: 218mm, Page Width: 154mm, Film: Digital
CONSUMER: CURRENT AFFAIRS & POLITICS

JOURNAL OF THEORETICAL POLITICS
47334U82-89_5
Editorial Address: 1 Oliver's Yard, 55 City Road, LONDON, EC1Y 1SP **Tel:** 020 7324 8500 **Fax:** 020 7324 8600
Advertising Address: As above.
Web site: http://www.sagepub.co.uk
ISSN: 0951-6928
Publisher: Sage Publications
Date Established: 1989
Frequency: Quarterly
Annual Sub.: £48.00
Circulation: 525 (Publisher's Statement)
Usual Pagination: 144
Editor: Keith Dowding; **Advertising Manager:** Sheena Karim
Summary of Content: International journal which aims to foster the development of theory in the study of the political process. Includes analytical articles on theoretical topics and presents new theoretical work in an accessible form for social scientists.
Readership/Target Audience: Aimed at those interested in theoretical politics.
ADVERTISING RATES:
Full Page Mono £400.00
Agency Commission: 5%
Mechanical Data: Film: Digital, Col Length: 210mm, Page Width: 140mm, Type Area: 210 x 140mm
CONSUMER: CURRENT AFFAIRS & POLITICS

JOY MAGAZINE
47729U87-153
Editorial Address: PO Box 777, NOTTINGHAM, NG1 6ZZ
Tel: 01158 240777 **Fax:** 0115 984 5251
Email: editorial@newlife.co.uk
Advertising Address: As above. **Tel:** 0115 921 7280
Email: sales@newlifepublishing.co.uk
Web site: http://www.newlifepublishing.co.uk
Publisher: New Life Publishing Company
Date Established: 1924
Frequency: Monthly
Cover Price: £1.75
Annual Sub.: £22.00
Circulation: 4,700 (Publisher's Statement)
Usual Pagination: 48
Editor: Peter Wreford; **Advertising Manager:** Barry Wilson
Summary of Content: Official journal of the Assemblies of God covering news and views of its members.
Readership/Target Audience: Aimed at members of the Assemblies of God in Great Britain and Ireland.
ADVERTISING RATES:
Full Page Colour £620.00
SCC £8.00
Agency Commission: 10%
Mechanical Data: Bleed Size: 321 x 246mm, Trim Size: 315 x 240mm, Film: Digital, Type Area: 287 x 213mm, Col Length: 287mm, Page Width: 213mm
Copy instructions: Copy Date: 2 months prior to publication date
Average advertising content per issue: 30%
CONSUMER: RELIGIOUS

THE JUDGE DREDD MEGAZINE
717984U79L-140
Formerly: The Judge Dredd Magazine
Editorial Address: Riverside House, Osney Mead, OXFORD, OX2 0ES **Tel:** 01865 792201 **Fax:** 01865 792254
Email: matt.smith@rebellion.co.uk
Advertising Address: As above. **Fax:** 01865 200610
Email: keith.richardson@rebellion.co.uk
Web site: http://www.2000adonline.com
ISSN: 0960-1813
Publisher: Rebellion
Date Established: 1990
Frequency: 13 issues yearly
Cover Price: £2.99
Circulation: 15,000 (Publisher's Statement)
Usual Pagination: 64
Editor: Matt Smith; **Advertising Manager:** Keith Richardson
Summary of Content: Magazine featuring a mixture of classic, new UK Sci-fi comic strips and Judge Dredd. Plus archive classics and features on cult comics, characters, films, TV and more.
Readership/Target Audience: Aimed at comic enthusiasts between 18 and 45 years of age.
ADVERTISING RATES:
Full Page Colour £1200.00
Agency Commission: 10%
Mechanical Data: Bleed Size: 282 x 216mm, Trim Size: 276 x 210mm, Film: Digital
Copy instructions: Copy Date: 4 weeks prior to publication date
CONSUMER: HOBBIES & DIY: Fantasy Games & Science Fiction

Consumer Magazines

JUKE BLUES MAGAZINE
46163U76D-349

Editorial Address: PO Box 4083, BATH, BA1 0FA
Tel: 01225 758375 **Fax:** 01225 758375
Email: juke@jukeblues.com
Advertising Address: As above.
Email: juke@jukeblues.com
Web site: http://www.jukeblues.com
ISSN: 1351-5551
Publisher: Juke Blues Magazine
Date Established: 1985
Frequency: 3 issues yearly - Published in April, August and December
Cover Price: £5.00
Circulation: 8,000 (Publisher's Statement)
Usual Pagination: 80
Editor: Cilla Huggins; **Advertising Manager:** Cilla Huggins;
Publisher: Cilla Huggins
Summary of Content: Magazine focusing on black American blues, vintage R&B, soul, gospel, zydeco and blue-jazz music. Mixes academic research and popular coverage with interviews, biographies, discography, CD, DVD and book reviews.
Readership/Target Audience: Aimed at enthusiasts of blues, soul, vintage R&B and gospel.
ADVERTISING RATES:
Full Page Mono £320.00
Full Page Colour £500.00
Agency Commission: 10%
Mechanical Data: Type Area: 270 x 187mm, Col Length: 270mm, Print Process: Litho, Film: Digital, Bleed Size: 303 x 216mm, Trim Size: 297 x 210mm, Page Width: 187mm
Average advertising content per issue: 10%
CONSUMER: MUSIC & PERFORMING ARTS: Music

JUMBO CROSS
46678U79F-28

Editorial Address: Zetland House, 5-25 Scrutton Street, LONDON, EC2A 4HJ **Tel:** 020 7613 7477
Fax: 020 7168 7956
Advertising Address: As above.
Email: justine@accoladepublishing.co.uk
Publisher: Accolade Publishing
Frequency: 13 issues yearly
Cover Price: £1.99
Circulation: 41,000 (Publisher's Statement)
Usual Pagination: 68
Editor: Justine Wall; **Advertising Manager:** Justine Wall;
Group Editor: Sarah Grummett; **Publisher:** Justine Wall
Summary of Content: Magazine containing crossword puzzles.
Readership/Target Audience: Aimed mainly at women over the age of 35 years old.
ADVERTISING: Rates on application
Agency Commission: 10%
Copy instructions: Copy Date: 1 month prior to publication date
CONSUMER: HOBBIES & DIY: Games & Puzzles

JUMBO CROSS COLLECTION
1622544U79F-72

Editorial Address: Zetland House, 5-25 Scrutton Street, LONDON, EC2A 4HJ **Tel:** 020 7613 7477
Fax: 020 7168 7956
Email: puzzles@accoladepublishing.co.uk
Advertising Address: As above.
Email: justine@accoladepublishing.co.uk
Publisher: Accolade Publishing
Frequency: 10 issues yearly
Annual Sub.: £21.60
Usual Pagination: 116
Editor: Lee Graham; **Advertising Manager:** Justine Wall;
Group Editor: Sarah Grummett; **Publisher:** Justine Wall
Summary of Content: Publication containing big value collection of giant grid crosswords.
Readership/Target Audience: Aimed mainly at women over the age of 35.
ADVERTISING: Rates on application
Agency Commission: 10%
Mechanical Data: Type Area: 240 x 165mm, Bleed Size: 270 x 190mm, Trim Size: 260 x 180mm, Col Length: 240mm, Film: Digital, Page Width: 165mm
Copy instructions: Copy Date: 4 weeks prior to publication date
Average advertising content per issue: 1%
CONSUMER: HOBBIES & DIY: Games & Puzzles

JUMP
1859010U74D-676

Editorial Address: 1st Floor, Mermaid House, 2 Puddle Dock, LONDON, EC4V 3DS **Tel:** 020 7332 2000
Fax: 020 7332 2001
Email: cate@programmemaster.com
Web site: http://www.bounty.com
Publisher: Programmemaster Ltd
Date Established: 2008
Frequency: Quarterly
Free to qualifying individuals
Circulation: 100,000 (Publisher's Statement)
Editor: Cate Langmuir; **Managing Editor:** Stephen Mitchell

Summary of Content: Magazine covering topics of importance to families from health, sport and travel to finance, entertainment and fashion. Also features parenting advice and product reviews.
Readership/Target Audience: Aimed at parents of pre-school children.
CONSUMER: WOMEN'S INTEREST CONSUMER MAGAZINES: Child Care

JUNGLEDRUMS MAGAZINE
1828266U90-1018

Formerly: Jungle Drums
Editorial Address: PO Box 49713, LONDON, WC1X 8WW
Tel: 020 7242 5140 **Fax:** 020 7242 5140
Email: editor@jungledrums.org
Advertising Address: As above.
Email: ad@jungledrums.org
Web site: http://www.jungledrumsonline.com
Publisher: Jungle Drums Ltd
Date Established: 2002
Frequency: Monthly
Cover Price: Free
Circulation: 20,000 (Publisher's Statement)
Usual Pagination: 72
Editor: Fernando Duarte
Summary of Content: Lifestyle magazine covering Brazilian and Latin culture, events, exhibitions and concerts as well as environmental and social issues.
Readership/Target Audience: Aimed at Brazilians in the UK and thus with an interest in Brazil and Latin America.
ADVERTISING RATES:
Full Page Colour £850.00
Mechanical Data: Trim Size: 270 x 213mm, Film: Digital
Editions:
Jungle Trips
CONSUMER: ETHNIC

JUNIOR
45321U74D-268

Editorial Address: 15-18 White Lion Street, Islington, LONDON, N1 9PD **Tel:** 020 7843 8800
Email: editorial@juniormagazine.co.uk
Advertising Address: As above. **Tel:** 01689 899200
Email: james.burton@magicalia.com
Web site: http://www.juniormagazine.co.uk
ISSN: 1461-362X
Publisher: Magicalia Ltd
Date Established: 1998
Frequency: Monthly
Cover Price: £3.50
Annual Sub.: £26.00
Circulation: 52,500 (Publisher's Statement)
Usual Pagination: 132
Editor: Catherine O'Dolan; **Features Editor:** Celia Morgan;
Managing Editor: Suzanne Milne; **Advertising Director:** James Burton
Summary of Content: Magazine focusing on health and development, as well as travel, lifestyle and children's designer fashion.
Readership/Target Audience: Aimed predominantly at men and women with children between 0 and 8 years old.
ADVERTISING RATES:
Full Page Colour £4100.00
Agency Commission: 10%
Mechanical Data: Film: Digital
Copy instructions: Copy Date: 4 weeks prior to publication date
Average advertising content per issue: 40%
Supplement(s): Junior Briefing - 12xY, JuniorLondon - 12xY
CONSUMER: WOMEN'S INTEREST CONSUMER MAGAZINES: Child Care

JUNIOR PREGNANCY & BABY
767710U74D-553

Editorial Address: 15-18 White Lion Street, Islington, LONDON, N1 9PG **Tel:** 020 7843 8800
Email: editorial@juniormagazine.co.uk
Advertising Address: Berwick House, 8-10 Knoll Rise, ORPINGTON, BR6 0EL **Tel:** 01689 899200
Email: nicola.gleghorn@magicalia.com
Web site: http://www.juniormagazine.co.uk
Publisher: Magicalia Ltd
Date Established: 2002
Frequency: 6 issues yearly
Cover Price: £4.90
Circulation: 12,688 (Publisher's Statement)
Usual Pagination: 146
Editor: Suzanne Milne; **Advertising Manager:** Nicola Gleghorn; **Managing Editor:** Suzanne Milne
Summary of Content: Magazine containing consumer and health articles from conception to six months old. Also includes shopping, interiors, fashion, lifestyle, health and beauty features.
Readership/Target Audience: Aimed at mothers-to-be and new mothers.
ADVERTISING RATES:
Full Page Colour £3400.00
Agency Commission: 10%

Mechanical Data: Type Area: 280 x 203mm, Col Length: 280mm, Page Width: 203mm, Bleed Size: 306 x 228mm, Trim Size: 300 x 222mm
Average advertising content per issue: 40%
CONSUMER: WOMEN'S INTEREST CONSUMER MAGAZINES: Child Care

JUNIOR PUZZLES
46662U79F-30

Formerly: Junior Puzzle Wonderland
Editorial Address: Stonecroft, 69 Station Road, REDHILL, RH1 1EY **Tel:** 01737 378700 **Fax:** 01737 781800
Email: reception@puzzlermedia.com
Advertising Address: As above.
Email: brian.ainge@puzzlermedia.com
Web site: http://www.puzzler.co.uk
Publisher: Puzzler Media Ltd
Frequency: 6 issues yearly
Cover Price: £2.40
Circulation: 53,086 (Publisher's Statement)
Usual Pagination: 114
Editor: Mike Murphy
Summary of Content: Magazine includes puzzles, activity pages and competitions.
Readership/Target Audience: Read by children aged between 7 and 11 years old.
ADVERTISING: Rates on application
CONSUMER: HOBBIES & DIY: Games & Puzzles

JUNO
1851431U74D-673

Editorial Address: PO Box 592, Ashurst Wood, EAST GRINSTEAD, RH19 3AQ **Tel:** 01342 823771
Email: editor@junomagazine.com
Web site: http://www.junomagazine.com
Frequency: 3 issues yearly
Cover Price: £3.50
Circulation: 10,000 (Publisher's Statement)
Usual Pagination: 64
Editor: Patricia Patterson-Vanegas
Summary of Content: Magazine covering conscious parenting, sustainability, social justice, non-violence and a commitment to personal growth and spiritual awareness with features, interviews, reviews, personal stories, crafts and celebrations.
Readership/Target Audience: Aimed at families with children of all ages including childminders, teachers, aunts and uncles and grandparents.
CONSUMER: WOMEN'S INTEREST CONSUMER MAGAZINES: Child Care

K9 MAGAZINE
1641728U81B-302

Formerly: K9
Editorial Address: 21 High Street, Warsop, MANSFIELD, NG20 0AA **Tel:** 0870 011 4115
Email: editorial@k9magazine.com
Advertising Address: As above.
Email: advertising@k9media.net
Web site: http://www.k9magazine.com
ISSN: 1740-9608
Publisher: K9 Media Ltd
Date Established: 2001
Frequency: Quarterly
Cover Price: £3.95
Circulation: 60,000 (Print Run)
Usual Pagination: 100
Editor: Ryan O'Meara; **Advertising Manager:** Kim Bruce;
Managing Editor: Sean O'Meara
Summary of Content: Lifestyle magazine covering health, product reviews, hints and tips from the Animal Advisory Panel, reviews of pet friendly cars, celebrity interviews, home and garden features and holiday features.
Readership/Target Audience: Aimed at modern dog owners.
ADVERTISING RATES:
Full Page Colour £1265.00
Agency Commission: 10%
Mechanical Data: Trim Size: 297 x 210mm, Type Area: 270 x 190mm, Bleed Size: 303 x 216mm, Col Length: 270mm, Page Width: 190mm, Film: Digital
Copy instructions: Copy Date: 4 weeks prior to publication date
Average advertising content per issue: 45%
CONSUMER: ANIMALS & PETS: Dogs

KARTING
46502U77R-250

Editorial Address: 15 Moorfield Road, ORPINGTON, BR6 0XD **Tel:** 01689 897123 **Fax:** 01689 890998
Email: support@kartingmagazine.com
Advertising Address: As above.
Email: support@kartingmagazine.com
Web site: http://www.kartingmagazine.com
ISSN: 0022-913X
Publisher: Lodgemark Press
Date Established: 1959
Frequency: Monthly

Cover Price: £3.80
Annual Sub.: £36.00
Circulation: 12,800 (Publisher's Statement)
Usual Pagination: 100
Advertising Manager: James Brown
Summary of Content: Magazine covering technical articles and race reports on kart racing.
Readership/Target Audience: Read by karting enthusiasts.
ADVERTISING RATES:
Full Page Mono £550.00
Full Page Colour £750.00
Agency Commission: 10%
Mechanical Data: Type Area: 270 x 200mm, Bleed Size: 290 x 220mm, Trim Size: 280 x 210mm, Col Length: 270mm, Film: Digital, Page Width: 200mm
Copy instructions: Copy Date: 3 weeks prior to publication date
Average advertising content per issue: 40%
CONSUMER: MOTORING & CYCLING: Motoring & Cycling Related

KEEP THE FAITH MAGAZINE   1792508U90-1002

Formerly: Keep the Faith
Editorial Address: PO Box 574, BURY ST. EDMUNDS, IP33 9BW **Tel:** 01284 760033 **Fax:** 0845 193 4438
Email: editorial@keepthefaith.co.uk
Advertising Address: As above. **Tel:** 0845 193 4431
Web site: http://www.keepthefaith.co.uk
Publisher: Black UK Publications Ltd
Date Established: 2005
Frequency: 10 issues yearly
Free to qualifying individuals
Annual Sub.: £10.00
Circulation: 50,000 (Publisher's Statement)
Usual Pagination: 32
Editor: Shirley McGreal; **News Editor:** Mike Best;
Advertising Manager: Shirley McGreal; **Publisher:** Shirley McGreal
Summary of Content: News and lifestyle magazine with a Christian theme.
Readership/Target Audience: Aimed predominantly at black and minority ethnic communities in the UK through churches, community groups and hairdressers.
ADVERTISING RATES:
Full Page Colour £1300.00
Agency Commission: 10%
Mechanical Data: Bleed Size: 307 x 220mm, Trim Size: 297 x 210mm, Film: Digital
Copy instructions: Copy Date: 6th of the month prior to publication date
Average advertising content per issue: 30%
CONSUMER: ETHNIC

KENNEL GAZETTE   47105U81B-130

Editorial Address: 1-5 Clarges Street, Piccadilly, LONDON, W1J 8AB **Tel:** 020 7518 1038 **Fax:** 020 7518 1028
Email: kennelgazette@thekennelclub.org.uk
Advertising Address: Mainline Media Ltd, Oakley Hay Lodge, Great Fold Road, CORBY, NN18 9AS
Tel: 01536 747333 **Fax:** 01536 746565
Email: tricia.mcdougall@mainlinemedia.co.uk
Web site: http://www.thekennelclub.org.uk
Publisher: The Kennel Club
Date Established: 1880
Frequency: Monthly
Cover Price: £2.25
Free to qualifying individuals
Annual Sub.: £20.00
Circulation: 9,500 (Publisher's Statement)
Usual Pagination: 46
Editor: Daniela Tranquada
Summary of Content: Magazine containing articles on training, breeding and care of pedigree dogs and profiles on breeds from the Kennel Club.
Readership/Target Audience: Aimed at dog owners and dog breeders.
ADVERTISING RATES:
Full Page Mono £465.00
Full Page Colour £880.00
SCC £10.00
Mechanical Data: No. of Columns (Display): 4, Type Area: 272 x 185mm, Col Length: 272mm, Page Width: 185mm, Bleed Size: 303 x216mm, Trim Size: 297 x 210mm
CONSUMER: ANIMALS & PETS: Dogs

KENSINGTON & CHELSEA EXCLUSIVE
1892649U80C-5495
Editorial Address: For all contact details see main edition, Exclusive (London)
Frequency: 10 issues yearly
Cover Price: Free
Circulation: 7,500 (Publisher's Statement)
ADVERTISING: Rates on application
Edition of: Exclusive (London)
CONSUMER: RURAL & REGIONAL INTEREST: Regional Interest English Counties

KENT COUNTY MAGAZINE   629867U80C-1930

Formerly: Kent Advertiser
Editorial Address: For all contact details see main edition, The County Magazine
Date Established: 1996
Frequency: Monthly
Circulation: 30,000 (Publisher's Statement)
Usual Pagination: 6
ADVERTISING RATES:
Full Page Colour £780.00
Edition of: The County Magazine
CONSUMER: RURAL & REGIONAL INTEREST: Regional Interest English Counties

KENT LIFE   46928U80C-1950

Editorial Address: 28 Teville Road, WORTHING, BN11 1UG
Tel: 01622 762818 **Fax:** 01622 663294
Email: sarah.sturt@kent-life.co.uk
Advertising Address: 25A Pudding Lane, MAIDSTONE, ME14 1PA **Tel:** 01622 763633 **Fax:** 01622 663294
Email: sales@kent-life.co.uk
Web site: http://www.kent-life.co.uk
Publisher: Archant Life
Date Established: 1962
Frequency: Monthly
Cover Price: £2.95
Annual Sub.: £30.00
Circulation: 15,000 (Publisher's Statement)
Usual Pagination: 196
Editor: Sarah Sturt
Summary of Content: Magazine covering all aspects of county life. Includes personalities, nostalgia, crafts and contemporary events. Also covers property, food, arts, antiques, interiors, books, gardening, fashion and sport.
Readership/Target Audience: Aimed at those aged between 30 and 55 years old living and working in Kent.
ADVERTISING RATES:
Full Page Colour £1610.00
Mechanical Data: Bleed Size: 306 x 226mm, Trim Size: 300 x 220mm, Type Area: 271 x 199mm, No. of Columns (Display): 4, Col Length: 271mm, Page Width: 199mm, Film: Digital
Copy instructions: Copy Date: 4 weeks prior to publication date
Average advertising content per issue: 50%
CONSUMER: RURAL & REGIONAL INTEREST: Regional Interest English Counties

KENT PROFILE   46929U80C-1955

Editorial Address: The Old Courthouse, New Road Avenue, CHATHAM, ME4 6BE **Tel:** 01444 831512 **Fax:** 01444 831512
Email: sunnycroftclose@btinternet.com
Advertising Address: As above.
Email: kentprofile@pop3.poptel.org.uk
Web site: http://www.kentprofile.com
ISSN: 1369-6270
Publisher: Prolific Publications Ltd
Date Established: 1996
Frequency: 6 issues yearly
Cover Price: Free
Circulation: 20,000 (Publisher's Statement)
Usual Pagination: 40
Editor: Rex Cooper; **Advertising Manager:** Sarah Leigh
Summary of Content: County lifestyle magazine containing topics like regeneration, 'green' issues, sustainable living, higher education, property development, business matters, tourism, local produce, features, financial advice, gardening, major features on sectors and sections of Kent and a 60 day county-wide entertainment guide.
Readership/Target Audience: Aimed at residents and visitors of Kent aged over 30 years old.
ADVERTISING RATES:
Full Page Colour £1040.00
Agency Commission: 10%
Mechanical Data: Type Area: 268 x 184mm, Trim Size: 297 x 210mm, Col Length: 268mm, Page Width: 184mm, Film: Digital
Copy instructions: Copy Date: 15th of the month prior to publication date
Average advertising content per issue: 40%
CONSUMER: RURAL & REGIONAL INTEREST: Regional Interest English Counties

KENTISH WAYS   1655737U80C-5136

Editorial Address: Rye House, 15 North Street, ASHFORD, TN25 8LF **Tel:** 01233 650888 **Fax:** 01233 650888
Email: editor.kwmedia@virgin.net
Advertising Address: 2 Pond Cottages, The Street, BETHERSDEN, TN26 3AD **Tel:** 01233 820036
Email: nickrandolph.mhm@virgin.net
Publisher: K W Media Ltd
Date Established: 2003
Frequency: Monthly
Cover Price: Free
Circulation: 10,000 (Publisher's Statement)
Usual Pagination: 36

Editor: Lea White; **Advertising Manager:** Nick Randolph;
Publisher: Nick Randolph
Summary of Content: Lifestyle magazine covering restaurants, wine, cars, gardening, nature and fashion as well as historical features and veterinary features.
Readership/Target Audience: Aimed at affluent, rural households in Weald and East Kent.
ADVERTISING RATES:
Full Page Colour £890.00
Agency Commission: 10%
Mechanical Data: Film: Digital
Copy instructions: Copy Date: 7 days prior to publication date
Average advertising content per issue: 40%
CONSUMER: RURAL & REGIONAL INTEREST: Regional Interest English Counties

KERRANG!   46239U76E-160

Editorial Address: Mappin House, 4 Winsley Street, LONDON, W1W 8HF **Tel:** 020 7182 8000
Fax: 020 7312 8910
Email: feedback@kerrang.com
Advertising Address: Endeavour House, 189 Shaftesbury Avenue, LONDON, WC2H 8JG **Tel:** 020 7295 5000
Fax: 020 7295 5466
Email: marco.soares@baueradvertising.co.uk
Web site: http://www.kerrang.com
Publisher: Bauer Consumer Media Ltd (Mappin House)
Date Established: 1981
Frequency: Weekly
Cover Price: £2.10
Annual Sub.: £75.00
Circulation: 43,253 (ABC 01/01/2009 to 30/06/2009)
Usual Pagination: 64
Editor: Simon Young; **News Editor:** Simon Young; **Editor-in-Chief:** Phil Alexander
Summary of Content: Magazine containing news, features gig guides and reviews of metal, rock & punk music.
Readership/Target Audience: Aimed at metal, rock & punk music fans.
ADVERTISING RATES:
Full Page Colour £4785.00
Agency Commission: 10%
Mechanical Data: Page Width: 190mm, Type Area: 265 x 190mm, Col Length: 265mm, Trim Size: 285 x 210mm, Bleed Size: 291 x 216mm, Film: Digital
Copy instructions: Copy Date: 6 days prior to publication date
Average advertising content per issue: 40%
CONSUMER: MUSIC & PERFORMING ARTS: Pop Music

KEW MAGAZINE   48565U93-55

Formerly: Kew
Editorial Address: Royal Botanic Gardens, Kew, RICHMOND, TW9 3AB **Tel:** 020 8332 5000
Email: magazine@kew.org
Advertising Address: Cultureshock Media, 27B Tradescant Road, LONDON, SW8 1XD **Tel:** 020 7735 9263
Email: oli@cultureshockmedia.co.uk
Web site: http://www.kew.org
ISSN: 0961-4141
Publisher: Kew Magazine
Date Established: 1990
Frequency: Quarterly
Cover Price: £3.95
Annual Sub.: £20.00
Circulation: 34,989 (ABC 01/01/2008 to 31/12/2008)
Usual Pagination: 60
Editor: Christina Harrison; **Advertising Manager:** Oliver Dillon
Summary of Content: Magazine containing information on plants, gardens, the environment and conservation.
Readership/Target Audience: Aimed at the Friends of the Royal Botanic Gardens, Kew and those with an interest in plants, horticulture, the environment and conservation.
ADVERTISING: Rates on application
Agency Commission: 10%
Average advertising content per issue: 40%
CONSUMER: GARDENING

KEYBOARD PLAYER   46164U76D-350

Editorial Address: 100 Birkbeck Road, ENFIELD, EN2 0ED
Tel: 020 8241 3695
Email: steve@keyboardplayer.com
Advertising Address: 48 Mereway Road, TWICKENHAM, TW2 6RG **Tel:** 020 8241 3695
Email: paul@keyboardplayer.com
Web site: http://www.keyboardplayer.com
ISSN: 0269-3836
Publisher: Keyboard Player
Date Established: 1979
Frequency: Monthly
Cover Price: £2.95
Annual Sub.: £35.40
Circulation: 9,000 (Publisher's Statement)
Usual Pagination: 56

Editor: Steve Miller; **Advertising Manager:** Paul Cohen;
Publisher: Steve Miller
Summary of Content: Magazine covering news, products
and reviews of keyboard instruments.
Readership/Target Audience: Aimed at the home and
semi-professional musician.
ADVERTISING RATES:
Full Page Mono £420.00
Full Page Colour £750.00
Agency Commission: 10%
Mechanical Data: Bleed Size: 303 x 216mm, Trim Size: 297
x 210mm, Film: Digital, Print Process: Litho
Copy instructions: Copy Date: 10th of the month prior to
publication date
Average advertising content per issue: 25%
CONSUMER: MUSIC & PERFORMING ARTS: Music

THE KEYS OF PETER   47822U87-154
Editorial Address: 157 Vicarage Road, Leyton, LONDON,
E10 5DU **Tel:** 020 8539 3876 **Fax:** 020 8539 3876
Email: keys@fsmail.net
Web site: http://www.smartgroups.com/groups/keys
Publisher: Delane Press
Date Established: 1969
Frequency: 6 issues yearly
Cover Price: £1.00
Annual Sub.: £5.00
Usual Pagination: 20
Editor: Ronald King
Summary of Content: Journal containing a review of
Catholic and international affairs.
Language(s): Afrikaans; Dutch; English; French; Latin
Readership/Target Audience: Aimed at members of the
Catholic church.
ADVERTISING: No Advertising taken
CONSUMER: RELIGIOUS

KICK   1739997U75B-282
Editorial Address: Unit 1.08 Clerkenwell Workshops, 31
Clerkenwell Close, LONDON, EC1R 0AT **Tel:** 020 7014 3775
Fax: 020 7014 3776
Email: ashleigh@atticmedianetwork.com
Advertising Address: As above. **Tel:** 020 7014 3777
Email: nigel@atticmedianetwork.com
Publisher: Attic Media Network
Date Established: 2006
Frequency: Monthly
Cover Price: £2.40
Circulation: 62,285 (ABC 01/01/2009 to 30/06/2009)
Usual Pagination: 52
Editor: Ian Pollard; **Advertising Manager:** Nigel Standley
Summary of Content: Magazine covering the lifestyle of
star football players and behind the scene gossip in the big
clubs in the premiership and championship as well as
interviews with players, posters and competitions.
Readership/Target Audience: Aimed at boys aged 6 to 13
years old.
ADVERTISING RATES:
Full Page Colour £3500.00
Agency Commission: 15%
Mechanical Data: Type Area: 265 x 200mm, Bleed Size:
281 x 216mm, Trim Size: 275 x 210mm, Col Length: 265mm,
Page Width: 200mm, Film: Digital
Copy instructions: Copy Date: 4 weeks prior to publication
date
Average advertising content per issue: 40%
CONSUMER: SPORT: Football

KIDAROUND MAGAZINE LTD 1667267U74D-596
Formerly: KidAround
Editorial Address: 1st Floor, Dolphin House, 126 Hythe Hill,
COLCHESTER, CO1 2NP **Tel:** 01206 863737
Fax: 05601 126250
Email: lisa.ward@kidaround.biz
Advertising Address: As above.
Email: ann.crossman@kidaround.biz
Web site: http://www.kidaround.biz
Publisher: KidAround Ltd
Date Established: 2000
Frequency: Quarterly
Cover Price: Free
Circulation: 91,000 (Publisher's Statement)
Usual Pagination: 56
Editor: Lisa Ward; **Publisher:** Tracy Thomas
Summary of Content: Magazine covering listings and
information, events, extra curricular activities, nurseries, pre-
schools, toddler groups, after school clubs and baby clinics.
Readership/Target Audience: Aimed at parents of children
0 to 12 years old and distributed through primary schools,
nurseries, libraries, doctors' surgeries and health visitors.
ADVERTISING RATES:
Full Page Colour £1078.00
Mechanical Data: Trim Size: 297 x 210mm, Film: Digital
Editions:
KidAround Central Essex

KidAround North East Essex
CONSUMER: WOMEN'S INTEREST CONSUMER
MAGAZINES: Child Care

KIDS ALIVE!   48462U91D-80
Editorial Address: 101 Newington Causeway, LONDON,
SE1 6BN **Tel:** 020 7367 4911 **Fax:** 020 7367 4710
Email: kidsalive@salvationarmy.org.uk
Web site: http://www.salvationarmy.org.uk/kids
ISSN: 1363-5662
Publisher: The Salvation Army
Date Established: 1996
Frequency: Weekly
Cover Price: £0.50
Circulation: 21,000 (Publisher's Statement)
Usual Pagination: 16
Editor: Justin Reeves
Summary of Content: Children's magazine containing
entertaining, educational and evangelical articles.
Readership/Target Audience: Aimed at children between 7
and 12 years old.
ADVERTISING: No Advertising taken
CONSUMER: RECREATION & LEISURE: Children & Youth

KIDZ LIFE   1832954U74D-666
Editorial Address: Enterprise House, 127 Bute Street,
CARDIFF, CF10 5LE **Tel:** 029 2045 0532 **Fax:** 029 2045 0533
Email: info@citypublications.org
Advertising Address: As above.
Email: sarah@citypublications.org
Web site: http://www.kidzlifeuk.com
Publisher: City Publications
Date Established: 2007
Frequency: Quarterly
Cover Price: Free
Circulation: 30,000 (Publisher's Statement)
Usual Pagination: 32
Editor: Alison Tucker
Summary of Content: Magazine covering health issues,
special needs, educational features, children's fashion,
nutrition, toys, games and gadgets, puzzles and celebrity
interviews.
Readership/Target Audience: Aimed at parents and
children aged 2 to 12 years old.
ADVERTISING RATES:
Full Page Colour £595.00
Agency Commission: 10%
Mechanical Data: Bleed Size: 246 x 176mm, Film: Digital
Copy instructions: Copy Date: 2 weeks prior to publication
date
Average advertising content per issue: 40%
CONSUMER: WOMEN'S INTEREST CONSUMER
MAGAZINES: Child Care

KINDRED SPIRIT   48694U94X-72
Editorial Address: Room 101, The Perfume Factory, 140
Wales Farm Road, LONDON, W3 6UG **Tel:** 020 8752 8125
Email: tania.ahsan@metropolis.co.uk
Advertising Address: Unit 2, Lynher House, 3 Bush Park,
PLYMOUTH, PL6 7RG **Tel:** 01752 762970
Fax: 01752 772107
Email: nigel.moore@metropolis.co.uk
Web site: http://www.kindredspirit.co.uk
ISSN: 0955-7067
Publisher: Kindred Spirit Ltd
Date Established: 1987
Frequency: 6 issues yearly
Cover Price: £3.60
Annual Sub.: £21.00
Circulation: 40,000 (Publisher's Statement)
Usual Pagination: 102
Editor: Tania Ahsan; **Advertising Manager:** Nigel Moore
Summary of Content: Holistic journal covering spiritual and
personal development, health, healing, medicine and natural
products, environmental issues and travel.
Readership/Target Audience: Aimed at women between
25 and 55 years old with an interest in holistic medicine and
spiritual and personal development.
ADVERTISING RATES:
Full Page Mono £1235.00
Full Page Colour £1400.00
Agency Commission: 10%
Mechanical Data: Film: Digital, Trim Size: 297 x 210mm
Copy instructions: Copy Date: 6 weeks prior to publication
date
Average advertising content per issue: 38%
CONSUMER: OTHER CLASSIFICATIONS: Miscellaneous

KING POLE CIRCUS MAGAZINE 48695U94X-73
Editorial Address: Fir Tree Cottage, Little Hormead,
BUNTINGFORD, SG9 0LU **Tel:** 01763 289543
Email: david.jamieson@btinternet.com
Advertising Address: As above.
Email: david.jamieson@btinternet.com
Web site: http://www.circusfriends.co.uk.

Publisher: Circus Friends Association of Great Britain
Date Established: 1934
Frequency: 5 issues yearly
Cover Price: £5.50
Annual Sub.: £27.00
Circulation: 700 (Publisher's Statement)
Usual Pagination: 56
Editor: David Jamieson; **Advertising Manager:** David
Jamieson
Summary of Content: Magazine containing news, reviews,
historical articles and profiles of the world of circus.
Readership/Target Audience: Read by members of the
Circus Friends Association of Great Britain, circus directors
and artists.
ADVERTISING RATES:
Full Page Mono £125.00
Full Page Colour £325.00
Mechanical Data: Bleed Size: 303 x 216mm, Trim Size: 297
x 210mm
Average advertising content per issue: 15%
Supplement(s): Circus Directory of the British Isles - 1xY
CONSUMER: OTHER CLASSIFICATIONS: Miscellaneous

KINGPIN   46663U79F-35
Editorial Address: 54 Hamilton Road, OXFORD, OX2 7PZ
Tel: 01865 559509
Email: jon_manley@msn.com
Advertising Address: As above.
Email: jon_manley@msn.com
Web site: http://www.chesscenter.com/kingpin/Kingpin
ISSN: 0969-2150
Publisher: Kingpin
Frequency: 3 issues yearly - Published in March, August
and November
Cover Price: £4.95
Annual Sub.: £14.00
Circulation: 2,000 (Publisher's Statement)
Usual Pagination: 64
Editor: Jonathan Manley; **Managing Director:** Jonathan
Manley; **Advertising Manager:** Anne Kidson; **Publisher:**
Jonathan Manley
Summary of Content: Magazine covering interviews,
tournament reports and leading masters' advice. Also covers
tips on improving one's game, book reviews and satire.
Readership/Target Audience: Aimed at chess players of all
levels.
ADVERTISING: Rates on application
Agency Commission: 15%
CONSUMER: HOBBIES & DIY: Games & Puzzles

KINGPIN SKATEBOARDING EUROPA
1667003U75L-811
Editorial Address: 1 West Smithfield, LONDON, EC1A 9JU
Tel: 020 7332 9700 **Fax:** 020 7332 9799
Email: info@factorymedia.com
Advertising Address: As above.
Email: harry.scott@factorymedia.com
Web site: http://www.kingpinmag.com
Publisher: Factory Media
Date Established: 2003
Frequency: Monthly
Cover Price: £3.20
Circulation: 85,000 (Print Run)
Usual Pagination: 164
Editor: Niall Neeson; **Advertising Manager:** Harry Scott
Summary of Content: Magazine covering skateboarding
throughout Europe with news, reviews of equipment,
accessories and clothing, events and competitions.
Readership/Target Audience: Aimed at skateboarders and
fans of skateboarding throughout Europe.
ADVERTISING RATES:
Full Page Colour EUR5000.00
Mechanical Data: Film: Digital, Trim Size: 280 x 230mm,
Bleed Size: 286 x 236mm
Copy instructions: Copy Date: 6 weeks prior to publication
date
CONSUMER: SPORT: Outdoor

KING'S LYNN PINK LOCAL DIRECTORY
48186U89C-153
Editorial Address: St. Augustines House, St. Augustines
Way, South Wootton, KING'S LYNN, PE30 3TE.
Tel: 01553 675885 **Fax:** 01553 670007
Advertising Address: As above.
Web site: http://www.pinklocaldirectory.co.uk
Publisher: Pink Local Directory Ltd
Date Established: 1988
Frequency: Annual - Published in June
Cover Price: Free
Circulation: 27,750 (Publisher's Statement)
Usual Pagination: 128
Editor: Lucan King; **Advertising Manager:** Lucan King;
Publisher: Lucan King

Summary of Content: Directory of all local business, containing business classified and alphabetical listings and local information.
Readership/Target Audience: Aimed at residents of Kings Lynn.
ADVERTISING: Rates on application
Copy instructions: Copy Date: End of April
CONSUMER: HOLIDAYS & TRAVEL: Entertainment Guides

KINGSTON MAGAZINE
1665924U80C-5217

Editorial Address: Unit A4, Kingsway Business Park, Oldfield Road, HAMPTON, TW12 2HD **Tel:** 020 8939 5601
Fax: 020 8941 7615
Email: editorial@sheengate.co.uk
Advertising Address: As above. **Tel:** 020 8939 5600
Fax: 020 8939 5610
Email: cathy@sheengate.co.uk
Publisher: Sheengate Publishing Ltd
Frequency: Monthly
Cover Price: Free
Circulation: 40,600 (Publisher's Statement)
Usual Pagination: 64
Editor: Richard Nye; **Advertising Manager:** Catherine Woods
Summary of Content: Magazine with lifestyle and local interest articles including fashion, beauty, art, history, motoring, property and interviews.
Readership/Target Audience: Aimed at households in Kinston-Upon-Thames and surrounding areas.
ADVERTISING RATES:
Full Page Mono £1155.00
Full Page Colour £1155.00
Agency Commission: 10%
CONSUMER: RURAL & REGIONAL INTEREST: Regional Interest English Counties

KIRBY COMMENT
1824871U80C-5433

Editorial Address: Parish Council Office, Station Road, Kirby Muxloe, LEICESTER, LE9 2EN **Tel:** 0116 238 6408
Fax: 0116 238 6408
Email: clerk@kirbymuxloepc.wanadoo.co.uk
Advertising Address: As above.
Email: clerk@kirbymuxloepc.wanadoo.co.uk
Web site: http://www.kirbymuxloeparishcouncil.org.uk
Publisher: Parish Council (Kirby Muxloe)
Frequency: 3 issues yearly - Published in March, July and November
Cover Price: Free
Circulation: 3,000 (Publisher's Statement)
Usual Pagination: 24
Editor: Yvonne Waters
Summary of Content: Magazine covering local, social and industrial matters, women, health and beauty, radio and TV, children, toys, books, puzzles, entertainment, CDs, videos, travel and recreational activities.
Readership/Target Audience: Aimed at residents and visitors to Kirby Muxloe in Leicestershire.
ADVERTISING: Rates on application
CONSUMER: RURAL & REGIONAL INTEREST: Regional Interest English Counties

KIT CAR
46504U77R-270

Editorial Address: 11 Meadow Close, HOVE, BN3 6QQ
Tel: 01273 555910
Email: info@kit-cars.com
Advertising Address: 14 Victoria Road, SUTTON, SM1 4RT
Tel: 020 8395 2653 **Fax:** 020 8395 2653
Email: info@kit-cars.com
Web site: http://www.kit-cars.com
Publisher: Kit Cars International Ltd
Frequency: Monthly
Cover Price: £4.30
Annual Sub.: £45.00
Circulation: 12,000 (Publisher's Statement)
Usual Pagination: 164
Editor: Ian Hyne; **Advertising Manager:** Tom Saunders
Summary of Content: Magazine covering all aspects of building and driving kit-cars. Includes technical information and roadtests.
Readership/Target Audience: Aimed at kit car enthusiasts.
ADVERTISING RATES:
Full Page Mono £600.00
Full Page Colour £600.00
SCC £100.00
Agency Commission: 10%
Mechanical Data: Film: Digital, Trim Size: 297 x 210mm, Bleed Size: 303 x 216mm, Type Area: 260 x 180mm, Col Length: 260mm, Page Width: 180mm
Copy instructions: Copy Date: 3 weeks prior to publication date
Average advertising content per issue: 50%
CONSUMER: MOTORING & CYCLING: Motoring & Cycling Related

THE KITCHEN GARDEN
48566U93-57

Editorial Address: Media Centre, Morton Way, HORNCASTLE, LN9 6JR **Tel:** 01507 529396
Fax: 01507 529499
Email: sott@mortons.co.uk
Advertising Address: As above. **Tel:** 01507 529300
Email: hrmartin@mortons.co.uk
Web site: http://www.kitchengarden.co.uk
Publisher: Mortons Media Group Ltd
Date Established: 1997
Frequency: Monthly
Cover Price: £3.50
Annual Sub.: £36.00
Circulation: 38,000 (Publisher's Statement)
Usual Pagination: 108
Editor: Steve Ott
Summary of Content: Magazine about growing fruit, vegetables and herbs used in the home kitchen.
Readership/Target Audience: Aimed at gardening and allotment enthusiasts.
ADVERTISING RATES:
Full Page Colour £1545.00
Agency Commission: 10%
Mechanical Data: Type Area: 270x 188mm, Bleed Size: 307 x 220mm, Trim Size: 297 x 210mm, Page Width: 188mm, Col Length: 270mm, Film: Digital, Col Widths (Display): 44mm, No. of Columns (Display): 4
Copy instructions: Copy Date: 6 weeks prior to publication date
Average advertising content per issue: 20%
CONSUMER: GARDENING

KITCHENS BEDROOMS & BATHROOMS MAGAZINE
45273U74C-268

Editorial Address: Equitable House, Lyon Road, HARROW, HA1 2EW **Tel:** 020 8515 2000 **Fax:** 020 8515 2006
Email: jackiedaly@taylistmedia.com
Advertising Address: As above.
Email: maggielister@taylistmedia.com
Web site: http://www.kbbmagazine.com
ISSN: 0966-4114
Publisher: Taylist Media
Date Established: 1990
Frequency: Monthly
Cover Price: £3.99
Annual Sub.: £45.00
Circulation: 27,000 (Publisher's Statement)
Usual Pagination: 176
Editor: Jackie Daly; **Advertising Manager:** Maggie Lister
Summary of Content: Magazine focusing on kitchen, bedroom and bathroom interiors, design and products.
Readership/Target Audience: Aimed at those who are about to make a purchasing decision on their kitchen, bedroom or bathroom.
ADVERTISING RATES:
Full Page Colour £2810.00
Agency Commission: 15%
Mechanical Data: Col Length: 275mm, Page Width: 208mm, Trim Size: 300 x 230mm, Type Area: 275 x 208mm, Bleed Size: 306 x 236mm, Film: Digital
Copy instructions: Copy Date: 3 weeks prior to publication date
Average advertising content per issue: 40%
CONSUMER: WOMEN'S INTEREST CONSUMER MAGAZINES: Home & Family

KITE WORLD
1645784U75X-1717

Editorial Address: 5 St. Georges Place, BRIGHTON, BN1 4GA **Tel:** 01273 808601
Email: jim@kiteworldmag.com
Advertising Address: As above.
Email: seb@kiteworldmag.com
Web site: http://www.kiteworldmag.com
Publisher: 328 Media
Frequency: 6 issues yearly
Cover Price: £3.75
Annual Sub.: £24.95
Circulation: 30,000 (Publisher's Statement)
Usual Pagination: 132
Editor: Jim Gaunt; **Advertising Manager:** Seb Hempstead
Summary of Content: Lifestyle magazine covering kite-surfing and snow-kiting with equipment reviews, interviews, news and stories.
Readership/Target Audience: Aimed predominantly at men aged between 20 and 50 years old who are involved in the sport.
ADVERTISING RATES:
Full Page Colour £969.00
Mechanical Data: Type Area: 270 x 215mm, Bleed Size: 286 x 236mm, Trim Size: 280 x 230mm, Col Length: 270mm, Page Width: 215mm, Film: Digital
Copy instructions: Copy Date: 3 weeks prior to publication date
Average advertising content per issue: 40%
CONSUMER: SPORT: Other Sport

KITESURF MAGAZINE
762876U75M-991

Editorial Address: The Blue Barns, Tew Lane, Wootton, WOODSTOCK, OX20 1HA **Tel:** 01993 811181
Fax: 01993 811481
Email: rou@kitesurf-magazine.co.uk
Advertising Address: As above.
Email: dan@kitesurf-magazine.co.uk
Web site: http://www.kitesurf-magazine.co.uk
Publisher: Arcwind Ltd
Date Established: 2001
Frequency: 6 issues yearly
Cover Price: £4.00
Annual Sub.: £20.00
Circulation: 18,000 (Publisher's Statement)
Usual Pagination: 132
Editor: Dom Moore; **Advertising Manager:** Dan Beechener
Summary of Content: Magazine covering all aspects of kitesurfing with news, reviews of products, places to go, tips, techniques and interviews.
Readership/Target Audience: Aimed at professional and recreational kitesurfers.
ADVERTISING RATES:
Full Page Colour £1165.00
Agency Commission: 10%
Mechanical Data: Bleed Size: 291 x 236mm, Trim Size: 285 x 230mm, Type Area: 261 x 206mm, Col Length: 261mm, Page Width: 206mm, Film: Digital, Print Process: Sheet-fed offset litho
Copy instructions: Copy Date: 8 weeks prior to publication date
Average advertising content per issue: 40%
CONSUMER: SPORT: Water Sports

KMAG
46240U76E-165

Formerly: Knowledge Magazine
Editorial Address: PO Box 56556, LONDON, SW18 9EP
Tel: 020 7183 0468
Email: colin@kmag.co.uk
Advertising Address: As above. **Fax:** 020 7183 2468
Email: rachel@kmag.co.uk
Web site: http://www.kmag.co.uk
ISSN: 1464-1453
Publisher: Pheonix Publishing
Date Established: 1994
Frequency: 10 issues yearly
Cover Price: £4.00
Annual Sub.: £31.50
Circulation: 25,000 (Publisher's Statement)
Usual Pagination: 100
Editor: Colin Steven; **News Editor:** Colin Steven; **Advertising Manager:** Rachel Patey; **Publisher:** Colin Steven
Summary of Content: Magazine covering drum & bass, breaks and hip-hop music and lifestyle issues. Includes articles on street culture, fashion, art, music technology, Internet, design and travel.
Readership/Target Audience: Aimed at 18 to 28 year olds who enjoy clubbing, travel, socialising, fashion, mixing and producing.
ADVERTISING RATES:
Full Page Colour £1200.00
Agency Commission: 10%
Mechanical Data: Bleed Size: 303 x 216mm, Trim Size: 297 x 210mm, Film: Digital
Copy instructions: Copy Date: 4 weeks prior to publication date
Average advertising content per issue: 40%
CONSUMER: MUSIC & PERFORMING ARTS: Pop Music

KNAVE
47609U86A-80

Editorial Address: PO Box 312, WITHAM, CM8 3SZ
Tel: 01376 534558 **Fax:** 01376 534546
Email: dougie.heard.dh@galaxy.co.uk
Advertising Address: Freebournes House, Freebournes Road, WITHAM, CM8 3US **Tel:** 01376 534534
Fax: 01376 534531
Email: sales@galaxy.co.uk
Web site: http://www.knave.co.uk
Publisher: Galaxy Publications
Date Established: 1968
Frequency: 6 issues yearly
Cover Price: £2.99
Circulation: 30,000 (Publisher's Statement)
Usual Pagination: 100
Editor: Matt Elliot; **Advertising Manager:** Anne Hanley
Summary of Content: Adult magazine containing glamour photography and male interest articles.
Readership/Target Audience: Read by men of all ages.
ADVERTISING RATES:
Full Page Colour £600.00
Agency Commission: 10%
Mechanical Data: Trim Size: 148 x 210mm, Film: Digital
Average advertising content per issue: 25%
CONSUMER: ADULT & GAY MAGAZINES: Adult Magazines

KNIT & STITCH TODAY
1705248U74E-698

Editorial Address: Little Cutmadoc, Jasons Hill, CHESHAM, HP5 3QP
Publisher: Angus Bird Publishing
Frequency: 6 issues yearly
Cover Price: £3.50
Circulation: 10,500 (Publisher's Statement)
Editor: Heather Cook
Summary of Content: Magazine covering knitting, stitching, patchwork, quilting and embroidery.
Readership/Target Audience: Aimed at knitters and stitchers of all ages and abilities.
ADVERTISING: Rates on application
CONSUMER: WOMEN'S INTEREST CONSUMER MAGAZINES: Crafts

KNIT TODAY
1748511U74E-699

Editorial Address: 9th Floor, Tower House, Fairfax Street, BRISTOL, BS1 3BN **Tel:** 0117 927 9009 **Fax:** 0117 934 9008
Email: marieparry@originpublishing.co.uk
Advertising Address: As above. **Fax:** 0117 927 9008
Email: shanellej@originpublishing.co.uk
Web site: http://www.knit-today.co.uk
ISSN: 1751-3774
Publisher: Origin Publishing Ltd
Date Established: 2006
Frequency: Monthly
Cover Price: £3.99
Circulation: 50,000 (Print Run)
Usual Pagination: 100
Editor: Elizabeth Leight
Summary of Content: Magazine covering knitting, patterns, products, book reviews and designer profiles.
Readership/Target Audience: Aimed at the enthusiastic knitter predominantly women aged between 25 and 50 years old.
ADVERTISING RATES:
Full Page Colour £800.00
Mechanical Data: Type Area: 280 x 202mm, Bleed Size: 306 x 226mm, Trim Size: 300 x 220mm, Col Length: 280mm, Page Width: 202mm, Film: Digital
CONSUMER: WOMEN'S INTEREST CONSUMER MAGAZINES: Crafts

THE KNITTER
1863457U74E-708

Editorial Address: 30 Monmouth Street, BATH, BA1 2BW
Tel: 01225 442244
Email: juliet.bernard@futurenet.com
Web site: http://www.theknitter.co.uk
Publisher: Future Publishing Ltd
Date Established: 2009
Frequency: 13 issues yearly
Cover Price: £5.99
Editor: Helen Spedding; **Publisher:** Kerry Lawrence
Summary of Content: Magazine covering knitting, fashions and trends, lifestyle, home, crafts and gadgets.
Readership/Target Audience: Aimed at experienced knitters.
CONSUMER: WOMEN'S INTEREST CONSUMER MAGAZINES: Crafts

KNITTING
1638229U74E-682

Editorial Address: 86 High Street, LEWES, BN7 1XN
Tel: 01273 477374
Email: emmak@thegmcgroup.com
Advertising Address: As above. **Tel:** 01273 402869
Fax: 01273 402849
Web site: http://www.thegmcgroup.com
ISSN: 1740-6943
Publisher: GMC Publications Ltd
Date Established: 2003
Frequency: 13 issues yearly
Cover Price: £3.99
Free to qualifying individuals
Circulation: 40,000 (Publisher's Statement)
Usual Pagination: 100
Editor: Emma Brown; **Publisher:** Simon McKeown
Summary of Content: Consumer magazine for hand knitters featuring patterns, news, products, reviews and events. Also includes feature articles on yarns, sources, techniques and designers and some crochet patterns.
Readership/Target Audience: Aimed at knitters of all ages.
ADVERTISING RATES:
Full Page Colour £800.00
CONSUMER: WOMEN'S INTEREST CONSUMER MAGAZINES: Crafts

KNOWSLEY NEWS
1666042U80C-5219

Editorial Address: PO Box 21, Archway Road, Huyton, LIVERPOOL, L36 9YU **Tel:** 0151 443 3397
Fax: 0151 443 3507
Email: knowsleynews@knowsley.gov.uk
Publisher: Knowsley Borough Council
Frequency: 6 issues yearly

Cover Price: Free
Circulation: 70,000 (Publisher's Statement)
Usual Pagination: 32
Editor: Stephen Roberts
Summary of Content: Magazine covering local information including news articles, what's on, music, sport, events, education and community news.
Readership/Target Audience: Aimed at residents of all ages in the Borough of Knowsley.
ADVERTISING: No Advertising taken
CONSUMER: RURAL & REGIONAL INTEREST: Regional Interest English Counties

KOI
1646015U81E-151

Formerly: Koi, Ponds & Gardens
Editorial Address: 9th Floor, Tower House, Fairfax Street, BRISTOL, BS1 3BN **Tel:** 0117 927 9009 **Fax:** 0117 934 9008
Email: beckierodgers@originpublishing.co.uk
Advertising Address: As above.
Email: tonyrobinson@originpublishing.co.uk
Web site: http://www.koimag.co.uk
ISSN: 1465-4075
Publisher: Origin Publishing Ltd
Date Established: 1999
Frequency: 13 issues yearly
Cover Price: £3.95
Annual Sub.: £43.50
Circulation: 15,000 (Publisher's Statement)
Usual Pagination: 116
Editor: Beckie Rodgers; **Advertising Manager:** Tony Robinson
Summary of Content: Magazine containing a practical guide to Koi keeping, water gardening and pond management.
Readership/Target Audience: Aimed at Koi enthusiasts at all levels of the hobby.
ADVERTISING RATES:
Full Page Colour £970.00
Mechanical Data: Type Area: 281 x 195mm, Bleed Size: 303 x 216mm, Trim Size: 297 x 210mm, Col Length: 281mm, Page Width: 195mm, Film: Digital
Average advertising content per issue: 55%
CONSUMER: ANIMALS & PETS: Fish

THE KOP
45764U75B-142

Editorial Address: PO Box 48, Old Hall Street, LIVERPOOL, L69 3EB **Tel:** 0151 285 8442 **Fax:** 0151 285 8466
Email: kop@sportmedia-tm.com
Advertising Address: As above. **Tel:** 0151 227 2000
Email: neil.johnson@liverpool.com
Web site: http://www.icliverpool.co.uk
Publisher: Liverpool Daily Post & Echo Ltd
Frequency: Monthly
Cover Price: £1.50
Circulation: 10,500 (Publisher's Statement)
Usual Pagination: 28
Editor: Paul Dove
Summary of Content: Magazine dedicated to Liverpool Football Club. An independent fanzine style publication.
Readership/Target Audience: Aimed at supporters of the club.
ADVERTISING RATES:
Full Page Colour £1000.00
Agency Commission: 10%
Mechanical Data: Col Length: 360mm, Type Area: 360 x 280mm, No. of Columns (Display): 8, Page Width: 280mm, Col Widths (Display): 35mm, Film: Digital
Copy instructions: Copy Date: 1 week prior to publication date
Average advertising content per issue: 10%
CONSUMER: SPORT: Football

KRISS KROSS
46664U79F-40

Editorial Address: Stonecroft, 69 Station Road, REDHILL, RH1 1EY **Tel:** 01737 378700 **Fax:** 01737 781800
Email: reception@puzzlermedia.com
Advertising Address: As above. **Fax:** 01737 378888
Email: brian.ainge@puzzlermedia.co.uk
Web site: http://www.puzzler.com
Publisher: Puzzler Media Ltd
Date Established: 1976
Frequency: 13 issues yearly
Cover Price: £1.95
Circulation: 67,369 (ABC 01/01/2008 to 31/12/2008)
Usual Pagination: 100
Editor: Sarah Johnson; **Managing Director:** Mel Lewis
Summary of Content: Puzzle magazine.
Readership/Target Audience: Aimed at women aged 40 and over.
ADVERTISING: Rates on application
CONSUMER: HOBBIES & DIY: Games & Puzzles

KUDOS
1664688U84B-360

Formerly: Competitions Bulletin
Editorial Address: 17 Greenhow Avenue, WIRRAL, CH48 5EL **Tel:** 0151 625 1446
Email: carolebaldock@hotmail.com
Advertising Address: As above.
Email: carolebaldock@hotmail.com
Web site: http://www.kudoswriting.wordpress.com
ISSN: 1468-487X
Publisher: Carole Baldock
Date Established: 1999
Frequency: 6 issues yearly
Cover Price: £2.50
Annual Sub.: £15.00
Circulation: 500 (Publisher's Statement)
Usual Pagination: 30
Editor: Carole Baldock; **Advertising Manager:** Carole Baldock
Summary of Content: Magazine with listings for literary competitions.
Readership/Target Audience: Aimed at those entering or organising literary competitions.
ADVERTISING RATES:
Full Page Mono £40.00
Mechanical Data: Film: Digital
Copy instructions: Copy Date: 15th of the month prior to publication date
CONSUMER: THE ARTS & LITERARY: Literary

LABEL
47405U83-23_50

Editorial Address: Ashby Road, LOUGHBOROUGH, LE11 3TT **Tel:** 01509 635000 **Fax:** 01509 635003
Email: label@lborosu.org.uk
Advertising Address: As above.
Email: amyleong@lborosu.org.uk
Web site: http://www.loughborough.net
Publisher: Loughborough Students' Union
Frequency: 28 issues yearly - Published weekly during term time
Cover Price: Free
Circulation: 3,500 (Publisher's Statement)
Usual Pagination: 20
Summary of Content: Magazine covering news, arts reviews, features, sport, style, fashion, music and listings.
Readership/Target Audience: Aimed at students of Loughborough University.
ADVERTISING RATES:
Full Page Colour £575.00
Agency Commission: 10%
Mechanical Data: Bleed Size: 281 x 216mm, Film: Digital, Trim Size: 275 x 210mm
Copy instructions: Copy Date: 10 days prior to publication date
Average advertising content per issue: 25%
CONSUMER: STUDENT PUBLICATIONS

LACROSSE TALK
46014U75X-560

Editorial Address: The Belle Vue Centre, Pink Bank Lane, Longsight, MANCHESTER, M12 5GL **Tel:** 0161 227 3626
Fax: 0161 227 3625
Email: c.royle@englishlacrosse.co.uk
Advertising Address: As above.
Email: c.royle@englishlacrosse.co.uk
Web site: http://www.englishlacrosse.co.uk
Publisher: English Lacrosse Association
Frequency: Quarterly
Annual Sub.: £25.00
Circulation: 10,000 (Publisher's Statement)
Usual Pagination: 32
Editor: Carolyn Royle; **Advertising Manager:** Carolyn Royle; **Publisher:** Paige Fast
Summary of Content: Magazine covering all aspects of lacrosse including men's, women's and mixed. Includes the latest news, features, articles and match reports.
Readership/Target Audience: Read by lacrosse players of all ages.
ADVERTISING RATES:
Full Page Mono £750.00
Full Page Colour £1000.00
Agency Commission: 10%
Mechanical Data: Type Area: 252 x 178mm, Bleed Size: +3mm, Trim Size: 297 x 210mm, Film: Digital, Col Length: 252mm, Page Width: 178mm
Copy instructions: Copy Date: 3 weeks prior to publication date
Average advertising content per issue: 20%
CONSUMER: SPORT: Other Sport

LADIES FIRST
45181U74A-250

Editorial Address: 1 Kings Road, CARDIFF, CF11 9BZ
Tel: 029 2039 6600 **Fax:** 029 2039 6611
Email: edits@ladiesfirst.co.uk
Advertising Address: As above.
Email: sales@ladiesfirst.co.uk
Web site: http://www.ladiesfirst.co.uk
Publisher: Hils Publications Ltd

Date Established: 1986
Frequency: Quarterly
Free to qualifying individuals
Annual Sub.: £12.00
Circulation: 37,151 (ABC 01/01/2009 to 30/06/2009)
Usual Pagination: 120
Editor: Victoria Patterson; **Managing Director:** Hilary Ferda
Summary of Content: Magazine covering fashion, beauty, health, features, careers, travel, home, garden and lifestyle.
Readership/Target Audience: Read by women between 20 and 45 years old.
ADVERTISING RATES:
Full Page Colour £875.00
Agency Commission: 10%
Mechanical Data: Page Width: 181mm, Type Area: 266 x 181mm, Col Length: 266mm, Film: Positive, right reading, emulsion side down. Digital, Screen: 60 lpc
Copy instructions: Copy Date: 5 weeks prior to publication date
Editions:
Ladies First Bucks, Berks & Oxfordshire
Ladies First SE and West Wales
CONSUMER: WOMEN'S INTEREST CONSUMER MAGAZINES: Women's Interest

THE LADY
45182U74A-280

Editorial Address: 39-40 Bedford Street, LONDON, WC2E 9ER **Tel:** 020 7379 4717 **Fax:** 020 7836 4620
Email: editors@lady.co.uk
Advertising Address: As above. **Fax:** 020 7497 2137
Web site: http://www.lady.co.uk
ISSN: 0023-7167
Publisher: The Lady Ltd
Date Established: 1885
Frequency: Weekly
Cover Price: £1.50
Annual Sub.: £70.00
Circulation: 28,721 (ABC 01/01/2009 to 30/06/2009)
Usual Pagination: 80
Editor: Rachel Johnson; **Features Editor:** Janina Pogorzelski
Summary of Content: Magazine containing articles on travel, the countryside, beauty, fashion, animals, gardening, history, culture, exhibitions, the arts and human interest.
Readership/Target Audience: Aimed at woman who are looking for holidays, property and placements as nannies and domestic staff but mainly aimed at woman aged 40 years and over.
ADVERTISING RATES:
Full Page Mono £1130.00
Full Page Colour £1565.00
Agency Commission: 15%
Mechanical Data: Page Width: 190mm, Col Widths (Display): 44mm, No. of Columns (Display): 4, Type Area: 270 x 190mm, Bleed Size: 303 x 213mm, Trim Size: 297 x 210mm, Col Length: 270mm, Print Process: Web-fed offset litho, Film: Digital
Copy instructions: Copy Date: 2 weeks prior to publication date
CONSUMER: WOMEN'S INTEREST CONSUMER MAGAZINES: Women's Interest

LADY GOLFER
45820U75D-175

Editorial Address: 1st Floor, 18-22 Market Street, CLECKHEATON, BD19 5AJ **Tel:** 01274 851323
Fax: 01274 852687
Email: editorial@sportspub.co.uk
Advertising Address: As above.
Email: mark_k@sportspub.co.uk
Web site: http://www.ladygolferonline.co.uk
ISSN: 1369-4790
Publisher: Sports Publications Ltd.
Date Established: 1997
Frequency: Monthly
Cover Price: £2.75
Free to qualifying individuals
Annual Sub.: £27.50
Circulation: 25,000 (Publisher's Statement)
Usual Pagination: 92
Editor: Dan Murphy; **Advertising Manager:** Richard Holt
Summary of Content: Magazine featuring celebrity interviews, news, tips and advice, travel, fashion and competitions.
Readership/Target Audience: Aimed at female golfers.
ADVERTISING RATES:
Full Page Colour £1139.40
Agency Commission: 10%
Mechanical Data: Trim Size: 297 x 210mm, Film: Digital
CONSUMER: SPORT: Golf

THE LAITY
47818U87-154_2

Editorial Address: 157 Vicarage Road, Leyton, LONDON, E10 5DU **Tel:** 020 8539 3876 **Fax:** 020 8539 3876
Email: keys@fsmail.net
Publisher: Delane Press
Date Established: 1974
Frequency: Quarterly

Cover Price: £1.00
Usual Pagination: 20
Editor: Ronald King
Summary of Content: Publication covering the study of Freemasonry and comparative religion.
Language(s): Afrikaans; Dutch; English; French; Latin
Readership/Target Audience: Aimed at those interested in Freemasonry.
ADVERTISING: No Advertising taken
CONSUMER: RELIGIOUS

LAKE DISTRICT LIFE
1834016U80C-5441

Editorial Address: 3 Tustin Court, Port Way, Ashton-on-Ribble, PRESTON, PR2 2YQ **Tel:** 01772 722022
Fax: 01772 760905
Email: paul.mackenzie@archant.co.uk
Web site: http://www.lakedistrict-life.co.uk
Publisher: Archant Life (North) PLC
Date Established: 2004
Frequency: 6 issues yearly
Cover Price: £2.45
Circulation: 13,000 (Publisher's Statement)
Usual Pagination: 116
Editor: Paul Mackenzie
Summary of Content: Magazine containing coverage of town and villages in Cumbria, the county's history and heritage, features about life in the county, property, antiques, fashion, interiors, gardening, food and wine and motoring.
Readership/Target Audience: Aimed at residents, businesses and visitors to Cumbria.
CONSUMER: RURAL & REGIONAL INTEREST: Regional Interest English Counties

LAKELAND EXTRA
47064U80F-100

Editorial Address: 8-10 East Bridge Street, ENNISKILLEN, BT74 7BT **Tel:** 028 6632 4422 **Fax:** 028 6632 5047
Email: ssanderson@impartialreporter.com
Advertising Address: As above. **Tel:** 028 6632 4425
Fax: 028 6632 5969
Email: jclarke@impartialreporter.com
Web site: http://www.impartialreporter.com
Publisher: William Trimble Ltd
Frequency: 10 issues yearly - Published on the 3rd Monday of the month
Cover Price: Free
Circulation: 24,500 (Publisher's Statement)
Usual Pagination: 24
Editor: Denzil McDaniel; **Advertising Manager:** June Clarke
Summary of Content: Lifestyle magazine featuring local celebrities and reviews.
Readership/Target Audience: Aimed at local people and businesses in the Fermanagh and South Tyrone areas.
ADVERTISING RATES:
Full Page Mono £531.00
Full Page Colour £658.00
SCC £2.30
Mechanical Data: Col Widths (Display): 35mm, No. of Columns (Display): 7, Type Area: 330 x 260mm, Col Length: 330mm, Page Width: 260mm, Film: Digital
Copy instructions: Copy Date: 4 weeks prior to publication date
Average advertising content per issue: 75%
CONSUMER: RURAL & REGIONAL INTEREST: Regional Interest Northern Ireland

LAKELAND WALKER
45926U75L-350

Editorial Address: The Maltings, West Street, BOURNE, PE10 9PH **Tel:** 01778 391126 **Fax:** 01778 425437
Email: michaelcowton@btinternet.com
Advertising Address: As above. **Tel:** 01778 391000
Fax: 01778 392422
Email: clairem@warnersgroup.co.uk
ISSN: 1369-4553
Publisher: Warners Group Publications plc
Date Established: 1997
Frequency: 6 issues yearly
Cover Price: £3.10
Circulation: 12,000 (Publisher's Statement)
Usual Pagination: 56
Editor: Michael Cowton; **Publisher:** Rob McDonnell
Summary of Content: Magazine containing Lake District news, countryside features, where to stay, walks and gear features.
Readership/Target Audience: Aimed at walkers and backpackers in the Lake District.
ADVERTISING RATES:
Full Page Mono £775.00
Full Page Colour £1140.00
SCC £12.00
Agency Commission: 10%
Mechanical Data: Page Width: 190mm, Type Area: 275 x 190mm, Bleed Size: 303 x 216mm, Trim Size: 297 x 210mm, Col Length: 275mm, Film: Digital
CONSUMER: SPORT: Outdoor

LANCASHIRE LIFE
46931U80C-2000

Formerly: Lancashire Life and Lake District Life
Editorial Address: 3 Tustin Court, Port Way, Ashton-on-Ribble, PRESTON, PR2 2YQ **Tel:** 01772 722022
Fax: 01772 760905
Email: enquiries@lancashirelife.co.uk
Advertising Address: As above. **Fax:** 01772 736496
Email: jan.robinson@lancashirelife.co.uk
Web site: http://www.lancashirelife.co.uk
Publisher: Archant Life (North) PLC
Date Established: 1947
Frequency: Monthly
Cover Price: £2.95
Annual Sub.: £12.00
Circulation: 23,496 (ABC 01/01/2008 to 31/12/2008)
Usual Pagination: 250
Editor: Roger Borrell
Summary of Content: Magazine containing coverage of towns, villages, the county's history and heritage, features about life in the county, property, antiques, fashion, interior design, gardening, food and wine and motoring.
Readership/Target Audience: Aimed at residents of Lancashire.
ADVERTISING RATES:
Full Page Mono £1840.00
Full Page Colour £2105.00
Mechanical Data: Page Width: 198mm, Trim Size: 300 x 220mm, Bleed Size: 306 x 226mm, Film: Digital, Print Process: Sheet-fed litho, Type Area: 275 x 198mm, Col Length: 275mm
Copy instructions: Copy Date: 18th of the month prior to publication date
CONSUMER: RURAL & REGIONAL INTEREST: Regional Interest English Counties

LANCASHIRE MAGAZINE
46932U80C-5353

Editorial Address: Unit 200, Oyston Mill, Strand Road, PRESTON, PR1 8UR **Tel:** 01772 761277 **Fax:** 01772 739202
Email: anthony.s@lancashiremagazine.co.uk
Advertising Address: As above.
Email: info@lancashiremagazine.co.uk
ISSN: 0960-5886
Publisher: Ridings Publishing Co.
Date Established: 1977
Frequency: Monthly
Cover Price: £1.95
Annual Sub.: £10.00
Circulation: 20,013 (ABC 01/07/2008 to 31/12/2008)
Usual Pagination: 200
Editor: Anthony Skinner; **Features Editor:** Richard Fulford-Brown
Summary of Content: Magazine covering features about Lancashire, arts, antiques, health and beauty, restaurants, gardening and the great outdoors.
Readership/Target Audience: Aimed at Lancashire residents and Lancastrians overseas.
ADVERTISING RATES:
Full Page Colour £1500.00
Agency Commission: 15%
Mechanical Data: Col Length: 270mm, Type Area: 270 x 183mm, Print Process: Litho, Bleed Size: 303 x 216mm, Trim Size: 297 x 210mm, Film: Digital, Page Width: 183mm
Copy instructions: Copy Date: 5 weeks prior to publication date
Average advertising content per issue: 45%
CONSUMER: RURAL & REGIONAL INTEREST: Regional Interest English Counties

LANCASHIRE SPIN
1655733U75K-852

Editorial Address: County Ground, Brian Statham Way, Old Trafford, MANCHESTER, M16 0PX **Tel:** 0161 282 4000
Fax: 0161 282 4064
Email: kgrime@lccc.co.uk
Advertising Address: As above. **Tel:** 0161 282 4049
Email: kgrime@lccc.co.uk
Web site: http://www.lccc.co.uk
Publisher: Lancashire County Cricket Club
Date Established: 2000
Frequency: 3 issues yearly - Published in April, July and November
Cover Price: £2.00
Free to qualifying individuals
Circulation: 10,000 (Publisher's Statement)
Usual Pagination: 36
Editor: Rebecca Trbojevich; **Advertising Manager:** Ken Grime
Summary of Content: Magazine covering Lancashire Cricket Club activities, players, player interviews and features as well as International matches played at Old Trafford.
Readership/Target Audience: Aimed at fans of Lancashire County Cricket Club.
ADVERTISING RATES:
Full Page Colour £600.00
Mechanical Data: Bleed Size: 303 x 216mm, Trim Size: 297 x 210mm
Average advertising content per issue: 25%
CONSUMER: SPORT: Cricket

Consumer Magazines

LAND BUSINESS
47047U80E-70

Formerly: Landowning in Scotland
Editorial Address: Studio 2001, Mile End, Abbey Mill
Business Centre, PAISLEY, PA1 1JS **Tel:** 0141 561 0300
Fax: 0141 561 0400
Email: info@connectcommunications.co.uk
Advertising Address: SRPBA, 18 Muirpark, Eskbank,
DALKEITH, EH22 3JE **Tel:** 0131 467 3977
Fax: 0131 225 9760
Email: kirstin@kirstinnorrie.co.uk
Publisher: SRPBA
Frequency: 6 issues yearly
Cover Price: Free
Circulation: 3,200 (Publisher's Statement)
Usual Pagination: 48
Editor: Wendy Fenemore; **Advertising Manager:** Kirstin
Norrie; **Managing Editor:** Wendy Fenemore
Summary of Content: Magazine covering the maintenance
of buildings and land. Includes articles on law and taxation,
buying and selling, finance, agriculture, forestry, mineral
development, diversification and conservation.
Readership/Target Audience: Aimed at members of the
Scottish Landowners' Federation.
ADVERTISING RATES:
Full Page Colour £650.00
Agency Commission: 10%
Mechanical Data: Bleed Size: 300 x 213mm, Col Length:
297mm, Type Area: 297 x 210mm, Page Width: 210mm,
Film: Digital
Copy instructions: Copy Date: 4 weeks prior to publication
date
Average advertising content per issue: 40%
CONSUMER: RURAL & REGIONAL INTEREST: Regional
Interest Scotland

LAND ROVER ENTHUSIAST
749728U77E-189

Editorial Address: 40 Stapeley Avenue, EDINBURGH, EH7
6QP **Tel:** 0131 669 7465
Email: editorial@landroverenthusiast.com
Advertising Address: 5 Cross Street, EYE, IP23 7AD
Tel: 01379 870645 **Fax:** 01379 871188
Email: debe.stocks@landroverenthusiast.com
Web site: http://www.landroverenthusiast.com
ISSN: 1471-7077
Publisher: LRE Media Ltd
Date Established: 2000
Frequency: Monthly
Cover Price: £3.80
Annual Sub.: £36.00
Usual Pagination: 180
Editor: James Taylor; **Publisher:** Bruce Skivington
Summary of Content: Magazine containing news, advice
and features on Land Rover vehicles of all ages.
Readership/Target Audience: Aimed at Land Rovers,
Discovery, Freelander and Range Rover enthusiasts.
ADVERTISING RATES:
Full Page Colour £450.00
Agency Commission: 10%
Mechanical Data: Type Area: 270 x 190mm, Bleed Size:
301 x 215mm, Film: Digital, Col Length: 270mm, Trim Size:
297 x 210mm, Page Width: 190mm
Copy instructions: Copy Date: 3 weeks prior to publication
date
Average advertising content per issue: 45%
CONSUMER: MOTORING & CYCLING: Club Cars

LAND ROVER ONELIFE
761538U77E-502

Editorial Address: 7 St. Martin's Place, LONDON, WC2N
4HA **Tel:** 020 7747 0745 **Fax:** 020 7747 0629
Email: zac.assemakis@redwoodgroup.net
Web site: http://www.redwoodgroup.net
Publisher: Redwood
Frequency: Half-yearly - Published in March and September
Free to qualifying individuals
Circulation: 150,000 (Publisher's Statement)
Usual Pagination: 64
Editor: Zac Assemakis
Summary of Content: Magazine covering travel and
adventure with details on new Land Rover product
developments and services.
Language(s): Arabic; English; Flemish; French; Italian;
Portuguese; Spanish
Readership/Target Audience: Read by Land Rover owners
and prospective purchasers.
ADVERTISING: No Advertising taken
CONSUMER: MOTORING & CYCLING: Club Cars

LAND ROVER OWNER INTERNATIONAL
MAGAZINE
46465U77E-190

Formerly: Land Rover Owner Magazine
Editorial Address: Media House, Lynchwood, Peterborough
Business Park, PETERBOROUGH, PE2 6EA
Tel: 01733 468000 **Fax:** 01733 468888
Email: landrover.owner@bauermedia.co.uk
Advertising Address: As above. **Fax:** 01733 468670
Email: sarah.dodd@bauerconsumer.co.uk

Web site: http://www.lro.com
ISSN: 0954-1403
Publisher: Bauer Consumer Media Ltd (Media House)
Date Established: 1987
Frequency: 13 issues yearly
Cover Price: £3.95
Annual Sub.: £49.40
Circulation: 40,033 (ABC 01/07/2008 to 31/12/2008)
Usual Pagination: 204
Editor: Mark Saville; **Features Editor:** Mark Saville; **Editor-
in-Chief:** John Pearson
Summary of Content: Magazine containing news, features
and accessories on all types of Land Rovers from series one
through to the new Range Rover.
Readership/Target Audience: Read by Land Rover and
4x4 enthusiasts.
ADVERTISING RATES:
Full Page Colour £1800.00
Mechanical Data: Type Area: 274 x 184mm, Bleed Size:
302 x 215mm, Trim Size: 297 x 210mm, Col Length: 274mm,
Film: Digital, Page Width: 184mm
Copy instructions: Copy Date: 5 weeks prior to publication
date
CONSUMER: MOTORING & CYCLING: Club Cars

LAND ROVER WORLD
46466U77E-192

Editorial Address: Cudham Tithe Barn, Berrys Hill, Berrys
Green, Cudham, WESTERHAM, TN16 3AG
Tel: 01959 543530
Email: lrw.ed@kelsey.co.uk
Advertising Address: Leon House, 233 High Street,
CROYDON, CR9 1HZ **Tel:** 020 8726 8000
Fax: 020 8726 8399
Email: lauren_george@ipcmedia.com
Web site: http://www.landroverworld.co.uk
Publisher: Kelsey Publishing Ltd
Date Established: 1994
Frequency: Monthly
Cover Price: £3.80
Circulation: 30,000 (Publisher's Statement)
Usual Pagination: 148
Editor: John Carroll; **Publisher:** Richard Marcroft
Summary of Content: Magazine about new, old and
modified Land Rover vehicles.
Readership/Target Audience: Aimed at Land Rover, Range
Rover and Discovery owners and enthusiasts.
ADVERTISING RATES:
Full Page Mono £485.00
Full Page Colour £590.00
Agency Commission: 10%
Mechanical Data: Type Area: 277 x 190mm, Film: Digital,
Trim Size: 297 x 210mm, Bleed Size: 303 x 216mm, Col
Length: 277mm, Page Width: 190mm
Copy instructions: Copy Date: 5 weeks prior to publication
date
CONSUMER: MOTORING & CYCLING: Club Cars

LANGUAGE TESTING
30068U88F-100

Editorial Address: 1 Oliver's Yard, 55 City Road, LONDON,
EC1Y 1SP **Tel:** 020 7324 8500 **Fax:** 020 7324 8600
Email: market@sagepub.co.uk
Advertising Address: As above.
Email: advertising@sagepub.co.uk
Web site: http://www.sagepub.co.uk
ISSN: 0265-5322
Publisher: Sage Publications
Date Established: 1984
Frequency: Quarterly
Annual Sub.: £360.00
Usual Pagination: 128
Editor: Catherine Elder; **Advertising Manager:** Sheena
Karim
Summary of Content: Academic publication providing a
forum for the exchange of ideas and information between
people working in the fields of first and second language
testing and assessment.
Readership/Target Audience: Read by those involved in
the linguistics and foreign languages fields.
ADVERTISING RATES:
Full Page Mono £500.00
Agency Commission: 5%
Mechanical Data: Page Width: 130mm, Type Area: 205 x
130mm, Col Length: 205mm
Copy instructions: Copy Date: 12 weeks prior to
publication date
CONSUMER: EDUCATION: Teachers

LARGE MANCHESTER
1905770U80C-5508

Editorial Address: 60 Port Street, MANCHESTER, M1 2EQ
Tel: 0161 235 7270 **Fax:** 0871 115 3137
Email: editor@largemanchester.com
Web site: http://www.largemanchester.com
Publisher: Large Publishing Ltd
Date Established: 2009
Frequency: Monthly
Circulation: 15,000 (Publisher's Statement)

Editor: Kelly Byrne; **Advertising Manager:** Alex Moore
Summary of Content: Lifestyle community magazine for
Manchester focusing on engaging the city centre
community.
Readership/Target Audience: Aimed at those living or
working in Manchester.
CONSUMER: RURAL & REGIONAL INTEREST: Regional
Interest English Counties

LARGE STUDENTS
1925406U83-315

Editorial Address: 60 Port Street, MANCHESTER, M1 2EQ
Tel: 0161 235 7270
Email: editor@largemanchester.com
Web site: http://www.largemanchester.com
Publisher: Large Publishing Ltd
Date Established: 2009
Frequency: Monthly
Cover Price: Free
Circulation: 10,000 (Publisher's Statement)
Usual Pagination: 64
Editor: Kelly Byrne
Summary of Content: Student guide to living in
Manchester, events, lifestyle, health and fitness and food.
Readership/Target Audience: Aimed at students aged 18-
25.
CONSUMER: STUDENT PUBLICATIONS

LATEST 7
1666405U89C-1036

Editorial Address: Unit 1, Level 5 North, New England
House, New England Street, BRIGHTON, BN1 4GH
Tel: 01273 818150 **Fax:** 01273 818152
Email: editorial@thelatest.co.uk
Advertising Address: Unit 6, Level 5 North, New England
House, New England Street, BRIGHTON, BN1 4GH
Tel: 01273 818150 **Fax:** 01273 818152
Email: marie@thelatest.co.uk
Publisher: Latest Media Ltd
Date Established: 2001
Frequency: Weekly
Cover Price: Free
Circulation: 120,000 (Publisher's Statement)
Usual Pagination: 200
Editor: Rachel Pegg; **Advertising Manager:** Marie Viviani;
Managing Editor: Bill Smith
Summary of Content: Magazine covering entertainment,
listings, fashion and beauty.
Readership/Target Audience: Aimed at readers of Latest
Homes magazine.
ADVERTISING RATES:
Full Page Mono £450.00
Full Page Colour £450.00
Agency Commission: 10%
Mechanical Data: Type Area: 277 x 190mm, Bleed Size:
303 x 216mm, Trim Size: 297 x 210mm, Col Length: 277mm,
Page Width: 190mm, Film: Digital
Copy instructions: Copy Date: 2 weeks prior to publication
date
CONSUMER: HOLIDAYS & TRAVEL: Entertainment Guides

LATEST HOMES
48104U89C-160

Formerly: The Latest
Editorial Address: Unit 1, Level 5 North, New England
House, New England Street, BRIGHTON, BN1 4GH
Tel: 01273 818150 **Fax:** 01273 818152
Email: editorial@thelatest.co.uk
Advertising Address: Unit 6, Level 5 North, New England
House, New England Street, BRIGHTON, BN1 4GH
Tel: 01273 818150 **Fax:** 01273 818152
Email: lynne@thelatest.co.uk
Web site: http://www.latest.co.uk
Publisher: Latest Homes Ltd
Date Established: 1988
Frequency: Weekly
Cover Price: Free
Circulation: 120,000 (Publisher's Statement)
Usual Pagination: 190
Editor: Lynne Edwards; **Managing Editor:** Bill Smith;
Advertising Director: Lynne Edwards
Summary of Content: Magazine covering property, news,
views, arts, retail, fashion, culture and listings.
Readership/Target Audience: Aimed at those living in
Sussex or thinking of moving to Sussex.
ADVERTISING RATES:
Full Page Colour £450.00
Agency Commission: 10%
Mechanical Data: Film: Digital
Copy instructions: Copy Date: 1 week prior to publication
date
CONSUMER: HOLIDAYS & TRAVEL: Entertainment Guides

LAZY TOWN
1800449U91D-956

Editorial Address: Titan House, 144 Southwark Street,
LONDON, SE1 0UP **Tel:** 020 7620 0200 **Fax:** 020 7620 0032
Email: toby.orton@titanemail.com

Advertising Address: As above. **Fax:** 020 7803 1803
Email: james.willmott@titanemail.com
Web site: http://www.tots.titanmagazine.co.uk
Publisher: Titan Magazines
Date Established: 2007
Frequency: 17 issues yearly
Cover Price: £1.85
Circulation: 31,601 (ABC 01/01/2009 to 30/06/2009)
Usual Pagination: 36
Editor: Toby Orton; **Advertising Manager:** James Willmott
Summary of Content: Children's magazine with puzzles, activities, stories and games based on the TV programme Lazy Town.
Readership/Target Audience: Aimed at boys and girls aged 4 to 7 years old.
ADVERTISING RATES:
Full Page Colour £4600.00
Agency Commission: 10%
Mechanical Data: Bleed Size: 303 x 236mm, Trim Size: 297 x 230mm, Film: Digital
Copy instructions: Copy Date: 6 weeks prior to publication date
CONSUMER: RECREATION & LEISURE: Children & Youth

LEAGUE WEEKLY
764945U75C-451
Formerly: The New League Weekly
Editorial Address: 1 Oates Street, DEWSBURY, WF13 1BB
Tel: 01924 666433
Email: editor@league-weekly.com
Advertising Address: As above. **Tel:** 01924 454448
Fax: 01924 457994
Email: editor@league-weekly.com
ISSN: 1477-7649
Publisher: League Weekly
Date Established: 2002
Frequency: Weekly - Published on Monday
Cover Price: £1.20
Circulation: 12,000 (Publisher's Statement)
Usual Pagination: 32
Editor: Rebecca Smith; **Advertising Manager:** Danny Lockwood; **Publisher:** Danny Lockwood
Summary of Content: Magazine covering rugby league news, features, scores, club news, reviews and interviews.
Readership/Target Audience: Read by supporters, officials, fans and players of rugby league.
ADVERTISING RATES:
Full Page Colour £750.00
SCC £3.50
Agency Commission: 15%
Mechanical Data: Type Area: 360 x 268mm, Col Length: 360mm, Film: Digital, Page Width: 268mm
Copy instructions: Copy Date: Thursday 5pm prior to publication date
CONSUMER: SPORT: Rugby

THE LEEDS GUIDE
48105U89C-165
Editorial Address: 80 North Street, LEEDS, LS2 7PN
Tel: 0113 244 1007 **Fax:** 0113 244 1002
Email: editor@leedsguide.co.uk
Advertising Address: As above. **Tel:** 0113 244 1000
Email: sales@leedsguide.co.uk
Web site: http://www.leedsguide.co.uk
ISSN: 1460-6429
Publisher: Leeds Guide Ltd
Date Established: 1997
Frequency: 26 issues yearly
Cover Price: £1.90
Circulation: 15,000 (Publisher's Statement)
Usual Pagination: 68
Editor: Tom Goodhand
Summary of Content: Fortnightly lifestyle & listings magazine for West Yorkshire covering eating out, shopping, bars, clubs, property, music, art, museums, books, cafes, travel, comedy, dance, films and music. Includes larger features, previews, reviews and interviews.
Readership/Target Audience: Aimed at 18 to 34 year olds with high disposable incomes, living in Leeds and West Yorkshire.
ADVERTISING RATES:
Full Page Colour £850.00
Agency Commission: 10%
Mechanical Data: Type Area: 277 x 190mm, Film: Digital, Col Length: 277mm, Bleed Size: 303 x 216mm, Trim Size: 297 x 210mm, Page Width: 190mm
Copy instructions: Copy Date: 1 week prior to publication date
Average advertising content per issue: 30%
CONSUMER: HOLIDAYS & TRAVEL: Entertainment Guides

THE LEEDS GUIDE STUDENT GUIDE
47406U83-27
Editorial Address: 80 North Street, LEEDS, LS2 7PN
Tel: 0113 244 1000 **Fax:** 0113 244 1002
Email: editor@leedsguide.co.uk
Advertising Address: As above.
Email: sales@leedsguideco.uk

Web site: http://www.leedsguide.co.uk
ISSN: 1465-7821
Publisher: Leeds Guide Ltd
Date Established: 1999
Frequency: Annual - Published in September
Cover Price: £2.00
Free to qualifying individuals
Circulation: 50,000 (Publisher's Statement)
Usual Pagination: 132
Editor: Ali Schofield
Summary of Content: Guide covering all aspects of student life. Includes articles on clubs, accommodation, live music, money, careers, eating and drinking, shopping, entertainment and celebrity interviews, centred on Leeds.
Readership/Target Audience: Aimed at students in West Yorkshire.
ADVERTISING RATES:
Full Page Mono £995.00
Full Page Colour £995.00
Agency Commission: 10%
Mechanical Data: Col Length: 277mm, No. of Columns (Display): 4, Bleed Size: 303 x 216mm, Trim Size: 297 x 210mm, Film: Digital, Type Area: 277 x 190mm, Col Widths (Display): 45mm, Page Width: 190mm
Copy instructions: Copy Date: September 5th
Average advertising content per issue: 40%
CONSUMER: STUDENT PUBLICATIONS

LEEDS LEEDS LEEDS
45765U75B-143_50
Editorial Address: 36 Worbeck Road, LONDON, SE20 7SW
Tel: 07973 720278
Email: neil.jeffries@LLLmagazine.co.uk
Advertising Address: Leeds Football Club, Elland Road, LEEDS, LS11 0ES **Tel:** 0113 367 6213
Email: paul.dews@leedsunited.com
Web site: http://www.leedsunited.com
ISSN: 1465-4660
Publisher: Ignition Publications
Date Established: 1998
Frequency: 6 issues yearly
Cover Price: £3.00
Free to qualifying individuals
Annual Sub.: £36.00
Circulation: 25,000 (Publisher's Statement)
Usual Pagination: 68
Editor: Neil Jeffries; **Advertising Manager:** Paul Dews; **Publisher:** Ian Guildford
Summary of Content: Official magazine of Leeds United AFC. Includes articles covering all aspects of the club, interviews with past and present players and fan related features.
Readership/Target Audience: Read by members and supporters worldwide.
ADVERTISING: Rates on application
CONSUMER: SPORT: Football

LEEDS STUDENT
47407U83-30
Editorial Address: PO Box 157, LEEDS, LS1 1UH
Tel: 0113 380 1450 **Fax:** 0113 380 1453
Email: editor@leedsstudent.org
Advertising Address: As above. **Tel:** 0113 380 1394
Fax: 0113 380 1205
Email: s.l.thornewill@leeds.ac.uk
Web site: http://www.leedsstudent.org.uk
Publisher: Leeds Student Union
Date Established: 1946
Frequency: 24 issues yearly - Weekly during term time
Cover Price: Free
Circulation: 17,000 (Publisher's Statement)
Usual Pagination: 48
Summary of Content: Magazine covering news, arts, music, TV and sport.
Readership/Target Audience: Read by students of Leeds Metropolitan University, The University of Leeds Students' Unions and the colleges of Leeds.
ADVERTISING RATES:
Full Page Mono £600.00
Full Page Colour £800.00
Mechanical Data: Film: Digital, Type Area: 322.5 x 274mm, Col Length: 322.5mm, Page Width: 274mm
Copy instructions: Copy Date: 7 days prior to publication date
CONSUMER: STUDENT PUBLICATIONS

LEGION
48583U94A-60
Editorial Address: 17 Britton Street, LONDON, EC1M 5TP
Tel: 020 7880 6200 **Fax:** 020 7880 7691
Email: editorial@legion-magazine.co.uk
Advertising Address: As above. **Tel:** 020 7880 6220
Fax: 020 7880 7553
Email: steve.grice@redactive.co.uk
Publisher: Redactive Media Group
Frequency: Quarterly
Free to qualifying individuals
Circulation: 367,895 (ABC 01/01/2008 to 31/12/2008)
Usual Pagination: 66

Editor: Steve Smethurst; **Advertising Manager:** Steve Grice; **Publisher:** Jason Grant
Summary of Content: Official magazine of the Royal British Legion. Includes regular news features relating to the ex-service community.
Readership/Target Audience: Aimed at members of the Royal British Legion and ex-servicemen and women.
ADVERTISING RATES:
Full Page Colour £8350.00
Agency Commission: 10%
Mechanical Data: Col Length: 279mm, Type Area: 272 x 180mm, Bleed Size: 303 x 216mm, Trim Size: 297 x 210mm, Film: Digital, Print Process: Web-fed offset litho, Page Width: 195mm
Average advertising content per issue: 45%
CONSUMER: OTHER CLASSIFICATIONS: War Veterans

LEICESTER LINK
46939U80C-2110
Editorial Address: New Walk Centre, Welford Place, LEICESTER, LE1 6ZG **Tel:** 0116 252 6394
Fax: 0116 254 5391
Email: link@leicester.gov.uk
Advertising Address: As above.
Email: bally.singh@leicester.gov.uk
Web site: http://www.leicester.gov.uk/link
Publisher: Leicester City Council
Date Established: 1987
Frequency: 6 issues yearly
Cover Price: Free
Circulation: 131,000 (Publisher's Statement)
Usual Pagination: 20
Editor: Nick Thornton
Summary of Content: Civic magazine covering news of the City Council's policies and services in Leicester.
Readership/Target Audience: Aimed at householders in the city of Leicester.
ADVERTISING: Rates on application
CONSUMER: RURAL & REGIONAL INTEREST: Regional Interest English Counties

LEICESTERSHIRE & RUTLAND LIFE
1645702U80C-5125
Editorial Address: St. George Street, LEICESTER, LE1 9FQ
Tel: 0116 222 4627 **Fax:** 0116 222 4669
Email: info@leicestershireandrutlandlife.co.uk
Advertising Address: As above. **Tel:** 0116 222 4793
Email: julienaylor@leicestershireandrutlandlife.co.uk
Publisher: Leicester Mercury Media Group Ltd
Date Established: 2004
Frequency: Monthly
Cover Price: £2.70
Free to qualifying individuals
Circulation: 9,000 (Publisher's Statement)
Usual Pagination: 176
Editor: Alex Dawson
Summary of Content: Lifestyle magazine covering interviews with local people. Local places, food and drink, health and beauty, motoring, fashion, travel, homes, gardens and interiors, auctions and antiques, business and personal finance.
Readership/Target Audience: Aimed at affluent, high achievers in Leicestershire and Rutland.
ADVERTISING RATES:
Full Page Colour £875.00
Agency Commission: 10%
Mechanical Data: Type Area: 297 x 210mm, Bleed Size: +3mm, Col Length: 297mm, Page Width: 210mm, Film: Digital
Copy instructions: Copy Date: 2 months prior to publication date
Average advertising content per issue: 30%
CONSUMER: RURAL & REGIONAL INTEREST: Regional Interest English Counties

THE LEICESTERSHIRE MAGAZINE
1786082U80C-5372
Editorial Address: 61 Friar Gate, DERBY, DE1 1DJ
Tel: 0116 222 9213
Email: carol.burns@leicestershiremagazine.co.uk
Advertising Address: As above. **Tel:** 01332 227850
Email: beverley.bearder@archant.co.uk
Web site: http://www.leicestershiremagazine.co.uk
Publisher: Archant Life (North) PLC
Date Established: 2006
Frequency: Quarterly
Cover Price: £1.50
Circulation: 8,000 (Print Run)
Usual Pagination: 96
Editor: Carol Burns
Summary of Content: Magazine covering property, homes and gardens, food and drink, society, people and places.
Readership/Target Audience: Aimed at those who enjoy the finer things in life and with an active interest in the county of Leicestershire.
ADVERTISING RATES:
Full Page Colour £750.00

Agency Commission: 10%
Copy instructions: Copy Date: 4 weeks prior to publication date
CONSUMER: RURAL & REGIONAL INTEREST: Regional Interest English Counties

LEISURE PAINTER
46784U79R-50

Editorial Address: 63-65 High Street, TENTERDEN, TN30 6BD **Tel:** 01580 763315 **Fax:** 01580 765411
Email: ingrid@tapc.co.uk
Advertising Address: As above.
Email: linde@tapc.co.uk
Web site: http://www.leisurepainter.co.uk
ISSN: 0024-0710
Publisher: The Artists' Publishing Company Ltd
Date Established: 1967
Frequency: Monthly - Published on the 12th of the month prior to cover date
Cover Price: £3.25
Annual Sub: £29.50
Usual Pagination: 68
Editor: Ingrid Lyon; **Managing Director:** Sally Bulgin;
Advertising Manager: Linde Ovington-Lee; **Publisher:** Sally Bulgin
Summary of Content: Magazine providing guidance and inspiration with step-by-step instruction. Includes set projects, working methods, helpful tips and ideas.
Readership/Target Audience: Read by amateur painters of all ages, particularly beginners.
ADVERTISING RATES:
Full Page Colour £1170.00
Agency Commission: 10%
Mechanical Data: No. of Columns (Display): 4, Type Area: 265 x 190mm, Bleed Size: 305 x 215mm, Trim Size: 297 x 210mm, Col Length: 265mm, Print Process: Web-fed offset litho, Film: Digital, Page Width: 190mm, Col Widths (Display): 45mm
Copy instructions: Copy Date: 10th of the month prior to publication date
Average advertising content per issue: 35%
CONSUMER: HOBBIES & DIY: Hobbies & DIY Related

LEOPARD MAGAZINE
47048U80E-90

Editorial Address: Auld Logie, Pitcaple, INVERURIE, AB51 5EE **Tel:** 01467 681678
Email: editor@leopardmag.co.uk
Advertising Address: The Old School House, Inverkeithny, HUNTLY, AB54 7XB **Tel:** 01466 730776 **Fax:** 01466 730776
Email: leopard.mag@talktalk.net
Web site: http://www.leopardmag.co.uk
Publisher: Leopard Magazine Ltd
Date Established: 1974
Frequency: 10 issues yearly
Cover Price: £3.20
Annual Sub: £40.00
Circulation: 9,000 (Publisher's Statement)
Usual Pagination: 52
Editor: Lindy Cheyne; **Advertising Manager:** Walter Miller; **Publisher:** Ian Hamilton
Summary of Content: Magazine covering all aspects of Scottish culture. Includes articles on archaeology, local history, place names, environment, the arts, gardens, sport, motoring, crosswords, diary, book reviews and family history.
Language(s): English; Scots
Readership/Target Audience: Read by residents, ex-patriots and visitors to Scotland.
ADVERTISING RATES:
Full Page Mono £285.00
Full Page Colour £400.00
Agency Commission: 10%
Mechanical Data: Film: Digital, Type Area: 280 x 214mm, Col Length: 280mm, Film: 214mm, Bleed Size: 286 x 220mm
Copy instructions: Copy Date: 16th of the month prior to publication date
Average advertising content per issue: 30%
CONSUMER: RURAL & REGIONAL INTEREST: Regional Interest Scotland

LET THEM EAT CAKE
1849967U74B-738

Editorial Address: Unit 206, Colourworks, 22-24 Abbot Street, LONDON, E8 3DP **Tel:** 07711 256182
Email: press@letthemeatcakemagazine.com
Advertising Address: As above.
Email: nnea@letthemeatcakemagazine.com
Web site: http://www.letthemeatcakemagazine.com
Publisher: Let Them Eat Cake Ltd
Date Established: 2006
Frequency: Quarterly
Cover Price: £3.50
Usual Pagination: 132
Editor: Cheryl Leung; **Features Editor:** Christina Rozakis;
Editor-in-Chief: Njide Ugboma; **Advertising Manager:** Nneka Ugboma
Summary of Content: Magazine covering fashion and style news, fashion editorial, arts, features, music and digital-online films.

Readership/Target Audience: Aimed predominantly at women aged between 15 and 35 years old.
ADVERTISING: Rates on application
CONSUMER: WOMEN'S INTEREST CONSUMER MAGAZINES: Women's Interest - Fashion

LET'S GO WITH THE CHILDREN IN BRISTOL, BATH, GLOS, WILTS (COTSWOLDS, FOREST OF DEAN)
48182U89C-166

Formerly: LET'S GO with the CHILDREN in Bristol, Bath, Glos & Wilts
Editorial Address: Manor House, Manor Park, ALDERSHOT, GU12 4JU **Tel:** 01252 368325
Fax: 01252 368385
Email: info@boomerangfamily.co.uk
Advertising Address: As above. **Tel:** 01252 322771
Fax: 01252 332772
Email: enquiries@cubepublications.co.uk
Web site: http://www.letsgowiththechildren.co.uk
Publisher: Boomberg
Date Established: 1988
Frequency: Annual - Published in February
Cover Price: £3.99
Circulation: 15,000 (Publisher's Statement)
Usual Pagination: 80
Editor: Maureen Cuthbert; **Advertising Manager:** Maureen Cuthbert
Summary of Content: Directory of attractions and leisure facilities.
Readership/Target Audience: Aimed at families, schools and grandparents.
ADVERTISING RATES:
Full Page Colour £695.00
Agency Commission: 10%
Editions:
Lets Go with the Children in Beds, Bucks, Herts, Northants & adjacent London Boroughs
Lets Go with the Children in Berks, Bucks, Oxon & adjacent London Boroughs
Lets Go with the Children in East Anglia
Lets Go with the Children in East Midlands
Lets Go with the Children in Hants, Dorset, & the Isle of Wight
Lets Go with the Children in Kent & adjacent London Boroughs
Lets Go with the Children in Surrey & adjacent London Boroughs
Lets Go with the Children in Sussex
Lets Go with the Children in the Heart of England
Lets Go with the Children in the North East
Lets Go with the Children in the North West & Yorkshire
Lets Go with the Children in the South West
CONSUMER: HOLIDAYS & TRAVEL: Entertainment Guides

LET'S GROW VEG
1809599U93-200

Editorial Address: 25 Phoenix Court, Hawkins Road, COLCHESTER, CO2 8JY **Tel:** 01206 505900
Email: jeannine@aceville.co.uk
Advertising Address: As above.
Email: teresa.tudge@aceville.co.uk
Web site: http://www.growfruitandveg.co.uk
Publisher: Aceville Publications Ltd
Date Established: 2007
Frequency: 5 issues yearly
Cover Price: £7.99
Usual Pagination: 68
Editor: Lucy Halsall; **Advertising Manager:** Teresa Tudge;
Group Editor: Jeannine McAndrew
Summary of Content: Magazine covering how to grow your own organic fruit and vegetables.
Readership/Target Audience: Aimed at kitchen gardeners.
ADVERTISING: Rates on application
CONSUMER: GARDENING

LET'S KNIT
1826309U74E-704

Editorial Address: 25 Phoenix Court, Hawkins Road, COLCHESTER, CO2 8JY **Tel:** 01206 505900
Fax: 01206 505945
Email: sarah.neal@aceville.co.uk
Advertising Address: As above.
Email: info@letsknit.co.uk
Web site: http://www.letsknit.co.uk
Publisher: Aceville Publications Ltd
Date Established: 2007
Frequency: Monthly
Cover Price: £4.99
Usual Pagination: 100
Editor: Sarah Neal
Summary of Content: Magazine including fashionable and fun to knit patterns, features, shopping, practical advice and a strong community element.
Readership/Target Audience: Aimed at a new generation of knitters of all ages and ability.
ADVERTISING RATES:
Full Page Colour £950.00

Agency Commission: 10%
Mechanical Data: Type Area: 276 x 211mm, Bleed Size: 308 x 238mm, Trim Size: 300 x 230mm, Col Length: 276mm, Page Width: 211mm, Film: Digital
Copy instructions: Copy Date: 2 weeks prior to publication date
Average advertising content per issue: 40%
CONSUMER: WOMEN'S INTEREST CONSUMER MAGAZINES: Crafts

LET'S MAKE CARDS
1789454U88D-41

Editorial Address: 25 Phoenix Court, Hawkins Road, COLCHESTER, CO2 8JY **Tel:** 01206 505994
Fax: 01206 505945
Email: holly.markham@aceville.co.uk
Advertising Address: As above. **Tel:** 01206 505940
Email: info@letsmakecards.co.uk
Web site: http://www.letsmakecards.com
Publisher: Aceville Publications Ltd
Date Established: 2006
Frequency: 9 issues yearly
Cover Price: £7.99
Usual Pagination: 68
Editor: Holly Markham; **Advertising Manager:** Craig De Souza
Summary of Content: Magazine with 50 card designs and ideas to be made up with a kit that comes with the magazine as well as features on how to improve your card making, card designers, the latest products, practical advice and step by step techniques.
Readership/Target Audience: Aimed at card makers at all levels of skill.
ADVERTISING RATES:
Full Page Colour £1100.00
Agency Commission: 10%
Mechanical Data: Type Area: 270 x 190mm, Bleed Size: 309 x 222mm, Trim Size: 297 x 210mm, Col Length: 270mm, Page Width: 190mm, Film: Digital
Copy instructions: Copy Date: 3 weeks prior to publication date
Average advertising content per issue: 22%
CONSUMER: EDUCATION: Crafts

LET'S TALK!
767370U74N-161

Formerly: Let's Talk! Norfolk
Editorial Address: Prospect House, Rouen Road, NORWICH, NR1 1RE **Tel:** 01603 628311 **Fax:** 01603 615343
Email: letstalk@archant.co.uk
Advertising Address: As above. **Fax:** 01603 615903
Email: wendy.wright@archant.co.uk
Web site: http://www.letstalk24.co.uk
Publisher: Archant Norfolk
Date Established: 2002
Frequency: Monthly - Published the 2nd Thursday of the month
Cover Price: £1.50
Circulation: 19,079 (ABC 01/01/2009 to 30/06/2009)
Usual Pagination: 132
Editor: Anne Gould; **Advertising Manager:** Judy Welsh
Summary of Content: Magazine featuring health, gardening, puzzles, nostalgia, food and competitions with features relevant to today.
Readership/Target Audience: Aimed at the active over 50s retired community in Norfolk, Suffolk, North Essex and East Cambridgeshire.
ADVERTISING RATES:
Full Page Colour £1020.00
Agency Commission: 10%
Mechanical Data: Type Area: 264 x 182mm, Col Length: 264mm, Page Width: 182mm, Trim Size: 297 x 210mm, Bleed Size: 303 x 216mm
Copy instructions: Copy Date: 2 weeks prior to publication date
Average advertising content per issue: 25%
CONSUMER: WOMEN'S INTEREST CONSUMER MAGAZINES: Retirement

LEXUS
45639U74Q-487

Editorial Address: 15B St. Georges Mews, Primrose Hill, LONDON, NW1 8XE **Tel:** 020 7449 1500 **Fax:** 020 7722 1851
Email: amar.patel@storyworldwide.com
Advertising Address: As above.
Email: phillip.every@storyworldwide.com
Publisher: Story Worldwide
Date Established: 2000
Frequency: Quarterly
Cover Price: Free
Circulation: 80,000 (Publisher's Statement)
Usual Pagination: 52
Editor: Amar Patel
Summary of Content: Magazine carrying arts, lifestyle and travel features, motoring, luxury product news, innovation, tech and eco elements.
Readership/Target Audience: Aimed at Lexus clients.
ADVERTISING RATES:
Full Page Colour £6750.00
Agency Commission: 10%

Mechanical Data: Type Area: 270 x 200mm, Col Length: 270mm, Page Width: 200mm, Bleed Size: 306 x 236mm, Trim Size: 300 x 230mm, Film: Digital
Copy instructions: Copy Date: 4 weeks prior to publication date
Average advertising content per issue: 15%
CONSUMER: WOMEN'S INTEREST CONSUMER MAGAZINES: Lifestyle

THE LIBERAL
1659645U82-260
Editorial Address: 208-210A High Road, LONDON, N2 9AY
Tel: 020 8444 1944 **Fax:** 020 8444 5413
Email: editor@theliberal.co.uk
Advertising Address: As above. **Fax:** 020 8444 1944
Email: advertising@theliberal.co.uk
Web site: http://www.theliberal.co.uk
ISSN: 1744-8573
Publisher: The Liberal Publications Limited
Date Established: 2004
Frequency: Quarterly
Cover Price: £3.99
Annual Sub.: £12.00
Circulation: 35,000 (Publisher's Statement)
Usual Pagination: 64
Editor: Benjamin Ramm; **Advertising Manager:** Benjamin Ramm
Summary of Content: Magazine devoted to politics and the arts. Publishes poetry, music, short fiction, photography, political and philosophical essays addressing a broad spectrum of subjects.
Readership/Target Audience: Aimed at the liberally-inclined community, well educated professionals in the legal, financial and commercial sectors, universities, the literary community and political think tanks.
ADVERTISING RATES:
Full Page Colour £1245.00
Copy instructions: Copy Date: 1 week prior to publication date
Average advertising content per issue: 15%
CONSUMER: CURRENT AFFAIRS & POLITICS

LIBERAL DEMOCRAT NEWS
47245U82-108
Editorial Address: 4 Cowley Street, LONDON, SW1P 3NB
Tel: 020 7222 7999 **Fax:** 020 7222 7904
Email: ldn@libdems.org.uk
Advertising Address: As above. **Fax:** 020 8020 1547
Email: ldn@libdems.org.uk
Web site: http://www.libdems.org.uk
ISSN: 0954-5735
Publisher: Liberal Democrats
Frequency: Weekly
Annual Sub.: £30.00
Circulation: 10,000 (Publisher's Statement)
Usual Pagination: 8
Editor: Deirdre Razzall; **Advertising Manager:** Jayne Martin-Kaye
Summary of Content: Newspaper of the Liberal Democrats containing information on current affairs, Parliament and party matters.
Readership/Target Audience: Aimed at supporters and members of the Liberal Democrats.
ADVERTISING RATES:
Full Page Mono £1367.00
Full Page Colour £1777.00
Mechanical Data: Type Area: 359 x 270mm, Col Length: 359mm, Col Widths (Display): 51mm, Page Width: 270mm, Film: Digital, No. of Columns (Display): 5
Copy instructions: Copy Date: 7 days prior to publication date
CONSUMER: CURRENT AFFAIRS & POLITICS

THE LIFE
1626411U87-2021
Editorial Address: 207-209 Queensway, Bletchley, MILTON KEYNES, MK2 2EB **Tel:** 01908 856000 **Fax:** 01908 856111
Email: media@scriptureunion.org.uk
Web site: http://www.scriptureunion.org.uk/thelife
Publisher: Scripture Union
Date Established: 2002
Frequency: Quarterly
Cover Price: Free
Circulation: 28,000 (Publisher's Statement)
Usual Pagination: 16
Editor: Christina Farley
Summary of Content: Magazine containing news, human interest stories and features related to Scripture Union England and Wales.
Readership/Target Audience: Read by Christians interested in the work of Scripture Union England and Wales.
ADVERTISING: No Advertising taken
CONSUMER: RELIGIOUS

LIFE!
622806U89C-74
Formerly: The Big Blackpool Guide
Editorial Address: Avroe House, Avroe Crescent, Blackpool Business Park, BLACKPOOL, FY4 2DP **Tel:** 01253 361833
Fax: 01253 361870
Email: life@blackpoolgazette.co.uk
Advertising Address: As above. **Tel:** 01253 400888
Fax: 01253 406600
Email: ava.makepeace@blackpoolgazette.co.uk
Web site: http://www.blackpoolgazette.co.uk
Publisher: Johnston Press plc
Date Established: 2002
Frequency: Weekly - Published every Saturday
Cover Price: Free
Circulation: 38,000 (Publisher's Statement)
Usual Pagination: 40
Editor: Steve Singleton
Summary of Content: Lifestyle magazine covering cinema, travel, fashion, music, health, TV listings, show-biz features and events.
Readership/Target Audience: Read by visitors and residents of Blackpool and the surrounding area.
ADVERTISING RATES:
Full Page Mono £917.00
Full Page Colour £1193.00
Agency Commission: 10%
Mechanical Data: Type Area: 335 x 273mm, Film: Digital, Col Length: 335mm, Page Width: 273mm
Copy instructions: Copy Date: 2 weeks prior to publication date
Supplement to: The Gazette (Blackpool)
CONSUMER: HOLIDAYS & TRAVEL: Entertainment Guides

LIFE AND WORK
47730U87-155
Editorial Address: 121 George Street, EDINBURGH, EH2 4YN **Tel:** 0131 225 5722 **Fax:** 0131 240 2207
Email: magazine@lifeandwork.org
Advertising Address: 15 Newton Terrace, GLASGOW, G3 7PJ **Tel:** 0141 204 2042 **Fax:** 0141 204 2043
Email: info@contactpublicity.co.uk
Web site: http://www.lifeandwork.org
Publisher: Church of Scotland Publications
Date Established: 1879
Frequency: Monthly
Cover Price: £1.60
Circulation: 34,002 (Publisher's Statement)
Usual Pagination: 60
Editor: Thomas Baldwin
Summary of Content: Publication of the Church of Scotland. Includes features on worldwide Christian ideas and Scottish church life, bible teaching, faith, ethics, politics and culture.
Language(s): English; Gaelic
Readership/Target Audience: Aimed at church members around the world.
ADVERTISING RATES:
Full Page Mono £1400.00
Full Page Colour £2250.00
Agency Commission: 10%
Mechanical Data: Trim Size: 297 x 210mm, Type Area: 265 x 185mm, Bleed Size: 303 x 213mm, Col Length: 265mm, Page Width: 185mm, Film: Digital
CONSUMER: RELIGIOUS

LIFE TIMES
1703580U87-2039
Editorial Address: Providence House, Ardenlee Street, BELFAST, BT6 8QJ **Tel:** 028 9045 0010
Email: samuellowry@aol.com
Advertising Address: 6 Cennick Grove, Gracehill, BALLYMENA, BT42 2AY **Tel:** 028 2564 6647
Email: leslie@gracehill.freeserve.co.uk
Web site: http://www.ambassador-productions.com
Publisher: Ambassador Productions Ltd
Frequency: 10 issues yearly
Cover Price: £2.95
Circulation: 30,000 (Publisher's Statement)
Usual Pagination: 96
Editor: Gillian Graham
Summary of Content: Christian lifestyle magazine with human interest stories and profiles of people who have suffered adversity as well as lifestyle, cooking, gardening and parenting.
Readership/Target Audience: Aimed at Christians in the evangelical community.
ADVERTISING RATES:
Full Page Colour £500.00
Agency Commission: 10%
Mechanical Data: Type Area: 265 x 185mm, Bleed Size: 303 x 216mm, Trim Size: 297 x 210mm, Col Length: 265mm, Page Width: 185mm, Film: Digital
Copy instructions: Copy Date: 7th of month prior to publication date
CONSUMER: RELIGIOUS

LIFESCAPE
1740171U74A-1007
Editorial Address: PO Box 456, POTTERS BAR, EN6 9DS
Tel: 01707 859805
Email: editor@lifescapemag.com
Advertising Address: As above.
Email: jaynen@warnersgroup.co.uk
Web site: http://www.lifescapemag.com
Publisher: Lifescape Magazine Ltd
Date Established: 2005
Frequency: 6 issues yearly
Cover Price: £2.95
Circulation: 40,000 (Publisher's Statement)
Usual Pagination: 96
Editor: Rajasana Otiende; **Features Editor:** Alexia Weeks
Summary of Content: Lifestyle magazine covering resources for vegetarians including holidays, meals, restaurants, fashion, beauty and alternative medicines.
Readership/Target Audience: Aimed at women aged between 25 and 34 years old.
ADVERTISING RATES:
Full Page Colour £900.00
Agency Commission: 10%
Mechanical Data: Bleed Size: 286 x 231mm, Trim Size: 280 x 225mm, Film: Digital
Copy instructions: Copy Date: 2 weeks prior to publication date
CONSUMER: WOMEN'S INTEREST CONSUMER MAGAZINES: Women's Interest

LIFESTYLE
764977U74Q-1121
Editorial Address: Haymarket Court, Hinson Street, BIRKENHEAD, CH41 5BX **Tel:** 0151 906 3000
Fax: 0151 906 3048
Email: cmanning@wirral-globe.co.uk
Advertising Address: As above. **Fax:** 0151 906 3049
Email: smorris@wirral-globe.co.uk
Web site: http://www.thisiswirral.co.uk
Publisher: Newsquest (Northwest) Ltd
Frequency: 6 issues yearly
Cover Price: £1.50
Circulation: 10,000 (Publisher's Statement)
Editor: Leigh Marles
Summary of Content: Magazine covering lifestyle, motoring, property and education.
Readership/Target Audience: Aimed at those living in and around the Wirral peninsula.
ADVERTISING: Rates on application
Agency Commission: 10%
CONSUMER: WOMEN'S INTEREST CONSUMER MAGAZINES: Lifestyle

LIFESTYLE
1744945U74Q-1311
Editorial Address: Crossford Court, Dane Road, SALE, M33 7BZ **Tel:** 0161 908 3380 **Fax:** 0161 908 3403
Email: sam.editorial@messengergrp.co.uk
Advertising Address: As above. **Tel:** 0161 908 3374
Fax: 0161 908 3402
Email: jfletcher@messengergrp.co.uk
Publisher: Newsquest (Northwest) Ltd
Frequency: Quarterly
Cover Price: Free
Circulation: 15,200 (Publisher's Statement)
Usual Pagination: 116
Editor: Carla Flynn
Summary of Content: Lifestyle magazine covering topics including fashion, beauty, travel, motoring and health.
Readership/Target Audience: Aimed at residents and visitors to Cheshire and Manchester.
ADVERTISING: Rates on application
Mechanical Data: Type Area: 277 x 190mm, Bleed Size: 307 x 220mm, Trim Size: 297 x 210mm, Col Length: 277mm, Page Width: 190mm, Film: Digital
Copy instructions: Copy Date: 2 weeks prior to publication date
CONSUMER: WOMEN'S INTEREST CONSUMER MAGAZINES: Lifestyle

LIFESTYLE
1664667U74Q-1451
Tel: 020 7938 6000 **Fax:** 020 7937 4463
Email: nicky.dawson@dailymail.co.uk
Frequency: Weekly - Published within the Daily Mail on Monday
Editor: Nicola Dawson
Summary of Content: Section covering Lifestyle features, fashion, beauty and health.
ADVERTISING: Rates on application
Part of Series, see entry for: Daily Mail
CONSUMER: WOMEN'S INTEREST CONSUMER MAGAZINES: Lifestyle

LIFESTYLE
48642U94F-580
Formerly: Motability Lifestyle
Editorial Address: 22 Stephenson Way, LONDON, NW1 2HD **Tel:** 020 7383 2335

Consumer Magazines

Email: mbewick@big-publishing.com
Advertising Address: Square 7 Media Ltd, 1st Floor, 3 More London Riverside, LONDON, SE1 2RE **Tel:** 020 3283 4055
Fax: 020 3282 4069
Email: mark@square7media.co.uk
Web site: http://www.lifestylemag.co.uk
Publisher: Big Publishing
Date Established: 1993
Frequency: Quarterly
Free to qualifying individuals
Annual Sub.: £10.00
Circulation: 394,766 (Publisher's Statement)
Usual Pagination: 76
Editor: Martin Bewick; **Advertising Manager:** Mark Toland
Summary of Content: Lifestyle magazine covering news of the Motability Scheme and disability related features.
Readership/Target Audience: Aimed at those with disabilities.
ADVERTISING RATES:
Full Page Colour £11150.00
Agency Commission: 10%
Mechanical Data: Type Area: 277 x 185mm, Bleed Size: 303 x 216mm, Trim Size: 297 x 210mm, Col Length: 277mm, Page Width: 185mm, Film: Digital
Copy instructions: Copy Date: 6 weeks prior to publication date
Average advertising content per issue: 60%
CONSUMER: OTHER CLASSIFICATIONS: Disability

LIFESTYLE DIRECTORY   1616282U74Q-1148
Editorial Address: 6 Freskyn Place, East Mains Industrial Estate, BROXBURN, EH52 5NF **Tel:** 01506 508001
Fax: 01506 508002
Email: root@capitalgroupuk.com
Advertising Address: As above.
Email: root@capitalgroupuk.com
Web site: http://www.capitalgroupuk.com
Publisher: Capital Publishing
Date Established: 2003
Frequency: Quarterly
Cover Price: Free
Circulation: 30,000 (Publisher's Statement)
Usual Pagination: 48
Editor: Lawrence Service
Summary of Content: Magazine featuring sport, health, beauty, fashion and lifestyle content.
Readership/Target Audience: Aimed at anyone between 20 and 49 years old.
ADVERTISING RATES:
Full Page Mono £1080.00
Full Page Colour £1200.00
Agency Commission: 10%
Average advertising content per issue: 80%
CONSUMER: WOMEN'S INTEREST CONSUMER MAGAZINES: Lifestyle

LIFETIME   45582U74N-110_50
Formerly: Prime Time
Editorial Address: Richmond Hill, BOURNEMOUTH, BH2 6HH **Tel:** 01202 554601 **Fax:** 01202 551246
Email: kevin.nash@bournemouthecho.co.uk
Advertising Address: As above. **Tel:** 01202 411252
Email: angela.boyer@bournemouthecho.co.uk
Web site: http://www.dailyecho.co.uk
Publisher: Newsquest (Media Group) Ltd
Date Established: 1994
Frequency: Monthly
Cover Price: Free
Circulation: 30,000 (Publisher's Statement)
Usual Pagination: 24
Editor: Kevin Nash; **Advertising Manager:** Angela Boyer
Summary of Content: Newspaper containing local news, food and drink, competitions, law and finance, antiques, gardening, women's interest, property, health and information concerning men and women in the prime of their life.
Readership/Target Audience: Aimed at the over fifties in Dorset, Hampshire and South Wiltshire.
ADVERTISING RATES:
Full Page Colour £500.00
Agency Commission: 10%
Mechanical Data: Film: Digital, Trim Size: 297 x 210mm
Copy instructions: Copy Date: 1st of the month prior to publication date
CONSUMER: WOMEN'S INTEREST CONSUMER MAGAZINES: Retirement

LIGHT AVIATION   45967U75N-300
Formerly: Popular Flying
Editorial Address: 9 The Mill Courtyard, Copley Hill Business Park, Babraham, CAMBRIDGE, CB22 3GN
Tel: 01280 846786
Email: bfjjodel@talktalk.net
Advertising Address: As above.
Email: victoria@laa.uk.com
Web site: http://www.pfa.org.uk

Publisher: Loop Publishing (UK) Ltd
Date Established: 1946
Frequency: Monthly
Free to qualifying individuals
Circulation: 8,500 (Publisher's Statement)
Usual Pagination: 60
Editor: Brian Hope; **Advertising Manager:** Victoria Griffiths;
Publisher: Sam Spurdens
Summary of Content: Publication containing features on building, restoring and operating vintage, classic and home built aircraft.
Readership/Target Audience: Aimed at recreational flying enthusiasts.
ADVERTISING RATES:
Full Page Colour £1000.00
Copy instructions: Copy Date: 1 week prior to publication date
CONSUMER: SPORT: Flight

LIGHTER LIFE   1644135U74G-267
Editorial Address: Sea Containers House, 20 Upper Ground, LONDON, SE1 9PD **Tel:** 020 7775 5777
Email: lighterlife@sevensquared.co.uk
Web site: http://www.lighterlife.com
Publisher: Seven Squared
Date Established: 2006
Frequency: 9 issues yearly
Cover Price: £3.20
Circulation: 35,566 (Publisher's Statement)
Usual Pagination: 116
Editor: Carole Hamilton
Summary of Content: Magazine covering psychology, fitness and health as well as lifestyle articles covering careers, relationships, fashion, travel and technology.
Readership/Target Audience: Aimed at women aged 30 and over who want to lose weight.
ADVERTISING: No Advertising taken
CONSUMER: WOMEN'S INTEREST CONSUMER MAGAZINES: Slimming & Health

LIMITED EDITION   46927U80C-1957
Editorial Address: Mega House, Crest View Drive, Petts Wood, ORPINGTON, BR5 1BT **Tel:** 01689 885792
Fax: 01689 875367
Email: le@london.newsquest.co.uk
Advertising Address: As above. **Tel:** 01689 885661
Fax: 01689 890253
Email: limitededitionsales@london.newsquest.co.uk
Web site: http://www.newsshopper.co.uk/limitededition
Publisher: Newsquest (South London)
Frequency: Monthly
Cover Price: Free
Circulation: 50,000 (Publisher's Statement)
Usual Pagination: 84
Editor: Heather Ramsden
Summary of Content: Local magazine covering fashion, health and beauty, the arts, travel and motoring, food and drink, property, homes and gardens.
Readership/Target Audience: Aimed at those with a high disposable income within the South East London and North Kent areas.
ADVERTISING RATES:
Full Page Colour £992.00
Agency Commission: 10%
Mechanical Data: Film: Digital, Type Area: 270 x 183mm, Trim Size: 297 x 210mm, Bleed Size: 303 x 216mm, Col Length: 270mm, Page Width: 183mm, No. of Columns (Display): 4, Print Process: Web-fed offset litho
Copy instructions: Copy Date: 2 weeks prior to publication date
Average advertising content per issue: 70%
CONSUMER: RURAL & REGIONAL INTEREST: Regional Interest English Counties

LIMITED EDITION   761781U80C-3660
Editorial Address: 44 St. James Street, TAUNTON, TA1 1JR **Tel:** 01823 365101 **Fax:** 01823 365200
Email: newsdesk@countygazette.co.uk
Advertising Address: As above. **Tel:** 01823 365211
Email: bethany.rowsell@countygazette.co.uk
Publisher: Newsquest (Media Group) Ltd
Date Established: 2001
Frequency: Monthly
Cover Price: £1.50
Free to qualifying individuals
Circulation: 15,000 (Publisher's Statement)
Usual Pagination: 76
Editor: Alex Cameron
Summary of Content: Local magazine covering social events, fashion, health and beauty, leisure, theatre and the arts along with restaurants, wine, travel, motoring, property and home interest.
Readership/Target Audience: Aimed at those with a high disposable income in the Somerset area.
ADVERTISING RATES:
Full Page Colour £911.00

Mechanical Data: Bleed Size: 303 x 216mm, Page Width: 190mm, Type Area: 270 x 190mm, Col Length: 270mm, Trim Size: 297 x 210mm, Film: Digital
Copy instructions: Copy Date: 2nd Friday of the publication month
CONSUMER: RURAL & REGIONAL INTEREST: Regional Interest English Counties

LIMITED EDITION (BOLTON)   704760U80C-1543
Editorial Address: Newspaper House, Churchgate, BOLTON, BL1 1DE **Tel:** 01204 537262 **Fax:** 01204 365068
Email: iheger@theboltonnews.co.uk
Advertising Address: As above. **Tel:** 01204 522345
Web site: http://www.thisisbolton.co.uk
Publisher: Newsquest (Lancs)
Date Established: 2001
Frequency: 6 issues yearly
Cover Price: Free
Circulation: 15,000 (Publisher's Statement)
Usual Pagination: 130
Editor: Irma Heger; **Advertising Manager:** Trish Waddington
Summary of Content: Magazine covering the best of fashion, food, home and rural pursuits and local features.
Readership/Target Audience: Aimed at those visiting or living in the area.
ADVERTISING RATES:
Full Page Colour £600.00
Mechanical Data: No. of Columns (Display): 6, Film: Digital, Trim Size: 297 x 210mm
Average advertising content per issue: 40%
CONSUMER: RURAL & REGIONAL INTEREST: Regional Interest English Counties

LIMITED EDITION NORTH   1804888U80C-5413
Editorial Address: 5 High Street, BROMSGROVE, B61 8AJ **Tel:** 01527 889032 **Fax:** 01527 889045
Email: carol.hinett@midlands.newsquest.co.uk
Advertising Address: As above.
Email: carol.hinett@midlands.newsquest.co.uk
Web site: http://www.limitededition-worcs.co.uk/north.html
Publisher: Newsquest Midlands South Ltd (Stourbridge)
Date Established: 1998
Frequency: 6 issues yearly
Cover Price: £1.50
Free to qualifying individuals
Annual Sub.: £9.00
Circulation: 23,300 (Publisher's Statement)
Usual Pagination: 108
Editor: Carol Hinett; **Advertising Manager:** Carol Hinett
Summary of Content: Local lifestyle magazine covering events, news, fashion, motoring, beauty, health, gardening, golf, bridge, travel, homes and interiors.
Readership/Target Audience: Aimed at affluent households in North Worcestershire.
ADVERTISING RATES:
Full Page Colour £760.00
Agency Commission: 10%
Mechanical Data: Type Area: 270 x 192mm, Col Length: 270mm, Page Width: 192mm, Film: Digital
Copy instructions: Copy Date: 2 weeks prior to publication date
Average advertising content per issue: 50%
CONSUMER: RURAL & REGIONAL INTEREST: Regional Interest English Counties

LIMITED EDITION SOUTH   1804889U80C-5414
Editorial Address: Berrows House, Hylton Road, WORCESTER, WR2 5JX **Tel:** 01905 748200
Fax: 01905 742277
Email: kevin.ward@midlands.newsquest.co.uk
Advertising Address: As above.
Email: emma.meacham@midlands.newsquest.co.uk
Web site: http://www.limitededition-worcs.co.uk/south.html
Publisher: Newsquest Midlands South Ltd (Worcester)
Frequency: 6 issues yearly
Cover Price: Free
Usual Pagination: 116
Editor: Kevin Ward; **Publisher:** Kevin Ward
Summary of Content: Magazine covering local news and events, fashion, travel, motoring, lifestyle, interiors and property.
Readership/Target Audience: Aimed at affluent households in South Worcestershire and The Cotswolds.
ADVERTISING RATES:
Full Page Colour £515.00
Agency Commission: 10%
Mechanical Data: Type Area: 270 x 192mm, Col Length: 270mm, Page Width: 192mm, Film: Digital
Average advertising content per issue: 35%
CONSUMER: RURAL & REGIONAL INTEREST: Regional Interest English Counties

LIMITED EDITION THE MAGAZINE FOR ESSEX
629127U80C-1410_50

Editorial Address: Oriel House, 43 North Hill, COLCHESTER, CO1 1TZ **Tel:** 01206 508270
Fax: 01206 508274
Email: claire.borley@nqe.com
Advertising Address: Wickham House, 1 Northgate Street, COLCHESTER, CO1 1HA **Tel:** 01206 508351
Fax: 01206 508199
Email: cheryl.ross@nqe.com
Web site: http://www.gazette-news.co.uk
Publisher: Newsquest (Essex) Ltd
Date Established: 2000
Frequency: Monthly
Cover Price: Free
Circulation: 25,000 (Publisher's Statement)
Usual Pagination: 98
Editor: Claire Borley; **Advertising Manager:** Cheryl Ross
Summary of Content: Magazine covering local interest and business stories with lifestyle features including wine, fashion, travel, theatre, health, beauty and profile interviews.
Readership/Target Audience: Aimed at adults aged 45 years old and over who have a high income living across Essex.
ADVERTISING RATES:
Full Page Colour £595.00
Agency Commission: 10%
Mechanical Data: Film: Digital, Type Area: 217 x 150mm, Col Length: 217mm, Trim Size: 235 x 170mm, Bleed Size: +5mm, No. of Columns (Display): 4, Page Width: 150mm, Col Widths (Display): 35mm
Copy instructions: Copy Date: 4 weeks prior to publication date
Average advertising content per issue: 37%
CONSUMER: RURAL & REGIONAL INTEREST: Regional Interest English Counties

LIMITED EDITION THE MAGAZINE FOR HERTFORDSHIRE
29257U80C-1794

Editorial Address: Observer House, Caxton Court, Caxton Way, Watford Business Park, WATFORD, WD18 8RJ
Tel: 01923 216216 **Fax:** 01923 243738
Email: lbilgorri@london.newsquest.co.uk
Advertising Address: As above. **Fax:** 01923 229745
Email: aeconomou@london.newsquest.co.uk
Web site: http://www.lemagazine.co.uk
Publisher: Newsquest (North London)
Frequency: Monthly
Cover Price: Free
Circulation: 26,283 (Publisher's Statement)
Usual Pagination: 76
Editor: Lindi Bilgorri
Summary of Content: Magazine containing features on local interest issues, motoring, food and drink, homes and gardens, interiors, crafts, fashion, celebrities, health and beauty.
Readership/Target Audience: Aimed at affluent householders in Hertfordshire, Middlesex and North London.
ADVERTISING RATES:
Full Page Colour £900.00
Agency Commission: 10%
Mechanical Data: Type Area: 270 x 186mm, Bleed Size: 307 x 220mm, Trim Size: 297 x 210mm, Col Length: 270mm, Col Widths (Display): 43mm, No. of Columns (Display): 4, Page Width: 186mm, Film: Digital
Copy instructions: Copy Date: 2 weeks prior to publication date
Average advertising content per issue: 50%
Editions:
Limited Edition The Magazine for Middlesex (Harrow and Hillingdon)
Limited Edition The Magazine for North London (London Borough)
CONSUMER: RURAL & REGIONAL INTEREST: Regional Interest English Counties

'LINCOLNSHIRE IN FOCUS'
760255U80C-2199

Editorial Address: Upper Spring Street, GRIMSBY, DN31 1QP **Tel:** 01472 359036 **Fax:** 01472 599910
Email: editor@waltonspublications.com
Advertising Address: As above.
Email: lif@waltonspublications.com
Web site: http://www.waltonspublications.com
Publisher: W.M. Walton & Co Ltd
Date Established: 2000
Frequency: Monthly
Cover Price: Free
Usual Pagination: 52
Editor: Nicole Tinmurth; **Managing Director:** T. Clive Aspinall
Summary of Content: Magazine covering county news, fashion, places of interest, leisure, local events, designer outlets and property.
Readership/Target Audience: Aimed at those with an average to high disposable income within the Lincolnshire region.
ADVERTISING RATES:
Full Page Mono £942.00

Full Page Colour £1149.00
Agency Commission: 10%
Mechanical Data: Film: Digital, Col Length: 270mm, Page Width: 186mm, Trim Size: 297 x 210mm, Type Area: 270 x 186mm, Bleed Size: +4mm
Copy instructions: Copy Date: 3 weeks prior to publication date
CONSUMER: RURAL & REGIONAL INTEREST: Regional Interest English Counties

LINCOLNSHIRE LIFE
46941U80C-2200

Editorial Address: County House, 9 Checkpoint Court, Sadler Road, LINCOLN, LN6 3PW **Tel:** 01522 527127
Fax: 01522 500880
Email: editorial@lincolnshirelife.co.uk
Advertising Address: As above. **Fax:** 01522 842000
Email: m.gage@lincolnshirelife.co.uk
Web site: http://www.lincolnshirelife.co.uk
ISSN: 0024-371X
Publisher: County Life Ltd
Date Established: 1961
Frequency: Monthly
Cover Price: £2.25
Circulation: 10,000 (Publisher's Statement)
Usual Pagination: 96
Editor: Josie Thurston; **Executive Editor:** Josie Thurston; **Managing Director:** Caroline Bingham; **Advertising Manager:** Michelle Gage; **Managing Editor:** Geoff Manners; **Publisher:** Caroline Bingham
Summary of Content: County magazine containing features on county life past and present, people, places, culture and heritage.
Readership/Target Audience: Read by Lincolnshire residents and ex-patriots aged 45 years old and over.
ADVERTISING RATES:
Full Page Mono £655.00
Full Page Colour £820.00
Agency Commission: 10%
Mechanical Data: Film: Digital, Type Area: 267 x 175mm, Col Length: 267mm, Page Width: 175mm, Bleed Size: 303 x 216mm, Trim Size: 297 x 210mm
Copy instructions: Copy Date: 3 weeks prior to publication date
Average advertising content per issue: 50%
CONSUMER: RURAL & REGIONAL INTEREST: Regional Interest English Counties

LINCOLNSHIRE TODAY
46942U80C-2205

Editorial Address: Armstrong House, Armstrong Street, GRIMSBY, DN31 2QE **Tel:** 01472 310305
Fax: 01472 310317
Email: lincs-today@blmgroup.co.uk
Advertising Address: As above. **Tel:** 01472 310302
Fax: 01472 310312
Email: k.collins@blmgroup.co.uk
Web site: http://www.blmgroup.co.uk
ISSN: 1366-1299
Publisher: Haychart Ltd
Date Established: 1996
Frequency: Monthly
Cover Price: £1.95
Circulation: 12,500 (Publisher's Statement)
Usual Pagination: 132
Editor: Steve Fisher; **Managing Director:** Steve Fisher; **Advertising Manager:** Kim Collins; **Publisher:** Steve Fisher
Summary of Content: Magazine containing articles on hair and beauty, towns, travel, hotels and restaurants, motoring, leisure, heritage, antiques, outdoor pursuits, health and fitness, holidays, fashion and celebrities.
Readership/Target Audience: Aimed at those living in Lincolnshire and Yorkshire.
ADVERTISING RATES:
Full Page Mono £795.00
Full Page Colour £1045.00
Agency Commission: 10%
Mechanical Data: Type Area: 277 x 190mm, Col Length: 277mm, Page Width: 190mm, Bleed Size: 303 x 216mm, Trim Size: 297 x 210mm, Film: Digital
Copy instructions: Copy Date: 4 weeks prior to publication date
Average advertising content per issue: 60%
CONSUMER: RURAL & REGIONAL INTEREST: Regional Interest English Counties

LINEDANCER
46289U76G-300

Editorial Address: Clare House, 166 Lord Street, SOUTHPORT, PR9 0QA **Tel:** 01704 392300
Fax: 01704 501678
Email: editor@linedancermagazine.com
Advertising Address: As above.
Email: chris.chew@linedancermagazine.com
Web site: http://www.linedancermagazine.com
ISSN: 1366-6509
Publisher: Champion Media Group
Date Established: 1996
Frequency: Monthly
Cover Price: £3.00

Annual Sub.: £30.00
Circulation: 25,000 (Publisher's Statement)
Usual Pagination: 84
Editor: Laurent Saletto; **Advertising Manager:** Chris Chew; **Managing Editor:** Laurent Saletto; **Publisher:** E. Drummond
Summary of Content: Magazine covering all aspects of line dancing including music reviews and star interviews.
Readership/Target Audience: Aimed at line dancers of all levels including instructors and associated businesses worldwide.
ADVERTISING RATES:
Full Page Mono £630.00
Full Page Colour £820.00
Agency Commission: 10%
Mechanical Data: Page Width: 190mm, Col Length: 277mm, Type Area: 277 x 190mm, Film: Digital, Bleed Size: 305 x 218mm, Trim Size: 297 x 210mm
Copy instructions: Copy Date: 4 weeks prior to publication date
Average advertising content per issue: 35%
CONSUMER: MUSIC & PERFORMING ARTS: Dance

LINUX FORMAT
624243U78E-14

Editorial Address: 30 Monmouth Street, BATH, BA1 2BW
Tel: 01225 442244
Email: paul.hudson@futurenet.com
Advertising Address: As above. **Fax:** 01225 822885
Email: sigoe@futurenet.com
Web site: http://www.linuxformat.co.uk
Publisher: Future Publishing Ltd
Date Established: 2000
Frequency: 13 issues yearly
Cover Price: £6.49
Annual Sub.: £60.00
Circulation: 28,734 (ABC 01/01/2008 to 31/12/2008)
Editor: Paul Hudson; **Advertising Director:** Sean Igoe
Summary of Content: Magazine covering all aspects of Linux, including news, developments, tutorials, products, technical advice, software and reviews.
Readership/Target Audience: Aimed at Linux users of all levels from business professionals to enthusiasts.
ADVERTISING RATES:
Full Page Colour £2500.00
Agency Commission: 10%
Mechanical Data: Type Area: 280 x 203mm, Bleed Size: 306 x 228mm, Trim Size: 300 x 222mm, Col Length: 280mm, Page Width: 203mm, Film: Digital
Copy instructions: Copy Date: 3 weeks prior to publication date
Average advertising content per issue: 20%
CONSUMER: CONSUMER ELECTRONICS: Home Computing

THE LIST
48106U89C-170

Editorial Address: 14 High Street, EDINBURGH, EH1 1TE
Tel: 0131 550 3050 **Fax:** 0131 557 8500
Email: editor@list.co.uk
Advertising Address: As above.
Email: ads@list.co.uk
Web site: http://www.list.co.uk
ISSN: 0959-1915
Publisher: The List Ltd
Date Established: 1985
Frequency: 26 issues yearly - Weekly issues in August to cover the Edinburgh Festival, otherwise fortnightly
Cover Price: £2.20
Annual Sub.: £45.00
Circulation: 8,493 (ABC 01/01/2008 to 31/12/2008)
Usual Pagination: 128
Editor: Mark Robertson; **News Editor:** Anna Millar; **Publisher:** Robin Hodge
Summary of Content: Entertainment and lifestyle guide for Glasgow and Edinburgh. Covers film, music, theatre, clubs, books, food and contemporary issues.
Readership/Target Audience: Aimed at 18 to 35 year olds.
ADVERTISING RATES:
Full Page Mono £660.00
Full Page Colour £930.00
Agency Commission: 10%
Mechanical Data: Col Length: 271mm, Page Width: 189mm, Type Area: 271 x 189mm, Trim Size: 297 x 210mm, Bleed Size: 305 x 218mm, Film: Digital
Copy instructions: Copy Date: 7 days prior to publication date
Average advertising content per issue: 30%
Supplement(s): Deli and Good Food Directory - 1xY, Edinburgh Festival - 1xY, Glasgow Green Music Festival - 1xY, The List Bar Guide - 1xY, The List Club Guide - 1xY, The List Eating and Drinking Guide - 1xY, The List Student Guide - 1xY, T in the Park Music Festival - 1xY
CONSUMER: HOLIDAYS & TRAVEL: Entertainment Guides

LITERARY REVIEW
47546U84B-80

Editorial Address: 44 Lexington Street, LONDON, W1F 0LW
Tel: 020 7437 9392 **Fax:** 020 7734 1844
Email: editorial@literaryreview.co.uk
Advertising Address: As above.

Email: terry@literaryreview.co.uk
Web site: http://www.literaryreview.co.uk
ISSN: 0144-4360
Publisher: Literary Review
Date Established: 1979
Frequency: 11 issues yearly
Cover Price: £3.00
Annual Sub.: £32.00
Circulation: 15,000 (Publisher's Statement)
Usual Pagination: 64
Editor: Nancy Sladek; **Advertising Manager:** Terry Finnegan
Summary of Content: Magazine covering literary book reviews, short stories, poetry and cartoons.
Readership/Target Audience: Read by those interested in literature.
ADVERTISING RATES:
Full Page Mono £1800.00
Full Page Colour £1995.00
Agency Commission: 10%
Mechanical Data: Type Area: 243 x 185mm, Col Length: 243mm, Trim Size: 279 x 209mm, Bleed Size: 289 x 219mm, Film: Digital, Page Width: 185mm
Copy instructions: Copy Date: 10th of the month prior to publication date
Average advertising content per issue: 15%
CONSUMER: THE ARTS & LITERARY: Literary

THE LITTLE SHIP
48377U91A-70
Editorial Address: Bell Wharf Lane, Upper Thames Street, LONDON, EC4R 3TB **Tel:** 020 8480 1683
Email: rachel@wildstrawberry.uk.com
Advertising Address: Pinegen Ltd, 95 Brighton Road, SURBITON, KT6 5NF **Tel:** 020 8335 1100
Fax: 020 8399 6374
Email: richard@pinegen.co.uk
Publisher: The Little Ship Club (Members) Ltd
Frequency: 3 issues yearly - Published in March, August and December
Cover Price: Free
Circulation: 1,500 (Publisher's Statement)
Usual Pagination: 46
Editor: Rachel Hedley; **Advertising Manager:** Richard Talbott; **Managing Editor:** Rachel Hedley
Summary of Content: Magazine covering news on sail and engine-driven yachts.
Readership/Target Audience: Read by members of The Little Ship Club and by boating and yachting enthusiasts.
ADVERTISING: Rates on application
CONSUMER: RECREATION & LEISURE: Boating & Yachting

LITTLE WHITE LIES MAGAZINE
1663816U76A-177
Formerly: Little White Lies
Editorial Address: Studio 209, Curtain House, 134-146 Curtain Road, LONDON, EC2A 3AR **Tel:** 020 7729 3675
Email: editorial@littlewhitelies.co.uk
Advertising Address: As above. **Tel:** 020 7689 9001
Email: Steph@littlewhitelies.co.uk
Web site: http://www.littlewhitelies.co.uk
ISSN: 1745-9168
Publisher: Story Publishing Ltd
Date Established: 2005
Frequency: 6 issues yearly
Cover Price: £3.75
Circulation: 14,000 (Publisher's Statement)
Usual Pagination: 116
Editor: Danny Miller; **Advertising Manager:** Danny Miller; **Publisher:** Danny Miller
Summary of Content: Film and lifestyle magazine.
Readership/Target Audience: Aimed at those interested in talking about films and life.
ADVERTISING RATES:
Full Page Colour £800.00
Mechanical Data: Bleed Size: 251x 206mm, Trim Size: 245 x 200mm
Copy instructions: Copy Date: 2 weeks prior to publication date
CONSUMER: MUSIC & PERFORMING ARTS: Cinema

LIV
46484U77E-380
Formerly: Volvo Magazine
Editorial Address: 7 St. Martin's Place, LONDON, WC2N 4HA **Tel:** 020 7747 0700 **Fax:** 020 7747 0629
Email: aarati.caria@redwoodgroup.net
Advertising Address: As above. **Fax:** 020 7747 0699
Email: andrew.hillier@redwoodgroup.net
Web site: http://www.redwoodgroup.net
Publisher: Redwood
Date Established: 1994
Frequency: Half-yearly - Published in April and September Free to qualifying individuals
Circulation: 1,500,000 (Publisher's Statement)
Usual Pagination: 68
Editor: Bill Dunn; **Advertising Manager:** Gordon Armstrong

Summary of Content: Magazine covering travel, outdoor activities, ownership experiences, fashion, design and the environment.
Language(s): Danish; Dutch; English; Flemish; French; German; Greek; Hungarian; Italian; Polish; Russian; Spanish; Turkish
Readership/Target Audience: Aimed at those who have bought a Volvo car within the last 5 years.
ADVERTISING: Rates on application
CONSUMER: MOTORING & CYCLING: Club Cars

LIVE CHESHIRE
1843558U80C-5464
Editorial Address: 623 Stretford Road, MANCHESTER, M16 0QA **Tel:** 0161 877 6437 **Fax:** 0161 876 0771
Email: lc@runwildmedia.com
Advertising Address: As above. **Fax:** 0161 876 4141
Email: s.rust@runwildgroup.com
Web site: http://runwildmedia.com
Publisher: Run Wild Media Ltd - Manchester
Date Established: 2007
Frequency: Monthly
Cover Price: Free
Circulation: 30,000 (Publisher's Statement 1998)
Usual Pagination: 132
Editor: Louisa Castle
Summary of Content: Luxury lifestyle magazine with features on homes and interiors, fashion, beauty, holidays, travel, business, arts, motoring, property and local personalities.
Readership/Target Audience: Aimed at residents in Cheshire.
ADVERTISING RATES:
Full Page Colour £2100.00
Mechanical Data: Bleed Size: 303 x 216mm, Trim Size: 297 x 210mm
Copy instructions: Copy Date: 15th of the month prior to publication date
CONSUMER: RURAL & REGIONAL INTEREST: Regional Interest English Counties

LIVE IT, THE CONRAN MAGAZINE
45604U74P-480
Formerly: Eat The Conran Food Magazine
Editorial Address: 11 Plough Yard, LONDON, EC2A 3LP **Tel:** 020 7684 7111 **Fax:** 020 7684 7122
Email: paul_keers@axonpublish.com
Advertising Address: As above.
Email: paul_keers@axonpublish.com
Web site: http://www.conran.com
Publisher: Axon Publishing Ltd
Date Established: 1999
Frequency: Half-yearly - Published in April and September Free to qualifying individuals
Circulation: 50,000 (Publisher's Statement)
Usual Pagination: 112
Editor: Paul Keers; **Advertising Manager:** Paul Keers
Summary of Content: Magazine containing features on contemporary metropolitan living, incorporating food, interior design, home products, travel, fashion and entertaining.
Readership/Target Audience: Aimed at Conran customers.
ADVERTISING: Rates on application
Copy instructions: Copy Date: 3 weeks prior to publication date
CONSUMER: WOMEN'S INTEREST CONSUMER MAGAZINES: Food & Cookery

LIVE MANCHESTER
1843557U80C-5463
Editorial Address: 623 Stretford Road, MANCHESTER, M16 0QA **Tel:** 0161 877 6437 **Fax:** 0161 876 0771
Email: lc@runwildmedia.com
Advertising Address: As above. **Fax:** 0161 876 4141
Email: s.rust@runwildgroup.com
Web site: http://www.runwildmedia.com
Publisher: Run Wild Media Ltd - Manchester
Date Established: 2007
Frequency: Monthly
Cover Price: Free
Circulation: 25,000 (Publisher's Statement)
Usual Pagination: 132
Editor: Louisa Castle
Summary of Content: Luxury lifestyle magazine with features on homes and interiors, fashion, beauty, holidays, business, arts, motoring, property and local personalities.
Readership/Target Audience: Aimed at residents in Manchester.
ADVERTISING RATES:
Full Page Colour £2100.00
Mechanical Data: Trim Size: 297 x 210mm, Bleed Size: 303 x 216mm
Copy instructions: Copy Date: 15th of the month prior to publication date
CONSUMER: RURAL & REGIONAL INTEREST: Regional Interest English Counties

LIVERPOOL MONTHLY
45766U75B-145
Editorial Address: Suite 2.1, Level 2, Renslade House, Bonhay Road, EXETER, EX4 3AY **Tel:** 01392 664141
Fax: 01392 221794
Email: jo@lcdpublishing.co.uk
Publisher: LCD Publishing
Date Established: 1996
Frequency: Monthly
Cover Price: £1.75
Circulation: 40,000 (Publisher's Statement)
Usual Pagination: 32
Editor: Joanne Trump; **Advertising Manager:** Joanne Trump
Summary of Content: Magazine covering football news and reviews concerning Liverpool FC.
Readership/Target Audience: Aimed at those who support the club.
ADVERTISING: No Advertising taken
CONSUMER: SPORT: Football

LIVERPOOL STUDENT
47410U83-32_50
Editorial Address: PO Box 187, Guild of Students, Liverpool University, 160 Mount Pleasant, LIVERPOOL, L69 7BR
Tel: 0151 794 4125 **Fax:** 0151 794 4174
Email: lseditor@liv.ac.uk
Advertising Address: BAM, 2nd Floor, 8 Castle Square, SWANSEA, SA1 1DW **Tel:** 0845 130 0667
Fax: 0845 130 0668
Email: ap@bamuk.com
Web site: http://www.liverpoolstudentnewspaper.co.uk
Publisher: Liverpool Student Media
Date Established: 1999
Frequency: Monthly - Published fortnightly during term time
Cover Price: Free
Circulation: 8,000 (Publisher's Statement)
Usual Pagination: 28
Summary of Content: Student publication including articles on news, opinion, features, entertainment, films, clubs, art, books, fashion, music, sport and student lifestyle.
Readership/Target Audience: Students of Liverpool, primarily from University of Liverpool.
ADVERTISING: Rates on application
CONSUMER: STUDENT PUBLICATIONS

LIVERPOOL.COM
1792736U89C-1096
Editorial Address: PO Box 48, Old Hall Street, LIVERPOOL, L69 3EB **Tel:** 0151 330 4932 **Fax:** 0151 472 2474
Advertising Address: As above. **Tel:** 0151 227 2000
Email: stephen.smith@liverpool.com
Web site: http://www.liverpool.com
Publisher: Trinity Mirror
Date Established: 2006
Frequency: Monthly
Cover Price: Free
Circulation: 25,000 (Publisher's Statement)
Usual Pagination: 64
Editor: Patricia Caliskan; **Features Editor:** Patricia Caliskan
Summary of Content: Magazine covering arts, entertainment and events across Merseyside, Cheshire and North East Wales.
Readership/Target Audience: Aimed at 18 to 45 year olds interested in going out and about in the region.
ADVERTISING RATES:
Full Page Colour £1500.00
Mechanical Data: Trim Size: 297 x 210mm, Film: Digital
Copy instructions: Copy Date: 2 weeks prior to publication date
Average advertising content per issue: 40%
CONSUMER: HOLIDAYS & TRAVEL: Entertainment Guides

LIVEWIRE
48255U89E-142
Editorial Address: Central Point, 45 Beech Street, LONDON, EC2Y 8AD **Tel:** 020 7805 5555
Fax: 020 7805 5911
Email: laura.richardson@iln.co.uk
Advertising Address: As above.
Email: marzia.ghiselli@iln.co.uk
Web site: http://www.iln.co.uk
Publisher: The Illustrated London News Ltd
Frequency: Quarterly
Cover Price: Free
Circulation: 121,200 (ABC 01/01/2008 to 31/12/2008)
Usual Pagination: 48
Editor: Laura Richardson; **Managing Director:** Lisa Barnard; **Advertising Manager:** Marzia Ghiselli
Summary of Content: Magazine featuring news, information and a guide to activities and events.
Readership/Target Audience: Aimed at Great North Eastern Railway travellers.
ADVERTISING RATES:
Full Page Colour £3000.00
Agency Commission: 10%
Mechanical Data: Bleed Size: 303 x 216mm, Trim Size: 297 x 210mm, Type Area: 269 x 185mm, Col Length: 269mm, Page Width: 185mm, Film: Digital

Copy instructions: Copy Date: 3 weeks prior to publication date
Average advertising content per issue: 35%
CONSUMER: HOLIDAYS & TRAVEL: Holidays

LIVING
46997U80C-3515

Editorial Address: Floor 6, Fort Dunlop, Fort Parkway, BIRMINGHAM, B24 9FF **Tel:** 0121 234 5653
Email: livingmag@birminghampost.net
Advertising Address: 103-106 High Green Court, Newhall Street, CANNOCK, WS11 1AB **Tel:** 01543 501777
Fax: 01543 501759
Web site: http://www.livingseries.co.uk
Publisher: Bpm Media (Midlands)
Frequency: Monthly
Cover Price: Free
Circulation: 50,200 (Publisher's Statement)
Usual Pagination: 96
Editor: Jon Perks; **Editor-in-Chief:** Jon Perks; **Advertising Manager:** Jo Bailey
Summary of Content: Lifestyle magazine covering interiors, property, wining and dining, travel, motoring and fashion.
Readership/Target Audience: Aimed predominantly at intellectual women between 35 and 55 years old.
ADVERTISING RATES:
Full Page Colour £2472.00
Agency Commission: 10%
Mechanical Data: No. of Columns (Display): 4, Film: Digital, Bleed Size: 360 x 285mm, Trim Size: 320 x 246mm
CONSUMER: RURAL & REGIONAL INTEREST: Regional Interest English Counties

LIVING ABROAD
1667149U74K-731

Editorial Address: 21 Royal Circus, EDINBURGH, EH3 6TL **Tel:** 0131 226 7766 **Fax:** 0131 225 4567
Email: sue.hitchen@gmail.com
Advertising Address: As above.
Email: jking.media@googlemail.com
Web site: http://www.livingabroadmagazine.com
Publisher: The Media Company
Date Established: 2005
Frequency: Monthly
Cover Price: £3.70
Circulation: 40,000 (Print Run)
Usual Pagination: 180
Editor: Sue Hitchen; **Advertising Manager:** James King; **Publisher:** Sue Hitchen
Summary of Content: Magazine covering real life stories of people who have moved overseas, advice on emigrating and buying a second home and advice on investing in property.
Readership/Target Audience: Aimed those considering buying a property or living overseas.
ADVERTISING RATES:
Full Page Colour £2950.00
Agency Commission: 10%
Mechanical Data: Type Area: 272 x 193mm, Bleed Size: 306 x 226mm, Trim Size: 300 x 220mm, Col Length: 272mm, Page Width: 193mm, Film: Digital
Average advertising content per issue: 40%
CONSUMER: WOMEN'S INTEREST CONSUMER MAGAZINES: Home Purchase

LIVING EARTH
37771U74P-485

Editorial Address: South Plaza, Marlborough Street, BRISTOL, BS1 3NX **Tel:** 0117 914 2434 **Fax:** 0117 314 5001
Email: ewinkler@soilassociation.org
Advertising Address: Think Scotland, Woodside House, Woodside Place, GLASGOW, G3 7SD **Tel:** 0141 582 1280
Fax: 0141 582 1484
Email: jacqueline@thinkpublishing.co.uk
Web site: http://www.soilassociation.org
ISSN: 1360-1741
Publisher: Soil Association
Date Established: 1946
Frequency: 3 issues yearly - Published in April, August and November
Cover Price: £2.00
Free to qualifying individuals
Annual Sub.: £24.00
Circulation: 25,000 (Publisher's Statement)
Usual Pagination: 36
Editor: Tim Young
Summary of Content: Official membership magazine of the Soil Association. Contains articles on organic food including genetic modification (which is incompatible with organic farming), organic farming, animal welfare, nutrition, food production and environmental issues.
Readership/Target Audience: Aimed at Soil Association members and the general public.
ADVERTISING RATES:
Full Page Colour £1950.00
Agency Commission: 10%
Mechanical Data: Type Area: 185 x 255mm, Col Length: 185mm, Page Width: 255mm, Film: Digital, Trim Size: 297 x 210mm

Average advertising content per issue: 14%
CONSUMER: WOMEN'S INTEREST CONSUMER MAGAZINES: Food & Cookery

LIVING FRANCE
45492U74K-225

Editorial Address: Archant House, Oriel Road, CHELTENHAM, GL50 1BB **Tel:** 01242 216050
Fax: 01242 216094
Email: editorial@livingfrance.com
Advertising Address: As above. **Tel:** 01242 216099
Email: debbie.macleod@archant.co.uk
Web site: http://www.livingfrance.com
Publisher: Archant Life
Date Established: 1989
Frequency: 13 issues yearly
Cover Price: £3.99
Annual Sub: £42.00
Circulation: 17,830 (Publisher's Statement)
Usual Pagination: 132
Editor: Liz Thorold
Summary of Content: Guide to France and French property, including regional information, advice on taxation, readers' experiences and other matters relevant to living in France. Also contains articles on French food, wine and travel.
Readership/Target Audience: Read by people who are interested in purchasing property in and travellers to France.
ADVERTISING RATES:
Full Page Colour £1350.00
Agency Commission: 10%
Mechanical Data: Col Widths (Display): 45mm, No. of Columns (Display): 4, Print Process: Web-fed offset, Bleed Size: 303 x 216mm, Trim Size: 265 x 182mm
Copy instructions: Copy Date: 3 weeks prior to publication date
Average advertising content per issue: 35%
CONSUMER: WOMEN'S INTEREST CONSUMER MAGAZINES: Home Purchase

LIVING NORTH
46951U80C-2452

Editorial Address: 5 Cattle Market, HEXHAM, NE46 1NJ **Tel:** 01434 609933 **Fax:** 01434 600066
Email: livingnorth@btconnect.com
Advertising Address: As above.
Email: livingnorth@btconnect.com
Web site: http://www.livingnorth.com
Publisher: Kensington West Productions Ltd
Date Established: 1999
Frequency: Monthly
Cover Price: £2.95
Annual Sub.: £29.50
Circulation: 15,500 (Publisher's Statement)
Usual Pagination: 300
Editor: Janet Blair; **Advertising Manager:** Mike Kearney; **Publisher:** Julian West
Summary of Content: Regional interest and lifestyle magazine covering shopping, motoring, leisure, people and property in the North East of England. Also contains a what's on section.
Readership/Target Audience: Aimed at those aged 25 years old and over who live in the North East of England.
ADVERTISING RATES:
Full Page Colour £775.00
Agency Commission: 10%
Copy instructions: Copy Date: 2 weeks prior to publication date
Average advertising content per issue: 35%
CONSUMER: RURAL & REGIONAL INTEREST: Regional Interest English Counties

LIVING SOUTH
46831U80B-125_55

Editorial Address: Unit F3, Battersea Studios, 80 Silverthorne Road, LONDON, SW8 3XA **Tel:** 020 7978 3490
Fax: 020 7978 3498
Email: victoria.purcell@archant.co.uk
Advertising Address: As above. **Tel:** 020 7978 3499
Email: danny.zahra-lee@archant.co.uk
Web site: http://www.archantlife.co.uk
Publisher: Archant Life
Date Established: 1992
Frequency: Monthly
Cover Price: Free
Circulation: 55,000 (Publisher's Statement)
Usual Pagination: 92
Editor: Victoria Purcell; **Advertising Manager:** Danny Zahra-Lee
Summary of Content: Lifestyle magazine covering news, views, interviews and events.
Readership/Target Audience: Aimed at those who live or work in the surrounding areas.
ADVERTISING RATES:
Full Page Colour £1478.00
Agency Commission: 10%
Mechanical Data: Type Area: 270 x 190mm, Col Length: 270mm, Page Width: 190mm, Bleed Size: 303 x 216mm, Film: Digital, Trim Size: 297 x 210mm

Copy instructions: Copy Date: 10 days prior to publication date
Average advertising content per issue: 70%
CONSUMER: RURAL & REGIONAL INTEREST: Regional Interest Greater London

LIVING SPAIN
1640074U89E-213

Editorial Address: 7 Southern Street, Islington, LONDON, N1 9AY **Tel:** 07719 328325
Email: editor@livingspain.co.uk
Advertising Address: R&J Offices, New Cut East, IPSWICH, IP3 0EA **Tel:** 01473 214444 **Fax:** 01473 214088
Email: advertising@livingspain.co.uk
Web site: http://www.livingspain.co.uk
Publisher: Albany Publishing
Frequency: 6 issues yearly
Cover Price: £3.99
Circulation: 9,004 (Publisher's Statement)
Editor: John McManus; **Advertising Manager:** Sue Lewis
Summary of Content: Magazine covering travel features, property purchase, living and working in Spain, financial issues, fiestas, food and wine.
Readership/Target Audience: Aimed at those travelling to Spain or considering purchasing a property, living or working in Spain.
ADVERTISING RATES:
Full Page Colour £1960.00
SCC £16.00
Agency Commission: 10%
Mechanical Data: Type Area: 267 x 183mm, Bleed Size: 306 x 236mm, Trim Size: 300 x 230mm, Col Length: 267mm, Page Width: 183mm, Film: Digital
Average advertising content per issue: 30%
CONSUMER: HOLIDAYS & TRAVEL: Holidays

THE LIVING TRADITION
46167U76D-351_57

Editorial Address: PO Box 1026, KILMARNOCK, KA2 0LG **Tel:** 01563 571220
Email: admin@livingtradition.co.uk
Advertising Address: As above.
Email: adverts@folkmusic.net
Web site: http://www.folkmusic.net
ISSN: 1351-4105
Publisher: The Living Tradition Ltd
Date Established: 1993
Frequency: 6 issues yearly
Cover Price: £3.25
Annual Sub.: £18.00
Circulation: 10,000 (Publisher's Statement)
Usual Pagination: 68
Editor: Peter Heywood; **Managing Director:** Peter Heywood; **Advertising Manager:** Peter Heywood
Summary of Content: Magazine covering traditional music of the British Isles and beyond. Contains news, reviews, interviews and a wide range of features.
Readership/Target Audience: Aimed at all enthusiasts of traditional music including players and listeners.
ADVERTISING RATES:
Full Page Mono £345.00
Full Page Colour £575.00
Agency Commission: 15%
Mechanical Data: Page Width: 190mm, Type Area: 275 x 190mm, Col Length: 275mm, Trim Size: 297 x 210mm, Film: Digital, Bleed Size: 303 x 216mm
Copy instructions: Copy Date: 1 month prior to publication date
Average advertising content per issue: 30%
CONSUMER: MUSIC & PERFORMING ARTS: Music

LIVINGEDGE
46870U80C-665

Editorial Address: 22A Victoria Road, Hale, ALTRINCHAM, WA15 9AD **Tel:** 0161 928 0333 **Fax:** 0161 929 8656
Advertising Address: As above.
Email: info@livingedge.co.uk
ISSN: 1464-2034
Publisher: Archant Life (North) PLC
Date Established: 1998
Frequency: Monthly
Cover Price: Free
Circulation: 42,000 (Publisher's Statement)
Usual Pagination: 128
Editor: Claire Cooper
Summary of Content: Lifestyle magazine covering local news with features on food, fashion, motoring and interiors.
Readership/Target Audience: Aimed at affluent professionals in Cheshire and Manchester.
ADVERTISING RATES:
Full Page Mono £970.00
Full Page Colour £970.00
Agency Commission: 10%
Mechanical Data: Type Area: 270 x 188mm, Bleed Size: 306 x 226mm, Trim Size: 300 x 220mm, Col Length: 270mm, Page Width: 188mm, Film: Digital
Copy instructions: Copy Date: 2 weeks prior to publication date

Consumer Magazines

Average advertising content per issue: 40%
CONSUMER: RURAL & REGIONAL INTEREST: Regional Interest English Counties

LIVING-ETC
45276U74C-290

Editorial Address: Blue Fin Building, 110 Southwark Street, LONDON, SE1 0SU Tel: 020 3148 7443 Fax: 020 3148 8121
Email: livingetc@ipcmedia.com
Advertising Address: As above. Tel: 020 3148 5000
Email: james_zaman@ipcmedia.com
Web site: http://www.livingetc.com
Publisher: IPC Southbank
Date Established: 1998
Frequency: Monthly
Cover Price: £3.50
Circulation: 90,877 (ABC 01/01/2009 to 30/06/2009)
Usual Pagination: 174
Editor: Suzanne Imre; News Editor: Bethan Ryder;
Advertising Manager: James Zaman; Managing Editor: Sara Norrman; Publisher: Lynsey Bushell
Summary of Content: Homes magazine covering relaxed modern living featuring gorgeous homes, offering style and decorating inspiration as well as shopping, food and travel. Twitter: https://twitter.com/Livingetc.
Readership/Target Audience: Aimed at those with an interest in relaxed modern style.
ADVERTISING RATES:
Full Page Colour £5775.00
Agency Commission: 10%
Mechanical Data: Bleed Size: 295 x 231mm, Trim Size: 289 x 225mm, Type Area: 260 x 205mm, Col Length: 260mm, Page Width: 196mm, Print Process: Web off-set litho, Film: Digital
Copy instructions: Copy Date: 4 weeks prior to publication date
Average advertising content per issue: 40%
CONSUMER: WOMEN'S INTEREST CONSUMER MAGAZINES: Home & Family

LLAFAR GWLAD (WELSH FOLKLORE)
47036U80D-90

Editorial Address: 12 Iard Yr Orsaf, Conwy, LLANRWST, LL26 0EH Tel: 01492 642031 Fax: 01492 641502
Email: llyfraud@carreg-gwalch.com
Web site: http://www.carreg-gwalch.com
ISSN: 1356-3777
Publisher: Gwasg Carreg Gwalch
Date Established: 1983
Frequency: Quarterly
Cover Price: £1.50
Annual Sub.: £8.00
Circulation: 2,000 (Publisher's Statement)
Usual Pagination: 24
Editor: Myrddin ap Dafydd; Publisher: Myrddin ap Dafydd
Summary of Content: Magazine written in Welsh covering Welsh, Celtic and international folklore.
Language(s): Welsh
Readership/Target Audience: Aimed at those interested in Welsh, Celtic and international folklore.
ADVERTISING: No Advertising taken
CONSUMER: RURAL & REGIONAL INTEREST: Regional Interest Wales

LOADED
47657U86C-350

Editorial Address: Blue Fin Building, 110 Southwark Street, LONDON, SE1 0SU Tel: 020 3148 5000 Fax: 020 3148 8107
Advertising Address: As above.
Email: chris_dicker@ipcmedia.com
Web site: http://www.loaded.co.uk
ISSN: 1353-3479
Publisher: IPC ignite!
Date Established: 1994
Frequency: Monthly
Cover Price: £2.50
Annual Sub.: £36.00
Circulation: 72,679 (ABC 01/01/2009 to 30/06/2009)
Editor: Andy Sherwood; Managing Director: Eric Fuller
Summary of Content: Magazine covering music, sex, sport, humour and general lifestyle.
Readership/Target Audience: Aimed at single men between 18 and 30 years old.
ADVERTISING RATES:
Full Page Colour £10415.00
Agency Commission: 10%
Mechanical Data: Film: Digital, Type Area: 269 x 177mm, Bleed Size: 295 x 216mm, Trim Size: 289 x 210mm, Col Length: 269mm, Page Width: 177mm
Average advertising content per issue: 30%
CONSUMER: ADULT & GAY MAGAZINES: Men's Lifestyle Magazines

LOBSTER MAGAZINE
1659845U73-9006

Editorial Address: 214 Westbourne Avenue, Princes Avenue, HULL, HU5 3JB Tel: 01482 447558
Email: robin@lobster.karoo.co.uk

Web site: http://www.lobster-magazine.co.uk
ISSN: 0946-0436
Publisher: Robin Ramsay
Date Established: 1983
Frequency: Half-yearly - Published in June and December
Cover Price: £4.00
Circulation: 1,200 (Publisher's Statement)
Usual Pagination: 48
Editor: Robin Ramsay
Summary of Content: Magazine covering politics, parapolitics, contemporary history and conspiracy theories.
Readership/Target Audience: Aimed at academics and journalists.
ADVERTISING: No Advertising taken
CONSUMER: NATIONAL & INTERNATIONAL PERIODICALS

THE LOCAL FOCAL
1820088U80C-5430

Editorial Address: Suites 1 & 7, Albion Mills, BRADFORD, BD10 9TQ Tel: 01274 420091 Fax: 01274 347291
Email: editor@madpublications.co.uk
Advertising Address: As above.
Email: editor@madpublications.co.uk
Publisher: Mad Publications Ltd
Date Established: 2005
Frequency: Monthly
Cover Price: Free
Circulation: 6,000 (Publisher's Statement)
Usual Pagination: 32
Editor: Angela Riches; Advertising Manager: Angela Riches
Summary of Content: Local business directory for the Leeds and Bradford border area. Also includes restaurant reviews, features on local area and competitions.
Readership/Target Audience: Aimed at high income homes on the Leeds and Bradford borders.
ADVERTISING: Rates on application
CONSUMER: RURAL & REGIONAL INTEREST: Regional Interest English Counties

LOCAL HISTORY MAGAZINE
48696U94X-75

Editorial Address: 56 Alcester Road, STUDLEY, B80 7LG
Tel: 01527 854228 Fax: 01527 852746
Email: admin@localhistorymag.com
Advertising Address: As above.
Email: enquiries@brewinbooks.com
Web site: http://www.localhistorymag.com
ISSN: 1471-1885
Publisher: Brewin Books Ltd
Date Established: 1984
Frequency: 6 issues yearly
Annual Sub.: £22.50
Circulation: 1,000 (Publisher's Statement)
Usual Pagination: 32
Editor: Alistair Brewin; Advertising Manager: Alan Brewin
Summary of Content: Magazine containing advice and information on local history research, including book and periodical reviews.
Readership/Target Audience: Aimed at local historians and those with an interest in local history, also professionals in archives, education, libraries and museums.
ADVERTISING RATES:
Full Page Mono £250.00
Full Page Colour £375.00
Agency Commission: 10%
Mechanical Data: Col Length: 262mm, No. of Columns (Display): 3, Type Area: 262 x 180mm, Film: Digital, Trim Size: 270 x 192mm, Page Width: 180mm, Print Process: Offset litho
Copy instructions: Copy Date: 15th of the month prior to publication date
Average advertising content per issue: 10%
CONSUMER: OTHER CLASSIFICATIONS: Miscellaneous

LOCALRIDER MAGAZINE
1667011U81D-361

Formerly: Local Rider Magazine
Editorial Address: Cudham Tithe Barn, Berrys Hill, Berrys Green, Cudham, WESTERHAM, TN16 3AG
Tel: 01959 541444
Email: fiona@localrider.co.uk
Advertising Address: 1 Crown Yard, Bedgebury Estate, Goudhurst, TUNBRIDGE WELLS, TN17 2QZ
Tel: 0870 066 8324 Fax: 0870 066 8196
Email: lr.ed@kelsey.co.uk
Web site: http://www.localrider.co.uk
Publisher: Kelsey Publishing Ltd
Date Established: 2002
Frequency: Monthly
Cover Price: £2.70
Circulation: 22,000 (Publisher's Statement)
Usual Pagination: 100
Editor: Fiona Rafferty; Advertising Manager: Melanie Crouch
Summary of Content: Magazine covering local and national equestrian events, equipment reviews, topical editorial, new products as well as amateur and professional rider profiles.

Readership/Target Audience: Aimed at amateur competition, pony club, riding club and professional riders.
ADVERTISING RATES:
Full Page Colour £650.00
Agency Commission: 10%
Mechanical Data: Film: Digital
CONSUMER: ANIMALS & PETS: Horses & Ponies

LOGIC PROBLEMS
46665U79F-50

Editorial Address: Stonecroft, 69 Station Road, REDHILL, RH1 1EY Tel: 01737 378700 Fax: 01737 767248
Email: reception@puzzlermedia.com
Advertising Address: As above. Fax: 01737 378888
Email: brian.ainge@puzzlermedia.co.uk
Web site: http://www.puzzler.co.uk
Publisher: Puzzler Media Ltd
Frequency: 13 issues yearly
Cover Price: £1.75
Circulation: 48,037 (Publisher's Statement)
Usual Pagination: 66
Editor: Sarah Brown; Managing Director: Mel Lewis;
Publisher: David Sergeant
Summary of Content: Publication containing crosswords and puzzles.
Readership/Target Audience: Aimed at puzzle enthusiasts.
ADVERTISING: Rates on application
CONSUMER: HOBBIES & DIY: Games & Puzzles

LOGICAL CHALLENGE
46681U79F-49

Editorial Address: Zetland House, 5-25 Scrutton Street, LONDON, EC2A 4HJ Tel: 020 7613 7477
Fax: 020 7168 7956
Email: justine@accoladepublishing.co.uk
Advertising Address: As above.
Email: justine.wall@accoladepublishing.co.uk
Web site: http://www.totalpuzzles.co.uk
Publisher: Accolade Publishing
Frequency: 13 issues yearly
Cover Price: £1.99
Usual Pagination: 64
Editor: Sarah Grummett; Advertising Manager: Justine Wall; Group Editor: Sarah Grummett; Publisher: Justine Wall
Summary of Content: Magazine containing a variety of logical problems.
Readership/Target Audience: Aimed at professional puzzle enthusiasts.
ADVERTISING: Rates on application
Agency Commission: 10%
Copy instructions: Copy Date: 1 month prior to publication date
CONSUMER: HOBBIES & DIY: Games & Puzzles

LONDON ARCHAEOLOGIST
48697U94X-78

Editorial Address: Institute of Archaeology, 31-34 Gordon Square, LONDON, WC1H 0PY Tel: 020 7679 4749
Fax: 020 7383 2572
Email: cliveorton@btinternet.com
Advertising Address: 44 Tantallon Road, LONDON, SW12 8DG Tel: 020 8673 1901
Email: becky.wallower@dial.pipex.com
Web site: http://www.londonarchaeologist.org.uk
ISSN: 0024-5984
Publisher: The London Archaeologist Association
Date Established: 1968
Frequency: Quarterly
Cover Price: £4.50
Circulation: 1,000 (Publisher's Statement)
Usual Pagination: 28
Editor: Clive Orton; Advertising Manager: Becky Wallower
Summary of Content: Magazine containing reports on current aspects of archaeology and allied history within the London region.
Readership/Target Audience: Aimed at those interested in archaeology.
ADVERTISING RATES:
Full Page Mono £150.00
Full Page Colour £150.00
Agency Commission: 10%
Mechanical Data: Type Area: 279 x 210mm, No. of Columns (Display): 2, Col Length: 279mm, Page Width: 210mm, Col Widths (Display): 90mm, Film: Digital
Copy instructions: Copy Date: 1 month prior to publication date
Average advertising content per issue: 5%
Supplement(s): London Fieldwork - 1xY, Publication Round-up - 1xY
CONSUMER: OTHER CLASSIFICATIONS: Miscellaneous

LONDON COMMUNITY POST
1841065U90-1028

Editorial Address: 117 Green Lanes, LONDON, N16 9DA
Tel: 020 7354 4424 Fax: 020 7354 0313
Email: info@toplumpostasi.net
Advertising Address: As above.
Email: info@toplumpostasi.net

Web site: http://www.toplumpostasi.net
Publisher: Toplum Postasi
Frequency: Weekly - Published on Thurday
Cover Price: Free
Circulation: 27,000 (Publisher's Statement)
Editor: Alkan Chaglar; **Advertising Manager:** Ali Keskin
Summary of Content: Newspaper with news from the UK, Cyprus, Turkey and the EU with current affairs, commentary, business, education and sport.
Readership/Target Audience: Aimed at 2nd and 3rd generation Cypriots in the UK.
ADVERTISING RATES:
Full Page Mono £450.00
Full Page Colour £1000.00
CONSUMER: ETHNIC

LONDON CYCLIST
46397U77C-780

Editorial Address: 2 Newhams Row, LONDON, SE1 3UZ
Tel: 020 7234 9310 **Fax:** 020 7234 9319
Email: office@lcc.org.uk
Advertising Address: 2 Lonsdale Road, LONDON, NW6 6RD **Tel:** 020 7306 0300 **Fax:** 020 7306 0301
Email: lcc@mongoosemedia.com
Web site: http://www.lcc.org.uk
Publisher: London Cycling Campaign Ltd
Frequency: 6 issues yearly
Free to qualifying individuals
Annual Sub.: £32.00
Circulation: 11,000 (Publisher's Statement)
Usual Pagination: 50
Editor: Mike Cavenett
Summary of Content: Magazine of the London Cycling Campaign. Includes articles on cycling, politics, safety, bikes, accessories, clothing, books, routes, health and fitness.
Readership/Target Audience: Read predominantly by members and Londoners of all ages who use bicycles to get to commute, for work and for leisure.
ADVERTISING RATES:
Full Page Colour £1250.00
Agency Commission: 10%
Mechanical Data: Trim Size: 297 x 210mm, Bleed Size: 303 x 216mm, Film: Digital
Copy instructions: Copy Date: 6 weeks prior to publication date
Average advertising content per issue: 15%
CONSUMER: MOTORING & CYCLING: Cycling

LONDON DRINKER
1685809U74P-928

Editorial Address: Press releases by email only
Fax: 020 8481 3699
Email: geoff@coherent-tech.co.uk
Advertising Address: 13 Lydd Close, SIDCUP, DA14 6RH
Tel: 020 8300 7693
Email: peter.tonge@googlemail.com
Web site: http://www.londondrinker.org.uk
Publisher: Campaign for Real Ale Ltd
Date Established: 1979
Frequency: 6 issues yearly
Cover Price: Free
Circulation: 46,000 (Publisher's Statement)
Usual Pagination: 60
Editor: Tony Hedger; **News Editor:** Tony Hedger
Summary of Content: Magazine with articles, listings and advertisements relating to real ale, cider and perry and pubs where they are available.
Readership/Target Audience: Aimed at discerning beer and cider drinkers and pub-goers generally.
ADVERTISING RATES:
Full Page Mono £240.00
Full Page Colour £300.00
Agency Commission: 10%
Mechanical Data: Col Length: 190mm, Page Width: 132mm, Type Area: 190 x 132mm, Bleed Size: 210 x 148mm, Film: Digital
Copy instructions: Copy Date: 4 weeks prior to publication date
Average advertising content per issue: 45%
CONSUMER: WOMEN'S INTEREST CONSUMER MAGAZINES: Food & Cookery

---

LONDON HOTEL MAGAZINE
48057U89B-150

Editorial Address: Suite 58, 235 Earls Court Road, LONDON, SW5 9FE **Tel:** 020 7373 7282 **Fax:** 020 7373 3215
Email: editorgoodlife@bethere.co.uk
Advertising Address: As above.
Email: goodlife.media@virgin.net
Web site: http://www.london-hotelmagazine.co.uk
Publisher: Goodlife Media PR and Promotions Ltd
Frequency: 5 issues yearly
Cover Price: £2.00
Free to qualifying individuals
Annual Sub.: £16.00
Circulation: 50,000 (Publisher's Statement)
Usual Pagination: 68

Editor: Eileen Spence; **Advertising Manager:** Eileen Spence; **Publisher:** Eileen Spence
Summary of Content: Lifestyle magazine including articles on health and beauty, property and interiors, fashion shoots, social pages and restaurant reviews.
Readership/Target Audience: Read by guests staying in four and five star hotels in London.
ADVERTISING RATES:
Full Page Mono £2475.00
Full Page Colour £3000.00
Agency Commission: 10%
Mechanical Data: Type Area: 273 x 186mm, Bleed Size: 303 x 216mm, Trim Size: 297 x 210mm, Film: Digital, No. of Columns (Display): 4, Col Length: 273mm, Page Width: 186mm, Print Process: Web
Copy instructions: Copy Date: 6 weeks prior to publication date
Average advertising content per issue: 40%
CONSUMER: HOLIDAYS & TRAVEL: Hotel Magazines

LONDON INSIGHTS
1626268U80B-409

Editorial Address: 3 Springfield Cottages, Bletchinglye Lane, Rotherfield, CROWBOROUGH, TN6 3NN
Tel: 01892 852096
Email: michael@michaelwrennpublishing.co.uk
Advertising Address: 1 Heath Street, LONDON, NW3 6TP
Tel: 020 7504 0340
Email: rwason@g-h.co.uk
Web site: http://www.g-h.co.uk/insights
Publisher: Goldschmidt & Howland
Frequency: Half-yearly - Published in Spring and Autumn
Cover Price: £3.00
Free to qualifying individuals
Circulation: 80,000 (Publisher's Statement)
Usual Pagination: 100
Editor: Michael Wrenn; **Advertising Manager:** Romer Wason; **Managing Editor:** Michael Wrenn
Summary of Content: Magazine of Goldschmidt & Howland covering lifestyle, travel, fashion, health, beauty, shopping and diary dates.
Readership/Target Audience: Aimed at affluent residents and wannabes in Central and North West London.
CONSUMER: RURAL & REGIONAL INTEREST: Regional Interest Greater London

---

LONDON LOOP
1704994U89C-1057

Editorial Address: 84-86 Regent Street, LONDON, W1B 5RR **Tel:** 020 7734 2303 **Fax:** 020 7494 2570
Email: london.loop@theforwardgroup.com
Advertising Address: As above. **Tel:** 020 7292 5572
Email: adrian.farr@theforwardgroup.com
Publisher: The Forward Group
Date Established: 2005
Frequency: Quarterly
Cover Price: Free
Circulation: 300,000 (Publisher's Statement)
Usual Pagination: 48
Editor: Bella Chapman; **Advertising Manager:** Adrian Farr
Summary of Content: Magazine with travel information about the whole of London Transport as well as feature articles on dining, music, theatre, art and the lesser-known joys of life in London.
Readership/Target Audience: Aimed at those living or working in London who use the bus and Tube networks.
ADVERTISING RATES:
Full Page Colour £5000.00
Agency Commission: 10%
Mechanical Data: Type Area: 230 x 160mm, Bleed Size: 250 x 180mm, Trim Size: 240 x 170mm, Col Length: 230mm, Page Width: 160mm, Film: Digital
Copy instructions: Copy Date: 8 weeks prior to publication date
Average advertising content per issue: 20%
CONSUMER: HOLIDAYS & TRAVEL: Entertainment Guides

LONDON MACADAM
1704998U74Q-1290

Formerly: London Macadam media group
Editorial Address: Suite 239, 2 Old Brompton Road, LONDON, SW7 3DQ **Tel:** 020 7602 2773
Fax: 020 7602 2527
Email: caroline@londonmacadam.com
Advertising Address: As above. **Tel:** 020 7603 2773
Email: londonmacadam@googlemail.com
Web site: http://www.londonmacadam.com
Publisher: London Macadam Ltd
Date Established: 2002
Frequency: 5 issues yearly
Cover Price: Free
Circulation: 30,000 (Publisher's Statement)
Editor: Caroline Sivilia; **Advertising Manager:** Caroline Sivilia
Summary of Content: Lifestyle magazine covering fashion, beauty, people and shopping.
Language(s): English; French
Readership/Target Audience: Aimed at the French community in London.

ADVERTISING RATES:
Full Page Colour £1200.00
Agency Commission: 10%
CONSUMER: WOMEN'S INTEREST CONSUMER MAGAZINES: Lifestyle

THE LONDON MAGAZINE
46832U80B-126

Editorial Address: 85 Strand, LONDON, WC2R 0DW
Tel: 020 7550 8000 **Fax:** 020 7550 8250
Email: thelondonmagazine@cedarcom.co.uk
Advertising Address: As above.
Email: oliver.hoare@cedarcom.co.uk
Web site: http://www.cedarcom.co.uk
Publisher: Cedar Communications
Date Established: 1991
Frequency: Monthly
Cover Price: £3.30
Circulation: 90,000 (Publisher's Statement)
Editor: Zoe Baty; **Managing Director:** Clare Broadbent
Summary of Content: Magazine containing news, reviews and interviews in and around London. Includes articles on fashion, style and property.
Readership/Target Audience: Aimed at householders with a high disposable income.
ADVERTISING RATES:
Full Page Colour £4056.00
Agency Commission: 10%
Mechanical Data: Film: Digital, Bleed Size: 306 x 240mm, Trim Size: 300 x 232mm
Copy instructions: Copy Date: 3 weeks prior to publication date
Average advertising content per issue: 30%
CONSUMER: RURAL & REGIONAL INTEREST: Regional Interest Greater London

---

THE LONDON MAGAZINE
1642285U84B-354

Editorial Address: 32 Addison Grove, LONDON, W4 1ER
Tel: 020 8400 5882 **Fax:** 020 8994 1713
Email: admin@thelondonmagazine.net
Advertising Address: As above.
Email: admin@thelondonmagazine.net
Web site: http://www.thelondonmagazine.net
ISSN: 0024-6805
Publisher: The London Magazine & Associated Publications Ltd
Date Established: 1732
Frequency: 6 issues yearly
Cover Price: £6.95
Annual Sub.: £33.00
Circulation: 1,200 (Publisher's Statement)
Usual Pagination: 128
Editor: Sara-Mae Tuson; **Advertising Manager:** Christopher Arkell
Summary of Content: Magazine covering a review of literature and the arts.
Readership/Target Audience: Aimed at the general, literate, reading public.
ADVERTISING RATES:
Full Page Mono £150.00
Full Page Colour £200.00
Mechanical Data: Trim Size: 195 x 139mm, Film: Digital
CONSUMER: THE ARTS & LITERARY: Literary

LONDON P.A.
1641009U74J-151

Editorial Address: Willow Walk Business Centre, 8-11 Willow Walk, Farmborough, ORPINGTON, BR6 7AA
Tel: 01843 282500 **Fax:** 01843 282501
Email: london@pa-magazine.co.uk
Advertising Address: 10A Millway, LONDON, NW7 3RE
Tel: 020 8906 9011 **Fax:** 020 3209 7010
Email: info@lyonsdown.co.uk
Web site: http://www.lyonsdown.co.uk
Publisher: The Graham Cumming Group
Date Established: 2004
Frequency: Quarterly
Cover Price: £3.00
Circulation: 12,000 (Publisher's Statement)
Usual Pagination: 48
Editor: Julian Lucas; **Advertising Manager:** Bradley Schesser
Summary of Content: Magazine containing articles on lifestyle and human interest as well as profession related sections and forums dealing with PA issues.
Readership/Target Audience: Aimed at PAs working for blue chip companies with an annual turnover of above £20 million.
ADVERTISING RATES:
Full Page Mono £3000.00
Full Page Colour £3000.00
Mechanical Data: Trim Size: 297 x 210mm
CONSUMER: WOMEN'S INTEREST CONSUMER MAGAZINES: Secretary & PA

Consumer Magazines

LONDON PHILATELIST
46638U79C-30

Editorial Address: 41 Devonshire Place, LONDON, W1G 6JY **Tel:** 020 7486 1044 **Fax:** 020 7486 0803
Email: lpeditor@rpsl.org.uk
Advertising Address: As above.
Email: secretary@rpsl.org.uk
Web site: http://www.rpsl.org.uk
ISSN: 0024-6131
Publisher: The Royal Philatelic Society
Date Established: 1869
Frequency: 10 issues yearly
Annual Sub.: £20.00
Circulation: 1,900 (Publisher's Statement)
Usual Pagination: 40
Editor: Micheal Pitt-Payne; **Advertising Manager:** Alex Wieck
Summary of Content: Magazine focusing on stamp collecting and postal history.
Readership/Target Audience: Aimed at philatelists.
ADVERTISING RATES:
Full Page Mono £242.00
Full Page Colour £430.00
Mechanical Data: Type Area: 220 x 152mm, Col Length: 220mm, Page Width: 152mm, Bleed Size: +3mm, Trim Size: 272 x 195mm, Film: Digital
Copy instructions: Copy Date: 4 weeks prior to publication date
Average advertising content per issue: 5%
CONSUMER: HOBBIES & DIY: Philately

LONDON PLANNER
48111U89C-190

Editorial Address: 233 High Holborn, LONDON, WC1V 7DN **Tel:** 020 7242 5222 **Fax:** 020 7242 4184
Email: london.planner@morriseurope.com
Advertising Address: As above.
Email: andrew.turner@morriseurope.com
ISSN: 0265-8437
Publisher: MVP Europe
Date Established: 1984
Frequency: Monthly
Cover Price: Free
Annual Sub.: £22.00
Circulation: 120,000 (Publisher's Statement)
Usual Pagination: 100
Editor: Hermione Barnett
Summary of Content: Listings magazine covering theatre, dance and music, sightseeing, museums and galleries, shopping, eating out and travel accommodation.
Readership/Target Audience: Aimed at tourists visiting London.
ADVERTISING RATES:
Full Page Colour £1790.00
Agency Commission: 10%
Mechanical Data: Col Length: 190mm, Film: Digital, No. of Columns (Display): 2, Type Area: 190 x 118mm, Bleed Size: 220 x 147mm, Trim Size: 210 x 137mm, Page Width: 118mm, Col Widths (Display): 91mm
Average advertising content per issue: 40%
CONSUMER: HOLIDAYS & TRAVEL: Entertainment Guides

LONDON PROPERTY
1899482U74K-796

Editorial Address: PR By email only **Tel:** 07879 012344
Email: editorial@ltppublications.com
Publisher: LTP Publications
Date Established: 2009
Frequency: Monthly
Free to qualifying individuals
Editor: Alastair Moxey; **Managing Director:** Lyndon Tiller
Summary of Content: Magazine featuring news, comment and in-depth articles on the capital's homes for sale and rent, house prices, market trends, celebrity moves and up and coming postcodes.
Readership/Target Audience: Aimed at those buying property in London.
Editions:
London Property Central & South
London Property Islington, City & Docklands
London Property North West & Central
CONSUMER: WOMEN'S INTEREST CONSUMER MAGAZINES: Home Purchase

LONDON REVIEW OF BOOKS
47547U84B-100

Editorial Address: 28 Little Russell Street, LONDON, WC1A 2HN **Tel:** 020 7209 1101 **Fax:** 020 7209 1102
Email: edit@lrb.co.uk
Advertising Address: As above. **Tel:** 020 7209 1131
Fax: 020 7209 1151
Email: ads@lrb.co.uk
Web site: http://www.lrb.co.uk
ISSN: 0260-9592
Publisher: LRB Ltd
Date Established: 1979
Frequency: 24 issues yearly - Published on Thursdays
Cover Price: £3.20
Annual Sub.: £70.80
Circulation: 48,265 (ABC 01/01/2008 to 31/12/2008)

Usual Pagination: 40
Editor: Mary-Kay Wilmers; **Advertising Director:** David Rose; **Publisher:** Nicholas Spice
Summary of Content: Magazine featuring the latest releases of books.
Readership/Target Audience: Aimed at intellectuals, writers, broadcasters, academics and philosophers.
ADVERTISING RATES:
Full Page Colour £4760.00
SCC £38.70
Mechanical Data: Type Area: 330 x 246mm, Col Length: 330mm, Trim Size: 372 x 274mm, Bleed Size: 380 x 278mm, Film: Digital, Page Width: 246mm
Copy instructions: Copy Date: 2 weeks prior to publication date
CONSUMER: THE ARTS & LITERARY: Literary

LONDON STUDENT
47411U83-34

Editorial Address: Malet Street, LONDON, WC1E 7HY **Tel:** 020 7664 2057
Email: editor@london-student.net
Advertising Address: BAM UK, 2nd Floor Offices, 8 Castle Square, SWANSEA, SA1 1DW **Tel:** 0845 130 0667
Fax: 0845 130 0668
Email: ad@bamuk.com
Publisher: University of London Union
Date Established: 1979
Frequency: 26 issues yearly
Cover Price: Free
Circulation: 10,000 (Print Run)
Usual Pagination: 36
Editor: Kat Lay
Summary of Content: Publication covering sport, arts, music, films and future careers.
Readership/Target Audience: Aimed at students in the London area.
ADVERTISING RATES:
Full Page Mono £980.00
Full Page Colour £980.00
Agency Commission: 10%
Mechanical Data: Film: Digital, Type Area: 369 x 272mm, Col Length: 369mm, Page Width: 272mm
Copy instructions: Copy Date: 1 week prior to publication date
Average advertising content per issue: 15%
CONSUMER: STUDENT PUBLICATIONS

THE LONDON VISITOR MAGAZINE
1745610U89C-1077

Formerly: The London Visitor
Editorial Address: 7-8 St. Stephens Mews, LONDON, W2 5QZ **Tel:** 020 7727 8000 **Fax:** 020 7221 6212
Email: nickb@valepublishing.co.uk
Advertising Address: As above.
Email: johnn@valepublishing.co.uk
Web site: http://www.thelondonvisitor.com
ISSN: 1751-293X
Publisher: Vale Publishing
Date Established: 2006
Frequency: Monthly
Cover Price: Free
Circulation: 100,000 (Print Run per month)
Usual Pagination: 100
Editor: Nick Buglione; **Managing Director:** Simon Haisman
Summary of Content: Magazine covering listings for theatre, music, dance, events, attractions, museums, art galleries, shopping, dining, pubs, clubs, accommodation and travel as well as feature articles, interviews and reviews.
Readership/Target Audience: Aimed at international and domestic visitors to London as well as London residents.
ADVERTISING RATES:
Full Page Mono £1320.00
Full Page Colour £1740.00
Mechanical Data: Type Area: 190 x 118mm, Bleed Size: 216 x 143mm, Trim Size: 210 x 137mm, Col Length: 190mm, Page Width: 118mm, Film: Digital
Average advertising content per issue: 40%
CONSUMER: HOLIDAYS & TRAVEL: Entertainment Guides

LONDON'S OWN
1794035U89C-1097

Editorial Address: Media House, 5 Broadway Court, High Street, CHESHAM, HP5 1EG **Tel:** 01494 771144
Fax: 01494 771277
Email: info@bpcmagazines.com
Advertising Address: As above.
Email: copy@bpcmagazines.com
Web site: http://www.bpcmagazines.com
Publisher: BPC Magazines
Date Established: 2005
Frequency: 3 issues yearly - Published in March, June and December
Cover Price: Free
Circulation: 30,000 (Publisher's Statement)
Usual Pagination: 48
Editor: Clare George; **Advertising Manager:** Stella Adams

Summary of Content: Magazine covering Irish related news, events, sport and places to go in London and the South East. Construction news in London, travel to and around Ireland, holidays in Northern Ireland and the Republic of Ireland, Irish pubs and restaurants and Irish food and drink. Irish business news, community news, charity news and events.
Readership/Target Audience: Aimed at Irish community living and working in London and South East.
ADVERTISING RATES:
Full Page Mono £1000.00
Full Page Colour £1000.00
Mechanical Data: Type Area: 277 x 190mm, Bleed Size: 303 x 216mm, Trim Size: 297 x 210, Film: Digital, Col Length: 277mm, Page Width: 190mm
CONSUMER: HOLIDAYS & TRAVEL: Entertainment Guides

LONDRA GAZETE
48315U90-957

Formerly: Toplum
Editorial Address: 177 Green Lanes, Palmers Green, LONDON, N13 4UR **Tel:** 020 8889 5025 **Fax:** 020 8889 5101
Email: news@londragazete.com
Advertising Address: As above.
Web site: http://www.londragazete.com
Publisher: Londra Gazete Ltd
Date Established: 1983
Frequency: Weekly - Published on Thursday
Cover Price: Free
Circulation: 22,500 (Publisher's Statement)
Usual Pagination: 56
Editor: Sanem Sahin
Summary of Content: Newspaper covering news, features, photos and sport concerning Turkish-speaking people in London and UK and summary of London, UK, Turkey and Cyprus news.
Language(s): English; Turkish
Readership/Target Audience: Aimed at the Turkish-speaking communities in Britain.
CONSUMER: ETHNIC

LONELY PLANET MAGAZINE
1855643U89A-751

Editorial Address: Media Centre, 201 Wood Lane, LONDON, W12 7TQ **Tel:** 020 8433 2000
Email: rory.goulding@bbc.com
Advertising Address: As above.
Email: arianne.salter@bbc.com
Publisher: BBC Worldwide Publishing
Date Established: 2008
Frequency: Monthly
Circulation: 40,702 (ABC 01/01/2009 to 30/06/2009)
Editor: Rory Goulding; **Features Editor:** Orla Thomas
Summary of Content: Magazine covering worldwide travel.
Readership/Target Audience: Aimed predominantly at frequent travellers with the time and means to indulge their passion.
ADVERTISING RATES:
SCC £50.00
CONSUMER: HOLIDAYS & TRAVEL: Travel

LOOK
1796543U74A-1029

Editorial Address: Blue Fin Building, 110 Southwark Street, LONDON, SE1 0SU **Tel:** 020 3148 5000 **Fax:** 020 3148 8112
Email: lookeditorial@ipcmedia.com
Advertising Address: As above.
Email: lindsay_dean@ipcmedia.com
Web site: http://www.look.co.uk
Publisher: IPC Connect Ltd
Date Established: 2007
Frequency: Weekly
Cover Price: £1.30
Circulation: 315,410 (ABC 01/01/2009 to 30/06/2009)
Usual Pagination: 108
Editor: Helen Francis; **News Editor:** Jonathan Bown; **Features Editor:** Jenny Wood; **Managing Director:** Fiona Dent; **Advertising Manager:** Lindsay Dean; **Managing Editor:** Duncan Baizley; **Publisher:** Tammi Iley
Summary of Content: Magazine covering high street fashion, celebrity style and gossip.
Twitter: https://twitter.com/Lookmagazine.
Readership/Target Audience: Aimed at women aged 18 to 30 years old.
ADVERTISING RATES:
Full Page Colour £14000.00
CONSUMER: WOMEN'S INTEREST CONSUMER MAGAZINES: Women's Interest

LOOK IT UP
1663954U80C-5209

Editorial Address: PO Box 29, 76-86 Walmgate, YORK, YO1 9YN **Tel:** 01904 653051 **Fax:** 01904 612853
Email: lynne.martin@thepress.co.uk
Advertising Address: As above. **Fax:** 01904 611488
Email: display@ycp.co.uk
Web site: http://www.yorkpress.co.uk
Publisher: York & County Press

Frequency: Monthly
Cover Price: Free
Circulation: 35,000 (Publisher's Statement)
Usual Pagination: 20
Editor: Lynne Martin; **Advertising Manager:** Louisa McCoy
Summary of Content: Magazine with local information, where to go with the children in the school holidays, health, beauty and local facts as well as competitions, puzzles and prizes.
Readership/Target Audience: Aimed at local families.
ADVERTISING RATES:
Full Page Colour £1100.00
Agency Commission: 10%
Mechanical Data: Trim Size: 260 x 180mm, Film: Digital
Copy instructions: Copy Date: 4 weeks prior to publication date
Average advertising content per issue: 50%
CONSUMER: RURAL & REGIONAL INTEREST: Regional Interest English Counties

LOONEY TUNES PRESENTS 1638847U91D-873
Formerly: Looney Tunes Comic
Editorial Address: Brockbourne House, Mount Ephraim, TUNBRIDGE WELLS, TN4 8BS **Tel:** 01892 500100
Fax: 01892 545666
Email: kvrhead@gmail.com
Advertising Address: Orange20 Ltd, Station House, Bunbury Way, EPSOM, KT17 4JP **Tel:** 01372 802800
Fax: 01372 723322
Email: michelle@o20.co.uk
Publisher: Panini UK Ltd
Date Established: 2004
Frequency: Quarterly
Cover Price: £2.50
Circulation: 50,000 (Publisher's Statement)
Usual Pagination: 52
Editor: Kate Rhead; **Advertising Manager:** Michelle Fairlamb
Summary of Content: Children's comic containing strip stories and activities featuring Looney Tunes characters.
Readership/Target Audience: Aimed at boys and girls aged 5 to 8 years old.
ADVERTISING RATES:
Full Page Colour £1500.00
CONSUMER: RECREATION & LEISURE: Children & Youth

LOTHIAN LEADER 47049U80E-100
Editorial Address: PO Box 6, HADDINGTON, EH41 3NQ
Tel: 01620 822578 **Fax:** 01620 822578
Email: allscotnews@btinternet.com
Advertising Address: As above.
Email: allscotnews@btinternet.com
Publisher: Rae-Lin Communications
Frequency: Monthly
Cover Price: £2.50
Annual Sub.: £30.00
Circulation: 1,200 (Publisher's Statement)
Usual Pagination: 18
Editor: Richard Brown; **Advertising Manager:** Richard Brown
Summary of Content: Magazine covering news, events and articles of local interest.
Readership/Target Audience: Read by residents in the Lothian area.
ADVERTISING: Rates on application
CONSUMER: RURAL & REGIONAL INTEREST: Regional Interest Scotland

LOUD 1692650U83-269
Editorial Address: The Busworks, United House, North Road, LONDON, N7 9DP **Tel:** 020 7609 4254
Fax: 020 7609 4424
Email: jude@fullonmag.co.uk
Advertising Address: As above.
Email: nosheen@fullonmag.co.uk
Web site: http://www.fullonmag.co.uk
Publisher: Full On Publications Ltd
Date Established: 2005
Frequency: 5 issues yearly
Cover Price: Free
Circulation: 50,000 (Publisher's Statement)
Usual Pagination: 68
Editor: Jude Schofield; **Advertising Manager:** Nosheen Riaz
Summary of Content: Magazine covering higher education as well as career choices, music, films, games and fashion.
Readership/Target Audience: Aimed at 16 to 19 year old students.
ADVERTISING: Rates on application
Agency Commission: 10%
Average advertising content per issue: 40%
CONSUMER: STUDENT PUBLICATIONS

LOVE IT! 1706910U74A-1006
Editorial Address: 2nd Floor, Swan House, 37-39 High Holborn, LONDON, WC1V 6AA **Tel:** 020 7421 5400
Email: yourstories@loveit.co.uk
Advertising Address: 2 Chelsea Manor Gardens, LONDON, SW3 5PN **Tel:** 020 7198 3000 **Fax:** 020 7198 3020
Email: harriet.edery@bauer.co.uk
Publisher: Hubert Burda Media UK
Date Established: 2006
Frequency: Weekly
Cover Price: £0.60
Circulation: 308,304 (ABC 01/01/2009 to 30/06/2009)
Editor: Siobhan Wykes; **Managing Director:** Luke Patten;
Advertising Manager: Harriet Edery
Summary of Content: Magazine covering real life stories, celebrity, sex and surgery.
Readership/Target Audience: Aimed at women 18 to 35 years old.
ADVERTISING RATES:
Full Page Colour £9000.00
Mechanical Data: Bleed Size: 306 x 226mm, Trim Size: 300 x 220mm, Film: Digital
Copy instructions: Copy Date: 2 weeks prior to publication date
Average advertising content per issue: 10%
CONSUMER: WOMEN'S INTEREST CONSUMER MAGAZINES: Women's Interest

LOVE MAGAZINE 1864961U74B-740
Editorial Address: 2nd Floor, Jamieson House, 146-148 Clerkenwell Road, LONDON, EC1R 5DG **Tel:** 020 7499 9080
Email: tim.cliftongreen@condenast.co.uk
Date Established: 2009
Frequency: Half-yearly
Circulation: 120,000 (Print Run)
Editor: Katie Grand
Summary of Content: Magazine featuring fashion news, reviews and luxury fashion.
Readership/Target Audience: Aimed at lovers of fashion.
CONSUMER: WOMEN'S INTEREST CONSUMER MAGAZINES: Women's Interest - Fashion

LRM LAND ROVER MONTHLY 46464U77E-188
Editorial Address: 2 Brickfield Business Park, Woolpit, BURY ST. EDMUNDS, IP30 9QS **Tel:** 01359 240066
Fax: 01359 244221
Email: editorial@lrm.co.uk
Advertising Address: As above. **Tel:** 01359 241444
Email: nick@lrm.co.uk
Web site: http://www.lrm.co.uk
ISSN: 1463-1202
Publisher: Golden Gate Production Company Ltd
Date Established: 1998
Frequency: Monthly
Cover Price: £3.95
Annual Sub.: £39.00
Circulation: 22,000 (Publisher's Statement)
Usual Pagination: 228
Editor: Francine Carrel; **Advertising Manager:** Nick King
Summary of Content: Magazine containing features on travel, technical aspects, innovations, tests, technology, special vehicles, classics, off-road sports and models.
Readership/Target Audience: Aimed at Land Rover, Range Rover, Discovery and Freelander enthusiasts.
ADVERTISING RATES:
Full Page Colour £600.00
Agency Commission: 10%
Mechanical Data: Type Area: 265 x 185mm, Bleed Size: 305 x 218mm, Trim Size: 297 x 210mm, Col Length: 265mm, Film: Digital, Page Width: 185mm
Copy instructions: Copy Date: 4 weeks prior to publication date
Average advertising content per issue: 40%
CONSUMER: MOTORING & CYCLING: Club Cars

LUCKY BAG COMIC 767606U91D-862
Editorial Address: Office Block 1, Southlink Business Park, Hamilton Street, OLDHAM, OL4 1DE **Tel:** 0161 624 0414
Fax: 0161 628 4655
Email: james.hill@toontastticpublishing.com
ISSN: 1477-3548
Publisher: Toontastic Publishing
Date Established: 2002
Frequency: Monthly
Cover Price: £2.99
Circulation: 30,000 (Publisher's Statement)
Usual Pagination: 32
Editor: James Hill; **Editor-in-Chief:** James Hill
Summary of Content: Children's magazine featuring original comic strip stories, jokes, puzzles, competitions and reviews. Features lifestyle content including movie previews/reviews, and movie merchandise prize give-aways.
Readership/Target Audience: Aimed at children between 6 and 12 years old.
ADVERTISING: No Advertising taken
CONSUMER: RECREATION & LEISURE: Children & Youth

LUCKY BREAK 1642462U79F-79
Editorial Address: 2nd Floor, Barclay House, 242-254 Banbury Road, OXFORD, OX2 7BY **Tel:** 01865 515840
Fax: 01865 556588
Email: alastair@prizemags.co.uk
Advertising Address: As above.
Email: tony@prizemags.co.uk
Web site: http://www.prizemagazines.com
Publisher: Prize Magazines
Frequency: 6 issues yearly
Annual Sub.: £21.00
Circulation: 60,000 (Publisher's Statement)
Usual Pagination: 52
Editor: Alastair Fry; **Advertising Manager:** Tony Lane
Summary of Content: Magazine covering crosswords and puzzles as well as entertainment reviews and gadgets.
Readership/Target Audience: Aimed at puzzle enthusiasts aged 25 years old plus.
ADVERTISING: Rates on application
Average advertising content per issue: 3%
CONSUMER: HOBBIES & DIY: Games & Puzzles

LUSSO 1660041U74Q-1237
Editorial Address: Suite 115, St Williams Court, 1 Gifford Street, LONDON, N1 0GN **Tel:** 0845 643 9651
Email: editorial@lussoluxury.com
Advertising Address: As above. **Tel:** 0845 643 9652
Email: dsharp@swrmedia.co.uk
Web site: http://www.lussoluxury.com
ISSN: 1745-6092
Publisher: SWR Media Ltd
Date Established: 2004
Frequency: Quarterly
Cover Price: £4.40
Annual Sub.: £16.00
Circulation: 15,222 (ABC 01/07/2008 to 31/12/2008)
Usual Pagination: 108
Editor: Greg Nasmyth; **Advertising Manager:** Daniel Sharp;
Publisher: Daniel Sharp
Summary of Content: Luxury lifestyle magazine covering motoring, yachting, flight, property, fashion, accessories, travel, sports, business, design, technology and the arts.
Readership/Target Audience: Aimed at 25 to 55 year old high earners, frequent travellers with an interest in expensive hobbies.
ADVERTISING RATES:
Full Page Colour £3960.00
Agency Commission: 10%
Mechanical Data: Type Area: 260 x 210mm, Col Length: 260mm, Page Width: 210mm, Bleed Size: 290 x 240mm, Trim Size: 280 x 230mm
Average advertising content per issue: 10%
CONSUMER: WOMEN'S INTEREST CONSUMER MAGAZINES: Lifestyle

LUTON & DUNSTABLE AT LARGE 1660393U80C-5211
Editorial Address: The Treacle Factory, 2A Reginald Street, LUTON, LU2 7QZ **Tel:** 01582 416171 **Fax:** 01582 416328
Email: editor@luton-at-large.co.uk
Advertising Address: As above.
Email: ian@luton-at-large.co.uk
Web site: http://www.luton-at-large.co.uk
Publisher: JNB Publishing
Frequency: Monthly
Cover Price: Free
Circulation: 10,000 (Publisher's Statement)
Usual Pagination: 32
Editor: Jeremy Brown; **Advertising Manager:** Ian Abrahams; **Publisher:** Ian Abrahams
Summary of Content: Magazine covering local news and events, bars, pubs, eating out, entertainment, DVD, video and cinema reviews.
Readership/Target Audience: Aimed at residents and visitors to Luton and Dunstable.
ADVERTISING RATES:
Full Page Colour £800.00
Agency Commission: 10%
Mechanical Data: Type Area: 291 x 204mm, Bleed Size: 301 x 214mm, Trim Size: 297 x 210mm, Col Length: 291mm, Page Width: 204mm, Film: Digital
Copy instructions: Copy Date: 15th of the month prior to publication
Average advertising content per issue: 40%
CONSUMER: RURAL & REGIONAL INTEREST: Regional Interest English Counties

LUX MAGAZINE 1800031U74Q-1349
Editorial Address: Durley House, 115 Sloane Street, LONDON, SW1X 9PJ **Tel:** 07775 532236
Email: jdgreyfriars@hotmail.co.uk
Advertising Address: C/ Camp Franc 2, 07194 Puigpuyent, MALLORCA **Tel:** 97 16 14 210 **Fax:** 97 16 14 234
Email: advertising@lux-mag.com
Web site: http://www.thesteingroup.com
Publisher: Lux Magazine Ltd

Consumer Magazines

Frequency: Quarterly
Cover Price: Free
Circulation: 24,000 (Publisher's Statement)
Usual Pagination: 126
Editor: Jim Dunn
Summary of Content: Lifestyle magazine covering watches, cars, travel, property, interiors, gardens and personal finance.
Readership/Target Audience: Aimed at customers of the Stein Group of 5 star hotels across Europe in city locations, resorts and country estates.
ADVERTISING: Rates on application
CONSUMER: WOMEN'S INTEREST CONSUMER MAGAZINES: Lifestyle

LUXOS
1685813U74Q-1413

Editorial Address: 1st Floor, 11 Poland Street, LONDON, W1F 8QA
Email: james@luxos.com
Advertising Address: Via Pietrasanta, 12, 20141, MILAN
Tel: 2 87 387 400
Email: james@luxos.com
Publisher: Luxe Publishing Ltd
Date Established: 2005
Frequency: Half-yearly - Published in April and September
Cover Price: Free
Circulation: 40,000 (Publisher's Statement)
Usual Pagination: 100
Editor: James Hill; **Advertising Manager:** James Hill;
Publisher: James Hill
Summary of Content: Magazine covering luxury travel and accommodation, luxury brands, restaurants and places to go.
Language(s): English; Italian; Spanish
Readership/Target Audience: Aimed at high end international and domestic travellers, business professionals, celebrities and cash rich but time poor individuals who stay in the best hotels in Italy and Spain.
ADVERTISING: Rates on application
Agency Commission: 10%
Average advertising content per issue: 25%
CONSUMER: WOMEN'S INTEREST CONSUMER MAGAZINES: Lifestyle

LUXX
1835479U74Q-1364

Editorial Address: 1 Pennington Street, LONDON, E98 1ST
Tel: 020 7782 5000 **Fax:** 020 7782 5075
Email: laura.lovett@thetimes.co.uk
Web site: http://www.timesonline.co.uk
Publisher: Times Newspapers Ltd
Date Established: 2007
Frequency: 6 issues yearly
Editor: Laura Lovett; **Executive Editor:** Gill Morgan
Summary of Content: Luxury lifestyle magazine covering beauty, fashion, style, shopping, travel and men's and women's interests.
Readership/Target Audience: Aimed at men and women readers of The Times aged 25 years old plus, with high disposable incomes.
Supplement to: The Times
CONSUMER: WOMEN'S INTEREST CONSUMER MAGAZINES: Lifestyle

MACCLESFIELD & DISTRICT LIFESTYLE MAGAZINE
46871U80C-675

Editorial Address: Summerhill Cottages, Macclesfield Road, ALDERLEY EDGE, SK9 7BG **Tel:** 01625 599909
Fax: 01625 599919
Email: ianlambert2000@aol.com
Advertising Address: As above.
Email: ianlambert2000@aol.com
Web site: http://www.macclesfieldlifestyle.co.uk
Publisher: Lambert and Tutton Colour Productions
Frequency: Quarterly
Cover Price: Free
Circulation: 20,000 (Publisher's Statement)
Editor: Ian Lambert; **Advertising Manager:** Ian Lambert
Summary of Content: Lifestyle magazine containing features of interest to local homes and businesses.
Readership/Target Audience: Aimed at AB income homes and businesses in villages throughout the Macclesfield area.
ADVERTISING RATES:
Full Page Mono £890.00
SCC £5.50
Agency Commission: 10%
Mechanical Data: Type Area: 297 x 210mm, Col Length: 297mm, Page Width: 210mm
Average advertising content per issue: 50%
CONSUMER: RURAL & REGIONAL INTEREST: Regional Interest English Counties

MACFORMAT
36171U78E-7

Editorial Address: 30 Monmouth Street, BATH, BA1 2BW
Tel: 01225 442244 **Fax:** 01225 732295

Email: macformat@futurenet.com
Advertising Address: As above. **Fax:** 01225 822885
Email: andrew.tilbury@futurenet.com
Web site: http://www.macformat.co.uk
ISSN: 1353-8519
Publisher: Future Publishing Ltd
Date Established: 1993
Frequency: 13 issues yearly - Published 1 month prior to cover date
Cover Price: £5.99
Annual Sub.: £49.95
Circulation: 29,447 (ABC 01/07/2008 to 31/12/2008)
Usual Pagination: 132
Editor: Graham Barlow; **Managing Director:** Robert Price;
Advertising Manager: Andrew Tilbury; **Publisher:** Stuart Anderton
Summary of Content: Magazine covering all aspects of Apple Mac computers. Includes news, reviews, product guides and other information relating to the industry.
Readership/Target Audience: Read by users of Apple Mac computers and those with an interest in computer hardware and software.
ADVERTISING RATES:
Full Page Colour £1825.00
Agency Commission: 10%
Mechanical Data: Film: Digital, Type Area: 280 x 213mm, Bleed Size: 306 x 238mm, Trim Size: 300 x 232mm, Col Length: 280mm, Page Width: 213mm
Copy instructions: Copy Date: 4 weeks prior to publication date
CONSUMER: CONSUMER ELECTRONICS: Home Computing

MACHINE KNITTING MONTHLY
45361U74E-240

Editorial Address: PO Box 1479, MAIDENHEAD, SL6 9YX
Tel: 01628 783080 **Fax:** 01628 633250
Email: mail@machineknittingmonthly.net
Advertising Address: As above.
Email: mail@machineknittingmonthly.net
Web site: http://www.machineknittingmonthly.net
ISSN: 0269-9761
Publisher: RPA Publishing Limited
Date Established: 1986
Frequency: Monthly
Cover Price: £3.25
Free to qualifying individuals
Annual Sub.: £39.00
Usual Pagination: 64
Editor: Anne Smith; **Advertising Manager:** Anne Smith
Summary of Content: Magazine covering all aspects of machine knitting. Includes patterns and product reviews.
Readership/Target Audience: Aimed at machine knitters of all ages.
ADVERTISING RATES:
Full Page Mono £464.00
Full Page Colour £512.00
Agency Commission: 20%
Mechanical Data: Type Area: 266 x 180mm, Col Length: 266mm, Trim Size: 297 x 210mm, Bleed Size: 303 x 213mm, Print Process: Web-fed offset litho, Page Width: 180mm, Film: Digital
Copy instructions: Copy Date: 1st of the second month prior to publication date
CONSUMER: WOMEN'S INTEREST CONSUMER MAGAZINES: Crafts

MACUSER
36172U78E-10

Editorial Address: 30 Cleveland Street, LONDON, W1T 4JD
Tel: 020 7907 6000
Email: nik@nikrawlinson.com
Advertising Address: As above. **Fax:** 020 7907 6600
Email: guy_scott-wilson@dennis.co.uk
Web site: http://www.macuser.co.uk
Publisher: Dennis Publishing Ltd
Frequency: 25 issues yearly
Cover Price: £3.99
Circulation: 13,249 (ABC 01/01/2008 to 31/12/2008)
Usual Pagination: 120
Editor: Nik Rawlinson
Summary of Content: Journal covering Mac news, reviews, buying information and technical advice.
Readership/Target Audience: Aimed at Mac users and computer specifiers in the business sector.
ADVERTISING RATES:
Full Page Colour £2952.00
Agency Commission: 10%
Mechanical Data: Page Width: 185mm, Film: Digital, Trim Size: 297 x 210mm, Type Area: 275 x 185mm, Col Length: 275mm, Bleed Size: 303 x 216mm
Copy instructions: Copy Date: 3 weeks prior to publication date
CONSUMER: CONSUMER ELECTRONICS: Home Computing

MACWORLD
36173U78E-15

Editorial Address: 4th Floor, 101 Euston Road, LONDON, NW1 2RA **Tel:** 020 7756 2877
Email: news@macworld.co.uk
Advertising Address: As above. **Tel:** 020 7756 2800
Fax: 020 7756 2838
Email: advertising@macworld.co.uk
Web site: http://www.macworld.co.uk
ISSN: 1356-9503
Publisher: IDG (International Data Group)
Date Established: 1989
Frequency: 14 issues yearly
Cover Price: £5.99
Circulation: 20,466 (ABC 01/01/2008 to 31/12/2008)
Usual Pagination: 130
Editor: Karen Haslam; **Editor-in-Chief:** Mark Hattersley;
Advertising Manager: James Poulson; **Publisher:** Mustafa Mustafa
Summary of Content: Magazine covering news, features and reviews on Macintosh computers.
Readership/Target Audience: Aimed at Mac-dedicated users and corporate purchasers.
ADVERTISING RATES:
Full Page Colour £3585.00
Agency Commission: 10%
Mechanical Data: Type Area: 275 x 185mm, Col Length: 275mm, Page Width: 185mm, Trim Size: 297 x 210mm, Bleed Size: 303 x 216mm, Film: Digital
Copy instructions: Copy Date: 10 days prior to publication date
Average advertising content per issue: 40%
CONSUMER: CONSUMER ELECTRONICS: Home Computing

MADE IN LEEDS
1824282U80C-5432

Editorial Address: Mill 7, Mabgate Mill, LEEDS, LS9 7DZ
Tel: 0113 244 3169 **Fax:** 0113 243 5903
Email: info@made-mag.co.uk
Advertising Address: As above.
Email: nina@made-mag.co.uk
Web site: http://www.made-mag.co.uk
Publisher: Made Publishing Ltd
Date Established: 2007
Frequency: 6 issues yearly
Cover Price: Free
Circulation: 30,000 (Publisher's Statement)
Usual Pagination: 132
Editor: Jason Daniel; **Advertising Manager:** Nina Ricks;
Publisher: Jason Daniel
Summary of Content: Lifestyle magazine covering fashion, health and beauty, interiors, business, property, music, entertainment, bars, restaurants, food and wine, hotels, travel and local news.
Readership/Target Audience: Aimed at residents, businesses and visitors to Leeds.
ADVERTISING: Rates on application
CONSUMER: RURAL & REGIONAL INTEREST: Regional Interest English Counties

THE MAGAZINE
46101U76C-242

Editorial Address: Media Wales, Park Street, CARDIFF, CF10 1XR **Tel:** 029 2058 3683 **Fax:** 029 2058 3652
Email: hannah.jones@mediawales.co.uk
Advertising Address: Western Mail, Thomson House, Havelock Street, CARDIFF, CF10 1XR **Tel:** 029 2058 3701
Fax: 029 2058 3495
Email: charlotte.payne@mediawales.co.uk
Web site: http://www.walesonline.co.uk
Publisher: Trinity Mirror
Frequency: Weekly - Published on Saturday, See main record for circulation figure
Free to qualifying individuals
Usual Pagination: 64
Editor: Hannah Jones; **Advertising Manager:** Charlotte Payne
Summary of Content: Magazine containing a guide to television programmes for Wales. Includes articles on fashion, food and drink, shopping, travel and book reviews.
Readership/Target Audience: Aimed at home entertainment enthusiasts.
ADVERTISING RATES:
Full Page Colour £960.00
Agency Commission: 10%
Mechanical Data: Bleed Size: 307 x 220mm, Trim Size: 266 x 185mm, Film: Digital
Copy instructions: Copy Date: 2 weeks prior to publication date
Average advertising content per issue: 50%
Supplement to: Western Mail (Cardiff)
CONSUMER: MUSIC & PERFORMING ARTS: TV & Radio

THE MAGDALEN
47457U83-77_90

Formerly: Student Times
Editorial Address: University of Dundee, Students Association, Airlie Place, DUNDEE, DD1 4HP
Tel: 01382 386060 **Fax:** 01382 386061

Email: vpc@dusa.co.uk
Advertising Address: As above.
Email: vpc@dusa.co.uk
Web site: http://www.dusa.co.uk
Publisher: Dundee University Publications Board
Frequency: Monthly
Cover Price: Free
Circulation: 4,000 (Publisher's Statement)
Usual Pagination: 28
Editor: Dave MacLeod; **Advertising Manager:** Martin Gribbon
Summary of Content: Magazine covering news around the campus, arts and culture, sport, music and general interest.
Readership/Target Audience: Distributed to the University and Art College in Dundee.
ADVERTISING RATES:
Full Page Colour £400.00
Agency Commission: 10%
Mechanical Data: Trim Size: 297 x 210mm, Bleed Size: 303 x 216mm
CONSUMER: STUDENT PUBLICATIONS

THE MAGHREB REVIEW
601240U90-92

Editorial Address: 45 Burton Street, LONDON, WC1H 9AL
Tel: 020 7388 1840 **Fax:** 020 7388 1840
Email: maghreb@maghrebreview.com
Advertising Address: As above.
Email: maghreb@maghrebreview.com
Web site: http://www.maghrebreview.com
ISSN: 0309-457X
Publisher: The Maghreb Review
Date Established: 1976
Frequency: Quarterly
Annual Sub.: £250.00
Circulation: 10,000 (Publisher's Statement)
Usual Pagination: 144
Editor: Mohamed Ben-Madani; **Advertising Manager:** Mohamed Ben-Madani
Summary of Content: Journal containing scholarly articles, review articles and thesis abstracts on all aspects of North Africa, Middle East and Africa from 600 AD to the present.
Language(s): English; French
Readership/Target Audience: Aimed at academics, students and specialists.
ADVERTISING RATES:
Full Page Mono £285.00
Mechanical Data: Film: Digital, Type Area: 245 x 172mm, Col Length: 245mm, Page Width: 172mm
CONSUMER: ETHNIC

THE MAGIC CIRCULAR (MAGAZINE)
46773U79L-200

Formerly: The Magic Circle
Editorial Address: 5 Folkington Corner, Woodside Park, LONDON, N12 7BH **Tel:** 020 8445 7607 **Fax:** 020 8445 7607
Advertising Address: As above.
Publisher: The Magic Circle
Date Established: 1906
Frequency: Monthly
Free to qualifying individuals
Usual Pagination: 40
Editor: Alan Snowden; **Advertising Manager:** Scott Penrose
Summary of Content: Magazine covering the history of magic, magic tricks and international magic news and events.
Readership/Target Audience: Aimed at magicians, members of the Magic Circle in 40 countries and those interested in joining the Magic Circle.
ADVERTISING RATES:
Full Page Mono £100.00
Full Page Colour £175.00
Mechanical Data: Type Area: 297 x 211mm, Col Length: 297mm, Page Width: 211mm
Copy instructions: Copy Date: 1 month prior to publication date
Average advertising content per issue: 10%
CONSUMER: HOBBIES & DIY: Fantasy Games & Science Fiction

MAGNET
46989U80C-3210

Formerly: Magnet -The Village Communicator
Editorial Address: 18 Silver Oaks Farm, Waldron, HEATHFIELD, TN21 0RS **Tel:** 0845 872 2885
Fax: 01435 810472
Email: magnet@magnetpublications.com
Advertising Address: As above.
Email: magnet@magnetpublications.com
Web site: http://www.magnetpublications.com
Publisher: Magnet Publications
Date Established: 1987
Frequency: Monthly
Cover Price: Free
Circulation: 30,000 (Publisher's Statement)
Usual Pagination: 48

Editor: Adele Trathan; **Advertising Manager:** Mary Hillyar
Summary of Content: Local interest magazine featuring events listings, lifestyle articles and news.
Readership/Target Audience: Read by the older, affluent generation, living in country areas of East Sussex and Kent.
ADVERTISING RATES:
Full Page Colour £850.00
Agency Commission: 10%
Mechanical Data: Film: Digital, Type Area: 270 x 184mm, Col Length: 270mm, No. of Columns (Display): 4, Page Width: 184mm
Copy instructions: Copy Date: 15th of the month prior to publication date
Average advertising content per issue: 50%
CONSUMER: RURAL & REGIONAL INTEREST: Regional Interest English Counties

MAILOUT
47503U84A-305

Editorial Address: 87 New Square, CHESTERFIELD, S40 1AH **Tel:** 01246 207070 **Fax:** 01246 238319
Email: editor@e-mailout.org
Advertising Address: As above.
Email: info@e-mailout.org
Web site: http://www.e-mailout.org
Publisher: The Mailout Trust
Date Established: 1986
Frequency: 6 issues yearly
Cover Price: £4.00
Annual Sub.: £18.00
Circulation: 1,300 (Publisher's Statement)
Usual Pagination: 32
Editor: Rob Howell
Summary of Content: Magazine covering news, events and features on participatory arts. Includes articles on music projects, dance, theatre, art and funding.
Readership/Target Audience: Read by those interested in participatory arts.
ADVERTISING RATES:
Full Page Mono £330.00
Agency Commission: 10%
Mechanical Data: Type Area: 277 x 190mm, Col Length: 277mm, Film: Digital, Page Width: 190mm
Copy instructions: Copy Date: 1 month prior to publication date
Average advertising content per issue: 9%
CONSUMER: THE ARTS & LITERARY: Arts

MAJESTY
45643U74Q-1120

Editorial Address: 64 Charlotte Street, LONDON, W1T 4QD
Tel: 020 7436 4006 **Fax:** 020 7436 3458
Email: joelittle@majestymagazine.com
Advertising Address: 89 Warren Road, ORPINGTON, BR6 6JE **Tel:** 01689 860082 **Fax:** 01689 860136
Email: majestyads@aol.com
Web site: http://www.majestymagazine.com
ISSN: 0144-6932
Publisher: Rex Publications Ltd
Date Established: 1980
Frequency: Monthly
Cover Price: £2.95
Circulation: 60,000 (Publisher's Statement)
Usual Pagination: 66
Editor: Joe Little; **Editor-in-Chief:** Ingrid Seward; **Managing Director:** Cliff Moulder; **Managing Editor:** Joe Little
Summary of Content: Magazine containing articles about the personalities and lifestyles of the British and worldwide royal families.
Readership/Target Audience: Aimed at those interested in the monarchy in Britain and worldwide.
ADVERTISING RATES:
Full Page Colour £2000.00
Agency Commission: 10%
Mechanical Data: Trim Size: 297 x 210mm, Bleed Size: 303 x 216mm
CONSUMER: WOMEN'S INTEREST CONSUMER MAGAZINES: Lifestyle

MAKING JEWELLERY
1895903U88D-42

Editorial Address: 86 High Street, LEWES, BN7 1XN
Tel: 01273 477374 **Fax:** 01273 487692
Email: heatherg@gmcgroup.com
Advertising Address: As above.
Web site: http://www.makingjewellery.com
Publisher: GMC Publications Ltd
Frequency: Monthly
Annual Sub.: £47.00
Circulation: 25,000 (Publisher's Statement)
Editor: Joan Gordon
Summary of Content: Magazine featuring projects, techniques, inspiration and expert guidance to make jewellery.
Readership/Target Audience: Aimed at anybody with an interest in jewellery making.
CONSUMER: EDUCATION: Crafts

MAN ABOUT TOWN
1824364U86C-741

Editorial Address: 133 Notting Hill Gate, LONDON, W11 3LB **Tel:** 020 7243 9966 **Fax:** 020 7243 9967
Advertising Address: As above.
Email: job@wonderlandmagazine.com
Web site: http://www.manabouttownonline.com
Publisher: Visual Talent Ltd
Date Established: 2007
Frequency: Half-yearly - Published in September and February
Cover Price: £5.00
Circulation: 140,000 (Publisher's Statement)
Editor: Lauren Blane; **Advertising Director:** Job Musters
Summary of Content: Magazine covering fashion, style, art, film and design.
Readership/Target Audience: Aimed at men with a high disposable income.
ADVERTISING RATES:
Full Page Mono £7000.00
Full Page Colour £7000.00
Agency Commission: 15%
Mechanical Data: Film: Digital
Copy instructions: Copy Date: 3 weeks prior to publication date
Average advertising content per issue: 35%
CONSUMER: ADULT & GAY MAGAZINES: Men's Lifestyle Magazines

MANCHESTER CITY MAGAZINE
45768U75B-147

Editorial Address: 1 Scott Place, Hardman Street, MANCHESTER, M3 3RN **Tel:** 0161 211 2301
Fax: 0161 834 9122
Email: david.clayton@men-news.co.uk
Advertising Address: As above. **Fax:** 0161 832 0345
Email: david.hendry@menmediasales.co.uk
Web site: http://www.mcfc.co.uk
Publisher: Manchester Evening News Ltd
Date Established: 1995
Frequency: Monthly
Cover Price: £2.50
Circulation: 16,000 (Publisher's Statement)
Usual Pagination: 68
Editor: David Clayton; **Editor-in-Chief:** Peter Spencer
Summary of Content: Official magazine of the Manchester City Football Club. Covers all club affairs including new signings, match reports and previews with player features.
Readership/Target Audience: Aimed at fans of the Club.
ADVERTISING RATES:
Full Page Colour £875.00
Agency Commission: 15%
Mechanical Data: Page Width: 186mm, Film: Digital, Type Area: 273 x 186mm, Trim Size: 297 x 210mm, Bleed Size: 303 x 213mm, Col Length: 273mm
Copy instructions: Copy Date: 1 week prior to publication date
Average advertising content per issue: 15%
CONSUMER: SPORT: Football

MANX TAILS
48212U80H-71

Editorial Address: Media House, Cronkbourne, DOUGLAS, IM4 4SB **Tel:** 01624 696565 **Fax:** 01624 625623
Email: simonrichardson@manninmedia.co.im
Advertising Address: As above.
Email: johntaylor@manninmedia.co.uk
Web site: http://www.manninmedia.co.im
Publisher: Executive Publications
Frequency: Monthly
Cover Price: Free
Circulation: 37,000 (Publisher's Statement)
Usual Pagination: 72
Editor: Simon Richardson
Summary of Content: Magazine covering news and events on the Isle of Man.
Readership/Target Audience: Read by residents of the Isle of Man.
ADVERTISING RATES:
Full Page Colour £695.00
Agency Commission: 10%
Mechanical Data: Col Length: 186mm, No. of Columns (Display): 2, Type Area: 186 x 124mm, Bleed Size: 216 x 154mm, Page Width: 124mm, Film: Digital
Copy instructions: Copy Date: 3 weeks prior to publication date
Average advertising content per issue: 40%
CONSUMER: RURAL & REGIONAL INTEREST: Regional Interest Isle of Man

MAP
1666935U84A-441

Editorial Address: 13 Perth Road, DUNDEE, DD1 4HT
Tel: 01382 381018
Email: editor@mapmagazine.co.uk
Advertising Address: As above. **Fax:** 0131 557 8500
Email: advertising@mapmagazine.co.uk
Web site: http://www.mapmagazine.co.uk
ISSN: 1745-4484

Consumer Magazines

Publisher: Map Magazine Ltd
Date Established: 2005
Frequency: Quarterly
Cover Price: £4.95
Circulation: 5,000 (Print Run)
Usual Pagination: 64
Editor: Alice Bain; **Advertising Manager:** Georgina Le Breuilly
Summary of Content: Contemporary art magazine with features on artists in Scotland and those with a particular connection to Scotland with features and profiles of artists, reviews of UK and international events and exhibitions, news and special commissions from artists.
Readership/Target Audience: Aimed at artists and art professionals as well as those with an interest in visual arts.
ADVERTISING RATES:
Full Page Colour £590.00
Agency Commission: 10%
Mechanical Data: Type Area: 247 x 193mm, Bleed Size: 283 x 227mm, Trim Size: 277 x 221mm, Col Length: 247mm, Page Width: 193mm, Film: Digital
Average advertising content per issue: 20%
CONSUMER: THE ARTS & LITERARY: Arts

MARIE CLAIRE
45183U74A-320
Editorial Address: Blue Fin Building, 110 Southwark Street, LONDON, SE1 0SU **Tel:** 020 3148 5000 **Fax:** 020 3148 8120
Email: marieclaire@ipcmedia.com
Advertising Address: As above.
Email: helen_walsh@ipcmedia.com
Web site: http://www.marieclaire.co.uk
Publisher: IPC Southbank
Date Established: 1988
Frequency: Monthly
Cover Price: £3.40
Circulation: 285,307 (ABC 01/01/2009 to 30/06/2009)
Usual Pagination: 350
Editor: Trish Halpin
Summary of Content: Magazine containing articles on fashion, beauty, health, interiors and worldwide socio-political issues.
Twitter: http://twitter.com/marieclaireuk
Readership/Target Audience: Read by professional women aged 20 years and over.
ADVERTISING RATES:
Full Page Colour £18975.00
Agency Commission: 15%
Mechanical Data: Type Area: 239 x 183mm, Col Length: 239mm, Page Width: 183mm, Bleed Size: 276 x 219mm, Trim Size: 269 x 213mm, Film: Digital, Print Process: Web-fed offset litho
Copy instructions: Copy Date: 8 weeks prior to publication date
CONSUMER: WOMEN'S INTEREST CONSUMER MAGAZINES: Women's Interest

MARINE MODELLING INTERNATIONAL
46597U79B-30
Editorial Address: Traplet House, Pendragon Close, MALVERN, WR14 1GA **Tel:** 01684 588500
Fax: 01684 578558
Email: mmi@traplet.com
Advertising Address: As above. **Tel:** 01684 595500
Email: advertising@traplet.com
Web site: http://www.marinemodelmagazine.com
ISSN: 1746-8590
Publisher: Traplet Publications Ltd
Date Established: 1985
Frequency: Monthly - Published the last Thursday of every month
Cover Price: £3.50
Annual Sub.: £34.95
Usual Pagination: 84
Editor: Barrie Stevens; **Managing Director:** Tony Stephenson; **Advertising Manager:** Vivienne Hill
Summary of Content: Magazine containing an overall view of marine modelling.
Readership/Target Audience: Aimed at amateur model makers and professionals.
ADVERTISING RATES:
Full Page Mono £336.00
Full Page Colour £653.00
SCC £12.00
Agency Commission: 10%
Mechanical Data: Type Area: 270 x 184mm, Col Length: 270mm, Page Width: 184mm, Trim Size: 297 x 210mm, Film: Digital
Copy instructions: Copy Date: 6 weeks prior to publication date
CONSUMER: HOBBIES & DIY: Models & Modelling

THE MARSHWOOD VALE MAGAZINE
1623325U80C-5062
Editorial Address: Lower Atrim, BRIDPORT, DT6 5PX
Tel: 01308 423031
Email: info@marshwoodvale.com

Advertising Address: As above.
Email: sales@marshwoodvale.com
Web site: http://www.marshwoodvale.com
Publisher: Marshwood Vale Ltd
Date Established: 2000
Frequency: Monthly
Cover Price: Free
Circulation: 23,000 (Publisher's Statement)
Usual Pagination: 88
Editor: Fergus Byrne; **Advertising Manager:** Fergus Byrne
Summary of Content: Magazine for the community covering local events, arts and entertainment, food, dining, house, gardens, health and environment.
Readership/Target Audience: Aimed predominantly at people aged over 30 years old in Devon, Dorset and Somerset.
ADVERTISING RATES:
Full Page Mono £310.00
Full Page Colour £310.00
SCC £2.75
Agency Commission: 10%
Mechanical Data: No. of Columns (Display): 5
Copy instructions: Copy Date: Middle of the month prior to publication date
Average advertising content per issue: 50%
CONSUMER: RURAL & REGIONAL INTEREST: Regional Interest English Counties

MARTIAL ARTS ILLUSTRATED
45990U75Q-400
Editorial Address: Revenue Chambers, St. Peter's Street, HUDDERSFIELD, HD1 1DL **Tel:** 01484 435011
Fax: 01484 422177
Email: martialartsltd@btconnect.com
Advertising Address: As above.
Email: martialartsltd@btconnect.com
Web site: http://www.martialartsltd.co.uk
ISSN: 0955-5447
Publisher: Martial Arts Ltd
Date Established: 1988
Frequency: Monthly
Cover Price: £3.75
Annual Sub.: £39.95
Circulation: 30,000 (Publisher's Statement)
Usual Pagination: 164
Editor: Bob Sykes
Summary of Content: Magazine covering articles on techniques, tournament results and martial arts profiles.
Readership/Target Audience: Aimed at beginners to black belt.
ADVERTISING RATES:
Full Page Colour £400.00
Agency Commission: 10%
Mechanical Data: Bleed Size: + 3mm, Film: Positive, right reading, emulsion side down, Type Area: 271 x 186mm, Col Length: 271mm, Page Width: 186mm, Trim Size: 297 x 210mm
Copy instructions: Copy Date: 6 weeks prior to publication date
CONSUMER: SPORT: Combat Sports

MARY HICKMOTT'S NEW STITCHES
27750U74E-270
Editorial Address: Well Oast, Brenley Lane, Boughton-under-Blean, FAVERSHAM, ME13 9LY **Tel:** 01227 750215
Fax: 01227 750813
Email: janice@ccpuk.co.uk
Advertising Address: Ewell House, Graveney Road, FAVERSHAM, ME13 8UP **Tel:** 01795 542417
Fax: 01795 542401
Email: melanier@deeson.co.uk
Web site: http://www.newstitches.com
ISSN: 0967-5884
Publisher: Creative Crafts Publishing Ltd
Date Established: 1991
Frequency: Monthly
Cover Price: £3.99
Annual Sub.: £39.95
Usual Pagination: 76
Editor: Janice Broadstock; **Advertising Manager:** Melanie Richards; **Publisher:** Iain Bowers
Summary of Content: Magazine containing needlework designs and reviews.
Readership/Target Audience: Aimed at women aged 25 years old and over.
ADVERTISING RATES:
Full Page Mono £600.00
Full Page Colour £600.00
Agency Commission: 10%
Average advertising content per issue: 20%
CONSUMER: WOMEN'S INTEREST CONSUMER MAGAZINES: Crafts

MARYLEBONE JOURNAL
1911484U80B-476
Editorial Address: Unit 11 La Gare, 51 Surrey Row, LONDON, SE1 0BZ **Tel:** 020 7401 7297
Email: mark@lscpublishing.com

Advertising Address: As above. **Tel:** 020 7401 2772
Email: donna@lscpublishing.com
Web site: http://www.themarylebonejournal.com
Publisher: LSC Publishing
Date Established: 2005
Frequency: 6 issues yearly
Free to qualifying individuals
Annual Sub.: £12.00
Circulation: 20,000 (Publisher's Statement)
Editor: Mark Riddaway
Summary of Content: Journal featuring articles covering the culture, history, food, architecture, property and shops of Marylebone.
Readership/Target Audience: Aimed at those living in or around Marylebone and those who shop and relax there.
ADVERTISING RATES:
Full Page Colour £1100.00
CONSUMER: RURAL & REGIONAL INTEREST: Regional Interest Greater London

MASSIVE
47412U83-37_20
Editorial Address: City University, Northampton Square, LONDON, EC1V 0HB **Tel:** 020 7040 5606
Fax: 020 7040 5601
Email: vpcomms@city.ac.uk
Advertising Address: As above.
Email: vpcomms@city.ac.uk
Web site: http://www.cusuonline.org
Publisher: City University Students' Union
Frequency: 6 issues yearly
Cover Price: Free
Circulation: 5,000 (Publisher's Statement)
Usual Pagination: 24
Editor: Marcus Mikely; **Advertising Manager:** Mudassar Aras
Summary of Content: Student magazine for the City University, covering national news and items of interest.
Readership/Target Audience: Aimed at students of City University.
ADVERTISING RATES:
Full Page Colour £400.00
Mechanical Data: Film: Digital, Bleed Size: 307 x 220mm, Trim Size: 297 x 210mm
Copy instructions: Copy Date: 3 weeks prior to publication date
CONSUMER: STUDENT PUBLICATIONS

MASTER & MULTITUDE
47830U87-156_20
Editorial Address: 4 Harrier Court, Woodside Road, Slip End, LUTON, LU1 4DQ **Tel:** 01582 841141
Fax: 01582 841145
Email: oamission@btinternet.com
Web site: http://www.oamission.com
Publisher: Open Air Mission
Date Established: 1853
Frequency: Quarterly
Cover Price: Free
Circulation: 5,800 (Publisher's Statement)
Usual Pagination: 16
Editor: Andy Banton
Summary of Content: Publication containing reports of evangelical work done by the Mission.
Language(s): English; Welsh
Readership/Target Audience: Aimed at present and prospective supporters.
ADVERTISING: No Advertising taken
CONSUMER: RELIGIOUS

MASTER DETECTIVE
31038U94X-80
Editorial Address: PO Box 735, LONDON, SE26 5NQ
Tel: 020 8778 0514 **Fax:** 020 8776 8260
Email: enquiries@truecrimelibrary.com
Advertising Address: As above.
Email: declan@truecrimelibrary.com
Web site: http://www.truecrimelibrary.com
Publisher: Magazine Design & Publishing Co Ltd
Date Established: 1945
Frequency: Monthly
Cover Price: £2.20
Annual Sub.: £20.40
Circulation: 30,000 (Publisher's Statement)
Usual Pagination: 54
Editor: Mike James; **Advertising Manager:** Declan Meehan
Summary of Content: Magazine covering all aspects of criminology.
Readership/Target Audience: Aimed at those interested in criminology.
ADVERTISING: Rates on application
CONSUMER: OTHER CLASSIFICATIONS: Miscellaneous

MATCH
45770U75B-150
Editorial Address: Media House, Lynchwood, Peterborough Business Park, PETERBOROUGH, PE2 6EA
Tel: 01733 468000

Email: match.magazine@bauermedia.co.uk
Advertising Address: Endeavour House, 189 Shaftesbury Avenue, LONDON, WC2H 8JG **Tel:** 020 7437 9011
Fax: 020 7295 5400
Email: nima.shahraz@baueradvertising.co.uk
Web site: http://www.matchmag.co.uk
Publisher: Bauer Consumer Media Ltd (Media House)
Frequency: Weekly
Cover Price: £1.80
Circulation: 100,007 (ABC 01/01/2008 to 31/12/2008)
Usual Pagination: 68
Editor: James Bandy; **Features Editor:** Matt Read; **Managing Director:** Rob Munro-Hall; **Advertising Manager:** Nima Shahraz
Summary of Content: Football magazine covering interviews, match descriptions, colour photos, posters, quizzes, facts and figures.
Readership/Target Audience: Aimed at boys between 9 and 15 who play and watch football.
ADVERTISING RATES:
Full Page Mono £6053.00
Full Page Colour £6554.00
Agency Commission: 10%
Mechanical Data: Type Area: 281 x 194mm, Bleed Size: 303 x 216mm, Trim Size: 297 x 210mm, Col Length: 281mm, Page Width: 194mm, Film: Digital
Copy instructions: Copy Date: 1 week prior to publication date
CONSUMER: SPORT: Football

MATCH FISHING MAGAZINE
48535U92-79
Editorial Address: 2 Stephenson Close, Drayton Fields Industrial Estate, DAVENTRY, NN11 8RF **Tel:** 01327 311999
Fax: 01327 311190
Email: dave.harrell@dhpub.co.uk
Advertising Address: As above. **Fax:** 01327 312418
Web site: http://www.total-fishing.com
ISSN: 0958-9023
Publisher: David Hall Publishing Ltd
Date Established: 1985
Frequency: Monthly
Cover Price: £3.25
Annual Sub.: £37.80
Circulation: 20,000 (Publisher's Statement)
Usual Pagination: 132
Editor: Dave Harrell
Summary of Content: Magazine containing technical advice, match fishing news and new product reviews.
Readership/Target Audience: Aimed at competitive anglers.
ADVERTISING: Rates on application
CONSUMER: ANGLING & FISHING

MATCH OF THE DAY MAGAZINE
1835415U75B-294
Editorial Address: Media Centre, 201 Wood Lane, LONDON, W12 7TQ **Tel:** 020 8433 2926 **Fax:** 020 8433 3294
Email: shout@motdmag.com
Web site: http://www.motdmag.com
Publisher: BBC Magazines
Date Established: 2008
Frequency: Weekly
Cover Price: £1.90
Usual Pagination: 68
Editor: Ian Foster
Summary of Content: Magazine covering football skills, features on players, news and gossip as well as competitions, posters and quizzes.
Readership/Target Audience: Aimed at girls and boys aged 8 to 14 years old.
CONSUMER: SPORT: Football

MATCHBOX
1746022U74Q-1321
Editorial Address: Studio 3C, 249-251 Kensal Road, LONDON, W10 5DB **Tel:** 020 8969 3069 **Fax:** 020 8969 3069
Email: editorial@matchboxmag.com
Advertising Address: As above.
Email: advertising@matchboxmag.com
Web site: http://www.matchboxmag.com
ISSN: 1747-9983
Publisher: Vie Europe Ltd
Date Established: 2006
Frequency: Monthly
Cover Price: Free
Circulation: 35,000 (Publisher's Statement)
Usual Pagination: 86
Editor: Laura Creal; **Advertising Director:** Chris Jenkin
Summary of Content: West London's monthly entertainment and lifestyle guide covering events, style, music, film, arts, food, travel, property and interiors.
Readership/Target Audience: Aimed at cultivated men and women aged 25 to 46 years old with a high disposable income.
ADVERTISING RATES:
Full Page Colour £1260.00
Agency Commission: 10%

Mechanical Data: Type Area: 245 x 175mm, Bleed Size: 271 x 201mm, Trim Size: 265 x 195mm, Col Length: 245mm, Page Width: 175mm, Print Process: Sheet-fed litho, Film: Digital
Average advertising content per issue: 30%
CONSUMER: WOMEN'S INTEREST CONSUMER MAGAZINES: Lifestyle

MATSIDE MAGAZINE
1706770U75Q-851
Editorial Address: Suite B, Loughborough Technology Centre, Epinal Way, LOUGHBOROUGH, LE11 3GE
Tel: 01509 631695 **Fax:** 01509 631680
Email: nicola.turner@britishjudo.org.uk
Advertising Address: As above.
Email: nicola.turner@britishjudo.org.uk
Web site: http://www.britishjudo.org.uk
Publisher: The British Judo Association
Frequency: Quarterly
Free to qualifying individuals
Annual Sub.: £16.00
Circulation: 28,000 (Publisher's Statement)
Usual Pagination: 40
Editor: Nicola Turner
Summary of Content: Magazine with news and updates from all aspects of world, European and British judo as well as training methods, fitness regimes and lifestyle issues.
Readership/Target Audience: Aimed at members of the British Judo Association and those who practice judo.
ADVERTISING RATES:
Full Page Colour £750.00
Mechanical Data: Trim Size: 297 x 210mm
Average advertising content per issue: 20%
CONSUMER: SPORT: Combat Sports

MATURE TIMES
1654782U74N-167
Editorial Address: Highwood House, Winters Lane, Redhill, BRISTOL, BS40 5SH **Tel:** 01275 331932 **Fax:** 01934 861028
Email: editorial@maturetimes.co.uk
Advertising Address: Landmark Publishing Services Ltd, 2 Windmill Street, LONDON, W1T 2HX **Tel:** 020 7692 9292
Fax: 020 7692 9393
Email: amf@lms.co.uk
Web site: http://www.maturetimes.co.uk
Publisher: Highwood House Publishing Ltd
Date Established: 1991
Frequency: Monthly
Free to qualifying individuals
Annual Sub.: £17.00
Circulation: 200,000 (Publisher's Statement)
Usual Pagination: 24
Editor: Tony Watts; **Advertising Manager:** Anne Marie Fox; **Managing Editor:** Tony Watts
Summary of Content: Magazine covering campaigns on issues such as ageism, council tax, pensions and healthcare as well as sections dedicated to lifestyle issues of genuine interest to mature readers including finance, health and beauty, property, motoring, holidays and leisure, the home, mobility, pets, crosswords, puzzles and competitions.
Readership/Target Audience: Aimed at the over 50s.
ADVERTISING RATES:
Full Page Colour £5250.00
SCC £22.00
Agency Commission: 10%
Mechanical Data: Type Area: 360 x 277mm, Col Length: 360mm, Page Width: 277mm, Col Widths (Display): 28mm, No. of Columns (Display): 9, Film: Digital
CONSUMER: WOMEN'S INTEREST CONSUMER MAGAZINES: Retirement

MAURICE MAGAZINE
1825711U84A-462
Editorial Address: Studio 4, 94 Dalston Lane, LONDON, E8 1NG
Email: louise@mauricemagazine.com
Web site: http://www.mauricemagazine.com
Publisher: Readymade Magazine
Date Established: 2006
Frequency: Quarterly
Cover Price: £3.00
Free to qualifying individuals
Circulation: 10,000 (Publisher's Statement)
Usual Pagination: 40
Editor: Louise Stern
Summary of Content: Magazine covering contemporary art.
Readership/Target Audience: Aimed at children aged 7 to 11 years old.
CONSUMER: THE ARTS & LITERARY: Arts

MAURITIUS NEWS
48320U90-95
Editorial Address: 583 Wandsworth Road, LONDON, SW8 3JD **Tel:** 020 7498 3066 **Fax:** 020 7498 3066
Email: peter@mauritiusnews.co.uk
Advertising Address: As above.
Email: editor@mauritiusnews.co.uk
Web site: http://www.mauritiusnews.co.uk
ISSN: 0953-2706

Publisher: Mauritius Publishers Co Ltd
Date Established: 1983
Frequency: Monthly
Annual Sub.: £15.00
Circulation: 5,000 (Publisher's Statement)
Usual Pagination: 24
Editor: Peter Chellen; **Managing Director:** Peter Chellen; **Advertising Manager:** Peter Chellen
Summary of Content: Newspaper containing general, business and international news.
Language(s): English; French
Readership/Target Audience: Aimed at Mauritians living in the UK and Europe.
ADVERTISING RATES:
Full Page Colour £600.00
Agency Commission: 10%
Mechanical Data: Bleed Size: +3mm, Type Area: 365 x 250mm, Col Length: 365mm, Page Width: 250mm, Film: Digital
Copy instructions: Copy Date: 10th of the month prior to publication date
Average advertising content per issue: 10%
CONSUMER: ETHNIC

MAVERICK
1606842U76D-757
Editorial Address: 24 Bray Gardens, MAIDSTONE, ME15 9TR **Tel:** 01622 744481
Email: editor@maverick-country.com
Advertising Address: As above.
Email: advertising@maverick-country.com
Web site: http://www.maverick-country.com
Publisher: AAG Publishing Ltd
Date Established: 2002
Frequency: 10 issues yearly
Cover Price: £3.50
Free to qualifying individuals
Annual Sub.: £40.00
Circulation: 10,000 (Publisher's Statement)
Usual Pagination: 96
Editor: Alan Cackett; **Advertising Manager:** Laura Bethell
Summary of Content: Magazine covering Americana country and roots music news including album reviews, tour dates, gig reports and artist profiles.
Readership/Target Audience: Aimed at enthusiasts of country and roots music.
ADVERTISING RATES:
Full Page Colour £435.00
Agency Commission: 10%
Mechanical Data: Trim Size: 297 x 210mm, Film: Digital, Bleed Size: +5mm, Col Length: 275mm, Page Width: 185mm, Type Area: 275 x 185mm
Copy instructions: Copy Date: 3 weeks prior to publication date
Average advertising content per issue: 30%
CONSUMER: MUSIC & PERFORMING ARTS: Music

MAX POWER
46505U77A-280
Editorial Address: Media House, Lynchwood, Peterborough Business Park, PETERBOROUGH, PE2 6EA
Tel: 01733 468000 **Fax:** 01733 468217
Email: max.power@bauermedia.co.uk
Advertising Address: Endeavour House, 189 Shaftesbury Avenue, LONDON, WC2H 8JG **Tel:** 020 7295 8597
Fax: 0207 7295 5400
Email: nima.shahraz@baueradvertising.co.uk
Web site: http://www.maxpower.co.uk
Publisher: Bauer Consumer Media Ltd (Media House)
Frequency: Monthly
Cover Price: £4.35
Annual Sub.: £51.35
Circulation: 30,076 (ABC 01/01/2008 to 31/12/2008)
Usual Pagination: 300
Editor: Leise Enright; **Advertising Manager:** Nima Shahraz
Summary of Content: Magazine covering modified production vehicles which are still street legal.
Readership/Target Audience: Aimed at men between 15 and 25 years old with an interest in modified vehicles.
ADVERTISING RATES:
Full Page Colour £5000.00
Agency Commission: 10%
Mechanical Data: Type Area: 270 x 197mm, Col Length: 270mm, Page Width: 197mm, Bleed Size: 305 x 220mm, Trim Size: 297 x 210mm, Film: Digital
Copy instructions: Copy Date: 3 weeks prior to publication date
Average advertising content per issue: 50%
CONSUMER: MOTORING & CYCLING: Motoring

MAYBOURNE STYLE MAGAZINE
718513U89B-340
Formerly: Style Magazine
Editorial Address: 6-8 Old Bond Street, LONDON, W1S 4PH **Tel:** 020 7499 9080 **Fax:** 020 7493 3758
Email: serena.hamilton@condenast.co.uk
Advertising Address: As above.
Email: nicola.anderson@condenast.co.uk

Consumer Magazines

Web site: http://www.maybourne.com
Publisher: Conde Nast Publications Ltd
Date Established: 2001
Frequency: 3 issues yearly - Published in April, September and December
Cover Price: Free
Circulation: 40,000 (Publisher's Statement)
Usual Pagination: 54
Editor: Serena Hamilton; **Managing Editor:** Serena Hamilton; **Advertising Director:** Nicola Anderson
Summary of Content: Themed lifestyle magazine with theatre reviews, features on new shops, interviews with celebrities and information on the Maybourne Group Hotels.
Readership/Target Audience: Read by customers and hotel guests of the Maybourne Group, including The Berkeley, Claridges, and The Connaught.
ADVERTISING RATES:
Full Page Colour £7000.00
Agency Commission: 15%
Mechanical Data: Trim Size: 225 x 225mm, Bleed Size: 231 x 231mm, Page Width: 195mm, Type Area: 198 x 195mm, Col Length: 198mm, Film: Digital
Copy instructions: Copy Date: 8 weeks prior to publication date
Average advertising content per issue: 25%
CONSUMER: HOLIDAYS & TRAVEL: Hotel Magazines

MAYFAIR   47610U86A-100
Editorial Address: 2 Archer Street, LONDON, W1D 7AW
Tel: 020 7292 8000 **Fax:** 020 7734 5030
Email: mayfair@paulraymond.com
Advertising Address: As above. **Fax:** 020 7292 8009
Email: nickys@paulraymond.com
Web site: http://www.sexclub.co.uk
ISSN: 0025-6161
Publisher: Paul Raymond Publications Ltd
Frequency: 13 issues yearly
Cover Price: £3.20
Usual Pagination: 100
Editor: David Rider; **Advertising Manager:** Nicola Swift
Summary of Content: Magazine covering adult glamour, video, male interest features, motorsports, technology, cars and motorcycles.
Readership/Target Audience: Aimed at men 18 years old and over.
ADVERTISING RATES:
Full Page Colour £3000.00
SCC £35.00
Mechanical Data: Page Width: 222mm, Col Length: 300mm, Film: Digital, Type Area: 300 x 222mm
Copy instructions: Copy Date: 1 month prior to publication date
Average advertising content per issue: 20%
CONSUMER: ADULT & GAY MAGAZINES: Adult Magazines

MAYFAIR TIMES   46833U80B-163
Editorial Address: Blandel Bridge House, 56 Sloane Square, LONDON, SW1W 8AX **Tel:** 020 7259 1050
Fax: 020 7901 9042
Email: mayfair.times@pubbiz.com
Advertising Address: As above.
Email: sam@pubbiz.com
Web site: http://www.mayfairtimes.co.uk
Publisher: Publishing Business
Date Established: 1985
Frequency: Monthly
Cover Price: £3.00
Free to qualifying individuals
Circulation: 21,000 (Publisher's Statement)
Usual Pagination: 76
Editor: Selma Day; **Advertising Director:** Sam Bradshaw
Summary of Content: Lifestyle magazine containing news, celebrity interviews, fashion, health and beauty, food and drink, art and antiques, events, theatre and business in and around the West End of London.
Readership/Target Audience: Aimed at residents, visitors and businesses in Mayfair and St. James.
ADVERTISING RATES:
Full Page Colour £1550.00
SCC £12.50
Agency Commission: 10%
Mechanical Data: Film: Digital, Bleed Size: 306 x 238mm, Trim Size: 300 x 232mm
Copy instructions: Copy Date: 20th of the month prior to the publication date
Average advertising content per issue: 50%
CONSUMER: RURAL & REGIONAL INTEREST: Regional Interest Greater London

THE MAYHEW   47076U81A-25
Formerly: Animal Rescue
Editorial Address: Trenmar Gardens, Kensal Green, LONDON, NW10 6BJ **Tel:** 020 8969 7110
Fax: 020 8969 3902
Email: pr@mayhewanimalhome.org
Advertising Address: 1078 Harrow Road, LONDON, NW10 5NL **Tel:** 020 8969 7110 **Fax:** 020 8969 3902

Email: pr@mayhewanimalhome.org
Web site: http://www.mayhewanimalhome.org
Publisher: The Mayhew Animal Home
Date Established: 1999
Frequency: 3 issues yearly - Published in April, June and October
Cover Price: £1.00
Free to qualifying individuals
Circulation: 15,000 (Publisher's Statement)
Usual Pagination: 32
Editor: Sarah Dickinson; **Advertising Manager:** Vicki Howard
Summary of Content: Magazine of the Mayhew Animal Home, containing features about animal welfare and events.
Readership/Target Audience: Aimed at those interested in the larger issues of animal welfare and in the Mayhew Animal Home in particular.
ADVERTISING RATES:
Full Page Colour £1500.00
Agency Commission: 10%
Mechanical Data: Bleed Size: +3mm, Film: Digital, Trim Size: 297 x 210mm
Copy instructions: Copy Date: 4 weeks prior to publication date
Average advertising content per issue: 10%
CONSUMER: ANIMALS & PETS: Animals & Pets Protection

MAZDA MAGAZINE   1647209U77E-513
Editorial Address: 7 St. Martin's Place, LONDON, WC2N 4HA **Tel:** 020 7747 0700
Advertising Address: As above.
Email: janine.goldblatt@redwoodgroup.net
Publisher: Redwood
Frequency: 3 issues yearly - Published in June, October and February
Cover Price: £4.00
Free to qualifying individuals
Circulation: 200,000 (Publisher's Statement)
Usual Pagination: 68
Editor: Janine Goldblatt; **Publisher:** Janine Goldblatt
Summary of Content: Magazine covering Mazda cars and features relevant to Mazda customers including travel and extreme sports.
Readership/Target Audience: Aimed at prospective purchasers and owners of Mazda cars.
ADVERTISING: Rates on application
Agency Commission: 10%
Copy instructions: Copy Date: 6 weeks prior to publication date
CONSUMER: MOTORING & CYCLING: Club Cars

MBR   46400U77C-803
Editorial Address: Leon House, 233 High Street, CROYDON, CR9 1HZ **Tel:** 020 8726 8451
Fax: 020 8726 8499
Email: mbr@ipcmedia.com
Advertising Address: As above. **Tel:** 020 8726 8467
Fax: 020 8726 8294
Email: jonathan_emery@ipcmedia.com
Web site: http://www.mbr.co.uk
ISSN: 1367-0824
Publisher: IPC Inspire
Date Established: 1997
Frequency: 13 issues yearly
Cover Price: £4.00
Circulation: 33,918 (ABC 01/01/2008 to 31/12/2008)
Usual Pagination: 174
Editor: Andy Waterman; **Managing Director:** Niall Clarkson; **Advertising Manager:** Jonathan Emery; **Publisher:** Keith Foster
Summary of Content: Magazine featuring the latest bikes available, mountain bike sports plus news and features.
Readership/Target Audience: Aimed at active mountain bikers between 18 and 50 years old.
ADVERTISING RATES:
Full Page Mono £1600.00
Full Page Colour £1600.00
Agency Commission: 10%
Mechanical Data: Page Width: 180mm, Type Area: 253 x 180mm, Col Length: 253mm, Trim Size: 275 x 210mm, Bleed Size: 281 x 216mm, Film: Digital
Copy instructions: Copy Date: 3 weeks prior to publication date
CONSUMER: MOTORING & CYCLING: Cycling

MCN MOTOR CYCLE NEWS   46365U77B-498
Editorial Address: Media House, Lynchwood, Peterborough Business Park, PETERBOROUGH, PE2 6EA
Tel: 01733 468000 **Fax:** 01733 468028
Email: mcn@motorcyclenews.com
Advertising Address: As above. **Fax:** 01733 468867
Email: chris.winters@bauermedia.co.uk
Web site: http://www.motorcyclenews.com
Publisher: Bauer Consumer Media Ltd (Media House)
Frequency: Weekly
Cover Price: £1.80

Annual Sub.: £120.00
Circulation: 120,002 (ABC 01/01/2008 to 31/12/2008)
Editor: Marc Potter; **Executive Editor:** Phil West; **Managing Director:** Rob Munro-Hall; **Publisher:** Will Hattam
Summary of Content: Newspaper focusing on the motorcycling world. Includes articles on equipment, events and road tests.
Readership/Target Audience: Read predominantly by men and women in their thirties who are motorcycling enthusiasts.
ADVERTISING RATES:
Full Page Colour £5420.00
Agency Commission: 10%
Mechanical Data: Trim Size: 357 x 276mm, Film: Digital
Copy instructions: Copy Date: 2 weeks prior to publication date
CONSUMER: MOTORING & CYCLING: Motorcycling

MEARNS PRESS   1809920U80E-369
Editorial Address: Unit 3, 47 Back Sneddon Street, PAISLEY, PA3 2DD **Tel:** 0141 842 1010 **Fax:** 0141 887 7122
Email: david@newvisionpublishing.co.uk
Advertising Address: Unit 7, 42 Back Sneddon Street, PAISLEY, PA3 2DD **Tel:** 0141 842 1010 **Fax:** 0141 887 7122
Email: enquiries@newvisionpublishing.co.uk
Web site: http://www.newvisionpublishing.co.uk
Publisher: New Vision Print & Publishing Ltd
Date Established: 2001
Frequency: 10 issues yearly
Cover Price: Free
Circulation: 15,000 (Publisher's Statement)
Usual Pagination: 32
Editor: David Wilson
Summary of Content: Magazine with local stories and lifestyle features including business, personal, sports, health, beauty, recipes, gardening, housing, finance, legal and books.
Readership/Target Audience: Aimed at residents of Newton Mearns.
ADVERTISING RATES:
Full Page Colour £400.00
Mechanical Data: Type Area: 267 x 190mm, Trim Size: 297 x 210mm, Col Length: 267mm, Page Width: 190mm, Film: Digital
Copy instructions: Copy Date: 10 days prior to publication date
CONSUMER: RURAL & REGIONAL INTEREST: Regional Interest Scotland

MED LIFE   1655346U89D-512
Editorial Address: 3-5 Spafield Street, LONDON, EC1R 4QB **Tel:** 020 7841 0340
Email: danny@touchline.com
Advertising Address: Copywrite, C.C. El Capricho, Of. 8, Km 179, E-29600 MARBELLA **Tel:** 95 28 27 000
Fax: 95 28 22 946
Email: medlife@copywrite.es
Web site: http://www.touchline.com
Publisher: Touchline Publishing
Date Established: 2003
Frequency: Quarterly
Cover Price: Free
Circulation: 28,000 (Publisher's Statement)
Usual Pagination: 162
Editor: Danielle Green; **Advertising Manager:** Edward Hill
Summary of Content: GB Airways in-flight magazine covering travel, lifestyle, celebrity interviews, fashion, culture, art and sport.
Readership/Target Audience: Aimed at passengers on GB Airways flights to the southern Mediterranean and North Africa.
ADVERTISING RATES:
Full Page Colour £2995.00
Agency Commission: 10%
Mechanical Data: Type Area: 260 x 182mm, Bleed Size: 298 x 220mm, Trim Size: 288 x 210mm, Col Length: 260mm, Page Width: 182mm, Film: Digital
Average advertising content per issue: 50%
CONSUMER: HOLIDAYS & TRAVEL: In-Flight Magazines

MEDAL NEWS   46748U79K-750
Editorial Address: Orchard House, Duchy Road, Heathpark, HONITON, EX14 1YD **Tel:** 01404 46972 **Fax:** 01404 44788
Email: info@tokenpublishing.com
Advertising Address: As above. **Tel:** 01404 44167
Email: celia@tokenpublishing.com
Web site: http://www.tokenpublishing.com
ISSN: 0958-4986
Publisher: Token Publishing Ltd
Date Established: 1981
Frequency: 10 issues yearly
Cover Price: £3.50
Annual Sub.: £32.00
Circulation: 5,000 (Publisher's Statement)
Usual Pagination: 60
Editor: John Mussell

Summary of Content: Magazine containing information on the market scene, profiles on medals and those they were awarded to, a badges section and a medal tracker service that allows readers to locate lost medals.
Readership/Target Audience: Aimed at medallists, military historians, collectors and dealers.
ADVERTISING RATES:
Full Page Mono £315.00
Full Page Colour £640.00
Agency Commission: 10%
Mechanical Data: Type Area: 272 x 185mm, Print Process: Offset litho, Bleed Size: 307 x 215mm, Trim Size: 297 x 210mm, Col Length: 272mm, Film: Digital, Page Width: 185mm
Copy instructions: Copy Date: 1st of the month prior to publication date
Average advertising content per issue: 40%
CONSUMER: HOBBIES & DIY: Collectors Magazines

MEDWAY MATTERS
1639593U80C-5082
Editorial Address: Gun Wharf, Dock Road, CHATHAM, ME4 4TR **Tel:** 01634 332782 **Fax:** 01634 332829
Email: medway.matters@medway.gov.uk
Advertising Address: As above. **Fax:** 01634 332743
Email: medway.matters@medway.gov.uk
Web site: http://www.medway.gov.uk
Publisher: Medway Council
Date Established: 1998
Frequency: 6 issues yearly
Cover Price: Free
Circulation: 111,437 (Publisher's Statement)
Usual Pagination: 16
Editor: John Staples; **Advertising Manager:** Fay Coffin
Summary of Content: Magazine containing council information and news about services in Medway.
Readership/Target Audience: Aimed at those living in the Medway area.
ADVERTISING RATES:
Full Page Colour £1980.00
Agency Commission: 10%
Mechanical Data: Film: Digital
Copy instructions: Copy Date: 6 weeks prior to publication date
Average advertising content per issue: 40%
CONSUMER: RURAL & REGIONAL INTEREST: Regional Interest English Counties

MEMORIAL FLIGHT
1655804U79H-164
Editorial Address: 2 Village Street, Careby, STAMFORD, PE9 4EA **Tel:** 01780 410016 **Fax:** 01780 410016
Email: tom.allett@btinternet.com
Web site: http://www.lincs-lancaster.com
Publisher: Lincolnshire Lancaster Association
Date Established: 1973
Frequency: Half-yearly - Published in April and November
Cover Price: £3.50
Free to qualifying individuals
Annual Sub.: £8.00
Circulation: 5,800 (Publisher's Statement)
Usual Pagination: 40
Editor: Tom Allett
Summary of Content: Magazine covering World War II aviation.
Readership/Target Audience: Aimed at members of the Lincolnshire Lancaster Association.
ADVERTISING: No Advertising taken
CONSUMER: HOBBIES & DIY: Military History

MEN MATTERS
47868U87-240
Formerly: World Outlook
Editorial Address: 10 Amity Street, READING, RG1 3LP
Tel: 07985 413641
Email: editor@baptistmen.org.uk
Advertising Address: As above.
Email: editor@baptistmen.org.uk
Web site: http://www.baptistmen.org.uk
Publisher: Baptist Men's Movement
Date Established: 1918
Frequency: Quarterly
Cover Price: £1.00
Circulation: 3,000 (Publisher's Statement)
Usual Pagination: 24
Editor: Phil Creighton; **Advertising Manager:** Phil Creighton
Summary of Content: Journal of worldwide Christian interest.
Readership/Target Audience: Aimed at members of the Baptist Men's Movement, plus other Baptists and Christians.
ADVERTISING RATES:
Full Page Mono £30.00
Mechanical Data: Trim Size: 210 x 148mm, No. of Columns (Display): 2, Print Process: Litho, Film: Digital
Average advertising content per issue: 12%
CONSUMER: RELIGIOUS

MEN ONLY
47611U86A-110
Editorial Address: 2 Archer Street, LONDON, W1D 7AW
Tel: 020 7292 8000 **Fax:** 020 7734 5030
Email: menonly@paulraymond.com
Advertising Address: As above. **Fax:** 020 7292 8009
Email: nickys@paulraymond.com
Web site: http://www.paulraymond.com
Publisher: Paul Raymond Publications Ltd
Frequency: 13 issues yearly
Cover Price: £2.95
Usual Pagination: 100
Editor: Neil Aldis; **Managing Director:** Mark Quinn;
Advertising Manager: Nicola Swift
Summary of Content: Magazine containing male interest photography and articles.
Readership/Target Audience: Aimed at men between 20 and 50 years old.
ADVERTISING RATES:
Full Page Colour £3000.00
Mechanical Data: Type Area: 300 x 222mm, Col Length: 300mm, Film: Digital, Page Width: 222mm, Bleed Size: +3mm
Average advertising content per issue: 20%
CONSUMER: ADULT & GAY MAGAZINES: Adult Magazines

THE MENDIP TIMES
1819047U80C-5426
Editorial Address: Coombe Lodge, Bourne Lane, Blagdon, BRISTOL, BS40 7RG **Tel:** 01761 463888 **Fax:** 01761 463890
Email: news@mendiptimes.co.uk
Advertising Address: As above.
Email: advertising@mendiptimes.co.uk
Web site: http://www.mendiptimes.co.uk
Publisher: Mendip Times Ltd
Date Established: 2005
Frequency: Monthly
Cover Price: Free
Annual Sub.: £15.00
Circulation: 19,000 (Publisher's Statement)
Usual Pagination: 68
Editor: Steve Egginton; **Advertising Manager:** Alice Jones;
Publisher: Steve Egginton
Summary of Content: Free monthly glossy magazine celebrating life on the Mendips and surrounding areas covering local news and people, local history, events and lifestyle.
Readership/Target Audience: Aimed at residents and visitors to the Mendip Hills area.
ADVERTISING RATES:
Full Page Colour 719.00
Mechanical Data: Bleed Size: 303 x 216mm, Trim Size: 275 x 190mm, Film: Digital
CONSUMER: RURAL & REGIONAL INTEREST: Regional Interest English Counties

MENEVIA NEWS
29313U87-156_25
Editorial Address: PO Box 8455, NEWARK, NG23 5WX
Tel: 01636 525607
Email: menevianews@ntlworld.com
Advertising Address: As above.
Email: johnclawson@xln.co.uk
Publisher: Bellcourt Limited
Date Established: 1996
Frequency: Monthly
Cover Price: Free
Circulation: 5,000 (Publisher's Statement)
Usual Pagination: 12
Editor: Arthur Meredith; **Advertising Manager:** John Clawson; **Publisher:** John Clawson
Summary of Content: Magazine covering religious topics, events, news and opinions.
Language(s): English; Welsh
Readership/Target Audience: Read by those concerned with religious issues, particularly Roman Catholics in South Wales.
ADVERTISING: Rates on application
CONSUMER: RELIGIOUS

MENORAH
1863350U87-2054
Editorial Address: 12 Conisborough Place, Whitefield, MANCHESTER, M45 6EJ **Tel:** 0161 766 6479
Email: martin.newman@armymail.mod.uk
Advertising Address: 1st Floor, Tailby House, Bath Road, KETTERING, NN16 8NL **Tel:** 01536 512624
Fax: 01536 515481
Email: christina@lancepublishing.co.uk
Publisher: Lance Publishing Ltd
Date Established: 1947
Frequency: Half-yearly
Cover Price: Free
Circulation: 2,000 (Publisher's Statement)
Usual Pagination: 36
Editor: Martin Newman; **Publisher:** Mike Urban
Summary of Content: Magazine covering military, religious and culture topics. Includes features on lifestyle, food and drink, travel, books and community news.

Readership/Target Audience: Aimed at all members of the Jewish faith serving HM forces and civil servants in defence.
ADVERTISING RATES:
Full Page Colour £720.00
Agency Commission: 10%
Mechanical Data: Type Area: 270 x 190mm, Bleed Size: 303 x 216mm, Trim Size: 297 x 210mm, Col Length: 270mm, Page Width: 190mm, Film: Digital
CONSUMER: RELIGIOUS

MEN'S FITNESS
45978U75P-390
Editorial Address: 30 Cleveland Street, LONDON, W1T 4JD
Tel: 020 7907 6000 **Fax:** 020 7907 6516
Email: mensfitness@dennis.co.uk
Advertising Address: As above. **Fax:** 020 7907 6601
Email: rick_asiyani@dennis.co.uk
Publisher: Dennis Publishing Ltd
Date Established: 1999
Frequency: Monthly
Cover Price: £3.70
Annual Sub.: £29.80
Circulation: 67,987 (ABC 01/01/2009 to 30/06/2009)
Usual Pagination: 156
Editor: Peter Muir; **Features Editor:** Joel Snape; **Managing Director:** James Tye; **Managing Editor:** Chris Miller;
Publisher: Simon Clark
Summary of Content: Magazine covering men's physical, mental, emotional and sexual fitness. Contains product reviews and features on sport, travelling, training and healthy eating.
Readership/Target Audience: Aimed at men in their early thirties with a high disposable income.
ADVERTISING RATES:
Full Page Colour £3500.00
Agency Commission: 15%
Mechanical Data: Film: Digital, Type Area: 269 x 182mm, Trim Size: 297 x 210mm, Col Length: 269mm, Page Width: 182mm, Bleed Size: 303 x 216mm
Copy instructions: Copy Date: 3 weeks prior to publication date
Average advertising content per issue: 30%
CONSUMER: SPORT: Fitness/Bodybuilding

MEN'S HEALTH
47661U86C-420
Editorial Address: 33 Broadwick Street, LONDON, W1F 0DQ **Tel:** 020 7339 4400 **Fax:** 020 7339 4444
Email: nicky.williams@natmag-rodale.co.uk
Advertising Address: As above. **Fax:** 020 7339 4455
Email: luke.robins@natmag-rodale.co.uk
Web site: http://www.menshealth.co.uk
ISSN: 1356-7438
Publisher: NatMag Rodale Ltd
Date Established: 1995
Frequency: 11 issues yearly
Cover Price: £3.80
Annual Sub.: £27.97
Circulation: 250,247 (ABC 01/01/2009 to 30/06/2009)
Editor: Nicky Williams; **Advertising Manager:** Luke Robins
Summary of Content: Magazine covering health and fashion issues.
Twitter: https://twitter.com/MensHealthMag.
Readership/Target Audience: Read by men between 25 and 45 years old.
ADVERTISING RATES:
Full Page Mono £9250.00
Full Page Colour £9250.00
Agency Commission: 15%
Mechanical Data: Film: Digital, Type Area: 270 x 200mm, Bleed Size: 286 x 221mm, Trim Size: 280 x 215mm, Col Length: 270mm, Page Width: 200mm
Copy instructions: Copy Date: 5 weeks prior to publication date
Average advertising content per issue: 40%
CONSUMER: ADULT & GAY MAGAZINES: Men's Lifestyle Magazines

MENSA MAGAZINE
48699U94X-90
Editorial Address: St. Johns House, St. Johns Square, WOLVERHAMPTON, WV2 4AH **Tel:** 01904 492233
Fax: 01904 492233
Email: b.page@btinternet.com
Advertising Address: As above. **Tel:** 01902 772771
Fax: 01902 392500
Email: bobby@mensa.org.uk
Web site: http://www.mensa.org.uk
Publisher: British Mensa Ltd
Frequency: Monthly
Free to qualifying individuals
Circulation: 24,500 (Publisher's Statement)
Usual Pagination: 44
Editor: Brian Page; **Advertising Manager:** Bobby Raikhy
Summary of Content: Journal of Mensa, the high IQ society. Includes news, puzzles, features and information.
Readership/Target Audience: Aimed at members of Mensa.
ADVERTISING RATES:
Full Page Mono £600.00

Consumer Magazines

Full Page Colour £750.00
Agency Commission: 10%
Mechanical Data: Type Area: 277 x 190mm, Bleed Size: 305 x 218mm, Trim Size: 297 x 210mm, Col Length: 277mm, Page Width: 190mm, Film: Digital
Copy instructions: Copy Date: 20th of the month prior to publication date
Average advertising content per issue: 10%
CONSUMER: OTHER CLASSIFICATIONS: Miscellaneous

MENSWORLD
1637488U86A-182
Editorial Address: 2 Archer Street, LONDON, W1D 7AW
Tel: 020 7292 8000 **Fax:** 020 7734 5030
Email: mensworld@paulraymond.com
Advertising Address: As above. **Fax:** 020 7292 8009
Email: nickys@paulraymond.com
Web site: http://www.sexclub.co.uk
Publisher: Paul Raymond Publications Ltd
Frequency: 13 issues yearly
Cover Price: £3.50
Usual Pagination: 100
Editor: Alistair Puddick; **Advertising Manager:** Nicola Swift
Summary of Content: Magazine covering adult glamour, video, male interest features, technology, motorsports, cars and motorcycles.
Readership/Target Audience: Aimed at men aged 18 years and over.
ADVERTISING RATES:
Full Page Colour £2500.00
Mechanical Data: Type Area: 300 x 222mm, Bleed Size: +3mm, Col Length: 300mm, Page Width: 222mm, Film: Digital
Average advertising content per issue: 20%
CONSUMER: ADULT & GAY MAGAZINES: Adult Magazines

MERCEDES ENTHUSIAST
718422U77E-192_60
Editorial Address: Sundial House, 17 Wickham Road, BECKENHAM, BR3 5JS **Tel:** 020 8639 4405
Fax: 020 8639 4411
Email: editorial@mercedesenthusiast.co.uk
Advertising Address: As above. **Tel:** 020 8639 4406
Email: ads@sundialmagazines.co.uk
Web site: http://www.mercedesenthusiast.co.uk
ISSN: 1474-7030
Publisher: Sundial Magazines Ltd
Date Established: 2001
Frequency: Monthly - Published on the 3rd Friday of the cover month
Cover Price: £3.80
Annual Sub.: £40.60
Circulation: 40,000 (Publisher's Statement)
Usual Pagination: 116
Editor: Lizzie Pope; **Publisher:** Peter Warwick
Summary of Content: Magazine covering all aspects of Mercedes cars including related products, events, motorsports and buying information.
Readership/Target Audience: Aimed at owners, enthusiasts and buyers of classic and contemporary Mercedes cars.
ADVERTISING RATES:
Full Page Colour £1095.00
Agency Commission: 10%
Mechanical Data: Type Area: 272 x 188mm, Bleed Size: 303 x 213mm, Col Length: 272mm, Page Width: 188mm, Print Process: Web-fed offset litho, Film: Digital, Trim Size: 297 x 210mm
Copy instructions: Copy Date: 4 weeks prior to publication date
Average advertising content per issue: 25%
CONSUMER: MOTORING & CYCLING: Club Cars

MERCEDES OWNER
767764U77E-504
Editorial Address: Langton Road, Langton Green, TUNBRIDGE WELLS, TN3 0EG **Tel:** 01892 860927
Email: ian.campbell@mercedesclub.org.uk
Advertising Address: Space Marketing, c/o Mercedes Owner, 10 Clayfield Mews, Newcomen Road, TUNBRIDGE WELLS, TN4 9PA **Tel:** 01892 677740 **Fax:** 01892 677743
Email: robq@spacemarketing.co.uk
Web site: http://www.mercedesclub.org.uk
Publisher: MBO
Frequency: Monthly
Cover Price: £3.00
Free to qualifying individuals
Annual Sub.: £35.00
Circulation: 8,000 (Publisher's Statement)
Usual Pagination: 56
Editor: Ian Campbell; **Advertising Manager:** Rob Quinnell
Summary of Content: Magazine covering news and events in the world of Mercedes-Benz including historical pieces, technical information and reviews. Also features a non-motoring section covering show previews, restaurants and holiday guide.
Readership/Target Audience: Aimed at owners and potential owners of Mercedes cars.
ADVERTISING RATES:
Full Page Colour £745.00

SCC £12.00
Agency Commission: 10%
Mechanical Data: Type Area: 270 x 180mm, Col Length: 270mm, Print Process: Sheet-fed litho, Film: Digital, Trim Size: 297 x 210mm, Bleed Size: 303 x 216mm, Page Width: 180mm
Copy instructions: Copy Date: 4 weeks prior to publication date
Average advertising content per issue: 60%
CONSUMER: MOTORING & CYCLING: Club Cars

MERCEDESMAGAZINE
46468U77E-192_50
Formerly: Mercedes
Editorial Address: Impact Press & PR, Wixford Park, George's Elm Lane, Wixford, ALCESTER, B50 4JS
Tel: 01789 490530 **Fax:** 01789 490465
Email: eric@impactpr.co.uk
Advertising Address: Mongoose Media Ltd, Mongoose House, Lonsdale Road, LONDON, NW6 6RD
Tel: 020 7306 0300 **Fax:** 020 7306 0301
Email: jpriest@mongoosemedia.com
Publisher: Mercedes-Benz(UK) Ltd
Date Established: 1993
Frequency: Quarterly
Cover Price: £3.50
Free to qualifying individuals
Circulation: 2,300,000 (Publisher's Statement)
Usual Pagination: 84
Editor: Eric Lafone; **Advertising Manager:** James Priest
Summary of Content: Magazine featuring company news, designs, road tests, travel and lifestyle articles.
Readership/Target Audience: Read by Mercedes-Benz owners.
ADVERTISING RATES:
Full Page Colour £4950.00
Mechanical Data: Trim Size: 280 x 215mm, Film: Digital, Bleed Size: 286 x 221mm
Copy instructions: Copy Date: 3 weeks prior to publication date
CONSUMER: MOTORING & CYCLING: Club Cars

MERGE MAGAZINE
765466U74Q-1122
Editorial Address: 3rd Floor, 27 Old Compton Street, LONDON, W1D 5JP **Tel:** 020 7494 4550 **Fax:** 020 7494 2918
Email: bradleyquinn@usa.net
Web site: http://www.mergemag.com
Publisher: Merge Magazine Ltd
Date Established: 1998
Frequency: Quarterly
Cover Price: £4.50
Annual Sub.: £18.00
Circulation: 8,000 (Print Run)
Usual Pagination: 84
Editor: Bradley Quinn
Summary of Content: Lifestyle magazine covering art, music, architecture, design, film, fashion and culture.
Readership/Target Audience: Aimed at a cultural audience.
CONSUMER: WOMEN'S INTEREST CONSUMER MAGAZINES: Lifestyle

MERIDIAN MAGAZINE
46834U80B-163_50
Formerly: Meridian Line
Editorial Address: 8 The Village, Charlton, LONDON, SE7 8UD **Tel:** 020 8319 0555 **Fax:** 020 8319 4555
Email: enquiries@meridian-magazine.co.uk
Advertising Address: As above.
Email: advertising@meridian-magazine.co.uk
Web site: http://www.meridian-magazine.co.uk
Publisher: Meridian Line Publishing Ltd
Date Established: 1996
Frequency: Monthly
Cover Price: Free
Circulation: 50,000 (Publisher's Statement)
Usual Pagination: 64
Editor: Valerie Breese; **Advertising Manager:** Ben Watt
Summary of Content: Local interest magazine covering news features in and around Greenwich, Blackheath and Docklands.
Readership/Target Audience: Aimed at residents of Greenwich, Blackheath and Docklands.
ADVERTISING RATES:
Full Page Colour £1450.00
Agency Commission: 10%
Mechanical Data: Film: Positive, right reading, emulsion side down, Type Area: 277 x 192mm, Bleed Size: 307x 215mm, Trim Size: 297 x 210mm, Col Length: 277mm, Page Width: 192mm
Copy instructions: Copy Date: 14 days prior to publication date
Average advertising content per issue: 60%
CONSUMER: RURAL & REGIONAL INTEREST: Regional Interest Greater London

MESSENGER
47832U87-156_30
Editorial Address: Alma Park, GRANTHAM, NG31 9SL
Tel: 01476 591700 **Fax:** 01476 577144
Email: editordnm@mac.com
Web site: http://www.adventist.org.uk
ISSN: 0309-3654
Publisher: Stanborough Press Ltd
Date Established: 1894
Frequency: 26 issues yearly
Cover Price: Free
Circulation: 12,000 (Publisher's Statement)
Usual Pagination: 16
Editor: David Marshall
Summary of Content: Seventh Day Adventist news magazine.
Readership/Target Audience: Aimed at Christians.
ADVERTISING: No Advertising taken
CONSUMER: RELIGIOUS

METAL HAMMER
46245U76E-225
Editorial Address: 2 Balcombe Street, LONDON, NW1 6NW
Tel: 020 7042 4000
Email: alexander.milas@futurenet.com
Advertising Address: As above. **Fax:** 020 7042 4471
Email: ian.williamson@futurenet.co.uk
Web site: http://www.metalhammer.co.uk
Publisher: Future Publishing Limited
Frequency: 13 issues yearly
Cover Price: £3.99
Circulation: 46,004 (ABC 01/01/2009 to 30/06/2009)
Usual Pagination: 148
Editor: Alexander Milas; **Features Editor:** Caren Gibson; **Advertising Manager:** Ian Williamson; **Managing Editor:** Alex Burrows
Summary of Content: Magazine covering the latest news, reviews and features on hard rock and metal bands from around the world. Includes events, lifestyle features, skate boarding and articles on tattoos and body piercing.
Readership/Target Audience: Aimed at traditional and contemporary metal band enthusiasts between 16 and 24 years old.
ADVERTISING RATES:
Full Page Colour £2680.00
Agency Commission: 10%
Mechanical Data: Type Area: 280 x 203mm, Bleed Size: 306 x 228mm, Trim Size: 300 x 222mm, Col Length: 280mm, Page Width: 203mm, Film: Digital
Copy instructions: Copy Date: 3 weeks prior to publication date
Average advertising content per issue: 30%
CONSUMER: MUSIC & PERFORMING ARTS: Pop Music

METHODIST RECORDER
47733U87-157
Editorial Address: 122 Golden Lane, LONDON, EC1Y 0TL
Tel: 020 7251 8414 **Fax:** 020 7608 3490
Email: editorial1@methodistrecorder.co.uk
Advertising Address: As above. **Fax:** 020 7251 8600
Email: ads@methodistrecorder.co.uk
Web site: http://www.methodistrecorder.co.uk
Publisher: Methodist Newspaper Co. Ltd.
Date Established: 1861
Frequency: Weekly
Cover Price: £1.30
Annual Sub.: £47.00
Circulation: 25,000 (Publisher's Statement)
Usual Pagination: 24
Editor: Moira Sleight; **Managing Editor:** Moira Sleight
Summary of Content: Newspaper featuring home and worldwide news, articles, reviews and resources for the Methodist church.
Readership/Target Audience: Aimed at Methodist church members, clergy and lay people.
ADVERTISING RATES:
SCC £13.00
Agency Commission: 10%
Mechanical Data: Col Length: 380mm, Type Area: 380 x 266mm, Page Width: 266mm, No. of Columns (Display): 6, Film: Digital, Col Widths (Display): 42mm
Copy instructions: Copy Date: 3 days prior to publication date
Average advertising content per issue: 10%
CONSUMER: RELIGIOUS

METROCENTRE MAGAZINE
1775047U74Q-1331
Editorial Address: Centre Management Offices, MetroCentre, GATESHEAD, NE11 9YG **Tel:** 0191 493 0200
Fax: 0191 493 2756
Email: nicola-redhead@capshop.co.uk
Advertising Address: As above.
Email: nicola-redhead@capshop.co.uk
Web site: http://www.metrocentre.uk.com
Publisher: CSC MetroCentre Ltd
Frequency: Half-yearly - Published in June and October
Cover Price: Free
Circulation: 380,000 (Publisher's Statement)
Usual Pagination: 42

Editor: Nicola Redhead; **Advertising Manager:** Debi Coldwell
Summary of Content: Shopping magazine covering the latest trends, fashion, home-wares, leisure and restaurants.
Readership/Target Audience: Aimed at shoppers in the MetroCentre.
ADVERTISING RATES:
Full Page Colour £1800.00
Mechanical Data: Bleed Size: 288 x 233mm, Trim Size: 285 x 230mm, Film: Digital
Copy instructions: Copy Date: April 2nd 2008
Average advertising content per issue: 50%
CONSUMER: WOMEN'S INTEREST CONSUMER MAGAZINES: Lifestyle

MF MICROLIGHT FLYING
36437U75N-280

Editorial Address: 4-6 Lansil Way, Caton Road, LANCASTER, LA1 3QY **Tel:** 01524 841010
Fax: 01524 841578
Email: dbremner@f2s.com
Advertising Address: As above.
Email: mf@pagefast.co.uk
Web site: http://www.bmaa.org
Publisher: British Microlight Aircraft Association
Date Established: 1980
Frequency: 6 issues yearly
Free to qualifying individuals
Circulation: 4,200 (Publisher's Statement)
Usual Pagination: 64
Editor: David Bremner; **Advertising Manager:** Paul Henry
Summary of Content: Magazine covering all aspects of microlight flying. Includes articles on microlight attire, specialist headgear, aviation maps and instrumentation.
Readership/Target Audience: Read by microlight pilots.
ADVERTISING RATES:
Full Page Colour £478.00
Agency Commission: 10%
Mechanical Data: Type Area: 252 x 178mm, Trim Size: 297 x 210mm, Film: Digital, Col Length: 252mm, Page Width: 178mm, Bleed Size: 303 x 216mm, No. of Columns (Display): 2, Col Widths (Display): 86mm, Print Process: Offset litho
Copy instructions: Copy Date: 1st of the month prior to publication date
Average advertising content per issue: 33%
CONSUMER: SPORT: Flight

MG ENTHUSIAST MAGAZINE
46425U77E-192_90

Editorial Address: 171 Eagle Way, Hampton Vale, PETERBOROUGH, PE7 8EL **Tel:** 01733 246500
Fax: 01733 246527
Email: tracy@mgenthusiast.com
Advertising Address: As above.
Email: madeleine@mgenthusiast.com
Web site: http://www.mg-enthusiast.com
Publisher: Hothouse Publishing Ltd
Frequency: Monthly
Cover Price: £3.75
Annual Sub.: £33.60
Circulation: 11,800 (Publisher's Statement)
Usual Pagination: 100
Editor: Tracy Scowen; **Advertising Manager:** Madeleine Lillywhite; **Publisher:** Geoff Love
Summary of Content: Magazine with news and information about MG cars.
Readership/Target Audience: Aimed at MG enthusiasts.
ADVERTISING RATES:
Full Page Mono £600.00
Full Page Colour £1800.00
Agency Commission: 10%
Mechanical Data: Film: Digital, Type Area: 270 x 182mm, Col Length: 270mm, Trim Size: 297 x 210mm, Bleed Size: 303 x 216mm, Page Width: 182mm
Copy instructions: Copy Date: 26th of the month prior to cover month
Average advertising content per issue: 40%
CONSUMER: MOTORING & CYCLING: Club Cars

MHA MAGAZINE
1836259U80B-432

Editorial Address: PO Box 39450, LONDON, N10 1WJ
Tel: 07934 630287
Email: editor@mhamagazine.com
Advertising Address: As above.
Email: advertising@mhamagazine.com
Web site: http://www.mhamagazine.com
ISSN: 1757-3572
Publisher: Imperative Media Ltd
Date Established: 2008
Frequency: Annual - Varies
Cover Price: Free
Cover Price: £3.50
Circulation: 10,000 (Print Run)
Usual Pagination: 60
Editor: Joy Coker
Summary of Content: Lifestyle magazine covering travel, property, local news and events, technology, business, films,

books, theatre, music, restaurant reviews, food and drink and a classified business directory.
Readership/Target Audience: Aimed at high income households in North London.
CONSUMER: RURAL & REGIONAL INTEREST: Regional Interest Greater London

MICRO MART
36175U78E-11

Formerly: Micro Computer Mart
Editorial Address: 30 Cleveland Street, LONDON, W1T 4JD
Tel: 020 7907 6000 **Fax:** 020 7907 6020
Email: simon_brew@dennis.co.uk
Advertising Address: As above.
Email: matthew_sullivan@dennis.co.uk
Web site: http://www.micromart.co.uk
ISSN: 0956-3881
Publisher: Dennis Publishing Ltd
Frequency: Weekly - Published on Thursday
Cover Price: £2.00
Circulation: 17,552 (ABC 01/01/2008 to 31/12/2008)
Usual Pagination: 140
Editor: Simon Brew; **Advertising Manager:** Matthew Sullivan-Pond; **Managing Editor:** Simon Brew
Summary of Content: Magazine covering product news, features, tips and computer reviews.
Readership/Target Audience: Aimed at the price conscious intermediate user of home and small business computers.
ADVERTISING RATES:
Full Page Colour £700.00
Agency Commission: 10%
Mechanical Data: Type Area: 270 x 190mm, Bleed Size: 307 x 220mm, Trim Size: 297 x 210mm, Film: Digital, Col Length: 270mm, Page Width: 190mm
Copy instructions: Copy Date: 1 week prior to publication date
Average advertising content per issue: 20%
CONSUMER: CONSUMER ELECTRONICS: Home Computing

MICROSOFT WINDOWS XP: THE OFFICIAL MAGAZINE
762662U78R-481

Editorial Address: 30 Monmouth Street, BATH, BA1 2BW
Tel: 01225 442244
Email: charlie.coles@futurenet.com
Advertising Address: As above.
Email: steve.grigg@futurenet.co.uk
Web site: http://www.windowsxpmagazine.co.uk
Publisher: Future Publishing Ltd
Date Established: 2001
Frequency: 13 issues yearly
Cover Price: £6.49
Circulation: 20,309 (Publisher's Statement)
Usual Pagination: 116
Editor: Charlie Coles; **Advertising Manager:** Steve Grigg; **Publisher:** Charlotte Morgan
Summary of Content: Magazine featuring articles on improving your PC, adding new components and making the most of your PC with reviews on the latest software and games.
Readership/Target Audience: Read by Windows XP users who want to get more from their PC.
ADVERTISING RATES:
Full Page Colour £1200.00
Mechanical Data: Film: Digital
Copy instructions: Copy Date: 4 weeks prior to publication date
CONSUMER: CONSUMER ELECTRONICS: Consumer Electronics Related

MID SUSSEX MATTERS
601251U80C-3215

Editorial Address: Oaklands, Oaklands Road, HAYWARDS HEATH, RH16 1SS **Tel:** 01444 477387 **Fax:** 01444 477507
Email: msm@midsussex.gov.uk
Advertising Address: 46 Parkside, SHOREHAM-BY-SEA, BN43 6HA **Tel:** 07946 638490
Email: vincebamford@btopenworld.com
Web site: http://www.midsussex.gov.uk
Publisher: Mid Sussex District Council
Date Established: 1995
Frequency: 3 issues yearly
Cover Price: Free
Circulation: 67,000 (Publisher's Statement)
Usual Pagination: 16
Editor: Martin Faulconbridge; **Advertising Manager:** Vince Bamford
Summary of Content: Magazine providing local government and community information.
Readership/Target Audience: Aimed at residents and businesses in Sussex.
ADVERTISING: Rates on application
CONSUMER: RURAL & REGIONAL INTEREST: Regional Interest English Counties

THE MIDDLE EAST
47248U82-115

Editorial Address: 7 Coldbath Square, LONDON, EC1R 4LQ **Tel:** 020 7841 3210 **Fax:** 020 7841 3211
Email: editorial@africasia.com
Advertising Address: As above. **Tel:** 020 7713 7711
Fax: 020 7713 7898
Email: sales@africasia.com
Web site: http://www.africasia.co.uk/themiddleeast
ISSN: 0305-0734
Publisher: IC Publications Ltd
Date Established: 1974
Frequency: 11 issues yearly - Published on the 3rd Friday of the month prior to cover date
Cover Price: £2.70
Circulation: 25,213 (ABC 01/01/2008 to 31/12/2008)
Usual Pagination: 68
Editor: Pat Lancaster; **Advertising Manager:** Omar Ben Yedder
Summary of Content: Magazine reporting on current affairs, business and finance issues, country reports, industry surveys and book reviews from the Middle East region and the Arab world.
Readership/Target Audience: Read by government officials, business professionals, researchers, academics and students around the world.
ADVERTISING RATES:
Full Page Colour £5700.00
Agency Commission: 15%
Mechanical Data: Bleed Size: 276 x 216mm, Trim Size: 270 x 210mm, Type Area: 242 x 186mm, Col Length: 242mm, Film: Digital, Page Width: 186mm
Copy instructions: Copy Date: 2 weeks prior to publication date
Average advertising content per issue: 15%
CONSUMER: CURRENT AFFAIRS & POLITICS

THE MIDDLE EAST IN EUROPE
1657704U90-941

Formerly: The Middle East in London
Editorial Address: Suite 207, Parkway House, Sheen Lane, LONDON, SW14 8LS **Tel:** 020 8392 1122
Fax: 020 8392 1422
Email: sajidrizvi@eapgroup.com
Advertising Address: As above.
Email: adsales@eapgroup.com
Web site: http://www.meenet.info
ISSN: 1749-8627
Publisher: EAP Group Business Media
Date Established: 2004
Frequency: 6 issues yearly - Published on the 1st of the cover month
Cover Price: £3.00
Free to qualifying individuals
Annual Sub.: £30.00
Circulation: 9,500 (Publisher's Statement)
Usual Pagination: 40
Editor: Sajid Rizvi; **Executive Editor:** Shirley Rizvi; **Editor-in-Chief:** Sajid Rizvi; **Advertising Manager:** Sybil Bernier-Hart
Summary of Content: Magazine covering politics, finance, current affairs, business, motoring, science and technology, art and culture, fashion and high life, film, music, theatre and going out with special reference to the Middle Eastern communities in Europe.
Readership/Target Audience: Aimed at those doing business in the Middle East and those in the Middle East doing business in Europe.
ADVERTISING RATES:
Full Page Colour £2995.00
Agency Commission: 10%
Mechanical Data: Type Area: 260 x 175mm, Bleed Size: 303 x 216mm, Trim Size: 297 x 210mm, Col Length: 260mm, Page Width: 175mm, Film: Digital
Copy instructions: Copy Date: 20 days prior to publication date
Average advertising content per issue: 35%
CONSUMER: ETHNIC

THE MIDDLE EAST IN LONDON
1789866U90-997

Editorial Address: SOAS, University of London, Thornhaugh Street, Russell Square, LONDON, WC1H 0XG
Tel: 020 7898 4271 **Fax:** 020 7898 4269
Email: sr47@soas.ac.uk
Advertising Address: As above. **Tel:** 020 7898 4442
Fax: 020 7898 4329
Email: lh2@soas.ac.uk
Web site: http://www.lmei.soas.ac.uk
Publisher: The London Middle East Institute
Frequency: 10 issues yearly
Cover Price: £3.00
Circulation: 750 (Publisher's Statement)
Usual Pagination: 34
Editor: Sahar Rad; **Advertising Manager:** Louise Hosking
Summary of Content: Magazine covering current Middle Eastern events in the UK, current affairs and opinion pieces as well as a news section, book, film and travel reviews.
Readership/Target Audience: Aimed at academics, students and businesses.

Copy instructions: Copy Date: 15th of the cover month
CONSUMER: ETHNIC

MIDLANDS HOMES & INTERIORS

1637771U80C-5068

Editorial Address: 5th Floor, White House, 111 New Street, BIRMINGHAM, B2 4EU **Tel:** 0121 631 6101
Email: sarah@malthusmedia.co.uk
Advertising Address: As above. **Fax:** 0121 336 1936
Email: leah@modamedia.co.uk
Web site: http://www.modamedia.co.uk
ISSN: 1741-7848
Publisher: Moda Media
Date Established: 2003
Frequency: 6 issues yearly
Cover Price: Free
Circulation: 20,000 (Publisher's Statement)
Usual Pagination: 68
Editor: Sarah Drew Jones
Summary of Content: Magazine covering homes and interiors, property, investment, personal finance, shopping, makeovers, art, gardening, food and new products.
Readership/Target Audience: Aimed at affluent households in the Midlands.
ADVERTISING RATES:
Full Page Colour £1200.00
Agency Commission: 10%
Average advertising content per issue: 40%
CONSUMER: RURAL & REGIONAL INTEREST: Regional Interest English Counties

MIDLANDS WHAT'S ON

48113U89C-265

Editorial Address: 4-5 Dogpole, SHREWSBURY, SY1 1EN
Tel: 01743 281708 **Fax:** 01743 248256
Email: davina@whatsonlive.co.uk
Advertising Address: As above. **Tel:** 01743 281777
Fax: 01743 281744
Email: sales@whatsonlive.co.uk
Publisher: What's On Magazine Group
Frequency: Monthly
Cover Price: £1.50
Free to qualifying individuals
Annual Sub.: £24.00
Circulation: 56,000 (Publisher's Statement)
Usual Pagination: 64
Editor: Davina Evans; **Managing Director:** Paul Oliver;
Advertising Manager: Paul Oliver
Summary of Content: Entertainment guide to what's on in the Midlands and North West areas.
Readership/Target Audience: Aimed at those living in and around the area.
ADVERTISING RATES:
Full Page Colour £3375.00
Agency Commission: 10%
Mechanical Data: Col Length: 277mm, Page Width: 190mm, Type Area: 277 x 190mm, Bleed Size: 303 x 216mm, Trim Size: 297 x 210mm, No. of Columns (Display): 6, Film: Digital
Copy instructions: Copy Date: 3rd Friday of the month prior to publication date
Average advertising content per issue: 50%
Editions:
Midlands What's On Black Country Edition
Midlands What's On Central Edition
Midlands What's On South Staffordshire Edition
What's On West Midlands 24:7
CONSUMER: HOLIDAYS & TRAVEL: Entertainment Guides

MIDLANDS ZONE

48117U89C-268

Editorial Address: 4-5 Dogpole, SHREWSBURY, SY1 1EN
Tel: 01743 281777 **Fax:** 01743 281744
Email: info@zonemag.com
Advertising Address: As above. **Fax:** 01743 248256
Email: info@zonemag.com
Web site: http://www.zonemag.com
ISSN: 1462-7043
Publisher: What's On Magazine Group
Date Established: 1996
Frequency: Monthly
Cover Price: £1.00
Free to qualifying individuals
Circulation: 20,000 (Publisher's Statement)
Usual Pagination: 80
Editor: Paul Oliver; **Managing Director:** Paul Oliver;
Advertising Manager: Paul Oliver
Summary of Content: What's on magazine covering news, film, theatre, music, videos, travel, events and holidays.
Readership/Target Audience: Aimed at the gay, lesbian and bisexual community in the Midlands.
ADVERTISING RATES:
Full Page Mono £1030.50
Full Page Colour £1145.00
SCC £14.50
Agency Commission: 10%

Mechanical Data: Col Length: 265mm, Film: Digital, Bleed Size: 291 x 216mm, Type Area: 265 x 190mm, Page Width: 190mm, Trim Size: 285 x 210mm
Copy instructions: Copy Date: 2 weeks prior to publication date
Average advertising content per issue: 50%
CONSUMER: HOLIDAYS & TRAVEL: Entertainment Guides

M.I.L. MATCHMAKER

48316U90-93

Formerly: Matchmaker Magazine
Editorial Address: PO Box 430, PINNER, HA5 2TW
Tel: 020 8868 1879
Email: mktg@perfect-partner.com
Advertising Address: As above.
Email: mktg@perfect-partner.com
Web site: http://www.perfect-partner.com
ISSN: 1750-4260
Publisher: Matchmaker International Ltd
Date Established: 1995
Frequency: 3 issues yearly - Published in March, July and October
Cover Price: £1.50
Free to qualifying individuals
Annual Sub.: £9.00
Circulation: 20,000 (Publisher's Statement)
Usual Pagination: 44
Editor: Bharat Raithatha; **Advertising Manager:** Bharat Raithatha
Summary of Content: Asian contact and introductions magazine including articles on health, beauty, fashion, travel, astrology, financial planning, property and classified business.
Readership/Target Audience: Aimed at Asians seeking partners.
ADVERTISING RATES:
Full Page Mono £150.00
Full Page Colour £300.00
Agency Commission: 20%
Mechanical Data: Trim Size: 297 x 210mm, Bleed Size: 303 x 216mm, Film: Digital
Average advertising content per issue: 40%
CONSUMER: ETHNIC

MILITARY ILLUSTRATED

46696U79H-80

Editorial Address: 1B Leigh Road, LONDON, N5 1ST
Tel: 01525 222573
Email: timn@fsmail.net
Advertising Address: Doolittle Mill, Doolittle Lane, Totternhoe, DUNSTABLE, LU6 1QX **Tel:** 01525 222573
Fax: 01525 222574
Email: colin@adhpublishing.com
Publisher: ADH Publishing
Frequency: Monthly
Cover Price: £3.85
Annual Sub.: £40.00
Circulation: 15,000 (Publisher's Statement)
Usual Pagination: 58
Editor: Tim Newark
Summary of Content: Magazine covering history of warfare, weapons, units, battles and personalities from ancient times to the present.
Readership/Target Audience: Read by dedicated military history enthusiasts.
ADVERTISING RATES:
Full Page Colour £950.00
Agency Commission: 10%
Mechanical Data: Col Length: 267mm, Page Width: 190mm, Trim Size: 297 x 210mm, Type Area: 267 x 190mm, Bleed Size: 303 x 216mm, Film: Digital
Copy instructions: Copy Date: 6 weeks prior to publication date
Average advertising content per issue: 12%
CONSUMER: HOBBIES & DIY: Military History

MILITARY IN SCALE

46600U79B-45

Editorial Address: Traplet House, Pendragon Close, MALVERN, WR14 1GA **Tel:** 01684 588500
Fax: 01684 578558
Email: mis@traplet.com
Advertising Address: As above.
Email: stephanie.hill@traplet.com
Web site: http://www.traplet.com
ISSN: 0967-7062
Publisher: Traplet Publications Ltd
Date Established: 1992
Frequency: Monthly
Cover Price: £3.50
Annual Sub.: £39.00
Usual Pagination: 68
Editor: Spencer Pollard; **Advertising Manager:** Stephanie Hill
Summary of Content: Magazine covering military modelling, from tanks and armoured fighting vehicles to figures and aircraft.
Readership/Target Audience: Read by model makers.
ADVERTISING RATES:
Full Page Mono £300.00

Full Page Colour £350.00
Agency Commission: 10%
Mechanical Data: Page Width: 184mm, Bleed Size: 303 x 216mm, Trim Size: 297 x 210mm, Type Area: 270 x 184mm, Col Length: 270mm, Film: Digital
Copy instructions: Copy Date: 4 weeks prior to publication date
CONSUMER: HOBBIES & DIY: Models & Modelling

MILITARY MACHINES INTERNATIONAL

764913U79K-992

Editorial Address: Unit 5, Chiltern Business Centre, 63-65 Woodside Road, AMERSHAM, HP6 6AA **Tel:** 01494 433453
Fax: 01494 433468
Email: military.machines@virgin.net
Advertising Address: As above. **Tel:** 01684 311514
Email: adverts@modelactivitypress.com
Web site: http://www.modelactivitypress.com
Publisher: Model Activity Press Ltd
Frequency: Monthly - Published on the 1st Thursday of each month
Cover Price: £3.80
Annual Sub.: £35.00
Circulation: 18,000 (Publisher's Statement)
Usual Pagination: 78
Editor: Ian Young; **Advertising Manager:** Lisa Dawson;
Publisher: Tony Dowdeswell
Summary of Content: Magazine written by military vehicle enthusiasts covering information on the purchase and restoration of all types of military vehicles.
Readership/Target Audience: Aimed at enthusiasts and those with aspirations of owning their own military vehicle.
ADVERTISING: Rates on application
Copy instructions: Copy Date: 4 weeks prior to publication
CONSUMER: HOBBIES & DIY: Collectors Magazines

MILITARY MODELCRAFT INTERNATIONAL

46598U79B-35

Editorial Address: Unit 3, Enigma building, Bilton Road, Bletchley, MILTON KEYNES, MK1 1HW **Tel:** 01908 270400
Fax: 01908 270614
Advertising Address: As above.
Email: reg@regallitho.co.uk
Web site: http://www.militarymodelcraftinternational.co.uk
Publisher: Guideline Publications Ltd
Date Established: 1996
Frequency: Monthly - Published on the 1st Thursday of each month
Cover Price: £3.95
Annual Sub.: £40.50
Circulation: 8,000 (Publisher's Statement)
Usual Pagination: 64
Editor: Tony Little; **Advertising Manager:** Regis Auckland;
Publisher: Regis Auckland
Summary of Content: Magazine focusing on military modelcraft covering armoured fighting vehicles and military figures, toy soldier figures and figurines.
Readership/Target Audience: Aimed at military model craft enthusiasts.
ADVERTISING RATES:
Full Page Mono £160.00
Full Page Colour £180.00
Mechanical Data: Col Length: 270mm, Bleed Size: 303 x 216mm, Type Area: 270 x 185mm, Trim Size: 297 x 210mm, Page Width: 185mm
Copy instructions: Copy Date: 4 weeks prior to publication date
CONSUMER: HOBBIES & DIY: Models & Modelling

MILITARY MODELLING

46599U79B-40

Editorial Address: PO Box 6017, LEIGHTON BUZZARD, LU7 2FA **Tel:** 01525 370389 **Fax:** 01525 370389
Email: ken.jones@myhobbystore.com
Advertising Address: Berwick House, 8-10 Knoll Rise, ORPINGTON, BR6 0EL **Tel:** 01689 899200
Email: huseyin.huseyin@magicalia.com
Web site: http://www.militarymodelling.com
ISSN: 0026-4083
Publisher: My Hobby Store Media
Date Established: 1971
Frequency: 15 issues yearly
Cover Price: £3.95
Circulation: 12,343 (Publisher's Statement)
Usual Pagination: 84
Editor: Ken Jones
Summary of Content: Modelling magazine covering miniature military vehicles and model soldiers.
Readership/Target Audience: Aimed at enthusiasts of military models.
ADVERTISING RATES:
Full Page Colour £695.00
Agency Commission: 10%
Mechanical Data: Page Width: 184mm, Film: Digital, Bleed Size: 303 x 213mm, Trim Size: 297 x 210mm, Type Area: 267 x 184mm, Col Length: 267mm

Copy instructions: Copy Date: 4 weeks prior to publication date
Average advertising content per issue: 30%
CONSUMER: HOBBIES & DIY: Models & Modelling

MILLENNIUM - JOURNAL OF INTERNATIONAL STUDIES
47250U82-119

Editorial Address: Room D701, London School of Economics and Political Science, Houghton Street, LONDON, WC2A 2AE **Tel:** 020 7955 6232
Fax: 020 7955 7438
Email: millennium@lse.ac.uk
Advertising Address: As above.
Email: millennium.manager@lse.ac.uk
Web site: http://www.e-millennium.ac
ISSN: 0305-8298
Publisher: Millennium Publishing Group
Date Established: 1971
Frequency: 3 issues yearly
Annual Sub.: £50.00
Circulation: 2,000 (Publisher's Statement)
Usual Pagination: 250
Editor: Rashmi Singh; **Advertising Manager:** Rashmi Singh
Summary of Content: Journal featuring international relations and affairs, politics and political economy, foreign policy analysis and diplomatic history.
Readership/Target Audience: Read by academics.
ADVERTISING RATES:
Full Page Mono £200.00
CONSUMER: CURRENT AFFAIRS & POLITICS

MILLIONAIRE LIFESTYLE
1827693U74Q-1357

Editorial Address: Press releases by email only
Tel: 020 7183 7330
Email: seans@mlmagazine.com
Advertising Address: Contact by email or phone only
Tel: 07918 937437
Email: seans@mlmagazine.com
Web site: http://www.mlmagazine.com
Publisher: Millionnaire Lifestyle Media Ltd
Date Established: 2006
Frequency: 6 issues yearly
Free to qualifying individuals
Circulation: 40,000 (Publisher's Statement)
Usual Pagination: 116
Editor: Miesha Headen; **Managing Editor:** Miesha Headen
Summary of Content: Luxury lifestyle magazine covering exotic boutique travel destinations, hotels, resorts and spas to the latest in fashion, jewellery, time pieces, luxury automobiles, yachts, and wellness.
Readership/Target Audience: Aimed at high net worth consumers.
ADVERTISING RATES:
Full Page Mono £4000.00
Full Page Colour £4000.00
Agency Commission: 20%
Mechanical Data: Trim Size: 297 x 210mm, Bleed Size: 305 x 218mm, Film: Digital
Copy instructions: Copy Date: 2 weeks prior to publication date
Average advertising content per issue: 40%
CONSUMER: WOMEN'S INTEREST CONSUMER MAGAZINES: Lifestyle

MINERVA. THE INTERNATIONAL REVIEW OF ANCIENT ART AND ARCHAEOLOGY
31044U94X-95

Formerly: Minerva
Editorial Address: 14 Old Bond Street, LONDON, W1S 4PP
Tel: 020 7495 2590 **Fax:** 020 7491 1595
Email: minerva@minervamagazine.com
Advertising Address: As above.
Email: advertising@minervamagazine.com
Web site: http://www.minervamagazine.com
ISSN: 0957-7718
Publisher: Aurora Publications Ltd
Date Established: 1990
Frequency: 6 issues yearly
Cover Price: £4.00
Circulation: 10,000 (Publisher's Statement)
Usual Pagination: 64
Editor: Mark Merrony; **Advertising Manager:** Mark Merrony
Summary of Content: Magazine containing museum and gallery exhibitions, auction previews and reviews, numismatic reviews, ancient art, book reviews, excavation announcements and archaeological tours.
Readership/Target Audience: Aimed at practising archaeologists, the general public and those interested in ancient art, archaeology, antiquities and museums.
ADVERTISING RATES:
Full Page Colour £1000.00
Agency Commission: 10%
Mechanical Data: Bleed Size: 303 x 216mm, Trim Size: 297 x 210mm, Film: Digital
Copy instructions: Copy Date: 4 weeks prior to publication date

Average advertising content per issue: 15%
CONSUMER: OTHER CLASSIFICATIONS: Miscellaneous

MINI MAGAZINE
46469U77E-194

Editorial Address: 30 Monmouth Street, BATH, BA1 2BW
Tel: 01225 442244
Email: mark.robinson@futurenet.com
Advertising Address: As above. **Fax:** 01225 732206
Email: eoin.hare@futurenet.co.uk
Web site: http://www.minimag.co.uk
ISSN: 1362-7252
Publisher: Future Publishing Ltd
Date Established: 1996
Frequency: 13 issues yearly
Cover Price: £3.99
Circulation: 15,000 (Publisher's Statement)
Usual Pagination: 148
Editor: Mark Robinson; **Features Editor:** Jeff Ruggles
Summary of Content: Magazine providing a mix of readers' car profiles, technical advice, aftermarket product reviews, show reports and news.
Readership/Target Audience: Aimed at Mini enthusiasts.
ADVERTISING RATES:
Full Page Colour £810.00
Agency Commission: 10%
Mechanical Data: Bleed Size: 309 x 222mm, Trim Size: 297 x 210mm, Film: Digital, Type Area: 277 x 190mm, Col Length: 277mm, Page Width: 190mm
Copy instructions: Copy Date: 4 weeks prior to publication date
Average advertising content per issue: 30%
CONSUMER: MOTORING & CYCLING: Club Cars

MINIATURE WARGAMES
46601U79B-50

Editorial Address: Main Street, Strelley Hall, NOTTINGHAM, NG8 6PE **Tel:** 0115 906 1218
Email: andrew@miniwargames.com
Advertising Address: As above. **Fax:** 0115 906 1251
Email: andrew@miniwargames.com
Web site: http://www.miniwargames.com
ISSN: 0266-3228
Publisher: Pireme Publishing Ltd
Date Established: 1983
Frequency: Monthly
Cover Price: £3.70
Annual Sub.: £43.00
Circulation: 8,500 (Publisher's Statement)
Usual Pagination: 48
Editor: Andrew Hubback; **Advertising Manager:** Andrew Hubback; **Publisher:** Andrew Hubback
Summary of Content: Publication featuring war games in all periods of history and all parts of the world plus fantasy and science fiction.
Readership/Target Audience: Aimed at male readers aged 20 years old and over.
ADVERTISING RATES:
Full Page Mono £302.00
Full Page Colour £393.00
Agency Commission: 10%
Mechanical Data: Col Widths (Display): 90mm, Print Process: Sheet-fed litho, Page Width: 185mm, Type Area: 270 x 185mm, Col Length: 270mm, No. of Columns (Display): 2, Film: Digital, Trim Size: 297 x 210mm, Bleed Size: 303 x 213mm
Copy instructions: Copy Date: 4 weeks prior to publication date
Average advertising content per issue: 20%
CONSUMER: HOBBIES & DIY: Models & Modelling

MINIWORLD
46470U77E-195

Editorial Address: Leon House, 233 High Street, CROYDON, CR9 1HZ **Tel:** 020 8726 8364
Fax: 020 8726 8398
Email: miniworld@ipcmedia.com
Advertising Address: As above. **Tel:** 020 8726 8000
Fax: 020 8726 8399
Email: ian_james@ipcmedia.com
Web site: http://www.miniworld.co.uk
ISSN: 0936-1186
Publisher: IPC Inspire
Date Established: 1991
Frequency: 13 issues yearly
Cover Price: £3.85
Annual Sub.: £40.80
Circulation: 25,000 (Publisher's Statement)
Usual Pagination: 148
Editor: Karen Drury; **Features Editor:** Stephen Colbran; **Advertising Manager:** Ian James
Summary of Content: Magazine covering original Mini tuning, conversions, rallying, clubs and news around the world. Does not cover the BMW Mini.
Readership/Target Audience: Aimed at Mini enthusiasts.
ADVERTISING RATES:
Full Page Colour £1139.00
Agency Commission: 10%
Mechanical Data: Type Area: 266 x 190mm, Bleed Size: 303 x 216mm, Trim Size: 297 x 210mm, Print Process: Web-

fed offset litho, Film: Digital, Col Length: 266mm, Page Width: 190mm
Copy instructions: Copy Date: 6 weeks prior to publication date
Average advertising content per issue: 36%
CONSUMER: MOTORING & CYCLING: Club Cars

MINOR MONTHLY
46495U77F-250

Editorial Address: Middle Farm, Middle Farm Way, Poundbury, DORCHESTER, DT1 3RS **Tel:** 01305 266360
Fax: 01305 756395
Email: russ@poundbury.co.uk
Advertising Address: As above. **Fax:** 01305 262760
Email: alison.hall@alisonhall-pr.co.uk
Web site: http://www.minormonthly.com
ISSN: 1358-829X
Publisher: Poundbury Publishing Ltd
Date Established: 1995
Frequency: Monthly
Cover Price: £2.40
Annual Sub.: £24.00
Circulation: 11,500 (Publisher's Statement)
Usual Pagination: 48
Editor: Russ Harvey; **Managing Director:** Peter Shaw; **Publisher:** Peter Shaw
Summary of Content: Magazine containing features on buying, maintenance and restoration of Morris Minors.
Readership/Target Audience: Read by Morris Minor enthusiasts.
ADVERTISING RATES:
Full Page Mono £550.00
Full Page Colour £755.00
Agency Commission: 10%
Mechanical Data: Type Area: 285 x 190mm, Trim Size: 295 x 210mm, Film: Digital, Col Length: 285mm, Page Width: 190mm
Copy instructions: Copy Date: 3 weeks prior to publication date
Average advertising content per issue: 40%
CONSUMER: MOTORING & CYCLING: Veteran Cars

MIXMAG
46169U76E-239

Editorial Address: 90-92 Pentonville Road, LONDON, N1 9HS **Tel:** 020 7078 8417 **Fax:** 020 7833 9900
Email: mixmag@mixmag.net
Advertising Address: As above. **Tel:** 020 7520 8625
Email: juliet.cromwell@developmenthell.co.uk
Web site: http://www.mixmag.net
Publisher: Development Hell Ltd
Frequency: Monthly
Cover Price: £3.95
Circulation: 30,159 (ABC 01/07/2008 to 31/12/2008)
Usual Pagination: 156
Editor: Nick Stevenson; **News Editor:** Nick Stevenson; **Features Editor:** Duncan Dick; **Editor-in-Chief:** Andrew Harrison; **Advertising Manager:** Juliet Cromwell; **Managing Editor:** James Mowbray
Summary of Content: Dance music magazine with fashion, record reviews and lifestyle features.
Readership/Target Audience: Aimed at dance music fans and clubbers generally.
ADVERTISING RATES:
Full Page Colour £4005.00
Agency Commission: 10%
Mechanical Data: Type Area: 275 x 200mm, Bleed Size: 306 x 236mm, Trim Size: 300 x 230mm, Col Length: 275mm, Page Width: 200mm, Film: Digital
Copy instructions: Copy Date: 4 weeks prior to publication date
Average advertising content per issue: 40%
CONSUMER: MUSIC & PERFORMING ARTS: Pop Music

MIZZ
45392U74F-363_50

Editorial Address: Brockbourne House, Mount Ephraim, TUNBRIDGE WELLS, TN4 8BS **Tel:** 01892 500100
Fax: 01892 545666
Email: mizz@panini.co.uk
Advertising Address: Orange 20 Limited, 20 Orange Street, LONDON, WC2H 7EF **Tel:** 020 7321 0701
Fax: 01372 723322
Email: panini.adsales@o20.co.uk
Web site: http://www.mizz.com
ISSN: 0955-0119
Publisher: Panini UK Ltd
Date Established: 1985
Frequency: 26 issues yearly
Cover Price: £2.10
Circulation: 54,068 (ABC 01/01/2009 to 30/06/2009)
Usual Pagination: 84
Editor: Lucy Saxton; **Features Editor:** Lucy Saxton; **Managing Director:** Mike Riddell; **Managing Editor:** Alan O'Keefe
Summary of Content: Magazine containing fashion advice, features, problem pages, career orientated section and gossip.
Readership/Target Audience: Aimed at fashion and beauty conscious girls between 10 and 14 years old.

ADVERTISING RATES:
Full Page Colour £3600.00
Mechanical Data: Type Area: 277 x 190mm, Bleed Size: 307 x 220mm, Trim Size: 297 x 210mm, Col Length: 277mm, Page Width: 190mm, Film: Digital
CONSUMER: WOMEN'S INTEREST CONSUMER MAGAZINES: Teenage

MMM MOTORCARAVAN MOTORHOME MONTHLY
48425U91B-134

Editorial Address: PO Box 88, TIVERTON, EX16 7ZN
Tel: 01778 392439
Email: mmmeditor@warnersgroup.co.uk
Advertising Address: The Maltings, West Street, BOURNE, PE10 9PH **Tel:** 01778 391000 **Fax:** 01778 425437
Email: helent@warnersgroup.co.uk
Web site: http://www.outandaboutlive.co.uk
ISSN: 0141-9269
Publisher: Warners Group Publications plc
Date Established: 1966
Frequency: Monthly
Cover Price: £3.40
Annual Sub.: £34.99
Circulation: 38,000 (ABC 01/01/2008 to 31/12/2008)
Usual Pagination: 350
Editor: Mike Jago
Summary of Content: Publication containing road test reports, new product news, travel articles, readers' letters, a buyer's guide and DIY information.
Readership/Target Audience: Aimed at motorcaravan and motorhome owners.
ADVERTISING RATES:
Full Page Mono £1290.00
Full Page Colour £1755.00
Agency Commission: 10%
Mechanical Data: Bleed Size: 303 x 216mm, Trim Size: 297 x 210mm, Type Area: 275 x 190mm, Col Length: 275mm, Film: Digital, Page Width: 190mm
Average advertising content per issue: 55%
Supplement(s): MMM Mobility Annual - 1xY
CONSUMER: RECREATION & LEISURE: Camping & Caravanning

MO
1640584U89B-342

Editorial Address: 6-8 Old Bond Street, LONDON, W1S 4PH **Tel:** 020 7499 9080 **Fax:** 020 7152 3899
Email: swright@condenast.co.uk
Advertising Address: As above. **Fax:** 020 7495 9662
Email: nicola.anderson@condenast.co.uk
Web site: http://www.condenast.co.uk
Publisher: Conde Nast Publications Ltd
Date Established: 2004
Frequency: Half-yearly - Published in May and November
Cover Price: Free
Circulation: 33,500 (Print Run)
Usual Pagination: 64
Editor: Serena Hamilton; **Managing Editor:** Serena Hamilton
Summary of Content: Luxury lifestyle magazine covering travel, design, fashion, food and drink, beauty and people.
Readership/Target Audience: Aimed at customers of the Mandarin Oriental Hotel Group.
ADVERTISING RATES:
Full Page Colour £6218.00
Agency Commission: 15%
Mechanical Data: Film: Digital, Col Length: 283mm, Page Width: 207mm, Bleed Size: 309 x 233mm, Trim Size: 303 x 227mm, Type Area: 283 x 207mm
Copy instructions: Copy Date: 8 weeks prior to publication date
Average advertising content per issue: 25%
CONSUMER: HOLIDAYS & TRAVEL: Hotel Magazines

MOBILISE
1791397U94F-1013

Editorial Address: The Maltings, West Street, BOURNE, PE10 9PH **Tel:** 01778 391000 **Fax:** 01778 394748
Email: editor@mobilise.info
Advertising Address: As above. **Fax:** 01778 392079
Email: sarahh@warnersgroup.co.uk
Web site: http://www.mobilise.info
Publisher: Warners Group Publications plc
Date Established: 2006
Frequency: Monthly
Cover Price: £2.95
Free to qualifying individuals
Circulation: 25,000 (Publisher's Statement)
Usual Pagination: 40
Editor: Lisa Crosby; **Advertising Manager:** Sarah Hubbard; **Managing Editor:** Nicky Rogers
Summary of Content: Magazine covering issues involved in motoring and mobility as well as sport, travel and other issues which affect disabled people.
Readership/Target Audience: Aimed at members of the Mobilise organisation.
ADVERTISING RATES:
Full Page Colour £1750.00

Agency Commission: 10%
Mechanical Data: Trim Size: 275 x 190mm, Bleed Size: 303 x 216mm, Film: Digital
Copy instructions: Copy Date: 3 weeks prior to publication date
Average advertising content per issue: 38%
CONSUMER: OTHER CLASSIFICATIONS: Disability

MOC MAGAZINE
1799099U86B-181

Editorial Address: Unit 14, 20 Palmers Road, LONDON, E2 0SY **Tel:** 0845 077 2887
Email: editorial@ukmoc.com
Advertising Address: As above. **Tel:** 0845 302 2968
Email: editorial@ukmoc.com
Web site: http://www.ukmoc.com
ISSN: 1750-8401
Publisher: VSM Media Ltd.
Date Established: 2005
Frequency: Monthly
Free to qualifying individuals
Annual Sub.: £29.00
Circulation: 20,000 (Publisher's Statement)
Usual Pagination: 48
Editor: Von Shaw; **Advertising Manager:** Von Shaw
Summary of Content: Magazine focusing on entertainment, health and lifestyle issues.
Readership/Target Audience: Aimed at gay, bisexual and transgender men of colour.
ADVERTISING RATES:
Full Page Colour £800.00
Mechanical Data: Bleed Size: 307 x 220mm, Trim Size: 297 x 210mm, Film: Digital
CONSUMER: ADULT & GAY MAGAZINES: Gay & Lesbian Magazines

MODEL AIRCRAFT MONTHLY
761539U79B-55

Editorial Address: Media House, 21 Kingsway, BEDFORD, MK42 9BJ **Tel:** 0870 733 3733 **Fax:** 0870 733 3744
Email: neil@sampublications.com
Advertising Address: As above.
Email: sophie@sampublications.com
Web site: http://www.sampublications.com
Publisher: Sam Ltd
Date Established: 2002
Frequency: Monthly
Cover Price: £3.80
Annual Sub.: £38.00
Circulation: 28,000 (Publisher's Statement)
Usual Pagination: 64
Editor: Neil Robinson; **Advertising Manager:** Sophie Elliot; **Publisher:** Steve Elliott
Summary of Content: Magazine providing reference material including scale plans and information on a variety of aviation subjects.
Readership/Target Audience: Read by aviation construction kit modellers.
ADVERTISING RATES:
Full Page Mono £800.00
Full Page Colour £980.00
Agency Commission: 10%
Mechanical Data: Page Width: 190mm, Type Area: 274 x 190mm, Col Length: 274mm, Trim Size: 297 x 210mm, Bleed Size: +3mm, Print Process: Web-fed offset litho, Film: Digital
Copy instructions: Copy Date: 1st week of the month prior to publication date
Average advertising content per issue: 30%
CONSUMER: HOBBIES & DIY: Models & Modelling

MODEL AIRPLANE INTERNATIONAL
1693878U79B-199

Editorial Address: Doolittle Mill, Doolittle Lane, Totternhoe, DUNSTABLE, LU6 1QX **Tel:** 01525 222573
Fax: 01525 222574
Email: editorial@modelairplaneinternational.com
Advertising Address: As above.
Email: adcopy@adhpublishing.com
Web site: http://www.modelairplaneinternational.com
Publisher: ADH Publishing
Date Established: 2005
Frequency: Monthly
Cover Price: £3.55
Circulation: 30,000 (Print Run)
Usual Pagination: 84
Editor: Richard Franks; **Advertising Manager:** Colin Spinner
Summary of Content: Magazine covering information on the latest models, gadgets and accessories as well as competitions, information on new product releases and local shows.
Readership/Target Audience: Aimed at enthusiasts of static model airplanes.
ADVERTISING RATES:
Full Page Colour £860.00
Agency Commission: 10%

Mechanical Data: Type Area: 287 x 200mm, Bleed Size: 303 x 216mm, Trim Size: 297 x 210mm, Col Length: 287mm, Page Width: 200mm, Film: Digital
Copy instructions: Copy Date: 5 weeks prior to publication date
Average advertising content per issue: 23%
CONSUMER: HOBBIES & DIY: Models & Modelling

MODEL BOATS
46603U79B-60

Editorial Address: PO Box 9890, BRENTWOOD, CM14 9EF
Tel: 01277 849927
Email: editor@modelboats.co.uk
Advertising Address: Berwick House, 8-10 Knoll Rise, ORPINGTON, BR6 0EL **Tel:** 01689 899253
Fax: 01689 899266
Email: andy.cross@magicalia.com
Web site: http://www.modelboats.co.uk
ISSN: 0144-2910
Publisher: My Hobby Store Media
Date Established: 1965
Frequency: Monthly
Cover Price: £3.85
Usual Pagination: 84
Editor: Paul Freshney
Summary of Content: Magazine covering all aspects of model boating from radio controlled warships to stately galleons, as well as projects, news of the latest developments and new products, free plans and plan features and kit reviews. Also includes coverage of model boat shows and exhibitions in the UK and abroad.
Readership/Target Audience: Aimed at model boat and yachting enthusiasts around the world.
ADVERTISING RATES:
Full Page Colour £550.00
SCC £17.00
Agency Commission: 10%
Mechanical Data: Page Width: 184mm, Col Widths (Display): 45mm, Film: Digital, Type Area: 267 x 184mm, Trim Size: 297 x 210mm, Bleed Size: 303 x 213mm, Col Length: 267mm, No. of Columns (Display): 4
Copy instructions: Copy Date: 6 weeks prior to publication date
Average advertising content per issue: 20%
CONSUMER: HOBBIES & DIY: Models & Modelling

MODEL COLLECTOR
46604U79B-70

Editorial Address: Leon House, 233 High Street, CROYDON, CR9 1HZ **Tel:** 020 8726 8000
Fax: 020 8276 8299
Email: modelcollector@ipcmedia.com
Web site: http://www.modelcollector.com
ISSN: 0951-6840
Publisher: IPC Inspire
Date Established: 1987
Frequency: 13 issues yearly
Cover Price: £3.40
Circulation: 9,593 (ABC 01/01/2008 to 31/12/2008)
Usual Pagination: 92
Editor: Lindsey Amrani
Summary of Content: Magazine containing articles predominantly on die cast and tin plate transport models, plus price guides and updates on new releases.
Readership/Target Audience: Read by die cast and tin plate model collectors.
ADVERTISING: No Advertising taken
CONSUMER: HOBBIES & DIY: Models & Modelling

MODEL ENGINEER
46605U79B-200

Editorial Address: Berwick House, 8-10 Knoll Rise, ORPINGTON, BR6 0PS **Tel:** 01689 899200
Fax: 01689 899266
Email: david.carpenter@myhobbystore.com
Advertising Address: As above.
Email: clare.hiscock@magicalia.com
ISSN: 0026-7325
Publisher: My Hobby Store Media
Date Established: 1898
Frequency: 26 issues yearly
Cover Price: £2.75
Usual Pagination: 60
Editor: David Carpenter
Summary of Content: Magazine covering all aspects of model engineering with articles on workshop equipment, tools and processes, internal combustion engines, rally and exhibition reports, clock-making, steam engine and locomotive construction, traction engines and related topics.
Readership/Target Audience: Aimed at model engineers.
ADVERTISING RATES:
Full Page Mono £620.00
Full Page Colour £850.00
Agency Commission: 10%
Mechanical Data: Trim Size: 297 x 210mm, Bleed Size: 303 x 213mm, Type Area: 267 x 184mm, Col Length: 267mm, Page Width: 184mm, Film: Digital
Copy instructions: Copy Date: 3 weeks prior to publication date

Average advertising content per issue: 25%
CONSUMER: HOBBIES & DIY: Models & Modelling

MODEL ENGINEERS' WORKSHOP
46606U79B-81

Editorial Address: Berwick House, 8-10 Knoll Rise, ORPINGTON, BR6 0EL **Tel:** 0844 412 2262
Email: david.clark@myhobbystore.com
Advertising Address: As above. **Tel:** 01689 899200
Email: duncan.armstrong@myhobbystore.com
ISSN: 0959-6909
Publisher: My Hobby Store Media
Date Established: 1990
Frequency: 13 issues yearly
Cover Price: £3.99
Circulation: 20,000 (Publisher's Statement)
Usual Pagination: 66
Editor: David Clark
Summary of Content: Magazine providing workshop activities from selecting the right machines and tools to producing finished model engineering items.
Readership/Target Audience: Aimed at amateur workshop operators and model engineers of all levels of experience.
ADVERTISING RATES:
Full Page Mono £620.00
Full Page Colour £820.00
Agency Commission: 10%
Mechanical Data: Bleed Size: 303 x 213mm, Trim Size: 297 x 210mm, Type Area: 267 x 184mm, Col Length: 267mm, Film: Digital, Page Width: 184mm
Copy instructions: Copy Date: 4 weeks prior to publication date
Average advertising content per issue: 33%
CONSUMER: HOBBIES & DIY: Models & Modelling

MODEL HELICOPTER WORLD
46607U79B-83

Editorial Address: Traplet House, Pendragon Close, MALVERN, WR14 1GA **Tel:** 01684 588500
Fax: 01684 578588
Email: mhw@traplet.com
Advertising Address: As above. **Fax:** 01684 578558
Email: advertising@traplet.com
Web site: http://www.modelheliworld.com
ISSN: 0953-7880
Publisher: Traplet Publications Ltd
Date Established: 1988
Frequency: Monthly - Published 2nd Thursday of every month
Cover Price: £4.25
Annual Sub.: £42.00
Circulation: 17,000 (Publisher's Statement)
Usual Pagination: 84
Editor: Jon Tanner; **Managing Director:** Tony Stephenson
Summary of Content: Magazine containing kit reviews, detailed articles and general information on model helicopters.
Readership/Target Audience: Aimed at model helicopter enthusiasts.
ADVERTISING RATES:
Full Page Colour £789.00
SCC £12.00
Agency Commission: 10%
Mechanical Data: Trim Size: 297 x 210mm, Bleed Size: 303 x 216mm, Film: Digital
Copy instructions: Copy Date: 5 weeks prior to publication date
CONSUMER: HOBBIES & DIY: Models & Modelling

MODEL RAIL
46608U79B-87

Editorial Address: Bushfield House, Orton Centre, PETERBOROUGH, PE2 5UW **Tel:** 01733 237111
Fax: 01733 288163
Email: ben.jones@bauermedia.co.uk
Advertising Address: As above. **Fax:** 01733 465897
Email: rachael.sheriff@bauerconsumer.co.uk
Web site: http://www.model-rail.com
Publisher: Bauer Media Ltd (Orton)
Date Established: 1997
Frequency: 13 issues yearly
Cover Price: £3.20
Annual Sub.: £41.60
Circulation: 28,925 (ABC 01/01/2008 to 31/12/2008)
Editor: Ben Jones
Summary of Content: Magazine covering railway layout and construction, including reports on what's new in model railways.
Readership/Target Audience: Read by those with an interest in modelling.
ADVERTISING RATES:
Full Page Colour £835.00
Agency Commission: 10%
Mechanical Data: No. of Columns (Display): 4, Trim Size: 297 x 210mm, Bleed Size: 303 x 216mm, Type Area: 270 x 185mm, Col Length: 270mm, Film: Digital, Col Widths (Display): 42mm

Average advertising content per issue: 30%
CONSUMER: HOBBIES & DIY: Models & Modelling

MODEL SHIPWRIGHT
46612U79B-105

Editorial Address: 10 Southcombe Street, LONDON, W14 0RA **Tel:** 020 7605 1400 **Fax:** 020 7605 1505
Email: modelshipwright@anovabooks.com
Advertising Address: As above.
Email: modelshipwright@anovabooks.com
Web site: http://www.anovabooks.com
ISSN: 0264-2220
Publisher: Conway Maritime Press
Date Established: 1972
Frequency: Quarterly
Annual Sub.: £27.50
Circulation: 4,000 (Publisher's Statement)
Usual Pagination: 80
Editor: John Lee; **Advertising Manager:** Komal Patel;
Publisher: John Lee
Summary of Content: Journal containing a mixture of articles, reviews and comment from modelmakers as well as plans, diagrams, photographs and a large scale modeller's draught.
Readership/Target Audience: Aimed at maritime model enthusiasts.
ADVERTISING RATES:
Full Page Mono £160.00
Mechanical Data: Trim Size: 240 x 185mm, Film: Digital
Copy instructions: Copy Date: 6 weeks prior to publication date
Average advertising content per issue: 1%
CONSUMER: HOBBIES & DIY: Models & Modelling

MODEL TRACTOR
1826784U79B-203

Editorial Address: 30 Hallow Lane, Lower Broadheath, WORCESTER, WR2 6QL **Tel:** 01905 640306
Email: vtmag@tiscali.co.uk
Advertising Address: As above.
Email: green-phil@ntlworld.com
Web site: http://www.vtmag.co.uk
Publisher: Vintage Tractor
Date Established: 2007
Frequency: Quarterly
Cover Price: £3.00
Annual Sub.: £10.00
Circulation: 20,000 (Print Run)
Editor: Tim Bolton; **Advertising Manager:** Phil Green
Summary of Content: Magazine covering model tractors, construction and farmyard equipment.
Readership/Target Audience: Aimed at model enthusiasts.
ADVERTISING RATES:
Full Page Colour £225.00
Agency Commission: 10%
Average advertising content per issue: 10%
CONSUMER: HOBBIES & DIY: Models & Modelling

MODERN MINI
1791014U77E-523

Editorial Address: Cudham Tithe Barn, Berrys Hill, Berrys Green, Cudham, WESTERHAM, TN16 3AG
Tel: 01959 541444 **Fax:** 01959 541400
Email: mm.ed@kelsey.co.uk
Advertising Address: 1st Floor, South Wing, Broadway Court, PETERBOROUGH, PE1 1RP **Tel:** 01733 347557
Fax: 01733 891342
Email: mm.adsales@kelsey.co.uk
Web site: http://www.modernmini.co.uk
Publisher: Kelsey Publishing Ltd
Date Established: 2006
Frequency: Monthly
Cover Price: £3.60
Circulation: 10,000 (Publisher's Statement)
Usual Pagination: 68
Editor: Phil Weeden
Summary of Content: Magazine dedicated to the new BMW Mini with news, reviews, road tests and profiles of modifications.
Readership/Target Audience: Aimed at Mini owners and prospective buyers.
ADVERTISING RATES:
Full Page Colour £900.00
Agency Commission: 10%
Mechanical Data: Type Area: 277 x 190mm, Bleed Size: 303 x 216mm, Trim Size: 297 x 210mm, Col Length: 277mm, Page Width: 190mm, Film: Digital
Copy instructions: Copy Date: 3 weeks prior to publication date
Average advertising content per issue: 25%
CONSUMER: MOTORING & CYCLING: Club Cars

MODERN MUM
1644412U74D-564

Editorial Address: 3 Woodfield Grove, NEWTOWNABBEY, BT37 0ZP **Tel:** 028 9086 2777 **Fax:** 028 9086 5000
Email: editorial@modernmum.co.uk
Advertising Address: As above.
Email: modernmum@btconnect.com

Web site: http://www.modernmum.co.uk
Publisher: Lindberg Delaney Publications
Date Established: 2004
Frequency: Quarterly
Cover Price: £2.50
Circulation: 30,000 (Print Run)
Usual Pagination: 150
Editor: Debbie Orme; **Advertising Manager:** Maureen Delaney
Summary of Content: Magazine covering health, beauty, fashion, child development and family lifestyle.
Readership/Target Audience: Aimed at parents of children aged between 0 and 8 years old as well as women aged 20 to 50 years old.
ADVERTISING RATES:
Full Page Mono £950.00
Full Page Colour £1200.00
Agency Commission: 15%
Mechanical Data: Film: Digital, Bleed Size: 306 x 231mm, Trim Size: 300 x 225mm
Copy instructions: Copy Date: 2 weeks prior to publication date
CONSUMER: WOMEN'S INTEREST CONSUMER MAGAZINES: Child Care

MOJO
46247U76E-250

Editorial Address: Mappin House, 4 Winsley Street, LONDON, W1W 8HF **Tel:** 020 7182 8616
Fax: 020 7182 8596
Email: mojo@bauermedia.co.uk
Advertising Address: Endeavour House, 189 Shaftesbury Avenue, LONDON, WC2H 8JG **Tel:** 020 7295 5000
Fax: 020 7295 5400
Email: marco.soares@bauermedia.co.uk
Web site: http://www.mojo4music.com
Publisher: Bauer Consumer Media Ltd (Mappin House)
Date Established: 1993
Frequency: Monthly
Cover Price: £4.30
Circulation: 97,722 (ABC 01/01/2009 to 30/06/2009)
Usual Pagination: 150
Editor: Phil Alexander; **News Editor:** Ian Harrison; **Editor-in-Chief:** Phil Alexander
Summary of Content: In depth coverage of popular music past and present.
Readership/Target Audience: Aimed at fans of music.
ADVERTISING RATES:
Full Page Colour £4890.00
Agency Commission: 15%
Mechanical Data: Type Area: 277 x 190mm, Bleed Size: 303 x 216mm, Trim Size: 297 x 210mm, Col Length: 277mm, Page Width: 190mm, Film: Digital
CONSUMER: MUSIC & PERFORMING ARTS: Pop Music

MONEY MARKET
1692801U74M-418

Editorial Address: 126 Wigmore Street, LONDON, W1U 3RZ **Tel:** 01428 684355
Email: ksteiner.uk@ausbanc.com
Advertising Address: C/Altamirano 33, 28008 MADRID
Tel: 965 21 63 40
Email: emanzanero.uk@ausbanc.com
Web site: http://www.find.co.uk/moneymarket
Publisher: Ausbanc
Frequency: Monthly
Cover Price: £3.00
Free to qualifying individuals
Circulation: 60,000 (Publisher's Statement)
Usual Pagination: 32
Editor: Katherine Steiner-Dicks; **Advertising Manager:** Elena Manzanero
Summary of Content: Newspaper covering personal finance including mortgages, investments, current accounts, savings, insurance and consumer affairs.
Readership/Target Audience: Aimed at those interested in their personal finances and those providing personal finance products.
ADVERTISING: Rates on application
CONSUMER: WOMEN'S INTEREST CONSUMER MAGAZINES: Personal Finance

MONEY OBSERVER
45552U74M-150

Editorial Address: 1st Floor, Standon House, 21 Mansell Street, LONDON, E1 8AA **Tel:** 020 7680 3660
Email: editorial@moneyobserver.com
Advertising Address: As above. **Tel:** 020 7680 3600
Email: trevor.leek@moneyobserver.com
Web site: http://www.moneyobserver.com
ISSN: 0263-7669
Publisher: Moneywise Publishing
Date Established: 1979
Frequency: Monthly - Published on the last Thursday of the month prior to cover date
Cover Price: £4.25
Annual Sub.: £44.00
Circulation: 20,081 (ABC 01/01/2008 to 31/12/2008)
Usual Pagination: 116

Consumer Magazines

Editor: Andrew Pitts; **Advertising Director:** Trevor Leek
Summary of Content: Magazine focusing on all aspects of investment, personal finance and money matters.
Readership/Target Audience: Aimed at discerning private investors who want to maximise the return on their investments.
ADVERTISING RATES:
Full Page Colour £4100.00
Copy instructions: Copy Date: 3 weeks prior to publication date
CONSUMER: WOMEN'S INTEREST CONSUMER MAGAZINES: Personal Finance

MONEYWISE
45553U74M-155
Editorial Address: Standon House, 21 Mansell Street, LONDON, E1 8AA **Tel:** 020 7680 3600
Email: nathalie.bonney@moneywise.co.uk
Advertising Address: As above. **Fax:** 020 7702 0710
Email: chris.sorrell@moneywise.co.uk
Web site: http://www.moneywise.co.uk
Publisher: Moneywise Publishing
Date Established: 1990
Frequency: Monthly - Published in the 3rd of the month
Cover Price: £4.25
Circulation: 23,028 (ABC 01/01/2008 to 31/12/2008)
Usual Pagination: 100
Editor: Liam Tarry; **News Editor:** Rebecca Atkinson;
Advertising Manager: Chris Sorrell; **Publisher:** Jeremy King
Summary of Content: Magazine covering all aspects of personal finance in the UK. Includes features on the stock market, pensions, insurance, investments, banking, borrowing and tax.
Readership/Target Audience: Aimed at people with an interest in personal finance.
ADVERTISING RATES:
Full Page Mono £4850.00
Full Page Colour £4850.00
Agency Commission: 10%
Mechanical Data: Type Area: 268 x 181mm, Bleed Size: 306 x 216mm, Trim Size: 300 x 210mm, Film: Digital, Col Length: 268mm, Page Width: 181mm
Average advertising content per issue: 40%
CONSUMER: WOMEN'S INTEREST CONSUMER MAGAZINES: Personal Finance

MONITORING MONTHLY
1739401U79D-171
Editorial Address: 43 Award Road, WIMBORNE, BH21 7NT
Tel: 0845 193 3600 **Fax:** 0845 193 3602
Email: kevin.nice@monitoringmonthly.co.uk
Advertising Address: As above. **Fax:** 08451 933 602
Email: jh@monitoringmonthly.co.uk
Web site: http://www.monitoringmonthly.co.uk
Publisher: Nice One Publishing Ltd
Date Established: 2006
Frequency: 13 issues yearly
Cover Price: £4.25
Circulation: 16,000 (Print Run)
Usual Pagination: 100
Editor: Kevin Nice; **Advertising Manager:** John Herbert
Summary of Content: Magazine covering hobby related subjects including scanners, short-wave radios, software defined radio, digital communications and systems, aviation, emergency communications, historical, amateur radio, multi-activities, remote satellite images, data communications and long distant television.
Readership/Target Audience: Aimed at radio enthusiasts.
ADVERTISING: Rates on application
CONSUMER: HOBBIES & DIY: Radio Electronics

MONMOUTHSHIRE COUNTY LIFE
1645904U80D-506
Editorial Address: Cardiff Road, NEWPORT, NP20 3QN
Tel: 01633 777420
Email: jo.barnes@gwent-wales.co.uk
Advertising Address: As above. **Tel:** 01633 777285
Fax: 01633 777082
Email: sharon.hutchinson@gwent-wales.co.uk
Web site: http://www.monmouthcountrylife.co.uk
Publisher: Newsquest Wales & Gloucestershire
Date Established: 2004
Frequency: 6 issues yearly
Cover Price: Free
Circulation: 10,000 (Publisher's Statement)
Usual Pagination: 64
Editor: Jo Barnes; **Advertising Manager:** Sharon Hutchinson
Summary of Content: Magazine covering fashion, food and drink, gardens, health and beauty, motors, antiques, property, restaurants, entertainment and travel.
Readership/Target Audience: Aimed at affluent residents and visitors to Monmouthshire.
ADVERTISING RATES:
Full Page Colour £800.00
Agency Commission: 10%
Mechanical Data: Film: Digital, Type Area: 277 x 185mm, Bleed Size: 303 x 211mm, Trim Size: 297 x 210mm

Copy instructions: Copy Date: 2 weeks prior to publication date
CONSUMER: RURAL & REGIONAL INTEREST: Regional Interest Wales

MONOCLE
1790179U82-274
Editorial Address: 20 Boston Place, Marylebone, LONDON, NW1 6ER **Tel:** 020 7725 4343 **Fax:** 020 7725 5711
Email: info@monocle.com
Advertising Address: As above.
Email: trs@monocle.com
Web site: http://www.monocle.com
Publisher: Winkontent
Date Established: 2007
Frequency: 10 issues yearly
Cover Price: £5.00
Usual Pagination: 248
Editor: Saul Taylor; **Editor-in-Chief:** Tyler Brûlé;
Advertisement Director: Tamsyn Spires; **Publisher:** Pamela Mullinger
Summary of Content: Magazine covering focusing on geopolitical affairs, business, culture and design.
Readership/Target Audience: Aimed at affluent, well travelled, well informed readers that work across a range of industries - in particular finance, media, IT, manufacturing, retail and hospitality. Aged between 25 and 55 years old who regularly travel for work and play, and are interested in current affairs, business concerns and good design.
ADVERTISING RATES:
Full Page Mono £10750.00
Full Page Colour £10750.00
Mechanical Data: Type Area: 249 x 184mm, Bleed Size: 271 x 206mm, Trim Size: 265 x 200mm, Col Length: 249mm, Page Width: 184mm, Film: Digital
CONSUMER: CURRENT AFFAIRS & POLITICS

THE MONTEBURY MAGAZINE
1900116U86C-758
Editorial Address: 15 Alexandra Road, LONDON, SW19 7JZ **Tel:** 020 8123 0475
Email: editorial@the-montebury.com
Web site: http://www.the-montebury.com
Date Established: 2009
Frequency: Monthly
Cover Price: Free
Editor: Benoit Durand
Summary of Content: Magazine providing news, interviews and features from the world of men's luxury fashion.

Readership/Target Audience: Aimed at males aged between 25 and 49 with an interest in fashion.
CONSUMER: ADULT & GAY MAGAZINES: Men's Lifestyle Magazines

THE MONTH (INCORPORATING EAST WINDOW)
624809U87-89_60
Formerly: East Window
Editorial Address: 1 Bouchiers Place, Messing, COLCHESTER, CO5 9TY **Tel:** 01621 810341
Fax: 01621 819443
Email: jmelongman@aol.com
Web site: http://www.chelmsford.anglican.org
Publisher: Diocese of Chelmsford
Date Established: 1987
Frequency: Monthly
Cover Price: Free
Circulation: 50,000 (Publisher's Statement)
Usual Pagination: 12
Editor: Jon Longman
Summary of Content: Newsletter covering church news, local events and issues, charity news and items of interest to church goers.
Readership/Target Audience: Aimed at parishioners of the Anglican Church.
ADVERTISING: No Advertising taken
CONSUMER: RELIGIOUS

THE MONTHLY RECORD OF FREE CHURCH OF SCOTLAND
47837U87-162
Editorial Address: 15 North Bank Street, EDINBURGH, EH1 2LS **Tel:** 0131 226 5286 **Fax:** 0131 220 0597
Email: edrecord@blueyonder.co.uk
Web site: http://www.freechurch.org
ISSN: 0016-0334
Publisher: Free Church of Scotland Communications Committee
Frequency: 11 issues yearly - Joint issue July and August
Cover Price: £1.25
Circulation: 4,000 (Publisher's Statement)
Usual Pagination: 24
Editor: David Robertson
Summary of Content: Reformed theology applied to current issues.

Language(s): English; Gaelic
Readership/Target Audience: Aimed at Christians and interested non-Christians.
ADVERTISING: No Advertising taken
CONSUMER: RELIGIOUS

MORE
45186U74A-340
Editorial Address: Endeavour House, 189 Shaftesbury Avenue, LONDON, WC2H 8JG **Tel:** 020 7208 3165
Fax: 020 7208 3595
Email: more.letters@moremagazine.co.uk
Advertising Address: As above. **Tel:** 020 7295 5000
Fax: 020 7295 5400
Email: suosan.williams@baueradvertising.co.uk
Web site: http://www.moremagazine.co.uk
ISSN: 0955-0348
Publisher: Bauer Media
Date Established: 1988
Frequency: Weekly - Published on Tuesday
Circulation: 190,708 (ABC 01/01/2009 to 30/06/2009)
Usual Pagination: 132
Editor: Abbie Pethullis; **News Editor:** Leigh Purves;
Features Editor: Helen Bownass; **Managing Director:** David Davies; **Managing Editor:** Alison Williams
Summary of Content: Magazine covering celebrity gossip, beauty, fashion, real life, music and films.
Twitter: https://twitter.com/moremagazine.
Readership/Target Audience: Aimed at women between 18 and 25 years old.
ADVERTISING RATES:
Full Page Colour £13060.00
Agency Commission: 15%
Mechanical Data: Bleed Size: 281 x 216mm, Trim Size: 275 x 210mm, Col Widths (Display): 255mm, Page Width: 192mm, Type Area: 255 x 192mm
Average advertising content per issue: 40%
CONSUMER: WOMEN'S INTEREST CONSUMER MAGAZINES: Women's Interest

MORNING STAR
41721U82-119_35
Editorial Address: William Rust House, 52 Beachey Road, LONDON, E3 2NS **Tel:** 020 8510 0815 **Fax:** 020 8986 5694
Email: newsed@peoples-press.com
Advertising Address: As above. **Fax:** 020 8525 6997
Email: starads@peoples-press.com
Web site: http://www.morningstaronline.co.uk
Publisher: Peoples Press Printing Society
Frequency: Daily
Cover Price: £0.60
Circulation: 25,000 (Publisher's Statement)
Usual Pagination: 12
Editor: John Haylett; **News Editor:** Daniel Coysh; **Features Editor:** Richard Bagley; **Advertising Manager:** Richard Mann
Summary of Content: Newspaper covering news and current affairs.
Readership/Target Audience: Aimed at the labour movement.
ADVERTISING RATES:
Full Page Mono £1337.53
Full Page Colour £1337.53
Agency Commission: 15%
Mechanical Data: Col Widths (Display): 41mm, Col Length: 381mm, Print Process: Web-fed offset litho, Type Area: 381 x 265mm, No. of Columns (Display): 6, Page Width: 265mm, Film: Digital
Copy instructions: Copy Date: 1 day prior to publication date
Average advertising content per issue: 10%
CONSUMER: CURRENT AFFAIRS & POLITICS

MORRISONS
1896803U74P-968
Editorial Address: 1 Liverpool Street, LONDON, EC2M 7QD
Tel: 020 7956 2792
Email: info@morrisonsmagazine.co.uk
Web site: http://www.morrisons.co.uk
Publisher: Result Customer Communications
Date Established: 2008
Frequency: Quarterly
Cover Price: Free
Circulation: 1,100,000 (ABC 01/01/2009 to 31/03/2009)
Usual Pagination: 92
Editor: Jo Wooderson; **Features Editor:** Lucy Battersby;
Managing Editor: Karen Bray
Summary of Content: Magazine featuring health tips, inspiring food and recipes and information about offers in store.
Readership/Target Audience: Aimed at Morrisons customers.
CONSUMER: WOMEN'S INTEREST CONSUMER MAGAZINES: Food & Cookery

MOTHER & BABY
45324U74D-340
Editorial Address: Endeavour House, 189 Shaftesbury Avenue, LONDON, WC2H 8JG **Tel:** 020 7295 5560

Email: mother&baby@bauerconsumer.co.uk
Advertising Address: As above. **Tel:** 020 7437 9011
Email: fiona.senior@bauerconsumer.co.uk
Web site: http://www.askamum.co.uk
Publisher: Bauer Media
Frequency: Monthly
Cover Price: £2.60
Circulation: 60,008 (ABC 01/01/2009 to 30/06/2009)
Usual Pagination: 145
Editor: Lucy Quick; **Features Editor:** Lola Borg; **Managing Editor:** Danielle O'Connell
Summary of Content: Magazine covering pregnancy, birth, baby care and the early years of a child's life, with features on health and consumer issues.
Readership/Target Audience: Aimed at expectant mothers and those with children between 0 and 3 years old.
ADVERTISING RATES:
Full Page Colour £5996.00
SCC £52.00
Agency Commission: 15%
Mechanical Data: Page Width: 186mm, Bleed Size: 303 x 216mm, Trim Size: 297 x 210mm, Type Area: 270 x 186mm, Col Length: 270mm, Film: Digital
Copy instructions: Copy Date: 8 weeks prior to publication date
Average advertising content per issue: 50%
CONSUMER: WOMEN'S INTEREST CONSUMER MAGAZINES: Child Care

MOTO MAGAZINE
1639505U77D-467
Editorial Address: 1 West Smithfield, LONDON, EC1A 9JU
Tel: 01202 606118
Email: ray@motomagazine.co.uk
Advertising Address: As above. **Tel:** 020 7332 9700
Email: jonathan.vincent@factorymedia.com
Web site: http://www.motomagazine.co.uk
Publisher: Factory Media Ltd
Date Established: 2004
Frequency: Monthly
Cover Price: £3.20
Circulation: 35,000 (Print Run)
Usual Pagination: 132
Editor: Jeff Perritt; **Advertising Manager:** Jonathan Vincent
Summary of Content: Magazine with international coverage of motocross, supercross, supermoto, racing, testing, equipment reviews and lifestyle.
Readership/Target Audience: Aimed at predominantly male, 14 to 44 year old motocross riders and enthusiasts.
ADVERTISING RATES:
Full Page Colour £1385.00
Agency Commission: 10%
Mechanical Data: Trim Size: 300 x 230mm, Bleed Size: 303 x 233mm, Film: Digital
Copy instructions: Copy Date: 4 weeks prior to publication date
Average advertising content per issue: 40%
CONSUMER: MOTORING & CYCLING: Motor Sports

MOTOPIA
1826307U77A-607
Editorial Address: 24 Beamont Way, Amesbury, SALISBURY, SP4 7UA **Tel:** 07500 978201
Fax: 01980 590997
Email: melissa@motopia.co.uk
Advertising Address: As above. **Tel:** 01980 590997
Email: melissa@motopia.co.uk
Web site: http://www.motopia.co.uk
Publisher: Motopia Creative Ltd
Date Established: 2007
Frequency: 6 issues yearly
Cover Price: Free
Circulation: 10,000 (Publisher's Statement)
Usual Pagination: 28
Editor: Melissa Terry; **Advertising Manager:** Melissa Terry
Summary of Content: Magazine covering all aspects of motoring including local and national motoring news, local motor sports, classic and new car reviews and accessories.
Readership/Target Audience: Aimed at motorists in general in the Salisbury and Amesbury areas.
ADVERTISING RATES:
Full Page Mono £295.00
Full Page Colour £295.00
Agency Commission: 10%
Mechanical Data: Type Area: 277 x 190mm, Bleed Size: 303 x 216mm, Trim Size: 297 x 210mm, Col Length: 277mm, Page Width: 190mm, No. of Columns (Display): 4, Col Widths (Display): 44.5mm, Film: Digital
Copy instructions: Copy Date: 2 weeks prior to publication date
Average advertising content per issue: 50%
CONSUMER: MOTORING & CYCLING: Motoring

MOTOR BOAT & YACHTING
48380U91A-80
Editorial Address: Blue Fin Building, 110 Southwark Street, LONDON, SE1 0SU **Tel:** 020 3148 4651 **Fax:** 020 3148 8127
Email: mby@ipcmedia.com

Advertising Address: As above. **Tel:** 020 3148 4900
Fax: 020 3148 8523
Email: michael_wills@ipcmedia.com
Web site: http://www.mby.com
Publisher: IPC Inspire
Date Established: 1904
Frequency: Monthly - Published on the 1st Thursday of the month prior to cover date
Cover Price: £4.30
Free to qualifying individuals
Annual Sub.: £34.99
Circulation: 17,346 (ABC 01/01/2008 to 31/12/2008)
Usual Pagination: 200
Editor: Sue Goddard; **Publisher:** Steve Kendall
Summary of Content: Magazine containing boat reports, equipment tests, advice on navigation and cruise accounts.
Readership/Target Audience: Aimed at those aged 35 years old and over with an interest in motor boats.
ADVERTISING RATES:
Full Page Mono £1767.00
Full Page Colour £3723.00
Agency Commission: 10%
Mechanical Data: Type Area: 285 x 215mm, Col Length: 285mm, Page Width: 215mm, Trim Size: 300 x 230mm, Bleed Size: 308 x 238mm, Film: Digital
Copy instructions: Copy Date: 15 working days prior to publication date
CONSUMER: RECREATION & LEISURE: Boating & Yachting

MOTOR BOATS MONTHLY
48381U91A-87
Editorial Address: 9th Floor, Blue Fin Building, 110 Southwark Street, LONDON, SE1 0SU **Tel:** 020 3148 5000
Fax: 020 3148 8128
Email: mbm@ipcmedia.com
Advertising Address: Blue Fin Building, 110 Southwark Street, LONDON, SE1 0SU **Tel:** 020 3148 5000
Fax: 020 3148 8523
Email: michael_wills@ipcmedia.com
Web site: http://www.mbmclub.com
Publisher: IPC Inspire
Date Established: 1987
Frequency: Monthly
Cover Price: £4.20
Circulation: 16,117 (ABC 01/01/2008 to 31/12/2008)
Usual Pagination: 164
Editor: Carl Richardson; **Publisher:** Steve Kendall
Summary of Content: Magazine containing features on motor boats between 18 and 60ft. Includes motor boating news, boat reports, product tests, cruising advice, DIY projects and a boat buying guide.
Readership/Target Audience: Aimed at those with an interest in motor boats.
ADVERTISING RATES:
Full Page Mono £1403.00
Full Page Colour £2922.00
Agency Commission: 10%
Mechanical Data: Type Area: 272 x 187mm, Col Length: 272mm, Page Width: 187mm, Trim Size: 297 x 215mm, Bleed Size: 303 x 221mm, Film: Digital
Copy instructions: Copy Date: 15 days prior to publication date
Average advertising content per issue: 50%
CONSUMER: RECREATION & LEISURE: Boating & Yachting

MOTOR CARAVAN MAGAZINE
48423U91B-105
Editorial Address: Leon House, 233 High Street, CROYDON, CR9 1HZ **Tel:** 020 8726 8000
Fax: 020 8726 8000
Email: motorcaravan@ipcmedia.com
Advertising Address: As above. **Fax:** 020 8726 8298
Email: sue_tannat@ipcmedia.com
Web site: http://www.motorcaravanmagazine.co.uk
ISSN: 0268-6120
Publisher: IPC Inspire
Date Established: 1986
Frequency: Monthly
Cover Price: £2.99
Annual Sub.: £35.40
Circulation: 10,000 (Publisher's Statement)
Usual Pagination: 164
Editor: Victoria Bentley; **Group Editor:** Victoria Bentley; **Publisher:** Clive Birch
Summary of Content: Magazine containing test reports and touring features, site reports, general advice, van and equipment reviews.
Readership/Target Audience: Aimed at motor caravanning enthusiasts.
ADVERTISING RATES:
Full Page Mono £992.00
Full Page Colour £1339.00
Agency Commission: 10%
Mechanical Data: Type Area: 278 x 190mm, Col Length: 278mm, Page Width: 190mm, Trim Size: 298 x 210mm, Bleed Size: 304 x 216mm, Print Process: Web-fed offset litho
Copy instructions: Copy Date: 6 weeks prior to publication date

Average advertising content per issue: 40%
CONSUMER: RECREATION & LEISURE: Camping & Caravanning

MOTOR CARAVANNER
48424U91B-130
Editorial Address: 27 Norwich Road, HALESWORTH, IP19 8BX **Tel:** 01986 834250 **Fax:** 01986 834255
Email: simon@artsindustry.co.uk
Advertising Address: As above.
Email: david@micropress.co.uk
Web site: http://www.motorcaravanner.eu
Publisher: BC Publications
Date Established: 1960
Frequency: Monthly
Cover Price: Free
Circulation: 7,500 (Publisher's Statement)
Usual Pagination: 40
Editor: Simon Tooth
Summary of Content: For members of the Motor Caravanners Association who are all owners of motor caravans.
Readership/Target Audience: Aimed at the motor caravanning enthusiast.
ADVERTISING RATES:
Full Page Colour £525.00
Agency Commission: 10%
Mechanical Data: Type Area: 270 x 188mm, Col Length: 270mm, Page Width: 188mm, Bleed Size: 303 x 214mm, Trim Size: 297 x 210mm
Copy instructions: Copy Date: 3 weeks prior to publication date
Average advertising content per issue: 50%
CONSUMER: RECREATION & LEISURE: Camping & Caravanning

MOTOR CYCLE MONTHLY
1927084U77B-731
Editorial Address: Media Centre, Morton Way, HORNCASTLE, LN9 6JR **Tel:** 01507 529529
Fax: 01507 529495
Email: editor@motorcyclemonthly.co.uk
Advertising Address: As above. **Tel:** 01507 529004
Email: glarkin@mortons.co.uk
Web site: http://www.motorcyclemonthly.co.uk
Publisher: Mortons Media Group Ltd
Frequency: Monthly
Free to qualifying individuals
Annual Sub.: £12.00
Circulation: 72,000 (Print Run)
Usual Pagination: 40
Editor: John Carroll; **Advertising Manager:** Gemma Larkin
Summary of Content: Publication featuring real stories about real bikers, a what, where, when section, BSB and WSB racing, manufacturers news and information on the latest riding laws and ride out details.
Readership/Target Audience: Aimed at motorcyclists.
ADVERTISING RATES:
Full Page Colour £1795.00
CONSUMER: MOTORING & CYCLING: Motorcycling

MOTOR EXCHANGE
1894842U77A-615
Editorial Address: 213-215 Town Street, Bramley, LEEDS, LS13 3JL **Tel:** 0113 320 0666 **Fax:** 0113 320 2044
Email: tony@parklanepublishing.co.uk
Web site: http://www.motorexchangeonline.com
ISSN: 1759-7242
Publisher: Park Lane Publishing Ltd
Date Established: 2008
Frequency: 26 issues yearly
Cover Price: Free
Circulation: 40,000 (Publisher's Statement)
Usual Pagination: 64
Editor: Tony Mite
Summary of Content: Magazine covering vehicle road tests, safety, new vehicle releases and second hand and new vehicles for sale.
Readership/Target Audience: Aimed at anyone shopping at the top supermarket chains.
CONSUMER: MOTORING & CYCLING: Motoring

MOTOR SPORT
46427U77D-300
Editorial Address: 38 Chelsea Wharf, 15 Lots Road, LONDON, W10 0QJ **Tel:** 020 7349 3150 **Fax:** 020 7349 3160
Email: editorial@motorsportmagazine.co.uk
Advertising Address: 26-30 Old Church Street, Chelsea, LONDON, SW3 5BY **Tel:** 020 7349 3150 **Fax:** 020 7349 3160
Email: richard.stillman@motorsportmagazine.co.uk
Web site: http://www.motorsportmagazine.co.uk
Publisher: Stratfield Ltd
Date Established: 1924
Frequency: Monthly
Cover Price: £4.95
Annual Sub.: £49.70
Circulation: 33,210 (ABC 01/01/2008 to 31/12/2008)
Usual Pagination: 130

Editor: Damien Smith; **Advertising Manager:** Richard Stillman; **Publisher:** Martin Nott
Summary of Content: Magazine covering international motor sport with additional sport, featuring material on Formula 1 and sports car racing, the veteran and vintage racing scene and speed record attempts.
Readership/Target Audience: Aimed at motor sport enthusiasts.
ADVERTISING RATES:
Full Page Mono £2475.00
Full Page Colour £2475.00
Agency Commission: 10%
Mechanical Data: Col Length: 250mm, Page Width: 196mm, Type Area: 250 x 196mm, Bleed Size: 291 x 236mm, Trim Size: 285 x 230mm, Film: Digital
Average advertising content per issue: 40%
CONSUMER: MOTORING & CYCLING: Motor Sports

MOTOR SPORTS NOW!   46428U77D-380
Formerly: Motorsports Now!
Editorial Address: MSA, Riverside Park, Colnbrook, SLOUGH, SL3 0HG **Tel:** 01753 765000 **Fax:** 01753 682938
Email: adean-lewis@msauk.org
Advertising Address: Winchester Court, 1 Forum Place, Fiddlebridge Lane, HATFIELD, AL10 0RN **Tel:** 01707 273999
Fax: 01707 252705
Email: dan@trmg.co.uk
Web site: http://www.msauk.org
Publisher: TRMG Ltd
Date Established: 1998
Frequency: Quarterly
Cover Price: £3.00
Free to qualifying individuals
Circulation: 43,000 (Publisher's Statement)
Usual Pagination: 60
Editor: Chris Hough; **Publisher:** Jonathon Fellows
Summary of Content: Magazine containing actual and proposed regulation changes, general news and competitor information.
Readership/Target Audience: Read by motorsport competition licence holders, club members, officials, team members and manufacturers.
ADVERTISING RATES:
Full Page Colour £2500.00
Agency Commission: 10%
Mechanical Data: Page Width: 195mm, Film: Digital, Trim Size: 297 x 210mm, Bleed Size: 303 x 216mm, Type Area: 279 x 195mm, Col Length: 279mm
CONSUMER: MOTORING & CYCLING: Motor Sports

MOTORCYCLE RACER   46368U77B-701
Editorial Address: Media Centre, Morton Way, HORNCASTLE, LN9 6JR **Tel:** 01507 529529
Fax: 01507 529495
Email: larry@motorcycleracer.com
Advertising Address: As above. **Tel:** 01507 524004
Fax: 01507 529499
Email: tglover-brown@mortons.co.uk
ISSN: 1461-3778
Publisher: Mortons Media Group Ltd
Date Established: 1962
Frequency: 11 issues yearly
Cover Price: £3.75
Annual Sub.: £36.00
Circulation: 24,301 (Publisher's Statement)
Usual Pagination: 100
Editor: Larry Carter; **Advertising Manager:** Tracy Glover-Brown
Summary of Content: Magazine covering British and American road racing and world superbikes. Includes news and features on race results, new products, developments and profiles of racing stars.
Readership/Target Audience: Aimed at motorcycle racing enthusiasts.
ADVERTISING RATES:
Full Page Colour £1000.00
Agency Commission: 10%
Mechanical Data: Type Area: 277 x 190mm, Col Length: 277mm, Page Width: 190mm, Bleed Size: 303 x 216mm, Trim Size: 297 x 210mm, Film: Digital
Average advertising content per issue: 40%
CONSUMER: MOTORING & CYCLING: Motorcycling

MOTORCYCLE RIDER   46369U77B-570
Editorial Address: Schipol Way, Humberside International Airport, Kirmington, ULCEBY, DN39 6GB **Tel:** 01652 680060
Fax: 01652 680070
Email: andy@rbplimited.co.uk
Web site: http://www.bmf.co.uk
Publisher: RBP Ltd
Frequency: 6 issues yearly
Cover Price: £2.50
Circulation: 25,000 (Publisher's Statement)
Usual Pagination: 64
Editor: Andy Dukes

Summary of Content: Journal of the British Motorcyclists Federation. Includes political, regional, commercial and leisure information.
Readership/Target Audience: Aimed at BMF members and those with an interest in the future of motorcycling.
ADVERTISING: No Advertising taken
CONSUMER: MOTORING & CYCLING: Motorcycling

MOTORCYCLE SPORT AND LEISURE   46370U77B-575
Editorial Address: Media Centre, Morton Way, HORNCASTLE, LN9 6JR **Tel:** 01507 529300
Fax: 01507 529495
Email: tcarter@mortons.co.uk
Advertising Address: As above. **Tel:** 01507 524004
Fax: 01507 529499
Email: swoodhouse@mortons.co.uk
Web site: http://www.mslmagazine.co.uk
Publisher: Mortons Media Group Ltd
Date Established: 1962
Frequency: Monthly
Cover Price: £3.30
Annual Sub.: £34.00
Circulation: 43,504 (Publisher's Statement)
Usual Pagination: 116
Editor: Tony Carter
Summary of Content: Magazine with in depth reviews of the latest super sport, sport, custom and touring motorcycles and accessories. Product, industry and European news, touring features, general motorcycling articles, book reviews and humour.
Readership/Target Audience: Aimed at mature leisure and sporting motorcycle owners and buyers.
ADVERTISING RATES:
Full Page Colour £1595.00
Agency Commission: 10%
Mechanical Data: Type Area: 277 x 180mm, No. of Columns (Display): 4, Trim Size: 297 x 210mm, Col Length: 277mm, Page Width: 180mm, Film: Digital, Bleed Size: 303 x 216mm
Average advertising content per issue: 30%
CONSUMER: MOTORING & CYCLING: Motorcycling

MOTORHOME MONTHLY   48426U91B-137
Editorial Address: Andrew House, Granville Road, SIDCUP, DA14 4BN **Tel:** 020 8302 6069 **Fax:** 020 8300 2315
Email: mhm2007@stoneleisure.com
Advertising Address: DRG Building, Longmoor Lane, Breaston, DERBY, DE72 3BQ **Tel:** 01332 874731
Fax: 01332 874732
Email: stephanie@stoneleisure.com
Web site: http://www.stoneleisure.com
ISSN: 1363-8971
Publisher: Stone Leisure Ltd
Frequency: 11 issues yearly
Cover Price: £2.50
Annual Sub.: £12.00
Circulation: 39,088 (ABC 01/01/2008 to 31/12/2008)
Usual Pagination: 100
Editor: Bob Griffiths; **Advertising Manager:** Stephanie Walker
Summary of Content: Magazine covering all aspects of motor caravanning.
Readership/Target Audience: Aimed at owners, first-time buyers, enthusiasts and organisers of motor home shows.
ADVERTISING RATES:
Full Page Mono £850.00
Full Page Colour £1140.00
Agency Commission: 10%
Mechanical Data: Bleed Size: 303 x 216mm, Trim Size: 297 x 210mm, Film: Digital
Copy instructions: Copy Date: 3 weeks prior to publication date
CONSUMER: RECREATION & LEISURE: Camping & Caravanning

MOTORSPORT NEWS   46321U77D-325
Formerly: Motoring News
Editorial Address: Teddington Studios, Broom Road, TEDDINGTON, TW11 9BE **Tel:** 020 8267 5385
Fax: 020 8267 5322
Email: mn.letters@haymarket.com
Advertising Address: As above. **Tel:** 020 8267 5000
Fax: 020 8267 5855
Email: simon.grayson@haymarket.com
Web site: http://www.motorsport-news.co.uk
Publisher: Haymarket Autosport and Classic Publications
Date Established: 1955
Frequency: Weekly
Cover Price: £2.50
Annual Sub.: £46.80
Circulation: 18,206 (ABC 01/01/2008 to 31/12/2008)
Usual Pagination: 56
Editor: Matt Burt

Summary of Content: Magazine containing national and international motorsport news, race reports and track reviews.
Readership/Target Audience: Aimed at British motorsport enthusiasts.
ADVERTISING RATES:
Full Page Mono £2436.00
Full Page Colour £3696.00
Agency Commission: 10%
Mechanical Data: Col Widths (Display): 42mm, Type Area: 357 x 267mm, Col Length: 357mm, No. of Columns (Display): 6, Film: Digital, Page Width: 267mm
Copy instructions: Copy Date: Friday prior to publication date
Average advertising content per issue: 25%
CONSUMER: MOTORING & CYCLING: Motor Sports

MOTOX   1810687U77B-722
Editorial Address: Alexander House, 38 Forehill, ELY, CB7 4ZA **Tel:** 01353 616104
Email: andy@motoxmag.co.uk
Advertising Address: As above.
Email: andy@motoxmag.co.uk
Web site: http://www.motoxmag.co.uk
Publisher: Motoplay Ltd
Date Established: 2003
Frequency: Monthly
Cover Price: £3.20
Circulation: 30,000 (Publisher's Statement)
Editor: Andrew Field; **Advertising Manager:** Andrew Field
Summary of Content: Magazine covering all aspects of motorcycling including product reviews, bike tests and interviews with riders.
Readership/Target Audience: Aimed at those with a interest in motorcycling.
ADVERTISING RATES:
Full Page Colour £904.00
Agency Commission: 10%
Mechanical Data: Type Area: 277 x 185mm, Bleed Size: 303 x 216mm, Trim Size: 297 x 210mm, Col Length: 277mm, Page Width: 185mm, Film: Digital
Copy instructions: Copy Date: 10 days prior to publication date
Average advertising content per issue: 30%
CONSUMER: MOTORING & CYCLING: Motorcycling

MOUNTAIN BIKING UK   46402U77C-810
Editorial Address: 30 Monmouth Street, BATH, BA1 2BW **Tel:** 01225 442244 **Fax:** 01225 822793
Email: mbuk@futurenet.com
Advertising Address: As above. **Fax:** 01225 446019
Email: chawkins@futurenet.co.uk
Web site: http://www.bikeradar.com
ISSN: 0954-8690
Publisher: Future Publishing Ltd
Date Established: 1988
Frequency: 13 issues yearly
Cover Price: £3.99
Annual Sub.: £33.00
Circulation: 45,983 (ABC 01/01/2008 to 31/12/2008)
Usual Pagination: 212
Editor: Ric McLaughlin
Summary of Content: Magazine covering all aspects of mountain biking as a sport in the UK.
Readership/Target Audience: Aimed at mountain bike enthusiasts.
ADVERTISING RATES:
Full Page Colour £1825.00
Agency Commission: 10%
Mechanical Data: Type Area: 270 x 190mm, Film: Digital, Trim Size: 297 x 210mm, Bleed Size: 303 x 216mm, Col Length: 270mm, Page Width: 190mm
Copy instructions: Copy Date: 3 weeks prior to publication date
Average advertising content per issue: 40%
CONSUMER: MOTORING & CYCLING: Cycling

MOVIE CLUB NEWS   46051U76A-35_50
Editorial Address: Orchardton Hall, Auchencairn, CASTLE DOUGLAS, DG7 1QL **Tel:** 0845 658 8329
Email: daveb@movieclubnews.co.uk
Advertising Address: As above. **Tel:** 0845 130 6249
Email: advert@bnw.demon.co.uk
Web site: http://www.movieclubnews.co.uk
Publisher: Brave New World International Ltd
Date Established: 1991
Frequency: Quarterly
Cover Price: £0.90
Circulation: 400,000 (Publisher's Statement)
Editor: Dave Burbidge; **Managing Director:** Susan Foster; **Advertising Manager:** Susan Foster; **Group Editor:** Dave Burbidge
Summary of Content: Magazine covering film reviews, cinema listings, celebrities and festivals.
Readership/Target Audience: Aimed at cinemagoers and businesses in the cinema industry.

ADVERTISING RATES:
Full Page Colour £1500.00
CONSUMER: MUSIC & PERFORMING ARTS: Cinema

MOVIE MAG INTERNATIONAL 1643461U76A-172

Editorial Address: 20 Station Road, Hanwell, LONDON, W7 3JE **Tel:** 020 8567 3662 **Fax:** 020 8567 9861
Email: sunny@moviemag.net
Advertising Address: As above.
Email: info@moviemag.net
Web site: http://www.moviemag.net
ISSN: 1467-7365
Publisher: Movie Mag International UK
Frequency: Monthly
Cover Price: £2.00
Annual Sub.: £24.00
Circulation: 32,500 (Publisher's Statement)
Usual Pagination: 116
Editor: Bharathi Pradhan; **Advertising Manager:** Sundeep Suri; **Managing Editor:** Bharathi Pradhan; **Publisher:** Sundeep Suri
Summary of Content: Magazine covering Asian entertainment, celebrities, films and music.
Readership/Target Audience: Aimed at Asian communities in the UK.
ADVERTISING RATES:
Full Page Colour £1600.00
Agency Commission: 10%
Mechanical Data: Bleed Size: 281 x 216mm, Trim Size: 275 x 210mm, Film: Digital
Copy instructions: Copy Date: 4 weeks prior to publication date
Average advertising content per issue: 30%
CONSUMER: MUSIC & PERFORMING ARTS: Cinema

MOVING HOUSE MAGAZINE 1637928U74K-675

Editorial Address: RMC House, Broadfield Court, Broadfield Business Park, SHEFFIELD, S8 0XF
Tel: 0114 250 6300 **Fax:** 0114 255 5881
Email: chris.wilson@regionalmagazine.co.uk
Advertising Address: As above. **Fax:** 0114 250 6320
Email: john.murphy@regionalmagazine.co.uk
Web site: http://www.northernlifestyle.com
Publisher: Regional Magazine Company
Frequency: Monthly
Cover Price: Free
Circulation: 20,000 (Publisher's Statement)
Usual Pagination: 70
Editor: Chris Wilson
Summary of Content: Magazine covering prestige property and luxury living.
Readership/Target Audience: Aimed at affluent home movers.
ADVERTISING RATES:
Full Page Colour £1311.00
Agency Commission: 10%
Mechanical Data: Film: Digital
Copy instructions: Copy Date: 2 weeks prior to publication date
Average advertising content per issue: 45%
CONSUMER: WOMEN'S INTEREST CONSUMER MAGAZINES: Home Purchase

MS MATTERS 48640U94F-520

Editorial Address: 372 Edgware Road, LONDON, NW2 6ND
Tel: 020 8438 0700 **Fax:** 020 8438 0701
Email: msmatters@mssociety.org.uk
Advertising Address: Mongoose Media Ltd, 2 Lonsdale Road, LONDON, NW6 6RD **Tel:** 020 7306 0300
Fax: 020 7306 0301
Email: msmatters@mongoosemedia.com
Web site: http://www.mssociety.org.uk
Publisher: MS Society
Date Established: 1995
Frequency: 6 issues yearly
Annual Sub.: £5.00
Circulation: 45,000 (Publisher's Statement)
Usual Pagination: 32
Editor: Debbie Reeves
Summary of Content: Magazine covering research and articles of interest to those with multiple sclerosis.
Readership/Target Audience: Aimed at people with MS, their families and carers, as well as health professionals.
ADVERTISING RATES:
Full Page Colour £2758.00
Agency Commission: 10%
Mechanical Data: Type Area: 278 x 186mm, Trim Size: 297 x 210mm, Col Length: 278mm, Bleed Size: 303 x 216mm, Film: Digital, Page Width: 186mm
Copy instructions: Copy Date: 6 weeks prior to publication date
Average advertising content per issue: 20%
CONSUMER: OTHER CLASSIFICATIONS: Disability

MSAFIRI 48214U89D-220

Editorial Address: 4 Rycote Lane Farm, Milton Common, OXFORD, OX9 2NZ **Tel:** 01844 278883 **Fax:** 01844 278893
Email: msafiri@travelafricamag.com
Advertising Address: Laurel Cottage, BROUGHTON-IN-FURNESS, LA20 6HU **Tel:** 01229 776575
Email: carol.ibb@btinternet.com
Publisher: Travel Africa Ltd
Date Established: 1971
Frequency: Quarterly
Cover Price: Free
Circulation: 60,000 (Publisher's Statement)
Usual Pagination: 192
Editor: Craig Rix; **Advertising Manager:** Carol Filby; **Publisher:** Craig Rix
Summary of Content: In-flight magazine of Kenya Airways containing news, travel and fashion features, sport, entertainment and business.
Readership/Target Audience: Aimed at national and international government officials, business and leisure travellers to Africa, Europe, the Middle East, Asia and the Far East.
ADVERTISING RATES:
Full Page Mono £3222.00
Full Page Colour £3580.00
Agency Commission: 15%
Mechanical Data: Type Area: 277 x 190mm, Trim Size: 297 x 210mm, Bleed Size: 305 x 215mm, Print Process: Web-fed offset litho, Film: Digital, Page Width: 190mm, Col Length: 277mm
Copy instructions: Copy Date: 1 month prior to publication date
Average advertising content per issue: 50%
CONSUMER: HOLIDAYS & TRAVEL: In-Flight Magazines

MSLEXIA 47548U84B-130

Editorial Address: Holy Jesus Hospital, City Road, NEWCASTLE UPON TYNE, NE1 2AS **Tel:** 0191 233 3860
Fax: 0191 233 3882
Email: postbag@mslexia.co.uk
Advertising Address: As above. **Tel:** 0191 261 6656
Fax: 0191 261 6636
Email: sarah@mslexia.co.uk
Web site: http://www.mslexia.co.uk
ISSN: 1473-9399
Publisher: Mslexia Publications Ltd
Date Established: 1999
Frequency: Quarterly
Cover Price: £5.50
Annual Sub.: £21.75
Circulation: 30,000 (Publisher's Statement)
Usual Pagination: 68
Editor: Wendy Macdonald; **Advertising Manager:** Sarah Mitchell
Summary of Content: Magazine containing features, interviews, reviews and news on writing, poetry and prose. Also covers literature events, jobs, publications, courses and venues around the country.
Readership/Target Audience: Aimed predominantly at self-improving women who write, want to write, teach creative writing or have a special interest in women's literature.
ADVERTISING RATES:
Full Page Mono £875.00
Full Page Colour £1050.00
Mechanical Data: Film: Digital, Trim Size: 297 x 210mm, Bleed Size: +3mm, Col Widths (Display): 85mm
Copy instructions: Copy Date: 2 weeks prior to publication date
Average advertising content per issue: 40%
CONSUMER: THE ARTS & LITERARY: Literary

MUD 47426U83-40

Editorial Address: Cat Hill, BARNET, EN4 8HT
Tel: 020 8411 6473 **Fax:** 020 8411 6473
Email: g.pluck@mdx.ac.uk
Advertising Address: As above.
Email: g.pluck@mdx.ac.uk
Web site: http://www.musu.mdx.ac.uk
Publisher: Middlesex University Students' Union
Frequency: 6 issues yearly - Published monthly during term time
Cover Price: Free
Circulation: 3,000 (Publisher's Statement)
Usual Pagination: 32
Editor: Gary Pluck; **Advertising Manager:** Gary Pluck
Summary of Content: Newspaper covering sport, news stories, jokes, art, music, film and video reviews and events.
Readership/Target Audience: Aimed at students of Middlesex University.
ADVERTISING RATES:
Full Page Colour £335.00
Agency Commission: 10%
Mechanical Data: Type Area: 297 x 210mm, Col Length: 297mm, Page Width: 210mm, Bleed Size: +3mm
Copy instructions: Copy Date: 2 weeks prior to publication date
Average advertising content per issue: 5%
CONSUMER: STUDENT PUBLICATIONS

MULTIHULL REVIEW 1813541U91A-295

Editorial Address: Regus House, Southampton International Business Park, George Curl Way, SOUTHAMPTON, SO18 2RZ **Tel:** 023 8030 2028 **Fax:** 023 8030 2001
Email: mark@multihullreview.co.uk
Advertising Address: As above.
Email: mark@multihullreview.co.uk
Web site: http://www.multihullreview.co.uk
Publisher: Multihull Review Ltd
Date Established: 2005
Frequency: 6 issues yearly
Annual Sub.: £18.00
Usual Pagination: 52
Editor: Mark Orr; **Features Editor:** Lia Ditton; **Advertising Manager:** Mark Orr
Summary of Content: Magazine covering boat reviews, yachting products, boat tests, sailing features and boating news.
Readership/Target Audience: Aimed at multihull sailors and those interested in multihulls.
ADVERTISING: Rates on application
CONSUMER: RECREATION & LEISURE: Boating & Yachting

MUM PLUS ONE 1824294U74D-661

Editorial Address: 134 Liverpool Road, LONDON, N1 1LA
Tel: 020 7665 1111 **Fax:** 020 7609 5837
Email: editorial@cwcomms.com
Advertising Address: As above.
Email: andy.roberts@cwcomms.com
Publisher: CW Publishing Group
Frequency: Half-yearly - Published in January and July
Cover Price: Free
Circulation: 250,000 (Publisher's Statement)
Usual Pagination: 140
Editor: Trisha Doyle; **Advertising Manager:** Sema Demir
Summary of Content: Magazine covering baby and parenting topics including nutrition, motoring, finance, insurance, travel, photography and health.
Readership/Target Audience: Aimed at new mothers at the time of birth through their midwife.
ADVERTISING: Rates on application
CONSUMER: WOMEN'S INTEREST CONSUMER MAGAZINES: Child Care

MUSCLE & FITNESS 45980U75P-450

Editorial Address: 10 Windsor Court, Clarence Drive, HARROGATE, HG1 2PE **Tel:** 01423 504516
Fax: 01423 561494
Email: ukpub@weideruk.com
Advertising Address: As above.
Email: slund@weideruk.com
Web site: http://www.muscle-fitness.co.uk
ISSN: 0955-1387
Publisher: Weider Publishing Ltd
Date Established: 1987
Frequency: Monthly
Cover Price: £3.60
Annual Sub.: £29.97
Circulation: 30,000 (Publisher's Statement)
Usual Pagination: 196
Editor: Chris Lund; **Managing Director:** Martin Cheifetz
Summary of Content: Magazine covering all aspects of super fitness primarily strength and fitness training and nutrition.
Language(s): Dutch; English; French; German; Italian
Readership/Target Audience: Aimed at dedicated fitness enthusiasts.
ADVERTISING RATES:
Full Page Mono £972.00
Full Page Colour £1470.00
Agency Commission: 15%
Mechanical Data: Type Area: 237 x 170mm, Trim Size: 267 x 200mm, Bleed Size: 273 x 206mm, Print Process: Web-fed offset litho, Film: Digital, Col Length: 237mm, Page Width: 170mm
Copy instructions: Copy Date: 8 weeks prior to publication date
Average advertising content per issue: 30%
CONSUMER: SPORT: Fitness/Bodybuilding

MUSCLEMAG INTERNATIONAL 45981U75P-802

Editorial Address: Fort Dunlop, Fort Parkway, BIRMINGHAM, B24 9FE **Tel:** 0845 345 0916
Fax: 0845 345 0917
Email: sophie@tropicanahealthandfitness.com
Web site: http://www.emusclemag.com
Publisher: Tropicana Health and Fitness
Frequency: Monthly
Circulation: 360,000 (Publisher's Statement)
Usual Pagination: 196
Editor: Sophie Adey
Summary of Content: Magazine covering all aspects of bodybuilding and fitness including training routine, nutrition, exercise, profiles, events and new products.

Consumer Magazines

Readership/Target Audience: Read by bodybuilding enthusiasts.
CONSUMER: SPORT: Fitness/Bodybuilding

AL MUSHAHID ASSIYASI
48288U90-17

Editorial Address: 25-27 Mossop Street, LONDON, SW3 2LY **Tel:** 020 7052 9600 **Fax:** 020 7052 9609
Email: almushahid@btinternet.com
Advertising Address: As above. **Fax:** 020 7731 6412
Email: wdaas@almushahid.com
Web site: http://www.almushahidassiyasi.com
ISSN: 1364-5323
Publisher: Media World Services Ltd
Frequency: Weekly
Annual Sub.: £80.00
Circulation: 40,282 (Publisher's Statement)
Usual Pagination: 66
Editor: Hisham Aldiwan; **Managing Director:** Mazen Koubrously; **Advertising Manager:** Walid Daas
Summary of Content: Pan-Arabian magazine covering mainstream topics such as film and book reviews, music and the arts, current affairs and international news stories.
Language(s): Arabic
Readership/Target Audience: Aimed at an Arabic readership.
ADVERTISING RATES:
Full Page Mono £3000.00
Full Page Colour £6000.00
Agency Commission: 15%
Mechanical Data: Film: Digital
Copy instructions: Copy Date: Tuesday prior to publication date
CONSUMER: ETHNIC

MUSIC TECH MAGAZINE
1614320U76D-762

Editorial Address: Suite 6, Piccadilly House, London Road, BATH, BA1 6PL **Tel:** 01225 489984 **Fax:** 01225 489980
Email: editorial@anthem-publishing.com
Advertising Address: As above.
Email: simon.lewis@anthem-publishing.com
Web site: http://www.musictechmag.co.uk
ISSN: 1479-4187
Publisher: Anthem Publishing Ltd
Date Established: 2003
Frequency: Monthly
Cover Price: £5.99
Free to qualifying individuals
Annual Sub.: £60.00
Circulation: 15,046 (Publisher's Statement)
Usual Pagination: 116
Editor: Lewis Brangwyn; **Advertising Director:** Simon Lewis
Summary of Content: Magazine covering technology and techniques used in musical performance, creation and recording.
Language(s): English; Spanish
Readership/Target Audience: Aimed at producers, engineers and recording musicians.
ADVERTISING RATES:
Full Page Colour £650.00
Agency Commission: 10%
Mechanical Data: Type Area: 270 x 190mm, Trim Size: 297 x 210mm, Bleed Size: 303 x 216mm, Film: Digital, Col Length: 297mm, Page Width: 190mm
Copy instructions: Copy Date: 4 weeks prior to publication date
Average advertising content per issue: 30%
CONSUMER: MUSIC & PERFORMING ARTS: Music

MUSICAL OPINION
46171U76D-365

Editorial Address: 1 Exford Road, LONDON, SE12 9HD
Tel: 020 8857 1582
Email: editor@musicalopinion.com
Advertising Address: Musical Opinion, Woodman Works, 204 Durnsford Road, LONDON, SW19 8DR
Tel: 020 8971 8450 **Fax:** 020 8971 8480
Email: lana@cabbell.co.uk
Web site: http://www.musicalopinion.com
ISSN: 0027-4623
Publisher: Musical Opinion Ltd
Date Established: 1877
Frequency: 6 issues yearly
Cover Price: £4.50
Annual Sub.: £28.00
Circulation: 8,500 (Publisher's Statement)
Usual Pagination: 68
Editor: Robert Matthew-Walker
Summary of Content: Magazine covering concerts, festivals, opera and dance featuring articles on new music, anniversaries and personalities. Includes video, DVD, book, concert, opera and music reviews. Annual features include education in music, summer schools and music festivals.
Readership/Target Audience: Aimed at music lovers, professionals, students, performers and members of orchestral and choral societies.
ADVERTISING RATES:
Full Page Colour £950.00
Agency Commission: 10%

Mechanical Data: Page Width: 180mm, Film: Digital, Bleed Size: 305 x 216mm, Trim Size: 297 x 210mm, Type Area: 260 x 180mm, Col Length: 260mm
Average advertising content per issue: 15%
CONSUMER: MUSIC & PERFORMING ARTS: Music

THE MUSICAL QUARTERLY
601510U76D-377

Editorial Address: Great Clarendon Street, OXFORD, OX2 6DP **Tel:** 01865 556767 **Fax:** 01865 353985
Email: jnls.cust.serv@oxfordjournals.org
Advertising Address: As above. **Tel:** 01865 353329
Email: jnlsadvertising@oxfordjournals.com
Web site: http://www.oup.co.uk/jnls
ISSN: 0027-4631
Publisher: OUP
Date Established: 1915
Frequency: Quarterly
Annual Sub.: £92.00
Circulation: 3,000 (Publisher's Statement)
Usual Pagination: 200
Editor: Leon Botstien; **Publisher:** Trish Thomas
Summary of Content: Journal features an American showcase for informed writing on all aspects of music.
Readership/Target Audience: Aimed at leading composers, critics, and scholars from America and around the world.
ADVERTISING RATES:
Full Page Mono £360.00
Agency Commission: 10%
Mechanical Data: Film: Digital, Page Width: 130mm, Type Area: 200 x 130mm, Col Length: 200mm
CONSUMER: MUSIC & PERFORMING ARTS: Music

MUSICAL STAGES
46073U76B-110

Editorial Address: PO Box 8365, LONDON, W14 0GL
Tel: 020 7603 2227 **Fax:** 020 7603 2221
Email: editor@musicalstages.co.uk
Advertising Address: As above. **Tel:** 020 7603 2221
Email: editor@musicalstages.co.uk
Web site: http://www.musicalstages.co.uk
ISSN: 1361-3693
Publisher: Musical Stages
Date Established: 1995
Frequency: Quarterly
Cover Price: £4.00
Annual Sub.: £20.00
Circulation: 5,000 (Publisher's Statement)
Usual Pagination: 32
Editor: Lynda Trapnell; **Advertising Manager:** Michael Tornay
Summary of Content: Magazine dedicated to musical theatre, featuring interviews, features and competitions, as well as news, reviews and listings.
Readership/Target Audience: Read by theatre-goers and performers.
ADVERTISING: Rates on application
Copy instructions: Copy Date: 31st of the month prior to publication date
CONSUMER: MUSIC & PERFORMING ARTS: Theatre

MUSIC-ZINE
1779105U76D-821

Editorial Address: PO Box 9080, BISHOPS STORTFORD, CM23 4XW **Tel:** 01279 865070 **Fax:** 0870 486 0812
Email: simon@music-zine.com
Advertising Address: As above.
Email: yvette@music-zine.com
Web site: http://www.music-zine.com
ISSN: 1753-576X
Publisher: Music-zine Ltd
Date Established: 2006
Frequency: 6 issues yearly
Cover Price: Free
Circulation: 10,000 (Publisher's Statement)
Usual Pagination: 42
Editor: Simon Baker; **Advertising Manager:** Yvette Chivers
Summary of Content: Magazine covering local band and established bands playing in the area as well as an events diary, interviews, reviews and news.
Readership/Target Audience: Aimed at music lovers within the M11 corridor.
ADVERTISING RATES:
Full Page Mono £250.00
Full Page Colour £400.00
Agency Commission: 10%
Copy instructions: Copy Date: 20th of the month prior to publication date
Average advertising content per issue: 20%
CONSUMER: MUSIC & PERFORMING ARTS: Music

THE MUSLIM NEWS
48323U90-105

Editorial Address: PO Box 380, HARROW, HA2 6LL
Tel: 020 8863 8586 **Fax:** 020 8863 9370
Email: editor@muslimnews.co.uk
Advertising Address: As above.
Email: advert@muslimnews.co.uk

Web site: http://www.muslimnews.co.uk
ISSN: 0956-5027
Publisher: Visitcrest Ltd
Date Established: 1989
Frequency: Monthly
Free to qualifying individuals
Annual Sub.: £12.00
Circulation: 30,000 (Publisher's Statement)
Usual Pagination: 16
Editor: Ahmed Versi; **Advertising Manager:** Tahera Versi
Summary of Content: Newspaper covering political and community affairs from the UK and abroad, education, social, ethical, legal, environment, science, cultural affairs and sports.
Readership/Target Audience: Aimed at the Muslim community, non-Muslims and policy makers aged 16 to 45 years old.
ADVERTISING RATES:
Full Page Mono £2890.00
Full Page Colour £2990.00
Agency Commission: 15%
Mechanical Data: Type Area: 380 x 266mm, Trim Size: 420 x 297mm, No. of Columns (Display): 5, Film: Digital, Col Length: 380mm, Page Width: 266mm
Copy instructions: Copy Date: 10 days prior to publication date
Average advertising content per issue: 50%
CONSUMER: ETHNIC

THE MUSLIM WEEKLY
1638668U90-921

Editorial Address: 117 Whitechapel Road, LONDON, E1 1DT **Tel:** 0870 350 1492 **Fax:** 020 7377 5004
Email: editor@themuslimweekly.com
Advertising Address: As above. **Tel:** 020 7377 1919
Fax: 0871 714 6451
Email: advertising@themuslimweekly.com
Web site: http://www.themuslimweekly.com
Publisher: SNS Publications
Date Established: 2003
Frequency: Weekly
Cover Price: £0.50
Circulation: 50,000 (Publisher's Statement)
Usual Pagination: 32
Editor: Ahmed Malik; **News Editor:** Hamza Bajwa; **Editor-in-Chief:** Ahmed Malik; **Advertising Manager:** A. Hoq
Summary of Content: Newspaper covering issues affecting Muslims in Britain and around the world with local and international news, current affairs, lifestyle, personalities, local communities and people, sport and Islamic art and culture all from an Islamic perspective.
Readership/Target Audience: Aimed mainly at Muslims and other minority communities.
ADVERTISING RATES:
Full Page Mono £2000.00
Full Page Colour £2500.00
Agency Commission: 10%
Mechanical Data: Bleed Size: +5mm, Trim Size: 388 x 264mm, Film: Digital
Copy instructions: Copy Date: 3 days prior to publication date
CONSUMER: ETHNIC

MUSO
766856U76D-759

Editorial Address: 2nd Floor, Century House, 11 St. Peters Square, MANCHESTER, M2 3DN **Tel:** 0161 236 9526
Email: editorial@musolife.com
Advertising Address: As above. **Fax:** 0161 247 7978
Email: advertising@muso-adverts.com
Web site: http://www.musolife.com
ISSN: 1476-9212
Publisher: Impromptu Publishing Ltd
Date Established: 2002
Frequency: 6 issues yearly
Cover Price: £3.50
Circulation: 13,000 (Publisher's Statement)
Usual Pagination: 76
Editor: Claire Jackson; **Publisher:** Marcus Netherwood
Summary of Content: Magazine covering all aspects of classical music, including news, events and equipment with competitions and artist profiles.
Readership/Target Audience: Aimed at young musicians between 16 and 30 years old.
ADVERTISING RATES:
Full Page Colour £1495.00
Agency Commission: 10%
Mechanical Data: Type Area: 270 x 202mm, Col Length: 270mm, Bleed Size: 298 x 240mm, Trim Size: 290 x 232mm, Film: Digital, Page Width: 202mm
Average advertising content per issue: 33%
CONSUMER: MUSIC & PERFORMING ARTS: Music

MY BRENT CROSS
1775130U74B-721

Formerly: Addiction
Editorial Address: Spitfire Studios, 61 Collier Street, LONDON, N1 9BE **Tel:** 020 7833 7410 **Fax:** 020 7833 7411
Email: salena.noel@northstarpublishing.com

Publisher: Northstar Publishing Ltd
Date Established: 2007
Frequency: Half-yearly
Cover Price: Free
Circulation: 100,000 (Publisher's Statement)
Usual Pagination: 36
Summary of Content: Magazine covering fashion that is available in Brent Cross Shopping Centre and competitions.
Readership/Target Audience: Aimed at women aged 25 to 45 years old.
ADVERTISING: No Advertising taken
CONSUMER: WOMEN'S INTEREST CONSUMER MAGAZINES: Women's Interest - Fashion

MY HOME IN THE SUN
1693227U74K-734

Editorial Address: Publishing House. 3 Bridgebank Industrial Estate, Taylor Street, Horwich, BOLTON, BL6 7PD
Tel: 0161 909 0909 **Fax:** 0161 909 0919
Email: clive.entwistle@bigspark.co.uk
Advertising Address: As above. **Tel:** 020 7831 1131
Fax: 020 7242 0832
Email: lee@petershampublishing.co.uk
Web site: http://www.myhomeinthesunshine.co.uk
Publisher: The Big Spark
Date Established: 2005
Frequency: Quarterly
Cover Price: Free
Circulation: 89,175 (Publisher's Statement)
Usual Pagination: 68
Editor: Clive Entwistle; **Managing Director:** Jack Durkin;
Advertising Manager: Lee Scott; **Publisher:** Stuart Parker
Summary of Content: Magazine covering property worldwide including villas and apartments to buy, sell or let as well as financial advice.
Readership/Target Audience: Aimed at Tesco's customers with a high disposable income.
ADVERTISING RATES:
Full Page Colour £2950.00
Agency Commission: 10%
Mechanical Data: Type Area: 275 x 190mm, Bleed Size: 317 x 215mm, Trim Size: 297 x 210mm, Col Length: 275mm, Page Width: 190mm
Copy instructions: Copy Date: 3 weeks prior to publication date
CONSUMER: WOMEN'S INTEREST CONSUMER MAGAZINES: Home Purchase

MY MERTON
1626346U80B-390

Editorial Address: Merton Civic Centre, London Road, MORDEN, SM4 5DX **Tel:** 020 8545 3327
Fax: 020 8545 0446
Email: mymerton@merton.gov.uk
Advertising Address: As above. **Fax:** 020 8545 3273
Email: andy.thompson@merton.gov.uk
Web site: http://www.merton.gov.uk/mymerton
Publisher: London Borough of Merton
Date Established: 2003
Frequency: 6 issues yearly
Cover Price: Free
Circulation: 86,000 (Publisher's Statement)
Usual Pagination: 24
Editor: Emma Henderson; **Advertising Manager:** Andy Thompson
Summary of Content: Community magazine covering news, views and issues across the Borough of Merton. Includes a comprehensive what's on listings guide.
Readership/Target Audience: Aimed at those who live, work and learn in the London Borough of Merton.
ADVERTISING RATES:
Full Page Colour £1650.00
Mechanical Data: Trim Size: 297 x 210mm, Film: Digital
Average advertising content per issue: 8%
CONSUMER: RURAL & REGIONAL INTEREST: Regional Interest Greater London

MY WEEKLY
45188U74A-370

Editorial Address: 80 Kingsway East, DUNDEE, DD4 8SL
Tel: 01382 223131 **Fax:** 01382 452491
Email: myweekly@dcthomson.co.uk
Advertising Address: 2 Albert Square, DUNDEE, DD1 9QJ
Tel: 01382 223131 **Fax:** 01382 454599
Email: advertising-meadowside@dcthomson.co.uk
Web site: http://www.jbwb.co.uk/weekly.html
Publisher: D.C. Thomson & Co Ltd
Date Established: 1910
Frequency: Weekly
Cover Price: £0.80
Circulation: 145,676 (ABC 01/01/2009 to 30/06/2009)
Usual Pagination: 64
Editor: Fiona Brown; **Features Editor:** Jennifer McEwan;
Managing Director: Andrew Thomson; **Advertising Manager:** Carol Horn
Summary of Content: Magazine covering beauty, fashion, cookery, fiction and human interest articles.
Readership/Target Audience: Aimed at women aged 50 years and over.

ADVERTISING RATES:
Full Page Mono £4060.00
Full Page Colour £6100.00
Agency Commission: 15%
Mechanical Data: Film: Positive, right reading, emulsion side down, Type Area: 270 x 200mm, Col Length: 270mm, Bleed Size: 301 x 231mm, Trim Size: 295 x 225mm, Page Width: 200mm
Copy instructions: Copy Date: 4 weeks prior to publication date
CONSUMER: WOMEN'S INTEREST CONSUMER MAGAZINES: Women's Interest

MYHOME
1824296U74C-872

Editorial Address: 134 Liverpool Road, LONDON, N1 1LA
Tel: 020 7665 1111 **Fax:** 020 7609 5837
Email: editorial@cwcomms.com
Advertising Address: As above.
Email: andy.roberts@cwcomms.com
Publisher: CW Publishing Group
Date Established: 2007
Frequency: Half-yearly - Published in October and March
Cover Price: Free
Circulation: 25,000 (Publisher's Statement)
Editor: Trisha Doyle; **Advertising Manager:** Sema Demir
Summary of Content: Homes and lifestyle magazine covering interiors, travel, finance, spring cleaning, motoring, recipes, wine, gardens and book reviews.
Readership/Target Audience: Aimed at men and women with a high disposable income.
ADVERTISING: Rates on application
CONSUMER: WOMEN'S INTEREST CONSUMER MAGAZINES: Home & Family

N16: THE MAGAZINE AT THE HEART OF STOKE NEWINGTON
1638154U80B-401

Editorial Address: PO Box 44624, LONDON, N16 5WN
Tel: 020 7249 9943 **Fax:** 020 7249 9943
Email: info@n16mag.com
Advertising Address: As above.
Email: info@n16mag.com
Web site: http://www.n16mag.com
Publisher: N16 Publishing Ltd
Date Established: 1999
Frequency: Quarterly
Cover Price: Free
Circulation: 35,000 (Publisher's Statement)
Usual Pagination: 44
Editor: Rab MacWilliam; **Advertising Manager:** Rab MacWilliam; **Publisher:** Rab MacWilliam
Summary of Content: Magazine with items of local interest, history, planning, property, arts, entertainment, celebrity, restaurants, bars and clubs.
Readership/Target Audience: Aimed at those living and working in London N16 and surrounding areas.
ADVERTISING: Rates on application
CONSUMER: RURAL & REGIONAL INTEREST: Regional Interest Greater London

NAAPSNEWS
1911413U90-1035

Editorial Address: NAAPS HQ, Room 102A, 1st Floor, Mitre House, 223-237 Borough High Street, LONDON, SE1 1JD
Tel: 020 7740 8563
Email: kunal.mehta@london.probation.gsi.gov.uk
Frequency: Quarterly
Cover Price: £6.00
Circulation: 13,000 (Publisher's Statement)
Editor: Kunal Mehta
Summary of Content: Magazine covering Asian perspectives in the probation and prison service, British Asian current affairs and healthcare.
Readership/Target Audience: Aimed at British Asians with an interest in Asian perspectives.
CONSUMER: ETHNIC

NADFAS REVIEW
47506U84A-325

Formerly: NADFAS News
Editorial Address: NADFAS House, 8 Guilford Street, LONDON, WC1N 1DA **Tel:** 020 7430 0730
Fax: 020 7242 0686
Email: nadfasreview@nadfas.org.uk
Advertising Address: As above.
Email: nadfasreview@nadfas.org.uk
Web site: http://www.nadfas.org.uk
Publisher: NADFAS Enterprises Ltd
Frequency: Quarterly
Cover Price: £2.50
Free to qualifying individuals
Circulation: 78,331 (ABC 01/01/2008 to 31/12/2008)
Usual Pagination: 64
Editor: Judith Quiney; **Advertising Manager:** Judith Quiney;
Publisher: Judith Quiney
Summary of Content: Magazine of the National Association of Decorative and Fine Arts Societies.

Readership/Target Audience: Aimed at members and those interested in fine arts.
ADVERTISING RATES:
Full Page Colour £2130.00
Agency Commission: 10%
Mechanical Data: Type Area: 262 x 202mm, Col Length: 262mm, No. of Columns (Display): 2, Bleed Size: 303 x 238mm, Trim Size: 297 x 232mm, Film: Digital, Page Width: 202mm
Copy instructions: Copy Date: 8 weeks prior to publication date
CONSUMER: THE ARTS & LITERARY: Arts

NANG!
1777136U74Q-1335

Editorial Address: Ground Floor, 24-26 Fournier Street, LONDON, E1 6QE **Tel:** 020 7183 3222
Email: nangmagazine@hotmail.co.uk
Advertising Address: As above.
Email: liz.millar@summeruni.org
Web site: http://www.summeruni.org/nang
Publisher: Tower Hamlets Summer University
Date Established: 2001
Frequency: Quarterly
Cover Price: Free
Circulation: 10,500 (Publisher's Statement)
Usual Pagination: 48
Editor: Liz Millar; **Advertising Manager:** Liz Millar;
Managing Editor: Liz Millar
Summary of Content: Magazine covering fashion, sport, health, real life, music, film, DVD and book reviews, careers, celebrity interviews and events.
Readership/Target Audience: Aimed at 16 to 21 year old students and distributed through sixth forms, colleges and universities in London.
ADVERTISING: Rates on application
CONSUMER: WOMEN'S INTEREST CONSUMER MAGAZINES: Lifestyle

NAPOLEON
48805U94X-100

Editorial Address: 157 Vicarage Road, Leyton, LONDON, E10 5DU **Tel:** 020 8539 3876 **Fax:** 020 8539 3876
ISSN: 0027-7825
Publisher: Delane Press
Date Established: 1969
Frequency: Quarterly
Cover Price: Free
Editor: Ronald King
Summary of Content: Magazine covering the history of France 1789-1945. Published on behalf of the Napoleonic Society.
Language(s): Dutch; English; French
Readership/Target Audience: Aimed at those with an interest in the history of France.
ADVERTISING: No Advertising taken
CONSUMER: OTHER CLASSIFICATIONS: Miscellaneous

NARROW GAUGE WORLD
46705U79J-44

Editorial Address: 83 Parkanaur Avenue, SOUTHEND-ON-SEA, SS1 3JA **Tel:** 01702 580409 **Fax:** 01702 588970
Email: dawjoy@aol.com
Advertising Address: As above.
Email: ja@atlanticpublishers.com
Web site: http://www.atlanticpublishers.com
ISSN: 1466-0180
Publisher: Atlantic Publishers
Frequency: 6 issues yearly
Cover Price: £3.95
Annual Sub.: £27.50
Circulation: 4,000 (Publisher's Statement)
Editor: David Joy; **Advertising Manager:** Juliet Arthur
Summary of Content: Magazine containing features and reports on narrow gauge railways across the world.
Readership/Target Audience: Aimed at railway enthusiasts and travellers.
ADVERTISING RATES:
Full Page Mono £214.00
Full Page Colour £267.00
Agency Commission: 10%
Mechanical Data: Film: Digital, Bleed Size: 307 x 220mm, Page Width: 192mm, Type Area: 266 x 192mm, Col Length: 266mm, Trim Size: 297 x 210mm
Copy instructions: Copy Date: 8834 weeks prior to publication date
Average advertising content per issue: 30%
CONSUMER: HOBBIES & DIY: Rail Enthusiasts

NATIONAL CLUB GOLFER
45821U75D-180

Editorial Address: 1st Floor, 18-22 Market Street, CLECKHEATON, BD19 5AJ **Tel:** 01274 851323
Fax: 01274 852687
Email: editorial@sportspub.co.uk
Advertising Address: As above.
Email: mark_k@sportspub.co.uk
Web site: http://www.nationalclubgolfer.com
ISSN: 1354-2532

Consumer Magazines

Publisher: Sports Publications Ltd.
Date Established: 1994
Frequency: Monthly
Cover Price: Free
Circulation: 70,000 (Publisher's Statement)
Usual Pagination: 172
Editor: Dan Murphy; **Advertising Manager:** Richard Holt
Summary of Content: Magazine focusing on golf clubs, courses and players. Includes news, instruction, reviews, travel and celebrity interviews.
Readership/Target Audience: Aimed at members of golf clubs and driving ranges.
ADVERTISING RATES:
Full Page Colour £2253.96
Agency Commission: 10%
Mechanical Data: Trim Size: 297 x 210mm, Film: Digital
Copy instructions: Copy Date: 4 weeks prior to publication date
CONSUMER: SPORT: Golf

NATIONAL DEAF CHILDREN'S SOCIETY MAGAZINE
48653U94F-845

Formerly: TALK
Editorial Address: 15 Dufferin Street, LONDON, EC1Y 8UR
Tel: 020 7490 8656
Email: jane.fookes@ndcs.org.uk
Advertising Address: As above.
Email: advertising@ndcs.org.uk
Web site: http://www.ndcs.org.uk
ISSN: 0049-2906
Publisher: The National Deaf Children's Society
Date Established: 1948
Frequency: Quarterly
Cover Price: Free
Circulation: 14,500 (Publisher's Statement)
Usual Pagination: 44
Editor: Jane Fookes
Summary of Content: Magazine of The National Deaf Children's Society. Covers society news, benefits, health, fundraising, technology and events, parents and young people's experiences. Also highlights issues affecting deaf children and their families.
Readership/Target Audience: Aimed at members of The National Deaf Children's Society and professionals working with families of deaf children.
ADVERTISING: Rates on application
CONSUMER: OTHER CLASSIFICATIONS: Disability

NATIONAL GEOGRAPHIC KIDS
1786259U91D-950

Editorial Address: Unit 1.08 Clerkenwell Workshops, 31 Clerkenwell Close, LONDON, EC1R 0AT **Tel:** 020 7014 3777
Fax: 020 7014 3776
Email: lauren@atticmedianetwork.com
Advertising Address: As above.
Email: nigel@atticmedianetwork.com
Web site: http://www.ngkids.co.uk
Publisher: Attic Media Network
Date Established: 2006
Frequency: Monthly
Cover Price: £2.99
Circulation: 130,000 (Print Run)
Usual Pagination: 52
Editor: Lauren Jarvis; **Features Editor:** Tim Herbert;
Advertising Manager: Nigel Standley
Summary of Content: Children's magazine covering wildlife, science and technology, world events and the environment as well as quizzes, competitions, sport and reviews of games, movies and music.
Readership/Target Audience: Aimed at girls and boys aged 6 to 14 years old.
ADVERTISING RATES:
Full Page Mono £4500.00
Full Page Colour £4500.00
Agency Commission: 15%
Mechanical Data: Type Area: 265 x 200mm, Bleed Size: 281 x 216mm, Trim Size: 275 x 210mm, Col Length: 265mm, Page Width: 200mm, Film: Digital
Copy instructions: Copy Date: 3 weeks prior to publication date
Average advertising content per issue: 30%
CONSUMER: RECREATION & LEISURE: Children & Youth

NATIONAL HORSEMART
47141U80A-162

Formerly: Horsemart
Editorial Address: London Road, Sayers Common, HASSOCKS, BN6 9HS **Tel:** 01273 217837
Email: editorial@horsemart.co.uk
Advertising Address: As above. **Tel:** 01273 837807
Fax: 01273 837976
Email: tracy.potter@horsemart.co.uk
Web site: http://www.horsemart.co.uk
Publisher: Friday Holdings Ltd
Date Established: 2006
Frequency: Monthly - Published end of each previous month

Free to qualifying individuals
Annual Sub.: £30.10
Circulation: 82,715 (Publisher's Statement)
Usual Pagination: 256
Editor: Jo Metcalfe
Summary of Content: Equestrian magazine containing news, product news, tried and tested reviews, editorial competitions, editorial features, classified ads, advertising features, events, diary, results and items of general interest.
Readership/Target Audience: Aimed at equestrians and those who live, work and play in the countryside.
ADVERTISING RATES:
Full Page Colour £500.00
Agency Commission: 10%
Mechanical Data: Film: Digital, No. of Columns (Display): 5, Col Widths (Display): 40mm, Bleed Size: 290 x 215mm
Copy instructions: Copy Date: Friday prior to publication date
CONSUMER: RURAL & REGIONAL INTEREST: Rural Interest

NATIONAL HORSEMART
1748240U81D-371

Formerly: National Horsemart Weekly
Editorial Address: London Road, Sayers Common, HASSOCKS, BN6 9HS **Tel:** 01273 837807
Fax: 01273 837976
Email: jo.metcalfe@horsemart.co.uk
Advertising Address: As above. **Tel:** 0870 127 4308
Email: tracy.potter@horsemart.co.uk
Web site: http://www.horsemart.co.uk
Publisher: Friday Holdings Ltd
Date Established: 2006
Frequency: Monthly
Cover Price: £2.95
Circulation: 25,000 (Print Run)
Editor: Jo Metcalfe
Summary of Content: Magazine covering buying and selling of horses, horse-boxes, trailers, tack and other equestrian items as well as editorial features.
Readership/Target Audience: Aimed at those looking to buy or sell horses and equestrian related equipment.
ADVERTISING RATES:
Full Page Colour £500.00
Agency Commission: 10%
Mechanical Data: Bleed Size: 310 x 240mm, Trim Size: 300 x 230mm, Film: Digital
Copy instructions: Copy Date: 1 week prior to publication date
Average advertising content per issue: 50%
CONSUMER: ANIMALS & PETS: Horses & Ponies

NATIONAL RIFLE ASSOCIATION JOURNAL
45860U75F-85

Editorial Address: Bisley Camp, Brookwood, WOKING, GU24 0PB **Tel:** 01483 797777 **Fax:** 01483 797285
Email: karen@bang.u-net.com
Advertising Address: Print Rite, 31 Parklands, Freeland, WITNEY, OX29 8HX **Tel:** 01993 881662 **Fax:** 01993 881662
Email: colinjudge38@btinternet.com
Web site: http://www.nra.org.uk
Publisher: National Rifle Association
Frequency: 3 issues yearly - Published in February, May and October
Free to qualifying individuals
Circulation: 6,000 (Publisher's Statement)
Editor: Karen Robertson; **Advertising Manager:** Colin Judge
Summary of Content: Journal covering all aspects of rifle and pistol target shooting, book and product reviews, features, event meetings and profiles.
Readership/Target Audience: Aimed at members of the National Rifle Association.
ADVERTISING RATES:
Full Page Mono £290.00
Full Page Colour £480.00
Mechanical Data: No. of Columns (Display): 2, Print Process: Litho, Bleed Size: 303 x 213mm, Trim Size: 297 x 210mm, Film: Positive, right reading, emulsion side down. Digital
Copy instructions: Copy Date: 5 weeks prior to publication date
Average advertising content per issue: 9%
CONSUMER: SPORT: Shooting

THE NATIONAL STUDENT
1824325U83-291

Editorial Address: 58 High Street, LINCOLN, LN5 8AH
Tel: 01522 521521
Email: editor@national-student.co.uk
Advertising Address: As above. **Tel:** 01522 524400
Fax: 01522 522929
Email: advertising@national-student.co.uk
Web site: http://www.national-student.co.uk
Publisher: Defender Newspapers
Date Established: 2003
Frequency: 7 issues yearly
Cover Price: Free

Circulation: 100,000 (Publisher's Statement)
Usual Pagination: 36
Editor: James Thornhill; **Advertising Manager:** James Thornhill
Summary of Content: Newspaper covering student news, sport, features and entertainment with comment and analysis on issues relating to student life and higher education.
Readership/Target Audience: Aimed at students predominantly aged 18 to 24 years old.
ADVERTISING RATES:
Full Page Colour £2000.00
Mechanical Data: Type Area: 350 x 264mm, Col Length: 350mm, Page Width: 264mm, Film: Digital
Supplement(s): The National Student Magazine - 8xY
CONSUMER: STUDENT PUBLICATIONS

THE NATIONAL STUDENT MAGAZINE
1824327U83-292

Editorial Address: PO BOX 7731, DERBY, DE1 0RW
Tel: 0845 463 0046
Email: magazine@thenationalstudent.co.uk
Advertising Address: As above. **Tel:** 01522 524400
Fax: 01522 522929
Email: advertising@national-student.co.uk
Web site: http://www.thenationalstudent.co.uk/magazine
Publisher: Defender Newspapers
Date Established: 2003
Frequency: 8 issues yearly
Cover Price: Free
Circulation: 100,000 (Publisher's Statement)
Usual Pagination: 12
Editor: James Thornhill; **Advertising Manager:** James Thornhill
Summary of Content: Magazine covering entertainment including music, film, TV, web, theatre, art, literature, comedy and gaming.
Readership/Target Audience: Aimed at students predominantly aged 18 to 24 years old.
ADVERTISING RATES:
Full Page Colour £2000.00
Mechanical Data: Type Area: 350 x 264mm, Col Length: 350mm, Page Width: 264mm, Film: Digital
Copy instructions: Copy Date: 5 days prior to publication date
Supplement to: The National Student
CONSUMER: STUDENT PUBLICATIONS

NATIONAL THEATRE PROGRAMMES
46084U76B-132

Formerly: Royal National Theatre Programmes
Editorial Address: Upper Ground, LONDON, SE1 9PX
Tel: 020 7452 3251 **Fax:** 020 7452 3244
Advertising Address: Woodman Works, 204 Durnsford Road, LONDON, SW19 8DR **Tel:** 020 8971 8450
Fax: 020 8971 8480
Email: bill@cabbell.co.uk
Web site: http://www.nationaltheatre.org.uk
Publisher: Cabbell Publishing Ltd
Date Established: 1963
Frequency: Quarterly
Cover Price: £2.50
Circulation: 400,000 (Publisher's Statement)
Usual Pagination: 72
Editor: Lyn Haill; **Advertising Manager:** Bill Sheehan
Summary of Content: Magazine containing cast lists, editorial, cast biographies and advertising.
Readership/Target Audience: Read by visitors and ticket buyers to National Theatre productions.
ADVERTISING RATES:
Full Page Colour £5500.00
Agency Commission: 10%
Mechanical Data: Col Length: 224mm, Page Width: 124mm, Film: Digital, Type Area: 224 x 124mm, Bleed Size: 246 x 146mm, Trim Size: 240 x 140mm
Copy instructions: Copy Date: 5th of the month prior to publication date
Average advertising content per issue: 20%
CONSUMER: MUSIC & PERFORMING ARTS: Theatre

THE NATIONAL TRUST MAGAZINE
46806U80A-135

Editorial Address: Heelis, Kemble Drive, SWINDON, SN2 2NA **Tel:** 01793 817716
Email: magazine@nationaltrust.org.uk
Advertising Address: Madison Bell Ltd, 20 Orange Street, LONDON, WC2H 7EF **Tel:** 020 7389 0802
Fax: 020 7839 6719
Email: info@madisonbell.com
Web site: http://www.nationaltrust.org.uk
ISSN: 0266-6006
Publisher: The National Trust
Date Established: 1968
Frequency: 3 issues yearly - Published in January, May and September
Free to qualifying individuals

Circulation: 1,752,636 (ABC 01/01/2008 to 31/12/2008)
Usual Pagination: 96
Editor: Sue Herdman; **Advertising Director:** Wesley Tatton
Summary of Content: Magazine covering the conservation of buildings, countryside and coastal areas in the care of the National Trust.
Readership/Target Audience: Aimed at National Trust members.
ADVERTISING RATES:
Full Page Colour £2131.50
Agency Commission: 15%
Mechanical Data: Type Area: 276 x 204mm, Bleed Size: 306 x 231mm, Trim Size: 300 x 228mm, Print Process: Web-fed offset litho, Film: Digital, Col Length: 276mm, Page Width: 204mm
CONSUMER: RURAL & REGIONAL INTEREST: Rural Interest

NATIONWIDE BOWLER   767169U75X-1701
Formerly: Scottish Bowler
Editorial Address: 50 High Craighall Road, GLASGOW, G4 9UD **Tel:** 0141 353 2222 **Fax:** 0141 332 3811
Email: paul@bunkered.co.uk
Advertising Address: As above. **Fax:** 0141 332 3839
Email: sales@nationwidebowler.co.uk
Web site: http://www.scottishbowler.co.uk
Publisher: PSP Publishing Ltd
Date Established: 2001
Frequency: Quarterly
Cover Price: £2.95
Annual Sub.: £9.99
Circulation: 10,000 (Publisher's Statement)
Usual Pagination: 66
Editor: Paul Grant; **Publisher:** Paul Grant
Summary of Content: Magazine including reports on competitions and coming events as well as articles on coaching and umpiring.
Readership/Target Audience: Aimed at bowlers of all ages.
ADVERTISING RATES:
Full Page Colour £1050.00
Agency Commission: 10%
Mechanical Data: Type Area: 267 x 180mm, Bleed Size: 303 x 216mm, Trim Size: 297 x 210mm, Col Length: 267mm, Page Width: 180mm, Film: Digital
CONSUMER: SPORT: Other Sport

THE NATIVE PONY   1605876U81D-353
Editorial Address: 26 Blairs Road, Letham, FORFAR, DD8 2PE **Tel:** 0845 130 7669 **Fax:** 01307 818919
Email: info@thenativepony.com
Advertising Address: As above. **Tel:** 01307 818919
Email: susan@snequestrian.com
Web site: http://www.thenativepony.com
ISSN: 1474-3639
Publisher: Hillaine Publishing Ltd
Date Established: 2001
Frequency: 6 issues yearly
Cover Price: £3.50
Annual Sub.: £20.00
Circulation: 5,000 (Publisher's Statement)
Usual Pagination: 40
Editor: Helen Crighton; **News Editor:** Elena Sandidge; **Advertising Manager:** Susan Cox; **Managing Editor:** Helen Crighton
Summary of Content: Magazine covering British native breeds with breed and stud profiles, news from the breed societies, as well as articles on habitats, genetics, behaviour, veterinary subjects, breeding, showing, winners' gallery and a children's page.
Readership/Target Audience: Aimed at native pony enthusiasts.
ADVERTISING RATES:
Full Page Mono £250.00
Full Page Colour £300.00
Agency Commission: 10%
Mechanical Data: Trim Size: 297 x 210mm, Type Area: 276 x 192mm, Col Length: 276mm, Page Width: 192mm, Bleed Size: 303 x 216mm, Film: Digital
Copy instructions: Copy Date: 10th of the month prior to publication date
CONSUMER: ANIMALS & PETS: Horses & Ponies

NATURAL HEALTH   .627223U74G-39_85
Formerly: Natural Health & Beauty
Editorial Address: 25 Phoenix Court, Hawkins Road, COLCHESTER, CO2 8JY **Tel:** 01206 508616
Fax: 01206 505985
Email: claire.garnham@aceville.co.uk
Advertising Address: 2nd Floor, Ewer House, 44-46 Crouch Street, COLCHESTER, CO3 3HH **Tel:** 01206 505944
Fax: 01206 500183
Email: joy.palmer@aceville.co.uk
Web site: http://www.naturalhealthmagazine.co.uk
Publisher: Aceville Publications Ltd
Date Established: 2000
Frequency: Monthly

Cover Price: £3.25
Annual Sub.: £27.95
Circulation: 60,000 (Publisher's Statement)
Usual Pagination: 132
Editor: Sarah Ivory; **Advertising Manager:** Joy Palmer; **Group Editor:** Charlotte Smith
Summary of Content: Magazine covering alternative health issues, beauty, children, fitness and well-being.
Readership/Target Audience: Aimed predominantly at women aged between 25 and 55.
ADVERTISING RATES:
Full Page Colour £1950.00
SCC £39.00
Agency Commission: 10%
Mechanical Data: Page Width: 190mm, Bleed Size: 303 x 216mm, Trim Size: 297 x 210mm, Type Area: 270 x 190mm, Col Length: 270mm, No. of Columns (Display): 4, Film: Digital, Col Widths (Display): 44mm
Copy instructions: Copy Date: 3rd week of the month prior to publication date
Average advertising content per issue: 40%
CONSUMER: WOMEN'S INTEREST CONSUMER MAGAZINES: Slimming & Health

---

NATURAL LIFESTYLE MAGAZINE
1609377U74G-230
Editorial Address: The Old Dairy, Hudsons Farm, Fieldgate Lane, Ugley Green, BISHOP'S STORTFORD, CM22 6HJ
Tel: 01279 816300 **Fax:** 01279 816496
Email: editor@nat-lifestyle.com
Advertising Address: As above.
Email: ruth.dodsley@targetpublishing.com
Web site: http://www.nat-lifestyle.com
Publisher: Target Publishing Ltd
Date Established: 2003
Frequency: Monthly
Cover Price: Free
Circulation: 100,000 (Publisher's Statement)
Usual Pagination: 32
Editor: Rachel Symonds
Summary of Content: Magazine covering all aspects of a natural lifestyle, advising on prevention as well as cure, looking at long-term health, through diet, supplementation, exercise and positive mental attitude.
Readership/Target Audience: Aimed at health-conscious consumers shopping in independent health food stores.
ADVERTISING RATES:
Full Page Colour £2795.00
Agency Commission: 10%
Mechanical Data: Type Area: 268 x 180mm, Trim Size: 297 x 210mm, Bleed Size: 303 x 216mm, Col Length: 268mm, Page Width: 180mm, Film: Digital
Copy instructions: Copy Date: 7 weeks prior to publication date
Average advertising content per issue: 50%
CONSUMER: WOMEN'S INTEREST CONSUMER MAGAZINES: Slimming & Health

---

NB   47841U87-166
Editorial Address: 1 Bouchiers Place, Messing, COLCHESTER, CO5 9TY **Tel:** 01621 810341
Fax: 01621 819443
Email: jmelongman@aol.com
Web site: http://www.chelmsford.anglican.org
Publisher: Diocese of Chelmsford
Date Established: 1999
Frequency: 6 issues yearly
Cover Price: Free
Circulation: 40,000 (Publisher's Statement)
Usual Pagination: 4
Editor: Jon Longman
Summary of Content: Magazine containing information for clergy, church officers and congregations.
Readership/Target Audience: Aimed at clergy and church officers.
ADVERTISING: No Advertising taken
CONSUMER: RELIGIOUS

NB   48643U94F-1005
Formerly: New Beacon
Editorial Address: 105 Judd Street, LONDON, WC1H 9NE
Tel: 020 7391 2018
Email: martyn.harris@rnib.org.uk
Web site: http://www.rnib.org.uk
ISSN: 0028-4270
Publisher: Royal National Institute of Blind People
Date Established: 2006
Frequency: Monthly
Annual Sub.: £28.80
Circulation: 2,000 (Publisher's Statement)
Usual Pagination: 62
Editor: Martyn Harris
Summary of Content: Magazine covering the latest developments in eye health, social care and policy. News, features by leading experts, case histories and personal

views, advice, letters, products, conferences, training and job adverts in the field of sight loss and eye health.
Readership/Target Audience: Aimed at all sight loss and eye health professionals.
ADVERTISING: No Advertising taken
CONSUMER: OTHER CLASSIFICATIONS: Disability

NEGESYDD   1645229U80D-516
Editorial Address: Cross Community Centre, 1 High Street, Pontardawe, SWANSEA, SA8 4HU **Tel:** 01792 864949
Email: menter@micnpt.org
Web site: http://www.mentrau-iaith.com
Publisher: South West Wales Media Ltd
Date Established: 2002
Frequency: 6 issues yearly
Editor: Alun Pugh
Summary of Content: Welsh and English language community newspaper covering local news and events with articles on sport, schools, local authorities, the Welsh language, and Welsh language learners.
Language(s): English; Welsh
Readership/Target Audience: Aimed at those who speak Welsh and those who are learning the language.
ADVERTISING: No Advertising taken
Supplement to: The Courier Series (Neath & Port Talbot)
CONSUMER: RURAL & REGIONAL INTEREST: Regional Interest Wales

NEO   1702740U76A-190
Editorial Address: B10 Arena Business Centre, Holyrood Close, POOLE, BH17 7BA **Tel:** 01202 606385
Fax: 01202 606386
Email: gemma@uncookedmedia.com
Advertising Address: As above. **Fax:** 01202 606385
Email: tarik@uncookedmedia.com
Web site: http://www.neomag.co.uk
Publisher: Uncooked Media Ltd
Date Established: 2004
Frequency: 13 issues yearly
Cover Price: £3.99
Circulation: 25,000 (Publisher's Statement)
Usual Pagination: 100
Editor: Gemma Cox; **Advertising Manager:** Rob Cox
Summary of Content: Magazine covering new wave action entertainment features, news and reviews of the latest anime, manga, film and games releases.
Readership/Target Audience: Aimed at 15 to 30 year old fans of action entertainment.
ADVERTISING RATES:
Full Page Colour £2495.00
Agency Commission: 10%
Mechanical Data: Type Area: 287 x 200mm, Bleed Size: 303 x 216mm, Trim Size: 297 x 210mm, Col Length: 287mm, Page Width: 200mm, Film: Digital
Copy instructions: Copy Date: 3 weeks prior to publication date
CONSUMER: MUSIC & PERFORMING ARTS: Cinema

NERVE   1668039U84A-443
Editorial Address: 85-89 Duke Street, LIVERPOOL, L1 5AP
Tel: 0151 709 9948
Email: mail@catalystmedia.org.uk
Advertising Address: As above.
Email: mail@catalystmedia.org.uk
Web site: http://www.catalystmedia.org.uk
Publisher: Catalyst Creative Media
Date Established: 2003
Frequency: Quarterly
Cover Price: Free
Circulation: 3,000 (Publisher's Statement)
Usual Pagination: 32
Editor: Colin Serjent; **Advertising Manager:** Colin Serjent
Summary of Content: Magazine promoting grass roots art and culture, artists' profiles, visual arts, film, theatre and poetry as well as political and social issues in Merseyside, major political issues, international affairs and public issues such as ID cards and homelessness.
Readership/Target Audience: Aimed at discerning readers looking for something a bit different.
ADVERTISING RATES:
Full Page Colour £400.00
Mechanical Data: Type Area: 270 x 190mm, Trim Size: 297 x 210mm, Film: Digital
CONSUMER: THE ARTS & LITERARY: Arts

NERVE MAGAZINE   1622946U83-258
Editorial Address: Talbot Campus, Fern Barrow, POOLE, BH12 5BB **Tel:** 01202 965653 **Fax:** 01202 535990
Email: suprint@bournemouth.ac.uk
Advertising Address: As above. **Tel:** 01202 965765
Email: susales@bournemouth.ac.uk
Web site: http://www.nervemedia.net
Publisher: SUBU
Date Established: 1990
Frequency: 8 issues yearly

Cover Price: Free
Usual Pagination: 64
Editor: Chrissy Backer; **Advertising Manager:** Ed Reacher
Summary of Content: Magazine covering any topic that is relevant or interesting to students. Covering everything from student issues (fees) to music, film, features articles and interviews.
Readership/Target Audience: Aimed mainly at Bournemouth University students between 18 and 24 years old.
ADVERTISING RATES:
Full Page Colour £600.00
Agency Commission: 10%
Mechanical Data: Trim Size: 297 x 210mm, Bleed Size: +3mm, Film: Digital
Copy instructions: Copy Date: 4 weeks prior to publication date
Average advertising content per issue: 15%
CONSUMER: STUDENT PUBLICATIONS

NETBALL MAGAZINE
46016U75X-600
Editorial Address: Netball House, 9 Paynes Park, HITCHIN, SG5 1EH **Tel:** 01462 442344 **Fax:** 01462 442343
Email: editor@englandnetball.co.uk
Advertising Address: As above.
Email: commercial@englandnetball.co.uk
Web site: http://www.englandnetball.co.uk
Publisher: All England Netball Association Ltd
Date Established: 1933
Frequency: 6 issues yearly
Cover Price: £2.50
Annual Sub.: £15.00
Circulation: 63,000 (Publisher's Statement)
Usual Pagination: 40
Editor: Nikki Richardson; **Advertising Manager:** Reena Lathia
Summary of Content: Magazine featuring coaching, competition results, international and national events, umpiring queries, club news and advice on injury treatment.
Readership/Target Audience: Aimed at members of the All England Netball Association, clubs and schools.
ADVERTISING RATES:
Full Page Colour £1800.00
Agency Commission: 10%
Mechanical Data: Bleed Size: +3mm, Film: Digital, Page Width: 185mm, Type Area: 271 x 185mm, Trim Size: 297 x 210mm, Col Length: 271mm
Copy instructions: Copy Date: 4 weeks prior to publication date
Average advertising content per issue: 25%
CONSUMER: SPORT: Other Sport

NEW!
1614564U74Q-1140
Editorial Address: The Northern & Shell Building, 10 Lower Thames Street, LONDON, EC3R 6EN **Tel:** 0871 520 7016
Fax: 0871 434 2763
Email: karmel.doughty@express.co.uk
Advertising Address: As above. **Fax:** 0871 434 7616
Email: nicky.noble@express.co.uk
Web site: http://www.new-magazine.co.uk
Publisher: Express Newspapers Ltd
Date Established: 2003
Frequency: Weekly
Cover Price: £0.85
Circulation: 400,189 (ABC 01/01/2009 to 30/06/2009)
Usual Pagination: 92
Editor: Karmel Doughty; **Features Editor:** David Bell
Summary of Content: Magazine covering celebrity gossip, pictures, what they are up to, fashion, trends and interviews. Twitter: https://twitter.com/new_magazine.
Readership/Target Audience: Aimed at anyone with an interest in celebrities predominantly women aged between 18 and 30 years old.
ADVERTISING RATES:
Full Page Colour £13475.00
Agency Commission: 15%
Mechanical Data: Trim Size: 300 x 215mm, Bleed Size: 306 x 221mm, Film: Digital, Type Area: 280 x 195mm, Col Length: 280mm, Page Width: 195mm
Copy instructions: Copy Date: 10 days prior to publication date
Average advertising content per issue: 30%
CONSUMER: WOMEN'S INTEREST CONSUMER MAGAZINES: Lifestyle

NEW AFRICAN
47252U82-119_60
Editorial Address: 7 Coldbath Square, LONDON, EC1R 4LQ **Tel:** 020 7841 3210 **Fax:** 020 7841 3211
Email: b.ankomah@africasia.com
Advertising Address: As above. **Tel:** 020 7713 7711
Fax: 020 7713 7898
Email: sales@africasia.com
Web site: http://www.africasia.com
ISSN: 0142-9345
Publisher: IC Publications Ltd
Date Established: 1966

Frequency: 11 issues yearly - Published at the end of the cover month
Cover Price: £2.70
Circulation: 48,033 (ABC 01/01/2008 to 31/12/2008)
Usual Pagination: 68
Editor: Baffour Ankomah; **Advertising Manager:** Omar Ben Yedder
Summary of Content: Magazine specialising in African political comment, economic and financial analysis, articles on culture, social affairs, including art, music, fashion and sport.
Readership/Target Audience: Aimed at business professionals, government officials and those with an interest in African affairs.
ADVERTISING RATES:
Full Page Colour £5900.00
Agency Commission: 15%
Mechanical Data: Bleed Size: 276 x 216mm, Trim Size: 270 x 210mm, Type Area: 242 x 186mm, Col Length: 242mm, Film: Digital, Page Width: 186mm
Copy instructions: Copy Date: 3 weeks prior to publication date
Average advertising content per issue: 15%
CONSUMER: CURRENT AFFAIRS & POLITICS

NEW DAY
47839U87-167_2
Editorial Address: Goldhay Way, Orton Goldhay, PETERBOROUGH, PE2 5GZ **Tel:** 01733 370505
Fax: 01733 404880
Email: clairet@tlmew.org.uk
Web site: http://www.leprosymission.org.uk
Publisher: The Leprosy Mission
Date Established: 1896
Frequency: Half-yearly - Published in January and August
Cover Price: Free
Circulation: 160,000 (Publisher's Statement)
Usual Pagination: 16
Editor: Claire Tuck
Summary of Content: Magazine containing development stories and feature articles on the work of The Leprosy Mission.
Readership/Target Audience: Aimed at church-based supporters of all ages and those interested in helping others defeat leprosy.
ADVERTISING: No Advertising taken
CONSUMER: RELIGIOUS

NEW FOREST EXCLUSIVE
1911894U74Q-1431
Editorial Address: Old Rectory Cottage, Park Lane, ABBOTS WORTHY, SO21 1DT **Tel:** 01202 765988
Email: lizfreelance@hotmail.com
Web site: http://www.bh-publications.co.uk
Publisher: BH Publications
Frequency: Half-yearly - Published in April and November
Cover Price: Free
Circulation: 30,000 (Publisher's Statement)
Usual Pagination: 116
Editor: Liz Kavanagh
Summary of Content: Luxury lifestyle magazine covering property, fine food, travel, designer fashion, celebrities, motoring and interiors.
Readership/Target Audience: Aimed at an AB1 audience living in the New Forest area of Southern England.
CONSUMER: WOMEN'S INTEREST CONSUMER MAGAZINES: Lifestyle

NEW GROUND
47254U82-119_90
Editorial Address: 1 London Bridge, 2nd Floor, Downstream Buildings, LONDON, SE1 9BG
Tel: 020 7022 1985
Email: melanie.smallman@sera.org.uk
Web site: http://www.serauk.org.uk
Publisher: Socialist Environment & Resources Association
Frequency: Half-yearly - Published in September and April
Cover Price: Free
Circulation: 2,000 (Publisher's Statement)
Usual Pagination: 20
Editor: Melanie Smallman
Summary of Content: Magazine devoted to the search for a greener socialism and the integration of equality and justice into environmental thinking.
Readership/Target Audience: Aimed at environmentalists, socialists and campaigners.
ADVERTISING: No Advertising taken
CONSUMER: CURRENT AFFAIRS & POLITICS

NEW HOMES
31272U74K-265
Editorial Address: Albion House, Broad Street, BRISTOL, BS1 2HL **Tel:** 0117 929 2990 **Fax:** 0117 929 2655
Email: editor@newhomesforsale.co.uk
Advertising Address: As above.
Email: julie.zahringer@newhomesforsale.co.uk
Web site: http://www.homeselector.co.uk
Publisher: Property Papers Ltd

Date Established: 1998
Frequency: 24 issues yearly
Cover Price: Free
Circulation: 15,000 (Publisher's Statement)
Usual Pagination: 32
Editor: David Collett
Summary of Content: Newspaper containing a guide to newly-built properties. Covers new houses and developments, mortgages, legal concerns, area features and purchasing information.
Readership/Target Audience: Aimed at new home buyers in the West Country.
ADVERTISING RATES:
Full Page Colour £1100.00
SCC £7.00
Agency Commission: 10%
Mechanical Data: Col Length: 380mm, Film: Digital, No. of Columns (Display): 8, Type Area: 380 x 253mm, Col Widths (Display): 29mm, Page Width: 253mm
Copy instructions: Copy Date: 6 days prior to publication date
Average advertising content per issue: 64%
Editions:
New Homes Eastern Region
New Homes North Midlands
New Homes North West
New Homes South Midlands
New Homes South Wales
New Homes West Country
CONSUMER: WOMEN'S INTEREST CONSUMER MAGAZINES: Home Purchase

NEW HOMES WALES AND THE SOUTH WEST
45495U74K-250
Editorial Address: 254 Cowbridge Road East, CARDIFF, CF5 1GZ **Tel:** 029 2040 2743 **Fax:** 029 2040 2744
Email: cardiff.advertiser@virgin.net
Advertising Address: As above. **Tel:** 029 2040 2740
Email: cardiff.advertiser@virgin.net
Publisher: Hot Press Publications
Date Established: 1997
Frequency: 10 issues yearly
Cover Price: Free
Circulation: 29,800 (Publisher's Statement)
Usual Pagination: 36
Editor: David Hynes; **Advertising Manager:** Cheryl Willis
Summary of Content: Magazine featuring new homes in South Wales and Bristol. Covers articles on all aspects of homes and related features such as design, gardens and furniture.
Readership/Target Audience: Aimed at those considering buying new properties and improving their current property.
ADVERTISING RATES:
Full Page Colour £950.00
Agency Commission: 10%
Mechanical Data: Col Length: 265mm, Page Width: 190mm, Type Area: 265 x 190mm, Film: Digital, Trim Size: 297 x 210mm
Copy instructions: Copy Date: 3 weeks prior to publication date
Average advertising content per issue: 60%
CONSUMER: WOMEN'S INTEREST CONSUMER MAGAZINES: Home Purchase

NEW HOUSES
708208U74K-270
Editorial Address: The Forge, 13B Lisburn Road, Moira, CRAIGAVON, BT67 0JR **Tel:** 028 9261 2990
Fax: 028 9261 2091
Email: newhouses@kmpltd.co.uk
Advertising Address: As above.
Email: donna@kmpltd.co.uk
Web site: http://www.kmpltd.co.uk
Publisher: KMP Ltd
Date Established: 2000
Frequency: Quarterly
Cover Price: £2.00
Circulation: 10,000 (Publisher's Statement)
Usual Pagination: 100
Editor: Adam Hassin; **Advertising Manager:** Donna McClelland
Summary of Content: Magazine containing a guide to new developments in Northern Ireland with features on interior design, exteriors, gardens and house styles. Includes news, financial advice, book reviews, tips and articles on kitchens and bathrooms.
Readership/Target Audience: Aimed at those interested in purchasing new homes.
ADVERTISING RATES:
Full Page Colour £1045.00
Agency Commission: 10%
Mechanical Data: Page Width: 190mm, Type Area: 257 x 190mm, Col Length: 257mm, Bleed Size: 307 x 240mm, Trim Size: 297 x 230mm, Film: Digital
Copy instructions: Copy Date: 2 weeks prior to publication date
Average advertising content per issue: 40%
CONSUMER: WOMEN'S INTEREST CONSUMER MAGAZINES: Home Purchase

NEW HUMANIST
47255U82-120

Editorial Address: 1 Gower Street, LONDON, WC1E 6HD
Tel: 020 7436 1171 **Fax:** 020 7079 3588
Email: press.releases@newhumanist.org.uk
Advertising Address: As above. **Tel:** 020 7436 1151
Email: info@newhumanist.org.uk
Web site: http://www.newhumanist.org.uk
ISSN: 0306-512X
Publisher: Rationalist Association
Date Established: 1899
Frequency: 6 issues yearly
Cover Price: £3.90
Annual Sub.: £21.00
Circulation: 10,000 (Publisher's Statement)
Usual Pagination: 52
Editor: Caspar Melville; **Advertising Manager:** Paul Sims
Summary of Content: Magazine reporting on current issues from a humanist standpoint. Subjects covered include philosophy, literature and science.
Readership/Target Audience: Read by professionals and those with an interest in human issues.
ADVERTISING RATES:
Full Page Mono £300.00
Full Page Colour £600.00
Agency Commission: 10%
Mechanical Data: Col Length: 270mm, Type Area: 270 x 210mm, Page Width: 210mm, Film: Digital, Bleed Size: +3mm
Copy instructions: Copy Date: 1 week prior to publication date
Average advertising content per issue: 10%
CONSUMER: CURRENT AFFAIRS & POLITICS

THE NEW IMBIBER
1743226U74P-944

Editorial Address: 16 Mount Street, LEWES, BN7 1HL
Tel: 01273 486787 **Fax:** 01273 486787
Email: ronaldatkins1@aol.com
Advertising Address: 42B Madeira Road, VENTNOR, PO38 1QS **Tel:** 01983 854696 **Fax:** 01983 854696
Email: michael.hammersley@btinternet.com
Publisher: The New Imbiber
Frequency: 6 issues yearly
Cover Price: £1.50
Annual Sub.: £10.00
Circulation: 1,000 (Publisher's Statement)
Usual Pagination: 24
Editor: Ronald Atkins; **Advertising Manager:** Michael Hammersley
Summary of Content: Magazine covering beer in general but real ale in particular. Detailing new beers and breweries in the UK and from around the world.
Readership/Target Audience: Aimed at lovers of good beer.
ADVERTISING RATES:
Full Page Mono £150.00
Mechanical Data: Type Area: 194 x 132mm, Col Length: 194mm, Page Width: 132mm, Film: Digital
Copy instructions: Copy Date: End of the 2nd week of the month prior to publication date
Average advertising content per issue: 5%
CONSUMER: WOMEN'S INTEREST CONSUMER MAGAZINES: Food & Cookery

NEW INTERNATIONALIST
47256U82-125

Editorial Address: 55 Rectory Road, OXFORD, OX4 1BW
Tel: 01865 811400 **Fax:** 01865 793152
Email: ni@newint.org
Advertising Address: 3 Forest Way, ASHTEAD, KT21 1JN
Tel: 01372 276233 **Fax:** 0870 705 1901
Email: tslock@terrylockmediasales.co.uk
Web site: http://www.newint.org
ISSN: 0305-9529
Publisher: New Internationalist Publications Ltd.
Date Established: 1973
Frequency: 11 issues yearly - Combined issue January/February
Cover Price: £3.25
Annual Sub.: £32.85
Circulation: 40,000 (Publisher's Statement)
Usual Pagination: 40
Editor: David Ransom; **Advertising Manager:** Terry Lock
Summary of Content: Magazine focusing attention on world poverty and the fight for world development.
Language(s): English; Greek; Japanese
Readership/Target Audience: Aimed at those wanting a guide to important international issues.
ADVERTISING RATES:
Full Page Mono £3000.00
Full Page Colour £3000.00
Agency Commission: 10%
Mechanical Data: Type Area: 270 x 188mm, Bleed Size: 307 x 220mm, Trim Size: 297 x 210mm, Film: Digital, Col Length: 270mm, Page Width: 188mm
Copy instructions: Copy Date: 4 weeks prior to publication date
Average advertising content per issue: 25%
CONSUMER: CURRENT AFFAIRS & POLITICS

NEW LEFT REVIEW
47258U82-130

Editorial Address: 6 Meard Street, LONDON, W1F 0EG
Tel: 020 7734 8830 **Fax:** 020 7439 3869
Email: mail@newleftreview.org
Advertising Address: As above.
Email: mail@newleftreview.org
Web site: http://www.newleftreview.org
ISSN: 0028-6060
Publisher: New Left Review Ltd
Date Established: 1960
Frequency: 6 issues yearly
Cover Price: £6.00
Annual Sub.: £32.00
Circulation: 8,000 (Publisher's Statement)
Usual Pagination: 160
Editor: Kheya Bag; **Advertising Manager:** Kheya Bhe
Summary of Content: Magazine containing articles on politics, culture, history, economics and sociology.
Language(s): English; Spanish
Readership/Target Audience: Aimed at academics, writers, thinkers, students and the politically active.
ADVERTISING RATES:
Full Page Mono £400.00
Mechanical Data: Page Width: 106mm, Type Area: 186 x 106mm, Col Length: 186mm, Film: Digital
Copy instructions: Copy Date: 1st of the month prior to publication date
CONSUMER: CURRENT AFFAIRS & POLITICS

NEW LIFE NEWSPAPER
47735U87-168

Formerly: New Life
Editorial Address: PO Box 777, NOTTINGHAM, NG11 6ZZ
Tel: 0115 921 7285 **Fax:** 0115 984 5251
Email: editor@newlife.co.uk
Advertising Address: As above.
Email: ads@newlifepublishing.co.uk
Web site: http://www.newlifepublishing.co.uk
Publisher: New Life Publishing Company
Date Established: 1983
Frequency: Monthly
Cover Price: £0.40
Circulation: 65,000 (Publisher's Statement)
Usual Pagination: 12
Editor: Peter Wreford; **Editor-in-Chief:** Peter Wreford; **Managing Director:** Peter Wreford; **Advertising Manager:** Barry Wilson
Summary of Content: Inter-denominational Christian tabloid newspaper with news and features of interest.
Readership/Target Audience: Aimed at non-Christians with some interest in spiritual matters.
ADVERTISING RATES:
Full Page Colour £695.00
SCC £8.00
Agency Commission: 10%
Mechanical Data: Film: Digital, No. of Columns (Display): 6, Col Widths (Display): 41mm, Type Area: 355 x 290mm, Col Length: 355mm, Page Width: 290mm
Copy instructions: Copy Date: 30th of the month prior to publication date
Average advertising content per issue: 20%
CONSUMER: RELIGIOUS

NEW NATION
48326U90-114

Editorial Address: Unit 2, Whitechapel Technology Centre, 65 Whitechapel Road, LONDON, E1 1DU
Tel: 020 7650 2000 **Fax:** 020 7650 2001
Email: newsdesk@newnation.co.uk
Advertising Address: As above. **Fax:** 020 7650 2020
Email: dean@ethnicmedia.co.uk
Web site: http://www.ethnicmedia.co.uk
ISSN: 1365-7496
Publisher: Ethnic Media Group
Frequency: Weekly
Cover Price: £0.65
Circulation: 22,081 (Publisher's Statement)
Usual Pagination: 56
Editor: Lester Holloway; **News Editor:** Lester Holloway; **Features Editor:** Adenike Adenitire; **Publisher:** Wayne Bower
Summary of Content: Newspaper covering the arts, music, entertainment, sport and news.
Readership/Target Audience: Aimed at the black community in the United Kingdom.
ADVERTISING RATES:
Full Page Mono £4012.00
Full Page Colour £4814.40
Agency Commission: 10%
Mechanical Data: Type Area: 340 x 260mm, No. of Columns (Display): 8, Page Width: 260mm, Col Length: 340mm, Film: Digital, Col Widths (Display): 30mm
Copy instructions: Copy Date: Friday prior to publication date
Average advertising content per issue: 40%
Supplement(s): The F Word - 52xY, Pulse - 52xY
CONSUMER: ETHNIC

NEW PATHWAYS
624165U94F-660

Editorial Address: 7 Peartree Business Centre, Peartree Road, Stanway, COLCHESTER, CO3 0JN
Tel: 01206 505444 **Fax:** 01206 505449
Email: newpathways@msrc.co.uk
Advertising Address: As above.
Email: info@msrc.co.uk
Web site: http://www.msrc.co.uk
Publisher: The Multiple Sclerosis Resource Centre
Date Established: 2000
Frequency: 6 issues yearly
Free to qualifying individuals
Annual Sub.: £15.00
Circulation: 6,000 (Publisher's Statement)
Usual Pagination: 54
Editor: Helen Yates; **Advertising Manager:** Tony West
Summary of Content: Magazine containing news and features relating to multiple sclerosis. Includes information on complementary therapies, healthy eating, therapy centres, holidays and advice on rights and benefits, sharing ideas and life stories.
Readership/Target Audience: Aimed at those affected by MS, their families, friends, GPs and professionals in the field.
ADVERTISING: Rates on application
CONSUMER: OTHER CLASSIFICATIONS: Disability

NEW SHOOTS DIRECTORY
1777329U74C-859

Formerly: New Shoots
Editorial Address: 2 Bexley Cottages, The Street, Horton Kirby, DARTFORD, DA4 9BU **Tel:** 01322 860100
Fax: 01322 860200
Email: francisbaldwin@hotmail.co.uk
Advertising Address: As above.
Email: karendefries@hotmail.com
Publisher: County Magazine Publications Ltd
Date Established: 2006
Frequency: Annual - Published in September
Cover Price: Free
Circulation: 20,000 (Publisher's Statement)
Usual Pagination: 64
Editor: Sharon Spirling
Summary of Content: Magazine with information covering weddings, parenting, buying, a news house, interiors and gardens.
Readership/Target Audience: Aimed at those in West Kent and South East London getting married, starting a family, buying a new home or planning a new garden.
ADVERTISING RATES:
Full Page Colour £670.00
Agency Commission: 10%
Mechanical Data: Type Area: 200 x 136mm, Bleed Size: 216 x 155mm, Trim Size: 216 x 136mm, Col Length: 200mm, Page Width: 136mm, Col Widths (Display): 66mm, No. of Columns (Display): 2, Print Process: Web-fed offset litho, Film: Digital
Copy instructions: Copy Date: 19th September
Average advertising content per issue: 40%
CONSUMER: WOMEN'S INTEREST CONSUMER MAGAZINES: Home & Family

NEW STATESMAN
45152U73-255

Editorial Address: 7th Floor, John Carpenter House, John Carpenter Street, LONDON, EC4Y 0AN **Tel:** 020 7730 3444
Fax: 020 7336 5203
Email: info@newstatesman.co.uk
Advertising Address: 1st Floor, Boundary House, 91-93 Charterhouse Street, LONDON, EC1M 6HR
Tel: 020 7881 5651 **Fax:** 020 7259 0181
Email: richard@newstatesman.co.uk
Web site: http://www.newstatesman.com
ISSN: 1364-7431
Publisher: New Statesman Ltd
Date Established: 1913
Frequency: Weekly
Cover Price: £2.95
Circulation: 23,128 (ABC 01/01/2008 to 31/12/2008)
Usual Pagination: 64
Editor: Jason Cowley; **Advertising Manager:** Richard Rowe; **Publisher:** Spencer Neal
Summary of Content: Magazine covering news, book reviews, arts, current affairs and politics, science and the environment.
Twitter: https://twitter.com/NewStatesman.
Readership/Target Audience: Read by politicians, academics and highly influential, educated opinion-formers such as media professionals and broadcasters.
ADVERTISING RATES:
Full Page Mono £2640.00
Full Page Colour £2640.00
Agency Commission: 10%
Mechanical Data: Page Width: 206mm, Film: Digital, Col Widths (Display): 83mm, No. of Columns (Display): 2, Bleed Size: 296 x 240mm, Type Area: 258 x 206mm, Col Length: 258mm, Trim Size: 286 x 230mm
Copy instructions: Copy Date: Tuesday prior to publication date
Average advertising content per issue: 30%
CONSUMER: NATIONAL & INTERNATIONAL PERIODICALS

NEW STYLE
1826778U90-1015

Editorial Address: 12 Devereux Court, 215 Strand, LONDON, WC2R 1AP **Tel:** 020 7353 5370
Email: tatiana@russianmedia.co.uk
Web site: http://www.newstyle-mag.com
Publisher: Russian Media House
Frequency: Monthly
Cover Price: £2.50
Circulation: 20,000 (Publisher's Statement)
Usual Pagination: 108
Editor: Tatiana Rodionova
Summary of Content: Lifestyle magazine covering fashion, cars, interviews with celebrities, entertainment, property, travel, restaurants, clubs, theatre and cinema.
Language(s): Russian
Readership/Target Audience: Aimed at Russian speakers in the London in particular but also in Europe through airlines and hotels.
CONSUMER: ETHNIC

NEW THEATRE QUARTERLY
46074U76B-120

Editorial Address: Oldstairs, Oldstairs Road, Kingsdown, DEAL, CT14 8ES **Tel:** 01304 373448 **Fax:** 01304 373448
Email: simontrussler@btinternet.com
Advertising Address: The Edinburgh Building, Shaftesbury Road, CAMBRIDGE, CB2 2RU **Tel:** 01223 325757
Fax: 01223 315052
Email: ad_sales@cambridge.org
Web site: http://journals.cambridge.org/jid_ntq
ISSN: 0266-464X
Publisher: Cambridge University Press
Frequency: Quarterly
Annual Sub: £33.00
Circulation: 1,250 (Publisher's Statement)
Editor: Simon Trussler
Summary of Content: Magazine providing an international forum where theatrical scholarship and practice can meet. Containing news, analysis and debate within the field of theatre studies.
Readership/Target Audience: Aimed at teachers and students, national and regional arts authorities, arts administrators and actors. Also playwrights, critics and theatre-goers worldwide with an interest in the affairs of world drama.
ADVERTISING RATES:
Full Page Mono £440.00
Copy instructions: Copy Date: 8 weeks prior to the 1st of the month of publication
CONSUMER: MUSIC & PERFORMING ARTS: Theatre

NEW VISION
40113U87-2045

Editorial Address: Bosham House, Main Road, Bosham, CHICHESTER, PO18 8PJ **Tel:** 01243 572109
Fax: 01243 572109
Email: office@thehamblinvision.org.uk
Advertising Address: As above.
Email: office@thehamblinvision.org.uk
Web site: http://www.thehamblintrust.org.uk
ISSN: 1460-2660
Publisher: The Hamblin Vision
Date Established: 1921
Frequency: 6 issues yearly
Cover Price: £18.00
Free to qualifying individuals
Circulation: 700 (Publisher's Statement)
Usual Pagination: 28
Editor: Elizabeth Medler; **Advertising Manager:** Elizabeth Medler
Summary of Content: Journal concerning mysticism, philosophy, positive thinking, healing and spirituality.
Readership/Target Audience: Aimed at readers of all ages interested in spirituality.
ADVERTISING: Rates on application
CONSUMER: RELIGIOUS

NEW WELSH REVIEW
47549U84B-140

Editorial Address: PO Box 170, ABERYSTWYTH, SY23 1WZ **Tel:** 01970 628410 **Fax:** 01970 628410
Email: editor@newwelshreview.com
Advertising Address: As above.
Email: admin@newwelshreview.com
Web site: http://www.newwelshreview.com
ISSN: 0954-2116
Publisher: New Welsh Review Ltd
Date Established: 1988
Frequency: Quarterly
Cover Price: £5.40
Annual Sub: £20.00
Circulation: 3,500 (Publisher's Statement)
Usual Pagination: 120
Editor: Sue Fisher; **Advertising Manager:** Sue Fisher
Summary of Content: Magazine containing articles of literary, cultural and political interest. Includes poetry, reviews, stories and features on Welsh theatre criticism and art criticism.

Readership/Target Audience: Aimed at those with an interest in books by Welsh authors of literary and cultural merit and in the arts.
ADVERTISING RATES:
Full Page Mono £110.00
Full Page Colour £135.00
Mechanical Data: Type Area: 189 x 121mm, Col Length: 189mm, Page Width: 121mm, Film: Digital
Average advertising content per issue: 5%
CONSUMER: THE ARTS & LITERARY: Literary

NEW WORLD
1614055U90-907

Editorial Address: 234 Holloway Road, LONDON, N7 8DA
Tel: 020 7700 2673 **Fax:** 020 7607 6706
Email: dhiren.newworld@blueyonder.co.uk
Advertising Address: As above.
Email: dhiren.newworld@blueyonder.co.uk
Publisher: New World Weekly Ltd
Date Established: 2000
Frequency: 26 issues yearly
Cover Price: £0.60
Circulation: 10,000 (Print Run)
Editor: Dhiren Basu; **Editor-in-Chief:** Dhiren Basu;
Advertising Manager: Dhiren Basu
Summary of Content: Newspaper covering local and international issues, with features on politics, economics, books and motoring.
Readership/Target Audience: Aimed at Asians and multicultural people.
ADVERTISING: Rates on application
CONSUMER: ETHNIC

NEW WORLD
600884U94X-120

Editorial Address: 64B Grange Road, SUTTON, SM2 6SN
Tel: 020 8643 3967 **Fax:** 020 8286 0468
Email: admin@glow-stream.com
Advertising Address: As above.
Email: new.world@lineone.net
Web site: http://www.new-world.ws
ISSN: 1461-3220
Publisher: New World Press
Date Established: 1999
Frequency: 6 issues yearly
Cover Price: £3.95
Annual Sub: £32.00
Circulation: 21,000 (Publisher's Statement)
Usual Pagination: 48
Editor: Jide Adefope; **Advertising Manager:** Matt Fopson
Summary of Content: Magazine featuring articles on topical issues relating to science, philosophy and culture.
Readership/Target Audience: Aimed at people interested in science, philosophy and culture.
ADVERTISING RATES:
Full Page Mono £675.00
Full Page Colour £850.00
Agency Commission: 15%
Mechanical Data: Print Process: Web-fed offset litho, Film: Positive, right reading, emulsion side down. Negative, wrong reading, emulsion side up. Digital, Trim Size: 275 x 210mm, Bleed Size: 281 x 216mm, Type Area: 241 x 176mm, Col Length: 241mm, Page Width: 176mm
Copy instructions: Copy Date: 3 weeks prior to publication date
Average advertising content per issue: 21%
CONSUMER: OTHER CLASSIFICATIONS: Miscellaneous

NEW ZEALAND INSPIRED
48328U90-116_5

Formerly: New Zealand News UK
Editorial Address: Suite 5, Eden House, 59 Fulham High Street, LONDON, SW6 3JJ **Tel:** 020 7731 0202
Email: moana.burt@newzealandinspired.info
Advertising Address: Quadrant House, 250 Kennington Lane, LONDON, SE11 5RD **Tel:** 0845 270 7907
Fax: 0845 270 7904
Email: janine.brinsdon@nzinspired.info
Web site: http://www.nznewsuk.co.uk
Publisher: New Zealand Ltd
Date Established: 1927
Frequency: 6 issues yearly
Cover Price: Free
Circulation: 14,000 (Print Run)
Usual Pagination: 16
Editor: Moana Burt
Summary of Content: Publication covering news, jobs, business, recruitment, migration, lifestyle, entertainment and sport.
Readership/Target Audience: Aimed at New Zealanders living and working in the UK and Britons considering emigration.
ADVERTISING RATES:
Full Page Colour £1555.00
Agency Commission: 10%
Mechanical Data: Film: Digital, Trim Size: 290 x 220mm, Page Width: 220mm, Col Length: 290mm
Average advertising content per issue: 42%
CONSUMER: ETHNIC

NEW ZEALAND OUTLOOK
48258U89E-144

Editorial Address: 13 London Road, BEXHILL-ON-SEA, TN39 3JR **Tel:** 01424 223111 **Fax:** 01424 224992
Email: shirley@consylpublishing.co.uk
Advertising Address: As above.
Email: consylpublishing@btconnect.com
Web site: http://www.consylpublishing.co.uk
Publisher: Consyl Publishing & Publicity Ltd
Frequency: Monthly
Cover Price: £0.85
Annual Sub: £15.50
Circulation: 5,000 (Publisher's Statement per month)
Usual Pagination: 28
Editor: Shirley Gilbertson; **Advertising Manager:** Shirley Gilbertson
Summary of Content: Newspaper covering employment, government and migration policy, housing, taxation, education and travelling.
Readership/Target Audience: Read predominantly by potential migrants and visitors to New Zealand.
ADVERTISING RATES:
Full Page Mono £780.00
Full Page Colour £950.00
Agency Commission: 10%
Mechanical Data: Type Area: 360 x 264mm, Col Length: 360mm, Page Width: 264mm, Film: Digital
CONSUMER: HOLIDAYS & TRAVEL: Holidays

NEW ZEALAND TIMES
1743621U90-982

Editorial Address: Unit 7, Commodore House, Juniper Drive, LONDON, SW18 1TW **Tel:** 0845 456 4910
Fax: 0845 456 4912
Email: editor@newzealandtimes.co.uk
Advertising Address: As above.
Email: wernerh@blueskygroup.co.uk
Web site: http://www.newzealandtimes.co.uk
Publisher: Blue Sky Publications Ltd
Date Established: 2005
Frequency: Weekly
Cover Price: Free
Annual Sub: £42.00
Circulation: 15,000 (Publisher's Statement)
Usual Pagination: 16
Editor: Frances Paddick
Summary of Content: Magazine covering New Zealand news as well as London life, events, travel, finance and property, recruitment and sport.
Language(s): English; Maori
Readership/Target Audience: Aimed at New Zealanders living in London.
ADVERTISING RATES:
Full Page Colour £350.00
Agency Commission: 10%
Mechanical Data: Type Area: 350 x 266mm, Col Length: 350mm, Page Width: 266mm, Film: Digital
Copy instructions: Copy Date: 1 week prior to publication date
Average advertising content per issue: 50%
CONSUMER: ETHNIC

NEWBOOKS
1648570U84B-355

Formerly: newBOOKSmag
Editorial Address: 4 Froxfield Close, WINCHESTER, SO22 6JW **Tel:** 01962 620320
Email: guy@newbooksmag.com
Advertising Address: As above.
Email: guy@newbooksmag.com
Web site: http://www.newbooksmag.com
Publisher: Guise Marketing
Date Established: 2000
Frequency: 6 issues yearly
Cover Price: £1.60
Free to qualifying individuals
Annual Sub: £11.50
Circulation: 17,000 (Publisher's Statement)
Usual Pagination: 64
Editor: Guy Pringle; **Advertising Manager:** Guy Pringle
Publisher: Guy Pringle
Summary of Content: Magazine covering book extracts and author information plus reviews by subscribers.
Readership/Target Audience: Aimed at readers and members of reading groups, predominantly women aged 40 and upwards who are passionate about their reading choices.
ADVERTISING RATES:
Full Page Colour £1450.00
Mechanical Data: Film: Digital, Type Area: 267 x 195mm, Col Length: 267mm, Page Width: 195mm, Bleed Size: 303 x 231mm
Average advertising content per issue: 10%
CONSUMER: THE ARTS & LITERARY: Literary

NEWGEN
760589U74D-365

Formerly: New Generation
Editorial Address: Alexandra House, Oldham Terrace, LONDON, W3 6NH **Tel:** 0844 243 6000 **Fax:** 0844 243 6001

Email: newgeneditor@nct.org.uk
Advertising Address: Mongoose Media, 2 Lonsdale Road, LONDON, NW6 6RD **Tel:** 020 7306 0300
Fax: 020 7306 0301
Email: nct@mongoosemedia.com
Web site: http://www.nct.org.uk
Publisher: The NCT
Date Established: 1982
Frequency: Quarterly
Cover Price: Free
Circulation: 48,000 (Publisher's Statement)
Usual Pagination: 28
Editor: Kay Doragh; **Advertising Manager:** Ben Shoesmith
Summary of Content: Magazine featuring information from the National Childbirth Trust. Includes information, pregnancy and parenting research news.
Readership/Target Audience: Read by members of the NCT - new parents, health professionals and midwives.
ADVERTISING RATES:
Full Page Mono £2400.00
Full Page Colour £2400.00
Agency Commission: 10%
Mechanical Data: Type Area: 270 x 185mm, Bleed Size: 303 x 216mm, Trim Size: 297 x 210mm, Col Length: 270mm, Page Width: 185mm
Copy instructions: Copy Date: 3 weeks prior to publication date
Average advertising content per issue: 30%
CONSUMER: WOMEN'S INTEREST CONSUMER MAGAZINES: Child Care

THE NEWHAM MAG
46835U80B-168

Formerly: Newham Magazine
Editorial Address: Newham Town Hall, East Ham, LONDON, E6 2RP **Tel:** 020 8430 4533 **Fax:** 020 8430 1549
Email: newham.mag@newham.gov.uk
Advertising Address: As above.
Email: julie.brown@newham.gov.uk
Web site: http://www.newham.gov.uk
Publisher: London Borough of Newham
Date Established: 2000
Frequency: 24 issues yearly
Cover Price: Free
Circulation: 108,600 (Publisher's Statement)
Usual Pagination: 32
Editor: Anita Plaha
Summary of Content: Community magazine covering local news, lifestyle, events and local features.
Readership/Target Audience: Aimed at residents of the borough of Newham.
ADVERTISING RATES:
Full Page Colour £2150.00
Agency Commission: 10%
Mechanical Data: Film: Digital, Trim Size: 297 x 230mm, Bleed Size: 305 x 238mm
Copy instructions: Copy Date: 10 days prior to publication date
Average advertising content per issue: 40%
CONSUMER: RURAL & REGIONAL INTEREST: Regional Interest Greater London

NEWS & VIEWS
48702U94X-111

Editorial Address: 19 Queen Elizabeth Street, LONDON, SE1 2LP **Tel:** 020 7403 8783 **Fax:** 020 7403 8815
Email: info@ssafa.org.uk
Web site: http://www.ssafa.org.uk
ISSN: 1460-0447
Publisher: SSAFA Forces Help
Date Established: 1997
Frequency: Half-yearly - Published in June and October
Cover Price: Free
Circulation: 15,000 (Publisher's Statement)
Usual Pagination: 16
Editor: Alex Bozeat
Summary of Content: Magazine of the Soldiers, Sailors, Airmen and Families Association-Forces Help. Provides advice and information.
Readership/Target Audience: Aimed at serving and ex-service men, women and their families.
ADVERTISING: No Advertising taken
CONSUMER: OTHER CLASSIFICATIONS: Miscellaneous

NEWS ON THE BLOCK
1601721U74K-665

Editorial Address: 8 Canfield Place, LONDON, NW6 3BT
Tel: 0870 060 0663 **Fax:** 0870 060 0664
Email: nic@newsontheblock.com
Advertising Address: As above.
Email: tony@newsontheblock.com
Web site: http://www.newsontheblock.com
ISSN: 1476-766X
Publisher: Adrenaline Media
Date Established: 2002
Frequency: 6 issues yearly
Cover Price: £3.35
Free to qualifying individuals
Annual Sub.: £38.00

Circulation: 8,608 (ABC 01/07/2007 to 30/06/2008)
Usual Pagination: 64
Editor: Nicolas Shulman; **Managing Director:** Nicolas Shulman
Summary of Content: Magazine covering leasehold property management and law.
Readership/Target Audience: Aimed at those interested in investment, property and management, solicitors, surveyors, property industry.
ADVERTISING RATES:
Full Page Colour £1500.00
Mechanical Data: Trim Size: 275 x 210mm
CONSUMER: WOMEN'S INTEREST CONSUMER MAGAZINES: Home Purchase

THE NEWSPAPER
1633009U74F-754

Editorial Address: PO Box 400, BRIDGWATER, TA6 9DT
Tel: 0845 094 0646
Email: phil@young-media.co.uk
Advertising Address: As above.
Email: phil@young-media.co.uk
Web site: http://www.thenewspaper.org.uk
Publisher: Young Media Holdings Ltd
Date Established: 2000
Frequency: 6 issues yearly
Free to qualifying individuals
Annual Sub.: £12.00
Circulation: 42,000 (Publisher's Statement)
Usual Pagination: 32
Editor: Phil Wood; **Advertising Manager:** Phil Wood;
Managing Editor: Phil Wood
Summary of Content: National children's newspaper covering news, sport, environment, science, games, books, film releases, fashion and music.
Readership/Target Audience: Aimed at 8 to 14 year olds.
ADVERTISING RATES:
Full Page Colour £1800.00
Agency Commission: 10%
Mechanical Data: Type Area: 360 x 265mm, Col Length: 360mm, Page Width: 265mm
Copy instructions: Copy Date: 2 weeks prior to publication date
Average advertising content per issue: 30%
CONSUMER: WOMEN'S INTEREST CONSUMER MAGAZINES: Teenage

THE NEWSPAPER
1656818U87-2027

Editorial Address: The Palace, HEREFORD, HR4 9BL
Tel: 01432 373300 **Fax:** 01432 352952
Email: a.holden@hereford.anglican.org
Advertising Address: Admag Newspapers Ltd, Priebie Building, Red Barn Drive, HEREFORD, HR4 9QL
Tel: 01432 376121 **Fax:** 01432 353231
Email: hereford.telesales@admagnewspapers.co.uk
Web site: http://www.hereford.anglican.org
Publisher: Dioceses of Hereford
Date Established: 1998
Frequency: Quarterly
Cover Price: Free
Circulation: 16,000 (Publisher's Statement)
Usual Pagination: 20
Editor: Anni Holden
Summary of Content: Newspaper reviewing and previewing events and issues that affect the church and community in the counties of Hereford and Shropshire.
Readership/Target Audience: Aimed at households in Hereford and Shropshire.
ADVERTISING RATES:
SCC £3.70
Mechanical Data: Col Widths (Display): 30mm, No. of Columns (Display): 8, Film: Digital
Copy instructions: Copy Date: 1 week prior to publication date
CONSUMER: RELIGIOUS

NEWSQUEST HERTFORDSHIRE, BUCKINGHAMSHIRE & MIDDLESEX
1666300U74K-727

Formerly: What's Your Property Worth
Editorial Address: Observer House, Caxton Court, Caxton Way, Watford Business Park, WATFORD, WD18 8RJ
Tel: 01923 216216 **Fax:** 01923 243738
Email: l.bilgorri@london.newsquest.co.uk
Advertising Address: As above. **Fax:** 01923 235201
Email: swestwood@london.newsquest.co.uk
Publisher: Newsquest (North London)
Frequency: Annual - Published in April
Cover Price: Free
Circulation: 66,000 (Publisher's Statement)
Editor: Lindi Bilgorri; **Features Editor:** Lindi Bilgorri;
Advertising Manager: Sabrina Westwood
Summary of Content: Magazine covering property prices and value statistics.
Readership/Target Audience: Aimed at homeowners.
ADVERTISING RATES:
Full Page Colour £400.00

Mechanical Data: Type Area: 350 x 206mm, Col Length: 350mm, Page Width: 206mm, No. of Columns (Display): 9, Film: Digital
Supplement to: Watford Observer Series
CONSUMER: WOMEN'S INTEREST CONSUMER MAGAZINES: Home Purchase

NEWSWEEK
45153U73-260

Editorial Address: Academy House, 36 Poland Street, LONDON, W1F 7LU **Tel:** 020 7851 9750
Advertising Address: As above. **Tel:** 020 7851 9777
Fax: 020 7851 9798
Email: john.pentin@newsweek.com
Web site: http://www.newsweek.com
ISSN: 0163-7053
Publisher: Washington Post Co
Frequency: Weekly
Cover Price: £2.40
Annual Sub.: £38.30
Circulation: 73,052 (Publisher's Statement)
Usual Pagination: 70
Editor: Sophie Grove; **Advertising Director:** John Pentin
Summary of Content: Magazine covering news, politics and current affairs.
Readership/Target Audience: Aimed at managers and professionals who travel frequently.
ADVERTISING RATES:
Full Page Colour £2815.00
Agency Commission: 15%
Mechanical Data: Page Width: 178mm, Col Widths (Display): 54mm, Bleed Size: 273 x 206mm, Trim Size: 267 x 200mm, Film: Digital, Type Area: 254 x 178mm, Col Length: 254mm, No. of Columns (Display): 3
Copy instructions: Copy Date: 3 weeks prior to publication date
Average advertising content per issue: 30%
CONSUMER: NATIONAL & INTERNATIONAL PERIODICALS

NEXUS
48607U94D-110

Editorial Address: Advertiser House, 19 Bartlett Street, SOUTH CROYDON, CR2 6TB **Tel:** 020 8256 0311
Fax: 020 8256 0312
Email: sheila.hare@expatnetwork.com
Advertising Address: As above.
Email: linda.taylor@expatnetwork.com
Web site: http://www.expatnetwork.com
Publisher: Expat Network Ltd
Date Established: 1989
Frequency: 11 issues yearly
Annual Sub.: £66.00
Circulation: 8,000 (Publisher's Statement)
Usual Pagination: 36
Editor: Sheila Hare; **Advertising Director:** Linda Taylor
Summary of Content: Magazine containing overseas employment information, location reports, lifestyle and financial advice.
Readership/Target Audience: Aimed at expatriates.
ADVERTISING RATES:
Full Page Mono £825.00
Full Page Colour £1045.00
SCC £12.00
Agency Commission: 10%
Mechanical Data: Col Length: 267mm, Film: Digital, Type Area: 267 x 190mm, Bleed Size: 303 x 216mm, Trim Size: 297 x 210mm, No. of Columns (Display): 4, Page Width: 190mm
Copy instructions: Copy Date: 16th of the month prior to publication date
Average advertising content per issue: 33%
CONSUMER: OTHER CLASSIFICATIONS: Expatriates

NEXUS MAGAZINE
30734U94E-47

Editorial Address: 55 Queens Road, EAST GRINSTEAD, RH19 1BG **Tel:** 01342 322854 **Fax:** 01342 324574
Email: nexus@ukoffice.u-net.com
Advertising Address: As above.
Email: nexus@ukoffice.u-net.com
Web site: http://www.nexusmagazine.com
ISSN: 1039-0170
Publisher: Nexus Magazine Pty Ltd
Date Established: 1987
Frequency: 6 issues yearly
Cover Price: £2.95
Annual Sub.: £18.00
Circulation: 18,000 (Publisher's Statement)
Usual Pagination: 104
Editor: Marcus Allen; **Advertising Manager:** Alex Allen;
Publisher: Marcus Allen
Summary of Content: Magazine covering alternative medicine, hidden history, conspiracies, future science, 'Behind the News', UFOs and the unexplained.
Language(s): English; French; Greek; Italian; Japanese; Korean; Polish; Russian; Swedish
Readership/Target Audience: Aimed at those with an interest in alternative news and hard to get information overlooked by the mainstream.

Consumer Magazines

ADVERTISING RATES:
Full Page Mono £500.00
Agency Commission: 10%
Mechanical Data: Page Width: 180mm, Film: Digital, Type Area: 240 x 180mm, Col Length: 240mm, Bleed Size: 286 x 212mm, Trim Size: 280 x 206mm, No. of Columns (Display): 3, Col Widths (Display): 58mm, Print Process: Web-fed offset litho
Copy instructions: Copy Date: 4 weeks prior to publication date
Average advertising content per issue: 20%
CONSUMER: OTHER CLASSIFICATIONS: Paranormal

NGAMER
1772529U78D-329
Editorial Address: 30 Monmouth Street, BATH, BA1 2BW **Email:** martin.kitts@futurenet.com
Advertising Address: 2 Balcombe Street, LONDON, NW1 6NW **Tel:** 020 7042 4000
Email: emma.cull@futurenet.co.uk
Web site: http://www.ngamermagazine.com
Publisher: Future Publishing Ltd
Date Established: 2006
Frequency: 13 issues yearly
Cover Price: £4.99
Circulation: 17,801 (ABC 01/07/2008 to 31/12/2008)
Usual Pagination: 114
Editor: Martin Kitts; **Advertising Manager:** Emma Cull
Summary of Content: Magazine covering new and retro Nintendo games with product reviews, features, news and previews.
Readership/Target Audience: Aimed at Nintendo gamers of all ages.
ADVERTISING RATES:
Full Page Colour £2850.00
Agency Commission: 10%
Mechanical Data: Type Area: 270 x 190mm, Bleed Size: 303 x 216mm, Trim Size: 297 x 210mm, Col Length: 270mm, Page Width: 190mm, Film: Digital
Copy instructions: Copy Date: 4 weeks prior to publication date
Average advertising content per issue: 15%
CONSUMER: CONSUMER ELECTRONICS: Games

NI HOMES & LIFESTYLE
1806116U74C-867
Editorial Address: 57A Prospect Road, BANGOR, BT20 5DF **Tel:** 028 9147 8703 **Fax:** 028 9147 2045
Email: editorial@nihomes.net
Advertising Address: As above.
Email: robert@nihomes.net
Publisher: Bayview Publishing Ltd
Date Established: 2006
Frequency: 11 issues yearly
Cover Price: £3.25
Circulation: 6,029 (ABC 01/07/2008 to 31/12/2008)
Usual Pagination: 164
Editor: Judith Robinson
Summary of Content: Magazine covering homes, interiors and lifestyle including arts and crafts, people and places, food and wine, travel, motoring and local homes.
Readership/Target Audience: Aimed at women aged 25 to 50 years old.
ADVERTISING RATES:
Full Page Colour £1350.00
Agency Commission: 15%
Mechanical Data: Trim Size: 297 x 230mm, Bleed Size: 303 x 236mm, Film: Digital
Copy instructions: Copy Date: 2 weeks prior to publication date
Average advertising content per issue: 30%
CONSUMER: WOMEN'S INTEREST CONSUMER MAGAZINES: Home & Family

NITRO
1656201U91D-900
Formerly: Jetix Magazine
Editorial Address: 30 Monmouth Street, BATH, BA1 2BW **Tel:** 01225 442244 **Fax:** 01225 446109
Email: nitro@futurenet.co.uk
Advertising Address: 2 Balcombe Street, LONDON, NW1 6NW **Tel:** 020 7042 4000
Email: emma.cull@futurenet.co.uk
Web site: http://www.jetix.co.uk/themag
Publisher: Future Publishing Ltd
Date Established: 2004
Frequency: 15 issues yearly
Cover Price: £2.99
Circulation: 70,000 (Publisher's Statement)
Usual Pagination: 48
Editor: Richard Owen; **Advertising Manager:** Emma Cull
Summary of Content: Children's magazine of Jetix Network with features, comic strips and activities.
Readership/Target Audience: Aimed at boys aged 7 to 11 years old.
ADVERTISING RATES:
Full Page Colour £1650.00
Agency Commission: 10%

Mechanical Data: Type Area: 280 x 203mm, Bleed Size: 306 x 228mm, Trim Size: 300 x 232mm, Col Length: 280mm, Page Width: 213mm, Film: Digital
Average advertising content per issue: 10%
CONSUMER: RECREATION & LEISURE: Children & Youth

NME
46251U76E-260
Editorial Address: 4th Floor, Blue Fin Building, 110 Southwark Street, LONDON, SE1 0SU **Tel:** 020 3148 5000
Fax: 020 3148 8107
Email: news@nme.com
Advertising Address: Blue Fin Building, 110 Southwark Street, LONDON, SE1 0SU **Tel:** 020 3148 5000
Fax: 020 3148 8108
Email: neil_mcsteen@ipcmedia.com
Web site: http://www.nme.com
ISSN: 0028-6362
Publisher: IPC ignite!
Date Established: 1952
Frequency: Weekly
Cover Price: £2.20
Circulation: 40,948 (ABC 01/01/2009 to 30/06/2009)
Editor: Paul Stokes; **News Editor:** Paul Stokes; **Managing Director:** Eric Fuller; **Advertising Manager:** Neil McSteen; **Publisher:** Faith Hill
Summary of Content: Magazine covering news and reviews on music, films and videos.
Readership/Target Audience: Aimed at young rock and pop enthusiasts.
ADVERTISING RATES:
Full Page Colour £6920.00
Agency Commission: 10%
Mechanical Data: Page Width: 225mm, Film: Digital, Type Area: 285 x 225mm, Col Length: 285mm, Bleed Size: 321 x 261mm, Trim Size: 315 x 255mm
Copy instructions: Copy Date: Wednesday 10 days prior to publication date
Editions:
New Musical Express Ireland
CONSUMER: MUSIC & PERFORMING ARTS: Pop Music

NO.1
1745218U74A-1011
Editorial Address: 50 High Craighall Road, GLASGOW, G4 9UD **Tel:** 0141 353 2222 **Fax:** 0141 332 3811
Email: nadine.hawkins@psp.uk.net
Advertising Address: As above.
Email: ann.liddle@psp.uk.net
Web site: http://www.no1magazine.co.uk
Publisher: PSP Publishing Ltd
Date Established: 2006
Frequency: 17 issues yearly
Cover Price: £1.95
Editor: Nadine Hawkins; **Advertising Manager:** Ann Liddle
Summary of Content: Lifestyle and celebrity magazine covering fashion, beauty, travel, health, interiors, horoscope, restaurants reviews, beauty and interiors.
Readership/Target Audience: Aimed at women aged between 25 and 55 years old.
ADVERTISING RATES:
Full Page Colour £1795.00
Agency Commission: 10%
Mechanical Data: Type Area: 220 x 210mm, Bleed Size: 336 x 246mm, Trim Size: 330 x 240mm, Col Length: 220mm, Page Width: 210mm, Film: Digital
Copy instructions: Copy Date: 3 weeks prior to publication date
Average advertising content per issue: 28%
CONSUMER: WOMEN'S INTEREST CONSUMER MAGAZINES: Women's Interest

NODDY
30619U91D-851
Editorial Address: Titan House, 144 Southwark Street, LONDON, SE1 0UP **Tel:** 020 7620 0200 **Fax:** 020 7620 0803
Email: anne.stewart@titanemail.com
Advertising Address: As above. **Fax:** 020 7803 1803
Email: james.willmott@titanemail.com
Publisher: Titan Magazines
Frequency: Monthly
Cover Price: £2.15
Circulation: 18,385 (Publisher's Statement)
Usual Pagination: 24
Editor: Anne Ewart; **Advertising Manager:** James Willmott
Summary of Content: Children's magazine featuring Noddy and his friends. Includes stories, activities, colouring and competitions.
Readership/Target Audience: Aimed at 3 to 5 year olds.
ADVERTISING RATES:
Full Page Colour £3250.00
Agency Commission: 10%
Mechanical Data: Col Length: 277mm, Page Width: 210mm, Trim Size: 297 x 230mm, Film: Digital, Type Area: 277 x 210mm, Bleed Size: 303 x 236mm
Average advertising content per issue: 10%
CONSUMER: RECREATION & LEISURE: Children & Youth

NON LEAGUE TODAY
1827156U75B-292
Editorial Address: 27 John Street, LONDON, WC1N 2BX
Tel: 020 7269 8900 **Fax:** 020 7269 8909
Email: nonleaguedaily@bmt-uk.com
Advertising Address: As above.
Email: rosemary.nolte@ipgonline.cc
Web site: http://www.nonleaguedaily.com
Publisher: IPG
Date Established: 2007
Frequency: Weekly
Cover Price: £2.00
Circulation: 30,000 (Publisher's Statement)
Usual Pagination: 56
Editor: David Watters; **Advertising Manager:** Rosemary Nolte
Summary of Content: Newspaper covering results, match reports and reaction from the big games in the non-league as well as comment, interviews and reader feedback.
Readership/Target Audience: Aimed at football fans.
ADVERTISING RATES:
Full Page Colour £1950.00
Agency Commission: 10%
Mechanical Data: Type Area: 338 x 269mm, Col Length: 338mm, Page Width: 269mm, Col Widths (Display): 35mm, No. of Columns (Display): 7, Film: Digital
Copy instructions: Copy Date: Friday prior to publication date
CONSUMER: SPORT: Football

THE NON-LEAGUE PAPER
1703076U75B-281
Formerly: Football Paper
Editorial Address: Lower Ground Floor, Tuition House, St. Georges Road, LONDON, SW19 4EU **Tel:** 020 8971 4333
Fax: 020 8971 4366
Email: nlp@greenwaysmedia.co.uk
Advertising Address: As above.
Email: andy.mcnulty@greenwaysmedia.co.uk
Web site: http://www.thenonleaguefootballpaper.com
Publisher: The Football Paper Ltd
Date Established: 2000
Frequency: Weekly - Published on Sunday
Cover Price: £1.50
Circulation: 36,000 (Publisher's Statement)
Usual Pagination: 56
Editor: John Lyons; **News Editor:** John Lyons; **Editor-in-Chief:** David Emery
Summary of Content: Newspaper covering football from the Conference to the bottom of the football pyramid with match reports, features, news, statistics, player profiles and guest columns.
Readership/Target Audience: Aimed at football fans, chairmen, managers, players and coaches.
ADVERTISING RATES:
Full Page Colour £1995.00
Agency Commission: 10%
Mechanical Data: Type Area: 332 x 263mm, Col Length: 332mm, Page Width: 263mm, Col Widths (Display): 35mm, No. of Columns (Display): 7, Film: Digital
Copy instructions: Copy Date: Thursday 1pm prior to publication date
CONSUMER: SPORT: Football

NORTH EAST HOMES
1697031U74C-845
Formerly: Exclusive Homes
Editorial Address: Echo House, Pennywell, SUNDERLAND, SR4 9ER **Tel:** 0191 501 5800 **Fax:** 0191 543 5975
Email: alison.goulding@northeast-press.co.uk
Advertising Address: As above. **Fax:** 0191 534 6687
Email: property@northeast-press.co.uk
Web site: http://www.exclusivehomes.co.uk
Publisher: Northeast Press Ltd
Date Established: 2005
Frequency: Monthly
Cover Price: £0.50
Usual Pagination: 52
Editor: Alison Goulding
Summary of Content: Magazine covering all aspects of exclusive homes including interiors, architectural design, kitchen, bathrooms, property news, homes for sale, legal issues, mortgages and personal finance.
Readership/Target Audience: Aimed at affluent consumers in the North East of England looking to move house or upgrade their existing property.
ADVERTISING RATES:
Full Page Colour £825.00
Copy instructions: Copy Date: 3 weeks prior to publication date
CONSUMER: WOMEN'S INTEREST CONSUMER MAGAZINES: Home & Family

NORTH EAST LIFE
1837340U80C-5445
Editorial Address: PO Box 164, HEXHAM, NE46 9AG
Tel: 01772 722022
Email: anne.graham@archant.co.uk
Advertising Address: As above.
Email: mark.scandle@archant.co.uk

Web site: http://www.northeast-life.co.uk
Publisher: Archant Life (North) PLC
Date Established: 2008
Frequency: Monthly
Cover Price: £1.95
Circulation: 20,000 (Print Run)
Usual Pagination: 164
Editor: Andrew Smith
Summary of Content: Magazine celebrating all the finer things in life including people, places, property, food and wine, interiors, fashion, motoring and what's on.
Readership/Target Audience: Aimed at those with a passion for the North East with high disposable incomes.
ADVERTISING RATES:
Full Page Colour £1400.00
Agency Commission: 10%
CONSUMER: RURAL & REGIONAL INTEREST: Regional Interest English Counties

NORTH MAGAZINE
46816U80B-5

Formerly: Alley Magazine
Editorial Address: Unit 2, Whitehorse Yard, 78 Liverpool Road, LONDON, N1 0QD **Tel:** 020 7359 5500
Fax: 020 7359 6001
Email: mark.kebble@archant.co.uk
Advertising Address: As above.
Email: karen.brodie@archant.co.uk
Web site: http://www.northmag.co.uk
Publisher: Archant Life
Frequency: Monthly
Cover Price: Free
Circulation: 52,635 (Publisher's Statement)
Usual Pagination: 48
Editor: Mark Kebble; **Managing Director:** Jeremy Moreton
Summary of Content: Magazine covering local news, travel, property, shopping and leisure.
Readership/Target Audience: Aimed at those who live and work in North London.
ADVERTISING RATES:
Full Page Colour £1804.00
Agency Commission: 10%
Mechanical Data: Trim Size: 300 x 230mm, Film: Digital, Bleed Size: 306 x 236mm, Type Area: 273 x 200mm, Col Length: 273mm, Page Width: 200mm
Copy instructions: Copy Date: 3 weeks prior to publication date
Average advertising content per issue: 40%
CONSUMER: RURAL & REGIONAL INTEREST: Regional Interest Greater London

THE NORTH STAFFORDSHIRE MAGAZINE
1826775U80C-5436

Editorial Address: Sentinel House, Etruria, STOKE-ON-TRENT, ST1 5SS **Tel:** 01782 602525
Email: nsmagazine@thesentinel.co.uk
Advertising Address: As above.
Email: sandra.kinsey@thesentinel.co.uk
Publisher: Staffordshire Sentinel News & Media Ltd
Date Established: 2007
Frequency: Monthly
Cover Price: £1.50
Circulation: 12,000 (Publisher's Statement)
Usual Pagination: 140
Editor: Jenny Amphlett; **Advertising Manager:** Sandra Kinsey
Summary of Content: Magazine covering lifestyle, homes, gardens, food, style, fashion, health, beauty, motors and travel.
Readership/Target Audience: Aimed at households in Staffordshire and South Cheshire.
ADVERTISING RATES:
Full Page Colour £650.00
Agency Commission: 10%
Mechanical Data: Trim Size: 297 x 220mm, Bleed Size: 303 x 226mm, Film: Digital
Copy instructions: Copy Date: 2 weeks prior to publication date
Average advertising content per issue: 30%
CONSUMER: RURAL & REGIONAL INTEREST: Regional Interest English Counties

NORTHEAST HOUSE HUNTER
634518U74K-275

Editorial Address: 5-11 Causey Street, Gosforth, NEWCASTLE UPON TYNE, NE3 4DJ **Tel:** 0191 284 9994
Fax: 0191 284 9995
Email: richard.holmes@accentmagazines.co.uk
Advertising Address: As above.
Email: jacqui.lyon@accentmagazines.co.uk
ISSN: 1473-2459
Publisher: Accent Magazines Ltd
Date Established: 2001
Frequency: Weekly
Cover Price: £1.00
Free to qualifying individuals
Circulation: 12,000 (Publisher's Statement)
Usual Pagination: 72

Editor: Richard Holmes
Summary of Content: Magazine covering information on interior design, DIY, mortgage news and property finance.
Readership/Target Audience: Aimed at property market enthusiasts and those looking for ideas for the interiors of their homes.
ADVERTISING RATES:
SCC £7.00
Agency Commission: 10%
Mechanical Data: Bleed Size: 426 x 303mm, Type Area: 390 x 277mm, Col Length: 390mm, Film: Digital, Page Width: 277mm, No. of Columns (Display): 7, Col Widths (Display): 36mm
Copy instructions: Copy Date: Friday of the week prior to publication date
Average advertising content per issue: 60%
CONSUMER: WOMEN'S INTEREST CONSUMER MAGAZINES: Home Purchase

NORTHERN CROSS
47737U87-180

Editorial Address: St. Joseph's Parish Centre, St. Paul's Road, HARTLEPOOL, TS26 9EY **Tel:** 01429 274305
Fax: 01429 274328
Email: norcross@btconnect.com
Advertising Address: 11 Foxcover Lane, SUNDERLAND, SR3 3TQ **Tel:** 0191 511 0050 **Fax:** 0191 511 0050
Email: norcrossads@yahoo.com
Web site: http://www.nor-cross.co.uk
Publisher: Northern Cross Trustees
Date Established: 1956
Frequency: Monthly
Cover Price: £0.80
Circulation: 5,845 (Publisher's Statement)
Usual Pagination: 28
Editor: Andrew Smith; **Advertising Manager:** Bryan Taylor
Summary of Content: Catholic newspaper for the RC Diocese of Hexham and Newcastle, linking 179 parishes and promoting Christian activities and opinions, with news and features on parish and diocesan events in the North East of England with interests in the rest of the Church in Britain and worldwide.
Readership/Target Audience: Aimed at Christians, predominantly Roman Catholics, and other faith readers in the North East of England, particularly Hexham and Newcastle RC diocese.
ADVERTISING RATES:
Full Page Mono £520.00
SCC £3.30
Mechanical Data: Col Length: 345mm, No. of Columns (Display): 7, Print Process: Web-fed offset litho, Type Area: 345 x 275mm, Page Width: 275mm, Col Widths (Display): 35mm, Film: Digital
Copy instructions: Copy Date: 15th of the month prior to publication date
Average advertising content per issue: 15%
CONSUMER: RELIGIOUS

NORTHERN EARTH
48613U94E-45

Editorial Address: 10 Jubilee Street, Mytholmroyd, HEBDEN BRIDGE, HX7 5NP **Tel:** 01422 882441
Fax: 01422 882441
Email: editor@northernearth.co.uk
Advertising Address: As above.
Email: editor@northernearth.co.uk
Web site: http://www.northernearth.co.uk
ISSN: 0268-8476
Publisher: Northern Earth
Date Established: 1979
Frequency: Quarterly
Cover Price: £1.95
Annual Sub.: £7.50
Circulation: 650 (Publisher's Statement)
Usual Pagination: 36
Editor: John Billingsley; **Advertising Manager:** John Billingsley
Summary of Content: Neo-antiquarian journal covering earth mysteries, sacred landscapes, traditions, folk cultures and fortean topics. Includes folklore, archaeology, landscape and place studies, prehistoric religion and paranormal events.
Readership/Target Audience: Aimed at those with an antiquarian interest in ancient sites and times.
ADVERTISING RATES:
Full Page Mono £32.00
SCC £1.00
Mechanical Data: Film: Digital
Copy instructions: Copy Date: 6 weeks prior to publication date
CONSUMER: OTHER CLASSIFICATIONS: Paranormal

NORTHERN IRELAND INTERIORS & LIVING
1732885U74C-856

Editorial Address: 9 Lakeland Manor, HILLSBOROUGH, BT26 6RE **Tel:** 028 9268 8577 **Fax:** 028 9268 8655
Email: info@nimedia.net
Advertising Address: As above.
Email: info@nimedia.net

ISSN: 1748-2445
Publisher: N.I. Media Ltd
Date Established: 2001
Frequency: Quarterly
Cover Price: £2.95
Circulation: 11,000 (Publisher's Statement)
Usual Pagination: 144
Editor: Shane Smith; **Managing Director:** Shane Smith; **Advertising Manager:** Shane Smith
Summary of Content: Magazine covering interiors and lifestyle with features on readers' homes, tips on how to make your home more functional and attractive, technology in the home, recipes, restaurant reviews, fitness and health and local artists.
Readership/Target Audience: Aimed at women in their 20s to late 40s who want to improve their existing home or move house.
ADVERTISING RATES:
Full Page Colour £995.00
Agency Commission: 10%
Mechanical Data: Bleed Size: 307 x 240mm, Trim Size: 297 x 230mm, Film: Digital
Copy instructions: Copy Date: 2 weeks prior to publication date
Average advertising content per issue: 25%
CONSUMER: WOMEN'S INTEREST CONSUMER MAGAZINES: Home & Family

NORTHERN IRELAND TRAVEL NEWS
47964U89A-380

Formerly: Northern Ireland Travel and Leisure News
Editorial Address: Unit 1, Windsor Business Park, 16-18 Lower Windsor Avenue, BELFAST, BT9 7DW
Tel: 028 9066 6151 **Fax:** 028 9068 3819
Email: brian@nitravelnews.com
Advertising Address: As above.
Email: jonathan@nitravelnews.com
Web site: http://www.nitravelnews.com
Publisher: Northern Ireland Travel and Leisure News
Frequency: 11 issues yearly
Cover Price: £0.50
Annual Sub.: £14.00
Circulation: 23,000 (Publisher's Statement)
Usual Pagination: 38
Editor: Brian Ogle
Summary of Content: Newspaper covering travel, leisure and tourism for Northern Ireland.
Readership/Target Audience: Read by those interested in the travel industry and travellers to Northern Ireland.
ADVERTISING RATES:
Full Page Colour £1750.00
SCC £6.10
Agency Commission: 10%
Mechanical Data: Type Area: 370 x 262mm, Col Length: 370mm, Page Width: 262mm, Film: Digital
Copy instructions: Copy Date: Last Tuesday of the month prior to publication date
CONSUMER: HOLIDAYS & TRAVEL: Travel

NORTHERN IRELAND VISITORS JOURNAL
47965U89A-385

Editorial Address: Penton House, 38 Heron Road, Sydenham Business Park, BELFAST, BT3 9LE
Tel: 028 9045 7457 **Fax:** 028 9045 6611
Email: info@pentonpublications.co.uk
Advertising Address: As above.
Email: info@nivisitorsjournal.com
Publisher: Penton Publications Ltd
Date Established: 1997
Frequency: Half-yearly - Published in March and July
Cover Price: £3.50
Free to qualifying individuals
Circulation: 45,000 (Publisher's Statement)
Usual Pagination: 150
Editor: Tara Craig; **Managing Director:** Bill Penton; **Publisher:** Bill Penton
Summary of Content: Comprehensive reference guide to Northern Ireland's leisure, entertainment and holiday facilities.
Readership/Target Audience: Aimed at those visiting Northern Ireland, and the home tourist.
ADVERTISING RATES:
Full Page Mono £1450.00
Full Page Colour £1795.00
Agency Commission: 10%
Mechanical Data: Print Process: Sheet-fed litho, No. of Columns (Display): 3, Film: Digital, Bleed Size: 303 x 216mm, Trim Size: 297 x 210mm
Copy instructions: Copy Date: Middle of the month prior to publication date
Average advertising content per issue: 30%
CONSUMER: HOLIDAYS & TRAVEL: Travel

THE NORTHERN JOURNAL
1666401U90-953

Editorial Address: Chapeltown Enterprise Centre, 231 Chapeltown Road, LEEDS, LS7 3DX **Tel:** 0113 262 6333

Consumer Magazines

Email: bmf@cec-resources.co.uk
Advertising Address: As above.
Email: bmf@cec-resources.co.uk
Web site: http://www.bmf-leeds.co.uk
ISSN: 1745-5987
Publisher: Gbakhanda Publishing
Date Established: 2004
Frequency: Quarterly
Cover Price: £5.95
Circulation: 6,000 (Publisher's Statement)
Usual Pagination: 40
Editor: Carl Hylton; **Executive Editor:** Carl Hylton;
Advertising Manager: Paul Auber
Summary of Content: Magazine covering issues that affect black minority groups including self-identity, health, education and training areas.
Readership/Target Audience: Aimed at black minority groups in schools, universities, colleges, business who are social policy makers and practitioners and social activists.
ADVERTISING RATES:
Full Page Mono £700.00
Full Page Colour £1000.00
Mechanical Data: Film: Digital
CONSUMER: ETHNIC

NORTHERN LIFE KIDS
1826070U74D-663
Editorial Address: 43 Scotland Road, NELSON, BB9 7UT
Tel: 01282 604387 **Fax:** 01282 604326
Email: karen@looppublishing.co.uk
Advertising Address: As above.
Email: lee@looppublishing.co.uk
Web site: http://www.northernlifekids.co.uk
Publisher: Loop Publishing Ltd
Date Established: 2006
Frequency: 6 issues yearly
Cover Price: Free
Circulation: 15,000 (Publisher's Statement)
Usual Pagination: 68
Editor: Olivia Foster; **Editor-in-Chief:** Karen Shaw;
Advertising Manager: Lee Banks
Summary of Content: Magazine covering family life, what's on, cooking, health and fitness, competitions, puzzles, readers' gallery, fashion, education and bedtime stories.
Readership/Target Audience: Aimed at parents, carers and teachers of children aged 2 to 10 years old in East Lancashire and West Yorkshire.
ADVERTISING RATES:
Full Page Colour £1250.00
Agency Commission: 10%
Mechanical Data: Bleed Size: 297 x 210mm, Film: Digital
Copy instructions: Copy Date: 2 weeks prior to publication date
CONSUMER: WOMEN'S INTEREST CONSUMER MAGAZINES: Child Care

NORTHERN LIFE MAGAZINE
1674055U80C-5225
Editorial Address: The Northern Life Centre, 43 Scotland Road, NELSON, BB9 7UT **Tel:** 01282 604387
Fax: 01282 604326
Email: karen@looppublishing.co.uk
Advertising Address: 43 Scotland Road, NELSON, BB9 7UT **Tel:** 01282 877108 **Fax:** 01282 604326
Email: paula@looppublishing.co.uk
Web site: http://www.looppublishing.co.uk
Publisher: Loop Publishing Ltd
Date Established: 2005
Frequency: 6 issues yearly
Cover Price: Free
Circulation: 25,000 (Publisher's Statement)
Usual Pagination: 80
Editor: Karen Shaw; **Advertising Manager:** Paula Smith
Summary of Content: Magazine providing local information concerning life in the north including a what's on guide to theatre, arts and places to visit in the area.
Readership/Target Audience: Aimed at affluent people in Lancashire and Yorkshire.
ADVERTISING RATES:
Full Page Colour £1250.00
Agency Commission: 10%
Mechanical Data: Bleed Size: +6mm, Trim Size: 297 x 210mm, Film: Digital
Average advertising content per issue: 40%
CONSUMER: RURAL & REGIONAL INTEREST: Regional Interest English Counties

NORTHERN WOMAN
45189U74A-373
Formerly: NW Northern Woman
Editorial Address: 5B Edgewater Business Park, Belfast Harbour Estate, BELFAST, BT3 9JQ **Tel:** 028 9078 3200
Fax: 028 9078 3210
Email: lynpalmer@greerpublications.com
Advertising Address: As above.
Email: soniatohani@greerpublications.com
Web site: http://www.greerpublications.com/northern_woman.htm
Publisher: Greer Publications Ltd

Frequency: 10 issues yearly
Cover Price: £1.95
Annual Sub.: £25.00
Circulation: 13,000 (Publisher's Statement)
Usual Pagination: 124
Editor: Lyn Palmer; **Advertising Manager:** Sonia Tohani
Summary of Content: Magazine covering lifestyle, fashion and health and beauty features.
Readership/Target Audience: Aimed at women between 18 and 45 years old.
ADVERTISING RATES:
Full Page Colour £1520.00
Agency Commission: 15%
Mechanical Data: Type Area: 252 x 192mm, Bleed Size: 290 x 235mm, Trim Size: 280 x 225mm, Col Length: 252mm, Page Width: 192mm
Average advertising content per issue: 40%
CONSUMER: WOMEN'S INTEREST CONSUMER MAGAZINES: Women's Interest

NORTHSIDE NEWS
1824605U80E-376
Editorial Address: For all contact details see main edition, Southside News
Frequency: Monthly
Cover Price: Free
Circulation: 10,000 (Publisher's Statement)
Edition of: Southside News
CONSUMER: RURAL & REGIONAL INTEREST: Regional Interest Scotland

NORTHUMBRIA STUDENT
1685462U83-274
Editorial Address: 2 Sandyford Road, NEWCASTLE UPON TYNE, NE1 8SB **Tel:** 0191 227 3737 **Fax:** 0191 227 3760
Email: su.newspaper@unn.ac.uk
Advertising Address: As above. **Tel:** 0191 227 4757
Email: maeve.conway@unn.ac.uk
Web site: http://www.mynsu.co.uk
Publisher: Northumbria Students' Union
Frequency: 6 issues yearly
Cover Price: Free
Circulation: 7,000 (Publisher's Statement)
Advertising Manager: Maeve Conway
Summary of Content: Newspaper covering student life including news, music, DVDs, clubs, pubs, bars and gigs.
Readership/Target Audience: Aimed at Students at Northumbria University.
ADVERTISING: Rates on application
CONSUMER: STUDENT PUBLICATIONS

THE NORTHUMBRIAN
46952U80C-2456
Editorial Address: Unit 17, St. Peters Wharf, NEWCASTLE UPON TYNE, NE6 1TZ **Tel:** 0191 265 0244
Fax: 0191 265 0040
Email: northumbrian@powdene.com
Advertising Address: As above. **Tel:** 0191 265 0040
Fax: 0191 275 2609
Email: geraldine@powdene.com
Web site: http://www.northumbrian.co.uk
Publisher: Powdene Publicity Ltd
Date Established: 1987
Frequency: 6 issues yearly
Cover Price: £3.25
Circulation: 18,000 (Publisher's Statement)
Usual Pagination: 74
Editor: Stewart Bonney; **Advertising Manager:** Geraldine Oliver
Summary of Content: Local interest magazine covering people, places and events and gardening.
Readership/Target Audience: Aimed at residents and ex-pats of Northumbria who enjoy the countryside.
ADVERTISING RATES:
Full Page Mono £740.00
Full Page Colour £900.00
Agency Commission: 10%
Mechanical Data: Bleed Size: 305 x 218mm, Trim Size: 297 x 210mm, Type Area: 265 x 180mm, Col Length: 265mm, Col Widths (Display): 85mm, Film: Digital, No. of Columns (Display): 2, Page Width: 180mm
Copy instructions: Copy Date: 3 weeks prior to publication date
CONSUMER: RURAL & REGIONAL INTEREST: Regional Interest English Counties

NORTHWEST MAGAZINE
46838U80B-171
Formerly: NW magazine
Editorial Address: Unit 2, White Horse Yard, 78 Liverpool Road, LONDON, N1 0QD **Tel:** 020 7359 5500
Fax: 020 7359 6001
Email: mark.kebble@archant.co.uk
Advertising Address: As above.
Email: karen.brody@archant.co.uk
Web site: http://www.northwestmag.co.uk
Publisher: Archant Life
Date Established: 1997

Frequency: Monthly
Cover Price: Free
Circulation: 34,000 (Publisher's Statement)
Usual Pagination: 100
Editor: Mark Kebble; **Managing Director:** Jeremy Moreton;
Advertising Manager: Karen Brody
Summary of Content: Local interest magazine covering news, reviews, interviews, issues and events in North West London.
Readership/Target Audience: Aimed at residents.
ADVERTISING RATES:
Full Page Colour £1640.00
Agency Commission: 10%
Mechanical Data: Col Length: 280mm, Bleed Size: 306 x 236mm, Trim Size: 300 x 230mm, Type Area: 280 x 210mm, Page Width: 210mm, Film: Digital
Copy instructions: Copy Date: 2 weeks prior to publication date
Average advertising content per issue: 60%
CONSUMER: RURAL & REGIONAL INTEREST: Regional Interest Greater London

NOTES & QUERIES
47550U84B-160
Editorial Address: Pembroke College, OXFORD, OX1 1DW
Tel: 01865 276463
Email: notes.queries@oup.com
Advertising Address: Great Clarendon Street, OXFORD, OX2 6DP **Tel:** 01865 353329
Email: jnlsadvertising@oxfordjournals.org
Web site: http://www.oup.co.uk/notesj
ISSN: 0029-3970
Publisher: OUP
Date Established: 1849
Frequency: Quarterly
Annual Sub.: £95.00
Circulation: 1,475 (Publisher's Statement)
Usual Pagination: 144
Editor: Sue Charkin
Summary of Content: Journal with emphasis on the factual rather than the speculative, with book reviews and readers' queries.
Readership/Target Audience: Aimed at academics, teachers and those with an interest in literature.
ADVERTISING RATES:
Full Page Mono £340.00
Agency Commission: 10%
Mechanical Data: Type Area: 210 x 135mm, Col Length: 210mm, Page Width: 135mm, Film: Digital
CONSUMER: THE ARTS & LITERARY: Literary

NOTEWORTHY
1805770U83-288
Editorial Address: 11 Plough Yard, LONDON, EC2A 3LP
Tel: 020 7684 7111 **Fax:** 020 7864 7122
Email: ella_johnston@axonpublish.com
Publisher: Axon Publishing Ltd
Date Established: 2007
Frequency: 3 issues yearly - Published in February, June and October
Cover Price: Free
Circulation: 40,000 (Print Run)
Editor: Ella Johnston
Summary of Content: Magazine covering events, alumni news and catching up with old friends.
Readership/Target Audience: Aimed at alumni of the University of Bedfordshire.
ADVERTISING: No Advertising taken
CONSUMER: STUDENT PUBLICATIONS

NOTICIAS LATIN AMERICA
48331U90-116_26
Editorial Address: PO Box 34783, LONDON, N7 7WD
Tel: 020 7686 1633 **Fax:** 020 7686 1662
Email: informacion@noticias.co.uk
Advertising Address: As above.
Email: karla@noticias.co.uk
Web site: http://www.noticias.co.uk
ISSN: 1467-601X
Publisher: Noticias Latin America
Date Established: 1992
Frequency: Monthly
Cover Price: Free
Circulation: 30,000 (Publisher's Statement)
Usual Pagination: 32
Editor: Luis Mario Tasama; **News Editor:** Alberto Rojas
Summary of Content: Newspaper providing opinion and analysis on news and culture from Latin America.
Language(s): Spanish
Readership/Target Audience: Aimed at the Latin American community living in the UK and Europeans with an interest in Latin America.
ADVERTISING RATES:
Full Page Mono £580.00
Full Page Colour £720.00
Agency Commission: 10%
Mechanical Data: Col Widths (Display): 40mm, Film: Digital, No. of Columns (Display): 6

Copy instructions: Copy Date: 10 days prior to publication date
Average advertising content per issue: 40%
Supplement(s): Community - 12xY
CONSUMER: ETHNIC

NOTION
1660327U76D-791

Formerly: Klub Knowledge
Editorial Address: 4th Floor, 2 Plough Yard, LONDON, EC2A 3LP **Tel:** 0870 046 6622 **Fax:** 0870 046 6611
Email: editorial@musichqmedia.com
Advertising Address: As above.
Email: olly@musichqmedia.com
Web site: http://www.planetnotion.com
Publisher: Music HQ Ltd
Date Established: 2004
Frequency: 6 issues yearly
Cover Price: £3.95
Circulation: 18,000 (Publisher's Statement)
Usual Pagination: 130
Advertising Manager: Olly Wetzig
Summary of Content: Magazine covering music, lifestyle, culture, fashion and reviews.
Readership/Target Audience: Aimed at trend setters, 18 to 30 year old men and women.
ADVERTISING RATES:
Full Page Colour £1150.00
Agency Commission: 10%
Mechanical Data: Type Area: 278 x 212mm, Bleed Size: 304 x 238mm, Trim Size: 298 x 232mm, Col Length: 278mm, Page Width: 212mm, Film: Digital
Copy instructions: Copy Date: 4 weeks prior to publication date
CONSUMER: MUSIC & PERFORMING ARTS: Music

NOTTINGHAMSHIRE TODAY
46955U80C-2530

Editorial Address: Castle Wharf House, NOTTINGHAM, NG1 7EU **Tel:** 0115 948 2000
Email: jeremy.lewis@nottinghameveningpost.co.uk
Advertising Address: As above. **Tel:** 0115 910 2182
Fax: 0115 964 4097
Email: today@nottinghameveningpost.co.uk
Publisher: Nottingham Post Media Group Ltd
Date Established: 1964
Frequency: Monthly
Cover Price: £2.95
Circulation: 8,500 (Publisher's Statement)
Usual Pagination: 180
Editor: Jeremy Lewis; **Advertising Manager:** Nicola West
Summary of Content: General interest, social and business publication. Contains features on fashion, weddings, travel, motoring, home and garden, antiques and wining and dining.
Readership/Target Audience: Aimed at those with a high disposable income aged 30 and over who work and live in Nottinghamshire.
ADVERTISING RATES:
Full Page Mono £950.00
Full Page Colour £950.00
Agency Commission: 10%
Mechanical Data: Type Area: 270 x 186mm, Col Length: 270mm, Trim Size: 297 x 210mm, Bleed Size: 307 x 216mm, Film: Digital, Page Width: 186mm
Copy instructions: Copy Date: 2 weeks prior to publication date
Average advertising content per issue: 40%
CONSUMER: RURAL & REGIONAL INTEREST: Regional Interest English Counties

NOTUN DIN BENGALI NEWSWEEKLY
48332U90-116_27

Editorial Address: 46G Greatorex Street, LONDON, E1 5NP
Tel: 020 7247 6280 **Fax:** 020 7247 0789
Email: news@notundin.com
Advertising Address: As above.
Email: admin@notundin.com
Web site: http://www.notundin.com
Publisher: Gold Prize Media Ltd
Frequency: Weekly
Cover Price: £0.50
Annual Sub.: £39.00
Circulation: 20,000 (Publisher's Statement)
Usual Pagination: 52
Editor: Mohib Chowdhury; **Executive Editor:** Taysir Mahmud; **Advertising Manager:** Daysir Mahmud
Summary of Content: Newspaper containing features on health, sports, finance, women's interest and films.
Language(s): Bengali
Readership/Target Audience: Read by Bengali speakers and the Bangladeshi community in the UK and Europe.
ADVERTISING RATES:
Full Page Mono £1900.00
Full Page Colour £2300.00
Agency Commission: 10%
Mechanical Data: Type Area: 380 x 260mm, Col Length: 380mm, Page Width: 260mm, Trim Size: 420 x 297mm, Film: Digital

NOUSE (UNIVERSITY OF YORK STUDENT NEWSPAPER)
47418U83-50_5

Editorial Address: Grimston House, Vanbrugh College, University of York, Heslington, YORK, YO10 5DD
Tel: 01904 434425 **Fax:** 01904 434425
Email: socs12@york.ac.uk
Advertising Address: As above.
Web site: http://www.nouse.co.uk
Publisher: Nouse Newspapers
Date Established: 1964
Frequency: 9 issues yearly - Published three times a term
Cover Price: Free
Circulation: 3,500 (Publisher's Statement)
Usual Pagination: 36
Summary of Content: Newspaper for the University of York.
Readership/Target Audience: Aimed at students of the University.
CONSUMER: STUDENT PUBLICATIONS

NOVELTY MAGAZINE
1830370U90-1022

Editorial Address: 203B Island Business Centre, 18-36 Wellington Street, LONDON, SE18 6PS **Tel:** 0844 884 3384
Fax: 020 8854 1484
Email: info@noveltymagazine.com
Web site: http://www.noveltymagazine.com
Publisher: Life Changers
Date Established: 2008
Frequency: Monthly
Circulation: 500,000 (Publisher's Statement)
Usual Pagination: 110
Editor: Sheri Adegbesan; **Publisher:** Sheri Adegbesan
Summary of Content: Magazine covering lifestyle and fashion from a western point of view, relationships and culture.
Readership/Target Audience: Aimed at Africans living in Europe and Africa.
CONSUMER: ETHNIC

NOW
45193U74A-386

Editorial Address: Blue Fin Building, 110 Southwark Street, LONDON, SE1 0SU **Tel:** 020 3148 5000 **Fax:** 020 3148 8110
Advertising Address: As above.
Email: lindsay_dean@ipcmedia.com
Web site: http://www.nowmagazine.co.uk
Publisher: IPC Connect Ltd
Frequency: Weekly
Cover Price: £1.10
Circulation: 384,356 (ABC 01/01/2009 to 30/06/2009)
Usual Pagination: 100
Editor: Corrine Barraclough; **News Editor:** Chris White; **Features Editor:** Kasie Davies; **Managing Director:** Fiona Dent; **Publisher:** Emily Hutchings
Summary of Content: Magazine covering show business and celebrity interviews as well as features on beauty and fashion.
Twitter: https://twitter.com/Nowmagazine.
Readership/Target Audience: Aimed at women between 16 and 35 years old.
ADVERTISING RATES:
Full Page Colour £18000.00
Agency Commission: 15%
Mechanical Data: Print Process: Web-fed offset litho, Type Area: 282 x 200mm, Bleed Size: 306 x 226mm, Trim Size: 300 x 220mm, Col Length: 282mm, Film: Positive, right reading, emulsion side down. Digital, Screen: Mono 40 lpc Colour 54 lpc, Page Width: 200mm
Copy instructions: Copy Date: 21 working days prior to publication date
Average advertising content per issue: 24%
CONSUMER: WOMEN'S INTEREST CONSUMER MAGAZINES: Women's Interest

NOW & THEN
1655744U94X-270

Editorial Address: 17 North Street, MIDDLESBROUGH, TS2 1JP **Tel:** 01642 252023 **Fax:** 01642 230657
Email: editor@nowandthenmag.co.uk
Advertising Address: As above.
Email: quoinpublishing@yahoo.co.uk
Web site: http://www.nowandthenmag.co.uk
Publisher: Quoin Publishing
Date Established: 2003
Frequency: 6 issues yearly
Cover Price: Free
Circulation: 78,000 (Publisher's Statement)
Usual Pagination: 96
Editor: Peter Cook
Summary of Content: Magazine that looks at major events and stories that have happened in the past and present.

Copy instructions: Copy Date: Tuesday prior to publication date
Average advertising content per issue: 40%
CONSUMER: ETHNIC

Readership/Target Audience: Aimed at those of all ages that have an interest in past events in the North East of England.
ADVERTISING RATES:
Full Page Colour £290.00
Agency Commission: 10%
Mechanical Data: Type Area: 198 x 136mm, Bleed Size: 216 x 154mm, Trim Size: 210 x 148mm, Film: Digital, No. of Columns (Display): 2, Col Length: 198mm, Page Width: 136mm
Copy instructions: Copy Date: 2 weeks prior to publication date
Average advertising content per issue: 60%
CONSUMER: OTHER CLASSIFICATIONS: Miscellaneous

N.PARADOXA
626125U84A-320

Editorial Address: 38 Bellot Street, East Greenwich, LONDON, SE10 0AQ **Tel:** 020 8858 3331
Fax: 020 8858 3331
Email: k.deepwell@ukonline.co.uk
Advertising Address: As above.
Email: ktpress@ktpress.co.uk
Web site: http://www.ktpress.co.uk
ISSN: 1461-0434
Publisher: KT Press
Date Established: 1998
Frequency: Half-yearly - Published in January and July
Annual Sub.: £18.00
Circulation: 2,500 (Publisher's Statement)
Usual Pagination: 96
Editor: Katy Deepwell; **Advertising Manager:** Katy Deepwell
Summary of Content: Journal on international feminist art (visual arts), containing thematic issues with articles, interviews and features by women about the relationship between feminist theory and contemporary women's art practices worldwide.
Readership/Target Audience: Aimed at academics, curators, artists and museums of contemporary and modern art.
ADVERTISING RATES:
Full Page Mono £800.00
Mechanical Data: Page Width: 185mm, Col Length: 250mm, No. of Columns (Display): 2, Type Area: 250 x 185mm
Copy instructions: Copy Date: 2 months prior to publication date
Average advertising content per issue: 4%
CONSUMER: THE ARTS & LITERARY: Arts

NREVOLUTION
1785495U78D-332

Formerly: Revolution
Editorial Address: Richmond House, 33 Richmond Hill, BOURNEMOUTH, BH2 6EZ **Tel:** 01202 586200
Email: nrevolution@imagine-publishing.co.uk
Advertising Address: As above.
Email: james.hanslip@imagine-publishing.co.uk
Web site: http://www.nrev-mag.co.uk
Publisher: Imagine Publishing
Date Established: 2006
Frequency: 13 issues yearly
Cover Price: £4.99
Circulation: 40,000 (Print Run)
Usual Pagination: 116
Editor: Simon Miller
Summary of Content: Magazine covering Nintendo Wii, Nintendo DS and virtual console with tips, previews, news, reviews and features.
Readership/Target Audience: Aimed at owners of Nintendo Wii consoles, predominantly aged between 18 and 28 years old.
ADVERTISING: Rates on application
CONSUMER: CONSUMER ELECTRONICS: Games

NUCLEAR FREE SCOTLAND
47260U82-140

Editorial Address: 15 Barrland Street, GLASGOW, G41 1QH **Tel:** 0141 423 1222
Email: scnd@banthebomb.org
Advertising Address: As above.
Email: scnd@banthebomb.org
Web site: http://www.banthebomb.org
Publisher: Scottish CND
Frequency: 3 issues yearly - Published in February, June and November
Free to qualifying individuals
Circulation: 2,000 (Publisher's Statement)
Usual Pagination: 16
Editor: Alan Mackinnon; **Advertising Manager:** Alan Mackinnon
Summary of Content: Magazine of Scottish CND. Includes articles on nuclear weapons and peace issues.
Readership/Target Audience: Read by CND members and supporters.
ADVERTISING: Rates on application
CONSUMER: CURRENT AFFAIRS & POLITICS

NUDE
1685367U84A-442

Editorial Address: PO Box 587, LONDON, WC1H 9WB
Tel: 020 7833 0050
Email: info@nudemagazine.co.uk
Advertising Address: As above.
Email: info@nudemagazine.co.uk
Web site: http://www.nudemagazine.co.uk
Publisher: Poke-in-the-Eye Publishing Ltd
Date Established: 2003
Frequency: Quarterly
Cover Price: £3.95
Circulation: 10,000 (Publisher's Statement)
Usual Pagination: 100
Editor: Suzy Prince; **Advertising Manager:** Suzy Prince
Summary of Content: Alternative arts magazine covering graphics, literature, music, comics and films.
Readership/Target Audience: Aimed at men and women aged between 20 and 45 years old.
ADVERTISING RATES:
Full Page Colour £500.00
Mechanical Data: Bleed Size: +3mm, Trim Size: 210 x 210mm, Film: Digital
Average advertising content per issue: 20%
CONSUMER: THE ARTS & LITERARY: Arts

LE NURB
47436U83-68_10

Formerly: Route 66
Editorial Address: Cleveland Road, UXBRIDGE, UB8 3PH
Tel: 01895 269269 **Fax:** 01895 269699
Email: media.officer@brunel.ac.uk
Advertising Address: As above.
Email: bonnie.crate@brunel.ac.uk
Publisher: Union of Brunel Students
Date Established: 1990
Frequency: 10 issues yearly - Published every four weeks
Cover Price: Free
Circulation: 5,000 (Publisher's Statement)
Usual Pagination: 20
Advertising Manager: Bonnie Crate
Summary of Content: Magazine covering campus news and sports, features and discussions.
Readership/Target Audience: Aimed at students on campus.
ADVERTISING RATES:
Full Page Mono £150.00
Mechanical Data: Bleed Size: +3mm, No. of Columns (Display): 3, Page Width: 210mm
Average advertising content per issue: 20%
CONSUMER: STUDENT PUBLICATIONS

NUTRITION & HEALING
45414U74G-40_10

Formerly: New Health Revelations
Editorial Address: Sea Containers House, 7th Floor, 20 Upper Ground, LONDON, SE1 9JD **Tel:** 020 7633 3630
Email: nhr@agorapub.co.uk
Web site: http://www.thehealthierlife.co.uk
Publisher: Agora Lifestyles Ltd
Date Established: 1996
Frequency: Monthly
Annual Sub.: £67.00
Circulation: 8,500 (Publisher's Statement)
Usual Pagination: 8
Editor: Andrew Miller
Summary of Content: Publication focusing on complementary health treatments, nutrition and advice on overcoming weight problems.
Readership/Target Audience: Aimed at men and women interested in diet and health.
ADVERTISING: No Advertising taken
CONSUMER: WOMEN'S INTEREST CONSUMER MAGAZINES: Slimming & Health

NUTS
1640031U86C-714

Editorial Address: Blue Fin Building, 110 Southwark Street, LONDON, SE1 0SU **Tel:** 020 3148 5000
Email: nutsmagazine@ipcmedia.com
Advertising Address: As above. **Fax:** 020 3148 8108
Email: chris_dicker@ipcmedia.com
Web site: http://www.nuts.co.uk
Publisher: IPC Media Ltd
Date Established: 2004
Frequency: Weekly
Annual Sub.: £81.60
Circulation: 188,532 (ABC 01/01/2009 to 30/06/2009)
Usual Pagination: 100
Editor: Louise Prior; **Publisher:** Clair Porteous
Summary of Content: Magazine covering sport, TV, features and news.
Twitter: https://twitter.com/nuts_website.
Readership/Target Audience: Aimed at men aged 16 to 40 years old.
ADVERTISING RATES:
Full Page Colour £10120.00
Agency Commission: 10%

Mechanical Data: Type Area: 282 x 204mm, Bleed Size: 306 x 228mm, Trim Size: 300 x 225mm, Col Length: 282mm, Page Width: 204mm
Copy instructions: Copy Date: 10 days prior to publication date
Average advertising content per issue: 15%
CONSUMER: ADULT & GAY MAGAZINES: Men's Lifestyle Magazines

THE OBSERVER FOOD MONTHLY
707169U74P-520

Editorial Address: Kings Place, 90 York Way, LONDON, N1 9GU **Tel:** 020 3353 2000
Email: rebecca.seal@observer.co.uk
Advertising Address: As above. **Tel:** 020 7239 9735
Fax: 020 7279 1449
Web site: http://www.observer.co.uk
Publisher: Guardian Media Group plc
Date Established: 2001
Frequency: Monthly - See main record for circulation figure
Cover Price: Free
Usual Pagination: 74
Editor: Rebecca Seal; **Advertising Manager:** Clive Jones
Summary of Content: Magazine featuring the culture of eating and drinking. Includes in-depth features, food news, interviews and celebrity-led items.
Readership/Target Audience: Aimed at those who read the Observer.
ADVERTISING RATES:
Full Page Mono £11000.00
Full Page Colour £11000.00
Mechanical Data: Type Area: 260 x 198mm, Col Length: 260mm, Page Width: 198mm, Bleed Size: 301 x 232mm, Trim Size: 291 x 222mm
Copy instructions: Copy Date: 4pm 10 days prior to publication date
Supplement to: The Observer
CONSUMER: WOMEN'S INTEREST CONSUMER MAGAZINES: Food & Cookery

OBSERVER MUSIC MONTHLY
1627065U76D-770

Editorial Address: Kings Place, 90 York Way, LONDON, N1 9GU **Tel:** 020 3353 2000
Email: omm@observer.co.uk
Advertising Address: 119 Farringdon Road, LONDON, EC1R 3ER **Tel:** 020 7278 2332 **Fax:** 020 7278 1449
Email: alexandra.turner@guardian.co.uk
Web site: http://www.guardian.co.uk/theobserver/ musicmonthly
Publisher: Guardian Media Group plc
Frequency: Monthly
Cover Price: Free
Circulation: 450,000 (Publisher's Statement)
Usual Pagination: 74
Editor: Caspar Llewellyn-Smith; **Advertising Manager:** Alexandra Turner
Summary of Content: Magazine covering all types of music with a bias towards popular music. Also includes celebrity interviews.
Readership/Target Audience: Aimed at readers of The Observer.
ADVERTISING RATES:
Full Page Colour £13120.00
Mechanical Data: Film: Digital
Supplement to: The Observer
CONSUMER: MUSIC & PERFORMING ARTS: Music

THE OBSERVER SPORT MONTHLY
624142U75A-600

Editorial Address: Kings Place, 90 York Way, LONDON, N1 9GU **Tel:** 020 3353 2000
Email: osm@observer.co.uk
Advertising Address: 119 Farringdon Road, LONDON, EC1R 3ER **Tel:** 020 7239 9735
Email: nicola.warren@guardian.co.uk
Web site: http://www.observer.co.uk/osm
Publisher: Guardian Media Group plc
Date Established: 2000
Frequency: Monthly - Published on the first Sunday of the month. See main record for circulation figure
Cover Price: Free
Usual Pagination: 66
Editor: Tim Lewis
Summary of Content: Magazine containing news and features on sport. Includes a guide to the month's sporting fixtures.
Readership/Target Audience: Read by sports enthusiasts.
ADVERTISING RATES:
Full Page Colour £11000.00
Copy instructions: Copy Date: 10 working days prior to publication date
Supplement to: The Observer
CONSUMER: SPORT

OCEAN VIEW
760952U74Q-75

Editorial Address: Park View House, 19 The Avenue, EASTBOURNE, BN21 3YD **Tel:** 01323 411601
Fax: 01323 411654
Email: linda@parkview-publishing.co.uk
Advertising Address: As above.
Email: linda@parkview-publishing.co.uk
Publisher: Park View Publishing Ltd
Date Established: 2002
Frequency: Quarterly
Cover Price: Free
Circulation: 35,000 (Publisher's Statement)
Editor: Linda Grace; **Advertising Manager:** Linda Grace;
Publisher: Lee Mansfield
Summary of Content: Lifestyle magazine featuring travel reviews, fashion, food and drink, motoring, health, money, film, theatre, TV, music, photography and entertainment.
Readership/Target Audience: Aimed at men and women aged 45 years old and over.
ADVERTISING RATES:
Full Page Colour £2050.00
Agency Commission: 10%
Mechanical Data: Film: Digital, Bleed Size: 264 x 196mm, Trim Size: 258 x 190mm
Average advertising content per issue: 40%
CONSUMER: WOMEN'S INTEREST CONSUMER MAGAZINES: Lifestyle

OCTANE
1623403U77E-511

Editorial Address: 1 Tower Court, Irchester Road, Wollaston, WELLINGBOROUGH, NN29 7PJ
Tel: 020 7907 6000 **Fax:** 01933 663367
Email: info@octane-magazine.com
Advertising Address: 19 Highfield Lane, MAIDENHEAD, SL6 3AN **Tel:** 01628 510080 **Fax:** 01628 510090
Email: sanjay@octane-magazine.co.uk
Web site: http://www.octane-magazine.com
Publisher: Dennis Publishing Ltd
Date Established: 2003
Frequency: Monthly
Cover Price: £3.95
Circulation: 30,500 (Publisher's Statement)
Usual Pagination: 188
Editor: David Lillywhite; **Managing Director:** Peter Wootton;
Managing Editor: David Lillywhite; **Advertising Director:** Sanjay Seetanah
Summary of Content: Magazine covering the world's greatest cars and the people involved with them as well as accessories, art and automobilia, auctions, events and rallies, books and literature, car insurance and specialist services.
Readership/Target Audience: Aimed at enthusiasts of classic cars and modern supercars.
ADVERTISING RATES:
Full Page Colour £2150.00
Agency Commission: 10%
Mechanical Data: Type Area: 256 x 196mm, Bleed Size: 295 x 232mm, Trim Size: 285 x 222mm, No. of Columns (Display): 3, Col Length: 256mm, Page Width: 196mm
Average advertising content per issue: 35%
CONSUMER: MOTORING & CYCLING: Club Cars

OCTOPUSH NEWS
1685689U75M-1000

Editorial Address: 31 Burroway Road, Langley, SLOUGH, SL3 8EH **Tel:** 01753 542810
Email: hockey@arnoldstrategy.com
Advertising Address: As above.
Email: tim.arnold@blueyonder.co.uk
Web site: http://www.gbuwh.co.uk
Publisher: Arnold Strategy
Date Established: 1971
Frequency: Quarterly
Free to qualifying individuals
Circulation: 1,500 (Publisher's Statement)
Usual Pagination: 16
Editor: Tim Arnold; **Advertising Manager:** Tim Arnold
Summary of Content: Magazine of the British Octopush Association covering events, results, coaching and clubs.
Readership/Target Audience: Aimed at players and officials involved with underwater hockey.
ADVERTISING RATES:
Full Page Colour £1200.00
Agency Commission: 10%
Mechanical Data: Trim Size: 297 x 210mm, Film: Digital
Copy instructions: Copy Date: 30 days prior to publication date
Average advertising content per issue: 20%
CONSUMER: SPORT: Water Sports

ODEON MAGAZINE
1826246U76A-212

Editorial Address: 2 Balcombe Street, LONDON, NW1 6NW
Tel: 020 7042 4000
Email: cassie.whittell@futurenet.co.uk
Advertising Address: 30 Monmouth Street, BATH, BA1 2BW **Tel:** 01225 442244 **Fax:** 01225 732206
Email: craithby@futurenet.co.uk

Publisher: Future Publishing Limited
Date Established: 2007
Frequency: Monthly
Cover Price: Free
Circulation: 199,880 (ABC 01/01/2009 to 30/06/2009)
Usual Pagination: 36
Editor: Cassie Whittell; **Advertising Director:** Clair Raithby
Summary of Content: Magazine covering current film releases.
Readership/Target Audience: Aimed at customers of Odeon cinemas.
ADVERTISING RATES:
Full Page Colour £4000.00
CONSUMER: MUSIC & PERFORMING ARTS: Cinema

OE OUTDOOR ENTHUSIAST
1663374U75L-808
Editorial Address: The Old Dairy, Hudsons Farm, Fieldgate Lane, Ugley Green, BISHOP'S STORTFORD, CM22 6HJ
Tel: 01279 816300 **Fax:** 01279 816496
Email: rebecca@yahoo.co.uk
Advertising Address: As above.
Email: kathryn.howe@oe-mag.com
Web site: http://www.oe-mag.com
Publisher: Target Publishing Ltd
Date Established: 2004
Frequency: Quarterly
Cover Price: £3.50
Annual Sub.: £18.00
Circulation: 17,500 (Publisher's Statement)
Usual Pagination: 140
Editor: Rebecca Corbally; **Managing Director:** David Cam
Summary of Content: Magazine covering outdoor sports and activities including walking, climbing, diving, cycling and photography.
Readership/Target Audience: Aimed at outdoor sports enthusiasts.
ADVERTISING RATES:
Full Page Colour £2120.00
Agency Commission: 10%
Mechanical Data: Trim Size: 297 x 210mm, Bleed Size: 303 x 216mm, Film: Digital
Copy instructions: Copy Date: 4 weeks prior to publication date
CONSUMER: SPORT: Outdoor

OFFICE PROFESSIONAL
45472U74J-40
Formerly: Career Secretary
Editorial Address: Suite 464, 24-28 St. Leonards Road, WINDSOR, SL4 3BB **Tel:** 0844 800 0182 **Fax:** 01753 775798
Email: iqps@cfa.uk.com
Advertising Address: As above.
Email: office@iqps.org
Web site: http://www.iqps.org
Publisher: IQPS Ltd
Date Established: 1985
Frequency: Quarterly
Free to qualifying individuals
Annual Sub.: £70.00
Circulation: 2,000 (Publisher's Statement)
Usual Pagination: 26
Editor: Kerrie Fuller
Summary of Content: Quarterly magazine of the Institute of Qualified Professional Secretaries offering advice on continued professional development, technology advances, career moves, HR plus contributions from local network.
Readership/Target Audience: Aimed at qualified office professional who are members of IQPS.
ADVERTISING: Rates on application
CONSUMER: WOMEN'S INTEREST CONSUMER MAGAZINES: Secretary & PA

THE OFFICIAL ELVIS PRESLEY FAN CLUB MAGAZINE
46273U76E-270
Editorial Address: PO Box 4, LEICESTER, LE1 3ZL
Tel: 0844 800 6881 **Fax:** 0844 800 6883
Email: sendtotodd@aol.com
SSN: 1361-6870
Publisher: HRC Leicester Ltd
Frequency: 6 issues yearly
Annual Sub.: £15.00
Circulation: 20,000 (Publisher's Statement)
Usual Pagination: 64
Editor: Todd Slaughter; **Publisher:** Todd Slaughter
Summary of Content: Magazine featuring historical, biographical and social articles relating to Elvis Presley.
Readership/Target Audience: Aimed at Elvis fans and collectors.
ADVERTISING: No Advertising taken
CONSUMER: MUSIC & PERFORMING ARTS: Pop Music

THE OFFICIAL FERRARI MAGAZINE
1852531U77E-526
Editorial Address: Vogue House, 1 Hanover Square, LONDON, W1S 1JU **Tel:** 020 7499 9080 **Fax:** 020 7439 1345

Publisher: Conde Nast Publications Ltd
Date Established: 2008
Frequency: Quarterly
Free to qualifying individuals
Annual Sub.: EUR250.00
Circulation: 30,000 (Publisher's Statement)
Usual Pagination: 180
Editor: Jason Barlow
Summary of Content: Magazine covering Ferrari news, Formula 1, interviews with celebrated Ferrari owners and luxury lifestyle.
Readership/Target Audience: Aimed at Ferrari owners worldwide.
CONSUMER: MOTORING & CYCLING: Club Cars

THE OFFICIAL GUIDE TO INTERNATIONAL WOMEN'S MONTH
1644307U90-930
Editorial Address: 102 Mallinson Road, Battersea, LONDON, SW11 1BN **Tel:** 020 7207 2734
Fax: 020 7207 6503
Email: livelistings@aol.com
Advertising Address: As above.
Email: all3mags@yahoo.co.uk
Web site: http://www.livelistingsmag.com
Publisher: Barb Wire Enterprises Ltd
Date Established: 2004
Frequency: Annual - Published in March
Cover Price: Free
Circulation: 50,000 (Publisher's Statement)
Editor: Barbara Campbell; **Advertising Manager:** Barbara Campbell
Summary of Content: Multicultural magazine covering profiles of women and women's achievements as well as news and entertainment.
Readership/Target Audience: Aimed at women aged 15 to 45 years old and distributed through schools, colleges and universities.
ADVERTISING RATES:
Full Page Colour £2900.00
Mechanical Data: Type Area: 262 x 185mm, Bleed Size: 297 x 210mm, Col Length: 262mm, Page Width: 185mm
CONSUMER: ETHNIC

THE OFFICIAL LFC MAGAZINE
45767U75B-271
Editorial Address: PO Box 48, Old Hall Street, LIVERPOOL, L69 3EB **Tel:** 0151 227 2000 **Fax:** 0151 285 8466
Email: stevehanrahan@sportmedia-tm.com
Advertising Address: As above.
Email: neil.johnson@liverpool.com
Publisher: Trinity Mirror
Date Established: 2002
Frequency: Weekly
Cover Price: £1.95
Circulation: 17,000 (Publisher's Statement)
Editor: Steve Hanrahan; **Executive Editor:** Ken Rogers
Summary of Content: Official magazine of Liverpool Football Club with weekly coverage of LFC news and action as well as interviews with past and present players.
Readership/Target Audience: Aimed at supporters of the club.
ADVERTISING RATES:
Full Page Colour £1950.00
Agency Commission: 10%
Mechanical Data: Trim Size: 297 x 210mm, Bleed Size: 307 x 220mm, Film: Digital
Copy instructions: Copy Date: Monday 5pm 1 week prior to publication date
Average advertising content per issue: 30%
CONSUMER: SPORT: Football

OFFICIAL NINTENDO MAGAZINE
46539U78D-205
Formerly: Nintendo Official Magazine
Editorial Address: 2 Balcombe Street, LONDON, NW1 6NW
Tel: 020 7042 4000
Email: neil.long@futurenet.com
Advertising Address: As above.
Email: emma.cull@futurenet.co.uk
Web site: http://www.officialnintendomagazine.co.uk
ISSN: 0965-4240
Publisher: Future Publishing Limited
Date Established: 1992
Frequency: 13 issues yearly
Cover Price: £3.99
Circulation: 58,795 (ABC 01/07/2008 to 31/12/2008)
Usual Pagination: 132
Editor: Neil Long; **Advertising Manager:** Emma Cull; **Publisher:** Lee Nutter
Summary of Content: Magazine containing news and features on Nintendo games and hardware.
Readership/Target Audience: Aimed predominantly at teenage males and those who enjoy playing Nintendo consoles.

ADVERTISING RATES:
Full Page Colour .... £4000.00.
Agency Commission: 10%
Mechanical Data: Col Length: 280mm, Page Width: 213mm, Film: Digital, Type Area: 280 x 213mm, Bleed Size: 306 x 238mm, Trim Size: 300 x 232mm
Copy instructions: Copy Date: 4 weeks prior to publication date
Average advertising content per issue: 20%
CONSUMER: CONSUMER ELECTRONICS: Games

OFFICIAL PLAYSTATION MAGAZINE
1790363U78D-334
Editorial Address: 30 Monmouth Street, BATH, BA1 2BW
Tel: 01225 442244
Email: tim.clark@futurenet.com
Advertising Address: 2 Balcombe Street, LONDON, NW1 6NW **Tel:** 020 7042 4000
Email: emma.cull@futurenet.co.uk
Publisher: Future Publishing Ltd
Date Established: 2006
Frequency: Monthly
Editor: Tim Clark; **News Editor:** Rachel Penny; **Editor-in-Chief:** Tim Clark; **Advertising Manager:** Emma Cull
Summary of Content: Magazine covering all 3 PlayStation formats.
Readership/Target Audience: Aimed at owners of PlayStation consoles.
ADVERTISING RATES:
Full Page Mono £7000.00
Full Page Colour £7000.00
Agency Commission: 10%
Mechanical Data: Type Area: 270 x 190mm, Bleed Size: 303 x 216mm, Trim Size: 297 x 210mm, Col Length: 270mm, Page Width: 190mm, Film: Digital
Copy instructions: Copy Date: 4 weeks prior to publication date
Average advertising content per issue: 30%
CONSUMER: CONSUMER ELECTRONICS: Games

THE OFFICIAL TOUR DE FRANCE GUIDE
1663370U77C-952
Editorial Address: 2 Balcombe Street, LONDON, NW1 6NW
Tel: 020 7042 4000
Email: pcossins@futurenet.co.uk
Advertising Address: Beauford Court, 30 Monmouth Street, BATH, BA1 2BW **Tel:** 01225 442244 **Fax:** 01225 822885
Email: shulbert@futurenet.co.uk
Web site: http://www.procycling.com
Publisher: Future Publishing Limited
Date Established: 2000
Frequency: Annual - Published in June
Cover Price: £7.50
Circulation: 40,000 (Publisher's Statement)
Usual Pagination: 190
Editor: Peter Cossins
Summary of Content: Official Tour de France Guide which showcases this annual sporting event, interviews with cyclists, full details of each day's racing, insight, rider profiles and equipment reviews.
Readership/Target Audience: Aimed at active and armchair sports enthusiasts.
ADVERTISING RATES:
Full Page Mono £4000.00
Full Page Colour £4000.00
Agency Commission: 10%
Mechanical Data: No. of Columns (Display): 4, Type Area: 280 x 210mm, Bleed Size: 306 x 236mm, Trim Size: 300 x 230mm, Col Length: 280mm, Page Width: 210mm, Film: Digital
Copy instructions: Copy Date: May 14th
Average advertising content per issue: 35%
CONSUMER: MOTORING & CYCLING: Cycling

OFFSTAGE
754226U84A-421
Editorial Address: PO Box 46288, Ealing Green, LONDON, W5 5WZ **Tel:** 0870 199 8493 **Fax:** 07092 342376
Email: editorial@off-stage.com
Advertising Address: As above.
Email: advertising@off-stage.com
Web site: http://www.off-stage.com
Publisher: OffStage Publications Ltd
Date Established: 1998
Frequency: Monthly
Cover Price: £2.50
Free to qualifying individuals
Circulation: 45,000 (Publisher's Statement)
Usual Pagination: 96
Editor: Martin Bevan; **Advertising Manager:** Christopher Ager; **Managing Editor:** Martin Bevan; **Publisher:** Christopher Ager
Summary of Content: Magazine covering arts, leisure, theatre, opera, ballet, musicals, drama and travel.
Readership/Target Audience: Aimed at drama groups, societies, corporate entertainment and theatre goers.
ADVERTISING: Rates on application

Consumer Magazines

Copy instructions: Copy Date: End of 1st week prior to publication date
CONSUMER: THE ARTS & LITERARY: Arts

OINK!　　　　　　　　　　　　1626457U91D-874
Editorial Address: 7 Hampstead Gate, 1A Frognal, LONDON, NW3 6AL **Tel:** 0870 755 0820 **Fax:** 020 8994 9265
Email: tsp@piggybank.co.uk
Advertising Address: As above.
Email: tsp@piggybank.co.uk
Web site: http://www.piggybank.co.uk
ISSN: 1479-2923
Publisher: Oink News Corporation Ltd
Date Established: 2002
Frequency: Monthly
Cover Price: £0.60
Free to qualifying individuals
Circulation: 100,000 (Publisher's Statement)
Usual Pagination: 12
Editor: Thura Soe-Paing; **Advertising Manager:** Thura Soe-Paing
Summary of Content: Newspaper covering money matters for kids including celebrity interviews, sport, fashion, films, music reviews by CBBC's Adrian Dickson, computer games, pets, quizzes, comic strips and competitions.
Readership/Target Audience: Aimed at those aged between 7 and 12 years old and their parents and teachers.
ADVERTISING RATES:
Full Page Colour £4000.00
Agency Commission: 15%
Copy instructions: Copy Date: Last Friday of the month prior to publication date
CONSUMER: RECREATION & LEISURE: Children & Youth

OK!　　　　　　　　　　　　45648U74Q-685
Editorial Address: 10 Lower Thames Street, LONDON, EC3R 6EN **Tel:** 0871 434 1010
Email: natalie.posner@express.co.uk
Advertising Address: As above.
Email: sam.how@express.co.uk
Web site: http://www.ok-magazine.com
Publisher: Northern & Shell plc
Date Established: 1996
Frequency: Weekly
Cover Price: £2.50
Circulation: 599,847 (ABC 01/01/2009 to 30/06/2009)
Usual Pagination: 212
Editor: Marcia Moody; **News Editor:** Christian Guiltenane; **Features Editor:** Marcia Moody; **Managing Director:** Martin Ellice; **Advertising Manager:** Sam How; **Publisher:** Richard Desmond
Summary of Content: Magazine containing photo features and articles on the lives of the stars, the rich and the famous. Twitter: https://twitter.com/OK_Magazine.
Readership/Target Audience: Aimed at women of all ages.
ADVERTISING RATES:
Full Page Colour £16170.00
Agency Commission: 15%
Mechanical Data: Film: Digital
Copy instructions: Copy Date: 12 days prior to publication date
Supplement(s): Hot Stars - 52xY
CONSUMER: WOMEN'S INTEREST CONSUMER MAGAZINES: Lifestyle

OLAY NEWSPAPER　　　　　　1666597U90-956
Editorial Address: 100 Green Lanes, LONDON, N16 9EH
Tel: 020 7923 9090 **Fax:** 020 7923 9080
Email: info@olaygazete.co.uk
Advertising Address: As above.
Email: info@olaygazete.co.uk
Web site: http://www.olaygazete.co.uk
Publisher: Olay Newspaper Ltd
Date Established: 1989
Frequency: 104 issues yearly
Cover Price: £1.00
Free to qualifying individuals
Circulation: 30,000 (Publisher's Statement)
Usual Pagination: 72
Editor: Nesin Fehmi
Summary of Content: Newspaper published in Turkish, with articles of interest to the local community as well as politics, economics, sport, entertainment, education and health.
Language(s): Turkish
Readership/Target Audience: Aimed at the Turkish community in London.
ADVERTISING: Rates on application
CONSUMER: ETHNIC

OLD GLORY　　　　　　　　　46785U79R-90
Editorial Address: Media Centre, Morton Way, HORNCASTLE, LN9 6JR **Tel:** 01507 529306
Fax: 01507 529495
Email: editor@mortons.co.uk
Advertising Address: As above. **Fax:** 01507 529499

Email: abruce@mortons.co.uk
Web site: http://www.oldglory.co.uk
ISSN: 0956-5922
Publisher: Mortons Media Group Ltd
Date Established: 1988
Frequency: Monthly
Cover Price: £3.60
Annual Sub.: £36.00
Circulation: 28,000 (Publisher's Statement)
Usual Pagination: 100
Editor: Colin Tyson
Summary of Content: Magazine covering news and club information on steam traction engines and other (non-railway) steam-powered machinery. Including agricultural tractors, old buses, commercial vehicles, mills, canals and steam boats.
Readership/Target Audience: Aimed at steam enthusiasts.
ADVERTISING RATES:
Full Page Colour £939.00
Agency Commission: 10%
Mechanical Data: Page Width: 188mm, Col Length: 270mm, Film: Digital, Type Area: 270 x 188mm, Bleed Size: 307 x 220mm, Trim Size: 297 x 210mm
Average advertising content per issue: 25%
CONSUMER: HOBBIES & DIY: Hobbies & DIY Related

THE OLDIE　　　　　　　　　45154U73-265
Editorial Address: 65 Newman Street, LONDON, W1T 3EG
Tel: 020 7436 8801 **Fax:** 020 7436 8804
Email: editorial@theoldie.co.uk
Advertising Address: Mongoose Media, Mongoose House, 2 Lonsdale Road, LONDON, NW6 6RD **Tel:** 020 7306 0300
Fax: 020 7306 0301
Email: theoldie@mongoosemedia.com
Web site: http://www.theoldie.co.uk
ISSN: 0965-2507
Publisher: Oldie Publications Ltd
Date Established: 1992
Frequency: 13 issues yearly
Cover Price: £3.50
Annual Sub.: £32.50
Circulation: 34,310 (ABC 01/01/2009 to 30/06/2009)
Usual Pagination: 76
Editor: Claire Daly; **Publisher:** James Pembroke
Summary of Content: Magazine covering humour, satire, current interest articles, books, film and theatre. Includes articles on music, radio and television reviews and cartoons.
Readership/Target Audience: Aimed at those aged 50 years old and over.
ADVERTISING RATES:
Full Page Colour £1590.00
Agency Commission: 10%
Mechanical Data: Type Area: 277 x 185mm, Col Length: 277mm, Trim Size: 297 x 210mm, Bleed Size: 303 x 216mm, Film: Digital, Page Width: 185mm, No. of Columns (Display): 4, Col Widths (Display): 61mm
CONSUMER: NATIONAL & INTERNATIONAL PERIODICALS

OLIVE　　　　　　　　　　　1638778U74P-912
Editorial Address: Media Centre, 201 Wood Lane, LONDON, W12 7TQ **Tel:** 020 8433 2000 **Fax:** 020 8433 3499
Advertising Address: Garden Centre, 201 Wood Lane, LONDON, W12 7TQ **Tel:** 020 8433 2000 **Fax:** 020 8433 3824
Email: gemma.baldwin@bbc.com
Web site: http://www.olivemagazine.co.uk
Publisher: BBC Worldwide Publishing
Date Established: 2003
Frequency: Monthly
Cover Price: £3.20
Circulation: 86,117 (ABC 01/01/2009 to 30/06/2009)
Editor: Danielle Theunissen; **Features Editor:** Jessica Gunn; **Advertising Manager:** Gemma Baldwin
Summary of Content: Magazine covering food, restaurants and travel.
Readership/Target Audience: Aimed at women aged between 25 and 44 years old.
ADVERTISING RATES:
Full Page Colour £4950.00
Agency Commission: 15%
Mechanical Data: Col Length: 265mm, Page Width: 220mm, Type Area: 265 x 220mm, Trim Size: 275 x 230mm, Bleed Size: 281 x 236mm, Film: Digital
Copy instructions: Copy Date: 7 weeks prior to publication date
Average advertising content per issue: 40%
CONSUMER: WOMEN'S INTEREST CONSUMER MAGAZINES: Food & Cookery

ON BUSINESS　　　　　　　　48215U89D-240
Editorial Address: Prospect House, Rouen Road, NORWICH, NR3 1RE **Tel:** 01603 772528 **Fax:** 01603 627823
Email: zoe.francis@archantdialogue.co.uk
Advertising Address: As above. **Tel:** 01603 772520
Email: samantha.overton@archantdialogue.co.uk
Web site: http://www.archantdialogue.co.uk
Publisher: Archant Norfolk

Frequency: Quarterly
Cover Price: Free
Circulation: 30,000 (Publisher's Statement)
Usual Pagination: 52
Editor: Tom Smith; **Managing Director:** Bob Crawley; **Advertising Manager:** Samantha Overton
Summary of Content: Magazine with news and features on topical issues facing the international business travel organiser.
Readership/Target Audience: Read by clients of Business Travel International - UK.
ADVERTISING RATES:
Full Page Colour £3500.00
Agency Commission: 10%
Mechanical Data: Trim Size: 297 x 210mm, Bleed Size: 303 x 216mm, Film: Digital
Copy instructions: Copy Date: 4 weeks prior to publication date
Average advertising content per issue: 40%
CONSUMER: HOLIDAYS & TRAVEL: In-Flight Magazines

ONBOARD　　　　　　　　　　1687433U75G-656
Editorial Address: 1 West Smithfield, LONDON, EC1A 9JU
Tel: 020 7332 9700 **Fax:** 020 7332 9799
Email: danny@onboardmag.com
Advertising Address: As above.
Email: craig.scrivener@factorymedia.com
Web site: http://www.onboardmag.com
Publisher: Factory Media
Frequency: 8 issues yearly
Cover Price: £3.30
Circulation: 21,032 (Publisher's Statement)
Editor: Danny Burrows; **Editor-in-Chief:** Danny Burrows; **Advertising Manager:** Craig Scrivener
Summary of Content: Magazine covering information on the European snowboarding scene; includes interviews with snowboarding personalities, travel, events, fashion, music, film and lifestyle.
Readership/Target Audience: Aimed at men and women aged 16 to 25 years old with a high disposable income.
ADVERTISING RATES:
Full Page Colour £5665.00
Agency Commission: 10%
Mechanical Data: Trim Size: 300 x 230mm, Bleed Size: 306 x 236mm, Film: Digital
CONSUMER: SPORT: Winter Sports

ONE80NEWS　　　　　　　　1835843U86B-183
Editorial Address: 4 Steine Street, BRIGHTON, BN2 1TE
Tel: 0870 620 1360 **Fax:** 01273 676201
Email: editor@one80news.co.uk
Advertising Address: As above.
Email: advertising@one80news.co.uk
Web site: http://www.one80news.co.uk
Publisher: Marble Media Publishing Ltd
Date Established: 2007
Frequency: 26 issues yearly
Cover Price: Free
Circulation: 12,000 (Publisher's Statement)
Usual Pagination: 32
Editor: Niall McMurray
Summary of Content: Newspaper covering up to date news, arts, entertainment, listings for the scene, theatre, restaurant reviews and local politics.
Readership/Target Audience: Aimed at the LGBT communities in Brighton and Hove.
ADVERTISING RATES:
Full Page Colour £875.00
Mechanical Data: Type Area: 350 x 275mm, Col Length: 350mm, Page Width: 275mm
CONSUMER: ADULT & GAY MAGAZINES: Gay & Lesbian Magazines

ONE IN SEVEN MAGAZINE　　48644U94F-665
Editorial Address: 19-23 Featherstone Street, LONDON, EC1Y 8SL **Tel:** 020 7296 8000 **Fax:** 020 7296 8021
Email: membership@rnid.org.uk
Web site: http://www.rnid.org.uk
ISSN: 1460-0811
Publisher: The RNID
Date Established: 1997
Frequency: 6 issues yearly
Free to qualifying individuals
Annual Sub.: £19.50
Circulation: 35,500 (Publisher's Statement)
Usual Pagination: 64
Editor: Dawn Dimond; **News Editor:** Tim Russell
Summary of Content: RNID membership magazine covering reviews, news, celebrity interviews and advice on tinnitus and hearing loss and tinnitus. Includes RNID campaigns information, features on new products and the latest on hearing aids.
Readership/Target Audience: Aimed at deaf and hard of hearing people.
ADVERTISING: No Advertising taken
CONSUMER: OTHER CLASSIFICATIONS: Disability

ONE PHILIPPINES
1831463U90-1024

Editorial Address: Suite 19-20, Network Business Centre, 329-339 Putney Bridge Road, LONDON, SW15 2PG
Tel: 020 8780 3152
Email: publisher@onephilippines.co.uk
Advertising Address: As above.
Email: advert@onephilippines.co.uk
Web site: http://www.onephilippines.co.uk
Publisher: Pinoy Services Ltd
Date Established: 2007
Frequency: Monthly
Cover Price: Free
Circulation: 30,000 (Publisher's Statement)
Usual Pagination: 36
Editor: Gen Ashley
Summary of Content: Newspaper covering developments back home, the latest health products, business venture opportunities, fashion, film, TV, music, theatre, restaurant and club reviews as well as travel, legal opinion and advice and corporate events and issues.
Readership/Target Audience: Aimed at Filipinos living or working in the UK.
ADVERTISING RATES:
Full Page Colour £475.00
Mechanical Data: Type Area: 355 x 270mm, Bleed Size: 380 x 299mm, Col Length: 355mm, Page Width: 270mm, Film: Digital
Copy instructions: Copy Date: 20th of the month prior to publication date
CONSUMER: ETHNIC

OPEN CHAMPIONSHIP MAGAZINE
45823U75D-190

Editorial Address: Herberts House, High Laver, ONGAR, CM5 0DZ **Tel:** 01732 750650
Advertising Address: As above.
Email: info@highpointmedia.co.uk
Publisher: Highpoint Media
Date Established: 1992
Frequency: Annual - Published in June
Cover Price: £3.95
Circulation: 58,000 (Publisher's Statement)
Usual Pagination: 138
Editor: Alan White; **Advertising Manager:** Alan White;
Publisher: Alan White
Summary of Content: Magazine previewing the Open Championship, endorsed by the Royal and Ancient Golf Club of St. Andrews.
Readership/Target Audience: Aimed at golf enthusiasts aged 30 years and over especially those who visit the Open Championship.
ADVERTISING RATES:
Full Page Colour £8950.00
Average advertising content per issue: 35%
CONSUMER: SPORT: Golf

OPEN GOAL
1826777U75B-291

Editorial Address: St Peter's Gate, Sunderland Science Park, Charles Street, SUNDERLAND, SR6 0AN
Tel: 0191 556 1050
Email: richard.stonehouse@opengoalmagazine.net
Advertising Address: 24 Stafford Rise, CATERHAM, CR3 6JY **Tel:** 01883 720162
Email: michael.james@opengoalmagazine.net
Web site: http://www.opengoalmagazine.co.uk
Publisher: Rich Media Ltd
Date Established: 2008
Frequency: Monthly
Cover Price: Free
Circulation: 250,000 (Print Run)
Usual Pagination: 64
Editor: Alfred Barnacle; **Managing Editor:** Richard Stonehouse
Summary of Content: Football magazine with an emphasis on humour and reflecting the true feelings of the games supporters.
Readership/Target Audience: Aimed at football fans and distributed at premier league ground.
ADVERTISING RATES:
Full Page Colour £8500.00
Agency Commission: 10%
Mechanical Data: Bleed Size: 221 x 141mm, Trim Size: 215 x 135mm, Film: Digital
Copy instructions: Copy Date: 10th of the month prior to publication date
CONSUMER: SPORT: Football

OPERA
46277U76F-200

Editorial Address: 36 Black Lion Lane, LONDON, W6 9BE
Tel: 020 8563 8893 **Fax:** 020 8563 8635
Email: editor@opera.co.uk
Advertising Address: Cabbell Publishing Ltd, Woodman Works, 204 Durnsford Road, LONDON, SW19 8DR
Tel: 020 8971 8479 **Fax:** 020 8971 8480
Email: jane@cabbell.co.uk
Web site: http://www.opera.co.uk

ISSN: 0030-3526
Publisher: Opera Magazine Ltd
Date Established: 1950
Frequency: 13 issues yearly
Cover Price: £4.60
Annual Sub.: £53.00
Circulation: 12,000 (Publisher's Statement)
Usual Pagination: 128
Editor: John Allison; **Advertising Manager:** Jane Stoggles
Summary of Content: Magazine covering opera music and opera events worldwide.
Readership/Target Audience: Aimed at opera-goers and performers.
ADVERTISING RATES:
Full Page Mono £1625.00
Full Page Colour £2250.00
Agency Commission: 10%
Mechanical Data: Type Area: 184 x 116mm, Trim Size: 210 x 148mm, Col Length: 184mm, Bleed Size: 218 x 156mm, Page Width: 116mm, Film: Digital
Copy instructions: Copy Date: 1 month prior to publication date
Average advertising content per issue: 20%
CONSUMER: MUSIC & PERFORMING ARTS: Opera

OPERA NOW
46278U76F-215

Editorial Address: 241 Shaftesbury Avenue, LONDON, WC2H 8TF **Tel:** 020 7333 1740 **Fax:** 020 7333 1769
Email: opera.now@rhinegold.co.uk
Advertising Address: As above. **Tel:** 020 7333 1720
Fax: 020 7333 1736
Email: opera.now@rhinegold.co.uk
Web site: http://www.rhinegold.co.uk
Publisher: Rhinegold Publishing Ltd
Date Established: 1989
Frequency: 6 issues yearly
Cover Price: £5.95
Annual Sub.: £34.00
Circulation: 20,000 (Publisher's Statement)
Usual Pagination: 130
Editor: Ashutosh Khandekar; **Managing Director:** Sarah Williams; **Advertising Manager:** Sebastianq Harris;
Publisher: Derek Smith
Summary of Content: Magazine containing features, live reviews, interviews, profiles and listings.
Readership/Target Audience: Aimed at opera lovers and professionals.
ADVERTISING RATES:
Full Page Mono £2050.00
Full Page Colour £2950.00
Agency Commission: 10%
Mechanical Data: Bleed Size: 303 x 216mm, Trim Size: 297 x 210mm, Film: Digital
Copy instructions: Copy Date: 2 weeks prior to publication date
Average advertising content per issue: 25%
CONSUMER: MUSIC & PERFORMING ARTS: Opera

OPTIMA MAGAZINE
46922U80C-1798

Formerly: Optima
Editorial Address: 20 Sparrows Herne, BUSHEY, WD23 1FX **Tel:** 020 8420 4488 **Fax:** 020 8386 4141
Email: editorial@optimamagazine.co.uk
Advertising Address: As above.
Email: ads@optimamagazine.co.uk
Web site: http://www.optimamagazine.co.uk
Publisher: Optima Magazine Ltd
Date Established: 1990
Frequency: 25 issues yearly
Cover Price: Free
Circulation: 42,000 (Publisher's Statement)
Usual Pagination: 72
Editor: Jill Glenn; **Advertising Manager:** Anthony Mitchell
Summary of Content: Magazine covering lifestyle matters, homes and gardens, restaurants, recruitment, the arts, leisure and articles of general interest.
Readership/Target Audience: Read by home owners of South West Hertfordshire and Middlesex aged 30 years old and over.
ADVERTISING RATES:
Full Page Colour £1155.00
Agency Commission: 10%
Mechanical Data: No. of Columns (Display): 6, Type Area: 265 x 190mm, Bleed Size: 302 x 216mm, Col Length: 265mm, Page Width: 190mm, Print Process: Web-fed litho
Average advertising content per issue: 65%
CONSUMER: RURAL & REGIONAL INTEREST: Regional Interest English Counties

OPTIMUM NUTRITION
1641993U74G-244

Formerly: The Institute for Optimum Nutrition
Editorial Address: Studio 111, Finsbury Business Centre, 40 Bowling Green Lane, LONDON, EC1R 0NE
Tel: 020 7415 7100 **Fax:** 020 7415 7002
Email: info@mediamarkpublishing.com

Advertising Address: Avalon House, 72 Lower Mortlake Road, RICHMOND, TW9 2JY **Tel:** 020 8614 7808
Web site: http://www.ion.ac.uk/journal.htm
ISSN: 1475-8725
Publisher: Mediamark Ltd
Date Established: 1984
Frequency: Quarterly
Cover Price: £3.30
Free to qualifying individuals
Circulation: 10,000 (Publisher's Statement)
Usual Pagination: 76
Editor: Pip Jones; **Advertising Manager:** Suzanne Bryson
Summary of Content: Magazine with features on food, health and nutrition by health journalists, with information and advice on the correct nutrition needed for living a healthy lifestyle as well as recipes, reviews and competitions, offers and discounts.
Readership/Target Audience: Aimed at those who want to find out more about food, nutrition and healthy living.
ADVERTISING RATES:
Full Page Colour £1155.00
Mechanical Data: Trim Size: 210 x 148mm, Film: Digital
Copy instructions: Copy Date: 1 month prior to publication date
CONSUMER: WOMEN'S INTEREST CONSUMER MAGAZINES: Slimming & Health

THE ORACLE CHELTENHAM
1789816U80C-5375

Editorial Address: Archant House, Oriel Road, CHELTENHAM, GL50 1BB **Tel:** 01242 216050
Fax: 01242 255116
Email: tara.walker@archant.co.uk
Advertising Address: As above.
Email: charlotte.davis@archant.co.uk
Web site: http://www.cheltenhamoracle.co.uk
Publisher: Archant Life
Date Established: 2005
Frequency: 6 issues yearly
Cover Price: Free
Circulation: 10,000 (Publisher's Statement)
Usual Pagination: 196
Editor: Tara Walker
Summary of Content: Magazine championing Cheltenham which includes editorial on the town and local people, food reviews, competitions, entertainment, social pages and fashion.
Readership/Target Audience: Aimed at residents and businesses in Cheltenham and the surrounding area.
ADVERTISING RATES:
Full Page Mono £295.00
Full Page Colour £295.00
Agency Commission: 10%
Mechanical Data: Type Area: 227 x 149mm, Bleed Size: 251 x 174mm, Trim Size: 245 x 168mm, Col Length: 227mm, Page Width: 149mm, Film: Digital
Copy instructions: Copy Date: 1st of the month prior to publication date
Average advertising content per issue: 50%
CONSUMER: RURAL & REGIONAL INTEREST: Regional Interest English Counties

THE ORACLE GLOUCESTER
1789817U80C-5376

Editorial Address: Archant House, Oriel Road, CHELTENHAM, GL50 1BB **Tel:** 01242 216050
Fax: 01242 255116
Email: tara.walker@archant.co.uk
Advertising Address: As above.
Email: jennifer.barnard@archant.co.uk
Web site: http://www.gloucesteroracle.co.uk
Publisher: Archant Life
Date Established: 2006
Frequency: 6 issues yearly
Cover Price: Free
Circulation: 10,000 (Publisher's Statement)
Usual Pagination: 130
Editor: Tara Walker
Summary of Content: Magazine championing Gloucester which includes editorial on the city and local people plus food reviews, competitions, entertainment, social scene and fashion.
Readership/Target Audience: Aimed at residents and businesses in Gloucester and the surrounding area.
ADVERTISING RATES:
Full Page Mono £295.00
Full Page Colour £295.00
Agency Commission: 10%
Mechanical Data: Type Area: 227 x 149mm, Bleed Size: 251 x 174mm, Trim Size: 245 x 168mm, Col Length: 227mm, Page Width: 149mm, Film: Digital
Copy instructions: Copy Date: 1st of the month prior to publication date
Average advertising content per issue: 50%
CONSUMER: RURAL & REGIONAL INTEREST: Regional Interest English Counties

Consumer Magazines

ORANGE STANDARD
1687722U87-2038

Editorial Address: Schomberg House, 368 Cregagh Road, BELFAST, BT6 9EY **Tel:** 028 9070 1122 **Fax:** 028 9040 3700
Email: info@grandorangelodge.co.uk
Advertising Address: As above.
Email: info@grandorangelodge.co.uk
Web site: http://www.grandorangelodge.co.uk
Publisher: The Grand Orange Lodge of Ireland
Date Established: 1973
Frequency: 11 issues yearly
Cover Price: £0.70
Circulation: 5,500 (Publisher's Statement)
Usual Pagination: 20
Editor: David Hume; **Advertising Manager:** David Hume
Summary of Content: Magazine of The Grand Orange Lodge of Ireland covering religion, culture, charity and politics.
Readership/Target Audience: Aimed at members of the Orange Order worldwide.
ADVERTISING: Rates on application
Copy instructions: Copy Date: 10 days prior to publication date
CONSUMER: RELIGIOUS

ORBIS INTERNATIONAL LITERARY JOURNAL
1664689U84B-361

Formerly: Orbis
Editorial Address: 17 Greenhow Avenue, WIRRAL, CH48 5EL **Tel:** 0151 625 1446
Email: carolebaldock@hotmail.com
Advertising Address: As above.
Email: carolebaldock@hotmail.com
Web site: http://www.kudoswritingcompetitions.com
ISSN: 0300-4452
Publisher: Carole Baldock
Date Established: 1969
Frequency: Quarterly
Cover Price: £4.00
Free to qualifying individuals
Annual Sub.: £15.00
Circulation: 1,000 (Publisher's Statement)
Usual Pagination: 84
Editor: Carole Baldock; **Advertising Manager:** Carole Baldock
Summary of Content: Literary journal with poetry, prose, translations, reviews, features, articles and letters as well as information about writing opportunities.
Readership/Target Audience: Aimed at those with an interest in literature.
ADVERTISING RATES:
Full Page Mono £40.00
Mechanical Data: Film: Digital
Copy instructions: Copy Date: 15th of the month prior to publication date
CONSUMER: THE ARTS & LITERARY: Literary

THE ORBITAL
47421U83-58

Editorial Address: Royal Holloway College, Student Union, University of London, EGHAM, TW20 0EX
Tel: 01784 486300 **Fax:** 01784 486312
Email: orbital@su.rhul.ac.uk
Advertising Address: As above. **Tel:** 01784 414621
Email: orbital@su.rhul.ac.uk
Web site: http://www.theorbital.co.uk
Publisher: Premier Colour
Date Established: 1994
Frequency: 7 issues yearly - Once a month during term-time
Cover Price: Free
Circulation: 3,000 (Publisher's Statement)
Usual Pagination: 38
Editor: Nick Stylianou; **Advertising Manager:** David Cummins
Summary of Content: Student magazine of the Students' union Royal Holloway, University of London.
Readership/Target Audience: Aimed at students and college staff.
ADVERTISING RATES:
Full Page Colour £400.00
Mechanical Data: Trim Size: 270 x 200mm, Film: Digital
CONSUMER: STUDENT PUBLICATIONS

THE ORCHID REVIEW
38136U93-171

Editorial Address: 9 Port Henderson, GAIRLOCH, IV21 2AS
Tel: 01445 741228
Email: orchidrevieweditor@rhs.org.uk
Advertising Address: 4th Floor, Churchgate, New Road, PETERBOROUGH, PE1 1TT **Tel:** 0845 260 0909
Fax: 01733 341633
Email: louise.bowering@rhspublications.co.uk
Web site: http://www.rhs.org.uk/learning/publications/orchidreview
ISSN: 0030-4476
Publisher: RHS Media
Frequency: 6 issues yearly
Free to qualifying individuals

Annual Sub.: £29.00
Circulation: 1,600 (Publisher's Statement)
Editor: Isobyl la Croix; **Advertising Manager:** Louise Bowering
Summary of Content: Journal containing studies on particular genera, reports on exhibition and information on plants in their habitats as well as show dates and reports, descriptions of new species, readers' letters, book reviews, orchid websites and Society news.
Readership/Target Audience: Aimed at breeders and hybridists worldwide.
ADVERTISING RATES:
Full Page Mono £357.00
Full Page Colour £357.00
Agency Commission: 10%
Mechanical Data: Type Area: 208 x 152mm, Bleed Size: 246 x 176mm, Trim Size: 240 x 170mm, Col Length: 208mm, Page Width: 152mm, Film: Digital, No. of Columns (Display): 2
CONSUMER: GARDENING

THE ORGAN
46174U76D-385

Editorial Address: 1 Exford Road, LONDON, SE12 9HD
Tel: 020 8857 1582
Email: editor@theorganmag.com
Advertising Address: Woodman Works, 204 Durnsford Road, LONDON, SW19 8DR **Tel:** 020 8971 8451
Fax: 020 8971 8480
Email: gordon@cabbell.co.uk
Web site: http://www.theorganmag.com
ISSN: 0030-4883
Publisher: Musical Opinion Ltd
Date Established: 1921
Frequency: Quarterly
Cover Price: £4.50
Annual Sub.: £20.00
Circulation: 8,500 (Publisher's Statement)
Usual Pagination: 68
Editor: Robert Matthew-Walker; **Advertising Manager:** Gordon Roland-Adams
Summary of Content: International journal containing articles on pipe and digital organs, church organs and organ building. Also features festival news, education, recitals and competitions.
Readership/Target Audience: Read by organists, organ builders, members of cathedrals and churches, students and teachers, directors of music and organ music enthusiasts.
ADVERTISING RATES:
Full Page Colour £825.00
Agency Commission: 10%
Mechanical Data: Page Width: 180mm, Trim Size: 297 x 210mm, Bleed Size: 305 x 216mm, Film: Digital, Type Area: 260 x 180mm, Col Length: 260mm
Average advertising content per issue: 15%
CONSUMER: MUSIC & PERFORMING ARTS: Music

ORGANIC GARDEN AND HOME
48570U93-67

Formerly: Organic Gardening
Editorial Address: Media Centre, Morton Way, HORNCASTLE, LN9 6JR **Tel:** 01507 529448
Email: spalmer@mortons.co.uk
Advertising Address: As above. **Tel:** 01507 529300
Fax: 01507 529499
Email: hrmartin@mortons.co.uk
Web site: http://www.organicgardeningmagazine.co.uk
ISSN: 0953-7465
Publisher: Mortons Media Group Ltd
Date Established: 1988
Frequency: Monthly
Cover Price: £3.10
Annual Sub.: £29.95
Circulation: 13,500 (Publisher's Statement)
Usual Pagination: 60
Editor: Sarah Palmer
Summary of Content: Magazine featuring all areas of gardening based on organic methods which rely on organic soil enrichment.
Readership/Target Audience: Aimed at amateur gardeners.
ADVERTISING RATES:
Full Page Colour £844.00
Agency Commission: 10%
Mechanical Data: Film: Digital, Trim Size: 297 x 210mm, Bleed Size: 307 x 216mm, Type Area: 270 x 188mm, Col Length: 270mm, Page Width: 188mm
Copy instructions: Copy Date: 3 weeks prior to publication date
Average advertising content per issue: 15%
CONSUMER: GARDENING

ORGANISTS' REVIEW
46175U76D-388

Editorial Address: 12 Broadfields Road, BIRMINGHAM, B23 5TL **Tel:** 0121 373 0285
Email: sarah@organistsreview.com
Advertising Address: Rose Cottage, Brigg Road, South Kelsey, MARKET RASEN, LN7 6PQ **Tel:** 01652 678230
Fax: 01652 678230

Email: jane@iao.org.uk
Web site: http://www.organistsreview.com
Publisher: Incorporated Association of Organists
Date Established: 1913
Frequency: Quarterly
Cover Price: £5.45
Circulation: 6,000 (Publisher's Statement)
Usual Pagination: 112
Editor: Sarah Beedle; **Advertising Manager:** Jane Beeson; **Managing Editor:** Fiona Chryssides
Summary of Content: Magazine containing features on organs, organ music and organists. Contains special review sections.
Readership/Target Audience: Aimed at organists, choirmasters, clergy, organ builders and lovers of classical organ music and instruments.
ADVERTISING RATES:
Full Page Mono £375.00
Full Page Colour £375.00
Agency Commission: 10%
Mechanical Data: Type Area: 252 x 185mm, Col Length: 252mm, Trim Size: 297 x 210mm, Page Width: 185mm, Film: Digital
Copy instructions: Copy Date: 8 weeks prior to publication date
Average advertising content per issue: 33%
CONSUMER: MUSIC & PERFORMING ARTS: Music

ORGANIZATION
47531U84A-325_20

Editorial Address: 1 Oliver's Yard, 55 City Road, LONDON, EC1Y 1SP **Tel:** 020 7324 8500 **Fax:** 020 7324 8600
Email: claire.lazzeri@sagepub.co.uk
Advertising Address: As above.
Email: advertising@sagepub.co.uk
Web site: http://www.sagepub.co.uk
ISSN: 1350-5084
Publisher: Sage Publications
Date Established: 1994
Frequency: 6 issues yearly
Annual Sub.: £56.00
Circulation: 675 (Publisher's Statement)
Usual Pagination: 640
Editor: Glenn Morgan; **Advertising Manager:** Sheena Karim
Summary of Content: Major forum for scholarly dialogue and innovation in organisation studies.
Readership/Target Audience: Aimed at those interested in organisation studies.
Agency Commission: 5%
CONSUMER: THE ARTS & LITERARY: Arts

ORYX - THE INTERNATIONAL JOURNAL OF CONSERVATION
47192U81X-180

Editorial Address: Flora & Fauna International, 4th Floor, Jupiter House, Station Road, CAMBRIDGE, CB1 2JD
Tel: 01223 571000 **Fax:** 01223 461481
Email: oryx@fauna-flora.org
Advertising Address: The Edinburgh Building, Shaftesbury Road, CAMBRIDGE, CB2 8RU **Tel:** 01223 326070
Fax: 01223 325150
Email: ad_sales@cambridge.org
Web site: http://journals.cambridge.org/jid_oryx
ISSN: 0030-6053
Publisher: Cambridge University Press
Date Established: 1903
Frequency: Quarterly
Annual Sub.: £240.00
Circulation: 2,700 (Publisher's Statement)
Usual Pagination: 96
Editor: Elizabeth Allen
Summary of Content: Journal providing a comprehensive view of the conservation of wild species of fauna and flora.
Readership/Target Audience: Aimed at conservation professionals, members of academic institutions specialising in wildlife conservation, government departments and non-governmental conservation organisations. Also students in conservation-related disciplines and those with an interest.
ADVERTISING RATES:
Full Page Mono £545.00
Full Page Colour £1395.00
Mechanical Data: Page Width: 170mm, Type Area: 250 x 170mm, Col Length: 250mm, Film: Digital
Copy instructions: Copy Date: 8 weeks prior to publication date
CONSUMER: ANIMALS & PETS

OS MAGAZINE
36796U74J-120

Editorial Address: 15 Grangers Place, WITNEY, OX28 4BS
Tel: 01993 775545 **Fax:** 01993 778884
Email: paul.ormond@peeblesmedia.com
Advertising Address: As above.
Email: paul.ormond@peeblesmedia.com
Web site: http://www.osmagazine.co.uk
Publisher: Peebles Media Group Ltd
Date Established: 1975
Frequency: 6 issues yearly
Free to qualifying individuals

Annual Sub.: £31.00
Circulation: 22,520 (ABC 01/07/2008 to 30/06/2009)
Usual Pagination: 50
Editor: Paul Ormond; **Advertising Manager:** Paul Ormond
Summary of Content: Magazine covering personal development, trends in modern working, career planning, personal finance, travel, health and well-being, beauty, motoring and lifestyle.
Readership/Target Audience: Aimed at executive and senior secretaries, PAs and office managers.
ADVERTISING RATES:
Full Page Mono £3600.00
Full Page Colour £3600.00
Agency Commission: 10%
Mechanical Data: Page Width: 185mm, Type Area: 270 x 185mm, Trim Size: 297 x 210mm, Bleed Size: 303 x 216mm, Col Length: 270mm, Film: Digital
Copy instructions: Copy Date: 2 weeks prior to publication date
Average advertising content per issue: 25%
CONSUMER: WOMEN'S INTEREST CONSUMER MAGAZINES: Secretary & PA

OSTEOPOROSIS NEWS
1645560U94F-994

Editorial Address: NOS, Skinners Hill, Camerton, BATH, BA2 0PJ **Tel:** 01761 471771 **Fax:** 01761 479271
Email: d.hall@nos.org.uk
Advertising Address: As above. **Tel:** 01761 471777
Fax: 01761 471104
Email: media@nos.org.uk
Web site: http://www.nos.org.uk
Publisher: National Osteoporosis Society
Frequency: Quarterly
Free to qualifying individuals
Circulation: 25,000 (Publisher's Statement)
Usual Pagination: 24
Editor: Dom Hall; **Advertising Manager:** Siobhan Hallmark
Summary of Content: Magazine of the National Osteoporosis Society providing news and information on the activities of the Society as well as covering a range of goods, services and editorial on osteoporosis issues.
Readership/Target Audience: Aimed at men and women with osteoporosis.
ADVERTISING RATES:
Full Page Colour £2510.00
Mechanical Data: Film: Digital, Print Process: Web-fed offset litho, Type Area: 279 x 195mm, Trim Size: 297 x 216mm, Col Length: 279mm, Page Width: 195mm
CONSUMER: OTHER CLASSIFICATIONS: Disability

THE OTHER SIDE
1810701U89C-1102

Editorial Address: 20 Hollickwood Avenue, LONDON, N12 0LT **Tel:** 07939 938805
Email: editor@theothersidemag.co.uk
Advertising Address: As above.
Email: info@tosmag.co.uk
Web site: http://www.theothersidemag.co.uk
Publisher: The Other Side Magazine
Date Established: 2007
Frequency: Monthly
Cover Price: Free
Circulation: 25,000 (Print Run)
Usual Pagination: 16
Editor: Sam Lassman Watts
Summary of Content: Magazine covering things going on around the Northern Line with comment, reviews and features.
Readership/Target Audience: Aimed at passengers on Northern Line tube trains.
ADVERTISING RATES:
Full Page Mono £800.00
Full Page Colour £950.00
Agency Commission: 10%
Mechanical Data: Film: Digital
Copy instructions: Copy Date: 1st of the month
Average advertising content per issue: 5%
CONSUMER: HOLIDAYS & TRAVEL: Entertainment Guides

OUR BEST FRIENDS
1897647U81-1

Editorial Address: 21 The Maltings, Bures, SUFFOLK, CO8 5EJ **Tel:** 01787 228027
Email: rescue@jspmedia.co.uk
Web site: http://rescueapet.co.uk
Publisher: Jennifer Prowse Media Services Ltd
Editor: Jennifer Prowse
Summary of Content: Magazine featuring animal rescue and re-homing.
Readership/Target Audience: Aimed at individuals who are interested in adopting a rescue animal.
CONSUMER: ANIMALS & PETS

OUR DIOCESAN FAMILY
1841175U87-2053

Editorial Address: PO Box 8455, NEWARK, NG23 5WX
Tel: 01636 525607

Email: johnclawson@xln.co.uk
Advertising Address: As above.
Email: johnclawson@xln.co.uk
Publisher: Bellcourt Limited
Frequency: 6 issues yearly
Cover Price: Free
Circulation: 9,000 (Publisher's Statement)
Usual Pagination: 12
Editor: John Clawson; **Managing Director:** John Clawson; **Advertising Manager:** John Clawson
Summary of Content: Newspaper covering religious topics, events, news and opinion.
Readership/Target Audience: Aimed at Roman Catholic churchgoers in the Diocese of East Anglia.
ADVERTISING: Rates on application
CONSUMER: RELIGIOUS

OUR DOGS
47107U81B-150

Editorial Address: 1 Lund Street, MANCHESTER, M16 9EJ
Tel: 0870 731 6500 **Fax:** 0870 731 6501
Email: editorial@ourdogs.co.uk
Advertising Address: As above. **Tel:** 0161 236 2660
Fax: 0870 731 6699
Email: adverts@ourdogs.co.uk
Web site: http://www.ourdogs.co.uk
Publisher: Our Dogs Centenary Ltd
Date Established: 1895
Frequency: Weekly
Cover Price: £2.00
Circulation: 18,000 (Publisher's Statement)
Usual Pagination: 64
Editor: Alison Smith; **News Editor:** Leanne Ridgley; **Managing Director:** Vince Hogan; **Advertising Manager:** John Holden; **Publisher:** David Cavill
Summary of Content: Magazine containing breeding and exhibiting news, plus show reports.
Readership/Target Audience: Read by owners of all breeds of dog.
ADVERTISING RATES:
Full Page Mono £576.00
Full Page Colour £795.00
SCC £5.50
Agency Commission: 10%
Mechanical Data: Col Length: 365mm, Film: Negative, right reading, emulsion side down. Digital, No. of Columns (Display): 6, Type Area: 365 x 265mm, Page Width: 265mm, Print Process: Web-fed offset litho, Trim Size: 400 x 289mm, Col Widths (Display): 41mm
Copy instructions: Copy Date: Friday 2pm prior to publication date
Average advertising content per issue: 25%
CONSUMER: ANIMALS & PETS: Dogs

OUR LADY'S NEWSLETTER
47846U87-182_5

Editorial Address: St. Benedicts, 1 Manor Road, Kemp Town, BRIGHTON, BN2 5EA **Tel:** 01273 680720
Fax: 01273 680527
Email: osb@graceandcompassion.co.uk
Web site: http://www.graceandcompassion.co.uk
Publisher: Our Lady's Newsletter
Date Established: 1956
Frequency: 3 issues yearly - Published at Easter, autumn and Christmas
Annual Sub.: £5.00
Circulation: 5,000 (Publisher's Statement)
Usual Pagination: 24
Editor: Peter McMenemy
Summary of Content: Newsletter of the Congregation of the Grace and Compassion Benedictines.
Readership/Target Audience: Aimed at Roman Catholics, and other supporters of the charity.
ADVERTISING: No Advertising taken
CONSUMER: RELIGIOUS

OUR TIME
1641678U74N-188

Editorial Address: Winship Road, Milton, CAMBRIDGE, CB24 6PP **Tel:** 01223 434409 **Fax:** 01223 434415
Email: chris.elliott@cambridge-news.co.uk
Advertising Address: As above. **Tel:** 01223 434434
Fax: 01223 434222
Email: caroline.harland@cambridge-news.co.uk
Web site: http://www.cambridge-news.co.uk
ISSN: 1743-4114
Publisher: Cambridge Newspapers Ltd
Date Established: 2004
Frequency: Quarterly
Cover Price: £1.50
Circulation: 10,000 (Print Run)
Usual Pagination: 68
Editor: Chris Elliott; **Advertising Manager:** Caroline Harland
Summary of Content: Magazine covering nostalgia, local news and some international news and puzzles.
Readership/Target Audience: Aimed at the over 50s in Cambridgeshire and the surrounding area.
ADVERTISING RATES:
Full Page Colour £500.00

Mechanical Data: Type Area: 330 x 255mm, Col Length: 330mm, Page Width: 255mm, Film: Digital
Average advertising content per issue: 15%
CONSUMER: WOMEN'S INTEREST CONSUMER MAGAZINES: Retirement

OUT & ABOUT
48126U89C-320

Formerly: Out & About Berkshire
Editorial Address: Newspaper House, Faraday Road, NEWBURY, RG14 2DW **Tel:** 01635 564530
Fax: 01635 522922
Email: out&about@newburynews.co.uk
Advertising Address: As above. **Tel:** 01635 550444
Fax: 01635 46052
Email: advert@newburynews.co.uk
Web site: http://www.newburytoday.co.uk
Publisher: NWN (Printers) Ltd
Date Established: 1986
Frequency: Monthly
Cover Price: Free
Circulation: 28,000 (Publisher's Statement)
Usual Pagination: 64
Editor: Katherine Broomfield; **Managing Director:** Adrian Martin
Summary of Content: Magazine covering leisure facilities, entertainment, features, travel, events and local interest. Also includes property and special themed features.
Readership/Target Audience: Aimed at those interested in local events.
ADVERTISING RATES:
Full Page Colour £510.00
Agency Commission: 10%
Mechanical Data: Film: Digital, Type Area: 282 x 200mm, Bleed Size: 307 x 220mm, Page Width: 200mm, Col Length: 282mm
Copy instructions: Copy Date: 3 weeks prior to publication date
Average advertising content per issue: 70%
Supplement to: Newbury Weekly News Series
CONSUMER: HOLIDAYS & TRAVEL: Entertainment Guides

OUT IN THE CITY
1812714U86B-182

Editorial Address: 37 Ivor Place, LONDON, NW1 6EA
Tel: 020 7258 1777 **Fax:** 020 7258 1787
Email: hudson@outmag.co.uk
Advertising Address: As above.
Email: dan@g3mag.co.uk
Web site: http://www.outmag.co.uk
Publisher: Square Peg Media
Date Established: 2006
Frequency: Monthly
Cover Price: Free
Circulation: 40,000 (Publisher's Statement)
Usual Pagination: 116
Editor: David Hudson; **Publisher:** Linda Riley
Summary of Content: Lifestyle magazine covering arts, music, film, fashion, travel, health and property.
Readership/Target Audience: Aimed at gay men in London.
ADVERTISING RATES:
Full Page Colour £2500.00
Agency Commission: 10%
Mechanical Data: Bleed Size: 303 x 216mm, Trim Size: 297 x 210mm, Film: Digital
Average advertising content per issue: 50%
CONSUMER: ADULT & GAY MAGAZINES: Gay & Lesbian Magazines

OUT OF HAND
1674207U89C-1039

Editorial Address: Hebron House, Sion Road, BRISTOL, BS3 3BD **Tel:** 0117 953 6363 **Fax:** 0117 953 6364
Email: editor@outofhand.co.uk
Advertising Address: As above.
Email: ads@outofhand.co.uk
Web site: http://www.outofhand.co.uk
Publisher: Out of Hand Ltd
Frequency: Monthly
Cover Price: Free
Circulation: 30,000 (Publisher's Statement)
Usual Pagination: 68
Editor: Melanie Joslin; **Advertising Manager:** William Long
Summary of Content: Entertainment magazine featuring regional and national entertainment news, interviews, film and album reviews, competitions, club, gig and comedy previews and listings.
Readership/Target Audience: Aimed at people aged between 18 and 35 years old.
ADVERTISING RATES:
Full Page Mono £540.00
Full Page Colour £540.00
Mechanical Data: Type Area: 230 x 158mm, Col Length: 230mm, Page Width: 158mm, Film: Digital
CONSUMER: HOLIDAYS & TRAVEL: Entertainment Guides

OUTDOOR ADVENTURE GUIDE
1663245U75L-807

Editorial Address: South Wing, Broadway Court, Broadway, PETERBOROUGH, PE1 1RP **Tel:** 01733 293250
Fax: 01733 293269
Email: hannah@fall-line.co.uk
Advertising Address: As above. **Fax:** 01733 293263
Email: georgie@fall-line.co.uk
Web site: http://www.outdooradventureguide.co.uk
Publisher: Fall Line Media Limited
Date Established: 2004
Frequency: Annual - Published in June
Circulation: 25,000 (Print Run)
Usual Pagination: 156
Editor: Richard Fincher; **Advertising Manager:** Georgie Horgan; **Publisher:** Richard Fincher
Summary of Content: Magazine covering outdoor adventure sport including mountain biking, climbing, golf, white water rafting, safaris, sky-diving, fishing and trekking as well as where to go and what to do, weekend adventure breaks, family trips, gear tests, travel, tips, news and updates.
Readership/Target Audience: Aimed at 30 to 45 year old men and women with a high disposable income.
ADVERTISING RATES:
Full Page Colour £1600.00
Agency Commission: 10%
Mechanical Data: Type Area: 275 x 190mm, Bleed Size: 303 x 216mm, Trim Size: 297 x 210mm, Col Length: 275mm, Page Width: 190mm, Film: Digital
Average advertising content per issue: 30%
CONSUMER: SPORT: Outdoor

OUTDOOR PHOTOGRAPHY
624149U85A-125

Editorial Address: 86 High Street, LEWES, BN7 1XN
Tel: 01273 477374 **Fax:** 01273 402849
Email: stevew@thegmcgroup.com
Advertising Address: As above. **Tel:** 01234 477374
Email: ads@thegmcgroup.com
Web site: http://www.gmcpubs.com
ISSN: 0965-9463
Publisher: GMC Publications Ltd
Date Established: 2000
Frequency: 13 issues yearly
Cover Price: £3.75
Annual Sub.: £40.50
Circulation: 35,000 (Print Run)
Usual Pagination: 112
Editor: Steve Watkins
Summary of Content: Magazine focusing on outdoor photography. Covers landscape, wildlife, nature, architecture and outdoor events.
Readership/Target Audience: Aimed at photographers with a passion for outdoor photography.
ADVERTISING RATES:
Full Page Colour £1064.00
Agency Commission: 10%
Mechanical Data: Type Area: 268 x 195mm, Bleed Size: 303 x 236mm, Trim Size: 297 x 230mm, Film: Digital, Col Length: 268mm, Page Width: 195mm
Copy instructions: Copy Date: 4 weeks prior to publication date
Average advertising content per issue: 25%
CONSUMER: PHOTOGRAPHY & FILM MAKING: Photography

OUTLOOK
47842U87-182_7

Editorial Address: Collard House, School Lane, Hadlow, TONBRIDGE, TN11 0EH **Tel:** 01732 850850
ISSN: 0969-1049
Publisher: Seminar Books
Date Established: 1992
Frequency: Half-yearly - Published in February and August
Cover Price: Free
Circulation: 2,500 (Print Run)
Usual Pagination: 12
Editor: G. Roland Smith; **Circulation Manager:** David Friend
Summary of Content: Journal covering spiritual and religious matters.
Readership/Target Audience: Aimed at those who form ideas or opinions relating to religious and spiritual matters.
ADVERTISING: No Advertising taken
CONSUMER: RELIGIOUS

OUTNORTHWEST
1694447U86B-170

Editorial Address: Princess House, 105-107 Princess Street, MANCHESTER, M1 6DD **Tel:** 0161 235 8035
Fax: 0161 235 8036
Email: grahame@lgf.org.uk
Advertising Address: As above. **Tel:** 0161 235 8021
Email: jo@lgf.org.uk
Web site: http://www.lgf.org.uk
Publisher: The Lesbian & Gay Foundation
Date Established: 2003
Frequency: Monthly

Cover Price: Free
Circulation: 15,000 (Publisher's Statement)
Usual Pagination: 72
Editor: Grahame Robertson
Summary of Content: Lesbian, gay, bisexual and transgender magazine covering community news, health, scene, lifestyle and culture.
Readership/Target Audience: Aimed at the LGBT of the North West of England.
ADVERTISING RATES:
Full Page Colour £650.00
Agency Commission: 10%
Mechanical Data: Type Area: 277 x 190mm, Col Length: 277mm, Page Width: 190mm, Bleed Size: 307 x 220mm, Trim Size: 297 x 210mm, Film: Digital
Copy instructions: Copy Date: 1 week prior to publication date
Average advertising content per issue: 25%
CONSUMER: ADULT & GAY MAGAZINES: Gay & Lesbian Magazines

OUTRAGE
47086U81A-140

Editorial Address: The Old Chapel, Bradford Street, TONBRIDGE, TN9 1AW **Tel:** 01732 364546
Fax: 01732 366533
Email: info@animalaid.org.uk
Advertising Address: As above.
Email: info@animalaid.org.uk
Web site: http://www.animalaid.org.uk
ISSN: 1466-206X
Publisher: Animal Aid
Date Established: 1977
Frequency: Quarterly
Free to qualifying individuals
Annual Sub.: £18.00
Circulation: 14,500 (Publisher's Statement)
Usual Pagination: 24
Editor: Mark Gold; **Advertising Manager:** Richard Mountford
Summary of Content: Magazine covering news and articles about the use and abuse of animals.
Readership/Target Audience: Read by Animal Aid members.
ADVERTISING RATES:
Full Page Mono £550.00
Full Page Colour £550.00
SCC £12.00
Agency Commission: 10%
Mechanical Data: Type Area: 265 x 195mm, Col Length: 265mm, Page Width: 195mm
Copy instructions: Copy Date: 6 weeks prior to publication date
Average advertising content per issue: 8%
CONSUMER: ANIMALS & PETS: Animals & Pets Protection

OVERSEAS
48704U94X-138

Editorial Address: Over-Seas House, Park Place, St. James's Street, LONDON, SW1A 1LR **Tel:** 020 7408 0214
Fax: 020 7499 6738
Email: swhitaker@rosl.org.uk
Advertising Address: As above.
Web site: http://www.rosl.org.uk
ISSN: 00307424
Publisher: Royal Over-Seas League
Date Established: 1915
Frequency: Quarterly
Free to qualifying individuals
Circulation: 21,000 (Publisher's Statement)
Usual Pagination: 30
Editor: Miranda Moore
Summary of Content: Journal of the Royal Over-Seas League. Contains feature articles on Commonwealth countries and reports of League activities and events.
Readership/Target Audience: Read by members of the Royal Over-Seas League.
ADVERTISING RATES:
Full Page Mono £690.00
Full Page Colour £920.00
Mechanical Data: Film: Digital
CONSUMER: OTHER CLASSIFICATIONS: Miscellaneous

OVERSEAS PROPERTY TRADER
1849797U74K-790

Editorial Address: Bury Business Park, Kay Street, BURY, BL9 6BU **Tel:** 0161 909 0909 **Fax:** 0161 909 0919
Email: dave.beevers@bigspark.co.uk
Web site: http://www.overseaspropertytrader.co.uk
Publisher: Simple World Ltd
Frequency: Quarterly
Cover Price: Free
Circulation: 105,000 (Publisher's Statement)
Usual Pagination: 68
Editor: Dave Beevers
Summary of Content: Magazine covering property worldwide including villas and apartments to buy, sell or let as well as financial advice.

Readership/Target Audience: Aimed at affluent supermarket shoppers.
CONSUMER: WOMEN'S INTEREST CONSUMER MAGAZINES: Home Purchase

THE OXFORD STUDENT
47422U83-59

Editorial Address: Thomas Hull House, New Inn Hall Street, OXFORD, OX1 2DH **Tel:** 01865 288657 **Fax:** 01865 288450
Email: editors@oxfordstudent.com
Advertising Address: As above. **Tel:** 01865 288450
Fax: 01865 288453
Email: business@ousu.org
Web site: http://www.oxfordstudent.com
Publisher: Oxford University Student Union
Date Established: 1990
Frequency: 24 issues yearly - 8 editions published weekly during Oxford University term time
Cover Price: Free
Circulation: 4,000 (Publisher's Statement)
Usual Pagination: 36
Advertising Manager: Dave Green
Summary of Content: Magazine containing news, features, sport, letters, comment, drama, film, books, music, fashion and columns. Strong focus on Oxford-related news and features, with reviews of local and national arts and music.
Readership/Target Audience: Aimed at students.
ADVERTISING RATES:
Full Page Colour £1100.00
Agency Commission: 10%
Mechanical Data: Type Area: 348 x 274mm, Col Length: 348mm, Page Width: 274mm
Copy instructions: Copy Date: Friday preceding publication date
Average advertising content per issue: 20%
CONSUMER: STUDENT PUBLICATIONS

OXFORDSHIRE HOMES
1692971U74K-742

Editorial Address: Newspaper House, Osney Mead, OXFORD, OX2 0EJ **Tel:** 01865 425262 **Fax:** 01865 425554
Email: tim.metcalfe@nqo.com
Advertising Address: As above. **Fax:** 01865 425334
Email: mvale@nqo.com
Web site: http://www.thisisoxfordshire.co.uk
Publisher: Newsquest (Oxfordshire) Ltd
Frequency: Quarterly
Cover Price: Free
Circulation: 26,860 (Publisher's Statement)
Usual Pagination: 40
Editor: Geoffrey Hedge; **Advertising Manager:** Maureen Vale
Summary of Content: Magazine covering property in Oxfordshire, interiors, news, buying online and overseas property.
Readership/Target Audience: Aimed at readers of the Oxford Times.
ADVERTISING RATES:
Full Page Colour £500.00
Agency Commission: 10%
Mechanical Data: Type Area: 270 x 190mm, Bleed Size: 303 x 216mm, Col Length: 270mm, Page Width: 190mm, Film: Digital, Trim Size: 297 x 210mm
Copy instructions: Copy Date: 2 weeks prior to publication date
Average advertising content per issue: 40%
Supplement to: The Oxford Times
CONSUMER: WOMEN'S INTEREST CONSUMER MAGAZINES: Home Purchase

OXFORDSHIRE LIMITED EDITION
46957U80C-2630

Formerly: Limited Edition (Oxfordshire)
Editorial Address: Newspaper House, Osney Mead, OXFORD, OX2 0EJ **Tel:** 01865 425470 **Fax:** 01865 425554
Email: tim.metcalfe@nqo.com
Advertising Address: As above. **Tel:** 01865 425262
Fax: 01865 425557
Email: lisa.hurren@nqo.com
Web site: http://www.thisislimitededition.co.uk
Publisher: Newsquest (Oxfordshire) Ltd
Frequency: Monthly
Cover Price: Free
Circulation: 34,000 (Publisher's Statement)
Usual Pagination: 108
Editor: Tim Metcalfe; **Advertising Manager:** Lisa Hurren
Summary of Content: Magazine containing general interest county news and lifestyle features including beauty and fashion features.
Readership/Target Audience: Aimed at residents and visitors to Oxfordshire.
ADVERTISING RATES:
Full Page Colour £990.00
Agency Commission: 10%
Mechanical Data: Type Area: 270 x 190mm, Trim Size: 297 x 210mm, Col Length: 270mm, Page Width: 190mm, Film: Digital, Bleed Size: 303 x 216mm

Copy instructions: Copy Date: 2 weeks prior to publication date
Average advertising content per issue: 40%
Supplement to: Herald and Times Series Oxon
Supplement(s): Limited Edition (Oxfordshire) Grow - 1xY, Limited Edition (Oxfordshire) Imago - 1xY, Limited Edition (Oxfordshire) Interiors - 1xY
CONSUMER: RURAL & REGIONAL INTEREST: Regional Interest English Counties

OXFORDSHIRE LIVING
1693387U80C-5274
Editorial Address: 9-11 Cholswell Court, ABINGDON, OX13 6HX **Tel:** 01235 553444
Email: john@youroxfordshire.co.uk
Advertising Address: As above. **Fax:** 01253 554465
Email: fil@youroxfordshire.co.uk
Web site: http://www.youroxfordshire.co.uk
Publisher: Tri Media Group
Date Established: 2004
Frequency: Monthly
Cover Price: Free
Circulation: 20,000 (Publisher's Statement)
Usual Pagination: 68
Editor: John Stanley; **Features Editor:** John Stanley
Summary of Content: Lifestyle magazine featuring property, food, travel, arts, gardens, motoring, fashion, beauty, health and fitness, shopping, business and entertainment as well as people places and events.
Readership/Target Audience: Aimed at households in Oxfordshire as well as local businesses.
ADVERTISING RATES:
Full Page Colour £900.00
Agency Commission: 10%
Mechanical Data: Type Area: 262 x 177mm, Bleed Size: 303 x 216mm, Trim Size: 297 x 210mm, Col Length: 262mm, Page Width: 177mm, Film: Digital
Copy instructions: Copy Date: 1 week prior to publication date
Average advertising content per issue: 40%
CONSUMER: RURAL & REGIONAL INTEREST: Regional Interest English Counties

THE PAKISTAN POST
1778649U90-999
Editorial Address: 779 High Road, Leytonstone, LONDON, E11 4QS **Tel:** 020 8558 9127 **Fax:** 020 8558 2247
Email: hazratpk@hotmail.com
Advertising Address: As above.
Email: kash@theasianpost.co.uk
Publisher: Hussain Media
Date Established: 2000
Frequency: Weekly
Cover Price: £0.70
Free to qualifying individuals
Circulation: 40,000 (Publisher's Statement)
Usual Pagination: 28
Editor: Murtaza Ali; **Advertising Manager:** Kash Hussain
Summary of Content: Newspaper covering news mainly on issues concerned with Muslims and British Pakistani communities in the UK, Pakistan and the wider world.
Readership/Target Audience: Aimed at Pakistani communities in the UK.
ADVERTISING RATES:
Full Page Mono £4000.00
Full Page Colour £5600.00
Agency Commission: 10%
Mechanical Data: Type Area: 480 x 370mm, Col Length: 480mm, Page Width: 370mm, Film: Digital
Copy instructions: Copy Date: 1 week prior to publication date
CONSUMER: ETHNIC

PAN
46176U76D-388_10
Editorial Address: 1 Doveridge Gardens, LONDON, N13 5BJ **Tel:** 020 8882 2627 **Fax:** 020 8882 2728
Email: editor@bfs.org.uk
Advertising Address: 27 Eskdale Gardens, PURLEY, CR8 1ET **Tel:** 020 8668 3360
Email: secretary@bfs.org.uk
Web site: http://www.bfs.org.uk
ISSN: 1360-1563
Publisher: British Flute Society
Date Established: 1983
Frequency: Quarterly
Annual Sub.: £25.00
Circulation: 2,000 (Publisher's Statement)
Usual Pagination: 64
Editor: Robert Bigio; **Advertising Manager:** Anna Munks
Summary of Content: Magazine of the British Flute Society containing articles on all aspects of the flute and flute playing. Includes a guide to the latest flute news, listings of concerts, courses and reviews of new music, books and recordings.
Readership/Target Audience: Read by members of the British Flute Society and those interested in the flute.
ADVERTISING RATES:
Full Page Mono £295.00
Full Page Colour £370.00

Agency Commission: 10%
Mechanical Data: Bleed Size: 252 x 195mm, Trim Size: 246 x 189mm, Film: Digital
Copy instructions: Copy Date: 8 weeks prior to publication date
CONSUMER: MUSIC & PERFORMING ARTS: Music

PANJAB TIMES INTERNATIONAL
48338U90-118
Formerly: Punjab Times International
Editorial Address: 21 Cotton Brook Road, Sir Francis Ley Industrial Park, DERBY, DE23 8YJ **Tel:** 01332 372851
Fax: 01332 372833
Email: panjabtimes@gmail.com
Advertising Address: As above.
Email: panjabtimes@aol.com
Publisher: PTI Derby Ltd
Date Established: 1965
Frequency: Weekly
Cover Price: £1.40
Annual Sub.: £85.00
Circulation: 42,000 (Publisher's Statement)
Usual Pagination: 68
Editor: Rajinder Purewal; **Advertising Manager:** Sulakhan Singh
Summary of Content: Publication covering news and features from Northern India and Pakistan.
Language(s): English; Punjabi
Readership/Target Audience: Aimed at the Punjabi community in Britain.
ADVERTISING RATES:
Full Page Mono £862.00
Full Page Colour £1232.00
Agency Commission: 15%
Mechanical Data: Film: Digital, Type Area: 334 x 230mm, No. of Columns (Display): 4, Page Width: 230mm, Col Length: 334mm
Copy instructions: Copy Date: 5 days prior to publication date
CONSUMER: ETHNIC

PAPERCRAFT ESSENTIALS
1696016U74E-695
Formerly: Craft Essentials
Editorial Address: Unit 1 Adlington Court, Adlington Industrial Estate, Adlington, MACCLESFIELD, SK10 4NL
Tel: 0844 561 1202 **Fax:** 01625 855011
Email: info@practicalpublishing.co.uk
Advertising Address: As above.
Email: danny.bowler@practicalpublishing.co.uk
Web site: http://www.practicalpublishing.co.uk/papercraftessentials
ISSN: 1744-8411
Publisher: Practical Publishing International Ltd
Frequency: Monthly
Cover Price: £3.99
Circulation: 20,000 (Publisher's Statement)
Usual Pagination: 100
Editor: Melanie Tickle; **Advertising Manager:** Lisa Sturgeon
Summary of Content: Magazine covering predominantly papercraft as well as general craft with hints, tips, ideas, money saving suggestions and step by step instructions.
Readership/Target Audience: Aimed at anyone with an interest in papercraft.
ADVERTISING RATES:
Full Page Colour £900.00
Agency Commission: 10%
Mechanical Data: Type Area: 275 x 210mm, Bleed Size: 303 x 236mm, Trim Size: 297 x 230mm, Col Length: 275mm, Page Width: 210mm, Film: Digital
Copy instructions: Copy Date: 3 weeks prior to publication date
Average advertising content per issue: 20%
CONSUMER: WOMEN'S INTEREST CONSUMER MAGAZINES: Crafts

PAPERCRAFT INSPIRATIONS
1650614U79R-151
Editorial Address: 30 Monmouth Street, BATH, BA1 2BW
Tel: 01225 442244
Email: papercraft@futurenet.com
Advertising Address: As above. **Fax:** 01225 732206
Email: amanda.haughey@futurenet.com
Web site: http://www.papercraftinspirationsmagazine.co.uk
Publisher: Future Publishing Ltd
Date Established: 2004
Frequency: 13 issues yearly
Cover Price: £3.99
Circulation: 39,309 (ABC 01/01/2008 to 31/12/2008)
Usual Pagination: 100
Editor: Jenny Dixon; **Advertising Manager:** Amanda Haughey
Summary of Content: Magazine covering cards, papercrafts and scrapbooking.
Readership/Target Audience: Aimed at women aged between 35 and 55 years old.
ADVERTISING RATES:
Full Page Mono £1290.00

Full Page Colour £1290.00
Agency Commission: 10%
Mechanical Data: Type Area: 270 x 190mm, Bleed Size: 303 x 216mm, Trim Size: 297 x 210mm, Col Length: 270mm, Page Width: 190mm, Film: Digital
Copy instructions: Copy Date: 4 weeks prior to publication date
Average advertising content per issue: 10%
CONSUMER: HOBBIES & DIY: Hobbies & DIY Related

PAPERS OF THE BRITISH SCHOOL AT ROME
48810U94X-140
Editorial Address: The British Academy, 10 Carlton House Terrace, LONDON, SW1Y 5AH **Tel:** 020 7969 5202
Fax: 020 7969 5401
Email: bsr@britac.ac.uk
Web site: http://www.bsr.ac.uk
ISSN: 0068-2462
Publisher: The British School at Rome
Date Established: 1902
Frequency: Annual - Published in November
Annual Sub.: £50.00
Circulation: 850 (Publisher's Statement)
Usual Pagination: 360
Editor: Gill Clark
Summary of Content: Publication covering archaeology, classics and history including ancient, medieval, modern and art history relating to Italy and the Mediterranean.
Language(s): English; Italian
Readership/Target Audience: Aimed at academic institutions, students partaking in Higher Education and researchers.
ADVERTISING: No Advertising taken
CONSUMER: OTHER CLASSIFICATIONS: Miscellaneous

DES PARDES
48296U90-47_80
Editorial Address: 8 The Crescent, SOUTHALL, UB1 1BE
Tel: 020 8571 1127 **Fax:** 020 8571 2604
Email: despardesuk@btconnect.com
Advertising Address: As above.
Email: despardesuk@btconnect.com
Web site: http://www.despardesweekly.co.uk
Publisher: C.V Publishers ltd
Date Established: 1965
Frequency: Weekly
Cover Price: £1.50
Annual Sub.: £110.00
Circulation: 34,000 (Publisher's Statement)
Usual Pagination: 68
Editor: Gurbax Virk; **Managing Director:** R. S. Chandan; **Advertising Manager:** Shukla Kochar; **Publisher:** R. S. Chandan
Summary of Content: Magazine covering Indian, UK, European and local news.
Language(s): English; Punjabi
Readership/Target Audience: Aimed at Indian expatriates in UK and Europe.
ADVERTISING RATES:
Full Page Mono £800.00
Full Page Colour £1500.00
Agency Commission: 15%
Mechanical Data: Trim Size: 380 x 250mm, Film: Digital, Type Area: 350 x 230mm, Col Length: 350mm, Page Width: 230mm, No. of Columns (Display): 4
Copy instructions: Copy Date: 7 days prior to publication date
CONSUMER: ETHNIC

PARENT TALK
45338U74D-435
Editorial Address: Horton House, 8 Ditton Street, ILMINSTER, TA19 0BQ **Tel:** 01460 259673
Fax: 01460 259678
Email: sales@parenttalk.biz
Advertising Address: As above.
Email: sales@parenttalk.biz
Publisher: Parent Talk
Date Established: 1997
Frequency: 11 issues yearly - Combined issue in July or August
Free to qualifying individuals
Annual Sub.: £13.00
Circulation: 33,000 (Publisher's Statement)
Usual Pagination: 16
Editor: Tamsin Humphrey; **Advertising Manager:** Juliet Young
Summary of Content: Magazine containing information, competitions and features on education, health, the home, fashion and events.
Readership/Target Audience: Aimed at parents of pre-teen children in Somerset.
ADVERTISING RATES:
Full Page Colour £1000.00
Mechanical Data: Type Area: 358 x 272mm, Col Length: 358mm, Page Width: 272mm
Copy instructions: Copy Date: 10 days prior to publication date

Consumer Magazines

Average advertising content per issue: 80%
CONSUMER: WOMEN'S INTEREST CONSUMER MAGAZINES: Child Care

THE PARENTS GUIDE UK   1773122U74D-645
Editorial Address: Cranes Point, Gardiners Lane South, BASILDON, SS14 3AP Tel: 01268 286070
Fax: 01268 280770
Email: paulmcdonald@focusmediauk.com
Advertising Address: As above.
Email: info@focusmediauk.com
Web site: http://www.theparentsguideuk.com
Publisher: Focus Media Publications Ltd
Date Established: 2005
Frequency: Quarterly
Cover Price: Free
Circulation: 80,000 (Publisher's Statement)
Editor: Paul McDonald; Advertising Manager: Paul McDonald
Summary of Content: Magazine covering education, health, leisure and lifestyle.
Readership/Target Audience: Aimed at parents of children aged 0 to 17 years old. Distributed direct to parents in primary schools, pre-schools, libraries, health centres and supermarkets in Essex.
ADVERTISING RATES:
Full Page Colour £1000.00
Agency Commission: 10%
Mechanical Data: Type Area: 277 x 190mm, Bleed Size: 303 x 216mm, Trim Size: 297 x 210mm, Col Length: 277mm, Page Width: 190mm, Film: Digital
Copy instructions: Copy Date: 2 weeks prior to publication date
Average advertising content per issue: 30%
CONSUMER: WOMEN'S INTEREST CONSUMER MAGAZINES: Child Care

PARENTS NEWS   48128U89C-339
Editorial Address: 10 The Manor Drive, WORCESTER PARK, KT4 7LG Tel: 020 8337 6337 Fax: 020 8337 8363
Email: editorial@parents-news.co.uk
Advertising Address: As above. Fax: 020 8715 2842
Email: fergus@parents-news.co.uk
Web site: http://www.parents-news.co.uk
ISSN: 1362-5551
Publisher: Parents News UK
Date Established: 1993
Frequency: 11 issues yearly
Free to qualifying individuals
Annual Sub.: £13.00
Circulation: 192,000 (Publisher's Statement)
Usual Pagination: 20
Editor: Penny McCarthy; Advertising Manager: Fergus McCarthy
Summary of Content: What's on guide for families. Includes seasonal themes and also covers health, safety, fitness, education, financial planning, dance, drama, music and holidays.
Readership/Target Audience: Aimed at parents of children aged 2 to 14 years old.
ADVERTISING: Rates on application
Agency Commission: 10%
Mechanical Data: Col Length: 350mm, Film: Digital, Type Area: 350 x 265mm, Print Process: Web-fed offset litho, Page Width: 265mm, No. of Columns (Display): 6, Col Widths (Display): 40mm
Copy instructions: Copy Date: 12 days prior to publication date
Average advertising content per issue: 50%
Editions:
Parents News Kent outside the M25
Parents News London, South East Surrey and West Kent
Parents News South West London and Surrey
CONSUMER: HOLIDAYS & TRAVEL: Entertainment Guides

PARENTS' WORLD   1646149U74D-572
Formerly: Parents' Guide
Editorial Address: 1 Chartwell Lodge, 9 Brackley Road, BECKENHAM, BR3 1SW
Email: parents_guide@hotmail.co.uk
Advertising Address: As above. Tel: 020 8663 1604
Email: parents_guide@hotmail.co.uk
Web site: http://www.parents-world.com
Publisher: Lighthouse Publishing
Date Established: 2004
Frequency: 6 issues yearly
Cover Price: Free
Circulation: 150,000 (Publisher's Statement)
Usual Pagination: 80
Editor: Richard Allen; Advertising Manager: Richard Allen
Summary of Content: Magazine covering childcare and education as well as information about nurseries, independent schools, colleges and universities, adoption and fostering, nannies and au pairs, health and food issues. Also covers music, dance, out of school clubs and places to visit.

Readership/Target Audience: Aimed primarily at all parents. Distributed through hotels, high street shops like Mothercare, hospitals, selected high street chemists, nurseries, schools, local libraries, museums, amusement arcaded and selected Sainsbury and Tesco stores.
ADVERTISING: Rates on application
Agency Commission: 15%
Copy instructions: Copy Date: 2 weeks prior to publication date
Average advertising content per issue: 65%
CONSUMER: WOMEN'S INTEREST CONSUMER MAGAZINES: Child Care

PARIKIAKI   48335U90-116_50
Editorial Address: 140 Falkland Road, LONDON, N8 0NP
Tel: 020 8341 0751 Fax: 020 8341 9391
Email: greek.section@parikiaki.com
Advertising Address: As above. Fax: 020 8347 8102
Email: english.section@parikiaki.com
Web site: http://www.parikiaki.net
Publisher: Parikiaki
Date Established: 1974
Frequency: Weekly - Published on Thursday
Cover Price: £0.50
Annual Sub.: £55.00
Circulation: 10,000 (Publisher's Statement)
Usual Pagination: 40
Editor: Bambos Charalambous; Managing Director: Bambos Charalambous; Advertising Manager: Emilia Zannetou
Summary of Content: Publication covering news, arts, travel and sport.
Language(s): English; Greek
Readership/Target Audience: Aimed at the Cypriot community in Britain.
ADVERTISING RATES:
Full Page Mono £480.00
Full Page Colour £590.00
SCC £2.00
Agency Commission: 10%
Mechanical Data: Col Widths (Display): 42mm, No. of Columns (Display): 6, Film: Digital
Copy instructions: Copy Date: 4 days prior to publication date
Average advertising content per issue: 15%
CONSUMER: ETHNIC

PARK & HOLIDAY HOMES   1641730U91B-302
Editorial Address: The Maltings, West Street, BOURNE, PE10 9PH Tel: 01778 392436 Fax: 01778 392422
Email: mikep@warnersgroup.co.uk
Advertising Address: As above. Tel: 01778 391119
Email: darrenw@warnersgroup.co.uk
Web site: http://www.parkandholidayhomes.co.uk
Publisher: Warners Group Publications plc
Date Established: 2004
Frequency: Monthly
Cover Price: £2.80
Circulation: 20,000 (Print Run)
Usual Pagination: 108
Editor: Mike Parker; Publisher: Rob McDonnell
Summary of Content: Magazine covering park and holiday home ownership including new homes, places to live, and holiday, and ideas on refurbishment as well as advice on buying and selling, DIY, gardening, legal and medical matters and lifestyle.
Readership/Target Audience: Aimed at owners and those looking to buy, rent or use holiday homes and residential park homes.
ADVERTISING RATES:
Full Page Mono £885.00
Full Page Colour £1100.00
Agency Commission: 10%
Mechanical Data: Type Area: 275 x 190mm, Trim Size: 297 x 210mm, Film: Digital, Col Length: 275mm, Page Width: 190mm
CONSUMER: RECREATION & LEISURE: Camping & Caravanning

PARK HOME & HOLIDAY CARAVAN   48427U91B-140
Editorial Address: Leon House, 233 High Street, CROYDON, CR9 1HZ Tel: 020 8726 8253
Fax: 020 8726 8299
Email: alex_melvin@ipcmedia.com
Advertising Address: As above. Tel: 020 8726 8000
Fax: 020 8726 8298
Email: sue_chambers@ipcmedia.com
Web site: http://www.phhc.co.uk
ISSN: 0268-4594
Publisher: IPC Inspire
Date Established: 1960
Frequency: 13 issues yearly - Every fourth Friday
Cover Price: £2.90
Annual Sub.: £39.90
Circulation: 14,000 (Publisher's Statement)
Usual Pagination: 148

Editor: Alex Melvin; Publisher: Olive Birch
Summary of Content: Magazine focusing on new and established sites for park homes and caravan holiday homes. Also includes reviews of new models and equipment.
Readership/Target Audience: Aimed at residents and owners of park homes, caravan holiday homes and prospective purchasers.
ADVERTISING RATES:
Full Page Mono £1185.00
Full Page Colour £1945.00
SCC £26.00
Agency Commission: 10%
Mechanical Data: Col Length: 278mm, Type Area: 278 x 190mm, Print Process: Web offset litho, Bleed Size: 304 x 216mm, Trim Size: 298 x 210mm, Page Width: 190mm
Copy instructions: Copy Date: 6 weeks prior to publication date
Supplement(s): Residential Parks Guide - 1xY, What Holiday Caravan - 1xY
CONSUMER: RECREATION & LEISURE: Camping & Caravanning

PARKER'S CAR PRICE GUIDE   1666684U77A-567
Editorial Address: Media House, Lynchwood, Peterborough Business Park, PETERBOROUGH, PE2 6EA
Tel: 01733 468000 Fax: 01733 468650
Email: feedback@parkers.co.uk
Advertising Address: As above. Fax: 01733 468890
Email: katherine.barratt@bauerconsumer.co.uk
Web site: http://www.parkers.co.uk
ISSN: 0958-0662
Publisher: Bauer Consumer Media Ltd (Media House)
Frequency: Monthly
Cover Price: £4.20
Annual Sub.: £75.00
Circulation: 25,462 (ABC 01/01/2008 to 31/12/2008)
Usual Pagination: 340
Editor: Kieren Puffett
Summary of Content: Magazine covering buying and selling advice on new, nearly new and used cars as well as price listings.
Readership/Target Audience: Aimed at those looking to buy a new or used car.
ADVERTISING RATES:
Full Page Colour £1650.00
Agency Commission: 10%
Mechanical Data: Type Area: 200 x 128mm, Bleed Size: 226 x 154mm, Trim Size: 220 x 148mm, Col Length: 200mm, Page Width: 128mm, Film: Digital
Copy instructions: Copy Date: 3 weeks prior to publication date
CONSUMER: MOTORING & CYCLING: Motoring

THE PARKINSON MAGAZINE   48646U94F-700
Editorial Address: 215 Vauxhall Bridge Road, LONDON, SW1V 1EJ Tel: 020 7931 8080 Fax: 020 7233 9908
Email: kmoss@parkinsons.org.uk
Web site: http://www.parkinsons.org.uk
Publisher: Parkinson's Disease Society of the UK
Date Established: 1969
Frequency: Quarterly
Free to qualifying individuals
Annual Sub.: £4.00
Circulation: 24,500 (Publisher's Statement)
Usual Pagination: 40
Editor: Katie Moss
Summary of Content: Magazine of the Parkinson's Disease Society of the UK. Contains news and features on Parkinson's research, treatment, therapies, equipment and views and tips from readers.
Readership/Target Audience: Read by those with Parkinson's disease, their families, carers and professionals involved in the field.
ADVERTISING: No Advertising taken
CONSUMER: OTHER CLASSIFICATIONS: Disability

THE PARLIAMENTARIAN   47347U82-145_60
Editorial Address: Suite 700, Westminster House, Millbank, LONDON, SW1P 3JA Tel: 020 7799 1460
Fax: 020 7222 6073
Email: andrew@cpahq.org
Advertising Address: As above.
Email: andrew@cpahq.org
Web site: http://www.cpahq.org
ISSN: 0031-2282
Publisher: Commonwealth Parliamentary
Date Established: 1920
Frequency: Quarterly
Free to qualifying individuals
Annual Sub.: £34.00
Circulation: 17,000 (Publisher's Statement)
Usual Pagination: 104
Editor: Andrew Imlach; Advertising Manager: Andrew Imlach
Summary of Content: Publication covering all aspects of the Parliaments of the Commonwealth.

Readership/Target Audience: Aimed at those interested in parliamentary systems and international politics.
ADVERTISING RATES:
Full Page Colour £2500.00
Agency Commission: 10%
Mechanical Data: Type Area: 274 x 178mm, Col Length: 274mm, Page Width: 178mm, Bleed Size: 296 x 208mm, Film: Digital
Copy instructions: Copy Date: 1st of the month prior to the month of publication
CONSUMER: CURRENT AFFAIRS & POLITICS

PARLIAMENTARY BRIEF
47264U82-146

Editorial Address: 26 York Street, LONDON, W1U 6PZ
Tel: 020 7381 1611
Email: editor@thepolitician.org
Advertising Address: As above.
Email: roderick@thepolitician.org
Web site: http://www.thepolitician.org
ISSN: 1354-5507
Publisher: Lexington Press Ltd
Date Established: 1992
Frequency: Monthly
Free to qualifying individuals
Annual Sub.: £55.00
Circulation: 2,152 (Publisher's Statement)
Usual Pagination: 32
Editor: Roderick Crawford; **Advertising Manager:** Roderick Crawford
Summary of Content: Magazine containing detailed special reports on specific political subjects. Includes articles on business, education, transport, health care, regeneration, local government and foreign policy.
Readership/Target Audience: Aimed at members of the House of Commons, the House of Lords, Regional Assemblies, Local Government, MEPs, think tanks, academics, the media and opinion formers in and around the government.
ADVERTISING RATES:
Full Page Mono £3950.00
Full Page Colour £3950.00
Agency Commission: 10%
Mechanical Data: Film: Digital, Col Length: 245mm, Type Area: 245 x 180mm, Bleed Size: 275 x 207mm, Trim Size: 267 x 203mm, Page Width: 180mm, No. of Columns (Display): 3
Average advertising content per issue: 25%
Supplement(s): CSR - 1xY, Secondary Schools - 1xY
CONSUMER: CURRENT AFFAIRS & POLITICS

PARROTS
626339U81F-280

Editorial Address: The Old Cart House, Applesham Farm, COOMBES, BN15 0RP **Tel:** 01273 464777
Fax: 01273 463999
Email: parrots@imaxweb.co.uk
Advertising Address: As above.
Email: advertising@imaxweb.co.uk
Web site: http://www.parrotmag.com
ISSN: 1356-3386
Publisher: Imax Ltd
Date Established: 1995
Frequency: Monthly
Cover Price: £3.25
Annual Sub.: £35.75
Usual Pagination: 68
Editor: John Catchpole
Summary of Content: Magazine covering all aspects of keeping of parrots. Includes articles on breeding, general care, veterinarian advice, conservation issues and readers' stories.
Readership/Target Audience: Aimed at parrot keepers and breeders worldwide and those involved with conservation.
ADVERTISING RATES:
Full Page Mono £850.00
Full Page Colour £850.00
SCC £10.50
Agency Commission: 10%
Mechanical Data: Col Length: 262mm, Page Width: 186mm, Type Area: 262 x 186mm, Bleed Size: 305 x 218mm, Film: Digital, Trim Size: 297 x 210mm
Average advertising content per issue: 40%
CONSUMER: ANIMALS & PETS: Birds

PARTY POLITICS
47339U82-148

Editorial Address: 1 Oliver's Yard, 55 City Road, LONDON, EC1Y 1SP **Tel:** 020 7324 8500 **Fax:** 020 7324 8600
Email: market@sagepub.co.uk
Advertising Address: As above.
Email: sheena.karim@sagepub.co.uk
Web site: http://www.sagepub.co.uk
ISSN: 1354-0688
Publisher: Sage Publications
Date Established: 1995
Frequency: 6 issues yearly
Free to qualifying individuals
Annual Sub.: £46.00
Circulation: 600 (Publisher's Statement)

Editor: David Farrell; **Advertising Manager:** Sheena Karim
Summary of Content: Publication providing an important new forum for discussion of the character and organisation of political parties, and their role within various national political systems.
Readership/Target Audience: Aimed at those who research political parties and organisations.
ADVERTISING RATES:
Full Page Mono £400.00
Agency Commission: 5%
Mechanical Data: Col Length: 205mm, Page Width: 130mm, Film: Digital, Type Area: 205 x 130mm
Average advertising content per issue: 3%
CONSUMER: CURRENT AFFAIRS & POLITICS

PASSION
625431U84B-169_30

Editorial Address: PO Box 393, MAIDSTONE, ME14 5XU
Tel: 01622 729593
Email: cresmopub@yahoo.co.uk
Web site: http://www.crescentmoon.org.uk
ISSN: 1352-3473
Publisher: Crescent Moon Publishing
Date Established: 1994
Frequency: Quarterly
Cover Price: £2.50
Annual Sub.: £10.00
Circulation: 200 (Publisher's Statement)
Usual Pagination: 60
Editor: Jeremy Robinson
Summary of Content: Magazine containing collections of poetry, fiction, reviews and essays on fine art, cinema, music, politics, philosophy, the media and feminism.
Readership/Target Audience: Aimed at those interested in literature and the arts.
ADVERTISING: No Advertising taken
CONSUMER: THE ARTS & LITERARY: Literary

THE PASTORAL REVIEW
47743U87-191

Formerly: Priests & People
Editorial Address: St. Mary's University College, Waldegrave Road, Strawberry Hill, TWICKENHAM, TW1 4SX
Tel: 020 8240 4191 **Fax:** 020 8240 2362
Email: hayesm@smuc.ac.uk
Advertising Address: 1 King Street Cloisters, Clifton Walk, LONDON, W6 OGY **Tel:** 01638 741549 **Fax:** 01638 744190
Email: mbeaman@thepastoralreview.co.uk
Web site: http://www.thepastoralreview.org
Publisher: Tablet Publishing Co. Ltd.
Date Established: 1931
Frequency: 6 issues yearly
Cover Price: £6.10
Annual Sub.: £31.00
Circulation: 4,000 (Publisher's Statement)
Usual Pagination: 96
Editor: Michael Hayes; **Advertising Manager:** Margaret Beaman; **Publisher:** Ignatius Kusiak
Summary of Content: Magazine containing pastoral theology and practical advice.
Readership/Target Audience: Aimed at priests and laypeople within parish communities.
ADVERTISING RATES:
Full Page Mono £290.00
Full Page Colour £350.00
SCC £15.00
Agency Commission: 15%
Mechanical Data: Type Area: 216 x 149mm, Col Length: 216mm, Page Width: 149mm, Film: Digital
Copy instructions: Copy Date: 4 weeks prior to publication date
Average advertising content per issue: 10%
CONSUMER: RELIGIOUS

PATCHWORK & QUILTING
45364U74E-345

Editorial Address: Traplet House, Pendragon Close, MALVERN, WR14 1GA **Tel:** 01684 588500
Fax: 01684 578588
Email: pq@traplet.com
Advertising Address: As above. **Fax:** 01684 578558
Email: advertising@traplet.com
Web site: http://www.pandqmagazine.com
ISSN: 0268-5620
Publisher: Traplet Publications Ltd
Date Established: 1985
Frequency: Monthly
Cover Price: £3.95
Annual Sub.: £47.00
Usual Pagination: 100
Editor: Dianne Huck; **Managing Director:** Tony Stephenson
Summary of Content: Magazine covering all levels of patchwork and quilting skills. Includes DIY projects, an events diary and exhibition reports.
Readership/Target Audience: Read by patchwork and quilting enthusiasts of all levels.
ADVERTISING RATES:
Full Page Colour £795.00

Agency Commission: 10%
CONSUMER: WOMEN'S INTEREST CONSUMER MAGAZINES: Crafts

PATEK PHILIPPE
47507U84A-325_50

Editorial Address: 84-86 Regent Street, LONDON, W1B 5RR **Tel:** 020 7734 2303 **Fax:** 020 7494 2570
Email: casey.jones@theforwardgroup.com
Web site: http://www.patek.com
Publisher: The Forward Group
Date Established: 1996
Frequency: Half-yearly - Published in April and October
Cover Price: Free
Circulation: 140,000 (Publisher's Statement)
Usual Pagination: 75
Editor: Casey Jones; **Circulation Manager:** Mainna Moreau
Summary of Content: Magazine of Patek Philippe. Includes articles on the arts, culture and horology worldwide.
Language(s): Chinese; English; French; German; Italian; Japanese; Spanish
Readership/Target Audience: Aimed at luxury market timepiece owners interested in art, culture, history and horology.
ADVERTISING: No Advertising taken
CONSUMER: THE ARTS & LITERARY: Arts

THE PAVEMENT
1687301U82-265

Editorial Address: PO Box 43675, LONDON, SE22 8YL
Web site: http://www.thepavement.org.uk
Date Established: 2005
Frequency: 10 issues yearly
Cover Price: Free
Circulation: 5,500 (Print Run)
Usual Pagination: 36
Editor: Richard Burdett; **News Editor:** Catherine Neilan
Summary of Content: Magazine with news, health and legal advice, issues such as ASBOs and the Vagrancy Law and cartoons.
Readership/Target Audience: Aimed at the homeless in Central London and Glasgow and Edinburgh.
ADVERTISING: No Advertising taken
CONSUMER: CURRENT AFFAIRS & POLITICS

PAWS
623220U81X-190

Editorial Address: Battersea Dogs & Cats Home, 4 Battersea Park Road, LONDON, SW8 4AA
Tel: 020 7622 3626 **Fax:** 020 7622 6451
Email: paws@battersea.org.uk
Advertising Address: As above.
Web site: http://www.battersea.org.uk
Publisher: William Joseph
Date Established: 1999
Frequency: Quarterly
Cover Price: £2.00
Free to qualifying individuals
Circulation: 53,000 (Publisher's Statement)
Usual Pagination: 40
Editor: Siobhan Wakely
Summary of Content: Magazine containing up to date news and articles on Battersea Dogs & Cats Home as well as pet care and training advice.
Readership/Target Audience: Aimed at those who have given a home to a Battersea dog or cat, also patrons and supporters of the Battersea Dogs & Cats Home.
ADVERTISING RATES:
Full Page Colour £1500.00
Agency Commission: 10%
Mechanical Data: Film: Digital, Type Area: 292 x 205mm, Bleed Size: 305 x 218mm, Trim Size: 297 x 210mm, Col Length: 292mm, Page Width: 205mm
Copy instructions: Copy Date: 6 weeks prior to publication date
Average advertising content per issue: 35%
CONSUMER: ANIMALS & PETS

PC ADVISOR
36178U78E-21

Editorial Address: 4th Floor, 101 Euston Road, LONDON, NW1 2RA **Tel:** 020 7756 2800
Email: letters@pcadvisor.co.uk
Advertising Address: As above. **Fax:** 020 7756 2838
Email: daniel_shaw@idg.co.uk
Web site: http://www.pcadvisor.co.uk
ISSN: 1359-8040
Publisher: IDG (International Data Group)
Date Established: 1995
Frequency: Monthly
Cover Price: £3.99
Annual Sub.: £23.97
Circulation: 41,905 (ABC 01/01/2008 to 31/12/2008)
Usual Pagination: 256
Editor: Paul Trotter; **Managing Director:** Kit Gould;
Advertising Manager: Daniel Shaw; **Managing Editor:** Matt Egan

Summary of Content: Technology magazine containing buying and productivity advice, all aspects of home and small business computing. Includes news, hardware and software reviews, top 10 charts, features, troubleshooting and practical workshops and a reader-driven helpline.
Readership/Target Audience: Aimed at consumers and small businesses.
ADVERTISING RATES:
Full Page Colour £3950.00
Agency Commission: 15%
Mechanical Data: Type Area: 275 x 185mm, Col Length: 275mm, Page Width: 185mm, Trim Size: 297 x 210mm, Film: Digital, Bleed Size: 303 x 216mm
Copy instructions: Copy Date: 3 weeks prior to publication date
Average advertising content per issue: 30%
CONSUMER: CONSUMER ELECTRONICS: Home Computing

PC ANSWERS
36118U78E-17
Editorial Address: 30 Monmouth Street, BATH, BA1 2BW
Tel: 01225 442244 **Fax:** 01225 732295
Email: pcanswers@futurenet.co.uk
Advertising Address: As above. **Fax:** 01225 882885
Email: mpyatt@futurenet.co.uk
Web site: http://www.pcanswers.co.uk
Publisher: Future Publishing Ltd
Date Established: 1991
Frequency: 13 issues yearly
Cover Price: £5.99
Annual Sub.: £44.99
Circulation: 13,915 (ABC 01/01/2008 to 31/12/2008)
Usual Pagination: 148
Editor: Christian Hall; **Managing Director:** Robert Price; **Publisher:** Stuart Anderton
Summary of Content: Magazine covering hardware, software and technical details for home PC users.
Readership/Target Audience: Aimed at home PC enthusiasts.
ADVERTISING RATES:
Full Page Colour £1350.00
Agency Commission: 10%
Mechanical Data: Film: Digital, Page Width: 190mm, Type Area: 270 x 190mm, Col Length: 270mm, Trim Size: 297 x 210mm
Copy instructions: Copy Date: 3 weeks prior to publication date
CONSUMER: CONSUMER ELECTRONICS: Home Computing

PC FORMAT
46542U78D-211_50
Editorial Address: 30 Monmouth Street, BATH, BA1 2BW
Tel: 01225 442244 **Fax:** 01225 732295
Email: dave.james@futurenet.com
Advertising Address: As above. **Fax:** 01225 732206
Email: mpyatt@futurenet.co.uk
Web site: http://www.pcformat.co.uk
Publisher: Future Publishing Ltd
Date Established: 1991
Frequency: 13 issues yearly - Published in the middle of the month prior to cover date
Cover Price: £4.99 (DVD edition)
Circulation: 18,003 (ABC 01/01/2008 to 31/12/2008)
Editor: Alan Dexter; **Publisher:** Stuart Anderton
Summary of Content: Magazine guide to personal leisure computing. Includes news, reviews, tutorials, competitions plus DVD and Internet features.
Readership/Target Audience: Read by men between 18 and 44 who own a PC.
ADVERTISING RATES:
Full Page Colour £2387.00
Agency Commission: 10%
Mechanical Data: Type Area: 280 x 203mm, Col Length: 280mm, Trim Size: 300 x 222mm, Bleed Size: 310 x 232mm, Film: Digital, Page Width: 203mm
Copy instructions: Copy Date: 4 weeks prior to publication date
CONSUMER: CONSUMER ELECTRONICS: Games

PC GAMER
46543U78D-211_60
Editorial Address: 30 Monmouth Street, BATH, BA1 2BW
Tel: 01225 442244 **Fax:** 01225 732275
Email: pcgamer@futurenet.co.uk
Advertising Address: 2 Balcombe Street, LONDON, NW1 6NW **Tel:** 020 7042 4000 **Fax:** 020 7042 4159
Email: emma.cull@futurenet.com
Web site: http://www.pcgamer.co.uk
Publisher: Future Publishing Ltd
Frequency: 13 issues yearly
Cover Price: £5.99
Circulation: 32,619 (ABC 01/01/2008 to 31/12/2008)
Editor: Craig Pearson; **News Editor:** Craig Pearson; **Advertising Manager:** Emma Cull; **Publisher:** Richard Keith
Summary of Content: Magazine covering news, reviews and previews of PC games and products.
Readership/Target Audience: Aimed at those interested in PC gaming.

ADVERTISING RATES:
Full Page Mono £3580.00
Full Page Colour £3580.00
Agency Commission: 10%
Mechanical Data: Type Area: 270 x 190mm, Col Length: 270mm, Trim Size: 297 x 210mm, Bleed Size: 303 x 216mm, Film: Digital, Page Width: 190mm
Copy instructions: Copy Date: 4 weeks prior to publication date
Average advertising content per issue: 30%
CONSUMER: CONSUMER ELECTRONICS: Games

PC PILOT
600928U78D-211_85
Editorial Address: PO Box 100, STAMFORD, PE9 1XQ
Tel: 01780 755131
Email: Derek@pcpilot.net
Advertising Address: As above. **Fax:** 01780 751323
Email: andrew.mason@keypublishing.com
Web site: http://www.pcpilot.net
Publisher: Key Publishing Ltd
Date Established: 1999
Frequency: 7 issues yearly
Cover Price: £4.99
Annual Sub.: £34.95
Circulation: 18,636 (ABC 01/01/2008 to 31/12/2008)
Usual Pagination: 100
Editor: Derek Davis
Summary of Content: Magazine containing news, advice and views on all aspects of flight simulation.
Readership/Target Audience: Aimed at all levels of PC aviation and flight simulation enthusiasts.
ADVERTISING RATES:
Full Page Colour £1575.00
SCC £15.00
Agency Commission: 10%
Mechanical Data: Type Area: 287 x 200mm, Bleed Size: 307 x 220mm, Trim Size: 297 x 210mm, Col Length: 287mm, Film: Digital, Page Width: 200mm
Copy instructions: Copy Date: 3 weeks prior to publication date
CONSUMER: CONSUMER ELECTRONICS: Games

PC PLUS
36181U78E-20
Editorial Address: 30 Monmouth Street, BATH, BA1 2BW
Tel: 01225 442244
Email: pcplus@futurenet.com
Advertising Address: As above. **Fax:** 01225 822885
Email: mpyatt@futurenet.co.uk
Web site: http://www.pcplus.co.uk
Publisher: Future Publishing Ltd
Date Established: 1986
Frequency: 13 issues yearly
Cover Price: £6.49
Circulation: 22,162 (ABC 01/01/2008 to 31/12/2008)
Usual Pagination: 242
Editor: Martin Cooper; **News Editor:** Alex Cox; **Features Editor:** Richard Cobbett; **Publisher:** Stuart Anderton
Summary of Content: Publication covering all aspects of computing.
Readership/Target Audience: Aimed at PC enthusiasts, regular users and small to medium sized businesses.
ADVERTISING RATES:
Full Page Colour £1837.50
Agency Commission: 10%
Mechanical Data: Bleed Size: 303 x 216mm, Col Widths (Display): 45mm, No. of Columns (Display): 4, Type Area: 270 x 190mm, Col Length: 270mm, Trim Size: 297 x 210mm, Page Width: 190mm, Film: Digital
Copy instructions: Copy Date: 4 weeks prior to publication date
CONSUMER: CONSUMER ELECTRONICS: Home Computing

PC PRO
36119U78E-23
Editorial Address: 30 Cleveland Street, LONDON, W1T 4JD
Tel: 020 7907 6000 **Fax:** 020 7907 6304
Email: news@pcpro.co.uk
Advertising Address: As above. **Fax:** 020 7907 6600
Email: ben_topp@dennis.co.uk
Web site: http://www.pcpro.co.uk
Publisher: Dennis Publishing Ltd
Frequency: Monthly
Cover Price: £3.99
Circulation: 75,438 (ABC 01/01/2008 to 31/12/2008)
Usual Pagination: 300
Editor: Barry Collins; **Advertising Manager:** Ben Topp
Summary of Content: Computing and technology magazine covering the latest news, features and laboratory-based testing.
Readership/Target Audience: Aimed at PC professionals involved in buying computer equipment and PC enthusiasts.
ADVERTISING RATES:
Full Page Colour £4425.00
Agency Commission: 10%
Mechanical Data: Type Area: 277 x 190mm, Bleed Size: 303 x 216mm, Col Length: 277mm, Page Width: 190mm, Trim Size: 297 x 210mm, Film: Digital

Copy instructions: Copy Date: 3 weeks prior to publication date
Average advertising content per issue: 50%
CONSUMER: CONSUMER ELECTRONICS: Home Computing

PC TOOLS
1647510U78D-312
Editorial Address: Unit 1, Adlington Court, London Road, Adlington Park, MACCLESFIELD, SK10 4NL
Tel: 01625 855036 **Fax:** 01625 855039
Email: ianb@magnesiummedia.com
Advertising Address: As above.
Email: nounas@magnesiummedia.com
Web site: http://www.pctoolsmagazine.co.uk
ISSN: 1477-514X
Publisher: Magnesium Media Ltd
Date Established: 2001
Frequency: 8 issues yearly
Cover Price: £5.49
Circulation: 18,000 (Publisher's Statement)
Usual Pagination: 68
Editor: Ian Barker
Summary of Content: Magazine covering themed collections of software.
Readership/Target Audience: Aimed at hobbyists and enthusiasts.
ADVERTISING RATES:
Full Page Colour £1495.00
Agency Commission: 10%
Mechanical Data: Type Area: 275 x 190mm, Bleed Size: 303 x 216mm, Trim Size: 297 x 210mm, Col Length: 275mm, Page Width: 190mm, Film: Digital
Copy instructions: Copy Date: 4 weeks prior to publication date
CONSUMER: CONSUMER ELECTRONICS: Games

PC UTILITIES
626738U78E-16
Editorial Address: Unit 1, Adlington Court, London Road, Adlington Park, MACCLESFIELD, SK10 4NL
Tel: 01625 855036 **Fax:** 01625 855039
Email: gavinb@magnesiummedia.com
Advertising Address: As above.
Email: nounes@magnesiummedia.com
Web site: http://www.magnesiummedia.com
ISSN: 1469-042X
Publisher: Magnesium Media Ltd
Date Established: 2000
Frequency: 13 issues yearly
Cover Price: £5.99
Circulation: 24,000 (Publisher's Statement)
Usual Pagination: 100
Editor: Gavin Burrell
Summary of Content: Magazine covering news, advice and reviews of hardware and software. Includes workshops, cover disc tutorials, how-to tutorials and problem solving.
Readership/Target Audience: Aimed at home users who want to get the most out of their PCs.
ADVERTISING RATES:
Full Page Colour £1495.00
Agency Commission: 10%
Mechanical Data: Type Area: 275 x 190mm, Col Length: 275mm, Page Width: 190mm, Trim Size: 297 x 210mm, Bleed Size: 303 x 216mm, Film: Digital
Copy instructions: Copy Date: 4 weeks prior to publication date
CONSUMER: CONSUMER ELECTRONICS: Home Computing

PC ZONE
46550U78D-213
Editorial Address: 2 Balcombe Street, LONDON, NW1 6NW
Tel: 020 7042 4000
Advertising Address: As above.
Email: emma.cull@futurenet.com
Web site: http://www.pczone.co.uk
Publisher: Future Publishing Limited
Date Established: 1993
Frequency: 13 issues yearly - Published on the 2nd Thursday of the month prior to cover date
Cover Price: £5.99
Annual Sub.: £51.95
Circulation: 19,023 (ABC 01/01/2008 to 31/12/2008)
Usual Pagination: 116
Editor: Steve Hogarty; **Advertising Manager:** Emma Cull
Summary of Content: Guide to the world of PC gaming.
Readership/Target Audience: Read by 20 to 40 year old PC games and leisure enthusiasts.
ADVERTISING RATES:
Full Page Colour £2850.00
Agency Commission: 10%
Mechanical Data: Page Width: 185mm, Bleed Size: 303 x 216mm, Trim Size: 297 x 210mm, Type Area: 275 x 185mm, Film: Digital, Col Length: 275mm
CONSUMER: CONSUMER ELECTRONICS: Games

PEACE NEWS
47266U82-150

Editorial Address: 5 Caledonian Road, LONDON, N1 9DY
Tel: 020 7278 3344 **Fax:** 020 7278 0444
Email: editorial@peacenews.info
Advertising Address: As above.
Email: promos@peacenews.info
Web site: http://www.peacenews.info
ISSN: 0031-3548
Publisher: Peace News Limited
Date Established: 1936
Frequency: 10 issues yearly
Cover Price: £1.00
Annual Sub.: £10.00
Circulation: 5,000 (Publisher's Statement)
Usual Pagination: 16
Editor: Emily Johns; **Advertising Manager:** Nik Gorecki
Summary of Content: Magazine campaigning for international non-violent action.
Readership/Target Audience: Aimed at peace and environmental movements.
ADVERTISING RATES:
Full Page Mono £500.00
Full Page Colour £750.00
SCC £5.00
Mechanical Data: No. of Columns (Display): 5, Col Widths (Display): 48.5mm, Film: Digital, Type Area: 335 x 265mm, Col Length: 335mm, Page Width: 265mm, Bleed Size: +3mm
Copy instructions: Copy Date: 15th of the month prior to publication date
Average advertising content per issue: 5%
CONSUMER: CURRENT AFFAIRS & POLITICS

PEAK DISTRICT LIFE
1685817U80C-5242

Editorial Address: 61 Friar Gate, DERBY, DE1 1DJ
Tel: 01332 227850 **Fax:** 01332 227860
Email: joy.hales@archant.co.uk
Advertising Address: 1200 Century Way, Thorpe Park, LEEDS, LS15 8ZA **Tel:** 0113 251 5027
Email: les.banton@archant.co.uk
Web site: http://www.peakdistrictlife.co.uk
Publisher: Archant Life (North) PLC
Date Established: 2004
Frequency: 6 issues yearly
Cover Price: £1.95
Circulation: 8,000 (Print Run)
Features Editor: Penny Oldham; **Publisher:** Amanda Hamilton
Summary of Content: Magazine covering people, places, food and drink, gardens, homes, local history and local wildlife.
Readership/Target Audience: Aimed at residents and visitors to the Derbyshire Peak District.
ADVERTISING RATES:
Full Page Colour £805.00
Agency Commission: 10%
Mechanical Data: Type Area: 271 x 199mm, Bleed Size: 306 x 226mm, Trim Size: 300 x 220mm, Col Length: 271mm, Page Width: 199mm, Film: Digital
Copy instructions: Copy Date: 28th of the month prior to publication date
Average advertising content per issue: 37%
CONSUMER: RURAL & REGIONAL INTEREST: Regional Interest English Counties

PEERAGE MAGAZINE
1685739U74Q-1262

Editorial Address: PO Box 5135, Strand-on-the-Green, Chiswick, LONDON, W4 3WN **Tel:** 020 8560 0897
Fax: 020 8560 0897
Email: peerage@aol.com
Advertising Address: As above.
Email: thepeeragegroup@yahoo.co.uk
Publisher: The Peerage Group Ltd
Frequency: Quarterly
Cover Price: £5.00
Circulation: 18,000 (Publisher's Statement)
Editor: Sara Marden-King; **Advertising Manager:** Bruce Duncan
Summary of Content: Magazine covering lifestyle, travel, hotels, food, motoring and fashion.
Readership/Target Audience: Aimed at those with a high disposable income.
ADVERTISING RATES:
Full Page Mono 900.00
Full Page Colour 1250.00
Mechanical Data: Type Area: 274 x 185mm, Bleed Size: 303 x 214mm, Trim Size: 297 x 210mm, Col Length: 274mm, Page Width: 185mm, Film: Digital
Copy instructions: Copy Date: 6 weeks prior to publication date
Average advertising content per issue: 25%
CONSUMER: WOMEN'S INTEREST CONSUMER MAGAZINES: Lifestyle

PEGASUS
1622827U81D-359

Editorial Address: Regency House, 6-7 Elwick Road, ASHFORD, TN23 1PD **Tel:** 01233 628496
Fax: 01233 663294
Email: info@pegasusmagazine.com
Advertising Address: As above.
Email: info@pegasusmagazine.com
Web site: http://www.pegasusmagazine.com
Publisher: Pegasus
Date Established: 1993
Frequency: Monthly
Cover Price: Free
Circulation: 25,000 (Publisher's Statement)
Usual Pagination: 64
Editor: Nick Salmon; **Advertising Manager:** Nick Salmon
Summary of Content: Magazine featuring articles on fencing, health, feeds, tack and show results.
Readership/Target Audience: Aimed at the equine market.
ADVERTISING RATES:
Full Page Mono £361.90
Full Page Colour £450.00
Agency Commission: 10%
Mechanical Data: Type Area: 275 x 194mm, Col Length: 275mm, Page Width: 194mm, Film: Digital
Copy instructions: Copy Date: 16th of the month prior to publication date
Average advertising content per issue: 80%
CONSUMER: ANIMALS & PETS: Horses & Ponies

PELL-MELL AND WOODCOTE
47663U86C-500

Editorial Address: 89 Pall Mall, LONDON, SW1Y 5HS
Tel: 020 7747 3295 **Fax:** 020 7976 1086
Email: pellmell@royalautomobileclub.co.uk
Advertising Address: As above. **Fax:** 020 7451 9988
Email: sarahw@royalautomobileclub.co.uk
Web site: http://www.royalautomobileclub.co.uk
Publisher: Wordwide Communications
Date Established: 1976
Frequency: Quarterly
Cover Price: Free
Circulation: 16,000 (Publisher's Statement)
Usual Pagination: 44
Editor: Angela Everitt
Summary of Content: Journal of The Royal Automobile Club containing news, features on sports, social activities and club news.
Readership/Target Audience: Aimed at members of The Royal Automobile Club.
ADVERTISING RATES:
Full Page Mono £900.00
Full Page Colour £1295.00
Mechanical Data: Type Area: 214 x 150mm, Col Length: 214mm, Page Width: 150mm
CONSUMER: ADULT & GAY MAGAZINES: Men's Lifestyle Magazines

PEN PEOPLE UK
1642428U79R-149

Editorial Address: 113 High Street, NEWCASTLE-UNDER-LYME, ST5 1PS **Tel:** 01782 611628
Email: editors@penpeople.org.uk
Web site: http://www.penpeople.org.uk
Publisher: Pen People UK
Date Established: 2002
Frequency: Quarterly
Annual Sub.: £15.00
Circulation: 250 (Publisher's Statement)
Usual Pagination: 40
Editor: Trevor Miles
Summary of Content: Magazine covering subjects of interest to the calligrapher, information and news, topics to think about penning and calligraphy.
Readership/Target Audience: Aimed at enthusiastic calligraphers of all levels and abilities.
ADVERTISING: No Advertising taken
CONSUMER: HOBBIES & DIY: Hobbies & DIY Related

PENDRO MAGAZINE
1789455U90-995

Editorial Address: 31B Gaskell Street, Stockton Heath, WARRINGTON, WA4 2UN **Tel:** 01925 262839
Email: info@pendro-magazine.com
Advertising Address: As above. **Fax:** 01925 438026
Email: info@pendro-magazine.com
Web site: http://www.pendro-magazine.com
Publisher: Desirable Fish Marketing
Date Established: 2005
Frequency: 6 issues yearly
Cover Price: £1.50
Free to qualifying individuals
Circulation: 10,000 (Publisher's Statement)
Usual Pagination: 36
Editor: Louise Hunt; **Advertising Manager:** Louise Hunt
Summary of Content: Magazine covering health, news, music, sport, education and articles affecting French-speaking Africans.
Language(s): French

Readership/Target Audience: Aimed at communities from the Democratic Republic of Congo, Angola and Congo Brazzaville and other French-speaking Africans living in the UK, Europe and central Africa.
ADVERTISING RATES:
Full Page Colour £1600.00
Agency Commission: 20%
Mechanical Data: Bleed Size: 303 x 216mm, Trim Size: 297 x 210mm, Film: Digital
Average advertising content per issue: 30%
CONSUMER: ETHNIC

THE PENINSULA TIMES
1894678U80C-5501

Editorial Address: Admirals Offices, The Historic Dockyard, CHATHAM, ME4 4TZ **Tel:** 01634 812530
Email: office@heronmedia.biz
Web site: http://www.heronmedia.biz
Publisher: Heron Media Ltd
Frequency: Monthly
Cover Price: Free
Circulation: 18,500 (Publisher's Statement)
Editor: Sue Wood
Summary of Content: Magazine covering lifestyle features, local event listings, motoring, film reviews, travel features and village news.
Readership/Target Audience: Aimed at residents and businesses of Hoo peninsula and surrounding areas.
ADVERTISING RATES:
Full Page Colour £545
CONSUMER: RURAL & REGIONAL INTEREST: Regional Interest English Counties

PENNANT
45579U74N-107

Editorial Address: 68 South Lambeth Road, Vauxhall, LONDON, SW8 1RL **Tel:** 020 7582 0469 **Fax:** 020 7820 7583
Email: beverleym@forpen.co.uk
Advertising Address: As above. **Tel:** 020 7820 8225
Email: maria@forpen.co.uk
Web site: http://www.forpen.co.uk
Publisher: The Forces Pension Society
Date Established: 1949
Frequency: Half-yearly - Published in May and November
Cover Price: £4.95
Free to qualifying individuals
Circulation: 33,000 (Publisher's Statement)
Usual Pagination: 88
Editor: Beverley McBean; **Advertising Manager:** Maria Donaire
Summary of Content: Magazine of the Forces' Pension Society. Includes pension information and rates, activities, events and articles of a military theme.
Readership/Target Audience: Read by serving and retired forces personnel of all ranks and their families.
ADVERTISING RATES:
Full Page Mono £725.00
Full Page Colour £825.00
Mechanical Data: Type Area: 260 x 180mm, Col Length: 260mm, Page Width: 180mm, Film: Digital, Bleed Size: 303 x 216mm, Trim Size: 297 x 210mm
Average advertising content per issue: 45%
CONSUMER: WOMEN'S INTEREST CONSUMER MAGAZINES: Retirement

PEOPLE WEEKLY MAGAZINE
45652U74Q-740

Editorial Address: Blue Fin Building, 110 Southwark Street, LONDON, SE1 0SU **Tel:** 020 3148 3000 **Fax:** 020 3148 8506
Email: simon_perry@peoplemag.com
Advertising Address: As above. **Tel:** 020 3148 3050
Web site: http://www.people.com
Publisher: Time Inc.
Date Established: 1974
Frequency: Weekly
Cover Price: $2.99
Circulation: 4,000,000 (Publisher's Statement)
Usual Pagination: 130
Editor: Simon Perry; **Advertising Manager:** Simon Perry
Summary of Content: Magazine containing articles on celebrity and human interest issues, lifestyle and events.
Readership/Target Audience: Read by those interested in celebrity news.
ADVERTISING: Rates on application
Agency Commission: 10%
CONSUMER: WOMEN'S INTEREST CONSUMER MAGAZINES: Lifestyle

PEOPLE'S FRIEND
45194U74A-440

Editorial Address: 80 Kingsway East, DUNDEE, DD4 8SL
Tel: 01382 462276 **Fax:** 01382 452491
Email: peoplesfriend@dcthomson.co.uk
Advertising Address: 2 Albert Square, DUNDEE, DD1 9QJ
Tel: 01382 223131 **Fax:** 01382 454599
Email: advertising-meadowside@dcthomson.co.uk
Web site: http://www.jbwb.co.uk/pfguidelines.htm
Publisher: D.C. Thomson & Co Ltd

Consumer Magazines

Date Established: 1869
Frequency: Weekly
Cover Price: £0.70
Annual Sub.: £54.08
Circulation: 313,711 (ABC 01/01/2009 to 30/06/2009)
Usual Pagination: 64
Editor: Angela Gilchrist; **Advertising Manager:** Arthur McEwan
Summary of Content: Magazine with items of interest including cookery, knitting, crafts and extracts from books.
Readership/Target Audience: Aimed at women of all ages.
ADVERTISING RATES:
Full Page Mono £4390.00
Full Page Colour £6500.00
Agency Commission: 15%
Mechanical Data: Film: Positive, right reading, emulsion side down, Type Area: 276 x 200mm, Screen: 70 lpc, Bleed Size: 301 x 231mm, Trim Size: 295 x 225mm, Col Length: 276mm, No. of Columns (Display): 4, Page Width: 200mm
Copy instructions: Copy Date: 5 weeks prior to publication date
CONSUMER: WOMEN'S INTEREST CONSUMER MAGAZINES: Women's Interest

PERDESAN MONTHLY
48336U90-117
Editorial Address: 21 Cotton Brook Road, Sir Francis Ley Industrial Park, DERBY, DE23 8YJ **Tel:** 01332 372851
Fax: 01332 372833
Email: panjabtimes@aol.com
Advertising Address: As above.
Email: panjabtimes@aol.com
Publisher: PTI Derby Ltd
Frequency: Monthly
Cover Price: £1.75
Annual Sub.: £25.00
Circulation: 18,600 (Publisher's Statement)
Usual Pagination: 58
Editor: Rajinder Purewal; **Advertising Manager:** Sulakhan Singh
Summary of Content: Magazine containing general news of interest to readers of Punjabi.
Language(s): Punjabi
Readership/Target Audience: Aimed at Punjabi readers in the UK and Europe.
ADVERTISING RATES:
Full Page Mono £500.00
Full Page Colour £800.00
SCC £6.00
Agency Commission: 15%
Mechanical Data: Trim Size: 334 x 230mm, Film: Digital
Copy instructions: Copy Date: 5 days prior to publication date
Average advertising content per issue: 50%
CONSUMER: ETHNIC

PERFECT HAIR
764885U74H-301
Editorial Address: 211 Old Street, LONDON, EC1V 9NR
Tel: 020 7608 6300
Email: robert@style-media.net
Advertising Address: As above. **Tel:** 020 7436 9766
Fax: 020 7436 9957
Publisher: Scissorhands Media
Date Established: 2002
Frequency: 6 issues yearly
Cover Price: £1.99
Annual Sub.: £11.94
Circulation: 56,368 (ABC 01/01/2009 to 30/06/2009)
Usual Pagination: 196
Editor: Robert Hough; **Advertising Manager:** Robert Hough
Summary of Content: Magazine containing over 500 different hair styles as well as features on celebrity styles and recreating the look at home.
Readership/Target Audience: Read by women between 16 and 35 years old who are looking for a new hairstyle.
ADVERTISING RATES:
Full Page Mono £1400.00
Full Page Colour £1750.00
Agency Commission: 10%
Mechanical Data: Film: Digital
CONSUMER: WOMEN'S INTEREST CONSUMER MAGAZINES: Hair & Beauty

PERFECT WEDDING
1797201U74L-258
Editorial Address: 9th Floor, Tower House, Fairfax Street, BRISTOL, BS1 3BN **Tel:** 0117 927 9009 **Fax:** 0117 934 9008
Email: helenwebster@originpublishing.co.uk
Advertising Address: As above. **Tel:** 01179 279009
Email: sarahmurray@originpublishing.co.uk
Web site: http://www.perfectweddingmag.com
Publisher: Origin Publishing Ltd
Date Established: 2007
Frequency: 13 issues yearly
Cover Price: £2.99
Circulation: 30,000 (Publisher's Statement)
Usual Pagination: 260
Editor: Helen Webster

Summary of Content: Magazine covering all aspects of weddings including fashion, hair, beauty, venues, planning and real life weddings.
Readership/Target Audience: Aimed at brides to be.
ADVERTISING RATES:
Full Page Mono £2000.00
Full Page Colour £2000.00
SCC £25.00
Agency Commission: 10%
Mechanical Data: Type Area: 212 x 158mm, Bleed Size: 241 x 186mm, Trim Size: 235 x 180mm, Col Length: 212mm, Page Width: 158mm, Film: Digital
Copy instructions: Copy Date: 5 weeks prior to publication date
Average advertising content per issue: 40%
CONSUMER: WOMEN'S INTEREST CONSUMER MAGAZINES: Brides

PERFORMANCE BIKES
46372U77B-585
Editorial Address: Media House, Lynchwood, Peterborough Business Park, PETERBOROUGH, PE2 6EA
Tel: 01733 468099 **Fax:** 01733 68092
Email: perf.bikes@bauermedia.co.uk
Advertising Address: As above. **Tel:** 01733 468000
Fax: 01733 468867
Email: sarah.nunn@bauerconsumer.co.uk
Web site: http://www.performancebikes.co.uk
Publisher: Bauer Consumer Media Ltd (Media House)
Frequency: Monthly
Cover Price: £2.99
Annual Sub.: £35.88
Circulation: 24,694 (ABC 01/01/2008 to 31/12/2008)
Usual Pagination: 132
Editor: Matt Wildee; **Features Editor:** Matt Wildee;
Advertising Manager: Sarah Nunn
Summary of Content: Magazine covering road tests on high performance bikes. Includes reports on motorcycle sport and articles on modified motorcycles owned and built by readers.
Language(s): Dutch; English
Readership/Target Audience: Aimed at owners of performance motorbikes.
ADVERTISING RATES:
Full Page Colour £3276.00
Agency Commission: 10%
Mechanical Data: Col Length: 274mm, Film: Digital, No. of Columns (Display): 4, Type Area: 274 x 184mm, Bleed Size: 303 x 216mm, Trim Size: 297 x 210mm, Page Width: 184mm
Copy instructions: Copy Date: 4 weeks prior to publication date
Average advertising content per issue: 30%
CONSUMER: MOTORING & CYCLING: Motorcycling

PERFORMANCE BMW
46327U77E-210
Editorial Address: Becket House, Vestry Road, SEVENOAKS, TN14 5EJ **Tel:** 01732 748000
Fax: 01732 748001
Email: pbmw@unity-media.com
Advertising Address: As above.
Email: lbrooker@unity-media.com
Web site: http://www.performancebmwmag.com
ISSN: 1353-7954
Publisher: Unity Media plc
Date Established: 1998
Frequency: Monthly
Cover Price: £4.20
Annual Sub.: £50.40
Circulation: 50,000 (Publisher's Statement)
Usual Pagination: 132
Editor: Louise Woodhams; **Managing Director:** Dennis Taylor; **Publisher:** Colin Wilkinson
Summary of Content: Magazine focusing on modified performance BMW cars. Covers performance tuning and aftermarket car accessories including wheels, suspension, body styling and in-car hi-fi systems.
Readership/Target Audience: Aimed at BMW owners and enthusiasts aged 17 to 35 years old.
ADVERTISING RATES:
Full Page Mono £950.00
Full Page Colour £950.00
Agency Commission: 10%
Mechanical Data: Col Length: 266mm, Type Area: 266 x 190mm, Trim Size: 297 x 210mm, Bleed Size: 303 x 216mm, Film: Digital, Page Width: 190mm
Copy instructions: Copy Date: 5 weeks prior to publication date
Average advertising content per issue: 40%
CONSUMER: MOTORING & CYCLING: Club Cars

PERFORMANCE CAR
1829403U77A-609
Editorial Address: Becket House, Vestry Road, SEVENOAKS, TN14 5EJ **Tel:** 01732 748000
Fax: 01732 748001
Email: performancecar@unity-media.com
Advertising Address: As above.
Email: dclarke@unity-media.com
Web site: http://www.performancecarmagazine.co.uk

Publisher: Unity Media plc
Date Established: 2008
Frequency: Monthly
Cover Price: £4.00
Circulation: 15,605 (ABC 01/01/2009 to 30/06/2009)
Editor: Chris Knapman
Summary of Content: Magazine covering affordable new performance cars with road tests, first drives, drive stories, news and product reviews and buying guides retrospectives on older models.
Readership/Target Audience: Aimed predominantly at men aged 20 to 50 who enjoy spending money on cars.
ADVERTISING RATES:
Full Page Colour £3800.00
Mechanical Data: Type Area: 270 x 210mm, Bleed Size: 306 x 236mm, Trim Size: 300 x 230mm, Col Length: 270mm, Page Width: 210mm, Film: Digital
Copy instructions: Copy Date: 5 weeks prior to publication date
CONSUMER: MOTORING & CYCLING: Motoring

PERFORMANCE FORD
46328U77A-360
Editorial Address: Becket House, Vestry Road, SEVENOAKS, TN14 5EJ **Tel:** 01732 748000
Fax: 01732 748001
Email: pfordmag@unity-media.com
Advertising Address: As above.
Email: moneill@unity-media.com
Web site: http://www.performancefordmag.com
ISSN: 0955-0526
Publisher: Unity Media plc
Frequency: Monthly
Cover Price: £3.99
Annual Sub.: £47.88
Circulation: 30,000 (Publisher's Statement)
Usual Pagination: 180
Editor: Luke Wood; **Features Editor:** Chris Pollitt;
Managing Director: Dennis Taylor; **Advertising Manager:** Melanie O'Neill; **Publisher:** Colin Wilkinson
Summary of Content: Magazine focusing on modified Ford vehicles. Includes articles on performance and engine modifications.
Readership/Target Audience: Aimed at Ford car enthusiasts.
ADVERTISING RATES:
Full Page Mono £935.00
Full Page Colour £1400.00
Agency Commission: 10%
Mechanical Data: Trim Size: 297 x 210mm, Bleed Size: 303 x 216mm, Type Area: 266 x 190mm, Film: Digital, Col Length: 266mm, Page Width: 190mm
Copy instructions: Copy Date: 5 weeks prior to publication date
Average advertising content per issue: 40%
CONSUMER: MOTORING & CYCLING: Motoring

PERFORMANCE FRENCH CARS
1640859U77E-509
Formerly: Performance GTI French Cars
Editorial Address: 1st Floor, South Wing, Broadway Court, PETERBOROUGH, PE1 1RP **Tel:** 01733 353353
Fax: 01733 891342
Email: pfc.adsales@kelseypb.co.uk
Advertising Address: As above.
Email: pfc.ads@kelsey.co.uk
Publisher: Kelsey Publishing Ltd
Date Established: 2002
Frequency: Monthly
Cover Price: £4.20
Annual Sub.: £43.80
Circulation: 35,000 (Publisher's Statement)
Usual Pagination: 100
Editor: Ian Cushway; **Publisher:** Phil Weeden
Summary of Content: Magazine covering modified French cars, tuning and accessories.
Readership/Target Audience: Aimed at French performance car owners and enthusiasts.
ADVERTISING RATES:
Full Page Colour £950.00
Agency Commission: 10%
Mechanical Data: Type Area: 266 x 190mm, Bleed Size: 303 x 216mm, Trim Size: 297 x 210mm, Film: Digital, Col Length: 266mm, Page Width: 190mm
Copy instructions: Copy Date: 5 weeks prior to publication date
Average advertising content per issue: 30%
CONSUMER: MOTORING & CYCLING: Club Cars

PERFORMANCE RESEARCH JOURNAL
625709U84A-325_75
Editorial Address: 4 Park Square, Milton Park, ABINGDON, OX14 4RN **Tel:** 020 7017 6000 **Fax:** 020 7017 6336
Email: performance-research@dartington.ac.uk
Advertising Address: As above. **Tel:** 020 7017 6413
Email: jenna.johnston@tandf.co.uk
Web site: http://www.tandf.co.uk

ISSN: 1352-8165
Publisher: Routledge, Taylor & Francis
Frequency: Quarterly
Annual Sub.: £61.00
Circulation: 800 (Publisher's Statement)
Editor: Richard Gough; **Managing Editor:** Stacey Gubb
Summary of Content: Journal covering theatre, dance, music and live art. Includes peer review articles and material from renowned artists and scholars.
Readership/Target Audience: Read by academics, practitioners, critics and students interested in the exchange between performance practice and research.
ADVERTISING: Rates on application
CONSUMER: THE ARTS & LITERARY: Arts

PERFORMANCE VW
46329U77A-363

Editorial Address: Becket House, Vestry Road, SEVENOAKS, TN14 5EJ **Tel:** 01732 748000
Fax: 01732 748001
Email: pvw@unity-media.com
Advertising Address: As above.
Email: pvw@unity-media.com
Web site: http://www.performancevwmag.com
ISSN: 1462-3110
Publisher: Unity Media plc
Frequency: Monthly
Cover Price: £4.20
Annual Sub.: £50.40
Circulation: 35,000 (Publisher's Statement)
Usual Pagination: 130
Editor: Elliott Roberts; **Managing Director:** Dennis Taylor; **Advertising Manager:** Sarah Church; **Publisher:** Colin Wilkinson
Summary of Content: Independent magazine containing information and features on engine tuning, body kits, ICE, wheels, suspension and car security.
Readership/Target Audience: Aimed at VW owners, drivers and enthusiasts.
ADVERTISING RATES:
Full Page Colour £950.00
Agency Commission: 10%
Mechanical Data: Col Length: 266mm, Page Width: 190mm, Type Area: 266 x 190mm, Trim Size: 297 x 210mm, Film: Digital
Copy instructions: Copy Date: 5 weeks prior to publication date
Average advertising content per issue: 40%
CONSUMER: MOTORING & CYCLING: Motoring

PERFORMING MUSICIAN
46170U76D-375

Formerly: Music Mart
Editorial Address: Media House, Trafalgar Way, Bar Hill, CAMBRIDGE, CB23 8SQ **Tel:** 01954 789888
Email: dave@soundonsound.com
Advertising Address: As above. **Fax:** 01954 789895
Email: patrick@performing-musician.com
Web site: http://www.performing-musician.com
Publisher: SOS Publications Ltd
Date Established: 1987
Frequency: Monthly
Cover Price: £2.95
Circulation: 15,000 (Publisher's Statement)
Usual Pagination: 160
Editor: David Lockwood; **Advertising Manager:** Patrick Shelley
Summary of Content: Publication containing news and reviews of musical instruments, equipment and accessories.
Readership/Target Audience: Aimed at performing musicians, and sound reinforcement (PA) operators.
ADVERTISING RATES:
Full Page Colour £740.00
Agency Commission: 10%
Mechanical Data: Type Area: 270 x 190mm, Col Length: 270mm, No. of Columns (Display): 4, Trim Size: 297 x 210mm, Page Width: 190mm, Bleed Size: 303 x 216mm
Copy instructions: Copy Date: 4 weeks prior to publication
CONSUMER: MUSIC & PERFORMING ARTS: Music

PERIOD HOUSE
45365U74E-359

Editorial Address: The Tower, Phoenix Square, Wyncolls Road, Severalls Industrial Park, COLCHESTER, CO4 9HU **Tel:** 01206 851117 **Fax:** 01206 849078
Email: sarah.mills@burdamagazines.co.uk
Advertising Address: As above. **Fax:** 01206 849079
Email: dale.macpherson@burdamagazines.co.uk
Web site: http://www.periodhouse.net
ISSN: 0966-1530
Publisher: Hubert Burda Media UK
Frequency: Monthly
Cover Price: £3.50
Circulation: 48,500 (Publisher's Statement)
Usual Pagination: 144
Editor: Sarah Mills; **Managing Director:** Luke Patten
Summary of Content: Magazine including features and new ideas for homes with character, also covers gardens and expert advice.

Readership/Target Audience: Aimed at owners of period properties, designers and period house enthusiasts.
ADVERTISING RATES:
Full Page Colour £2750.00
Agency Commission: 10%
Mechanical Data: Film: Digital, Type Area: 276 x 206mm, Bleed Size: 306 x 236mm, Trim Size: 300 x 230mm, Col Length: 276mm, Page Width: 206mm
CONSUMER: WOMEN'S INTEREST CONSUMER MAGAZINES: Crafts

PERIOD IDEAS
639472U74C-367

Formerly: Period Ideas for your Home
Editorial Address: 25 Phoenix Court, Hawkins Road, COLCHESTER, CO2 8JY **Tel:** 01206 505976
Fax: 01206 505945
Email: jeannine@aceville.co.uk
Advertising Address: 21-23 Phoenix Court, Hawkins Road, COLCHESTER, CO2 8JY **Tel:** 01206 505900
Fax: 01206 505953
Email: info@periodideas.com
Web site: http://www.periodideas.com
Publisher: Aceville Publications Ltd
Date Established: 2000
Frequency: Monthly
Cover Price: £3.50
Circulation: 38,000 (Publisher's Statement)
Usual Pagination: 180
Editor: Jeannine McAndrew; **Advertising Manager:** Daniel Lodge
Summary of Content: Magazine containing inspiration and practical advice on decorating and renovating period homes. Includes sections on property and gardening as well as monthly special features devoted to specific areas of the home such as the kitchen and bathroom.
Readership/Target Audience: Aimed at homeowners with an interest in older properties and traditional style.
ADVERTISING RATES:
Full Page Colour £1645.00
SCC £27.00
Agency Commission: 10%
Mechanical Data: Type Area: 270 x 190mm, Bleed Size: 305 x 233mm, Trim Size: 297 x 225mm, Col Length: 270mm, Film: Digital, Print Process: Web-fed offset litho, Page Width: 190mm
Copy instructions: Copy Date: 3 weeks prior to publication date
Average advertising content per issue: 35%
Supplement(s): Covermounted Books - 3xY
CONSUMER: WOMEN'S INTEREST CONSUMER MAGAZINES: Home & Family

PERIOD LIVING
45282U74C-370

Formerly: Period Living & Traditional Homes
Editorial Address: St. Giles House, 50 Poland Street, LONDON, W1F 7AX **Tel:** 020 7970 4433 **Fax:** 020 7970 4438
Email: period.living@centaur.co.uk
Advertising Address: As above. **Tel:** 020 7970 4000
Email: emma.farrington@centaur.co.uk
Web site: http://www.periodliving.co.uk
Publisher: Centaur Communications Ltd
Date Established: 1990
Frequency: Monthly
Cover Price: £3.40
Annual Sub.: £34.20
Circulation: 52,834 (ABC 01/06/2007 to 31/12/2007)
Usual Pagination: 170
Editor: Sarah Whelan; **Features Editor:** Naomi Jones; **Editor-in-Chief:** Michael Holmes; **Managing Director:** Peter Harris; **Advertising Manager:** Emma Farrington
Summary of Content: Magazine containing features on traditional homes and furnishings.
Readership/Target Audience: Aimed at those who enjoy stylish period living and homes with character.
ADVERTISING RATES:
Full Page Colour £3800.00
Agency Commission: 10%
Mechanical Data: Bleed Size: 303 x 236mm, Trim Size: 297 x 230mm, Col Length: 277mm, Page Width: 210mm, Film: Digital, Type Area: 277 x 210mm
Average advertising content per issue: 30%
CONSUMER: WOMEN'S INTEREST CONSUMER MAGAZINES: Home & Family

PET OWNER
1703197U81X-505

Editorial Address: Park View House, 19 The Avenue, EASTBOURNE, BN21 3YD **Tel:** 01323 411601
Fax: 01323 734909
Email: laura.l@parkview-publishing.co.uk
Advertising Address: As above. **Fax:** 01323 411654
Email: carole.l@parkview-publishing.co.uk
Web site: http://www.parkview-publishing.co.uk
Publisher: Park View Publishing Ltd
Frequency: 9 issues yearly
Cover Price: £1.50
Circulation: 30,000 (Publisher's Statement)
Usual Pagination: 32

Editor: Linda Grace; **Advertising Manager:** Linda Grace
Summary of Content: Magazine covering training, health, nutrition, new products and general news.
Readership/Target Audience: Aimed at pet owners who want the best for their pets.
ADVERTISING RATES:
Full Page Colour £995.00
Agency Commission: 10%
Mechanical Data: Type Area: 220 x 150mm, Bleed Size: 245 x 173mm, Trim Size: 242 x 170mm, Col Length: 220mm, Page Width: 150mm, Film: Digital
Average advertising content per issue: 40%
CONSUMER: ANIMALS & PETS

PET PEOPLE
1667152U81B-304

Formerly: Petpatter
Editorial Address: Studio 7, 3rd Floor, Enterprise House, 1-2 Hatfields, LONDON, SE1 9PG **Tel:** 020 7793 2460
Fax: 020 7793 2461
Email: oliver@sundaypublishing.com
Advertising Address: As above.
Email: ruth@sundaypublishing.com
Web site: http://www.sundaypublishing.com
Publisher: Sunday Publishing
Date Established: 2008
Frequency: Half-yearly - Published in May and November
Cover Price: Free
Circulation: 524,476 (ABC 01/01/2008 to 31/12/2008)
Usual Pagination: 52
Editor: Oliver Parsons
Summary of Content: Magazine with general advice, tips and new products related to dogs, cats and rabbits.
Readership/Target Audience: Aimed at customers of Pet Plan Insurers.
ADVERTISING RATES:
Full Page Colour £12000.00
Mechanical Data: Type Area: 285 x 198mm, Bleed Size: 303 x 216mm, Trim Size: 297 x 210mm, Col Length: 285mm, Page Width: 198mm, Film: Digital
CONSUMER: ANIMALS & PETS: Dogs

PETFOCUS
1654974U81X-503

Editorial Address: Elmtree Business Park, Elmswell, BURY ST. EDMUNDS, IP30 9HR **Tel:** 01359 243400
Fax: 01359 242921
Email: pet-editor@visionline.co.uk
Advertising Address: As above.
Email: amanda.smith@visionline.co.uk
Web site: http://www.petfocus.com
ISSN: 1744-6562
Publisher: Vision Online
Date Established: 2004
Frequency: Quarterly
Cover Price: £2.75
Annual Sub.: £10.00
Circulation: 15,000 (Publisher's Statement)
Usual Pagination: 56
Editor: Amanda Smith; **Advertising Manager:** Amanda Smith
Summary of Content: Magazine promoting responsible pet ownership covering all aspects of keeping dogs, cats, small pets, birds, reptiles and fish including health, behaviour and general news.
Readership/Target Audience: Aimed at pet owners.
ADVERTISING RATES:
Full Page Mono £650.00
Full Page Colour £1000.00
Agency Commission: 10%
Mechanical Data: Film: Digital
Copy instructions: Copy Date: 4 weeks prior to publication date
Average advertising content per issue: 25%
CONSUMER: ANIMALS & PETS

PETS WELCOME!
48007U89A-396

Editorial Address: Abbey Mill Business Centre, Seedhill, PAISLEY, PA1 1TJ **Tel:** 0141 887 0428 **Fax:** 0141 889 7204
Email: editorial@fhguides.com
Advertising Address: As above.
Email: dorothy@fhguides.com
Web site: http://www.holidayguides.com
Publisher: FHG Guides
Date Established: 1961
Frequency: Half-yearly - Published in April and October
Cover Price: £8.99
Circulation: 35,000 (Publisher's Statement)
Usual Pagination: 450
Editor: Anne Cuthbertson
Summary of Content: Publication featuring hotels, guesthouses, self-catering, farms, caravans and camping sites that cater for pets and their owners.
Readership/Target Audience: Aimed at pet owners.
ADVERTISING RATES:
Full Page Mono £789.00
Full Page Colour £1379.00
Agency Commission: 10%

Mechanical Data: Type Area: 190 x 118mm, Col Length: 190mm, Film: Digital, Bleed Size: +3mm, Page Width: 118mm
CONSUMER: HOLIDAYS & TRAVEL: Travel

PETUARIA PRESS
622780U80C-1392

Editorial Address: 43 Station Road, BROUGH, HU15 1DZ
Tel: 07980 072860
Email: petuariapress@googlemail.com
Publisher: Elloughton-cum-Brough Parish Council
Date Established: 1999
Frequency: Quarterly
Cover Price: Free
Circulation: 4,000 (Publisher's Statement)
Usual Pagination: 4
Editor: Justine McMillan
Summary of Content: Publication covering developments, events and lifestyle stories only relevant to the area.
Readership/Target Audience: Aimed at residents in the Elloughton and Brough areas of East Yorkshire.
ADVERTISING: No Advertising taken
CONSUMER: RURAL & REGIONAL INTEREST: Regional Interest English Counties

PEVEREL LIFE AND STYLE
622954U74N-110_15

Formerly: Peverel News
Editorial Address: Queensway House, 11 Queensway, NEW MILTON, BH25 5NR **Tel:** 01425 638863 **Fax:** 01425 638838
Email: peverelnews@peverel.co.uk
Advertising Address: As above.
Email: advertising@peverel.co.uk
Web site: http://www.peverel.co.uk
Publisher: The Peverel Group
Date Established: 1987
Frequency: 3 issues yearly - Published in April, August and December
Cover Price: Free
Circulation: 100,000 (Publisher's Statement)
Usual Pagination: 56
Editor: Ria Wilcox; **Advertising Manager:** Ria Wilcox
Summary of Content: Magazine covering retirement homes, health, finance, property, news and gardening.
Readership/Target Audience: Aimed at those in, or planning to move to a private retirement property.
ADVERTISING RATES:
Full Page Colour £2120.00
Agency Commission: 10%
Mechanical Data: Film: Digital
Copy instructions: Copy Date: 5 weeks prior to publication date
Average advertising content per issue: 30%
CONSUMER: WOMEN'S INTEREST CONSUMER MAGAZINES: Retirement

THE PGA PROFESSIONAL
45824U75D-200

Formerly: PGA Profile
Editorial Address: Centenary House, The Belfry, SUTTON COLDFIELD, B76 9PT **Tel:** 01675 470333
Fax: 01675 477888
Email: editor@pga.org.uk
Advertising Address: 45 Woodside Gardens, SITTINGBOURNE, ME10 1SG **Tel:** 01795 424631
Fax: 01795 555707
Email: graham@prosportmedia.co.uk
Web site: http://www.pga.info
Publisher: ProSport Media Ltd
Date Established: 1919
Frequency: Monthly - Published the second week of each month
Free to qualifying individuals
Circulation: 7,500 (Publisher's Statement)
Usual Pagination: 44
Editor: Lee McLaughlan; **Advertising Manager:** Roger Murphy
Summary of Content: Official magazine of The Professional Golfers' Association.
Readership/Target Audience: Read by members of the association.
ADVERTISING RATES:
Full Page Mono £1034.00
Full Page Colour £1335.00
Agency Commission: 10%
Mechanical Data: No. of Columns (Display): 3, Page Width: 276mm, Type Area: 276 x 190mm, Col Length: 190mm, Trim Size: 297 x 210mm, Bleed Size: 303 x 216mm, Film: Digital, Col Widths (Display): 59mm
Copy instructions: Copy Date: 2 weeks prior to publication date
Average advertising content per issue: 40%
CONSUMER: SPORT: Golf

THE PHILATELIC EXPORTER
46630U79C-40

Editorial Address: 7 Parkside, Christchurch Road, RINGWOOD, BH24 3SH **Tel:** 01425 472363
Fax: 01425 470247

Email: exportereditor@aol.com
Advertising Address: As above. **Tel:** 01903 604335
Fax: 01903 537321
Email: advertising@philatelicexporter.com
Web site: http://www.philatelicexporter.com
ISSN: 0031-7381
Publisher: Philatelic Exporter
Date Established: 1945
Frequency: Monthly - Published the last week of the month prior to cover date
Annual Sub.: £29.00
Circulation: 1,700 (Publisher's Statement)
Usual Pagination: 56
Editor: Graham Phillips
Summary of Content: Publication covering the international postage stamp trade.
Language(s): English; French; German
Readership/Target Audience: Aimed at stamp dealers, philatelic professionals, postal administrators and others with an interest in the postage stamp trade.
ADVERTISING RATES:
Full Page Mono £324.00
Full Page Colour £485.00
Agency Commission: 10%
Mechanical Data: Col Length: 270mm, Bleed Size: 303 x 216mm, Type Area: 270 x 190mm, Trim Size: 297 x 210mm, Page Width: 190mm, Film: Digital
Copy instructions: Copy Date: 5th of the month prior to publication date
CONSUMER: HOBBIES & DIY: Philately

THE PHILOSOPHERS' MAGAZINE
1775743U94X-290

Editorial Address: Dunstan House, 14A St. Cross Street, LONDON, EC1N 8XA **Tel:** 020 7841 1959
Fax: 020 7242 1474
Email: editor@philosophers.co.uk
Advertising Address: As above. **Tel:** 020 7387 8558
Email: matthew@philosophersnet.com
Web site: http://www.philosophersmag.com
ISSN: 1354-814X
Publisher: Philosophy Press Ltd
Date Established: 1998
Frequency: Quarterly
Cover Price: £5.99
Circulation: 6,000 (Publisher's Statement)
Usual Pagination: 128
Editor: Julian Baggini; **Advertising Manager:** Matthew Humphrys
Summary of Content: Magazine covering serious philosophy for the masses.
Readership/Target Audience: Aimed at educated non-professional philosophers and students.
ADVERTISING: Rates on application
CONSUMER: OTHER CLASSIFICATIONS: Miscellaneous

PHILOSOPHY NOW
48705U94X-143

Editorial Address: 43A Jerningham Road, LONDON, SE14 5NQ **Tel:** 020 7639 7314 **Fax:** 020 7639 7314
Email: rick.lewis@philosophynow.org
Advertising Address: As above.
Email: jay.sanders@philosophynow.org
Web site: http://www.philosophynow.org
ISSN: 0961-5970
Publisher: Anja Publications Ltd
Date Established: 1991
Frequency: 6 issues yearly
Cover Price: £3.20
Annual Sub.: £14.35
Circulation: 14,000 (Publisher's Statement)
Usual Pagination: 56
Editor: Richard Lewis; **Advertising Manager:** Jay Sanders; **Publisher:** Richard Lewis
Summary of Content: Magazine covering all aspects of philosophy.
Readership/Target Audience: Aimed at amateur philosophers, general educated members of the public and philosophy students.
ADVERTISING RATES:
Full Page Mono £628.00
Full Page Colour £835.00
Agency Commission: 10%
Mechanical Data: Type Area: 263 x 187mm, Bleed Size: 286 x 216mm, Trim Size: 280 x 210mm, Col Length: 263mm, Page Width: 187mm, Film: Digital
Average advertising content per issue: 10%
CONSUMER: OTHER CLASSIFICATIONS: Miscellaneous

PHOTO PLUS
1820148U85A-214

Editorial Address: 30 Monmouth Street, BATH, BA1 2BW
Tel: 01225 442244
Advertising Address: As above. **Fax:** 01225 822885
Email: chris.burgess@futurenet.co.uk
Web site: http://www.futurenet.co.uk
Publisher: Future Publishing Ltd

Date Established: 2007
Frequency: 13 issues yearly
Cover Price: £3.99
Circulation: 31,255 (ABC 01/07/2008 to 31/12/2008)
Usual Pagination: 132
Editor: Geoff Harris
Summary of Content: Magazine with features, tutorials, product reviews and a video disc with Photoshop tutorials.
Readership/Target Audience: Aimed at owners of Canon digital SLR cameras.
ADVERTISING RATES:
Full Page Colour £1875.00
Agency Commission: 10%
Mechanical Data: Type Area: 255 x 215mm, Bleed Size: 281 x 238mm, Trim Size: 275 x 232mm, Col Length: 255mm, Page Width: 215mm, Film: Digital
Copy instructions: Copy Date: 3 weeks prior to publication date
Average advertising content per issue: 10%
CONSUMER: PHOTOGRAPHY & FILM MAKING: Photography

PHOTO PRO MAGAZINE
1789974U85A-208

Formerly: Digital Photo Pro
Editorial Address: Bright House, 82 High Street, Sawston, CAMBRIDGE, CB22 3HJ **Tel:** 01223 499450
Email: terryhope@bright-publishing.com
Advertising Address: As above. **Fax:** 01223 839953
Email: mattsnow@bright-publishing.com
Web site: http://www.dppro.co.uk
Publisher: Bright Publishing Ltd
Date Established: 2006
Frequency: Monthly
Cover Price: £3.70
Circulation: 16,000 (Publisher's Statement)
Editor: Terry Hope; **News Editor:** Charlotte Griffiths;
Features Editor: Charlotte Griffiths; **Advertising Manager:** Matt Snow
Summary of Content: Magazine covering tests and reports on the latest pro cameras, systems and accessories including software, flash systems, memory cards and storage devices, studio gear, frames and albums as well as features of importance to the contemporary pro.
Readership/Target Audience: Aimed at professional photographers and those who are professionally minded in their approach to photography.
ADVERTISING RATES:
Full Page Colour £1750.00
Agency Commission: 10%
Mechanical Data: Bleed Size: 303 x 216mm, Trim Size: 297 x 210mm, Film: Digital
Average advertising content per issue: 20%
CONSUMER: PHOTOGRAPHY & FILM MAKING: Photography

PHOTOGRAPHICA WORLD
46749U79K-785

Editorial Address: Ware Lodge, Ware, LYME REGIS, DT7 3RH **Tel:** 01297 443469 **Fax:** 01297 442883
Email: john@tapestry.org.uk
Advertising Address: 5 Buntingford Road, Puckeridge, WARE, SG11 1RT **Tel:** 01920 821831 **Fax:** 01920 821611
Email: drbalfour@hotmail.com
Web site: http://www.pccgb.org
ISSN: 0953-4067
Publisher: The Photographic Collectors Club International Ltd.
Date Established: 1977
Frequency: Quarterly
Free to qualifying individuals
Annual Sub.: £25.00
Circulation: 1,700 (Publisher's Statement)
Usual Pagination: 42
Editor: John Marriage; **Advertising Manager:** David Balfour
Summary of Content: Journal of the Photographic Collectors Club of Great Britain. Contains research articles, book and exhibition reviews related to history of photography.
Readership/Target Audience: Read by members, museums, collectable-photographic dealers and traders.
ADVERTISING RATES:
Full Page Mono £140.00
Full Page Colour £200.00
Mechanical Data: Trim Size: 297 x 210mm
Copy instructions: Copy Date: 6 weeks prior to publication date
CONSUMER: HOBBIES & DIY: Collectors Magazines

PHOTOGRAPHY MONTHLY
711576U85A-140

Editorial Address: The Mill, Bearwalden Business Park, Wendens Ambo, SAFFRON WALDEN, CB11 4GB
Tel: 0845 650 1065
Email: photography.monthly@photographymonthly.co.uk
Advertising Address: As above. **Tel:** 01799 544200
Fax: 01799 544202
Email: sam.scottsmith@archant.co.uk
Web site: http://www.photographymonthly.com
ISSN: 1473-4966

Publisher: Archant Specialist Ltd (Saffron Walden)
Date Established: 2001
Frequency: Monthly - Published on the third Thursday of every month
Cover Price: £3.40
Annual Sub.: £37.20
Circulation: 33,052 (ABC 01/01/2008 to 31/12/2008)
Usual Pagination: 152
Editor: Roger Payne; **Advertising Director:** Sam Scott-Smith
Summary of Content: Magazine containing technique advice, interviews, a buying guide and reader images.
Readership/Target Audience: Aimed at the enthusiastic photographer.
ADVERTISING RATES:
Full Page Colour £2935.00
Agency Commission: 10%
Mechanical Data: Trim Size: 297 x 210mm, Bleed Size: 303 x 216mm, Film: Digital
Copy instructions: Copy Date: 3 weeks prior to publication date
Average advertising content per issue: 27%
CONSUMER: PHOTOGRAPHY & FILM MAKING: Photography

PHOTOSHOP CREATIVE

1695158U85A-204

Editorial Address: Richmond House, 33 Richmond Hill, BOURNEMOUTH, BH2 6EZ **Tel:** 01202 586200
Email: pcr@imagine-publishing.co.uk
Advertising Address: As above.
Email: hannah.bradshaw@imagine-publishing.co.uk
Web site: http://www.pshopcreative.co.uk
Publisher: Imagine Publishing
Date Established: 2005
Frequency: 13 issues yearly
Cover Price: £6.00
Circulation: 35,000 (Print Run)
Usual Pagination: 100
Editor: Rosie Tanner; **Editor-in-Chief:** Jo Cole
Summary of Content: Magazine with step by step tutorial for using Adobe Photoshop.
Readership/Target Audience: Aimed at creative Mac and PC users.
ADVERTISING RATES:
Full Page Colour £2000.00
Agency Commission: 10%
Mechanical Data: Type Area: 260 x 210mm, Bleed Size: 290 x 240mm, Trim Size: 280 x 230mm, Col Length: 260mm, Page Width: 210mm, Film: Digital
Copy instructions: Copy Date: 4 weeks prior to publication date
Average advertising content per issue: 20%
CONSUMER: PHOTOGRAPHY & FILM MAKING: Photography

PI

47423U83-60_4

Editorial Address: University College, London Union, 25 Gordon Street, LONDON, WC1H 0AH **Tel:** 020 7679 7985
Fax: 020 7916 8533
Email: cs.officer@ucl.ac.uk
Advertising Address: As above.
Email: mc.officer@ucl.ac.uk
Web site: http://www.pimagazine.net
Publisher: University College London
Date Established: 1946
Frequency: 7 issues yearly - Published monthly during term time
Cover Price: Free
Circulation: 20,000 (Publisher's Statement)
Usual Pagination: 36
Editor: Sean Clothier; **Advertising Manager:** Sean Clothier
Summary of Content: Magazine covering national and university news, music, interviews, gaming, sport, food, listings and arts including theatre.
Readership/Target Audience: Read by students and staff at the University College London.
ADVERTISING RATES:
Full Page Colour £1000.00
Mechanical Data: Bleed Size: +5mm, Film: Digital, Trim Size: 297 x 210mm
Copy instructions: Copy Date: 2 weeks prior to publication date
Average advertising content per issue: 10%
CONSUMER: STUDENT PUBLICATIONS

PIANIST

764865U76D-751

Editorial Address: 6 Warrington Crescent, LONDON, W9 1EL **Tel:** 020 7266 0760 **Fax:** 020 7286 0748
Email: editor@pianistmagazine.com
Advertising Address: As above.
Email: ads@pianistmagazine.com
Web site: http://www.pianistmagazine.com
ISSN: 1475-1348
Publisher: Warners Group Publications plc
Date Established: 2001
Frequency: 6 issues yearly

Cover Price: £4.95
Annual Sub.: £27.00
Circulation: 15,000 (Publisher's Statement)
Usual Pagination: 84
Editor: Erica Worth; **Advertising Manager:** Erica Worth
Summary of Content: Magazine covering music news, reviews, music scores, playing tips and techniques as well as features on famous piano performers.
Readership/Target Audience: Read by those who enjoy playing the piano from beginners to advanced players.
ADVERTISING: Rates on application
CONSUMER: MUSIC & PERFORMING ARTS: Music

PIANO

46177U76D-388_20

Editorial Address: 241 Shaftesbury Avenue, LONDON, WC2H 8TF **Tel:** 020 7333 1744 **Fax:** 020 7333 1769
Email: piano@rhinegold.co.uk
Advertising Address: As above. **Tel:** 020 7333 1733
Fax: 020 7333 1736
Email: charles.pinkham@rhinegold.co.uk
Publisher: Rhinegold Publishing Ltd
Frequency: 6 issues yearly
Cover Price: £3.50
Free to qualifying individuals
Circulation: 10,000 (Publisher's Statement)
Usual Pagination: 42
Editor: Jonathan Wikeley
Summary of Content: Magazine that covers news and features on pianos and piano music.
Readership/Target Audience: Aimed at pianists and lovers of piano music.
ADVERTISING RATES:
Full Page Mono £990.00
Full Page Colour £1575.00
Agency Commission: 10%
Mechanical Data: No. of Columns (Display): 4, Type Area: 278 x 190mm, Trim Size: 297 x 210mm, Bleed Size: 303 x 216mm, Col Length: 278mm, Film: Digital, Page Width: 190mm
CONSUMER: MUSIC & PERFORMING ARTS: Music

PICK ME UP

1664421U74A-984

Editorial Address: Blue Fin Building, 110 Southwark Street, LONDON, SE1 0SU **Tel:** 020 3148 5000 **Fax:** 020 3148 8112
Email: pickmeup@ipcmedia.com
Advertising Address: As above.
Email: richard_smith@ipcmedia.com
Web site: http://www.pickmeupmagazine.com
Publisher: IPC Connect Ltd
Date Established: 2005
Frequency: Weekly
Cover Price: £0.68
Circulation: 323,171 (ABC 01/01/2009 to 30/06/2009)
Usual Pagination: 68
Editor: Rachel Tompkins; **Features Editor:** Heather Bishop;
Managing Director: Fiona Dent; **Advertising Manager:** Richard Smith; **Publisher:** Simon Denny
Summary of Content: Magazine with real life stories. Also covers health, puzzles, competitions, problem pages and horoscopes.
Readership/Target Audience: Aimed at women of all ages with a certain outlook on life.
ADVERTISING RATES:
Full Page Colour £8900.00
Agency Commission: 15%
Copy instructions: Copy Date: 3 weeks prior to publication date
CONSUMER: WOMEN'S INTEREST CONSUMER MAGAZINES: Women's Interest

PICTURE POSTCARD MONTHLY

46750U79K-800

Editorial Address: 15 Debdale Lane, Keyworth, NOTTINGHAM, NG12 5HT **Tel:** 0115 937 4079
Fax: 0115 937 6197
Email: reflections@postcardcollecting.co.uk
Advertising Address: As above.
Email: reflections@postcardcollecting.co.uk
Web site: http://www.postcardcollecting.co.uk
ISSN: 0144-8137
Publisher: Reflections of a Bygone Age
Frequency: Monthly - Published on the 24th of the month prior to cover date
Cover Price: £2.40
Annual Sub.: £28.00
Circulation: 4,000 (Publisher's Statement)
Usual Pagination: 60
Editor: Brian Lund; **Advertising Manager:** Mary Lund
Summary of Content: Magazine with a focus on picture postcards. Contains features, artist profiles, auctions and prices, also club news, views and a diary.
Readership/Target Audience: Aimed at collectors of old and modern postcards.
ADVERTISING RATES:
Full Page Mono £175.00
Full Page Colour £262.00

Mechanical Data: Type Area: 272 x 184mm, Col Length: 272mm, Bleed Size: 306 x 216mm, Trim Size: 300 x 210mm, Page Width: 184mm, Film: Digital
Copy instructions: Copy Date: 10th of the month prior to publication date
Average advertising content per issue: 25%
CONSUMER: HOBBIES & DIY: Collectors Magazines

PIKE & PREDATORS

48536U92-82

Editorial Address: 18 Haverbreaks Place, LANCASTER, LA1 5BH **Tel:** 01524 60713 **Fax:** 01524 60713
Email: editor@predatorpublications.co.uk
Advertising Address: 5 Pilley Hill, Pilley, LYMINGTON, SO41 5QF **Tel:** 01590 678400 **Fax:** 01590 678400
Email: chris.ball2@virgin.net
Web site: http://www.totalcoarsefishing.com
Publisher: Predator Publications Ltd
Date Established: 1996
Frequency: Monthly
Cover Price: £2.75
Circulation: 12,000 (Publisher's Statement)
Usual Pagination: 68
Editor: Neville Fickling
Summary of Content: Magazine focusing on predatory fishing in the UK. Contains articles on all aspects of pike, catfish, zander and eel fishing.
Readership/Target Audience: Aimed at anglers who enjoy predatory fishing.
ADVERTISING RATES:
Full Page Mono £260.00
Full Page Colour £370.00
Agency Commission: 10%
Mechanical Data: Film: Digital, Type Area: 262 x 185mm, Print Process: Sheet-fed litho, Col Length: 262mm, Trim Size: 297 x 210mm, Page Width: 185mm
Copy instructions: Copy Date: 20th of the month prior to publication date
Average advertising content per issue: 30%
CONSUMER: ANGLING & FISHING

PILOT

21480U75N-751

Editorial Address: The Mill, Bearwalden Business Park, Wendens Ambo, SAFFRON WALDEN, CB11 4GB
Tel: 01799 544200 **Fax:** 01799 544204
Email: nick.bloom@archant.co.uk
Advertising Address: As above. **Tel:** 01799 544343
Email: tim.price@pilotweb.co.uk
Web site: http://www.pilotweb.aero
Publisher: Archant Specialist Ltd (Saffron Walden)
Date Established: 1965
Frequency: Monthly
Cover Price: £3.80
Annual Sub.: £39.00
Circulation: 18,705 (ABC 01/01/2008 to 31/12/2008)
Usual Pagination: 132
Editor: Nick Bloom
Summary of Content: Magazine covering all aspects of general aviation including flight testing of old and new aircraft, product tests for light aircraft, general news and book reviews.
Readership/Target Audience: Aimed at affluent men with a passion for aviation, commercial pilots and those with a private pilot's licence.
ADVERTISING RATES:
Full Page Colour £2200.00
Agency Commission: 10%
Mechanical Data: Type Area: 277 x 185mm, Trim Size: 297 x 215mm, Bleed Size: 303 x 219mm, Col Length: 277mm, Page Width: 185mm, Film: Digital
Copy instructions: Copy Date: 4 weeks prior to publication date
Average advertising content per issue: 30%
CONSUMER: SPORT: Flight

PIMP

1743275U84A-454

Editorial Address: Studio 52, Old Truman Brewery, 91 Brick Lane, LONDON, E1 6QL **Tel:** 020 7655 0995
Email: press@pimpguides.com
Advertising Address: As above.
Email: nosca@pimpguides.com
Web site: http://www.pimpguides.com
ISSN: 1749-1143
Publisher: Partners in Media Publishing
Date Established: 2004
Frequency: 6 issues yearly
Cover Price: Free
Annual Sub.: £16.00
Circulation: 40,000 (Publisher's Statement)
Usual Pagination: 100
Editor: Kate Darcy; **Features Editor:** Kate Darcy;
Advertising Manager: Nosca Northfield
Summary of Content: Magazine covering art, music, fashion and culture.
Readership/Target Audience: Aimed at global style hunters aged 17-30.
ADVERTISING RATES:
Full Page Colour £1200.00

Consumer Magazines

Agency Commission: 10%
Mechanical Data: Type Area: 260 x 195mm, Col Length: 260mm, Page Width: 195mm, Bleed Size: 276 x 211mm, Trim Size: 270 x 205mm
Copy instructions: Copy Date: 2 weeks prior to publication date
Average advertising content per issue: 30%
CONSUMER: THE ARTS & LITERARY: Arts

PIN HIGH! 601183U75D-205

Editorial Address: 1st Floor, 18-22 Market Street, CLECKHEATON, BD19 5AJ **Tel:** 01274 851323
Fax: 01274 852687
Email: mark_k@sportspub.co.uk
Advertising Address: As above. **Tel:** 0161 428 1221
Fax: 0161 428 6413
Email: paul.wilson@thegolfersclub.co.uk
Web site: http://www.thegolfersclub.co.uk
Publisher: Sports Publications Ltd.
Date Established: 1999
Frequency: Half-yearly - Published in November and June
Cover Price: Free
Circulation: 30,000 (Publisher's Statement)
Usual Pagination: 32
Editor: Mark Kilburn
Summary of Content: Magazine covering golfing news, analysis and advice with celebrity interviews.
Readership/Target Audience: Read by members of the Golfers Club UK.
ADVERTISING RATES:
Full Page Colour £2500.00
SCC £24.00
Agency Commission: 10%
Mechanical Data: Film: Digital, Trim Size: 297 x 210mm, Bleed Size: 303 x 216mm
Copy instructions: Copy Date: 1 month prior to publication date
CONSUMER: SPORT: Golf

PINK PAPER 47630U86B-169

Editorial Address: Unit M, Spectrum House, 32-34 Gordon House Road, LONDON, NW5 1LP **Tel:** 020 7424 7400
Fax: 020 7424 7401
Email: news@pinkpaper.com
Advertising Address: As above.
Email: marianna@millivres.co.uk
Web site: http://www.pinkpaper.com
Publisher: Millivres-Prowler Ltd
Frequency: 25 issues yearly
Cover Price: Free
Circulation: 100,000 (Publisher's Statement)
Usual Pagination: 48
Editor: Tris Reid-Smith; **News Editor:** Peter Lloyd; **Features Editor:** Darren Scott; **Advertising Manager:** Marianna Virides
Summary of Content: Website covering all aspects of health, culture, politics and entertainment as well as news and lifestyle.
Readership/Target Audience: Read by lesbians and gay men between 18 and 80 years old.
ADVERTISING RATES:
Full Page Colour £2040.00
SCC £10.00
Agency Commission: 10%
Mechanical Data: Trim Size: 297 x 210mm, Film: Digital, Page Width: 277mm, Col Length: 344mm, Col Widths (Display): 44mm, No. of Columns (Display): 6, Type Area: 344 x 277mm
Copy instructions: Copy Date: 2 days prior to publication date
CONSUMER: ADULT & GAY MAGAZINES: Gay & Lesbian Magazines

PINK RIBBON 1623518U74A-957

Editorial Address: 41 Green Lane, LONDON, SE9 2AF
Tel: 07900 267988 **Fax:** 020 8859 3664
Email: info@pinkribbon.co.uk
Advertising Address: As above.
Email: info@pinkribbon.co.uk
Web site: http://www.pinkribbon.co.uk
ISSN: 1466-0059
Publisher: Gerard Dugdill
Date Established: 1999
Frequency: Annual - Published in September/October
Cover Price: £3.45
Free to qualifying individuals
Circulation: 42,000 (Publisher's Statement)
Usual Pagination: 200
Editor: Gerard Dugdill; **Advertising Manager:** Gerard Dugdill; **Publisher:** Gerard Dugdill
Summary of Content: Lifestyle magazine covering issues on breast cancer awareness and the Awareness Month in a positive and upbeat style.
Readership/Target Audience: Aimed at women of any age.

ADVERTISING: Rates on application
CONSUMER: WOMEN'S INTEREST CONSUMER MAGAZINES: Women's Interest

---

THE PINK SOUTHAMPTON 45706U75A-640

Editorial Address: Newspaper House, Test Lane, Redbridge, SOUTHAMPTON, SO16 9JX **Tel:** 023 8042 4777
Fax: 023 8042 4550
Email: echosport@dailyecho.co.uk
Advertising Address: As above.
Email: kate.freeman@dailyecho.co.uk
Web site: http://www.thisishampshire.net
ISSN: 0969-5702
Publisher: Newsquest (Media Group) Ltd
Frequency: Weekly
Cover Price: £0.50
Circulation: 6,000 (Publisher's Statement)
Editor: Simon Straker; **Advertising Manager:** Kate Freeman
Summary of Content: Saturday evening sports supplement to the Southern Daily Echo.
Readership/Target Audience: Aimed at sport enthusiasts.
ADVERTISING RATES:
Full Page Mono £756.00
SCC £2.40
Mechanical Data: Type Area: 350 x 264mm, No. of Columns (Display): 9, Col Length: 350mm, Page Width: 264mm
Supplement to: The Southern Daily Echo (Southampton)
CONSUMER: SPORT

THE PINK 'UN (NORWICH) 45701U75A-657

Editorial Address: Prospect House, Rouen Road, NORWICH, NR1 1RE **Tel:** 01603 772440 **Fax:** 01603 219060
Email: richard.willner@archant.co.uk
Advertising Address: As above. **Tel:** 01603 628311
Fax: 01603 615343
Email: lee.todd@archant.co.uk
Web site: http://www.pinkun.com
Publisher: Archant Norfolk
Date Established: 1913
Usual Pagination: 12
Editor: Richard Willner; **Advertising Manager:** Lee Todd
Summary of Content: Football Supplement of Eastern Daily Press.
Readership/Target Audience: Aimed at football enthusiasts.
ADVERTISING RATES:
Full Page Mono £600.00
Full Page Colour £800.00
Agency Commission: 10%
Mechanical Data: Col Length: 360mm, Type Area: 360 x 270mm, Print Process: Offset litho, Page Width: 270mm, Film: Digital
Copy instructions: Copy Date: Thursday 12pm prior to publication date
Average advertising content per issue: 20%
Supplement to: Eastern Daily Press (Norwich)
CONSUMER: SPORT

PIPING TODAY 1616501U76D-773

Editorial Address: National Piping Centre, 30-34 McPhater Street, Cowcaddens, GLASGOW, G4 0HW
Tel: 0141 353 0220 **Fax:** 0141 353 1570
Email: mikepaterson@mac.com
Advertising Address: As above.
Web site: http://www.thepipingcentre.co.uk
ISSN: 1479-7143
Publisher: National Piping Centre
Date Established: 2002
Frequency: 6 issues yearly
Cover Price: £2.95
Annual Sub.: £15.00
Circulation: 5,000 (Publisher's Statement)
Usual Pagination: 50
Editor: Roddy MacLeod; **Advertising Manager:** Paul Warren
Summary of Content: Magazine of the National Piping Centre promoting the music, history and study of the bagpipes worldwide. Also containing current news, features and profiles, new product listings, scholarly contributions, etc.
Readership/Target Audience: Those interested in the Highland bagpipes and related instruments.
CONSUMER: MUSIC & PERFORMING ARTS: Music

THE PISTE 1666942U75G-653

Editorial Address: 27 Norwich Road, HALESWORTH, IP19 8BX **Tel:** 01986 834216 **Fax:** 01986 834270
Email: barry.spouge@snowsportengland.org.uk
Advertising Address: As above.
Email: barry.spouge@micropress.co.uk
Web site: http://www.snowsportengland.org.uk
Publisher: Countrywide Publications
Date Established: 2003

Frequency: Quarterly
Cover Price: £2.50
Free to qualifying individuals
Circulation: 12,500 (Publisher's Statement)
Usual Pagination: 24
Editor: Barry Spouge; **Advertising Manager:** Barry Spouge
Summary of Content: Magazine covering all aspects of snow sports including skiing, snow-boarding and snow blades.
Readership/Target Audience: Aimed at around 21,000 snow sports enthusiasts and members of Snowsport England.
ADVERTISING RATES:
Full Page Mono £475.00
Full Page Colour £500.00
Agency Commission: 10%
Mechanical Data: Film: Digital, Type Area: 268 x 185mm, Col Length: 268mm, Page Width: 185mm, Trim Size: 297 x 210mm, No. of Columns (Display): 4, Print Process: Litho
Copy instructions: Copy Date: 3 weeks prior to publication date
Average advertising content per issue: 30%
CONSUMER: SPORT: Winter Sports

PITPILOT 1646394U75M-994

Editorial Address: PO Box 441, NEWQUAY, TR7 2XQ
Tel: 01637 878140
Email: info@pitpilotmag.co.uk
Advertising Address: As above. **Tel:** 01637 878149
Email: nick@pitpilotmag.co.uk
Web site: http://www.pitpilotmag.co.uk
ISSN: 1745-6037
Publisher: Arcwind Ltd
Date Established: 2003
Frequency: 6 issues yearly
Cover Price: £3.80
Annual Sub.: £20.00
Circulation: 14,000 (Publisher's Statement)
Usual Pagination: 132
Editor: Greg Martin; **Advertising Manager:** Nick Lloyd; **Publisher:** Mark Kasprowicz
Summary of Content: Magazine covering all aspects of surfing in Britain as well as rock music, skate boarding, extreme sports, interviews and product reviews.
Readership/Target Audience: Aimed at the British surfing community.
ADVERTISING RATES:
Full Page Colour £550.00
Agency Commission: 10%
Mechanical Data: Bleed Size: 266 x 206mm, Trim Size: 260 x 200mm, Film: Digital, Type Area: 250 x 190mm, Col Length: 250mm, Page Width: 190mm
Average advertising content per issue: 30%
CONSUMER: SPORT: Water Sports

PLAIN TRUTH 47739U87-183

Editorial Address: PO Box 4421, WORTHING, BN14 8WQ
Tel: 01638 741549 **Fax:** 01638 744190
Email: editor@plaintruth.co.uk
Advertising Address: CPO, Garcia Estate, Canterbury Road, WORTHING, BN13 1BW **Tel:** 01903 602100
Fax: 01903 537321
Email: paulataylor@cpo.org.uk
Web site: http://www.plain-truth.org.uk
Publisher: The Plain Truth Ltd
Date Established: 1953
Frequency: 5 issues yearly
Cover Price: Free
Circulation: 9,000 (Publisher's Statement)
Usual Pagination: 24
Editor: Mary Hammond; **Advertising Manager:** Paula Taylor
Summary of Content: Magazine covering contemporary Christian issues.
Readership/Target Audience: Aimed at those interested in religion.
ADVERTISING RATES:
Full Page Mono £995.00
Full Page Colour £1095.00
Agency Commission: 10%
Mechanical Data: Type Area: 270 x 182mm, Trim Size: 297 x 210mm, Page Width: 182mm, Col Length: 270mm, Film: Digital, Bleed Size: +3mm
Copy instructions: Copy Date: 1 month prior to publication date
CONSUMER: RELIGIOUS

PLANET 4X4 1750019U77A-597

Editorial Address: 151 Station Street, BURTON-ON-TRENT, DE14 1BG **Tel:** 01283 742950 **Fax:** 01283 742957
Email: editorial@toronline.co.uk
Advertising Address: As above.
Email: ian.sharpe@wwonline.co.uk
Publisher: WW Magazines
Date Established: 2006
Frequency: Monthly
Cover Price: £3.75
Usual Pagination: 100

Editor: Alan Kidd; **Advertising Manager:** Ian Sharpe
Summary of Content: Magazine covering new and used 4x4s and off road adventure with news, road tests group tests and stories about adventure travel.
Readership/Target Audience: Aimed at anyone interested in buying and or owning a 4x4.
ADVERTISING RATES:
Full Page Colour £975.00
Agency Commission: 10%
Mechanical Data: Type Area: 267 x 190mm, Bleed Size: 303 x 216mm, Trim Size: 297 x 210mm, Col Length: 267mm, Page Width: 190mm, Film: Digital
Copy instructions: Copy Date: 6 weeks prior to publication date
CONSUMER: MOTORING & CYCLING: Motoring

PLANET PHILIPPINES
1647093U90-967
Editorial Address: 313 Brompton Road, LONDON, SW3 2DY **Tel:** 020 7581 8100 **Fax:** 020 7581 9194
Email: philservicecorp@aol.com
Advertising Address: As above.
Email: philservicecorp@aol.com
Publisher: Philippine Service Corporation
Frequency: Monthly
Cover Price: Free
Circulation: 15,000 (Publisher's Statement)
Usual Pagination: 40
Editor: Rina Reyes; **Advertising Manager:** Camille Lazaro
Summary of Content: Magazine covering the lifestyle and culture of the Philippines as well as stories of celebrities and achievers.
Readership/Target Audience: Aimed at the Filipino communities in the UK.
ADVERTISING: Rates on application
CONSUMER: ETHNIC

PLANET - THE WELSH INTERNATIONALIST
47268U82-153_50
Editorial Address: PO Box 44, ABERYSTWYTH, SY23 3ZZ
Tel: 01970 611255 **Fax:** 01970 611197
Email: planet.enquiries@planetmagazine.org.uk
Advertising Address: As above.
Email: dafydd.prys@planetmagazine.org.uk
Web site: http://www.planetmagazine.org.uk
ISSN: 0048-4288
Publisher: Berw Cyf
Date Established: 1970
Frequency: 6 issues yearly
Cover Price: £4.00
Annual Sub.: £22.00
Circulation: 1,300 (Publisher's Statement)
Usual Pagination: 128
Editor: Helle Michelsen; **Advertising Manager:** Dafydd Prys
Summary of Content: Magazine containing features on literature, art, politics, science and the environment.
Readership/Target Audience: Aimed at those interested in Welsh affairs and global issues.
ADVERTISING RATES:
Full Page Mono £100.00
Full Page Colour £150.00
Agency Commission: 10%
Mechanical Data: Film: Digital, Page Width: 135mm, Type Area: 175 x 135mm, Trim Size: 210 x 160mm, Col Length: 175mm
Copy instructions: Copy Date: 4 weeks prior to publication date
Average advertising content per issue: 5%
CONSUMER: CURRENT AFFAIRS & POLITICS

PLASTIQUE
1800023U74B-728
Editorial Address: Suite 13, 93 Shepperton Road, LONDON, N1 3DF **Tel:** 020 7288 1828 **Fax:** 020 7288 1828
Email: info@plastiquemagazine.com
Advertising Address: As above.
Email: idalina@plastiquemagazine.com
Web site: http://www.plastiquemagazine.com
Publisher: Plastique Magazine Ltd
Date Established: 2007
Frequency: Quarterly
Cover Price: £5.00
Circulation: 25,000 (Publisher's Statement)
Usual Pagination: 240
Editor: Siobhan Witter; **Editor-in-Chief:** Brylie Fowler; **Advertising Director:** Idalina Leandro
Summary of Content: Magazine covering fashion and accessories.
Readership/Target Audience: Aimed at women aged 25 to 35 years old.
ADVERTISING RATES:
Full Page Colour £6500.00
Mechanical Data: Film: Digital, Trim Size: 285 x 220mm, Bleed Size: 295 x 230mm
CONSUMER: WOMEN'S INTEREST CONSUMER MAGAZINES: Women's Interest - Fashion

PLATFORM
761555U83-61_50
Editorial Address: Byron House, Shakespeare Street, NOTTINGHAM, NG1 4GH **Tel:** 0115 848 6244
Fax: 0115 848 6201
Email: platform@su.ntu.ac.uk
Advertising Address: As above.
Email: simon.rhodes@su.ntu.ac.uk
Web site: http://www.trentstudents.org
Publisher: Nottingham Trent University Students' Union
Frequency: 15 issues yearly
Cover Price: Free
Circulation: 20,000 (Publisher's Statement)
Usual Pagination: 40
Advertising Manager: Simon Rhodes
Summary of Content: Student newspaper covering sport, music, cinema and student life in general.
Readership/Target Audience: Read by students at Nottingham Trent University.
ADVERTISING RATES:
Full Page Colour £450.00
Agency Commission: 10%
Mechanical Data: Film: Digital, Bleed Size: 246 x 176mm, Trim Size: 240 x 170mm
Copy instructions: Copy Date: 1 week prior to publication date
Average advertising content per issue: 15%
CONSUMER: STUDENT PUBLICATIONS

PLAY
46554U78D-213_40
Editorial Address: Richmond House, 33 Richmond Hill, BOURNEMOUTH, BH2 6EZ **Tel:** 01202 586200
Email: play@imagine-publishing.co.uk
Advertising Address: As above.
Email: james.hanslip@imagine-publishing.co.uk
Web site: http://www.play-mag.co.uk
ISSN: 1358-9474
Publisher: Imagine Publishing
Frequency: 13 issues yearly
Cover Price: £4.99
Circulation: 26,464 (ABC 01/01/2008 to 31/12/2008)
Usual Pagination: 132
Editor: Nick Jones; **Features Editor:** Tom Le Clerk; **Editor-in-Chief:** Nick Jones; **Managing Director:** Damian Butt
Summary of Content: Magazine featuring games available on the PlayStation 2 system.
Readership/Target Audience: Aimed at the serious games player, predominantly male between 14 and 26 years old.
ADVERTISING RATES:
Full Page Colour £3500.00
Mechanical Data: Film: Digital, Type Area: 277 x 210mm, Page Width: 210mm, Col Length: 277mm, Trim Size: 297 x 230mm, Bleed Size: 307 x 240mm
CONSUMER: CONSUMER ELECTRONICS: Games

THE PLAYER
1668057U75D-538
Editorial Address: 5 Alford Street, LONDON, W1K 2AF
Tel: 020 7493 2030 **Fax:** 020 7493 2020
Email: andie@theplayer.co.uk
Advertising Address: As above.
Email: andie@theplayer.co.uk
Web site: http://www.theplayer.co.uk
Publisher: Lazy Cats Media Ltd
Date Established: 2005
Frequency: Quarterly
Annual Sub.: £199.00
Circulation: 37,000 (Publisher's Statement)
Usual Pagination: 202
Editor: Andrew Jones; **Editor-in-Chief:** Andrew Jones; **Advertising Director:** Andie Jones
Summary of Content: Magazine covering a luxury lifestyle including golf courses, spas, resorts, travel, top marques cars, boyz toys and gadgets, polo, powerboats and high finance. Also covers fine wines, cognacs, brandies, champagne, cigars, watches, men's accessories and men's fashion.
Language(s): English; Russian
Readership/Target Audience: Distributed in the UK, Russia, Ukraine, Dubai, Bahrain, Qatar and New York through the European PGA Seniors Tour, UK Football Clubs, Spectrum Finance Clientele, plus individuals who belong to the Player Club.
ADVERTISING RATES:
Full Page Colour £15000.00
Mechanical Data: Type Area: 330 x 240mm, Bleed Size: +6mm, Col Length: 330mm, Page Width: 240mm, Film: Digital
CONSUMER: SPORT: Golf

PLAYERS CLUB
1895430U74Q-1375
Editorial Address: Valley House, Trimpley, BEWDLEY, DY12 1PG **Tel:** 07980 770701
Email: chris.jordan@cj-media.co.uk
Web site: http://www.givemefootball.com/pfa/commercial/players-club
Publisher: CJ Media
Frequency: 5 issues yearly

Cover Price: Free
Circulation: 4,000 (Publisher's Statement)
Editor: Chris Jordan; **Publisher:** Chris Jordan
Summary of Content: Magazine covering lifestyle, fashion, motors, investment, Professional Footballers Association news and interviews with celebrities associated with football.
Readership/Target Audience: Aimed at PFA members in England and Wales.
ADVERTISING RATES:
Full Page Colour £1960
CONSUMER: WOMEN'S INTEREST CONSUMER MAGAZINES: Lifestyle

PLAYLIST
1623040U89C-954
Formerly: Knowledge
Editorial Address: 1 Pennington Street, LONDON, E98 1TE
Tel: 020 7782 5000
Email: playlist@thetimes.co.uk
Advertising Address: As above. **Fax:** 020 7782 7107
Email: sarah.walker@newsint.co.uk
Web site: http://www.timesonline.co.uk/theknowledge
Publisher: Times Newspapers Ltd
Date Established: 2003
Frequency: Weekly - See The Times for circulation figure
Cover Price: Free
Usual Pagination: 64
Editor: James Jackson; **Advertising Manager:** Sarah Walker
Summary of Content: Magazine covering features, interviews and previews on arts and entertainment nationwide, including gadgets and games. Plus kids, general events and a TV guide.
ADVERTISING RATES:
Full Page Colour £12600.00
SCC £110.00
Agency Commission: 10%
Mechanical Data: Type Area: 260 x 225mm, Col Length: 260mm, Page Width: 225mm, Film: Digital
Copy instructions: Copy Date: 2 Wednesday's prior to publication date
Supplement to: The Times
CONSUMER: HOLIDAYS & TRAVEL: Entertainment Guides

PLAYMUSIC PICKUP
1820138U76D-835
Editorial Address: Webster House, Dudley Road, TUNBRIDGE WELLS, TN1 1LE **Tel:** 01892 533456
Fax: 01892 535417
Email: tim@standfirst-media.com
Advertising Address: As above.
Email: nick@just-play.com
Web site: http://www.playmusicpickup.co.uk
ISSN: 1752-1017
Publisher: Standfirst Media Limited
Frequency: Monthly
Cover Price: Free
Circulation: 25,000 (Publisher's Statement)
Usual Pagination: 92
Editor: Tim Slater
Summary of Content: Magazine with reviews of musical instruments as well as reviews and features of signed and unsigned bands.
Readership/Target Audience: Aimed at music fans aged 15 to 25 years old.
ADVERTISING RATES:
Full Page Mono £700.00
Full Page Colour £700.00
Agency Commission: 10%
Mechanical Data: Type Area: 261 x 174mm, Bleed Size: 303 x 216mm, Trim Size: 297 x 210mm, Col Length: 261mm, Page Width: 174mm, Film: Digital
Copy instructions: Copy Date: 1 week prior to publication date
Average advertising content per issue: 40%
CONSUMER: MUSIC & PERFORMING ARTS: Music

PLAYS INTERNATIONAL
46076U76B-130
Editorial Address: 33A Lurline Gardens, LONDON, SW11 4DD **Tel:** 020 7720 1950 **Fax:** 020 7720 1950
ISSN: 0268-2028
Publisher: Performing Arts Trust
Frequency: 6 issues yearly
Cover Price: £2.99
Annual Sub.: £35.00
Circulation: 12,000 (Publisher's Statement)
Usual Pagination: 48
Editor: Peter Roberts
Summary of Content: Magazine covering play reviews and news of the theatre world.
Readership/Target Audience: Aimed at regular theatre-goers.
ADVERTISING: No Advertising taken
CONSUMER: MUSIC & PERFORMING ARTS: Theatre

Consumer Magazines

PLUK
1664535U85A-203

Editorial Address: 13 Masons Yard, LONDON, SW1Y 6BU
Tel: 020 7839 9300 **Fax:** 020 7321 0496
Email: info@plukmagazine.com
Advertising Address: As above.
Email: advertising@plukmagazine.com
Web site: http://www.plukmagazine.com
ISSN: 1473-9933
Publisher: Pluk
Date Established: 2001
Frequency: Quarterly
Cover Price: £4.95
Circulation: 16,000 (Publisher's Statement)
Usual Pagination: 100
Editor: Anna Smith; **Advertising Manager:** Anna Smith;
Managing Editor: Anna Smith
Summary of Content: Magazine covering photography
containing up-to-date interviews, previews of exhibitions and
events, profiles of the latest books and concise and
informative articles on the market, the scene and the people.
Readership/Target Audience: Aimed at the general public
with photography or art interests, photographers and
dealers.
ADVERTISING RATES:
Full Page Mono £550.00
Full Page Colour £738.00
Mechanical Data: Type Area: 185 x 100mm, Bleed Size:
206 x 126mm, Trim Size: 200 x 120mm, Col Length: 185mm,
Page Width: 100mm, Film: Digital
CONSUMER: PHOTOGRAPHY & FILM MAKING:
Photography

PLUS & EAGLE WINGS
48490U91D-87_10

Formerly: Plus Comic & Eagle Wings
Editorial Address: The Barn, Flaxlands Manor Farm,
Flaxlands, Wootton Bassett, SWINDON, SN4 8DY
Tel: 01793 850589
Email: editor@pluseagleswings.org
Web site: http://www.pluseagleswings.org
Publisher: Hayes Press
Date Established: 1910
Frequency: 10 issues yearly
Cover Price: £0.85
Annual Sub.: £8.50
Circulation: 8,000 (Publisher's Statement)
Usual Pagination: 8
Editor: K. Hickling
Summary of Content: Children's magazine containing
picture strips, children's interest features and puzzles.
Readership/Target Audience: Aimed at children between 7
and 11 years old.
ADVERTISING: No Advertising taken
CONSUMER: RECREATION & LEISURE: Children & Youth

PLUSH
1696058U80C-5278

Editorial Address: 80 North Street, LEEDS, LS2 7PN
Tel: 0113 244 1007 **Fax:** 0113 244 1002
Email: ali.schofield@leedsguide.co.uk
Advertising Address: As above. **Tel:** 0113 244 1000
Email: jessica.bradley@leedsguide.co.uk
Web site: http://www.leedsguide.co.uk
Publisher: Leeds Guide Ltd
Date Established: 2005
Frequency: Monthly
Free to qualifying individuals
Annual Sub.: £20.00
Circulation: 10,000 (Publisher's Statement)
Usual Pagination: 52
Editor: Ali Schofield; **Advertising Manager:** Jessica
Bradley; **Managing Editor:** Jessica Bradley
Summary of Content: Lifestyle magazine covering
restaurants, entertainment, culture, fashion, health and
beauty, motors, theatre, live music, clubs, arts and kids.
Readership/Target Audience: Aimed at residents and
visitors to Harrogate.
ADVERTISING RATES:
Full Page Colour £850.00
Agency Commission: 10%
Mechanical Data: Type Area: 277 x 190mm, Trim Size: 297
x 210mm, Bleed Size: 303 x 216mm, Col Length: 277mm,
Page Width: 190mm, Film: Digital
Copy instructions: Copy Date: 17th of the month prior to
publication date
CONSUMER: RURAL & REGIONAL INTEREST: Regional
Interest English Counties

PLUTO
47427U83-62_50

Editorial Address: University of Central Lancashire
Students Union, Fylde Road, PRESTON, PR1 2TQ
Tel: 01772 894875
Email: sucommunication@uclan.ac.uk
Advertising Address: As above. **Fax:** 01772 894970
Email: suinformation@uclan.ac.uk
Web site: http://www.pluto-online.co.uk
Publisher: UCLAN Students Union
Date Established: 1991

Frequency: Monthly - Published fortnightly during term time
Cover Price: Free
Circulation: 4,000 (Publisher's Statement)
Usual Pagination: 36
Editor: Ed Walker; **Advertising Manager:** Joanna Bibby
Summary of Content: Magazine containing student news
and features on music, film, theatre and university sporting
events.
Readership/Target Audience: Read by students at the
University of Central Lancashire.
ADVERTISING RATES:
Full Page Mono £620.00
Full Page Colour £875.00
Mechanical Data: Bleed Size: 356 x 270mm, Trim Size: 350
x 264mm, Film: Digital
Copy instructions: Copy Date: 1 week prior to publication
date
Average advertising content per issue: 12%
CONSUMER: STUDENT PUBLICATIONS

THE PLYMOUTH DIARY
1894225U80C-5499

Editorial Address: 22 Mary Seacole Road, PLYMOUTH,
PL1 3JY **Tel:** 01752 510061
Email: caroline@plymouthdiary.co.uk
Web site: http://www.plymouthdiary.co.uk
Publisher: Synchro Publishing UK Ltd
Frequency: 6 issues yearly
Cover Price: £2.00
Free to qualifying individuals
Circulation: 30,000 (Publisher's Statement)
Editor: Caroline Tiernan-Locke; **Publisher:** Elaine Elliott
Summary of Content: Magazine covering community,
sports, entertainment events.
Readership/Target Audience: Aimed at people and visitors
in Plymouth.
CONSUMER: RURAL & REGIONAL INTEREST: Regional
Interest English Counties

THE PLYMOUTH MAGAZINE
1659053U80C-5157

Editorial Address: 28 Old Park Road, Peverell, PLYMOUTH,
PL3 4PY **Tel:** 01752 225623 **Fax:** 01752 673441
Email: info@theplymouthmagazine.com
Advertising Address: As above.
Email: tessa@cornerstonevision.com
Web site: http://www.theplymouthmagazine.com
Publisher: Cornerstone Vision
Date Established: 2004
Frequency: Monthly
Cover Price: Free
Circulation: 42,000 (Publisher's Statement)
Usual Pagination: 48
Editor: Chris Girdler; **Publisher:** Chris Girdler
Summary of Content: Magazine covering lifestyle including
interior design, property, personal finance, events guide,
eating out, health and welfare.
Readership/Target Audience: Aimed at home owners in
Plymouth.
ADVERTISING RATES:
Full Page Colour £525.00
Agency Commission: 10%
Mechanical Data: Type Area: 277 x 190mm, Col Length:
277mm, Page Width: 190mm, Film: Digital, Bleed Size: 303 x
216mm, Trim Size: 297 x 210mm
Copy instructions: Copy Date: 10 days prior to publication
date
CONSUMER: RURAL & REGIONAL INTEREST: Regional
Interest English Counties

POCKET LONDON
601161U89C-347

Editorial Address: 3 Stewart's Court, 218-220 Stewart's
Road, LONDON, SW8 4UB **Tel:** 020 7720 1166
Fax: 020 7720 1177
Email: info@pocketlondon.com
Advertising Address: As above.
Email: rupert@pocketlondon.com
Web site: http://www.pocketlondon.com
ISSN: 1369-3492
Publisher: Pocket London Ltd
Date Established: 1997
Frequency: Quarterly
Cover Price: Free
Circulation: 300,000 (Publisher's Statement)
Usual Pagination: 60
Editor: Julia Starkey; **Managing Director:** Rupert Saunders;
Advertising Manager: Rupert Saunders
Summary of Content: Guide to what's on and what's new
in London. Covering sights and attractions, museums and
galleries, music and theatre, eating, drinking and shopping.
Each entry is cross referenced with precise maps of Central
London.
Readership/Target Audience: Aimed at business and
tourist visitors to London.
ADVERTISING: Rates on application
CONSUMER: HOLIDAYS & TRAVEL: Entertainment Guides

POCKET WORDSEARCH
46684U79F-59

Editorial Address: Stonecroft, 69 Station Road, REDHILL,
RH1 1EY **Tel:** 01737 378700 **Fax:** 01737 781800
Email: reception@puzzlermedia.com
Advertising Address: As above. **Fax:** 01737 781888
Email: brian.ainge@puzzlermedia.com
Web site: http://www.puzzler.com
Publisher: Puzzler Media Ltd
Frequency: Monthly
Cover Price: £1.10
Circulation: 80,000 (Publisher's Statement)
Editor: Maggie Ayers; **Advertising Director:** Brian Ainge
Summary of Content: Publication containing puzzles with
words hidden in a grid of jumbled letters.
Readership/Target Audience: Read by middle or older
aged people, 80% of whom are female.
ADVERTISING RATES:
Full Page Mono £700.00
Full Page Colour £950.00
Agency Commission: 10%
Mechanical Data: Trim Size: 255 x 180mm, Film: Digital
CONSUMER: HOBBIES & DIY: Games & Puzzles

POETRY REVIEW
47551U84B-170

Editorial Address: 22 Betterton Street, LONDON, WC2H
9BX **Tel:** 020 7420 9880 **Fax:** 020 7240 4818
Email: poetryreview@poetrysociety.org.uk
Advertising Address: As above.
Email: marketing@poetrysociety.org.uk
Web site: http://www.poetrysociety.org.uk
Publisher: The Poetry Society
Frequency: Quarterly
Cover Price: £7.95
Annual Sub.: £30.00
Circulation: 4,000 (Publisher's Statement)
Usual Pagination: 96
Editor: Fiona Sampson; **Advertising Manager:** Lisa Roberts
Summary of Content: Magazine containing poems, reviews
and features on all aspects of poetry and the work of poets.
Readership/Target Audience: Aimed at poets, teachers,
students and general readers of poetry.
ADVERTISING RATES:
Full Page Mono £370.00
Agency Commission: 10%
Mechanical Data: Film: Digital, Trim Size: 240 x 170mm
Copy instructions: Copy Date: 4 weeks prior to publication
date
Average advertising content per issue: 12%
CONSUMER: THE ARTS & LITERARY: Literary

POETRY WALES
47552U84B-172

Editorial Address: 57 Nolton Street, BRIDGEND, CF31 3AE
Tel: 01656 663018 **Fax:** 01656 649226
Email: poetrywales@seren-books.com
Advertising Address: As above.
Email: poetrywales@seren-books.com
Web site: http://www.poetrywales.co.uk
ISSN: 0332-2202
Publisher: Poetry Wales Press Ltd
Date Established: 1965
Frequency: Quarterly
Cover Price: £4.00
Annual Sub.: £16.00
Circulation: 800 (Publisher's Statement)
Usual Pagination: 72
Editor: Zoe Skoulding; **Advertising Manager:** Penny
Thomas
Summary of Content: Literary magazine publishing poetry,
reviews and critical articles, focusing on Wales, but with a
broad interest in contemporary cultural issues.
Readership/Target Audience: Aimed at poets, students,
teachers and all who enjoy poetry.
ADVERTISING RATES:
Full Page Mono £125.00
Full Page Colour 150.00
Mechanical Data: Trim Size: 248 x 174mm, Film: Digital
Average advertising content per issue: 5%
CONSUMER: THE ARTS & LITERARY: Literary

POKEMON WORLD
628703U91D-952

Editorial Address: Richmond House, 33 Richmond Hill,
BOURNEMOUTH, BH2 6EZ **Tel:** 01202 586219
Email: nick.roberts@imagine-publishing.co.uk
Web site: http://www.pokemon-world.co.uk
Publisher: Imagine Publishing
Date Established: 2000
Frequency: 10 issues yearly
Cover Price: £3.99
Circulation: 25,000 (Publisher's Statement)
Usual Pagination: 52
Editor: Nick Roberts; **Publisher:** Nick Roberts
Summary of Content: Children's magazine covering all
aspects of Pokemon, including news, puzzles, video games,
Pokemon Trading Card Game and tips plus other multi-
format video games, toys and books.

Readership/Target Audience: Aimed at 6 to 14 year olds.
CONSUMER: RECREATION & LEISURE: Children & Youth

POKER EUROPA
1804958U79F-107

Editorial Address: 33 Parkhurst Road, TORQUAY, TQ1 4EW **Tel:** 01803 313013 **Fax:** 01803 313013
Email: ElizaB@PokerEuropa.co.uk
Advertising Address: As above. **Tel:** 01803 390736
Email: evesz@pokereuropa.co.uk
Web site: http://www.pokereuropa.net
Date Established: 1999
Frequency: Monthly
Cover Price: Free
Circulation: 15,000 (Publisher's Statement)
Usual Pagination: 96
Editor: Eliza Burnett; **Managing Editor:** Nic Szeremeta
Summary of Content: Magazine covering poker news and reports from across Europe. Information and educational poker material, features and interviews.
Language(s): English; French; German
Readership/Target Audience: Aimed at poker players and potential poker players.
ADVERTISING RATES:
Full Page Colour EUR1440.00
Agency Commission: 10%
Mechanical Data: Bleed Size: 307 x 220mm, Trim Size: 297 x 210mm, Film: Digital
CONSUMER: HOBBIES & DIY: Games & Puzzles

POKER PLAYER
1695648U79F-92

Editorial Address: 30 Cleveland Street, LONDON, W1T 4JD
Tel: 020 7907 6000 **Fax:** 020 7907 6282
Email: dave_woods@dennis.co.uk
Advertising Address: As above. **Fax:** 020 7907 6600
Email: russell_blackman@dennis.co.uk
Publisher: Dennis Publishing Ltd
Date Established: 2005
Frequency: Monthly
Cover Price: £2.25
Circulation: 17,240 (Publisher's Statement)
Editor: Dave Woods
Summary of Content: Magazine with tips, strategies, opinions and features as well as chances to play with the top Poker professionals.
Readership/Target Audience: Aimed at poker players at all levels of skill.
ADVERTISING RATES:
Full Page Colour £6454.00
Agency Commission: 10%
Mechanical Data: Type Area: 263 x 190mm, Bleed Size: 281 x 216mm, Trim Size: 275 x 210mm, Col Length: 263mm, Page Width: 190mm, Film: Digital
Copy instructions: Copy Date: 2nd Thursday of month prior to publication date
Average advertising content per issue: 25%
CONSUMER: HOBBIES & DIY: Games & Puzzles

POLICY & POLITICS
47269U82-155

Editorial Address: Policy & Politics, School for Policy Studies, University of Bristol, 8 Priory Road, BRISTOL, BS8 1TZ **Tel:** 0117 954 6755 **Fax:** 0117 954 6756
Email: tpp-pp@bristol.ac.uk
Advertising Address: Beacon House, 4th Floor, Queen's Road, BRISTOL, BS8 1QU **Tel:** 0117 331 4054
Fax: 0117 331 4093
Email: kathryn.king@bristol.ac.uk
Web site: http://www.policypress.org.uk
ISSN: 0305-5736
Publisher: The Policy Press
Date Established: 1972
Frequency: Quarterly - Published in January, April, July and October
Annual Sub.: £65.00
Circulation: 500 (Publisher's Statement)
Usual Pagination: 130
Editor: Geetanjali Gangoli; **Advertising Manager:** Kathryn King
Summary of Content: Publication containing an insight into the origins, implementation and impact of public policy, focusing increasingly on European and international policy debates.
Readership/Target Audience: Aimed at central and local government, university departments, academic libraries, health, education and housing departments.
ADVERTISING RATES:
Full Page Mono £350.00
Mechanical Data: Type Area: 207 x 134mm, Col Length: 207mm, Page Width: 134mm
Copy instructions: Copy Date: 8 weeks prior to publication date
CONSUMER: CURRENT AFFAIRS & POLITICS

POLISH EXPRESS
1745163U90-984

Editorial Address: 603 Cumberland House, 80 Scrubs Lane, LONDON, NW10 6RF **Tel:** 020 8964 4488
Fax: 020 8960 7737
Email: info@polishexpress.co.uk
Advertising Address: As above.
Email: i.zajaczkowska@fortismedia.uk
Web site: http://www.polishexpress.co.uk
Publisher: Polish Express
Date Established: 2003
Frequency: Weekly
Cover Price: £1.00
Free to qualifying individuals
Circulation: 60,000 (Publisher's Statement)
Usual Pagination: 64
Editor: Tomasz Kmiecik; **Advertising Manager:** Isabella Zajaczkowska
Summary of Content: Newspaper covering culture, entertainment and life from a Polish perspective.
Language(s): English; Polish
Readership/Target Audience: Aimed at Polish communities in the UK.
ADVERTISING: Rates on application
Agency Commission: 3%
Average advertising content per issue: 35%
CONSUMER: ETHNIC

POLO TIMES
46018U75X-630

Editorial Address: East End Farm, East End, North Leigh, WITNEY, OX29 6PX **Tel:** 01993 886885 **Fax:** 01993 882660
Email: admin@polotimes.co.uk
Advertising Address: As above.
Email: ads@polotimes.co.uk
Web site: http://www.polotimes.co.uk
ISSN: 1461-4685
Publisher: Dallas Brett Publishing
Date Established: 1993
Frequency: 10 issues yearly
Cover Price: £5.00
Annual Sub.: £50.00
Circulation: 2,000 (Publisher's Statement)
Usual Pagination: 68
Editor: Yolanda Carslaw; **Publisher:** Margie Brett
Summary of Content: Magazine covering polo around the world. Includes information from clubs and associations, tournament and team news, polo reports, social news, polo destination features and player profiles.
Readership/Target Audience: Aimed at both spectators and players.
ADVERTISING RATES:
Full Page Colour £1200.00
Agency Commission: 10%
Mechanical Data: Trim Size: 297 x 210mm, Bleed Size: 303 x 216mm, Film: Digital
Copy instructions: Copy Date: 3 weeks prior to publication date
Average advertising content per issue: 35%
CONSUMER: SPORT: Other Sport

PONY MAGAZINE
47137U81D-200

Editorial Address: Headley House, Headley Road, Grayshott, HINDHEAD, GU26 6TU **Tel:** 01428 601020
Fax: 01428 601027
Email: djm@djmurphy.co.uk
Advertising Address: As above. **Fax:** 01428 601030
Email: andrea@djmurphy.co.uk
Web site: http://www.ponymag.com
Publisher: D.J. Murphy (Publishers) Ltd
Date Established: 1949
Frequency: 13 issues yearly
Cover Price: £2.70
Annual Sub.: £35.10
Circulation: 242,219 (Publisher's Statement)
Usual Pagination: 76
Editor: Janet Rising; **Advertisement Director:** Andrea Moffatt
Summary of Content: Magazine containing features to help improve readers' riding and horse care knowledge, including tips from famous riders and trainers.
Readership/Target Audience: Aimed at children and teenage riding enthusiasts.
ADVERTISING RATES:
Full Page Colour £2360.00
SCC £31.00
Agency Commission: 10%
Mechanical Data: Type Area: 273 x 186mm, Bleed Size: 307 x 220mm, Trim Size: 297 x 210mm, Col Length: 273mm, Page Width: 186mm, Film: Digital
Copy instructions: Copy Date: 4 weeks prior to publication date
Average advertising content per issue: 20%
CONSUMER: ANIMALS & PETS: Horses & Ponies

POPULAR PATCHWORK
45367U74E-370

Editorial Address: Berwick House, 8-10 Knoll Rise, ORPINGTON, BR6 0EL **Tel:** 01689 899200
Fax: 01689 899266
Email: jane.rae@myhobbystore.com
Advertising Address: As above.
Email: louise.hodgson@magicalia.com
ISSN: 0969-6945
Publisher: My Hobby Store Media
Date Established: 1993
Frequency: 13 issues yearly
Cover Price: £3.50
Annual Sub.: £32.00
Usual Pagination: 76
Editor: Jane Rae
Summary of Content: Magazine covering articles on traditional and contemporary quilts and information on quilt makers. Includes designs and ideas for patchwork, quilting and appliqué, exhibition reviews and competitions.
Readership/Target Audience: Read by people interested in patchwork, quilting and appliqué as well as educators and students.
ADVERTISING RATES:
Full Page Colour £600.00
Agency Commission: 10%
Mechanical Data: Type Area: 267 x 184mm, Bleed Size: 303 x 213mm, Trim Size: 297 x 210mm, No. of Columns (Display): 4, Film: Digital, Col Length: 267mm, Col Widths (Display): 42mm, Page Width: 184mm
Copy instructions: Copy Date: 4 weeks prior to publication date
Average advertising content per issue: 20%
CONSUMER: WOMEN'S INTEREST CONSUMER MAGAZINES: Crafts

PORSCHE POST
46472U77E-215

Editorial Address: Cornbury House, Cotswold Business Village, London Road, MORETON-IN-MARSH, GL56 0JQ
Tel: 01608 652911 **Fax:** 01608 652944
Email: publications@porscheclubgb.com
Advertising Address: Hine Marketing, Regency House, 19 Suffolk Road, CHELTENHAM, GL50 2AF **Tel:** 01242 222996
Fax: 01242 222077
Email: nick@hinemarketing.co.uk
Web site: http://www.porscheclubgb.com
ISSN: 1743-3452
Publisher: Porsche Club Great Britain
Date Established: 1961
Frequency: Monthly
Annual Sub.: £59.00
Circulation: 16,000 (Publisher's Statement)
Usual Pagination: 140
Editor: Stephen Mummery; **Advertising Manager:** Nick Hine
Summary of Content: Publication containing Porsche-related articles, news and features from the Porsche Club of Great Britain.
Readership/Target Audience: Aimed at members and Porsche enthusiasts.
ADVERTISING RATES:
Full Page Colour £925.00
SCC £10.00
Agency Commission: 10%
Mechanical Data: Col Length: 262mm, Type Area: 262 x 190mm, Bleed Size: 303 x 231mm, Trim Size: 297 x 225mm, Film: Digital, Page Width: 190mm
Average advertising content per issue: 50%
CONSUMER: MOTORING & CYCLING: Club Cars

THE PORTMAN
1648839U80B-411

Editorial Address: Blandel Bridge House, 56 Sloane Square, LONDON, SW1W 8AX **Tel:** 020 7259 1050
Fax: 020 7901 9042
Email: portman@pubbiz.com
Advertising Address: As above. **Tel:** 020 7259 1051
Email: sam@pubbiz.com
Web site: http://www.pubbiz.com/portman.html
Publisher: Publishing Business
Frequency: Quarterly
Cover Price: Free
Circulation: 17,000 (Publisher's Statement)
Usual Pagination: 52
Editor: Erik Brown; **Advertisement Director:** Sam Bradshaw
Summary of Content: Lifestyle magazine covering local and community news as well as food, drink, fashion property and the arts.
Readership/Target Audience: Aimed at residents, businesses and visitors to Marylebone.
ADVERTISING RATES:
Full Page Colour £1550.00
Agency Commission: 10%
Mechanical Data: Bleed Size: 246 x 174mm, Trim Size: 240 x 168mm, Film: Digital
CONSUMER: RURAL & REGIONAL INTEREST: Regional Interest Greater London

Consumer Magazines

PORTSMOUTH & DISTRICT POST

1657244U80C-5286

Editorial Address: 120 London Road, North End, PORTSMOUTH, PO2 0NB **Tel:** 02392 656910
Fax: 02392 656910
Email: molly@portsmouthpost.com
Advertising Address: As above.
Email: molly@portsmouthpost.com
Web site: http://www.portsmouthpost.com
Publisher: Portsmouth & District Post
Date Established: 2003
Frequency: 6 issues yearly
Cover Price: Free
Circulation: 40,000 (Publisher's Statement)
Usual Pagination: 124
Editor: Molly Wilson; **Advertising Manager:** Molly Wilson
Summary of Content: Magazine covering local news, views and interviews as well as entertainment, education, health and beauty, history, home design, eating out and competitions.
Readership/Target Audience: Aimed at residents and visitors of all ages to Portsmouth and the surrounding areas.
ADVERTISING: Rates on application
CONSUMER: RURAL & REGIONAL INTEREST: Regional Interest English Counties

PORTSMOUTH PEOPLE

47740U87-184

Editorial Address: Park Place Pastoral Centre, Winchester Road, Wickham, FAREHAM, PO17 5HA **Tel:** 01329 835583
Email: editor@portsmouthdiocese.org.uk
Advertising Address: As above.
Email: editor@portsmouthdiocese.org.uk
Web site: http://www.portsmouthdiocese.org.uk
Publisher: Cornerstone Vision
Date Established: 1989
Frequency: 10 issues yearly - Not published in January or August
Cover Price: Free
Circulation: 19,000 (Publisher's Statement)
Usual Pagination: 16
Editor: Leo Patrick; **Advertising Manager:** Leo Patrick
Summary of Content: Magazine of the Diocese of Portsmouth covering general news, real-life stories and events.
Readership/Target Audience: Read predominantly by Roman Catholics.
ADVERTISING: Rates on application
CONSUMER: RELIGIOUS

PORTUGUESE STUDIES

47577U84B-172_50

Editorial Address: Kings College London, Strand, LONDON, WC2R 2LS **Tel:** 020 7848 2507
Fax: 020 7848 2787
Email: portuguesestudiesjournal@kcl.ac.uk
ISSN: 0267-5315
Publisher: Modern Humanities Research Association
Date Established: 1985
Frequency: Annual - Published in October
Cover Price: Free
Usual Pagination: 250
Editor: David Treece
Summary of Content: Journal containing articles on Portuguese culture, language, history and literature.
Readership/Target Audience: Aimed at researchers and scholars.
ADVERTISING: No Advertising taken
CONSUMER: THE ARTS & LITERARY: Literary

POSITIVE NEWS FROM AROUND THE WORLD

48706U94X-144

Editorial Address: Unit 5-6, Bicton Enterprise Centre, Bicton, Clun, CRAVEN ARMS, SY7 8NF **Tel:** 01588 640022
Fax: 01588 640033
Email: shauna@positivenews.org.uk
Advertising Address: As above. **Tel:** 0845 458 0014
Email: adverts@positivenews.org.uk
Web site: http://www.positivenews.org.uk
ISSN: 1464-7044
Publisher: Positive News Publishing Ltd
Date Established: 1993
Frequency: Quarterly
Free to qualifying individuals
Annual Sub.: £15.00
Circulation: 75,000 (Publisher's Statement)
Usual Pagination: 20
Editor: Shauna Crockett-Burrows; **Editor-in-Chief:** Shauna Crockett-Burrows; **Advertising Manager:** Francis Smith
Summary of Content: Newspaper covering positive environmental news from around the world. Includes news on health, education, organic food, economics and business, new products, alternative transport and the environment.
Readership/Target Audience: Aimed at environmentalists, educationalists and those interested in alternative health issues, organic, safe foods and world issues.

POST GRADUATE GUIDE

1779192U88A-234

Editorial Address: 150-152 King Street, LONDON, W6 0QU
Tel: 020 8600 5307
Email: ed.colley@hotcourses.com
Advertising Address: As above. **Tel:** 020 8600 5300
Email: peter.lynch@hotcourses.com
Web site: http://www.hotcourses.com
Publisher: Hotcourses
Frequency: Annual - Published in May
Cover Price: £4.95
Free to qualifying individuals
Circulation: 30,000 (Publisher's Statement)
Editor: Ed Colley; **Managing Editor:** Jessie-May Murphy
Summary of Content: Magazine covering funding and course information.
Readership/Target Audience: Aimed at students looking to study at postgraduate level.
ADVERTISING: Rates on application
CONSUMER: EDUCATION

POST OFFICE MOTORING MAGAZINE

46473U77E-220

Editorial Address: Unit 15F, Follingsby Avenue, GATESHEAD, NE10 8HQ **Tel:** 0191 418 3970
Email: fairbairnmarquees@totalise.co.uk
Advertising Address: As above.
Email: fairbairnmarquees@totalise.co.uk
Publisher: Alan Fairbairn Promotions
Date Established: 1971
Frequency: Quarterly
Cover Price: £2.00
Free to qualifying individuals
Circulation: 25,000 (Publisher's Statement)
Usual Pagination: 50
Editor: Alan Fairbairn; **Advertising Manager:** Alan Fairbairn
Summary of Content: Magazine covering articles on car and touring news, new car tests, accessories, information and events.
Readership/Target Audience: Aimed at members of the Post Office Auto Club Ltd.
ADVERTISING: Rates on application
Copy instructions: Copy Date: 3 weeks prior to publication date
Average advertising content per issue: 20%
CONSUMER: MOTORING & CYCLING: Club Cars

POTRIKA

48337U90-117_60

Editorial Address: 218 Jubilee Street, LONDON, E1 3BS
Tel: 020 7423 9270 **Fax:** 020 7423 9122
Email: info@potrika.co.uk
Advertising Address: As above. **Tel:** 020 7423 9220
Email: potrika@btconnect.co.uk
Publisher: Samad Publications Ltd
Date Established: 1997
Frequency: Weekly - No publication the week of Christmas
Cover Price: £0.50
Free to qualifying individuals
Annual Sub.: 45.00
Circulation: 15,000 (Publisher's Statement)
Usual Pagination: 28
Editor: Mohammed Chowdhury; **Advertising Manager:** K. Chowdhury
Summary of Content: Independent publication covering news from Bangladesh.
Language(s): Bengali
Readership/Target Audience: Aimed at Bangladeshi people living in the UK.
ADVERTISING RATES:
Full Page Mono £1800.00
Full Page Colour £2000.00
Agency Commission: 15%
Mechanical Data: Trim Size: 520 x 340mm, Film: Digital
Copy instructions: Copy Date: Friday before noon prior to publication date
CONSUMER: ETHNIC

POWER RANGERS

1667582U91D-925

Editorial Address: 239 Kensington High Street, LONDON, W8 6SA **Tel:** 020 7761 3500 **Fax:** 020 7761 3510
Email: jmillen@euk.egmont.com
Advertising Address: As above.
Email: aallen@euk.egmont.com
Web site: http://www.egmont.com
Publisher: Egmont Magazines UK
Date Established: 2005
Frequency: Monthly
Cover Price: £1.99
Circulation: 52,004 (ABC 01/01/2009 to 30/06/2009)
Usual Pagination: 32
Editor: Julia Millen
Summary of Content: Children's magazine covering Power Rangers with puzzles, stories, games, posters and colouring.
Readership/Target Audience: Aimed at boys aged between 4 and 7 years old.
ADVERTISING RATES:
Full Page Colour £1800.00
Agency Commission: 10%
Mechanical Data: Film: Digital, Type Area: 282 x 202mm, Col Length: 282mm, Page Width: 202mm, Trim Size: 300 x 220mm, Bleed Size: 306 x 226mm
Copy instructions: Copy Date: 4 weeks prior to publication date
Average advertising content per issue: 10%
CONSUMER: RECREATION & LEISURE: Children & Youth

POWERKITE

1620689U75X-1702

Editorial Address: The Blue Barns, Tew Lane, Wootton, WOODSTOCK, OX20 1HA **Tel:** 01993 811181
Fax: 01993 811481
Email: noserider@corduroylines.com
Advertising Address: As above.
Email: dan@arcwind.co.uk
Publisher: Arcwind Ltd
Frequency: 6 issues yearly
Cover Price: £3.20
Circulation: 26,000 (Publisher's Statement)
Usual Pagination: 84
Editor: Simon Mitchell; **Advertising Manager:** Dan Beechener
Summary of Content: Magazine covering powerkiting and the range of things you can do with two or four lines as well as all styles of kiting and the way kites are flown around the world.
Readership/Target Audience: Aimed at kite flyers from beginners to experts.
ADVERTISING RATES:
Full Page Colour £1165.00
Agency Commission: 10%
Mechanical Data: Trim Size: 285 x 230mm, Type Area: 261 x 206mm, Col Length: 261mm, Page Width: 206mm, Film: Digital, Bleed Size: +3mm
Copy instructions: Copy Date: 3 weeks prior to publication date
Average advertising content per issue: 40%
CONSUMER: SPORT: Other Sport

POWERPLAY

45873U75G-250

Editorial Address: 28 Saville Road, Westwood, PETERBOROUGH, PE3 7PR **Tel:** 01733 331500
Fax: 01733 331511
Email: editorial@powerplaymagazine.com
Advertising Address: As above.
Email: info@powerplaymagazine.com
Web site: http://www.powerplaymagazine.com
Publisher: Keyprint
Date Established: 1992
Frequency: 35 issues yearly - Published weekly from September to March and monthly April to August
Cover Price: £3.00
Annual Sub.: £65.00
Circulation: 3,000 (Publisher's Statement)
Usual Pagination: 32
Editor: Steve Clarke; **Advertising Manager:** Steve Clarke
Summary of Content: Magazine covering all aspects of British ice hockey and inline skating.
Readership/Target Audience: Aimed at ice hockey supporters, coaches, players and officials.
ADVERTISING RATES:
Full Page Colour £250.00
Mechanical Data: Page Width: 192mm, Col Length: 275mm, Film: Digital, Type Area: 275 x 192mm, Print Process: Sheet-fed litho, Bleed Size: +3mm, Trim Size: 297 x 210mm
Copy instructions: Copy Date: 10 days prior to publication date
Average advertising content per issue: 20%
CONSUMER: SPORT: Winter Sports

POWERSTATION

46561U78D-214_50

Editorial Address: Richmond House, 33 Richmond Hill, BOURNEMOUTH, BH2 6EZ **Tel:** 01202 586200
Email: henrietta.rowlatt@imagine-publishing.co.uk
Advertising Address: As above.
Email: ben.taylor@imagine-publishing.co.uk
Web site: http://www.cheat-machine.co.uk
ISSN: 1362-5047
Publisher: Imagine Publishing
Date Established: 1995
Frequency: 13 issues yearly
Cover Price: £3.99
Circulation: 15,171 (Publisher's Statement)

Usual Pagination: 132

Editor: Henrietta Rowlatt; **Editor-in-Chief:** Nick Jones

Summary of Content: Magazine providing playing tips for the Sony PlayStation 1 and 2. Includes solutions, guides, passwords, cheats and tips for the latest games.

Readership/Target Audience: Aimed at serious game players.

ADVERTISING RATES:

Full Page Colour £3200.00

Agency Commission: 10%

Mechanical Data: Bleed Size: 307 x 240mm, Trim Size: 297 x 230mm, Film: Digital

Copy instructions: Copy Date: 4 weeks prior to publication date

Average advertising content per issue: 20%

CONSUMER: CONSUMER ELECTRONICS: Games

POYNTON POST
46872U80C-700

Editorial Address: PO Box 174, Poynton, STOCKPORT, SK12 1WF **Tel:** 01625 874164 **Fax:** 01625 858847

Email: poynton.post@virgin.net

Advertising Address: As above.

Email: poynton.post@virgin.net

Publisher: Poynton Post

Date Established: 1961

Frequency: Monthly

Cover Price: Free

Circulation: 10,000 (Publisher's Statement)

Usual Pagination: 28

Editor: Jill Keating; **Advertising Manager:** Jill Keating

Summary of Content: Newspaper covering local news and events.

Readership/Target Audience: Aimed at residents in the Poynton area.

ADVERTISING RATES:

Full Page Mono £450.00

SCC £3.00

Agency Commission: 10%

Mechanical Data: Trim Size: 420 x 297mm, Type Area: 390 x 276mm, Page Width: 276mm, Film: Digital, Col Length: 390mm

CONSUMER: RURAL & REGIONAL INTEREST: Regional Interest English Counties

---

PRACTICAL BOAT OWNER
48384U91A-110

Editorial Address: Westover House, West Quay Road, POOLE, BH15 1JG **Tel:** 01202 440820 **Fax:** 01202 440860

Email: pbo@ipcmedia.com

Advertising Address: Blue Fin Building, 110 Southwark Street, LONDON, SE1 0SU **Tel:** 020 3148 5000

Fax: 020 3148 8128

Email: john_gaylard@ipcmedia.com

Web site: http://www.ybw.com

ISSN: 0032-6348

Publisher: IPC Inspire

Date Established: 1967

Frequency: Monthly

Cover Price: £3.80

Circulation: 47,406 (ABC 01/01/2008 to 31/12/2008)

Usual Pagination: 180

Editor: Sarah Norbury; **News Editor:** Rob Melotti; **Advertising Manager:** John Gaylard

Summary of Content: In-depth, hands-on information about boats and gear, maintenance, pilotage and seamanship.

Readership/Target Audience: Aimed at boating enthusiasts.

ADVERTISING RATES:

Full Page Mono £1700.00

Full Page Colour £3130.00

Agency Commission: 10%

Mechanical Data: Page Width: 187mm, Type Area: 275 x 187mm, Col Length: 275mm, Trim Size: 300 x 214mm, Bleed Size: 306 x 220mm, Film: Digital

Copy instructions: Copy Date: 1st week of the month prior to publication date

Average advertising content per issue: 55%

CONSUMER: RECREATION & LEISURE: Boating & Yachting

PRACTICAL CARAVAN
48429U91B-150

Editorial Address: Teddington Studios, Broom Road, TEDDINGTON, TW11 9BE **Tel:** 020 8267 5629

Fax: 020 8267 5725

Email: practical.caravan@haymarket.com

Advertising Address: As above. **Tel:** 020 8267 5656

Fax: 020 8267 5717

Email: chris.woods@haymarket.com

Web site: http://www.practicalcaravan.com

Publisher: Haymarket Consumer Media

Frequency: 13 issues yearly

Cover Price: £3.60

Circulation: 41,515 (ABC 01/01/2008 to 31/12/2008)

Usual Pagination: 180

Editor: Nigel Donnelly; **Features Editor:** Mark Bigault; **Managing Director:** Bob McDowell

Summary of Content: Magazine covering caravan and product tests, touring features, towcars and real-life caravanning experiences.

Readership/Target Audience: Aimed at touring caravanners.

ADVERTISING RATES:

Full Page Colour £3586.00

Agency Commission: 10%

Mechanical Data: Type Area: 272 x 192mm, Bleed Size: 304 x 222mm, Trim Size: 298 x 216mm, Col Widths (Display): 44mm, No. of Columns (Display): 4, Col Length: 272mm, Page Width: 192mm, Film: Digital

Copy instructions: Copy Date: 4 weeks prior to publication date

Average advertising content per issue: 40%

CONSUMER: RECREATION & LEISURE: Camping & Caravanning

PRACTICAL CLASSICS
46496U77F-340

Formerly: Practical Classics inc. Popular Classics

Editorial Address: Media House, Lynchwood, Peterborough Business Park, PETERBOROUGH, PE2 6EA

Tel: 01733 468000 **Fax:** 01733 468888

Email: practical.classics@bauermedia.co.uk

Advertising Address: As above. **Fax:** 01733 468670

Email: louise.rizzo@bauerconsumer.co.uk

Web site: http://www.practicalclassics.co.uk

ISSN: 0957-6975

Publisher: Bauer Consumer Media Ltd (Media House)

Date Established: 1980

Frequency: 13 issues yearly

Cover Price: £3.99

Annual Sub: £50.70

Circulation: 57,936 (ABC 01/01/2009 to 30/06/2009)

Usual Pagination: 180

Editor: Matt Wright; **Features Editor:** Matthew Jones

Summary of Content: Magazine covering all aspects of classic cars including product tests and accessories.

Readership/Target Audience: Aimed at owners who are interested in restoring, maintaining and running cars made in the 1930s to the 1980s.

ADVERTISING RATES:

Full Page Mono £1161.00

Full Page Colour £1890.00

Agency Commission: 10%

Mechanical Data: Col Length: 271mm, Page Width: 186mm, Film: Digital, Type Area: 271 x 186mm, Bleed Size: 307 x 220mm, Trim Size: 297 x 210mm

Copy instructions: Copy Date: 3 weeks prior to publication date

Average advertising content per issue: 40%

CONSUMER: MOTORING & CYCLING: Veteran Cars

PRACTICAL FAMILY HISTORY
752923U94X-144_10

Editorial Address: 61 Great Whyte, Ramsey, HUNTINGDON, PE26 1HJ **Tel:** 01487 814050

Fax: 01487 711361

Email: belinda.g@abmpublishing.co.uk

Advertising Address: As above.

Email: paulat@warnersgroup.co.uk

Web site: http://www.family-tree.co.uk

ISSN: 1367-1669

Publisher: ABM Publishing Ltd

Date Established: 1997

Frequency: 13 issues yearly

Cover Price: £3.75

Annual Sub: £44.00

Circulation: 27,000 (Publisher's Statement)

Usual Pagination: 100

Editor: Belinda Griffin

Summary of Content: Magazine featuring family history, advice on starting a family tree including computer based resources and useful addresses and websites.

Readership/Target Audience: Aimed at those with an interest in starting their family history.

ADVERTISING RATES:

Full Page Colour £550.00

Agency Commission: 10%

Mechanical Data: Bleed Size: 303 x 216mm, Trim Size: 297 x 210mm, Film: Digital, Type Area: 260 x 190mm, Col Length: 260mm, Page Width: 190mm, Col Widths (Display): 45mm, No. of Columns (Display): 4

Copy instructions: Copy Date: 1st of the month 2 months prior to publication date

CONSUMER: OTHER CLASSIFICATIONS: Miscellaneous

PRACTICAL FISHKEEPING
47158U81E-100

Editorial Address: Bushfield House, Orton Centre, PETERBOROUGH, PE2 5UW **Tel:** 01733 237111

Email: matt.clarke@bauermedia.co.u

Advertising Address: As above. **Fax:** 01733 288005

Email: rebecca.mee@bauerconsumer.co.uk

Web site: http://www.practicalfishkeeping.co.uk

Publisher: Bauer Media Ltd (Orton)

Date Established: 1981

Frequency: 13 issues yearly

Cover Price: £3.50

Circulation: 15,401 (ABC 01/01/2008 to 31/12/2008)

Usual Pagination: 124

Editor: Matt Clarke; **Managing Director:** Rob Croxall

Summary of Content: Magazine providing guidance on aquariums, ponds and their inhabitants.

Readership/Target Audience: Aimed at fish keepers of all levels of experience.

ADVERTISING RATES:

Full Page Colour £2700.00

Agency Commission: 10%

Mechanical Data: Type Area: 270 x 185mm, Bleed Size: 303 x 216mm, Trim Size: 297 x 210mm, Col Length: 270mm, Page Width: 185mm, Film: Digital

Copy instructions: Copy Date: 4 weeks prior to publication date

Average advertising content per issue: 30%

CONSUMER: ANIMALS & PETS: Fish

PRACTICAL MOTORHOME
714765U91B-160

Editorial Address: Teddington Studios, Broom Road, TEDDINGTON, TW11 9BE **Tel:** 020 8267 5629

Fax: 020 8267 5725

Email: practical.motorhome@haymarket.com

Advertising Address: As above. **Tel:** 020 8267 5656

Fax: 020 8267 5717

Web site: http://www.practicalmotorhome.com

Publisher: Haymarket Consumer Media

Date Established: 2001

Frequency: Monthly

Cover Price: £3.40

Circulation: 15,825 (ABC 01/01/2008 to 31/12/2008)

Usual Pagination: 228

Editor: Rob Ganley; **Managing Director:** Bob McDowell

Summary of Content: Magazine covering all aspects of motorhomes including travel sites, technical matters, improvements, new models and buying information.

Readership/Target Audience: Aimed at motorhome owners and those considering buying.

ADVERTISING RATES:

Full Page Mono £1581.00

Full Page Colour £1797.00

SCC £30.00

Mechanical Data: Bleed Size: 304 x 222mm, Trim Size: 298 x 216mm, Film: Digital, Col Length: 272mm, Page Width: 192mm, Type Area: 272 x 192mm, No. of Columns (Display): 4

Copy instructions: Copy Date: 5 weeks prior to publication date

CONSUMER: RECREATION & LEISURE: Camping & Caravanning

PRACTICAL PARENTING
45339U74D-475

Editorial Address: 15 - 18 White Lion Street, Islington, LONDON, N1 9PD **Tel:** 020 7843 8800

Email: roisin.johnson@magicalia.com

Advertising Address: Berwick House, 8-10 Knoll Rise, ORPINGTON, BR6 0EL **Tel:** 01689 899200

Email: michelle.coley@magicalia.com

Web site: http://www.practicalparenting.co.uk

ISSN: 0954-9846

Publisher: Magicalia Ltd

Date Established: 1986

Frequency: Monthly

Cover Price: £2.70

Circulation: 28,095 (ABC 01/01/2009 to 30/06/2009)

Editor: Roisin Johnson; **Advertising Manager:** Nicola Gleghorn

Summary of Content: Magazine covering all aspects of being a parent including pregnancy as well as beauty and lifestyle.

Readership/Target Audience: Aimed at pregnant women and parents with children aged up to three and a half years old.

ADVERTISING: Rates on application

CONSUMER: WOMEN'S INTEREST CONSUMER MAGAZINES: Child Care

PRACTICAL PERFORMANCE CAR
1779769U77A-601

Editorial Address: Crown Lane, Tinwell, STAMFORD, PE9 3UF **Tel:** 01780 758800

Email: will@ppcmag.co.uk

Advertising Address: As above. **Fax:** 01780 489215

Email: advertising@ppcmag.co.uk

Web site: http://www.ppcmag.co.uk

Publisher: Blockhead Media Ltd

Date Established: 2004

Frequency: Monthly

Cover Price: £4.20

Circulation: 15,000 (Publisher's Statement)

Usual Pagination: 156

Editor: Will Holman

Summary of Content: Magazine covering affordable performance cars, driving adventures and technical features.

Readership/Target Audience: Aimed at car enthusiasts.

Consumer Magazines

ADVERTISING RATES:
Full Page Colour £540.00
Agency Commission: 10%
Mechanical Data: Bleed Size: +4mm, Trim Size: 297 x 210mm, Film: Digital
Average advertising content per issue: 30%
CONSUMER: MOTORING & CYCLING: Motoring

PRACTICAL PHOTOGRAPHY 47597U85A-150

Editorial Address: Media House, Lynchwood, Peterborough Business Park, PETERBOROUGH, PE2 6EA
Tel: 01733 468000 **Fax:** 01733 465246
Email: practical.photography@bauermedia.co.uk
Advertising Address: As above. **Fax:** 01733 468387
Email: jayne.phillips@bauerconsumer.co.uk
Web site: http://www.practicalphotography.co.uk
ISSN: 0032-6445
Publisher: Bauer Consumer Media Ltd (Media House)
Frequency: 13 issues yearly
Cover Price: £3.90
Circulation: 56,003 (ABC 01/01/2008 to 31/12/2008)
Usual Pagination: 154
Editor: Ben Hawkins; **Editor-in-Chief:** Andrew James
Summary of Content: Magazine covering techniques, equipment reviews and competitions.
Readership/Target Audience: Aimed at amateur and serious photographers.
ADVERTISING RATES:
Full Page Mono £3893.00
Full Page Colour £3893.00
Agency Commission: 10%
Mechanical Data: Page Width: 194mm, Type Area: 281 x 194mm, Col Length: 281mm, Film: Digital, Bleed Size: 303 x 216mm, Trim Size: 297 x 210mm
Average advertising content per issue: 30%
CONSUMER: PHOTOGRAPHY & FILM MAKING: Photography

PRACTICAL REPTILE KEEPING 1898893U81-2

Editorial Address: Cudham tithe Barn, Berrys Hill, CUDHAM, TN16 3AG **Tel:** 01959 541444 **Fax:** 01959 541000
Email: prk.ed@kelsey.co.uk
Web site: http://www.practicalreptilekeeping.co.uk
Publisher: Kelsey Publishing Ltd
Frequency: Monthly
Cover Price: £3.00
Annual Sub.: £33.00
Editor: David Alderton
Summary of Content: Magazine covering all aspects of reptiles care including news, places to visit and health advice.
Readership/Target Audience: Aimed at reptile owners.
CONSUMER: ANIMALS & PETS

PRACTICAL WIRELESS 46644U79D-140

Editorial Address: Arrowsmith Court, Station Approach, BROADSTONE, BH18 8PW **Tel:** 0845 803 1979
Fax: 01202 659950
Email: pwnews@pwpublishing.ltd.uk
Advertising Address: As above.
Email: roger@pwpublishing.ltd.uk
Web site: http://www.pwpublishing.ltd.uk
Publisher: PW Publishing Ltd
Date Established: 1932
Frequency: Monthly - Published on the 2nd Thursday of the month prior to cover date
Cover Price: £3.50
Annual Sub.: £38.00
Circulation: 18,000 (Publisher's Statement)
Usual Pagination: 80
Editor: Rob Mannion; **Managing Director:** Roger Hall;
Advertising Manager: Roger Hall
Summary of Content: Magazine containing new product and technology news, articles on techniques, construction and operation.
Readership/Target Audience: Aimed at radio enthusiasts.
ADVERTISING RATES:
Full Page Mono £775.00
Full Page Colour £880.00
Agency Commission: 10%
Mechanical Data: Type Area: 270 x 182mm, Bleed Size: 303 x 216mm, Trim Size: 297 x 210mm, Print Process: Web-fed offset litho, Film: Positive, right reading, emulsion side down. Digital, Col Length: 270mm, Page Width: 182mm
Copy instructions: Copy Date: 6 weeks prior to publication date
Average advertising content per issue: 27%
CONSUMER: HOBBIES & DIY: Radio Electronics

PRACTICAL WOODWORKING 46578U79A-150

Editorial Address: Berwick House, 8-10 Knoll Rise, ORPINGTON, BR6 0EL **Tel:** 01689 899200
Fax: 01689 899266
Email: neilmead@freeuk.com
Advertising Address: As above.

Email: clare.hiscock@magicalia.com
Web site: http://www.getwoodworking.com
ISSN: 0032-6488
Publisher: My Hobby Store Media
Date Established: 1966
Frequency: 6 issues yearly
Cover Price: £4.99
Circulation: 9,436 (Publisher's Statement)
Usual Pagination: 108
Editor: Neil Mead
Summary of Content: Magazine featuring woodworking projects and techniques, product tests and news.
Readership/Target Audience: Aimed at woodworking improvers and enthusiasts.
ADVERTISING RATES:
Full Page Colour £720.00
Agency Commission: 10%
Mechanical Data: Bleed Size: 303 x 213mm, Trim Size: 297 x 210mm, Type Area: 267 x 184mm, Col Length: 267mm, Page Width: 184mm, Film: Digital
Copy instructions: Copy Date: 6 weeks prior to publication date
CONSUMER: HOBBIES & DIY

PRAYER BOOK SOCIETY JOURNAL
1626477U87-2022

Editorial Address: The Studio, Copyhold Farm, Goring Heath, READING, RG8 7RT **Tel:** 0118 984 5220
Email: pbs.admin@pbs.org.uk
Advertising Address: As above. **Tel:** 0118 984 2582
Fax: 0118 984 5220
Email: pbs.admin@prayerbook.org.uk
Web site: http://www.pbs.org.uk
ISSN: 1479-215X
Publisher: Prayer Book Society
Frequency: 3 issues yearly
Cover Price: Free
Circulation: 7,000 (Publisher's Statement)
Usual Pagination: 32
Advertising Manager: Clare Fox
Summary of Content: Magazine of the Prayer Book Society whose aim it is to safeguard the tradition of the Book of Common Prayer. Includes reviews, reports of Society events past and present, reviews of Church music and lists of Society branches in the UK and overseas.
Readership/Target Audience: Aimed at members of the Prayer Book Society, the Church of England and the General Synod.
ADVERTISING: Rates on application
CONSUMER: RELIGIOUS

PREDICTION 48614U94E-50

Editorial Address: Leon House, 233 High Street, CROYDON, CR9 1HZ **Tel:** 020 8726 8000
Fax: 020 8726 8299
Email: prediction@ipcmedia.com
Advertising Address: As above. **Fax:** 020 8726 8298
Email: joanne_o'brien@ipcmedia.com
Web site: http://www.predictionmagazine.co.uk
ISSN: 0032-7182
Publisher: IPC Inspire
Date Established: 1936
Frequency: 13 issues yearly
Cover Price: £2.95
Annual Sub.: £33.60
Circulation: 14,646 (ABC 01/01/2008 to 31/12/2008)
Usual Pagination: 84
Editor: Marion Williamson
Summary of Content: Magazine focusing on astrology, the mind, body, spirit and alternative health. Also covers news, tarot, dreams, reviews, psychics, the paranormal, spiritual travel and other divination.
Readership/Target Audience: Aimed at those interested in horoscopes and mind, body and spirit.
Mechanical Data: No. of Columns (Display): 4, Type Area: 278 x 190mm, Film: Positive, right reading, emulsion side down. Digital, Col Length: 278mm, Page Width: 190mm
CONSUMER: OTHER CLASSIFICATIONS: Paranormal

PREDICTION ANNUAL 48618U94E-60

Editorial Address: Leon House, 233 High Street, CROYDON, CR9 1HZ **Tel:** 020 8726 8000
Email: prediction@ipcmedia.com
Advertising Address: As above. **Tel:** 020 8726 8231
Fax: 020 8726 8298
Email: cheryl_townsend@ipcmedia.com
Web site: http://www.predictionmagazine.co.uk
ISSN: 0079-4953
Publisher: IPC Inspire
Frequency: Annual - Published in September
Cover Price: £6.50
Usual Pagination: 196
Editor: Marion Williamson; **Advertising Manager:** Cheryl Townsend
Summary of Content: Publication containing articles on astrology, divination and forecasts for the year ahead.

Readership/Target Audience: Read by those interested in astrology, tarots, dreams, psychic phenomena and alternative therapies.
ADVERTISING RATES:
Full Page Mono £1020.00
Full Page Colour £1515.00
Agency Commission: 10%
Mechanical Data: Type Area: 188 x 122mm, Bleed Size: 216 x 154mm, Trim Size: 210 x 148mm, Col Length: 188mm, Page Width: 122mm, Film: Digital
Average advertising content per issue: 30%
CONSUMER: OTHER CLASSIFICATIONS: Paranormal

PREGNANCY & BIRTH 45348U74D-485

Formerly: Your Complete Guide to Pregnancy & Birth
Editorial Address: Endeavour House, 189 Shaftesbury Avenue, LONDON, WC2H 8JG **Tel:** 020 7295 5563
Email: jessica.powell@bauermedia.co.uk
Advertising Address: As above. **Tel:** 020 7437 9011
Fax: 020 7520 6565
Email: fiona.senior@bauerconsumer.co.uk
Web site: http://www.askamum.co.uk
Publisher: Bauer Media
Frequency: Monthly
Cover Price: £2.70
Circulation: 38,778 (ABC 01/01/2009 to 30/06/2009)
Usual Pagination: 108
Editor: Jessica Powell; **Managing Director:** Nick Morgan
Summary of Content: Magazine covering all aspects of pregnancy and birth. Includes advice, features on fashion, beauty, new products and health.
Readership/Target Audience: Aimed at expectant mothers of all ages.
ADVERTISING RATES:
Full Page Colour £5821.00
Agency Commission: 15%
Mechanical Data: Page Width: 186mm, Type Area: 270 x 186mm, Bleed Size: 303 x 216mm, Trim Size: 297 x 210mm, Col Length: 270mm, Film: Digital
Copy instructions: Copy Date: 4 weeks prior to publication date
Average advertising content per issue: 40%
CONSUMER: WOMEN'S INTEREST CONSUMER MAGAZINES: Child Care

PRESBYTERIAN HERALD 47742U87-189

Editorial Address: Church House, Fisherwick Place, BELFAST, BT1 6DW **Tel:** 028 9032 2284 **Fax:** 028 9041 7307
Email: herald@presbyterianireland.org
Advertising Address: As above.
Email: herald@presbyterianireland.org
Web site: http://www.presbyterianireland.org/herald
Publisher: Presbyterian Church in Ireland
Date Established: 1943
Frequency: 10 issues yearly - Combined issues December/January and July/August
Cover Price: £0.80
Circulation: 14,000 (Publisher's Statement)
Usual Pagination: 38
Editor: Stephen Lynas; **Advertising Manager:** Anne McCully
Summary of Content: Magazine of the Presbyterian Church in Ireland. Includes news, events and views.
Readership/Target Audience: Aimed at Presbyterian Church members.
ADVERTISING RATES:
Full Page Mono £450.00
Full Page Colour £450.00
SCC £6.00
Agency Commission: 15%
Mechanical Data: Col Length: 255mm, No. of Columns (Display): 4, Type Area: 255 x 183mm, Trim Size: 284 x 210mm, Page Width: 183mm
Copy instructions: Copy Date: 1st of the month prior to publication date
CONSUMER: RELIGIOUS

PRETTY PONY CLUB 48503U91D-89

Editorial Address: Office Block 1, Southlink Business Park, Hamilton Street, OLDHAM, OL4 1DE **Tel:** 0161 624 0414
Fax: 0161 628 4655
Email: nicola.littlejohn@toontasticpublishing.com
Publisher: Toontastic Publishing
Date Established: 1998
Frequency: 13 issues yearly
Cover Price: £2.60
Circulation: 25,000 (Publisher's Statement)
Usual Pagination: 32
Editor: Nicola Littlejohn; **Editor-in-Chief:** James Hill;
Publisher: Alan Young
Summary of Content: Children's magazine containing games, competitions and stories relating to ponies.
Readership/Target Audience: Aimed at girls between 3 and 12 years old.
ADVERTISING: No Advertising taken
CONSUMER: RECREATION & LEISURE: Children & Youth

PREVIEW GLASGOW MUSEUMS MAGAZINE
47508U84A-326

Editorial Address: Glasgow Museums Resource Centre, 200 Woodhead Road, GLASGOW, G4 0PX
Tel: 0141 276 9300 **Fax:** 0141 271 8354
Email: susan.pacitti@csglasgow.org
Advertising Address: Contact Publicity, 15 Newton Terrace, GLASGOW, G3 7PJ **Tel:** 0141 204 2042 **Fax:** 0141 204 2043
Email: val@contactpublicity.co.uk
Web site: http://www.glasgowmuseums.com
ISSN: 0962-2470
Publisher: Culture and Sport Glasgow
Date Established: 1990
Frequency: Quarterly
Cover Price: Free
Circulation: 30,000 (Publisher's Statement)
Usual Pagination: 28
Editor: Susan Pacitti; **Managing Editor:** Susan Pacitti
Summary of Content: Magazine containing listings, news and features about Glasgow City Council's museums.
Readership/Target Audience: Read by those with an interest in the arts, museums and galleries.
ADVERTISING: Rates on application
CONSUMER: THE ARTS & LITERARY: Arts

PRIDE MAGAZINE
45195U74A-450

Editorial Address: Hamilton House, 55 Battersea Bridge Road, LONDON, SW11 3AX **Tel:** 020 7228 3110
Fax: 020 7228 3121
Email: info@pridemagazine.com
Advertising Address: As above.
Email: michelle@pridemagazine.com
Web site: http://www.pridemagazine.com
ISSN: 0963-1720
Publisher: Pride Magazine Ltd
Date Established: 1991
Frequency: Monthly
Cover Price: £2.80
Circulation: 50,000 (Publisher's Statement)
Usual Pagination: 146
Editor: Keysha Davis; **Features Editor:** Cynthia Lawrence; **Advertising Manager:** Michelle Bertin; **Publisher:** Carl Cushnie
Summary of Content: Magazine containing features on fashion and beauty, plus celebrity profiles.
Readership/Target Audience: Aimed at second generation African-Caribbean women between 18 and 35 years old.
ADVERTISING RATES:
Full Page Mono £2400.00
Full Page Colour £2400.00
Agency Commission: 10%
Mechanical Data: Type Area: 250 x 190mm, Trim Size: 270 x 210mm, Bleed Size: +5mm, Col Length: 250mm, Page Width: 190mm, Film: Digital
CONSUMER: WOMEN'S INTEREST CONSUMER MAGAZINES: Women's Interest

PRIDE OF BRITAIN MAGAZINE
48061U89B-300

Formerly: Pride of Britain
Editorial Address: 20 Orange Street, LONDON, WC2H 7EF
Tel: 020 7389 0808 **Fax:** 020 7839 6719
Email: info@freewaymedia.com
Advertising Address: As above. **Tel:** 020 7389 0800
Fax: 020 7490 3476
Email: myles@freewaymedia.com
Web site: http://www.freewaymedia.com
Publisher: Freeway Media Ltd
Date Established: 1996
Frequency: Half-yearly - Published in April and November
Cover Price: Free
Circulation: 60,000 (Publisher's Statement)
Usual Pagination: 68
Editor: Sophie Mackenzie; **Advertising Manager:** Myles Poulton
Summary of Content: Magazine with features on the very best of British traditions, countryside, cuisine and sporting pursuits.
Readership/Target Audience: Aimed at guests of Pride of Britain hotels.
ADVERTISING RATES:
Full Page Colour £2800.00
Agency Commission: 10%
Mechanical Data: Type Area: 264 x 182mm, Col Length: 264mm, Trim Size: 297 x 210mm, Bleed Size: 303 x 216mm, Film: Digital, Page Width: 182mm
Copy instructions: Copy Date: 21 days prior to publication date
Average advertising content per issue: 4%
CONSUMER: HOLIDAYS & TRAVEL: Hotel Magazines

PRIMA
45196U74A-460

Editorial Address: National Magazine House, 72 Broadwick Street, LONDON, W1F 9EP **Tel:** 020 7439 5000
Fax: 020 7312 4100
Email: prima@natmags.co.uk

Advertising Address: As above. **Tel:** 020 7312 3931
Fax: 020 7312 3717
Email: lewis.hammond@natmags.co.uk
Web site: http://www.allaboutyou.com/prima
ISSN: 0951-8622
Publisher: National Magazine Company Ltd
Date Established: 1986
Frequency: Monthly
Cover Price: £2.50
Annual Sub.: £26.40
Circulation: 274,063 (ABC 01/01/2009 to 30/06/2009)
Usual Pagination: 170
Editor: Karen Swayne; **Features Editor:** Karen Swayne; **Publisher:** Matthew Salmon
Summary of Content: Magazine covering ideas for home cookery, patterns, craft, fashion, beauty, health and features.
Twitter: https://twitter.com/primamagazine.
Readership/Target Audience: Aimed at women.
ADVERTISING RATES:
Full Page Colour £19465.00
Agency Commission: 15%
Mechanical Data: Trim Size: 297 x 210mm, Film: Digital
Copy instructions: Copy Date: 6th of the month prior to publication date
CONSUMER: WOMEN'S INTEREST CONSUMER MAGAZINES: Women's Interest

PRIMA BABY & PREGNANCY
45342U74D-490

Formerly: Prima Baby
Editorial Address: National Magazine House, 72 Broadwick Street, LONDON, W1F 9EP **Tel:** 020 7439 5000
Fax: 020 7312 3744
Email: info@babyexpert.co.uk
Advertising Address: As above. **Fax:** 020 7312 3717
Email: claire.campbell@natmags.co.uk
Web site: http://www.babyexpert.com
ISSN: 1362-8607
Publisher: National Magazine Company Ltd
Date Established: 1996
Frequency: Monthly
Cover Price: £2.50
Circulation: 46,014 (ABC 01/01/2009 to 30/06/2009)
Usual Pagination: 140
Editor: Elaine Griffiths; **Advertising Manager:** Claire Campbell
Summary of Content: Magazine providing practical advice on pregnancy, health issues, mother and baby care.
Readership/Target Audience: Aimed at pregnant women, especially first time mothers and those with babies.
ADVERTISING RATES:
Full Page Colour £6210.00
Agency Commission: 15%
Mechanical Data: Film: Digital, Type Area: 266 x 192mm, Bleed Size: 292 x 221mm, Trim Size: 286 x 215mm, Col Length: 266mm, Page Width: 192mm
Copy instructions: Copy Date: 4 weeks prior to publication date
Average advertising content per issue: 40%
CONSUMER: WOMEN'S INTEREST CONSUMER MAGAZINES: Child Care

PRIMARY TIMES GLASGOW & WEST OF SCOTLAND
1645626U74D-567

Formerly: Primary Times in Glasgow North
Editorial Address: 11 Blackadder Place, East Kilbride, GLASGOW, G75 8YT **Tel:** 01355 234413 **Fax:** 01355 521638
Email: lindasturrock@blueyonder.co.uk
Advertising Address: As above.
Email: lindaprimarytimes@blueyonder.co.uk
Web site: http://www.primarytimes.net
Publisher: Primary Times
Date Established: 2003
Frequency: 6 issues yearly
Free to qualifying individuals
Annual Sub.: £10.00
Circulation: 60,000 (Publisher's Statement)
Usual Pagination: 24
Editor: Linda Sturrock; **Advertising Manager:** Linda Sturrock
Summary of Content: Magazine covering current educational issues and family matters as well as a what's on and where to go guide.
Readership/Target Audience: Aimed at teachers, parents and primary school children in the Glasgow and West of Scotland area.
ADVERTISING RATES:
Full Page Colour £1320.00
Mechanical Data: Trim Size: 297 x 210mm, Type Area: 273 x 184mm, Col Length: 273mm, Page Width: 184mm
Copy instructions: Copy Date: 2 weeks prior to publication date
CONSUMER: WOMEN'S INTEREST CONSUMER MAGAZINES: Child Care

PRIMARY TIMES IN AVON
45327U74D-490_20

Formerly: OSM (Avon) Our Schools Magazine
Editorial Address: Temple Way, BRISTOL, BS99 7HD
Tel: 0117 934 3742 **Fax:** 0117 934 3755
Email: h.mottram@bepp.co.uk
Advertising Address: As above. **Tel:** 0117 934 3000
Fax: 0117 934 3577
Email: kathyg@bepp.co.uk
Web site: http://www.primarytimes.net
Publisher: Bristol News and Media
Date Established: 1988
Frequency: 7 issues yearly
Cover Price: Free
Circulation: 70,000 (Publisher's Statement)
Usual Pagination: 32
Editor: Harry Mottram; **Advertising Manager:** Kathy Gould
Summary of Content: Magazine covering current educational issues and forthcoming events.
Readership/Target Audience: Read by parents, teachers and children in Avon.
Mechanical Data: Trim Size: 297 x 210mm, Type Area: 272 x 187mm, Col Length: 272mm, Page Width: 187mm
Copy instructions: Copy Date: 2 weeks prior to publication date
Editions:
Primary Times in Gloucestershire
Primary Times in Wiltshire
CONSUMER: WOMEN'S INTEREST CONSUMER MAGAZINES: Child Care

PRIMARY TIMES IN BEDFORDSHIRE & LUTON
765002U74D-552

Editorial Address: The Artworks, The Mill, Free Church Passage, ST. IVES, PE27 5AY **Tel:** 01480 495663
Fax: 01480 495665
Email: editorial@sundial.co.uk
Advertising Address: As above.
Email: artworks@sundial.co.uk
Web site: http://www.sundial.co.uk
Publisher: Primary Times
Date Established: 2002
Frequency: 7 issues yearly
Free to qualifying individuals
Annual Sub.: £10.00
Circulation: 40,000 (Publisher's Statement)
Usual Pagination: 24
Editor: Jerry Hills
Summary of Content: Magazine covering educational issues, news and family matters. Includes a what's on and where to go guide and book reviews.
Readership/Target Audience: Read by teachers, children and parents of 4 to 11 year olds.
ADVERTISING: Rates on application
Copy instructions: Copy Date: 2 weeks prior to publication date
CONSUMER: WOMEN'S INTEREST CONSUMER MAGAZINES: Child Care

PRIMARY TIMES IN BELFAST, COUNTIES ANTRIM, DOWN & ARMAGH
1692171U74D-605

Formerly: Primary Times in Belfast, County Antrim & Co Down
Editorial Address: 2 Slievedarragh Park, BELFAST, BT14 8JA **Tel:** 028 9336 2436 **Fax:** 028 9336 2436
Email: henry@primarytimesni.co.uk
Advertising Address: As above. **Tel:** 028 9072 1352
Fax: 028 9072 1352
Email: henry@primarytimesni.co.uk
Web site: http://www.primarytimes.net
Publisher: Primary Times
Date Established: 2005
Frequency: 7 issues yearly - Linked to school terms in Northern Ireland
Cover Price: Free
Circulation: 35,000 (Publisher's Statement)
Usual Pagination: 40
Editor: Henry Ardis; **Advertising Manager:** Henry Ardis
Summary of Content: Magazine covering educational issues, news and family matters as well as a what's on guide, where to go guide and book reviews.
Readership/Target Audience: Read by teachers, children and parents of children aged between 4 and 12 years old.
ADVERTISING RATES:
Full Page Colour £999.00
Mechanical Data: Type Area: 277 x 190mm, Col Length: 277mm, Page Width: 190mm, Film: Digital, Trim Size: 297 x 210mm
Copy instructions: Copy Date: 2 weeks prior to publication date
Average advertising content per issue: 50%
CONSUMER: WOMEN'S INTEREST CONSUMER MAGAZINES: Child Care

PRIMARY TIMES IN BERKSHIRE

45328U74D-490_25

Formerly: OSM (Berkshire) Our Schools Magazine
Editorial Address: 33 Wood Lane, Sonning Common, READING, RG4 9SJ **Tel:** 0845 880 1777 **Fax:** 0845 880 1770
Email: office@primarytimesmag.com
Advertising Address: As above.
Email: office@primarytimesmag.com
Publisher: Moonscape Media Ltd
Date Established: 1998
Frequency: 7 issues yearly
Cover Price: Free
Circulation: 57,000 (Publisher's Statement)
Usual Pagination: 32
Editor: Michelle Dilger; **Publisher:** Richard Dilger
Summary of Content: Magazine covering current educational and social issues and forthcoming events. Includes theatre listings, competitions and book reviews.
Readership/Target Audience: Read by teachers, parents and children in Berkshire. Distributed throughout primary schools.
ADVERTISING RATES:
Full Page Colour £1350.00
Mechanical Data: Type Area: 272 x 187mm, Trim Size: 297 x 210mm, Col Length: 272mm, Page Width: 187mm
Copy instructions: Copy Date: 2 weeks prior to publication date
Editions:
Primary Times in Cheshire & Greater Manchester
Primary Times in Northamptonshire
CONSUMER: WOMEN'S INTEREST CONSUMER MAGAZINES: Child Care

PRIMARY TIMES IN CAMBRIDGESHIRE

749719U74D-490_27

Editorial Address: PO Box 357, Warboys, HUNTINGDON, PE28 2XY **Tel:** 01487 710489 **Fax:** 01487 710489
Email: ptimes.cambs@btinternet.com
Advertising Address: As above. **Fax:** 01487 740238
Email: ptimes.cambs@btinternet.com
Publisher: Primary Times
Date Established: 2001
Frequency: 6 issues yearly
Cover Price: Free
Circulation: 35,000 (Publisher's Statement)
Usual Pagination: 24
Editor: Ashley Hill; **Advertising Manager:** Ashley Hill
Summary of Content: Magazine covering current educational issues and family matters with a what's on and where to go guide.
Readership/Target Audience: Aimed at primary school children, parents and teachers in Cambridgeshire and Norfolk.
ADVERTISING: Rates on application
Copy instructions: Copy Date: 2 weeks prior to publication date
CONSUMER: WOMEN'S INTEREST CONSUMER MAGAZINES: Child Care

PRIMARY TIMES IN CARDIFF & SOUTH WALES

714065U74D-490_30

Editorial Address: 4 The Courtyard, Michaelston le Pit, Vale of Glamorgan, CARDIFF, CF64 4HE **Tel:** 029 2051 5444
Email: mail@primarypub.co.uk
Advertising Address: As above. **Tel:** 01446 719797
Fax: 01446 719798
Email: mail@primarypub.co.uk
Web site: http://www.primarytimes.net
Publisher: Primary Times
Date Established: 1999
Frequency: 6 issues yearly
Cover Price: Free
Circulation: 50,000 (Publisher's Statement)
Usual Pagination: 32
Editor: Kristin Litton; **Advertising Manager:** Kristin Litton
Summary of Content: Magazine covering current educational issues and family matters with a what's on and where to go guide.
Readership/Target Audience: Read by teachers, parents and children in Cardiff and the Vale of Glamorgan.
ADVERTISING RATES:
Full Page Colour £1300.00
CONSUMER: WOMEN'S INTEREST CONSUMER MAGAZINES: Child Care

PRIMARY TIMES IN DERBYSHIRE

1605935U74D-554

Formerly: Primary Times in Derby
Editorial Address: 5th Floor, White House, 111 New Street, BIRMINGHAM, B2 4EU **Tel:** 01332 513355
Fax: 0121 336 1936
Email: lin@modomedia.co.uk
Advertising Address: As above. **Tel:** 01332 291177
Fax: 01332 595598
Email: lwinfield@derbytelegraph.co.uk

Web site: http://www.primarytimes.net
Publisher: Moda Media
Date Established: 2002
Frequency: 7 issues yearly
Cover Price: Free
Circulation: 31,000 (Publisher's Statement)
Usual Pagination: 24
Editor: Lin Woodhouse; **Advertising Manager:** Leah Winfield
Summary of Content: Magazine covering current educational issues and family matters with a what's on and where to go guide.
Readership/Target Audience: Read by school teachers, parents and primary school children in Derbyshire.
ADVERTISING: Rates on application
Copy instructions: Copy Date: 2 weeks prior to publication date
CONSUMER: WOMEN'S INTEREST CONSUMER MAGAZINES: Child Care

PRIMARY TIMES IN DEVON

45330U74D-491

Formerly: OSM (Devon) Our Schools Magazine
Editorial Address: The Forge, Fore Street, Kenton, EXETER, EX6 8LF **Tel:** 0845 260 0803 **Fax:** 0845 260 0804
Email: office@razzpublications.co.uk
Advertising Address: As above. **Tel:** 01626 891944
Fax: 01626 891936
Email: office@primary-times.co.uk
Web site: http://www.primarytimes.net
Publisher: Razz UK Ltd
Date Established: 1993
Frequency: 7 issues yearly - Published prior to school holidays
Cover Price: Free
Circulation: 77,000 (Publisher's Statement)
Usual Pagination: 32
Editor: Ceri Lee; **Advertising Manager:** Ceri Lee
Summary of Content: What's on guide for families of primary school aged children featuring educational issues and forthcoming events.
Readership/Target Audience: Read by parents, teachers and children in Devon.
ADVERTISING RATES:
Full Page Colour £680.00
Mechanical Data: Trim Size: 297 x 210mm, Bleed Size: 303 x 206mm
Editions:
Primary Times in Cornwall
Primary Times in Dorset
CONSUMER: WOMEN'S INTEREST CONSUMER MAGAZINES: Child Care

PRIMARY TIMES IN EDINBURGH & THE LOTHIANS

1645652U74D-569

Editorial Address: The Forge, Fore Street, Kenton, EXETER, EX6 8LF **Tel:** 0131 477 1471 **Fax:** 0131 477 1471
Email: flyingstarts@murdies.co.uk
Advertising Address: 16 Briarbank Terrace, EDINBURGH, EH11 1ST **Tel:** 0131 477 1471
Email: ceri@primary-times.co.uk
Publisher: Primary Times
Date Established: 2002
Frequency: 6 issues yearly
Cover Price: Free
Circulation: 30,000 (Publisher's Statement)
Usual Pagination: 24
Editor: Ceri Lee; **Advertising Manager:** Ceri Lee
Summary of Content: Magazine covering current educational issues and family matters as well as a what's on and where to go guide.
Readership/Target Audience: Aimed at teachers, parents and primary school children in Edinburgh and the Lothians.
ADVERTISING RATES:
Full Page Colour £1150.00
Mechanical Data: Trim Size: 272 x 190mm, Bleed Size: 303 x 216mm
CONSUMER: WOMEN'S INTEREST CONSUMER MAGAZINES: Child Care

PRIMARY TIMES IN ESSEX

714069U74D-491_5

Editorial Address: Dagnets Farm, Dagnets Lane, Black Notley, BRAINTREE, CM77 8QP **Tel:** 01245 362822
Fax: 0845 280 2286
Email: mail@ptessex.co.uk
Advertising Address: As above. **Tel:** 01245 362882
Fax: 01245 361700
Email: ceri@primary-times.co.uk
Web site: http://www.primarytimes.net
Publisher: Primary Times
Frequency: 6 issues yearly
Cover Price: Free
Circulation: 85,000 (Publisher's Statement)
Usual Pagination: 32
Editor: Rachel Keir; **Advertising Manager:** Nick Cousins;
Publisher: Nick Cousins

Summary of Content: Magazine covering current educational issues with a what's on and where to go guide.
Readership/Target Audience: Read by teachers, parents and children in Essex.
ADVERTISING: Rates on application
Copy instructions: Copy Date: 2 weeks prior to publication date
Editions:
Primary Times in North and Mid Essex
Primary Times in South and West Essex
CONSUMER: WOMEN'S INTEREST CONSUMER MAGAZINES: Child Care

PRIMARY TIMES IN FIFE, TAYSIDE & CENTRAL SCOTLAND

1645625U74D-566

Editorial Address: 4 Glamis Place, Dalgety Bay, DUNFERMLINE, KY11 9UA **Tel:** 01383 820364
Email: maureen@ptimes.co.uk
Advertising Address: As above.
Email: ceri@primary-times.co.uk
Web site: http://www.primarytimes.net
Publisher: Primary Times
Date Established: 2003
Frequency: 6 issues yearly
Free to qualifying individuals
Annual Sub.: £10.00
Circulation: 41,000 (Publisher's Statement)
Usual Pagination: 24
Editor: Maureen Smith; **Advertising Manager:** Maureen Smith
Summary of Content: Magazine covering current educational issues and family matters as well as a what's on and where to go guide.
Readership/Target Audience: Aimed at teachers, parents and primary school children in Fife, Tayside and central Scotland.
ADVERTISING: Rates on application
Copy instructions: Copy Date: 2 weeks prior to publication date
CONSUMER: WOMEN'S INTEREST CONSUMER MAGAZINES: Child Care

PRIMARY TIMES IN HAMPSHIRE

45333U74D-491_10

Formerly: OSM (Hampshire)
Editorial Address: Chinadale, Churchinford, TAUNTON, TA3 7PW **Tel:** 01823 601188 **Fax:** 01823 601199
Email: primarytimes.eyrie@tiscali.co.uk
Advertising Address: As above.
Email: primarytimes.eyrie@tiscali.co.uk
Web site: http://www.primarytimes.net
Date Established: 1997
Frequency: 6 issues yearly - Published just before each school holiday commences
Cover Price: Free
Circulation: 57,000 (Publisher's Statement)
Usual Pagination: 32
Editor: Debbie Williams; **Advertising Manager:** Alan Williams; **Publisher:** Debbie Williams
Summary of Content: Magazine covering current educational issues and family matters with a what's on and where to go guide.
Readership/Target Audience: Aimed at parents, teachers and children of primary school age in Hampshire.
ADVERTISING: Rates on application
Copy instructions: Copy Date: 2 weeks prior to publication date
Editions:
Primary Times in Somerset
CONSUMER: WOMEN'S INTEREST CONSUMER MAGAZINES: Child Care

PRIMARY TIMES IN HERTFORDSHIRE

714063U74D-491_20

Formerly: OSM Hertfordshire
Editorial Address: PO Box 39047, LONDON, E4 8YZ
Tel: 020 8529 7982 **Fax:** 0870 051 0279
Email: office@primary-times.com
Advertising Address: As above.
Email: office@primarytimes.demon.co.uk
Web site: http://www.primarytimes.net
Publisher: Primary Times
Date Established: 1999
Frequency: 6 issues yearly - Published two weeks prior to school holidays
Cover Price: Free
Circulation: 50,000 (Publisher's Statement)
Usual Pagination: 32
Editor: Paul Hardy; **Advertising Manager:** Sarah Bates; **Publisher:** Paul Hardy
Summary of Content: Magazine covering educational issues, health, bringing up children and forthcoming events.
Readership/Target Audience: Read by teachers and parents of primary school pupils in Hertfordshire.
ADVERTISING RATES:
Full Page Colour £1075.00

Mechanical Data: Type Area: 272 x 187mm, Bleed Size: 307 x 220mm, Trim Size: 297 x 210mm, Col Length: 272mm, Page Width: 187mm, Print Process: Web-fed offset litho, Film: Positive, right reading, emulsion side down. Digital
Copy instructions: Copy Date: 2 weeks prior to publication date
CONSUMER: WOMEN'S INTEREST CONSUMER MAGAZINES: Child Care

PRIMARY TIMES IN LANCASHIRE
714082U74D-581
Editorial Address: 12 Roche Gardens, Cheadle Hulme, CHEADLE, SK8 7QT **Tel:** 0161 439 4694
Fax: 0161 439 4694
Email: belinda.primarytimeslancashire@ntlworld.com
Advertising Address: As above.
Email: ceri@primary-times.co.uk
Web site: http://www.primarytimes.net
Publisher: It's Manchester Ltd
Frequency: 7 issues yearly
Cover Price: Free
Circulation: 40,000 (Publisher's Statement)
Usual Pagination: 24
Editor: Belinda Harman-Craddock; **Advertising Manager:** Belinda Harman-Craddock
Summary of Content: Magazine covering current educational issues and family matters with a what's on and where to go guide.
Readership/Target Audience: Read by teachers, parents and children in Lancashire.
ADVERTISING: Rates on application
Copy instructions: Copy Date: 2 weeks prior to publication date
CONSUMER: WOMEN'S INTEREST CONSUMER MAGAZINES: Child Care

PRIMARY TIMES IN LEICESTERSHIRE & RUTLAND
1796258U74D-651
Editorial Address: PO Box 39047, LONDON, E4 8YZ
Tel: 020 8529 7982 **Fax:** 0870 051 0279
Email: news@primary-times.com
Advertising Address: As above.
Email: office@primarytimes.demon.co.uk
Web site: http://www.primarytimes.net
Publisher: Primary Times
Frequency: 6 issues yearly
Cover Price: Free
Circulation: 45,000 (Publisher's Statement)
Usual Pagination: 24
Editor: Paul Hardy; **Advertising Manager:** Sarah Bates; **Publisher:** Paul Hardy
Summary of Content: Magazine covering educational issues, health, bringing up children and forth-coming events.
Readership/Target Audience: Aimed at teachers and parents of primary school children in Leicestershire and Rutland.
ADVERTISING RATES:
Full Page Colour £1075.00
Mechanical Data: Type Area: 272 x 187mm, Bleed Size: 307 x 220mm, Trim Size: 297 x 210mm, Col Length: 272mm, Page Width: 187mm, Print Process: Web-fed offset litho, Film: Positive, right reading, emulsion side down. Digital
Copy instructions: Copy Date: 2 weeks prior to publication date
CONSUMER: WOMEN'S INTEREST CONSUMER MAGAZINES: Child Care

PRIMARY TIMES IN MERSEYSIDE
1806121U74D-655
Editorial Address: Ashill Court, Ashill, CULLOMPTON, EX15 3NQ **Tel:** 01884 822886 **Fax:** 01884 840994
Email: ptmerseyside@btinternet.com
Advertising Address: As above. **Tel:** 01884 840994
Email: pt-merseyside@btinternet.com
Web site: http://www.primarytimes.net
Publisher: Primary Times Liverpool
Frequency: 7 issues yearly
Cover Price: Free
Circulation: 32,000 (Publisher's Statement)
Usual Pagination: 24
Editor: Judi Foster; **Advertising Manager:** Judi Foster
Summary of Content: Magazine covering current educational issues and family matters as well as what's on, where to go, book reviews and local and national features.
Readership/Target Audience: Aimed at teachers, parents and careers of primary school children in Merseyside.
ADVERTISING: Rates on application
CONSUMER: WOMEN'S INTEREST CONSUMER MAGAZINES: Child Care

PRIMARY TIMES IN NEWCASTLE, NORTH TYNESIDE & NORTHUMBERLAND
1646144U74D-580
Formerly: Primary Times in Newcastle & North Tyneside
Editorial Address: 1 Denehead Cottages, Hexham Road, Wabottle, NEWCASTLE UPON TYNE, NE15 9RX
Tel: 0191 264 5909
Email: jan@primarytimesne.co.uk
Advertising Address: As above.
Email: jan@primary-timesne.co.uk
Web site: http://www.primarytimes.net
Publisher: Round Sun Ltd
Date Established: 2004
Frequency: 7 issues yearly
Cover Price: Free
Circulation: 68,000 (Publisher's Statement)
Usual Pagination: 24
Editor: Jan Stewart; **Advertising Manager:** Jan Stewart
Summary of Content: Magazine covering current educational issues and family matters as well as a what's on and where to go guide.
Readership/Target Audience: Aimed at teachers, parents and primary school children in the North East.
ADVERTISING: Rates on application
Copy instructions: Copy Date: 2 weeks prior to publication date
CONSUMER: WOMEN'S INTEREST CONSUMER MAGAZINES: Child Care

PRIMARY TIMES IN NEWPORT & MONMOUTHSHIRE
1657703U74D-579
Editorial Address: 38 Pencisely Rise, CARDIFF, CF5 1DY
Tel: 029 2065 2311 **Fax:** 029 2065 2311
Email: primarytimes.newport@ntlworld.com
Advertising Address: As above.
Email: primarytimes.newport@ntlworld.com
Web site: http://www.primarytimes.net
Publisher: Primary Times Newport & Monmouthshire
Date Established: 2004
Frequency: 7 issues yearly
Cover Price: Free
Circulation: 40,000 (Publisher's Statement)
Usual Pagination: 32
Editor: Alison White; **Advertising Manager:** Alison White
Summary of Content: Magazine covering current educational issues and family matters. A what's on and where to go guide as well as competitions, library page, book reviews and further education for parents wanting to go back to work.
Language(s): English; Welsh
Readership/Target Audience: Aimed at teachers, parents and primary school children.
ADVERTISING: Rates on application
Copy instructions: Copy Date: 2 weeks prior to publication date
CONSUMER: WOMEN'S INTEREST CONSUMER MAGAZINES: Child Care

PRIMARY TIMES IN NORTH LONDON
714085U74D-491_40
Editorial Address: Islington Business Centre, 14-22 Coleman Fields, LONDON, N1 7AD **Tel:** 020 7748 2214
Email: liz.pt@btinternet.com
Advertising Address: As above. **Fax:** 020 7748 2214
Email: ptnl@btinternet.com
Web site: http://www.primarytimes.net
Publisher: Primary Times
Date Established: 2001
Frequency: 7 issues yearly
Cover Price: Free
Circulation: 40,000 (Publisher's Statement)
Usual Pagination: 32
Editor: Liz Gold; **Advertising Manager:** Liz Gold
Summary of Content: Magazine covering current educational issues and forthcoming events.
Readership/Target Audience: Read by teachers, parents and children in North London.
ADVERTISING RATES:
Full Page Mono £1300.00
Full Page Colour £1300.00
Mechanical Data: Type Area: 277 x 190mm, Bleed Size: 307 x 220mm, Trim Size: 297 x 210mm, Col Length: 277mm, Page Width: 190mm, Film: Digital
Copy instructions: Copy Date: 2 weeks prior to publication date
CONSUMER: WOMEN'S INTEREST CONSUMER MAGAZINES: Child Care

PRIMARY TIMES IN NORTH YORKSHIRE
1745162U74D-637
Editorial Address: 10 Meadow Park, DAWLISH, EX7 9BS
Tel: 0845 450 6178 **Fax:** 01626 895958
Email: belinda@primarytimesnorthyorks.com
Advertising Address: As above.

Email: sales@primarytimesnorthyorks.com
Web site: http://www.primarytimes.net
Publisher: Primary Times North Yorkshire
Frequency: 7 issues yearly
Cover Price: Free
Circulation: 40,000 (Publisher's Statement)
Usual Pagination: 24
Editor: Belinda Collins; **Advertising Manager:** Kathy Gould
Summary of Content: Magazine containing a what's on, what to do and where to go guide.
Readership/Target Audience: Read by children, parents and teachers in the State primary school sector.
ADVERTISING: Rates on application
CONSUMER: WOMEN'S INTEREST CONSUMER MAGAZINES: Child Care

PRIMARY TIMES IN NOTTINGHAMSHIRE
1645901U74D-571
Editorial Address: 81 Chestnut Crescent, Chudleigh, NEWTON ABBOT, TQ13 0PT **Tel:** 01626 853734
Email: kathygould@sky.com
Advertising Address: As above. **Tel:** 0116 286 6136
Fax: 0116 286 9083
Email: primarytimesnotts@btconnect.com
Web site: http://www.primarytimes.net
Publisher: Primary Times Nottingham
Date Established: 2003
Frequency: 7 issues yearly
Cover Price: Free
Circulation: 65,000 (Publisher's Statement)
Usual Pagination: 24
Editor: Kathy Gould; **Advertising Manager:** Kathy Gould
Summary of Content: Magazine covering current educational issues and family matters as well as a what's on and where to go guide.
Readership/Target Audience: Aimed at teachers, parents and primary school children.
ADVERTISING: Rates on application
Copy instructions: Copy Date: 2 weeks prior to publication date
Editions:
Primary Times in Staffordshire
CONSUMER: WOMEN'S INTEREST CONSUMER MAGAZINES: Child Care

PRIMARY TIMES IN OXFORDSHIRE
718013U74D-491_45
Editorial Address: Office 2, 4 Heath Court, Queen Street, Hook Norton, BANBURY, OX15 5EG **Tel:** 01608 737850
Advertising Address: As above. **Fax:** 01608 730323
Email: ceri@primary-times.co.uk
Publisher: Primary Times
Date Established: 1999
Frequency: 6 issues yearly - Published at the end of term and half term
Cover Price: Free
Circulation: 37,500 (Publisher's Statement)
Usual Pagination: 24
Editor: Ian Buchanan; **Advertising Manager:** Ian Buchanan; **Publisher:** Ian Buchanan
Summary of Content: Magazine containing news and feature articles and a what's on and where to go guide.
Readership/Target Audience: Aimed at pupils, parents, teachers and governors of state primary schools.
ADVERTISING: Rates on application
Copy instructions: Copy Date: 2 weeks prior to publication date
Editions:
Primary Times in Buckinghamshire & Milton Keynes
CONSUMER: WOMEN'S INTEREST CONSUMER MAGAZINES: Child Care

PRIMARY TIMES IN SOUTH EAST LONDON
749722U74D-491_50
Editorial Address: 2 Southbrook Mews, LONDON, SE12 8LG **Tel:** 020 8318 0400
Email: peter@primarytimes.biz
Advertising Address: As above.
Email: sales@primarytimes.biz
Web site: http://www.primarytimes.net
Publisher: Primary Times
Date Established: 2002
Frequency: 7 issues yearly
Cover Price: Free
Circulation: 43,000 (Publisher's Statement)
Usual Pagination: 40
Editor: Peter Watson; **Advertising Manager:** Peter Watson; **Publisher:** Alison Watson
Summary of Content: Magazine containing a what's on and where to go guide as well as features on education and family matters.
Readership/Target Audience: Read by primary school children, parents and teachers.
ADVERTISING RATES:
Full Page Colour £1360.00

Consumer Magazines

Agency Commission: 10%
Mechanical Data: Type Area: 277 x 190mm, Bleed Size: 307 x 220mm, Trim Size: 297 x 210mm, Col Length: 277mm, Page Width: 190mm
Copy instructions: Copy Date: 2 weeks prior to publication date
Editions:
Primary Times in East Kent
Primary Times in East Sussex
Primary Times in North/West Kent
Primary Times in West Sussex
CONSUMER: WOMEN'S INTEREST CONSUMER MAGAZINES: Child Care

PRIMARY TIMES IN SOUTH LONDON
749720U74D-491_55
Editorial Address: 1354 London Road, LONDON, SW16 4DA **Tel:** 020 8764 4411 **Fax:** 020 8764 4433
Email: primarytimes@topemediagroup.com
Advertising Address: As above.
Email: luke@topemediagroup.com
Web site: http://www.primarytimes.net
Publisher: Primary Times
Frequency: 7 issues yearly
Cover Price: Free
Circulation: 40,000 (Publisher's Statement)
Usual Pagination: 24
Editor: Luke Tope; **Advertising Manager:** Luke Tope; **Publisher:** Luke Tope
Summary of Content: Magazine containing a what's on and where to go guide as well as features on education, health and safety and family matters.
Readership/Target Audience: Aimed at primary school children, parents and teachers.
ADVERTISING: Rates on application
Copy instructions: Copy Date: 2 weeks prior to publication date
CONSUMER: WOMEN'S INTEREST CONSUMER MAGAZINES: Child Care

PRIMARY TIMES IN SUNDERLAND & DURHAM
1794515U74D-649
Editorial Address: 1 Denehead Cottages, Hexham Road, Wabottle, NEWCASTLE UPON TYNE, NE15 9RX
Tel: 0191 264 5909
Email: jan@primarytimesne.co.uk
Advertising Address: As above.
Email: jan@primarytimesne.co.uk
Web site: http://www.primarytimes.net
Publisher: Round Sun Ltd
Date Established: 2006
Frequency: 7 issues yearly
Cover Price: Free
Circulation: 40,000 (Publisher's Statement)
Usual Pagination: 24
Editor: Jan Stewart; **Advertising Manager:** Jan Stewart
Summary of Content: Magazine covering current educational issues and family matters as well as a what's on and where to go guide.
Readership/Target Audience: Aimed at teachers, parents and primary school children in Sunderland and Durham.
ADVERTISING RATES:
Full Page Colour £945.00
Mechanical Data: Type Area: 272 x 187mm, Bleed Size: 307 x 220mm, Trim Size: 297 x 210mm, Col Length: 272mm, Page Width: 187mm, Print Process: Web-fed offset litho, Film: Positive, right reading, emulsion side down. Digital
Copy instructions: Copy Date: 2 weeks prior to publication date
CONSUMER: WOMEN'S INTEREST CONSUMER MAGAZINES: Child Care

PRIMARY TIMES IN SURREY
714064U74D-491_70
Editorial Address: Richardson House, 21-24 New Street, WORCESTER, WR1 2DP **Tel:** 01905 723011
Fax: 01905 612039
Email: dawn@pw-media.co.uk
Advertising Address: As above.
Email: dawn@pw-media.co.uk
Web site: http://www.primarytimes.net
Publisher: PW Media & Publishing Ltd
Date Established: 1999
Frequency: 7 issues yearly
Cover Price: Free
Circulation: 45,000 (Publisher's Statement)
Usual Pagination: 40
Editor: Dawn Pardoe; **Advertising Manager:** Dawn Pardoe
Summary of Content: Magazine which aims to inform families and children of current educational issues and forthcoming events.
Readership/Target Audience: Read by teachers, parents and children in Surrey, Herefordshire and Worcestershire.
ADVERTISING RATES:
Full Page Colour £1120.00

Mechanical Data: Type Area: 277 x 190mm, Bleed Size: 307 x 220mm, Trim Size: 297 x 210mm, Col Length: 277mm, Page Width: 190mm
Editions:
Primary Times in Hereford & Worcester
CONSUMER: WOMEN'S INTEREST CONSUMER MAGAZINES: Child Care

PRIMARY TIMES IN THE TEES VALLEY
1645675U74D-570
Editorial Address: PO Box 676, STOCKTON-ON-TEES, TS19 7WT **Tel:** 01642 586214 **Fax:** 01642 585410
Email: office@primarytimes.info
Advertising Address: As above.
Email: office@primarytimes.info
Web site: http://www.primarytimes.net
Publisher: Primary Times
Date Established: 2002
Frequency: 7 issues yearly
Cover Price: Free
Circulation: 65,000 (Publisher's Statement)
Usual Pagination: 32
Editor: Russel Warnock; **Advertising Manager:** Russel Warnock
Summary of Content: Magazine covering current educational issues and family matters as well as a what's on and where to go guide.
Readership/Target Audience: Aimed at teachers, parents and primary school children.
ADVERTISING: Rates on application
CONSUMER: WOMEN'S INTEREST CONSUMER MAGAZINES: Child Care

PRIMARY TIMES IN WEST YORKSHIRE
45335U74D-492_25
Editorial Address: The Old Bulls Head, Dun Street, SHEFFIELD, S3 8SL **Tel:** 0114 279 9793 **Fax:** 0114 279 9792
Email: mandymail@btconnect.com
Advertising Address: As above. **Tel:** 0113 307 0114
Email: primary@planet-group.co.uk
Web site: http://www.primarytimes.net
Publisher: Primary Times
Date Established: 1998
Frequency: 7 issues yearly
Cover Price: Free
Circulation: 30,000 (Publisher's Statement)
Usual Pagination: 24
Editor: Mandy Mellor; **Advertising Manager:** Margaret Gough
Summary of Content: Magazine containing a what's on and where to go guide covering educational news, articles, puzzles, book reviews and children's work.
Readership/Target Audience: Read by primary school children, parents and teachers in Yorkshire.
ADVERTISING RATES:
Full Page Colour £960.00
Mechanical Data: Type Area: 273 x 184mm, Bleed Size: 303 x 216mm, Col Length: 273mm, Page Width: 184mm
CONSUMER: WOMEN'S INTEREST CONSUMER MAGAZINES: Child Care

PRIMARY TIMES WEST MIDLANDS AND BLACK COUNTRY
1646145U74D-578
Formerly: Primary Times in the West Midlands
Editorial Address: 5th Floor, White House, 111 New Street, BIRMINGHAM, B2 4EU **Tel:** 0121 631 6101
Email: mikedav@ic24.net
Advertising Address: As above. **Fax:** 0121 336 1936
Email: leah@modamedia.co.uk
Web site: http://www.primarytimes.net
Publisher: Moda Media
Frequency: 7 issues yearly
Cover Price: Free
Circulation: 70,000 (Publisher's Statement)
Usual Pagination: 32
Summary of Content: Magazine covering current educational issues and family matters as well as a what's on and where to go guide.
Readership/Target Audience: Aimed at teachers, parents and primary school children in the West Midlands.
ADVERTISING RATES:
Full Page Colour £1900.00
Agency Commission: 10%
Mechanical Data: Type Area: 272 x 180mm, Col Length: 272mm, Page Width: 180mm, Film: Digital
Average advertising content per issue: 40%
CONSUMER: WOMEN'S INTEREST CONSUMER MAGAZINES: Child Care

PRIME OF LIFE
45581U74N-110_25
Editorial Address: The Tindle Suite, Webbs House, The Parade, LISKEARD, PL14 6AH **Tel:** 01579 342174
Fax: 01579 341851
Email: ct.edit@internet-today.co.uk

Advertising Address: As above. **Fax:** 01579 341852
Email: primeoflife@internet-today.co.uk
Publisher: Cornish Times Group
Frequency: Monthly
Cover Price: Free
Circulation: 35,000 (Publisher's Statement)
Editor: John Noble; **Advertising Manager:** Hazel Bradley
Summary of Content: Magazine containing news, holidays, leisure, health, views and ideas. Also includes articles on nostalgia, gardening, antiques, competitions, TV, books, food and drink.
Readership/Target Audience: Aimed at those aged over 50 years old.
ADVERTISING RATES:
Full Page Mono £1785.00
Full Page Colour £1785.00
SCC £6.20
Agency Commission: 10%
Mechanical Data: Type Area: 360 X 272mm, Col Length: 360mm, Page Width: 272mm, No. of Columns (Display): 8, Col Widths (Display): 32mm, Film: Digital
Average advertising content per issue: 50%
CONSUMER: WOMEN'S INTEREST CONSUMER MAGAZINES: Retirement

PRIVATE EYE
45155U73-270
Editorial Address: 6 Carlisle Street, LONDON, W1D 3BN
Tel: 020 7437 4017 **Fax:** 020 7437 0705
Email: strobes@private-eye.co.uk
Web site: http://www.private-eye.co.uk
Publisher: Pressdram Ltd
Date Established: 1961
Frequency: 26 issues yearly
Cover Price: £1.50
Annual Sub.: £28.00
Circulation: 206,550 (ABC 01/01/2009 to 30/06/2009)
Usual Pagination: 40
Editor: Ian Hislop
Summary of Content: Magazine covering political satire, investigative journalism, gossip and jokes, plus business news.
Readership/Target Audience: Aimed at those with an interest in news.
ADVERTISING: No Advertising taken
CONSUMER: NATIONAL & INTERNATIONAL PERIODICALS

PRIZE QUEST
1642763U79F-81
Editorial Address: 2nd Floor, Barclay House, 242-254 Banbury Road, OXFORD, OX2 7BY **Tel:** 01865 515840
Fax: 01865 556588
Email: alastair@prizemags.co.uk
Advertising Address: As above.
Email: tony@prizemags.co.uk
Web site: http://www.prizemagazines.com
Publisher: Prize Magazines
Frequency: 6 issues yearly
Annual Sub.: £21.00
Circulation: 60,000 (Publisher's Statement)
Usual Pagination: 52
Editor: Alastair Fry; **Advertising Manager:** Tony Lane
Summary of Content: Magazine with crosswords and puzzles as well as entertainment reviews, gadgets and travel.
Readership/Target Audience: Aimed at puzzle enthusiasts aged 25 years old plus.
ADVERTISING: Rates on application
Average advertising content per issue: 3%
CONSUMER: HOBBIES & DIY: Games & Puzzles

PRIZES & PUZZLES SPECIAL
1642609U79F-80
Editorial Address: 2nd Floor, Barclay House, 242-254 Banbury Road, OXFORD, OX2 7BY **Tel:** 01865 515840
Fax: 01865 556588
Email: tony@prizemags.co.uk
Web site: http://www.prizemagazine.com
Publisher: Prize Magazines
Frequency: Quarterly
Annual Sub.: £14.00
Circulation: 25,000 (Publisher's Statement)
Usual Pagination: 68
Editor: Tony Lane
Summary of Content: Magazine containing crosswords, puzzles and promotional competitions.
Readership/Target Audience: Aimed at puzzle enthusiasts aged 25 years old plus.
ADVERTISING: No Advertising taken
CONSUMER: HOBBIES & DIY: Games & Puzzles

PRIZES GALORE
46668U79F-60
Editorial Address: 2nd Floor, Barclay House, 242-254 Banbury Road, OXFORD, OX2 7BY **Tel:** 01865 515840
Fax: 01865 556588
Email: alastair@prizemags.co.uk
Advertising Address: As above.

Email: tony@prizemags.co.uk
Web site: http://www.prizemagazines.com
Publisher: Prize Magazines
Frequency: Monthly
Annual Sub.: £36.00
Circulation: 100,000 (Publisher's Statement)
Usual Pagination: 60
Editor: Alastair Fry; **Advertising Manager:** Tony Lane;
Publisher: Tony Lane
Summary of Content: Competition magazine, covering home, leisure, holidays, travel, money, health and beauty.
Readership/Target Audience: Read by those who enjoy competitions.
ADVERTISING RATES:
Full Page Colour £3000.00
SCC £35.00
Agency Commission: 15%
Mechanical Data: Film: Digital, Trim Size: 275 x 205mm, Bleed Size: 281 x 211mm, Type Area: 250 x 185mm, Col Length: 250mm, Col Widths (Display): 44mm, No. of Columns (Display): 4, Print Process: Web-fed offset litho, Page Width: 185mm
Copy instructions: Copy Date: 1st of the month prior to publication date
CONSUMER: HOBBIES & DIY: Games & Puzzles

PROBUS MAGAZINE
45594U74N-111
Editorial Address: 2 Wychbold Farm Barns, Crown Lane, Wychbold, DROITWICH, WR9 0BX **Tel:** 01527 861066
Fax: 01527 861066
Email: juliak@probustrading.com
Advertising Address: Jessmond, New Wood, STOURBRIDGE, DY7 6RX **Tel:** 01384 394803
Fax: 01384 394803
Email: mj.mann@btinternet.com
Publisher: Probus Trading
Frequency: Quarterly
Circulation: 45,000 (Publisher's Statement)
Usual Pagination: 40
Editor: Julia Kyte; **Advertising Manager:** Michelle Mann
Summary of Content: Magazine of the Probus club. Includes news, leisure, travel, finance and motoring.
Readership/Target Audience: Aimed at members.
ADVERTISING RATES:
Full Page Mono £1000.00
Full Page Colour £1100.00
Agency Commission: 10%
Mechanical Data: Film: Digital, Trim Size: 297 x 210mm, Type Area: 277 x 190mm, Col Length: 277mm, Bleed Size: 303 x 216mm, Page Width: 190mm
Copy instructions: Copy Date: 5 weeks prior to publication date
Average advertising content per issue: 50%
CONSUMER: WOMEN'S INTEREST CONSUMER MAGAZINES: Retirement

PROCEEDINGS OF WESLEY HISTORICAL SOCIETY
47850U87-191_50
Editorial Address: 26 Roe Cross Green, Mottram, HYDE, SK14 6LP **Tel:** 01457 763485 **Fax:** 01457 763485
Advertising Address: As above.
Web site: http://www.wesleyhistoricalsociety.org.uk
ISSN: 0043-2873
Publisher: Wesley Historical Society
Date Established: 1897
Frequency: 3 issues yearly - Published in February, May and October
Annual Sub.: £12.00
Circulation: 850 (Publisher's Statement)
Usual Pagination: 40
Editor: Edward Rose; **Advertising Manager:** D. Ryan
Summary of Content: Magazine focusing on the study of the history and literature of all the branches of Methodism.
Readership/Target Audience: Aimed at members and those throughout the world interested in Methodism.
ADVERTISING RATES:
Full Page Mono £40.00
Mechanical Data: Page Width: 110mm
Copy instructions: Copy Date: 1st of the month prior to publication date
Average advertising content per issue: 2%
CONSUMER: RELIGIOUS

PROCYCLING
46405U77C-845
Editorial Address: 2 Balcombe Street, LONDON, NW1 6NW **Tel:** 020 7042 4000
Email: procycling@futurenet.com
Advertising Address: 30 Monmouth Street, BATH, BA1 2BW **Tel:** 01225 442244
Email: steve.hulbert@futurenet.com
Web site: http://www.procycling.com
ISSN: 1465-7198
Publisher: Future Publishing Limited
Frequency: 13 issues yearly
Cover Price: £3.99
Circulation: 30,000 (Publisher's Statement)

Usual Pagination: 148
Editor: Cam Winstanley; **Advertising Manager:** Steve Hulbert
Summary of Content: Magazine covering all aspects of international cycling. Contains news, features, interviews and bike tests.
Readership/Target Audience: Aimed at people with an interest in the professional race scene, from the active cyclist to the armchair fan.
ADVERTISING RATES:
Full Page Colour £1700.00
Agency Commission: 10%
Mechanical Data: Type Area: 270 x 190mm, Bleed Size: 296 x 216mm, Trim Size: 290 x 210mm, Col Length: 270mm, Page Width: 190mm, Film: Digital
Copy instructions: Copy Date: 4 weeks prior to publication date
Average advertising content per issue: 35%
CONSUMER: MOTORING & CYCLING: Cycling

PROFILE
1740126U80C-5332
Formerly: Elite
Editorial Address: 121 Newgate Lane, MANSFIELD, NG18 2PA **Tel:** 01623 456789 **Fax:** 01623 464647
Email: newsdesk@chad.co.uk
Advertising Address: As above.
Email: haroldine.lockwood@chad.co.uk
Web site: http://www.mansfieldtoday.co.uk
Publisher: Wilfred Edmunds
Date Established: 2005
Frequency: Quarterly
Cover Price: Free
Circulation: 20,000 (Publisher's Statement)
Editor: Ashley Booker; **News Editor:** Ashley Booker;
Advertising Manager: Haroldine Lockwood
Summary of Content: Magazine covering interiors, gardens, out and about, eating out, leisure, property, travel, fashion, arts and antiques, sport, health and beauty.
Readership/Target Audience: Aimed at high income households in Mansfield.
ADVERTISING: Rates on application
CONSUMER: RURAL & REGIONAL INTEREST: Regional Interest English Counties

PROFILE (SHEFFIELD)
47016U80C-3700
Editorial Address: York Street, SHEFFIELD, S1 1PU **Tel:** 0114 276 7676 **Fax:** 0114 272 5978
Email: martin.smith@sheffieldnewspapers.co.uk
Advertising Address: As above. **Fax:** 0114 252 1227
Email: melinda.gore@sheffieldnewspapers.co.uk
Publisher: Sheffield Newspapers Ltd
Date Established: 1998
Frequency: Monthly
Cover Price: £1.95
Free to qualifying individuals
Circulation: 17,208 (Publisher's Statement)
Usual Pagination: 80
Editor: Martin Smith; **Advertising Director:** Melinda Gore
Summary of Content: Lifestyle magazine covering fashion, food and drink, motoring and leisure.
Readership/Target Audience: Aimed at 25 to 55 year olds.
ADVERTISING: Rates on application
Agency Commission: 10%
Copy instructions: Copy Date: 2nd Friday of the month prior to publication date
Average advertising content per issue: 50%
CONSUMER: RURAL & REGIONAL INTEREST: Regional Interest English Counties

PROFIT WATCH RECOMMENDS
1794238U74M-426
Editorial Address: 7th Floor, Sea Containers House, 20 Upper Ground, LONDON, SE1 9JD **Tel:** 020 7633 3600
Fax: 020 7633 3740
Email: pwr@f-s-p.co.uk
Web site: http://www.fleetstreetpublications.co.uk
Publisher: Fleet Street Publications Ltd
Frequency: Monthly
Annual Sub.: £39.00
Circulation: 1,000 (Publisher's Statement)
Usual Pagination: 8
Editor: Frank Hemsley; **Managing Editor:** Frank Hemsley
Summary of Content: Newsletter featuring regular wealth-building share recommendations.
Readership/Target Audience: Aimed at private investors.
ADVERTISING: No Advertising taken
CONSUMER: WOMEN'S INTEREST CONSUMER MAGAZINES: Personal Finance

PROFYLE
1831468U74Q-1362
Editorial Address: Galleon House, Glengarnock Avenue, Tower Hamlets, LONDON, E14 3DL **Tel:** 020 7987 9862
Fax: 020 7987 9862
Email: profyle@profylemagazine.com

Web site: http://www.profylemagazine.com
Publisher: Profyle Magazine Ltd
Date Established: 2008
Frequency: Monthly
Cover Price: £3.50
Circulation: 30,000 (Publisher's Statement)
Editor: Cindy Okwera; **Features Editor:** Marsha Blake
Summary of Content: Lifestyle magazine covering fashion, beauty, entertainment, property, travel and celebrity gossip.
Readership/Target Audience: Aimed at young, ambitious men and women between the ages of 18 to 35 years old.
CONSUMER: WOMEN'S INTEREST CONSUMER MAGAZINES: Lifestyle

THE PROGRAMME BOOKS
45379U75E-271
Editorial Address: Weatherbys Thoroughbred Ltd, Sanders Road, WELLINGBOROUGH, NN8 4BX **Tel:** 01933 304787
Fax: 01933 440807
Email: editorial@weatherbys.co.uk
Advertising Address: As above. **Tel:** 01933 440077
Fax: 01933 270300
Email: marketing@wetherbys.co.uk
Publisher: British Horseracing Board
Frequency: Quarterly
Cover Price: £44.00
Circulation: 1,500 (Publisher's Statement)
Usual Pagination: 700
Editor: Karen Osborne
Summary of Content: Booklet giving information on all races to be run in Great Britain. Includes race conditions, prize money and distances.
Readership/Target Audience: Aimed at all racehorse trainers in Great Britain, leading foreign trainers and leading owners worldwide.
ADVERTISING: Rates on application
CONSUMER: SPORT: Horse Racing

PROGRESS
1697685U94F-1001
Editorial Address: PO Box 173, PETERBOROUGH, PE2 6WS **Tel:** 0845 702 3153
Email: editorial@rnib.org.uk
Advertising Address: As above.
Email: cjames@rnib.org.uk
Publisher: Royal National Institute of Blind People
Frequency: Monthly
Cover Price: £0.57
Circulation: 400 (Publisher's Statement)
Editor: Chris James; **Advertising Manager:** Chris James
Summary of Content: Magazine featuring general interest articles, short stories and crosswords.
Readership/Target Audience: Aimed at visually impaired adults of all ages.
ADVERTISING: Rates on application
CONSUMER: OTHER CLASSIFICATIONS: Disability

PROGRESS IN HUMAN GEOGRAPHY
30947U94X-144_15
Editorial Address: 1 Oliver's Yard, 55 City Road, LONDON, EC1Y 1SP **Tel:** 020 7324 8500 **Fax:** 020 7324 8600
Email: market@sagepub.co.uk
Advertising Address: As above.
Email: sheena.karim@sagepub.co.uk
Web site: http://www.sagepub.co.uk
ISSN: 0309-1325
Publisher: Sage Publications
Date Established: 1977
Frequency: 6 issues yearly
Annual Sub.: £477.00
Usual Pagination: 176
Editor: Roger Lee; **Managing Editor:** Roger Lee
Summary of Content: Academic publication providing an appraisal of geographical work in the social sciences and humanities.
Readership/Target Audience: Aimed at academics and students in the field of social, economic, political and cultural geography and related disciplines.
ADVERTISING RATES:
Full Page Mono £450.00
Agency Commission: 5%
Mechanical Data: Trim Size: 246 x 189mm, Page Width: 160mm, Film: Digital, Bleed Size: 254 x 195mm, Screen: Mono 52 lpc Colour 60 lpc, Print Process: Sheet-fed litho, Type Area: 215 x 160mm, Col Length: 215mm
Copy instructions: Copy Date: 12 weeks prior to publication date
Average advertising content per issue: 1%
CONSUMER: OTHER CLASSIFICATIONS: Miscellaneous

PROGRESS IN PHYSICAL GEOGRAPHY
30796U94X-144_20
Editorial Address: 1 Oliver's Yard, 55 City Road, LONDON, EC1Y 1SP **Tel:** 020 7324 8500 **Fax:** 020 7324 8600
Email: market@sagepub.co.uk

Consumer Magazines

Advertising Address: As above.
Email: advertising@sagepub.co.uk
Web site: http://www.sagepub.co.uk
ISSN: 0909-1333
Publisher: Sage Publications
Date Established: 1977
Frequency: 6 issues yearly
Annual Sub.: £477.00
Usual Pagination: 160
Editor: Bruce Atkinson; **Advertising Manager:** Sheena Karim
Summary of Content: International publication providing a forum for geographical work in the natural and environmental sciences, reviewing current research and theoretical developments.
Readership/Target Audience: Read by physical geographers, students and lecturers.
ADVERTISING RATES:
Full Page Mono £450.00
Agency Commission: 5%
Mechanical Data: Type Area: 215 x 160mm, Col Length: 215mm, Page Width: 160mm, Print Process: Sheet-fed offset litho, Film: Digital
Copy instructions: Copy Date: 12 weeks prior to publication date
CONSUMER: OTHER CLASSIFICATIONS: Miscellaneous

PROM
1895960U74F-778
Editorial Address: 25 Phoenix Court, Hawkins Road, COLCHESTER, CO2 8JY **Tel:** 01206 505900
Email: naomi@aceville.co.uk
Web site: http://www.prom-magazine.com
Publisher: Maze Media (2000) Ltd
Date Established: 2009
Frequency: Annual - Published in March
Cover Price: £4.99
Circulation: 60,000 (Publisher's Statement)
Editor: Naomi Abeykoon
Summary of Content: Magazine featuring information and advice on outfits, hair and makeup for going to a prom.
Readership/Target Audience: Aimed at those attending a prom.
ADVERTISING: Rates on application
CONSUMER: WOMEN'S INTEREST CONSUMER MAGAZINES: Teenage

THE PROPERTY GUIDE
1664419U74K-723
Editorial Address: Alewater, Lilliesleaf, MELROSE, TD6 9EL **Tel:** 01835 825921 **Fax:** 01835 870570
Email: real@alewater.com
Advertising Address: 22 Chester Street, EDINBURGH, EH3 7RA **Tel:** 0131 467 3977
Email: kirstin@kirstennorrie.co.uk
Web site: http://www.theonlinepropertyguide.com
Publisher: Hawthorne Publishing
Date Established: 1986
Frequency: Monthly
Cover Price: Free
Circulation: 25,000 (Publisher's Statement)
Usual Pagination: 32
Editor: Helen Narracott; **Advertising Manager:** Kirstin Norrie
Summary of Content: Magazine covering new, re-sale and rental properties in Edinburgh, the Lothians and the Scottish Borders.
Readership/Target Audience: Aimed at house-buyers, tenants, estate agents, letting agent and private landlords.
ADVERTISING RATES:
Full Page Colour £895.00
Agency Commission: 10%
Mechanical Data: Type Area: 275 x 190mm, Bleed Size: 310 x 224mm, Trim Size: 297 x 210mm, Col Length: 275mm, Page Width: 190mm, Film: Digital
Copy instructions: Copy Date: 2 weeks prior to publication date
CONSUMER: WOMEN'S INTEREST CONSUMER MAGAZINES: Home Purchase

PROPERTY MART
1789964U74K-762
Editorial Address: Media House, 539 High Road, ILFORD, IG1 1UD **Tel:** 020 8478 4444
Advertising Address: 46 High Street, ROMFORD, RM1 1HR **Tel:** 01708 771500 **Fax:** 01708 771521
Email: tony.meston@archant.co.uk
Web site: http://www.homes24.co.uk
Publisher: Archant London
Frequency: 25 issues yearly
Cover Price: Free
Circulation: 160,000 (Publisher's Statement)
Usual Pagination: 36
Advertising Manager: Tony Meston
Summary of Content: Magazine with local property advertising for property to sell or rent.
Readership/Target Audience: Aimed at estate agents and the general public looking to buy, sell or rent property in London or Essex.

ADVERTISING RATES:
Full Page Colour £672.00
Copy instructions: Copy Date: 1 week prior to publication date
Editions:
Property Mart Docklands
Property Mart East London
Property Mart South Essex
Property Mart West Esssex
CONSUMER: WOMEN'S INTEREST CONSUMER MAGAZINES: Home Purchase

PROPERTY NEWS
1601535U74K-664
Formerly: Property News (Cambridge Evening News)
Editorial Address: Winship Road, Milton, CAMBRIDGE, CB24 6PP **Tel:** 01223 434434 **Fax:** 01223 434415
Email: jennifer.shelton@cambridge-news.co.uk
Advertising Address: As above. **Tel:** 01223 434231
Fax: 01223 434222
Email: property@cambridge-news.co.uk
Web site: http://www.cambridge-news.co.uk
ISSN: 1463-5399
Publisher: Cambridge Newspapers Ltd
Frequency: Weekly
Cover Price: £1.00
Free to qualifying individuals
Circulation: 20,000 (Publisher's Statement)
Usual Pagination: 132
Editor: Jennifer Shelton
Summary of Content: Magazine featuring news on all aspects of residential property in Cambridgeshire, including property for sale and to rent.
Readership/Target Audience: Aimed at people buying or selling houses in Cambridgeshire.
ADVERTISING RATES:
SCC £7.50
Agency Commission: 10%
Mechanical Data: Col Length: 270mm, No. of Columns (Display): 4, Type Area: 270 x 209mm, Page Width: 209mm, Film: Digital
Copy instructions: Copy Date: Monday 12 noon prior to publication date
Average advertising content per issue: 97%
Supplement to: Cambridge News
CONSUMER: WOMEN'S INTEREST CONSUMER MAGAZINES: Home Purchase

PROPERTY SOUTH EAST
1814270U74K-783
Editorial Address: Cowden Close, Horns Road, Hawkhurst, CRANBROOK, TN18 4QT **Tel:** 01580 753322
Fax: 01580 754104
Email: property@wealdenad.co.uk
Web site: http://www.wealdenproperty.co.uk
Publisher: The Wealden Advertiser
Frequency: Weekly
Cover Price: Free
Circulation: 37,500 (Publisher's Statement)
Usual Pagination: 36
Editor: Melanie Payne; **Managing Editor:** Graham Thorn
Summary of Content: Magazine covering all aspects of property including lettings, residential, commercial and agricultural property.
Readership/Target Audience: Aimed as perspective purchasers and vendors of property in Kent and East Sussex.
ADVERTISING: No Advertising taken
CONSUMER: WOMEN'S INTEREST CONSUMER MAGAZINES: Home Purchase

PROPHETIC WITNESS
47745U87-192_20
Editorial Address: 6 Bushcombe Close, Woodmancote, CHELTENHAM, GL52 9HX **Tel:** 01242 678989
Fax: 01242 678989
Email: revglyntaylor@btinternet.com
Advertising Address: PO Box 109, LEYLAND, PR25 1WB **Tel:** 01772 452846 **Fax:** 01772 452846
Email: colin.lenoury@virgin.net
Web site: http://www.pwmi.org
Publisher: Prophetic Witness Movement International
Frequency: Monthly
Cover Price: £1.75
Annual Sub.: £18.00
Circulation: 2,500 (Publisher's Statement)
Usual Pagination: 24
Editor: Glyn L. Taylor; **Advertising Manager:** Colin Le Noury
Summary of Content: Journal highlighting aspects of the Bible relating to the future and time prophesy.
Readership/Target Audience: Read by those interested in prophetic interpretations of the scriptures.
ADVERTISING RATES:
Full Page Mono £200.00
Full Page Colour £300.00
Agency Commission: 15%
Mechanical Data: Trim Size: 297 x 210mm, Film: Digital
Copy instructions: Copy Date: 1st of the month prior to publication date

Average advertising content per issue: 20%
CONSUMER: RELIGIOUS

PROSPECT
45156U73-275
Editorial Address: 2 Bloomsbury Place, LONDON, WC1A 2QA **Tel:** 020 7255 1281 **Fax:** 020 7255 1279
Email: editorial@prospect-magazine.co.uk
Advertising Address: As above.
Email: advertising@prospect-magazine.co.uk
Web site: http://www.prospect-magazine.co.uk
ISSN: 1359-5024
Publisher: Prospect Publishing Ltd
Date Established: 1995
Frequency: Monthly
Cover Price: £4.50
Annual Sub.: £54.00
Circulation: 27,645 (ABC 01/01/2009 to 30/06/2009)
Usual Pagination: 96
Editor: David Goodhart; **Executive Editor:** Hilly Janes; **Advertising Manager:** Jenny Shramenko; **Publisher:** David Hanger
Summary of Content: Magazine covering politics, international affairs, social and cultural issues and the arts.
Readership/Target Audience: Read by company directors, politicians, journalists and academics.
ADVERTISING RATES:
Full Page Colour £2600.00
Agency Commission: 10%
Mechanical Data: No. of Columns (Display): 2, Type Area: 246 x 174mm, Col Length: 246mm, Film: Digital, Trim Size: 275 x 210mm, Bleed Size: 281 x 216mm, Page Width: 174mm
Copy instructions: Copy Date: 14 days prior to publication date
CONSUMER: NATIONAL & INTERNATIONAL PERIODICALS

PROSPERITY
627287U82-157_50
Editorial Address: 268 Bath Street, GLASGOW, G2 4JR **Tel:** 0141 332 2214 **Fax:** 0141 353 6900
Email: contactus@prosperityuk.com
Web site: http://www.prosperityuk.com
Publisher: Alistair McConnachie
Date Established: 2000
Frequency: Quarterly
Annual Sub.: £10.00
Circulation: 2,500 (Publisher's Statement)
Usual Pagination: 4
Editor: Alistair McConnachie; **Publisher:** Alistair McConnachie
Summary of Content: Magazine focusing on the advocacy of state-created debt free money spent into society via public spending projects.
Readership/Target Audience: Aimed at political activists, academics and opinion formers.
ADVERTISING: No Advertising taken
CONSUMER: CURRENT AFFAIRS & POLITICS

PROTESTANT TRUTH
47746U87-192_50
Editorial Address: 184 Fleet Street, LONDON, EC4A 2HJ **Tel:** 020 7405 4960 **Fax:** 020 7405 4960
Email: ptslondon@btconnect.com
Advertising Address: As above.
Email: ptslondon@btconnect.com
Web site: http://www.protestant-truth.org
Publisher: Protestant Truth Society (Inc.)
Date Established: 1846
Frequency: 6 issues yearly
Cover Price: £1.00
Annual Sub.: £7.50
Circulation: 2,500 (Publisher's Statement)
Usual Pagination: 20
Editor: Gordon Murray; **Advertising Manager:** George Rae
Summary of Content: Publication containing Protestant and Evangelical news and issues.
Readership/Target Audience: Aimed at those interested in religion.
ADVERTISING RATES:
Full Page Mono £70.00
Full Page Colour £70.00
Mechanical Data: Film: Digital
Copy instructions: Copy Date: 4 weeks prior to publication date
Average advertising content per issue: 10%
CONSUMER: RELIGIOUS

PSM3
1640546U78D-311
Formerly: PSM2
Editorial Address: 30 Monmouth Street, BATH, BA1 2BW **Tel:** 01225 442244 **Fax:** 01225 732384
Email: daniel.dawkins@futurenet.co.uk
Advertising Address: 2 Balcombe Street, LONDON, NW1 6NW **Tel:** 020 7042 4000
Email: emma.cull@futurenet.com
Web site: http://www.futurenet.co.uk
ISSN: 1471-4965

Publisher: Future Publishing Ltd
Frequency: 13 issues yearly
Cover Price: £4.99
Circulation: 26,202 (ABC 01/07/2008 to 31/12/2008)
Usual Pagination: 132
Editor: Daniel Dawkins; **Advertising Manager:** Emma Cull
Summary of Content: Magazine with news, previews and reviews of the latest PS3 games.
Readership/Target Audience: Aimed at 13 to 30 year old games enthusiasts.
ADVERTISING RATES:
Full Page Colour £3000.00
Mechanical Data: Type Area: 270 x 190mm, Bleed Size: 303 x 216mm, Trim Size: 297 x 210mm, Col Length: 270mm, Page Width: 190mm, Film: Digital
CONSUMER: CONSUMER ELECTRONICS: Games

PSYCHIC NEWS
48615U94E-80

Editorial Address: The Coach House, Stansted Hall, Burton End, STANSTED, CM24 8UD **Tel:** 01279 817050
Fax: 01279 817051
Email: pnadverts@btconnect.com
Advertising Address: As above.
Email: pnadverts@btconnect.com
Web site: http://www.psychicnews.org.uk
ISSN: 0033-2801
Publisher: Psychic Press (1995) Ltd
Date Established: 1932
Frequency: Weekly - A double issue at Christmas
Cover Price: £0.65
Annual Sub.: £55.10
Circulation: 40,000 (Publisher's Statement)
Usual Pagination: 12
Editor: Paul Brett; **Advertising Manager:** Paul Brett
Summary of Content: Magazine covering healing, life after death, mediums and all other aspects of the paranormal.
Readership/Target Audience: Aimed at those interested in spiritualism and the paranormal.
ADVERTISING RATES:
Full Page Mono £850.00
Full Page Colour £1275.00
SCC £5.59
Agency Commission: 10%
Mechanical Data: No. of Columns (Display): 5, Film: Digital
Copy instructions: Copy Date: 10 days prior to publication date
CONSUMER: OTHER CLASSIFICATIONS: Paranormal

PSYCHIC WORLD
40085U94E-352

Editorial Address: PO Box 14, GREENFORD, UB6 0UF
Tel: 020 8903 1993 **Fax:** 020 8903 1987
Email: ray.pw@virgin.net
Advertising Address: As above.
Email: ray.pw@virgin.net
ISSN: 1352-8394
Publisher: Psychic World Publishing
Date Established: 1946
Frequency: Monthly
Cover Price: £0.60
Annual Sub.: £10.00
Usual Pagination: 16
Editor: Ray Taylor; **Advertising Manager:** Ray Taylor
Summary of Content: Publication providing articles on spiritualism and the paranormal.
Readership/Target Audience: Read by spiritualists and those interested in the paranormal and psychic research.
ADVERTISING RATES:
Full Page Mono £500.00
SCC £3.00
Mechanical Data: No. of Columns (Display): 4, Page Width: 260mm, Film: Digital, Type Area: 380 x 260mm, Col Length: 380mm
Copy instructions: Copy Date: 1st of the month prior to publication date
Average advertising content per issue: 40%
CONSUMER: OTHER CLASSIFICATIONS: Paranormal

PSYCHOLOGIES
1685481U74A-991

Editorial Address: 64 North Row, LONDON, W1K 7LL
Tel: 020 7150 7000 **Fax:** 020 7150 7675
Email: sarah.neish@hf-uk.com
Advertising Address: As above.
Email: ann.oneil@hf-uk.com
Web site: http://www.psychologies.co.uk
Publisher: Hachette Filipacchi (UK) Ltd
Date Established: 2005
Frequency: Monthly
Cover Price: £3.20
Circulation: 130,101 (Print Run)
Editor: Sarah Neish; **Features Editor:** Rebecca Alexander
Summary of Content: Magazine covering a psychology and positive living for a mainstream consumer audience: How you think, feel, connect and communicate as well as beauty, travel, food, wine and home.
Readership/Target Audience: Aimed at women aged 30 and over.

ADVERTISING RATES:
Full Page Colour £6000.00
Agency Commission: 15%
Mechanical Data: Type Area: 255 x 195mm, Bleed Size: 285 x 225mm, Trim Size: 275 x 215mm, Col Length: 255mm, Page Width: 195mm, Film: Digital
Average advertising content per issue: 30%
CONSUMER: WOMEN'S INTEREST CONSUMER MAGAZINES: Women's Interest

PUBLIC POLICY RESEARCH
47253U82-119_85

Formerly: New Economy
Editorial Address: IPPR, 30-32 Southampton Street, LONDON, WC2E 7RA **Tel:** 020 7470 6100
Fax: 020 7470 6111
Advertising Address: 9600 Garsington Road, Cowley, OXFORD, OX4 2DQ **Tel:** 01865 776868 **Fax:** 01865 714951
Email: craig.pickett@wiley.com
Web site: http://www.ippr.org
ISSN: 1070-3535
Publisher: Wiley-Blackwell Publishing
Frequency: Quarterly
Annual Sub.: £32.00
Editor: Georgina Kyriacou; **Advertising Manager:** Craig Pickett
Summary of Content: Journal of the Institute for Public Policy Research. Aims to contribute to public understanding of social, economic and political issues.
Readership/Target Audience: Read by academics in politics and economics, politicians, practitioners and think tanks.
ADVERTISING RATES:
Full Page Mono £445.00
Agency Commission: 10%
Mechanical Data: Type Area: 205 x 135mm, Col Length: 205mm, Page Width: 135mm, Film: Digital
CONSUMER: CURRENT AFFAIRS & POLITICS

PULL!
45861U75F-90

Editorial Address: Ewell House, Graveney Road, Goodstone, FAVERSHAM, PE9 1RB **Tel:** 01795 535468
Fax: 01795 535469
Email: enquiries@deeson.co.uk
Advertising Address: Deeson Group, Ewell House, Graveney Road, Goodstone, FAVERSHAM, ME13 8UP **Tel:** 01795 535468 **Fax:** 01795 535469
Email: ads@pull-magazine.co.uk
Web site: http://www.deeson.co.uk
Publisher: GTC
Frequency: 10 issues yearly
Cover Price: £3.00
Free to qualifying individuals
Circulation: 27,000 (Publisher's Statement)
Usual Pagination: 82
Editor: James Buzzel; **Advertising Manager:** Robert Aspin
Summary of Content: Official journal of the Clay Pigeon Shooting Association featuring reports, product reviews, fixtures and results.
Readership/Target Audience: Read by members of the Clay Pigeon Shooting Association.
ADVERTISING RATES:
Full Page Colour £1450.00
Agency Commission: 10%
Mechanical Data: Col Length: 276mm, Bleed Size: 305 x 215mm, Trim Size: 297 x 210mm, Page Width: 184mm, Type Area: 276 x 184mm, Film: Digital
CONSUMER: SPORT: Shooting

THE PULSE EDINBURGH
1827918U80E-380

Editorial Address: 108 Holyrood Road, EDINBURGH, EH8 8AS **Tel:** 0131 620 8416 **Fax:** 0131 523 0241
Email: the.pulse@scotsman.com
Advertising Address: As above. **Fax:** 0131 523 0373
Email: srobertson@scotsman.com
Web site: http://www.scotsman.com/thepulse
Publisher: The Scotsman Publications Ltd
Date Established: 2007
Frequency: Quarterly
Cover Price: Free
Circulation: 15,000 (Publisher's Statement)
Usual Pagination: 84
Editor: Gabe Stewart
Summary of Content: Lifestyle magazine covering fashion, health and beauty, eating out, entertainment, travel and celebrity interviews.
Readership/Target Audience: Aimed at men and women in Edinburgh aged 30 to 50 years old and with a high disposable income.
ADVERTISING RATES:
Full Page Colour £1350.00
Copy instructions: Copy Date: 2 weeks prior to publication date
CONSUMER: RURAL & REGIONAL INTEREST: Regional Interest Scotland

THE PULSE SUSSEX
47430U83-63_35

Editorial Address: Falmer House, Falmer, BRIGHTON, BN1 9QF **Tel:** 01273 678152 **Fax:** 01273 873329
Email: pulse@ussu.sussex.ac.uk
Advertising Address: As above. **Tel:** 0845 130 0667
Fax: 0845 130 0668
Email: gc@bamuk.com
Web site: http://www.ussu.info/pulse/
Publisher: Sussex University Students' Union
Frequency: 3 issues yearly - Published monthly during each academic term
Cover Price: Free
Circulation: 3,000 (Publisher's Statement)
Usual Pagination: 16
Editor: Natalie Peck; **Advertising Manager:** Gavin Crewe
Summary of Content: Magazine covering political, social and cultural issues. Includes entertainment, photography, fashion, music and the arts in the Brighton area.
Readership/Target Audience: Read by university students and local residents.
ADVERTISING RATES:
Full Page Mono £450.00
Full Page Colour £595.00
Agency Commission: 10%
Mechanical Data: Film: Digital, Trim Size: 346 x 270mm, Bleed Size: 356 x 280mm, Col Length: 335mm, Page Width: 259mm, Type Area: 335 x 259mm
Copy instructions: Copy Date: 10 days prior to publication date
CONSUMER: STUDENT PUBLICATIONS

PULSE UK
1826779U90-1016

Editorial Address: 12 Devereux Court, 215 Strand, LONDON, WC2R 1AP **Tel:** 020 7353 5370
Fax: 020 7353 5375
Email: editor@pulse-uk.org.uk
Web site: http://www.pulse-uk.org.uk
Publisher: Russian Media House
Frequency: Weekly
Cover Price: Free
Circulation: 20,000 (Publisher's Statement)
Editor: Elena Osipova
Summary of Content: Newspaper covering what's on in London and the UK in general.
Language(s): Russian
Readership/Target Audience: Aimed at Russian speakers in London.
CONSUMER: ETHNIC

PURE BUXTON
1841340U80C-5448

Editorial Address: 1 Paradise Square, SHEFFIELD, S1 2DE
Tel: 0114 275 8840
Email: editor@purebuxton.co.uk
Advertising Address: As above.
Email: sales@purebuxton.co.uk
Web site: http://www.purebuxton.co.uk
Publisher: Merit Publications Ltd
Date Established: 2007
Frequency: Quarterly
Cover Price: Free
Circulation: 10,000 (Publisher's Statement)
Usual Pagination: 60
Editor: Steve Caddy; **Advertising Manager:** Steve Caddy
Summary of Content: Magazine covering local news and lifestyle including events, arts, music, property, businesses and restaurants.
Readership/Target Audience: Aimed at residents and visitors to Buxton and the High Peak area of the Peak District.
ADVERTISING RATES:
Full Page Colour £575.00
Mechanical Data: Type Area: 277 x 185mm, Col Length: 277mm, Page Width: 185mm, Bleed Size: 303 x 216mm
CONSUMER: RURAL & REGIONAL INTEREST: Regional Interest English Counties

PURE WEDDINGS
1732183U74L-245

Editorial Address: 3 Tustin Court, Port Way, Ashton-on-Ribble, PRESTON, PR2 2YQ **Tel:** 01772 722022
Fax: 01772 736496
Email: amanda.griffiths@archant.co.uk
Advertising Address: As above.
Email: jackie.allen@cheshirelife.co.uk
Web site: http://www.pureweddingsnorth.co.uk
Publisher: Archant Life (North) PLC
Date Established: 2005
Frequency: Quarterly
Cover Price: £3.00
Usual Pagination: 226
Editor: Amanda Griffiths; **Advertising Manager:** Jackie Allen
Summary of Content: Magazine covering all aspects of weddings including venues, jewellery, fashion, beauty, flowers, cakes, honeymoons, grooms' wear and real life weddings.

Readership/Target Audience: Aimed at brides and grooms in the North West of England.
ADVERTISING RATES:
Full Page Colour £1595.00
Agency Commission: 10%
Mechanical Data: Type Area: 271 x 199mm, Bleed Size: 306 x 226mm, Trim Size: 300 x 220mm, Col Length: 271mm, Page Width: 199mm, Film: Digital
CONSUMER: WOMEN'S INTEREST CONSUMER MAGAZINES: Brides

PURPLE
1644419U74G-246

Editorial Address: Third Floor, Weston House, 246 High Holborn, LONDON, WC1V 7EX **Tel:** 020 7025 2470
Email: purple@breakthrough.org.uk
Web site: http://www.breakthrough.org.uk
Publisher: Breakthrough Breast Cancer
Frequency: Quarterly
Cover Price: Free
Circulation: 30,000 (Publisher's Statement)
Usual Pagination: 44
Editor: Ned Collier
Summary of Content: Magazine covering the latest news and developments in breast cancer research as well as personal stories.
Readership/Target Audience: Aimed at supporters of the Breakthrough Breast Cancer Charity and those with or recovering from breast cancer.
ADVERTISING: No Advertising taken
CONSUMER: WOMEN'S INTEREST CONSUMER MAGAZINES: Slimming & Health

PUSH
1742994U75X-1711

Editorial Address: 17A South Street, LANCING, BN15 8AE
Tel: 0870 803 4891
Email: editor@pushhockey.co.uk
Advertising Address: PO Box 5166, HOVE, BN52 9GX
Tel: 0870 803 4891
Email: jeremy@pushhockey.co.uk
Web site: http://www.pushhockey.co.uk
ISSN: 1749-4214
Publisher: Push Hockey Ltd
Date Established: 2006
Frequency: 6 issues yearly
Cover Price: £4.20
Annual Sub.: £25.00
Circulation: 25,000 (Publisher's Statement)
Usual Pagination: 60
Editor: Tom Cooper; **Advertising Manager:** Jeremy Subedar; **Publisher:** Jeremy Subedar
Summary of Content: Magazine covering hockey in the UK including interviews with prominent sports personnel, product testing, coaching, the grass roots of the game, tours and festivals as well as lifestyle, health and fitness, beauty, horoscopes, alternative therapies and an agony aunt.
Readership/Target Audience: Aimed at players, coaches, umpires, officials and volunteers aged between 16 and 65 years old.
ADVERTISING RATES:
Full Page Colour £1100.00
Agency Commission: 10%
Mechanical Data: Bleed Size: 303 x 213mm, Trim Size: 297 x 210mm, Film: Digital
Copy instructions: Copy Date: 4 weeks prior to publication date
Average advertising content per issue: 25%
CONSUMER: SPORT: Other Sport

PUSH AND PULL
46706U79J-50

Editorial Address: Keighley & Worth Valley Railway, The Railway Station, Haworth, KEIGHLEY, BD22 8NJ
Tel: 01535 645214 **Fax:** 01535 647317
Email: admin@kwvr.co.uk
Advertising Address: As above.
Email: admin@kwvr.co.uk
Web site: http://www.kwvr.co.uk
Publisher: Keighley & Worth Valley Railway Preservation Society
Date Established: 1964
Frequency: Quarterly
Cover Price: £2.50
Circulation: 4,300 (Publisher's Statement)
Usual Pagination: 60
Editor: Jim Shipley; **Advertising Manager:** Jim Shipley
Summary of Content: Magazine of the Keighley & Worth Valley Railway Preservation Society.
Readership/Target Audience: Read by society members and steam railway enthusiasts.
ADVERTISING: Rates on application
CONSUMER: HOBBIES & DIY: Rail Enthusiasts

PUZZLE COMPENDIUM
29052U79F-62

Editorial Address: Stonecroft, 69 Station Road, REDHILL, RH1 1EY **Tel:** 01737 378700 **Fax:** 01737 781800
Email: birgitta.bingham@puzzlermedia.com

Advertising Address: As above. **Fax:** 01731 781888
Email: brian.ainge@puzzlermedia.com
Web site: http://www.puzzler.co.uk
Publisher: Puzzler Media Ltd
Frequency: 10 issues yearly
Cover Price: £2.05
Circulation: 66,387 (Publisher's Statement)
Editor: Sarah Brown
Summary of Content: Magazine containing a mix of puzzles and games.
Readership/Target Audience: Read by women 40 years and over.
ADVERTISING: Rates on application
CONSUMER: HOBBIES & DIY: Games & Puzzles

PUZZLE CORNER SPECIAL
46687U79F-64

Editorial Address: Stonecroft, 69 Station Road, REDHILL, RH1 1EY **Tel:** 01737 378700 **Fax:** 01737 781800
Email: reception@puzzlermedia.com
Advertising Address: The Insert House Ltd, 3rd Floor, 118 Commercial Street, LONDON, E1 6NF **Tel:** 020 7426 5060
Fax: 020 7092 9176
Email: parry.jones@theinserthouse.com
Web site: http://www.puzzler.co.uk
Publisher: Puzzler Media Ltd
Frequency: 10 issues yearly
Cover Price: £2.40
Circulation: 115,000 (Publisher's Statement)
Usual Pagination: 116
Editor: Deborah Hardy; **Advertising Manager:** Parry Jones
Summary of Content: Magazine containing a mix of puzzles and games.
Readership/Target Audience: Aimed predominantly at women aged 45 years old and over.
ADVERTISING: Rates on application
Agency Commission: 10%
CONSUMER: HOBBIES & DIY: Games & Puzzles

PUZZLE MONTHLY
46688U79F-65

Editorial Address: Zetland House, 5-25 Scrutton Street, LONDON, EC2A 4HJ **Tel:** 020 7613 7477
Fax: 020 7168 7956
Advertising Address: As above.
Email: justine@accoladepublishing.co.uk
Publisher: Accolade Publishing
Date Established: 1974
Frequency: 13 issues yearly
Cover Price: £1.99
Usual Pagination: 68
Editor: Justine Wall; **Advertising Manager:** Justine Wall; **Group Editor:** Sarah Grummett; **Publisher:** Justine Wall
Summary of Content: Magazine includes competition based puzzles and teasers, mainly crosswords, with cash, books and pens as prizes.
Readership/Target Audience: Aimed at puzzle enthusiasts.
ADVERTISING: Rates on application
Agency Commission: 10%
Copy instructions: Copy Date: 4 weeks prior to publication date
CONSUMER: HOBBIES & DIY: Games & Puzzles

PUZZLE MONTHLY COLLECTION
46689U79F-65_50

Editorial Address: Zetland House, 5-25 Scrutton Street, LONDON, EC2A 4HJ **Tel:** 020 7613 7477
Fax: 020 7168 7956
Advertising Address: As above.
Email: justine@accoladepublishing.co.uk
Web site: http://www.totalpuzzles.co.uk
Publisher: Accolade Publishing
Frequency: Monthly
Cover Price: £2.20
Usual Pagination: 100
Editor: Justine Wall; **Advertising Manager:** Justine Wall; **Group Editor:** Sarah Grummett; **Publisher:** Justine Wall
Summary of Content: Magazine featuring puzzles.
Readership/Target Audience: Aimed mainly at women over the age of 35.
ADVERTISING: Rates on application
CONSUMER: HOBBIES & DIY: Games & Puzzles

Q MAGAZINE
46252U76E-290

Formerly: Q
Editorial Address: Mappin House, 4 Winsley Street, LONDON, W1W 8HF **Tel:** 020 7436 1515
Fax: 020 7182 5457
Email: qmag@qthemusic.com
Advertising Address: Endeavour House, 189 Shaftesbury Avenue, LONDON, WC2H 8JG **Tel:** 020 7437 9011
Fax: 020 7295 5400
Email: marco.soares@baueradvertising.co.uk
Web site: http://www.q4music.com
ISSN: 0955-4955
Publisher: Bauer Consumer Media Ltd (Mappin House)

Frequency: Monthly
Cover Price: £3.90
Annual Sub.: £34.80
Circulation: 100,172 (ABC 01/01/2009 to 30/06/2009)
Editor: Nasarene Asghar; **Editor-in-Chief:** Paul Rees; **Managing Editor:** Simon McEwen
Summary of Content: Magazine of modern music featuring reviews, interviews and news about music and pop stars.
Readership/Target Audience: Aimed at those between 18 and 35 years old.
ADVERTISING RATES:
Full Page Colour £9340.00
Mechanical Data: Page Width: 190mm, Film: Digital, Type Area: 265 x 190mm, Bleed Size: 291 x 216mm, Trim Size: 285 x 210mm, Col Length: 265mm
Copy instructions: Copy Date: 4 weeks prior to publication date
CONSUMER: MUSIC & PERFORMING ARTS: Pop Music

QEFI QUIET & ELECTRIC FLIGHT INTERNATIONAL
46593U79B-120

Editorial Address: Traplet House, Pendragon Close, MALVERN, WR14 1GA **Tel:** 01684 588500
Fax: 01684 578588
Email: qefi@traplet.com
Advertising Address: As above. **Fax:** 01684 578558
Email: advertising@traplet.com
Web site: http://www.traplet.com
ISSN: 1355-2228
Publisher: Traplet Publications Ltd
Date Established: 1994
Frequency: Monthly - Published the last Friday of every month
Cover Price: £3.25
Annual Sub.: £39.00
Usual Pagination: 100
Editor: Mike Nott; **Managing Director:** Tony Stephenson
Summary of Content: Magazine focusing on modelling aircraft, particularly electrically controlled model aircraft.
Readership/Target Audience: Aimed at makers of model aircraft.
ADVERTISING RATES:
Full Page Mono £505.00
Full Page Colour £760.00
SCC £4.86
Agency Commission: 10%
Mechanical Data: Page Width: 184mm, Type Area: 260 x 184mm, Bleed Size: 303 x 216mm, Trim Size: 297 x 210mm, Film: Digital, Col Length: 260mm
Copy instructions: Copy Date: 6 weeks prior to publication date
CONSUMER: HOBBIES & DIY: Models & Modelling

QP
1616194U79K-998

Editorial Address: 3rd Floor, Commonwealth House, 1 New Oxford Street, LONDON, WC1A 1NU **Tel:** 020 7759 2904
Fax: 020 7759 2951
Email: david.stone@qpmagazine.com
Advertising Address: As above. **Tel:** 020 7759 2999
Fax: 020 7759 2901
Email: james@qpmagazine.com
Web site: http://www.qpmagazine.com
ISSN: 1479-4837
Publisher: AS&K Skylight
Date Established: 2003
Frequency: 6 issues yearly
Cover Price: £6.50
Annual Sub.: £39.00
Circulation: 15,000 (Publisher's Statement)
Usual Pagination: 96
Editor: David Stone; **Advertising Manager:** James Gurney
Summary of Content: Magazine looking at active watch brands, covers collecting, technical aspects and background reports, provides analysis and opinion from auction house experts and profiles famous collectors and industry personalities.
Readership/Target Audience: Aimed at the interested as well as the specialist knowledgeable collectors, industry insiders and those new to the world of fine horology.
ADVERTISING RATES:
Full Page Colour £3250.00
Agency Commission: 15%
Mechanical Data: Bleed Size: 291 x 221mm, Trim Size: 285 x 220mm, Col Length: 255mm, Page Width: 200mm, Print Process: Offset litho, Type Area: 255 x 200mm
Copy instructions: Copy Date: 4 weeks prior to publication date
Average advertising content per issue: 15%
CONSUMER: HOBBIES & DIY: Collectors Magazines

QUAD
1668129U77B-711

Editorial Address: 6 Kendal Court, Railway Road, NEWHAVEN, BN9 0AY **Tel:** 01273 616040
Fax: 01273 514417
Email: andy@quad.tv
Advertising Address: As above.
Email: ads@quad.tv

Web site: http://www.quad.tv
Publisher: ME Publishing
Date Established: 2004
Frequency: Monthly
Cover Price: £3.00
Annual Sub.: £30.00
Circulation: 17,000 (Print Run)
Usual Pagination: 100

Editor: Andrew Foulkes; **Advertising Manager:** Alison Payne; **Publisher:** Andrew Foulkes
Summary of Content: Magazine dedicated to the 4 wheel market covering sport, leisure, safety and training advice, safety and work, machine tests, event reports, features, new products and a buyers' guide section.
Readership/Target Audience: Aimed at enthusiasts of quad bikes.
ADVERTISING RATES:
Full Page Colour £700.00
Agency Commission: 10%
Mechanical Data: Bleed Size: 303 x 216mm, Trim Size: 297 x 210mm, Film: Digital
Average advertising content per issue: 40%
CONSUMER: MOTORING & CYCLING: Motorcycling

THE QUARTERLY
1660039U74Q-1242

Editorial Address: Ground Floor, 1-2 Ravey Street, LONDON, EC2A 4QP **Tel:** 020 3222 0101
Fax: 020 7739 1369
Email: info@showmedia.net
Advertising Address: 30 Cleveland Street, LONDON, W1T 4JD **Tel:** 020 7907 6000 **Fax:** 020 7907 6001
Email: dan_reeves@dennis.co.uk
Web site: http://www.showmedia.net
Publisher: Show Media Ltd
Frequency: Quarterly
Cover Price: £3.50
Free to qualifying individuals
Circulation: 100,000 (Publisher's Statement)
Editor: Joanne Glasbey
Summary of Content: Lifestyle magazine covering fashion, motoring, gadgets, features and travel.
Readership/Target Audience: Aimed mainly at readers of The Week.
ADVERTISING RATES:
Full Page Colour £8777.00
Agency Commission: 10%
Mechanical Data: Type Area: 275 x 185mm, Col Length: 275mm, Page Width: 185mm, Bleed Size: 303 x 216mm, Trim Size: 297 x 210mm, Film: Digital
Copy instructions: Copy Date: 3 weeks prior to publication date
Average advertising content per issue: 34%
Supplement to: The Week
CONSUMER: WOMEN'S INTEREST CONSUMER MAGAZINES: Lifestyle

QUEST
48707U94X-144_50

Editorial Address: 1 Church Lane, Whittlesford, CAMBRIDGE, CB22 4NX **Tel:** 01223 499880
Fax: 01223 499889
Email: bruce.hodge@questonline.co.uk
Advertising Address: As above.
Email: info@questonline.co.uk
Web site: http://www.questonline.co.uk
Publisher: Bulldog Publishing
Date Established: 1999
Frequency: Monthly
Cover Price: Free
Circulation: 25,000 (Publisher's Statement)
Usual Pagination: 88
Editor: Donald Campbell; **Advertising Manager:** Bruce Hodge
Summary of Content: Magazine providing assistance and help, including education, resettlement and recruitment information.
Readership/Target Audience: Aimed at members of the armed forces and their families.
ADVERTISING RATES:
Full Page Mono £3650.00
Full Page Colour £3650.00
Agency Commission: 10%
Mechanical Data: Trim Size: 297 x 210mm, Type Area: 265 x 185mm, Col Length: 265mm, Page Width: 185mm
Copy instructions: Copy Date: 2 weeks prior to publication date
Average advertising content per issue: 70%
CONSUMER: OTHER CLASSIFICATIONS: Miscellaneous

QUICK & EASY GUIDE
1849710U78R-526

Editorial Address: 30 Monmouth Street, BATH, BA1 2BW
Tel: 01225 442244
Advertising Address: As above.
Publisher: Future Publishing Ltd
Date Established: 2008
Frequency: 6 issues yearly
Cover Price: £5.99

Usual Pagination: 292
Editor: Charlotte Morgan; **Publisher:** Charlotte Morgan
Summary of Content: Magazine with tips, tricks and hints for getting the most from Windows Vista operating system.
Readership/Target Audience: Aimed at users of Windows Vista.
CONSUMER: CONSUMER ELECTRONICS: Consumer Electronics Related

QUICK CARDS MADE EASY
1657869U74E-686

Editorial Address: 14th Floor, Tower House, Fairfax Street, BRISTOL, BS1 3BN **Tel:** 0117 927 9009 **Fax:** 0117 934 9008
Email: sarahbostock@originpublishing.co.uk
Advertising Address: 9th Floor, Tower House, Fairfax Street, BRISTOL, BS1 3BN **Tel:** 0117 927 9009
Fax: 0117 934 9008
Email: davidmanson@originpublishing.co.uk
Web site: http://www.cardmakingandpapercraft.com
Publisher: Origin Publishing Ltd
Date Established: 2004
Frequency: 13 issues yearly
Cover Price: £3.65
Circulation: 20,304 (ABC 01/01/2008 to 31/12/2008)
Usual Pagination: 92
Editor: Sarah Bostock; **Advertising Manager:** David Manson
Summary of Content: Magazine covering cards that are quick and easy to make with easy paper craft card designs, great ideas, tips and tricks.
Readership/Target Audience: Aimed at card makers of all levels but particularly those who are short of time.
ADVERTISING RATES:
Full Page Colour £1050.00
Agency Commission: 10%
Mechanical Data: Type Area: 281 x 195mm, Bleed Size: 303 x 216mm, Trim Size: 297 x 210mm, Col Length: 281mm, Page Width: 195mm
Copy instructions: Copy Date: 6 weeks prior to publication date
Average advertising content per issue: 20%
CONSUMER: WOMEN'S INTEREST CONSUMER MAGAZINES: Crafts

QUIZKIDS
46669U79F-66

Editorial Address: Stonecroft, 69 Station Road, REDHILL, RH1 1EY **Tel:** 01737 378700 **Fax:** 01737 781800
Email: reception@puzzlermedia.com
Web site: http://www.puzzler.com
Publisher: Puzzler Media Ltd
Frequency: 6 issues yearly
Cover Price: £2.40
Usual Pagination: 84
Editor: Jackie Guthrie
Summary of Content: Educational puzzle and features magazine. Includes games, puzzles and competitions.
Readership/Target Audience: Aimed at 7 to 11 year olds.
ADVERTISING: No Advertising taken
CONSUMER: HOBBIES & DIY: Games & Puzzles

QX MAGAZINE
47631U86B-105

Editorial Address: 2nd Floor, 23 Denmark Street, LONDON, WC2H 8NH **Tel:** 020 7379 7887 **Fax:** 020 7379 7525
Email: editorial@qxmagazine.com
Advertising Address: As above.
Email: stephen@qxmagazine.com
Web site: http://www.qxmagazine.com
ISSN: 1356-6903
Publisher: Firststar Ltd
Date Established: 1994
Frequency: Weekly
Cover Price: Free
Circulation: 25,000 (Publisher's Statement)
Usual Pagination: 88
Editor: Cliff Joannou; **Advertising Manager:** Stephen Vowles
Summary of Content: Magazine covering the gay lifestyle scene. Includes articles on music, travel, politics, arts and club reviews.
Readership/Target Audience: Aimed at socially active gay men aged between 18 and 65 years old.
ADVERTISING RATES:
Full Page Colour £550.00
Agency Commission: 10%
Mechanical Data: Film: Digital, Type Area: 252 x 196mm, Trim Size: 275 x 210mm, Bleed Size: 281 x 216mm, Col Length: 252mm, Page Width: 196mm
Copy instructions: Copy Date: Thursday 5.00pm prior to publication date
Average advertising content per issue: 65%
CONSUMER: ADULT & GAY MAGAZINES: Gay & Lesbian Magazines

RA MAGAZINE
47509U84A-330

Editorial Address: Royal Academy of Arts, Burlington House, Piccadilly, LONDON, W1J 0BD **Tel:** 020 7300 5820
Fax: 020 7300 8032
Email: ramagazine@royalacademy.org.uk
Advertising Address: As above. **Tel:** 020 7300 8000
Email: jane.grylls@royalacademy.org.uk
Web site: http://www.ramagazine.org.uk
Publisher: RA Publications
Date Established: 1983
Frequency: Quarterly
Cover Price: £4.95
Free to qualifying individuals
Annual Sub.: £20.00
Circulation: 100,000 (Publisher's Statement)
Usual Pagination: 100
Editor: Nigel Billen; **Advertising Manager:** Jane Grylls; **Publisher:** Nick Tite
Summary of Content: Magazine of the Royal Academy of Arts. Includes articles on the exhibitions of the Royal Academy, Royal Academicians, schools, as well as more general arts features.
Readership/Target Audience: Read by friends and sponsors of the Royal Academy.
ADVERTISING RATES:
Full Page Mono £2900.00
Full Page Colour £3800.00
Agency Commission: 10%
Mechanical Data: Type Area: 260 x 202mm, Bleed Size: 306 x 235mm, Trim Size: 300 x 229mm, Col Length: 260mm, Page Width: 202mm, Film: Digital, No. of Columns (Display): 2
Copy instructions: Copy Date: 6 weeks prior to publication date
Average advertising content per issue: 50%
CONSUMER: THE ARTS & LITERARY: Arts

THE RABBIT
752810U83-63_50

Editorial Address: Wivenhoe Park, COLCHESTER, CO4 3SQ **Tel:** 01206 863211 **Fax:** 01206 870915
Email: rabbit@essex.ac.uk
Advertising Address: As above.
Email: rabbit@essex.ac.uk
Web site: http://www.essexstudent.com
Publisher: University of Essex Students Union
Date Established: 2001
Frequency: Monthly - Published fortnightly during term time
Cover Price: Free
Circulation: 5,000 (Publisher's Statement)
Usual Pagination: 24
Editor: Alex Reily
Summary of Content: Newspaper covering news, comment, community, music, film, arts, creative writing, lifestyle, games, technology, travel, societies, sport and listings.
Readership/Target Audience: Aimed at students and staff of the University of Essex and the Colchester Institute.
ADVERTISING: Rates on application
CONSUMER: STUDENT PUBLICATIONS

RABBITING ON
712153U81X-350

Editorial Address: 17 Inverewe Place, DUNFERMLINE, KY11 8FH **Tel:** 01383 626216 **Fax:** 01383 626216
Email: rabbitingon@fsmail.net
Advertising Address: Hollybush Park, Culm Head, TAUNTON, TA3 7EA **Tel:** 01823 421515
Email: rae@hollybushpark.wanadoo.co.uk
ISSN: 1472-8095
Publisher: Rabbit Welfare Association
Date Established: 1997
Frequency: Quarterly
Cover Price: £4.00
Annual Sub.: £17.50
Circulation: 4,500 (Publisher's Statement)
Usual Pagination: 48
Editor: Carina Norris; **Advertising Manager:** Rachael Todd
Summary of Content: Magazine about pet rabbits, including features on care, behaviour and health advice.
Readership/Target Audience: Read by pet rabbit owners, veterinary professionals and members of the Rabbit Welfare Association.
ADVERTISING: Rates on application
Agency Commission: 10%
Average advertising content per issue: 20%
CONSUMER: ANIMALS & PETS

RACE & CLASS
30538U82-158

Editorial Address: 2-6 Leeke Street, LONDON, WC1X 9HS
Tel: 020 7837 0041 **Fax:** 020 7278 0623
Email: info@irr.org.uk
Advertising Address: Institute of Race Relations, 1 Oliver's Yard, 55 City Road, LONDON, EC1Y 1SP
Tel: 020 7324 8500 **Fax:** 020 7324 8600
Email: advertising@sagepub.co.uk
Web site: http://www.irr.org.uk
ISSN: 0306-3968

Publisher: Institute of Race Relations
Frequency: Quarterly
Cover Price: £7.00
Annual Sub.: £26.00
Circulation: 5,000 (Publisher's Statement)
Usual Pagination: 120
Editor: Arun Kundnani
Summary of Content: Publication containing race and third world issues.
Readership/Target Audience: Read by those concerned with current affairs including students and academics.
ADVERTISING RATES:
Full Page Mono £400.00
Agency Commission: 5%
Mechanical Data: Type Area: 215 x 145mm, Col Length: 215mm, Page Width: 145mm, Film: Digital
Copy instructions: Copy Date: 12 weeks prior to publication date
Average advertising content per issue: 5%
CONSUMER: CURRENT AFFAIRS & POLITICS

RACE TECH   46430U77D-395

Editorial Address: 841 High Road, Finchley, LONDON, N12 8PT **Tel:** 020 8446 2100 **Fax:** 020 8446 2191
Email: info@racetechmag.com
Advertising Address: As above.
Email: info@racetechmag.com
Web site: http://www.racetechmag.com
ISSN: 1356-2975
Publisher: Racecar Graphic Ltd
Date Established: 1995
Frequency: Monthly
Cover Price: £4.50
Circulation: 25,000 (Publisher's Statement)
Usual Pagination: 92
Editor: William Kimberley; **Publisher:** Soheila Kimberley
Summary of Content: Magazine covering the techniques and technology of amateur and professional motorsport. Contains in-depth coverage of car design and development, driving skills and new products for racers.
Language(s): English; Japanese
Readership/Target Audience: Aimed at engineers, designers, drivers, teams, team managers, suppliers, race circuit owners and the informed enthusiast.
ADVERTISING RATES:
Full Page Mono £1200.00
Full Page Colour £1800.00
Agency Commission: 10%
Mechanical Data: Col Length: 277mm, Page Width: 190mm, Type Area: 277 x 190mm, Trim Size: 297 x 210mm, Bleed Size: 303 x 216mm, Film: Digital
Copy instructions: Copy Date: 2 weeks prior to publication date
CONSUMER: MOTORING & CYCLING: Motor Sports

RACEFORM UPDATE   45842U75E-220

Editorial Address: 1 Canada Square, LONDON, E14 5AP **Tel:** 020 7293 2474 **Fax:** 020 7293 3193
Email: update@raceform.co.uk
Advertising Address: As above. **Tel:** 020 7293 3271
Fax: 020 7293 3320
Email: damian.mears@racingpost.co.uk
Web site: http://www.raceform.co.uk
Publisher: Raceform Ltd
Frequency: Weekly - Two specials in March and June
Cover Price: £2.30
Circulation: 12,500 (Publisher's Statement)
Usual Pagination: 88
Editor: Bernie Ford; **Advertising Manager:** Damian Mears
Summary of Content: Tabloid racing newspaper with details of weekend racing, last week's results and other statistics.
Readership/Target Audience: Aimed at racing, football and sports betting enthusiasts.
ADVERTISING RATES:
Full Page Mono £1224.00
Full Page Colour £1530.00
Agency Commission: 10%
Mechanical Data: Type Area: 340 x 262mm, Col Length: 340mm, Film: Digital, Page Width: 262mm
Copy instructions: Copy Date: Monday prior to publication date
CONSUMER: SPORT: Horse Racing

RACER READY   1659844U75G-652

Editorial Address: 27 The Brambles, CROWTHORNE, RG45 6EF **Tel:** 07509 005670
Email: editorial@racer-ready.co.uk
Advertising Address: As above.
Email: neil@racer-ready.co.uk
Web site: http://www.racer-ready.co.uk
Publisher: Alternative Sports Media
Date Established: 2001
Frequency: Quarterly
Cover Price: £3.00
Annual Sub.: £20.00

Circulation: 1,000 (Publisher's Statement)
Usual Pagination: 36
Editor: Neil McQuoid; **Advertising Manager:** Neil McQuoid
Summary of Content: Magazine covering winter sports including ski racing, snowboarding, freestyle, jumping and ski bike racing.
Readership/Target Audience: Aimed at competitive winter sports enthusiasts.
ADVERTISING RATES:
Full Page Mono £350.00
Full Page Colour £450.00
Mechanical Data: Film: Digital, Type Area: 271 x 189mm, Bleed Size: 305 x 218mm, Trim Size: 297 x 210mm, Col Length: 271mm, Page Width: 189mm
Copy instructions: Copy Date: 2 weeks prior to publication date
Average advertising content per issue: 30%
CONSUMER: SPORT: Winter Sports

RACING AHEAD MAGAZINE   1827696U75E-277

Editorial Address: Office 113, Imperial Court, Exchange Street East, LIVERPOOL, L3 2AB **Tel:** 0845 638 0704
Email: editorial@racingahead.net
Advertising Address: e4 Media Management Ltd, South Fens Business Centre, Fenton Way, CHATTERIS, PE16 6TT **Tel:** 0845 226 0477
Email: graham@racingahead.net
Web site: http://www.racingahead.net
Publisher: Racing Ahead Ltd
Frequency: 11 issues yearly
Cover Price: £2.70
Circulation: 15,000 (Publisher's Statement)
Usual Pagination: 64
Editor: Stephen Mullen; **Advertising Manager:** Gareth MacFarlane; **Publisher:** Anne Grondah
Summary of Content: Magazine containing interviews with trainers, horses to follow, statistics and betting tips.
Readership/Target Audience: Aimed at people who bet on horse racing.
ADVERTISING RATES:
Full Page Colour £1000.00
Mechanical Data: Trim Size: 297 x 210mm, Film: Digital
CONSUMER: SPORT: Horse Racing

RACING AHEAD WEEKEND   1827697U75E-278

Editorial Address: The Old Brewery, Priory Lane, BURFORD, OX18 4SG **Tel:** 01993 822811
Email: editorial@racingahead.net
Advertising Address: e4 Media Management Ltd, South Fens Business Centre, Fenton Way, CHATTERIS, PE16 6TT **Tel:** 0845 226 0477
Email: graham@racingahead.net
Web site: http://www.racingahead.net
Publisher: Racing Ahead Weekend Ltd
Date Established: 2007
Frequency: Weekly
Cover Price: £1.00
Circulation: 30,000 (Publisher's Statement)
Editor: Stephen Mullen; **Advertising Manager:** Gareth MacFarlane; **Publisher:** Anne Grondah
Summary of Content: Newspaper which features colour race cards, form guides and tips for Saturday and Sunday racing as well as coverage of major sporting events including greyhound racing.
Readership/Target Audience: Aimed at betting fans.
ADVERTISING RATES:
Full Page Colour £1000.00
Mechanical Data: Type Area: 345 x 269mm, Col Length: 345mm, Page Width: 269mm, Film: Digital
CONSUMER: SPORT: Horse Racing

RACING & FOOTBALL OUTLOOK

                               45843U75E-250
Editorial Address: 1 Canada Square, Canary Wharf, LONDON, E14 5AP **Tel:** 020 7293 3586 **Fax:** 020 7510 6457
Email: rfo@rfoutlook.co.uk
Advertising Address: As above. **Tel:** 020 7293 2852
Fax: 020 7293 3320
Email: damian.mears@racingpost.co.uk
Publisher: Raceform Ltd
Date Established: 1909
Frequency: Weekly
Cover Price: £1.60
Circulation: 30,000 (Publisher's Statement)
Usual Pagination: 44
Editor: Sean Gollogly; **Managing Director:** Alan Burn; **Advertising Manager:** Damian Mears
Summary of Content: Journal containing horse racing and football pools coverage, plus greyhounds and other betting sports including golf.
Readership/Target Audience: Aimed at those interested in betting on sports.
ADVERTISING RATES:
Full Page Mono £1836.00
Full Page Colour £2295.00
SCC £12.00

Agency Commission: 15%
Mechanical Data: Col Length: 340mm, No. of Columns (Display): 6, Type Area: 340 x 262mm, Page Width: 262mm, Col Widths (Display): 40mm, Film: Digital, Print Process: Web-fed offset litho
Copy instructions: Copy Date: Friday prior to publication date
Average advertising content per issue: 8%
CONSUMER: SPORT: Horse Racing

RACING CALENDAR   622702U77C-460

Formerly: British Cycling
Editorial Address: National Cycling Centre, Stuart Street, MANCHESTER, M11 4DQ **Tel:** 0161 274 2035
Email: pressoffice@britishcycling.org.uk
Advertising Address: Blueleaf, The Old Barn, Whitchurch Road, Spurstow, TARPORLEY, CW6 9TD **Tel:** 01829 260600
Fax: 0870 441 6528
Email: sarah@blue-leaf.co.uk
Web site: http://www.britishcycling.org.uk
ISSN: 1466-4887
Publisher: British Cycling
Date Established: 1999
Frequency: Quarterly
Cover Price: £2.50
Free to qualifying individuals
Circulation: 15,729 (Publisher's Statement)
Usual Pagination: 44
Editor: Philip Ingham; **Advertising Manager:** Sarah Evans
Summary of Content: Magazine covering federation news, equipment testing and competitions.
Readership/Target Audience: Aimed at members of the British Cycling Federation and racing cyclists.
ADVERTISING: Rates on application
CONSUMER: MOTORING & CYCLING: Cycling

RACING INTERNATIONAL   45844U75E-255

Editorial Address: 54 Alderley Road, WILMSLOW, SK9 1NY **Tel:** 01625 535081 **Fax:** 01625 537487
Email: mikeg@sportingpublications.com
Advertising Address: As above.
Email: mikeg@sportingpublications.com
Publisher: Worldwide Sporting Publications
Frequency: Annual - Published in December
Cover Price: £5.00
Circulation: 47,000 (Publisher's Statement)
Editor: Mike Gallemore; **Advertising Manager:** Mike Gallemore
Summary of Content: Racing magazine covering news, features and information about the international racing industry.
Readership/Target Audience: Aimed at owners, trainers and those working in the international racing industry.
ADVERTISING RATES:
Full Page Colour £7750.00
Mechanical Data: Trim Size: 297 x 210mm, Film: Digital
CONSUMER: SPORT: Horse Racing

RACING POST   45845U75E-260

Editorial Address: 1 Canada Square, Canary Wharf, LONDON, E14 5AP **Tel:** 020 7293 3000 **Fax:** 020 7293 3758
Email: editor@racingpost.co.uk
Advertising Address: As above. **Fax:** 020 7293 3320
Email: robert.brown@racingpost.co.uk
Web site: http://www.racingpost.co.uk
Publisher: Trinity Mirror
Date Established: 1986
Frequency: Daily
Cover Price: £1.50
Circulation: 60,363 (ABC 03/08/2009 to 30/08/2009)
Usual Pagination: 80
Editor: Chris Smith; **Features Editor:** Mark Blackman; **Managing Director:** Alan Byrne; **Advertising Manager:** Robert Brown
Summary of Content: Newspaper containing horse and greyhound racing news and betting information.
Readership/Target Audience: Read by those within the betting industry and racing enthusiasts.
ADVERTISING RATES:
Full Page Mono £6120.00
Full Page Colour £10200.00
SCC £30.00
Agency Commission: 15%
Mechanical Data: Type Area: 340 x 262mm, Col Length: 340mm, Film: Digital, Page Width: 262mm
Copy instructions: Copy Date: 1 day prior to publication date
Average advertising content per issue: 9%
Supplement(s): RPSport - 52xY
CONSUMER: SPORT: Horse Racing

RACING POST WEEKENDER   45846U75E-270

Editorial Address: 1 Canada Square, Canary Wharf, LONDON, E14 5AP **Tel:** 020 7293 2740 **Fax:** 020 7293 3758
Email: fleur.cushman@racingpost.com

Advertising Address: As above. **Tel:** 020 7293 2001
Fax: 020 7293 3320
Email: damian.mears@racingpost.co.uk
Publisher: Trinity Mirror
Frequency: Weekly
Cover Price: £2.30
Circulation: 19,181 (Publisher's Statement)
Usual Pagination: 88
Editor: Fleur Cushman
Summary of Content: Newspaper covering weekend racing in Britain and Ireland focusing on statistics and results. Includes features from racing journalists, news from the training centres and comprehensive previews, reviews and results section for point to point in the UK and Ireland.
Readership/Target Audience: Aimed at those in the betting industry and racing enthusiasts.
ADVERTISING RATES:
Full Page Colour £1900.00
Mechanical Data: Col Length: 340mm, Page Width: 262mm, No. of Columns (Display): 6, Col Widths (Display): 40mm, Type Area: 340 x 262mm, Film: Digital
Copy instructions: Copy Date: 1 day prior to publication date
CONSUMER: SPORT: Horse Racing

RADAR NEW BULLETIN   48650U94F-800
Formerly: RADAR Bulletin
Editorial Address: 12 City Forum, 250 City Road, LONDON, EC1V 8AF **Tel:** 020 7250 3222 **Fax:** 020 7250 0212
Email: radar@radar.org.uk
Advertising Address: As above.
Email: agnes.fletcher@radar.org.uk
Web site: http://www.radar.org.uk
ISSN: 0954-237X
Publisher: Royal Association for Disability & Rehabilitation
Frequency: 6 issues yearly
Free to qualifying individuals
Annual Sub.: £24.00
Circulation: 2,000 (Publisher's Statement)
Usual Pagination: 28
Editor: John Stanford
Summary of Content: Publication reporting on issues affecting disabled people.
Readership/Target Audience: Aimed at those involved in disability organisations, disabled people, professionals associated with disability, policy-makers and opinion formers.
ADVERTISING: Rates on application
Copy instructions: Copy Date: 2 months prior to publication date
CONSUMER: OTHER CLASSIFICATIONS: Disability

RADICAL ECONOMICS   47259U82-135
Editorial Address: 3 Jonathan Street, LONDON, SE11 5NH
Tel: 020 7820 6300 **Fax:** 020 7820 6301
Email: info@neweconomics.org
Advertising Address: As above.
Email: corrina.cordon@neweconomics.org
Web site: http://www.neweconomics.org
ISSN: 1466-2264
Publisher: nef (New Economics Foundation)
Date Established: 1986
Frequency: Quarterly
Free to qualifying individuals
Annual Sub.: £25.00
Circulation: 2,000 (Publisher's Statement)
Usual Pagination: 8
Editor: David Boyle
Summary of Content: Newspaper of the New Economics Foundation. Covers local, national and international alternative economic news, views and events.
Readership/Target Audience: Aimed at politicians, community groups, activists and individuals with an interest in alternative economics.
ADVERTISING: Rates on application
Agency Commission: 10%
CONSUMER: CURRENT AFFAIRS & POLITICS

RADIO BYGONES   639453U79D-146
Editorial Address: Sequoia House, 398A Ringwood Road, FERNDOWN, BH22 9AU **Tel:** 01202 873872
Fax: 01202 874562
Email: editorial@wimborne.co.uk
Advertising Address: As above.
Email: stewart.kearn@wimborne.co.uk
Web site: http://www.radiobygones.co.uk
ISSN: 0956-974X
Publisher: Wimborne Publishing Limited
Date Established: 1989
Frequency: 6 issues yearly
Cover Price: £3.70
Annual Sub.: £21.00
Circulation: 2,000 (Publisher's Statement)
Usual Pagination: 36
Editor: Mike Kenward; **Advertising Manager:** Stewart Kearn; **Publisher:** Mike Kenward

Summary of Content: Magazine looking at the technology of radio from the start of the century. Includes articles on radio restoration and repairs, histories, circuit diagrams, nostalgic memories and adverts by specialists.
Readership/Target Audience: Read by vintage radio enthusiasts.
ADVERTISING RATES:
Full Page Mono £115.00
Agency Commission: 10%
Mechanical Data: Trim Size: 297 x 210mm, Type Area: 262 x 180mm, Col Length: 262mm, Film: Digital, Page Width: 180mm
Copy instructions: Copy Date: 4 weeks prior to publication date
Average advertising content per issue: 30%
CONSUMER: HOBBIES & DIY: Radio Electronics

RADIO CONTROL CAR RACER   713788U79B-145
Editorial Address: Doolittle Mill, Doolittle Lane, Totternhoe, DUNSTABLE, LU6 1QX **Tel:** 01525 222573
Fax: 01525 222574
Email: racermag@aol.com
Advertising Address: ADH Publishing Ltd, Doolittle Mill, Doolittle Lane, Totternhoe, BEDFORDSHIRE, LU6 1QX
Tel: 01525 222573 **Fax:** 01525 222574
Email: adcopy@adhpublishing.com
Web site: http://www.rcracer.com
ISSN: 1366-6916
Publisher: ADH Publishing
Date Established: 1997
Frequency: Monthly
Cover Price: £3.75
Annual Sub.: £33.00
Circulation: 24,000 (Publisher's Statement)
Usual Pagination: 140
Editor: Matt Benfield; **Publisher:** Alan Harman
Summary of Content: Magazine containing features on the latest radio control car models, race reports, interviews and road tests.
Readership/Target Audience: Read by radio control car model enthusiasts.
ADVERTISING RATES:
Full Page Mono £725.00
Full Page Colour £725.00
Agency Commission: 10%
Mechanical Data: Type Area: 287 x 193mm, Bleed Size: 303 x 216mm, Trim Size: 297 x 210mm, Col Length: 287mm, Film: Digital, Page Width: 193mm
Copy instructions: Copy Date: 6 weeks prior to publication date
Average advertising content per issue: 45%
CONSUMER: HOBBIES & DIY: Models & Modelling

RADIO CONTROL JET INTERNATIONAL
46614U79B-150
Editorial Address: Traplet House, Pendragon Close, MALVERN, WR14 1GA **Tel:** 01684 588500
Fax: 01684 578554
Email: rcji@traplet.com
Advertising Address: As above. **Fax:** 01684 576348
Email: advertising@traplet.com
Web site: http://www.traplet.com
ISSN: 0968-3291
Publisher: Traplet Publications Ltd
Date Established: 1993
Frequency: 6 issues yearly - Published the last Thursday of every other month
Cover Price: £3.50
Annual Sub.: £21.00
Usual Pagination: 76
Editor: John Wright; **Managing Director:** Tony Stephenson
Summary of Content: Magazine dedicated to radio control model jet aircraft.
Readership/Target Audience: Aimed at radio control jet aircraft enthusiasts.
ADVERTISING RATES:
Full Page Mono £505.00
Full Page Colour £760.00
SCC £12.00
Agency Commission: 10%
CONSUMER: HOBBIES & DIY: Models & Modelling

RADIO CONTROL MODEL FLYER
713433U79B-82
Formerly: Model Flyer
Editorial Address: Doolittle Mill, Doolittle Lane, Totternhoe, DUNSTABLE, LU6 1QX **Tel:** 01525 222573
Fax: 01525 222574
Email: modflymag@aol.com
Advertising Address: As above. **Tel:** 01622 670434
Fax: 01622 670434
Email: john@modelglasses.com
Web site: http://www.modelflymagazine.com
ISSN: 1467-7741
Publisher: ADH Publishing
Date Established: 1999

Frequency: Monthly
Cover Price: £3.25
Annual Sub.: £33.00
Circulation: 28,000 (Publisher's Statement)
Usual Pagination: 100
Editor: Ken Sheppard; **Publisher:** Alan Harman
Summary of Content: Magazine covering all disciplines of aero-modelling including free flight, control line and radio control.
Readership/Target Audience: Read predominantly by men aged 20 years old and above.
ADVERTISING RATES:
Full Page Colour £400.00
Agency Commission: 10%
Mechanical Data: Type Area: 270 x 190mm, Bleed Size: 303 x 216mm, Col Length: 270mm, Page Width: 190mm, Trim Size: 297 x 210mm, Film: Digital
Copy instructions: Copy Date: 6 weeks prior to publication date
Average advertising content per issue: 30%
CONSUMER: HOBBIES & DIY: Models & Modelling

RADIO CONTROL MODEL WORLD
46615U79B-160
Editorial Address: Traplet House, Pendragon Close, MALVERN, WR14 1GA **Tel:** 01684 588500
Fax: 01684 578588
Email: rcmw@traplet.com
Advertising Address: As above. **Fax:** 01684 588600
Email: advertising@traplet.com
Web site: http://www.traplet.com
Publisher: Traplet Publications Ltd
Date Established: 1984
Frequency: Monthly
Cover Price: £3.95
Annual Sub.: £47.40
Usual Pagination: 132
Editor: Tony van Gefen; **Managing Director:** Tony Stephenson
Summary of Content: Magazine covering radio-controlled model aircraft, with features on building and flying and product news and reviews.
Readership/Target Audience: Read by radio-controlled model aircraft enthusiasts.
ADVERTISING RATES:
Full Page Mono £548.00
Full Page Colour £767.00
Agency Commission: 10%
Copy instructions: Copy Date: 5 weeks prior to publication date
CONSUMER: HOBBIES & DIY: Models & Modelling

RADIO CONTROL MODELS & ELECTRONICS
46616U79B-170
Editorial Address: Berwick House, 8-10 Knoll Rise, ORPINGTON, BR6 0EL **Tel:** 01689 899200
Fax: 01689 899266
Email: david.ashby@myhobbystore.com
Advertising Address: As above.
Email: andy.cross@magicalia.com
Web site: http://www.modelflying.co.uk
ISSN: 0269-8307
Publisher: My Hobby Store Media
Date Established: 1960
Frequency: 13 issues yearly
Cover Price: £3.80
Circulation: 17,994 (Publisher's Statement)
Usual Pagination: 124
Editor: David Ashby; **Advertising Manager:** Andy Cross
Summary of Content: Magazine containing all aspects of radio controlled model aircraft.
Readership/Target Audience: Aimed at beginners and experts of all ages.
ADVERTISING RATES:
Full Page Colour £675.00
Agency Commission: 10%
Mechanical Data: Type Area: 267 x 184mm, Bleed Size: 303 x 213mm, Trim Size: 297 x 210mm, Col Length: 267mm, Page Width: 184mm, Film: Digital
Copy instructions: Copy Date: 3 weeks prior to publication date
Average advertising content per issue: 26%
CONSUMER: HOBBIES & DIY: Models & Modelling

RADIO RACE CAR INTERNATIONAL
46617U79B-179
Editorial Address: Traplet House, Pendragon Close, MALVERN, WR14 1GA **Tel:** 01684 588500
Fax: 01684 578558
Email: rrci@traplet.com
Advertising Address: As above.
Email: advertising@traplet.com
Web site: http://www.traplet.com
ISSN: 0268-3334
Publisher: Traplet Publications Ltd
Date Established: 1981

Consumer Magazines

Frequency: Monthly - Published the 1st Thursday of every month
Cover Price: £3.25
Annual Sub.: £35.40
Usual Pagination: 150
Editor: Dez Chand; **News Editor:** Dez Chand; **Managing Director:** Tony Stephenson
Summary of Content: Magazine featuring radio-controlled model cars, covering model car racing worldwide.
Readership/Target Audience: Aimed at enthusiasts of radio-controlled model cars, spanning all levels of skill and interest.
ADVERTISING RATES:
Full Page Mono £481.00
Full Page Colour £770.00
SCC £12.00
Agency Commission: 10%
Mechanical Data: Col Length: 270mm, Page Width: 184mm, Film: Digital, Type Area: 270 x 184mm, Bleed Size: 303 x 216mm, Trim Size: 297 x 210mm
Copy instructions: Copy Date: 6 weeks prior to publication date
CONSUMER: HOBBIES & DIY: Models & Modelling

RADIO TIMES
46103U76C-320

Editorial Address: Room MC1 D4, Media Centre, 201 Wood Lane, LONDON, W12 7TQ **Tel:** 020 8433 3878
Fax: 020 8433 3160
Email: radio.times@bbc.co.uk
Advertising Address: Garden House, 201 Wood Lane, LONDON, W12 7TQ **Tel:** 020 8433 3000 **Fax:** 020 8433 3002
Email: paul.kombou@bbc.com
Web site: http://www.radiotimes.com
Publisher: BBC Worldwide Publishing
Date Established: 1923
Frequency: Weekly
Cover Price: £1.05
Circulation: 966,098 (ABC 01/01/2009 to 30/06/2009)
Usual Pagination: 148
Editor: Ben Preston; **News Editor:** Terry Payne; **Features Editor:** Kim Newson; **Advertising Manager:** Paul Kombou
Summary of Content: Guide to BBC-TV, BBC-Radio, ITV, C4, C5, Satellite, Cable and Digital Television. Twitter: https://twitter.com/radiotimes
Readership/Target Audience: Aimed at people interested in TV and radio.
ADVERTISING RATES:
Full Page Colour £23100.00
Agency Commission: 15%
Mechanical Data: Type Area: 270 x 210mm, Trim Size: 300 x 226mm, Bleed Size: 312 x 238mm, Film: Digital, Col Length: 270mm, Page Width: 210mm
Copy instructions: Copy Date: 1 week prior to publication date
Average advertising content per issue: 25%
CONSUMER: MUSIC & PERFORMING ARTS: TV & Radio

RADIO USER
1739403U79D-172

Editorial Address: Arrowsmith Court, Station Approach, BROADSTONE, BH18 8PW **Tel:** 0845 803 1979
Fax: 01202 659950
Email: ru@pwpublishing.ltd.uk
Advertising Address: As above.
Email: roger@pwpublishing.ltd.uk
Web site: http://www.pwpublishing.ltd.uk
Publisher: PW Publishing Ltd
Date Established: 2006
Frequency: Monthly
Cover Price: £3.50
Circulation: 12,000 (Publisher's Statement)
Usual Pagination: 84
Editor: Roger Hall
Summary of Content: Magazine covering hobby radio communication. Includes equipment reviews, CB news, short-wave listening, amateur, scanning, DAB digital radio and air band listening.
Readership/Target Audience: Aimed at radio enthusiasts.
ADVERTISING RATES:
Full Page Mono £583.00
Full Page Colour £583.00
Agency Commission: 10%
Mechanical Data: Type Area: 270 x 182mm, Bleed Size: 303 x 216mm, Trim Size: 297 x 210mm, Col Length: 270mm, Page Width: 182mm, Film: Digital
Copy instructions: Copy Date: 6 weeks prior to publication date
Average advertising content per issue: 40%
CONSUMER: HOBBIES & DIY: Radio Electronics

RAIL
46707U79J-60

Editorial Address: Bushfield House, Orton Centre, PETERBOROUGH, PE2 5UW **Tel:** 01733 237111
Fax: 01733 288163
Email: rail@bauermedia.co.uk
Advertising Address: As above. **Fax:** 01733 465897
Email: kirsty.warren@bauerconsumer.co.uk
ISSN: 0953-4563

Publisher: Bauer Media Ltd (Orton)
Frequency: 26 issues yearly
Cover Price: £3.20
Annual Sub.: £83.20
Circulation: 21,019 (ABC 01/01/2008 to 31/12/2008)
Usual Pagination: 80
Editor: Philip Haigh; **Features Editor:** Richard Clinnick; **Managing Director:** Rob Croxall; **Managing Editor:** Nigel Harris
Summary of Content: Magazine covering railway information and news.
Readership/Target Audience: Read by railway professionals and enthusiasts.
ADVERTISING RATES:
Full Page Colour £1950.00
Agency Commission: 10%
Mechanical Data: Trim Size: 297 x 210mm, Bleed Size: 303 x 216mm, Page Width: 185mm, Film: Digital, Type Area: 270 x 185mm, Col Length: 270mm
Copy instructions: Copy Date: 1 week prior to publication date
Average advertising content per issue: 20%
CONSUMER: HOBBIES & DIY: Rail Enthusiasts

RAIL EXPRESS
46708U79J-65

Editorial Address: 20 Park Street, Kings Cliffe, PETERBOROUGH, PE8 6XN **Tel:** 01780 470086
Fax: 01780 470060
Email: editors@railexpress.co.uk
Advertising Address: As above.
Email: editor@railexpress.co.uk
Web site: http://www.railexpress.co.uk
ISSN: 1362-234X
Publisher: Foursight Publications Ltd
Date Established: 1996
Frequency: Monthly
Cover Price: £3.75
Circulation: 17,000 (Publisher's Statement)
Usual Pagination: 76
Editor: Philip Sutton; **Advertising Manager:** Philip Sutton
Summary of Content: Magazine covering British railway news.
Readership/Target Audience: Read by those with general railway interest plus railway industry professionals and enthusiasts.
ADVERTISING RATES:
Full Page Colour £750.00
Agency Commission: 10%
Mechanical Data: Film: Digital, Bleed Size: 303 x 215mm, Trim Size: 297 x 210mm, Type Area: 270 x 190mm, Print Process: Web-fed offset litho, Col Length: 270mm, Page Width: 190mm
Copy instructions: Copy Date: 15th of the month prior to publication date
Average advertising content per issue: 20%
CONSUMER: HOBBIES & DIY: Rail Enthusiasts

RAILWATCH
48710U94X-145_50

Editorial Address: 4 Christchurch Square, LONDON, E9 7HU **Tel:** 020 8985 8548
Email: editor@railwatch.org.uk
Advertising Address: As above. **Fax:** 020 8985 8212
Email: editor@railwatch.org.uk
Web site: http://www.railwatch.org.uk
ISSN: 0267-5943
Publisher: Railfuture
Frequency: Quarterly
Cover Price: £1.50
Free to qualifying individuals
Circulation: 4,000 (Publisher's Statement)
Usual Pagination: 20
Editor: Ray King; **Advertising Manager:** Ray King
Summary of Content: Magazine focusing on rail service issues. Covers new developments, line re-openings, campaigns, new stations and revisions in service.
Readership/Target Audience: Aimed at rail users and members of Railfuture.
ADVERTISING RATES:
Full Page Colour £190.00
Mechanical Data: Col Length: 280mm, Film: Digital, Trim Size: 297 x 210mm, Type Area: 280 x 197mm, Page Width: 197mm
Copy instructions: Copy Date: 3 weeks prior to publication date
Average advertising content per issue: 10%
CONSUMER: OTHER CLASSIFICATIONS: Miscellaneous

THE RAILWAY MAGAZINE
46709U79J-70

Editorial Address: Blue Fin Building, 110 Southwark Street, LONDON, SE1 0SU **Tel:** 020 3148 5000 **Fax:** 020 3148 8122
Email: railway@ipcmedia.com
Advertising Address: As above. **Fax:** 020 3148 8155
Email: lee_morris@ipcmedia.com
Web site: http://www.railwaymagazine.co.uk
ISSN: 0033-8923
Publisher: IPC Inspire

Date Established: 1897
Frequency: Monthly
Cover Price: £3.35
Circulation: 35,100 (ABC 01/01/2008 to 31/12/2008)
Usual Pagination: 108
Advertising Manager: Lee Morris
Summary of Content: Magazine focusing on rail practice and performance, with photo and feature articles on locomotives, train operating companies, underground systems, steam, heritage and preservation.
Readership/Target Audience: Aimed at those with an interest in railway performance.
ADVERTISING RATES:
Full Page Mono £551.00
Full Page Colour £948.00
Agency Commission: 10%
Mechanical Data: Col Length: 279mm, Bleed Size: 295 x 216mm, Type Area: 279 x 185mm, Trim Size: 289 x 210mm, Film: Digital, Page Width: 185mm
Copy instructions: Copy Date: 3 weeks prior to publication date
Average advertising content per issue: 17%
CONSUMER: HOBBIES & DIY: Rail Enthusiasts

RAILWAY MODELLER
46618U79B-180

Editorial Address: Underleys, Beer, SEATON, EX12 3NA **Tel:** 01297 20580 **Fax:** 01297 20229
Email: railway-modeller@btconnect.com
Advertising Address: As above.
Email: pecopubs@btconnect.com
Web site: http://www.peco-uk.com
ISSN: 0033-8931
Publisher: Peco Publications & Publicity Ltd.
Date Established: 1949
Frequency: Monthly
Cover Price: £3.25
Annual Sub.: £33.60
Circulation: 43,194 (ABC 01/01/2008 to 31/12/2008)
Usual Pagination: 124
Editor: Steve Flint; **Managing Director:** Michael Pritchard; **Advertising Manager:** John King
Summary of Content: Magazine covering the construction and operation of railway models in the smaller scales. Includes scale-drawings, trade reports, planning and historical articles.
Readership/Target Audience: Aimed at railway enthusiasts of all ages.
ADVERTISING RATES:
Full Page Colour £690.00
Agency Commission: 10%
Mechanical Data: Type Area: 268 x 204mm, Col Length: 268mm, Page Width: 204mm, Film: Digital
Copy instructions: Copy Date: 5 weeks prior to publication date
Average advertising content per issue: 60%
CONSUMER: HOBBIES & DIY: Models & Modelling

RAILWAY PHILATELY
46722U79J-72

Editorial Address: 5 Garth Lane, Widdrington, MORPETH, NE61 5EN **Tel:** 01670 760252
Email: f.will.taylor@btinternet.com
Advertising Address: As above.
Email: f.will.taylor@btinternet.com
Web site: http://www.geocities.com/tonygoodbody
ISSN: 0951-886X
Publisher: Railway Philatelic Group
Date Established: 1966
Frequency: Quarterly
Annual Sub.: £10.00
Circulation: 500 (Publisher's Statement)
Usual Pagination: 52
Editor: Frederick Taylor; **Advertising Manager:** Frederick Taylor
Summary of Content: Journal covering all aspects of railways and the post.
Readership/Target Audience: Aimed at those interested in stamp collecting related to railways.
ADVERTISING RATES:
Full Page Mono £50.00
Mechanical Data: Trim Size: 210 x 148mm, Film: Digital, Type Area: 175 x 115mm, Col Length: 175mm, Page Width: 115mm, No. of Columns (Display): 2
Copy instructions: Copy Date: 3 weeks prior to publication date
Average advertising content per issue: 5%
CONSUMER: HOBBIES & DIY: Rail Enthusiasts

RAILWAYS ILLUSTRATED
1611043U79J-331

Editorial Address: PO Box 1162, Spalding, PETERBOROUGH, PE11 9BD **Tel:** 01775 723849
Email: pip.dunn@eastfieldmedia.com
Advertising Address: Mallard, 6 Sunningdale Avenue, SPALDING, PE11 2SP **Tel:** 01775 767184
Web site: http://www.railwaysillustrated.com
ISSN: 1479-2230
Publisher: Ian Allan Publishing Ltd
Date Established: 2003

Frequency: Monthly
Cover Price: £3.50
Annual Sub.: £40.20
Usual Pagination: 96
Editor: Pip Dunn; **Advertising Manager:** David Smith
Summary of Content: Magazine covering railway companies, train operators and infrastructure functions as well as main line steam operations, private railway heritage sites and the National Railway Museum.
Readership/Target Audience: Aimed at railway enthusiasts.
ADVERTISING RATES:
Full Page Colour £650.00
Mechanical Data: Film: Digital
Copy instructions: Copy Date: 10th of month prior to publication date
CONSUMER: HOBBIES & DIY: Rail Enthusiasts

RALLYACTION UK
765060U77D-461
Formerly: Rally Action
Editorial Address: 20A Swan Street, BRECHIN, DD9 6EF
Tel: 01356 625080 **Fax:** 01356 622214
Email: editorial@rallyactionuk.com
Advertising Address: As above.
Email: bill@scotmaps.co.uk
Web site: http://www.rallyactionuk.com
Publisher: Select Publications
Frequency: 6 issues yearly
Cover Price: £4.00
Annual Sub.: £40.00
Circulation: 12,100 (Publisher's Statement)
Usual Pagination: 70
Editor: Bill Sturrock; **Advertising Manager:** Bill Sturrock;
Publisher: Bill Sturrock
Summary of Content: Magazine covering all aspects of UK rallying with a focus on clubman level rallying. Includes advice on getting involved in the sport, building cars and technical information as well as race reports, women in motor sports and comparisons of rally cars.
Readership/Target Audience: Aimed at motor sport enthusiasts.
ADVERTISING: Rates on application
Mechanical Data: Page Width: 190mm, Type Area: 277 x 190mm, Trim Size: 297 x 210mm, Bleed Size: 303 x 216mm, Col Length: 277mm, Film: Digital
Copy instructions: Copy Date: Last working day of the month prior to publication date
CONSUMER: MOTORING & CYCLING: Motor Sports

RANDOM MAGAZINE
1852047U74B-739
Editorial Address: 67-69 Sutherland Road, LONDON, E17 6BH **Tel:** 0845 260 1236 **Fax:** 0845 230 5256
Email: info@random-magazine.com
Web site: http://www.random-magazine.com
Publisher: Peckish Media Ltd
Date Established: 2008
Frequency: Half-yearly - Published in October and April
Cover Price: £6.00
Circulation: 40,000 (Publisher's Statement)
Editor: Rivkie Baum; **Editor-in-Chief:** Tom Kembery
Summary of Content: Magazine offering in-depth interviews, backstage insight, professional profiles, stunning photo shoots, fashion, beauty, music, art and food.
Readership/Target Audience: Aimed at inspired people who enjoy the finer things in life.
CONSUMER: WOMEN'S INTEREST CONSUMER MAGAZINES: Women's Interest - Fashion

RANGERS NEWS
45775U75B-190
Editorial Address: 1st Floor, Argyle House, Ibrox Stadium, GLASGOW, G51 2XD **Tel:** 0141 580 8797
Fax: 0141 580 8799
Email: editor@rangers.co.uk
Advertising Address: The Old Brewery, Priory Lane, BURFORD, OX18 4SG **Tel:** 01993 822811
Fax: 01993 825928
Email: pgeddes@cre8ing.com
Web site: http://www.rangers.co.uk
Publisher: CRE8
Date Established: 1972
Frequency: 46 issues yearly
Cover Price: £2.25
Circulation: 10,000 (Publisher's Statement)
Usual Pagination: 72
Editor: Lindsay Herron
Summary of Content: Official newspaper of Rangers Football Club.
Readership/Target Audience: Aimed at supporters of Rangers Football Club.
ADVERTISING RATES:
Full Page Colour £900.00
Agency Commission: 10%
Mechanical Data: Film: Digital, Trim Size: 297 x 210mm
Copy instructions: Copy Date: Friday prior to publication date

Average advertising content per issue: 40%
CONSUMER: SPORT: Football

RAPPORT
45656U74Q-902
Editorial Address: Clifton Heights, Triangle West, BRISTOL, BS8 1EJ **Tel:** 0117 925 1696 **Fax:** 0117 925 1808
Email: karen.ellison@specialistuk.com
Publisher: Specialist (UK) Ltd
Frequency: 3 issues yearly
Free to qualifying individuals
Circulation: 250,000 (Publisher's Statement)
Usual Pagination: 60
Editor: Karen Ellison
Summary of Content: Magazine includes features on motoring issues, lifestyle, travel and sport.
Readership/Target Audience: Aimed at new Peugeot car owners.
ADVERTISING: No Advertising taken
CONSUMER: WOMEN'S INTEREST CONSUMER MAGAZINES: Lifestyle

RAVERS DVD
47618U86A-120
Formerly: Ravers
Editorial Address: PO Box 312, WITHAM, CM8 3SZ
Tel: 01376 534534 **Fax:** 01376 534546
Email: ravers@galaxy.co.uk
Advertising Address: As above. **Fax:** 01376 534531
Email: anne.hanley@freebournes.com
Web site: http://www.ravers.co.uk
Publisher: Galaxy Publications
Frequency: Monthly
Cover Price: £5.95
Circulation: 30,000 (Publisher's Statement)
Usual Pagination: 100
Editor: Matthew Elliott; **Advertising Manager:** Anne Hanley
Summary of Content: Magazine containing erotic material.
Readership/Target Audience: Aimed at men over 18 years old.
ADVERTISING: Rates on application
CONSUMER: ADULT & GAY MAGAZINES: Adult Magazines

RAW VISION
47511U84A-337
Editorial Address: 1 Watford Road, RADLETT, WD7 8LA
Tel: 01923 856644 **Fax:** 01923 859897
Email: info@rawvision.com
Advertising Address: PO Box 44, WATFORD, WD25 8LN
Tel: 01923 856644 **Fax:** 01923 859897
Email: info@rawvision.com
Web site: http://www.rawvision.com
ISSN: 0955-1182
Publisher: Raw Vision Ltd
Date Established: 1989
Frequency: Quarterly
Cover Price: £6.95
Annual Sub.: £24.00
Circulation: 11,000 (Publisher's Statement)
Usual Pagination: 80
Editor: John Maizels; **Advertising Manager:** John Maizels
Summary of Content: International magazine and web site covering a variety of styles of art, particularly outsider art and contemporary folk art.
Readership/Target Audience: Aimed at those interested in art.
ADVERTISING RATES:
Full Page Colour £1155.00
Mechanical Data: Bleed Size: 307 x 230mm, Type Area: 272 x 187mm, Col Length: 272mm, Page Width: 187mm, Film: Digital, Trim Size: 297 x 210mm
CONSUMER: THE ARTS & LITERARY: Arts

READER'S DIGEST
45158U73-300
Editorial Address: 11 Westferry Circus, Canary Wharf, LONDON, E14 4HE **Tel:** 020 7715 8000 **Fax:** 020 7715 8716
Email: theeditor@readersdigest.co.uk
Advertising Address: As above. **Fax:** 020 7715 8701
Email: flora_macmillan@readersdigest.co.uk
Web site: http://www.readersdigest.co.uk
Publisher: Reader's Digest Association Ltd
Date Established: 1938
Frequency: Monthly
Cover Price: £2.95
Annual Sub.: £42.00
Circulation: 541,282 (ABC 01/01/2009 to 30/06/2009)
Editor: Simon Hartley; **Executive Editor:** Simon Hartley;
Features Editor: Stuart Reid; **Managing Director:** Chris Spratling; **Managing Editor:** Catherine Haughney;
Advertising Director: Flora Macmillan
Summary of Content: Magazine focusing on articles of universal interest, specially commissioned, or reprinted from British and foreign publications.
Twitter: https://twitter.com/readersdigest.
Language(s): Danish; English; Finnish; French; German; Norwegian; Portuguese; Spanish; Swedish

Readership/Target Audience: Aimed at men and women of all ages.
ADVERTISING RATES:
Full Page Colour £24500.00
Agency Commission: 15%
Mechanical Data: Trim Size: 184 x 134mm, Page Width: 121mm, Type Area: 171 x 121mm, Col Length: 171mm, Bleed Size: 190 x 140mm, Film: Digital
Copy instructions: Copy Date: 4 weeks prior to publication date
Average advertising content per issue: 20%
CONSUMER: NATIONAL & INTERNATIONAL PERIODICALS

REAL HOLIDAYS
1613626U89E-205
Editorial Address: 85 Strand, LONDON, WC2R 0DW
Tel: 020 7550 8000 **Fax:** 020 7550 8250
Email: alison.crampin@cedarcom.co.uk
Advertising Address: As above.
Email: ben.williamson@cedarcom.co.uk
Web site: http://www.yourrealholidays.co.uk
Publisher: Cedar Communications
Date Established: 2002
Frequency: Half-yearly - Published in May and December
Free to qualifying individuals
Circulation: 250,000 (Publisher's Statement)
Usual Pagination: 68
Editor: Alison Crampin
Summary of Content: Magazine covering travel destinations, advice and information on new holiday resorts.
Readership/Target Audience: Aimed at customers of TUI, Thomson, Lunn Poly, Portland Holidays Direct, Crystal Holidays and Magic Travel Group.
ADVERTISING RATES:
Full Page Colour £6250.00
Agency Commission: 10%
Mechanical Data: Trim Size: 265 x 210mm, Film: Digital, Bleed Size: 271 x 216mm, Type Area: 250 x 195mm, Col Length: 250mm, Page Width: 195mm
Copy instructions: Copy Date: 6 weeks prior to publication date
CONSUMER: HOLIDAYS & TRAVEL: Holidays

REAL HOMES MAGAZINE
45284U74C-415
Editorial Address: 2 Sugar Brook Court, Aston Road, BROMSGROVE, B60 3EX **Tel:** 01527 834400
Fax: 01527 574388
Email: caron.bronson@centaur.co.uk
Advertising Address: As above. **Tel:** 01537 834400
Email: gill.grimshaw@centaur.co.uk
Web site: http://www.realhomesmagazine.co.uk
ISSN: 1464-4061
Publisher: Centaur Special Interest Media
Date Established: 1998
Frequency: Monthly
Cover Price: £2.50
Circulation: 68,005 (ABC 01/07/2008 to 31/12/2008)
Usual Pagination: 180
Editor: Caron Bronson; **Managing Director:** Peter Harris;
Advertising Director: Gill Grimshaw
Summary of Content: Magazine covering all aspects of homes and lifestyle. Includes articles on makeovers, homes abroad, style tips and food.
Readership/Target Audience: Aimed at people interested in the home and interior design.
ADVERTISING RATES:
Full Page Colour £3100.00
Mechanical Data: Type Area: 270 x 193mm, Bleed Size: 296 x 219mm, Trim Size: 290 x 213mm, Film: Digital, Col Length: 270mm, Page Width: 193mm
CONSUMER: WOMEN'S INTEREST CONSUMER MAGAZINES: Home & Family

REAL PEOPLE
1692281U74A-1005
Editorial Address: 33 Broadwick Street, LONDON, W1F 0DQ **Tel:** 020 7439 5000 **Fax:** 020 7339 4650
Email: features@realpeoplemag.co.uk
Advertising Address: As above. **Fax:** 020 7339 4527
Email: james.graham@natmags.co.uk
Web site: http://www.realpeoplemag.co.uk
Publisher: ACP-NatMag
Date Established: 2006
Frequency: Weekly
Cover Price: £0.68
Circulation: 201,960 (ABC 01/01/2009 to 30/06/2009)
Usual Pagination: 60
Editor: Samm Taylor
Summary of Content: Magazine covering real life stories, health, fashion and beauty as well as including money off vouchers.
Twitter: http://twitter.com/RealPeopleMag.
Readership/Target Audience: Aimed at women of all ages who enjoy real life stories.
ADVERTISING RATES:
Full Page Colour £8900.00
Agency Commission: 10%

Consumer Magazines

Mechanical Data: Type Area: 275 x 212mm, Bleed Size: 296 x 236mm, Trim Size: 290 x 230mm, Col Length: 275mm, Page Width: 212mm, Film: Digital
Copy instructions: Copy Date: 10 days prior to publication date
Average advertising content per issue: 10%
CONSUMER: WOMEN'S INTEREST CONSUMER MAGAZINES: Women's Interest

REAL TRAVEL
1743219U89A-731

Editorial Address: 15-16 Lower Park Row, BRISTOL, BS1 5BN **Tel:** 0117 929 7462 **Fax:** 0117 927 6535
Email: hfu@realtravelmag.com
Advertising Address: As above.
Email: caroline@realtravelmag.com
Web site: http://www.realtravelmag.com
Publisher: Create Publishing
Date Established: 2006
Frequency: 13 issues yearly
Cover Price: £3.50
Circulation: 27,000 (Publisher's Statement)
Usual Pagination: 114
Editor: Hfu Reisenhofer; **Advertising Manager:** Caroline Harding
Summary of Content: Magazine covering independent world travel from weekend city breaks to year out career trips.
Readership/Target Audience: Aimed at 20 to 50 year olds who are looking to travel outside the normal package tour.
ADVERTISING RATES:
Full Page Colour £1895.00
SCC £25.00
Agency Commission: 10%
Mechanical Data: Type Area: 275 x 205mm, Bleed Size: 291 x 221mm, Trim Size: 285 x 215mm, Col Length: 275mm, Page Width: 205mm, Film: Digital
Copy instructions: Copy Date: 3 weeks prior to publication date
Average advertising content per issue: 30%
CONSUMER: HOLIDAYS & TRAVEL: Travel

REAL WORLD
754843U88C-178

Editorial Address: 22-26 Albert Embankment, LONDON, SE1 7TJ **Tel:** 020 7735 2111 **Fax:** 020 7840 0443
Email: dee@realworldmagazine.com
Advertising Address: As above. **Tel:** 020 7735 4900
Email: paul@realworldmagazine.com
Web site: http://www.realworldmagazine.com
Publisher: Cherry Publishing
Frequency: Monthly
Cover Price: Free
Circulation: 42,888 (Publisher's Statement)
Usual Pagination: 64
Editor: Dee Pilgrim; **Advertising Manager:** Paul Wade; **Publisher:** Darius Norell
Summary of Content: Magazine covering advice and information on careers after university.
Readership/Target Audience: Read by students and graduates of UK universities.
ADVERTISING RATES:
Full Page Colour £4000.00
Agency Commission: 10%
Mechanical Data: Trim Size: 297 x 210mm, Bleed Size: 303 x 216mm, Type Area: 280 x 190mm, Col Length: 280mm, Page Width: 190mm, Film: Digital
Copy instructions: Copy Date: 2 weeks prior to publication date
Average advertising content per issue: 35%
CONSUMER: EDUCATION: Careers

RECOMMENDED INNS & PUBS OF BRITAIN
48012U89A-405

Formerly: Recommended Country Inns & Pubs of Britain
Editorial Address: Abbey Mill Business Centre, Seedhill, PAISLEY, PA1 1TJ **Tel:** 0141 887 0428 **Fax:** 0141 889 7204
Email: editorial@fhguides.co.uk
Advertising Address: As above.
Email: dorothy@fhguides.co.uk
Web site: http://www.holidayguides.com
Publisher: FHG Guides
Date Established: 1975
Frequency: Annual - Published in December
Annual Sub.: £6.99
Circulation: 10,000 (Publisher's Statement)
Usual Pagination: 160
Editor: Anne Cuthbertson; **Advertising Manager:** Dorothy Clements
Summary of Content: Magazine featuring articles on pubs, inns and small hotels for day trips, weekend breaks and touring holidays.
Readership/Target Audience: Read by those planning a holiday in Britain.
ADVERTISING RATES:
Full Page Colour £739.00
Agency Commission: 10%

Mechanical Data: Page Width: 118mm, Trim Size: 210 x 145mm, Bleed Size: +3mm, Type Area: 190 x 118mm, Col Length: 190mm, Film: Digital
Copy instructions: Copy Date: 4 weeks prior to publication date
Average advertising content per issue: 40%
CONSUMER: HOLIDAYS & TRAVEL: Travel

RECOMMENDED SHORT BREAK HOLIDAYS IN BRITAIN
48011U89A-402

Editorial Address: Abbey Mill Business Centre, Seedhill, PAISLEY, PA1 1TJ **Tel:** 0141 887 0428 **Fax:** 0141 889 7204
Email: editorial@fhguides.co.uk
Advertising Address: As above.
Email: dorothy@fhguides.co.uk
Web site: http://www.holidayguides.com
Publisher: FHG Guides
Frequency: Annual - Published in October
Cover Price: £6.99
Circulation: 15,000 (Publisher's Statement)
Editor: Anne Cuthbertson
Summary of Content: Magazine containing addresses and contacts for bargain breaks all year round.
Readership/Target Audience: Aimed at those who are planning a holiday in Britain.
ADVERTISING RATES:
Full Page Colour £739.00
Agency Commission: 10%
Mechanical Data: Page Width: 118mm, Type Area: 190 x 118mm, Col Length: 190mm, Film: Digital
Copy instructions: Copy Date: August 18th
CONSUMER: HOLIDAYS & TRAVEL: Travel

RECORD COLLECTOR
46253U76E-310

Editorial Address: Unit 101, 140 Wales Farm Road, Acton, LONDON, W3 6UG **Tel:** 0870 732 8080 **Fax:** 0870 732 6060
Email: alan.lewis@metropolis.co.uk
Advertising Address: As above. **Tel:** 020 8752 8181
Fax: 020 8752 8185
Email: rcads@metropolis.co.uk
Web site: http://www.recordcollectormag.com
Publisher: Diamond Publishing Ltd
Date Established: 1980
Frequency: 13 issues yearly
Cover Price: £3.90
Circulation: 35,000 (Publisher's Statement)
Usual Pagination: 164
Editor: Alan Lewis; **News Editor:** Tim Jones; **Editor-in-Chief:** Alan Lewis
Summary of Content: Magazine celebrating the history of popular music from 1950s to the present day, includes news, reviews, interviews, discographies and record values.
Readership/Target Audience: Aimed at record collectors and general music fans.
ADVERTISING RATES:
Full Page Mono £885.00
Full Page Colour £1085.00
Agency Commission: 15%
Mechanical Data: Trim Size: 297 x 210mm, Page Width: 185mm, Film: Digital, Bleed Size: 303 x 216mm, Type Area: 271 x 185mm, Col Length: 271mm
Copy instructions: Copy Date: 4 weeks prior to publication date
Average advertising content per issue: 40%
CONSUMER: MUSIC & PERFORMING ARTS: Pop Music

THE RECORDER MAGAZINE
46178U76D-388_50

Editorial Address: Scout Bottom Farm, Mytholmroyd, HEBDEN BRIDGE, HX7 5JS **Tel:** 01422 882751
Fax: 01422 886157
Email: helen.shabetai@ntlworld.com
Advertising Address: As above.
Email: advertising@recordermail.demon.co.uk
Web site: http://www.recordermail.co.uk
ISSN: 0961-3544
Publisher: Peacock Press
Date Established: 1935
Frequency: Quarterly
Annual Sub.: £25.00
Circulation: 2,800 (Publisher's Statement)
Usual Pagination: 44
Editor: Helen Shahbetai; **Managing Director:** Ruth Burbidge; **Advertising Manager:** Jeremy Burbidge; **Publisher:** Jeremy Burbidge
Summary of Content: Magazine containing articles, reports and reviews on all aspects of the recorder and its music. Includes tips on improving technique, as well as features on the history of the recorder, interviews with players and makers, and concert and book reviews.
Readership/Target Audience: Aimed at recorder players and teachers.
ADVERTISING: Rates on application
Agency Commission: 10%
Copy instructions: Copy Date: 1 month prior to publication date
CONSUMER: MUSIC & PERFORMING ARTS: Music

RECUSANT HISTORY
48814U94X-146_50

Editorial Address: c/o 12 Melbourne Place, WOLSINGHAM, DL13 3EH **Tel:** 01388 527747
Web site: http://www.catholic-history.org.uk/crs
ISSN: 0034-1937
Publisher: The Catholic Record Society
Date Established: 1952
Frequency: Half-yearly - Published in May and October
Annual Sub.: £20.00
Circulation: 780 (Publisher's Statement)
Usual Pagination: 150
Editor: V. A. McClelland
Summary of Content: Journal of the Catholic Record Society. Includes articles on post reformation English and Welsh Catholic history.
Readership/Target Audience: Aimed at those interested in the history and culture of British Catholics.
ADVERTISING: No Advertising taken
CONSUMER: OTHER CLASSIFICATIONS: Miscellaneous

RED
45197U74A-500

Editorial Address: 64 North Row, LONDON, W1K 7LL
Tel: 020 7150 7600 **Fax:** 020 7150 7684
Email: saska.graville@redmagazine.co.uk
Advertising Address: As above. **Tel:** 020 7150 7000
Fax: 020 7150 7001
Email: claire.cearney@hf-uk.com
Web site: http://www.redmagazine.co.uk
Publisher: Hachette Filipacchi (UK) Ltd
Date Established: 1998
Frequency: Monthly
Cover Price: £3.50
Annual Sub.: £40.80
Circulation: 218,726 (ABC 01/01/2009 to 30/06/2009)
Usual Pagination: 282
Editor: Saska Graville
Summary of Content: Magazine covering a variety of topics including fashion, beauty, food and lifestyle.
Readership/Target Audience: Aimed at women aged 30 years and over.
ADVERTISING RATES:
Full Page Colour £12197.00
Agency Commission: 15%
Mechanical Data: Col Length: 280mm, Page Width: 210mm, Bleed Size: 306 x 236mm, Trim Size: 300 x 230mm, Film: Digital, Type Area: 280 x 210mm
Copy instructions: Copy Date: 8 weeks prior to publication date
CONSUMER: WOMEN'S INTEREST CONSUMER MAGAZINES: Women's Interest

THE RED BULLETIN
1882018U86C-747

Editorial Address: 14 Soho Square, LONDON, W1D 3QG
Tel: 020 7434 8600
Email: adam.phillips@uk.redbulletin.com
Advertising Address: As above.
Email: adam.phillips@uk.redbulletin.com
Web site: http://uk.redbulletin.com
Publisher: Red Bulletin
Date Established: 2009
Frequency: Monthly - Published first Tuesday of the month within the Independent
Cover Price: Free
Circulation: 540,000 (Publisher's Statement)
Usual Pagination: 100
Editor: Adam Phillips
Summary of Content: Lifestyle magazine featuring articles on sport, culture, music and interviews with Red Bull heroes.
Readership/Target Audience: Aimed predominantly at readers aged 16 to 35 years old.
ADVERTISING RATES:
Full Page Colour £6395.00
Mechanical Data: Trim Size: 276 x 202mm, Bleed Size: +3mm
CONSUMER: ADULT & GAY MAGAZINES: Men's Lifestyle Magazines

RED HANDED
1623672U86C-716

Editorial Address: 24 Stacey Road, CARDIFF, CF24 1DU
Tel: 029 2019 0224 **Fax:** 029 2019 0226
Email: editorial@conroymedia.co.uk
Advertising Address: As above.
Email: redhanded@conroymedia.co.uk
Web site: http://www.redhandedmagazine.co.uk
Publisher: Conroy Media
Date Established: 2003
Frequency: Quarterly
Cover Price: Free
Circulation: 28,862 (ABC 01/01/2008 to 31/12/2008)
Usual Pagination: 96
Advertising Manager: Paul Mulligan; **Publisher:** Paul Mulligan
Summary of Content: Magazine covering issues that matter to men in Wales.

Readership/Target Audience: Aimed at men in Wales aged between 18 and 40 years old. Distributed through sports venues, fashion retailers, bars, clubs and car dealers.
ADVERTISING RATES:
Full Page Colour £1045.00
Agency Commission: 10%
Mechanical Data: Bleed Size: +3mm, Trim Size: 297 x 210mm, Film: Digital
Copy instructions: Copy Date: 2 weeks prior to publication date
Average advertising content per issue: 35%
CONSUMER: ADULT & GAY MAGAZINES: Men's Lifestyle Magazines

RED PEPPER
47271U82-160
Editorial Address: 1B Waterlow Road, LONDON, N19 5NJ
Tel: 020 7281 7024 **Fax:** 020 7263 9345
Email: mail2009@redpepper.org.uk
Advertising Address: As above.
Email: ads@redpepper.org.uk
Web site: http://www.redpepper.org.uk
ISSN: 1353-7024
Publisher: Socialist Newspaper Publications
Date Established: 1995
Frequency: 6 issues yearly
Cover Price: £3.95
Annual Sub.: £29.00
Circulation: 10,320 (Publisher's Statement)
Usual Pagination: 70
Editor: Tamana Kalhar; **Advertising Manager:** Fiona Osler
Summary of Content: Magazine covering domestic and international issues including articles on the arts, book reviews and leisure.
Readership/Target Audience: Aimed at politically aware individuals.
ADVERTISING: Rates on application
CONSUMER: CURRENT AFFAIRS & POLITICS

REDAN FUN TO LEARN BARNEY MAGAZINE
48467U91D-90
Editorial Address: Suite 2, Prospect House, Belle Vue Road, SHREWSBURY, SY3 7NR **Tel:** 01743 364433
Fax: 01743 271528
Email: info@redan.com
Advertising Address: As above.
Email: info@redan.com
Web site: http://www.redan.co.uk
Publisher: Redan Publishing
Date Established: 1996
Frequency: Monthly
Cover Price: £1.99
Circulation: 55,000 (Publisher's Statement)
Usual Pagination: 36
Editor: Lee Bishop; **Advertising Manager:** Emily Bell
Summary of Content: Children's magazine covering the adventures of Barney including stories and activities.
Readership/Target Audience: Aimed at 3 to 7 year olds reading with their parents.
ADVERTISING RATES:
Full Page Colour £1550.00
Agency Commission: 10%
Mechanical Data: Film: Digital, Type Area: 272 x 185mm, Trim Size: 297 x 210mm, Bleed Size: 304 x 216mm, Col Length: 272mm, Page Width: 185mm
Copy instructions: Copy Date: 8 weeks prior to publication date
CONSUMER: RECREATION & LEISURE: Children & Youth

REDAN FUN TO LEARN DISCOVERY
1646100U91D-884
Editorial Address: Suite 2, Prospect House, Belle Vue Road, SHREWSBURY, SY3 7NR **Tel:** 01743 364433
Fax: 01743 271528
Email: info@redan.com
Advertising Address: As above.
Email: info@redan.com
Web site: http://www.redan.co.uk
Publisher: Redan Publishing
Frequency: Half-yearly - Published in April and October
Cover Price: £1.99
Circulation: 35,000 (Publisher's Statement)
Usual Pagination: 36
Editor: Lee Bishop; **Advertising Manager:** Emily Bell
Summary of Content: Children's magazine with fun, themed stories and activities.
Readership/Target Audience: Aimed at boys and girls aged 3 to 7 years old.
ADVERTISING RATES:
Full Page Colour £1300.00
Agency Commission: 10%
Mechanical Data: Type Area: 272 x 185mm, Bleed Size: 304 x 216mm, Trim Size: 297 x 210mm, Col Length: 272mm, Page Width: 185mm, Film: Digital
Copy instructions: Copy Date: 8 weeks prior to publication date
CONSUMER: RECREATION & LEISURE: Children & Youth

REDAN FUN TO LEARN FAVOURITES
48468U91D-92
Editorial Address: Suite 2, Prospect House, Belle Vue Road, SHREWSBURY, SY3 7NR **Tel:** 01743 364433
Fax: 01743 271528
Email: info@redan.com
Advertising Address: As above.
Email: info@redan.com
Web site: http://www.redan.co.uk
Publisher: Redan Publishing
Date Established: 1998
Frequency: 26 issues yearly
Cover Price: £2.35
Circulation: 48,314 (ABC 01/01/2009 to 30/06/2009)
Usual Pagination: 52
Editor: Emily Bell; **Advertising Manager:** Emily Bell
Summary of Content: Children's magazine containing stories, activities and puzzles based on popular children's characters.
Readership/Target Audience: Aimed at 3 to 7 year olds reading with their parents.
ADVERTISING RATES:
Full Page Colour £2000.00
Agency Commission: 10%
Mechanical Data: Film: Digital, Type Area: 270 x 190mm, Bleed Size: 306 x 226mm, Trim Size: 300 x 220mm, Col Length: 270mm, Page Width: 190mm
CONSUMER: RECREATION & LEISURE: Children & Youth

REDBRICK
47432U83-65
Editorial Address: The Guild Of Students, Edgbaston Park Road, Edgbaston, BIRMINGHAM, B15 2TU
Tel: 0121 251 2462
Email: redbrick@guild.bham.ac.uk
Advertising Address: As above. **Tel:** 0121 251 2533
Fax: 0121 251 2526
Email: media@guild.bham.ac.uk
Web site: http://www.bugs.bham.ac.uk/redbrick
Publisher: Birmingham University Guild of Students
Date Established: 1936
Frequency: 22 issues yearly - Published weekly during term time
Cover Price: Free
Circulation: 20,000 (Publisher's Statement)
Usual Pagination: 28
Advertising Manager: Emily Badger
Summary of Content: Publication covering student news, the arts and sport at local and national level.
Readership/Target Audience: Aimed at students and staff at Birmingham university.
ADVERTISING RATES:
Full Page Mono £635.00
Full Page Colour £895.00
Agency Commission: 10%
Mechanical Data: Film: Digital
Copy instructions: Copy Date: 10 days prior to publication date
CONSUMER: STUDENT PUBLICATIONS

REDLINE
46332U77A-383
Editorial Address: 30 Monmouth Street, BATH, BA1 2BW
Tel: 01225 442244 **Fax:** 01225 732301
Email: redline@futurenet.com
Advertising Address: As above. **Fax:** 01225 822885
Email: phil.jones@futurenet.co.uk
Web site: http://www.redlinemag.com
ISSN: 1462-463X
Publisher: Future Publishing Ltd
Frequency: 13 issues yearly
Cover Price: £3.99
Circulation: 19,297 (ABC 01/01/2008 to 31/12/2008)
Usual Pagination: 196
Editor: Davy Lewis; **Advertising Manager:** Phil Jones;
Publisher: Richard Schofield
Summary of Content: Magazine focusing on the enjoyment of modified and performance cars. Covers the modified car scene, men's lifestyle, motoring news and tuning, styling and in-car entertainment accessories. Includes in-car TV, video, DVD, music and consoles.
Readership/Target Audience: Aimed at men between 21 and 40 years old.
ADVERTISING RATES:
Full Page Colour £1795.00
Agency Commission: 10%
Mechanical Data: Film: Digital
Copy instructions: Copy Date: 4 weeks prior to publication date
Average advertising content per issue: 40%
CONSUMER: MOTORING & CYCLING: Motoring

REFEREEING
45756U75B-286
Formerly: Refereeing Today
Editorial Address: 25 Soho Square, LONDON, W1D 4FA
Tel: 020 7745 4545 **Fax:** 020 7745 5684
Email: cassandra.rees@thefa.com
Publisher: The Football Association

Frequency: 3 issues yearly
Cover Price: Free
Circulation: 30,000 (Publisher's Statement)
Usual Pagination: 64
Editor: Cassandra Rees
Summary of Content: Official publication of The Referees' Association featuring news and views about football refereeing and current advice for today's referee.
Readership/Target Audience: Read by association football referees, assistant referees and those interested in the game of football.
ADVERTISING: No Advertising taken
CONSUMER: SPORT: Football

REFLECTIONS
1685736U80C-5239
Editorial Address: 118 Saltergate, CHESTERFIELD, S40 1NG **Tel:** 01246 550488 **Fax:** 01246 555420
Email: editor@reflections-magazine.com
Advertising Address: As above.
Email: mikes@bannisterpublications.co.uk
Web site: http://www.reflections-magazine.com
ISSN: 1466-9803
Publisher: Bannister Publications
Date Established: 1992
Frequency: Monthly
Cover Price: £1.00
Free to qualifying individuals
Circulation: 19,000 (Publisher's Statement)
Usual Pagination: 100
Editor: Tom Blyth; **Advertising Manager:** Mike Snow
Summary of Content: Magazine covering local history, current events and features of local interest.
Readership/Target Audience: Aimed at residents and tourists to North Derbyshire.
ADVERTISING RATES:
Full Page Colour £625.00
Agency Commission: 10%
Mechanical Data: Type Area: 270 x 190mm, Trim Size: 297 x 210mm, Col Length: 270mm, Page Width: 190mm, Film: Digital
Average advertising content per issue: 50%
CONSUMER: RURAL & REGIONAL INTEREST: Regional Interest English Counties

---

REFLECTIVE IMAGE
1810890U80B-429
Editorial Address: Churchill House, Stirling Way, BOREHAMWOOD, WD6 2HP **Tel:** 020 8736 0077
Fax: 020 8736 0078
Email: info@reflective-image.com
Advertising Address: As above.
Email: rita@reflective-image.com
Web site: http://www.reflective-image.com
Frequency: Monthly
Cover Price: £2.50
Free to qualifying individuals
Circulation: 40,000 (Publisher's Statement)
Usual Pagination: 84
Editor: Jo Bates; **Advertising Manager:** Rita Murphy
Summary of Content: Magazine covering health, travel, interiors, fashion, beauty, sport and cars as well as local news and events.
Readership/Target Audience: Aimed at households in North London and Middlesex.
ADVERTISING: Rates on application
Average advertising content per issue: 50%
CONSUMER: RURAL & REGIONAL INTEREST: Regional Interest Greater London

---

REFORM
47747U87-193
Editorial Address: 86 Tavistock Place, LONDON, WC1H 9RT **Tel:** 020 7916 8630 **Fax:** 020 7916 2021
Email: reform@urc.org.uk
Advertising Address: Impact, Media House, 55 Old Road, LEIGHTON BUZZARD, LU7 2RB **Tel:** 01525 370013
Fax: 01525 382487
Email: jo@impact-now.co.uk
Web site: http://www.urc.org.uk
ISSN: 0306-7262
Publisher: The United Reformed Church (London)
Date Established: 1972
Frequency: 11 issues yearly
Cover Price: £1.70
Annual Sub.: £18.70
Circulation: 13,000 (Publisher's Statement)
Usual Pagination: 44
Editor: Kay Parris; **Managing Director:** Martin Hazell
Summary of Content: Magazine of the United Reformed Church. Covers religious news, events and views.
Readership/Target Audience: Aimed at people with an interest in and members of the United Reformed Church.
ADVERTISING: Rates on application
CONSUMER: RELIGIOUS

Consumer Magazines

REFORMER (CON)
47272U82-162

Editorial Address: 83 Victoria Street, LONDON, SW1H 0HW
Tel: 020 3008 4991 **Fax:** 07092 879366
Email: trg@trg.org.uk
Advertising Address: As above.
Email: trg@trg.org.uk
Web site: http://www.trg.org.uk
ISSN: 1463-077X
Publisher: Tory Reform Group
Date Established: 1976
Frequency: Half-yearly - Published in the Spring and Autumn
Cover Price: £4.00
Free to qualifying individuals
Annual Sub.: £8.00
Circulation: 2,000 (Publisher's Statement)
Usual Pagination: 20
Editor: Clare Whelan; **Advertising Manager:** Clare Whelan
Summary of Content: Journal covering debate within the Conservative Party.
Readership/Target Audience: Read by Tory Reform Group members, Conservative Party members and supporters.
ADVERTISING: Rates on application
Agency Commission: 15%
Average advertising content per issue: 10%
CONSUMER: CURRENT AFFAIRS & POLITICS

REFRESH
766552U86B-164

Editorial Address: 22A Iliffe Yard, LONDON, SE17 3QA
Tel: 020 7277 4517 **Fax:** 020 7703 8718
Email: refresh@wildpublishing.com
Advertising Address: As above. **Tel:** 01322 225023
Email: rory@wildpublishing.com
Web site: http://www.refreshmag.co.uk
ISSN: 1478-1816
Publisher: Wild Publishing Ltd
Date Established: 2002
Frequency: 6 issues yearly
Cover Price: £4.25
Circulation: 50,000 (Publisher's Statement)
Usual Pagination: 132
Editor: Remy Le Fevre; **Editor-in-Chief:** David Tickner;
Advertising Manager: Rory Cameron
Summary of Content: Magazine covering gay lifestyle with a core focus on culture and the arts, travel, fashion and lifestyle.
Readership/Target Audience: Aimed at affluent, professional, gay men between 25 and 35 years old.
ADVERTISING RATES:
Full Page Colour £2495.00
Agency Commission: 10%
Mechanical Data: Film: Digital, Type Area: 330 x 230mm, Bleed Size: 346 x 246mm, Trim Size: 340 x 240mm, Col Length: 330mm, Page Width: 230mm
Copy instructions: Copy Date: 2 weeks prior to publication date
Average advertising content per issue: 40%
CONSUMER: ADULT & GAY MAGAZINES: Gay & Lesbian Magazines

REFUGEE SURVEY QUARTERLY
29553U82-164

Editorial Address: Great Clarendon Street, OXFORD, OX2 6DP **Tel:** 01865 267907
Email: jnls.cust.serv@oxfordjournals.org
Advertising Address: As above. **Tel:** 01865 353329
Email: jnlsadvertising@oxfordjournals.org
Web site: http://www.oup.co.uk/refqtl
ISSN: 1020-4067
Publisher: OUP
Date Established: 1982
Frequency: Quarterly
Annual Sub.: £119.00
Circulation: 700 (Publisher's Statement)
Usual Pagination: 232
Editor: Vincent Chetail; **Editor-in-Chief:** Vincent Chetail
Summary of Content: Publication containing country reports and literature and featuring articles on refugee and human rights and how they relate to legal documentation.
Language(s): English; French; Spanish
Readership/Target Audience: Aimed at NGOs and people with an interest in refugees and their problems.
ADVERTISING RATES:
Full Page Mono £270.00
Agency Commission: 10%
Mechanical Data: Type Area: 200 x 130mm, Col Length: 200mm, Page Width: 130mm, Film: Digital
CONSUMER: CURRENT AFFAIRS & POLITICS

THE REGISTER - NWR NATIONAL MAGAZINE
45217U74A-505

Editorial Address: 23 Vulcan House, Vulcan Road North, NORWICH, NR6 6AQ **Tel:** 01603 406767 **Fax:** 01603 407003
Email: office@nwr.org.uk
Advertising Address: As above. **Tel:** 0845 450 0287
Email: office@nwr.org.uk
Web site: http://www.nwr.org.uk

Publisher: National Women's Register
Date Established: 1966
Frequency: Half-yearly - Published in June and November
Free to qualifying individuals
Annual Sub.: £16.00
Circulation: 7,400 (Publisher's Statement)
Usual Pagination: 12
Editor: Mary Dodkins
Summary of Content: Magazine containing views and opinions of NWR members, reports on conferences and workshops, plus national stories of relevance to women.
Readership/Target Audience: Aimed at NWR members.
ADVERTISING RATES:
Full Page Colour £1000.00
Mechanical Data: Print Process: Offset litho, Type Area: 261 x 183mm, Col Length: 261mm, Page Width: 183mm
Copy instructions: Copy Date: End of cover month
Average advertising content per issue: 10%
CONSUMER: WOMEN'S INTEREST CONSUMER MAGAZINES: Women's Interest

RELAX
1696251U74Q-1280

Editorial Address: Publishing House, 3 Bridgebank Industrial Estate, Taylor Street, Horwich, BOLTON, BL6 7PD
Tel: 0161 909 0909 **Fax:** 0161 909 0919
Email: clive.entwistle@belfastcitylife.com
Advertising Address: As above.
Email: jeremy.bladon@bigspark.co.uk
Publisher: The Big Spark
Date Established: 2005
Frequency: Quarterly
Cover Price: £3.95
Free to qualifying individuals
Circulation: 40,000 (Publisher's Statement)
Usual Pagination: 100
Editor: Clive Entwistle; **Advertising Director:** Jeremy Bladon
Summary of Content: Lifestyle magazine covering fashion, hunting, shooting, fishing, high end travel and cars, boats and profiles of 5 star hotels.
Readership/Target Audience: Aimed at those staying in 5 star hotels around the world with a high net worth.
ADVERTISING RATES:
Full Page Mono £1950.00
Full Page Colour £2950.00
Agency Commission: 10%
Mechanical Data: Trim Size: 297 x 210mm, Film: Digital
Copy instructions: Copy Date: 8 weeks prior to publication date
Average advertising content per issue: 30%
CONSUMER: WOMEN'S INTEREST CONSUMER MAGAZINES: Lifestyle

RELIGIOUS STUDIES
1895915U87-2055

Editorial Address: Department of Theology & Religious Studies, University of London, King's College, LONDON, WC2R 2LS **Tel:** 01223 326070
Email: peter.byrne@kcl.ac.uk
Web site: http://journals.cambridge.org/action/displayJournal?jid=RES
Publisher: Cambridge University Press
Frequency: Quarterly
Annual Sub.: £56.00
Editor: P. Byrne
Summary of Content: Journal devoted to the problems of the philosophy of religion as they arrive out of classical and contemporary discussion and from varied religious traditions. Also contains an extensive book review section.
Readership/Target Audience: Aimed at religious studies students.
CONSUMER: RELIGIOUS

RENAISSANCE STUDIES
30829U94X-254

Editorial Address: 9600 Garsington Road, Cowley, OXFORD, OX4 2DQ **Tel:** 01865 776868 **Fax:** 01865 714591
Advertising Address: As above.
Email: craig.pickett@oxon.blackwellpublishing.com
Web site: http://www.blackwellpublishing.com/journals/rest
ISSN: 0269-1213
Publisher: Wiley-Blackwell Publishing
Date Established: 1987
Frequency: 5 issues yearly
Annual Sub.: £128.00
Circulation: 1,000 (Publisher's Statement)
Usual Pagination: 640
Editor: Andrew Hadfield; **Advertising Manager:** Craig Pickett
Summary of Content: Journal containing articles on all aspects of Renaissance history and culture, art, architecture and the languages of Europe during the Renaissance period.
Readership/Target Audience: Aimed at students and academics with an interest in the Renaissance period.
ADVERTISING RATES:
Full Page Mono £445.00
Agency Commission: 10%

Mechanical Data: Type Area: 190 x 112mm, Col Length: 190mm, Film: Digital, Page Width: 112mm
CONSUMER: OTHER CLASSIFICATIONS: Miscellaneous

THE RENAULT MAGAZINE
46475U77E-240

Editorial Address: The Courtyard, Ladycross Farm, Hollow Lane, Dormansland, LINGFIELD, RH7 6PB
Tel: 01342 870409
Email: vicky.stewart@streampublishing.net
Publisher: Stream Publishing Ltd
Frequency: Half-yearly
Cover Price: Free
Circulation: 209,891 (Publisher's Statement)
Usual Pagination: 96
Editor: Vicky Stewart; **Managing Director:** Darren Styles
Summary of Content: Magazine covering articles on Renault cars and light commercial vehicles, accessories, services, travel and leisure activities and lifestyle features.
Readership/Target Audience: Read by Renault owners and enthusiasts.
ADVERTISING: No Advertising taken
CONSUMER: MOTORING & CYCLING: Club Cars

REPERTOIRE
48133U89C-360

Editorial Address: Upper Floor, Finnieston House, 1 Stables Yard, 1103 Argyle Street, GLASGOW, G3 8ND
Tel: 0141 221 6965 **Fax:** 0141 221 6561
Email: gemma@mediaworldltd.com
Advertising Address: As above. **Fax:** 0141 221 7641
Email: lynne@mediaworldltd.com
Web site: http://www.barbrowser.co.uk
ISSN: 1470-2428
Publisher: Media World Ltd
Frequency: Monthly
Cover Price: £1.50
Free to qualifying individuals
Circulation: 8,500 (Publisher's Statement)
Usual Pagination: 40
Editor: Gemma Scott
Summary of Content: Magazine covering Scotland's bar and restaurant industry. Includes new products, venues, music, fashion and drinks.
Readership/Target Audience: Aimed at 18 to 35 year olds.
ADVERTISING RATES:
Full Page Colour £900.00
Agency Commission: 10%
Mechanical Data: Type Area: 225 x 178mm, Film: Digital, Col Length: 225mm, Page Width: 178mm
Copy instructions: Copy Date: 10th of the month prior to publication date
CONSUMER: HOLIDAYS & TRAVEL: Entertainment Guides

REPTILE CARE
1637557U81X-502

Editorial Address: 126-128 Gloucester Road North, Filton, BRISTOL, BS34 7BQ **Tel:** 0117 969 3013
Email: pb@reptilecare-magazine.co.uk
Advertising Address: Ad Ventures Worldwide, Inc, 1312 SE 32nd Street, CAPE CORAL, FL 33904 **Tel:** 239 542 8123
Fax: 239 542 7353
Email: reptilecare@aol.com
Web site: http://www.reptilecaremagazine.com
Publisher: Reptile Care UK Ltd
Date Established: 2003
Frequency: 6 issues yearly
Cover Price: £3.25
Annual Sub.: £16.00
Circulation: 20,000 (Publisher's Statement)
Usual Pagination: 100
Editor: Pete Blake; **Advertising Director:** Dana Roseberry
Summary of Content: Magazine containing advice on and care for reptiles of both commonly kept animals and their more exotic wild cousins.
Readership/Target Audience: Aimed at pet owners and professionals as well as specialist retailers of reptiles and pet shops.
ADVERTISING RATES:
Full Page Mono £795.00
Full Page Colour £795.00
Mechanical Data: Bleed Size: 303 x 216mm, Trim Size: 297 x 210mm, No. of Columns (Display): 3, Film: Digital
Copy instructions: Copy Date: 45 days prior to publication date
Average advertising content per issue: 20%
CONSUMER: ANIMALS & PETS

THE RESIDENT (LONDON)
46840U80B-173_50

Editorial Address: 5th Floor, Avon House, Kensington Village, Avonmore Road, LONDON, W14 8TS
Tel: 020 7605 2275
Email: amanda.constance@archant.co.uk
Advertising Address: As above. **Tel:** 020 7605 2200
Fax: 020 7605 2201
Email: amanda.ramsay@archant.co.uk
Web site: http://www.theresident.co.uk
Publisher: Archant Life

Date Established: 1993
Frequency: Monthly
Cover Price: Free
Circulation: 55,000 (Publisher's Statement)
Usual Pagination: 120
Editor: Amanda Constance
Summary of Content: Magazine covering all aspects of London life.
Readership/Target Audience: Aimed at residents in the Kensington, Chelsea and Central London areas.
ADVERTISING RATES:
Full Page Colour £1875.00
Agency Commission: 10%
Mechanical Data: Type Area: 280 x 210mm, Bleed Size: 306 x 236mm, Page Width: 210mm, Col Length: 280mm, Film: Digital, Trim Size: 300 x 230mm
Copy instructions: Copy Date: 1 week prior to publication date
Average advertising content per issue: 65%
CONSUMER: RURAL & REGIONAL INTEREST: Regional Interest Greater London

RESIDENTIAL ESSENTIALS
1685820U83-268

Editorial Address: 87 Loopland Drive, Castlereagh Road, BELFAST, BT6 9DW **Tel:** 028 9073 8008 **Fax:** 028 9045 5684
Email: gill@imagine8withus.com
Advertising Address: As above.
Email: gill@imagine8withus.com
Web site: http://www.imagine8withus.com
Publisher: Imagine 8 International Ltd
Date Established: 2005
Frequency: Annual - Published in July
Cover Price: Free
Circulation: 10,000 (Publisher's Statement)
Usual Pagination: 52
Editor: Garath Kennedy
Summary of Content: Magazine covering accommodation for students, student life, events and university news.
Readership/Target Audience: Aimed at students at the University of Ulster.
ADVERTISING RATES:
Full Page Mono £700.00
Full Page Colour £700.00
Agency Commission: 10%
Mechanical Data: Bleed Size: +4mm, Print Process: Litho, Type Area: 210 x 148mm, Col Length: 210mm, Page Width: 148mm, Film: Digital
Copy instructions: Copy Date: 30th July
Average advertising content per issue: 45%
CONSUMER: STUDENT PUBLICATIONS

RESURGENCE
48712U94X-148

Editorial Address: Ford House, Hartland, BIDEFORD, EX39 6EE **Tel:** 01237 441293 **Fax:** 01237 441203
Email: editorial@resurgence.org
Advertising Address: As above.
Email: advert@resurgence.org
Web site: http://www.resurgence.org
ISSN: 0034-5970
Publisher: Resurgence Ltd
Date Established: 1966
Frequency: 6 issues yearly
Cover Price: £4.95
Annual Sub.: £30.00
Circulation: 12,000 (Publisher's Statement)
Usual Pagination: 72
Editor: Lorna Howarth; **Advertising Manager:** Gwydion Batten
Summary of Content: Holistic magazine specialising in ecology, sustainability and spirituality.
Readership/Target Audience: Aimed at those interested in ecology and sustainable living.
ADVERTISING RATES:
Full Page Mono £960.00
Full Page Colour £1104.00
Mechanical Data: Type Area: 276 x 188mm, Col Length: 276mm, Trim Size: 297 x 210mm, Page Width: 188mm, Film: Digital, No. of Columns (Display): 3
Copy instructions: Copy Date: 8 weeks prior to publication date
Average advertising content per issue: 15%
CONSUMER: OTHER CLASSIFICATIONS: Miscellaneous

RETAIL THERAPY
1665708U88C-169

Editorial Address: Northcliffe House, 2 Derry Street, LONDON, W8 5TT **Tel:** 020 7005 2000 **Fax:** 020 7005 2273
Email: retailtherapy@independent.co.uk
Advertising Address: As above. **Tel:** 020 7005 2283
Fax: 020 7005 2922
Email: p.watkins@independent.co.uk
Web site: http://www.independent.co.uk
Publisher: Independent News and Media (UK) Ltd
Frequency: Half-yearly
Cover Price: Free
Circulation: 10,000 (Publisher's Statement)
Usual Pagination: 36

Editor: Dan Poole; **Advertising Manager:** Philippa Watkins
Summary of Content: Lifestyle magazine encouraging young people to get a career in the retail sector, career information and advice.
Readership/Target Audience: Aimed at school leavers aged 16 plus and career centres.
ADVERTISING RATES:
Full Page Colour £3480.00
Mechanical Data: Type Area: 280 x 210mm, Col Length: 280mm, Page Width: 210mm, Film: Digital
CONSUMER: EDUCATION: Careers

RETRO FORD
1745157U77E-521

Editorial Address: Becket House, Vestry Road, SEVENOAKS, TN14 5EJ **Tel:** 01732 748000
Fax: 01732 748001
Email: bmorley@unity-media.com
Advertising Address: As above.
Email: snorwood@unity-media.com
Web site: http://www.unity-media.co.uk
Publisher: Unity Media plc
Date Established: 2006
Frequency: Monthly
Cover Price: £3.95
Annual Sub.: £38.00
Circulation: 60,000 (Print Run)
Usual Pagination: 140
Editor: Ben Morley; **Features Editor:** James Gambles;
Advertising Manager: Sarah Norwood
Summary of Content: Magazine covering modified street and track, pre 1980s Ford cars.
Readership/Target Audience: Aimed at enthusiasts of classic Fords.
ADVERTISING RATES:
Full Page Colour £950.00
Mechanical Data: Type Area: 266 x 190mm, Bleed Size: 303 x 216mm, Trim Size: 297 x 210mm, Col Length: 266mm, Page Width: 190mm, Film: Digital
Copy instructions: Copy Date: 4 weeks prior to publication date
Average advertising content per issue: 30%
CONSUMER: MOTORING & CYCLING: Club Cars

RETRO GAMER
1641401U78D-324

Editorial Address: Richmond House, 33 Richmond Hill, BOURNEMOUTH, BH2 6E **Tel:** 01202 586200
Email: darran.jones@imagine-publishing.co.uk
Advertising Address: As above.
Email: ben.taylor@imagine-publishing.co.uk
Web site: http://www.retrogamer.net
Publisher: Imagine Publishing
Date Established: 2004
Frequency: 13 issues yearly
Cover Price: £4.99
Circulation: 25,000 (Publisher's Statement)
Usual Pagination: 116
Editor: Darran Jones; **Editor-in-Chief:** Nick Jones
Summary of Content: Magazine covering classic games, computers and consoles.
Readership/Target Audience: Aimed at predominantly male, 20 to 35 year old, retro games enthusiasts.
ADVERTISING RATES:
Full Page Colour £3200.00
Agency Commission: 10%
Mechanical Data: Film: Digital, Type Area: 275 x 210mm, Bleed Size: 303 x 236mm, Trim Size: 297 x 230mm, Col Length: 275mm, Page Width: 210mm
Copy instructions: Copy Date: 4 weeks prior to publication date
Average advertising content per issue: 15%
CONSUMER: CONSUMER ELECTRONICS: Games

THE RETURN OF MARES
47150U81D-357

Editorial Address: Sanders Road, Finedon Road Industrial Estate, WELLINGBOROUGH, NN8 4BX **Tel:** 01933 440077
Fax: 01933 304758
Advertising Address: As above. **Fax:** 01933 304785
Email: scheney@weatherbys.co.uk
Publisher: Weatherbys Ventures Ltd
Date Established: 1971
Frequency: Annual - Published in November
Cover Price: £40.00
Circulation: 1,000 (Publisher's Statement)
Editor: Di Harvey; **Advertising Manager:** Steve Cheney
Summary of Content: Journal containing foaling results of thoroughbred and non-thoroughbred mares.
Readership/Target Audience: Aimed at racehorse breeders.
ADVERTISING RATES:
Full Page Mono £400.00
Full Page Colour £700.00
Agency Commission: 15%
Mechanical Data: Col Length: 273mm, Type Area: 273 x 175mm, Bleed Size: 303 x 216mm, Screen: Mono 54 lpc Colour 70 lpc, Print Process: Litho, Film: Positive, right

reading, emulsion side down, Trim Size: 297 x 210mm, Page Width: 175mm
Copy instructions: Copy Date: October 13th
CONSUMER: ANIMALS & PETS: Horses & Ponies

REVEAL
1649843U74A-973

Formerly: Project Buzz
Editorial Address: National Magazine House, 33 Broadwick Street, LONDON, W1F 0DQ **Tel:** 020 7439 5000
Fax: 020 7339 4529
Email: rosalind.sack@natmags.co.uk
Advertising Address: As above. **Tel:** 020 7339 4566
Fax: 020 7439 5595
Email: jessica.cain@natmags.co.uk
Web site: http://www.revealblog.co.uk
Publisher: National Magazine Company Ltd
Date Established: 2004
Frequency: Weekly
Cover Price: £0.99
Circulation: 315,660 (ABC 01/01/2009 to 30/06/2009)
Usual Pagination: 100
Editor: Rosalind Sack; **Features Editor:** Nicole Carmichael
Summary of Content: Magazine covering celebrities real-life stories, fashion, beauty, travel, cookery and television listings.
Readership/Target Audience: Aimed at women aged 20 to 40 years old.
ADVERTISING RATES:
Full Page Colour £15570.00
Agency Commission: 10%
Mechanical Data: Type Area: 283 x 204mm, Col Length: 283mm, Page Width: 204mm, Bleed Size: 306 x 228mm, Trim Size: 300 x 222mm, Film: Digital
Copy instructions: Copy Date: 5 days prior to publication date
Average advertising content per issue: 20%
CONSUMER: WOMEN'S INTEREST CONSUMER MAGAZINES: Women's Interest

REVERBERATIONS
46588U79R-156

Editorial Address: 87 The Woodfields, Sanderstead, SOUTH CROYDON, CR2 0HJ **Tel:** 020 8651 2663
Fax: 020 8651 2663
Email: info@hrgb.org.uk
Advertising Address: Gilman House, Swinscoe, Ashbourne, DERBY, DE6 2BW **Tel:** 01335 300506
Web site: http://www.hrgb.org
ISSN: 0263-452X
Publisher: Handbell Ringers of Great Britain
Frequency: Half-yearly - Published in April and September
Annual Sub.: £7.00
Circulation: 3,200 (Publisher's Statement)
Usual Pagination: 90
Editor: Sandra Winter; **Advertising Manager:** Lindsay Trevarthen
Summary of Content: Publication containing news and articles on hand-bell ringing from a small set of 1.5 diatonic octaves to a full set of 6 octaves, and from a standard staff notation to a tablature system.
Readership/Target Audience: Aimed at those interested in playing music on hand-bells.
ADVERTISING RATES:
Full Page Mono £60.00
Mechanical Data: Type Area: 190 x 128.5mm, Trim Size: 210 x 148.5mm, Col Length: 190mm, Col Widths (Display): 58mm, No. of Columns (Display): 2, Page Width: 128.5mm, Film: Positive, right reading, emulsion side down. Digital, Print Process: Offset litho
Average advertising content per issue: 17%
CONSUMER: HOBBIES & DIY: Hobbies & DIY Related

REVIEW OF INTERNATIONAL STUDIES
47274U82-165

Editorial Address: Department of International Relations, University of St. Andrews, ST. ANDREWS, KY16 9AL
Email: njr3@st-andrews.ac.uk
Advertising Address: The Edinburgh Building, Shaftesbury Road, CAMBRIDGE, CB2 2RU **Tel:** 01223 326070
Fax: 01223 325150
Email: ad_sales@cambridge.org
Web site: http://journals.cambridge.org/jid_ris
ISSN: 0260-2105
Publisher: Cambridge University Press
Date Established: 1975
Frequency: Quarterly - Special issue in December
Annual Sub.: £49.00
Circulation: 1,700 (Publisher's Statement)
Usual Pagination: 176
Editor: Nick Rengger
Summary of Content: Official journal of The British International Studies Association, promoting the analysis and understanding of international relations and international politics.
Readership/Target Audience: Aimed at students and scholars interested in every aspect of international studies.

ADVERTISING RATES:
Full Page Mono £465.00
Mechanical Data: Page Width: 135mm, Type Area: 200 x 135mm, Col Length: 200mm; Film: Digital
Copy instructions: Copy Date: 8 weeks prior to publication date
CONSUMER: CURRENT AFFAIRS & POLITICS

RHYTHM
46179U76D-398
Editorial Address: 30 Monmouth Street, BATH, BA1 2BW
Tel: 01225 442244 **Fax:** 01225 732353
Email: phil.ascott@futurenet.com
Advertising Address: As above. **Fax:** 01225 7322206
Email: tweeks@futurenet.co.uk
Web site: http://www.futurenet.co.uk
Publisher: Future Publishing Ltd
Date Established: 1985
Frequency: 13 issues yearly
Cover Price: £4.75
Circulation: 9,472 (ABC 01/01/2008 to 31/12/2008)
Usual Pagination: 116
Editor: Christopher Barnes; **Publisher:** Rob Last
Summary of Content: Drum and percussion magazine containing comprehensive features, technique articles, gear reviews and interviews with famous and up and coming drummers. Comes complete with tuitional Rhythm CD.
Readership/Target Audience: Aimed at percussionists, drummers and drum programmers.
ADVERTISING RATES:
Full Page Colour £1235.00
Agency Commission: 10%
Mechanical Data: Film: Digital, Page Width: 190mm, Type Area: 270 x 190mm, Trim Size: 297 x 210mm, Bleed Size: 303 x 216mm, Col Length: 270mm
CONSUMER: MUSIC & PERFORMING ARTS: Music

RIB INTERNATIONAL
48385U91A-112
Editorial Address: Oyster House, Hunters Lodge, Kentisbeare, CULLOMPTON, EX15 2DY **Tel:** 01884 266100
Fax: 01884 266101
Email: hms@ribmagazine.com
Advertising Address: As above.
Email: neil@ribmagazine.com
Web site: http://www.ribmagazine.com
ISSN: 1360-9408
Publisher: RIB International Ltd
Date Established: 1994
Frequency: 6 issues yearly
Cover Price: £3.95
Circulation: 10,000 (Publisher's Statement)
Usual Pagination: 100
Editor: Hugo Montgomery-Swan; **Managing Director:** Hugo Montgomery-Swan
Summary of Content: Magazine dedicated to all aspects of the rigid inflatable boat.
Readership/Target Audience: Aimed at those with an interest in rigid inflatable boats and their worldwide market.
ADVERTISING RATES:
Full Page Colour £1350.00
Agency Commission: 10%
Mechanical Data: Type Area: 262 x 184mm, Col Length: 262mm, Page Width: 184mm
Copy instructions: Copy Date: 1st of the month prior to publication date
CONSUMER: RECREATION & LEISURE: Boating & Yachting

THE RICHMOND MAGAZINE
46841U80B-174
Editorial Address: Unit A4, Kingsway Business Park, Oldfield Road, HAMPTON, TW12 2HD **Tel:** 020 8939 5601
Fax: 020 8941 7615
Email: editorial@sheengate.co.uk
Advertising Address: As above. **Tel:** 020 8939 5600
Fax: 020 8939 5610
Email: richmond@sheengate.co.uk
Web site: http://www.sheengate.co.uk
Publisher: Sheengate Publishing Ltd
Date Established: 1998
Frequency: Monthly
Cover Price: Free
Circulation: 32,000 (Publisher's Statement)
Usual Pagination: 72
Editor: Richard Nye; **Advertising Manager:** Terry Hayden
Summary of Content: Magazine containing mainly lifestyle and local interest articles. Includes features on fashion, beauty, art, history, motoring, property and interviews.
Readership/Target Audience: Aimed at households in the London Borough of Richmond.
ADVERTISING RATES:
Full Page Colour £1155.00
Agency Commission: 10%
Mechanical Data: Type Area: 270 x 180mm, Bleed Size: 307 x 230mm, Trim Size: 297 x 210mm, Col Length: 270mm, Page Width: 180mm, Film: Digital
Copy instructions: Copy Date: 2 weeks prior to publication date

---

Average advertising content per issue: 65%
CONSUMER: RURAL & REGIONAL INTEREST: Regional Interest Greater London

---

RICKMANSWORTH EXCLUSIVE
1892642U80C-5489
Editorial Address: For all contact details see main edition, Exclusive (Chilterns)
Frequency: 10 issues yearly
Cover Price: Free
Circulation: 5,000 (Publisher's Statement)
ADVERTISING: Rates on application
Edition of: Exclusive (Chilterns)
CONSUMER: RURAL & REGIONAL INTEREST: Regional Interest English Counties

---

RIDE
46373U77B-592
Editorial Address: Media House, Lynchwood, Peterborough Business Park, PETERBOROUGH, PE2 6EA
Tel: 01733 468081 **Fax:** 01733 468092
Email: ride@bauermedia.co.uk
Advertising Address: As above. **Tel:** 01733 468000
Fax: 01733 468867
Email: sarah.nunn@bauerconsumer.co.uk
Web site: http://www.ride.co.uk
Publisher: Bauer Consumer Media Ltd (Media House)
Date Established: 1995
Frequency: Monthly
Cover Price: £3.80
Circulation: 45,844 (ABC 01/01/2008 to 31/12/2008)
Usual Pagination: 148
Editor: Emma Franklin; **Advertising Manager:** Sarah Nunn
Summary of Content: Magazine with features on new and used motorcycles and product tests. Provides information on how to get the best value out of a motorcycle.
Readership/Target Audience: Aimed at motorcycle enthusiasts.
ADVERTISING RATES:
Full Page Colour £3024.00
Agency Commission: 10%
Mechanical Data: Type Area: 267 x 181mm, Col Length: 267mm, Bleed Size: 303 x 220mm, Trim Size: 297 x 210mm, Page Width: 181mm, Film: Digital
Copy instructions: Copy Date: 4 weeks prior to publication date
Average advertising content per issue: 30%
CONSUMER: MOTORING & CYCLING: Motorcycling

RIDE BMX MAGAZINE
46406U77C-851
Editorial Address: 1 West Smithfield, LONDON, EC1A 9JU
Tel: 07968 238371
Advertising Address: As above. **Tel:** 020 7332 9700
Fax: 020 7332 9799
Email: ian.gunner@factorymedia.com
Web site: http://www.4130.com
Publisher: Factory Media Ltd
Date Established: 1992
Frequency: Monthly
Cover Price: £3.20
Annual Sub.: £24.50
Circulation: 56,250 (Publisher's Statement)
Usual Pagination: 196
Editor: Steve Bancroft; **Advertising Manager:** Ian Gunner
Summary of Content: Magazine covering all aspects of BMX riding, bicycle freestyle, dirt jumping and street riding. Coverage of events worldwide, interviews, riders, road trips, bike tests and product reviews.
Readership/Target Audience: Aimed at BMX riders between 10 to 30 years old.
ADVERTISING: Rates on application
Agency Commission: 10%
Copy instructions: Copy Date: 6 weeks prior to publication date
Average advertising content per issue: 45%
CONSUMER: MOTORING & CYCLING: Cycling

RIDERS
718217U81D-330
Formerly: West Country Riders
Editorial Address: Temple Way, BRISTOL, BS99 7HD
Tel: 0117 934 3000
Email: k.edser@bepp.co.uk
Advertising Address: As above. **Tel:** 0117 934 3434
Fax: 0117 934 3755
Email: t.dyer@bepp.co.uk
Web site: http://www.westerndailypress.co.uk/riders
Publisher: Bristol News and Media
Date Established: 1998
Frequency: Weekly
Cover Price: £0.40
Circulation: 54,000 (Publisher's Statement)
Usual Pagination: 12
Editor: Kate Edser
Summary of Content: Magazine covering all aspects of equestrianism in the West Country including reports on local

---

shows, rider interviews, training tips, news and competitions.
Readership/Target Audience: Aimed at horse owners in the region.
ADVERTISING RATES:
Full Page Colour £1000.00
Agency Commission: 10%
Mechanical Data: Film: Digital
Average advertising content per issue: 50%
Supplement to: Western Daily Press Bristol
CONSUMER: ANIMALS & PETS: Horses & Ponies

RIDGEWAY RIDER
1698879U81D-366
Editorial Address: Unit 2, Devizes Trade Centre, Hopton Park, DEVIZES, SN10 2EH **Tel:** 0845 644 2236
Fax: 0845 430 8678
Email: sales@redpin.co.uk
Advertising Address: As above. **Fax:** 01380 730899
Email: lisadure@redpin.co.uk
Web site: http://www.redpin.co.uk
Publisher: Redpin Publishing Ltd
Frequency: Monthly
Cover Price: Free
Circulation: 15,000 (Publisher's Statement)
Editor: Sara Haines
Summary of Content: Magazine covering all-round equestrian interests and disciplines, feature articles, product reviews and events.
Readership/Target Audience: Aimed at riders in South West England.
ADVERTISING: Rates on application
CONSUMER: ANIMALS & PETS: Horses & Ponies

RIGHT START
45344U74D-500
Editorial Address: 9 Savoy Street, LONDON, WC2E 7HR
Tel: 020 7878 2338 **Fax:** 020 7379 6261
Email: lynette.lowthian@tenalpspublishing.com
ISSN: 0957-3704
Publisher: Ten Alps Publishing
Date Established: 1989
Frequency: 6 issues yearly
Cover Price: £2.50
Annual Sub.: £10.90
Circulation: 56,000 (Publisher's Statement)
Usual Pagination: 76
Editor: Lynette Lowthian; **Publisher:** Tony Morbin
Summary of Content: Magazine covering advice on health, behaviour, child development and learning at home and school.
Readership/Target Audience: Aimed at parents with children aged 6 months to 7 years.
ADVERTISING: No Advertising taken
Supplement(s): The Best Toy Guide - 1xY
CONSUMER: WOMEN'S INTEREST CONSUMER MAGAZINES: Child Care

RINGING & MIGRATION
47173U81F-300
Editorial Address: The Nunnery, THETFORD, IP24 2PU
Tel: 01842 750050 **Fax:** 01842 750030
Email: ringing@bto.org
Web site: http://www.bto.org
ISSN: 0307-8698
Publisher: BTO
Date Established: 1975
Frequency: Half-yearly - Published in June and December
Annual Sub.: £13.50
Circulation: 2,500 (Publisher's Statement)
Usual Pagination: 88
Editor: Chris Redfern; **Managing Editor:** Jacquie Clark
Summary of Content: Magazine consisting of ornithological papers and reviews pertinent to the ringing and migration of birds.
Readership/Target Audience: Aimed at amateur and professional ornithologists.
ADVERTISING: No Advertising taken
CONSUMER: ANIMALS & PETS: Birds

THE RINGING WORLD
48715U94X-150
Editorial Address: Eagleside House, 7-9 Chantry Street, ANDOVER, SP10 1DE **Tel:** 01264 366620
Fax: 01264 360594
Email: editor@ringingworld.co.uk
Advertising Address: As above.
Email: notices@ringingworld.co.uk
Web site: http://www.ringingworld.co.uk
Publisher: The Ringing World Ltd
Date Established: 1911
Frequency: Weekly
Cover Price: £1.60
Annual Sub.: £52.00
Circulation: 4,000 (Publisher's Statement)
Usual Pagination: 24
Editor: Robert Lewis; **Advertising Manager:** Chris Darvill

Summary of Content: Magazine of the Central Council of Church Bell Ringers. Includes news, peal reports, safety issues and events.
Readership/Target Audience: Read by church bell ringers.
ADVERTISING RATES:
Full Page Mono £416.93
Full Page Colour £722.93
Mechanical Data: Col Length: 255mm, No. of Columns (Display): 3, Col Widths (Display): 59mm
Copy instructions: Copy Date: Thursday 9am 15 days prior to publication date
Average advertising content per issue: 5%
CONSUMER: OTHER CLASSIFICATIONS: Miscellaneous

RIPPLE
47435U83-68
Editorial Address: Percy Gee Building, University of Leicester, University Road, LEICESTER, LE1 7RH
Tel: 0116 223 1216 **Fax:** 0116 223 1112
Email: ripple@le.ac.uk
Advertising Address: As above. **Fax:** 0116 223 1150
Email: ai40@le.ac.uk
Web site: http://www.leicesterstudent.org/pages/groups_and_sports/media/the_ripple.html
Publisher: University of Leicester Students Union
Date Established: 1957
Frequency: Monthly - Published fortnightly during term time
Cover Price: Free
Circulation: 4,000 (Publisher's Statement)
Usual Pagination: 48
Editor: Emily Key
Summary of Content: Newspaper including news, features and sport. Includes sections covering film, arts, music and listings.
Readership/Target Audience: Read by University of Leicester students and staff.
ADVERTISING RATES:
Full Page Colour £600.00
CONSUMER: STUDENT PUBLICATIONS

THE RITZ
625429U89B-330
Editorial Address: Oyster Wharf, 18 Lombard Road, Battersea, LONDON, SW11 3RR **Tel:** 020 7223 6331
Fax: 020 7223 9206
Email: juliane@ifpr.co.uk
Advertising Address: New Barn, Fanhams Grange, Fanhams Hall Road, WARE, SG12 7QA **Tel:** 01920 467492
Fax: 01920 460149
Email: deborah@fms.co.uk
Publisher: FMS Publishing
Date Established: 2000
Frequency: Half-yearly - Published in June and December
Cover Price: Free
Circulation: 41,000 (Publisher's Statement)
Usual Pagination: 100
Editor: Juliane Fischer; **Managing Editor:** Ann Marie McGrath
Summary of Content: Magazine covering travel information, gambling, design, fashion, style, motoring, business, technology and food and drink.
Readership/Target Audience: Read by visitors to The Ritz Hotel. Also mailed internationally to all members of the Ritz Club as well as selected individuals.
ADVERTISING RATES:
Full Page Colour £7175.00
Mechanical Data: Col Length: 315mm, Page Width: 230mm, Type Area: 315 x 230mm, Bleed Size: 331 x 246mm, Trim Size: 325 x 240mm, Film: Digital
Copy instructions: Copy Date: 4 weeks prior to publication date
CONSUMER: HOLIDAYS & TRAVEL: Hotel Magazines

ROAD RACING IRELAND
1693632U77B-714
Editorial Address: 26 The Oaks, NEWTOWNARDS, BT23 8GZ **Tel:** 028 9182 8211 **Fax:** 028 9182 7463
Email: info@roadracingireland.com
Advertising Address: As above. **Tel:** 028 9042 5777
Fax: 028 9042 5888
Email: info@roadracingireland.com
Web site: http://www.roadracingireland.com
ISSN: 0960-6424
Publisher: Rollins Promotions Ltd
Frequency: 11 issues yearly
Cover Price: £3.95
Circulation: 32,000 (Publisher's Statement)
Editor: Leslie Moore; **Advertising Director:** Gillian Rollins
Summary of Content: Magazine covering major motorcycle road races as well as in-depth interviews with top riders, product reviews and results.
Readership/Target Audience: Aimed at motorcycle racing fans.
ADVERTISING RATES:
Full Page Colour £2095.00
Agency Commission: 10%
Mechanical Data: Type Area: 272 x 190mm, Bleed Size: 303 x 213mm, Trim Size: 297 x 210mm, Col Length: 272mm, Page Width: 190mm, Film: Digital

Copy instructions: Copy Date: 2 weeks prior to publication date
CONSUMER: MOTORING & CYCLING: Motorcycling

ROAD RECORD
46334U77A-395
Editorial Address: One Central Quay, GLASGOW, G3 8DA
Tel: 0141 309 3000 **Fax:** 0141 309 3340
Email: b.caven@dailyrecord.co.uk
Advertising Address: As above.
Email: d.giblin@dailyrecord.co.uk
Web site: http://www.dailyrecord.co.uk
Publisher: Trinity Mirror
Frequency: Weekly - Published on Fridays
Circulation: 561,419 (Publisher's Statement)
Usual Pagination: 36
Editor: Bill Caven; **Advertising Manager:** Danny Giblin
Summary of Content: Magazine covering general motoring issues including product testing of accessories and motorcycle wear.
Readership/Target Audience: Aimed at those with an interest in cars and motorcycles.
ADVERTISING RATES:
Full Page Mono £14490.00
Full Page Colour £18846.00
SCC £53.30
Agency Commission: 15%
Mechanical Data: Type Area: 340 x 265mm, Col Length: 340mm, No. of Columns (Display): 7, Page Width: 265mm, Film: Digital
Average advertising content per issue: 70%
Supplement to: Daily Record
CONSUMER: MOTORING & CYCLING: Motoring

ROCHDALE STYLE
1840311U80C-5446
Editorial Address: 26 Sandown Road, Hazel Grove, STOCKPORT, SK7 4SH **Tel:** 0161 483 1790
Email: colin@rochdalestyle.com
Advertising Address: 115 Shawclough Way, ROCHDALE, OL12 6EE **Tel:** 01706 710810
Email: advertising@rochdalestyle.com
Web site: http://www.rochdalestyle.com
Publisher: EM & EN Media
Frequency: Quarterly
Cover Price: Free
Circulation: 30,000 (Publisher's Statement)
Usual Pagination: 64
Summary of Content: Magazine covering lifestyle, fashion, eating out, local sport, what's on and features about Rochdale.
Readership/Target Audience: Aimed at residents of Rochdale and the surrounding areas.
ADVERTISING RATES:
Full Page Colour £750.00
CONSUMER: RURAL & REGIONAL INTEREST: Regional Interest English Counties

ROCHESTER LINK
601139U87-201
Editorial Address: 57 Neal Road, West Kingsdown, SEVENOAKS, TN15 6DG **Tel:** 01474 852474
Email: link@church-media.co.uk
Advertising Address: 57 Century Road, Rainham, GILLINGHAM, ME8 0BQ **Tel:** 01634 401611
Fax: 01634 306368
Email: m.silver@breathe.com
Web site: http://www.church-media.co.uk
Publisher: Kent Christian Press
Date Established: 1991
Frequency: 10 issues yearly - Published on the last week of the month except January and August
Cover Price: Free
Circulation: 20,000 (Publisher's Statement)
Usual Pagination: 12
Editor: Bryan Harris; **Advertising Manager:** Mike Silver
Summary of Content: Church of England newspaper covering news, listings and book reviews relevant to churchgoers. Also contains articles featuring community issues of relevance.
Readership/Target Audience: Aimed at churchgoers within the Diocese of Rochester.
ADVERTISING: Rates on application
CONSUMER: RELIGIOUS

ROCK SOUND
46257U76E-315_50
Editorial Address: Unit 22, Jack's Place, 6 Corbet Place, LONDON, E1 6NN **Tel:** 020 7877 8770 **Fax:** 020 7377 0455
Email: darren.taylor@rock-sound.net
Advertising Address: As above. **Tel:** 020 7873 0455
Email: ben.crudgington@rock-sound.net
Web site: http://www.rocksound.tv
Publisher: Rock Sound Ltd
Date Established: 1999
Frequency: 13 issues yearly
Cover Price: £3.60

Annual Sub.: £29.97
Circulation: 20,011 (ABC 01/07/2008 to 31/12/2008)
Usual Pagination: 132
Editor: Darren Taylor; **News Editor:** Darren Sadler;
Features Editor: Darren Sadler; **Advertising Manager:** Ben Crudgington; **Publisher:** Patrick Napier
Summary of Content: Magazine concentrating on rock, metal, indie and alternative music. Includes the latest news and features, album, single, live reviews and fashion related items.
Readership/Target Audience: Aimed at 15 to 24 year olds with a passion for music and the lifestyle associated with it.
ADVERTISING RATES:
Full Page Colour £1815.00
Agency Commission: 10%
Mechanical Data: Page Width: 190mm, Type Area: 277 x 190mm, Col Length: 277mm, Trim Size: 297 x 210mm, Bleed Size: 303 x 216mm, Film: Digital, Print Process: Web-fed offset litho
Copy instructions: Copy Date: 4 weeks prior to publication date
Average advertising content per issue: 23%
CONSUMER: MUSIC & PERFORMING ARTS: Pop Music

ROCK'N'REEL
1793870U76D-827
Editorial Address: PO Box 38, CLEATOR MOOR, CA25 5WA **Tel:** 01946 812496
Email: sean.mcg1@btinternet.com
Advertising Address: Derw Mill North, Pentre-Cwrt, LLANDYSUL, SA44 5DB **Tel:** 01559 363190
Fax: 01559 363186
Email: joan@rock-n-reel.co.uk
Web site: http://www.rock-n-reel.co.uk
Publisher: Hand to Mouth Publishing Ltd
Date Established: 1988
Frequency: 6 issues yearly
Cover Price: £4.25
Circulation: 10,000 (Publisher's Statement)
Usual Pagination: 100
Editor: Sean McGhee; **Advertising Manager:** Joan Franclova
Summary of Content: Magazine covering up-and-coming acts alongside respected artists across a broad range of music genres with interviews with groups, performers, singers and songwriters as well as reviews of albums, DVDs, books and live events.
Readership/Target Audience: Aimed predominantly at men aged 35 to 55 years old who go to festivals and buy CDs.
ADVERTISING RATES:
Full Page Colour £800.00
Mechanical Data: Type Area: 277 x 190mm, Bleed Size: 309 x 222mm, Trim Size: 297 x 210mm, Col Length: 277mm, Page Width: 190mm, Film: Digital
Average advertising content per issue: 20%
CONSUMER: MUSIC & PERFORMING ARTS: Music

THE ROSE
48571U93-150
Editorial Address: Articulate Studio, 14c North Street, EMSWORTH, PO10 7DG **Tel:** 01243 374523
Fax: 01243 378194
Email: mjsis@waitrose.com
Advertising Address: As above.
Web site: http://www.rosesociety.org.uk
ISSN: 0951-0982
Publisher: The Royal National Rose Society
Frequency: Quarterly
Free to qualifying individuals
Circulation: 8,000 (Publisher's Statement)
Usual Pagination: 32
Editor: Marilyn Stevens; **Advertising Manager:** Marilyn Stevens
Summary of Content: Publication featuring general interest articles on roses, plus show reports, book reviews and competitions.
Readership/Target Audience: Read by members of the Royal National Rose Society.
ADVERTISING: Rates on application
Agency Commission: 10%
Average advertising content per issue: 20%
CONSUMER: GARDENING

ROSEMARY CONLEY DIET & FITNESS MAGAZINE
45444U74G-44
Editorial Address: Quorn House, Meeting Street, Quorn, LOUGHBOROUGH, LE12 8EX **Tel:** 01509 620444
Fax: 01509 620555
Email: magazine@rosemaryconley.com
Advertising Address: 36 St Albans Crescent, LONDON, N22 5NB **Tel:** 020 8881 2521
Email: diana@dianadavid.co.uk
Web site: http://www.rosemaryconley.com
Publisher: Quorn House Publishing Ltd
Date Established: 1996
Frequency: 9 issues yearly
Cover Price: £2.55
Annual Sub.: £19.99

Consumer Magazines

Circulation: 108,716 (Publisher's Statement)
Usual Pagination: 112
Editor: Nicky Dorril; **Editor-in-Chief:** Rosemary Conley;
Advertising Manager: Diana David
Summary of Content: Magazine covering articles on diet, health, fitness and beauty.
Readership/Target Audience: Aimed at women interested in diet, fitness and improving their image.
ADVERTISING RATES:
Full Page Colour £6500.00
Agency Commission: 10%
Mechanical Data: Film: Digital, Trim Size: 275 x 195mm, Bleed Size: 283 x 203mm, Type Area: 241 x 160mm, Col Length: 241mm, Page Width: 160mm
Copy instructions: Copy Date: 1 month prior to publication date
Average advertising content per issue: 20%
CONSUMER: WOMEN'S INTEREST CONSUMER MAGAZINES: Slimming & Health

ROSSENDALE PROPERTY NEWS

762869U74K-661

Editorial Address: Banner House, Briar Close, EVESHAM, WR11 4XA **Tel:** 01386 765832 **Fax:** 01386 40650
Email: sara@ppsprint.co.uk
Advertising Address: As above. **Fax:** 01386 49164
Email: info@rossendalehomes.co.uk
Web site: http://www.rossendalehomes.co.uk
Publisher: PPS
Date Established: 2001
Frequency: Monthly
Cover Price: Free
Circulation: 10,000 (Publisher's Statement)
Usual Pagination: 20
Editor: Vernon Pethard; **Advertising Manager:** Sara Cresswell
Summary of Content: Publication covering local news and features homes to buy and let.
Readership/Target Audience: Aimed at homebuyers, renters and sellers.
ADVERTISING: Rates on application
Copy instructions: Copy Date: 5 days prior to publication date
Average advertising content per issue: 90%
CONSUMER: WOMEN'S INTEREST CONSUMER MAGAZINES: Home Purchase

ROTHWELL AND DISTRICT RECORD

1745158U80C-5334

Editorial Address: 19 Marsh Street, Rothwell, LEEDS, LS26 0AG **Tel:** 0113 282 6661 **Fax:** 0113 288 7429
Email: news@rothwellrecord.co.uk
Web site: http://www.rothwellrecord.co.uk
Publisher: Stephen Ward Photography (Leeds) Ltd
Frequency: 11 issues yearly
Cover Price: £1.20
Circulation: 4,500 (Publisher's Statement)
Editor: Pam Gamble
Summary of Content: Magazine covering local services, entertainment, events, sport, fundraising and the environment.
Readership/Target Audience: Aimed at residents and visitors to Rothwell and the surrounding areas.
ADVERTISING: No Advertising taken
CONSUMER: RURAL & REGIONAL INTEREST: Regional Interest English Counties

ROUND & ABOUT OXFORDSHIRE

46958U80C-2640

Editorial Address: The Old Coach House, The Street, Crowmarsh Gifford, WALLINGFORD, OX10 8EH
Tel: 01491 837621 **Fax:** 01491 826809
Email: psavage@roundandabout.co.uk
Advertising Address: As above.
Email: sales@roundandabout.co.uk
Web site: http://www.roundandabout.co.uk
Publisher: Round and About Publications Ltd.
Date Established: 1994
Frequency: Monthly
Cover Price: Free
Circulation: 136,000 (Publisher's Statement)
Usual Pagination: 64
Editor: Peter Savage; **Managing Director:** Peter Savage;
Advertising Manager: Luke Maitland; **Publisher:** Peter Savage
Summary of Content: County magazine featuring the highlights of living in Oxfordshire. Includes articles on fashion, travel and what's on in the local area.
Readership/Target Audience: Aimed at those living in the South Oxfordshire, North Berks and West Bucks area.
ADVERTISING RATES:
Full Page Colour £3500.00
Agency Commission: 10%
Mechanical Data: Trim Size: 220 x 165mm, Type Area: 210 x 155mm, Film: Digital, Col Length: 210mm, Page Width:

155mm, Bleed Size: 226 x 171mm, Col Widths (Display): 62mm, No. of Columns (Display): 2
Copy instructions: Copy Date: 1st of the month prior to publication date
Average advertising content per issue: 50%
CONSUMER: RURAL & REGIONAL INTEREST: Regional Interest English Counties

ROWING & REGATTA

45949U75M-600

Formerly: Regatta
Editorial Address: 6 Lower Mall, Hammersmith, LONDON, W6 9DJ **Tel:** 0870 060 7100 **Fax:** 0870 060 7101
Email: info@ara-rowing.org
Advertising Address: Cabbell Ltd, Woodman Works, 204 Durnsford Road, LONDON, SW19 8DR **Tel:** 020 8971 8450
Fax: 020 8971 8480
Email: george.miller@cabbell.co.uk
Web site: http://www.ara-rowing.org
Publisher: Amateur Rowing Association
Date Established: 1987
Frequency: 9 issues yearly
Cover Price: £3.00
Free to qualifying Individuals
Annual Sub.: £25.00
Circulation: 22,131 (ABC 01/01/2007 to 31/12/2007)
Usual Pagination: 64
Editor: Wendy Kewley; **Advertising Manager:** George Miller
Summary of Content: Magazine covering news and reviews about rowing in the UK and around the world.
Readership/Target Audience: Read by members and those with an interest in rowing.
ADVERTISING RATES:
Full Page Colour £1550.00
Agency Commission: 10%
Mechanical Data: Page Width: 205mm, Type Area: 280 x 205mm, Bleed Size: 300 x 236mm, Trim Size: 300 x 230mm, Col Length: 280mm, Film: Digital
Copy instructions: Copy Date: 4 weeks prior to publication date
Average advertising content per issue: 50%
CONSUMER: SPORT: Water Sports

ROYAL NAVAL SAILING ASSOCIATION JOURNAL

48387U91A-120

Editorial Address: 10 Haslar Marina, Haslar Road, GOSPORT, PO12 1NU **Tel:** 023 9252 1100
Fax: 023 9252 1122
Email: depgensecrnsa@btconnect.com
Advertising Address: As above.
Email: depgensecrnsa@btconnect.com
Web site: http://www.rnsa.net
Publisher: RNSA
Frequency: Half-yearly - Published in May and December
Free to qualifying individuals
Circulation: 6,500 (Publisher's Statement)
Usual Pagination: 130
Editor: Chris Rezek-Clark; **Advertising Manager:** Chris Rezek-Clark
Summary of Content: Journal of the Royal Naval Sailing Association. Containing articles from members on racing, regattas and sailing.
Readership/Target Audience: Read by members, clubs and firms around the world.
ADVERTISING RATES:
Full Page Mono £560.00
Full Page Colour £700.00
Agency Commission: 10%
Mechanical Data: Type Area: 254 x 170mm, Trim Size: 297 x 210mm, Film: Digital, Col Length: 254mm, Page Width: 170mm, Bleed Size: 303 x 216mm
Copy instructions: Copy Date: End of March and September prior to publication
Average advertising content per issue: 10%
CONSUMER: RECREATION & LEISURE: Boating & Yachting

ROYAL OPERA HOUSE NIGHTLY PROGRAMME BOOK

46085U76B-133

Formerly: Royal Opera House Daily Programme Book
Editorial Address: Royal Opera House, Covent Garden, LONDON, WC2E 9DD **Tel:** 020 7212 9100
Email: john.snelson@roh.org.uk
Advertising Address: As above. **Tel:** 020 7212 9455
Fax: 020 7212 9525
Email: helen.ball@roh.org.uk
Web site: http://www.roh.org.uk
Publisher: The Royal Opera House Covent Garden Ltd.
Frequency: 40 issues yearly
Cover Price: £6.00
Circulation: 250,000 (Publisher's Statement)
Usual Pagination: 48
Editor: John Snelson
Summary of Content: Opera and ballet synopses, background notes, pictures and biographies.
Readership/Target Audience: Read by patrons of the Royal Opera House.

ADVERTISING RATES:
Full Page Colour £8200.00
Agency Commission: 10%
Mechanical Data: Film: Digital, Bleed Size: 254 x 194mm, Trim Size: 246 x 186mm
Average advertising content per issue: 20%
CONSUMER: MUSIC & PERFORMING ARTS: Theatre

ROYAL WINGS

1832462U89D-532

Editorial Address: 13-16 Jacobs Well Mews, LONDON, W1U 3DY **Tel:** 020 7906 2001 **Fax:** 020 7906 2003
Email: clewis@spafax.com
Advertising Address: As above.
Email: agreen@spafax.com
Web site: http://www.rj.com
Publisher: Spafax
Date Established: 1999
Frequency: 6 issues yearly
Cover Price: Free
Circulation: 25,000 (Publisher's Statement)
Usual Pagination: 132
Editor: Clare Lewis
Summary of Content: In-flight magazine covering travel news, lifestyle and entertainment features.
Language(s): Arabic; English
Readership/Target Audience: Aimed at passengers travelling with Royal Jordanian Airlines.
ADVERTISING RATES:
Full Page Colour £3050.00
Agency Commission: 15%
Mechanical Data: Bleed Size: 307 x 240mm, Trim Size: 297 x 230mm, Film: Digital
Copy instructions: Copy Date: 35 days prior to publication date
Average advertising content per issue: 40%
CONSUMER: HOLIDAYS & TRAVEL: In-Flight Magazines

ROYALTY

45659U74Q-916

Editorial Address: PO Box 3278, 805 Finchley Road, LONDON, NW11 8DP **Tel:** 020 8201 9978
Fax: 020 8201 9965
Email: info@royalty-magazine.com
Advertising Address: As above.
Email: ad@royalty-magazine.com
Web site: http://www.royalty-magazine.com
ISSN: 0950-3439
Publisher: Sena Julia Publicatus Ltd
Date Established: 1981
Frequency: Monthly
Cover Price: £3.20
Annual Sub.: £29.00
Circulation: 83,000 (Publisher's Statement)
Usual Pagination: 84
Editor: Marco Houston; **Advertising Manager:** James Davis
Summary of Content: Magazine containing features and news on royal families around the world.
Readership/Target Audience: Read by those with an interest in royalty.
ADVERTISING RATES:
Full Page Mono £1550.00
Full Page Colour £2750.00
Agency Commission: 15%
Mechanical Data: Film: Digital, Print Process: Web-fed litho, Trim Size: 276 x 230mm, Bleed Size: 282 x 236mm, Type Area: 260 x 220mm, Col Length: 260mm, Page Width: 220mm
Copy instructions: Copy Date: 4 weeks prior to publication date
Average advertising content per issue: 15%
CONSUMER: WOMEN'S INTEREST CONSUMER MAGAZINES: Lifestyle

RSA JOURNAL

47510U84A-335

Editorial Address: 8 John Adam Street, LONDON, WC2N 6EZ **Tel:** 020 7930 5115
Email: editor@rsa.org.uk
Web site: http://www.thersa.org
ISSN: 0958-0433
Publisher: Wardour Publishing and Design
Date Established: 1852
Frequency: Quarterly
Free to qualifying individuals
Annual Sub.: £140.00
Circulation: 28,000 (Publisher's Statement)
Usual Pagination: 68
Editor: Sophie Charles
Summary of Content: Magazine of the Royal Society for the encouragement of Arts, Manufactures and Commerce. Covers RSA project work and lectures in the fields of art, design, education, environment, manufactures and commerce.
Readership/Target Audience: Read by RSA fellows and opinion leaders in business, industry, art, design, education and the environment.
ADVERTISING: No Advertising taken
CONSUMER: THE ARTS & LITERARY: Arts

RUBBISH
1740674U74B-718

Editorial Address: 326 Kensal Road, LONDON, NW10 5BZ
Tel: 020 8960 8263
Email: catherine@rubbishmag.com
Advertising Address: As above. **Tel:** 020 8968 8386
Email: info@rubbishmag.com
Web site: http://www.rubbishmag.com
Publisher: Rubbish
Date Established: 2006
Frequency: Annual - Published in February/March
Cover Price: £23.45
Usual Pagination: 250
Editor: Catherine Bullman; **Managing Director:** Jana Dowling; **Advertising Manager:** Jason Bold
Summary of Content: Magazine covering fashion, confectionery, teens, music and books from a humorous viewpoint.
Readership/Target Audience: Aimed at those who like a satirical spin on all things sartorial.
ADVERTISING RATES:
Full Page Colour £5000.00
CONSUMER: WOMEN'S INTEREST CONSUMER MAGAZINES: Women's Interest - Fashion

RUGBY LEAGUE WORLD
45796U75C-305

Editorial Address: Wellington House, Briggate, BRIGHOUSE, HD6 1DN **Tel:** 01484 401895
Fax: 01484 401995
Email: newsdesk@totalrl.com
Advertising Address: As above. **Tel:** 01484 404924
Email: honor@totalrl.com
Web site: http://www.totalrl.com
ISSN: 1466-0105
Publisher: League Publications Ltd
Date Established: 1976
Frequency: Monthly
Cover Price: £3.50
Annual Sub.: £35.00
Circulation: 25,000 (Publisher's Statement)
Usual Pagination: 82
Editor: Richard De La Riviere; **Managing Director:** Tim Butcher; **Advertising Manager:** Honor James; **Publisher:** Martyn Sadler
Summary of Content: Magazine providing worldwide coverage of the rugby game and rugby league with a particular emphasis on the game in Great Britain.
Readership/Target Audience: Read by fans, players and administrators of rugby league.
ADVERTISING RATES:
Full Page Colour £1800.00
SCC £5.00
Agency Commission: 10%
Mechanical Data: Trim Size: 297 x 210mm, Film: Digital, Type Area: 268 x 188mm, Col Length: 268mm, Page Width: 188mm, Bleed Size: +5mm, Col Widths (Display): 55mm, No. of Columns (Display): 3
Average advertising content per issue: 25%
CONSUMER: SPORT: Rugby

RUGBY LEAGUER & LEAGUE EXPRESS
45795U75C-453

Formerly: Rugby League Express
Editorial Address: Wellington House, Briggate, BRIGHOUSE, HD6 1DN **Tel:** 01484 401895
Fax: 01484 401995
Email: newsdesk@totalrl.com
Advertising Address: As above.
Email: honor@totalrl.com
Web site: http://www.totalrl.com
ISSN: 0962-1547
Publisher: League Publications Ltd
Date Established: 1990
Frequency: Weekly
Cover Price: £1.30
Circulation: 45,000 (Publisher's Statement)
Usual Pagination: 36
Editor: Honor James; **Advertising Manager:** Honor James; **Managing Editor:** Martyn Sadler
Summary of Content: Newspaper containing rugby league news features, scores, club news, reviews and interviews.
Readership/Target Audience: Read by supporters, officials, fans and players.
ADVERTISING RATES:
Full Page Mono £800.00
Full Page Colour £900.00
Agency Commission: 10%
Mechanical Data: Type Area: 348 x 264mm, Col Length: 348mm, Page Width: 264mm, Col Widths (Display): 50mm, No. of Columns (Display): 5, Film: Digital, Trim Size: 420 x 297mm
Copy instructions: Copy Date: Thursday 12pm prior to publication date
Average advertising content per issue: 15%
CONSUMER: SPORT: Rugby

RUGBY TIMES
767792U75C-452

Editorial Address: Wellington House, Briggate, BRIGHOUSE, HD6 1DN **Tel:** 01484 404920
Fax: 01484 401995
Email: newsdesk@rugbytimes.com
Advertising Address: Winchester Court, 1 Forum Place, HATFIELD, AL10 0RN **Tel:** 01707 273999
Fax: 01707 252705
Email: dan@trmg.co.uk
Web site: http://www.rugbytimes.com
ISSN: 1478-4513
Publisher: League Publications Ltd
Date Established: 2002
Frequency: 40 issues yearly
Cover Price: £1.70
Circulation: 20,000 (Publisher's Statement)
Usual Pagination: 32
Editor: Jonathan Newcombe; **Advertising Manager:** Dan Grainger; **Publisher:** Martyn Sadler
Summary of Content: Newspaper covering rugby news, player features, reports and previews of games in the Zurich Premiership as well as games, results and fixtures in the national leagues.
Readership/Target Audience: Read by Rugby Union players and fans.
ADVERTISING RATES:
Full Page Colour £1000.00
Agency Commission: 10%
Mechanical Data: No. of Columns (Display): 5, Trim Size: 419 x 289mm, Film: Digital
Copy instructions: Copy Date: Monday 5pm prior to publication date
Average advertising content per issue: 10%
CONSUMER: SPORT: Rugby

RUGBY WORLD
45799U75C-330

Editorial Address: Blue Fin Building, 110 Southwark Street, LONDON, SE1 0SU **Tel:** 020 3148 5000
Email: paul_morgan@ipcmedia.com
Advertising Address: As above. **Tel:** 020 3148 4240
Fax: 020 3148 8130
Email: andrew_boxer@ipcmedia.com
Web site: http://www.rugbyworld.com
Publisher: IPC Inspire
Date Established: 1960
Frequency: Monthly - Published on the 1st Tuesday of the month prior to publication date
Cover Price: £3.90
Circulation: 46,047 (ABC 01/01/2008 to 31/12/2008)
Usual Pagination: 148
Editor: Paul Morgan; **Features Editor:** Sarah Mockford
Summary of Content: Magazine offering a comprehensive round-up of rugby action, results and fixtures.
Readership/Target Audience: Aimed at rugby enthusiasts.
ADVERTISING RATES:
Full Page Colour £2995.00
Agency Commission: 10%
Mechanical Data: Type Area: 258 x 196mm, Trim Size: 300 x 230mm, Bleed Size: 306 x 236mm, Film: Digital, No. of Columns (Display): 4, Col Length: 258mm, Page Width: 196mm
Copy instructions: Copy Date: 5 weeks prior to publication date
Average advertising content per issue: 40%
CONSUMER: SPORT: Rugby

RUGRATS
30629U91D-860

Editorial Address: Office Block 1, Southlink Business Park, Hamilton Street, OLDHAM, OL4 1DE **Tel:** 0161 624 0414
Fax: 0161 628 4655
Email: james.hill@toontasticpublishing.com
Publisher: Toontastic Publishing
Frequency: Monthly
Cover Price: £2.99
Circulation: 30,000 (Publisher's Statement)
Usual Pagination: 32
Editor: James Hill; **Editor-in-Chief:** James Hill; **Publisher:** Alan Young
Summary of Content: Children's magazine featuring comic strip stories of the Rugrats, wild Thornberries and All Grown Up Kids. Regular competitions and prize giveaways of new, exciting products, DVDs, books, toys and games.
Readership/Target Audience: Aimed at children between 5 and 10 years old.
ADVERTISING: No Advertising taken
CONSUMER: RECREATION & LEISURE: Children & Youth

RUNNER'S WORLD
45901U75J-550

Editorial Address: 33 Broadwick Street, LONDON, W1F 0DQ **Tel:** 020 7339 4400 **Fax:** 020 7339 4420
Email: rwedit@natmag-rodale.co.uk
Advertising Address: As above. **Tel:** 020 7339 4401
Email: rwsales@natmag-rodale.co.uk
Web site: http://www.runnersworld.co.uk
ISSN: 1350-7745
Publisher: NatMag Rodale Ltd
Frequency: Monthly
Cover Price: £3.99
Annual Sub.: £42.00
Circulation: 94,456 (ABC 01/01/2008 to 31/12/2008)
Usual Pagination: 136
Editor: Andy Dixon; **Managing Editor:** Catherine Lee; **Advertising Director:** Jason Elson
Summary of Content: Magazine focusing on how to improve your lifestyle through the sport of running. Contains information and advice with achievable fitness and performance goals. Includes opinions and tips from professional runners and articles on nutrition.
Readership/Target Audience: Aimed at people interested in running, jogging and general fitness.
ADVERTISING RATES:
Full Page Mono £2485.00
Full Page Colour £3595.00
Agency Commission: 10%
Mechanical Data: Type Area: 278 x 185mm, Col Length: 278mm, Page Width: 185mm, Film: Digital, Trim Size: 290 x 215mm
Copy instructions: Copy Date: 10th of the month prior to publication date
Average advertising content per issue: 45%
CONSUMER: SPORT: Athletics

RUNNING FITNESS
45902U75J-600

Formerly: Today's Runner
Editorial Address: 14 Priestgate, PETERBOROUGH, PE1 1JA **Tel:** 01733 353356 **Fax:** 01733 891342
Email: rf.ed@kelseypb.co.uk
Advertising Address: 1st Floor, South Wing, Broadway Court, PETERBOROUGH, PE1 1RP **Tel:** 01733 347559
Fax: 01733 891342
Email: mark.wilson@kelseypb.co.uk
Web site: http://www.runningfitness.mag
Publisher: Kelsey Publishing Ltd
Date Established: 2000
Frequency: Monthly
Cover Price: £4.00
Annual Sub.: £36.30
Circulation: 22,000 (Publisher's Statement)
Usual Pagination: 116
Editor: David Castle; **Advertising Manager:** Mark Wilson; **Publisher:** Matt Skelton
Summary of Content: Magazine focusing on information and advice on running. With articles covering adventure racing, canoeing, biking and general fitness.
Readership/Target Audience: Read by runners of all abilities.
ADVERTISING RATES:
Full Page Colour £1500.00
Agency Commission: 10%
Mechanical Data: Film: Digital, Type Area: 274 x 186mm, No. of Columns (Display): 4, Bleed Size: 306 x 216mm, Trim Size: 297 x 210mm, Col Length: 274mm, Page Width: 186mm
Average advertising content per issue: 30%
CONSUMER: SPORT: Athletics

RUNNINGFREE MAGAZINE
1902577U75P-801

Editorial Address: Webster House, Dudley Road, TUNBRIDGE WELLS, TN1 1LE **Tel:** 01892 533456
Web site: http://www.runningfreemag.co.uk/
Publisher: Standfirst Media Limited
Cover Price: Free
Editor: Julia Buckley
Summary of Content: Magazine containing hints, tips, features and news about sport and running.
Readership/Target Audience: Aimed at anyone who likes to run.
ADVERTISING: Rates on application
CONSUMER: SPORT: Fitness/Bodybuilding

RURAL WALES
754660U80D-160

Editorial Address: Ty Gwyn, 31 High Street, WELSHPOOL, SY21 7YD **Tel:** 01938 552525 **Fax:** 01938 552741
Email: peter@cprwmail.org.uk
Advertising Address: As above.
Email: charlotte@cprwmail.org.uk
Web site: http://www.cprw.org.uk
Publisher: CPRW
Frequency: 3 issues yearly - Published in March, June and November
Free to qualifying individuals
Circulation: 3,000 (Publisher's Statement)
Usual Pagination: 30
Editor: Peter Ogden; **Advertising Manager:** Charlotte Mansell
Summary of Content: Magazine providing advice and information upon matters affecting protection, conservation and improvement of the environment in rural Wales.
Language(s): English; Welsh
Readership/Target Audience: Read by CPRW members and affiliated organisations, planning officers, members of

the Welsh Assembly, MPs and organisations concerned with the environment of rural Wales.
ADVERTISING: Rates on application
CONSUMER: RURAL & REGIONAL INTEREST: Regional Interest Wales

RWD
1642448U76D-778

Editorial Address: Unit 10-13, The Leather Market, Weston Street, LONDON, SE1 3ER **Tel:** 020 7939 7600
Fax: 020 7407 7090
Email: hattie@rwdmag.com
Advertising Address: As above. **Fax:** 020 7367 6184
Email: sales@rwdmag.com
Web site: http://www.rwdmag.com
Publisher: Rewind Creative Media
Date Established: 2001
Frequency: Monthly
Cover Price: Free
Circulation: 77,560 (ABC 01/01/2009 to 30/06/2009)
Usual Pagination: 116
Editor: Hattie Collins; **Advertising Manager:** Nigel Wells
Summary of Content: Magazine covering urban music including UK garage, hip hop, R&B, drum n bass and US house as well as fashion, artist interviews, reviews of new artists and competitions.
Readership/Target Audience: Aimed at 15 to 24 year olds who are passionate about urban music.
ADVERTISING RATES:
Full Page Colour £2650.00
Mechanical Data: Film: Digital, Bleed Size: 216 x 152mm, Trim Size: 210 x 148mm, Type Area: 200 x 138mm, Col Length: 200mm, Page Width: 138mm
Copy instructions: Copy Date: 2 weeks prior to publication date
CONSUMER: MUSIC & PERFORMING ARTS: Music

RYA MAGAZINE
48386U91A-115

Editorial Address: RYA House, Ensign Way, Hamble, SOUTHAMPTON, SO31 4YA **Tel:** 023 8060 4100
Fax: 023 8060 4293
Email: deborah.cornick@rya.org.uk
Web site: http://www.rya.org.uk
Publisher: Royal Yachting Association
Frequency: Quarterly
Free to qualifying individuals
Circulation: 88,881 (ABC 01/01/2008 to 31/12/2008)
Usual Pagination: 72
Editor: Deborah Cornick
Summary of Content: Magazine of the Royal Yachting Association. Includes news, government regulations affecting boaters, plus cruising, training and racing articles.
Readership/Target Audience: Read by RYA members, clubs and boat owners.
ADVERTISING: No Advertising taken
CONSUMER: RECREATION & LEISURE: Boating & Yachting

RYANAIR MAGAZINE
1800037U89D-528

Editorial Address: 141-143 Shoreditch High Street, LONDON, E1 6JE **Tel:** 020 7613 8777 **Fax:** 020 7613 6985
Email: ramsay.short@ink-publishing.com
Advertising Address: As above. **Fax:** 020 7613 8778
Email: jeffrey.lindstrom@ink-publishing.com
Web site: http://www.ryanairmag.com
Publisher: Ink Publishing
Date Established: 2007
Frequency: Monthly
Cover Price: Free
Circulation: 350,000 (Publisher's Statement)
Usual Pagination: 132
Editor: Ramsay Short
Summary of Content: Magazine covering destination reviews, product reviews and fashion.
Readership/Target Audience: Aimed at passengers on Ryanair.
ADVERTISING RATES:
Full Page Colour £11494.00
Agency Commission: 10%
Mechanical Data: Type Area: 260 x 200mm, Col Length: 260mm, Page Width: 200mm, Bleed Size: +3mm; Film: Digital
Copy instructions: Copy Date: 2 weeks prior to publication date
Average advertising content per issue: 45%
CONSUMER: HOLIDAYS & TRAVEL: In-Flight Magazines

SA TIMES
48346U90-1034

Formerly: South African Times UK
Editorial Address: 14-15 Child's Place, Earls Court, LONDON, SW5 9RX **Tel:** 0845 270 7885 **Fax:** 020 8947 4527
Advertising Address: As above. **Tel:** 020 8946 0108
Fax: 0845 270 7962
Email: mike@jath.co.za
Web site: http://www.southafricantimes.co.uk
Publisher: TNT Publishing

Frequency: Monthly
Cover Price: Free
Circulation: 34,500 (Publisher's Statement)
Usual Pagination: 20
Summary of Content: Newspaper covering news and business events, political, social and financial developments and major sports in South Africa, plus coverage of events involving South Africans in the UK.
Language(s): Afrikaans; English
Readership/Target Audience: Aimed at South Africans living in London, travellers, expatriates and those with an interest in South Africa.
ADVERTISING RATES:
Full Page Colour £829.00
Agency Commission: 10%
Mechanical Data: Type Area: 350 x 276mm, Film: Digital, Bleed Size: +5mm, Col Length: 350mm, Page Width: 276mm
Copy instructions: Copy Date: Thursday 12pm prior to publication date
Average advertising content per issue: 40%
CONSUMER: ETHNIC

SAAB DRIVER
46476U77E-503

Editorial Address: Gorsey Field House, Birtle, BURY, BL9 6UD **Tel:** 01706 368724 **Fax:** 01706 368724
Advertising Address: KJS Advertising, 16 Throstle Nest Close, OTLEY, LS21 2RR **Tel:** 01943 461679
Fax: 01943 461679
Email: kjsadvertising@btinternet.com
Web site: http://www.saabclub.co.uk
ISSN: 1477-2604
Publisher: Saab Owners Club of GB
Date Established: 1963
Frequency: 6 issues yearly - Published in the 1st week of cover month
Cover Price: £5.00
Free to qualifying individuals
Circulation: 5,500 (Publisher's Statement)
Usual Pagination: 64
Editor: Dave Garnett
Summary of Content: Official magazine of the Saab Owners Club of Great Britain. Contains news, views, technical information and letters.
Readership/Target Audience: Aimed at members, UK Saab dealers and clubs worldwide.
ADVERTISING RATES:
Full Page Mono £415.00
Full Page Colour £528.00
Agency Commission: 10%
Mechanical Data: Film: Digital, Bleed Size: 303 x 216mm, Col Length: 263mm, Page Width: 176mm, Type Area: 263 x 176mm, Trim Size: 297 x 210mm
Copy instructions: Copy Date: 4 weeks prior to publication date
Average advertising content per issue: 25%
CONSUMER: MOTORING & CYCLING: Club Cars

SAAB MAGAZINE
45660U74Q-920

Editorial Address: Prospect House, Rouen Road, NORWICH, NR1 1RE **Tel:** 01603 664242 **Fax:** 01603 627723
Email: zoe.francis@archantdialogue.co.uk
Advertising Address: As above. **Fax:** 01603 627823
Email: samantha.overton@archantdialogue.co.uk
Web site: http://www.archantdialogue.co.uk
Publisher: Archant Dialogue
Date Established: 1989
Frequency: Half-yearly - Published in March and September
Cover Price: Free
Circulation: 600,000 (Publisher's Statement)
Usual Pagination: 64
Editor: Zoe Francis
Summary of Content: Magazine covering Saab products and company features. Includes lifestyle features on holidays, sport, fashion, technology, design, art and cultural events.
Language(s): Danish; Dutch; English; Finnish; French; German; Hungarian; Italian; Korean; Norwegian; Russian; Spanish
Readership/Target Audience: Read by Saab owners and affluent professionals with active lifestyles.
ADVERTISING RATES:
Full Page Colour £2500.00
Agency Commission: 10%
Mechanical Data: Page Width: 187mm, Film: Digital, Type Area: 265 x 187mm, Print Process: Sheet-fed offset litho, Bleed Size: 291 x 216mm, Trim Size: 285 x 210mm, Col Length: 265mm
Copy instructions: Copy Date: 2 months prior to publication date
Average advertising content per issue: 12%
CONSUMER: WOMEN'S INTEREST CONSUMER MAGAZINES: Lifestyle

SACRED HOOP
1637736U87-2023

Editorial Address: BCM Sacred Hoop, LONDON, WC1N 3XX **Tel:** 01239 628029 **Fax:** 0870 054 8946
Email: nick@sacredhoop.org

Advertising Address: As above. **Tel:** 01239 682029
Email: nick@sacredhoop.org
Web site: http://www.sacredhoop.org
ISSN: 1364-2219
Publisher: Sacred Hoop
Date Established: 1993
Frequency: Quarterly
Cover Price: £3.50
Annual Sub.: £14.00
Circulation: 5,000 (Publisher's Statement)
Usual Pagination: 52
Editor: Nicholas Breeze Wood; **Advertising Manager:** Nicholas Breeze Wood
Summary of Content: Magazine covering the integration of shamanic and animistic spirituality as held by indigenous peoples to contribute to a balanced and sustainable lifestyle in today's world.
Readership/Target Audience: Aimed at those wanting to learn about the shamanic and animistic spiritual teachings of indigenous peoples.
ADVERTISING RATES:
Full Page Colour £710.00
Agency Commission: 10%
Mechanical Data: Bleed Size: 303 x 216mm, Trim Size: 297 x 210mm, Film: Digital
Copy instructions: Copy Date: 1st of the month prior to publication date
CONSUMER: RELIGIOUS

SAFETY FAST!
46477U77E-260

Editorial Address: Kimber House, PO Box 251, ABINGDON, OX14 1FF **Tel:** 01235 555552 **Fax:** 01235 533755
Email: andyknott@mgcc.co.uk
Web site: http://www.mgcc.co.uk
Publisher: MG Car Club Ltd
Date Established: 1959
Frequency: Monthly
Free to qualifying individuals
Annual Sub.: £36.00
Circulation: 15,000 (Publisher's Statement)
Usual Pagination: 100
Editor: Andy Knott
Summary of Content: Magazine covering all aspects of MG cars.
Readership/Target Audience: Read by MG Car Club members.
ADVERTISING: No Advertising taken
CONSUMER: MOTORING & CYCLING: Club Cars

SAGA MAGAZINE
45585U74N-120

Editorial Address: Saga Building, Enbrook Park, FOLKESTONE, CT20 3SE **Tel:** 01303 771111
Fax: 01303 776699
Email: editor@saga.co.uk
Advertising Address: 85 Buckingham Gate, LONDON, SW1E 6PD **Tel:** 020 7233 1157 **Fax:** 020 7233 1158
Email: adsales@saga.co.uk
Web site: http://www.saga.co.uk
Publisher: Saga Publishing Ltd
Date Established: 1984
Frequency: Monthly
Cover Price: £2.50
Annual Sub.: £24.95
Circulation: 653,930 (ABC 01/01/2009 to 30/06/2009)
Usual Pagination: 228
Editor: Maria Abobeleira; **Features Editor:** David Allsop
Summary of Content: Magazine covering celebrity profiles, health, food, savings, gardening and broad views on lifestyle.
Readership/Target Audience: Aimed at those over 50 years old.
ADVERTISING RATES:
Full Page Colour £11250.00
Agency Commission: 15%
Mechanical Data: Type Area: 240 x 174mm, Bleed Size: 266 x 296mm, Trim Size: 260 x 190mm, Film: Digital, Col Length: 240mm, Page Width: 174mm
Average advertising content per issue: 40%
Supplement(s): Saga fm - 4xY
CONSUMER: WOMEN'S INTEREST CONSUMER MAGAZINES: Retirement

SAHB TIMES
1873294U77A-614

Editorial Address: 55 Howletts Lane, RUISLIP, HA4 7SA
Tel: 01895 630893
Email: tonybeadle@gmail.com
Web site: http://www.autohistory.org.uk
Publisher: Society of Automotive Historians in Britain
Cover Price: Free
Editor: Tony Beadle
Summary of Content: Magazine covering the history of the development of the automobile and related subjects from inception to the present day.

Readership/Target Audience: Aimed at professional writers, archivists, curators, private collectors or literature and automobilia enthusiasts.
CONSUMER: MOTORING & CYCLING: Motoring

SAILING TODAY
48389U91A-130

Editorial Address: Swanwick Marina, Lower Swanwick, SOUTHAMPTON, SO31 1ZL **Tel:** 01489 585225
Fax: 01489 565054
Email: rodger.witt@sailingtoday.co.uk
Advertising Address: As above.
Email: jayne.bennett@sailingtoday.co.uk
Web site: http://www.sailingtoday.co.uk
Publisher: Edisea Ltd
Date Established: 1997
Frequency: Monthly - Published on the 1st Thursday of each month
Cover Price: £3.50
Annual Sub.: £29.99
Circulation: 20,000 (Publisher's Statement)
Usual Pagination: 186
Editor: Rodger Witt
Summary of Content: Magazine containing regular features which include new and used boat testing, equipment tests, sailing skills, boat improvements and chartering.
Readership/Target Audience: Aimed at sailing enthusiasts interested in the latest news and features on the boating industry.
ADVERTISING RATES:
Full Page Colour £2433.00
Agency Commission: 10%
Mechanical Data: Col Length: 280mm, Type Area: 280 x 203mm, Bleed Size: 310 x 232mm, Trim Size: 300 x 222mm, Film: Digital, Page Width: 203mm
Average advertising content per issue: 60%
CONSUMER: RECREATION & LEISURE: Boating & Yachting

SAILPLANE & GLIDING
45969U75N-500

Editorial Address: Kimberley House, Vaughan Way, LEICESTER, LE1 4SE **Tel:** 0116 253 1051
Email: editor@sailplaneandgliding.co.uk
Advertising Address: As above. **Fax:** 0116 251 5939
Email: debbie@gliding.co.uk
Web site: http://www.gliding.co.uk
Publisher: British Gliding Association Ltd
Date Established: 1955
Frequency: 6 issues yearly
Cover Price: £3.95
Annual Sub.: £22.50
Circulation: 5,500 (Print Run)
Usual Pagination: 68
Editor: Susan Newby; **Advertising Manager:** Debbie Carr
Summary of Content: Magazine covering all aspects of gliding.
Readership/Target Audience: Aimed at existing and prospective glider pilots.
ADVERTISING RATES:
Full Page Mono £391.00
Full Page Colour £674.00
Agency Commission: 10%
Mechanical Data: Trim Size: 247 x 189mm
Average advertising content per issue: 10%
CONSUMER: SPORT: Flight

SAINSBURY'S FRESH IDEAS
1700421U74P-935

Editorial Address: Sea Containers House, 20 Upper Ground, LONDON, SE1 9PD **Tel:** 020 7775 5777
Email: freshideas@sevensquared.co.uk
Advertising Address: As above. **Tel:** 020 7775 5543
Fax: 020 7928 8157
Email: millie.bustard@sevensquared.co.uk
Web site: http://www.sevensquared.co.uk
Publisher: Seven Squared
Date Established: 2005
Frequency: Quarterly
Cover Price: Free
Circulation: 1,499,499 (ABC 01/01/2009 to 30/06/2009)
Usual Pagination: 100
Editor: Maxine Briggs; **Advertising Manager:** Millie Bustard
Summary of Content: Magazine covering food, lifestyle, fashion, beauty, health and nutrition.
Readership/Target Audience: Aimed at Sainsbury's Nectar-card customers in three customised versions for readers at different stages of life.
ADVERTISING RATES:
Full Page Colour £20590.00
Agency Commission: 15%
Mechanical Data: Type Area: 244 x 190mm, Bleed Size: 276 x 221mm, Trim Size: 270 x 215mm, Col Length: 244mm, Page Width: 190mm, Film: Digital
Average advertising content per issue: 40%
CONSUMER: WOMEN'S INTEREST CONSUMER MAGAZINES: Food & Cookery

SAINSBURY'S FRESH IDEAS FOR YOUNG FAMILIES
1829676U74P-958

Editorial Address: Sea Containers House, 20 Upper Ground, LONDON, SE1 9PD **Tel:** 020 7775 5777
Email: lauren.hoffman@sevensquared.co.uk
Advertising Address: As above.
Email: martin.short@sevensquared.co.uk
Publisher: Seven Squared
Date Established: 2007
Frequency: Quarterly
Cover Price: Free
Circulation: 299,625 (ABC 01/07/2008 to 31/12/2008)
Editor: Lauren Hoffman
Summary of Content: Magazine with food ideas for the whole family but especially toddlers and babies.
Readership/Target Audience: Aimed at young families with Nectar cards.
ADVERTISING RATES:
Full Page Colour £16000.00
Agency Commission: 15%
Copy instructions: Copy Date: 4 weeks prior to publication date
Average advertising content per issue: 25%
CONSUMER: WOMEN'S INTEREST CONSUMER MAGAZINES: Food & Cookery

SAINSBURY'S MAGAZINE
45613U74P-600

Formerly: Sainsbury's The Magazine
Editorial Address: Sea Containers House, 20 Upper Ground, LONDON, SE1 9PD **Tel:** 020 7775 7775
Fax: 020 7775 7705
Email: gillian.rhys@sevensquared.co.uk
Advertising Address: As above. **Tel:** 020 7775 5543
Fax: 020 7928 8157
Email: millie.bustard@7publishing.co.uk
ISSN: 0054-6652
Publisher: Seven Publishing
Date Established: 1993
Frequency: Monthly
Cover Price: £1.40
Annual Sub.: £24.00
Circulation: 301,842 (ABC 01/01/2009 to 30/06/2009)
Usual Pagination: 200
Editor: Gillian Rhys; **Advertising Manager:** Millie Bustard
Summary of Content: Magazine covering articles on food, wine, health, beauty, home, gardens, travel and celebrity interviews.
Readership/Target Audience: Aimed at customers of Sainsbury's supermarkets.
ADVERTISING RATES:
Full Page Colour £11760.00
Agency Commission: 15%
Mechanical Data: Film: Digital, Type Area: 276 x 196mm, Bleed Size: 306 x 226mm, Trim Size: 300 x 220mm, Col Length: 276mm, Page Width: 196mm
Copy instructions: Copy Date: 6 weeks prior to publication date
Average advertising content per issue: 40%
CONSUMER: WOMEN'S INTEREST CONSUMER MAGAZINES: Food & Cookery

THE SAINT
47438U83-68_30

Editorial Address: Students' Association Building, St. Mary's Place, ST. ANDREWS, KY16 9UZ **Tel:** 01334 422737
Email: thesaint@st-andrews.ac.uk
Web site: http://www.thesaintonline.co.uk
Publisher: The Saint
Frequency: 10 issues yearly
Cover Price: Free
Circulation: 5,000 (Publisher's Statement)
Usual Pagination: 32
Editor: Robert Williams
Summary of Content: Newspaper with local news, features, society events, sport and arts coverage from across Scotland and the UK.
Readership/Target Audience: Read by students at the University of St Andrews, also staff and graduate subscribers.
ADVERTISING: No Advertising taken
CONSUMER: STUDENT PUBLICATIONS

ST. ALBANS DIOCESAN DIRECTORY
47856U87-213_5

Editorial Address: Holywell Lodge, 41 Holywell Hill, ST. ALBANS, AL1 1HE **Tel:** 01727 854532 **Fax:** 01727 846469
Email: mail@stalbans.anglican.org
Advertising Address: As above.
Email: cbrown@stalbans.anglican.org
Web site: http://www.stalbans.anglican.org
Publisher: St. Albans Diocese
Date Established: 1877
Frequency: Annual - Published in October
Cover Price: £7.00
Circulation: 1,400 (Publisher's Statement)
Usual Pagination: 170
Editor: Susan Pope; **Advertising Manager:** Claudia Brown
Summary of Content: Journal covering news, information and contacts of church officers.
Readership/Target Audience: Aimed at clergy, church officers, parochial church councils and supplies officers in Bedfordshire and Hertfordshire.
ADVERTISING RATES:
Full Page Mono £160.00
Full Page Colour £220.00
Mechanical Data: Film: Digital, Trim Size: 210 x 148mm
Copy instructions: Copy Date: 8 weeks prior to publication date
CONSUMER: RELIGIOUS

THE SAINTS MAGAZINE
45776U75B-210

Editorial Address: Newspaper House, Test Lane, Redbridge, SOUTHAMPTON, SO16 9JX **Tel:** 023 8042 4520
Email: simon.carter@dailyecho.co.uk
Advertising Address: As above. **Tel:** 023 8042 4777
Email: carol.eades@dailyecho.co.uk
Web site: http://www.dailyecho.co.uk
Publisher: Newsquest (Media Group) Ltd
Frequency: Quarterly - Bi-monthly during the football season
Cover Price: £2.50
Circulation: 5,000 (Publisher's Statement)
Usual Pagination: 68
Editor: Simon Carter
Summary of Content: Official magazine of Southampton Football Club. Includes player interviews, exclusive stories and original photographs.
Readership/Target Audience: Read by supporters of the Southampton football team around the world.
ADVERTISING RATES:
Full Page Colour £396.00
Mechanical Data: Bleed Size: 307 x 220mm, Type Area: 287 x 200mm, Col Length: 287mm, Page Width: 200mm, Film: Digital, Trim Size: 297 x 210mm
Average advertising content per issue: 20%
CONSUMER: SPORT: Football

THE SALISBURY AND STONEHENGE VISITORS GUIDE
48187U89C-317

Formerly: The Guide
Editorial Address: 3 Rollestone Street, SALISBURY, SP1 1DX **Tel:** 01722 434238 **Fax:** 01722 434440
Email: medtmail@salisbury.gov.uk
Web site: http://www.visitsalisbury.com
Publisher: Salisbury District Council
Date Established: 1996
Frequency: Annual - Published in December
Cover Price: £1.00
Free to qualifying individuals
Circulation: 55,000 (Publisher's Statement)
Usual Pagination: 84
Editor: Bryn Jones
Summary of Content: Visitor guide to all there is to see and do in the area including accommodation.
Readership/Target Audience: Aimed at potential and current visitors to the area.
ADVERTISING: No Advertising taken
CONSUMER: HOLIDAYS & TRAVEL: Entertainment Guides

SALISBURY LIFE
1665743U80C-5213

Editorial Address: Circus Mews House, Circus Mews, BATH, BA1 2PW **Tel:** 01225 475800
Email: nicola.cunningham@mediaclash.co.uk
Advertising Address: As above. **Fax:** 01225 475801
Email: richard.booth@mediaclash.co.uk
Web site: http://www.salisburylifemagazine.co.uk
Publisher: Media Clash
Date Established: 2003
Frequency: 17 issues yearly
Cover Price: £2.50
Free to qualifying individuals
Annual Sub.: £30.00
Circulation: 10,000 (Publisher's Statement)
Usual Pagination: 84
Editor: Nicola Cunningham; **Advertising Manager:** Richard Booth
Summary of Content: Property and lifestyle magazine covering food, arts, out and about, fashion, beauty and gardening.
Readership/Target Audience: Aimed at affluent home owners in Salisbury and surrounding villages.
ADVERTISING: Rates on application
Agency Commission: 10%
Copy instructions: Copy Date: 1 week prior to publication date
Average advertising content per issue: 30%
CONSUMER: RURAL & REGIONAL INTEREST: Regional Interest English Counties

Consumer Magazines

SALISBURY SPORT
1786302U75A-1027

Editorial Address: Home Close, Teffont, SALISBURY, SP3 5QY **Tel:** 01722 716268 **Fax:** 01722 716781
Email: davidoparker@aol.com
Advertising Address: As above.
Email: karlos200885@aol.com
Publisher: Kingsley House (Publishing)
Frequency: Quarterly
Cover Price: Free
Circulation: 2,000 (Publisher's Statement)
Usual Pagination: 16
Editor: David Parker; **Advertising Manager:** Karl Plaskett
Summary of Content: Magazine covering local sport, school sport and international events.
Readership/Target Audience: Aimed at sports clubs in Salisbury and those with a general interest in sport.
ADVERTISING RATES:
Full Page Colour £50.00
CONSUMER: SPORT

SALVATION ARMY YEAR BOOK
47858U87-2012_50

Editorial Address: 101 Queen Victoria Street, LONDON, EC4V 4EH **Tel:** 020 7332 8086 **Fax:** 020 7332 8076
Publisher: Salvation Army (International)
Date Established: 1906
Frequency: Annual - Published in November
Cover Price: £5.50
Circulation: 12,000 (Publisher's Statement)
Usual Pagination: 350
Editor: Trevor Howes; **Editor-in-Chief:** Charles King
Summary of Content: Reference Book covering all aspects of the work of The Salvation Army worldwide.
Readership/Target Audience: Aimed at worldwide membership of The Salvation Army and all others who have an interest in the organisation's activities.
ADVERTISING: No Advertising taken
CONSUMER: RELIGIOUS

SANDMAN
1665951U76D-792

Formerly: Sandman Sheffield
Editorial Address: PO Box 4250, SHEFFIELD, S8 2EL
Tel: 0114 278 6727
Web site: http://www.sandmanmagazine.co.uk
Publisher: Sandman Magazine
Frequency: Monthly
Cover Price: Free
Circulation: 10,000 (Publisher's Statement)
Usual Pagination: 60
Editor: Mark Roberts
Summary of Content: Magazine covering local music news and features, gig reviews, gig guides, nightlife, new releases and interviews.
Readership/Target Audience: Aimed at bands, musicians, gig-goers and music lovers.
ADVERTISING: Rates on application
CONSUMER: MUSIC & PERFORMING ARTS: Music

SARKY CUTT
47439U83-68_50

Editorial Address: Cooper Building, King William Walk, Greenwich, LONDON, SE10 9JH **Tel:** 020 8331 8479
Fax: 020 8331 7628
Email: aspire@bexley.ac.uk
Advertising Address: Students' Union, University of Greenwich, Bath Way, Woolwich, LONDON, SE18 6QX
Tel: 020 8331 9964 **Fax:** 020 8331 8591
Web site: http://www.suug.co.uk/main/sarky
Publisher: Students Union University of Greenwich
Frequency: 5 issues yearly
Cover Price: Free
Circulation: 4,000 (Publisher's Statement)
Usual Pagination: 48
Summary of Content: Newspaper of the Students' Union of the University of Greenwich containing student related news stories and entertainment reviews.
Readership/Target Audience: Aimed at students of all ages attending the university.
CONSUMER: STUDENT PUBLICATIONS

THE SARUM LINK
47750U87-202

Editorial Address: Church House, Crane Street, SALISBURY, SP1 2QB **Tel:** 01722 438652
Fax: 01722 411990
Email: sarum.link@salisbury.anglican.org
Advertising Address: 28 Old Park Road, Peverell, PLYMOUTH, PL3 4PY **Tel:** 01752 225623
Fax: 01752 673441
Email: diocesan@cornerstonevision.com
Web site: http://www.salisbury.anglican.org
Publisher: Cornerstone Vision
Date Established: 1988
Frequency: Monthly
Cover Price: Free

Circulation: 31,000 (Publisher's Statement)
Usual Pagination: 16
Editor: Nicky Davies
Summary of Content: Newspaper for the Diocese of Salisbury.
Readership/Target Audience: Aimed at the church and community in the Diocese of Salisbury.
ADVERTISING RATES:
SCC £5.75
Average advertising content per issue: 40%
CONSUMER: RELIGIOUS

SCALE AVIATION MODELLER INTERNATIONAL
601051U79B-184

Editorial Address: Media House, 21 Kingsway, BEDFORD, MK42 9BJ **Tel:** 0870 733 3373 **Fax:** 0870 733 3744
Email: neil@sampublications.com
Advertising Address: As above. **Tel:** 0870 733 3733
Email: sophie@sampublications.com
Web site: http://www.sampublications.com
Publisher: Sam Ltd
Date Established: 1994
Frequency: Monthly
Cover Price: £3.95
Annual Sub.: £38.00
Circulation: 49,000 (Publisher's Statement)
Usual Pagination: 100
Editor: Gary Hatcher; **Advertising Manager:** Sophie Elliot; **Managing Editor:** Neil Robinson; **Publisher:** Steve Elliott
Summary of Content: Magazine focusing on all forms of static scale aviation model making.
Readership/Target Audience: Aimed at aviation and aviation model enthusiasts.
ADVERTISING RATES:
Full Page Colour £995.00
Agency Commission: 10%
Mechanical Data: Bleed Size: +4mm, Page Width: 190mm, Type Area: 274 x 190mm, Col Length: 274mm, Film: Digital, Print Process: Web-fed offset litho, Trim Size: 297 x 210mm
Copy instructions: Copy Date: 2 weeks prior to publication date
Average advertising content per issue: 30%
CONSUMER: HOBBIES & DIY: Models & Modelling

SCALE MODELS COLLECTOR INTERNATIONAL
46620U79B-186

Formerly: Scale Models International
Editorial Address: Media House, 21 Kingsway, BEDFORD, MK42 9BJ **Tel:** 0870 733 3733 **Fax:** 0870 733 3744
Email: andyevans@sampublications.com
Advertising Address: As above.
Email: sophie@sampublications.com
Web site: http://www.sampublications.com
Publisher: Sam Ltd
Date Established: 1969
Frequency: Monthly
Cover Price: £3.80
Annual Sub.: £38.00
Circulation: 30,000 (Publisher's Statement)
Usual Pagination: 80
Editor: Andy Evans; **Advertising Manager:** Sophie Elliot; **Publisher:** Steve Elliott
Summary of Content: Magazine covering all forms of static scale model making.
Readership/Target Audience: Read by modelling enthusiasts.
ADVERTISING RATES:
Full Page Colour £980.00
Agency Commission: 10%
Mechanical Data: Bleed Size: + 3mm, Page Width: 190mm, Type Area: 274 x 190mm, Col Length: 274mm, Film: Positive, right reading, emulsion side down. Digital, Print Process: Web-fed offset litho, Trim Size: 294 x 210mm
Copy instructions: Copy Date: 1st week of the month prior to publication date
Average advertising content per issue: 40%
CONSUMER: HOBBIES & DIY: Models & Modelling

SCAN
47440U83-69

Editorial Address: Slaidburn House, Bailrigg, LANCASTER, LA1 4YA **Tel:** 01524 592613 **Fax:** 01524 846732
Email: scan@lancaster.ac.uk
Advertising Address: As above.
Email: m.ennis@lancaster.ac.uk
Web site: http://www.lusu.co.uk/scan
Publisher: Lancaster University Students' Union
Date Established: 1967
Frequency: 17 issues yearly - Published fortnightly during term time
Cover Price: Free
Circulation: 3,000 (Publisher's Statement)
Usual Pagination: 40
Advertising Manager: Martin Ennis
Summary of Content: Student newspaper of Lancaster University containing news and features from the University,

Lancaster area and national student sources. Covers a wide range of arts, sport, music and comment.
Readership/Target Audience: Read by local college and university students and those living in and around Lancaster.
ADVERTISING RATES:
Full Page Mono £400.00
Full Page Colour £550.00
Agency Commission: 10%
Mechanical Data: Trim Size: 340 x 266mm, Film: Digital, No. of Columns (Display): 4
Copy instructions: Copy Date: 1 week prior to publication date
Average advertising content per issue: 33%
CONSUMER: STUDENT PUBLICATIONS

SCARLET
1655406U74A-970

Editorial Address: 107 Graham Road, LONDON, SW19 3SP
Tel: 020 8543 3172
Email: editorial@scarletmagazine.co.uk
Advertising Address: Lawrence House, Morrell Street, LEAMINGTON SPA, CV32 5SZ **Tel:** 01926 3339898
Email: simon@scarletmagazine.co.uk
Web site: http://www.scarletmagazine.co.uk
Publisher: Blaze Publishing Limited
Date Established: 2004
Frequency: Monthly
Cover Price: £2.95
Annual Sub.: £30.00
Circulation: 30,000 (Publisher's Statement)
Usual Pagination: 114
Editor: Sarah Hedley; **Advertising Manager:** Simon La Thangue; **Publisher:** Wesley Stanton
Summary of Content: Magazine covering sex, lifestyle, news and politics.
Readership/Target Audience: Aimed at fearless and feisty women aged between 25 and 35 years old.
ADVERTISING RATES:
Full Page Colour £2850.00
Mechanical Data: Type Area: 263 x 195mm, Col Length: 263mm, Page Width: 195mm, Bleed Size: 279 x 211mm, Trim Size: 273 x 205mm, Film: Digital
CONSUMER: WOMEN'S INTEREST CONSUMER MAGAZINES: Women's Interest

THE SCHMIDT REPORT
45560U74M-280

Editorial Address: 17 Fleet Street, LONDON, EC4Y 1AA
Tel: 020 7353 7300
Web site: http://www.schmidtreport.co.uk
ISSN: 1356-4544
Publisher: Wentworth Publishing Ltd
Date Established: 1995
Frequency: 10 issues yearly
Annual Sub.: £98.00
Circulation: 3,000 (Publisher's Statement)
Usual Pagination: 16
Editor: Nathaniel Litman; **Managing Director:** Justin Power; **Publisher:** Claire Hutchinson
Summary of Content: Magazine covering news and information on managing tax affairs. Includes advice on how to save on tax bills.
Readership/Target Audience: Aimed at those interested in personal finance management.
ADVERTISING: No Advertising taken
CONSUMER: WOMEN'S INTEREST CONSUMER MAGAZINES: Personal Finance

SCHNEWS
47275U82-172

Editorial Address: SchNews c/o Community Base, 113 Queens Road, BRIGHTON, BN1 3XG **Tel:** 01273 685913
Email: schnews@brighton.co.uk
Web site: http://www.schnews.org.uk
Publisher: Justice
Date Established: 1994
Frequency: Weekly
Cover Price: Free
Circulation: 60,000 (Publisher's Statement)
Editor: Jo Makepeace
Summary of Content: Magazine covering the collective action taken by people against the power of the state and against environmental destruction.
Readership/Target Audience: Aimed at information centres, libraries, schools, radical bookshops, peace centres and parliament.
ADVERTISING: No Advertising taken
CONSUMER: CURRENT AFFAIRS & POLITICS

SCHOOL HOUSE MAGAZINE
1872677U88A-235

Editorial Address: The Studio, 1 Linver Road, LONDON, SW6 3RA **Tel:** 020 7731 9470
Email: penny.dash@deepermedia.co.uk
Web site: http://www.countryandtownhouse.co.uk
Publisher: Country and Town House Ltd
Frequency: Half-yearly - Published in March and September
Cover Price: Free
Circulation: 100,000 (Publisher's Statement)

Usual Pagination: 144
Editor: Penny Dash
Summary of Content: Magazine covering a guide to the best of London and country schools.
Readership/Target Audience: Aimed at Londoners.
CONSUMER: EDUCATION

SCIENCE & CHRISTIAN BELIEF
47859U87-204

Editorial Address: 77 Beaumont Road, CAMBRIDGE, CB1 8PX **Tel:** 01223 246696
Email: dra24@hermes.cam.ac.uk
Web site: http://www.scienceandchristianbelief.org
ISSN: 0954-4194
Publisher: Authentic Media
Date Established: 1989
Frequency: Half-yearly - Published in April and October
Free to qualifying individuals
Annual Sub.: £22.80
Circulation: 1,800 (Publisher's Statement)
Usual Pagination: 96
Editor: Denis Alexander
Summary of Content: Journal containing major articles and abstracts on science and religion.
Readership/Target Audience: Aimed at scientists and theologians who are interested in the relationship between these disciplines.
ADVERTISING: No Advertising taken
CONSUMER: RELIGIOUS

SCIFI NOW
1800021U79L-387

Editorial Address: Richmond House, 33 Richmond Hill, BOURNEMOUTH, BH2 6EZ **Tel:** 01202 586200
Fax: 01202 294032
Email: scifinow@imagine-publishing.co.uk
Advertising Address: As above.
Email: layla.ibrahim@imagine-publishing.co.uk
Web site: http://www.imagine-publishing.co.uk
Publisher: Imagine Publishing
Date Established: 2007
Frequency: 13 issues yearly
Cover Price: £4.00
Circulation: 50,000 (Print Run)
Usual Pagination: 148
Editor: Aaron Asadi; **News Editor:** James Rundle;
Advertising Manager: Layla Ibrahim
Summary of Content: Magazine covering scifi fantasy, horror and cult TV.
Readership/Target Audience: Aimed at fans of the genre predominantly men between 25 and 45 years of age.
ADVERTISING RATES:
Full Page Colour £1850.00
Agency Commission: 10%
Mechanical Data: Type Area: 277 x 210mm, Bleed Size: 307 x 240mm, Trim Size: 297 x 230mm, Col Length: 277mm, Page Width: 210mm, Film: Digital
Copy instructions: Copy Date: 4 weeks prior to publication date
Average advertising content per issue: 20%
CONSUMER: HOBBIES & DIY: Fantasy Games & Science Fiction

THE SCILLONIAN
1775321U80J-1

Editorial Address: The Paper Shop, Hugh Street, St. Mary's, ISLES OF SCILLY, TR21 0LL **Tel:** 01720 422438
Email: clive@clivemumford.wanadoo.co.uk
Advertising Address: As above. **Fax:** 01720 422127
Email: clive@clivemumford.wanadoo.co.uk
Publisher: The Scillonian
Frequency: Half-yearly - Published in February and August
Cover Price: £3.99
Circulation: 2,000 (Publisher's Statement)
Editor: Clive Tregarthen Mumford; **Advertising Manager:** Clive Tregarthen Mumford
Summary of Content: Magazine covering local news, views, opinion and events.
Readership/Target Audience: Aimed at residents and visitors to the Isles of Scilly.
ADVERTISING RATES:
Full Page Mono £75.00
Copy instructions: Copy Date: 4 weeks prior to publication date
CONSUMER: RURAL & REGIONAL INTEREST: Regional Interest Scilly Isles

SCOOBY DOO
1664287U91D-916

Editorial Address: Brockbourne House, Mount Ephraim, TUNBRIDGE WELLS, TN4 8BS **Tel:** 01892 500100
Email: ecaruana@panini.co.uk
Advertising Address: Orange20 Ltd, Station House, Bunbury Way, EPSOM, KT17 4JP **Tel:** 01372 802800
Fax: 01372 723322
Email: panini.adsales@o20.co.uk
Web site: http://www.paninicomics.co.uk
Publisher: Panini UK Ltd

Date Established: 2003
Frequency: 17 issues yearly
Cover Price: £1.99
Circulation: 40,695 (ABC 01/07/2008 to 31/12/2008)
Usual Pagination: 36
Editor: Ed Caruana; **Advertising Manager:** Michelle Fairlamb
Summary of Content: Children's magazine covering the adventures of Scooby Doo with competitions, prizes and activities.
Readership/Target Audience: Aimed at boys and girls aged 6 to 9 years old.
ADVERTISING RATES:
Full Page Colour £2500.00
Mechanical Data: Type Area: 277 x 190mm, Bleed Size: 307 x 220mm, Trim Size: 297 x 210mm, Col Length: 277mm, Page Width: 190mm
CONSUMER: RECREATION & LEISURE: Children & Youth

SCOOTERING
46374U77B-596_50

Editorial Address: PO Box 99, HORNCASTLE, LN9 6LZ **Tel:** 01507 529300 **Fax:** 01507 529499
Email: agillard@mortons.co.uk
Advertising Address: As above. **Tel:** 01507 524004
Fax: 01507 525772
Email: gthomas@mortons.co.uk
Web site: http://www.scootering.com
ISSN: 0268-7194
Publisher: Mortons Media Group Ltd
Date Established: 1985
Frequency: Monthly
Cover Price: £3.50
Annual Sub.: £36.00
Circulation: 35,000 (Publisher's Statement)
Usual Pagination: 144
Editor: Andy Gillard; **Advertising Manager:** Gary Thomas
Summary of Content: Magazine covering all aspects of scooters and scootering.
Readership/Target Audience: Aimed at Mod revivalists, rally-going scooterists, scooter racing fans and vintage scooter enthusiasts in Britain and around the world.
ADVERTISING RATES:
Full Page Mono £525.00
Full Page Colour £625.00
Agency Commission: 10%
Mechanical Data: Col Length: 270mm, Page Width: 188mm, Type Area: 270 x 188mm, Trim Size: 297 x 210mm, Bleed Size: 308 x 220, Film: Digital
Copy instructions: Copy Date: 1st Friday of publication month
CONSUMER: MOTORING & CYCLING: Motorcycling

SCORECARD
1826011U75K-855

Editorial Address: 22 Dene Avenue, HOUNSLOW, TW3 3AH **Tel:** 020 8570 5434
Email: puckett@middxlge.fsnet.co.uk
Advertising Address: As above.
Email: puckett@middxlge.fsnet.co.uk
Publisher: Middlesex Cricket Club
Frequency: Quarterly
Cover Price: Free
Circulation: 1,500 (Publisher's Statement)
Editor: Charlie Puckett; **Advertising Manager:** Charlie Puckett
Summary of Content: Magazine of the Middlesex Cricket Board Covering women's and colt's cricket as well as advice, competition results, CRB clearance, league cricket for Middlesex clubs, cup cricket involving Middlesex clubs, umpiring and legal issues.
Readership/Target Audience: Aimed at players, officials and supporters.
ADVERTISING: Rates on application
CONSUMER: SPORT: Cricket

SCOTLAND AND NORTH OF ENGLAND PARKS GUIDE
752963U91B-165

Formerly: Pure & Simple - The Scottish Parks Guide
Editorial Address: Suite 7, Buko Tower, Dalton Road, GLENROTHES, KY6 2SS **Tel:** 01592 610421
Fax: 01592 755315
Email: bob@scottishcaravanner.com
Advertising Address: As above.
Email: bob@scottishcaravanner.com
Web site: http://www.scottishcaravanner.com
Publisher: Scottish Caravanner
Date Established: 1998
Frequency: Annual - Published in October
Cover Price: £2.95
Circulation: 38,000 (Publisher's Statement)
Usual Pagination: 132
Editor: Bob Mather; **Advertising Manager:** Bob Mather;
Managing Editor: Bob Mather
Summary of Content: Magazine containing a complete guide to every caravan park in Scotland and the North of England.

Readership/Target Audience: Aimed at those planning a caravan holiday in Scotland.
ADVERTISING: Rates on application
CONSUMER: RECREATION & LEISURE: Camping & Caravanning

SCOTLAND: CARAVAN & CAMPING, WHERE TO STAY GUIDE
48438U91B-190

Formerly: Scotland: Camping & Caravan Parks
Editorial Address: Ocean Point One, 94 Ocean Drive, EDINBURGH, EH6 6JH **Tel:** 0131 332 2433
Email: wendy.bell@visitscotland.com
Web site: http://www.visitscotland.com
Publisher: VisitScotland
Frequency: Annual - Published in November
Cover Price: £4.99
Circulation: 10,500 (Publisher's Statement)
Usual Pagination: 110
Editor: Gwen Raez
Summary of Content: Directory showing sites for caravans and tents in Scotland.
Readership/Target Audience: Aimed at potential visitors from the UK and overseas.
ADVERTISING: No Advertising taken
CONSUMER: RECREATION & LEISURE: Camping & Caravanning

SCOTLAND: HOTELS & GUEST HOUSES, WHERE TO STAY GUIDE
48003U89A-430

Formerly: Scotland: Where to Stay Hotels & Guest Houses
Editorial Address: Ocean Point One, 94 Ocean Drive, EDINBURGH, EH6 6JH **Tel:** 0131 472 2222
Fax: 0131 472 2250
Email: gwen.raez@visitscotland.com
Web site: http://www.visitscotland.com
Publisher: VisitScotland
Frequency: Annual - Published in November
Cover Price: £8.99
Circulation: 12,000 (Publisher's Statement)
Usual Pagination: 280
Editor: Gwen Raez
Summary of Content: Accommodation guide to hotels and guest houses in Scotland.
Readership/Target Audience: Aimed at potential tourists and visitors looking for a place to stay.
ADVERTISING: No Advertising taken
CONSUMER: HOLIDAYS & TRAVEL: Travel

SCOTLAND IN TRUST
1647213U80E-361

Editorial Address: 91 East London Street, EDINBURGH, EH7 4BQ **Tel:** 0131 556 2220
Email: editor@scotlandintrust.co.uk
Advertising Address: As above. **Fax:** 0131 556 3300
Email: kirsti@scotlandintrust.co.uk
Web site: http://www.scotlandintrust.co.uk
ISSN: 1479-0424
Publisher: CMYK Design
Date Established: 2002
Frequency: 3 issues yearly - Published in March, June and September
Cover Price: Free
Circulation: 181,803 (ABC 01/01/2008 to 31/12/2008)
Usual Pagination: 76
Editor: Iain Gale; **Advertising Manager:** Kirsti Thomson
Summary of Content: Magazine covering the works of the National Trust Scotland with features on its properties and conservation work in the built heritage, gardens and open countryside. It also promotes the products and services, provided by the Trust for its members, through news and features about holidays and retail and provides background information to new appeals launched by the charity.
Readership/Target Audience: Aimed at anyone who has an interest in, or passion for, Scottish heritage, gardens, buildings, countryside and culture.
ADVERTISING RATES:
Full Page Colour £3195.00
Agency Commission: 10%
Mechanical Data: Type Area: 251 x 180mm, Bleed Size: 281 x 216mm, Trim Size: 275 x 210mm, Col Length: 251mm, Page Width: 180mm, Film: Digital
CONSUMER: RURAL & REGIONAL INTEREST: Regional Interest Scotland

SCOTLAND MAGAZINE
755504U80E-165

Editorial Address: St. Faiths House, Mountergate, NORWICH, NR1 1PY **Tel:** 01603 633808 **Fax:** 01603 632808
Email: sally@paragraphpublishing.co.uk
Advertising Address: As above.
Email: paulholmes@paragraphpublishing.co.uk
Web site: http://www.scotlandmag.co.uk
ISSN: 1475-5505
Publisher: Paragraph Publishing
Date Established: 2002
Frequency: 6 issues yearly

Consumer Magazines

Cover Price: £3.75
Circulation: 45,000 (Publisher's Statement)
Usual Pagination: 76
Editor: Sally Toms
Summary of Content: Magazine covering all things Scottish including local news, entertainment, travel, famous personalities, style, culture and a leisure directory.
Language(s): English; French; Japanese
Readership/Target Audience: Read by those who are passionate about all things Scottish.
ADVERTISING RATES:
Full Page Colour £2760.00
Agency Commission: 10%
Mechanical Data: Bleed Size: 291 x 221mm, Trim Size: 285 x 215mm, Film: Digital
Copy instructions: Copy Date: 6 weeks prior to publication date
Average advertising content per issue: 20%
CONSUMER: RURAL & REGIONAL INTEREST: Regional Interest Scotland

SCOTLAND: SELF CATERING, WHERE TO STAY GUIDE
48013U89A-420
Formerly: Scotland: Self Catering
Editorial Address: Ocean Point One, 94 Ocean Drive, EDINBURGH, EH6 6JH **Tel:** 0131 332 2433
Email: wendy.bell@visitscotland.com
Web site: http://www.visitscotland.com
Publisher: VisitScotland
Frequency: Annual - Published in November
Cover Price: £5.99
Circulation: 8,000 (Publisher's Statement)
Usual Pagination: 310
Editor: Wendy Bell
Summary of Content: Guide covering all aspects of self catering accommodation.
Readership/Target Audience: Aimed at potential visitors from the UK and overseas.
ADVERTISING: No Advertising taken
CONSUMER: HOLIDAYS & TRAVEL: Travel

SCOTLAND'S NEW HOMEBUYER
600825U74K-430
Editorial Address: 9 Gayfield Square, EDINBURGH, EH1 3NT **Tel:** 0131 556 9702 **Fax:** 0131 557 4701
Email: helen@pinpoint-scotland.com
Advertising Address: As above.
Email: helen@pinpoint-scotland.com
Web site: http://www.snhb.co.uk
ISSN: 1478-3789
Publisher: Pinpoint Scotland Ltd
Date Established: 1985
Frequency: Quarterly
Cover Price: Free
Circulation: 17,000 (Publisher's Statement)
Usual Pagination: 80
Editor: Anna Baird; **Advertising Manager:** Helen Stuart
Summary of Content: Magazine focusing on new-build houses and apartments in Scotland. Includes information on mortgages, solicitors advice, interior design ideas and National House Building Council updates. Also covers articles on self-build, gardening tips and listings of new developments.
Readership/Target Audience: Aimed at new homebuyers in Scotland.
ADVERTISING RATES:
Full Page Colour £2054.00
Agency Commission: 10%
Mechanical Data: Type Area: 270 x 178mm, Bleed Size: 303 x 216mm, Trim Size: 297 x 210mm, Col Length: 270mm, Film: Digital, Page Width: 178mm
Copy instructions: Copy Date: 1st of the month prior to publication date
Average advertising content per issue: 50%
CONSUMER: WOMEN'S INTEREST CONSUMER MAGAZINES: Home Purchase

SCOTS INDEPENDENT
47052U80E-371
Editorial Address: 51 Cowane Street, STIRLING, FK8 1JW
Tel: 01259 730099 **Fax:** 0131 334 1739
Email: comment@scotsindependent.org
Advertising Address: As above.
Email: denholm@scotsindependent.org
Web site: http://www.scotsindependent.org
Publisher: Scots Independent (Newspapers) Ltd
Date Established: 1926
Frequency: Monthly
Cover Price: £1.50
Annual Sub.: £24.00
Circulation: 6,000 (Publisher's Statement)
Usual Pagination: 12
Editor: Jim Lynch; **Advertising Manager:** Thomas Christie
Summary of Content: Magazine covering all aspects of Scottish life and culture, including self-government for Scotland.

Readership/Target Audience: Read by all those interested in Scottish culture and politics.
ADVERTISING: Rates on application
CONSUMER: RURAL & REGIONAL INTEREST: Regional Interest Scotland

THE SCOTS MAGAZINE
47053U80E-190
Editorial Address: 2 Albert Square, DUNDEE, DD1 9QJ
Tel: 01382 223131 **Fax:** 01382 322214
Email: mail@scotsmagazine.com
Advertising Address: 80 Kingsway East, DUNDEE, DD4 8SL **Tel:** 01382 223131 **Fax:** 01382 454599
Email: advertising-kingsway@dcthomson.co.uk
Web site: http://www.scotsmagazine.com
Publisher: D.C. Thomson & Co Ltd
Date Established: 1739
Frequency: Monthly
Cover Price: £1.70
Annual Sub.: £24.00
Circulation: 34,691 (ABC 01/01/2009 to 30/06/2009)
Usual Pagination: 112
Editor: Christina Dolen; **Advertising Manager:** Dorothy Hume
Summary of Content: Magazine focusing on walking and climbing, history and traditions, wildlife, environmental issues, books and music.
Readership/Target Audience: Read by those who have a special interest in and an affection for Scotland.
ADVERTISING RATES:
Full Page Mono £856.00
Full Page Colour £1244.00
SCC £23.50
Agency Commission: 15%
Mechanical Data: Bleed Size: 220 x 141mm, Trim Size: 214 x 141mm, Type Area: 187 x 114mm, Col Length: 187mm, No. of Columns (Display): 2, Film: Positive, right reading, emulsion side down, Print Process: Offset litho, Col Widths (Display): 55mm, Page Width: 114mm
Copy instructions: Copy Date: 7 weeks prior to publication date
CONSUMER: RURAL & REGIONAL INTEREST: Regional Interest Scotland

SCOTSGAY
47632U86B-125
Editorial Address: PO Box 666, EDINBURGH, EH7 5YW
Tel: 0131 539 0666 **Fax:** 0131 539 2999
Email: editorial@scotsgay.co.uk
Advertising Address: As above. **Tel:** 07722 388903
Email: advertising@scotsgay.co.uk
Web site: http://www.scotsgay.co.uk
ISSN: 1357-0595
Publisher: Pageprint Publishing Limited
Frequency: Monthly
Cover Price: £1.00
Circulation: 6,000 (Publisher's Statement)
Usual Pagination: 32
Editor: John Hein; **Advertising Manager:** Jean Genie; **Publisher:** John Hein
Summary of Content: Magazine containing news, views, gossip, reviews and features on the media, travel and holidays.
Readership/Target Audience: Aimed at the lesbian, gay and bisexual community in Scotland.
ADVERTISING RATES:
Full Page Colour £460.00
Agency Commission: 10%
Mechanical Data: Trim Size: 297 x 210mm, Film: Digital
Average advertising content per issue: 25%
CONSUMER: ADULT & GAY MAGAZINES: Gay & Lesbian Magazines

THE SCOTTISH AND NORTHERN EQUESTRIAN
1605878U81D-354
Formerly: The Scottish Equestrian
Editorial Address: 26 Blairs Road, Letham, FORFAR, DD8 2PE **Tel:** 0845 130 7669 **Fax:** 0845 130 7669
Email: info@snequestrian.com
Advertising Address: As above. **Tel:** 01307 818919
Fax: 01307 818919
Email: susan@snequestrian.com
Web site: http://www.snequestrian.com
ISSN: 1742-7312
Publisher: Hillaine Publishing Ltd
Date Established: 1998
Frequency: 11 issues yearly
Cover Price: £3.10
Annual Sub.: £29.00
Circulation: 10,000 (Publisher's Statement)
Usual Pagination: 100
Editor: Helen Crighton; **Advertising Manager:** Susan Cox; **Managing Editor:** Helen Crighton
Summary of Content: Official magazine for the Scottish Equestrian Association, which is recognised by Sportscotland and the Scottish Executive. Covering features, articles and reports on a wide spectrum of

equestrian activity from grassroots to international competition.
Readership/Target Audience: Aimed at all active equestrian enthusiasts of all ages, disciplines and levels.
ADVERTISING RATES:
Full Page Colour £575.00
Agency Commission: 10%
Mechanical Data: Trim Size: 297 x 210mm, Bleed Size: 303 x 216mm, Film: Digital, Type Area: 275 x 190mm, Page Width: 190mm, Col Length: 275mm
Copy instructions: Copy Date: 10th of the month prior to publication date
CONSUMER: ANIMALS & PETS: Horses & Ponies

SCOTTISH CARAVANNER
625506U91B-200
Editorial Address: Suite 7, Buko Tower, Dalton Road, GLENROTHES, KY6 2SS **Tel:** 01592 610421
Fax: 01592 755315
Email: bob@scottishcaravanner.com
Advertising Address: As above.
Email: bob@scottishcaravanner.com
Web site: http://www.scottishcaravanner.com
Publisher: Scottish Caravanner
Date Established: 1998
Frequency: Quarterly
Cover Price: £2.25
Free to qualifying individuals
Circulation: 8,000 (Publisher's Statement)
Usual Pagination: 96
Editor: Bob Mather; **Advertising Manager:** Bob Mather; **Managing Editor:** Bob Mather
Summary of Content: Magazine offering a guide to caravan and camping news in Scotland and regular reviews on all manufacture of caravans and motorhomes in the UK.
Readership/Target Audience: Aimed at Scottish caravanners and potential caravanners in Scotland.
ADVERTISING RATES:
Full Page Colour £595.00
Agency Commission: 10%
Mechanical Data: Trim Size: 297 x 210mm
Average advertising content per issue: 45%
CONSUMER: RECREATION & LEISURE: Camping & Caravanning

SCOTTISH CATHOLIC OBSERVER
47753U87-207
Editorial Address: 19 Waterloo Street, GLASGOW, G2 6BT
Tel: 0141 221 4956 **Fax:** 0141 221 4546
Email: editor@scottishcatholicobserver.org.uk
Advertising Address: As above.
Email: advertising@scottishcatholicobserver.com
Web site: http://www.scottishcatholicobserver.com
Publisher: Catholic Herald Ltd
Frequency: Weekly
Cover Price: £0.80
Circulation: 17,000 (Publisher's Statement)
Usual Pagination: 24
Editor: Liz Leydon; **Advertising Manager:** Rebecca Rigg
Summary of Content: National Catholic newspaper of Scotland.
Readership/Target Audience: Read by Catholics.
ADVERTISING RATES:
Full Page Mono £1132.20
Full Page Colour £1415.25
Agency Commission: 10%
Mechanical Data: Page Width: 265mm, Type Area: 360 x265mm, Film: Digital, Col Length: 360mm, No. of Columns (Display): 6, Col Widths (Display): 41mm
Copy instructions: Copy Date: Friday 5pm prior to publication date
Average advertising content per issue: 25%
CONSUMER: RELIGIOUS

SCOTTISH CLUB GOLFER
1665558U75D-541
Editorial Address: 50 High Craighall Road, GLASGOW, G4 9UD **Tel:** 0141 353 2222 **Fax:** 0141 332 3811
Email: martin.dempster@psp.uk.net
Advertising Address: As above.
Web site: http://www.bunkered.co.uk
Publisher: PSP Publishing Ltd
Date Established: 2003
Frequency: 6 issues yearly
Cover Price: Free
Circulation: 25,000 (Publisher's Statement)
Editor: Martin Dempster
Summary of Content: Magazine covering amateur golf in Scotland including fixtures, results, player profiles and interviews and equipment reviews.
Readership/Target Audience: Aimed at amateur golfers in Scotland.
ADVERTISING RATES:
Full Page Colour £1695.00
Agency Commission: 10%
Mechanical Data: Bleed Size: 366 x 286mm, Trim Size: 360 x 280mm, Film: Digital

Average advertising content per issue: 35%
CONSUMER: SPORT: Golf

THE SCOTTISH CURLER
45874U75G-280

Editorial Address: Skip Cottage, Wamphray, MOFFATT, DG10 9NG **Tel:** 01576 470650 **Fax:** 01383 737040
Advertising Address: Pitreavie Business Park, Queensferry Road, DUNFERMLINE, KY11 8QS **Tel:** 01383 728201
Fax: 01383 737040
Email: advertising@dunfermlinepress.co.uk
Web site: http://www.dunfermlinepress.com
Publisher: The Dunfermline Press Group
Date Established: 1954
Frequency: 8 issues yearly - Published monthly from October to April
Annual Sub.: £15.75
Usual Pagination: 24
Advertising Manager: Janet Richards
Summary of Content: Magazine covering all aspects of the curling sport in Scotland.
Readership/Target Audience: Aimed at club secretaries and curlers nationwide, with an emphasis on Scotland.
ADVERTISING RATES:
Full Page Mono £859.00
Full Page Colour £1040.00
Agency Commission: 10%
Mechanical Data: Col Length: 267mm, Film: Digital, Type Area: 267 x 180mm, Print Process: Sheet fed litho, Trim Size: 297 x 210mm, Bleed Size: +3mm, Page Width: 180mm
Copy instructions: Copy Date: 12th of the month, prior to publication date
CONSUMER: SPORT: Winter Sports

SCOTTISH DIVER
45950U75M-700

Editorial Address: The Cockburn Centre, 40 Bogmoor Place, GLASGOW, G51 4TQ **Tel:** 0141 425 1021
Fax: 0141 425 1021
Email: editor@scotsac.com
Advertising Address: 5 Craighall House, 58A High Craighall Road, GLASGOW, G4 9UD **Tel:** 0141 332 3933
Email: freetime@tfti.demon.co.uk
Web site: http://www.scotsac.com
ISSN: 0308-7379
Publisher: The Scottish Sub-Aqua Club
Frequency: 6 issues yearly
Cover Price: £2.50
Free to qualifying individuals
Annual Sub.: £9.95
Circulation: 3,000 (Publisher's Statement)
Usual Pagination: 40
Editor: Jack Morrison
Summary of Content: Magazine of the Scottish Sub-Aqua Club containing news updates and features on local clubs, diving abroad, equipment, techniques, new products and diving destinations in Scotland.
Readership/Target Audience: Read by members and anyone with an interest in diving.
ADVERTISING RATES:
Full Page Colour £340.00
Agency Commission: 10%
Mechanical Data: Page Width: 185mm, Type Area: 267 x 185mm, Trim Size: 297 x 210mm, Bleed Size: 307 x 220mm, Col Length: 267mm, Film: Digital
Copy instructions: Copy Date: 19 days prior to publication date
Average advertising content per issue: 45%
CONSUMER: SPORT: Water Sports

THE SCOTTISH EQUESTRIAN DIRECTORY
1605872U81D-352

Editorial Address: 26 Blairs Road, Letham, FORFAR, DD8 2PE **Tel:** 0845 130 7669 **Fax:** 0845 130 7669
Email: info@snequestrian.com
Advertising Address: As above. **Tel:** 01307 818919
Fax: 01307 818919
Email: susan@snequestrian.com
Web site: http://www.snequestrian.com
Publisher: Hillaine Publishing Ltd
Date Established: 2001
Frequency: Annual - Published in February
Cover Price: Free
Circulation: 20,000 (Publisher's Statement)
Usual Pagination: 164
Editor: Helen Crighton; **Advertising Manager:** Susan Cox
Summary of Content: Directory covering useful sources of information to all involved in equestrian life, from complete beginners to the most knowledgeable.
Readership/Target Audience: Aimed at anyone interested and/or involved in equestrianism.
ADVERTISING RATES:
Full Page Colour £575.00
Agency Commission: 15%
Mechanical Data: Trim Size: 210 x 148mm, Film: Digital, Type Area: 187 x 124.5mm, Col Length: 187mm, Page Width: 124.5mm
Copy instructions: Copy Date: January 10th

Average advertising content per issue: 45%
CONSUMER: ANIMALS & PETS: Horses & Ponies

SCOTTISH FIELD
47054U80E-220

Editorial Address: Craigcrook Castle, Craigcrook Road, EDINBURGH, EH4 3PE **Tel:** 0131 312 4550
Fax: 0131 312 4551
Email: editor@scottishfield.co.uk
Advertising Address: As above.
Email: adverts@scottishfield.co.uk
Web site: http://www.scottishfield.co.uk
ISSN: 0036-9209
Publisher: Wyvex Media Group
Date Established: 1903
Frequency: Monthly
Cover Price: £3.40
Annual Sub.: £40.80
Circulation: 13,905 (ABC 01/01/2008 to 31/12/2008)
Usual Pagination: 128
Editor: Archie Mackenzie; **Advertising Manager:** Brian Cameron
Summary of Content: Magazine covering Scottish contemporary life, including people, style, culture, landscape, natural history and attractions, plus history and heritage.
Readership/Target Audience: Aimed at people with a high disposable income who are interested in Scottish lifestyle.
ADVERTISING RATES:
Full Page Colour £2175.00
Agency Commission: 10%
Mechanical Data: Film: Digital, Type Area: 267 x 190mm, Bleed Size: 303 x 216mm, Trim Size: 297 x 210mm, Col Length: 267mm, Page Width: 190mm
Copy instructions: Copy Date: 3 weeks prior to publication date
Average advertising content per issue: 35%
CONSUMER: RURAL & REGIONAL INTEREST: Regional Interest Scotland

SCOTTISH HOME & COUNTRY
47055U80E-230

Editorial Address: 42 Heriot Row, EDINBURGH, EH3 6ES
Tel: 0131 225 1724 **Fax:** 0131 225 8129
Email: magazine@swri.demon.co.uk
Advertising Address: As above.
Email: magazine@swri.demon.co.uk
Web site: http://www.swri.org.uk
Publisher: Scottish Women's Rural Institutes
Date Established: 1924
Frequency: Monthly
Cover Price: £1.00
Annual Sub.: £18.50
Circulation: 10,000 (Publisher's Statement)
Usual Pagination: 54
Editor: Liz Ferguson; **Features Editor:** Liz Ferguson; **Managing Director:** Anne Peacock; **Advertising Manager:** Liz Ferguson
Summary of Content: Magazine of the Scottish Women's Rural Institutes covering rural interests and activities, health, cookery, gardening, women's issues and general interest.
Readership/Target Audience: Read by SWRI members, predominantly with rural backgrounds.
ADVERTISING RATES:
Full Page Mono £174.00
Full Page Colour £347.00
Agency Commission: 10%
Mechanical Data: Trim Size: 210 x 148mm, Type Area: 177 x 127mm, Col Length: 177mm, Page Width: 127mm, Film: Digital
Copy instructions: Copy Date: 4 weeks prior to publication date
CONSUMER: RURAL & REGIONAL INTEREST: Regional Interest Scotland

SCOTTISH HOSTELLER
48441U91C-100

Editorial Address: 7 Glebe Crescent, STIRLING, FK8 2JA
Tel: 01786 891400 **Fax:** 01786 891333
Email: hosteller@syha.org.uk
Advertising Address: Pro Sports Ltd, 50 High Craighall Road, GLASGOW, G4 9UD **Tel:** 0141 950 2216
Fax: 0141 950 1330
Email: print@prosportsltd.co.uk
Web site: http://www.syha.org.uk
Publisher: SYHA
Frequency: Half-yearly - Published in March and September
Cover Price: Free
Circulation: 40,000 (Publisher's Statement)
Editor: Nicola McCrae
Summary of Content: Magazine containing information on outdoor equipment and travel, activities and youth hostelling holidays north of the border.
Readership/Target Audience: Read by members of SYHA and outdoor clubs as well as those involved in the tourism industry.
ADVERTISING RATES:
Full Page Colour £950.00
Agency Commission: 10%

Mechanical Data: Trim Size: 297 x 210mm, Bleed Size: 303 x 216mm, Type Area: 274 x 182mm, Page Width: 182mm, Col Length: 274mm, Film: Digital
Average advertising content per issue: 40%
CONSUMER: RECREATION & LEISURE: Hostelling

SCOTTISH ISLANDS EXPLORER
1772595U89A-733

Editorial Address: Bay Street Cottage, The Street, Dallington, HEATHFIELD, TN21 9NH **Tel:** 07828 978328
Email: info@scottishislandsexplorer.com
Advertising Address: As above.
Email: john@gettingon.com
Web site: http://www.scottishislandsexplorer.com
Publisher: Silver Sea Press
Frequency: 6 issues yearly
Cover Price: £3.25
Circulation: 6,000 (Publisher's Statement)
Usual Pagination: 48
Editor: Jeremy Smith; **Publisher:** Jeremy Smith
Summary of Content: Magazine with articles about the Scottish Islands including wildlife, culture, environment, archaeology, lifestyle, history, travel and current affairs.
Readership/Target Audience: Aimed at those interested in the Scottish Islands.
ADVERTISING RATES:
Full Page Colour £520.00
Mechanical Data: Type Area: 267 x 182mm, Bleed Size: 303 x 213mm, Trim Size: 297 x 210mm, Col Length: 267mm, Page Width: 182mm, Film: Digital
Copy instructions: Copy Date: 28th of the month prior to publication date
CONSUMER: HOLIDAYS & TRAVEL: Travel

SCOTTISH JOBS
48717U94X-182

Editorial Address: 200 Renfield Street, GLASGOW, G2 3QB
Tel: 0141 302 6191 **Fax:** 0141 302 6363
Advertising Address: As above. **Tel:** 0141 302 6123
Fax: 0141 302 6252
Email: recruitment@glasgow.newsquest.co.uk
Publisher: Newsquest (Herald and Times) Ltd
Frequency: Weekly
Cover Price: £0.70
Circulation: 20,000 (Publisher's Statement)
Usual Pagination: 26
Advertising Manager: Stephen Connelly
Summary of Content: Newspaper covering jobs in Scotland, includes articles on how to apply for a job, career training and employment initiatives.
Readership/Target Audience: Aimed at employment seekers or those looking for a career change.
ADVERTISING RATES:
Full Page Mono £453.00
Full Page Colour £483.00
SCC £2.40
Mechanical Data: Film: Digital
Copy instructions: Copy Date: Friday, 12pm prior to publication date
CONSUMER: OTHER CLASSIFICATIONS: Miscellaneous

SCOTTISH LEGION NEWS
48584U94A-120

Editorial Address: New Haig House, Logie Green Road, EDINBURGH, EH7 4HR **Tel:** 0131 557 2782
Fax: 0131 557 5819
Email: publicity@ehfs.org.uk
Advertising Address: As above.
Email: rblspublicity@poppyscotland.org.uk
Publisher: Royal British Legion Scotland
Frequency: 5 issues yearly
Annual Sub.: £6.00
Circulation: 16,000 (Publisher's Statement)
Usual Pagination: 32
Editor: Neil Griffiths; **Advertising Manager:** Neil Griffiths
Summary of Content: Magazine covering all matters of interest to the ex-service community.
Readership/Target Audience: Read by members of the Royal British Legion Scotland, ex-service people and serving personnel.
ADVERTISING RATES:
Full Page Colour £900.00
Mechanical Data: Type Area: 390 x 260mm, Col Length: 390mm, Page Width: 260mm, Film: Digital
Average advertising content per issue: 30%
Official Journal of: The Royal British Legion Scotland
CONSUMER: OTHER CLASSIFICATIONS: War Veterans

SCOTTISH MEMORIES
48718U94X-183

Editorial Address: Strathclyde Business Centre, 120 Carstairs Street, GLASGOW, G40 4JD **Tel:** 0141 554 9944
Fax: 0141 554 9955
Email: scottishmemories@aol.com
Advertising Address: As above. **Tel:** 0141 946 8708
Fax: 0141 946 8708
Email: scottishmemories@yahoo.co.uk

Web site: http://www.scottish-memories.co.uk
ISSN: 0968-7874
Publisher: Lang Syne Publishers Ltd
Date Established: 1993
Frequency: Monthly
Cover Price: £2.95
Annual Sub.: £36.00
Circulation: 18,000 (Publisher's Statement)
Usual Pagination: 52
Editor: George Forbes; **Managing Director:** Ken Laird;
Advertising Manager: Alison Fraser; **Publisher:** Ken Laird
Summary of Content: Magazine covering all aspects of
Scotland's national history, classic history and nostalgia.
Readership/Target Audience: Aimed at households and
those interested in history and nostalgia aged 30 years and
over.
ADVERTISING RATES:
Full Page Colour £895.00
Agency Commission: 10%
Mechanical Data: Film: Digital, Type Area: 273 x 190mm,
Page Width: 190mm, Trim Size: 297 x 210mm, Bleed Size:
307 x 220mm, Col Length: 273mm
Copy instructions: Copy Date: 2 weeks prior to publication
date
Average advertising content per issue: 30%
CONSUMER: OTHER CLASSIFICATIONS: Miscellaneous

SCOTTISH MOUNTAINEER   767172U75L-802

Editorial Address: Old Granary, West Mill Street, PERTH,
PH1 5QP **Tel:** 01738 638227 **Fax:** 01738 442095
Email: kev@mountaineering-scotland.org.uk
Advertising Address: 50 High Craighall Road, GLASGOW,
G4 9UD **Tel:** 0141 353 2222 **Fax:** 0141 332 3811
Email: ann.liddle@psp.uk.net
Web site: http://www.mountaineering-scotland.org.uk
Publisher: Newsquest (Herald and Times) Ltd
Date Established: 1992
Frequency: Quarterly
Cover Price: £3.25
Circulation: 15,000 (Publisher's Statement)
Usual Pagination: 100
Editor: Kevin Howett; **Advertising Manager:** Ann Liddle
Summary of Content: Magazine covering all aspects of
mountaineering, climbing, hill walking and cross-country
skiing in Scotland.
Readership/Target Audience: Aimed at walkers, climbers
and mountaineers with skis, with an interest in hill walking
and mountaineering.
ADVERTISING RATES:
Full Page Colour £995.00
SCC £18.00
Agency Commission: 10%
Mechanical Data: Film: Digital, Type Area: 274 x 186mm,
Col Length: 274mm, Page Width: 186mm, Bleed Size: 303 x
216mm, Trim Size: 297 x 210mm
Copy instructions: Copy Date: 5 weeks prior to publication
date
Average advertising content per issue: 30%
CONSUMER: SPORT: Outdoor

SCOTTISH SPCA NEWS   766923U81A-252

Formerly: Scottish SPCA
Editorial Address: 603 Queensferry Road, EDINBURGH,
EH4 6EA **Tel:** 0131 339 0222 **Fax:** 0131 339 4777
Email: ben.supple@scottishspca.org
Web site: http://www.scottishspca.org
ISSN: 1360-8207
Publisher: Scottish SPCA
Frequency: Quarterly
Cover Price: Free
Circulation: 45,000 (Publisher's Statement)
Editor: Ben Supple
Summary of Content: Magazine providing the latest news
on the Scottish Society for the Prevention of Cruelty to
Animals featuring animal-related issues, events and animal
welfare news.
Readership/Target Audience: Read by members of the
SSPCA and contributors to the society.
ADVERTISING: No Advertising taken
CONSUMER: ANIMALS & PETS: Animals & Pets Protection

THE SCOTTISH SPORTING GAZETTE & INTERNATIONAL TRAVELLER

                                              1648724U80A-165
Editorial Address: Roebuck House, 33 Broad Street,
STAMFORD, PE9 1RB **Tel:** 01780 754900
Fax: 01780 766416
Email: j.buzzel@bournepublishinggroup.co.uk
Advertising Address: As above. **Fax:** 01780 754774
Web site: http://www.scottishsporting.co.uk
ISSN: 1364-0526
Publisher: BPG (Stamford) Ltd
Frequency: Annual - Published in December
Cover Price: £4.95
Circulation: 20,000 (Publisher's Statement)
Usual Pagination: 132

Editor: James Buzzel
Summary of Content: Magazine covering country pursuits
in Scotland including fishing, stalking and game shooting as
well as hotels, whisky and restaurants.
Readership/Target Audience: Aimed at those interested in
sporting holidays in Scotland.
ADVERTISING RATES:
Full Page Colour £2050.00
Agency Commission: 10%
Mechanical Data: Type Area: 269 x 196mm, Col Length:
269mm, Page Width: 196mm, Bleed Size: 309 x 236mm,
Trim Size: 297 x 224mm, Film: Digital, No. of Columns
(Display): 2, Print Process: Web-fed litho
CONSUMER: RURAL & REGIONAL INTEREST: Rural
Interest

THE SCOTTISH WEDDING DIRECTORY

                                              761832U74L-160
Editorial Address: Unit 26, 6 Harmony Row, GLASGOW,
G51 3BA **Tel:** 0141 445 5545 **Fax:** 0141 445 4468
Email: info@scottishweddingdirectory.co.uk
Advertising Address: As above.
Email: craig@scottishweddingdirectory.co.uk
Web site: http://www.scottishweddingdirectory.co.uk
Publisher: The Scottish Wedding Directory
Date Established: 1995
Frequency: Half-yearly - Published in January and July
Cover Price: £3.95
Circulation: 25,000 (Publisher's Statement)
Usual Pagination: 552
Editor: Ros Nash; **Managing Director:** Lorna Leckie
Summary of Content: Magazine includes features on bridal
wear, wedding receptions, beauty, travel, furnishing and
decor.
Readership/Target Audience: Aimed at Scottish couples
intending to marry in the near future.
ADVERTISING RATES:
Full Page Mono £1140.00
Full Page Colour £1140.00
Agency Commission: 10%
Mechanical Data: Trim Size: 297 x 220mm, Bleed Size: 303
x 226mm, Film: Digital
Average advertising content per issue: 65%
Supplement(s): Scottish Wedding Venues - 2xY
CONSUMER: WOMEN'S INTEREST CONSUMER
MAGAZINES: Brides

SCOTTISH WILDLIFE   761391O U81A-256

Editorial Address: Cramond House, 3 Kirk Cramond,
EDINBURGH, EH4 6HZ **Tel:** 0131 312 7765
Fax: 0131 312 8705
Email: editor@swt.org.uk
Advertising Address: 7-8 Saunders Street, EDINBURGH,
EH3 6TU **Tel:** 0131 226 5364
Email: daniel@danielevans.co.uk
Web site: http://www.swt.org.uk
Publisher: Scottish Wildlife Trust
Date Established: 1987
Frequency: 3 issues yearly - Published in March, August
and November
Cover Price: £2.50
Free to qualifying individuals
Circulation: 18,500 (Publisher's Statement)
Usual Pagination: 36
Editor: Clara Govier; **Advertising Manager:** Daniel Evans
Summary of Content: Magazine covering the latest wildlife
news, species profiles, wildlife articles and book reviews.
Readership/Target Audience: Aimed at members of the
Scottish Wildlife Trust.
ADVERTISING RATES:
Full Page Mono £490.00
Full Page Colour £750.00
Mechanical Data: Type Area: 270 x 195mm, Trim Size: 297
x 210mm, Col Length: 270mm, Page Width: 195mm, Film:
Digital
Copy instructions: Copy Date: 6 weeks prior to publication
date
CONSUMER: ANIMALS & PETS: Animals & Pets Protection

SCOTTISH WOMAN   1638722U80E-354

Editorial Address: PO Box 2012, LIVINGSTON, EH54 0BD
Tel: 01506 200890 **Fax:** 01506 203419
Email: maria@scottishwomanmagazine.com
Advertising Address: As above.
Email: maria@scottishwomanmagazine.com
Web site: http://www.scottishwomanmagazine.com
Publisher: Haxton Marketing Ltd
Date Established: 2003
Frequency: 6 issues yearly
Cover Price: £2.95
Circulation: 100,000 (Publisher's Statement)
Usual Pagination: 120
Editor: Maria Morrison-Barnett; **Managing Director:** Maria
Morrison-Barnett; **Advertising Manager:** Maria Morrison-
Barnett; **Publisher:** Maria Morrison-Barnett

Summary of Content: Magazine covering hair, health,
beauty and fashion.
Readership/Target Audience: Aimed at women in
Scotland.
ADVERTISING: Rates on application
CONSUMER: RURAL & REGIONAL INTEREST: Regional
Interest Scotland

SCOUTING   48475U91D-100

Formerly: Scouting Magazine
Editorial Address: Gilwell Park, Chingford, LONDON, E4
7QW **Tel:** 020 8433 7100 **Fax:** 020 8433 7103
Email: scouting.magazine@scout.org.uk
Advertising Address: Think Publishing Ltd, The Pall Mall
Deposit, 124-128 Barlby Road, LONDON, W10 6BL
Tel: 020 8962 3020 **Fax:** 020 8962 8689
Email: michael@thinkpublishing.co.uk
Web site: http://www.scouts.org.uk
ISSN: 0036-9489
Publisher: The Scout Association
Date Established: 1909
Frequency: 6 issues yearly
Free to qualifying individuals
Circulation: 84,000 (Publisher's Statement)
Usual Pagination: 100
Editor: Elis Matthews
Summary of Content: Magazine providing the exchange of
news and views from all sections of the Scout Movement.
Readership/Target Audience: Aimed at those interested in
the Scout Movement.
ADVERTISING RATES:
Full Page Colour £2500.00
Mechanical Data: Type Area: 195 x 131mm, Col Length:
195mm, Page Width: 131mm, Trim Size: 210 x 146mm,
Bleed Size: 216 x 152mm, Film: Digital
CONSUMER: RECREATION & LEISURE: Children & Youth

SCRAPBOOK INSPIRATIONS   1667446U74E-692

Editorial Address: 30 Monmouth Street, BATH, BA1 2BW
Tel: 01225 442244
Email: scrapbookinspirations@futurenet.com
Advertising Address: As above.
Email: rhobbs@futurenet.com
Web site: http://www.scrapbookinspirationsmagazine.co.uk
Publisher: Future Publishing Ltd
Date Established: 2005
Frequency: 13 issues yearly
Cover Price: £3.99
Circulation: 60,000 (Print Run)
Usual Pagination: 100
Editor: Rosie Waddicor; **Advertising Manager:** Robert
Hobbs
Summary of Content: Magazine giving inspiration for new
layouts with advice and tips from top designers on how to
achieve them and the materials to use.
Readership/Target Audience: Aimed at scrapbookers of all
abilities.
ADVERTISING RATES:
Full Page Mono £1290.00
Full Page Colour £1290.00
Agency Commission: 10%
Mechanical Data: Type Area: 270 x 190mm, Bleed Size:
303 x 216mm, Trim Size: 297 x 210mm, Col Length: 270mm,
Page Width: 190mm, Film: Digital
CONSUMER: WOMEN'S INTEREST CONSUMER
MAGAZINES: Crafts

SCRAPBOOK MAGAZINE   1648790U79R-150

Editorial Address: Unit 1 Adlington Court, Adlington
Industrial Estate, Adlington, MACCLESFIELD, SK10 4NL
Tel: 0844 561 1202 **Fax:** 01625 855071
Email: info@practicalpublishing.co.uk
Advertising Address: As above. **Tel:** 0870 242 7038
Fax: 01625 855011
Email: lisa.sturgeon@practicalpublishing.co.uk
Web site: http://www.practicalpublishing.co.uk/scrapbook
ISSN: 1743-4335
Publisher: Practical Publishing International Ltd
Date Established: 2004
Frequency: 8 issues yearly
Cover Price: £3.99
Annual Sub.: £21.55
Circulation: 15,000 (Publisher's Statement)
Usual Pagination: 84
Editor: Lee Jepson; **Advertising Manager:** Lisa Sturgeon
Summary of Content: Magazine covering the craft of scrap
booking including how to use paint, stamps, computer
software and photography, paper cutting and journaling as
well as events listings.
Readership/Target Audience: Aimed at those who want to
create a keepsake for the family as well as paper crafters,
photographers and card makers.
ADVERTISING RATES:
Full Page Colour £900.00
Agency Commission: 10%

Mechanical Data: Type Area: 275 x 190mm, Bleed Size: 303 x 216mm, Trim Size: 297 x 210mm, Col Length: 275mm, Page Width: 190mm, Film: Digital
Copy instructions: Copy Date: 3 weeks prior to publication date
Average advertising content per issue: 18%
CONSUMER: HOBBIES & DIY: Hobbies & DIY Related

SCREEN
46056U76A-45

Editorial Address: Gilmorehill Centre, University of Glasgow, GLASGOW, G12 8QQ **Tel:** 0141 330 5035
Fax: 0141 330 3515
Email: screen@arts.gla.ac.uk
Advertising Address: 60 Upper Broadmoor Road, CROWTHORNE, RG45 7DE **Tel:** 01344 779945
Fax: 01344 779945
Email: lhann@lhms.fsnet.co.uk
Web site: http://www.screen.arts.gla.ac.uk
ISSN: 0036-9543
Publisher: OUP
Date Established: 1959
Frequency: Quarterly
Annual Sub.: £46.00
Circulation: 1,100 (Publisher's Statement)
Usual Pagination: 120
Editor: Caroline Beven
Summary of Content: Journal of screen studies covering all aspects of contemporary and historical film including video art, popular television, Hollywood, art cinema and British film finance. Each issue contains scholarly essays, reports and debates, current research and book reviews.
Readership/Target Audience: Read by those interested in film and television studies as an academic discipline.
ADVERTISING RATES:
Full Page Mono £340.00
Agency Commission: 10%
CONSUMER: MUSIC & PERFORMING ARTS: Cinema

THE SCRUM
1828669U75C-474

Editorial Address: 34 Bernard Street, EDINBURGH, EH6 6PR **Tel:** 0131 554 1129 **Fax:** 0131 555 1622
Email: gary@scrummagazine.com
Advertising Address: As above.
Email: john@belljohnstone.co.uk
Web site: http://www.scrummagazine.com
Publisher: Bell Johnstone Communications
Date Established: 2007
Frequency: Monthly
Cover Price: £3.00
Circulation: 11,000 (Publisher's Statement)
Usual Pagination: 56
Editor: Gary Heatly
Summary of Content: Magazine covering rugby union with news, club features, kit reviews, interviews with players and lifestyle articles.
Readership/Target Audience: Aimed at rugby union fans 15 to 30 years old and distributed through clubs and schools.
Mechanical Data: Type Area: 270 x 190mm, Bleed Size: 303 x 216mm, Trim Size: 297 x 210mm, Col Length: 270mm, Page Width: 190mm, Film: Digital
CONSUMER: SPORT: Rugby

SEA ANGLER
48539U92-90

Editorial Address: Bushfield House, Orton Centre, PETERBOROUGH, PE2 5UW **Tel:** 01733 465759
Fax: 01733 465658
Email: mel.russ@bauermedia.co.uk
Advertising Address: As above. **Tel:** 01733 237111
Fax: 01733 288005
Email: kimberley.smith@bauerconsumer.co.uk
Web site: http://www.gofishing.co.uk
Publisher: Bauer Media Ltd (Orton)
Frequency: 13 issues yearly
Cover Price: £3.25
Circulation: 37,359 (ABC 01/01/2008 to 31/12/2008)
Usual Pagination: 148
Editor: Mel Russ
Summary of Content: Magazine covering all aspects of the sea fishing scene, with equipment reviews and location reports.
Readership/Target Audience: Aimed at sea anglers.
ADVERTISING RATES:
Full Page Colour £2995.00
Agency Commission: 10%
Mechanical Data: Type Area: 275 x 185mm, Col Length: 275mm, Page Width: 185mm, Trim Size: 297 x 210mm, Bleed Size: 303 x 216mm, Film: Digital
Copy instructions: Copy Date: 4 weeks prior to publication date
Average advertising content per issue: 45%
CONSUMER: ANGLING & FISHING

SEA ANGLING NEWS
1872712U92-114

Editorial Address: 27 Lower Bere Wood, WATERLOOVILLE, PO7 7NQ **Tel:** 023 9226 5445 **Fax:** 023 9226 5445
Email: seaangling@aol.com
Web site: http://www.seaanglingnews.co.uk
Publisher: Sea Angling News Ltd
Date Established: 1998
Frequency: Monthly
Cover Price: Free
Circulation: 10,000 (Publisher's Statement)
Usual Pagination: 24
Editor: Norman Berry
Summary of Content: Magazine covering sea angling, boat and shore, match fishing and political issues pertaining to sea angling.
Readership/Target Audience: Aimed at pleasure, leisure and match anglers.
CONSUMER: ANGLING & FISHING

SEAFARER
48410U91A-288

Editorial Address: 202 Lambeth Road, LONDON, SE1 7JW **Tel:** 020 7654 7000 **Fax:** 020 7928 8914
Email: info@ms-sc.org
Advertising Address: As above.
Email: bmacgibbon@ms-sc.org
Web site: http://www.ms-sc.org
ISSN: 0037-007X
Publisher: The Marine Society & Sea Cadets
Date Established: 1934
Frequency: 3 issues yearly - Published in February, June and October
Cover Price: £3.00
Free to qualifying individuals
Annual Sub.: £10.00
Circulation: 8,000 (Publisher's Statement)
Usual Pagination: 36
Editor: Catherine Page; **Advertising Manager:** Rebecca MacGibbon
Summary of Content: Nautical, maritime and shipping magazine covering technology, history and culture as well as articles written by seafarers, profiles and book reviews.
Readership/Target Audience: Aimed at those with an interest in the maritime sector.
ADVERTISING: Rates on application
CONSUMER: RECREATION & LEISURE: Boating & Yachting

SEAHORSE INTERNATIONAL SAILING
48390U91A-140

Editorial Address: 5 Britannia Place, Station Street, LYMINGTON, SO41 3BA **Tel:** 01590 671899
Fax: 01590 671116
Email: info@seahorse.co.uk
Advertising Address: As above.
Email: info@seahorse.co.uk
Web site: http://www.seahorsemagazine.com
ISSN: 0143-246X
Publisher: Fairmead Communications Ltd
Frequency: Monthly
Cover Price: £3.95
Annual Sub.: £56.00
Circulation: 20,000 (Publisher's Statement)
Usual Pagination: 68
Editor: Andrew Hurst; **Advertising Manager:** Graeme Beeson
Summary of Content: Official magazine of the Royal Ocean Racing Club, covering international sailing news and races. Includes articles on various technical sailing topics.
Readership/Target Audience: Read by those with an interest in top level yacht racing, boat owners, investors and participants.
ADVERTISING RATES:
Full Page Colour £3122.00
Agency Commission: 10%
Mechanical Data: Page Width: 188mm, Type Area: 270 x 188mm, Bleed Size: 303 x 216mm, Trim Size: 297 x 210mm, Film: Digital, Col Length: 270mm
Copy instructions: Copy Date: 3 weeks prior to publication date
Average advertising content per issue: 50%
CONSUMER: RECREATION & LEISURE: Boating & Yachting

SECOND LANGUAGE RESEARCH
30086U88R-40

Editorial Address: 1 Oliver's Yard, 55 City Road, LONDON, EC1Y 1SP **Tel:** 020 7324 8500 **Fax:** 020 7324 8600
Email: market@sagepub.co.uk
Advertising Address: As above.
Email: sheena.karim@sagepub.co.uk
Web site: http://www.sagepub.co.uk
ISSN: 0267-6583
Publisher: Sage Publications
Date Established: 1985
Frequency: Quarterly
Annual Sub.: £318.00
Editor: Roger Hawkins

Summary of Content: Academic publication containing theoretical and experimental papers concerned with second language acquisition and performance.
Readership/Target Audience: Aimed at investigators in the field of non-native language learning, acquisition studies, neurolinguistics, theoretical linguistics and first language developmental psycholinguistics.
ADVERTISING RATES:
Full Page Mono £400.00
Agency Commission: 5%
Mechanical Data: Trim Size: 234 x 156mm, Type Area: 205 x 130mm, Col Length: 205mm, Page Width: 130mm, Film: Digital, Bleed Size: 242 x 262mm
CONSUMER: EDUCATION: Education Related

SECURITY DIALOGUE
47340U82-173

Editorial Address: 1 Oliver's Yard, 55 City Road, LONDON, EC1Y 1SP **Tel:** 020 7324 8500 **Fax:** 020 7324 8600
Email: market@sagepub.co.uk
Advertising Address: As above.
Email: advertising@sagepub.co.uk
Web site: http://www.sagepub.co.uk
ISSN: 0967-0106
Publisher: Sage Publications
Frequency: Quarterly
Annual Sub.: £42.00
Circulation: 800 (Publisher's Statement)
Editor: Peter Burgess; **Advertising Manager:** Matthew Schlag
Summary of Content: Journal covering contemporary international and inter-group affairs, searching for solutions to conflict situations in the light of general peace research theory.
Readership/Target Audience: Aimed at those with an interest in issues of security in the modern day society.
ADVERTISING RATES:
Full Page Mono £400.00
Agency Commission: 5%
Mechanical Data: Col Length: 210mm, Page Width: 140mm, Type Area: 210 x 140mm
Copy instructions: Copy Date: 12 weeks prior to publication date
CONSUMER: CURRENT AFFAIRS & POLITICS

SELAMTA
48217U89D-265

Editorial Address: 32 Friars Walk, LONDON, N14 5LP **Tel:** 020 8361 2942
Email: camerapixuk@btinternet.com
Advertising Address: As above.
Email: carol.ibb@btinternet.com
Web site: http://www.camerapix.com
Publisher: Camerapix Magazines Ltd
Date Established: 1984
Frequency: Quarterly
Cover Price: £4.00
Annual Sub.: £16.00
Circulation: 65,000 (Publisher's Statement)
Usual Pagination: 80
Editor: Azra Chaudhry; **Advertising Manager:** Carol Filby
Summary of Content: In-flight magazine of Ethiopian Airlines containing features on Ethiopia, where to stay and sites to see.
Readership/Target Audience: Aimed at passengers of Ethiopian Airlines.
ADVERTISING RATES:
Full Page Mono £2810.00
Full Page Colour £3640.00
Agency Commission: 15%
Mechanical Data: Col Length: 250mm, Film: Digital, No. of Columns (Display): 3, Type Area: 250 x 180mm, Print Process: Web-fed offset litho, Bleed Size: 285 x 212mm, Trim Size: 283 x 210mm, Page Width: 180mm
Copy instructions: Copy Date: 1st week of month prior to publication date
Average advertising content per issue: 28%
CONSUMER: HOLIDAYS & TRAVEL: In-Flight Magazines

SELF BUILD, EXTEND & RENOVATE
1667240U79A-178

Editorial Address: 119 Cahard, Saintfield, CO.DOWN, BT24 7LA **Tel:** 028 9751 0570 **Fax:** 028 9751 0576
Email: info@selfbuild.ie
Advertising Address: As above.
Email: info@selfbuild.ie
Web site: http://www.selfbuild.ie
ISSN: 1477-724X
Publisher: SelfBuild Ireland Ltd
Date Established: 2001
Frequency: Quarterly
Cover Price: £3.50
Free to qualifying individuals
Circulation: 17,127 (ABC 01/01/2008 to 31/12/2008)
Usual Pagination: 180
Editor: Gillian Corry
Summary of Content: Irish Magazine covering suppliers, prices, conditions, rules and regulations, case studies,

Consumer Magazines

technical information, reviews, feature articles and local people.
Readership/Target Audience: Aimed at those looking to build their own home, renovate or extend their existing one in Ireland.
ADVERTISING RATES:
Full Page Colour £1300.00
Agency Commission: 10%
Mechanical Data: Type Area: 261 x 194mm, Bleed Size: 303 x 236mm, Trim Size: 297 x 230mm, Col Length: 261mm, Page Width: 194mm, Film: Digital
Copy instructions: Copy Date: 5 weeks prior to publication date
Average advertising content per issue: 33%
CONSUMER: HOBBIES & DIY

SELFBUILD AND DESIGN
46582U79A-163

Formerly: Self Build and Design
Editorial Address: 151 Station Street, BURTON-ON-TRENT, DE14 1BG **Tel:** 01283 742950 **Fax:** 01283 742957
Email: ross.stokes@sbdonline.co.uk
Advertising Address: 1 Edward Mews, WARWICK, CV34 4JF **Tel:** 01926 493337
Email: david.melville@sbdonline.co.uk
Web site: http://www.sbdonline.co.uk
ISSN: 1368-2830
Publisher: WW Magazines
Date Established: 1997
Frequency: Monthly
Cover Price: £3.99
Circulation: 16,000 (Publisher's Statement)
Usual Pagination: 144
Editor: Louise Parkin; **Advertising Manager:** David Melville; **Publisher:** Peter Johns
Summary of Content: Magazine featuring the complexities of home construction. Provides practical information, covering the options available and their cost implications.
Readership/Target Audience: Aimed at people who would like to have a property built to their own design and specification.
ADVERTISING RATES:
Full Page Colour £1550.00
Agency Commission: 10%
Mechanical Data: Page Width: 190mm, Bleed Size: 306 x 236mm, Type Area: 267 x 190mm, Trim Size: 300 x 230mm, Col Length: 267mm, Film: Digital
Copy instructions: Copy Date: 6 weeks prior to publication date
CONSUMER: HOBBIES & DIY

SELFBUILDER & HOMEMAKER
1623835U79A-177

Editorial Address: Cointronic House, Station Road, HEATHFIELD, TN21 8DF **Tel:** 01435 865797
Fax: 0870 855 5491
Email: editorial@netmagmedia.eu
Advertising Address: As above. **Tel:** 01435 863500
Fax: 01435 863897
Email: sheehan@sbhonline.eu
Web site: http://www.parkerellis.eu
Publisher: Parker Ellis Publishing Ltd
Date Established: 2003
Frequency: 6 issues yearly
Cover Price: Free
Circulation: 9,997 (ABC 01/07/2008 to 30/06/2009)
Usual Pagination: 32
Editor: Patricia Percival
Summary of Content: Product guide with features to help consumers to complete their self-build or renovation projects.
Readership/Target Audience: Aimed at consumers who have been granted planning permission for a self build or renovation project.
ADVERTISING RATES:
Full Page Colour £1425.00
Agency Commission: 10%
Mechanical Data: Type Area: 277 x 190mm, Col Length: 277mm, Page Width: 190mm, Film: Digital, Trim Size: 297 x 210mm, Bleed Size: 303 x 216mm
Average advertising content per issue: 70%
CONSUMER: HOBBIES & DIY

SELVEDGE
1638579U74E-683

Editorial Address: PO Box 40038, LONDON, N6 5UW
Tel: 020 8341 9721 **Fax:** 020 8341 9721
Email: editor@selvedge.org
Advertising Address: 14 Milton Park, Highgate, LONDON, N6 5QA **Tel:** 020 8341 9721 **Fax:** 020 8341 9721
Email: advertising@selvedge.org
Web site: http://www.selvedge.org
ISSN: 1742-254X
Publisher: Selvedge
Date Established: 2004
Frequency: 6 issues yearly - Published in the 1st week of each month
Cover Price: £8.50

Circulation: 10,729 (Publisher's Statement)
Usual Pagination: 100
Editor: Polly Leonard; **Advertising Manager:** Julie Wu
Summary of Content: Magazine covering textile art, design and craft with features on contemporary textile art, internationally renowned makers and ethnographic textiles as well as travel, shopping, future trends and the history and social history of textiles. Also includes book reviews, exhibitions and listings.
Readership/Target Audience: Aimed at women aged 17 to 70 years old interested in arts, craft and design.
ADVERTISING RATES:
Full Page Colour £1500.00
Mechanical Data: Trim Size: 238 x 238mm, Bleed Size: 241 x 241mm, Page Width: 218mm, Film: Digital
Copy instructions: Copy Date: 8 weeks prior to publication date
CONSUMER: WOMEN'S INTEREST CONSUMER MAGAZINES: Crafts

SEREN
47443U83-69_50

Editorial Address: University of Wales, Deiniol Road, BANGOR, LL57 2TH **Tel:** 01248 388017
Email: editor@seren.bangor.ac.uk
Advertising Address: As above.
Email: editor@seren.bangor.ac.uk
Web site: http://www.seren.bangor.ac.uk
Publisher: Students Union Bangor
Date Established: 1980
Frequency: 6 issues yearly - Monthly during term time
Cover Price: Free
Circulation: 2,000 (Publisher's Statement)
Usual Pagination: 20
Editor: Georgia Mannion; **Advertising Manager:** Georgia Mannion
Summary of Content: Students' Union newspaper of the University of Bangor.
Readership/Target Audience: Read by students.
ADVERTISING RATES:
Full Page Colour £300.00
Mechanical Data: Trim Size: 297 x 210mm, Bleed Size: 303 x 216mm, Film: Digital
CONSUMER: STUDENT PUBLICATIONS

SESAME
47444U88B-151

Editorial Address: Walton Hall, MILTON KEYNES, MK7 6AA
Tel: 01908 653011 **Fax:** 01908 652247
Email: sesame@open.ac.uk
Advertising Address: Tulip House, 70 Borough High Street, LONDON, SE1 1XF **Tel:** 020 7864 9995
Email: mark@square7media.co.uk
Web site: http://www.open.ac.uk/sesame
ISSN: 0267-033X
Publisher: The Open University
Frequency: Quarterly
Free to qualifying individuals
Circulation: 450,000 (Publisher's Statement)
Usual Pagination: 48
Editor: Tracy Buchanan
Summary of Content: Magazine of The Open University.
Readership/Target Audience: Aimed at students and staff of the university.
ADVERTISING RATES:
Full Page Colour £7385.00
SCC £40.00
Agency Commission: 10%
Mechanical Data: Type Area: 287 x 200mm, Col Length: 287mm, Page Width: 200mm, Film: Digital, Col Widths (Display): 42mm, No. of Columns (Display): 4
Copy instructions: Copy Date: 5 weeks prior to publication date
Average advertising content per issue: 40%
Supplement(s): OU Student - 4xY
CONSUMER: EDUCATION: Adult Education

SEW
1902243U74E-713

Editorial Address: 21-23 Phoenix Court, Hawkins Road, COLCHESTER, CO2 8JY **Tel:** 01206 505900
Email: laura.cruickshank@aceville.co.uk
Web site: http://www.sewmag.co.uk
Publisher: Aceville Publications Ltd
Frequency: Monthly
Cover Price: £5.99
Circulation: 25,000 (Publisher's Statement)
Editor: Laura Cruickshank; **Group Editor:** Lynn Martin
Summary of Content: Magazine covering hint and tips, features and stories of how to sew.
Readership/Target Audience: Aimed at those with an interest in sewing.
CONSUMER: WOMEN'S INTEREST CONSUMER MAGAZINES: Crafts

SEW TODAY
45369U74E-480

Formerly: Sewing Today
Editorial Address: New Lane, HAVANT, PO9 2ND
Tel: 0870 777 9966 **Fax:** 023 9249 2769
Email: marilyn@sewtoday.co.uk
Advertising Address: As above.
Email: tracey@butterick-vogue.co.uk
Web site: http://www.sewdirect.com
ISSN: 0950-3625
Publisher: Butterick Company Ltd
Date Established: 1866
Frequency: 10 issues yearly
Cover Price: £3.95
Circulation: 16,000 (Publisher's Statement)
Usual Pagination: 96
Editor: Marilyn Stevens; **Managing Director:** Keith Jones
Summary of Content: Magazine containing sewing patterns reflecting looks from the fashion runway, fabric forecasts, Editor's picks, what's new section, book reviews, diary dates, advice from experts and readers offers.
Readership/Target Audience: Aimed at fashion sewers, home decor and needlecraft enthusiasts of all ages and skill levels.
ADVERTISING RATES:
Full Page Colour £1595.00
Agency Commission: 10%
Mechanical Data: Bleed Size: 303 x 216mm, Type Area: 266 x 182mm, Col Length: 266mm, Page Width: 182mm, Film: Digital, Trim Size: 297 x 210mm
Copy instructions: Copy Date: 4 weeks prior to publication date
CONSUMER: WOMEN'S INTEREST CONSUMER MAGAZINES: Crafts

SEW TODAY'S SEW BRIDAL
45351U74E-640

Formerly: Sew Bridal
Editorial Address: New Lane, HAVANT, PO9 2ND
Tel: 01243 374523
Email: marilyn@sewtoday.co.uk
Advertising Address: As above. **Tel:** 0870 777 9955
Fax: 023 9249 2769
Email: tracey@sewtoday.co.uk
Web site: http://www.sewbridal.co.uk
ISSN: 1352-9358
Publisher: Butterick Company Ltd
Date Established: 2003
Frequency: Annual - Published in January
Cover Price: £3.25
Circulation: 25,000 (Publisher's Statement)
Usual Pagination: 96
Editor: Marilyn Stevens; **Managing Director:** Keith Jones
Summary of Content: Magazine containing patterns by leading international designers for traditional weddings, avant-garde and second time around ceremonies.
Readership/Target Audience: Aimed at sewing enthusiasts and professional dressmakers.
ADVERTISING RATES:
Full Page Mono £1350.00
Full Page Colour £1595.00
SCC £7.00
Agency Commission: 10%
Mechanical Data: Type Area: 266 x 182mm, Col Length: 266mm, Trim Size: 297 x 210mm, Bleed Size: 303 x 216mm, Page Width: 182mm, Film: Digital
Copy instructions: Copy Date: 4 weeks prior to publication date
CONSUMER: WOMEN'S INTEREST CONSUMER MAGAZINES: Crafts

SEWING WORLD
45370U74E-520

Editorial Address: Traplet House, Pendragon Close, MALVERN, WR14 1GA **Tel:** 01684 588500
Fax: 01684 578588
Email: sw@traplet.com
Advertising Address: As above. **Fax:** 01684 578558
Email: advertising@traplet.co.uk
Web site: http://www.sewingworldmagazine.com
Publisher: Traplet Publications Ltd
Date Established: 1987
Frequency: Monthly
Cover Price: £3.95
Annual Sub.: £39.95
Circulation: 20,000 (Publisher's Statement)
Usual Pagination: 92
Editor: Wendy Gardiner; **Advertising Manager:** Stephanie Hill
Summary of Content: Magazine covering machine sewing skills, dressmaking, projects and techniques.
Readership/Target Audience: Aimed at sewing enthusiasts.
ADVERTISING RATES:
Full Page Mono £655.00
Full Page Colour £835.00
SCC £12.00
Agency Commission: 10%
Mechanical Data: Bleed Size: 303 x 216mm, Trim Size: 297 x 210mm, Film: Digital

Copy instructions: Copy Date: 6 weeks prior to publication date
Average advertising content per issue: 23%
Supplement(s): Pattern Supplement - 4xY
CONSUMER: WOMEN'S INTEREST CONSUMER MAGAZINES: Crafts

SFX
46765U79L-306
Editorial Address: 30 Monmouth Street, BATH, BA1 2BW
Tel: 01225 442244
Email: sfx@futurenet.com
Advertising Address: As above.
Web site: http://www.sfx.co.uk
Publisher: Future Publishing Ltd
Date Established: 1995
Frequency: 13 issues yearly
Cover Price: £3.99
Circulation: 31,327 (ABC 01/01/2008 to 31/12/2008)
Usual Pagination: 132
Editor: David Bradley; **News Editor:** Richard Edwards; **Features Editor:** Nick Setchfield; **Advertising Manager:** Adrian Hill
Summary of Content: Science fiction and fantasy magazine covering films, TV, books, video, comics and games.
Readership/Target Audience: Aimed at enthusiasts of science fiction and fantasy.
ADVERTISING RATES:
Full Page Colour £1995.00
Mechanical Data: Type Area: 280 x 203mm, Bleed Size: 306 x 228mm, Trim Size: 300 x 222mm, Col Length: 280mm, Page Width: 203mm, Film: Digital
CONSUMER: HOBBIES & DIY: Fantasy Games & Science Fiction

SHAKESPEARE AT THE CENTRE
1606167U84A-422
Editorial Address: Shakespeare Centre, Henley Street, STRATFORD-UPON-AVON, CV37 6QW **Tel:** 01789 204016
Fax: 01789 296083
Email: magazine@shakespeare.org.uk
Advertising Address: As above.
Email: info@shakespeare.org.uk
Web site: http://www.shakespeare.org.uk
ISSN: 1475-7141
Publisher: The Shakespeare Birthplace Trust
Date Established: 2001
Frequency: Half-yearly - Published April and October
Cover Price: £1.50
Free to qualifying individuals
Circulation: 20,000 (Publisher's Statement)
Usual Pagination: 20
Editor: Jacqueline Green; **Advertising Manager:** Elizabeth Woledge
Summary of Content: Magazine of the world's premier Shakespeare charity, covering academic performance and historical aspects of the world's Shakespeare heritage.
Readership/Target Audience: Aimed at friends of the trust, students, academics and all those interested in the history and current practice of Shakespeare in performance.
ADVERTISING RATES:
Full Page Colour £800.00
Mechanical Data: Page Width: 190mm, Type Area: 275 x 190mm, Trim Size: 295 x 210mm, Col Length: 275mm, Film: Digital
CONSUMER: THE ARTS & LITERARY: Arts

SHARE
47844U87-209_50
Editorial Address: Allen Gardiner Cottage, Pembury Road, TUNBRIDGE WELLS, TN2 3QU **Tel:** 01892 538647
Fax: 01892 525797
Email: med@samsgb.org
Web site: http://www.samsgb.org
ISSN: 1367-6741
Publisher: South American Mission Society
Date Established: 1867
Frequency: Quarterly
Cover Price: Free
Circulation: 7,500 (Publisher's Statement)
Usual Pagination: 16
Editor: Robert Lunt
Summary of Content: Publication providing news and features about the church and matters concerning the church in South America and Iberia for Anglicans in the UK.
Language(s): English; Spanish
Readership/Target Audience: Read by those who wish to be involved in the society or are interested in spiritual growth in South America.
ADVERTISING: No Advertising taken
CONSUMER: RELIGIOUS

SHARE INTERNATIONAL
47276U82-175
Editorial Address: PO Box 3677, LONDON, NW5 1RU
Tel: 020 7482 1113 **Fax:** 020 7267 2881
Web site: http://www.share-international.org
ISSN: 0169-1341

Publisher: Share International
Date Established: 1982
Frequency: 10 issues yearly
Cover Price: £2.75
Annual Sub.: £24.00
Usual Pagination: 28
Editor: Benjamin Creme
Summary of Content: Publication containing articles about the current economic, political and spiritual changes occurring in the world. Also covers third world development.
Language(s): Dutch; English; French; German; Japanese; Romanian; Spanish
Readership/Target Audience: Aimed at individuals and groups of all religions with an interest in global spiritual developments and who believe in the emergence and return of the world teacher.
ADVERTISING: No Advertising taken
CONSUMER: CURRENT AFFAIRS & POLITICS

SHAREIT!
47845U87-209_75
Formerly: Share It
Editorial Address: Marlowe House, 109 Station Road, SIDCUP, DA15 7AD **Tel:** 020 8309 9991 **Fax:** 020 8309 3500
Email: comms@churcharmy.org.uk
Web site: http://www.churcharmy.org.uk
Publisher: Church Army
Date Established: 1993
Frequency: Half-yearly - Published in April and August
Cover Price: Free
Circulation: 20,000 (Publisher's Statement)
Usual Pagination: 16
Editor: David Coleman
Summary of Content: Magazine containing practical church features, church army resources, activities and developments as a result of prayer.
Readership/Target Audience: Aimed at church members and leaders and Church Army supporters throughout the United Kingdom.
ADVERTISING: No Advertising taken
CONSUMER: RELIGIOUS

SHE
45198U74A-520
Editorial Address: National Magazine House, 72 Broadwick Street, LONDON, W1F 9EP **Tel:** 020 7439 5000
Fax: 020 7312 3940
Email: contact@shemagazine.co.uk
Advertising Address: As above. **Fax:** 020 7312 3779
Email: alexandra.heath@natmags.co.uk
Web site: http://www.allaboutyou.com
ISSN: 0037-3370
Publisher: National Magazine Company Ltd
Date Established: 2005
Frequency: Monthly
Cover Price: £3.30
Circulation: 148,860 (ABC 01/01/2009 to 30/06/2009)
Editor: Marie Campbell; **Features Editor:** Sarah Gooding; **Managing Director:** Jessica Burley; **Advertising Manager:** Alexandra Heath
Summary of Content: Magazine covering home, fashion, beauty and health.
Twitter: https://twitter.com/SheMag.
Readership/Target Audience: Aimed at confident, educated women over 35 years old.
ADVERTISING RATES:
Full Page Colour £10000.00
Agency Commission: 15%
Mechanical Data: Bleed Size: 296 x 221mm, Type Area: 270 x 192mm, Col Length: 270mm, Page Width: 192mm, Trim Size: 290 x 215mm, Film: Digital
Copy instructions: Copy Date: 4 weeks prior to publication date
Average advertising content per issue: 35%
CONSUMER: WOMEN'S INTEREST CONSUMER MAGAZINES: Women's Interest

SHEFFIELD SIXER
1637929U80C-5098
Editorial Address: RMC House, Broadfield Court, Broadfield Business Park, SHEFFIELD, S8 0XF
Tel: 0114 250 6300 **Fax:** 0114 255 5881
Email: chris.wilson@regionalmagazine.co.uk
Advertising Address: As above. **Fax:** 0114 250 6320
Email: simon.moreman@regionalmagazine.co.uk
Web site: http://www.northernlifestyle.com
Publisher: Regional Magazine Company
Frequency: Monthly
Cover Price: Free
Circulation: 20,000 (Publisher's Statement)
Usual Pagination: 48
Editor: Chris Wilson; **Advertising Manager:** Simon Moreman
Summary of Content: Magazine covering lifestyle and leisure, local issues, local people, fashion, motoring and travel.
Readership/Target Audience: Aimed at residents of Sheffield.

ADVERTISING RATES:
Full Page Colour £1000.00
Agency Commission: 10%
Mechanical Data: Type Area: 260 x 185mm, Bleed Size: 303 x 216mm, Trim Size: 297 x 210mm, Col Length: 260mm, Page Width: 185mm, Film: Digital
Copy instructions: Copy Date: 3 weeks prior to publication date
CONSUMER: RURAL & REGIONAL INTEREST: Regional Interest English Counties

SHETLAND LIFE
47057U80E-240
Editorial Address: Gremista Industrial Estate, Gremista, Lerwick, SHETLAND, ZE1 0PX **Tel:** 01595 693622
Fax: 01595 694637
Email: shetlandlife@shetland-times.co.uk
Advertising Address: As above.
Web site: http://www.shetlandtoday.co.uk
Publisher: The Shetland Times Ltd
Date Established: 1980
Frequency: Monthly
Cover Price: £2.30
Circulation: 2,600 (Publisher's Statement)
Usual Pagination: 48
Editor: Malachy Tallach; **Advertising Manager:** Vivienne Henderson
Summary of Content: Local interest magazine for the Shetland Islands.
Readership/Target Audience: Aimed at residents of the Shetland Islands and expatriates.
ADVERTISING RATES:
Full Page Colour £320.00
Agency Commission: 10%
Mechanical Data: Col Length: 240mm, Type Area: 240 x 185mm, Trim Size: 270 x 220mm, Page Width: 185mm, Col Widths (Display): 3, Film: Digital
Copy instructions: Copy Date: 20th of the month prior to publication date
Average advertising content per issue: 20%
CONSUMER: RURAL & REGIONAL INTEREST: Regional Interest Scotland

THE SHETLAND PONY STUD-BOOK SOCIETY MAGAZINE
47147U81D-240
Editorial Address: 22 York Place, PERTH, PH2 8EH
Tel: 01738 623471 **Fax:** 01738 442274
Email: jane@kerswellshetlands.co.uk
Advertising Address: As above.
Email: enquiries@shetlandponystudbooksociety.co.uk
Web site: http://www.shetlandponystudbooksociety.co.uk
Publisher: The Shetland Pony Stud-Book Society
Frequency: Annual - Published in March
Cover Price: £10.00
Circulation: 1,500 (Publisher's Statement)
Usual Pagination: 200
Editor: Jane Dennis
Summary of Content: Magazine containing information on Shetland ponies.
Readership/Target Audience: Aimed at members of the Shetland Pony Stud-Book Society.
ADVERTISING: Rates on application
Copy instructions: Copy Date: End of October
CONSUMER: ANIMALS & PETS: Horses & Ponies

SHIATSU SOCIETY NEWS
45447U74G-47
Editorial Address: PO Box 4580, RUGBY, CV21 9EL
Tel: 0845 130 4560 **Fax:** 01788 555052
Email: admin@shiatsusociety.org
Advertising Address: As above.
Email: admin@shiatsusociety.org
Web site: http://www.shiatsusociety.org
ISSN: 1366-2813
Publisher: Shiatsu Society
Date Established: 1981
Frequency: Quarterly
Annual Sub.: £43.00
Circulation: 1,800 (Publisher's Statement)
Usual Pagination: 40
Editor: Samantha Haywood; **Advertising Manager:** Samantha Haywood
Summary of Content: Newsletter includes information on developments within the Society, courses and articles on shiatsu and related issues.
Readership/Target Audience: Aimed at Shiatsu Society members and those interested in Shiatsu.
ADVERTISING RATES:
Full Page Mono £265.00
Full Page Colour £318.00
SCC £25.00
Copy instructions: Copy Date: 48 days prior to publication date
Average advertising content per issue: 30%
CONSUMER: WOMEN'S INTEREST CONSUMER MAGAZINES: Slimming & Health

Consumer Magazines

SHINDIG
1831347U76D-836

Editorial Address: 5 Altmore, Cherry Garden Lane, MAIDENHEAD, SL6 3QG **Tel:** 01628 825652
Fax: 01628 821148
Email: info@shindig-magazine.com
Advertising Address: As above.
Web site: http://www.shindig-magazine.com
Publisher: Volcano Publishing
Date Established: 2007
Frequency: 6 issues yearly
Cover Price: £4.25
Circulation: 10,000 (Publisher's Statement)
Usual Pagination: 84
Editor: Jon Mills; **Publisher:** Slim Smith
Summary of Content: Magazine specializing in psychedelic, garage, beat, powerpop, soul and folk music.
Readership/Target Audience: Aimed at the older music fan keen on classic pop music.
CONSUMER: MUSIC & PERFORMING ARTS: Music

SHIVERS
46058U76A-47

Editorial Address: 9-10 Blades Court, Deodar Road, LONDON, SW15 2NU **Tel:** 020 8875 1520
Fax: 020 8875 1588
Email: shivers@visimag.com
Advertising Address: As above. **Tel:** 020 8875 7400
Email: mclarke@visimag.com
Web site: http://www.visimag/shivers
ISSN: 0965-8238
Publisher: Visual Imagination Ltd
Date Established: 1992
Frequency: 8 issues yearly
Cover Price: £3.99
Annual Sub.: £29.00
Circulation: 25,000 (Publisher's Statement)
Usual Pagination: 84
Editor: Stuart Weightman; **Advertising Manager:** Martin Clarke; **Group Editor:** Jan Vincent-Rudzki
Summary of Content: Magazine covering horror in films, dark fantasy, videos and books.
Readership/Target Audience: Read by fans of horror movies and television, between 15 and 25 years old.
ADVERTISING RATES:
Full Page Colour £950.00
Agency Commission: 10%
Mechanical Data: Film: Digital, Bleed Size: 307 x 230mm, Trim Size: 297 x 220mm, Page Width: 192mm, Type Area: 270 x 192mm, Col Length: 270mm
Copy instructions: Copy Date: 3 weeks prior to publication date
Average advertising content per issue: 20%
CONSUMER: MUSIC & PERFORMING ARTS: Cinema

SHOOTING & CONSERVATION
45862U75F-210

Formerly: Voiceofshooting.com
Editorial Address: Marford Mill, Rossett, WREXHAM, LL12 0HL **Tel:** 01244 573032 **Fax:** 01244 573040
Email: jeffrey.olstead@basc.org.uk
Advertising Address: Fair Oak Close, Exeter Airport Business Park, Clyst Honiton, EXETER, EX5 2UL
Tel: 01392 888555 **Fax:** 01392 888470
Email: anna.merritt@archant.co.uk
Web site: http://www.basc.org.uk
Publisher: Archant South West
Frequency: 6 issues yearly
Cover Price: £4.25
Free to qualifying individuals
Circulation: 127,000 (Publisher's Statement)
Usual Pagination: 92
Editor: Jeffrey Olstead; **Advertising Manager:** Anna Merritt
Summary of Content: Official journal of the British Association for Shooting and Conservation. Covers articles on shooting, practical conservation, land management, equipment, clothing and firearms.
Readership/Target Audience: Read by members of the Association.
ADVERTISING: Rates on application
Agency Commission: 10%
Average advertising content per issue: 45%
CONSUMER: SPORT: Shooting

THE SHOOTING GAZETTE
45863U75F-125

Editorial Address: PO Box 225, STAMFORD, PE9 2HS
Tel: 01780 485350 **Fax:** 01780 485390
Email: will_hetherington@ipcmedia.com
Advertising Address: Blue Fin Building, 110 Southwark Street, LONDON, SE1 0SU **Tel:** 020 3148 5000
Fax: 020 3148 8130
Email: toby_drought@ipcmedia.com
Web site: http://www.ipcmedia.com
Publisher: IPC Inspire
Date Established: 1989
Frequency: Monthly
Cover Price: £3.60
Annual Sub.: £37.00

Circulation: 16,313 (ABC 01/01/2008 to 31/12/2008)
Usual Pagination: 140
Editor: Will Hetherington; **Advertising Manager:** Toby Drought
Summary of Content: Magazine covering game, rough shooting, gun dogs and stalking.
Readership/Target Audience: Aimed at pure game shooters.
ADVERTISING RATES:
Full Page Mono £2325.00
Full Page Colour £3115.00
Agency Commission: 15%
Mechanical Data: Col Length: 269mm, Bleed Size: 303 x 230mm, Trim Size: 297 x 224mm, Print Process: Digital, Page Width: 196mm, Type Area: 269 x 196mm
Copy instructions: Copy Date: 3 months prior to publication date
Average advertising content per issue: 40%
CONSUMER: SPORT: Shooting

SHOOTING SPORTS
31211U75F-140

Editorial Address: 21-23 Phoenix Court, Hawkins Road, COLCHESTER, CO2 8JY **Tel:** 01206 525697
Email: peter.moore403@ntlworld.com
Advertising Address: 2nd Floor, Ewer House, 44-46 Crouch Street, COLCHESTER, CO3 3HH **Tel:** 01206 506248
Fax: 01206 500226
Email: shootingsports@aceville.co.uk
Web site: http://www.shooting-sports.net
Publisher: Maze Media (2000) Ltd
Date Established: 1997
Frequency: Monthly
Cover Price: £3.30
Circulation: 25,000 (Publisher's Statement)
Usual Pagination: 100
Editor: Peter Moore; **Advertising Manager:** Vanessa Green
Summary of Content: Magazine containing articles on all aspects of shooting, including product reviews and accessories.
Readership/Target Audience: Aimed at gun enthusiasts.
ADVERTISING RATES:
Full Page Colour £550.00
Agency Commission: 10%
Mechanical Data: Page Width: 190mm, No. of Columns (Display): 4, Type Area: 270 x 190mm, Bleed Size: 307 x 220mm, Trim Size: 297 x 210mm, Col Length: 270mm, Film: Digital
Copy instructions: Copy Date: 4 weeks prior to publication date
Average advertising content per issue: 40%
CONSUMER: SPORT: Shooting

SHOOTING TIMES AND COUNTRY MAGAZINE
45864U75F-160

Editorial Address: Blue Fin Building, 110 Southwark Street, LONDON, SE1 0SU **Tel:** 020 3148 4741 **Fax:** 020 3148 8175
Email: steditorial@ipcmedia.com
Advertising Address: As above. **Tel:** 020 3148 5000
Fax: 020 3148 8130
Email: toby_drought@ipcmedia.com
Web site: http://www.shootingtimes.co.uk
Publisher: IPC Inspire
Frequency: Weekly
Cover Price: £2.10
Circulation: 26,071 (ABC 01/01/2008 to 31/12/2008)
Usual Pagination: 68
Editor: Selena Masson; **News Editor:** Selena Masson
Summary of Content: Magazine covering all disciplines of shooting including game, rough and stalking. Includes coverage on issues of conservation and land management.
Readership/Target Audience: Aimed at shooting sportsmen.
ADVERTISING RATES:
Full Page Mono £1875.00
Full Page Colour £2500.00
Agency Commission: 10%
Mechanical Data: Type Area: 274 x 200mm, Bleed Size: 306 x 226mm, Trim Size: 300 x 220mm, Col Length: 274mm, Film: Digital, Page Width: 200mm
Copy instructions: Copy Date: 1 week prior to publication date
Average advertising content per issue: 35%
CONSUMER: SPORT: Shooting

SHORT CIRCUIT MAGAZINE
46431U77D-440

Editorial Address: York House, 22 Frederick Street, BIRMINGHAM, B1 3HE **Tel:** 0121 233 3468
Fax: 0121 236 4230
Email: info@shortcircuitmag.com
Advertising Address: As above.
Email: info@shortcircuitmag.com
Publisher: YBA Publications
Frequency: Monthly
Cover Price: £3.00
Annual Sub.: £36.00
Circulation: 5,000 (Publisher's Statement)

Editor: Mark Haddleton; **Advertising Manager:** Mark Haddleton
Summary of Content: Magazine covering race reports, driver profiles and interviews, news from trade suppliers and information on general oval racing.
Readership/Target Audience: Aimed at car racing enthusiasts.
ADVERTISING RATES:
Full Page Mono £260.00
Full Page Colour £320.00
Agency Commission: 15%
Copy instructions: Copy Date: Middle of the month prior to publication date
CONSUMER: MOTORING & CYCLING: Motor Sports

SHORTCUT CONFIDENTIAL
45557U74M-220

Formerly: Personal & Finance Confidential
Editorial Address: Sea Containers House, 7th Floor, 20 Upper Ground, LONDON, SE1 9JD **Tel:** 020 7633 3600
Fax: 020 7447 4041
Email: glenn.fisher@f-s-p.co.uk
Web site: http://www.shortcutbulletin.co.uk
ISSN: 1365-6384
Publisher: Agora Lifestyles Ltd
Date Established: 1996
Frequency: Monthly
Annual Sub.: £29.00
Circulation: 14,000 (Publisher's Statement)
Usual Pagination: 12
Editor: Glenn Fisher
Summary of Content: Guide to making the correct decisions on finance, business opportunities, career development and personal development.
Readership/Target Audience: Read predominantly by affluent men aged over 45 years old who are interested in personal and professional improvement.
ADVERTISING: No Advertising taken
CONSUMER: WOMEN'S INTEREST CONSUMER MAGAZINES: Personal Finance

SHORTLIST
1823892U86C-740

Editorial Address: 6-8 Emerald Street, LONDON, WC1N 3QA **Tel:** 020 7611 9700 **Fax:** 020 7611 9701
Email: andrew.lowry@shortlist.com
Advertising Address: As above.
Email: jo.fraser@shortlist.com
Web site: http://www.shortlist.com
Publisher: Shortlist Media Ltd
Date Established: 2007
Frequency: Weekly
Cover Price: Free
Circulation: 510,720 (ABC 01/01/2009 to 30/06/2009)
Usual Pagination: 46
Editor: Andrew Lowry; **News Editor:** Lucy Foster;
Advertising Manager: Chris Healy; **Advertising Director:** Jo Fraser
Summary of Content: Magazine covering entertainment, technology, careers and money, going out, style, driving, sport, travel, grooming and business.
Readership/Target Audience: Aimed at men aged 25 to 35 years old.
ADVERTISING RATES:
Full Page Mono £18145.00
Full Page Colour £18145.00
Agency Commission: 15%
Mechanical Data: Type Area: 296 x 251mm, Bleed Size: 316 x 271mm, Trim Size: 310 x 265mm, Col Length: 296mm, Page Width: 251mm, Film: Digital
Copy instructions: Copy Date: 7 days prior to publication date
Average advertising content per issue: 25%
CONSUMER: ADULT & GAY MAGAZINES: Men's Lifestyle Magazines

SHOUT!
47633U86B-140

Editorial Address: PO Box YR46, LEEDS, LS9 6XG
Tel: 0113 248 5700 **Fax:** 0113 295 6097
Email: shout.magazine@ntlworld.com
Advertising Address: As above.
Email: shout.magazine@ntlworld.com
Web site: http://www.shoutweb.co.uk
Publisher: Shout! Publications
Date Established: 1995
Frequency: 11 issues yearly - Not published in January
Free to qualifying individuals
Annual Sub.: £10.00
Circulation: 7,000 (Publisher's Statement)
Usual Pagination: 24
Editor: Mark Michalowski; **Advertising Manager:** Mark Michalowski
Summary of Content: Publication featuring news, arts, health, politics and events both national and local.
Readership/Target Audience: Aimed at the lesbian, gay, bisexual and transgender community.
ADVERTISING RATES:
Full Page Mono £295.00

Agency Commission: 10%
Mechanical Data: Type Area: 260 x 180mm, Film: Digital,
Col Length: 260mm, Page Width: 180mm
Copy instructions: Copy Date: 2 weeks prior to publication
date
Average advertising content per issue: 40%
CONSUMER: ADULT & GAY MAGAZINES: Gay & Lesbian
Magazines

SHOUT MAGAZINE
45395U74F-600

Editorial Address: 2 Albert Square, DUNDEE, DD1 9QJ
Tel: 01382 223131 **Fax:** 01382 200880
Email: mwelch@shoutmag.co.uk
Advertising Address: Orange 20, 20 Orange Street,
LONDON, WC2H 7EF **Tel:** 020 7321 0701
Fax: 020 7839 6993
Email: robin@o20.co.uk
Web site: http://www.shoutmag.co.uk
Publisher: D.C. Thomson & Co Ltd
Date Established: 1993
Frequency: 26 issues yearly
Cover Price: £2.20
Annual Sub.: £57.20
Circulation: 76,568 (ABC 01/01/2009 to 30/06/2009)
Usual Pagination: 100
Editor: Laura Brown; **Features Editor:** Lynn Cameron
Summary of Content: Magazine covering beauty, fashion,
music, films and celebrities.
Readership/Target Audience: Aimed at girls between 11
and 14 years old.
ADVERTISING RATES:
Full Page Colour £3885.00
Agency Commission: 15%
Mechanical Data: Trim Size: 225 x 170mm, Col Length:
202mm, Film: Positive, right reading, emulsion side down.
Digital, No. of Columns (Display): 4, Type Area: 202 x
154mm, Bleed Size: 231 x 176mm, Page Width: 154mm
Copy instructions: Copy Date: 4 weeks prior to publication
date
Average advertising content per issue: 10%
CONSUMER: WOMEN'S INTEREST CONSUMER
MAGAZINES: Teenage

SHOWING WORLD
1633084U81D-356

Editorial Address: PO Box 793, Badley, IPSWICH, IP6 8WN
Tel: 01449 722505
Email: info@showingworldonline.co.uk
Advertising Address: As above.
Email: tracy@showingworldonline.co.uk
Web site: http://www.showingworldonline.co.uk
Publisher: Robin Altwood Publications
Frequency: 6 issues yearly
Free to qualifying individuals
Annual Sub.: £9.99
Circulation: 10,000 (Publisher's Statement)
Usual Pagination: 78
Editor: Sandy Lee-Wooderson; **Advertising Manager:**
Tracy Robinson
Summary of Content: Magazine covering all aspects of
showing horses and ponies, club news, new products, care
and maintenance and show reports.
Readership/Target Audience: Aimed at those interested in
keeping and showing horses and ponies.
ADVERTISING: Rates on application
Agency Commission: 10%
Copy instructions: Copy Date: 1st of the month prior to
publication date
Average advertising content per issue: 40%
CONSUMER: ANIMALS & PETS: Horses & Ponies

SHOWTIME
1808697U91D-964

Formerly: Showtime Weekly
Editorial Address: Brockbourne House, Mount Ephraim,
TUNBRIDGE WELLS, TN4 8BS **Tel:** 01892 500100
Email: tomalley@panini.co.uk
Advertising Address: Orange 20 Ltd, 20 Orange Street,
LONDON, WC2H 7EF **Tel:** 020 7389 0800
Fax: 01372 723322
Email: sales@o20.co.uk
Web site: http://www.paninicomics.co.uk
Publisher: Panini UK Ltd
Date Established: 2007
Frequency: Monthly
Cover Price: £1.75
Circulation: 150,000 (Print Run)
Usual Pagination: 32
Editor: Tom O'Malley; **Advertising Manager:** Robin
Johnson
Summary of Content: Children's magazine based on a
mixture of pre-school shows with activities, stories and
competitions.
Readership/Target Audience: Aimed at boys and girls
aged 2 to 5 years old.
ADVERTISING RATES:
Full Page Colour £2500.00
Agency Commission: 10%

Copy instructions: Copy Date: 4 weeks prior to publication
date
CONSUMER: RECREATION & LEISURE: Children & Youth

SHROPSHIRE LIFE
1658583U80C-5169

Editorial Address: PO Box 3106, STOKE-ON-TRENT, ST4
9JB **Tel:** 01782 850539
Email: joanne.goodwin@archant.co.uk
Advertising Address: 23 Lloyd Street, OSWESTRY, SY11
1NL **Tel:** 07702 674025
Email: david.gregory@archant.co.uk
Publisher: Archant Life (Midlands) Ltd
Frequency: Monthly
Cover Price: £2.50
Circulation: 10,000 (Print Run)
Editor: Joanne Goodwin
Summary of Content: Magazine covering art,
entertainment, celebrity interviews, food and drink, interiors,
fashion, beauty, travel, social events and local interest
stories.
Readership/Target Audience: Aimed at residents in
Shropshire.
ADVERTISING: Rates on application
CONSUMER: RURAL & REGIONAL INTEREST: Regional
Interest English Counties

THE SHROPSHIRE MAGAZINE
46959U80C-2700

Editorial Address: Waterloo Road, Ketley, TELFORD, TF1
5HU **Tel:** 01952 242424 **Fax:** 01952 254605
Email: nthomas@shropshirestar.co.uk
Advertising Address: As above. **Fax:** 01952 288820
Email: gwilliams@shropshirestar.co.uk
Web site: http://www.shropshiremagazine.com
Publisher: Shropshire Newspapers Ltd
Frequency: Monthly
Cover Price: £2.50
Free to qualifying individuals
Circulation: 19,500 (Publisher's Statement)
Usual Pagination: 140
Editor: Neil Thomas; **Editor-in-Chief:** Sarah-Jane Smith;
Managing Director: Steve Brown
Summary of Content: Magazine containing articles on
personalities, book reviews, wining and dining, antiques,
education, festivals and family histories. Also features local
culture, a social diary, extensive live entertainment listings
for the area and a regular horse racing diary.
Readership/Target Audience: Aimed at affluent
households in Shropshire and surrounding areas.
ADVERTISING RATES:
Full Page Colour £1150.00
Agency Commission: 15%
Mechanical Data: Col Length: 270mm, Film: Positive, right
reading, emulsion side down. Digital, No. of Columns
(Display): 4, Type Area: 270 x 199mm, Bleed Size: 307 x
229mm, Page Width: 199mm, Col Widths (Display): 45mm
Copy instructions: Copy Date: 2nd Friday of the month
prior to publication date
Average advertising content per issue: 40%
CONSUMER: RURAL & REGIONAL INTEREST: Regional
Interest English Counties

THE SHROPSHIRE REVIEW
46960U80C-2730

Editorial Address: Media House, Building 9, Stanmore
Industrial Estate, BRIDGNORTH, WV15 5HR
Tel: 01746 766848 **Fax:** 01746 764226
Email: editorial@reviewmedia.com
Advertising Address: As above. **Fax:** 01746 767780
Email: info@reviewmedia.com
ISSN: 1473-4028
Publisher: Review Media Ltd.
Date Established: 1984
Frequency: 6 issues yearly
Cover Price: Free
Circulation: 25,900 (Publisher's Statement)
Usual Pagination: 100
Editor: Peter Wooldridge; **Advertising Manager:** Martin
Edwards; **Publisher:** Martin Edwards
Summary of Content: Magazine containing local news,
events, fashion, lifestyle, health, beauty, history, motoring,
property, sport, travel and features on the county of
Shropshire.
Readership/Target Audience: Aimed at every home and
business within south-east Shropshire and home buyers
within the Shropshire county.
ADVERTISING RATES:
Full Page Colour £975.00
Agency Commission: 10%
Mechanical Data: Film: Digital, Type Area: 210 x 128mm,
Bleed Size: 236 x 154mm, Trim Size: 230 x 148mm, Col
Length: 210mm, Page Width: 128mm, No. of Columns
(Display): 4
Copy instructions: Copy Date: 3 weeks prior to publication
date
Average advertising content per issue: 40%
CONSUMER: RURAL & REGIONAL INTEREST: Regional
Interest English Counties

SHU PRINT
47437U83-68_20

Formerly: S Press
Editorial Address: The Hubs, Paternoster Row,
SHEFFIELD, S1 2QQ **Tel:** 0114 225 4808
Fax: 0114 225 4140
Advertising Address: As above. **Tel:** 0114 225 4144
Email: g.burton@shu.ac.uk
Web site: http://www.shumedia.co.uk
Publisher: Hallam Students Union
Date Established: 1983
Frequency: 7 issues yearly - Published monthly during term
time
Cover Price: Free
Circulation: 4,820 (Publisher's Statement)
Usual Pagination: 36
Editor: Katie Johnson; **Advertising Manager:** Grace Burton
Summary of Content: Magazine containing features on the
local area, student life, university news and developments.
Includes articles on music, theatre, the arts, cinema and a
variety of student issues.
Readership/Target Audience: Aimed at students of
Sheffield Hallam University.
ADVERTISING RATES:
Full Page Colour £400.00
Mechanical Data: Type Area: 232 x 164mm, Col Length:
232mm, Page Width: 164mm, Film: Digital
CONSUMER: STUDENT PUBLICATIONS

SIDEWALK SKATEBOARDING MAGAZINE
46024U75X-820

Formerly: Sidewalk Surfer
Editorial Address: 1 West Smithfield, LONDON, EC1A 9JU
Tel: 020 7332 9700 **Fax:** 020 7332 9799
Email: ben@sidewalkmag.com
Advertising Address: As above.
Email: harry.scott@factorymedia.com
Web site: http://www.sidewalkmag.com
Publisher: Factory Media
Date Established: 1995
Frequency: Monthly
Cover Price: £3.95
Circulation: 32,000 (Publisher's Statement)
Usual Pagination: 156
Editor: Ben Powell; **Advertising Manager:** Harry Scott
Summary of Content: Magazine covering skateboarding,
related sports and their cultures including skate park guide,
trick tips, events, new products, graffiti art and music.
Readership/Target Audience: Read by skateboarders of all
ages.
ADVERTISING RATES:
Full Page Colour £1385.00
Agency Commission: 10%
Mechanical Data: Bleed Size: 268 x 218mm, Trim Size: 260
x 210mm, Film: Digital
Copy instructions: Copy Date: 4 weeks prior to publication
date
Average advertising content per issue: 50%
CONSUMER: SPORT: Other Sport

SIGHT & SOUND
46059U76A-50

Editorial Address: 21 Stephen Street, LONDON, W1T 1LN
Tel: 020 7255 1444 **Fax:** 020 7436 2327
Email: s&s@bfi.org.uk
Advertising Address: As above.
Email: ronnie.hackston@bfi.org.uk
Web site: http://www.bfi.org.uk/sightandsound
ISSN: 0037-4806
Publisher: British Film Institute
Date Established: 1932
Frequency: Monthly
Cover Price: £3.95
Annual Sub.: £47.00
Circulation: 19,733 (ABC 01/01/2008 to 31/12/2008)
Usual Pagination: 72
Editor: Nick James; **Publisher:** Rob Winter
Summary of Content: Magazine contains features,
comment and news on films, both new and classic, by
leading writers.
Readership/Target Audience: Read by movie enthusiasts,
film studies students and the media industry.
ADVERTISING RATES:
Full Page Mono £1575.00
Full Page Colour £2250.00
Agency Commission: 10%
Mechanical Data: Bleed Size: 306 x 228mm, Trim Size: 300
x 222mm, Film: Digital, Type Area: 277 x 196mm, Page
Width: 196mm, Col Length: 277mm
Copy instructions: Copy Date: 3 weeks prior to publication
date
Average advertising content per issue: 25%
CONSUMER: MUSIC & PERFORMING ARTS: Cinema

THE SIGN
47756U87-210

Editorial Address: 77 Verulam Road, ST. ALBANS, AL3 4DJ
Tel: 01727 833400
Email: terence@harrowweald.org

Consumer Magazines

Advertising Address: 13-17 Long Lane, LONDON, EC1A 9PN **Tel:** 020 7776 1060
Email: stephen@churchtimes.co.uk
ISSN: 1471-6267
Publisher: Hymns ancient & modern
Date Established: 1891
Frequency: Monthly
Circulation: 65,000 (Publisher's Statement)
Usual Pagination: 16
Editor: Terence Handley-MacMath; **Managing Editor:** Paul Handley
Summary of Content: Insert for parish magazines covering all aspects of Christian life. Includes features on the church, arts, family issues and book reviews.
Readership/Target Audience: Aimed at those with an interest in Christian community life.
ADVERTISING RATES:
SCC £25.00
Agency Commission: 10%
Mechanical Data: Type Area: 190 x 125mm, Col Length: 190mm, Page Width: 125mm, No. of Columns (Display): 3, Col Widths (Display): 40mm, Print Process: Web offset, Film: Digital
Copy instructions: Copy Date: 8 weeks prior to publication date
Average advertising content per issue: 20%
CONSUMER: RELIGIOUS

SILHOUETTE
48218U89D-270
Editorial Address: 32 Friars Walk, LONDON, N14 5LP
Tel: 020 8361 2942
Email: camerapixuk@btinternet.com
Advertising Address: As above.
Email: camerapixuk@btinternet.com
Web site: http://www.camerapix.com
Publisher: Camerapix Magazines Ltd
Date Established: 1989
Frequency: Half-yearly - Published in January and July
Cover Price: £4.00
Annual Sub.: £16.00
Circulation: 35,000 (Publisher's Statement)
Usual Pagination: 96
Editor: Azra Chaudhry; **Advertising Manager:** Roger Barnard
Summary of Content: In-flight magazine of Air Seychelles, with travel articles and general features.
Language(s): English; French
Readership/Target Audience: Read by customers of Air Seychelles.
ADVERTISING RATES:
Full Page Mono £2810.00
Full Page Colour £3640.00
Agency Commission: 15%
Mechanical Data: Col Length: 250mm, Film: Digital, No. of Columns (Display): 3, Type Area: 250 x 180mm, Print Process: Web-fed offset litho, Bleed Size: 285 x 212mm, Trim Size: 283 x 210mm, Page Width: 180mm
Average advertising content per issue: 30%
CONSUMER: HOLIDAYS & TRAVEL: In-Flight Magazines

THE SIMMARIAN
47445U83-72
Editorial Address: St. Mary's College, Waldegrave Road, Strawberry Hill, TWICKENHAM, TW1 4SX
Tel: 020 8240 4039 **Fax:** 020 8240 4255
Email: kendelk@smuc.ac.uk
Web site: http://www.smuc.ac.uk
Publisher: St Mary's College
Date Established: 1905
Frequency: Annual - Published in August
Cover Price: Free
Circulation: 18,000 (Publisher's Statement)
Usual Pagination: 12
Editor: Karen Kendel-Smith
Summary of Content: Magazine featuring articles about St Mary's college and its former students.
Readership/Target Audience: Aimed at former students and staff of St Mary's.
ADVERTISING: No Advertising taken
CONSUMER: STUDENT PUBLICATIONS

SIMPLY CARDS & PAPERCRAFT
1696017U74E-696
Editorial Address: Unit 1 Adlington Court, Adlington Industrial Estate, Adlington, MACCLESFIELD, SK10 4NL
Tel: 0870 242 7038 **Fax:** 01625 855071
Email: lindsey.hopkins@practicalpublishing.co.uk
Advertising Address: As above. **Tel:** 0844 561 1202
Fax: 01625 855011
Email: lisa.sturgeon@practicalpublishing.co.uk
Web site: http://www.practicalpublishing.co.uk/simplycards
ISSN: 1745-1221
Publisher: Practical Publishing International Ltd
Frequency: 13 issues yearly
Cover Price: £3.35
Circulation: 60,000 (Publisher's Statement)

Editor: Lindsey Hopkins-Westbrook; **Advertising Manager:** Lisa Sturgeon
Summary of Content: Magazine covering cards and papercraft.
Readership/Target Audience: Aimed predominantly at intermediate and advance paper crafters.
ADVERTISING RATES:
Full Page Colour £900.00
Agency Commission: 10%
Mechanical Data: Type Area: 275 x 190mm, Bleed Size: 303 x 216mm, Trim Size: 297 x 210mm, Col Length: 275mm, Page Width: 190mm, Film: Digital
Copy instructions: Copy Date: 3 weeks prior to publication date
Average advertising content per issue: 20%
CONSUMER: WOMEN'S INTEREST CONSUMER MAGAZINES: Crafts

SIMPLY KNITTING
1665343U74E-690
Editorial Address: 30 Monmouth Street, BATH, BA1 2BW
Tel: 01225 442244 **Fax:** 01225 822793
Email: simplyknitting@futurenet.com
Advertising Address: As above. **Fax:** 01225 822885
Email: amanda.haughey@futurenet.co.uk
Web site: http://www.simplyknitting.co.uk
Publisher: Future Publishing Ltd
Date Established: 2005
Frequency: 13 issues yearly
Cover Price: £4.49
Circulation: 45,459 (ABC 01/01/2008 to 31/12/2008)
Usual Pagination: 100
Editor: Elizabeth Bagwell; **Advertising Manager:** Amanda Haughey
Summary of Content: Magazine covering knitting and crochet, practical fashion for all the family, toys and home furnishings.
Readership/Target Audience: Aimed at women aged 18 to 50 years old.
ADVERTISING RATES:
Full Page Colour £1170.00
Agency Commission: 10%
Mechanical Data: Type Area: 280 x 213mm, Bleed Size: 306 x 238mm, Trim Size: 300 x 232mm, Col Length: 280mm, Page Width: 213mm, No. of Columns (Display): 4, Film: Digital
CONSUMER: WOMEN'S INTEREST CONSUMER MAGAZINES: Crafts

SIMPSONS COMIC
48491U91D-108
Editorial Address: Titan House, 144 Southwark Street, LONDON, SE1 0UP **Tel:** 020 7620 0200 **Fax:** 020 7803 1803
Advertising Address: As above. **Tel:** 020 7803 1922
Email: james.willmott@titanemail.com
Web site: http://www.titanmagazines.com
ISSN: 1365-8298
Publisher: Titan Magazines
Frequency: 15 issues yearly
Cover Price: £2.60
Circulation: 119,720 (ABC 01/01/2007 to 01/07/2007)
Editor: Ned Hartley; **Advertising Manager:** James Willmott; **Publisher:** Nick Landau
Summary of Content: Magazine featuring comic strips and articles on the cult television show.
Readership/Target Audience: Aimed at fans of the television show.
ADVERTISING RATES:
Full Page Colour £5000.00
Agency Commission: 10%
Mechanical Data: Film: Digital, Type Area: 272 x 200mm, Col Length: 272mm, Trim Size: 297 x 230mm, Bleed Size: 305 x 238mm, Page Width: 200mm
Copy instructions: Copy Date: 6 weeks prior to publication date
CONSUMER: RECREATION & LEISURE: Children & Youth

SING TAO DAILY (EUROPEAN EDITION)
48344U90-156
Editorial Address: 1st Floor, Unit 3, Technology Park, Colindeep Lane, LONDON, NW9 6BX **Tel:** 020 8732 7628
Fax: 020 8732 7630
Email: editor@singtao.co.uk
Advertising Address: As above.
Email: sales@singtao.co.uk
Web site: http://www.singtaoeu.com
ISSN: 0260-342X
Publisher: Sing Tao (UK) Ltd
Date Established: 1975
Frequency: 310 issues yearly - Saturday and Sunday combined issue
Cover Price: £1.00
Annual Sub.: £298.00
Circulation: 35,000 (Publisher's Statement)
Usual Pagination: 24
Editor: Alego Poon; **Executive Editor:** Siu Mui Poon
Summary of Content: Newspaper covering national and international news.

Language(s): Chinese
Readership/Target Audience: Aimed at the Chinese community in Europe.
ADVERTISING RATES:
Full Page Mono £2520.00
Full Page Colour £3600.00
SCC £5.45
Agency Commission: 10%
Mechanical Data: Type Area: 520 x 330mm, Col Length: 520mm, Film: Digital, No. of Columns (Display): 10, Page Width: 330mm, Col Widths (Display): 33mm
Copy instructions: Copy Date: 1 week prior to publication date
Average advertising content per issue: 15%
Supplement(s): East Week - 52xY
CONSUMER: ETHNIC

SINGLETRACK
626404U77C-750
Formerly: Go Far
Editorial Address: Singletrack, Lockside Mill, Dale Street, TODMORDEN, OL14 5PX **Tel:** 01706 813344
Fax: 01706 813356
Email: editor@singletrackworld.com
Advertising Address: As above.
Email: ads@singletrackworld.com
Web site: http://www.singletrackworld.com
Publisher: GoFar Enterprises
Date Established: 2001
Frequency: 8 issues yearly
Cover Price: £4.25
Circulation: 22,000 (Publisher's Statement)
Usual Pagination: 148
Editor: Chipps Chippendale; **News Editor:** Ben Haworth
Summary of Content: Magazine covering all aspects of mountain biking including photography from around the world, travel features, bike reviews and route guides.
Readership/Target Audience: Aimed at serious mountain bikers between 25 and 40 years old.
ADVERTISING RATES:
Full Page Colour £1045.00
Agency Commission: 10%
Mechanical Data: Trim Size: 297 x 210mm, Type Area: 267 x 183mm, Col Length: 267mm, Bleed Size: +3mm, Page Width: 183mm
Average advertising content per issue: 25%
CONSUMER: MOTORING & CYCLING: Cycling

SJ (SPAGHETTI JUNCTION)
47380U83-73_25
Formerly: Spaghetti Junction
Editorial Address: Union of Students, Franchise Street, Perry Barr, BIRMINGHAM, B42 2SZ **Tel:** 0121 331 6812
Fax: 0121 331 6802
Email: union.comms@bcu.ac.uk
Advertising Address: Birmingham Students' Union, Franchise Street, Perry Barr, BIRMINGHAM, B42 2EN
Tel: 0121 331 6801 **Fax:** 0121 331 6802
Email: donna.powell@uce.ac.uk
Web site: http://www.uceunion.com
Publisher: Birmingham City University
Frequency: 6 issues yearly
Cover Price: Free
Circulation: 15,000 (Publisher's Statement)
Usual Pagination: 32
Advertising Manager: Marianna Nicolaidou
Summary of Content: Magazine containing Union news, sport, previews and reviews of gigs and plays, listings, feature stories and competitions.
Readership/Target Audience: Read by students.
ADVERTISING RATES:
Full Page Colour £525.00
Agency Commission: 10%
Mechanical Data: Bleed Size: +3mm, Trim Size: 297 x 210mm, Film: Digital
Copy instructions: Copy Date: 2 weeks prior to publication date
Average advertising content per issue: 20%
CONSUMER: STUDENT PUBLICATIONS

THE SKEPTIC
1775742U94E-362
Editorial Address: Anomalistic Psychology Research Unit, Dept. Psychology, Goldsmiths College, University of London, LONDON, SE14 6NW **Tel:** 020 7919 7882
Fax: 020 7919 7973
Email: edit@skeptic.org.uk
Web site: http://www.skeptic.org.uk
Publisher: CSI
Date Established: 1987
Frequency: Quarterly
Annual Sub.: £20.00
Circulation: 350 (Publisher's Statement)
Usual Pagination: 28
Editor: Chris French
Summary of Content: Magazine which takes a sceptical look at pseudoscience and claims of the paranormal and unusual phenomena.

Readership/Target Audience: Aimed at journalists, teachers, psychologists, and inquisitive people of all ages who yearn to discover the truth behind the many extraordinary claims of paranormal and unusual phenomena.
ADVERTISING: No Advertising taken
CONSUMER: OTHER CLASSIFICATIONS: Paranormal

SKI+BOARD
45877U75G-340
Formerly: Ski and Board
Editorial Address: The White House, 57-63 Church Road, Wimbledon, LONDON, SW19 5SB **Tel:** 020 8410 2000
Fax: 0845 458 0781
Email: editor@skiclub.co.uk
Advertising Address: Publicom Ltd, Battersea Studios, 80 Silverthorne Road, LONDON, SW8 3HE **Tel:** 0870 803 4271
Fax: 020 7627 5026
Email: ski@publicom-uk.com
Web site: http://www.skiclub.co.uk
ISSN: 0955-8225
Publisher: Ski Club of GB
Frequency: Quarterly - Published monthly September to December/January
Cover Price: £3.75
Free to qualifying individuals
Annual Sub.: £15.00
Circulation: 21,164 (ABC 01/01/2008 to 31/12/2008)
Usual Pagination: 132
Editor: Arnie Wilson
Summary of Content: Magazine featuring action and adventure resorts. Includes articles on equipment, clothes, technique, touring news, reviews, fitness, safety, celebrities and gossip.
Readership/Target Audience: Aimed at members of the Ski Club of Great Britain and those who want to keep up to date with developments in the snow sports world.
ADVERTISING RATES:
Full Page Colour £2500.00
Agency Commission: 10%
Mechanical Data: Bleed Size: +3mm, Col Length: 280mm, Page Width: 200mm, Film: Digital, Trim Size: 300 x 230mm, Type Area: 280 x 200mm
Copy instructions: Copy Date: 4 weeks prior to publication date
CONSUMER: SPORT: Winter Sports

THE SKIER AND SNOWBOARDER MAGAZINE
45878U75G-350
Editorial Address: PO Box 386, SEVENOAKS, TN13 1AQ
Tel: 0845 310 8303
Email: frank.baldwin@skierandsnowboarder.co.uk
Advertising Address: Space Marketing, 10 Clayfield Mews, Newcomen Road, TUNBRIDGE WELLS, TN4 9PA
Tel: 01892 677740 **Fax:** 01892 677743
Email: sharonm@spacemarketing.co.uk
Web site: http://www.skierandsnowboarder.co.uk
ISSN: 0951-5941
Publisher: Mountain Marketing Ltd
Date Established: 1980
Frequency: Quarterly - Only published during the skiing season September to April
Cover Price: £2.00
Free to qualifying individuals
Annual Sub.: £10.00
Circulation: 30,000 (Publisher's Statement)
Usual Pagination: 36
Editor: Frank Baldwin; **Managing Director:** Frank Baldwin; **Publisher:** Frank Baldwin
Summary of Content: Magazine covering all aspects of winter sports.
Readership/Target Audience: Aimed at ski and snowboarding enthusiasts.
ADVERTISING RATES:
Full Page Colour £2000.00
Agency Commission: 10%
Mechanical Data: Page Width: 277mm, Film: Digital, Type Area: 380 x 277mm, Bleed Size: 430 x 307mm, Trim Size: 420 x 297mm, Col Length: 380mm
Copy instructions: Copy Date: 3 weeks prior to publication date
Average advertising content per issue: 35%
CONSUMER: SPORT: Winter Sports

SKIN DEEP
1694385U94X-280
Editorial Address: The Old School, Higher Kinnerton, CHESTER, CH4 9AJ **Tel:** 01244 663410 **Fax:** 01244 660611
Email: editor@skindeep.co.uk
Advertising Address: As above. **Tel:** 01244 663400
Email: advertising@skindeep.co.uk
Web site: http://www.skindeep.co.uk
Publisher: Jazz Publishing
Date Established: 1994
Frequency: 13 issues yearly
Cover Price: £3.95
Free to qualifying individuals
Usual Pagination: 70
Editor: Neil Dalleywater; **Publisher:** Stuart Mears

Summary of Content: Magazine covering tattooing worldwide with practical advice about the art of tattooing and piercing as well as covering health and safety issues. Interviews with tattooed celebrities and profiles on top tattooists.
Readership/Target Audience: Aimed at anyone over the age of 18 with an interest in tattooing and piercing.
ADVERTISING RATES:
Full Page Colour £710.00
Mechanical Data: Trim Size: 297 x 210mm, Film: Digital
Copy instructions: Copy Date: 2 weeks prior to publication date
Average advertising content per issue: 20%
CONSUMER: OTHER CLASSIFICATIONS: Miscellaneous

SKIN TWO
626100U86A-180
Editorial Address: BCM Box 2071, LONDON, WC1N 3XX
Tel: 020 8487 9528
Email: mail@twpublishing.co.uk
Advertising Address: As above. **Fax:** 020 8878 8123
Email: ads@twpublishing.co.uk
Web site: http://www.skintwo.com
Publisher: Tim Woodward Publishing Ltd
Date Established: 1984
Frequency: Quarterly
Cover Price: £10.00
Annual Sub.: £35.00
Circulation: 15,000 (Publisher's Statement)
Usual Pagination: 116
Editor: Liz Tray; **Advertising Manager:** Mark Rodgers
Summary of Content: Magazine covering all aspects of the fetish industry including fashion, products and events.
Readership/Target Audience: Aimed at fetishists and clubbers worldwide.
ADVERTISING RATES:
Full Page Colour £950.00
Agency Commission: 10%
Mechanical Data: Bleed Size: +5mm, Trim Size: 297 x 210mm
Copy instructions: Copy Date: 4 weeks prior to publication date
CONSUMER: ADULT & GAY MAGAZINES: Adult Magazines

THE SKINNY
1895210U89C-1133
Editorial Address: The Drill Hall, 30 -38 Dalmeny Street, EDINBURGH, EH6 8RG **Tel:** 0131 467 4630
Email: rupert@theskinny.co.uk
Advertising Address: As above.
Web site: http://www.theskinny.co.uk
Publisher: Radge Media Limited
Frequency: Monthly
Cover Price: Free
Circulation: 28,592 (Publisher's Statement)
Editor: Rupert Thomson
Summary of Content: Magazine featuring interviews and articles on music, art, film, comedy and other aspects of Scottish culture.
Readership/Target Audience: Anybody living in Scotland with an interest in cultural events.
CONSUMER: HOLIDAYS & TRAVEL: Entertainment Guides

SKIPTON LIFE
627194U74M-283
Editorial Address: 4-8 Rodney Street, LONDON, N199JH
Tel: 020 7841 8721
Email: helen.monks@word-wide.co.uk
Publisher: Wordwide Communications
Date Established: 2000
Frequency: Half-yearly - Published in March and September
Cover Price: Free
Circulation: 100,000 (Publisher's Statement)
Usual Pagination: 68
Editor: Helen Monks
Summary of Content: Magazine for Skipton Building Society investors. Includes money advice and comment, lifestyle features, celebrity interviews, food & drink, travel features, interior design, gardening, reader offers and competitions.
Readership/Target Audience: Aimed at the top 100,000 investors with Skipton Building Society.
ADVERTISING: No Advertising taken
CONSUMER: WOMEN'S INTEREST CONSUMER MAGAZINES: Personal Finance

SKIRMISH
48719U94X-185
Editorial Address: Dane Mill Business Centre, Broadhurst Lane, CONGLETON, CW12 1LA **Tel:** 01260 291536
Email: rachel@skirmishmagazine.co.uk
Advertising Address: As above.
Email: advertising@skirmishmagazine.com
Web site: http://www.skirmishmagazine.co.uk
ISSN: 1466-8068
Publisher: Dragoon Publishing Ltd
Date Established: 1999
Frequency: 10 issues yearly

Cover Price: £2.00
Annual Sub.: £15.00
Circulation: 30,000 (Publisher's Statement)
Usual Pagination: 52
Editor: Rachel Evans; **Advertising Manager:** Sophie Flawn
Summary of Content: Magazine covering all aspects of re-enactment and living history including events, film and television work, societies, costume and weapons.
Readership/Target Audience: Aimed at historical re-enactors and history and heritage enthusiasts.
ADVERTISING RATES:
Full Page Mono £275.00
Full Page Colour £395.00
Agency Commission: 10%
Mechanical Data: Trim Size: 306 x 219mm, Col Length: 275mm, No. of Columns (Display): 3, Film: Digital, Bleed Size: +3mm, Type Area: 275 x 188mm, Page Width: 188mm
Copy instructions: Copy Date: 3 weeks prior to publication date
Average advertising content per issue: 40%
CONSUMER: OTHER CLASSIFICATIONS: Miscellaneous

SKY KIDS MAGAZINE
1643497U91D-879
Editorial Address: 136-142 Bramley Road, LONDON, W10 6SR **Tel:** 020 7565 3000 **Fax:** 020 7565 3094
Email: helen.ward@johnbrowngroup.co.uk
Advertising Address: As above. **Tel:** 020 7565 3103
Fax: 020 7565 3358
Email: annie.jarvis@johnbrowngroup.co.uk
Web site: http://www.sky.com/skykids
Publisher: John Brown Group
Date Established: 2004
Frequency: 10 issues yearly - October/November and May/June combined
Cover Price: Free
Circulation: 755,141 (ABC 01/01/2009 to 30/06/2009)
Usual Pagination: 36
Editor: Jo Brennan; **Group Editor:** Helen Ward
Summary of Content: Children's magazine covering everything that's great about kids TV and available on the Sky TV platform.
Readership/Target Audience: Aimed at kids aged 6 to 12 years old who live in a household with Sky TV.
ADVERTISING RATES:
Full Page Colour £8500.00
Agency Commission: 10%
Mechanical Data: Trim Size: 210 x 148mm
Average advertising content per issue: 5%
CONSUMER: RECREATION & LEISURE: Children & Youth

SKY MAG
46108U76C-454
Formerly: Sky The Magazine
Editorial Address: 14 Floodwalk, LONDON, SW3 5RG
Tel: 020 7990 1999
Email: skyeditorial@bskyb.com
Advertising Address: As above. **Tel:** 020 7198 3000
Fax: 020 7198 3020
Email: gemma.ridgwell@bskyb.com
Web site: http://www.sky.com
Publisher: BSKYB Publications Ltd
Date Established: 2002
Frequency: Monthly
Cover Price: Free
Circulation: 7,545,510 (ABC 01/01/2009 to 30/06/2009)
Usual Pagination: 110
Editor: Nick Chalmers
Summary of Content: TV listings magazine covering Sky digital satellite television.
Readership/Target Audience: Read by subscribers of Sky digital television.
ADVERTISING RATES:
Full Page Colour £32200.00
Agency Commission: 10%
Mechanical Data: Type Area: 245 x 190mm, Bleed Size: 271 x 216mm, Trim Size: 265 x 210mm, Col Length: 245mm, Page Width: 190mm, Film: Digital
Copy instructions: Copy Date: 4 weeks prior to publication date
Average advertising content per issue: 30%
CONSUMER: MUSIC & PERFORMING ARTS: TV & Radio

SKY MOVIES
1789570U76A-211
Editorial Address: 2 Balcombe Street, LONDON, NW1 6NW
Tel: 020 7042 4000
Email: alistair.gray@futurenet.co.uk
Advertising Address: Chelsea Towers, No 2 Chelsea Manor Gardens, LONDON, SW3 5PN **Tel:** 020 7198 3000
Email: mcourt@newsmagazines.co.uk
Publisher: Future Publishing Limited
Date Established: 2006
Frequency: Monthly
Circulation: 4,200,000 (Publisher's Statement)
Usual Pagination: 56
Editor: Ali Gray; **Advertising Manager:** Mat Court
Summary of Content: Magazine covering films.

Readership/Target Audience: Aimed at Sky Movies customers.
ADVERTISING: Rates on application
CONSUMER: MUSIC & PERFORMING ARTS: Cinema

SKY SPORTS MAGAZINE
1791912U75A-1029

Formerly: Sky Sports
Editorial Address: Teddington Studios, Broom Road, TEDDINGTON, TW11 9BE **Tel:** 020 8267 5000
Email: simon.kanter@haymarket.com
Advertising Address: As above. **Fax:** 020 8267 5815
Email: david.goodman@haymarket.com
Publisher: Haymarket Network
Date Established: 2007
Frequency: Monthly
Cover Price: Free
Circulation: 5,100,000 (Publisher's Statement)
Editor: Ryan Herman; **Managing Editor:** Colin Hubbuck
Summary of Content: Magazine covering all sport including football, cricket, boxing, golf, rugby union. rugby league and tennis as well as a guide to the month ahead on Sky Sports.
Readership/Target Audience: Aimed at subscribers to Sky Sports.
ADVERTISING RATES:
Full Page Colour £32000.00
Agency Commission: 10%
Mechanical Data: Type Area: 225 x 174mm, Bleed Size: 243 x 196mm, Trim Size: 237 x 190mm, Col Length: 225mm, Page Width: 174mm, Film: Digital
Copy instructions: Copy Date: 4 weeks prior to publication date
Average advertising content per issue: 25%
CONSUMER: SPORT

SKYDIVE MAG
45971U75N-600

Formerly: Sport Parachutist
Editorial Address: 5 Station Road, Ailsworth, PETERBOROUGH, PE5 7AH **Tel:** 01733 380568
Fax: 01733 380568
Email: editor@skydivemag.com
Advertising Address: The Maltings, West Street, BOURNE, PE10 9PH **Tel:** 01778 391000 **Fax:** 01778 392079
Email: rosso@warnersgroup.co.uk
Web site: http://www.skydivemag.com
Publisher: Warners Group Publications plc
Date Established: 1960
Frequency: 6 issues yearly
Annual Sub.: £22.00
Circulation: 6,000 (Publisher's Statement)
Usual Pagination: 88
Editor: Lesley Gale
Summary of Content: Official magazine of the British Parachute Association. Carries features, events, competitions, news, clubs, topical issues and educational articles.
Readership/Target Audience: Read by members of the British Parachute Association and interested parties.
ADVERTISING RATES:
Full Page Mono £270.00
Full Page Colour £636.00
Agency Commission: 10%
Mechanical Data: Page Width: 188mm, Type Area: 267 x 188mm, Trim Size: 297 x 210mm, Bleed Size: 303 x 216mm, Col Length: 267mm, Film: Positive, right reading, emulsion side down. Digital, Print Process: Web-fed offset litho
Copy instructions: Copy Date: 3 weeks prior to publication date
Supplement(s): Skydive Starter - 1xY
CONSUMER: SPORT: Flight

SKYWINGS
45970U75N-700

Editorial Address: 39 London Road, HARLESTON, IP20 9BH **Tel:** 01379 855021 **Fax:** 01379 855021
Email: skywings@bhpa.co.uk
Advertising Address: Fargher Design Ltd., Killane House, Ballaugh, ISLE OF MAN, IM7 5BD **Tel:** 020 7193 9133
Email: sales@skywingsmag.com
Web site: http://www.skywingsmag.com
Publisher: British Hang Gliding and Paragliding Association
Date Established: 1975
Frequency: Monthly
Annual Sub.: £32.00
Circulation: 8,000 (Publisher's Statement)
Usual Pagination: 68
Editor: Joe Schofield; **Advertising Manager:** Colin Fargher
Summary of Content: Magazine containing British and world news on hang gliding and paragliding. Covers technical, competitions, travel and equipment information.
Readership/Target Audience: Read by members of the British Hang Gliding and Paragliding Association.
ADVERTISING RATES:
Full Page Colour £627.00
Agency Commission: 10%
Mechanical Data: Print Process: Litho, Col Widths (Display): 92mm, Page Width: 188mm, Trim Size: 297 x 210mm, Type

Area: 268 x 188mm, Bleed Size: 303 x 216mm, Col Length: 268mm, Film: Digital, No. of Columns (Display): 2
Copy instructions: Copy Date: 14th of the month prior to publication date
Average advertising content per issue: 30%
CONSUMER: SPORT: Flight

SLIM AT HOME
45448U74G-50

Formerly: Slimmer
Editorial Address: 25 Phoenix Court, Hawkins Road, COLCHESTER, CO2 8JY **Tel:** 01206 505972
Email: beverley@aceville.co.uk
Advertising Address: 2nd Floor, Ewer House, 44-46 Crouch Street, COLCHESTER, CO3 3HH **Tel:** 01206 505946
Fax: 01206 500183
Email: joy.palmer@aceville.co.uk
Web site: http://www.slimathome.co.uk
Publisher: Aceville Publications Ltd
Date Established: 2007
Frequency: 10 issues yearly
Cover Price: £2.60
Circulation: 115,000 (Publisher's Statement)
Usual Pagination: 116
Editor: Laura Jones; **Advertising Manager:** Joy Palmer
Summary of Content: Magazine covering advice on slimming, fitness, fashion, beauty, health and nutrition.
Readership/Target Audience: Aimed at overweight women between 25 to 45 interested in a healthy lifestyle and losing weight but who are disillusioned with clubs and gyms and want to slim independently.
ADVERTISING RATES:
Full Page Colour £1950.00
SCC £39.00
Agency Commission: 10%
Mechanical Data: Trim Size: 278 x 203mm, Bleed Size: 288 x 213mm, Type Area: 248 x 183mm, Col Length: 248mm, No. of Columns (Display): 4, Page Width: 183mm, Film: Digital
Copy instructions: Copy Date: 5 weeks prior to publication date
Average advertising content per issue: 25%
CONSUMER: WOMEN'S INTEREST CONSUMER MAGAZINES: Slimming & Health

---

SLIMMING WORLD
45450U74G-72

Editorial Address: Clover Nook Road, Somercotes, ALFRETON, DE55 4RF **Tel:** 01773 546071
Email: editorial@slimmingworld.com
Advertising Address: As above. **Tel:** 0870 070 7222
Fax: 0870 442 9935
Email: julian.oiller@slimming-world.com
Web site: http://www.slimmingworldmagazine.co.uk
Publisher: Miles-Bramwell Executive Services Ltd
Date Established: 1998
Frequency: 7 issues yearly
Cover Price: £2.65
Circulation: 291,730 (ABC 01/01/2009 to 30/06/2009)
Usual Pagination: 120
Editor: Elise Wells; **Features Editor:** Sarah Davison;
Managing Director: Caryl Richards; **Advertising Manager:** Julian Oiller; **Publisher:** Jan Boxshall; **Circulation Manager:** Tim Harris
Summary of Content: Magazine covering slimming success stories, cookery, wearable fashion and achievable fitness. Twitter: http://twitter.com/SlimmingWorldPR.
Readership/Target Audience: Read by members of the Slimming World organisation and those with an interest in slimming and a healthy lifestyle.
ADVERTISING RATES:
Full Page Colour £4200.00
Agency Commission: 10%
Mechanical Data: Film: Digital, Type Area: 270 x 192mm, Bleed Size: 296 x 218mm, Trim Size: 290 x 215mm, Col Length: 270mm, Page Width: 192mm
Copy instructions: Copy Date: 5 weeks prior to publication date
Average advertising content per issue: 25%
CONSUMER: WOMEN'S INTEREST CONSUMER MAGAZINES: Slimming & Health

---

SLOANE SQUARE
1648840U80B-412

Editorial Address: Blandel Bridge House, 56 Sloane Square, LONDON, SW1W 8AX **Tel:** 020 7259 1050
Fax: 020 7901 9042
Email: erik.brown@pubbiz.com
Advertising Address: As above.
Email: sam@pubbiz.com
Web site: http://www.pubbiz.com
Publisher: Publishing Business
Date Established: 1999
Frequency: 6 issues yearly
Cover Price: Free
Circulation: 28,000 (Publisher's Statement)
Usual Pagination: 24
Editor: Erik Brown; **Advertising Manager:** Sam Bradshaw

Summary of Content: Lifestyle magazine covering local news as well as food, drink, fashion, property and the arts.
Readership/Target Audience: Aimed at residents, businesses and visitors to Chelsea.
ADVERTISING RATES:
Full Page Colour £2200.00
Agency Commission: 10%
Mechanical Data: Bleed Size: 276 x 236mm, Trim Size: 270 x 230mm, Film: Digital
CONSUMER: RURAL & REGIONAL INTEREST: Regional Interest Greater London

---

SM SQUARE MILE MAGAZINE
1698265U86C-725

Editorial Address: 4 Tun Yard, Peardon Street, LONDON, SW8 3HT **Tel:** 020 7819 9999 **Fax:** 020 7819 9840
Email: editorial@squaremilemagazine.co.uk
Advertising Address: As above.
Email: info@squaremilemagazine.co.uk
Web site: http://www.squaremileclub.co.uk
Publisher: Square Up Media Ltd
Date Established: 2005
Frequency: 10 issues yearly
Cover Price: Free
Circulation: 26,867 (ABC 01/01/2009 to 30/06/2009)
Editor: Martin Deeson; **Advertising Manager:** Stephen Murphy; **Publisher:** Stephen Murphy
Summary of Content: Magazine covering travel, motors, property, interiors and health and fitness.
Readership/Target Audience: Aimed at professional men in the square mile of London with a high disposable income.
ADVERTISING RATES:
Full Page Colour £5995.00
Agency Commission: 10%
Mechanical Data: Type Area: 264 x 194mm, Bleed Size: 286 x 216mm, Trim Size: 280 x 210mm, Col Length: 264mm, Page Width: 194mm, Film: Digital
Copy instructions: Copy Date: 3 weeks prior to publication date
Average advertising content per issue: 40%
CONSUMER: ADULT & GAY MAGAZINES: Men's Lifestyle Magazines

SMALL WORLD
1789574U89A-737

Editorial Address: The Minories, STRATFORD-UPON-AVON, CV37 6NF **Tel:** 0870 879 3743
Email: info@smallworldmagazine.co.uk
Advertising Address: As above. **Fax:** 0870 879 3781
Email: mike@liaisoncommunications.com
Web site: http://www.smallworldmagazine.co.uk
ISSN: 1750-4201
Publisher: Great Explorers Ltd
Date Established: 2006
Frequency: 6 issues yearly
Cover Price: £3.25
Annual Sub.: £19.00
Circulation: 25,000 (Publisher's Statement)
Usual Pagination: 100
Editor: Jeanette Davey; **Advertising Manager:** Mike Mikunda; **Publisher:** Jeanette Davey
Summary of Content: Magazine dedicated to family travel and outdoor leisure. Includes long and short haul travel, UK travel, expats and sabbaticals, special needs, medical, gear tests, London 2012, the natural world, news and reviews.
Readership/Target Audience: Aimed at affluent parents of children from birth to gap year.
ADVERTISING RATES:
Full Page Colour £1526.00
CONSUMER: HOLIDAYS & TRAVEL: Travel

SMART INVESTOR
1659560U74M-409

Editorial Address: 84-86 Regent Street, LONDON, W1B 5RR **Tel:** 020 7734 2303 **Fax:** 020 7494 2570
Publisher: The Forward Group
Date Established: 2004
Frequency: 3 issues yearly - Published in February, June and October
Cover Price: Free
Circulation: 100,000 (Publisher's Statement)
Usual Pagination: 16
Editor: Nick Kirby
Summary of Content: Magazine with articles on how to invest in stock markets, funds, other instruments as well as covering investment strategies.
Readership/Target Audience: Aimed at clients of Barclays Stockbrokers.
ADVERTISING: No Advertising taken
CONSUMER: WOMEN'S INTEREST CONSUMER MAGAZINES: Personal Finance

---

SMART PA
45477U74J-145

Formerly: Smart PA incorporating Smart European Business Travel
Editorial Address: Western House, St. James Place, High Street, CRANLEIGH, GU6 8RL **Tel:** 01483 276788
Fax: 01483 277646

Email: smartpa@btinternet.com
Advertising Address: As above.
Email: smartpa@btinternet.com
Web site: http://www.smartgroup.eu.com
ISSN: 1464-3340
Publisher: Smart Group
Date Established: 1998
Frequency: 6 issues yearly
Cover Price: £4.99
Circulation: 150,000 (Publisher's Statement)
Usual Pagination: 48
Editor: Tony Williams; **Features Editor:** Zoe Thompkins-Jones; **Advertising Manager:** Zoe Halstead; **Managing Editor:** Tony Williams
Summary of Content: Magazine covering office products, conference and events facilities, business travel, including features on health, beauty, business and motoring.
Readership/Target Audience: Aimed at secretaries and PAs.
ADVERTISING RATES:
Full Page Colour £1650.00
Agency Commission: 10%
Mechanical Data: Trim Size: 297 x 210mm, Bleed Size: 303 x 216mm, Film: Digital, Type Area: 273 x 182mm, Col Length: 273mm, Page Width: 182mm
Copy instructions: Copy Date: 6 weeks prior to publication date
Average advertising content per issue: 50%
CONSUMER: WOMEN'S INTEREST CONSUMER MAGAZINES: Secretary & PA

SMARTLIFE INTERNATIONAL   624930U78R-370

Editorial Address: 21-23 Phoenix Court, Hawkins Road, COLCHESTER, CO2 8JY **Tel:** 01206 505924
Fax: 01206 505929
Email: stuart@smartlifeint.com
Advertising Address: 9 Gloucester Mews, South Street, EASTBOURNE, BN21 4XH **Tel:** 01323 636000
Fax: 01273 719911
Email: richard@partridgeltd.co.uk
Web site: http://www.smartlifeint.com
Publisher: Partridge Publications (2000) Ltd
Date Established: 2000
Frequency: 10 issues yearly
Cover Price: £3.95
Circulation: 18,080 (ABC 01/01/2008 to 31/12/2008)
Usual Pagination: 148
Editor: Stuart Pritchard; **Editor-in-Chief:** Stuart Pritchard; **Advertising Manager:** Richard Davies
Summary of Content: Magazine containing lifestyle and consumer technology, centred around the idea of the intelligent house, but also enveloping all areas of consumer technology, design, motoring and travel.
Readership/Target Audience: Aimed at professionals with a real interest in technological innovation and high end living in all its forms and with the necessary income to possess it.
ADVERTISING RATES:
Full Page Colour £2995.00
Agency Commission: 10%
Copy instructions: Copy Date: 3 weeks prior to publication date
Average advertising content per issue: 40%
CONSUMER: CONSUMER ELECTRONICS: Consumer Electronics Related

SMARTPHONE & PDA ESSENTIALS

758602U78R-330
Formerly: PDA Essentials & GPS Advisor
Editorial Address: Richmond House, 33 Richmond Hill, BOURNEMOUTH, BH2 6EZ **Tel:** 01202 586200
Email: pdaessentials@imagine-publishing.co.uk
Advertising Address: As above. **Fax:** 01202 294032
Email: natalie.stainer@imagine-publishing.co.uk
Web site: http://www.smartphonedaily.co.uk
ISSN: 2040-2007
Publisher: Imagine Publishing
Date Established: 2001
Frequency: 13 issues yearly
Cover Price: £5.99
Circulation: 13,471 (ABC 01/01/2004 to 31/12/2004)
Usual Pagination: 116
Editor: Andy Betts
Summary of Content: Magazine focusing on hand-held electronic personal organizers and GPS devices, featuring a buyer's guide and product reviews.
Readership/Target Audience: Aimed at men 25 years old and over who are users of hand held computers and smart phones.
ADVERTISING RATES:
Full Page Colour £2300.00
Agency Commission: 10%
Mechanical Data: Page Width: 205mm, Type Area: 270 x 205mm, Col Length: 270mm, Trim Size: 297 x 230mm, Bleed Size: 307 x 240mm, Film: Digital
Copy instructions: Copy Date: 4 weeks prior to publication date

Average advertising content per issue: 10%
CONSUMER: CONSUMER ELECTRONICS: Consumer Electronics Related

SMILEGUIDE   1789776U74G-276

Editorial Address: Clifton Heights, Triangle West, BRISTOL, BS8 1EJ **Tel:** 0117 925 1696 **Fax:** 0117 925 1808
Email: mark.cherry@specialistuk.com
Web site: http://www.specialistuk.com
Publisher: Specialist (UK) Ltd
Frequency: Annual - Published in October
Cover Price: Free
Circulation: 1,400,000 (Publisher's Statement)
Usual Pagination: 24
Editor: Mark Cherry; **Publisher:** Mark Cherry
Summary of Content: Magazine covering all aspects of dental care and lifestyle.
Readership/Target Audience: Aimed at Denplan clients.
ADVERTISING: No Advertising taken
CONSUMER: WOMEN'S INTEREST CONSUMER MAGAZINES: Slimming & Health

---

THE SMOKE   47447U83-73_50

Editorial Address: 35 Marylebone Road, LONDON, NW1 5LS **Tel:** 020 7911 5000
Email: vpcomms@wmin.ac.uk
Advertising Address: As above. **Fax:** 020 7911 5793
Email: vpcomms@wmin.ac.uk
Web site: http://www.uwsu.com
Publisher: University of Westminster Student Union
Frequency: 10 issues yearly - Published monthly during term time
Cover Price: Free
Circulation: 22,000 (Publisher's Statement)
Usual Pagination: 48
Editor: Rob Watson; **Advertising Manager:** Vanessa Patel
Summary of Content: Magazine covering University news and features of general interest. Includes articles on music and cinema.
Readership/Target Audience: Read by students in Central London and Harrow.
ADVERTISING RATES:
Full Page Mono £600.00
Full Page Colour £800.00
Mechanical Data: Type Area: 350 x 264mm, Col Length: 350mm, Page Width: 264mm
CONSUMER: STUDENT PUBLICATIONS

SNAKE TORQUE   46478U77E-280

Editorial Address: 18 Neptune Road, FAREHAM, PO15 6SW **Tel:** 01329 312011
Email: peter.snaketorque@ntlworld.com
Advertising Address: As above.
Email: peter.snaketorque@ntlworld.com
Web site: http://www.cobraclub.com
Publisher: UK Cobra Replica Club Ltd
Date Established: 1988
Frequency: 6 issues yearly
Cover Price: £2.90
Circulation: 1,500 (Publisher's Statement)
Usual Pagination: 36
Editor: Peter Jones; **Advertising Manager:** Peter Jones
Summary of Content: Magazine containing current vehicle legislation for kit cars, technical advice, regional reports, annual diary of events and company profiles. Also covers modifications, members build articles, road trips, accessories and kit car shows.
Readership/Target Audience: Read by members of the Cobra Replica club.
ADVERTISING RATES:
Full Page Mono £100.00
Full Page Colour £150.00
Mechanical Data: Film: Digital
CONSUMER: MOTORING & CYCLING: Club Cars

SNOOKER SCENE   46025U75X-910

Formerly: Snooker Scene Incorporating Pot Black
Editorial Address: Hayley Green Court, 130 Hagley Road, Hayley Green, HALESOWEN, B63 1DY **Tel:** 0121 585 9188
Fax: 0121 585 7117
Email: clive.everton@talk21.com
Advertising Address: As above.
Email: clive.everton@talk21.com
Web site: http://www.snookersceneonline.com
Publisher: Everton's News Agency
Date Established: 1971
Frequency: Monthly - Published on the 1st Wednesday of the cover month
Cover Price: £2.75
Annual Sub.: £30.00
Circulation: 10,000 (Publisher's Statement)
Usual Pagination: 40
Editor: Clive Everton; **Advertising Manager:** Clive Everton

Summary of Content: Publication containing news and features on snooker and other cue sports.
Readership/Target Audience: Read by snooker and billiards enthusiasts.
ADVERTISING RATES:
Full Page Mono £650.00
Full Page Colour £925.00
Agency Commission: 15%
Mechanical Data: Trim Size: 297 x 210mm, Film: Digital
Copy instructions: Copy Date: 17th of the month prior to publication date
Average advertising content per issue: 30%
CONSUMER: SPORT: Other Sport

SNOW   1638180U75G-651

Editorial Address: 1 Victoria Villas, RICHMOND, TW9 2GW **Tel:** 020 8332 8440 **Fax:** 020 8332 9307
Email: christine.ottery@circlepublishing.net
Advertising Address: As above.
Email: graeme.spratley@circlepublishing.net
Web site: http://www.snowmagazine.com
Publisher: Circle Publishing
Date Established: 2003
Frequency: 5 issues yearly
Cover Price: Free
Circulation: 40,000 (Publisher's Statement)
Usual Pagination: 68
Editor: Rob McKinlay; **Editor-in-Chief:** Rupert Mellor
Summary of Content: Magazine with news and features on skiing, snowboarding and mountain lifestyle.
Readership/Target Audience: Aimed at those interested in skiing and snowboarding.
ADVERTISING RATES:
Full Page Colour £2200.00
Agency Commission: 10%
Mechanical Data: Bleed Size: 310 x 240mm, Trim Size: 300 x 230mm, Type Area: 280 x 210mm, Col Length: 280mm, Page Width: 210mm, Film: Digital
Copy instructions: Copy Date: 10 days prior to publication date
Average advertising content per issue: 30%
CONSUMER: SPORT: Winter Sports

SO ESTEEM   1829668U74A-1043

Editorial Address: 16 Stratford Place, LONDON, W1C 1BF **Tel:** 0870 765 6110 **Fax:** 0870 765 6120
Email: admin@soesteem.co.uk
Advertising Address: As above.
Email: jeff@soesteem.co.uk
Web site: http://www.soesteem.co.uk
Publisher: So Esteem Ltd
Date Established: 2007
Frequency: 6 issues yearly
Cover Price: Free
Circulation: 10,000 (Publisher's Statement)
Usual Pagination: 68
Editor: Angela Barclay
Summary of Content: Magazine covering plus size fashion, beauty, lifestyle, image, readers' letters, competitions, book reviews and healthy option recipes.
Readership/Target Audience: Aimed at plus size women.
ADVERTISING: Rates on application
CONSUMER: WOMEN'S INTEREST CONSUMER MAGAZINES: Women's Interest

---

SO TUNBRIDGE WELLS   1843168U80C-5462

Editorial Address: 14B Chapel Place, High Street, TUNBRIDGE WELLS, TN1 1YQ **Tel:** 01892 616103
Fax: 01892 513547
Email: richard.moore@sotunbridgewells.co.uk
Advertising Address: As above.
Email: sharon.lacey@sotunbridgewells.co.uk
Web site: http://www.sotunbridgewells.co.uk
Publisher: The Magazine People
Date Established: 2008
Frequency: Monthly
Cover Price: £1.50
Circulation: 22,000 (Publisher's Statement)
Usual Pagination: 108
Editor: Richard Moore; **Publisher:** Nick Moore
Summary of Content: Lifestyle magazine with local features, fashion, beauty, property and celebrities.
Readership/Target Audience: Aimed at residents in Tunbridge Wells and the surrounding area.
ADVERTISING RATES:
Full Page Colour £1173.00
Agency Commission: 10%
Mechanical Data: Type Area: 247 x 155mm, Bleed Size: 303 x 216mm, Trim Size: 297 x 210mm, Col Length: 247mm, Page Width: 155mm
Average advertising content per issue: 40%
CONSUMER: RURAL & REGIONAL INTEREST: Regional Interest English Counties

Consumer Magazines

SOAPLIFE
714504U76C-460

Editorial Address: Blue Fin Building, 110 Southwark Street, LONDON, SE1 0SU **Tel:** 020 3148 5000
Email: hellen_gardner@ipcmedia.com
Advertising Address: As above.
Email: richard_smith@ipcmedia.com
Publisher: IPC TX
Date Established: 1999
Frequency: 26 issues yearly
Cover Price: £1.50
Circulation: 117,966 (ABC 01/01/2009 to 30/06/2009)
Usual Pagination: 68
Editor: Hellen Gardner; **Advertising Manager:** Richard Smith
Summary of Content: Magazine with the big soap stories and pictures from the soaps, plus, celebrity news and gossip, celebrity fashion and real-life celebrity interviews.
Readership/Target Audience: Read by women who are interested in soaps.
ADVERTISING RATES:
Full Page Colour £3000.00
Agency Commission: 15%
Mechanical Data: Type Area: 253 x 190mm, Bleed Size: 286 x 216mm, Trim Size: 280 x 210mm, Film: Digital, Col Length: 253mm, Page Width: 190mm
Copy instructions: Copy Date: 2 weeks prior to publication date
CONSUMER: MUSIC & PERFORMING ARTS: TV & Radio

SOBORNOST (INCORPORATING EASTERN CHURCHES REVIEW)
47857U87-211

Editorial Address: 1 Canterbury Road, OXFORD, OX2 6LU
Tel: 01865 552991 **Fax:** 01865 316700
Email: gensec@sobornost.org
Web site: http://www.sobornost.org
ISSN: 0144-8722
Publisher: Fellowship of St Alban & St Sergius
Date Established: 1933
Frequency: Half-yearly - Published in June and November
Annual Sub.: £20.00
Circulation: 1,500 (Publisher's Statement)
Usual Pagination: 100
Editor: Stephen Platt
Summary of Content: Publication featuring articles dealing with liturgy, history and art of the eastern and oriental orthodox world, especially in interaction with Western Christianity. Reports on ecumenical work, conferences and exhibitions and includes book reviews.
Readership/Target Audience: Aimed at Christians and those interested in ecumenical work involving eastern orthodox and oriental orthodox churches, in particular members of the Fellowship of St Alban and St Sergius.
ADVERTISING: No Advertising taken
CONSUMER: RELIGIOUS

SOCIALIST REVIEW
47278U82-180

Editorial Address: PO Box 42184, LONDON, SW8 2WD
Tel: 020 7819 1176
Email: office@socialistreview.org.uk
Web site: http://www.socialistreview.org.uk
ISSN: 0141-2442
Publisher: Sherborne Publishing
Date Established: 1978
Frequency: 11 issues yearly
Cover Price: £3.00
Annual Sub.: £30.00
Circulation: 12,000 (Publisher's Statement)
Usual Pagination: 36
Editor: Christophe Chataigne
Summary of Content: Magazine covering socialism, anti-capitalism and anti-imperialism today. Contains news, various articles, theatre, film and book reviews.
Readership/Target Audience: Read by members of the Socialist Workers Party and anti-war and anti-capitalist activists.
ADVERTISING: No Advertising taken
CONSUMER: CURRENT AFFAIRS & POLITICS

SOCIETY GOLF
45827U75D-240

Editorial Address: P.O. Box 1252, BRIGHTON, BN1 2YN
Tel: 0870 600 5566
Email: golforganiser@aol.com
Advertising Address: 9F Bedford Towers, Kings Road, BRIGHTON, BN1 2JG **Tel:** 0870 600 5566
Email: golforganiser@aol.com
Web site: http://www.golforganiser.com
Publisher: Society Golf Magazine Ltd
Date Established: 1984
Frequency: Annual - Published in February
Cover Price: £3.50
Circulation: 85,000 (Publisher's Statement)
Usual Pagination: 100
Editor: Fred Moghadam; **Advertising Manager:** Fred Moghadam; **Publisher:** Fred Moghadam

Summary of Content: Magazine covering all aspects of golf. Includes news and articles on tournaments.
Readership/Target Audience: Aimed at members of all golf societies in the UK.
ADVERTISING RATES:
Full Page Mono £3000.00
Full Page Colour £5500.00
Agency Commission: 15%
Mechanical Data: Film: Digital, Bleed Size: 303 x 216mm, Trim Size: 297 x 210mm
Copy instructions: Copy Date: Last day of November
Average advertising content per issue: 50%
CONSUMER: SPORT: Golf

SOCIETY TODAY
1664422U82-261

Editorial Address: 17-21 Wyfold Road, LONDON, SW6 6SE
Tel: 020 7385 6137
Email: editorial@society-today.com
Advertising Address: As above.
Email: advertising@society-today.com
Web site: http://www.society-today.com
ISSN: 1744-2966
Publisher: Books & Life Ltd
Date Established: 2005
Frequency: 6 issues yearly
Cover Price: £2.50
Free to qualifying individuals
Circulation: 20,000 (Publisher's Statement)
Usual Pagination: 48
Editor: Hom Paribag; **News Editor:** Prakash Khanal; **Advertising Manager:** Luiz Faulin
Summary of Content: Magazine covering social issues including religion, social and ethnic issues, the economy and the environment as well as book, film, theatre and music reviews as well as policy related issues.
Readership/Target Audience: Aimed at the general public aged between 25 and 65 years old as well as policy makers, decision makers, those working in charities, rights activists, religious and ethnic contacts, students, teachers and professionals.
ADVERTISING RATES:
Full Page Mono £1200.00
Full Page Colour £2000.00
Mechanical Data: Type Area: 260 x 184mm, Trim Size: 275 x 210mm, Bleed Size: 290 x 220mm, Col Length: 260mm, Page Width: 184mm, Film: Positive, right reading, emulsion side down. Digital
Copy instructions: Copy Date: 2 weeks prior to publication date
CONSUMER: CURRENT AFFAIRS & POLITICS

SOLDIERS OF THE QUEEN
46698U79H-140

Editorial Address: PO Box 5837, NEWBURY, RG14 7FJ
Tel: 01635 48628
Email: vmsdan@msn.com
Advertising Address: As above.
Web site: http://www.victorianmilitarysociety.org.uk
Publisher: Victorian Military Society
Date Established: 1974
Frequency: Quarterly
Annual Sub.: £20.00
Circulation: 2,000 (Publisher's Statement)
Usual Pagination: 32
Editor: Andy Smith; **Advertising Manager:** Beverley Allen
Summary of Content: Features original research articles on the military history of all nations and races in the period 1837- 1914. Includes book reviews.
Readership/Target Audience: Aimed at members of the Victorian Military Society and associated organisations throughout the world.
CONSUMER: HOBBIES & DIY: Military History

SOLDIERS SMALL BOOK
46699U79H-150

Editorial Address: PO Box 5837, NEWBURY, RG14 7FJ
Tel: 01635 48628
Advertising Address: As above.
Email: vmsdan@msn.com
Web site: http://www.victorianmilitarysociety.org.uk
Publisher: Victorian Military Society
Date Established: 1974
Frequency: Quarterly
Annual Sub.: £20.00
Circulation: 2,000 (Publisher's Statement)
Usual Pagination: 4
Editor: Dan Allen; **Advertising Manager:** Beverley Allen
Summary of Content: Newsletter giving details of society activities, auction reports, "what's on", notes & queries, members' classified adverts and details of forthcoming military history publications.
Readership/Target Audience: Aimed at members of the Victorian Military Society and associated organisations throughout the world.
ADVERTISING: Rates on application

Copy instructions: Copy Date: 1st of month prior to publication date
CONSUMER: HOBBIES & DIY: Military History

THE SOMERFIELD MAGAZINE
45616U74P-650

Editorial Address: Phoenix House, 1 Queen Square, BRISTOL, BS1 4LJ **Tel:** 0117 989 7800 **Fax:** 0117 930 4805
Email: letters@psprarepublishing.co.uk
Advertising Address: 3rd Floor, 21 Great Sutton Street, LONDON, EC1V 0DY **Tel:** 020 7566 9910
Fax: 020 7490 1723
Email: dan.jefferson@psprarepublishing.co.uk
Web site: http://www.somerfield.co.uk
Publisher: PSP Rare Publishing
Frequency: 13 issues yearly
Cover Price: Free
Circulation: 1,003,795 (ABC 01/01/2009 to 30/06/2009)
Usual Pagination: 76
Editor: Matt Robinson; **Managing Director:** Kim Conchie; **Advertising Manager:** Dan Jefferson
Summary of Content: Magazine of Somerfield Stores Ltd. Includes articles on cookery, the home and entertainment.
Readership/Target Audience: Read by Somerfield customers.
ADVERTISING RATES:
Full Page Colour £19950.00
Agency Commission: 10%
Mechanical Data: Film: Digital, Col Length: 227mm, Page Width: 186mm, Trim Size: 270 X 210mm, Type Area: 227 x 186mm, Bleed Size: +3mm, Print Process: Web-fed offset litho
Copy instructions: Copy Date: 4 weeks prior to publication date
Average advertising content per issue: 40%
CONSUMER: WOMEN'S INTEREST CONSUMER MAGAZINES: Food & Cookery

SOMERSET COUNTY NEWS
1828229U80C-5435

Formerly: Somerset Advertiser
Editorial Address: Publishing House, 3 Bridgebank Industrial Estate, Taylor Street, Horwich, BOLTON, BL6 7PD
Tel: 0161 909 0909 **Fax:** 0161 909 0919
Email: info@bigspark.co.uk
Advertising Address: As above.
Web site: http://www.somersetadvertiser.co.uk
Publisher: The Big Spark
Date Established: 2007
Frequency: Monthly
Cover Price: £0.60
Circulation: 18,000 (Publisher's Statement)
Usual Pagination: 40
Editor: Dave Beevers; **Publisher:** Stuart Parker
Summary of Content: Newspaper covering local news and events in Somerset.
Readership/Target Audience: Aimed at households in Somerset.
CONSUMER: RURAL & REGIONAL INTEREST: Regional Interest English Counties

THE SON NEWSPAPER
1668045U87-2037

Editorial Address: PO Box 3070, LITTLEHAMPTON, BN17 6WX **Tel:** 01903 732190 **Fax:** 01903 733492
Email: hugh.southon1@btinternet.com
Advertising Address: As above.
Email: leggsteve@aol.com
Web site: http://www.theson.org.uk
Publisher: The Son Newspaper
Date Established: 2004
Frequency: Quarterly
Cover Price: £0.35
Circulation: 200,000 (Publisher's Statement)
Usual Pagination: 20
Editor: Chris Girdler; **Advertising Manager:** Steve Legg; **Publisher:** Steve Legg
Summary of Content: Magazine aiming to put Jesus back as the centre of society. Also contains celebrity interviews, football, TV, movies and regular columnists.
Readership/Target Audience: Aimed at the public at large.
ADVERTISING RATES:
Full Page Colour £1200.00
Agency Commission: 10%
Mechanical Data: Type Area: 360 x 260mm, Page Width: 260mm, Col Length: 360mm, Film: Digital
Copy instructions: Copy Date: 1 month prior to publication date
Average advertising content per issue: 20%
CONSUMER: RELIGIOUS

SONGLINES
1792507U76D-825

Editorial Address: PO Box 54209, LONDON, W14 0WU
Tel: 020 7371 2777 **Fax:** 020 7371 2220
Email: editor@songlines.co.uk

Advertising Address: Unit F5, Shepherds Studios, Rockley Road, LONDON, W14 0DA **Tel:** 020 7371 2834
Fax: 020 7371 2220
Email: james@songlines.co.uk
Web site: http://www.songlines.co.uk
ISSN: 1464-8113
Publisher: Songlines Publications Ltd
Date Established: 1999
Frequency: 8 issues yearly
Cover Price: £4.25
Circulation: 25,000 (Publisher's Statement)
Usual Pagination: 112
Editor: Jo Frost
Summary of Content: Magazine covering music from traditional and popular to contemporary and fusion with CD reviews, artist interviews, guides to world music traditions, concert listings and travel stories.
Readership/Target Audience: Aimed at world music lovers.
ADVERTISING RATES:
Full Page Mono £1152.00
Full Page Colour £1524.00
Agency Commission: 10%
Mechanical Data: Type Area: 277 x 200mm, Bleed Size: 303 x 226mm, Trim Size: 297 x 220mm, Col Length: 277mm, Page Width: 200mm, Film: Digital
Average advertising content per issue: 20%
CONSUMER: MUSIC & PERFORMING ARTS: Music

SONY MAGAZINE
1830173U78R-524
Editorial Address: Teddington Studios, Broom Road, TEDDINGTON, TW11 9BE **Tel:** 020 8267 5000
Email: kerry.thompson@haymarket.com
Advertising Address: As above.
Web site: http://www.sonymagazine.co.uk
Publisher: Haymarket Network
Date Established: 2007
Frequency: Quarterly
Cover Price: £3.50
Free to qualifying individuals
Circulation: 200,000 (Print Run)
Usual Pagination: 100
Editor: Kerry Thompson; **Executive Editor:** Niall Hampton
Summary of Content: Magazine covering film and TV, music, technology, games and celebrity interviews.
Readership/Target Audience: Aimed at predominantly men aged 25 to 45 years old with a high disposable income.
CONSUMER: CONSUMER ELECTRONICS: Consumer Electronics Related

SORTED
1837393U86C-745
Editorial Address: PO Box 3070, LITTLEHAMPTON, BN17 6WX **Tel:** 01903 732190 **Fax:** 01903 733492
Email: hugh.southon1@btinternet.com
Advertising Address: As above.
Email: leggsteve@aol.com
Web site: http://www.sorted-magazine.com
Publisher: The Son Newspaper
Date Established: 2007
Frequency: 6 issues yearly
Cover Price: £2.50
Annual Sub.: £15.00
Circulation: 20,000 (Publisher's Statement)
Usual Pagination: 60
Editor: Hugh Southon; **Advertising Manager:** Steve Legg; **Publisher:** Steve Legg
Summary of Content: Men's lifestyle magazine covering motoring, gadgets, finance, films, finance, fitness, faith, sport and features.
Readership/Target Audience: Aimed at men of all ages.
ADVERTISING RATES:
Full Page Mono £500.00
Full Page Colour £500.00
CONSUMER: ADULT & GAY MAGAZINES: Men's Lifestyle Magazines

SOTHACH (ROCK MAGAZINE)
46260U76E-340
Editorial Address: Ffordd Llanllechid, Llanllechid, BANGOR, LL57 3EE **Tel:** 01248 602267 **Fax:** 01248 602267
Email: emyrpierce@hotmail.com
Publisher: Cytgord
Frequency: 6 issues yearly
Cover Price: Free
Circulation: 3,500 (Publisher's Statement)
Editor: Emyr Pierce
Summary of Content: Magazine containing features and news on the rock and pop industry.
Language(s): Welsh
Readership/Target Audience: Aimed at music fans in their teens to late twenties, researchers for BBC Radio Wales and Welsh language chart compilers.
ADVERTISING: No Advertising taken
CONSUMER: MUSIC & PERFORMING ARTS: Pop Music

SOUL & SPIRIT
1830091U94X-299
Editorial Address: 25 Phoenix Court, Hawkins Road, COLCHESTER, CO2 8JY **Tel:** 01206 508628
Email: katy.evans@aceville.co.uk
Advertising Address: 2nd Floor, Ewer House, 44-46 Crouch Street, COLCHESTER, CO3 3HH **Tel:** 01206 505944
Fax: 01206 500183
Email: joy.palmer@aceville.co.uk
Web site: http://www.soulandspiritmagazine.com
Publisher: Aceville Publications Ltd
Date Established: 2008
Frequency: Monthly
Cover Price: £3.25
Usual Pagination: 116
Editor: Katy Evans; **Advertising Manager:** Joy Palmer; **Group Editor:** Charlotte Smith
Summary of Content: Magazine covering astrology, energy therapies, divination, life coaching, psychology, meditation, personality quizzes and wellbeing.
Readership/Target Audience: Aimed at women aged between 25 and 60 years old.
ADVERTISING RATES:
Full Page Colour £1395.00
Agency Commission: 10%
Mechanical Data: Type Area: 276 x 211mm, Bleed Size: 308 x 238mm, Trim Size: 300 x 230mm, Col Length: 276mm, Page Width: 211mm, Film: Digital
Average advertising content per issue: 20%
CONSUMER: OTHER CLASSIFICATIONS: Miscellaneous

SOULSTAR CHATBUSTERS
1666681U76D-799
Formerly: Chat Busters
Editorial Address: Home Close, Teffont, SALISBURY, SP3 5QY **Tel:** 01722 716268 **Fax:** 01722 716781
Email: davidoparker@aol.com
Advertising Address: As above.
Email: davidoparker@aol.com
Web site: http://www.soulstarmagazine.co.uk
Publisher: Kingsley House (Publishing)
Date Established: 2000
Frequency: 6 issues yearly
Cover Price: £3.95
Free to qualifying individuals
Circulation: 1,000 (Publisher's Statement)
Usual Pagination: 28
Editor: David Parker; **Advertising Manager:** Karl Plaskett
Summary of Content: Magazine featuring interviews, reviews, show dates and news of Motown music and artists.
Readership/Target Audience: Aimed at fans of music from the 50s, 60s and 70s.
ADVERTISING RATES:
Full Page Mono £100.00
Full Page Colour £200.00
Agency Commission: 20%
Mechanical Data: Type Area: 270 x 190mm, Bleed Size: 307 x 220mm, Trim Size: 297 x 210mm, Col Length: 270mm, Page Width: 190mm, Film: Digital
Average advertising content per issue: 30%
CONSUMER: MUSIC & PERFORMING ARTS: Music

SOUND ON SOUND
46182U76D-405
Editorial Address: Media House, Trafalgar Way, Bar Hill, CAMBRIDGE, CB23 8SQ **Tel:** 01954 789888
Fax: 01954 789895
Email: sos.feedback@soundonsound.com
Advertising Address: As above.
Email: adsales@soundonsound.com
Web site: http://www.soundonsound.com
ISSN: 0951-6816
Publisher: SOS Publications Ltd
Date Established: 1985
Frequency: Monthly
Cover Price: £4.99
Annual Sub.: £48.00
Circulation: 30,000 (Publisher's Statement)
Usual Pagination: 272
Editor: Chris Mayes-Wright; **News Editor:** Chris Mayes-Wright; **Features Editor:** Sam Inglis; **Editor-in-Chief:** Paul White; **Publisher:** David Lockwood
Summary of Content: Magazine covering all aspects of hi-tech music and recording technology.
Readership/Target Audience: Aimed at professional and semi-professional musicians interested in music recording.
ADVERTISING RATES:
Full Page Colour £2000.00
Agency Commission: 10%
Mechanical Data: Type Area: 277 x 190mm, Trim Size: 297 x 210mm, Bleed Size: 303 x 216mm, Film: Digital, Col Length: 277mm, Page Width: 190mm
Copy instructions: Copy Date: 6 weeks prior to publication date
Average advertising content per issue: 45%
CONSUMER: MUSIC & PERFORMING ARTS: Music

SOUNDAROUND
48651U94F-825
Editorial Address: 74 Glentham Road, Barnes, LONDON, SW13 9JJ **Tel:** 0800 917 6008
Email: nigel@soundaround.org
Advertising Address: As above.
Email: nigel@soundaround.org
Web site: http://www.soundaround.org
Publisher: Soundaround Associations
Date Established: 1975
Frequency: Monthly
Cover Price: Free
Circulation: 5,000 (Publisher's Statement per month)
Editor: Nigel Verbeek; **Advertising Manager:** Nigel Verbeek
Summary of Content: Participation magazine for blind and visually impaired listeners throughout the English speaking world, covering news and general topics of interest.
Readership/Target Audience: Aimed at those who are blind or visually impaired.
ADVERTISING: Rates on application
CONSUMER: OTHER CLASSIFICATIONS: Disability

THE SOURCE
48480U91D-135
Formerly: UK Youth
Editorial Address: Avon Tyrrell, Bransgore, CHRISTCHURCH, BH23 8EE **Tel:** 01425 672347
Fax: 01425 822537
Email: alan@alanrogers.org
Advertising Address: 27 Norwich Road, HALESWORTH, IP19 8BX **Tel:** 01986 834250 **Fax:** 01986 834255
Email: david@micropress.co.uk
Web site: http://www.ukyouth.org
Publisher: UK Youth
Frequency: Monthly
Cover Price: Free
Circulation: 6,000 (Publisher's Statement)
Usual Pagination: 22
Editor: Alan Rogers; **Advertising Manager:** David Burns
Summary of Content: Magazine containing articles on how to manage youth work and informal education.
Readership/Target Audience: Aimed at youth workers and managers who work with young people.
ADVERTISING RATES:
Full Page Colour £800.00
Agency Commission: 10%
Mechanical Data: Type Area: 270 x 188mm, Col Length: 270mm, Trim Size: 297 x 210mm, Bleed Size: 304 x 214mm, Page Width: 188mm, Film: Digital
Copy instructions: Copy Date: 4 weeks prior to publication date
Average advertising content per issue: 30%
CONSUMER: RECREATION & LEISURE: Children & Youth

SOUTH AFRICAN
1666678U90-959
Editorial Address: Unit 7, Commodore House, Juniper Drive, LONDON, SW18 1TW **Tel:** 0845 456 4910
Fax: 0845 456 4912
Email: editor@southafrican.co.uk
Advertising Address: As above.
Email: wernerh@blueskygroup.com
Web site: http://www.southafrican.co.uk
Publisher: Blue Sky Publications Ltd
Frequency: Weekly
Free to qualifying individuals
Annual Sub.: £42.00
Circulation: 30,000 (Publisher's Statement)
Usual Pagination: 24
Editor: Frances Paddick
Summary of Content: Newspaper covering South African news as well as events, travel, recruitment, property, business and sport.
Readership/Target Audience: Aimed at South Africans living in London.
ADVERTISING RATES:
Full Page Colour £750.00
Agency Commission: 10%
Mechanical Data: Type Area: 350 x 266mm, Col Length: 350mm, Page Width: 266mm, Film: Digital
Copy instructions: Copy Date: 1 week prior to publication date
Supplement(s): Everything SA - 6xY
CONSUMER: ETHNIC

SOUTH BELFAST LIFE
1790173U80F-208
Editorial Address: 39 Boucher Road, BELFAST, BT12 6UT **Tel:** 028 9066 3311 **Fax:** 028 9038 1915
Email: edit@ulstertatler.com
Advertising Address: As above.
Email: william.sale@ulstertatler.com
Web site: http://www.ulstertatler.com
ISSN: 1745-4417
Publisher: Ulster Journals Ltd
Date Established: 2003
Frequency: 3 issues yearly - Published in spring, summer and winter
Cover Price: £2.00
Free to qualifying individuals

Usual Pagination: 96
Editor: Christopher Sherry
Summary of Content: Magazine covering women's and men's fashion, local events profiles of local people and businesses, interiors, art, property, health and beauty.
Readership/Target Audience: Aimed at households in South Belfast.
ADVERTISING RATES:
Full Page Colour £900.00
Agency Commission: 15%
Mechanical Data: Bleed Size: 225 x 310mm, Trim Size: 215 x 300mm, Film: Digital
Average advertising content per issue: 40%
CONSUMER: RURAL & REGIONAL INTEREST: Regional Interest Northern Ireland

SOUTH CAMBS MAGAZINE   1605150U80C-5046

Editorial Address: South Cambridgeshire Hall, Cambourne Business Park, CAMBRIDGE, CB3 6EA **Tel:** 0845 045 0500
Fax: 01954 713149
Email: scdc@scambs.gov.uk
Advertising Address: The Irwin Centre, Scotland Road, Dry Drayton, CAMBRIDGE, CB3 8AR **Tel:** 01954 212906
Fax: 01954 212105
Email: info@manpublishing.co.uk
Web site: http://www.scambs.gov.uk
ISSN: 1741-8852
Publisher: Manning Publishing Ltd
Date Established: 1992
Frequency: Quarterly
Cover Price: Free
Circulation: 61,000 (Publisher's Statement)
Usual Pagination: 48
Editor: Georgina Hayward; **Publisher:** Debbie Johnson
Summary of Content: Magazine covering community and village issues, environmental health, planning, housing, sport, art, sustainability, waste collection and recycling.
Readership/Target Audience: Aimed at residents and businesses in South Cambridgeshire.
ADVERTISING RATES:
Full Page Colour £1595.00
Agency Commission: 10%
Mechanical Data: Bleed Size: 305 x 218mm, Trim Size: 297 x 210mm, Film: Digital, Type Area: 277 x 190mm, Col Length: 277mm, Page Width: 190mm
Copy instructions: Copy Date: 2 weeks prior to publication date
Average advertising content per issue: 35%
CONSUMER: RURAL & REGIONAL INTEREST: Regional Interest English Counties

SOUTH DOWNS LIVING   1777456U80C-5360

Editorial Address: 48 Keymer Road, HASSOCKS, BN6 8AR **Tel:** 01273 842550 **Fax:** 01273 842597
Email: editorial@southdownsliving.com
Advertising Address: As above. **Fax:** 01273 842550
Email: sales@southdownsliving.com
Web site: http://www.southdownsliving.com
Publisher: Roger Booth Studios Ltd
Date Established: 2005
Frequency: Monthly
Cover Price: Free
Circulation: 18,000 (Publisher's Statement)
Usual Pagination: 46
Editor: Roger Booth
Summary of Content: Magazine including articles of local interest with upcoming events across the villages to history and local heritage. All editorial locally derived and directed.
Readership/Target Audience: Aimed at residents of Ditchling, Hassocks and Hurstpierpoint and surrounding countryside.
ADVERTISING RATES:
Full Page Colour £750.00
Agency Commission: 10%
Mechanical Data: Type Area: 260 x 190mm, Bleed Size: 303 x 216mm, Trim Size: 297 x 210mm, Col Length: 260mm, Page Width: 190mm, Film: Digital
Copy instructions: Copy Date: 7th of the month
Average advertising content per issue: 50%
CONSUMER: RURAL & REGIONAL INTEREST: Regional Interest English Counties

SOUTH EAST BIKER   1927082U77B-730

Editorial Address: Wirral Acre, Eridge Road, CROWBOROUGH, TN6 2SP **Tel:** 01892 610808
Email: peter@southeastbiker.co.uk
Web site: http://www.southeastwalker.co.uk
Publisher: South East Biker
Frequency: Monthly
Editor: Peter Kamios
Summary of Content: Magazine covering news and features for motorcyclists in the South East area.
Readership/Target Audience: Aimed at motorcyclists in the South East area.
CONSUMER: MOTORING & CYCLING: Motorcycling

SOUTH EAST WALKER   45931U75L-600

Formerly: South East Rambler
Editorial Address: 8 Faircroft, 37 St. Andrews Grove, LONDON, N16 5NJ **Tel:** 020 8809 2338
Email: dougramb@yahoo.co.uk
Publisher: Mortons Media Group Ltd
Frequency: Quarterly
Cover Price: £2.95
Free to qualifying individuals
Annual Sub.: £10.50
Circulation: 19,000 (Publisher's Statement)
Usual Pagination: 68
Editor: Les Douglas
Summary of Content: Regional newsletter reporting on Ramblers' Association activities.
Readership/Target Audience: Aimed at Ramblers' Association members living in the South East of England.
ADVERTISING: No Advertising taken
CONSUMER: SPORT: Outdoor

SOUTH WALES GOLFER   1665707U75D-527

Editorial Address: Cardiff Road, NEWPORT, NP20 3QN **Tel:** 01633 777133 **Fax:** 01633 777160
Email: steve.davies@gwent-wales.co.uk
Advertising Address: As above.
Email: steve.davies@gwent-wales.co.uk
Web site: http://www.southwalesgolfer.co.uk
Publisher: Newsquest Wales & Gloucestershire
Frequency: Monthly
Cover Price: Free
Circulation: 12,000 (Publisher's Statement)
Usual Pagination: 24
Editor: Steve Davies; **Advertising Manager:** Steve Davies
Summary of Content: Magazine covering news, course reviews, player profiles, golf equipment reviews and golfing holidays.
Readership/Target Audience: Aimed at ladies, men and junior golfers in South Wales.
ADVERTISING RATES:
Full Page Mono £1440.00
Full Page Colour £1440.00
Mechanical Data: Type Area: 320 x 259mm, Col Length: 320mm, Page Width: 259mm, Film: Digital, No. of Columns (Display): 9, Col Widths (Display): 27mm
CONSUMER: SPORT: Golf

SOUTH WEST COAST PATH ANNUAL GUIDE   45936U75L-625

Formerly: South West Coast Path
Editorial Address: Windlestraw, Penquit, ERMINGTON, PL21 0LU **Tel:** 01752 698048 **Fax:** 01752 893654
Email: info@swcp.org.uk
Web site: http://www.swcp.org.uk
Publisher: South West Coast Path Association
Date Established: 1975
Frequency: Annual - Published in February
Cover Price: £8.50
Circulation: 7,000 (Publisher's Statement)
Usual Pagination: 176
Editor: Eric Wallis
Summary of Content: Guide to walking the South West Coast Path. Includes trail information, tide tables, accommodation and railway, bus and sea transport services.
Readership/Target Audience: Aimed at walkers and ramblers.
ADVERTISING: No Advertising taken
CONSUMER: SPORT: Outdoor

SOUTHAMPTON CITY VIEW   46916U80C-1700

Editorial Address: Corporate Communications, Southampton City Council, Civic Centre, SOUTHAMPTON, SO14 7LY **Tel:** 023 8083 2095 **Fax:** 023 8023 4537
Email: cityview@southampton.gov.uk
Advertising Address: As above. **Tel:** 023 8083 4086
Fax: 023 8083 3836
Email: amanda.hill@southampton.gov.uk
Web site: http://www.southampton.gov.uk/cityview
Publisher: Southampton City Council
Date Established: 1985
Frequency: 10 issues yearly
Cover Price: Free
Circulation: 111,000 (Publisher's Statement)
Usual Pagination: 24
Editor: Amanda Hill; **Advertising Manager:** Amanda Hill
Summary of Content: Magazine containing, council, leisure, community, business and environmental news.
Readership/Target Audience: Aimed at people living and working in Southampton.
ADVERTISING RATES:
Full Page Mono £1600.00
Full Page Colour £1600.00
Agency Commission: 25%

Mechanical Data: Type Area: 267 x 190mm, Bleed Size: 300 x 213mm, Trim Size: 297 x 210mm, Col Length: 267mm, Page Width: 190mm
Copy instructions: Copy Date: 6 weeks prior to publication
Average advertising content per issue: 30%
CONSUMER: RURAL & REGIONAL INTEREST: Regional Interest English Counties

SOUTHERN PROPERTY ADVERTISER   45503U74K-470

Formerly: Southern Property & Homes
Editorial Address: Newspaper House, Test Lane, Redbridge, SOUTHAMPTON, SO16 9JX **Tel:** 023 8042 4422 **Fax:** 023 8042 4508
Email: property@dailyecho.co.uk
Advertising Address: As above. **Tel:** 023 8042 4777
Email: property@dailyecho.co.uk
Web site: http://www.dailyecho.co.uk/homes
Publisher: Newsquest Media Group
Frequency: Weekly
Cover Price: Free
Circulation: 129,329 (Publisher's Statement)
Usual Pagination: 40
Editor: Ian Murray
Summary of Content: Magazine covering property prices and features.
Readership/Target Audience: Read by those looking to re-locate to the South of the country.
ADVERTISING RATES:
Full Page Mono £2313.36
Full Page Colour £2570.40
Agency Commission: 10%
Mechanical Data: Film: Digital, No. of Columns (Display): 9, Col Length: 350mm
Copy instructions: Copy Date: Friday 12 noon prior to publication date
Average advertising content per issue: 80%
CONSUMER: WOMEN'S INTEREST CONSUMER MAGAZINES: Home Purchase

SOUTHSIDE NEWS   1824603U80E-374

Editorial Address: 2nd Floor, 73 Robertson Street, GLASGOW, G2 8QD **Tel:** 0141 248 6331
Fax: 0141 248 6472
Email: john.maclean@premierpublishing.co.uk
Advertising Address: As above.
Email: stuart@premierpublishing.co.uk
Web site: http://www.premierpublishing.co.uk
Publisher: Premier Publishing Ltd
Date Established: 2007
Frequency: 26 issues yearly
Cover Price: Free
Circulation: 20,000 (Publisher's Statement)
Usual Pagination: 28
Editor: John Maclean
Summary of Content: Newspaper covering news, views and interviews about Glasgow and the people who live and work there. Includes guides to local issues and events and features entertainment, property, health and beauty, financial matters motoring and sport.
Readership/Target Audience: Aimed at those living and working in Glasgow.
ADVERTISING RATES:
SCC £6.00
Agency Commission: 10%
Copy instructions: Copy Date: Friday prior to publication date
Average advertising content per issue: 40%
Editions:
City Centre News
East End News
Inverclyde News
Northside News
West End News
CONSUMER: RURAL & REGIONAL INTEREST: Regional Interest Scotland

SOUTHWEST   46842U80B-175

Editorial Address: Battersea Studios, 80 Silverthorne Road, LONDON, SW8 3HE **Tel:** 020 7978 3484 **Fax:** 020 7978 3498
Email: lorraine.crighton-smith@archant.co.uk
Advertising Address: As above. **Tel:** 020 7978 3488
Email: grant.elgin@archant.co.uk
Web site: http://www.southwestmag.co.uk
Publisher: Archant Life
Frequency: Monthly
Cover Price: Free
Circulation: 94,000 (Publisher's Statement)
Editor: Lorraine Crighton-Smith; **Advertising Manager:** Grant Elgin
Summary of Content: Magazine with articles on local events, personalities and places. Includes features on art and property.
Readership/Target Audience: Aimed at residents of South-West London and people who work in the area.

ADVERTISING RATES:
Full Page Colour £1792.00
Agency Commission: 10%
Mechanical Data: Trim Size: 297 x 210mm, Type Area: 270 x 190mm, Bleed Size: 303 x 216mm, Film: Digital, Col Length: 270mm, Page Width: 190mm
Copy instructions: Copy Date: 1 week prior to publication date
Average advertising content per issue: 70%
CONSUMER: RURAL & REGIONAL INTEREST: Regional Interest Greater London

SOVEREIGNTY
627286U82-182_50
Editorial Address: 268 Bath Street, GLASGOW, G2 4JR
Tel: 0141 332 2214 **Fax:** 0141 353 6900
Email: contactus@sovereignity.org.uk
Web site: http://www.sovereign.org.uk
Publisher: Alistair McConnachie
Date Established: 1999
Frequency: Monthly
Annual Sub.: £15.00
Circulation: 2,500 (Publisher's Statement)
Usual Pagination: 8
Editor: Alistair McConnachie; **Publisher:** Alistair McConnachie
Summary of Content: Journal containing articles on campaigning for self determination on a national, local and personal level.
Readership/Target Audience: Aimed at those with an interest in the UK's independence, political, economic and ecological issues.
ADVERTISING: No Advertising taken
CONSUMER: CURRENT AFFAIRS & POLITICS

THE SOWER
47757U87-212
Editorial Address: Maryvale House, Old Oscott Hill, BIRMINGHAM, B44 9AG **Tel:** 0121 360 8118
Fax: 0121 366 6786
Email: maryvale.institute@dial.pipex.com
Advertising Address: As above.
Email: enquiries@maryvale.ac.uk
Web site: http://www.maryvale.ac.uk
ISSN: 1462-1576
Publisher: Maryvale Institute
Date Established: 1919
Frequency: Quarterly
Cover Price: £4.95
Annual Sub.: £18.00
Circulation: 2,500 (Publisher's Statement)
Usual Pagination: 36
Editor: Petroc Willey; **Advertising Manager:** Petroc Willey
Summary of Content: Journal focusing on religious education and educational issues in the home, parish and schools.
Readership/Target Audience: Circulated to schools, parishes, homes, colleges and universities.
ADVERTISING RATES:
Full Page Colour £300.00
Agency Commission: 10%
Mechanical Data: Film: Digital
Copy instructions: Copy Date: 3 weeks prior to publication date
Average advertising content per issue: 12%
CONSUMER: RELIGIOUS

SOZVEZDIE
1808488U90-1010
Editorial Address: 89 Cressfield Close, LONDON, NW5 4BN **Tel:** 07960 329525
Email: stman4u@hotmail.com
Advertising Address: As above.
Email: stman4u@hotmail.com
Date Established: 2007
Frequency: 6 issues yearly
Circulation: 20,000 (Publisher's Statement)
Usual Pagination: 450
Editor: Stephen Mahoney; **Advertising Manager:** Stephen Mahoney
Summary of Content: Magazine covering fashion as well as cultural, sport and financial activities.
Readership/Target Audience: Aimed at cultural, finance and sports ministers in the CIS.
ADVERTISING: Rates on application
CONSUMER: ETHNIC

SP
47664U86C-535
Editorial Address: PO Box 173, PETERBOROUGH, PE2 6WS **Tel:** 01733 375107 **Fax:** 01733 371001
Email: john.whycock@rnib.org.uk
Web site: http://www.rnib.org.uk
Publisher: Royal National Institute of Blind People
Date Established: 1998
Frequency: Monthly
Cover Price: £0.70
Usual Pagination: 60
Editor: John Whytock

Summary of Content: Lifestyle magazine covering fashion, music, sex and entertainment with additional features on eye health and related topics.
Readership/Target Audience: Read by blind and partially sighted men between the ages of 18 and 29 years old.
ADVERTISING: No Advertising taken
CONSUMER: ADULT & GAY MAGAZINES: Men's Lifestyle Magazines

SPA SECRETS MAGAZINE
1744319U74G-273
Formerly: SpaSecrets Magazine
Editorial Address: 197-199 City Road, LONDON, EC1V 1JN
Tel: 020 7553 7384 **Fax:** 020 7253 9907
Email: editor@spasecretsmagazine.com
Advertising Address: As above.
Email: nicola@spasecretsmagazine.com
Web site: http://www.spasecretsmagazine.com
Publisher: Absolute Publishing Ltd
Date Established: 2005
Frequency: Quarterly
Cover Price: £3.75
Free to qualifying individuals
Annual Sub.: £17.99
Circulation: 30,000 (Publisher's Statement)
Usual Pagination: 100
Editor: Jo Gardner; **Advertising Manager:** Nicola Brookes
Summary of Content: Magazine covering spa lifestyle, health and fitness with features on spa holidays, new products, nutrition and cosmetic surgery.
Readership/Target Audience: Aimed at spa users and fitness club members.
ADVERTISING RATES:
Full Page Colour £4400.00
Agency Commission: 10%
Mechanical Data: Type Area: 265 x 200mm, Bleed Size: 291 x 226mm, Trim Size: 285 x 200mm, Col Length: 265mm, Page Width: 200mm
CONSUMER: WOMEN'S INTEREST CONSUMER MAGAZINES: Slimming & Health

SPA WELLBEING
1646397U74G-249
Editorial Address: 29 Hacketts Lane, WOKING, GU22 8PP
Tel: 01932 400800 **Fax:** 01932 346201
Email: editor@spawellbeing.com
Advertising Address: As above.
Email: info@spawellbeing.com
ISSN: 1744-9243
Publisher: Discovery Books & Publications
Date Established: 2005
Frequency: Quarterly
Cover Price: Free
Circulation: 20,000 (Publisher's Statement)
Usual Pagination: 56
Editor: Catherine Beattie; **Advertising Manager:** Catherine Beattie; **Managing Editor:** Catherine Beattie
Summary of Content: Consumer magazine covering spas, health, well-being, spa services and treatments, therapies, fitness, food and travel.
Readership/Target Audience: Aimed at those interested in spas, health and wellbeing.
ADVERTISING RATES:
Full Page Colour £1850.00
Agency Commission: 10%
Mechanical Data: Bleed Size: 303 x 213mm, Trim Size: 250 x 174mm, Film: Digital
Copy instructions: Copy Date: 8 weeks prior to publication date
Average advertising content per issue: 25%
CONSUMER: WOMEN'S INTEREST CONSUMER MAGAZINES: Slimming & Health

SPA WORLD
1615587U74G-237
Editorial Address: 5-7 The Shambles, WETHERBY, LS22 6NG **Tel:** 01937 585800
Email: terri@spaworldmagazine.com
Advertising Address: As above. **Tel:** 01943 851400
Fax: 01943 851401
Email: sylvia@spaworldmagazine.com
Web site: http://www.spaworldmagazine.com
Publisher: Spa World Magazine Ltd
Date Established: 2003
Frequency: 6 issues yearly
Cover Price: £3.75
Free to qualifying individuals
Annual Sub.: £22.00
Circulation: 30,000 (Publisher's Statement)
Usual Pagination: 100
Editor: Terri Fleeman-Hardwick; **Editor-in-Chief:** Terri Fleeman-Hardwick
Summary of Content: Magazine covering health, beauty, fitness, diet, healthy living, travel, spas, health farms, complementary medicine and alternative therapies.
Readership/Target Audience: Aimed at both men and women aged 25 plus.
ADVERTISING RATES:
Full Page Colour £3000.00

Agency Commission: 10%
Mechanical Data: Print Process: Digital, Bleed Size: 303 x 216mm, Trim Size: 297 x 210mm
Copy instructions: Copy Date: 1 week prior to publication date
Average advertising content per issue: 35%
CONSUMER: WOMEN'S INTEREST CONSUMER MAGAZINES: Slimming & Health

SPAIN MAGAZINE
755522U89E-156_25
Editorial Address: 21 Royal Circus, EDINBURGH, EH3 6TL
Tel: 0131 226 7766 **Fax:** 0131 225 4567
Email: sue.hitchen@gmail.com
Advertising Address: As above.
Email: carlos.spainmag@gmail.com
Web site: http://www.spainmagazine.co.uk
Publisher: The Media Company
Date Established: 2002
Frequency: Monthly
Cover Price: £3.70
Circulation: 40,000 (Publisher's Statement)
Usual Pagination: 164
Editor: Sue Hitchen; **Advertising Manager:** Carlos Plazas; **Publisher:** Sue Hitchen
Summary of Content: Lifestyle magazine focusing on Spain. Features exhibitions, art galleries, fashion, sport, food and wine and property. Includes celebrity interviews, traditions, articles and practical advice on living and visiting Spain.
Readership/Target Audience: Aimed at those interested in Spain including visitors and those who have moved there, have a second home there or are thinking of going there.
ADVERTISING RATES:
Full Page Colour £2950.00
Agency Commission: 10%
Mechanical Data: Film: Digital, Type Area: 272 x 193mm, Col Length: 272mm, Page Width: 193mm, Bleed Size: 306 x 226mm, Trim Size: 300 x 220mm
Copy instructions: Copy Date: 2 weeks prior to publication date
Average advertising content per issue: 40%
CONSUMER: HOLIDAYS & TRAVEL: Holidays

SPAREROOM
1895112U74K-795
Editorial Address: Lomber Hay Farm, Andrew Lane, High Lane, STOCKPORT, SK6 8HY **Tel:** 07834 158483
Email: matt@spareroom.co.uk
Web site: http://www.spareroom.co.uk
Publisher: PPS
Date Established: 2009
Frequency: 26 issues yearly
Editor: Matt Hutchinson
Summary of Content: Magazine covering London property news and any flatshare related news.
Readership/Target Audience: Aimed at those looking to live in shared accommodation in London.
CONSUMER: WOMEN'S INTEREST CONSUMER MAGAZINES: Home Purchase

THE SPARK
601031U74Q-928
Editorial Address: 86 Colston Street, BRISTOL, BS1 5BB
Tel: 0117 914 3434 **Fax:** 0117 914 3444
Email: darryl@thespark.co.uk
Advertising Address: As above.
Email: sales@thespark.co.uk
Web site: http://www.thespark.co.uk
Publisher: Blue Sax Publishing Ltd
Date Established: 1993
Frequency: Quarterly
Annual Sub.: £10.00
Circulation: 32,000 (Publisher's Statement)
Usual Pagination: 60
Editor: Darryl Bullock
Summary of Content: Magazine dedicated to positive change and alternative lifestyles. Includes environmental issues, health and personal development, training, travel, spirituality and leisure.
Readership/Target Audience: Read predominantly by women in their thirties.
ADVERTISING RATES:
Full Page Mono £1035.00
Full Page Colour £1200.00
Mechanical Data: Trim Size: 420 x 297mm, Film: Digital
CONSUMER: WOMEN'S INTEREST CONSUMER MAGAZINES: Lifestyle

SPARK*
47448U83-74
Formerly: Spark
Editorial Address: Reading University Students Union, PO Box 230, Whiteknights, READING, RG6 6AZ
Tel: 0118 986 5140
Email: editor.spark@reading.ac.uk
Advertising Address: As above. **Tel:** 0118 986 5115
Fax: 0118 975 5283

Consumer Magazines

Email: spark@reading.ac.uk
Web site: http://www.rusu.co.uk/spark
Publisher: RUSU
Date Established: 1934
Frequency: 30 issues yearly - Published fortnightly during term time
Cover Price: Free
Circulation: 16,000 (Publisher's Statement)
Usual Pagination: 32
Editor: Claire Taylor
Summary of Content: Student newspaper covering local, national and student news. Also includes reviews of music, films, videos, books and computer games, plus features on entertainment and sport.
Readership/Target Audience: Aimed at students and staff of Reading University.
ADVERTISING RATES:
Full Page Mono £250.00
Full Page Colour £450.00
Agency Commission: 10%
Mechanical Data: Type Area: 346 x 277mm, Col Length: 346mm, No. of Columns (Display): 6, Page Width: 277mm, Film: Digital
Copy instructions: Copy Date: 1 week prior to publication
Average advertising content per issue: 10%
CONSUMER: STUDENT PUBLICATIONS

SPARKLE WORLD
1646103U91D-886

Editorial Address: Suite 2, Prospect House, Belle Vue Road, SHREWSBURY, SY3 7NR **Tel:** 01743 364433
Fax: 01743 271528
Email: info@redan.com
Advertising Address: As above.
Email: emily@redan.com
Web site: http://www.redan.co.uk
Publisher: Redan Publishing
Frequency: 17 issues yearly
Cover Price: £2.45
Circulation: 63,863 (ABC 01/01/2009 to 30/06/2009)
Usual Pagination: 48
Editor: Lee Bishop; **Advertising Manager:** Emily Bell
Summary of Content: Children's magazine with fun stories and activities based around popular children's characters including Polly Pocket, My Little Pony, Rainbow Magic and Strawberry Shortcake.
Readership/Target Audience: Aimed at girls aged 3 to 7 years old.
ADVERTISING RATES:
Full Page Colour £1800.00
Agency Commission: 10%
Mechanical Data: Type Area: 220 x 190mm, Trim Size: 250 x 220mm, Bleed Size: 256 x 226mm, Col Length: 220mm, Page Width: 190mm, Film: Digital
Copy instructions: Copy Date: 8 weeks prior to publication date
CONSUMER: RECREATION & LEISURE: Children & Youth

SPECTACULAR SPIDERMAN
1663404U91D-903

Editorial Address: Brockbourne House, Mount Ephraim, TUNBRIDGE WELLS, TN4 8BS **Tel:** 01892 500100
Fax: 01892 545666
Email: pbishop@panini.co.uk
Advertising Address: Orange20 Ltd, Station House, Bunbury Way, EPSOM, KT17 4JP **Tel:** 01372 802800
Fax: 01372 723322
Email: robin@o20.co.uk
Web site: http://www.paninicomics.co.uk
Publisher: Panini UK Ltd
Frequency: 17 issues yearly
Cover Price: £1.99
Circulation: 33,351 (ABC 01/01/2009 to 30/06/2009)
Usual Pagination: 36
Editor: Patrick Bishop; **Advertising Manager:** Robin Johnson
Summary of Content: Children's magazine covering all things Spiderman with comic strips, features, fact files and competitions.
Readership/Target Audience: Aimed predominantly at boys aged 5 to 10 years old.
ADVERTISING RATES:
Full Page Colour £2500.00
CONSUMER: RECREATION & LEISURE: Children & Youth

THE SPECTATOR
45159U73-330

Editorial Address: 22 Old Queen Street, LONDON, SW1H 9HP **Tel:** 020 7961 0200
Email: editor@spectator.co.uk
Advertising Address: As above. **Fax:** 020 7961 0020
Email: advertising@spectator.co.uk
Web site: http://www.spectator.co.uk
ISSN: 0038-6952
Publisher: Pressholdings
Date Established: 1828
Frequency: Weekly
Cover Price: £2.95
Annual Sub.: £103.00

Circulation: 75,095 (ABC 01/01/2009 to 30/06/2009)
Usual Pagination: 70
Editor: Fraser Nelson
Summary of Content: Magazine covering politics, current affairs and the arts.
Readership/Target Audience: Aimed at those interested in politics, the art world, theatre and culture.
ADVERTISING RATES:
Full Page Colour £4836.00
SCC £75.00
Agency Commission: 10%
Mechanical Data: Type Area: 250 x 185mm, Col Length: 250mm, Page Width: 185mm, Bleed Size: 282 x 216mm, Trim Size: 276 x 210mm, No. of Columns (Display): 3, Col Widths (Display): 59mm, Film: Digital
Copy instructions: Copy Date: 8 days prior to publication date
Average advertising content per issue: 35%
CONSUMER: NATIONAL & INTERNATIONAL PERIODICALS

SPEEDSCENE
46433U77D-450

Editorial Address: 42B Edwards Avenue, RUISLIP, HA4 6UT **Tel:** 020 8845 9491 **Fax:** 020 8845 9491
Email: editor@hillclimbandsprint.co.uk
Advertising Address: 2 Julius Road, BRISTOL, BS7 8EU **Tel:** 0117 942 2687 **Fax:** 0117 924 5691
Email: advertising@hillclimbandsprint.co.uk
Web site: http://www.hillclimbandsprint.co.uk
Publisher: Hillclimb & Sprint Association
Frequency: 5 issues yearly
Cover Price: £4.00
Free to qualifying individuals
Annual Sub.: £23.00
Circulation: 1,000 (Publisher's Statement)
Editor: Martin Price; **Advertising Manager:** Fryth Crosse
Summary of Content: Magazine of the Hillclimb and Sprint Association containing reports, articles, photographs and features covering all aspects of sprinting and speed hill climbing.
Readership/Target Audience: Aimed at members of the Hillclimb & Sprint Association.
ADVERTISING RATES:
Full Page Mono £150.00
Full Page Colour £225.00
Mechanical Data: Trim Size: 297 x 210mm, Bleed Size: 307 x 220mm, Film: Digital
Average advertising content per issue: 20%
CONSUMER: MOTORING & CYCLING: Motor Sports

SPEEDWAY STAR
46375U77B-599

Editorial Address: 9 Coppergate Mews, Brighton Road, SURBITON, KT6 5NE **Tel:** 020 8335 1100
Fax: 020 8399 6374
Email: star@pinegen.co.uk
Advertising Address: As above. **Fax:** 020 8333 1117
Email: dave@pinegen.co.uk
Web site: http://www.speedwaystar.net
Publisher: Pinegen Ltd
Date Established: 1952
Frequency: Weekly
Cover Price: £2.60
Annual Sub.: £104.00
Circulation: 20,000 (Publisher's Statement)
Usual Pagination: 48
Editor: Richard Clark; **Managing Director:** Philip Rising;
Publisher: Philip Rising
Summary of Content: Magazine covering news from the speedway racing circuit.
Readership/Target Audience: Read by speedway supporters, officials and riders.
ADVERTISING RATES:
Full Page Colour £420.00
Mechanical Data: Trim Size: 297 x 210mm, Film: Digital
Copy instructions: Copy Date: Friday 12 noon prior to publication date
CONSUMER: MOTORING & CYCLING: Motorcycling

SPHERE
48259U89E-145

Formerly: Orient-Express Magazine
Editorial Address: Central Point, 45 Beech Street, LONDON, EC2Y 8AD **Tel:** 020 7805 5555
Fax: 020 7805 5911
Email: iln@iln.co.uk
Advertising Address: As above.
Email: sphere@iln.co.uk
Web site: http://www.orient-express.com
ISSN: 1350-9012
Publisher: The Illustrated London News Ltd
Frequency: Quarterly
Free to qualifying individuals
Annual Sub.: £19.00
Circulation: 74,697 (ABC 01/01/2007 to 31/12/2007)
Usual Pagination: 120
Editor: Sam Villis; **Managing Director:** Lisa Barnard; **Group Editor:** Alison Booth; **Publisher:** Lisa Barnard

Summary of Content: Magazine containing features on arts, fashion, cuisine and shopping with profiles of those in the international spotlight. Also includes a guide to events around each Orient-Express hotel, train or cruise ship.
Readership/Target Audience: Read by travellers on the Venice Simplon-Orient-Express and in Orient-Express Hotels worldwide.
ADVERTISING RATES:
Full Page Colour £6150.00
Agency Commission: 15%
Mechanical Data: Bleed Size: 303 x 226mm, Trim Size: 297 x 220mm, Film: Digital
Copy instructions: Copy Date: 3 weeks prior to publication date
Average advertising content per issue: 40%
Supplement(s): Gourmet Voyager - 2xY, Pulse - 1xY
CONSUMER: HOLIDAYS & TRAVEL: Holidays

SPHERE ASIA
48235U89E-84

Formerly: Orient-Express Eastern & Oriental Magazine
Editorial Address: Central Point, 45 Beech Street, LONDON, EC2Y 8AD **Tel:** 020 7805 5555
Fax: 020 7805 5911
Email: iln@iln.co.uk
Advertising Address: As above.
Email: daphne.capelr@iln.co.uk
Web site: http://www.iln.co.uk
Publisher: The Illustrated London News Ltd
Date Established: 1982
Frequency: Quarterly
Cover Price: Free
Circulation: 35,000 (Publisher's Statement)
Usual Pagination: 120
Editor: Alison Booth; **Managing Director:** Lisa Barnard;
Advertising Manager: Daphne Capel; **Group Editor:** Alison Booth
Summary of Content: Magazine covering travel, fashion, art, celebrities, theatre and entertainment.
Readership/Target Audience: Read by passengers on the Eastern and Orient Express and guests at Orient Express hotels. Also distributed on Malaysia and Cathay Pacific Airlines in first and business classes.
ADVERTISING RATES:
Full Page Mono £4000.00
Full Page Colour £4000.00
Agency Commission: 15%
Mechanical Data: Type Area: 263 x 181mm, Bleed Size: 303 x 226mm, Trim Size: 297 x 220mm, Film: Digital, Col Length: 263mm, Page Width: 181mm
Copy instructions: Copy Date: 4 weeks prior to publication date
Average advertising content per issue: 40%
CONSUMER: HOLIDAYS & TRAVEL: Holidays

SPIDERMAN & FRIENDS
1779863U91D-949

Editorial Address: Brockbourne House, Mount Ephraim, TUNBRIDGE WELLS, TN4 8BS **Tel:** 01892 500100
Fax: 01892 545666
Email: sfrith@panini.co.uk
Advertising Address: Orange20 Ltd, 20 Orange Street, LONDON, WC2H 7EF **Tel:** 020 7389 0800
Fax: 01372 723322
Email: michelle@o20.co.uk
Web site: http://www.paninicomics.co.uk
Publisher: Panini UK Ltd
Date Established: 2006
Frequency: 13 issues yearly
Cover Price: £1.85
Circulation: 80,000 (Print Run)
Usual Pagination: 24
Editor: Simon Frith; **Advertising Manager:** Michelle Fairlamb
Summary of Content: Children's magazine with free gift, activity book, stories and super-hero themed activities.
Readership/Target Audience: Aimed at boys aged 3 to 5 years old.
ADVERTISING RATES:
Full Page Colour £2500.00
Agency Commission: 10%
Mechanical Data: Type Area: 277 x 190mm, Bleed Size: 307 x 220mm, Trim Size: 297 x 210mm, Col Length: 277mm, Page Width: 190mm, Film: Digital
Average advertising content per issue: 15%
CONSUMER: RECREATION & LEISURE: Children & Youth

SPIKES
1849651U75J-606

Editorial Address: Teddington Studios, Broom Road, TEDDINGTON, TW11 9BE **Tel:** 020 8267 5000
Email: spikescontactus@haymarket.com
Web site: http://www.spikesmag.com
Publisher: Haymarket Network
Date Established: 2008
Frequency: 3 issues yearly - Published in April, July and September
Cover Price: Free
Circulation: 70,000 (Print Run)
Editor: David Hall

Summary of Content: Magazine of the IAAF with stories about athletes, their achievements and athletics news.
Readership/Target Audience: Aimed at sports fans.
ADVERTISING: No Advertising taken
CONSUMER: SPORT: Athletics

SPIN
1774990U75K-854

Editorial Address: 3-7 Sunnyhill Road, LONDON, SW16 2UG **Tel:** 020 8696 6200
Email: editors@spincricket.com
Advertising Address: 151 Station Street, BURTON-ON-TRENT, DE14 1BG **Tel:** 01283 742950
Email: ted.tomlin@spincricket.com
Web site: http://www.spincricket.com
Publisher: WW Magazines
Frequency: Monthly
Cover Price: £3.75
Circulation: 40,000 (Print Run)
Usual Pagination: 100
Editor: Duncan Steer; **Advertising Manager:** Ted Tomlin
Summary of Content: Magazine covering all aspects of the cricket world from star interviews to game analysis.
Readership/Target Audience: Aimed at cricket fans.
ADVERTISING RATES:
Full Page Colour £2100.00
Agency Commission: 10%
Mechanical Data: Type Area: 267 x 190mm, Bleed Size: 303 x 216mm, Trim Size: 297 x 210mm, Col Length: 267mm, Page Width: 190mm, Film: Digital
Copy instructions: Copy Date: 5 weeks prior to publication date
Average advertising content per issue: 9%
CONSUMER: SPORT: Cricket

SPIRIT & DESTINY
767336U94E-356

Editorial Address: Academic House, 24-28 Oval Road, LONDON, NW1 7DT **Tel:** 020 7241 8000 **Fax:** 020 7241 8056
Email: spirit.destiny@bauer.co.uk
Advertising Address: The Publishing Consultancy, 8 Upper St. Martin's Lane, LONDON, WC2H 9DW
Tel: 020 7240 9400 **Fax:** 020 7240 9040
Email: lisac@tpc-london.com
Publisher: H. Bauer Publishing
Date Established: 2002
Frequency: Monthly
Cover Price: £2.90
Circulation: 61,537 (ABC 01/01/2009 to 30/06/2009)
Usual Pagination: 108
Editor: Rhiannon Powell; **Features Editor:** Emma Hibbs; **Advertising Manager:** Lisa Carver
Summary of Content: Magazine covering astrology, alternative therapies, self discovery and spiritual self improvement.
Readership/Target Audience: Aimed at women aged between 25 and 50 years old.
ADVERTISING RATES:
Full Page Colour £5400.00
Agency Commission: 15%
Mechanical Data: Type Area: 254 x 195mm, Bleed Size: 293 x 229mm, Trim Size: 285 x 225mm, Film: Digital, Col Length: 254mm, Page Width: 195mm
Copy instructions: Copy Date: 3 weeks prior to publication date
CONSUMER: OTHER CLASSIFICATIONS: Paranormal

SPONGEBOB SQUAREPANTS
1664055U91D-911

Editorial Address: Titan House, 144 Southwark Street, LONDON, SE1 0UP **Tel:** 020 7620 0200 **Fax:** 020 7620 0032
Email: rona.simpson@titanemail.com
Advertising Address: As above. **Tel:** 020 7803 1922
Fax: 020 7803 1803
Email: james.willmott@titanemail.com
Web site: http://www.titanmagazines.com
Publisher: Titan Magazines
Date Established: 2004
Frequency: 17 issues yearly
Cover Price: £2.60
Circulation: 34,163 (ABC 01/01/2009 to 30/06/2009)
Usual Pagination: 52
Editor: Rona Simpson; **Advertising Manager:** James Willmott
Summary of Content: Children's magazine made up of repackaged information from Tokyo Pop and Nickelodeon.
Readership/Target Audience: Aimed at boys and girls aged 4 to 11 years old.
ADVERTISING RATES:
Full Page Colour £4000.00
Agency Commission: 10%
Mechanical Data: Bleed Size: 303 x 236mm, Trim Size: 297 x 230mm, Film: Digital, Type Area: 277 x 210mm, Col Length: 277mm, Page Width: 210mm
Copy instructions: Copy Date: 6 weeks prior to publication date
Average advertising content per issue: 10%
CONSUMER: RECREATION & LEISURE: Children & Youth

SPORTDIVER
45952U75M-800

Editorial Address: The Mill, Bearwalden Business Park, Wendens Ambo, SAFFRON WALDEN, CB11 4GB
Tel: 01799 544243 **Fax:** 01799 544204
Email: mark.evans@sportdiver.co.uk
Advertising Address: As above. **Tel:** 01799 544200
Email: dave.pritchett@sportdiver.co.uk
Web site: http://www.divedestinations.co.uk
ISSN: 0958-9007
Publisher: Archant Specialist Ltd (Saffron Walden)
Date Established: 1992
Frequency: Monthly
Cover Price: £3.80
Annual Sub.: £32.00
Circulation: 9,124 (ABC 01/01/2008 to 31/12/2008)
Usual Pagination: 108
Editor: Mark Evans; **Publisher:** Tina Cronin
Summary of Content: The official magazine of the PADI Diving Society. Includes features on diving both in the UK and abroad, unbiased equipment tests, comprehensive news section, underwater photography, marine biology and medical questions and answers columns.
Readership/Target Audience: Aimed at divers and those specifically interested in diving abroad, underwater photography and marine life.
ADVERTISING RATES:
Full Page Mono £1430.00
Full Page Colour £1430.00
Agency Commission: 10%
Mechanical Data: Page Width: 190mm, No. of Columns (Display): 4, Col Length: 277mm, Col Widths (Display): 42mm, Film: Digital, Type Area: 277 x 190mm, Bleed Size: 303 x 216mm, Trim Size: 297 x 210mm
Copy instructions: Copy Date: 30th of the month prior to publication date
Average advertising content per issue: 40%
CONSUMER: SPORT: Water Sports

SPORTING BLUE
45711U75A-750

Editorial Address: St. George Street, LEICESTER, LE1 9FQ
Tel: 0116 222 4627 **Fax:** 0116 253 0645
Email: sportsdesk@leicestermercury.co.uk
Advertising Address: As above. **Fax:** 0116 262 4608
Email: adverts@leicestermercury.co.uk
Web site: http://www.thisisleicestershire.co.uk
Publisher: Leicester Mercury Media Group Ltd
Frequency: Weekly
Cover Price: £0.50
Editor: Chris Goddard
Summary of Content: Sports paper for Leicestershire readers.
Readership/Target Audience: Read by sports enthusiasts in the Leicester area.
ADVERTISING RATES:
Full Page Mono £849.60
Full Page Colour £1062.00
Agency Commission: 15%
Mechanical Data: Col Widths (Display): 32mm, No. of Columns (Display): 8, Page Width: 277mm, Trim Size: 420 x 297mm, Type Area: 360 x 277mm, Col Length: 360mm, Film: Digital
Copy instructions: Copy Date: 4 weeks prior to publication date
Average advertising content per issue: 20%
CONSUMER: SPORT

SPORTING GUN
45865U75F-180

Editorial Address: PO Box 157, STAMFORD, PE9 9FU
Tel: 01780 485370 **Fax:** 01780 485390
Email: sportinggun@ipcmedia.com
Advertising Address: Blue Fin Building, 110 Southwark Street, LONDON, SE1 0SU **Tel:** 020 3148 5000
Fax: 020 3148 8130
Email: toby_drought@ipcmedia.com
Web site: http://www.ipcmedia.co.uk
Publisher: IPC Inspire
Date Established: 1978
Frequency: Monthly
Cover Price: £3.20
Annual Sub.: £33.00
Circulation: 32,886 (ABC 01/01/2008 to 31/12/2008)
Usual Pagination: 132
Editor: Mary Bremner; **Advertising Manager:** Toby Drought
Summary of Content: Magazine containing shooting instruction, gun-care and maintenance. Includes game shoots, antique guns, pigeon and clay shooting, wildfowling, gun dog training, shooting fixtures, news and results.
Readership/Target Audience: Aimed at shotgun and shooting enthusiasts.
ADVERTISING RATES:
Full Page Mono £2275.00
Full Page Colour £3045.00
Agency Commission: 10%
Mechanical Data: Page Width: 183mm, Type Area: 274 x 183mm, Bleed Size: 303 x 216mm, Trim Size: 297 x 210mm, Col Length: 274mm, Film: Digital
Copy instructions: Copy Date: 2 weeks prior to publication date

Average advertising content per issue: 35%
CONSUMER: SPORT: Shooting

SPORTING SHOOTER
1637994U75F-211

Editorial Address: 3 The Courtyard, Denmark Street, WOKINGHAM, RG40 2AZ **Tel:** 0118 989 7212
Email: james@sportingshooter.co.uk
Advertising Address: As above. **Tel:** 0118 989 7264
Fax: 0118 977 2903
Email: neil.dyson@archant.co.uk
Web site: http://www.sportingshooter.co.uk
ISSN: 1741-1939
Publisher: Archant Specialist Ltd
Date Established: 2003
Frequency: Monthly
Cover Price: £3.40
Circulation: 22,603 (ABC 01/01/2008 to 31/12/2008)
Usual Pagination: 148
Editor: James Marchington
Summary of Content: Magazine covering shooting sports especially game shooting, pigeons, gun dogs, gun trade, clay pigeons and game keeping as well as associated activities such as beating, 4x4s, game cookery, etc.
Readership/Target Audience: Aimed at those interested in shooting.
ADVERTISING RATES:
Full Page Colour £850.00
SCC £13.00
Agency Commission: 10%
Mechanical Data: Trim Size: 300 x 230mm, Col Widths (Display): 45mm, No. of Columns (Display): 4, Print Process: Offset litho, Bleed Size: 308 x 238mm, Type Area: 270 x 200mm, Film: Digital, Col Length: 270mm, Page Width: 200mm
Copy instructions: Copy Date: 2nd Monday of publication month
Average advertising content per issue: 45%
CONSUMER: SPORT: Shooting

SPORTS MAIL (PORTSMOUTH)
45720U75A-820

Editorial Address: The News Centre, Hilsea, PORTSMOUTH, PO2 9SX **Tel:** 023 9266 4488
Fax: 023 9265 1136
Email: sport@thenews.co.uk
Advertising Address: As above. **Fax:** 023 9269 0544
Email: sue.kent@thenews.co.uk
Web site: http://www.portsmouth.co.uk
Publisher: Johnston Press plc
Date Established: 1903
Frequency: Weekly
Cover Price: £0.40
Circulation: 12,000 (Publisher's Statement)
Usual Pagination: 32
Editor: Howard Frost
Summary of Content: Sports newspaper for the Portsmouth area.
Readership/Target Audience: Read by sports enthusiasts.
ADVERTISING RATES:
SCC £4.68
Agency Commission: 10%
Mechanical Data: Type Area: 340 x 277mm, Col Length: 340mm, Page Width: 277mm, Film: Digital, No. of Columns (Display): 9, Col Widths (Display): 29mm
Copy instructions: Copy Date: 4 days prior to publication date
Supplement to: The News (Portsmouth)
CONSUMER: SPORT

SPORTSBOAT & RIB MAGAZINE
48392U91A-158

Formerly: Sportsboat
Editorial Address: Alliance House, 49 Sidney Street, CAMBRIDGE, CB2 3JF **Tel:** 01223 460490
Fax: 01223 315960
Email: editor@sportsboat.co.uk
Advertising Address: As above.
Email: chris@sportsboat.co.uk
Web site: http://www.sportsboat.co.uk
Publisher: CSL Publishing Ltd
Frequency: Monthly
Cover Price: £3.20
Circulation: 12,000 (Publisher's Statement)
Usual Pagination: 118
Editor: Alex Smith; **Advertising Manager:** Chris Lawrence
Summary of Content: Magazine featuring performance sport boats, RIBs and water-skiing, boats up to 35 feet and where and how to use them and a section on extreme watersports.
Readership/Target Audience: Aimed at those aged 30 years and upwards with a high disposable income.
ADVERTISING RATES:
Full Page Colour £1570.00
SCC £19.00
Agency Commission: 10%

Mechanical Data: Type Area: 258 x 200mm, Col Length: 258mm, Page Width: 200mm, Trim Size: 300 x 232mm, Bleed Size: 306 x 238mm, Film: Digital
Copy instructions: Copy Date: 15th of the month prior to publication date
Average advertising content per issue: 55%
CONSUMER: RECREATION & LEISURE: Boating & Yachting

SPROUTS
1804949U74D-656
Editorial Address: St Aidens, 1 Yarmouth Road, Ditchingham, BUNGAY, NR35 2PF **Tel:** 01986 892335
Email: denice@sproutsmagazine.com
Advertising Address: PO Box 1143, NORWICH, NR15 1WR **Tel:** 01295 780244
Email: jpbristowbristow@btinternet.com
Web site: http://www.sproutsmagazine.co.uk
Publisher: Sprouts
Date Established: 2006
Frequency: 6 issues yearly
Cover Price: Free
Circulation: 30,000 (Publisher's Statement)
Usual Pagination: 56
Editor: Denice Currie
Summary of Content: General lifestyle magazine covering all aspects relating to pre-school children.
Readership/Target Audience: Aimed at parents of children under 5 years old.
ADVERTISING RATES:
Full Page Colour £520.00
Mechanical Data: Type Area: 277 x 185mm, Col Length: 277mm, Page Width: 185mm, Film: Digital
Copy instructions: Copy Date: End of the month prior to publication date
CONSUMER: WOMEN'S INTEREST CONSUMER MAGAZINES: Child Care

THE SQUARE
622890U94X-186
Editorial Address: Riverdene Business Park, Molesey Road, HERSHAM, KT12 4RG **Tel:** 020 7436 3678
Fax: 01932 266601
Email: leozanelli@aol.com
Advertising Address: 17 Litchfield Avenue, MORDEN, SM4 5QS **Tel:** 01780 484630
ISSN: 1369-068X
Publisher: Ian Allan Publishing Ltd
Date Established: 1975
Frequency: Quarterly
Cover Price: £2.75
Annual Sub.: £11.00
Usual Pagination: 64
Editor: Leo Zanelli; **Advertising Director:** David Lane
Summary of Content: Magazine covering news and features on the Masonic way of life.
Readership/Target Audience: Aimed at Freemasons and fraternal societies.
ADVERTISING RATES:
Full Page Mono £200.00
Full Page Colour £300.00
Agency Commission: 10%
Mechanical Data: Col Length: 178mm, Page Width: 122mm, Type Area: 178 x 122mm, Trim Size: 212 x 150mm, Film: Digital
Copy instructions: Copy Date: 5th of the month prior to publication date
Average advertising content per issue: 25%
CONSUMER: OTHER CLASSIFICATIONS: Miscellaneous

SQUARE MEAL LIFESTYLE
48663U94G-230
Formerly: Square Meal The Magazine
Editorial Address: Quadrant House, 250 Kennington Lane, LONDON, SE11 5RD **Tel:** 020 7582 0222
Fax: 020 7582 5444
Advertising Address: As above.
Email: advertising@squaremeal.co.uk
Web site: http://www.squaremeal.co.uk
Publisher: Monomax Ltd
Date Established: 1997
Frequency: Quarterly
Cover Price: £3.50
Free to qualifying individuals
Circulation: 54,777 (ABC 01/01/2007 to 31/12/2007)
Usual Pagination: 232
Editor: Ben McCormack; **Managing Director:** Simon White; **Publisher:** Mark de Wesselow
Summary of Content: Magazine covering restaurant news plus features on food, travel, weekends, sport, art, motoring, fashion and leisure.
Readership/Target Audience: Aimed at City and London executives.
ADVERTISING RATES:
Full Page £5000.00
Agency Commission: 10%
Mechanical Data: Trim Size: 290 x 215mm, Bleed Size: 296 x 221mm, Film: Digital
Copy instructions: Copy Date: 3 weeks prior to publication date

Average advertising content per issue: 40%
CONSUMER: OTHER CLASSIFICATIONS: Restaurant Guides

SQUARE-GO
1849767U78R-527
Formerly: Fidget
Editorial Address: The Drill Hall, 30-38 Dalmeny Street, EDINBURGH, EH6 8RG **Tel:** 07929 381197
Email: josh@square-go.com
Advertising Address: As above.
Web site: http://www.square-go.com
Publisher: Fidget Ltd
Date Established: 2008
Frequency: Monthly
Cover Price: Free
Circulation: 10,000 (Publisher's Statement)
Usual Pagination: 24
Editor: Josh Wilson
Summary of Content: Magazine covering the new generation of video games encompassing all of the new platforms including consoles, hand-helds, pcs, mobile phones, i-phones, ipods, web browsers and anything else that will allow you to play games.
Readership/Target Audience: Aimed at everyone who has ever tried a video game.
CONSUMER: CONSUMER ELECTRONICS: Consumer Electronics Related

THE SQUASH PLAYER
45887U75H-770
Formerly: Squash & Racketball - The Magazine
Editorial Address: Longhouse, 460 Bath Road, Longford, WEST DRAYTON, UB7 0EB **Tel:** 01753 775511
Fax: 01753 775512
Email: mail@squashplayer.co.uk
Advertising Address: As above.
Email: spadverts@aol.com
Web site: http://www.squashplayer.co.uk
ISSN: 1356-7780
Publisher: McKenzie Publishing Ltd
Frequency: 6 issues yearly
Annual Sub.: £24.00
Circulation: 9,000 (Publisher's Statement)
Usual Pagination: 40
Editor: Ian McKenzie; **Managing Director:** Ian McKenzie; **Advertising Manager:** Joseph Laredo; **Publisher:** Ian McKenzie
Summary of Content: Magazine providing reports and news from the squash world.
Readership/Target Audience: Aimed at those with an interest in squash.
ADVERTISING RATES:
Full Page Colour £300.00
Agency Commission: 10%
Mechanical Data: Bleed Size: 302 x 216mm, Trim Size: 297 x 210mm, Print Process: Sheet-fed litho, Film: Digital, Type Area: 255 x 181mm, No. of Columns (Display): 4, Page Width: 181mm, Col Length: 255mm
Copy instructions: Copy Date: 1st of the month prior to publication date
Average advertising content per issue: 20%
CONSUMER: SPORT: Racquet Sports

THE SQUASH PLAYER - ENGLAND SQUASH PLAYER EDITION
45886U75H-775
Formerly: The Squash Player - SRA Edition
Editorial Address: Longhouse, 460 Bath Road, Longford, WEST DRAYTON, UB7 0EB **Tel:** 01753 775511
Fax: 01753 775512
Email: mail@squashplayer.co.uk
Advertising Address: As above.
Email: spadverts@aol.com
Web site: http://www.squashplayer.co.uk
ISSN: 1469-431X
Publisher: McKenzie Publishing Ltd
Date Established: 1971
Frequency: 6 issues yearly
Cover Price: £2.50
Circulation: 35,156 (ABC 01/01/2008 to 31/12/2008)
Usual Pagination: 40
Editor: Ian McKenzie; **Advertising Manager:** Joseph Laredo
Summary of Content: Official journal of the Squash Rackets Association.
Readership/Target Audience: Read by members of English and Scottish SRA.
ADVERTISING RATES:
Full Page Colour £1000.00
Agency Commission: 10%
Mechanical Data: Film: Digital, No. of Columns (Display): 3, Trim Size: 210 x 148mm
Average advertising content per issue: 20%
CONSUMER: SPORT: Racquet Sports

ST ALBANS EXCLUSIVE
1892644U80C-5491
Editorial Address: For all contact details see main edition, Exclusive (Chilterns)
Frequency: 10 issues yearly
Cover Price: Free
Circulation: 5,000 (Publisher's Statement)
ADVERTISING: Rates on application
Edition of: Exclusive (Chilterns)
CONSUMER: RURAL & REGIONAL INTEREST: Regional Interest English Counties

ST FASHION
1824542U74B-735
Editorial Address: Ground Floor, 1-2 Ravey Street, LONDON, EC2A 4QP **Tel:** 020 3222 0101
Fax: 020 7739 1369
Email: info@showmedia.net
Advertising Address: Telegraph Media Group, 111 Buckingham Palace Road, LONDON, SW1W 0DT **Tel:** 020 7931 2000 **Fax:** 020 7931 3377
Email: lucy.flanagan@telegraph..co.uk
Publisher: Show Media Ltd
Date Established: 2007
Frequency: Half-yearly - Published in September and March
Circulation: 300,000 (Publisher's Statement)
Editor: Peter Howarth
Summary of Content: Magazine covering fashion, beauty and accessories.
Readership/Target Audience: Aimed at women readers of The Sunday Telegraph in London and the South East.
ADVERTISING: Rates on application
Supplement to: The Sunday Telegraph
CONSUMER: WOMEN'S INTEREST CONSUMER MAGAZINES: Women's Interest - Fashion

ST MEN
1833111U86C-743
Editorial Address: Ground Floor, 1-2 Ravey Street, LONDON, EC2A 4QP **Tel:** 020 3222 0101
Fax: 020 7739 1369
Email: info@showmedia.net
Advertising Address: Telegraph Media Group, 111 Buckingham Palace Road, LONDON, SW1W 0DT **Tel:** 020 7931 2000 **Fax:** 020 7931 3377
Email: lucy.flanagan@telegraph.co.uk
Web site: http://www.showmedia.net
Publisher: Show Media Ltd
Date Established: 2008
Frequency: Half-yearly - Published in April and September
Cover Price: Free
Circulation: 300,000 (Publisher's Statement)
Usual Pagination: 100
Editor: Peter Howarth
Summary of Content: Magazine covering high end men's fashion.
Readership/Target Audience: Aimed at affluent, fashion conscious men.
ADVERTISING: Rates on application
Supplement to: The Sunday Telegraph
CONSUMER: ADULT & GAY MAGAZINES: Men's Lifestyle Magazines

STAFFORDSHIRE COUNTY
46970U80C-2890
Formerly: Staffordshire Quality
Editorial Address: PO Box 3106, STOKE-ON-TRENT, ST4 9JB **Tel:** 01782 850539
Email: joanne.goodwin@archant.co.uk
Advertising Address: 1 Yeoman Way, Armitage, RUGELEY, WS15 4UY **Tel:** 07841 492655
Email: sue.burke@archant.co.uk
Publisher: Archant Life
Date Established: 1995
Frequency: Monthly
Cover Price: £2.50
Annual Sub.: £25.00
Usual Pagination: 132
Editor: Joanne Goodwin; **Advertising Manager:** Susan Burke
Summary of Content: Magazine covering county features, profiles, local producers, home interests, gardens, fashion, motoring, social events and personalities.
Readership/Target Audience: Aimed at those living in or visiting the Staffordshire area.
ADVERTISING RATES:
Full Page Colour £995.00
Agency Commission: 10%
Mechanical Data: Film: Digital, Print Process: Litho, Trim Size: 300 x 200mm, Bleed Size: 306 x 226mm, Type Area: 271 x 199mm, Col Length: 271mm, Page Width: 199mm
Copy instructions: Copy Date: 10th of month prior to publication date
Average advertising content per issue: 40%
CONSUMER: RURAL & REGIONAL INTEREST: Regional Interest English Counties

STAFFORDSHIRE LIFE
46969U80C-2880

Editorial Address: The Publishing Centre, Derby Street, STAFFORD, ST16 2DT **Tel:** 01785 257700
Fax: 01785 253287
Email: editor@staffordshirelife.co.uk
Advertising Address: As above.
Email: advertising@staffordshirelife.co.uk
Web site: http://www.staffordshirelife.co.uk
Publisher: Staffordshire Newspapers Ltd
Date Established: 1980
Frequency: Monthly
Cover Price: £2.00
Free to qualifying individuals
Circulation: 17,000 (Publisher's Statement)
Usual Pagination: 120
Editor: Louise Elliott; **Features Editor:** Bryony Vale
Summary of Content: County magazine containing news and features on local people, places and events. Covers fashion and beauty, homes and gardens, travel and entertainment.
Readership/Target Audience: Aimed at high income households in Staffordshire.
ADVERTISING RATES:
Full Page Mono £925.00
Full Page Colour £1270.00
Agency Commission: 10%
Mechanical Data: Film: Digital, Bleed Size: 303 x 216mm, Trim Size: 297 x 210mm, Type Area: 270 x 190mm, Col Length: 270mm, Page Width: 190mm
Copy instructions: Copy Date: 3 weeks prior to publication date
Average advertising content per issue: 40%
Supplement(s): Antiques Life - 11xY, Gourmet Life - 11xY, Homes and Gardens Life - 11xY, Independent Education - 2xY, Property Life - 11xY, Staffordshire Life Brides - 2xY
CONSUMER: RURAL & REGIONAL INTEREST: Regional Interest English Counties

STAFFORDSHIRE LIVING
1657192U80C-5141

Editorial Address: Park Hall Works, Sutherland Road, STOKE-ON-TRENT, ST3 1HB **Tel:** 01782 597500
Fax: 01782 318537
Email: editorial@staffsmedia.com
Advertising Address: As above.
Email: ryan@staffsmedia.com
Web site: http://www.staffordshireliving.com
Publisher: Staffordshire Media Ltd
Date Established: 2004
Frequency: 6 issues yearly
Cover Price: £1.95
Circulation: 25,000 (Publisher's Statement)
Usual Pagination: 132
Editor: Lisa Black; **Advertising Manager:** Ryan Yates
Summary of Content: Magazine covering home, leisure, events, health, fitness, travel, fashion, property, motoring and finance.
Readership/Target Audience: Aimed at residents of Staffordshire.
ADVERTISING RATES:
Full Page Colour £1095.00
Mechanical Data: Type Area: 256 x 170mm, Trim Size: 297 x 210mm, Col Length: 256mm, Page Width: 170mm
CONSUMER: RURAL & REGIONAL INTEREST: Regional Interest English Counties

STAFFORDSHIRE WHAT'S ON
48121U89C-315

Formerly: North West What's On
Editorial Address: 4-5 Dogpole, SHREWSBURY, SY1 1EN
Tel: 01743 281708 **Fax:** 01743 248256
Email: davina@whatsonmag.co.uk
Advertising Address: As above. **Tel:** 01743 281777
Fax: 01743 281744
Email: info@whatsonlive.co.uk
Publisher: What's On Magazine Group
Date Established: 1985
Frequency: Monthly
Cover Price: £1.50
Free to qualifying individuals
Circulation: 10,000 (Publisher's Statement)
Usual Pagination: 64
Editor: Davina Evans; **Managing Director:** Paul Oliver;
Advertising Manager: Paul Oliver
Summary of Content: Entertainment guide for North Staffordshire.
Readership/Target Audience: Aimed at those in and around the North Staffordshire area.
ADVERTISING RATES:
Full Page Colour £1350.00
Agency Commission: 10%
Mechanical Data: Col Length: 277mm, Film: Digital, Type Area: 277 x 190mm, Bleed Size: 303 x 216mm, Page Width: 190mm, Trim Size: 297 x 210mm
Copy instructions: Copy Date: 1 week prior to publication date
Average advertising content per issue: 50%
CONSUMER: HOLIDAYS & TRAVEL: Entertainment Guides

THE STAGE
46077U76B-135

Formerly: The Stage inc. Television Today
Editorial Address: Stage House, 47 Bermondsey Street, LONDON, SE1 3XT **Tel:** 020 7403 1818 **Fax:** 020 7357 9287
Email: newsdesk@thestage.co.uk
Advertising Address: As above. **Fax:** 020 7378 0480
Email: niki@thestage.co.uk
Web site: http://www.thestage.co.uk
ISSN: 0038-9099
Publisher: The Stage Newspaper Ltd
Date Established: 1888
Frequency: Weekly
Cover Price: £1.20
Annual Sub.: £54.00
Circulation: 18,611 (ABC 01/07/2008 to 30/06/2009)
Usual Pagination: 42
Editor: Cyrila Pereira; **News Editor:** Alistair Smith;
Managing Director: Catherine Comerford; **Advertising Manager:** Niki Lancaster
Summary of Content: Newspaper for the entertainment industry, featuring new openings and jobs.
Readership/Target Audience: Aimed at professional actors, entertainers, agents, producers, companies and individuals in the industry.
ADVERTISING RATES:
Full Page Mono £2574.00
Full Page Colour £3088.80
SCC £13.00
Agency Commission: 10%
Mechanical Data: Film: Digital
Copy instructions: Copy Date: 3 days prior to publication date
Average advertising content per issue: 45%
CONSUMER: MUSIC & PERFORMING ARTS: Theatre

THE STALLION BOOK
47152U81D-300

Editorial Address: Sanders Road, Finedon Road Industrial Estate, WELLINGBOROUGH, NN8 4BX **Tel:** 01933 440077
Fax: 01933 304785
Email: scheney@weatherbys.co.uk
Advertising Address: As above.
Email: scheney@weatherbys.co.uk
Web site: http://www.weatherbys.co.uk
Publisher: Weatherbys Ventures Ltd
Date Established: 1984
Frequency: Annual - Published in November/December
Free to qualifying individuals
Annual Sub.: £56.00
Circulation: 6,000 (Publisher's Statement)
Usual Pagination: 800
Editor: Steve Cheney; **Advertising Manager:** Steve Cheney
Summary of Content: Journal showing thoroughbred stallions represented in posed photograph, with full pedigree, racing and stud details.
Readership/Target Audience: Aimed at thoroughbred horse breeders, bloodstock agents, racing and breeding enthusiasts worldwide.
ADVERTISING: Rates on application
Agency Commission: 15%
Average advertising content per issue: 80%
CONSUMER: ANIMALS & PETS: Horses & Ponies

STAMFORD LIVING
1655738U80C-5137

Editorial Address: PO Box 208, STAMFORD, PE9 9FY
Tel: 01780 765571 **Fax:** 01780 765571
Email: localliving@btopenworld.com
Advertising Address: As above. **Tel:** 01780 480409
Email: claudia@stamfordliving.fsnet.co.uk
Web site: http://www.stamfordliving.co.uk
Publisher: Local Living Ltd
Date Established: 2002
Frequency: Monthly
Cover Price: £1.50
Free to qualifying individuals
Circulation: 10,000 (Publisher's Statement)
Usual Pagination: 48
Editor: Nicholas Rudd-Jones; **Advertising Manager:** Claudia Bayley; **Publisher:** Nicholas Rudd-Jones
Summary of Content: Magazine covering food, drink, home, garden, fashion, beauty and freetime as well as local information.
Readership/Target Audience: Aimed at households with a high disposable income in Stamford, Peterborough, Rutland, Oundle, Market Harborough and North Norfolk.
ADVERTISING RATES:
Full Page Colour £750.00
Agency Commission: 10%
Mechanical Data: Film: Digital, Trim Size: 297 x 210mm
Copy instructions: Copy Date: 2 weeks prior to publication date
Average advertising content per issue: 50%
Editions:
Nene Valley Living
North Norfolk Living
Rutland & Market Harborough Living
CONSUMER: RURAL & REGIONAL INTEREST: Regional Interest English Counties

STAMP & COIN MART
46631U79C-53

Editorial Address: 5th Floor, 31-32 Park Row, LEEDS, LS1 5JD **Tel:** 0113 200 2925
Email: mhill@writersnews.co.uk
Advertising Address: As above. **Fax:** 0113 200 2928
Email: brendas@writersnews.co.uk
Web site: http://www.stampmart.co.uk
Publisher: Warners Group Publications plc
Frequency: Monthly
Cover Price: £2.95
Annual Sub.: £24.00
Circulation: 12,000 (Publisher's Statement)
Usual Pagination: 130
Editor: Matthew Hill
Summary of Content: Magazine containing informative, topical articles on stamps and coins as well as a New Issues section and buy and sell section.
Readership/Target Audience: Aimed at the established stamp and coin collector and newcomers to the hobby.
ADVERTISING RATES:
Full Page Colour £532.40
Agency Commission: 10%
Mechanical Data: Film: Digital, Type Area: 274 x 190mm, Bleed Size: 303 x 216mm, Trim Size: 297 x 210mm, Col Length: 274mm, Page Width: 190mm
Copy instructions: Copy Date: 3 weeks prior to publication date
Average advertising content per issue: 60%
CONSUMER: HOBBIES & DIY: Philately

STAMP MAGAZINE
46633U79C-188

Editorial Address: Leon House, 233 High Street, CROYDON, CR9 1HZ **Tel:** 020 8726 8000
Fax: 020 8726 8299
Email: guy_thomas@ipcmedia.com
Advertising Address: As above. **Tel:** 020 8726 8228
Fax: 020 8726 8298
Email: jay_jones@ipcmedia.com
Web site: http://www.stampmagazine.co.uk
ISSN: 0951-6840
Publisher: IPC Inspire
Frequency: Monthly
Cover Price: £3.35
Annual Sub.: £37.80
Circulation: 23,000 (Publisher's Statement)
Usual Pagination: 140
Editor: Julia Lee
Summary of Content: Magazine focusing on philately. Covers auctions, exhibitions and thematic collecting.
Readership/Target Audience: Read by stamp collectors of all ages.
ADVERTISING RATES:
Full Page Mono £715.00
Full Page Colour £980.00
Agency Commission: 10%
Mechanical Data: Type Area: 265 x 181mm, Col Length: 265mm, Page Width: 181mm, Trim Size: 297 x 210mm, Bleed Size: 303 x 216mm, Film: Digital
Copy instructions: Copy Date: 3-4 weeks prior to publication date
Average advertising content per issue: 45%
CONSUMER: HOBBIES & DIY: Philately

STANDPOINT
1840889U82-280

Editorial Address: 11 Manchester Square, LONDON, W1U 3PW **Tel:** 020 7563 9840 **Fax:** 020 7563 9841
Email: mmosbacher@standpointmag.co.uk
Advertising Address: As above.
Email: fdhew@standpointmag.co.uk
Web site: http://www.standpointmag.co.uk
ISSN: 1757-1111
Publisher: Social Affairs Unit Magazines Ltd
Date Established: 2008
Frequency: Monthly
Cover Price: £4.50
Circulation: 30,000 (Print Run)
Usual Pagination: 84
Editor: Michael Mosbacher; **Advertising Manager:** Fletcher Dhew; **Managing Editor:** Michael Mosbacher
Summary of Content: Magazine covering culture, politics, arts and books.
Readership/Target Audience: Aimed at affluent, well educated readers of all ages.
ADVERTISING RATES:
Full Page Colour £2990.00
Mechanical Data: Type Area: 262 x 190mm, Col Length: 262mm, Page Width: 190mm, Bleed Size: 303 x 231mm, Trim Size: 297 x 225mm
CONSUMER: CURRENT AFFAIRS & POLITICS

STAR
1639084U74Q-1165

Editorial Address: 10 Lower Thames Street, LONDON, EC3R 6EN **Tel:** 0871 434 1010 **Fax:** 0871 434 7505
Email: starmagazine@express.co.uk
Advertising Address: As above.
Email: sam.how@express.co.uk

Publisher: Northern & Shell plc
Date Established: 2003
Frequency: Weekly
Cover Price: £0.99
Circulation: 317,940 (ABC 01/01/2009 to 30/06/2009)
Usual Pagination: 132
Editor: Elizabeth Gardiner; **Advertising Manager:** Sam How
Summary of Content: Magazine covering celebrity news, gossip, fashion, beauty, travel, TV listings and reviews.
Readership/Target Audience: Aimed at women 20 to 35 years old.
ADVERTISING RATES:
Full Page Colour £12100.00
Agency Commission: 15%
Mechanical Data: Film: Digital
Copy instructions: Copy Date: Thursday 5pm prior to publication date
CONSUMER: WOMEN'S INTEREST CONSUMER MAGAZINES: Lifestyle

STAR GIRL MAGAZINE   713845U74F-619_50

Editorial Address: Suite 2.1, Level 2, Renslade House, Bonhay Road, EXETER, EX4 3AY **Tel:** 01392 664141
Fax: 01392 221794
Email: jo@lcdpublishing.co.uk
Advertising Address: As above.
Email: jo@lcdpublishing.co.uk
Publisher: LCD Publishing
Date Established: 1998
Frequency: Monthly
Cover Price: £1.75
Circulation: 80,000 (Publisher's Statement)
Usual Pagination: 32
Editor: Joanne Trump; **Advertising Manager:** Joanne Trump
Summary of Content: Magazine covering fashion, films and news.
Readership/Target Audience: Aimed primarily at girls between 8 and 10 years old.
ADVERTISING: Rates on application
Agency Commission: 10%
Copy instructions: Copy Date: 1 month prior to publication date
CONSUMER: WOMEN'S INTEREST CONSUMER MAGAZINES: Teenage

THE STAR GREEN 'UN (SHEFFIELD)
                                              45724U75A-870
Editorial Address: York Street, SHEFFIELD, S1 1PU
Tel: 0114 276 7676 **Fax:** 0114 272 5978
Email: ian.vickers@sheffieldnewspapers.co.uk
Advertising Address: As above. **Fax:** 0114 252 1377
Email: gary.armstrong@sheffieldnewspapers.co.uk
Web site: http://www.sheffieldtoday.net
Publisher: Sheffield Newspapers Ltd
Date Established: 1907
Frequency: Weekly
Cover Price: £0.50
Circulation: 51,585 (Publisher's Statement)
Usual Pagination: 36
Editor: Ian Vickers
Summary of Content: Newspaper containing articles on local football, racing, greyhounds, cricket, basketball, ice hockey, rugby and angling.
Readership/Target Audience: Read by those in the Sheffield area with an interest in local sport.
ADVERTISING: Rates on application
CONSUMER: SPORT

STAR TREK MAGAZINE   46766U79L-310

Formerly: Star Trek Monthly
Editorial Address: Titan House, 144 Southwark Street, LONDON, SE1 0UP **Tel:** 020 7620 0200 **Fax:** 020 7803 1803
Email: startrekmail@titanemail.com
Advertising Address: As above.
Email: james.willmott@titanemail.com
Web site: http://www.titanmagazines.com
ISSN: 1357-3880
Publisher: Titan Magazines
Date Established: 1995
Frequency: 6 issues yearly
Cover Price: £4.99
Circulation: 27,000 (Publisher's Statement)
Usual Pagination: 100
Editor: Paul Simpson; **Advertising Manager:** James Willmott; **Publisher:** Nick Landau
Summary of Content: Official Star Trek magazine offering exclusive news, interviews and features.
Readership/Target Audience: Read by fans of science fiction.
ADVERTISING RATES:
Full Page Colour $4000.00
Agency Commission: 10%
Mechanical Data: Print Process: Web-fed offset, Trim Size: 297 x 230mm, Bleed Size: 303 x 236mm, Film: Digital

Copy instructions: Copy Date: 6 weeks prior to publication date
CONSUMER: HOBBIES & DIY: Fantasy Games & Science Fiction

STAR WARS INSIDER   46767U79L-315

Formerly: Star Wars Magazine
Editorial Address: Titan House, 144 Southwark Street, LONDON, SE1 0UP **Tel:** 020 7620 0200 **Fax:** 020 7803 1803
Email: starwarsmail@titanemail.com
Advertising Address: As above.
Email: james.willmott@titanemail.com
ISSN: 1361-5211
Publisher: Titan Magazines
Frequency: 8 issues yearly
Cover Price: £4.99
Annual Sub.: £29.90
Circulation: 80,000 (Publisher's Statement)
Usual Pagination: 100
Editor: Jonathan Wilkins; **Managing Director:** Nick Landau
Advertising Manager: James Willmott; **Publisher:** Nick Landau
Summary of Content: Official magazine containing exclusive news, interviews and features.
Readership/Target Audience: Aimed at Star Wars enthusiasts.
ADVERTISING RATES:
Full Page Colour £2000.00
Agency Commission: 10%
Mechanical Data: Page Width: 180mm, Trim Size: 276 x 200mm, Bleed Size: 282 x 206mm, Film: Digital, Type Area: 256 x 180mm, Col Length: 256mm
Copy instructions: Copy Date: 4 weeks prior to publication date
Average advertising content per issue: 12%
CONSUMER: HOBBIES & DIY: Fantasy Games & Science Fiction

STARBURST   46768U79L-320

Editorial Address: 9-10 Blades Court, Deodar Road, LONDON, SW15 2NU **Tel:** 020 8875 1520
Fax: 020 8875 1588
Advertising Address: As above. **Tel:** 020 8875 7400
Email: adverts@visimag.com
Web site: http://www.visimag.com
ISSN: 0955-114X
Publisher: Visual Imagination Ltd
Frequency: 13 issues yearly
Cover Price: £3.99
Circulation: 39,500 (Publisher's Statement)
Usual Pagination: 82
Editor: Stephen Payne; **Advertising Manager:** John Paul Garlick; **Group Editor:** Stephen Payne
Summary of Content: Magazine about science fiction, covering film, television, video and books.
Readership/Target Audience: Aimed at people with an interest in all areas of science fiction.
ADVERTISING RATES:
Full Page Colour £750.00
Agency Commission: 10%
Mechanical Data: Bleed Size: 310 x 232mm, Trim Size: 300 x 222mm, Film: Digital, Type Area: 270 x 192mm, Col Length: 270mm, Page Width: 192mm
CONSUMER: HOBBIES & DIY: Fantasy Games & Science Fiction

STARBURST SPECIAL   46769U79L-330

Editorial Address: 9-10 Blades Court, Deodar Road, LONDON, SW15 2NU **Tel:** 020 8875 1520
Fax: 020 8875 1588
Email: starburst@visimag.com
Advertising Address: As above. **Tel:** 020 8875 7400
Email: adverts@visimag.com
Web site: http://www.visimag.com
ISSN: 0958-7128
Publisher: Visual Imagination Ltd
Frequency: 6 issues yearly
Cover Price: £4.99
Circulation: 39,500 (Publisher's Statement)
Usual Pagination: 100
Editor: Stephen Payne; **Advertising Manager:** Martin Clarke; **Group Editor:** Stephen Payne
Summary of Content: Science fiction magazine with a focus on television and film.
Readership/Target Audience: Aimed at science fiction enthusiasts.
ADVERTISING RATES:
Full Page Colour £950.00
Mechanical Data: Page Width: 192mm, Type Area: 270 x 192mm, Bleed Size: 307 x 230mm, Trim Size: 297 x 220mm, Col Length: 270mm, Film: Digital
CONSUMER: HOBBIES & DIY: Fantasy Games & Science Fiction

STARDUST INTERNATIONAL   46060U76A-60

Editorial Address: PO Box 5095, LONDON, W1A 7WG
Tel: 020 7486 8409
Email: stardustmag@aol.com
Advertising Address: As above.
Email: stardustmag@aol.com
Web site: http://www.stardustindia.com
Publisher: Magna Publishing Co. (UK) Ltd
Frequency: Monthly
Cover Price: £2.00
Annual Sub.: £24.00
Circulation: 35,000 (Publisher's Statement)
Usual Pagination: 132
Editor: Ami Kadakia; **Managing Director:** Nari Hira;
Advertising Manager: Vikram Hira
Summary of Content: Magazine covering the Indian film industry. Includes reviews and celebrity gossip.
Readership/Target Audience: Aimed at those interested in Bollywood.
ADVERTISING RATES:
Full Page Mono £1200.00
Full Page Colour £2500.00
Agency Commission: 10%
Mechanical Data: Page Width: 185mm, Type Area: 245 x 185mm, Bleed Size: 271 x 211mm, Trim Size: 265 x 205mm, Col Length: 245mm, Film: Digital
Average advertising content per issue: 40%
CONSUMER: MUSIC & PERFORMING ARTS: Cinema

STARGATE   1778560U91D-948

Editorial Address: Titan House, 144 Southwark Street, LONDON, SE1 0UP **Tel:** 020 7620 0200 **Fax:** 020 7620 0032
Email: emma.matthews@titanemail.com
Advertising Address: As above.
Email: james.willmott@titanemail.com
Web site: http://www.titanmagazines.co.uk
Publisher: Titan Magazines
Frequency: 6 issues yearly
Cover Price: £3.75
Circulation: 10,000 (Publisher's Statement)
Usual Pagination: 68
Editor: Emma Matthews; **Advertising Manager:** James Willmott
Summary of Content: Magazine covering Stargate 1 and its sister series Stargate Atlanta with stories, interviews, features, quizzes and competitions.
Readership/Target Audience: Aimed at Stargate fans.
ADVERTISING RATES:
Full Page Colour $4000.00
Mechanical Data: Bleed Size: 303 x 221mm, Trim Size: 297 x 215mm, Film: Digital
CONSUMER: RECREATION & LEISURE: Children & Youth

STARTLINE   46434U77D-460

Editorial Address: Thruxton Circuit, ANDOVER, SP11 8PN
Tel: 01264 882200 **Fax:** 01264 882233
Email: info@barc.net
Advertising Address: As above.
Email: tswettenham@barc.net
Web site: http://www.barc.net
Publisher: British Automobile Racing Club
Date Established: 1988
Frequency: 6 issues yearly
Cover Price: £2.75
Free to qualifying individuals
Circulation: 4,500 (Publisher's Statement)
Usual Pagination: 36
Editor: Dennis Carter; **Advertising Manager:** Trevor Swettenham
Summary of Content: Magazine containing news, views and information from the British Automobile Racing Club.
Readership/Target Audience: Read by members and friends of the club.
ADVERTISING RATES:
Full Page Mono £250.00
Full Page Colour £375.00
Agency Commission: 10%
Mechanical Data: Print Process: Offset litho, Trim Size: 297 x 210mm, Film: Digital
Copy instructions: Copy Date: 4 weeks prior to publication date
CONSUMER: MOTORING & CYCLING: Motor Sports

STATIONARY ENGINE   28957U79K-995

Editorial Address: Cudham Tithe Barn, Berrys Hill, Berrys Green, Cudham, WESTERHAM, TN16 3AG
Tel: 01959 541444 **Fax:** 01959 541400
Email: se.info@kelsey.co.uk
Advertising Address: As above. **Tel:** 01959 543500
Email: graham@kelsey.co.uk
Web site: http://www.stationaryengine.com
Publisher: Kelsey Publishing Ltd
Date Established: 2002
Frequency: Monthly
Cover Price: £2.85
Annual Sub.: £30.24

Circulation: 6,700 (Publisher's Statement)
Usual Pagination: 48
Editor: Gordon Wright
Summary of Content: Magazine covering restoration, buying and selling and the history of stationary engines.
Readership/Target Audience: Aimed at owners, restorers and collectors of stationary engines.
ADVERTISING RATES:
Full Page Colour £485.00
Agency Commission: 10%
Mechanical Data: Page Width: 188mm, Film: Digital, Trim Size: 297 x 210mm, Type Area: 270 x 188mm, Bleed Size: 303 x 216mm, Col Length: 270mm, No. of Columns (Display): 2
Copy instructions: Copy Date: 10th of the month prior to publication date
Average advertising content per issue: 30%
CONSUMER: HOBBIES & DIY: Collectors Magazines

STEAM DAYS
46711U79J-80
Editorial Address: PO Box 2471, BOURNEMOUTH, BH7 7WF **Tel:** 01202 304849 **Fax:** 01202 304849
Email: red.gauntlett@btconnect.com
Advertising Address: As above.
Email: red.gauntlett@btconnect.com
Web site: http://www.steamdaysmag.co.uk
ISSN: 0269-0020
Publisher: Redgauntlet Publications Ltd
Date Established: 1986
Frequency: Monthly
Cover Price: £3.85
Annual Sub.: £41.00
Circulation: 14,000 (Publisher's Statement)
Usual Pagination: 64
Editor: Rex Kennedy; **Managing Director:** Rex Kennedy;
Advertising Manager: Rex Kennedy
Summary of Content: Magazine covering the history and nostalgia of steam railways.
Readership/Target Audience: Aimed at steam railway enthusiasts.
ADVERTISING RATES:
Full Page Mono £275.00
Full Page Colour £425.00
Agency Commission: 10%
Mechanical Data: Film: Digital
Copy instructions: Copy Date: 6 weeks prior to publication date
Average advertising content per issue: 5%
CONSUMER: HOBBIES & DIY: Rail Enthusiasts

STEAM HERITAGE MUSEUMS AND RALLY GUIDE
46712U79J-85
Editorial Address: The Fosse, Fosse Way, LEAMINGTON SPA, CV31 1XN **Tel:** 01926 614101 **Fax:** 01926 614293
Email: info@teepublishing.com
Advertising Address: As above.
Email: info@teepublishing.co.uk
Web site: http://www.fotec.co.uk/mehs/tee
ISSN: 0269-2368
Publisher: TEE Publishing Ltd
Date Established: 1965
Frequency: Annual - Published in March
Annual Sub.: £3.95
Circulation: 15,000 (Publisher's Statement)
Usual Pagination: 100
Editor: C L Deith; **Managing Director:** C L Deith;
Advertising Manager: Avril Spence; **Publisher:** C L Deith
Summary of Content: Guide to the preservation scene containing information on museums, preserved railways, steam centres, places of interest and related events.
Readership/Target Audience: Aimed at those planning a day out in the UK.
ADVERTISING RATES:
Full Page Mono £360.00
Full Page Colour £500.00
Agency Commission: 10%
Mechanical Data: Col Length: 190mm, Type Area: 190 x 124mm, Page Width: 124mm
Copy instructions: Copy Date: January 13th
CONSUMER: HOBBIES & DIY: Rail Enthusiasts

STEAM RAILWAY
46713U79J-90
Editorial Address: Bushfield House, Orton Centre, PETERBOROUGH, PE2 5UW **Tel:** 01733 237111
Fax: 01733 288163
Email: steam.railway@bauermedia.co.uk
Advertising Address: As above. **Tel:** 01733 288066
Fax: 01733 465897
Email: natalie.coe@bauerconsumer.co.uk
Web site: http://www.steamrailway.co.uk
Publisher: Bauer Media Ltd (Orton)
Date Established: 1979
Frequency: 13 issues yearly
Cover Price: £3.50
Annual Sub.: £40.30
Circulation: 32,124 (ABC 01/01/2008 to 31/12/2008)

Usual Pagination: 108
Editor: Danny Hopkins; **News Editor:** Gary Boyd-Hope
Summary of Content: Magazine covering steam engines, preserved railways and the history of steam.
Readership/Target Audience: Aimed at those interested in steam traction.
ADVERTISING RATES:
Full Page Colour £1050.00
Agency Commission: 10%
Mechanical Data: Page Width: 185mm, Type Area: 270 x 185mm, Col Length: 270mm, Trim Size: 297 x 210mm, Bleed Size: 303 x 216mm, Film: Digital
CONSUMER: HOBBIES & DIY: Rail Enthusiasts

STEAM WORLD
46715U79J-200
Editorial Address: 1st Floor, 2 King Street, PETERBOROUGH, PE1 1LT **Tel:** 01733 555123
Fax: 01733 427500
Email: steamworld@choicemag.co.uk
Advertising Address: Action In Media, Church View Office, 15A St. Mary's Street, STAMFORD, PE9 2DF
Tel: 01780 763200 **Fax:** 01780 757718
Email: paula@actioninmedia.co.uk
Publisher: Steam World Publishing
Date Established: 1987
Frequency: Monthly - Published on the 3rd Friday of the month prior to publication date
Cover Price: £3.70
Annual Sub.: £41.20
Circulation: 20,000 (Publisher's Statement)
Usual Pagination: 68
Editor: Mel Holley; **Advertising Director:** Paula Scott;
Publisher: Clive Nicholls
Summary of Content: Magazine covering steam on Britain's railways pre-1968.
Readership/Target Audience: Read by those interested in UK railway history, largely post-war.
ADVERTISING RATES:
Full Page Mono £620.00
Full Page Colour £870.00
SCC £15.00
Agency Commission: 10%
Mechanical Data: Page Width: 185mm, Col Length: 270mm, Film: Digital, Type Area: 270 x 185mm, Bleed Size: 300 x 215mm, Trim Size: 297 x 210mm
Copy instructions: Copy Date: 5th of the month prior to publication date
Average advertising content per issue: 10%
CONSUMER: HOBBIES & DIY: Rail Enthusiasts

STEP AHEAD
1795332U74D-650
Editorial Address: 1st Floor, 299-301 London Road, BENFLEET, SS7 2BN **Tel:** 01702 555990 **Fax:** 01702 555880
Email: editor@stepaheadmagazine.co.uk
Advertising Address: As above.
Email: sarah@stepaheadmagazine.co.uk
Web site: http://www.stepaheadmagazine.co.uk
Publisher: Step Ahead Ltd
Date Established: 2004
Frequency: 11 issues yearly
Cover Price: Free
Circulation: 47,000 (Publisher's Statement)
Usual Pagination: 48
Editor: Kim Kimbler
Summary of Content: Magazine covering modern family life including health, education, food, what's happening in schools, charity, competitions, activities and quizzes as well as seasonal features.
Readership/Target Audience: Aimed predominantly at ABC1 families in Essex.
ADVERTISING: Rates on application
CONSUMER: WOMEN'S INTEREST CONSUMER MAGAZINES: Child Care

STEPPE
1791402U90-1005
Editorial Address: Manor Farm, High Street, Nettlebed, HENLEY-ON-THAMES, RG9 5DA **Tel:** 01491 641914
Email: info@steppemagazine.com
Advertising Address: As above.
Email: lucy@kelaart.com
Web site: http://www.steppemagazine.com
Publisher: Steppe International Ltd
Date Established: 2006
Frequency: Half-yearly - Published in April and October
Cover Price: £10.00
Circulation: 10,000 (Print Run)
Editor: Lucy Kelaart; **Advertising Manager:** Lucy Kelaart
Summary of Content: Magazine covering the arts, culture, history and people of Central Asia.
Readership/Target Audience: Aimed at those with an interest in Central Asia.
ADVERTISING RATES:
Full Page Colour £2000.00
Mechanical Data: Trim Size: 270 x 230mm, Bleed Size: 276 x 236mm, Film: Digital
CONSUMER: ETHNIC

STITCH WITH THE EMBROIDERERS' GUILD
622773U74E-560
Editorial Address: 9 The Meadows, PEEBLES, EH45 9HZ
Tel: 01721 722658
Email: kathy.troup@btopenworld.com
Advertising Address: Mongoose Media, 2 Lonsdale Road, LONDON, NW6 6RD **Tel:** 020 7306 0300
Email: embroiderersguild@mongoosemedia.com
Web site: http://www.embroiderersguild.com/stitch
ISSN: 1467-6648
Publisher: E.G. Enterprises Ltd
Date Established: 1999
Frequency: 6 issues yearly
Cover Price: £3.95
Annual Sub.: £23.70
Circulation: 19,500 (Publisher's Statement)
Usual Pagination: 68
Editor: Kathy Troup
Summary of Content: Magazine containing designs and ideas for creative needlework projects. Includes features on contemporary and traditional embroidery, designers, products, community needlework projects, competitions and book reviews.
Readership/Target Audience: Aimed at beginners and experienced stitchers.
ADVERTISING RATES:
Full Page Colour £1100.00
Agency Commission: 10%
Mechanical Data: Type Area: 270 x 185mm, Col Length: 270mm, Page Width: 185mm, Bleed Size: 303 x 216mm, Trim Size: 297 x 210mm, Film: Digital
Copy instructions: Copy Date: 4 weeks prior to publication date
Average advertising content per issue: 20%
CONSUMER: WOMEN'S INTEREST CONSUMER MAGAZINES: Crafts

THE STOCKPORT DIARY
1708237U89C-1072
Editorial Address: Environmental & Economy Directorate, Lower Ground, Stopford House, Piccadilly, STOCKPORT, SK1 3XE **Tel:** 0161 474 4480
Email: alison.farthing@stockport.gov.uk
Advertising Address: 5-6 Shoplatch, SHREWSBURY, SY1 1HF **Tel:** 01743 281777 **Fax:** 01743 248256
Email: paul@whatsonmag.com
Web site: http://www.stockport.gov.uk
Publisher: What's On Magazine Group
Frequency: 6 issues yearly
Cover Price: Free
Circulation: 15,000 (Publisher's Statement)
Usual Pagination: 16
Editor: Alison Farthing; **Advertising Manager:** Paul Oliver
Summary of Content: Listings guide covering theatre, dance, music, visual arts, kids activities and attractions and film reviews.
Readership/Target Audience: Aimed at residents of all ages in Stockport.
ADVERTISING RATES:
Full Page Colour ....,............................ £4190.00
Agency Commission: 10%
Mechanical Data: Type Area: 265 x 190mm, Bleed Size: 295 x 215mm, Trim Size: 285 x 210mm, Col Length: 265mm, Page Width: 190mm, Film: Digital
Copy instructions: Copy Date: 2 weeks prior to publication date
Average advertising content per issue: 30%
CONSUMER: HOLIDAYS & TRAVEL: Entertainment Guides

STOCKTON NEWS
47017U80C-3720
Editorial Address: PO Box 11, Church Road, STOCKTON-ON-TEES, TS18 1LD **Tel:** 01642 393020 **Fax:** 01642 393026
Email: communications@stockton.gov.uk
Advertising Address: As above. **Fax:** 01642 526166
Email: erika.mason@stockton.gov.uk
Web site: http://www.stockton.gov.uk
Publisher: Stockton Borough Council
Date Established: 1982
Frequency: Quarterly
Cover Price: Free
Circulation: 75,000 (Publisher's Statement)
Usual Pagination: 40
Editor: Vince Rutland; **Advertising Manager:** Erika Mason
Summary of Content: Magazine containing community news and information of local interest.
Readership/Target Audience: Aimed at all residents and visitors in the Borough of Stockton-on-Tees.
ADVERTISING RATES:
Full Page Mono £995.00
Full Page Colour £995.00
Mechanical Data: Type Area: 273 x 186mm, Trim Size: 297 x 210mm, Col Length: 273mm, Page Width: 186mm
Average advertising content per issue: 12%
CONSUMER: RURAL & REGIONAL INTEREST: Regional Interest English Counties

Consumer Magazines

STOPGAP
47284U82-189

Formerly: Towards Equality
Editorial Address: 1-3 Berry Street, LONDON, EC1V 0AA
Tel: 020 7253 2598 **Fax:** 020 7253 2599
Email: rosanna.downes@fawcettsociety.org.uk
Advertising Address: As above.
Email: rowena.lewis@fawcettsociety.org.uk
Web site: http://www.fawcettsociety.org.uk
Publisher: The Fawcett Society
Frequency: 3 issues yearly - Published in March, July and October
Cover Price: £2.50
Free to qualifying individuals
Annual Sub.: £20.00
Circulation: 3,500 (Publisher's Statement)
Usual Pagination: 20
Editor: Rosanna Downes; **Advertising Manager:** Rowena Lewis
Summary of Content: Magazine of the Fawcett Society, which campaigns for equality between women and men.
Readership/Target Audience: Aimed at members of the Fawcett Society.
ADVERTISING: Rates on application
CONSUMER: CURRENT AFFAIRS & POLITICS

THE STOUR & AVON MAGAZINE
762704U80C-3765

Formerly: The Community Magazine
Editorial Address: 1A Princes Court, Princes Road, FERNDOWN, BH22 9JG **Tel:** 01202 896966
Fax: 01202 855411
Email: mbarber@bvmedia.co.uk
Advertising Address: As above.
Email: gweeks@bvmedia.co.uk
Publisher: Blackmore Vale Media
Frequency: Weekly
Cover Price: Free
Circulation: 53,000 (Publisher's Statement)
Usual Pagination: 64
Editor: Marilyn Barber; **News Editor:** Marilyn Barber; **Group Editor:** Fanny Charles
Summary of Content: Magazine covering local news, current affairs, arts, planning, environment, health and education.
Readership/Target Audience: Aimed at those living in Ferndown, Wimbourne and the surrounding area.
ADVERTISING RATES:
Full Page Mono £690.00
Full Page Colour £830.00
Agency Commission: 10%
Mechanical Data: No. of Columns (Display): 5, Col Widths (Display): 37mm, Film: Digital
Copy instructions: Copy Date: Tuesday 12pm prior to publication date
Average advertising content per issue: 65%
CONSUMER: RURAL & REGIONAL INTEREST: Regional Interest English Counties

STOWMARKET COMMUNITY NEWS
48138U89C-370

Editorial Address: 101 Thunder Lane, NORWICH, NR7 0JG
Tel: 01603 433972
Email: fords@onetel.com
Advertising Address: As above.
Publisher: Profile Publishing & Design
Frequency: Monthly
Cover Price: £2.00
Free to qualifying individuals
Circulation: 10,000 (Publisher's Statement)
Usual Pagination: 8
Editor: Alan Geere; **Advertising Manager:** Steven Ford
Summary of Content: Newspaper containing book, record and video reviews, local news and events guide and motoring features.
Readership/Target Audience: Aimed at those living in Stowmarket and the surrounding areas.
ADVERTISING: Rates on application
CONSUMER: HOLIDAYS & TRAVEL: Entertainment Guides

THE STRAD
46183U76D-410

Editorial Address: 2nd Floor, 30 Cannon Street, LONDON, EC4M 6YJ **Tel:** 020 7618 3456 **Fax:** 020 7618 3483
Email: thestrad@orpheuspublications.com
Advertising Address: As above.
Email: advertising@orpheuspublications.com
Web site: http://www.thestrad.com
ISSN: 0039-2049
Publisher: Orpheus Portfolio at Newsquest Specialist Media Ltd
Date Established: 1890
Frequency: Monthly
Cover Price: £3.75
Annual Sub.: £40.95
Circulation: 17,500 (Publisher's Statement)
Usual Pagination: 120

Editor: Ariane Todes; **Managing Editor:** David Kettle
Summary of Content: Magazine covering bowed string instruments. Includes concert and CD reviews and profiles of famous string artists.
Language(s): English; Korean
Readership/Target Audience: Aimed at musicians, instrument makers and lovers of string music.
ADVERTISING RATES:
Full Page Mono £1990.00
Full Page Colour £1990.00
Agency Commission: 10%
Mechanical Data: Page Width: 180mm, Type Area: 255 x 180mm, Bleed Size: 303 x 216mm, Trim Size: 297x 210mm, Col Length: 255mm, Film: Digital
Copy instructions: Copy Date: 4 weeks prior to publication date
Average advertising content per issue: 15%
Supplement(s): Degrees - 1xY, London International String Quartet Competition Programme - 1xY, SummerPlus - 1xY
CONSUMER: MUSIC & PERFORMING ARTS: Music

STRANGER
1660330U74Q-1246

Editorial Address: The Ground Floor, 1 South Harbour, Harbour Village, PENRYN, TR10 8LR **Tel:** 01326 376500
Email: editorial@stranger-mag.com
Advertising Address: As above.
Email: editorial@stranger-mag.com
Web site: http://www.stranger-mag.com
ISSN: 1750-7987
Publisher: Helen Gilchrist
Date Established: 2004
Frequency: Half-yearly - Published in June and November
Circulation: 15,000 (Publisher's Statement)
Editor: Clare Howdle; **Advertising Manager:** Helen Gilchrist
Summary of Content: Magazine with a southwest-inspired flavour covering lifestyle, environment, music, graphic arts, surf, skateboarding, fashion and current affairs.
Readership/Target Audience: Aimed at 18 to 35 year old men and women.
ADVERTISING: Rates on application
CONSUMER: WOMEN'S INTEREST CONSUMER MAGAZINES: Lifestyle

STRATHCLYDE TELEGRAPH
47452U83-76

Editorial Address: Strathclyde Student Association, 90 John Street, GLASGOW, G1 1JH **Tel:** 0141 567 5054
Fax: 0141 567 5092
Email: editor@theunion.strath.ac.uk
Web site: http://www.s-t.org.uk
Publisher: Strathclyde University Students Association
Date Established: 1960
Frequency: 17 issues yearly
Cover Price: Free
Circulation: 12,000 (Publisher's Statement)
Usual Pagination: 36
Summary of Content: Student newspaper covering student issues, university news and sport, general arts and music.
Readership/Target Audience: Aimed at students of Strathclyde University.
ADVERTISING: No Advertising taken
CONSUMER: STUDENT PUBLICATIONS

STREETFIGHTERS
46376U77B-605

Editorial Address: 1 Canada Square, 19th Floor, Canary Wharf, LONDON, E14 5AP **Tel:** 020 7772 8300
Fax: 020 7772 8585
Email: will.jobbins@oceanmedia.co.uk
Advertising Address: As above. **Tel:** 020 7293 3000
Email: justin_driver@oceanmedia.co.uk
Web site: http://www.streetfightersmag.com
Publisher: Ocean Media Group Ltd
Frequency: Monthly
Cover Price: £3.40
Circulation: 24,031 (Publisher's Statement)
Editor: Will Jobbins; **Managing Editor:** Stu Garland
Summary of Content: Magazine covering streetfighter motorbikes.
Readership/Target Audience: Aimed at those with an interest in all bikes.
ADVERTISING RATES:
Full Page Colour £1260.00
Agency Commission: 10%
Mechanical Data: Bleed Size: 303 x 216mm, Trim Size: 297 x 210mm, Type Area: 287 x 200mm, Film: Digital, Col Length: 287mm, Page Width: 200mm
Copy instructions: Copy Date: 3 weeks prior to publication date
Average advertising content per issue: 30%
CONSUMER: MOTORING & CYCLING: Motorcycling

STROKE NEWS
45663U94F-840

Editorial Address: Stroke House, 240 City Road, LONDON, EC1V 2PR **Tel:** 020 7566 0300 **Fax:** 020 7490 2686
Email: strokenews@stroke.org.uk

Advertising Address: Redactive Media Group, 17 Britton Street, LONDON, EC1M 5TP **Tel:** 020 7880 6200
Fax: 020 7880 7553
Email: emmalouise.renton@redactive.co.uk
Web site: http://www.stroke.org.uk
Publisher: The Stroke Association
Frequency: Quarterly
Cover Price: Free
Circulation: 81,000 (Publisher's Statement)
Usual Pagination: 36
Editor: Rachel Tonkin
Summary of Content: Magazine from The Stroke Association.
Readership/Target Audience: Read by people and families who have been affected by strokes and health professionals working with people affected by stroke.
ADVERTISING RATES:
Full Page Colour £2645.00
SCC £25.00
Agency Commission: 10%
Mechanical Data: Type Area: 253 x 180mm, Col Length: 253mm, Page Width: 180mm, Film: Digital
Average advertising content per issue: 35%
CONSUMER: OTHER CLASSIFICATIONS: Disability

STUDENT DIRECT
47429U83-77_20

Editorial Address: University of Manchester, Student Union, Oxford Road, MANCHESTER, M13 9PR **Tel:** 0161 275 2943
Fax: 0161 275 2936
Email: editor@student-direct.co.uk
Advertising Address: University House, The Crescent, SALFORD, M5 4WT **Tel:** 0161 351 5402 **Fax:** 0161 737 1633
Email: studentdirect@salford.ac.uk
Web site: http://www.student-direct.co.uk
Publisher: Student Direct Ltd
Date Established: 1909
Frequency: 22 issues yearly - Published during term time
Cover Price: Free
Circulation: 20,000 (Publisher's Statement)
Usual Pagination: 36
Editor: Dominic Koole
Summary of Content: Official student newspaper of Greater Manchester. Covers news, features, lifestyle, travel, sport, music and art. Also includes clubbing, film and television, culture and the Internet.
Readership/Target Audience: Read by students at Manchester University, The University of Salford and Bolton University.
ADVERTISING RATES:
Full Page Mono £1139.00
Full Page Colour £1458.00
Agency Commission: 10%
Mechanical Data: Trim Size: 340 x 265mm, Film: Digital
Copy instructions: Copy Date: 6 days prior to publication date
Average advertising content per issue: 10%
CONSUMER: STUDENT PUBLICATIONS

STUDENT IMPACT
47449U83-15

Formerly: Impact (Bath)
Editorial Address: University of Bath, Claverton Down, BATH, BA2 7AY **Tel:** 01225 386151 **Fax:** 01225 444061
Email: editor@bathimpact.com
Advertising Address: As above. **Tel:** 01225 826883
Fax: 01225 826562
Email: h.freeman@bath.ac.uk
Web site: http://www.bathimpact.com
Publisher: University of Bath Students' Union
Date Established: 2000
Frequency: 14 issues yearly - Published term-time only
Cover Price: Free
Circulation: 2,500 (Publisher's Statement)
Usual Pagination: 28
Editor: Tim Leigh; **Editor-in-Chief:** Tim Leigh; **Advertising Manager:** Helen Freeman
Summary of Content: Newspaper covering articles on student lifestyle, events that affect the student population, music, travel, books, fashion, jobs, computer games and sport.
Readership/Target Audience: Aimed at students of the University of Bath.
ADVERTISING RATES:
Full Page Mono £360.00
Full Page Colour £675.00
Agency Commission: 10%
Mechanical Data: Type Area: 350 x 264mm, Col Length: 350mm, Page Width: 264mm, Film: Digital
CONSUMER: STUDENT PUBLICATIONS

STUDENT TIMES
1746606U83-276

Editorial Address: Studio 4, Hiltongrove, 14 Southgate Road, LONDON, N1 3LY **Tel:** 020 7407 7747
Fax: 020 7407 6800
Email: info@sugarmedia.co.uk
Advertising Address: As above.
Email: Ian@sugarmedia.co.uk

Web site: http://www.studenttimes.org
Publisher: Sugar Media Ltd
Frequency: Quarterly
Cover Price: Free
Circulation: 100,000 (Publisher's Statement)
Usual Pagination: 24
Editor: Isabel Appio; **Advertising Manager:** Ian Thomas
Summary of Content: Magazine covering national and global issues affecting students as well as entertainment and sport.
Readership/Target Audience: Aimed at students aged between 16 and 25 years old.
ADVERTISING RATES:
Full Page Mono £3000.00
Full Page Colour £3000.00
Agency Commission: 10%
Mechanical Data: Type Area: 338 x 260mm, Col Length: 338mm, Page Width: 260mm
Copy instructions: Copy Date: 2 weeks prior to publication date
Average advertising content per issue: 40%
CONSUMER: STUDENT PUBLICATIONS

STUDIES IN THE HISTORY OF GARDENS & DESIGNED LANDSCAPES
48573U93-160

Editorial Address: 4 Park Square, Milton Park, ABINGDON, OX14 4RN **Tel:** 01235 828600 **Fax:** 01235 828900
Email: jessica.feinstein@tandf.co.uk
Advertising Address: As above. **Tel:** 020 7017 6000
Fax: 020 7017 6713
Email: jenna.johnston@tandf.co.uk
Web site: http://www.tandf.co.uk
ISSN: 1460-1176
Publisher: Routledge, Taylor & Francis
Frequency: Quarterly
Annual Sub.: £132.00 (Individual)
Editor: Jennifer Roberts; **Advertising Manager:** Jenna Johnston
Summary of Content: Academic journal about the history of gardening through the ages.
Readership/Target Audience: Read by garden and cultural historians.
ADVERTISING RATES:
Full Page Mono £300.00
Agency Commission: 10%
Mechanical Data: Trim Size: 297 x 210mm, Film: Digital, Type Area: 240 x 190mm, Col Length: 240mm, Page Width: 190mm
CONSUMER: GARDENING

STUDY OVERSEAS
47879U88A-100

Formerly: Trans-World Education Magazine
Editorial Address: 101 Southwark Street, LONDON, SE1 0JF **Tel:** 020 7401 7333 **Fax:** 020 7401 7233
Email: editor@srmedia.net
Advertising Address: Dominion House, 101 Southwark Street, LONDON, SE1 0JF **Tel:** 020 7401 7333
Fax: 020 7401 7233
Email: luke@srmedia.net
Web site: http://www.studyoverseas.com
Publisher: SR Media Ltd
Date Established: 1976
Frequency: 6 issues yearly
Cover Price: Free
Circulation: 100,000 (Publisher's Statement)
Usual Pagination: 300
Editor: Emma Salt; **Features Editor:** Harry Byford; **Managing Director:** Luke Turnell; **Advertising Director:** Luke Turnell
Summary of Content: Magazine providing informative features on educational opportunities for international students.
Readership/Target Audience: Read by international students.
ADVERTISING RATES:
Full Page Colour £3900.00
Agency Commission: 10%
Mechanical Data: Bleed Size: 303 x 216mm, Trim Size: 297 x 210mm, Film: Digital, Type Area: 253 x 180mm, Col Length: 253mm, Page Width: 180mm
Copy instructions: Copy Date: 4 weeks prior to publication date
CONSUMER: EDUCATION

STUFF
47666U86C-560

Editorial Address: Teddington Studios, Broom Road, TEDDINGTON, TW11 9BE **Tel:** 020 8267 5036
Fax: 020 8267 5019
Email: stuff@haymarket.com
Advertising Address: As above. **Tel:** 020 8267 5000
Email: mike.walsh@haymarket.com
Web site: http://www.stuff.tv
Publisher: Haymarket Consumer Media
Frequency: Monthly
Cover Price: £3.99
Annual Sub.: £32.40

Circulation: 84,565 (ABC 01/01/2009 to 30/06/2009)
Usual Pagination: 160
Editor: Tom Wiggins; **News Editor:** Tom Wiggins;
Managing Director: Kevin Costello; **Managing Editor:** Nic Shaw
Summary of Content: Men's lifestyle magazine with a focus on gadgets and innovation.
Readership/Target Audience: Aimed at men between 25 and 34 years of age.
ADVERTISING RATES:
Full Page Colour £7325.00
Agency Commission: 10%
Mechanical Data: Type Area: 272 x 200mm, Bleed Size: 303 x 226mm, Trim Size: 297 x 229mm, Film: Digital, Col Length: 272mm, Page Width: 200mm
Average advertising content per issue: 40%
CONSUMER: ADULT & GAY MAGAZINES: Men's Lifestyle Magazines

STYLE
762619U74Q-1118

Editorial Address: Winship Road, Milton, CAMBRIDGE, CB24 6PP **Tel:** 01223 434409 **Fax:** 01223 434415
Email: debbietweedie@cambridge-news.co.uk
Advertising Address: As above. **Tel:** 01223 434434
Email: sue.walden@cambridge-news.co.uk
Publisher: Cambridge Newspapers Ltd
Date Established: 2002
Frequency: Monthly
Cover Price: Free
Circulation: 15,000 (Publisher's Statement)
Usual Pagination: 60
Editor: Debbie Tweedie; **Advertising Manager:** Sue Walden
Summary of Content: Magazine featuring articles on homes and gardens, food and drink, fashion, sport, travel, health and beauty.
Readership/Target Audience: Aimed at those living in Cambridgeshire.
ADVERTISING RATES:
Full Page Colour £1500.00
Agency Commission: 10%
Mechanical Data: Trim Size: 297 x 210mm, Film: Digital, Bleed Size: 307 x 215mm, Col Widths (Display): 44.5mm, No. of Columns (Display): 4
Copy instructions: Copy Date: 2 weeks prior to publication date
Average advertising content per issue: 30%
CONSUMER: WOMEN'S INTEREST CONSUMER MAGAZINES: Lifestyle

STYLE WEDDINGS
1799611U74L-260

Formerly: East Anglian Weddings
Editorial Address: Winship Road, Milton, CAMBRIDGE, CB24 6PP **Tel:** 01223 434409 **Fax:** 01223 434415
Email: debbietweedie@cambridge-news.co.uk
Advertising Address: As above. **Tel:** 01223 434434
Email: sue.walden@cambridge-news.co.uk
Publisher: Cambridge Newspapers Ltd
Date Established: 2006
Frequency: Half-yearly - Published in March and September
Cover Price: £2.95
Free to qualifying individuals
Circulation: 15,000 (Publisher's Statement)
Usual Pagination: 120
Editor: Debbie Tweedie; **Advertising Manager:** Sue Walden
Summary of Content: Magazine covering all aspects of weddings including fashion, beauty, hair, venues, honeymoons, accessories, mother of the bride, grooms, gifts and photography.
Readership/Target Audience: Aimed at brides to be in East Anglia.
ADVERTISING RATES:
Full Page Colour £700.00
Agency Commission: 10%
Mechanical Data: Type Area: 270 x 190mm, Bleed Size: 307 x 215mm, Trim Size: 297 x 210mm, Col Length: 270mm, Page Width: 190mm, Film: Digital
Copy instructions: Copy Date: 22nd February
CONSUMER: WOMEN'S INTEREST CONSUMER MAGAZINES: Brides

SUBLIME
1774732U74Q-1327

Editorial Address: 167 Southwood Lane, Highgate, LONDON, N6 5TA **Tel:** 020 8374 7695
Email: editorial@sublimemagazine.com
Advertising Address: As above.
Email: info@sublimemagazine.com
Web site: http://www.sublimemagazine.com
Publisher: Sublime Magazine Ltd
Date Established: 2006
Frequency: 6 issues yearly
Cover Price: £4.95
Circulation: 55,000 (Publisher's Statement)
Usual Pagination: 128
Editor: Damian Santamaria; **Advertising Manager:** Damian Santamaria

Summary of Content: Lifestyle magazine covering culture, music, architecture, fashion, food, travel, environment, soul and sustainable living.
Readership/Target Audience: Aimed at men and women aged between 20 and 45 years old.
ADVERTISING RATES:
Full Page Colour £7000.00
Agency Commission: 10%
Mechanical Data: Bleed Size: 304 x 236mm, Trim Size: 298 x 230mm, Film: Digital
Copy instructions: Copy Date: 10 days prior to publication date
Average advertising content per issue: 8%
CONSUMER: WOMEN'S INTEREST CONSUMER MAGAZINES: Lifestyle

SUDOKU
1694394U79F-89

Editorial Address: Stonecroft, 69 Station Road, REDHILL, RH1 1EY **Tel:** 01737 378700 **Fax:** 01737 781800
Advertising Address: 3rd Floor, 118 Commercial Street, LONDON, E1 6NF **Tel:** 020 7426 5060 **Fax:** 020 7092 9176
Email: garywhyte@theinserthouse.com
Web site: http://www.puzzler.com
Publisher: Puzzler Media Ltd
Date Established: 2005
Frequency: Monthly
Cover Price: £2.00
Circulation: 131,636 (Publisher's Statement)
Usual Pagination: 48
Editor: Ariane Blok; **Advertising Manager:** Gary Whyte
Summary of Content: Magazine of hand-made Sudoku puzzles.
Language(s): English; French; German; Spanish
Readership/Target Audience: Aimed at puzzle fans.
ADVERTISING: Rates on application
CONSUMER: HOBBIES & DIY: Games & Puzzles

SUFFOLK NORFOLK LIFE
46975U80C-2940

Editorial Address: The Publishing House, Station Road, Framlingham, WOODBRIDGE, IP13 9EE **Tel:** 01728 622030
Fax: 01728 622031
Email: todaymagazines@btopenworld.com
Advertising Address: As above.
Email: todaymagazines@btopenworld.com
Web site: http://www.suffolknorfolklife.com
ISSN: 1359-2408
Publisher: Today Magazines Ltd
Date Established: 1989
Frequency: Monthly - Published in the penultimate week of the month prior to cover date
Cover Price: £1.90
Annual Sub.: £24.00
Circulation: 19,000 (Publisher's Statement)
Usual Pagination: 84
Editor: William Locks; **Publisher:** Kevin Davis
Summary of Content: Magazine containing local news and features on food, wine, property, motoring, health, finance, travel and county events.
Readership/Target Audience: Aimed at residents and visitors to Suffolk and Norfolk.
ADVERTISING RATES:
Full Page Mono £750.00
Full Page Colour £800.00
Agency Commission: 10%
Mechanical Data: Col Length: 278mm, Col Widths (Display): 42mm, Film: Digital, No. of Columns (Display): 4, Bleed Size: 305 x 215mm, Trim Size: 297 x 210mm
Copy instructions: Copy Date: 3 weeks prior to publication date
Average advertising content per issue: 30%
CONSUMER: RURAL & REGIONAL INTEREST: Regional Interest English Counties

SUGAR
45396U74F-620

Editorial Address: 64 North Row, LONDON, W1K 7LL
Tel: 020 7150 7087 **Fax:** 020 7150 7678
Email: sugarreaders@sugarmagazine.co.uk
Advertising Address: As above. **Tel:** 020 7150 7000
Fax: 020 7150 7685
Email: carole.best@hf-uk.com
Web site: http://www.sugarscape.com
ISSN: 1355-9672
Publisher: Hachette Filipacchi (UK) Ltd
Frequency: Monthly
Cover Price: £2.30
Circulation: 140,599 (ABC 01/01/2009 to 30/06/2009)
Usual Pagination: 124
Editor: Kate Wills; **Features Editor:** Laura MacBeth
Summary of Content: Magazine covering fashion, beauty, lifestyle and entertainment.
Readership/Target Audience: Aimed at girls and young women between 13 and 17 years old.
ADVERTISING: Rates on application
Agency Commission: 15%

Consumer Magazines

Copy instructions: Copy Date: 4 weeks prior to publication date
CONSUMER: WOMEN'S INTEREST CONSUMER MAGAZINES: Teenage

SUIT YOURSELF MAGAZINE   1804501U80C-5404
Editorial Address: 17 Eastwood Road, BRISTOL, BS4 4RN **Tel:** 0117 370 2722
Email: info@suityourselfmagazine.co.uk
Advertising Address: As above.
Email: info@suityourselfmagazine.co.uk
Web site: http://www.suityourselfmagazine.co.uk
Publisher: Suit Yourself Ltd
Date Established: 2005
Frequency: Quarterly
Cover Price: Free
Circulation: 50,000 (Publisher's Statement)
Usual Pagination: 80
Editor: Matt Whittle; **Advertising Manager:** Faye Westrop
Summary of Content: Magazine covering music, fashion, beauty, arts and creative pursuits, sports, charities and local issues, events and going out.
Readership/Target Audience: Aimed at 18 to 35 year olds in Bristol and the surrounding area.
ADVERTISING RATES:
Full Page Mono £250.00
Full Page Colour £250.00
Average advertising content per issue: 30%
CONSUMER: RURAL & REGIONAL INTEREST: Regional Interest English Counties

SUMMIT   45932U75L-650
Editorial Address: 177-179 Burton Road, MANCHESTER, M20 2BB **Tel:** 0161 445 6111 **Fax:** 0161 445 4500
Email: summit@thebmc.co.uk
Advertising Address: The Maltings, West Street, BOURNE, PE10 9PH **Tel:** 01778 393313 **Fax:** 01778 392079
Email: emmahowl@warnersgroup.co.uk
Web site: http://www.thebmc.co.uk
Publisher: British Mountaineering Council
Date Established: 1996
Frequency: Quarterly
Cover Price: £3.50
Free to qualifying individuals
Circulation: 33,000 (Publisher's Statement)
Usual Pagination: 78
Editor: Alex Messenger
Summary of Content: Official magazine of the British Mountaineering Council covering climbing, hill walking, mountaineering and travel.
Readership/Target Audience: Aimed at members of the BMC and all those interested in climbing and mountaineering.
ADVERTISING RATES:
Full Page Mono £1050.00
Full Page Colour £1600.00
SCC £34.00
Agency Commission: 10%
Mechanical Data: Col Length: 273mm, Type Area: 273 x 190mm, Trim Size: 297 x 210mm, Page Width: 190mm, Bleed Size: 303 x 216mm, Film: Digital
Copy instructions: Copy Date: 4 weeks prior to publication date
Average advertising content per issue: 30%
CONSUMER: SPORT: Outdoor

SUMMIT   1779440U89B-348
Editorial Address: The Pall Mall Deposit, 124-128 Barlby Road, LONDON, W10 6BL **Tel:** 020 8962 3020
Fax: 020 8962 8689
Email: editorial@thinkpublishing.co.uk
Advertising Address: As above.
Email: adam@thinkpublishing.co.uk
Web site: http://www.thinkpublishing.co.uk
Publisher: Think Publishing Ltd
Date Established: 2006
Frequency: Half-yearly - Published in March and October
Cover Price: Free
Circulation: 55,000 (Publisher's Statement)
Usual Pagination: 98
Editor: Sarah Notton
Summary of Content: Luxury magazine covering travel, entertainment and culture.
Readership/Target Audience: Aimed at high end business travellers through Summit Hotels worldwide.
ADVERTISING RATES:
Full Page Colour $12000.00
Agency Commission: 10%
Mechanical Data: Bleed Size: 303 x 238mm, Trim Size: 297 x 232mm
Average advertising content per issue: 40%
CONSUMER: HOLIDAYS & TRAVEL: Hotel Magazines

THE SUNDAY TIMES TRAVEL MAGAZINE   1605109U89A-704
Editorial Address: Level 4, 1 Pennington Street, LONDON, E98 1ST **Tel:** 020 7782 7200
Email: travelmag@sundaytimes.co.uk
Advertising Address: As above. **Tel:** 020 7198 3000
Fax: 020 7198 3232
Email: dinah.williams@newsmagazines.co.uk
Web site: http://www.timesonline.co.uk/tol/travel/magazine/article1305929.ece
Publisher: News International Ltd
Date Established: 2003
Frequency: Monthly
Cover Price: £3.50
Circulation: 67,461 (ABC 01/01/2009 to 30/06/2009)
Usual Pagination: 180
Editor: Ed Grenby; **Features Editor:** Katie Bowman
Summary of Content: Travel lifestyle magazine looking at all aspects of holiday and foreign travel, including fashion, sport, motoring, food and drink. Also looking at travel industry news.
Readership/Target Audience: Aimed at holiday-makers.
ADVERTISING RATES:
Full Page Colour £6950.00
SCC £45.00
Agency Commission: 10%
Mechanical Data: Type Area: 280 x 200mm, Bleed Size: 306 x 226mm, Trim Size: 300 x 220mm, Col Length: 280mm, Page Width: 200mm, Film: Digital
Copy instructions: Copy Date: 4 weeks prior to publication date
Average advertising content per issue: 30%
CONSUMER: HOLIDAYS & TRAVEL: Travel

SUNRISE   707915U80C-3723
Formerly: Sunderland City News
Editorial Address: Chief Executives Directorate, Sunderland City Council, Civic Centre, SUNDERLAND, SR2 7DN **Tel:** 0191 561 1181 **Fax:** 0191 561 1138
Email: louise.darby@sunderland.gov.uk
Advertising Address: As above. **Fax:** 0191 553 1138
Email: louise.darby@sunderland.gov.uk
Date Established: 1997
Frequency: 5 issues yearly
Cover Price: Free
Circulation: 125,000 (Publisher's Statement)
Usual Pagination: 24
Editor: Louise Darby; **Advertising Manager:** Louise Darby
Summary of Content: Council magazine covering issues and services concerning residents of the City of Sunderland.
Readership/Target Audience: Aimed at residents in the city of Sunderland.
ADVERTISING: Rates on application
CONSUMER: RURAL & REGIONAL INTEREST: Regional Interest English Counties

SUNSEEKER   1843180U74Q-1366
Editorial Address: New Barn, Fanhams Grange, Fanhams Hall Road, WARE, SG12 7QA **Tel:** 01920 467492
Fax: 01920 460149
Advertising Address: As above.
Email: tracey@fms.co.uk
Web site: http://www.fmspublishing.co.uk
Publisher: FMS Publishing
Frequency: Quarterly
Cover Price: Free
Circulation: 40,000 (Publisher's Statement)
Usual Pagination: 110
Editor: Irene Mateides
Summary of Content: Luxury lifestyle magazine covering travel, motoring, fashion, watches, jewellery, gastronomy and sport.
Readership/Target Audience: Aimed at owners of Sunseeker yachts.
ADVERTISING RATES:
Full Page Colour £6950.00
Agency Commission: 10%
Mechanical Data: Trim Size: 327 x 239mm
Average advertising content per issue: 30%
CONSUMER: WOMEN'S INTEREST CONSUMER MAGAZINES: Lifestyle

SUNSHINE MAGAZINE HILLINGDON   1665820U74D-594
Editorial Address: PO Box 800, UXBRIDGE, UB8 2YY **Tel:** 01895 812594
Email: cathy@sunshinemagazine.org.uk
Advertising Address: As above.
Email: cathy@sunshinemagazine.org.uk
Web site: http://www.sunshinemagazine.org.uk
Publisher: Sunshine Publishing
Date Established: 2002
Frequency: 3 issues yearly - Published in February, June and October
Cover Price: Free

Circulation: 17,000 (Publisher's Statement)
Usual Pagination: 52
Editor: Cathy Ranson; **Advertising Manager:** Cathy Ranson
Summary of Content: Magazine covering parenting, education, health, fun, out and about, local information and advice to make family life more enjoyable and a little bit easier.
Readership/Target Audience: Aimed at parents and carers of children aged 0 to 11 years old.
ADVERTISING RATES:
Full Page Colour £660.00
Mechanical Data: Type Area: 246 x 190mm, Col Length: 246mm, Page Width: 190mm, Film: Digital, Print Process: Offset litho
Copy instructions: Copy Date: 4 weeks prior to publication date
Average advertising content per issue: 40%
CONSUMER: WOMEN'S INTEREST CONSUMER MAGAZINES: Child Care

THE SUPER SUPER   1706836U74Q-1297
Editorial Address: 2nd Floor, 182 Commercial Road, LONDON, E1 2JY **Tel:** 020 3002 7923
Email: info@thesupersuper.com
Advertising Address: As above. **Tel:** 020 3004 9770
Email: luc@thesupersuper.com
Web site: http://www.thesupersuper.com
Publisher: Super Super Media Ltd
Date Established: 2006
Frequency: 6 issues yearly
Circulation: 62,000 (Publisher's Statement)
Editor: Emma Davies; **Advertising Manager:** Luc Le Corre
Summary of Content: Magazine covering style, fashion and music.
Readership/Target Audience: Aimed at men and women aged between 15 and 30 years old.
ADVERTISING RATES:
Full Page Mono £3500.00
Full Page Colour £3500.00
Agency Commission: 15%
Mechanical Data: Type Area: 340x 245mm, Col Length: 340mm, Page Width: 245mm, Film: Digital
Average advertising content per issue: 15%
CONSUMER: WOMEN'S INTEREST CONSUMER MAGAZINES: Lifestyle

SUPER YACHT WORLD   1841120U91A-303
Editorial Address: Blue Fin Building, 110 Southwark Street, LONDON, SE1 0SU **Tel:** 020 3148 5000
Email: syw@ipcmedia.com
Advertising Address: As above. **Fax:** 020 3148 8523
Email: syw@ipcmedia.com
Web site: http://www.superyachtworld.com
Publisher: IPC Inspire
Date Established: 2008
Frequency: 6 issues yearly
Cover Price: £5.00
Circulation: 22,000 (Publisher's Statement)
Editor: Hugo Andreae; **Editor-in-Chief:** Hugo Andreae
Summary of Content: Magazine covering super yachts over 30 metres, both sail and power, and the lifestyle that goes with yachting.
Readership/Target Audience: Aimed at owners and captains.
ADVERTISING RATES:
Full Page Colour £3525.00
Agency Commission: 10%
Mechanical Data: Type Area: 255 x 210mm, Col Length: 255mm, Page Width: 210mm, Trim Size: 285 x 240mm
CONSUMER: RECREATION & LEISURE: Boating & Yachting

SUPERBIKE   46377U77B-610
Editorial Address: Leon House, 233 High Street, CROYDON, CR9 1HZ **Tel:** 020 8726 8445
Fax: 020 8726 8499
Email: superbike_letters@ipcmedia.com
Advertising Address: As above. **Tel:** 020 3148 5000
Fax: 020 8726 8294
Email: susan_bann@ipcmedia.com
Web site: http://www.superbike.co.uk
ISSN: 0262-8456
Publisher: IPC Inspire
Date Established: 1974
Frequency: 13 issues yearly
Cover Price: £4.00
Circulation: 38,951 (ABC 01/01/2008 to 31/12/2008)
Usual Pagination: 132
Editor: Kenny Pryde; **Features Editor:** Simon Roots
Summary of Content: Magazine featuring tests, racing coverage and features on sports orientated motorcycling as well as Race reports and product features.
Language(s): Afrikaans; English; Hungarian; Italian; Polish
Readership/Target Audience: Aimed at owners of sports bikes between 15 and 55 years old as well as more general motorbike enthusiasts with a sense of humour.

ADVERTISING RATES:
Full Page Colour £3060.00
Agency Commission: 10%
Mechanical Data: Page Width: 190mm, Type Area: 266 x 190mm, Col Length: 266mm, Trim Size: 297 x 216mm, Bleed Size: 303 x 224mm, Film: Digital
Average advertising content per issue: 38%
CONSUMER: MOTORING & CYCLING: Motorcycling

SUPERMAN LEGENDS
1800450U91D-957

Editorial Address: Titan House, 144 Southwark Street, LONDON, SE1 0UP **Tel:** 020 7620 0200 **Fax:** 020 7620 0032
Email: ned.hartley@titanemail.com
Advertising Address: As above. **Fax:** 020 7803 1803
Email: james.willmott@titanemail.com
Web site: http://www.tots.titanmagazine.co.uk
Publisher: Titan Magazines
Date Established: 2007
Frequency: 13 issues yearly
Cover Price: £2.60
Circulation: 30,000 (Print Run)
Usual Pagination: 84
Editor: Ned Hartley; **Advertising Manager:** James Willmott
Summary of Content: Children's magazine with re-prints of DC Comics comic strips.
Readership/Target Audience: Aimed at boys and girls aged 8 to 12 years old.
ADVERTISING RATES:
Full Page Colour £1500.00
Agency Commission: 10%
Mechanical Data: Bleed Size: 264 x 176mm, Trim Size: 258 x 170mm, Film: Digital
Copy instructions: Copy Date: 6 weeks prior to publication date
CONSUMER: RECREATION & LEISURE: Children & Youth

SUPERMOTO MAGAZINE
1625972U77B-708

Editorial Address: PO Box 9845, LONDON, W13 9WP
Tel: 020 8840 4760 **Fax:** 020 8840 5066
Email: info@supermotomag.co.uk
Advertising Address: As above. **Tel:** 020 8840 6848
Fax: 020 8840 6848
Email: mel@trailbikemag.com
Web site: http://www.supermotomag.co.uk
Publisher: Extreme Publishing Ltd
Date Established: 2002
Frequency: Annual
Cover Price: £4.95
Usual Pagination: 120
Editor: James Barnicoat; **Advertising Manager:** Melanie Falconer; **Publisher:** Si Melber
Summary of Content: Magazine containing motorbike features, race information and race reviews.
Readership/Target Audience: Aimed at supermoto enthusiasts.
ADVERTISING RATES:
Full Page Mono £1800.00
Full Page Colour £1800.00
Agency Commission: 10%
Mechanical Data: Type Area: 280 x 215mm, Col Length: 280mm, Page Width: 215mm, Bleed Size: +3mm, Film: Digital
CONSUMER: MOTORING & CYCLING: Motorcycling

SUPERNATURAL MAGAZINE
1827911U76C-836

Editorial Address: Titan House, 144 Southwark Street, LONDON, SE1 0UP **Tel:** 020 7620 0200 **Fax:** 020 7620 0032
Email: supernaturalmag@titanemail.com
Advertising Address: As above. **Fax:** 020 7803 1803
Email: james.willmott@titanemail.com
Web site: http://www.titanmagazines.com
Publisher: Titan Magazines
Date Established: 2007
Frequency: 6 issues yearly
Cover Price: £3.75
Editor: Neil Edwards; **Advertising Manager:** James Willmott
Summary of Content: Magazine covering the TV programme Supernatural with cast interviews, behind the scenes stories, competitions and posters.
Readership/Target Audience: Aimed at fans of the TV programme.
ADVERTISING RATES:
Full Page Colour £2500.00
Mechanical Data: Trim Size: 276 x 200mm, Film: Digital
CONSUMER: MUSIC & PERFORMING ARTS: TV & Radio

SUPERSAIL WORLD
1837388U91A-301

Editorial Address: Blue Fin Building, 110 Southwark Street, LONDON, SE1 0SU **Tel:** 020 3148 5000
Email: david_glenn@ipcmedia.com
Advertising Address: As above.
Web site: http://www.yachtingworld.com
Publisher: IPC Inspire
Date Established: 2007

Frequency: Half-yearly - Published in June and October. See manin record for circulation figure
Editor: David Glenn
Summary of Content: Magazine dedicated to sailing boats over 24 metres with no upper size limit, covering super yacht regattas, new launches and designs yet to be built.
Readership/Target Audience: Aimed at owners, skippers and crews of the world's super-sailing yacht fleet.
Supplement to: Yachting World
CONSUMER: RECREATION & LEISURE: Boating & Yachting

SURF EUROPE
1687356U75M-996

Editorial Address: 1 West Smithfield, LONDON, EC1A 9JU
Tel: 020 7332 9700 **Fax:** 020 7332 9799
Email: paul@surfeuropemag.com
Advertising Address: As above.
Email: oliver.tappin@factorymedia.com
Web site: http://www.surfeuropemag.com
Publisher: Factory Media
Frequency: 8 issues yearly
Cover Price: £3.20
Circulation: 21,700 (Publisher's Statement)
Editor: Paul Evans; **Advertising Manager:** Oliver Tappin
Summary of Content: Magazine covering the surfing scene in Europe with news and interviews, product reviews and competitions.
Readership/Target Audience: Aimed at surfing enthusiasts throughout Europe.
ADVERTISING RATES:
Full Page Colour £4700.00
Agency Commission: 10%
Mechanical Data: Trim Size: 300 x 230mm, Bleed Size: 306 x 236mm, Film: Digital
CONSUMER: SPORT: Water Sports

SURF GIRL
1691567U75M-997

Editorial Address: Berry Road Studios, Berry Road, NEWQUAY, TR7 1AT **Tel:** 01637 878074 **Fax:** 01637 850226
Email: louise@orcasurf.co.uk
Advertising Address: As above.
Email: steve@carvemag.co.uk
Web site: http://www.surfgirlmag.com
Publisher: Orca Publications
Date Established: 2003
Frequency: 5 issues yearly
Cover Price: Free
Circulation: 36,000 (Publisher's Statement)
Usual Pagination: 92
Editor: Louise Searle; **Advertising Manager:** Steve England
Summary of Content: Magazine covering surfing profiles, fashion, health and beauty, techniques and advice.
Readership/Target Audience: Aimed at fit surfer girls who are into the sport and the lifestyle.
ADVERTISING RATES:
Full Page Colour £1680.00
Agency Commission: 10%
Mechanical Data: Bleed Size: +3mm, Trim Size: 265 x 205mm, Film: Digital
Average advertising content per issue: 35%
CONSUMER: SPORT: Water Sports

THE SURFER'S PATH
45956U75M-860

Editorial Address: 1 West Smithfield, LONDON, EC1A 9JU
Tel: 020 7332 9700 **Fax:** 020 7332 9799
Email: info@surferspath.com
Advertising Address: As above.
Email: oliver.tappin@factorymedia.com
Web site: http://www.surferspath.com
Publisher: Factory Media
Date Established: 1998
Frequency: 6 issues yearly
Cover Price: £4.50
Circulation: 30,000 (Publisher's Statement)
Usual Pagination: 132
Editor: Alex Dick-Read; **Managing Director:** Darryl Newton; **Publisher:** Darryl Newton
Summary of Content: Magazine covering travel, the art of surfing and environmental issues that relate to surfing, plus the latest information on the worldwide surf scene.
Readership/Target Audience: Aimed at surfers.
ADVERTISING RATES:
Full Page Mono £1895.00
Full Page Colour £2187.00
Agency Commission: 10%
Mechanical Data: Trim Size: 280 x 230mm, Bleed Size: 286 x 236mm, Film: Digital, Type Area: 274 x 224mm, Col Length: 274mm, Page Width: 224mm
Copy instructions: Copy Date: 4 weeks prior to publication date
Average advertising content per issue: 25%
CONSUMER: SPORT: Water Sports

SURMA
48349U90-170

Formerly: Surma Bangla Newsweekly
Editorial Address: Unit 10B Quaker Street, LONDON, E1 6SZ **Tel:** 020 7377 9787 **Fax:** 020 7377 9717
Email: info@surmanewsgroup.co.uk
Advertising Address: As above.
Email: info@surmanewsgroup.co.uk
Web site: http://www.surmanewsgroup.co.uk
Publisher: Surma News Group Ltd
Frequency: Weekly
Cover Price: £0.50
Annual Sub.: £40.00
Circulation: 15,500 (Publisher's Statement)
Usual Pagination: 68
Editor: Syed Mynsur; **Advertising Manager:** Sarz Ahmed
Summary of Content: Newspaper covering national and community news and cultural reviews.
Language(s): Bengali
Readership/Target Audience: Aimed at Bangla-speaking people.
ADVERTISING RATES:
Full Page Mono £3200.00
Full Page Colour £4000.00
SCC £18.00
Agency Commission: 10%
Mechanical Data: Type Area: 380 x 260mm, Col Length: 380mm, Page Width: 260mm, Film: Positive, right reading, emulsion side down. Digital, No. of Columns (Display): 6, Col Widths (Display): 40mm
Copy instructions: Copy Date: Wednesday 5pm prior to publication date
CONSUMER: ETHNIC

SURREY LIFE
46981U80C-3050

Formerly: Surrey County Magazine
Editorial Address: Holmesdale House, 46 Croydon Road, REIGATE, RH2 0NH **Tel:** 01737 240419
Email: editor@surreylife.co.uk
Advertising Address: As above. **Tel:** 01737 247188
Fax: 01737 246596
Email: sales@archant.co.uk
Web site: http://www.surreylife.com
Publisher: Archant Norfolk
Date Established: 1970
Frequency: Monthly
Cover Price: £2.95
Circulation: 15,000 (Publisher's Statement)
Usual Pagination: 188
Editor: Caroline Harrap; **Advertising Manager:** Rhiannon Wragg
Summary of Content: Magazine covering art, antiques, food & drink, eating out, farmers' markets, local produce, pubs, places to go, local history, the environment, fashion, interiors, health and beauty, gardening, property and what's on.
Readership/Target Audience: Aimed at residents of Surrey.
ADVERTISING RATES:
Full Page Colour £1800.00
Agency Commission: 10%
Mechanical Data: Col Length: 271mm, Trim Size: 300 x 220mm, Bleed Size: 306 x 226mm, Type Area: 271 x 199mm, Page Width: 199mm, Film: Digital
Copy instructions: Copy Date: 4 weeks prior to publication date
Average advertising content per issue: 50%
CONSUMER: RURAL & REGIONAL INTEREST: Regional Interest English Counties

SURREY NATURE
47085U81A-150

Formerly: Surrey Nature Line
Editorial Address: 14 Clarice Way, WALLINGTON, SM6 9LD **Tel:** 020 8669 0686 **Fax:** 020 8669 3678
Email: surreynature@woodcote-communications.co.uk
Advertising Address: Space Marketing, 10 Clayfield Mews, Newcomen Road, TUNBRIDGE WELLS, TN4 9PA
Tel: 01892 677740 **Fax:** 01892 677743
Email: sales@spacemarketing.co.uk
Web site: http://www.surreywildlifetrust.co.uk
Publisher: Surrey Wildlife Trust
Date Established: 1959
Frequency: 3 issues yearly - Published in April/March, July, October
Cover Price: Free
Circulation: 11,000 (Publisher's Statement)
Usual Pagination: 28
Editor: Lindy Margach
Summary of Content: Magazine produced by Surrey Wildlife Trust. Contains news, articles and information about Trust activities and the activities of kindred organisations in Surrey, management and general information about Surrey Wildlife Trust reserves, details of conservation work and general environmental and wildlife issues.
Readership/Target Audience: Aimed at Trust members and all who love and respect Surrey's countryside.
ADVERTISING RATES:
Full Page Mono £590.00
Full Page Colour £650.00

Consumer Magazines

Agency Commission: 10%
Mechanical Data: Film: Digital, Print Process: Sheet-fed offset litho, Type Area: 260 x 186mm, Col Length: 260mm, Page Width: 186mm
Copy instructions: Copy Date: 42 days prior to publication date
CONSUMER: ANIMALS & PETS: Animals & Pets Protection

SURREY OCCASIONS
46982U80C-3060

Editorial Address: Hillrising House, 115 Potters Lane, Send, WOKING, GU23 7AW Tel: 01483 750692 Fax: 01483 750692
Advertising Address: As above.
Email: surreyoccasions@btconnect.com
Publisher: Lamont Publications
Date Established: 1986
Frequency: 10 issues yearly
Cover Price: £3.00
Circulation: 20,000 (Publisher's Statement)
Usual Pagination: 56
Editor: Martin Gates; Advertising Manager: Mary Conisbee; Publisher: Mary Conisbee
Summary of Content: Lifestyle magazine containing local news and leisure features.
Readership/Target Audience: Aimed at those with a disposable income aged 30 to 60 years old.
ADVERTISING RATES:
Full Page Colour £1050.00
Agency Commission: 10%
Mechanical Data: Page Width: 190mm, Trim Size: 297 x 210mm, Type Area: 270 x 190mm, Bleed Size: 303 x 216mm, Col Length: 270mm, Film: Digital
Copy instructions: Copy Date: 4 weeks prior to publication date
Average advertising content per issue: 40%
CONSUMER: RURAL & REGIONAL INTEREST: Regional Interest English Counties

SURVIVAL
47280U82-183

Editorial Address: 4 Park Square, Milton Park, ABINGDON, OX14 4RN Tel: 020 7017 6000 Fax: 020 7017 6336
Web site: http://www.tandf.co.uk/journals
ISSN: 0039-6338
Publisher: Routledge, Taylor & Francis
Date Established: 1959
Frequency: 6 issues yearly
Annual Sub.: £279.00
Circulation: 4,250 (Publisher's Statement)
Usual Pagination: 240
Editor: Dana H. Allin; Publisher: Richard Delahunty
Summary of Content: Journal of the International Institute of Strategic Studies. Covers book reviews, articles and original documents, providing a forum for both policy debate and academic discussion.
Readership/Target Audience: Aimed at the IISS membership and subscribers from both the academic and professional sphere.
ADVERTISING: Rates on application
CONSUMER: CURRENT AFFAIRS & POLITICS

SUSSEX LIFE
46991U80C-3250

Editorial Address: 28 Teville Road, WORTHING, BN11 1UG Tel: 01903 703730 Fax: 01903 703770
Email: jonathan.keeble@archant.co.uk
Advertising Address: As above.
Email: sales@sussexlife.co.uk
Web site: http://www.sussexlife.co.uk
Publisher: Archant Life
Frequency: Monthly
Cover Price: £3.20
Circulation: 18,000 (Publisher's Statement)
Usual Pagination: 240
Editor: Jonathan Keeble
Summary of Content: Magazine containing features on property, fashion, books, food, antiques, gardening, interiors, wildlife, environment, health and beauty, finance and the arts.
Readership/Target Audience: Aimed at affluent residents of East and West Sussex.
ADVERTISING RATES:
Full Page Colour £2118.00
Agency Commission: 10%
Mechanical Data: Type Area: 271 x 199mm, Col Length: 271mm, Bleed Size: 306 x 226mm, Trim Size: 300 x 220mm, Page Width: 199mm, Film: Digital
Copy instructions: Copy Date: 6th of the month prior to publication date
CONSUMER: RURAL & REGIONAL INTEREST: Regional Interest English Counties

SWEET MAGAZINE
1834260U74G-291

Editorial Address: 3 East Avenue, BOURNEMOUTH, BH3 7BW Tel: 01789 842305
Email: editor@sweetmagazine.org
Advertising Address: PO Box 6337, BOURNEMOUTH, BH1 9EH Tel: 01202 586848

Email: felicity@selectps.com
Web site: http://www.sweetmagazine.org
Publisher: Select Publisher Services
Date Established: 2008
Frequency: 7 issues yearly
Cover Price: £2.95
Circulation: 80,000 (Print Run)
Editor: Sarah Moran
Summary of Content: Magazine containing everyday fitness, weight management help, health and psychology issues.
Readership/Target Audience: Aimed at men and women of all ages who have diabetes or are at risk of diabetes.
ADVERTISING RATES:
Full Page Colour £2400.00
Mechanical Data: Trim Size: 280 x 210mm, Film: Digital
Copy instructions: Copy Date: 3 weeks prior to publication date
CONSUMER: WOMEN'S INTEREST CONSUMER MAGAZINES: Slimming & Health

SWIMMING TIMES MAGAZINE
45958U75M-900

Formerly: Swimming Magazine
Editorial Address: 41 Granby Street, LOUGHBOROUGH, LE11 3DU Tel: 01509 632230 Fax: 01509 632233
Email: swimmingtimes@swimming.org
Advertising Address: As above. Tel: 01509 632231
Email: advertising@swimming.org
Web site: http://www.britishswimming.org
ISSN: 1750-581X
Publisher: Swimming Times Ltd
Frequency: Monthly - Published 3rd week of the month prior to cover date
Cover Price: £2.50
Annual Sub.: £22.00
Circulation: 18,000 (Publisher's Statement)
Usual Pagination: 64
Editor: Peter Hassall
Summary of Content: Official journal of the Amateur Swimming Association and the Institute of Swimming Teachers and Coaches. Includes articles on coaching, teaching and events.
Readership/Target Audience: Aimed at swimming clubs, professional coaches, local authorities and those involved in the administrative side of the sport.
ADVERTISING RATES:
Full Page Mono £664.00
Full Page Colour £778.00
Agency Commission: 10%
Mechanical Data: Type Area: 268 x 186mm, Trim Size: 297 x 210mm, Col Length: 268mm, Film: Digital, Page Width: 186mm
CONSUMER: SPORT: Water Sports

SWINDON LINK MAGAZINE
47003U80C-3547

Formerly: The Link (Swindon)
Editorial Address: 71 Basepoint, Rivermead Drive, Westlea, SWINDON, SN5 7EX Tel: 01793 608840
Email: publisher@swindonlink.com
Advertising Address: As above.
Email: publisher@swindonlink.com
Web site: http://www.swindonlink.com
Publisher: Swindon Publications Ltd
Date Established: 1979
Frequency: Monthly
Cover Price: Free
Circulation: 27,000 (Publisher's Statement)
Usual Pagination: 48
Editor: Roger Ogle; Advertising Manager: Nicola Norridge; Publisher: Roger Ogle
Summary of Content: Publication covering local news, events, views and information.
Readership/Target Audience: Aimed at residents in the areas of North and West Swindon.
ADVERTISING RATES:
Full Page Mono £750.00
Full Page Colour £878.00
Agency Commission: 10%
Mechanical Data: Type Area: 276 x 190mm, Trim Size: 297 x 210mm, Col Length: 276mm, Page Width: 190mm, Print Process: Web-fed offset litho
Copy instructions: Copy Date: 4th of the month prior to publication date
Average advertising content per issue: 60%
CONSUMER: RURAL & REGIONAL INTEREST: Regional Interest English Counties

SWING
1742498U75D-554

Editorial Address: Victory House, 14 Leicester Place, Leicester Square, LONDON, WC2H 7BZ Tel: 020 7306 0304
Fax: 020 7306 0314
Email: eburgass@riverltd.co.uk
Advertising Address: As above.
Email: eburgass@riverltd.co.uk
Web site: http://www.riverltd.co.uk
Publisher: River Publishing Ltd

Date Established: 2006
Frequency: 6 issues yearly
Cover Price: £2.50
Circulation: 50,000 (Publisher's Statement)
Usual Pagination: 132
Editor: Ed Burgass
Summary of Content: Magazine covering golf equipment, tuition, golf travel, star profiles and player tips.
Readership/Target Audience: Aimed at customers of the golf shops American Golf.
ADVERTISING: Rates on application
CONSUMER: SPORT: Golf

THE SWORD
46026U75X-960

Editorial Address: Pyndar Lodge, Hanley Swan, WORCESTER, WR8 0DN Tel: 01684 311197
Fax: 01684 311250
Email: malcolm.fare@crossword.demon.co.uk
Advertising Address: Baron's Gate, 33 Rothschild Road, LONDON, W4 5HT Tel: 020 8742 3032 Fax: 020 8742 3033
Email: nosheen.khan@britishfencing.co.uk
Publisher: British Fencing Association
Date Established: 1948
Frequency: Quarterly
Free to qualifying individuals
Annual Sub.: £20.00
Circulation: 8,000 (Publisher's Statement)
Editor: Malcolm Fare; Advertising Manager: Nosheen Khan
Summary of Content: Magazine containing news and features about fencing at home and abroad.
Readership/Target Audience: Aimed at fencing enthusiasts at all levels.
ADVERTISING RATES:
Full Page Colour £400.00
Mechanical Data: Bleed Size: +3mm, Trim Size: 297 x 210mm, Film: Digital
Copy instructions: Copy Date: 6 weeks prior to publication date
Average advertising content per issue: 50%
CONSUMER: SPORT: Other Sport

SWORD
47744U87-192

Formerly: Prophecy Today
Editorial Address: Workspace House, 28-29 Maxwell Road, PETERBOROUGH, PE2 7JE Tel: 01733 239090
Fax: 01733 239090
Email: editorial@swordpdp.com
Web site: http://www.swordpdp.com
ISSN: 1752-1653
Publisher: Present Day Publishing Limited
Date Established: 1985
Frequency: 6 issues yearly
Cover Price: £3.50
Annual Sub.: £20.00
Circulation: 8,000 (Publisher's Statement)
Usual Pagination: 40
Editor: David Andrew
Summary of Content: Magazine offering a Christian perspective on current world events.
Readership/Target Audience: Aimed at Christian believers.
ADVERTISING: No Advertising taken
CONSUMER: RELIGIOUS

T3 THE GADGET MAGAZINE
46516U78A-500

Formerly: T3 The World's Number One Gadget Magazine
Editorial Address: 2 Balcombe Street, LONDON, NW1 6NW Tel: 020 7042 4000
Email: t3@futurenet.co.uk
Advertising Address: As above. Fax: 020 7042 4471
Email: stephen.mckeon@futurenet.co.uk
Web site: http://www.t3.co.uk
Publisher: Future Publishing Limited
Date Established: 1997
Frequency: 13 issues yearly
Cover Price: £3.99
Annual Sub.: £35.96
Circulation: 60,127 (ABC 01/01/2008 to 31/12/2008)
Usual Pagination: 168
Editor: Michael Brook; News Editor: Joe Svetlik;
Advertising Manager: Stephen McKeon; Publisher: Nial Ferguson
Summary of Content: Magazine containing news, reviews and features on all aspects of consumer-orientated technology and electronics. Includes articles on cameras, camcorders, cars, computers, hi-fi and home cinema equipment, electronic gadgets, mobile phones, motorbikes and PDAs.
Readership/Target Audience: Aimed at 25 to 45 year old males with an interest in technology and consumer electronics.
ADVERTISING RATES:
Full Page Colour £4400.00
Agency Commission: 10%
Mechanical Data: Col Length: 280mm, Bleed Size: 306 x 228mm, Trim Size: 300 x 222mm, Type Area: 280 x 203mm, Page Width: 203mm, Film: Digital

Average advertising content per issue: 40%
CONSUMER: CONSUMER ELECTRONICS: Hi-Fi & Recording

TA NEA
1665813U90-183

Editorial Address: 167c Stroud Green Road, LONDON, N4 3PZ **Tel:** 020 7272 9702 **Fax:** 020 7272 9704
Email: ta.nea@btconnect.com
Advertising Address: As above.
Email: ta.nea@btconnect.com
Publisher: Teamprint Ltd
Frequency: 26 issues yearly
Cover Price: £0.40
Circulation: 8,500 (Publisher's Statement)
Usual Pagination: 24
Editor: Louis Vrakas; **Advertising Manager:** Louis Vrakas
Summary of Content: Newspaper with general interest articles and news stories.
Language(s): English; Greek
Readership/Target Audience: Read by London's Greek community.
ADVERTISING: Rates on application
CONSUMER: ETHNIC

TABLE TENNIS ILLUSTRATED
1665813U75H-914

Editorial Address: 11 Limes Paddock, Dorrington, SHREWSBURY, SY5 7LF **Tel:** 01743 718739
Fax: 01743 719120
Email: imarshall@ittf.com
Advertising Address: 2211 Riverside Drive, Suite 405, Ottawa, ON, K1S 7X5 **Tel:** 613 733 2987 **Fax:** 613 733 4603
Email: cv@tmsin.com
Web site: http://www.ittf.com
Publisher: ITTF
Date Established: 1996
Frequency: Quarterly
Cover Price: $6.00
Circulation: 15,000 (Publisher's Statement)
Usual Pagination: 64
Editor: Ian Marshall; **Advertising Manager:** Christian Veronese
Summary of Content: Magazine covering events, fixtures, player profiles, technical help and product reviews.
Readership/Target Audience: Aimed at anyone interested in table tennis particularly members of the ITTF.
ADVERTISING RATES:
Full Page Colour $765.00
Mechanical Data: Type Area: 277 x 190mm, Col Length: 277mm, Page Width: 190mm, Trim Size: 297 x 210mm, Bleed Size: 303 x 216mm, Film: Digital
CONSUMER: SPORT: Racquet Sports

TABLE TENNIS NEWS
45889U75H-850

Editorial Address: Queensbury House, 3rd Floor, Havelock Road, HASTINGS, TN34 1HF **Tel:** 01424 456217
Email: richard.pettit@etta.co.uk
Advertising Address: As above. **Tel:** 01424 722525
Fax: 01424 422103
Email: richard.pettit@etta.co.uk
Web site: http://www.etta.co.uk
Publisher: ETTA The English Table Tennis Association Ltd
Date Established: 1966
Frequency: 8 issues yearly
Cover Price: £2.95
Annual Sub.: £21.00
Circulation: 1,500 (Publisher's Statement)
Usual Pagination: 48
Editor: Richard Pettit
Summary of Content: Magazine of The English Table Tennis Association.
Readership/Target Audience: Aimed at table tennis players, administrators and umpires.
ADVERTISING RATES:
Full Page Mono £300.00
Full Page Colour £400.00
Agency Commission: 15%
Mechanical Data: Film: Digital, Type Area: 275 x 190mm, Col Length: 275mm, Trim Size: 297 x 210mm, Bleed Size: 303 x 216mm, Page Width: 190mm
CONSUMER: SPORT: Racquet Sports

THE TABLET
47758U87-214

Editorial Address: 1 King Street Cloisters, Clifton Walk, LONDON, W6 0GY **Tel:** 020 8748 8484 **Fax:** 020 8748 1550
Email: thetablet@thetablet.co.uk
Advertising Address: As above. **Fax:** 020 8563 7644
Email: advertising@thetablet.co.uk
Web site: http://www.thetablet.co.uk
ISSN: 0039-8837
Publisher: Tablet Publishing Co. Ltd.
Date Established: 1842
Frequency: Weekly
Cover Price: £2.40

Circulation: 22,402 (ABC 01/01/2009 to 30/06/2009)
Usual Pagination: 44
Editor: Elena Curti; **Advertising Manager:** John Burnyeat
Summary of Content: Catholic publication covering religion, politics, society, ethical issues, books and the arts. Also includes news concerning the work of the church at home and abroad.
Readership/Target Audience: Aimed at Catholics and the wider church.
ADVERTISING RATES:
Full Page Mono £890.00
Full Page Colour £1090.00
SCC £17.00
Agency Commission: 15%
Mechanical Data: Col Length: 264mm, Bleed Size: 303 x 216mm, No. of Columns (Display): 3, Col Widths (Display): 59mm, Type Area: 264 x 185mm, Film: Digital, Page Width: 185mm, Trim Size: 297 x 210mm
Copy instructions: Copy Date: 9 days prior to publication date
Average advertising content per issue: 25%
CONSUMER: RELIGIOUS

TAEKWONDO & KOREAN MARTIAL ARTS MAGAZINE
45992U75Q-750

Editorial Address: Unit 20, Maybrook Business Park, Maybrook Road, Sutton Coldfield, BIRMINGHAM, B76 1BE
Tel: 0121 351 6930 **Fax:** 0121 356 7300
Email: combat.magazine@btclick.com
Advertising Address: As above. **Tel:** 0121 344 3737
Email: combat.magazine@btclick.com
Web site: http://www.taekwondomag.co.uk
Publisher: Martial Arts Publications Ltd
Date Established: 1996
Frequency: Monthly
Cover Price: £3.50
Annual Sub.: £38.95
Circulation: 80,000 (Publisher's Statement)
Usual Pagination: 100
Editor: Paul Clifton; **Managing Director:** Paul Clifton;
Advertising Manager: Paul Clifton; **Publisher:** Paul Clifton
Summary of Content: Magazine covering all aspects of Korean martial arts, including articles on techniques, advice, profiles, interviews, events, schools and associations.
Readership/Target Audience: Read by instructors and enthusiasts of Taekwondo and Korean martial arts in general.
ADVERTISING RATES:
Full Page Colour £587.50
Agency Commission: 10%
Mechanical Data: Type Area: 240 x 205mm, Print Process: Web-fed offset litho, Page Width: 205mm, Col Length: 240mm, Film: Digital
Copy instructions: Copy Date: 2nd Thursday of 2 months prior to publication date
Average advertising content per issue: 38%
CONSUMER: SPORT: Combat Sports

TAKE A BREAK
45200U74A-560

Editorial Address: Academic House, 24-28 Oval Road, LONDON, NW1 7DT **Tel:** 020 7241 8000 **Fax:** 020 7241 8052
Email: tab.features@bauer.co.uk
Advertising Address: As above. **Fax:** 020 7075 0786
Email: sales@tpc.bauer.co.uk
Web site: http://www.takeabreak.co.uk
Publisher: H. Bauer Publishing
Date Established: 1990
Frequency: Weekly
Cover Price: £0.76
Circulation: 920,060 (ABC 01/01/2009 to 30/06/2009)
Usual Pagination: 70
Editor: Julia Sidwell; **Advertising Manager:** Harriet Edery
Summary of Content: General features magazine covering cookery, beauty, fashion, travel and competitions.
Twitter: http://twitter.com/takeabreakmag.
Readership/Target Audience: Aimed mainly at women.
ADVERTISING RATES:
Full Page Colour £22920.00
Agency Commission: 15%
Mechanical Data: Type Area: 266 x 207mm, Col Length: 266mm, Page Width: 207mm, Trim Size: 290 x 230mm, Bleed Size: 298 x 238mm, Film: Digital
Copy instructions: Copy Date: 2 weeks prior to publication date
Average advertising content per issue: 20%
CONSUMER: WOMEN'S INTEREST CONSUMER MAGAZINES: Women's Interest

TAKE A BREAK SPECIALS
1745731U74A-1013

Editorial Address: Academic House, 24-28 Oval Road, LONDON, NW1 7DT **Tel:** 020 7241 8000
Email: tab.specials@bauer.co.uk
Advertising Address: Publishing Consultancy, 8 Upper St. Martin's Lane, LONDON, WC2H 9DW **Tel:** 020 7759 8967
Fax: 020 7240 9040
Email: harriete@tpc-london.com
Publisher: H. Bauer Publishing

Frequency: 8 issues yearly
Cover Price: £1.65
Editor: Margaret Nicholls; **Advertising Manager:** Harriet Edery
Summary of Content: A series of seasonal specials with true life features for the season.
Readership/Target Audience: Aimed at women of all ages.
ADVERTISING RATES:
Full Page Colour £22920.00
Agency Commission: 15%
Average advertising content per issue: 5%
CONSUMER: WOMEN'S INTEREST CONSUMER MAGAZINES: Women's Interest

TALIESIN
47553U84B-175

Editorial Address: 3ydd Llawr, Ty Mount Stuart, Sgwar Mount Stuart, CARDIFF, CF10 5FQ **Tel:** 029 2047 2266
Fax: 029 2049 2930
Email: manonrhys@aol.com
Advertising Address: As above. **Fax:** 029 2047 0691
Email: post@academi.org
Web site: http://www.academi.org
ISSN: 0049-2884
Publisher: Yr Academi Gymreig
Date Established: 1959
Frequency: 3 issues yearly - Published in March, July and December
Cover Price: £4.00
Annual Sub.: £11.00
Circulation: 1,000 (Publisher's Statement)
Usual Pagination: 176
Editor: Manon Rhys; **Advertising Manager:** Petra Bennett; **Publisher:** Peter Finch
Summary of Content: Academic literary magazine containing poetry, short stories and literary criticism.
Language(s): Welsh
Readership/Target Audience: Read by people in Wales interested in literature.
ADVERTISING RATES:
Full Page Mono £80.00
Copy instructions: Copy Date: 2 months prior to publication date
Average advertising content per issue: 5%
CONSUMER: THE ARTS & LITERARY: Literary

TALKING SENSE
48654U94F-850

Editorial Address: 101 Pentonville Road, LONDON, N1 9LG
Tel: 084 5127 0060 **Fax:** 084 5127 0061
Email: colin.anderson@sense.org.uk
Web site: http://www.sense.org.uk
ISSN: 1367-4064
Publisher: Sense, National Deafblind & Rubella Association
Date Established: 1955
Frequency: 3 issues yearly - April, August and December Free to qualifying individuals
Annual Sub.: £15.00
Circulation: 5,000 (Publisher's Statement)
Usual Pagination: 48
Editor: Colin Anderson
Summary of Content: Magazine of Sense featuring experiences, expertise and information around issues facing deafblind and multiple disabled children and adults.
Readership/Target Audience: Read by families and professionals.
ADVERTISING: No Advertising taken
CONSUMER: OTHER CLASSIFICATIONS: Disability

TALYLLYN NEWS
46724U79J-250

Editorial Address: Talyllyn Railway, Wharf Station, TYWYN, LL36 9EY **Tel:** 01654 710472 **Fax:** 01654 711755
Email: editor@talyllyn.co.uk
Web site: http://www.talyllyn.co.uk
ISSN: 0300-3272
Publisher: Talyllyn Railway Preservation Society
Date Established: 1953
Frequency: Quarterly
Cover Price: £3.00
Free to qualifying individuals
Annual Sub.: £25.00
Circulation: 2,300 (Publisher's Statement)
Usual Pagination: 56
Editor: Nicholas Newble
Summary of Content: Publication containing news of the Talyllyn Railway and Talyllyn Railway Preservation Society. Includes features on the history of the railway and experiences of volunteer members working on the line.
Readership/Target Audience: Aimed at all TRPS members.
ADVERTISING: No Advertising taken
CONSUMER: HOBBIES & DIY: Rail Enthusiasts

TAMIYA MODEL MAGAZINE INTERNATIONAL
28968U79B-187

Editorial Address: Doolittle Mill, Doolittle Lane, Totternhoe, DUNSTABLE, LU6 1QX **Tel:** 01525 222573
Fax: 01525 222574
Email: editor@tamiyamodelmagazine.com
Advertising Address: As above.
Web site: http://www.tamiyamodelmagazine.com
Publisher: ADH Publishing
Date Established: 1985
Frequency: Monthly
Cover Price: £3.95
Free to qualifying individuals
Circulation: 30,000 (Publisher's Statement)
Usual Pagination: 68
Editor: Marcus Nicholls; **Publisher:** Alan Harman
Summary of Content: Magazine containing general information on model building and kit reviews, new modelling related books, products and events.
Readership/Target Audience: Read by model kit enthusiasts.
ADVERTISING RATES:
Full Page Colour £950.00
Agency Commission: 10%
Mechanical Data: Type Area: 270 x 190mm, Bleed Size: 303 x 216mm, Trim Size: 297 x 210mm, Col Length: 270mm, Page Width: 190mm, Film: Digital
Copy instructions: Copy Date: 6 weeks prior to publication date
CONSUMER: HOBBIES & DIY: Models & Modelling

TANK
712293U74Q-935_75

Editorial Address: Princess House, 50-60 Eastcastle Street, LONDON, W1W 8EA **Tel:** 020 7323 3475
Fax: 020 7631 4280
Email: mail@tankmagazine.com
Advertising Address: As above. **Fax:** 020 7434 9232
Email: ian@thorleymedia.com
Web site: http://www.tankmagazine.com
ISSN: 1464-3472
Publisher: Tank Publications Ltd
Date Established: 1998
Frequency: Quarterly
Cover Price: £5.00
Annual Sub.: £30.00
Circulation: 60,000 (Publisher's Statement)
Usual Pagination: 208
Editor: Masoud Golsorkhi; **Editor-in-Chief:** Masoud Golsorkhi; **Advertising Director:** Victoria Greaves
Summary of Content: Magazine containing fashion and photography features, art, architecture and short stories.
Readership/Target Audience: Aimed at design orientated professional men and women between 18 and 40 years old.
ADVERTISING RATES:
Full Page Colour £5250.00
Mechanical Data: Trim Size: 310 x 248mm, Bleed Size: 316 x 254mm, Print Process: Sheet-fed offset litho
CONSUMER: WOMEN'S INTEREST CONSUMER MAGAZINES: Lifestyle

TASTE
630132U89A-468

Editorial Address: 4 Kemp House, Sewardstone Road, LONDON, E2 9JL **Tel:** 020 8980 8635
Email: tim@tastemagazine.co.uk
Advertising Address: As above.
Email: tim@tastemagazine.co.uk
Publisher: Create UK
Date Established: 2001
Frequency: Quarterly
Cover Price: £4.95
Free to qualifying individuals
Circulation: 220,000 (Publisher's Statement)
Usual Pagination: 136
Editor: Tim Hirschmann; **Advertising Manager:** Tim Hirschmann
Summary of Content: Magazine covering UK and worldwide travel with reviews on restaurants, bars, wine, eating out and eating in, recipes and hotels.
Readership/Target Audience: Aimed at those aged between 25 and 50 years old with a high disposable income.
ADVERTISING RATES:
Full Page Colour £3000.00
CONSUMER: HOLIDAYS & TRAVEL: Travel

TASTE ITALIA
1789333U74P-949

Editorial Address: Suite 6, Piccadilly House, London Road, BATH, BA1 6PL **Tel:** 01225 489984 **Fax:** 01225 489980
Email: simon.lewis@anthem-publishing.com
Advertising Address: As above.
Email: leah.fitz-henry@anthem-publishing.com
Web site: http://www.tasteitaliamag.com
Publisher: Anthem Publishing Ltd
Date Established: 2006
Frequency: Monthly
Cover Price: £3.50

Circulation: 45,000 (Print Run)
Usual Pagination: 116
Editor: Becky Ambury
Summary of Content: Magazine covering Italian food and drink profiling Italian recipes, restaurant reviews and interviews with chefs.
Readership/Target Audience: Aimed at lovers of Italian food.
ADVERTISING RATES:
Full Page Colour £1150.00
Agency Commission: 10%
CONSUMER: WOMEN'S INTEREST CONSUMER MAGAZINES: Food & Cookery

TASTE SHROPSHIRE & THE MARCHES
1793369U74P-953

Formerly: Taste Shropshire
Editorial Address: 18 Princess Street, SHREWSBURY, SY1 1LP **Tel:** 01743 232181
Email: hello@tasteextra.com
Advertising Address: As above. **Tel:** 01743 718331
Email: mail@redbarnpublications.com
Web site: http://www.tasteshropshire.com
ISSN: 1752-3648
Publisher: Red Barn Publications Ltd
Date Established: 2006
Frequency: Quarterly
Cover Price: Free
Circulation: 10,000 (Print Run)
Usual Pagination: 48
Editor: Bruce McMichael; **Advertising Manager:** Bruce McMichael
Summary of Content: Magazine promoting food tourism, local food and drink, producers and suppliers as well as places to eat, stay and shop.
Readership/Target Audience: Aimed at the general public, food producers, growers, suppliers and vendors including delis and farm shops as well as staff in the hospitality industry including hotel and restaurant proprietors and chefs.
ADVERTISING RATES:
Full Page Colour £695.00
Agency Commission: 15%
Mechanical Data: Bleed Size: 303 x 216mm, Trim Size: 297 x 210mm, Film: Digital
Copy instructions: Copy Date: 3 weeks prior to publication date
Average advertising content per issue: 40%
CONSUMER: WOMEN'S INTEREST CONSUMER MAGAZINES: Food & Cookery

TATE ETC
47514U84A-427

Formerly: Tate Magazine
Editorial Address: Tate Britian, Millbank, LONDON, SW1P 4RG **Tel:** 020 7887 8724 **Fax:** 020 7887 3940
Email: tateetc@tate.org.uk
Advertising Address: As above. **Tel:** 020 7887 8606
Email: advertising@tate.org.uk
Web site: http://www.tate.org.uk/tateetc
ISSN: 1743-8853
Publisher: Tate Enterprises Ltd
Date Established: 1993
Frequency: 3 issues yearly - Published in January, May and September
Cover Price: £5.00
Annual Sub.: £15.00
Circulation: 100,000 (Publisher's Statement)
Usual Pagination: 112
Editor: Simon Grant; **Advertising Manager:** Naomi Richmond-Swift; **Publisher:** Naomi Richmond-Swift
Summary of Content: International art magazine offering a fresh perspective on historic, modern and contemporary art from outstanding writers and artists.
Readership/Target Audience: Aimed at a culturally sophisticated audience that is passionate about the visual arts.
ADVERTISING RATES:
Full Page Colour £3750.00
Agency Commission: 10%
Mechanical Data: Film: Digital, Type Area: 250 x 190mm, Col Length: 250mm, Bleed Size: 276 x 216mm, Page Width: 190mm, Trim Size: 270 x 210mm, Print Process: Web-fed offset litho
Copy instructions: Copy Date: 5 weeks prior to publication date
Average advertising content per issue: 30%
CONSUMER: THE ARTS & LITERARY: Arts

TATLER
45160U73-350

Editorial Address: Vogue House, 1 Hanover Square, LONDON, W1S 1JU **Tel:** 020 7499 9080 **Fax:** 020 7409 0451
Advertising Address: As above. **Fax:** 020 7493 1962
Email: victoria.higgins@condenast.co.uk
Web site: http://www.tatler.co.uk
Publisher: Conde Nast Publications Ltd
Date Established: 1707

Frequency: Monthly
Cover Price: £3.70
Circulation: 85,064 (ABC 01/01/2009 to 30/06/2009)
Editor: Catherine Ostler; **Executive Editor:** Annabel Rivkin; **Features Editor:** Ticky Hedley-Dent; **Managing Director:** Nicholas Coleridge; **Advertising Manager:** Emma Samuel; **Managing Editor:** Ahlya Fateh; **Publisher:** Patricia Stevenson
Summary of Content: Magazine featuring property, restaurants, motoring, shopping, fashion and celebrity interviews.
Readership/Target Audience: Read by affluent socialites.
ADVERTISING RATES:
Full Page Mono £10200.00
Full Page Colour £10200.00
Agency Commission: 15%
Mechanical Data: Type Area: 265 x 200mm, Bleed Size: 291 x 226mm, Trim Size: 285 x 220mm, Col Length: 265mm, Page Width: 200mm
Copy instructions: Copy Date: 5 weeks prior to publication date
Average advertising content per issue: 46%
CONSUMER: NATIONAL & INTERNATIONAL PERIODICALS

TEA BREAK QUICKIE CROSSWORDS
46692U79F-68

Editorial Address: Zetland House, 5-25 Scrutton Street, LONDON, EC2A 4HJ **Tel:** 020 7613 7477
Fax: 020 7168 7956
Advertising Address: As above.
Email: justine@accoladepublishing.co.uk
Web site: http://www.totalpuzzles.co.uk
Publisher: Accolade Publishing
Frequency: 13 issues yearly
Cover Price: £1.99
Annual Sub.: £25.90
Usual Pagination: 68
Editor: Justine Wall; **Advertising Manager:** Justine Wall; **Group Editor:** Liz Osler; **Publisher:** Justine Wall
Summary of Content: Publication containing part cryptic crosswords.
Readership/Target Audience: Aimed at women over the age of 35.
ADVERTISING: Rates on application
Agency Commission: 10%
Copy instructions: Copy Date: 4 weeks prior to publication date
Average advertising content per issue: 2%
CONSUMER: HOBBIES & DIY: Games & Puzzles

TECHNOLOGY HORIZONS
1753062U88C-176

Editorial Address: St. Giles House, 50 Poland Street, LONDON, W1F 7AX **Tel:** 020 7970 4000 **Fax:** 020 7970 4189
Email: sean.marshall@centaur.co.uk
Advertising Address: As above. **Fax:** 020 7970 4193
Email: moh.lalani@centaur.co.uk
Web site: http://www.technologyhorizons.co.uk
Publisher: Centaur Media plc
Date Established: 2006
Frequency: Quarterly
Cover Price: Free
Circulation: 25,000 (Print Run)
Usual Pagination: 60
Editor: Sean Marshall; **Advertising Manager:** Moh Lalani; **Publisher:** Sean Marshall
Summary of Content: Magazine covering a mixture of news, features and analysis describing emerging technologies, role models, industry overviews and job opportunities in science and technology.
Readership/Target Audience: Aimed at graduate engineering technology communities.
ADVERTISING RATES:
Full Page Colour £3500.00
Agency Commission: 15%
Mechanical Data: Type Area: 255 x 185mm, Bleed Size: 286 x 216mm, Trim Size: 270 x 200mm, Col Length: 255mm, Page Width: 185mm, Film: Digital
Copy instructions: Copy Date: 4 weeks prior to publication date
Average advertising content per issue: 29%
CONSUMER: EDUCATION: Careers

THE TEDDY BEAR CLUB INTERNATIONAL
46754U79K-920

Editorial Address: Ancient Lights, 19 River Road, ARUNDEL, BN18 9EY **Tel:** 01903 884988
Fax: 01903 885514
Email: kirste@ashdown.co.uk
Advertising Address: As above.
Email: krystyna@ashdown.co.uk
Web site: http://www.planet-teddybear.com
ISSN: 0961-0944
Publisher: Ashdown.co.uk Ltd
Date Established: 1990
Frequency: Monthly
Cover Price: £3.95

Annual Sub.: £44.00
Circulation: 25,000 (Publisher's Statement)
Usual Pagination: 76
Editor: Kirste McCool; **Managing Director:** David King;
Advertising Manager: Krystyna Semlekan
Summary of Content: Magazine covering the collection of
teddy bears. Includes artist's profiles, patterns, news and
events.
Readership/Target Audience: Aimed at teddy bear
collectors and enthusiasts.
ADVERTISING RATES:
Full Page Mono £475.00
Full Page Colour £870.00
Agency Commission: 10%
Mechanical Data: Film: Digital, Type Area: 263 x 185mm,
Trim Size: 297 x 210mm, Bleed Size: 303 x 216mm, Col
Length: 263mm, Page Width: 185mm
Copy instructions: Copy Date: 6 weeks prior to publication
date
CONSUMER: HOBBIES & DIY: Collectors Magazines

TEESSIDE HIGHLIGHTS
1655747U88R-58

Editorial Address: 45 Atkinson Gardens, Aycliffe, NEWTON
AYCLIFFE, DL5 6LH **Tel:** 01325 304360 **Fax:** 01325 314283
Email: sue@cherrington.onyxnet.co.uk
Advertising Address: As above.
Email: sue@cherrington.onyxnet.co.uk
Publisher: Cherrington Advertising Ltd
Frequency: Annual
Cover Price: Free
Circulation: 1,000 (Publisher's Statement)
Usual Pagination: 68
Editor: Sue Riney-Smith; **Advertising Manager:** Sue Riney-
Smith
Summary of Content: Magazine covering the school year at
Teesside High School.
Readership/Target Audience: Aimed at parents of children
who attend the school.
ADVERTISING: Rates on application
CONSUMER: EDUCATION: Education Related

THE TELEGRAPH
48611U94D-290

Formerly: The Weekly Telegraph
Editorial Address: 111 Buckingham Palace Road,
LONDON, SW1W 0DT **Tel:** 020 7931 2000
Fax: 020 7538 6109
Email: weeklyt@telegraph.co.uk
Advertising Address: As above. **Fax:** 020 7931 3373
Email: julie.bridge@telegraph.co.uk
Web site: http://www.expat.telegraph.co.uk
Publisher: Telegraph Media Group Ltd
Date Established: 1991
Frequency: Weekly
Annual Sub.: £125.00
Circulation: 82,000 (Publisher's Statement)
Editor: Will Holder
Summary of Content: Publication produced by The Daily
Telegraph and Sunday Telegraph covering news from
Britain.
Readership/Target Audience: Aimed at British expatriates.
ADVERTISING RATES:
Full Page Mono £5200.00
Full Page Colour £6700.00
SCC £38.00
Agency Commission: 10%
Mechanical Data: Print Process: Web-fed offset litho, Col
Widths (Display): 39mm, Film: Digital, Type Area: 330 x
254mm, Col Length: 330mm, No. of Columns (Display): 6,
Page Width: 254mm
Copy instructions: Copy Date: 6 days prior to publication
date
Average advertising content per issue: 20%
CONSUMER: OTHER CLASSIFICATIONS: Expatriates

TELLY-TIME FAVOURITES
48514U91D-131

Formerly: Telly-Time
Editorial Address: Suite 2.1, Level 2, Renslade House,
Bonhay Road, EXETER, EX4 3AY **Tel:** 01392 664141
Fax: 01392 221794
Email: jo@lcdpublishing.co.uk
ISSN: 1465-2498
Publisher: LCD Publishing
Frequency: Monthly
Cover Price: £1.95
Circulation: 40,000 (Publisher's Statement)
Usual Pagination: 32
Editor: Joanne Trump
Summary of Content: Children's educational comic
containing puzzles and stories on TV characters.
Readership/Target Audience: Aimed at children up to the
age of 4 years old.
ADVERTISING: No Advertising taken
CONSUMER: RECREATION & LEISURE: Children & Youth

TEMPO
46185U76D-415

Editorial Address: PO Box 171, Herne Bay, KENT, CT6
6WD **Tel:** 01223 312393 **Fax:** 01453 821575
Email: macval@compuserve.com
Advertising Address: The Edinburgh Building, Shaftesbury
Road, CAMBRIDGE, CB2 2RU **Tel:** 01223 325757
Fax: 01223 315052
Email: ad_sales@cambridge.org
Web site: http://journals.cambridge.org/jid_tem
ISSN: 0040-2982
Publisher: Cambridge University Press
Date Established: 1939
Frequency: Quarterly
Annual Sub.: £22.00
Circulation: 800 (Publisher's Statement)
Usual Pagination: 64
Editor: Calum MacDonald; **Advertising Manager:** Rebecca
Roberts
Summary of Content: Journal focusing on 20th century and
contemporary concert music featuring literate and scholarly
articles, music examples, interviews with contemporary
composers, a news section and reviews of recent
recordings, books and first performances.
Readership/Target Audience: Aimed at musicians, music
journalists, researchers and teachers in music, composers
and performers, music librarians, music historians, critics,
listeners and concert goers.
ADVERTISING RATES:
Full Page Mono £275.00
Mechanical Data: Page Width: 138mm, Type Area: 210 x
138mm, Col Length: 210mm, Film: Digital
Copy instructions: Copy Date: 8 weeks prior to publication
date
OONSUMER: MUSIC & PERFORMING ARTS: Music

TENBY TIMES
629153U80D-200

Editorial Address: Tindle House, Warren Street, TENBY,
SA70 7JY **Tel:** 01834 843262 **Fax:** 01834 844774
Email: tenbytimes@thetenbyobserver.co.uk
Advertising Address: As above.
Email: advertising@thetenbyobserver.co.uk
Web site: http://www.tenby-today.co.uk
Publisher: Tindle Newspapers Ltd
Date Established: 2000
Frequency: 11 issues yearly
Cover Price: Free
Circulation: 5,000 (Publisher's Statement)
Usual Pagination: 14
Editor: Patrick Ovenden
Summary of Content: Newspaper covering pictures from
the past and stories from the archives with an emphasis on
local history and heritage.
Readership/Target Audience: Aimed at the residents of
Tenby, exiles and regular visitors who become part of the
community.
ADVERTISING RATES:
Full Page Mono £150.00
Full Page Colour £187.50
SCC £1.00
Agency Commission: 10%
Mechanical Data: Col Length: 360mm, Col Widths (Display):
35mm, No. of Columns (Display): 7, Type Area: 360 x
272mm, Page Width: 272mm
Copy instructions: Copy Date: Friday prior to 1st
Wednesday of the month prior to publication date
Average advertising content per issue: 40%
CONSUMER: RURAL & REGIONAL INTEREST: Regional
Interest Wales

TENNIS TODAY
45891U75H-910

Editorial Address: Cedar Lodge, Howe Road,
WATLINGTON, OX49 5ER **Tel:** 01491 612042
Fax: 01491 614104
Email: henry@tennistodayltd.co.uk
Advertising Address: 14 Sykes Lane, Balderton, NEWARK,
NG24 3LT **Tel:** 01636 689169 **Fax:** 01636 707952
Email: ian@tennistodayltd.co.uk
Web site: http://www.tennis-today.net
Publisher: Tennis Today Ltd
Date Established: 1996
Frequency: 6 issues yearly
Cover Price: £3.00
Free to qualifying individuals
Annual Sub.: £18.00
Circulation: 6,500 (Publisher's Statement)
Usual Pagination: 40
Editor: Henry Wancke; **Advertising Manager:** Ian Beswick
Summary of Content: Magazine about tennis at
International club and regional level, including regular
features for club administrators.
Readership/Target Audience: Aimed at tennis players at all
levels.
ADVERTISING RATES:
Full Page Colour £693.00
Agency Commission: 10%
Mechanical Data: Type Area: 271 x 190mm, Bleed Size:
303 x 216mm, Trim Size: 297 x 210mm, Col Length: 271mm,
Page Width: 190mm, Film: Digital

Copy instructions: Copy Date: 1 month prior to publication
date
Average advertising content per issue: 40%
CONSUMER: SPORT: Racquet Sports

TERRORIZER
46265U76E-380

Editorial Address: Unit 36, 10-50 Willow Street, LONDON,
EC2A 4BH **Tel:** 020 7729 7666 **Fax:** 020 7739 0544
Email: editorial@terrorizer.com
Advertising Address: As above.
Email: john@terrorizer.com
Web site: http://www.terrorizer.com
Publisher: Dark Arts Ltd
Frequency: 13 issues yearly
Cover Price: £3.50
Annual Sub.: £36.00
Circulation: 13,786 (ABC 01/01/2008 to 31/12/2008)
Usual Pagination: 100
Editor: Louise Brown; **Advertising Manager:** John
Biscomb; **Publisher:** Miranda Yardley
Summary of Content: Music magazine covering metal,
hardcore and industrial music.
Readership/Target Audience: Aimed at metal, hardcore
and industrial music fans.
ADVERTISING RATES:
Full Page Colour £2000.00
Agency Commission: 10%
Mechanical Data: Trim Size: 297 x 220mm, Bleed Size:
+3mm, Film: Digital
Copy instructions: Copy Date: 4 weeks prior to publication
date
CONSUMER: MUSIC & PERFORMING ARTS: Pop Music

TES CYMRU
1647017U88A-218

Editorial Address: Sophia House, 28 Cathedral Road,
CARDIFF, CF11 9LJ **Tel:** 029 2066 0201 **Fax:** 029 2066 0207
Email: cymru@tes.co.uk
Web site: http://www.tes.co.uk/cymru
Publisher: TSL Education Ltd
Date Established: 2004
Frequency: Weekly
Cover Price: £1.40
Circulation: 3,500 (Publisher's Statement)
Usual Pagination: 6
Summary of Content: Journal covering education news,
opinion, analysis, research, curriculum and resources, book
reviews, arts, teaching aids and computer programs.
Language(s): English; Welsh
Readership/Target Audience: Read by the educational
community at local and national level in Wales.
ADVERTISING: No Advertising taken
CONSUMER: EDUCATION

THE TES MAGAZINE
1791019U88A-233

Editorial Address: 26 Red Lion Square, LONDON, WC1R
4HQ **Tel:** 020 3194 3000 **Fax:** 020 3194 3200
Email: features@tes.co.uk
Advertising Address: As above. **Fax:** 020 3194 3405
Email: kelly.andrews@tsleducation.com
Publisher: TSL Education Ltd
Date Established: 2006
Frequency: Weekly - See main publication for circulation
figure
Circulation: 80,000 (Publisher's Statement)
Usual Pagination: 64
Editor: Jo Faragher; **Advertising Manager:** Kelly Andrews
Summary of Content: Magazine covering education news,
features, lifestyle and classroom ideas.
Readership/Target Audience: Aimed at readers of The
Times Educational Supplement.
ADVERTISING RATES:
Full Page Colour £4280.00
Copy instructions: Copy Date: 10 days prior to publication
date
Supplement to: TES The Times Educational Supplement
CONSUMER: EDUCATION

TES THE TIMES EDUCATIONAL
SUPPLEMENT
47877U88A-95

Editorial Address: 26 Red Lion Square, LONDON, WC1R
4HQ **Tel:** 020 3194 3000 **Fax:** 020 3194 3200
Email: features@tes.co.uk
Advertising Address: As above. **Fax:** 020 3194 3405
Email: kelly.andrews@tsleducation.com
Web site: http://www.tes.co.uk
Publisher: TSL Education Ltd
Date Established: 1910
Frequency: Weekly
Cover Price: £1.40
Circulation: 58,045 (ABC 01/01/2009 to 30/06/2009)
Editor: Gerard Kelly; **News Editor:** Ed Dorrell
Summary of Content: Journal covering news, opinion,
analysis, research, features, curriculum and resources, book
reviews, arts, teaching aids and computer programmes.

Consumer Magazines

Readership/Target Audience: Read by the educational community at local and national levels.
ADVERTISING RATES:
Full Page Mono £5457.00
Full Page Colour £6366.50
Agency Commission: 10%
Mechanical Data: Film: Digital
Copy instructions: Copy Date: 7 days prior to publication date
Supplement(s): FE Focus - 52xY, TES Jobs - 52xY, The TES Magazine - 51xY
CONSUMER: EDUCATION

TESCO BABY & TODDLER CLUB

45313U74D-520

Formerly: Tesco Baby Club
Editorial Address: 84-86 Regent Street, LONDON, W1B 5RR Tel: 020 7734 2303 Fax: 020 7494 2570
Advertising Address: As above.
Email: adrian.farr@theforwardgroup.com
Publisher: The Forward Group
Frequency: Monthly
Cover Price: Free
Circulation: 500,000 (Publisher's Statement)
Usual Pagination: 28
Editor: Rebecca Hersey
Summary of Content: Magazine published on behalf of Tesco and featuring issues relating to the different stages throughout pregnancy and early motherhood.
Readership/Target Audience: Aimed at pregnant women and parents with children up to the age of 5 years old.
ADVERTISING RATES:
Full Page Colour £11000.00
Agency Commission: 10%
Mechanical Data: Type Area: 215 x 160mm, Col Length: 215mm, Page Width: 160mm, Trim Size: 225 x 170mm, Bleed Size: 235 x 180mm, Film: Digital
Average advertising content per issue: 25%
CONSUMER: WOMEN'S INTEREST CONSUMER MAGAZINES: Child Care

TESCO: THE MAGAZINE

1640950U74A-966

Editorial Address: 85 Strand, LONDON, WC2R 0DW
Tel: 020 7550 8000 Fax: 020 7550 8250
Email: emma.oliver@cedarcom.co.uk
Advertising Address: Tesco Stores Ltd, Cirrus A, Shire Park, WELWYN GARDEN CITY, AL7 1ZR Tel: 01707 360065
Fax: 01992 649964
Email: tom.glenister@uk.tesco.com
Web site: http://www.tesco.com/todayattesco/index.shtml
Publisher: Cedar Communications
Frequency: 6 issues yearly
Cover Price: Free
Circulation: 2,000,000 (Publisher's Statement)
Managing Director: Clare Broadbent; Advertising Manager: Tom Glenister
Summary of Content: Lifestyle magazine covering food, fashion, health, beauty, travel, gardening, the home, product reviews, book, CD, computer games and DVD reviews and a celebrity columns list.
Readership/Target Audience: Aimed at women aged between 25 and 45 years old who lead busy lives.
ADVERTISING RATES:
Full Page Colour £26500.00
Agency Commission: 15%
Mechanical Data: Film: Digital
Copy instructions: Copy Date: 6 weeks prior to publication date
Average advertising content per issue: 30%
CONSUMER: WOMEN'S INTEREST CONSUMER MAGAZINES: Women's Interest

TESS

47878U88A-90

Formerly: TES Scotland The Times Educational Supplement
Editorial Address: 21-23 Thistle Street, EDINBURGH, EH2 1DF Tel: 0131 624 8333 Fax: 0131 624 8350
Email: scoted@tes.co.uk
Advertising Address: As above. Tel: 0131 624 8344
Email: tesscotscopy@tes.co.uk
Web site: http://www.tes.co.uk/scotland
Publisher: TSL Education Ltd
Frequency: Weekly
Circulation: 18,000 (Print Run)
Editor: Neil Munro; News Editor: Elizabeth Buie;
Advertising Manager: Natalie Smith
Summary of Content: Newspaper supplement covering all aspects of education in Scotland.
Readership/Target Audience: Read by people in Scotland interested in education.
ADVERTISING RATES:
Full Page Mono £4080.00
Full Page Colour £4930.00
SCC £20.00
Agency Commission: 12.5%
Mechanical Data: No. of Columns (Display): 5, Print Process: Litho, Col Length: 340mm, Film: Digital, Type Area:

340 x 265mm, Page Width: 265mm, Col Widths (Display): 40mm
Copy instructions: Copy Date: 10 days prior to publication date
Average advertising content per issue: 40%
CONSUMER: EDUCATION

TFT - THE FEMALE TOUCH

1686714U74A-992

Editorial Address: 37A Mapleleaf House, Canterbury Road, WORTHING, BN13 1AN Tel: 0870 190 0220
Fax: 0870 190 0210
Email: steve@camcentral.co.uk
Advertising Address: As above.
Email: vicki@camcentral.co.uk
Web site: http://www.tftmag.co.uk
Publisher: CAM Publishing
Date Established: 2005
Frequency: Quarterly
Cover Price: Free
Circulation: 30,000 (Publisher's Statement)
Usual Pagination: 68
Editor: Steve Cusack; Advertising Director: Vicki Fairman
Summary of Content: Magazine covering seasonal fashion, food and recipes, health and fitness, diet and exercise, homes, shopping, gardens, motoring, travel, property, competitions and giveaways.
Readership/Target Audience: Aimed at dynamic and intelligent women living in Sussex.
ADVERTISING RATES:
Full Page Colour £1100.00
Agency Commission: 10%
Mechanical Data: Bleed Size: 306 x 236mm, Col Widths (Display): 48mm, No. of Columns (Display): 4, Film: Digital
Average advertising content per issue: 40%
CONSUMER: WOMEN'S INTEREST CONSUMER MAGAZINES: Women's Interest

TGO THE GREAT OUTDOORS

48430U75L-803

Editorial Address: 200 Renfield Street, GLASGOW, G2 3QB
Tel: 0141 302 7700 Fax: 0141 302 7799
Email: cameron.mcneish@tgomagazine.co.uk
Advertising Address: As above.
Email: ranjit.gill@tgomagazine.co.uk
Web site: http://www.tgomagazine.co.uk
ISSN: 0140-7570
Publisher: Newsquest Herald & Times Ltd
Date Established: 1978
Frequency: Monthly
Annual Sub.: £36.00
Circulation: 9,891 (ABC 01/01/2008 to 31/12/2008)
Usual Pagination: 120
Editor: Cameron McNeish; Advertising Manager: Ranjit Gill; Publisher: Darren Bruce
Summary of Content: Journal containing in-depth features on hill walking and backpacking in the UK and overseas.
Readership/Target Audience: Aimed at hill walkers, backpackers and overseas trekkers.
ADVERTISING RATES:
Full Page Colour £1828.00
SCC £22.00
Agency Commission: 10%
Mechanical Data: Trim Size: 297 X 210mm, Film: Digital, Type Area: 267 x 188mm, Bleed Size: 305 x 215mm, Col Length: 267mm, Page Width: 188mm
Copy instructions: Copy Date: 3 weeks prior to publication date
Average advertising content per issue: 30%
CONSUMER: SPORT: Outdoor

THAMES VALLEY SECRETARY

1704992U74J-152

Editorial Address: 10-12 Queens Road, Portishead, BRISTOL, BS20 8HT Tel: 01275 815497 Fax: 01275 815490
Email: admin@mediawest.co.uk
Advertising Address: As above. Tel: 01275 845846
Fax: 01275 817585
Email: steve@mediawest.co.uk
Publisher: Media West 2001 Ltd
Date Established: 2006
Frequency: Quarterly
Cover Price: Free
Circulation: 7,000 (Publisher's Statement)
Usual Pagination: 32
Editor: Dan Lawton
Summary of Content: Magazine containing features on fashion, beauty, restaurants, training, office equipment, conference facilities, hotels and job vacancies.
Readership/Target Audience: Aimed at PAs, secretaries and office managers in the Thames Valley area.
ADVERTISING RATES:
Full Page Colour £1500.00
Agency Commission: 10%
Mechanical Data: Trim Size: 297 x 210mm, Film: Digital
Copy instructions: Copy Date: 1 month prior to publication date

Average advertising content per issue: 60%
CONSUMER: WOMEN'S INTEREST CONSUMER MAGAZINES: Secretary & PA

THATCHED LIVING

45291U74C-540

Editorial Address: 6 The Rickyard, Clifton Reynes, OLNEY, MK43 5LQ Tel: 01234 714644 Fax: 01234 714633
Email: newsdesk@thatchedliving.co.uk
Advertising Address: As above. Tel: 01234 714404
Email: sales@thatchedliving.co.uk
Web site: http://www.thatchedliving.co.uk
Publisher: Pickwick Swales Ltd
Date Established: 1996
Frequency: Quarterly
Annual Sub.: £27.00
Circulation: 20,000 (Publisher's Statement)
Usual Pagination: 52
Editor: Anthony Bush; Publisher: Karen Pickwick
Summary of Content: Magazine offering practical hints, furnishing ideas and tips on thatched house and garden maintenance. Includes conservation issues, heritage matters, holidays and gardening features.
Readership/Target Audience: Aimed at owners and prospective owners of thatched property and those with an interest in the market.
ADVERTISING RATES:
Full Page Colour £1200.00
Agency Commission: 10%
Mechanical Data: Type Area: 270 x 195mm, Col Length: 270mm, Page Width: 195mm, Bleed Size: 303 x 216mm, Trim Size: 297 x 210mm, Film: Digital
Copy instructions: Copy Date: 3 weeks prior to publication date
Average advertising content per issue: 20%
CONSUMER: WOMEN'S INTEREST CONSUMER MAGAZINES: Home & Family

THAT'S LIFE

45201U74A-580

Editorial Address: Academic House, 24-28 Oval Road, LONDON, NW1 7DT Tel: 020 7241 8000 Fax: 020 7241 8008
Email: jennifer.fletcher@bauer.co.uk
Advertising Address: 8 Upper St. Martins Lane, LONDON, WC2H 9DW Tel: 020 7240 9400 Fax: 020 7240 9040
Email: harriete@tpc-london.com
Web site: http://www.thatslife.co.uk
Publisher: H. Bauer Publishing
Date Established: 1995
Frequency: Weekly
Cover Price: £0.68
Circulation: 386,875 (ABC 01/01/2009 to 30/06/2009)
Usual Pagination: 48
Editor: Jennifer Fletcher; Features Editor: Tiffany Sherlock;
Managing Director: David Goodchild; Advertising Manager: Harriet Edery
Summary of Content: Magazine featuring real life stories, health, beauty, cookery, fashion and fiction.
Twitter: http://twitter.com/ThatsLifeMag.
Readership/Target Audience: Aimed at 20 to 60 year olds.
ADVERTISING RATES:
Full Page Colour £10900.00
Agency Commission: 15%
Mechanical Data: Type Area: 260 x 190mm, Bleed Size: 288 x 218mm, Trim Size: 280 x 210mm, Film: Digital, Col Length: 260mm, Page Width: 190mm
Copy instructions: Copy Date: 4 weeks prior to publication date
CONSUMER: WOMEN'S INTEREST CONSUMER MAGAZINES: Women's Interest

THEATRE RECORD

46078U76B-250

Editorial Address: 131 Sherringham Avenue, LONDON, N17 9RU Tel: 020 8808 3656 Fax: 020 8350 0211
Email: editor@theatrerecord.com
Advertising Address: As above.
Email: editor@theatrerecord.com
Web site: http://www.theatrerecord.com
ISSN: 0962-1792
Publisher: Theatre Record
Date Established: 1981
Frequency: 26 issues yearly
Cover Price: £6.50
Annual Sub.: £150.00
Usual Pagination: 72
Editor: Ian Shuttleworth; Advertising Manager: Ian Shuttleworth; Publisher: Ian Shuttleworth
Summary of Content: Magazine containing a running archive of the English stage. Reprints all the reviews of the national newspaper drama critics with photographs and cast lists. Also lists forthcoming premieres.
Readership/Target Audience: Aimed at professionals in the theatre and as a reference source for scholars.
ADVERTISING RATES:
Full Page Mono £250.00
Agency Commission: 15%
Mechanical Data: Type Area: 270 x 170mm, Col Length: 270mm, Trim Size: 298 x 210mm, No. of Columns (Display): 4, Page Width: 170mm

Copy instructions: Copy Date: 14 days prior to publication date
Average advertising content per issue: 5%
Supplement(s): Theatre Index - 1xY
CONSUMER: MUSIC & PERFORMING ARTS: Theatre

THEATRE RESEARCH INTERNATIONAL
29679U84A-390

Editorial Address: The Edinburgh Building, Shaftesbury Road, CAMBRIDGE, CB2 2RU **Tel:** 01223 325801
Fax: 01223 325801
Email: journals@cambridge.org
Advertising Address: As above. **Tel:** 01223 326070
Fax: 01223 325150
Email: ad_sales@cambridge.org
Web site: http://journals.cambridge.org/jid_tri
ISSN: 0307-8833
Publisher: Cambridge University Press
Date Established: 1958
Frequency: 3 issues yearly - Published March, July and October
Annual Sub.: £28.00
Circulation: 1,000 (Publisher's Statement)
Editor: Adam Hooper; **Advertising Manager:** Rebecca Roberts
Summary of Content: Journal covering the historical, critical and theoretical study of documentation of drama. Publishes original articles on performance, acting and production techniques, theatre architecture, and actors' social conditions.
Readership/Target Audience: Aimed at academics and people with a specific interest in theatre.
ADVERTISING RATES:
Full Page Mono £440.00
Mechanical Data: Page Width: 135mm, Type Area: 200 x 135mm, Col Length: 200mm, Film: Digital
Copy instructions: Copy Date: 8 weeks preceding 1st of publication month
CONSUMER: THE ARTS & LITERARY: Arts

THEOLOGY
47759U87-214_1

Editorial Address: 36 Causton Street, LONDON, SW1P 4ST
Tel: 020 7592 3900 **Fax:** 020 7592 3939
Email: theology@spck.org.uk
Advertising Address: As above.
Email: theology@spck.org.uk
Web site: http://www.spck.org.uk
ISSN: 0040-571X
Publisher: SPCK
Date Established: 1920
Frequency: 6 issues yearly
Cover Price: £5.25
Annual Sub.: £27.50
Circulation: 1,500 (Publisher's Statement)
Usual Pagination: 80
Editor: Stephen Plant; **Advertising Manager:** Karen Beerman
Summary of Content: Journal containing book reviews, letters and articles covering the major moral, ethical and religious issues and trends in contemporary thinking.
Readership/Target Audience: Aimed at those who want to develop and deepen their knowledge of theology.
ADVERTISING RATES:
Full Page Mono £200.00
Mechanical Data: Col Length: 195mm, Page Width: 120mm, Type Area: 195 x 120mm
Copy instructions: Copy Date: 9 weeks prior to publication date
CONSUMER: RELIGIOUS

THE THEORIST
1657567U94E-358

Editorial Address: 35 Overdale Road, CHESHAM, HP5 2DZ
Tel: 01494 782831
Publisher: Angus Bird Publishing
Date Established: 2002
Frequency: Monthly
Annual Sub.: £30.00
Circulation: 1,500 (Publisher's Statement)
Editor: Roger Katt
Summary of Content: Magazine reporting on the latest conspiracy theories and UFO sightings from around the world.
Readership/Target Audience: Aimed at those with an interest in UFOs and alternative news stories.
ADVERTISING: No Advertising taken
CONSUMER: OTHER CLASSIFICATIONS: Paranormal

THERE'S MORE TO LIFE
1668009U74N-180

Editorial Address: 1 St. Cross Road, WINCHESTER, S023 9JA **Tel:** 01962 868545 **Fax:** 01962 870957
Email: mail@ageconcernhampshire.org.uk
Advertising Address: Suite 20, Cavendish Centre, WINCHESTER, SO23 0LB **Tel:** 01962 859559
Fax: 01962 870957

Email: rich@observerrecruitment.co.uk
Web site: http://www.hantsmedia.co.uk
Publisher: Hampshire Media Ltd
Frequency: Quarterly
Cover Price: Free
Circulation: 13,000 (Publisher's Statement)
Usual Pagination: 20
Editor: Chris Perry; **Advertising Manager:** Richard Peake
Summary of Content: Newspaper of Age Concern covering holidays, advice on discrimination, pensions, inheritance tax, long term illness, health and social security.
Readership/Target Audience: Aimed at the over 50s in Hampshire.
ADVERTISING RATES:
Full Page Mono £816.00
Full Page Colour £816.00
Agency Commission: 10%
Mechanical Data: Film: Digital, Trim Size: 340 x 262mm, Col Widths (Display): 31mm, No. of Columns (Display): 8
Copy instructions: Copy Date: 1 week prior to publication date
Average advertising content per issue: 40%
CONSUMER: WOMEN'S INTEREST CONSUMER MAGAZINES: Retirement

THETFORD & BRANDON PINK LOCAL DIRECTORY
48188U89C-395

Editorial Address: St. Augustines House, St. Augustines Way, South Wootton, KING'S LYNN, PE30 3TE
Tel: 01553 675885 **Fax:** 01553 670007
Advertising Address: As above.
Email: sales@pinklocaldirectory.co.uk
Web site: http://www.pinklocaldirectory.co.uk
Publisher: Pink Local Directory Ltd
Date Established: 1990
Frequency: Annual
Cover Price: Free
Circulation: 20,435 (Publisher's Statement)
Usual Pagination: 64
Editor: Lucan King; **Advertising Manager:** Lucan King
Summary of Content: Provides a directory of all local businesses. Contains business classified and information sections.
Readership/Target Audience: Aimed at local residents and businesses.
ADVERTISING RATES:
Full Page Mono £839.00
Mechanical Data: Type Area: 192 x 126mm, Col Length: 192mm, Page Width: 126mm
CONSUMER: HOLIDAYS & TRAVEL: Entertainment Guides

THIRD TEXT
47528U84A-400

Editorial Address: 2G Crusader House, 289 Cricklewood Broadway, LONDON, NW2 6NX **Tel:** 020 8830 7803
Email: thirdtext@btconnect.com
Web site: http://www.tandf.co.uk/journals
ISSN: 0952-8822
Publisher: Routledge, Taylor & Francis
Date Established: 1987
Frequency: 6 issues yearly
Cover Price: £12.00
Annual Sub.: £68.00
Circulation: 1,000 (Publisher's Statement)
Usual Pagination: 130
Editor: Rasheed Araeen
Summary of Content: Magazine covering critical perspectives on contemporary art and culture, art criticism and art history. Includes articles on film, book, television, theatre and literature reviews.
Readership/Target Audience: Aimed at artists, academics, art historians, cultural critics, PhD students, film makers and those with an interest in contemporary art and culture.
ADVERTISING: Rates on application
CONSUMER: THE ARTS & LITERARY: Arts

THIRD WAY
47760U87-214_5

Editorial Address: 13-17 Long Lane, LONDON, EC1A 9PN
Tel: 020 7776 1071
Email: editor@thirdway.org.uk
Advertising Address: As above. **Fax:** 020 7776 1017
Email: stephen@churchtimes.co.uk
Web site: http://www.thirdway.org.uk
ISSN: 0309-3492
Publisher: Hymns ancient & modern
Date Established: 1977
Frequency: 10 issues yearly - Double issues in Summer/Winter
Cover Price: £2.90
Annual Sub.: £29.00
Circulation: 4,500 (Publisher's Statement)
Usual Pagination: 32
Editor: Simon Jones; **Features Editor:** Nick Thorpe;
Advertising Manager: Stephen Dutton
Summary of Content: Publication featuring Christian comment on the political, social and cultural issues of the day.

Readership/Target Audience: Aimed at Christians.
ADVERTISING RATES:
Full Page Colour £375.00
Agency Commission: 10%
Mechanical Data: Film: Digital
Copy instructions: Copy Date: 1st Friday of the month prior to publication date
CONSUMER: RELIGIOUS

THIS IS ANFIELD
1613654U75B-272

Editorial Address: PO Box 48, Old Hall Street, LIVERPOOL, L69 3EB **Tel:** 0151 227 2000 **Fax:** 0151 285 8466
Email: stevehanrahan@sportmedia-tm.com
Advertising Address: As above. **Tel:** 0151 285 8412
Email: neil.johnson@liverpool.com
Publisher: Trinity Mirror
Date Established: 2002
Frequency: 24 issues yearly - Published for each home game
Cover Price: £3.00
Circulation: 20,000 (Publisher's Statement)
Editor: Steve Hanrahan; **Advertising Manager:** Neil Johnson
Summary of Content: Official matchday programme of Liverpool Football Club with features based on the days match as well as interviews with past and present players.
Readership/Target Audience: Aimed at supporters of Liverpool Football Club.
ADVERTISING RATES:
Full Page Colour £3950.00
Agency Commission: 10%
Mechanical Data: Trim Size: 245 x 167mm, Bleed Size: 255 x 177mm, Film: Digital
Copy instructions: Copy Date: 5pm 8 working days prior to publication date
Average advertising content per issue: 20%
CONSUMER: SPORT: Football

THIS IS BATH
1852760U80C-5469

Editorial Address: Westpoint, James Street West, BATH, BA1 2DA **Tel:** 01225 322322
Email: thisiseditor@westnews.co.uk
Advertising Address: As above. **Fax:** 01225 429743
Email: s.murrant@
Publisher: Bath News & Media
Date Established: 2008
Frequency: Weekly
Cover Price: Free
Circulation: 10,000 (Publisher's Statement)
Editor: Tom Bradshaw
Summary of Content: Magazine featuring events, eating out, entertainment, fashion, home improvements, celebrity news and social comment.
Readership/Target Audience: Aimed at residents and visitors to Bath.
ADVERTISING RATES:
Full Page Colour £300.00
Agency Commission: 30%
Mechanical Data: Type Area: 290 x 204mm, Trim Size: 297 x 210mm, Film: Digital
Copy instructions: Copy Date: 1 week prior to publication date
Average advertising content per issue: 10%
CONSUMER: RURAL & REGIONAL INTEREST: Regional Interest English Counties

THIS IS LONDON
48144U89C-420

Editorial Address: 42 Conduit Street, LONDON, W1R 9FB
Tel: 020 7434 1281 **Fax:** 020 7287 0592
Email: editorial@til.com
Advertising Address: As above.
Email: editorial@til.com
Web site: http://www.til.com
Publisher: This is London Magazine Ltd
Date Established: 1956
Frequency: Weekly
Cover Price: Free
Circulation: 10,000 (Publisher's Statement)
Usual Pagination: 28
Editor: Jan Gardner; **Advertising Manager:** Jan Gardener; **Publisher:** Julie Jones
Summary of Content: Magazine featuring arts, entertainment and restaurant information.
Readership/Target Audience: Aimed at businessmen and visitors to London.
ADVERTISING RATES:
Full Page Mono £695.00
Full Page Colour £795.00
Agency Commission: 10%
Mechanical Data: No. of Columns (Display): 3, Trim Size: 210 x 148mm, Film: Digital
Copy instructions: Copy Date: 1 week prior to publication date
CONSUMER: HOLIDAYS & TRAVEL: Entertainment Guides

THOMAS & FRIENDS
1846241U91D-977

Editorial Address: 239 Kensington High Street, LONDON, W8 6SA **Tel:** 020 7761 3500 **Fax:** 020 7761 3510
Email: jtarrant@euk.egmont.com
Web site: http://www.egmont.co.uk
ISSN: 0954-9390
Publisher: Egmont Magazines UK
Frequency: 24 issues yearly
Cover Price: £1.99
Circulation: 37,458 (ABC 01/01/2009 to 30/06/2009)
Usual Pagination: 32
Editor: Jane Tarrant
Summary of Content: Magazine with stories, facts, information, stories and puzzles based on Thomas the Tank Engine.
Readership/Target Audience: Aimed at boys aged 3 to 6 years old.
CONSUMER: RECREATION & LEISURE: Children & Youth

THOMAS & FRIENDS PLAY & LEARN
623048U91D-86

Formerly: Play and Learn Thomas the Tank Engine & Friends
Editorial Address: 239 Kensington High Street, LONDON, W8 6SA **Tel:** 020 7761 3500 **Fax:** 020 7761 3510
Email: jtarrant@euk.egmont.com
Advertising Address: As above.
Email: aallen@euk.egmont.com
Web site: http://www.egmont.co.uk
ISSN: 1468-1730
Publisher: Egmont Magazines UK
Date Established: 2000
Frequency: 24 issues yearly
Cover Price: £2.10
Circulation: 38,033 (ABC 01/01/2009 to 30/06/2009)
Usual Pagination: 28
Editor: Jane Tarrant
Summary of Content: Children's magazine full of activities and stories designed to teach children basic moral and social skills.
Readership/Target Audience: Aimed at children between 3 and 7 years old.
ADVERTISING RATES:
Full Page Colour £1800.00
Agency Commission: 10%
Mechanical Data: Film: Digital, Type Area: 282 x 202mm, Col Length: 282mm, Bleed Size: 306 x 226mm, Trim Size: 300 x 220mm, Page Width: 202mm
Copy instructions: Copy Date: 4 weeks prior to publication date
Average advertising content per issue: 10%
CONSUMER: RECREATION & LEISURE: Children & Youth

THOMAS COOK TRAVEL MAGAZINE
766810U89D-503

Formerly: Thomas Cook Air
Editorial Address: 141-143 Shoreditch High Street, LONDON, E1 6JE **Tel:** 020 7613 8777 **Fax:** 020 7613 8776
Email: tobi.cohen@ink-publishing.com
Advertising Address: As above. **Fax:** 020 7613 8778
Email: stuart.wass@ink-publishing.com
Publisher: Ink Publishing
Date Established: 2006
Frequency: Quarterly
Cover Price: Free
Circulation: 400,000 (Publisher's Statement)
Usual Pagination: 182
Editor: Tobi Cohen; **Advertising Manager:** Stuart Wass
Summary of Content: Customer magazine of Thomas Cook Airlines covering travel, lifestyle, food, gadgets, fashion, beauty and sport.
Readership/Target Audience: Aimed at travellers on Thomas Cook Airlines.
ADVERTISING RATES:
Full Page Colour £9995.00
Agency Commission: 10%
CONSUMER: HOLIDAYS & TRAVEL: In-Flight Magazines

THOROUGHBRED OWNER & BREEDER
45839U75E-284

Formerly: Pacemaker
Editorial Address: First Floor Suite, 65 The Broadway, HAYWARDS HEATH, RH16 3AS **Tel:** 01444 440540
Email: editor@ownerbreeder.co.uk
Advertising Address: The Litten, Newtown Road, NEWBURY, RG14 7BB **Tel:** 01635 35599
Fax: 01635 845811
Email: advertising@pacemakerworld.co.uk
Web site: http://www.ownerbreeder.co.uk
Publisher: Dunwoody Marketing Communications
Date Established: 1977
Frequency: Monthly
Cover Price: £4.95
Annual Sub.: £40.00

Circulation: 15,000 (Publisher's Statement)
Usual Pagination: 124
Editor: Richard Griffiths
Summary of Content: Magazine covering horseracing, including race information and breeding of horses.
Readership/Target Audience: Aimed at breeders, owners, trainers and other enthusiasts in the UK and overseas.
ADVERTISING RATES:
Full Page Colour £1870.00
Agency Commission: 10%
Mechanical Data: Film: Digital, Type Area: 277 x 180mm, Col Length: 277mm, Page Width: 180mm, Trim Size: 297 x 210mm, Bleed Size: 303 x 216mm
Average advertising content per issue: 40%
CONSUMER: SPORT: Horse Racing

THREE WEEKS
1741354U89C-1075

Editorial Address: 3rd Floor, Unicorn House, 221-222 Shoreditch High Street, LONDON, E14 9YT
Tel: 0870 744 2643 **Fax:** 070 9231 4982
Email: editor@threeweeks.co.uk
Advertising Address: As above.
Email: ads@unlimitedmedia.co.uk
Web site: http://www.threeweeks.co.uk
Publisher: UnLimited Media
Date Established: 1996
Frequency: Quarterly - Published weekly and daily in Edinburgh during August and Brighton during May
Cover Price: Free
Circulation: 40,000 (Publisher's Statement)
Usual Pagination: 20
Editor: Chris Cooke; **Advertising Manager:** Chris Cooke; **Publisher:** Chris Cooke
Summary of Content: Magazine covering cover all aspects of the Edinburgh and Brighton Festivals, focusing in particular on the artists, acts, events and performers.
Readership/Target Audience: Aimed at visitors to the festivals or those interested in festivals.
ADVERTISING RATES:
Full Page Colour £1000.00
Agency Commission: 10%
Mechanical Data: Bleed Size: 341 x 276mm, Trim Size: 335 x 270mm, Film: Digital
Copy instructions: Copy Date: 2 weeks prior to publication date
Average advertising content per issue: 25%
CONSUMER: HOLIDAYS & TRAVEL: Entertainment Guides

THREESIXTY BODYBOARDING MAGAZINE
45959U75M-930

Editorial Address: Berry Road Studios, Berry Road, NEWQUAY, TR7 1AT **Tel:** 01637 878074 **Fax:** 01637 850226
Email: rob@orcasurf.co.uk
Advertising Address: As above.
Email: rob@orcasurf.co.uk
Web site: http://www.orcasurf.co.uk
ISSN: 1352-9471
Publisher: Orca Publications
Frequency: Quarterly
Cover Price: £2.85
Annual Sub.: £13.70
Circulation: 10,000 (Publisher's Statement)
Usual Pagination: 72
Editor: Rob Barber; **Advertising Manager:** Rob Barber; **Managing Editor:** Mike Searle
Summary of Content: Magazine featuring the latest techniques, travel information, competitions and interviews with professional bodyboarders.
Readership/Target Audience: Aimed at 14 to 22 year old men interested in bodyboarding.
ADVERTISING RATES:
Full Page Colour £630.00
Agency Commission: 10%
Mechanical Data: Page Width: 210mm, Bleed Size: 286 x 236mm, Trim Size: 280 x 230mm, Type Area: 260 x 210mm, Col Length: 260mm, Film: Digital
Copy instructions: Copy Date: 3 weeks prior to publication date
Average advertising content per issue: 30%
CONSUMER: SPORT: Water Sports

TIARA
1626284U74L-218

Editorial Address: 1 Kings Road, CARDIFF, CF11 9BZ
Tel: 029 2039 6600 **Fax:** 029 2039 6611
Email: edits@ladiesfirst.co.uk
Advertising Address: As above.
Email: info@ladiesfirst.co.uk
Web site: http://www.ladiesfirst.co.uk
Publisher: Hils Publications Ltd
Frequency: 3 issues yearly - Published in January, April and September
Cover Price: Free
Circulation: 13,000 (Publisher's Statement)
Usual Pagination: 76
Editor: Hilary Ferda; **Advertising Manager:** Hilary Ferda

Summary of Content: Bridal magazine covering fashion, beauty, venues, photography, flowers, cakes and cards.
Readership/Target Audience: Aimed at those getting married and their families.
ADVERTISING RATES:
Full Page Colour £665.00
Agency Commission: 10%
Mechanical Data: Trim Size: 297 x 210mm, Bleed Size: 303 x 216mm, Type Area: 278 x 216mm, Col Length: 278mm, Page Width: 216mm, Film: Digital
Copy instructions: Copy Date: 5 weeks prior to publication date
CONSUMER: WOMEN'S INTEREST CONSUMER MAGAZINES: Brides

THE TICKET
48063U89C-50

Formerly: The A List Incorporating Mirror Screen
Editorial Address: 1 Canada Square, Canary Wharf, LONDON, E14 5AP **Tel:** 020 7293 3000 **Fax:** 020 7293 2293
Advertising Address: As above. **Fax:** 020 7293 3077
Web site: http://www.mirror.co.uk
Publisher: Trinity Mirror
Frequency: Weekly - Published on Fridays
Cover Price: Free
Usual Pagination: 26
Editor: Alun Palmer; **Advertising Manager:** Michael Burne
Summary of Content: Magazine covering listings and reviews on all forms of entertainment for London and the South East.
Readership/Target Audience: Aimed at 15 to 45 year olds.
ADVERTISING RATES:
Full Page Mono £33300.00
Full Page Colour £42300.00
Agency Commission: 15%
Mechanical Data: Film: Digital, No. of Columns (Display): 7, Type Area: 340 x 265mm, Col Length: 340mm, Page Width: 265mm
Copy instructions: Copy Date: 7 days prior to publication date
Supplement to: Daily Mirror
CONSUMER: HOLIDAYS & TRAVEL: Entertainment Guides

TIDE TIMES
48415U91A-160

Editorial Address: Befferlands Farm Workshop, Charmouth, DORSET, DT6 6RD **Tel:** 01297 561577 **Fax:** 01297 561577
Email: mail@njcpublications.co.uk
Advertising Address: As above.
Email: penny@njcpublications.co.uk
Web site: http://www.njcpublications.co.uk
Publisher: Nigel J. Clarke Publications
Date Established: 1979
Frequency: Annual - Published in November
Cover Price: £1.40
Circulation: 35,000 (Publisher's Statement)
Usual Pagination: 40
Editor: Penny Hall; **Advertising Manager:** Penny Hall; **Publisher:** Nigel Clarke
Summary of Content: Magazine containing 8 tables showing tidal predictions for the south coast of England.
Readership/Target Audience: Aimed at sailors, divers, walkers, Coastal engineers, Port and Harbour authorities, environment agency, Marine Coastguard Agency.
ADVERTISING RATES:
Full Page Mono £99.00
Mechanical Data: Col Length: 140mm, Print Process: Web-fed offset litho, Bleed Size: 165 x 110mm, Type Area: 140 x 95mm, Page Width: 95mm, Film: Digital
Copy instructions: Copy Date: September 1st
Average advertising content per issue: 33%
CONSUMER: RECREATION & LEISURE: Boating & Yachting

TILLLATE
46241U76E-198

Formerly: M8
Editorial Address: 111 Bell Street, GLASGOW, G4 0TQ
Tel: 0141 553 0500 **Fax:** 0141 553 5800
Email: kevin@tilllatemag.com
Advertising Address: As above.
Email: lynne@tilllatemag.com
Web site: http://www.tilllatemagazine.com
ISSN: 0954-6898
Publisher: Music Scotland Ltd
Date Established: 1988
Frequency: Monthly
Cover Price: £1.00
Circulation: 30,000 (Publisher's Statement)
Usual Pagination: 100
Editor: Kevin McFarlane; **Advertising Manager:** Lynne McDermott; **Publisher:** David Faulds
Summary of Content: Youth magazine covering club culture, lifestyle, photography, flowers and music.
Readership/Target Audience: Aimed at young people between 18 and 30 years.
ADVERTISING RATES:
Full Page Colour £2500.00
Agency Commission: 10%

Mechanical Data: Trim Size: 297 x 210mm, Bleed Size: 303 x 216mm, Film: Digital
CONSUMER: MUSIC & PERFORMING ARTS: Pop Music

TIME & LEISURE CLAPHAM, BATTERSEA AND FULHAM
1777441U80B-424

Editorial Address: 14 The Apprentice Shop, Merton Abbey Mills, LONDON, SW19 2RD **Tel:** 020 8545 6777
Fax: 020 8545 6778
Email: fiona@timeandleisure.co.uk
Advertising Address: As above.
Email: marie@timeandleisure.co.uk
Web site: http://www.timeandleisure.co.uk
Publisher: Time & Leisure
Date Established: 2004
Frequency: Monthly
Cover Price: Free
Circulation: 45,000 (Publisher's Statement)
Usual Pagination: 52
Editor: Fiona Razvi
Summary of Content: Magazine covering arts, music, theatre, cinema, fashion, books, interiors, food, eating out and local issues as well as an entertainment and listings guide. Includes interviews with local celebrities, authors, designers and entertainers.
Readership/Target Audience: Aimed at residents of Clapham, Battersea and Fulham.
ADVERTISING RATES:
Full Page Colour £1300.00
Mechanical Data: Type Area: 273 x 186mm, Bleed Size: 307 x 220mm, Trim Size: 297 x 210mm, Col Length: 273mm, Page Width: 186mm, Film: Digital
CONSUMER: RURAL & REGIONAL INTEREST: Regional Interest Greater London

TIME & LEISURE EPSOM AND SUTTON
1777447U80B-426

Editorial Address: 14 The Apprentice Shop, Merton Abbey Mills, 12 Watermill Way, LONDON, SW19 2RD
Tel: 020 8540 3653 **Fax:** 020 8542 3652
Email: chris@timeandleisure.co.uk
Advertising Address: As above. **Tel:** 020 8545 6777
Fax: 020 8545 6778
Email: karen@timeandleisure.co.uk
Web site: http://www.timeandleisure.co.uk
Publisher: Time & Leisure
Frequency: Monthly
Cover Price: Free
Circulation: 155,000 (Publisher's Statement)
Usual Pagination: 52
Editor: Chris Wood
Summary of Content: Magazine covering arts, music, cinema, theatre, food, eating out and local issues as well as an entertainment and listings guide.
Readership/Target Audience: Aimed at residents in Epsom and Sutton.
ADVERTISING RATES:
Full Page Colour £1100.00
Mechanical Data: Type Area: 273 x 186mm, Bleed Size: 307 x 220mm, Trim Size: 297 x 210mm, Col Length: 273mm, Page Width: 186mm, Film: Digital
CONSUMER: RURAL & REGIONAL INTEREST: Regional Interest Greater London

TIME & LEISURE KINGSTON
1777443U80B-425

Editorial Address: 14 The Apprentice Shop, Merton Abbey Mills, 12 Watermill Way, LONDON, SW19 2RD
Tel: 020 8540 3653 **Fax:** 020 8542 3652
Email: sara@timeandleisure.co.uk
Advertising Address: As above. **Tel:** 020 8545 6777
Email: caroline@timeandleisure.co.uk
Web site: http://www.timeandleisure.co.uk
Publisher: Time & Leisure
Frequency: Monthly
Cover Price: Free
Circulation: 30,000 (Publisher's Statement)
Usual Pagination: 56
Editor: Sara Warshawski
Summary of Content: Magazine covering arts, music, theatre, cinema, food, eating out and local issues as well as an entertainment and listings guide.
Readership/Target Audience: Aimed at residents of Kingston.
ADVERTISING RATES:
Full Page Colour £1100.00
Mechanical Data: Type Area: 273 x 186mm, Bleed Size: 307 x 220mm, Trim Size: 297 x 210mm, Col Length: 273mm, Page Width: 186mm, Film: Digital
CONSUMER: RURAL & REGIONAL INTEREST: Regional Interest Greater London

TIME & LEISURE, WIMBLEDON, PUTNEY & WANDSWORTH
623218U80B-423

Formerly: Wimbledon and Putney Time & Leisure
Editorial Address: 14 The Apprentice Shop, Merton Abbey Mills, 12 Watermill Way, LONDON, SW19 2RD
Tel: 020 8540 3653 **Fax:** 020 8545 6778
Email: editor@timeandleisure.co.uk
Advertising Address: As above. **Tel:** 020 8540 6777
Email: mike@timeandleisure.co.uk
Web site: http://www.timeandleisure.co.uk
Publisher: Time & Leisure
Date Established: 1998
Frequency: Monthly
Cover Price: Free
Circulation: 50,000 (Publisher's Statement)
Usual Pagination: 76
Editor: Tony Kane; **Managing Director:** Lucy Kane
Summary of Content: Lifestyle magazine covering the arts, music, theatre, cinema, food, eating out and local issues with an entertainment and listings guide.
Readership/Target Audience: Aimed at residents in Wimbledon, Putney and Wandsworth.
ADVERTISING RATES:
Full Page Colour £1400.00
Mechanical Data: Type Area: 273 x 186mm, Bleed Size: 307 x 210mm, Trim Size: 297 x 210mm, Col Length: 273mm, Page Width: 186mm, Film: Digital
CONSUMER: RURAL & REGIONAL INTEREST: Regional Interest Greater London

TIME FOR U
1666197U74R-551

Formerly: Time For You
Editorial Address: 87 Loopland Drive, Castlereagh Road, BELFAST, BT6 9DW **Tel:** 028 9073 8008 **Fax:** 028 9045 5684
Email: editorial@imagine8withus.com
Advertising Address: As above.
Email: gill@imagine8withus.com
Web site: http://www.imagine8withus.com
ISSN: 1746-5915
Publisher: Imagine 8 International Ltd
Date Established: 2005
Frequency: Quarterly
Cover Price: Free
Circulation: 10,000 (Publisher's Statement)
Usual Pagination: 100
Editor: Sharon Gillespie; **Advertising Manager:** Sharon Gillespie
Summary of Content: Magazine with a positive and pro-active slant for women who want to change their lives including health, job prospects, travel and motivation.
Readership/Target Audience: Aimed at women over 40 years old who want to improve or change their lifestyle, relationships or education.
ADVERTISING RATES:
Full Page Colour £700.00
Agency Commission: 15%
Mechanical Data: Trim Size: 223 x 168mm, Bleed Size: 229 x 174mm, Film: Digital
Copy instructions: Copy Date: End of each quarter per calendar year
Average advertising content per issue: 40%
CONSUMER: WOMEN'S INTEREST CONSUMER MAGAZINES: Women's Interest Related

TIME MAGAZINE
45161U73-360

Editorial Address: 8th Floor, Blue Fin Building, 110 Southwark Street, LONDON, SE1 0SU **Tel:** 020 3148 3000
Fax: 020 3148 8514
Email: edit_office@timemagazine.com
Advertising Address: Blue Fin Building, 110 Southwark Street, LONDON, SE1 0SU **Tel:** 020 3148 3000
Fax: 020 3148 8514
Email: tim_howat@timemagazine.com
Web site: http://www.time.com
ISSN: 0928-8430
Publisher: TIME Magazines Europe Limited
Date Established: 1923
Frequency: Weekly
Cover Price: £2.80
Circulation: 527,501 (ABC 01/01/2009 to 30/06/2009)
Usual Pagination: 80
Editor: Simon Robinson; **Advertising Director:** Tim Howat
Summary of Content: International news magazine covering current affairs, reviews and politics. Twitter: http://twitter.com/TIME.
Readership/Target Audience: Read by adults with an interest in world news.
ADVERTISING RATES:
Full Page Mono EUR46304.00
Full Page Colour EUR71000.00
Mechanical Data: Film: Digital, Bleed Size: 273 x 206mm, Trim Size: 267 x 200mm, Type Area: 254 x 178mm, No. of Columns (Display): 3, Col Length: 254mm, Page Width: 178mm
Copy instructions: Copy Date: 1 month prior to publication date

Average advertising content per issue: 35%
CONSUMER: NATIONAL & INTERNATIONAL PERIODICALS

TIME OUT LONDON
48146U89C-460

Formerly: Time Out Magazine
Editorial Address: Universal House, 251 Tottenham Court Road, LONDON, W1T 7AB **Tel:** 020 7813 3000
Fax: 020 7813 6001
Advertising Address: As above. **Fax:** 020 7813 6100
Email: advertising@timeout.com
Web site: http://www.timeout.com
ISSN: 0049-3910
Publisher: Time Out Group Ltd
Date Established: 1968
Frequency: Weekly
Cover Price: £2.95
Circulation: 64,712 (ABC 01/01/2009 to 30/06/2009)
Usual Pagination: 188
Editor: Mark Frith; **News Editor:** Rebecca Taylor; **Features Editor:** Nina Caplan; **Managing Director:** Mark Elliott; **Advertising Manager:** Phil Peachey; **Managing Editor:** Claire Hojem
Summary of Content: London's listings magazine. News, features and guide to the London entertainment scene.
Readership/Target Audience: Aimed at those who are visiting or live in London.
ADVERTISING RATES:
Full Page Mono £3880.00
Full Page Colour £4625.00
Agency Commission: 10%
Mechanical Data: Film: Digital, Type Area: 249 x 185mm, Col Length: 249mm, Page Width: 185mm, Trim Size: 273 x 206mm, Bleed Size: 283 x 216mm
Copy instructions: Copy Date: 7 days prior to publication date
Average advertising content per issue: 40%
CONSUMER: HOLIDAYS & TRAVEL: Entertainment Guides

TIME OUT LONDON SHOPS & SERVICES
46845U80B-240

Formerly: Time Out Shopping Guide
Editorial Address: Universal House, 251 Tottenham Court Road, LONDON, W1T 7AB **Tel:** 020 7813 3000
Fax: 020 7813 6153
Email: guides@timeout.com
Advertising Address: As above. **Tel:** 020 7813 6020
Fax: 020 7813 6100
Email: guidesadvertising@timeout.com
Web site: http://www.timeout.com
Publisher: Time Out Group Ltd
Date Established: 1994
Frequency: Annual - Published in October
Cover Price: £9.99
Circulation: 35,000 (Publisher's Statement)
Usual Pagination: 304
Editor: Holly Pick
Summary of Content: Magazine containing a guide to shops and services in London, from fashion to flowers, and pets to photography.
Readership/Target Audience: Aimed at people living in or visiting London.
ADVERTISING RATES:
Full Page Mono £2395.00
Full Page Colour £2800.00
Agency Commission: 10%
Mechanical Data: Type Area: 254 x 178mm, Film: Digital, Col Length: 254mm, Page Width: 178mm
Copy instructions: Copy Date: 4 weeks prior to publication date
CONSUMER: RURAL & REGIONAL INTEREST: Regional Interest Greater London

THE TIMES BOOKS
1697686U84B-370

Formerly: Books
Editorial Address: 1 Pennington Street, LONDON, E98 1TT **Tel:** 020 7782 5169 **Fax:** 020 7782 5126
Email: books@thetimes.co.uk
Advertising Address: 1 Virginia Street, LONDON, E98 1PL **Tel:** 020 7782 7608
Email: sarah.walker@newsint.co.uk
Frequency: Weekly - See main record for circulation figure
Editor: Tom Gatti
Summary of Content: Supplement covering book and related industry news with book reviews and features.
ADVERTISING RATES:
SCC £64.00
Mechanical Data: Type Area: 325 x 264mm, Col Length: 325mm, Page Width: 264mm, Col Widths (Display): 40mm, No. of Columns (Display): 6, Film: Digital
Copy instructions: Copy Date: 3 working days prior to publication date
Supplement to: The Times
CONSUMER: THE ARTS & LITERARY: Literary

TIMES GONE BY
1664183U94X-276

Editorial Address: 19 Getliffes Yard, Derby Street, LEEK, ST13 6HU **Tel:** 01538 371800 **Fax:** 01538 371810
Email: harry.gottschalk@staffordshirenewspapers.co.uk
Advertising Address: As above.
Email: awynne@staffordshirenewsletter.co.uk
Publisher: Your Leek Paper
Frequency: Quarterly
Cover Price: £2.50
Circulation: 1,650 (Publisher's Statement)
Usual Pagination: 32
Editor: Harry Gottschalk; **Advertising Manager:** Angela Wynne
Summary of Content: Magazine covering the history of the Leek and Staffordshire moors, people and events.
Readership/Target Audience: Aimed at those interested in local history predominantly 25 years old and over.
ADVERTISING RATES:
Full Page Colour £300.00
Mechanical Data: Type Area: 290 x 203mm, Col Length: 290mm, Page Width: 203mm, Film: Digital
CONSUMER: OTHER CLASSIFICATIONS: Miscellaneous

TIMES HIGHER EDUCATION
47904U88B-75

Formerly: The Times Higher Education Supplement
Editorial Address: 26 Red Lion Square, LONDON, WC1R 4HQ **Tel:** 020 3194 3000 **Fax:** 020 3194 3300
Email: editor@tsleducation.com
Advertising Address: As above. **Fax:** 020 3194 3405
Email: melanie.garcia@tsleducation.com
Web site: http://www.timeshighereducation.co.uk
ISSN: 0049-3929
Publisher: TSL Education Ltd
Date Established: 1972
Frequency: Weekly
Cover Price: £1.95
Annual Sub.: £55.00
Circulation: 21,140 (ABC 01/01/2007 to 31/12/2007)
Usual Pagination: 56
Editor: Phil Baty; **News Editor:** Phil Baty; **Managing Director:** Louise Rogers
Summary of Content: Newspaper containing national and international news about higher education.
Readership/Target Audience: Aimed at adults involved in higher education.
ADVERTISING RATES:
Full Page Colour £5880.00
Mechanical Data: Film: Digital, No. of Columns (Display): 5, Type Area: 282 x 212mm, Col Length: 282mm, Page Width: 212mm
Copy instructions: Copy Date: 10 days prior to publication date
CONSUMER: EDUCATION: Adult Education

THE TIMES LITERARY SUPPLEMENT
47554U84B-189

Editorial Address: Times House, 1 Pennington Street, LONDON, E98 1BS **Tel:** 020 7782 5000 **Fax:** 020 7782 4966
Email: letters@the-tls.co.uk
Advertising Address: As above. **Tel:** 020 7782 4974
Email: lucy.smart@newsint.co.uk
Web site: http://www.the-tls.co.uk
Publisher: Times Literary Supplement Ltd
Date Established: 1902
Frequency: Weekly - Published every Friday
Cover Price: £2.70
Annual Sub.: £92.00
Circulation: 31,958 (ABC 01/01/2009 to 30/06/2009)
Usual Pagination: 36
Editor: Will Eaves; **Managing Director:** James MacManus; **Managing Editor:** Robert Potts
Summary of Content: Supplement covering forty to fifty book reviews every week.
Readership/Target Audience: Read by the general and academic reader.
ADVERTISING RATES:
Full Page Mono £2910.40
Full Page Colour £3274.20
Agency Commission: 12.5%
Mechanical Data: Col Length: 340mm, Col Widths (Display): 63mm, Type Area: 340 x 264mm, Film: Digital, No. of Columns (Display): 4, Page Width: 264mm
Copy instructions: Copy Date: 8 days prior to publication date
Average advertising content per issue: 30%
CONSUMER: THE ARTS & LITERARY: Literary

TINKER BELL
1752933U91D-945

Formerly: Tinkerbell
Editorial Address: 239 Kensington High Street, LONDON, W8 6SA **Tel:** 020 7761 3500 **Fax:** 020 7761 3510
Email: jmillen@euk.egmont.com
Advertising Address: As above.
Email: svernon@euk.egmont.com
Publisher: Egmont Magazines UK

Date Established: 2006
Frequency: Monthly
Cover Price: £2.25
Circulation: 25,543 (ABC 01/01/2008 to 30/06/2008)
Usual Pagination: 36
Editor: Julia Millen
Summary of Content: Children's magazine covering the magical world of fairies based around Tinkerbell and her friends as well as puzzles, activities and stories.
Readership/Target Audience: Aimed at girls aged 5 to 7 years old.
ADVERTISING RATES:
Full Page Colour £1800.00
Mechanical Data: Type Area: 282 x 202mm, Bleed Size: 306 x 226mm, Trim Size: 300 x 220mm, Col Length: 282mm, Page Width: 202mm, Film: Digital
Copy instructions: Copy Date: 4 weeks prior to publication date
Average advertising content per issue: 15%
CONSUMER: RECREATION & LEISURE: Children & Youth

TIP STATION
1640541U78D-325

Editorial Address: Unit 1, Adlington Court, London Road, Adlington Park, MACCLESFIELD, SK10 4NL
Tel: 01625 855036 **Fax:** 01625 855039
Email: iainw@magnesiummedia.com
Advertising Address: As above.
Email: nounes@magnesiummedia.com
Web site: http://www.magnesiummedia.com
ISSN: 1476-8356
Publisher: Magnesium Media Ltd
Date Established: 2002
Frequency: Quarterly
Cover Price: £2.99
Circulation: 17,000 (Publisher's Statement)
Usual Pagination: 84
Editor: Iain Warde
Summary of Content: Magazine covering PlayStation2, PS3, Xbox, Xbox 360, PSP cheats, guides and walk throughs.
Readership/Target Audience: Aimed at 8 to 80 year old games enthusiasts.
ADVERTISING RATES:
Full Page Colour £1495.00
Agency Commission: 10%
Mechanical Data: Trim Size: 297 x 210mm, Film: Digital, Type Area: 275 x 190mm, Col Length: 275mm, Page Width: 190mm, Bleed Size: 303 x 216mm
Copy instructions: Copy Date: 4 weeks prior to publication date
CONSUMER: CONSUMER ELECTRONICS: Games

TIPS & ADVICE INTERNET
707463U78E-27

Editorial Address: Calgarth House, 39-41 Bank Street, ASHFORD, TN23 1DQ **Tel:** 01233 653507
Fax: 01233 647200
Email: editorial@indicator.co.uk
Web site: http://www.indicator.co.uk
Publisher: Indicator Limited
Date Established: 1998
Frequency: 22 issues yearly
Annual Sub.: £96.00
Circulation: 5,000 (Publisher's Statement)
Usual Pagination: 12
Editor: Duncan Callow; **Editor-in-Chief:** John Chapman; **Managing Editor:** Duncan Callow
Summary of Content: Newsletter covering information on new sites, Internet software and tips on how to make the most of your time surfing the Internet.
Readership/Target Audience: Aimed at Internet surfers looking for efficiency and profitability.
ADVERTISING: No Advertising taken
CONSUMER: CONSUMER ELECTRONICS: Home Computing

TKC MAG
1639649U77E-527

Formerly: totalkitcar
Editorial Address: 52 Sunnybank, WARLINGHAM, CR6 9SS
Tel: 01883 372085 **Fax:** 01883 624964
Email: steve_h@sportscar.fsbusiness.co.uk
Advertising Address: As above. **Fax:** 01833 624694
Email: nats@carpr.net
Web site: http://www.totalkitcar.com
Publisher: CAR PR Ltd
Date Established: 2003
Frequency: 6 issues yearly
Cover Price: £4.95
Circulation: 20,000 (Publisher's Statement)
Usual Pagination: 124
Editor: Steve Hole
Summary of Content: Magazine covering news, viewpoints, road tests, what's on and old kit cars.
Readership/Target Audience: Aimed at those interested in specialist cars.
ADVERTISING RATES:
Full Page Colour £500.00
Agency Commission: 10%

Mechanical Data: Type Area: 272 x 188mm, Bleed Size: 303 x 216mm, Trim Size: 297 x 210mm, Col Length: 272mm, Page Width: 188mm, Film: Digital
CONSUMER: MOTORING & CYCLING: Club Cars

TNT MAGAZINE
48350U90-182

Editorial Address: 14-15 Child's Place, Earls Court, LONDON, SW5 9RX **Tel:** 020 7373 3377
Email: tnteditor@tntmagazine.com
Advertising Address: As above. **Fax:** 020 7512 2719
Email: enquiries@tntmagazine.com
Web site: http://www.tntmagazine.com
Publisher: TNT Publishing
Date Established: 1983
Frequency: Weekly
Cover Price: Free
Circulation: 67,000 (Publisher's Statement)
Usual Pagination: 220
Editor: Samantha Baden; **News Editor:** Erin Miller; **Advertising Manager:** Kirsty Bourne
Summary of Content: Magazine covering Australian, South African and New Zealand news, sport and lifestyle. Includes London listings, entertainment and travel.
Readership/Target Audience: Aimed at nationals of Australia, New Zealand and South Africa who are living and working in the UK.
ADVERTISING RATES:
Full Page Colour £3250.90
SCC £34.02
Agency Commission: 10%
Mechanical Data: Film: Digital, No. of Columns (Display): 4, Type Area: 260 x 186mm, Col Length: 260mm, Page Width: 186mm, Col Widths (Display): 34mm, Trim Size: 297 x 210mm
Copy instructions: Copy Date: Noon 1 week prior to publication date
Average advertising content per issue: 70%
CONSUMER: ETHNIC

TODAY KENT & SUSSEX
1658472U80C-5188

Editorial Address: Longfield Road, TUNBRIDGE WELLS, TN2 3HL **Tel:** 01892 681000
Email: editor@today-magazine.co.uk
Advertising Address: As above. **Fax:** 01892 543181
Email: marian.wright@today-magazine.co.uk
Web site: http://www.thisiscourier.co.uk/today
Publisher: Courier Media Group Ltd
Frequency: Monthly
Cover Price: Free
Circulation: 34,000 (Publisher's Statement)
Usual Pagination: 88
Editor: Tony Durrant; **Advertising Manager:** Marian Wright
Summary of Content: Magazine covering women's lifestyle including fashion, beauty, shopping, interiors, property, gardening, health and fitness, travel and local lifestyle.
Readership/Target Audience: Aimed at women aged 35 to 55 years old in Kent and East Sussex.
ADVERTISING RATES:
Full Page Colour £1183.00
Copy instructions: Copy Date: 2 weeks prior to publication date
CONSUMER: RURAL & REGIONAL INTEREST: Regional Interest English Counties

TODAY TOMORROW
1640034U77E-508

Formerly: IF
Editorial Address: Studio 7, 3rd Floor, Enterprise House, 1-2 Hatfields, LONDON, SE1 9PG **Tel:** 020 7793 2460
Fax: 020 7953 7056
Email: oliver@sundaypublishing.com
Publisher: Sunday Publishing
Date Established: 2003
Frequency: 3 issues yearly
Cover Price: Free
Circulation: 320,000 (Publisher's Statement)
Usual Pagination: 52
Editor: Oliver Parsons
Summary of Content: Magazine published on behalf of Toyota UK with motoring and product based articles.
Readership/Target Audience: Aimed at Toyota customers in the UK.
ADVERTISING: No Advertising taken
CONSUMER: MOTORING & CYCLING: Club Cars

TODAY'S GOLFER
45830U75D-250

Editorial Address: Media House, Lynchwood, Peterborough Business Park, PETERBOROUGH, PE2 6EA
Tel: 01733 468000 **Fax:** 01733 468671
Email: editorial@todaysgolfer.co.uk
Advertising Address: As above.
Email: mark.thompson@bauerconsumer.co.uk
Web site: http://www.todaysgolfer.co.uk
Publisher: Bauer Consumer Media Ltd (Media House)
Date Established: 1988

Frequency: 13 issues yearly
Cover Price: £3.90
Annual Sub: £48.75
Circulation: 77,069 (ABC 01/01/2009 to 30/06/2009)
Usual Pagination: 180
Editor: Andy Calton; **Editor-in-Chief:** Andy Calton;
Managing Director: Steve Prentice
Summary of Content: Magazine with tips on improving your game, courses to play, equipment reviews and interviews.
Readership/Target Audience: Read by golfers.
ADVERTISING RATES:
Full Page Colour £4372.00
Agency Commission: 10%
Mechanical Data: Col Length: 267mm, Type Area: 267 x 178mm, Bleed Size: 303 x 216mm, Trim Size: 297 x 210mm, Film: Digital, Page Width: 178mm
Copy instructions: Copy Date: 4 weeks prior to publication date
Average advertising content per issue: 35%
CONSUMER: SPORT: Golf

TODAY'S PILOT
629561U75N-750
Editorial Address: PO Box 100, STAMFORD, PE9 1XQ
Tel: 01780 755131 **Fax:** 01780 757261
Email: dave.unwin@keypublishing.com
Advertising Address: As above.
Email: rhona.york@keypublishing.com
Web site: http://www.todayspilot.co.uk
ISSN: 1465-6337
Publisher: Key Publishing Ltd
Date Established: 2000
Frequency: Monthly
Cover Price: £3.80
Usual Pagination: 116
Editor: Dave Unwin; **Managing Director:** Adrian Cox;
Advertising Manager: Rhona York; **Publisher:** Adrian Cox
Summary of Content: Magazine covering all aspects of flying. Includes articles on microlights, gliders, paragliders, balloons, helicopters, vintage and kit planes.
Readership/Target Audience: Aimed at private pilots.
ADVERTISING RATES:
Full Page Colour £1900.00
SCC £13.00
Agency Commission: 10%
Mechanical Data: Bleed Size: 307 x 220mm, Col Widths (Display): 87mm, No. of Columns (Display): 2, Page Width: 180mm, Film: Digital, Type Area: 267 x 180mm, Col Length: 267mm, Trim Size: 297 x 210mm
Copy instructions: Copy Date: 4 weeks prior to publication date
Average advertising content per issue: 25%
CONSUMER: SPORT: Flight

TODAY'S RAILWAYS UK
760043U79J-16
Formerly: Entrain
Editorial Address: 3 Wyvern House, Sark Road, SHEFFIELD, S2 4HG **Tel:** 0114 255 2625
Fax: 0114 255 2471
Email: editorial@platform5.com
Advertising Address: As above.
Email: andrew.dyson@platform5.com
ISSN: 1475-9713
Publisher: Platform 5 Publishing Ltd
Date Established: 2002
Frequency: Monthly
Cover Price: £3.75
Circulation: 8,000 (Publisher's Statement)
Usual Pagination: 84
Editor: Peter Fox; **Advertising Manager:** Andrew Dyson
Summary of Content: Magazine covering railways and LRT systems throughout the UK.
Readership/Target Audience: Read by consumers, enthusiasts and industry members.
ADVERTISING: Rates on application
CONSUMER: HOBBIES & DIY: Rail Enthusiasts

TOM AND JERRY
48504U91D-132
Editorial Address: Brockbourne House, Mount Ephraim, TUNBRIDGE WELLS, TN4 8BS **Tel:** 01892 500100
Fax: 01892 545666
Email: ecaruana@panini.co.uk
Advertising Address: Orange20 Ltd, Station House, Bunbury Way, EPSOM, KT17 4JP **Tel:** 01372 802800
Fax: 01372 723322
Email: panini.adsales@o20.co.uk
Web site: http://www.paninicomics.co.uk
ISSN: 1358-9539
Publisher: Panini UK Ltd
Frequency: 13 issues yearly
Cover Price: £1.99
Circulation: 30,000 (Publisher's Statement)
Usual Pagination: 36
Editor: Ed Caruana; **Advertising Manager:** Michelle Fairlamb
Summary of Content: Children's magazine featuring cartoon fun and games from Tom and Jerry.

Readership/Target Audience: Aimed at children aged 5 to 9 years old.
ADVERTISING RATES:
Full Page Colour £1500.00
CONSUMER: RECREATION & LEISURE: Children & Youth

TONI & GUY MAGAZINE
1623440U74H-303
Editorial Address: 58-60 Stamford Street, LONDON, SE1 9LX **Tel:** 020 7921 9019 **Fax:** 020 7921 9145
Advertising Address: As above. **Tel:** 020 7921 9000
Email: rcaverhill@fstcomms.com
Publisher: FST
Date Established: 2003
Frequency: 3 issues yearly
Cover Price: £2.00
Free to qualifying individuals
Circulation: 100,000 (Publisher's Statement)
Usual Pagination: 100
Editor: Alex Ashcroft; **Advertising Manager:** Rebecca Caverhill
Summary of Content: Lifestyle magazine covering hair, fashion and beauty.
Readership/Target Audience: Aimed predominantly at women between 18 and 50 years old.
ADVERTISING: Rates on application
Copy instructions: Copy Date: 4 weeks prior to publication date
CONSUMER: WOMEN'S INTEREST CONSUMER MAGAZINES: Hair & Beauty

TOP OF THE POPS
46267U76E-401
Editorial Address: Media Centre, 201 Wood Lane, LONDON, W12 7TQ **Tel:** 020 8433 3910 **Fax:** 020 8433 2763
Email: claire.blindell@bbc.com
Advertising Address: Garden House, 201 Wood Lane, LONDON, W12 7TQ **Tel:** 020 8433 2000
Email: claire.stidwell@bbc.com
Web site: http://www.totpmag.com
Publisher: BBC Worldwide Publishing
Frequency: Monthly
Cover Price: £2.25
Circulation: 119,739 (ABC 01/01/2009 to 30/06/2009)
Usual Pagination: 88
Editor: Claire Blindell; **Managing Director:** Peter Phippen;
Advertising Manager: Claire Stidwell
Summary of Content: Magazine focusing on pop music. Contains interviews with pop stars, album reviews, concert dates and competitions.
Readership/Target Audience: Aimed at 10 to 16 year olds.
ADVERTISING RATES:
Full Page Colour £9050.00
Agency Commission: 10%
Mechanical Data: Col Length: 265mm, Page Width: 190mm, Type Area: 265 x 190mm, Trim Size: 285 x 210mm, Bleed Size: 293 x 218mm, Film: Digital
Copy instructions: Copy Date: 4 weeks prior to publication date
CONSUMER: MUSIC & PERFORMING ARTS: Pop Music

TOP REVIEW
46062U76A-90
Formerly: Top Review Magazine
Editorial Address: Orchardton Hall, Auchencairn, CASTLE DOUGLAS, DG7 1QL **Tel:** 0845 130 6249
Fax: 0845 658 8329
Email: edit@bnw.demon.co.uk
Advertising Address: As above.
Email: topreview@bnw.demon.co.uk
Web site: http://www.topreview.net
Publisher: Brave New World International Ltd
Frequency: Half-yearly - Published in July and December
Cover Price: £0.90
Circulation: 50,000 (Publisher's Statement)
Usual Pagination: 64
Editor: Roy Osbourne; **Managing Director:** Susan Foster;
Advertising Manager: Susan Foster; **Group Editor:** Dave Burbidge
Summary of Content: Review magazine with entertainment features and video, film, car and book reviews.
Readership/Target Audience: Read by those between 16 and 40 years old with a high disposable income.
ADVERTISING RATES:
Full Page Colour £1500.00
Agency Commission: 15%
Mechanical Data: Trim Size: 297 x 210mm
Copy instructions: Copy Date: 3 weeks prior to publication date
CONSUMER: MUSIC & PERFORMING ARTS: Cinema

TOP SANTE HEALTH & BEAUTY
45452U74G-76
Editorial Address: Endeavour House, 189 Shaftesbury Avenue, LONDON, WC2H 8JG **Tel:** 020 7437 9011
Email: fiona.embleton@bauermedia.com
Advertising Address: As above.
Email: amanda.campbell@bauerconsumer.co.uk

Publisher: Bauer Media
Date Established: 1993
Frequency: Monthly
Cover Price: £2.80
Annual Sub: £19.00
Circulation: 85,074 (ABC 01/01/2009 to 30/06/2009)
Usual Pagination: 132
Editor: Fiona Embleton; **Advertising Director:** Amanda Campbell
Summary of Content: Magazine covering all aspects of health and beauty.
Readership/Target Audience: Read by women of all ages.
ADVERTISING RATES:
Full Page Colour £7123.00
Mechanical Data: Type Area: 255 x 192mm, Col Length: 255mm, Page Width: 192mm, Film: Digital, Trim Size: 278 x 213mm, Bleed Size: 286 x 219mm
Copy instructions: Copy Date: 3 weeks prior to publication date
CONSUMER: WOMEN'S INTEREST CONSUMER MAGAZINES: Slimming & Health

TOP YACHTS
1834301U91A-300
Editorial Address: Blue Fin Building, 110 Southwark Street, LONDON, SE1 0SU **Tel:** 020 3148 5000
Email: elaine@elainebunting.com
Advertising Address: As above.
Web site: http://www.ybw.com/topyachts
Publisher: IPC Inspire
Frequency: Annual - Published in July
Cover Price: £3.50
Circulation: 30,000 (Publisher's Statement)
Editor: Elaine Bunting
Summary of Content: Guide to new yachts from the world's most important builders.
Readership/Target Audience: Aimed at those looking to buy boats of up to 60 feet long.
CONSUMER: RECREATION & LEISURE: Boating & Yachting

TOPLUM POSTASI
1841064U90-1027
Editorial Address: 117 Green Lanes, LONDON, N16 9DA
Tel: 020 7354 4424 **Fax:** 020 7354 0313
Email: info@toplumpostasi.net
Advertising Address: As above.
Email: info@toplumpostasi.net
Web site: http://www.toplumpostassi.net
Publisher: Toplum Postasi
Frequency: Weekly - Published on Thursday
Cover Price: Free
Circulation: 27,000 (Publisher's Statement)
Editor: Alkan Chaglar; **Advertising Manager:** Ali Keskin
Summary of Content: Newspaper covering news from the UK, Cyprus, Turkey and the EU with current affairs, commentary, business, education and sport.
Language(s): Turkish
Readership/Target Audience: Aimed at first generation, Turkish speaking people including Cypriots, Turks and Kurds.
ADVERTISING RATES:
Full Page Mono £450.00
Full Page Colour £1000.00
CONSUMER: ETHNIC

TOPMBA CAREER GUIDE
47915U88C-60
Formerly: The MBA Career Guide
Editorial Address: 1 Tranley Mews, Fleet Road, LONDON, NW3 2DG **Tel:** 020 7284 7200 **Fax:** 020 7284 7201
Email: ross@qsnetwork.com
Advertising Address: As above. **Tel:** 020 7284 7221
Fax: 020 7284 7203
Email: kamran@qsnetwork.com
Web site: http://www.topmba.com
ISSN: 1060-4669
Publisher: QS Quacquarelli Symonds Ltd
Date Established: 1993
Frequency: Half-yearly - Published in March and September
Cover Price: £15.95
Circulation: 30,000 (Publisher's Statement)
Usual Pagination: 250
Editor: Nunzio Quacquarelli; **Advertising Manager:** Kamran Ahmed; **Managing Editor:** Ross Geraghty; **Publisher:** Nunzio Quacquarelli
Summary of Content: International magazine providing business schools with a forum for communication with MBA applicants and students.
Readership/Target Audience: Aimed at MBA students, graduates and recruiters.
ADVERTISING RATES:
Full Page Colour £2500.00
Agency Commission: 10%
Mechanical Data: Type Area: 272 x 184mm, Bleed Size: 303 x 216mm, Trim Size: 297 x 210mm, Col Length: 272mm, Page Width: 184mm, Film: Digital
Average advertising content per issue: 15%
CONSUMER: EDUCATION: Careers

Consumer Magazines

TORCHWOOD
1832672U74F-773

Editorial Address: Titan House, 144 Southwark Street, LONDON, SE1 0UP **Tel:** 020 7620 0200 **Fax:** 020 7620 0032
Email: torchwoodmagazine@titanemail.com
Advertising Address: As above. **Fax:** 020 7803 1803
Email: james.willmott@titanemail.com
Web site: http://www.titanmagazines.com
Publisher: Titan Magazines
Date Established: 2008
Frequency: 13 issues yearly
Cover Price: £3.75
Editor: Simon Hugo; **Advertising Manager:** James Willmott
Summary of Content: Magazine based on the TV programme Torchwood with behind the scenes reporting, celebrity interviews, step by step information on special effects and comic strips.
Readership/Target Audience: Aimed at fans of the show of all ages.
ADVERTISING RATES:
Full Page Colour £2500.00
Mechanical Data: Trim Size: 276 x 200mm, Film: Digital
CONSUMER: WOMEN'S INTEREST CONSUMER MAGAZINES: Teenage

TOTAL 911
1668010U77E-516

Editorial Address: Richmond House, 33 Richmond Hill, BOURNEMOUTH, BH2 6EZ **Tel:** 01202 586200
Email: phil.raby@imagine-publishing.co.uk
Advertising Address: As above.
Email: darren@total911.co.uk
Web site: http://www.total911.com
ISSN: 1746-613X
Publisher: Imagine Publishing
Date Established: 2005
Frequency: 13 issues yearly
Cover Price: £4.25
Circulation: 35,000 (Publisher's Statement)
Usual Pagination: 116
Editor: Philip Raby
Summary of Content: Magazine covering all aspects and all models of the Porsche 911.
Readership/Target Audience: Aimed at Porsche enthusiasts.
ADVERTISING RATES:
Full Page Colour £1250.00
Agency Commission: 10%
Copy instructions: Copy Date: 2 weeks prior to publication date
CONSUMER: MOTORING & CYCLING: Club Cars

TOTAL BMW
633828U77E-295

Editorial Address: Cudham Tithe Barn, Berrys Hill, Berrys Green, Cudham, WESTERHAM, TN16 3AG
Tel: 01959 541444
Email: bmw.ed@kelsey.co.uk
Advertising Address: 1st Floor, South Wing, Broadway Court, Broadway, PETERBOROUGH, PE1 1RP
Tel: 01733 347559 **Fax:** 01733 891342
Email: matt.carson@kelseypb.co.uk
Web site: http://www.kelsey.co.uk
ISSN: 1471-4299
Publisher: Kelsey Publishing Ltd
Date Established: 2000
Frequency: Monthly
Cover Price: £4.25
Circulation: 12,000 (Publisher's Statement)
Usual Pagination: 132
Editor: Paul Wager; **Advertising Director:** Matt Carson; **Publisher:** Phil Weeden
Summary of Content: Magazine covering all aspects of BMW cars. Includes product news, show reports, technical articles and features on the BMW racing team.
Readership/Target Audience: Aimed at BMW owners and enthusiasts.
ADVERTISING RATES:
Full Page Colour £800.00
Agency Commission: 10%
Mechanical Data: Film: Digital, Type Area: 277 x 188mm, Col Length: 277mm, Trim Size: 297 x 210mm, Bleed Size: 303 x 216mm, Page Width: 188mm
Copy instructions: Copy Date: 3 weeks prior to publication date
CONSUMER: MOTORING & CYCLING: Club Cars

TOTAL CARP
601081U92-94

Editorial Address: 2 Stephenson Close, Drayton Fields Industrial Estate, DAVENTRY, NN11 8RF **Tel:** 01327 311999
Fax: 01327 311190
Email: marccoulson@dhpub.co.uk
Advertising Address: As above. **Fax:** 01327 312418
Email: garth.ethelston@dhpub.co.uk
Web site: http://www.totalcarpmagazine.com
ISSN: 1467-7938
Publisher: David Hall Publishing Ltd
Date Established: 1999
Frequency: Monthly

Cover Price: £3.40
Annual Sub.: £43.30
Circulation: 22,524 (Publisher's Statement)
Usual Pagination: 196
Editor: Marc Coulson; **Advertising Manager:** Garth Ethelston; **Publisher:** David Hall
Summary of Content: Magazine covering all aspects of carp fishing.
Readership/Target Audience: Aimed at carp fishing enthusiasts and newcomers to the sport.
ADVERTISING: Rates on application
CONSUMER: ANGLING & FISHING

TOTAL CATHOLIC
47763U87-215

Formerly: The Universe
Editorial Address: 4th Floor, Landmark House, Station Road, Cheadle Hulme, CHEADLE, SK8 7JH
Tel: 0161 488 1700
Email: newsdesk@totalcatholic.com
Advertising Address: As above. **Fax:** 0161 488 1782
Email: advertising@totalcatholic.net
Web site: http://www.totalcatholic.com
Publisher: Gabriel Communications Ltd
Frequency: Weekly
Cover Price: £1.00
Annual Sub.: £52.00
Circulation: 36,000 (Publisher's Statement)
Editor: Lee Siggs; **News Editor:** Lee Siggs; **Features Editor:** Emma Clancy
Summary of Content: Newspaper covering news, campaigns and Catholic concerns and issues.
Readership/Target Audience: Aimed at Roman Catholics.
ADVERTISING RATES:
Full Page Mono £4755.00
Full Page Colour £5943.75
SCC £19.98
Agency Commission: 10%
Mechanical Data: Col Length: 340mm, No. of Columns (Display): 7, Type Area: 340 x 265mm, Print Process: Web-fed offset litho, Screen: 60 lpc, Page Width: 265mm
Copy instructions: Copy Date: Thursday 2 weeks prior to publication date
Average advertising content per issue: 60%
CONSUMER: RELIGIOUS

TOTAL COARSE FISHING
1773979U92-109

Editorial Address: 2 Stephenson Close, Drayton Fields Industrial Estate, DAVENTRY, NN11 8RF **Tel:** 01327 311999
Fax: 01327 311190
Email: gareth@dhpub.co.uk
Advertising Address: As above.
Email: garth.ethelston@dhpub.co.uk
Web site: http://www.total-fishing.com
Publisher: David Hall Publishing Ltd
Date Established: 2006
Frequency: Monthly
Cover Price: £2.85
Circulation: 35,000 (Publisher's Statement)
Usual Pagination: 148
Editor: Gareth Purnell
Summary of Content: Magazine covering fresh water coarse fishing including instruction, tackle reviews, competitions, interviews and overseas adventure angling.
Readership/Target Audience: Aimed at all round pleasure anglers who like to keep their angling varied.
ADVERTISING RATES:
Full Page Colour £835.00
Agency Commission: 10%
Mechanical Data: Bleed Size: 303 x 216mm, Trim Size: 297 x 210mm, Film: Digital, Type Area: 273 x 185mm, Col Length: 273mm, Page Width: 185mm
Copy instructions: Copy Date: 2nd Wednesday of the month prior to publication date
Average advertising content per issue: 25%
CONSUMER: ANGLING & FISHING

TOTAL FILM
46063U76A-100

Editorial Address: 2 Balcombe Street, LONDON, NW1 6NW
Tel: 020 7042 4000 **Fax:** 020 7042 4839
Email: totalfilm@futurenet.co.uk
Advertising Address: As above. **Fax:** 020 7042 4471
Email: rachel.sinclair@futurenet.co.uk
Web site: http://www.totalfilm.com
Publisher: Future Publishing Limited
Date Established: 1997
Frequency: 13 issues yearly
Cover Price: £3.90
Circulation: 85,031 (ABC 01/01/2009 to 30/06/2009)
Usual Pagination: 164
Editor: Aubrey Day; **News Editor:** Rosie Fletcher; **Editor-in-Chief:** Aubrey Day
Summary of Content: Film magazine featuring news, reviews and articles on all current and future video, film, book, soundtrack and multimedia releases.
Readership/Target Audience: Aimed at male and female readers aged between 15 and 35 years old.

ADVERTISING RATES:
Full Page Colour £4620.00
Agency Commission: 10%
Mechanical Data: No. of Columns (Display): 4, Bleed Size: 306 x 228mm, Trim Size: 300 x 222mm, Type Area: 280 x 203mm, Col Length: 280mm, Film: Digital, Page Width: 203mm
Average advertising content per issue: 30%
CONSUMER: MUSIC & PERFORMING ARTS: Cinema

TOTAL FLYFISHER
1626011U92-101

Formerly: Today's flyfisher
Editorial Address: 2 Stephenson Close, Drayton Fields Industrial Estate, DAVENTRY, NN11 8RF **Tel:** 01327 311999
Fax: 01327 311190
Email: steve.cullen@dhpub.co.uk
Advertising Address: As above. **Tel:** 01327 315401
Email: sue@dhpub.co.uk
Web site: http://www.dhponline.com
Publisher: David Hall Publishing Ltd
Frequency: Monthly
Cover Price: £2.80
Annual Sub.: £32.40
Circulation: 18,000 (Publisher's Statement)
Usual Pagination: 132
Editor: Steve Cullen; **Advertising Manager:** Sue Shaw; **Publisher:** David Hall
Summary of Content: Instructional magazine covering all aspects of fly fishing. Includes advice, tackle, fishing destinations and problem solving solutions.
Readership/Target Audience: Aimed at fly fishing enthusiasts of all levels.
ADVERTISING RATES:
Full Page Colour £650.00
SCC £15.00
Agency Commission: 10%
Mechanical Data: Type Area: 273 x 185mm, Bleed Size: 303 x 216mm, Trim Size: 297 x 210mm, Col Length: 273mm, Page Width: 185mm, Film: Digital
CONSUMER: ANGLING & FISHING

TOTAL GUITAR
46186U76D-425

Editorial Address: 30 Monmouth Street, BATH, BA1 2BW
Tel: 01225 442244
Email: totalguitar@futurenet.com
Advertising Address: As above. **Fax:** 01225 732396
Email: martin.hughes@futurenet.co.uk
Web site: http://www.totalguitar.co.uk
ISSN: 1355-5049
Publisher: Future Publishing Ltd
Date Established: 1994
Frequency: 13 issues yearly
Cover Price: £4.99
Circulation: 42,171 (ABC 01/01/2008 to 31/12/2008)
Usual Pagination: 156
Editor: Stephen Lawson; **News Editor:** Nick Cracknell
Summary of Content: Magazine covering all aspects of guitars and guitar playing.
Readership/Target Audience: Aimed at amateur guitarists.
ADVERTISING RATES:
Full Page Colour £1640.00
Agency Commission: 10%
Mechanical Data: Film: Digital, Type Area: 270 x 190mm, Col Length: 270mm, Trim Size: 297 x 210mm, Bleed Size: 303 x 216mm, Page Width: 190mm
CONSUMER: MUSIC & PERFORMING ARTS: Music

TOTAL OFF-ROAD
767353U77A-504

Editorial Address: 151 Station Street, BURTON-ON-TRENT, DE14 1BG **Tel:** 01283 742950 **Fax:** 01283 742957
Email: editorial@toronline.co.uk
Advertising Address: Wenallt Fawr, Rhydcymerau, LLANDEILO, SA19 7RL **Tel:** 01558 685383
Fax: 01558 685228
Email: sylvia.maskelyne@toronline.co.uk
Publisher: WW Magazines
Date Established: 2002
Frequency: Monthly
Cover Price: £3.75
Usual Pagination: 116
Editor: Alan Kidd; **Advertising Manager:** Sylvia Maskelyne
Summary of Content: Magazine covering 4x4s and off-roading of all types in UK and abroad.
Readership/Target Audience: Aimed at recreational off-roaders and 4x4 owners.
ADVERTISING RATES:
Full Page Colour £956.00
Agency Commission: 10%
Mechanical Data: Type Area: 267 x 190mm, Col Length: 267mm, Trim Size: 297 x 210mm, Bleed Size: 303 x 213mm, Film: Digital, Page Width: 190mm
CONSUMER: MOTORING & CYCLING: Motoring

TOTAL PC GAMING
1826938U78D-337

Editorial Address: Richmond House, 33 Richmond Hill, BOURNEMOUTH, BH2 6EZ **Tel:** 01202 586200
Email: dave.harfield@imagine-publishing.co.uk
Advertising Address: As above. **Fax:** 01202 294032
Email: jordan.quinn@imagine-publishing.co.uk
ISSN: 1755-7623
Publisher: Imagine Publishing
Date Established: 2007
Frequency: 13 issues yearly
Cover Price: £3.99
Circulation: 30,000 (Print Run)
Usual Pagination: 148
Editor: David Harfield; **Editor-in-Chief:** David Harfield
Summary of Content: Magazine covering all aspects of contemporary PC gaming with a special focus on MMORPG, retro gaming and hardware as well as previews and reviews of the latest.
Readership/Target Audience: Aimed at hardcore gamers.
ADVERTISING RATES:
Full Page Colour £1850.00
Mechanical Data: Type Area: 277 x 210mm, Bleed Size: 307 x 240mm, Trim Size: 297 x 230mm, Col Length: 277mm, Page Width: 210mm, Film: Digital
CONSUMER: CONSUMER ELECTRONICS: Games

TOTAL POLITICS
764911U82-279

Editorial Address: 7 Cowley Street, LONDON, SW1P 3NB **Tel:** 020 7654 5567
Email: http://sarah.mackinlay@totalpolitics.com
Web site: http://www.totalpolitics.com
ISSN: 1757-0492
Publisher: Biteback Media
Date Established: 2008
Frequency: Monthly
Cover Price: £3.99
Free to qualifying individuals
Annual Sub.: £38.30
Circulation: 25,456 (Publisher's Statement)
Usual Pagination: 64
Editor: Ben Duckworth; **Executive Editor:** Shane Greer; **Publisher:** Iain Dale
Summary of Content: Magazine covering cross party politics including campaigning, interviews, features, cartoons and humour.
Readership/Target Audience: Aimed at elected politicians in Britain and those with an interest in politics.
CONSUMER: CURRENT AFFAIRS & POLITICS

TOTAL PRODUCTION INTERNATIONAL
46079U76B-270

Formerly: Total Production
Editorial Address: 19 Princes Street, SOUTHEND-ON-SEA, SS1 1QA **Tel:** 01702 333003 **Fax:** 01702 333005
Email: m.cunningham@mondiale.co.uk
Advertising Address: Waterloo Place, Watson Square, STOCKPORT, SK1 3AZ **Tel:** 0161 476 5580
Fax: 0161 429 7214
Email: h.eakins@mondiale.co.uk
Web site: http://www.mondiale.co.uk
ISSN: 1461-3786
Publisher: Mondiale Publishing Ltd
Date Established: 1998
Frequency: Monthly - Published in the 1st week of the cover month
Cover Price: £3.50
Circulation: 25,000 (Publisher's Statement)
Usual Pagination: 68
Editor: Mark Cunningham; **Advertising Manager:** Hannah Eakins
Summary of Content: Magazine containing news and reviews on all aspects of live performance production, including sound, lighting, set design and video.
Readership/Target Audience: Aimed at those involved in the production of theatre shows, festivals and concerts.
ADVERTISING RATES:
Full Page Colour £1890.00
Mechanical Data: Page Width: 190mm, Type Area: 277 x 190mm, Bleed Size: 303 x 213mm, Trim Size: 297 x 210mm, Col Length: 277mm, Film: Digital
CONSUMER: MUSIC & PERFORMING ARTS: Theatre

TOTAL SEA FISHING
48540U92-96_80

Editorial Address: 2 Stephenson Close, Drayton Fields Industrial Estate, DAVENTRY, NN11 8RF **Tel:** 01327 311999
Tel: 01327 311190
Email: barney.wright@dhpub.co.uk
Advertising Address: As above. **Fax:** 01327 315435
Email: trevor@dhpub.co.uk
Web site: http://www.totalseamagazine.com
ISSN: 1461-622X
Publisher: David Hall Publishing Ltd
Date Established: 1998
Frequency: Monthly
Cover Price: £2.60

Annual Sub.: £31.20
Circulation: 24,000 (Publisher's Statement)
Usual Pagination: 116
Editor: Barney Wright; **Publisher:** David Hall
Summary of Content: Instructional magazine covering all aspects of sea fishing including beach, pier, match and boat fishing.
Readership/Target Audience: Aimed at the general sea angler.
ADVERTISING RATES:
Full Page Colour £575.00
Agency Commission: 10%
Mechanical Data: Trim Size: 297 x 210mm, Bleed Size: 307 x 220mm, No. of Columns (Display): 4, Film: Digital, Type Area: 273 x 185mm, Col Length: 273mm, Page Width: 185mm
Copy instructions: Copy Date: 2nd Wednesday of every month prior to publication date
Average advertising content per issue: 40%
CONSUMER: ANGLING & FISHING

TOTAL SUDOKU
1696579U79F-93

Editorial Address: Zetland House, 5-25 Scrutton Street, LONDON, EC2A 4HJ **Tel:** 020 7613 7477
Fax: 020 7168 7956
Email: sarah@accoladepublishing.co.uk
ISSN: 1748-5622
Publisher: Accolade Publishing
Date Established: 2005
Frequency: 13 issues yearly
Cover Price: £2.10
Circulation: 40,000 (Publisher's Statement)
Usual Pagination: 68
Editor: Justine Wall; **Publisher:** Justine Wall
Summary of Content: Magazine containing Sudoku puzzles.
Readership/Target Audience: Aimed generally at men and women aged 25 years old plus.
ADVERTISING: No Advertising taken
CONSUMER: HOBBIES & DIY: Games & Puzzles

TOTAL TATTOO
1664184U74Q-1244

Editorial Address: PO Box 10038, Sudbury, SUFFOLK, CO10 7WL **Tel:** 01787 242100 **Fax:** 01787 242161
Email: editor@totaltattoo.co.uk
Advertising Address: As above.
Email: advertising@totaltattoo.co.uk
Web site: http://www.totaltattoo.co.uk
Publisher: KMT Publishing Ltd
Date Established: 2004
Frequency: Monthly
Cover Price: £4.20
Circulation: 25,000 (Print Run)
Usual Pagination: 84
Editor: Sally Feldt
Summary of Content: Magazine covering tattoos, interviews with top tattoo artists and up and coming talent, features on tattoo history worldwide, opinion columns, conventions, fashion spreads with tattooed models as well as news and views.
Readership/Target Audience: Aimed at discerning tattoo enthusiasts.
ADVERTISING RATES:
Full Page Colour £750.00
Mechanical Data: Type Area: 275 x 190mm, Bleed Size: 303 x 216mm, Trim Size: 297 x 210mm, Col Length: 275mm, Page Width: 190mm, Film: Digital
Copy instructions: Copy Date: 15 days prior to the publication date
Average advertising content per issue: 20%
CONSUMER: WOMEN'S INTEREST CONSUMER MAGAZINES: Lifestyle

TOTAL TV GUIDE
1637568U76C-824

Editorial Address: Academic House, 24-28 Oval Road, LONDON, NW1 7DT **Tel:** 020 7241 8000 **Fax:** 020 7241 8042
Email: total.tvletters@bauer.co.uk
Advertising Address: As above. **Fax:** 020 7075 0786
Email: lisa.carver@bauer.co.uk
Web site: http://www.bauer.co.uk
Publisher: H. Bauer Publishing
Date Established: 2003
Frequency: Weekly
Cover Price: £0.98
Circulation: 107,681 (ABC 01/01/2009 to 30/06/2009)
Usual Pagination: 98
Editor: Ben Lawrence; **Features Editor:** Sue Malins; **Advertising Manager:** Lisa Carver
Summary of Content: TV guide with digital and satellite listings as well as features, celebrity interviews and entertainment documentaries.
Readership/Target Audience: Aimed at users of multi-channel TV with a core readership of men and women aged 25 to 44.
ADVERTISING RATES:
Full Page Colour £7000.00

Agency Commission: 15%
Mechanical Data: Type Area: 280 x 205mm, Col Length: 280mm, Page Width: 205mm, Trim Size: 300 x 225mm, Bleed Size: 310 x 235mm, Print Process: Web-fed offset litho
CONSUMER: MUSIC & PERFORMING ARTS: TV & Radio

TOTAL VAUXHALL
713436U77A-430

Editorial Address: 30 Monmouth Street, BATH, BA1 2BW
Tel: 01225 442244 **Fax:** 01225 446019
Email: dougie.rankine@futurenet.co.uk
Advertising Address: As above. **Fax:** 01225 732206
Email: steve.roberts@futurenet.co.uk
Web site: http://www.totalvauxhall.co.uk
ISSN: 1474-1393
Publisher: Future Publishing Ltd
Date Established: 2001
Frequency: 13 issues yearly
Cover Price: £3.99
Annual Sub.: £39.99
Circulation: 28,000 (Publisher's Statement)
Usual Pagination: 164
Summary of Content: Magazine containing expert technical advice, modified cars, step-by-step DIY features, buying guides and the latest ICE systems and products.
Readership/Target Audience: Aimed at owners, drivers and enthusiasts of Vauxhall cars.
ADVERTISING RATES:
Full Page Colour £488.00
Agency Commission: 10%
Mechanical Data: Type Area: 278 x 188mm, Trim Size: 297 x 210mm, Bleed Size: 303 x 216mm, Col Length: 278mm, Page Width: 188mm
Copy instructions: Copy Date: 3 weeks prior to publication date
Average advertising content per issue: 33%
CONSUMER: MOTORING & CYCLING: Motoring

TOTAL YOUTH FOOTIE
1825930U75B-290

Editorial Address: The Old Brewery, Priory Lane, BURFORD, OX18 4SG **Tel:** 01993 822811
Email: editorial@tyfootie.com
Advertising Address: As above. **Fax:** 01993 825928
Email: robin@totalyouthfootball.com
Web site: http://www.tyfootie.com
Publisher: O Publishing
Date Established: 2007
Frequency: Monthly
Cover Price: £1.50
Free to qualifying individuals
Circulation: 50,000 (Publisher's Statement)
Usual Pagination: 44
Editor: Tim Beynon
Summary of Content: Magazine with football news, education, health, nutrition, lifestyle features and competitions.
Readership/Target Audience: Aimed at youth football players, both boys and girls, aged 10 to 14 years old through their clubs and schools.
ADVERTISING RATES:
Full Page Colour £1575.00
Mechanical Data: Bleed Size: 253 x 180mm, Trim Size: 245 x 172mm, Film: Digital
CONSUMER: SPORT: Football

TOTALLY MEDIA LTD
1745161U80C-5338

Formerly: Totally
Editorial Address: The Brewery House, 74 High Street, MARLOW, SL7 1AH **Tel:** 01628 488388 **Fax:** 01628 481877
Email: enquiries@totallymedia.net
Advertising Address: As above.
Email: enquiries@totallymedia.net
Web site: http://www.totallymedia.net
Publisher: Totally Media Ltd
Date Established: 2005
Frequency: Monthly
Cover Price: Free
Circulation: 60,000 (Publisher's Statement)
Usual Pagination: 60
Editor: Angela Meredith; **Advertising Manager:** Tony Light; **Publisher:** Tony Light
Summary of Content: Local society magazine covering local events and editorial features as well as fashion, health and beauty, technology, travel, motoring and property.
Readership/Target Audience: Aimed at those aged between 20 and 50 years old in high net worth towns in SW London, The Thames Valley and South West Midlands.
ADVERTISING RATES:
Full Page Colour £713.00
Mechanical Data: Type Area: 277 x 190mm, Bleed Size: 303 x 216mm, Trim Size: 297 x 210mm, Col Length: 277mm, Page Width: 190mm, Film: Digital
Copy instructions: Copy Date: 1 week prior to publication date

Consumer Magazines

Average advertising content per issue: 33%
CONSUMER: RURAL & REGIONAL INTEREST: Regional Interest English Counties

TOUCHDOWN BRITISH AIRWAYS
45588U74N-140

Editorial Address: Waterside (HCB3), PO Box 365, Harmondsworth, WEST DRAYTON, UB7 0GB
Tel: 020 8738 5100 **Fax:** 020 8738 9838
Email: ian.lynch@ba.com
Advertising Address: Publicom Ltd, Battersea Studios, 80 Silverthorne Road, LONDON, SW8 3HE **Tel:** 020 7978 2544
Email: dsandalls@publicom-uk.com
Publisher: British Airways Communications Department
Frequency: Half-yearly
Cover Price: Free
Circulation: 44,000 (Publisher's Statement)
Usual Pagination: 32
Editor: Ian Lynch
Summary of Content: Magazine covering company news, staff associations, books, gardening, letters and details of forthcoming events.
Readership/Target Audience: Read by retired British Airways staff.
ADVERTISING RATES:
Full Page Mono £2500.00
Full Page Colour £2500.00
SCC £18.00
Agency Commission: 10%
Mechanical Data: Type Area: 293 x 235mm, Page Width: 235mm, No. of Columns (Display): 4, Col Length: 293mm, Trim Size: 333 x 260mm, Bleed Size: 339 x 266mm, Film: Digital
Average advertising content per issue: 40%
CONSUMER: WOMEN'S INTEREST CONSUMER MAGAZINES: Retirement

TOWN AND COUNTRY NEWS NORTH NORFOLK & BROADLAND
46946U80C-2340

Formerly: North Norfolk & Broadland Town and Country News
Editorial Address: Unit 5, Bank Street, Stalham, NORWICH, NR12 9BA **Tel:** 01692 582287
Email: editorial@leisurepublishing.co.uk
Advertising Address: As above. **Fax:** 01692 580994
Email: sales@leisurepublishing.co.uk
Web site: http://www.townandcountrynews.co.uk
Publisher: Leisure Publishing
Date Established: 1989
Frequency: Monthly
Cover Price: Free
Circulation: 33,000 (Publisher's Statement)
Usual Pagination: 32
Editor: Laurence Watts; **Managing Director:** Laurence Watts; **Advertising Manager:** Clare Storey
Summary of Content: Community newspaper covering local news, events and general interest articles.
Readership/Target Audience: Aimed at householders in the North Norfolk and Norfolk Broads area.
ADVERTISING RATES:
Full Page Mono £370.00
Full Page Colour £481.00
SCC £3.53
Agency Commission: 10%
Mechanical Data: Print Process: Web-fed offset litho, Type Area: 340 x 265mm, Col Length: 340mm, No. of Columns (Display): 8, Page Width: 265mm, Film: Digital
Copy instructions: Copy Date: 1 week prior to publication date
CONSUMER: RURAL & REGIONAL INTEREST: Regional Interest English Counties

TOWN & COUNTRY POST
1814269U89C-1103

Editorial Address: 6A Station Road, LONGFIELD, DA3 7QD
Tel: 01474 705899 **Fax:** 01474 705808
Email: info@townandcountrypost.co.uk
Advertising Address: As above.
Email: info@townandcountrypost.co.uk
Web site: http://www.townandcountrypost.co.uk
Publisher: The Wealden Advertiser
Frequency: Monthly
Cover Price: Free
Circulation: 28,500 (Publisher's Statement)
Usual Pagination: 64
Editor: Colin Senneck; **Managing Editor:** Graham Thorn
Summary of Content: Community magazine covering what's on and where as well as events reports.
Readership/Target Audience: Aimed at the general public in Kent.
ADVERTISING RATES:
Full Page Colour £320.00
Copy instructions: Copy Date: Middle of the month prior to publication date
CONSUMER: HOLIDAYS & TRAVEL: Entertainment Guides

TOWN & VILLAGE COMMUNITY MAGAZINE
1656407U80C-5139

Formerly: Town & Village Times
Editorial Address: 6 Whittle Road, Ferndown Industrial Estate, WIMBORNE, BH21 7RU **Tel:** 01202 870270
Fax: 01202 870370
Email: mags@mags4dorset.co.uk
Advertising Address: As above.
Email: tavt@btconnect.com
Web site: http://www.mags@mags4dorset.co.uk
Publisher: Page & Pulford
Date Established: 2003
Frequency: Monthly
Cover Price: Free
Annual Sub.: £15.00
Circulation: 20,000 (Publisher's Statement)
Usual Pagination: 32
Editor: Janine Pulford; **Advertising Manager:** Val O'Neill
Summary of Content: Magazine covering community issues as well as sport, motoring, clubs, restaurants, home improvements, education and events.
Readership/Target Audience: Aimed at residents in Dorset and Hampshire.
ADVERTISING RATES:
Full Page Colour £650.00
SCC £6.60
Agency Commission: 5%
Mechanical Data: Type Area: 270 x 195mm, Col Length: 270mm, Page Width: 195mm, Bleed Size: 311 x 226mm, Trim Size: 295 x 210mm, Film: Digital, No. of Columns (Display): 5, Col Widths (Display): 35mm
Copy instructions: Copy Date: 10 days prior to publication date
Average advertising content per issue: 50%
CONSUMER: RURAL & REGIONAL INTEREST: Regional Interest English Counties

TOWNSWOMAN
45292U74A-590

Editorial Address: Agriculture House, North Gate, Uppingham, OAKHAM, LE15 9PL **Tel:** 01572 824683
Fax: 01572 824646
Email: christine.moss@associa.co.uk
Advertising Address: As above. **Tel:** 01572 824600
Fax: 01572 824600
Email: mandy.frisby@associa.co.uk
Web site: http://www.townswomen.org.uk
ISSN: 0266-8491
Publisher: Associa Ltd
Date Established: 1933
Frequency: Quarterly
Free to qualifying individuals
Circulation: 35,000 (Publisher's Statement)
Usual Pagination: 52
Editor: Christine Moss; **Advertising Manager:** Mandy Frisby
Summary of Content: Official magazine of the Townswomen's Guilds. Includes arts, cookery, health, crafts, fashion, lifestyle and political and social issues. Also covers individual Guild news and national Townswomen's Guilds news.
Readership/Target Audience: Read by members of the Townswomen's Guild.
ADVERTISING RATES:
Full Page Colour £2200.00
Agency Commission: 10%
Mechanical Data: Trim Size: 297 x 210mm, Bleed Size: 303 x 216mm, Type Area: 277 x 190mm, Col Length: 277mm, Film: Digital, Page Width: 190mm
Copy instructions: Copy Date: 2 weeks prior to publication date
Average advertising content per issue: 40%
CONSUMER: WOMEN'S INTEREST CONSUMER MAGAZINES: Women's Interest

TOWPATH TALK
1696118U91R-160

Editorial Address: Media Centre, Morton Way, HORNCASTLE, LN9 6JR **Tel:** 01507 529529
Fax: 01507 529495
Email: thoyland@mortons.co.uk
Advertising Address: As above. **Tel:** 01507 529459
Fax: 01507 529499
Email: dtaylor@mortons.co.uk
Web site: http://www.towpathtalk.co.uk
ISSN: 1749-866X
Publisher: Mortons Media Group Ltd
Frequency: Monthly
Free to qualifying individuals
Annual Sub.: £10.00
Circulation: 23,477 (Publisher's Statement)
Usual Pagination: 40
Editor: Sarah Palmer
Summary of Content: Newspaper covering life and leisure around Britain's canals with insights into life on the canals and places to explore from English pubs to quaint villages and historic pubs.
Readership/Target Audience: Aimed at those living on or planning a holiday on Britain's canals.
ADVERTISING RATES:
Full Page Colour £721.00

Agency Commission: 10%
Mechanical Data: Bleed Size: +3mm, Type Area: 339 x 265mm, Col Length: 339mm, Page Width: 265mm, Film: Digital
Copy instructions: Copy Date: 2 weeks prior to publication date
Average advertising content per issue: 30%
CONSUMER: RECREATION & LEISURE: Recreation & Leisure Related

TOXIC
767925U91D-858

Editorial Address: 239 Kensington High Street, LONDON, W8 6SA **Tel:** 020 7761 3500
Email: adavidson@euk.egmont.com
Advertising Address: As above. **Fax:** 020 7761 3510
Email: svernon@euk.egmont.com
Web site: http://www.toxicmag.co.uk
Publisher: Egmont Magazines UK
Frequency: 26 issues yearly
Cover Price: £2.50
Circulation: 49,005 (ABC 01/01/2009 to 30/06/2009)
Editor: Andy Davidson; **Advertising Manager:** Lisa Crichlow
Summary of Content: Children's magazine covering games, movies and sport.
Readership/Target Audience: Aimed at boys between 9 and 12 years old.
ADVERTISING RATES:
Full Page Colour £2400.00
Agency Commission: 10%
Mechanical Data: Film: Digital, Bleed Size: 306 x 226mm, Trim Size: 300 x 220mm, Type Area: 282 x 202mm, Col Length: 282mm, Page Width: 202mm
Copy instructions: Copy Date: 4 weeks prior to publication date
Average advertising content per issue: 15%
CONSUMER: RECREATION & LEISURE: Children & Youth

TOYBOX
1647276U91D-887

Editorial Address: Meia Centre, 201 Wood Lane, LONDON, W12 7TQ **Tel:** 020 8433 2000 **Fax:** 020 8433 2941
Email: stephanie.cooper@bbc.com
Advertising Address: The Garden House, 201 Wood Lane, LONDON, W12 7TQ **Tel:** 020 8433 2000
Email: sophie.dennis@bbc.com
Publisher: BBC Children's Magazines
Frequency: 17 issues yearly
Cover Price: £0.99
Annual Sub.: £15.50
Circulation: 41,582 (ABC 01/01/2009 to 30/06/2009)
Editor: Stephanie Cooper
Summary of Content: Children's magazine with stories, things to make, puzzles, board games, colouring and competitions.
Readership/Target Audience: Aimed at children from 3 to 5 years old.
ADVERTISING: Rates on application
CONSUMER: RECREATION & LEISURE: Children & Youth

TRACE
1648405U74Q-1191

Editorial Address: 2nd Floor, Farringdon House, 105-107 Farringdon Road, LONDON, EC1R 3BU **Tel:** 020 7014 9549
Fax: 020 7251 8051
Email: ben@trace44.com
Advertising Address: As above. **Fax:** 020 7168 5727
Email: christopher@trace44.com
Web site: http://www.trace212.com
Publisher: Alliance Trace Media Ltd
Date Established: 1995
Frequency: 10 issues yearly
Cover Price: £3.95
Annual Sub.: £17.50
Circulation: 64,000 (Publisher's Statement)
Usual Pagination: 132
Editor: Melissa Simpemba; **Advertising Manager:** Christopher Keeling; **Publisher:** Ben Martin
Summary of Content: Trans-cultural style magazine with features on street fashion, music, art, design and new ideas.
Readership/Target Audience: Aimed at men and women aged between 16 and 30 years old of all races.
ADVERTISING RATES:
Full Page Colour £4000.00
Agency Commission: 15%
Mechanical Data: Bleed Size: 306 x 236mm, Trim Size: 300 x 230mm, Film: Digital
Copy instructions: Copy Date: 3 weeks prior to publication date
Average advertising content per issue: 25%
CONSUMER: WOMEN'S INTEREST CONSUMER MAGAZINES: Lifestyle

TRACK & RACE CARS
1637572U77D-464

Editorial Address: 194A Upper Richmond Road West, LONDON, SW14 8AN **Tel:** 020 8296 5467
Email: trc@motorshoot.com

Advertising Address: Silverback Media Solutions Ltd, Silverstone Innovation Centre, Silverstone Circuit, Silverstone, TOWCESTER, NN12 8GX **Tel:** 01327 856136 **Fax:** 01327 856001
Email: advertising@trcmagazine.com
Web site: http://www.trcmagazine.com
Publisher: P1 Media Ltd
Date Established: 2003
Frequency: Monthly
Cover Price: £3.99
Circulation: 40,000 (Publisher's Statement)
Editor: Keith Wood; **Advertising Manager:** Steve Lysandrou; **Managing Editor:** Andrew Brown
Summary of Content: Magazine covering track-tested race cars and timed-track day cars as well as in-depth technical insights on the motor sport industry and its products.
Readership/Target Audience: Aimed at men and women aged 25 and over who are motor sports enthusiasts and those involved in the motor sports industry.
ADVERTISING: Rates on application
CONSUMER: MOTORING & CYCLING: Motor Sports

TRACK DRIVER
46419U77D-163
Formerly: Circuit Driver
Editorial Address: 194A Upper Richmond Road West, LONDON, SW14 8AN **Tel:** 01379 897200 **Fax:** 01379 897211
Email: mark@circuitdriver.com
Advertising Address: Silverback Media Solutions Ltd, Silverstone Innovation Centre, Silverstone Circuit, Silverstone, TOWCESTER, NN12 8GX **Tel:** 01327 856136
Fax: 01327 856001
Email: advertising@trcmagazine.com
Web site: http://www.circuitdriver.com
ISSN: 1478-3916
Publisher: P1 Media Ltd
Date Established: 1999
Frequency: Monthly
Annual Sub.: £35.88
Circulation: 10,000 (Publisher's Statement)
Usual Pagination: 64
Editor: Charys Wycombe; **Advertising Manager:** Steve Lysandrou
Summary of Content: Magazine covering all aspects of track driving and circuit racing. Includes dates of track days and general test days.
Readership/Target Audience: Aimed at track drivers, circuit racers and performance car enthusiasts.
ADVERTISING: Rates on application
CONSUMER: MOTORING & CYCLING: Motor Sports

TRACTION
46717U79J-330
Editorial Address: The Maltings, West Street, BOURNE, PE10 9PH **Tel:** 01778 391160 **Fax:** 01778 425437
Email: davidb@warnersgroup.co.uk
Advertising Address: As above. **Tel:** 01778 391000
Email: patsisko@warnersgroup.co.uk
Web site: http://www.traction.co.uk
Publisher: Warners Group Publications plc
Date Established: 1994
Frequency: Monthly
Cover Price: £3.75
Annual Sub.: £45.00
Circulation: 6,341 (Publisher's Statement)
Usual Pagination: 64
Editor: David Brown; **Managing Editor:** David Brown; **Publisher:** John Greenwood
Summary of Content: Magazine covering classic diesels and electrics railway motive power past and present. Contains news, nostalgia features, railway work insight, heritage scene, reviews of books, models and videos.
Readership/Target Audience: Aimed at rail enthusiasts.
ADVERTISING RATES:
Full Page Mono £270.00
Full Page Colour £350.00
Agency Commission: 10%
Mechanical Data: Bleed Size: 303 x 216mm, Trim Size: 297 x 210mm, Type Area: 275 x 190mm, Col Length: 275mm, Page Width: 190mm, Film: Positive, right reading, emulsion side down. Digital
Copy instructions: Copy Date: 1st of the month prior to publication date
Average advertising content per issue: 16%
CONSUMER: HOBBIES & DIY: Rail Enthusiasts

TRACTOR
1667506U79R-154
Formerly: Tractor & Farming Heritage
Editorial Address: Media Centre, Morton Way, HORNCASTLE, LN9 6JR **Tel:** 01507 529529
Fax: 01507 529490
Email: pkelly@mortons.co.uk
Advertising Address: PO Box 43, HORNCASTLE, LN9 6JR
Tel: 01507 529300 **Fax:** 01507 529499
Email: rsinclair@mortons.co.uk
Web site: http://www.tractorheritage.co.uk
ISSN: 1749-866X
Publisher: Mortons Media Group Ltd

Frequency: Monthly
Cover Price: £3.40
Circulation: 30,104 (Publisher's Statement)
Usual Pagination: 140
Editor: Peter Kelly
Summary of Content: Magazine covering farming life and the tractors and machinery that worked them over the past hundred years. From seed time to harvest, dairy to stockyard, our farming heritage is as important as the tractors themselves. Featuring the rare as well as the famous names, with archive and colour pictures of restored machines.
Readership/Target Audience: Aimed at those with an interest in farming heritage.
ADVERTISING RATES:
Full Page Colour £688.00
Copy instructions: Copy Date: 2 weeks prior to publication date
CONSUMER: HOBBIES & DIY: Hobbies & DIY Related

TRACTOR & MACHINERY
46788U79R-147
Editorial Address: Cudham Tithe Barn, Berrys Hill, Berrys Green, Cudham, WESTERHAM, TN16 3AG
Tel: 01959 541444 **Fax:** 01959 541400
Email: martin.oldaker@kelsey.co.uk
Advertising Address: As above. **Fax:** 01959 543585
Email: tm.adsales@kelsey.co.uk
Web site: http://www.kelsey.co.uk/tractor
Publisher: Kelsey Publishing Ltd
Date Established: 1994
Frequency: Monthly
Cover Price: £3.50
Annual Sub.: £38.52
Circulation: 50,299 (ABC 01/01/2008 to 31/12/2008)
Usual Pagination: 212
Editor: Martin Oldaker; **Advertisement Director:** David Lerpiniere; **Publisher:** Stephen Curtis
Summary of Content: Magazine covering antique and classic tractors and machinery around the world. Includes features on history and restoration projects, vintage news, sales, models, toys, for sales section and monthly price guide. Also looks at the modern scene.
Readership/Target Audience: Read by farmers, vintage and classic collectors and tractor enthusiasts throughout the world.
ADVERTISING RATES:
Full Page Colour £900.00
Agency Commission: 10%
Mechanical Data: Type Area: 272 x 188mm, Col Length: 272mm, Trim Size: 297 x 210mm, Bleed Size: 303 x 216mm, Film: Digital, No. of Columns (Display): 3, Page Width: 188mm
CONSUMER: HOBBIES & DIY: Hobbies & DIY Related

TRACTOR TOM
1663413U91D-908
Editorial Address: Brockbourne House, Mount Ephraim, TUNBRIDGE WELLS, TN4 8BS **Tel:** 01892 500100
Fax: 01892 545666
Email: tractortom@panini.co.uk
Advertising Address: Orange20 Ltd, Station House, Bunbury Way, EPSOM, KT17 4JP **Tel:** 01372 802800
Fax: 01372 723322
Email: panini.adsales@o20.co.uk
Web site: http://www.paninicomics.co.uk
Publisher: Panini UK Ltd
Frequency: 13 issues yearly
Cover Price: £1.85
Circulation: 60,000 (Publisher's Statement)
Usual Pagination: 24
Editor: Patrick Bishop; **Advertising Manager:** Michelle Fairlamb
Summary of Content: Children's magazine based on the TV programme Tractor Tom with stories, puzzles, competitions and games.
Readership/Target Audience: Aimed at pre-school boys and girls aged 3 to 5 years old.
ADVERTISING RATES:
Full Page Colour £1500.00
Mechanical Data: Type Area: 280 x 205mm, Trim Size: 300 x 225mm, Bleed Size: 310 x 235mm, Col Length: 280mm, Page Width: 205mm
CONSUMER: RECREATION & LEISURE: Children & Youth

TRADITIONAL BOATS & TALL SHIPS
48393U91A-170
Editorial Address: 22A Iliffe Yard, LONDON, SE17 3QA
Tel: 020 7277 4517 **Fax:** 020 7703 8718
Email: tallship@wildpublishing.co.uk
Advertising Address: As above.
Email: tallship@wildpublishing.co.uk
Web site: http://www.tallship.co.uk
ISSN: 1466-2477
Publisher: Wild Publishing Ltd
Date Established: 1999
Frequency: Quarterly
Cover Price: £3.65

Annual Sub.: £35.00
Circulation: 20,000 (Publisher's Statement)
Usual Pagination: 68
Editor: David Tickner; **Editor-in-Chief:** David Tickner; **Advertising Manager:** David Tickner
Summary of Content: Magazine looking at sailing, maritime history, warfare under sail, ports and sailor profiles.
Readership/Target Audience: Aimed at traditional boat and tall ship enthusiasts, those involved in the industry, related businesses and event organisers.
ADVERTISING RATES:
Full Page Colour £750.00
Agency Commission: 10%
Mechanical Data: Trim Size: 340 x 240mm, Bleed Size: 346 x 246mm, Film: Digital, Type Area: 330 x 230mm, Col Length: 230mm, Page Width: 330mm
Copy instructions: Copy Date: 3 weeks prior to publication date
CONSUMER: RECREATION & LEISURE: Boating & Yachting

TRADITIONAL HOMES & INTERIORS
628730U74C-550
Editorial Address: Unit 5, The Oast, 62 Bell Road, SITTINGBOURNE, ME10 4HC **Tel:** 01795 599191
Fax: 01795 599282
Email: vicki@cplmedia.co.uk
Advertising Address: As above.
Email: jo@cplmedia.co.uk
ISSN: 1467-7758
Publisher: CPL Media Ltd
Date Established: 2000
Frequency: 11 issues yearly
Cover Price: £3.20
Circulation: 60,000 (Publisher's Statement)
Usual Pagination: 120
Editor: Vicki Watson; **Publisher:** Colin Woolley
Summary of Content: Magazine covering homes and gardening, with advice and features on lifestyle and travel.
Readership/Target Audience: Aimed at women with an interest in traditional style home furnishing.
ADVERTISING RATES:
Full Page Colour £2795.00
Agency Commission: 10%
Mechanical Data: Film: Digital, Trim Size: 297 x 210mm, Bleed Size: 303 x 216mm
Copy instructions: Copy Date: 4 weeks prior to publication date
Average advertising content per issue: 40%
CONSUMER: WOMEN'S INTEREST CONSUMER MAGAZINES: Home & Family

TRADITIONAL KARATE
45993U75Q-800
Editorial Address: Unit 20, Maybrook Business Park, Maybrook Road, SUTTON COLDFIELD, B76 1BE
Tel: 0121 351 6930
Email: trad@martialartsinprint.com
Advertising Address: As above. **Tel:** 0121 344 3737
Fax: 0121 356 7300
Email: paul@martialartsinprint.com
Web site: http://www.martialartsinprint.com
Publisher: Martial Arts Publications Ltd
Date Established: 1986
Frequency: Monthly
Cover Price: £3.50
Annual Sub.: £38.95
Usual Pagination: 100
Advertising Manager: Paul Clifton; **Publisher:** Paul Clifton
Summary of Content: Magazine with news and features about karate including techniques, advice, profiles, events and associations and students.
Readership/Target Audience: Read by karate enthusiasts, instructors and heads of associations.
ADVERTISING RATES:
Full Page Colour £795.00
Agency Commission: 10%
Mechanical Data: Trim Size: 297 x 210mm, Print Process: Web-fed offset litho, Film: Digital
Copy instructions: Copy Date: 5 weeks prior to publication date
Average advertising content per issue: 37%
CONSUMER: SPORT: Combat Sports

Y TRAETHODYDD (THE ESSAYIST)
47555U84B-250
Editorial Address: Gwasg y Bwthyn, Lon Ddewi, CAERNARFON, LL55 1ER **Tel:** 01286 672018
Fax: 01286 677823
Email: gwasgybwthyn@btconnect.com
ISSN: 0969-8930
Publisher: Gwasg Pantycelyn
Date Established: 1845
Frequency: Quarterly
Annual Sub.: £12.00
Circulation: 500 (Publisher's Statement)
Usual Pagination: 64
Editor: B. Roberts

Consumer Magazines

Summary of Content: Cultural magazine featuring literary history and criticism, theology, non-specialist philosophy, social issues and book reviews.
Language(s): Welsh
Readership/Target Audience: Read by those living in Wales and those who speak Welsh.
ADVERTISING: No Advertising taken
CONSUMER: THE ARTS & LITERARY: Literary

THE TRAFFORD MAGAZINE
623219U74Q-937
Editorial Address: Management Suite, Trafford Centre, MANCHESTER, M17 8AA **Tel:** 0161 746 7777
Fax: 0161 749 1599
Email: cbell@traffordcentre.co.uk
Advertising Address: As above. **Fax:** 0161 749 1550
Email: drhodes@traffordcentre.co.uk
Web site: http://www.babersmith.co.uk
Publisher: Trafford Centre
Frequency: Half-yearly - Published in March and September
Cover Price: Free
Circulation: 70,000 (Publisher's Statement)
Usual Pagination: 40
Editor: Catrin Bell; **Advertising Manager:** Diane Rhodes
Summary of Content: Magazine covering news and features on fashion and lifestyle.
Readership/Target Audience: Aimed at customers of the Trafford shopping centre.
ADVERTISING RATES:
Full Page Colour £1100.00
Mechanical Data: Film: Digital, Trim Size: 297 x 105mm
Copy instructions: Copy Date: 5 weeks prior to publication date
Average advertising content per issue: 15%
CONSUMER: WOMEN'S INTEREST CONSUMER MAGAZINES: Lifestyle

TRAIL
45933U75L-700
Editorial Address: Media House, Lynchwood, Peterborough Business Park, PETERBOROUGH, PE2 6EA
Tel: 01733 468000 **Fax:** 01733 468387
Email: trail@bauermedia.co.uk
Advertising Address: As above. **Fax:** 01733 468048
Email: justin.gould@bauermedia.com
Web site: http://www.trailroutes.com
ISSN: 1361-9748
Publisher: Bauer Consumer Media Ltd (Media House)
Date Established: 1990
Frequency: Monthly - 10th of the month prior to cover date
Cover Price: £3.40
Circulation: 40,531 (ABC 01/01/2008 to 31/12/2008)
Usual Pagination: 148
Editor: Matt Swaine; **Features Editor:** Simon Ingram;
Editor-in-Chief: Guy Procter; **Managing Director:** Edward Beale; **Publisher:** Mel Bagnall
Summary of Content: Magazine covering routes for walking, climbing, scrambling, mountain biking and trail running. Also contains outdoor clothing and equipment tests, personality profiles and advice on fitness, diet and health.
Readership/Target Audience: Aimed at enthusiasts of outdoor activities.
ADVERTISING RATES:
Full Page Colour £2950.00
Agency Commission: 10%
Mechanical Data: Page Width: 184mm, Type Area: 275 x 184mm, Col Length: 275mm, Film: Digital, Bleed Size: 303 x 216mm, Trim Size: 297 x 210mm
Average advertising content per issue: 22%
CONSUMER: SPORT: Outdoor

TRAILBIKE AND ENDURO MAGAZINE
46379U77B-620
Editorial Address: PO Box 9845, LONDON, W13 9WP
Tel: 020 8840 4760 **Fax:** 020 8840 6848
Advertising Address: 191A Uxbridge Road, LONDON, W13 9AA **Tel:** 020 8840 4760
Email: clark@trailbikemag.com
Web site: http://www.trailbikemag.com
ISSN: 1359-0324
Publisher: Extreme Publishing Ltd
Date Established: 1995
Frequency: Monthly
Cover Price: £3.20
Circulation: 18,000 (Publisher's Statement)
Usual Pagination: 140
Editor: James Barnicoat; **Managing Director:** Si Melber;
Advertising Manager: Melanie Falconer; **Publisher:** Si Melber
Summary of Content: Magazine covering on and off road motorcycling. Includes news, reviews, features and maintenance tips.
Readership/Target Audience: Aimed at trailbike sports enthusiasts.
ADVERTISING RATES:
Full Page Colour £850.00
Agency Commission: 10%

Mechanical Data: Trim Size: 210 x 148mm, Film: Digital, Bleed Size: 216 x 154mm, Type Area: 200 x 138mm, Col Length: 200mm, Page Width: 138mm
CONSUMER: MOTORING & CYCLING: Motorcycling

TRAMP
1810046U74Q-1353
Editorial Address: 72 New Bond Street, LONDON, W1S 1RR **Tel:** 020 7514 9990 **Fax:** 020 7514 5811
Email: info@trampmagazine.com
Advertising Address: As above.
Email: enrico@trampmagazine.com
Web site: http://www.trampmagazine.com
Publisher: Tramp Media Ltd
Date Established: 2007
Frequency: 10 issues yearly
Cover Price: £4.99
Circulation: 25,000 (Publisher's Statement)
Usual Pagination: 148
Editor: Sam Williams; **Advertising Manager:** Sam Williams
Summary of Content: Magazine covering the lifestyle of socialites from around the world based in and around London as well as lifestyle features including luxury hotels, elite restaurants, VIP night clubs, fashion, art and music.
Readership/Target Audience: Aimed at the affluent, flamboyant jet set and individuals who love luxury.
ADVERTISING RATES:
Full Page Colour £5000.00
Agency Commission: 10%
Mechanical Data: Film: Digital, Trim Size: 297 x 210mm, Bleed Size: 303 x 216mm
Copy instructions: Copy Date: 3 weeks prior to publication date
Average advertising content per issue: 25%
CONSUMER: WOMEN'S INTEREST CONSUMER MAGAZINES: Lifestyle

TRANSLATION & LITERATURE
47582U84B-255
Editorial Address: Dept. of English Literature, University of Glasgow, GLASGOW, G12 8QQ **Tel:** 0141 330 5296
Fax: 0141 330 4601
Email: s.gillespie@englit.arts.gla.ac.uk
Advertising Address: 22 George Square, EDINBURGH, EH8 9LF **Tel:** 0131 650 4220 **Fax:** 0131 662 0053
Email: journals@eup.ed.ac.uk
Web site: http://www.eupjournals.com/journal/tal
ISSN: 0968-1361
Publisher: Edinburgh University Press Ltd
Date Established: 1992
Frequency: Half-yearly
Annual Sub.: £36.00
Circulation: 500 (Publisher's Statement)
Usual Pagination: 144
Editor: Stuart Gillespie; **Advertising Manager:** Wendy Gardiner; **Publisher:** Ann Larsson
Summary of Content: Scholarly journal publishing articles, notes and reviews on literary translation of all kinds and periods, focusing on English literature in its foreign relations.
Readership/Target Audience: Aimed at academics.
ADVERTISING RATES:
Full Page Mono £250.00
Agency Commission: 5%
Mechanical Data: Type Area: 210 x 115mm, Col Length: 210mm, Trim Size: 234 x 152mm, Page Width: 115mm
Average advertising content per issue: 1%
CONSUMER: THE ARTS & LITERARY: Literary

TRAVEL AFRICA MAGAZINE
48263U89E-157_20
Editorial Address: 4 Rycote Lane Farm, Milton Common, OXFORD, OX9 2NZ **Tel:** 01844 278883 **Fax:** 01844 278893
Email: matt@travelafricamag.com
Advertising Address: As above.
Email: craig@travelafricamag.com
Web site: http://www.travelafricamag.com
ISSN: 1561-2783
Publisher: Travel Africa Ltd
Date Established: 1997
Frequency: Quarterly
Cover Price: £3.95
Annual Sub.: £15.00
Circulation: 22,000 (Publisher's Statement)
Usual Pagination: 160
Editor: Matt Phillips; **Advertising Manager:** Craig Rix;
Publisher: Craig Rix
Summary of Content: Magazine featuring African travel destinations, wildlife and culture. Includes coverage of national parks, cities and tribes.
Readership/Target Audience: Aimed at those wanting to travel in Africa with a broad interest in wildlife, landscape and culture.
ADVERTISING RATES:
Full Page Colour £1530.00
Mechanical Data: Type Area: 275 x 185mm, Bleed Size: 305 x 218mm, Col Length: 275mm, Page Width: 185mm
Copy instructions: Copy Date: 4 weeks prior to publication date

Average advertising content per issue: 25%
CONSUMER: HOLIDAYS & TRAVEL: Holidays

THE TRAVEL & LEISURE MAGAZINE
47973U89A-754
Editorial Address: First Floor, 114 Cranbrook Road, ILFORD, IG1 4LZ **Tel:** 020 8554 4456
Email: peter@ellegard.co.uk
Advertising Address: As above. **Fax:** 020 8554 4443
Email: darrenp@tlmags.com
Web site: http://www.tlmags.com
Publisher: Travel & Leisure Magazines Ltd
Date Established: 1993
Frequency: 6 issues yearly
Cover Price: Free
Cover Price: £2.00
Annual Sub.: £5.00
Circulation: 100,000 (Publisher's Statement)
Usual Pagination: 64
Editor: Peter Ellegard
Summary of Content: Magazine providing independent information on holidays, short breaks and leisure activities, including health and well being, gardening and food and drink.
Readership/Target Audience: Aimed at consumers looking to book their next holiday or break.
ADVERTISING RATES:
Full Page Colour £1895.00
Agency Commission: 15%
Mechanical Data: Type Area: 275 x 186mm, Film: Digital, Col Length: 275mm, Page Width: 186mm, Trim Size: 297 x 210mm, Bleed Size: 303 x 216mm
Copy instructions: Copy Date: 8 weeks prior to publication date
Average advertising content per issue: 50%
CONSUMER: HOLIDAYS & TRAVEL: Travel

TRAVEL AUSTRALIA & NEW ZEALAND
48264U89E-157_50
Formerly: Travel Australia
Editorial Address: 13 London Road, BEXHILL-ON-SEA, TN39 3JR **Tel:** 01424 223111 **Fax:** 01424 224992
Email: shirley@consylpublishing.co.uk
Advertising Address: As above.
Email: consylpublishing@btconnect.com
Web site: http://www.consylpublishing.co.uk
Publisher: Consyl Publishing & Publicity Ltd
Date Established: 1983
Frequency: Half-yearly - Published in February and September
Cover Price: £1.50
Free to qualifying individuals
Circulation: 30,000 (Publisher's Statement)
Usual Pagination: 48
Editor: Shirley Gilbertson; **Advertising Manager:** Shirley Gilbertson
Summary of Content: Newspaper covering holidays, resorts, trips, activities, sports, visas, weather conditions and medical advice.
Readership/Target Audience: Aimed at potential working holiday makers, travellers and visitors to Australia and New Zealand.
ADVERTISING RATES:
Full Page Mono £1100.00
Full Page Colour £1500.00
Mechanical Data: Type Area: 360 x 264mm, Col Length: 360mm, Page Width: 264mm, Film: Digital
Supplement(s): Go Australia & New Zealand - 2xY
CONSUMER: HOLIDAYS & TRAVEL: Holidays

THE TRAVEL MAGAZINE
753217U89E-165
Formerly: Travel News Magazine
Editorial Address: 19 Morley Crescent, EDGWARE, HA8 8XE **Tel:** 020 8905 4851 **Fax:** 020 8933 4307
Email: travel@thetravelmagazine.net
Advertising Address: As above.
Email: sharron@thetravelmagazine.co.uk
Web site: http://www.thetravelmagazine.net
ISSN: 1751-3073
Publisher: Travel Publications
Date Established: 2001
Frequency: Quarterly
Cover Price: £2.00
Free to qualifying individuals
Annual Sub.: £8.00
Circulation: 40,000 (Publisher's Statement)
Usual Pagination: 72
Editor: Sharron Livingston
Summary of Content: Magazine covering features, articles, news, previews of new hotels, reviews of destinations and events worldwide.
Readership/Target Audience: Aimed at travellers.
ADVERTISING RATES:
Full Page Colour £1300.00
Agency Commission: 10%

Mechanical Data: Bleed Size: 302 x 215mm, Trim Size: 297 x 210mm, Type Area: 290 x 200mm, Col Length: 290mm, Film: Digital, Page Width: 200mm
Copy instructions: Copy Date: 3 weeks prior to publication date
Average advertising content per issue: 20%
CONSUMER: HOLIDAYS & TRAVEL: Holidays

TRAVEL TALES (TALL AND TRUE)
1666479U89A-720

Editorial Address: 45 Salford Road, Aspley Guise, MILTON KEYNES, MK17 8HZ **Tel:** 01908 282363 **Fax:** 01908 282363
Email: editorial@traveltalestallandtrue.com
Advertising Address: As above.
Email: editorial@traveltalestallandtrue.com
Web site: http://www.traveltalestallandtrue.com
Publisher: Travel Tales
Date Established: 2005
Frequency: 3 issues yearly - Varies
Editor: Catherine Malcolm; **Advertising Manager:** Catherine Malcolm
Summary of Content: Magazine with a combination of quirky travel stories and travel facts.
Readership/Target Audience: Aimed at erudite travellers who are familiar with exotic destinations.
ADVERTISING RATES:
Full Page Colour £1800.00
SCC £30.00
Agency Commission: 10%
Mechanical Data: Film: Digital
Copy instructions: Copy Date: 4 weeks prior to publication date
CONSUMER: HOLIDAYS & TRAVEL: Travel

TRAVELLER
48265U89E-160

Editorial Address: 45-49 Brompton Road, Knightsbridge, LONDON, SW3 1DE **Tel:** 020 7589 0500 **Fax:** 020 7581 8476
Advertising Address: As above.
Email: joe.legate@wexas.com
Web site: http://www.traveller.org.uk
ISSN: 0262-2726
Publisher: Wexas
Date Established: 1970
Frequency: Quarterly
Cover Price: £4.95
Free to qualifying individuals
Annual Sub.: £19.80
Circulation: 21,204 (ABC 01/01/2008 to 31/12/2008)
Usual Pagination: 116
Editor: Duncan Mills; **Advertising Manager:** Joe Legate
Summary of Content: Magazine containing travel features and news, plus book and travel product reviews.
Readership/Target Audience: Aimed at UK residents interested in travel and members of WEXAS.
ADVERTISING RATES:
Full Page Colour £2450.00
Agency Commission: 10%
Mechanical Data: Type Area: 266 x 180mm, Bleed Size: 303 x 216mm, Print Process: Web-fed offset litho, Trim Size: 297 x 210mm, Col Length: 266mm, Page Width: 180mm
CONSUMER: HOLIDAYS & TRAVEL: Holidays

TRAVELLER IN FRANCE
1638127U89E-207

Editorial Address: Unit 3, The Old Estate Yard, North Stoke Lane, Upton Cheyney, BRISTOL, BS30 6ND
Tel: 01225 329381 **Fax:** 01225 786801
Email: justin.postlethwaite@edpltd.co.uk
Advertising Address: Lincoln House, 300 High Holborn, LONDON, WC1V 7JH **Tel:** 09068 244123
Fax: 020 7061 6646
Email: claire.kaletka@franceguide.com
Web site: http://www.franceguide.com
Publisher: Evolve Digital Publishing
Date Established: 1924
Frequency: Half-yearly - Published in March and September
Cover Price: Free
Circulation: 83,000 (Publisher's Statement)
Usual Pagination: 80
Editor: Justin Postlethwaite; **Advertising Manager:** Claire Kaletka
Summary of Content: Magazine covering all forms of travel to France including short breaks, city breaks and winter sun.
Readership/Target Audience: Aimed at those with an interest in France.
ADVERTISING RATES:
Full Page Colour £6940.00
Mechanical Data: Film: Digital, Trim Size: 297 x 210mm, Bleed Size: 303 x 216mm, Type Area: 270 x 185mm, Col Length: 270mm, Page Width: 185mm
CONSUMER: HOLIDAYS & TRAVEL: Holidays

TREASURE HUNTING
46649U79E-185

Editorial Address: 119 Newland Street, WITHAM, CM8 1WF
Tel: 01376 521900 **Fax:** 01376 521901

Email: info@treasurehunting.co.uk
Advertising Address: As above.
Email: info@treasurehunting.co.uk
Web site: http://www.treasurehunting.co.uk
ISSN: 0140-4539
Publisher: Greenlight Publishing
Date Established: 1972
Frequency: Monthly
Cover Price: £3.60
Annual Sub.: £43.20
Circulation: 15,000 (Publisher's Statement)
Usual Pagination: 84
Editor: Greg Payne; **Managing Director:** Daniel Golbourn;
Advertising Manager: Alan Golbourn
Summary of Content: Magazine carrying metal detector and ancillary equipment tests, historical articles and site guides.
Readership/Target Audience: Aimed at the detecting enthusiast.
ADVERTISING RATES:
Full Page Mono £550.00
Full Page Colour £745.00
Agency Commission: 10%
Mechanical Data: Col Length: 268mm, Page Width: 190mm, Film: Digital, Type Area: 268 x 190mm, Print Process: Web-fed offset litho, Trim Size: 297 x 210mm, Bleed Size: 307 x 220mm
Copy instructions: Copy Date: 4 weeks prior to publication date
Average advertising content per issue: 40%
CONSUMER: HOBBIES & DIY: Numismatics

TREND
1827153U80E-379

Editorial Address: The Bank, 292 Rosemount Place, ABERDEEN, AB25 2YA **Tel:** 01224 631141
Fax: 01224 622288
Email: gill@trendmagazine.co.uk
Advertising Address: As above.
Email: sarah@trendmagazine.co.uk
Web site: http://www.trendmagazine.co.uk
Publisher: Trend Publications Ltd
Date Established: 2007
Frequency: 6 issues yearly
Cover Price: Free
Circulation: 15,000 (Publisher's Statement)
Usual Pagination: 72
Editor: Niki Tennant
Summary of Content: Lifestyle magazine covering restaurants, delis, wine, fashion, beauty, property, motoring and interviews with local personalities.
Readership/Target Audience: Aimed at professional men and women aged 25 years old and over with a high disposable income in Aberdeen and Aberdeenshire.
ADVERTISING RATES:
Full Page Mono £1500.00
Full Page Colour £1500.00
Agency Commission: 10%
Mechanical Data: Type Area: 196 x 140mm, Bleed Size: 216 x 171mm, Trim Size: 210 x 165mm, Col Length: 196mm, Page Width: 140mm, Film: Digital, Print Process: Litho
Copy instructions: Copy Date: 2 weeks prior to publication date
Average advertising content per issue: 40%
CONSUMER: RURAL & REGIONAL INTEREST: Regional Interest Scotland

TRIALS & MOTOCROSS NEWS
46380U77B-630

Editorial Address: 12 Victoria Street, MORECAMBE, LA4 4AG **Tel:** 01524 833111 **Fax:** 01524 425469
Email: john.dickinson@tmxnews.co.uk
Advertising Address: As above. **Tel:** 01524 834030
Fax: 01524 834045
Email: tmx.ads@tmxnews.co.uk
Web site: http://www.tmxnews.co.uk
Publisher: Johnston Press Off Road Portfolio
Date Established: 1977
Frequency: Weekly - Published on Friday
Cover Price: £2.00
Circulation: 20,000 (Publisher's Statement)
Usual Pagination: 72
Editor: John Dickinson; **Managing Director:** Mike Harper;
Advertising Manager: Sue Murgatroyd
Summary of Content: Specialist newspaper covering all aspects of off-road motorcycling with emphasis on trials, motocross and enduro.
Readership/Target Audience: Aimed at those with a interest in all forms of off road motorcycling, motocross, trials, enduro and supermoto.
ADVERTISING RATES:
Full Page Colour £1365.44
Agency Commission: 10%
Mechanical Data: Page Width: 273mm, Col Length: 340mm, No. of Columns (Display): 7, Type Area: 340 x 273mm, Film: Digital, Col Widths (Display): 36mm
Copy instructions: Copy Date: 1 week prior to publication date
Average advertising content per issue: 60%
CONSUMER: MOTORING & CYCLING: Motorcycling

TRIATHLON PLUS
1892599U75J-607

Editorial Address: 30 Monmouth Street, BATH, BA1 2BW
Tel: 01225 442244 **Fax:** 01225 822836
Email: triathlonplus@futurenet.com
Publisher: Future Publishing Ltd
Date Established: 2009
Frequency: Monthly
Cover Price: £3.99
Circulation: 50,000 (Print Run)
Editor: Mat Brett
Summary of Content: Magazine focusing on the triathlon sports of running, cycling and swimming. Includes tutorials, features and reviews of events and equipment.
Readership/Target Audience: Aimed at enthusiasts at all levels.
ADVERTISING: Rates on application
CONSUMER: SPORT: Athletics

TRIBUNE
47285U82-190

Editorial Address: 9 Arkwright Road, LONDON, NW3 6AN
Tel: 020 7433 6410 **Fax:** 020 7433 6419
Email: keith.richmond@tribunemagazine.co.uk
Advertising Address: As above.
Email: tribuneweb@btconnect.com
Web site: http://www.tribunemagazine.co.uk
Publisher: Tribune Publications Ltd
Date Established: 1937
Frequency: Weekly
Cover Price: £2.00
Annual Sub.: £64.00
Circulation: 15,000 (Publisher's Statement)
Usual Pagination: 28
Editor: Keith Richmond; **Advertising Manager:** Marcus Papadopoulos
Summary of Content: Newspaper of the Labour Party covering policy debates, issues and campaigns.
Readership/Target Audience: Aimed at Labour supporters.
ADVERTISING RATES:
Full Page Mono £980.00
Full Page Colour £1100.00
Agency Commission: 10%
Mechanical Data: Page Width: 185mm, Type Area: 270 x 185mm, Col Length: 270mm, Bleed Size: 303 x 216mm, Trim Size: 297 x 210mm, Film: Digital
Copy instructions: Copy Date: Tuesday 2pm prior to publication date
Average advertising content per issue: 10%
CONSUMER: CURRENT AFFAIRS & POLITICS

TRIUMPH WORLD
46481U77E-310

Editorial Address: PO Box 978, PETERBOROUGH, PE1 9FL **Tel:** 01733 347559 **Fax:** 01733 557235
Email: tw.ed@kelseypb.co.uk
Advertising Address: 1st Floor, South Wing, Broadway Court, Broadway, PETERBOROUGH, PE1 1RP
Tel: 01733 353362 **Fax:** 01733 891342
Email: matt.carson@kelseypb.co.uk
Web site: http://www.triumph-world.co.uk
ISSN: 1357-4248
Publisher: Kelsey Publishing Ltd
Date Established: 1995
Frequency: Monthly
Cover Price: £3.70
Circulation: 26,000 (Publisher's Statement)
Usual Pagination: 68
Editor: Simon Goldsworthy; **Advertising Manager:** Matt Carson; **Managing Editor:** Peter Simpson
Summary of Content: Motoring magazine devoted to Triumph and Standard cars and Triumph-based specials with features on all aspects of the cars from restoring to maintaining, historical articles, interviews with ex-factory personnel, owners reports and listings of triumph clubs and events around the world.
Readership/Target Audience: Aimed at classic car enthusiasts.
ADVERTISING RATES:
Full Page Mono £880.00
Full Page Colour £980.00
Agency Commission: 10%
Mechanical Data: Page Width: 190mm, Type Area: 266 x 190mm, Col Length: 266mm, Trim Size: 297 x 210mm, Bleed Size: 306 x 216mm, Film: Digital
Copy instructions: Copy Date: 3 weeks prior to publication date
Average advertising content per issue: 40%
CONSUMER: MOTORING & CYCLING: Club Cars

TROUT AND SALMON
48542U92-100

Editorial Address: Bushfield House, Orton Centre, PETERBOROUGH, PE2 5UW **Tel:** 01733 237111
Fax: 01733 465820
Email: andrew.flitcroft@bauerconsumer.co.uk
Advertising Address: As above. **Fax:** 01733 288047
Email: donna.harris@bauerconsumer.co.uk
Web site: http://www.trout-and-salmon.com
Publisher: Bauer Media Ltd (Orton)

Consumer Magazines

Date Established: 1955
Frequency: Monthly
Cover Price: £3.20.
Circulation: 31,800 (ABC 01/01/2008 to 31/12/2008)
Usual Pagination: 140
Editor: Andrew Flitcroft; **Managing Director:** Steve Prentice
Summary of Content: Magazine covering all aspects of trout and salmon fishing. Includes information and advice, reports and news updates.
Readership/Target Audience: Aimed at fly-fishermen.
ADVERTISING RATES:
Full Page Colour £1820.00
Agency Commission: 10%
Mechanical Data: Page Width: 202mm, Type Area: 275 x 202mm, Col Length: 275mm, Trim Size: 297 x 222mm, Bleed Size: 300 x 225mm, Film: Digital
Copy instructions: Copy Date: 3 weeks prior to publication date
Average advertising content per issue: 40%
CONSUMER: ANGLING & FISHING

TROUT FISHERMAN
48541U92-97

Editorial Address: Bushfield House, Orton Centre, PETERBOROUGH, PE2 5UW **Tel:** 01733 237111
Fax: 01733 465820
Email: russell.hill@bauermedia.co.uk
Advertising Address: As above. **Tel:** 01733 288051
Fax: 01733 288025
Email: donna.harris@bauerconsumer.co.uk
Web site: http://www.troutfisherman.co.uk
Publisher: Bauer Media Ltd (Orton)
Frequency: 13 issues yearly
Cover Price: £3.10
Circulation: 22,146 (ABC 01/01/2008 to 31/12/2008)
Usual Pagination: 124
Editor: Russell Hill; **Features Editor:** Jeffrey Prest;
Managing Editor: Steve Prentice
Summary of Content: Magazine covering all aspects of stillwater fly-fishing. Includes features on fishing tackle, advice on tactics and trout articles.
Readership/Target Audience: Aimed predominantly at stillwater trout fishermen as well as novice and experienced fly anglers.
ADVERTISING RATES:
Full Page Colour £1800.00
Agency Commission: 10%
Mechanical Data: Type Area: 275 x 184mm, Col Length: 275mm, Bleed Size: 307 x 215mm, Trim Size: 297 x 210mm, Film: Digital, Page Width: 184mm
Average advertising content per issue: 40%
CONSUMER: ANGLING & FISHING

TRUCK MODEL WORLD
46623U79B-190

Editorial Address: Traplet House, Pendragon Close, MALVERN, WR14 1GA **Tel:** 01684 588500
Fax: 01684 578558
Email: peter.white@traplet.com
Advertising Address: As above.
Email: debbie.smith@traplet.com
Web site: http://www.traplet.com
Publisher: Traplet Publications Ltd
Date Established: 1992
Frequency: Monthly
Cover Price: £3.50
Annual Sub.: £42.00
Circulation: 5,000 (Publisher's Statement)
Usual Pagination: 48
Editor: Peter White
Summary of Content: Magazine dedicated to building and collecting truck models. Includes reviews of new models, kits and accessories plus news of people and events.
Readership/Target Audience: Aimed at model collectors and truck enthusiasts.
ADVERTISING RATES:
Full Page Mono £205.00
Full Page Colour £338.00
Agency Commission: 10%
Mechanical Data: Page Width: 190mm, Type Area: 277 x 190mm, Col Length: 277mm, Trim Size: 297 x 210mm, Bleed Size: 303 x 216mm, Film: Digital
Copy instructions: Copy Date: 3rd week of the month prior to publication date
CONSUMER: HOBBIES & DIY: Models & Modelling

TRUE CRIME
31059U94X-191

Editorial Address: PO Box 735, LONDON, SE26 5NQ
Tel: 020 8778 0514 **Fax:** 020 8776 8260
Email: enquiries@truecrimelibrary.com
Advertising Address: As above.
Email: advertising@truecrimelibrary.com
Web site: http://www.truecrimelibrary.com
Publisher: Magazine Design & Publishing Co Ltd
Frequency: Monthly
Cover Price: £2.60
Annual Sub.: £26.00
Circulation: 35,000 (Publisher's Statement)

Usual Pagination: 50
Editor: Mike James; **Advertising Manager:** Declan Meehan
Summary of Content: Magazine covering the area of criminology.
Readership/Target Audience: Aimed at males and females between 35 and 75 years old.
ADVERTISING: Rates on application
CONSUMER: OTHER CLASSIFICATIONS: Miscellaneous

THE TRUMPET
1647282U90-936

Editorial Address: 44A Selby Road, Leytonstone, LONDON, E11 3LT **Tel:** 020 8522 6600 **Fax:** 020 8522 6699
Email: info@the-trumpet.com
Advertising Address: As above.
Email: adverts@the-trumpet.com
Web site: http://www.the-trumpet.com
ISSN: 1477-3392
Publisher: The Trumpet
Date Established: 1995
Frequency: 26 issues yearly
Cover Price: Free
Annual Sub.: £30.00
Circulation: 26,031 (ABC 01/07/2002 to 31/12/2002)
Usual Pagination: 20
Editor: Femi Okutubo; **Editor-in-Chief:** Femi Okutubo;
Advertising Manager: Femi Okutubo; **Publisher:** Femi Okutubo
Summary of Content: Newspaper covering articles of interest to the African community including general news, sport, arts, features and finance.
Readership/Target Audience: Aimed at the African community in the UK.
ADVERTISING RATES:
Full Page Mono £3040.00
Full Page Colour £3648.00
SCC £10.00
Agency Commission: 10%
Mechanical Data: Type Area: 380 x 254mm, Col Length: 380mm, Page Width: 254mm, No. of Columns (Display): 8, Film: Digital
Copy instructions: Copy Date: 5 days prior to publication date
CONSUMER: ETHNIC

TRUST
1694387U74M-416

Editorial Address: Studio 111, Finsbury Business Centre, 40 Bowling Green Lane, LONDON, EC1R 0NE
Tel: 020 7415 7100 **Fax:** 020 7415 7002
Email: info@mediamark.co.uk
Publisher: Mediamark Ltd
Frequency: Half-yearly - Published in March and September
Cover Price: Free
Circulation: 48,000 (Publisher's Statement)
Editor: Heather Farmbrough
Summary of Content: Magazine covering investment platforms that Baillie Gifford support including investment trusts, OEICS, ISAs, PEPs, children's savings plans, share plans and self invested personal pensions.
Readership/Target Audience: Aimed at customers of the investment house Baillie Gifford.
ADVERTISING: No Advertising taken
CONSUMER: WOMEN'S INTEREST CONSUMER MAGAZINES: Personal Finance

TV & SATELLITE WEEK
46110U76C-500

Editorial Address: Blue Fin Building, 110 Southwark Street, LONDON, SE1 0SU **Tel:** 020 3148 5532 **Fax:** 020 3148 8115
Email: tv&satweek@ipcmedia.com
Advertising Address: As above. **Tel:** 020 3148 5000
Email: richard_smith@ipcmedia.com
Web site: http://www.ipcmedia.com/brands/tvsatweek
Publisher: IPC TX
Frequency: Weekly
Cover Price: £1.10
Circulation: 183,929 (ABC 01/01/2009 to 30/06/2009)
Usual Pagination: 102
Editor: Judy Ewens; **Features Editor:** Judy Ewens;
Advertising Manager: Richard Smith
Summary of Content: Magazine providing a comprehensive guide to TV and satellite listings.
Readership/Target Audience: Aimed at those aged 30 to 45.
ADVERTISING RATES:
Full Page Colour £5715.00
Agency Commission: 5%
Mechanical Data: Type Area: 282 x 200mm, Bleed Size: 306 x 226mm, Trim Size: 300 x 220mm, Col Length: 282mm, Page Width: 200mm, Film: Digital, Print Process: Web-fed offset litho
Copy instructions: Copy Date: 15 working days prior to publication date
Average advertising content per issue: 9%
CONSUMER: MUSIC & PERFORMING ARTS: TV & Radio

TV EASY
1683724U76C-830

Editorial Address: Blue Fin Building, 110 Southwark Street, LONDON, SE1 0SU **Tel:** 020 3148 5720
Email: tveasy@ipcmedia.com
Advertising Address: As above. **Tel:** 020 3148 5000
Email: richard_smith@ipcmedia.com
Web site: http://www.ipcmedia.com/brands/tveasy
Publisher: IPC TX
Date Established: 2005
Frequency: Weekly
Cover Price: £0.47
Circulation: 201,728 (ABC 01/01/2009 to 30/06/2009)
Usual Pagination: 100
Editor: Richard Clark; **Advertising Manager:** Richard Smith;
Managing Editor: Claire Ruck; **Publisher:** Mark Winterton
Summary of Content: TV listings magazine with features on soaps, drama, true life stories and entertainment TV as well as a film guide.
Readership/Target Audience: Aimed at the mass market.
ADVERTISING RATES:
Full Page Colour £7172.00
Mechanical Data: Type Area: 208 x 160mm, Bleed Size: 231 x 179mm, Trim Size: 225 x 173mm, Col Length: 208mm, Page Width: 160mm, Film: Digital
CONSUMER: MUSIC & PERFORMING ARTS: TV & Radio

THE TV MAG
46112U76C-550

Editorial Address: 1 Virginia Street, LONDON, E98 1SN
Tel: 020 7782 4377 **Fax:** 020 7782 4351
Email: jonathan.worsnop@the-sun.co.uk
Advertising Address: As above. **Fax:** 020 7782 7714
Email: clare.greenslade@the-sun.co.uk
Web site: http://www.thesun.co.uk
Publisher: News Group Newspapers Ltd
Frequency: Weekly - Published on Saturday. See main record for circulation figure
Cover Price: Free
Usual Pagination: 88
Editor: Jon Worsnop
Summary of Content: Magazine containing listings for all terrestrial, satellite and digital channels as well as features on upcoming TV programmes, actors and actresses, features cinema and DVD rental reviews, TV secrets and a gossip page.
Readership/Target Audience: Read by the readers of The Sun newspaper.
ADVERTISING RATES:
Full Page Colour £31000.00
Agency Commission: 10%
Mechanical Data: Type Area: 269 x 215mm, Col Length: 269mm, Page Width: 215mm, Bleed Size: 293 x 235mm, Trim Size: 283 x 225mm, Film: Digital
Copy instructions: Copy Date: 2 weeks prior to publication date
Average advertising content per issue: 25%
Supplement to: The Sun
CONSUMER: MUSIC & PERFORMING ARTS: TV & Radio

TV QUICK
46113U76C-701

Editorial Address: Academic House, 24-28 Oval Road, LONDON, NW1 7DT **Tel:** 020 7241 8000 **Fax:** 020 7241 8020
Email: carmen.o'boyle@bauer.co.uk
Advertising Address: As above. **Fax:** 020 7075 0786
Email: lisa.carver@bauer.co.uk
Web site: http://www.tvquick.co.uk
Publisher: H. Bauer Publishing
Date Established: 1991
Frequency: Weekly - Published on Tuesday
Cover Price: £0.80
Circulation: 144,270 (ABC 01/01/2009 to 30/06/2009)
Usual Pagination: 74
Editor: Carmen O'Boyle; **Features Editor:** Marie-Anne Hamilton; **Editor-in-Chief:** Jon Peake; **Managing Director:** David Goodchild; **Advertising Manager:** Lisa Carver
Summary of Content: TV listings magazine with soap and celebrity linked features.
Readership/Target Audience: Aimed at those between 18 and 45 years old.
ADVERTISING RATES:
Full Page Colour £11500.00
Agency Commission: 15%
Mechanical Data: Page Width: 190mm, Film: Digital, Type Area: 260 x 190mm, Bleed Size: 288 x 218mm, Trim Size: 280 x 210mm, Print Process: Web-fed offset litho, Col Length: 260mm
Average advertising content per issue: 11%
CONSUMER: MUSIC & PERFORMING ARTS: TV & Radio

TV TIMES
46114U76C-703

Editorial Address: Blue Fin Building, 110 Southwark Street, LONDON, SE1 0SU **Tel:** 020 3148 5615 **Fax:** 020 3148 8115
Email: tvtimes_letters@ipcmedia.com
Advertising Address: As above. **Tel:** 020 3148 5000
Email: richard_smith@ipcmedia.com
Web site: http://www.ipcmedia.com/brands/tvtimes
Publisher: IPC TX

Date Established: 1955
Frequency: Weekly
Cover Price: £1.05
Circulation: 311,307 (ABC 01/01/2009 to 30/06/2009)
Usual Pagination: 100
Editor: Ian Abbott; **Features Editor:** Robert Hiley;
Advertising Manager: Richard Smith
Summary of Content: Magazine containing previews of TV, satellite and radio programmes. Includes TV news, gossip and behind-the-scenes features. Also includes film reviews, video and cinema releases and celebrity interviews.
Readership/Target Audience: Aimed at those interested in TV and radio programmes.
ADVERTISING RATES:
Full Page Colour £16450.00
Agency Commission: 15%
Mechanical Data: Type Area: 282 x 200mm, Bleed Size: 306 x 226mm, Trim Size: 300 x 220mm, Col Length: 282mm, Film: Digital, Page Width: 200mm, Print Process: Web-fed offset litho
Copy instructions: Copy Date: 15 days prior to publication date
Average advertising content per issue: 15%
CONSUMER: MUSIC & PERFORMING ARTS: TV & Radio

TV ZONE
46117U76C-710
Editorial Address: 9-10 Blades Court, Deodar Road, LONDON, SW15 2NU **Tel:** 020 8875 1520
Fax: 020 8875 1588
Email: tvzone@visimag.com
Advertising Address: As above.
Email: adverts@visimag.com
Web site: http://www.visimag.com
ISSN: 0957-3844
Publisher: Visual Imagination Ltd
Frequency: 13 issues yearly
Cover Price: £3.99
Annual Sub.: £41.00
Circulation: 38,500 (Publisher's Statement)
Usual Pagination: 100
Editor: Anthony Brown; **Advertising Manager:** Martin Clarke; **Group Editor:** Stephen Payne
Summary of Content: Magazine covering cult TV shows, concentrating on sci-fi and fantasy.
Readership/Target Audience: Aimed at 15 to 35 year old cult TV enthusiasts.
ADVERTISING RATES:
Full Page Colour £950.00
Agency Commission: 10%
Mechanical Data: Film: Digital, Bleed Size: 310 x 232mm, Trim Size: 300 x 222mm, Type Area: 270 x 192mm, Col Length: 270mm, Page Width: 192mm
Copy instructions: Copy Date: 2 weeks prior to publication date
Average advertising content per issue: 25%
CONSUMER: MUSIC & PERFORMING ARTS: TV & Radio

TVCHOICE
600976U76C-503
Editorial Address: Academic House, 24-28 Oval Road, LONDON, NW1 7DT **Tel:** 020 7241 8000 **Fax:** 020 7241 8020
Email: tvchoice@bauer.co.uk
Advertising Address: 8 Upper St. Martin's Lane, LONDON, WC2H 9DW **Tel:** 020 7240 9400 **Fax:** 020 7241 9040
Email: tim.collins@bauer.co.uk
Web site: http://www.tvchoicemagazine.co.uk
Publisher: H. Bauer Publishing
Date Established: 1999
Frequency: Weekly - Published on Tuesday
Cover Price: £0.40
Circulation: 1,335,894 (ABC 01/01/2009 to 30/06/2009)
Usual Pagination: 76
Editor: Carmen O'Boyle; **Features Editor:** Elaine Penn;
Editor-in-Chief: Jon Peake; **Managing Director:** David Goodchild
Summary of Content: Magazine containing TV listings, focusing on the terrestrial TV channels, including a film guide, horoscopes and show-biz news.
Readership/Target Audience: Aimed at those who have an interest in show-biz news.
ADVERTISING RATES:
Full Page Colour £17000.00
Mechanical Data: Page Width: 190mm, Film: Digital, Type Area: 260 x 190mm, Col Length: 260mm
Copy instructions: Copy Date: 1 week prior to publication date
CONSUMER: MUSIC & PERFORMING ARTS: TV & Radio

TW MAGAZINE
1789572U80B-427
Editorial Address: 26 York Street, LONDON, W1U 6PZ
Tel: 020 7788 7547
Email: enquiries@twmagazine.co.uk
Advertising Address: As above.
Email: enquiries@twmagazine.co.uk
Web site: http://www.twmagazine.co.uk
Publisher: LVC Ltd
Date Established: 2006
Frequency: Monthly

Cover Price: Free
Circulation: 30,000 (Publisher's Statement)
Usual Pagination: 40
Editor: Jaz Walia; **Publisher:** Jaz Walia
Summary of Content: Magazine covering movies, restaurants, theatre, fashion, gadgets, health, beauty, property, travel, shopping and events.
Readership/Target Audience: Aimed at residents and visitors to the London TW postcode areas.
ADVERTISING RATES:
Full Page Colour £1250.00
Agency Commission: 10%
Mechanical Data: Trim Size: 270 x 210mm, Film: Digital
Average advertising content per issue: 50%
CONSUMER: RURAL & REGIONAL INTEREST: Regional Interest Greater London

TWINS TRIPLETS AND MORE MAGAZINE
45345U74D-530
Editorial Address: 12 Danescourt Road, WOLVERHAMPTON, WV6 9BG **Tel:** 01902 751565
Fax: 01902 751588
Email: jelwilliams@btinternet.com
Advertising Address: 2 The Willows, Gardner Road, GUILDFORD, GU1 4PG **Tel:** 0870 770 3305
Fax: 0870 770 3303
Email: advertising@tamba.org.uk
ISSN: 0967-8867
Publisher: TAMBA
Date Established: 1990
Frequency: Quarterly
Cover Price: £2.50
Free to qualifying individuals
Circulation: 15,000 (Publisher's Statement)
Usual Pagination: 32
Editor: Jane Williams
Summary of Content: Magazine covering details on personal experiences and human-interest features of those with twins, triplets and more. Also contains advice on childcare and parenting issues, travel guide for families and a product testing page.
Readership/Target Audience: Read by members of the Twins and Multiple Births Association. Also aimed at twin club members, parents of twins or more and health education professionals.
ADVERTISING RATES:
Full Page Colour £450.00
Mechanical Data: Bleed Size: 303 x 216mm, Trim Size: 297 x 210mm, Film: Positive, right reading, emulsion side down, No. of Columns (Display): 3
Copy instructions: Copy Date: 8 weeks prior to publication date
Average advertising content per issue: 10%
CONSUMER: WOMEN'S INTEREST CONSUMER MAGAZINES: Child Care

TWIST & GO MAGAZINE
628704U77B-635
Formerly: TAG Magazine
Editorial Address: PO Box 99, HORNCASTLE, LN9 6LZ
Tel: 01507 525771 **Fax:** 01507 525499
Email: info@twistngo.co.uk
Advertising Address: As above. **Tel:** 01507 524004
Fax: 01507 529499
Email: mpercival@mortons.co.uk
Web site: http://www.twistngo.com
ISSN: 1471-0501
Publisher: Mortons Media Group Ltd
Date Established: 2000
Frequency: 6 issues yearly
Cover Price: £3.50
Free to qualifying individuals
Circulation: 27,000 (Publisher's Statement)
Usual Pagination: 116
Editor: Mau Spencer; **Features Editor:** Chris Pearson
Summary of Content: Magazine covering commuter and automatic scooters. Includes road tests, product reviews, price guides and articles on tuning and workshops along with quads and learner legal motorcycles.
Readership/Target Audience: Read by scooter riders and potential purchasers of a scooter along with first time motorcycle riders.
ADVERTISING RATES:
Full Page Mono £525.00
Full Page Colour £650.00
Agency Commission: 10%
Mechanical Data: Page Width: 181mm, No. of Columns (Display): 4, Col Widths (Display): 44mm, Type Area: 270 x 181mm, Col Length: 270mm, Trim Size: 297 x 210mm, Bleed Size: 307 x 220mm, Film: Digital
CONSUMER: MOTORING & CYCLING: Motorcycling

TWO WHEELS ONLY
711560U77B-637
Editorial Address: 15-18 White Lion Street, Islington, LONDON, N1 9PD **Tel:** 020 7843 8800
Email: mail@two.tv

Advertising Address: Berwick House, 8-10 Knoll Rise, ORPINGTON, BR6 0EL **Tel:** 01689 899200
Email: andy@two.tv
Web site: http://www.visordown.com
Publisher: Magicalia Ltd
Date Established: 2000
Frequency: Monthly
Cover Price: £3.95
Circulation: 24,730 (ABC 01/01/2008 to 31/12/2008)
Usual Pagination: 148
Editor: John Cantlie; **Features Editor:** John Hogan
Summary of Content: Magazine covering all aspects of motorcycles. Includes reviews, products, racing, road tests and gadgets.
Readership/Target Audience: Read by motorcycle enthusiasts aged 30 years old and over.
ADVERTISING RATES:
Full Page Mono £1885.00
Full Page Colour £1885.00
Agency Commission: 10%
Mechanical Data: Type Area: 257 x 200mm, Col Length: 257mm, Trim Size: 295 x 220mm, Bleed Size: 301 x 226mm, Film: Digital, Col Widths (Display): 47mm, No. of Columns (Display): 4, Page Width: 200mm
Copy instructions: Copy Date: 3 weeks prior to publication date
Average advertising content per issue: 35%
CONSUMER: MOTORING & CYCLING: Motorcycling

U3A NEWS
47903U88B-110
Editorial Address: 19 East Street, BROMLEY, BR1 1QE
Tel: 020 8349 9194 **Fax:** 020 8346 9506
Email: national.office@u3a.org.uk
Advertising Address: 41 St James Gardens, WESTCLIFF-ON-SEA, SS0 0BU **Tel:** 01702 342573 **Fax:** 01702 342573
Email: gerald.brigg@talktalk.net
Web site: http://www.u3a.org.uk
Publisher: Third Age Trust
Frequency: Quarterly
Cover Price: Free
Circulation: 170,000 (Publisher's Statement)
Usual Pagination: 36
Editor: Francis Beckett; **Advertising Manager:** Gerald Brigg
Summary of Content: House magazine for the Universities of the Third Age. Covers news, events, interviews with personalities and information on courses and groups.
Readership/Target Audience: Aimed at members of the University of the Third Age and those no longer in full time employment interested in lifelong learning.
ADVERTISING RATES:
Full Page Colour £1559.00
Agency Commission: 10%
Mechanical Data: Page Width: 182mm, Film: Digital, Type Area: 272 x 182mm, Col Length: 272mm, Col Widths (Display): 58mm, No. of Columns (Display): 3, Print Process: Web-fed offset litho, Bleed Size: 303 x 213mm, Trim Size: 297 x 210mm
Copy instructions: Copy Date: 4 weeks prior to publication date
Average advertising content per issue: 40%
CONSUMER: EDUCATION: Adult Education

UK CARP
1800801U92-110
Editorial Address: Bushfield House, Orton Centre, PETERBOROUGH, PE2 5UW **Tel:** 01733 23711
Email: steve.broad@bauermedia.co.uk
Advertising Address: As above. **Tel:** 01733 237111
Fax: 01733 288005
Email: donna.harris@bauerconsumer.co.uk
Web site: http://www.anglingtimes.co.uk
Publisher: Bauer Media Ltd (Orton)
Date Established: 2006
Frequency: Monthly
Cover Price: £3.50
Circulation: 50,000 (Publisher's Statement)
Usual Pagination: 132
Editor: Steve Broad
Summary of Content: Magazine covering all aspects of carp fishing including product reviews and fishing lifestyle.
Readership/Target Audience: Aimed at carp fishing enthusiasts.
ADVERTISING RATES:
Full Page Colour £600.00
Agency Commission: 10%
Mechanical Data: Trim Size: 297 x 210mm, Film: Digital
Copy instructions: Copy Date: 1 week prior to publication date
CONSUMER: ANGLING & FISHING

UK ROCK
1776463U76D-820
Editorial Address: PO Box 2113, LEIGH-ON-SEA, SS9 5WW **Tel:** 01702 512512
Email: ukrockmagazine@aol.com
Advertising Address: As above.
Email: ukrockmagazine@aol.com
Web site: http://www.ukrock.net

Section 4 (c) Consumer Magazines

Consumer Magazines

Publisher: Southern Rock Ltd
Date Established: 1994
Frequency: Monthly
Cover Price: £2.50
Circulation: 3,000 (Publisher's Statement)
Usual Pagination: 48
Editor: John Howard; **Advertising Manager:** Ken Major
Summary of Content: Magazine covering 50s rock and roll music and 50s lifestyle with gig reviews, live music listings, CD and book reviews, previews and interviews with the stars.
Readership/Target Audience: Aimed at rock and roll music fans.
ADVERTISING RATES:
Full Page Mono £100.00
Full Page Colour £300.00
Agency Commission: 10%
Mechanical Data: Type Area: 275 x 190mm, Bleed Size: 307 x 220mm, Trim Size: 297 x 210mm, Col Length: 275mm, Page Width: 190mm, Film: Digital, Print Process: Offset litho, No. of Columns (Display): 3, Col Widths (Display): 60mm
Copy instructions: Copy Date: 20th of the month prior to publication date
Average advertising content per issue: 40%
CONSUMER: MUSIC & PERFORMING ARTS: Music

ULSTER AIRSHOW PROGRAMME
1686814U75N-752
Editorial Address: Media House, 5 Broadway Court, High Street, CHESHAM, HP5 1EG **Tel:** 01494 771144
Fax: 01494 771177
Email: info@bpcmagazines.com
Advertising Address: As above.
Email: copy@bpcmagazines.com
Web site: http://www.bpcmagazines.com
Publisher: BPC Magazines
Frequency: Annual - Published in May
Circulation: 3,000 (Publisher's Statement)
Editor: Stella Adams; **Advertising Manager:** Clare George;
Publisher: Robert Adams
Summary of Content: Programme providing a showcase for companies associated with the Air Show.
Readership/Target Audience: Aimed at the general public and those attending the Air Show.
ADVERTISING: Rates on application
CONSUMER: SPORT: Flight

ULSTER BRIDE
1659803U74L-231
Editorial Address: 39 Boucher Road, BELFAST, BT12 6UT
Tel: 028 9066 3311 **Fax:** 028 9038 1915
Email: larasalmon@ulstertatler.com
Advertising Address: As above.
Email: ccorr@ulsterbride.com
Web site: http://www.ulstertatler.com
Publisher: Ulster Journals Ltd
Frequency: Quarterly
Cover Price: £3.95
Circulation: 44,000 (Publisher's Statement)
Usual Pagination: 288
Editor: Lara Salmon
Summary of Content: Magazine covering all aspects of weddings including fashion, beauty, honeymoons, photography, hotels, receptions, transport, men's wear, entertainment, mother of the bride and interiors.
Readership/Target Audience: Aimed at brides and grooms and all those connected with the weddings in Ireland.
ADVERTISING RATES:
Full Page Colour £1240.00
Agency Commission: 15%
Mechanical Data: Type Area: 270 x 187mm, Bleed Size: 310 x 225mm, Trim Size: 300 x 215mm, Col Length: 270mm, Page Width: 187mm, Film: Digital
Copy instructions: Copy Date: 1st of the month prior to publication date
CONSUMER: WOMEN'S INTEREST CONSUMER MAGAZINES: Brides

ULSTER ROAD RACING IN FOCUS
1732054U77B-717
Editorial Address: 6 Parkland Avenue, LISBURN, BT28 3JW
Tel: 028 9266 4336 **Fax:** 028 9266 4336
Advertising Address: As above.
Email: ulsterspeed@btinternet.com
Publisher: Ulster Speed Promotions
Frequency: 3 issues yearly - Published in May, August and November
Cover Price: £3.00
Circulation: 12,000 (Publisher's Statement)
Usual Pagination: 52
Editor: William Johnston; **Advertising Manager:** Eddie Mateer
Summary of Content: Magazine highlighting and promoting motorcycle tarmac racing, events, profiles of riders and historic races.

Readership/Target Audience: Aimed at those interested in road and track motorcycle racing.
ADVERTISING: Rates on application
CONSUMER: MOTORING & CYCLING: Motorcycling

ULSTER TATLER
47067U80F-200
Editorial Address: 39 Boucher Road, BELFAST, BT12 6UT
Tel: 028 9066 3311 **Fax:** 028 9038 1915
Email: arlene.lattimer@ulstertatler.com
Advertising Address: As above.
Email: advertising@ulstertatler.com
Web site: http://www.ulstertatler.com
Publisher: Ulster Journals Ltd
Frequency: Monthly
Cover Price: £2.95
Circulation: 10,549 (ABC 01/01/2008 to 31/12/2008)
Usual Pagination: 250
Editor: Christopher Sherry; **Features Editor:** Arlene Lattimer
Summary of Content: Magazine containing features on social coverage, sport and leisure, food & drink, property, health, fashion and holidays.
Readership/Target Audience: Aimed at high income men and women living in Northern Ireland.
ADVERTISING RATES:
Full Page Colour £1370.00
Agency Commission: 15%
Mechanical Data: Trim Size: 300 x 215mm, Type Area: 270 x 187mm, Bleed Size: +5mm, No. of Columns (Display): 4, Film: Digital, Col Length: 270mm, Page Width: 187mm
Copy instructions: Copy Date: 3 weeks prior to publication date
Average advertising content per issue: 50%
Supplement(s): Director's Chair - 4xY, Ulster Tatler Woman - 12xY
CONSUMER: RURAL & REGIONAL INTEREST: Regional Interest Northern Ireland

ULSTER TATLER INTERIORS
1796257U74C-864
Formerly: Living Design
Editorial Address: 39 Boucher Road, BELFAST, BT12 6UT
Tel: 028 9066 3311 **Fax:** 028 9038 1915
Email: edit@ulstertatler.com
Advertising Address: As above.
Email: arlene.lattimer@ulstertatler.com
Web site: http://www.ulstertatler.com
Publisher: Ulster Journals Ltd
Date Established: 2006
Frequency: Half-yearly - Published in Summer and Winter
Cover Price: EUR7.00
Free to qualifying individuals
Circulation: 8,000 (Print Run)
Usual Pagination: 96
Editor: Graeme Kelly; **Managing Editor:** Christopher Sherry
Summary of Content: Magazine covering architect designed homes in Northern Ireland.
Readership/Target Audience: Aimed at individuals and professionals who are interested in local architecture.
ADVERTISING RATES:
Full Page Colour £995.00
Agency Commission: 10%
Average advertising content per issue: 30%
CONSUMER: WOMEN'S INTEREST CONSUMER MAGAZINES: Home & Family

ULSTER TATLER INTERIORS
47066U80F-155
Formerly: Portrait
Editorial Address: 39 Boucher Road, BELFAST, BT12 6UT
Tel: 028 9066 3311 **Fax:** 028 9038 1915
Email: gkelly@ulstertatler.com
Advertising Address: As above. **Fax:** 028 9068 1915
Email: gkelly@ulstertatler.com
Web site: http://www.ulstertatler.com
Publisher: Ulster Journals Ltd
Frequency: Quarterly
Cover Price: £2.50
Circulation: 10,000 (Publisher's Statement)
Editor: Graeme Kelly; **Features Editor:** Graeme Kelly;
Advertising Manager: Graeme Kelly
Summary of Content: Publication featuring interior design for the home.
Readership/Target Audience: Aimed at the local community and tourists to the area.
ADVERTISING RATES:
Full Page Colour £850.00
Mechanical Data: Film: Digital
CONSUMER: RURAL & REGIONAL INTEREST: Regional Interest Northern Ireland

THE ULSTER TIPPLER
1696951U89C-1055
Editorial Address: 5 University Street, BELFAST, BT7 1FY
Tel: 028 9024 6624 **Fax:** 028 9024 6936
Email: info@admanpublishing.com
Advertising Address: As above.
Email: info@admanpublishing.com

Web site: http://www.admanpublishing.com
Publisher: Adman Publishing Ltd
Frequency: Annual - Published in March
Cover Price: Free
Circulation: 30,000 (Publisher's Statement)
Usual Pagination: 112
Editor: Henry Davidson; **Advertising Manager:** Mary McCaffrey; **Publisher:** Henry Davidson
Summary of Content: Magazine covering good pubs in Ulster.
Readership/Target Audience: Aimed at tourists, tourist information centres, Belfast Welcome Centre and Bord Failte.
ADVERTISING RATES:
Full Page Colour £486.50
Agency Commission: 15%
Mechanical Data: Film: Digital
Copy instructions: Copy Date: 2 weeks prior to publication date
Average advertising content per issue: 100%
CONSUMER: HOLIDAYS & TRAVEL: Entertainment Guides

ULTIMATE DVD
626557U78B-420
Editorial Address: 9-10 Blades Court, Deodar Road, LONDON, SW15 2NU **Tel:** 020 8875 1520
Fax: 020 8875 1588
Email: ultimatedvd@visimag.com
Advertising Address: As above.
Email: adverts@visimag.com
Web site: http://www.visimag.com
Publisher: Visual Imagination Ltd
Date Established: 1999
Frequency: Monthly
Cover Price: £3.99
Annual Sub.: £43.00
Circulation: 35,000 (Publisher's Statement)
Usual Pagination: 132
Editor: Stuart Weightman
Summary of Content: Magazine covering news and reviews of the latest DVD releases and DVD players.
Readership/Target Audience: Read by people of all ages with an interest in DVDs.
ADVERTISING RATES:
Full Page Colour £1150.00
Agency Commission: 10%
Mechanical Data: Page Width: 192mm, Type Area: 270 x 192mm, Bleed Size: 307 x 230mm, Trim Size: 297 x 220mm, Col Length: 270mm, Film: Digital
Copy instructions: Copy Date: 2 weeks prior to publication date
Average advertising content per issue: 20%
CONSUMER: CONSUMER ELECTRONICS: Video & DVD

ULTRA VW
1639386U77E-506
Editorial Address: Nimax House, 20 Ullswater Crescent, Ullswater Business Park, COULSDON, CR5 2HR
Tel: 01702 526531
Email: ultravw@chpltd.com
Advertising Address: As above. **Tel:** 020 8655 6400
Fax: 020 8763 1001
Email: ads@chpltd.com
Web site: http://www.ultravw.com
Publisher: CH Publications Ltd
Date Established: 2003
Frequency: Monthly
Cover Price: £3.90
Annual Sub.: £34.00
Circulation: 35,000 (Publisher's Statement)
Usual Pagination: 100
Editor: Paul Knight; **Advertising Manager:** Frank Archer;
Managing Editor: Keith Seume
Summary of Content: Magazine covering air-cooled VWs, water cooled new Beetles and the new Transporters as well as classic and vintage Porsches.
Readership/Target Audience: Aimed at vintage, performance and general VW enthusiasts of all ages.
ADVERTISING RATES:
Full Page Mono £880.00
Full Page Colour £980.00
Mechanical Data: Type Area: 267 x 190mm, Bleed Size: 300 x 222mm, Trim Size: 297 x 220mm, Col Length: 267mm, Page Width: 190mm, Film: Digital
Copy instructions: Copy Date: 2 weeks prior to publication date
CONSUMER: MOTORING & CYCLING: Club Cars

ULTRA-FIT MAGAZINE
45984U75P-800
Formerly: Ultra-Fit
Editorial Address: Champions House, 5 Princes Street, PENZANCE, TR18 2NL **Tel:** 01736 350204
Fax: 01736 368587
Advertising Address: As above.
Email: adsales@ultra-fitmagazine.com
Web site: http://www.ultra-fitmagazine.com
ISSN: 0957-0616
Publisher: Ultra-fit Publications Ltd

Date Established: 1989
Frequency: 9 issues yearly
Cover Price: £3.99
Annual Sub.: £33.59
Circulation: 45,000 (Publisher's Statement)
Usual Pagination: 114
Editor: John Shepherd; **Advertising Manager:** Niggy Rowe
Summary of Content: Magazine covering news and information on fitness training. Includes outdoor activities, sports clothing, footwear, fitness equipment, clubs and workshops, sports nutrition and exercise products.
Readership/Target Audience: Aimed at fitness enthusiasts, professional sportsmen and women and those interested in living a healthy lifestyle.
ADVERTISING RATES:
Full Page Colour £2000.00
Agency Commission: 15%
Mechanical Data: Type Area: 268 x 180mm, Trim Size: 297 x 210mm, Col Length: 268mm, Film: Digital, Page Width: 180mm, Bleed Size: 303 x 216mm
Copy instructions: Copy Date: 4 weeks prior to publication date
CONSUMER: SPORT: Fitness/Bodybuilding

ULTRATRAVEL
1663900U89A-717

Editorial Address: 111 Buckingham Palace Road, LONDON, SW1W 0DT **Tel:** 020 7931 2381
Email: traveldesk@telegraph.co.uk
Advertising Address: As above. **Tel:** 020 7931 2000
Fax: 01494 678612
Email: nick@ultra.travel
Web site: http://www.telegraph.co.uk
Publisher: Telegraph Media Group Ltd
Date Established: 2004
Frequency: Quarterly
Cover Price: Free
Circulation: 60,000 (Publisher's Statement)
Usual Pagination: 68
Editor: Graham Boynton; **Advertising Manager:** Nick Perry
Summary of Content: Magazine covering luxury travel including how to fly, where to stay and what's new in hotels, travel accessories, travel trends and where and when to go as well as competitions.
Readership/Target Audience: Aimed at aspirational travellers with a high disposable income.
ADVERTISING RATES:
Full Page Colour £11880.00
Agency Commission: 15%
Mechanical Data: Type Area: 338 x 244mm, Bleed Size: 390 x 285mm, Trim Size: 380 x 280mm, Col Length: 338mm, Page Width: 244mm, Film: Digital
Copy instructions: Copy Date: 5 weeks prior to publication date
Average advertising content per issue: 40%
Supplement to: The Daily Telegraph
CONSUMER: HOLIDAYS & TRAVEL: Travel

UNCUT
46269U76E-530

Editorial Address: Blue Fin Building, 110 Southwark Street, LONDON, SE1 0SU **Tel:** 020 3148 5000 **Fax:** 020 3148 8170
Email: farah_ishaq@ipcmedia.com
Advertising Address: As above. **Fax:** 020 3148 8108
Email: neil_mcsteen@ipcmedia.com
Web site: http://www.uncut.co.uk
ISSN: 1368-0722
Publisher: IPC ignite!
Date Established: 1997
Frequency: Monthly
Cover Price: £4.20
Annual Sub.: £37.80
Circulation: 76,526 (ABC 01/01/2009 to 30/06/2009)
Usual Pagination: 184
Editor: Farah Ishaq; **Advertising Manager:** Neil McSteen;
Publisher: Faith Hill
Summary of Content: Magazine providing in-depth coverage of the latest developments in the world of music and film.
Readership/Target Audience: Aimed at men between 25 and 45 years old.
ADVERTISING RATES:
Full Page Mono £3020.00
Full Page Colour £4190.00
Agency Commission: 10%
Mechanical Data: Col Length: 275mm, Type Area: 275 x 200mm, Print Process: Web-fed offset, Bleed Size: 306 x 236mm, Trim Size: 300 x 230mm, Page Width: 200mm, Film: Digital
Average advertising content per issue: 35%
CONSUMER: MUSIC & PERFORMING ARTS: Pop Music

UNDER 5
47948U88R-55

Formerly: Under 5 Contact
Editorial Address: Fitzpatrick Building, 188 York Way, LONDON, N7 9AD **Tel:** 020 7697 2500 **Fax:** 020 7697 8607
Email: editor.U5@pre-school.org.uk

Advertising Address: Mongoose Media Ltd, Mongoose House, 2 Lonsdale Road, LONDON, NW6 6RD
Tel: 020 7306 0300 **Fax:** 020 7306 0301
Email: underfive@mongoosemedia.com
Web site: http://www.pre-school.org.uk
ISSN: 0969-9481
Publisher: Pre-school Learning Alliance
Date Established: 1963
Frequency: 10 issues yearly
Free to qualifying individuals
Annual Sub.: £30.00
Circulation: 16,500 (Publisher's Statement)
Usual Pagination: 24
Editor: Mandy Murphy; **Advertising Manager:** Rachel Dadds
Summary of Content: Journal covering practical advice on the care and education of babies and young children in nursery, toddler, playgroup and pre-school settings.
Readership/Target Audience: Membership magazine also aimed at pre-school staff and parents.
ADVERTISING RATES:
Full Page Colour £1885.00
SCC £20.00
Agency Commission: 10%
Mechanical Data: Type Area: 269 x 190mm, Bleed Size: 301 x 214mm, Trim Size: 295 x 208mm
CONSUMER: EDUCATION: Education Related

UNILEVER MAGAZINE
48828U94X-192

Editorial Address: PO Box 68, Unilever House, LONDON, EC4P 4BQ **Tel:** 020 7822 5252 **Fax:** 020 7822 5128
Publisher: Unilever Plc
Date Established: 1972
Frequency: Quarterly
Cover Price: Free
Circulation: 55,000 (Publisher's Statement)
Usual Pagination: 40
Editor: Steven Golding
Summary of Content: A global internal magazine.
Readership/Target Audience: Aimed at Unilever managers.
ADVERTISING: No Advertising taken
CONSUMER: OTHER CLASSIFICATIONS: Miscellaneous

UNION
47462U83-92

Editorial Address: University of Sheffield, Union of Students, Western Bank, SHEFFIELD, S10 2TG
Tel: 0114 222 8540 **Fax:** 0114 222 8542
Email: thestudentconnection@sheffield.ac.uk
Advertising Address: As above.
Email: studentconnection@sheffield.ac.uk
Web site: http://www.sheffieldunion.com
Publisher: Union of Students
Frequency: Annual - Published in August
Cover Price: Free
Circulation: 5,000 (Print Run)
Usual Pagination: 24
Editor: Libby de Frain; **Advertising Manager:** James Eardley
Summary of Content: Magazine providing a complete overview of all the Union's activities.
Readership/Target Audience: Aimed at present and prospective students of the University of Sheffield.
ADVERTISING RATES:
Full Page Colour £750.00
Agency Commission: 10%
Mechanical Data: Type Area: 240 x 180mm, Col Length: 240mm, Page Width: 180mm, Bleed Size: +3mm, Film: Digital
Copy instructions: Copy Date: July 1st
Average advertising content per issue: 5%
CONSUMER: STUDENT PUBLICATIONS

UNITE MAGAZINE
45589U74N-155

Formerly: Unite
Editorial Address: Unit 6, Imperial Court, Laporte Way, LUTON, LU4 8FE **Tel:** 01582 721652 **Fax:** 01582 450906
Email: info@pensioneronline.com
Advertising Address: Mainline Media Ltd, The Barn, 8 Oakley Hay Lodge Business Park, Great Fold Road, CORBY, NN18 9AS **Tel:** 01536 747333 **Fax:** 01536 746565
Email: lynn.newman@mainlinemedia.co.uk
Web site: http://www.pensioneronline.com
Publisher: UNITE
Date Established: 1930
Frequency: 8 issues yearly
Cover Price: £1.10
Free to qualifying individuals
Circulation: 100,000 (Publisher's Statement)
Usual Pagination: 36
Editor: Lee Wilson; **Advertising Manager:** Lynn Newman;
Managing Editor: Roger Turner
Summary of Content: Magazine containing articles on politics, travel, music, books, health, computing, gadgets and gardening. Includes competitions, finance, legal and pension issues.

Readership/Target Audience: Read by members of UNITE, the largest occupational Pensioner group in the UK, with members from BT Pensioners, British Steel Pensioners and Rolls Royce and Bentley Pensioners.
ADVERTISING RATES:
Full Page Mono £2175.00
Full Page Colour £2460.00
Agency Commission: 10%
Mechanical Data: Trim Size: 297 x 210mm, Bleed Size: 307 x 220mm, Film: Digital, Type Area: 266 x 184mm, Col Length: 266mm, Page Width: 184mm
Copy instructions: Copy Date: 3 weeks prior to publication date
Average advertising content per issue: 25%
CONSUMER: WOMEN'S INTEREST CONSUMER MAGAZINES: Retirement

UNITED REVIEW
1613623U75B-268

Editorial Address: Teddington Studios, Broom Road, TEDDINGTON, TW11 9BE **Tel:** 020 8267 5000
Fax: 020 8267 5194
Email: unitedreview@haymarket.com
Advertising Address: As above. **Fax:** 020 8267 5815
Email: kavita.brown@haymarket.com
Web site: http://www.haymarket.com
Publisher: Haymarket Network
Date Established: 2002
Frequency: 30 issues yearly - New issue produced for every Manchester United home match in all competitions
Cover Price: £3.00
Usual Pagination: 68
Editor: Ian McLeish; **Editor-in-Chief:** Ian McLeish
Summary of Content: Official match day programme of Manchester United Football Club.
Readership/Target Audience: Aimed at supporters of Manchester United.
ADVERTISING: Rates on application
CONSUMER: SPORT: Football

UNITY
624748U87-214_70

Editorial Address: PO Box 8455, NEWARK, NG23 5WX
Tel: 01636 525607
Email: johnclawson@xln.co.uk
Advertising Address: As above. **Tel:** 01636 535607
Email: johnclawson@xln.co.uk
Web site: http://www.bellcourtltd.co.uk
Publisher: Bellcourt Limited
Date Established: 1999
Frequency: Monthly
Cover Price: Free
Circulation: 5,000 (Publisher's Statement)
Usual Pagination: 12
Editor: John Clawson; **Managing Director:** John Clawson; **Advertising Manager:** David Lodge
Summary of Content: Magazine featuring religious articles and interviews with an ecumenical flavour. The main emphasis is on news, events and stories relating to Devon and Cornwall.
Readership/Target Audience: Aimed at church goers of all denominations from late teens and upwards.
ADVERTISING RATES:
SCC £3.85
Agency Commission: 10%
Mechanical Data: Col Length: 350mm, No. of Columns (Display): 7, Type Area: 350 x 270mm, Print Process: Litho, Page Width: 270mm
Copy instructions: Copy Date: 30th of the month 8 weeks prior to publication date
Average advertising content per issue: 25%
CONSUMER: RELIGIOUS

UNIVERSITY OF READING MAGAZINE
47431U83-64

Formerly: Reading: reading
Editorial Address: DARO, Blandford Lodge, PO Box 217, READING, RG6 6AH **Tel:** 0118 378 8006
Fax: 0118 378 6587
Email: alumni@reading.ac.uk
Web site: http://www.reading.ac.uk
Publisher: The University of Reading
Date Established: 1985
Frequency: Half-yearly - Published in May and November
Cover Price: Free
Circulation: 80,000 (Publisher's Statement)
Usual Pagination: 24
Editor: Liz Hinde
Summary of Content: Magazine of The University of Reading.
Readership/Target Audience: Aimed at the alumni of The University of Reading, The Friends of the University, staff, local councillors and local business people.
ADVERTISING: No Advertising taken
CONSUMER: STUDENT PUBLICATIONS

UP FRONT THE OFFICIAL MAGAZINE OF GLOUCESTER RUGBY CLUB
1667163U75C-470

Editorial Address: Kingsholm Stadium, Kingsholm Road, GLOUCESTER, GL1 3AX **Tel:** 01452 300951
Fax: 01452 416300
Email: alastairdowney@gloucesterrugby.co.uk
Advertising Address: As above.
Email: alastairdowney@gloucesterrugby.co.uk
Publisher: Dunwoody Marketing Communications
Date Established: 2005
Frequency: Quarterly
Cover Price: £2.75
Circulation: 10,000 (Publisher's Statement)
Usual Pagination: 52
Editor: Alastair Downey; **Advertising Manager:** Alastair Downey
Summary of Content: Official magazine of Gloucester Rugby Football Club, includes interviews with players, rugby related and lifestyle focused articles as well as regular features including profiles on local clubs and product led features.
Readership/Target Audience: Aimed at fans of Gloucester Rugby Club.
ADVERTISING: Rates on application
Average advertising content per issue: 15%
CONSUMER: SPORT: Rugby

UPDATE
763513U76D-750

Formerly: Seven Update
Editorial Address: PO Box 89, SLOUGH, SL1 8NA
Tel: 01628 667124 **Fax:** 01628 605246
Email: update@dmcworld.com
Advertising Address: 3 Progress Business Centre, Whittle Parkway, Burnham, SLOUGH, SL1 6DQ **Tel:** 01628 667124
Fax: 01628 605246
Web site: http://www.dmcupdate.com
Publisher: DMC Publishing Ltd
Date Established: 2002
Frequency: Weekly
Cover Price: £0.75
Annual Sub.: £40.00
Circulation: 40,000 (Publisher's Statement)
Usual Pagination: 16
Editor: Martin Madigan; **Advertising Manager:** Martin Madigan; **Publisher:** Christine Prince
Summary of Content: Magazine featuring dance music news, reviews, news and chart music information.
Readership/Target Audience: Aimed at dance music DJs, producers and professional record buyers.
ADVERTISING: Rates on application
CONSUMER: MUSIC & PERFORMING ARTS: Music

UPTOWN MAGAZINE
1626410U74C-816

Editorial Address: Unit 13, 10 High Craighall Road, GLASGOW, G4 9UD **Tel:** 0141 581 2646
Fax: 0141 588 1410
Email: lynne@uptownmagazine.co.uk
Advertising Address: As above.
Email: kathy@uptownmagazine.co.uk
Web site: http://www.uptownmagazine.co.uk
Publisher: greatroom Ltd
Date Established: 2003
Frequency: 6 issues yearly
Cover Price: £2.95
Circulation: 20,000 (Print Run)
Usual Pagination: 196
Editor: Rosalind Erskine
Summary of Content: Magazine covering interiors, design and architecture as well as lifestyle, holidays, cars, food, arts and exhibitions.
Readership/Target Audience: Aimed at men and women aged 25 years old plus in Northern England and Scotland.
ADVERTISING RATES:
Full Page Mono £1900.00
Full Page Colour £2200.00
SCC £20.00
Agency Commission: 10%
Mechanical Data: Film: Digital, Type Area: 262 x 180mm, Col Length: 262mm, Bleed Size: 303 x 216mm, Trim Size: 297 x 210mm, No. of Columns (Display): 4, Page Width: 180mm
Copy instructions: Copy Date: Middle of month prior to publication date
CONSUMER: WOMEN'S INTEREST CONSUMER MAGAZINES: Home & Family

URBAN LIFE
1659589U80B-415

Editorial Address: 10 Greycoat Place, LONDON, SW1P 1SB **Tel:** 0871 989 8206 **Fax:** 0871 989 8207
Email: info@urbanlife-magazine.com
Advertising Address: As above.
Email: info@urbanlife-magazine.com
Web site: http://www.urbanlife-magazine.com
Publisher: Westside Communications Ltd
Date Established: 2004

Frequency: Quarterly
Cover Price: Free
Circulation: 35,000 (Publisher's Statement)
Usual Pagination: 68
Editor: Ataur Rahman; **Editor-in-Chief:** Ataur Rahman;
Advertising Manager: James Tan
Summary of Content: Magazine covering fashion, health and beauty, motoring, technology, travel, nightlife, arts and culture, competitions, celebrity interviews, profiles and reviews.
Readership/Target Audience: Aimed at 20 to 45 year old affluent, stylish, outgoing, well travelled, ambitious and discerning Londoners.
ADVERTISING RATES:
Full Page Colour £3900.00
Agency Commission: 15%
Mechanical Data: Trim Size: 297 x 210mm, Bleed Size: 303 x 216mm, Film: Digital
Copy instructions: Copy Date: 4 weeks prior to publication date
Average advertising content per issue: 40%
CONSUMER: RURAL & REGIONAL INTEREST: Regional Interest Greater London

URBAN LIFE
1840357U80C-5447

Editorial Address: 1 Scott Place, MANCHESTER, M3 3RN
Tel: 0161 832 7200 **Fax:** 0161 832 0155
Email: mark.burrow@urban-life.co.uk
Advertising Address: As above.
Email: natalie.young@urban-life.co.uk
Web site: http://www.urban-life.co.uk
Publisher: MEN Media
Date Established: 2008
Frequency: Weekly
Cover Price: Free
Circulation: 18,000 (Publisher's Statement)
Editor: Mark Burrow; **Advertising Manager:** Natalie Young
Summary of Content: Magazine covering local news, property and entertainment as well as lifestyle features on fashion, sport and TV.
Readership/Target Audience: Aimed at those living or working in Manchester city centre.
ADVERTISING: Rates on application
CONSUMER: RURAL & REGIONAL INTEREST: Regional Interest English Counties

USED BIKE GUIDE
46381U77B-640

Editorial Address: Media Centre, Morton Way, HORNCASTLE, LN9 6JR **Tel:** 01507 523456
Fax: 01507 529499
Email: igrainger@mortons.co.uk
Advertising Address: As above. **Tel:** 01507 524004
Email: deveritt@mortons.co.uk
Web site: http://www.usedbikeguide.co.uk
Publisher: Mortons Media Group Ltd
Date Established: 1988
Frequency: 6 issues yearly
Cover Price: £2.95
Free to qualifying individuals
Circulation: 23,000 (Publisher's Statement)
Usual Pagination: 196
Editor: Ian Grainger
Summary of Content: Magazine containing practical tips on maintaining, riding and buying used and new motorcycles, technical features, touring, kit, equipment, useful tips and advice.
Readership/Target Audience: Aimed at riders of second hand motorcycles.
ADVERTISING RATES:
Full Page Colour £514.00
Agency Commission: 10%
Mechanical Data: Type Area: 190 x 130mm, Col Length: 190mm, Page Width: 130mm, Film: Digital
Average advertising content per issue: 7%
CONSUMER: MOTORING & CYCLING: Motorcycling

UTILITAS
48829U94X-192_5

Editorial Address: London School of Economics, Houghton Street, LONDON, WC2A 2AE
Email: p.j.kelly@lse.ac.uk
Advertising Address: The Edinburgh Building, Shaftesbury Road, CAMBRIDGE, CB2 8RU **Tel:** 01223 326070
Fax: 01223 325801
Email: ad_sales@cambridge.org
Web site: http://www.utilitas.org.uk
ISSN: 0953-8208
Publisher: Cambridge University Press
Date Established: 1989
Frequency: Quarterly
Annual Sub.: £40.00
Circulation: 450 (Publisher's Statement)
Usual Pagination: 126
Editor: Paul Kelly; **Advertising Manager:** Rebecca Curtis;
Publisher: Pam O'Connor

Summary of Content: Pioneering interdisciplinary journal of moral and political philosophy, economic theory, jurisprudence and intellectual history.
Readership/Target Audience: Aimed at academic philosophers and interested lay people.
ADVERTISING RATES:
Full Page Mono £325.00
Agency Commission: 10%
Mechanical Data: Type Area: 200 x 135mm, Col Length: 200mm, Page Width: 135mm
Copy instructions: Copy Date: 8 weeks prior to publication date
CONSUMER: OTHER CLASSIFICATIONS: Miscellaneous

UTOPIA KITCHEN & BATHROOM
1810044U74C-869

Editorial Address: The Old School, Colchester Road, Wakes Colne, COLCHESTER, CO6 2BY **Tel:** 01787 221396
Fax: 01787 221394
Email: editorial@propub.co.uk
Advertising Address: As above.
Email: clara@propub.co.uk
Web site: http://www.utopiamag.co.uk
ISSN: 1753-9684
Publisher: Pro Publishing Ltd
Date Established: 2007
Frequency: Monthly
Cover Price: £3.99
Circulation: 18,000 (Publisher's Statement)
Usual Pagination: 140
Editor: Sally Narraway
Summary of Content: Magazine covering high end, luxury kitchens and bathrooms.
Readership/Target Audience: Aimed at homeowners with a high disposable income, independent professional women, ladies that lunch, interior designers and architects.
ADVERTISING RATES:
Full Page Colour £3350.00
Mechanical Data: Type Area: 280 x 210mm, Bleed Size: 306 x 236mm, Trim Size: 300 x 230mm, Col Length: 280mm, Page Width: 210mm, Film: Digital
Copy instructions: Copy Date: 6 weeks prior to publication date
CONSUMER: WOMEN'S INTEREST CONSUMER MAGAZINES: Home & Family

V&A MAGAZINE
1626932U84A-428

Editorial Address: Victoria and Albert Museum, Cromwell Road, LONDON, SW7 2RL **Tel:** 020 7942 2276
Email: newseditor@vam.ac.uk
Advertising Address: 27B Tradescant Road, LONDON, SW8 1XD **Tel:** 020 7735 9263 **Fax:** 020 7735 5052
Email: emilypalmer@cultureshockmedia.co.uk
Web site: http://www.vam.ac.uk
ISSN: 1465-8291
Publisher: Cultureshock Media Ltd
Date Established: 2003
Frequency: 3 issues yearly - Published in February, June and October
Cover Price: £4.00
Free to qualifying individuals
Circulation: 25,000 (Publisher's Statement)
Usual Pagination: 112
Editor: Kate Jazwinski; **Advertising Manager:** Emily Palmer
Summary of Content: Magazine covers all aspects of the visual arts -architecture, design, craft, photography, fashion and fine art - taking the V&A's exhibition and display programme as its starting point. V&A Magazine aims to be accessible, intelligent, entertaining and visually appealing as the museum itself.
Readership/Target Audience: Aimed at members of the museum and those planning a visit to the museum.
ADVERTISING RATES:
Full Page Colour £4000.00
Mechanical Data: Type Area: 225 x 185mm, Trim Size: 255 x 215mm, Film: Digital, Col Length: 225mm, Page Width: 185mm
Copy instructions: Copy Date: 1 month prior to publication date
CONSUMER: THE ARTS & LITERARY: Arts

V - THE VAUXHALL MAGAZINE
46338U77A-457

Formerly: VM The Vauxhall Magazine
Editorial Address: The Courtyard, Ladycross Farm, Hollow Lane, Dormansland, LINGFIELD, RH7 6PB
Tel: 01342 870409
Email: vicky.stewart@streampublishing.net
Advertising Address: As above. **Tel:** 01737 786800
Fax: 01737 786801
Email: tim.bostel@brooklandsgroup.com
Web site: http://www.vmonline.co.uk
ISSN: 1469-2236
Publisher: Stream Publishing Ltd
Date Established: 1996
Frequency: 3 issues yearly - Published in February, July and November
Cover Price: Free

Circulation: 396,294 (ABC 01/01/2007 to 31/12/2007)
Usual Pagination: 52
Editor: Vicky Stewart; **Managing Director:** Darren Styles
Summary of Content: Magazine focusing on Vauxhall products, motoring related and related lifestyle articles.
Readership/Target Audience: Read by motorists.
ADVERTISING RATES:
Full Page Colour £6500.00
Agency Commission: 10%
Mechanical Data: Bleed Size: 264 x 188mm, Trim Size: 256 x 180mm, Film: Digital
Copy instructions: Copy Date: 6 weeks prior to publication date
CONSUMER: MOTORING & CYCLING: Motoring

VAISAKHI UK
1628219U90-914

Editorial Address: Eton House, 66 Eton Avenue, WEMBLEY, HA0 3AU **Tel:** 0845 013 8401
Fax: 0845 013 8402
Email: amit@memediagroup.com
Advertising Address: As above.
Email: info@memediagroup.com
Web site: http://www.memediagroup.com
Publisher: ME Media Ltd
Date Established: 2001
Frequency: Annual - Published in April
Cover Price: Free
Circulation: 50,000 (Publisher's Statement)
Usual Pagination: 60
Editor: Amit Daryanani; **Advertising Manager:** Neena Kent
Summary of Content: Magazine with information on religious resources, entertainment and profiles of prominent Sikhs that are of interest to the community.
Readership/Target Audience: Aimed at Sikh communities in the UK.
ADVERTISING: Rates on application
CONSUMER: ETHNIC

VALLEY NEWS
1786301U80C-5371

Editorial Address: Home Close, Teffont, SALISBURY, SP3 5QY **Tel:** 01722 716268 **Fax:** 01722 716781
Email: yourvalleynews@aol.com
Advertising Address: As above.
Email: yourvalleynews@aol.com
Web site: http://www.kingsleyhousepublishers.com
Publisher: Kingsley House (Publishing)
Date Established: 2005
Frequency: Monthly - Published 1st day of the month
Free to qualifying individuals
Annual Sub.: £12.00
Circulation: 7,500 (Publisher's Statement)
Usual Pagination: 48
Editor: David Parker; **Advertising Manager:** Karl Plaskett
Summary of Content: Magazine covering community news, events and sport.
Readership/Target Audience: Aimed at households in Wiltshire villages.
ADVERTISING RATES:
Full Page Mono £135.00
Full Page Colour £190.00
Copy instructions: Copy Date: 20th of the month prior to publication date
CONSUMER: RURAL & REGIONAL INTEREST: Regional Interest English Counties

VANITY FAIR
45202U74A-600

Editorial Address: Vogue House, 1 Hanover Square, LONDON, W1S 1JU **Tel:** 020 7499 9080 **Fax:** 020 7409 0783
Email: annabel.davidson@condenast.co.uk
Advertising Address: As above. **Tel:** 020 7152 9080
Fax: 020 7489 0783
Web site: http://www.vanityfair.co.uk
Publisher: Conde Nast Publications Ltd
Frequency: Monthly
Cover Price: £3.90
Circulation: 101,698 (ABC 01/01/2009 to 30/06/2009)
Usual Pagination: 204
Editor: Annabel Davidson; **Advertising Manager:** Francesca Boys; **Advertising Director:** Polly Beynon
Summary of Content: Magazine covering politics, culture, crime, media, travel and fashion.
Readership/Target Audience: Aimed at professional men and women.
ADVERTISING RATES:
Full Page Colour £10270.00
Agency Commission: 15%
Mechanical Data: Page Width: 178mm, Type Area: 254 x 178mm, Col Length: 254mm, Trim Size: 276 x 203mm, Bleed Size: 282 x 209mm, Film: Digital
Copy instructions: Copy Date: 1 month prior to publication date
Average advertising content per issue: 35%
CONSUMER: WOMEN'S INTEREST CONSUMER MAGAZINES: Women's Interest

VARIANT
1614819U84A-444

Editorial Address: 1/2 189B Maryhill Road, GLASGOW, G20 7XJ **Tel:** 0141 333 9522
Email: variantmag@btinternet.com
Advertising Address: As above.
Email: variantmag@btinternet.com
Web site: http://www.variant.org.uk
ISSN: 0954-8815
Publisher: Variant
Date Established: 1996
Frequency: 3 issues yearly - Published in March, June and October
Cover Price: Free
Annual Sub.: £15.00
Circulation: 15,000 (Publisher's Statement)
Usual Pagination: 36
Editor: Leigh French; **Advertising Manager:** Leigh French
Summary of Content: Magazine covering video, television and film, music, new art initiatives, performances, cultural and media studies, philosophy, critical thinking, popular culture and social movements. Includes feature articles, reviews, reports, insights, interviews, letters, comments and artists pages.
Readership/Target Audience: Aimed at those with an awareness of social, political and cultural issues.
ADVERTISING RATES:
Full Page Mono £900.00
Full Page Colour £1080.00
Mechanical Data: Type Area: 352 x 252mm, Col Length: 352mm, Page Width: 252mm, Film: Digital
CONSUMER: THE ARTS & LITERARY: Arts

VAROOM
1748503U84A-455

Editorial Address: 2nd Floor, Back Building, 150 Curtain Road, LONDON, EC2A 3AT **Tel:** 020 7324 7225
Fax: 020 7613 4417
Email: derek@varoom-mag.com
Advertising Address: As above. **Tel:** 020 7613 4328
Email: derek@varoom-mag.com
Web site: http://www.varoom-mag.com
ISSN: 1750-483X
Publisher: Association of Illustrators
Date Established: 2006
Frequency: 3 issues yearly - Published in March, May and November
Cover Price: £12.00
Free to qualifying individuals
Annual Sub.: £30.00
Circulation: 4,500 (Publisher's Statement)
Usual Pagination: 86
Editor: Derek Brazell; **Advertising Manager:** Derek Brazell; **Publisher:** Ramon Blomfield
Summary of Content: Journal of illustration culture and society, featuring interviews with leading illustrators and image-makers and exploring the attitude behind their designs. It looks at influential movements in illustration as well as covering new talent, features from acclaimed design critics and will review exhibitions, events and publications.
Readership/Target Audience: Aimed at designers, illustrators, students and the general public interested in current visual culture.
ADVERTISING RATES:
Full Page Colour £450.00
Mechanical Data: Type Area: 277 x 180mm, Bleed Size: 307 x 220mm, Trim Size: 297 x 210mm, Col Length: 277mm, Page Width: 180mm, Print Process: Offset litho, Film: Digital
Average advertising content per issue: 6%
CONSUMER: THE ARTS & LITERARY: Arts

VARSITY
47465U83-95

Editorial Address: Old Examination Hall, Free School Lane, CAMBRIDGE, CB2 3RF **Tel:** 01223 337575
Fax: 01223 352913
Email: editor@varsity.co.uk
Advertising Address: As above. **Fax:** 01223 760949
Email: business@varsity.co.uk
Web site: http://www.varsity.co.uk
Publisher: Varsity Publications Ltd
Date Established: 1947
Frequency: 22 issues yearly - Published weekly during term
Cover Price: Free
Circulation: 10,000 (Publisher's Statement)
Usual Pagination: 32
Advertising Manager: Michael Derringer
Summary of Content: Publication providing news and sports coverage, plus features on a range of arts.
Readership/Target Audience: Aimed at Cambridge University students.
ADVERTISING RATES:
Full Page Colour £1320.00
Agency Commission: 10%
Mechanical Data: Col Length: 370mm, Page Width: 265mm, Type Area: 370 x 265mm, Film: Digital, Col Widths (Display): 50mm, Print Process: Web-fed offset litho
Copy instructions: Copy Date: 5 days prior to publication date
Average advertising content per issue: 25%
CONSUMER: STUDENT PUBLICATIONS

THE VEGAN
45620U74P-800

Editorial Address: 21 Hylton Street, Hockley, BIRMINGHAM, B18 6HJ **Tel:** 0121 523 1730
Email: editor@vegansociety.com
Advertising Address: As above. **Tel:** 0121 523 1733
Fax: 0121 523 1739
Email: adverts@vegansociety.com
Web site: http://www.vegansociety.com
ISSN: 0307-4811
Publisher: The Vegan Society Ltd
Date Established: 1944
Frequency: Quarterly
Cover Price: £2.50
Free to qualifying individuals
Annual Sub.: £10.00
Circulation: 5,500 (Publisher's Statement)
Usual Pagination: 44
Editor: Rosamund Raha; **Advertising Manager:** Dave Palmer
Summary of Content: Magazine focusing on vegan issues, from animal rights to ecology, with food news and recipes from the national society.
Readership/Target Audience: Aimed at vegetarians and vegans.
ADVERTISING RATES:
Full Page Mono £305.00
Full Page Colour £425.00
SCC £15.00
Agency Commission: 10%
Mechanical Data: Bleed Size: 303 x 216mm, Trim Size: 297 x 210mm, No. of Columns (Display): 4, Film: Digital
Copy instructions: Copy Date: 10th of the month prior to publication date
Average advertising content per issue: 28%
CONSUMER: WOMEN'S INTEREST CONSUMER MAGAZINES: Food & Cookery

THE VEGETARIAN
45621U74P-820

Editorial Address: Parkdale, Dunham Road, ALTRINCHAM, WA14 4QG **Tel:** 0161 925 2000 **Fax:** 0161 926 9182
Email: editor@vegsoc.org
Advertising Address: As above.
Email: graham@vegsoc.org
Web site: http://www.vegsoc.org
ISSN: 1475-3413
Publisher: The Vegetarian Society
Date Established: 1849
Frequency: Quarterly
Cover Price: Free
Circulation: 15,000 (Publisher's Statement)
Usual Pagination: 62
Editor: Jane Bowler
Summary of Content: In-house magazine of the Vegetarian Society. Covers cookery, nutrition, animal welfare, the environment, lifestyle and philosophy.
Readership/Target Audience: Aimed at vegetarians.
ADVERTISING RATES:
Full Page Colour £1150.00
Agency Commission: 10%
Mechanical Data: Bleed Size: 303 x 216mm, Trim Size: 297 x 210mm, Film: Positive, right reading, emulsion side down. Digital, Page Width: 180mm, Type Area: 260 x 180mm, Col Length: 260mm, Screen: 54 lpc
Copy instructions: Copy Date: 6 weeks prior to publication date
CONSUMER: WOMEN'S INTEREST CONSUMER MAGAZINES: Food & Cookery

VEGGIETIMES
1792511U74P-959

Editorial Address: Independent House, Radford Business Centre, Radford Way, BILLERICAY, CM12 0BZ
Tel: 01277 627300
Email: media@theenquirer.co.uk
Advertising Address: As above.
Web site: http://www.veggietimes.co.uk
Publisher: Typestyle Ltd
Frequency: Monthly - See main record for circulation figure
Free to qualifying individuals
Annual Sub.: £12.00
Editor: Karin Ridgers
Summary of Content: Newspaper covering vegetarian living with recipes, celebrity interviews, products and events.
Readership/Target Audience: Aimed at those interested in a healthy lifestyle.
Supplement to: Essex Enquirer Series
CONSUMER: WOMEN'S INTEREST CONSUMER MAGAZINES: Food & Cookery

VELOCITY - VLM INFLIGHT MAGAZINE
1647211U89D-510

Editorial Address: 141-143 Shoreditch High Street, LONDON, E1 6JE **Tel:** 020 7613 8777 **Fax:** 020 7613 8776
Email: steve.watson@ink-publishing.com
Advertising Address: As above. **Tel:** 020 7613 8779
Fax: 020 7613 8778
Email: keith.martin@ink-publishing.com

Consumer Magazines

Web site: http://www.vlmmagazine.com
Publisher: Ink Publishing
Date Established: 2004
Frequency: 6 issues yearly
Cover Price: Free
Circulation: 30,000 (Publisher's Statement)
Usual Pagination: 100
Editor: Steve Watson; **Advertising Manager:** Keith Martin
Summary of Content: Magazine with business news and features, sports stories, tips on doing business abroad and free time guides.
Readership/Target Audience: Aimed at passengers of VLM Airlines.
ADVERTISING RATES:
Full Page Colour £4537.00
Mechanical Data: Bleed Size: 271 x 216mm, Trim Size: 265 x 210mm, Film: Digital
Copy instructions: Copy Date: 1 month prior to publication date
CONSUMER: HOLIDAYS & TRAVEL: In-Flight Magazines

VENTURE
1800334U89A-740

Editorial Address: 40 Earls Court Road, LONDON, W8 6EJ
Tel: 0800 092 9595 **Fax:** 020 7937 6664
Email: venture@kumuka.com
Web site: http://www.venturemag.net
Publisher: Kumuka Worldwide
Date Established: 2006
Frequency: Quarterly
Cover Price: Free
Circulation: 90,000 (Publisher's Statement)
Usual Pagination: 32
Editor: Ozkan Ozbuluter; **Managing Director:** Ozkan Ozbuluter
Summary of Content: Magazine covering worldwide destinations for soft adventure travel and adventure tours for families.
Readership/Target Audience: Aimed at soft adventure travellers.
ADVERTISING: No Advertising taken
CONSUMER: HOLIDAYS & TRAVEL: Travel

VENUE
48149U89C-500

Editorial Address: 2nd Floor, Bristol News & Media, Temple Way, BRISTOL, BS99 7HD **Tel:** 0117 942 8491
Fax: 0117 934 3566
Email: editor@venue.co.uk
Advertising Address: As above.
Email: sales@venue.co.uk
Web site: http://www.venue.co.uk
Publisher: Venue Publishing
Date Established: 1982
Frequency: Weekly
Cover Price: £1.50
Circulation: 12,000 (Publisher's Statement)
Usual Pagination: 112
Editor: Joe Spurgeon; **Group Editor:** David Higgitt
Summary of Content: Guide to the arts and entertainment, which includes listings for Bristol and Bath.
Readership/Target Audience: Aimed at young, professional people.
ADVERTISING RATES:
Full Page Colour £1100.00
Agency Commission: 10%
Mechanical Data: Type Area: 273 x 184mm, Col Length: 273mm, Page Width: 184mm, Trim Size: 297 x 210mm, Bleed Size: 301 x 214mm, Film: Digital
Copy instructions: Copy Date: Wednesday prior to publication date
Average advertising content per issue: 40%
Supplement(s): Eating Out West - 1xY, Inside Out - 4xY, Venue Student Pages - 1xY
CONSUMER: HOLIDAYS & TRAVEL: Entertainment Guides

THE VERWOOD & WIMBOURNE VIEWPOINT
1779101U80C-5361

Formerly: Viewpoint
Editorial Address: 6 Whittle Road, Ferndown Industrial Estate, WIMBORNE, BH21 7RU **Tel:** 01202 870270
Email: mags@mags4dorset.co.uk
Advertising Address: As above.
Email: tavt@btconnect.com
Publisher: Page & Pulford
Frequency: Monthly
Cover Price: Free
Circulation: 25,000 (Publisher's Statement)
Editor: Janine Pulford
Summary of Content: Magazine covering local news and events.
Readership/Target Audience: Aimed at homes and businesses in Wimborne, Ferndown and Verwood.
ADVERTISING RATES:
Full Page Colour £361.00
Mechanical Data: Trim Size: 297 x 210mm

Copy instructions: Copy Date: 8th of the month prior to publication
CONSUMER: RURAL & REGIONAL INTEREST: Regional Interest English Counties

VETERAN CAR
46497U77F-430

Editorial Address: Jessamine Court, 15 High Street, Ashwell, BALDOCK, SG7 5NL **Tel:** 01462 742818
Fax: 01462 742997
Email: hq@vccofgb.co.uk
Advertising Address: As above.
Email: hq@vccofgb.co.uk
Publisher: Veteran Car Services Ltd
Date Established: 1930
Frequency: 6 issues yearly
Circulation: 1,800 (Publisher's Statement)
Editor: June Cutchie; **Advertising Manager:** June Cutchie
Summary of Content: Magazine covering the events of the Veteran Car Club of Great Britain. Includes historical articles on pre-1919 cars, museums, services and restorations.
Readership/Target Audience: Read by members.
ADVERTISING: Rates on application
Average advertising content per issue: 16%
CONSUMER: MOTORING & CYCLING: Veteran Cars

VICE MAGAZINE
766921U74Q-1129

Editorial Address: Ground Floor, 77 Leonard Street, LONDON, EC2A 4QS **Tel:** 020 7613 5981
Fax: 020 7729 6884
Email: andy@viceuk.com
Advertising Address: As above.
Email: matt@viceuk.com
Web site: http://www.viceland.com
Publisher: Vice UK Ltd
Date Established: 2002
Frequency: 15 issues yearly
Cover Price: Free
Circulation: 85,000 (Publisher's Statement)
Editor: Andy Capper; **Advertising Manager:** Matt Elek; **Publisher:** Matt Elak
Summary of Content: Magazine covering youth culture including music, events, politics and fashion.
Readership/Target Audience: Aimed at young adults.
ADVERTISING RATES:
Full Page Colour £3500.00
Agency Commission: 10%
CONSUMER: WOMEN'S INTEREST CONSUMER MAGAZINES: Lifestyle

THE VICTORIAN
48592U94B-200

Editorial Address: 1 Priory Gardens, Bedford Park, LONDON, W4 1TT **Tel:** 020 8994 1019 **Fax:** 020 8747 5899
Email: director@victoriansociety.org.uk
Advertising Address: Hall-McCartney Limited, Heritage House, PO Box 21, BALDOCK, SG7 5SH **Tel:** 01462 896688
Fax: 01462 896677
Email: victoriansociety@hall-mccartney.co.uk
Web site: http://www.victoriansociety.org.uk
ISSN: 1467-7970
Publisher: The Victorian Society
Date Established: 1999
Frequency: 3 issues yearly - Published in March, July and November
Annual Sub.: £33.00
Circulation: 3,500 (Publisher's Statement)
Usual Pagination: 32
Editor: Elizabeth Robinson; **Advertising Manager:** Geoff Connelly
Summary of Content: Magazine containing information on the current campaigns and research of the Victorian Society containing articles on decorative arts, architecture and the social history of the period.
Readership/Target Audience: Aimed at members of the society.
ADVERTISING RATES:
Full Page Mono £352.00
Full Page Colour £475.00
Agency Commission: 10%
Mechanical Data: Bleed Size: 303 x 216mm, Trim Size: 297 x 210mm, Type Area: 270 x 190mm, Col Length: 270mm, Film: Digital, Page Width: 190mm
Copy instructions: Copy Date: 6 weeks prior to publication date
Average advertising content per issue: 25%
CONSUMER: OTHER CLASSIFICATIONS: Historic Buildings

VIEWS
718631U74Q-406

Formerly: Health, Beauty & Fitness
Editorial Address: Fair Oak Close, Exeter Airport Business Park, Clyst Honiton, EXETER, EX5 2UL **Tel:** 01392 888482
Fax: 01392 888499
Email: magazines.devon@archant.co.uk
Advertising Address: As above. **Tel:** 01395 888482
Fax: 01392 888470

Email: nicky.webber@archant.co.uk
Publisher: Archant South West
Date Established: 2001
Frequency: Quarterly
Cover Price: Free
Circulation: 18,000 (Publisher's Statement)
Usual Pagination: 76
Editor: Andrew Coley; **Group Editor:** Phil Griffin
Summary of Content: Lifestyle magazine covering the people and places of East Devon, plus health, beauty, fitness, education, motoring and art.
Readership/Target Audience: Aimed at readers of the Sidmouth Herald and Exmouth Journal.
ADVERTISING: Rates on application
Agency Commission: 10%
Copy instructions: Copy Date: 5 weeks prior to publication date
Average advertising content per issue: 15%
Supplement to: Sidmouth Herald Series
CONSUMER: WOMEN'S INTEREST CONSUMER MAGAZINES: Lifestyle

THE VILLAGE
1606166U80C-5051

Editorial Address: 16 The Square, Alvechurch, BIRMINGHAM, B48 7LA **Tel:** 0121 445 6757
Fax: 0870 705 3041
Email: mail@villageonline.co.uk
Advertising Address: As above. **Fax:** 0870 705 1627
Email: sales@platformpublishing.co.uk
Web site: http://www.villageonline.co.uk
ISSN: 1466-3376
Publisher: Platform Publishing & Media Ltd
Date Established: 1998
Frequency: 10 issues yearly - Joint issues July/August and December/January
Cover Price: £2.50
Free to qualifying individuals
Annual Sub.: £20.00
Circulation: 11,000 (Publisher's Statement)
Usual Pagination: 68
Editor: Richard Peach; **Publisher:** Richard Peach
Summary of Content: Local news magazine covering health and beauty, fashion, motoring, travel, entertainment, restaurants and property.
Readership/Target Audience: Aimed at those living in and visitors to North Worcestershire, Birmingham and Solihull.
ADVERTISING RATES:
Full Page Colour £600.00
Mechanical Data: Col Length: 235mm, Page Width: 162mm, Type Area: 235 x 162mm, Bleed Size: +3mm, Trim Size: 245 x 172mm, Col Widths (Display): 77mm, No. of Columns (Display): 2
Average advertising content per issue: 35%
CONSUMER: RURAL & REGIONAL INTEREST: Regional Interest English Counties

THE VILLAGE ECHO
629562U80C-300

Editorial Address: 114-115 West Street, FARNHAM, GU9 7HL **Tel:** 01252 899297
Email: echo.news@internet-today.co.uk
Advertising Address: As above. **Fax:** 01252 899257
Email: planning.herald@internet-today.co.uk
Publisher: Farnham Castle Publications
Date Established: 1997
Frequency: Monthly
Cover Price: Free
Circulation: 12,000 (Publisher's Statement)
Usual Pagination: 40
Editor: Tony Short; **Advertising Manager:** Beverley Blanche
Summary of Content: Village focused news magazine covering community news, features, photographs, sports, entertainment, leisure, diary, listings, crosswords, letters and general news.
Readership/Target Audience: Aimed at residents of villages in parts of the Thames Valley, South Bucks and surrounding areas.
ADVERTISING RATES:
Full Page Colour £250.00
Agency Commission: 10%
Mechanical Data: Trim Size: 297 x 210mm, Film: Digital
Copy instructions: Copy Date: 1 week prior to publication date
Average advertising content per issue: 40%
CONSUMER: RURAL & REGIONAL INTEREST: Regional Interest English Counties

THE VINE
1841174U87-2052

Editorial Address: PO Box 8455, NEWARK, NG23 5WX
Tel: 01636 525607
Email: johnclawson@xln.co.uk
Advertising Address: As above.
Email: johnclawson@xln.co.uk
Publisher: Bellcourt Limited
Frequency: Monthly
Cover Price: Free
Circulation: 8,000 (Publisher's Statement)

Editor: John Clawson; **Managing Director:** John Clawson;
Advertising Manager: John Clawson
Summary of Content: Newspaper covering religious topic,
events, news and opinion.
Readership/Target Audience: Aimed at Roman Catholic
churchgoers in the Diocese of Northampton.
ADVERTISING: Rates on application
CONSUMER: RELIGIOUS

VINTAGE ROADSCENE
46340U77F-450
Editorial Address: PO Box 10, Foundry Road, STAMFORD,
PE9 2PP **Tel:** 01768 351053 **Fax:** 01768 353558
Email: paul.appleton@ianallanpublishing.co.uk
Advertising Address: As above.
Email: kevin@transpenninepublishing.co.uk
Web site: http://www.ianallanpublishing.co.uk
ISSN: 0266-8947
Publisher: Ian Allan Publishing Ltd
Date Established: 1984
Frequency: Monthly
Cover Price: £3.25
Circulation: 12,000 (Publisher's Statement)
Usual Pagination: 64
Advertising Manager: Kevin Bradley
Summary of Content: Magazine covering news and
features on the restoration of vintage and commercial
vehicles of yesteryear.
Readership/Target Audience: Read by enthusiasts of
commercial vehicles, buses, trams and light commercials
from the outset of motoring history up to 25-years ago.
ADVERTISING RATES:
Full Page Mono £390.00
Full Page Colour £390.00
Agency Commission: 10%
Mechanical Data: Col Length: 265mm, Page Width:
185mm, Bleed Size: 303 x 216mm, Trim Size: 297 x 210mm,
Film: Digital, Type Area: 265 x 185mm
CONSUMER: MOTORING & CYCLING: Veteran Cars

VINTAGE SPIRIT
1641354U77F-453
Editorial Address: 151 Station Street, BURTON-ON-
TRENT, DE14 1BG **Tel:** 01283 742950 **Fax:** 01483 542901
Email: brian.gooding@vintagespirit.co.uk
Advertising Address: As above. **Fax:** 01283 742966
Email: ian.sharpe@vintagespirit.co.uk
Web site: http://www.vintagespirit.co.uk
Publisher: WW Magazines
Date Established: 2002
Frequency: Monthly
Cover Price: £3.50
Usual Pagination: 100
Editor: Brian Gooding; **News Editor:** Ken Rimell;
Advertising Manager: Ted Tomlin
Summary of Content: Magazine covering vintage or
heritage transport including road steam engines, old lorries
and vintage machinery as well as industrial heritage.
Readership/Target Audience: Aimed at those interested in
vintage machinery.
ADVERTISING RATES:
Full Page Mono £825.00
Full Page Colour £825.00
Agency Commission: 10%
Mechanical Data: Type Area: 267 x 190mm, Col Length:
267mm, Page Width: 190mm, Bleed Size: 303 x 216mm,
Trim Size: 297 x 210mm, Film: Digital
Copy instructions: Copy Date: 5 weeks prior to publication
date
CONSUMER: MOTORING & CYCLING: Veteran Cars

VINTAGE TRACTOR
1667823U79R-153
Editorial Address: 30 Hallow Lane, Lower Broadheath,
WORCESTER, WR2 6QL **Tel:** 01905 640306
Email: info@vtmag.co.uk
Advertising Address: As above.
Email: green-phil@ntlworld.co.uk
Web site: http://www.vtmag.co.uk
Publisher: Vintage Tractor
Frequency: 6 issues yearly
Cover Price: £3.80
Circulation: 15,000 (Publisher's Statement)
Usual Pagination: 52
Editor: Tim Bolton; **Advertising Manager:** Phil Green;
Publisher: Tim Bolton
Summary of Content: Magazine covering vintage and
classic tractors of all ages and types with articles on
preservation, collecting, storing, buying and selling as well
as a section on vintage and classic plant.
Readership/Target Audience: Aimed at vintage and classic
tractor enthusiasts aged from 9 to 99 years old.
ADVERTISING RATES:
Full Page Colour £395.00
Agency Commission: 10%
Average advertising content per issue: 10%
CONSUMER: HOBBIES & DIY: Hobbies & DIY Related

VIRGIN MOBILE BITES
1654976U74Q-1193
Editorial Address: Exmouth House, 3 Pine Street,
LONDON, EC1R 0JH **Tel:** 020 7278 9584
Fax: 020 7278 9659
Email: marie@que-pasa.co.uk
Web site: http://www.virginmobile.com/bites
Publisher: Que Pasa Communications Ltd
Date Established: 2004
Frequency: Annual
Cover Price: Free
Circulation: 300,000 (Publisher's Statement)
Usual Pagination: 28
Editor: Marie Ahsun; **Managing Director:** Mark Maddox
Summary of Content: Magazine covering indie, urban and
dance music, celebrity news and gossip, humour, sport,
recommendations of the newest products from gadgets to
fragrances and clothing.
Readership/Target Audience: Aimed at owners of Virgin
mobile phones.
ADVERTISING: No Advertising taken
CONSUMER: WOMEN'S INTEREST CONSUMER
MAGAZINES: Lifestyle

VISION
1704772U94F-1014
Editorial Address: 105 Judd Street, LONDON, WC1H 9NE
Tel: 020 7391 2018
Email: martyn.harris@rnib.org.uk
Web site: http://www.rnib.org.uk
Publisher: Royal National Institute of the Blind
Date Established: 2002
Frequency: 6 issues yearly
Free to qualifying individuals
Circulation: 10,000 (Publisher's Statement)
Usual Pagination: 28
Editor: Martyn Harris
Summary of Content: Lifestyle magazine for people with
sight problems.
Readership/Target Audience: Aimed at blind and partially
sighted people.
ADVERTISING: No Advertising taken
CONSUMER: OTHER CLASSIFICATIONS: Disability

THE VISITOR
46967U80C-2840
Editorial Address: PO Box 1, CASTLE CARY, BA7 7BG
Tel: 01963 351256 **Fax:** 01963 350552
Email: info@thevisitormagazine.co.uk
Advertising Address: As above.
Email: info@thevisitormagazine.co.uk
Publisher: Badger Publications
Date Established: 1983
Frequency: Monthly
Cover Price: Free
Circulation: 33,000 (Publisher's Statement)
Usual Pagination: 64
Editor: Helen Dunion; **Advertising Manager:** Michelle
Trulock
Summary of Content: Magazine of general interest covering
current events, history, house and home, gardening and
leisure.
Readership/Target Audience: Aimed at people in the West
Country.
ADVERTISING RATES:
Full Page Mono £360.00
SCC £4.20
Agency Commission: 10%
Mechanical Data: Page Width: 192mm, Col Widths
(Display): 45mm, Film: Digital, Col Length: 282mm, No. of
Columns (Display): 4, Type Area: 282 x 192mm, Trim Size:
297 x 210mm
Copy instructions: Copy Date: 10 days prior to publication
date
Average advertising content per issue: 65%
CONSUMER: RURAL & REGIONAL INTEREST: Regional
Interest English Counties

VITA
1665387U80D-512
Editorial Address: 11 The Bulwark, BRECON, LD3 7AE
Tel: 01874 610111 **Fax:** 01874 624097
Email: theeditor@brecon-radnor.co.uk
Advertising Address: As above. **Fax:** 01874 624359
Email: sales@brecon-radnor.co.uk
Publisher: Brecon and Radnor Express Ltd
Date Established: 2004
Frequency: Quarterly
Cover Price: Free
Circulation: 15,000 (Publisher's Statement)
Usual Pagination: 16
Editor: Julie Chappell; **News Editor:** Twm Owen
Summary of Content: Magazine with lifestyle features,
restaurants, shops and local personalities.
Readership/Target Audience: Aimed at 20 to 60 year olds
in Breconshire and Radnorshire.
ADVERTISING RATES:
Full Page Colour £400.00
Agency Commission: 10%

Mechanical Data: Type Area: 345 x 260mm, Col Length:
345mm, Page Width: 260mm, Col Widths (Display): 32.5mm,
No. of Columns (Display): 8, Film: Digital
Copy instructions: Copy Date: 2 weeks prior to publication
date
Average advertising content per issue: 45%
CONSUMER: RURAL & REGIONAL INTEREST: Regional
Interest Wales

VIVO MAGAZINE
1800303U80C-5401
Editorial Address: 21 High Street, Warsop, MANSFIELD,
NG20 0AA **Tel:** 0870 011 4115
Email: editorial@vivomagazine.co.uk
Advertising Address: As above.
Email: kim@k9media.net
Web site: http://www.vivomagazine.co.uk
Publisher: K9 Media Ltd
Date Established: 2006
Frequency: Quarterly
Cover Price: Free
Circulation: 5,000 (Publisher's Statement)
Editor: Sean O'Meara; **Advertising Manager:** Kim Bruce
Summary of Content: Magazine covering homes and
gardens, cars, property at home and abroad, financial
advice, health and beauty, cuisine, technology and local
news and events.
Readership/Target Audience: Aimed at residents and
businesses in Ravenshead.
ADVERTISING RATES:
Full Page Colour £640.00
Agency Commission: 10%
Mechanical Data: Type Area: 270 x 188mm, Bleed Size:
307 x 220mm, Trim Size: 297 x 210mm, Col Length: 270mm,
Page Width: 188mm, Film: Digital
Copy instructions: Copy Date: 4 weeks prior to publication
date
Average advertising content per issue: 40%
CONSUMER: RURAL & REGIONAL INTEREST: Regional
Interest English Counties

VIYA
1820084U74L-267
Editorial Address: 18 Salisbury Road, LONDON, E10 5RG
Tel: 020 8279 0831
Email: info@viyamagazine.com
Advertising Address: As above.
Email: info@viyamagazine.com
Web site: http://www.viyamagazine.com
Publisher: Bo Publications Ltd
Frequency: Half-yearly - Published in spring/summer and
autumn/winter
Cover Price: £4.95
Circulation: 25,000 (Publisher's Statement)
Usual Pagination: 320
Editor: Samina Saeed; **Advertising Manager:** Zulika Bibi
Summary of Content: Wedding magazine covering all
aspects of Asian weddings as well as fashion and beauty.
Readership/Target Audience: Aimed at brides to be.
ADVERTISING: Rates on application
CONSUMER: WOMEN'S INTEREST CONSUMER
MAGAZINES: Brides

VIZ
48724U94X-194
Editorial Address: PO Box 656, NEWCASTLE UPON TYNE,
NE30 4EZ **Tel:** 020 7907 6000
Email: viz@viz.co.uk
Advertising Address: 30 Cleveland Street, LONDON, W1T
4JD **Tel:** 020 7907 6000 **Fax:** 020 7907 6601
Email: james_clements@dennis.co.uk
Web site: http://www.viz.co.uk
ISSN: 0952-7966
Publisher: Dennis Publishing Ltd
Date Established: 1979
Frequency: 10 issues yearly
Cover Price: £3.00
Circulation: 82,241 (ABC 01/01/2008 to 31/12/2008)
Usual Pagination: 52
Editor: Russell Blackman; **Publisher:** Russell Blackman
Summary of Content: Magazine containing cartoons, letters
and tabloid spoof editorial.
Readership/Target Audience: Aimed mainly at the 16 to 40
age group.
ADVERTISING RATES:
Full Page Colour £6750.00
Agency Commission: 10%
Mechanical Data: Col Length: 278mm, Film: Digital, Type
Area: 278 x 206mm, Bleed Size: 306 x 236mm, Trim Size:
300 x 230mm, Page Width: 206mm, No. of Columns
(Display): 5
Copy instructions: Copy Date: 4 weeks prior to publication
date
Average advertising content per issue: 20%
CONSUMER: OTHER CLASSIFICATIONS: Miscellaneous

Consumer Magazines

LA VOCE DEGLI ITALIANI
48354U90-183_75

Editorial Address: 20 Brixton Road, LONDON, SW9 6BU
Tel: 020 7735 5164 **Fax:** 020 7793 0385
Email: ziliotto@scalabrini.co.uk
Advertising Address: As above.
Email: ziliotto@scalabrini.co.uk
Publisher: Scalabrini Fathers
Date Established: 1948
Frequency: Monthly
Cover Price: £0.50
Annual Sub.: £20.00
Circulation: 10,000 (Publisher's Statement)
Usual Pagination: 12
Editor: Giandomenico Ziliotto; **Advertising Manager:** Giandomenico Ziliotto
Summary of Content: Newspaper covering news and general interest.
Language(s): English; Italian
Readership/Target Audience: Aimed at Italians living in Britain.
ADVERTISING RATES:
Full Page Mono £250.00
Agency Commission: 10%
Mechanical Data: Type Area: 380 x 270mm, Col Length: 380mm, Page Width: 270mm
Copy instructions: Copy Date: 4 weeks prior to publication date
Average advertising content per issue: 35%
CONSUMER: ETHNIC

VOGUE
45232U74B-610

Editorial Address: Vogue House, 1 Hanover Square, LONDON, W1S 1JU **Tel:** 020 7499 9080 **Fax:** 020 7408 0559
Email: vogue.com.editor@condenast.co.uk
Advertising Address: As above. **Fax:** 020 7152 3881
Email: flora.king@condenast.co.uk
Web site: http://www.vogue.co.uk
Publisher: Conde Nast Publications Ltd
Date Established: 1916
Frequency: Monthly
Cover Price: £3.70
Circulation: 210,435 (ABC 01/01/2009 to 30/06/2009)
Editor: Nina Godfrey; **Features Editor:** Jo Ellison;
Managing Director: Nicholas Coleridge; **Managing Editor:** Frances Bentley
Summary of Content: Magazine containing features on fashion and beauty.
Twitter: http://twitter.com/VOGUEfashion
Readership/Target Audience: Read by professional women between 20 and 44 years old.
ADVERTISING RATES:
Full Page Colour £22200.00
Mechanical Data: Page Width: 200mm, Type Area: 265 x 200mm, Bleed Size: 291 x 226mm, Trim Size: 285 x 220mm, Col Length: 265mm, Film: Digital
CONSUMER: WOMEN'S INTEREST CONSUMER MAGAZINES: Women's Interest - Fashion

THE VOICE
48355U90-184

Editorial Address: Northern and Shell Tower, 6th Floor, 4 Selsdon Way, LONDON, E14 9GL **Tel:** 020 7510 0340
Fax: 020 7510 0341
Email: newsdesk@gvmedia.co.uk
Advertising Address: As above. **Tel:** 020 7510 0352
Email: advertising@gvmedia.co.uk
Web site: http://www.voice-online.co.uk
Publisher: GV Media Ltd
Date Established: 1982
Frequency: Weekly
Cover Price: £0.85
Circulation: 40,000 (Publisher's Statement)
Usual Pagination: 60
Editor: George Ruddock; **Features Editor:** Rodney Hinds;
Advertising Manager: Edwin Efa; **Group Editor:** Ope Bankole
Summary of Content: Newspaper covering news, features, music and sport.
Readership/Target Audience: Aimed at members of the black community between 18 and 35 years old.
ADVERTISING RATES:
Full Page Mono £4428.00
Full Page Colour £5757.00
SCC £19.95
Agency Commission: 10%
Mechanical Data: Trim Size: 420 x 297mm, Film: Digital, No. of Columns (Display): 8, Type Area: 370 x 262mm, Col Length: 370mm, Page Width: 262mm
Copy instructions: Copy Date: Friday 4pm prior to publication date
Average advertising content per issue: 40%
Supplement(s): 24 Seven - 51xY, V2 Jobs - 51xY, Woman2Woman - 11xY
CONSUMER: ETHNIC

VOICE OF THE ARAB WORLD
47287U82-200

Editorial Address: The Studio, 143 Lavender Hill, LONDON, SW11 5QJ **Tel:** 020 7228 1060 **Fax:** 020 7228 1191
Email: voice@mia.gb.com
ISSN: 0954-5697
Publisher: Morris International Associates Ltd
Date Established: 1986
Frequency: Quarterly
Annual Sub.: £60.00
Circulation: 5,000 (Publisher's Statement)
Usual Pagination: 60
Editor: Ann Morris; **Managing Director:** Daniel Donovan;
Managing Editor: Daniel Donovan
Summary of Content: Magazine covering UK news and current affairs relating to Arab Gulf countries.
Readership/Target Audience: Aimed at diplomats, politicians, business people and academics.
ADVERTISING: No Advertising taken
CONSUMER: CURRENT AFFAIRS & POLITICS

VOLKSWAGEN CAMPER AND COMMERCIAL
764975U77A-502

Editorial Address: The Old School, Higher Kinnerton, CHESTER, CH4 9AJ **Tel:** 01244 663400 **Fax:** 01244 660611
Email: editor@volkswagencamper.co.uk
Advertising Address: As above.
Email: advertising@volkswagencamper.co.uk
Web site: http://www.volkswagencamper.co.uk/
Publisher: Jazz Publishing
Frequency: 6 issues yearly
Cover Price: £3.33
Annual Sub.: £15.80
Circulation: 11,000 (Publisher's Statement)
Usual Pagination: 64
Editor: David Eccles; **Advertising Manager:** Emma McCindle; **Publisher:** Stuart Mears
Summary of Content: Magazine covering all aspects of buying, owning and running a VW Transporter.
Readership/Target Audience: Aimed at Camper enthusiasts.
ADVERTISING RATES:
Full Page Colour £630.00
Agency Commission: 10%
Mechanical Data: Trim Size: 297 x 210mm, Bleed Size: +3mm, Film: Digital
Copy instructions: Copy Date: 2 weeks prior to publication date
Average advertising content per issue: 30%
CONSUMER: MOTORING & CYCLING: Motoring

VOLKSWAGEN DRIVER
46483U77E-315

Formerly: Volkswagen Audi Car
Editorial Address: Campion House, 1 Greenfield Road, Westoning, BEDFORD, MK45 5JD **Tel:** 01525 750500
Fax: 01525 750700
Email: mail@autometrix.co.uk
Advertising Address: As above.
Email: sales@autometrix.co.uk
Web site: http://www.volkswagendrivermag.co.uk
ISSN: 1470-3785
Publisher: AutoMetrix Publications
Date Established: 2000
Frequency: Monthly
Cover Price: £3.95
Annual Sub.: £38.00
Circulation: 20,000 (Publisher's Statement)
Usual Pagination: 84
Editor: Neil Birkitt; **Advertising Manager:** Debbie Forbes; **Publisher:** Paul Harris
Summary of Content: Publication containing road tests of new Volkswagen models, owner profiles, technical developments and car prices. Includes information on performance tuning, equipment, accessories and motor sport coverage.
Readership/Target Audience: Aimed at owners and enthusiasts of Volkswagen cars.
ADVERTISING RATES:
Full Page Colour £650.00
Agency Commission: 10%
Mechanical Data: Bleed Size: 303 x 213mm, Trim Size: 297 x 210mm, Type Area: 260 x 182mm, Film: Digital, Col Length: 260mm, Page Width: 182mm
Copy instructions: Copy Date: 3 weeks prior to publication date
Average advertising content per issue: 30%
CONSUMER: MOTORING & CYCLING: Club Cars

VOLKSWAGEN GOLF+
46455U77E-154_75

Formerly: Golf+
Editorial Address: PO Box 13, Berrys Green, WESTERHAM, TN16 3WT **Tel:** 01959 541444
Fax: 020 8726 8399
Email: golf.ed@kelsey.co.uk
Advertising Address: As above.
Email: matt.carson@kelsey.co.uk
Web site: http://www.thegolf.co.uk

ISSN: 1359-4982
Publisher: Kelsey Publishing Ltd
Date Established: 1995
Frequency: Monthly
Cover Price: £3.90
Circulation: 3,000 (Publisher's Statement)
Usual Pagination: 116
Editor: Ian Cushway
Summary of Content: Magazine covering the latest VW Golfs including new product news and technical advice as well as Seats, Skodas and Audis.
Readership/Target Audience: Read by Volkswagen Audi Group car enthusiasts.
ADVERTISING RATES:
Full Page Colour £705.00
Agency Commission: 10%
Mechanical Data: Col Length: 277mm, Film: Digital, Type Area: 277 x 190mm, Bleed Size: 303 x 216mm, Trim Size: 297 x 210mm, No. of Columns (Display): 5, Page Width: 190mm
Copy instructions: Copy Date: 4 weeks prior to publication date
CONSUMER: MOTORING & CYCLING: Club Cars

VOLKSWORLD
46482U77E-320

Editorial Address: Leon House, 233 High Street, CROYDON, CR9 1HZ **Tel:** 020 8726 8000
Email: volksworld@ipcmedia.com
Advertising Address: As above. **Fax:** 020 8726 8399
Email: kara_goodwin@ipcmedia.com
Web site: http://www.volksworld.com
Publisher: IPC Inspire
Frequency: 13 issues yearly
Cover Price: £4.10
Circulation: 36,000 (Publisher's Statement)
Usual Pagination: 116
Editor: Jon Gilbert
Summary of Content: Magazine containing news, events, products and features.
Readership/Target Audience: Aimed at air-cooled Volkswagen enthusiasts.
ADVERTISING RATES:
Full Page Mono £715.00
Full Page Colour £1200.00
Agency Commission: 10%
Mechanical Data: Film: Digital, No. of Columns (Display): 2, Bleed Size: 303 x 216mm, Trim Size: 297 x 210mm
Copy instructions: Copy Date: 6 weeks prior to publication date
Average advertising content per issue: 40%
CONSUMER: MOTORING & CYCLING: Club Cars

VOLKSWORLD CAMPER & BUS
1745689U77E-522

Editorial Address: Leon House, 233 High Street, CROYDON, CR9 1HZ **Tel:** 020 8726 8354
Fax: 020 8726 8333
Email: volksworld@ipcmedia.com
Advertising Address: As above. **Tel:** 020 8726 8000
Fax: 020 8726 8399
Email: kara_goodwin@ipcmedia.com
Publisher: IPC Inspire
Date Established: 2005
Frequency: 13 issues yearly
Cover Price: £3.95
Circulation: 30,000 (Print Run)
Usual Pagination: 100
Editor: James Peene; **Managing Editor:** Ivan McCutcheon
Summary of Content: Magazine containing news, products and features about Volkswagen camper vans and buses.
Readership/Target Audience: Aimed at enthusiasts of Volkswagen camper vans.
ADVERTISING RATES:
Full Page Colour £1380.00
Agency Commission: 10%
Mechanical Data: Type Area: 266 x 190mm, Bleed Size: 303 x 216mm, Trim Size: 297 x 210mm, Col Length: 266mm, Page Width: 190mm, Film: Digital
Copy instructions: Copy Date: 4 weeks prior to publication date
Average advertising content per issue: 35%
CONSUMER: MOTORING & CYCLING: Club Cars

VOYAGER
48222U89D-500

Editorial Address: 141-143 Shoreditch High Street, LONDON, E1 6JE **Tel:** 020 7613 8777 **Fax:** 020 7613 8778
Email: robina.dam@ink-publishing.com
Advertising Address: As above. **Tel:** 020 7613 8779
Fax: 0845 280 9898
Email: stefan@electricink.net
Web site: http://www.bmivoyager.com
ISSN: 1358-8907
Publisher: Ink Publishing
Date Established: 1990
Frequency: Monthly

Cover Price: Free
Circulation: 65,928 (Publisher's Statement)
Usual Pagination: 84
Editor: Robina Dam; **Advertising Manager:** Stefan Bartsch
Summary of Content: In-flight magazine of bmi - British Midland. Includes features on business and leisure travel, lifestyle, wellbeing, sports, telecoms, technology, celebrity and sport.
Readership/Target Audience: Read by passengers between 25 to 50 years old.
ADVERTISING RATES:
Full Page Colour £7150.00
Agency Commission: 10%
Mechanical Data: Film: Digital
Copy instructions: Copy Date: 6th of month prior to publication month
Average advertising content per issue: 33%
CONSUMER: HOLIDAYS & TRAVEL: In-Flight Magazines

VV MAGAZINE
1896804U74Q-1381

Editorial Address: 48 Langham Street, LONDON, W1W 7AY
Tel: 027 768 425 766
Email: editor@vvmag.com
Advertising Address: As above.
Email: oksanal@vv-media.com
Web site: http://www.vvmag.com
Publisher: V V Media
Date Established: 2005
Frequency: Quarterly
Circulation: 15,000 (Publisher's Statement)
Editor: Matt Morley
Summary of Content: Guide to the world of luxury.
Language(s): English; Russian
Readership/Target Audience: Magazine uniting all Russian-speaking elite representatives in the world.
ADVERTISING RATES:
Full Page Colour £1750.00
CONSUMER: WOMEN'S INTEREST CONSUMER MAGAZINES: Lifestyle

W
45234U74B-700

Editorial Address: 20 Shorts Gardens, LONDON, WC2H 9AU **Tel:** 020 7240 0420 **Fax:** 020 7240 0290
Email: nina.jones@fairchildpub.com
Advertising Address: Conde Nast, 750 3rd Avenue, NEW YORK, 10017 **Tel:** 212 630 4000 **Fax:** 212 63 04 919
Email: david_anekstein@condenast.com
Web site: http://www.fairchildpub.com
Publisher: Fairchild Publications
Frequency: Monthly
Annual Sub.: $90.00
Circulation: 450,000 (Publisher's Statement)
Usual Pagination: 410
Editor: Samantha Conti; **Advertising Manager:** David Anekstein
Summary of Content: Magazine covering news on fashion and lifestyle trends.
Readership/Target Audience: Aimed at the contemporary woman interested in lifestyle.
ADVERTISING RATES:
Full Page Mono $59260.00
Full Page Colour $74560.00
Mechanical Data: Film: Digital
CONSUMER: WOMEN'S INTEREST CONSUMER MAGAZINES: Women's Interest - Fashion

---

W1 MAGAZINE
1703865U80B-420

Editorial Address: 26 York Street, LONDON, W1U 6PZ
Tel: 020 7788 7547
Email: enquiries@w1magazine.co.uk
Advertising Address: As above.
Email: enquiries@w1magazine.co.uk
Web site: http://www.w1magazine.co.uk
Publisher: LVC Ltd
Date Established: 2005
Frequency: Monthly
Cover Price: Free
Circulation: 30,000 (Publisher's Statement)
Usual Pagination: 40
Editor: Jaz Walia; **Features Editor:** Allegra Winton; **Publisher:** Jaz Walia
Summary of Content: Magazine covering movies, restaurants, theatre, fashion, gadgets, health, beauty, property, travel, shopping and events.
Readership/Target Audience: Aimed at affluent residents, businesses and visitors to London's West End.
ADVERTISING RATES:
Full Page Colour £1250.00
Mechanical Data: Trim Size: 270 x 210mm, Film: Digital
CONSUMER: RURAL & REGIONAL INTEREST: Regional Interest Greater London

---

WAG
47087U81A-155

Editorial Address: 17 Wakley Street, LONDON, EC1V 7RQ
Tel: 020 7837 0006 **Fax:** 020 7713 8151
Email: wag@dogstrust.org.uk
Web site: http://www.dogstrust.org.uk
Publisher: Dogs Trust
Date Established: 1997
Frequency: 3 issues yearly - Published in February, July and October
Cover Price: Free
Circulation: 640,000 (Publisher's Statement)
Usual Pagination: 20
Editor: Deana Selby
Summary of Content: Magazine of the Dogs Trust covering the activities of the charity and issues concerning dog welfare.
Readership/Target Audience: Aimed at all supporters of Dogs Trust, the UK's largest dog welfare charity.
ADVERTISING: No Advertising taken
CONSUMER: ANIMALS & PETS: Animals & Pets Protection

WAITROSE FOOD ILLUSTRATED
45623U74P-900

Editorial Address: 136-142 Bramley Road, LONDON, W10 6SR **Tel:** 020 7565 3000 **Fax:** 020 7565 3076
Email: food@johnbrownmedia.com
Advertising Address: As above. **Fax:** 020 7565 3358
Email: food@johnbrowngroup.co.uk
Web site: http://www.waitrose.com/wfi
ISSN: 1461-7838
Publisher: John Brown Group
Date Established: 1999
Frequency: Monthly
Cover Price: £2.50
Free to qualifying individuals
Circulation: 321,886 (ABC 01/01/2009 to 30/06/2009)
Usual Pagination: 106
Editor: Amber Dalton; **Features Editor:** Katy Salter; **Advertising Director:** Anna Lahiri; **Publisher:** Sarah Arthur
Summary of Content: Magazine covering all aspects of food. Includes articles on restaurants, chefs, farmers and producers.
Readership/Target Audience: Aimed at 30 to 50 year olds.
ADVERTISING RATES:
Full Page Mono £12500.00
Full Page Colour £12500.00
Agency Commission: 15%
Copy instructions: Copy Date: 6 weeks prior to publication date
Average advertising content per issue: 30%
CONSUMER: WOMEN'S INTEREST CONSUMER MAGAZINES: Food & Cookery

---

WALK
45930U75L-500

Formerly: The Rambler
Editorial Address: 2nd Floor, Camelford House, 87-90 Albert Embankment, LONDON, SE1 7TW
Tel: 020 7339 8540 **Fax:** 020 7339 8501
Email: dominic.bates@ramblers.org.uk
Advertising Address: Unit 29, The Pall Mall Deposit, 124-128 Barlby Road, LONDON, W10 6BL **Tel:** 020 8962 3020
Fax: 020 8962 8689
Email: adam@thinkpublishing.co.uk
Web site: http://www.walkmag.co.uk
ISSN: 1752-7293
Publisher: The Ramblers' Association
Date Established: 2003
Frequency: Quarterly
Cover Price: £3.50
Free to qualifying individuals
Circulation: 104,476 (ABC 01/01/2008 to 31/12/2008)
Usual Pagination: 100
Editor: Dominic Bates
Summary of Content: Magazine covering reports and features on walking and countryside issues including walking, hiking, outdoors, environment, health issues and travel.
Readership/Target Audience: Aimed at Ramblers' Association members, potential members, walkers, hikers and the outdoor industry.
ADVERTISING RATES:
Full Page Colour £4500.00
SCC £43.27
Agency Commission: 10%
Mechanical Data: Page Width: 190mm, Type Area: 262 x 190mm, Col Length: 262mm, Film: Digital
Copy instructions: Copy Date: 6 weeks prior to publication date
Average advertising content per issue: 40%
CONSUMER: SPORT: Outdoor

WALKING WALES
1743237U75L-812

Editorial Address: 3 Glantwymyn Village Workshop, Cemmaes Road, MACHYNLLETH, SY20 8LY
Tel: 01650 511314 **Fax:** 01650 511314
Email: perrographics@btconnect.com

Advertising Address: The Maltings, West Street, BOURNE, PE10 9PH **Tel:** 01778 391179 **Fax:** 01778 392422
Email: clairem@warnersgroup.co.uk
ISSN: 1460-1028
Publisher: Walking Wales Ltd
Frequency: Quarterly
Cover Price: £3.25
Circulation: 4,000 (Publisher's Statement)
Usual Pagination: 72
Editor: Chris Barber
Summary of Content: Magazine covering walking in Wales with equipment reviews, general interest articles, walks, local history, folk law, countryside issues, personality profiles and book reviews.
Readership/Target Audience: Aimed at those with an interest in Wales.
ADVERTISING RATES:
Full Page Mono £250.00
Full Page Colour £250.00
Mechanical Data: Bleed Size: 210 x 148.50mm, Film: Digital
Average advertising content per issue: 15%
CONSUMER: SPORT: Outdoor

WALLPAPER*
45293U74C-554

Editorial Address: Blue Fin Building, 7th Floor, 110 Southwark Street, LONDON, SE1 0SU **Tel:** 020 3148 5000
Fax: 020 3148 8119
Email: contact@wallpaper.com
Advertising Address: As above. **Tel:** 020 3148 7720
Email: advertising@wallpaper.com
Web site: http://www.wallpaper.com
ISSN: 1364-4475
Publisher: IPC Media Ltd
Date Established: 1997
Frequency: 11 issues yearly
Cover Price: £4.00
Circulation: 108,050 (ABC 01/01/2008 to 31/12/2008)
Usual Pagination: 180
Editor: Apphia Michael; **Editor-in-Chief:** Tony Chambers; **Managing Editor:** Jessica Diamond; **Advertising Director:** Paula Cain; **Publisher:** Ben Giles
Summary of Content: International lifestyle magazine covering interiors, architecture, industrial design, entertaining and travel.
Twitter: http://twitter.com/wallpapermag.
Readership/Target Audience: Read by adults aged between 25 and 35 years old with high disposable incomes.
ADVERTISING RATES:
Full Page Colour £11200.00
Agency Commission: 15%
Mechanical Data: Type Area: 276 x 204mm, Col Length: 276mm, Trim Size: 300 x 220mm, Bleed Size: 306 x 226mm, Film: Digital, Print Process: Offset, Page Width: 204mm
Copy instructions: Copy Date: 5 weeks prior to publication date
Average advertising content per issue: 40%
CONSUMER: WOMEN'S INTEREST CONSUMER MAGAZINES: Home & Family

WANDERLUST
48269U89E-175

Editorial Address: 1 Leworth Place, Mellor Walk, Bachelors Acre, WINDSOR, SL4 1EB **Tel:** 01753 620426
Fax: 01753 620474
Email: info@wanderlust.co.uk
Advertising Address: As above. **Fax:** 01753 753479
Email: sales@wanderlust.co.uk
Web site: http://www.wanderlust.co.uk
ISSN: 1351-4733
Publisher: Wanderlust Publications
Date Established: 1993
Frequency: 8 issues yearly - Published 4 weeks prior to cover date
Cover Price: £3.80
Circulation: 37,500 (Publisher's Statement)
Usual Pagination: 154
Editor: Dan Linstead; **Editor-in-Chief:** Lyn Hughes; **Advertising Manager:** Graham Keutenius
Summary of Content: Magazine covering worldwide destinations and travel related topics, including health and eco-tourism.
Readership/Target Audience: Aimed at affluent and avid travel consumers seeking soft-adventure or cultural experiences other than the conventional package holiday.
ADVERTISING RATES:
Full Page Colour £2900.00
Agency Commission: 10%
Mechanical Data: Type Area: 272 x 189mm, Bleed Size: 307 x 230mm, Trim Size: 297 x 220mm, Film: Digital, Col Length: 272mm, Page Width: 189mm
Copy instructions: Copy Date: 4 weeks prior to publication date
Average advertising content per issue: 30%
CONSUMER: HOLIDAYS & TRAVEL: Holidays

THE WAR CRY
47764U87-223

Editorial Address: 101 Newington Causeway, LONDON, SE1 6BN **Tel:** 020 7367 4900 **Fax:** 020 7367 4710

Consumer Magazines

Email: warcry@salvationarmy.org.uk
Web site: http://www.salvationarmy.org.uk/warcry
Publisher: The Salvation Army
Date Established: 1879
Frequency: Weekly
Cover Price: £0.20
Circulation: 55,000 (Publisher's Statement)
Usual Pagination: 8
Editor: Nigel Bovey; **Publisher:** Shaw Clifton
Summary of Content: Newspaper of the Salvation Army providing Christian comment on topical issues.
Readership/Target Audience: Aimed at the general public.
ADVERTISING: No Advertising taken
CONSUMER: RELIGIOUS

WAR IN HISTORY
30837U94X-194_50

Editorial Address: 1 Oliver's Yard, 55 City Road, LONDON, EC1Y 1SP **Tel:** 020 7324 8500 **Fax:** 020 7324 8600
Email: market@sagepub.com
Advertising Address: As above.
Email: sheena.karim@sagepub.co.uk
Web site: http://www.sagepub.co.uk
ISSN: 0968-3445
Publisher: Sage Publications
Date Established: 1944
Frequency: Quarterly
Annual Sub.: £265.00
Usual Pagination: 128
Editor: Hew Strachan
Summary of Content: Journal focusing on all aspects of war, considering the economic, social and political issues in addition to military.
Readership/Target Audience: Aimed at historians.
ADVERTISING RATES:
Full Page Mono £400.00
Agency Commission: 10%
Mechanical Data: Bleed Size: +4mm, Screen:, Print Process: Sheet-fed litho, Page Width: 130mm, Trim Size: 234 x 156mm, Type Area: 205 x 130mm, Film: Digital, Col Length: 205mm
Copy instructions: Copy Date: 12 weeks prior to publication date
Average advertising content per issue: 2%
CONSUMER: OTHER CLASSIFICATIONS: Miscellaneous

WARSHIP WORLD
46790U79H-160

Editorial Address: Lodge Hill, LISKEARD, PL14 4EL
Tel: 01579 343663 **Fax:** 01579 346747
Email: warshipworld@navybooks.com
Advertising Address: As above.
Email: sales@navybooks.com
Web site: http://www.navybooks.com
ISSN: 1464-0511
Publisher: Maritime Books
Date Established: 1985
Frequency: 6 issues yearly
Cover Price: £2.75
Annual Sub.: £19.50
Circulation: 4,500 (Publisher's Statement)
Usual Pagination: 32
Editor: Steven Bush; **Managing Director:** Mike Critchley; **Advertising Manager:** Steven Bush; **Publisher:** Mike Critchley
Summary of Content: Magazine covering all aspects of the old and new Royal Navy, including ship preservation, disposals, news on the RFA and RMAS and an overseas section.
Readership/Target Audience: Aimed at ex-members of the Royal Navy and those with an interest in naval matters.
ADVERTISING: Rates on application
Agency Commission: 10%
Copy instructions: Copy Date: 4 weeks prior to publication date
Average advertising content per issue: 20%
CONSUMER: HOBBIES & DIY: Military History

WARWICKSHIRE LIFE
1657762U80C-5373

Editorial Address: PO Box 219, Cleeve Prior, EVESHAM, WR11 8WJ **Tel:** 01789 778568
Email: jane.sullivan@archant.co.uk
Advertising Address: PO Box 14581, BROMSGROVE, B60 9ET **Tel:** 01527 831733 **Fax:** 01527 979646
Email: marisha.arthur@archant.co.uk
Web site: http://www.warwickshirelife.co.uk
ISSN: 1478-1751
Publisher: Archant Life
Frequency: Monthly
Cover Price: £2.50
Circulation: 12,000 (Publisher's Statement)
Editor: Jane Sullivan
Summary of Content: Lifestyle magazine covering fashion, beauty, restaurants, interiors, travel, art, motoring and property.
Readership/Target Audience: Aimed at affluent householders in Warwickshire.

ADVERTISING RATES:
Full Page Colour £1200.00
Agency Commission: 10%
Mechanical Data: Type Area: 271 x 199mm, Bleed Size: 306 x 226mm, Trim Size: 300 x 220mm, Col Length: 271mm, Page Width: 199mm, Film: Digital
Copy instructions: Copy Date: 1 month prior to publication date
Average advertising content per issue: 40%
CONSUMER: RURAL & REGIONAL INTEREST: Regional Interest English Counties

WARWICKSHIRE LIVING
1791016U80C-5380

Editorial Address: Unit 28B Harris Business Park, Hanbury Road, Stoke Prior, BROMSGROVE, B60 4DJ
Tel: 01527 871747 **Fax:** 01527 882501
Email: jackycook@gmx.com
Advertising Address: As above.
Email: allan@warwickshireliving.co.uk
Web site: http://www.warwickshireliving.co.uk
Publisher: Bee3 Ltd
Date Established: 2006
Frequency: Monthly
Cover Price: Free
Circulation: 16,000 (Publisher's Statement)
Usual Pagination: 100
Editor: Jacky Cook
Summary of Content: Lifestyle magazine covering fashion, health and beauty, property, homes and gardens, motoring, food and drink, local news and events.
Readership/Target Audience: Aimed at residents and visitors to Warwickshire with high disposable incomes.
ADVERTISING RATES:
Full Page Colour £950.00
Agency Commission: 10%
Mechanical Data: Bleed Size: 306 x 236mm, Trim Size: 300 x 230mm, Film: Digital
Copy instructions: Copy Date: 5th of the month prior to publication date
Average advertising content per issue: 30%
CONSUMER: RURAL & REGIONAL INTEREST: Regional Interest English Counties

WASAFIRI
626098U84A-420

Editorial Address: Open University in London, 1-11 Hawley Street, Camden Town, LONDON, NW2 8NP
Tel: 020 7556 6110 **Fax:** 020 7556 6187
Email: wasafiri@open.ac.uk
Web site: http://www.wasafiri.org
Publisher: Routledge, Taylor & Francis
Frequency: Quarterly
Cover Price: £7.00
Annual Sub.: £21.00
Circulation: 6,000 (Publisher's Statement)
Usual Pagination: 80
Editor: Teresa Palmiero
Summary of Content: Journal of international literature containing contemporary African-Asian, Asian, Black-British and Caribbean fiction, poetry, articles, reviews, art, film, theatre and literature.
Readership/Target Audience: Read by academics, scholars, teachers, students and lecturers and all those interested in literature.
ADVERTISING: No Advertising taken
CONSUMER: THE ARTS & LITERARY: Arts

WATERFRONT
1828228U74Q-1359

Editorial Address: 4 Stable Court, Water Lane, Tarbock Green, PRESCOT, L35 1RD **Tel:** 0151 487 6900
Fax: 0151 487 5300
Email: editorial@waterfrontmagazines.co.uk
Advertising Address: Bury Business Park, Kay Street, BURY, BL9 6BU **Tel:** 0151 487 6900 **Fax:** 0151 487 5300
Email: sales@waterfrontmagazines.co.uk
Web site: http://www.waterfrontmagazines.co.uk
Publisher: Waterfront Magazines Ltd
Date Established: 2008
Frequency: Monthly
Free to qualifying individuals
Annual Sub.: £36.00
Circulation: 22,000 (Print Run)
Usual Pagination: 68
Editor: Jane Harris; **Managing Director:** Phil Harris; **Advertising Manager:** Phil Harris
Summary of Content: Luxury lifestyle magazine covering fashion, motors, travel, homes, events and happenings.
Readership/Target Audience: Aimed at the discerning wealthy and distributed to homes valued in excess of £750,000 in Lancashire, Merseyside, Wirral and North Cheshire and South Manchester homes valued above £1,000,000.
ADVERTISING RATES:
Full Page Colour £1950.00
Mechanical Data: Trim Size: 300 x 230mm, Bleed Size: 310 x 240mm, Film: Digital
CONSUMER: WOMEN'S INTEREST CONSUMER MAGAZINES: Lifestyle

WATERLIFE
47088U81A-170

Formerly: Wildfowl & Wetlands
Editorial Address: Slimbridge, GLOUCESTER, GL2 7BT
Tel: 0870 334 4000 **Fax:** 01453 890827
Email: waterlife@wwt.org.uk
Advertising Address: The Pall Mall Deposit, 124-128 Barlby Road, LONDON, W10 6BL **Tel:** 020 8962 3020
Fax: 020 8962 8689
Email: victor@thinkpublishing.co.uk
Web site: http://www.wwt.org.uk
ISSN: 0960-4421
Publisher: Think Publishing Ltd
Date Established: 1950
Frequency: Quarterly
Cover Price: £3.75
Free to qualifying individuals
Circulation: 79,931 (ABC 01/01/2008 to 31/12/2008)
Usual Pagination: 44
Editor: Malcom Tate
Summary of Content: Magazine of the Wildfowl & Wetlands Trust with news of conservation work, research and educational activities relating to ducks, geese, swans and other water-birds and freshwater wetlands.
Readership/Target Audience: Read by members of WWT, visitors to WWT's nine wetlands centres around the UK, and those with an interest in wildfowl, wetlands or conservation.
ADVERTISING RATES:
Full Page Colour £4500.00
Agency Commission: 10%
Mechanical Data: Film: Digital, Type Area: 250 x 180mm, Print Process: Offset litho, Bleed Size: 266x 196mm, Col Length: 250mm, Page Width: 180mm, Trim Size: 260 x 190mm
Average advertising content per issue: 20%
CONSUMER: ANIMALS & PETS: Animals & Pets Protection

WATERSTONE'S BOOKS QUARTERLY
712857U84B-325

Editorial Address: Sea Containers House, 20 Upper Ground, LONDON, SE1 9PD **Tel:** 020 7775 5777
Fax: 020 7775 5711
Email: ed.wood@sevensquared.co.uk
Advertising Address: As above.
Email: brett.walker@sevensquared.co.uk
Web site: http://www.subscribeonline.com/wbq
ISSN: 1474-4260
Publisher: Seven Squared
Date Established: 2001
Frequency: Quarterly
Cover Price: £2.50
Free to qualifying individuals
Circulation: 155,000 (Publisher's Statement)
Usual Pagination: 100
Editor: Keeley Young; **Advertising Manager:** Brett Walker; **Publisher:** Keeley Young
Summary of Content: Magazine about books, includes new titles, reviews, news, jacket design and recommendations.
Readership/Target Audience: Aimed at medium to heavy book buyers and book enthusiasts.
ADVERTISING RATES:
Full Page Colour £4450.00
Agency Commission: 10%
Mechanical Data: Type Area: 280 x 200mm, Col Length: 280mm, Trim Size: 300 x 220mm, Bleed Size: 306 x 226mm, Page Width: 200mm, Print Process: Web-fed offset litho
Average advertising content per issue: 30%
CONSUMER: THE ARTS & LITERARY: Literary

WATERWAYS
48395U91A-190

Editorial Address: 151 Station Street, BURTON-ON-TRENT, DE14 1BG **Tel:** 01283 742950
Email: k.goss@wwonline.co.uk
Advertising Address: As above.
Email: tony.preston@wwonline.co.uk
Web site: http://www.waterways.org.uk
ISSN: 0969-0654
Publisher: Inland Waterways Association
Date Established: 1946
Frequency: Quarterly
Free to qualifying individuals
Annual Sub.: £25.00
Circulation: 20,000 (Publisher's Statement)
Usual Pagination: 40
Editor: Keith Goss; **Advertising Manager:** Tony Preston
Summary of Content: Reports on the conservation, restoration and development of Britain's inland waterway system for commercial and recreational use.
Readership/Target Audience: Aimed at anyone who uses or is interested in the waterways of Britain including boaters, walkers, anglers and industrial archaeologists.
ADVERTISING RATES:
Full Page Colour £695.00
Mechanical Data: Film: Digital, Trim Size: 297 x 210mm
Copy instructions: Copy Date: 4 weeks prior to publication date
CONSUMER: RECREATION & LEISURE: Boating & Yachting

WATERWAYS WORLD
48396U91A-210

Editorial Address: 151 Station Street, BURTON-ON-TRENT, DE14 1BG **Tel:** 01283 742950 **Fax:** 01283 742957
Email: editorial@waterwaysworld.com
Advertising Address: As above. **Tel:** 01283 742966
Email: ian.sharpe@wwonline.co.uk
Web site: http://www.waterwaysworld.com
ISSN: 0309-1422
Publisher: WW Magazines
Date Established: 1972
Frequency: Monthly
Cover Price: £3.50
Circulation: 15,246 (ABC 01/01/2008 to 31/12/2008)
Usual Pagination: 176
Editor: Richard Fairhurst; **Features Editor:** Keith Goss;
Managing Director: Peter Johns; **Publisher:** Peter Johns
Summary of Content: Magazine covering inland waterways at home and abroad. Includes cruising, boats and boating and history.
Readership/Target Audience: Read by people owning or interested in narrowboats and river cruisers.
ADVERTISING RATES:
Full Page Colour £709.00
Agency Commission: 10%
Mechanical Data: Type Area: 262 x 183mm, Col Length: 262mm, Bleed Size: 303 x 216mm, Trim Size: 297 x 210mm, Page Width: 183mm, Film: Digital
Copy instructions: Copy Date: 4 weeks prior to publication date
Average advertising content per issue: 40%
CONSUMER: RECREATION & LEISURE: Boating & Yachting

WAVE
600890U74Q-1170

Editorial Address: Unit 1, Level 5 North, New England House, New England Street, BRIGHTON, BN1 4GH
Tel: 01273 818150 **Fax:** 01273 818152
Email: wave@thelatest.co.uk
Advertising Address: As above.
Email: jason@thelatest.co.uk
Web site: http://www.wavemagazine.co.uk
Publisher: Latest Homes Ltd
Date Established: 1998
Frequency: Monthly
Free to qualifying individuals
Annual Sub.: £18.00
Circulation: 50,000 (Publisher's Statement)
Usual Pagination: 48
Editor: Pearl Bates; **Publisher:** Bill Smith
Summary of Content: Alternative lifestyle magazine covering personal development, holistic and complementary medicine, holistic holidays, organic gardening, books, music, arts and events. Also includes food and drink, ethical finance and natural health and beauty.
Readership/Target Audience: Read predominantly by 25 to 50 year old women.
ADVERTISING: Rates on application
Agency Commission: 10%
Copy instructions: Copy Date: 4 weeks prior to publication date
Average advertising content per issue: 33%
CONSUMER: WOMEN'S INTEREST CONSUMER MAGAZINES: Lifestyle

WAVELENGTH
45961U75M-960

Editorial Address: Harmsworth House, City Wharf, Malpas Road, TRURO, TR1 1QH **Tel:** 01872 247456
Email: tim@wavelengthmag.co.uk
Advertising Address: As above. **Tel:** 01872 247546
Fax: 01872 247434
Email: andrew@wavelengthmag.co.uk
Web site: http://www.wavelengthmag.co.uk
Publisher: Cornwall & Devon Media Limited
Date Established: 1981
Frequency: 9 issues yearly - Joint issues in October and November, December and January and February and March
Cover Price: £3.20
Circulation: 16,000 (Publisher's Statement)
Usual Pagination: 116
Editor: Tim Nunn; **Advertising Manager:** Andrew Dunstan
Summary of Content: Surfing magazine covering all aspects of the British and international surf scene.
Readership/Target Audience: Read by surfing enthusiasts of all ages.
ADVERTISING RATES:
Full Page Colour £960.00
Agency Commission: 10%
Mechanical Data: Trim Size: 297 x 210mm, Film: Digital
Copy instructions: Copy Date: 4 weeks prior to publication date
Average advertising content per issue: 40%
CONSUMER: SPORT: Water Sports

WAVENEY PROFILE
46947U80C-2350

Editorial Address: 101 Thunder Lane, NORWICH, NR7 0JG
Tel: 01603 433972
Email: profilepublishing@hotmail.co.uk

Advertising Address: As above.
Email: profilepublishing@hotmail.co.uk
Publisher: Profile Publishing & Design
Frequency: Quarterly
Cover Price: Free
Circulation: 5,000 (Publisher's Statement)
Usual Pagination: 24
Editor: Steven Ford; **Advertising Manager:** Nick James
Summary of Content: Magazine containing news on towns and villages in the North Suffolk and South Norfolk area.
Readership/Target Audience: Read by locals in the Suffolk and Norfolk areas.
ADVERTISING RATES:
Full Page Mono £395.00
Full Page Colour £500.00
SCC £2.50
Agency Commission: 10%
Mechanical Data: Type Area: 270 x 209mm, Col Length: 270mm, Page Width: 209mm, No. of Columns (Display): 4, Print Process: Offset litho
Average advertising content per issue: 45%
CONSUMER: RURAL & REGIONAL INTEREST: Regional Interest English Counties

WAY TO GO
1739470U88R-62

Editorial Address: 24 Lancaster Street, Summerhill, NEWCASTLE UPON TYNE, NE4 6EU **Tel:** 0191 478 8300
Fax: 0191 298 3561
Email: john.graham@distinctivepublishing.co.uk
Advertising Address: As above. **Tel:** 0191 298 3571
Email: ewan.waterhouse@distinctivepublishing.co.uk
Publisher: Distinctive Publishing
Date Established: 2005
Frequency: 6 issues yearly
Cover Price: Free
Circulation: 24,000 (Publisher's Statement)
Usual Pagination: 72
Editor: John Graham
Summary of Content: Magazine covering training, education and enterprise with tips and advice on how young people can better their situations.
Readership/Target Audience: Aimed at 15 to 19 year olds and distributed through schools, colleges and other education establishments in the north east of England.
ADVERTISING: Rates on application
CONSUMER: EDUCATION: Education Related

WAYBULOO
1896753U91D-983

Editorial Address: Media Centre, 201 Wood Lane, LONDON, W12 7TQ **Tel:** 020 8433 1027 **Fax:** 020 8433 3867
Email: waybuloomagazine@bbc.com
Web site: http://www.bbc.co.uk/cbeebies
Publisher: BBC Children's Magazines
Date Established: 2009
Frequency: 26 issues yearly
Cover Price: £2.35
Editor: Stephanie Cooper; **Publisher:** Pauline Cooke
Summary of Content: Magazine focusing on the development of children's social and emotional learning. Based around the TV programme Waybuloo.
Readership/Target Audience: Aimed at 3-5 year olds.
CONSUMER: RECREATION & LEISURE: Children & Youth

WE LOVE BEDFORDSHIRE
629397U80C-195

Formerly: Beds
Editorial Address: County Hall, Cauldwell Street, BEDFORD, MK42 9AP **Tel:** 01234 228675
Email: jane.sneesby@bedscc.gov.uk
Web site: http://www.bedscc.gov.uk
Publisher: Bedfordshire County Council
Date Established: 2000
Frequency: 6 issues yearly
Cover Price: Free
Circulation: 166,000 (Publisher's Statement)
Usual Pagination: 16
Editor: Jane Sneesby
Summary of Content: Magazine covering county issues, lifestyle and business news for Bedfordshire.
Readership/Target Audience: Aimed at residents of Bedfordshire.
ADVERTISING: No Advertising taken
CONSUMER: RURAL & REGIONAL INTEREST: Regional Interest English Counties

WE LOVE TELLY!
1626331U76C-823

Editorial Address: 1 Canada Square, Canary Wharf, LONDON, E14 5AP **Tel:** 020 7293 3000 **Fax:** 020 7293 2655
Email: welovetelly@mirror.co.uk
Advertising Address: As above. **Tel:** 020 7293 3329
Fax: 020 7293 3285
Web site: http://www.trinity-mirror.co.uk
Publisher: Trinity Mirror
Date Established: 2003
Frequency: Weekly - See main record for circulation figure

Cover Price: Free
Usual Pagination: 54
Editor: Cecile Metcalf; **Features Editor:** Jennifer Rodger;
Advertising Manager: Claire Greenslade
Summary of Content: Magazine covering TV listings, previews and celebrity interviews.
Readership/Target Audience: Aimed at readers of the Daily Mirror.
ADVERTISING RATES:
Full Page Colour £31250.00
Agency Commission: 15%
Mechanical Data: Trim Size: 297 x 210mm, Film: Digital
Copy instructions: Copy Date: 2 weeks prior to publication date
Average advertising content per issue: 22%
Supplement to: Daily Mirror
CONSUMER: MUSIC & PERFORMING ARTS: TV & Radio

THE WEALDEN ADVERTISER
1814060U94X-294

Editorial Address: Cowden Close, Horns Road, Hawkhurst, CRANBROOK, TN18 4QT **Tel:** 01580 753322
Fax: 01580 754104
Email: graham.thorn@wealdenad.co.uk
Advertising Address: As above.
Email: advertise@wealdenad.co.uk
Web site: http://www.wealdenad.co.uk
Publisher: The Wealden Advertiser
Frequency: Weekly
Cover Price: Free
Circulation: 37,500 (Publisher's Statement)
Usual Pagination: 56
Editor: Graham Thorn
Summary of Content: Magazine with adverts for vehicles, property and situations vacant to plumbers, builders and domestic appliances.
Readership/Target Audience: Aimed at the general public.
ADVERTISING RATES:
Full Page Mono £515.00
Full Page Colour £700.00
SCC £6.45
Mechanical Data: Type Area: 302 x 207mm, Col Length: 302mm, Page Width: 207mm, Film: Digital
Copy instructions: Copy Date: Mono Monday 5pm prior to publication date Colour Friday 12 noon prior to publication date
CONSUMER: OTHER CLASSIFICATIONS: Miscellaneous

WEALDEN TIMES
1646444U80C-5127

Editorial Address: 21 Stone Street, CRANBROOK, TN17 3HF **Tel:** 01580 714705 **Fax:** 01580 715983
Email: info@wealdentimes.co.uk
Advertising Address: As above.
Email: hayley.biddulph@wealdentimes.co.uk
Web site: http://www.wealdentimes.co.uk
Publisher: JPS Media Limited
Date Established: 2001
Frequency: Monthly
Free to qualifying individuals
Annual Sub.: £12.00
Circulation: 33,000 (Publisher's Statement)
Usual Pagination: 132
Editor: Julie Simpson
Summary of Content: Magazine covering homes, gardens, education, health and beauty, locally grown food and drink and a monthly French feature.
Readership/Target Audience: Aimed at residents and visitors to Kent and East Sussex Weald.
ADVERTISING RATES:
Full Page Colour £915.00
Agency Commission: 10%
Mechanical Data: Bleed Size: +3mm, Type Area: 265 x 185mm, Trim Size: 297 x 210mm, Col Length: 265mm, Page Width: 185mm, Film: Digital
Copy instructions: Copy Date: 1 week prior to publication date
Average advertising content per issue: 60%
CONSUMER: RURAL & REGIONAL INTEREST: Regional Interest English Counties

THE WEALTH COLLECTION
1691978U74Q-1298

Editorial Address: Brunel House, 55-57 North Wharf Road, LONDON, W2 1LA **Tel:** 020 7915 9600 **Fax:** 020 7915 9757
Email: christopherkanal@spgmedia.com
Advertising Address: As above. **Fax:** 020 7915 9773
Email: nathanpark@spgmedia.com
Web site: http://www.wealthcollection.com
Publisher: SPG Media Ltd
Date Established: 2004
Frequency: Half-yearly - Published in March and September
Cover Price: Free
Circulation: 10,000 (ABC 01/01/2008 to 31/12/2008)
Usual Pagination: 60
Editor: Christopher Kanal; **Publisher:** William Crocker
Summary of Content: Lifestyle magazine encompassing all aspects of luxurious living from charitable giving, property

and finance to interior design, travel, food and wine, the arts, fashion, motoring and technology.
Readership/Target Audience: Aimed at individuals representing the most affluent sectors of society.
ADVERTISING RATES:
Full Page Colour £6900.00
Copy instructions: Copy Date: 6 weeks prior to publication date
Average advertising content per issue: 33%
CONSUMER: WOMEN'S INTEREST CONSUMER MAGAZINES: Lifestyle

WEB DESIGNER
36255U78E-31

Formerly: Practical Internet Web Designer
Editorial Address: Richmond House, 33 Richmond Hill, BOURNEMOUTH, BH2 6EZ **Tel:** 01202 586200
Email: webdesigner@imagine-publishing.co.uk
Advertising Address: As above. **Fax:** 01202 789966
Email: hannah.bradshaw@imagine-publishing.co.uk
Web site: http://www.webdesignermag.co.uk
ISSN: 1366-7661
Publisher: Imagine Publishing
Date Established: 1996
Frequency: 13 issues yearly
Cover Price: £5.99
Annual Sub.: £62.30
Circulation: 13,265 (Publisher's Statement)
Usual Pagination: 148
Editor: Mark Billen; **Features Editor:** Steven Jenkins; **Group Editor:** David Harfield
Summary of Content: Magazine providing advice and practical information on all aspects of Internet web design.
Readership/Target Audience: Aimed at advanced web designers.
ADVERTISING RATES:
Full Page Colour £2000.00
Agency Commission: 10%
Mechanical Data: Trim Size: 297 x 230mm, Bleed Size: 307 x 240mm, Type Area: 277 x 210mm, Col Length: 277mm, Page Width: 210mm, Film: Digital
Copy instructions: Copy Date: 4 weeks prior to publication date
CONSUMER: CONSUMER ELECTRONICS: Home Computing

WEB USER
704675U78R-460

Editorial Address: Blue Fin Building, 110 Southwark Street, LONDON, SE1 0SU **Tel:** 020 3148 5000 **Fax:** 020 3148 8122
Email: webuser@ipcmedia.com
Advertising Address: As above. **Fax:** 020 3148 4130
Email: nicola_ponting@ipcmedia.com
Web site: http://www.web-user.co.uk
ISSN: 1473-7094
Publisher: IPC Media Ltd
Date Established: 2001
Frequency: 26 issues yearly
Cover Price: £2.00
Circulation: 33,589 (ABC 01/01/2008 to 31/12/2008)
Usual Pagination: 76
Editor: Ben Camm-Jones; **News Editor:** Ben Camm-Jones; **Features Editor:** Robert Irvine; **Advertising Manager:** Nicola Ponting; **Publisher:** Alex Robb
Summary of Content: Magazine offering advice and tips on how to make the most of your time on the Internet. Covers features, news and product/software reviews.
Readership/Target Audience: Aimed at web users of all ages and levels of ability.
ADVERTISING RATES:
Full Page Colour £3565.00
Agency Commission: 10%
Mechanical Data: Film: Digital, Type Area: 272 x 186mm, Col Length: 272mm, Page Width: 186mm, Bleed Size: 303 x 216mm, Trim Size: 297 x 210mm
Copy instructions: Copy Date: 10 days prior to publication date
Average advertising content per issue: 25%
CONSUMER: CONSUMER ELECTRONICS: Consumer Electronics Related

WEDDING
45535U74L-190_50

Formerly: Wedding and Home
Editorial Address: Blue Fin Building, 110 Southwark Street, LONDON, SE1 0SU **Tel:** 020 3148 7800
Email: weddingweb@ipcmedia.com
Advertising Address: As above. **Tel:** 020 3148 5000
Email: nicola_moore@ipcmedia.com
Web site: http://www.wedding-magazine.co.uk
Publisher: IPC Southbank
Frequency: 6 issues yearly
Cover Price: £4.70
Circulation: 39,277 (ABC 01/01/2008 to 31/12/2008)
Usual Pagination: 250
Editor: Catherine Westwood; **Advertising Manager:** Nicola Moore
Summary of Content: Magazine providing inspirational ideas for modern brides.

Readership/Target Audience: Aimed at brides-to-be, bridegrooms and their families.
ADVERTISING RATES:
Full Page Colour £5050.00
Mechanical Data: Type Area: 260 x 186mm, Bleed Size: 295 x 221mm, Trim Size: 289 x 215mm, Film: Digital, Col Length: 260mm, Page Width: 186mm
CONSUMER: WOMEN'S INTEREST CONSUMER MAGAZINES: Brides

WEDDING CAKES - A DESIGN SOURCE
45536U74L-191

Formerly: Wedding Cakes
Editorial Address: Alfred House, Hones Business Park, FARNHAM, GU9 8BB **Tel:** 0845 225 5671
Fax: 0845 225 5673
Email: editorial@squires-group.co.uk
Advertising Address: As above.
Email: advertising@squires-group.co.uk
Web site: http://www.squires-group.co.uk
ISSN: 1465-1998
Publisher: Squires Kitchen Magazine Publishing
Date Established: 1999
Frequency: Quarterly
Cover Price: £4.99
Circulation: 40,000 (Publisher's Statement)
Usual Pagination: 128
Editor: Natalie Chivers; **Advertising Manager:** Natalie Chivers
Summary of Content: Magazine covering all aspects of wedding cakes including design, recipes and ideas.
Readership/Target Audience: Aimed at brides, professional and amateur cake makers and designers.
ADVERTISING RATES:
Full Page Mono £900.00
Full Page Colour £1600.00
Agency Commission: 10%
Mechanical Data: Trim Size: 297 x 210mm, Page Width: 190mm, Film: Digital, Type Area: 260 x 190mm, Col Length: 260mm
Copy instructions: Copy Date: 2 months prior to publication date
Average advertising content per issue: 5%
CONSUMER: WOMEN'S INTEREST CONSUMER MAGAZINES: Brides

WEDDING DAY
1682051U74L-230

Editorial Address: Messenger House, New Hythe Lane, Larkfield, AYLESFORD, ME20 6SG **Tel:** 01622 794672
Fax: 01622 715225
Email: deales@thekmgroup.co.uk
Advertising Address: 6-7 Middle Row, MAIDSTONE, ME14 1TG **Tel:** 01622 695777 **Fax:** 01622 664988
Email: maidstoneads@thekmgroup.co.uk
Publisher: Kent Messenger Group
Date Established: 1999
Frequency: Annual - Published in January
Cover Price: Free
Circulation: 30,000 (Publisher's Statement)
Usual Pagination: 60
Editor: Debbie Eales; **Advertising Manager:** Joy Adams
Summary of Content: Magazine covering all aspects of getting married in Kent, including bridal gowns, accessories, mother of the bride fashion, lingerie, flowers, stationery, jewellery, make-up, hair, receptions, venues, gift lists, trousseaus, photography, videos, honeymoons and travel as well as human interest stories.
Readership/Target Audience: Aimed at brides and all those involved in organising weddings.
ADVERTISING: Rates on application
CONSUMER: WOMEN'S INTEREST CONSUMER MAGAZINES: Brides

WEDDING DRESSES - A DESIGN SOURCE
766924U74L-213

Editorial Address: Alfred House, Hones Business Park, FARNHAM, GU9 8BB **Tel:** 0845 225 5671
Fax: 0845 225 5673
Email: publishing@squires-group.co.uk
Advertising Address: As above.
Email: advertising@squires-group.co.uk
Web site: http://www.squires-group.co.uk
Publisher: Squires Kitchen Magazine Publishing
Date Established: 2003
Frequency: Annual
Cover Price: £4.99
Circulation: 22,000 (Publisher's Statement)
Usual Pagination: 128
Editor: Natalie Chivers; **Advertising Manager:** Natalie Chivers
Summary of Content: Magazine focusing on wedding dresses. An inspirational visual resource for brides-to-be. Features collections from many bridal wear designers from ready to wear labels to haute couture names.
Readership/Target Audience: Aimed at brides to be and the wedding party.

ADVERTISING: Rates on application
CONSUMER: WOMEN'S INTEREST CONSUMER MAGAZINES: Brides

WEDDING FLOWERS MAGAZINE
1697080U74L-243

Editorial Address: Blue Fin Building, 110 Southwark Street, LONDON, SE1 0SU **Tel:** 020 3148 5000
Email: weddingflowers@ipcmedia.com
Advertising Address: As above.
Email: nicola_moore@ipcmedia.com
Web site: http://www.ipcmedia.com
Publisher: IPC Southbank
Frequency: 6 issues yearly
Cover Price: £4.60
Usual Pagination: 132
Editor: Catherine Westwood; **Advertising Manager:** Nicola Moore
Summary of Content: Magazine covering all aspects of planning wedding flowers including the bride's bouquet, reception flowers and fashion.
Readership/Target Audience: Aimed at brides-to-be.
ADVERTISING RATES:
Full Page Colour £5050.00
Agency Commission: 10%
Mechanical Data: Type Area: 260 x 191mm, Bleed Size: 295 x 216mm, Trim Size: 289 x 210mm, Col Length: 260mm, Page Width: 191mm, Film: Digital
Copy instructions: Copy Date: 4 weeks prior to publication date
Average advertising content per issue: 20%
CONSUMER: WOMEN'S INTEREST CONSUMER MAGAZINES: Brides

WEDDING IDEAS
1637635U74L-219

Editorial Address: 8 Hammet Street, TAUNTON, TA1 1RZ **Tel:** 01823 288344 **Fax:** 01823 288239
Email: rachelm@weddingideasmagazine.co.uk
Advertising Address: As above.
Email: pippaward@gjraffe-media.co.uk
Web site: http://www.weddingideasmagazine.co.uk
Publisher: Giraffe Media Ltd
Date Established: 2004
Frequency: 13 issues yearly
Circulation: 28,107 (ABC 01/01/2008 to 31/12/2008)
Usual Pagination: 200
Editor: Rachel Moschke; **Publisher:** Rachel Southwood
Summary of Content: Magazine covering all aspects of getting married including dresses, caterers, venues, honeymoons, flowers, hair and beauty.
Readership/Target Audience: Aimed at 25 to 35 year old first time brides who are planning their weddings.
ADVERTISING RATES:
Full Page Colour £2000.00
Mechanical Data: Trim Size: 210 x 148mm
Average advertising content per issue: 10%
CONSUMER: WOMEN'S INTEREST CONSUMER MAGAZINES: Brides

WEDDING VENUES & SERVICES MAGAZINE
623708U74L-209

Editorial Address: 215 London Road, HEMEL HEMPSTEAD, HP3 9SE **Tel:** 01442 260178
Fax: 01442 266940
Email: info@weddingvenues.co.uk
Advertising Address: As above.
Email: info@weddingvenues.co.uk
Web site: http://www.weddingvenues.co.uk
ISSN: 1473-1002
Publisher: Wedding Venues Ltd
Date Established: 1998
Frequency: Quarterly
Cover Price: £4.50
Circulation: 30,000 (Publisher's Statement)
Usual Pagination: 288
Editor: Abigael Sullivan; **Managing Director:** Alan Radcliffe; **Publisher:** Abigael Sullivan
Summary of Content: Magazine containing the latest information on wedding venues in the UK. Includes articles on themed real weddings with regular pages on gifts, honeymoons, venues, receptions, fashion and beauty and a directory of wedding suppliers.
Readership/Target Audience: Aimed at those planning a wedding.
ADVERTISING RATES:
Full Page Mono £1450.00
Full Page Colour £1450.00
Agency Commission: 15%
Mechanical Data: Trim Size: 290 x 215mm, Bleed Size: 296 x 221mm, Type Area: 270 x 195mm, Col Length: 270mm, Page Width: 195mm, Film: Digital
Copy instructions: Copy Date: 4 weeks prior to publication date
CONSUMER: WOMEN'S INTEREST CONSUMER MAGAZINES: Brides

WEDDINGS ETC
1647460U74L-220

Formerly: When you say 'I Do'
Editorial Address: 48 Bell Street, MAIDENHEAD, SL6 1HX
Tel: 01628 678240 **Fax:** 01628 678245
Email: janes@baylismedia.co.uk
Advertising Address: As above. **Tel:** 01628 678215
Fax: 01628 682700
Email: janed@maidenads.co.uk
Web site: http://www.maidenhead-advertiser.co.uk
Publisher: Baylis & Co.
Frequency: Half-yearly - Published in February and September
Cover Price: Free
Circulation: 30,000 (Publisher's Statement)
Usual Pagination: 60
Editor: Jane Stevens
Summary of Content: Magazine covering venues, beauty, make-up, photography, stationery, bridal wear, accessories and transport.
Readership/Target Audience: Aimed at brides-to-be.
ADVERTISING RATES:
Full Page Colour £500.00
Agency Commission: 10%
Mechanical Data: Type Area: 277 x 190mm, Col Length: 277mm, Page Width: 190mm, Film: Digital
Average advertising content per issue: 40%
Supplement to: Maidenhead Advertiser Series
CONSUMER: WOMEN'S INTEREST CONSUMER MAGAZINES: Brides

WEED WORLD
1640280U74Q-1171

Editorial Address: PO Box 1332, COVENTRY, CV8 3YA
Tel: 01974 821518 **Fax:** 01974 821518
Email: info@weedworld.co.uk
Advertising Address: As above.
Email: info@weedworld.co.uk
Web site: http://www.weedworld.co.uk
Publisher: Weed World
Date Established: 1994
Frequency: 6 issues yearly
Cover Price: £3.50
Annual Sub.: £28.00
Circulation: 140,000 (Publisher's Statement)
Usual Pagination: 132
Editor: Phil Kilvington; **Advertising Manager:** Phil Kilvington
Summary of Content: Magazine covering all aspects of marijuana, cannabis, the geo-political climate in the UK and worldwide, medical aspects and grow your own advice as well as lifestyle, music, DVD reviews and video games.
Readership/Target Audience: Aimed at music and leisure enthusiasts between 18 and 45 years old.
ADVERTISING RATES:
Full Page Colour £1300.00
Agency Commission: 10%
Mechanical Data: Trim Size: 297 x 210mm, Film: Digital, Bleed Size: +3mm
Copy instructions: Copy Date: 4 weeks prior to publication date
Average advertising content per issue: 15%
CONSUMER: WOMEN'S INTEREST CONSUMER MAGAZINES: Lifestyle

THE WEEK
45162U73-430

Editorial Address: 6th Floor, Compass House, 22 Redan Place, LONDON, W2 4SA **Tel:** 020 7907 6180
Fax: 020 7221 1803
Email: editorialadmin@theweek.co.uk
Advertising Address: 30 Cleveland Street, LONDON, W1T 4JD **Tel:** 020 7907 6000 **Fax:** 020 7907 6601
Email: dan_reeves@dennis.co.uk
Web site: http://www.theweek.co.uk
ISSN: 1362-3435
Publisher: Dennis Publishing Ltd
Frequency: Weekly
Cover Price: £2.35
Circulation: 165,609 (ABC 01/01/2009 to 30/06/2009)
Usual Pagination: 46
Editor: Caroline Law
Summary of Content: Magazine containing a digest of the best items from the British and foreign media, including theatre, forthcoming events and exhibitions.
Readership/Target Audience: Aimed at professional adults working and living in and around London.
ADVERTISING RATES:
Full Page Colour £8777.00
Agency Commission: 10%
Mechanical Data: Film: Digital, Bleed Size: 303 x 216mm, Trim Size: 297 x 210mm, Type Area: 275 x 185mm, Col Length: 275mm, Page Width: 185mm
Copy instructions: Copy Date: Monday 5.30pm prior to publication date
Average advertising content per issue: 25%
Supplement(s): The Quarterly - 4xY
CONSUMER: NATIONAL & INTERNATIONAL PERIODICALS

WEEKEND
1627027U74G-238

Formerly: Body & Soul
Editorial Address: 1 Pennington Street, LONDON, E98 1TT
Tel: 020 7782 7531
Email: weekend@thetimes.co.uk
Advertising Address: As above. **Tel:** 020 7782 5000
Email: sevda.gurpinar@newsint.co.uk
Web site: http://www.timesonline.co.uk
Publisher: Times Newspapers Ltd
Frequency: Weekly - See The Times for circulation figure
Cover Price: Free
Editor: Lesley Thomas
Summary of Content: Magazine covering health, science, beauty and wellbeing.
Readership/Target Audience: Aimed at readers of The Times.
ADVERTISING RATES:
Full Page Mono £14994.00
Full Page Colour £25466.00
Mechanical Data: Type Area: 325 x 264mm, Col Length: 325mm, Page Width: 264mm, no. of Columns (Display): 7, Col Widths (Display): 34mm, Film: Digital
Copy instructions: Copy Date: Wednesday 1pm prior to publication date
Supplement to: The Times
CONSUMER: WOMEN'S INTEREST CONSUMER MAGAZINES: Slimming & Health

WEEKENDER
1827158U89E-256

Editorial Address: Zetland House, 5-25 Scrutton Street, LONDON, EC2A 4HJ **Tel:** 020 7749 3300
Fax: 020 7749 3325
Email: donna.hardie@augustmedia.com
Web site: http://www.bigweekends.com
Publisher: August Media
Date Established: 2007
Frequency: Quarterly
Cover Price: Free
Circulation: 180,000 (Print Run)
Usual Pagination: 36
Editor: Donna Hardie
Summary of Content: Magazine covering Butlins weekend breaks with celebrity interviews, what's on at Butlins, fashion and entertainment.
Readership/Target Audience: Aimed at Butlins customers.
ADVERTISING: No Advertising taken
CONSUMER: HOLIDAYS & TRAVEL: Holidays

THE WEEKLY GLEANER
48356U90-225

Editorial Address: Northern and Shell Tower, 6th Floor, 4 Selsdon Way, LONDON, E14 9GL **Tel:** 020 7510 0340
Fax: 020 7510 0341
Email: steve.pope@gvmedia.co.uk
Advertising Address: As above.
Email: edwin.efa@gvmedia.co.uk
Web site: http://www.jamaica-gleaner.com
ISSN: 0962-8606
Publisher: GV Media Ltd
Date Established: 1950
Frequency: Weekly
Cover Price: £0.65
Circulation: 12,300 (Publisher's Statement)
Usual Pagination: 28
Editor: Steve Pope; **Managing Director:** George Ruddock;
Advertising Manager: Edwin Efa
Summary of Content: Publication containing current affairs, news and an entertainment guide of interest to the Jamaica and Caribbean communities in the UK.
Readership/Target Audience: Aimed at the Caribbean and Jamaican communities and people of Caribbean and Jamaican heritage living in the UK.
ADVERTISING RATES:
Full Page Mono £2040.00
Full Page Colour £2652.00
SCC £12.00
Agency Commission: 10%
Mechanical Data: Col Widths (Display): 40mm, No. of Columns (Display): 5, Film: Digital
Copy instructions: Copy Date: Friday 1pm prior to publication date
CONSUMER: ETHNIC

WEEKLY JOURNEY
48357U90-250

Editorial Address: 7-8 Market Place, LONDON, W1W 8AG
Tel: 020 7307 3210 **Fax:** 020 7307 3218
Email: lina@japanjournals.com
Advertising Address: As above.
Email: info@japanjournals.com
Web site: http://www.japanjournals.com
Publisher: Japan Journals Ltd
Date Established: 1998
Frequency: Weekly - Double issue over Christmas and New Year
Free to qualifying individuals
Annual Sub.: £55.00
Circulation: 11,600 (Publisher's Statement)

Usual Pagination: 48
Editor: Lina Panchal; **Advertising Manager:** Lina Panchal
Summary of Content: Journal containing news and current affairs from Japan. Covers politics, the economy, social affairs, entertainment and sport.
Language(s): Japanese
Readership/Target Audience: Read by Japanese people living in Britain.
ADVERTISING RATES:
Full Page Mono £890.00
Full Page Colour £970.00
Agency Commission: 10%
Mechanical Data: Col Length: 310mm, Type Area: 310 x 214mm, Film: Digital, Page Width: 214mm, Bleed Size: 339 x 236mm, Trim Size: 333 x 230mm
Copy instructions: Copy Date: 2 weeks prior to publication date
Average advertising content per issue: 45%
CONSUMER: ETHNIC

THE WEEKLY NEWS
45163U73-450

Editorial Address: 2 Albert Square, DUNDEE, DD1 9QJ
Tel: 01382 223131 **Fax:** 01382 201390
Email: weeklynews@dcthomson.co.uk
Advertising Address: As above. **Fax:** 01382 454599
Email: advertising-meadowside@dcthomson.co.uk
Web site: http://www.dcthomson.co.uk
Publisher: D.C. Thomson & Co Ltd
Date Established: 1855
Frequency: Weekly
Cover Price: £0.70
Circulation: 56,688 (ABC 01/01/2009 to 30/06/2009)
Usual Pagination: 48
Editor: David Burness; **Advertising Manager:** Arthur McEwan
Summary of Content: Newspaper covering human interest articles, television profiles, health awareness, sport, current affairs, puzzles, competitions and gardening.
Readership/Target Audience: Read by adults primarily 35 years old and over.
ADVERTISING RATES:
Full Page Mono £5232.00
Full Page Colour £6278.00
SCC £22.60
Agency Commission: 10%
Mechanical Data: Type Area: 350 x 264mm, Col Length: 350mm, Film: Digital, Page Width: 264mm, No. of Columns (Display): 7, Print Process: Web-offset
Average advertising content per issue: 15%
CONSUMER: NATIONAL & INTERNATIONAL PERIODICALS

WEEKLY WORKER
47288U82-215

Editorial Address: BCM Box 928, LONDON, WC1N 3XX
Tel: 020 7254 8444
Email: weeklyworker@cpgb.org.uk
Web site: http://www.cpgb.org.uk
Publisher: November Publications Ltd
Date Established: 1993
Frequency: Weekly
Cover Price: £1.00
Annual Sub.: £50.00
Circulation: 25,000 (Publisher's Statement)
Usual Pagination: 12
Editor: Peter Manson
Summary of Content: Newspaper of the Communist Party of Great Britain. Covers news items and analysis of current world events.
Readership/Target Audience: Aimed at trade unionists and political activists.
ADVERTISING: No Advertising taken
CONSUMER: CURRENT AFFAIRS & POLITICS

WEIGHT WATCHERS MAGAZINE
45453U74G-110

Editorial Address: 3rd Floor, 1 Neal Street, LONDON, WC2H 9QL **Tel:** 020 7306 0304
Advertising Address: As above. **Tel:** 020 7413 9362
Email: msimpson@riverltd.co.uk
Publisher: River Publishing Ltd
Frequency: Monthly
Cover Price: £2.60
Annual Sub.: £30.00
Circulation: 244,231 (ABC 01/07/2006 to 31/12/2006)
Usual Pagination: 116
Editor: Charlotte Bailey; **Features Editor:** Sian Merrylees;
Advertising Manager: Matthew Simpson
Summary of Content: Magazine covering diet and nutrition, celebrity profiles, general women's interest features and low fat recipes.
Readership/Target Audience: Read by members of Weight Watchers and those interested in slimming.
ADVERTISING RATES:
Full Page Colour £5500.00
Agency Commission: 10%
Mechanical Data: Print Process: Web-fed offset litho, Type Area: 270 x 195mm, Bleed Size: 296 x 221mm, Trim Size:

Consumer Magazines

290 x 215mm, Page Width: 195mm, Col Length: 270mm, Film: Digital
Copy instructions: Copy Date: 3 weeks prior to publication date
Average advertising content per issue: 40%
CONSUMER: WOMEN'S INTEREST CONSUMER MAGAZINES: Slimming & Health

WELCOME ABOARD
1666206U89E-238

Editorial Address: 87 Loopland Drive, Castlereagh Road, BELFAST, BT6 9DW **Tel:** 028 9073 8008 **Fax:** 028 9045 5684
Email: gill@imagine8withus.com
Advertising Address: As above.
Email: jim@imagine8withus.com
Web site: http://www.imagine8withus.com
Publisher: Imagine 8 International Ltd
Date Established: 1999
Frequency: Quarterly
Cover Price: Free
Circulation: 10,000 (Publisher's Statement)
Usual Pagination: 100
Editor: Sharon Gillespie
Summary of Content: Magazine covering travel, business, arts, celebrity profiles, lifestyle and events.
Readership/Target Audience: Aimed at passengers on P&O Irish Sea Ferries and also distributed through Tourist Information Centres.
ADVERTISING RATES:
Full Page Colour £1200.00
Agency Commission: 15%
Mechanical Data: Bleed Size: +4mm, Print Process: Litho, Trim Size: 297 x 210mm, Film: Digital
Average advertising content per issue: 40%
CONSUMER: HOLIDAYS & TRAVEL: Holidays

WELCOME TO LONDON
48152U89C-1087

Editorial Address: 197-199 City Road, LONDON, EC1V 1JN
Tel: 020 7253 9906
Email: editorial@welcometolondon.com
Advertising Address: As above. **Tel:** 020 7253 9909
Fax: 020 7250 0955
Email: coletteoregan@absolutepublishing.com
ISSN: 1368-4493
Publisher: Absolute Publishing Ltd
Date Established: 1997
Frequency: Quarterly
Cover Price: Free
Circulation: 43,768 (Publisher's Statement)
Usual Pagination: 84
Editor: Jo Gardner; **Advertising Manager:** Colette O'Regan
Summary of Content: Magazine and entertainment guide containing features and listings for places to go, restaurants, theatre, historical and commercial attractions in London and across the UK.
Readership/Target Audience: Aimed at short stay tourist visitors to London.
ADVERTISING RATES:
Full Page Colour £1950.00
Agency Commission: 10%
Mechanical Data: Trim Size: 210 x 148mm, Film: Digital
Average advertising content per issue: 30%
CONSUMER: HOLIDAYS & TRAVEL: Entertainment Guides

WELLBEING MAGAZINE
1895963U74G-298

Editorial Address: 2 The Hall, Turners Green Road, WADHURST, TN5 6TR **Tel:** 01892 782697
Email: rachel@wellbeingmagazine.com
Web site: http://www.wellbeingmagazine.com
Publisher: Wellbeing Magazine Ltd
Date Established: 2006
Frequency: 6 issues yearly
Cover Price: Free
Circulation: 23,500 (Combined Circulation)
Editor: Rachel Scriven; **Publisher:** Lenette Howard
Summary of Content: Magazine looking at the food we eat, how to look after our bodies and minds as well as our home and working environment. Editorial features are centred around women's and men's health, mental health, fitness, weightloss, posture, beauty, eco products and wellness travel features. Also includes tried and tested products and treatments and information on illnesses such as diabetes, asthma, heart conditions and cancer and readers offers, competitions and book reviews.
Readership/Target Audience: Aimed at those interested in taking responsibility for their own health and wellbeing as well as for their families.
Editions:
East Sussex Edition
Gwent Edition
North Kent Edition
West Kent Edition
CONSUMER: WOMEN'S INTEREST CONSUMER MAGAZINES: Slimming & Health

WELLINGTON NEWS
31295U80C-2745

Editorial Address: 2 Crown Street, Wellington, TELFORD, TF1 1LP **Tel:** 01952 415334 **Fax:** 01952 245077
Email: martin.scholes@wellnews.co.uk
Advertising Address: As above.
Email: marlane.wilkes@ppmedia.co.uk
Web site: http://www.thewellingtonnews.co.uk
Publisher: Partnership Publishing Limited
Date Established: 1999
Frequency: Monthly
Cover Price: £0.25
Free to qualifying individuals
Annual Sub.: £15.00
Circulation: 60,000 (Publisher's Statement)
Usual Pagination: 64
Editor: Martin Scholes; **Group Editor:** Martin Scholes
Summary of Content: Magazine containing local news, events, places to go, competitions, recipes, leisure and features on the history of Shropshire's oldest market town, Wellington.
Readership/Target Audience: Read by residents in Wellington and the Telford area.
ADVERTISING RATES:
Full Page Mono £485.00
Full Page Colour £625.00
Agency Commission: 10%
Mechanical Data: Type Area: 276 x 198mm, Col Length: 276mm, No. of Columns (Display): 6, Film: Digital, Page Width: 198mm
Average advertising content per issue: 40%
CONSUMER: RURAL & REGIONAL INTEREST: Regional Interest English Counties

WELSH BOWLER
1703374U75X-1710

Editorial Address: PO Box 280, GRAVESEND, DA13 9WB
Tel: 01634 256794 **Fax:** 01634 256798
Email: bljournals@tiscali.co.uk
Advertising Address: As above. **Tel:** 01474 535399
Fax: 01474 535390
Email: bljournals@tiscali.co.uk
Web site: http://www.bljournals.co.uk
Publisher: B.L. Journals
Date Established: 1996
Frequency: Quarterly
Cover Price: Free
Circulation: 9,000 (Publisher's Statement)
Usual Pagination: 20
Editor: Dave Peters; **Advertising Manager:** Dave Peters; **Publisher:** Dave Peters
Summary of Content: Magazine covering all news, technical items and product editorial relating to bowling in Wales.
Readership/Target Audience: Aimed at Welsh bowlers and association officials.
ADVERTISING RATES:
Full Page Mono £695.00
Agency Commission: 10%
Mechanical Data: Bleed Size: 303 x 216mm, Trim Size: 297 x 210mm, Film: Digital
Copy instructions: Copy Date: 1 week prior to publication date
CONSUMER: SPORT: Other Sport

WELSH CLUB GOLFER
1685508U75D-542

Editorial Address: 50 High Craighall Road, GLASGOW, G4 9UD **Tel:** 0141 353 2222 **Fax:** 0141 332 3811
Email: martin.dempster@psp.uk.net
Advertising Address: As above.
Web site: http://www.bunkered.co.uk
Publisher: PSP Publishing Ltd
Date Established: 2005
Frequency: Quarterly
Cover Price: Free
Circulation: 15,000 (Publisher's Statement)
Editor: Martin Dempster
Summary of Content: Magazine covering amateur golf in Wales including fixtures, results, player profiles and interviews and equipment reviews.
Readership/Target Audience: Aimed at amateur golfers in Wales.
ADVERTISING RATES:
Full Page Colour £950.00
Agency Commission: 10%
Mechanical Data: Trim Size: 360 x 280mm, Film: Digital
Average advertising content per issue: 35%
CONSUMER: SPORT: Golf

WELSH COUNTRY
1655119U80D-505

Editorial Address: Aberbanc, Penrhiwllan, LLANDYSUL, SA44 5NP **Tel:** 01559 372010 **Fax:** 01559 371995
Email: kath@welshcountry.co.uk
Advertising Address: As above.
Email: ian@welshcountry.co.uk
Web site: http://www.welshcountry.co.uk
Publisher: Equine Marketing Ltd
Date Established: 2004

Frequency: 6 issues yearly
Cover Price: £2.95
Circulation: 19,658 (Publisher's Statement)
Usual Pagination: 68
Editor: Kath Rhodes; **Advertising Manager:** Ian Mole
Summary of Content: Magazine covering areas of interest to Welsh people and those living and visiting Wales. Features covered include wildlife, property, Welsh food as well as recipes, farmers markets, farm shops, eating out, fishing, places to stay, interviews, gardening, rural and country matters, book reviews, CD review, wine, motoring, diary dates, green issues, conservation and horoscopes.
Readership/Target Audience: Aimed at those living in Wales or born in Wales, the Welsh living abroad as well as tourists, visitors and anyone with a passion or soft spot for Wales.
ADVERTISING RATES:
Full Page Colour £1150.00
SCC £10.00
Agency Commission: 10%
Mechanical Data: Trim Size: 297 x 210mm, Bleed Size: 300 x 219mm, No. of Columns (Display): 4, Col Widths (Display): 45mm, Film: Digital
Copy instructions: Copy Date: 6th of the month prior to publication date
Average advertising content per issue: 33%
CONSUMER: RURAL & REGIONAL INTEREST: Regional Interest Wales

WELSH RIDER
1743751U81D-369

Editorial Address: Unit 2, Devizes Trade Centre, Hopton Park, DEVIZES, SN10 2EH **Tel:** 0845 644 2236
Email: sales@redpin.co.uk
Advertising Address: As above.
Email: lisadure@redpin.co.uk
Web site: http://www.welshrider.co.uk
Publisher: Redpin Publishing Ltd
Frequency: Monthly
Cover Price: Free
Circulation: 9,000 (Publisher's Statement)
Editor: Sara Haines
Summary of Content: Magazine covering all-round equestrian interests and disciplines, feature articles, product reviews and events.
Readership/Target Audience: Aimed at riders in Wales.
ADVERTISING: Rates on application
CONSUMER: ANIMALS & PETS: Horses & Ponies

WESSEX SCENE
47469U83-105

Editorial Address: S.U. Southampton University, University Road, Highfield, SOUTHAMPTON, SO17 1BJ
Tel: 023 8059 5226 **Fax:** 023 8059 5252
Email: editor@soton.ac.uk
Advertising Address: As above. **Fax:** 023 8059 5416
Email: james@susu.org
Web site: http://www.wessexscene.co.uk
Publisher: Wessex Scene
Date Established: 1926
Frequency: 9 issues yearly - Once every 3 weeks during term time
Cover Price: Free
Circulation: 23,000 (Publisher's Statement)
Usual Pagination: 44
Summary of Content: Newspaper covering sport, travel, music, arts, cinemas, union news, letters, local news, support and welfare.
Readership/Target Audience: Aimed at members of Southampton University Students' Union.
ADVERTISING RATES:
Full Page Colour £650.00
Agency Commission: 10%
Mechanical Data: Trim Size: 347 x 265mm, Film: Digital
Copy instructions: Copy Date: 2 days prior to publication date
Supplement(s): The Edge - 9xY
CONSUMER: STUDENT PUBLICATIONS

WEST COUNTRY LIFE
622621U80C-360

Formerly: WestLife
Editorial Address: Temple Way, BRISTOL, BS99 7HD
Tel: 0117 934 3338 **Fax:** 0117 934 3574
Email: wcl@bepp.co.uk
Web site: http://www.westpress.co.uk
Publisher: Bristol News & Media Ltd
Frequency: Weekly
Cover Price: Free
Circulation: 48,127 (Publisher's Statement)
Usual Pagination: 48
Editor: Rachael Sugden
Summary of Content: Magazine covering lifestyle, fashion, gardening, food and wine, interiors, books, design, travel and general interest. Includes TV and radio listings.
Readership/Target Audience: Aimed at residents and visitors to the West Country.
ADVERTISING: No Advertising taken

Supplement to: Western Daily Press Bristol
CONSUMER: RURAL & REGIONAL INTEREST: Regional
Interest English Counties

WEST END DIRECTORY
1903417U80-6240

Editorial Address: PO Box 198, DARLINGTON, DL1 9FW
Tel: 01325 250985
Email: westenddirectory@gmail.com
Web site: http://www.westenddirectory.co.uk
Publisher: Beona Publishing
Frequency: 6 issues yearly
Cover Price: Free
Circulation: 6,000 (Print Run)
Editor: Theresa Stinson
Summary of Content: Magazine containing local
information, news and entertainment listings.
Readership/Target Audience: Aimed at people living in the
Darlington area.
CONSUMER: RURAL & REGIONAL INTEREST

WEST END NEWS
1824604U80E-375

Editorial Address: For all contact details see main edition,
Southside News
Frequency: Monthly
Cover Price: Free
Circulation: 20,000 (Publisher's Statement)
Edition of: Southside News
CONSUMER: RURAL & REGIONAL INTEREST: Regional
Interest Scotland

WEST END REVIEW
1703356U74Q-1286

Editorial Address: 77 Oxford Street, LONDON, W1D 2ES
Tel: 020 7659 2728 **Fax:** 01483 480462
Email: westendreview@abbeystirling.co.uk
Advertising Address: As above.
Email: westendreview@aol.com
Web site: http://www.westendreview.com
Publisher: West End Review
Date Established: 2001
Frequency: 3 issues yearly
Cover Price: Free
Circulation: 20,000 (Publisher's Statement)
Usual Pagination: 52
Editor: Abbey Stirling; **Advertising Manager:** Peter Burt;
Publisher: Peter Burt
Summary of Content: Lifestyle magazine covering
entertainment, fashion, property, music, dining and travel.
Readership/Target Audience: Aimed at residents,
businesses and hotels in the West End of London.
ADVERTISING RATES:
Full Page Colour £1100.00
Agency Commission: 15%
Mechanical Data: Type Area: 277 x 190mm, Bleed Size:
303 x 216mm, Trim Size: 297 x 210mm, Col Length: 277mm,
Page Width: 190mm, Film: Digital
Copy instructions: Copy Date: 3 weeks prior to publication
date
Average advertising content per issue: 60%
CONSUMER: WOMEN'S INTEREST CONSUMER
MAGAZINES: Lifestyle

WEST ESSEX LIFE
1779310U80C-5366

Editorial Address: 28 Teville Road, WORTHING, BN11 1UG
Tel: 020 8504 0455 **Fax:** 020 8504 0488
Email: editor@archant.co.uk
Advertising Address: As above.
Email: chris.boosey@archant.co.uk
Publisher: Archant South East
Date Established: 2003
Frequency: Monthly
Cover Price: Free
Circulation: 32,000 (Publisher's Statement)
Usual Pagination: 100
Editor: Julian Read; **Publisher:** Robyn Bechelet
Summary of Content: Magazine covering leisure, lifestyle,
motoring, property, interiors, men's and women's fashion,
food and drink, events and exhibitions.
Readership/Target Audience: Aimed at residents and
businesses in West Essex.
ADVERTISING RATES:
Full Page Colour £1250.00
Agency Commission: 10%
Mechanical Data: Bleed Size: 306 x 226mm, Trim Size: 271
x 199mm
Average advertising content per issue: 60%
CONSUMER: RURAL & REGIONAL INTEREST: Regional
Interest English Counties

WEST PARK
1655745U94X-271

Editorial Address: 45 Atkinson Gardens, Aycliffe, NEWTON
AYCLIFFE, DL5 6LH **Tel:** 01325 304360 **Fax:** 01325 314283
Email: sue@cherrington.onyxnet.co.uk
Advertising Address: As above.

Email: sue@cherrington.onyxnet.co.uk
Publisher: Cherrington Advertising Ltd
Date Established: 2004
Frequency: Annual
Cover Price: Free
Circulation: 58,000 (Publisher's Statement)
Usual Pagination: 12
Editor: Sue Riney-Smith; **Advertising Manager:** Sue Riney-
Smith
Summary of Content: Magazine covering the West Park
development in Darlington, shops, homes, parkland and
hospital as well as features on those involved with the site.
Readership/Target Audience: Aimed at households and
businesses in Darlington.
ADVERTISING: Rates on application
CONSUMER: OTHER CLASSIFICATIONS: Miscellaneous

WEST PARK DIRECTORY
1903506U80-6241

Editorial Address: PO Box 198, DARLINGTON, DL1 9FW
Tel: 01325 250985
Email: westparkdirectory@gmail.com
Publisher: Beona Publishing
Frequency: 6 issues yearly
Cover Price: Free
Circulation: 1,500 (Print Run)
Editor: Theresa Stinson
Summary of Content: Magazine containing community
news, local information and entertainment listings.
Readership/Target Audience: Aimed at those living in the
Darlington area.
CONSUMER: RURAL & REGIONAL INTEREST

WEST WEDDINGS
601343U74L-52

Formerly: Weddings incorporating Beautiful Brides
Editorial Address: 1 Clarence Parade, CHELTENHAM,
GL50 3NY **Tel:** 0117 934 3742 **Fax:** 0117 934 3755
Email: tanya.gledhill@glosmedia.co.uk
Advertising Address: As above. **Tel:** 0117 934 3136
Fax: 0117 934 3577
Email: j.lewis@bepp.co.uk
Web site: http://www.thisisbristol.co.uk/beautifulbrides
Publisher: Gloucestershire Media
Date Established: 1995
Frequency: Quarterly
Cover Price: Free
Circulation: 15,000 (Publisher's Statement)
Usual Pagination: 60
Editor: Tanya Gledhill
Summary of Content: Magazine covering all aspects of
weddings and honeymoons with an emphasis on wedding
gowns, make-up and hotels.
Readership/Target Audience: Aimed at brides-to-be in the
Bristol, Bath, Weston-Super-Mare and North East Somerset
region.
ADVERTISING RATES:
Full Page Colour £926.00
Agency Commission: 10%
Mechanical Data: Trim Size: 297 x 210mm, Bleed Size:
+5mm, Type Area: 260 x 187mm, Col Length: 260mm, Page
Width: 187mm, Film: Digital
Copy instructions: Copy Date: 3 weeks prior to publication
date
Average advertising content per issue: 50%
CONSUMER: WOMEN'S INTEREST CONSUMER
MAGAZINES: Brides

THE WESTENDER
46846U80B-350

Editorial Address: 25 Horsell Road, LONDON, N5 1XL
Tel: 020 7607 6060 **Fax:** 020 7607 2299
Advertising Address: As above. **Tel:** 020 7607 6070
Publisher: The Westender
Date Established: 1988
Frequency: Monthly
Cover Price: Free
Circulation: 40,000 (Publisher's Statement)
Usual Pagination: 24
Editor: Eileen Martin; **Advertising Manager:** Danny
Connolley; **Publisher:** Danny Connolley
Summary of Content: Newspaper covering news of
London's West End.
Readership/Target Audience: Aimed at workers, residents
and visitors to central London.
ADVERTISING RATES:
Full Page Mono £1944.00
Full Page Colour £2235.00
SCC £9.00
Agency Commission: 15%
Mechanical Data: Col Length: 360mm, No. of Columns
(Display): 6, Type Area: 360 x 273mm, Page Width: 273mm,
Film: Digital
Copy instructions: Copy Date: 25th of the month prior to
publication date
CONSUMER: RURAL & REGIONAL INTEREST: Regional
Interest Greater London

WESTMINSTER RECORD
1827025U87-2048

Editorial Address: 147A Leighton Road, LONDON, NW5
2RB **Tel:** 020 7267 3616
Email: news@indcatholicnews.com
Advertising Address: CathCom, Unit L4, Blois Meadow
Business Park, Steeple Bumpstead, HAVERHILL, CB9 7BN
Tel: 0870 228 4266 **Fax:** 0870 312 6134
Email: westminsterrecord@cathcom.org
Publisher: Gabriel Communications Ltd
Date Established: 1980
Frequency: Monthly
Cover Price: £0.50
Free to qualifying individuals
Circulation: 14,000 (Publisher's Statement)
Usual Pagination: 16
Advertising Manager: Nick Layton
Summary of Content: Newspaper covering diocesan news
for the Diocese of Westminster.
Readership/Target Audience: Aimed at catholic
parishioners.
ADVERTISING RATES:
Full Page Mono £1515.00
Full Page Colour £1742.00
Agency Commission: 10%
Mechanical Data: Type Area: 319 x 265mm, Col Length:
319mm, Page Width: 265mm, Col Widths (Display): 49mm,
No. of Columns (Display): 5, Film: Digital
Copy instructions: Copy Date: 3 weeks prior to publication
date
Average advertising content per issue: 20%
CONSUMER: RELIGIOUS

WESTMINSTER YEAR BOOK
47864U87-225_20

Editorial Address: Archbishop's House, Ambrosden
Avenue, LONDON, SW1P 1QJ **Tel:** 020 7798 9055
Fax: 020 7798 9077
Email: poa@rcdow.org.uk
Advertising Address: As above. **Tel:** 07981 770478
Email: nick@cathcom.org
Web site: http://www.westminsteryearbook.org.uk
ISSN: 1468-8549
Publisher: Lonsdale Press
Date Established: 1952
Frequency: Annual - Published in December
Cover Price: £3.00
Circulation: 12,000 (Publisher's Statement)
Usual Pagination: 288
Editor: Eddie Tulasiewicz; **Advertising Manager:** Nick
Layton
Summary of Content: Roman Catholic yearbook giving
details of the Catholic community throughout the
Westminster diocese.
Readership/Target Audience: Read by those in the
Catholic community.
ADVERTISING RATES:
Full Page Mono £500.00
Full Page Colour £550.00
Mechanical Data: Film: Digital, Type Area: 195 x 113mm,
Col Length: 195mm, Page Width: 113mm
Copy instructions: Copy Date: September 22nd
CONSUMER: RELIGIOUS

WESTONE EXCLUSIVE
1892647U80C-5493

Editorial Address: For all contact details see main edition,
Exclusive (London)
Frequency: 10 issues yearly
Cover Price: Free
Circulation: 7,500 (Publisher's Statement)
ADVERTISING: Rates on application
Edition of: Exclusive (London)
CONSUMER: RURAL & REGIONAL INTEREST: Regional
Interest English Counties

WESTSIDE MAGAZINE
1626233U80B-391

Editorial Address: Avon House, 5th Floor, Kensington
Village, LONDON, W14 8TS **Tel:** 020 7605 2271
Email: lucy.jenkins@archant.co.uk
Advertising Address: As above. **Tel:** 020 7792 2626
Email: mathew@archant.co.uk
Publisher: Archant Life
Date Established: 2003
Frequency: Monthly
Cover Price: Free
Circulation: 47,000 (Print Run)
Usual Pagination: 84
Editor: Lucy Jenkins
Summary of Content: Magazine covering local news and
events, local history and celebrity interviews as well as
lifestyle features including interiors, food and drink,
gardening, motoring, travel, property, fashion, health and
fitness, book, film and theatre reviews, diary listings and
family-interest and children's pages.
Readership/Target Audience: Aimed at those living and
working in West London.
ADVERTISING RATES:
Full Page Colour £1625.00

Agency Commission: 10%
Copy instructions: Copy Date: 3 weeks prior to publication date
Average advertising content per issue: 50%
CONSUMER: RURAL & REGIONAL INTEREST: Regional Interest Greater London

WESTSIDE MAGAZINE
46884U80C-1050

Editorial Address: RMC House, Broadfield Court, Broadfield Business Park, SHEFFIELD, S8 0XF
Tel: 0114 250 6300 **Fax:** 0114 255 5881
Email: chris.wilson@regionalmagazine.co.uk
Advertising Address: As above. **Fax:** 0114 250 6320
Email: amanda.roy@regionalmagazine.co.uk
Web site: http://www.northernlifestyle.com
Publisher: Regional Magazine Company
Date Established: 1986
Frequency: Monthly
Cover Price: Free
Circulation: 20,103 (Publisher's Statement)
Usual Pagination: 92
Editor: Chris Wilson; **Advertising Manager:** Amanda Roy;
Managing Editor: Chris Wilson
Summary of Content: Magazine covering lifestyle, food, travel, fashion, gardening, entertainment, restaurants, motoring and local news.
Readership/Target Audience: Aimed at people living in Derbyshire and Sheffield.
ADVERTISING RATES:
Full Page Colour £1311.00
Agency Commission: 10%
Mechanical Data: Bleed Size: 303 x 216mm, Trim Size: 297 x 210mm, Film: Digital, Type Area: 260 x 185mm, Col Length: 260mm, Page Width: 185mm
Copy instructions: Copy Date: 6th of the month prior to publication
Average advertising content per issue: 60%
Editions:
Eastside Magazine
Northside Magazine
Southside Magazine
CONSUMER: RURAL & REGIONAL INTEREST: Regional Interest English Counties

WESTWORLD
47470U83-115

Editorial Address: Univ. of West of England S.U., Coldharbour Lane, Frenchay Campus, BRISTOL, BS16 1QY
Tel: 0117 328 2842 **Fax:** 0117 344 2986
Email: western.eye@uwe.ac.uk
Advertising Address: As above. **Tel:** 0117 328 2096
Fax: 0117 328 2986
Email: sumarketing@uwe.ac.uk
Web site: http://www.uwesu.org/westworld
Publisher: UWESU Student Publications
Date Established: 1972
Frequency: 3 issues yearly
Cover Price: Free
Circulation: 4,000 (Publisher's Statement)
Usual Pagination: 12
Summary of Content: Magazine containing arts, music, film and general features.
Readership/Target Audience: Distributed to students of the University of West England and available to further education colleges in Bristol.
ADVERTISING: Rates on application
CONSUMER: STUDENT PUBLICATIONS

THE WEY
1657043U87-2031

Formerly: The Herald
Editorial Address: Diocesan House, Quarry Street, GUILDFORD, GU1 3XG **Tel:** 01483 790347
Fax: 01483 790311
Email: editorial@cofeguildford.org.uk
Advertising Address: 28 Old Park Road, Peverell, PLYMOUTH, PL3 4PY **Tel:** 01752 225623
Fax: 01752 673441
Email: ian@cornerstonevision.com
Web site: http://www.cofeguildford.org.uk
Publisher: Cornerstone Vision
Date Established: 2006
Frequency: 10 issues yearly - No separate January and August editions
Cover Price: Free
Circulation: 27,000 (Publisher's Statement)
Usual Pagination: 16
Editor: Emma Nutbrown
Summary of Content: Magazine of the Diocese of Guildford covering news and events affecting the Anglican community in Surrey and North Hampshire.
Readership/Target Audience: Aimed at the people in the parishes.
ADVERTISING RATES:
Full Page Colour £1250.00
SCC £5.75
Agency Commission: 10%

Mechanical Data: Type Area: 345 x 261mm, Col Length: 345mm, Page Width: 261mm, Bleed Size: +5mm, Film: Digital
Copy instructions: Copy Date: 3 weeks prior to publication date
Average advertising content per issue: 40%
CONSUMER: RELIGIOUS

WHAT BIKE?
46382U77B-660

Editorial Address: Media House, Lynchwood, Peterborough Business Park, PETERBOROUGH, PE2 6EA
Tel: 01733 468000 **Fax:** 01733 468092
Email: whatbike@bauermedia.co.uk
Advertising Address: As above. **Fax:** 01733 468377
Email: sarah.nunn@bauerconsumer.co.uk
Publisher: Bauer Consumer Media Ltd (Media House)
Date Established: 1985
Frequency: Quarterly
Cover Price: £4.95
Circulation: 35,000 (Publisher's Statement)
Usual Pagination: 276
Editor: Stefan Bartlett; **Advertising Manager:** Sarah Nunn;
Managing Editor: Stefan Bartlett
Summary of Content: Magazine covering all aspects of motorcycling. Contains a full buyer's guide to all new bikes, road tests of new models and a products section, as well as features on training and insurance.
Readership/Target Audience: Aimed at motorcycling enthusiasts and newcomers alike.
ADVERTISING RATES:
Full Page Colour £1575.00
Agency Commission: 10%
Mechanical Data: Col Length: 274mm, Film: Digital, No. of Columns (Display): 2, Type Area: 274 x 184mm, Bleed Size: 303 x 216mm, Trim Size: 297 x 210mm, Page Width: 184mm
Copy instructions: Copy Date: 5 weeks prior to publication date
Average advertising content per issue: 30%
CONSUMER: MOTORING & CYCLING: Motorcycling

WHAT CAR?
46342U77A-475

Editorial Address: Teddington Studios, Broom Road, TEDDINGTON, TW11 9BE **Tel:** 020 8267 5688
Fax: 020 8267 5750
Email: editorial@whatcar.com
Advertising Address: As above. **Tel:** 020 8267 5715
Fax: 020 8267 5717
Email: whatcar@haymarket.com
Web site: http://www.whatcar.com
ISSN: 0307-2991
Publisher: Haymarket Media Group Ltd
Date Established: 1973
Frequency: 13 issues yearly
Cover Price: £4.35
Circulation: 87,220 (ABC 01/01/2009 to 30/06/2009)
Usual Pagination: 394
Editor: Steve Fowler; **Managing Director:** Kevin Costello;
Advertising Manager: Sean Costa; **Group Editor:** Steve Fowler
Summary of Content: Magazine with news and specifications on the latest cars, plus advice on purchasing secondhand and new cars. Features include road tests, safety and security tips and information on used cars.
Readership/Target Audience: Aimed at prospective car buyers.
ADVERTISING RATES:
Full Page Colour £13019.00
Agency Commission: 10%
Mechanical Data: Type Area: 280 x 196mm, Bleed Size: 306 x 224mm, Trim Size: 300 x 218mm, Film: Digital, Page Width: 196mm, Col Length: 280mm
Copy instructions: Copy Date: 3 weeks prior to publication date
Average advertising content per issue: 40%
CONSUMER: MOTORING & CYCLING: Motoring

WHAT DIESEL
46312U77A-145

Formerly: What Diesel Car
Editorial Address: 211 Old Street, LONDON, EC1V 9NR
Tel: 020 7608 6500
Email: ian.robertson@trojanpublishing.co.uk
Advertising Address: Ground Floor, 211 Old Street, LONDON, EC1V 9NR **Tel:** 020 7608 6300
Email: phil.curran@trojanpublishing.co.uk
Web site: http://www.whatdiesel.co.uk
ISSN: 1361-9446
Publisher: Trojan Publishing
Date Established: 1988
Frequency: 13 issues yearly
Cover Price: £4.25
Annual Sub.: £32.50
Circulation: 27,000 (Publisher's Statement)
Usual Pagination: 148
Editor: Ian Robertson; **Advertising Manager:** Philip Curran

Summary of Content: Magazine containing road tests, new Diesel-engine cars, technical features, data listings, environmental and transport issues.
Readership/Target Audience: Read by private and business users of diesel cars, especially the growing number of diesel enthusiasts.
ADVERTISING RATES:
Full Page Colour £1900.00
Mechanical Data: Film: Digital, Type Area: 275 x 190mm, Col Length: 275mm, Trim Size: 297 x 210mm, Bleed Size: 307 x 220mm, Page Width: 190mm
CONSUMER: MOTORING & CYCLING: Motoring

WHAT DIGITAL CAMERA
38805U85A-213

Editorial Address: Blue Fin Building, 110 Southwark Street, LONDON, SE1 0SU **Tel:** 020 3148 5000
Email: wdc@ipcmedia.com
Advertising Address: As above. **Tel:** 020 7261 5000
Email: dave_stone@ipcmedia.com
Web site: http://www.whatdigitalcamera.com
Publisher: IPC Inspire
Date Established: 1997
Frequency: 13 issues yearly
Cover Price: £3.99
Circulation: 24,011 (ABC 01/01/2008 to 31/12/2008)
Usual Pagination: 200
Editor: Paul Nuttall; **News Editor:** Paul Nuttall; **Advertising Manager:** Dave Stone
Summary of Content: Magazine covering all aspects of digital imaging hardware, software and technique. Includes a section for readers' test reports of latest equipment and comment on each others' photos.
Readership/Target Audience: Aimed at photography enthusiasts and business users of digital imaging technology.
ADVERTISING RATES:
Full Page Mono £1057.00
Full Page Colour £1761.00
Agency Commission: 10%
Mechanical Data: Type Area: 270 x 190mm, Bleed Size: 303 x 216mm, Trim Size: 297 x 210mm, Film: Digital, Col Length: 270mm, Page Width: 190mm
Copy instructions: Copy Date: 5 weeks prior to publication date
Average advertising content per issue: 25%
CONSUMER: PHOTOGRAPHY & FILM MAKING: Photography

WHAT DOCTORS DON'T TELL YOU
45454U74G-160

Editorial Address: Unit 10, Woodman Works, 204 Durnsford Road, LONDON, SW19 8DR **Tel:** 020 8944 9555
Fax: 020 8944 9888
Email: info@wddty.co.uk
Advertising Address: Cabbell Publishing Ltd, Woodman Works, 204 Durnsford Road, LONDON, SW19 8DR
Tel: 020 8971 8454 **Fax:** 020 8971 8480
Email: jenny.scott@cabbell.co.uk
Web site: http://www.wddty.com
ISSN: 1352-1241
Publisher: What Doctors Don't Tell You Plc
Date Established: 1989
Frequency: Monthly
Annual Sub.: £59.00
Circulation: 17,000 (Publisher's Statement)
Usual Pagination: 24
Editor: Lynne McTaggart; **Advertising Manager:** Jenny Scott; **Publisher:** Bryan Hubbard
Summary of Content: Newsletter covering alternative approaches to orthodox medicine.
Readership/Target Audience: Aimed at the general health consumer and alternative practitioner.
ADVERTISING RATES:
Full Page Colour £1500.00
Agency Commission: 10%
Mechanical Data: Type Area: 271 x 188mm, Bleed Size: 303 x 216mm, Trim Size: 297 x 210mm, Col Length: 271mm, Page Width: 188mm, Film: Digital
Copy instructions: Copy Date: 14th of the month prior to publication date
Average advertising content per issue: 35%
CONSUMER: WOMEN'S INTEREST CONSUMER MAGAZINES: Slimming & Health

WHAT GUN
1665816U75F-212

Editorial Address: 21-23 Phoenix Court, Hawkins Road, COLCHESTER, CO2 8JY **Tel:** 01702 479724
Email: pat_farey@tiscali.com
Advertising Address: 2nd Floor, Ewer House, 44-46 Crouch Street, COLCHESTER, CO3 3HH **Tel:** 01206 506247
Fax: 01206 500226
Email: gunmart@aceville.co.uk
Publisher: Aceville Publications Ltd
Frequency: Annual - Published in September
Cover Price: £3.95
Editor: Pat Farey; **Publisher:** Anthony Phelps

Summary of Content: Magazine covering all shooting guns and equipment available on the market.
Readership/Target Audience: Aimed at all shooting enthusiasts, whatever their shooting discipline.
ADVERTISING RATES:
Full Page Mono £300.00
Full Page Colour £500.00
Mechanical Data: Type Area: 270 x 190mm, Bleed Size: 313 x 220mm, Trim Size: 303 x 210mm, Col Length: 270mm, Page Width: 190mm, Film: Digital
Copy instructions: Copy Date: 1st Friday in August
CONSUMER: SPORT: Shooting

WHAT HI-FI? SOUND AND VISION
46517U78A-600

Editorial Address: Teddington Studios, Broom Road, TEDDINGTON, TW11 9BE **Tel:** 020 8267 5000
Fax: 020 8267 5019
Email: whfanswers@haymarket.com
Advertising Address: As above. **Fax:** 020 8267 5866
Email: katie.frame@haymarket.com
Web site: http://www.whathifi.com
ISSN: 0309-3336
Publisher: Haymarket Consumer Media
Date Established: 1976
Frequency: 13 issues yearly
Cover Price: £4.10
Circulation: 59,147 (ABC 01/01/2007 to 31/12/2007)
Usual Pagination: 220
Editor: Richard Melville; **News Editor:** Joe Cox; **Managing Director:** Kevin Costello
Summary of Content: Magazine containing technical features and reviews of the latest hi-fi and home cinema equipment for the home.
Readership/Target Audience: Aimed at people aged 16 years and upwards interested in the latest hi-fi and home cinema.
ADVERTISING RATES:
Full Page Mono £4352.00
Full Page Colour £6405.00
Agency Commission: 10%
Mechanical Data: Type Area: 272 x 182mm, Bleed Size: 303 x 216mm, Trim Size: 297 x 210mm, Film: Digital, Col Length: 272mm, Page Width: 182mm
Copy instructions: Copy Date: 4 weeks prior to publication date
Average advertising content per issue: 50%
Supplement(s): Ultimate Guide to ... - 6xY
CONSUMER: CONSUMER ELECTRONICS: Hi-Fi & Recording

WHAT INVESTMENT
45562U74M-300

Editorial Address: Octavia House, 50 Banner Street, LONDON, EC1Y 8ST **Tel:** 020 7250 7010
Fax: 020 7250 7011
Email: jenny.lowe@vitessemedia.co.uk
Advertising Address: As above.
Email: darren.griffin@vitessemedia.co.uk
Web site: http://www.whatinvestment.co.uk
ISSN: 0263-953X
Publisher: Vitesse Media plc
Date Established: 1982
Frequency: Monthly - Published on the last Saturday of the month prior to cover date
Cover Price: £3.95
Annual Sub.: £35.95
Circulation: 16,320 (ABC 01/01/2008 to 31/12/2008)
Usual Pagination: 100
Editor: Jennifer Lowe; **Publisher:** Sara Williams
Summary of Content: Magazine focusing on all aspects of personal finance and investment.
Readership/Target Audience: Aimed at the individual investor.
ADVERTISING RATES:
Full Page Colour £3500.00
Agency Commission: 10%
Mechanical Data: Type Area: 269 x 187mm, Bleed Size: 303 x 216mm, Trim Size: 297 x 210mm, Page Width: 187mm, Film: Digital, Col Length: 269mm
Copy instructions: Copy Date: 2 weeks prior to publication date
Average advertising content per issue: 35%
Supplement(s): What Investment Trust - 4xY
CONSUMER: WOMEN'S INTEREST CONSUMER MAGAZINES: Personal Finance

WHAT INVESTMENT TRUST
1665511U74M-432

Editorial Address: For all contact details see main record, What Investment
Date Established: 1993
Frequency: Quarterly
Advertising Manager: Darren Griffin
ADVERTISING RATES:
Full Page Colour £3500.00
Mechanical Data: Type Area: 269 x 187mm, Bleed Size: 303 x 216mm, Trim Size: 297 x 210mm, Col Length: 269mm, Page Width: 187mm, Film: Digital

Supplement to: What Investment
CONSUMER: WOMEN'S INTEREST CONSUMER MAGAZINES: Personal Finance

WHAT LAPTOP
36201U78E-13

Formerly: What Laptop & Handheld PC
Editorial Address: 2 Balcombe Street, LONDON, NW1 6NW
Tel: 020 7042 4000
Email: alex.bentley@futurenet.co.uk
Advertising Address: Beauford Court, 30 Monmouth Street, BATH, BA1 2BW **Tel:** 01225 442244
Email: steve.griggs@futurenet.com
Web site: http://www.whatlaptop.co.uk
Publisher: Future Publishing Limited
Date Established: 1999
Frequency: 13 issues yearly
Cover Price: £3.99
Annual Sub.: £28.20
Circulation: 10,756 (ABC 01/01/2008 to 31/12/2008)
Usual Pagination: 144
Editor: Alex Bentley
Summary of Content: Magazine containing a guide to notebook PCs and electronic PDAs, with news, reviews, features and practical tips.
Readership/Target Audience: Aimed at owners of, and those interested in buying a portable computer.
ADVERTISING RATES:
Full Page Colour £2740.00
Agency Commission: 10%
Mechanical Data: Bleed Size: 303 x 216mm, Trim Size: 297 x 210mm, Type Area: 287 x 195mm, Col Length: 287mm, Page Width: 195mm, Film: Digital
CONSUMER: CONSUMER ELECTRONICS: Home Computing

WHAT MOBILE
37523U78R-480

Editorial Address: 3rd Floor, 102-108 Clerkenwell Road, LONDON, EC1M 5SA **Tel:** 020 7324 3500
Fax: 020 7324 3511
Email: editorial@whatmobile.net
Advertising Address: As above.
Email: advertising@whatmobile.net
Web site: http://www.whatmobile.net
Publisher: Clark White Publishing Ltd
Date Established: 1993
Frequency: 13 issues yearly
Cover Price: £3.95
Annual Sub.: £39.96
Circulation: 23,500 (Publisher's Statement)
Usual Pagination: 100
Editor: Jonathan Morris; **Advertising Manager:** Mark Sennett
Summary of Content: Consumer buyers' guide to mobile phones and portable gadgets.
Readership/Target Audience: Aimed at mobile phone users and buyers.
ADVERTISING RATES:
Full Page Colour £2100.00
Agency Commission: 10%
Mechanical Data: Type Area: 280 x 210mm, Bleed Size: 306 x 236mm, Trim Size: 300 x 230mm, Col Length: 280mm, Page Width: 210mm, Film: Digital
Copy instructions: Copy Date: 2 weeks prior to publication date
Average advertising content per issue: 15%
CONSUMER: CONSUMER ELECTRONICS: Consumer Electronics Related

WHAT MORTGAGE
45507U74K-570

Editorial Address: 6th Floor, Davis House, 2 Robert Street, CROYDON, CR0 1QQ **Tel:** 020 8253 8600
Fax: 020 8253 4603
Email: ben.wilkie@metropolis.co.uk
Advertising Address: As above.
Email: mike.harrison@metropolis.co.uk
Web site: http://www.whatmortgage.co.uk
ISSN: 0263-8525
Publisher: Metropolis International Group Ltd
Date Established: 1982
Frequency: Monthly - Published the 3rd Thursday prior to cover date
Cover Price: £3.75
Circulation: 30,000 (Publisher's Statement)
Usual Pagination: 84
Editor: Ben Wilkie; **Managing Director:** Kevin Crook
Summary of Content: Magazine providing information on mortgages and home buying related products. Includes mortgage comparison tables with detailed information on the mortgage deals currently available.
Readership/Target Audience: Aimed at first-time buyers and those buying as an investment, re-mortgaging or for any other aspect of the purchasing chain.
ADVERTISING RATES:
Full Page Colour £2522.00
Agency Commission: 10%

Mechanical Data: Type Area: 269 x 187mm, Film: Digital, Col Length: 269mm, Page Width: 187mm, Trim Size: 297 x 210mm, Bleed Size: 303 x 216mm
Copy instructions: Copy Date: 4 weeks prior to publication date
CONSUMER: WOMEN'S INTEREST CONSUMER MAGAZINES: Home Purchase

WHAT MOUNTAIN BIKE
623964U77C-950

Editorial Address: 30 Monmouth Street, BATH, BA1 2BW
Tel: 01225 442244 **Fax:** 01225 822793
Email: justin.loretz@futurenet.com
Advertising Address: As above. **Fax:** 01225 446019
Email: chawkins@futurenet.co.uk
Web site: http://www.whatmtb.com
Publisher: Future Publishing Ltd
Date Established: 2000
Frequency: 13 issues yearly
Cover Price: £3.99
Annual Sub.: £29.99
Circulation: 17,351 (ABC 01/07/2008 to 31/12/2008)
Usual Pagination: 186
Editor: Justin Loretz; **Publisher:** Richard Schofield
Summary of Content: Product led mountain bike magazine containing guides, bike tests, news, reviews and features.
Readership/Target Audience: Aimed at mountain bike enthusiasts.
ADVERTISING RATES:
Full Page Colour £1300.00
Agency Commission: 10%
Mechanical Data: Type Area: 270 x 190mm, Col Length: 270mm, Page Width: 190mm, Film: Digital, Bleed Size: 303 x 216mm, Trim Size: 297 x 210mm
Average advertising content per issue: 40%
CONSUMER: MOTORING & CYCLING: Cycling

WHAT PLASMA AND LCD TV
1642287U76C-826

Editorial Address: 2 Balcombe Street, LONDON, NW1 6NW
Tel: 020 7042 4000
Email: rob.lane@futurenet.com
Advertising Address: As above. **Fax:** 020 7042 4471
Email: angela.brown@futurenet.co.uk
Publisher: Future Publishing Limited
Date Established: 2004
Frequency: 13 issues yearly
Cover Price: £4.50
Usual Pagination: 132
Editor: Rob Lane; **Advertising Manager:** Angela Brown
Summary of Content: Magazine with reviews, features and news on plasma and LCD televisions. Also contains a buyers' guide.
Readership/Target Audience: Aimed at those looking to buy a new technology television.
ADVERTISING RATES:
Full Page Colour £2480.00
Mechanical Data: Type Area: 266 x 181mm, Bleed Size: 307 x 215mm, Trim Size: 297 x 210mm, Col Length: 266mm, Page Width: 181mm, Film: Digital
Copy instructions: Copy Date: 3 weeks prior to publication date
CONSUMER: MUSIC & PERFORMING ARTS: TV & Radio

WHAT POOL & HOT TUB
1660077U74C-836

Formerly: Home Pools & Hot Tubs
Editorial Address: PO Box 874, Taunton, SOMERSET, TA1 9HB
Email: alan.lewis@gopublishing.com
Advertising Address: As above. **Tel:** 020 7637 5900
Email: edward@manpublishing.co.uk
Publisher: Go Publishing Ltd
Date Established: 2004
Frequency: Half-yearly - Published in May and October
Cover Price: £4.00
Free to qualifying individuals
Circulation: 47,000 (Publisher's Statement)
Usual Pagination: 100
Editor: Alan Lewis; **Publisher:** Alan Lewis
Summary of Content: Magazine covering home, swimming and outdoor living including, swimming pools, spas, hot tubs, saunas and related products.
Readership/Target Audience: Aimed at home owners in the UK.
ADVERTISING RATES:
Full Page Colour £1250.00
Mechanical Data: Type Area: 277 x 190mm, Bleed Size: 305 x 218mm, Trim Size: 297 x 210mm, Col Length: 277mm, Page Width: 190mm, Film: Digital
CONSUMER: WOMEN'S INTEREST CONSUMER MAGAZINES: Home & Family

Consumer Magazines

WHAT SATELLITE & DIGITAL TV

46121U76C-800

Formerly: What Satellite TV
Editorial Address: 2 Balcombe Street, LONDON, NW1 6NW
Tel: 020 7042 4000
Email: wotsat@futurenet.com
Advertising Address: As above. **Fax:** 020 7042 4471
Email: angela.brown@futurenet.co.uk
Web site: http://www.wotsat.com
ISSN: 1470-1960
Publisher: Future Publishing Limited
Date Established: 1986
Frequency: Monthly
Cover Price: £3.99
Annual Sub.: £35.80
Circulation: 20,000 (Publisher's Statement)
Usual Pagination: 180
Editor: Stephen Graves; **Managing Director:** Robert Price;
Advertising Manager: Angela Brown; **Publisher:** Andy Ford
Summary of Content: Magazine covering buying advice on
digital TV, Freeview, Sky digital, satellite TV developments
and monthly programming.
Readership/Target Audience: Read by those with an
interest in satellite and digital television.
ADVERTISING RATES:
Full Page Colour £1940.00
Agency Commission: 10%
Mechanical Data: Col Length: 266mm, Page Width:
181mm, Type Area: 266 x 181mm, Trim Size: 297 x 210mm,
Bleed Size: 307 x 215mm, Film: Digital
Copy instructions: Copy Date: 3 weeks prior to publication
CONSUMER: MUSIC & PERFORMING ARTS: TV & Radio

WHAT VAN?

46508U77A-476

Editorial Address: 16 Dean Road, HAMPTON, TW12 3JL
Tel: 020 8941 8263
Email: neil@mcintee.co.uk
Advertising Address: Progressive House, 2 Maidstone
Road, Foots Cray, SIDCUP, DA14 5HZ **Tel:** 020 8269 7856
Fax: 020 7324 2378
Email: l.dehoog@progressivemediagroup.com
Web site: http://www.whatvan.co.uk
ISSN: 1350-6404
Publisher: Progressive Media Publications
Date Established: 1987
Frequency: 11 issues yearly - Published on the 3rd
Wednesday of the month prior to cover date
Cover Price: £3.95
Free to qualifying individuals
Annual Sub.: £31.00
Circulation: 20,000 (Publisher's Statement)
Usual Pagination: 76
Editor: Neil McIntee
Summary of Content: Guide to buying new vans. Includes
prices, reviews and accessories.
Readership/Target Audience: Aimed at users, operators
and owners of vans.
ADVERTISING RATES:
Full Page Colour £2030.00
Agency Commission: 10%
Mechanical Data: Page Width: 190mm, Film: Digital, Type
Area: 272 x 190mm, Bleed Size: 303 x 216mm, Trim Size:
297 x 210mm, Col Length: 272mm
Copy instructions: Copy Date: 3 weeks prior to publication
date
CONSUMER: MOTORING & CYCLING: Motoring

WHAT VIDEO AND HIGH-DEFINITION TV

46525U78B-650

Formerly: What Video and Widescreen TV
Editorial Address: 2 Balcombe Street, LONDON, NW1 6NW
Tel: 020 7042 4000
Email: jday-williams@futurenet.com
Advertising Address: As above. **Fax:** 020 7042 4471
Email: angela.brown@futurenet.co.uk
Web site: http://www.whatvideotv.com
ISSN: 1352-6162
Publisher: Future Publishing Limited
Date Established: 1980
Frequency: 13 issues yearly
Cover Price: £3.99
Annual Sub.: £39.99
Circulation: 10,514 (ABC 01/01/2007 to 01/07/2007)
Usual Pagination: 172
Editor: Jake Day-Williams; **Advertising Manager:** Angela
Brown; **Publisher:** Andy Ford
Summary of Content: Magazine specialising in features and
tests on new televisions, video recorders, DVD decks,
plasma TV, LCD screens and home cinema systems.
Readership/Target Audience: Aimed at first time buyers,
those looking to upgrade and those that have a keen
interest.
ADVERTISING RATES:
Full Page Colour £2480.00
Agency Commission: 10%

Mechanical Data: Page Width: 181mm, Type Area: 266 x
181mm, Col Length: 266mm, Trim Size: 297 x 210mm, Bleed
Size: 307 x 215mm, Film: Digital
Copy instructions: Copy Date: 3 weeks prior to publication
date
Average advertising content per issue: 40%
CONSUMER: CONSUMER ELECTRONICS: Video & DVD

WHATBOAT?

1902266U91A-308

Editorial Address: Northam Road, Drivers Wharf,
SOUTHAMPTON, S014 0PF **Tel:** 0845 686 0645
Email: pcox@whatboat.com
Web site: http://www.whatboat.com
Publisher: Cox Publications
Frequency: 6 issues yearly
Cover Price: £3.49
Free to qualifying individuals
Circulation: 12,000 (Print Run)
Usual Pagination: 64
Editor: Philip Cox
Summary of Content: Magazine covering marine activity in
power and sails.
Readership/Target Audience: Aimed at people active with
boats.
ADVERTISING: Rates on application
CONSUMER: RECREATION & LEISURE: Boating & Yachting

WHAT'S BREWING

36510U94X-210

Editorial Address: 230 Hatfield Road, ST. ALBANS, AL1
4LW **Tel:** 01727 798454 **Fax:** 01727 848795
Email: tom.stainer@camra.org.uk
Advertising Address: Think Publishing Ltd, The Pall Mall
Deposit, 124-128 Barlby Road, LONDON, W10 6BL
Tel: 020 8962 1258 **Fax:** 020 8962 8689
Email: advertising@camra.org.uk
Web site: http://www.camra.org.uk
Publisher: Campaign for Real Ale Ltd
Date Established: 1973
Frequency: Monthly - Published first week of the month
Free to qualifying individuals
Annual Sub.: £22.00
Circulation: 90,000 (Publisher's Statement)
Usual Pagination: 16
Editor: Tom Stainer
Summary of Content: Newspaper containing brewing
reports, beer (real ale) and cider news. Includes articles on
traditional draught beer and regular features on
microbrewers, pub preservation, home brewing, bottles
beers, cooking with beer and campaigns.
Readership/Target Audience: Aimed at members of
CAMRA.
ADVERTISING RATES:
Full Page Mono £1925.00
Full Page Colour £2950.00
Agency Commission: 10%
Mechanical Data: Type Area: 380 x 262mm, Col Length:
380mm, Print Process: Web-fed offset litho, No. of Columns
(Display): 6, Film: Digital, Page Width: 262mm, Col Widths
(Display): 40mm
Copy instructions: Copy Date: 1st of month prior to
publication date
Average advertising content per issue: 45%
CONSUMER: OTHER CLASSIFICATIONS: Miscellaneous

WHAT'S ON

48154U89C-510

Editorial Address: Messenger House, New Hythe Lane,
Larkfield, AYLESFORD, ME20 6SG **Tel:** 01622 717880
Fax: 01622 715225
Email: whatsoneditor@thekmgroup.co.uk
Advertising Address: As above. **Fax:** 01622 719637
Email: jrutherford@thekmgroup.co.uk
Web site: http://www.kentonline.co.uk
Publisher: Kent Messenger Group
Frequency: Weekly
Cover Price: Free
Circulation: 1,000,000 (Publisher's Statement)
Usual Pagination: 36
Editor: Digby Kennard
Summary of Content: Magazine covering, events, celebrity
interviews, the arts, cinema and book reviews, previews
club, music and leisure in Kent as well as a weekly TV guide,
and What's On across the channel.
Readership/Target Audience: Aimed at Kent residents and
visitors to Kent.
ADVERTISING RATES:
SCC £16.95
Agency Commission: 10%
Mechanical Data: Col Widths (Display): 31mm, No. of
Columns (Display): 8, Type Area: 340 x 276mm, Col Length:
340mm, Page Width: 276mm
Copy instructions: Copy Date: Tuesday 11am prior to
publication date
CONSUMER: HOLIDAYS & TRAVEL: Entertainment Guides

WHAT'S ON & WHERE IN KENT

48189U89C-511

Editorial Address: 108 Wick Street, LITTLEHAMPTON,
BN17 7JS **Tel:** 0845 450 6605 **Fax:** 0845 450 6606
Email: studio@rwpgroup.com
Advertising Address: As above. **Tel:** 01903 732590
Fax: 01903 732592
Email: johnh@rwpgroup.com
Publisher: Real World Publishing Ltd
Frequency: Annual - Published in March
Cover Price: £2.00
Free to qualifying individuals
Circulation: 33,000 (Publisher's Statement)
Editor: Julia Elvidge; **Advertising Manager:** John Hollands
Summary of Content: Guide covering what to see and
where to eat, drink, stay, shop and travel. Includes a fold-out
map at the back, an events section, competitions and
listings.
Readership/Target Audience: Aimed at holiday makers
and local residents.
ADVERTISING RATES:
Full Page Colour £760.00
Agency Commission: 20%
Mechanical Data: Bleed Size: 216 x 154mm, Trim Size: 210
x 148mm, Film: Digital
Copy instructions: Copy Date: End of January prior to
publication date
Average advertising content per issue: 35%
CONSUMER: HOLIDAYS & TRAVEL: Entertainment Guides

WHAT'S ON & WHERE IN SUSSEX

48190U89C-512

Editorial Address: 108 Wick Street, LITTLEHAMPTON,
BN17 7JS **Tel:** 01903 732590 **Fax:** 01903 732592
Email: studio@realworldpublishing.com
Advertising Address: As above.
Email: info@rwpgroup.com
Web site: http://www.wowsussex.co.uk
Publisher: Real World Publishing Ltd
Frequency: Annual - Published in March
Cover Price: £2.00
Free to qualifying individuals
Circulation: 33,000 (Publisher's Statement)
Editor: Julia Elvidge
Summary of Content: Magazine covering tourist attractions
around Sussex including where to go, what to see, places to
eat, drink, shop and travel.
Readership/Target Audience: Aimed at holiday makers
and local residents.
ADVERTISING RATES:
Full Page Mono £594.00
Full Page Colour £660.00
Agency Commission: 20%
Mechanical Data: Trim Size: 210 x 148mm, Bleed Size: 216
x 154mm, Film: Digital
Copy instructions: Copy Date: 3 weeks prior to publication
date
Average advertising content per issue: 50%
CONSUMER: HOLIDAYS & TRAVEL: Entertainment Guides

WHAT'S ON AND WHERE TO GO - A NATIONWIDE GUIDE

713784U89C-514

Formerly: What's On and Where To Go in Northern England
and Wales
Editorial Address: 150 Burnley Road, ACCRINGTON, BB5
6DW **Tel:** 01254 390066 **Fax:** 01254 390077
Email: editorial@euromedia-al.com
Advertising Address: Unit 8, Chorley West Business Park,
Ackhurst Road, CHORLEY, PR7 1NL **Tel:** 0870 444 8955
Fax: 0870 444 8956
Email: sales@euromedia-al.com
ISSN: 0959-7375
Publisher: Euromedia Associates Ltd
Date Established: 1990
Frequency: Half-yearly - Published in spring and summer
Cover Price: £0.90
Free to qualifying individuals
Circulation: 30,000 (Publisher's Statement)
Usual Pagination: 130
Editor: Richard Cheesbrough; **Advertising Manager:** Emma
Higham
Summary of Content: Magazine providing tourist
information including where to stay and places of interest.
Special features on holiday and day out hotspots and
focuses on major tourist areas as well as small enterprises.
Readership/Target Audience: Aimed at tourists and
visitors to the north of England and Wales.
ADVERTISING RATES:
Full Page Mono £1150.00
Full Page Colour £1300.00
Agency Commission: 10%
Mechanical Data: Trim Size: 280 x 190mm, Film: Digital
Average advertising content per issue: 40%
CONSUMER: HOLIDAYS & TRAVEL: Entertainment Guides

WHAT'S ON EDINBURGH & LOTHIANS

48156U89C-535

Editorial Address: 208-210 Great Junction Street, EDINBURGH, EH6 5LW **Tel:** 0131 555 6667
Email: events@whatson-scotland.co.uk
Advertising Address: As above. **Fax:** 0131 555 2888
Email: sales@whatson-scotland.co.uk
Web site: http://www.whatson-scotland.co.uk
Publisher: What's On Publications
Date Established: 1984
Frequency: Monthly
Free to qualifying individuals
Annual Sub.: £10.00
Circulation: 40,000 (Publisher's Statement)
Usual Pagination: 40
Editor: Tom Hogarth; **Advertising Manager:** Tom Hogarth;
Publisher: Tom Hogarth
Summary of Content: Guide to events in Edinburgh and the Lothians.
Readership/Target Audience: Aimed at visitors and residents.
ADVERTISING RATES:
Full Page Colour £825.00
SCC £25.00
Agency Commission: 10%
Mechanical Data: Page Width: 138mm, Col Length: 195mm, Type Area: 195 x 138mm, Film: Digital
Copy instructions: Copy Date: 15 days prior to publication date
Average advertising content per issue: 40%
Editions:
What's on Angus and Dundee
What's on Loch Lomond, Stirling, The Trossachs & Forth Valley
What's on Perthshire
CONSUMER: HOLIDAYS & TRAVEL: Entertainment Guides

WHAT'S ON IN CHESTER & CHESHIRE GUIDE

1749881U89C-1079

Formerly: Welcome to Chester & Cheshire Guide
Editorial Address: Chester City Council, The Forum, CHESTER, CH1 2HS **Tel:** 01244 402150 **Fax:** 01244 315789
Email: g.tattum@chester.gov.uk
Advertising Address: As above. **Tel:** 01244 402445
Email: stephanie.jones@chester.gov.uk
Web site: http://www.chestertourism.gov.uk
Publisher: Chester City Council
Date Established: 2005
Frequency: Monthly
Cover Price: Free
Circulation: 20,000 (Publisher's Statement)
Usual Pagination: 36
Editor: Gerald Tattum
Summary of Content: Listings and lifestyle magazine covering eating out, shopping, things to see and do, fashion, beauty, news, where to stay, travel and leisure.
Readership/Target Audience: Aimed at visitors and residents of Chester and Cheshire.
ADVERTISING: Rates on application
Agency Commission: 10%
Copy instructions: Copy Date: 15th of the month prior to publication date
Average advertising content per issue: 50%
CONSUMER: HOLIDAYS & TRAVEL: Entertainment Guides

WHAT'S ON IN DORSET & THE NEW FOREST

48158U89C-575

Editorial Address: Lantern House, Lodge Drove, Woodfalls, SALISBURY, SP5 2NH **Tel:** 01725 512200
Email: whatson@phoenix-2.co.uk
Advertising Address: As above.
Email: whatson@phoenix-2.co.uk
Web site: http://www.whatsonindorset.info
Publisher: Phoenix 2
Date Established: 1980
Frequency: Half-yearly - Published in May and July
Cover Price: Free
Circulation: 100,000 (Publisher's Statement)
Usual Pagination: 20
Editor: Amanda Walker; **Advertising Manager:** Amanda Walker; **Publisher:** Amanda Walker
Summary of Content: Events, entertainment and attractions guide for Dorset, South Wiltshire and Hampshire.
Readership/Target Audience: Aimed at visitors to Dorset, South Wiltshire and Hampshire and residents of the area.
ADVERTISING RATES:
Full Page Mono £2625.00
Full Page Colour £2992.00
Agency Commission: 10%
Mechanical Data: Film: Digital, No. of Columns (Display): 6, Col Widths (Display): 44mm
Copy instructions: Copy Date: 4 weeks prior to publication date
Average advertising content per issue: 25%
CONSUMER: HOLIDAYS & TRAVEL: Entertainment Guides

WHAT'S ON IN EAST ANGLIA

48159U89C-580

Editorial Address: 101 Thunder Lane, NORWICH, NR7 0JG
Tel: 01603 433972
Email: profilepublishing@hotmail.co.uk
Advertising Address: As above.
Email: profilepublishing@hotmail.co.uk
Publisher: Profile Publishing & Design
Date Established: 1968
Frequency: Monthly
Cover Price: Free
Circulation: 12,000 (Publisher's Statement)
Editor: Steven Ford; **Features Editor:** Carolyn Norfolk-Smith; **Advertising Manager:** Nick Stevens
Summary of Content: County leisure and entertainment magazine for East Anglia. Covers book, video and record reviews, motoring and home features and fashion news.
Readership/Target Audience: Aimed at those living in East Anglia.
ADVERTISING RATES:
Full Page Mono £600.00
Full Page Colour £750.00
Agency Commission: 10%
Mechanical Data: Col Length: 270mm, Type Area: 270 x 190mm, No. of Columns (Display): 2, Print Process: Sheet-fed offset, Page Width: 190mm, Film: Digital
Copy instructions: Copy Date: 3rd week of month prior to publication date
Average advertising content per issue: 55%
CONSUMER: HOLIDAYS & TRAVEL: Entertainment Guides

WHAT'S ON SOMERSET

1832704U89C-1107

Editorial Address: 56 Station Road, TAUNTON, TA1 1NS
Tel: 01823 279008 **Fax:** 01823 279011
Email: whatsonsomerset@btinternet.com
Advertising Address: As above. **Tel:** 01823 2790008
Email: gilesadams@btinternet.com
Web site: http://www.whatsonsomerset.com
Publisher: Character Graphics
Date Established: 2007
Frequency: Quarterly
Cover Price: Free
Circulation: 20,000 (Publisher's Statement)
Usual Pagination: 32
Editor: Giles Adams; **Advertising Manager:** Giles Adams
Summary of Content: Magazine covering a wide variety of entertainment listings and features about interesting people and activities in Somerset.
Readership/Target Audience: Aimed at residents and visitors to Somerset.
ADVERTISING RATES:
Full Page Colour £998.00
Agency Commission: 15%
Mechanical Data: Trim Size: 297 x 210mm, Film: Digital
CONSUMER: HOLIDAYS & TRAVEL: Entertainment Guides

WHAT'S ON STAGE

626541U89C-385

Formerly: Theatregoer
Editorial Address: 5th Floor, Palace Theatre, 109-113 Shaftsbury Avenue, LONDON, W1V 5AY **Tel:** 020 7317 9104
Email: editorial@whatsonstage.com
Advertising Address: As above. **Tel:** 020 7907 7043
Fax: 0871 661 8591
Email: richard@whatsonstage.com
Web site: http://www.whatsonstage.com
Publisher: Bandwidth Communications Ltd.
Date Established: 2000
Frequency: 10 issues yearly
Free to qualifying individuals
Annual Sub.: £30.00
Circulation: 80,000 (Publisher's Statement)
Usual Pagination: 48
Editor: Roger Foss
Summary of Content: Magazine covering London and UK theatre news, reviews, interviews and previews.
Readership/Target Audience: Aimed at UK theatre and performing arts and audiences.
ADVERTISING RATES:
Full Page Colour £1800.00
Agency Commission: 10%
Mechanical Data: Bleed Size: 216 x 151mm, Trim Size: 210 x 148mm, Film: Digital, Type Area: 190 x 128mm, Col Length: 190mm, Page Width: 128mm
Average advertising content per issue: 30%
CONSUMER: HOLIDAYS & TRAVEL: Entertainment Guides

WHAT'S ON TV

46122U76C-820

Editorial Address: Blue Fin Building, 110 Southwark Street, LONDON, SE1 0SU **Tel:** 020 3148 5000
Email: colin_tough@ipcmedia.com
Advertising Address: As above.
Email: richard_smith@ipcmedia.com
Web site: http://www.whatsontv.co.uk
Publisher: IPC TX
Date Established: 1991
Frequency: Weekly
Cover Price: £0.47

Circulation: 1,272,586 (ABC 01/01/2009 to 30/06/2009)
Usual Pagination: 92
Editor: Colin Tough; **Features Editor:** Jo Lewis; **Advertising Manager:** Richard Smith
Summary of Content: Magazine covering TV listings, TV features, celebrity gossip and reviews.
Readership/Target Audience: Aimed at those interested in TV and radio programmes.
ADVERTISING RATES:
Full Page Colour £21260.00
Agency Commission: 15%
Mechanical Data: Film: Digital
CONSUMER: MUSIC & PERFORMING ARTS: TV & Radio

WHATSONUK GUIDES

749623U74Q-979

Editorial Address: PO Box 6160, BIRMINGHAM, B16 8XA
Tel: 0121 245 0000 **Fax:** 0121 245 0009
Email: editorial@whatson.uk.com
Advertising Address: As above.
Email: sales@whatson.uk.com
Web site: http://www.whatson.uk.com
ISSN: 1356-9023
Publisher: City Guides Ltd
Date Established: 1989
Frequency: Monthly
Cover Price: £2.50
Free to qualifying individuals
Circulation: 50,000 (Publisher's Statement)
Usual Pagination: 40
Editor: Peter Harris; **Advertising Manager:** Sam Alim
Summary of Content: Series of guides covering clubs, fashion, multicultural issues, politics, festivals, student issues and homosexual interests.
Readership/Target Audience: Aimed at young, pro-active people interested in contemporary and pop culture between 18 to 25 years old.
ADVERTISING RATES:
Full Page Colour £1800.00
Agency Commission: 15%
Copy instructions: Copy Date: 15th of the month prior to publication date
CONSUMER: WOMEN'S INTEREST CONSUMER MAGAZINES: Lifestyle

WHEN SATURDAY COMES

45784U75B-250

Editorial Address: 17A Perseverance Works, 38 Kingsland Road, LONDON, E2 8DD **Tel:** 020 7729 1110
Fax: 020 7729 9417
Email: editorial@wsc.co.uk
Advertising Address: Space Matters Ltd, 7 Burgess Mews, 38 Wycliffe Road, LONDON, SW19 1UF **Tel:** 020 8543 4445
Fax: 020 8540 6661
Email: georgey@spacematters.co.uk
Web site: http://www.wsc.co.uk
ISSN: 0959-0048
Publisher: When Saturday Comes Ltd
Date Established: 1986
Frequency: Monthly
Cover Price: £2.50
Circulation: 19,026 (ABC 01/01/2008 to 31/12/2008)
Usual Pagination: 48
Editor: Andy Lyons; **Advertising Manager:** George Young;
Publisher: Richard Guy
Summary of Content: Magazine containing articles on football culture from the supporters' viewpoint.
Readership/Target Audience: Aimed at men between 18 and 34 years old.
ADVERTISING RATES:
Full Page Colour £2100.00
SCC £20.00
Agency Commission: 10%
Mechanical Data: Film: Digital, Bleed Size: 303 x 216mm, Trim Size: 297 x 210mm
Copy instructions: Copy Date: 2 weeks prior to publication date
Average advertising content per issue: 10%
CONSUMER: SPORT: Football

WHERE LONDON

48168U89C-660

Editorial Address: 233 High Holborn, LONDON, WC1V 7DN
Tel: 020 7242 5222 **Fax:** 020 7242 4184
Email: sandrae.lawrence@morriseurope.com
Advertising Address: As above.
Email: andrew.turner@morriseurope.com
Web site: http://wheretraveler.com/classic/intl/uk/london/
ISSN: 0951-323X
Publisher: MVP Europe
Date Established: 1974
Frequency: Monthly
Free to qualifying individuals
Annual Sub.: £48.00
Circulation: 72,735 (Publisher's Statement)
Usual Pagination: 76
Editor: Sandrae Lawrence
Summary of Content: Magazine covering dining, shopping, entertainment etc information in London.

Consumer Magazines

Readership/Target Audience: Aimed at travelers that are planning to visit London.
ADVERTISING RATES:
Full Page Colour £3385.00
Agency Commission: 10%
Mechanical Data: Bleed Size: +3mm, Film: Digital
Copy instructions: Copy Date: 6th of the month prior to publication date
Average advertising content per issue: 50%
Supplement(s): Society of the Golden Keys Map - 1xY, Where London Dining - 1xY
CONSUMER: HOLIDAYS & TRAVEL: Entertainment Guides

WHICH?
45295U74C-560
Editorial Address: 2 Marylebone Road, LONDON, NW1 4DF
Tel: 020 7770 7000 **Fax:** 020 7770 7655
Email: brcpress@which.co.uk
Web site: http://www.which.co.uk
Publisher: Which? Ltd
Frequency: Monthly
Cover Price: £6.25
Annual Sub.: £75.00
Circulation: 516,000 (Publisher's Statement)
Editor: Chris Matthews
Summary of Content: Magazine containing product tests and campaigns for improvements in goods and services.
Readership/Target Audience: Aimed at consumers who want the best products and services.
ADVERTISING: No Advertising taken
CONSUMER: WOMEN'S INTEREST CONSUMER MAGAZINES: Home & Family

WHICH CARAVAN
48420U91B-30
Formerly: Caravan Life
Editorial Address: The Maltings, West Street, BOURNE, PE10 9PH **Tel:** 01778 391000 **Fax:** 01778 425437
Email: sallyp@warnersgroup.co.uk
Advertising Address: As above.
Email: saml@warnersgroup.co.uk
Web site: http://www.whichcaravan.co.uk
ISSN: 0957-6282
Publisher: Warners Group Publications plc
Date Established: 1987
Frequency: Monthly
Cover Price: £3.15
Annual Sub.: £29.99
Circulation: 11,000 (Publisher's Statement)
Usual Pagination: 104
Editor: Sally Pepper; **Managing Director:** Stephen Warner; **Advertising Manager:** Sam Lewis; **Publisher:** John Greenwood
Summary of Content: Magazine covering all aspects of caravanning including new and second-hand caravans, product testing, tow car reports and site reports.
Readership/Target Audience: Read by caravanning enthusiasts.
ADVERTISING RATES:
Full Page Mono £950.00
Full Page Colour £1410.00
Agency Commission: 10%
Mechanical Data: Type Area: 275 x 190mm, Bleed Size: 303 x 216mm, Trim Size: 297 x 210mm, Col Length: 275mm, Page Width: 190mm, Film: Digital
Copy instructions: Copy Date: 3 weeks prior to publication date
Average advertising content per issue: 60%
CONSUMER: RECREATION & LEISURE: Camping & Caravanning

WHICH? COMPUTING
624663U78E-35
Formerly: Computing Which?
Editorial Address: 2 Marylebone Road, LONDON, NW1 4DF
Tel: 020 7770 7000 **Fax:** 020 7770 7671
Email: computing@which.co.uk
Publisher: Which? Ltd
Date Established: 2000
Frequency: 6 issues yearly
Annual Sub.: £31.00
Circulation: 150,000 (Publisher's Statement)
Usual Pagination: 68
Editor: Sarah Kidner
Summary of Content: Magazine covering computers and the internet with sections - news, advice, buying and testing.
Readership/Target Audience: Aimed at home computer owners.
ADVERTISING: No Advertising taken
CONSUMER: CONSUMER ELECTRONICS: Home Computing

WHICH COURSE?
47924U88C-150
Editorial Address: Northcliffe House, 2 Derry Street, LONDON, W8 5TT **Tel:** 020 7005 2000 **Fax:** 020 7005 2273
Email: whichcourse@independent.co.uk
Advertising Address: As above. **Fax:** 020 7005 2922
Email: m.simmons@independent.co.uk

Web site: http://www.independent.co.uk
Publisher: Independent News and Media (UK) Ltd
Frequency: Half-yearly
Cover Price: Free
Circulation: 20,000 (Publisher's Statement)
Usual Pagination: 36
Editor: Dan Poole; **Advertising Manager:** Marcus Simmons
Summary of Content: Publication providing advice and information on higher and further education.
Readership/Target Audience: Aimed at the 16 to 19 year old age group.
ADVERTISING RATES:
Full Page Colour £3480.00
Agency Commission: 10%
Mechanical Data: Trim Size: 280 x 210mm, Bleed Size: 286 x 216mm, Film: Digital, Type Area: 253 x 190mm
Average advertising content per issue: 40%
CONSUMER: EDUCATION: Careers

WHICH? HOLIDAY
47961U89A-345
Formerly: Holiday Which?
Editorial Address: 2 Marylebone Road, LONDON, NW1 4DF
Tel: 020 7770 7000 **Fax:** 020 7770 7663
Email: lorna.cowan@which.co.uk
Web site: http://www.which.co.uk/holiday
Publisher: Which? Ltd
Date Established: 1974
Frequency: Quarterly
Annual Sub.: £24.00
Usual Pagination: 60
Editor: Lorna Cowan
Summary of Content: Magazine containing reports on holiday destinations and related consumer issues.
Readership/Target Audience: Read by discerning members of the general public.
ADVERTISING: No Advertising taken
CONSUMER: HOLIDAYS & TRAVEL: Travel

WHICH? MONEY
1804123U74M-438
Editorial Address: 2 Marylebone Road, LONDON, NW1 4DF
Tel: 020 7770 7000 **Fax:** 020 7770 7655
Email: james.daley@which.co.uk
Web site: http://www.which.co.uk
Publisher: Which? Ltd
Frequency: Monthly
Cover Price: £3.00
Editor: James Daley
Summary of Content: Independent source of information on personal finance.
Readership/Target Audience: Aimed at consumers.
CONSUMER: WOMEN'S INTEREST CONSUMER MAGAZINES: Personal Finance

WHICH MOTORCARAVAN
48431U91B-300
Editorial Address: The Maltings, West Street, BOURNE, PE10 9PH **Tel:** 01778 391118 **Fax:** 01778 425437
Email: peterv@warnersgroup.co.uk
Advertising Address: As above. **Tel:** 01778 391027
Email: fleurb@warnersgroup.co.uk
Web site: http://www.outandaboutlive.co.uk
ISSN: 0950-9291
Publisher: Warners Group Publications plc
Date Established: 1986
Frequency: Monthly
Cover Price: £3.25
Annual Sub.: £35.40
Circulation: 7,199 (ABC 01/01/2008 to 31/12/2008)
Usual Pagination: 180
Editor: Peter Vaughan; **Publisher:** John Greenwood
Summary of Content: Magazine containing road tests, reviews of new equipment and ideas for motor caravan holidays.
Readership/Target Audience: Aimed at buyers of new and second hand motor caravans.
ADVERTISING RATES:
Full Page Mono £495.00
Full Page Colour £715.00
Agency Commission: 10%
Mechanical Data: Bleed Size: 303 x 216mm, Trim Size: 297 x 210mm, Type Area: 275 x 190mm, Col Length: 275mm, Page Width: 190mm, Film: Positive, right reading, emulsion side down. Digital
CONSUMER: RECREATION & LEISURE: Camping & Caravanning

WHISKY MAGAZINE
45296U74P-903
Editorial Address: St. Faiths House, Mountergate, NORWICH, NR1 1PY **Tel:** 01603 633808 **Fax:** 01603 632808
Email: editorial@whiskymag.com
Advertising Address: As above.
Email: info@whiskymag.com
Web site: http://www.whiskymag.com
Publisher: Paragraph Publishing
Date Established: 1998

Frequency: 8 issues yearly
Cover Price: £4.25
Annual Sub.: £34.00
Circulation: 30,000 (Publisher's Statement)
Usual Pagination: 84
Editor: Rob Allanson
Summary of Content: Magazine covering news, products, celebrity interviews, whisky tasting plus events and features from around the world.
Readership/Target Audience: Aimed at whisky connoisseurs, enthusiasts and novices.
ADVERTISING RATES:
Full Page Colour £4845.00
Agency Commission: 10%
Mechanical Data: Type Area: 258 x 180mm, Page Width: 180mm, Col Length: 258mm, Film: Digital, Bleed Size: 291 x 221mm, Trim Size: 285 x 215mm
Copy instructions: Copy Date: 4 weeks prior to publication date
Average advertising content per issue: 40%
CONSUMER: WOMEN'S INTEREST CONSUMER MAGAZINES: Food & Cookery

WHITE DWARF
46770U79L-380
Editorial Address: Willow Road, Lenton, NOTTINGHAM, NG7 2WS **Tel:** 0115 916 8000 **Fax:** 0115 916 8001
Email: mark.latham@games-workshop.co.uk
Web site: http://www.games-workshop.co.uk
ISSN: 0265-8712
Publisher: Games Workshop Ltd
Date Established: 1977
Frequency: Monthly
Cover Price: £4.00
Circulation: 55,000 (Publisher's Statement)
Usual Pagination: 128
Editor: Mark Latham; **Circulation Manager:** Andy Jones
Summary of Content: Magazine covering all aspects of science fiction and fantasy war gaming. Includes painting guides, models, new products and Games Workshop's own range of game systems.
Language(s): English; French; German; Italian; Spanish
Readership/Target Audience: Aimed at those with an interest in fantasy war games.
ADVERTISING: No Advertising taken
CONSUMER: HOBBIES & DIY: Fantasy Games & Science Fiction

WHITE LINES SNOWBOARD MAGAZINE
45882U75G-650
Formerly: White Lines Snowboarding Magazine
Editorial Address: 1 West Smithfield, LONDON, EC1A 9JU
Tel: 020 7332 9700 **Fax:** 020 7332 9799
Email: info@whitelines.com
Advertising Address: As above.
Email: craig.scrivener@factorymedia.com
Web site: http://www.network26.com
Publisher: Factory Media
Date Established: 1995
Frequency: 6 issues yearly - Published monthly from October to March
Cover Price: £4.95
Annual Sub.: £27.95
Circulation: 30,000 (Publisher's Statement)
Usual Pagination: 164
Editor: Ed Blomfield; **Advertising Manager:** Craig Scrivener; **Publisher:** Darryl Newton
Summary of Content: Magazine covering all aspects of snowboarding.
Readership/Target Audience: Aimed at snowboarding enthusiasts aged between 13 and 35 years old.
ADVERTISING RATES:
Full Page Colour £1600.00
Agency Commission: 10%
Mechanical Data: Bleed Size: 286 x 236mm, Trim Size: 280 x 230mm, Film: Digital, Print Process: Sheet-fed litho, Type Area: 274 x 224mm, Col Length: 274mm, Page Width: 224mm
Copy instructions: Copy Date: 1st week of the month prior to the publication date
Average advertising content per issue: 40%
CONSUMER: SPORT: Winter Sports

WHITE WEDDING PAGES
1820182U74L-266
Editorial Address: 90 Main Street, Saintfield, BALLYNAHINCH, BT24 7AB **Tel:** 028 9751 2665
Fax: 028 9751 1030
Email: info@whiteweddingpages.net
Advertising Address: As above.
Email: info@whiteweddingpages.net
Web site: http://www.whiteweddingpages.net
Publisher: White Wedding Pages Ltd
Date Established: 2006
Frequency: Quarterly
Cover Price: £3.95
Circulation: 10,172 (Publisher's Statement)

Editor: Anna Bailie; **Advertising Manager:** Mairead Hendry; **Publisher:** Tanya Doory
Summary of Content: Magazine covering all aspects of weddings from bridal gowns to balloons and men's hire to Mum's hat.
Readership/Target Audience: Aimed at those planning a wedding.
ADVERTISING RATES:
Full Page Colour £800.00
Mechanical Data: Trim Size: 285 x 220mm, Bleed Size: 291 x 226mm
CONSUMER: WOMEN'S INTEREST CONSUMER MAGAZINES: Brides

WHO'S JACK
1799750U76D-831
Editorial Address: 93 Barker Drive, Camden, LONDON, NW1 0JG **Tel:** 07595 366196
Email: louise@whos-jack.co.uk
Advertising Address: As above. **Tel:** 07789 393118
Email: louise@whos-jack.co.uk
Web site: http://www.whos-jack.co.uk
Publisher: Who's Jack
Frequency: 6 issues yearly
Cover Price: Free
Circulation: 10,000 (Publisher's Statement)
Usual Pagination: 52
Editor: Louise Orcheston-Findlay; **Advertising Manager:** Louise Orcheston-Findlay
Summary of Content: Magazine covering new grassroots upwards music, fashion, art, the London scene and opinion.
Readership/Target Audience: Aimed at men and women aged 18 to 30 years old.
ADVERTISING RATES:
Full Page Colour £600.00
Mechanical Data: Bleed Size: +3mm, Film: Digital
Copy instructions: Copy Date: 2 weeks prior to publication date
Average advertising content per issue: 30%
CONSUMER: MUSIC & PERFORMING ARTS: Music

WI LIFE
1800093U74A-1031
Editorial Address: 104 New King's Road, Fulham, LONDON, SW6 4LY **Tel:** 020 7731 5777 **Fax:** 020 7736 4061
Email: n.maidment@nfwi.org.uk
Advertising Address: As above. **Fax:** 020 7371 0912
Email: d.ebejer@nfwi.org.uk
Web site: http://www.thewi.org.uk
Publisher: National Federation of Women's Institutes
Date Established: 2007
Frequency: 8 issues yearly
Free to qualifying individuals
Circulation: 202,898 (ABC 01/07/2008 to 31/12/2008)
Usual Pagination: 76
Editor: Neal Maidment; **Features Editor:** Sheila Purcell
Summary of Content: Magazine covering national and county WI news and members and their activities as well as cookery, gardening, books, health and crafts.
Readership/Target Audience: Aimed at members of the WI in England and Wales.
ADVERTISING RATES:
Full Page Colour £11775.00
Agency Commission: 10%
Mechanical Data: Type Area: 265 x 185mm, Bleed Size: 303 x 213mm, Trim Size: 297 x 210mm, Col Length: 265mm, Page Width: 185mm, Print Process: Web-fed offset litho, Film: Digital
Average advertising content per issue: 30%
CONSUMER: WOMEN'S INTEREST CONSUMER MAGAZINES: Women's Interest

WI NEWS (ESSEX)
45219U74A-615
Editorial Address: The Publishing House, Station Road, Framlingham, WOODBRIDGE, IP13 9EE **Tel:** 01728 622030
Fax: 01728 622031
Advertising Address: As above.
Publisher: Today Magazines Ltd
Frequency: Monthly
Circulation: 12,500 (Publisher's Statement)
Usual Pagination: 16
Editor: Brenda Davis; **Advertising Manager:** Tracy Pyke; **Publisher:** Brenda Davis
Summary of Content: Magazine featuring news and views of The Women's Institutes.
Readership/Target Audience: Aimed at Women's Institute members in Essex.
ADVERTISING: Rates on application
Agency Commission: 10%
Copy instructions: Copy Date: 2nd of the month prior to publication date
Average advertising content per issue: 40%
CONSUMER: WOMEN'S INTEREST CONSUMER MAGAZINES: Women's Interest

WI NEWS MAGAZINE (SUFFOLK EAST)
45221U74A-616
Formerly: WI Newws Magazine (Suffolk East)
Editorial Address: The Publishing House, Station Road, Framlingham, WOODBRIDGE, IP13 9EE **Tel:** 01728 622030
Fax: 01728 622031
Email: todaymagazines@btopenworld.com
Advertising Address: As above. **Tel:** 01782 622030
Fax: 01782 622031
Email: info@todaymagazines.co.uk
Publisher: Today Magazines Ltd
Date Established: 1989
Frequency: Monthly
Circulation: 5,500 (Publisher's Statement)
Usual Pagination: 16
Editor: Jenny Wilkinson; **Publisher:** Brenda Davis
Summary of Content: Magazine featuring news and views of The Women's Institutes.
Readership/Target Audience: Aimed at Women's Institute members in East Suffolk.
ADVERTISING: Rates on application
Copy instructions: Copy Date: 2 weeks prior to publication date
CONSUMER: WOMEN'S INTEREST CONSUMER MAGAZINES: Women's Interest

WI NEWS MAGAZINE (SUFFOLK WEST)
45222U74A-617
Editorial Address: The Publishing House, Station Road, Framlingham, WOODBRIDGE, IP13 9EE **Tel:** 01728 622030
Fax: 01728 622031
Advertising Address: As above.
Publisher: Today Magazines Ltd
Date Established: 1989
Frequency: Monthly
Circulation: 5,500 (Publisher's Statement)
Usual Pagination: 16
Editor: Brenda Davis; **Advertising Manager:** Brenda Davis; **Publisher:** Brenda Davis
Summary of Content: Magazine featuring news and views of The Women's Institutes.
Readership/Target Audience: Aimed at Women's Institute members in West Suffolk.
ADVERTISING RATES:
Full Page Colour £834.00
Agency Commission: 10%
Mechanical Data: Trim Size: 297 x 210mm, Type Area: 278 x 185mm, Col Length: 278mm, Page Width: 185mm
Copy instructions: Copy Date: 6th of the month prior to publication date
Average advertising content per issue: 40%
CONSUMER: WOMEN'S INTEREST CONSUMER MAGAZINES: Women's Interest

WI NEWS MAGAZINE (WEST KENT)
45223U74A-618
Editorial Address: The Publishing House, Station Road, Framlingham, WOODBRIDGE, IP13 9EE **Tel:** 01728 622030
Fax: 01728 622031
Advertising Address: As above.
Publisher: Today Magazines Ltd
Date Established: 1995
Frequency: Monthly
Circulation: 10,500 (Publisher's Statement)
Usual Pagination: 16
Editor: Anne France; **Advertising Manager:** Brenda Davis; **Publisher:** Brenda Davis
Summary of Content: Magazine featuring news and views of The Women's Institute.
Readership/Target Audience: Aimed at members in West Kent.
ADVERTISING RATES:
Full Page Colour £834.50
Agency Commission: 10%
Mechanical Data: Page Width: 185mm, Type Area: 278 x 185mm, Trim Size: 297 x 210mm, Col Length: 278mm
Copy instructions: Copy Date: 4th of the month prior to publication date
Average advertising content per issue: 40%
CONSUMER: WOMEN'S INTEREST CONSUMER MAGAZINES: Women's Interest

WIGAN COURIER
1657032U80C-5468
Editorial Address: Suite 116, The Standish Centre, Cross Street, Standish, WIGAN, WN6 0HQ **Tel:** 01257 400026
Fax: 01257 400078
Email: info@courier-online.net
Advertising Address: As above.
Email: info@courier-online.net
Web site: http://www.wigancourier.co.uk
Publisher: Standish Media Services Ltd
Date Established: 1998
Frequency: 18 issues yearly
Cover Price: Free
Circulation: 32,400 (Publisher's Statement)

Usual Pagination: 80
Editor: Michelle Hafez
Summary of Content: Newspaper which published good local news as well as entertainment, business, property, classifieds, body and soul, weddings and cinema.
Readership/Target Audience: Aimed at households in Wigan and the surrounding areas.
ADVERTISING RATES:
Full Page Colour £680.00
SCC £5.00
Agency Commission: 10%
Mechanical Data: Type Area: 340 x 266mm, Col Length: 340mm, Page Width: 266mm, Col Widths (Display): 30.6mm, No. of Columns (Display): 8, Film: Digital, Print Process: Web-fed offset litho
Average advertising content per issue: 65%
CONSUMER: RURAL & REGIONAL INTEREST: Regional Interest English Counties

WILDLIFE (SUSSEX WILDLIFE TRUST)
712282U81A-185
Formerly: Wildlife (Sussex)
Editorial Address: Woods Mill, Shoreham Road, HENFIELD, BN5 9SD **Tel:** 01273 492630 **Fax:** 01273 494500
Email: amandasolomon@sussexwt.org.uk
Advertising Address: Space Marketing, 10 Clayfield Mews, Newcomen Road, TUNBRIDGE WELLS, TN4 9PA
Tel: 01892 677740 **Fax:** 01892 677743
Email: sales@spacemarketing.co.uk
Web site: http://www.sussexwt.org.uk
Publisher: Sussex Wildlife Trust
Date Established: 1961
Frequency: 3 issues yearly - Published in January, April and September
Free to qualifying individuals
Circulation: 25,000 (Publisher's Statement)
Usual Pagination: 32
Editor: Amanda Solomon; **Advertising Manager:** Brian Shilling
Summary of Content: Magazine covering wildlife conservation in Sussex including a diary of events.
Readership/Target Audience: Aimed at members of the Trust in Sussex.
ADVERTISING RATES:
Full Page Mono £494.00
Full Page Colour £605.00
Agency Commission: 10%
Mechanical Data: Col Widths (Display): 89mm, No. of Columns (Display): 2, Film: Digital, Col Length: 260mm, Page Width: 186mm, Type Area: 260 x 186mm
Average advertising content per issue: 17%
CONSUMER: ANIMALS & PETS: Animals & Pets Protection

WILDSCAPE
1616016U94X-260
Editorial Address: Greenways, Bridge Road, Lower Hardres, CANTERBURY, CT4 7AG **Tel:** 01227 464739
Email: info@wildscapemag.co.uk
Advertising Address: As above.
Email: info@wildscapemag.co.uk
Web site: http://www.wildscapemag.co.uk/
Publisher: Darwin Publishing
Date Established: 2001
Frequency: Quarterly
Cover Price: £3.50
Annual Sub.: £20.00
Circulation: 2,000 (Publisher's Statement)
Usual Pagination: 36
Editor: Ken Stroud; **Advertising Manager:** Roger Diamond; **Publisher:** Ken Stroud
Summary of Content: Magazine focusing on the interests of wildlife and animal artists. Covering a wide variety of subjects including conservation issues and containing, all art mediums, photography and in-depth and informative articles by some of the leading exponents of the genre, also includes competitions.
Readership/Target Audience: Aimed at artists and collectors of animal artworks and those interested in wildlife art and conservation.
ADVERTISING RATES:
Full Page Mono £400.00
Full Page Colour £400.00
Agency Commission: 10%
Mechanical Data: Col Length: 276mm, Type Area: 276 x 191mm, Print Process: Offset litho, Bleed Size: 303 x 216mm, Trim Size: 297 x 210mm, No. of Columns (Display): 2, Col Widths (Display): 93mm, Page Width: 191mm
Copy instructions: Copy Date: 1st week of the month prior to publication date
Average advertising content per issue: 10%
CONSUMER: OTHER CLASSIFICATIONS: Miscellaneous

WILTSHIRE LIFE
47004U80C-3570
Editorial Address: Jesses Farm, Snow Hill, Dinton, SALISBURY, SP3 5HN **Tel:** 01722 716996
Fax: 01722 716926
Email: wl@markallengroup.co.uk
Advertising Address: As above.

Consumer Magazines

Email: lisa.s@markallengroup.co.uk
Web site: http://www.wiltshirelife.co.uk
Publisher: A & D Media Ltd
Date Established: 1946
Frequency: Monthly
Cover Price: £3.99
Annual Sub.: £50.00
(Publisher's Statement)
Usual Pagination: 90
Editor: Claire Waring; **Advertising Manager:** Lisa Saunders;
Managing Editor: Claire Waring; **Publisher:** Fiona Richards
Summary of Content: Regional magazine with features on village life, walking, local history, food and drink, local issues, gardening and arts and crafts. Each month it focuses on different towns and villages throughout Wiltshire and special features include subjects such as independent schools, weddings, interiors, restaurants, days out, motoring and healthy living.
Readership/Target Audience: Read by Wiltshire residents and those living on the borders and ex-pats.
ADVERTISING RATES:
Full Page Colour £835.00
Agency Commission: 10%
Mechanical Data: Type Area: 263 x 195mm, Bleed Size: 303 x 236mm, Trim Size: 297 x 230mm, Col Length: 263mm, Film: Digital, Page Width: 195mm
Copy instructions: Copy Date: 2nd Friday of the cover month
Average advertising content per issue: 45%
CONSUMER: RURAL & REGIONAL INTEREST: Regional Interest English Counties

WILTSHIRE SOCIETY
713388U80C-1680

Formerly: Limited Edition (South Wiltshire and West Hampshire)
Editorial Address: Rollestone House, 8-12 Rollestone Street, SALISBURY, SP1 1DY **Tel:** 01722 426506
Fax: 01722 321854
Email: sarah.mcquillen@salisburyjournal.co.uk
Advertising Address: As above. **Tel:** 01722 426570
Fax: 01722 426591
Email: eleanor.sillett@salisburyjournal.co.uk
Web site: http://www.salisburyjournal.co.uk
Publisher: Salisbury Newspapers Ltd
Frequency: Monthly
Cover Price: Free
Circulation: 31,000 (Publisher's Statement)
Usual Pagination: 100
Editor: Sarah McQuillen
Summary of Content: Magazine covering local issues and including features on fashion, beauty, travel, shopping, entertainment and places of local interest.
Readership/Target Audience: Aimed primarily at women, living in AB1 households in the South Wiltshire and West Hampshire area.
ADVERTISING RATES:
Full Page Colour £475.00
Mechanical Data: Type Area: 273 x 186mm, Col Length: 273mm, Trim Size: 297 x 210mm, Film: Digital, Page Width: 186mm, Bleed Size: 303 x 216mm
Copy instructions: Copy Date: 2 weeks prior to publication date
Average advertising content per issue: 50%
CONSUMER: RURAL & REGIONAL INTEREST: Regional Interest English Counties

WINDOWS VISTA: THE OFFICIAL MAGAZINE
1789970U78E-54

Editorial Address: 30 Monmouth Street, BATH, BA1 2BW
Tel: 01225 442244
Email: windowsvistamagazine@futurenet.com
Advertising Address: As above. **Fax:** 01225 822885
Email: steve.grigg@futurenet.co.uk
Web site: http://www.windowsvistamagazine.co.uk
Publisher: Future Publishing Ltd
Date Established: 2006
Frequency: 13 issues yearly
Cover Price: £4.99
Circulation: 22,017 (ABC 01/07/2008 to 31/12/2008)
Editor: Adam Isans; **Advertising Manager:** Steve Grigg
Summary of Content: Magazine inspiring consumers to get more from their interests and activities using Windows technology.
Readership/Target Audience: Aimed at home computer users.
ADVERTISING RATES:
Full Page Mono £3500.00
Full Page Colour £3500.00
Agency Commission: 10%
Mechanical Data: Type Area: 270 x 190mm, Bleed Size: 303 x 216mm, Trim Size: 297 x 210mm, Col Length: 270mm, Page Width: 190mm, Film: Digital
Copy instructions: Copy Date: 4 weeks prior to publication date
CONSUMER: CONSUMER ELECTRONICS: Home Computing

WINDS
46188U76D-450

Editorial Address: Y Fron, Llansadwrn, MENAI BRIDGE, LL59 5SL **Tel:** 01248 811285
Email: windsmagazine@btinternet.com
Advertising Address: As above.
Email: windsmagazine@btinternet.com
Web site: http://www.basbwe.org
ISSN: 1470-563X
Publisher: BASBWE
Date Established: 1981
Frequency: Quarterly
Cover Price: £3.95
Free to qualifying individuals
Annual Sub.: £12.00
Circulation: 1,000 (Publisher's Statement)
Usual Pagination: 32
Editor: Richard Edwards; **Advertising Manager:** Richard Edwards
Summary of Content: Journal of the British Association of Symphonic Bands and Wind Ensembles. Includes music and book reviews, composer interviews, band profiles and articles on teaching and conducting.
Readership/Target Audience: Aimed at members and wind band conductors.
ADVERTISING RATES:
Full Page Mono £360.00
Full Page Colour £500.00
Mechanical Data: Page Width: 186mm, Type Area: 270 x 186mm, Col Length: 270mm, Trim Size: 297 x 210mm, Bleed Size: 303 x 216mm, Film: Digital
Copy instructions: Copy Date: 4 weeks prior to publication date
Average advertising content per issue: 25%
CONSUMER: MUSIC & PERFORMING ARTS: Music

WINDSURF MAGAZINE
45962U75M-980

Editorial Address: The Blue Barns, Tew Lane, Wootton, WOODSTOCK, OX20 1HA **Tel:** 01993 811181
Fax: 01993 811481
Email: sarah@windsurf.co.uk
Advertising Address: As above.
Email: dan@windsurf.co.uk
Web site: http://www.windsurf.co.uk
ISSN: 0958-5500
Publisher: Arcwind Ltd
Date Established: 1980
Frequency: 10 issues yearly - Combined issues November/December and January/February
Cover Price: £4.10
Free to qualifying individuals
Annual Sub.: £34.00
Circulation: 22,070 (Publisher's Statement)
Usual Pagination: 124
Editor: Sarah Cotton; **Features Editor:** Sarah Cotton; **Publisher:** Mark Kasprowicz
Summary of Content: Magazine covering all aspects of windsurfing, including new products, equipment and techniques.
Readership/Target Audience: Aimed at windsurfing enthusiasts.
ADVERTISING RATES:
Full Page Colour £1165.00
SCC £15.00
Agency Commission: 10%
Mechanical Data: Trim Size: 285 x 230mm, Type Area: 261 x 206mm, Bleed Size: 292 x 242mm, Col Length: 261mm, Film: Digital, Page Width: 206mm, Col Widths (Display): 100mm, No. of Columns (Display): 2
Copy instructions: Copy Date: 4 weeks prior to publication date
Average advertising content per issue: 40%
CONSUMER: SPORT: Water Sports

WINE & DINE IN NORTHERN IRELAND
601134U94G-300

Editorial Address: 39 Boucher Road, BELFAST, BT12 6UT
Tel: 028 9066 3311 **Fax:** 028 9038 1915
Email: edit@ulstertatler.com
Advertising Address: As above.
Email: ccorr@ulstertatler.com
Web site: http://www.ulstertatler.com
Publisher: Ulster Journals Ltd
Frequency: Annual - Published in April
Cover Price: £1.50
Circulation: 10,000 (Publisher's Statement)
Usual Pagination: 100
Editor: James Sherry
Summary of Content: Magazine containing a comprehensive guide to all the top restaurants, hotels and bars in Northern Ireland.
Readership/Target Audience: Aimed at the discerning diner.
ADVERTISING RATES:
Full Page Colour £750.00
Agency Commission: 15%
Mechanical Data: Film: Digital

Average advertising content per issue: 50%
CONSUMER: OTHER CLASSIFICATIONS: Restaurant Guides

THE WIRE
46189U76D-550

Editorial Address: 23 Jack's Place, 6 Corbet Place, LONDON, E1 6NN **Tel:** 020 7422 5010 **Fax:** 020 7422 5011
Email: info@thewire.co.uk
Advertising Address: As above. **Tel:** 020 7422 5014
Email: ads@thewire.co.uk
Web site: http://www.thewire.co.uk
ISSN: 0952-0686
Publisher: The Wire Magazine Ltd
Date Established: 1982
Frequency: Monthly
Cover Price: £3.90
Annual Sub.: £39.00
Circulation: 30,000 (Publisher's Statement)
Usual Pagination: 106
Editor: Chris Bohn; **Editor-in-Chief:** Tony Herrington; **Advertising Manager:** Andy Tait; **Publisher:** Tony Herrington
Summary of Content: Independent music magazine covering the more leftfield areas of rock, electronic, jazz, improvised, modern classical and global music.
Readership/Target Audience: Aimed at music fans of all kinds of specialist music from the ages of 20 to 70 years old.
ADVERTISING RATES:
Full Page Mono £995.00
Full Page Colour £1450.00
Agency Commission: 10%
Mechanical Data: Bleed Size: 285 x 235mm, Trim Size: 280 x 230mm, Type Area: 270 x 220mm, Col Length: 270mm, Film: Digital, Page Width: 220mm
Copy instructions: Copy Date: 3 weeks prior to publication date
Average advertising content per issue: 20%
CONSUMER: MUSIC & PERFORMING ARTS: Music

WISBECH PINK LOCAL DIRECTORY
1691864U89C-1042

Editorial Address: St. Augustines House, St. Augustines Way, South Wootton, KING'S LYNN, PE30 3TE
Tel: 01553 675885 **Fax:** 01553 670007
Email: info@pinklocaldirectory.co.uk
Advertising Address: As above.
Email: info@pinklocaldirectory.co.uk
Web site: http://www.pinklocaldirectory.co.uk
Publisher: Pink Local Directory Ltd
Frequency: Annual - Published in November
Cover Price: Free
Circulation: 23,150 (Publisher's Statement)
Editor: Lucan King; **Advertising Manager:** Lucan King
Summary of Content: Directory of local businesses containing business, classified and alphabetical listings as well as local information.
Readership/Target Audience: Aimed at residents and businesses in Wisbech and the surrounding villages.
ADVERTISING RATES:
Full Page Mono £839.00
Mechanical Data: Type Area: 192 x 126mm, Trim Size: 210 x 148mm, Col Length: 192mm, Page Width: 126mm, Film: Digital
CONSUMER: HOLIDAYS & TRAVEL: Entertainment Guides

THE WISDEN CRICKETER
45912U75K-850

Formerly: Wisden Cricket Monthly
Editorial Address: 2nd Floor, 123 Buckingham Palace Road, LONDON, SW1W 9SL **Tel:** 020 7705 4911
Email: twc@wisdencricketer.com
Advertising Address: As above. **Tel:** 020 7921 9195
Email: colin.ackehurst@wisdencricketer.com
Web site: http://www.cricinfo.com
ISSN: 1740-9519
Publisher: Wisden Cricketer Publishing Ltd
Date Established: 2003
Frequency: Monthly
Cover Price: £3.75
Circulation: 36,000 (Publisher's Statement)
Usual Pagination: 100
Editor: John Stern; **Publisher:** Lynda Wheeler
Summary of Content: Magazine covering international and first class cricket throughout the world. Includes comment, interviews, up-to-date test match analysis, book reviews, obituaries, statistics, TV and radio cricket listings.
Readership/Target Audience: Read by cricket lovers of all ages.
ADVERTISING RATES:
Full Page Colour £2500.00
Agency Commission: 10%
Mechanical Data: Page Width: 198mm, Film: Digital, Type Area: 260 x 198mm, Col Length: 260mm, Bleed Size: 291 x 226mm, Trim Size: 285 x 220mm
Copy instructions: Copy Date: 3 weeks prior to publication date

Average advertising content per issue: 25%
CONSUMER: SPORT: Cricket

WISH   1796307U74D-652
Editorial Address: PO Box 158, BROMLEY, BR1 4YH
Tel: 020 8289 3410 **Fax:** 020 8325 8352
Email: katechubb@xcessmedia.co.uk
Advertising Address: As above.
Email: lisaa@xcessmedia.co.uk
ISSN: 1742-6804
Publisher: Xcess Media Ltd
Date Established: 2005
Frequency: 3 issues yearly - Published in spring, summer and winter
Cover Price: £2.50
Free to qualifying individuals
Circulation: 30,000 (Publisher's Statement)
Usual Pagination: 132
Editor: Kate Chubb; **Advertising Director:** Lisa Allen;
Publisher: Kate Chubb
Summary of Content: Magazine covering all aspects of parenting as well as kids fashion, leisure, DVD reviews, films, health, beauty and travel.
Readership/Target Audience: Aimed at parents of children aged 0 to 8 years old.
ADVERTISING RATES:
Full Page Colour £5000.00
Agency Commission: 10%
Mechanical Data: Type Area: 260 x 185mm, Bleed Size: 296 x 216mm, Trim Size: 290 x 210mm, Col Length: 260mm, Page Width: 185mm, Film: Digital
Average advertising content per issue: 40%
CONSUMER: WOMEN'S INTEREST CONSUMER MAGAZINES: Child Care

WIZZIT   1698524U89D-522
Editorial Address: 141-143 Shoreditch High Street, LONDON, E1 6JE **Tel:** 020 7613 8777 **Fax:** 020 7613 6985
Email: edward.chamberlin@ink-publishing.com
Advertising Address: As above. **Fax:** 020 7613 8778
Email: mark.duke@ink-publishing.com
Web site: http://www.wizzmagazine.com
Publisher: Ink Publishing
Date Established: 2005
Frequency: 6 issues yearly
Cover Price: Free
Circulation: 800,000 (Publisher's Statement)
Usual Pagination: 156
Editor: Edward Chamberlin; **Advertising Manager:** Mark Duke
Summary of Content: Magazine with city guides for all Wizz Air's destinations plus news and features linked to cities to which Wizz flies. Topics include food and drink, people, sights, culture, nightlife, business, property and sport.
Language(s): English; Hungarian; Polish
Readership/Target Audience: Aimed at passengers of Wizz Air.
ADVERTISING RATES:
Full Page Colour EUR6950.00
Agency Commission: 15%
Mechanical Data: Bleed Size: 259 x 183mm, Trim Size: 253 x 177mm
CONSUMER: HOLIDAYS & TRAVEL: In-Flight Magazines

WM   45203U74A-630
Editorial Address: 6 Park Street, CARDIFF, CF10 1XR
Tel: 029 2024 3773
Email: charlotte.laing@mediawales.co.uk
Advertising Address: As above. **Tel:** 029 2022 3333
Email: lucinda.lynas@mediawales.co.uk
Web site: http://www.icwales.co.uk
Publisher: Media Wales Ltd
Date Established: 1998
Frequency: Quarterly
Cover Price: Free
Circulation: 33,145 (ABC 01/01/2009 to 30/06/2009)
Usual Pagination: 164
Editor: Charlotte Laing; **Editor-in-Chief:** Margaret O'Reilly;
Advertising Manager: Lucinda Lynas
Summary of Content: Magazine covering fashion, lifestyle, health and beauty, interior design, holidays and interviews.
Readership/Target Audience: Aimed at women between 28 and 55 years old.
ADVERTISING RATES:
Full Page Colour £960.00
Mechanical Data: Film: Digital, Page Width: 175mm, Bleed Size: 265 x 225mm, Type Area: 255 x 175mm, Col Length: 255mm
Copy instructions: Copy Date: 4 weeks prior to publication date
Supplement to: Western Mail (Cardiff)
CONSUMER: WOMEN'S INTEREST CONSUMER MAGAZINES: Women's Interest

---

WM BRIDE   1840072U74L-268
Editorial Address: 6 Park Street, CARDIFF, CF10 1XR
Tel: 029 2024 3771
Email: lydia.whitfield@mediawales.co.uk
Advertising Address: As above. **Tel:** 029 2022 3333
Email: lucinda.lynas@mediawales.co.uk
Web site: http://www.icwales.co.uk
Publisher: Media Wales Ltd
Frequency: 3 issues yearly - Published in January, April and August
Cover Price: Free
Circulation: 17,000 (Publisher's Statement)
Editor: Lydia Whitfield; **Advertising Manager:** Lucinda Lynas
Summary of Content: Magazine covering all aspects of weddings focusing on real life weddings and gowns.
Readership/Target Audience: Aimed at brides in South and West Wales.
ADVERTISING RATES:
Full Page Colour £960.00
CONSUMER: WOMEN'S INTEREST CONSUMER MAGAZINES: Brides

WM HOME   1840073U74C-876
Editorial Address: 6 Park Street, CARDIFF, CF10 1XR
Tel: 029 2022 3333
Email: rin.simpson@mediawales.co.uk
Advertising Address: As above.
Email: lucinda.lynas@mediawales.co.uk
Web site: http://www.icwales.co.uk
Publisher: Media Wales Ltd
Frequency: 3 issues yearly - Published in February, May and October
Cover Price: Free
Circulation: 17,000 (Publisher's Statement)
Editor: Rin Simpson; **Advertising Manager:** Lucinda Lynas
Summary of Content: Magazine covering homes and interiors.
Readership/Target Audience: Aimed at home owners, those looking to enter the housing market and those planning to upgrade their existing property.
ADVERTISING RATES:
Full Page Colour £790.00
CONSUMER: WOMEN'S INTEREST CONSUMER MAGAZINES: Home & Family

THE WOKING LIFESTYLE MAGAZINE
    1668011U80C-5224
Editorial Address: Unit A4, Kingsway Business Park, Oldfield Road, HAMPTON, TW12 2HD **Tel:** 020 8939 5600
Fax: 020 8939 5610
Email: editorial@sheengate.co.uk
Advertising Address: As above.
Email: leon@sheengate.co.uk
Web site: http://www.sheengate.co.uk
Publisher: Sheengate Publishing Ltd
Frequency: Monthly
Cover Price: Free
Usual Pagination: 64
Editor: Maggie Walsh; **Advertising Manager:** Leon Cook
Summary of Content: Lifestyle magazine covering local interest articles and interviews as well as features on fashion, theatre, education, shopping and property.
Readership/Target Audience: Aimed at households in Woking and the surrounding area.
ADVERTISING RATES:
Full Page Colour £1155.00
Agency Commission: 10%
Mechanical Data: Type Area: 270 x 180mm, Bleed Size: 307 x 220mm, Trim Size: 297 x 210mm, Col Length: 270mm, Page Width: 180mm, Film: Digital
Average advertising content per issue: 60%
CONSUMER: RURAL & REGIONAL INTEREST: Regional Interest English Counties

---

THE WOKING MAGAZINE   48165U89C-650
Formerly: What's On in Woking
Editorial Address: Woking Borough Council, Civic Offices, Gloucester Square, WOKING, GU21 6YL **Tel:** 01483 755855
Fax: 01483 725318
Advertising Address: As above. **Tel:** 01483 743024
Fax: 01483 743055
Email: dory.merriman@woking.gov.uk
Web site: http://www.woking.gov.uk
Publisher: Woking Borough Council
Date Established: 2004
Frequency: Quarterly
Cover Price: Free
Circulation: 45,000 (Publisher's Statement)
Usual Pagination: 8
Editor: Karen Porter
Summary of Content: Magazine published by Woking Borough Council. Covers news and listings of arts and entertainment events and articles of local interest.

Readership/Target Audience: Aimed at residents of Woking and the surrounding areas.
ADVERTISING RATES:
Full Page Mono £900.00
Full Page Colour £900.00
Agency Commission: 10%
Mechanical Data: Type Area: 270 x 185mm, Col Length: 270mm, Page Width: 185mm, Trim Size: 297 x 210mm, Bleed Size: 303 x 216mm, Film: Digital
Copy instructions: Copy Date: 6 weeks prior to publication date
Average advertising content per issue: 25%
CONSUMER: HOLIDAYS & TRAVEL: Entertainment Guides

WOLVERINE AND DEADPOOL   1663409U91D-906
Editorial Address: Brockbourne House, Mount Ephraim, TUNBRIDGE WELLS, TN4 8BS **Tel:** 01892 500100
Fax: 01892 545666
Email: collectorsed@panini.co.uk
Advertising Address: Orange20 Ltd, Station House, Bunbury Way, EPSOM, KT17 4JP **Tel:** 01372 802800
Fax: 01732 723322
Email: robin@o20.co.uk
Web site: http://www.paninicomics.co.uk
Publisher: Panini UK Ltd
Frequency: 13 issues yearly
Cover Price: £2.50
Usual Pagination: 76
Editor: Scott Gray; **Advertising Manager:** Robin Johnson
Summary of Content: Magazine with Marvel comic reprints. Comic strip adventures with heroes and villains.
Readership/Target Audience: Aimed at comic enthusiasts 12 years old and over.
ADVERTISING RATES:
Full Page Colour £1000.00
CONSUMER: RECREATION & LEISURE: Children & Youth

WOMAN   45204U74A-640
Editorial Address: Blue Fin Building, 110 Southwark Street, LONDON, SE1 0SU **Tel:** 020 3148 5000 **Fax:** 020 3148 8113
Email: woman@ipcmedia.com
Advertising Address: As above.
Email: richard_smith@ipcmedia.com
Web site: http://www.ipcmedia.com
Publisher: IPC Connect Ltd
Date Established: 1937
Frequency: Weekly
Cover Price: £0.90
Circulation: 331,065 (ABC 01/01/2009 to 30/06/2009)
Usual Pagination: 84
Editor: Tracey Baldwin; **Features Editor:** Anna Kingsley;
Managing Director: Fiona Dent; **Advertising Manager:** Richard Smith; **Publisher:** Sue Coffin
Summary of Content: Magazine with show-biz, home, cookery, fashion, beauty and health features, fiction, consumer affairs and human interest features.
Readership/Target Audience: Aimed at women between 15 to 65 years old plus.
ADVERTISING RATES:
Full Page Colour £19050.00
Mechanical Data: Page Width: 207mm, Type Area: 267 x 207mm, Bleed Size: 290 x 228mm, Trim Size: 284 x 225mm, Col Length: 267mm, Film: Digital, Screen: 60 lpc
Supplement(s): Family Health - 1xY, Family Matters - 1xY, Makeover Special - 1xY, Summer Special - 1xY
CONSUMER: WOMEN'S INTEREST CONSUMER MAGAZINES: Women's Interest

---

WOMAN ALIVE   47768U87-227
Editorial Address: CPO, Garcia Estate, Canterbury Road, WORTHING, BN13 1BW **Tel:** 01903 264556
Fax: 01903 821081
Email: womanalive@cpo.org.uk
Advertising Address: As above. **Tel:** 01903 602102
Fax: 01903 537321
Email: advertising@womanalive.org.uk
Web site: http://www.womanalive.co.uk
Publisher: Christian Publishing & Outreach Ltd
Date Established: 1982
Frequency: Monthly
Cover Price: £2.40
Circulation: 10,000 (Publisher's Statement)
Usual Pagination: 52
Editor: Jackie Stead
Summary of Content: Magazine with articles which inspire, encourage and resource women in their faith, alongside general health and lifestyle articles.
Readership/Target Audience: Aimed at Christian women.
ADVERTISING RATES:
Full Page Colour £950.00
Agency Commission: 10%
Mechanical Data: No. of Columns (Display): 4, Col Widths (Display): 42mm, Type Area: 270 x 182mm, Col Length: 270mm, Page Width: 182mm, Trim Size: 297 x 210mm, Bleed Size: 303 x 216mm, Film: Digital
Copy instructions: Copy Date: 15th of the month prior to publication date

Consumer Magazines

Average advertising content per issue: 15%
CONSUMER: RELIGIOUS

WOMAN&HOME
45298U74C-660
Formerly: Woman & Home
Editorial Address: Blue Fin Building, 110 Southwark Street, LONDON, SE1 0SU **Tel:** 020 3148 5000 **Fax:** 020 3148 8168
Email: w&hmail@ipcmedia.com
Advertising Address: As above.
Email: lisa_frost@ipcmedia.com
Web site: http://www.womanandhome.com
Publisher: IPC Media Ltd
Date Established: 1926
Frequency: Monthly
Cover Price: £3.40
Annual Sub.: £36.00
Circulation: 350,212 (ABC 01/01/2009 to 30/06/2009)
Usual Pagination: 242
Editor: Sue James; **Advertising Director:** Lisa Frost; **Publisher:** Ilka Schmitt
Summary of Content: Magazine containing features on fashion, beauty, health, home decor and gardening. Includes articles on travel, fiction, relationships and people.
Twitter: http://twitter.com/womanandhome.
Readership/Target Audience: Aimed at women aged 35 years old and over.
ADVERTISING RATES:
Full Page Colour £12000.00
Agency Commission: 15%
Mechanical Data: Type Area: 260 x 196mm, Bleed Size: 295 x 231mm, Trim Size: 289 x 225mm, Col Length: 260mm, Film: Digital
Average advertising content per issue: 30%
CONSUMER: WOMEN'S INTEREST CONSUMER MAGAZINES: Home & Family

WOMAN'S HEALTH
1665788U74G-257
Formerly: Woman's World Health
Editorial Address: 8 Forge Close, FARNHAM, GU9 9PX
Tel: 01252 712233
Email: penny.kitchen@btopenworld.com
Publisher: Atalink Ltd
Date Established: 2005
Frequency: Annual - Published in January
Free to qualifying individuals
Circulation: 25,000 (Publisher's Statement)
Editor: Penny Kitchen
Summary of Content: Magazine covering health features, news and products relating to women.
Readership/Target Audience: Aimed at WI Members.
ADVERTISING: No Advertising taken
CONSUMER: WOMEN'S INTEREST CONSUMER MAGAZINES: Slimming & Health

WOMAN'S OWN
45206U74A-690
Editorial Address: Blue Fin Building, 110 Southwark Street, LONDON, SE1 0SU **Tel:** 020 3148 5000 **Fax:** 020 3148 8112
Email: womansown@ipcmedia.com
Advertising Address: As above.
Email: richard_smith@ipcmedia.com
Web site: http://www.ipcmedia.com/brands/womansown
Publisher: IPC Media Ltd
Date Established: 1932
Frequency: Weekly
Cover Price: £0.90
Circulation: 307,407 (ABC 01/01/2009 to 30/06/2009)
Usual Pagination: 68
Editor: Anna Wharton; **Features Editor:** Anna Wharton; **Managing Director:** Fiona Dent; **Advertising Manager:** Richard Smith
Summary of Content: Magazine containing features on fashion, beauty and home decor. Includes makeovers, fiction, real-life stories and interviews.
Twitter: http://twitter.com/WomansOwn.
Readership/Target Audience: Aimed at women over 35 years old.
ADVERTISING RATES:
Full Page Colour £23650.00
Mechanical Data: Page Width: 207mm, Type Area: 262 x 207mm, Bleed Size: 285 x 231mm, Trim Size: 279 x 225mm, Col Length: 262mm, Film: Digital
Copy instructions: Copy Date: 3 weeks prior to publication date
Average advertising content per issue: 14%
CONSUMER: WOMEN'S INTEREST CONSUMER MAGAZINES: Women's Interest

WOMAN'S WEEKLY
45208U74A-750
Editorial Address: Blue Fin Building, 110 Southwark Street, LONDON, SE1 0SU **Tel:** 020 3148 5000
Email: womansweeklypostbag@ipcmedia.com
Advertising Address: As above.
Email: richard_smith@ipcmedia.com
Web site: http://www.ipcmedia.com/brands/womansweekly

ISSN: 0955-9418
Publisher: IPC Media Ltd
Frequency: Weekly
Cover Price: £0.82
Circulation: 335,118 (ABC 01/01/2009 to 30/06/2009)
Usual Pagination: 68
Editor: Sue Pilkington; **Features Editor:** Sue Pilkington; **Advertising Manager:** Richard Smith; **Publisher:** Sue Coffin
Summary of Content: General interest magazine with an emphasis towards practical skills including knitting, craft and cookery, also romantic fiction.
Twitter: http://twitter.com/wonmensweekly.
Readership/Target Audience: Aimed at women over 40 years old.
ADVERTISING RATES:
Full Page Colour £12400.00
Mechanical Data: Type Area: 262 x 207mm, Bleed Size: 285 x 231mm, Trim Size: 279 x 225mm, Col Length: 262mm, Film: Digital, Page Width: 207mm
Copy instructions: Copy Date: 3 weeks prior to publication date
CONSUMER: WOMEN'S INTEREST CONSUMER MAGAZINES: Women's Interest

WOMAN'S WORLD
1616320U74A-955
Editorial Address: 8 Forge Close, FARNHAM, GU9 9PX
Tel: 01252 712233
Email: penny.kitchen@btopenworld.com
Advertising Address: 40 Bowling Green Lane, LONDON, EC1R 0NE **Tel:** 020 7074 7700 **Fax:** 020 7837 6135
Email: mark@atalink.co.uk
Web site: http://www.atalink.co.uk
Publisher: Atalink Ltd
Date Established: 1996
Frequency: Annual - Published every Autumn
Circulation: 26,000 (Publisher's Statement)
Usual Pagination: 280
Editor: Penny Kitchen
Summary of Content: Magazine covering articles on topics of interest to WI members - food and wine, travel, environment, arts and crafts, gardening, fashion and beauty, literature, celebrity interviews, social and historical issues, personal finance and health and fitness.
Readership/Target Audience: Aimed at members of the WI and their families.
ADVERTISING RATES:
Full Page Colour £4450.00
Mechanical Data: Type Area: 272 x 185mm, Col Length: 272mm, Page Width: 185mm, Film: Digital, Bleed Size: 303 x 216mm, Trim Size: 297 x 210mm
Copy instructions: Copy Date: 6 weeks prior to publication date
Average advertising content per issue: 25%
CONSUMER: WOMEN'S INTEREST CONSUMER MAGAZINES: Women's Interest

WOMEN & GOLF
45833U75D-500
Editorial Address: 5th Floor, Telford Plaza 2, Ironmasters Way, TELFORD, TF3 4NT **Tel:** 020 8498 0428
Fax: 020 7261 7240
Email: alison.root@womansgolfnetwork.co.uk
Advertising Address: As above. **Tel:** 020 7370 8491
Fax: 020 7370 8499
Email: peter.goodman@gemininetworkmedia.co.uk
Publisher: Gemini Network Media
Date Established: 1991
Frequency: 9 issues yearly - Published on the 2nd Friday of each month prior to cover date
Cover Price: £2.90
Circulation: 15,000 (Publisher's Statement)
Usual Pagination: 84
Editor: Alison Root; **Advertising Manager:** Peter Goodman
Summary of Content: Magazine containing articles about golf, including instructions, fashion and travel.
Readership/Target Audience: Aimed at female golf players.
ADVERTISING RATES:
Full Page Colour £1600.00
SCC £14.76
Mechanical Data: Type Area: 271 x 188mm, Col Length: 271mm, Trim Size: 297 x 210mm, Bleed Size: 303 x 216mm, Film: Digital, Page Width: 188mm
Copy instructions: Copy Date: 6 weeks prior to publication date
CONSUMER: SPORT: Golf

WOMEN'S FITNESS
761534U74G-226
Formerly: Personal Trainer For Women
Editorial Address: Ground Floor, 211 Old Street, LONDON, EC1V 9NR **Tel:** 020 7608 6500 **Fax:** 020 7608 6380
Email: joanna.knight@trojanpublishing.co.uk
Advertising Address: As above. **Tel:** 020 7608 6443
Email: kirsty.clark@trojanpublishing.co.uk
Publisher: Trojan Publishing
Date Established: 2002
Frequency: 13 issues yearly

Cover Price: £3.25
Circulation: 37,604 (ABC 01/01/2009 to 30/06/2009)
Usual Pagination: 116
Editor: Joanna Knight; **Features Editor:** Louise Pyne; **Advertising Manager:** Heidi Wilson; **Advertising Director:** Ricky Boggia
Summary of Content: Magazine covering fitness including working out at home and in the gym.
Readership/Target Audience: Aimed at women interested in fitness.
ADVERTISING: Rates on application
Agency Commission: 10%
Copy instructions: Copy Date: 4 weeks prior to publication date
Average advertising content per issue: 25%
CONSUMER: WOMEN'S INTEREST CONSUMER MAGAZINES: Slimming & Health

WOMEN'S NEWS
1695530U74A-996
Editorial Address: Cathedral Quarter Managed Workspace, 109-113 Royal Avenue, BELFAST, BT1 1FF
Tel: 028 9032 2823 **Fax:** 028 9043 8788
Email: editorwomensnews@btconnect.com
Advertising Address: As above.
Email: financewomensnews@btconnect.com
Web site: http://www.womensnewsmagazine.org
Publisher: Women's News
Date Established: 1984
Frequency: 6 issues yearly
Cover Price: £1.75
Circulation: 800 (Publisher's Statement)
Usual Pagination: 36
Editor: Roisin Davis; **Advertising Manager:** Cathy Donnelly
Summary of Content: Magazine covering feminist issues including local and world events and how they impact on women's lives.
Readership/Target Audience: Aimed at women.
ADVERTISING RATES:
Full Page Colour £250.00
Mechanical Data: Trim Size: 297 x 210mm
Copy instructions: Copy Date: 3 weeks prior to publication date
CONSUMER: WOMEN'S INTEREST CONSUMER MAGAZINES: Women's Interest

WONDERLAND
1666486U74Q-1250
Editorial Address: 133 Notting Hill Gate, LONDON, W11 3LB **Tel:** 020 7243 9966 **Fax:** 020 7243 9967
Email: info@wonderlandmagazine.com
Advertising Address: As above.
Email: adam@wonderlandmagazine.com
Web site: http://www.wonderlandmagazine.com
Publisher: Visual Talent Ltd
Date Established: 2005
Frequency: 6 issues yearly
Cover Price: £3.95
Circulation: 140,000 (Publisher's Statement)
Usual Pagination: 50
Editor: Lauren Blane; **Advertising Manager:** Adam Thompson
Summary of Content: Magazine covering fashion, luxury goods, visual culture, beauty, people, celebrities, parties, art, film and music.
Readership/Target Audience: Aimed at affluent men and women aged between 18 and 40 with a high disposable income.
ADVERTISING RATES:
Full Page Colour £7000.00
Agency Commission: 15%
Mechanical Data: Bleed Size: 306 x 233mm, Trim Size: 300 x 230mm, Film: Digital
Average advertising content per issue: 25%
CONSUMER: WOMEN'S INTEREST CONSUMER MAGAZINES: Lifestyle

WOODBRIDGE AND MELTON COMMUNITY NEWS
48192U89C-680
Editorial Address: 27 Norwich Road, HALESWORTH, IP19 8BX **Tel:** 01986 834200 **Fax:** 01986 834270
Email: communitynews@micropress.co.uk
Advertising Address: As above. **Tel:** 01986 834228
Fax: 01986 843270
Email: donna@micropress.co.uk
Publisher: Micropress
Date Established: 1975
Frequency: Monthly
Cover Price: Free
Circulation: 6,100 (Publisher's Statement)
Usual Pagination: 20
Editor: Dennis Perkins; **Advertising Manager:** Karen Taylor
Summary of Content: Publication containing local news and events listings.
Readership/Target Audience: Read by residents of Woodbridge and Melton.
ADVERTISING RATES:
Full Page Mono £330.00

Full Page Colour £575.00
SCC £2.20
Agency Commission: 10%
Mechanical Data: Film: Digital, Col Length: 400mm, Col Widths (Display): 35mm, No. of Columns (Display): 7, Page Width: 268mm, Type Area: 400 x 268mm
Copy instructions: Copy Date: 10 days prior to publication date
Average advertising content per issue: 50%
CONSUMER: HOLIDAYS & TRAVEL: Entertainment Guides

WOODCARVING
46584U79A-173
Editorial Address: 86 High Street, LEWES, BN7 1XN
Tel: 01273 477374
Email: micheller@thegmcgroup.com
Advertising Address: As above. **Tel:** 01273 487535
Fax: 01273 487692
Email: rhonab@thegmcgroup.com
Web site: http://www.woodworkersinstitute.com
ISSN: 0965-9463
Publisher: GMC Publications Ltd
Frequency: 6 issues yearly
Cover Price: £3.50
Annual Sub.: £21.00
Circulation: 15,000 (Print Run)
Usual Pagination: 80
Editor: Michelle Robertson; **Publisher:** Simon McKeown
Summary of Content: Magazine covering projects, technical advice, features, tool tests, galleries, profiles, new products and reviews.
Readership/Target Audience: Aimed at beginner and expert woodcarvers.
ADVERTISING RATES:
Full Page Colour £825.00
Agency Commission: 10%
Mechanical Data: Type Area: 268 x 186mm, Col Length: 268mm, Bleed Size: 305 x 218mm, Trim Size: 297 x 210mm, Film: Digital, Page Width: 186mm
Copy instructions: Copy Date: 7 weeks prior to publication date
Average advertising content per issue: 30%
CONSUMER: HOBBIES & DIY

THE WOODWORKER
46585U79A-175
Editorial Address: Berwick House, 8-10 Knoll Rise, ORPINGTON, BR6 0EL **Tel:** 0844 412 2262
Email: ralph@ralphlaughton.com
Advertising Address: As above. **Tel:** 01689 899200
Fax: 01689 899266
Email: clare.hiscock@magicalia.com
Web site: http://www.getwoodworking.com
ISSN: 0043-776X
Publisher: My Hobby Store Media
Date Established: 1901
Frequency: 13 issues yearly
Cover Price: £3.40
Annual Sub.: £38.40
Circulation: 14,894 (Publisher's Statement)
Usual Pagination: 100
Editor: Ralph Laughton; **Managing Director:** Owen Davies
Summary of Content: Magazine featuring woodworking projects, techniques and equipment news.
Readership/Target Audience: Aimed at intermediate to skilled woodworkers.
ADVERTISING RATES:
Full Page Colour £800.00
Agency Commission: 10%
Mechanical Data: Film: Digital, Type Area: 267 x 184mm, Col Length: 267mm, Page Width: 184mm, Bleed Size: 303 x 213mm, Trim Size: 297 x 210mm
Copy instructions: Copy Date: 3 weeks prior to publication date
Average advertising content per issue: 25%
CONSUMER: HOBBIES & DIY

WOODWORKING PLANS & PROJECTS
623961U79A-176
Formerly: New Woodworking
Editorial Address: 86 High Street, LEWES, BN7 1XN
Tel: 01273 402897 **Fax:** 01273 487692
Email: markc@thegmcgroup.com
Advertising Address: As above.
Email: rhonab@thegmcgroup.com
Web site: http://www.thegmcgroup.com
ISSN: 1476 4016
Publisher: GMC Publications Ltd
Date Established: 2000
Frequency: 13 issues yearly
Cover Price: £3.40
Circulation: 20,000 (Publisher's Statement)
Usual Pagination: 96
Editor: Mark Baker; **Advertising Manager:** Rhona Bolger; **Group Editor:** Mark Baker; **Publisher:** Simon McKeown
Summary of Content: Woodworking magazine containing project ideas, technical tips, product tests and industry contacts.

Readership/Target Audience: Aimed at those who enjoy the practical and recreational side of woodworking and DIY.
ADVERTISING RATES:
Full Page Mono £850.00
Full Page Colour £1150.00
Agency Commission: 10%
Mechanical Data: Page Width: 186mm, Type Area: 268 x 186mm, Col Length: 268mm, Bleed Size: 305 x 218mm, Trim Size: 297 x 210mm, Film: Digital
Average advertising content per issue: 30%
CONSUMER: HOBBIES & DIY

WORCESTERSHIRE LIFE
1657764U80C-5374
Editorial Address: PO Box 219, Cleeve Prior, EVESHAM, WR11 8WJ **Tel:** 01527 558470 **Fax:** 01527 558477
Email: jane.sullivan@archant.co.uk
Advertising Address: Archant House, Oriel Road, CHELTENHAM, GL50 1BB **Tel:** 01527 831733
Email: joanne.walker@archant.co.uk
Web site: http://www.worcestershirelife.co.uk
ISSN: 1742-0679
Publisher: Archant Life (Midlands) Ltd
Frequency: Monthly
Cover Price: £2.50
Circulation: 14,500 (Publisher's Statement)
Usual Pagination: 156
Editor: Jane Sullivan; **Advertising Manager:** Joanne Walker
Summary of Content: Magazine covering local celebrity interviews, news, features, homes, gardens, dining out, food and drink, health, beauty, property, countryside matters, events, motoring, travel and Worcestershire society.
Readership/Target Audience: Aimed at affluent households in Worcestershire.
ADVERTISING RATES:
Full Page Colour £1200.00
Agency Commission: 10%
Mechanical Data: Type Area: 271 x 199mm, Bleed Size: 306 x 226mm, Trim Size: 300 x 220mm, Col Length: 271mm, Page Width: 199mm, Film: Digital
Copy instructions: Copy Date: 1st of the month prior to publication date
Average advertising content per issue: 40%
CONSUMER: RURAL & REGIONAL INTEREST: Regional Interest English Counties

WORCESTERSHIRE LIVING
1791015U80C-5379
Editorial Address: The Round House, Butters Bank, Croxton, STAFFORD, ST21 6NN **Tel:** 01527 871747
Fax: 01527 882501
Email: sallyannbloomer@btinternet.com
Advertising Address: Unit 28B Harris Business Park, Hanbury Road, Stoke Prior, BROMSGROVE, B60 4DJ
Tel: 01527 871747 **Fax:** 01527 882501
Email: allan@warwickshireliving.co.uk
Web site: http://www.worcestershireliving.co.uk
Publisher: Bee3 Ltd
Date Established: 2006
Frequency: Monthly
Cover Price: Free
Circulation: 16,000 (Publisher's Statement)
Usual Pagination: 132
Editor: Sally-Ann Bloomer
Summary of Content: Lifestyle magazine covering fashion, health and beauty, property, homes and gardens, motoring, food and drink, local news and events.
Readership/Target Audience: Aimed at residents and visitors to Worcestershire with high disposable incomes.
ADVERTISING RATES:
Full Page Colour £950.00
Agency Commission: 10%
Mechanical Data: Bleed Size: 306 x 236mm, Trim Size: 300 x 230mm, Film: Digital
Copy instructions: Copy Date: 5th of the month prior to publication date
Average advertising content per issue: 30%
CONSUMER: RURAL & REGIONAL INTEREST: Regional Interest English Counties

THE WORD
1613617U76D-758
Editorial Address: 90-92 Pentonville Road, LONDON, N1 9HS **Tel:** 020 7520 8625 **Fax:** 020 7833 9900
Email: mail@wordmagazine.co.uk
Advertising Address: As above.
Email: juliet.cromwell@developmenthell.co.uk
Web site: http://www.wordmagazine.co.uk
Publisher: Development Hell Ltd
Frequency: Monthly
Cover Price: £4.50
Circulation: 40,000 (Publisher's Statement)
Usual Pagination: 132
Editor: Mark Ellen; **Advertising Manager:** Juliet Cromwell; **Publisher:** Jerry Perkins
Summary of Content: Website covering music, entertainment, books and DVDs.
Readership/Target Audience: Aimed at men and women aged 18 to 55 years old.

ADVERTISING RATES:
Full Page Colour £3500.00
Agency Commission: 15%
Mechanical Data: Col Length: 275mm, Page Width: 200mm, Trim Size: 300 x 230mm, Type Area: 275 x 200mm, Bleed Size: 306 x 236mm, Film: Digital
Copy instructions: Copy Date: 3 weeks prior to publication date
CONSUMER: MUSIC & PERFORMING ARTS: Music

WORD SEARCH
46670U79F-70
Editorial Address: Stonecroft, 69 Station Road, REDHILL, RH1 1EY **Tel:** 01737 378700 **Fax:** 01737 781800
Email: reception@puzzlermedia.com
Advertising Address: As above. **Fax:** 01737 781888
Email: brian.ainge@puzzlermedia.com
Web site: http://www.puzzler.com
ISSN: 0956-1633
Publisher: Puzzler Media Ltd
Frequency: 13 issues yearly
Cover Price: £2.00
Circulation: 92,359 (ABC 01/01/2008 to 31/12/2008)
Usual Pagination: 100
Editor: Rosemary Banfield; **Managing Editor:** Rosemary Banfield
Summary of Content: Magazine containing mainly word search puzzles, other puzzles and a monthly competition.
Readership/Target Audience: Read by word search enthusiasts.
ADVERTISING: Rates on application
CONSUMER: HOBBIES & DIY: Games & Puzzles

WORKBOX
45374U74E-650
Editorial Address: PO Box 25, LISKEARD, PL14 6XX
Tel: 01579 340100 **Fax:** 01579 340400
Email: workbox@ebony.co.uk
Advertising Address: As above.
Email: paul@ebony.co.uk
Web site: http://www.ebony.co.uk/workbox
ISSN: 0269-5175
Publisher: Ebony Media Ltd
Date Established: 1982
Frequency: 6 issues yearly
Cover Price: £3.25
Circulation: 20,000 (Publisher's Statement)
Usual Pagination: 64
Editor: Carole D'Silva; **Advertising Manager:** Paul Elkin
Summary of Content: Magazine covering all aspects of needlecraft and textiles.
Readership/Target Audience: Read by enthusiasts, amateurs and professionals.
ADVERTISING RATES:
Full Page Mono £660.00
Full Page Colour £792.00
Agency Commission: 10%
Mechanical Data: Bleed Size: 303 x 216mm, Trim Size: 297 x 210mm, Type Area: 260 x 180mm, Col Length: 260mm, Page Width: 180mm, Film: Digital
Copy instructions: Copy Date: 6 weeks prior to publication date
CONSUMER: WOMEN'S INTEREST CONSUMER MAGAZINES: Crafts

WORKING TOGETHER
1790383U80C-5377
Editorial Address: Bryer Ash Business Park, Bradford Road, TROWBRIDGE, BA14 8RT **Tel:** 01225 715913
Fax: 01225 715950
Email: workingtogether@selwoodhousing.com
Web site: http://www.selwoodhousing.com
Publisher: Selwood Housing Society
Date Established: 2005
Frequency: Quarterly
Cover Price: Free
Circulation: 5,500 (Publisher's Statement)
Usual Pagination: 24
Editor: Mandy Hole
Summary of Content: Newsletter covering issues affecting people in West Wiltshire from community and housing issues to consumer products.
Readership/Target Audience: Aimed at social housing tenants in West Wiltshire.
ADVERTISING: No Advertising taken
CONSUMER: RURAL & REGIONAL INTEREST: Regional Interest English Counties

WORLD BIRDWATCH
712141U81A-190
Editorial Address: Wellbrook Court, Girton Road, CAMBRIDGE, CB3 0NA **Tel:** 01223 277318
Fax: 01223 277200
Email: birdlife@birdlife.org
Advertising Address: The Chocolate Factory, 5 Clarendon Road, LONDON, N22 6XJ **Tel:** 020 8881 0550
Fax: 020 8881 0990
Email: advertising@birdwatch.co.uk
Web site: http://www.birdlife.org

ISSN: 0144-4476
Publisher: BirdLife International
Date Established: 1986
Frequency: Quarterly
Annual Sub.: £28.00
Circulation: 8,200 (Publisher's Statement)
Usual Pagination: 32
Editor: Martin Fowlie; **Publisher:** Martin Fowlie
Summary of Content: Magazine covering birds and bird conservation around the world.
Readership/Target Audience: Aimed at those with an interest in birds and conservation.
ADVERTISING RATES:
Full Page Mono £525.00
Full Page Colour £850.00
Agency Commission: 10%
Mechanical Data: Type Area: 270 x 192mm, Bleed Size: 305 x 218mm, Trim Size: 297 x 210mm, Col Length: 270mm, Film: Digital, Page Width: 192mm
Copy instructions: Copy Date: 1 month prior to publication date
Average advertising content per issue: 10%
CONSUMER: ANIMALS & PETS: Animals & Pets Protection

THE WORLD IN
1704064U73-9007
Editorial Address: 25 St. James's Street, LONDON, SW1A 1HG **Tel:** 020 7830 7000 **Fax:** 020 7925 0651
Email: worldineditor@economist.com
Advertising Address: As above.
Email: harywhitbread@economist.com
Web site: http://www.theworldin.com
Publisher: The Economist Newspaper Ltd
Frequency: Annual - Published in November
Cover Price: £4.95
Editor: Harriet Ziegler; **Managing Editor:** Harriet Ziegler
Summary of Content: Magazine compilation of forecasts and predictions for the year ahead from The Economist. Written by journalists from The Economist Group and distinguished outside contributors.
Readership/Target Audience: Aimed at an intelligent, internationally minded audience.
ADVERTISING RATES:
Full Page Colour £17450.00
Agency Commission: 15%
Copy instructions: Copy Date: October 20th
CONSUMER: NATIONAL & INTERNATIONAL PERIODICALS

THE WORLD OF CROSS STITCHING
45375U74E-680
Editorial Address: 9th Floor, Tower House, Fairfax Street, BRISTOL, BS1 3BN **Tel:** 0117 927 9009 **Fax:** 0117 934 9008
Email: hannahbellis@originpublishing.co.uk
Advertising Address: 5th Floor, Tower House, Fairfax Street, BRISTOL, BS1 3BN **Tel:** 0117 927 9009
Email: melanieharris@originpublishing.co.uk
Web site: http://www.cross-stitching.com
Publisher: Origin Publishing Ltd
Date Established: 1977
Frequency: 13 issues yearly
Cover Price: £3.75
Circulation: 42,022 (ABC 01/01/2008 to 31/12/2008)
Usual Pagination: 100
Editor: Eleanor Morris
Summary of Content: Magazine covering cross stitch, designs and practical information.
Readership/Target Audience: Aimed at all levels of cross stitchers.
ADVERTISING RATES:
Full Page Colour £1050.00
Agency Commission: 10%
Mechanical Data: Type Area: 281 x 195mm, Bleed Size: 303 x 216mm, Trim Size: 297 x 210mm, Page Width: 195mm, Film: Digital
Copy instructions: Copy Date: 5 weeks prior to publication date
CONSUMER: WOMEN'S INTEREST CONSUMER MAGAZINES: Crafts

WORLD OF CRUISING
1660654U89E-235
Editorial Address: Softec House, London Road, Albourne, HASSOCKS, BN6 9BN **Tel:** 0870 429 2686
Fax: 0870 429 2683
Email: woc@cruiseline.co.uk
Advertising Address: As above.
Web site: http://www.worldofcruisingmagazine.com
Publisher: World of Cruising Ltd
Date Established: 1997
Frequency: Quarterly
Cover Price: £3.75
Annual Sub.: £15.00
Circulation: 20,000 (Publisher's Statement)
Usual Pagination: 88
Editor: Simon Veness; **Advertisement Director:** Richard Partridge
Summary of Content: Magazine with up to date news and articles on leading cruise lines as well as top hotel and spas.

Readership/Target Audience: Aimed at affluent regular cruisers with a high disposable income.
ADVERTISING RATES:
Full Page Colour £3250.00
Mechanical Data: Type Area: 252 x 175mm, Bleed Size: 306 x 215mm, Col Length: 252mm, Page Width: 175mm, Film: Digital
CONSUMER: HOLIDAYS & TRAVEL: Holidays

THE WORLD OF FINE WINE
1642318U74P-914
Editorial Address: 226 City Road, LONDON, EC1V 2TT
Tel: 020 7812 8673 **Fax:** 020 7253 4370
Email: info@finewinemag.com
Advertising Address: As above. **Tel:** 020 7812 8675
Fax: 020 7253 4437
Email: sarab@finewinemag.com
Web site: http://www.finewinemag.com
ISSN: 1743-503X
Publisher: Quarto Magazines Ltd
Date Established: 2004
Frequency: Quarterly
Cover Price: £30.00
Circulation: 5,000 (Publisher's Statement)
Usual Pagination: 216
Advertising Manager: Sara Morley; **Publisher:** Sara Morley
Summary of Content: Magazine with features and articles on fine wine, book reviews and cultural and historical articles with an emphasis on fine wine.
Readership/Target Audience: Aimed at lovers of fine wine internationally.
ADVERTISING RATES:
Full Page Colour £2250.00
Mechanical Data: Type Area: 256 x 170mm, Bleed Size: 303 x 213mm, Trim Size: 297 x 210mm, Col Length: 256mm, Page Width: 170mm, Film: Digital
CONSUMER: WOMEN'S INTEREST CONSUMER MAGAZINES: Food & Cookery

THE WORLD OF INTERIORS
45299U74C-700
Editorial Address: Vogue House, 1 Hanover Square, LONDON, W1S 1JU **Tel:** 020 7499 9080 **Fax:** 020 7493 4013
Email: woi-editorial@condenast.co.uk
Advertising Address: As above. **Fax:** 020 7493 4723
Email: katharine.atkinson@condenast.co.uk
Web site: http://www.worldofinteriors.co.uk
ISSN: 0264-083X
Publisher: Conde Nast Publications Ltd
Date Established: 1981
Frequency: Monthly
Cover Price: £4.10
Annual Sub.: £43.20
Circulation: 62,016 (ABC 01/01/2009 to 30/06/2009)
Usual Pagination: 100
Editor: Nathalie Wilson; **Advertising Manager:** Katharine Atkinson; **Publisher:** Emma Redmayne
Summary of Content: Magazine highlighting elaborate home and garden designs and art events.
Readership/Target Audience: Aimed at men and women who have an interest in all kinds of design.
ADVERTISING RATES:
Full Page Colour £9900.00
Mechanical Data: Page Width: 190mm, Type Area: 255 x 190mm, Col Length: 255mm, Trim Size: 279 x 216mm, Bleed Size: 285 x 222mm, Film: Digital
Copy instructions: Copy Date: 6 weeks prior to publication date
CONSUMER: WOMEN'S INTEREST CONSUMER MAGAZINES: Home & Family

WORLD OF PROPERTY MAGAZINE
45508U74K-580
Editorial Address: 1 Commercial Road, EASTBOURNE, BN21 3XQ **Tel:** 01323 726040 **Fax:** 01323 649249
Email: news@outboundmedia.co.uk
Advertising Address: As above. **Fax:** 01323 735002
Email: steve.jeanes@outboundmedia.co.uk
Web site: http://www.worldofproperty.co.uk
ISSN: 1357-0269
Publisher: Outbound Media and Exhibitions
Frequency: Annual - Published in January
Cover Price: Free
Circulation: 25,000 (Publisher's Statement)
Usual Pagination: 84
Editor: David Fuller; **Group Editor:** Paul Beasley
Summary of Content: Magazine containing profiles of properties for sale outside of the UK. Features destinations, legal and tax issues and property news.
Readership/Target Audience: Aimed at people looking to purchase a second home abroad.
ADVERTISING: Rates on application
Agency Commission: 10%
Copy instructions: Copy Date: 6 weeks prior to publication date
CONSUMER: WOMEN'S INTEREST CONSUMER MAGAZINES: Home Purchase

WORLD SIKH FOUNDATION INCORPORATING THE SIKH COURIER
48343U90-300
Editorial Address: 33 Wargrave Road, HARROW, HA2 8LL
Tel: 020 8864 9228
Advertising Address: As above.
Email: bablibharara@hotmail.com
ISSN: 0037-511X
Publisher: The World Sikh Foundation
Date Established: 1961
Frequency: Half-yearly - Published in January and August
Annual Sub.: £10.00
Circulation: 3,000 (Publisher's Statement)
Usual Pagination: 50
Editor: Babli Bharara; **Advertising Manager:** Babli Bharara; **Managing Editor:** Babli Bharara; **Publisher:** Babli Bharara
Summary of Content: Magazine containing cultural and religious subjects on the Sikh religion from the UK and throughout the world.
Readership/Target Audience: Aimed at the Sikh community.
ADVERTISING RATES:
Full Page Mono £120.00
Mechanical Data: Film: Digital, Trim Size: 210 x 148mm
Copy instructions: Copy Date: 4 weeks prior to publication date
CONSUMER: ETHNIC

WORLD SKI GUIDE
1667889U75G-654
Editorial Address: Parman House, 30-36 Fife Road, KINGSTON UPON THAMES, KT1 1SY **Tel:** 020 8547 9822
Email: info@goodholidayideas.com
Advertising Address: As above. **Tel:** 01372 468140
Email: gideon@goodholidayideas.com
Web site: http://www.goodskiguide.com
Publisher: Mountain Leisure Ltd
Frequency: 7 issues yearly
Cover Price: £3.95
Circulation: 80,000 (Publisher's Statement)
Usual Pagination: 120
Editor: John Hill; **Advertising Manager:** Gideon Reeves
Summary of Content: Magazine covering low cost ski resorts worldwide, hotels and equipment.
Readership/Target Audience: Aimed at skiers and snowboarders of all abilities.
ADVERTISING: Rates on application
CONSUMER: SPORT: Winter Sports

WORLD SOCCER
45785U75B-260
Editorial Address: Blue Fin Building, 110 Southwark Street, LONDON, SE1 0SU **Tel:** 020 3148 5000 **Fax:** 020 3148 8128
Email: world_soccer@ipcmedia.com
Advertising Address: As above. **Tel:** 020 3148 4241
Fax: 020 3148 8130
Email: simon_gerard@ipcmedia.com
Web site: http://www.worldsoccer.com
Publisher: IPC Inspire
Frequency: 13 issues yearly
Cover Price: £3.60
Circulation: 44,003 (ABC 01/01/2008 to 31/12/2008)
Usual Pagination: 92
Editor: Gavin Hamilton; **Advertising Manager:** Dave Stone
Summary of Content: Magazine containing news, interviews and features on World Association football.
Readership/Target Audience: Aimed at people interested in football.
ADVERTISING RATES:
Full Page Colour £2670.00
Agency Commission: 10%
Mechanical Data: Film: Digital, Page Width: 190mm, Type Area: 270 x 190mm, Col Length: 270mm, Trim Size: 286 x 210mm, Bleed Size: 292 x 216mm, No. of Columns (Display): 4
Copy instructions: Copy Date: 12 days prior to publication date
Average advertising content per issue: 10%
CONSUMER: SPORT: Football

THE WORLD TODAY
1605574U82-253
Editorial Address: Chatham House, 10 St. James's Square, LONDON, SW1Y 4LE **Tel:** 020 7957 5712
Fax: 020 9757 5710
Email: wt@chathamhouse.org.uk
Advertising Address: As above. **Fax:** 020 7957 5710
Email: wt@chathamhouse.org.uk
Web site: http://www.theworldtoday.org
Publisher: The Royal Institute of International Affairs
Date Established: 1945
Frequency: 11 issues yearly
Annual Sub.: £35.00
Circulation: 10,000 (Publisher's Statement)
Usual Pagination: 32
Editor: Alison Couldridge; **Advertising Manager:** Alison Couldridge

Summary of Content: Magazine with analysis of international issues.
Readership/Target Audience: Aimed at academics, policy makers, schools and universities, governments, businesses, the media, charities and laymen.
ADVERTISING RATES:
Full Page Colour £1000.00
Agency Commission: 10%
Mechanical Data: Trim Size: 297 x 210mm, Bleed Size: +3mm
Average advertising content per issue: 10%
CONSUMER: CURRENT AFFAIRS & POLITICS

WORLDWIDE GOLF
1641321U75D-509
Editorial Address: 54 Alderley Road, WILMSLOW, SK9 1NY
Tel: 01625 535081 **Fax:** 01625 537487
Email: rickb@sportingpublications.com
Advertising Address: As above.
Email: mikeg@sportingpublications.com
Web site: http://www.wwgolf.biz
Publisher: Worldwide Sporting Publications
Date Established: 1999
Frequency: 11 issues yearly - Combined issues July/August
Cover Price: £2.00
Free to qualifying individuals
Circulation: 500,000 (Print Run)
Usual Pagination: 76
Editor: Richard Bevan; **Editor-in-Chief:** Mike Gallemore;
Advertising Manager: Mike Gallemore
Summary of Content: Golf magazine with features on equipment, interviews with players, coverage of the European and PGA tournaments and reviews of new courses.
Readership/Target Audience: Aimed at golf enthusiasts worldwide.
ADVERTISING RATES:
Full Page Colour £2500.00
Agency Commission: 15%
Mechanical Data: Type Area: 271 x 185mm, Col Length: 271mm, Page Width: 185mm, Trim Size: 297 x 210mm, Bleed Size: 303 x 216mm, Film: Digital
Copy instructions: Copy Date: 10 days prior to publication date
Average advertising content per issue: 30%
CONSUMER: SPORT: Golf

WRVS ACTION
45686U74R-550
Editorial Address: Garden House, Milton Hill, Steventon, ABINGDON, OX13 6AD **Tel:** 01235 442900
Fax: 01235 861166
Email: enquires@wrvs.org.uk
Advertising Address: Think Publishing, The Pall Mall Deposit, 124-128 Barlby Road, LONDON, W10 6BL
Tel: 020 8962 3020 **Fax:** 020 8962 8689
Email: victor@thinkpublishing.co.uk
Web site: http://www.wrvs.org.uk
Publisher: Women's Royal Voluntary Service
Date Established: 1996
Frequency: Half-yearly - Published in Spring and Autumn
Cover Price: Free
Circulation: 65,000 (Publisher's Statement)
Usual Pagination: 68
Editor: Alison Phillips
Summary of Content: Magazine covering news and events relating to WRVS, volunteering, older people's issues and lifestyle.
Readership/Target Audience: Read by volunteers and supporters.
ADVERTISING RATES:
Full Page Colour £3500.00
Agency Commission: 10%
Mechanical Data: Film: Digital, Type Area: 236 x 166mm, Bleed Size: 266 x 196mm, Trim Size: 260 x 190mm, Col Length: 236mm, Page Width: 166mm
Copy instructions: Copy Date: 4 weeks prior to publication date
Average advertising content per issue: 40%
CONSUMER: WOMEN'S INTEREST CONSUMER MAGAZINES: Women's Interest Related

WWF ACTION
48725U81A-200
Formerly: WWF News
Editorial Address: Panda House, Weyside Park, GODALMING, GU7 1XR **Tel:** 01483 426444
Fax: 01483 426409
Email: wwf-uk-news@wwf.org.uk
Web site: http://www.wwf.org.uk
ISSN: 0952-3170
Publisher: WWF-UK
Date Established: 1962
Frequency: 3 issues yearly - Published in February, June and October
Free to qualifying individuals
Circulation: 120,000 (Publisher's Statement)
Usual Pagination: 32
Editor: Guy Jowett

Summary of Content: Magazine covering environmental and wildlife issues.
Readership/Target Audience: Read by members of WWF.
ADVERTISING: No Advertising taken
CONSUMER: ANIMALS & PETS: Animals & Pets Protection

X360
1702312U78D-321
Editorial Address: Richmond House, 33 Richmond Hill, BOURNEMOUTH, BH2 6EZ **Tel:** 01202 586200
Email: X360@imagine-publishing.co.uk
Advertising Address: As above.
Email: james.haley@imagine-publishing.co.uk
Web site: http://www.360magazine.co.uk
Publisher: Imagine Publishing
Date Established: 2005
Frequency: 13 issues yearly
Cover Price: £4.99
Circulation: 26,098 (ABC)
Usual Pagination: 132
Editor: Simon Miller
Summary of Content: Magazine covering the XBox 360 games console with new generation games reviews, XBox live, DVD, music, book and hardware reviews.
Readership/Target Audience: Aimed at men aged between 18 and their late 20s who are hardcore gamers.
ADVERTISING RATES:
Full Page Colour £3200.00
Agency Commission: 10%
Mechanical Data: Type Area: 277 x 210mm, Col Length: 277mm, Page Width: 210mm, Bleed Size: 307 x 240mm, Trim Size: 297 x 230mm, Film: Digital
Average advertising content per issue: 20%
CONSUMER: CONSUMER ELECTRONICS: Games

XBOX 360 THE OFFICIAL XBOX MAGAZINE
1695438U78D-319
Formerly: The Official Xbox 360 Magazine
Editorial Address: 2 Balcombe Street, LONDON, NW1 6NW
Tel: 020 7042 4000
Email: ben.talbot@futurenet.co.uk
Advertising Address: As above. **Fax:** 020 7042 4259
Email: emma.cull@futurenet.co.uk
Web site: http://www.oxm.co.uk
Publisher: Future Publishing Limited
Date Established: 2005
Frequency: 13 issues yearly
Cover Price: £5.99
Circulation: 60,000 (Print Run)
Editor: Jon Hicks; **Advertising Manager:** Emma Cull
Summary of Content: Magazine covering the Xbox 360 games console and games.
Readership/Target Audience: Aimed at the Xbox 360 community.
ADVERTISING RATES:
Full Page Colour £6000.00
Agency Commission: 10%
Mechanical Data: Type Area: 270 x 190mm, Bleed Size: 303 x 216mm, Trim Size: 297 x 210mm, Col Length: 270mm, Page Width: 190mm
Copy instructions: Copy Date: 4 weeks prior to publication date
CONSUMER: CONSUMER ELECTRONICS: Games

XBOX WORLD 360
1616375U78D-299
Formerly: Xbox World
Editorial Address: 30 Monmouth Street, BATH, BA1 2BW
Tel: 01225 442244
Email: xbw@futurenet.com
Advertising Address: 2 Balcombe Street, LONDON, NW1 6NW **Tel:** 020 7042 4000 **Fax:** 020 7042 4259
Email: emma.cull@futurenet.co.uk
Publisher: Future Publishing Ltd
Date Established: 2003
Frequency: 13 issues yearly
Cover Price: £4.99
Circulation: 31,030 (ABC 01/07/2008 to 31/12/2008)
Editor: Tim Weaver; **Advertising Manager:** Emma Cull;
Publisher: James Binns
Summary of Content: Magazine for the Xbox console featuring game reviews and tips.
Readership/Target Audience: Aimed at those with an Xbox console.
ADVERTISING RATES:
Full Page Colour £2850.00
Agency Commission: 10%
Mechanical Data: Film: Digital, Type Area: 270 x 190mm, Bleed Size: 303 x 216mm, Trim Size: 297 x 210mm, Col Length: 270mm, Page Width: 190mm
Copy instructions: Copy Date: 5 weeks prior to publication date
Average advertising content per issue: 15%
CONSUMER: CONSUMER ELECTRONICS: Games

XK GAZETTE
46485U77E-500
Editorial Address: PO Box 2, TENBURY WELLS, WR15 8XX
Tel: 01584 781588 **Fax:** 01584 781630
Email: philip@xkclub.com
Advertising Address: As above.
Email: mary@xkclub.com
Web site: http://www.xkclub.com
Publisher: Porter & Porter Ltd
Date Established: 1997
Frequency: Monthly
Annual Sub.: £48.00
Circulation: 2,000 (Publisher's Statement)
Usual Pagination: 48
Editor: Philip Porter; **Advertising Manager:** Mary Fulford-Talbot
Summary of Content: Magazine focusing on XK Jaguar cars. Contains features, events, practical and technical advice, historical articles, interviews, profiles and reports from around the world.
Readership/Target Audience: Aimed at XK owners and devotees.
ADVERTISING: Rates on application
CONSUMER: MOTORING & CYCLING: Club Cars

XPOSÉ
46065U76A-170
Formerly: Xposé Special
Editorial Address: 9-10 Blades Court, Deodar Road, LONDON, SW15 2NU **Tel:** 020 8875 1520
Fax: 020 8875 1588
Email: xpose@visimag.com
Advertising Address: As above.
Email: mclarke@visimag.com
Web site: http://www.visimag.com
ISSN: 1363-8289
Publisher: Visual Imagination Ltd
Date Established: 1996
Frequency: 8 issues yearly
Cover Price: £3.99
Annual Sub.: £32.00
Circulation: 36,500 (Publisher's Statement)
Usual Pagination: 68
Editor: Anthony Brown; **Group Editor:** Stephen Payne
Summary of Content: Film and TV magazine focusing on science fiction, fantasy, horror and the paranormal.
Language(s): English; German
Readership/Target Audience: Read by film and TV enthusiasts and others with an interest in this area.
ADVERTISING RATES:
Full Page Colour £1150.00
Agency Commission: 10%
Mechanical Data: Bleed Size: 307 x 230mm, Trim Size: 297 x 220mm, Film: Digital, Type Area: 270 x 192mm, Col Length: 270mm, Page Width: 192mm
Copy instructions: Copy Date: 3 weeks prior to publication date
CONSUMER: MUSIC & PERFORMING ARTS: Cinema

X-PRESS
714141U74F-725
Editorial Address: 4 Newhams Row, LONDON, SE1 3UZ
Tel: 020 7939 8280 **Fax:** 020 7939 8300
Email: x-press@ippf.org
Web site: http://www.ippf.org/x-press
ISSN: 1607-145X
Publisher: International Planned Parenthood Federation
Date Established: 2000
Frequency: Annual - Published in October
Cover Price: Free
Circulation: 6,000 (Publisher's Statement)
Usual Pagination: 8
Editor: Upeka De Silva
Summary of Content: Newsletter containing information on sexual and reproductive health.
Language(s): English; French; Spanish
Readership/Target Audience: Aimed at young people worldwide.
ADVERTISING: No Advertising taken
CONSUMER: WOMEN'S INTEREST CONSUMER MAGAZINES: Teenage

YACHTING LIFE
48398U91A-250
Editorial Address: Wheatsheaf House, Montgomery Street, The Village, East Kilbride, GLASGOW, G74 4JS
Tel: 01355 279077 **Fax:** 01355 279088
Email: info@yachtinglife.co.uk
Advertising Address: As above.
Email: info@yachtinglife.co.uk
Web site: http://www.yachtinglife.co.uk
ISSN: 0958-6393
Publisher: KAV Publicity Ltd
Date Established: 1977
Frequency: Monthly - Published on the 24th of the month prior to cover month
Cover Price: £2.50
Annual Sub.: £25.00
Circulation: 9,500 (Publisher's Statement)
Usual Pagination: 64

Consumer Magazines

Editor: Alistair Vallance; **Advertising Manager:** Alistair Vallance
Summary of Content: Magazine dealing with local issues at yacht club level as well as reporting on local heroes on the race circuit, with an emphasis on Scotland, the North of England and Northern Ireland.
Readership/Target Audience: Aimed at yachting skippers and crews.
ADVERTISING RATES:
Full Page Mono £675.00
Full Page Colour £990.00
SCC £8.00
Agency Commission: 10%
Mechanical Data: Type Area: 275 x 183mm, Bleed Size: 305 x 215mm, Trim Size: 297 x 210mm, Print Process: Web-fed offset litho, Col Length: 275mm, Film: Digital, Page Width: 183mm
Copy instructions: Copy Date: 1st week of the month prior to publication date
Average advertising content per issue: 30%
CONSUMER: RECREATION & LEISURE: Boating & Yachting

YACHTING MONTHLY
48399U91A-260
Editorial Address: Blue Fin Building, 110 Southwark Street, LONDON, SE1 0SU **Tel:** 020 3148 5000
Email: yachting_monthly@ipcmedia.com
Advertising Address: As above. **Fax:** 020 3148 8128
Email: john_gaylard@ipcmedia.com
Web site: http://www.yachtingmonthly.com
ISSN: 0043-9983
Publisher: IPC Inspire
Date Established: 1906
Frequency: Monthly
Cover Price: £3.70
Circulation: 34,103 (ABC 01/01/2008 to 31/12/2008)
Usual Pagination: 210
Editor: Paul Gelder; **News Editor:** Dick Durham; **Features Editor:** Dick Durham; **Advertising Manager:** John Gaylard
Summary of Content: Magazine featuring all aspects of cruising under sail, including reviews, seamanship and boat handling.
Readership/Target Audience: Aimed at anyone interested in leisurely sailing.
ADVERTISING RATES:
Full Page Mono £1700.00
Full Page Colour £3130.00
Agency Commission: 10%
Mechanical Data: Type Area: 275 x 187mm, Col Length: 275mm, Page Width: 187mm, Trim Size: 300 x 214mm, Bleed Size: 306 x 220mm, Film: Digital
Copy instructions: Copy Date: 1st week of the month prior to publication date
Average advertising content per issue: 55%
CONSUMER: RECREATION & LEISURE: Boating & Yachting

YACHTING WORLD
48400U91A-270
Formerly: Yachting World International
Editorial Address: Blue Fin Building, 110 Southwark Street, LONDON, SE1 0SU **Tel:** 020 3148 5000 **Fax:** 020 3148 8127
Email: yachting_world@ipcmedia.com
Advertising Address: As above. **Fax:** 020 3148 8128
Email: alan_warren@ipcmedia.com
Web site: http://www.yachtingworld.com
Publisher: IPC Inspire
Date Established: 1894
Frequency: Monthly
Cover Price: £4.20
Annual Sub.: £50.40
Circulation: 27,649 (ABC 01/01/2008 to 31/12/2008)
Usual Pagination: 180
Editor: Andrew Bray; **Features Editor:** Elaine Bunting; **Advertising Manager:** Alan Warren
Summary of Content: Magazine containing information on events, cruising, techniques and equipment.
Readership/Target Audience: Aimed at the international yachtsman.
ADVERTISING RATES:
Full Page Mono £1983.00
Full Page Colour £3654.00
Agency Commission: 10%
Mechanical Data: Film: Digital, Type Area: 270 x 200mm, Col Length: 270mm, Page Width: 200mm, Trim Size: 300 x 230mm, Bleed Size: 306 x 236mm
Copy instructions: Copy Date: 4 weeks prior to publication date
Average advertising content per issue: 60%
Supplement(s): Supersail World - 2xY
CONSUMER: RECREATION & LEISURE: Boating & Yachting

YACHTS AND YACHTING
48401U91A-280
Editorial Address: 196 Eastern Esplanade, SOUTHEND-ON-SEA, SS1 3AB **Tel:** 01702 582245 **Fax:** 01702 588434
Email: editorial@yachtsandyachting.com
Advertising Address: As above.
Email: james@yachtsandyachting.com
Web site: http://www.yachtsandyachting.com
ISSN: 0044-0000

Publisher: Yachting Press Ltd
Date Established: 1947
Frequency: Monthly
Cover Price: £3.99
Circulation: 22,000 (Publisher's Statement)
Usual Pagination: 144
Editor: Gael Pawson; **Managing Director:** John Heyes; **Advertising Manager:** Fred Willis
Summary of Content: Publication covering UK and international sailing as well as performance tips, personality profiles and gossip.
Readership/Target Audience: Aimed at sailing enthusiasts.
ADVERTISING RATES:
Full Page Colour £3029.00
Agency Commission: 10%
Mechanical Data: Type Area: 258 x 179mm, Col Length: 258mm, Bleed Size: 306 x 236mm, Trim Size: 300 x 230mm, Film: Digital, Page Width: 179mm
Copy instructions: Copy Date: 6 weeks prior to publication date
Average advertising content per issue: 35%
CONSUMER: RECREATION & LEISURE: Boating & Yachting

YACHTWORLD.COM MAGAZINE
1839991U91A-302
Editorial Address: 8-10 Furzehall Farm, Wickham Road, FAREHAM, PO16 7JH **Tel:** 01329 222300
Fax: 01329 222301
Email: clare@yachtworldmagazine.com
Web site: http://www.yachtworld.com
ISSN: 1756-3828
Date Established: 2008
Frequency: Monthly
Cover Price: Free
Circulation: 12,000 (Publisher's Statement)
Usual Pagination: 100
Editor: Clare Willison
Summary of Content: Magazine offering practical advice on buying and selling yachts, news and views and article covering charter, cruising, brokerage industry, product launches and regulation changes.
Readership/Target Audience: Aimed at those buying or selling yachts over £100,000.
CONSUMER: RECREATION & LEISURE: Boating & Yachting

YARN FORWARD
1846555U74E-707
Editorial Address: Units 6-8 87 Trowbridge Road, BRADFORD ON AVON, BA15 1EG **Tel:** 07818 082818
Email: lou@kalmedia.co.uk
Web site: http://www.yarnforwardmagazine.co.uk
Publisher: KAL Media
Date Established: 2006
Frequency: Monthly
Cover Price: £4.50
Circulation: 3,000 (Publisher's Statement)
Editor: Louise Butt
Summary of Content: Magazine covering all aspects of knitting, crochet and yarns.
Readership/Target Audience: Aimed at knitters with some previous experience.
CONSUMER: WOMEN'S INTEREST CONSUMER MAGAZINES: Crafts

YEAHBABY
1744835U89D-525
Editorial Address: 141-143 Shoreditch High Street, LONDON, E1 6JE **Tel:** 020 7613 8777 **Fax:** 020 7613 8776
Email: bmibaby@ink-publishing.com
Advertising Address: As above. **Fax:** 020 7613 8778
Email: stefan.bartsch@ink-publishing.com
Web site: http://www.bmibabymagazine.com
Publisher: Ink Publishing
Frequency: 6 issues yearly
Cover Price: Free
Circulation: 750,000 (Publisher's Statement)
Usual Pagination: 100
Editor: Ginny Cumming; **Advertising Manager:** Stefan Bartsch
Summary of Content: In-flight magazine of bmi baby.
Readership/Target Audience: Aimed at passengers on bmi baby flights.
ADVERTISING RATES:
Full Page Colour £4795.00
Agency Commission: 10%
Mechanical Data: Type Area: 255 x 195mm, Col Length: 255mm, Trim Size: 275 x 215mm, Page Width: 195mm
Copy instructions: Copy Date: 7th of the month prior to publication date
CONSUMER: HOLIDAYS & TRAVEL: In-Flight Magazines

YOGA AND HEALTH
45456U74G-200
Editorial Address: 101 Matilda House, St. Katherine's Way, LONDON, E1W 9LF **Tel:** 020 7480 5456 **Fax:** 020 7480 5456
Email: janesill@aol.com

Advertising Address: SDB Marketing, Unit 28, The Old Town Hall, 142 Albion Street, Southwick, BRIGHTON, BN42 4AX **Tel:** 01273 594455 **Fax:** 01273 594458
Email: simon@sdbmarketing.co.uk
Web site: http://www.yogaandhealthmag.com
Publisher: Yoga Today Ltd
Date Established: 1974
Frequency: Monthly - Published on the 1st of the month
Cover Price: £2.30
Annual Sub.: £22.00
Circulation: 15,000 (Publisher's Statement)
Usual Pagination: 50
Editor: Jane Sill; **Advertising Manager:** Simon Briant
Summary of Content: Magazine covering all aspects of yoga and health subjects such as health foods, nutrition and holistic approaches to health, ecology and green issues.
Readership/Target Audience: Read by adults interested in yoga, relaxation and a healthy life.
ADVERTISING: Rates on application
CONSUMER: WOMEN'S INTEREST CONSUMER MAGAZINES: Slimming & Health

YOGA MAGAZINE (MIND BODY SPIRIT)
1626019U74G-236
Formerly: Yoga Magazine
Editorial Address: 233 Bethnal Green Road, LONDON, E2 6AB **Tel:** 020 7729 5454 **Fax:** 020 7739 0025
Email: halima@yogamagazine.co.uk
Advertising Address: Mongoose Media, Mongoose House, Lonsdale Road, LONDON, NW6 6RD **Tel:** 020 7306 0300
Fax: 020 7306 0301
Email: yoga@mongoosemedia.com
Web site: http://www.yogamagazine.co.uk
ISSN: 1478-9671
Publisher: YOGA Magazine Ltd
Frequency: Monthly
Cover Price: £2.95
Annual Sub.: £
Circulation: 90,000 (Publisher's Statement)
Usual Pagination: 100
Editor: Halima Malik; **Advertising Manager:** Bhupinder Ran
Summary of Content: Magazine covering all aspects of yoga as well as articles on mind, body and spirit issues fashion, travel, reviews, advice and shopping.
Readership/Target Audience: Aimed predominantly at women between 20 and 55 years old of all yoga levels.
ADVERTISING RATES:
Full Page Colour £1117.00
Agency Commission: 10%
Mechanical Data: Bleed Size: 303 x 216mm, Trim Size: 297 x 210mm, Type Area: 275 x 190mm, Col Length: 275mm, Page Width: 190mm, Film: Digital
Copy instructions: Copy Date: 3 weeks prior to publication date
CONSUMER: WOMEN'S INTEREST CONSUMER MAGAZINES: Slimming & Health

THE YORK FREE GUIDE
48172U89C-925
Editorial Address: PO Box 29, 76-86 Walmgate, YORK, YO1 9YN **Tel:** 01904 567141 **Fax:** 01904 612853
Email: lynne.martin@thepress.co.uk
Advertising Address: As above. **Tel:** 01904 653051
Fax: 01904 611488
Email: cpsales@ycp.co.uk
Web site: http://www.yorkpress.co.uk
Publisher: Newsquest Yorkshire and North East (York)
Date Established: 1998
Frequency: Monthly
Cover Price: Free
Circulation: 10,000 (Publisher's Statement)
Usual Pagination: 36
Editor: Lynne Martin; **Advertising Manager:** Alyson Liversedge
Summary of Content: Guide to events and places of interest including exhibitions, museums, the theatre and historical attractions.
Readership/Target Audience: Aimed at visitors to York and the surrounding area.
ADVERTISING RATES:
Full Page Colour £275.00
Agency Commission: 10%
Mechanical Data: Film: Digital, Trim Size: 790 x 190mm
Copy instructions: Copy Date: 4 weeks prior to publication date
Average advertising content per issue: 30%
CONSUMER: HOLIDAYS & TRAVEL: Entertainment Guides

THE YORK NEWS & TIMES
1834348U80C-5442
Editorial Address: Oaktree Farm, The Moor, Haxby, YORK, YO32 2LH **Tel:** 01904 767881 **Fax:** 01904 764843
Email: info@yourlocallink.co.uk
Advertising Address: As above.
Email: tracy@yourlocallink.co.uk
Web site: http://www.yourlocalweblink.co.uk
Publisher: Your Local Link Ltd
Date Established: 2008

Frequency: Monthly
Cover Price: Free
Circulation: 87,900 (Publisher's Statement)
Usual Pagination: 40
Editor: Tracy Outram; **Advertising Manager:** Tracy Outram
Summary of Content: Magazine featuring recruitment, housing, finance and local issues.
Readership/Target Audience: Aimed at people living or working in York.
ADVERTISING RATES:
SCC £14.00
Mechanical Data: Film: Digital, Col Widths (Display): 40mm, No. of Columns (Display): 6
CONSUMER: RURAL & REGIONAL INTEREST: Regional Interest English Counties

YORK TWENTY4SEVEN
48090U89C-142_25
Formerly: Friday Night Fever
Editorial Address: PO Box 29, 76-86 Walmgate, YORK, YO1 9YN **Tel:** 01904 653051 **Fax:** 01904 612853
Email: features@thepress.co.uk
Advertising Address: As above. **Fax:** 01904 676400
Email: entertainments@ycp.co.uk
Web site: http://www.thepress.co.uk
Publisher: York & County Press
Date Established: 2003
Frequency: Weekly
Cover Price: Free
Circulation: 33,000 (Publisher's Statement)
Usual Pagination: 20
Editor: Julian Cole; **Advertising Manager:** Sally Trousdale
Summary of Content: Guide to what's on in York and the local region, TV Listings and weekly TV review.
Readership/Target Audience: Aimed at those living in and around York.
ADVERTISING RATES:
Full Page Mono £2754.80
Full Page Colour £3442.50
Mechanical Data: Film: Digital, Type Area: 340 x 259mm, Col Length: 340mm, Page Width: 259mm
Copy instructions: Copy Date: Tuesday 5pm prior to publication date
Supplement to: The Press (York)
CONSUMER: HOLIDAYS & TRAVEL: Entertainment Guides

YORK WHAT'S ON
48173U89C-950
Editorial Address: 20 George Hudson Street, YORK, YO1 6WR **Tel:** 01904 554455 **Fax:** 01904 554460
Email: rn@visityork.org
Advertising Address: As above. **Tel:** 01904 554464
Email: rn@visityork.org
Web site: http://www.whatsonyork.com
Publisher: Visit York
Frequency: 11 issues yearly - Combined issues December/January
Cover Price: Free
Circulation: 25,000 (Publisher's Statement)
Usual Pagination: 16
Editor: Kay Hyde; **Advertising Manager:** Rachel Norris
Summary of Content: Guide for visitors and residents to exhibitions and entertainment in the local area.
Readership/Target Audience: Aimed at residents and visitors of York.
ADVERTISING RATES:
Full Page Colour £300.00
Mechanical Data: Type Area: 187 x 133mm, Bleed Size: 216 x 154mm, Trim Size: A5, Col Length: 187mm, Page Width: 133mm
Copy instructions: Copy Date: 10th of month prior to publication date
Average advertising content per issue: 50%
CONSUMER: HOLIDAYS & TRAVEL: Entertainment Guides

THE YORKER
47466U83-97
Formerly: York Vision
Editorial Address: Grimston House, University of York, Heslington, YORK, YO10 5DD **Tel:** 01904 433720
Fax: 01904 433720
Email: editor@theyorker.co.uk
Advertising Address: As above.
Email: managinged@yorkvision.ac.uk
Web site: http://www.theyorker.co.uk
Publisher: York University Students' Union
Date Established: 1986
Frequency: 9 issues yearly - Three times a term
Cover Price: Free
Circulation: 3,000 (Publisher's Statement)
Usual Pagination: 44
Editor: Marie Thouaille; **News Editor:** Antonia Moura; **Features Editor:** Victoria Walvis; **Advertising Manager:** Alex Richman
Summary of Content: Student paper featuring current news stories and interviews. Includes features on politics, film, books, lifestyle, food and drink, the arts and sport.
Readership/Target Audience: Aimed at York University students and staff.

ADVERTISING RATES:
Full Page Mono £500.00
Full Page Colour £650.00
Agency Commission: 10%
Mechanical Data: Type Area: 350 x 263mm, Col Length: 350mm, Page Width: 263mm, Film: Digital
Copy instructions: Copy Date: 1 week prior to publication date
Average advertising content per issue: 15%
CONSUMER: STUDENT PUBLICATIONS

YORKSHIRE ADVERTISER (RYEDALE AND NORTH YORK MOORS)
47018U80C-3735
Editorial Address: Kirkdale Road, Kirkbymoorside, YORK, YO62 6YB **Tel:** 01751 434609 **Fax:** 01751 432536
Advertising Address: As above.
Email: yorkshireadvertiser@ryedalegroup.co.uk
ISSN: 1470-1634
Publisher: The Ryedale Group
Date Established: 1986
Frequency: 11 issues yearly - December and January is a double issue
Cover Price: Free
Circulation: 15,000 (Publisher's Statement)
Usual Pagination: 48
Editor: Emma Brackley; **Managing Director:** John Buffoni; **Advertising Manager:** Jessica Loughran
Summary of Content: Local and regional interest magazine covering home, gardens and leisure features in Ryedale, Hambletons and the North Yorkshire Moors.
Readership/Target Audience: Aimed at tourists and residents of the North Yorkshire Moors, Hambletons and Ryedale area.
ADVERTISING RATES:
Full Page Mono £220.00
Full Page Colour £276.00
Agency Commission: 10%
Mechanical Data: Film: Positive, right reading, emulsion side down
Copy instructions: Copy Date: 7th of the month prior to publication date
Average advertising content per issue: 60%
CONSUMER: RURAL & REGIONAL INTEREST: Regional Interest English Counties

YORKSHIRE LIFE
47020U80C-3750
Editorial Address: PO Box 163, RIPON, HG4 9AG
Tel: 0113 251 5027 **Fax:** 0113 251 5100
Email: esther.leach@yorkshirelife.co.uk
Advertising Address: As above.
Email: rebecca.baird@yorkshirelife.co.uk
Web site: http://www.yorkshirelife.co.uk
Publisher: Archant Norfolk
Date Established: 1946
Frequency: Monthly
Cover Price: £2.75
Annual Sub.: £29.00
Circulation: 22,644 (ABC 01/01/2008 to 31/12/2008)
Usual Pagination: 212
Editor: Esther Leach; **Publisher:** Andy Phelan; **Circulation Manager:** Robert Hughes
Summary of Content: Magazine containing features on personalities, food and drink, gardening, property, the arts and town and village profiles.
Readership/Target Audience: Read by residents of Yorkshire and those who enjoy the finer things in life.
ADVERTISING RATES:
Full Page Colour £2005.00
Agency Commission: 10%
Mechanical Data: Page Width: 199mm, Trim Size: 300 x 220mm, Bleed Size: 306 x 226mm, Film: Digital, Type Area: 271 x 199mm, Col Length: 271mm
Copy instructions: Copy Date: 2 weeks prior to publication date
Average advertising content per issue: 40%
CONSUMER: RURAL & REGIONAL INTEREST: Regional Interest English Counties

YORKSHIRE LIVING
1806073U80C-5424
Editorial Address: PO Box 29, 76-86 Walmgate, YORK, YO1 9YN **Tel:** 01904 653051
Email: francine.clee@ycp.co.uk
Advertising Address: As above. **Fax:** 01904 611488
Email: charlotte.baker@ycp.co.uk
Publisher: Newsquest Yorkshire and North East (York)
Frequency: Monthly
Cover Price: Free
Circulation: 20,000 (Print Run)
Usual Pagination: 116
Editor: Francine Clee
Summary of Content: Magazine covering property, leisure, luxury and lifestyle in North and East Yorkshire.
Readership/Target Audience: Aimed at residents in North and East Yorkshire.
ADVERTISING RATES:
Full Page Colour £1000.00

Agency Commission: 10%
Mechanical Data: Bleed Size: 305 x 215mm, Trim Size: 267 x 188mm, Film: Digital
Copy instructions: Copy Date: 2 weeks prior to publication date
Average advertising content per issue: 50%
CONSUMER: RURAL & REGIONAL INTEREST: Regional Interest English Counties

YORKSHIRE LIVING BRIDES
1663953U74L-227
Formerly: Yorkshire Weddings
Editorial Address: PO Box 29, 76-86 Walmgate, YORK, YO1 9YN **Tel:** 01904 653051 **Fax:** 01904 612853
Email: lynne.martin@thepress.co.uk
Advertising Address: As above. **Tel:** 01904 567170
Fax: 01904 611488
Email: alyson.liversedge@ycp.co.uk
Web site: http://www.yorkpress.co.uk
Publisher: York & County Press
Frequency: Half-yearly - Published in April and August
Cover Price: Free
Circulation: 35,000 (Publisher's Statement)
Usual Pagination: 60
Editor: Lynne Martin; **Advertising Manager:** Alyson Liversedge
Summary of Content: Magazine covering everything for the bride to be including fashion, hair, flowers, lingerie, venues, catering, gifts, honeymoons, jewellery, hen nights and invitations.
Readership/Target Audience: Aimed at brides to be.
ADVERTISING RATES:
Full Page Colour £600.00
Agency Commission: 10%
Mechanical Data: Film: Digital, Trim Size: 297 x 210mm, Type Area: 267 x 188mm, Col Length: 267mm, Page Width: 188mm
Copy instructions: Copy Date: 4 weeks prior to publication date
Average advertising content per issue: 30%
CONSUMER: WOMEN'S INTEREST CONSUMER MAGAZINES: Brides

YORKSHIRE RELISH
1804891U80C-5415
Editorial Address: 1200 Century Way, Thorpe Park, LEEDS, LS15 8ZA **Tel:** 0113 251 5027 **Fax:** 0113 251 5100
Email: esther.leach@yorkshirelife.co.uk
Advertising Address: As above. **Tel:** 01772 722022
Fax: 01772 736496
Email: les.banton@archant.co.uk
Web site: http://www.yorkshirelife.co.uk
Publisher: Archant Norfolk
Frequency: Half-yearly - Published in June and November
Editor: Esther Leach; **Publisher:** Chris Jennings
Summary of Content: Magazine covering food and wine and places to eat, drink and stay.
Readership/Target Audience: Aimed at residents and visitors to Yorkshire.
ADVERTISING RATES:
Full Page Colour £1495.00
Agency Commission: 10%
Mechanical Data: Type Area: 271 x 199mm, Bleed Size: 306 x 226mm, Trim Size: 300 x 220mm, Col Length: 271mm, Page Width: 199mm, Film: Digital, Col Widths (Display): 46mm
CONSUMER: RURAL & REGIONAL INTEREST: Regional Interest English Counties

YORKSHIRE RIDINGS MAGAZINE
47021U80C-3760
Editorial Address: Unit 200, Oystons Mill, Strand Road, PRESTON, PR1 8UR **Tel:** 01772 761277 **Fax:** 01772 739202
Email: info@lancashiremagazine.co.uk
Advertising Address: As above.
Email: janet.m@yorkshireridingsmagazine.co.uk
ISSN: 0960-0000
Publisher: Ridings Publishing Co.
Date Established: 1964
Frequency: Monthly
Cover Price: £1.40
Annual Sub.: £10.00
Circulation: 12,175 (ABC 01/07/2008 to 31/12/2008)
Usual Pagination: 100
Editor: Anthony Skinner; **Circulation Manager:** Peter Fisher
Summary of Content: County magazine featuring furnishings, art and antiques, health, eating out, gardening, kitchen corner, fashion, the outdoors and country shopping.
Readership/Target Audience: Aimed at residents of Yorkshire and those with an interest in Yorkshire.
ADVERTISING RATES:
Full Page Colour £1200.00
Agency Commission: 10%
Mechanical Data: Col Length: 278mm, Print Process: Sheet-fed litho, Trim Size: 297mm x 210mm, Type Area: 278 x 200mm, Page Width: 200mm, Film: Digital
Copy instructions: Copy Date: 2 months prior to publication date

Consumer Magazines

Average advertising content per issue: 30%
CONSUMER: RURAL & REGIONAL INTEREST: Regional
Interest English Counties

YORKSHIRE SPORT
45729U75A-990

Editorial Address: PO Box 168, Wellington Street, LEEDS,
LS1 1RF **Tel:** 0113 243 2701 **Fax:** 0113 238 8536
Email: yep.sport@ypn.co.uk
Advertising Address: As above. **Fax:** 0113 383 1356
Email: christopher.tremlett@ypn.co.uk
Web site: http://www.yorkshireeveningpost.co.uk
Publisher: Yorkshire Post Newspapers Ltd
Date Established: 1997
Frequency: Weekly - Published on Sunday
Cover Price: £0.85
Circulation: 10,000 (Publisher's Statement)
Usual Pagination: 44
Editor: Mark Absolon
Summary of Content: Newspaper covering sports in
Yorkshire. Includes a round-up of results and league tables.
Readership/Target Audience: Aimed at people interested
in Yorkshire sport.
ADVERTISING RATES:
Full Page Mono £336.06
Full Page Colour £437.58
Agency Commission: 10%
Mechanical Data: Film: Digital, Type Area: 340 x 265mm,
Page Width: 265mm, Col Length: 340mm, No. of Columns
(Display): 9
Copy instructions: Copy Date: Friday 12 noon prior to
publication date
Average advertising content per issue: 20%
CONSUMER: SPORT

YORKSHIRE TODAY
1704766U80C-5292

Editorial Address: Armstrong House, Armstrong Street,
GRIMSBY, DN31 2QE **Tel:** 01472 310305
Fax: 01472 310317
Email: s.williams@blmgroup.co.uk
Advertising Address: As above. **Fax:** 01472 310312
Email: t.cooper@blmgroup.co.uk
Web site: http://www.yorkshiretoday.net
ISSN: 1740-3472
Publisher: Haychart Ltd
Date Established: 2003
Frequency: Monthly
Cover Price: £2.25
Circulation: 17,500 (Publisher's Statement)
Usual Pagination: 100
Editor: Steve Fisher; **Circulation Manager:** Dawn Cook
Summary of Content: Regional lifestyle magazine
containing articles on places of interest in Yorkshire, what's
on, travel, motoring, restaurants, hotels, leisure, heritage,
antiques, hair, beauty, health and fitness, fashion and
celebrities.
Readership/Target Audience: Aimed at residents in
Yorkshire aged between 25 and 50 years old.
ADVERTISING RATES:
Full Page Mono £865.00
Full Page Colour £1150.00
Agency Commission: 10%
Mechanical Data: Type Area: 277 x 190mm, Col Length:
277mm, Page Width: 190mm, Film: Digital
Copy instructions: Copy Date: 2 weeks prior to publication
date
Average advertising content per issue: 30%
CONSUMER: RURAL & REGIONAL INTEREST: Regional
Interest English Counties

YORKSHIRE WOMEN'S LIFE MAGAZINE
765782U74Q-1123

Formerly: Yorkshire Womans Life Magazine
Editorial Address: PO Box 113, LEEDS, LS8 2WX
Tel: 0113 262 1409 **Fax:** 0113 240 7199
Email: ywlmagenquiries@btinternet.com
Advertising Address: As above.
Email: ywladvertising@btinternet.com
Web site: http://www.yorkshirewomenslife.co.uk
ISSN: 1476-4601
Publisher: Yorkshire Women's Life Magazine
Date Established: 2001
Frequency: 3 issues yearly - Published in March/April, July/
August and November/December
Annual Sub.: £9.25
Circulation: 15,000 (Publisher's Statement)
Usual Pagination: 30
Editor: Anna Jenkins; **Advertising Manager:** Anna Jenkins
Summary of Content: Handbag sized women's magazine
covering lifestyle, regional and international news, women
focus issues, art and travel.
Readership/Target Audience: Aimed at professional career
women aged 30 years old and over.
ADVERTISING RATES:
Full Page Mono £455.00
Full Page Colour £580.00
Agency Commission: 15%

Mechanical Data: Film: Digital, Col Widths (Display): 44mm,
Bleed Size: 303 x 216mm, Type Area: 258 x 185mm, Col
Length: 258mm, Page Width: 185mm, Print Process: Litho
print
Copy instructions: Copy Date: 3 weeks prior to publication
date
Average advertising content per issue: 30%
CONSUMER: WOMEN'S INTEREST CONSUMER
MAGAZINES: Lifestyle

YOU & YOUR FAMILY
1824293U74D-660

Editorial Address: 134 Liverpool Road, LONDON, N1 1LA
Tel: 020 7665 1111 **Fax:** 020 7609 5837
Email: trisha.doyle@ashville.com
Advertising Address: As above.
Email: andy.roberts@cwcomms.com
Web site: http://www.youandyourfamily.com
Publisher: CW Publishing Group
Date Established: 2008
Frequency: Half-yearly - Published in January and July
Cover Price: Free
Circulation: 250,000 (Print Run)
Usual Pagination: 180
Editor: Trisha Doyle; **Advertising Manager:** Sema Demir
Summary of Content: Magazine covering pregnancy and
baby issue up to a year old.
Readership/Target Audience: Aimed at pregnant women in
their second trimester through their midwife.
ADVERTISING: Rates on application
CONSUMER: WOMEN'S INTEREST CONSUMER
MAGAZINES: Child Care

YOU & YOUR WEDDING
45541U74L-210

Editorial Address: National Magazine House, 72 Broadwick
Street, LONDON, W1F 9EP **Tel:** 020 7439 5000
Fax: 020 7439 2985
Email: yywinfo@natmags.co.uk
Advertising Address: As above. **Fax:** 020 7287 8655
Email: katie.rose@natmags.co.uk
Web site: http://www.youandyourwedding.co.uk
ISSN: 0267-2391
Publisher: National Magazine Company Ltd
Frequency: 6 issues yearly
Cover Price: £4.60
Circulation: 58,046 (ABC 01/01/2008 to 31/12/2008)
Usual Pagination: 350
Editor: Colette Harris; **Advertising Manager:** Katie Rose;
Publisher: Matt Salmon
Summary of Content: Magazine containing everything for
the modern young bride, from wedding outfits to honeymoon
destinations and setting up home.
Readership/Target Audience: Aimed at brides-to-be
between 25 and 34 years old.
ADVERTISING RATES:
Full Page Colour £9865.00
Agency Commission: 15%
Mechanical Data: Film: Positive, right reading, emulsion
side down. Digital, Bleed Size: 291 x 226mm, Trim Size: 285
x 220mm, Type Area: 265 x 204mm, Col Length: 265mm,
Page Width: 204mm
Copy instructions: Copy Date: 8 weeks prior to publication
date
CONSUMER: WOMEN'S INTEREST CONSUMER
MAGAZINES: Brides

YOU CAN!
47905U88B-150

Editorial Address: Rosehill, New Barn Lane,
CHELTENHAM, GL52 3LZ **Tel:** 01242 544873
Fax: 01242 544806
Email: youcan@ucas.ac.uk
Advertising Address: Independent House, 191 Marsh Wall,
LONDON, E14 9RS **Tel:** 020 7005 2600 **Fax:** 020 7005 2156
Email: m.simmons@independent.co.uk
Web site: http://www.ucas.com
Publisher: UCAS
Frequency: 3 issues yearly - Published in May, September
and November
Cover Price: Free
Circulation: 140,000 (Publisher's Statement)
Usual Pagination: 42
Editor: Chris Dry; **Editor-in-Chief:** Anthony McClaran;
Advertising Manager: Marcus Simmons; **Managing Editor:**
Darren Barker
Summary of Content: Magazine containing advice and
information on further education.
Readership/Target Audience: Aimed at students choosing
and entering higher education.
ADVERTISING RATES:
Full Page Colour £9500.00
Agency Commission: 15%
Mechanical Data: Type Area: 231 x 189mm, Bleed Size:
262 x 219mm, Trim Size: 256 x 213mm, Col Length: 231mm,
Page Width: 189mm, Film: Digital
Copy instructions: Copy Date: 3 weeks prior to publication
date
CONSUMER: EDUCATION: Adult Education

YOU FOOD
1856860U74P-962

Editorial Address: 16 Lower Road, Higher Denham,
UXBRIDGE, UB9 5EA **Tel:** 01895 832259
Email: tracyreader@you-food.co.uk
Web site: http://www.you-food.co.uk
Publisher: You Food Ltd
Date Established: 2008
Frequency: Quarterly
Cover Price: Free
Circulation: 18,000 (Publisher's Statement)
Usual Pagination: 24
Editor: Tracy Reader
Summary of Content: Magazine covering all food related
topics. Information on shopping, cooking, eating out, where
to find local, free-range, organic, healthy, budget,
convenience and gourmet food.
Readership/Target Audience: Aimed at local residents in
South Buckinghamshire and North West London.
CONSUMER: WOMEN'S INTEREST CONSUMER
MAGAZINES: Food & Cookery

YOU ME BABY
1900158U74G-303

Editorial Address: The Coach House, Calehill Park, Little
Chart, ASHFORD, TN27 0QG **Tel:** 0845 862 2344
Email: kathy.carter@youmebaby.co.uk
Web site: http://www.youmebaby.co.uk
Publisher: You Me Baby LTD
Frequency: Monthly
Cover Price: Free
Circulation: 43,170 (Publisher's Statement)
Editor: Kathy Carter; **Publisher:** Sean Kane
CONSUMER: WOMEN'S INTEREST CONSUMER
MAGAZINES: Slimming & Health

YOUNG PERFORMER
1829669U84A-464

Editorial Address: 9 Savoy Street, LONDON, WC2E 7HR
Tel: 020 7878 2300
Email: liz.granirer@gmail.com
Web site: http://www.youngperformer.co.uk
Publisher: Ten Alps Publishing plc
Frequency: 6 issues yearly
Cover Price: £1.99
Circulation: 34,000 (Publisher's Statement)
Usual Pagination: 44
Editor: Liz Granirer; **Advertising Manager:** Georgia Samuel-
Camps
Summary of Content: Magazine with features about TV,
film, the stage, singing, music and dance, as well as
competitions, interviews and news of what's happening in
the world of performing arts. Published for Stagecoach
Theatre Arts.
Readership/Target Audience: Aimed at young people for
whom acting, singing and dancing is a passion.
CONSUMER: THE ARTS & LITERARY: Arts

YOUNG SCOT PORTAL
45399U74F-750

Formerly: Young Scot Magazine
Editorial Address: Rosebery House, 9 Haymarket Terrace,
EDINBURGH, EH12 5EZ **Tel:** 0131 313 2488
Fax: 0131 313 6800
Email: info@youngscot.org
Web site: http://www.youngscot.org
Publisher: Young Scot Magazine
Date Established: 2001
Frequency: Quarterly - See main record for circulation figure
Cover Price: Free
Circulation: 590,000 (Publisher's Statement)
Usual Pagination: 16
Editor: Martin Dewar
Summary of Content: Magazine of Young Scot the national
youth information and discount charity. Includes information
and ideas for young people in Scotland.
Readership/Target Audience: Read by 11 to 26 year olds
in Scotland.
ADVERTISING: No Advertising taken
Supplement to: Daily Record
CONSUMER: WOMEN'S INTEREST CONSUMER
MAGAZINES: Teenage

YOUNG VOICES
1638424U90-924

Editorial Address: Northern and Shell Tower, 6th Floor, 4
Selsdon Way, LONDON, E14 9GL **Tel:** 020 7510 0340
Fax: 020 7510 0341
Email: newsdesk@gvmedia.co.uk
Advertising Address: As above. **Fax:** 020 7738 5361
Email: advertising@the-voice.co.uk
Web site: http://www.young-voices.co.uk
Publisher: GV Media Ltd
Date Established: 2003
Frequency: Monthly
Cover Price: £2.40
Circulation: 40,000 (Print Run)
Usual Pagination: 68

Editor: Dionne Grant; **News Editor:** Andrew Clunis; **Features Editor:** Rodney Hinds; **Advertising Manager:** Ope Bankole; **Circulation Manager:** Laurence White
Summary of Content: Magazine covering urban music and fashion.
Readership/Target Audience: Aimed at those aged between 11 to 16 years old.
ADVERTISING RATES:
Full Page Colour £2500.00
Agency Commission: 10%
Mechanical Data: Trim Size: 297 x 210mm, Bleed Size: 303 x 216mm, Type Area: 280 x 190mm, Film: Digital, Col Length: 280mm, Page Width: 190mm
Copy instructions: Copy Date: 7 days prior to publication date
Average advertising content per issue: 35%
CONSUMER: ETHNIC

YOUR BABY
1833991U74D-668

Editorial Address: Dephna House, 24-26 Arcadia Avenue, LONDON, N3 2JU **Tel:** 020 8349 7192 **Fax:** 020 8349 7193
Email: yourkids@lyonsdown.co.uk
Web site: http://www.lyonsdown.co.uk/pub_title_cosmetic.php?sortby=Y&pubid=38
Publisher: Lyonsdown Ltd
Date Established: 2007
Frequency: Annual - Published on the 6th October
Cover Price: Free
Editor: Anthony Wilks
Summary of Content: Magazine promoting the physical and emotional well-being of babies.
Readership/Target Audience: Aimed at parents of babies and expectant mums.
Supplement to: The Guardian
CONSUMER: WOMEN'S INTEREST CONSUMER MAGAZINES: Child Care

YOUR BERKS & BUCKS WEDDING
1790468U74L-257

Formerly: Berks & Bucks Your Wedding
Editorial Address: Broseley House, Newlands Drive, WITHAM, CM8 2UL **Tel:** 01376 514000 **Fax:** 01376 514555
Email: editorial@countyweddingmagazines.com
Advertising Address: As above. **Tel:** 0870 609 1628
Email: scottb@countyweddingmagazines.com
Web site: http://www.berksandbuckswedding.com
ISSN: 1751-7087
Publisher: Kline Davis Ltd
Date Established: 2006
Frequency: 6 issues yearly
Cover Price: £2.95
Circulation: 5,000 (Publisher's Statement)
Usual Pagination: 100
Editor: Rowena Marella-Daw; **Features Editor:** Rowena Marella-Daw; **Group Editor:** Emma Cant
Summary of Content: Magazine covering all aspects of weddings including venues, grooms, fashion, real weddings, honeymoons, grooms, cakes, catering, news, events, give-aways, letters and question and answers.
Readership/Target Audience: Aimed at brides and grooms in Berkshire and Buckinghamshire.
ADVERTISING RATES:
Full Page Colour £900.00
Agency Commission: 10%
Mechanical Data: Bleed Size: 303 x 216mm, Trim Size: 297 x 210mm, Film: Digital
Copy instructions: Copy Date: 2 weeks prior to publication date
Average advertising content per issue: 40%
CONSUMER: WOMEN'S INTEREST CONSUMER MAGAZINES: Brides

YOUR CAMDEN
1626025U80B-406

Formerly: Camden Living
Editorial Address: Room 303, Town Hall, Judd Street, LONDON, WC1H 9JE **Tel:** 020 7974 6021
Fax: 020 7974 5718
Email: yourcamden@camden.gov.uk
Advertising Address: As above. **Tel:** 020 7974 5573
Email: yourcamden@camden.gov.uk
Web site: http://www.camden.gov.uk/yourcamden
Publisher: The London Borough of Camden
Date Established: 2006
Frequency: 11 issues yearly - Double issue December/January
Cover Price: Free
Circulation: 105,000 (Publisher's Statement)
Usual Pagination: 24
Editor: Colette Smith; **Advertising Manager:** Ashley Wilcox
Summary of Content: Magazine covering council and local news, vox pops, campaigns, competitions, events, entertainment listings and services.
Language(s): Bengali; English; Somali
Readership/Target Audience: Aimed at those living, working and studying in Camden.

ADVERTISING RATES:
Full Page Colour £1750.00
Mechanical Data: Bleed Size: 306 x 238mm, Film: Digital, Type Area: 290 x 222mm, Col Length: 290mm, Page Width: 222mm
Copy instructions: Copy Date: Beginning of the month prior to publication date
Average advertising content per issue: 17%
CONSUMER: RURAL & REGIONAL INTEREST: Regional Interest Greater London

YOUR CAT
47117U81C-500

Editorial Address: Roebuck House, 33 Broad Street, STAMFORD, PE9 1RB **Tel:** 01780 766199
Fax: 01780 766416
Email: yourcat@bournepublishinggroup.co.uk
Advertising Address: As above. **Fax:** 01780 754774
Email: a.desborough@bournepublishinggroup.co.uk
Web site: http://www.yourcat.co.uk
Publisher: BPG (Stamford) Ltd
Date Established: 1994
Frequency: Monthly
Cover Price: £3.10
Annual Sub.: £37.20
Circulation: 20,000 (Publisher's Statement)
Usual Pagination: 100
Editor: Sue Parslow; **Publisher:** Alison Queenborough
Summary of Content: Magazine containing practical information on behaviour, grooming and all aspects of healthcare. Includes lifestyle features, interviews, cat shopping, fashion and celebrities and a buyers' guide to practical products.
Readership/Target Audience: Aimed at all cat lovers.
ADVERTISING RATES:
Full Page Colour £1935.00
Agency Commission: 10%
Mechanical Data: No. of Columns (Display): 2, Bleed Size: 307 x 215mm, Trim Size: 297 x 210mm, Film: Digital, Col Length: 276mm, Page Width: 185mm, Type Area: 276 x 185mm
Copy instructions: Copy Date: 8 weeks prior to publication date
CONSUMER: ANIMALS & PETS: Cats

YOUR DOG
47109U81B-300

Editorial Address: Roebuck House, 33 Broad Street, STAMFORD, PE9 1RB **Tel:** 01780 766199
Fax: 01780 766416
Email: s.wright@bournepublishinggroup.co.uk
Advertising Address: As above. **Fax:** 01780 754774
Email: b.kane@bournepublishinggroup.co.uk
Web site: http://www.yourdog.co.uk
ISSN: 1355-7386
Publisher: BPG (Stamford) Ltd
Date Established: 1995
Frequency: Monthly
Cover Price: £3.35
Annual Sub.: £37.20
Circulation: 30,552 (ABC 01/01/2009 to 30/06/2009)
Usual Pagination: 116
Editor: Sarah Wright; **Publisher:** Alison Queenborough
Summary of Content: Magazine focusing on canine health and care issues.
Readership/Target Audience: Aimed at pet owners.
ADVERTISING RATES:
Full Page Mono £2068.00
Full Page Colour £2068.00
Agency Commission: 10%
Mechanical Data: Film: Digital, Bleed Size: 307 x 215mm, Trim Size: 297 x 210mm, Type Area: 296 x 196mm, Col Length: 296mm, Page Width: 196mm
Copy instructions: Copy Date: 1st week of two months prior to publication date
CONSUMER: ANIMALS & PETS: Dogs

YOUR FAMILY TREE
1637639U94X-265

Editorial Address: 30 Monmouth Street, BATH, BA1 2BW
Tel: 01225 442244
Email: aray@futurenet.com
Advertising Address: As above. **Fax:** 01225 732341
Email: rachael.unsworth@futurenet.com
Web site: http://www.yourfamilytreemag.co.uk
Publisher: Future Publishing Ltd
Date Established: 2003
Frequency: 13 issues yearly
Cover Price: £4.99
Circulation: 20,413 (ABC 01/01/2008 to 31/12/2008)
Usual Pagination: 100
Editor: Lara Glasspool; **Advertising Manager:** Rachael Unsworth
Summary of Content: Magazine with advice on how to trace your family history, tips from genealogy experts, guidance on using historical sources, case studies and the latest news for family historians.
Readership/Target Audience: Aimed at amateur genealogists and family historians.

ADVERTISING RATES:
Full Page Colour £900.00
Agency Commission: 10%
Mechanical Data: Type Area: 280 x 203mm, Col Length: 280mm, Page Width: 203mm, Trim Size: 300 x 222mm, Bleed Size: 306 x 228mm, No. of Columns (Display): 4, Col Widths (Display): 49mm, Film: Digital
Average advertising content per issue: 20%
CONSUMER: OTHER CLASSIFICATIONS: Miscellaneous

YOUR HAIR
628900U74H-300

Editorial Address: 9th Floor, Tower House, Fairfax Street, BRISTOL, BS1 3BN **Tel:** 0117 927 9009 **Fax:** 0117 934 9008
Email: sophiejordan@originpublishing.co.uk
Advertising Address: As above.
Email: tyronejones@originpublishing.co.uk
Web site: http://www.yourhair.co.uk
Publisher: Origin Publishing Ltd
Frequency: Monthly
Cover Price: £2.99
Circulation: 30,727 (ABC 01/01/2009 to 30/06/2009)
Usual Pagination: 132
Editor: Sarah Trevor; **Publisher:** Alison Worthington
Summary of Content: Magazine covering hair care, includes advice and new hairstyle ideas in each issue.
Readership/Target Audience: Aimed at women between 16 and 30 years old.
ADVERTISING RATES:
Full Page Colour £2422.00
Agency Commission: 10%
Mechanical Data: Page Width: 194mm, Type Area: 281 x 194mm, Col Length: 281mm, Trim Size: 297 x 210mm, Bleed Size: 303 x 216mm, Film: Digital
Average advertising content per issue: 10%
CONSUMER: WOMEN'S INTEREST CONSUMER MAGAZINES: Hair & Beauty

YOUR HAMPSHIRE WEDDING
1800804U74L-263

Editorial Address: Broseley House, Newland Drive, WITHAM, CM8 2UL **Tel:** 01376 535611 **Fax:** 01376 514555
Email: demelzar@klinedavis.com
Advertising Address: As above. **Tel:** 0870 609 1628
Email: katet@countyweddingmagazines.com
Web site: http://www.yourhampshirewedding.com
ISSN: 1753-0903
Publisher: Kline Davis Ltd
Date Established: 2007
Frequency: 6 issues yearly
Cover Price: £2.95
Circulation: 5,000 (Publisher's Statement)
Usual Pagination: 108
Editor: Rowena Marella-Daw; **Features Editor:** Rowena Marella-Daw; **Group Editor:** Emma Cant
Summary of Content: Magazine covering all aspects of weddings including venues, fashion, real weddings, honeymoons, grooms, cakes, catering, news, events, giveaways and questions and answers.
Readership/Target Audience: Aimed at brides and grooms in Hampshire.
ADVERTISING RATES:
Full Page Colour £900.00
Agency Commission: 10%
Mechanical Data: Bleed Size: 303 x 216mm, Trim Size: 297 x 210mm, Film: Digital
Copy instructions: Copy Date: 2 weeks prior to publication date
Average advertising content per issue: 40%
CONSUMER: WOMEN'S INTEREST CONSUMER MAGAZINES: Brides

YOUR HEALTH
712475U75P-225

Formerly: Fitness First
Editorial Address: 3rd Floor, 2-4 St. Georges Road, Wimbledon, LONDON, SW19 4DP **Tel:** 020 8181 5594
Fax: 020 8247 3820
Email: ianmackie@btconnect.com
Advertising Address: As above.
Email: lancem@wppl.biz
Publisher: Weybridge Press and Promotions Ltd
Date Established: 2001
Frequency: Annual - Published in January
Free to qualifying individuals
Circulation: 500,000 (Publisher's Statement)
Usual Pagination: 116
Editor: Ian Mackie
Summary of Content: Covering health, fitness and personal training, fashion, beauty, travel and food.
Readership/Target Audience: Aimed predominantly at members of Fitness First health clubs.
ADVERTISING RATES:
Full Page Colour £9950.00
Agency Commission: 10%
Mechanical Data: Film: Digital, Bleed Size: +3mm, Trim Size: 297 x 210mm
CONSUMER: SPORT: Fitness/Bodybuilding

Consumer Magazines

YOUR HERTS & BEDS WEDDING
1800802U74L-262

Editorial Address: Broseley House, Newland Drive, WITHAM, CM8 2UL **Tel:** 01376 535609 **Fax:** 01376 514555
Email: danielleh@klinedavis.com
Advertising Address: As above. **Tel:** 0870 609 1628
Fax: 0870 609 1652
Email: lindag@klinedavis.com
Web site: http://www.countyweddingmagazines.com
Publisher: Kline Davis Ltd
Frequency: 6 issues yearly
Cover Price: £2.95
Annual Sub.: £15.00
Circulation: 4,000 (Publisher's Statement)
Usual Pagination: 108
Editor: Lisa Morgan; **Group Editor:** Emma Cant
Summary of Content: Magazine covering all aspects of weddings including venues, fashion, real weddings, honeymoons, grooms, cakes, catering, news, events, give-aways and questions and answers.
Readership/Target Audience: Aimed at brides and grooms in Hertfordshire and Bedfordshire.
ADVERTISING RATES:
Full Page Colour £900.00
Mechanical Data: Bleed Size: 303 x 216mm, Trim Size: 297 x 210mm, Film: Digital
CONSUMER: WOMEN'S INTEREST CONSUMER MAGAZINES: Brides

YOUR HOME
45377U74C-805

Editorial Address: The Tower, Phoenix Square, Wyncolls Road, Severalls Industrial Park, COLCHESTER, CO4 9HU
Tel: 01206 851117 **Fax:** 01206 849078
Email: yourhome@burdamagazines.co.uk
Advertising Address: Herbert Burda Media UK, 6th Floor, Swan House, 37-39 High Holborn, LONDON, WC1V 6AA
Tel: 0845 481 0661 **Fax:** 0845 481 0662
Email: lenka@essentialpublishing.co.uk
Web site: http://www.yhmag.co.uk
ISSN: 1367-0727
Publisher: Hubert Burda Media UK
Date Established: 1997
Frequency: 11 issues yearly - Combined issue December/January
Cover Price: £1.99
Circulation: 114,542 (ABC 01/01/2009 to 30/06/2009)
Usual Pagination: 144
Editor: Anna-Lisa De'Ath; **Features Editor:** Lisa Hibberd; **Managing Director:** Luke Patten
Summary of Content: Magazine focusing on the home with features on real life homes, makeovers and gardens, decorating and DIY, furnishing and renovation.
Twitter: https://twitter.com/your_home.
Readership/Target Audience: Aimed at homeowners aged between 25 and 45 years old.
ADVERTISING RATES:
Full Page Colour £3950.00
Agency Commission: 10%
Mechanical Data: Type Area: 270 x 192mm, Bleed Size: 296 x 218mm, Trim Size: 290 x 221mm, Col Length: 270mm, Page Width: 192mm, Film: Digital
Copy instructions: Copy Date: 4 weeks prior to publication date
Average advertising content per issue: 25%
CONSUMER: WOMEN'S INTEREST CONSUMER MAGAZINES: Home & Family

YOUR HORSE
47143U81D-350

Editorial Address: Bushfield House, Orton Centre, PETERBOROUGH, PE2 5UW **Tel:** 01733 465644
Email: julie.brown@bauermedia.co.uk
Advertising Address: As above. **Tel:** 01733 237111
Fax: 01733 288005
Email: lucy.obrien@bauerconsumer.co.uk
Web site: http://www.yourhorse.co.uk
Publisher: Bauer Media Ltd (Orton)
Date Established: 1983
Frequency: 13 issues yearly
Cover Price: £3.70
Circulation: 33,052 (ABC 01/01/2008 to 31/12/2008)
Usual Pagination: 164
Editor: Julie Brown
Summary of Content: Magazine containing ideas, techniques and inspiration for horse owners and riders.
Readership/Target Audience: Aimed at horse owners and riders.
ADVERTISING RATES:
Full Page Colour £2550.00
Agency Commission: 10%
Mechanical Data: Col Length: 275mm, Bleed Size: 307 x 215mm, Trim Size: 297 x 210mm, Page Width: 184mm, Film: Digital, Type Area: 275 x 184mm
Copy instructions: Copy Date: 3 weeks prior to publication date
Average advertising content per issue: 33%
CONSUMER: ANIMALS & PETS: Horses & Ponies

YOUR KENT WEDDING
1790462U74L-255

Editorial Address: Broseley House, Newland Drive, WITHAM, CM8 2UL **Tel:** 01376 514000 **Fax:** 01376 514555
Email: editor@yourkentwedding.com
Advertising Address: As above. **Tel:** 0870 609 1628
Email: amyw@countyweddingmagazines.com
Web site: http://www.yourkentwedding.com
ISSN: 1746-9384
Publisher: Kline Davis Ltd
Date Established: 2005
Frequency: 6 issues yearly
Cover Price: £2.95
Circulation: 5,000 (Publisher's Statement)
Usual Pagination: 100
Editor: Demelza Rayner; **Group Editor:** Demelza Rayner
Summary of Content: Magazine covering all aspects of weddings including venues, fashion, real weddings, honeymoons, grooms, cakes, catering, news, events, give-aways, letters and questions and answers.
Readership/Target Audience: Aimed at brides and grooms in Kent.
ADVERTISING RATES:
Full Page Colour £900.00
Agency Commission: 10%
Mechanical Data: Bleed Size: 303 x 216mm, Trim Size: 297 x 210mm, Film: Digital
Copy instructions: Copy Date: 2 weeks prior to publication date
Average advertising content per issue: 40%
CONSUMER: WOMEN'S INTEREST CONSUMER MAGAZINES: Brides

YOUR M&S MAGAZINE
45277U74C-310

Formerly: Marks and Spencer Magazine
Editorial Address: 7 St. Martin's Place, LONDON, WC2N 4HA **Tel:** 020 7747 0952 **Fax:** 020 7747 0879
Email: alice.makoni@redwoodgroup.net
Advertising Address: As above. **Tel:** 020 7747 0700
Fax: 020 7747 0883
Email: minal.bhima@redwoodgroup.net
Web site: http://www.redwoodgroup.net
ISSN: 0954-2868
Publisher: Redwood
Frequency: 6 issues yearly
Cover Price: £1.20
Free to qualifying individuals
Circulation: 1,000,000 (Publisher's Statement)
Usual Pagination: 132
Editor: Alice Makoni; **Managing Editor:** Michelle George; **Advertisement Director:** Minal Bhima
Summary of Content: Magazine providing a comprehensive coverage of the goods and services available from Marks & Spencer together with lifestyle and travel features.
Readership/Target Audience: Aimed at Marks & Spencer's customers and charge card holders.
ADVERTISING RATES:
Full Page Colour £24220.00
Agency Commission: 15%
Mechanical Data: Bleed Size: 306 x 234mm, Film: Digital
Copy instructions: Copy Date: 6 weeks prior to publication date
Average advertising content per issue: 30%
CONSUMER: WOMEN'S INTEREST CONSUMER MAGAZINES: Home & Family

YOUR MONEY
45563U74M-400

Formerly: Your Money: Savings and Investments
Editorial Address: Haymarket House, 28-29 Haymarket, LONDON, SW1Y 4RX **Tel:** 020 7484 9700
Fax: 020 7484 9900
Email: pauline.mccallion@incisivemedia.com
Advertising Address: As above. **Fax:** 020 7004 7544
Email: paul.bedwell@incisivemedia.com
Web site: http://www.yourmoney.com
ISSN: 1369-6910
Publisher: Incisive Media Investments
Date Established: 1996
Frequency: 3 issues yearly - Published in February, June and September
Cover Price: £3.50
Circulation: 35,000 (Publisher's Statement)
Usual Pagination: 60
Editor: Barney McCarthy; **Editor-in-Chief:** Paula John; **Managing Director:** Jonathan Whiteley; **Advertising Manager:** Paul Bedwell; **Managing Editor:** Ben Marquand
Summary of Content: Magazine covering savings and investments, and all other personal finance products.
Readership/Target Audience: Aimed at consumers of financial products and intelligent, curious laypeople.
ADVERTISING RATES:
Full Page Colour £3000.00
Agency Commission: 10%
Mechanical Data: Bleed Size: 303 x 216mm, Trim Size: 297 x 210mm, Film: Digital
Average advertising content per issue: 40%
CONSUMER: WOMEN'S INTEREST CONSUMER MAGAZINES: Personal Finance

YOUR MORTGAGE
45510U74K-600

Editorial Address: Haymarket House, 28-29 Haymarket, LONDON, SW1Y 4RX **Tel:** 020 7484 9700
Email: yourmortgage@incisivemedia.com
Advertising Address: As above. **Fax:** 020 7004 7544
Email: jamie.hurst@incisivemedia.com
Web site: http://www.yourmortgage.co.uk
ISSN: 1357-4353
Publisher: Incisive Media Investments
Date Established: 1987
Frequency: Monthly
Cover Price: £3.75
Circulation: 20,000 (Publisher's Statement)
Usual Pagination: 82
Editor: Paula John; **Editor-in-Chief:** Paula John; **Managing Editor:** Ben Marquand
Summary of Content: Magazine covering all aspects of the housing and mortgage markets. Includes features on home interest as well as advice on choosing the most suitable mortgage.
Readership/Target Audience: Aimed at homeowners and buyers, re-mortgagers and those interested in buying property to let.
ADVERTISING RATES:
Full Page Mono £5292.00
Full Page Colour £5292.00
Agency Commission: 10%
Mechanical Data: Type Area: 269 x 186mm, Page Width: 186mm, Film: Digital, Bleed Size: 303 x 216mm, Trim Size: 297 x 210mm, Col Length: 269mm, No. of Columns (Display): 2
Copy instructions: Copy Date: 3 weeks prior to publication date
Average advertising content per issue: 35%
Supplement(s): Property Prices - 6xY
CONSUMER: WOMEN'S INTEREST CONSUMER MAGAZINES: Home Purchase

YOUR MOVE
1655125U80C-5132

Editorial Address: 36 Henry Street, LIVERPOOL, L1 5BS
Tel: 0151 709 3871 **Fax:** 0151 707 1678
Email: post@movepublishing.co.uk
Advertising Address: As above.
Email: fiona@movepublishing.co.uk
Web site: http://www.yourmovemagazine.com
Publisher: Move Publishing
Date Established: 1999
Frequency: 26 issues yearly
Cover Price: Free
Circulation: 50,000 (Publisher's Statement)
Usual Pagination: 90
Editor: Lucy Oliver; **Advertising Director:** Fiona Barnett
Summary of Content: Magazine covering property, lifestyle, motoring, theatre, the arts, music, days out and events.
Readership/Target Audience: Aimed at residents and visitors to Liverpool.
ADVERTISING RATES:
Full Page Colour £1155.00
Agency Commission: 10%
Mechanical Data: Type Area: 265 x 190mm, Trim Size: 285 x 210mm, Col Length: 265mm, Page Width: 190mm, Film: Digital, Bleed Size: 295 x 220mm
Copy instructions: Copy Date: 1 week prior to publication date
Average advertising content per issue: 25%
CONSUMER: RURAL & REGIONAL INTEREST: Regional Interest English Counties

YOUR NEW HOME
45511U74K-650

Editorial Address: 60 Churchill Square, Kings Hill, WEST MALLING, ME19 4YU **Tel:** 01732 525800
Fax: 01732 525801
Email: info@yournewhome.co.uk
Advertising Address: As above.
Email: kim@yournewhome.co.uk
Web site: http://www.yournewhome.co.uk
Publisher: NCG Media
Date Established: 1997
Frequency: 6 issues yearly
Cover Price: £2.95
Circulation: 32,000 (Publisher's Statement)
Usual Pagination: 160
Editor: Karen Keeman; **Managing Director:** David Rossiter
Summary of Content: Magazine containing comprehensive advice on general lifestyle, interiors and buying a brand new home. Also includes a location directory.
Readership/Target Audience: Aimed at house buyers, new home owners, investors and foreign buyers.
ADVERTISING RATES:
Full Page Colour £1800.00
Agency Commission: 10%
Mechanical Data: Type Area: 270 x 190mm, Bleed Size: 303 x 216mm, Trim Size: 297 x 210mm, Col Length: 270mm, Page Width: 190mm, Film: Digital
Average advertising content per issue: 40%
Supplement(s): Mortgage Matters - 4xY
CONSUMER: WOMEN'S INTEREST CONSUMER MAGAZINES: Home Purchase

YOUR OVERSEAS PROPERTY 1792573U74K-775
Formerly: Overseas Property TV Magazine
Editorial Address: 60 Churchill Square, Kings Hill, WEST MALLING, ME19 4YU **Tel:** 01732 525800
Fax: 01732 525801
Email: stuart.humphrey@ncgmedia.co.uk
Advertising Address: As above. **Tel:** 01444 451996
Fax: 01444 473534
ISSN: 1751-8865
Publisher: NCG Media
Date Established: 2006
Frequency: 6 issues yearly
Circulation: 32,000 (Publisher's Statement)
Editor: Stuart Humphrey
Summary of Content: Magazine covering all aspects of buying a property abroad with legal and financial advice, profiles of regions and destinations.
Language(s): English; Spanish
Readership/Target Audience: Aimed at those considering buying a property overseas.
ADVERTISING RATES:
Full Page Colour £1650.00
Mechanical Data: Trim Size: 297 x 210mm, Film: Digital, Type Area: 272 x 178mm, Col Length: 272mm, Page Width: 178mm, Bleed Size: 303 x 216mm, Col Widths (Display): 85mm, No. of Columns (Display): 2
Copy instructions: Copy Date: 1 week prior to publication date
Average advertising content per issue: 7%
CONSUMER: WOMEN'S INTEREST CONSUMER MAGAZINES: Home Purchase

YOUR SURREY WEDDING 1790460U74L-254
Editorial Address: Broseley House, Newland Drive, WITHAM, CM8 2UL **Tel:** 01376 514000 **Fax:** 01376 514555
Email: editor@yoursurreywedding.com
Advertising Address: As above. **Tel:** 0870 609 1628
Email: melissag@countyweddingmagazines.com
Web site: http://www.yoursurreywedding.com
ISSN: 1751-7095
Publisher: Kline Davis Ltd
Date Established: 2006
Frequency: 6 issues yearly
Cover Price: £2.95
Circulation: 5,000 (Publisher's Statement)
Usual Pagination: 116
Editor: Danielle Harvey; **Features Editor:** Danielle Harvey; **Group Editor:** Emma Cant
Summary of Content: Magazine covering all aspects of weddings including venues, fashion, real weddings, honeymoons, grooms, cakes, catering, news, events, give-aways, letters and questions and answers.
Readership/Target Audience: Aimed at brides and grooms in the Surrey area and surrounds.
ADVERTISING RATES:
Full Page Colour £900.00
Agency Commission: 10%
Mechanical Data: Bleed Size: 303 x 216mm, Trim Size: 297 x 210mm, Film: Digital
Copy instructions: Copy Date: 2 weeks prior to publication date
Average advertising content per issue: 40%
CONSUMER: WOMEN'S INTEREST CONSUMER MAGAZINES: Brides

YOUR SUSSEX WEDDING 1790456U74L-253
Editorial Address: Broseley House, Newlands Drive, WITHAM, CM8 2UL **Tel:** 01376 514000 **Fax:** 01376 514555
Email: editor@yoursussexwedding.com
Advertising Address: As above. **Tel:** 0870 609 1628
Email: rachelc@countyweddingmagazines.com
Web site: http://www.yoursussexwedding.com
ISSN: 1750-3477
Publisher: Kline Davis Ltd
Date Established: 2006
Frequency: 6 issues yearly
Cover Price: £2.95
Circulation: 5,000 (Publisher's Statement)
Usual Pagination: 100
Editor: Demelza Rayner; **Group Editor:** Demelza Rayner
Summary of Content: Magazine covering all aspects of weddings including venues, fashion, real weddings, honeymoons, grooms, cakes, catering, news, events, give-aways, letters and questions and answers.
Readership/Target Audience: Aimed at brides and grooms in the sussex area.
ADVERTISING RATES:
Full Page Colour £900.00
Agency Commission: 10%
Mechanical Data: Bleed Size: 303 x 216mm, Trim Size: 297 x 210mm, Film: Digital
Copy instructions: Copy Date: 2 weeks prior to publication date
Average advertising content per issue: 40%
CONSUMER: WOMEN'S INTEREST CONSUMER MAGAZINES: Brides

YOUR TRAVEL 1665238U89A-718
Formerly: My Travel
Editorial Address: The Press Association, PA Entertainment, 292 Vauxhall Bridge Road, LONDON, SW1V 1AE **Tel:** 020 7963 7256
Email: claire.spreadbury@pa-entertainment.co.uk
Advertising Address: Mediaforce Ltd, 1 Gunpowder Square, Fleet Street, LONDON, EC4A 3EP
Tel: 020 7583 2100 **Fax:** 020 75832111
Email: sgill@mediaforce.co.uk
Web site: http://www.pacustomerpublishing.co.uk
Publisher: Johnston Press plc
Date Established: 2005
Frequency: Annual - Published in January
Cover Price: Free
Circulation: 1,200,000
Editor: Claire Spreadbury; **Advertising Manager:** Scott Gill
Summary of Content: Lifestyle magazine covering travel.
Readership/Target Audience: Aimed at readers of Johnston press regional newspapers.
ADVERTISING: Rates on application
CONSUMER: HOLIDAYS & TRAVEL: Travel

YOUR WEDDING 1753421U74L-247
Editorial Address: The Old Library, Church Green West, REDDITCH, B97 4DU **Tel:** 01527 453726 **Fax:** 01527 453724
Email: vanessa@osdesign.net
Advertising Address: As above.
Email: vanessa@osdesign.net
Web site: http://www.osdesign.net
Publisher: Observer Standard Newspapers Magazine Division
Frequency: Annual - Published in January
Cover Price: Free
Circulation: 30,000 (Publisher's Statement)
Usual Pagination: 68
Editor: Vanessa Bradford
Summary of Content: Magazine covering all aspects of weddings as well as local features.
Readership/Target Audience: Aimed at brides to be in Warwickshire, Worcestershire and South Birmingham.
ADVERTISING RATES:
Full Page Colour £900.00
Agency Commission: 10%
Mechanical Data: Bleed Size: 303 x 216mm, Trim Size: 297 x 210mm, Film: Digital
Copy instructions: Copy Date: 1 week prior to publication date
Average advertising content per issue: 60%
CONSUMER: WOMEN'S INTEREST CONSUMER MAGAZINES: Brides

YOURS 45592U74N-160
Editorial Address: Media House, Lynchwood, Peterborough Business Park, PETERBOROUGH, PE2 6EA
Tel: 01733 468000 **Fax:** 01733 465266
Email: yours@bauermedia.co.uk
Advertising Address: Endeavour House, 189 Shaftesbury Avenue, LONDON, WC2H 8JG **Tel:** 020 7437 9011
Email: michael.kalli@emap.com
Web site: http://www.yours.co.uk
Publisher: Bauer Consumer Media Ltd (Media House)
Date Established: 1974
Frequency: 26 issues yearly
Cover Price: £1.40
Annual Sub.: £33.80
Circulation: 301,089 (ABC 01/01/2009 to 30/06/2009)
Usual Pagination: 148
Editor: Sharon Reid; **Advertising Manager:** Michael Kalli
Summary of Content: Journal containing advice on a variety of topics including entertainment, health, cooking, personal finance, gardening, housing and social security benefits and celebrity features.
Readership/Target Audience: Read by men and women over 50 years old.
ADVERTISING RATES:
Full Page Colour £13140.00
Agency Commission: 10%
Mechanical Data: Page Width: 180mm, Type Area: 267 x 180mm, Col Length: 267mm, Trim Size: 297 x 210mm, Bleed Size: 309 x 222mm, Film: Digital
Copy instructions: Copy Date: 4 weeks prior to publication date
Average advertising content per issue: 40%
CONSUMER: WOMEN'S INTEREST CONSUMER MAGAZINES: Retirement

YOUTH LIVE 1833995U83-296
Editorial Address: 50-54 Mount Pleasant, LIVERPOOL, L3 5SD **Tel:** 0151 702 6960
Email: news@youthlive.co.uk
Advertising Address: As above.
Email: news@youthlive.co.uk
Web site: http://www.youthlive.co.uk
Publisher: Youth Communications Network CIC
Date Established: 2007

Frequency: Quarterly
Cover Price: £0.90
Free to qualifying individuals
Circulation: 6,000 (Print Run)
Usual Pagination: 24
Editor: Richard Horscraft; **Managing Editor:** Richard Horscraft
Summary of Content: Magazine covering educational topics, political and social awareness, social commentary, health information, leisure, entertainment and sport. Written by students.
Readership/Target Audience: Aimed at male and female students in Merseyside, aged 13 to 19 years old.
ADVERTISING RATES:
Full Page Colour £530.00
Mechanical Data: Trim Size: 297 x 210mm, Film: Digital
Copy instructions: Copy Date: 3rd week of the month
CONSUMER: STUDENT PUBLICATIONS

YOUTHWORK 48481U91D-200
Editorial Address: Premier Media Group, 22 Chapter Street, LONDON, SW1P 4NP **Tel:** 020 7316 1450
Fax: 020 7316 1453
Email: youthwork@premier.org.uk
Advertising Address: Broadway House, The Broadway, CROWBOROUGH, TN6 1HQ **Tel:** 020 7316 1456
Fax: 01892 663329
Email: candy.odonovan@premier.org.uk
Web site: http://www.youthwork.co.uk
ISSN: 0966-2855
Publisher: CCP Ltd
Date Established: 1991
Frequency: Monthly - 15th of preceding month
Cover Price: £3.00
Annual Sub.: £30.00
Circulation: 9,000 (Publisher's Statement)
Usual Pagination: 56
Editor: Martin Saunders
Summary of Content: Publication featuring articles on youthwork, session planning and related information.
Readership/Target Audience: Aimed predominantly at Christian youth workers.
ADVERTISING RATES:
Full Page Mono £780.00
Full Page Colour £780.00
SCC £7.22
Agency Commission: 10%
Mechanical Data: Col Length: 270mm, Type Area: 270 x 186mm, Bleed Size: 303 x 216mm, Trim Size: 297 x 210mm, Page Width: 186mm, Film: Digital
Copy instructions: Copy Date: 1 month prior to publication date
Average advertising content per issue: 25%
CONSUMER: RECREATION & LEISURE: Children & Youth

YQ MAGAZINE 1743267U74Q-1304
Formerly: Your Quarter
Editorial Address: RMC House, Broadfield Court, Broadfield Business Park, SHEFFIELD, S8 0XF
Tel: 0114 250 6300 **Fax:** 0845 255 5881
Email: chris.wilson@regionalmagazine.co.uk
Advertising Address: As above. **Tel:** 0845 200 8369
Fax: 0845 200 8367
Email: peter@yqnorthwest.com
Web site: http://www.yqmagazine.co.uk
Publisher: Regional Magazine Company
Date Established: 2004
Frequency: Monthly
Cover Price: £1.95
Circulation: 30,000 (Publisher's Statement)
Usual Pagination: 138
Editor: Chris Wilson; **Managing Director:** Peter Lever
Summary of Content: Lifestyle magazine covering local news and events, property & interiors, fashion, beauty & health, food, motoring, music, travel, fitness, gardening, gadgets, sport and horoscopes.
Readership/Target Audience: Aimed at young professionals aged 25 to 40 years old in Lancashire, Cheshire, Manchester and Merseyside with high disposable incomes.
ADVERTISING RATES:
Full Page Colour £1250.00
Agency Commission: 10%
Mechanical Data: Bleed Size: 303 x 223mm, Trim Size: 300 x 220mm, Film: Digital, Print Process: 4 colour
Copy instructions: Copy Date: 2 weeks prior to publication date
Average advertising content per issue: 40%
CONSUMER: WOMEN'S INTEREST CONSUMER MAGAZINES: Lifestyle

ZEE MAGAZINE 1642461U90-927
Editorial Address: 1st Floor, Mermaid House, 2 Puddle Dock, LONDON, EC4V 3DS **Tel:** 020 7332 2000
Fax: 020 7332 2001
Email: cate@programmemaster.com
Advertising Address: As above.

Email: steve@programmemaster.com
Web site: http://www.zeetvmagazine.co.uk
Publisher: Programmemaster Ltd
Date Established: 2004
Frequency: Quarterly
Cover Price: Free
Circulation: 150,000 (Publisher's Statement)
Usual Pagination: 128
Editor: Cate Langmuir
Summary of Content: Magazine covering fashion, property, finance, art, music, sport, food, travel and comedy as well as previews of Zee TV and celebrity interviews.
Readership/Target Audience: Aimed at three generations of Asian communities.
ADVERTISING RATES:
Full Page Colour £12950.00
Mechanical Data: Trim Size: 297 x 210mm, Film: Digital
CONSUMER: ETHNIC

ZEST
45211U74A-950

Editorial Address: National Magazine House, 72 Broadwick Street, LONDON, W1F 9EP **Tel:** 020 7439 5000
Fax: 020 7312 3750
Email: caroline.hamman@natmags.co.uk
Advertising Address: As above. **Tel:** 020 7312 3834
Fax: 020 7312 3779
Email: andrea.sullivan@natmags.co.uk
Web site: http://www.zest.co.uk
Publisher: National Magazine Company Ltd
Date Established: 1994
Frequency: Monthly
Cover Price: £3.30
Annual Sub.: £19.98
Circulation: 96,754 (ABC 01/01/2009 to 30/06/2009)
Usual Pagination: 154
Editor: Kate Langrish; **Features Editor:** Zoe McDonald;
Advertising Director: Andrea Sullivan
Summary of Content: Magazine covering health, beauty, fashion and exercise.
Twitter: https://twitter.com/ZESTmagazine.
Readership/Target Audience: Read by women between 20 and 40 years old.
ADVERTISING RATES:
Full Page Colour £5480.00
Agency Commission: 15%
Mechanical Data: Type Area: 266 x 192mm, Bleed Size: 292 x 221mm, Trim Size: 286 x 215mm, Film: Digital
Copy instructions: Copy Date: 1 month prior to publication date

Average advertising content per issue: 30%
CONSUMER: WOMEN'S INTEREST CONSUMER
MAGAZINES: Women's Interest

THE ZIMBABWEAN
1665754U90-950

Editorial Address: PO Box 248, HYTHE, SO45 4WX
Tel: 023 8084 5271
Email: news@thezimbabwean.co.uk
Advertising Address: As above.
Email: mbanga@thezimbabwean.co.uk
Web site: http://www.thezimbabwean.co.uk
Publisher: The Zimbabwean Ltd
Date Established: 2005
Frequency: Weekly
Cover Price: £0.60
Circulation: 88,000 (Publisher's Statement)
Usual Pagination: 24
Editor: Wilf Mbanga; **Advertising Manager:** Trish Mbanga;
Publisher: Wilf Mbanga
Summary of Content: Newspaper covering politics, sports, opinions, human rights and letters to the Editor as well as general news and features.
Readership/Target Audience: Aimed at Zimbabweans at home and abroad.
ADVERTISING RATES:
Full Page Mono £650.00
Full Page Colour £720.00
SCC £7.00
Agency Commission: 30%
Mechanical Data: Type Area: 350 x 250mm, Col Length: 350mm, Page Width: 250mm, Film: Digital
Copy instructions: Copy Date: 14 days prior to publication date
Average advertising content per issue: 33%
CONSUMER: ETHNIC

ZONEAST
600873U90-900

Editorial Address: Unit 1, Dolphin House, Smugglers Way, LONDON, SW18 1DE **Tel:** 020 8870 7088
Email: zoneastmarketing@yahoo.com
Advertising Address: As above.
Email: zoneastmarketing@yahoo.com
Publisher: Zoneast Production
Date Established: 1999
Frequency: Monthly
Free to qualifying individuals
Annual Sub.: £12.00

Circulation: 20,000 (Publisher's Statement)
Usual Pagination: 60
Editor: Michelle Chua; **Advertising Manager:** Michelle Chua
Summary of Content: Magazine covering news and entertainment from Europe and the Far East.
Language(s): Chinese; English
Readership/Target Audience: Aimed at the Chinese population living and working in Europe, especially in the UK.
ADVERTISING RATES:
Full Page Colour £1300.00
Agency Commission: 10%
Mechanical Data: Bleed Size: 303 x 216mm, Trim Size: 297 x 210mm, Film: Digital
CONSUMER: ETHNIC

ZOO
1639949U86C-713

Editorial Address: Mappin House, 4 Winsley Street, LONDON, W1W 8HF **Tel:** 020 7182 8000
Fax: 020 7182 8300
Email: info@zootoday.com
Advertising Address: Endeavour House, 189 Shaftesbury Avenue, LONDON, WC2H 8JG **Tel:** 020 7295 5000
Fax: 020 7295 5444
Email: rob.henderson@baueradvertising.co.uk
Web site: http://www.zootoday.com
Publisher: Bauer Consumer Media Ltd (Mappin House)
Date Established: 2004
Frequency: Weekly
Cover Price: £1.50
Circulation: 111,012 (ABC 01/01/2009 to 30/06/2009)
Editor: Natalie Cornish; **News Editor:** Gavin Brett; **Features Editor:** Richard Innes; **Managing Director:** Geoff Campbell
Summary of Content: Magazine covering news, sport, humour, female celebrities and general male interests.
Twitter: http://twitter.com/ZooToday.
Readership/Target Audience: Aimed at men aged between 16 and 30 years old.
ADVERTISING RATES:
Full Page Colour £8800.00
Agency Commission: 15%
Mechanical Data: Type Area: 280 x 200mm, Bleed Size: 306 x 226mm, Trim Size: 300 x 220mm, Col Length: 280mm, Page Width: 200mm, Film: Digital
Copy instructions: Copy Date: 1 week prior to publication date
Average advertising content per issue: 20%
CONSUMER: ADULT & GAY MAGAZINES: Men's Lifestyle Magazines

Willings Volume 1
Section 5

Internet Media

Internet media includes unique electronic magazines found on the world wide web, electronically delivered newsletters and online versions of consumer magazines, business magazines and national, regional and local newspapers.

Internet Media

.NET MAGAZINE
626206U78E-39

Formerly: .net online
Editorial Address: 30 Monmouth Street, BATH, BA1 2BW
Tel: 01225 442244
Email: oliver.lindberg@futurenet.com
Web site: http://www.netmag.co.uk
Publisher: Future Publishing Ltd
Date Launched: 1994
Frequency of update: Daily
Website Access: Free
Traffic Figures: 40,000 Unique Users (per week Publisher's Statement)
Editor: Oliver Lindberg
Summary of Content: Website containing Internet news, advice and tips on how to make the best use of the World Wide Web and web building.
Readership/Target Audience: Aimed at people wishing to learn how to use the net and intermediate net users. Also for those who want build a website.
Other Features: Features include an online discussion forum, tutorials, reviews, features, competitions and archiving.
CONSUMER: CONSUMER ELECTRONICS: Home Computing

'007' MAGAZINE ONLINE
1625901U79K-999

Formerly: '007' Magazine
Editorial Address: 6 New Street, Lydd, ROMNEY MARSH, TN29 9DJ **Tel:** 01797 322007
Email: editor@007magazine.co.uk
Web site: http://www.007magazine.co.uk
Date Launched: 1979
Frequency of update: Monthly
Website Access: Paid
Traffic Figures: 15,000 Unique Users (Publisher's Statement)
Editor: Graham Rye
Summary of Content: Website covering each new James Bond film on its release, interviews with characters past and present including never before seen photographs.
Readership/Target Audience: Aimed at James Bond enthusiasts of all ages around the world.
CONSUMER: HOBBIES & DIY: Collectors Magazines

160 CHARACTERS
1665163U18B-1961

Editorial Address: 10 Upper Close, FOREST ROW, RH18 5DX **Tel:** 01342 825169
Email: press@160characters.org
Web site: http://www.160characters.org
Date Launched: 2001
Frequency of update: Daily
Website Access: Free
Traffic Figures: 5,149 Unique Users (Publisher's Statement)
Editor: Mike Grenville
Summary of Content: Website covering all aspects of mobile messaging and content delivery including usage stats and case studies.
Readership/Target Audience: Aimed at mobile messaging professionals.
Other Features: Weekly newsletter, Conference diary
BUSINESS: ELECTRONICS: Telecommunications

21ST CENTURY WORKER
36810U14A-318_50

Formerly: Teleworker
Editorial Address: Swan House, Darvel, AYERSHIRE, KA17 0LP **Tel:** 0800 616008
Email: shirley@telework.org.uk
Web site: http://www.telework.org.uk
Publisher: The Telework Association
Frequency of update: Quarterly
Website Access: Paid
Traffic Figures: 1,200 Unique Users (Publisher's Statement)
Editor: Shirley Borrett
Summary of Content: Electronically delivered magazine of the Teleworkers Association. Covers news, business advice, surveys and equipment reviews.
Readership/Target Audience: Aimed at teleworkers, designers, engineers and computer professionals. Also those involved in telecentres and telecottages.
BUSINESS: COMMERCE, INDUSTRY & MANAGEMENT

4CAR
623581U77A-8

Editorial Address: Kensington Village, Avonmore Road, LONDON, W14 8RF **Tel:** 020 7013 4000 **Fax:** 020 7013 4001
Email: contact4car@channel4.com
Web site: http://www.channel4.com/4car
Publisher: IWC Media
Date Launched: 2000
Frequency of update: Daily
Website Access: Free

Traffic Figures: 850,000 Unique Users (per month Publisher's Statement)
Editor: Tim Bowdler
Summary of Content: Website focusing on new car road tests, competitions, features, buying and selling information and daily news.
Readership/Target Audience: Aimed at upwardly mobile males, car enthusiasts and those looking to purchase a car. Readership reflects Channel 4 ABC viewer profile.
Other Features: Features include a buyer's guide, chat forum and new car browsing.
CONSUMER: MOTORING & CYCLING: Motoring

4HOMES
767168U74K-663

Editorial Address: 124 Horseferry Road, LONDON, SW1P 2TX **Tel:** 020 7396 4444
Email: lferro@channel4.co.uk
Web site: http://www.channel4.com/4homes
Frequency of update: Daily
Website Access: Free
Editor: Lelia Ferro
Summary of Content: Website covering homes, property, home decor, styling, home finance, DIY and home entertainment services.
Readership/Target Audience: Aimed at people looking to buy, sell, build or renovate properties.
CONSUMER: WOMEN'S INTEREST CONSUMER MAGAZINES: Home Purchase

4THEGAME.COM
763352U75B-264

Editorial Address: 12th Floor, Sunlight House, Quay Street, MANCHESTER, M3 3JZ **Tel:** 0161 835 3444
Fax: 0161 835 3488
Email: stephen.omalley@fastwebmedia.com
Web site: http://www.4thegame.com
Publisher: Sportech PLC
Date Launched: 1995
Frequency of update: Daily
Website Access: Free
Traffic Figures: 1,000,000 Unique Users (per month Publisher's Statement)
Editor: Stephen O'Malley
Summary of Content: Website focusing on Premiership football featuring news, statistics, results, fixtures and blogs.
Readership/Target Audience: Aimed at all Premier League football fans.
Other Features: Features include archiving, events and an email newsletter.
CONSUMER: SPORT: Football

50CONNECT.CO.UK
712170U74N-10

Editorial Address: Morley House, Badminton Court, Church Street, AMERSHAM, HP7 0DD **Tel:** 01494 736130
Fax: 0800 634 2250
Web site: http://www.50connect.co.uk
Publisher: 50Connect Ltd
Date Launched: 1999
Frequency of update: Daily
Website Access: Free
Traffic Figures: 2,100,100 Unique Users (per month Publisher's Statement)
Summary of Content: Website focusing on lifestyle issues for those over 45 years old. Covers finance, health, beauty, travel, leisure, sport, home and garden, food and drink, retirement, relationships and entertainment.
Readership/Target Audience: Aimed at mature men and women.
Other Features: Features include chat forums, an e-mail newsletter and competitions.
CONSUMER: WOMEN'S INTEREST CONSUMER MAGAZINES: Retirement

ABERDEENSHIRE MATTERS
1881583U72J-326

Email: comments@aberdeenshire-matters.co.uk
Web site: http://www.aberdeenshire-matters.co.uk
Frequency of update: Daily
Summary of Content: This website was created to help people who care about local issues. Whether you need access to useful information, want to highlight a particular topic to other people, discuss ideas with like-minded people or just show your support and keep up to date with current affairs in your area, Aberdeenshire Matters is the place for you.
Readership/Target Audience: Aimed at residents in the local area of Aberdeenshire.
LOCAL NEWSPAPERS: Community Newsletters

THE ABINGDON HERALD
44223U72B-2720_110

Editorial Address: Market Place, Didcot, OXFORDSHIRE, OX11 7LE **Tel:** 01235 813417 **Fax:** 01235 813316

Email: abingdon@nqo.com
Web site: http://www.heraldseries.co.uk
Frequency of update: Daily
Website Access: Paid
(02/07/2007 To 30/12/2007 ABC)
Summary of Content: Website covering news, sport and leisure for Abingdon, Didcot, Wantage, Wallingford.
Readership/Target Audience: Aimed at people living in this area.
LOCAL NEWSPAPERS: Local Newspapers English Counties

ABOUTMYAREA
1800272U80C-5399

Editorial Address: TS2 Pinewood Business Park, Coleshill Road, Marston Green, BIRMINGHAM, B37 7HG
Tel: 0870 062 2212
Email: kerris@aboutmyarea.co.uk
Web site: http://www.aboutmyarea.co.uk
Frequency of update: Daily
Website Access: Free
Traffic Figures: 150,000 Unique Users (per month Publisher's Statement)
Editor: Kerris Morgan
Summary of Content: Website covering local news and information, events, things for the family to do, sport, schools and businesses.
Readership/Target Audience: Aimed at residents and businesses in local communities across the nation.
CONSUMER: RURAL & REGIONAL INTEREST: Regional Interest English Counties

ABOUTMYAREA RG14
1805241U80C-5416

Editorial Address: 1 Pumping Station, Ilsley Road, Compton, NEWBURY, RG20 7PH **Tel:** 01635 578051
Fax: 01635 578051
Email: eddylerpiniere@aboutmyarea.co.uk
Web site: http://www.aboutmyarea.co.uk/rg14
Date Launched: 2007
Frequency of update: Daily
Website Access: Free
Editor: Eddy Lerpiniere
Summary of Content: Web based magazine covering local news, useful numbers, business directory, charities, events, fashion, motoring and health.
Readership/Target Audience: Aimed at residents and businesses in Newbury and surrounding areas.
CONSUMER: RURAL & REGIONAL INTEREST: Regional Interest English Counties

ABOUTMYAREA SOUTH NORFOLK & NORTH SUFFOLK
1800273U80C-5400

Editorial Address: 89 The Street, Costessey, NORWICH, NR8 5DF **Tel:** 07906 189835
Email: jamesduffell@aboutmyarea.co.uk
Web site: http://www.aboutmyarea.co.uk
Date Launched: 2007
Frequency of update: Daily
Website Access: Free
Editor: James Duffell
Summary of Content: Website covering local news, events, recipes, things to do with the family, sports, schools and businesses.
Readership/Target Audience: Aimed at residents and businesses in South Norfolk and North Suffolk.
Other Features: Newsletter.
CONSUMER: RURAL & REGIONAL INTEREST: Regional Interest English Counties

ABOUTMYGENERATION
1793918U74Q-1368

Editorial Address: Kingfisher House, 21-23 Elmfield Road, BROMLEY, BR1 1LT **Tel:** 020 8315 6682
Fax: 020 8315 6555
Email: christine.hurley@btinternet.com
Web site: http://www.aboutmygeneration.com
Publisher: AMG Ltd
Date Launched: 2006
Frequency of update: Weekly
Website Access: Free
Editor: Christine Hurley
Summary of Content: Website covering health, diet and lifestyle, exercise, hobbies, restaurants, books, anti-aging remedies, cosmetic surgery, relationships, theatre, film, concerts, music, exhibitions, gigs, TV and radio, travel, food and drink, gadgets and personal finance.
Readership/Target Audience: Aimed at men and women aged 45 to 65 years old.
Other Features: Competitions, partner search, photo galleries, blogs, groups and forums.
CONSUMER: WOMEN'S INTEREST CONSUMER MAGAZINES: Lifestyle

ABOUTPROPERTY.CO.UK
1666797U74C-840

Editorial Address: South Quay Plaza, 183 Marsh Wall, LONDON, E14 9SH **Tel:** 020 7517 2225 **Fax:** 020 7517 2229
Email: news@aboutproperty.co.uk
Web site: http://www.aboutproperty.co.uk
Publisher: Adfero
Date Launched: 2004
Frequency of update: Daily
Website Access: Free
Traffic Figures: 30,000 Unique Users (per month Publisher's Statement)
Editor: Daniel Barnes
Summary of Content: Website covering homes and property news including house prices, home improvements, gardens, house finances, planning, buying and selling property, property investment and overseas property.
Readership/Target Audience: Aimed at first-time buyers, homeowners and property investors.
CONSUMER: WOMEN'S INTEREST CONSUMER MAGAZINES: Home & Family

ACCOUNTANCYAGE.COM
626209U1B-15_1

Editorial Address: 32-34 Broadwick Street, LONDON, W1A 2HG **Tel:** 020 7316 9000 **Fax:** 020 7316 9250
Email: news@accountancyage.com
Web site: http://www.accountancyage.com
Publisher: Incisive Media
Date Launched: 1969
Frequency of update: Daily
Website Access: Free
Editor: Rachael Singh
Summary of Content: Website covering business, financial and careers news for primarily UK based accountancy professionals.
Readership/Target Audience: Aimed at part and fully qualified accountants throughout the UK.
BUSINESS: FINANCE & ECONOMICS: Accountancy

ACCOUNTANCYMAGAZINE.COM
626208U1B-16

Formerly: Accountancy Online
Editorial Address: 145 London Road, KINGSTON UPON THAMES, KT2 6SR **Tel:** 020 8247 1389 **Fax:** 020 8247 1424
Email: accountancynews@cch.co.uk
Web site: http://www.accountancymagazine.com
Publisher: Wolters Kluwer (UK) Ltd
Date Launched: 2000
Frequency of update: 260 times a year
Website Access: Paid
Editor: Penny Sukhraj
Summary of Content: Website covering the latest accountancy headline news.
Readership/Target Audience: Aimed at accountants and accounting practitioners worldwide.
BUSINESS: FINANCE & ECONOMICS: Accountancy

ACCOUNTINGANDFINANCE365
1615478U1B-317

Editorial Address: 32-34 Broadwick Street, LONDON, W1A 2HG **Tel:** 020 7316 9000 **Fax:** 020 7316 9250
Web site: http://www.accountingandfinance365.com
Publisher: Incisive Media
Date Launched: 2002
Frequency of update: Daily
Website Access: Free
Summary of Content: Online exhibition providing the latest news and information regarding accounting and financial software.
Readership/Target Audience: Aimed at enterprise end users of accounting and financial software.
BUSINESS: FINANCE & ECONOMICS: Accountancy

ACCOUNTINGWEB.CO.UK
622860U1B-45

Editorial Address: 100 Victoria Street, BRISTOL, BS1 6HZ **Tel:** 0117 915 8657 **Fax:** 0117 915 9630
Email: editor@accountingweb.co.uk
Web site: http://www.accountingweb.co.uk
Publisher: Sift Media Ltd
Frequency of update: 260 times a year
Website Access: Free
Editor: Steve Roth
Summary of Content: Website consisting of a professional online community covering tax, accountancy news, comment and technical data.
Readership/Target Audience: Aimed at accountants in business and practice.
Other Features: Weekly e-mail bulletins.
BUSINESS: FINANCE & ECONOMICS: Accountancy

ACI BRIEFING
625174U1A-9

Editorial Address: Suite 26, London Fruit Exchange, Brushfield Street, LONDON, E1 6EU **Tel:** 020 7377 6716
Fax: 020 7426 0727
Email: colin_lambert@profit-loss.com
Web site: http://www.profit-loss.com
Publisher: P & L Services
Date Launched: 1999
Frequency of update: 10 times a year
Website Access: Paid
Traffic Figures: 16,000 Unique Users (Publisher's Statement)
Editor: Colin Lambert
Summary of Content: Online newsletter featuring articles about wholesale financial markets around the world.
Readership/Target Audience: Read by members of ACI - The Financial Markets Association.
BUSINESS: FINANCE & ECONOMICS

ACTION FOR CHILDREN
629035U1P-83_70

Formerly: NCH
Editorial Address: 85 Highbury Park, LONDON, N5 1UD
Tel: 01579 346998 **Fax:** 020 7704 7134
Web site: http://www.actionforchildren.org.uk
Date Launched: 1998
Frequency of update: Daily
Website Access: Free
Traffic Figures: 85,000 Unique Users (per month Publisher's Statement)
Editor: Richard Saunders
Summary of Content: Website focusing on the work of the NCH charity.
Readership/Target Audience: Aimed at those working within children's charities as well as other professionals such as social workers.
BUSINESS: FINANCE & ECONOMICS: Fundraising

ACTIVE AND INTELLIGENT PACK NEWS
1664906U35-365

Editorial Address: Cleeve Road, LEATHERHEAD, KT22 7RU **Tel:** 01372 802269
Email: joe.thompson@pira-international.com
Web site: http://www.piranet.com
Publisher: PIRA International
Frequency of update: 26 times a year
Website Access: Paid
Editor: Joe Thompson
Summary of Content: Electronically delivered newsletter covering active and intelligent packaging technology.
Readership/Target Audience: Aimed at print and packaging suppliers, brand owners and retailers.
BUSINESS: PACKAGING & BOTTLING

ADOPTION UK
1739878U74D-634

Editorial Address: 46 The Green, South Bar Street, BANBURY, OX16 9AB **Tel:** 01295 752240
Fax: 01295 752241
Email: jonathan@adoptionuk.org.uk
Web site: http://www.adoptionuk.org
Date Launched: 2003
Frequency of update: Daily
Website Access: Free
Traffic Figures: 9,000 Unique Users (Publisher's Statement)
Editor: Clive Griffiths
Summary of Content: Website covering all aspects of adoption with the latest news, advice on the adoption process, events, message boards and shop.
Readership/Target Audience: Aimed at those looking to adopt, adoptive parents and those working in adoption.
CONSUMER: WOMEN'S INTEREST CONSUMER MAGAZINES: Child Care

ADRENALINTRIP.NET
1849713U75X-1721

Editorial Address: 1 West Smithfield, LONDON, EC1A 9JU
Tel: 020 7332 9700 **Fax:** 020 7332 9799
Email: paul.moore@factorymedia.com
Web site: http://www.adrenalintrip.net
Publisher: Factory Media
Frequency of update: Daily
Website Access: Free
Traffic Figures: 80,000 Unique Users (per month Publisher's Statement)
Editor: Paul Moore
Summary of Content: Website covering action sports including motor cross, snowboarding and mountain biking.
Readership/Target Audience: Aimed at anyone with an interest of action sports.
CONSUMER: SPORT: Other Sport

ADVANCED-TELEVISION.COM
1614209U2D-134

Editorial Address: Bondway Commercial Centre, 4th Floor, Unit 4.01, 71 Bondway, LONDON, SW8 1SQ
Tel: 020 7793 8855 **Fax:** 020 7793 9955
Email: colin.mann@advanced-television.com
Web site: http://www.advanced-television.com
Publisher: Advanced Television Limited
Date Launched: 2000
Frequency of update: Daily
Website Access: Free
Traffic Figures: 30,000 Unique Users (Publisher's Statement)
Editor: Colin Mann; **Editor-in-Chief:** Nick Snow
Summary of Content: Website covering developments in media with a focus on TV, business and technology.
Readership/Target Audience: Aimed at those involved in the broadcasting industry.
BUSINESS: COMMUNICATIONS, ADVERTISING & MARKETING: Broadcasting

ADVENTURE CORNWALL
1750018U75X-1712

Editorial Address: St Josephs, St. Mawgan, NEWQUAY, TR8 4EN **Tel:** 01637 860031
Email: info@adventure-cornwall.co.uk
Web site: http://www.adventure-cornwall.co.uk
Publisher: Coast Publishing Ltd
Date Launched: 2006
Frequency of update: Weekly
Website Access: Free
Editor: Elliot Walker
Summary of Content: Website covering adventure sports including surfing, sailing, kite surfing, mountain boarding, mountain biking and hiking with news, activity reviews, gear guides, destination features, centre profiles and expert tips.
Readership/Target Audience: Read by 18 to 40 year-old, adventurous people with boundless energy and the means to enjoy an active lifestyle. Enjoyed by residents and visitors, male and female, predominantly professionals and skilled workers.
CONSUMER: SPORT: Other Sport

AEN NEWS DIARY
1658832U90-946

Editorial Address: For all contact details see main edition, The Asian Express Newspaper
Frequency of update: 26 times a year
CONSUMER: ETHNIC

AERBT AN EXECUTIVE REVIEW OF BUSINESS TRAVEL
1899400U50-249

Editorial Address: PO Box 1315, POTTERS BAR, EN6 1PU
Tel: 01707 665454
Email: info@aerbt.co.uk
Web site: http://www.aerbt.co.uk
Date Launched: 2009
Frequency of update: Weekly
Website Access: Free
Traffic Figures: 26,500 Unique Users (Publisher's Statement)
Editor: Malcolm Ginsberg
Summary of Content: Global review available by email and on the web featuring comment, 20 news stories, a feature item on an aspect of travel and travel related humour.
Readership/Target Audience: Aimed at travel suppliers, travel organisers and regular travellers.
BUSINESS: TRAVEL & TOURISM

AEROSPACE INDUSTRY DIRECTORY
1912912U6A-227

Editorial Address: 18 Generator Hall, Electric Wharf, COVENTRY, CV1 4JL **Tel:** 0870 199 4044
Fax: 0870 777 4360
Email: enquires@industrydirectory.co.uk
Web site: http://www.industrydirectory.co.uk/
Publisher: Simply Marcomms
Frequency of update: Daily
Website Access: Free
Editor: Kirstie Colledge
Summary of Content: Directory containing the latest news stories for the UK Aerospace industry. Includes news archives.
Readership/Target Audience: Aimed at the aerospace professionals, suppliers to the aerospace industry, aerospace PR & Marketing firms.
BUSINESS: AVIATION & AERONAUTICS

AEROSPACE TECHNOLOGY
1616231U6D-503

Editorial Address: Brunel House, 55-57 North Wharf Road, LONDON, W2 1LA **Tel:** 020 7915 9957 **Fax:** 020 7915 9720

Internet Media

Email: production@spgmedia.com
Web site: http://www.aerospace-technology.com
Publisher: SPG Media Ltd
Date Launched: 1999
Frequency of update: Daily
Website Access: Paid
Traffic Figures: 114,022 Unique Users (Publisher's Statement)
Editor: Duncan West
Summary of Content: Website covering international aerospace technology projects both in production and under development.
Readership/Target Audience: Aimed at aerospace industry professionals.
BUSINESS: AVIATION & AERONAUTICS: Aviation Engineering Equipment

AGE AGENDA BULLETIN
40292U56B-5

Formerly: Age Concern Information Bulletin
Editorial Address: Astral House, 1268 London Road, LONDON, SW16 4ER Tel: 020 8765 7200
Fax: 020 8764 6594
Email: diana.fawcett@ace.org.uk
Web site: http://www.ageconcern.org.uk
Publisher: Age Concern England
Date Launched: 2007
Frequency of update: Monthly
Website Access: Free
Traffic Figures: 1,280 Unique Users (Publisher's Statement)
Editor: Diana Fawcett
Summary of Content: Web page covering issues concerning older people, offering information for those looking after older people and coverage of policy, legislation news and new reports.
Readership/Target Audience: Aimed at those working with and for older people.
BUSINESS: HEALTH & MEDICAL: Nursing

AGENDA
35315U1F-500

Formerly: Utilities Journal
Editorial Address: Park Central, 40-41 Park End Street, OXFORD, OX1 1JD Tel: 01865 253000 Fax: 01865 251172
Email: enquiries@oxera.com
Web site: http://www.oxera.com
Publisher: OXERA
Date Launched: 2005
Frequency of update: Monthly
Website Access: Free
Traffic Figures: 6,000 Unique Users (Publisher's Statement)
Editor: Kerry Hughes
Summary of Content: Online publication providing expert analysis and comment on economic thinking and applying it to business, law and regulation.
Readership/Target Audience: Aimed at senior executives in regulated industries, trade associations, government departments and regulators.
BUSINESS: FINANCE & ECONOMICS: Investment

AGRICULTURE INDUSTRY DIRECTORY
1912914U21A-1120

Editorial Address: 18 Generator Hall, Electric Wharf, COVENTRY, CV1 4JL Tel: 0870 199 4044
Fax: 0870 777 4360
Email: enquiries@industrydirectory.co.uk
Web site: http://www.industrydirectory.co.uk
Publisher: Simply Marcomms
Frequency of update: Daily
Website Access: Free
Editor: Kirstie Colledge
Summary of Content: Directory containing the latest news stories for the UK agriculture industry. Includes news archive.
Readership/Target Audience: Aimed at Agriculture professionals, suppliers to the Agriculture industry, Agricultural PR & Marketing firms.
BUSINESS: AGRICULTURE & FARMING

AIME
629096U5E-2010

Formerly: NOC
Editorial Address: 28 Foundry Street, BRIGHTON, BN1 4AT
Tel: 0844 582 8828
Email: andrew@aimelink.org
Web site: http://www.aimelink.org
Publisher: Association for Interactive Media & Entertainment
Date Launched: 1998
Frequency of update: Monthly
Website Access: Paid
Traffic Figures: 12,000 Unique Users (Publisher's Statement)
Editor: Andrew Darling

Summary of Content: Website focusing on the interactive services and entertainment industry. Includes AIME forums and initiatives, industry news, industry events diary and members area.
Readership/Target Audience: Aimed at those working in the interactive media value chain from telco, mobile and fixed network operators, service providers, ISPs, content providers, media groups and technology providers.
BUSINESS: COMPUTERS & AUTOMATION: Data Transmission

AIR & BUSINESS TRAVEL NEWS
36321U50-211

Editorial Address: Cardinal House, 39-40 Albemarle Street, LONDON, W1S 4TE Tel: 020 7647 6330 Fax: 020 7647 6331
Email: editorial@panaceapublishing.co.uk
Web site: http://www.abtn.co.uk
Publisher: Panacea Publishing
Frequency of update: Daily
Website Access: Free
Traffic Figures: 37,000 Unique Users (per month Publisher's Statement)
Editor: Tom Otley
Summary of Content: A review covering the weeks news in the air travel business and associated travel interests including airlines, hotels, rail, car hire and ground transport.
Readership/Target Audience: Aimed at the business traveller, the suppliers, the travel management companies and the travel buyers.
Other Features: E-newsletters, archive and jobs
BUSINESS: TRAVEL & TOURISM

AIR TRANSPORT INTELLIGENCE
36327U6A-33

Editorial Address: Quadrant House, The Quadrant, SUTTON, SM2 5AS Tel: 020 8652 3837 Fax: 020 8652 3892
Email: atirelease@flightglobal.com
Web site: http://www.rati.com
Publisher: Reed Business Information
Date Launched: 1997
Frequency of update: Daily
Website Access: Paid
Editor: Kieran Daly
Summary of Content: Website covering real-time news and data for the air industry.
Readership/Target Audience: Aimed at airlines, manufacturers and other air transport professionals.
BUSINESS: AVIATION & AERONAUTICS

AIRFORCE TECHNOLOGY
1616232U40-420

Editorial Address: Brunel House, 55-57 North Wharf Road, LONDON, W2 1LA Tel: 020 7915 9957 Fax: 020 7915 9720
Email: production@spgmedia.com
Web site: http://www.airforce-technology.com
Publisher: SPG Media Ltd
Date Launched: 1996
Frequency of update: Daily
Website Access: Free
Traffic Figures: 347,710 Unique Users (Publisher's Statement)
Editor: Duncan West
Summary of Content: Website covering bombers, fighters, surveillance and patrol aircraft, training aircraft, tankers and transporters, support and naval helicopters.
Readership/Target Audience: Aimed at aerospace and defence industry professionals.
BUSINESS: DEFENCE

AIRFRAMER
1684381U6D-505

Editorial Address: 134 South Street, BISHOP'S STORTFORD, CM23 3BQ Tel: 01279 714505
Fax: 01279 714519
Email: jenny@airframer.com
Web site: http://www.airframer.com
Publisher: Stansted News Ltd
Date Launched: 2005
Frequency of update: Weekly
Website Access: Paid
Editor: Jenny Parker
Summary of Content: Online journal providing news of the latest innovations and techniques in the aircraft manufacturing industry.
Readership/Target Audience: Aimed at aircraft manufacturing executives and managers, designers and engineers, parts and systems suppliers, government officials, academics, and the media.
BUSINESS: AVIATION & AERONAUTICS: Aviation Engineering Equipment

AIRLINE INDUSTRY INFORMATION
36421U6F-73

Editorial Address: PR by email only Tel: 020 7047 0200
Email: m2pw@m2.com
Web site: http://www.m2.com
Publisher: M2 Communications Ltd
Frequency of update: 260 times a year
Website Access: Paid
Editor: Jamie Ayres
Summary of Content: E-mail newsletter providing information on the airline industry, travel and related events.
Readership/Target Audience: Aimed at the commercial sector of the airline industry.
BUSINESS: AVIATION & AERONAUTICS: Airlines

AIRPORT INTERNATIONAL
1640535U6R-158

Editorial Address: 100 Chapel Street, TIVERTON, EX16 6BU Tel: 01884 244670 Fax: 01884 244671
Email: info@copybook.com
Web site: http://www.copybook.com/airportdirectory.asp
Publisher: Copybook Solutions Ltd
Date Launched: 1999
Frequency of update: Monthly
Website Access: Free
Editor: James Armstrong
Summary of Content: Online portal covering the latest developments, technologies and suppliers in the airport industry.
Readership/Target Audience: Aimed at decision-makers within the airport industry.
BUSINESS: AVIATION & AERONAUTICS: Aviation Related

AIRPORT TECHNOLOGY
21472U6B-351

Editorial Address: Brunel House, 55-57 North Wharf Road, LONDON, W2 1LA Tel: 020 7915 9957 Fax: 020 7915 9720
Email: production@spgmedia.com
Web site: http://www.airport-technology.com
Publisher: SPG Media Ltd
Date Launched: 1998
Frequency of update: Daily
Website Access: Free
Traffic Figures: 115,095 Unique Users (per month Publisher's Statement)
Editor: Duncan West
Summary of Content: Website covering airport technology projects both in production and under development.
Readership/Target Audience: Aimed at airport and aviation professionals.
BUSINESS: AVIATION & AERONAUTICS: Airports

AKHBAR LIBYA
1749432U90-988

Editorial Address: PO Box 268, SOUTH CROYDON, CR2 0EB Tel: 0845 370 1102 Fax: 0845 370 1103
Email: aasmedia@hotmail.com
Web site: http://www.akhbar-libya.com
Publisher: Akhbar Libya Cultural Ltd
Date Launched: 2001
Frequency of update: Daily
Website Access: Free
Editor: Ashur Shamis
Summary of Content: Website covering new and analysis of Libyan affairs as well as politics, society and culture.
Readership/Target Audience: Aimed at Libyans worldwide and other Arab countries.
CONSUMER: ETHNIC

ALBEMARLE OF LONDON
707280U76B-60

Editorial Address: 5th Floor, Medius House, 63-69 New Oxford Street, LONDON, WC1A 1DG Tel: 020 7579 5118
Fax: 020 7379 8829
Email: trevor@albemarle-london.com
Web site: http://www.albemarle-london.com
Date Launched: 1997
Frequency of update: Daily
Website Access: Free
Editor: Trevor Baughan
Summary of Content: Website focusing on being a theatre guide to London's West End. Also provides information about ballet, opera, musicals and events.
Readership/Target Audience: Aimed at those who love the theatre, tourists and prospective visitors to London.
Other Features: Features include archiving.
CONSUMER: MUSIC & PERFORMING ARTS: Theatre

ALBOURNE VILLAGE
1773260U1F-622

Editorial Address: Garden House, Cloisters Business Centre, 8 Battersea Park Road, LONDON, SW8 4BG
Tel: 020 7720 9201 Fax: 020 7720 9202
Email: editors@village.albourne.com

Web site: http://www.village.albourne.com
Frequency of update: Daily
Website Access: Free
Traffic Figures: 50,000 Unique Users (Publisher's Statement)
Editor: Marwa Younes
Summary of Content: Website providing daily news and articles on alternative investment with coverage of jobs, conferences, courses, strategy and forecasts and a directory of contacts within the industry.
Readership/Target Audience: Aimed at anyone with an interest in hedge funds and alternative investment.
BUSINESS: FINANCE & ECONOMICS: Investment

ALIVE.CO.UK
1834259U89C-1109
Editorial Address: 80 New North Road, HUDDERSFIELD, HD1 5NE **Tel:** 01484 451730 **Fax:** 01484 451729
Email: steve@alive.co.uk
Web site: http://www.alive.co.uk
Publisher: Sound Culture Ltd
Date Launched: 1993
Frequency of update: Monthly
Website Access: Free
Traffic Figures: 35,000 Unique Users (per month Publisher's Statement)
Editor: Steve Barr
Summary of Content: Website covering in-depth monthly listings for live music, theatre, comedy and nightclubs.
Readership/Target Audience: Aimed at anyone who like to go out.
Other Features: Other features include reviews, previews, interviews and competitions.
CONSUMER: HOLIDAYS & TRAVEL: Entertainment Guides

ALL4HORSES.TV
1820117U81D-372
Editorial Address: Big Red Office, 101 Princess Street, MANCHESTER, M1 6DD **Tel:** 0161 237 9994
Fax: 0845 299 1419
Email: alex.kapp@all4horses.tv
Web site: http://www.all4horses.tv
Publisher: KOAN Ltd
Date Launched: 2007
Frequency of update: Daily
Website Access: Free
Traffic Figures: 7,000 Unique Users (Publisher's Statement)
Editor: Alex Kapp; **Web Editor:** Alex Kapp
Summary of Content: Website covering all things equine with new, expert commentary, jobs, holidays, horses for sale, features and product reviews.
Readership/Target Audience: Aimed at horse enthusiasts, owners and lovers of all ages.
CONSUMER: ANIMALS & PETS: Horses & Ponies

ALL THAT WOMEN WANT
626144U74A-3_40
Editorial Address: 125 Elmore, Eldene, SWINDON, SN3 3TN
Email: editor@allthatwomenwant.com
Web site: http://www.allthatwomenwant.com
Publisher: All That Women Want
Date Launched: 1999
Frequency of update: Daily
Website Access: Free
Traffic Figures: 88,000 Unique Users (per month Publisher's Statement)
Editor: Colleen Moulding; **Web Editor:** Colleen Moulding
Summary of Content: Website providing information on parenting, entertainment, crafts, food, shopping, money, working from home, women's business, antiques, fashion, home decorating and children's sites.
Readership/Target Audience: Aimed at women of all ages.
Other Features: Features include archiving, newsletter, arts and crafts, food, homemaking, interior design, books, software, games and new products.
CONSUMER: WOMEN'S INTEREST CONSUMER MAGAZINES: Women's Interest

ALLABOUTYOU
1752941U74A-1016
Editorial Address: 5th Floor, 7 Swallow Place, LONDON, W1B 2AG **Tel:** 020 7292 0020 **Fax:** 020 7499 8945
Email: adrienne.wyper@allaboutyou.com
Web site: http://www.allaboutyou.com
Publisher: Handbag Publishing Group
Date Launched: 2006
Frequency of update: Daily
Website Access: Free
Traffic Figures: 449,681 Unique Users (01/09/2008 To 30/09/2008 ABC/Electronic)
Editor: Adrienne Wyper
Summary of Content: Website covering fashion, beauty, relationships, parenting, food and entertaining, diet and health, travel and careers.

Readership/Target Audience: Aimed at women aged 30 to 50 years old with children.
CONSUMER: WOMEN'S INTEREST CONSUMER MAGAZINES: Women's Interest

ALLABOUTYOU.COM/ GOODHOUSEKEEPING
1789979U74C-862
Editorial Address: National Magazine House, 72 Broadwick Street, LONDON, W1F 9EP **Tel:** 020 7439 5000
Email: editor@allaboutyou.com
Web site: http://www.allaboutyou.com/goodhousekeeping
Publisher: National Magazine Company Ltd
Frequency of update: Daily
Website Access: Paid
Traffic Figures: 10,000 Unique Users (per week Publisher's Statement)
Editor: Bernadette Fallon
Summary of Content: Website containing features on family, health and beauty, relationships, food, fashion and working mothers as well as readers' experiences, home and design, travel and fiction.
Readership/Target Audience: Aimed at women aged 35 plus with partners and children living comfortable lifestyles.
CONSUMER: WOMEN'S INTEREST CONSUMER MAGAZINES: Home & Family

ALTASSETS
1708615U1R-375
Editorial Address: Burleigh House, 357 Strand, LONDON, WC2R 0HS **Tel:** 020 7845 7590 **Fax:** 020 7845 7599
Email: editorial@altassets.com
Web site: http://www.altassets.net
Publisher: Almeida Capital Limited
Date Launched: 2001
Frequency of update: Daily
Website Access: Free
Traffic Figures: 440,363 Unique Users (per month Publisher's Statement)
Summary of Content: Website providing news and research on the private equity industry.
Readership/Target Audience: Aimed at private equity, venture capital and alternative asset investment professionals.
BUSINESS: FINANCE & ECONOMICS: Financial Related

AMBULANCE ASSESSMENT
40507U56P-4
Editorial Address: 6 The Old Brewery, Charlton Estate, SHEPTON MALLET, BA4 5QE **Tel:** 0870 167 0999
Fax: 01749 342042
Email: enquiries@apap.uk.net
Web site: http://www.apap.org.uk
Publisher: APAP
Frequency of update: Daily
Website Access: Paid
Editor: Bernard Peacher
Summary of Content: Website of the Association of Professional Ambulance Personnel. Covers all aspects of the ambulance world.
Readership/Target Audience: Read by all ambulance staff.
BUSINESS: HEALTH & MEDICAL: Casualty & Emergency

AMMO WEEKLY BULLETIN
1858707U2A-699
Editorial Address: 45 Fouberts Place, LONDON, W1F 7QH
Tel: 020 7575 1940 **Fax:** 020 7575 1931
Email: matthew@ammo.xtremeinformation.com
Web site: http://www.ammoweeklybulletin.co.uk
Publisher: Xtreme Information
Date Launched: 1991
Frequency of update: Weekly. Published on Friday
Website Access: Paid
Traffic Figures: 500 Unique Users (Publisher's Statement)
Editor: Matthew Carlton
Summary of Content: Bulletin tracking advertising sales leads.
Readership/Target Audience: Aimed at media sales teams and business development units as a tool for generating and developing media sales.
BUSINESS: COMMUNICATIONS, ADVERTISING & MARKETING

ANGLING NEWS
711752U92-20
Editorial Address: Combermere Cottage, Old Woodhouses, Broughall, WHITCHURCH, SY13 4EH **Tel:** 01948 871399
Fax: 01948 871392
Email: andy@anglingnews.net
Web site: http://www.anglingnews.net
Date Launched: 2000
Frequency of update: Daily
Website Access: Free

Traffic Figures: 100,000 Unique Users (per week Publisher's Statement)
Editor: Andy Nicholson; **Webmaster:** Juliette Moran; **Online Journalist:** Andy Nicholson
Summary of Content: Website containing angling news, reviews and reports. Includes information on where to fish, accommodation, holidays, tackle suppliers, books, videos, ghillies and guides. Also repair services, angling boards, agencies and bodies, tourist boards, clubs and associations.
Readership/Target Audience: Aimed at anglers of all levels.
CONSUMER: ANGLING & FISHING

ANGLOFILE
39713U50-12
Editorial Address: Thames Tower, Blacks Road, LONDON, W6 9EL **Tel:** 020 8563 3351 **Fax:** 020 8563 3029
Email: anglofile@visitbritain.org
Web site: http://www.enjoyengland.com/presscentre
Publisher: VisitBritain
Frequency of update: Monthly
Website Access: Free
Traffic Figures: 1,000 Unique Users (Publisher's Statement)
Editor: Tess Sullivan
Summary of Content: Website focusing on holidays, travel and leisure in England.
Readership/Target Audience: Aimed at the British and Irish travel journalist.
BUSINESS: TRAVEL & TOURISM

ANGLOGERMANTRADE.COM
718850U14C-7
Editorial Address: PR by email only **Tel:** 0870 759 3688
Email: contactagt1@anglogermantrade.com
Web site: http://www.anglogermantrade.com
Publisher: EFE International
Date Launched: 2001
Frequency of update: Daily
Website Access: Free
Editor: Editorial Department
Summary of Content: Website providing industry, technology, tender information and news, an events calendar, a vendor directory, jobs, education and career opportunities, a travel and destination directory and expatriate information.
Readership/Target Audience: Aimed at directors, managers, business development and marketing executives of corporates, trade associations and government bodies.
BUSINESS: COMMERCE, INDUSTRY & MANAGEMENT: International Commerce

ANIMALS WRITE
626262U81X-20
Editorial Address: Orchardton Hall, Auchencairn, CASTLE DOUGLAS, DG7 1QL **Tel:** 0845 130 6249
Email: animal@bnw.demon.co.uk
Web site: http://www.animalswrite.com
Publisher: Brave New World International Ltd
Date Launched: 1996
Frequency of update: Weekly
Website Access: Free
Editor: Susan Foster
Summary of Content: Website focusing on domestic pets and containing real life stories. Includes reviews of new products for pets and charities that help animals.
Readership/Target Audience: Aimed at animal lovers.
Other Features: Features include a buyer's guide and an events calendar.
CONSUMER: ANIMALS & PETS

THE ANNUAL BUYER'S GUIDE
1665698U14F-252
Editorial Address: For all contact details see main record, e.learning age
Web site: http://www.elearningage.co.uk/productsandservices
Frequency of update: Annual
Website Access: Paid
BUSINESS: COMMERCE, INDUSTRY & MANAGEMENT: Training & Recruitment

ANORAK
47201U82-2_22
Editorial Address: 4 Water Gardens, STANMORE, HA7 3QA
Tel: 07980 578831
Email: editor@anorak.co.uk
Web site: http://www.anorak.co.uk
Publisher: Anorak UK Ltd
Date Launched: 1995
Frequency of update: Daily. News updated throughout the week
Website Access: Free
Traffic Figures: 250,000 Unique Users (per month Publisher's Statement)
Editor: Paul Sorene

Summary of Content: Website reviewing the UK and US press. Includes a review of the tabloids, broadsheets and glossy show-biz magazines. Also features a daily poll and weekly quiz.
Readership/Target Audience: Aimed at 20 to 40 year-old Internet surfers with an appetite for news with attitude.
Other Features: Features include an e-mail newsletter and archiving.
CONSUMER: CURRENT AFFAIRS & POLITICS

ANTIQUE DEALER & COLLECTORS GUIDE
36440U7-80

Editorial Address: 16 Dartmouth Court, Dartmouth Grove, LONDON, SE10 8AS **Tel:** 020 8691 4820
Fax: 020 8691 2489
Email: philipbartlam@tiscali.co.uk
Web site: http://www.antiquecollectorsguide.co.uk
Publisher: Philip Bartlam
Date Launched: 1946
Frequency of update: Monthly
Website Access: Free
Editor: Philip Bartlam
Summary of Content: Website featuring prices and information on all facets of the antiques world. Includes fairs calendar, book reviews and news items.
Readership/Target Audience: Aimed at the amateur and the professional collector and dealer.
BUSINESS: ANTIQUES

ANTIQUES TRADE GAZETTE
626599U7-100_1

Editorial Address: 115 Shaftesbury Avenue, LONDON, WC2H 8AD **Tel:** 020 7420 6600 **Fax:** 020 7420 6605
Email: editorial@antiquestradegazette.com
Web site: http://www.antiquestradegazette.com
Publisher: Metropress Ltd.
Date Launched: 1997
Frequency of update: Daily
Website Access: Free
Editor: Roland Arkell; **Editor-in-Chief:** Mark Bridge; **Web Editor:** Carl Nestor
Summary of Content: Website providing information about the sale of art and antiques worldwide.
Readership/Target Audience: Aimed at auctioneers, dealers and collectors worldwide.
BUSINESS: ANTIQUES

ANTIQUESNEWS
634540U7-86

Formerly: Antiques and Art Independent Online
Editorial Address: PO Box 3369, CHIPPENHAM, SN15 9DU
Tel: 01225 742240
Email: mail@antiquesnews.co.uk
Web site: http://www.antiquesnews.co.uk
Publisher: Antiques News
Date Launched: 2000
Frequency of update: Weekly
Website Access: Free
Editor: Gail Mcleod
Summary of Content: Website reporting on the news and views of the British antiques trade.
Readership/Target Audience: Aimed at serious buyers, sellers, dealers and those with an interest in the antiques and art trade.
BUSINESS: ANTIQUES

THE APPLE
39580U49A-123

Formerly: Going Green
Editorial Address: 68 High Street, WEYBRIDGE, KT13 8RS
Tel: 0845 389 1010 **Fax:** 0845 389 1015
Email: news@eta.co.uk
Web site: http://www.eta.co.uk
Publisher: ETA Services Ltd
Frequency of update: Daily
Website Access: Free
Traffic Figures: 15,000 Unique Users (per week Publisher's Statement)
Editor: Yannick Read
Summary of Content: Website covering UK environmental issues relating to transport.
Readership/Target Audience: Aimed at anyone concerned about the impact of transport on the environment in the UK.
BUSINESS: TRANSPORT

THE ARAB
1834019U90-1025

Editorial Address: 27 Old Gloucester Street, LONDON, WC1N 3AX **Tel:** 020 7100 6017
Email: info@the-arab.com
Web site: http://www.the-arab.com
Publisher: The Arab Magazine
Date Launched: 2008

Frequency of update: Weekly
Website Access: Paid
Traffic Figures: 8,000 Unique Users (Publisher's Statement)
Editor: Anna Costin
Summary of Content: Online magazine with original stories from across the Middle East and North Africa, pan-Arab issues and pressing issues from individual states as well as culture, business, human interest features, regional analysis, interviews and topical issues.
Readership/Target Audience: Aimed at reasonably educated people with a general interest in current affairs of the Middle East and North Africa.
CONSUMER: ETHNIC

ARCHITECTSJOURNAL.CO.UK
706689U4A-12

Formerly: aj Plus
Editorial Address: Greater London House, Hampstead Road, LONDON, NW1 7EJ **Tel:** 020 7728 5000
Email: richard.waite@emap.com
Web site: http://www.architectsjournal.co.uk
Publisher: EMAP Insight
Date Launched: 2000
Frequency of update: Daily
Website Access: Paid
Editor: Richard Waite
Summary of Content: Website containing real-time news, information and competitions for the architectural industry. In-depth information on buildings and technical issues and an archive of The Architect's Journal.
Readership/Target Audience: Aimed at architects.
BUSINESS: ARCHITECTURE & BUILDING: Architecture

THE ARGUS ONLINE
629006U80C-3252

Formerly: This is Brighton and Hove
Editorial Address: Argus House, Crowhurst Road, Hollingbury, BRIGHTON, BN1 8AR **Tel:** 01273 544544
Fax: 01273 566114
Email: news@theargus.co.uk
Web site: http://www.theargus.co.uk
Date Launched: 1881
Frequency of update: Daily
Website Access: Free
Traffic Figures: 243,000 Unique Users (Publisher's Statement)
Editor: Emma Shotton
Summary of Content: Website covering local news, information and an entertainment guide for the Brighton and Hove area.
Readership/Target Audience: Aimed at local people, expats and tourists to the area.
Other Features: Features include archiving, a buyer's guide, recruitment and discussion forums.
CONSUMER: RURAL & REGIONAL INTEREST: Regional Interest English Counties

ARMED FORCES INTERNATIONAL
1640536U40-440

Editorial Address: 100 Chapel Street, TIVERTON, EX16 6BU **Tel:** 01884 244670 **Fax:** 01884 244671
Email: info@copybook.com
Web site: http://www.copybook.com/militarydirectory.asp
Publisher: Copybook Solutions Ltd
Date Launched: 1999
Frequency of update: Monthly
Website Access: Free
Editor: James Armstrong
Summary of Content: Internet portal providing information on companies, products and services related to the defence sector.
Readership/Target Audience: Aimed at suppliers, purchasers and key decision makers within the defence sector.
BUSINESS: DEFENCE

ARMY TECHNOLOGY
626495U40-421

Editorial Address: Brunel House, 55-57 North Wharf Road, LONDON, W2 1LA **Tel:** 020 7915 9957 **Fax:** 020 7915 9720
Email: production@spgmedia.com
Web site: http://www.army-technology.com
Publisher: SPG Media Ltd
Date Launched: 1996
Frequency of update: Daily
Website Access: Free
Traffic Figures: 549,555 Unique Users (Publisher's Statement)
Editor: Duncan West
Summary of Content: Website covering main battle tanks, armoured fighting vehicles, artillery systems, missile systems, attack and support helicopters.

Readership/Target Audience: Aimed at defence industry professionals.
BUSINESS: DEFENCE

AROUND CANTERBURY
48064U89C-60

Editorial Address: Crossdykes, The Street, Wickhambreaux, CANTERBURY, CT3 1RP
Tel: 01227 722133
Email: around@cantweb.co.uk
Web site: http://www.aroundcanterbury.co.uk
Publisher: Around Kent Publications
Date Launched: 1982
Frequency of update: Daily
Website Access: Free
Traffic Figures: 2,000 Unique Users (per month Publisher's Statement)
Editor: Steve Disleris-Beck
Summary of Content: Website covering activities and events in the Canterbury area.
Readership/Target Audience: Read by visitors to North Kent.
CONSUMER: HOLIDAYS & TRAVEL: Entertainment Guides

ARTS.TELEGRAPH.CO.UK
1615668U84A-423

Editorial Address: 111 Buckingham Palace Road, LONDON, SW1W 0DT **Tel:** 020 7931 2000
Email: florence.waters@telegraph.co.uk
Web site: http://www.arts.telegraph.co.uk
Publisher: Telegraph Media Group Ltd
Frequency of update: 313 times a year. Not updated on Sundays
Website Access: Free
Traffic Figures: 70,000 Unique Users (per week Publisher's Statement)
Editor: Florence Waters
Summary of Content: Website providing news and information on selected reviews and features on the arts.
Readership/Target Audience: Aimed at anyone with an interest in the arts.
CONSUMER: THE ARTS & LITERARY: Arts

ARTWORK ONLINE
629025U84A-152

Editorial Address: PO Box 3, ELLON, AB41 9EA
Tel: 01651 842429 **Fax:** 01651 842180
Web site: http://www.artwork.co.uk
Date Launched: 2000
Frequency of update: 26 times a year
Website Access: Free
Editor: Eleanor Stewart
Summary of Content: Website focusing on art reviews and features, with video interviews and comprehensive art listings.
Readership/Target Audience: Aimed at those with a critical interest in art.
Other Features: Features include an events calendar.
CONSUMER: THE ARTS & LITERARY: Arts

ASBESTOS INDUSTRY DIRECTORY
1818152U57-157

Editorial Address: 18 Generator Hall, Electric Wharf, COVENTRY, CV1 4JL **Tel:** 0870 199 4044
Fax: 0870 777 4360
Email: enquiries@industrydirectory.co.uk
Web site: http://www.industrydirectory.co.uk/asbestos
Publisher: Simply Marcomms
Frequency of update: Daily
Website Access: Free
Editor: Kirstie Colledge
Summary of Content: Directory containing the latest news stories for the UK asbestos industry. Includes a news archive.
Readership/Target Audience: Aimed at professionals in the building and construction industry particularly those in the asbestos industry.
BUSINESS: ENVIRONMENT & POLLUTION

ASE.NETWORK
626428U89B-10

Editorial Address: Derlwyn, Hayscastle, HAVERFORDWEST, SA62 5PW **Tel:** 01437 741543
Fax: 01437 741129
Web site: http://www.ase.net
Publisher: Accommodation Search Engine
Date Launched: 1995
Frequency of update: Daily
Website Access: Free
Traffic Figures: 84,548 Unique Users (per month Publisher's Statement)
Editor: Martin Drew

Summary of Content: Website providing a list of accommodation and lodgings available worldwide.
Readership/Target Audience: Aimed at those looking for accommodation of all types.
Other Features: Features include an e-mail newsletter.
CONSUMER: HOLIDAYS & TRAVEL: Hotel Magazines

ASIAN NEWS
48285U90-33

Editorial Address: Observer Buildings, Drake Street, ROCHDALE, OL16 1PH **Tel:** 01706 357086
Fax: 01706 341595
Email: asiannews@menwn.co.uk
Web site: http://www.theasiannews.co.uk
Publisher: Guardian Media Group plc
Date Launched: 1997
Frequency of update: Daily
Website Access: Free
Traffic Figures: 47,337 Unique Users (01/01/2009 To 30/06/2009 ABC/Electronic)
Editor: Shelina Begum
Summary of Content: Website covering local news, features, heritage, culture, business, sport and events.
Readership/Target Audience: Aimed at Asians living in Manchester, Accrington, Bury, Oldham, Rochdale, Tameside, Trafford, Bolton and Blackburn.
CONSUMER: ETHNIC

ASIAN SOCIETY
626152U90-34

Editorial Address: 37 Hampshire Drive, BIRMINGHAM, B15 3NY **Tel:** 07973 198066
Email: info@asiansociety.co.uk
Web site: http://www.asiansociety.co.uk
Publisher: New Asian Media
Date Launched: 1996
Frequency of update: Monthly
Website Access: Free
Traffic Figures: 50,000 Unique Users (per month Publisher's Statement)
Editor: Sam Samra
Summary of Content: Website providing news and information for the British Asian society.
Readership/Target Audience: Aimed at the Asian community as a whole.
Other Features: Features include an events calendar, a recruitment board, a buyer's guide and a discussion forum and archiving.
CONSUMER: ETHNIC

ASSETS WORLD
1753013U74Q-1320

Editorial Address: PR by email only, LONDON
Tel: 07976 205185
Email: rehna@assetsworld.com
Web site: http://www.assetsworld.com
Publisher: Britain's Asian Assets
Date Launched: 2006
Frequency of update: Daily
Website Access: Free
Editor: Rehna Azim
Summary of Content: Website covering show business, entertainment and lifestyle including celebrity news, current affairs, health and beauty, interviews, movies, music, reviews and television.
Readership/Target Audience: Aimed at women of all ages.
CONSUMER: WOMEN'S INTEREST CONSUMER MAGAZINES: Lifestyle

ASSETSWORLD
1646154U90-934

Formerly: Britain's Asian Assets
Editorial Address: PR by email only **Tel:** 07976 205185
Email: editor@assetsworld.com
Web site: http://www.assetsworld.com
Publisher: Britain's Asian Assets
Date Launched: 2006
Frequency of update: Weekly
Website Access: Free
Editor: Rehna Azim
Summary of Content: Website covering celebrity and lifestyle interests including current affairs, social comment, media and general lifestyle.
Readership/Target Audience: Aimed at high achieving professionals.
Other Features: Message and comment board.
CONSUMER: ETHNIC

AUTO EXPRESS ONLINE
600852U77A-21

Editorial Address: 30 Cleveland Street, LONDON, W1T 4JD
Tel: 020 7907 6000 **Fax:** 020 7907 6020
Email: webmaster.autoexpress@dennis.co.uk
Web site: http://www.autoexpress.co.uk
Publisher: Dennis Publishing Ltd

Frequency of update: Daily
Website Access: Free
Traffic Figures: 1,000,000 Unique Users (per month Publisher's Statement)
Editor: Dan Strong; **Editor-in-Chief:** David Johns
Summary of Content: Website covering news on new cars, road tests, previews, used car prices, product tests, car care tips, crash tests, spy video footage and car purchase advice.
Readership/Target Audience: Aimed primarily at 25 to 44 year old male drivers.
Other Features: Features include car finder service, forums, picture galleries, recruitment and archiving.
CONSUMER: MOTORING & CYCLING: Motoring

AUTO TRADER
626216U77A-45

Formerly: Autotrader
Editorial Address: 41-47 Hartfield Road, Wimbledon, LONDON, SW19 3RQ **Tel:** 020 8544 7000
Fax: 020 8879 1879
Email: stuart.milne@autotrader.co.uk
Web site: http://www.autotrader.co.uk
Publisher: TNT Publishing
Date Launched: 1997
Frequency of update: Daily
Website Access: Free
Traffic Figures: 10,319,057 Unique Users (01/03/2008 To 31/03/2008 ABC/Electronic)
Editor: Stuart Milne
Summary of Content: Website featuring online classifieds, motoring news and road tests plus auxiliary motoring centres including insurance and finance.
Readership/Target Audience: Aimed at all UK car buyers.
Other Features: Features include a buyer's guide, board, car valuation tool and email newsletter.
CONSUMER: MOTORING & CYCLING: Motoring

AUTOMOTIVE BUSINESS REVIEW
1794992U31A-396

Editorial Address: Brunel House, 55-57 North Wharf Road, LONDON, W2 1LA **Tel:** 020 7915 9931
Email: jsharp@industryreview.com
Web site: http://www.automotive-business-review.com
Publisher: Ovum
Frequency of update: Weekly
Summary of Content: Electronic newsletter focusing on automobile distribution, vehicle manufacturing, fleet management and aftermarket services.
Readership/Target Audience: Aimed at vehicle and components manufacturers and service providers.
BUSINESS: MOTOR TRADE: Motor Trade Accessories

AUTOMOTIVE INDUSTRY DIRECTORY
1912915U31R-74

Editorial Address: 18 Generator Hall, Electric Wharf, COVENTRY, CV1 4JL **Tel:** 0870 199 4044
Fax: 0870 777 4360
Email: enquries@simplymarcomms.co.uk
Web site: http://www.industrydirectory.co.uk
Publisher: Simply Marcomms
Frequency of update: Daily
Editor: Kirstie Colledge
Summary of Content: Directory containing the latest news stories for the UK automotive industry. Includes news archives.
Readership/Target Audience: Aimed at Automotive professionals, suppliers to the Automotive industry, Automotive PR & Marketing firms.
BUSINESS: MOTOR TRADE: Motor Trade Related

AUTOMOTIVEWORLD.COM
1870992U31R-67

Editorial Address: 14 Great College Street, Westminster, LONDON, SW1P 3RX **Tel:** 020 7878 1030
Fax: 020 7878 1031
Email: editorial@automotiveworld.com
Web site: http://www.automotiveworld.com
Frequency of update: Daily
Traffic Figures: 61,000 Unique Users (Publisher's Statement)
Editor: Colin Whitbread
Summary of Content: Website providing a detailed focus analysis on individual automotive sectors, companies and markets in the form of regular news stories, features, e-newsletters and reports.
Readership/Target Audience: Aimed at anyone within the automotive industry.
BUSINESS: MOTOR TRADE: Motor Trade Related

AUTOPRESSPOINT.COM
626412U31R-17_50

Editorial Address: 43-44 North Bar House, North Bar, BANBURY, OX16 0TH **Tel:** 01295 277050
Fax: 01295 277030
Email: becky.curry@m-eng.com
Web site: http://www.autopresspoint.com
Date Launched: 2000
Frequency of update: Daily
Website Access: Free
Traffic Figures: 450 Unique Users (Publisher's Statement)
Editor: Rebecca Curry
Summary of Content: Online information service covering the international automotive technology, manufacturing, aftermarket and related industries.
Readership/Target Audience: Aimed at journalists and PR consultants.
BUSINESS: MOTOR TRADE: Motor Trade Related

AUTOSPORT.COM
629228U77D-90_5

Editorial Address: Teddington Studios, Broom Road, TEDDINGTON, TW11 89BE **Tel:** 020 8267 5263
Fax: 020 8267 5922
Email: news@autosport.com
Web site: http://www.autosport.com
Publisher: Haymarket Media Group Ltd
Date Launched: 1995
Frequency of update: Daily
Website Access: Paid
Traffic Figures: 646,023 Unique Users (per month ABC/Electronic)
Editor: David Harris
Summary of Content: Website delivering a comprehensive coverage of Formula One and international motor sport including an up-to-date news service; exclusive interviews, columns and features, photos, results and stats.
Readership/Target Audience: Aimed at F1 and motor sports professionals and enthusiasts.
Other Features: Classified ads for jobs in the motor sport industry, daily newsletter, fans bulletin board.
CONSUMER: MOTORING & CYCLING: Motor Sports

AUTOVENDING
626162U11B-30_1

Editorial Address: Rephoto House, Plough Road, Smallfield, HORLEY, RH6 9EZ **Tel:** 01342 844444
Fax: 01342 844488
Email: amanda-roberts@btconnect.com
Web site: http://www.auto-vending.co.uk
Publisher: Rephoto Publishing Ltd
Date Launched: 1991
Frequency of update: Monthly
Website Access: Paid
Traffic Figures: 7,800 Unique Users (Publisher's Statement)
Editor: Amanda Roberts
Summary of Content: Website covering news and information about all aspects the vending industry. Covers machines, products, accessories, new technology, vending users and specifiers.
Readership/Target Audience: Aimed at vending equipment manufacturers, service operators, vending specifiers, users and trade bodies across a wide sector of industries.
BUSINESS: CATERING: Vending Machines

AUTOWIRED
601663U31A-19

Editorial Address: 1 Princes Road, WEYBRIDGE, KT13 9TU
Tel: 01932 823787 **Fax:** 01932 823798
Email: editor@autowired.co.uk
Web site: http://www.autowired.co.uk
Publisher: Glass's Information
Date Launched: 1999
Frequency of update: Daily
Website Access: Free
Traffic Figures: 5,500 Unique Users (Publisher's Statement)
Editor: Janet Palmer
Summary of Content: Website featuring the latest developments in the motor industry. Includes company news, views, industry events and product reviews. Also covers marketing campaigns.
Readership/Target Audience: Aimed at motor dealers, retailers, independent garages and manufacturers of motor cars and accessories.
BUSINESS: MOTOR TRADE: Motor Trade Accessories

AV INTERACTIVE
1800799U2D-152

Editorial Address: 174 Hammersmith Road, LONDON, W6 7JP **Tel:** 020 8267 8005 **Fax:** 020 8267 8008
Email: bhavna.mistry@haymarket.com
Web site: http://www.avinteractive.co.uk
Publisher: Haymarket Specialist Publications
Frequency of update: Daily
Website Access: Free
Traffic Figures: 8,000 Unique Users (Publisher's Statement)

Editor: Bhavna Mistry
Summary of Content: Website focusing on audio-visual applications in industry and education. Includes interactive downloads.
Readership/Target Audience: Read by managers within the audio-visual communications industry and regular end-user companies.
BUSINESS: COMMUNICATIONS, ADVERTISING & MARKETING: Broadcasting

AV INTERNATIONAL NEWSLETTER
1639992U2D-136

Editorial Address: 174 Hammersmith Road, LONDON, W6 7JP **Tel:** 020 8267 8005 **Fax:** 020 8267 8008
Email: avnewsdesk@haymarket.com
Web site: http://www.avinteractive.co.uk
Publisher: Haymarket Business Media Ltd
Date Launched: 2003
Frequency of update: Daily
Website Access: Free
Traffic Figures: 10,000 Unique Users (Publisher's Statement)
Editor: Bhavna Mistry
Summary of Content: Newsletter covering audio-visual applications in industry and education within Europe.
Readership/Target Audience: Read by managers within the audio-visual communications industry and regular end user companies.
BUSINESS: COMMUNICATIONS, ADVERTISING & MARKETING: Broadcasting

AVREVIEW.CO.UK
1739874U78R-508

Editorial Address: 15-18 White Lion Street, ISLINGTON, N1 9PG **Tel:** 020 7843 8851
Email: dave@avreview.co.uk
Web site: http://www.avreview.co.uk
Publisher: Magicalia Ltd
Date Launched: 2004
Frequency of update: Daily
Website Access: Free
Traffic Figures: 230,000 Unique Users (per month Publisher's Statement)
Editor: Dave Oliver
Summary of Content: Website covering AV and hi-fi news, reviews and features.
Readership/Target Audience: Aimed at 20 to 60 year old enthusiasts of audio visual and hi-fi.
CONSUMER: CONSUMER ELECTRONICS: Consumer Electronics Related

AWARENESS MAGAZINE
1746607U80C-5337

Editorial Address: PO Box 18727, ABERDEEN, AB25 2ZU **Tel:** 0845 338 0373 **Fax:** 0845 338 0373
Email: kim@awarenessmagazine.co.uk
Web site: http://www.awarenessmagazine.co.uk
Publisher: Awareness Magazine Ltd
Date Launched: 2005
Frequency of update: Daily
Website Access: Free
Editor: Kimberley Grant
Summary of Content: Website covering health and fitness, diet, complementary and alternative therapies, personal growth, environment and local news.
Readership/Target Audience: Aimed at households in Aberdeen and also available through community centres and libraries.
CONSUMER: RURAL & REGIONAL INTEREST: Regional Interest English Counties

AXIOM
39123U44-147

Editorial Address: DMC House, Pullman Business Park, Pullman Way, RINGWOOD, BH24 1HD **Tel:** 020 7503 0163
Email: grahamcoult@blueyonder.co.uk
Web site: http://www.axiom-magazine.co.uk
Publisher: Ourebi Ltd
Date Launched: 1996
Frequency of update: Monthly
Website Access: Paid
Traffic Figures: 2,000 Unique Users (Publisher's Statement)
Editor: Graham Coult
Summary of Content: Magazine covering business management issues for the legal profession. Includes articles on IT, business, marketing, education, training and people development.
Readership/Target Audience: Aimed at heads of IT, heads of marketing, heads of practice in legal firms, heads of business, managing partners, training partners and heads of personnel.
BUSINESS: LEGAL

AXM
47622U86B-12

Editorial Address: Unit M, Spectrum House, 32-34 Gordon House Road, LONDON, NW5 1LP **Tel:** 020 7424 7400
Fax: 020 7424 7401
Email: matt@axm-mag.com
Web site: http://www.axm-mag.com
Publisher: Millivres-Prowler Ltd
Date Launched: 1997
Frequency of update: Monthly
Website Access: Paid
Traffic Figures: 82,500 Unique Users (Publisher's Statement)
Editor: Matthew Miles
Summary of Content: Health and lifestyle digital magazine covering fashion, arts, music, film, grooming, property and interiors.
Readership/Target Audience: Aimed at gay men between 20 and 45 years old.
CONSUMER: ADULT & GAY MAGAZINES: Gay & Lesbian Magazines

AYLESBURY TODAY
629888U67B-3

Formerly: Aylesbury on-line
Editorial Address: The Gatehouse, Gatehouse Road, AYLESBURY, HP19 8ED **Tel:** 01296 619700
Fax: 01296 619760
Email: editorial@bucksherald.co.uk
Web site: http://www.bucksherald.co.uk
Publisher: Central Counties Newspapers South Ltd
Date Launched: 1998
Frequency of update: Daily
Website Access: Free
Traffic Figures: 20,500 Unique Users (per month Publisher's Statement)
Editor: Ellen Campbell
Summary of Content: Website containing news, sport, information and features about Aylesbury.
Readership/Target Audience: Read by residents and visitors to the local area.
Other Features: Features include recruitment, a chat forum and archiving.
REGIONAL DAILY & SUNDAY NEWSPAPERS: Regional Daily Newspapers

B4 MAGAZINE
1895846U63B-2597

Editorial Address: PR by email only **Tel:** 01865 742211
Fax: 01865 741391
Email: info@b4-business.com
Web site: http://www.b4-business.com
Date Launched: 2006
Frequency of update: Quarterly
Website Access: Paid
Traffic Figures: 7,500 Unique Users (Publisher's Statement)
Editor: Richard Rosser
Summary of Content: Online magazine covering Oxfords business community and showcasing what they do.
Readership/Target Audience: Aimed at business decision makers in Oxfordshire from key organisations, business parks, university departments, professional organisations, independent businesses, council departments leading education establishments, PR agencies and subscribers.
BUSINESS: REGIONAL BUSINESS: Regional Business English Counties

THE BABY DIRECTORY
1655842U74D-576

Editorial Address: 7 Eurolink Business Centre, Effra Road, LONDON, SW2 1BZ **Tel:** 020 7733 0088 **Fax:** 020 7733 4988
Email: editor@babydirectory.com
Web site: http://www.babydirectory.com
Publisher: Brockwell Publishing
Date Launched: 1996
Frequency of update: Daily
Website Access: Free
Traffic Figures: 90,000 Unique Users (per month Publisher's Statement)
Editor: Clare Flawn-Thomas
Summary of Content: Listings magazine with reviews and features on education, health, travel, days out, food, books, videos, music, clothes, toys, baby goods and fashion.
Readership/Target Audience: Aimed at pregnant women, and mothers with babies and children under 5 years old in London.
Other Features: Nanny Finder.
CONSUMER: WOMEN'S INTEREST CONSUMER MAGAZINES: Child Care

BABYCENTRE
1655120U74D-575

Editorial Address: The Genome Centre, Norwich Research Park, Colney, NORWICH, NR4 7UH **Tel:** 01603 450984
Fax: 01603 450986
Email: editor@babycentre.co.uk
Web site: http://www.babycentre.co.uk

Publisher: Content Consultants
Date Launched: 2000
Frequency of update: Daily
Website Access: Free
Editor: Emma Woolfenden
Summary of Content: Website covering medical information about pre-pregnancy and birth, child development and family life including travel, buying for baby and baby equipment.
Readership/Target Audience: Aimed at those trying to conceive, pregnant women and parents of children up to 3 years old.
CONSUMER: WOMEN'S INTEREST CONSUMER MAGAZINES: Child Care

BABYEXPERT.COM
1752604U74D-640

Formerly: babyexpert.co.uk
Editorial Address: National Magazine House, 72 Broadwick Street, LONDON, W1F 9EP **Tel:** 020 7439 5000
Email: info@babyexpert.co.uk
Web site: http://www.babyexpert.co.uk
Publisher: National Magazine Company Ltd
Date Launched: 2006
Frequency of update: Daily
Website Access: Free
Traffic Figures: 268,288 Unique Users (01/11/2008 To 30/11/2008 ABC/Electronic)
Editor: Alison Alexander; **Web Editor:** Alison Alexander
Summary of Content: Website offering expert advice, product reviews, shopping advice, offers and competitions.
Readership/Target Audience: Aimed at pregnant women and new mums.
Other Features: Baby namer tool, good birth guide, sex predictor chart and newsletter.
CONSUMER: WOMEN'S INTEREST CONSUMER MAGAZINES: Child Care

BABYGOES2
1626380U89A-706

Editorial Address: 50 Hampstead Road, BRIGHTON, BN1 5NG **Tel:** 01273 230669
Email: press@babygoes2.com
Web site: http://www.babygoes2.com
Frequency of update: Daily
Website Access: Free
Traffic Figures: 75,000 Unique Users (per month Publisher's Statement)
Editor: Debi Green
Summary of Content: Website covering travel with children including destinations, accommodation, advice, toys, books and equipment.
Readership/Target Audience: Aimed at those intending to travel with a baby or child.
CONSUMER: HOLIDAYS & TRAVEL: Travel

BABYWORLD.CO.UK
626153U74D-558

Formerly: babyworld
Editorial Address: The Slate Barn, Mongewell Park Farm, Mongewell, WALLINGFORD, OX10 8BY **Tel:** 01491 821879
Email: editor@babyworld.co.uk
Web site: http://www.babyworld.co.uk
Publisher: Babyworld.com Ltd
Date Launched: 1997
Frequency of update: Daily
Website Access: Free
Traffic Figures: 518,327 Unique Users (01/03/2009 To 31/03/2009 ABC/Electronic)
Editor: Debbie Bird
Summary of Content: Website focusing on trying for a baby, pregnancy, birth and general parenting issues, with a focus on those relevant to the UK.
Readership/Target Audience: Aimed at those planning for a baby, mums-to-be and parents of babies and toddlers up to 2 years old.
Other Features: Name finder/gender predictor/buyers guide/message board/mailing list/newsletter.
CONSUMER: WOMEN'S INTEREST CONSUMER MAGAZINES: Child Care

BAD NEWS
1667982U14H-418

Editorial Address: 1st Floor, Northumbria House, 5 Delta Bank Road, Metro Riverside Park, GATESHEAD, NE11 9DJ **Tel:** 0191 461 8000 **Fax:** 0191 461 8001
Email: badnews@cobwebinfo.com
Web site: http://www.cobwebinfo.com/index.php?module=bad
Publisher: Cobweb Information Ltd
Date Launched: 1998
Frequency of update: Weekly. Published on Tuesday
Website Access: Free
Traffic Figures: 20,000 Unique Users (Publisher's Statement)
Editor: Julia Stockdale

Summary of Content: Electronically delivered bulletin looking at key issues affecting small businesses in the UK. Topics covered include business round-up, HR, import/export tax, finance, legal, IT, e-commerce, HR, employment and health and safety. Also covers sector based news affecting small businesses.
Readership/Target Audience: Aimed at business advisers, consultants and professionals.
BUSINESS: COMMERCE, INDUSTRY & MANAGEMENT: Small Business

BANBURY CAKE
44211U72B-2677

Editorial Address: 13 Market Place, BANBURY, OX16 5LG
Tel: 01295 256111 **Fax:** 01295 268544
Email: banbury@nqo.com
Web site: http://www.banburycake.net
Publisher: Newsquest (Media Group) Ltd
Date Launched: 1973
Frequency of update: Daily
(02/07/2007 To 30/12/2007 VFD)
Editor: Derek Holmes
Summary of Content: Website covering Banbury news, sports, leisure.
Readership/Target Audience: Aimed at people living in and near Banbury.
LOCAL NEWSPAPERS: Local Newspapers English Counties

BANBURY GUARDIAN.CO.UK
629898U72B-4155

Formerly: Banbury GUARDIAN On-Line
Editorial Address: 7 North Bar, BANBURY, OX16 0TQ
Tel: 01295 227799 **Fax:** 01295 270734
Email: editorial@banburyguardian.co.uk
Web site: http://www.banburyguardian.co.uk
Date Launched: 1838
Frequency of update: Daily
Website Access: Free
Editor: Jason Gibbins
Summary of Content: Website containing news, sport, information and features about Banbury.
Readership/Target Audience: Read by residents and visitors to the local area.
Other Features: Features include recruitment, a chat forum and archiving.
LOCAL NEWSPAPERS: Local Newspapers English Counties

BARKING AND DAGENHAM MATTERS
1881584U72J-327

Email: comments@barkinganddagenham-matters.co.uk
Web site: http://www.barkinganddagenham-matters.co.uk
Frequency of update: Daily
Summary of Content: This website was created to help people who care about local issues. Whether you need access to useful information, want to highlight a particular topic to other people, discuss ideas with like-minded people or just show your support and keep up to date with current affairs in your area, Barking and Dagenham Matters is the place for you.
Readership/Target Audience: Aimed at residents in the local area of Barking and Dagenham.
LOCAL NEWSPAPERS: Community Newsletters

BARNET MATTERS
1881585U72J-328

Email: comments@barnet-matters.co.uk
Web site: http://www.barnet-matters.co.uk
Frequency of update: Daily
Summary of Content: This website was created to help people who care about local issues. Whether you need access to useful information, want to highlight a particular topic to other people, discuss ideas with like-minded people or just show your support and keep up to date with current affairs in your area, Barnet Matters is the place for you.
Readership/Target Audience: Aimed at residents in the local area of Barnet.
LOCAL NEWSPAPERS: Community Newsletters

BBC ANTIQUES
1659693U79K-1002

Editorial Address: For all contact details see main edition, BBC Lifestyle
CONSUMER: HOBBIES & DIY: Collectors Magazines

BBC BIRMINGHAM
1640949U80C-5113

Formerly: BBC Where I Live Birmingham
Editorial Address: The Mailbox, 102-108 Wharfside Street, Birmingham, BIRMINGHAM, B1 1AY **Tel:** 0121 567 6000
Email: birmingham@bbc.co.uk
Web site: http://www.bbc.co.uk/birmingham

Frequency of update: Daily
Website Access: Free
Editor: Jill Ella
Summary of Content: Website covering local news and information, sport, travel, going out, entertainment and student life.
Readership/Target Audience: Aimed at residents and visitors to Birmingham and the Black Country.
Other Features: Archiving, message board, mailing list, newsletter.
CONSUMER: RURAL & REGIONAL INTEREST: Regional Interest English Counties

BBC BLACK COUNTRY
1666510U80C-5293

Editorial Address: For all contact details see main edition, BBC Birmingham
Frequency of update: Daily
CONSUMER: RURAL & REGIONAL INTEREST: Regional Interest English Counties

BBC GARDENING
1659699U93-189

Editorial Address: For all contact details see main edition, BBC Lifestyle
CONSUMER: GARDENING

BBC HEALTH
1659700U74G-254

Editorial Address: For all contact details see main edition, BBC Lifestyle
CONSUMER: WOMEN'S INTEREST CONSUMER MAGAZINES: Slimming & Health

BBC HOLIDAYS
1659698U89E-234

Editorial Address: For all contact details see main edition, BBC Lifestyle
CONSUMER: HOLIDAYS & TRAVEL: Holidays

BBC LANCASHIRE
1640352U80C-5088

Formerly: BBC Where I Live Lancashire
Editorial Address: Darwen Street, BLACKBURN, BB2 2EA
Tel: 01254 262411 **Fax:** 01254 680821
Email: lancashire@bbc.co.uk
Web site: http://www.bbc.co.uk/lancashire
Frequency of update: Daily
Website Access: Free
Editor: Emma Stanley
Summary of Content: Website covering local news, sport, travel, weather, people and places in Lancashire.
Readership/Target Audience: Aimed at residents and visitors to Lancashire.
CONSUMER: RURAL & REGIONAL INTEREST: Regional Interest English Counties

BBC LIFESTYLE
1638231U74Q-1163

Formerly: BBCi Lifestyle
Editorial Address: Room 2406, 201 Wood Lane, LONDON, W12 7TS **Tel:** 020 8752 5252
Web site: http://www.bbc.co.uk/lifestyle
Publisher: BBC
Frequency of update: Daily
Website Access: Free
Editor: Camilla Phelps
Summary of Content: Lifestyle website covering food, homes, parenting, health, fashion, antiques, motoring, gardening and holidays.
Readership/Target Audience: Aimed at those interested in improving their lifestyle.
Other Features: Other features include Community (Virtual Sofa), TV presenters, personal shopping rules, virtual garden design and newsletters.
CONSUMER: WOMEN'S INTEREST CONSUMER MAGAZINES: Lifestyle

BBC LIVING THE DREAM
1659695U74Q-1227

Editorial Address: For all contact details see main edition, BBC Lifestyle
Web site: http://www.bbc.co.uk/lifestyle/livingthedream
Frequency of update: Daily
CONSUMER: WOMEN'S INTEREST CONSUMER MAGAZINES: Lifestyle

BBC LOCAL BEDS, HERTS AND BUCKS
1642424U80C-5182

Formerly: BBC Where I Live Beds, Herts and Bucks
Editorial Address: 1 Hastings Street, LUTON, LU1 5XL
Tel: 01582 637400
Email: threecounties@bbc.co.uk
Web site: http://www.bbc.co.uk/threecounties
Frequency of update: Daily
Website Access: Free
Editor: Katy Lewis
Summary of Content: Website covering local news and information, sport, travel, entertainment, history, nature, people and places.
Readership/Target Audience: Aimed at residents and visitors to Beds, Herts and Bucks.
CONSUMER: RURAL & REGIONAL INTEREST: Regional Interest English Counties

BBC LOCAL ESSEX
1640724U80C-5103

Formerly: BBC Where I Live Essex
Editorial Address: PO Box 765, CHELMSFORD, CM2 9XB
Tel: 01245 616000 **Fax:** 01245 492983
Email: essex.online@bbc.co.uk
Web site: http://www.bbc.co.uk/essex
Frequency of update: Daily
Website Access: Free
Editor: Claire Whiteman
Summary of Content: Website covering local news and information, sport, travel, films, music, clubs, restaurants and student life.
Readership/Target Audience: Aimed at residents and visitors to Essex.
CONSUMER: RURAL & REGIONAL INTEREST: Regional Interest English Counties

BBC LOCAL GLOUCESTERSHIRE
1640685U80C-5094

Formerly: BBC Where I Live Gloucestershire
Editorial Address: London Road, GLOUCESTER, GL1 1SW
Tel: 01452 308585
Email: gloucestershire@bbc.co.uk
Web site: http://www.bbc.co.uk/gloucestershire
Frequency of update: Daily
Website Access: Free
Editor: Chris Sandys
Summary of Content: Website covering local news and information, sport, travel, entertainment, music, clubbing, videos and student life.
Readership/Target Audience: Aimed at 18 to 35 year old residents and visitors to Gloucestershire.
CONSUMER: RURAL & REGIONAL INTEREST: Regional Interest English Counties

BBC LOCAL HAMPSHIRE
1640719U80C-5096

Formerly: BBC Where I Live Hampshire
Editorial Address: Broadcasting House, Havelock Road, SOUTHAMPTON, SO14 7PU **Tel:** 023 8063 1311
Email: hampshire@bbc.co.uk
Web site: http://www.bbc.co.uk/hampshire
Frequency of update: Daily
Website Access: Free
Editor: Indy Almroth-Wright; **Online Journalist:** Indy Almroth-Wright
Summary of Content: Website covering local news and information, sport, travel, films, music and clubs.
Readership/Target Audience: Aimed at 15 to 35 year old residents and visitors to Hampshire, Dorset and the Isle of Wight.
CONSUMER: RURAL & REGIONAL INTEREST: Regional Interest English Counties

BBC LOCAL HUMBERSIDE
1643595U80C-5119

Formerly: BBC Local Humber
Editorial Address: Queen's Court, HULL, HU1 3RH
Tel: 01482 323232 **Fax:** 01482 621450
Email: humber.online@bbc.co.uk
Web site: http://www.bbc.co.uk/humber
Publisher: BBC
Frequency of update: Daily
Website Access: Free
Editor: Derek McGill
Summary of Content: Website covering local news and information, sport, travel, unsigned music, people, places, history and audience derived content.
Readership/Target Audience: Aimed at residents and visitors to East Yorkshire and North Lincolnshire.
CONSUMER: RURAL & REGIONAL INTEREST: Regional Interest English Counties

Internet Media

BBC LOCAL KENT
1640684U80C-5093

Formerly: BBC Where I Live Kent
Editorial Address: Great Hall Arcade, Mount Pleasant Road, TUNBRIDGE WELLS, TN1 1QQ **Tel:** 01892 670000
Email: kent@bbc.co.uk
Web site: http://www.bbc.co.uk/kent
Frequency of update: Daily
Website Access: Free
Editor: Will Roffey
Summary of Content: Website covering local news and information, sport, travel, food, entertainment, gardening and weather.
Readership/Target Audience: Aimed at 18 to 35 year old residents and visitors to Kent.
CONSUMER: RURAL & REGIONAL INTEREST: Regional Interest English Counties

BBC LOCAL LIVERPOOL
1641589U80C-5107

Formerly: BBC Where I Live Liverpool
Editorial Address: PO Box 95.8, LIVERPOOL, L69 1ZJ
Tel: 0151 794 0980 **Fax:** 0151 794 0909
Email: liverpool@bbc.co.uk
Web site: http://www.bbc.co.uk/liverpool
Frequency of update: Daily
Website Access: Free
Editor: Paul Coslett
Summary of Content: Website covering local news and information, sport, travel, music, theatre, film, arts, clubs and videos.
Readership/Target Audience: Aimed at residents and visitors to Merseyside.
CONSUMER: RURAL & REGIONAL INTEREST: Regional Interest English Counties

BBC LOCAL MANCHESTER
1640359U80C-5117

Formerly: BBC Where I Live Manchester
Editorial Address: New Broadcasting House, Oxford Road, MANCHESTER, M60 1SJ **Tel:** 0161 200 2020
Fax: 0161 236 5804
Email: manchester.online@bbc.co.uk
Web site: http://www.bbc.co.uk/manchester
Frequency of update: Daily
Website Access: Free
Editor: Richard Turner
Summary of Content: Website covering local news and information, lifestyle, going out, sport, travel, music, arts, films and religion.
Readership/Target Audience: Aimed at residents and visitors to Manchester.
CONSUMER: RURAL & REGIONAL INTEREST: Regional Interest English Counties

BBC LOCAL NORFOLK
1640582U80C-5089

Formerly: BBC Where I Live Norfolk
Editorial Address: The Forum, Millennium Plain, NORWICH, NR2 1BH **Tel:** 01603 617411
Email: norfolk@bbc.co.uk
Web site: http://www.bbc.co.uk/norfolk
Frequency of update: Daily
Website Access: Free
Editor: Phil Daly
Summary of Content: Website covering local news and information, sport, travel, entertainment, music, films and weather.
Readership/Target Audience: Aimed at residents and visitors to Norfolk.
CONSUMER: RURAL & REGIONAL INTEREST: Regional Interest English Counties

BBC LOCAL NORTHAMPTONSHIRE
1640398U80C-5110

Formerly: BBC Where I Live Northamptonshire
Editorial Address: Broadcasting House, Abington Street, NORTHAMPTON, NN1 2BH **Tel:** 01604 239100
Fax: 01604 737654
Email: northamptonshire@bbc.co.uk
Web site: http://www.bbc.co.uk/northamptonshire
Publisher: BBC
Date Launched: 2002
Frequency of update: Daily
Website Access: Free
Traffic Figures: 130,000 Unique Users (per month Publisher's Statement)
Editor: Mark Whall
Summary of Content: Website covering local news and information, sport, travel, cinema, films, music and entertainment.

Readership/Target Audience: Aimed at residents and visitors to Northamptonshire predominantly aged between 18 and 40 years old.
CONSUMER: RURAL & REGIONAL INTEREST: Regional Interest English Counties

BBC LOCAL OXFORD
1640681U80C-5091

Formerly: BBC Where I Live Oxford
Editorial Address: 269 Banbury Road, OXFORD, OX2 7DW
Tel: 0845 931 1444
Email: oxford@bbc.co.uk
Web site: http://www.bbc.co.uk/oxford
Frequency of update: Daily
Website Access: Free
Editor: Tim Bearder
Summary of Content: Website covering local news and information, sport, travel, entertainment, films, music and computer games.
Readership/Target Audience: Aimed at residents and visitors to Oxfordshire.
CONSUMER: RURAL & REGIONAL INTEREST: Regional Interest English Counties

BBC LOCAL STAFFORDSHIRE
1640583U80C-5090

Formerly: BBC Where I Live Staffordshire
Editorial Address: Cheapside, Hanley, STOKE-ON-TRENT, ST1 1JJ **Tel:** 01782 208080 **Fax:** 01782 289115
Email: stoke@bbc.co.uk
Web site: http://www.bbc.co.uk/staffordshire
Frequency of update: Daily
Website Access: Free
Editor: Mark Stewart
Summary of Content: Website covering local news and information, sport, travel, entertainment, music, films and weather.
Readership/Target Audience: Aimed at residents and visitors to Staffordshire.
CONSUMER: RURAL & REGIONAL INTEREST: Regional Interest English Counties

BBC LOCAL TEES
1640913U80C-5101

Formerly: BBC Where I Live Tees
Editorial Address: Broadcasting House, Newport Road, MIDDLESBROUGH, TS1 5DG **Tel:** 01642 340654
Fax: 01642 211356
Email: tees@bbc.co.uk
Web site: http://www.bbc.co.uk/tees
Frequency of update: Daily
Website Access: Free
Editor: Kerry Sillett
Summary of Content: Website covering local news and information, sport, travel, entertainment, films, music and clubs.
Readership/Target Audience: Aimed at residents and visitors to Teeside and the Tees Valley.
CONSUMER: RURAL & REGIONAL INTEREST: Regional Interest English Counties

BBC LOCAL WALES
1642426U80D-504

Formerly: BBC Where I Live Wales
Editorial Address: Room M2001, Ty Oldfield, Llantrisant, CARDIFF, CF5 2YQ **Tel:** 029 2032 2312
Email: sian.davies@bbc.co.uk
Web site: http://www.bbc.co.uk/wales/whereilive
Frequency of update: Daily
Website Access: Free
Editor: Sian Davies
Summary of Content: Website covering local news and information, sport, travel, film, going out and local history.
Readership/Target Audience: Aimed at residents and visitors to Wales.
CONSUMER: RURAL & REGIONAL INTEREST: Regional Interest Wales

BBC LOCAL WEAR
1640761U80C-5099

Formerly: BBC Where I Live Wear
Editorial Address: Broadcasting Centre, Barrack Road, NEWCASTLE UPON TYNE, NE99 1RN **Tel:** 0191 232 4141
Email: wear@bbc.co.uk
Web site: http://www.bbc.co.uk/wear
Frequency of update: Daily
Website Access: Free
Editor: Francesca Williams
Summary of Content: Website covering local news and information, sport, travel, films, music, clubs, theatre and religion.

Readership/Target Audience: Aimed at residents and visitors to Wearside and County Durham.
CONSUMER: RURAL & REGIONAL INTEREST: Regional Interest English Counties

BBC LOCAL YORKSHIRE
1640357U80C-5109

Formerly: BBC Where I Live North Yorkshire
Editorial Address: 20 Bootham Row, YORK, YO30 7BR
Tel: 01904 540314
Email: northyorkshire@bbc.co.uk
Web site: http://www.bbc.co.uk/northyorkshire
Frequency of update: Daily
Website Access: Free
Editor: Matthew Seymour
Summary of Content: Website covering local news and information, lifestyle, sport, travel, music and films.
Readership/Target Audience: Aimed at residents and visitors to North Yorkshire.
CONSUMER: RURAL & REGIONAL INTEREST: Regional Interest English Counties

BBC MOTORING
1659691U77A-541

Editorial Address: For all contact details see main edition, BBC Lifestyle
CONSUMER: MOTORING & CYCLING: Motoring

BBC PARENTING
1659696U74D-586

Editorial Address: For all contact details see main edition, BBC Lifestyle
CONSUMER: WOMEN'S INTEREST CONSUMER MAGAZINES: Child Care

BBC PATRIKA
1785566U90-994

Editorial Address: Room 410 NE, Central Block, Bush House, Strand, LONDON, WC2B 4BH **Tel:** 020 7557 1777
Fax: 020 7497 0297
Email: hindi.letters@bbc.co.uk
Web site: http://www.bbc.co.uk/hindi/entertainment
Date Launched: 2006
Frequency of update: Daily
Website Access: Free
Editor: Salma Zaidi
Summary of Content: Internet magazine covering entertainment, fashion, picture galleries, features, fiction, stories, poems and travel-logs.
Readership/Target Audience: Aimed at Indians worldwide.
CONSUMER: ETHNIC

BBC RELATIONSHIPS
1659697U74Q-1228

Editorial Address: For all contact details see main edition, BBC Lifestyle
Frequency of update: Daily
CONSUMER: WOMEN'S INTEREST CONSUMER MAGAZINES: Lifestyle

BBC SOMERSET
1640718U80C-5095

Formerly: BBC Where I Live Somerset
Editorial Address: Broadcasting House, Park Street, TAUNTON, TA1 4DA **Tel:** 01823 323956 **Fax:** 01823 332539
Email: somerset@bbc.co.uk
Web site: http://www.bbc.co.uk/somerset
Date Launched: 2003
Frequency of update: Daily
Website Access: Free
Traffic Figures: 49,000 Unique Users (05/01/2009 To 28/06/2009 RAJAR/Ipsos-RSL)
Editor: Tammy McAllister
Summary of Content: Website covering local news and information, sport, travel, weather, entertainment, music, clubs, student life, tourism, going out and community features.
Readership/Target Audience: Aimed at 15 to 35 year old residents and visitors to Somerset.
Other Features: Message board, mailing list and newsletter.
CONSUMER: RURAL & REGIONAL INTEREST: Regional Interest English Counties

BBC STYLE
1659694U74B-710

Editorial Address: For all contact details see main edition, BBC Lifestyle
CONSUMER: WOMEN'S INTEREST CONSUMER MAGAZINES: Women's Interest - Fashion

BBC SURREY
1640725U80C-5111

Formerly: BBC Southern Counties
Editorial Address: Broadcasting Centre, GUILDFORD, GU2 7AP **Tel:** 01483 734330
Email: surrey@bbc.co.uk
Web site: http://www.bbc.co.uk/surrey
Frequency of update: Daily
Website Access: Free
Editor: Heather Driscoll
Summary of Content: Website covering local news and information, travel, sport, music, clubs, entertainment and films.
Readership/Target Audience: Aimed at residents and visitors to Surrey and Sussex.
CONSUMER: RURAL & REGIONAL INTEREST: Regional Interest English Counties

BBC SUSSEX
1898733U80C-5503

Editorial Address: Broadcasting House, Queens Road, BRIGHTON, BN1 3XB **Tel:** 01273 320401
Email: sussex@bbc.co.uk
Web site: http://news.bbc.co.uk/local/sussex/hi
Summary of Content: Website covering local news and information, travel, sport, music, clubs, entertainment and films.
Readership/Target Audience: Aimed at residents and visitors to Sussex.
CONSUMER: RURAL & REGIONAL INTEREST: Regional Interest English Counties

BBC TYNE
1640795U80C-5100

Formerly: BBC Local Tyne
Editorial Address: Broadcasting Centre, Barrack Road, NEWCASTLE UPON TYNE, NE99 1RN **Tel:** 0191 232 4141
Email: tyne@bbc.co.uk
Web site: http://www.bbc.co.uk/tyne
Frequency of update: Daily
Website Access: Free
Editor: Joanne Carruthers
Summary of Content: Website covering local news and information, travel, sport, people, places, nature, history, faith, and weather.
Readership/Target Audience: Aimed at residents and visitors to Tyneside and Northumberland.
CONSUMER: RURAL & REGIONAL INTEREST: Regional Interest English Counties

BBC WATCHDOG
713573U74C-50

Formerly: BBCi Watchdog
Editorial Address: Room G509, 201 Wood Lane, LONDON, W12 7TS **Tel:** 020 8743 8000 **Fax:** 020 8752 5820
Email: watchdog@bbc.co.uk
Web site: http://www.bbc.co.uk/watchdog
Publisher: BBC
Date Launched: 1997
Frequency of update: Weekly
Website Access: Free
Traffic Figures: 20,627 Unique Users (per week Publisher's Statement)
Editor: Rob Unsworth
Summary of Content: Website focusing on consumer complaints regarding poor goods and or services. Includes reports, consumer guides and a quiz.
Readership/Target Audience: Aimed at consumers of all ages.
Other Features: Features include a buyer's guide and an e-mail newsletter.
CONSUMER: WOMEN'S INTEREST CONSUMER MAGAZINES: Home & Family

BBC WHERE I LIVE CAMBRIDGESHIRE
1640686U80C-5104

Formerly: BBC Cambridgeshire
Editorial Address: 104 Hills Road, CAMBRIDGE, CB2 1LQ
Tel: 01223 259696
Email: cambridgeshire@bbc.co.uk
Web site: http://www.bbc.co.uk/cambridgeshire
Frequency of update: Daily
Website Access: Free
Editor: Helen Burchell; **Online Journalist:** Helen Burchell
Summary of Content: Website covering local news and information, community issues, sport, travel, entertainment, going out, theatre, and student life.
Readership/Target Audience: Aimed at residents and visitors to Cambridgeshire.
CONSUMER: RURAL & REGIONAL INTEREST: Regional Interest English Counties

BBC WHERE I LIVE CORNWALL
1642438U80C-5116

Formerly: BBC Cornwall
Editorial Address: Phoenix Wharf, TRURO, TR1 1UA
Tel: 01872 275421 **Fax:** 01872 240679
Email: cornwall@bbc.co.uk
Web site: http://www.bbc.co.uk/cornwall
Date Launched: 2001
Frequency of update: Daily
Website Access: Free
Editor: Matthew Shepherd
Summary of Content: Website covering local news and information, sport, travel, films, music, clubs, art, theatre, Cornwall features, village profiles, video nation and surfing etc.
Readership/Target Audience: Aimed at residents and visitors to Cornwall.
CONSUMER: RURAL & REGIONAL INTEREST: Regional Interest English Counties

BBC WHERE I LIVE COVENTRY & WARWICKSHIRE
1640916U80C-5102

Formerly: BBC Coventry and Warwickshire
Editorial Address: Priory Place, COVENTRY, CV1 5SQ
Tel: 024 7653 9226
Email: coventry@bbc.co.uk
Web site: http://www.bbc.co.uk/coventry
Frequency of update: Daily
Website Access: Free
Editor: Martin Winch
Summary of Content: Website covering local news, information, sport, travel, music, films, arts, local history and student life.
Readership/Target Audience: Aimed at residents and visitors to Coventry and Warwickshire.
CONSUMER: RURAL & REGIONAL INTEREST: Regional Interest English Counties

BBC WHERE I LIVE CUMBRIA
1640580U80C-5108

Formerly: BBC Cumbria
Editorial Address: Annetwell Street, CARLISLE, CA3 8BB
Tel: 01228 592444 **Fax:** 01228 511195
Email: cumbria@bbc.co.uk
Web site: http://www.bbc.co.uk/cumbria
Frequency of update: Daily
Website Access: Free
Editor: Mark Robertson
Summary of Content: Website covering local news and information, sport, travel, weather, entertainment, music and films.
Readership/Target Audience: Aimed at residents and visitors to Cumbria.
CONSUMER: RURAL & REGIONAL INTEREST: Regional Interest English Counties

BBC WHERE I LIVE DERBY
1641578U80C-5105

Formerly: BBC Derby
Editorial Address: 56 St. Helens Street, DERBY, DE1 3HY
Tel: 01332 361111
Email: derby@bbc.co.uk
Web site: http://www.bbc.co.uk/derby
Date Launched: 2001
Frequency of update: Daily
Website Access: Free
Editor: Simon Cornes
Summary of Content: Website covering local news and information, sport, travel, music, theatre, cinema and religion.
Readership/Target Audience: Aimed at residents and visitors to Derbyshire aged between 18 and 35 years old.
CONSUMER: RURAL & REGIONAL INTEREST: Regional Interest English Counties

BBC WHERE I LIVE GUERNSEY
1641580U80C-5106

Formerly: BBC Guernsey
Editorial Address: Broadcasting House, Bulwer Avenue, St. Sampson, GUERNSEY, GY2 4LA **Tel:** 01481 200600
Email: guernsey@bbc.co.uk
Web site: http://www.bbc.co.uk/guernsey
Frequency of update: Daily
Website Access: Free
Editor: Tom Girard
Summary of Content: Website covering local news and information, sport, travel, weather, entertainment, films, music, clubs, surfing, what's on, local history, unsigned bands, local government, picture galleries and features.
Readership/Target Audience: Aimed at residents and visitors of the Bailiwick of Guernsey.

Other Features: Other features on site including message boards.
CONSUMER: RURAL & REGIONAL INTEREST: Regional Interest English Counties

BBC WHERE I LIVE HEREFORD AND WORCESTER
1640682U80C-5092

Formerly: BBC Hereford and Worcester
Editorial Address: Hylton Road, WORCESTER, WR2 5WW
Tel: 01905 748485
Email: worcester@bbc.co.uk
Web site: http://www.bbc.co.uk/herefordandworcester
Frequency of update: Daily
Website Access: Free
Editor: Jerry Chester
Summary of Content: Website covering local news and information, sport, travel, entertainment, films, music, videos and student life.
Readership/Target Audience: Aimed at residents and visitors to Hereford and Worcester.
CONSUMER: RURAL & REGIONAL INTEREST: Regional Interest English Counties

BBC WHERE I LIVE LINCOLNSHIRE
1640362U80C-5085

Formerly: BBC Lincolnshire
Editorial Address: Radion Building, Newport, LINCOLN, LN1 3XY **Tel:** 01522 511411 **Fax:** 01522 511058
Email: lincolnshire@bbc.co.uk
Web site: http://www.bbc.co.uk/lincolnshire
Frequency of update: Daily
Website Access: Free
Traffic Figures: 20,000 Unique Users (per week Publisher's Statement)
Editor: Paul Sims
Summary of Content: Website covering local news and information, lifestyle, sport, travel and entertainment.
Readership/Target Audience: Aimed at residents and visitors to Lincolnshire generally aged between 18 and 35 years old.
CONSUMER: RURAL & REGIONAL INTEREST: Regional Interest English Counties

BBC WHERE I LIVE LONDON
1644038U80C-5122

Formerly: BBC London
Editorial Address: 35 Marylebone High Street, LONDON, W1U 4QA **Tel:** 020 7224 2424
Email: yourlondon@bbc.co.uk
Web site: http://www.bbc.co.uk/london
Frequency of update: Daily
Website Access: Free
Editor: Claire Timms
Summary of Content: Website covering local news and information, travel, weather sport, entertainment, games, TV and Radio.
Readership/Target Audience: Aimed at those who work in London as well as residents and visitors.
CONSUMER: RURAL & REGIONAL INTEREST: Regional Interest English Counties

BBC WHERE I LIVE NOTTINGHAM
1640360U80C-5086

Formerly: BBC Nottingham
Editorial Address: London Road, NOTTINGHAM, NG2 4UU
Tel: 0115 902 1933
Web site: http://www.bbc.co.uk/nottingham
Date Launched: 2001
Frequency of update: Daily
Website Access: Free
Editor: Nigel Bell; **Web Editor:** Nigel Bell
Summary of Content: Website covering local news and information, lifestyle, travel, sport, films, music and culture.
Readership/Target Audience: Aimed at residents, former residents and visitors to Nottingham aged from teens to 45 years old.
CONSUMER: RURAL & REGIONAL INTEREST: Regional Interest English Counties

BBC WHERE I LIVE WALES MID
1657843U80D-507

Editorial Address: For all contact details see main edition, BBC Local Wales
Frequency of update: Daily
Website Access: Free
CONSUMER: RURAL & REGIONAL INTEREST: Regional Interest Wales

Internet Media

BBC WHERE I LIVE WALES NORTH EAST

1657844U80D-508

Editorial Address: For all contact details see main edition, BBC Local Wales
Frequency of update: Daily
Website Access: Free
CONSUMER: RURAL & REGIONAL INTEREST: Regional Interest Wales

BBC WHERE I LIVE WALES NORTH WEST

1657845U80D-509

Editorial Address: For all contact details see main edition, BBC Local Wales
Frequency of update: Daily
Website Access: Free
CONSUMER: RURAL & REGIONAL INTEREST: Regional Interest Wales

BBC WHERE I LIVE WALES SOUTH EAST

1657841U80D-510

Editorial Address: For all contact details see main edition, BBC Local Wales
Frequency of update: Daily
Website Access: Free
CONSUMER: RURAL & REGIONAL INTEREST: Regional Interest Wales

BBC WHERE I LIVE WALES SOUTH WEST

1657842U80D-511

Editorial Address: For all contact details see main edition, BBC Local Wales
Frequency of update: Daily
Website Access: Free
CONSUMER: RURAL & REGIONAL INTEREST: Regional Interest Wales

BBC WHERE I LIVE WILTSHIRE

1640690U80C-5120

Formerly: BBC Wiltshire
Editorial Address: Broadcasting House, 56-58 Prospect Place, SWINDON, SN1 3RW **Tel:** 01793 513626
Email: wiltshire@bbc.co.uk
Web site: http://www.bbc.co.uk/wiltshire
Frequency of update: Daily
Website Access: Free
Editor: Shelley Keen
Summary of Content: Website covering local news and information, sport, travel, entertainment, films, music, clubs and bars.
Readership/Target Audience: Aimed at residents and visitors to Wiltshire aged between 18 and 35 years old.
CONSUMER: RURAL & REGIONAL INTEREST: Regional Interest English Counties

BBCGOODFOOD.COM

1789425U74P-950

Editorial Address: Media Centre, 201 Wood Lane, LONDON, W12 7TQ **Tel:** 020 8433 2000
Email: goodfoodwebsite@bbc.co.uk
Web site: http://www.bbcgoodfood.com
Publisher: BBC Worldwide Publishing
Date Launched: 2006
Frequency of update: Daily
Website Access: Free
Traffic Figures: 833,187 Unique Users (01/02/2009 To 28/02/2009 ABC/Electronic)
Editor: Caroline Hire; **Web Editor:** Caroline Hire
Summary of Content: Website featuring 5 years of recipes from the BBC Good Food and Olive Magazines, independent editorial on food related, eco- and wellbeing issues, postcode search for local and seasonal food.
Readership/Target Audience: Aimed at anyone with an interest in food particularly home cooks.
CONSUMER: WOMEN'S INTEREST CONSUMER MAGAZINES: Food & Cookery

BBCWHODOYOUTHINKYOUARE.COM

1824047U94X-296

Editorial Address: 9th Floor, Tower House, Fairfax Street, BRISTOL, BS1 3BN **Tel:** 0117 927 9009
Email: dancossins.@bbcmagazinesbristol.com
Web site: http://www.bbcwhodoyouthinkyouare.com
Publisher: BBC Magazines Bristol
Date Launched: 2007
Frequency of update: Weekly
Website Access: Free
Editor: Dan Cossins

Summary of Content: Website with celebrity TV content including unseen footage and family history tutorials.
Readership/Target Audience: Aimed at those interested in family history.
CONSUMER: OTHER CLASSIFICATIONS: Miscellaneous

BCW

1609294U5B-9003

Formerly: ITreviewed
Editorial Address: 55 Millbrook Drive, Shenstone, LICHFIELD, WS14 0JL **Tel:** 07542 921922
Email: christian@harrismarketing.net
Web site: http://www.businesscomputingworld.co.uk
Publisher: Black Letter Publishing
Date Launched: 2003
Frequency of update: Daily
Website Access: Free
Traffic Figures: 100,000 Unique Users (per month Publisher's Statement)
Editor: Christian Harris
Summary of Content: Website covering the latest IT news for technology enthusiasts and product buyers.
Readership/Target Audience: Aimed at early adopters and technology enthusiasts.
Other Features: Reviews, buyers guides, opinion pieces, price comparison search, jobs
BUSINESS: COMPUTERS & AUTOMATION: Data Processing

THE BDAILY NEWS

1664724U63B-2534

Formerly: bdaily
Editorial Address: 6 Charlotte Square, NEWCASTLE UPON TYNE, NE1 4XF **Tel:** 0191 261 1333 **Fax:** 0191 261 6012
Email: editor@bdaily.info
Web site: http://www.bdaily.info
Publisher: The bgroup
Date Launched: 2001
Frequency of update: 260 times a year
Website Access: Free
Traffic Figures: 9,000 Unique Users (Publisher's Statement)
Editor: Robert Perry
Summary of Content: Electronically delivered publication covering business news, enterprise, culture, law, job vacancies, events and technology across the North East.
Readership/Target Audience: Aimed at those who are operating in, or have an interest in business in the North East region.
BUSINESS: REGIONAL BUSINESS: Regional Business English Counties

BEAUTY4MEDIA.COM

1842852U15A-205

Editorial Address: Unit 11, The Chandlery, 50 Westminster Bridge Road, LONDON, SE1 7QY **Tel:** 020 7953 7504
Fax: 020 7953 8773
Email: news.desk@beauty4media.com
Web site: http://www.beauty4media.com
Publisher: News4Media Ltd
Date Launched: 2008
Frequency of update: Daily
Website Access: Free
Traffic Figures: 5,000 Unique Users (per month Publisher's Statement)
Editor: Cherise Williams
Summary of Content: Website covering all aspects of news from the beauty industry.
Readership/Target Audience: Aimed at those working in the beauty trade at all levels.
BUSINESS: COSMETICS & HAIRDRESSING: Cosmetics

BEAUTYANDTHEDIRT.CO.UK

714006U74A-10

Editorial Address: 46A Carnaby Street, LONDON, W1F 9PS **Tel:** 020 7292 9779
Email: krista@beautyandthedirt.com
Web site: http://www.beautyandthedirt.co.uk
Publisher: Mimi Media
Date Launched: 2001
Frequency of update: Daily
Website Access: Free
Traffic Figures: 500,000 Unique Users (per month Publisher's Statement)
Editor: Krista Madden
Summary of Content: Website providing gossip and advice and information on beauty, fashion, shopping, travel and London night life.
Readership/Target Audience: Aimed at women aged 14 to 40 years old and men aged over 18.
CONSUMER: WOMEN'S INTEREST CONSUMER MAGAZINES: Women's Interest

BEAUTYBIBLE.COM

1813427U74H-307

Editorial Address: 2 Fore Street, Thorncombe, CHARD, TA20 4PP **Tel:** 01460 30072
Email: s.stacey@you.co.uk
Web site: http://www.beautybible.com
Editor: Sarah Stacey
Summary of Content: Online magazine covering beauty information, tips, questions and answers, prize draws and exclusive offers.
Readership/Target Audience: Aimed at women of all ages.
CONSUMER: WOMEN'S INTEREST CONSUMER MAGAZINES: Hair & Beauty

BEDFORDSHIRE MATTERS

1881586U72J-329

Email: comments@bedfordshire-matters.co.uk
Web site: http://www.bedfordshire-matters.co.uk
Frequency of update: Daily
Summary of Content: This website was created to help people who care about local issues. Whether you need access to useful information, want to highlight a particular topic to other people, discuss ideas with like-minded people or just show your support and keep up to date with current affairs in your area, Bedfordshire Matters is the place for you.
Readership/Target Audience: Aimed at residents in the local area of Bedfordshire.
LOCAL NEWSPAPERS: Community Newsletters

BEER TODAY

1741345U74P-943

Editorial Address: 3 Curnows Road, HAYLE, TR27 4RZ **Tel:** 07867 585395
Email: darren@beertoday.co.uk
Web site: http://www.beertoday.co.uk
Date Launched: 2004
Frequency of update: Daily
Website Access: Free
Editor: Darren Norbury
Summary of Content: Website covering real ale news mainly from around the UK, with brewery and ale listings and news of events and beer festivals. Also highlights the best places for good pints and a specialist interest in matching beer with food.
Readership/Target Audience: Aimed at beer drinkers in general but particularly real ale enthusiasts.
CONSUMER: WOMEN'S INTEREST CONSUMER MAGAZINES: Food & Cookery

BELFAST MATTERS

1881587U72J-330

Email: comments@belfast-matters.co.uk
Web site: http://www.belfast-matters.co.uk
Frequency of update: Daily
Summary of Content: This website was created to help people who care about local issues. Whether you need access to useful information, want to highlight a particular topic to other people, discuss ideas with like-minded people or just show your support and keep up to date with current affairs in your area, Belfast Matters is the place for you.
Readership/Target Audience: Aimed at residents in the local area of Belfast.
LOCAL NEWSPAPERS: Community Newsletters

BELPER TODAY

629814U72B-685

Formerly: Belper NEWS On-Line
Editorial Address: The Courtyard, 8 Market Place, BELPER, DE56 1FZ **Tel:** 01773 881100 **Fax:** 01773 822428
Email: editor@belpernews.co.uk
Web site: http://www.belpernews.co.uk
Publisher: Johnston Press plc
Frequency of update: Daily
Website Access: Free
Traffic Figures: 4,460 Unique Users (per month Publisher's Statement)
Editor: Amanda Hatfield
Summary of Content: Website containing news, sport, information and features about Belper.
Readership/Target Audience: Read by residents and visitors to the local area.
Other Features: Features include recruitment, a buyer's guide, a discussion forum and archiving.
LOCAL NEWSPAPERS: Local Newspapers English Counties

BERKSHIRE MATTERS

1881588U72J-331

Email: comments@berkshire-matters.co.uk
Web site: http://www.berkshire-matters.co.uk
Frequency of update: Daily
Summary of Content: This website was created to help people who care about local issues. Whether you need access to useful information, want to highlight a particular topic to other people, discuss ideas with like-minded people

or just show your support and keep up to date with current affairs in your area, Berkshire Matters is the place for you.
Readership/Target Audience: Aimed at residents in the local area of Berkshire.
LOCAL NEWSPAPERS: Community Newsletters

BERRY BROS. & RUDD
628952U9C-10

Editorial Address: Hamilton Close, Houndmills, BASINGSTOKE, RG21 6YB **Tel:** 01256 323566
Fax: 01256 340157
Email: charlie.bennett@bbr.com
Web site: http://www.bbr.com
Date Launched: 1994
Frequency of update: Daily
Website Access: Free
Traffic Figures: 33,000 Unique Users (per week Publisher's Statement)
Editor: Charlie Bennett
Summary of Content: Website focusing on wines of the world including an online shopping facility, news and a wine pronunciation guide.
Readership/Target Audience: Aimed at wine lovers worldwide.
BUSINESS: DRINKS & LICENSED TRADE: Licensed Trade, Wines & Spirits

BEXHILL TODAY
634143U67B-25

Formerly: BEXHILL-ON-SEA Observer
Editorial Address: 18 Sackville Road, BEXHILL-ON-SEA, TN39 3JL **Tel:** 01424 730555 **Fax:** 01424 730832
Email: bexobs@trbeckett.co.uk
Web site: http://www.bexhilltoday.co.uk
Date Launched: 2001
Frequency of update: Daily
Website Access: Free
Traffic Figures: 11,236 Unique Users (per month Publisher's Statement)
Editor: Newsdesk
Summary of Content: Website containing news, sport, information and features about the local area.
Readership/Target Audience: Read by local residents, visitors and expatriates.
Other Features: Features include recruitment, a chat forum, a calendar of events and archiving.
REGIONAL DAILY & SUNDAY NEWSPAPERS: Regional Daily Newspapers

BEXLEY MATTERS
1881589U72J-332

Email: comments@bexley-matters.co.uk
Web site: http://www.bexley-matters.co.uk
Frequency of update: Daily
Summary of Content: Website created to help people who care about local issues. Whether you need access to useful information, want to highlight a particular topic to other people, discuss ideas with like-minded people or just show your support and keep up to date with current affairs in your area, Bexley Matters is the place for you.
Readership/Target Audience: Aimed at residents in the local area of Bexley.
LOCAL NEWSPAPERS: Community Newsletters

BIA NEWSCAST
623868U55-34

Editorial Address: 14-15 Belgrave Square, LONDON, SW1X 8PS **Tel:** 020 7565 7190
Email: rwinder@bioindustry.org
Web site: http://www.bioindustry.org
Publisher: BioIndustry Association
Date Launched: 1999
Frequency of update: Weekly
Website Access: Paid
Traffic Figures: 2,000 Unique Users (Publisher's Statement)
Editor: Robert Winder
Summary of Content: Electronically sent newsletter which contains feature articles on biotechnology, political, financial and corporate news, as well as information on BIA activities.
Readership/Target Audience: Aimed at bioscience professionals.
BUSINESS: APPLIED SCIENCE & LABORATORIES

BIBENDUM
628985U9C-15

Editorial Address: 113 Regents Park Road, LONDON, NW1 8UR **Tel:** 020 7722 5577 **Fax:** 020 7722 7354
Email: sales@bibendum-wine.co.uk
Web site: http://www.bibendum-wine.co.uk
Frequency of update: Daily
Website Access: Free
Editor: Ben Smith
Summary of Content: Website covering wines from around the world, with updated news and an online shopping facility.

Readership/Target Audience: Aimed at retailers and consumers.
BUSINESS: DRINKS & LICENSED TRADE: Licensed Trade, Wines & Spirits

BICESTER ADVERTISER
44215U72B-2700

Editorial Address: 50 Market Square, BICESTER, OX26 7AJ
Tel: 01869 327182 **Fax:** 01869 322977
Email: bicester@nqo.com
Web site: http://www.bicesteradvertiser.net
Publisher: Newsquest (Oxfordshire) Ltd
Frequency of update: Daily
Website Access: Paid
(02/07/2007 To 30/12/2007 ABC)
Editor: Sam McGregor
Summary of Content: Website covering news, sports and leisure in Bicester.
Readership/Target Audience: Aimed at people living in this area.
LOCAL NEWSPAPERS: Local Newspapers English Counties

BIG CITY REDNECK
1753012U76A-198

Editorial Address: 98 Douglas Buildings, Marshalsea Road, LONDON, SE1 1JW **Tel:** 020 7407 1310
Email: big_city_redneck@yahoo.co.uk
Web site: http://www.bigcityredneck.co.uk
Date Launched: 2006
Frequency of update: 26 times a year
Website Access: Free
Traffic Figures: 2,000 Unique Users (per month Publisher's Statement)
Editor: Rose Dennen
Summary of Content: Website covering music, arts and film.
Readership/Target Audience: Aimed at aspirers aged between 17 and 40 years old.
CONSUMER: MUSIC & PERFORMING ARTS: Cinema

BIKEMAGIC
626539U77C-455

Editorial Address: 8th Floor, Caxton House, 2 Farringdon Road, LONDON, EC1M 3HP **Tel:** 01373 813413
Fax: 020 7861 9899
Email: editor@bikemagic.com
Web site: http://www.bikemagic.com
Publisher: Magicalia Ltd
Date Launched: 1998
Frequency of update: Daily
Website Access: Free
Traffic Figures: 252,000 Unique Users (per month Publisher's Statement)
Editor: Mike Davis
Summary of Content: Website focusing on all aspects of cycling. Includes cycling events, reviews, places to visit, cycling clubs, contacts and products.
Readership/Target Audience: Aimed at cyclists.
CONSUMER: MOTORING & CYCLING: Cycling

BIKERADAR.COM
1814379U77C-953

Editorial Address: 30 Monmouth Street, BATH, BA1 2BW
Tel: 01225 442244
Email: bikeradar@bikeradar.com
Web site: http://www.bikeradar.com
Publisher: Future Publishing Ltd
Date Launched: 2007
Frequency of update: Daily
Website Access: Free
Editor: Jeff Jones
Summary of Content: Website covering all aspects of cycling both on and off-road with bike and gear reviews, race news, health and fitness and roots.
Readership/Target Audience: Aimed at on and off-road cyclists of all ages and abilities worldwide.
CONSUMER: MOTORING & CYCLING: Cycling

BIOCENTURY INTERNATIONAL
39948U55-35_50

Editorial Address: Cranbrook House, 287-291 Banbury Road, OXFORD, OX2 7JQ **Tel:** 01865 512184
Email: mward@biocentury.com
Web site: http://www.biocentury.com
Publisher: Bio-Century Publications Inc
Frequency of update: Daily
Website Access: Paid
Editor: Mike Ward
Summary of Content: Newsletter covering the worldwide biotechnology business. Includes news, clinical results, analysis and comment on events, issues, deals, partnerships, R&D and financial and clinical results.

Readership/Target Audience: Aimed at scientists, investors, accountants, lawyers and business intelligence units.
BUSINESS: APPLIED SCIENCE & LABORATORIES

BIOFUEL REVIEW
1775585U58-180

Editorial Address: Windmill Oast, Benenden Road, Rolvenden, CRANBROOK, TN17 4PF **Tel:** 01580 240055
Email: giles@biofuelreview.com
Web site: http://www.biofuelreview.com
Publisher: Bishop Rock Publishing
Date Launched: 2006
Frequency of update: Daily
Website Access: Free
Editor: Giles Clark
Summary of Content: Web-site providing business news for the bio fuel industry, whilst also covering the commerce, politics and technology of the biofuel sector.
Readership/Target Audience: Aimed at all those involved professionally in the bio fuel markets including market analysts, bankers, politicians, executives, technologists and scientists.
Other Features: Weekly newsletter.
BUSINESS: ENERGY, FUEL & NUCLEAR

BIOWORLD INTERNATIONAL
39953U55-40

Editorial Address: 11A Sycamore Close, Audlem, CREWE, CW3 0EZ **Tel:** 01270 812775
Email: nuala@merebrook.demon.co.uk
Web site: http://www.bioworld.com
Publisher: Thomson Healthcare
Frequency of update: Weekly
Website Access: Paid
Editor: Nuala Moran
Summary of Content: Website covering the biotechnology industry worldwide.
Readership/Target Audience: Read by biotech investors and pharmaceutical companies and professionals in the biotech industry.
BUSINESS: APPLIED SCIENCE & LABORATORIES

BIRMINGHAM 101
719353U74Q-9

Editorial Address: 214 Brandwood Road, Kings Heath, BIRMINGHAM, B14 6LD **Tel:** 0121 444 4723
Email: vanessa@birmingham101.com
Web site: http://www.birmingham101.com
Publisher: Birmingham101
Date Launched: 2000
Frequency of update: Daily
Website Access: Free
Traffic Figures: 95,000 Unique Users (per month Publisher's Statement)
Editor: Vanessa Houghton
Summary of Content: Online lifestyle magazine covering local news and events. Also provides information on entertainment, motors, what's on, live music, places to stay and property to rent in the Midlands area as well as many competitions and features of general interest.
Readership/Target Audience: Aimed at anyone living in the Midlands area, visitors and expatriates.
Other Features: Features include a calendar of events and archiving.
CONSUMER: WOMEN'S INTEREST CONSUMER MAGAZINES: Lifestyle

BIRMINGHAM INDEPENDENT
1654828U80C-5131

Formerly: Ads & Info
Editorial Address: The Old School Room, 358 Old Birmingham Road, Lickey, BIRMINGHAM, B45 8ES
Tel: 0121 445 0668
Email: editor@birminghamindependent.co.uk
Web site: http://www.birminghamindependent.co.uk
Publisher: Mybrum.tv
Date Launched: 2005
Frequency of update: Weekly
Website Access: Free
Traffic Figures: 85,019 Unique Users (Publisher's Statement)
Editor: Paul Blair
Summary of Content: Website focusing on topics and issues relevant to the local community as well as business and pleasure contact details.
Readership/Target Audience: Aimed at households in North and South Birmingham.
CONSUMER: RURAL & REGIONAL INTEREST: Regional Interest English Counties

Internet Media

BIRMINGHAM MATTERS
1881590U72J-333

Email: comments@birmingham-matters.co.uk
Web site: http://www.birmingham-matters.co.uk
Frequency of update: Daily
LOCAL NEWSPAPERS: Community Newsletters

BIT-TECH.NET
1867235U78R-529

Editorial Address: 30 Cleveland Street, LONDON, W1T 4JD
Tel: 020 7907 6000
Email: press@bit-tech.net
Web site: http://www.bit-tech.net
Publisher: Dennis Publishing Ltd
Date Launched: 2001
Frequency of update: Daily
Website Access: Free
Traffic Figures: 1,000,000 Unique Users (per month Publisher's Statement)
Editor: Tim Smalley
Summary of Content: Website covering hardware reviews and features, case modification, enthusiast gaming as well as news and editorial opinion.
Readership/Target Audience: Aimed at computer enthusiasts and early adopters.
CONSUMER: CONSUMER ELECTRONICS: Consumer Electronics Related

BITWISE MAGAZINE
1800038U5C-915

Editorial Address: PR by email only **Tel:** 01237 441527
Email: editor@bitwisemag.com
Web site: http://www.bitwisemag.com
Publisher: Dark Neon Ltd
Date Launched: 2005
Frequency of update: Monthly
Website Access: Free
Traffic Figures: 30,000 Unique Users (Publisher's Statement)
Editor: Huw Collingbourne
Summary of Content: Online magazine covering programming, mathematical and scientific software, computer hardware, video, audio and DVD.
Readership/Target Audience: Aimed at technically literate computer users.
BUSINESS: COMPUTERS & AUTOMATION: Professional Personal Computers

BIZASIA.CO.UK
1834387U2B-204

Editorial Address: PR by email only **Tel:** 07852 334711
Web site: http://www.bizasia.co.uk
Publisher: Media 247
Frequency of update: Daily
Website Access: Free
Traffic Figures: 12,000 Unique Users (Publisher's Statement)
Editor: Raj Baddhan
Summary of Content: Website featuring breaking UK Asian media news and information.
Readership/Target Audience: Aimed at the media industry and consumers.
Other Features: Asian media recruitment in Asian, Asian TV listings, weekly mailing list, Directory of Asian media.
BUSINESS: COMMUNICATIONS, ADVERTISING & MARKETING: Press

BJHCIM (THE BRITISH JOURNAL OF HEALTHCARE COMPUTING & INFORMATION MANAGEMENT)
40145U56A-52_20

Formerly: The British Journal of Healthcare Computing & Information Management
Editorial Address: 29 Pinewood Park, FARNBOROUGH, GU14 9LB **Tel:** 01252 691590
Email: harry.wood@bjhcim.co.uk
Web site: http://www.bjhcim.co.uk
Publisher: The Birchley Hall Press
Date Launched: 1984
Frequency of update: Monthly. Published around the 1st week of the cover month
Website Access: Free
Traffic Figures: 30,000 Unique Users (Publisher's Statement)
Editor: Harry Wood
Summary of Content: News, case studies, analysis and comment on healthcare informatics issues in the UK.
Readership/Target Audience: Aimed at healthcare professionals, healthcare information managers, healthcare IT managers, healthcare managers, social services, and healthcare IT suppliers.
BUSINESS: HEALTH & MEDICAL

BJPONLINE
626555U38-10_1

Editorial Address: 32-34 Broadwick Street, LONDON, W1A 2HG **Tel:** 020 7316 9658 **Fax:** 020 7316 9000
Email: diane.smyth@incisivemedia.com
Web site: http://www.bjp-online.com
Publisher: Incisive Media
Date Launched: 1998
Frequency of update: Weekly
Website Access: Free
Editor: Simon Bainbridge
Summary of Content: Website focusing on all aspects of photography. Online edition of the British Journal of Photography.
Readership/Target Audience: Aimed at professional photographers.
BUSINESS: PHOTOGRAPHIC TRADE

BLACK INFORMATION LINK
626329U90-40

Editorial Address: Suite 12, Winchester House, 9 Cranmer Road, LONDON, SW9 6EJ **Tel:** 020 7582 1990
Fax: 020 7793 8269
Email: editor@blink.org.uk
Web site: http://www.blink.org.uk
Publisher: The 1990 Trust
Date Launched: 1995
Frequency of update: Daily
Website Access: Free
Traffic Figures: 68,000 Unique Users (per month Publisher's Statement)
Editor: Davis Mukasa
Summary of Content: Website of the 1990 Trust, it is a black news site focusing on news and information affecting the lives of black and other minority ethnic communities.
Readership/Target Audience: Aimed at the minority communities in the UK and those interested in promoting race relations.
Other Features: Features include discussion forums, an e-mail newsletter and recruitment.
CONSUMER: ETHNIC

BLACK UK ONLINE
1792509U90-1003

Editorial Address: PO Box 574, BURY ST. EDMUNDS, IP33 9BW **Tel:** 01284 760033 **Fax:** 0845 280 0845
Email: editorial@blackukonline.com
Web site: http://www.blackukonline.com
Publisher: Black UK Publications Ltd
Date Launched: 2003
Frequency of update: Daily
Website Access: Free
Traffic Figures: 179,000 Unique Users (per month Publisher's Statement)
Editor: Shirley McGreal
Summary of Content: Online magazine reflecting the multicultural Britain that we live in today with news sport, business directory, overseas news African news, jobs, education, music, arts and cultures as well as women's, men's and youth section.
Readership/Target Audience: Aimed at black and minority ethnic communities in the UK.
CONSUMER: ETHNIC

BLACKNET UK
629485U90-40_50

Formerly: BLACKNET
Editorial Address: 61 Caroline Street, Jewellery Quarter, BIRMINGHAM, B1 1HF **Tel:** 020 8305 6779
Fax: 020 8692 9755
Email: junior@blacknet.co.uk
Web site: http://www.blacknet.co.uk
Frequency of update: Daily
Website Access: Free
Editor: Junior Wilson
Summary of Content: Website covering news, entertainment and general lifestyle information. Includes a media pack, forums, games, beauty, a what's on guide, business, black history, recipes and education.
Readership/Target Audience: Aimed primarily at ethnic communities and also people who would like to learn more about and understand other cultures.
Other Features: Features include chat rooms, discussion forums, employment, training and business information, an e-mail newsletter, an events calendar, search engine and archiving.
CONSUMER: ETHNIC

BLOWOUT
629244U14L-530

Formerly: OILC
Editorial Address: 49 Carmelite Street, ABERDEEN, AB11 6NQ **Tel:** 01224 210118 **Fax:** 01224 210095
Email: blowout@oilc.org
Web site: http://www.oilc.org
Publisher: OILC

Date Launched: 1989
Frequency of update: Quarterly
Website Access: Paid
Traffic Figures: 3,300 Unique Users (per quarter Publisher's Statement)
Editor: Jake Molloy
Summary of Content: Website focusing on Trade Union news and information about the offshore industry.
Readership/Target Audience: Read by professional offshore oil and gas personnel.
BUSINESS: COMMERCE, INDUSTRY & MANAGEMENT: Trade Unions

BLUE DOME
626435U75L-70

Editorial Address: 6 Anselms Court, Werneth, OLDHAM, OL8 4EG **Tel:** 0161 628 3885
Email: editorial@bluedome.co.uk
Web site: http://www.bluedome.co.uk
Publisher: Blue Dome
Date Launched: 1995
Frequency of update: Daily
Website Access: Free
Traffic Figures: 50,000 Unique Users (per month Publisher's Statement)
Editor: David Lynch
Summary of Content: Website covering UK outdoor information. Includes an outdoors job section, archery, caving, climbing, mountain biking, orienteering, sky sports, sub aqua, trekking, water sports and gear reviews.
Readership/Target Audience: Aimed at anyone interested in outdoor leisure, events and expeditions.
Other Features: Features include recruitment, an industry buyer's guide and discussion forums.
CONSUMER: SPORT: Outdoor

BMI DIAMOND CLUB MAGAZINE
1626065U89D-505

Editorial Address: Oliver House, 54 Edward Road, West Bridgford, NOTTINGHAM, NG2 5GB **Tel:** 0115 981 4421
Email: sarah.able@darkhorsepr.co.uk
Web site: http://www.flybmi.com/yourdiamondclub
Publisher: Dark Horse PR
Frequency of update: Quarterly
Website Access: Paid
Traffic Figures: 478,047 Unique Users (Publisher's Statement)
Editor: Sarah Able
Summary of Content: Website covering bmi news, features on European cities, hotels and travel related products as well as allowing customers to redeem their points, take advantage of exclusive offers and enter competitions.
Readership/Target Audience: Aimed exclusively at bmi diamond club members.
CONSUMER: HOLIDAYS & TRAVEL: In-Flight Magazines

BMJ.COM
707622U56A-45

Editorial Address: BMA House, Tavistock Square, LONDON, WC1H 9JR **Tel:** 020 7387 4499
Fax: 020 7383 6418
Email: tdelamothe@bmj.com
Web site: http://www.bmj.com
Publisher: BMJ Publishing Group
Date Launched: 1995
Frequency of update: Daily
Website Access: Paid
Traffic Figures: 1,376,090 Unique Users (01/10/2008 To 31/10/2008 ABC/Electronic)
Editor: Annabel Ferriman; **Web Editor:** David Payne
Summary of Content: Website containing articles and information on medical topics.
Readership/Target Audience: Aimed at professionals in the medical industry.
BUSINESS: HEALTH & MEDICAL

BOATING CORNWALL
1776192U91A-290

Editorial Address: 3 Falmouth Business Park, Bickland Water Road, FALMOUTH, TR11 4SZ **Tel:** 01326 213333
Fax: 01326 212108
Email: steve.ivall@packetseries.co.uk
Web site: http://www.boatingcornwall.co.uk
Publisher: Newsquest Media Group
Date Launched: 2006
Frequency of update: Daily
Website Access: Free
Editor: Stephen Ivall
Summary of Content: Website covering all aspects of boating and water based activities.
Readership/Target Audience: Aimed at those interested in boating and water sports.
CONSUMER: RECREATION & LEISURE: Boating & Yachting

BOOKREVIEW ONLINE
626187U84B-27

Formerly: Bookmark Online
Editorial Address: Orchardton Hall, Auchencairn, CASTLE DOUGLAS, DG7 1QL **Tel:** 0845 130 6249
Fax: 0845 658 8329
Email: edit@bnw.demon.co.uk
Web site: http://www.bookreviewonline.co.uk
Publisher: Brave New World International Ltd
Date Launched: 2001
Frequency of update: Weekly
Website Access: Free
Traffic Figures: 220,000 Unique Users (Publisher's Statement)
Editor: Susan Foster
Summary of Content: Website focusing on a wide variety of book reviews and some book news, competitions and features.
Readership/Target Audience: Aimed at people of all ages interested in books.
CONSUMER: THE ARTS & LITERARY: Literary

BOOKS MONTHLY
1844556U84B-371

Formerly: gatewaymonthly.co.uk
Editorial Address: 40 Nelson Road, SHERINGHAM, NR26 8BU **Tel:** 01603 873768
Email: editor@booksmonthly.co.uk
Web site: http://www.booksmonthly.co.uk
Frequency of update: Monthly
Website Access: Free
Editor: Paul Norman
Summary of Content: Website covering books reviews, features articles, original stories and competitions.
Readership/Target Audience: Aimed at anyone who likes books.
CONSUMER: THE ARTS & LITERARY: Literary

THE BOOKSELLER.COM
626197U60A-25_1

Editorial Address: 5th Floor, Endeavour House, 189 Shaftesbury Avenue, LONDON, WC2H 8TJ
Tel: 020 7420 6000 **Fax:** 020 7420 6103
Email: webeditor@bookseller.co.uk
Web site: http://www.thebookseller.com
Publisher: Bookseller Publications
Date Launched: 1997
Frequency of update: Daily
Website Access: Free
Traffic Figures: 20,000 Unique Users (per month Publisher's Statement)
Editor: Philip Jones
Summary of Content: Website covering developments in the book publishing industry.
Readership/Target Audience: Aimed at individuals in both the book retailing and book publishing industries.
Other Features: Features include an online recruitment board, a discussion forum and archiving.
BUSINESS: PUBLISHING: Publishing & Book Trade

BPF WEEKLY NEWSLETTER
1696671U39-157

Editorial Address: 6 Bath Place, Rivington Street, LONDON, EC2A 3JE **Tel:** 020 7457 5000
Fax: 020 7457 5045
Email: press@bpf.co.uk
Web site: http://www.bpf.co.uk
Publisher: British Plastics Federation
Frequency of update: Weekly
Website Access: Paid
Traffic Figures: 750 Unique Users (Publisher's Statement)
Editor: Stephen Hunt
Summary of Content: Electronically delivered newsletter focusing on issues surrounding the plastics industry.
Readership/Target Audience: Aimed at BPF members.
BUSINESS: PLASTICS & RUBBER

BRADFORD MATTERS
1881591U72J-334

Email: comments@bradford-matters.co.uk
Web site: http://www.bradford-matters.co.uk
Frequency of update: Daily
Summary of Content: Website created to help people who care about local issues. Whether you need access to useful information, want to highlight a particular topic to other people, discuss ideas with like-minded people or just show your support and keep up to date with current affairs in your area, Bradford Matters is the place for you.
Readership/Target Audience: Aimed at,residents in the local area of Bradford.
LOCAL NEWSPAPERS: Community Newsletters

BRADMANS.COM
1647212U89A-711

Formerly: Bradman's Business Travel Guides
Editorial Address: 141-143 Shoreditch High Street, LONDON, E1 6JE **Tel:** 020 7613 8777 **Fax:** 020 7613 8776
Email: michael.keating@ink-publishing.com
Web site: http://www.bradmans.com
Publisher: Ink Publishing
Frequency of update: Quarterly
Website Access: Free
Editor: Michael Keating
Summary of Content: Business travel guides covering all aspects of business travel and doing business.
Readership/Target Audience: Aimed at corporate and entrepreneurial business travellers.
CONSUMER: HOLIDAYS & TRAVEL: Travel

BRAND PROTECTION NEWS
1664908U35-364

Editorial Address: Cleeve Road, LEATHERHEAD, KT22 7RU **Tel:** 01372 802000
Email: sara.ver-bruggen@pira-international.com
Web site: http://www.intertechpira.com
Publisher: PIRA International
Frequency of update: 10 times a year
Website Access: Paid
Editor: Sara Ver-Bruggen; **Editor-in-Chief:** Sara Ver-Bruggen
Summary of Content: Electronically delivered newsletter covering strategies and technologies being used to combat brand attacks worldwide.
Readership/Target Audience: Aimed at brand owners and those providing the legal and technological security solutions.
BUSINESS: PACKAGING & BOTTLING

BRAND REPUBLIC
761884U2A-551

Editorial Address: 174 Hammersmith Road, LONDON, W6 7JP **Tel:** 020 8267 4547 **Fax:** 020 8267 4175
Email: editor@brandrepublic.com
Web site: http://www.brandrepublic.com
Publisher: Haymarket Business Media Ltd
Date Launched: 2001
Frequency of update: Daily
Website Access: Free
Traffic Figures: 489,000 Unique Users (01/10/2007 To 31/10/2007 ABC/Electronic)
Editor: Rich Sutcliffe
Summary of Content: Portal containing advertising, marketing and media news including market reports, media statistics and circulation figures.
Readership/Target Audience: Aimed at media and marketing personnel.
BUSINESS: COMMUNICATIONS, ADVERTISING & MARKETING

BRAVE
37116U14H-17

Formerly: BRAVE Magazine
Editorial Address: The Coach House Small Business Centre, 2 Upper York Street, BRISTOL, BS2 8QN
Tel: 0117 944 5330 **Fax:** 0117 944 5661
Email: lizs@brave.org.uk
Web site: http://www.brave.org.uk
Publisher: BRAVE Enterprise Agency
Frequency of update: Daily
Website Access: Free
Editor: Liz Sands
Summary of Content: Website for those starting a business or already trading in the Greater Bristol area.
Readership/Target Audience: Aimed at entrepreneurs and owners of small businesses.
BUSINESS: COMMERCE, INDUSTRY & MANAGEMENT: Small Business

BREAKING TRAVEL NEWS
1666057U50-214

Editorial Address: 1A Northumberland Avenue, LONDON, WC2N 5BW **Tel:** 020 7925 0000 **Fax:** 020 7925 2552
Email: pressbox@breakingtravelnews.com
Web site: http://www.breakingtravelnews.com
Publisher: World Group
Frequency of update: Daily
Website Access: Free
Editor: Mary Aziz
Summary of Content: Online magazine covering news, events and insights into the travel and tourism sector. Topics covered include technology, hotels, spas and airlines.
Readership/Target Audience: Aimed at those working within the travel and tourism trade.
BUSINESS: TRAVEL & TOURISM

BREAKINGVIEWS
629516U1F-67

Editorial Address: 1st Floor, 16 St. Helen's Place, LONDON, EC3A 6DF **Tel:** 020 7256 9333
Fax: 020 7256 5880
Email: newseditor@breakingviews.com
Web site: http://www.breakingviews.com
Date Launched: 2000
Frequency of update: Daily
Website Access: Paid
Traffic Figures: 13,636 Unique Users (Publisher's Statement)
Editor: Hugo Dixon
Summary of Content: Website containing views on the latest financial business stories including features and the latest FTSE changes.
Readership/Target Audience: Aimed at professionals in the investment and financial industries.
BUSINESS: FINANCE & ECONOMICS: Investment

BRENT MATTERS
1881592U72J-335

Email: comments@brent-matters.co.uk
Web site: http://www.brent-matters.co.uk
Frequency of update: Daily
Summary of Content: Website created to help people who care about local issues. Whether you need access to useful information, want to highlight a particular topic to other people, discuss ideas with like-minded people or just show your support and keep up to date with current affairs in your area, Brent Matters is the place for you.
Readership/Target Audience: Aimed at residents in the local area of Brent.
LOCAL NEWSPAPERS: Community Newsletters

BRIDESMAGAZINE.CO.UK
1809962U74L-264

Editorial Address: 25 Maddox Street, LONDON, W1S 2QN
Tel: 020 7499 9080
Email: dolly.jones@condenast.co.uk
Web site: http://www.bridesmagazine.co.uk
Publisher: Conde Nast Interactive
Date Launched: 2006
Frequency of update: Daily
Website Access: Free
Traffic Figures: 40,000 Unique Users (per month Publisher's Statement)
Editor: Dolly Jones
Summary of Content: Online bridal magazine with a 12 month checklist, a budget calculator and instructions on how to plan a wedding reception as well as an address book for cakes, photographers, make-up artists and honeymoon planners. Also includes a wedding style section with wedding dresses and suits.
Readership/Target Audience: Aimed at brides-to-be, their partners, family and friends.
CONSUMER: WOMEN'S INTEREST CONSUMER MAGAZINES: Brides

BRIGHTON MATTERS
1881593U72J-336

Email: comments@brighton-matters.co.uk
Web site: http://www.brighton-matters.co.uk
Frequency of update: Daily
Summary of Content: Website created to help people who care about local issues. Whether you need access to useful information, want to highlight a particular topic to other people, discuss ideas with like-minded people or just show your support and keep up to date with current affairs in your area, Brighton Matters is the place for you.
Readership/Target Audience: Aimed at residents in the local area of Brighton.
LOCAL NEWSPAPERS: Community Newsletters

BRISTOL MATTERS
1881594U72J-337

Email: comments@bristol-matters.co.uk
Web site: http://www.bristol-matters.co.uk
Frequency of update: Daily
Summary of Content: Website created to help people who care about local issues. Whether you need access to useful information, want to highlight a particular topic to other people, discuss ideas with like-minded people or just show your support and keep up to date with current affairs in your area, Bristol Matters is the place for you.
Readership/Target Audience: Aimed at the residents in the local area of Bristol.
LOCAL NEWSPAPERS: Community Newsletters

BRISTOL RUGBY
1663658U75C-458

Formerly: Bristol Shoguns
Editorial Address: Clifton RFC, Station Road, Henbury, BRISTOL, BS10 7TT **Tel:** 0117 958 1630 **Fax:** 0117 958 1631
Email: duncan@bristolrugby.co.uk
Web site: http://www.bristolrugby.co.uk

Internet Media

Frequency of update: Daily
Website Access: Free
Editor: Duncan Wood
Summary of Content: Website covering fixtures, results, match reports, player, coach and management profiles as well as ticket and merchandise sales.
Readership/Target Audience: Aimed at fans of Bristol Rugby Club.
CONSUMER: SPORT: Rugby

BRITAIN CALLING
39715U50-13

Editorial Address: Thames Tower, Blacks Road, LONDON, W6 9EL **Tel:** 020 8563 3262 **Fax:** 020 8563 3028
Email: britaincalling@visitbritain.org
Web site: http://www.visitbritain.com/presscentre
Publisher: VisitBritain
Frequency of update: 10 times a year. Combined issues for August/September and December/January
Website Access: Free
Traffic Figures: 900 Unique Users (Publisher's Statement)
Editor: Patricia Yates
Summary of Content: Website focusing on tourism in Britain.
Readership/Target Audience: Aimed at the press overseas.
BUSINESS: TRAVEL & TOURISM

BRITFLICKS.COM
1785676U76A-202

Editorial Address: 80 Surrenden Road, FOLKESTONE, CT19 4AG **Tel:** 07757 169938
Email: contacts@britflicks.com
Web site: http://www.britflicks.com
Date Launched: 2006
Frequency of update: Weekly
Website Access: Free
Traffic Figures: 11,000 Unique Users (Publisher's Statement)
Editor: John Baker
Summary of Content: Website covering British films including what's on where, DVD releases, previews, British film news, competitions and letters to the editor.
Readership/Target Audience: Aimed at film lovers.
Other Features: Archiving, message board and newsletter.
CONSUMER: MUSIC & PERFORMING ARTS: Cinema

THE BRITISH THEATRE GUIDE
1834264U76B-353

Editorial Address: 62 Sandringham Road, SUNDERLAND, SR6 9QZ **Tel:** 0191 548 7482
Email: peter@britishtheatreguide.info
Web site: http://www.britishtheatreguide.info
Date Launched: 2001
Frequency of update: Daily
Website Access: Free
Traffic Figures: 50,000 Unique Users (per week Publisher's Statement)
Editor: Peter Lathan
Summary of Content: Website covering theatre news, reviews, book reviews, interviews and feature articles.
Readership/Target Audience: Aimed at industry professionals and keen theatregoers.
Other Features: Other features on site include archiving of all news stories, reviews, interviews and features, weekly email newsletter, message board and blog.
CONSUMER: MUSIC & PERFORMING ARTS: Theatre

BRITXBOX
1871215U78D-381

Formerly: Forums.britxbox.co.uk
Email: mike@britxbox.co.uk
Web site: http://forums.britxbox.co.uk
Frequency of update: Daily
Traffic Figures: 40,000 Unique Users (per month Publisher's Statement)
Editor: Mike Rossell
Summary of Content: Website covering video games news and features, and providing forum of UK's Xbox players.
Readership/Target Audience: Aimed at Xbox lovers.
CONSUMER: CONSUMER ELECTRONICS: Games

BROADBAND TV NEWS
1655115U43C-101

Editorial Address: PO Box 499, CAMBRIDGE, CB1 0AH
Tel: 01223 475381
Email: news@broadbandtvnews.com
Web site: http://www.broadbandtvnews.com
Publisher: Broadband TV News
Date Launched: 2003
Frequency of update: Daily
Website Access: Free

Traffic Figures: 74,563 Unique Users (Publisher's Statement)
Editor: Julian Clover
Summary of Content: Website covering current events in digital, satellite and cable TV.
Readership/Target Audience: Aimed at those working within the TV industry.
BUSINESS: ELECTRICAL RETAIL TRADE: TV

BROADBAND-HELP
711916U78E-28

Editorial Address: 51 Hermitage Drive, Twyford, READING, RG10 9HT **Tel:** 01189 344740
Email: rowland.oconnor@broadband-help.com
Web site: http://www.broadband-help.com
Date Launched: 2000
Frequency of update: Daily
Website Access: Free
Traffic Figures: 1,500 Unique Users (per month Publisher's Statement)
Editor: Rowland O'Connor
Summary of Content: Website providing a central reference for anyone wishing to acquire or switch broadband. Also contains ISP reviews, diagnostic tools, helpful articles and relevant news.
Readership/Target Audience: Aimed at broadband consumers.
CONSUMER: CONSUMER ELECTRONICS: Home Computing

THE BROADCASTER'S BULLETIN
35665U2D-53_80

Editorial Address: 3 New Burlington Place, LONDON, W1S 2HR **Tel:** 020 7851 0828
Email: paul.baker@broadcastersbulletin.co.uk
Web site: http://www.broadcastersbulletin.co.uk
Publisher: MDS Studio Ltd
Date Launched: 1994
Frequency of update: Daily
Website Access: Free
Traffic Figures: 5,000 Unique Users (Publisher's Statement)
Editor: Paul Baker
Summary of Content: Online magazine used as a source for radio production ideas.
Readership/Target Audience: Aimed at people working at all levels on radio stations in the UK and Ireland.
BUSINESS: COMMUNICATIONS, ADVERTISING & MARKETING: Broadcasting

BROADCASTNOW
601268U2D-83_23

Formerly: Produxion.com
Editorial Address: Greater London House, Hampstead Road, LONDON, NW1 7EJ **Tel:** 020 7728 5512
Fax: 020 7728 5555
Email: will.hurrell@emap.com
Web site: http://www.broadcastnow.co.uk
Publisher: EMAP Insight
Date Launched: 2000
Frequency of update: Daily
Website Access: Free
Traffic Figures: 40,000 Unique Users (Publisher's Statement)
Editor: Will Hurrell
Summary of Content: Website containing comprehensive online information for the UK television production industry.
Readership/Target Audience: Aimed at TV producers, commissioners, editors, technicians and suppliers.
BUSINESS: COMMUNICATIONS, ADVERTISING & MARKETING: Broadcasting

BROKER ZONE
707874U1C-79

Editorial Address: 2 Woodborough Road, MANSFIELD, NG19 6DT **Tel:** 01623 656264 **Fax:** 0871 433 6920
Email: paul@moneymart.co.uk
Web site: http://www.broker-zone.co.uk
Date Launched: 2001
Frequency of update: Daily
Traffic Figures: 3,000 Unique Users (per day Publisher's Statement)
Editor: Paul Rhodes
Summary of Content: Website providing information and advice regarding mortgages, loans and insurance to finance professionals.
Readership/Target Audience: Aimed at UK mortgage brokers, independent financial advisers and finance professionals.
BUSINESS: FINANCE & ECONOMICS: Banking

BROMLEY MATTERS
1881595U72J-338

Email: comments@bromley-matters.co.uk
Web site: http://www.bromley-matters.co.uk
Frequency of update: Daily
Summary of Content: Website created to help people who care about local issues. Whether you need access to useful information, want to highlight a particular topic to other people, discuss ideas with like-minded people or just show your support and keep up to date with current affairs in your area, Bromley Matters is the place for you.
Readership/Target Audience: Aimed at residents in the local area of Bromley.
LOCAL NEWSPAPERS: Community Newsletters

BRSCC RACING NEWS
46415U77D-140

Formerly: British Racing News
Editorial Address: The Old Bakery, 55A Belmont Road, WALLINGTON, SM6 8TE **Tel:** 020 8773 3404
Fax: 020 8773 3704
Email: racingnews@xenogamy-plc.co.uk
Web site: http://www.brscc.co.uk
Publisher: Xenogamy Limited
Date Launched: 2006
Frequency of update: Monthly
Website Access: Paid
Traffic Figures: 3,000 Unique Users (per year Publisher's Statement)
Editor: Martin Sharp
Summary of Content: Electronically delivered newsletter published on behalf of the British Racing & Sports Car Club Limited covering club news and a racing diary.
Readership/Target Audience: Aimed at competitors, club members and motor sport enthusiasts.
CONSUMER: MOTORING & CYCLING: Motor Sports

BRUSH EXPERT
629558U16B-3

Formerly: brushexpert.com
Editorial Address: 44 Boleyn Close, Maidenbower, CRAWLEY, RH10 7QJ **Tel:** 01293 884103 **Fax:** 5 49 29 03 08
Email: alice@brushexpert.com
Web site: http://www.brushexpert.com
Publisher: Brush Expert Ltd
Date Launched: 2000
Frequency of update: 104 times a year
Website Access: Free
Traffic Figures: 2,440 Unique Users (per day Publisher's Statement)
Editor: Alice Castle
Summary of Content: Website focusing on news, views and information about the brush, broom and mop industry, including a directory of industry related companies.
Readership/Target Audience: Aimed at professionals who work in the brush trade.
BUSINESS: DECORATING & PAINT: Paint - Technical Manufacture

BUCKINGHAM TODAY
629885U67B-134

Formerly: Buckingham on-line
Editorial Address: 61-62 Well Street, BUCKINGHAM, MK18 1EN **Tel:** 01280 827940 **Fax:** 01280 823729
Email: editorial@buckinghamadvertiser.co.uk
Web site: http://www.buckinghamtoday.co.uk
Frequency of update: Daily
Website Access: Free
Traffic Figures: 72,048 Unique Users (per month Publisher's Statement)
Editor: Rob Gibbard
Summary of Content: Website containing news, sport, information and features concerning Buckingham.
Readership/Target Audience: Read by residents and visitors to the local area.
Other Features: Features include recruitment, a chat forum and archiving.
REGIONAL DAILY & SUNDAY NEWSPAPERS: Regional Daily Newspapers

BUCKINGHAMSHIRE MATTERS
1881596U72J-339

Email: comments@buckinghamshire-matters.co.uk
Web site: http://www.buckinghamshire-matters.co.uk
Frequency of update: Daily
Summary of Content: Website created to help people who care about local issues. Whether you need access to useful information, want to highlight a particular topic to other people, discuss ideas with like-minded people or just show your support and keep up to date with current affairs in your area, Buckinghamshire Matters is the place for you.
Readership/Target Audience: Aimed at residents in the local area of Buckinghamshire.
LOCAL NEWSPAPERS: Community Newsletters

BUDDYPOWER.NET
1795408U74G-279

Formerly: FatHappens.com
Editorial Address: 40 Bowling Green Lane, LONDON, EC1R 0NE **Tel:** 0700 030 0707 **Fax:** 020 7415 7074
Email: tony@fathappens.com
Web site: http://www.buddypower.net
Publisher: TFA Group
Frequency of update: Daily
Website Access: Free
Traffic Figures: 20,000 Unique Users (Publisher's Statement)
Editor: Tony Fitzpatrick
Summary of Content: Website containing a range of national and international news on obesity and obesity related health stories with members helping one another share tips and support to lose and manage their weight.
Readership/Target Audience: Aimed at members of Anne Diamond's Weight Management site.
CONSUMER: WOMEN'S INTEREST CONSUMER MAGAZINES: Slimming & Health

BUILDING DESIGN NEWS
1794337U4E-442

Editorial Address: Hill Farm, Linton Hill, Linton, MAIDSTONE, ME17 4AL **Tel:** 01622 745333
Fax: 01622 746444
Email: enquiries@arundel-jones.co.uk
Web site: http://www.buildingdesign-news.co.uk
Frequency of update: Daily
Website Access: Free
Editor: Lawrence France
Summary of Content: Website and newsletter covering all aspects of building design and construction projects.
Readership/Target Audience: Aimed at building specifiers, buyers and end users including architects, contractors, facility managers, interior designers and building services engineers.
BUSINESS: ARCHITECTURE & BUILDING: Building

BUILDINGTALK
1606902U4E-405

Editorial Address: PR by email only **Tel:** 020 7970 4920
Email: news@buildingtalk.com
Web site: http://www.buildingtalk.com
Publisher: Pro-Talk Ltd
Date Launched: 2002
Frequency of update: Daily
Website Access: Free
Traffic Figures: 102,921 Unique Users (per month Publisher's Statement)
Editor: Howard Chapman
Summary of Content: Website covering building and construction including news, policy and regulations, IT, site preparation, security and fire prevention, plant and equipment hire, buildings, bridges, tunnelling, ground engineering and landfill.
Readership/Target Audience: Aimed at professionals in the building and construction industries.
Other Features: Newsletter, media pack.
BUSINESS: ARCHITECTURE & BUILDING: Building

BURYFREEPRESS (ON-LINE)
629841U67B-137

Editorial Address: Kings Road, BURY ST. EDMUNDS, IP33 3ET **Tel:** 01284 768911 **Fax:** 01284 755619
Email: lesley.anslow@buryfreepress.co.uk
Web site: http://www.buryfreepress.co.uk
Publisher: Anglia Newspapers
Date Launched: 1999
Frequency of update: Daily
Website Access: Free
Traffic Figures: 39,000 Unique Users (per month Publisher's Statement)
Editor: Lesley Anslow
Summary of Content: Website containing news, sport, jobs, property, classifieds, what's on information and features about Bury St. Edmunds and West Suffolk.
Readership/Target Audience: Read by residents, expats and visitors to the local area.
Other Features: Features include a chat forum, recruitment, e-mail updates and news archiving.
REGIONAL DAILY & SUNDAY NEWSPAPERS: Regional Daily Newspapers

BUSINESS4MEDIA.COM
1851099U1R-384

Editorial Address: Unit 11, The Chandlery, 50 Westminster Bridge Road, LONDON, SE1 7QY **Tel:** 020 7953 8770
Fax: 020 7953 8773
Email: news.desk@business4media.com
Web site: http://www.business4media.com
Publisher: News4Media Ltd
Date Launched: 2008
Frequency of update: Daily
Website Access: Free

Traffic Figures: 5,000 Unique Users (per month Publisher's Statement)
Editor: Henry Hemming
Summary of Content: Website covering all aspects of news from the business industry.
Readership/Target Audience: Aimed at those working in the business and financial sectors.
BUSINESS: FINANCE & ECONOMICS: Financial Related

BUSINESS7
1911124U63D-726

Editorial Address: Onesixty, 160 Dundee Street, EDINBURGH, EH11 1DQ **Tel:** 0131 535 5550
Fax: 0131 220 1203
Email: editor@business7.co.uk
Web site: http://www.business7.co.uk
Publisher: Scottish Daily Record & Sunday Mail Ltd
Frequency of update: Daily
Website Access: Free
Editor: Greig Cameron
Summary of Content: Website focusing on Scottish company news.
Readership/Target Audience: Aimed at middle managers and leading decision makers.
BUSINESS: REGIONAL BUSINESS: Regional Business Scotland

BUSINESS CAR MANAGER
1840797U49A-423

Editorial Address: 95 Station Road, HAMPTON, TW12 2BD
Tel: 020 8783 0999
Email: editor@businesscarmanager.co.uk
Web site: http://www.businesscarmanager.co.uk
Publisher: Business Car Manager Ltd
Date Launched: 2006
Frequency of update: 24 times a year
Website Access: Free
Traffic Figures: 35,000 Unique Users (per month Publisher's Statement)
Editor: Ralph Morton
Summary of Content: Online business motoring magazine. Features include new car news, new legislation, special reports on running business vehicles, road tests, tax and legislation advice.
Readership/Target Audience: Aimed at small businesses.
BUSINESS: TRANSPORT

BUSINESS CREDIT MANAGEMENT UK
629102U1G-8

Formerly: Business Credit News UK
Editorial Address: 24 Nelsons Gardens, Hedge End, SOUTHAMPTON, SO30 2NE **Tel:** 0845 226 1842
Fax: 01489 787541
Email: jarnold@creditman.co.uk
Web site: http://www.creditman.co.uk
Date Launched: 1997
Frequency of update: Daily
Website Access: Free
Traffic Figures: 7,500 Unique Users (Publisher's Statement)
Editor: John Arnold
Summary of Content: Website containing business credit management and debt information.
Readership/Target Audience: Aimed at those interested in credit management and the UK business news.
BUSINESS: FINANCE & ECONOMICS: Credit Trading

BUSINESS LEADER
41219U63A-67

Formerly: North London Chamber of Commerce Newsletter
Editorial Address: Enfield Business Centre, 201 Hertford Road, ENFIELD, EN3 5JH **Tel:** 020 8443 4464
Fax: 020 8443 3822
Web site: http://www.nlcc.co.uk
Publisher: North London Chamber of Commerce
Frequency of update: Monthly
Website Access: Paid
Traffic Figures: 3,500 Unique Users (Publisher's Statement)
Editor: Huw Jones
Summary of Content: Electronically delivered newsletter for the North London Chamber of Commerce containing a calendar of events, news and company reviews.
Readership/Target Audience: Aimed at members of the North London Chamber of Commerce.
BUSINESS: REGIONAL BUSINESS: Regional Business Greater London

BUSINESS MANAGEMENT ZONE
1622838U14A-513

Editorial Address: 100 Victoria Street, BRISTOL, BS1 6HZ
Tel: 0117 915 9600 **Fax:** 0117 915 9630
Email: editor@businessmanagementzone.co.uk
Web site: http://www.businessmanagementzone.co.uk

Publisher: Sift Media Ltd
Date Launched: 2002
Frequency of update: Daily
Website Access: Paid
Editor: Dan Martin
Summary of Content: Website covering issues concerning those responsible for the management and costs and savings of a business.
Readership/Target Audience: Aimed at financial directors, financial controllers, management accountants, managing directors and company secretaries.
BUSINESS: COMMERCE, INDUSTRY & MANAGEMENT

BUSINESS MONEY (ONLINE)
626597U1A-52

Editorial Address: Bowdens Business Centre, Hambridge, LANGPORT, TA10 0BP **Tel:** 01458 253536
Fax: 01458 253538
Email: editor@business-money.com
Web site: http://www.business-money.com
Publisher: Business Money Ltd
Date Launched: 1993
Frequency of update: Monthly
Website Access: Free
Editor: Robert Lefroy
Summary of Content: Website covering the UK and international commercial funding industry. Includes regular commentary on commercial mortgages, business banking, factoring, invoice discounting and all asset finance.
Readership/Target Audience: Aimed at senior management in commercial lending, accountants, bankers, solicitors, financial advisers, insurers, estate agents, surveyors, commercial valuers, company chief executives, company secretaries and finance directors.
Other Features: Features include daily business news via e-mail, recruitment, a buyer's guide and archiving.
BUSINESS: FINANCE & ECONOMICS

BUSINESS VAN MANAGER
1849648U49D-363

Editorial Address: 95 Station Road, HAMPTON, TW12 2BD
Tel: 020 8783 0999
Email: ralph@businessvanmanager.co.uk
Web site: http://www.businessvanmanager.co.uk
Publisher: Business Car Manager Ltd
Date Launched: 2008
Frequency of update: Monthly
Website Access: Free
Traffic Figures: 13,000 Unique Users (Publisher's Statement)
Editor: Mark Bursa
Summary of Content: Online business van magazine. Features include news, special reports, road tests and an advice centre.
Readership/Target Audience: Aimed at small business van operators.
BUSINESS: TRANSPORT: Commercial Vehicles

BUSINESSESFORSALE.COM
1706661U14H-427

Editorial Address: Dynamis House, 6-8 Sycamore Street, LONDON, EC1Y 0SW **Tel:** 020 7324 1949
Fax: 020 7324 1931
Email: dandrage@dynamis.co.uk
Web site: http://www.businessesforsale.com
Publisher: Dynamis plc
Date Launched: 1996
Frequency of update: Daily
Website Access: Free
Traffic Figures: 570,671 Unique Users (per month ABC/Electronic)
Editor: Adam Bannister
Summary of Content: Website covering all aspects of buying and selling a business including case studies of people who have already bought and sold businesses, general articles on business buying and relocation guides by country.
Readership/Target Audience: Aimed at anyone thinking of buying or selling a business.
Other Features: Monthly newsletters for registered buyers, a buyer networking forum, message boards, email alerts and RSS feeds.
BUSINESS: COMMERCE, INDUSTRY & MANAGEMENT: Small Business

BUSINESS-FOCUS.NET
1787946U14A-580

Formerly: bizportal.co.uk
Editorial Address: 123 Sutherland Street, COVENTRY, CV5 7NH **Tel:** 0560 132 6260 **Fax:** 0871 733 5046
Email: editor@business-focus.net
Web site: http://www.business-focus.net
Publisher: Proteus Media
Date Launched: 2002
Frequency of update: Daily
Website Access: Free

Internet Media

Traffic Figures: 15,000 Unique Users (per month Publisher's Statement)
Editor: Stephen Peters; **Editor-in-Chief:** Alan Bramton
Summary of Content: Business related website covering management, marketing, finance, legislation, IT, law, telecommunications, commercial property, energy and environment, government trade, human resources, exhibitions and events, transportation and logistics.
Readership/Target Audience: Aimed at senior decision makers in business.
BUSINESS: COMMERCE, INDUSTRY & MANAGEMENT

BUSINESSGREEN.COM
1833962U57-160
Formerly: Business Green
Editorial Address: 32-34 Broadwick Street, LONDON, W1A 2HG **Tel:** 020 7316 9000
Email: james.s.murray@incisivemedia.com
Web site: http://www.businessgreen.com
Publisher: Incisive Media
Date Launched: 2007
Frequency of update: Daily
Website Access: Free
Traffic Figures: 145,140 Unique Users (per month Publisher's Statement)
Editor: James Murray
Summary of Content: Online publication covering green companies. Featuring news, forum, blog and advice to companies on environmental issues.
Readership/Target Audience: Aimed at firms intent on improving their environmental credentials.
BUSINESS: ENVIRONMENT & POLLUTION

BUSINESSWEEK
36741U14A-65
Editorial Address: 20 Canada Square, LONDON, E14 5LH
Tel: 020 7176 6060 **Fax:** 020 7176 6070
Web site: http://www.businessweek.com
Publisher: The McGraw-Hill Companies
Frequency of update: Daily
Website Access: Paid
Editor: Andy Renihardt
Summary of Content: Website providing in-depth coverage and analysis of business, industrial and economic news events around the world.
Readership/Target Audience: Aimed at managers worldwide.
BUSINESS: COMMERCE, INDUSTRY & MANAGEMENT

BUSINESSWINGS.CO.UK
1786555U14A-578
Formerly: Businessinacan.com
Editorial Address: Dynamis House, 6-8 Sycamore Street, LONDON, EC1Y 0SW **Tel:** 020 7324 1947
Fax: 020 7324 1931
Email: adam@dynamis.co.uk
Web site: http://www.businesswings.co.uk
Publisher: Dynamis plc
Date Launched: 2006
Frequency of update: Daily
Website Access: Free
Editor: Adam Bannister
Summary of Content: Website providing advice and help on all aspects of starting a business or franchise.
Readership/Target Audience: Aimed at aspiring entrepreneurs and first time business buyers.
BUSINESS: COMMERCE, INDUSTRY & MANAGEMENT

BUSINESSZONE
626226U14H-29_80
Editorial Address: 100 Victoria Street, BRISTOL, BS1 6HZ
Tel: 0117 915 9600 **Fax:** 0117 915 9630
Email: editor@businesszone.co.uk
Web site: http://www.businesszone.co.uk
Publisher: Sift Media Ltd
Date Launched: 1998
Frequency of update: Daily
Website Access: Free
Traffic Figures: 7,000 Unique Users (per month Publisher's Statement)
Editor: Dan Martin
Summary of Content: Website focusing on the small business communities with news and reference materials.
Readership/Target Audience: Aimed at small businesses in the UK.
BUSINESS: COMMERCE, INDUSTRY & MANAGEMENT: Small Business

BYTESTART.CO.UK
1805026U14H-437
Editorial Address: 6 Sonic Court, 21 Woodbridge Road, GUILDFORD, GU1 1DZ
Email: editor@bytestart.co.uk
Web site: http://www.bytestart.co.uk

Publisher: Bytestart Ltd
Frequency of update: Daily
Website Access: Free
Traffic Figures: 125,000 Unique Users (per month Publisher's Statement)
Editor: James Leckie
Summary of Content: Portal providing advice about start-ups and existing small businesses. Features business guides, planning, marketing, selling, finance, insurance and legal issues.
Readership/Target Audience: Aimed at people starting up or running a small business.
BUSINESS: COMMERCE, INDUSTRY & MANAGEMENT: Small Business

CAERPHILLY MATTERS
1881597U72J-340
Email: comments@caerphilly-matters.co.uk
Web site: http://www.caerphilly-matters.co.uk
Frequency of update: Daily
Summary of Content: Website created to help people who care about local issues. Whether you need access to useful information, want to highlight a particular topic to other people, discuss ideas with like-minded people or just show your support and keep up to date with current affairs in your area, Caerphilly Matters is the place for you.
Readership/Target Audience: Aimed at residents of the local area of Caerphilly.
LOCAL NEWSPAPERS: Community Newsletters

CAITHNESS BUSINESS PAGES
711413U63D-70
Editorial Address: 19 March Road, WICK, KW1 5TY
Tel: 01955 604648 **Fax:** 01955 606498
Email: bill@caithness.org
Web site: http://www.caithness-business.co.uk
Date Launched: 2001
Frequency of update: Daily
Website Access: Free
Traffic Figures: 100,000 Unique Users (Publisher's Statement)
Editor: Bill Fernie; **Webmaster:** Niall Fernie
Summary of Content: Website providing a wide range of information about the Caithness, Sutherland and to a lesser extent North of Scotland. Includes topics such as local businesses, tourism, transport, public services, leisure and retail.
Readership/Target Audience: Aimed at those living in and/ or interested in the Caithness area, particularly its businesses, also tourists and visitors.
BUSINESS: REGIONAL BUSINESS: Regional Business Scotland

CALL CENTRE HELPER
1732942U18B-1969
Formerly: Call Centre Helper.com
Editorial Address: Trevethin, Dixton Road, MONMOUTH, NP25 3PR **Tel:** 01600 714546
Email: newsdesk@callcentrehelper.com
Web site: http://www.callcentrehelper.com
Publisher: Call Centre Helper
Date Launched: 2003
Frequency of update: Weekly
Website Access: Free
Traffic Figures: 27,000 Unique Users (per month Publisher's Statement)
Editor: Jonty Pearce
Summary of Content: Website covering news, technology, call care hints and tips, multi-skilling, over coming jargon and staff motivation.
Readership/Target Audience: Aimed at call centre managers and decision makers in the UK and globally.
BUSINESS: ELECTRONICS: Telecommunications

CALL-CENTRES.COM
1808391U18B-1975
Editorial Address: 1 Wood Street, STRATFORD-UPON-AVON, CV37 6JE **Tel:** 0845 468 5627
Email: info@call-centres.com
Web site: http://www.call-centres.com
Publisher: Info Valley Ltd
Date Launched: 2004
Frequency of update: Weekly
Website Access: Free
Traffic Figures: 8,500 Unique Users (Publisher's Statement)
Editor: Rob O'Malley
Summary of Content: Electronic newsletter focusing on call-centres, including news, best practice, training advice and recruitment.
Readership/Target Audience: Aimed at key decision makers in the UK call centre industry.
Other Features: Buyers guide, message board, recruitment.
BUSINESS: ELECTRONICS: Telecommunications

CALM ZONE
1745681U86C-731
Editorial Address: PO Box 52490, LONDON, NW3 9DW
Tel: 0870 609 4601
Email: janepowell@thecalmzone.net
Web site: http://www.thecalmzone.net
Date Launched: 2006
Frequency of update: Daily
Website Access: Free
Editor: Jane Powell
Summary of Content: Website of C.A.L.M. the charity offering advice and information on issues that affect young men as well as lifestyle including music, sport, art, comedy and games.
Readership/Target Audience: Aimed at men aged between 15 and 35 years old suffering from depression or the onset of depression.
CONSUMER: ADULT & GAY MAGAZINES: Men's Lifestyle Magazines

CAMBRIDGESHIRE MATTERS
1881598U72J-341
Email: comments@cambridgeshire-matters.co.uk
Web site: http://www.cambridgeshire-matters.co.uk
Frequency of update: Daily
Summary of Content: Website created to help people who care about local issues. Whether you need access to useful information, want to highlight a particular topic to other people, discuss ideas with like-minded people or just show your support and keep up to date with current affairs in your area, Cambridgeshire Matters is the place for you.
Readership/Target Audience: Aimed at residents in the local area of Cambridgeshire.
LOCAL NEWSPAPERS: Community Newsletters

CAMDEN MATTERS
1881599U72J-342
Email: comments@camden-matters.co.uk
Web site: http://www.camden-matters.co.uk
Frequency of update: Daily
Summary of Content: Website created to help people who care about local issues. Whether you need access to useful information, want to highlight a particular topic to other people, discuss ideas with like-minded people or just show your support and keep up to date with current affairs in your area, Camden Matters is the place for you.
Readership/Target Audience: Aimed at residents in the local area of Camden.
LOCAL NEWSPAPERS: Community Newsletters

CAR DESIGN NEWS
1858772U31R-66
Editorial Address: Lamb House, Church Street, LONDON, W4 2PD **Tel:** 020 8987 0900 **Fax:** 020 8987 0948
Email: editor@cardesignnews.com
Web site: http://www.cardesignnews.com
Publisher: Ultima Media Ltd
Frequency of update: Daily
Website Access: Paid
Editor: Eric Gallina
Summary of Content: Online magazine giving a global overview of automotive design news, coverage of major autoshows and student design exhibitions, design reviews and feature articles on design processes.
Readership/Target Audience: Aimed at automotive design industry professionals, transportation design students and design enthusiasts worldwide.
BUSINESS: MOTOR TRADE: Motor Trade Related

CAR NEWS INTERNATIONAL
46308U77A-121
Editorial Address: Orchardton Hall, Auchencairn, CASTLE DOUGLAS, DG7 1QL **Tel:** 0845 130 6249
Fax: 0845 658 8329
Email: lauren@motornews.co.uk
Web site: http://www.motornews.co.uk
Publisher: Brave New World International Ltd
Date Launched: 1997
Frequency of update: Weekly
Website Access: Free
Traffic Figures: 225,000 Unique Users (per month Publisher's Statement)
Editor: Lauren Courtney
Summary of Content: Website covering a variety of news and information related to cars, including test drive reviews.
Readership/Target Audience: Aimed at 18 to 40 year olds.
CONSUMER: MOTORING & CYCLING: Motoring

CAR NEWS PORTAL
1840803U31R-63
Editorial Address: Britannia House, 11 Glenthorne Road, LONDON, W6 0LH **Tel:** 0870 745 3380
Email: editorial@carnewsportal.co.uk
Web site: http://www.carnewsportal.co.uk
Publisher: Areza Ltd

Date Launched: 2006
Frequency of update: Daily
Website Access: Free
Traffic Figures: 50,000 Unique Users (per month WebTrends)
Editor: Charles Clark
Summary of Content: Car and automotive portal covering news and articles on all types of cars as well as motorbikes, vans, trucks, lorries, caravans and motorhomes.
Readership/Target Audience: Aimed at car enthusiasts, organisations looking to buy a new or used car, car dealers and providers of services to the car industry.
Other Features: Directory and classifieds.
BUSINESS: MOTOR TRADE: Motor Trade Related

THE CARBONNEUTRAL COMPANY

711361U57-30_31

Formerly: FUTURE FORESTS
Editorial Address: Bravington House, 2 Bravington Walk, Regent Quarter, Kings Cross, LONDON, N1 9AF
Tel: 020 7833 6000 **Fax:** 020 7833 6049
Email: sharon.corrigan@carbonneutral.com
Web site: http://www.carbonneutral.com
Date Launched: 1997
Frequency of update: Daily
Website Access: Free
Traffic Figures: 28,498 Unique Users (per month Publisher's Statement)
Editor: Sharon Corrigan
Summary of Content: Website promoting awareness and the benefits of forests and climate friendly technologies against the battle of rising levels of carbon dioxide and generating finance for schemes to facilitate this.
Readership/Target Audience: Aimed at individuals and companies interested in reducing and offsetting the emissions of carbon dioxide and helping to combat global warming.
BUSINESS: ENVIRONMENT & POLLUTION

Y CARDI BACH

761631U72J-40

Editorial Address: Bro Gronw, Cwmfelin Mynach, WHITLAND, SA34 0DH **Tel:** 01994 448283
Fax: 01994 448283
Publisher: Gwasg Aeron Printers
Frequency of update: Monthly. Published in the last week of the month
Website Access: Paid
Traffic Figures: 1,150 Unique Users (Publisher's Statement)
Editor: Rhoswen Llewellyn
Summary of Content: Welsh language community newspaper featuring local news, concert listings and interviews with local residents.
Readership/Target Audience: Aimed at Welsh speaking readers with an interest in the local community.
LOCAL NEWSPAPERS: Community Newsletters

CARDIFF MATTERS

1881600U72J-343

Email: comments@cardiff-matters.co.uk
Web site: http://www.cardiff-matters.co.uk
Frequency of update: Daily
Summary of Content: Website created to help people who care about local issues. Whether you need access to useful information, want to highlight a particular topic to other people, discuss ideas with like-minded people or just show your support and keep up to date with current affairs in your area, Cardiff Matters is the place for you.
Readership/Target Audience: Aimed at residents in the local area of Cardiff.
LOCAL NEWSPAPERS: Community Newsletters

CAREERSCOPE

47913U88C-55

Formerly: ISCO CareerScope
Editorial Address: 1st Floor, St. George's House, Knoll Road, CAMBERLEY, GU15 3SY **Tel:** 01276 687500
Fax: 01276 28258
Email: info@inspiringfutures.org.uk
Web site: http://www.careerscope.org.uk
Publisher: The Inspiring Futures Foundation
Date Launched: 1956
Frequency of update: 3 times a year. Updated in January, April and September
Website Access: Paid
Traffic Figures: 100,000 Unique Users (Publisher's Statement)
Editor: Richard Scott-Clark
Summary of Content: Online magazine covering all aspects of higher education and career choice including study, work, gap year and international study.
Readership/Target Audience: Aimed at post 15 students and university students, parents, school advisors and management teams.
CONSUMER: EDUCATION: Careers

CAREWEEK

38485U32G-83

Formerly: Nursing Care Home Business
Editorial Address: Park View House, 19 The Avenue, EASTBOURNE, BN21 3YD **Tel:** 01323 411601
Email: l.knight@parkview-publishing.co.uk
Web site: http://viewer.zmags.com/showmag.php?mid=hphgd
Publisher: Park View Publishing Ltd
Date Launched: 1997
Frequency of update: Weekly
Website Access: Paid
Traffic Figures: 18,000 Unique Users (Publisher's Statement)
Editor: Laura Knight
Summary of Content: Online publication covering the daily running and organisation of nursing home businesses, nursing/care and residential homes nationwide.
Readership/Target Audience: Aimed at owners and managers of nursing homes.
BUSINESS: LOCAL GOVERNMENT, LEISURE & RECREATION: Community Care & Social Services

CARGO WORLD - THE NEWSLETTER

39632U49C-27

Formerly: Cargo Tomorrow
Editorial Address: Suite 2, 85 Western Road, ROMFORD, RM1 3LS **Tel:** 01708 735295 **Fax:** 01708 735225
Email: info@ichcainternational.co.uk
Web site: http://www.ichcainternational.co.uk
Publisher: ICHCA International
Date Launched: 1995
Frequency of update: 6 times a year
Website Access: Paid
Traffic Figures: 3,500 Unique Users (Publisher's Statement)
Editor: Rosemary Neilson
Summary of Content: Newsletter covering commercial and economic developments in the cargo handling industry worldwide.
Readership/Target Audience: Aimed at those involved in cargo handling.
BUSINESS: TRANSPORT: Freight

CARKEYS

707870U77A-118

Editorial Address: An Garadh, Gallachoille, TAYVALLICH, PA31 8PG **Tel:** 01546 870356
Email: pdrmail@aol.com
Web site: http://www.carkeys.co.uk
Publisher: PDR Online Ltd.
Date Launched: 1999
Frequency of update: Daily
Website Access: Free
Editor: David Finlay
Summary of Content: Website containing news and information on road tests, car launches, features, columns and motorsports.
Readership/Target Audience: Aimed at those interested in new car launches and cars in general.
Other Features: Buying guides, glossary, RSS feed, newsletter, gallery, video tests.
CONSUMER: MOTORING & CYCLING: Motoring

CARMARTHENSHIRE MATTERS

1881601U72J-344

Email: comments@carmarthenshire-matters.co.uk
Web site: http://www.carmarthenshire-matters.co.uk
Frequency of update: Daily
Summary of Content: Website created to help people who care about local issues. Whether you need access to useful information, want to highlight a particular topic to other people, discuss ideas with like-minded people or just show your support and keep up to date with current affairs in your area, Carmarthenshire Matters is the place for you.
Readership/Target Audience: Aimed at residents in the local area of Carmarthenshire.
LOCAL NEWSPAPERS: Community Newsletters

CARSOURCE

749382U77A-128

Editorial Address: 2-3 The Academy Suite, Sheffield United Academy, Firshill Crescent, SHEFFIELD, S4 7DR
Tel: 0114 281 5760 **Fax:** 0114 281 5767
Email: info@carsource.co.uk
Web site: http://www.carsource.co.uk
Publisher: Data Media and Research Ltd.
Date Launched: 1996
Frequency of update: Daily
Website Access: Free
Editor: Patrick Cull; **Webmaster:** John O'Connell
Summary of Content: Website providing news and information about purchasing a car. Includes new and used car guides and articles on finance and insurance.

Readership/Target Audience: Aimed at potential car buyers.
Other Features: Features include a buyer's guide, an e-mail newsletter and archiving.
CONSUMER: MOTORING & CYCLING: Motoring

CASINO WORLD

45676U74Q-109

Editorial Address: The Maltings, 50 Bath Street, GRAVESEND, DA11 0DF **Tel:** 01474 335087
Email: info@casinoworld.co.uk
Web site: http://www.casinoworld.co.uk
Publisher: R.G. Enterprises Ltd
Frequency of update: Daily
Website Access: Free
Editor: Roger Melling
Summary of Content: Website containing information on the newest technology, products and industry news on casinos and gaming.
Readership/Target Audience: Aimed at those interested in casinos, casino products and industry news.
CONSUMER: WOMEN'S INTEREST CONSUMER MAGAZINES: Lifestyle

CASUALGAMING.BIZ

1893895U5R-696

Editorial Address: Saxon House, 6A St. Andrew Street, HERTFORD, SG14 1JA **Tel:** 01992 535646
Fax: 01992 535648
Email: ben.parfitt@intentmedia.co.uk
Web site: http://www.casualgaming.biz
Publisher: Intent Media
Frequency of update: Daily
Website Access: Free
Editor: Ben Parfitt
Summary of Content: Website focusing on casual games. Providing market and sales data, news, research and interviews.
Readership/Target Audience: Aimed at games retailers and buyers, casual games publishers, developers of casual games, portals and aggregators.
BUSINESS: COMPUTERS & AUTOMATION: Computers Related

CAT WORLD ONLINE

629483U81C-190_10

Editorial Address: Ancient Lights, 19 River Road, ARUNDEL, BN18 9EY **Tel:** 01903 884988
Fax: 01903 885514
Email: laura@ashdown.co.uk
Web site: http://www.catworld.co.uk
Publisher: Ashdown.co.uk Ltd
Date Launched: 1998
Frequency of update: Daily
Website Access: Free
Editor: Laura Quiggan
Summary of Content: Website focusing on cat breeds and care with general news and information.
Readership/Target Audience: Aimed at those with an interest in cats as well as breeders and owners.
Other Features: Features include archiving, a buyer's guide and discussion forums.
CONSUMER: ANIMALS & PETS: Cats

CATERERSEARCH.COM

713837U11A-18

Formerly: Caterer-Online.com
Editorial Address: Quadrant House, The Quadrant, SUTTON, SM2 5AS **Tel:** 020 8652 4424 **Fax:** 020 8652 8973
Email: info@caterersearch.com
Web site: http://www.caterersearch.com
Publisher: Reed Business Information
Date Launched: 1999
Frequency of update: Daily
Website Access: Free
Traffic Figures: 180,000 Unique Users (Publisher's Statement)
Editor: Amanda Afiya; **Web Editor:** Amanda Afiya
Summary of Content: Website containing information and news for the hospitality industry.
Readership/Target Audience: Aimed at managers in hotels, restaurants and catering companies.
BUSINESS: CATERING: Catering, Hotels & Restaurants

CATFLAP

1824346U75B-288

Editorial Address: 9 Arundel Mews, 13-18 Arundel Place, BRIGHTON, BN2 1GD **Tel:** 01273 819826
Fax: 01273 547029
Email: info@catflapmag.com
Web site: http://www.catflapmag.com
Publisher: Made Up Media
Date Launched: 2007
Frequency of update: Weekly
Website Access: Free

Internet Media

Editor: Gavin Neesham
Summary of Content: Website covering football with an angle on humour including interviews and interactive areas.
Readership/Target Audience: Aimed at football fans aged 16 to 35 years old.
CONSUMER: SPORT: Football

CAVYRESCUE.CO.UK
1615978U81X-501
Editorial Address: 10 College Gardens, Westgate-On-Sea, CT8 8EY **Tel:** 07932 750271
Email: cavyrescue@yahoo.co.uk
Web site: http://www.cavyrescue.co.uk
Publisher: Cavyrescue
Date Launched: 2001
Frequency of update: Daily
Website Access: Free
Traffic Figures: 45,000 Unique Users (Publisher's Statement)
Editor: Stella Hulott; **Web Editor:** Jason Hulott; **Online Journalist:** Stella Hulott
Summary of Content: Website covering small animal healthcare including rats, rabbits, chinchillas, hamsters, guinea pigs and gerbils.
Readership/Target Audience: Aimed at small animal lovers.
Other Features: Archived newsletter.
CONSUMER: ANIMALS & PETS

CBI SUSTAINABILITY UPDATE
40634U57-20_45
Formerly: EHS Update
Editorial Address: Centre Point, 103 New Oxford Street, LONDON, WC1A 1DU **Tel:** 020 7395 8264
Fax: 020 7497 2597
Email: alice.hume@cbi.org.uk
Web site: http://www.cbi.org.uk/climate
Publisher: CBI London
Date Launched: 1997
Frequency of update: 26 times a year
Website Access: Free
Traffic Figures: 3,000 Unique Users (Publisher's Statement)
Editor: Sam Corry
Summary of Content: Email newsletter providing a summary of the latest developments in the environment, health and safety policy and management.
Readership/Target Audience: Read by members of the Confederation of British Industry.
BUSINESS: ENVIRONMENT & POLLUTION

CELLULAR NEWS
1702736U18B-1966
Editorial Address: 89 Naxos Building, Hutchings Street, LONDON, E14 8LE
Email: press@cellular-news.com
Web site: http://www.cellular-news.com
Date Launched: 1998
Frequency of update: Daily
Website Access: Paid
Editor: Ian Mansfield
Summary of Content: Website covering wireless telecommunications from a global perspective.
Readership/Target Audience: Aimed at industry professionals.
BUSINESS: ELECTRONICS: Telecommunications

CERAMICNEWS
753023U12A-28
Editorial Address: Queens Road, Penkhull, STOKE-ON-TRENT, ST4 7LQ **Tel:** 01782 764326 **Fax:** 01782 412331
Email: mandy.rymill@ceram.com
Web site: http://www.ceramicnews.com
Publisher: CERAM Research Ltd
Date Launched: 2000
Frequency of update: Weekly
Website Access: Free
Editor: Mandy Rymill; **Web Editor:** Mandy Rymill
Summary of Content: Website dedicated to ceramics latest industry news and materials. Includes company activities, new ventures, product launches, economic trends and market statistics.
Readership/Target Audience: Aimed at ceramic sector companies, manufacturers, suppliers and end users.
Other Features: Features include archiving.
BUSINESS: CERAMICS, POTTERY & GLASS: Ceramics & Pottery

CHAMPIONS365
1888277U75A-1036
Formerly: www.champions365.com
Web site: http://www.champions365.com
Frequency of update: Daily
Traffic Figures: 3,695 Unique Users (ABC/Electronic)

Summary of Content: Independent global sports community website highlighting the very best of international sport. Live news feeds on all major events are coupled with extensive community applications, discussion boards, expert comments, multimedia and fantasy sports.
CONSUMER: SPORT

CHANNEL EMEA
1835484U5R-689
Editorial Address: 32 Scarletts Road, COLCHESTER, CO1 2HA **Tel:** 01206 503502
Email: pr@channelemea.com
Web site: http://www.channelemea.com
Date Launched: 2008
Frequency of update: Daily
Website Access: Free
Editor: Stuart Wilson
Summary of Content: Content portal featuring news, comment and analysis in the ICT and consumer electronics channel.
Readership/Target Audience: Aimed at channel professionals.
BUSINESS: COMPUTERS & AUTOMATION: Computers Related

CHARITY TIMES ONLINE
629004U1P-74
Editorial Address: 6th Floor, 3 London Wall Buildings, LONDON, EC2M 5PD **Tel:** 020 7562 2401
Email: andrew.holt@charitytimes.com
Web site: http://www.charitytimes.com
Frequency of update: Daily
Website Access: Free
Editor: Andrew Holt
Summary of Content: Website providing news and information for UK charities.
Readership/Target Audience: Aimed at managers and directors of charities, trustees and fundraisers.
BUSINESS: FINANCE & ECONOMICS: Fundraising

CHEMICALS INDUSTRY DIRECTORY
1912916U13-207
Editorial Address: 18 Generator Hall, Electric Wharf, COVENTRY, CV1 4JL **Tel:** 0870 199 4044
Fax: 0870 777 4360
Email: enquries@industrydirectory.co.uk
Web site: http://www.industrydirectory.co.uk
Publisher: Simply Marcomms
Frequency of update: Daily
Website Access: Free
Editor: Kirstie Colledge
Summary of Content: Directory containing the latest news stories for the UK chemicals industry. Includes news archives.
Readership/Target Audience: Aimed at Chemicals professionals, suppliers to the Chemicals industry, Chemicals Industry PR & Marketing firms.
BUSINESS: CHEMICALS

CHEMICALS TECHNOLOGY
1616578U13-192
Editorial Address: Brunel House, 55-57 North Wharf Road, LONDON, W2 1LA **Tel:** 020 7915 9957 **Fax:** 020 7915 9720
Email: production@spgmedia.com
Web site: http://www.chemicals-technology.com
Publisher: SPG Media Ltd
Date Launched: 1999
Frequency of update: Daily
Website Access: Free
Traffic Figures: 51,175 Unique Users (per month Publisher's Statement)
Editor: Duncan West
Summary of Content: Website covering chemicals technology projects both in production and under development as well as general news, products and services and exhibitions and conferences.
Readership/Target Audience: Aimed at those working in the chemicals industries.
BUSINESS: CHEMICALS

CHEMIST + DRUGGIST
626507U37-22_70
Formerly: dotPharmacy
Editorial Address: Riverbank House, Angel Lane, TONBRIDGE, TN9 1SE **Tel:** 01732 364422
Fax: 01732 367065
Email: thawkins@cmpmedica.com
Web site: http://www.chemistanddruggist.co.uk
Publisher: UBM Information (Tonbridge)
Date Launched: 1995
Frequency of update: Daily
Website Access: Free
Editor: Tom Hawkins

Summary of Content: Website delivering the latest news, information, educational articles and data to UK community pharmacists.
Readership/Target Audience: Aimed at pharmacists, pharmaceutical manufacturers and wholesalers.
BUSINESS: PHARMACEUTICAL & CHEMISTS

CHESHIRE MATTERS
1881602U72J-345
Email: comments@cheshire-matters.co.uk
Web site: http://www.cheshire-matters.co.uk
Frequency of update: Daily
Summary of Content: Website created to help people who care about local issues. Whether you need access to useful information, want to highlight a particular topic to other people, discuss ideas with like-minded people or just show your support and keep up to date with current affairs in your area, Cheshire Matters is the place for you.
Readership/Target Audience: Aimed at residents in the local area of Cheshire.
LOCAL NEWSPAPERS: Community Newsletters

THE CHIC GEEK
1914462U86C-760
Editorial Address: 32 Aldwick Road, BEDDINGTON, CR0 4PL
Web site: http://www.thechicgeek.co.uk
Frequency of update: Daily
Summary of Content: Website covering men's fashion tips and information.
Readership/Target Audience: Aimed at men interested in fashion and appearance.
CONSUMER: ADULT & GAY MAGAZINES: Men's Lifestyle Magazines

CHICKENDINNER.CO.UK
1810480U79F-108
Editorial Address: 36 Eastcastle Street, LONDON, W1W 8DP **Tel:** 020 7580 7744
Email: michael@grandparade.co.uk
Web site: http://www.chickendinner.co.uk
Date Launched: 2007
Frequency of update: Daily
Website Access: Free
Editor: Ed Needham
Summary of Content: Website covering research and information on all types of sports and cultural events so that the reader betting on them can make smarter decisions.
Readership/Target Audience: Aimed at those who bet on sport and cultural events.
CONSUMER: HOBBIES & DIY: Games & Puzzles

CHILDFRIENDLY.NET
1739971U74D-635
Editorial Address: 32A Shelburne Road, CALNE, SN11 8ER
Email: press@childfriendly.net
Web site: http://www.childfriendly.net
Date Launched: 2003
Frequency of update: Daily
Website Access: Free
Traffic Figures: 12,040 Unique Users (per day Publisher's Statement)
Editor: Emma Shipman
Summary of Content: Electronic database covering child friendly places in the UK including shops, restaurants, hotels, cafes and events.
Readership/Target Audience: Aimed at parents of children under 10 years old.
CONSUMER: WOMEN'S INTEREST CONSUMER MAGAZINES: Child Care

CHILDREN & YOUNG PEOPLE NOW
1859793U32G-181
Editorial Address: 174 Hammersmith Road, LONDON, W6 7JP **Tel:** 020 8267 4210
Email: ruth.smith@haymarket.com
Web site: http://www.cypnow.co.uk
Publisher: Haymarket Professional Publications Ltd
Frequency of update: Daily
Website Access: Free
Editor: Ruth Smith
Summary of Content: Website of the magazine Children and Young People Now. Features forums, blogs, events, jobs and careers.
Readership/Target Audience: Aimed at multi-agency professionals who need to be kept up-to-date with news and information across children and youth services.
BUSINESS: LOCAL GOVERNMENT, LEISURE & RECREATION: Community Care & Social Services

CHILDREN FIRST FOR HEALTH
1695597U74D-614

Editorial Address: GOSH marketing and communications, 40 Bernard Street, LONDON, WC1N 1LE **Tel:** 020 7239 3000
Email: mcevoym@gosh.nhs.uk
Web site: http://www.childrenfirst.nhs.uk
Publisher: Great Ormond Street Hospital
Date Launched: 2001
Frequency of update: Weekly
Website Access: Free
Traffic Figures: 85,000 Unique Users (per month Publisher's Statement)
Editor: Ben Holt
Summary of Content: Health promotion website run by Great Ormond Street Hospital giving generic health and hospital information and responding to young people's health enquiries. Content is clinically approved by Great Ormand Street Hospital experts.
Readership/Target Audience: Resource with section aimed at teenagers, children and family.
CONSUMER: WOMEN'S INTEREST CONSUMER MAGAZINES: Child Care

CHINA CONFIDENTIAL
1893962U1F-664

Editorial Address: 1 Southwark Bridge, LONDON, SE1 9HL
Tel: 020 7873 3000
Email: editorial.ftchinaconfidential@ft.com
Web site: http://www.ftchinaconfidential.com
Publisher: Financial Times
Date Launched: 2009
Frequency of update: 26 times a year
Website Access: Paid
Editor: James Kynge
Summary of Content: Electronic newsletter and website reporting on investment trends and highlighting investment opportunities in China. Also focusing on China's political environment in relation to business and finance.
Readership/Target Audience: Aimed at analysts, fund managers, researchers and investors.
BUSINESS: FINANCE & ECONOMICS: Investment

CI ONLINE
1703583U45A-514

Editorial Address: Informa House, 69-77 Paul Street, LONDON, EC2A 4LQ **Tel:** 020 7017 4891
Fax: 020 7017 4976
Email: enquiries@ci-online.co.uk
Web site: http://www.ci-online.co.uk
Publisher: Informa Plc
Date Launched: 1967
Frequency of update: Daily
Website Access: Paid
Traffic Figures: 10,500 Unique Users (Publisher's Statement)
Editor: Mike Wackett
Summary of Content: Website covering news and information on the container industry.
Readership/Target Audience: Aimed at shippers, analysts, bankers, PRs and port and terminal operators.
BUSINESS: MARINE & SHIPPING

THE CIBSE ELECTRONIC NEWSLETTER
625118U4R-360

Editorial Address: 222 Balham High Road, LONDON, SW12 9BS **Tel:** 020 8675 5211 **Fax:** 020 8675 5449
Email: enquiries@cibse.org
Web site: http://www.cibse.org
Publisher: CIBSE
Frequency of update: Monthly
Traffic Figures: 15,000 Unique Users (Publisher's Statement)
Editor: Richard Howard
Summary of Content: E-mail newsletter covering new products and services.
Readership/Target Audience: Read by members of the Chartered Institute of Building Services Engineers.
BUSINESS: ARCHITECTURE & BUILDING: Building Related

CIMA INSIGHT
1639878U1B-320

Editorial Address: 26 Chapter Street, LONDON, SW1P 4NP
Tel: 01234 325522 **Fax:** 020 8849 2453
Email: tim.cooper@cimaglobal.com
Web site: http://www.cimaglobal.com/insight
Publisher: Chartered Institute of Management Accountants
Date Launched: 2003
Frequency of update: Monthly
Website Access: Free
Traffic Figures: 124,000 Unique Users (Publisher's Statement)
Editor: Tim Cooper

Summary of Content: Email newsletter covering accountancy in business. Includes articles on budgeting, forecasting, performance measurement, corporate governance and accounting standards.
Readership/Target Audience: Aimed at professional accountants in business.
Other Features: Archives, jobs and careers and training and development.
BUSINESS: FINANCE & ECONOMICS: Accountancy

CIMA SYNERGY
1646018U1B-319

Editorial Address: 26 Chapter Street, LONDON, SW1P 4NP
Tel: 01234 325522 **Fax:** 020 8849 2453
Email: tim.cooper@cimaglobal.com
Web site: http://www.cimaglobal.com/synergy
Publisher: Chartered Institute of Management Accountants
Date Launched: 2003
Frequency of update: 6 times a year
Website Access: Paid
Traffic Figures: 5,400 Unique Users (Publisher's Statement)
Editor: Tim Cooper
Summary of Content: Website for CIMA's employer partners covering recruiting, retraining, training, supporting and developing Chartered Management Accountants.
Readership/Target Audience: Aimed at employers of management accountants.
Other Features: Archives, and 'Meet the Employer Support Team'.
BUSINESS: FINANCE & ECONOMICS: Accountancy

CIMA VELOCITY
1866559U1B-333

Editorial Address: 26 Chapter Street, LONDON, SW1P 4NP
Tel: 01234 325522 **Fax:** 020 8849 2453
Email: tim.cooper@cimaglobal.com
Web site: http://www.cimaglobal.com/velocity
Publisher: Chartered Institute of Management Accountants
Frequency of update: Monthly
Website Access: Free
Traffic Figures: 84,000 Unique Users (Publisher's Statement)
Editor: Tim Cooper
Summary of Content: E-magazine aiming to help CIMA students get through their studies and advance to membership as quickly as possible. Contains news and features, important notices about exams and study and a careers and development section.
Readership/Target Audience: Aimed at CIMA students.
BUSINESS: FINANCE & ECONOMICS: Accountancy

CISION MEDIA UPDATES - UK
1745540U2A-685

Formerly: Cision Media Bulletin
Editorial Address: Chess House, 34 Germain Street, CHESHAM, HP5 1SJ **Tel:** 01494 797225 **Fax:** 01494 797278
Email: research.europe@cision.com
Web site: http://uk.cision.com
Publisher: Cision UK Ltd
Date Launched: 2005
Frequency of update: Weekly
Website Access: Free
Traffic Figures: 8,000 Unique Users (Publisher's Statement)
Editor: Joanna Bowles
Summary of Content: Electronic newsletter covering editorial changes within the media industry as well as rankings and changes within social media.
Readership/Target Audience: Aimed at those interested in changes within the media, including public relations professionals, journalists and bloggers.
BUSINESS: COMMUNICATIONS, ADVERTISING & MARKETING

CITYTECH
1732056U5R-686

Editorial Address: 8F Blackburnes Mews, LONDON, W1K 2LG **Tel:** 020 7495 1697 **Fax:** 020 7487 4776
Email: kjones@j-p-c.tv
Web site: http://www.citytechmag.com
Publisher: JPC
Date Launched: 2005
Frequency of update: 10 times a year
Website Access: Free
Traffic Figures: 2,000 Unique Users (per week Publisher's Statement)
Editor: Karen Jones
Summary of Content: Electronically delivered newsletter covering US and UK law technology news, features, white papers, case studies and people moves.
Readership/Target Audience: Aimed at senior IT directors and law firm management.
BUSINESS: COMPUTERS & AUTOMATION: Computers Related

CITYWEALTH
1732055U1R-377

Editorial Address: 8F Blackburnes Mews, LONDON, W1K 2LG **Tel:** 020 7495 1697 **Fax:** 020 7487 4776
Email: kjones@j-p-c.tv
Web site: http://www.citywealthmag.com
Publisher: JPC
Frequency of update: Monthly
Website Access: Paid
Traffic Figures: 2,800 Unique Users (per week Publisher's Statement)
Editor: Karen Jones
Summary of Content: Electronically delivered newsletter covering features on banks, trust companies, accountants and lawyers working in the area of wealth management around the world, including events, people, pictures, interviews, lifestyle, travel restaurants and spas.
Readership/Target Audience: Aimed at bankers, lawyers and accountants with salaries between £280,000 and £2,000,000.
BUSINESS: FINANCE & ECONOMICS: Financial Related

CITYWIRE
623338U1F-121_50

Editorial Address: 1st Floor, 87 Vauxhall Walk, LONDON, SE11 5HJ **Tel:** 020 7840 2250
Email: news@citywire.co.uk
Web site: http://www.citywire.co.uk
Publisher: Citywire
Date Launched: 2000
Frequency of update: Daily
Website Access: Free
Traffic Figures: 110,000 Unique Users (Publisher's Statement)
Editor: Charlie Parker; **Editor-in-Chief:** Gavin Lumsden
Summary of Content: Website covering advice and opinion on funds, investments and corporate activity.
Readership/Target Audience: Aimed at private investors with a keen interest in making money.
BUSINESS: FINANCE & ECONOMICS: Investment

CLASSIC CHARTER & CRUISE
1645678U91A-283

Editorial Address: PO Box 72, CALDICOT, NP26 3ZG
Tel: 01633 889419 **Fax:** 0870 787 7413
Email: editor@classiccharterandcruise.com
Web site: http://www.classiccharterandcruise.com
Publisher: Alfa Media Group
Date Launched: 2004
Frequency of update: Daily
Website Access: Free
Editor: William Loram
Summary of Content: Website covering chartered opportunities, sailing and corporate entertainment, film locations, ships, motor-boats and yachts.
Readership/Target Audience: Aimed at sailing enthusiasts and holiday makers.
CONSUMER: RECREATION & LEISURE: Boating & Yachting

THE CLASSIC MOTORCYCLE
626353U77B-493_1

Editorial Address: Media Centre, Morton Way, HORNCASTLE, LN9 6JR **Tel:** 01507 529300
Fax: 01507 529495
Email: info@classicmotorcycle.co.uk
Web site: http://www.classicmotorcycle.co.uk
Publisher: Mortons Media Group Ltd
Date Launched: 1996
Frequency of update: Monthly
Website Access: Free
Traffic Figures: 11,650 Unique Users (per month Publisher's Statement)
Editor: James Robinson
Summary of Content: Website covering the full spectrum of the classic and vintage period of motorcycling.
Readership/Target Audience: Aimed at vintage and classic motorcycle enthusiasts.
CONSUMER: MOTORING & CYCLING: Motorcycling

CLASSIC RACER ONLINE
718517U77B-493_7

Editorial Address: Media Centre, Morton Way, HORNCASTLE, LN9 6JR **Tel:** 01507 529300
Fax: 01507 529495
Email: mwheeler@mortons.co.uk
Web site: http://www.classicracer.co.uk
Publisher: Mortons Media Group Ltd
Date Launched: 1982
Frequency of update: 6 times a year
Website Access: Free
Traffic Figures: 41,926 Unique Users (per month Publisher's Statement)
Editor: Malcolm Wheeler; **Webmaster:** Jason Williams
Summary of Content: Website containing the latest news, coverage of the motorcycle sporting festivals and reports on all aspects of the current vintage and classic racing scene.

Internet Media

Readership/Target Audience: Aimed at classic racing enthusiasts.
Other Features: Features include archiving.
CONSUMER: MOTORING & CYCLING: Motorcycling

CLEANZINE
1753061U4F-107

Editorial Address: 155 Hook Road, EPSOM, KT19 8TU
Tel: 01372 811307 **Fax:** 01580 754669
Email: news@thecleanzine.com
Web site: http://www.thecleanzine.com
Publisher: b2bzines.net
Date Launched: 2002
Frequency of update: Weekly
Website Access: Free
Traffic Figures: 80,000 Unique Users (Publisher's Statement)
Editor: Jan Hobbs
Summary of Content: Emailed bulletin covering all aspects of cleaning and hygiene including related health and safety information, legislation and personnel and logistics issues.
Readership/Target Audience: Aimed at contract cleaners and distributors/suppliers of cleaning products and equipment, together with those whose role it is to source and purchase cleaning products, equipment and services, manage health and safety and solve cleaning-related problems.
BUSINESS: ARCHITECTURE & BUILDING: Cleaning & Maintenance

CLEAR PROFIT
1606948U1F-576

Tel: 01273 311289
Email: phil.cain@clear-profit.com
Web site: http://www.clear-profit.com
Publisher: Vital Publishing
Date Launched: 2001
Frequency of update: Monthly
Website Access: Free
Traffic Figures: 1,500 Unique Users (Publisher's Statement)
Editor: Phil Cain
Summary of Content: Electronic newsletter featuring coverage of efforts to align investment decisions with social, environmental and ethical concerns.
Readership/Target Audience: Read by the managers of ethically guided funds, IFAs, high net worth individuals, senior practitioners in the field of ethical and social investment. It is also a trusted source for their potential investors.
BUSINESS: FINANCE & ECONOMICS: Investment

CLEVELAND MATTERS
1881603U72J-346

Email: comments@cleveland-matters.co.uk
Web site: http://www.cleveland-matters.co.uk
Frequency of update: Daily
Summary of Content: Website created to help people who care about local issues. Whether you need access to useful information, want to highlight a particular topic to other people, discuss ideas with like-minded people or just show your support and keep up to date with current affairs in your area, Cleveland Matters is the place for you.
Readership/Target Audience: Aimed at residents in the local area of Cleveland.
LOCAL NEWSPAPERS: Community Newsletters

CLICKMUSIC
626410U76D-303_7

Editorial Address: 3rd Floor, 74 Great Eastern Street, LONDON, EC2A 3JL **Tel:** 020 7613 0997
Email: becky@clickmusic.com
Web site: http://www.clickmusic.co.uk
Publisher: Sonic Network
Date Launched: 1999
Frequency of update: Daily
Website Access: Free
Traffic Figures: 200,000 Unique Users (per month Publisher's Statement)
Editor: Becky Reed
Summary of Content: Website focusing on the latest music. Contains news, reviews, new releases, downloads, competitions and gig listings.
Readership/Target Audience: Aimed at anyone interested in music and the music industry.
Other Features: Features include an email newsletter and polls.
CONSUMER: MUSIC & PERFORMING ARTS: Music

CLICKWALLA.COM
767415U90-902

Editorial Address: Eton House, 66 Eton Avenue, WEMBLEY, HA0 3AU **Tel:** 0845 013 8401
Email: info@memediagroup.com
Web site: http://www.clickwalla.com
Publisher: ME Media Ltd

Frequency of update: Daily
Website Access: Free
Traffic Figures: 120,000 Unique Users (Publisher's Statement)
Editor: Neena Kent
Summary of Content: Website covering Asian news, entertainment, lifestyle, shopping and business. Contains an Asian business directory and features on Bollywood films and Asian music.
Readership/Target Audience: Aimed at UK Asians.
CONSUMER: ETHNIC

CLOCKERZ
1800371U78R-518

Editorial Address: 38 Rawson Street, Farnworth, BOLTON, BL4 7RJ **Tel:** 01204 437433
Email: eripmav@clockerz.org
Web site: http://www.clockerz.org
Date Launched: 2000
Frequency of update: Daily
Website Access: Free
Editor: Dan Muir; **Editor-in-Chief:** Dan Muir
Summary of Content: Website with reviews of games, gadgets, computer hardware, films and music.
Readership/Target Audience: Aimed at those aged 14 to 60 years old.
CONSUMER: CONSUMER ELECTRONICS: Consumer Electronics Related

CLOSERDIETS.COM
1774776U74G-281

Editorial Address: Endeavour House, 189 Shaftesbury Avenue, LONDON, WC2H 8JG **Tel:** 020 7295 5000
Fax: 020 7208 3245
Email: olivia.ebeling@closermag.co.uk
Web site: http://www.closerdiets.com
Publisher: Bauer Media
Date Launched: 2006
Frequency of update: Daily
Website Access: Paid
Traffic Figures: 97,000 Unique Users (per month Publisher's Statement)
Summary of Content: Website offering personalised diet plans as well as diet and fitness news and celebrity diets.
Readership/Target Audience: Aimed at women aged 18 to 45 years old.
CONSUMER: WOMEN'S INTEREST CONSUMER MAGAZINES: Slimming & Health

CLOSERONLINE.CO.UK
1798724U74A-1028

Editorial Address: Endeavour House, 189 Shaftesbury Avenue, LONDON, WC2H 8JG **Tel:** 020 7859 8454
Fax: 020 7859 8600
Email: olivia.ebeling@closermag.co.uk
Web site: http://www.closeronline.co.uk
Publisher: Bauer Media
Date Launched: 2006
Frequency of update: Daily
Website Access: Free
Traffic Figures: 115,000 Unique Users (per month Publisher's Statement)
Summary of Content: Website covering celebrity gossip, diet, health, real life features and competitions.
Readership/Target Audience: Aimed at women aged 18 to 45 years old.
CONSUMER: WOMEN'S INTEREST CONSUMER MAGAZINES: Women's Interest

CLOSE-UP FILM
1745987U76A-201

Editorial Address: The Yard, North Lane, Sandgate, FOLKESTONE, CT20 3AS **Tel:** 01304 812382
Email: editor@close-upfilm.com
Web site: http://www.close-upfilm.com
Frequency of update: Daily
Website Access: Free
Traffic Figures: 15,000 Unique Users (per month Publisher's Statement)
Editor: Jean Lynch
Summary of Content: Website covering films from the latest blockbuster release to independent art house releases with film reviews, interviews, practical advice on film making and events.
Readership/Target Audience: Aimed at active film lovers.
CONSUMER: MUSIC & PERFORMING ARTS: Cinema

CMC MARKETS
1924663U1F-681

Editorial Address: 66 Prescot Street, LONDON, E1 8HG
Tel: 020 7170 8201 **Fax:** 020 7170 8498
Email: editorial@cmcmarkets.co.uk
Web site: http://www.cmcmarkets.co.uk
Frequency of update: Daily
Website Access: Paid

Summary of Content: Website covering financial spread betting, CFD and Forex trading with CMC Markets, a global leader in online derivatives trading.
Readership/Target Audience: Targets investors and stockbrokers.
BUSINESS: FINANCE & ECONOMICS: Investment

CML NEWS & VIEWS
35376U1J-10

Editorial Address: North West Wing, Bush House, Aldwych, LONDON, WC2B 4PJ **Tel:** 020 7438 8923
Fax: 0845 373 6778
Email: bernard.clarke@cml.org.uk
Web site: http://www.cml.org.uk
Publisher: Council of Mortgage Lenders
Date Launched: 1997
Frequency of update: 24 times a year
Website Access: Free
Editor: Bernard Clarke
Summary of Content: Electronic newsletter from the Council of Mortgage Lenders which provides a digest of opinions and perspectives on current issues in the mortgage and housing markets.
Readership/Target Audience: Aimed at those with an interest in mortgage lending.
BUSINESS: FINANCE & ECONOMICS: Building Societies

CMU DAILY
623062U61-505

Formerly: CMU The Update
Editorial Address: 3rd Floor, Unicorn House, 221-222 Shoreditch High Street, LONDON, E1 6PJ
Tel: 0870 744 2643 **Fax:** 070 9231 4982
Email: musicnews@unlimitedmedia.co.uk
Web site: http://www.cmumusicnetwork.co.uk
Publisher: UnLimited Media
Date Launched: 1998
Frequency of update: 250 times a year. Every weekday, excluding UK bank holidays
Website Access: Paid
Traffic Figures: 12,500 Unique Users (per day Publisher's Statement)
Editor: Chris Cooke
Summary of Content: Email newsletter giving reviews of forthcoming albums and single releases, the latest music industry and music media news, interviews with new and innovative bands and music and media professionals.
Readership/Target Audience: Aimed at those working in music media (national, regional and college radio, TV and press) as well as those working in the UK music industry.
BUSINESS: MUSIC TRADE

CN PLUS
706688U42A-15

Editorial Address: Greater London House, LONDON, NW1 7EJ **Tel:** 020 7728 4633 **Fax:** 020 7391 3435
Email: lisa.glancy@emap.com
Web site: http://www.cnplus.co.uk
Date Launched: 2000
Frequency of update: Daily
Website Access: Paid
Editor: Lisa Glancy
Summary of Content: Website focusing on being business-to-business portal for the construction industry. Includes real-time news, legal information and new product information.
Readership/Target Audience: Aimed at contractors in the construction industry.
BUSINESS: CONSTRUCTION

CNET.CO.UK
1685615U78R-500

Editorial Address: 5-11 Lavington Street, LONDON, SE1 0NZ **Tel:** 020 7021 1000 **Fax:** 020 7021 1308
Email: edit@cnet.com
Web site: http://www.cnet.co.uk
Publisher: CBS Interactive
Date Launched: 2005
Frequency of update: Daily
Website Access: Free
Traffic Figures: 2,500,000 Unique Users (Publisher's Statement)
Editor: Jason Jenkins
Summary of Content: Personal technology website with news and reviews of televisions, mobile phones, laptops, MP3 players and digital music, digital cameras, camcorders, digital radios, DVD and PVR, handhelds, monitors, printers and accessories.
Readership/Target Audience: Aimed at people who are passionate about consumer electronics.
Other Features: Video, Podcast, newsletter and forums.
CONSUMER: CONSUMER ELECTRONICS: Consumer Electronics Related

CNTRAVELLER
626243U89A-95

Editorial Address: 25 Maddox Street, LONDON, W1S 2QN
Tel: 020 7499 9080 **Fax:** 020 7493 1469
Email: emma.lundin@condenast.co.uk
Web site: http://www.cntraveller.com
Publisher: Conde Nast Publications Ltd
Date Launched: 1997
Frequency of update: Daily
Website Access: Free
Traffic Figures: 270,000 Unique Users (per month
Publisher's Statement)
Summary of Content: Website providing an in-depth travel
guide to various destinations. Includes a top ten holiday
destinations and activity holidays guide, a readers' travel
awards section, travellers' tales and a what's new section.
Readership/Target Audience: Aimed at those looking for
high quality holiday ideas and discerning travellers in
general.
Other Features: Features include archiving and an e-mail
newsletter.
CONSUMER: HOLIDAYS & TRAVEL: Travel

COALINTERNATIONAL
719337U30-28

Editorial Address: British Fields, Ollerton Road, Tuxford,
NEWARK, NG22 0PQ **Tel:** 01777 871007 **Fax:** 01777 872271
Email: info@tradelinkpub.co.uk
Web site: http://www.mqworld.com
Date Launched: 1998
Frequency of update: Daily
Website Access: Paid
Traffic Figures: 6,500 Unique Users (per month Publisher's
Statement)
Editor: Trevor Barratt
Summary of Content: Website providing worldwide news
and information on the coal mining industry. Includes a
search engine and information on mining journals. Also
provides links to coal producers and coal mining equipment.
Readership/Target Audience: Aimed at the mining industry
professionals worldwide.
BUSINESS: MINING & QUARRYING

COAST
1902880U74A-1065

Editorial Address: 72 Broadwick Street, LONDON, W1F
9EP **Tel:** 020 7439 5000
Email: enquiries.coast@natmags.co.uk
Web site: http://www.allaboutyou.com
Publisher: Hearst Digital
Frequency of update: Daily
Website Access: Free
Editor: Bernadette Fallon
Summary of Content: Website covering lifestyle features.
Readership/Target Audience: Aimed at women of all ages.
CONSUMER: WOMEN'S INTEREST CONSUMER
MAGAZINES: Women's Interest

CODEJUNKIES
601108U78D-70

Formerly: codejunkies.com
Editorial Address: Datel, Stone Business Park, Stafford
Road, STONE, ST15 0DG **Tel:** 01785 810816
Fax: 01785 810840
Email: ian.osborne@datel.co.uk
Web site: http://www.codejunkies.com
Publisher: Datel/Thin Ice Media
Date Launched: 1999
Frequency of update: Daily
Website Access: Free
Traffic Figures: 50,000 Unique Users (per week Publisher's
Statement)
Editor: Ian Osborne
Summary of Content: Website in association with PSi-2
print magazine, for the latest on PlayStation 2, GameCube,
Sega Dreamcast, Microsoft Xbox and all next generation
consoles and gadgets.
Readership/Target Audience: Aimed at those who play
games, watch DVDs and buy gadgets.
Other Features: Features include a chat forum, a buyer's
guide, an e-mail newsletter, Action Replay cheat codes and
archiving.
CONSUMER: CONSUMER ELECTRONICS: Games

COFFEE INTERNATIONAL DIRECTORY
37995U22A-75

Editorial Address: Office 8, Unit 1-2 Wyvern Estate,
Beverley Way, NEW MALDEN, KT3 4PH **Tel:** 020 8949 0088
Fax: 020 8949 0160
Email: info@siemex.biz
Web site: http://www.coffeeandcocoa.net
Publisher: Siemex International Ltd
Frequency of update: Daily
Website Access: Paid
Editor: Andrew Kingsley

Summary of Content: Electronic publication containing
essential statistics, list of soluble manufacturers and
processors, importers, exporters, brokers and agents,
bankers, national coffee associations and state coffee
agencies, plant and machinery manufacturers, suppliers of
ancillary equipment shipping and warehousing and services
to the industry.
Readership/Target Audience: Aimed at growers,
exporters, roasters, importers, retailers and process and
handling machinery manufacturers.
BUSINESS: FOOD

COLD STORE NEWS
1659058U3C-202

Editorial Address: For all contact details see main record,
Cold Chain News
Frequency of update: 3 times a year
Website Access: Paid
BUSINESS: HEATING & VENTILATION: Refrigeration &
Ventilation

COLDSWELL.COM
634816U75M-110

Editorial Address: 54 Hoole Street, SHEFFIELD, S6 2WR
Tel: 07740 197485
Email: gav@coldswell.com
Web site: http://www.coldswell.com
Publisher: Pipe Ten Ltd
Date Launched: 1999
Frequency of update: Monthly
Website Access: Paid
Traffic Figures: 20,000 Unique Users (per month Publisher's
Statement)
Editor: Gavin Kimpton
Summary of Content: Website focusing on news and
information on surfing in the UK and Ireland. Includes surf
checks, webcams, links, weather charts and a beach guide.
Readership/Target Audience: Read by surfing enthusiasts.
Other Features: News/Events/Product reviews.
CONSUMER: SPORT: Water Sports

COMBICHEM.NET
1665980U13-197

Editorial Address: Woodview, Bull Lane Industrial Estate,
Bull Lane, Acton, SUDBURY, CO10 0BD **Tel:** 01787 319234
Fax: 01787 319235
Email: editor@technologynetworks.net
Web site: http://www.combichem.net
Publisher: Technology Networks Limited
Date Launched: 1999
Frequency of update: Daily
Website Access: Free
Traffic Figures: 26,000 Unique Users (Publisher's
Statement)
Editor: Val Mann
Summary of Content: Website dedicated to combinatorial
and medicinal chemistry including, news, supplier listings,
forum, events listing and product information, scientific
posters and conference presentations.
Readership/Target Audience: Aimed at professionals in the
field of combinatorial and medicinal chemistry.
Other Features: eNewsletters every fortnight.
BUSINESS: CHEMICALS

COMMODITIES NOW ONLINE
707468U1L-4

Editorial Address: 39 Thurloe Place, LONDON, SW7 2HP
Tel: 020 7584 0000 **Fax:** 020 7584 0022
Email: gish@commodities-now.com
Web site: http://www.commodities-now.com
Publisher: Isherwood Production
Date Launched: 1997
Frequency of update: Quarterly
Website Access: Paid
Traffic Figures: 10,000 Unique Users (per month Publisher's
Statement)
Editor: Guy Isherwood
Summary of Content: Website containing news, views and
data across the commodity markets as well as an events
and links library.
Readership/Target Audience: Aimed at people employed
within the commodities industry.
BUSINESS: FINANCE & ECONOMICS: Commodities

COMPANY CAR DRIVER
1861594U49D-365

Editorial Address: Media House, Lynchwood, Peterborough
Business Park, PETERBOROUGH, PE2 6EA
Tel: 01733 468000
Email: sharon.sim@bauermedia.co.uk
Web site: http://www.companycardriver.co.uk
Publisher: Bauer Consumer Media Ltd (Media House)
Frequency of update: Daily
Website Access: Free
Editor: Sharon Sim

Summary of Content: Website containing company car
news, information, road tests and services.
Readership/Target Audience: Aimed at company car
drivers and businesses using company cars.
BUSINESS: TRANSPORT: Commercial Vehicles

COMPANY.CO.UK
1642357U74A-965

Formerly: getlippy.com
Editorial Address: 5th Floor, 7 Swallow Place, LONDON,
W1B 2AG **Tel:** 020 3312 3775 **Fax:** 020 7499 8945
Email: editor@company.co.uk
Web site: http://www.company.co.uk
Publisher: NatMag Rodale Ltd
Date Launched: 2004
Frequency of update: Daily
Website Access: Free
Traffic Figures: 421,000 Unique Users (per month
Publisher's Statement)
Editor: Clare Gill
Summary of Content: Website covering fashion, beauty,
celebrity, relationships and entertainment.
Readership/Target Audience: Aimed at women aged
between 18 and 30 years old.
CONSUMER: WOMEN'S INTEREST CONSUMER
MAGAZINES: Women's Interest

COMPLEMENTARY THERAPISTS
ASSOCIATION
1732869U15A-200

Formerly: Embody Professional
Editorial Address: PO Box 6955, TOWCESTER, NN12 6WZ
Tel: 0870 201 1912 **Fax:** 0844 779 8899
Email: nixon@emsv.co.uk
Web site: http://www.complementary.assoc.org.uk
Frequency of update: Weekly
Website Access: Free
Traffic Figures: 3,000 Unique Users (per day Publisher's
Statement)
Editor: Martyn Nixon
Summary of Content: Website and membership club
covering how to find work, improve your skills and enjoy
your profession.
Readership/Target Audience: Aimed at health and beauty
professionals.
BUSINESS: COSMETICS & HAIRDRESSING: Cosmetics

COMPLINET
749388U1C-110

Editorial Address: 3rd Floor, Vinter's Place, Upper Thames
Street, LONDON, EC4V 3BJ **Tel:** 0870 042 6400
Fax: 0870 8661 5879
Email: editorial@complinet.com
Web site: http://www.complinet.com
Publisher: Complinet
Date Launched: 1997
Frequency of update: Daily
Website Access: Paid
Traffic Figures: 100,000 Unique Users (Publisher's
Statement)
Editor: Alex Viall; **Editor-in-Chief:** Alex Viall
Summary of Content: Website providing regulatory news
and information for the financial services sector. Includes
information on securities and banking, insurance, sanctions
and enforcement and money laundering. Also includes an
HR section.
Readership/Target Audience: Aimed at compliance
professionals, money laundering reporting officers and
human resources departments within the financial services
sector.
BUSINESS: FINANCE & ECONOMICS: Banking

COMPOUNDING WORLD
1882056U39-159

Editorial Address: AMI House, 45-47 Stokes Croft,
BRISTOL, BS1 3QP **Tel:** 0117 924 9442
Email: editorial@compoundingworld.com
Web site: http://www.compoundingworld.com
Publisher: Applied Market Information Ltd
Date Launched: 2008
Frequency of update: Monthly. Published in the first week
of the month
Website Access: Free
Traffic Figures: 13,312 Unique Users (Publisher's
Statement)
Editor: Andy Beevers
Summary of Content: Digital magazine covering key
technical developments, market trends, strategic business
issues, legislative announcements, company profiles and
new product launches.
Readership/Target Audience: Aimed at polymer
compounders and masterbach producers.
BUSINESS: PLASTICS & RUBBER

Internet Media

COMPUTER ACTIVE ONLINE
629030U78E-44

Editorial Address: 32-34 Broadwick Street, LONDON, W1A 2HG **Tel:** 020 7316 9000 **Fax:** 020 7316 9520
Email: news@computeractive.co.uk
Web site: http://www.computeractive.co.uk
Publisher: Incisive Media
Date Launched: 1998
Frequency of update: Daily
Website Access: Free
Traffic Figures: 200,307 Unique Users (per month)
Editor: Dinah Greek
Summary of Content: Website covering advice and information for PC users.
Readership/Target Audience: Aimed at beginners and intermediate home PC users.
CONSUMER: CONSUMER ELECTRONICS: Home Computing

COMPUTER ARTS ONLINE
626212U78E-40

Editorial Address: 30 Monmouth Street, BATH, BA1 2BW
Tel: 01225 442244
Email: jim.mccauley@futurenet.co.uk
Web site: http://www.computerarts.co.uk
Publisher: Future Publishing Ltd
Date Launched: 1997
Frequency of update: Daily
Website Access: Free
Traffic Figures: 19,758 Unique Users (per month Publisher's Statement)
Editor: Jim McCauley
Summary of Content: Website focusing on web and graphic design.
Readership/Target Audience: Aimed at professional and aspiring web and graphic designers.
CONSUMER: CONSUMER ELECTRONICS: Home Computing

COMPUTER MUSIC (ONLINE)
629073U76D-797

Editorial Address: 30 Monmouth Street, BATH, BA1 2BW
Tel: 01225 442244 **Fax:** 01225 822793
Email: ronan.macdonald@futurenet.com
Web site: http://www.computermusic.co.uk
Publisher: Future Publishing Ltd
Date Launched: 1998
Frequency of update: Daily
Website Access: Free
Editor: Ronan MacDonald
Summary of Content: Website containing news, reviews and advice on computer music.
Readership/Target Audience: Aimed at those interested in making music using the latest technology.
CONSUMER: MUSIC & PERFORMING ARTS: Music

COMPUTER SHOPPER.CO.UK
626247U78E-45

Editorial Address: 30 Cleveland Street, LONDON, W1T 4JD
Tel: 020 7907 6000
Email: news@computershopper.co.uk
Web site: http://www.computershopper.co.uk
Publisher: Dennis Publishing Ltd
Date Launched: 1997
Frequency of update: Daily
Website Access: Free
Editor: David Ludlow
Summary of Content: Website covering the daily world of personal computing, with software and hardware reviews, features and news on the PC marketplace.
Readership/Target Audience: Aimed at computer enthusiasts and buyers of new software and hardware.
CONSUMER: CONSUMER ELECTRONICS: Home Computing

COMPUTERWEEKLY.COM
707595U5B-59

Formerly: cw360
Editorial Address: Quadrant House, The Quadrant, SUTTON, SM2 5AS **Tel:** 020 8652 3500 **Fax:** 020 8652 8088
Email: cwnews@rbi.co.uk
Web site: http://www.computerweekly.com
Publisher: Reed Business Information
Date Launched: 2001
Frequency of update: Daily
Website Access: Free
Traffic Figures: 142,000 Unique Users (per month Publisher's Statement)
Editor: James Garner; **Web Editor:** Joe O'Halloran
Summary of Content: Website designed to help IT professionals and resellers meet the challenges of the new economy. Offers business and technical information alongside independent analysis and views on technology, strategy and careers.

Readership/Target Audience: Aimed at IT professionals.
BUSINESS: COMPUTERS & AUTOMATION: Data Processing

COMPUTERWORLD UK
1828667U5B-9021

Editorial Address: 4th Floor, 101 Euston Road, LONDON, NW1 2RA **Tel:** 020 7071 3615
Email: cwuknews@idg.co.uk
Web site: http://www.computerworlduk.com
Publisher: IDG (International Data Group)
Date Launched: 2007
Frequency of update: Daily
Website Access: Free
Editor: Mike Simons
Summary of Content: Website providing news, analysis and opinions about the latest IT issues, new products and technology trends. Also provides a forum for discussion on a range of current issues and topics.
Readership/Target Audience: Aimed at IT managers and professionals in medium to large companies.
BUSINESS: COMPUTERS & AUTOMATION: Data Processing

COMSEUROPA
1706831U18B-1968

Formerly: TelecomsEurope
Editorial Address: PR by email only
Email: editorial@morianamediagroup.com
Web site: http://www.mcubedigital.com
Publisher: Moriana Media Group
Date Launched: 2006
Frequency of update: 6 times a year. Published in the 3rd week of the 1st cover month
Website Access: Free
Traffic Figures: 10,000 Unique Users (Publisher's Statement)
Editor: John Williamson
Summary of Content: Magazine focused on wireless practitioners with features and reports on current trends and developments within the global wireless community.
Readership/Target Audience: Aimed at higher management within the global wireless community including operators, vendors and service providers.
BUSINESS: ELECTRONICS: Telecommunications

CONFERENCE CALENDAR
35632U2C-40

Editorial Address: 123 Adams Gardens, LONDON, SE16 4JH **Tel:** 020 7237 9777
Email: info@confcal.com
Web site: http://www.confcal.com
Publisher: Fleming Information Services
Date Launched: 1997
Frequency of update: 104 times a year
Website Access: Paid
Editor: John Nosworthy
Summary of Content: Listings of conferences, awards and affiliated exhibitions in the UK and overseas.
Readership/Target Audience: E-zine aimed at libraries, educational and training organisations and staff, government, associations and institutions, industry, marketing and PR companies.
BUSINESS: COMMUNICATIONS, ADVERTISING & MARKETING: Conferences & Exhibitions

CONFERENCE VENUE MARKETPLACE
1842231U2C-520

Editorial Address: 29A Market Square, BIGGLESWADE, SG18 8AQ **Tel:** 01767 316255 **Fax:** 01767 316430
Email: info@eou.org.uk
Web site: http://www.eou.org.uk
Publisher: The Meetings Forum
Date Launched: 2008
Frequency of update: 6 times a year
Website Access: Free
Traffic Figures: 5,000 Unique Users (Publisher's Statement)
Editor: Peter Cotterell
Summary of Content: Electronic newsletter covering news and features about conference venues.
Readership/Target Audience: Aimed at organisers of conferences.
BUSINESS: COMMUNICATIONS, ADVERTISING & MARKETING: Conferences & Exhibitions

CONFETTI.CO.UK
1665563U74L-229

Editorial Address: 80-81 Tottenham Court Road, LONDON, W1T 4TE **Tel:** 020 7291 7600 **Fax:** 020 7291 7601
Email: carolr@confetti.co.uk
Web site: http://www.confetti.co.uk
Publisher: Confetti Network
Frequency of update: Daily

Website Access: Free
Traffic Figures: 729,061 Unique Users (01/01/2006 To 30/01/2006 ABC/Electronic)
Editor: Carol Richardson
Summary of Content: Website covering celebrations including weddings, birthdays, anniversaries and parties.
Readership/Target Audience: Aimed at those planning a celebration.
CONSUMER: WOMEN'S INTEREST CONSUMER MAGAZINES: Brides

CONFIDENT LIFE
1740082U74R-552

Editorial Address: High View Farm, Folley Road, Ackleton, WOLVERHAMPTON, WV6 7JL **Tel:** 0845 838 1014
Fax: 0845 838 1653
Email: info@confidentlife.com
Web site: http://www.confidentlife.com
Date Launched: 2005
Frequency of update: Monthly
Website Access: Paid
Traffic Figures: 900 Unique Users (per month Publisher's Statement)
Editor: Jill Mytton
Summary of Content: Social Networking site, online and offline, covering events, networking and chat as well as lifestyle features.
Readership/Target Audience: Aimed at men and women aged 35 years and over.
Other Features: Newsletter.
CONSUMER: WOMEN'S INTEREST CONSUMER MAGAZINES: Women's Interest Related

CONNECT2U
707752U60C-25

Editorial Address: Wakefield House, Pipers Way, SWINDON, SN3 1RF **Tel:** 0845 123 0000 **Fax:** 01793 542088
Email: kerrie.colford@smithsnews.co.uk
Web site: http://www.connect2u.co.uk
Publisher: Smiths News
Date Launched: 2000
Frequency of update: Daily. News updated continuously
Website Access: Free
Traffic Figures: 2,000 Unique Users (per month Publisher's Statement)
Editor: Kerrie Colford
Summary of Content: Website covering information and order management for Smith News customers. Includes product information including magazine catalogue, magazine rankings, product launches and promotions, and industry information.
Readership/Target Audience: Aimed at retailers of newspapers and magazines, mainly independent retailers but also some multiple groups.
BUSINESS: PUBLISHING: Newsagents

CONNECTING INDUSTRY
633875U19A-583

Formerly: CONNECTING INDUSTRY online
Editorial Address: 15A London Road, MAIDSTONE, ME16 8LY **Tel:** 01622 687031 **Fax:** 01622 757646
Email: mfrancis@datateam.co.uk
Web site: http://www.connectingindustry.com
Publisher: Datateam Publishing Ltd
Date Launched: 2000
Frequency of update: Daily
Website Access: Free
Editor: Matt Francis
Summary of Content: Website serving seven industrial market sectors within the UK manufacturing industry. Markets include automation, electrical engineering, electronics, factory equipment, instrumentation, OEM design, process and control.
Readership/Target Audience: Aimed at engineers, buyers, manufacturers and those who purchase industrial equipment.
BUSINESS: ENGINEERING & MACHINERY

CONSTRUCTION BIBLE
1775665U42A-238

Editorial Address: The Quadrus Centre, Woodstock Way, Boldon Business Park, BOLDON COLLIERY, NE35 9PF
Tel: 0191 519 7268 **Fax:** 0191 519 7201
Email: andyb@resultsnetwork.co.uk
Web site: http://www.constructionbible.co.uk
Publisher: Construction Bible Ltd
Date Launched: 2006
Frequency of update: Daily
Traffic Figures: 15,000 Unique Users (per month Publisher's Statement)
Editor: Andy Barker
Summary of Content: Website covering all aspects of construction, building and utility news also includes construction training news.

Readership/Target Audience: Aimed at senior managers in construction, specifiers, architects, project managers and buyers.
Other Features: Message board and forum.
BUSINESS: CONSTRUCTION

CONSTRUCTION INDUSTRY DIRECTORY

1912917U42A-251

Editorial Address: 18 Generator Hall, Electric Wharf, COVENTRY, CV1 4JL **Tel:** 0870 199 4044
Fax: 0870 777 4360
Email: enquiries@industrydirectory.co.uk
Web site: http://www.industrydirectory.co.uk
Publisher: Simply Marcomms
Frequency of update: Daily
Website Access: Free
Editor: Kirstie Colledge
Summary of Content: Directory containing the latest news stories for the UK construction industry. Includes news archives.
Readership/Target Audience: Aimed at construction professionals, suppliers to the construction industry, construction industry PR & Marketing firms.
BUSINESS: CONSTRUCTION

CONSTRUCTION NEWS PORTAL

1840802U42A-247

Editorial Address: Britannia House, 11 Glenthorne Road, LONDON, W6 0LH **Tel:** 0870 745 3380
Email: editorial@constructionnewsportal.com
Web site: http://www.constructionnewsportal.co.uk
Publisher: Areza Ltd
Date Launched: 2003
Frequency of update: Daily
Website Access: Free
Traffic Figures: 60,000 Unique Users (per month WebTrends)
Editor: Chris Mortimer
Summary of Content: Portal featuring news, case studies, research articles and market reports. Covering general construction, civil engineering, mining, roads, bridges and the building industry.
Readership/Target Audience: Aimed at contractors, end users, specifiers, manufacturers, rental companies and distributors of construction equipment, machines, services and solutions.
Other Features: Directory, jobs and classifieds.
BUSINESS: CONSTRUCTION

CONSTRUCTION NOW

1809324U4E-443

Editorial Address: Avian House, 87 Brook Street, Broughty Ferry, DUNDEE, DD5 1DJ **Tel:** 01382 427037
Fax: 01382 427006
Email: news@constructionnow.co.uk
Web site: http://www.constructionnow.co.uk
Date Launched: 2007
Frequency of update: 250 times a year
Website Access: Free
Traffic Figures: 40,000 Unique Users (Publisher's Statement)
Editor: Jonathan Brown; **Editor-in-Chief:** Jonathan Brown
Summary of Content: Electronic newsletter featuring construction news, planning applications, new housing developments, tenders and appointments.
Readership/Target Audience: Aimed at builders, architects, local authorities and housing associations.
BUSINESS: ARCHITECTURE & BUILDING: Building

CONSTRUCTION PRODUCTS INDUSTRY DIRECTORY

1818155U42A-242

Editorial Address: 18 Generator Hall, Electric Wharf, COVENTRY, CV1 4JL **Tel:** 0870 199 4044
Fax: 0870 777 4360
Email: enquiries@industrydirectory.co.uk
Web site: http://www.industrydirectory.co.uk/construction
Publisher: Simply Marcomms
Frequency of update: Daily
Website Access: Free
Editor: Kirstie Colledge
Summary of Content: Directory containing the latest news stories for the UK construction industry. Includes a news archive.
Readership/Target Audience: Aimed at professionals in the building and construction industry.
BUSINESS: CONSTRUCTION

CONTACTCENTREJOBS.CO.UK

1850115U14F-265

Editorial Address: 16 Rosewood Way, West End, WOKING, GU24 9PF **Tel:** 01296 857950
Email: lchuter@contactcentrelink.com
Web site: http://www.contactcentrejobs.co.uk
Publisher: Contact Centre Media Ltd
Frequency of update: Daily
Website Access: Free
Traffic Figures: 9,000 Unique Users (per month Publisher's Statement)
Editor: Louise Chuter
Summary of Content: Website covering recruitment in the call centre market.
Readership/Target Audience: Aimed at call centre managers and those looking for jobs in the call centre sector.
BUSINESS: COMMERCE, INDUSTRY & MANAGEMENT: Training & Recruitment

CONTACTCENTRELINK.COM

1646433U18B-1950

Editorial Address: The Paddock, 44 High Street, Cheddington, LEIGHTON BUZZARD, LU7 0RQ
Tel: 01296 660251
Email: paulskeldon@paulskeldon.com
Web site: http://www.contactcentrelink.com
Publisher: Contact Centre Media Ltd
Date Launched: 2003
Frequency of update: Weekly
Website Access: Free
Traffic Figures: 3,500 Unique Users (Publisher's Statement)
Editor: Paul Skeldon
Summary of Content: Electronically delivered newsletter covering contact centre industry news. Includes articles on technology, HR, training and recruitment.
Readership/Target Audience: Aimed at call centre managers.
BUSINESS: ELECTRONICS: Telecommunications

CONTENT MANAGEMENT 365

1665271U5C-909

Editorial Address: Ludgate House, 245 Blackfriars Road, LONDON, SE1 9UY **Tel:** 020 7955 3956 **Fax:** 020 7955 3945
Email: endaf.kerfoot@ubm.com
Web site: http://www.ubm.com
Publisher: United Business Media International Limited
Date Launched: 2003
Frequency of update: Daily
Website Access: Free
Traffic Figures: 27,000 Unique Users (Publisher's Statement)
Editor: Endaf Kerfoot
Summary of Content: Online exhibition concentrating on the web, enterprise content management, web content management, digital asset management and document management.
Readership/Target Audience: Aimed at those involved in assessing or buying any products or services related to content and document management.
Other Features: Archived white papers, case studies, press releases, regular bimonthly newsletters, buyers guide.
BUSINESS: COMPUTERS & AUTOMATION: Professional Personal Computers

CONTINGENCYTODAY.COM

1794292U54C-332

Formerly: Contingency Today
Editorial Address: PO Box 594, CAMBRIDGE, CB1 0FY
Tel: 07798 812253 **Fax:** 01223 279148
Email: jrush@contingencytoday.com
Web site: http://www.contingencytoday.com
Publisher: GEO:connexion Limited
Date Launched: 2007
Frequency of update: Daily. News updates daily, articles updated twice monthly
Website Access: Free
Editor: Jonathan Rush
Summary of Content: Web-based magazine focusing on Critical National Infrastructure protection and business continuity against industrial accidents, pandemics, climate change, floods, organised crime and terrorism.
Readership/Target Audience: Aimed at suppliers and decision makers engaged in emergency planning, disaster recovery and infrastructure protection.
Other Features: Archived articles and news items.
BUSINESS: SAFETY & SECURITY: Security

CONTINUITY CENTRAL

1633993U1R-355

Editorial Address: PO Box 1393, HUDDERSFIELD, HD1 9TN **Tel:** 01484 300750
Email: dhonour@continuitycentral.com
Web site: http://www.continuitycentral.com

Publisher: Portal Publishing Ltd
Date Launched: 2003
Frequency of update: Daily
Website Access: Free
Traffic Figures: 43,000 Unique Users (per month Publisher's Statement)
Editor: David Honour
Summary of Content: Website containing information for the business continuity management community and their suppliers with up-to-the-minute news and features.
Readership/Target Audience: Aimed at business continuity, disaster recovery, information security and business risk planners in the UK and US mainly.
BUSINESS: FINANCE & ECONOMICS: Financial Related

CONTRACTOR UK

711371U5B-57_10

Editorial Address: 1 Northumberland Avenue, LONDON, WC2N 5BW **Tel:** 020 7872 5448
Email: editor@contractoruk.com
Web site: http://www.contractoruk.com
Date Launched: 1998
Frequency of update: Daily
Website Access: Free
Editor: Helen James
Summary of Content: Website providing a wide range of information and news related to the IT industry. Includes an IT directory, insurance, mortgages, income protection, tax advice and information about IT training.
Readership/Target Audience: Aimed at IT contractors.
BUSINESS: COMPUTERS & AUTOMATION: Data Processing

CONVERGING MEDIA

624095U5E-473_50

Formerly: Broadband Markets
Editorial Address: Mortimer House, 37-41 Mortimer Street, LONDON, W1T 3JH **Tel:** 020 7017 5537
Email: steve.mullins@informa.com
Web site: http://www.informatm.com
Publisher: Informa Telecoms and Media Group
Date Launched: 2000
Frequency of update: 23 times a year
Website Access: Paid
Editor: Steve Mullins
Summary of Content: Online magazine covering global digital media content and digital convergence issues.
Readership/Target Audience: Aimed at studios, broadcasters, music companies, consultants, lawyers and investment bankers.
BUSINESS: COMPUTERS & AUTOMATION: Data Transmission

CORNWALL MATTERS

1881604U72J-347

Email: comments@cornwall-matters.co.uk
Web site: http://www.cornwall-matters.co.uk
Frequency of update: Daily
Summary of Content: Website created to help people who care about local issues. Whether you need access to useful information, want to highlight a particular topic to other people, discuss ideas with like-minded people or just show your support and keep up to date with current affairs in your area, Cornwall Matters is the place for you.
Readership/Target Audience: Aimed at residents in the local area of Cornwall.
LOCAL NEWSPAPERS: Community Newsletters

CORPORATE CLOTHING DIRECTOR-E

624192U47A-70

Editorial Address: South House 3A, Suite 4, Bond Estate, Bond Avenue, Bletchley, MILTON KEYNES, MK1 1SW
Tel: 0870 870 4578 **Fax:** 0870 870 4679
Email: hannah@director-e.com
Web site: http://www.director-e.com
Publisher: Marston Consulting Ltd TA director-e.com
Date Launched: 2000
Frequency of update: Daily
Website Access: Free
Traffic Figures: 92,000 Unique Users (per month Publisher's Statement)
Editor: Catherine Christie
Summary of Content: Online news and information service containing information relating to the corporate clothing and work wear industry including fabrics, work wear, PPE, school uniform, linings, designers, manufacturers, fastenings, accessories, packaging and transport.
Readership/Target Audience: Aimed at buyers and suppliers of corporate work wear clothing, PPE, footwear, promotional, equipment, fabric, technical, design, trends, manufacture and accessories.
BUSINESS: CLOTHING & TEXTILES

Internet Media

CORPORATE HOSPITALITY AND PARTY UPDATE
1810891U11A-225

Editorial Address: 29A Market Square, BIGGLESWADE, SG18 8AQ **Tel:** 01767 316255 **Fax:** 01767 316430
Email: info@eou.org.uk
Web site: http://www.eou.org.uk
Publisher: The Meetings Forum
Frequency of update: 6 times a year
Website Access: Free
Traffic Figures: 15,000 Unique Users (Publisher's Statement)
Editor: Peter Cotterell
Summary of Content: Electronic newsletter covering news and features about corporate entertainment and hospitality. Includes venues and events, catering, travel and diary.
Readership/Target Audience: Aimed at organisers of hospitality events and parties.
BUSINESS: CATERING: Catering, Hotels & Restaurants

CORPORATE REPORTS
626250U1A-81

Editorial Address: Technology Centre, Technology Drive, BATLEY, WF17 6ER **Tel:** 01924 500366 **Fax:** 01924 500355
Email: gwen@corpworld.co.uk
Web site: http://www.corpreports.co.uk
Publisher: NAK (UK) Limited
Date Launched: 1999
Frequency of update: Daily
Website Access: Paid
Traffic Figures: 19,000 Unique Users (per month Publisher's Statement)
Editor: Gwen Hawgate
Summary of Content: Website providing reports on ISPs, accounts and financial information.
Readership/Target Audience: Aimed at private investors, stockbrokers, relevant academics and accountants.
BUSINESS: FINANCE & ECONOMICS

COSMOPOLITAN.CO.UK
1789579U74A-1027

Editorial Address: National Magazine House, 72 Broadwick Street, LONDON, W1F 9EP **Tel:** 020 7439 5000
Email: info@cosmopolitan.co.uk
Web site: http://www.cosmopolitan.co.uk
Publisher: National Magazine Company Ltd
Frequency of update: Daily
Website Access: Free
Traffic Figures: 802,080 Unique Users (per month Publisher's Statement)
Editor: Bridget March
Summary of Content: Website covering fashion, beauty, relationships, travel and work as well as an online community.
Readership/Target Audience: Aimed at young professional women.
CONSUMER: WOMEN'S INTEREST CONSUMER MAGAZINES: Women's Interest

COSTAR GROUP
35201U1E-330

Formerly: Focus
Editorial Address: 10 Great Pulteney Street, LONDON, W1F 9NB **Tel:** 020 3214 0100 **Fax:** 020 3214 0126
Email: deals@costar.co.uk
Web site: http://www.costar.co.uk
Publisher: CoStar Ltd
Date Launched: 1984
Frequency of update: Daily
Website Access: Paid
Traffic Figures: 17,000 Unique Users (Publisher's Statement)
Editor: Caterina Rigoni
Summary of Content: Website providing an information service dealing with commercial property.
Readership/Target Audience: Aimed at commercial property professionals.
BUSINESS: FINANCE & ECONOMICS: Property

COUNTRY LIFE ONLINE
626149U80A-80_1

Editorial Address: Blue Fin Building, 110 Southwark Street, LONDON, SE1 0SU **Tel:** 020 3148 5000 **Fax:** 020 7261 5145
Email: countrylife@ipcmedia.com
Web site: http://www.countrylife.co.uk
Publisher: IPC Inspire
Date Launched: 1999
Frequency of update: Daily
Website Access: Free
Traffic Figures: 100,000 Unique Users (per month Publisher's Statement)
Editor: Mark Hedges
Summary of Content: Website featuring articles on the environment, wildlife and field sports, architecture, fine arts and antiques, an online property search for anyone looking to move to the country or buy a second home in the UK or abroad.
Readership/Target Audience: Aimed at 35 to 55 year olds who live in or have an interest in the countryside.
Other Features: Features include chat forums, an email newsletter and archiving.
CONSUMER: RURAL & REGIONAL INTEREST: Rural Interest

COUNTRY LIVING
1902873U74-2011

Editorial Address: 72 Broadwick Street, LONDON, W1F 9EP **Tel:** 020 7439 5000
Email: country.living@natmags.co.uk
Web site: http://www.allaboutyou.com
Publisher: Hearst Digital
Frequency of update: Daily
Website Access: Free
Editor: Bernadette Fallon
Summary of Content: Website covering homes, interiors and lifestyle features.
Readership/Target Audience: Aimed at women of all ages.
CONSUMER: WOMEN'S INTEREST CONSUMER MAGAZINES

COUNTRYDOCTOR.CO.UK
40154U56A-59_40

Formerly: Country Doctor
Editorial Address: 17 Symonds Road, HITCHIN, SG5 2JJ **Tel:** 01462 434515
Email: davidroberts@doctors.org.uk
Web site: http://www.countrydoctor.co.uk
Publisher: Country Doctor
Date Launched: 2000
Frequency of update: Daily
Website Access: Free
Editor: David Roberts; **Web Editor:** David Roberts
Summary of Content: Website focusing on all issues relating to medical practice especially in country areas, plus entertainment, travel, politics, finance and law, books, music and CD-Rom reviews, motoring, new product launches and trials, medical equipment, dispensing ethical and OTC products and clinical.
Readership/Target Audience: Read by NHS managers, politicians, doctors and GPs and staff in rural areas, and doctors living and working abroad. Also open to lay readers.
BUSINESS: HEALTH & MEDICAL

THE COUNTRYSIDE ALLIANCE
711785U80A-170

Formerly: countryside-alliance.org
Editorial Address: 367 Kennington Road, LONDON, SE11 4PT **Tel:** 020 7840 9220 **Fax:** 020 7793 8899
Email: info@countryside-alliance.org.uk
Web site: http://www.countryside-alliance.org.uk
Publisher: Countryside Alliance
Date Launched: 2000
Frequency of update: Daily
Website Access: Free
Editor: Jill Grieve
Summary of Content: Website containing general political and campaigning news relevant to the countryside and rural people.
Readership/Target Audience: Aimed at those interested in the countryside.
Other Features: Features include an e-mail newsletter, an events calendar, daily national and regional news stories, recruitment and archiving.
CONSUMER: RURAL & REGIONAL INTEREST: Rural Interest

COUNTY DURHAM MATTERS
1881605U72J-348

Email: comments@countydurham-matters.co.uk
Web site: http://www.countydurham-matters.co.uk
Frequency of update: Daily
Summary of Content: Website created to help people who care about local issues. Whether you need access to useful information, want to highlight a particular topic to other people, discuss ideas with like-minded people or just show your support and keep up to date with current affairs in your area, County Durham Matters is the place for you.
Readership/Target Audience: Aimed at residents in the local area of County Durham.
LOCAL NEWSPAPERS: Community Newsletters

COVENTRYTELEGRAPH.NET
707262U80C-3498

Formerly: icCoventry.co.uk
Editorial Address: PO Box 34, COVENTRY, CV1 1FP **Tel:** 024 7663 3633
Email: news@coventrytelegraph.net
Web site: http://www.coventrytelegraph.net
Date Launched: 2001
Frequency of update: Daily
Website Access: Free
Traffic Figures: 208,088 Unique Users (01/07/2008 To 31/12/2008 ABC/Electronic)
Editor: Martin Smith
Summary of Content: Website focusing on the latest news, sports, weather, TV and radio listings for the Coventry area.
Readership/Target Audience: Aimed at those living in and around the local area.
Other Features: Features include discussion forums, an e-mail newsletter, recruitment, an events calendar and archiving.
CONSUMER: RURAL & REGIONAL INTEREST: Regional Interest English Counties

CRAFTBUBBLE.COM
1864118U74E-709

Editorial Address: 9th Floor, Tower House, Fairfax Street, BRISTOL, BS1 3BN **Tel:** 0117 927 9009 **Fax:** 0117 934 9008
Email: annadavenport@originpublishing.co.uk
Web site: http://www.craftbubble.com
Publisher: Origin Publishing Ltd
Date Launched: 2008
Frequency of update: Daily
Website Access: Free
Editor: Anna Davenport
Summary of Content: Social networking website for craft enthusiasts to share their knowledge, meet fellow crafters and display their work.
Readership/Target Audience: Aimed at crafters from all disciplines looking to meet like minded crafters.
CONSUMER: WOMEN'S INTEREST CONSUMER MAGAZINES: Crafts

CRASH.NET
1648537U77D-468

Editorial Address: No 1 Silverstone Innovation Centre, Silverstone Circuit, SILVERSTONE, NN12 8GX **Tel:** 0870 350 5044 **Fax:** 0870 350 5088
Email: press@crash.net
Web site: http://www.crash.net
Publisher: Crash Media Group Ltd
Date Launched: 1996
Frequency of update: Daily
Website Access: Free
Traffic Figures: 1,000,000 Unique Users (per month Publisher's Statement)
Editor: Craig Llewellyn
Summary of Content: Global motor sport portal covering all forms of motor sport, including F1, WRC, MOTO GP, NASCAR, WSBK, BSB, BTCC and world super bikes.
Readership/Target Audience: Aimed at motor sports enthusiasts, motor sport professionals and those in the motor sports industry.
Other Features: Live news, images, Internet radio station, Babe.
CONSUMER: MOTORING & CYCLING: Motor Sports

CRAWLEY TODAY
629711U67B-190

Editorial Address: 12 The Boulevard, CRAWLEY, RH10 1XY **Tel:** 01293 562929 **Fax:** 01293 615589
Email: kirk.ward@sussexnewspapers.co.uk
Web site: http://www.crawleyobserver.co.uk
Frequency of update: Daily
Website Access: Free
Traffic Figures: 12,000 Unique Users (per month Publisher's Statement)
Editor: Kirk Ward
Summary of Content: Website containing news, sport, information and features about Crawley.
Readership/Target Audience: Read by residents and visitors to the local area.
Other Features: Features include recruitment and chat forums.
REGIONAL DAILY & SUNDAY NEWSPAPERS: Regional Daily Newspapers

CREATIVEMATCH
1623513U2A-664

Editorial Address: Building 3, Chiswick Park, 566 Chiswick High Road, LONDON, W4 5YA **Tel:** 0845 676 2250 **Fax:** 0845 676 2251
Email: editor@creativematch.co.uk
Web site: http://www.creativematch.co.uk
Publisher: Creativematch
Date Launched: 1996
Frequency of update: Daily
Website Access: Free (Publisher's Statement)
Editor: Mark Lesbirel
Summary of Content: Website focusing on the UK creative industry. Covers design, advertising, marketing, new media, PR, film, video and sound.

Readership/Target Audience: Aimed at those involved within creative organisations.
BUSINESS: COMMUNICATIONS, ADVERTISING & MARKETING

CREWECHRONICLE.CO.UK   1902250U72B-4162

Editorial Address: 32-34 Victoria Street, CREWE, CW1 2JE
Tel: 01270 255733
Email: crewe.news@cheshirenews.co.uk
Web site: http://www.crewechronicle.co.uk
Frequency of update: Daily
Website Access: Free
Editor: James Shepherd
Summary of Content: Website featuring local news and information.
Readership/Target Audience: Aimed at residents of the Crewe area.
LOCAL NEWSPAPERS: Local Newspapers English Counties

CRICINFO   626393U75K-30

Formerly: Wisden Cricinfo
Editorial Address: 3 Queen Caroline Street, Hammersmith, LONDON, W6 9PE **Tel:** 020 8222 1665
Email: andrew.miller@cricinfo.com
Web site: http://www.cricinfo.com
Publisher: Cricinfo
Date Launched: 1994
Frequency of update: Daily
Website Access: Free
Traffic Figures: 171,329 Unique Users (per month ABC/Electronic)
Editor: Andrew Miller
Summary of Content: Website covering news, information and features on cricket for the following countries: Australia, India, Pakistan, England, South Africa and the USA.
Readership/Target Audience: Aimed at cricket fans.
Other Features: Features include live coverage, a cricket shop, classifieds, a chat forum and archiving.
CONSUMER: SPORT: Cricket

CRICKET WORLD   712391U75K-43

Formerly: Cricket World.com
Editorial Address: 24-26 London Road, GRANTHAM, NG31 6EJ **Tel:** 01476 565569 **Fax:** 01476 572901
Email: as@cricketworld.com
Web site: http://www.cricketworld.com
Publisher: Cricket World Media Ltd
Date Launched: 1996
Frequency of update: Daily
Website Access: Free
Traffic Figures: 400,000 Unique Users (per month Publisher's Statement)
Editor: Alastair Symondson
Summary of Content: Website covering the cricket world. Includes news, reviews, women's cricket, youth and school cricket, laws, umpires and coaching.
Readership/Target Audience: Aimed at both male and female, active or armchair cricketers of all ages.
CONSUMER: SPORT: Cricket

CRIMESQUAD.COM   1667947U84B-362

Editorial Address: 82 Kenton Avenue, SUNBURY-ON-THAMES, TW16 5AR **Tel:** 01932 787373
Email: crimeonline@crimesquad.com
Web site: http://www.crimesquad.com
Date Launched: 2005
Frequency of update: Monthly
Website Access: Free
Editor: Chris Simmons
Summary of Content: Website reviewing crime fiction highlighting an author of the month and new crime fiction writers.
Readership/Target Audience: Aimed at crime fiction fans.
CONSUMER: THE ARTS & LITERARY: Literary

CRONER'S EMPLOYMENT CASE LAW INDEX   39265U44-469

Editorial Address: 145 London Road, KINGSTON UPON THAMES, KT2 6SR **Tel:** 020 8547 3333 **Fax:** 020 8547 2637
Email: john.herbert@croner.co.uk
Web site: http://www.croner.co.uk
Publisher: Wolters Kluwer (UK) Ltd
Frequency of update: Weekly
Website Access: Paid
Editor: John Herbert
Summary of Content: A summary of employment law cases in the UK.

Readership/Target Audience: Aimed at employment law professionals and lawyers.
BUSINESS: LEGAL

CROSS RHYTHMS ONLINE   626129U76D-310_50

Editorial Address: PO Box 1110, STOKE-ON-TRENT, ST1 1XR **Tel:** 0870 011 8008 **Fax:** 0870 011 7002
Email: admin@crossrhythms.co.uk
Web site: http://www.crossrhythms.co.uk
Publisher: Cross Rhythms
Date Launched: 1998
Frequency of update: Daily
Website Access: Free
Traffic Figures: 180,000 Unique Users (per month Publisher's Statement)
Editor: Heather Bellamy; **Web Editor:** Heather Bellamy
Summary of Content: Website focusing on contemporary Christian music with music reviews, news, articles and events info, plus an online radio station with webcam, chat room and an online shop. Includes prayer rooms, life articles and also weekly emailed Bible Studies written by national youth leaders.
Readership/Target Audience: Aimed at people interested in Christian music with emphasis on the United Kingdom and young people.
Other Features: Features include discussion forums and an e-mail newsletter.
CONSUMER: MUSIC & PERFORMING ARTS: Music

CROYDON MATTERS   1881606U72J-349

Email: comments@croydon-matters.co.uk
Web site: http://www.croydon-matters.co.uk
Frequency of update: Daily
Summary of Content: Website created to help people who care about local issues. Whether you need access to useful information, want to highlight a particular topic to other people, discuss ideas with like-minded people or just show your support and keep up to date with current affairs in your area, Croydon Matters is the place for you.
Readership/Target Audience: Aimed at residents in the local area of Croydon.
LOCAL NEWSPAPERS: Community Newsletters

THE CULINARY GUIDE   1692151U74P-929

Editorial Address: 4 Kemp House, Sewardstone Road, LONDON, E2 9JL **Tel:** 020 8980 8635
Email: ed@theculinaryguide.co.uk
Web site: http://www.theculinaryguide.co.uk
Publisher: Create UK
Date Launched: 2005
Frequency of update: Daily
Website Access: Free
Traffic Figures: 234,000 Unique Users (per month Publisher's Statement)
Editor: Tim Hirschmann
Summary of Content: Website covering food, drink and travel with recipes, restaurant reviews, hotel reviews, in depth travel features, food, drink and travel news, kitchenware and appliances, book reviews and competitions.
Readership/Target Audience: Aimed at affluent 25 to 40 year olds with a contemporary attitude towards food, drink and travel.
CONSUMER: WOMEN'S INTEREST CONSUMER MAGAZINES: Food & Cookery

CULTURE 24   1696195U84A-450

Formerly: 24 Hour Museum
Editorial Address: Office 4, 28 Kensington Street, BRIGHTON, BN1 4AJ **Tel:** 01273 623266
Email: newsdesk@culture24.org.uk
Web site: http://www.24hourmuseum.org.uk
Date Launched: 1999
Frequency of update: Daily
Website Access: Free
Traffic Figures: 300,000 Unique Users (per month Publisher's Statement)
Editor: Richard Moss
Summary of Content: Website covering the UK's museums, galleries and heritage attractions with arts and museums news and exhibition reviews.
Readership/Target Audience: Aimed at those interested in culture.
CONSUMER: THE ARTS & LITERARY: Arts

CUMBERLAND & WESTMORLAND HERALD ONLINE   629289U72B-608

Editorial Address: 14 King Street, PENRITH, CA11 7AH
Tel: 01768 862313 **Fax:** 01768 890363
Email: lizs@cwherald.com

Web site: http://www.cwherald.com
Publisher: Cumberland & Westmorland Herald
Date Launched: 1860
Frequency of update: Weekly
Website Access: Free
Editor: Colin Maughan
Summary of Content: Website focusing on news and information about Cumbria.
Readership/Target Audience: Aimed at residents in the Lake District area.
Other Features: Features include archiving.
LOCAL NEWSPAPERS: Local Newspapers English Counties

CUMBRIA MATTERS   1881607U72J-350

Email: comments@cumbria-matters.co.uk
Web site: http://www.cumbria-matters.co.uk
Frequency of update: Daily
Summary of Content: Website created to help people who care about local issues. Whether you need access to useful information, want to highlight a particular topic to other people, discuss ideas with like-minded people or just show your support and keep up to date with current affairs in your area, Cumbria Matters is the place for you.
Readership/Target Audience: Aimed at residents in the local area of Cumbria.
LOCAL NEWSPAPERS: Community Newsletters

CURRENT ARCHAEOLOGY   626231U94X-263

Editorial Address: Lamb House, Church Street, LONDON, W4 2PD **Tel:** 0845 644 7707 **Fax:** 0845 644 7708
Email: editor@archaeology.co.uk
Web site: http://www.archaeology.co.uk
Publisher: Current Publishing
Date Launched: 1995
Frequency of update: Daily
Website Access: Free
Editor: Andrew Selkirk
Summary of Content: Website covering developments in the world of archaeology.
Readership/Target Audience: Aimed at all those interested in archaeology.
Other Features: Features include an online directory of UK archaeology and archiving.
CONSUMER: OTHER CLASSIFICATIONS: Miscellaneous

CWN   711844U89C-129_25

Editorial Address: Pant Y Nos, Llanfair Clydogau, LAMPETER, SA48 8LH **Tel:** 0845 166 1366
Fax: 0845 166 1365
Email: editor@cwn.org.uk
Web site: http://www.cwn.org.uk
Date Launched: 1995
Frequency of update: Daily
Website Access: Free
Traffic Figures: 125,000 Unique Users (per month Publisher's Statement)
Editor: Chris Studman
Summary of Content: Website featuring news, information and what's on listings in Coventry and Warwickshire. Includes articles on sport, heritage, education, health, politics, crime, environment, business, tourism, motoring and religion.
Readership/Target Audience: Aimed at those living in, or with an interest in Coventry and Warwickshire.
Other Features: Features include recruitment and a chat forum.
CONSUMER: HOLIDAYS & TRAVEL: Entertainment Guides

DADS SPACE   1849780U74D-672

Editorial Address: 44-48 Wharf Road, LONDON, N1 7UX
Tel: 020 7490 8789
Email: editor@dads-space.com
Web site: http://www.dads-space.com
Publisher: BDP Media
Date Launched: 2008
Frequency of update: Daily
Website Access: Free
Editor: Jon Hamblin
Summary of Content: Website with help and advice for fathers as well as covering fun, entertainment, reviews of books, films and music, news and celebrity interviews.
Readership/Target Audience: Aimed at dads of children of all ages.
Other Features: Other features include newsletter, mailing list, message board, help desk and buyers guides.
CONSUMER: WOMEN'S INTEREST CONSUMER MAGAZINES: Child Care

Internet Media

THE DAILY DEAL
1812701U1A-341

Editorial Address: 107-111 Fleet Street, LONDON, EC4A 2AB **Tel:** 020 7936 9037
Email: lboard@thedeal.com
Web site: http://www.thedeal.com
Publisher: The Deal
Frequency of update: Daily
Website Access: Paid
Editor: Laura Board
Summary of Content: Electronic newsletter covering mergers, acquisitions, stock market flotations, private equity and venture capital transactions.
Readership/Target Audience: Aimed at investment bankers, corporate lawyers, venture capitalists, fund managers and board-level corporate executives.
BUSINESS: FINANCE & ECONOMICS

DAILY MAIL ONLINE
622752U65A-9001

Formerly: dailymail.co.uk
Editorial Address: Northcliffe House, 2 Derry Street, LONDON, W8 5TT **Tel:** 020 7938 6000
Email: websiteeditorial@dailymail.co.uk
Web site: http://www.dailymail.co.uk
Publisher: Associated Newspapers Ltd
Date Launched: 2001
Frequency of update: Daily
Website Access: Free
Traffic Figures: 21,842,107 Unique Users (01/02/2009 To 28/02/2009 ABC/Electronic)
Editor: Danny Groom
Summary of Content: Website covering news, sport, show-biz, finance, health, beauty, fashion, children, careers, homes, food, travel, shopping, reader comments and relationships.
Twitter: http://twitter.com/mailonline.
NATIONAL DAILY & SUNDAY NEWSPAPERS: National Daily Newspapers

DAILY RECORD DIGITAL
1656089U67B-9006

Editorial Address: 1 Central Quay, GLASGOW, G3 8DA
Tel: 0141 309 1460 **Fax:** 0141 309 3202
Email: webeditor@dailyrecord.co.uk
Web site: http://www.dailyrecord.co.uk
Publisher: Scottish Daily Record & Sunday Mail Ltd
Frequency of update: Daily
Website Access: Free
Traffic Figures: 400,000 Unique Users (Publisher's Statement)
Summary of Content: Daily Scottish news and sports coverage.
Other Features: Message boards, polls, games, shopping, readers offers and past month news archive.
REGIONAL DAILY & SUNDAY NEWSPAPERS: Regional Daily Newspapers

THE DAILY SAIL
628916U91A-75

Formerly: Madforsailing.com
Editorial Address: Unit 15, Upper Floor, Hamble Yacht Services, Port Hamble Marina, LONDON, S031 4NN
Tel: 023 8045 6997
Email: news@thedailysail.com
Web site: http://www.thedailysail.com
Publisher: Sailing Media Ltd.
Date Launched: 2000
Frequency of update: Daily. Updated 20 times a day
Website Access: Paid
Traffic Figures: 45,000 Unique Users (per month Publisher's Statement)
Editor: James Boyd
Summary of Content: Website covering news, features and photographs about performance yacht and dinghy racing in the UK and abroad.
Readership/Target Audience: Aimed at performance sailors and sailing enthusiasts globally.
Other Features: Features include experts discussion forums, a weekly pdf newsletter, an events calendar and archiving.
CONSUMER: RECREATION & LEISURE: Boating & Yachting

DAILY STAR ONLINE
1829838U65A-9003

Formerly: dailystar.co.uk
Editorial Address: The Northern & Shell Building, 10 Lower Thames Street, LONDON, EC3R 6EN **Tel:** 0871 434 1010
Email: web.help@dailystar.co.uk
Web site: http://www.dailystar.co.uk
Publisher: Express Newspapers Ltd
Frequency of update: Daily
Website Access: Free
Editor: Geoff Marsh

Summary of Content: Website of the Daily Star, featuring news stories, show-biz news and sport.
Twitter: http://twitter.com/daily_star.
NATIONAL DAILY & SUNDAY NEWSPAPERS: National Daily Newspapers

DAILYCANDY.COM
1743333U74B-731

Editorial Address: Unit 238, 22 Notting Hill Gate, LONDON, W11 3JE
Email: mdalamal@dailycandy.com
Web site: http://www.dailycandy.com
Date Launched: 2005
Frequency of update: 260 times a year
Website Access: Free
Traffic Figures: 2,600,000 Unique Users (per day Publisher's Statement)
Editor: Malika Dalamal
Summary of Content: Electronic newsletter covering fashion, beauty, food, travel, services and fun.
Readership/Target Audience: Aimed at all ages looking for insider news.
CONSUMER: WOMEN'S INTEREST CONSUMER MAGAZINES: Women's Interest - Fashion

DAILY/SUNDAY EXPRESS ONLINE
1813130U65A-9002

Formerly: Daily Express Online
Editorial Address: The Northern & Shell Building, 10 Lower Thames Street, LONDON, EC3R 6EN **Tel:** 020 8612 7783
Fax: 0871 434 2723
Email: web.help@express.co.uk
Web site: http://www.express.co.uk
Publisher: Express Newspapers Ltd
Frequency of update: Daily
Website Access: Free
Traffic Figures: 750,000 Unique Users (per month Publisher's Statement)
Editor: Geoff Marsh
Summary of Content: Website with breaking news, sport and showbiz from London-based newspaper.
Twitter: http://twitter.com/daily_express.
NATIONAL DAILY & SUNDAY NEWSPAPERS: National Daily Newspapers

DATA INSTALLER & SPECIFIER
1814453U18A-9037

Editorial Address: PR by email only
Email: info@data-installer.co.uk
Web site: http://www.data-installer.co.uk
Date Launched: 2007
Frequency of update: Daily
Website Access: Free
Traffic Figures: 2,000 Unique Users (Publisher's Statement)
Editor: D. Bryans
Summary of Content: Website focusing on data installers and specifiers including telecoms, fibre optics, VOIP, cable management, copper cabling, data centre, UPS and voice systems.
Readership/Target Audience: Aimed at professionals in the data installer, specifier and telecoms market.
Other Features: Produce and email newsletter.
BUSINESS: ELECTRONICS

DATACENTRE TIMES
1895117U5E-9008

Editorial Address: 15 Ravens Close, Knaphill, WOKING, GU21 2LD **Tel:** 01483 888378
Email: editor@datacentretimes.com
Web site: http://www.datacentretimes.com
Publisher: Synonym Ltd
Date Launched: 2008
Frequency of update: Daily
Website Access: Free
Traffic Figures: 5,500 Unique Users (per month Publisher's Statement)
Editor: Ian Murphy
Summary of Content: Website looking at all the technologies used in the datacentre, Includes news and articles about servers, operating systems, applications and rack systems, power and coding, ITSM and any other technology used in the datacentre.
Readership/Target Audience: Aimed at both vendors and IT departments.
BUSINESS: COMPUTERS & AUTOMATION: Data Transmission

DAVENTRY TODAY.CO.UK
633951U67B-205

Formerly: DAVENTRY EXPRESS.CO.UK
Editorial Address: 63 High Street, DAVENTRY, NN11 4BQ
Tel: 01327 703383 **Fax:** 01327 300416

Email: editorial@daventryexpress.co.uk
Web site: http://www.daventrytoday.co.uk
Publisher: Central Counties Newspapers South Ltd
Date Launched: 1998
Frequency of update: Daily
Website Access: Free
Traffic Figures: 10,041 Unique Users (per month WebTrends)
Editor: Chris Lillington
Summary of Content: Website containing news and information about the local area. Also includes a unique property search, motors, weddings and family announcements.
Readership/Target Audience: Read by local residents, visitors and expatriates.
Other Features: Features include an events calendar, recruitment, a chat forum and archiving.
REGIONAL DAILY & SUNDAY NEWSPAPERS: Regional Daily Newspapers

DAY TRIPPER
626275U89A-110

Editorial Address: 239 Stoke Newington, Church Street, LONDON, N16 9HP **Tel:** 020 7254 7772
Email: drash05@day-tripper.net
Web site: http://www.day-tripper.net
Publisher: Day Tripper
Date Launched: 1999
Frequency of update: Daily
Website Access: Free
Traffic Figures: 160,000 Unique Users (per month Publisher's Statement)
Editor: David Ash; **Webmaster:** David Ash
Summary of Content: Website covering news and information for shoppers and visitors to Calais and the Channel ports in France as well as Belgium.
Readership/Target Audience: Aimed at shoppers and tourists to Calais, Northern France and Belgium, as well as along the channel coast.
Other Features: Features include an e-mail newsletter.
CONSUMER: HOLIDAYS & TRAVEL: Travel

DAZED DIGITAL
1793310U76D-832

Editorial Address: 112-116 Old Street, LONDON, EC1V 9BG **Tel:** 020 7336 0766 **Fax:** 020 7336 0966
Email: info@dazeddigital.com
Web site: http://www.DazedDigital.com
Publisher: Waddell Ltd
Date Launched: 2006
Frequency of update: Daily
Website Access: Free
Editor: Susanna Lau
Summary of Content: Website covering art, fashion, books, film, music, events and ideas.
Readership/Target Audience: Aimed at 16 to 35 year old trend-setting, early adopters who influence their peer group.
Other Features: Have a weekly email newsletter.
CONSUMER: MUSIC & PERFORMING ARTS: Music

DEALREPORTER
1849139U1F-649

Editorial Address: 80 Strand, LONDON, WC2R 0RL
Tel: 020 7059 6100 **Fax:** 020 7059 6101
Email: ben.smith@mergermarket.com
Web site: http://www.dealreporter.com
Frequency of update: Daily
Website Access: Paid
Traffic Figures: 20,000 Unique Users (per day Publisher's Statement)
Editor: Ben Smith
Summary of Content: Online news, intelligence and data service.
Readership/Target Audience: Aimed at the investment market.
BUSINESS: FINANCE & ECONOMICS: Investment

DEBTWATCHDOG.CO.UK
1819082U74M-429

Editorial Address: 15 Livingston Lane, Cambuslang, GLASGOW, G72 8ST **Tel:** 0141 646 0847
Email: george.c@debtwatchdog.com
Web site: http://www.debtwatchdog.com
Date Launched: 2007
Frequency of update: Daily
Website Access: Free
Traffic Figures: 3,000 Unique Users (Publisher's Statement)
Editor: George Currie
Summary of Content: Website covering all issues surrounding debt and exploring avenues for resolving debt problems including debt consolidation, debt management, IVA, bankruptcy, protected trust deeds and sequestration as well as money saving tips, news and debt forums.

Readership/Target Audience: Aimed at those with debt problem and those wishing to control their spending.
CONSUMER: WOMEN'S INTEREST CONSUMER MAGAZINES: Personal Finance

DEFENSEFILE
1809949U40-439

Editorial Address: PR by email only
Email: info@defensefile.com
Web site: http://www.defensefile.com
Publisher: H40 Ltd
Date Launched: 2007
Frequency of update: Daily
Website Access: Free
Editor: Jerry Osborne
Summary of Content: Website covering aerospace, marine and navy, land, manufacturing, services for the defence industry, personnel and backup equipment. Features news and product announcements.
Readership/Target Audience: Aimed at procurement executives and others involved in specifying and purchasing defence-related goods and services.
BUSINESS: DEFENCE

DEHAVILLAND
626155U82-13_40

Editorial Address: Greater London House, Hampstead Road, LONDON, NW1 7EJ **Tel:** 020 7728 4410
Email: newsdesk@dehavilland.co.uk
Web site: http://www.dehavilland.co.uk
Publisher: DeHavilland
Date Launched: 1997
Frequency of update: Daily
Website Access: Paid
Editor: David Bowers; **Web Editor:** Jonathan Blanks
Summary of Content: Website providing complete political government and current affairs information to the desktops of customers, via their proprietary Internet enabled system.
Readership/Target Audience: Aimed at public affairs professionals.
CONSUMER: CURRENT AFFAIRS & POLITICS

DEMOLITION INDUSTRY DIRECTORY
1818156U42A-243

Editorial Address: 18 Generator Hall, Electric Wharf, COVENTRY, CV1 4JL **Tel:** 0870 199 4044
Fax: 0870 777 4360
Email: enquiries@industrydirectory.co.uk
Web site: http://www.industrydirectory.co.uk/demolition
Publisher: Simply Marcomms
Frequency of update: Daily
Website Access: Free
Editor: Kirstie Colledge
Summary of Content: Directory containing the latest news stories for the UK demolition industry.
Readership/Target Audience: Aimed at professionals in the building and construction industry particularly those in demolition.
BUSINESS: CONSTRUCTION

DENTAL PRODUCTS REPORT EUROPE
1847240U56D-206

Editorial Address: Advanstar House, Park West, Sealand Road, CHESTER, CH1 4RN **Tel:** 01244 378888
Fax: 01244 370011
Email: pbrook@advanstar.com
Web site: http://www.dpreurope.com
Publisher: Advanstar Communications (U.K.) Ltd
Date Launched: 1981
Frequency of update: Weekly. Newsletter is updated weekly, website is update every other day
Website Access: Paid
Traffic Figures: 9,000 Unique Users (Publisher's Statement)
Editor: Pamela Brook
Summary of Content: Website and e-newsletter featuring new products, exhibition news and instruction on techniques for using materials, instruments and equipment.
Readership/Target Audience: Aimed at dentists throughout Europe.
BUSINESS: HEALTH & MEDICAL: Dental

DENTISTRY.CO.UK
1911125U56D-208

Editorial Address: 1 Hertford House, Hugo Gryn Way, Farm Close, SHENLEY, WD7 9AB **Tel:** 01923 851777
Fax: 01923 851778
Email: info@dentistry.co.uk
Web site: http://www.dentistry.co.uk
Publisher: Finlayson Media Communications Ltd
Frequency of update: Daily
Website Access: Free
Editor: Guy Hiscott

Summary of Content: Website covering all aspects of the dental industry, including product updates and practical information.
Readership/Target Audience: Aimed at anyone associated with the dental industry.
BUSINESS: HEALTH & MEDICAL: Dental

DERBYSHIRE MATTERS
1881608U72J-351

Email: comments@derbyshire-matters.co.uk
Web site: http://www.derbyshire-matters.co.uk
Frequency of update: Daily
Summary of Content: Website created to help people who care about local issues. Whether you need access to useful information, want to highlight a particular topic to other people, discuss ideas with like-minded people or just show your support and keep up to date with current affairs in your area, Derbyshire Matters is the place for you.
Readership/Target Audience: Aimed at residents in the local area of Derbyshire.
LOCAL NEWSPAPERS: Community Newsletters

DERBYSHIRE TIMES
629795U72B-711

Formerly: Chesterfield Today
Editorial Address: Station Road, CHESTERFIELD, S41 7XD
Tel: 01246 504500 **Fax:** 01246 504579
Email: editorial@derbyshiretimes.co.uk
Web site: http://www.derbyshiretimes.co.uk
Frequency of update: 260 times a year
Website Access: Free
Editor: Mike Wilson
Summary of Content: Website containing news, sport, information and features about Derbyshire.
Readership/Target Audience: Read by residents and visitors to the local area.
Other Features: Features include recruitment and discussion forums.
LOCAL NEWSPAPERS: Local Newspapers English Counties

DERRY MATTERS
1881609U72J-352

Email: comments@derry-matters.co.uk
Web site: http://www.derry-matters.co.uk
Frequency of update: Daily
Summary of Content: Website created to help people who care about local issues. Whether you need access to useful information, want to highlight a particular topic to other people, discuss ideas with like-minded people or just show your support and keep up to date with current affairs in your area, Derry Matters is the place for you.
Readership/Target Audience: Aimed at residents in the local area of Derry.
LOCAL NEWSPAPERS: Community Newsletters

DESIGN & INNOVATION NEWS WIRE
37148U14J-70

Formerly: Design News Wire
Editorial Address: 9 Pavilion Parade, BRIGHTON, BN2 1RA
Tel: 01273 621378 **Fax:** 01273 622144
Email: info@britishdesigninnovation.org
Web site: http://www.britishdesigninnovation.org
Publisher: British Design Innovation
Date Launched: 1993
Frequency of update: Daily
Website Access: Free
Traffic Figures: 700,000 Unique Users (per year Publisher's Statement)
Editor: Maxine Horn
Summary of Content: Website focusing on all aspects of the design and innovation industry and its influence on business and export success.
Readership/Target Audience: Aimed at commercial design buyers, government, creative industries' policy makers and international trade advisors, universities, executives in design companies, art and design faculties and their graduates.
BUSINESS: COMMERCE, INDUSTRY & MANAGEMENT: Commercial Design

DESIGN WEEK
1867682U14J-553

Editorial Address: St Giles House, 50 Poland Street, LONDON, W1F 7AX **Tel:** 020 7970 4000 **Fax:** 020 7970 6730
Email: angus.montgomery@centaur.co.uk
Web site: http://www.designweek.co.uk
Publisher: Centaur Communications Ltd
Frequency of update: Daily
Website Access: Free
Editor: Angus Montgomery
Summary of Content: Website offering a broad range of news and features about the design industry.

Readership/Target Audience: Aimed at those in retail, graphic, product and interior design, both practising designers and clients.
BUSINESS: COMMERCE, INDUSTRY & MANAGEMENT: Commercial Design

DESIGNBUILD-NETWORK.COM
1689911U4A-312

Formerly: Intelligent Design and Build Innovations
Editorial Address: Brunel House, 55-57 North Wharf Road, LONDON, W2 1LA **Tel:** 020 7915 9600
Email: christopherkanal@spgmedia.com
Web site: http://www.designbuild-network.com
Publisher: SPG Media Ltd
Frequency of update: Daily
Website Access: Paid
Editor: Christopher Kanal
Summary of Content: Magazine focusing on architecture, interior design and construction.
Readership/Target Audience: Aimed at architects, building engineers, building surveyors, contractors and quantity surveyors.
BUSINESS: ARCHITECTURE & BUILDING: Architecture

DESIGNLIFE.TV
1849965U4B-190

Editorial Address: Studio 25, Royal Victoria Patriotic Building, Fitzhugh Grove, LONDON, SW18 3SX
Tel: 07716 723787
Email: jane@designlife.tv
Web site: http://www.designlife.tv
Date Launched: 2008
Frequency of update: Quarterly
Website Access: Free
Traffic Figures: 8,000 Unique Users (Publisher's Statement)
Editor: Jane Moriarty
Summary of Content: Website featuring interior design and architecture exhibitions and events, profiles of product areas. Each issue features an interior designer, architect and overseas project. Images are available for presentations.
Readership/Target Audience: Aimed at designers, retailers, manufacturers, architects and members of RIBA.
Other Features: Archiving
BUSINESS: ARCHITECTURE & BUILDING: Interior Design & Flooring

DEVON MATTERS
1881610U72J-353

Email: comments@devon-matters.co.uk
Web site: http://www.devon-matters.co.uk
Frequency of update: Daily
Summary of Content: Website created to help people who care about local issues. Whether you need access to useful information, want to highlight a particular topic to other people, discuss ideas with like-minded people or just show your support and keep up to date with current affairs in your area, Devon Matters is the place for you.
Readership/Target Audience: Aimed at residents in the local area of Devon.
LOCAL NEWSPAPERS: Community Newsletters

DIA DIWAN
1892651U74Q-1371

Editorial Address: Suite 9, 10 Melbury Road, LONDON, W14 8LW **Tel:** 07990 514929
Email: info@diadiwan.com
Web site: http://www.diadiwan.com
Date Launched: 2008
Frequency of update: Daily
Website Access: Free
Editor: Rasha Khouri
Summary of Content: Luxury content and e-commerce website catering to the Middle East's need for unique fashion and leisure, providing access to international brands, Arab and Middle Eastern designers, as well as expert advice and opinions from the region.
Readership/Target Audience: Aimed at people interested in international and Arab fashion and goods.
CONSUMER: WOMEN'S INTEREST CONSUMER MAGAZINES: Lifestyle

DIESELMOTORING.COM
1667700U77A-569

Editorial Address: Orchardton Hall, Auchencairn, CASTLE DOUGLAS, DG7 1QL **Tel:** 0845 130 6249
Fax: 0845 658 8329
Email: lauren@motornews.co.uk
Web site: http://www.dieselmotoring.com
Publisher: Brave New World International Ltd
Frequency of update: Daily
Website Access: Free
Editor: Lauren Courtney

Summary of Content: Website covering all aspects of diesel motoring from vans to cars including previews and road tests.
Readership/Target Audience: Aimed at the general public.
CONSUMER: MOTORING & CYCLING: Motoring

DIGITAL PHOTOGRAPHY NOW
1786179U85A-207

Editorial Address: Apsley Mills Cottage, London Road, Apsley, HEMEL HEMPSTEAD, HP3 9RL **Tel:** 01442 242960
Email: news@dpnow.com
Web site: http://www.dpnow.com
Publisher: The Write Technology Ltd
Date Launched: 2001
Frequency of update: Daily
Website Access: Free
Traffic Figures: 200,000 Unique Users (per week Publisher's Statement)
Editor: Julia Burley
Summary of Content: Website covering all aspects of digital photography including cameras, printers, scanners, software and accessories.
Readership/Target Audience: Aimed at users of digital photography equipment both professional and amateur.
Other Features: Forum, galleries and newsletter.
CONSUMER: PHOTOGRAPHY & FILM MAKING: Photography

DIGITAL TEXTILE
1647469U47A-571

Editorial Address: Perkin House, 1 Longlands Street, BRADFORD, BD1 2TP **Tel:** 01274 378819
Fax: 01274 378811
Email: jscrimshaw@world-textile.net
Web site: http://www.digital-textile.net
Publisher: World Textile Publications Ltd
Date Launched: 2004
Frequency of update: 6 times a year
Website Access: Paid
Traffic Figures: 3,500 Unique Users (Publisher's Statement)
Editor: John Scrimshaw
Summary of Content: Electronically delivered magazine dedicated wholly to textile applications in the rapidly developing field of digital printing.
Readership/Target Audience: Aimed at both users and suppliers of digital printing equipment.
BUSINESS: CLOTHING & TEXTILES

DIGITAL-LIFESTYLES.INFO
1657142U18B-1951

Editorial Address: 3rd Floor, 102 Dean Street, LONDON, W1D 3TQ **Tel:** 020 7870 7671
Email: news@digital-lifestyles.info
Web site: http://digital-lifestyles.info
Publisher: Meeja
Date Launched: 2001
Frequency of update: Daily
Website Access: Free
Editor: Simon Perry
Summary of Content: Website covering technology and the effect it has on the creation, distribution and consumption of media.
Readership/Target Audience: Aimed at media executives.
BUSINESS: ELECTRONICS: Telecommunications

DIGITALPUBLISHINGNEWS.NET
1685556U60R-102

Editorial Address: 4 Capulet Road, Stratford Sub Castle, SALISBURY, SP1 3JY **Tel:** 01722 341757
Email: nickhampshire@btinternet.com
Web site: http://www.digitalpublishingnews.net
Date Launched: 2005
Frequency of update: Weekly
Website Access: Free
Editor: Nick Hampshire
Summary of Content: Website focusing on electronic publishing including e-books, e-magazines and e-readers.
Readership/Target Audience: Aimed at the publishing industry, including corporate publishers.
BUSINESS: PUBLISHING: Publishing Related

DIGYORKSHIRE
1639503U80C-5076

Editorial Address: Studio 23/24, Leeds Design Innovation Centre, 46 The Calls, LEEDS, LS2 7EY **Tel:** 0113 320 0160
Fax: 0113 320 0161
Email: info@digyorkshire.com
Web site: http://www.digyorkshire.com
Date Launched: 2002
Frequency of update: Monthly
Website Access: Free

Traffic Figures: 95,000 Unique Users (per month Publisher's Statement)
Editor: Rory Ffoulkes
Summary of Content: Electronic what's-on guide covering music, cinema, theatre, clubs, museums, galleries and other attractions in Yorkshire.
Readership/Target Audience: Aimed at those living in or visiting Yorkshire.
Other Features: Monthly e-bulletin.
CONSUMER: RURAL & REGIONAL INTEREST: Regional Interest English Counties

DINE ONLINE
626296U94G-40

Editorial Address: 5 Azure Suites, Churchill Court, 112 The Street, Rustington, LITTLEHAMPTON, BN16 3DA
Tel: 01903 779538 **Fax:** 01903 856683
Email: dine@dine-online.co.uk
Web site: http://www.dine-online.co.uk
Publisher: Midascode Ltd
Date Launched: 1996
Frequency of update: Daily
Website Access: Free
Editor: Barry Dunlop
Summary of Content: Website reviewing and promoting the appreciation of fine dining and the use of good quality wines and ingredients. Also reviews international travel and hotels.
Readership/Target Audience: Aimed at those who love good food and wine and also international travel enthusiasts.
Other Features: Features include an online buyer's guide, a chat forum, an events calendar and archiving.
CONSUMER: OTHER CLASSIFICATIONS: Restaurant Guides

DIRECTOR OF FINANCE ONLINE
1821868U1R-380

Editorial Address: 40 Bowling Green Lane, LONDON, EC1R 0NE **Tel:** 020 7074 7768 **Fax:** 020 7837 6135
Email: gary@atalink.co.uk
Web site: http://www.dofonline.co.uk
Publisher: Atalink Ltd
Date Launched: 2007
Frequency of update: Daily
Website Access: Free
Editor: Gary Howes
Summary of Content: Website featuring information for senior UK financial professionals covering accounting, governance, strategic finance, economy, management and lifestyle.
Readership/Target Audience: Aimed at UK finance directors and senior financial decision makers.
Other Features: Recruitment, message boards, newsletter, news feeds and video
BUSINESS: FINANCE & ECONOMICS: Financial Related

DISTINGUISHED SPAS
1837384U89A-749

Editorial Address: Press releases by email only
Tel: 0871 989 8619
Email: editordir@distinguishedspas.com
Web site: http://www.DistinguishedSpas.com
Publisher: EFE International
Frequency of update: Daily
Website Access: Free
Summary of Content: Website featuring up-market spa resorts, hotels, thermal and medical spas, health and beauty farms, as well as attractive spa travel destinations, accommodation, tourism and travel information, as well as spa holidays, weekend breaks and pamper days.
Readership/Target Audience: Aimed at consumers with a high disposable income.
CONSUMER: HOLIDAYS & TRAVEL: Travel

DIVERNET
626510U75M-205

Editorial Address: 55 High Street, TEDDINGTON, TW11 8HA **Tel:** 020 8943 4288 **Fax:** 020 8943 4312
Email: steve@divermag.co.uk
Web site: http://www.divernet.com
Publisher: Eaton Publications
Date Launched: 1995
Frequency of update: Daily
Website Access: Free
Traffic Figures: 160,000 Unique Users (per month Publisher's Statement)
Editor: Steve Weinman
Summary of Content: Website covering the sport and business of scuba-diving worldwide. Includes articles on learning to dive, travel, wrecks, equipment, techniques, news and marine life.
Readership/Target Audience: Aimed at divers of all ages and abilities and those with a general interest.
Other Features: Features include recruitment and archiving.
CONSUMER: SPORT: Water Sports

DIY DOG
626137U79A-8

Editorial Address: Orchardton Hall, Auchencairn, CASTLE DOUGLAS, DG7 1QL **Tel:** 0845 130 6249
Email: bray@bnw.demon.co.uk
Web site: http://www.diydog.com
Publisher: Brave New World International Ltd
Frequency of update: Monthly
Website Access: Free
Editor: Susan Foster
Summary of Content: Website focusing on information and tips to make DIY easier.
Readership/Target Audience: Aimed at those interested in DIY.
Other Features: Features include archiving.
CONSUMER: HOBBIES & DIY

DNJ ONLINE
36059U5B-68

Editorial Address: 7 Unity Street, BRISTOL, BS1 5HH
Tel: 0117 930 0255
Email: dnj@mattmags.com
Web site: http://www.dnjonline.com
Publisher: Matt Publishing
Date Launched: 1997
Website Access: Free
Traffic Figures: 19,451 Unique Users (per month Publisher's Statement)
Editor: Matt Nicholson
Summary of Content: Website for software developers working with Microsoft technologies. Covers news, products, events and technology issues.
Readership/Target Audience: Aimed at software developers.
BUSINESS: COMPUTERS & AUTOMATION: Data Processing

DORSET MATTERS
1881611U72J-354

Email: comments@dorset-matters.co.uk
Web site: http://www.dorset-matters.co.uk
Frequency of update: Daily
Summary of Content: Website created to help people who care about local issues. Whether you need access to useful information, want to highlight a particular topic to other people, discuss ideas with like-minded people or just show your support and keep up to date with current affairs in your area, Dorset Matters is the place for you.
Readership/Target Audience: Aimed at residents in the local area of Dorset.
LOCAL NEWSPAPERS: Community Newsletters

DORSET ONLINE
629296U80C-1241

Editorial Address: 3A Poundbury Business Centre, Poundbury, DORCHESTER, DT1 3RS **Tel:** 01305 211842
Fax: 01305 211841
Email: bridget.swann@archant.co.uk
Web site: http://www.dorsetmag.co.uk
Publisher: Archant Norfolk
Date Launched: 1994
Frequency of update: Monthly
Website Access: Free
Editor: Bridget Swann
Summary of Content: Website covering news, reviews and information about Dorset.
Readership/Target Audience: Aimed at those who live in the area.
Other Features: Features include a what's on guide and archiving.
CONSUMER: RURAL & REGIONAL INTEREST: Regional Interest English Counties

DRAG, ROD & CLASSIC REVIEW
1663738U77R-751

Editorial ADDRESS: PO Box 753, Flackwell Heath, HIGH WYCOMBE, HP10 9XG **Tel:** 01628 530323
Email: andrew.kirk@kjpartnership.co.uk
Web site: http://www.drcreview.com
Publisher: K J Partnership Ltd
Date Launched: 2004
Frequency of update: Weekly
Website Access: Free
Traffic Figures: 89,176 Unique Users (Publisher's Statement)
Editor: Andrew Kirk
Summary of Content: Website dedicated to American automotive culture in the UK, focusing primarily on nostalgia drag racing, hot rodding plus new and classic American cars.
Readership/Target Audience: Aimed at American car enthusiasts in the UK, mainland Europe and the US.

Other Features: News, features, new product information and reviews
CONSUMER: MOTORING & CYCLING: Motoring & Cycling Related

DREAMWATCH
46098U79L-76

Editorial Address: Titan House, 144 Southwark Street, LONDON, SE1 0UP **Tel:** 020 7803 1831 **Fax:** 020 7803 1803
Email: dreamwatch@titanemail.com
Web site: http://www.dwscifi.com
Publisher: Titan Magazines
Date Launched: 1995
Frequency of update: Daily
Website Access: Free
Editor: Matt McAllister
Summary of Content: Website covering all popular science fiction including fantasy programmes on television, both current and archive.
Readership/Target Audience: Aimed at enthusiasts of science fiction and fantasy programmes.
CONSUMER: HOBBIES & DIY: Fantasy Games & Science Fiction

DRINKS INTERNATIONAL
1871106U9A-267

Editorial Address: Gateway House, 42A East Park, CRAWLEY, RH10 6AS **Tel:** 01293 590046
Email: lucy.britner@drinksint.com
Web site: http://www.drinksint.com
Publisher: Agile Media
Frequency of update: Daily
Website Access: Free
Editor: Lucy Britner
Summary of Content: Website covering International alcoholic drink products, marketing and trends.
Readership/Target Audience: Aimed at International buyers, distributors and agents of wines and spirits and other alcoholic drinks.
BUSINESS: DRINKS & LICENSED TRADE: Drinks, Licensed Trade, Wines & Spirits

DRIVERS-REPUBLIC.COM
1849709U77A-611

Editorial Address: The Forge, Blisworth Hill Farm, Stoke Road, BLISWORTH, NN7 3BD **Tel:** 01604 858524
Email: eds@drivers-republic.com
Web site: http://www.drivers-republic.com
Publisher: New Media Republic Ltd
Date Launched: 2008
Frequency of update: Daily
Website Access: Free
Editor: Jethro Bovingdon
Summary of Content: Electronic magazine covering the launch of new cars, in-depth features, accessories and motor sport.
Readership/Target Audience: Aimed at car enthusiasts at all levels.
CONSUMER: MOTORING & CYCLING: Motoring

DROWNEDINSOUND.COM
1786300U76D-823

Editorial Address: 1 Junction Mews, Paddington, LONDON, W2 1PN
Email: sean@drownedinsound.com
Web site: http://www.drownedinsound.com
Frequency of update: Daily
Website Access: Free
Traffic Figures: 500,000 Unique Users (per month Publisher's Statement)
Editor: Sean Adams
Summary of Content: Website with news, features and reviews on all types of music from indie rock to electronica.
Readership/Target Audience: Aimed at music fans of all genres.
CONSUMER: MUSIC & PERFORMING ARTS: Music

DVCAMERA.CO.UK
1795198U85A-212

Editorial Address: 20 Green Lane, CHISLEHURST, BR7 6AG **Tel:** 020 8467 2465
Email: vsoliver@aol.com
Web site: http://www.dvcamera.co.uk
Publisher: photo-i
Date Launched: 2007
Frequency of update: Daily
Website Access: Free
Editor: Vincent Oliver
Summary of Content: Website covering all aspects of digital video from taking to rendering.
Readership/Target Audience: Aimed at home users of digital video.
CONSUMER: PHOTOGRAPHY & FILM MAKING: Photography

DVD INTELLIGENCE
39110U43D-7

Editorial Address: 26 Windridge Close, ST. ALBANS, AL3 4JP **Tel:** 01727 851761 **Fax:** 01727 753454
Email: jeanluc.renaud@dvd-intelligence.com
Web site: http://www.dvd-intelligence.com
Publisher: Globalcom Ltd
Date Launched: 1997
Frequency of update: Daily
Website Access: Paid
Traffic Figures: 17,500 Unique Users (per month Publisher's Statement)
Editor: Jean-Luc Renaud
Summary of Content: Website covering news and analysis of the global market for DVD products with a focus on Europe.
Readership/Target Audience: Aimed at professionals interested in DVD in Europe.
BUSINESS: ELECTRICAL RETAIL TRADE: Video

DVD REVIEWER
711792U78B-68

Editorial Address: 99 Falmouth Avenue, LONDON, E4 9QR **Tel:** 020 8527 8935
Email: dvd@myreviewer.com
Web site: http://www.dvdreviewer.co.uk
Publisher: Reviewer Ltd
Date Launched: 1999
Frequency of update: Daily
Website Access: Free
Traffic Figures: 1,000,000 Unique Users (per month Publisher's Statement)
Editor: Robert Shepherd
Summary of Content: Website featuring news, reviews, hardware and technical articles, opinions and information on the world of DVDs.
Readership/Target Audience: Aimed at those interested in the latest DVD news and home cinema technology.
Other Features: Features include competitions and a chat forum.
CONSUMER: CONSUMER ELECTRONICS: Video & DVD

DVD TIMES
46224U78B-78

Editorial Address: 42 Bedhampton Way, HAVANT, PO9 2DP **Tel:** 07962 189196
Email: editorial@dvdtimes.co.uk
Web site: http://www.dvdtimes.co.uk
Publisher: DVD Times
Date Launched: 1999
Frequency of update: Daily
Website Access: Free
Traffic Figures: 500,000 Unique Users (per month Publisher's Statement)
Editor: Dave Foster
Summary of Content: Website covering DVD news, reviews and features.
Readership/Target Audience: Aimed at DVD users and those interested in DVDs.
Other Features: Features include discussion forums.
CONSUMER: CONSUMER ELECTRONICS: Video & DVD

DYINGTOTELL.CO.UK
1614218U74Q-1141

Formerly: DyingtoTell.com
Editorial Address: 2 The Laurels, BASINGSTOKE, RG21 4JP **Tel:** 01256 817063
Email: terry@dyingtotell.co.uk
Web site: http://www.dyingtotell.co.uk
Publisher: Mediadirect
Date Launched: 2003
Frequency of update: Monthly
Website Access: Free
Editor: Terry Lowndes; **Web Editor:** Terry Lowndes
Summary of Content: Website covering holidays and travel for those people wanting something more than a basic beach holiday package and those who are willing to make independent travel arrangements and are interested in activity holidays such as walking, riding and sailing.
Readership/Target Audience: Aimed mainly at women aged 35 to 80 years old.
CONSUMER: WOMEN'S INTEREST CONSUMER MAGAZINES: Lifestyle

E-ACCESS BULLETIN
1601044U56L-122

Editorial Address: 68 Middle Street, BRIGHTON, BN1 1AL **Tel:** 01273 267173 **Fax:** 01273 232179
Email: dan@headstar.com
Web site: http://www.headstar.com/eab
Publisher: Headstar
Date Launched: 2001
Frequency of update: Monthly
Website Access: Free
Traffic Figures: 6,000 Unique Users (per month Publisher's Statement)

Editor: Dan Jellinek
Summary of Content: Electronically delivered newsletter covering information technology for the visually impaired from consumer electronics to the Internet including design and access issues and technical developments.
Readership/Target Audience: Aimed at blind and visually impaired people, voluntary and charitable agencies, policy makers, the technology sector, local government IT managers or access officers and the media.
BUSINESS: HEALTH & MEDICAL: Disability & Rehabilitation

EALING MATTERS
1881612U72J-355

Email: comments@ealing-matters.co.uk
Web site: http://www.ealing-matters.co.uk
Frequency of update: Daily
Summary of Content: Website created to help people who care about local issues. Whether you need access to useful information, want to highlight a particular topic to other people, discuss ideas with like-minded people or just show your support and keep up to date with current affairs in your area, Ealing Matters is the place for you.
Readership/Target Audience: Aimed at residents in the local area of Ealing.
LOCAL NEWSPAPERS: Community Newsletters

EAST MIDLANDS MATTERS
1881613U72J-356

Email: comments@eastmidlands-matters.co.uk
Web site: http://www.eastmidlands-matters.co.uk
Frequency of update: Daily
Summary of Content: Website created to help people who care about local issues. Whether you need access to useful information, want to highlight a particular topic to other people, discuss ideas with like-minded people or just show your support and keep up to date with current affairs in your area, East Midlands Matters is the place for you.
Readership/Target Audience: Aimed at residents in the local area of East Midlands.
LOCAL NEWSPAPERS: Community Newsletters

EAST OF SCOTLAND GOLF
1665986U75D-530

Editorial Address: 207 Oakbank Road, PERTH, PH1 1DS **Tel:** 07982 827390
Email: graham.hood@eastofscotlandgolf.com
Web site: http://www.eastofscotlandgolf.com
Publisher: East of Scotland Golf Alliance
Frequency of update: Weekly
Website Access: Free
Editor: Graham Hood
Summary of Content: Website covering golf course reviews, tournament reports, golf holidays, accommodation details, competitions and special offers.
Readership/Target Audience: Aimed at those planning to play golf in the East of Scotland.
CONSUMER: SPORT: Golf

EAST SUSSEX MATTERS
1881614U72J-357

Email: comments@eastsussex-matters.co.uk
Web site: http://www.eastsussex-matters.co.uk
Frequency of update: Daily
Summary of Content: Website created to help people who care about local issues. Whether you need access to useful information, want to highlight a particular topic to other people, discuss ideas with like-minded people or just show your support and keep up to date with current affairs in your area, East Sussex Matters is the place for you.
Readership/Target Audience: Aimed at residents in the local area of East Sussex.
LOCAL NEWSPAPERS: Community Newsletters

EASTBOURNE TODAY
634141U67B-215

Editorial Address: Beckett House, 1 Commercial Road, EASTBOURNE, BN21 3XQ **Tel:** 01323 722091 **Fax:** 01323 431387
Email: eastbourne.herald@trbeckett.co.uk
Web site: http://www.eastbourneherald.co.uk
Frequency of update: Daily
Website Access: Free
Traffic Figures: 18,614 Unique Users (per month Publisher's Statement)
Editor: Laura Sonier
Summary of Content: Website containing news, information and features about the local area.
Readership/Target Audience: Local residents and visitors to this area.
Other Features: Features include recruitment, a chat forum and archiving.
REGIONAL DAILY & SUNDAY NEWSPAPERS: Regional Daily Newspapers

Internet Media

EASTERN ART REPORT ON LINE

36022U84A-222

Formerly: ArtByte
Editorial Address: PO Box 13666, LONDON, SW14 8WF
Tel: 020 8392 1122 **Fax:** 020 8392 1422
Email: ear@eapgroup.com
Web site: http://www.eapgroup.com
Publisher: EAPGroup International Media
Date Launched: 1997
Frequency of update: Weekly
Website Access: Free
Editor: Sajid Rizvi; **Editor-in-Chief:** Sajid Rizvi
Summary of Content: Website featuring online version of the Eastern Art Report print magazine, plus many original online features, including extensive listings. Includes topics such as multicultural art scene of Britain, the arts of Africa, the Near and Middle East, South and Southeast Asia, China and Japan, computer applications in art history, conservation and design. Also features interviews, exhibition and book reviews and news.
Readership/Target Audience: Aimed at artists, art collectors, art dealers and other art professionals, historians, designers and innovators.
Other Features: An art gallery, and online bookshop.
CONSUMER: THE ARTS & LITERARY: Arts

EASTERN VOICE

1813129U90-1011

Editorial Address: 160 Rolfe Street, SMETHWICK, B66 2AU
Tel: 0121 558 3020 **Fax:** 0121 275 6197
Email: info@emgonline.co.uk
Web site: http://www.emgonline.co.uk
Publisher: Eastern Media Group
Date Launched: 2006
Frequency of update: Daily
Website Access: Free
Editor: Gurjeet Kaur Bains
Summary of Content: Magazine covering real life issues and breaking news and addresses subjects which have always been considered controversial and contentious.
Readership/Target Audience: Aimed at Asian communities in the UK.
CONSUMER: ETHNIC

EAST.HOUSINGNEWS.CO.UK

1776298U4D-415

Editorial Address: For all contact details see main edition, housingnews.co.uk
Website Access: Free
BUSINESS: ARCHITECTURE & BUILDING: Planning & Housing

EASTMIDLANDS.HOUSINGNEWS.CO.UK

1776297U4D-414

Editorial Address: For all contact details see main edition, housingnews.co.uk
Website Access: Free
BUSINESS: ARCHITECTURE & BUILDING: Planning & Housing

EASYLIVINGMAGAZINE.COM

1825719U74A-1041

Editorial Address: Hanover House, 1 Hanover Square, LONDON, W1S 1JU **Tel:** 020 7499 9080
Email: emma.lundin@condenast.co.uk
Web site: http://www.easylivingmagazine.com
Publisher: Conde Nast Publications Ltd
Frequency of update: Daily
Website Access: Free
Traffic Figures: 100,000 Unique Users (per month Publisher's Statement)
Editor: Emma Lundin
Summary of Content: Website covering fashion, food, relationships, home, films, arts, health and beauty.
Readership/Target Audience: Aimed at women aged 25 to 55 years old.
CONSUMER: WOMEN'S INTEREST CONSUMER MAGAZINES: Women's Interest

EBONYONLINE

1743033U90-992

Editorial Address: Coopers Yard (Amani Training), Westow Hill, LONDON, SE19 1TQ **Tel:** 020 8670 8200
Email: info@ebonyonline.net
Web site: http://www.ebonyonline.net
Publisher: Ebonyonline Communications Ltd
Frequency of update: 6 times a year
Website Access: Free
Editor: Ade Idowu

Summary of Content: Website covering clubs, restaurants, celebrity interviews, business directory, music, concerts, fashion, lifestyle, family, education, the arts and events.
Readership/Target Audience: Aimed at minority, ethnic communities in the UK.
CONSUMER: ETHNIC

ECO FRIEND NEWS

1840805U57-162

Editorial Address: Britannia House, 11 Glenthorne Road, LONDON, W6 0LH **Tel:** 0870 745 3380
Email: editorial@ecofriendnews.com
Web site: http://www.ecofriendnews.com
Publisher: Areza Ltd
Date Launched: 2007
Frequency of update: Daily
Website Access: Free
Traffic Figures: 50,000 Unique Users (per month WebTrends)
Editor: Erik Edmundson
Summary of Content: Portal covering environmental technologies, sustainable and renewable energy, air, water, soil and waste technologies and recycling.
Readership/Target Audience: Aimed at end users, installers, specifiers, manufacturers and distributors of environmentally friendly products and solutions.
BUSINESS: ENVIRONMENT & POLLUTION

ECO-ECHO.COM

1647279U57-127

Formerly: Eco Echo
Editorial Address: The Mill House, Mill Lane, Earls Barton, NORTHAMPTON, NN6 0NR **Tel:** 01604 810507
Fax: 01604 810507
Email: rogerwolens@btconnect.com
Web site: http://www.eco-echo.com
Publisher: The Green Organisation
Date Launched: 2008
Frequency of update: Daily
Website Access: Free
Traffic Figures: 5,000 Unique Users (Publisher's Statement)
Editor: Roger Wolens
Summary of Content: Electronic magazine covering environmental news from commerce, industry and local authorities.
Readership/Target Audience: Aimed at environmental professionals.
BUSINESS: ENVIRONMENT & POLLUTION

ECOFORYOU

1862595U94X-304

Editorial Address: Suite 3.4, 111 Union Street, GLASGOW, G1 3TA **Tel:** 0141 248 5595 **Fax:** 0141 248 5596
Email: shaun@ecoforyou.co.uk
Web site: http://www.ecoforyou.co.uk
Publisher: Planet Ink Ltd
Date Launched: 2008
Frequency of update: Monthly
Website Access: Free
Editor: Shaun Milne
Summary of Content: Digital publication featuring news on the environment, green living and corporate social responsibility.
Readership/Target Audience: Aimed at those looking to make informed choices on green issues.
CONSUMER: OTHER CLASSIFICATIONS: Miscellaneous

THE ECOLOGIST ONLINE

629091U57-20_10

Editorial Address: Unit 102 Lana House Studios, 116-118 Commercial Street, Spitalfields, LONDON, E1 6NF
Tel: 020 7422 8100 **Fax:** 020 7422 8101
Email: press@theecologist.org
Web site: http://www.theecologist.org
Publisher: Ecosystems Ltd
Date Launched: 1970
Frequency of update: Daily
Website Access: Free
Editor: Mark Anslow
Summary of Content: Website containing environmental and current affairs news, information and features.
Readership/Target Audience: Aimed at those willing to challenge the current state of affairs.
BUSINESS: ENVIRONMENT & POLLUTION

ECONOMIST.COM

629557U73-9005

Formerly: Economist online
Editorial Address: 25 St. James's Street, LONDON, SW1A 1HG **Tel:** 020 7830 7000 **Fax:** 020 7930 5104
Email: barneysouthin@economist.com
Web site: http://www.economist.com
Date Launched: 2000
Frequency of update: Daily
Website Access: Paid

Traffic Figures: 1,608,979 Unique Users (per month Publisher's Statement)
Editor: Barney Southin
Summary of Content: Website covering business, political and financial news and information.
Readership/Target Audience: Aimed at professionals in business, finance and politics.
Other Features: Features include recruitment, an e-mail newsletter and archiving.
CONSUMER: NATIONAL & INTERNATIONAL PERIODICALS

THE ECONOMY NEWS

1902445U1A-755

Editorial Address: 29 Links Avenue, MORDEN, SM4 5AE
Tel: 07874 085952
Email: editor@economy-news.co.uk
Web site: http://www.economy-news.co.uk
Publisher: The Economy News
Date Launched: 2008
Frequency of update: Monthly
Website Access: Free
Traffic Figures: 12,500 Unique Users (per month Publisher's Statement)
Editor: Will Peters
Summary of Content: Website providing independent economic news and insight on the UK economy and the global economy.
Readership/Target Audience: Aimed at the UK investment community.
BUSINESS: FINANCE & ECONOMICS

EDGE ONLINE

1697290U78D-320

Editorial Address: 30 Monmouth Street, BATH, BA1 2BW
Tel: 01225 442244 **Fax:** 01225 732275
Web site: http://www.edge-online.co.uk
Publisher: Future Publishing Ltd
Frequency of update: Daily
Website Access: Free
Editor: Alex Wiltshire
Summary of Content: Website covering reviews and previews of video games across multiple formats. Also includes interviews and news on the latest technology.
Readership/Target Audience: Aimed at males over 25 years old.
CONSUMER: CONSUMER ELECTRONICS: Games

EDIE

626416U57-20_40

Editorial Address: Faversham House, 232A Addington Road, SOUTH CROYDON, CR2 8LE **Tel:** 020 8651 7161
Fax: 020 8651 7117
Email: newsdesk@edie.net
Web site: http://www.edie.net
Publisher: Faversham House Group Ltd
Date Launched: 1998
Frequency of update: Daily
Website Access: Free
Traffic Figures: 145,000 Unique Users (Publisher's Statement)
Editor: Sam Bond
Summary of Content: Website providing interactive news, information and communications for the water, waste and environment industry worldwide.
Readership/Target Audience: Aimed at professionals who work in the water, waste and environment industries worldwide.
BUSINESS: ENVIRONMENT & POLLUTION

EDINBURGH GUIDE.COM

626294U80E-42

Editorial Address: Braeside Cottage, Robertson Bank, GOREBRIDGE, EH23 4JT **Tel:** 01875 822694
Fax: 01875 822314
Email: editor@edinburghguide.com
Web site: http://www.edinburghguide.com
Publisher: Edinburgh Guide
Date Launched: 1997
Frequency of update: Daily
Website Access: Free
Traffic Figures: 225,000 Unique Users (per month Publisher's Statement)
Editor: John Ritchie; **Web Editor:** Robert Alstead
Summary of Content: Website providing up to date information on Scotland's capital city, including what's on guides, book, hotel and restaurant reviews, travel and tourism, general news and review coverage of the Edinburgh festival. Provides a comprehensive online directory for Edinburgh.
Readership/Target Audience: Aimed at those interested in Edinburgh and Scotland in general.
Other Features: Features include discussion forums, news boards and archiving.
CONSUMER: RURAL & REGIONAL INTEREST: Regional Interest Scotland

EDINBURGH MATTERS
1881615U72J-358

Email: comments@edinburgh-matters.co.uk
Web site: http://www.edinburgh-matters.co.uk
Frequency of update: Daily
Summary of Content: Website created to help people who care about local issues. Whether you need access to useful information, want to highlight a particular topic to other people, discuss ideas with like-minded people or just show your support and keep up to date with current affairs in your area, Edinburgh Matters is the place for you.
Readership/Target Audience: Aimed at residents in the local area of Edinburgh.
LOCAL NEWSPAPERS: Community Newsletters

EDINBURGHNEWS.COM
634896U67B-9038

Editorial Address: 108 Holyrood Road, EDINBURGH, EH8 8AS **Tel:** 0131 620 8620
Email: news_en@edinburghnews.com
Web site: http://www.edinburghnews.com
Publisher: Johnston Press plc
Date Launched: 1996
Frequency of update: Daily
Website Access: Free
Traffic Figures: 3,824,146 Unique Users (01/01/2007 To 28/01/2007 ABC/Electronic)
Editor: Alan Young
Summary of Content: Website containing news, sport, business and information on the city of Edinburgh.
Readership/Target Audience: Read by anyone interested in Edinburgh.
Other Features: Features include recruitment, an e-mail newsletter, a restaurant guide, a buyer's guide and archiving.
REGIONAL DAILY & SUNDAY NEWSPAPERS: Regional Daily Newspapers

EDUCATIONGUARDIAN.CO.UK
706988U88A-51

Editorial Address: 119 Farringdon Road, LONDON, EC1R 3DR **Tel:** 020 7713 9913
Email: education.editor@guardianunlimited.co.uk
Web site: http://educationguardian.co.uk
Date Launched: 1999
Frequency of update: Daily
Website Access: Free
Traffic Figures: 450,000 Unique Users (per month Publisher's Statement)
Editor: Polly Curtis
Summary of Content: Website focusing on education. Contains news, reports and information on education.
Readership/Target Audience: Read by teachers, parents and lecturers in higher education.
Other Features: Features include a discussion forum, archiving and recruitment.
CONSUMER: EDUCATION

EE TIMES EUROPE
1745410U18A-9044

Editorial Address: Ludgate House, 245 Blackfriars Road, LONDON, SE1 9UY **Tel:** 020 7921 8271 **Fax:** 020 7921 8499
Email: jwalko@techinsights.com
Web site: http://www.eetimes.eu
Publisher: Tech Insights Europe, United Business Media
Date Launched: 2005
Frequency of update: Daily
Website Access: Free
Editor: John Walko
Summary of Content: Website covering the development of communications systems and equipment including mobile phones, wireless base stations, internetworking systems, internet appliances, broadband modems and equipment and optical networking systems.
Readership/Target Audience: Aimed at OEM design engineers and technical managers.
BUSINESS: ELECTRONICS

EETIMES EUROPE
37346U18A-73

Formerly: EETimesUK
Editorial Address: PO Box 32444, LONDON, SE18 3ZP
Tel: 020 8319 1324 **Fax:** 0870 137 8812
Email: cholland@techinsights.com
Web site: http://www.eetimes.eu
Publisher: TechInsights Europe
Date Launched: 1979
Frequency of update: Daily
Website Access: Free
Traffic Figures: 120,000 Unique Users (Publisher's Statement)
Editor: Colin Holland
Summary of Content: Website covering electronic engineering.

Readership/Target Audience: Aimed at design engineers in the computer and electronics industries.
BUSINESS: ELECTRONICS

EFFICIENTENERGY.NET
1872678U58-198

Editorial Address: PR by email only **Tel:** 01892 615107
Email: editor@efficientenergy.net
Web site: http://www.efficientenergy.net
Publisher: Damte ltd
Date Launched: 2009
Frequency of update: Daily
Website Access: Free
Editor: David Keighley
Summary of Content: Business to business website providing a platform for suppliers to promote their products, equipment and services for energy efficient projects. Includes materials, components, products and systems.
Readership/Target Audience: Aimed at professionals in industrial, commercial and public sector organisations who need to make more efficient use of energy.
BUSINESS: ENERGY, FUEL & NUCLEAR

EFINANCIAL NEWS
623956U1F-155

Editorial Address: 2nd Floor, Stapleton House, 29-33 Scrutton Street, LONDON, EC2A 4HU **Tel:** 020 7426 3333
Fax: 020 7426 3329
Email: news@efinancialnews.com
Web site: http://www.efinancialnews.com
Publisher: Efinancialnews.com
Date Launched: 2000
Frequency of update: Daily
Website Access: Free
Traffic Figures: 35,000 Unique Users (per month Publisher's Statement)
Editor: Fareed Sahloul; **Online Journalist:** Fareed Sahloul
Summary of Content: Website providing news and information on European investment banking, fund management and security industries.
Readership/Target Audience: Aimed at European investors and the banking investment industry.
BUSINESS: FINANCE & ECONOMICS: Investment

EGI
35191U1E-143

Editorial Address: 1 Procter Street, LONDON, WC1V 6EU
Tel: 020 7911 1700 **Fax:** 020 7911 1900
Email: newsdesk@egi.co.uk
Web site: http://www.egi.co.uk
Publisher: Reed Business Information
Date Launched: 1996
Frequency of update: Daily
Website Access: Paid
Editor: Denis Hall
Summary of Content: Website featuring up-to-the-minute news, law reports and legal articles. Includes a research service and an online shop.
Readership/Target Audience: Aimed at professionals in the commercial property market.
BUSINESS: FINANCE & ECONOMICS: Property

EGOV MONITOR
763350U5B-451

Editorial Address: PR by email only
Email: editor@egovmonitor.com
Web site: http://www.egovmonitor.com
Publisher: Policy Dialogue International Limited
Frequency of update: Daily. News service updated daily, Newsletter updated weekly
Website Access: Free
Summary of Content: Roundup of key developments concerning electronic government and the public sector ICT marketplace, as well as the communication and technology markets.
Readership/Target Audience: Aimed at senior executives in government and the IT industry, ministers, MPs, consultants and analysts.
BUSINESS: COMPUTERS & AUTOMATION: Data Processing

E-GOVERNMENT BULLETIN
768340U32R-488

Editorial Address: 68 Middle Street, BRIGHTON, BN1 1AL
Tel: 01273 267173 **Fax:** 01273 232179
Email: egb@headstar.com
Web site: http://www.headstar.com/egb
Publisher: Headstar
Date Launched: 1996
Frequency of update: 24 times a year
Website Access: Free
Traffic Figures: 11,050 Unique Users (Publisher's Statement)
Editor: Dan Jellinek

Summary of Content: E-mail newsletter covering the use of the internet and other new technologies to improve public services and democracy.
Readership/Target Audience: Aimed at everyone in central and local government, the social sector and their private senior partners.
BUSINESS: LOCAL GOVERNMENT, LEISURE & RECREATION: Local Government Related

EGTV
1684378U1E-386

Editorial Address: 1 Procter Street, LONDON, WC1V 6EU
Tel: 020 7911 1821
Email: paul@hernesmedia.co.uk
Web site: http://www.eg.tv
Publisher: Reed Business Information
Date Launched: 2004
Frequency of update: 156 times a year
Website Access: Free
Traffic Figures: 24,000 Unique Users (per month Publisher's Statement)
Editor: Paul Yandall
Summary of Content: Internet TV channel covering all aspects of the commercial property sector.
Readership/Target Audience: Aimed at estate agents, surveyors, property developers, construction companies, local authorities and government departments.
BUSINESS: FINANCE & ECONOMICS: Property

E-HEALTH INSIDER
1693908U56A-193

Editorial Address: Southbank House, Black Prince Road, LONDON, SE1 7SJ **Tel:** 020 7785 6900 **Fax:** 020 7785 6908
Email: info@e-health-media.com
Web site: http://www.e-health-insider.com
Publisher: E-Health Media Ltd
Date Launched: 2001
Frequency of update: 260 times a year. Published around the 15th of the cover month
Website Access: Free
Editor: Jon Hoeksma
Summary of Content: Website covering news and features on healthcare information technology.
Readership/Target Audience: Aimed at IT staff in the NHS, IT suppliers and consultants working in healthcare, healthcare IT researchers, analysts, policy makers and clinical staff with an interest in IT.
BUSINESS: HEALTH & MEDICAL

E-HEALTH INSIDER PRIMARY CARE
1693911U56A-194

Editorial Address: Southbank House, Black Prince Road, LONDON, SE1 7SJ **Tel:** 020 7785 6900
Email: info@e-health-media.com
Web site: http://www.ehiprimarycare.com
Publisher: E-Health Media Ltd
Date Launched: 2005
Frequency of update: 260 times a year
Website Access: Free
Editor: Jon Hoeksma
Summary of Content: Website covering all aspects of IT in primary healthcare.
Readership/Target Audience: Aimed at GPs, IT staff in primary care trusts, clinical staff with an interest in IT, primary care IT suppliers and consultants, researchers, analysts and policy makers.
BUSINESS: HEALTH & MEDICAL

ELECTRICAL PORTAL
1840800U17-269

Editorial Address: Britannia House, 11 Glenthorne Road, LONDON, W6 0LH **Tel:** 0870 745 3380
Email: editor@electricalportal.co.uk
Web site: http://www.electricalportal.co.uk
Publisher: Areza Ltd
Date Launched: 2001
Frequency of update: Daily
Website Access: Free
Traffic Figures: 65,000 Unique Users (per month WebTrends)
Editor: Mark Crow
Summary of Content: Portal covering electrical distribution, lighting, power generation, automation, drives and control. Featuring news, case studies, research articles and market reports.
Readership/Target Audience: Aimed at electricians, electrical contractors, panel builders, specifiers and consultants, end users, maintenance engineers, electrical engineers, lighting designers, manufacturers, distributors and wholesalers, trade associations and industry bodies.
Other Features: Jobs forum, classifieds and online directory.
BUSINESS: ELECTRICAL

THE ELECTRONIC BRITISH LIBRARY JOURNAL
40898U60B-12_50

Formerly: British Library Journal
Editorial Address: 96 Euston Road, LONDON, NW1 2DB
Tel: 020 7412 7000 **Fax:** 020 7412 7577
Email: eblj@bl.uk
Web site: http://www.bl.uk/eblj
Publisher: British Library
Date Launched: 1975
Frequency of update: Quarterly
Website Access: Free
Editor: Barry Taylor
Summary of Content: Website containing articles on recent acquisitions and research on all aspects of the Library's collections.
Readership/Target Audience: Aimed at librarians, researchers and the general reader.
BUSINESS: PUBLISHING: Libraries

ELECTRONIC PAYMENTS INTERNATIONAL (EPI)
35076U1C-140

Formerly: Electronic Payments International
Editorial Address: The Colonnades, 34 Porchester Road, LONDON, W2 6ES **Tel:** 020 7563 5600 **Fax:** 020 7563 5601
Email: stafford.thomas@vrlknowledgebank.com
Web site: http://www.vrlpublishing.com
Publisher: VRL Knowledge Bank Ltd
Frequency of update: Daily
Website Access: Paid
Editor: Stafford Thomas
Summary of Content: E-newsletter offering benchmark intelligence on the funds transfer industry. Coverage includes strategic news, commentary, analysis, case studies and research about global electronic payments.
Readership/Target Audience: Aimed at those working in the senior-level payments industry.
BUSINESS: FINANCE & ECONOMICS: Banking

ELECTRONICS DISTRIBUTOR ON-LINE
1740080U18A-9035

Editorial Address: 31 High Street, Martin, LINCOLN, LN4 3QY **Tel:** 01526 378703
Email: editor@edimag.co.uk
Web site: http://www.edimag.co.uk
Publisher: Pathart Limited
Date Launched: 2005
Frequency of update: Daily
Website Access: Free
Traffic Figures: 8,500 Unique Users (per week Publisher's Statement)
Editor: Robin Paterson
Summary of Content: Electronically delivered magazine focusing on the development and availability of components to the UK electronics manufacturing industry.
Readership/Target Audience: Aimed at specifiers and purchasers in electronics manufacturing.
Other Features: Web Site Directory (of contributors).
BUSINESS: ELECTRONICS

ELECTRONICS MANUFACTURE AND TEST ONLINE
707488U18A-242

Editorial Address: Blair House, 184 High Street, TONBRIDGE, TN9 1BQ **Tel:** 01732 359990
Fax: 01732 770049
Email: tim.fryer@imlgroup.co.uk
Web site: http://www.emtworldwide.com
Date Launched: 1999
Frequency of update: Daily
Website Access: Free
Editor: Tim Fryer
Summary of Content: Website containing the latest news in the manufacturing industry.
Readership/Target Audience: Aimed at those involved in the electronics production quality assurance and test marketplace.
BUSINESS: ELECTRONICS

ELECTRONICSTALK
634080U18A-81

Formerly: Electronicstalk.com
Editorial Address: PR by email only **Tel:** 020 7970 4920
Email: news@electronicstalk.com
Web site: http://www.electronicstalk.com
Publisher: Pro-Talk Ltd
Date Launched: 2001
Frequency of update: Daily. E-mail newletter published weekly
Website Access: Free
Traffic Figures: 259,757 Unique Users (per month Publisher's Statement)
Editor: Dave Wilson

Summary of Content: Website containing the latest news and information about new electronic products.
Readership/Target Audience: Read by electronics engineers.
Other Features: Weekly editorial email newsletter.
BUSINESS: ELECTRONICS

ELECTRONICSWEEKLY.COM
626190U18A-83

Formerly: Electronics Weekly
Editorial Address: Quadrant House, The Quadrant, SUTTON, SM2 5AS **Tel:** 020 8652 8313 **Fax:** 020 8652 8956
Email: alun.williams@rbi.co.uk
Web site: http://www.electronicsweekly.com
Publisher: Reed Business Information
Date Launched: 1996
Frequency of update: Daily
Website Access: Free
Editor: Alun Williams; **Web Editor:** Alun Williams
Summary of Content: Website covering information and news for the UK electronics industry.
Readership/Target Audience: Aimed at professionals within the field.
BUSINESS: ELECTRONICS

ELECTROPAGES.COM
22277U18A-286_50

Formerly: Electropages
Editorial Address: Unit 4, The Axium Centre, POOLE, BH16 6FE **Tel:** 01202 632441
Email: info@electropages.com
Web site: http://www.electropages.com
Publisher: Electropages Limited
Date Launched: 1999
Website Access: Free
Traffic Figures: 62,000 Unique Users (per month Publisher's Statement)
Editor: Brian Butler
Summary of Content: Website providing information on new electronic products, services, an industry directory with hyperlinks.
Readership/Target Audience: Aimed at professionals that work within the electronics industry including electronic engineers, designers, specifiers and buyers.
BUSINESS: ELECTRONICS

ELIXIR NEWS
1729064U74G-268

Editorial Address: 7 Monroe House Regent's Park, LONDON, NW8 7JN **Tel:** 020 7569 8676 **Fax:** 020 7706 2438
Email: editor@elixirnews.com
Web site: http://www.elixirnews.com
Publisher: Elixir Press Ltd
Date Launched: 2005
Frequency of update: Daily
Website Access: Free
Traffic Figures: 1,500,000 Unique Users (Publisher's Statement)
Editor: Avril O'Connor
Summary of Content: Website covering health, anti-aging, product reviews and regeneration.
Readership/Target Audience: Aimed at people of all ages who would like to learn about how to stay healthy for longer.
Other Features: Archiving, Radio Show Interviews and Podcasts.
CONSUMER: WOMEN'S INTEREST CONSUMER MAGAZINES: Slimming & Health

ELLEUK.COM
1810539U74A-1035

Editorial Address: 64 North Row, LONDON, W1K 7LL
Tel: 020 7150 7000 **Fax:** 020 7150 7670
Email: elleonline@hf-uk.com
Web site: http://www.elleUK.com
Publisher: Hachette Filipacchi (UK) Ltd
Date Launched: 2007
Frequency of update: Daily
Website Access: Free
Traffic Figures: 371,000 Unique Users (per month Publisher's Statement)
Editor: Emma Sells
Summary of Content: Website covering fashion, catwalk, trends, celebrity style, beauty, news, shopping and style guides, TV, horoscopes, street style, spas and diets.
Readership/Target Audience: Aimed at women in the UK aged 18 to 40 years old.
CONSUMER: WOMEN'S INTEREST CONSUMER MAGAZINES: Women's Interest

EMBEDDED TECHNOLOGY JOURNAL UPDATE
1800033U18A-9043

Editorial Address: 34 North View, WINCHESTER, SO22 5EH **Tel:** 01962 853781
Email: pr@techfocusmedia.com
Web site: http://www.embeddedtechjournal.com
Publisher: Techfocus Media, Inc
Frequency of update: Weekly
Website Access: Paid
Editor: Dick Selwood
Summary of Content: Electronic newsletter featuring the latest articles and news.
Readership/Target Audience: Aimed at systems, hardware, and software engineers and engineering managers in systems companies developing electronic products involving embedded computing technology.
BUSINESS: ELECTRONICS

EMBEDDED.COM
707502U5B-8

Formerly: allEMBEDDED.COM
Editorial Address: PO Box 32444, LONDON, SE18 3ZP
Tel: 020 8319 1324
Email: es@colinholland.co.uk
Web site: http://www.embedded.com
Date Launched: 2000
Frequency of update: Daily
Website Access: Free
Editor: Colin Holland
Summary of Content: Website containing embedded industry news from across the EETimes network, conferences and seminars and a range of products.
Readership/Target Audience: Aimed at embedded designers and programmers.
BUSINESS: COMPUTERS & AUTOMATION: Data Processing

EMBODY FOR YOU
1732866U74G-270

Editorial Address: PO Box 6955, TOWCESTER, NN12 6WZ
Tel: 0 845 202 2941
Email: info@embodyforyou.com
Web site: http://www.embodyforyou.com
Publisher: Education and Media Services Ltd.
Frequency of update: Daily
Website Access: Free
Traffic Figures: 3,000 Unique Users (per day Publisher's Statement)
Editor: Martyn Nixon
Summary of Content: Website covering complementary health and beauty treatments, health and fitness, hair and beauty.
Readership/Target Audience: Aimed at those with and interest in leading a healthy lifestyle.
CONSUMER: WOMEN'S INTEREST CONSUMER MAGAZINES: Slimming & Health

EMMA MAGAZINE
1627071U90-913

Editorial Address: 67-69 Whitfield Street, LONDON, W1T 4HS **Tel:** 020 7636 1233 **Fax:** 020 7636 1255
Email: mail@emma.tv
Web site: http://www.emmainteractive.com
Publisher: EMMA Media
Frequency of update: Daily
Website Access: Free
Editor: Bobby Syed
Summary of Content: Website of the Ethnic Multicultural Media Awards covering achievements within the media and marketing fields by individuals from the ethnic minority sector.
Readership/Target Audience: Aimed at those attending the awards.
CONSUMER: ETHNIC

EMPIRE ONLINE
626528U76A-265

Editorial Address: Mappin House, 4 Winsley Street, LONDON, W1W 8HF **Tel:** 020 7859 8621
Email: james@empireonline.com
Web site: http://www.empireonline.com
Publisher: Bauer Consumer Media Ltd (Mappin House)
Date Launched: 1996
Frequency of update: Daily
Website Access: Free
Traffic Figures: 1,000,000 Unique Users (per month ABC/Electronic)
Editor: James Dyer
Summary of Content: Website breaking exclusive film news, reviews and features with a UK slant.
Readership/Target Audience: Aimed at movie fans.
Other Features: Features include a forum and archiving.
CONSUMER: MUSIC & PERFORMING ARTS: Cinema

EMPLOYMENT LAW BULLETIN 36905U14B-190

Formerly: Industrial Relations Law Bulletin
Editorial Address: Quadrant House, The Quadrant, SUTTON, SM2 5AS
Web site: http://www.xperthr.co.uk
Publisher: Reed Business Information
Date Launched: 1973
Frequency of update: 24 times a year
Website Access: Paid
Traffic Figures: 4,000 Unique Users (Publisher's Statement)
Editor: Joanna Stubbs
Summary of Content: Website and electronic newsletter covering all aspects of employment law.
Readership/Target Audience: Aimed at personnel and industrial relations managers, trade unions, legal professionals in private practice and companies and professional bodies.
BUSINESS: COMMERCE, INDUSTRY & MANAGEMENT: Industry & Factories

ENDS EUROPE DAILY 1685812U57-137

Editorial Address: 11-17 Wolverton Gardens, LONDON, W6 7DY **Tel:** 020 8267 5000 **Fax:** 020 8267 8150
Email: news@endseurope.com
Web site: http://www.endseuropedaily.com
Publisher: Haymarket Business Media Ltd
Date Launched: 1997
Frequency of update: 220 times a year
Website Access: Paid
Editor: Paul Kaye
Summary of Content: Electronically delivered newsletter covering news and analysis on EU and European environmental policy and legislation.
Readership/Target Audience: Aimed at policy makers, academics, PR agencies, environmental consultancies, government officials, media and NGO's.
BUSINESS: ENVIRONMENT & POLLUTION

ENERGY & ENVIRONMENT INDUSTRY DIRECTORY 1912919U57-251

Editorial Address: 18 Generator Hall, Electric Wharf, COVENTRY, CV1 4JL **Tel:** 0870 199 4044
Fax: 0870 777 4360
Email: enquries@industrydirectory.co.uk
Web site: http://www.industrydirectory.co.uk
Publisher: Simply Marcomms
Frequency of update: Daily
Website Access: Free
Editor: Kirstie Colledge
Summary of Content: Directory containing the latest news stories for the UK energy and environment industry. Includes news archives.
Readership/Target Audience: Aimed at Energy & Environment professionals, suppliers to the Energy & Environment industry, Energy & Environment Industry PR & Marketing firms.
BUSINESS: ENVIRONMENT & POLLUTION

ENERGY AND ENVIRONMENTAL MANAGEMENT MAGAZINE 25190U58-29

Formerly: Energy Resource Environmental and Sustainable Management
Editorial Address: Trelawney House, Chestergate, MACCLESFIELD, SK11 6DW **Tel:** 01625 613000
Fax: 01625 435078
Email: cathy.baldwin@tenalpspublishing.com
Web site: http://www.eaem.co.uk
Publisher: Ten Alps Publishing
Frequency of update: 6 times a year
Website Access: Free
Traffic Figures: 23,800 Unique Users (Publisher's Statement)
Editor: Cathy Baldwin
Summary of Content: Online journal published on behalf of the Department of the Environment, Food and Rural Affairs. Includes news, features, comment, best practice, case studies, research, new products, events and independent perspectives on sustainable development, including progress in energy and environmental management.
Readership/Target Audience: Aimed at directors and managers responsible for sustainable development, energy and environmental issues.
BUSINESS: ENERGY, FUEL & NUCLEAR

ENERGY BUSINESS REVIEW 1892613U58-199

Editorial Address: Brunel House, 55-57 North Wharf Road, LONDON, W2 1LA **Tel:** 020 7915 9931
Email: jsharp@industryreview.com
Web site: http://www.energy-business-review.com
Publisher: Progressive Media Group
Frequency of update: Daily

Website Access: Free
Editor: Jake Sharp
Summary of Content: Online newsletter covering energy including coal, gas, oil, power, solar, wind, hydro and green energy.
Readership/Target Audience: Aimed at those in the energy industry.
BUSINESS: ENERGY, FUEL & NUCLEAR

ENERGY EFFICIENCY NEWS 1926491U58-207

Editorial Address: 6 Orchard Bank, Great Rissington, CHELTENHAM, GL54 2LT **Tel:** 01451 810377
Fax: 0870 199 1100
Email: c.sealy@energyefficiencynews.com
Web site: http://www.energyefficiencynews.com
Publisher: Afion Media Ltd
Frequency of update: Daily
Website Access: Paid
Editor: Cordelia Sealy
Summary of Content: News website covering the latest developments and trends in all aspects of energy efficiency with an emphasis on global policy driven initiatives that have a major impact on the global use of energy.
Readership/Target Audience: Aimed at government officials, managers, architects and developers, consultants and researchers.
BUSINESS: ENERGY, FUEL & NUCLEAR

ENEWS 1808481U57-155

Editorial Address: 26-28 Underwood Street, LONDON, N1 7JQ **Tel:** 020 7490 1555 **Fax:** 020 7490 0881
Email: info@foe.co.uk
Web site: http://www.foe.co.uk
Publisher: Friends of the Earth
Frequency of update: Monthly
Website Access: Free
Traffic Figures: 28,000 Unique Users (Publisher's Statement)
Editor: John Hutchin
Summary of Content: Electronic newsletter containing campaign news, ideas on how to get involved, as well as simple tips for a greener lifestyle.
Readership/Target Audience: Aimed at members of Friends of the Earth and anybody interested in green issues.
BUSINESS: ENVIRONMENT & POLLUTION

ENEWSLETTER 37135U14H-78

Formerly: Newsletter
Editorial Address: Ruskin Chambers, Drury Lane, KNUTSFORD, WA16 6HA **Tel:** 01565 634467
Fax: 0870 241 9570
Email: production@fpb.org
Web site: http://www.fpb.org
Publisher: The Forum of Private Business
Frequency of update: Weekly
Website Access: Paid
Traffic Figures: 17,000 Unique Users (Publisher's Statement)
Editor: Sally Pigdon
Summary of Content: E-newsletter covering issues relevant to smaller businesses, including practical guidance, top tips, special offers aimed at smaller businesses and information about lobbying activities conducted on behalf of private businesses.
Readership/Target Audience: Read by businesses represented by the Forum of Private Business and other owner-managers of small and medium sized businesses.
BUSINESS: COMMERCE, INDUSTRY & MANAGEMENT: Small Business

ENFIELD MATTERS 1881616U72J-359

Email: comments@enfield-matters.co.uk
Web site: http://www.enfield-matters.co.uk
Frequency of update: Daily
Summary of Content: Website created to help people who care about local issues. Whether you need access to useful information, want to highlight a particular topic to other people, discuss ideas with like-minded people or just show your support and keep up to date with current affairs in your area, Enfield Matters is the place for you.
Readership/Target Audience: Aimed at residents in the local area of Enfield.
LOCAL NEWSPAPERS: Community Newsletters

THE ENGINEER ONLINE 633856U19A-178

Formerly: e4engineering
Editorial Address: St. Giles House, 50 Poland Street, LONDON, W1F 7AX **Tel:** 020 7970 4440 **Fax:** 020 7970 4459
Email: jason.ford@centaur.co.uk
Web site: http://www.theengineer.co.uk

Publisher: Centaur Media plc
Date Launched: 2000
Frequency of update: Daily
Website Access: Free
Traffic Figures: 45,000 Unique Users (per month Publisher's Statement)
Editor: Jason Ford
Summary of Content: Website containing the latest industry news and views, in-depth features and analysis, editorial comment, a comprehensive archive, engineering jobs, tendering vacancies and a searchable database of subcontractors.
Readership/Target Audience: Aimed at the engineering community.
BUSINESS: ENGINEERING & MACHINERY

ENGINEERING INDUSTRY DIRECTORY 1912918U19A-577

Editorial Address: 18 Generator Hall, Electric Wharf, COVENTRY, CV1 4JL **Tel:** 0870 199 4044
Fax: 0870 777 4360
Email: enquries@industrydirectory.co.uk
Web site: http://www.industrydirectory.co.uk
Publisher: Simply Marcomms
Frequency of update: Daily
Website Access: Free
Editor: Kirstie Colledge
Summary of Content: Directory containing the latest news stories for the UK engineering industry. Includes news archives.
Readership/Target Audience: Aimed at engineering professionals, engineering service providers, engineering PR & Marketing firms, suppliers to the engineering industry.
BUSINESS: ENGINEERING & MACHINERY

ENGINEERINGTALK 623299U19A-248_50

Formerly: engineeringtalk.com
Editorial Address: PR by email only **Tel:** 020 970 4920
Fax: 020 7970 4599
Email: news@engineeringtalk.com
Web site: http://www.engineeringtalk.com
Publisher: Pro-Talk Ltd
Date Launched: 2000
Frequency of update: Daily
Website Access: Free
Traffic Figures: 50,000 Unique Users (per month Publisher's Statement)
Editor: Dave Wilson
Summary of Content: Website containing product and company news and technical features.
Readership/Target Audience: Aimed at product design engineers and machine builders.
BUSINESS: ENGINEERING & MACHINERY

ENGINEERLIVE 762501U19A-541

Editorial Address: Europa House, 13-17 Ironmonger Row, LONDON, EC1V 3QG **Tel:** 020 7253 2545
Fax: 020 7608 1600
Email: editorial@setform.com
Web site: http://www.engineerlive.com
Publisher: Setform Ltd
Frequency of update: Daily
Editor: Paul Boughton
Summary of Content: Website covering latest engineering news through a combination of news stories and indepth features, also new major engineering developments and latest technologies.
Readership/Target Audience: Aimed at decision-makers involved in the engineering industry.
BUSINESS: ENGINEERING & MACHINERY

ENGLAND BASKETBALL 46034U75X-1706

Formerly: ZonePress Online
Editorial Address: PO Box 3971, SHEFFIELD, S9 9AZ **Tel:** 0114 223 5694 **Fax:** 0114 242 6419
Email: todd.stuart@englandbasketball.co.uk
Web site: http://www.englandbasketball.co.uk
Publisher: English Basketball Association
Date Launched: 1974
Frequency of update: Daily
Website Access: Paid
Traffic Figures: 24,567 Unique Users (per month Publisher's Statement)
Editor: Todd Stuart; **Web Editor:** Todd Stuart
Summary of Content: Website containing news, match reports and championship coverage. Official site of the England Basketball Association.
Readership/Target Audience: Aimed at clubs and those with an interest in basketball.
CONSUMER: SPORT: Other Sport

Internet Media

ENTERTAIN
1827096U89C-1110

Editorial Address: The Basement, Woodlands, 79 High Street, GREENHITHE, DA9 9RD **Tel:** 01322 386444
Fax: 01322 386660
Email: toni@expansivemedia.com
Web site: http://www.entertaindvd.com
Publisher: Expansive Media Ltd
Date Launched: 2007
Frequency of update: 6 times a year
Website Access: Paid
Traffic Figures: 60,000 Unique Users (Publisher's Statement)
Editor: Toni Wade
Summary of Content: Interactive entertainment magazine on DVD covering cinema and television including trailers, interviews, behind the scenes footage and features as well as trails of PC games, down loads, web links and reviews.
Readership/Target Audience: Aimed at men and women with an interest in films.
CONSUMER: HOLIDAYS & TRAVEL: Entertainment Guides

ENTERTAINMENT4MEDIA.COM
1776304U64K-653

Editorial Address: The Chandlery, 50 Westminster Bridge Road, LONDON, SE1 7QY **Tel:** 020 7953 8770
Fax: 020 7953 8773
Email: news.desk@entertainment4media.com
Web site: http://www.entertainment4media.com
Publisher: News4Media Ltd
Date Launched: 2006
Frequency of update: Daily
Website Access: Free
Traffic Figures: 10,000 Unique Users (Publisher's Statement)
Editor: Henry Hemming
Summary of Content: Online arts and entertainment news service covering film, TV, music, radio, celebrities, comedy, books, art, festivals, dvd and video, online and mobile and games.
Readership/Target Audience: Aimed at entertainment companies, organisations and PR companies.
BUSINESS: OTHER CLASSIFICATIONS: Cinema Entertainment

ENTERTAINMENT WISE
1870531U74Q-1406

Editorial Address: 60 Tabernacle Street, LONDON, EC2A 4NB **Tel:** 020 7336 0616
Email: cher@entertainmentwise.com
Web site: http://www.entertainmentwise.com
Date Launched: 2004
Frequency of update: Daily
Website Access: Free
Traffic Figures: 40,000 Unique Users (per day Publisher's Statement)
Editor: Cher Tippetts
Summary of Content: Web site covering entertainment, celebrities, movies, music, lifestyle and TV.
CONSUMER: WOMEN'S INTEREST CONSUMER MAGAZINES: Lifestyle

ENTS24.COM
1785450U76D-822

Editorial Address: PO Box 1379, BRISTOL, BS99 3HE
Tel: 0117 973 0548 **Fax:** 0117 973 0152
Email: events@ents24.com
Web site: http://www.ents24.com
Publisher: Ents24 Ltd
Date Launched: 1999
Frequency of update: Daily
Website Access: Free
Traffic Figures: 1,000,000 Unique Users (per month Publisher's Statement)
Editor: Sarah Barter
Summary of Content: Website covering entertainment throughout the UK including live music, clubbing, theatre, arts and stand-up comedy.
Readership/Target Audience: Aimed at fans of music, comedy and arts of all ages.
Other Features: Newsletter, tour date and ticket on sale alerts via email, message board.
CONSUMER: MUSIC & PERFORMING ARTS: Music

EPHOTOZINE
714942U85A-95

Editorial Address: The Turbine, Shireoaks Triangle Business Park, Coach Close, Shireoaks, WORKSOP, S81 8AP **Tel:** 01909 512111 **Fax:** 01909 512147
Email: info@ephotozine.com
Web site: http://www.ephotozine.com
Publisher: Magezine Publishing Ltd.
Date Launched: 2001
Frequency of update: Daily
Website Access: Free

Traffic Figures: 702,774 Unique Users (01/04/2009 To 30/04/2009 ABC/Electronic)
Editor: Peter Bargh
Summary of Content: Website focusing on photography. Includes techniques, equipment reviews, photo galleries and daily news.
Readership/Target Audience: Aimed at all levels of photographers and creative image makers.
Other Features: Features include a chat forum and archiving.
CONSUMER: PHOTOGRAPHY & FILM MAKING: Photography

EPOLITIX.COM
634635U82-21_50

Formerly: ePolitix
Editorial Address: Westminster Tower, 3rd Floor, 3 Albert Embankment, LONDON, SE1 7SP **Tel:** 020 7091 7530
Email: editorial@epolitix.com
Web site: http://www.epolitix.com
Publisher: Dods
Date Launched: 2000
Frequency of update: Daily
Website Access: Paid
Editor: Daniel Forman
Summary of Content: Website containing the latest political and parliamentary news at Westminster, the Scottish Parliament and the assemblies in Northern Ireland and Wales and also featuring coverage from London and Europe.
Readership/Target Audience: Read by MPs and professionals in the media and public affairs industry.
Other Features: Features include an events calendar, recruitment, e-mail newsletters and archives of news stories. Public affairs messages from organisations, MP links, legislation details and political blogs.
CONSUMER: CURRENT AFFAIRS & POLITICS

EQUESTRIAN
629233U75E-30

Editorial Address: Easons Barn, Easons Green, Framfield, UCKFIELD, TN22 5RB **Tel:** 01825 873444
Fax: 01825 873555
Email: editor@equestrian.co.uk
Web site: http://www.equestrian.co.uk
Publisher: Remus
Date Launched: 1996
Frequency of update: Daily
Website Access: Free
Traffic Figures: 50,000 Unique Users (per month Publisher's Statement)
Editor: Sarah Johnstone
Summary of Content: Website focusing on news and information regarding the UK competitive equestrian industry. Includes horses for sales and new product information.
Readership/Target Audience: Aimed at professional horse riders and enthusiasts.
CONSUMER: SPORT: Horse Racing

EQUINE WORLD UK
633884U75E-32

Editorial Address: 18 Shepherds Close, Grove, WANTAGE, OX12 0NX **Tel:** 01235 224633
Email: ewuk@acorn-internet-ltd.co.uk
Web site: http://www.equine-world.co.uk
Publisher: Acorn Internet Ltd
Date Launched: 2000
Frequency of update: Daily
Website Access: Free
Traffic Figures: 110,000 Unique Users (per month Publisher's Statement)
Editor: Lorraine Hill
Summary of Content: Equestrian resource and community website aimed at UK horse enthusiasts. Includes news and information, product news, equine care information and an online store.
Readership/Target Audience: Read by UK equestrians, enthusiasts and professional horse riders.
Other Features: Features include a forum events listings, product news, information section, pictures & videos.
CONSUMER: SPORT: Horse Racing

EQUITY BITES
1667970U1F-599

Editorial Address: PR by email only **Tel:** 020 7047 0200
Email: m2pw@m2.com
Web site: http://www.m2.com
Publisher: M2 Communications Ltd
Date Launched: 2004
Frequency of update: Daily
Website Access: Paid
Editor: Jamie Ayres
Summary of Content: Electronically delivered news service providing daily coverage of stories relating to companies in the FTSE 100, FTSE 250 and the S&P exchanges.

Readership/Target Audience: Aimed at industry professionals.
BUSINESS: FINANCE & ECONOMICS: Investment

EQUIWORLD.NET
628988U81D-52_50

Editorial Address: Hayfield, Hazelhead Park, ABERDEEN, AB15 8BB **Tel:** 01224 321132 **Fax:** 01224 321132
Email: press@equiworld.com
Web site: http://www.equiworld.net
Date Launched: 1994
Frequency of update: Daily
Website Access: Free
Traffic Figures: 6,500 Unique Users (per day Publisher's Statement)
Editor: Caroline Martin
Summary of Content: Website focusing on news and information about horses and all equestrian matters.
Readership/Target Audience: Aimed at anyone interested in horses.
Other Features: Features include archiving, discussion forums and an e-mail newsletter.
CONSUMER: ANIMALS & PETS: Horses & Ponies

ETHICAL CONSUMER
601352U74C-104

Formerly: ethicalconsumer.org
Editorial Address: Unit 21, 41 Old Birley Street, MANCHESTER, MI5 5RF **Tel:** 0161 226 2929
Fax: 0161 226 6277
Email: news@ethicalconsumer.org
Web site: http://www.ethicalconsumer.org
Publisher: ECRA Publishing Ltd
Date Launched: 1989
Frequency of update: 6 times a year
Website Access: Paid
Traffic Figures: 6,500 Unique Users (Publisher's Statement)
Editor: Jane Turner
Summary of Content: Website providing information on companies and products so consumers can vote with their wallets. Covers animal welfare, environmental sustainability, human rights, the organic movement and fair trade.
Readership/Target Audience: Aimed at consumers wanting to know more about ethical consumerism, with league tables of over 160 products on our buyers guide website.
Other Features: Features include a buyer's guide and archiving.
CONSUMER: WOMEN'S INTEREST CONSUMER MAGAZINES: Home & Family

E-TID.COM
39746U50-16_10

Formerly: Travel Industry Digest
Editorial Address: Julia House, 40-44 Newman Street, LONDON, W1T 1QD **Tel:** 020 7436 1088
Email: newsdesk@e-tid.com
Web site: http://www.e-tid.com
Publisher: EastCastle Publishing
Date Launched: 2000
Frequency of update: Daily
Website Access: Free
Traffic Figures: 15,000 Unique Users (Publisher's Statement)
Editor: Janine Murphy
Summary of Content: Website news service focusing on all aspects of the travel and hospitality industry.
Readership/Target Audience: Read by senior executives working in the travel and leisure industry.
BUSINESS: TRAVEL & TOURISM

EUROMONEY.COM
629301U1F-177_50

Editorial Address: Nestor House, Playhouse Yard, LONDON, EC4V 5EX **Tel:** 020 7779 8650
Fax: 020 7779 8345
Email: editorialassistant@euromoney.com
Web site: http://www.euromoney.com
Publisher: Euromoney Institutional Investor plc
Date Launched: 1996
Frequency of update: Daily
Website Access: Paid
Traffic Figures: 705,598 Unique Users (2008 Publisher's Statement)
Summary of Content: Business and investment magazine and website offering news, analysis and research. Focusing on the world's capital, equity and money markets.
Readership/Target Audience: Read by presidents of companies, directors, chairmen, corporate treasurers, institutional investors and investment and accounting personnel worldwide.
Other Features: Weekly newsletter, research, archive to 1996, breaking news updates.
BUSINESS: FINANCE & ECONOMICS: Investment

EUROPE AFRICA NEWSLETTER 38604U33-15

Formerly: Offshore Mediterranean and West Africa
Editorial Address: PO Box 2779, LONDON, W2 6ZW
Tel: 020 7386 5703
Email: info@offshore-intelligence.org.uk
Web site: http://www.offshore-intelligence.org.uk
Publisher: Offshore Intelligence
Frequency of update: Weekly
Website Access: Paid
Editor: Steve Garner
Summary of Content: Online report covering offshore oil and gas exploration in the Mediterranean, West Africa and the Western Caspian.
Readership/Target Audience: Aimed at people working within the gas and oil industry.
BUSINESS: OIL & PETROLEUM

EUROPEAN BUSINESS AIR NEWS 626219U6A-74

Editorial Address: 134 South Street, BISHOP'S STORTFORD, CM23 3BQ **Tel:** 01279 714505
Fax: 01279 714519
Email: rod@ebanmagazine.com
Web site: http://www.ebanmagazine.com
Publisher: Stansted News Ltd
Date Launched: 1990
Frequency of update: Daily
Website Access: Free
Traffic Figures: 23,345 Unique Users (per month Publisher's Statement)
Editor: Rod Smith
Summary of Content: Website covering the world of business flight and the European business aircraft industry.
Readership/Target Audience: Aimed at aviation operators and other business aircraft owners.
BUSINESS: AVIATION & AERONAUTICS

EUROPEAN DAILY CARBON MARKETS

1810732U58-186
Editorial Address: 1 Procter Street, Holborn, LONDON, WC1V 6EU **Tel:** 020 7911 1920 **Fax:** 020 7911 1851
Email: info@icisheren.com
Web site: http://www.heren.com
Date Launched: 2006
Frequency of update: 260 times a year
Website Access: Paid
Traffic Figures: 1,000 Unique Users (per month Publisher's Statement)
Editor: Isabelle Save
Summary of Content: Electronic newsletter covering the European carbon marketplace, EU Emissions Trading Scheme and the Kyoto Protocol.
Readership/Target Audience: Aimed at decision makers and traders within the power industry.
BUSINESS: ENERGY, FUEL & NUCLEAR

EUROPEAN EMPLOYMENT REVIEW

36951U14C-70_5
Formerly: European Industrial Relations Review
Editorial Address: Quadrant House, The Quadrant, Brighton Road, SUTTON, SM2 5AS **Tel:** 020 8652 2243
Fax: 020 8652 4394
Email: beatrice.harper@irseclipse.co.uk
Web site: http://www.irsonline.co.uk
Publisher: IRS
Date Launched: 1974
Frequency of update: Monthly
Website Access: Paid
Editor: Beatrice Harper
Summary of Content: Website covering industrial relations in Europe.
Readership/Target Audience: Read by directors, managers, trade union members, academics and personnel officers.
BUSINESS: COMMERCE, INDUSTRY & MANAGEMENT: International Commerce

EUROPEAN FRANCHISING 1667153U14A-543

Editorial Address: Franchise House, 56 Surrey Street, NORWICH, NR1 3FD **Tel:** 01603 620301 **Fax:** 01603 630174
Email: editorial@fdsltd.com
Web site: http://www.europeanfranchising.net
Publisher: Franchise Development Services Ltd
Date Launched: 2005
Frequency of update: Daily
Website Access: Free
Editor: Stuart Anderson
Summary of Content: Online publication promoting the availability of master franchise rights throughout Europe.

Readership/Target Audience: Aimed at individuals and organisations seeking to operate a master franchise.
BUSINESS: COMMERCE, INDUSTRY & MANAGEMENT

EUROPEAN NATURAL GAS 38078U24-8

Formerly: Financial Times Gas Daily Europe
Editorial Address: 20 Canada Square, Canary Wharf, LONDON, E14 5LH **Tel:** 020 7176 6268 **Fax:** 020 7176 6670
Email: power@platts.com
Web site: http://www.platts.com
Publisher: Platts
Date Launched: 1999
Frequency of update: 260 times a year
Website Access: Paid
Editor: Eloise Logan
Summary of Content: Electronically mailed news and pricing service covering the European gas market.
Readership/Target Audience: Aimed at gas traders, producers, consultants and marketers.
BUSINESS: GAS

EUROPEAN SPOT GAS MARKETS 38076U24-6

Formerly: British Spot Gas Markets
Editorial Address: 1 Procter Street, LONDON, WC1V 6EU
Tel: 020 7911 1920 **Fax:** 020 7911 1851
Email: info@icisheren.com
Web site: http://www.icis.com/heren
Publisher: ICIS Heren
Date Launched: 1994
Frequency of update: 240 times a year
Website Access: Paid
Editor: Ed Cox
Summary of Content: Market report covering news and analysis of European gas markets.
Readership/Target Audience: Aimed at those involved in the gas industry.
BUSINESS: GAS

EUROPROPERTY (ONLINE) 626457U1E-169_50

Editorial Address: 1 Procter Street, LONDON, WC1V 6EU
Tel: 020 7911 1845 **Fax:** 020 7911 1900
Email: mark.cooper@rbi.co.uk
Web site: http://www.europroperty.com
Publisher: Reed Business Information
Date Launched: 1996
Frequency of update: 22 times a year
Website Access: Paid
Editor: Mark Cooper
Summary of Content: Website covering news and information about the European commercial property market, as well as a searchable database.
Readership/Target Audience: Aimed at senior commercial property investors and developers working on an international level.
BUSINESS: FINANCE & ECONOMICS: Property

EVECARS.COM 1740120U77A-595

Editorial Address: Teddington Studios, Broom Road, TEDDINGTON, TW11 9BE **Tel:** 020 8267 5654
Fax: 020 8267 5750
Email: alexandra.jenner-fust@haymarket.com
Web site: http://www.evecars.com
Publisher: Haymarket Motoring
Date Launched: 2006
Frequency of update: Daily
Website Access: Free
Traffic Figures: 80,000 Unique Users (Publisher's Statement)
Editor: Iain Reid
Summary of Content: Online magazine offering advice to women about buying a car including car reviews, practical advice and information about finances.
Readership/Target Audience: Aimed at women of all ages and budgets who want help choosing which car to buy.
CONSUMER: MOTORING & CYCLING: Motoring

EVENT ORGANISERS UPDATE 1810842U2C-517

Editorial Address: 29A Market Square, BIGGLESWADE, SG18 8AQ **Tel:** 01767 316255
Email: info@eou.org.uk
Web site: http://www.eou.org.uk
Publisher: The Meetings Forum
Frequency of update: 6 times a year
Website Access: Free
Traffic Figures: 30,000 Unique Users (Publisher's Statement)
Editor: Peter Cotterell
Summary of Content: Electronic newsletter of the Society of Event Organisers featuring news and comment about the

sector including venues, restaurant reviews, technology and training advice.
Readership/Target Audience: Aimed at organisers of corporate and associated events.
BUSINESS: COMMUNICATIONS, ADVERTISING & MARKETING: Conferences & Exhibitions

EVERYINVESTOR.CO.UK 1808727U74M-428

Editorial Address: 1 Vincent Square, LONDON, SW1P 2PN
Tel: 020 7932 4158
Email: feedback@everyinvestor.co.uk
Web site: http://www.everyinvestor.co.uk
Publisher: Every Investor Ltd
Date Launched: 2003
Frequency of update: Daily
Website Access: Free
Traffic Figures: 500,000 Unique Users (Publisher's Statement)
Editor: Corin Vestey; **Editor-in-Chief:** Chris Gilchrist
Summary of Content: Website with best buy information on financial products including mortgages, personal loans, credit cards, savings accounts, ISAs, insurances, investment funds and pensions as well as personal finance editorial.
Readership/Target Audience: Aimed at individual investors and savers.
Other Features: Other features on the site Money Maker Newsletter and The Share Weekly Newsletter.
CONSUMER: WOMEN'S INTEREST CONSUMER MAGAZINES: Personal Finance

EVERYWOMAN.CO.UK 626258U74A-96

Formerly: Everywoman
Editorial Address: 17 Wootton Street, LONDON, SE1 8TG
Tel: 0870 746 1800
Email: editor@everywoman.co.uk
Web site: http://www.everywoman.co.uk
Date Launched: 1999
Frequency of update: Daily
Website Access: Free
Traffic Figures: 25,000 Unique Users (per month Publisher's Statement)
Editor: Ruth Jordan
Summary of Content: Website providing information and advice for women business owners and women interested in setting up their own business as well as women in senior corporate roles. Features include a conference programme, an awards programme and a support services programme.
Readership/Target Audience: Aimed at women aged between 20 to 55 years of age.
Other Features: Features include a bulletin board, e-mail newsletter mailing list and a marketplace where products and services can be promoted.
CONSUMER: WOMEN'S INTEREST CONSUMER MAGAZINES: Women's Interest

EWEEKEUROPE UK 1894026U5C-917

Editorial Address: 54 Poland Street, LONDON, W1F 7NJ
Tel: 020 7432 7254 **Fax:** 020 7681 1516
Email: pjudge@netmediaeurope.com
Web site: http://www.eweekeurope.co.uk
Publisher: NetMediaEurope
Date Launched: 2009
Frequency of update: Daily
Website Access: Free
Editor: Peter Judge
Summary of Content: Technology news site addressing the new corporate climate and covering sustainability and return on investment, efficient computing which can cut energy costs and other bills and flexible IT. Topics include mobility and wireless, security, networking and storage.
Readership/Target Audience: Aimed at all IT professionals.
BUSINESS: COMPUTERS & AUTOMATION: Professional Personal Computers

EXCLUSIVE LONDON 1746722U89C-1078

Editorial Address: Office 6231, 2nd Floor, 49 Greenwich High Road, LONDON, SE10 8JL **Tel:** 0845 299 7744
Email: editor@exclusivelondon.co.uk
Web site: http://www.exclusivelondon.co.uk
Publisher: Exclusive London Group
Date Launched: 2003
Frequency of update: Weekly
Website Access: Free
Traffic Figures: 200,000 Unique Users (per week Publisher's Statement)
Editor: Maryse Mignott
Summary of Content: Website covering London lifestyle and entertainment including clubs and bars, fashion, restaurants, cinema, finance, music, health and fitness, beauty, culture and gadgets.

Internet Media

Readership/Target Audience: Aimed at affluent young professionals aged between 21 and 35 years old living, working or visiting London.
CONSUMER: HOLIDAYS & TRAVEL: Entertainment Guides

EXEC UK
1825900U14A-589
Editorial Address: Grosvenor House, Prince of Wales Road, NORWICH, NR1 1NS **Tel:** 01603 217530 **Fax:** 01603 617082
Email: editor@whitedm.com
Web site: http://www.execdigital.co.uk
Publisher: White Digital Media Ltd
Date Launched: 2007
Frequency of update: Daily
Website Access: Paid
Traffic Figures: 170,000 Unique Users (per month Publisher's Statement)
Editor: Paul Pearce-Couch
Summary of Content: Online magazine covering men's fashion and health, retail, automotives, manufacturing, reviews, energy and executive lifestyle. Includes a diary and new appointments section, high-end domestic, commercial and overseas property.
Readership/Target Audience: Aimed at c-level business executives.
BUSINESS: COMMERCE, INDUSTRY & MANAGEMENT

EXECUTIVE TRAVELLER
1640565U50-210
Editorial Address: 33 Donkin House, Galleywall Road, LONDON, SE16 3PQ **Tel:** 07984 021973
Email: lyssiemay@executivetraveller.net
Web site: http://www.executivetraveller.net
Publisher: LNA Associates Ltd
Date Launched: 2003
Frequency of update: Quarterly
Website Access: Paid
Traffic Figures: 500,000 Unique Users (Publisher's Statement)
Editor: Lyssiemay Annoh
Summary of Content: Electronic magazine with monthly newsletters featuring economic features on the industry, including tourist and exclusive destinations, with detailed travel features from around the world, tried and tested gadgets as well as food and drink reviews.
Readership/Target Audience: Aimed at those who want to travel comfortably and eat well.
BUSINESS: TRAVEL & TOURISM

EXIT ONLINE
1895034U74Q-1373
Editorial Address: 205 Regent Street, LONDON, W1B 4HB **Tel:** 020 7734 5299 **Fax:** 020 7734 5392
Email: steve@exitmagazine.co.uk
Web site: http://www.exitmagazine.co.uk
Frequency of update: Daily
Website Access: Free
Editor: Stephen Toner
Summary of Content: Website featuring art, fashion, photography and travel features.
Readership/Target Audience: Aimed at men and women aged between 20 and 35 years old with a high disposable income.
CONSUMER: WOMEN'S INTEREST CONSUMER MAGAZINES: Lifestyle

EXPAT.TELEGRAPH
707447U94D-80
Formerly: Global Network
Editorial Address: 111 Buckingham Palace, LONDON, SW1W 0EG **Tel:** 020 7931 2796
Email: sirgut.yadeta@telegraph.co.uk
Web site: http://www.expat.telegraph.co.uk
Date Launched: 1998
Frequency of update: Daily
Website Access: Free
Traffic Figures: 500,000 Unique Users (per month Publisher's Statement)
Editor: Sirgut Yadeta
Summary of Content: Website containing information on personal finance, healthcare issues, property and education. Also contains news on sport.
Readership/Target Audience: Aimed at Britons living overseas and those interested in things British.
Other Features: Features include archiving, a buyer's guide, a discussion forum, classified ads, stories by expats, expert advice and an e-mail newsletter.
CONSUMER: OTHER CLASSIFICATIONS: Expatriates

EYEBROW
1826932U82-278
Editorial Address: 25C Upper Cheyne Row, LONDON, SW3 5JL **Tel:** 07940 176128
Email: rebecca@eyebrowmagazine.com
Web site: http://www.eyebrowmagazine.com

Date Launched: 2007
Frequency of update: Daily
Website Access: Free
Editor: Rebecca Thornton
Summary of Content: Online magazine covering worldwide current affairs and entertainment.
Readership/Target Audience: Aimed and those in their 20s and 30s.
Other Features: Newsletter, archiving, web forums, correspondence, polls and videos.
CONSUMER: CURRENT AFFAIRS & POLITICS

EYEFORTRANSPORT
749237U49A-102
Editorial Address: 7-9 Fashion Street, LONDON, E1 6PX
Tel: 020 7375 7500 **Fax:** 020 7375 7511
Email: pressrelease@eyefortransport.com
Web site: http://www.eyefortransport.com
Date Launched: 1998
Frequency of update: Daily
Website Access: Free
Traffic Figures: 300,000 Unique Users (per month Publisher's Statement)
Editor: Chris Saynor
Summary of Content: Website providing news for the transport industry. Includes research and reports, video and audio sections, and a glossary.
Readership/Target Audience: Aimed at freight industry professionals.
BUSINESS: TRANSPORT

EYEFORTRAVEL
749239U50-16_13
Editorial Address: 7/9 Fashion Street, LONDON, E1 6PX
Tel: 020 7375 7552 **Fax:** 020 7375 7511
Email: news@eyefortravel.com
Web site: http://www.eyefortravel.com
Date Launched: 1997
Frequency of update: Daily
Website Access: Free
Traffic Figures: 300,000 Unique Users (per month Publisher's Statement)
Editor: Simon Carkeek
Summary of Content: Website providing news and information for the travel industry.
Readership/Target Audience: Aimed at professionals within the travel industry in the USA and Europe.
BUSINESS: TRAVEL & TOURISM

FABRICDIRECTOR-E
1616379U47A-568
Editorial Address: South House 3A, Suite 4, Bond Estate, Bond Avenue, Bletchley, MILTON KEYNES, MK1 1SW
Tel: 0870 870 4578 **Fax:** 0870 870 4679
Email: hannah@director-e.com
Web site: http://www.fabricdirector-e.com
Publisher: Marston Consulting Ltd TA director-e.com
Date Launched: 2003
Frequency of update: Daily
Website Access: Free
Traffic Figures: 92,000 Unique Users (per month Publisher's Statement)
Editor: John Gibbon
Summary of Content: Online database and news service containing information relating to the fabric industry from underwear to outerwear. Generic searches of fabrics by type and fabrics by use, designers, manufacturers, suppliers. Features as well as corporate/work wear clothing manufacturers, contracts, jobs and surplus stock, industry standards and events.
Readership/Target Audience: Aimed at designers, trends forecast, fabric manufacturers and suppliers.
BUSINESS: CLOTHING & TEXTILES

FACILITIES MANAGEMENT & MAINTENANCE INDUSTRY DIRECTORY
1818157U4R-625
Editorial Address: 18 Generator Hall, Electric Wharf, COVENTRY, CV1 4JL **Tel:** 0870 199 4044
Fax: 0870 777 4360
Email: enquiries@industrydirectory.co.uk
Web site: http://www.industrydirectory.co.uk/maintenance
Publisher: Simply Marcomms
Frequency of update: Daily
Website Access: Free
Editor: Kirstie Colledge
Summary of Content: Directory containing the latest news stories for the facilities management and maintenance industry. Includes a news archive.
Readership/Target Audience: Aimed at professionals in the building and construction industry particularly those in facilities management and maintenance.
BUSINESS: ARCHITECTURE & BUILDING: Building Related

FACILITIES MANAGEMENT ONLINE
622873U4R-386_70
Formerly: FMO
Editorial Address: Cefn Tew, Tynlon, Llanddeusant, HOLYHEAD, LL65 4AU **Tel:** 01248 470477
Fax: 01248 470003
Email: copy@fmonline.co.uk
Web site: http://www.fmonline.co.uk
Publisher: Facilities Management Online Limited
Date Launched: 1999
Frequency of update: Daily
Website Access: Free
Traffic Figures: 50,000 Unique Users (per month Publisher's Statement)
Editor: James Brunson
Summary of Content: Bi-monthly targeted E-shot and website focusing mainly on being a service supplier and product locator directory for UK based companies. Provides a targeted newsletter service to UK Managing Directors and high net-worth decision maker contacts within the UK's largest corporations and SME market. Website and newsletter service provides advertisers with a targeted distribution channel to distribute their latest company profiles and monthly news and product stories or press releases.
Readership/Target Audience: Aimed at UK based Managing Directors in charge of purchasing goods and services for small to major blue chip UK based companies.
BUSINESS: ARCHITECTURE & BUILDING: Building Related

FACTORYEQUIPMENT.COM
1666070U19A-554
Editorial Address: PO Box 223, TUNBRIDGE WELLS, TN2 9HU **Tel:** 01892 619616 **Fax:** 01892 619616
Email: editorial@factoryequipment.com
Web site: http://www.factoryequipment.com
Publisher: Process and Control Today Ltd
Date Launched: 2005
Frequency of update: Daily
Website Access: Free
Traffic Figures: 37,428 Unique Users (Publisher's Statement)
Editor: John Houston
Summary of Content: Online journal covering product and business news for the industrial, manufacture and engineering sector.
Readership/Target Audience: Aimed at buyers/specifiers, engineers, managers and directors from end user and OEM markets.
BUSINESS: ENGINEERING & MACHINERY

FAIRWAY TO GREEN OXFORDSHIRE
1664341U75D-544
Editorial Address: For all contact details see main edition, Fairway to Green
Frequency of update: Monthly
Traffic Figures: 28,000 Unique Users (Publisher's Statement)
CONSUMER: SPORT: Golf

THE FALKIRK HERALD ON-LINE
629712U72D-1026
Editorial Address: Redbrae Road, Camelon, FALKIRK, FK1 4ZA **Tel:** 01324 638314 **Fax:** 01324 629792
Email: editorial@falkirkherald.co.uk
Web site: http://www.falkirktoday.co.uk
Date Launched: 1998
Frequency of update: Daily
Website Access: Free
Editor: Colin Hume
Summary of Content: Website containing news, sport, information, entertainment and features about Falkirk.
Readership/Target Audience: Read by residents and visitors to the local area.
Other Features: Features include recruitment, chat forums and archiving.
LOCAL NEWSPAPERS: Local Newspapers Scotland

FAMILY MOTORING
1772597U77A-599
Editorial Address: 39 Stoneleigh Road, OXTED, RH8 0TP
Tel: 01883 722468
Email: j.violet@virgin.net
Web site: http://www.familymotoring.co.uk
Date Launched: 2006
Frequency of update: Monthly
Website Access: Free
Editor: Jackie Violet
Summary of Content: Website covering manufacturers' news, car reviews, safety issues, family travel, insurance and environmental issues.

Readership/Target Audience: Aimed at families looking to buy a new car.
CONSUMER: MOTORING & CYCLING: Motoring

FAMILYFUN
1860290U74C-880

Editorial Address: 49 North Worple Way, Mortlake, LONDON, SW14 8PZ **Tel:** 020 8876 1948
Email: info@famfun.co.uk
Web site: http://www.famfun.co.uk
Date Launched: 2007
Frequency of update: Daily
Website Access: Free
Traffic Figures: 40,000 Unique Users (Publisher's Statement)
Editor: David Wright
Summary of Content: Website featuring ideas for fun days out for families in London, including culture, arts, sports and leisure activities.
Readership/Target Audience: Aimed predominantly at parents of children under 14 years old.
CONSUMER: WOMEN'S INTEREST CONSUMER MAGAZINES: Home & Family

FANSFC.COM
712070U75B-125_25

Formerly: fromtheterrace
Editorial Address: PO Box 24767, LONDON, SE13 6GY
Tel: 07003 470034
Email: joe@vitv.co.uk
Web site: http://www.fansfc.com
Date Launched: 1998
Frequency of update: Daily
Website Access: Free
Traffic Figures: 150,000 Unique Users (per day Publisher's Statement)
Editor: Joe Broadfoot
Summary of Content: Website containing the latest news, views and events in English and Scottish football. Includes statistics, a betting column, league tables and a daily quiz. Provides comprehensive analysis on every professional club in Britain.
Readership/Target Audience: Aimed at football enthusiasts.
Other Features: Features include a chat forum, an e-mail newsletter, book reviews and archiving.
CONSUMER: SPORT: Football

FARMERS WEEKLY INTERACTIVE
652170U21A-495

Formerly: FWI
Editorial Address: Quadrant House, The Quadrant, SUTTON, SM2 5AS **Tel:** 020 8652 4911 **Fax:** 020 8652 4005
Email: fwiinfo@rbi.co.uk
Web site: http://www.fwi.co.uk
Publisher: Reed Business Information
Date Launched: 1997
Frequency of update: Daily. News, prices, jobs, classified, forums, pictures and weather updated throughout the day
Website Access: Free
Traffic Figures: 300,000 Unique Users (per month Publisher's Statement)
Editor: Julian Gairdner
Summary of Content: Website covering UK, EU and worldwide agricultural news, market commentaries, discussion and weather. Also allows users to search for specific information published in a range of agricultural publications.
Readership/Target Audience: Aimed at the UK agricultural sector.
BUSINESS: AGRICULTURE & FARMING

FASHION156.COM
1779404U74B-723

Editorial Address: Number 1, 24 Old Royal Free Square, Liverpool Road, LONDON, NI 0YH **Tel:** 020 7359 3632
Email: info@fashion156.com
Web site: http://www.fashion156.com
Date Launched: 2006
Frequency of update: Daily
Website Access: Free
Editor: Guy Hipwell
Summary of Content: Website covering fashion shoots, style advice, thought provoking articles and beauty news as well as fashion, style and grooming tips and features for men.
Readership/Target Audience: Aimed at men and women aged predominantly between 20 and 40 years old.
CONSUMER: WOMEN'S INTEREST CONSUMER MAGAZINES: Women's Interest - Fashion

FASHION4MEDIA.COM
1834351U47A-590

Editorial Address: Unit 11, The Chandlery, 50 Westminster Bridge Road, LONDON, SE1 7QY **Tel:** 020 7953 8770
Email: news.desk@fashion4media.com
Web site: http://www.fashion4media.com
Publisher: News4Media Ltd
Frequency of update: Daily
Website Access: Free
Traffic Figures: 5,000 Unique Users (per day Publisher's Statement)
Editor: Henry Hemming
Summary of Content: Website covering breaking news from the fashion sector.
Readership/Target Audience: Aimed at fashion marketing and media professionals.
BUSINESS: CLOTHING & TEXTILES

FASHIONCAPITAL
1810521U47A-587

Editorial Address: FC House, 1st Floor, 28 Station Approach, Hayes, BROMLEY, BR2 7EH **Tel:** 020 8462 9620
Email: jenni@fashion-enter.com
Web site: http://www.fashioncapital.co.uk
Date Launched: 2003
Frequency of update: Daily
Website Access: Free
Traffic Figures: 2,000 Unique Users (per month Publisher's Statement)
Editor: Jenni Sutton
Summary of Content: Portal containing news and stories for the fashion industry. Features fashion from around the world, details of exhibitions, textiles, catwalk shows and interviews, business tips including marketing and retail advice.
Readership/Target Audience: Aimed at designers, stylists, retailers, manufacturers and members of the press.
BUSINESS: CLOTHING & TEXTILES

FASHION-ENTER
1810523U47A-588

Editorial Address: FC House, 1st Floor, 28 Station Approach, Hayes, BROMLEY, BR2 7EH **Tel:** 020 8462 9620
Email: vanessa@fashion-enter.com
Web site: http://www.fashion-enter.com
Date Launched: 2006
Frequency of update: Daily
Website Access: Paid
Traffic Figures: 300 Unique Users (per month Publisher's Statement)
Editor: Vanessa Camelia
Summary of Content: Website featuring fashion and product news, market trends, business information, links to specialists providing advice about pattern cutting, styling, business planning, marketing, sourcing and legal issues.
Readership/Target Audience: Aimed mainly at established designers, as well as new and emerging designers.
BUSINESS: CLOTHING & TEXTILES

FASHION.TELEGRAPH.CO.UK
713993U74B-125

Editorial Address: 111 Buckingham Palace Road, LONDON, SW1W 0DT **Tel:** 020 7931 2000
Email: kimberly.thrower@telegraph.co.uk
Web site: http://www.fashion.telegraph.co.uk
Publisher: Telegraph Media Group Ltd
Date Launched: 2001
Frequency of update: 260 times a year. Updated 5 times a week
Website Access: Free
Editor: Kimberly Thrower
Summary of Content: Website providing news and information about the fashion industry. Includes style, beauty, trendspotting, retail therapy sections and photo galleries.
Readership/Target Audience: Aimed at those interested in fashion.
Other Features: Features include an events calendar and email newsletter.
CONSUMER: WOMEN'S INTEREST CONSUMER MAGAZINES: Women's Interest - Fashion

FASHIONWEB.CO.UK
1810522U74B-729

Editorial Address: 15 Cottenham Road, Histon, CAMBRIDGE, CB24 9ES **Tel:** 0845 644 2284
Fax: 0845 126 0752
Email: info@fashionweb.co.uk
Web site: http://www.fashionweb.co.uk
Publisher: Fashion Web Ltd
Frequency of update: Daily
Website Access: Free
Editor: Jonathan Roth; **Webmaster:** Jonathan Roth
Summary of Content: Website covering jobs in the fashion industry, PR forum, fashion video clips, links to fashion sites, fashion news and fashion industry directory.

Readership/Target Audience: Aimed at those with an interest in fashion and those in the fashion industry.
CONSUMER: WOMEN'S INTEREST CONSUMER MAGAZINES: Women's Interest - Fashion

FAST-AUTOS.COM
1641225U77A-507

Editorial Address: 15 Forth Wynd, Port Seton, PRESTONPANS, EH32 0TL **Tel:** 01875 818988
Fax: 01875 818988
Email: fastautos@gmail.com
Web site: http://www.fast-autos.com
Publisher: Persimmon Publishing Ltd
Date Launched: 2002
Frequency of update: Weekly
Website Access: Free
Traffic Figures: 40,000 Unique Users (per month Publisher's Statement)
Editor: John Hartley
Summary of Content: Website containing articles on the latest and best high-performance cars from the very fastest near racing car to hot hatches as well as images and specifications for many more cars of this type are also included.
Readership/Target Audience: Aimed at those who own or are interested in high performance cars.
Other Features: Message board.
CONSUMER: MOTORING & CYCLING: Motoring

FASTCAR.CO.UK
1814102U77A-604

Editorial Address: 30 Monmouth Street, BATH, BA1 2BW
Tel: 01225 442244
Email: glenn.rowswell@futurenet.co.uk
Web site: http://www.fastcar.co.uk
Publisher: Future Publishing Ltd
Frequency of update: Daily
Website Access: Free
Traffic Figures: 125,000 Unique Users (per month Publisher's Statement)
Editor: Glenn Rowswell
Summary of Content: Website covering performance tuning, product information and tests as well as the latest street styles, music, people and their cars, glamour models, forums, interactive stories and classified advertisements.
Readership/Target Audience: Aimed at men aged 15 to 35 years old.
CONSUMER: MOTORING & CYCLING: Motoring

FASTENING SOLUTIONS
1639507U19A-558

Formerly: Fastening News
Editorial Address: Crendon House, Crendon Industrial Park, LONG CRENDON, HP18 9BB **Tel:** 01844 202027
Fax: 01844 202267
Email: mark@fastening-solutions.co.uk
Web site: http://www.fastening-solutions.co.uk
Publisher: NewbyCom Ltd
Frequency of update: Weekly
Website Access: Free
Editor: Mark Newby
Summary of Content: Website covering industrial fastening, fixing, adhesives and assembly.
Readership/Target Audience: Aimed at engineers and production professionals in the manufacturing industry.
BUSINESS: ENGINEERING & MACHINERY

FEED STATISTICS
37812U21B-160

Formerly: Feed Facts Quarterly
Editorial Address: Rye House, 47 Oakfield Avenue, Somersall, CHESTERFIELD, S40 3LE **Tel:** 01246 569967
Fax: 01246 567932
Email: simon@simonmounsey.com
Web site: http://www.simonmounsey.com
Publisher: Simon Mounsey Ltd
Date Launched: 1990
Frequency of update: Quarterly. Published annually and revised quarterly
Website Access: Paid
Traffic Figures: 1,050 Unique Users (Publisher's Statement)
Editor: Simon Mounsey
Summary of Content: Website report and analysis of UK and European animal feed production and ration formulation data, published annually and updated quarterly. Includes financial data on the leading 100 UK feed producers.
Readership/Target Audience: Aimed at animal feed manufacturers and their suppliers (especially of raw materials).
BUSINESS: AGRICULTURE & FARMING: Agriculture - Supplies & Services

Internet Media

FEMALEFIRST.CO.UK
1743227U74A-1009

Editorial Address: 69-71 Gerard Street, Ashton-in-Makerfield, WIGAN, WN4 9AG **Tel:** 01942 712000
Email: stephen.reay@femalefirst.co.uk
Web site: http://www.femalefirst.co.uk
Frequency of update: Daily
Website Access: Free
Traffic Figures: 3,000,000 Unique Users (per month Publisher's Statement)
Editor: Stephen Reay
Summary of Content: Website covering entertainment, celebrity gossip and interviews, DVD, music, movie and book reviews, TV, food and drink, health, home and garden, money, horoscopes, parenting, jobs, travel, weddings and competitions.
Readership/Target Audience: Aimed at women aged between 25 and 40 years old.
CONSUMER: WOMEN'S INTEREST CONSUMER MAGAZINES: Women's Interest

FENEWS.CO.UK
1703132U62F-955

Editorial Address: 6 Broad Street, Black Torrington, BEAWORTHY, EX21 5PT **Tel:** 0845 612 5750
Fax: 0845 612 0705
Email: editor@fenews.co.uk
Web site: http://www.fenews.co.uk
Date Launched: 2004
Frequency of update: Daily
Website Access: Free
Traffic Figures: 55,000 Unique Users (per month Publisher's Statement)
Editor: Jason Rainbow
Summary of Content: Website covering all aspects of further education and work based learning.
Readership/Target Audience: Aimed at principals, directors and CEOs, as well as tutors, assessors, teaching staff, government, colleges, learning providers and those interested in attending further education news.
BUSINESS: CHURCH & SCHOOL EQUIPMENT & EDUCATION: Adult Education

FHM (ONLINE)
47647U86C-193

Editorial Address: Mappin House, 4 Winsley Street, LONDON, W1W 8HF **Tel:** 020 7182 8028
Fax: 020 7182 8021
Email: general@fhm.com
Web site: http://www.fhm.com
Publisher: Bauer Consumer Media Ltd (Mappin House)
Frequency of update: Daily
Website Access: Free
Traffic Figures: 2,033,105 Unique Users (01/04/2008 To 30/04/2008 ABC/Electronic)
Editor: David Clack; **Editor-in-Chief:** Chris Mooney
Summary of Content: Website focusing on topics such as lifestyle, fashion, sport, sex, cover girls, games, bar room jokes and articles of interest. Includes access to FHM Web TV.
Readership/Target Audience: Aimed at men aged 16 years old and over.
Other Features: Features include a buyer's guide, an e-mail newsletter, competitions and archiving.
CONSUMER: ADULT & GAY MAGAZINES: Men's Lifestyle Magazines

THE FIELD ONLINE
626401U80A-110

Editorial Address: Blue Fin Building, 110 Southwark Street, LONDON, SE1 0SU **Tel:** 020 3148 5000 **Fax:** 020 3148 8179
Email: sarah_fitzpatrick@ipcmedia.com
Web site: http://www.thefield.co.uk
Publisher: IPC Inspire
Date Launched: 1998
Frequency of update: Weekly
Website Access: Free
Editor: Sarah Fitzpatrick; **Web Editor:** Jonathan Young
Summary of Content: Website covering news and features about country pursuits.
Readership/Target Audience: Aimed at those interested in all aspects of the countryside.
CONSUMER: RURAL & REGIONAL INTEREST: Rural Interest

FIFE MATTERS
1881618U72J-361

Email: comments@fife-matters.co.uk
Web site: http://www.fife-matters.co.uk
Frequency of update: Daily
Summary of Content: Website created to help people who care about local issues. Whether you need access to useful information, want to highlight a particular topic to other people, discuss ideas with like-minded people or just show your support and keep up to date with current affairs in your area, Fife Matters is the place for you.

Readership/Target Audience: Aimed at residents in the local area of Fife.
LOCAL NEWSPAPERS: Community Newsletters

FIFE TODAY
629697U80E-45

Formerly: Fife On-Line
Editorial Address: 23 Kirk Wynd, KIRKALDY, KY1 1EP
Tel: 01592 598811
Email: ffpnews@fifetoday.co.uk
Web site: http://www.fifetoday.co.uk
Publisher: Johnston Press plc
Date Launched: 1998
Frequency of update: 260 times a year. Updated every week day
Website Access: Free
Editor: Allan Crow
Summary of Content: Website containing news, sport, information and features about the Fife area.
Readership/Target Audience: Read by residents and visitors to the local area.
Other Features: Features include a chat forum.
CONSUMER: RURAL & REGIONAL INTEREST: Regional Interest Scotland

FIFTHGEAR.FIVE.TV
1828365U77A-608

Editorial Address: 2 Shad Thames, LONDON, SE1 2YU
Tel: 020 7234 0221 **Fax:** 020 7403 8096
Email: andy.pringle@mac.com
Web site: http://fifthgear.five.tv
Publisher: Spyder Redspy
Frequency of update: Daily
Website Access: Free
Editor: Andy Pringle
Summary of Content: Website backing up and promoting the television programme Fifth Gear with test drives, road tests and motoring news.
Readership/Target Audience: Aimed at anyone interested in cars.
CONSUMER: MOTORING & CYCLING: Motoring

FILM AND SHEET EXTRUSION
1882059U39-161

Editorial Address: AMI House, 45-47 Stokes Croft, BRISTOL, BS1 3QP **Tel:** 0117 924 9442 **Fax:** 0117 989 2128
Email: lou@filmandsheet.com
Web site: http://www.filmandsheet.com
Publisher: Applied Market Information Ltd
Date Launched: 2009
Frequency of update: 6 times a year. Published in the middle of the first month
Website Access: Free
Traffic Figures: 11,788 Unique Users (Publisher's Statement)
Editor: Lou Reade
Summary of Content: Digital magazine featuring technical developments, market trends, business news and legislative announcements for the producers of polymer film and sheets.
Readership/Target Audience: Aimed at producers of plastics, film and sheet.
BUSINESS: PLASTICS & RUBBER

FILM EDUCATION
1696018U62B-1409

Editorial Address: 91 Berwick Street, LONDON, W1F 0BP
Tel: 020 7292 7330 **Fax:** 020 7287 6970
Email: postbox@filmeducation.org
Web site: http://www.filmeducation.org
Frequency of update: 260 times a year
Website Access: Free
Traffic Figures: 60,000 Unique Users (per month Publisher's Statement)
Editor: Chris Bauer
Summary of Content: Website focusing on film related resources for schools.
Readership/Target Audience: Aimed at teachers.
BUSINESS: CHURCH & SCHOOL EQUIPMENT & EDUCATION: Education Teachers

FINANCE DAILY
1775366U74M-423

Editorial Address: Madeira House, Madeira Walk, WINDSOR, SL4 1EU **Tel:** 01753 860700
Email: dedwards@utmedia.co.uk
Web site: http://www.financedaily.co.uk
Publisher: UTMedia
Date Launched: 2006
Frequency of update: Daily
Website Access: Free
Traffic Figures: 800,000 Unique Users (Publisher's Statement)
Editor: Dan Edwards

Summary of Content: Website with personal finance news, advice, business and finance, columns and tips.
Readership/Target Audience: Aimed at the general public looking for financial advice and the latest finance or business news.
CONSUMER: WOMEN'S INTEREST CONSUMER MAGAZINES: Personal Finance

FINANCE INDUSTRY DIRECTORY
1912965U1R-405

Editorial Address: 18 Generator Hall, Electric Wharf, COVENTRY, CV1 4JL **Tel:** 0870 199 4044
Fax: 0870 777 4360
Email: enquires@industrydirectory.co.uk
Web site: http://www.industrydirectory.co.uk
Publisher: Simply Marcomms
Frequency of update: Daily
Website Access: Free
Editor: Kirstie Colledge
Summary of Content: Directory containing the latest news stories for the UK finance industry. Includes news archives.
Readership/Target Audience: Aimed at Finance professionals, suppliers to the Finance industry, Finance Industry PR & Marketing firms.
BUSINESS: FINANCE & ECONOMICS: Financial Related

FINANCIAL NEWS
1896319U1F-668

Editorial Address: 2nd Floor, Stapleton House, 29-33 Scrutton Street, LONDON, EC2A 4HU **Tel:** 020 7426 3333
Fax: 020 7426 3329
Web site: http://www.efinancialnews.com
Publisher: Efinancialnews.com
Frequency of update: Daily
Editor: Phillipa Leighton-Jones
Summary of Content: Financial website focusing on securities and investment banking.
Readership/Target Audience: Aimed at those involved in the securities and investment banking sector.
BUSINESS: FINANCE & ECONOMICS: Investment

FINDTHEFAIRWAYS.COM
1814205U75D-559

Editorial Address: Centaur House, Ancells Business Park, Ancells Road, FLEET, GU51 2UJ **Tel:** 07740 554261
Email: press@findthefairways.com
Web site: http://www.findthefairways.com
Date Launched: 2007
Frequency of update: Daily
Website Access: Free
Traffic Figures: 479,649 Unique Users (2008 Publisher's Statement)
Editor: Jonathan Ashworth
Summary of Content: Website covering all aspects of golf including golf tips, golf equipment, courses, holidays, golf tips videos, travel and breaking news.
Readership/Target Audience: Aimed at golfers of all abilities.
Other Features: Additional features include buyers' guide, newsletter, news and forum.
CONSUMER: SPORT: Golf

FINEXTRA
628973U5B-84_90

Editorial Address: 101 St. Martin's Lane, LONDON, WC2N 4AZ **Tel:** 020 3100 3670
Email: news@finextra.com
Web site: http://www.finextra.com
Publisher: Finextra Research
Date Launched: 2001
Frequency of update: Daily. Updated throughout every working day
Website Access: Free
Traffic Figures: 57,000 Unique Users (Publisher's Statement)
Editor: Paul Penrose
Summary of Content: Website providing worldwide financial technology news.
Readership/Target Audience: Aimed exclusively at financial technology professionals in financial markets, wholesale banking, retail banking and insurance.
BUSINESS: COMPUTERS & AUTOMATION: Data Processing

FIRA INTERNATIONAL LIMITED
749383U23A-19

Formerly: FIRA
Editorial Address: Maxwell Road, STEVENAGE, SG1 2EW
Tel: 01438 777700 **Fax:** 01438 777800
Email: info@fira.co.uk
Web site: http://www.askfira.co.uk
Publisher: FIRA International Ltd

Date Launched: 1998
Frequency of update: 120 times a year
Website Access: Paid
Traffic Figures: 8,500 Unique Users (per month Publisher's Statement)
Editor: Geoff Covey
Summary of Content: Website providing news and information for the furniture industry. Includes a database of furniture manufacturers, reports and publications, and a training database.
Readership/Target Audience: Aimed at manufacturers, retailers and suppliers in the furniture industry.
Other Features: Events and training update, standards updates, industry news and The Suppliers' Directory.
BUSINESS: FURNISHINGS & FURNITURE

FIRE
39847U54A-50
Formerly: Fire International
Editorial Address: PO Box 100, CHICHESTER, PO18 8HD
Tel: 01243 576444 **Fax:** 01243 576456
Email: andrew.lynch@keywaypublishing.co.uk
Web site: http://www.fire-magazine.com
Publisher: Keyways Publishing Limited
Frequency of update: Weekly
Website Access: Paid
Editor: Philip Mason
Summary of Content: Website covering fire protection and fire fighting throughout the world.
Readership/Target Audience: Read by international fire industry decision makers.
BUSINESS: SAFETY & SECURITY: Fire Fighting

FIRST4FARMING
1614903U21J-351
Formerly: First 4 Farming
Editorial Address: Dragon Hall, Whitchurch Road, Tattenhall, CHESTER, CH3 9DU **Tel:** 01829 771888
Fax: 01829 772420
Email: editor@first4farming.co.uk
Web site: http://www.first4farming.com
Date Launched: 2003
Frequency of update: Daily
Website Access: Free
Editor: James Loud
Summary of Content: Website covering the agricultural marketplace with agricultural and trading news.
Readership/Target Audience: Aimed at the agricultural industries, farmers and trade.
BUSINESS: AGRICULTURE & FARMING: Agriculture & Farming - Regional

THE FIRST POST
1744952U74Q-1312
Editorial Address: 6th Floor, Compass House, 22 Redan Place, LONDON, W2 4SA **Tel:** 020 7907 6000
Email: editorial@thefirstpost.co.uk
Web site: http://www.thefirstpost.co.uk
Publisher: Dennis Publishing Ltd
Date Launched: 2005
Frequency of update: Daily
Website Access: Free
Traffic Figures: 1,346,440 Unique Users (01/01/2008 To 31/01/2008 ABC/Electronic)
Editor: Mark Law
Summary of Content: Electronic lifestyle magazine covering the news, arts, movies, music, photography, fashion, motoring, sport, opinion and politics.
Readership/Target Audience: Aimed at thinking young professionals who appreciate a sideways look at the world.
CONSUMER: WOMEN'S INTEREST CONSUMER MAGAZINES: Lifestyle

FISHINGMAGIC
626547U92-57_90
Editorial Address: 2 Stephen's Way, Bignall End, STOKE-ON-TRENT, ST7 8PL **Tel:** 01782 721195
Email: editor@fishingmagic.com
Web site: http://www.fishingmagic.com
Publisher: Magicalia Ltd
Date Launched: 2000
Frequency of update: Daily
Website Access: Free
Traffic Figures: 100,000 Unique Users (Publisher's Statement)
Editor: Graham Marsden
Summary of Content: Website covering news, features and reviews on angling, angling products, travel, tackle and shopping. Also includes databases of local resources and information.
Readership/Target Audience: Aimed at anglers.
Other Features: Features include a shopping section, discussion forum, newsletter and a local resource search engine.
CONSUMER: ANGLING & FISHING

FISHINGWAREHOUSE
626131U92-57_95
Editorial Address: 69 Browmere Drive, Croft, WARRINGTON, WA3 7HS **Tel:** 01925 763572
Fax: 01925 763572
Email: paul@selman66.fsnet.co.uk
Web site: http://www.fishingwarehouse.co.uk
Publisher: Fishing Warehouse
Date Launched: 1999
Frequency of update: Daily
Website Access: Free
Traffic Figures: 200,000 Unique Users (per day Publisher's Statement)
Editor: Paul Selman
Summary of Content: Website covering online shopping, news, articles and information for all anglers.
Readership/Target Audience: Aimed at fishing enthusiasts.
Other Features: Features include a buyer's guide, gallery, editorial, links, on-line shops, discussion forums and archiving.
CONSUMER: ANGLING & FISHING

FIVE MINUTE LIFESTYLE
1813028U74Q-1355
Editorial Address: 11 Chiltern Court, Asheridge Road Industrial Estate, Asheridge Road, CHESHAM, HP5 2PX
Tel: 0845 127 4600
Email: info@iotamedia.co.uk
Web site: http://www.fiveminutelifestyle.com
Publisher: iotaMEDIA
Date Launched: 2007
Frequency of update: 26 times a year
Website Access: Free
Editor: Gordon O'Neill
Summary of Content: Website with fortnightly video podcasts covering beauty, health, fashion and lifestyle as well as a bi-weekly newsletter.
Readership/Target Audience: Aimed at women aged 18 to 35 years old.
CONSUMER: WOMEN'S INTEREST CONSUMER MAGAZINES: Lifestyle

FLAVORPILL LONDON
1743240U89C-1092
Formerly: Flavorpill LDN
Editorial Address: 10 Great Russell Street, LONDON, WC1B 3BQ
Email: london_events@flavorpill.com
Web site: http://www.flavorpill.com/london
Frequency of update: Weekly
Website Access: Free
Traffic Figures: 30,000 Unique Users (Publisher's Statement)
Editor: Kieran Wyatt
Summary of Content: E-magazine featuring a hand-picked selection of cultural happenings across art, music, film, theatre, dance, literature and DJ events.
Readership/Target Audience: Aimed at 18 to 40 year olds who love going out in London.
CONSUMER: HOLIDAYS & TRAVEL: Entertainment Guides

FLAVOUR MAGAZINE ONLINE
1925328U74Q-1448
Editorial Address: P.O. BOX 55748, LONDON, E16 3XY
Tel: 020 7511 1372
Email: info@flavourmag.co.uk
Web site: http://www.flavourmag.co.uk
Publisher: Flavour Magazine Ltd
Date Launched: 2008
Frequency of update: Daily
Traffic Figures: 61,000 Unique Users (per month Publisher's Statement)
Editor: Annika Allen
Summary of Content: Website of a magazine covering latest trends in fashion, lifestyle and entertainment.
Readership/Target Audience: Aimed at young and ambitious young people.
CONSUMER: WOMEN'S INTEREST CONSUMER MAGAZINES: Lifestyle

FLEET INDUSTRY CONFIDENTIAL (FIC)
1863537U49D-366
Editorial Address: 18 Alban Park, Hatfield Road, ST. ALBANS, AL4 0JJ **Tel:** 01727 739160 **Fax:** 01727 739169
Email: steve@stevemoodycommunications.co.uk
Web site: http://www.fleetworldgroup.co.uk
Publisher: Stag Publications Ltd
Date Launched: 2009
Frequency of update: Weekly. Published each Monday
Website Access: Free
Traffic Figures: 4,000 Unique Users (Publisher's Statement)
Editor: Steve Moody

Summary of Content: Electronic publication covering news, feature information, new car launches and statistical data on fleet motors.
Readership/Target Audience: Aimed at those working within the fleet industry in fleet departments of motor manufacturers, contract hire and leasing companies, fleet service suppliers, industry bodies and fleet consultancies.
BUSINESS: TRANSPORT: Commercial Vehicles

FLEET NEWS ONLINE
39575U49A-111
Formerly: Fleet NewsNet
Editorial Address: Media House, Lynchwood, Peterborough Business Park, PETERBOROUGH, PE2 6EA
Tel: 01733 468298 **Fax:** 01733 468296
Email: jeremy.bennett@bauermedia.co.uk
Web site: http://www.fleetnews.co.uk
Publisher: Bauer Consumer Media Ltd (Media House)
Date Launched: 1996
Frequency of update: Daily
Website Access: Free
Traffic Figures: 40,000 Unique Users (per month Publisher's Statement)
Editor: Jeremy Bennett
Summary of Content: Website containing fleet industry news and analysis, information on road tests, vehicle running costs, residual values, recall information and employment opportunities.
Readership/Target Audience: Aimed at fleet decision-makers and automotive professionals and drivers.
BUSINESS: TRANSPORT

FLEXIBLE - THE JOURNAL OF PLASTICS & PACKAGING TECHNOLOGY
1643667U35-368
Editorial Address: Cleeve Road, LEATHERHEAD, KT22 7RU **Tel:** 01372 802000 **Fax:** 01372 802243
Email: sara.ver-bruggen@pira-international.com
Web site: http://www.intertechpira.com
Publisher: PIRA International
Frequency of update: 10 times a year
Website Access: Paid
Editor: Sara Ver-Bruggen
Summary of Content: Online journal that gives information on what's happening in the world of plastics packaging. Topics include new ideas, new products being launched and recycling.
Readership/Target Audience: Membership only, available to anyone within the plastics packaging industry and anyone interested in plastics packaging.
BUSINESS: PACKAGING & BOTTLING

FLINTSHIRE MATTERS
1881619U72J-362
Email: comments@flintshire-matters.co.uk
Web site: http://www.flintshire-matters.co.uk
Frequency of update: Daily
Summary of Content: Website created to help people who care about their local issues. Whether you need access to useful information, want to highlight a particular topic to other people, discuss ideas with like-minded people or just show your support and keep up to date with current affairs in your area, Flintshire Matters is the place for you.
Readership/Target Audience: Aimed at residents in the local area of Flintshire.
LOCAL NEWSPAPERS: Community Newsletters

FLOREO COMMUNITY
1708434U94E-361
Formerly: Floreo News
Editorial Address: Brambletyne Close, Angmering, LITTLEHAMPTON, BN16 4DD **Tel:** 01903 774345
Email: euphrosene@floreo.org
Web site: http://www.euphroseneabon.com/modules/newbb
Publisher: Floreo 33
Date Launched: 2002
Frequency of update: Daily
Website Access: Free
Editor: Euphrosene Labon
Summary of Content: Mind, body and spirit website covering pragmatic and esoteric news, views and spiritual concepts, religion, spirituality, book reviews, business and personal development. Also includes items re contemporary spiritual art.
Readership/Target Audience: Aimed at those interested in mind body spirit, creative thinking including the general public, HR officers, training personnel, coaches and recruitment consultants.
Other Features: Newsletter, message board, sponsored advertising and mailing list.
CONSUMER: OTHER CLASSIFICATIONS: Paranormal

Internet Media

FLYER AIR-PORTAL
626252U6A-95_50

Formerly: Flyer Air Portal
Editorial Address: 9 Riverside Court, Lower Bristol Road, BATH, BA2 3DZ **Tel:** 01225 481440 **Fax:** 01225 481262
Email: martinlp@flyermag.co.uk
Web site: http://www.flyer.co.uk
Publisher: Seager Publishing Ltd
Date Launched: 1998
Frequency of update: Daily
Website Access: Free
Editor: Ian Waller; **Web Editor:** Martin Le Poidevin
Summary of Content: Portal covering information for pilots and those interested in aviation in the UK and Europe.
Readership/Target Audience: Aimed at pilots and aviation enthusiasts.
BUSINESS: AVIATION & AERONAUTICS

FMWF FINANCIAL MAIL WOMEN'S FORUM
1776152U74A-1022

Editorial Address: Northcliffe House, 2 Derry Street, LONDON, W8 5TT **Tel:** 020 7938 6000
Email: franco.capaldo@mailonsunday.co.uk
Web site: http://www.fmwf.com
Publisher: Associated Newspapers Ltd
Date Launched: 2006
Frequency of update: Weekly
Website Access: Free
Traffic Figures: 100,000 Unique Users (per month Publisher's Statement)
Summary of Content: Website covering women in business, news, profiles, features and business tools.
Readership/Target Audience: Aimed at professional women, female entrepreneurs and those researching women.
CONSUMER: WOMEN'S INTEREST CONSUMER MAGAZINES: Women's Interest

FOOD AND DRINK DIGITAL
1895433U22A-397

Editorial Address: Grovenor House, Prince of Wales Road, NORWICH, NR1 1NS **Tel:** 01603 217530 **Fax:** 01603 617082
Email: ben.lobel@whitedm.com
Web site: http://www.foodanddrinkdigital.com
Publisher: White Digital Media Ltd
Frequency of update: Daily
Editor: Ben Lobel
Summary of Content: Website exploring sector related issues and opportunities facing top executives, with news delivered daily.
BUSINESS: FOOD

FOODEPEDIA
1924474U11A-234

Editorial Address: 22 Carnaby Street, LONDON, W1F 7DB
Email: editorial@foodepedia.co.uk
Web site: http://www.foodepedia.co.uk
Frequency of update: Daily
Traffic Figures: 7,500 Unique Users (per month Publisher's Statement)
Editor: Nick Harman
Summary of Content: Website providing information on restaurants, on food, on wine, on breaks and sometimes even on breakfast.
BUSINESS: CATERING: Catering, Hotels & Restaurants

FOOTBALL INSIDER
38528U32H-108

Editorial Address: 292 Vauxhall Bridge Road, LONDON, SW1V 1AE **Tel:** 020 7963 7888 **Fax:** 020 7963 7894
Email: rory.squires@pa-sport.com
Web site: http://www.pa-sport.com
Publisher: Press Association Sport Services
Date Launched: 1998
Frequency of update: Daily
Website Access: Paid
Traffic Figures: 5,000 Unique Users (Publisher's Statement)
Editor: Rory Squires
Summary of Content: Daily bulletin containing interviews with those running world football, plus analysis of trends and commercial issues within the game.
Readership/Target Audience: Aimed at commercial managers and directors of football league and county football clubs, as well as manufacturing and supply companies targeting the football business.
BUSINESS: LOCAL GOVERNMENT, LEISURE & RECREATION: Leisure, Recreation & Entertainment

FOOTBALLAUDIO.COM
1800275U75B-285

Editorial Address: Broadcast Centre, Suite 16, The Linen House, 253 Kilburn Lane, LONDON, W10 4BQ
Tel: 020 8964 5522 **Fax:** 020 8964 6565
Email: jonny.gould@sportsmedia.co.uk

Web site: http://www.footballaudio.com
Publisher: Sports Media Broadcasting
Date Launched: 2006
Frequency of update: Daily
Website Access: Free
Traffic Figures: 350,000 Unique Users (per month Publisher's Statement)
Editor: Jonny Gould
Summary of Content: Website covering Premiership and Champions League football as well as player and manager interviews and podcasts.
Readership/Target Audience: Aimed at football fans.
CONSUMER: SPORT: Football

FORTEANTIMES ONLINE
628927U94E-31

Editorial Address: 30 Cleveland Street, LONDON, W1T 4JD
Tel: 020 7907 6235 **Fax:** 020 7907 6406
Email: david_sutton@dennis.co.uk
Web site: http://www.forteantimes.com
Publisher: Dennis Publishing Ltd
Date Launched: 1997
Frequency of update: Daily
Website Access: Free
Traffic Figures: 28,000 Unique Users (per month Publisher's Statement)
Editor: David Sutton; **Web Editor:** Jen Ogilvie
Summary of Content: Website focusing on news, reviews and research on strange phenomena and experiences, curiosities, prodigies and portents.
Readership/Target Audience: Aimed at people interested in strange phenomena and experiences.
CONSUMER: OTHER CLASSIFICATIONS: Paranormal

FRANCHISE INTERNATIONAL
36757U14A-120

Editorial Address: Franchise House, 56 Surrey Street, NORWICH, NR1 3FD **Tel:** 01603 620301 **Fax:** 01603 630174
Email: stuarta@fdsltd.com
Web site: http://www.franchise-international.net
Publisher: Franchise Development Services Ltd
Date Launched: 1993
Frequency of update: Daily
Editor: Stuart Anderson
Summary of Content: Website promoting the availability of master franchise rights worldwide.
Readership/Target Audience: Aimed at individuals and organisations seeking to operate a master franchise.
BUSINESS: COMMERCE, INDUSTRY & MANAGEMENT

FRANCHISESALES.COM
1772728U14A-570

Editorial Address: Dynamis House, Sycamore Street, LONDON, EC1Y 0SW **Tel:** 020 7324 1940
Fax: 020 7324 1931
Email: jcd@dynamis.co.uk
Web site: http://www.franchisesales.com
Publisher: Dynamis plc
Frequency of update: Daily. Articles are added to the site as and when they come in/are created
Website Access: Free
Traffic Figures: 20,000 Unique Users (per day Publisher's Statement)
Editor: Jo Dalton
Summary of Content: Website covering information and advice on franchising around the world. Franchise opportunities are available, as well as news, case studies, advice and more on how to get into and run a franchise..
Readership/Target Audience: Aimed at anyone thinking about going into business or franchising.
Other Features: Monthly newsletters.
BUSINESS: COMMERCE, INDUSTRY & MANAGEMENT

FREE FEATURES
1706772U60R-104

Editorial Address: 9A Station Avenue, CATERHAM, CR3 6LB **Tel:** 0870 950 3330 **Fax:** 0870 950 3331
Email: info@freefeatures.co.uk
Web site: http://www.freefeatures.co.uk
Date Launched: 2004
Frequency of update: Daily
Website Access: Free
Editor: Janet Kelly
Summary of Content: Website providing free editorial articles on a range of subjects from lifestyle, entertainment, gardens, property, fashion, travel, food, driving, beauty, music, cinema, business, recruitment, internet, technology, book reviews and TV and drama.
Readership/Target Audience: Aimed at publishers who require consumer targeted feature content.
BUSINESS: PUBLISHING: Publishing Related

FREE PINT
36835U14A-135

Editorial Address: 4-6 Station Approach, ASHFORD, TW15 2QN **Tel:** 0870 141 7474
Email: support@freepint.com
Web site: http://www.freepint.com
Publisher: Free Pint Limited
Date Launched: 1997
Frequency of update: 24 times a year
Website Access: Free
Traffic Figures: 78,000 Unique Users (Publisher's Statement)
Editor: Robin Neidorf
Summary of Content: Newsletter containing articles and reviews about performing serious business research on the Internet.
Readership/Target Audience: Aimed at librarians, business researchers, market researchers and information students.
BUSINESS: COMMERCE, INDUSTRY & MANAGEMENT

FREELANCE UK
1667946U60R-101

Editorial Address: 1 Northumberland Avenue, LONDON, WC2N 5BW **Tel:** 020 7872 5448
Email: editor@freelanceuk.com
Web site: http://www.freelanceuk.com
Date Launched: 2005
Frequency of update: Daily
Website Access: Free
Editor: Helen James
Summary of Content: Website offering news and advice to knowledge-based freelancers, specialising in the creative sectors.
Readership/Target Audience: Aimed at freelance journalists.
BUSINESS: PUBLISHING: Publishing Related

FRESH BUSINESS THINKING
1799658U14H-433

Editorial Address: 130 Shaftesbury Avenue, LONDON, W1D 5EU **Tel:** 0845 500 0328 **Fax:** 0845 500 1328
Email: editor@freshbusinessthinking.com
Web site: http://www.freshbusinessthinking.com
Date Launched: 2007
Frequency of update: Daily
Website Access: Free
Traffic Figures: 200,000 Unique Users (Publisher's Statement)
Editor: Claire West
Summary of Content: Electronic magazine focusing on business and lifestyle news and features. Includes profiles of successful business people, business and leisure travel, sales, HR, legal, finance and marketing articles.
Readership/Target Audience: Aimed at owners, directors and entrepreneurs starting up or running small and medium sized businesses.
BUSINESS: COMMERCE, INDUSTRY & MANAGEMENT: Small Business

FRESHTIES
1861422U94X-303

Editorial Address: 17 Hardwick Avenue, NEWARK, NG24 4AW **Tel:** 01636 678540
Email: penny@freshties.com
Web site: http://www.freshties.com
Frequency of update: Weekly
Website Access: Free
Traffic Figures: 7,000 Unique Users (per week Publisher's Statement)
Editor: Ash Poddar
Summary of Content: Online newspaper helping people share life skills, knowledge and resources. Featuring community news, charities and giving a voice to young people.
Readership/Target Audience: Aimed at those looking to connect with the community including businesses, charities and individuals.
CONSUMER: OTHER CLASSIFICATIONS: Miscellaneous

FRY ONLINE
1804555U11C-31

Editorial Address: Suite 1, Bexley House, 77 Bexley High Street, BEXLEY, DA5 1JX **Tel:** 01322 526089
Fax: 01322 528172
Email: pybuspromotions@btconnect.com
Web site: http://www.fry-online.co.uk
Publisher: Pybus Events and Publications Limited
Date Launched: 2007
Frequency of update: Daily
Website Access: Free
Editor: Reece Head
Summary of Content: Website featuring the latest industry news, events, businesses for sale, marketing tips and advice for new and existing outlets, weekly offers from suppliers and a comprehensive product and service directory.

Readership/Target Audience: Aimed at owners and managers of fish and chip shops and fast food outlets.
BUSINESS: CATERING: Fried Fish

FSBO.ORG.UK
1840487U74K-788

Editorial Address: Lomber Hay Farm, Andrew Lane, High Lane, STOCKPORT, SK6 8HY **Tel:** 07834 158483
Email: matt@fsbo.org.uk
Web site: http://www.fsbo.org.uk
Date Launched: 2007
Frequency of update: 104 times a year
Website Access: Free
Editor: Matt Hutchinson
Summary of Content: Website with property news and views which aim to educate people of the possibilities and pitfalls of selling without an estate agent.
Readership/Target Audience: Aimed at those looking to by or sell property.
Other Features: Other features on site include a property blog.
CONSUMER: WOMEN'S INTEREST CONSUMER MAGAZINES: Home Purchase

FSN
36079U5B-84_55

Formerly: Financial Systems News
Editorial Address: Clarendon House, 125 Shenley Road, BOREHAMWOOD, WD6 1AG **Tel:** 020 8445 2688
Fax: 020 8445 7172
Email: gary.simon@fsn.co.uk
Web site: http://www.fsn.co.uk
Publisher: FSN Publishing Ltd
Date Launched: 1996
Frequency of update: Weekly
Website Access: Free
Traffic Figures: 30,000 Unique Users (per month Publisher's Statement)
Editor: Gary Simon
Summary of Content: Electronically delivered newsletter covering news, products, supplier information, software articles and advice.
Readership/Target Audience: Read by senior finance professionals.
BUSINESS: COMPUTERS & AUTOMATION: Data Processing

FTADVISER.COM
634809U1F-205

Editorial Address: 1 Southwark Bridge, LONDON, SE1 9HL
Tel: 020 7775 6636
Email: gemma.westacott@ft.com
Web site: http://www.ftadviser.com
Publisher: FT Group
Date Launched: 2001
Frequency of update: 730 times a year
Website Access: Paid
Traffic Figures: 43,000 Unique Users (per month Publisher's Statement)
Editor: Gemma Westacott
Summary of Content: News website offering the latest breaking news and industry analysis for the UK intermediary market. The website combines content from FTAdviser along with that of the magazines Financial Adviser, Investment Adviser, Mortgage Adviser and Money Management.
Readership/Target Audience: Read by independent financial advisors, intermediaries, brokers and product providers in retail finance.
Other Features: Breaking News, Features, Industry Commentary, Blogs, Archive and recent magazines for Financial Adviser, Mortgage Adviser, Investment Adviser, Money Management, Up-to-date funds data, online jobs and recruitment site, online training, twice daily newsletter, breaking news e-mail alerts, results of FTAdviser, Financial Adviser and money Management industry awards.
BUSINESS: FINANCE & ECONOMICS: Investment

FT.COM
622829U65A-81

Editorial Address: 1 Southwark Bridge, LONDON, SE1 9HL
Tel: 020 7873 3000 **Fax:** 020 7873 3194
Email: ep.newsdesk@ft.com
Web site: http://www.ft.com
Publisher: Financial Times
Frequency of update: Daily. News updated constantly
Website Access: Paid
Traffic Figures: 11,396,926 Unique Users (01/03/2009 To 31/03/2009 ABC/Electronic)
Editor: Andrew Slade; **Web Editor:** Isolin Jorgensen
Summary of Content: Website version of the Financial Times. Includes business and financial news and analyses, market news, coverage of 14 key industries worldwide, each with its own homepage, a database of business people, careers advice and a 'Time Off' section containing lifestyle and entertainment features. FTpm is a financial news briefing

available in print and online every afternoon on subscription only.
Twitter: http://twitter.com/FinancialTImes.
NATIONAL DAILY & SUNDAY NEWSPAPERS: National Daily Newspapers

FTPM
1668185U65A-81_110

Editorial Address: For all contact details see main edition, Financial Times
Frequency of update: Daily
Website Access: Free
NATIONAL DAILY & SUNDAY NEWSPAPERS: National Daily Newspapers

FTYOURMONEY
601029U74M-70

Editorial Address: 1 Southwark Bridge, LONDON, SE1 9HL
Tel: 020 7873 3000 **Fax:** 020 7873 3195
Email: intomoney@ft.com
Web site: http://www.ft.com/yourmoney
Publisher: FT Finance
Date Launched: 1999
Frequency of update: Daily
Website Access: Free
Editor: Matthew Vincent
Summary of Content: Website providing guidance on how to select from a full range of financial products. Includes topical news and features on home buying, mortgages, pensions, insurance and tax. Covers articles on saving money, finding an advisor, education and retirement.
Readership/Target Audience: Aimed at those wishing to both manage and maximise their money.
CONSUMER: WOMEN'S INTEREST CONSUMER MAGAZINES: Personal Finance

FUK.CO.UK
45226U74B-150

Editorial Address: PO Box 38185, LONDON, W10 4WF
Tel: 020 7286 7660
Email: marian@fuk.co.uk
Web site: http://www.fuk.co.uk
Publisher: WideMedia Ltd
Date Launched: 1995
Frequency of update: Daily
Website Access: Free
Traffic Figures: 300,000 Unique Users (per month Publisher's Statement)
Editor: Marian Buckley
Summary of Content: Website focusing on UK street style, daily fashion news and catwalk coverage.
Readership/Target Audience: Aimed at fashion enthusiasts between 18 and 30 years old.
Other Features: Message board.
CONSUMER: WOMEN'S INTEREST CONSUMER MAGAZINES: Women's Interest - Fashion

FULHAM MATTERS
1881620U72J-363

Email: comments@fulham-matters.co.uk
Web site: http://www.fulham-matters.co.uk
Frequency of update: Daily
Summary of Content: Website created to help people who care about local issues. Whether you need access to useful information, want to highlight a particular topic to other people, discuss ideas with like-minded people or just show your support and keep up to date with current affairs in your area, Fulham Matters is the place for you.
Readership/Target Audience: Aimed at residents in the local area of Fulham.
LOCAL NEWSPAPERS: Community Newsletters

FUNCTIONALDRINKS
1692333U22R-761

Editorial Address: 7 Kingsmead Square, BATH, BA1 2AB
Tel: 01225 327900 **Fax:** 01225 327901
Email: jfoulds@zenithinternational.com
Web site: http://www.functionaldrinksnews.com
Publisher: Zenith International
Date Launched: 2001
Frequency of update: 25 times a year
Website Access: Paid
Editor: Jenny Foulds
Summary of Content: Newsletter focusing on the functional drinks market including analysis of current market trends, company strategies, new product launches, legislation and regulatory issues.
Readership/Target Audience: Aimed at soft drink companies, but also to other operators in entire non-alcoholic beverage industry.
BUSINESS: FOOD: Food Related

FUNKY
1645246U74Q-1184

Editorial Address: iBubble Ltd, Denny Lodge Business Park, Chittering, CAMBRIDGE, CB25 9PH
Tel: 01223 863843 **Fax:** 01223 864780
Email: editor@funky.co.uk
Web site: http://www.funky.co.uk
Frequency of update: Daily
Website Access: Free
Traffic Figures: 480,000 Unique Users (per month Publisher's Statement)
Editor: Peter Dabrowa
Summary of Content: Website covering style, beauty, music, entertainment, travel, housing, jobs, finance and student life.
Readership/Target Audience: Aimed at youths and students aged between 16 and 24 years old.
CONSUMER: WOMEN'S INTEREST CONSUMER MAGAZINES: Lifestyle

FUNKYFOGEY.COM
1743097U74N-187

Editorial Address: 67A Willowfield Road, EASTBOURNE, BN22 8AP **Tel:** 01323 411464 **Fax:** 01323 731136
Email: editor@funkyfogey.com
Web site: http://www.funkyfogey.com
Date Launched: 2002
Frequency of update: Monthly
Website Access: Free
Traffic Figures: 20,000 Unique Users (per month Publisher's Statement)
Editor: Andrew Wilson
Summary of Content: Website covering entertainment, health and fitness, holidays and travel, shopping, motors, sports and leisure, rambling and walking, books, property, gardening, wine, music and technology.
Readership/Target Audience: Aimed at men and women aged 50 years and older.
CONSUMER: WOMEN'S INTEREST CONSUMER MAGAZINES: Retirement

FUNNY.CO.UK
711828U94X-258

Editorial Address: PR by email only **Tel:** 07801 550541
Fax: 07092 122020
Email: simon@funny.co.uk
Web site: http://www.funny.co.uk
Date Launched: 1997
Frequency of update: Daily
Website Access: Free
Traffic Figures: 1,200,000 Unique Users (per month Publisher's Statement)
Editor: Simon Kimber
Summary of Content: Website focusing on comedy. Includes news, a joke book, a TV comedy guide, UK live comedy, a funny encyclopaedia and links to other comedy websites.
Readership/Target Audience: Aimed at those who enjoy comedy and jokes.
Other Features: Features include a chat forum, an e-mail newsletter, an events calendar and archiving.
CONSUMER: OTHER CLASSIFICATIONS: Miscellaneous

FUTURE HEALTH BULLETIN
1606947U56H-51

Editorial Address: 4th Floor, Intergen House, 65-67 Western Road, HOVE, BN3 2JQ **Tel:** 01273 311289
Email: phil@care-connection.com
Web site: http://www.care-connection.com
Publisher: Vital Publishing
Date Launched: 2001
Frequency of update: Monthly
Website Access: Free
Traffic Figures: 1,300 Unique Users (Publisher's Statement)
Editor: Phil Cain
Summary of Content: Electronic newsletter covering news and issues relating to technology and healthcare in the UK and worldwide.
Readership/Target Audience: Read by decision makers within the NHS.
BUSINESS: HEALTH & MEDICAL: Medical Engineering Technology

FYI
1682496U14H-420

Editorial Address: 2 Mornington Place, BELFAST, BT7 3LD
Tel: 028 9069 2334 **Fax:** 028 9069 2335
Email: editor@fyini.com
Web site: http://www.fyini.com
Publisher: OMNIA Media
Date Launched: 2004
Frequency of update: Monthly
Website Access: Free
Traffic Figures: 7,000 Unique Users (Publisher's Statement)
Editor: Anna Mooney

Internet Media

Summary of Content: Website featuring issues affecting small businesses in Northern Ireland.
Readership/Target Audience: Aimed at entrepreneurs and small business owners.
BUSINESS: COMMERCE, INDUSTRY & MANAGEMENT: Small Business

GADGET SPEAK
1775314U78R-513

Editorial Address: 40 Handside Lane, WELWYN GARDEN CITY, AL8 6SJ **Tel:** 01707 891840
Email: editor@gadgetspeak.com
Web site: http://www.gadgetspeak.com
Publisher: YellowHawk Ltd
Date Launched: 2003
Frequency of update: Daily
Website Access: Free
Traffic Figures: 100,000 Unique Users (per month Publisher's Statement)
Editor: Peter Wilson
Summary of Content: Website with product reviews of gadgets including cameras, entertainment, health and beauty, homes and gardens, laptops, personal computers and Apples, PDAs, phones, printers and scanners, software and wireless.
Readership/Target Audience: Aimed at gadget 'experts' that want to share their knowledge as well as those wishing to research products, look for gift ideas or just ask a question in the discussion forums target audience primarily UK.
Other Features: Competitions, member blogs, article comments, product search, vendor search.
CONSUMER: CONSUMER ELECTRONICS: Consumer Electronics Related

GAJ-IT
1850500U78R-528

Editorial Address: 50 Caledonian Road, DEWSBURY, WF12 9NT **Tel:** 07792 875625
Email: news@gaj-it.com
Web site: http://www.gaj-it.com
Frequency of update: Daily
Website Access: Free
Traffic Figures: 1,000 Unique Users (per day Publisher's Statement)
Editor: Riyas Patel
Summary of Content: Website with UK gadget news and reviews as well as a shopping blog.
Readership/Target Audience: Aimed at those of all ages interested in technology.
CONSUMER: CONSUMER ELECTRONICS: Consumer Electronics Related

GALA BINGO
1667948U79F-87

Editorial Address: New Castle House, Castle Boulevard, NOTTINGHAM, NG7 1FT **Tel:** 0115 948 5000
Fax: 0115 948 5116
Email: sarah.mercer@galacoral.com
Web site: http://www.galabingo.co.uk
Date Launched: 2005
Frequency of update: Daily
Website Access: Free
Editor: Sarah Mercer
Summary of Content: Website of Gala Bingo allowing bingo to be played online.
Readership/Target Audience: Aimed at Bingo enthusiasts.
CONSUMER: HOBBIES & DIY: Games & Puzzles

GALA GAMES
46661U79F-27

Formerly: Jamba
Editorial Address: New Castle House, Castle Boulevard, NOTTINGHAM, NG7 1FT **Tel:** 0115 948 5000
Fax: 020 948 5116
Email: sarah.mercer@galacoral.com
Web site: http://www.galagames.co.uk
Frequency of update: Daily
Website Access: Paid
(Publisher's Statement)
Editor: Sarah Mercer
Summary of Content: Website dedicated to trivia, games, prizes, competitions, puzzles and gambling - low fixed stakes.
Readership/Target Audience: Aimed at puzzle and games enthusiasts.
CONSUMER: HOBBIES & DIY: Games & Puzzles

GALAXY LIFE
1851523U74A-1056

Editorial Address: 5th Floor, The Triangle, MANCHESTER, M4 3TR **Tel:** 0161 279 0300 **Fax:** 0161 279 0390
Email: webcontroller@galaxyfm.co.uk
Web site: http://www.galaxymagazine.co.uk
Date Launched: 2008

Frequency of update: Quarterly
Website Access: Free
Traffic Figures: 340,000 Unique Users (Publisher's Statement)
Editor: David Farrar
Summary of Content: Online magazine covering lifestyle, fashion, beauty, style, showbiz interviews and competitions.
Readership/Target Audience: Aimed at women aged 20 to 29 years old.
CONSUMER: WOMEN'S INTEREST CONSUMER MAGAZINES: Women's Interest

GAMBLING.COM
1740119U79F-99

Editorial Address: 77 Queen Victoria Street, LONDON, EC4V 4AY **Tel:** 020 7618 9000 **Fax:** 020 7618 9001
Email: sara@gambling.com
Web site: http://www.gambling.com
Date Launched: 2006
Frequency of update: Daily
Website Access: Free
Traffic Figures: 18,500 Unique Users (per day Publisher's Statement)
Editor: Sara Vincent
Summary of Content: Website covering casino games and sports including card games, slots, video poker and bingo as well as a gaming specific search engine.
Readership/Target Audience: Aimed at those interested in online gaming.
CONSUMER: HOBBIES & DIY: Games & Puzzles

GAMERSDAILYNEWS.COM
1849366U78D-338

Editorial Address: 4 Moorcrest Road, HUDDERSFIELD, HD4 5PT **Tel:** 07913 148613
Email: ukpr@gamersdailynews.com
Web site: http://www.gamersdailynews.com
Publisher: GDN Media Group
Frequency of update: Daily
Website Access: Free
Traffic Figures: 120,000 Unique Users (per month Publisher's Statement)
Editor: Spanner Spencer
Summary of Content: Website covering news and reviews of all games formats.
Readership/Target Audience: Aimed at gamers aged predominantly 25 to 40 years old.
CONSUMER: CONSUMER ELECTRONICS: Games

GAMES INVESTOR
634872U5F-383

Editorial Address: 155 Holland Park Avenue, LONDON, W11 4UX **Tel:** 07889 144881
Email: info@gamesinvestor.com
Web site: http://www.gamesinvestor.co.uk
Date Launched: 1997
Frequency of update: Monthly
Website Access: Free
Editor: Nick Gibson
Summary of Content: Website providing potential and existing investors with regular news and analysis about the publicly quoted UK computer and video games companies.
Readership/Target Audience: Read by those who invest in computer and video game companies.
BUSINESS: COMPUTERS & AUTOMATION: Multimedia

GAMES PRESS
1638179U78D-303

Editorial Address: 255 Staines Road, Laleham, STAINES, TW18 2RS **Tel:** 020 7193 2246
Email: inbox@gamespress.com
Web site: http://www.gamespress.com
Publisher: Games Press Ltd
Date Launched: 2000
Frequency of update: 260 times a year
Website Access: Paid
Traffic Figures: 31,089 Unique Users (Publisher's Statement)
Editor: Jonathan Davies
Summary of Content: Trade website singularly covering video games news.
Readership/Target Audience: Aimed at journalists, PR personnel, retailers and distributors.
Other Features: Includes archiving, message board and Opt - in daily digest of latest content editions.
CONSUMER: CONSUMER ELECTRONICS: Games

GAMESINDUSTRY.BIZ
1698926U5R-683

Editorial Address: 18 Surrenden Crescent, BRIGHTON, BN1 6WF **Tel:** 07967 217388 **Fax:** 01273 555898
Email: news@gamesindustry.biz
Web site: http://www.gamesindustry.biz
Publisher: Eurogamer Network Ltd

Date Launched: 2002
Frequency of update: Daily
Website Access: Free
Traffic Figures: 419,554 Unique Users (per month Publisher's Statement)
Editor: Phil Elliott
Summary of Content: Trade website covering news and information on the global video games industry, from development through to retail.
Readership/Target Audience: Aimed at those involved with the design, development, publishing, marketing, distribution or retail of video games.
BUSINESS: COMPUTERS & AUTOMATION: Computers Related

GAMESPOT UK
1764851U78D-331

Editorial Address: 5-11 Lavington Street, LONDON, SE1 0NZ **Tel:** 020 7021 1000
Email: edit@gamespot.co.uk
Web site: http://uk.gamespot.com
Publisher: CBS Interactive
Date Launched: 2006
Frequency of update: Quarterly
Website Access: Paid
Traffic Figures: 4,548,455 Unique Users (01/12/2008 To 31/12/2008 ABC/Electronic)
Editor: Alex Coby
Summary of Content: Website covering PC and video games including breaking news, reviews, exclusive videos and hardware recommendations.
Readership/Target Audience: Aimed at gamers.
Other Features: GameSpot UK Downloads, GameSpot Trax and newsletters.
CONSUMER: CONSUMER ELECTRONICS: Games

GAMESRADAR
628951U78D-163

Formerly: gamesradar.com
Editorial Address: 30 Monmouth Street, BATH, BA1 2BW **Tel:** 01225 442244
Email: gamesradar@futurenet.com
Web site: http://www.gamesradar.com
Publisher: Future Publishing Ltd
Date Launched: 1999
Frequency of update: Daily. News updated several times a day
Website Access: Free
Traffic Figures: 850,000 Unique Users (per month Publisher's Statement)
Editor: Matt Cundy
Summary of Content: Website includes news, reviews and previews of computer games.
Readership/Target Audience: Aimed at male computer game enthusiasts between 16 and 30 years old.
Other Features: Features include a buyer's guide, a discussion forum, an e-mail newsletter and archiving.
CONSUMER: CONSUMER ELECTRONICS: Games

GAMING FLOOR
1626309U64A-173

Editorial Address: 72 New Bond Street, LONDON, W1S 1RR **Tel:** 0870 011 3020
Email: editorial@gamingfloor.com
Web site: http://www.gamingfloor.com
Publisher: Gaming floor.com ltd
Date Launched: 1999
Frequency of update: Daily
Website Access: Free
Traffic Figures: 40,000 Unique Users (per month Publisher's Statement)
Editor: Ian Sutton
Summary of Content: Website covering casino news, legal information and new products and developments within the casino industry.
Readership/Target Audience: Aimed at casino industry operators, suppliers, investors and gaming staff.
BUSINESS: OTHER CLASSIFICATIONS: Amusement Trade

GARDENERSWORLD.COM
1813759U93-198

Editorial Address: Media Centre, 201 Wood Lane, LONDON, W12 7TQ
Email: abbie.fereday@bbc.com
Web site: http://www.gardenersworld.com
Publisher: BBC Worldwide Publishing
Date Launched: 2007
Frequency of update: Daily
Website Access: Free
Traffic Figures: 220,356 Unique Users (01/05/2008 To 31/05/2008 ABC/Electronic)
Editor: Abbie Fereday
Summary of Content: Gardening website with how to projects, plant database, forums, blogs, scrapbook for personalising site, seven day bespoke gardening weather forecasts, wallpapers, video, problem solving, classified

gardening ads, gardenersworld offers, competitions, giveaways, gardening job checklists, free newsletter.
Readership/Target Audience: Aimed at gardeners of all ages and abilities.
CONSUMER: GARDENING

GARDENFORUM.CO.UK   712251U26C-35

Editorial Address: Stourton House, High Street, Stourton, WARMINSTER, BA12 6QF **Tel:** 01747 841457
Fax: 01747 841394
Email: info@gardenforum.co.uk
Web site: http://www.gardenforum.co.uk
Publisher: Gardenforum Ltd
Date Launched: 2000
Frequency of update: Daily
Website Access: Paid
Traffic Figures: 20,000 Unique Users (Publisher's Statement)
Editor: George Bullivant
Summary of Content: Website providing the latest industry news and advice on the garden industry. Also includes product news, companies' results, a directory of industry websites, jobs, companies for sale, landscape contracts and information about trade bargains and garden services.
Readership/Target Audience: Aimed at professionals within the garden industry.
Other Features: Monthly Buyers newsletter and Fortnightly briefing
BUSINESS: GARDEN TRADE

THE GARDENING WEBSITE   1804883U93-196

Editorial Address: Lilacs Thurston Road, Great Barton, BURY ST. EDMUNDS, IP31 2PL **Tel:** 01359 233404
Email: editor@thegardeningwebsite.co.uk
Web site: http://www.thergardeningwebsite.co.uk
Publisher: My WEBSITE Limited
Date Launched: 2004
Frequency of update: Daily
Website Access: Free
Editor: Robert Hale
Summary of Content: Website covering all aspects of gardening including garden design and build, gardens to visit, product reviews, show previews and reports, garden design, landscaping, maintenance, garden machinery garden tools, gardens and homes for sale, plants, garden centres and nurseries.
Readership/Target Audience: Aimed at the general public as well as horticulture and gardening businesses, garden designers, nurseries and manufacturers.
CONSUMER: GARDENING

GARDENING.TELEGRAPH.CO.UK
713972U93-23

Editorial Address: 111 Buckingham Palace Road, LONDON, SW1W 0DT **Tel:** 020 7931 2000
Fax: 020 7538 6158
Email: kylie.obrien@telegraph.co.uk
Web site: http://www.gardening.telegraph.co.uk
Publisher: Telegraph Media Group Ltd
Date Launched: 2001
Frequency of update: Daily
Website Access: Free
Editor: Kylie O'Brien
Summary of Content: Website focusing on gardening topics. Includes plant profiles, garden projects and tours, weather and an expert advice section.
Readership/Target Audience: Aimed at people interested in gardening.
Other Features: Features include an e-mail newsletter.
CONSUMER: GARDENING

GATESHEAD MATTERS   1881621U72J-364

Email: comments@gateshead-matters.co.uk
Web site: http://www.gateshead-matters.co.uk
Frequency of update: Daily
Summary of Content: Website created to help people who care about local issues. Whether you need access to useful information, want to highlight a particular topic to other people, discuss ideas with like-minded people or just show your support and keep up to date with current affairs in your area, Gateshead Matters is the place for you.
Readership/Target Audience: Aimed at residents in the local area of Gateshead.
LOCAL NEWSPAPERS: Community Newsletters

GATEWAY TO PORTSMOUTH AND THE SOLENT   629478U80C-1650

Editorial Address: The News Centre, Hilsea, PORTSMOUTH, PO2 9SX **Tel:** 023 9266 4488
Fax: 023 9267 3363

Email: newsdesk@thenews.co.uk
Web site: http://www.portsmouth.co.uk
Publisher: Johnston Press plc
Date Launched: 1997
Frequency of update: Daily
Website Access: Free
Editor: Graeme Patfield
Summary of Content: Website covering news, events and information for the Portsmouth area.
Readership/Target Audience: Aimed at local residents, visitors to the area and people interested in the area.
Other Features: Features include recruitment, a search engine and archiving.
CONSUMER: RURAL & REGIONAL INTEREST: Regional Interest English Counties

GAY BRITAIN NETWORK   626138U86B-28

Editorial Address: PO Box 6991, LEICESTER, LE1 6YS
Tel: 0870 345 5600 **Fax:** 0870 345 5584
Email: webmaster@gaybritain.co.uk
Web site: http://www.gaybritain.co.uk
Publisher: Gay Britain Network
Frequency of update: Daily
Website Access: Free
Editor: Simon Mallinson
Summary of Content: Website covering entertainment, lifestyle information and travel for the gay population.
Readership/Target Audience: Aimed at gay people over 18 years old.
Other Features: Features include an events calendar, a buyer's guide, an e-mail newsletter and archiving.
CONSUMER: ADULT & GAY MAGAZINES: Gay & Lesbian Magazines

GAY TO Z DIRECTORY   1796311U86B-179

Formerly: Gay to z
Editorial Address: 41 Cooks Road, LONDON, SE17 3NG
Tel: 0844 562 6006 **Fax:** 0844 562 6007
Email: info@gaytoz.com
Web site: http://www.gaytoz.com
Date Launched: 1994
Frequency of update: Daily
Website Access: Free
Traffic Figures: 450,000 Unique Users (per month Publisher's Statement)
Editor: Stephen Coote
Summary of Content: Web-based directory covering everything gay in the UK including LGBT business and community directory, what's on, hotels, bars, clubs and gay research.
Readership/Target Audience: Aimed at lesbian, gay, trans-sexual and bi-sexual men and women in the UK.
CONSUMER: ADULT & GAY MAGAZINES: Gay & Lesbian Magazines

GAY UK NEWS   1844885U86B-186

Formerly: UK Gay Guides
Editorial Address: 8 Bourne Hall, 2 Bourne Close, BOURNEMOUTH, BH2 6BW **Tel:** 0845 388 6328
Email: editor@gayuknews.com
Web site: http://www.ukgayguides.co.uk
Date Launched: 2006
Frequency of update: Daily
Website Access: Free
Traffic Figures: 8,000 Unique Users (Publisher's Statement)
Editor: Tom Faull
Summary of Content: Website with a gay and lesbian guide to the UK with the latest news, city guides, pride events listings and user forum.
Readership/Target Audience: Aimed at lgbt communities in the UK.
CONSUMER: ADULT & GAY MAGAZINES: Gay & Lesbian Magazines

GAYDARNATION   629031U86B-110

Formerly: RainbowNetwork
Editorial Address: 6th Floor, Queens House, 2 Holly Road, TWICKENHAM, TW1 4EG **Tel:** 020 8744 1287
Fax: 020 8744 1089
Email: stephen.beeny@qsoft.co.uk
Web site: http://www.gaydarnation.com
Date Launched: 1999
Frequency of update: Daily
Website Access: Free
Traffic Figures: 600,000 Unique Users (per month Publisher's Statement)
Editor: Stephen Beeny
Summary of Content: Website focusing on news and information for gays and lesbians.
Readership/Target Audience: Read by all ages of the gay and lesbian community.

Other Features: Features include archiving, a discussion forum, an e-mail newsletter, a buyer's guide, an events calendar and recruitment.
CONSUMER: ADULT & GAY MAGAZINES: Gay & Lesbian Magazines

GAZETTEHERALD.CO.UK   711376U72B-3646

Formerly: This is RYEDALE
Editorial Address: PO Box 29, 76-86 Walmgate, YORK, YO1 9YN **Tel:** 01904 653051 **Fax:** 01904 672371
Email: jon.butler@thepress.co.uk
Web site: http://www.gazetteherald.co.uk
Date Launched: 2001
Frequency of update: Daily
Website Access: Free
Editor: Jon Butler
Other Features: Features include a buyer's guide and recruitment.
LOCAL NEWSPAPERS: Local Newspapers English Counties

GAZETTELIVE.CO.UK   707265U80C-5421

Formerly: icTeesside.co.uk
Editorial Address: Evening Gazette, Borough Road, MIDDLESBROUGH, TS1 3AZ **Tel:** 01912 043364
Fax: 01912 043371
Email: helen.dalby@ncjmedia.co.uk
Web site: http://www.gazettelive.co.uk
Publisher: Gazette Media Company Ltd
Date Launched: 2001
Frequency of update: Daily
Website Access: Free
Traffic Figures: 273,500 Unique Users (01/07/2008 To 31/12/2008 ABC/Electronic)
Editor: Helen Dalby
Summary of Content: Website containing the latest news, sports, entertainment, business, travel and weather for the Teesside and North Yorkshire area.
Readership/Target Audience: Aimed at visitors and those living in the local area.
Other Features: Features include archiving, an e-mail newsletter, a calendar of events, discussion forums and recruitment.
CONSUMER: RURAL & REGIONAL INTEREST: Regional Interest English Counties

GB.GOLF   1644941U75D-511

Editorial Address: Westfield Lodge, Moreton Morrell, WARWICK, CV35 9DB **Tel:** 01926 650173
Email: david.morgan@warksgolf.co.uk
Web site: http://www.gbgolf.com
Publisher: FGA Ltd
Date Launched: 2008
Frequency of update: Monthly
Website Access: Paid
Editor: David Morgan
Summary of Content: Website covering excellence in golf including style, courses and players.
Readership/Target Audience: Aimed at golf club members.
Other Features: Newsletter.
CONSUMER: SPORT: Golf

G-CULTURE   1800267U86C-736

Editorial Address: 15 Alexandra Road, LONDON, SW19 7JZ **Tel:** 020 8123 0475 **Fax:** 020 8947 9036
Email: info@gculture.co.uk
Web site: http://www.gculture.co.uk
Date Launched: 2007
Frequency of update: Daily
Website Access: Free
Editor: Aaron Hales
Summary of Content: Electronic magazine with four sections: body, mind, indulgence and refinement. These sections cover such areas as fashion and grooming, business, health stage and screen, music, books, arts, technology, automotive, interiors and London and Paris based exhibitions.
Readership/Target Audience: Aimed at men aged between 25 and 49 years old with a high disposable income.
CONSUMER: ADULT & GAY MAGAZINES: Men's Lifestyle Magazines

GEAR WHEELS INCORPORATING WESSEX WHEELS   46341U77A-473

Formerly: Wessex Wheels-The Regional Motoring Magazine
Editorial Address: 26A Queens Road, SWANAGE, BH19 2ER **Tel:** 01929 421974 **Fax:** 01929 421974
Email: editor@gearwheelsmag.com
Web site: http://www.gearwheelsmag.co.uk
Publisher: DSA Publishing

Date Launched: 1998
Frequency of update: Daily
Website Access: Free
Editor: David Simpson
Summary of Content: Motoring website includes news, developments, events, road tests, clubs, classics and advice.
Readership/Target Audience: Aimed at those with an interest in vehicles and motoring aged 35 years and over.
CONSUMER: MOTORING & CYCLING: Motoring

GEEKANOIDS
1825899U78R-520

Editorial Address: Press releases by email only
Email: geekanoids@gmail.com
Web site: http://www.geekanoids.co.uk
Publisher: Wiki Design
Date Launched: 2005
Frequency of update: Daily
Website Access: Free
Traffic Figures: 65,000 Unique Users (per month Publisher's Statement)
Editor: Dave Cryer
Summary of Content: Website covering Macintosh technology and gadgets related news as well as reviews of computer software, hardware and peripherals.
Readership/Target Audience: Aimed at anyone interested in technology.
CONSUMER: CONSUMER ELECTRONICS: Consumer Electronics Related

GEOGRAPHICAL ONLINE
629097U82-25_51

Editorial Address: 1 Victoria Villas, RICHMOND, TW9 2GW
Tel: 020 8332 2713 **Fax:** 020 8332 9307
Email: magazine@geographical.co.uk
Web site: http://www.geographical.co.uk
Publisher: Circle Publishing
Date Launched: 1935
Frequency of update: Weekly
Website Access: Free
Traffic Figures: 6,000 Unique Users (per week Publisher's Statement)
Editor: Geordie Torr
Summary of Content: Website covering geographical issues worldwide, with information on education, travel and photography.
Readership/Target Audience: Aimed at those concerned with education, travel and human rights.
Other Features: Features include recruitment, discussion forums, an e-mail newsletter and archiving.
CONSUMER: CURRENT AFFAIRS & POLITICS

GET READY TO ROCK!
1825522U76E-780

Editorial Address: 34 Coniston Road, NESTON, CH64 0TD
Tel: 0151 336 6199 **Fax:** 0151 336 6199
Email: info@getreadytorock.com
Web site: http://www.getreadytorock.com
Publisher: Hotdigits New Media
Frequency of update: Daily
Website Access: Free
Traffic Figures: 250,000 Unique Users (per month Publisher's Statement)
Editor: David Randall
Summary of Content: Website covering news, interviews books, CDs, DVDs and live performance reviews about rock music and all sub-genres. Also includes features, competitions, downloads, radio show and podcast.
Readership/Target Audience: Aimed at music fans aged from 16 to 60 years old.
CONSUMER: MUSIC & PERFORMING ARTS: Pop Music

GETANIGHTLIFE.COM
1794228U89C-1099

Formerly: getanightlife
Editorial Address: 5 Siskin Road, SOUTHSEA, PO4 8UG
Tel: 07811 189055
Email: simon@getanightlife.com
Web site: http://www.getanightlife.com
Date Launched: 1999
Frequency of update: Daily
Website Access: Free
Editor: Simon Speller
Summary of Content: Website covering nightlife in Portsmouth, Bournemouth, Southampton and Brighton with reviews of clubs, pubs, cinema, DJ interviews and competitions.
Readership/Target Audience: Aimed at clubbers aged 18 to 30 years old.
CONSUMER: HOLIDAYS & TRAVEL: Entertainment Guides

GETWOODWORKING.COM
626220U79A-175_1

Editorial Address: Berwick House, 8-10 Knoll Rise, ORPINGTON, BR6 0PS **Tel:** 01689 899200
Fax: 01689 899266
Email: editor@getwoodworking.com
Web site: http://www.getwoodworking.com
Publisher: My Hobby Store Media
Date Launched: 1998
Frequency of update: Daily
Website Access: Free
Traffic Figures: 85,000 Unique Users (per month Publisher's Statement)
Editor: Ben Plewes
Summary of Content: Website focusing on woodworking as a hobby and pro woodworking. Includes techniques, tool tests, resources and ideas.
Readership/Target Audience: Aimed at woodworkers from amateur to professional.
CONSUMER: HOBBIES & DIY

GG2.NET
1796539U90-1006

Editorial Address: Garavi Gujarat House, 1 Silex Street, LONDON, SE1 0DW **Tel:** 020 7928 1234 **Fax:** 020 7261 0055
Email: ash@gg2.net
Web site: http://www.gg2.net
Publisher: Garavi Gujarat Publications Ltd
Date Launched: 2006
Frequency of update: Daily
Website Access: Free
Summary of Content: Website covering Asian lifestyle, travel, food, celebrities, sports, entertainment, real life stories, fashion, beauty and grooming.
Readership/Target Audience: Aimed at well educated Asian men and women aged between 18 and 44 years old.
CONSUMER: ETHNIC

GIFT OR PRESENT
1840807U94X-301

Editorial Address: Britannia House, 11 Glenthorne Road, LONDON, W6 0LH **Tel:** 0870 745 3380
Email: editorial@giftorpresent.co.uk
Web site: http://www.giftorpresent.co.uk
Publisher: Areza Ltd
Date Launched: 2005
Frequency of update: Daily
Website Access: Free
Traffic Figures: 45,000 Unique Users (per month WebTrends)
Editor: Daniel Dixons
Summary of Content: Portal covering gifts and presents for children, teenager, men and women, pets or the home.
Readership/Target Audience: Aimed at anyone looking for an original present for a special occasion.
CONSUMER: OTHER CLASSIFICATIONS: Miscellaneous

GIGWISE.COM
1775769U76D-818

Editorial Address: 60 Tabernacle Street, LONDON, EC2A 4NB **Tel:** 020 7336 0616
Email: gigwise@gigwise.com
Web site: http://www.gigwise.com
Date Launched: 2002
Frequency of update: Daily
Website Access: Free
Traffic Figures: 50,000 Unique Users (per day Publisher's Statement)
Editor: Scott Colothan
Summary of Content: Online music magazine with news, reviews, features and gig listings.
Readership/Target Audience: Aimed at music lovers aged 15 to 36 years old.
CONSUMER: MUSIC & PERFORMING ARTS: Music

GLAMOUR.COM
1626051U74B-702

Editorial Address: 25 Maddox Street, LONDON, W1S 2QN
Tel: 020 7152 3943 **Fax:** 020 7493 1469
Email: natasha.aitken@condenast.co.uk
Web site: http://www.glamourmagazine.co.uk
Publisher: Conde Nast Publications Ltd
Frequency of update: Daily
Website Access: Free
Traffic Figures: 500,000 Unique Users (per month Publisher's Statement)
Editor: Natasha Aitken
Summary of Content: Website covering celebrity gossip, beauty must haves and fashion.
Readership/Target Audience: Aimed at beauty and fashion conscious women between 18 and 34 years old.
CONSUMER: WOMEN'S INTEREST CONSUMER MAGAZINES: Women's Interest - Fashion

---

GLASGOW MATTERS
1881622U72J-365

Email: comments@glasgow-matters.co.uk
Web site: http://www.glasgow-matters.co.uk
Frequency of update: Daily
Summary of Content: Website created to help people who care about local issues. Whether you need access to useful information, want to highlight a particular topic to other people, discuss ideas with like-minded people or just show your support and keep up to date with current affairs in your area, Glasgow Matters is the place for you.
Readership/Target Audience: Aimed at residents in the local area of Glasgow.
LOCAL NEWSPAPERS: Community Newsletters

THE GL@ZINE
1614978U12B-76

Editorial Address: WATFORD **Tel:** 01727 752202
Email: theglazine@sky.com
Web site: http://www.theglazine.com
Publisher: E-Trade Media Ltd
Frequency of update: Daily
Website Access: Free (Publisher's Statement)
Editor: Tony Higgin
Summary of Content: Electronic newsletter covering products, standards and white papers as well as news and views from within the industry.
Readership/Target Audience: Aimed at the glass, glazing and fenestration industry.
BUSINESS: CERAMICS, POTTERY & GLASS: Glass

GLOBAL ASSETS
766464U1A-288

Editorial Address: PO Box 726, St. Helier, JERSEY, JE4 0XJ **Tel:** 01534 859006 **Fax:** 01534 853927
Email: ceo@financeoffshore.com
Web site: http://www.financeoffshore.com
Publisher: Finance Publications Offshore Ltd
Frequency of update: Quarterly
Website Access: Paid
Editor: Paul Mundy
Summary of Content: Electronic guide to offshore international finance.
Readership/Target Audience: Aimed at IFAs and professional advisors only.
BUSINESS: FINANCE & ECONOMICS

GLOBAL BUSINESS FOCUS
1658825U90-945

Editorial Address: For all contact details see main edition, The Asian Express Newspaper
CONSUMER: ETHNIC

GLOBAL PIPELINE MONTHLY
1629419U19G-201

Formerly: Pipeline World
Editorial Address: PO Box 21, BEACONSFIELD, HP9 1NS
Tel: 01494 675139 **Fax:** 01494 670155
Email: jtiratsoo@pipemag.com
Web site: http://www.pipemag.com
Publisher: Scientific Surveys Ltd
Date Launched: 2004
Frequency of update: Monthly
Website Access: Paid
Traffic Figures: 10,000 Unique Users (Publisher's Statement)
Editor: John Tiratsoo
Summary of Content: Website covering technological and operational developments in oil and gas pipeline design, construction, engineering, maintenance and servicing. Also covers news of activities, events and senior personnel.
Readership/Target Audience: Aimed at senior planning, operational and engineering management and procurement personnel responsible for planning, construction and operating pipelines and utilities.
BUSINESS: ENGINEERING & MACHINERY: Pipelines

GLOBALCOMMS DATABASE & COMMS UPDATE NEWS SERVICE
600908U18B-470

Formerly: GlobalComms Database
Editorial Address: 3 Colleton Crescent, EXETER, EX2 4DG
Tel: 01392 315567 **Fax:** 01392 315501
Email: tharvey@telegeography.com
Web site: http://www.telegeography.com
Publisher: TeleGeography
Frequency of update: Daily
Website Access: Paid
Editor: Tania Harvey
Summary of Content: Website providing in-depth analysis on the world's largest telecoms operators. Includes financial information, developments and company profiles.

Readership/Target Audience: Aimed at those interested in global telecoms markets.
BUSINESS: ELECTRONICS: Telecommunications

GLOBALINVESTOR.COM
1873238U1F-663

Editorial Address: 59 Addison Gardens, LONDON, W14 0DP **Tel:** 020 7603 3445
Email: david.williams@globalinvestor.com
Web site: http://www.globalinvestor.com
Frequency of update: Daily
Website Access: Free
Editor: David Williams
Summary of Content: Website providing investors with online information regarding funds, fund managers and emerging markets.
Readership/Target Audience: Aimed at investors looking at the emerging markets.
BUSINESS: FINANCE & ECONOMICS: Investment

GLOBALPENSIONS.COM
707462U1H-72_50

Formerly: International Pensions News
Editorial Address: Haymarket House, 28-29 Haymarket, LONDON, SW1Y 4RX **Tel:** 020 7484 9700
Email: alex.beveridge@incisivemedia.com
Web site: http://www.globalpensions.com
Publisher: Incisive Media
Date Launched: 2000
Frequency of update: Daily
Website Access: Free
Editor: Alex Beveridge
Summary of Content: Website containing up to the minute news on the pensions industry.
Readership/Target Audience: Aimed at professionals who work with pensions.
BUSINESS: FINANCE & ECONOMICS: Pensions

GLOUCESTER RUGBY.CO.UK
1663821U75C-467

Formerly: Gloucester Rugby Club.com
Editorial Address: Kingsholm Stadium, Kingsholm Road, GLOUCESTER, GL1 3AX **Tel:** 0871 871 8781
Email: alastairdowney@gloucesterrugby.co.uk
Web site: http://www.gloucesterrugby.co.uk
Frequency of update: Daily
Website Access: Free
Editor: Alastair Downey
Summary of Content: Official website of Gloucester Rugby Football Club with club news, fixtures, match reports, player interviews, fans services, fans forums and message board.
Readership/Target Audience: Aimed at fans, sponsors and corporate partners of Gloucester Rugby Club.
CONSUMER: SPORT: Rugby

GLOUCESTERSHIRE MATTERS
1881623U72J-366

Email: comments@gloucestershire-matters.co.uk
Web site: http://www.gloucestershire-matters.co.uk
Frequency of update: Daily
Summary of Content: Website created to help people who care about local issues. Whether you need access to useful information, want to highlight a particular topic to other people, discuss ideas with like-minded people or just show your support and keep up to date with current affairs in your area, Gloucestershire Matters is the place for you.
Readership/Target Audience: Aimed at residents in the local area of Gloucestershire.
LOCAL NEWSPAPERS: Community Newsletters

GMTV
1641071U74Q-1176

Formerly: GM.TV.
Editorial Address: The London Television Centre, Upper Ground, LONDON, SE1 9TT **Tel:** 020 7827 7000
Fax: 020 7827 7001
Email: feedback@gm.tv
Web site: http://www.gm.tv
Date Launched: 2000
Frequency of update: Daily
Website Access: Free
Traffic Figures: 1,600,000 Unique Users (per month Publisher's Statement)
Editor: Gareth Herincx
Summary of Content: Website covering GMTV's programming as well as dating, horoscopes, shopping, personal finance, competitions and children's content, exclusive celebrity web-chats, feature articles, in-depth topical news, competitions, lifestyle and advice.
Readership/Target Audience: Aimed at GMTV viewers predominantly women aged between 21 and 40 years old many of whom have children.
CONSUMER: WOMEN'S INTEREST CONSUMER MAGAZINES: Lifestyle

GO WITH KIDS.COM
1685557U89A-722

Editorial Address: Bowerhope House, St. Mary's Loch, SELKIRK, TD7 5LF **Tel:** 01750 42224
Email: gowithkids@supanet.com
Web site: http://www.gowithkids.com
Frequency of update: Half-yearly
Website Access: Free
Editor: Derek Mackenzie-Hook
Summary of Content: Website covering child friendly holidays including travel by air, sea, rail and road, accommodation, attractions and places to eat.
Readership/Target Audience: Aimed at parents planning a family holiday.
CONSUMER: HOLIDAYS & TRAVEL: Travel

GOLD AND PRECIOUS METALS
1840806U1L-90

Editorial Address: Britannia House, 11 Glenthorne Road, LONDON, W6 0LH **Tel:** 0870 745 3380
Email: editorial@goldpreciousmetals.com
Web site: http://www.goldpreciousmetals.com
Publisher: Areza Ltd
Date Launched: 2001
Frequency of update: Daily
Website Access: Free
Traffic Figures: 100,000 Unique Users (per month WebTrends)
Editor: Steve Sutton
Summary of Content: Portal covering gold, silver, platinum and other precious metals.
Readership/Target Audience: Aimed at investors in gold, silver and precious metals.
Other Features: Live and historic charts for gold, silver and precious metals in various currencies
BUSINESS: FINANCE & ECONOMICS: Commodities

GOLF BUSINESS NEWS.COM
41478U64C-25

Formerly: Golf Enterprise Europe
Editorial Address: 5-7 High Street, Dorchester-on-Thames, WALLINGFORD, OX10 7HH **Tel:** 01865 340759
Email: gbc@golfbusinesslinks.net
Web site: http://www.golfbusinessnews.com
Publisher: E.GolfBusiness.Com Ltd
Date Launched: 2000
Frequency of update: Daily
Website Access: Free
Traffic Figures: 8,600 Unique Users (per month Publisher's Statement)
Editor: Geoffrey Russell
Summary of Content: Website containing news and comment on products, innovations and developments in the golf industry.
Readership/Target Audience: Aimed at golf operators, developers, designers, landowners, leisure operators, planning and environmental institutions, golf professionals, retail outlets and green keepers.
Other Features: Features include newsletter, mailing list, message board, buyer's guide, recruitment and archiving.
BUSINESS: OTHER CLASSIFICATIONS: Clubs

GOLF TODAY
45813U75D-125

Editorial Address: 8 The Glen, Shepherdswell, DOVER, CT15 7PF **Tel:** 01304 832470
Email: info@golftodaynetwork.com
Web site: http://www.golftoday.co.uk
Publisher: Nexus Internet Ltd
Date Launched: 1996
Frequency of update: Daily
Website Access: Free
Traffic Figures: 500,000 Unique Users (per month Publisher's Statement)
Editor: Traviss Willcox
Summary of Content: Website providing golf scores worldwide, news and equipment updates.
Readership/Target Audience: Aimed at golfing enthusiasts.
Other Features: Features include a chat forum and a weekly newsletter.
CONSUMER: SPORT: Golf

GOLFANDTRAVELMAG.COM
1832517U75D-562

Editorial Address: PO Box 324, FLEET, GU51 3ZH **Tel:** 01252 621513
Email: info@golf-and-travel.com
Web site: http://www.golfandtravelmag.com
Publisher: VRA Media
Frequency of update: 6 times a year
Website Access: Free
Traffic Figures: 40,000 Unique Users (Publisher's Statement)
Editor: Vic Robbie
Summary of Content: Web-based magazine for adventurous golfers covering domestic and international golf

travel, advice on where to invest golfing property overseas, reviews of the world's best courses, interviews with stars, where to play competitive golf on holiday and where to see the top players in action.
Readership/Target Audience: Aimed at adventurous golfers.
CONSUMER: SPORT: Golf

GOLFEASTLOTHIAN.COM
1666038U75D-533

Editorial Address: Carlyle House, Lodge Street, HADDINGTON, EH41 3DX **Tel:** 01620 827282
Email: info@golfeastlothian.com
Web site: http://www.golfeastlothian.com
Frequency of update: Daily
Website Access: Free
Traffic Figures: 7,000 Unique Users (per month Publisher's Statement)
Editor: Allan Minto
Summary of Content: Website with reviews of East Lothian golf clubs, accommodation, events, leisure and travel.
Readership/Target Audience: Aimed at those planning to play golf in East Lothian.
CONSUMER: SPORT: Golf

GOLFMAGIC
626396U75D-105

Editorial Address: 16 Northwick Road, Ketton, STAMFORD, PE9 3SB **Tel:** 01780 721411
Email: editor@golfmagic.com
Web site: http://www.golfmagic.com
Publisher: Magicalia Ltd
Date Launched: 1999
Frequency of update: Daily
Website Access: Free
Traffic Figures: 80,000 Unique Users (per month Omniture)
Editor: Bob Warters
Summary of Content: Website covering the latest golf news, features and product and course reviews.
Readership/Target Audience: Aimed at golfers of all ages.
Other Features: Features include a weekly email newsletter, a chat forum, course and equipment reviews, equipment and tour news, instruction, micro-web-site facility for clubs, shopping and travel zone, personalisation of content and product reviews.
CONSUMER: SPORT: Golf

GOOD HOUSEKEEPING
1902866U74A-1063

Editorial Address: 72 Broadwick Street, LONDON, W1F 9EP **Tel:** 020 7439 5000
Email: goodh.mail@natmags.co.uk
Web site: http://www.allaboutyou.com
Publisher: Hearst Digital
Frequency of update: Daily
Website Access: Free
Editor: Bernadette Fallon
Summary of Content: Website covering. homes, cooking and lifestyle features.
Readership/Target Audience: Aimed at women of all ages.
CONSUMER: WOMEN'S INTEREST CONSUMER MAGAZINES: Women's Interest

GOODTOKNOW
1826063U74G-288

Editorial Address: Blue Fin Building, 110 Southwark Street, LONDON, SE1 0SU **Tel:** 020 3148 5000
Email: goodtoknow@ipcmedia.com
Web site: http://www.goodtoknow.co.uk
Publisher: IPC Connect Ltd
Date Launched: 2007
Frequency of update: Daily
Website Access: Free
Traffic Figures: 764,015 Unique Users (per month Publisher's Statement)
Editor: Jolene Akehurst
Summary of Content: Website covering health, diets, food and family.
Readership/Target Audience: Aimed at women of all ages.
CONSUMER: WOMEN'S INTEREST CONSUMER MAGAZINES: Slimming & Health

GQ ONLINE
47651U86C-260

Editorial Address: 25 Maddox Street, LONDON, W1S 2QN **Tel:** 020 7499 9080 **Fax:** 020 7493 1469
Email: jamie.millar@condenast.co.uk
Web site: http://www.gq.com
Publisher: Conde Nast Publications Ltd
Frequency of update: Daily
Website Access: Free
Traffic Figures: 500,000 Unique Users (per month Publisher's Statement)
Editor: Sarah Hecks

Internet Media

Summary of Content: Website covering style, fashion and lifestyle. Includes sport, entertainment, restaurant and bar reviews, competitions, daily news, quirky stories and comments.
Readership/Target Audience: Aimed at men between 18 and 45 years old.
CONSUMER: ADULT & GAY MAGAZINES: Men's Lifestyle Magazines

GRAMOPHONE ONLINE   752717U76D-321

Editorial Address: Teddington Studios, Broom Road, TEDDINGTON, TW11 9BE **Tel:** 020 8267 8000
Fax: 020 8267 5844
Email: gramophone@haymarket.com
Web site: http://www.gramophone.co.uk
Publisher: Haymarket Consumer Media
Date Launched: 2000
Frequency of update: Daily
Website Access: Free
Traffic Figures: 80,000 Unique Users (per month Publisher's Statement)
Editor: Martin Cullingford
Summary of Content: Website covering international classical music news, Gramofile (archive of over 33000 CD reviews), interviews, obituaries and competitions. The online presence of the Gramophone.
Readership/Target Audience: Aimed at those with an interest in classical music.
Other Features: An archive of over 33000 classical CD reviews, and message boards.
CONSUMER: MUSIC & PERFORMING ARTS: Music

GRANTHAM TODAY   629849U80C-2195

Editorial Address: 46 High Street, GRANTHAM, NG31 6NE **Tel:** 01476 562291 **Fax:** 01476 560564
Email: bob.hart@granthamjournal.co.uk
Web site: http://www.granthamtoday.co.uk
Publisher: Johnston Press plc
Date Launched: 1999
Frequency of update: Daily
Website Access: Free
Traffic Figures: 6,500 Unique Users (Publisher's Statement)
Editor: Bob Hart
Summary of Content: Website covering news, sport, information and features about Grantham.
Readership/Target Audience: Read by residents and visitors to the local area.
Other Features: Features include recruitment, a chat forum and archiving.
CONSUMER: RURAL & REGIONAL INTEREST: Regional Interest English Counties

GREEN ENGLAND   1861421U57-165

Editorial Address: 17 Hardwick Avenue, NEWARK, NG24 4AW **Tel:** 01636 678540
Email: enquiries@green-england.co.uk
Web site: http://www.green-england.co.uk
Frequency of update: Daily
Website Access: Free
Traffic Figures: 8,000 Unique Users (per month Publisher's Statement)
Editor: Penny Ritson
Summary of Content: Website providing a directory of organisations that provide green and ethical services and featuring information on days out.
Readership/Target Audience: Aimed at greener businesses and those concerned with green and ethical issues.
BUSINESS: ENVIRONMENT & POLLUTION

GREEN PLACES   626369U26D-70

Formerly: Green Places News
Editorial Address: Ewell House, Graveney Road, FAVERSHAM, ME13 8UP **Tel:** 01795 542436
Fax: 01795 535468
Email: editorial@green-places.co.uk
Web site: http://www.landscape.co.uk
Publisher: GTC
Date Launched: 2003
Frequency of update: 10 times a year
Website Access: Free
Traffic Figures: 3,000 Unique Users (Publisher's Statement)
Editor: Melanie Armstrong
Summary of Content: Newsletter dedicated to improving public space and focusing on its design, creation, use and management.
Readership/Target Audience: Aimed at all public space professionals, architects, parks managers, urban designers, planners, communities, local groups and local authorities.
BUSINESS: GARDEN TRADE: Garden Trade Horticulture

GREEN-CAR-GUIDE.COM   1789863U77R-753

Editorial Address: Barbour Square, High Street, Tattenhall, CHESTER, CH3 9RF **Tel:** 01244 401811
Email: paul.clarke@proenvironment.co.uk
Web site: http://www.green-car-guide.com
Publisher: Promote Environmental Communication
Date Launched: 2006
Frequency of update: Daily
Website Access: Free
Traffic Figures: 21,465 Unique Users (per month Publisher's Statement)
Editor: Paul Clarke
Summary of Content: Website providing news and information relating to green cars, cars and the environment.
Readership/Target Audience: Aimed at motorists looking to buy a green car or looking for information about environmentally friendly cars.
Other Features: News archiving, green car buyers guide, e-newsletter and free how to save money by greener driving tips.
CONSUMER: MOTORING & CYCLING: Motoring & Cycling Related

GREENEYE   1695409U77B-715

Editorial Address: Schipol Way, Humberside International Airport, Kirmington, ULCEBY, DN39 6GB **Tel:** 01652 680060
Fax: 01652 680070
Email: nina@rbplimited.co.uk
Web site: http://www.greeneyemag.co.uk
Publisher: RBP Ltd
Date Launched: 2005
Frequency of update: Quarterly
Website Access: Free
Editor: Nina Groves; **Editor-in-Chief:** Paul Farmer
Summary of Content: Website covering all Kawasaki leisure products including motorcycles, jet skis and quads as well as general lifestyle.
Readership/Target Audience: Aimed at men aged between 20 and 45 years old.
CONSUMER: MOTORING & CYCLING: Motorcycling

GREENHOTELIER   36569U11A-93

Editorial Address: 10 Fashion Street, LONDON, E1 6PX
Email: greenhoteliercontent@iln.co.uk
Web site: http://www.greenhotelier.org
Publisher: International Tourism Partnership
Date Launched: 1995
Frequency of update: Daily
Website Access: Free
Summary of Content: Communications portal and online newsletter covering responsible business in hotels and tourism, showcasing best practice amongst its members and the wider industry and providing the latest trends and insight in sustainable tourism.
Readership/Target Audience: Aimed at hoteliers and those interested in a sustainable future for the tourism industry.
BUSINESS: CATERING: Catering, Hotels & Restaurants

GREENWICH MATTERS   1881624U72J-367

Email: comments@greenwich-matters.co.uk
Web site: http://www.greenwich-matters.co.uk
Frequency of update: Daily
Summary of Content: Website created to help people who care about local issues. Whether you need access to useful information, want to highlight a particular topic to other people, discuss ideas with like-minded people or just show your support and keep up to date with current affairs in your area, Greenwich Matters is the place for you.
Readership/Target Audience: Aimed at residents in the local area of Greenwich.
LOCAL NEWSPAPERS: Community Newsletters

GROWINGBUSINESS.CO.UK   633814U1F-524

Formerly: GB Deals
Editorial Address: 2nd Floor, Westminster House, Kew Road, RICHMOND, TW9 2ND **Tel:** 020 8334 1653
Email: editor@crimsonbusiness.co.uk
Web site: http://www.growingbusiness.co.uk
Publisher: Crimson Business Ltd
Frequency of update: Daily
Website Access: Free
Traffic Figures: 50,000 Unique Users (per month Publisher's Statement)
Editor: Jon Card
Summary of Content: Website providing news and information for owner managers and entrepreneurs in the UK. Also contains news, guidance, features, introduction services, senior executive resources for venture capital-backed deals, business opportunities and services for small businesses.
Readership/Target Audience: Aimed at entrepreneurs, senior management, SMEs, venture capitalists, private

equity houses, banks, financial advisers, lawyers, accountants, consultants and service providers to the venture capital industry.
BUSINESS: FINANCE & ECONOMICS: Investment

GROWTH COMPANY INVESTOR ONLINE   629492U1F-226

Formerly: Growth Company Online
Editorial Address: Octavia House, 50 Banner Street, LONDON, EC1Y 8ST **Tel:** 020 7250 7010
Fax: 020 7250 7011
Email: editorial@growthcompany.co.uk
Web site: http://www.growthcompany.co.uk
Publisher: Vitesse Media plc
Frequency of update: Daily
Website Access: Paid
Traffic Figures: 100,000 Unique Users (Publisher's Statement)
Editor: Oliver Haill
Summary of Content: Website containing news, information and advice on fast-growing companies and buying or selling shares.
Readership/Target Audience: Aimed at small companies and private investors.
BUSINESS: FINANCE & ECONOMICS: Investment

GROWTHBUSINESS   1692639U1F-607

Editorial Address: Octavia House, 50 Banner Street, LONDON, EC1Y 8ST **Tel:** 020 7250 7010
Email: nicholas.britton@vitessemedia.co.uk
Web site: http://www.growthbusiness.co.uk
Publisher: Vitesse Media plc
Frequency of update: 260 times a year
Website Access: Free
Traffic Figures: 35,000 Unique Users (per month Publisher's Statement)
Editor: Nicholas Britton
Summary of Content: Website providing news and analysis for entrepreneurs investing in a growth company.
Readership/Target Audience: Aimed at venture capitalists, investors and entrepreneurs.
BUSINESS: FINANCE & ECONOMICS: Investment

GRUB4LIFE.ORG.UK   1851935U74D-674

Editorial Address: 40 Bowling Green Lane, LONDON, EC1R 0NE **Tel:** 020 7415 7070 **Fax:** 020 7415 7074
Email: tony@grub4life.org.uk
Web site: http://www.grub4life.org.uk
Publisher: TFA Group
Frequency of update: Daily
Website Access: Free
Traffic Figures: 5,000 Unique Users (Publisher's Statement)
Editor: Tony Fitzpatrick
Summary of Content: Online community covering nutrition for pre-school children.
Readership/Target Audience: Aimed at parents, teachers and carers of pre-school children.
CONSUMER: WOMEN'S INTEREST CONSUMER MAGAZINES: Child Care

GSQ   39799U53-56_14

Formerly: ECQ
Editorial Address: Staple Court, 11 Staple Inn Building, LONDON, WC1V 7QH **Tel:** 020 7092 3500
Fax: 020 7681 22290
Email: info@gs1uk.org
Web site: http://www.gs1uk.org
Publisher: GS1 UK
Date Launched: 1999
Frequency of update: Quarterly
Website Access: Free
Traffic Figures: 26,000 Unique Users (Publisher's Statement)
Editor: Marian Makram
Summary of Content: Official magazine of e centre, the association for standards and practices in electronic trade. Carries case studies of successful use of bar codes, scanning and electronic data interchange communications.
Readership/Target Audience: Aimed at users and potential users of electronic commerce.
BUSINESS: RETAILING & WHOLESALING

GTNEWS.COM   624166U1C-178

Editorial Address: 2nd Floor, Kenilworth House, 79-80 Margaret Street, LONDON, W1W 8TA **Tel:** 020 7079 2801
Fax: 020 7631 4792
Email: news@gtnews.com
Web site: http://www.gtnews.com
Publisher: C-Stream

Date Launched: 1997
Frequency of update: Weekly
Website Access: Free
Traffic Figures: 60,000 Unique Users (per quarter Publisher's Statement)
Editor: Ben Poole
Summary of Content: Website offering articles on banking, careers, cash management, capital markets, risk and treasury organisation, management information, payments and systems. Also features events and news, job listings and directories.
Readership/Target Audience: Aimed at corporate treasurers and banks.
BUSINESS: FINANCE & ECONOMICS: Banking

GUARDIAN.CO.UK   31265U65A-91
Formerly: Guardian Unlimited
Editorial Address: Kings Place, 90 York Way, LONDON, N1 9GU **Tel:** 020 3353 2000 **Fax:** 020 7713 4471
Email: editor@guardianunlimited.co.uk
Web site: http://www.guardian.co.uk
Publisher: Guardian Media Group plc
Date Launched: 1999
Frequency of update: Daily. Updated continuously
Website Access: Paid
Traffic Figures: 26,990,072 Unique Users (01/07/2009 To 31/07/2009 ABC/Electronic)
Editor: Sheila Pulham
Summary of Content: Online version of The Guardian. Includes a network of 13 sites covering books, film, shopping, news, football, sport, money, business, arts, travel plus stand-alone sites for the professional communities of media, education and society. Contains news from The Guardian and The Observer as well as original editorial content.
Twitter: http://twitter.com/guardian.
Readership/Target Audience: Aimed at those interested in current affairs, culture and sport.
Other Features: Features include message boards, audio reports and interactive guides.
NATIONAL DAILY & SUNDAY NEWSPAPERS: National Daily Newspapers

GUARDIAN.CO.UK/BOOKS   706991U84B-63
Formerly: Guardian Unlimited Books
Editorial Address: Kings Place, 90 York Way, LONDON, N1 9GU **Tel:** 020 7239 9870 **Fax:** 020 7713 4172
Email: michelle.pauli@guardian.co.uk
Web site: http://www.guardian.co.uk/books
Date Launched: 1999
Frequency of update: Daily
Website Access: Free
Traffic Figures: 1,170,000 Unique Users (per month Publisher's Statement)
Editor: Richard Lea
Summary of Content: Website focusing on books. Contains news and reviews, in-depth interviews with authors, games, competitions and quizzes, authors choosing their top ten books, first chapters and extracts, comprehensive bestseller charts, talkboards, celebrity online chats and an online reading group.
Readership/Target Audience: Aimed at those who love books.
Other Features: Features include a chat forum and archiving.
CONSUMER: THE ARTS & LITERARY: Literary

GUARDIAN.CO.UK/ENVIRONMENT
                                 1785503U94X-291
Formerly: Guardian Unlimited Environment
Editorial Address: 90 York Way, LONDON, N1 9GU
Tel: 020 3353 3213
Email: jessica.aldred@guardian.co.uk
Web site: http://www.guardian.co.uk/environment
Date Launched: 2006
Frequency of update: 260 times a year
Website Access: Free
(Controlled Circulation)
Editor: Jessica Aldred
Summary of Content: Website with news, features and comment pieces on climate change, conservation and renewable energy alongside practical guides to ethical living and having a more environmentally friendly lifestyle.
Readership/Target Audience: Aimed at the public in general.
CONSUMER: OTHER CLASSIFICATIONS: Miscellaneous

GUARDIAN.CO.UK/FILM   31262U76A-30
Formerly: Guardian Unlimited Film
Editorial Address: 119 Farringdon Road, LONDON, EC1R 3ER **Tel:** 020 7278 2332 **Fax:** 020 7713 4447
Email: catherine.shoard@guardian.co.uk

Web site: http://www.guardian.co.uk/film
Publisher: Guardian Media Group plc
Date Launched: 1999
Frequency of update: Daily
Website Access: Free
Traffic Figures: 1,200,000 Unique Users (per month Publisher's Statement)
Editor: Catherine Shoard
Summary of Content: Website providing film news, reviews and gossip.
Readership/Target Audience: Aimed at UK audiences between 25 and 35 years old.
CONSUMER: MUSIC & PERFORMING ARTS: Cinema

GUARDIAN.CO.UK/MONEY   706970U74M-75
Formerly: Guardian Unlimited Money
Editorial Address: Kings Place, 90 York Way, LONDON, N1 9GU **Tel:** 020 3353 3271 **Fax:** 020 7713 4171
Email: hilary.osborne@guardian.co.uk
Web site: http://www.guardian.co.uk/money
Date Launched: 2000
Frequency of update: Daily
Website Access: Free
Editor: Hilary Osborne
Summary of Content: Website focusing on personal financial issues. Includes topics such as buying a house, checking savings rates, creating a share portfolio, arranging a pension and starting your own business. You can also compare re-mortgage deals, find the best credit card or calculate the cost of moving home.
Readership/Target Audience: Aimed at those reviewing their personal financial situation.
Other Features: Features include special reports, cash clinics, factsheets, calculators, live share price feed and an experts question and answer facility.
CONSUMER: WOMEN'S INTEREST CONSUMER MAGAZINES: Personal Finance

GUARDIAN.CO.UK/POLITICS   707412U82-29
Formerly: Guardian Unlimited Politics
Editorial Address: Kings Place, 90 York Way, LONDON, N1 9GU **Tel:** 020 3353 3548 **Fax:** 020 7713 4033
Email: guardian.unlimited.politics@guardian.co.uk
Web site: http://www.guardian.co.uk/politics
Publisher: Guardian News and Media
Date Launched: 2001
Frequency of update: Daily. The site is updated regularly throughout the day
Website Access: Free
Traffic Figures: 5,910,000 Unique Users (per month Publisher's Statement)
Editor: Steve Busfield
Summary of Content: Website providing news, political commentary, analysis, games, gossip and 'Aristotle'- a unique database of political information.
Readership/Target Audience: Aimed at the general public interested in politics.
Other Features: Features include a chat forum, an e-mail newsletter, recruitment, an events calendar and archiving.
CONSUMER: CURRENT AFFAIRS & POLITICS

GUARDIAN.CO.UK/TRAVEL   1793622U89A-746
Formerly: Guardian Unlimited Travel
Editorial Address: Kings Place, 90 York Way, LONDON, N1 9GU **Tel:** 020 7131 7057
Email: travel.editor@guardianunlimited.co.uk
Web site: http://www.guardian.co.uk/travel
Publisher: Guardian Media Group plc
Frequency of update: Daily
Website Access: Free
Traffic Figures: 888,230 Unique Users (per month Publisher's Statement)
Editor: Georgia Brown
Summary of Content: Website covering travel news and features, readers tips and late offers.
Readership/Target Audience: Aimed at Aimed at international travellers.
CONSUMER: HOLIDAYS & TRAVEL: Travel

THE GUILD OF FOOD WRITERS
                                 629021U22A-210
Editorial Address: 255 Kent House Road, BECKENHAM, BR3 1JQ **Tel:** 020 8659 0422
Email: guild@gfw.co.uk
Web site: http://www.gfw.co.uk
Frequency of update: 6 times a year
Website Access: Free
Editor: Jonathan Woods
Summary of Content: Website focusing on bringing together professional food writers.

Readership/Target Audience: Read by professional food writers.
BUSINESS: FOOD

HABBO   1641356U74F-757
Formerly: Habbo Hotel
Editorial Address: Suite 104, Business Design Centre, 52 Upper Street, Islington, LONDON, N1 0QH
Tel: 020 7288 6689 **Fax:** 020 7288 6186
Email: oisin.lunny@sulake.com
Web site: http://www.habbo.co.uk
Date Launched: 2001
Frequency of update: Daily
Website Access: Paid
Traffic Figures: 920,000 Unique Users (per month Publisher's Statement)
Editor: Oisin Lunny
Summary of Content: Virtual world, online community, social network and website covering all teenage subjects.
Readership/Target Audience: Aimed at 11 to 20 year olds in the UK.
Other Features: Other features on site chat and online games.
CONSUMER: WOMEN'S INTEREST CONSUMER MAGAZINES: Teenage

HABIA NEWS   714057U15B-40
Formerly: Habia
Editorial Address: Oxford House, Sixth Avenue, Sky Business Park, Robin Hood Airport, DONCASTER, DN9 3GG
Tel: 0845 230 6080 **Fax:** 01302 774949
Email: mark.phillips@habia.org
Web site: http://www.habia.org.uk
Publisher: Habia
Date Launched: 2005
Frequency of update: 6 times a year
Website Access: Paid
Traffic Figures: 15,000 Unique Users (Publisher's Statement)
Editor: Mark Phillips
Summary of Content: Magazine focusing on training, education and business development right across the hair, beauty, nails and spa industries.
Readership/Target Audience: Aimed at hairdressers, beauty therapists, nail techs, spa therapists, barbers and African Caribbean hairdressers salon owners and managers, students, colleges and training centre educators, careers advisors, Government and regional bodies, corporate companies and organisations in hair, beauty and spa.
BUSINESS: COSMETICS & HAIRDRESSING: Hairdressing

HACKNEY MATTERS   1881625U72J-368
Email: comments@hackney-matters.co.uk
Web site: http://www.hackney-matters.co.uk
Frequency of update: Daily
Summary of Content: Website created to help people who care about local issues. Whether you need access to useful information, want to highlight a particular topic to other people, discuss ideas with like-minded people or just show your support and keep up to date with current affairs in your area, Hackney Matters is the place for you.
Readership/Target Audience: Aimed at residents in the local area of Hackney.
LOCAL NEWSPAPERS: Community Newsletters

HALI   1681783U7-302
Formerly: HALI.com
Editorial Address: Studio 30, Liddell Road, LONDON, NW6 2EW **Tel:** 020 7578 7228 **Fax:** 020 7578 7222
Email: info@hali.com
Web site: http://www.hali.com
Publisher: Hali Publications Ltd
Date Launched: 1978
Frequency of update: Weekly
Website Access: Free
Editor: Lucy Upward
Summary of Content: Website focusing on international carpets, textiles and tribal and Islamic art.
Readership/Target Audience: Aimed at professional traders, academics, museum curators, collectors, amateur enthusiasts and designers.
BUSINESS: ANTIQUES

HAM&HIGH   629292U80B-122_80
Editorial Address: 100A Avenue Road, Hampstead, LONDON, NW3 3HF **Tel:** 020 7433 0000 **Fax:** 020 7433 6229
Email: editorial@hamhigh.co.uk
Web site: http://www.hamhigh.co.uk
Frequency of update: Daily
Website Access: Free

Traffic Figures: 30,000 Unique Users (per month Publisher's Statement)
Editor: Ed Thomas
Summary of Content: Website covering news, sport, art and information concerning the Hampstead and Highgate area.
Readership/Target Audience: Aimed at citizens who live in the area.
CONSUMER: RURAL & REGIONAL INTEREST: Regional Interest Greater London

HAMMERSMITH MATTERS
1881626U72J-369

Email: comments@hammersmith-matters.co.uk
Web site: http://www.hammersmith-matters.co.uk
Frequency of update: Daily
Summary of Content: Website created to help people who care about local issues. Whether you need access to useful information, want to highlight a particular topic to other people, discuss ideas with like-minded people or just show your support and keep up to date with current affairs in your area, Hammersmith Matters is the place for you.
Readership/Target Audience: Aimed at residents in the local area of Hammersmith.
LOCAL NEWSPAPERS: Community Newsletters

HAMPSHIRE MATTERS
1881627U72J-370

Email: comments@hampshire-matters.co.uk
Web site: http://www.hampshire-matters.co.uk
Frequency of update: Daily
LOCAL NEWSPAPERS: Community Newsletters

HANDBAG.COM
601083U74A-145

Editorial Address: 72 Broadwick Street, LONDON, W1F 9EP **Tel:** 020 7439 5000
Email: marketing@hearstdigital.co.uk
Web site: http://www.handbag.com
Publisher: Hearst Digital
Date Launched: 1999
Frequency of update: Daily
Website Access: Free
Traffic Figures: 1,452,290 Unique Users (01/05/2007 To 31/07/2007 ABC/Electronic)
Editor: Debbie Djordjevic
Summary of Content: Online lifestyle magazine containing features on arts and entertainment, careers, education, beauty, celebrity gossip, family, fashion, health and fitness, travel, homes and property, food and drink, horoscopes, relationships and finance.
Readership/Target Audience: Aimed at women aged 24 to 45 years old.
Other Features: Features include archiving.
CONSUMER: WOMEN'S INTEREST CONSUMER MAGAZINES: Women's Interest

HAPPY FAMILIES ONLINE
626128U74C-185

Editorial Address: Orchardton Hall, Auchencairn, CASTLE DOUGLAS, DG7 1QL **Tel:** 0845 130 6249
Email: edit@happyfamiliesonline.com
Web site: http://www.happyfamiliesonline.com
Publisher: Brave New World International Ltd
Frequency of update: Weekly
Website Access: Free
Traffic Figures: 350,000 Unique Users (per month Publisher's Statement)
Editor: Dave Burbidge
Summary of Content: Website covering music, books, television and films.
Readership/Target Audience: Aimed at all the family.
Other Features: Features include archiving.
CONSUMER: WOMEN'S INTEREST CONSUMER MAGAZINES: Home & Family

HARBOROUGH TODAY
629842U72B-2116

Formerly: HARBOROUGH Mail On-Line
Editorial Address: 9 Northampton Road, MARKET HARBOROUGH, LE16 9HB **Tel:** 01858 436000
Fax: 01858 410097
Email: alex.blackwell@harboroughmail.co.uk
Web site: http://www.harboroughmail.co.uk
Publisher: Johnston Press plc
Date Launched: 1999
Frequency of update: Daily
Website Access: Free
Traffic Figures: 9,643 Unique Users (per month Publisher's Statement)
Editor: Alex Blackwell
Summary of Content: Website containing news, sport, information and features about Harborough and Lutterworth area.

Readership/Target Audience: Read by residents and visitors to the local area.
Other Features: Features include recruitment and a chat forum.
LOCAL NEWSPAPERS: Local Newspapers English Counties

HARINGAY MATTERS
1881628U72J-371

Email: comments@haringay-matters.co.uk
Web site: http://www.haringay-matters.co.uk
Frequency of update: Daily
LOCAL NEWSPAPERS: Community Newsletters

HARLEQUINS RUGBY LEAGUE
1663717U75C-461

Formerly: London Broncos
Editorial Address: Twickenham Stoop, Langhorn Drive, TWICKENHAM, TW2 7SX **Tel:** 020 8410 6072
Email: rlmedia@quins.co.uk
Web site: http://www.quins.co.uk
Frequency of update: Daily
Website Access: Free
Editor: Malcolm Cranmer
Summary of Content: Official site of Harlequins Rugby League Club covering fixtures, match reports, player profiles, community work and club news.
Readership/Target Audience: Aimed at fans of Harlequins Rugby.
CONSUMER: SPORT: Rugby

HARLOT
1799656U74A-1030

Editorial Address: Unit 503, Erico House, 93-99 Upper Richmond Road, LONDON, SW15 2TG **Tel:** 020 8785 5620
Fax: 020 8785 5658
Email: editorial@scarletmagazine.co.uk
Web site: http://www.harlotmagazine.co.uk
Publisher: Blaze Publishing Limited
Frequency of update: 24 times a year
Website Access: Free
Traffic Figures: 65,000 Unique Users (per week Publisher's Statement)
Editor: Andrea Wilde
Summary of Content: Electronic magazine covering celebrity gossip, fashion and erotic stories.
Readership/Target Audience: Aimed at women aged 25 to 45 years old with a high disposable income.
CONSUMER: WOMEN'S INTEREST CONSUMER MAGAZINES: Women's Interest

HARPERS WINE & SPIRIT
1868156U9A-268

Editorial Address: Broadfield Park, CRAWLEY, RH11 9RT **Tel:** 01293 613400
Email: richard.siddle@william-reed.co.uk
Web site: http://www.harpers.co.uk
Publisher: William Reed Business Media
Frequency of update: Daily
Website Access: Free
Editor: Richard Siddle
Summary of Content: Website dedicated to bringing worldwide drinks industry news, views and expert analysis from the wine, spirit, beer and cider markets.
Readership/Target Audience: Aimed at multiple and specialist retailers, sommeliers, hoteliers and those involved in the wine and spirit trade.
BUSINESS: DRINKS & LICENSED TRADE: Drinks, Licensed Trade, Wines & Spirits

HARPERSBAZAAR.CO.UK
1923358U74B-766

Editorial Address: National Magazine House, 72 Broadwick Street, LONDON, W1F 9EP **Tel:** 020 7439 5000
Fax: 020 7439 5506
Email: bazaar.webeditor@harpersbazaar.co.uk
Web site: http://www.harpersbazaar.co.uk
Publisher: National Magazine Company Ltd
Frequency of update: Daily
Traffic Figures: 80,000 Unique Users (per month Publisher's Statement)
Editor: Camilla Hume-Smith
Summary of Content: Website containing features on health, beauty, fashion, arts, interiors, gardening, food and current issues.
Readership/Target Audience: Aimed at upmarket, discerning adults.
CONSUMER: WOMEN'S INTEREST CONSUMER MAGAZINES: Women's Interest - Fashion

HARROGATEADVERTISER.NET
629280U72B-4059

Formerly: Harrogate Today
Editorial Address: 1 Cardale Park, Beckwith Head Road, HARROGATE, HG3 1RZ **Tel:** 01423 564321
Fax: 01423 501228
Email: ackrill.news@ypn.co.uk
Web site: http://www.harrogateadvertiser.net
Publisher: Ackrill Group Ltd
Date Launched: 1996
Frequency of update: Daily
Website Access: Free
Editor: Tom Hay
Other Features: Features include a discussion forum, recruitment and archiving.
LOCAL NEWSPAPERS: Local Newspapers English Counties

HARROW MATTERS
1881629U72J-372

Email: comments@harrow-matters.co.uk
Web site: http://www.harrow-matters.co.uk
Frequency of update: Daily
LOCAL NEWSPAPERS: Community Newsletters

HAVERING MATTERS
1881630U72J-373

Email: comments@havering-matters.co.uk
Web site: http://www.havering-matters.co.uk
Frequency of update: Daily
Summary of Content: Website created to help people who care about local issues. Whether you need access to useful information, want to highlight a particular topic to other people, discuss ideas with like-minded people or just show your support and keep up to date with current affairs in your area, Havering Matters is the place for you.
Readership/Target Audience: Aimed at residents in the local area of Havering.
LOCAL NEWSPAPERS: Community Newsletters

HC2D
1894028U56A-220

Editorial Address: Manor Farm Stables, Biddestone, CHIPPENHAM, SN14 7DH **Tel:** 01249 701100
Fax: 01249 715785
Email: mailbox@mayden.co.uk
Web site: http://www.hc2d.co.uk
Publisher: Mayden Health
Date Launched: 2005
Frequency of update: Daily
Website Access: Free
Traffic Figures: 10,000 Unique Users (per month Publisher's Statement)
Editor: Claire Tuckey
Summary of Content: Healthcare news resource covering the NHS, UK and world health news.
Readership/Target Audience: Aimed at managers, doctors, clinicians, acute trusts, PCTs, SHAs, private healthcare institutions and healthcare companies.
BUSINESS: HEALTH & MEDICAL

HCSTUFF
1698075U88A-231

Editorial Address: 150-152 King Street, LONDON, W6 0QU **Tel:** 020 8600 5307
Email: ed.colley@hotcourses.com
Web site: http://www.hcstuff.com
Publisher: Hotcourses
Date Launched: 2004
Frequency of update: Weekly
Website Access: Free
Traffic Figures: 100,000 Unique Users (per day Publisher's Statement)
Editor: Ed Colley
Summary of Content: Website providing a guide to UK undergraduate courses, universities and colleges. Also covers lifestyle, games, celebrity gossip, music and film reviews.
Readership/Target Audience: Aimed at 15 to 17 year olds who are thinking about their next career and education steps.
CONSUMER: EDUCATION

HD HOSPITAL DEVELOPMENT
1833060U56C-388

Editorial Address: Beechwood House, 2-3 Commercial Way, Christy Close, Southfields, BASILDON, SS15 6EF **Tel:** 01268 495600 **Fax:** 01268 495602
Email: joanne.makosinski@binleys.com
Web site: http://www.hdmagazine.co.uk
Publisher: Binleys
Date Launched: 2008
Website Access: Free

Editor: Joanne Makosinski
Summary of Content: Website covering design, construction, refurbishment, facilities management and maintenance in healthcare establishments.
Readership/Target Audience: Aimed at NHS management, decision makers involved in planning, estates and facilities management plus architects and consultants serving both the private and public healthcare markets.
BUSINESS: HEALTH & MEDICAL: Hospitals

HEALTH & SAFETY INDUSTRY DIRECTORY
1818361U54B-112

Editorial Address: 18 Generator Hall, Electric Wharf, COVENTRY, CV1 4JL **Tel:** 0870 199 4044
Fax: 0870 777 4360
Email: enquiries@industrydirectory.co.uk
Web site: http://www.industrydirectory.co.uk/safety
Publisher: Simply Marcomms
Frequency of update: Daily
Website Access: Free
Editor: Kirstie Colledge
Summary of Content: Directory containing the latest news stories for the health and safety industry. Includes a news archive.
Readership/Target Audience: Aimed at professionals in the building and construction industry particularly those in the health and safety industry.
BUSINESS: SAFETY & SECURITY: Safety

HEALTH4MEDIA.COM
1828545U56A-211

Editorial Address: Unit 11, The Chandlery, 50 Westminster Bridge Road, LONDON, SE1 7QY **Tel:** 020 7953 7435
Fax: 020 7953 8773
Email: news.desk@health4media.com
Web site: http://www.health4media.com
Publisher: News4Media Ltd
Date Launched: 2007
Frequency of update: Daily
Website Access: Paid
Traffic Figures: 5,000 Unique Users (Publisher's Statement)
Editor: Henry Hemming
Summary of Content: Online Publication covering men's, women's, children's, complementary, private, mental and clinical health, disease treatment, cosmetic surgery, pharmaceuticals, hospitals & clinics, products and accessories, events and publishing.
Readership/Target Audience: Aimed at health industry professionals.
BUSINESS: HEALTH & MEDICAL

HEALTHANDSAFETYZONE.COM
1622836U54B-102

Editorial Address: Heath House, Firfields, WEYBRIDGE, KT13 0UD **Tel:** 01932 830111
Email: editorial@healthandsafetyzone.com
Web site: http://www.healthandsafetyzone.com
Publisher: PersonnelZone
Date Launched: 1988
Frequency of update: Daily
Website Access: Paid
Traffic Figures: 8,500 Unique Users (per month Publisher's Statement)
Editor: Stewart Shepherd
Summary of Content: Website featuring reviews and articles for the Health and Safety industry. Contains a directory of health and safety suppliers in the EC, a bookstore and a list of training courses.
Readership/Target Audience: Aimed at health professionals and safety managers.
BUSINESS: SAFETY & SECURITY: Safety

HEALTH OUTCOMES COMMUNICATOR
1872683U56A-217

Editorial Address: 2 Long Barn, Pistyll Farm, Nercwys, MOLD, CH7 4EW **Tel:** 01352 706190 **Fax:** 01352 756260
Email: duncan.dibble@rxcomms.com
Web site: http://www.rxcomms.com/hocezine.asp
Publisher: Rx Communications
Frequency of update: Monthly
Website Access: Free
Traffic Figures: 1,000 Unique Users (Publisher's Statement)
Editor: Duncan Dibble
Summary of Content: E-newsletter covering health and pharmacal economics.
Readership/Target Audience: Aimed at healthcare economists and outcomes researchers.
BUSINESS: HEALTH & MEDICAL

HEALTHCAREREPUBLIC.COM
1789822U56A-206

Editorial Address: 174 Hammersmith Road, LONDON, W6 7JP **Tel:** 020 8267 4406
Email: pressreleases.hcr@haymarket.com
Web site: http://www.healthcarerepublic.com
Publisher: Haymarket Medical Publications Ltd
Frequency of update: Daily
Website Access: Free
Editor: Emilie Reymond
Summary of Content: Website covering issues for GPs and the primary healthcare sector with coverage of prescription, education, clinical and pharmaceutical industry trends.
Readership/Target Audience: Aimed at GPs and the primary healthcare sector.
BUSINESS: HEALTH & MEDICAL

HEALTHNET
628937U56A-66_70

Editorial Address: 18 Oxleasow Road, East Moons Moat, REDDITCH, B98 0RE **Tel:** 0871 220 0355
Fax: 0871 220 0356
Email: press@healthnet.co.uk
Web site: http://www.healthnet.co.uk
Frequency of update: Monthly
Website Access: Free
Editor: Yolande Saunders
Summary of Content: Website covering news and information about the healthcare industry, with online advice services.
Readership/Target Audience: Aimed at healthcare professionals in the UK.
Other Features: Features include news articles, product launches, recruitment, discussion forums, mailing list, an e-mail newsletter and archiving.
BUSINESS: HEALTH & MEDICAL

HEALTH.TELEGRAPH.CO.UK
713996U74G-21

Editorial Address: 111 Buckingham Palace Road, LONDON, SW1W 0DT **Tel:** 020 7931 2000
Email: kate.devlin@telegraph.co.uk
Web site: http://www.telegraph.co.uk/health
Publisher: Telegraph Media Group Ltd
Date Launched: 2001
Frequency of update: Daily
Website Access: Free
Traffic Figures: 100,000 Unique Users (per week Publisher's Statement)
Editor: Kate Devlin
Summary of Content: Website providing news and information about health and beauty. Includes specific sections for women, men, children and elders. Also covers diet and fitness.
Readership/Target Audience: Aimed predominantly at men and women with an interest in health and beauty.
CONSUMER: WOMEN'S INTEREST CONSUMER MAGAZINES: Slimming & Health

HEALTHYSOUL.CO.UK
1828081U74G-289

Editorial Address: PO Box 1073, COULSDON, CR5 3ZU
Tel: 01737 555322
Email: feedback@healthysoul.co.uk
Web site: http://www.healthysoul.co.uk
Publisher: Healthy Soul
Date Launched: 2005
Frequency of update: Weekly
Website Access: Free
Traffic Figures: 500 Unique Users (per month Publisher's Statement)
Editor: Frances Ive
Summary of Content: Website with news and features covering complementary medicine, nutrition and health.
Readership/Target Audience: Aimed at those interested in taking responsibility for their welbeing.
Other Features: Other features on site opportunity to buy products and monthly competition.
CONSUMER: WOMEN'S INTEREST CONSUMER MAGAZINES: Slimming & Health

HEART BEAT GUIDES
1732182U89E-249

Editorial Address: 4 David Street, St. Dogmaels, CARDIGAN, SA43 3HT **Tel:** 01239 612793
Email: tim.richards@virgin.net
Web site: http://www.heartbeatguides.com
Date Launched: 2006
Frequency of update: 24 times a year
Website Access: Free
Editor: Tim Richards
Summary of Content: Electronic travel guides with lively, evocative and informative, global destination reports for downloading onto personal computers and MP3 players.

Readership/Target Audience: Aimed at English-speaking travellers from back-packers to those going on luxury cruises.
Other Features: Free hotels download page.
CONSUMER: HOLIDAYS & TRAVEL: Holidays

HEATWORLD.COM
1810894U74A-1036

Editorial Address: Endeavour House, 189 Shaftesbury Avenue, LONDON, WC2H 8JG **Tel:** 020 7859 8657
Email: helen.wardman@bauermedia.co.uk
Web site: http://www.heatworld.com
Publisher: Bauer Media
Date Launched: 2007
Frequency of update: Daily
Website Access: Free
Traffic Figures: 140,000 Unique Users (per month Publisher's Statement)
Editor: Helen Wardman
Summary of Content: Website covering breaking celebrity news, behind the news footage and from shoots as well as fashion, beauty and discussion boards.
Readership/Target Audience: Aimed at those aged 18 to 40 years old.
CONSUMER: WOMEN'S INTEREST CONSUMER MAGAZINES: Women's Interest

HEBDEN BRIDGE WEB
47010U80C-3645

Editorial Address: 32 Windsor Road, HEBDEN BRIDGE, HX7 8LF **Tel:** 01422 843724
Email: webmaster@penninepens.co.uk
Web site: http://www.hebdenbridge.co.uk
Publisher: Pennine Pens
Frequency of update: Daily
Website Access: Free
Editor: Chris Ratcliffe
Summary of Content: Website covering local interest issues in and around the Hebden Bridge area. Includes news, photos and tourist information.
Readership/Target Audience: Aimed at those who live in the local area and tourists interested in visiting.
Other Features: Features include a discussion forum, an events calendar and archiving.
CONSUMER: RURAL & REGIONAL INTEREST: Regional Interest English Counties

HELICOPTER INTERNATIONAL
626491U6R-128

Editorial Address: 75 Elm Tree Road, Locking, WESTON-SUPER-MARE, BS24 8EL **Tel:** 01934 822524
Fax: 01934 822400
Email: editorial@aviapress.fsnet.co.uk
Web site: http://www.helidata.rotor.com
Publisher: Avia Press Associates
Date Launched: 1977
Frequency of update: 6 times a year
Website Access: Paid
Traffic Figures: 25,000 Unique Users (Publisher's Statement)
Editor: Elfan ap Rees; **Editor-in-Chief:** Elfan ap Rees
Summary of Content: Website focusing on news and information about the helicopter industry.
Readership/Target Audience: Aimed at the professional helicopter industry, operators and owners.
BUSINESS: AVIATION & AERONAUTICS: Aviation Related

HEMEL HEMPSTEAD TODAY
629890U80C-1785

Formerly: Hemel on-line
Editorial Address: 39 Marlowes, HEMEL HEMPSTEAD, HP1 1LH **Tel:** 01442 213211 **Fax:** 01442 261887
Email: editorial@hemelgazette.co.uk
Web site: http://www.hemelhempsteadtoday.co.uk
Frequency of update: Daily
Website Access: Free
Traffic Figures: 2,500 Unique Users (per week Publisher's Statement)
Editor: Adam Hollier
Summary of Content: Website containing news, sport, information and features about Hemel Hempstead.
Readership/Target Audience: Read by residents and visitors to the local area and also by former residents.
Other Features: Features include recruitment, a chat forum and archiving.
CONSUMER: RURAL & REGIONAL INTEREST: Regional Interest English Counties

HEMSCOTT
752998U74M-421

Editorial Address: 1st Floor, Castle House, 37-45 Paul Street, LONDON, EC2A 4LS **Tel:** 020 7763 8313
Email: editorial@hemscott.co.uk
Web site: http://www.hemscott.com
Frequency of update: Daily

Internet Media

Website Access: Paid
Summary of Content: Website providing data, news and comment on companies listed on the London Stock Market.
Readership/Target Audience: Aimed at private investors and companies.
CONSUMER: WOMEN'S INTEREST CONSUMER MAGAZINES: Personal Finance

HEREFORDSHIRE MATTERS
1881631U72J-374
Email: comments@herefordshire-matters.co.uk
Web site: http://www.herefordshire-matters.co.uk
Frequency of update: Daily
Summary of Content: Website created to help people who care about local issues. Whether you need access to useful information, want to highlight a particular topic to other people, discuss ideas with like minded individuals or just show your support and keep up to date with current affairs in your area, Herefordshire Matters is the place for you.
Readership/Target Audience: Aimed at residents in the local area of Herefordshire.
LOCAL NEWSPAPERS: Community Newsletters

HERTFORDSHIRE MATTERS
1881632U72J-375
Email: comments@hertfordshire-matters.co.uk
Web site: http://www.hertfordshire-matters.co.uk
Frequency of update: Daily
Summary of Content: Website created to help people who care about local issues. Whether you need access to useful information, want to highlight a particular topic to other people, discuss ideas with like minded individuals or just show your support and keep up to date with current affairs in your area, Hertfordshire Matters is the place for you.
Readership/Target Audience: Aimed at residents in the local area of Hertfordshire.
LOCAL NEWSPAPERS: Community Newsletters

HEXUS.NET
1695424U78R-503
Editorial Address: 37 High Street, Purton, SWINDON, SN5 4BE **Tel:** 07775 775115
Email: editorial@hexus.net
Web site: http://www.hexus.net
Publisher: Hexus Ltd.
Date Launched: 2000
Frequency of update: Daily
Website Access: Free
Traffic Figures: 1,800,000 Unique Users (per month Publisher's Statement)
Editor: Steve Kerrison
Summary of Content: Website covering new technology, solutions, components and turn key systems.
Readership/Target Audience: Aimed at tech savvy, early adopters and pc enthusiasts.
CONSUMER: CONSUMER ELECTRONICS: Consumer Electronics Related

HI~ARTS (NORTHINGS ONLINE ARTS JOURNAL)
1743225U84A-453
Formerly: Hi-Arts
Editorial Address: Ballantyne House, 84 Academy Street, INVERNESS, IV1 1LU
Email: fiona@hi-arts.co.uk
Web site: http://www.hi-arts.co.uk
Frequency of update: Daily
Website Access: Free
Editor: Fiona Fisher
Summary of Content: Website promoting and developing the arts within the Highlands and Islands covering what's on, events, music, visual arts and theatre.
Readership/Target Audience: Aimed at the general public and artists.
CONSUMER: THE ARTS & LITERARY: Arts

HIDDENWIRES
1685506U43A-62
Editorial Address: Great Brownings, College Road, LONDON, SE21 7HP **Tel:** 020 8761 1042
Email: info@hiddenwires.co.uk
Web site: http://www.hiddenwires.co.uk
Publisher: SYPHA
Date Launched: 2003
Frequency of update: Daily
Website Access: Free
Traffic Figures: 100,000 Unique Users (per month Publisher's Statement)
Editor: Yasmin Hashmi
Summary of Content: Website focusing on custom installed home automation and home entertainment.
Readership/Target Audience: Aimed at custom installers, builders, architects, designers, suppliers and consumers.
BUSINESS: ELECTRICAL RETAIL TRADE

HIGHFLYERS
600896U89E-127
Formerly: High Flyers
Editorial Address: Studio 111, Finsbury Business Centre, 40 Bowling Green Lane, LONDON, EC1R 0NE
Tel: 020 7415 7100
Email: tracyh@mediamarkpublishing.com
Web site: http://www.mediamarkpublishing.com
Publisher: Mediamark Ltd
Date Launched: 1997
Frequency of update: 3 times a year
Website Access: Free
Editor: Tracy Harvey
Summary of Content: British Midland's online loyalty magazine containing features on travel, destinations, shopping and lifestyle.
Readership/Target Audience: Aimed at members of the British Midland's flight bookers club.
CONSUMER: HOLIDAYS & TRAVEL: Holidays

HIGHLAND MATTERS
1881633U72J-376
Email: comments@highland-matters.co.uk
Web site: http://www.highland-matters.co.uk
Frequency of update: Daily
Summary of Content: Website created to help people who care about local issues. Whether you need access to useful information, want to highlight a particular topic to other people, discuss ideas with like minded individuals or just show your support and keep up to date with current affairs in your area, Highland Matters is the place for you.
Readership/Target Audience: Aimed at residents in the local area of Highland.
LOCAL NEWSPAPERS: Community Newsletters

HILLINGDON MATTERS
1881634U72J-377
Email: comments@hillingdon-matters.co.uk
Web site: http://www.hillingdon-matters.co.uk
Frequency of update: Daily
Summary of Content: Website created to help people who care about local issues. Whether you need access to useful information, want to highlight a particular topic to other people, discuss ideas with like minded individuals or just show your support and keep up to date with current affairs in your area, Hillingdon Matters is the place for you.
Readership/Target Audience: Aimed at residents in the local area of Hillingdon.
LOCAL NEWSPAPERS: Community Newsletters

HIP-HOP CONNECTION
46235U76E-140
Editorial Address: PO Box 392, CAMBRIDGE, CB1 3WH
Tel: 01223 210536 **Fax:** 01223 210536
Email: andyc@hiphop.com
Web site: http://www.hhcdigital.net.com
Publisher: Infamous Ink Ltd
Date Launched: 1988
Frequency of update: Daily
Website Access: Paid
Editor: Andy Cowan
Summary of Content: Website covering all aspects of Hip-Hop lifestyle and music.
Readership/Target Audience: Aimed at 13 to 30 year old rap and R&B fans.
CONSUMER: MUSIC & PERFORMING ARTS: Pop Music

HISTORIC-UK.COM
623137U94B-40
Editorial Address: PO Box 1510, RUGBY, CV22 6YE
Tel: 01788 522341 **Fax:** 01788 522341
Email: info@historic-uk.com
Web site: http://www.historic-uk.com
Publisher: Historic UK Ltd
Date Launched: 2000
Frequency of update: Daily
Website Access: Free
Traffic Figures: 300,000 Unique Users (per month Publisher's Statement)
Editor: Deborah Johnson
Summary of Content: Website featuring an accommodation guide in historic and heritage buildings in the UK and Europe and a magazine with articles on British history and culture. Also includes information on living history displays, re-enactments, destinations and marketplace for traditional goods.
Readership/Target Audience: Aimed at those interested in the history and culture of Britain and visiting and staying in historic buildings and hotels.
CONSUMER: OTHER CLASSIFICATIONS: Historic Buildings

HITCHED.CO.UK
1842311U74L-269
Editorial Address: Unit 7, Stanhope Gate, Stanhope Road, CAMBERLEY, GU15 3DW **Tel:** 0870 011 2545
Fax: 01276 28284

Email: francesca.moore@hitched.co.uk
Web site: http://www.hitched.co.uk
Traffic Figures: 350,000 Unique Users (per month Publisher's Statement)
Editor: Francesca Moore
Summary of Content: Website covering all aspects of weddings including venues, fashion, gifts, honeymoons and stag and hen nights.
Readership/Target Audience: Aimed at those planning a wedding.
CONSUMER: WOMEN'S INTEREST CONSUMER MAGAZINES: Brides

HKY WORLD
1839666U75X-1719
Editorial Address: 17A South Street, LANCING, BN15 8AE
Tel: 0870 803 4891
Email: editor@hkyworld.com
Web site: http://www.hkyworld.com
Publisher: Push Hockey Ltd
Date Launched: 2008
Frequency of update: Monthly
Website Access: Free
Traffic Figures: 150,000 Unique Users (per month Publisher's Statement)
Editor: Chris Henry
Summary of Content: Online magazine covering world hockey with interviews, the latest news, coaching, lifestyle and product reviews.
Readership/Target Audience: Aimed at hockey players, coaches, umpires and volunteers worldwide.
CONSUMER: SPORT: Other Sport

HOGMANAY.NET
767631U80E-352
Formerly: Hogmanay
Editorial Address: Braeside Cottage, Robertson Bank, GOREBRIDGE, EH23 4JT **Tel:** 01875 822694
Email: john@hogmanay.net
Web site: http://www.hogmanay.net
Publisher: Alstead Consulting
Date Launched: 1998
Frequency of update: Daily
Website Access: Free
Traffic Figures: 10,000,000 Unique Users (per year Publisher's Statement)
Editor: John Ritchie; **Webmaster:** Jonathan Alstead
Summary of Content: Website providing information on all of Scotland's Hogmanay parties and traditions.
Readership/Target Audience: Aimed at those interested in Scottish traditions and Hogmanay celebrations.
CONSUMER: RURAL & REGIONAL INTEREST: Regional Interest Scotland

HOLDTHEFRONTPAGE.CO.UK
704834U2B-54
Editorial Address: Northcliffe House, Meadow Road, Northcliffe House, DERBY, DE1 2BH **Tel:** 01332 228020
Email: paul.linford@and.co.uk
Web site: http://www.holdthefrontpage.co.uk
Publisher: Northcliffe Media Ltd
Date Launched: 2000
Frequency of update: Daily
Website Access: Free
Traffic Figures: 50,000 Unique Users (per month Publisher's Statement)
Editor: Paul Linford; **Online Journalist:** Tamlyn Jones
Summary of Content: Website containing news and job adverts for and about people in the regional newspaper industry.
Readership/Target Audience: Aimed at regional UK print and online journalists, newspaper photographers, sub-editors and editors, freelance writers and students interested in journalism as a career.
Other Features: Freelance directory, CV listings, journalism glossary, opt-in mailing list (daily mailings), newspaper database, story ideas, contacts directory, website reviews and six-year editorial archive.
BUSINESS: COMMUNICATIONS, ADVERTISING & MARKETING: Press

HOLYROOD TODAY
1690404U82-267
Editorial Address: 14-16 Holyrood Road, EDINBURGH, EH8 8AF **Tel:** 0131 270 7096 **Fax:** 0131 272 2116
Email: editor@holyrood.com
Web site: http://www.holyrood.com
Publisher: Holyrood Communications Ltd
Date Launched: 2005
Frequency of update: 260 times a year
Website Access: Free
Traffic Figures: 2,000 Unique Users (Publisher's Statement)
Editor: Mandy Rhodes
Summary of Content: Email news bulletin covering local authority news, Scottish Parliament, Executive and local

government news. Also covers Westminster and European news, where relevant to Scotland.
Readership/Target Audience: Aimed at business people, MSPs, MPs, Government Ministers, policy experts, civil servants and academics.
Other Features: Forums, jobs, business arenas, events.
CONSUMER: CURRENT AFFAIRS & POLITICS

HOMES4MEDIA
1826304U23C-96

Editorial Address: The Chandlery, 50 Westminster Bridge Road, LONDON, SE1 7QY **Tel:** 020 7953 7624
Fax: 020 7953 8773
Email: news.desk@homes4media.com
Web site: http://www.homes4media.com
Publisher: News4Media Ltd
Date Launched: 2007
Frequency of update: Daily
Website Access: Free
Traffic Figures: 12,000 Unique Users (Publisher's Statement)
Editor: Mark Inger
Summary of Content: Online homes and interiors service covering furniture, home technology, home improvements and homes and interiors events.
Readership/Target Audience: Aimed at homes and interiors companies, organisations and agencies.
BUSINESS: FURNISHINGS & FURNITURE: Furnishings & Furniture - Kitchens & Bathrooms

HOMES & INTERIORS SCOTLAND ONLINE
626264U74C-203_70

Editorial Address: Bergius House, 20 Clifton Street, GLASGOW, G3 7LA **Tel:** 0141 567 6000 **Fax:** 0141 331 1395
Email: editorial@peeblesmedia.com
Web site: http://www.homesandinteriorsscotland.com
Publisher: Peebles Media Group Ltd
Date Launched: 2000
Frequency of update: 6 times a year
Website Access: Free
Editor: Sandra Colamartino
Summary of Content: Website covering homes and interior design news, features and information on Scotland.
Readership/Target Audience: Aimed at those interested in home improvement and design in Scotland.
CONSUMER: WOMEN'S INTEREST CONSUMER MAGAZINES: Home & Family

HOMESANDPROPERTY.CO.UK
1813668U74K-782

Editorial Address: Northcliffe House, 2 Derry Street, LONDON, W8 5TT **Tel:** 020 7938 6713 **Fax:** 020 7938 7249
Email: sonia.brar@standard.co.uk
Web site: http://www.homesandproperty.co.uk
Publisher: Associated Newspapers Ltd
Date Launched: 2007
Frequency of update: Weekly
Website Access: Free
Editor: Sonia Brar
Summary of Content: Website covering all aspects of the property market in London and the home counties including news, trends, events, furnishings, accessories and buying overseas.
Readership/Target Audience: Aimed at people living and working in London.
CONSUMER: WOMEN'S INTEREST CONSUMER MAGAZINES: Home Purchase

HOT GOSSIP UK
626462U74Q-1174

Editorial Address: 3 St. Andrews Road, LONDON, W14 9SX
Tel: 020 7381 5735
Email: sally@hotgossip.co.uk
Web site: http://www.hotgossip.co.uk
Publisher: Knight International Ltd
Date Launched: 1995
Frequency of update: Monthly
Website Access: Free
Traffic Figures: 250,000 Unique Users (per month Publisher's Statement)
¹**Editor:** Sally Farmiloe-Neville
Summary of Content: Website covering music, fashion, fitness, beauty, gossip, celebrities, the arts, crime, launches, books, new products and services, restaurant reviews and travel.
Readership/Target Audience: Aimed at men and women of all ages.
CONSUMER: WOMEN'S INTEREST CONSUMER MAGAZINES: Lifestyle

HOTEL REVIEW EDINBURGH
1842271U89A-750

Editorial Address: 15 Leslie Place, EDINBURGH, EH4 1NF
Tel: 0131 343 2116
Email: vivien_devlin@tiscali.co.uk
Web site: http://www.hotelreviewedinburgh.com
Publisher: Hotel Review World
Date Launched: 2007
Frequency of update: Weekly
Website Access: Free
Summary of Content: Visitors guide covering where to stay, how to get there, hotels, travel, eating out, food and drink and places to go.
Readership/Target Audience: Aimed at weekender and leisure visitors to Edinburgh.
CONSUMER: HOLIDAYS & TRAVEL: Travel

HOTEL REVIEW MADEIRA
1685560U89A-724

Editorial Address: 15 Leslie Place, EDINBURGH, EH4 1NF
Tel: 0131 343 2116
Email: vivien_devlin@tiscali.co.uk
Web site: http://www.hotelreviewmadeira.com
Publisher: Hotel Review World
Date Launched: 2005
Frequency of update: Monthly
Website Access: Free
Summary of Content: Visitors guide covering where to stay, how to get there, hotels, travel, eating out, food and drink and places to go, golf and spas.
Readership/Target Audience: Aimed at the leisure and corporate travel market.
CONSUMER: HOLIDAYS & TRAVEL: Travel

HOTEL REVIEW SCOTLAND
1685561U89A-725

Editorial Address: 127 Broughton Road, EDINBURGH, EH7 4JH
Email: Info@HotelReviewScotland.com
Web site: http://www.hotelreviewedinburgh.com
Publisher: Hotel Review World
Date Launched: 2002
Frequency of update: Daily
Website Access: Free
Traffic Figures: 10,000 Unique Users (per day Publisher's Statement)
Summary of Content: Visitors guide covering where to stay, how to get there, hotels, travel, eating out, food and drink, golf and spas, wedding hotels and romantic breaks.
Readership/Target Audience: Aimed at the international leisure and corporate markets.
CONSUMER: HOLIDAYS & TRAVEL: Travel

HOTONLINE
633941U14F-34_55

Formerly: jobs in education
Editorial Address: Bowmont House, Kensington Village, Avonmore Road, LONDON, W14 8TS **Tel:** 0870 202 0121
Fax: 0870 202 0131
Email: marketing@hotonline.com
Web site: http://www.hotonline.com
Date Launched: 2000
Frequency of update: Daily
Website Access: Free
Traffic Figures: 1,067,323 Unique Users (Publisher's Statement)
Editor: Ann Johnson
Summary of Content: Website comprising a network of specialist recruitment sites, including jobsfinancial.com, planetrecruit.com, hotrecruit.com, jobsearcher.com and jobsineducation.co.uk
Readership/Target Audience: Aimed at employers and job seekers.
BUSINESS: COMMERCE, INDUSTRY & MANAGEMENT: Training & Recruitment

HOUNSLOW MATTERS
1881635U72J-378

Email: comments@hounslow-matters.co.uk
Web site: http://www.hounslow-matters.co.uk
Frequency of update: Daily
Summary of Content: Website created to help people who care about local issues. Whether you need access to useful information, want to highlight a particular topic to other people, discuss ideas with like minded individuals or just show your support and keep up to date with current affairs in your area, Hounslow Matters is the place for you.
Readership/Target Audience: Aimed at residents in the local area of Hounslow.
LOCAL NEWSPAPERS: Community Newsletters

HOUSE BEAUTIFUL
1902878U74A-1064

Editorial Address: 72 Broadwick Street, LONDON, W1F 9EP **Tel:** 020 7439 5000
Email: houseb.mail@natmags.co.uk

Web site: http://www.allaboutyou.com
Publisher: Hearst Digital
Frequency of update: Daily
Website Access: Free
Editor: Bernadette Fallon
Summary of Content: Website covering homes, interiors and lifestyle features.
Readership/Target Audience: Aimed at women of all ages.
CONSUMER: WOMEN'S INTEREST CONSUMER MAGAZINES: Women's Interest

HOUSETOHOME
1812751U74C-870

Editorial Address: Blue Fin Building, 110 Southwark Street, LONDON, SE1 0SU **Tel:** 020 3148 5000 **Fax:** 020 3148 8165
Email: housetohome@ipcmedia.com
Web site: http://www.housetohome.co.uk
Publisher: IPC Southbank
Date Launched: 2007
Frequency of update: Daily
Website Access: Free
Summary of Content: Website with expert advice and ideas for decorating with room, garden and colour planners, planning tips, room inspiration, interactive tool to paint a room and a find and buy product guide.
Readership/Target Audience: Aimed at those who are undertaking a decorating project.
CONSUMER: WOMEN'S INTEREST CONSUMER MAGAZINES: Home & Family

HOUSINGNEWS.CO.UK
1776245U4D-409

Editorial Address: Avian House, 87 Brook Street, Broughty Ferry, DUNDEE, DD5 1DJ **Tel:** 01382 427037
Fax: 01382 427006
Email: news@housingnews.co.uk
Web site: http://www.housingnews.co.uk
Publisher: Housing News Ltd
Date Launched: 2002
Frequency of update: Daily
Website Access: Free
Traffic Figures: 40,000 Unique Users (Publisher's Statement)
Editor: Jonathan Brown
Summary of Content: Daily electronic newsletter covering social housing news and jobs.
Readership/Target Audience: Aimed at those in the social housing sector including housing associations, councils and private developers.
BUSINESS: ARCHITECTURE & BUILDING: Planning & Housing

HOW-DO
1805235U2B-203

Editorial Address: PR by email only
Email: news@how-do.co.uk
Web site: http://www.how-do.co.uk
Date Launched: 2007
Frequency of update: Daily
Website Access: Free
Editor: Alan Johnstone
Summary of Content: Portal carrying daily industry news, features, profiles of companies and major industry figures and blogs.
Readership/Target Audience: Aimed at people working in public relations, press, marketing, broadcast, advertising, design and digital media in the North West.
BUSINESS: COMMUNICATIONS, ADVERTISING & MARKETING: Press

HOWTOLOOKGOOD
1641478U74A-964

Editorial Address: 90 Furness Road, LONDON, NW10 5UE
Tel: 020 8933 1659 **Fax:** 020 8933 1659
Email: info@howtolookgood.com
Web site: http://www.howtolookgood.com
Publisher: Brilliant Productions
Date Launched: 2002
Frequency of update: Monthly
Website Access: Free
Traffic Figures: 50,000 Unique Users (per month Publisher's Statement)
Editor: Caryn Franklin
Summary of Content: Website covering fashion and style advice as well as an online retail directory.
Readership/Target Audience: Aimed at mainstream consumers of fashion who want directory services and styling advice.
CONSUMER: WOMEN'S INTEREST CONSUMER MAGAZINES: Women's Interest

Internet Media

HR ZONE
1623036U14F-234

Formerly: HRZone
Editorial Address: 100 Victoria Street, BRISTOL, BS1 6HZ
Tel: 0117 915 8644 **Fax:** 0117 915 9630
Email: editor@hrzone.co.uk
Web site: http://www.hrzone.co.uk
Publisher: Sift Media Ltd
Date Launched: 2000
Frequency of update: Daily
Website Access: Free
Traffic Figures: 25,000 Unique Users (Publisher's Statement)
Editor: Lucie Mitchell
Summary of Content: Website focusing on HR. Features a community forum with questions and answers as well as all the latest news, features and information.
Readership/Target Audience: Aimed at HR professionals, mainly managers and directors.
BUSINESS: COMMERCE, INDUSTRY & MANAGEMENT: Training & Recruitment

HUCKNALL AND BULWELL DISPATCH
629831U80C-2490

Formerly: Hucknall Today and Bulwell Dispatch
Editorial Address: 1 Yorke Street, HUCKNALL, NG15 7BT
Tel: 0115 953 6552 **Fax:** 0115 953 6551
Email: newsdesk@hucknall-dispatch.co.uk
Web site: http://www.hucknalltoday.co.uk
Publisher: Wilfred Edmunds
Date Launched: 1903
Frequency of update: Weekly. Published on Friday
Website Access: Free
Traffic Figures: 9,000 Unique Users (Publisher's Statement)
Editor: Richard Silverwood
Summary of Content: Website containing news, sport, information and features about Hucknall and Bulwell.
Readership/Target Audience: Read by residents and visitors to the local area.
Other Features: Features include recruitment and chat forums.
CONSUMER: RURAL & REGIONAL INTEREST: Regional Interest English Counties

HUDDERSFIELD GIANTS
1663721U75C-464

Editorial Address: Galpharm Stadium, Stadium Way, Leeds Road, HUDDERSFIELD, HD1 6PG **Tel:** 0870 444 4677
Fax: 01484 531712
Email: enquiries@giantsrl.com
Web site: http://www.giantsrl.com
Frequency of update: Daily
Website Access: Free
Editor: James Brammar
Summary of Content: Official site of Huddersfield Giants Rugby League Club covering club news, fixtures, match previews, match reports, player profiles and club history.
Readership/Target Audience: Aimed at fans and sponsors of Huddersfield Giants.
CONSUMER: SPORT: Rugby

HUMBERSIDE MATTERS
1881636U72J-379

Email: comments@humberside-matters.co.uk
Web site: http://www.humberside-matters.co.uk
Frequency of update: Daily
Summary of Content: Website created to help people who care about local issues. Whether you need access to useful information, want to highlight a particular topic to other people, discuss ideas with like minded individuals or just show your support and keep up to date with current affairs in your area, Humberside Matters is the place for you.
Readership/Target Audience: Aimed at residents in the local area of Humberside.
LOCAL NEWSPAPERS: Community Newsletters

HVAC INDUSTRY DIRECTORY
1818360U3B-44

Editorial Address: 18 Generator Hall, Electric Wharf, COVENTRY, CV1 4JL **Tel:** 0870 199 4044
Fax: 0870 777 4360
Email: enquiries@industrydirectory.co.uk
Web site: http://www.industrydirectory.co.uk/hvac
Publisher: Simply Marcomms
Frequency of update: Daily
Website Access: Free
Editor: Kirstie Colledge
Summary of Content: Directory containing the latest news stories for the heating, ventilation and air conditioning industry. Includes a news archive.
Readership/Target Audience: Aimed at professionals in the building and construction industry particularly those in the heating, ventilation and air conditioning industry.
BUSINESS: HEATING & VENTILATION: Industrial Heating & Ventilation

HYDROCARBONS TECHNOLOGY
1616238U33-72

Editorial Address: Brunel House, 55-57 North Wharf Road, LONDON, W2 1LA **Tel:** 020 7915 9957 **Fax:** 020 7915 9720
Email: production@spgmedia.com
Web site: http://www.hydrocarbons-technology.com
Publisher: SPG Media Ltd
Frequency of update: Daily
Website Access: Free
Traffic Figures: 33,692 Unique Users (per month Publisher's Statement)
Editor: Duncan West
Summary of Content: Website covering hydrocarbons technology projects both in production and under development.
Readership/Target Audience: Aimed at those working within the hydrocarbons industry.
BUSINESS: OIL & PETROLEUM

I AM A PC GAMER
1863300U78D-340

Editorial Address: 8 Coblecrook Place, ALVA, FK12 5DX
Tel: 07508 624464
Email: news@iamapcgamer.com
Web site: http://www.iamapcgamer.com
Frequency of update: Daily
Editor: C.J. Rideout
Summary of Content: Website covering news and reviews on PC games and PC hardware.
Readership/Target Audience: Aimed at PC gamers.
CONSUMER: CONSUMER ELECTRONICS: Games

I & C ENERGY SNAPSHOT
38083U24-48

Formerly: The Heren Index
Editorial Address: 1 Procter Street, Hoburn, LONDON, WC1V 6EU **Tel:** 020 7911 1920
Email: info@heren.com
Web site: http://www.heren.com
Publisher: ICIS Heren
Frequency of update: Daily
Website Access: Paid
Editor: Louise Boddy
Summary of Content: Electronically delivered newsletter covering news on gas, power and electricity markets. Includes prices, finance and information.
Readership/Target Audience: Read by buyers and investors.
BUSINESS: GAS

IAIN
39432U45R-57

Formerly: IAIN Newsletter
Editorial Address: No 3 The Green, Ketton, STAMFORD, PE9 3RA **Tel:** 01780 721628 **Fax:** 01780 721980
Email: pridgway@globalnet.co.uk
Web site: http://www.iainav.org
Publisher: International Association of Institutes of Navigation IAIN
Frequency of update: Monthly
Website Access: Paid
Editor: Paul Ridgway
Summary of Content: Website of the IAIN, whose members represent navigators by land, sea, air and space in North America, Europe, Australia, the Arab world, the Far East, China and Russia.
Readership/Target Audience: Aimed at administrators, planners and manufacturers throughout the world.
BUSINESS: MARINE & SHIPPING: Marine Related

IAM-MAGAZINE
1903289U44-3062

Editorial Address: New Hibernia House, Winchester Walk, LONDON, SE1 9AG **Tel:** 020 7234 0606 **Fax:** 020 7234 0808
Email: jwild@iam-magazine.com
Web site: http://www.iam-magazine.com
Publisher: Globe White Page Ltd
Frequency of update: Daily
Website Access: Paid
Editor: Joff Wild
Summary of Content: Website covering business issues surrounding intellectual property and assets.
Readership/Target Audience: Aimed at CEOs, finance directors, CIOs, in-house lawyers, analysts and investors.
BUSINESS: LEGAL

IBEADMAG
1911405U52A-123

Editorial Address: Empirical Praxis Ltd, Tapton Park Innovation Centre, Brimington Road, CHESTERFIELD, S41 0TZ **Tel:** 01246 556988
Email: support@ibeadmag.com
Web site: http://ibeadmag.com/

Frequency of update: Daily
Editor: Allison Galpin
Summary of Content: Website covering beading and jewellery making.
Readership/Target Audience: Aimed at those interested in beading and jewellery making.
BUSINESS: GIFT TRADE: Jewellery

IBI
713142U45E-371

Editorial Address: Leon House, 233 High Street, CROYDON, CR9 1HZ **Tel:** 020 8726 8134
Fax: 020 8726 8196
Email: ed_slack@ipcmedia.com
Web site: http://www.ibinews.com
Publisher: IPC Inspire
Date Launched: 2001
Frequency of update: Daily
Website Access: Free
Editor: Ed Slack
Summary of Content: Website focusing on the international boating market on a country-by-country basis. Also includes a boat show calendar.
Readership/Target Audience: Aimed at boating professionals in the marine leisure industry.
Other Features: Features include an industry buyers guide, an e-mail newsletter and archiving.
BUSINESS: MARINE & SHIPPING: Boat Trade

ICBIRMINGHAM.CO.UK
707172U80C-3496

Editorial Address: Floor 6, Fort Dunlop, BIRMINGHAM, B24 9FF **Tel:** 0121 234 5057
Email: anna.jeys@birminghammail.net
Web site: http://www.icbirmingham.co.uk
Date Launched: 2000
Frequency of update: Daily
Website Access: Free
Editor: Anna Jays
Summary of Content: Website containing local, national, business, transport and sports news in Birmingham. Also includes TV listings, what's on at the cinema and weather in Birmingham.
Readership/Target Audience: Aimed at expatriates and those living in the Birmingham area.
Other Features: Features include a discussion forum, recruitment and archiving.
CONSUMER: RURAL & REGIONAL INTEREST: Regional Interest English Counties

ICCHESHIREONLINE.CO.UK
713694U80C-630

Formerly: icChesterOnline.co.uk
Editorial Address: Chronicle House, Commonhall Street, CHESTER, CH1 2AA **Tel:** 01244 606401
Email: digital@cheshirenews.co.uk
Web site: http://www.iccheshireonline.co.uk
Date Launched: 2000
Frequency of update: Daily
Website Access: Free
Traffic Figures: 40,000 Unique Users (per month Publisher's Statement)
Editor: James Shepherd
Summary of Content: Website covering local news, sport and business. Also includes a what's on guide, arts, entertainment and information about expatriates clubs.
Readership/Target Audience: Aimed predominantly at 15 to 45 year olds living in Cheshire, expatriates and people interested in the Cheshire area.
Other Features: Features include recruitment.
CONSUMER: RURAL & REGIONAL INTEREST: Regional Interest English Counties

ICHILD.CO.UK
1774730U74D-646

Formerly: iChild.tv
Editorial Address: 7th Floor, Artillery House, 11-19 Artillery Row, LONDON, SW1P 1RT **Tel:** 020 7227 3736
Fax: 020 7222 5949
Email: sara@ichild.co.uk
Web site: http://www.ichild.co.uk
Publisher: ichild
Date Launched: 2006
Frequency of update: Daily
Website Access: Free
Editor: Sara Maslin
Summary of Content: Online magazine featuring developmental and educational activities and covers parenting, child development, news, features and health.
Readership/Target Audience: Aimed at working mums of children aged 0 to 5 years old.
CONSUMER: WOMEN'S INTEREST CONSUMER MAGAZINES: Child Care

ICHUDDERSFIELD.CO.UK
707260U80C-3594

Editorial Address: Queen Street South, HUDDERSFIELD, HD1 3DU **Tel:** 01484 430000 **Fax:** 01484 437789
Email: editorial@examiner.co.uk
Web site: http://www.ichuddersfield.co.uk
Date Launched: 2001
Frequency of update: 260 times a year
Website Access: Free
Editor: Neil Atkinson
Summary of Content: Website focusing on news, sport and weather. Also includes a business search and a TV and radio listing for the Huddersfield area.
Readership/Target Audience: Aimed at expatriates and those living in and around Huddersfield.
Other Features: Features include an events calendar, message board forum, archiving and recruitment.
CONSUMER: RURAL & REGIONAL INTEREST: Regional Interest English Counties

ICIS NEWS
36653U13-54

Formerly: Chemical News & Intelligence
Editorial Address: Quadrant House, The Quadrant, SUTTON, SM2 5AS **Tel:** 020 8652 3214 **Fax:** 020 8652 3218
Email: icisnews.europe@icis.com
Web site: http://www.icis.com
Publisher: Reed Business Information
Frequency of update: Daily
Website Access: Paid
Editor: Graham Paterson
Summary of Content: Website covering the chemical and related industries.
Readership/Target Audience: Aimed at business executives, industry regulators, investment analysts, chemical traders and distributors.
BUSINESS: CHEMICALS

ICNEWCASTLE
707418U80C-5114

Formerly: icNewcastle.co.uk
Editorial Address: ncjMedia, Groat Market, NEWCASTLE UPON TYNE, NE1 1ED **Tel:** 0191 204 3366
Fax: 0191 204 3371
Email: graham.heslop@ncjmedia.co.uk
Web site: http://www.icnewcastle.co.uk
Date Launched: 2001
Frequency of update: Daily
Website Access: Free
Traffic Figures: 336,069 Unique Users (Publisher's Statement)
Editor: Graham Heslop
Summary of Content: Website covering news and information for the Newcastle area. Includes topics on sport, entertainment, business, health, fashion, travel and weather.
Readership/Target Audience: Aimed at those who live in or near Tyneside, Wearside, Northumberland and Durham.
Other Features: Features include an e-mail newsletter, a chat forum, recruitment and archiving.
CONSUMER: RURAL & REGIONAL INTEREST: Regional Interest English Counties

ICONS
713663U75B-132

Editorial Address: 168A Camden Street, LONDON, NW1 9PT **Tel:** 020 7267 4774 **Fax:** 020 7267 1119
Email: tom@icons.com
Web site: http://www.icons.com
Publisher: Zone Ltd
Date Launched: 2000
Frequency of update: 364 times a year
Website Access: Free
Editor: Alison Ratcliffe
Summary of Content: Website focusing on interviews with footballers, football managers and pundits. Home to over 50 football players' websites, competitions and an online shop selling signed football merchandise and memorabilia.
Readership/Target Audience: Aimed at football enthusiasts mainly men aged between 18 and 30 years old.
Other Features: Features include a fortnightly e-mail newsletter.
CONSUMER: SPORT: Football

ICSCOTLAND
628921U80E-60

Editorial Address: Press Buildings, Campbell Street, HAMILTON, ML3 6AX **Tel:** 01698 205196
Fax: 01698 891151
Email: rmooney@s-un.co.uk
Web site: http://www.icscotland.co.uk
Publisher: Scottish and Universal Newspapers Hamilton
Date Launched: 2000
Frequency of update: Daily
Website Access: Free
Traffic Figures: 90,000 Unique Users (per month Publisher's Statement)

Editor: Ritchie Mooney
Summary of Content: Website covering events and information for Scotland, as well as news and features.
Readership/Target Audience: Aimed at anyone interested in Scotland.
Other Features: Features include a buyer's guide, recruitment, discussion forums, an e-mail newsletter and archiving.
CONSUMER: RURAL & REGIONAL INTEREST: Regional Interest Scotland

ICT SPAGHETTI
761654U19J-55

Editorial Address: Pel House, 35 Station Square, ORPINGTON, BR5 1LZ **Tel:** 01689 873636
Fax: 01689 878070
Email: david.eaton@business-advantage.com
Web site: http://www.ictspaghetti.com
Publisher: Business Advantage Group
Date Launched: 2000
Frequency of update: Quarterly
Website Access: Free
Traffic Figures: 10,000 Unique Users (Publisher's Statement)
Editor: David Eaton
Summary of Content: Website covering market research into the needs and behaviour of global IT, telecommunications and CAD/CAM/CAE/EDM/PDM users as well as looking at the implications of worldwide news and developments within these fields.
Readership/Target Audience: Aimed at manufacturers, developers, distributors, dealers and resellers within the IT, telecommunications and technical computing sector.
BUSINESS: ENGINEERING & MACHINERY: CAD & CIM (Computer Integrated Manufacture)

ICWALES.CO.UK
713690U80D-89

Formerly: ic-Wales.co.uk
Editorial Address: 6 Park Street, CARDIFF, CF10 1XR
Tel: 029 2022 3333
Email: chris.glynn-jones@mediawales.co.uk
Web site: http://icwales.icnetwork.co.uk
Publisher: Media Wales Ltd
Date Launched: 2001
Frequency of update: Daily
Website Access: Free
Traffic Figures: 272,553 Unique Users (per month ABC/Electronic)
Editor: Chris Glynn-Jones
Summary of Content: The latest news, business and sport in Wales. Also includes sections on politics, local information, education, holidays, weather, ex-pats, TV and radio, classified advertising, motors, jobs and homes.
Readership/Target Audience: Aimed at residents of Wales, visitors to Wales and Welsh ex-pats around the world.
Other Features: Features include business listings, message board, archiving, votes, questionnaires, e-cards and ex-pats newsletter.
CONSUMER: RURAL & REGIONAL INTEREST: Regional Interest Wales

IDENTITY LOOP
1853138U54C-337

Editorial Address: 6 Cardiff Road, St. Fagans, CARDIFF, CF5 6EB **Tel:** 029 2056 0458 **Fax:** 029 2056 0458
Email: m.lockie@identityloop.com
Web site: http://www.identityloop.com
Date Launched: 2008
Frequency of update: Daily
Website Access: Free
Editor: Mark Lockie
Summary of Content: Website featuring global identity technology and application information. Covering biometrics, smart cards, RFID and brand protection technologies.
Readership/Target Audience: Aimed at companies within the industry and companies or governments seeking to implement such infrastructure.
BUSINESS: SAFETY & SECURITY: Security

IFAONLINE
34943U1A-194_50

Formerly: ifaonline.co.uk
Editorial Address: Haymarket House, 28-29 Haymarket, LONDON, SW1Y 4RX **Tel:** 020 7484 9700
Email: katrina.baugh@incisivemedia.com
Web site: http://www.ifaonline.co.uk
Publisher: Incisive Media Investments
Date Launched: 1998
Frequency of update: 364 times a year
Website Access: Free
Editor: Katrina Baugh
Summary of Content: Website providing rolling news, analysis, market reviews, portfolio management and events for the independent financial advisers' community.

Readership/Target Audience: Aimed at independent financial advisers.
BUSINESS: FINANCE & ECONOMICS

I-FM
26031U4R-420

Editorial Address: 18 Princess Park Manor, Royal Drive, LONDON, N11 3FL **Tel:** 020 7722 3820
Email: news@i-fm.net
Web site: http://www.i-fm.net
Publisher: Information Facilities Management Ltd.
Date Launched: 1999
Frequency of update: Daily
Website Access: Paid
Traffic Figures: 7,500 Unique Users (per month Publisher's Statement)
Editor: Elliott Chase
Summary of Content: Website containing facilities management information including news, features articles, reference listings, people, technology, workplaces, FM in Europe, sustainability channels, event and training listings.
Readership/Target Audience: Aimed at facilities management professionals.
BUSINESS: ARCHITECTURE & BUILDING: Building Related

IFYOUSKI.COM
626380U75G-240

Editorial Address: 29 Llanvair Drive, ASCOT, SL5 9HS
Tel: 01344 621475
Email: suz@ifyouski.com
Web site: http://www.ifyouski.com
Publisher: Ski Solutions Ltd
Date Launched: 1998
Frequency of update: Daily
Website Access: Free
Traffic Figures: 300,000 Unique Users (per month Omniture)
Editor: Susanne Hedges
Summary of Content: Website covering all aspects of skiing, snowboarding, ski holidays and winter sports. Includes articles on resorts, news, equipment and other snow sports.
Readership/Target Audience: Aimed at those interested in winter sports.
Other Features: Features include a ski holiday database listing chalets, apartments and hotels from Europe's top tour operators, a comprehensive ski resort guide including resort reviews, gear information, snow reports, webcams and ski news.
CONSUMER: SPORT: Winter Sports

IGIZMO
1833992U78R-525

Formerly: Gizmo
Editorial Address: 30 Cleveland Street, LONDON, W1T 4JD
Tel: 020 7907 6000
Email: press@igizmomag.co.uk
Web site: http://www.igizmomag.co.uk
Publisher: Dennis Publishing Ltd
Date Launched: 2008
Frequency of update: Daily
Website Access: Free
Traffic Figures: 187,016 Unique Users (01/07/2008 To 31/07/2008 ABC/Electronic)
Editor: Ross Burridge
Summary of Content: Website covering new products, technical news, video, lifestyle, entertainment and technology.
Readership/Target Audience: Aimed at predominantly men aged 25 to 45 with a high disposable income.
CONSUMER: CONSUMER ELECTRONICS: Consumer Electronics Related

ILIKEMUSIC.COM
752750U76D-334

Editorial Address: Unit 404, Solent Business Cnetre, Millbrook Road West, Millbrook, SOUTHAMPTON, SO15 0HW **Tel:** 0845 430 8651
Email: kim@ilikemusic.com
Web site: http://www.ilikemusic.com
Date Launched: 2001
Frequency of update: Daily
Website Access: Free
Traffic Figures: 10,000 Unique Users (per day Publisher's Statement)
Editor: Kim Hillyard
Summary of Content: Website containing music news, interviews and reviews. Also includes competitions, features, making music section, music careers information, a ticket shop and bookshelf.
Readership/Target Audience: Aimed at those interested in the latest music news.
Other Features: Newsletter.
CONSUMER: MUSIC & PERFORMING ARTS: Music

Internet Media

IMAGES
47500U84A-250

Editorial Address: The Town Hall, Kings Street, IPSWICH, IP1 1DH **Tel:** 01473 836448
Email: images@ipswich-arts.org.uk
Web site: http://www.ipswich-arts.org.uk
Publisher: Ipswich Arts Association
Frequency of update: Monthly
Website Access: Free
Editor: Joy Bounds
Summary of Content: Magazine covering music, dance, theatre, visual arts and literature.
Readership/Target Audience: Aimed at art lovers in Suffolk and North Essex.
CONSUMER: THE ARTS & LITERARY: Arts

IMAGINATION
1658929U79L-383

Editorial Address: 15 Ravens Close, Knaphill, WOKING, GU21 2LD **Tel:** 01483 888378
Email: imagination@online-mags.com
Web site: http://www.online-mags.com/Imagination/index.html
Date Launched: 2005
Frequency of update: 26 times a year
Website Access: Free
Editor: Ian Murphy
Summary of Content: Website with reviews of games, books, music, DVDs and videos covering the science fiction and horror genre.
Readership/Target Audience: Aimed at sci-fi and horror fans.
CONSUMER: HOBBIES & DIY: Fantasy Games & Science Fiction

IMOTOR
1849141U77A-610

Editorial Address: 30 Cleveland Street, LONDON, W1T 4JD
Tel: 020 7907 6000
Email: mat_watson@dennis.co.uk
Web site: http://www.imotormag.co.uk
Publisher: Dennis Publishing Ltd
Date Launched: 2008
Frequency of update: 26 times a year
Website Access: Free
Traffic Figures: 221,739 Unique Users (01/09/2008 To 30/09/2008 ABC/Electronic)
Editor: Mat Watson; **Editor-in-Chief:** Ben Raworth
Summary of Content: Digital magazine covering the latest news, videos and test drives of the hottest new cars.
Readership/Target Audience: Aimed at anyone who likes cars.
CONSUMER: MOTORING & CYCLING: Motoring

INCAPITALHEALTH
1872579U56A-216

Editorial Address: Catspring Farm, Oakley, AYLESBURY, HP18 9UL **Tel:** 01844 338000
Email: bob@incapitalhealth.co.uk
Web site: http://www.incapitalhealth.com
Publisher: inCapitalHealth Ltd
Date Launched: 2009
Frequency of update: Daily
Website Access: Free
Traffic Figures: 6,000 Unique Users (Publisher's Statement)
Editor: Bob Davidson
Summary of Content: Website featuring expert medical education for patients, includes updated editorial from senior London doctors covering all therapeutic areas.
Readership/Target Audience: Aimed at patients.
BUSINESS: HEALTH & MEDICAL

INCISOR
623996U18B-908

Editorial Address: Hampshire Gate, Langley, LISS, GU33 7JR **Tel:** 01730 895614 **Fax:** 0870 033 3104
Email: vholton@incisor.tv
Web site: http://www.incisor.tv
Publisher: Click IT Ltd
Date Launched: 1998
Frequency of update: Monthly
Website Access: Free
Traffic Figures: 30,000 Unique Users (Publisher's Statement)
Editor: Vince Holton; **Editor-in-Chief:** Vince Holton
Summary of Content: Electronic magazine and internet TV content covering all aspects of short range wireless technologies including Bluetooth, Wireless USB, UWB, ZigBee, WLAN/Wi-fi, RFID, NFC and WiMAX.
Readership/Target Audience: Aimed at wireless industry companies, private and public sector companies interested in wireless, academics, corporate and enterprise wireless users, investors and venture capitalists worldwide.
BUSINESS: ELECTRONICS: Telecommunications

INDEPENDENT CATHOLIC NEWS
1638256U87-2025

Editorial Address: 147A Leighton Road, LONDON, NW5 2RB **Tel:** 020 7267 3616
Email: news@indcatholicnews.com
Web site: http://www.indcatholicnews.com
Publisher: Independent Catholic News
Date Launched: 2000
Frequency of update: Daily
Website Access: Free
Traffic Figures: 800,000 Unique Users (Publisher's Statement)
Editor: Josephine Siedlecka
Summary of Content: Daily online Catholic news service covering all subjects of interest to Catholics and the wider Christian community. Includes articles by guest contributors.
Readership/Target Audience: Aimed at Catholics and those interested in religion.
Other Features: Features include a listings guide, classified ads and archiving.
CONSUMER: RELIGIOUS

INDEPENDENT HEALTHCARE
1698863U56A-200

Formerly: Healthcare Bi-Weekly
Editorial Address: Marble Arch Tower, 55 Bryanston Street, LONDON, W1H 7AJ **Tel:** 020 7868 8522 **Fax:** 020 7868 8744
Email: navtam@navtam.freeserve.co.uk
Web site: http://www.ihmltd.com
Publisher: Independent Healthcare Media Ltd
Date Launched: 2004
Frequency of update: 22 times a year
Website Access: Paid
Traffic Figures: 20,000 Unique Users (Publisher's Statement)
Editor: Navtam Gosai
Summary of Content: Online publication featuring news and information on the healthcare sector.
Readership/Target Audience: Aimed at care homes, private hospitals, charities and suppliers.
BUSINESS: HEALTH & MEDICAL

INDMIN.COM
749154U1L-37

Editorial Address: Nestor House, Playhouse Yard, LONDON, EC4V 5EX **Tel:** 020 7827 9977
Fax: 020 7827 6441
Email: edit@indmin.com
Web site: http://www.indmin.com
Publisher: Metal Bulletin plc
Frequency of update: Monthly
Website Access: Paid
Editor: Mike O'Driscoll
Summary of Content: Website covering non-fuel and non-metallic minerals. Includes business news, mineral production, processing and trade statistics.
Readership/Target Audience: Aimed at companies in all sectors of the non-fuel and non-metallic business.
BUSINESS: FINANCE & ECONOMICS: Commodities

INDUSTRIAL TECHNOLOGY
626346U19B-320_1

Editorial Address: PO Box 342, TONBRIDGE, TN10 4WD
Tel: 01732 773268 **Fax:** 01732 365676
Email: mark.simms@itmagazine.uk.com
Web site: http://www.industrialtechnology.co.uk/
Publisher: New Wave Publishing
Date Launched: 1988
Frequency of update: 10 times a year
Website Access: Free
Editor: Mark Simms
Summary of Content: Website with features on engineering components.
Readership/Target Audience: Aimed at product design engineers and machine builders.
BUSINESS: ENGINEERING & MACHINERY: Engineering - Design

INFANT
626530U56B-179

Formerly: Infant Online
Editorial Address: 134 South Street, BISHOP'S STORTFORD, CM23 3BQ **Tel:** 01279 714511
Fax: 01279 714519
Email: publishing@infantgrapevine.co.uk
Web site: http://www.infantgrapevine.co.uk
Publisher: Stansted News Ltd
Date Launched: 2005
Frequency of update: 6 times a year
Website Access: Paid
Traffic Figures: 5,000 Unique Users (Publisher's Statement)
Editor: Christine Bishop

Summary of Content: Review journal containing articles with a clinical or practical bias written by experts in the field.
Readership/Target Audience: Aimed at the multidisciplinary team caring for vulnerable, sick or premature babies in their first year of life, including neonatal nurses, neonatologists, paediatric intensive care nurses and doctors, paediatric A & E personnel and midwives.
Other Features: Features include recruitment, a discussion forum, archiving and a directory.
BUSINESS: HEALTH & MEDICAL: Nursing

INFLIGHT ONLINE
36429U6F-145

Formerly: Inflight
Editorial Address: 268 Bath Road, SLOUGH, SL1 4DX
Tel: 01753 727001 **Fax:** 01753 727002
Email: bg@shephard.co.uk
Web site: http://www.inflight-online.com
Publisher: The Shephard Group
Date Launched: 1994
Frequency of update: Daily
Website Access: Free
Traffic Figures: 3,915 Unique Users (per month Publisher's Statement)
Editor: Brendan Gallagher
Summary of Content: Website covering the in-flight passenger entertainment and passenger communications industry.
Readership/Target Audience: Aimed at aviation and telecoms authorities, equipment manufacturers, service providers and technical and marketing personnel in airlines and operators.
BUSINESS: AVIATION & AERONAUTICS: Airlines

INFO4SECURITY
1809598U54C-334

Editorial Address: Ludgate House, 245 Blackfriars Road, LONDON, SE1 9UY **Tel:** 020 7921 8289
Email: info@info4security.com
Web site: http://www.info4security.com
Publisher: UBM Information Ltd
Date Launched: 2007
Frequency of update: Daily
Website Access: Free
Editor: Anthony Hildebrand
Summary of Content: Website focusing on the security industry. Features security installation, security management, CCTV, IPN networks, guarding, intruder alarms and access control.
Readership/Target Audience: Aimed at security professionals at all levels.
BUSINESS: SAFETY & SECURITY: Security

INFORMATION MANAGEMENT & TECHNOLOGY (IM@T.ONLINE)
36228U60B-19_35

Formerly: IM@T.Online
Editorial Address: University of Hertfordshire, Innovation Centre, College Lane, HATFIELD, AL10 9AB
Tel: 01707 281060 **Fax:** 01707 281061
Email: r.n.broadhurst@herts.ac.uk
Web site: http://www.cimtech.co.uk
Publisher: CIMTECH Ltd
Date Launched: 1967
Frequency of update: 10 times a year. Published in the middle of the month. Combined issues Dec/Jan and Jul/Aug
Website Access: Paid
Traffic Figures: 800 Unique Users (Publisher's Statement)
Editor: Roger Broadhurst
Summary of Content: Electronic journal covering news, topical issues, articles, case studies, product reviews and events within electronic document, content and record management.
Readership/Target Audience: Aimed at information management professionals including document managers, content managers, records managers, archivists, librarians, information officers, product and services suppliers.
BUSINESS: PUBLISHING: Libraries

INFOVEST21
1840764U1F-648

Editorial Address: PR by email only **Tel:** 020 8444 1651
Email: lpeltz@infovest21.com
Web site: http://www.infovest21.com
Publisher: Infovest21
Frequency of update: Daily
Website Access: Paid
Editor: Neil Behrmann
Summary of Content: Information service for the hedge fund industry featuring news, manager interviews, white papers, surveys and industry events.
Readership/Target Audience: Aimed at qualified investors, institutional investors and alternative investment managers.
BUSINESS: FINANCE & ECONOMICS: Investment

INFRASTRUCTURE JOURNAL 1663945U42R-152

Editorial Address: Greater London House, Hampstead Road, LONDON, NW1 7EJ **Tel:** 020 7728 5407
Fax: 020 7938 3560
Email: a.melville@ijonline.com
Web site: http://www.ijonline.com
Publisher: EMAP Insight
Date Launched: 1997
Frequency of update: Daily
Website Access: Paid
Editor: Angus Leslie Melville
Summary of Content: Website covering key topics of importance for power, oil and gas, transport, telecommunications, water, PPP, infrastructure as well as policy and legal advice.
Readership/Target Audience: Aimed at government ministers and officials, developers, investors, financiers, lawyers and consultants.
BUSINESS: CONSTRUCTION: Construction Related

INPHARM.COM 38737U37-28

Editorial Address: The Atrium, Southern Gate, CHICHESTER, PO19 8SQ **Tel:** 01243 779777
Fax: 01243 772002
Email: amcconaghie@wiley.com
Web site: http://www.inpharm.com
Publisher: John Wiley & Sons Ltd
Date Launched: 1998
Frequency of update: Daily
Website Access: Free
Traffic Figures: 14,200 Unique Users (Publisher's Statement)
Editor: Brendan Haughey
Summary of Content: Website containing pharmaceutical and healthcare news, views, jobs and a directory of organisations and freelancers.
Readership/Target Audience: Aimed at professionals in the pharmaceutical and healthcare industries.
BUSINESS: PHARMACEUTICAL & CHEMISTS

INQUIRELIVE.CO.UK 1846564U83-297

Editorial Address: Mandela Building, University of Kent, CANTERBURY, CT2 7NZ **Tel:** 01227 824257
Fax: 01227 824219
Email: rr82@kent.ac.uk
Web site: http://www.inquirelive.co.uk
Publisher: University of Kent Students' Union
Date Launched: 2008
Frequency of update: Daily
Website Access: Free
Summary of Content: Website covering campus news, sport, art, music and reviews. Also features local events and regular blogs.
Readership/Target Audience: Aimed at students of the University of Kent.
CONSUMER: STUDENT PUBLICATIONS

THE INQUIRER 1657837U5R-662

Editorial Address: 32-34 Broadwick Street, LONDON, W1A 2HG **Tel:** 020 7316 9000 **Fax:** 020 7316 9313
Email: press.releases@theinquirer.net
Web site: http://www.theinquirer.net
Publisher: Incisive Media
Date Launched: 2001
Frequency of update: Daily
Website Access: Free
Traffic Figures: 2,500,000 Unique Users (per month Publisher's Statement)
Editor: Madeline Bennett
Summary of Content: Website covering all aspects of IT, including news and reviews.
Readership/Target Audience: Aimed at IT professionals and computing enthusiasts.
Other Features: Recruitment.
BUSINESS: COMPUTERS & AUTOMATION: Computers Related

INSIDE HOUSING ONLINE 629076U4D-135_10

Editorial Address: 1 Canada Square, Canary Wharf, LONDON, E14 5AP **Tel:** 020 7772 8300 **Fax:** 020 7772 8591
Email: editorial@insidehousing.co.uk
Web site: http://www.insidehousing.co.uk
Publisher: Ocean Media Group Ltd
Date Launched: 2000
Frequency of update: Weekly
Website Access: Free
Traffic Figures: 25,397 Unique Users (per month Publisher's Statement)
Editor: Martin Hilditch
Summary of Content: Website covering all aspects of housing including news, views and recruitment.

Readership/Target Audience: Read by managers who work in the housing industry and/or who work with local authorities.
BUSINESS: ARCHITECTURE & BUILDING: Planning & Housing

INSIDE SATELLITE TV 1654827U2D-140

Formerly: Inside Satellite
Editorial Address: 37 The Towers, Lower Mortlake Road, RICHMOND, TW9 2JR **Tel:** 020 8948 8561
Fax: 020 8940 6009
Email: chris@forrester-solutions.com
Web site: http://www.insidesatellite.com
Publisher: Broadgate Publications
Date Launched: 2004
Frequency of update: 25 times a year
Website Access: Paid
Editor: Chris Forrester
Summary of Content: Electronically delivered newsletter covering all aspects of the communications satellite business.
Readership/Target Audience: Aimed at senior executives in the broadcasting and satellite community.
BUSINESS: COMMUNICATIONS, ADVERTISING & MARKETING: Broadcasting

INSIDECLAPHAM.CO.UK 1849134U80B-436

Editorial Address: 149 Ramsden Road, LONDON, SW12 8RF **Tel:** 020 8675 7697
Email: richard@insideclapham.co.uk
Web site: http://www.insideclapham.co.uk
Publisher: Essential Local Marketing
Frequency of update: 150 times a year
Website Access: Free
Traffic Figures: 250 Unique Users (per day Publisher's Statement)
Editor: Richard Chumbley
Summary of Content: Online magazine covering local reviews, restaurant reviews, celebrity interviews, lifestyle articles, events previews, fashion, local organisations, markets and charities, recipes, local news, events listing and business directories.
Readership/Target Audience: Aimed at affluent households in South West London and Bournemouth.
CONSUMER: RURAL & REGIONAL INTEREST: Regional Interest Greater London

INSIDEDIVORCE.COM 1797549U74C-865

Editorial Address: Hereford House, 22-24 Smithfield Street, LONDON, EC1A 9LF **Tel:** 020 7332 2580
Fax: 020 7332 2599
Email: derekbedlow@insidedivorce.com
Web site: http://www.insidedivorce.com
Publisher: Polyview Media Ltd
Date Launched: 2007
Frequency of update: Daily
Website Access: Free
Traffic Figures: 300,000 Unique Users (per year Publisher's Statement)
Editor: Derek Bedlow
Summary of Content: Website with advice and information on relationship breakdowns and divorce including articles on legal issues, money, property, children, well-being and moving on.
Readership/Target Audience: Aimed at anyone going through a relationship breakdown, thinking of divorce, getting divorced or moving on afterwards.
Other Features: Weekly newsletters, quarterly magazine, discussion forums, services directory, interactive planner and checklist.
CONSUMER: WOMEN'S INTEREST CONSUMER MAGAZINES: Home & Family

INSIDER 719219U63D-180

Editorial Address: Onesixty, 160 Dundee Street, EDINBURGH, EH11 1DQ **Tel:** 0131 535 5555
Fax: 0131 220 1203
Email: editor@insider.co.uk
Web site: http://www.insider.co.uk
Publisher: Scottish Daily Record & Sunday Mail Ltd
Date Launched: 1984
Frequency of update: 11 times a year. Monthly but July and August combined
Website Access: Free
Editor: Alasdair Northrop
Summary of Content: Website focusing on business issues in Scotland. Includes topics on accountancy, law, politics, corporate finance, IT, commercial property, management issues and commercial market reviews. Innovation and corporate sections are also featured and a list of the top 500 Scottish companies.

Readership/Target Audience: Aimed at company directors and businesses based in Scotland.
BUSINESS: REGIONAL BUSINESS: Regional Business Scotland

INSIDERWEEKLY (EAST MIDLANDS) 1810702U63B-2581

Editorial Address: 4th Floor, Canterbury House, 85 Newhall Street, BIRMINGHAM, B3 1LH **Tel:** 0121 232 0980
Fax: 0121 232 0989
Email: eastmids@insiderweekly.co.uk
Web site: http://www.insiderweekly.co.uk
Publisher: Newsco Insider Ltd
Frequency of update: Weekly
Website Access: Free
Traffic Figures: 5,500 Unique Users (Publisher's Statement)
Editor: Kurt Jacobs
Summary of Content: Electronic newsletter containing business news and developments affecting the East Midlands.
Readership/Target Audience: Aimed at members of the business community in the East Midlands.
BUSINESS: REGIONAL BUSINESS: Regional Business English Counties

INSIDERWEEKLY (WEST MIDLANDS) 1810700U63B-2580

Editorial Address: 4th Floor, Canterbury House, 85 Newhall Street, BIRMINGHAM, B3 1LH **Tel:** 0121 232 0980
Fax: 0121 232 0989
Email: westmids@insiderweekly.co.uk
Web site: http://www.insiderweekly.co.uk
Publisher: Newsco Insider Ltd
Frequency of update: Weekly
Website Access: Free
Traffic Figures: 6,000 Unique Users (Publisher's Statement)
Editor: Kurt Jacobs
Summary of Content: Electronic newsletter containing business news and developments affecting the West Midlands.
Readership/Target Audience: Aimed at members of the business community in the West Midlands.
BUSINESS: REGIONAL BUSINESS: Regional Business English Counties

INSIGHT 629568U13-50_10

Formerly: Chemical Insight
Editorial Address: Quadrant House, The Quadrant, SUTTON, SM2 5AS **Tel:** 020 8652 3397 **Fax:** 020 8652 8952
Email: nigel.davis@icis.com
Web site: http://www.icis.com
Publisher: Reed Business Information
Frequency of update: Daily
Website Access: Paid
Editor: Nigel Davis
Summary of Content: Website with a daily comment and analysis on the global chemicals sector as part of ICIS news.
Readership/Target Audience: Read by senior professionals in the chemical industry.
Other Features: News, industry data, forums, blogs.
BUSINESS: CHEMICALS

INSTALLATION EUROPE 1925994U18A-9057

Editorial Address: 245 Blackfriars Road, LONDON, SE1 9UY **Tel:** 020 7921 8317 **Fax:** 020 7921 8302
Email: paddy.baker@ubm.com
Web site: http://installationeurope.com
Publisher: UBM Information Ltd
Frequency of update: Daily
Website Access: Free
Editor: Paddy Baker
Summary of Content: Website covering design and integration within the audio, video and lighting industries. Includes business and product news and features on management.
Readership/Target Audience: Aimed at systems integrators, installers, architects and project consultants.
BUSINESS: ELECTRONICS

INSURANCE DAY 35130U1D-184

Formerly: Lloyds' List Insurance Day
Editorial Address: Telephone House, 69-77 Paul Street, LONDON, EC2A 4LQ **Tel:** 020 7017 4155
Email: editorial@insuranceday.com
Web site: http://www.insuranceday.com/insday/news/home.htm
Publisher: Informa PLC
Frequency of update: Daily
Website Access: Paid

Internet Media

Traffic Figures: 1,556 Unique Users (01/07/2007 To 30/06/2008 ABC)
Editor: Richard Banks
Summary of Content: Online news and research service from Informa Maritime & Professional, delivering the latest insurance news, commentary and analysis online across eight key channels, covering international insurance and risk.
Readership/Target Audience: Read by directors, CFOs, risk carriers and service providers in the insurance industry.
BUSINESS: FINANCE & ECONOMICS: Insurance

INSURANCE NEWSLINK
1606543U1D-402
Editorial Address: 34 West Street, FARNHAM, GU9 7DR
Tel: 01252 724865 **Fax:** 01252 733772
Email: shillito@netcomuk.co.uk
Web site: http://www.insurancenewslink.com
Date Launched: 1993
Frequency of update: 104 times a year
Website Access: Paid
Editor: Douglas Shillito
Summary of Content: Website covering company news, information technology, e-commerce, research, regulatory and seminars within the worldwide insurance business as well as regular opinion and interviews.
Readership/Target Audience: Aimed at insurance company management and information technology suppliers and consultants.
BUSINESS: FINANCE & ECONOMICS: Insurance

INSURANCETIMES ONLINE
626359U1D-230_1
Editorial Address: 30 Cannon Street, LONDON, EC4M 6YJ
Tel: 020 7618 3498 **Fax:** 020 7618 3499
Email: news@instimes.co.uk
Web site: http://www.insurancetimes.co.uk
Publisher: Newsquest Specialist Media Ltd
Date Launched: 1999
Frequency of update: Daily
Website Access: Free
Traffic Figures: 45,902 Unique Users (01/11/2008 To 30/11/2008 ABC/Electronic)
Editor: Michael Faulkner
Summary of Content: Website covering business news for the UK insurance industry.
Readership/Target Audience: Aimed at UK-based insurance companies, brokers, intermediaries and their associated industries and suppliers.
BUSINESS: FINANCE & ECONOMICS: Insurance

INTELETEX
1647476U47A-570
Editorial Address: Perkin House, 1 Longlands Street, BRADFORD, BD1 2TP **Tel:** 01274 378800
Fax: 01274 378811
Email: athornton@world-textile.net
Web site: http://www.inteletex.com
Publisher: World Textile Publications Ltd
Date Launched: 2002
Frequency of update: Daily
Website Access: Free
Traffic Figures: 30,000 Unique Users (per month Publisher's Statement)
Editor: Andrew Thornton
Summary of Content: Website covering news and analysis on the textile industry.
Readership/Target Audience: Aimed at retailers, suppliers and manufacturers.
BUSINESS: CLOTHING & TEXTILES

INTERACTIVE INVESTOR
45547U74M-100
Formerly: Ample
Editorial Address: Standon House, 1st Floor, 21 Mansell Street, LONDON, E1 8AA **Tel:** 020 7680 3600
Email: veditor@iii.co.uk
Web site: http://www.iii.co.uk
Publisher: Interactive Investor Trading LTD
Date Launched: 1995
Frequency of update: Daily
Website Access: Free
Traffic Figures: 1,127,276 Unique Users (01/03/2009 To 31/03/2009 ABC/Electronic)
Editor: Richard Beddard
Summary of Content: Website covering personal finance issues. Contains news, features on investments, analysis and advice.
Readership/Target Audience: Aimed at private investors.
CONSUMER: WOMEN'S INTEREST CONSUMER MAGAZINES: Personal Finance

INTERIOR LINKS
1615060U4B-175
Editorial Address: Cointronic House, Station Road, HEATHFIELD, TN21 8DF **Tel:** 01435 865797
Fax: 01435 863897
Email: editorial@netmagmedia.eu
Web site: http://www.interiorlinks.eu
Publisher: Parker Ellis Publishing Ltd
Date Launched: 2003
Frequency of update: Daily
Website Access: Free
Editor: Patricia Percival
Summary of Content: Website covering all interior design products.
Readership/Target Audience: Aimed at interior design professionals.
BUSINESS: ARCHITECTURE & BUILDING: Interior Design & Flooring

INTERIORS HUB
1882346U4B-191
Editorial Address: 245 Blackfriars Road, LONDON, SE1 9UY **Tel:** 020 7921 8408 **Fax:** 020 7921 8450
Email: news@interiorshub.com
Web site: http://www.interiorshub.com
Publisher: UBM Live
Date Launched: 2009
Frequency of update: Daily
Website Access: Free
Editor: Grahame Morrison
Summary of Content: Website containing news, jobs and supplier details for those professionally involved in interiors projects. Covers interiors, interior design, house and home, bedrooms, furniture, fabrics, soft furnishings, lighting, flooring, kitchens and bathrooms.
Readership/Target Audience: Aimed at all interiors professionals including architects, interior designers, lighting designers, specialist kitchen, bedroom and bathroom designers and flooring professionals.
BUSINESS: ARCHITECTURE & BUILDING: Interior Design & Flooring

THE INTERNAL COMMS HUB
1799357U2R-187
Formerly: The Hub for Internal Communications
Editorial Address: 322B King Street, LONDON, W6 0AX
Tel: 020 8600 4670 **Fax:** 020 8741 9975
Email: annie.waite@melcrum.com
Web site: http://www.internalcommshub.com
Publisher: Melcrum Publishing Ltd
Date Launched: 2005
Frequency of update: Daily
Website Access: Paid
Summary of Content: Website focusing on internal communications and corporate communications. Contains advice and tips about and including improving survey effectiveness, communicating strategy, beginning an employee engagement initiative, setting a strategic communication plan, helping employees adapt to change and running focus groups. Provides a discussion forum for sharing experiences and runs member events.
Readership/Target Audience: Aimed mainly at people working in internal communications.
BUSINESS: COMMUNICATIONS, ADVERTISING & MARKETING: Communications Related

INTERNATIONAL EVENT ORGANISERS UPDATE
1810846U2C-518
Editorial Address: 29A Market Square, BIGGLESWADE, SG18 8AQ **Tel:** 01767 316255 **Fax:** 01767 316430
Email: info@eou.org.uk
Web site: http://www.eou.org.uk
Frequency of update: 6 times a year
Website Access: Free
Traffic Figures: 12,000 Unique Users (Publisher's Statement)
Editor: Peter Cotterell
Summary of Content: Electronic newsletter of the Society of Events Organisers featuring news and comment about the sector including details about international venues, technology, training courses and a conference diary.
Readership/Target Audience: Aimed at organisers of corporate and associated events and seminars.
BUSINESS: COMMUNICATIONS, ADVERTISING & MARKETING: Conferences & Exhibitions

INTERNATIONAL INSIDER
35083U1C-180
Editorial Address: 18 King William Street, LONDON, EC4N 7BP **Tel:** 020 7017 7006 **Fax:** 020 7017 7844
Email: helen.craig@intinsider.com
Web site: http://www.informa.com
Publisher: International Insider Publishing Co
Date Launched: 1972
Frequency of update: Weekly
Website Access: Paid

Editor: Helen Craig
Summary of Content: E-newsletter covering international banking, capital markets and emerging markets, including screen services via Reuter and Bloomberg providing news and commentary on international bond and loan markets.
Readership/Target Audience: Read by euromarket professionals, international bankers, brokers and fund managers. Also eurobond specialists and corporate investors.
BUSINESS: FINANCE & ECONOMICS: Banking

INTERNATIONAL JOURNAL OF BANK MARKETING
20209U1R-170
Editorial Address: Howard House, Wagon Lane, BINGLEY, BD16 1WA **Tel:** 01274 777700 **Fax:** 01274 785200
Email: rwhitfield@emeraldinsight.com
Web site: http://www.emeraldinsight.com/ijbm.htm
Publisher: Emerald Group Publishing Ltd
Frequency of update: 7 times a year
Website Access: Paid
Editor: Richard Whitfield
Summary of Content: Website featuring results of academic and practitioner research within the financial sector. Contains articles on all aspects of marketing as it relates to financial services in the Internet banking sector, branding, service quality and customer satisfaction.
Readership/Target Audience: Aimed at academic, market and financial institutions.
BUSINESS: FINANCE & ECONOMICS: Financial Related

INTERNATIONAL LAW OFFICE
753080U44-995
Editorial Address: New Hibernia House, Winchester Walk, LONDON, SE1 9AG **Tel:** 020 7234 0606 **Fax:** 020 7234 0808
Email: cboyle@gbp.co.uk
Web site: http://www.internationallawoffice.com
Publisher: Globe Business Publishing Ltd
Date Launched: 1998
Frequency of update: Daily
Website Access: Free
Editor: Carolyn Boyle
Summary of Content: Website covering legal developments, a directory of firms and partners, a database of the world's major deals and the legal advisors involved and a global news round-up.
Readership/Target Audience: Aimed at senior lawyers.
Other Features: Features include e-mail newsletters and archiving.
BUSINESS: LEGAL

INTERNATIONAL OIL DAILY
1744357U33-92
Editorial Address: 8th Floor, Holborn Tower, 137-144 High Holborn, LONDON, WC1V 6PW **Tel:** 020 7632 4700
Email: jcollin@energyintel.com
Web site: http://www.energyintel.com
Publisher: Energy Intelligence Group
Frequency of update: Daily
Website Access: Paid
Editor: Jane Collin
Summary of Content: Electronic newsletter providing coverage of the latest developments in the oil and gas business, including worldwide upstream and downstream developments, assessments of key market trends and prices, news on mergers and acquisitions and political changes that affect the industry.
Readership/Target Audience: Aimed at suppliers and distributors.
BUSINESS: OIL & PETROLEUM

INTERNATIONAL PESTICIDE DIRECTORY
36698U13-100
Editorial Address: Grenville Court, Britwell Road, Burnham, SLOUGH, SL1 8DF **Tel:** 01628 600499 **Fax:** 01628 600488
Email: info@researchinformation.co.uk
Web site: http://www.researchinformation.co.uk
Publisher: Research Information Ltd
Date Launched: 1982
Frequency of update: Annual. Published in January
Website Access: Paid
Traffic Figures: 1,000 Unique Users (Publisher's Statement)
Editor: Ras Patel
Summary of Content: Online access reference directory on trade-named pesticides, their active ingredients and the companies that manufacture and market them.
Readership/Target Audience: Aimed at managers in the pesticide industry.
BUSINESS: CHEMICALS

INTERNATIONAL PHARMACEUTICAL AGREEMENTS
38780U37-28_50

Editorial Address: Lincoln House, City Fields Business Park, City Fields Way, Tangmere, CHICHESTER, PO20 2FS
Tel: 01243 533322 **Fax:** 01243 533418
Email: healthcare@espicom.com
Web site: http://www.espicom.com
Publisher: Espicom Ltd
Date Launched: 1997
Frequency of update: Monthly
Website Access: Paid
Editor: Jeremy Webber
Summary of Content: Website covering information on over 2000 pharmaceutical company agreements every year.
Readership/Target Audience: Aimed at international executives in the pharmaceutical industry.
BUSINESS: PHARMACEUTICAL & CHEMISTS

INTERNATIONAL TEXTILE CALENDAR
39530U47A-199

Editorial Address: 1st Floor, St. James's Building, Oxford Street, MANCHESTER, M1 6FQ **Tel:** 0161 237 1188
Fax: 0161 236 1991
Email: escott@textileinst.org.uk
Web site: http://www.textileinstitute.org
Publisher: The Textile Institute
Frequency of update: Monthly
Website Access: Paid
Traffic Figures: 5,000 Unique Users (Publisher's Statement)
Editor: Emma Scott
Summary of Content: Website containing a listing of future conferences, exhibitions, seminars, short courses and other events. Covers textile science and technology, design and marketing, fibres, yarns, clothing and fashion.
Readership/Target Audience: Aimed at academic, industrial and general people interested in textiles.
BUSINESS: CLOTHING & TEXTILES

INTERNET BUSINESS NEWS
36233U5E-470

Editorial Address: PR by email only **Tel:** 020 7047 0200
Email: m2pw@m2.com
Web site: http://www.m2.com
Publisher: M2 Communications Ltd
Date Launched: 1994
Frequency of update: 104 times a year
Website Access: Paid
Editor: Jamie Ayres
Summary of Content: Website covering Internet business activity including commercial and development uses.
Readership/Target Audience: Aimed at people across the IT board.
BUSINESS: COMPUTERS & AUTOMATION: Data Transmission

INTHENEWS.CO.UK
1666798U76A-178

Editorial Address: South Quay Plaza, 183 Marsh Wall, LONDON, E14 9SH **Tel:** 020 7517 2200 **Fax:** 020 7517 2229
Email: nationalnews@adfero.co.uk
Web site: http://www.inthenews.co.uk
Publisher: Adfero
Date Launched: 2004
Frequency of update: Daily
Website Access: Free
Traffic Figures: 300,000 Unique Users (per month Publisher's Statement)
Editor: Matthew Champion
Summary of Content: Comprehensive news website, featuring headlines, sport, entertainment, health, science and money news daily.
Readership/Target Audience: Aimed at the general public.
Other Features: Comment section, archiving, Yahoo search.
CONSUMER: MUSIC & PERFORMING ARTS: Cinema

INTRODUCERUK
1847243U1R-383

Editorial Address: Jackson House, Burton Road, BLACKPOOL, FY4 4NW **Tel:** 0845 434 8544
Email: newsdesk@introduceruk.com
Web site: http://www.introduceruk.com
Frequency of update: Daily
Website Access: Paid
Editor: James Lucas
Summary of Content: Business to business networking site for the UK finances industry and services that serve the industry including mortgages.
Readership/Target Audience: Aimed at the financial services industry including IFAs, brokers, lenders, mortgage advisors and lead generators.
BUSINESS: FINANCE & ECONOMICS: Financial Related

INVERCLYDE NOW
1808934U72D-1025

Editorial Address: 120 Albert Road, GOUROCK, PA19 1BS
Tel: 01475 631100
Email: contact@inverclydenow.com
Web site: http://www.inverclydenow.com
Date Launched: 2004
Frequency of update: Daily
Website Access: Free
Editor: Jeremy Burrows
Summary of Content: Website covering local news and sport with photo galleries and a what's on guide.
LOCAL NEWSPAPERS: Local Newspapers Scotland

INVESTEGATE
1800332U1F-635

Editorial Address: 6th Floor, Roxburghe House, 273-287 Regent Street, LONDON, W1B 2HA **Tel:** 020 7408 8000
Fax: 020 7408 8001
Email: jonathan.boyd@financialexpress.net
Web site: http://www.investegate.co.uk
Publisher: Financial Express Limited
Frequency of update: Daily
Website Access: Free
Traffic Figures: 2,300,000 Unique Users (per month Publisher's Statement)
Editor: Jonathan Boyd; **Editor-in-Chief:** Jonathan Boyd
Summary of Content: Website featuring company and general investment news, including equities and collective investments.
Readership/Target Audience: Aimed at investors, financial intermediaries and institutional readers.
BUSINESS: FINANCE & ECONOMICS: Investment

INVESTMENTGUIDE.CO.UK
624167U1F-2

Formerly: AAA Investment Guide
Editorial Address: PR by email only
Email: media@investmentguide.co.uk
Web site: http://www.investmentguide.co.uk
Publisher: Wisebuy Publications
Date Launched: 1995
Frequency of update: Weekly
Website Access: Paid
Editor: David Lewis
Summary of Content: Website focusing on know-how investment for investors and savers.
Readership/Target Audience: Aimed at experts and beginners in financial planning.
BUSINESS: FINANCE & ECONOMICS: Investment

IOFILM
626185U76A-35_27

Formerly: insideout.co.uk
Editorial Address: 38 Craighall Road, EDINBURGH, EH6 4RU **Tel:** 0131 208 0633
Web site: http://www.iofilm.co.uk
Frequency of update: Daily
Website Access: Free
Traffic Figures: 280,000 Unique Users (per month Publisher's Statement)
Editor: Robert Alstead
Summary of Content: Website focusing on the world of films. Contains the latest UK film and DVD releases, coverage of film festivals, awards and news.
Readership/Target Audience: Aimed at film goers of all ages.
Other Features: Competitions.
CONSUMER: MUSIC & PERFORMING ARTS: Cinema

IPRA FRONTLINE
622845U2E-56

Formerly: Frontline 21
Editorial Address: International Public Relations Association, 12 Dunley Hill Court, Ranmore Common, DORKING, RH5 6SX **Tel:** 01483 280130 **Fax:** 01483 280131
Email: info@ipra.org
Web site: http://www.ipra.org
Publisher: IPRA Frontline Ltd
Date Launched: 1999
Frequency of update: 6 times a year
Website Access: Free
Traffic Figures: 1,000 Unique Users (Publisher's Statement)
Editor: Robert Gray
Summary of Content: Website focusing on PR issues and communications.
Readership/Target Audience: Aimed at PR executives, corporate leaders, politicians, academics and major institutions.
BUSINESS: COMMUNICATIONS, ADVERTISING & MARKETING: Public Relations

IPREMENSTRAL.COM
1851094U74A-1055

Editorial Address: 17 Illingworth Avenue, Altofts, NORMANTON, WF6 2LL **Tel:** 0844 561 0787
Fax: 0845 120 1037
Email: hello@ipremenstral.com
Web site: http://www.ipremenstral.com
Date Launched: 2008
Frequency of update: Daily
Website Access: Free
Editor: Star Lerthattasin
Summary of Content: Website covering indulgence for women at that time of the month as well as women's interest and lifestyle.
Readership/Target Audience: Aimed at women aged 18 to 40 years old.
CONSUMER: WOMEN'S INTEREST CONSUMER MAGAZINES: Women's Interest

IRS EMPLOYMENT REVIEW
37049U14F-24_85

Formerly: IRS Employment Trends
Editorial Address: Quadrant House, The Quadrant, SUTTON, SM2 5AS **Tel:** 020 8652 3500
Email: shelia.attwood@irseclipse.co.uk
Web site: http://www.xperthr.co.uk
Publisher: Reed Business Information
Date Launched: 1971
Frequency of update: Daily
Website Access: Paid
Editor: Sheila Attwood
Summary of Content: Online journal covering policy, practice and law in the workplace.
Readership/Target Audience: Aimed at HR managers and personnel managers, trade unions, industrial relations and employment academics.
BUSINESS: COMMERCE, INDUSTRY & MANAGEMENT: Training & Recruitment

ISLE OF MAN MATTERS
1881637U72J-380

Email: comments@isleofman-matters.co.uk
Web site: http://www.isleofman-matters.co.uk
Frequency of update: Daily
Summary of Content: Website created to help people who care about local issues. Whether you need access to useful information, want to highlight a particular topic to other people, discuss ideas with like minded individuals or just show your support and keep up to date with current affairs in your area, Isle of Man Matters is the place for you.
Readership/Target Audience: Aimed at residents in the local area of Isle of Man.
LOCAL NEWSPAPERS: Community Newsletters

ISLE OF MAN TODAY
629716U80H-30

Formerly: Isle of Man on-line
Editorial Address: Publishing House, Peel Road, DOUGLAS, IM1 5PZ **Tel:** 01624 695695 **Fax:** 01624 611149
Email: newsdesk@newsiom.co.im
Web site: http://www.iomtoday.co.im
Publisher: Isle of Man Newspapers Ltd
Date Launched: 2000
Frequency of update: Daily
Website Access: Free
Traffic Figures: 65,191 Unique Users (per month Publisher's Statement)
Editor: Richard Butt
Summary of Content: Website containing news, sport, information and features about the Isle of Man.
Readership/Target Audience: Aimed at expatriates, residents and visitors to the area.
Other Features: Features include a buyer's guide, an events calendar, recruitment, mailing list and archiving.
CONSUMER: RURAL & REGIONAL INTEREST: Regional Interest Isle of Man

ISLE OF WIGHT COUNTY PRESS ONLINE
629274U67B-435

Editorial Address: Brannon House, 123 Pyle Street, NEWPORT, PO30 1ST **Tel:** 01983 522210
Fax: 01983 528920
Email: editor@iwcp2.demon.co.uk
Web site: http://www.iwcp.co.uk
Publisher: Isle of Wight County Press Ltd
Date Launched: 1998
Frequency of update: Daily
Website Access: Free
Editor: Maurice Bower
Summary of Content: Website featuring news, sport, features and information on the local area, plus jobs, motoring, family announcements and property advertising.
Readership/Target Audience: Aimed at people who live on the Isle of Wight, plus expatriates and tourists.

Internet Media

Other Features: Features include a searchable news database, recruitment, car and property advertisements, weather and coastal conditions.
REGIONAL DAILY & SUNDAY NEWSPAPERS: Regional Daily Newspapers

ISLE OF WIGHT MATTERS
1881638U72J-381

Email: comments@isleofwight-matters.co.uk
Web site: http://www.isleofwight-matters.co.uk
Frequency of update: Daily
Summary of Content: Website created to help people who care about local issues. Whether you need access to useful information, want to highlight a particular topic to other people, discuss ideas with like minded individuals or just show your support and keep up to date with current affairs in your area, Isle of Wight Matters is the place for you.
Readership/Target Audience: Aimed at residents in the local area of Isle of Wight.
LOCAL NEWSPAPERS: Community Newsletters

ISLINGTON MATTERS
1881639U72J-382

Email: comments@islington-matters.co.uk
Web site: http://www.islington-matters.co.uk
Frequency of update: Daily
Summary of Content: Website created to help people who care about local issues. Whether you need access to useful information, want to highlight a particular topic to other people, discuss ideas with like minded individuals or just show your support and keep up to date with current affairs in your area, Islington Matters is the place for you.
Readership/Target Audience: Aimed at residents in the local area of Islington.
LOCAL NEWSPAPERS: Community Newsletters

ISPAL E-ZINE
1804557U32H-474

Editorial Address: Abbey House, 1650 Arlington Business Park, Theale, READING, RG7 4SA **Tel:** 0845 603 8734
Fax: 01491 874801
Email: editor@ispal.org.uk
Web site: http://www.ispal.org.uk
Publisher: Institute for Sport, Parks & Leisure
Date Launched: 2007
Frequency of update: Weekly
Website Access: Free
Traffic Figures: 3,000 Unique Users (Publisher's Statement)
Editor: Joanna Rota
Summary of Content: Electronic newsletter containing news and views from across the leisure industry. Includes health and fitness, children's play, sports, parks, arts and culture.
Readership/Target Audience: Aimed at members of ISPAL, CEOs of organisations, managers of fitness centres and people working in leisure facilities.
BUSINESS: LOCAL GOVERNMENT, LEISURE & RECREATION: Leisure, Recreation & Entertainment

ISPREVIEW.CO.UK
711749U5E-482

Formerly: ISP Review
Editorial Address: PR by email only **Fax:** 01202 622564
Email: m.jack@ispreview.co.uk
Web site: http://www.ispreview.co.uk
Date Launched: 1999
Frequency of update: 260 times a year
Website Access: Free
Traffic Figures: 3,500 Unique Users (per day Publisher's Statement)
Editor: Mark Jackson; **Editor-in-Chief:** Mark Jackson
Summary of Content: Website containing Internet service provider news, reviews, articles and discussions.
Readership/Target Audience: Aimed at Internet users.
BUSINESS: COMPUTERS & AUTOMATION: Data Transmission

IT INDUSTRY DIRECTORY
1912966U78R-558

Editorial Address: 18 Generator Hall, Electric Wharf, COVENTRY, CV1 4JL **Tel:** 0870 199 4044
Fax: 0870 777 4360
Email: enquiries@industrydirectory.co.uk
Web site: http://www.industrydirectory.co.uk
Publisher: Simply Marcomms
Frequency of update: Daily
Website Access: Free
Editor: Kirstie Colledge
Summary of Content: Directory containing the latest news stories for the UK I.T industry. Includes news archives.
Readership/Target Audience: Aimed at IT professionals, suppliers to the IT industry, IT Industry PR & Marketing firms.
CONSUMER: CONSUMER ELECTRONICS: Consumer Electronics Related

IT PRO
1774818U5B-9016

Editorial Address: 30 Cleveland Street, LONDON, W1T 4JD
Tel: 020 7907 6000
Email: maggie_holland@dennis.co.uk
Web site: http://www.itpro.co.uk
Publisher: Dennis Publishing Ltd
Frequency of update: Daily
Website Access: Free
Editor: Maggie Holland
Summary of Content: Website covering all aspects of business IT technology with news, features and reviews.
Readership/Target Audience: Aimed at business and IT managers.
BUSINESS: COMPUTERS & AUTOMATION: Data Processing

ITALIAN WINES & SPIRITS
36515U9C-100

Editorial Address: 21 South Square, LONDON, NW11 7AJ
Tel: 020 8458 4860 **Fax:** 020 8458 0994
Email: bruno@roncarati.com
Web site: http://www.iwines.it
Publisher: Editoriale Lariana
Date Launched: 1978
Frequency of update: Weekly
Website Access: Free
Traffic Figures: 15,000 Unique Users (per month Publisher's Statement)
Editor: Bruno Roncarati
Summary of Content: Website containing articles on the evolution of techniques and production of Italian wine and food.
Readership/Target Audience: Read by restaurateurs, wine importers and retailers.
BUSINESS: DRINKS & LICENSED TRADE: Licensed Trade, Wines & Spirits

ITALIAUK.NET
767871U11A-187

Formerly: Italia UK
Editorial Address: 3 Brooklands Place, Brooklands Road, SALE, M33 3SD **Tel:** 0161 976 1212 **Fax:** 0161 976 2888
Email: bev@italiauk.net
Web site: http://www.italiauk.net
Publisher: Italia UK Ltd
Date Launched: 2002
Frequency of update: Daily
Website Access: Free
Traffic Figures: 8,000 Unique Users (Publisher's Statement)
Editor: Glenn Routledge
Summary of Content: Website covering all aspects of the UK and Italian catering food sector, hospitality and food industries.
Readership/Target Audience: Aimed at the Italian business sector, Italian restaurants, takeaways, delicatessens, coffee shops, lifestyle bars, suppliers, importers, suppliers and distributors.
BUSINESS: CATERING: Catering, Hotels & Restaurants

IT-ANALYSIS.COM
626276U5R-139

Formerly: IT Analysis
Editorial Address: 8 Priors Park, Emerson Valley, MILTON KEYNES, MK4 2BT **Tel:** 01908 880760 **Fax:** 01908 880761
Web site: http://www.it-analysis.com
Publisher: IT Analysis Communications Ltd
Date Launched: 1999
Frequency of update: Daily
Website Access: Free
Traffic Figures: 25,000 Unique Users (Controlled Circulation)
Editor: Brian Smithson
Summary of Content: Website focusing on IT and e-business.
Readership/Target Audience: Aimed at executives within the IT sector.
BUSINESS: COMPUTERS & AUTOMATION: Computers Related

ITCHY CITY
1641847U89C-958

Editorial Address: Unit 2, White Horse Yard, 78 Liverpool Rd, LONDON, N1 0QQ **Tel:** 020 7288 9810
Fax: 020 7288 9815
Email: tracy@itchygroup.co.uk
Web site: http://www.itchycity.co.uk
Publisher: Itchy Group
Date Launched: 2002
Frequency of update: Daily
Website Access: Free
Traffic Figures: 400,000 Unique Users (Publisher's Statement)
Editor: Tracy Fitzgerald

Summary of Content: Website covering entertainment including eating, drinking, clubbing, activities, shopping, cinema, travel and accommodation.
Readership/Target Audience: Aimed at visitors to major cities predominantly aged between 18 and 35 years old.
Other Features: Online bookshop, noticeboards, competitions, music downloads, merchandise, flat finder, travel and restaurant booking engine.
CONSUMER: HOLIDAYS & TRAVEL: Entertainment Guides

IT-DIRECTOR.COM
626158U5R-139_15

Editorial Address: 8 Priors Park, Emerson Valley, MILTON KEYNES, MK4 2BT **Tel:** 01908 880760 **Fax:** 01908 880761
Web site: http://www.it-director.com
Publisher: IT Analysis Communications Ltd
Date Launched: 1999
Frequency of update: Daily
Website Access: Free
Traffic Figures: 30,000 Unique Users (Controlled Circulation)
Editor: Brian Smithson
Summary of Content: Website covering in-depth technology issues including news, analysis and interviews.
Readership/Target Audience: Aimed at IT directors.
BUSINESS: COMPUTERS & AUTOMATION: Computers Related

ITGIRL WORLD
1774820U74Q-1329

Editorial Address: Suite 5C Ashbridge Street, Marylebone, LONDON, NW8 8DQ **Tel:** 020 7723 1209
Email: chanel@itgirlworld.co.uk
Web site: http://www.itgirlworld.co.uk
Publisher: Unique Talent Management Ltd
Date Launched: 2006
Frequency of update: Weekly
Website Access: Free
Editor: Chanel Williams
Summary of Content: Website covering celebrity news, fashion and accessories, beauty, health, parties, nightclubs, films, books, hotels and restaurants, home, lifestyle and travel.
Readership/Target Audience: Aimed at women aged 18 to 35 years old who like to party.
CONSUMER: WOMEN'S INTEREST CONSUMER MAGAZINES: Lifestyle

ITPROPORTAL.COM
1685548U5D-337

Editorial Address: 4th Floor, 90-93 Cowcross Street, LONDON, EC1M 6BF **Tel:** 020 7291 0778
Fax: 020 7291 0771
Email: desire@itproportal.com
Web site: http://www.itproportal.com
Publisher: Net Communities Ltd
Date Launched: 1999
Frequency of update: Daily
Website Access: Free
Editor: France Desire Athow
Summary of Content: Website covering all aspects of IT including development, security, web services, applications, internet, storage, wireless, careers, networks, systems and data management.
Readership/Target Audience: Aimed at CEOs, IT managers and SMEs.
BUSINESS: COMPUTERS & AUTOMATION: Personal Computers

IVILLAGE UK
629721U74A-215

Formerly: iVillageuk
Editorial Address: Propect House, 80-110 New Oxford Street, LONDON, WC1A 1HB **Tel:** 020 7079 6000
Fax: 020 7079 6497
Email: editorial@email.ivillage.co.uk
Web site: http://www.ivillage.co.uk
Publisher: iVillage Ltd
Date Launched: 2000
Frequency of update: Daily
Website Access: Free
Traffic Figures: 2,114,556 Unique Users (per month ABC/ Electronic)
Summary of Content: Website focusing on lifestyle issues for women. Includes information on careers, computers, diet and fitness, health and beauty, parenting, money, news, entertainment, pregnancy, food and relationships.
Readership/Target Audience: Aimed at women of all ages.
Other Features: Features include recruitment, chat forums and archiving.
CONSUMER: WOMEN'S INTEREST CONSUMER MAGAZINES: Women's Interest

IZZIWIZZI KIDS
1851095U91D-979

Editorial Address: 17 Illingworth Avenue, Altofts, NORMANTON, WF6 2LL **Tel:** 0845 120 1036
Fax: 0845 120 1037
Email: alison.boxall@izziwizzikids.co.uk
Web site: http://www.izziwizzikids.co.uk
Date Launched: 2006
Frequency of update: Weekly
Website Access: Free
Traffic Figures: 21,000 Unique Users (per month Publisher's Statement)
Editor: Alison Boxall
Summary of Content: Website covering toys and gifts for the under 5s.
Readership/Target Audience: Aimed mainly at parents and grandparents of children under 5 years old.
CONSUMER: RECREATION & LEISURE: Children & Youth

JAFFE LEGAL NEWS SERVICE
1638068U44-3009

Editorial Address: Lloyd's Avenue House, 6 Lloyd's Avenue, LONDON, EC3N 3EH **Tel:** 020 7266 3020
Fax: 020 7266 3060
Email: jlns@jlns.com
Web site: http://www.jlns.com
Frequency of update: Weekly
Website Access: Free
Editor: Ronel Lehmann
Summary of Content: Website covering all the latest developments in the legal profession. Includes feature articles and a services guide.
Readership/Target Audience: Aimed at legal professionals.
BUSINESS: LEGAL

JANE'S AIR LAUNCHED WEAPONS
762792U40-401

Editorial Address: Sentinel House, 163 Brighton Road, COULSDON, CR5 2YH **Tel:** 020 8700 3700
Fax: 020 8763 1006
Email: rob@airlaunched.co.uk
Web site: http://jalw.janes.com
Publisher: Jane's Information Group
Frequency of update: Monthly
Website Access: Paid
Editor: Robert Hewson
Summary of Content: Guide detailing development programmes, system descriptions, users and contractors of the world's strategic weapon systems, including ballistic and cruise missiles, surface-to-air and anti-ballistic missile systems.
Readership/Target Audience: Read by researchers, developers and analysts within the defence and defence industry community.
BUSINESS: DEFENCE

JANE'S FOREIGN REPORT
626360U40-414

Editorial Address: Sentinel House, 163 Brighton Road, COULSDON, CR5 2YH **Tel:** 020 8700 3700
Email: christian.lemiere@janes.com
Web site: http://www.foreignreport.com
Publisher: Jane's Information Group
Frequency of update: Daily
Website Access: Paid
Editor: Christian LeMiere
Summary of Content: Source covering news and information on foreign politics.
Readership/Target Audience: Aimed at those with an interest in foreign political information, 'under the counter' intelligence and the political 'rumour mill'.
BUSINESS: DEFENCE

JANE'S INTELLIGENCE REVIEW
629106U40-161_80

Formerly: Jane's Intelligence Defence Review
Editorial Address: Sentinel House, 163 Brighton Road, COULSDON, CR5 2YH **Tel:** 020 8700 3700
Fax: 020 8763 1006
Email: jir@janes.com
Web site: http://jir.janes.com
Publisher: Jane's Information Group
Frequency of update: Daily
Website Access: Paid
Editor: Christian LeMiere
Summary of Content: Source covering intelligence and developments for the military and intelligence services worldwide.
Readership/Target Audience: Aimed at government, military and law enforcement officials.
BUSINESS: DEFENCE

JANE'S INTERNATIONAL DEFENCE REVIEW
629062U40-162_55

Editorial Address: Sentinel House, 163 Brighton Road, COULSDON, CR5 2YH **Tel:** 020 8700 3700
Fax: 020 8700 3846
Email: nick.brown@janes.com
Web site: http://idr.janes.com
Publisher: Jane's Information Group
Frequency of update: Daily
Website Access: Paid
Editor: Nick Brown
Summary of Content: Title focusing on the world of defence technology.
Readership/Target Audience: Aimed at professionals working in the defence industry.
BUSINESS: DEFENCE

JANE'S MISSILES & ROCKETS
626488U40-162_70

Editorial Address: Sentinel House, 163 Brighton Road, COULSDON, CR5 2YH **Tel:** 020 8700 3700
Fax: 020 8763 1007
Email: derichardson@textrix.co.uk
Web site: http://jmr.janes.com
Frequency of update: Daily
Website Access: Paid
Editor: Doug Richardson
Summary of Content: Website covering missile technology and new developments in the industry.
Readership/Target Audience: Aimed at government, military and industry officials.
BUSINESS: DEFENCE

JANE'S NAVAL CONSTRUCTION & RETROFIT MARKETS
23442U40-403

Editorial Address: Sentinel House, 163 Brighton Road, COULSDON, CR5 2YH **Tel:** 020 8700 3700
Fax: 020 8763 1006
Email: info@janes.com
Web site: http://jnc.janes.com
Publisher: Jane's Information Group
Frequency of update: Monthly
Website Access: Paid
Editor: Jurrien Noot
Summary of Content: Website covering specialised intelligence on the latest shipbuilding and modernisation programmes throughout the world. Contains expert forecasts on naval requirements worldwide for the next 10 to 15 years.
Readership/Target Audience: Aimed at the defence industry, ministries of defence, armed forces and academic institutions worldwide.
BUSINESS: DEFENCE

JANE'S NAVY INTERNATIONAL ONLINE
626490U40-163_10

Editorial Address: Sentinel House, 163 Brighton Road, COULSDON, CR5 2YH **Tel:** 020 8700 3700
Fax: 020 8763 1423
Email: jni@janes.com
Web site: http://jni.janes.com
Publisher: Jane's Information Group
Frequency of update: Daily
Website Access: Paid
Editor: Jon Rosamond
Summary of Content: Website containing news and analysis of maritime security.
Readership/Target Audience: Aimed at naval, government and military officials.
Other Features: Features include over 10 years of archiving.
BUSINESS: DEFENCE

JANE'S SIMULATION & TRAINING SYSTEMS
38901U40-163_70

Editorial Address: Sentinel House, 163 Brighton Road, COULSDON, CR5 2YH **Tel:** 020 8700 3700
Fax: 020 8763 1007
Email: info@janes.com
Web site: http://jsts.janes.com
Publisher: Jane's Information Group
Date Launched: 1988
Frequency of update: Daily
Website Access: Paid
Editor: Giles Ebbutt
Summary of Content: Website containing analysis and details of 3000 simulators and training packages for civil and military applications. Includes virtual reality and entertainment simulators.

Readership/Target Audience: Aimed at the transport and defence industry, ministries of defence, armed forces and academic institutions worldwide.
BUSINESS: DEFENCE

JANE'S UNDERWATER SECURITY SYSTEMS AND TECHNOLOGY
39452U45R-68

Formerly: Jane's Underwater Technology
Editorial Address: Sentinel House, 163 Brighton Road, COULSDON, CR5 2YH **Tel:** 020 8700 3700
Fax: 020 8763 1005
Email: info@janes.com
Web site: http://juwt.janes.com
Publisher: Jane's Information Group
Date Launched: 1998
Frequency of update: Daily
Website Access: Paid
Editor: Cliff Funnell
Summary of Content: Online guide to the current state of the underwater technology industry including harnessing tide energy and seabed surveying.
Readership/Target Audience: Aimed at armed forces, seabed mining organisations, government agencies, university libraries, conservation organisations and submersible manufacturers.
BUSINESS: MARINE & SHIPPING: Marine Related

JERSEY MATTERS
1881640U72J-383

Email: comments@jersey-matters.co.uk
Web site: http://www.jersey-matters.co.uk
Frequency of update: Daily
Summary of Content: Website created to help people who care about local issues. Whether you need access to useful information, want to highlight a particular topic to other people, discuss ideas with like minded individuals or just show your support and keep up to date with current affairs in your area, Jersey Matters is the place for you.
Readership/Target Audience: Aimed at residents in the local area of Jersey.
LOCAL NEWSPAPERS: Community Newsletters

JEWTASTIC
1826692U90-1023

Editorial Address: PO Box 585, EDGWARE, HA8 4DU
Tel: 020 7993 0092
Web site: http://www.jewtastic.com
Publisher: JMT Ventures Ltd
Frequency of update: Daily
Website Access: Free
Editor: Leslie Bunder
Summary of Content: Website covering Jewish pop culture, music, TV, film, food, fashion.
Readership/Target Audience: Aimed at Jewish communities in the UK.
CONSUMER: ETHNIC

JOURNALISM.CO.UK
629501U2B-30

Formerly: dotJournalism
Editorial Address: 68 Middle Street, BRIGHTON, BN1 1AL
Tel: 01273 384293 **Fax:** 01273 232179
Email: info@journalism.co.uk
Web site: http://www.journalism.co.uk
Publisher: Mousetrap Media Ltd
Date Launched: 2001
Frequency of update: Daily
Website Access: Paid
Traffic Figures: 100,000 Unique Users (per month ABC/Electronic)
Editor: Laura Oliver
Summary of Content: Online news site focusing on jobs, recruitment, industry news and freelance resources for journalists.
Readership/Target Audience: Aimed at journalists and media professionals.
BUSINESS: COMMUNICATIONS, ADVERTISING & MARKETING: Press

JUNKK.COM
1657091U94X-272

Editorial Address: Kyrle House, Edde Cross Street, ROSS-ON-WYE, HR9 7BZ **Tel:** 01989 762269
Email: editorial@junkk.com
Web site: http://www.junkk.com
Publisher: Junkk.com
Date Launched: 2004
Frequency of update: Daily
Website Access: Free
Traffic Figures: 150,000 Unique Users (per month Publisher's Statement)
Editor: Peter Martin

Internet Media

Summary of Content: Website covering environmental issues pertinent to the consumer, specifically in the area of recycling - local, regional, national and international.
Readership/Target Audience: Aimed at those with access to computer and Internet connections with a need for and interest in matters pertaining to recycling and environmental issues.
Other Features: Forum, blog, polls, ideas, matchmaking, articles.
CONSUMER: OTHER CLASSIFICATIONS: Miscellaneous

JUST-AUTO.COM
626288U31R-36

Editorial Address: Seneca House, Buntsford Hill Business Park, Buntsford Park Road, BROMSGROVE, B60 3DX
Tel: 01527 573600 **Fax:** 01527 577423
Email: editor@just-auto.com
Web site: http://www.just-auto.com
Publisher: Aroq Ltd
Date Launched: 1999
Frequency of update: Daily
Website Access: Paid
Traffic Figures: 130,000 Unique Users (per month Publisher's Statement)
Editor: Graeme Roberts
Summary of Content: Website containing business news and features covering all aspects of the automotive industry.
Readership/Target Audience: Aimed at business professionals within the automotive and allied industries.
Other Features: Job, events (e.g. auto industry conferences and similar).
BUSINESS: MOTOR TRADE: Motor Trade Related

JUSTCOMPETITIONS.CO.UK
1819083U79F-109

Editorial Address: Madeira House, Madeira Walk, WINDSOR, SL4 1EU **Tel:** 01753 850606
Email: dedwards@utmedia.co.uk
Web site: http://www.justcompetitions.co.uk
Publisher: UTMedia
Date Launched: 2007
Frequency of update: Daily
Website Access: Free
Editor: Dan Edwards
Summary of Content: Portal with competitions from the web in one easy spot covering holidays to cars, cash to CDs, DVDs to concert tickets and more.
Readership/Target Audience: Aimed at competition fans.
CONSUMER: HOBBIES & DIY: Games & Puzzles

JUST-DRINKS.COM
626287U22R-250

Editorial Address: Seneca House, Buntsford Hill Business Park, Buntsford Park Road, BROMSGROVE, B60 3DX
Tel: 01527 573600 **Fax:** 01527 577423
Email: editor@just-drinks.com
Web site: http://www.just-drinks.com
Publisher: Aroq Ltd
Date Launched: 1999
Frequency of update: Daily
Website Access: Paid
Traffic Figures: 100,000 Unique Users (per month Publisher's Statement)
Editor: Olly Wehring
Summary of Content: Website providing news and information about the drinks industry. Provides instant access to reports, books and research products from leading market information providers.
Readership/Target Audience: Aimed at business professionals from the global drinks industry.
BUSINESS: FOOD: Food Related

JUST-FOOD.COM
626290U22A-250

Editorial Address: Seneca House, Buntsford Hill Business Park, Buntsford Park Road, BROMSGROVE, B60 3DX
Tel: 01527 573600 **Fax:** 01527 577423
Email: editor@just-food.com
Web site: http://www.just-food.com
Publisher: Aroq Ltd
Date Launched: 1999
Frequency of update: Daily
Website Access: Paid
Traffic Figures: 82,655 Unique Users (per month Publisher's Statement)
Editor: Katy Humphries
Summary of Content: E-Zine featuring news and features covering all aspects of the food industry.
Readership/Target Audience: Aimed at business professionals in the food and allied industries.
BUSINESS: FOOD

JUSTOVERSEAS.CO.UK
1819086U74K-784

Editorial Address: Madeira House, Madeira Walk, WINDSOR, SL4 1EU **Tel:** 01753 860700
Email: dedwards@utmedia.co.uk
Web site: http://www.justoverseas.co.uk
Publisher: UTMedia
Date Launched: 2007
Frequency of update: Daily
Website Access: Free
Editor: Dan Edwards
Summary of Content: Website covering overseas property with features, news stories and property listings as well as a facility to list your own property.
Readership/Target Audience: Aimed at those looking to buy a property overseas.
CONSUMER: WOMEN'S INTEREST CONSUMER MAGAZINES: Home Purchase

JUST-STYLE.COM
623385U47A-230

Editorial Address: Seneca House, Buntsford Hill Business Park, Buntsford Park Road, BROMSGROVE, B60 3DX
Tel: 01527 573600 **Fax:** 01527 577423
Email: editor@just-style.com
Web site: http://www.just-style.com
Publisher: Aroq Ltd
Date Launched: 1999
Frequency of update: Daily
Website Access: Paid
Traffic Figures: 100,000 Unique Users (Publisher's Statement)
Editor: Leonie Barrie
Summary of Content: Website focusing on footwear and textile trade sites. Also provides reports, books and research products from leading market information providers.
Readership/Target Audience: Aimed at business professionals from the apparel, textile and footwear industries worldwide.
BUSINESS: CLOTHING & TEXTILES

THE K&BZINE
1641998U23C-91

Editorial Address: PO Box 46, HOCKHURST, TN18 4RD
Tel: 01580 755863
Email: johnausten@mac.com
Web site: http://www.thekbzine.com
Publisher: Zenius (Croydon) Ltd
Date Launched: 2001
Frequency of update: Weekly
Website Access: Free
Traffic Figures: 80,229 Unique Users (per year Publisher's Statement)
Editor: John Austin
Summary of Content: Electronic newsletter including the latest news, ideas and information about the people, products and issues for the kitchen, bathroom and bedroom industry.
Readership/Target Audience: Aimed primarily at kitchen and bathroom retailers.
BUSINESS: FURNISHINGS & FURNITURE: Furnishings & Furniture - Kitchens & Bathrooms

KEEP THE DOCTOR AWAY
1775363U74G-274

Editorial Address: Madeira House, Madeira Walk, WINDSOR, SL4 1EU **Tel:** 01753 860700
Email: newsdesk@utmedia.co.uk
Web site: http://www.keepthedoctoraway.co.uk
Publisher: UTMedia
Date Launched: 2006
Frequency of update: Daily
Website Access: Free
Traffic Figures: 800,000 Unique Users (Publisher's Statement)
Editor: Dan Edwards
Summary of Content: Website with health news and features on how to stay healthy, get fit, diet, lose weight and improve your health.
Readership/Target Audience: Aimed at people of all ages looking to find out more about staying healthy.
Other Features: Health competitions and reviews.
CONSUMER: WOMEN'S INTEREST CONSUMER MAGAZINES: Slimming & Health

KENSINGTON AND CHELSEA MATTERS
1881641U72J-384

Email: comments@kensingtonandchelsea-matters.co.uk
Web site: http://www.kensingtonandchelsea-matters.co.uk
Frequency of update: Daily
Summary of Content: Website created to help people who care about local issues. Whether you need access to useful information, want to highlight a particular topic to other people, discuss ideas with like minded individuals or just show your support and keep up to date with current affairs in your area, Kensington and Chelsea Matters is the place for you.
Readership/Target Audience: Aimed at residents in the local area of Kensington and Chelsea.
LOCAL NEWSPAPERS: Community Newsletters

KENT MATTERS
1881642U72J-385

Email: comments@kent-matters.co.uk
Web site: http://www.kent-matters.co.uk
Frequency of update: Daily
Summary of Content: Website created to help people who care about local issues. Whether you need access to useful information, want to highlight a particular topic to other people, discuss ideas with like minded individuals or just show your support and keep up to date with current affairs in your area, Kent Matters is the place for you.
Readership/Target Audience: Aimed at residents in the local area of Kent.
LOCAL NEWSPAPERS: Community Newsletters

KENT ONLINE
754925U67B-4

Editorial Address: Medway House, Sir Thomas Longley Road, Medway City Estate, ROCHESTER, ME2 4DU
Tel: 01622 717880 **Fax:** 01622 715225
Email: editor.kentonline@thekmgroup.co.uk
Web site: http://www.kentonline.co.uk
Publisher: Kent Messenger Group
Date Launched: 1999
Frequency of update: Daily
Website Access: Free
Traffic Figures: 286,585 Unique Users (01/02/2009 To 28/02/2009 ABC/Electronic)
Editor: Andy Winter
Summary of Content: Website containing the latest news for the Kent area. Includes sections on sport, home, jobs, motors, travel, education, eating out guides, dating and weather.
Readership/Target Audience: Aimed at those living in Kent.
Other Features: Features include recruitment, a directory and archiving.
REGIONAL DAILY & SUNDAY NEWSPAPERS: Regional Daily Newspapers

KEY PUBLISHING LTD AVIATION FORUMS
1871267U94X-2061

Formerly: Forum.keypublishing.co.uk
Email: webmaster@keypublishing.com
Web site: http://forum.keypublishing.co.uk
Frequency of update: Daily
Summary of Content: Website forum covering modern military aviation affairs relating to any country or aviation industry.
Readership/Target Audience: Aimed at people interested in aviation.
CONSUMER: OTHER CLASSIFICATIONS: Miscellaneous

KINGSTON UPON THAMES MATTERS
1881643U72J-386

Email: comments@kingstonuponthames-matters.co.uk
Web site: http://www.kingstonuponthames-matters.co.uk
Frequency of update: Daily
Summary of Content: Website created to help people who care about local issues. Whether you need access to useful information, want to highlight a particular topic to other people, discuss ideas with like-minded people or just show your support and keep up to date with current affairs in your area, Kingston upon Thames Matters is the place for you.
Readership/Target Audience: Aimed at residents in the local area of Kingston upon Thames.
LOCAL NEWSPAPERS: Community Newsletters

KIRKLEES MATTERS
1881644U72J-387

Email: comments@kirklees-matters.co.uk
Web site: http://www.kirklees-matters.co.uk
Frequency of update: Daily
Summary of Content: Website created to help people who care about local issues. Whether you need access to useful information, want to highlight a particular topic to other people, discuss ideas with like-minded people or just show your support and keep up to date with current affairs in your area, Kirklees Matters is the place for you.
Readership/Target Audience: Aimed at residents in the local area of Kirklees.
LOCAL NEWSPAPERS: Community Newsletters

KNITTING TRADE JOURNAL
1846834U47C-231

Editorial Address: 80 Featherstone Lane, Featherstone, PONTEFRACT, WF7 6LR **Tel:** 01977 708488
Fax: 0700 609 0531
Email: editor@knittingtradejournal.com
Web site: http://www.knittingtradejournal.com
Publisher: Mowbray Communications Ltd
Date Launched: 2008
Frequency of update: Daily
Website Access: Paid
Traffic Figures: 1,320 Unique Users (per week Publisher's Statement)
Editor: Haydn Davis
Summary of Content: Online magazine covering new fabrics, fibres, yarns, new machinery development and commercial news.
Readership/Target Audience: Aimed at the global knitwear manufacturers, knitted textile and knitwear producers and knitted fabric manufacturers.
BUSINESS: CLOTHING & TEXTILES: Knitwear

KRONIKA READING
1791399U72B-180_291

Editorial Address: For all contact details see main edition, Reading Chronicle Series
Web site: http://www.kronika.co.uk
Frequency of update: Weekly
Website Access: Paid
Traffic Figures: 5,000 Unique Users (Print Run)
LOCAL NEWSPAPERS: Local Newspapers English Counties

L&SI ONLINE (PLASA)
626321U4B-169

Formerly: PLASA
Editorial Address: Redoubt House, 1 Edward Road, EASTBOURNE, BN23 8AS **Tel:** 01323 524120
Fax: 01323 524121
Email: news@plasa.org
Web site: http://www.lsionline.co.uk
Publisher: PLASA
Date Launched: 1994
Frequency of update: 260 times a year
Website Access: Free
Traffic Figures: 20,000 Unique Users (Publisher's Statement)
Editor: Lee Baldock
Summary of Content: Website covering developments in lighting, sound, video and staging technology across all aspects of the global entertainment, leisure and presentation industries.
Readership/Target Audience: Aimed at those working within the field/sector of entertainment and installation technology worldwide.
Other Features: Recruitment, Bookshop, Events Listing, Magazine Archive, Classified Advertising.
BUSINESS: ARCHITECTURE & BUILDING: Interior Design & Flooring

LABORATORYTALK
1606351U55-9006

Editorial Address: PR by email only **Tel:** 020 7970 4920
Email: news@laboratorytalk.com
Web site: http://www.laboratorytalk.com
Publisher: Pro-Talk Ltd
Date Launched: 2001
Frequency of update: Daily
Website Access: Free
Editor: Russ Swan
Summary of Content: Website covering laboratory equipment, supplies and services.
Readership/Target Audience: Aimed at scientists and laboratory managers.
BUSINESS: APPLIED SCIENCE & LABORATORIES

LAFFERTY
707751U1A-229

Editorial Address: 1 Hammersmith Grove, LONDON, W6 0NB **Tel:** 020 3008 8420
Email: sadeek.varacchia@lafferty.com
Web site: http://www.lafferty.com
Date Launched: 1997
Frequency of update: Daily
Editor: Sadeek Varacchia
Summary of Content: Website providing international business intelligence to the banking, financial, insurance, accounting, consulting and related sectors.
Readership/Target Audience: Aimed at financial industry professionals.
BUSINESS: FINANCE & ECONOMICS

LAMBETH MATTERS
1881645U72J-388

Email: comments@lambeth-matters.co.uk
Web site: http://www.lambeth-matters.co.uk
Frequency of update: Daily
Summary of Content: Website created to help people who care about local issues. Whether you need access to useful information, want to highlight a particular topic to other people, discuss ideas with like-minded people or just show your support and keep up to date with current affairs in your area, Lambeth Matters is the place for you.
Readership/Target Audience: Aimed at residents in the local area of Lambeth.
LOCAL NEWSPAPERS: Community Newsletters

LANCASHIRE MATTERS
1881646U72J-389

Email: comments@lancashire-matters.co.uk
Web site: http://www.lancashire-matters.co.uk
Frequency of update: Daily
Summary of Content: Website created to help people who care about local issues. Whether you need access to useful information, want to highlight a particular topic to other people, discuss ideas with like minded individuals or just show your support and keep up to date with current affairs in your area, Lancashire Matters is the place for you.
Readership/Target Audience: Aimed at residents in the local area of Lancashire.
LOCAL NEWSPAPERS: Community Newsletters

LATEST IN BEAUTY
1839988U74H-308

Editorial Address: PO Box 62186, LONDON, SW11 6UU
Tel: 07720 887011
Email: info@latestinbeauty.com
Web site: http://www.latestinbeauty.com
Date Launched: 2008
Frequency of update: Daily
Website Access: Free
Traffic Figures: 10,000 Unique Users (Publisher's Statement)
Editor: Nort Janssen
Summary of Content: Website covering new beauty products coming to the market, fashion and trends as well as giving consumers have the choice to order trial size products free of charge to try at home.
Readership/Target Audience: Aimed at women of all ages.
Other Features: Other features include product sampling and consumer and shopper research.
CONSUMER: WOMEN'S INTEREST CONSUMER MAGAZINES: Hair & Beauty

LATIN AMERICAN INFORMES ESPECIALES
601210U14A-194_40

Editorial Address: 61 Old Street, LONDON, EC1V 9HW
Tel: 020 7251 0012 **Fax:** 020 7253 8193
Email: subs@latinnews.com
Web site: http://www.latinnews.com
Publisher: Intelligence Research Ltd
Date Launched: 1983
Frequency of update: Weekly
Website Access: Paid
Editor: Yolanda Drinot
Summary of Content: Magazine which covers areas of topical importance, a Spanish version of Special Reports.
BUSINESS: COMMERCE, INDUSTRY & MANAGEMENT

LATIN AMERICAN NEWSLETTERS
629560U82-106

Editorial Address: 61 Old Street, LONDON, EC1V 9HW
Tel: 020 7251 0012 **Fax:** 020 7253 8193
Email: latinnews@intelligenceresearch.com
Web site: http://www.latinnews.com
Publisher: Intelligence Research Ltd
Date Launched: 1967
Frequency of update: Daily
Website Access: Paid
Editor: Will Ollard
Summary of Content: Website containing economic and political news and information on Latin America.
Readership/Target Audience: Read by those interested in Latin America.
Other Features: Features include a daily e-mail newsletter.
CONSUMER: CURRENT AFFAIRS & POLITICS

LAW SOCIETY OF SCOTLAND
1674272U44-3018

Editorial Address: 26 Drumsheugh Gardens, EDINBURGH, EH3 7YR **Tel:** 0131 226 7411 **Fax:** 0131 476 8359
Email: angusmaclauchlan@lawscot.org.uk
Web site: http://www.lawscot.org.uk
Publisher: The Law Society of Scotland
Frequency of update: Daily
Website Access: Free
Traffic Figures: 10,000 Unique Users (Publisher's Statement)
Editor: Suzy Powell
Summary of Content: Information portal covering issues affecting the interests of the solicitor's profession in Scotland and the interests of the public in relation to the profession.
Readership/Target Audience: Aimed at solicitors and the general public.
BUSINESS: LEGAL

LAWANDMORE.CO.UK
1812840U74Q-1354

Editorial Address: 70 St. Mary Axe, LONDON, EC3A 8BD
Tel: 020 3102 4395
Email: vwozniak@lawandmore.co.uk
Web site: http://www.lawandmore.co.uk
Date Launched: 2008
Frequency of update: Daily
Website Access: Free
Editor: Vanessa Wozniak
Summary of Content: Lifestyle website covering hotels, travel, property, personal finance, beauty, fashion, music, cinema, theatre, motoring, home, style, shopping, gadgets, restaurants, pubs and clubs as well as recruitment for the legal industry.
Readership/Target Audience: Aimed at working legal professionals with a high disposable income from legal secretaries to barristers.
Other Features: Job Search
CONSUMER: WOMEN'S INTEREST CONSUMER MAGAZINES: Lifestyle

THE LAWYER.COM
626354U44-891

Editorial Address: St. Giles House, 50 Poland Street, LONDON, W1F 7AX **Tel:** 020 7970 4000 **Fax:** 020 7970 4699
Email: editorial@thelawyer.com
Web site: http://www.thelawyer.com
Publisher: Centaur Communications Ltd
Date Launched: 1999
Frequency of update: Daily
Website Access: Free
Traffic Figures: 240,703 Unique Users (01/03/2009 To 31/03/2009 ABC/Electronic)
Editor: Catrin Griffiths; **Web Editor:** Jon Parker
Summary of Content: Website covering the legal profession. Offers a range of both broad and specific information and services for lawyers.
Readership/Target Audience: Aimed at lawyers, students, marketing, IT personnel and recruitment consultants.
BUSINESS: LEGAL

THE LEARNING EXCHANGE
1748867U62A-510

Formerly: Schools ETC
Editorial Address: 31-33 Bondway, Vauxhall, LONDON, SW8 1SJ **Tel:** 020 7587 5080 **Fax:** 020 7735 4002
Email: paddy.odea@continyou.org.uk
Web site: http://www.learning-exchange.org.uk
Publisher: ContinYou
Frequency of update: Quarterly
Website Access: Paid
Editor: Paddy O'Dea
Summary of Content: Social networking website for professionals and practioners involved in all aspects of developing and delivering extended school services including projects and events.
Readership/Target Audience: Aimed at head teachers, LEAs and people working in community focused community schools, extended schools and lifelong learning.
BUSINESS: CHURCH & SCHOOL EQUIPMENT & EDUCATION: Education

LEARNTHINGS
624198U88A-53

Formerly: learn.co.uk
Editorial Address: 3-7 Herbal Hill, LONDON, EC1R 5EJ
Tel: 020 7713 4050
Email: learncontact@guardian.co.uk
Web site: http://www.learnthings.co.uk
Publisher: Guardian Media Group plc
Date Launched: 2000
Frequency of update: Daily
Website Access: Free
Traffic Figures: 343,563 Unique Users (Publisher's Statement)
Editor: Emily Drabble
Summary of Content: Website covering the whole of the national curriculum including revision guides, interactive testing and assessment facilities. Also covers educational news and features and trips.
Readership/Target Audience: Aimed at teachers, parents and children.
CONSUMER: EDUCATION

Internet Media

LEEDS MATTERS
1881647U72J-390

Email: comments@leeds-matters.co.uk
Web site: http://www.leeds-matters.co.uk
Frequency of update: Daily
Summary of Content: Website created to help people who care about local issues. Whether you need access to useful information, want to highlight a particular topic to other people, discuss ideas with like minded individuals or just show your support and keep up to date with current affairs in your area, Leeds Matters is the place for you.
Readership/Target Audience: Aimed at residents in the local area of Leeds.
LOCAL NEWSPAPERS: Community Newsletters

LEEDS RHINOS
1663659U75C-459

Editorial Address: Headingley Carnegie Stadium, St. Michaels Lane, Headingley, LEEDS, LS6 3BR
Tel: 0113 203 3281 **Fax:** 0845 070 0882
Email: phil.daly@leedsrugby.com
Web site: http://www.leedsrugby.com
Frequency of update: Daily
Website Access: Free
Editor: Phil Daly
Summary of Content: Official website of Leeds Rhinos, Leeds Carnegie and Headingley Carnegie Stadium covers both rugby league and rugby union, fixtures, player profiles and the club shop.
Readership/Target Audience: Aimed at fans of both rugby disciplines.
CONSUMER: SPORT: Rugby

LEEDSTODAY
629154U80C-3597

Formerly: thisisleeds
Editorial Address: PO Box 168, Wellington Street, LEEDS, LS1 1RF **Tel:** 0113 243 2701
Email: geoff.fox@ypn.co.uk
Web site: http://www.leedstoday.net
Publisher: Yorkshire Post Newspapers Ltd
Date Launched: 2000
Frequency of update: Daily
Website Access: Free
Traffic Figures: 71,654 Unique Users (per month Publisher's Statement)
Editor: Geoff Fox
Summary of Content: Website covering news, sport, information and features about Leeds.
Readership/Target Audience: Read by residents and visitors to the local area.
Other Features: Features include a buyer's guide, recruitment and archiving.
CONSUMER: RURAL & REGIONAL INTEREST: Regional Interest English Counties

LEGAL HUB
1808534U44-3048

Editorial Address: 100 Avenue Road, Swiss Cottage, LONDON, NW3 3PF **Tel:** 020 7393 7000 **Fax:** 020 7393 7790
Email: hub@legalhub.co.uk
Web site: http://www.legalhub.co.uk
Publisher: Sweet & Maxwell Ltd
Date Launched: 2007
Frequency of update: Weekly
Website Access: Free
Traffic Figures: 11,750 Unique Users (per month Publisher's Statement)
Editor: Anne Kemsley
Summary of Content: Online publication featuring legal directories, articles, events, listing and news.
Readership/Target Audience: Aimed at members of the legal profession.
BUSINESS: LEGAL

LEGAL TECHNOLOGY
1868561U44-3064

Editorial Address: Oak Lodge, Darrow Green Road, DENTON, HARLESTON, IP20 0AY **Tel:** 01986 788 666
Fax: 01986 788 808
Email: news@legaltechnology.com
Web site: http://www.legaltechnology.org
Frequency of update: Daily
Traffic Figures: 4,000 Unique Users (per month Publisher's Statement)
Editor: Charles Christian
Summary of Content: Web site of Legal Technology Insider newsletter being an online resource for the latest news about legal technology with extensive diary of forthcoming legal IT events, a jobs board for recruitment opportunities within the legal IT market and our definitive top 250 chart of which systems the UK's largest law firms are using.
BUSINESS: LEGAL

LEGAL-MOVES
1745995U44-3045

Editorial Address: 10 Tonbridge Chambers, Pembury Road, TONBRIDGE, TN9 2HZ **Tel:** 01732 358861
Fax: 01732 367947
Email: nick@biogs.co.uk
Web site: http://www.legalmoves.co.uk
Publisher: Biogs Ltd
Date Launched: 2005
Frequency of update: 22 times a year
Website Access: Paid
Editor: Nick Clark
Summary of Content: Current awareness publication which tracks lawyers and other professional staff as they move within the legal profession.
Readership/Target Audience: Aimed at law firms, barristers chambers and service providers to the legal profession.
BUSINESS: LEGAL

LEICESTER TIGERS
1663660U75C-460

Editorial Address: Aylestone Road, LEICESTER, LE2 7TR
Tel: 0116 217 1284
Email: tigers@tigers.co.uk
Web site: http://www.leicestertigers.com
Frequency of update: Daily
Website Access: Free
Traffic Figures: 81,000 Unique Users (per month Publisher's Statement)
Editor: Gary Sherrard
Summary of Content: Official site of Leicester Tigers Rugby Club covering fixtures, player interviews, match reports and general rugby news.
Readership/Target Audience: Aimed at fans of Leicester Tigers.
CONSUMER: SPORT: Rugby

LEICESTERSHIRE MATTERS
1881648U72J-391

Email: comments@leicestershire-matters.co.uk
Web site: http://www.leicestershire-matters.co.uk
Frequency of update: Daily
Summary of Content: Website created to help people who care about local issues. Whether you need access to useful information, want to highlight a particular topic to other people, discuss ideas with like minded individuals or just show your support and keep up to date with current affairs in your area, Leicestershire Matters is the place for you.
Readership/Target Audience: Aimed at residents in the local area of Leicestershire.
LOCAL NEWSPAPERS: Community Newsletters

LEISURETOURISM.COM
1627023U50-207

Editorial Address: Nosworthy Way, WALLINGFORD, OX10 8DE **Tel:** 01491 829434 **Fax:** 01491 829465
Email: leisuretourism@cabi.org
Web site: http://www.leisuretourism.com
Publisher: CABI
Frequency of update: Daily
Website Access: Paid
Editor: Janice Osborn
Summary of Content: Website covering reference materials for those working in leisure, recreation, sport tourism, hospitality and the cultural industries.
Readership/Target Audience: Aimed at university libraries, heads of schools, national tourism organisations and research consultancies.
BUSINESS: TRAVEL & TOURISM

LETS-DO-DIY.COM
1895879U79A-180

Editorial Address: The Old School House, St. Johns Court, South Parade, BATH, BA2 4AF **Tel:** 01225 316 940
Email: editor@lets-do-diy.com
Web site: http://www.lets-do-diy.com
Frequency of update: Daily
Website Access: Free
Traffic Figures: 10,000 Unique Users (Publisher's Statement)
Editor: Seb Mills
Summary of Content: Website featuring DIY tips, projects and advice.
Readership/Target Audience: Anyone with an interest in home improvements.
CONSUMER: HOBBIES & DIY

LETSRECYCLE.COM
711412U57-36_40

Editorial Address: Elizabeth House, 39 York Road, LONDON, SE1 7NQ **Tel:** 020 7633 4500 **Fax:** 020 7633 4519
Email: news@letsrecycle.com
Web site: http://www.letsrecycle.com
Publisher: letsrecycle.com
Date Launched: 2000
Frequency of update: Daily
Website Access: Free
Traffic Figures: 22,000 Unique Users (per month Publisher's Statement)
Editor: Caelia Quinault
Summary of Content: Website providing news and information including material prices for the local authority recycling business sector. Covers information about glass, metal, paper, plastics, textiles and wood recycling and transport. Also features legislation and official bodies responsible for recycling.
Readership/Target Audience: Aimed at those interested in and/or involved in recycling and waste management.
BUSINESS: ENVIRONMENT & POLLUTION

LEWISHAM MATTERS
1881649U72J-392

Email: comments@lewisham-matters.co.uk
Web site: http://www.lewisham-matters.co.uk
Frequency of update: Daily
Summary of Content: Website created to help people who care about local issues. Whether you need access to useful information, want to highlight a particular topic to other people, discuss ideas with like minded individuals or just show your support and keep up to date with current affairs in your area, Lewisham Matters is the place for you.
Readership/Target Audience: Aimed at residents in the local area of Lewisham.
LOCAL NEWSPAPERS: Community Newsletters

LGCNET
38376U32A-107

Editorial Address: Greater London House, Hampstead Road, LONDON, NW1 7EJ **Tel:** 020 7728 3774
Email: david.brownsey-joyce@emap.com
Web site: http://www.lgcplus.com
Publisher: EMAP Insight
Date Launched: 1994
Frequency of update: Daily
Website Access: Paid
Editor: David Brownsey-Joyce
Summary of Content: Website containing news, analysis and research information concerning local government.
Readership/Target Audience: Aimed at local government officers and elected members, along with the local government supply chain.
BUSINESS: LOCAL GOVERNMENT, LEISURE & RECREATION: Local Government

LIBRARY LINK
40867U60B-55

Formerly: Library Management
Editorial Address: Howard House, Wagon Lane, BINGLEY, BD16 1WA **Tel:** 01274 777700 **Fax:** 01274 785200
Email: lthorley@emeraldinsight.com
Web site: http://www.emeraldinsight.com/librarians/index.htm
Publisher: Emerald Group Publishing Ltd
Frequency of update: 6 times a year
Website Access: Free
Editor: Lynn Thorley
Summary of Content: Website discussing strategy and innovative developments in the management of libraries and information services.
Readership/Target Audience: Aimed at librarians and information professionals.
BUSINESS: PUBLISHING: Libraries

LIGHT READING
623226U5E-487

Editorial Address: 42 Hookfield, EPSOM, KT19 8JG
Tel: 020 8224 8268
Email: editors@lightreading.com
Web site: http://www.lightreading.com
Publisher: Light Reading Inc
Date Launched: 2000
Frequency of update: Daily
Website Access: Free
Traffic Figures: 700,000 Unique Users (per month Publisher's Statement)
Editor: Ray Le Maistre
Summary of Content: Website covering technologies used in the next generation Internet infrastructures.
Readership/Target Audience: Aimed at carriers, vendors and investors.
BUSINESS: COMPUTERS & AUTOMATION: Data Transmission

LINCOLNSHIRE MATTERS
1881650U72J-393

Email: comments@lincolnshire-matters.co.uk
Web site: http://www.lincolnshire-matters.co.uk
Frequency of update: Daily

Summary of Content: Website created to help people who care about local issues. Whether you need access to useful information, want to highlight a particular topic to other people, discuss ideas with like minded individuals or just show your support and keep up to date with current affairs in your area, Lincolnshire Matters is the place for you.
Readership/Target Audience: Aimed at residents in the local area of Lincolnshire.
LOCAL NEWSPAPERS: Community Newsletters

LIQUIDS AND GAS HANDLING
1775304U19F-686

Editorial Address: Hesketh House, 3 School Road, SALE, M33 7XY **Tel:** 01732 773268 **Fax:** 01732 365676
Email: it.marketing@itmagazine.uk.com
Web site: http://www.liquidsandgashandling.co.uk
Publisher: New Wave Publishing
Frequency of update: Weekly
Website Access: Free
Editor: Mark Simms
Summary of Content: Website covering the engineering components, mechanical and processing products involved in storage, packaging, handling and transportation of liquids and gas.
Readership/Target Audience: Aimed at those involved in manufacturing, processing, storage, handling and distribution of liquids or gas.
BUSINESS: ENGINEERING & MACHINERY: Production & Mechanical Engineering

LISBURN MATTERS
1881651U72J-394

Email: comments@lisburn-matters.co.uk
Web site: http://www.lisburn-matters.co.uk
Frequency of update: Daily
Summary of Content: Website created to help people who care about local issues. Whether you need access to useful information, want to highlight a particular topic to other people, discuss ideas with like minded individuals or just show your support and keep up to date with current affairs in your area, Lisburn Matters is the place for you.
Readership/Target Audience: Aimed at residents in the local area of Lisburn.
LOCAL NEWSPAPERS: Community Newsletters

THE LITERATEUR MAGAZINE
1895150U84A-470

Editorial Address: 35 Delta Road, WORCESTER PARK, KT4 7HP **Tel:** 07754 835344
Email: editor@literateur.com
Web site: http://www.literateur.com
Date Launched: 2009
Frequency of update: Quarterly
Website Access: Free
Editor: Kumiko Toda
Summary of Content: Online publication featuring interviews with major figures in the literary world, articles on a broad range of subjects, book reviews of recent publications and stories and poems.
Readership/Target Audience: Aimed at anyone with an interest in literature.
CONSUMER: THE ARTS & LITERARY: Arts

LIVE LISTINGS
1644304U90-929

Editorial Address: 102 Mallinson Road, Battersea, LONDON, SW11 1BN **Tel:** 020 7207 2734
Fax: 020 7207 6503
Email: all3mags@yahoo.co.uk
Web site: http://www.livelistingsmag.com
Publisher: Barb Wire Enterprises Ltd
Date Launched: 2000
Frequency of update: 6 times a year
Website Access: Free
Editor: Barbara Campbell
Summary of Content: Website covering features, events, news, business and entertainment, all with a mainstream and multicultural slant.
Readership/Target Audience: Aimed at men and women aged between 18 and 35 plus years old.
CONSUMER: ETHNIC

LIVERPOOL CONFIDENTIAL
1790416U80C-5378

Editorial Address: 208 Vanilla Factory, 39 Fleet Street, LIVERPOOL, L1 4AR **Tel:** 0151 708 0948
Email: angies@liverpoolconfidential.co.uk
Web site: http://www.liverpoolconfidential.com
Publisher: 2m Media
Date Launched: 2006
Frequency of update: Daily
Website Access: Free
Traffic Figures: 82,192 Unique Users (per month Publisher's Statement)
Editor: Angie Sammons

Summary of Content: Website covering bars, restaurants and cafes, childcare, clubs, events, health, hotels, lifestyle, property, shopping, competitions and offers.
Readership/Target Audience: Aimed at residents, visitors and businesses in Merseyside.
CONSUMER: RURAL & REGIONAL INTEREST: Regional Interest English Counties

LIVERPOOL MATTERS
1881652U72J-395

Email: comments@liverpool-matters.co.uk
Web site: http://www.liverpool-matters.co.uk
Frequency of update: Daily
Summary of Content: Website created to help people who care about local issues. Whether you need access to useful information, want to highlight a particular topic to other people, discuss ideas with like minded individuals or just show your support and keep up to date with current affairs in your area, Liverpool Matters is the place for you.
Readership/Target Audience: Aimed at residents in the local area of Liverpool.
LOCAL NEWSPAPERS: Community Newsletters

LIVERPOOL.COM
1792735U89C-1095

Editorial Address: PO Box 48, Old Hall Street, LIVERPOOL, L69 3EB **Tel:** 0151 330 4932 **Fax:** 0151 472 2474
Email: david.lloyd@liverpool.com
Web site: http://www.liverpool.com
Publisher: Trinity Mirror
Date Launched: 2006
Frequency of update: Daily
Website Access: Free
Editor: Patricia Caliskan
Summary of Content: Website covering arts, entertainment and events across Merseyside, Cheshire and North East Wales.
Readership/Target Audience: Aimed at 18 to 45 year olds interested in going out and about in the region.
CONSUMER: HOLIDAYS & TRAVEL: Entertainment Guides

LLM DIRECTORY
1896985U88-1

Editorial Address: Press releases by email only
Email: editordir@llmdirectory.com
Web site: http://www.LLMDirectory.com
Publisher: Edutech Media Ltd
Frequency of update: Daily
Website Access: Free
Editor: Editorial Department
Summary of Content: Website featuring a directory of Master of Laws and other law courses, law school profiles, news and articles on legal study and training; scholarship information, an events calendar, a career and jobs section, as well as a community forum.
Readership/Target Audience: Current and prospective students, graduates, alumni, human resource department, career advisors and recruiters.
CONSUMER: EDUCATION

LOAN DISTRIBUTOR
1820189U1A-342

Editorial Address: St. Giles House, 50 Poland Street, LONDON, W1F 7AX **Tel:** 020 7970 6319 **Fax:** 020 7970 4906
Email: natalie.martin@centaur.co.uk
Publisher: Centaur Media Plc
Date Launched: 2007
Frequency of update: Daily
Website Access: Paid
Editor: Natalie Martin
Summary of Content: Website covering secured lending, commercial and bridging finance and debt management.
Readership/Target Audience: Aimed at finance brokers, mortgage intermediaries and the secured loans industry.
BUSINESS: FINANCE & ECONOMICS

LOCAL GOVERNMENT CHRONICLE
1868586U32A-310

Formerly: LGC Local Government Chronicle
Editorial Address: Greater London House, Hampstead Road, LONDON, NW1 7EJ **Tel:** 020 7728 5000
Email: lgcnews@emap.com
Web site: http://www.lgcplus.com
Frequency of update: Daily
Traffic Figures: 27,000 Unique Users (per month Publisher's Statement)
Summary of Content: Provides local government news and local government jobs across England, Wales, Scotland and Northern Ireland: policy, social care, planning, finance, housing, environment.
BUSINESS: LOCAL GOVERNMENT, LEISURE & RECREATION: Local Government

LOCAL GOVERNMENT MANAGER
1668043U32A-258

Editorial Address: 1 Giltspur Street, LONDON, EC1A 9DD
Tel: 020 7294 2470 **Fax:** 020 7294 2402
Email: editorial@i-l-m.com
Web site: http://www.i-l-m.com
Publisher: Institute of Leadership & Management
Frequency of update: Monthly
Website Access: Paid
Editor: Jennifer Churchill
Summary of Content: Website focusing on leadership and management skills and issues faced by local government managers.
Readership/Target Audience: Aimed at managers in local government.
BUSINESS: LOCAL GOVERNMENT, LEISURE & RECREATION: Local Government

LOCAL HISTORY ONLINE
623099U94X-76

Formerly: Local History Magazine Online
Editorial Address: 3 Devonshire Promenade, Lenton, NOTTINGHAM, NG7 2DS **Tel:** 0115 970 6473
Email: news@local-history.co.uk
Web site: http://www.local-history.co.uk
Publisher: The Local History Press Ltd
Date Launched: 1997
Frequency of update: Weekly
Website Access: Free
Editor: Robert Howard
Summary of Content: Website covering local history, with regular updated news and calendar sections, directories of local history organisations and course providers and an online bookshop.
Readership/Target Audience: Aimed at anyone interested in becoming involved in local history.
Other Features: Features include archiving.
CONSUMER: OTHER CLASSIFICATIONS: Miscellaneous

LOCALMOTORING.COM
1825784U77A-605

Editorial Address: Newcastle House, 135 Liverpool Street, NEWCASTLE-UNDER-LYME, ST15 9HD **Tel:** 01782 626626
Email: john@localmotoring.com
Web site: http://www.localmotoring.com
Date Launched: 2007
Frequency of update: Daily
Website Access: Free
Editor: John Swift
Summary of Content: Website covering new and used cars, learner drivers, fleet and contract hire, motorbikes, caravans and motor homes, vans, car accessories, car repairs and garage services, insurance and car finance.
Readership/Target Audience: Aimed at those in need motor related information in the Midlands.
CONSUMER: MOTORING & CYCLING: Motoring

LOGISTICS & HANDLING
1850502U10-226

Editorial Address: Latimer House, 189 High Street, POTTERS BAR, EN6 5DA **Tel:** 01707 664200
Fax: 01707 664800
Email: editor@logisticshandling.com
Web site: http://www.logisticshandling.com
Publisher: Interactive Business Communications Ltd
Frequency of update: Daily
Website Access: Free
Traffic Figures: 35,000 Unique Users (per month Publisher's Statement)
Editor: Keith Saward
Summary of Content: Website covering the logistics and handling sector.
Readership/Target Audience: Aimed at professionals who specify, purchase and use material handling systems and other supporting products to automate their supply chains.
BUSINESS: MATERIALS HANDLING

LONDON CONSTRUCTION NOW
1809327U4E-444

Editorial Address: For all contact details see main record, Construction Now
Frequency of update: 250 times a year
BUSINESS: ARCHITECTURE & BUILDING: Building

LONDON DIARY ONLINE
1622330U89C-953

Formerly: London Diary
Editorial Address: Does not accept PR by mail.
Tel: 020 7121 0000
Email: news@londondiary.ltd.uk
Web site: http://www.londoneventslist.co.uk
Date Launched: 1998
Frequency of update: Daily

Internet Media

Website Access: Free
Editor: Michael Wint
Summary of Content: Website covering listings of events, parties, promotions and entertainment news.
Readership/Target Audience: Aimed at corporate, media people surfing the net during office hours.
CONSUMER: HOLIDAYS & TRAVEL: Entertainment Guides

LONDON ESSENCE MAGAZINE
1799438U80B-428

Editorial Address: 6 Forsyth Gardens, Kennington, LONDON, SE17 3NE **Tel:** 020 7582 2581
Email: info@londonessence.com
Web site: http://www.londonessence.com
Publisher: London Essence Magazine Ltd
Date Launched: 2007
Frequency of update: Monthly
Website Access: Free
Editor: Caroline Dubanchet
Summary of Content: Magazine covering new trends in London, events, festivals, fairs, theatre, art, music, culture, fashion, shopping, nightlife, food and drink, property, finance and sport.
Readership/Target Audience: Aimed at the European travellers and expatriates wanting to know more about London, its places of interest, new and alternative trends and sub-cultures.
CONSUMER: RURAL & REGIONAL INTEREST: Regional Interest Greater London

LONDON IRISH
1663830U75C-471

Editorial Address: The Avenue, SUNBURY-ON-THAMES, TW16 5EQ **Tel:** 01932 783034 **Fax:** 01932 784462
Email: paddy.lennon@london-irish.com
Web site: http://www.london-irish.com
Frequency of update: Daily
Website Access: Free
Traffic Figures: 34,000 Unique Users (per month Publisher's Statement)
Editor: Paddy Lennon
Summary of Content: Official site of London Irish Rugby Club covering fixtures, match reports, player profiles and general rugby union news.
Readership/Target Audience: Aimed at fans of London Irish and general rugby union fans.
CONSUMER: SPORT: Rugby

LONDON LOOP WEEKEND
1810699U89C-1101

Editorial Address: 84-86 Regent Street, LONDON, W1B 5RR **Tel:** 020 7734 2303
Email: editor@londonlloopweekend.com
Web site: http://londonloop.tfl.gov.uk/ezine
Publisher: The Forward Group
Date Launched: 2006
Frequency of update: Weekly. Sent out on Thursday
Website Access: Free
Editor: Alison Carswell
Summary of Content: Electronic newsletter covering weekly events in London and travel updates on the tube and buses.
Readership/Target Audience: Aimed at Londoners aged between 25 and 50 who use public transport.
CONSUMER: HOLIDAYS & TRAVEL: Entertainment Guides

THE LONDON MORNING PAPER
1668064U82-268

Editorial Address: 57 Nutbourne Street, LONDON, W10 4HW **Tel:** 020 8968 0742
Email: editor@london-morning-paper.co.uk
Web site: http://www.london-morning-paper.co.uk
Date Launched: 1999
Frequency of update: Daily
Website Access: Free
Traffic Figures: 2,690 Unique Users (per week Publisher's Statement)
Editor: James Beam van Etten
Summary of Content: Website covering the digital signage industry.
Readership/Target Audience: Aimed at those with an interest in digital marketing.
CONSUMER: CURRENT AFFAIRS & POLITICS

LONDON SALSA SCENE
1691980U76G-302

Editorial Address: 23 Padua Road, LONDON, SE20 8HF
Tel: 020 8778 2215
Email: editor@londonsalsascene.co.uk
Web site: http://www.londonsalsascene.co.uk
Publisher: Knightwriter Publishing
Date Launched: 2005

Frequency of update: Daily
Website Access: Free
Editor: Lee Knights
Summary of Content: Magazine about the London salsa scene covering dance, including the full range of dance genres, dance holidays, breaks, live and recorded music and lifestyle, night life, theatre, dancehalls, etc. Largely, but not exclusively Latin dance and music, open to a range of dance and musical genres, new releases, live gigs in London and outside, concerts, clubs, interviews, special events, restaurant reviews and eating out as well as related entertainment news.
Readership/Target Audience: Aimed at those interested in Latin music, eating out and the Latin lifestyle in London, the South East and beyond.
Other Features: Regular bi-monthly newsletters, dance, music, arts and eating out.
CONSUMER: MUSIC & PERFORMING ARTS: Dance

LONDON SE1
1613627U80B-387

Editorial Address: 27 Blackfriars Road, LONDON, SE1 8NY
Tel: 020 7633 0766 **Fax:** 020 7401 2521
Email: james.hatts@banksidepress.com
Web site: http://www.london-se1.co.uk
Publisher: Bankside Press
Date Launched: 1998
Frequency of update: Daily
Website Access: Free
Traffic Figures: 100,000 Unique Users (per month Publisher's Statement)
Editor: James Hatts
Summary of Content: Website covering news, exhibitions, eating out, entertainment, art, books, pubs, education, theatre, property, health, leisure and shopping.
Readership/Target Audience: Aimed at those living in or working in the SE1 area of London.
Other Features: Message board and email newsletter.
CONSUMER: RURAL & REGIONAL INTEREST: Regional Interest Greater London

THE LONDON SOURCE
1835839U11A-228

Editorial Address: Progressive House, 2 Maidstone Road, SIDCUP, DA14 5HZ **Tel:** 0845 000 2500
Email: news@thelondonsource.co.uk
Web site: http://www.thelondonsource.co.uk
Publisher: Dewberry Redpoint Ltd
Date Launched: 2006
Frequency of update: Daily
Website Access: Free
Editor: Clare Riley; **Web Editor:** Clare Riley
Summary of Content: Website covering top end restaurants, hotels and bars in London. Featuring menu monitors, recopies, design case studies and recruitment.
Readership/Target Audience: Aimed at restaurateurs, caterers, pub managers and hoteliers.
BUSINESS: CATERING: Catering, Hotels & Restaurants

THE LONDON THEATRE GUIDE
46082U76B-109_5

Editorial Address: 32 Rose Street, LONDON, WC2E 9ET
Tel: 020 7557 6700 **Fax:** 020 7557 6788
Email: enquiries@solttma.co.uk
Web site: http://www.officiallondontheatre.co.uk
Publisher: The Society of London Theatre
Frequency of update: 26 times a year
Website Access: Free
Traffic Figures: 175,000 Unique Users (Publisher's Statement)
Editor: Matthew Amer; **Web Editor:** Matthew Amer
Summary of Content: Website for the Society of London Theatre's listings of all current West End shows. Includes performance start and finishing times, price ranges, travel information, theatreland map and general information. Also current theatre and related products and services.
Readership/Target Audience: Aimed at theatre-goers.
Other Features: Other features include an email newsletter.
CONSUMER: MUSIC & PERFORMING ARTS: Theatre

LONDON WASPS
1663720U75C-463

Editorial Address: Twyford Avenue Sports Ground, Twyford Avenue, LONDON, W3 9QA **Tel:** 020 8896 4890
Fax: 020 8993 2621
Email: fiona.hackett@wasps.co.uk
Web site: http://www.wasps.co.uk
Frequency of update: Daily
Website Access: Free
Editor: Fiona Hackett
Summary of Content: Official site of London Wasps Rugby Union Club covering fixtures, match reports, player profiles and club news.
Readership/Target Audience: Aimed at fans of London Wasps.

Other Features: Message board, newsletter, On-line merchandising.
CONSUMER: SPORT: Rugby

LONDONDANCE.COM
1834263U76G-303

Editorial Address: Sadlers Wells, Rosebery Avenue, LONDON, EC1R 4TN **Tel:** 020 7863 8118
Email: editor@londondance.com
Web site: http://www.londondance.com
Date Launched: 2001
Frequency of update: Daily
Website Access: Free
Traffic Figures: 50,000 Unique Users (per month Publisher's Statement)
Editor: Carmel Smith
Summary of Content: Website covering all aspects of dance in London. Which includes performance listings, reviews, classes and workshops, video clips, directory of venues, companies, rehearsal spaces and dance organisations, job watch page and notice boards.
Readership/Target Audience: Aimed at those interested in dance both audiences and professionals.
CONSUMER: MUSIC & PERFORMING ARTS: Dance

LONDON-EATING
1789963U74P-952

Editorial Address: 23-25 Queen Elizabeth Street, LONDON, SE1 2LP **Tel:** 07971 200165 **Fax:** 020 7336 6656
Email: nick@city-eating.com
Web site: http://www.london-eating.co.uk
Frequency of update: Daily
Website Access: Free
Editor: Nick Harman
Summary of Content: Website covering restaurants in London and featuring reviews by members of the public and editorial house reviews, cookbook reviews, interviews with chefs, wine, special offers and competitions.
Readership/Target Audience: Aimed at London's diners.
CONSUMER: WOMEN'S INTEREST CONSUMER MAGAZINES: Food & Cookery

LONDON-GUIDES.CO.UK
1785448U89C-1089

Editorial Address: Brookcroft House, 26 Second Avenue, LONDON, E17 9QH **Tel:** 020 8923 0918 **Fax:** 020 8521 9548
Email: info@london-guides.co.uk
Web site: http://www.london-guides.co.uk
Frequency of update: Annual. Updated irregularly
Website Access: Free
Editor: Roy McKenzie
Summary of Content: Leisure and business guide to London.
Readership/Target Audience: Aimed at leisure and business travellers to London.
CONSUMER: HOLIDAYS & TRAVEL: Entertainment Guides

LONDON.HOUSINGNEWS.CO.UK
1776299U4D-416

Editorial Address: For all contact details see main edition, housingnews.co.uk
Website Access: Free
BUSINESS: ARCHITECTURE & BUILDING: Planning & Housing

LONDONKIDZ
1853590U74C-881

Editorial Address: PR by email only
Email: grownups@londonkidz.co.uk
Web site: http://www.londonkidz.co.uk
Publisher: City Kidz Media
Date Launched: 2003
Frequency of update: Daily
Website Access: Free
Traffic Figures: 10,000 Unique Users (per month Publisher's Statement)
Summary of Content: Website covering London area venues and events suitable for families and children.
Readership/Target Audience: Aimed at parents, carers and relatives in the London area.
Other Features: Newsletter, family friendly London area event listings including venue, date, time, text, picture and website
CONSUMER: WOMEN'S INTEREST CONSUMER MAGAZINES: Home & Family

LONDONNET
628926U80B-126_50

Editorial Address: Hopping Wood Farm, Robin Hood Way, LONDON, SW20 0AB **Tel:** 020 8949 5363
Fax: 020 8949 5364
Email: editorial@londonnet.co.uk
Web site: http://www.londonnet.co.uk

Publisher: London Net Limited
Date Launched: 1996
Frequency of update: Daily
Website Access: Free
Traffic Figures: 650,000 Unique Users (per month Publisher's Statement)
Editor: Peter Clee
Summary of Content: Website covering information for Greater London featuring entertainment, theatre, cinema and classical listings, travel, accommodation and events.
Readership/Target Audience: Aimed at those living in London and visitors to the city.
Other Features: Features include archiving, buyer's guide, recruitment, discussion forums and free classified advertising.
CONSUMER: RURAL & REGIONAL INTEREST: Regional Interest Greater London

LOVE FOOD LOVE DRINK
1893471U74P-965
Editorial Address: PR by email only **Tel:** 07504 472909
Email: consumer@lovefoodlovedrink.co.uk
Web site: http://www.lovefoodlovedrink.co.uk
Date Launched: 2008
Frequency of update: Daily. Newsletter 52xy
Website Access: Free
Traffic Figures: 18,000 Unique Users (Publisher's Statement)
Editor: Jamie Gandhi
Summary of Content: Website taking a fun and accessible look at the world of food. Covering food events, restaurant news and reviews, food and drink product news and reviews, competitions and special offers.
Readership/Target Audience: Aimed at those interested in innovative home dining and products as well as cool restaurants and events.
CONSUMER: WOMEN'S INTEREST CONSUMER MAGAZINES: Food & Cookery

LOVEYOURHAIR.COM
1862244U74H-309
Editorial Address: 9th Floor, Tower House, Fairfax Street, BRISTOL, BS1 3BN **Tel:** 0117 927 9009 **Fax:** 0117 934 9008
Email: news@yourhair.co.uk
Web site: http://www.loveyourhair.com
Publisher: Origin Publishing Ltd
Date Launched: 2008
Frequency of update: Daily
Website Access: Free
Editor: Michelle Tiernan
Summary of Content: Website covering interaction with top stylists, videos on insider secrets to great hair, celebrity style news, competitions and a search for hairstyles, salons and products.
Readership/Target Audience: Aimed at everyone interested in hair beauty and health, mainly at women.
CONSUMER: WOMEN'S INTEREST CONSUMER MAGAZINES: Hair & Beauty

LOYALTY MAGAZINE
35728U2F-42
Formerly: Loyalty Online
Editorial Address: 3A Market Place, UPPINGHAM, LE15 9QH **Tel:** 01572 820088 **Fax:** 01572 820099
Email: liam@cm-media.net
Web site: http://www.loyaltymagazine.com
Publisher: C&M Publications Ltd
Date Launched: 1995
Frequency of update: Daily
Website Access: Paid
Traffic Figures: 8,000 Unique Users (Publisher's Statement)
Editor: Liam McLoughlin
Summary of Content: Online magazine covering the latest news and issues on customer retention, loyalty schemes and customer relationship management (CRM) including business to business, net based programmes, e-commerce and employee loyalty.
Readership/Target Audience: Read by marketing and finance directors, managing directors, marketing personnel, IT call centre managers, data handling departments and customer retention managers in all sectors.
BUSINESS: COMMUNICATIONS, ADVERTISING & MARKETING: Selling

LUTON TODAY
634133U80C-3670
Formerly: luton online
Editorial Address: Media House, 39 Upper George Street, LUTON, LU1 2RD **Tel:** 01582 700666 **Fax:** 01582 700660
Email: editorial@heraldpost.co.uk
Web site: http://www.lutontoday.co.uk
Date Launched: 2000
Frequency of update: Daily
Website Access: Free
Editor: John Francis

Summary of Content: Website containing news, information and features about the local area.
Readership/Target Audience: Read by local residents, visitors and expatriates.
Other Features: Features include recruitment, a chat forum and archiving.
CONSUMER: RURAL & REGIONAL INTEREST: Regional Interest English Counties

M2PRESSWIRE
711356U18B-980
Editorial Address: PR by email only **Tel:** 020 7047 0200
Email: m2pw@m2.com
Web site: http://www.m2.com
Publisher: M2 Communications Ltd
Date Launched: 1994
Frequency of update: Daily
Website Access: Paid
Editor: Jamie Ayres
Summary of Content: Website providing daily news and information on the telecommunication industry and IT marketplace.
Readership/Target Audience: Aimed at telecommunication and IT industry professionals, users and buyers.
BUSINESS: ELECTRONICS: Telecommunications

MACHINEBUILDING.NET
1809579U19A-564
Editorial Address: PR by email only **Tel:** 01767 677620
Email: editor@machinebuilding.net
Web site: http://www.machinebuilding.net
Publisher: Damte ltd
Date Launched: 2006
Frequency of update: Daily
Website Access: Free
Traffic Figures: 40,000 Unique Users (per month Publisher's Statement)
Editor: Jonathan Severn
Summary of Content: Website featuring products and systems for machinery and industrial automation, focusing on new products and innovative applications. Offers guidance on product selection, industry issues and legislation.
Readership/Target Audience: Aimed at designers, design managers and engineers who design, build or modify machinery, including those working with specialist machine-building companies, system integrators and manufacturing companies with in-house facilities.
Other Features: Directory of suppliers, brochure requests and monthly email newsletter, also software and book reviews.
BUSINESS: ENGINEERING & MACHINERY

MACWORLD UK (ONLINE)
626299U78E-41
Editorial Address: 4th Floor, 101 Euston Road, LONDON, NW1 2RA **Tel:** 020 7071 3615
Email: news@macworld.co.uk
Web site: http://www.macworld.co.uk
Publisher: IDG (International Data Group)
Date Launched: 1995
Frequency of update: Daily
Website Access: Free
Editor: Nick Spence; **Editor-in-Chief:** Mark Hattersley
Summary of Content: Website covering all aspects of Mac hardware and software, including reviews, blogs and news.
Readership/Target Audience: Aimed at UK Mac users.
CONSUMER: CONSUMER ELECTRONICS: Home Computing

MAD.CO.UK
623900U2A-108_50
Editorial Address: St. Giles House, 50 Poland Street, LONDON, W1F 7AX **Tel:** 020 7970 4000 **Fax:** 020 7970 4925
Email: branwell.johnson@mad.co.uk
Web site: http://www.mad.co.uk
Publisher: Centaur Media Plc
Date Launched: 1999
Frequency of update: Daily
Website Access: Paid
Traffic Figures: 118,318 Unique Users (01/10/2007 To 31/10/2007 ABC/Electronic)
Editor: Branwell Johnson
Summary of Content: Website covering information, news, jobs and comment for the marketing, media, advertising and design industries.
Readership/Target Audience: Aimed at professionals in the marketing, media, advertising and design industries.
Other Features: Recruitment, advertising opportunities and blogs.
BUSINESS: COMMUNICATIONS, ADVERTISING & MARKETING

MAIZE ABSTRACTS
37818U21B-720
Editorial Address: Nosworthy Way, WALLINGFORD, OX10 8DE **Tel:** 01491 832111 **Fax:** 01491 829198
Email: cabi@cabi.org
Web site: http://www.cabi-publishing.org
Publisher: CABI
Frequency of update: Weekly
Website Access: Paid
Editor: Halina Dawson
Summary of Content: Website covering scientific literature regarding maize, genetics, breeding and genetic resources, biotechnology, taxonomy, agronomy, physiology, biochemistry, plant protection including pests, diseases and weeds, harvesting, storage, agricultural engineering, nutrition, food technology, economics and rural development.
Readership/Target Audience: Aimed at academic and government research institutes, seed, agro-chemical, oil-producing, snack food and plant breeding companies.
BUSINESS: AGRICULTURE & FARMING: Agriculture - Supplies & Services

MALEHEALTH
1732841U86C-728
Editorial Address: 32-36 Loman Street, LONDON, SE1 0EH **Tel:** 020 7922 7908 **Fax:** 020 7388 4477
Email: jim.pollard@menshealthforum.org.uk
Web site: http://www.malehealth.co.uk
Publisher: Men's Health Forum
Frequency of update: Weekly
Website Access: Free
Traffic Figures: 150,000 Unique Users (2007/2008 Publisher's Statement)
Editor: Jim Pollard
Summary of Content: Website offering free, independent health information for men of all ages covering the key health problems that affect males. With tips, expert advice and details of how men can check their own health and use health professionals more effectively.
Readership/Target Audience: Aimed at men wishing to lead healthier and happier lives.
CONSUMER: ADULT & GAY MAGAZINES: Men's Lifestyle Magazines

MANAGEMENT-ISSUES.COM
1682043U14A-546
Formerly: Management Issues
Editorial Address: New Broad Street House, 35 New Broad Street, LONDON, EC2M 1NH **Tel:** 020 7183 6000
Email: editor@management-issues.com
Web site: http://www.management-issues.com
Publisher: Management-Issues.com Ltd
Date Launched: 2000
Frequency of update: 260 times a year
Website Access: Free
Traffic Figures: 8,000 Unique Users (per day Publisher's Statement)
Editor: David Bosdet
Summary of Content: Online resource of information, news and views on workplace and management issues.
Readership/Target Audience: Aimed managers, directors and HR professionals.
Other Features: Weekly newsletter, e-books, white papers, podcasting and video.
BUSINESS: COMMERCE, INDUSTRY & MANAGEMENT

MANCHESTER MATTERS
1881654U72J-397
Email: comments@manchester-matters.co.uk
Web site: http://www.manchester-matters.co.uk
Frequency of update: Daily
Summary of Content: Website created to help people who care about local issues. Whether you need access to useful information, want to highlight a particular topic to other people, discuss ideas with like minded individuals or just show your support and keep up to date with current affairs in your area, Manchester Matters is the place for you.
Readership/Target Audience: Aimed at residents in the local area of Manchester.
LOCAL NEWSPAPERS: Community Newsletters

THE MANCHESTER REVIEW
1864962U84A-467
Editorial Address: University of Manchester, Oxford Road, MANCHESTER, M13 9PL **Tel:** 0161 275 3167
Email: simon.richardson@manchester.ac.uk
Web site: http://www.themanchesterreview.co.uk
Publisher: Centre for New Writing
Frequency of update: Half-yearly
Editor: Simon Richardson
Summary of Content: Website covering literary and art reviews with new music, public debates, video pieces, visual art, fiction and poetry.
Readership/Target Audience: Aimed at art enthusiasts.
CONSUMER: THE ARTS & LITERARY: Arts

Internet Media

MANCHESTERCONFIDENTIAL.COM
1697032U80C-5282

Formerly: Manchester Confidential
Editorial Address: 11-13 Spear Street, MANCHESTER, M1 1JU **Tel:** 0161 228 0044
Email: jonathans@planetconfidential.co.uk
Web site: http://www.manchesterconfidential.com
Publisher: 2M Media Ltd
Date Launched: 1994
Frequency of update: Daily
Website Access: Free
Traffic Figures: 135,000 Unique Users (per month Publisher's Statement)
Editor: Jonathan Schofield
Summary of Content: Website covering Manchester lifestyle, property, recruitment, health and beauty, what's on and food and drink.
Readership/Target Audience: Aimed at affluent consumers who live or work in Manchester.
CONSUMER: RURAL & REGIONAL INTEREST: Regional Interest English Counties

MANDADEALS.CO.UK
1808492U1A-340

Editorial Address: 154 Great Charles Street, Queensway, BIRMINGHAM, B3 3HN **Tel:** 0121 248 0464
Email: patrizia.rossi@vitessemedia.co.uk
Web site: http://www.mandadeals.co.uk
Publisher: Vitesse Media plc
Date Launched: 2007
Frequency of update: Daily
Website Access: Free
Editor: Patrizia Rossi
Summary of Content: Website featuring an updated real-time daily deal news service, features and deals listing, with the latest venture capital and private equity transactions. The site helps identify potential deals, deal teams and different funding methods.
Readership/Target Audience: Aimed at advisers, funders and management teams.
BUSINESS: FINANCE & ECONOMICS

MANSIZED
1744949U86C-730

Editorial Address: PO Box 55106, LONDON, N12 9WU **Tel:** 020 8445 8041
Email: will@mansized.co.uk
Web site: http://www.mansized.co.uk
Publisher: Soma Digital Ltd
Date Launched: 2006
Frequency of update: Daily
Website Access: Free
Traffic Figures: 127,000 Unique Users (per month Publisher's Statement)
Editor: Will Callaghan
Summary of Content: Online magazine for men with news updated as it happens, reviews of DVDs, movies, games and gadgets and answers from qualified experts.
Readership/Target Audience: Aimed at men aged 18 and over who have more than just sport, cars and girls on their minds.
Other Features: Message board and newsletter.
CONSUMER: ADULT & GAY MAGAZINES: Men's Lifestyle Magazines

MANUFACTURING CHEMIST
1925996U13-208

Editorial Address: Poulton House, 8 Shepherdess Walk, LONDON, N1 7LB **Tel:** 020 7490 0049 **Fax:** 020 7549 8622
Email: hilarya@hpcimedia.com
Web site: http://www.manufacturingchemist.com
Publisher: HPCi Media Ltd
Frequency of update: Daily
Website Access: Free
Summary of Content: Website covering all aspects of the pharmaceutical industry, including development, formulation, processing and outsourcing.
Readership/Target Audience: Aimed at manufacturers of pharmaceuticals.
BUSINESS: CHEMICALS

MANUFACTURING COMPUTER SOLUTIONS
37694U19J-96_50

Editorial Address: Hawley Mill, Hawley Road, DARTFORD, DA2 7TJ **Tel:** 01322 221144 **Fax:** 01322 221188
Email: btinham@findlay.co.uk
Web site: http://www.mcsolutions.co.uk
Publisher: Findlay Media Ltd
Frequency of update: Daily
Website Access: Free
Editor: Brian Tinham
Summary of Content: Website focusing on IT and computer systems used in manufacturing, engineering and process

companies for manufacturing, engineering and business management.
Readership/Target Audience: Read by directors, managers and senior engineers responsible for the IT implementation within UK manufacturing companies.
BUSINESS: ENGINEERING & MACHINERY: CAD & CIM (Computer Integrated Manufacture)

MANUFACTURING INDUSTRY DIRECTORY
1912967U19F-688

Editorial Address: 18 Generator Hall, Electric Wharf, COVENTRY, CV1 4JL **Tel:** 0870 199 4044
Fax: 0870 777 4360
Email: enquiries@industrydirectory.co.uk
Web site: http://www.industrydirectory.co.uk
Publisher: Simply Marcomms
Frequency of update: Daily
Website Access: Free
Editor: Kirstie Colledge
Summary of Content: Directory containing the latest news stories for the UK Manufacturing industry. Includes news archives.
Readership/Target Audience: Aimed at Manufacturing professionals, suppliers to the Manufacturing industry, Manufacturing Industry PR & Marketing firms.
BUSINESS: ENGINEERING & MACHINERY: Production & Mechanical Engineering

MANUFACTURINGTALK
652138U19F-673

Formerly: manufacturingtalk.com
Editorial Address: PR by email only **Tel:** 020 7970 4920
Email: news@manufacturingtalk.com
Web site: http://www.manufacturingtalk.com
Publisher: Pro-Talk Ltd
Date Launched: 2001
Frequency of update: Daily
Website Access: Free
Traffic Figures: 210,843 Unique Users (per month Publisher's Statement)
Editor: Mike Page
Summary of Content: Website containing the latest new product news for manufacturing, production and automation engineers.
Readership/Target Audience: Aimed at manufacturing, production and automation engineers.
BUSINESS: ENGINEERING & MACHINERY: Production & Mechanical Engineering

MARIECLAIRE.CO.UK
1829389U74A-1042

Editorial Address: Blue Fin Building, 110 Southwark Street, LONDON, SE1 0SU **Tel:** 020 3148 7472
Email: mconline@ipcmedia.com
Web site: http://www.marieclaire.co.uk
Publisher: IPC Southbank
Frequency of update: Daily
Website Access: Free
Traffic Figures: 468,000 Unique Users (per month Publisher's Statement)
Editor: Carla Bevan
Summary of Content: Website covering fashion, celebrity, beauty, health and news.
Readership/Target Audience: Aimed at professional women aged 20 years and over.
Other Features: Daily news letter.
CONSUMER: WOMEN'S INTEREST CONSUMER MAGAZINES: Women's Interest

THE MARINE CONSERVATION SOCIETY (MCS)
713841U57-36_70

Formerly: The Marine Conservation Society
Editorial Address: Unit 3, Wolf Business Park, ROSS-ON-WYE, HR9 5NB **Tel:** 01989 566017
Email: info@mcsuk.org
Web site: http://www.mcsuk.org
Date Launched: 2000
Frequency of update: Quarterly
Website Access: Free
(per day)
Editor: Richard Harrington
Summary of Content: Website covering information on the marine world. Includes projects, events, campaigns and links.
Readership/Target Audience: Aimed at marine biologists, scientists and those interested in marine life and science.
BUSINESS: ENVIRONMENT & POLLUTION

MARINER.CO.UK
48379U91A-77

Editorial Address: 12 Heathgate, Wickham Bishops, WITHAM, CM8 3NZ **Tel:** 01621 892755

Email: peter@travision.com
Web site: http://www.mariner.co.uk
Publisher: Travision Limited
Date Launched: 1997
Frequency of update: Daily
Website Access: Free
Editor: Peter Booth
Summary of Content: Website containing maritime news, information on clubs and associations and competition results. Also covers training, coastal and inland sailing activities web site hosting for Sailing Clubs and Class Associations.
Readership/Target Audience: Aimed at enthusiasts of water sports and activities.
CONSUMER: RECREATION & LEISURE: Boating & Yachting

MARKET PREDICT
1840765U1A-346

Editorial Address: PR by email only **Tel:** 020 8444 1651
Email: neil@marketpredict.com
Web site: http://www.marketpredict.com
Frequency of update: Daily
Website Access: Paid
Editor: Neil Behrmann
Summary of Content: Online publication covering financial markets including asset allocation, bonds, currencies, stocks, hedge funds and pensions.
Readership/Target Audience: Aimed at those working in the financial markets.
BUSINESS: FINANCE & ECONOMICS

MARKETING DIRECT
35527U2A-111_4

Editorial Address: 174 Hammersmith Road, LONDON, W6 7JP **Tel:** 020 8267 5000 **Fax:** 020 8267 4192
Email: noelle.mcelhatton@haymarket.com
Web site: http://www.brandrepublic.com/marketingdirect
Publisher: Haymarket Specialist Publications
Frequency of update: Daily
Website Access: Paid
Editor: Noelle McElhatton
Summary of Content: Website covering news and features on direct marketing.
Readership/Target Audience: Read by clients and direct marketing agency marketers.
BUSINESS: COMMUNICATIONS, ADVERTISING & MARKETING

MARKETING (UK)
1868703U2-1526

Editorial Address: 174 Hammersmith Road, LONDON, W6 8BS **Tel:** 020 8267 4567
Web site: http://www.marketingmagazine.co.uk
Frequency of update: Daily
Editor: Lucy Barrett
Summary of Content: Website covering information for its readers about the biggest and freshest news in the industry and delves into the issues behind the stories.
Readership/Target Audience: Aimed at readers who are interested in the marketing industry.
BUSINESS: COMMUNICATIONS, ADVERTISING & MARKETING

MARKETINGMAGAZINE.CO.UK
1895151U2A-706

Editorial Address: 174 Hammersmith Road, LONDON, W6 7JP **Tel:** 020 8267 5000
Email: bill.britt@haymarket.com
Web site: http://www.marketingmagazine.co.uk
Publisher: Haymarket Specialist Publications
Frequency of update: Daily
Website Access: Free
Traffic Figures: 80,000 Unique Users (per month Publisher's Statement)
Editor: Bill Britt
Summary of Content: Website covering news and features on key marketing issues.
Readership/Target Audience: Aimed at marketing directors and brand and product managers.
BUSINESS: COMMUNICATIONS, ADVERTISING & MARKETING

MARKETINGSERVICESTALK
1810479U2A-695

Editorial Address: PR by email only **Tel:** 020 7970 4920
Email: news@marketingservicestalk.com
Web site: http://www.marketingservicestalk.com
Publisher: Pro-Talk Ltd
Date Launched: 2007
Frequency of update: Daily
Website Access: Free
Editor: Lyndon White

Summary of Content: Website providing news and information for the marketing industry, features news releases, case studies and technical articles from manufacturers and service providers.
Readership/Target Audience: Aimed at marketing professionals worldwide.
Other Features: Email newsletter distributed on the 1st Monday of each month
BUSINESS: COMMUNICATIONS, ADVERTISING & MARKETING

MARKETWATCH
1691949U1R-369
Editorial Address: 10 Fleet Place, Limeburner Lane, LONDON, EC4M 7QN **Tel:** 020 7842 9424
Email: mwlondonbureau@dowjones.com
Web site: http://www.marketwatch.com
Frequency of update: Daily
Website Access: Free
Editor: Steve Goldstein
Summary of Content: Website covering financial market information and breaking business news.
Readership/Target Audience: Aimed at finance professionals and consumers.
BUSINESS: FINANCE & ECONOMICS: Financial Related

MARMALADYA.COM
1799102U80C-5397
Editorial Address: 65A Aylesford Street, LONDON, SW1V 3RJ **Tel:** 020 7834 0330
Email: info@marmaladya.com
Web site: http://www.marmaladya.com
Publisher: Marmaladya Ltd
Frequency of update: Weekly
Website Access: Free
Traffic Figures: 15,000 Unique Users (per week Publisher's Statement)
Editor: Lucy Hutchings
Summary of Content: Electronic newsletter covering women's lifestyle and local issues, people, bars and boutiques.
Readership/Target Audience: Aimed at women aged 25 to 40 years old in London as well as women in small businesses.
CONSUMER: RURAL & REGIONAL INTEREST: Regional Interest English Counties

MATLOCK MERCURY
629811U72B-751
Formerly: Matlock Today
Editorial Address: 4 Firs Parade, MATLOCK, DE4 3AS
Tel: 01629 762130 **Fax:** 01629 584270
Email: news@matlockmercury.co.uk
Web site: http://www.matlockmercury.co.uk
Publisher: Johnston Press plc
Frequency of update: Daily
Website Access: Free
Editor: News Desk
Summary of Content: Website containing news, sport, information and features about Matlock.
Readership/Target Audience: Read by residents and visitors to the local area.
Other Features: Features include recruitment and discussion forums.
LOCAL NEWSPAPERS: Local Newspapers English Counties

MAX POWER.CO.UK
713872U77A-282
Editorial Address: Media House, Lynchwood, Peterborough Business Park, PETERBOROUGH, PE2 6EA
Tel: 01733 468000 **Fax:** 01733 468217
Email: andrew.baxter@bauermedia.co.uk
Web site: http://www.maxpower.co.uk
Publisher: Bauer Consumer Media Ltd (Media House)
Date Launched: 2000
Frequency of update: Daily
Website Access: Free
Traffic Figures: 276,000 Unique Users (WebTrends)
Editor: Andrew Baxter; **Web Editor:** Andrew Baxter
Summary of Content: Website providing advice and information on how to modify your car, insurance and security and car components. Includes information on games, mobile phones and a cyber babes section.
Readership/Target Audience: Aimed at men between 18 to 35 years old interested in modified vehicles.
Other Features: Features include a chat forum, an e-mail newsletter, an events calendar and archiving.
CONSUMER: MOTORING & CYCLING: Motoring

MBA SPECTRUM
1786630U88C-177
Editorial Address: PR by email only **Tel:** 0871 989 8629
Email: editordir@mbaspectrum.com
Web site: http://www.mbaspectrum.com

Publisher: EFE International
Frequency of update: Daily
Website Access: Free
Summary of Content: Site covers MBA programs and higher education, MBA career and jobs, executive education and training, events calendar, student resources including scholarships, GMAT and language tests information, book reviews, computer store and other education and career related support.
Readership/Target Audience: Aimed at graduates, students, business professionals, personnel development managers, career advisors and university personnel.
Other Features: Course directory, study and university guide, events calendar and recruitment.
CONSUMER: EDUCATION: Careers

MBAINUK.COM
719197U14E-395
Editorial Address: PR by email only **Tel:** 0870 759 3697
Email: editordir@mbainuk.com
Web site: http://www.mbainuk.com
Publisher: EFE International
Date Launched: 1999
Frequency of update: Daily
Website Access: Free
Editor: Editorial Department
Summary of Content: Website containing information about MBA programmes and business courses, executive education and training courses, career tools, higher education fairs and events. Also covering aspects on leadership, entrepreneurship, global business, choosing the right career and other career related topics.
Readership/Target Audience: Aimed at business professionals and executives, students, university personnel, human resources managers, personnel development managers and career advisors.
BUSINESS: COMMERCE, INDUSTRY & MANAGEMENT: Work Study

MEANS OF ESCAPE
1745539U54A-233
Editorial Address: Wins House, Bentalls, Pipps Hill Industrial Estate, BASILDON, SS14 3BS **Tel:** 01268 242340
Fax: 01268 284046
Email: georgie.knight@means-of-escape.com
Web site: http://www.means-of-escape.com
Publisher: Means of Escape Publications Ltd
Date Launched: 1997
Frequency of update: Daily
Website Access: Free
Traffic Figures: 20,000 Unique Users (per month Publisher's Statement)
Editor: Georgie Knight
Summary of Content: Online publication covering all aspects of fire safety management, risk assessment, extinguishers and suppression systems, fire alarm, fire fighting, containment, prevention, protection, escape and training.
Readership/Target Audience: Aimed at responsible, nominated and competent persons within all organisations; fire and safety enforcement authorities; industrial fire officers, architects and approved building Inspectors; risk assessment consultants and fire protection supply, installation and maintenance organisations.
BUSINESS: SAFETY & SECURITY: Fire Fighting

MEAT TRADES JOURNAL ONLINE
1868721U22D-283
Formerly: Meat Trades Journal
Editorial Address: Broadfield Park, CRAWLEY, RH11 9RT
Tel: 01293 613400
Email: web.services@william-reed.co.uk
Web site: http://www.meatinfo.co.uk/index.php
Publisher: William Reed Business Media
Frequency of update: Daily
Traffic Figures: 10,000 Unique Users (per month Publisher's Statement)
Editor: Ed Bedington
Summary of Content: Website focused on meat trade industry news with platform for companies to promote their products & services to key decision-makers.
BUSINESS: FOOD: Meat Trade

MECHANICAL DESIGN (MCADONLINE)
37687U19J-105
Formerly: MCAD
Editorial Address: Ludgate House, 145 Blackfriars Road, LONDON, SE1 9UY **Tel:** 020 7921 5000
Email: mcad@technical-lucidity.co.uk
Web site: http://www.mcadonline.com
Publisher: Tech Insights Europe, United Business Media
Date Launched: 1980
Frequency of update: Daily
Website Access: Free

Traffic Figures: 228,416 Unique Users (Publisher's Statement)
Editor: Mark Fletcher
Summary of Content: Website and Website containing news, in-depth features, case studies and product stories relating to electromechanical systems design, machine and plant design, mechatronics and automation. Covering all aspects of mechanical and electrical interaction and integration, from a designers viewpoint.
Readership/Target Audience: Aimed at mechanical electromechanical engineers, technicians and designers at all levels within a company, across all facets of industry.
Other Features: Monthly newsletter.
BUSINESS: ENGINEERING & MACHINERY: CAD & CIM (Computer Integrated Manufacture)

MEDIA FINANCE
1640105U1R-357
Editorial Address: 292 Vauxhall Bridge Road, LONDON, SW1V 1AE **Tel:** 020 7963 7680 **Fax:** 020 7963 7682
Email: ed.ansell@mediafinance.com
Web site: http://www.telecomfinance.com
Publisher: PA Business
Date Launched: 2003
Frequency of update: 24 times a year
Website Access: Paid
Traffic Figures: 500 Unique Users (Publisher's Statement)
Editor: Ed Ansell
Summary of Content: Electronically delivered publication covering mergers and acquisitions, bank loans and equity.
Readership/Target Audience: Aimed at media bankers, law firms, consultants and private equity firms.
BUSINESS: FINANCE & ECONOMICS: Financial Related

MEDIAGUARDIAN.CO.UK
629515U2A-40
Editorial Address: Kings Place, 90 York Way, LONDON, N1 9GU **Tel:** 020 3353 2000 **Fax:** 020 3353 3179
Email: editor@mediaguardian.co.uk
Web site: http://www.mediaguardian.co.uk
Date Launched: 2000
Frequency of update: Daily
Website Access: Free
Traffic Figures: 8,000,000 Unique Users (Publisher's Statement)
Editor: Jason Deans
Summary of Content: Website providing daily news, commentary, analysis and key information for media professionals.
Readership/Target Audience: Read by professionals in the media industry.
BUSINESS: COMMUNICATIONS, ADVERTISING & MARKETING

MEDIATEL NEWSLINE
628931U2A-125
Editorial Address: 84-86 Regent Street, LONDON, W1B 5AJ **Tel:** 020 7439 7575 **Fax:** 020 7149 9943
Email: news@mediatel.co.uk
Web site: http://www.mediatel.co.uk
Date Launched: 1981
Frequency of update: Daily
Website Access: Paid
Traffic Figures: 3,000 Unique Users (per month Publisher's Statement)
Editor: Sam Howroyd
Summary of Content: Daily updated media news service.
Readership/Target Audience: Aimed at professionals within the media and advertising industry.
BUSINESS: COMMUNICATIONS, ADVERTISING & MARKETING

MEDIAWEEKJOBS.CO.UK
1837375U14F-264
Editorial Address: 174 Hammersmith Road, LONDON, W6 8SD **Tel:** 020 8267 5000
Email: paula.fox@haymarket.com
Web site: http://www.mediaweekjobs.co.uk
Publisher: Haymarket Business Media Ltd
Date Launched: 2008
Frequency of update: Daily
Website Access: Free
Editor: Paula Fox
Summary of Content: Website featuring jobs in the media sales industry.
Readership/Target Audience: Aimed at job seekers and recruiters in the media sales industry.
BUSINESS: COMMERCE, INDUSTRY & MANAGEMENT: Training & Recruitment

MEDICAL NEWS TODAY
1866809U56A-218
Editorial Address: PO Box 193, BEXHILL-ON-SEA, TN40 9BA **Tel:** 01625 415347 **Fax:** 0161 332 8215
Email: pressrelease@medicalnewstoday.com

Internet Media

Web site: http://www.medicalnewstoday.com
Publisher: MediLexicon International
Frequency of update: Daily
Website Access: Free
Traffic Figures: 1,800,000 Unique Users (per month Publisher's Statement)
Editor: Christian Nordqvist
Summary of Content: Independent health and medical news website updated with more than 150 articles on weekdays and 40 articles at the weekend.
Readership/Target Audience: Aimed at patients, carers and HCPs.
BUSINESS: HEALTH & MEDICAL

MEDICAL TECHNOLOGY BUSINESS EUROPE
1827404U56A-210
Formerly: MTB Europe
Editorial Address: 29 Pinewood Park, FARNBOROUGH, GU14 9LB **Tel:** 01252 691590
Email: harry.wood@mtbeurope.info
Web site: http://www.mtbeurope.info
Publisher: The Birchley Hall Press
Date Launched: 2005
Frequency of update: Daily
Website Access: Free
Traffic Figures: 90,000 Unique Users (Publisher's Statement)
Editor: Harry Wood
Summary of Content: Online publication covering electronic medical technologies.
Readership/Target Audience: Aimed at all medical professionals and suppliers of medical technology.
Other Features: Directory of suppliers, recruitment and newsletter.
BUSINESS: HEALTH & MEDICAL

MEDWIRENEWS
1819386U56A-208
Editorial Address: 11-12 Paul Street, LONDON, EC2A 4JU **Tel:** 020 7562 2957 **Fax:** 020 7562 2931
Email: lucy.piper@medwire-news.md
Web site: http://www.medwire-news.md
Publisher: Current Medicine Group Ltd
Date Launched: 2000
Frequency of update: Daily
Website Access: Free
Editor: Lucy Piper
Summary of Content: Online medical news service featuring healthcare professional news and consumer medical news.
Readership/Target Audience: Aimed at those with an interest in the latest medical research and clinical trials.
BUSINESS: HEALTH & MEDICAL

MEETINGS INDUSTRY NEWS
626225U2C-25
Formerly: BusinessMeetings.com
Editorial Address: 1-3 The Pavilions, Amber Close, TAMWORTH, B77 4RP **Tel:** 01827 61666 **Fax:** 01827 61661
Email: ken.clayton@reftech.co.uk
Web site: http://www.meetingsindustrynews.com
Publisher: Reference Technology
Date Launched: 1996
Frequency of update: Monthly
Website Access: Free
Traffic Figures: 20,000 Unique Users (per month Publisher's Statement)
Editor: Ken Clayton; **Web Editor:** Simon Clayton
Summary of Content: Website focusing on the business meetings industry worldwide. Also covers hotel industry news and association news.
Readership/Target Audience: Aimed at conference and event organisers and others involved in the meetings industry.
BUSINESS: COMMUNICATIONS, ADVERTISING & MARKETING: Conferences & Exhibitions

MEGASTAR
47660U86C-415
Editorial Address: 1.1.2 The Leather Market, 11 Weston Street, LONDON, SE1 3ER **Tel:** 020 7407 9351
Email: mark@edpic.com
Web site: http://www.megastar.co.uk
Publisher: Edpic
Date Launched: 1997
Frequency of update: Daily
Website Access: Free
Traffic Figures: 1,189,448 Unique Users (per month ABC/Electronic)
Editor: Mark Doyle
Summary of Content: UK's leading daily entertainment website for men with fun, showbiz, sports, gambling, music and movie news along with girls pictures and videos.

Readership/Target Audience: Aimed at those interested in news, sport, chat and showbiz gossip.
Other Features: Features include what's hot or not lists, viral emails, model pictures and archiving.
CONSUMER: ADULT & GAY MAGAZINES: Men's Lifestyle Magazines

MELTON TODAY
629843U72B-2178
Formerly: Melton Times On-Line
Editorial Address: 49 Nottingham Street, MELTON MOWBRAY, LE13 1NT **Tel:** 01664 410041
Fax: 01664 412515
Email: michael.cooke@meltontimes.co.uk
Web site: http://www.meltontoday.co.uk
Publisher: Johnston Press plc
Date Launched: 2000
Frequency of update: Weekly. Published on Thursday
Website Access: Free
Editor: Michael Cooke
Summary of Content: Website containing news, sport, information and features about Melton Mowbray, Syston and Vale of Belvoir.
Readership/Target Audience: Read by residents and visitors to the local area.
Other Features: Features include recruitment and a chat forum.
LOCAL NEWSPAPERS: Local Newspapers English Counties

MEMORABLETV.COM
1638719U76C-825
Editorial Address: 301 Narborough Road, LEICESTER, LE3 2RB
Email: peter@memorabletv.com
Web site: http://www.memorabletv.com
Date Launched: 2002
Frequency of update: Daily
Website Access: Free
Traffic Figures: 500,000 Unique Users (Publisher's Statement)
Editor: Peter Platts
Summary of Content: Website covering TV, DVD, book and film reviews.
Readership/Target Audience: Aimed at people aged 20 to 50 years old who are interested in classic to current TV. Also has features and reviews of music, related DVDs and books.
Other Features: Other features archive, TV encyclopaedia and music encyclopaedia.
CONSUMER: MUSIC & PERFORMING ARTS: TV & Radio

MEN'S HEALTH FORUM
1732840U56R-520
Editorial Address: 32-36 Loman Street, LONDON, SE1 0EH **Tel:** 020 7922 7908
Email: jim.pollard@menshealthforum.org.uk
Web site: http://www.malehealth.co.uk
Publisher: Men's Health Forum
Date Launched: 2006
Frequency of update: Weekly
Website Access: Free
Traffic Figures: 15,000 Unique Users (Publisher's Statement)
Editor: Jim Pollard
Summary of Content: The website of the Men's Health Forum, the UK voluntary organisation working to improve the health of men and boys.
Readership/Target Audience: Aimed at all those interested in or working in men's health and public health policy.
BUSINESS: HEALTH & MEDICAL: Health Medical Related

MENSHEALTH.CO.UK
634683U86C-421
Formerly: Men's Health Online
Editorial Address: 33 Broadwick Street, LONDON, W1F 0DQ **Tel:** 020 7339 4400 **Fax:** 020 7339 4455
Email: webeditor@menshealth.co.uk
Web site: http://www.menshealth.co.uk
Publisher: NatMag Rodale Ltd
Date Launched: 2000
Frequency of update: Daily
Website Access: Paid
Traffic Figures: 697,132 Unique Users (01/01/2009 To 31/01/2009 ABC/Electronic)
Editor: Abi Newman
Summary of Content: Website containing articles on health, fitness and muscle, style and grooming, nutrition, sex, relationships, weight loss and wealth. Includes gear, car, restaurant, hotel, food and wine reviews and recipes with weekly events listing, personal trainer function, message board, competitions, polls and a questions and answers section from qualified professionals and tips.
Readership/Target Audience: Aimed at 24 to 40 year old men.

Other Features: Features include message board, weekly newsletter, live web chats with experts, buyers guides and subscription offers for the magazine.
CONSUMER: ADULT & GAY MAGAZINES: Men's Lifestyle Magazines

MERGERMARKET.COM
626358U1A-245
Editorial Address: 1 Southwark Bridge, LONDON, SE1 9HL **Tel:** 020 7059 6100 **Fax:** 020 7059 6162
Email: cw@mergermarket.com
Web site: http://www.mergermarket.com
Date Launched: 2000
Frequency of update: Daily
Website Access: Paid
Editor: Charlie Welsh; **Editor-in-Chief:** Charlie Welsh
Summary of Content: Website covering mergers, deals, advice, news and real-time league tables.
Readership/Target Audience: Aimed at corporate executives and business advisors.
BUSINESS: FINANCE & ECONOMICS

MERSEY AND SOUTHPORT REPORTER SERIES
1629337U72B-3937
Editorial Address: 4A Post Office Avenue, SOUTHPORT, PR9 0US **Tel:** 01704 513569
Email: news24@merseyreporter.com
Web site: http://www.southportreporter.com
Publisher: PCBT Photography & PBT Media Relations Ltd.
Date Launched: 2000
Frequency of update: Weekly
Website Access: Free
Editor: Patrick Trollope
Summary of Content: News and information about events on Merseyside with film, music and gig reviews.
Readership/Target Audience: Aimed at people living in Merseyside.
Other Features: Recruitment, archive, message board and mailing lists.
LOCAL NEWSPAPERS: Local Newspapers English Counties

MERSEY REPORTER
1633034U72B-3937_100
Editorial Address: For all contact details see main record, Mersey and Southport Reporter Series
Frequency of update: Weekly
Website Access: Free
LOCAL NEWSPAPERS: Local Newspapers English Counties

MERSEYSIDE MATTERS
1881655U72J-398
Email: comments@merseyside-matters.co.uk
Web site: http://www.merseyside-matters.co.uk
Frequency of update: Daily
Summary of Content: Website created to help people who care about local issues. Whether you need access to useful information, want to highlight a particular topic to other people, discuss ideas with like-minded people or just show your support and keep up to date with current affairs in your area, Merseyside Matters is the place for you.
Readership/Target Audience: Aimed at residents in the local area of Merseyside.
LOCAL NEWSPAPERS: Community Newsletters

MERTON MATTERS
1881656U72J-399
Email: comments@merton-matters.co.uk
Web site: http://www.merton-matters.co.uk
Frequency of update: Daily
Summary of Content: Website created to help people who care about local issues. Whether you need access to useful information, want to highlight a particular topic to other people, discuss ideas with like minded individuals or just show your support and keep up to date with current affairs in your area, Merton Matters is the place for you.
Readership/Target Audience: Aimed at residents in the local area of Merton.
LOCAL NEWSPAPERS: Community Newsletters

METAL4LIFE
1805244U76E-778
Editorial Address: PO Box 13499, EDINBURGH, EH6 8YL **Tel:** 07966 389732
Email: info@metal4life.co.uk
Web site: http://www.metal4life.co.uk
Publisher: Zietgeist
Date Launched: 2007
Frequency of update: Daily
Website Access: Free
Traffic Figures: 55,000 Unique Users (per month Publisher's Statement)

Editor: Stuart Hamilton
Summary of Content: Independent portal covering heavy metal and heavy rock music.
Readership/Target Audience: Aimed at fans of the genre.
Other Features: Other features on site include competitions, downloads and chat forums.
CONSUMER: MUSIC & PERFORMING ARTS: Pop Music

METALBULLETIN.COM
626277U27-90_1

Editorial Address: Nestor House, Playhouse Yard, LONDON, EC4V 5EX **Tel:** 020 7827 9977
Fax: 020 7928 6892
Email: editorial@metalbulletin.com
Web site: http://www.metalbulletin.com
Publisher: Euromoney Institutional Investor plc
Date Launched: 1999
Frequency of update: Daily
Website Access: Paid
Traffic Figures: 6,500 Unique Users (Publisher's Statement)
Editor: Alex Harrison
Summary of Content: Website featuring news and analysis on the world metal and steel markets.
Readership/Target Audience: Aimed at producers, consumers and traders in the international metal and steel markets.
BUSINESS: METAL, IRON & STEEL

METRO.CO.UK
1793971U67B-9033

Editorial Address: Northcliffe House, 2 Derry Street, LONDON, W8 5TT **Tel:** 020 7651 5200 **Fax:** 020 7651 5342
Email: ryan.battles@ukmetro.co.uk
Web site: http://www.metro.co.uk
Publisher: Associated Newspapers Ltd
Frequency of update: Daily
Website Access: Free
Traffic Figures: 1,250,000 Unique Users (per month Publisher's Statement)
Editor: Ryan Battles
Summary of Content: Website of the Metro newspaper covering news, sport, entertainment, celebrities, travel, money and human interest stories.
Readership/Target Audience: Aimed at 20 to 40 year olds.
Other Features: Video content and Blogs.
REGIONAL DAILY & SUNDAY NEWSPAPERS: Regional Daily Newspapers

MG ENTHUSIAST
626459U77E-192_80

Formerly: MG Cars Enthusiasts
Editorial Address: 171 Eagle Way, Hampton Vale, PETERBOROUGH, PE7 8EL **Tel:** 01733 246500
Fax: 01733 246555
Email: simon@mgenthusiast.com
Web site: http://www.mgenthusiast.com
Publisher: Hothouse Publishing Ltd
Frequency of update: Daily
Website Access: Free
Editor: Simon Goldsworthy
Summary of Content: Website providing news and information for the MG car owner or enthusiast.
Readership/Target Audience: Aimed at people who drive or would like to own an MG car.
Other Features: Features include an events diary, classifieds and a bulletin board.
CONSUMER: MOTORING & CYCLING: Club Cars

THE MIDWEEK PINK
1663592U80C-5205

Editorial Address: Corporation Street, COVENTRY, CV1 1FP **Tel:** 024 7663 3633 **Fax:** 024 7625 2164
Email: midweekpink@coventrytelegraph.net
Web site: http://www.coventrytelegraph.net
Publisher: Midland Newspapers Ltd
Date Launched: 1997
Frequency of update: Weekly
Website Access: Free
Traffic Figures: 2,000 Unique Users (Publisher's Statement)
Editor: Rob Madill
Summary of Content: Website covering local grass roots sport including football, rugby, cricket and bowls with match reports and league tables.
Readership/Target Audience: Aimed at residents of Coventry and Warwickshire.
CONSUMER: RURAL & REGIONAL INTEREST: Regional Interest English Counties

MINING JOURNAL
719186U30-62

Editorial Address: Albert House, 1 Singer Street, LONDON, EC2A 4BQ **Tel:** 020 7216 6060 **Fax:** 020 7216 6050
Email: editorial@mining-journal.com
Web site: http://www.mining-journal.com

Publisher: Aspermont
Frequency of update: Weekly
Website Access: Paid
Traffic Figures: 2,000 Unique Users (Publisher's Statement)
Editor: Chris Hinde
Summary of Content: Website providing news and information for the mining industry. Covers profiles of mining industry companies around the world, information about mining projects, metal prices and equipment reviews. Also includes unit and currency conversions and research services.
Readership/Target Audience: Aimed at mining industry professionals.
BUSINESS: MINING & QUARRYING

MINING TECHNOLOGY
629303U30-151

Editorial Address: Brunel House, 55-57 North Wharf Road, LONDON, W2 1LA **Tel:** 020 7915 9957 **Fax:** 020 7915 9720
Email: production@spgmedia.com
Web site: http://www.mining-technology.com
Publisher: SPG Media Ltd
Date Launched: 1996
Frequency of update: Daily
Website Access: Free
Traffic Figures: 94,349 Unique Users (Publisher's Statement)
Editor: Duncan West
Summary of Content: Website covering mines extracting energy minerals, ferrous, base and precious metals, industrial minerals and gemstones.
Readership/Target Audience: Aimed at purchasers and decision makers within the mining industries.
Other Features: Recruitment, e-newsletter, white papers, buyers guide, daily news, and feature articles.
BUSINESS: MINING & QUARRYING

MINISTRY OF SOUND
628919U76D-353

Editorial Address: 103 Gaunt Street, LONDON, SE1 6DP **Tel:** 020 7740 8770 **Fax:** 020 7403 5348
Email: gleversuch@ministryofsound.com
Web site: http://www.ministryofsound.com
Publisher: Ministry of Sound
Date Launched: 1994
Frequency of update: Daily
Website Access: Free
Traffic Figures: 850,000 Unique Users (per month Publisher's Statement)
Editor: Gavin Leversuch
Summary of Content: Website covering news, features and information about the dance and club music scene. Also includes an online radio and TV station.
Readership/Target Audience: Aimed at 16 to 35 year olds interested in dance music.
Other Features: Features include recruitment, a chat forum and an e-mail newsletter.
CONSUMER: MUSIC & PERFORMING ARTS: Music

MKWEB
629556U80C-3678

Editorial Address: 1 Diamond Court, Fox Milne, MILTON KEYNES, MK15 0DU **Tel:** 01908 357037
Web site: http://www.mkweb.co.uk
Date Launched: 1999
Frequency of update: Daily. News updated throughout the day
Website Access: Free
Traffic Figures: 1,000,000 Unique Users (Publisher's Statement)
Editor: Debbie Sellers
Summary of Content: Website covering news and information for the Milton Keynes and North Buckinghamshire area.
Readership/Target Audience: Aimed at local residents and visitors.
Other Features: Features include archiving and discussion forums.
CONSUMER: RURAL & REGIONAL INTEREST: Regional Interest English Counties

MOBILE MARKETING MAGAZINE
1703764U2A-681

Editorial Address: 15 Loraine Gardens, ASHTEAD, KT21 1PD **Tel:** 01372 274059 **Fax:** 01372 274059
Email: editor@mobilemarketingmagazine.co.uk
Web site: http://www.mobilemarketingmagazine.co.uk
Publisher: Freelance.com Ltd
Date Launched: 2005
Frequency of update: Daily
Website Access: Free
Traffic Figures: 35,000 Unique Users (per month Publisher's Statement)
Editor: David Murphy

Summary of Content: Website focusing direct marketing to mobile devices.
Readership/Target Audience: Aimed at digital agencies, network operators and companies interested in mobile marketing.
BUSINESS: COMMUNICATIONS, ADVERTISING & MARKETING

MOBILECOMMS TECHNOLOGY
1616580U18B-1947

Editorial Address: Brunel House, 55-57 North Wharf Road, LONDON, W2 1LA **Tel:** 020 7915 9957 **Fax:** 020 7915 9720
Email: production@spgmedia.com
Web site: http://www.mobilecomms-technology.com
Publisher: SPG Media Ltd
Date Launched: 2000
Frequency of update: Daily
Website Access: Free
Traffic Figures: 57,615 Unique Users (per month Publisher's Statement)
Editor: Duncan West
Summary of Content: Website covering mobile and cellular communications technology as well as general news, products and services and exhibitions and conferences.
Readership/Target Audience: Aimed at those working within mobile communications.
BUSINESS: ELECTRONICS: Telecommunications

MOBILITYTODAY
48641U94F-550

Formerly: MobilityToday.co.uk
Editorial Address: 63 Amberley Slope, Werrington, PETERBOROUGH, PE4 6QQ **Tel:** 01733 571858
Email: clive.frusher@btinternet.com
Web site: http://www.mobilitytodaymagazine.com
Publisher: CFES Publishing
Date Launched: 2006
Frequency of update: Daily
Website Access: Free
Traffic Figures: 55,000 Unique Users
Editor: Clive Frusher
Summary of Content: Website covering all aspects of mobility for disabled people who can drive or be driven by a carer. Includes articles on motoring news, vehicle testing, travel and holiday details, information pages, letters and product analysis.
Readership/Target Audience: Aimed at disabled drivers and their carers.
CONSUMER: OTHER CLASSIFICATIONS: Disability

MODEL RAILWAY EXPRESS
46609U79B-90

Formerly: Model Railway Enthusiast
Editorial Address: PO Box 199, SCARBOROUGH, YO11 3GT **Tel:** 01723 506326
Email: pat@mremag.com
Web site: http://www.mremag.demon.co.uk
Publisher: Hammond Publishing
Date Launched: 1999
Frequency of update: 250 times a year
Website Access: Free
Traffic Figures: 40,000 Unique Users (per month Publisher's Statement)
Editor: Pat Hammond
Summary of Content: Website covering the history of model railway manufacturers from 1900 to the present day. Includes news and reviews of new railway and associated models and the manufacturing industry behind them, as well as daily updates of the model industry and book reviews.
Readership/Target Audience: Aimed at model railway enthusiasts.
Other Features: Readers' correspondence, model and book reviews, classified ads, database, forthcoming model railway shows, auctions and surveys.
CONSUMER: HOBBIES & DIY: Models & Modelling

MODERNSELLING.COM
1749924U2F-83

Editorial Address: Unit 2, Flag House, 47 Brunswick Court, LONDON, SE1 3LH **Tel:** 020 7939 0790 **Fax:** 01404 871663
Email: editor@modernselling.com
Web site: http://www.modernselling.com
Publisher: 2 N Media Ltd
Date Launched: 2006
Frequency of update: Daily
Website Access: Free
Traffic Figures: 7,772 Unique Users (per month ABC/Electronic)
Editor: Nick de Cent
Summary of Content: Online magazine covering items of interest to sales professionals including sales technique, management, training, cars, business travel, conferences, incentives, presentations, export issues, IT and telecoms, the economy, lifestyle and jobs.

Internet Media

Readership/Target Audience: Aimed at the sales profession from graduates and new recruits to senior sales people, sales managers and directors.
Other Features: Editorial archive, 5,000+ jobs, post/browse a CV, message board, interactive sales advice, comprehensive directory of products and services. New reader forum.
BUSINESS: COMMUNICATIONS, ADVERTISING & MARKETING: Selling

MOJO4MUSIC
714402U76D-357

Editorial Address: Mappin House, 4 Winsley Street, LONDON, W1W 8HF **Tel:** 020 7436 1515
Fax: 020 7312 8246
Email: editor@mojo4music.com
Web site: http://www.mojo4music.com
Publisher: Bauer Consumer Media Ltd (Mappin House)
Date Launched: 2001
Frequency of update: Daily
Website Access: Free
Traffic Figures: 80,000 Unique Users (per month Publisher's Statement)
Editor: Danny Eccleston
Summary of Content: Website focusing on popular music. Includes an enlightenment section for answering music fans questions.
Readership/Target Audience: Aimed at serious music lovers.
Other Features: Features include a message board and an e-mail newsletter.
CONSUMER: MUSIC & PERFORMING ARTS: Music

MONDAQ
626305U1A-250

Editorial Address: 16 West Barnes Lane, LONDON, SW20 0BU **Tel:** 020 8544 8300 **Fax:** 020 8946 8920
Email: enquiries@mondaq.com
Web site: http://www.mondaq.com
Publisher: Mondaq
Date Launched: 1995
Frequency of update: Daily
Website Access: Free
Traffic Figures: 300,000 Unique Users (per year Publisher's Statement)
Editor: Charles Aspinwall
Summary of Content: Website covering information on international trade and investment from the professional financial advisors' perspective.
Readership/Target Audience: Aimed at professional business advisors providing legal, regulatory and financial commentary and information.
BUSINESS: FINANCE & ECONOMICS

MONEY4MEDIA.COM
1851098U1F-650

Editorial Address: Unit 11, The Chandlery, 50 Westminster Bridge Road, LONDON, SE1 7QY **Tel:** 020 7953 8770
Fax: 020 7953 8773
Email: news.desk@money4media.com
Web site: http://www.money4media.com
Publisher: News4Media Ltd
Date Launched: 2008
Frequency of update: Daily
Website Access: Free
Traffic Figures: 5,000 Unique Users (per month Publisher's Statement)
Editor: Henry Hemming
Summary of Content: Website covering the money industry including mortgages, insurance and news.
Readership/Target Audience: Aimed at those working in the money sector.
BUSINESS: FINANCE & ECONOMICS: Investment

MONEY MART DIRECTORY
623654U74M-135

Formerly: Moneymart
Editorial Address: 2 Woodborough Road, MANSFIELD, NG19 6DT **Tel:** 01623 656264 **Fax:** 0871 433 6920
Email: admin@moneymart.co.uk
Web site: http://www.moneymart.co.uk
Date Launched: 1998
Frequency of update: Daily
Website Access: Free
Editor: Paul Rhodes
Summary of Content: Website covering financial advice and products.
Readership/Target Audience: Aimed at general consumers requiring financial advice.
CONSUMER: WOMEN'S INTEREST CONSUMER MAGAZINES: Personal Finance

MONEYEXTRA
45554U74M-175

Formerly: MX moneyextra
Editorial Address: 1st Floor, City Wharf, New Bailey Street, SALFORD, M3 5ER **Tel:** 0161 638 0200
Email: public.relations@moneyextra.com
Web site: http://www.moneyextra.com
Publisher: Moneyextra.com Ltd
Date Launched: 1995
Frequency of update: Daily
Website Access: Free
Traffic Figures: 536,000 Unique Users (per month Publisher's Statement)
Editor: Jennifer Rose
Summary of Content: Website containing news, facts and figures on mortgages, savings, insurance, annuities, credit cards, loans, ISAs and unit trusts.
Readership/Target Audience: Aimed at financially active individuals.
Other Features: Features include a bi-monthly newsletters.
CONSUMER: WOMEN'S INTEREST CONSUMER MAGAZINES: Personal Finance

MONEYHOSPITAL.CO.UK
1885871U1F-673

Formerly: moneyhospital.co.uk/blog/
Editorial Address: Merchants House North, Wapping Road, BRISTOL, BS1 4RW **Tel:** 0117 920 0038 **Fax:** 0117 920 0039
Email: heoffice@moneyhospital.co.uk
Web site: http://moneyhospital.co.uk/blog
Frequency of update: Daily
Traffic Figures: 196 Unique Users (ABC/Electronic)
Summary of Content: Website covering mortgages, loans, debt, credit cards, banking and insurance.
Readership/Target Audience: Aimed at people looking for information on finance.
BUSINESS: FINANCE & ECONOMICS: Investment

MONEYNET
35021U74M-140

Formerly: moneynet.co.uk
Editorial Address: Sussex House, 8-10 Homesdale Road, BROMLEY, BR2 9LZ **Tel:** 020 8313 9030
Fax: 020 8464 1971
Email: info@moneynet.co.uk
Web site: http://www.moneynet.co.uk
Date Launched: 1997
Frequency of update: Daily
Website Access: Free
Editor: Keith Goldson
Summary of Content: Website covering a comprehensive and independent overview of the products available in the personal finance sector. Includes comparison tools and online application facilities for mortgages, credit cards, loans, savings and current accounts and insurance products.
Readership/Target Audience: Aimed at those looking for personal finance guidance.
CONSUMER: WOMEN'S INTEREST CONSUMER MAGAZINES: Personal Finance

MONEYSAVINGEXPERT.COM
765754U74M-401

Editorial Address: G12.1, Shepherds Studios, Charecroft Way, Shepherds Bush, LONDON, W14 0DA
Tel: 020 7348 9103 **Fax:** 0870 831 7286
Email: editorial@moneysavingexpert.com
Web site: http://www.moneysavingexpert.com
Publisher: MoneySavingExpert.com
Date Launched: 2003
Frequency of update: Daily
Website Access: Free
Traffic Figures: 4,900,000 Unique Users (per month Publisher's Statement)
Editor: Jenny Keefe; **Web Editor:** Dan Plant
Summary of Content: Website containing research led articles and tips on the best buys and the top products across consumer finance.
Readership/Target Audience: Aimed at those looking to save money.
Other Features: Email newsletter, features include e-mail tips, profiles, product recommendations poll and chat forums, flightchecker, travel money maximiser, callcheckers phones and other comparisons.
CONSUMER: WOMEN'S INTEREST CONSUMER MAGAZINES: Personal Finance

MONEYWISE.CO.UK
1829667U74M-433

Editorial Address: Standon House, 21 Mansell Street, LONDON, E1 8AA **Tel:** 020 7680 3600
Email: rebecca.atkinson@moneywise.co.uk
Web site: http://www.moneywise.co.uk
Publisher: Moneywise Publishing
Frequency of update: Daily
Website Access: Free

Editor: Rebecca Atkinson
Summary of Content: Website with news, features and guides to all aspects of personal finance including pensions, insurance, banking, borrowing, tax and the stock market.
Readership/Target Audience: Aimed at those with an interest in personal finance.
Other Features: Forums, user blogs and financial tools and calculators.
CONSUMER: WOMEN'S INTEREST CONSUMER MAGAZINES: Personal Finance

MONKEY
1777379U86C-734

Editorial Address: 30 Cleveland Street, LONDON, W1T 4JD
Tel: 020 7907 6000
Email: leon_poultney@dennis.co.uk
Web site: http://www.monkeymag.co.uk
Publisher: Dennis Publishing Ltd
Date Launched: 2006
Frequency of update: Weekly
Website Access: Free
Traffic Figures: 1,009,298 Unique Users (01/09/2008 To 30/09/2008 ABC/Electronic)
Editor: Leon Poultney; **Editor-in-Chief:** Ben Raworth
Summary of Content: Online magazine with live video and music as well as covering cars, sport, humour, entertainment, gadgets and clothes.
Readership/Target Audience: Aimed at men aged 16 to 30 years old.
CONSUMER: ADULT & GAY MAGAZINES: Men's Lifestyle Magazines

MONKEYSLUM
1647612U74F-759

Editorial Address: 5th Floor, Fergusson House, 124-128 City Road, LONDON, EC1V 2NJ **Tel:** 020 7553 3360
Fax: 020 7490 4837
Email: matt@mykindaplace.com
Web site: http://www.monkeyslum.com
Publisher: Mykindaplace Ltd
Date Launched: 2004
Frequency of update: Daily
Website Access: Free
Traffic Figures: 250,000 Unique Users (Publisher's Statement)
Editor: Matthew Bagwell
Summary of Content: Website covering sport, girls, gadgets, fashion, gaming, motors, music, films and TV.
Readership/Target Audience: Aimed at boys aged 11 to 19 years old.
CONSUMER: WOMEN'S INTEREST CONSUMER MAGAZINES: Teenage

MONSTERSANDCRITICS.COM
1779374U82-273

Editorial Address: 4 Mossgiel Road, Newlands, GLASGOW, G43 2DF **Tel:** 0141 632 8875
Email: james.wray@monstersandcritics.com
Web site: http://www.monstersandcritics.com
Date Launched: 2004
Frequency of update: Daily
Website Access: Free
Traffic Figures: 1,653,529 Unique Users (per month Quantcast)
Editor: James Wray
Summary of Content: Website covering world news, people and movies as well as arts, books, DVDs, music, science and sport.
Readership/Target Audience: Aimed at college educated men and women predominantly under 44 years of age.
CONSUMER: CURRENT AFFAIRS & POLITICS

MOOD FOOD
762735U11A-145

Formerly: Menu Magazine
Editorial Address: PO Box 416, SURBITON, KT1 9BJ
Tel: 020 8399 4831
Email: editor@menumagazine.co.uk
Web site: http://www.moodfoodmag.com
Publisher: FSR
Date Launched: 1996
Frequency of update: Weekly. Published on the 19th of the cover month
Website Access: Free
Traffic Figures: 75,000 Unique Users (Publisher's Statement)
Editor: Peter Grove
Summary of Content: Online magazine covering news, reviews, recipes, food issues, history and interviews on multicultural food, drink and restaurants worldwide.
Readership/Target Audience: Read by restaurateurs and suppliers within the multicultural food and drink sector.
BUSINESS: CATERING: Catering, Hotels & Restaurants

MOORTOWN TODAY
1896762U67B-9084

Editorial Address: PO Box 168, Wellington Street, LEEDS, LS1 1RF **Tel:** 0113 243 2701
Email: moortown@ypn.co.uk
Web site: http://www.moortowntoday.co.uk
Publisher: Yorkshire Post Newspapers Ltd
Frequency of update: Daily
Website Access: Free
Editor: Suzanne McTaggart
Summary of Content: Website featuring news and events for the Moortown area of Leeds.
REGIONAL DAILY & SUNDAY NEWSPAPERS: Regional Daily Newspapers

MORE ONLINE
1614576U74A-954

Formerly: More!
Editorial Address: 4th Floor, Endeavor House, 189 Shaftesbury Avenue, LONDON, WC2H 8JG
Tel: 020 7859 8642 **Fax:** 020 7208 3595
Email: emma.ledger@moremagazine.co.uk
Web site: http://www.moremagazine.co.uk
Publisher: Bauer Media
Date Launched: 2003
Frequency of update: Daily
Website Access: Free
Traffic Figures: 60,000 Unique Users (per month Publisher's Statement)
Editor: Emma Ledger; **Web Editor:** Emma Ledger
Summary of Content: Website covering daily celebrity gossip, fashion, beauty, relationships, films and music.
Readership/Target Audience: Aimed at young women between 18 and 25 years old.
CONSUMER: WOMEN'S INTEREST CONSUMER MAGAZINES: Women's Interest

MOREINTELLIGENTLIFE.COM
1911607U73-9011

Editorial Address: 25 St. James Street, LONDON, SW1A 1HG **Tel:** 020 7830 7000 **Fax:** 020 7839 4092
Email: intelligentlife@economist.com
Web site: http://www.moreintelligentlife.com
Publisher: The Economist Newspaper Ltd
Frequency of update: Daily
Website Access: Free
Editor: Caroline Carter
Summary of Content: Website covering fashion, beauty, travel, cars, science and general interest features.
Readership/Target Audience: Aimed at affluent and successful men and women.
CONSUMER: NATIONAL & INTERNATIONAL PERIODICALS

THE MORNING BRIEFING
764935U2R-181

Editorial Address: Bridgegate, Howden, GOOLE, DN14 7AE
Tel: 01430 455777
Email: howard.foster@pressassociation.co.uk
Web site: http://www.pressassociation.com
Publisher: Press Association
Date Launched: 2000
Frequency of update: Daily
Editor: Howard Foster
Summary of Content: Newsletter focusing on the latest developments in the fast-converging broadcast, print, Internet and telecommunications sectors.
Readership/Target Audience: Read by senior executives in technology and law firms, finance houses, PR agencies, consulting groups, media companies and marketing services companies.
BUSINESS: COMMUNICATIONS, ADVERTISING & MARKETING: Communications Related

MORNING STAR ONLINE
629304U82-119_40

Editorial Address: William Rust House, 52 Beachy Road, LONDON, E3 2NS **Tel:** 020 8510 0815 **Fax:** 020 8986 5694
Email: webmaster@morningstaronline.co.uk
Web site: http://www.morningstaronline.co.uk
Date Launched: 1930
Frequency of update: Daily
Website Access: Paid
Traffic Figures: 30,000 Unique Users (Publisher's Statement)
Editor: Daniel Coysh; **Webmaster:** Carl Worswick
Summary of Content: Website focusing on issues that directly involve the working class and their organisations. Includes news, sport, culture and features.
Readership/Target Audience: Aimed at environmentalists, political activists, trade unionists and peace campaigners.
Other Features: Features include archiving from September 2004.
CONSUMER: CURRENT AFFAIRS & POLITICS

MORNINGSTAR
647131U1F-304_43

Editorial Address: 1 Oliver's Yard, 55-71 City Road, LONDON, EC1Y 1HQ **Tel:** 020 3107 0000
Fax: 020 3107 0001
Email: fundnews@morningstar.com
Web site: http://www.morningstar.co.uk
Date Launched: 2001
Frequency of update: Daily
Website Access: Free
Editor: Christopher Traulsen
Summary of Content: Website focusing on news, feature stories and data including information that will help private investors and intermediaries make better investment decisions.
Readership/Target Audience: Aimed at buyers of investment fund products, private investors and intermediaries.
BUSINESS: FINANCE & ECONOMICS: Investment

MOSTLY FOOD JOURNAL
1849419U74P-961

Editorial Address: 75 Strawberry Vale, TWICKENHAM, TW1 4SJ **Tel:** 020 8891 5659
Email: mostlyfood@yahoo.com
Web site: http://www.mostlyfood.co.uk
Date Launched: 2008
Frequency of update: 208 times a year
Website Access: Free
Traffic Figures: 70,000 Unique Users (per month Publisher's Statement)
Editor: Chrissie Walker
Summary of Content: Online magazine covering cookbook reviews, chef interviews, food and travel articles, restaurant reviews, food product reviews, food news and food event news.
Readership/Target Audience: Aimed at food and travel lovers.
CONSUMER: WOMEN'S INTEREST CONSUMER MAGAZINES: Food & Cookery

MOTHER@WORK
1625713U74A-956

Editorial Address: Premier House, 11 Marlborough Place, BRIGHTON, BN1 1UB **Tel:** 01273 670003
Fax: 0870 135 0302
Email: denise.tyler@motheratwork.co.uk
Web site: http://www.motheratwork.co.uk
Publisher: Tyler Publishing
Frequency of update: 11 times a year
Website Access: Free
Traffic Figures: 28,000 Unique Users (per month Publisher's Statement)
Editor: Denise Tyler
Summary of Content: Magazine featuring all aspects of a working mothers life. Includes articles on work life balance, finding time for yourself, inner health, family health, finance and government legislation, childcare, celebrity, motoring, and real-life interviews.
Readership/Target Audience: Aimed at working mothers with children of all ages.
CONSUMER: WOMEN'S INTEREST CONSUMER MAGAZINES: Women's Interest

THE MOTLEY FOOL
600979U74M-170

Formerly: The Motley Fool UK
Editorial Address: 18 Soho Square, LONDON, W1D 3QL
Tel: 020 7025 8057 **Fax:** 020 7025 8112
Email: uknews@fool.co.uk
Web site: http://www.fool.co.uk
Publisher: The Motley Fool UK
Date Launched: 1997
Frequency of update: Daily
Website Access: Free
Traffic Figures: 18,259 Unique Users (ABC/Electronic)
Editor: Stuart Watson
Summary of Content: Website covering personal financial news and information, including stock ideas and advice, online banking, retirement planning, ISAs, mortgages and pensions.
Readership/Target Audience: Aimed at consumers.
Other Features: Features include a daily/weekly e-mail newsletter, a chat forum and money reports.
CONSUMER: WOMEN'S INTEREST CONSUMER MAGAZINES: Personal Finance

MOTOR BOAT & YACHTING ONLINE
628966U91A-81

Editorial Address: Blue Fin Building, 110 Southwark Street, LONDON, SE1 0SU **Tel:** 020 3148 5000
Email: rob_peake@ipcmedia.com
Web site: http://www.mby.com
Publisher: IPC Inspire
Date Launched: 1997
Frequency of update: Daily
Website Access: Free
Editor: Rob Peake
Summary of Content: Website featuring boat tests, as well as keeping the market up-to-date with the latest innovations from the world of electronic navigation.
Readership/Target Audience: Aimed at sailing enthusiasts.
Other Features: Features include a buyer's guide, a chat forum, an e-mail newsletter, a marine company directory, classified listings, weather and tide information and archiving.
CONSUMER: RECREATION & LEISURE: Boating & Yachting

MOTOR BOATS MONTHLY ONLINE
31245U91A-88

Editorial Address: Blue Fin Building, 110 Southwark Street, LONDON, SE1 0SU **Tel:** 020 3148 5000 **Fax:** 020 3148 8128
Email: stewart_campbell@ipcmedia.com
Web site: http://www.mbmclub.com
Publisher: IPC Inspire
Date Launched: 1997
Frequency of update: Daily
Website Access: Free
Editor: Stewart Campbell
Summary of Content: Website covering all aspects of motor boats including news, boat reports, products and services.
Readership/Target Audience: Read by boat owners and people interested in motor cruising, yachting and sailing.
Other Features: Features include a buyer's guide, a chat forum, an e-mail newsletter, a marine company directory, classified listings, weather and tide information and archiving.
CONSUMER: RECREATION & LEISURE: Boating & Yachting

MOTOR NEWS
626429U77A-340

Editorial Address: Orchardton Hall, Auchencairn, CASTLE DOUGLAS, DG7 1QL **Tel:** 0845 130 6249
Fax: 0845 658 8329
Email: lauren@motornews.co.uk
Web site: http://www.motornews.co.uk
Publisher: Brave New World International Ltd
Date Launched: 1992
Frequency of update: Weekly
Website Access: Free
Editor: Lauren Courtney; **Web Editor:** Susan Foster
Summary of Content: Website covering news, reviews and features concerned with the international motor industry.
Readership/Target Audience: Aimed at motor enthusiasts between 18 and 60 years old.
CONSUMER: MOTORING & CYCLING: Motoring

MOTORBAR
629068U77A-310

Formerly: MotorBar.com
Editorial Address: 3 Cromers Road, SITTINGBOURNE, ME10 4HP **Tel:** 01795 425520
Email: editorial@motorbar.co.uk
Web site: http://www.motorbar.co.uk
Publisher: MotorBar
Date Launched: 2000
Frequency of update: Daily
Website Access: Free
Traffic Figures: 350,000 Unique Users (per month Publisher's Statement)
Editor: Dee Townsend
Summary of Content: Website focusing on new cars with first drives and in-depth road tests of the latest models. Includes general motoring and car-related news as well as details of the latest models and new consumer products and services. Also includes an expanding lifestyle and travel section, along with book, CD and DVD reviews.
Other Features: New cars, motoring, travel and lifestyle.
CONSUMER: MOTORING & CYCLING: Motoring

MOTORCARLOANS.COM
1641956U77A-508

Editorial Address: The Loading Bay, 12-18 Pollard Street, MANCHESTER, MA 7AJ **Tel:** 0800 019 7180
Email: info@netcars.co.uk
Web site: http://www.motorcarloans.com
Publisher: Netcars Ltd
Date Launched: 2004
Frequency of update: Daily
Website Access: Free
Traffic Figures: 5,000 Unique Users (per month Publisher's Statement)
Editor: Louis Rix
Summary of Content: Website covering information for motorists including independently written guides, news and reviews as well as access to ancillary products.
Readership/Target Audience: Aimed at those with an interest in motoring.
CONSUMER: MOTORING & CYCLING: Motoring

Internet Media

MOTORCYCLENEWS.COM
46366U77B-498_50

Formerly: MCW On-line
Editorial Address: Media House, Lynchwood, Peterborough Business Park, PETERBOROUGH, PE2 6EA
Tel: 01733 468000 **Fax:** 01733 468028
Email: mcn.online@bauerconsumer.co.uk
Web site: http://www.motorcyclenews.com
Publisher: Bauer Consumer Media Ltd (Media House)
Date Launched: 1998
Frequency of update: Daily
Website Access: Free
Editor: Samuel Pinney
Summary of Content: Website covering motorcycle news, products and classifieds.
Readership/Target Audience: Aimed at motorcycling enthusiasts.
Other Features: Features include recruitment, a buyers' guide, message boards and archiving.
CONSUMER: MOTORING & CYCLING: Motorcycling

MOTORING4MEDIA.COM
1842849U31R-65

Editorial Address: Unit 11, The Chandlery, 50 Westminster Bridge Road, LONDON, SE1 7QY **Tel:** 020 7953 8770
Fax: 020 7953 8773
Email: news.desk@motoring4media.com
Web site: http://www.motoring4media.com
Publisher: News4Media Ltd
Date Launched: 2008
Frequency of update: 2444 times a year
Website Access: Free
Traffic Figures: 5,000 Unique Users (per month Publisher's Statement)
Editor: Henry Hemming
Summary of Content: Website covering all aspects of news from the motoring industry.
Readership/Target Audience: Aimed at those working in the motoring industry at all levels.
BUSINESS: MOTOR TRADE: Motor Trade Related

MOTORMARQUES.COM
1743300U77F-456

Editorial Address: Unit 18, Greenwich Centre Business Park, 53 Norman Road, LONDON, SE10 9QF
Tel: 020 8293 0256
Email: john_sutton@btconnect.com
Web site: http://www.motormarques.com
Frequency of update: Daily
Website Access: Free
Traffic Figures: 15,000 Unique Users (per month Publisher's Statement)
Editor: John Sutton
Summary of Content: Website covering International auction results, historic car data, event reports and a drivers' database.
Readership/Target Audience: Aimed at classic car owners and enthusiasts worldwide.
CONSUMER: MOTORING & CYCLING: Veteran Cars

MPDCLICK
1810524U74B-730

Editorial Address: Unit 21-23, Home Farm Rural Industries, East Tytherley Road, Lockerley, ROMSEY, SO51 0JT
Tel: 01794 344040 **Fax:** 01794 344056
Email: sarah.wade@mudpie.co.uk
Web site: http://www.mpdclick.co.uk
Frequency of update: Daily
Website Access: Paid
Editor: Sarah Wade
Summary of Content: Online children's and youth fashion portal covering news and fashion events.
Readership/Target Audience: Aimed at men's and women's wear with an interest in fashion.
CONSUMER: WOMEN'S INTEREST CONSUMER MAGAZINES: Women's Interest - Fashion

MRWEB.COM
1793162U2A-691

Editorial Address: Langdale House, 11 Marshalsea Road, LONDON, SE1 1EN **Tel:** 020 7515 6040
Email: nick@mrweb.com
Web site: http://www.mrweb.com
Publisher: MrWeb.com
Date Launched: 1998
Frequency of update: Daily
Website Access: Free
Traffic Figures: 23,000 Unique Users (per month Publisher's Statement)
Editor: Nick Thomas
Summary of Content: Portal site covering items of interest for those working in the market research industry including news, jobs and directories.

Readership/Target Audience: Aimed at agency and clientside market research professionals and HR personnel working in the market research industry.
BUSINESS: COMMUNICATIONS, ADVERTISING & MARKETING

MSN CARS
707927U77A-130

Formerly: carview
Editorial Address: Cardinal Place, 100 Victoria Street, LONDON, SW1E 5JL **Tel:** 020 3139 6716
Email: msncars@live.co.uk
Web site: http://cars.uk.msn.com
Publisher: Microsoft Ltd.
Date Launched: 2001
Frequency of update: 156 times a year
Website Access: Free
Traffic Figures: 1,600,000 Unique Users (per month Publisher's Statement)
Editor: Tom Evans
Summary of Content: Website covering all aspects of the car industry. Includes information on car news, car prices, special offers, used car guide and research service, motor shows and road tests. Also articles on finance, insurance and used and new cars for sale.
Readership/Target Audience: Aimed at car buyers and all other people interested in motoring.
CONSUMER: MOTORING & CYCLING: Motoring

MSN TRAVEL
1794033U89A-739

Editorial Address: Cardinal Place, 100 Victoria Street, LONDON, SW1E 5JL
Email: abruce@microsoft.com
Web site: http://travel.uk.msn.com
Publisher: Microsoft Ltd.
Date Launched: 2006
Frequency of update: Daily
Website Access: Free
Traffic Figures: 750,000 Unique Users (per month Publisher's Statement)
Editor: Alastair Bruce
Summary of Content: Website covering all aspects of UK and foreign travel including destination guides, features, reviews and hotels as well as a booking functionality through Expedia and online travel resources.
Readership/Target Audience: Aimed at 25 to 44 year old frequent flyers.
Other Features: Destination guides, features, reviews and hotels as well as a booking functionality through Expedia.
CONSUMER: HOLIDAYS & TRAVEL: Travel

MT MANGEMENTTODAY.COM
626300U14A-210_1

Formerly: MANAGEMENTTODAY
Editorial Address: 174 Hammersmith Road, LONDON, W6 7JP **Tel:** 020 8267 4960 **Fax:** 020 8267 4966
Email: management.today@haymarket.com
Web site: http://www.mtmagazine.co.uk
Publisher: Haymarket Business Media Ltd
Date Launched: 2000
Frequency of update: Weekly
Website Access: Free
Editor: James Taylor
Summary of Content: Website providing management and business news.
Readership/Target Audience: Aimed at middle, senior and board level management in all businesses.
BUSINESS: COMMERCE, INDUSTRY & MANAGEMENT

MTV ONLINE UK & IRELAND
46242U76E-201

Editorial Address: 17-29 Hawley Crescent, Camden Town, LONDON, NW1 8TT **Tel:** 020 7284 6319 **Fax:** 020 7284 6461
Email: cullen.gavin@mtvne.com
Web site: http://www.mtv.co.uk
Publisher: MTV Networks Europe
Date Launched: 1994
Frequency of update: Daily
Website Access: Free
Editor: Gavin Cullen
Summary of Content: Website featuring music industry news, the latest charts and pages dedicated to individual shows.
Readership/Target Audience: Aimed at music fans in the UK and Ireland.
Other Features: Features include an events calendar.
CONSUMER: MUSIC & PERFORMING ARTS: Pop Music

MUMSNET
626171U74D-347

Editorial Address: Unit 6, Deane House Studios, Greenwood Place, Highgate Road, LONDON, NW5 1LB
Tel: 020 7609 3370 **Fax:** 0870 458 2616
Email: editorial@mumsnet.com
Web site: http://www.mumsnet.com
Date Launched: 2000
Frequency of update: Daily
Website Access: Free
Traffic Figures: 350,000 Unique Users (Publisher's Statement)
Editor: Justine Roberts
Summary of Content: Parenting website run by parents, for parents. Containing product reviews, local listings, social networking, competitions, parenting and childcare, forums for advice and support by other parents.
Readership/Target Audience: Aimed at parents of children from 0 to 18 years old.
Other Features: Product reviews and weekly newsletter.
CONSUMER: WOMEN'S INTEREST CONSUMER MAGAZINES: Child Care

MUSICOMH.COM
1741065U76D-812

Editorial Address: PR by email only
Email: info@musicOMH.com
Web site: http://www.musicomh.com
Date Launched: 1999
Frequency of update: Daily
Website Access: Free
Traffic Figures: 250,000 Unique Users (per month Publisher's Statement)
Editor: Michael Hubbard; **Editor-in-Chief:** Michael Hubbard
Summary of Content: Website including independent reviews and features, previewing a broad range of music releases and performances from gigs to opera. Includes interviews with new and established music acts and features. Organises occasional live music nights in London.
Readership/Target Audience: Aimed at fans of all types of music as well as opera, film and theatre audiences in the UK and beyond.
Other Features: Mailiong lists for all sections
CONSUMER: MUSIC & PERFORMING ARTS: Music

MUSICWEB INTERNATIONAL
1790895U76D-824

Editorial Address: 95 Arnold Avenue, COVENTRY, CV3 5ND **Tel:** 02476 419652
Email: len@musicweb-international.com
Web site: http://www.musicweb-international.com
Date Launched: 1997
Frequency of update: Daily
Website Access: Free
Traffic Figures: 110,000 Unique Users (per month Publisher's Statement)
Editor: Len Mullenger
Summary of Content: Website covering mainly classical music with CD and live concert reviews as well as film music, jazz, nostalgia, book reviews and interviews.
Readership/Target Audience: Aimed at music lovers.
CONSUMER: MUSIC & PERFORMING ARTS: Music

MY CHILD
1692406U74D-636

Editorial Address: 33-41 Dallington Street, LONDON, EC1V 0BB **Tel:** 0845 450 6414
Email: editorial@mychild.co.uk
Web site: http://www.mychild.co.uk
Publisher: Electric Words plc
Date Launched: 2005
Editor: Tara Gardner
Summary of Content: Website covering primary education at key stages 1, 2 and 3 as well as foundation. Also covers topics including parenting, family health and well-being, family nutrition and family finance.
Readership/Target Audience: Aimed at families with children aged between 3 and 13 years old.
CONSUMER: WOMEN'S INTEREST CONSUMER MAGAZINES: Child Care

MY MOVIES.NET
46053U76A-37_50

Editorial Address: 40 Oxford Drive, 7-25 Bermondsey Street, LONDON, SE1 2FB **Tel:** 020 7940 4910
Fax: 020 7403 0314
Email: andrew.dillon@mymovies.net
Web site: http://www.mymovies.net
Publisher: My Movies.net Ltd
Date Launched: 1999
Frequency of update: Daily
Website Access: Free
Traffic Figures: 2,490,000 Unique Users (WebTrends)
Editor: Andrew Dillon

Summary of Content: Website covering all aspects of movies including trailers, new releases, reviews, movie news, awards, videos, DVDs, media news and competitions.
Readership/Target Audience: Aimed at those aged between 20 and 40 years old.
CONSUMER: MUSIC & PERFORMING ARTS: Cinema

MY REVIEWER
1843682U78B-664

Editorial Address: 99 Falmouth Avenue, LONDON, E4 9QR
Tel: 020 8527 8935
Email: dvd@myreviewer.com
Web site: http://www.myreviewer.com
Publisher: Reviewer Ltd
Date Launched: 2008
Frequency of update: Daily
Website Access: Free
Editor: Robert Shepherd
Summary of Content: Website reviewing DVDs, music, video games, films and books.
Readership/Target Audience: Aimed at the public in general.
CONSUMER: CONSUMER ELECTRONICS: Video & DVD

MYBUSINESS.CO.UK
1605131U14H-409

Formerly: BusinessEurope.com
Editorial Address: Westminster House, Kew Road, RICHMOND, TW9 2ND **Tel:** 020 8334 1600
Fax: 020 8334 1601
Email: sarar@crimsonbusiness.co.uk
Web site: http://www.mybusiness.co.uk
Publisher: Crimson Business Ltd
Date Launched: 2000
Frequency of update: Daily
Website Access: Free
Traffic Figures: 70,000 Unique Users (per month Publisher's Statement)
Editor: Sara Rizk
Summary of Content: Website covering news, features and how to guides focused on small business issues.
Readership/Target Audience: Aimed at small business managers and entrepreneurs.
BUSINESS: COMMERCE, INDUSTRY & MANAGEMENT: Small Business

MYCHILTERNS.CO.UK
1800727U80C-5402

Editorial Address: 10 Rosetree Close, Prestwood, GREAT MISSENDEN, HP16 9EW **Tel:** 07901 552392
Email: info@mychilterns.co.uk
Web site: http://www.mychilterns.co.uk
Date Launched: 2006
Frequency of update: Daily
Website Access: Free
Traffic Figures: 8,500 Unique Users (per month Publisher's Statement)
Editor: Mike Knuckey
Summary of Content: Website focusing on the Chilterns including accommodation, beauty, crafts, property, getting about, cars and motorcycles, education, food and drink, health, sports and leisure, arts and media, entertainment, furniture, house and gardens professional services and weddings.
Readership/Target Audience: Aimed at affluent residents in the Chilterns region.
Other Features: Local buyers guide and directory, archived theatre reviews and tourism.
CONSUMER: RURAL & REGIONAL INTEREST: Regional Interest English Counties

MYCUSTOMER.COM
713698U14A-93

Formerly: CMC InsightExec - The Customer Management Community
Editorial Address: 100 Victoria Street, BRISTOL, BS1 6HZ
Tel: 0117 915 9600 **Fax:** 0117 915 9630
Email: ndavey@sift.com
Web site: http://www.mycustomer.com
Publisher: Sift Media Ltd
Date Launched: 1998
Frequency of update: Daily
Website Access: Free
Editor: Louise Druce
Summary of Content: Website containing up-to-date CRM (Customer Relationship Management) developments. Includes weekly updates on CRM related news, new products and a document library.
Readership/Target Audience: Aimed at CRM and marketing professionals working in the business consumer marketplace.
BUSINESS: COMMERCE, INDUSTRY & MANAGEMENT

MYDECO.COM
1817441U74C-874

Editorial Address: Newcombe House, 45 Notting Hill Gate, LONDON, W11 3LQ **Tel:** 020 3384 1332
Email: annie@mydeco.com
Web site: http://www.mydeco.com
Date Launched: 2008
Frequency of update: Daily
Website Access: Free
Editor: Annie Deakin
Summary of Content: Website covering all aspects and styles of decorating with features on style and trends as well as buying guides and product reviews.
Readership/Target Audience: Aimed at anyone looking to decorate their homes.
CONSUMER: WOMEN'S INTEREST CONSUMER MAGAZINES: Home & Family

MYFINANCES.CO.UK
1666796U74M-413

Editorial Address: South Quay Plaza, 183 Marsh Wall, LONDON, E14 9SH **Tel:** 020 7517 2200 **Fax:** 020 7517 2229
Email: news@myfinances.co.uk
Web site: http://www.myfinances.co.uk
Publisher: Adfero
Date Launched: 2004
Frequency of update: Daily
Website Access: Free
Traffic Figures: 180,000 Unique Users (Publisher's Statement)
Editor: Daniel Barnes
Summary of Content: News portal covering personal finance from household bills to savings and investments, loans, pensions and insurance.
Readership/Target Audience: Aimed at all those interested in their personal finances including savers, investors, borrowers, consumers, consumers, home owners and financial professionals.
Other Features: Ask the expert section, guides, reference material, product updates.
CONSUMER: WOMEN'S INTEREST CONSUMER MAGAZINES: Personal Finance

MY-HOSPITALITY.COM
1804630U11A-221

Editorial Address: 121 Dunkirk Lane, LEYLAND, PR26 7SQ
Tel: 0870 609 8045 **Fax:** 0871 522 7035
Email: editorial@my-hospitality.com
Web site: http://www.my-hospitality.com
Publisher: THG Publishing
Date Launched: 2007
Frequency of update: Weekly
Website Access: Free
Traffic Figures: 11,000 Unique Users (Publisher's Statement)
Editor: Shaun Turner
Summary of Content: Digital magazine for Northwest Hospitality Magazine covering local hospitality industry news, reviews, supplier directory, regional hospitality jobs, career advice and details of hospitality businesses for sale.
Readership/Target Audience: Aimed at people working in the hospitality industry in hotels, restaurants, bars and food destination pubs in the North West.
BUSINESS: CATERING: Catering, Hotels & Restaurants

MYKINDAPLACE.COM
626268U74F-370

Editorial Address: 5th Floor, Fergusson House, 124-128 City Road, LONDON, EC1V 2NJ **Tel:** 020 7705 4768
Fax: 020 7490 4837
Email: matthew@mykindaplace.com
Web site: http://www.mykindaplace.com
Publisher: Mykindaplace Ltd
Date Launched: 2000
Frequency of update: Daily
Website Access: Free
Editor: Matthew Bagwell
Summary of Content: Website with features on beauty, fashion, music and lifestyle issues.
Readership/Target Audience: Aimed at teenage girls between the ages of 11 and 18 years old.
CONSUMER: WOMEN'S INTEREST CONSUMER MAGAZINES: Teenage

MYMONEYDIVA.COM
1872530U74M-436

Editorial Address: 2 Harlakenden Cottages, Woodchurch, ASHFORD, TN26 3PS **Tel:** 01233 860265
Email: admin@mymoneydiva.com
Web site: http://www.mymoneydiva.com
Frequency of update: Daily
Website Access: Free
Editor: Alison Steed
Summary of Content: Website covering an easy guide of personal finance covering shopping, insurance, mobile phones, fashion, banking and more.

Readership/Target Audience: Aimed at women.
CONSUMER: WOMEN'S INTEREST CONSUMER MAGAZINES: Personal Finance

MYPADGATESHEAD.CO.UK
1805682U74K-777

Editorial Address: Keelman House, Fifth Avenue Business Park, Team Valley Trading Estate, GATESHEAD, NE11 0XA
Tel: 0191 433 5382 **Fax:** 0191 433 5354
Email: ianclarkin@gatesheadhousing.co.uk
Web site: http://www.mypadgateshead.co.uk
Publisher: The Gateshead Housing Company
Date Launched: 2006
Frequency of update: Daily
Website Access: Free
Editor: Ian Clarkin
Summary of Content: Website providing advice, information and guidance about housing services, rights and responsibilities as well as further contacts where people can get help from.
Readership/Target Audience: Aimed at 16 to 24 year olds in Gateshead and surrounding areas.
CONSUMER: WOMEN'S INTEREST CONSUMER MAGAZINES: Home Purchase

MYVILLAGE
1622947U80C-5067

Formerly: My Village
Editorial Address: The Workplace, 105 Ladbroke Grove, LONDON, W11 1PG **Tel:** 020 7792 0624
Email: editor@myvillage.co.uk
Web site: http://www.myvillage.com
Publisher: My Village Local
Frequency of update: Daily
Website Access: Free
Traffic Figures: 610,130 Unique Users (per month Publisher's Statement)
Editor: Laura Heaps
Summary of Content: Website covering lifestyle and fashion, clubs, arts, entertainment, restaurants, cinema, celebrity gossip, property, shopping and events.
Readership/Target Audience: Aimed at those living and working in British cities.
CONSUMER: RURAL & REGIONAL INTEREST: Regional Interest English Counties

NANOMATERIALS WORLD
1664912U35-362

Formerly: Nanomaterials News
Editorial Address: Cleeve Road, LEATHERHEAD, KT22 7RU **Tel:** 01372 802000 **Fax:** 01372 802079
Email: daniel.rogers@pira-international.com
Web site: http://www.intertechpira.com
Publisher: PIRA International
Frequency of update: 10 times a year
Website Access: Paid
Editor: Daniel Rogers
Summary of Content: Electronically delivered E-journal covering new developments and the use of nanotechnology to improve the performance of paper and plastic based packaging.
Readership/Target Audience: Aimed at paper and packaging manufacturers, retailers and brand owners.
BUSINESS: PACKAGING & BOTTLING

NATIONAL FEDERATION OF ANGLERS
704830U92-80

Editorial Address: National Water Sports Centre, Adbolton Lane, Holme Pierrepont, NOTTINGHAM, NG12 2LU
Tel: 0115 9813535 **Fax:** 0115 9819039
Email: tom.goldspink@nfadirect.com
Web site: http://www.nfadirect.com
Date Launched: 1997
Frequency of update: Daily
Website Access: Paid
Traffic Figures: 1,500 Unique Users (per day Publisher's Statement)
Editor: Tom Goldspink
Summary of Content: Website containing news and information on freshwater angling. Includes competitions, a list of regions and clubs. Includes pages for disabled people.
Readership/Target Audience: Aimed at angling enthusiasts.
Other Features: Features include an events calendar and archiving.
CONSUMER: ANGLING & FISHING

NATURE
628923U55-99

Editorial Address: The Macmillan Building, 4 Crinan Street, LONDON, N1 9XW **Tel:** 020 7833 4000 **Fax:** 020 7843 4596
Email: nature@nature.com
Web site: http://www.nature.com

Internet Media

Publisher: Nature Publishing Group
Date Launched: 1997
Frequency of update: Weekly
Website Access: Paid
Traffic Figures: 65,000 Unique Users (per day Publisher's Statement)
Editor: Philip Campbell; **Editor-in-Chief:** Philip Campbell
Summary of Content: Website focusing on all aspects of science.
Readership/Target Audience: Aimed at scientists, lecturers and doctors.
BUSINESS: APPLIED SCIENCE & LABORATORIES

NATURE REPORTS CLIMATE CHANGE
1837014U57-161
Editorial Address: The Macmillan Building, 4 Crinan Street, LONDON, N1 9XW **Tel:** 020 7833 4000 **Fax:** 020 7833 4563
Email: a.barnett@nature.com
Web site: http://www.nature.com/climate
Publisher: Nature Publishing Group
Date Launched: 2007
Frequency of update: Weekly
Website Access: Paid
Editor: Olive Heffernan
Summary of Content: Web portal covering climate change, energy, science, environment and policy.
Readership/Target Audience: Aimed at scientists, policy makers, journalists and lecturers.
BUSINESS: ENVIRONMENT & POLLUTION

NAVAL TECHNOLOGY
626497U40-215
Editorial Address: Brunel House, 55-57 North Wharf Road, LONDON, W2 1LA **Tel:** 020 7915 9957 **Fax:** 020 7915 9720
Email: production@spgmedia.com
Web site: http://www.naval-technology.com
Publisher: SPG Media Ltd
Date Launched: 1996
Frequency of update: 260 times a year
Website Access: Free
Traffic Figures: 229,011 Unique Users (Publisher's Statement)
Editor: Duncan West
Summary of Content: Website covering the naval defence industry with emphasis on current projects in the sector.
Readership/Target Audience: Aimed at naval defence sector professionals.
BUSINESS: DEFENCE

NAVY NEWS ONLINE
628936U40-211
Editorial Address: HMS Nelson, Queen Street, PORTSMOUTH, PO1 3HH **Tel:** 023 9272 4163
Fax: 023 9283 8845
Email: edit@navynews.co.uk
Web site: http://www.navynews.co.uk
Publisher: Navy News
Date Launched: 1999
Frequency of update: 260 times a year
Website Access: Free
Editor: Sarah Fletcher
Summary of Content: Website covering news and information about the UK Royal Navy.
Readership/Target Audience: Aimed at Royal Navy personnel and those with a general interest.
BUSINESS: DEFENCE

NCE
706682U42A-128
Formerly: NCE Plus
Editorial Address: Greater London House, Hampstead Road, LONDON, NW1 7EJ **Tel:** 020 7728 5000
Email: nceedit@construct.emap.com
Web site: http://www.nce.co.uk
Publisher: EMAP Insight
Date Launched: 2000
Frequency of update: Weekly
Website Access: Free
Traffic Figures: 57,000 Unique Users (Publisher's Statement)
Editor: Antony Oliver
Summary of Content: Website focusing on civil engineering. Includes real-time news, industry contacts, new product information and a weather guide.
Readership/Target Audience: Aimed at civil engineers.
BUSINESS: CONSTRUCTION

NEED2KNOW
1638259U74F-756
Editorial Address: 90 Red Square, Stoke, NEWINGTON, NA16 9AG **Tel:** 020 7324 7780 **Fax:** 020 7324 7781
Email: need2know@cimex.com
Web site: http://www.need2know.co.uk

Publisher: Cimex Media
Date Launched: 2003
Frequency of update: Daily
Website Access: Free
Editor: Kary Stewart
Summary of Content: Youth orientated website covering issues including leisure, health, relationships, bullying and law.
Readership/Target Audience: Aimed at 13 to 19 year olds.
CONSUMER: WOMEN'S INTEREST CONSUMER MAGAZINES: Teenage

NETCARS.CO.UK
1826242U77A-606
Editorial Address: The Loading Bay, 12-18 Pollard Street, MANCHESTER, M4 7AJ **Tel:** 0800 019 7180
Email: louis.rix@netcars.co.uk
Web site: http://www.netcars.co.uk
Publisher: Netcars Ltd
Frequency of update: Daily
Website Access: Free
Traffic Figures: 220,000 Unique Users (per month Publisher's Statement)
Editor: Louis Rix
Summary of Content: Website covering motoring with a used car search, car news and reviews, car insurance, loans and vehicle data checks.
Readership/Target Audience: Aimed at all UK residents.
CONSUMER: MOTORING & CYCLING: Motoring

NETIMPERATIVE
623426U14R-502
Editorial Address: Mare Street Studios, Unit 303, 203-213 Mare Street, LONDON, E8 3QE **Tel:** 020 8986 7797
Email: editorial@netimperative.com
Web site: http://www.netimperative.com
Publisher: The Net Imperative Limited
Date Launched: 1999
Frequency of update: Daily
Website Access: Free
Traffic Figures: 35,000 Unique Users (per month Publisher's Statement)
Editor: Robin Langford
Summary of Content: Website providing a range of services for businesses, consumers, observers and commentators interested in all aspects of digital business, including commentary, opinion, features, case studies, profiles, research, statistics, published reports and events concerning key digital sectors and industry issues.
Readership/Target Audience: Aimed at Internet and new media professionals.
BUSINESS: COMMERCE, INDUSTRY & MANAGEMENT: Commerce Related

NETLOANS.CO.UK
1826243U74M-430
Editorial Address: The Loading Bay, Albion Works, 12-18 Pollard Street, MANCHESTER, M4 7AJ **Tel:** 0800 019 7180
Email: louis.rix@netloans.co.uk
Web site: http://www.netloans.co.uk
Publisher: Net Loans Ltd
Frequency of update: Daily
Website Access: Free
Traffic Figures: 9,000 Unique Users (per month Publisher's Statement)
Editor: Louis Rix
Summary of Content: Website covering secured loans, bridging loans, tips and advice.
Readership/Target Audience: Aimed at home owners who want a secured loan and clients looking for bridging finance.
CONSUMER: WOMEN'S INTEREST CONSUMER MAGAZINES: Personal Finance

THE NEW BLACK MAGAZINE
1744320U90-983
Editorial Address: 15 Gardens Court, 231-232 Ladywood, Middleway, BIRMINGHAM, B16 8EU **Tel:** 07920 519316
Fax: 0121 454 2238
Email: editor@thenewblackmagazine.com
Web site: http://www.thenewblackmagazine.com
Publisher: The New Black Publishers
Date Launched: 2005
Frequency of update: Daily
Website Access: Free
Traffic Figures: 3,000,000 Unique Users (per year Publisher's Statement)
Editor: Shola Adenekan
Summary of Content: Website covering people, politics, businesses, careers, arts, media, books, literature, music, education and up-coming events.
Readership/Target Audience: Aimed at degree holders of Black origin from across the globe.
CONSUMER: ETHNIC

NEW CAR NET
626328U77A-345
Editorial Address: 39-51 Highgate Road, LONDON, NW5 1RT **Tel:** 020 7267 7002 **Fax:** 020 7267 7544
Email: newsdesk@newcarnet.co.uk
Web site: http://www.newcarnet.co.uk
Publisher: Netro42 Ltd
Date Launched: 1997
Frequency of update: Daily
Website Access: Free
Traffic Figures: 161,687 Unique Users (per month Publisher's Statement)
Editor: Massimo Pini; **Editor-in-Chief:** Massimo Pini
Summary of Content: Website covering researching, searching, choosing, buying, insuring, running and maintaining new cars. Includes classifieds, road tests and features backed up by advice and detailed information to help get the best motoring deals.
Readership/Target Audience: Aimed at UK motorists and new car buyers.
Other Features: Features include an e-mail newsletter, Car Trumps[®] game, side-by-side comparisons, road tests by women for women, used car classifieds and searchable archives.
CONSUMER: MOTORING & CYCLING: Motoring

NEW ENERGY FINANCE
1926495U58-209
Editorial Address: 2nd Floor, 283-288 High Holborn, LONDON, WC1V 7HP **Tel:** 020 7092 8800
Fax: 020 7092 0801
Web site: http://www.newenergyfinance.com
Publisher: New Energy Finance
Frequency of update: Daily
Website Access: Free
Editor: Angus McCrone
Summary of Content: Website covering clean energy, low carbon technologies and the carbon markets.
Readership/Target Audience: Aimed at investors, corporations and governments.
BUSINESS: ENERGY, FUEL & NUCLEAR

NEW ENERGY FOCUS
1840881U58-206
Editorial Address: Elizabeth House, 39 York Road, LONDON, SE1 7NQ **Tel:** 020 7633 4508
Email: news@newenergyfocus.com
Web site: http://www.newenergyfocus.com
Publisher: Medalyer Public Relations
Frequency of update: Daily
Website Access: Free
Editor: Steve Eminton
Summary of Content: Online publication covering renewable energy and low carbon issues in the UK.
Readership/Target Audience: Aimed at people with an interest in renewable energy.
BUSINESS: ENERGY, FUEL & NUCLEAR

NEW RENAISSANCE
48701U94X-105
Editorial Address: 3A Cazenove Road, LONDON, N16 6PA **Tel:** 020 8806 4250 **Fax:** 020 7502 0737
Email: newren@ru.org
Web site: http://www.ru.org
Publisher: Renaissance Universal
Date Launched: 1990
Frequency of update: Monthly
Website Access: Free
Editor: Paul Adams; **Webmaster:** Donald Nelson
Summary of Content: Website providing holistic coverage of social, spiritual, environmental, political and cultural concerns.
Readership/Target Audience: Aimed at 18 to 50 year olds.
CONSUMER: OTHER CLASSIFICATIONS: Miscellaneous

NEW START
1868971U32G-191
Editorial Address: The Workstation, Paternoster Row, SHEFFIELD, S1 2BX **Tel:** 0114 281 6133
Email: news@newstartmag.co.uk
Web site: http://www.newstartmag.co.uk
Publisher: New Start Publishing Ltd
Frequency of update: Monthly
Website Access: Free
Editor: Austin Macauley
Summary of Content: Website covering regeneration, economic development and sustainable communities.
Readership/Target Audience: Aimed at regeneration practitioners.
BUSINESS: LOCAL GOVERNMENT, LEISURE & RECREATION: Community Care & Social Services

NEW TELEVISION INSIDER
1655114U43C-102

Editorial Address: PO Box 499, CAMBRIDGE, CB1 0AH
Tel: 01223 475381
Email: news@broadbandtvnews.com
Web site: http://www.newtelevisioninsider.com
Publisher: Broadband TV News
Date Launched: 2003
Frequency of update: 24 times a year
Website Access: Paid
Editor: Julian Clover
Summary of Content: Electronically delivered newsletter covering analysis and insight on the delivery of multichannel television.
Readership/Target Audience: Aimed at senior executives.
BUSINESS: ELECTRICAL RETAIL TRADE: TV

NEWBORN TO TEEN
1840808U74D-670

Editorial Address: Britannia House, 11 Glenthorne Road, LONDON, W6 0LH **Tel:** 0870 745 3380
Email: editorial@newborntoteen.com
Web site: http://www.newborntoteen.com
Publisher: Areza Ltd
Date Launched: 2007
Frequency of update: Daily
Website Access: Free
Traffic Figures: 40,000 Unique Users (per month Publisher's Statement)
Editor: Natalie Turner
Summary of Content: Portal covering health, education, toys and games, and activities for all children from babies to teenagers.
Readership/Target Audience: Aimed at children and parents.
CONSUMER: WOMEN'S INTEREST CONSUMER MAGAZINES: Child Care

NEWCASTLE MATTERS
1881657U72J-400

Email: comments@newcastle-matters.co.uk
Web site: http://www.newcastle-matters.co.uk
Frequency of update: Daily
Summary of Content: Website created to help people who care about local issues. Whether you need access to useful information, want to highlight a particular topic to other people, discuss ideas with like-minded people or just show your support and keep up to date with current affairs in your area, Newcastle Matters is the place for you.
Readership/Target Audience: Aimed at residents in the local area of Newcastle.
LOCAL NEWSPAPERS: Community Newsletters

NEWHAM MATTERS
1881658U72J-401

Email: comments@newham-matters.co.uk
Web site: http://www.newham-matters.co.uk
Frequency of update: Daily
Summary of Content: Website created to help people who care about local issues. Whether you need access to useful information, want to highlight a particular topic to other people, discuss ideas with like minded individuals or just show your support and keep up to date with current affairs in your area, Newham Matters is the place for you.
Readership/Target Audience: Aimed at residents in the local area of Newham.
LOCAL NEWSPAPERS: Community Newsletters

NEWHAM.COM
1835431U80B-431

Editorial Address: London Borough of Newham, Communications Service, Barking Road, LONDON, E6 2RP
Tel: 020 8340 2272 **Fax:** 020 8430 1549
Email: info@newham.com
Web site: http://www.newham.com
Frequency of update: Daily
Website Access: Free
Traffic Figures: 5,000 Unique Users (per month Publisher's Statement)
Editor: Kulbinder Mann
Summary of Content: Website covering services and what's on in the area including art, culture, food and drink, entertainment and health.
Readership/Target Audience: Aimed at residents, visitors and businesses in Newham.
CONSUMER: RURAL & REGIONAL INTEREST: Regional Interest Greater London

NEW-MAGAZINE.CO.UK
1698610U74Q-1284

Formerly: Daily Snack
Editorial Address: The Northern & Shell Building, 10 Lower Thames Street, LONDON, EC3R 6EN **Tel:** 0871 434 1010
Fax: 0871 520 7766
Email: robert.spellman@express.co.uk
Web site: http://www.new-magazine.co.uk

Publisher: Express Newspapers Ltd
Date Launched: 2008
Frequency of update: Daily
Website Access: Free
Editor: Robert Spellman
Summary of Content: Website covering gossip, celebrity, sport, music, reviews, gig guide, health, food, travel, money, cars and shopping.
Readership/Target Audience: Aimed at 20 to 35 year olds interested in gossip and celebrity news.
CONSUMER: WOMEN'S INTEREST CONSUMER MAGAZINES: Lifestyle

NEWMINI.ORG
1645943U77E-525

Editorial Address: Leon House, 233 High Street, CROYDON, CR9 1HZ **Tel:** 020 8726 8364
Fax: 020 8726 8399
Email: newmini@ipcmedia.com
Web site: http://www.newmini.org
Publisher: IPC Inspire
Date Launched: 2004
Frequency of update: Daily
Website Access: Free
Editor: Karen Drury; **Editor-in-Chief:** Monty Watkins; **Webmaster:** Ben Clarke
Summary of Content: Website covering modifying, tuning, driving and enjoying the New Mini.
Readership/Target Audience: Aimed at enthusiasts of the new BMW Mini.
CONSUMER: MOTORING & CYCLING: Club Cars

NEWNET
1926497U58-210

Editorial Address: 357 Strand, LONDON, WC2R 0HS
Tel: 020 7845 7595
Email: editorial@newenergyworldnetwork.com
Web site: http://www.newenergyworldnetwork.com
Publisher: New Energy World Press Ltd
Frequency of update: Daily
Website Access: Free
Editor: Ben Chambers
Summary of Content: Magazine covering investment in innovation covering the latest news, views and analysis and by organising exclusive networking events between the leaders, experts and shapers of the industry.
Readership/Target Audience: Aimed at people with an interest in energy investment.
BUSINESS: ENERGY, FUEL & NUCLEAR

NEWPORT MATTERS
1881659U72J-402

Email: comments@newport-matters.co.uk
Web site: http://www.newport-matters.co.uk
Frequency of update: Daily
Summary of Content: Website created to help people who care about local issues. Whether you need access to useful information, want to highlight a particular topic to other people, discuss ideas with like-minded people or just show your support and keep up to date with current affairs in your area, Newport Matters is the place for you.
Readership/Target Audience: Aimed at residents in the local area of Newport.
LOCAL NEWSPAPERS: Community Newsletters

NEWS@ALL-ENERGY
1605013U58-164

Editorial Address: 34 Ellerker Gardens, RICHMOND, TW10 6AA **Tel:** 020 8241 1912 **Fax:** 020 8940 6211
Email: info@all-energy.co.uk
Web site: http://www.all-energy.co.uk
Publisher: Media Generation Events Ltd
Date Launched: 2001
Frequency of update: 26 times a year
Website Access: Free
Traffic Figures: 15,000 Unique Users (Publisher's Statement)
Editor: Judith Patten
Summary of Content: Electronic newsletter covering news about sources of renewable energy and the renewable energy industry.
Readership/Target Audience: Aimed at those with a professional/business interest in renewable energy.
Other Features: Full archive of back issues on website
BUSINESS: ENERGY, FUEL & NUCLEAR

NEWS OF THE WORLD ONLINE
623384U65B-11

Editorial Address: 1 Virginia Street, LONDON, E98 1NW
Tel: 020 7782 1001 **Fax:** 020 7782 4463
Email: newsdesk@notw.co.uk
Web site: http://www.newsoftheworld.co.uk
Publisher: News Group Newspapers Ltd
Frequency of update: Daily. News updated constantly
Website Access: Free

Traffic Figures: 493,530 Unique Users (per month Publisher's Statement)
Editor: News Desk
Summary of Content: Website version of News of the World. Covers news, sport, show-biz, motoring, travel, entertainment, gardening and personal finance.
Readership/Target Audience: Aimed at readers of the newspaper and those with Internet access.
NATIONAL DAILY & SUNDAY NEWSPAPERS: National Sunday Newspapers

NEWS WALES
711713U80D-57

Editorial Address: 17 Market Street, BUILTH WELLS, LD2 3EF **Tel:** 0845 260 2808
Email: newswales@goholidays.net
Web site: http://www.newswales.co.uk
Date Launched: 1998
Frequency of update: Daily
Website Access: Free
Traffic Figures: 40,000 Unique Users (per month Publisher's Statement)
Editor: Ken Whitmore
Summary of Content: Website containing a wide range of information about Wales, including local government, politics, business, agriculture, education, culture, environment, health, sport, tourism and transport.
Readership/Target Audience: Aimed at those living in and those who are interested in Wales.
Other Features: Features include an e-mail newsletter and archiving.
CONSUMER: RURAL & REGIONAL INTEREST: Regional Interest Wales

NEWSCIENTIST.COM
39993U55-108

Editorial Address: Lacon House, 84 Theobalds Road, LONDON, WC1X 8NS **Tel:** 020 7611 1206
Fax: 020 7611 1290
Email: webnews@newscientist.com
Web site: http://www.newscientist.com
Publisher: Reed Business Information
Frequency of update: Daily
Website Access: Paid
Traffic Figures: 3,173,373 Unique Users (01/03/2009 To 31/03/2009 ABC/Electronic)
Editor: Shaoni Bhattacharya
Summary of Content: Website focusing on news, features and opinions on the world of science, technology and the environment.
Readership/Target Audience: Aimed at professionals working within science or technology industries.
BUSINESS: APPLIED SCIENCE & LABORATORIES

NEWSTECH ON-LINE
707753U60A-45

Editorial Address: 8 Sovereign Park, Cleveland Way, HEMEL HEMPSTEAD, HP2 7DA **Tel:** 01442 233656
Fax: 01442 258853
Email: gary@cullumpublishing.co.uk
Web site: http://www.newstech.co.uk
Date Launched: 1999
Frequency of update: Monthly
Website Access: Free
Editor: Gary Cullum
Summary of Content: Website featuring news about newspaper production around the world. Also contains a series of invaluable resources about newspaper technology.
Readership/Target Audience: Aimed at professionals working for newspapers, suppliers and manufactures of equipment to the news publishing industry.
BUSINESS: PUBLISHING: Publishing & Book Trade

NEWSWIRELESS.NET
1685558U5R-681

Editorial Address: 38 Digby Crescent, LONDON, N4 2HR
Tel: 020 8809 0492
Email: guy.kewney@gmail.com
Web site: http://www.newswireless.net
Publisher: AuthorIT Publishing Ltd
Date Launched: 2001
Frequency of update: Daily
Website Access: Free
Editor: Guy Kewney
Summary of Content: Website focusing on mobile communication and technologies.
Readership/Target Audience: Aimed at IT professionals.
BUSINESS: COMPUTERS & AUTOMATION: Computers Related

NMA.CO.UK
707931U2A-550

Formerly: newmediazero
Editorial Address: St. Giles House, 50 Poland Street, LONDON, W1F 7AX **Tel:** 020 7970 4000 **Fax:** 020 7943 8169

Internet Media

Email: danielle.long@centaur.co.uk
Web site: http://www.nma.co.uk
Publisher: Centaur Media plc
Date Launched: 2001
Frequency of update: Weekly
Website Access: Paid
Editor: Danielle Long; Editor-in-Chief: Michael Nutley
Summary of Content: Website featuring new media news and comment, as well as the latest market research data and analysis.
Readership/Target Audience: Aimed at new media industry professionals.
BUSINESS: COMMUNICATIONS, ADVERTISING & MARKETING

NMK
1646148U2A-661

Editorial Address: Westmarc, University of Westminster, 115 New Cavendish Street, LONDON, W1W 6UW
Tel: 020 7911 5000 Fax: 020 7911 5812
Email: ian.delaney@nmk.co.uk
Web site: http://www.nmk.co.uk
Date Launched: 1998
Frequency of update: Daily
Website Access: Free
Editor; Ian Delaney
Summary of Content: Website covering all aspects of digital interactive media, including articles on marketing and project management.
Readership/Target Audience: Aimed at professionals working in the digital media industries.
BUSINESS: COMMUNICATIONS, ADVERTISING & MARKETING

NOBLESVENUES.COM
1665947U89B-346

Formerly: Noble's Venues Guides
Editorial Address: The Old Corn Store, Heartenoak Road, Hawkhurst, CRANBROOK, TN18 4DZ Tel: 01580 752404
Fax: 01580 752604
Email: noblepublishing@aol.com
Web site: http://www.noblesvenues.com
Publisher: The Noble Publishing Company
Date Launched: 2002
Frequency of update: Daily
Website Access: Free
Traffic Figures: 60,000 Unique Users (per month Publisher's Statement)
Editor: Janet Simpson
Summary of Content: Website covering information on venues and ideas for group activities and events from weddings and parties to business meetings and sports meetings. Also features a searchable database to find venues.
Readership/Target Audience: Aimed at those looking for a venue for a group of people, corporate or private.
Other Features: Notice boards for late availability, promotions and special events.
CONSUMER: HOLIDAYS & TRAVEL: Hotel Magazines

NON-LEAGUE-DAILY.COM
1640856U75B-275

Editorial Address: 27 John Street, LONDON, WC1N 2BX
Tel: 07876 568903
Email: enquiries@nonleaguedaily.com
Web site: http://www.nonleaguedaily.com
Publisher: IPG
Date Launched: 2003
Frequency of update: Daily
Website Access: Free
Traffic Figures: 51,000 Unique Users (Publisher's Statement)
Editor: Simon Lambert
Summary of Content: Website covering news, results and league tables for the non-league football pyramid as well as features on topical non-league events.
Readership/Target Audience: Aimed at followers of non-league football.
CONSUMER: SPORT: Football

NOOZZ.COM
1789820U1F-633

Editorial Address: 40 Grosvenor Gardens, LONDON, SW1W 0EB Tel: 020 7259 9000 Fax: 020 7259 9020
Email: info@noozz.com
Web site: http://www.noozz.com
Publisher: Noozz.com Ltd
Date Launched: 2004
Frequency of update: Daily
Website Access: Paid
Traffic Figures: 60,000 Unique Users (per month Publisher's Statement)
Summary of Content: Website focusing on individual emerging markets in the Middle East and providing a blend of news, commentary, analysis, research and business services.

Readership/Target Audience: Aimed at decision makers and higher level management.
BUSINESS: FINANCE & ECONOMICS: Investment

NORDIC BUSINESS REPORT
36971U14C-107_30

Editorial Address: PR by email only Tel: 020 7047 0200
Email: m2pw@m2.com
Web site: http://www.nordicbusinessreport.com
Publisher: M2 Communications Ltd
Frequency of update: Daily
Website Access: Paid
Editor: Jamie Ayres
Summary of Content: Website covering corporate, financial and general developments in the Nordic countries.
Readership/Target Audience: Aimed at those interested in business in the Nordic countries.
BUSINESS: COMMERCE, INDUSTRY & MANAGEMENT: International Commerce

NORFOLK MATTERS
1881660U72J-403

Email: comments@norfolk-matters.co.uk
Web site: http://www.norfolk-matters.co.uk
Frequency of update: Daily
Summary of Content: Website created to help people who care about local issues. Whether you need access to useful information, want to highlight a particular topic to other people, discuss ideas with like minded individuals or just show your support and keep up to date with current affairs in your area, Norfolk Matters is the place for you.
Readership/Target Audience: Aimed at residents in the local area of Norfolk.
LOCAL NEWSPAPERS: Community Newsletters

NORTH EAST AND YORKSHIRE CONSTRUCTION NOW
1809329U4E-446

Editorial Address: For all contact details see main record, Construction Now
Frequency of update: 250 times a year
BUSINESS: ARCHITECTURE & BUILDING: Building

NORTH LANARKSHIRE MATTERS
1881661U72J-404

Email: comments@northlanarkshire-matters.co.uk
Web site: http://www.northlanarkshire-matters.co.uk
Frequency of update: Daily
Summary of Content: Website created to help people who care about local issues. Whether you need access to useful information, want to highlight a particular topic to other people, discuss ideas with like minded individuals or just show your support and keep up to date with current affairs in your area, North Lanarkshire Matters is the place for you.
Readership/Target Audience: Aimed at residents in the local area of North Lanarkshire.
LOCAL NEWSPAPERS: Community Newsletters

NORTH SEA WEEKLY NEWSLETTER
38605U33-17

Formerly: Offshore Report NW Europe
Editorial Address: PO Box 2779, LONDON, W2 6ZW
Tel: 020 7386 5703
Email: info@offshore-intelligence.org.uk
Web site: http://www.offshore-intelligence.org.uk
Publisher: Offshore Intelligence
Frequency of update: Weekly
Website Access: Paid
Editor: Steve Garner
Summary of Content: Online publication reporting on offshore exploration around the North-Sea, including United Kingdom, Germany, Netherlands and Norway.
Readership/Target Audience: Aimed at those working within the oil and gas industries.
BUSINESS: OIL & PETROLEUM

NORTH WEST AND NORTH WALES CONSTRUCTION NOW
1809330U4E-447

Editorial Address: For all contact details see main record, Construction Now
Frequency of update: 250 times a year
BUSINESS: ARCHITECTURE & BUILDING: Building

NORTH YORKSHIRE MATTERS
1881662U72J-405

Email: comments@northyorkshire-matters.co.uk
Web site: http://www.northyorkshire-matters.co.uk

Frequency of update: Daily
Summary of Content: Website created to help people who care about local issues. Whether you need access to useful information, want to highlight a particular topic to other people, discuss ideas with like minded individuals or just show your support and keep up to date with current affairs in your area, North Yorkshire Matters is the place for you.
Readership/Target Audience: Aimed at residents in the local area of North Yorkshire.
LOCAL NEWSPAPERS: Community Newsletters

NORTHAMPTON SAINTS
1663718U75C-462

Editorial Address: Franklins Gardens, Weedon Road, NORTHAMPTON, NN5 5BG Tel: 01604 751543
Fax: 01604 599110
Email: chriswearmouth@northamptonsaints.co.uk
Web site: http://www.northamptonsaints.co.uk
Frequency of update: Daily
Website Access: Free
Editor: Chris Wearmouth
Summary of Content: Official site of the Northampton Saints Rugby Union Football Club with club news, fixtures, match reports and player profiles.
Readership/Target Audience: Aimed at fans and sponsors of Northampton Saints.
CONSUMER: SPORT: Rugby

NORTHAMPTONCHRON.CO.UK
629839U67B-445

Formerly: NorthantsNews.com
Editorial Address: Upper Mounts, NORTHAMPTON, NN1 3HR Tel: 01604 467032 Fax: 01604 467190
Email: editor@northantsnews.co.uk
Web site: http://www.northamptonchron.co.uk
Publisher: Northamptonshire Newspapers Ltd
Date Launched: 2000
Frequency of update: Daily
Website Access: Free
Editor: Richard Edmondson
Summary of Content: Website containing news, sport, information and features about Northampton.
Readership/Target Audience: Read by residents and visitors to the local area.
Other Features: Features include archiving, webcams, schools, database, property, motors, jobs, family notices, games and travel.
REGIONAL DAILY & SUNDAY NEWSPAPERS: Regional Daily Newspapers

NORTHAMPTONSHIRE MATTERS
1881663U72J-406

Email: comments@northamptonshire-matters.co.uk
Web site: http://www.northamptonshire-matters.co.uk
Frequency of update: Daily
Summary of Content: Website created to help people who care about local issues. Whether you need access to useful information, want to highlight a particular topic to other people, discuss ideas with like minded individuals or just show your support and keep up to date with current affairs in your area, Northamptonshire Matters is the place for you.
Readership/Target Audience: Aimed at residents in the local area of Northamptonshire.
LOCAL NEWSPAPERS: Community Newsletters

NORTHEAST.HOUSINGNEWS.CO.UK
1776294U4D-411

Editorial Address: For all contact details see main edition, housingnews.co.uk
Website Access: Free
BUSINESS: ARCHITECTURE & BUILDING: Planning & Housing

NORTHUMBERLAND MATTERS
1881664U72J-407

Email: comments@northumberland-matters.co.uk
Web site: http://www.northumberland-matters.co.uk
Frequency of update: Daily
Summary of Content: Website created to help people who care about local issues. Whether you need access to useful information, want to highlight a particular topic to other people, discuss ideas with like minded individuals or just show your support and keep up to date with current affairs in your area, Northumberland Matters is the place for you.
Readership/Target Audience: Aimed at residents in the local area of Northumberland.
LOCAL NEWSPAPERS: Community Newsletters

NORTHWEST.HOUSINGNEWS.CO.UK

1776295U4D-412

Editorial Address: For all contact details see main edition, housingnews.co.uk
Website Access: Free
BUSINESS: ARCHITECTURE & BUILDING: Planning & Housing

NOTTINGHAMSHIRE MATTERS

1881665U72J-408

Email: comments@nottinghamshire-matters.co.uk
Web site: http://www.nottinghamshire-matters.co.uk
Frequency of update: Daily
Summary of Content: Website created to help people who care about local issues. Whether you need access to useful information, want to highlight a particular topic to other people, discuss ideas with like minded individuals or just show your support and keep up to date with current affairs in your area, Nottinghamshire Matters is the place for you.
Readership/Target Audience: Aimed at residents in the local area of Nottinghamshire.
LOCAL NEWSPAPERS: Community Newsletters

NOWGAMER.COM

1892614U78D-341

Editorial Address: Richmond Hill, 33 Richmond Hill, BOURNEMOUTH, BH2 6EZ **Tel:** 01202 586200
Email: christopher.reynolds@imagine-publishing.co.uk
Web site: http://www.nowgamer.com
Publisher: Imagine Publishing
Date Launched: 2009
Frequency of update: Daily
Website Access: Free
Editor: Christopher Reynolds
Summary of Content: Website covering all current videgames formats - PS3, PSP, Xbox 360, Wii, DS, PC, Mac and iPhone.
Readership/Target Audience: Aimed primarily at 24-34 year old men.
CONSUMER: CONSUMER ELECTRONICS: Games

NOWMAGAZINE.CO.UK

1775721U74A-1023

Editorial Address: Blue Fin Building, 110 Southwark Street, LONDON, SE1 0SU **Tel:** 020 3148 6363
Email: nowletters@ipcmedia.com
Web site: http://www.nowmagazine.co.uk
Publisher: IPC Connect Ltd
Date Launched: 2006
Frequency of update: Daily
Website Access: Free
Traffic Figures: 55,000 Unique Users (01/02/2009 To 28/02/2009 Publisher's Statement)
Editor: Beverley Watts
Summary of Content: Website covering celebrity news, star style, beauty, fashion, celebrity, recipes, travel, health, competitions, horoscopes, shopping.
Readership/Target Audience: Aimed at those who love celebrity gossip and glamour.
Other Features: Newsletter.
CONSUMER: WOMEN'S INTEREST CONSUMER MAGAZINES: Women's Interest

NS NEWS

35619U2B-95

Editorial Address: St. Andrew's House, St. Andrew Street, LONDON, EC4A 3AY **Tel:** 020 7632 7424
Fax: 020 7632 7401
Email: sinkerp@newspapersoc.org.uk
Web site: http://www.newspapersoc.org.uk
Publisher: The Newspaper Society
Frequency of update: Weekly
Website Access: Free
Editor: Paul Sinker
Summary of Content: Electronically delivered newsletter covering Newspaper Society issues including research, lobbying, campaigns, events and publications.
Readership/Target Audience: Read by members of the Newspaper Society and media trade press.
BUSINESS: COMMUNICATIONS, ADVERTISING & MARKETING: Press

NUCLEAR INDUSTRY DIRECTORY

1912968U58-204

Editorial Address: 18 Generator Hall, Electric Wharf, COVENTRY, CV1 4JL **Tel:** 0870 199 4044
Fax: 0870 777 4360
Email: enquries@industrydirectory.co.uk
Web site: http://www.industrydirectory.co.uk
Publisher: Simply Marcomms
Frequency of update: Daily
Website Access: Free

Editor: Kirstie Colledge
Summary of Content: Directory containing the latest news stories for the UK Nuclear industry. Includes news archives.
Readership/Target Audience: Aimed at nuclear professionals, suppliers to the nuclear industry, nuclear Industry PR & Marketing firms.
BUSINESS: ENERGY, FUEL & NUCLEAR

NURSERY ONLINE

1839659U48C-123

Editorial Address: PR by email only **Tel:** 07736 180017
Email: cathy@nursery-online.com
Web site: http://www.nursery-online.com
Publisher: Nursery Online Ltd
Date Launched: 2008
Frequency of update: Daily
Website Access: Free
Editor: Cathy Bryan
Summary of Content: Website containing information on nursery products. Features include supplier contacts and a product finder.
Readership/Target Audience: Aimed at suppliers and retailers of nursery products.
BUSINESS: TOY TRADE & SPORTS GOODS: Toy Trade - Baby Goods

NURSERY WORLD

1859647U62C-746

Editorial Address: 22 Bute Gardens, LONDON, W6 7HN
Tel: 020 8267 8400
Email: liz.roberts@haymarket.com
Web site: http://www.nurseryworld.co.uk
Publisher: Haymarket Business Media Ltd
Frequency of update: Daily
Website Access: Free
Editor: Liz Roberts
Summary of Content: Website covering all aspects of baby and child care. Features news stories, forums and a bookshop.
Readership/Target Audience: Aimed at early year professionals.
BUSINESS: CHURCH & SCHOOL EQUIPMENT & EDUCATION: Junior Education

NUSSL TRADING DIRECTORY

37223U14L-500

Formerly: NUS Buyers Directory
Editorial Address: Snape Road, MACCLESFIELD, SK10 2NZ **Tel:** 01625 413200 **Fax:** 01625 413400
Email: customerservices@nussl.co.uk
Web site: http://www.nussl.co.uk
Publisher: NUS Services Ltd
Frequency of update: Annual. Published in April
Website Access: Free
Traffic Figures: 1,000 Unique Users (Publisher's Statement)
Editor: Nick Emms
Summary of Content: Directory listing companies wishing to supply student organisations.
Readership/Target Audience: Read by student union members.
BUSINESS: COMMERCE, INDUSTRY & MANAGEMENT: Trade Unions

NUTRITION REVIEW

1663591U56A-182

Editorial Address: 69 Wigmore Street, LONDON, W1U 1PZ
Tel: 020 7486 6660 **Fax:** 020 7486 6066
Email: chris@healthsquared.co.uk
Web site: http://www.nutritionreview.co.uk
Publisher: Health Squared Communications
Date Launched: 2004
Frequency of update: Weekly
Website Access: Free
Editor: Chris Sheppard
Summary of Content: Website covering news and information about nutrition issues from a dietary, scientific and political standpoint.
Readership/Target Audience: Aimed at health professionals.
BUSINESS: HEALTH & MEDICAL

THE OBSERVER.CO.UK

717690U65B-71

Editorial Address: Kings Place, 90 York Way, LONDON, N1 9GU **Tel:** 020 3353 2000
Email: susan.smillie@observer.co.uk
Web site: http://www.observer.co.uk
Publisher: Guardian Media Group plc
Date Launched: 1999
Frequency of update: Daily
Website Access: Free
Traffic Figures: 349,193 Unique Users (01/02/2009 To 28/02/2009 ABC)
Editor: Susan Smillie

Summary of Content: Website focusing on the latest UK and international news with an added focus on sports, business, travel and lifestyle issues. Also contains reviews and letters.
Readership/Target Audience: Aimed at those interested in the latest news and events.
NATIONAL DAILY & SUNDAY NEWSPAPERS: National Sunday Newspapers

OFF DUTY

38434U32F-260

Editorial Address: Colchester Business Centre, 1 George Williams Way, COLCHESTER, CO1 2JS **Tel:** 01206 369448
Fax: 01206 369437
Email: info@policelife.net
Web site: http://www.offduty.co.uk
Publisher: Occucom Ltd
Date Launched: 1996
Frequency of update: 260 times a year
Website Access: Free
Traffic Figures: 20,000 Unique Users (Publisher's Statement)
Editor: Martin Herman
Summary of Content: Website containing a wide range of information for serving and retired police officers.
Readership/Target Audience: Aimed at police officers and their families.
BUSINESS: LOCAL GOVERNMENT, LEISURE & RECREATION: Police

OFF LICENCE NEWS

1902859U9A-269

Editorial Address: Broadfield Park, CRAWLEY, RH11 9RT
Tel: 01293 613400
Email: rosie.davenport@william-reed.co.uk
Web site: http://www.offlicencenews.co.uk
Publisher: William Reed Business Media
Frequency of update: Daily
Website Access: Free
Editor: Rosie Davenport
Summary of Content: Website covering news from within major off licence outlets, including supermarkets, cash and carry stores and the wider drinks industry.
Readership/Target Audience: Aimed at managers and decision makers within major off licence outlets and head offices of drinks suppliers and producers.
BUSINESS: DRINKS & LICENSED TRADE: Drinks, Licensed Trade, Wines & Spirits

OFFICE JOTTER

768373U18A-9002

Editorial Address: 14 Amy Road, OXTED, RH8 0PX
Tel: 01883 713074 **Fax:** 0871 433 5581
Web site: http://www.office-futures.com/blog·
Publisher: Office Futures
Date Launched: 2002
Frequency of update: 125 times a year
Website Access: Free
Editor: Roger Whitehead
Summary of Content: Website covering major trends, activities and strategies involved in running an electronic business.
Readership/Target Audience: Aimed at IT directors and policy makers.
BUSINESS: ELECTRONICS

OFFSHORE TECHNOLOGY

629302U33-18

Editorial Address: Brunel House, 55-57 North Wharf Road, LONDON, W2 1LA **Tel:** 020 7915 9957 **Fax:** 020 7915 9720
Email: production@spgmedia.com
Web site: http://www.offshore-technology.com
Publisher: SPG Media Ltd
Date Launched: 2000
Frequency of update: 356 times a year
Website Access: Free
Traffic Figures: 126,987 Unique Users (Publisher's Statement)
Editor: Duncan West
Summary of Content: Website focusing on current projects and information for the offshore oil and gas industry. Includes projects, products and services, exhibitions and conferences and a complete listing of relevant organisations.
Readership/Target Audience: Aimed at specifiers and procurement managers within the offshore technology industry.
BUSINESS: OIL & PETROLEUM

OGILVIE'S E & P DAILY

38626U33-18_50

Formerly: Petroleum Monitor
Editorial Address: Quatro House, Lyon Way, FRIMLEY, GU16 7ER **Tel:** 01276 804508 **Fax:** 01276 804513
Email: shamlen@ogilviepub.com
Web site: http://www.ogilviepub.com

Internet Media

Publisher: Ogilvie Publishing Ltd
Frequency of update: 250 times a year
Website Access: Paid
Editor: Steve Hamlen
Summary of Content: Electronically delivered newsletter containing company news, government policy, ongoing and future projects, benchmark prices and business opportunities within the upstream oil and gas industry.
Readership/Target Audience: Aimed at upper management, business development executives and directors.
BUSINESS: OIL & PETROLEUM

OLD BIKE MART
626336U77B-583

Editorial Address: Media Centre, Morton Way, HORNCASTLE, LN9 6JR **Tel:** 01507 529529
Fax: 01507 529490
Email: editor@oldbikemart.co.uk
Web site: http://www.oldbikemart.co.uk
Publisher: Mortons Media Group Ltd
Date Launched: 1996
Frequency of update: Daily
Website Access: Free
Traffic Figures: 18,000 Unique Users (per month Publisher's Statement)
Editor: Nigel Clarke
Summary of Content: Website focusing on classic motorcycles.
Readership/Target Audience: Aimed at middle to retirement aged riders, collectors and enthusiasts of classic motorcycles.
CONSUMER: MOTORING & CYCLING: Motorcycling

OLDHAM CHRONICLE ONLINE
629570U67B-491

Editorial Address: PO Box 47, 172 Union Street, OLDHAM, OL1 1EQ **Tel:** 0161 633 2121 **Fax:** 0161 652 2111
Email: editorial@oldham-chronicle.co.uk
Web site: http://www.oldham-chronicle.co.uk
Publisher: Hirst Kidd & Rennie Ltd
Frequency of update: Daily
Website Access: Paid
Editor: Jim Williams
Summary of Content: Website containing news, sport and classifieds for the Oldham area and a point of contact for Oldham information and links.
Readership/Target Audience: Aimed at those who live in the local area and expatriates.
REGIONAL DAILY & SUNDAY NEWSPAPERS: Regional Daily Newspapers

---

OLÉ
1894845U34-207

Editorial Address: Suite 223, Business Design Centre, 52 Upper Street, LONDON, N1 0QH **Tel:** 020 7288 6833
Fax: 020 7288 6834
Email: julia.dennison@intelligentmedia.co.uk
Web site: http://www.olezine.co.uk
Publisher: Intelligent Media Solutions
Frequency of update: Monthly
Website Access: Free
Editor: Julia Dennison
Summary of Content: Magazine delivered by email covering office lifestyle features and articles.
Readership/Target Audience: Aimed at dealers to deliver to their customers.
BUSINESS: OFFICE EQUIPMENT

ON THE ROAD
39732U50-22

Editorial Address: Riverside Lodge, Collier Close, Camerton, BATH, BA2 0QB **Tel:** 01761 479645
Fax: 01761 479663
Email: info@chalkfarmpublishing.co.uk
Web site: http://www.ontheroad.co.uk
Publisher: On the Road
Date Launched: 1983
Frequency of update: Monthly
Website Access: Paid
Traffic Figures: 16,000 Unique Users (Publisher's Statement)
Editor: Alan Bennett
Summary of Content: Digital publication covering travel news, issues, events and reviews.
Readership/Target Audience: Aimed at people working in the inbound group tour industry into Europe, Britain and Ireland.
BUSINESS: TRAVEL & TOURISM

ONECLICKHR
629932U14F-50_40

Editorial Address: 2 Bromley Road, BECKENHAM, BR3 5JE **Tel:** 020 8663 1330 **Fax:** 020 8663 4550
Email: marketing@vizual.co.uk

Web site: http://www.oneclickhr.com
Date Launched: 2000
Frequency of update: Monthly
Website Access: Paid
Editor: Eamon Carney-Holland
Summary of Content: Website covering human resources and employee administration management issues, including health and safety, training and employment law.
Readership/Target Audience: Read by human resources and management professionals.
BUSINESS: COMMERCE, INDUSTRY & MANAGEMENT: Training & Recruitment

---

ONEUP
1732456U74D-638

Formerly: OneUp Magazine
Editorial Address: 18 Lower Holt Street, Earls Colne, COLCHESTER, CO6 2PH **Tel:** 01787 223557
Fax: 01787 221686
Email: editor@oneupezine.com
Web site: http://www.oneupmagazine.co.uk
Publisher: Oneup Magazine Ltd
Date Launched: 2006
Frequency of update: Weekly
Website Access: Free
Traffic Figures: 5,000 Unique Users (per month Publisher's Statement)
Editor: Jenny Shelley
Summary of Content: Website containing practical information on work, childcare, finances and legal matters, health and fitness, parenting, entertainment and real life stories.
Readership/Target Audience: Aimed at single and step parents.
CONSUMER: WOMEN'S INTEREST CONSUMER MAGAZINES: Child Care

THE ONLINE REPORTER
36253U5E-580

Editorial Address: PO Box 2077, Verney Park, BUCKINGHAM, MK18 1WQ **Tel:** 01280 820560
Fax: 01280 820554
Email: simon@riderresearch.com
Web site: http://www.riderresearch.com
Publisher: Information Express
Date Launched: 1996
Frequency of update: Weekly
Website Access: Paid
Traffic Figures: 2,000 Unique Users (Publisher's Statement)
Editor: Simon Thompson; **Editor-in-Chief:** Charles Hall
Summary of Content: Electronically delivered newsletter covering digital rights management (DRM), audio and video enabling technologies, internet music, copyright, media asset management, broadband issues, merging of PCs and home entertainment, internet security, privacy and wireless networking relevant to digital media.
Readership/Target Audience: Aimed at professionals in the telecoms, consumer electronics and media industry.
BUSINESS: COMPUTERS & AUTOMATION: Data Transmission

ONLINECASINONEWS.COM
1640364U79F-102

Editorial Address: 5th Floor, 124 Victoria Street, LONDON, 1E 5LA **Tel:** 020 7828 2244
Email: editor@onlinecasinonews.com
Web site: http://www.onlinecasinonews.com
Publisher: Lyceum Publishing
Frequency of update: Daily
Website Access: Free
Traffic Figures: 100,000 Unique Users (Publisher's Statement)
Editor: Michael Caselli
Summary of Content: Website covering gambling, casino and sports betting news, gambling odds and what you need to know to better your chances gambling online.
Readership/Target Audience: Aimed at online gamblers.
CONSUMER: HOBBIES & DIY: Games & Puzzles

OOZE ONLINE
1605511U81A-253

Editorial Address: Whistlers Cottage, The Ridge, Woldingham, CATERHAM, CR3 7AN **Tel:** 0845 127 9903
Fax: 01883 652854
Email: editor@oozemagazine.co.uk
Web site: http://www.oozemagazine.co.uk
Date Launched: 2001
Frequency of update: Monthly
Website Access: Free
Traffic Figures: 5,000 Unique Users (Publisher's Statement)
Editor: Frances Gavin; **Web Editor:** Frances Gavin; **Online Journalist:** Frances Gavin
Summary of Content: Website containing articles on animal, environmental and social issues.
Readership/Target Audience: Aimed at anyone interested in animal welfare.

Other Features: Features include a message board.
CONSUMER: ANIMALS & PETS: Animals & Pets Protection

OPEN FAIRWAYS
1667489U75D-555

Editorial Address: Unit 3, Teal Pavillion, Portside Business Park, 189 Airport Road West, BELFAST, BT3 9ED
Tel: 028 9073 1055 **Fax:** 028 9073 1780
Email: info@openfairways.com
Web site: http://www.openfairways.com
Frequency of update: Quarterly
Website Access: Free
Editor: Pauline McCabe
Summary of Content: Online directory with details and offers on golf courses throughout Ireland and the UK.
Readership/Target Audience: Aimed at golfers within Ireland and the UK.
CONSUMER: SPORT: Golf .

OPEN MAGAZINE
1819872U84A-460

Formerly: Open
Editorial Address: 12 Bemish Road, LONDON, SW15 1DG
Tel: 07946 476153
Email: contributors@openmagazine.co.uk
Web site: http://www.openmagazine.co.uk
Date Launched: 2007
Frequency of update: Daily
Website Access: Free
Editor: Loma-Ann Marks
Summary of Content: Online magazine covering high arts and popular culture including art, photography, theatre, dance, books, film, TV and fashion.
Readership/Target Audience: Aimed at professionals aged 20 - 45, members or affiliates of the arts and creative industries, established practitioners of the creative industries, socially, environmentally and culturally aware people.
CONSUMER: THE ARTS & LITERARY: Arts

OPP RUSSIA
1895153U1E-404

Editorial Address: 1 Lion House, Red Lion Street, RICHMOND, TW9 1RE **Tel:** 020 8332 4611
Email: ed@oppmag.ru
Web site: http://www.oppmag.ru
Publisher: Richmond Green Group
Date Launched: 2008
Frequency of update: Monthly
Website Access: Paid
Traffic Figures: 4,000 Unique Users (Publisher's Statement)
Editor: Dmitry Drozdov
Summary of Content: Online magazine covering industry news, country and regional features, legal issues, products and new developments.
Readership/Target Audience: Aimed at Russian property agents, developers targeting Russian buyers and agents, International property agents selling to Russian buyers and associated trade buyers.
BUSINESS: FINANCE & ECONOMICS: Property

ORTHOPAEDIC PRODUCT NEWS
626624U56A-107_60

Editorial Address: 2 Cheltenham Mount, HARROGATE, HG1 1DL **Tel:** 01423 569676 **Fax:** 01423 569677
Email: editor@pelgrp.com
Web site: http://www.opnews.com
Date Launched: 1984
Frequency of update: Daily
Website Access: Free
Traffic Figures: 8,000 Unique Users (per month Publisher's Statement)
Editor: Richard Redwin
Summary of Content: Website focusing on news and new product information for the orthopaedic industry.
Readership/Target Audience: Aimed at orthopaedic professionals.
BUSINESS: HEALTH & MEDICAL

OSS/BSS ANALYST
1846724U18B-1979

Editorial Address: Mortimer House, 37-41 Mortimer Street, LONDON, W1T 3JH **Tel:** 020 7017 5000
Email: peter.dykes@informa.com
Web site: http://shop.telecoms.com
Publisher: T&F Informa Group PLC
Frequency of update: Monthly
Website Access: Paid
Editor: Peter Dykes
Summary of Content: Online database of publicly announced contracts featuring statistical data on BSS and OSS contract wins.

Readership/Target Audience: Aimed at software vendors and network operators.
BUSINESS: ELECTRONICS: Telecommunications

OTAKU NEWS
1654776U79K-1000

Editorial Address: 22 Barnside Court, WELWYN GARDEN CITY, AL8 6TL **Tel:** 01707 395536
Email: webmaster@otakunews.com
Web site: http://www.otakunews.com
Date Launched: 2004
Frequency of update: Daily
Website Access: Free
Traffic Figures: 175,000 Unique Users (Publisher's Statement)
Editor: Joe Curzon
Summary of Content: Website covering anime, manga and Japanese culture.
Readership/Target Audience: Aimed at those interested in all things Japanese.
CONSUMER: HOBBIES & DIY: Collectors Magazines

OUCH!
767223U94F-995

Editorial Address: Room 2362A, BBC White City, 201 Wood Lane, LONDON, W12 7TS **Tel:** 020 8752 5444
Email: ouch@bbc.co.uk
Web site: http://www.bbc.co.uk/ouch
Date Launched: 2002
Frequency of update: Daily
Website Access: Free
Editor: Damon Rose
Summary of Content: Website reflecting the experiences of disabled people with news features, humour and opinions.
Readership/Target Audience: Aimed at those with an interest in disability.
CONSUMER: OTHER CLASSIFICATIONS: Disability

OUTDOORSMAGIC
626548U75L-463

Editorial Address: 126 St. Marys Road, GLOSSOP, SK13 8JB **Tel:** 020 7861 9856
Email: editor@outdoorsmagic.com
Web site: http://www.outdoorsmagic.com
Publisher: Magicalia Ltd
Date Launched: 2000
Frequency of update: Daily
Website Access: Free
Traffic Figures: 152,000 Unique Users (per month Omniture)
Editor: Jon Doran
Summary of Content: Website with news and features on outdoor pursuits such as scrambling, walking and climbing.
Readership/Target Audience: Aimed at outdoor enthusiasts.
Other Features: Features include a buyer's guide, classifieds, a message board, an e-mail newsletter, a local search facility and archiving.
CONSUMER: SPORT: Outdoor

OUT-LAW.COM
1645416U44-3011

Editorial Address: 123 St. Vincent Street, GLASGOW, G2 5EA **Tel:** 0141 249 5422 **Fax:** 0141 248 6655
Email: struan.robertson@out-law.com
Web site: http://www.out-law.com
Date Launched: 2000
Frequency of update: Daily
Website Access: Free
Traffic Figures: 150,000 Unique Users (Publisher's Statement)
Editor: Struan Robertson
Summary of Content: Website focusing on IT and e-commerce legal news and information.
Readership/Target Audience: Aimed at senior managers, directors and in-house lawyers.
BUSINESS: LEGAL

OVERSEAS PROPERTY PROFESSIONAL ONLINE
1705970U1E-391

Editorial Address: 1 Red Lion Street, RICHMOND, TW9 1RE **Tel:** 020 8332 4600 **Fax:** 020 8332 4639
Email: trevor.l@opp.org.uk
Web site: http://www.opp.org.uk
Publisher: PFI Media Ltd
Date Launched: 2006
Frequency of update: Daily
Website Access: Paid
Traffic Figures: 23,366 Unique Users (Publisher's Statement)
Editor: Alex Evans
Summary of Content: Website focusing on overseas property sales and marketing, international buyer trends plus global, national and regional property growth factors.

Readership/Target Audience: Aimed at international property agents, developers and associated professionals active in the residential overseas property industry all over the world.
Other Features: Searchable news and feature archive, industry reports, diary dates, directories, recruitment
BUSINESS: FINANCE & ECONOMICS: Property

OXFORDMAIL.CO.UK
629020U80C-2650

Formerly: oxfordmail.net
Editorial Address: Newspaper House, Osney Mead, OXFORD, OX2 0EJ **Tel:** 01865 425262 **Fax:** 01865 425554
Email: news@oxfordmail.co.uk
Web site: http://www.oxfordmail.co.uk
Publisher: Newsquest (Oxfordshire) Ltd
Date Launched: 2006
Frequency of update: Daily
Website Access: Free
Traffic Figures: 149,247 Unique Users (01/01/2009 To 30/06/2009 ABC/Electronic)
Editor: Jason Collie
Summary of Content: Website covering news, sport and information for the Oxford region.
Readership/Target Audience: Aimed at local residents and visitors to the area.
Other Features: Features include an events calendar, archiving, recruitment, property, motoring and discussion forums.
CONSUMER: RURAL & REGIONAL INTEREST: Regional Interest English Counties

OXFORDSHIRE MATTERS
1881666U72J-409

Email: comments@oxfordshire-matters.co.uk
Web site: http://www.oxfordshire-matters.co.uk
Frequency of update: Daily
Summary of Content: Website created to help people who care about local issues. Whether you need access to useful information, want to highlight a particular topic to other people, discuss ideas with like minded individuals or just show your support and keep up to date with current affairs in your area, Oxfordshire Matters is the place for you.
Readership/Target Audience: Aimed at residents in the local area of Oxfordshire.
LOCAL NEWSPAPERS: Community Newsletters

PA ENEWS
45476U74J-130

Editorial Address: Western House, St. James Place, High Street, CRANLEIGH, GU6 8RL **Tel:** 01483 276788
Fax: 01483 277646
Email: smartpa@btinternet.com
Web site: http://www.smartgroup.eu.com
Publisher: Smart Group
Date Launched: 2001
Frequency of update: Monthly
Website Access: Free
Traffic Figures: 50,000 Unique Users (Publisher's Statement)
Editor: Tony Williams
Summary of Content: Electronic newsletter covering business news, travel, conference venues and hotels. Includes articles on office products, hospitality and events.
Readership/Target Audience: Read predominantly by secretaries and PAs.
CONSUMER: WOMEN'S INTEREST CONSUMER MAGAZINES: Secretary & PA

PACKAGING INDUSTRY DIRECTORY
1912969U35-370

Editorial Address: 18 Generator Hall, Electric Wharf, COVENTRY, CV1 4JL **Tel:** 0870 199 4044
Fax: 0870 777 4360
Email: enquiries@industrydirectory.co.uk
Web site: http://www.industrydirectory.co.uk
Publisher: Simply Marcomms
Frequency of update: Daily
Website Access: Free
Editor: Kirstie Colledge
Summary of Content: Directory containing the latest news stories for the UK packaging industry. Includes news archives.
Readership/Target Audience: Aimed at Packaging professionals, suppliers to the Packaging industry, Packaging Industry PR & Marketing firms.
BUSINESS: PACKAGING & BOTTLING

PACKAGING-GATEWAY.COM
1863301U35-369

Editorial Address: Brunel House, 55-57 North Wharf Road, LONDON, W2 1LA **Tel:** 020 7915 9600
Email: pennyjones@spgmedia.com
Web site: http://www.packaging-gateway.com

Publisher: SPG Media Ltd
Frequency of update: Daily
Website Access: Free
Editor: Penny Jones
Summary of Content: Website covering packaging. Featuring company profiles, news, features, industry projects and white papers.
Readership/Target Audience: Aimed at packaging executives.
BUSINESS: PACKAGING & BOTTLING

PARENTS NEWS (ONLINE)
626452U74D-450

Editorial Address: 10 The Manor Drive, WORCESTER PARK, KT4 7LG **Tel:** 020 8337 6337 **Fax:** 020 8715 2842
Email: mccarthy@parents-news.co.uk
Web site: http://www.parents-news.co.uk
Publisher: Parents News UK
Date Launched: 1997
Frequency of update: 11 times a year
Website Access: Free
Editor: Penny McCarthy
Summary of Content: Website covering family orientated local events and information.
Readership/Target Audience: Aimed at parents in London and the South East of England.
CONSUMER: WOMEN'S INTEREST CONSUMER MAGAZINES: Child Care

PARENTS ONLINE
622854U74D-430

Editorial Address: 28 Holly Hill Lane, Sarisbury Green, SOUTHAMPTON, SO31 7AD **Tel:** 01489 559111
Email: editor@parents.org.uk
Web site: http://www.parents.org.uk
Publisher: Parents Online
Date Launched: 1999
Frequency of update: Daily
Website Access: Free
Traffic Figures: 89,000 Unique Users (per month Publisher's Statement)
Editor: Simon Lovesey
Summary of Content: Website containing news and information on all aspects of education, leisure activities and child healthcare.
Readership/Target Audience: Aimed at parents of primary school children aged 4 to 12 years old.
Other Features: Features include a discussion forum.
CONSUMER: WOMEN'S INTEREST CONSUMER MAGAZINES: Child Care

PARKER'S ONLINE
46325U77A-356

Editorial Address: Media House, Lynchwood, Peterborough Business Park, PETERBOROUGH, PE2 6EA
Tel: 01733 468000 **Fax:** 01733 468665
Email: daniel.harrison@bauermedia.co.uk
Web site: http://www.parkers.co.uk
Publisher: Bauer Consumer Media Ltd (Media House)
Date Launched: 1999
Frequency of update: Daily
Website Access: Paid
Traffic Figures: 1,204,198 Unique Users (01/03/2009 To 31/03/2009 ABC/Electronic)
Editor: Daniel Harrison
Summary of Content: Website offering advice on buying cars. Includes prices, reviews, buying guides, news and road test reports.
Readership/Target Audience: Aimed at anyone involved in the car buying, selling and owning process.
Other Features: Features include a buyer's guide and a chat forum.
CONSUMER: MOTORING & CYCLING: Motoring

PASSENGERTERMINALTODAY.COM
1895534U49A-425

Editorial Address: Abinger House, Church Street, DORKING, RH4 1DF **Tel:** 01306 743744 **Fax:** 01306 887546
Email: a.pickering@ukintpress.co
Web site: http://www.passengerterminaltoday.com
Publisher: UKIP Media & Events Ltd
Frequency of update: Daily
Website Access: Free
Editor: Andrew Pickering
Summary of Content: Website containing daily, real-time passenger terminal news and dealing with aspects of projects involving air, rail, sail and bus passenger terminals.
Readership/Target Audience: Aimed at key decision makers, engineers, designers and planners.
BUSINESS: TRANSPORT

Internet Media

PATIENT UK
628996U74G-40_60

Editorial Address: 25 Polwarth Crescent, NEWCASTLE UPON TYNE, NE3 2EE **Tel:** 0191 217 1536
Fax: 0191 217 1536
Email: tkenny101@btinternet.com
Web site: http://www.patient.co.uk
Date Launched: 1997
Frequency of update: Daily
Website Access: Free
Traffic Figures: 60,000 Unique Users (per day Publisher's Statement)
Editor: Tim Kenny
Summary of Content: Website providing information covering all aspects of health, disease and healthcare.
Readership/Target Audience: Aimed at patients, carers and health professionals.
CONSUMER: WOMEN'S INTEREST CONSUMER MAGAZINES: Slimming & Health

PAY AND BENEFITS BULLETIN
34958U1A-270

Editorial Address: Quadrant House, The Quadrant, SUTTON, SM2 5AS **Tel:** 020 8652 2251 **Fax:** 020 8652 4394
Email: sheila.attwood@rbi.co.uk
Web site: http://www.xperthr.co.uk
Publisher: Reed Business Information
Frequency of update: 24 times a year
Website Access: Paid
Editor: Sheila Attwood
Summary of Content: Electronic newsletter containing information on the current pay and benefits scene.
Readership/Target Audience: Aimed at unions, governments and employers.
BUSINESS: FINANCE & ECONOMICS

PC ADVISOR
626313U78E-26

Formerly: PC Advisor (Online)
Editorial Address: 4th Floor, 101 Euston Road, LONDON, NW1 2RA **Tel:** 020 7756 2800 **Fax:** 020 7071 3658
Email: letters@pcadvisor.co.uk
Web site: http://www.pcadvisor.co.uk
Publisher: IDG (International Data Group)
Date Launched: 1995
Frequency of update: Daily
Website Access: Free
Editor: Paul Trotter
Summary of Content: Website featuring articles and advice for business and consumer PC users as well as news, reviews, blogs, podcasts and forums.
Readership/Target Audience: Aimed at consumers, small business owners and PC proficient managers.
Other Features: Features include archiving.
CONSUMER: CONSUMER ELECTRONICS: Home Computing

PC ANSWERS ONLINE
749747U78E-36

Editorial Address: 30 Monmouth Street, BATH, BA1 2BW
Tel: 01225 442244
Email: pcanswers@futurenet.com
Web site: http://www.pcanswers.co.uk
Publisher: Future Publishing Ltd
Date Launched: 1998
Frequency of update: Daily
Website Access: Free
Editor: Christian Hall
Summary of Content: Website covering news on new software and hardware. Includes tips, upgrades, tutorials, guides and an ask the expert section.
Readership/Target Audience: Aimed at PC enthusiasts over 25 years old.
Other Features: Features include a buyer's guide, a chat forum, an e-mail newsletter and archiving.
CONSUMER: CONSUMER ELECTRONICS: Home Computing

PC FREAKS AND GEEKS
1799749U78R-517

Editorial Address: 3 Brades Rise, OLDBURY, B69 2HG
Tel: 0121 532 9319
Email: news@pcfrags.com
Web site: http://www.pcfrags.com
Date Launched: 2006
Frequency of update: Daily
Website Access: Free
Editor: Joanne Harris
Summary of Content: Website with reviews of products including pc hardware, gadgets, computer peripherals, MP3 players, wireless products, graphics cards and audio products.
Readership/Target Audience: Aimed at pc gamers and those thinking of buying computer peripherals.

Other Features: Public forums.
CONSUMER: CONSUMER ELECTRONICS: Consumer Electronics Related

PC PLUS ONLINE
628969U78E-37

Editorial Address: 30 Monmouth Street, BATH, BA1 2BW
Tel: 01225 442244 **Fax:** 01225 732295
Email: pcplus@futurenet.com
Web site: http://www.pcplus.co.uk
Publisher: Future Publishing Ltd
Date Launched: 1996
Frequency of update: Daily
Website Access: Free
Traffic Figures: 50,000 Unique Users (per month Publisher's Statement)
Editor: Ian Robson
Summary of Content: Website covering information and resources on personal computing for the intermediate level of expertise.
Readership/Target Audience: Aimed at PC users of all ages and abilities.
Other Features: Features include a buyer's guide, discussion forums, an e-mail newsletter and archiving.
CONSUMER: CONSUMER ELECTRONICS: Home Computing

PC PRO ONLINE
626317U78E-42

Editorial Address: 30 Cleveland Street, LONDON, W1T 4JD
Tel: 020 7907 6000
Email: barryc@pcpro.co.uk
Web site: http://www.pcpro.co.uk
Publisher: Dennis Publishing Ltd
Date Launched: 1997
Frequency of update: Daily
Website Access: Free
Traffic Figures: 1,000,000 Unique Users (per month Publisher's Statement)
Editor: Barry Collins
Summary of Content: Website with reviews and features of specialised computer hardware and software.
Readership/Target Audience: Aimed at professionals within the IT industry and advanced PC users.
CONSUMER: CONSUMER ELECTRONICS: Home Computing

PCZONE
46551U78D-213_2

Editorial Address: 2 Balcombe Street, LONDON, NW1 6NW
Tel: 020 7042 4000
Email: steve.hogarty@futurenet.co.uk
Web site: http://www.pczone.co.uk
Publisher: Future Publishing Limited
Date Launched: 1996
Frequency of update: Daily
Website Access: Free
Editor: Steve Hogarty
Summary of Content: Website focusing on PC game news, tips, reviews, previews, multiplays and downloads.
Readership/Target Audience: Aimed at PC game enthusiasts between 16 to 38 years old.
Other Features: Features include a chat forum, an e-mail newsletter and archiving.
CONSUMER: CONSUMER ELECTRONICS: Games

PEGITUP
1644940U75D-510

Editorial Address: Westfield Lodge, Moreton Morrell, WARWICK, CV35 9DB **Tel:** 01926 650173
Email: david.morgan@warksgolf.co.uk
Web site: http://www.pegitup.com
Publisher: FGA Ltd
Date Launched: 2004
Frequency of update: 324 times a year
Website Access: Free
Traffic Figures: 17,000 Unique Users (per month Publisher's Statement)
Editor: David Morgan
Summary of Content: Website covering equipment profiles, interviews with players, resorts, courses and championships.
Readership/Target Audience: Aimed at regular golfers of all standards.
Other Features: Newsletter.
CONSUMER: SPORT: Golf

PENSIONS WORLD ONLINE
626319U1H-75_25

Editorial Address: 2 Addiscombe Road, CROYDON, CR9 5AF **Tel:** 020 8686 9141 **Fax:** 020 8212 1970
Email: stephanie.hawthorne@lexisnexis.co.uk
Web site: http://www.pensionsworld.co.uk
Publisher: LexisNexis UK
Date Launched: 1998
Frequency of update: Monthly

Website Access: Free
Editor: Stephanie Hawthorne
Summary of Content: Website focusing on pensions for professionals. Includes news and a directory.
Readership/Target Audience: Read by members of the NAPF.
BUSINESS: FINANCE & ECONOMICS: Pensions

PENSIONSNEWS.COM
1749426U1H-95

Editorial Address: 1 Southwark Bridge, LONDON, SE1 9HL
Tel: 020 7775 6385 **Fax:** 020 7775 6414
Email: PensionsNews@FT.Com
Web site: http://www.pensionsnews.com
Publisher: FT Group
Frequency of update: Daily
Website Access: Paid
Summary of Content: Website covering all aspects of pension related news including fund management and investments.
Readership/Target Audience: Aimed at pension professionals, fund managers, pension scheme managers, trustees and pension lawyers.
BUSINESS: FINANCE & ECONOMICS: Pensions

PEOPLE MANAGEMENT
626381U14F-55_1

Formerly: People Management Online
Editorial Address: 17 Britton Street, LONDON, EC1M 5TP
Tel: 020 7324 2729 **Fax:** 020 7324 2791
Email: editorial@peoplemanagement.co.uk
Web site: http://www.peoplemanagement.co.uk
Publisher: Redactive Media Group
Frequency of update: 100 times a year
Traffic Figures: 68,927 Unique Users (01/04/2009 To 30/04/2009 ABC/Electronic)
Editor: Anna Scott
Summary of Content: Website covering human resources news. The official online magazine of the Chartered Institute of Personnel and Development.
Readership/Target Audience: Aimed at human resources professionals.
BUSINESS: COMMERCE, INDUSTRY & MANAGEMENT: Training & Recruitment

PEOPLEANDPLANET.NET
47267U82-153

Formerly: People & the Planet
Editorial Address: 60 Twisden Road, LONDON, NW5 1DN
Tel: 020 7485 3136 **Fax:** 020 7485 3136
Email: planet21@totalise.co.uk
Web site: http://www.peopleandplanet.net
Publisher: Planet 21
Date Launched: 2000
Frequency of update: Daily
Website Access: Free
Traffic Figures: 100,000 Unique Users (per month Publisher's Statement)
Editor: John Rowley; **Editor-in-Chief:** John Rowley
Summary of Content: Online information and educational resource, reporting on worldwide population, environment and sustainable development issues.
Readership/Target Audience: Aimed at schools, colleges, educationalists, policy-makers, media, non-governmental organisations and those with an interest.
Other Features: Features include archiving and picture gallery.
CONSUMER: CURRENT AFFAIRS & POLITICS

PERSONAL FINANCE & SAVINGS
45558U74M-240

Formerly: Personal Finance
Editorial Address: 6th Floor, Davis House, 2 Robert Street, CROYDON, CR0 1QQ **Tel:** 020 8253 8600
Fax: 020 8253 4603
Email: ben.wilkie@metropolis.co.uk
Web site: http://www.themoneypages.com
Publisher: Metropolis International Group Ltd
Date Launched: 1993
Frequency of update: Weekly
Website Access: Free
Traffic Figures: 35,000 Unique Users (per month Publisher's Statement)
Editor: Ben Wilkie
Summary of Content: Website covering all areas of personal finance. Includes savings and investments, mortgages, insurance, pensions, borrowing and alternative investments. Also covers stocks and shares, unit trusts, portfolio management and tax.
Readership/Target Audience: Aimed at private investors, borrowers and savers.

Other Features: Features on the site include, e-newsletter, borrowing tools, calculators, switching tools.
CONSUMER: WOMEN'S INTEREST CONSUMER MAGAZINES: Personal Finance

PERSONALISED EDUCATION NOW

1827916U62A-512

Editorial Address: 15 Campbell Close, WALSALL, WS4 2EJ
Tel: 01922 624097
Email: personalisededucationnow@blueyonder.co.uk
Web site: http://www.personalisededucationnow.org.uk/
Publisher: Personalised Education Now
Date Launched: 1988
Frequency of update: Monthly. Hard copy journal 2xy
Website Access: Free
Editor: Peter Humphreys
Summary of Content: E-briefing and journal covering comment, news and articles regarding personalised education and learning. Featuring conference and training listings, book reviews, journals and magazine listings, job listings, film and animation, links, provocations and think pieces.
Readership/Target Audience: Aimed at educationalists and educators of all levels from within and beyond mainstream settings.
Other Features: Archiving, back copies of e-briefings, journal and newsletters, links and listings to other organisations.
BUSINESS: CHURCH & SCHOOL EQUIPMENT & EDUCATION: Education

PERSONNELZONE

1622835U14F-233

Editorial Address: Heath House, Firfields, WEYBRIDGE, KT13 0UD **Tel:** 01932 830111 **Fax:** 01932 821592
Email: editorial@personnelzone.com
Web site: http://www.personnelzone.com
Publisher: PersonnelZone
Date Launched: 1998
Frequency of update: Monthly. Published around the middle of the month prior to the cover date
Website Access: Paid
Traffic Figures: 38,000 Unique Users (per month Publisher's Statement)
Editor: Stewart Shepherd
Summary of Content: Website featuring news, articles and reviews for the HR industry. Contains a directory of HR and training suppliers in the UK, plus training courses, an HR bookstore and a reference point for jobs in the HR sector.
Readership/Target Audience: Aimed at professional HR and training managers.
BUSINESS: COMMERCE, INDUSTRY & MANAGEMENT: Training & Recruitment

PETERBOROUGHTODAY

629855U80C-540

Formerly: peterboroughnow
Editorial Address: 57 Priestgate, PETERBOROUGH, PE1 1JW **Tel:** 01733 555111 **Fax:** 01733 313147
Email: eteditor@peterboroughtoday.co.uk
Web site: http://www.peterboroughtoday.co.uk
Publisher: East Midlands Newspapers Ltd
Date Launched: 2000
Frequency of update: Daily
Website Access: Free
Traffic Figures: 162,149 Unique Users (01/01/2009 To 30/06/2009 ABC/Electronic)
Editor: Rich Kendall; **Web Editor:** Rich Kendall
Summary of Content: Website containing local news, sport, business news, local information, entertainment guides and local business directory for the city of Peterborough.
Readership/Target Audience: Read by residents and visitors to the local area.
Other Features: Features include recruitment, property and cars for sale, a chat forum and archiving.
CONSUMER: RURAL & REGIONAL INTEREST: Regional Interest English Counties

PETHEALTHCARE.CO.UK

626135U81X-195

Editorial Address: 4 Frampton Way, Kings Worthy, WINCHESTER, SO23 7QE **Tel:** 07970 385250
Email: laura@pethealthcare.co.uk
Web site: http://www.pethealthcare.co.uk
Publisher: Hyper @ Fallon
Date Launched: 2000
Frequency of update: Monthly
Website Access: Free
Traffic Figures: 101,272 Unique Users (Publisher's Statement)
Editor: Laura Cannon
Summary of Content: Website covering all aspects of pet healthcare with news, database of common questions, vaccination reminder service, vet and rescue centre directories, guide to breeds and a interactive breed selector.

Readership/Target Audience: Aimed at pet owners, professionals and anyone with an interest in pets.
Other Features: Archiving of news and features, Message board, Newsletter - 6 weekly
CONSUMER: ANIMALS & PETS

PETPLANET.CO.UK

628929U81X-205

Formerly: Pets Park
Editorial Address: 10 Lindsay Square, Deans Industrial Estate, Deans, LIVINGSTON, EH54 8RL **Tel:** 0845 345 0723
Fax: 0845 601 2765
Email: kirsty@petplanet.co.uk
Web site: http://www.petplanet.co.uk
Publisher: PetPlanet.co.uk Ltd
Date Launched: 1999
Frequency of update: Daily
Website Access: Free
Traffic Figures: 650,000 Unique Users (per month Publisher's Statement)
Editor: Kirsty McNamara
Summary of Content: Website focusing on pets. Includes the latest news, what's new, health, welfare, charity information, animal behaviour and travel.
Readership/Target Audience: Aimed at pet owners and animal lovers.
Other Features: Features include an online shop, newsletter and chat forums.
CONSUMER: ANIMALS & PETS

PHARMACEUTICAL EXECUTIVE EUROPE

1666076U37-408

Formerly: European Pharmaceutical Executive
Editorial Address: 500 Chiswick High Road, LONDON, W4 5RG **Tel:** 020 8956 2660 **Fax:** 020 8956 2666
Email: jupton@advanstar.com
Web site: http://www.pharmexeceurope.com
Publisher: Advanstar Communications (U.K.) Ltd
Date Launched: 2004
Frequency of update: Daily
Website Access: Paid
Editor: Julian Upton
Summary of Content: Digital magazine focusing on strategic business and management issues within biopharmaceutical and pharmaceutical companies. Includes articles on business developments, sales and marketing strategies, corporate management, industry trends, new technologies, news and interviews with leading figures in the industry.
Readership/Target Audience: Aimed at senior corporate executives and sales, marketing and business professionals within the pharmaceutical industry and biopharmaceutical industries.
BUSINESS: PHARMACEUTICAL & CHEMISTS

PHARMACEUTICAL INDUSTRY DIRECTORY

1912970U37-436

Editorial Address: 18 Generator Hall, Electric Wharf, COVENTRY, CV1 4JL **Tel:** 0870 199 4044
Fax: 0870 777 4360
Email: enquries@industrydirectory.co.uk
Web site: http://www.industrydirectory.co.uk
Publisher: Simply Marcomms
Frequency of update: Daily
Website Access: Free
Editor: Kirstie Colledge
Summary of Content: Directory containing the latest news stories for the UK Pharmaceutical industry. Includes news archives.
Readership/Target Audience: Aimed at Pharmaceutical professionals, suppliers to the Pharmaceutical industry, Pharmaceutical Industry PR & Marketing firms.
BUSINESS: PHARMACEUTICAL & CHEMISTS

PHARMACEUTICAL TECHNOLOGY

1616275U37-405

Editorial Address: Brunel House, 55-57 North Wharf Road, LONDON, W2 1LA **Tel:** 020 7915 9957 **Fax:** 020 7915 9720
Email: production@spgmedia.com
Web site: http://www.pharmaceutical-technology.com
Publisher: SPG Media Ltd
Date Launched: 2000
Frequency of update: Daily
Website Access: Free
Traffic Figures: 56,438 Unique Users (per month Publisher's Statement)
Editor: Duncan West
Summary of Content: Website covering pharmaceutical technology projects both in production and under development.

Readership/Target Audience: Aimed at those working within pharmaceutical industries.
BUSINESS: PHARMACEUTICAL & CHEMISTS

PHARMALICENSING

711791U37-61_35

Editorial Address: Marlborough House, 1st Floor, Westminster Place, York Business Park, YORK, YO26 6RW
Tel: 01904 520460 **Fax:** 01904 520461
Email: info@pharmalicensing.com
Web site: http://www.pharmalicensing.com
Publisher: UTEK Europe
Date Launched: 1999
Frequency of update: Daily
Website Access: Paid
Traffic Figures: 310,000 Unique Users (per year Publisher's Statement)
Editor: Raveena Bhambra
Summary of Content: Online business development tool containing biopharmaceutical business news, partnering and business development directories, industry developments and information about pharmaceutical and biotech events. Also features a pharmaceutical professional services outsourcing directory.
Readership/Target Audience: Aimed at senior pharmaceutical, biotech licensing and business development executives.
BUSINESS: PHARMACEUTICAL & CHEMISTS

PHARMATIMES WORLD NEWS ONLINE

626522U37-61_58

Formerly: PharmaTimes News Online
Editorial Address: 173 Sheen Lane, East Sheen, LONDON, SW14 0NA **Tel:** 020 8878 8566 **Fax:** 020 8876 8834
Email: claire@pharmatimes.com
Web site: http://www.pharmatimes.com
Date Launched: 2000
Frequency of update: Weekly
Website Access: Free
Traffic Figures: 29,543 Unique Users (per month Publisher's Statement)
Editor: Claire Bowie
Summary of Content: Website focusing on news for the pharmaceutical industry.
Readership/Target Audience: Aimed at pharmaceutical professionals.
BUSINESS: PHARMACEUTICAL & CHEMISTS

PHARMIWEB.COM

1795203U37-432

Editorial Address: Clarendon House, Grenville Place, BRACKNELL, RG12 1BP **Tel:** 01344 677433
Fax: 01344 677434
Web site: http://www.pharmiweb.com
Publisher: PharmiWeb Solutions
Date Launched: 1999
Frequency of update: Daily
Website Access: Free
Traffic Figures: 100,000 Unique Users (Publisher's Statement)
Editor: Mike Wood
Summary of Content: Portal providing news, information and recruitment solutions for the pharmaceutical sector.
Readership/Target Audience: Aimed at pharmaceutical manufacturers.
BUSINESS: PHARMACEUTICAL & CHEMISTS

PHARMWEB

626180U37-61_60

Editorial Address: 3 Kilmory Fold, GLOSSOP, SK13 7PH
Tel: 07092 030763 **Fax:** 07092 030763
Email: info@pharmweb.com
Web site: http://www.pharmweb.net
Publisher: Pharmweb
Date Launched: 1994
Frequency of update: Daily
Website Access: Free
Traffic Figures: 40,000 Unique Users (per month Publisher's Statement)
Editor: Antony D'Emanuele
Summary of Content: Portal covering all aspects of the UK pharmaceutical industry.
Readership/Target Audience: Aimed at professionals within the pharmaceutical industry and health care related professionals.
BUSINESS: PHARMACEUTICAL & CHEMISTS

PHOTO-I

1791859U85A-211

Editorial Address: 20 Green Lane, CHISLEHURST, BR7 6AG **Tel:** 020 8467 2465
Email: vsoliver@aol.com
Web site: http://www.photo-i.co.uk

Internet Media

Date Launched: 2002
Frequency of update: Daily
Website Access: Free
Traffic Figures: 30,000 Unique Users (per day Publisher's Statement)
Editor: Vincent Oliver
Summary of Content: Website with inter-active reviews covering digital photography, printers, software, books, cameras and digital video.
Readership/Target Audience: Aimed at intermediate to advanced photographers who want more in-depth knowledge.
Other Features: Forum Board.
CONSUMER: PHOTOGRAPHY & FILM MAKING: Photography

PI DIRECTORY (POWDER INDUSTRY)

628858U10-100

Editorial Address: PO Box 1523, LONDON, N2 9HZ
Tel: 020 8442 0654 **Fax:** 020 8442 1640
Email: powderfax@btinternet.com
Web site: http://www.powderreporter.co.uk
Publisher: Salisbury Sarum Ltd
Date Launched: 2001
Frequency of update: Daily
Website Access: Free
Editor: Allan Davies
Summary of Content: Directory of companies and services within the powder processing and handling market.
Readership/Target Audience: Aimed at personnel in the pharmaceutical, chemical, mineral, food, animal feedstuffs and environmental sectors.
BUSINESS: MATERIALS HANDLING

PICK ME UP

1902822U74A-1061

Editorial Address: The Blue Fin Building, 110 Southwark Street, LONDON, SE1 0SU **Tel:** 020 3148 6432
Email: pickmeup@ipcmedia.com
Web site: http://www.pickmeupmagazine.co.uk
Publisher: IPC Media Ltd
Frequency of update: Daily
Traffic Figures: 53,228 Unique Users (per month Publisher's Statement)
Editor: June Smith-Sheppard
Summary of Content: Website covering real life, puzzles, competitions, problem pages and horoscopes.
Readership/Target Audience: Aimed at women with a certain outlook on life.
CONSUMER: WOMEN'S INTEREST CONSUMER MAGAZINES: Women's Interest

PINK WISHES

1833335U74A-1044

Editorial Address: Suite 103, Greenway Business Centre, Harlow Business Park, HARLOW, CM19 5QE
Tel: 01279 216441
Email: lynn@pinkwishes.co.uk
Web site: http://www.pinkwishes.co.uk
Date Launched: 2007
Frequency of update: Daily
Website Access: Free
Traffic Figures: 45,000 Unique Users (Nov2007-Jan2008 Publisher's Statement)
Editor: Lynn Culver
Summary of Content: Online magazine covering fashion including accessories, bags and lingerie, hair, beauty, food and drink, health and fitness, holidays, travel, celebrity interviews, events and what's on.
Readership/Target Audience: Aimed at women aged 25 to 60 years old.
Other Features: Other features include Post A Wish.
CONSUMER: WOMEN'S INTEREST CONSUMER MAGAZINES: Women's Interest

PINKE.BIZ

1858703U86B-187

Editorial Address: Senate House, Saxon Business Park, Hanbury Road, Stoke Prior, BROMSGROVE, B60 4AD
Tel: 0844 800 3628
Email: news@pinke.biz
Web site: http://www.pinke.biz
Frequency of update: Daily
Traffic Figures: 34,310 Unique Users (per month Publisher's Statement)
Editor: Robert Knox
Summary of Content: Website featuring a business directory covering topics such as travel, health and wellbeing, advice, weddings, events and search tools.
Readership/Target Audience: Aimed at the lesbian, gay, bisexual and transgender community.
CONSUMER: ADULT & GAY MAGAZINES: Gay & Lesbian Magazines

PINKNEWS.CO.UK

1746708U86B-171

Editorial Address: Phoenix Yard, 65 King's Cross Road, LONDON, WC1X 9LW **Tel:** 020 7239 4910
Email: news@pinknews.co.uk
Web site: http://www.pinknews.co.uk
Publisher: Pink Unlimited
Frequency of update: Daily
Website Access: Free
Traffic Figures: 34,207 Unique Users (per month ABC/Electronic)
Editor: Jessica Green
Summary of Content: Website covering anything of interest to gay people as well as lifestyle articles including grooming, motoring and high income luxury items.
Readership/Target Audience: Aimed at lesbians, bi-sexuals, gays and trans-sexuals aged 25 years and over.
CONSUMER: ADULT & GAY MAGAZINES: Gay & Lesbian Magazines

PIPE AND PROFILE EXTRUSION

1882058U39-160

Editorial Address: AMI House, 45-47 Stokes Croft, BRISTOL, BS1 3QP **Tel:** 0117 924 9442 **Fax:** 0117 989 2128
Email: lou@pipeandprofile.com
Web site: http://www.pipeandprofile.com
Publisher: Applied Market Information Ltd
Date Launched: 2009
Frequency of update: 6 times a year. Published in the middle of the first month
Website Access: Free
Traffic Figures: 9,774 Unique Users (Publisher's Statement)
Editor: Lou Reade
Summary of Content: Digital magazine covering technical developments, market trends, business news and legislative announcements.
Readership/Target Audience: Aimed at the producers of plastics, pipes and profiles.
BUSINESS: PLASTICS & RUBBER

PISTONHEADS.COM

633853U77D-390

Editorial Address: Teddington Studios, Broom Road, TEDDINGTON, TW11 9BE **Tel:** 020 8267 5000
Email: news@pistonheads.com
Web site: http://www.pistonheads.com
Publisher: Haymarket Consumer Media
Date Launched: 1998
Frequency of update: Daily
Website Access: Free
Traffic Figures: 2,545,411 Unique Users (01/03/2009 To 31/03/2009 ABC/Electronic)
Editor: Ollie Stallwood
Summary of Content: Website focusing on sports car news and features within the UK market.
Readership/Target Audience: Aimed at car enthusiasts, mostly males aged 25 to 45 years old.
Other Features: Features include classifieds, e-mail newsletters and a message board.
CONSUMER: MOTORING & CYCLING: Motor Sports

PLANT HIRE INDUSTRY DIRECTORY

1818199U42A-244

Editorial Address: 18 Generator Hall, Electric Wharf, COVENTRY, CV1 4JL **Tel:** 0870 199 4044
Fax: 0870 777 4360
Email: enquiries@industrydirectory.co.uk
Web site: http://www.industrydirectory.co.uk/plant
Publisher: Simply Marcomms
Frequency of update: Daily
Website Access: Free
Editor: Kirstie Colledge
Summary of Content: Directory containing the latest news stories for the plant hire industry. Includes a news archive.
Readership/Target Audience: Aimed at professionals in the building and construction industry particularly those in the plant hire industry.
BUSINESS: CONSTRUCTION

PLASTICS PACKAGING INNOVATIONS NEWS

1664913U35-361

Editorial Address: Cleeve Road, LEATHERHEAD, KT22 7RU **Tel:** 01372 802091 **Fax:** 01372 802079
Email: joe.thompson@pira-international.com
Web site: http://www.intertechpira.com
Publisher: PIRA International
Frequency of update: 10 times a year
Website Access: Paid
Editor: Joe Thompson
Summary of Content: Electronically delivered newsletter covering new developments in plastics packaging.

Readership/Target Audience: Aimed at brand owners, packaging, print and label suppliers.
BUSINESS: PACKAGING & BOTTLING

PLATINUM METALS REVIEW

38204U27-123

Editorial Address: Orchard Road, ROYSTON, SG8 5HE
Tel: 01763 256323 **Fax:** 01763 256359
Email: editor@matthey.com
Web site: http://www.platinummetalsreview.com
Publisher: Johnson Matthey plc
Date Launched: 1957
Frequency of update: Quarterly
Website Access: Free
Editor: Barry Copping
Summary of Content: Online journal offering a range of free material, including the PGM (platinum group metals) database, directories of people and organisations, events, links and questions and answers.
Readership/Target Audience: Aimed at industrial and academic users of the platinum metals.
BUSINESS: METAL, IRON & STEEL

PLUMBING PARK

624647U3D-90

Editorial Address: Britannia House, 11 Glenthorne Road, LONDON, W6 0LH **Tel:** 0870 745 3380
Email: editor@plumbingpark.co.uk
Web site: http://www.plumbingpark.co.uk
Publisher: Areza Ltd
Date Launched: 2000
Frequency of update: Daily. News updated several times a day
Website Access: Free
Traffic Figures: 60,000 Unique Users (Publisher's Statement)
Editor: John Cohen
Summary of Content: Business website with features on plumbing, heating, ventilation and air conditioning, bathroom and kitchen products and services in the UK.
Readership/Target Audience: Aimed at installers, users, designers, specifiers, merchants and distributors of plumbing, heating, ventilation and air conditioning (HVAC) products and equipment.
Other Features: Jobs forum, directory and classifieds.
BUSINESS: HEATING & VENTILATION: Heating & Plumbing

PLUMBINGPAGES.COM

1776142U3D-101

Editorial Address: 2 Millennium Court, Enterprise Way, Vale Park, EVESHAM, WR11 1GS **Tel:** 01386 768078
Fax: 01386 768494
Email: editor@plumbingpages.com
Web site: http://www.plumbingpages.com
Date Launched: 1999
Frequency of update: Daily
Website Access: Free
Traffic Figures: 9,000 Unique Users (per day Publisher's Statement)
Editor: James Hickman
Summary of Content: Website covering all aspects of plumbing, heating and energy efficiency including advice, legislation, regulations, news, bathrooms, showers, radiators, taps, sinks, plumbing courses and suppliers.
Readership/Target Audience: Aimed at the plumbing and heating industry.
Other Features: Discussion forum.
BUSINESS: HEATING & VENTILATION: Heating & Plumbing

PLUMBZINE

1893952U3D-105

Editorial Address: Becket House, Vestry Road, SEVENOAKS, TN14 5EJ **Tel:** 01732 748000
Fax: 01732 748001
Email: nfarrugia@unity-media.com
Web site: http://www.plumbzine.com
Publisher: Unity Media plc
Date Launched: 2009
Frequency of update: Daily. Plus weekly electronic newsletter
Website Access: Free
Editor: Nichola Farrugia
Summary of Content: Online publication covering the latest equipment, developments, methods and advice on instillation and specification.
Readership/Target Audience: Aimed at installers of domestic plumbing and air conditioning installers.
BUSINESS: HEATING & VENTILATION: Heating & Plumbing

PLUS NEWS

45683U91R-150

Editorial Address: 210 Commerce House, High Street, SUTTON COLDFIELD, B72 1AB **Tel:** 0870 879 4960
Email: plusnews@18plus.org.uk
Web site: http://www.18plus.org.uk

Publisher: National Federation of 18 Plus Groups
Date Launched: 1968
Frequency of update: Quarterly
Website Access: Free
Editor: Richard Mahhaffery
Summary of Content: Website of the National Federation of 18 Plus Groups. Contains articles on activities and events including sporting competitions and charity fundraisers.
Readership/Target Audience: Aimed at those between 18 to 35 years old.
CONSUMER: RECREATION & LEISURE: Recreation & Leisure Related

POCKETGAMER.CO.UK
1792572U78D-336
Editorial Address: 17 Wilmar Close, UXBRIDGE, UB8 1AS
Tel: 07811 135982
Email: joao@pocketgamer.co.uk
Web site: http://www.pocketgamer.co.uk
Publisher: Steel Media Ltd
Date Launched: 2006
Frequency of update: Daily
Website Access: Free
Traffic Figures: 450,000 Unique Users (per month Publisher's Statement)
Editor: Joao Diniz Sanches
Summary of Content: Website covering mobile and hand-held console games with news, reviews and features.
Readership/Target Audience: Aimed at a mainstream games audience.
Other Features: Other features include- calendar of new releases, games archive, buyers guide, forum, mailing list and newsletter, competitions and how to guides.
CONSUMER: CONSUMER ELECTRONICS: Games

POCKET-LINT.CO.UK
1705053U78R-506
Editorial Address: 3 Course Road, ASCOT, SL5 7HQ
Tel: 07968 420874
Email: stuart@pocket-lint.co.uk
Web site: http://www.pocket-lint.co.uk
Frequency of update: Daily
Website Access: Free
Traffic Figures: 1,000,000 Unique Users (Publisher's Statement)
Editor: Stuart Miles
Summary of Content: Website covering gadgets, gear and gizmo news and reviews. Everything from digital cameras and mobile phones to home appliances and boys toys.
Readership/Target Audience: Aimed at consumers with an interest in technology and the latest gadgets.
Other Features: Forums, Newsletter and Email Alerts.
CONSUMER: CONSUMER ELECTRONICS: Consumer Electronics Related

POCKETPICKS.CO.UK
1827909U78R-521
Editorial Address: 17 Wilmar Close, UXBRIDGE, UB8 1AS
Tel: 07944 829025
Email: news@pocketpicks.co.uk
Web site: http://www.pocketpicks.co.uk
Publisher: Steel Media Ltd
Date Launched: 2006
Frequency of update: Daily
Website Access: Free
Traffic Figures: 150,000 Unique Users (per month Publisher's Statement)
Summary of Content: Website covering mobile phones and content, providing news on new handsets, new services and new content types as well as hands on trials and how to guides.
Readership/Target Audience: Aimed at early adopters of mobile technology and services.
CONSUMER: CONSUMER ELECTRONICS: Consumer Electronics Related

POINTER
36910U14B-300
Editorial Address: Campsie House, 17 Park Circus Place, GLASGOW, G3 6AH **Tel:** 0141 332 9119 **Fax:** 0141 333 0039
Email: chris.watson@scdi.org.uk
Web site: http://www.scdi.org.uk
Publisher: The Scottish Council Development and Industry
Frequency of update: 17 times a year
Website Access: Paid
Traffic Figures: 200 Unique Users (Publisher's Statement)
Editor: Chris Watson
Summary of Content: Electronically delivered newsletter of The Scottish Council Development and Industry, covering Scottish industrial and commercial activity including new companies, takeovers, mergers, company plans, employment changes, contracts and other potential sales leads.

Readership/Target Audience: Read by Scottish businesses.
BUSINESS: COMMERCE, INDUSTRY & MANAGEMENT: Industry & Factories

POLICE AVIATION NEWS
1626375U6R-157
Editorial Address: 7 Windmill Close, WALTHAM ABBEY, EN9 3BQ **Tel:** 01992 714162
Email: editor@policeaviationnews.com
Web site: http://www.policeaviationnews.com
Publisher: Police Aviation Research
Date Launched: 1996
Frequency of update: Monthly
Website Access: Free
Traffic Figures: 7,000 Unique Users (per month Publisher's Statement)
Editor: Bryn Elliott
Summary of Content: Website covering news and views, new products and technical documents.
Readership/Target Audience: Aimed at airborne emergency services.
BUSINESS: AVIATION & AERONAUTICS: Aviation Related

POLITICS.CO.UK
1666801U82-264
Editorial Address: South Quay Plaza, 183 Marsh Wall, LONDON, E14 9SH **Tel:** 020 7517 2268 **Fax:** 020 7517 2233
Email: kate.webb@politics.co.uk
Web site: http://www.politics.co.uk
Publisher: Adfero
Frequency of update: Daily
Website Access: Free
Traffic Figures: 105,000 Unique Users (per month Publisher's Statement)
Editor: Ian Dunt
Summary of Content: Website covering the latest political developments. Coverage is in five sections: domestic policy, foreign policy, party politics, public services, and the economy.
Readership/Target Audience: Aimed at politicians, researchers, journalists, political activists, students, and voters.
CONSUMER: CURRENT AFFAIRS & POLITICS

POPBET
1826069U79F-110
Editorial Address: 36 Eastcastle Street, LONDON, W1W 8DP **Tel:** 020 7580 7744
Email: info@chickendinner.co.uk
Web site: http://www.popbet.com
Frequency of update: Daily
Website Access: Free
Traffic Figures: 50,000 Unique Users (per month Publisher's Statement)
Editor: Ed Needham
Summary of Content: Website covering cultural betting on reality TV, politics and celebrity.
Readership/Target Audience: Aimed at men and women aged 18 to 24 years old who are interested in gossip magazines and betting on their interests.
CONSUMER: HOBBIES & DIY: Games & Puzzles

POPCORN
1687142U76A-182
Editorial Address: Granada Television, Quay Street, MANCHESTER, M60 9EA **Tel:** 0161 952 1000
Email: greg.taylor@itv.com
Web site: http://www.popcorn.co.uk
Frequency of update: Daily
Website Access: Free
(Publisher's Statement)
Editor: Greg Taylor
Summary of Content: Website covering the latest films and DVDs as well as news, reviews and interviews, prizes, trailers and games.
Readership/Target Audience: Aimed at children and young teenagers from 8 to 16 years old.
Other Features: Monthly newsletter sent to subscribers
CONSUMER: MUSIC & PERFORMING ARTS: Cinema

PORT TALBOT MATTERS
1881667U72J-410
Email: comments@porttalbot-matters.co.uk
Web site: http://www.porttalbot-matters.co.uk
Frequency of update: Daily
Summary of Content: Website created to help people who care about local issues. Whether you need access to useful information, want to highlight a particular topic to other people, discuss ideas with like minded individuals or just show your support and keep up to date with current affairs in your area, Port Talbot Matters is the place for you.
Readership/Target Audience: Aimed at residents in the local area of Port Talbot.
LOCAL NEWSPAPERS: Community Newsletters

POWDEREPORTER ONLINE
36542U10-108
Editorial Address: PO Box 1523, LONDON, N2 9HZ
Tel: 020 8442 0654 **Fax:** 020 8442 1640
Email: powderfax@btinternet.com
Web site: http://www.powdereporter.co.uk
Publisher: Salisbury Sarum Ltd
Date Launched: 1998
Frequency of update: Daily
Website Access: Free
Editor: Allan Davies
Summary of Content: Website covering the latest advances taking place within the powder and bulk processing and handling market. Includes features on testing, analysis, packaging, quality, conveying, storage, processing, safety, environmental issues, academic and industrial research, training and education.
Readership/Target Audience: Read by professionals in the chemical, paint, pharmaceutical, plastics, ceramics, metals and mineral industries and those involved in agribusiness.
BUSINESS: MATERIALS HANDLING

POWER TECHNOLOGY
1616280U58-166
Editorial Address: Brunel House, 55-57 North Wharf Road, LONDON, W2 1LA **Tel:** 020 7915 9957 **Fax:** 020 7915 9720
Email: production@spgmedia.com
Web site: http://www.power-technology.com
Publisher: SPG Media Ltd
Date Launched: 2000
Frequency of update: Daily
Website Access: Free
Traffic Figures: 89,945 Unique Users (Publisher's Statement)
Editor: Jessica Stillman
Summary of Content: Website covering power technology projects both in production and under development as well as products and services, exhibitions and conferences.
Readership/Target Audience: Aimed at those working with the power industries.
BUSINESS: ENERGY, FUEL & NUCLEAR

PPAJOBS.CO.UK
1837373U14F-262
Editorial Address: Griffin House, 161 Hammersmith Road, LONDON, W6 8SD **Tel:** 020 8267 8038
Email: paula.fox@haymarket.com
Web site: http://www.ppajobs.co.uk
Publisher: Haymarket Brand Media
Date Launched: 2008
Frequency of update: Daily
Website Access: Free
Editor: Paula Fox
Summary of Content: Website covering magazine and business media job listings.
Readership/Target Audience: Aimed at job seekers and recruiters in the magazine and business media.
BUSINESS: COMMERCE, INDUSTRY & MANAGEMENT: Training & Recruitment

PPP BULLETIN
707405U1A-273_25
Formerly: PrivateFinance-i
Editorial Address: 20A Hillgate Place, 18-20 Balham Hill, LONDON, SW12 9ER **Tel:** 020 8675 8030
Fax: 020 8675 0950
Email: anicholls@pppbulletin.com
Web site: http://www.pppbulletin.com
Publisher: Rockcliffe Ltd
Date Launched: 1994
Frequency of update: Daily
Website Access: Paid
Editor: Amanda Nicholls
Summary of Content: Online and hardcopy publication focusing on news and information on the private finance sector.
Readership/Target Audience: Aimed at those who work within the government and financial industry.
BUSINESS: FINANCE & ECONOMICS

PPPFOCUS.COM
1637634U1A-292
Formerly: the PFI.net
Editorial Address: 40 Longshut Lane West, STOCKPORT, SK2 6RX **Tel:** 0845 310 1780 **Fax:** 0845 310 1781
Email: will.hudson@pppfocus.com
Web site: http://www.pppfocus.com
Publisher: Webnet Media
Date Launched: 2003
Frequency of update: Daily
Website Access: Free
Traffic Figures: 1,500 Unique Users (per week Publisher's Statement)
Editor: Will Hudson

Internet Media

Summary of Content: Website covering news, case studies and project updates relating to the UK private finance initiative.
Readership/Target Audience: Aimed at advisors, practitioners and project managers involved with PFI projects.
BUSINESS: FINANCE & ECONOMICS

PR & MARKETING INDUSTRY DIRECTORY
1912971U2A-743

Editorial Address: 18 Generator Hall, Electric Wharf, COVENTRY, CV1 4JL **Tel:** 0870 199 4044
Fax: 0870 777 4360
Email: enquries@simplymarcomms.co.uk
Web site: http://www.industrydirectory.co.uk
Publisher: Simply Marcomms
Frequency of update: Daily
Website Access: Free
Editor: Kirstie Colledge
Summary of Content: Directory containing the latest news stories for the UK PR & Marketing industry. Includes news archives.
Readership/Target Audience: Aimed at PR & Marketing professionals, suppliers to the PR & Marketing industry, PR & Marketing firms.
BUSINESS: COMMUNICATIONS, ADVERTISING & MARKETING

PRACTICAL FACILITIES MANAGEMENT
35974U4R-580

Editorial Address: 30 The Copse, St. Georges, WESTON-SUPER-MARE, BS22 7SL **Tel:** 01934 521224
Fax: 01934 521224
Email: newsdesk@practicalfm.co.uk
Web site: http://www.practicalfm.co.uk
Publisher: Practical Facilities Management
Date Launched: 1998
Frequency of update: 6 times a year
Website Access: Paid
Traffic Figures: 7,000 Unique Users (Publisher's Statement)
Editor: Anne Donald
Summary of Content: Magazine covering building administration and property services issues.
Readership/Target Audience: Aimed at facilities managers.
BUSINESS: ARCHITECTURE & BUILDING: Building Related

PRECIOUS ONLINE MAGAZINE AND NETWORK
1709242U90-979

Formerly: Precious
Editorial Address: 7 Crayford House, Staple Street, LONDON, SE1 4BU **Tel:** 07950 814371
Email: editorial@preciousonline.co.uk
Web site: http://www.preciousonline.co.uk
Publisher: Precious Online Magazine and Network
Date Launched: 1999
Frequency of update: Daily
Website Access: Free
Traffic Figures: 81,111 Unique Users (per month Publisher's Statement)
Editor: Foluke Akinlose
Summary of Content: Interactive lifestyle magazine and network covering lifestyle, careers and business, arts and entertainment, health and well-being, money, events, music, fashion, beauty, travel, food and drink, consumer technology and enterprise.
Readership/Target Audience: Aimed at independent and spirited women of colour who are ambitious and socially conscious aged between 21 and 38 years old.
Other Features: Newsletter, social networking, archive and recruitment.
CONSUMER: ETHNIC

PRESSWATCH SECTOR SUMMARIES
622928U2B-175

Editorial Address: 66 Wilson Street, LONDON, EC2A 2JX
Tel: 020 7868 6100
Email: info@presswatch.com
Web site: http://www.presswatch.com
Publisher: TNS Media
Date Launched: 1996
Frequency of update: Daily
Website Access: Paid
Traffic Figures: 11,000 Unique Users (Publisher's Statement)
Editor: Brian Merrion
Summary of Content: Precis of the national UK press covering a variety of sectors including the NHS, private healthcare, pharmaceutical, financial services, food and drink, travel and tourism and e-commerce.

Readership/Target Audience: Aimed at professionals, internal and external communications and public relations agencies within the business and occupational sectors.
BUSINESS: COMMUNICATIONS, ADVERTISING & MARKETING: Press

PRINTED AND DISPOSABLE ELECTRONICS NEWS
1664910U35-363

Editorial Address: Cleeve Road, LEATHERHEAD, KT22 7RU **Tel:** 01372 802048
Email: joe.thompson@pira-international.com
Web site: http://www.piranet.com
Publisher: PIRA International
Frequency of update: 26 times a year
Website Access: Paid
Editor: Joe Thompson
Summary of Content: Electronically delivered newsletter covering breakthroughs and developments in the nascent printed and disposable electronics industry.
Readership/Target Audience: Aimed at brand owners and print and packaging companies.
BUSINESS: PACKAGING & BOTTLING

PRINTINGTALK
1606899U41A-328

Editorial Address: PR by email only **Tel:** 020 7970 4920
Email: news@printingtalk.com
Web site: http://www.printingtalk.com
Publisher: Pro-Talk Ltd
Date Launched: 2003
Frequency of update: Daily
Website Access: Free
Traffic Figures: 117,332 Unique Users (per month Publisher's Statement)
Editor: Ian Mayor
Summary of Content: Website covering new products and services for and from the printing industry.
Readership/Target Audience: Aimed at printers and print buyers.
BUSINESS: PRINTING & STATIONERY: Printing

PRIVATE EQUITY ONLINE
633876U1F-330

Editorial Address: Sycamore House, Sycamore Street, LONDON, EC1Y 0SG **Fax:** 020 7566 5455
Email: amanda.j@peimedia.com
Web site: http://www.privateequityonline.com
Publisher: PEI Media Ltd
Date Launched: 2000
Frequency of update: Daily
Website Access: Free
Editor: Amanda Janis
Summary of Content: Website focusing on the world of private equity. Includes industry news from around the world, with a special focus on developments in Europe, video interviews with leading venture capitalists, fund managers, analysts and entrepreneurs, profiles of deals that are shaping the market and documentaries that take an in-depth look at sectors, countries and current trends.
Readership/Target Audience: Aimed at institutional investors and private equity professionals.
BUSINESS: FINANCE & ECONOMICS: Investment

PRIVATE EQUITY WIRE
1926494U1R-414

Editorial Address: 18 Hanover Square, LONDON, W1S 1HX
Tel: 20 3159 4000
Email: sunil.gopalan@globalfundmedia.com
Web site: http://www.privateequitywire.co.uk
Frequency of update: Daily
Website Access: Free
Editor: Sunil Gopalan
Summary of Content: Website covering information and news about private equity.
Readership/Target Audience: Aimed at people within the financial sector.
BUSINESS: FINANCE & ECONOMICS: Financial Related

PRIVATE HEALTHCARE UK
1814377U74G-284

Editorial Address: The Wilderness, 3 Churchgates, BERKHAMSTED, HP4 2UB **Tel:** 0870 777 0401
Fax: 01442 817818
Email: editorial@privatehealth.co.uk
Web site: http://www.privatehealthcare.co.uk
Publisher: Intuition Communication
Date Launched: 1996
Frequency of update: Daily
Website Access: Free
Traffic Figures: 370,000 Unique Users (Publisher's Statement)
Editor: Keith Pollard

Summary of Content: Website providing information about private healthcare services and providers featuring private hospitals, doctors and specialists, private medical insurance, cosmetic surgery, dentistry and care for the elderly.
Readership/Target Audience: Aimed at those seeking information about private treatment and healthcare services.
CONSUMER: WOMEN'S INTEREST CONSUMER MAGAZINES: Slimming & Health

---

PROCESS AND CONTROL TODAY
37560U19A-510

Editorial Address: PO Box 223, TUNBRIDGE WELLS, TN2 9HU **Tel:** 01892 619616 **Fax:** 01892 619616
Email: editorial@pandct.com
Web site: http://www.pandct.com
Publisher: Process and Control Today Ltd
Date Launched: 1998
Frequency of update: Daily
Website Access: Free
Traffic Figures: 368,922 Unique Users (per year Publisher's Statement)
Editor: John Houston
Summary of Content: Online eJournal featuring the latest developments in the process, control, automation and manufacturing industries including acquisitions, mergers, technological breakthroughs, case studies and new products. It also lists suppliers and products e.g. control, instrumentation, automation, drivers, pneumatics, hazardous area equipment, hydraulics and solids handling markets.
Readership/Target Audience: Aimed at buyers, specifiers, engineers, managers and directors, from the end user and OEM market within the process, control, automation and manufacturing industries.
BUSINESS: ENGINEERING & MACHINERY

PROCESSINGTALK
1606905U19A-546

Editorial Address: PR by email only
Email: news@processingtalk.com
Web site: http://www.processingtalk.com
Publisher: Pro-Talk Ltd
Date Launched: 2003
Frequency of update: Daily
Website Access: Free
Traffic Figures: 80,841 Unique Users (per month Publisher's Statement)
Editor: Nick Denbow
Summary of Content: Website covering new products and services for the process engineering sector.
Readership/Target Audience: Aimed at engineers and technical management.
BUSINESS: ENGINEERING & MACHINERY

PROFESSIONAL CRICKETERS' ASSOCIATION
1663240U75K-853

Formerly: Cricnet.com
Editorial Address: 5 Utopia Village, LONDON, NW1 8HL
Tel: 07866 241241 **Fax:** 020 7586 8520
Email: jhindson@thepca.co.uk
Web site: http://www.thepca.co.uk
Date Launched: 2000
Frequency of update: 260 times a year
Website Access: Free
Editor: Jimmy Hindson
Summary of Content: Website covering news, views and exclusive player content. Official site of the Professional Cricketers Association.
Readership/Target Audience: Aimed at cricket fans as well as members of the PCA and the media.
CONSUMER: SPORT: Cricket

PROFESSIONAL FITNESS MAGAZINE
38527U32H-258

Formerly: Professional Fitness
Editorial Address: Meridian Office Park, Osborn Way, HOOK, RG27 9HY **Tel:** 01256 748048
Email: pfmagazine@r3group.com
Web site: http://www.professional-fitness.co.uk
Publisher: R3 Group Ltd
Date Launched: 2008
Frequency of update: Monthly
Website Access: Free
Editor: Claire Ford
Summary of Content: Magazine covering fitness news from the industry plus choreography and exercise fitness fashions and training updates.
Readership/Target Audience: Aimed at professional fitness instructors and personal trainers.
BUSINESS: LOCAL GOVERNMENT, LEISURE & RECREATION: Leisure, Recreation & Entertainment

PROFINEWS
35993U5A-196

Editorial Address: 1 West Street, Titchfield, FAREHAM, PO14 4DH **Tel:** 01329 846166 **Fax:** 01329 512063
Email: geoff@ggh.co.uk
Web site: http://www.profibus.com
Publisher: Profibus Nutzerorganisation e. V.
Date Launched: 1995
Frequency of update: 6 times a year
Website Access: Free
Traffic Figures: 15,000 Unique Users (Publisher's Statement)
Editor: Geoff Hodgkinson
Summary of Content: Electronically delivered newsletter covering news and information supplied by companies who are members of PROFIBUS/PROFINET user groups around the world. Covers all aspects of the PROFIBUS and PROFINET vendor and user communities, including articles on new products, the implementation of PROFIBUS and PROFINET products in industry, reports from around the world and news from PI itself.
Readership/Target Audience: Read mainly by engineers and managers in automation.
BUSINESS: COMPUTERS & AUTOMATION: Automation & Instrumentation

PROFIT AND LOSS SQUAWKBOX
1687137U1F-612

Editorial Address: For all contact details see main edition, Profit and Loss
Frequency of update: Weekly
Website Access: Paid
BUSINESS: FINANCE & ECONOMICS: Investment

PROFIT WATCH
1805684U74M-427

Editorial Address: 7th Floor, Sea Containers House, 20 Upper Ground, LONDON, SE1 9JD **Tel:** 020 7633 3600 **Fax:** 020 7633 3740
Email: pwr@f-s-p.co.uk
Web site: http://www.fspinvest.co.uk
Publisher: Fleet Street Publications Ltd
Frequency of update: 150 times a year
Website Access: Free
Traffic Figures: 25,000 Unique Users (Publisher's Statement)
Editor: Frank Hemsley
Summary of Content: Electronic newsletter containing general investment ideas and information.
Readership/Target Audience: Aimed at private investors.
CONSUMER: WOMEN'S INTEREST CONSUMER MAGAZINES: Personal Finance

PROMOTIONS & INCENTIVES
35538U2A-167

Editorial Address: 174 Hammersmith Road, LONDON, W6 7JP **Tel:** 020 8267 4499
Email: james.quilter@haymarket.com
Web site: http://www.pandionline.com
Publisher: Haymarket Brand Media
Frequency of update: Daily. Published at the beginning of the cover month
Traffic Figures: 10,386 Unique Users (Publisher's Statement)
Summary of Content: Website covering news and features on consumer and trade promotions and incentives.
Readership/Target Audience: Aimed at clients and agencies involved in promotional marketing.
BUSINESS: COMMUNICATIONS, ADVERTISING & MARKETING

PROOF!
45442U74G-42

Editorial Address: Unit 10, Woodman Works, 204 Durnsford Road, LONDON, SW19 8DR **Tel:** 020 8944 9555
Fax: 020 8944 9888
Email: info@wddty.co.uk
Web site: http://www.wddty.co.uk
Publisher: Consumer Medical Reports Ltd
Date Launched: 1996
Website Access: Free
Editor: Lynne McTaggart
Summary of Content: Online journal covering all aspects of alternative therapies. Includes case studies, research news, mind and body, and product road-tests.
Readership/Target Audience: Aimed at practitioners and consumers interested in alternative medicine.
CONSUMER: WOMEN'S INTEREST CONSUMER MAGAZINES: Slimming & Health

PROPERTY4MEDIA.COM
1773985U74K-758

Editorial Address: The Chandlery, 50 Westminster Bridge Road, LONDON, SE1 7QY **Tel:** 020 7953 8770
Fax: 020 7953 8773
Email: news.desk@property4media.com
Web site: http://www.property4media.com
Publisher: News4Media Ltd
Date Launched: 2006
Frequency of update: Daily
Website Access: Free
Traffic Figures: 10,000 Unique Users (per day Publisher's Statement)
Editor: Henry Hemming
Summary of Content: Online news bulletin covering residential property, commercial property, online property, overseas property, new homes, construction, design, interiors, home improvements, gardens, professional services and financial services.
Readership/Target Audience: Aimed at those interested in homes and property.
CONSUMER: WOMEN'S INTEREST CONSUMER MAGAZINES: Home Purchase

PROPERTYWEEK.COM
1809957U1E-399

Editorial Address: Ludgate House, 245 Blackfriars Road, LONDON, SE1 9UY **Tel:** 020 7921 8561
Email: iain.oneil@ubm.com
Web site: http://www.propertyweek.com
Publisher: UBM Information Ltd
Date Launched: 1999
Frequency of update: Daily
Website Access: Free
Traffic Figures: 130,736 Unique Users (01/11/2008 To 30/11/2008 ABC/Electronic)
Editor: Giles Barrie; **Web Editor:** Iain O'Neil
Summary of Content: Website covering news, features, commentary and gossip about the UK and international commercial property market.
Readership/Target Audience: Aimed at property professionals.
BUSINESS: FINANCE & ECONOMICS: Property

PROSECURIZINE
1795205U54C-330

Editorial Address: PR by email only **Tel:** 01795 435913
Email: news@prosecurizine.com
Web site: http://www.proSecurizine.com
Publisher: Zenius (Croydon) Ltd
Date Launched: 2005
Frequency of update: Weekly
Website Access: Free
Traffic Figures: 7,500 Unique Users (Publisher's Statement)
Editor: Henry Lott
Summary of Content: Website and newsletter providing the latest private security and product news affecting the security industry.
Readership/Target Audience: Aimed at private security firms or anyone working for a large organisation and responsible for security.
BUSINESS: SAFETY & SECURITY: Security

PROTECTION INSURANCE
1696117U74M-419

Editorial Address: 10 College Gardens, Westgate-On-Sea, KENT, CT8 8EY **Tel:** 01843 831088
Email: mail@protection-insurance.com
Web site: http://www.protection-insurance.com
Publisher: Speedie Consultants Ltd
Date Launched: 2003
Frequency of update: Daily
Website Access: Free
Traffic Figures: 50,000 Unique Users (per month Publisher's Statement)
Editor: Jason Hulott
Summary of Content: Website covering personal insurance including car, home, life, women's, motorbike, pet, travel and private medical insurance.
Readership/Target Audience: Aimed at UK consumers of all ages.
CONSUMER: WOMEN'S INTEREST CONSUMER MAGAZINES: Personal Finance

PROVET
626261U81X-300

Editorial Address: Stable Cottage, Shaftesbury Road, East Knoyle, SALISBURY, SP3 6AT **Tel:** 07930 569948
Email: mike.davies@provet.co.uk
Web site: http://www.provet.co.uk
Date Launched: 1999
Frequency of update: Daily
Website Access: Free
Traffic Figures: 164,000 Unique Users (per month Publisher's Statement)
Editor: Mike Davies; **Web Editor:** John Brice
Summary of Content: Website containing news, products and information on animal health.
Readership/Target Audience: Aimed at pet owners, animal breeders, veterinary students, children, vets and those interested in animals.
Other Features: Features include a chat forum and archiving.
CONSUMER: ANIMALS & PETS

PSYCHOLOGIES
1926303U74A-1074

Editorial Address: 64 North Row, LONDON, W1K 7LL
Tel: 020 7150 7000 **Fax:** 020 7150 7675
Email: sarah.neish@hf-uk.com
Web site: http://www.psychologies.co.uk
Publisher: Hachette Filipacchi Magazines
Frequency of update: Daily
Website Access: Free
Editor: Sarah Neish
Summary of Content: Website covering a psychology and positive living for a mainstream consumer audience: How you think, feel, connect and communicate as well and beauty, travel, food, wine and home.
Readership/Target Audience: Aimed at women aged 30 and over.
CONSUMER: WOMEN'S INTEREST CONSUMER MAGAZINES: Women's Interest

PUBLIC
1647328U14A-527

Editorial Address: 3-7 Ray Street, LONDON, EC1R 3DR
Tel: 020 7278 2332
Email: public@guardian.co.uk
Web site: http://www.guardianpublic.co.uk
Publisher: Guardian Media Group plc
Date Launched: 2004
Frequency of update: Daily
Website Access: Paid
Traffic Figures: 12,672 Unique Users (Publisher's Statement)
Editor: Jane Dudman
Summary of Content: Website covering public sector management, finance, policy and technology.
Readership/Target Audience: Aimed at senior managers and influential decision makers across the UK public sector including local government, central government, health, education, NDPBs, executive agencies, voluntary sector, housing, police, fire and emergency services sector.
BUSINESS: COMMERCE, INDUSTRY & MANAGEMENT

THE PUBLICAN.COM
712406U9A-144_25

Editorial Address: 1st Floor, Ludgate House, 245 Blackfriars Road, LONDON, SE1 9UY **Tel:** 020 7955 3714
Fax: 020 7955 3756
Email: news@thepublican.com
Web site: http://www.thepublican.com
Publisher: UBM Live
Date Launched: 2001
Frequency of update: Daily. News updated hourly
Website Access: Free
Editor: Matt Eley; **Web Editor:** Roland Ellison
Summary of Content: Website providing existing pub industry people and newcomers with everything they need to build their business and careers. Also provides up-to-date news and city news with search and legal advice, The Publican's special reports, a listing of available properties and essential career information.
Readership/Target Audience: Aimed at those in the pub industry.
BUSINESS: DRINKS & LICENSED TRADE: Drinks, Licensed Trade, Wines & Spirits

PUBLICNET
601566U32A-214_5

Editorial Address: PO Box 7003, WESTCLIFF-ON-SEA, SS0 0TH **Tel:** 01702 343343 **Fax:** 01702 353588
Email: editor@publicnet.co.uk
Web site: http://www.publicnet.co.uk
Publisher: Knowshare Ltd
Date Launched: 1998
Frequency of update: Daily
Website Access: Free
Editor: Don Morley; **Online Journalist:** Bob Calver
Summary of Content: Website concerned with the modernisation of the entire public sector. Provides news and features relating to the governance and management of public services.
Readership/Target Audience: Aimed at governors and senior managers of public service organisations, consultants involved in the public sector and academics.
Other Features: Recruitment
BUSINESS: LOCAL GOVERNMENT, LEISURE & RECREATION: Local Government

Internet Media

PUBLICPRIVATEFINANCE.COM

633846U1F-306

Formerly: PFIOnline
Editorial Address: St. Giles House, 50 Poland Street, LONDON, W1F 7AX **Tel:** 020 7970 4822 **Fax:** 020 7970 4869
Email: michael.kapoor@centaur.co.uk
Web site: http://www.publicprivatefinance.com
Publisher: Centaur Media plc
Date Launched: 1999
Frequency of update: Daily
Website Access: Paid
Editor: Michael Kapoor
Summary of Content: Website containing information, news, data and analyses on private finance initiative projects and the companies involved in them.
Readership/Target Audience: Aimed at PFI professionals.
BUSINESS: FINANCE & ECONOMICS: Investment

PUFFTA.CO.UK

1779100U86B-175

Editorial Address: Unit M, Spectrum House, 32-34 Gordon House Road, LONDON, NW5 1LP **Tel:** 020 7424 7400
Fax: 020 7424 7401
Email: matt@axm-mag.com
Web site: http://www.puffta.co.uk
Publisher: Millivres-Prowler Ltd
Date Launched: 1999
Frequency of update: Daily
Website Access: Free
Traffic Figures: 30,000 Unique Users (Publisher's Statement)
Editor: Matt Myles
Summary of Content: Website focusing on gay lifestyle and entertainment, community and social responsibility.
Readership/Target Audience: Aimed at gay teens aged 13 to 21 years old.
Other Features: Newsletter, mobile.
CONSUMER: ADULT & GAY MAGAZINES: Gay & Lesbian Magazines

PULSE

1869319U56A-697

Editorial Address: Ludgate House, 245 Blackfriars Road, LONDON, SE1 9UY
Email: feedback@pulsetoday.co.uk
Web site: http://www.pulsetoday.co.uk
Frequency of update: Daily
Traffic Figures: 53,285 Unique Users (per month Publisher's Statement)
Summary of Content: Contains all of the content of Pulse magazine and more, with extra features such as practical downloadable resources, NHS and non-NHS fees and an Ask the Expert service allowing users to get their questions answered.
Readership/Target Audience: Targets GPs and other primary care professionals.
BUSINESS: HEALTH & MEDICAL

Q4MUSIC

630911U76E-290_1

Editorial Address: Mappin House, 4 Winsley Street, LONDON, W1W 8HF **Tel:** 020 7182 8342
Fax: 020 7312 8246
Email: editor@qthemusic.com
Web site: http://www.q4music.com
Publisher: Bauer Consumer Media Ltd (Mappin House)
Frequency of update: Daily
Website Access: Free
Traffic Figures: 130,000 Unique Users (per month Publisher's Statement)
Editor: Jo Pinkney
Summary of Content: Website providing magazine news, gig tickets, online radio & an events guide.
Readership/Target Audience: Aimed at music fans.
Other Features: Features include competitions, special offers, interviews, an e-mail newsletter and archiving.
CONSUMER: MUSIC & PERFORMING ARTS: Pop Music

QUANTASECURITY.COM

1810335U5R-690

Editorial Address: 9 River Valley Road, Chudleigh Knighton, Chudleigh, NEWTON ABBOT, TQ13 0HP **Tel:** 01626 854125
Email: kevin.townsend@quantumlabs.org
Web site: http://www.quantasecurity.com
Publisher: ITsecurity Ltd
Date Launched: 2007
Frequency of update: Daily
Website Access: Free
Editor: Kevin Townsend
Summary of Content: Website featuring infosec news, blogs, articles, white papers, alerts and product reviews.
Readership/Target Audience: Aimed at businessmen and home users interested in computer security.

Other Features: PENWARP, a closed community for journalists.
BUSINESS: COMPUTERS & AUTOMATION: Computers Related

THE R2 PROJECT

1615388U78B-657

Editorial Address: 6 Crosshill Terrace, Wormit, NEWPORT-ON-TAY, DD6 8PS **Tel:** 01382 345078 **Fax:** 01382 345509
Email: andy@r2-dvd.org
Web site: http://www.r2-dvd.org
Date Launched: 1998
Frequency of update: Daily
Website Access: Free
Traffic Figures: 35,000 Unique Users (Publisher's Statement)
Editor: Andy Cobley; **Web Editor:** Andy Cobley
Summary of Content: Website with news and reviews of all UK DVD releases.
Readership/Target Audience: Aimed at DVD buyers both trade and consumer.
CONSUMER: CONSUMER ELECTRONICS: Video & DVD

RAC PLUS

1896972U3C-205

Editorial Address: Greater London House, Hampstead Road, LONDON, NW1 7EJ **Tel:** 020 7728 4650
Email: andrew.gaved@emap.com
Web site: http://www.racplus.co.uk
Publisher: EMAP Inform
Frequency of update: Daily
Editor: Andrew Gaved
Summary of Content: Website covering the air conditioning and refrigeration industry.
Readership/Target Audience: Read by senior decision makers and buyers in the UK and overseas. Also aimed at installers, distributors, manufacturers and end users.
BUSINESS: HEATING & VENTILATION: Refrigeration & Ventilation

RACECAR

711970U77D-393

Editorial Address: Concept House, The Square Shere, GUILDFORD, GU5 9HG **Tel:** 01483 203781
Email: info@racecar.co.uk
Web site: http://www.racecar.co.uk
Date Launched: 1997
Frequency of update: Daily
Website Access: Free
Traffic Figures: 200,000 Unique Users (per month Publisher's Statement)
Editor: Jane Kuler
Summary of Content: Website containing daily news about the racecar world. Includes a photo gallery and features.
Readership/Target Audience: Aimed at racecar enthusiasts.
Other Features: Features include a chat forum, an e-mail newsletter, archiving and a parts board.
CONSUMER: MOTORING & CYCLING: Motor Sports

RACINGPOST.CO.UK

626449U75E-265

Formerly: Racing Post Online
Editorial Address: 1 Canada Square, Canary Wharf, LONDON, E14 5AP **Tel:** 020 7293 2389
Email: internet@racingpost.co.uk
Web site: http://www.racingpost.co.uk
Publisher: Trinity Mirror
Date Launched: 1999
Frequency of update: Daily
Website Access: Free
Traffic Figures: 30,000 Unique Users (per day Publisher's Statement)
Summary of Content: Website covering the world of sports betting, focusing particularly on horse racing. Includes news, results, statistics, future races and a betting exchange feature.
Readership/Target Audience: Aimed at horse-racing and sports betting enthusiasts.
CONSUMER: SPORT: Horse Racing

RADIOTIMES.COM

1806078U76C-834

Editorial Address: Media Centre, 201 Wood Lane, LONDON, W12 7TQ **Tel:** 020 8433 1272 **Fax:** 020 8433 1396
Email: helen.hackworthy@bbc.com
Web site: http://www.radiotimes.com
Publisher: BBC Worldwide Publishing
Date Launched: 1997
Frequency of update: Daily
Website Access: Free
Traffic Figures: 1,200,000 Unique Users (per month ABC/Electronic)
Editor: Helen Hackworthy

Summary of Content: Website covering TV and radio listings, programme features with episode guides and cast and crew information and information on downloading programmes, podcasting and online video. Plus blogs and technical guides to digital TV.
Readership/Target Audience: Aimed at TV viewers of all ages.
Other Features: Other features include newsletter, forums and shop (RT Direct).
CONSUMER: MUSIC & PERFORMING ARTS: TV & Radio

RAIL MANAGMENT

1638345U49E-251

Formerly: RailManager Online
Editorial Address: 25 Burges Close, DUNSTABLE, LU6 3EU
Tel: 01582 477886
Email: sim.harris@keepingtrack.co.uk
Web site: http://www.keepingtrack.co.uk
Publisher: KT Publications
Date Launched: 2003
Frequency of update: Weekly
Website Access: Free
Traffic Figures: 5,000 Unique Users (Publisher's Statement)
Editor: Sim Harris
Summary of Content: Electronic magazine in PDF format covering all aspects of the rail industry with a focus on political, legal and financial matters.
Readership/Target Audience: Aimed at middle to senior management involved within the rail industry.
BUSINESS: TRANSPORT: Railways

RAILWAY HERALD

1873237U49E-256

Editorial Address: PO Box 252, SCUNTHORPE, DN17 2WY
Tel: 01904 500175
Email: editor@railwayherald.co.uk
Web site: http://www.railwayherald.co.uk
Publisher: Railway Herald Ltd
Date Launched: 2005
Frequency of update: Weekly
Website Access: Paid
Traffic Figures: 27,564 Unique Users (Publisher's Statement)
Editor: Richard Tuplin
Summary of Content: Digital publication featuring news stories from the rail industry worldwide.
Readership/Target Audience: Aimed at railway managers and enthusiasts.
BUSINESS: TRANSPORT: Railways

RAILWAY TECHNOLOGY

629428U49E-212

Editorial Address: Brunel House, 55-57 North Wharf Road, LONDON, W2 1LA **Tel:** 020 7915 9957 **Fax:** 020 7915 9720
Email: production@spgmedia.com
Web site: http://www.railway-technology.com
Publisher: SPG Media Ltd
Frequency of update: 260 times a year
Website Access: Free
Traffic Figures: 160,000 Unique Users (Publisher's Statement)
Editor: Duncan West
Summary of Content: Website covering news, information and related projects for the railway technology industry, including project news, products and services, industry events, a complete listing of railway industry organisations and a free regular e-bulletin.
Readership/Target Audience: Aimed at executives in the international railway industry, electrical, mechanical engineers and CAD/CAM engineers.
BUSINESS: TRANSPORT: Railways

THE RAILWAYCENTRE.COM

1741358U79J-332

Editorial Address: PO Box 45, DAWLISH, EX7 9XY
Tel: 01626 862320
Email: cjmarsden@btopenworld.com
Web site: http://www.therailwaycentre.com
Publisher: TheRailwayCentre.com Ltd
Date Launched: 2006
Frequency of update: Daily
Website Access: Free
Editor: Colin Marsden
Summary of Content: Website covering news from the rail industry both in the UK and overseas as well as railway events.
Readership/Target Audience: Aimed at railway enthusiasts, serious rail transport followers and professional rail staff.
CONSUMER: HOBBIES & DIY: Rail Enthusiasts

RAISINGKIDS
1640170U74D-559

Formerly: raisingkids.co.uk
Editorial Address: Disney Interactive Media Group, MC2620, 3 Queen Caroline Street, LONDON, W6 9PE
Tel: 020 8222 3923
Email: catherine.hanly@disney.com
Web site: http://www.raisingkids.co.uk
Date Launched: 2001
Frequency of update: Daily
Website Access: Free
Traffic Figures: 180,000 Unique Users (September 2007 Publisher's Statement)
Editor: Catherine Hanly
Summary of Content: Website covering all aspects of parenting.
Readership/Target Audience: Aimed at parents of children aged 0 to 21 years old.
Other Features: Newsletter.
CONSUMER: WOMEN'S INTEREST CONSUMER MAGAZINES: Child Care

RALLYZONE
711972U77D-420

Formerly: rallyzone.com
Editorial Address: 37 North Parade, ILKLEY, LS29 8JN
Tel: 01943 817690
Email: richard@rallyzone.co.uk
Web site: http://www.rallyzone.co.uk
Date Launched: 1997
Frequency of update: Daily
Website Access: Free
Traffic Figures: 30,000 Unique Users (per month Publisher's Statement)
Editor: Richard Cockburn
Summary of Content: Website containing news, team information, competitions and photographs from the World and British Rally Championship.
Readership/Target Audience: Aimed at rally fans.
Other Features: Features include an events calendar, an e-mail newsletter and archiving.
CONSUMER: MOTORING & CYCLING: Motor Sports

THE RAMBLERS' ASSOCIATION
711850U75L-520

Editorial Address: 2nd Floor, Camelford House, 87-90 Albert Embankment, LONDON, SE1 7TW
Tel: 020 7339 8500 **Fax:** 020 7339 8501
Email: ramblers@london.ramblers.org.uk
Web site: http://www.ramblers.org.uk
Publisher: The Ramblers' Association
Date Launched: 1999
Frequency of update: Daily
Website Access: Free
Traffic Figures: 250,000 Unique Users (per month Publisher's Statement)
Editor: Paul Strong
Summary of Content: Website featuring news and information on walking in Great Britain. Includes news of campaigns and events, extensive practical advice and information on clothing and equipment, maps, long distance paths, public transport for walkers, accommodation, local walks, walking groups and a listing of useful addresses and links.
Readership/Target Audience: Aimed at those interested in walking.
CONSUMER: SPORT: Outdoor

RANDOMLYACCESSED.COM
1791194U78R-516

Editorial Address: 12 Jameson Road, Woolston, SOUTHAMPTON, SO19 2HY **Tel:** 07515 107395
Email: wastedhours@gmail.com
Web site: http://www.randomlyaccessed.com
Date Launched: 2006
Frequency of update: Daily
Website Access: Free
Editor: Steve Farnworth
Summary of Content: Website covering anything technical including kitchenware, MP3 players, computers and peripherals, DVD players and DVD reviews, mobile phones and video games.
Readership/Target Audience: Aimed at young males aged between 18 and 25 years old.
CONSUMER: CONSUMER ELECTRONICS: Consumer Electronics Related

RAPID TV NEWS
1851238U2D-155

Editorial Address: 37 The Towers, Lower Mortlake Road, RICHMOND, TW9 2JR **Tel:** 020 8948 8561
Fax: 020 8940 6009
Email: chris@forrester-solutions.com
Web site: http://www.rapidtvnews.com
Publisher: Broadgate Publications

Frequency of update: Daily
Website Access: Free
Editor: Chris Forrester
Summary of Content: Electronically delivered newsletter covering all aspects of the TV and communications satellite business.
Readership/Target Audience: Aimed at senior executives in the broadcasting and satellite community.
BUSINESS: COMMUNICATIONS, ADVERTISING & MARKETING: Broadcasting

READY STEADY BOOK
1750351U84A-463

Editorial Address: 40 Kings Place, Hamlet Gardens, Hammersmith, LONDON, W6 0RN **Tel:** 0 7736 772515
Email: info@readysteadybook.com
Web site: http://www.readysteadybook.com
Frequency of update: Daily
Website Access: Free
Editor: Mark Thwaite
Summary of Content: Online book review journal covering literary fiction, philosophy, history and poetry as well as a daily updated blog.
Readership/Target Audience: Aimed at well educated literary personnel generally broadsheet readers.
CONSUMER: THE ARTS & LITERARY: Arts

READYMEALSINFO
764669U22A-377

Editorial Address: PO Box 72, CALDICOT, NP26 3ZG
Tel: 01633 889419 **Fax:** 0870 787 7413
Email: editor@readymealsinfo.com
Web site: http://www.readymealsinfo.com
Publisher: Alfa Media Group
Date Launched: 2000
Frequency of update: Daily
Website Access: Free
Traffic Figures: 7,800 Unique Users (per week Publisher's Statement)
Editor: Bill Lewis; **Editor-in-Chief:** William Loram
Summary of Content: News and information portal covering all aspects of the UK ready meal sector, including business to business news, specialist information and research.
Readership/Target Audience: Aimed at producers and suppliers of the ready meals sector.
BUSINESS: FOOD

REAL FD
630681U1A-274

Formerly: Real Finance
Editorial Address: 198 Kings Road, LONDON, SW3 5XP
Tel: 020 7368 7100
Email: catherine@realfd.net
Web site: http://www.realfd.net
Publisher: Caspian Publishing
Date Launched: 2001
Frequency of update: Daily
Website Access: Paid
Editor: Catherine Woods
Summary of Content: Business-to-business web page covering all aspects of finance, news, features and advice.
Readership/Target Audience: Aimed at finance directors, CFOs, senior financial managers and senior executives with financial interests.
BUSINESS: FINANCE & ECONOMICS

REAL MOVIE NEWS
1685688U76A-181

Formerly: The Z Review
Editorial Address: 34 Hamilton Gardens, Armadale, BATHGATE, EH48 2JA **Tel:** 01501 731122
Email: gary@thezreview.co.uk
Web site: http://www.realmovienews.com
Date Launched: 2003
Frequency of update: Daily
Website Access: Free
Traffic Figures: 65,000 Unique Users (Publisher's Statement)
Editor: Gary Gray
Summary of Content: Website covering movie news, reviews and trailers, release dates, DVDs and interviews.
Readership/Target Audience: Aimed at men aged 18 to 25 years old.
CONSUMER: MUSIC & PERFORMING ARTS: Cinema

THE RECKLESS GARDENER
1706711U93-194

Editorial Address: Brant Lea, 2 Black Dyke Road, Arnside, CARNFORTH, LA5 0HH **Tel:** 01524 762653
Email: sandy@recklessgardener.co.uk
Web site: http://www.recklessgardener.co.uk
Publisher: Mill Cottage New Media
Date Launched: 2004
Frequency of update: Weekly

Website Access: Free
Summary of Content: Website providing basic help and advice with garden features, design ideas and designer profiles, jobs this month, garden visits, book reviews and show information and coverage (including major RHS shows). Including section on bed and breakfast for gardeners and online shop.
Readership/Target Audience: Aimed at amateur gardeners but also suitable for the more experienced gardener who wants to keep up to date with gardening news and shows.
Other Features: Newsletter and archiving.
CONSUMER: GARDENING

RECORD OF THE DAY
1613867U76D-760

Editorial Address: PO Box 49554, LONDON, E17 9WB
Tel: 020 8520 6646 **Fax:** 020 8520 2130
Email: paul@recordoftheday.com
Web site: http://www.recordoftheday.com
Publisher: Music Today Ltd
Date Launched: 2002
Frequency of update: 260 times a year
Website Access: Paid
Traffic Figures: 3,500 Unique Users (per day Publisher's Statement)
Editor: Nicola Slade
Summary of Content: Website providing access to a daily music industry newsletter and weekly electronic magazine. Includes information on media news, audio clips, statistics, business news and new artists.
Readership/Target Audience: Aimed at those involved within the music industry.
Other Features: Recruitment and a messageboard.
CONSUMER: MUSIC & PERFORMING ARTS: Music

RECRUITMENT & RETENTION
1648407U14F-239

Editorial Address: Quadrant House, The Quadrant, SUTTON, SM2 5AS **Tel:** 020 8212 1902
Email: neil.rankin@irseclipse.co.uk
Web site: http://www.xperthr.co.uk
Publisher: Reed Business Information
Frequency of update: 24 times a year
Website Access: Paid
Editor: Neil Rankin
Summary of Content: Online journal covering recruitment, selection and retention of staff.
Readership/Target Audience: Aimed at HR managers.
BUSINESS: COMMERCE, INDUSTRY & MANAGEMENT: Training & Recruitment

RECYCLING & WASTE INDUSTRY DIRECTORY
1818198U57-158

Editorial Address: 18 Generator Hall, Electric Wharf, COVENTRY, CV1 4JL **Tel:** 0870 199 4044
Fax: 0870 777 4360
Email: enquiries@industrydirectory.co.uk
Web site: http://www.industrydirectory.co.uk/recycling
Publisher: Simply Marcomms
Frequency of update: Daily
Website Access: Free
Editor: Kirstie Colledge
Summary of Content: Directory containing the latest news stories for the recycling and waste industry. Includes a news archive.
Readership/Target Audience: Aimed at professionals in the building and construction industry particularly those in the recycling and waste industry.
BUSINESS: ENVIRONMENT & POLLUTION

THE RED FERRET JOURNAL
1685824U78R-498

Editorial Address: 10 Baldwyn Gardens, LONDON, W3 6HH
Tel: 020 8992 1732
Email: red@redferret.net
Web site: http://www.redferret.net
Date Launched: 2000
Frequency of update: Daily
Website Access: Free
Traffic Figures: 350,000 Unique Users (per month Publisher's Statement)
Editor: Nigel Powell
Summary of Content: Website/weblog covering gadgets, software, websites and trivia.
Readership/Target Audience: Aimed at those interested in new technologies, software and legal music downloads.
CONSUMER: CONSUMER ELECTRONICS: Consumer Electronics Related

REDBRIDGE MATTERS
1881668U72J-411

Email: comments@redbridge-matters.co.uk
Web site: http://www.redbridge-matters.co.uk

Internet Media

Frequency of update: Daily
Summary of Content: Website created to help people who care about local issues. Whether you need access to useful information, want to highlight a particular topic to other people, discuss ideas with like-minded people or just show your support and keep up to date with current affairs in your area, Redbridge Matters is the place for you.
Readership/Target Audience: Aimed at residents in the local area of Redbridge.
LOCAL NEWSPAPERS: Community Newsletters

REDPEPPER ONLINE
629061U82-160_5

Editorial Address: 1B Waterlow Road, LONDON, N19 5NJ
Tel: 020 7281 7024 **Fax:** 020 7263 9345
Email: office@redpepper.org.uk
Web site: http://www.redpepper.org.uk
Publisher: Socialist Newspaper Publications
Date Launched: 1996
Frequency of update: Weekly
Website Access: Free
Editor: Oscar Reyes
Summary of Content: Website focusing on domestic and international current affairs.
Readership/Target Audience: Aimed at politically aware individuals.
Other Features: Features include an events calendar, archiving and recruitment.
CONSUMER: CURRENT AFFAIRS & POLITICS

REEL WORLD MAGAZINE
1861139U64K-657

Editorial Address: PR by email only **Tel:** 01273 276665
Email: steve@reel-show.tv
Web site: http://www.reel-show.tv
Frequency of update: Daily
Website Access: Free
Editor: Steve Parker
Summary of Content: Website covering film related information including film making and DVD making.
Readership/Target Audience: Aimed at film and broadcasting professionals.
BUSINESS: OTHER CLASSIFICATIONS: Cinema Entertainment

REFRESH
626245U74Q-902_30

Editorial Address: Unit 110, 334 Queenstown Road, LONDON, SW8 4NP **Tel:** 020 7099 5535
Email: jonathan@refresh.com
Web site: http://www.refresh.com
Date Launched: 1997
Frequency of update: Daily. Updated four times a day
Website Access: Free
Traffic Figures: 326,000 Unique Users (per month Publisher's Statement)
Editor: Jonathan Phillips
Summary of Content: Youth entertainment community site, featuring music videos, movie trailers, quizzes, message boards, games, fiction, horoscopes and lots more.
Readership/Target Audience: Aimed at 13-18 year olds.
CONSUMER: WOMEN'S INTEREST CONSUMER MAGAZINES: Lifestyle

THE REGISTER
36122U5B-155

Formerly: The Register Online
Editorial Address: 33 Glasshouse Street, LONDON, W1B 5DG **Tel:** 020 3178 6500 **Fax:** 020 3178 6484
Email: news@theregister.co.uk
Web site: http://www.theregister.co.uk
Publisher: Situation Publishing Ltd.
Date Launched: 1996
Frequency of update: 2704 times a year. Website can be updated up to 8 times a day
Website Access: Free
Traffic Figures: 5,203,619 Unique Users (01/11/2008 To 30/11/2008 ABC/Electronic)
Editor: Joe Fay
Summary of Content: Website focusing on computer and Internet related articles and reviews.
Readership/Target Audience: Aimed at the computing, semiconductor, networking, OEM and reseller markets.
BUSINESS: COMPUTERS & AUTOMATION: Data Processing

RESPONSIBLE INVESTOR
1926493U1F-682

Editorial Address: 30 Spalding Road, LONDON, SW17 9BW **Tel:** 020 8682 3638
Email: hugh@responsible-investor.com
Web site: http://www.responsible-investor.com
Frequency of update: Weekly
Website Access: Paid
Editor: Hugh Wheelan

Summary of Content: Online magazine and information resource which recognises the growing requirement to achieve investment returns within an environmental, social and corporate governance framework.
Readership/Target Audience: Aimed at those working in pension funds, public and government funds, central banks, endowments, foundations, charities, faith groups, family offices, investment consultants, asset managers, insurance companies, commercial banks, private banks, investment banks, custodian banks, index providers, associations, governments, regulators, bureaucrats, NGOs, trades unions, supra-nationals, lawyers, lobbyists, the media and others.
BUSINESS: FINANCE & ECONOMICS: Investment

THE RETAIL BULLETIN
1623259U53-678

Editorial Address: Priory House, 45-51 High Street, REIGATE, RH2 9AE **Tel:** 01737 648209
Email: news@theretailbulletin.com
Web site: http://www.theretailbulletin.com
Publisher: Retail Bulletin Media Ltd
Date Launched: 2002
Frequency of update: Daily
Website Access: Paid
Traffic Figures: 100,000 Unique Users (per month Publisher's Statement)
Editor: Matthew Valentine
Summary of Content: Website covering company news, breaking stories and summaries of media coverage of the retail sector.
Readership/Target Audience: Aimed at retailers, brand owners, suppliers and media covering the retail sector.
Other Features: Newsletter, archive.
BUSINESS: RETAILING & WHOLESALING

RETAIL DIRECTIONS
39819U53-295

Editorial Address: Martec House, 40 High Street, TAUNTON, TA1 3PN **Tel:** 01823 333469 **Fax:** 01823 332423
Email: frances_riseley@martec-international.com
Web site: http://www.martec-international.com
Publisher: Martec International Ltd
Date Launched: 1992
Frequency of update: 6 times a year
Website Access: Free
Traffic Figures: 12,000 Unique Users (Publisher's Statement)
Editor: Frances Riseley
Summary of Content: Electronically delivered newsletter covering all aspects of retailing, including articles on merchandise management, customer loyalty and supplier liaison.
Readership/Target Audience: Aimed at senior retail executives.
BUSINESS: RETAILING & WHOLESALING

RETAIL PROPERTY AND DEVELOPMENT
26034U4E-455

Editorial Address: Portland Buildings, 127-129 Portland Street, MANCHESTER, M1 4PZ **Tel:** 0161 236 2782
Fax: 0161 236 2783
Email: danielle.regan@excelpublishing.co.uk
Web site: http://www.retailpropertyanddevelopment.co.uk
Publisher: Excel Publishing Company Ltd
Date Launched: 2009
Frequency of update: Daily
Website Access: Free
Traffic Figures: 4,500 Unique Users (per month Publisher's Statement)
Editor: Danielle Regan
Summary of Content: Online magazine covering news and articles on retailers, leisure operators, shopfitters, designers, contractors, developers, property letting agents, property developments and estate management techniques.
Readership/Target Audience: Aimed at retailers, managing and letting agents, shop-fitters and interior designers. Also contractors, consultants and developers.
BUSINESS: ARCHITECTURE & BUILDING: Building

RETAIL TECHNOLOGY REVIEW
1850503U53-707

Editorial Address: Latimer House, 189 High Street, POTTERS BAR, EN6 5DA **Tel:** 01707 664200
Fax: 01707 664800
Email: editor@retailtechnologyreview.com
Web site: http://www.retailtechnologyreview.com
Publisher: Interactive Business Communications Ltd
Frequency of update: Daily
Website Access: Free
Traffic Figures: 30,000 Unique Users (per month Publisher's Statement)
Editor: Ed Holden
Summary of Content: Web portal dedicated to the products and solutions needs of end users within the retail sector.

Content includes mobile computing, RFID, printing and labelling, Epos systems, kiosk technology, surveillance and security, internet retailing, digital signage, current news, opinion articles and key events on the European retail calendar.
Readership/Target Audience: Aimed at end users in the retail sector.
BUSINESS: RETAILING & WHOLESALING

RETIREMENT MATTERS ONLINE
628970U74N-162

Editorial Address: 191 Nevill Avenue, HOVE, BN3 7NG
Tel: 01273 749990 **Fax:** 01273 725789
Email: mjacobs@retirement-matters.co.uk
Web site: http://www.retirement-matters.co.uk
Date Launched: 2000
Frequency of update: Weekly
Website Access: Free
Editor: Melanie Jacobs; **Web Editor:** Melanie Jacobs
Summary of Content: Website focusing on lifestyle and retirement issues.
Readership/Target Audience: Aimed at those aged over 50 years old.
Other Features: Competitions.
CONSUMER: WOMEN'S INTEREST CONSUMER MAGAZINES: Retirement

REUTERS CLUB
626500U74Q-907

Editorial Address: The Thomson Reuters Building, South Colonnade, LONDON, E14 5EP **Tel:** 020 7542 6856
Fax: 020 7542 5863
Email: mary.kitchen@thomsonreuters.com
Web site: http://www.reuters.com/club
Publisher: Thomson Reuters Ltd
Date Launched: 1999
Frequency of update: Monthly
Website Access: Paid
Traffic Figures: 25,000 Unique Users (per month Publisher's Statement)
Editor: Mary Kitchen
Summary of Content: Website covering a range of leisure competitions for financial markets professionals with a focus on golf.
Readership/Target Audience: Aimed at Reuters customers and members of the global financial community.
CONSUMER: WOMEN'S INTEREST CONSUMER MAGAZINES: Lifestyle

REUTERS.CO.UK/FOOTBALL
1820151U75B-287

Editorial Address: The Thomson Reuters Building, South Colonnade, LONDON, E14 5EP **Tel:** 020 7542 7934
Fax: 020 7542 9052
Email: sportsdesk@reuters.com
Web site: http://www.reuters.co.uk/football
Publisher: Thomson Reuters Ltd
Date Launched: 2007
Frequency of update: Daily
Website Access: Free
Editor: Jon Bramley; **Editor-in-Chief:** Miles Evans
Summary of Content: Website providing in-depth coverage of the UK Premier League, the Championship, Leagues one and two and the FA and Carling Cups as well as news from the major leagues and cup tournaments in Europe, North and South America, Africa and Asia. Also covers team news, listings, profiles, fixtures, tables and a Blog.
Readership/Target Audience: Aimed at football fans of all ages.
CONSUMER: SPORT: Football

REVEAL BLOG
1902820U74A-1060

Email: revealblog@natmags.co.uk
Web site: http://www.revealblog.co.uk
Frequency of update: Daily
Summary of Content: Website covering celebrity news.
Readership/Target Audience: Aimed at women with an interest in celebrities.
CONSUMER: WOMEN'S INTEREST CONSUMER MAGAZINES: Women's Interest

REVOLUTIONJOBS.CO.UK
1837374U14F-263

Editorial Address: 161 Hammersmith Road, LONDON, W6 8SD **Tel:** 020 8267 5000 **Fax:** 020 8267 4987
Email: paula.fox@haymarket.com
Web site: http://www.revolutionjobs.co.uk
Publisher: Haymarket Brand Media
Date Launched: 2008
Frequency of update: Daily
Website Access: Free
Editor: Paula Fox

Summary of Content: Website featuring jobs for professionals in the digital media industry.
Readership/Target Audience: Aimed at job seekers and recruiters in the digital media industry.
BUSINESS: COMMERCE, INDUSTRY & MANAGEMENT: Training & Recruitment

RFID TODAY
1666544U10-209

Editorial Address: 3 Todmore, Greatham, LISS, GU33 6AR
Tel: 01420 538196 **Fax:** 01420 538196
Email: rlewis@rfidtoday.co.uk
Web site: http://www.rfidtoday.co.uk
Date Launched: 2004
Frequency of update: 6 times a year
Website Access: Paid
Traffic Figures: 5,000 Unique Users (Publisher's Statement)
Editor: Roger Lewis
Summary of Content: Magazine focusing on the application of technologies associated with radio frequency identification.
Readership/Target Audience: Aimed at board members, CTOs, logistics, directors, BDMs and consultants.
BUSINESS: MATERIALS HANDLING

RHONDDA CYNON TAFF MATTERS
1881669U72J-412

Email: comments@rhonddacynontaff-matters.co.uk
Web site: http://www.rhonddacynontaff-matters.co.uk
Frequency of update: Daily
Summary of Content: Website created to help people who care about local issues. Whether you need access to useful information, want to highlight a particular topic to other people, discuss ideas with like-minded people or just show your support and keep up to date with current affairs in your area, Rhondda Cynon Taff Matters is the place for you.
Readership/Target Audience: Aimed at residents in the local area of Rhondda Cynon Taff.
LOCAL NEWSPAPERS: Community Newsletters

RICHMOND MATTERS
1881670U72J-413

Email: comments@richmond-matters.co.uk
Web site: http://www.richmond-matters.co.uk
Frequency of update: Daily
Summary of Content: Website created to help people who care about local issues. Whether you need access to useful information, want to highlight a particular topic to other people, discuss ideas with like-minded people or just show your support and keep up to date with current affairs in your area, Richmond Matters is the place for you.
Readership/Target Audience: Aimed at residents in the local area of Richmond.
LOCAL NEWSPAPERS: Community Newsletters

RIPLEY TODAY
629800U72B-761

Formerly: Ripley and Heanor NEWS On-Line
Editorial Address: 27 Grosvenor Road, RIPLEY, DE5 3JE
Tel: 01773 514150 **Fax:** 01773 570109
Email: news@rhnews.co.uk
Web site: http://www.ripleyandheanornews.co.uk
Frequency of update: 260 times a year
Website Access: Free
Editor: Julie Crouch
Summary of Content: Website containing news, sport, information and features about Ripley and Heanor.
Readership/Target Audience: Read by residents and visitors to the local area.
LOCAL NEWSPAPERS: Local Newspapers English Counties

THE RIVER THAMES GUIDE
760603U80B-381

Editorial Address: 100-102 George Lane, LONDON, E18 1AD **Tel:** 020 8989 2041
Email: riverthames@btconnect.com
Web site: http://www.riverthames.co.uk
Publisher: The River Thames Guide
Date Launched: 1997
Frequency of update: 364 times a year
Website Access: Free
Traffic Figures: 520,000 Unique Users (per year Publisher's Statement)
Editor: Jeannette Briggs
Summary of Content: Website containing a comprehensive guide to restaurants, pubs, hotels and B&Bs along the whole of the River Thames, conference and wedding venues, entertainment, watersports and festivals, boats, boating and boat trips, cultural and holiday information.
Readership/Target Audience: Aimed at tourists, residents, corporate clients and boat lovers.
CONSUMER: RURAL & REGIONAL INTEREST: Regional Interest Greater London

ROAD TRAFFIC TECHNOLOGY
1616308U42B-251

Editorial Address: Brunel House, 55-57 North Wharf Road, LONDON, W2 1LA **Tel:** 020 7915 9957 **Fax:** 020 7915 9720
Email: production@spgmedia.com
Web site: http://www.roadtraffic-technology.com
Publisher: SPG Media Ltd
Date Launched: 2002
Frequency of update: Daily
Website Access: Free
Traffic Figures: 37,865 Unique Users (per month Publisher's Statement)
Editor: Duncan West
Summary of Content: Website covering bridges, road systems, traffic management and tunnels including road traffic equipment, products, road traffic industry exhibitions, conferences and events.
Readership/Target Audience: Aimed at those working in the road construction and traffic management industries.
BUSINESS: CONSTRUCTION: Roads

ROADCYCLINGUK
1655345U77C-951

Editorial Address: 15-18 White Lion Street, Islington, LONDON, N1 9PG **Tel:** 020 7861 9862 **Fax:** 020 7861 9899
Email: editor@roadcyclinguk.com
Web site: http://www.roadcyclinguk.com
Publisher: Magicalia Ltd
Date Launched: 2004
Frequency of update: Daily
Website Access: Free
Traffic Figures: 165,000 Unique Users (per month Omniture)
Editor: Richard Hallett
Summary of Content: Website covering road cycling in the UK including racing, riding and events as well as cycling products.
Readership/Target Audience: Aimed at road cycling enthusiasts.
CONSUMER: MOTORING & CYCLING: Cycling

ROADTESTS.CO.UK
1655131U77A-512

Editorial Address: Bracken House, Queens Park Avenue, Dresden, STOKE-ON-TRENT, ST3 4AU **Tel:** 01782 312119 **Fax:** 01782 314152
Email: mail@roadtests.co.uk
Web site: http://www.roadtests.co.uk
Publisher: Nick Fletcher & Associates
Date Launched: 2002
Frequency of update: Monthly
Website Access: Free
Editor: Mark Slack
Summary of Content: Website covering news of all the latest vehicles, product matters relating to the motorist, the motor industry and road tests.
Readership/Target Audience: Aimed at car enthusiasts who want to know more about the latest models.
CONSUMER: MOTORING & CYCLING: Motoring

ROADTRANSPORT.COM
1804231U49C-506

Editorial Address: Quadrant House, The Quadrant, SUTTON, SM2 5AS
Email: editor@roadtransport.com
Web site: http://www.roadtransport.com
Publisher: Reed Business Information
Date Launched: 2007
Frequency of update: Daily
Website Access: Free
Editor: Toby Clark; **Web Editor:** Toby Clark
Summary of Content: Website providing news and updates on industry news and legislation. Includes used commercial vehicles for sale, transport jobs, information about new products and links to blogs.
Readership/Target Audience: Aimed at road transport professionals.
BUSINESS: TRANSPORT: Freight

ROCKSOUND.TV
754703U76D-392

Formerly: Rock-Sound.net
Editorial Address: Unit 22, Jack's Place, 6 Corbet Place, LONDON, E1 6NN **Tel:** 020 7877 8770 **Fax:** 020 7377 0455
Email: andy.kelham@rock-sound.net
Web site: http://www.rocksound.tv
Publisher: Rock Sound Ltd
Date Launched: 2001
Frequency of update: Daily
Website Access: Free
Traffic Figures: 105,000 Unique Users (per month Publisher's Statement)
Editor: Andy Kelham
Summary of Content: Website containing news round ups, forum, downloads, links to music sites, reviews, gig guides, letters and competitions.

Readership/Target Audience: Aimed at rock music enthusiasts between 15 and 24 years old.
Other Features: Archiving, e-mail newsletter and events calendar.
CONSUMER: MUSIC & PERFORMING ARTS: Music

ROOFING INDUSTRY DIRECTORY
1818197U4E-448

Editorial Address: 18 Generator Hall, Electric Wharf, COVENTRY, CV1 4JL **Tel:** 0870 199 4044
Fax: 0870 777 4360
Email: enquiries@industrydirectory.co.uk
Web site: http://www.industrydirectory.co.uk/roofing
Publisher: Simply Marcomms
Frequency of update: Daily
Website Access: Free
Editor: Kirstie Colledge
Summary of Content: Directory containing the latest news stories for the roofing industry. Includes a news archive.
Readership/Target Audience: Aimed at professionals in the building and construction industry particularly those in the roofing industry.
BUSINESS: ARCHITECTURE & BUILDING: Building

RSPCA
629259U81A-148

Editorial Address: Wilberforce Way, Southwater, HORSHAM, RH13 9RS **Tel:** 0300 123 0100
Fax: 0300 123 0048
Email: publications@rspca.org.uk
Web site: http://www.rspca.org.uk
Publisher: RSPCA
Frequency of update: Daily
Website Access: Free
Traffic Figures: 100,000 Unique Users (per month Publisher's Statement)
Editor: Sarah Evans
Summary of Content: Website focusing on pets and how to care for them covering campaigns, advice, news, international affairs and the history of the RSPCA.
Readership/Target Audience: Aimed at animal lovers, pet owners and anybody thinking of having a pet.
CONSUMER: ANIMALS & PETS: Animals & Pets Protection

RUCKUS
1745916U74F-765

Formerly: Ruckas
Editorial Address: Eastgate House, 19-23 Humberstone Road, LEICESTER, LE5 3GJ **Fax:** 0116 242 7444
Email: steveb@nya.org.uk
Web site: http://www.youthinformation.com/ruckus
Publisher: The National Youth Agency
Date Launched: 2006
Frequency of update: Quarterly
Website Access: Free
Traffic Figures: 15,000 Unique Users (per quarter Publisher's Statement)
Editor: Steve Beebee
Summary of Content: Electronic magazine covering anything of interest to young adults including games, celebrities, advice, opinion, paranormal, cars, gadgets, sport, relationships, fashion, reading, travel and lifestyle.
Readership/Target Audience: Aimed at young people and young adults aged 14 to 20 years old.
CONSUMER: WOMEN'S INTEREST CONSUMER MAGAZINES: Teenage

RUGBY ADVERTISER.CO.UK
629893U67B-1005

Formerly: RUGBY ADVERTISER On-Line
Editorial Address: 2 Albert Street, RUGBY, CV21 2RS
Tel: 01788 539977 **Fax:** 01788 539960
Email: editorial@rugbyadvertiser.co.uk
Web site: http://www.rugbyadvertiser.co.uk
Publisher: Rugby Advertiser
Date Launched: 1999
Frequency of update: Daily
Website Access: Free
Editor: Philip Hibble
Summary of Content: Website containing news, sport, information and features about the town of Rugby.
Readership/Target Audience: Read by residents and visitors to the local area.
Other Features: Features include recruitment, a chat forum and archiving.
REGIONAL DAILY & SUNDAY NEWSPAPERS: Regional Daily Newspapers

RUNNERSWORLD.CO.UK
1774726U75J-605

Editorial Address: 33 Broadwick Street, LONDON, W1F 0DQ **Tel:** 020 7339 4400 **Fax:** 020 7339 4420
Email: editor@runnersworld.co.uk

Web site: http://www.runnersworld.co.uk
Publisher: NatMag Rodale Ltd
Date Launched: 2002
Frequency of update: Daily
Website Access: Free
Traffic Figures: 370,000 Unique Users (Publisher's Statement)
Editor: Catherine Lee
Summary of Content: Website covering training events and discussion.
Readership/Target Audience: Aimed at runners of all levels.
CONSUMER: SPORT: Athletics

RUSSIAN LONDON.COM
1692013U90-968

Editorial Address: 124 New Bond Street, LONDON, W1S 1DX **Tel:** 020 7629 7707 **Fax:** 020 7629 7177
Email: info@russianlondon.com
Web site: http://www.russianlondon.com
Frequency of update: Daily
Website Access: Paid
Traffic Figures: 4,500 Unique Users (per day Publisher's Statement)
Editor: Olga Sirenko
Summary of Content: Website covering Russian and British news and Russian events in London.
Readership/Target Audience: Aimed at the Russian speaking community in London.
CONSUMER: ETHNIC

RUTLAND & STAMFORD MERCURY ON-LINE
629848U72B-2275

Editorial Address: Mercury House, 7 Sheepmarket, STAMFORD, PE9 2QZ **Tel:** 01733 555111
Fax: 01780 751371
Email: smeditor@stamfordmercury.co.uk
Web site: http://www.stamfordmercury.co.uk
Date Launched: 1999
Frequency of update: Weekly
Website Access: Free
Editor: Lisa Bruen
Summary of Content: Website containing news, sport, information and features about Rutland and Stamford.
Readership/Target Audience: Aimed at residents and visitors to the local area.
Other Features: Features include recruitment, classifieds, blogs and archiving.
LOCAL NEWSPAPERS: Local Newspapers English Counties

RYDER CUP MAGAZINE
1648579U75D-513

Editorial Address: Independent House, 191 Marsh Wall, LONDON, E14 9RS **Tel:** 020 7005 5073
Email: intrugby@indmags.co.uk
Publisher: Independent News & Media Group
Frequency of update: Annual. Published in June
Website Access: Paid
Traffic Figures: 44,000 Unique Users (Publisher's Statement)
Editor: Jon Edwards
Summary of Content: Magazine covering the Ryder Cup Golf Tournament.
Readership/Target Audience: Aimed at golf fans.
CONSUMER: SPORT: Golf

THE SAFE ENERGY JOURNAL
40781U58-69_20

Editorial Address: 24 Parkhead View, EDINBURGH, EH11 4RT **Tel:** 0131 444 1445 **Fax:** 0131 444 1445
Email: rochepete8@aol.com
Web site: http://www.no2nuclearpower.org.uk
Publisher: The Safe Energy Journal
Date Launched: 1977
Frequency of update: Quarterly
Website Access: Free
Traffic Figures: 350 Unique Users (Publisher's Statement)
Editor: Pete Roche
Summary of Content: Electronically mailed magazine covering trade developments within the nuclear industry.
Readership/Target Audience: Aimed at anti-nuclear activists, energy professionals and environmentalists.
BUSINESS: ENERGY, FUEL & NUCLEAR

SAFETY.CO.UK
1616005U54B-101

Editorial Address: Glaisdale Drive East, Bilborough, NOTTINGHAM, NG8 4JJ **Tel:** 0115 942 8912
Fax: 0115 929 0490
Email: patricia@tdk.co.uk
Web site: http://www.safety.co.uk
Publisher: TDK Business Technologies Ltd

Date Launched: 2002
Frequency of update: Daily
Website Access: Free
Editor: Patricia Cullen
Summary of Content: Website covering safety, security and fire equipment as well as services, events, education, associations and features.
Readership/Target Audience: Aimed at decision makers, safety officers, health and safety officers and general safety officers in offices.
BUSINESS: SAFETY & SECURITY: Safety

SAILPOWER.COM
623122U91A-126

Editorial Address: Blue Fin Building, 110 Southwark Street, LONDON, SE1 0SU **Tel:** 020 3148 4844 **Fax:** 020 3148 8127
Email: sue_pelling@ipcmedia.com
Web site: http://www.sailpower.com
Publisher: IPC Inspire
Date Launched: 2000
Frequency of update: Daily
Website Access: Free
Editor: Sue Pelling
Summary of Content: Website focusing on dinghy and small boat racing including results, video features, interviews and racing tips.
Readership/Target Audience: Aimed at beginners or high-performance racers in the boating world.
Other Features: Features include an events calender, free classified ads and archiving.
CONSUMER: RECREATION & LEISURE: Boating & Yachting

SAINT HELENS RUGBY LEAGUE
1663819U75C-466

Formerly: Saints
Editorial Address: St. Helens Rugby League Football Club, Dunriding Lane, ST. HELENS, WA10 4AD
Tel: 0870 756 5252 **Fax:** 0870 756 5277
Email: mike.appleton@saintsrlfc.com
Web site: http://www.saintsrlfc.com
Frequency of update: Daily
Website Access: Free
Editor: Mike Appleton
Summary of Content: Website covering club news, fixtures, match reports, player profiles and supporter features.
Readership/Target Audience: Aimed at St Helens Saints supporters and general rugby league and sports fans.
CONSUMER: SPORT: Rugby

SARACENS ONLINE
1663653U75C-468

Editorial Address: 160 Harpenden Road, ST. ALBANS, AL3 6BB **Tel:** 01727 792800
Email: mikehartwell@saracens.net
Web site: http://www.saracens.com
Frequency of update: Daily
Website Access: Free
Traffic Figures: 50,000 Unique Users (per month Publisher's Statement)
Editor: Mike Hartwell
Summary of Content: Official site of Saracens Rugby Club covering fixture updates, match reports, team news, player interviews, ticket updates, competitions and auctions.
Readership/Target Audience: Aimed at fans of Saracens Rugby Union club and rugby fans generally.
CONSUMER: SPORT: Rugby

SAVILEROW-STYLE.COM
47665U86C-545

Formerly: Savile Row
Editorial Address: Beacon House, 2 Beacon Hill, LONDON, N7 9LY **Tel:** 020 7609 5100
Email: scotay@gmail.com
Web site: http://www.savillerow-style.com
Publisher: Scott Taylor Publishing Ltd
Frequency of update: Quarterly
Website Access: Free
Editor: Marie Scott
Summary of Content: Website containing features on luxury goods, services, travel, quality clothes, wine, art, accessories and motoring.
Readership/Target Audience: Aimed at customers of Savile Row tailors.
CONSUMER: ADULT & GAY MAGAZINES: Men's Lifestyle Magazines

SCHOOLSNET.COM
601635U62A-445

Editorial Address: 150-152 King Street, LONDON, W6 0QU
Tel: 020 8600 5300
Email: greg.hadfield@hotcourses.com
Web site: http://www.schoolsnet.com
Frequency of update: Daily

Website Access: Free
Traffic Figures: 762,000 Unique Users (per month Publisher's Statement)
Editor: Greg Hadfield
Summary of Content: Website covering information about the UK education system.
Readership/Target Audience: Aimed at teachers, parents and pupils.
BUSINESS: CHURCH & SCHOOL EQUIPMENT & EDUCATION: Education

SCI STRUCTURED CREDIT INVESTOR
1776543U1F-631

Editorial Address: 507 Clarkenweel Workshops, 27-31 Clarkenwell Close, LONDON, EC1R 0AT **Tel:** 020 7438 1160
Fax: 020 7117 3664
Email: corinne.smith@structuredcreditinvestor.com
Web site: http://www.structuredcreditinvestor.com
Publisher: Cold Fountains Media
Date Launched: 2006
Frequency of update: Weekly
Website Access: Paid
Traffic Figures: 3,500 Unique Users (per week Publisher's Statement)
Editor: Corinne Smith
Summary of Content: Website covering all classes of credit derivatives and structured credit.
Readership/Target Audience: Aimed at hedge fund, asset and pensions managers.
BUSINESS: FINANCE & ECONOMICS: Investment

SCIENCE|BUSINESS
1697548U55-9023

Formerly: ScienceBusiness
Editorial Address: 11 Fulready Road, LONDON, E10 6DT
Tel: 020 8539 1052
Email: info@sciencebusiness.net
Web site: http://www.sciencebusiness.net
Publisher: Science Business Publishing Ltd
Date Launched: 2005
Frequency of update: 356 times a year
Website Access: Paid
Editor: Richard Hudson
Summary of Content: Website covering news, insight and trends in the business of science. Features a fortnightly e-mailed bulletin.
Readership/Target Audience: Aimed at key decision makers in the scientific enterprise.
BUSINESS: APPLIED SCIENCE & LABORATORIES

SCIENTIFIC COMPUTING WORLD
707495U55-158

Formerly: SCIENTIFIC COMPUTING WORLD Online
Editorial Address: The Spectrum Building, Michael Young Centre, Purbeck Road, CAMBRIDGE, CB2 8PD
Tel: 01223 211196 **Fax:** 01223 211107
Email: warren.clark@europascience.com
Web site: http://www.scientific-computing.com
Publisher: Europa Science Ltd
Date Launched: 2000
Frequency of update: Monthly
Website Access: Free
Editor: Warren Clark
Summary of Content: Website focusing on computer science. Includes news, events, developments, products and reviews of software.
Readership/Target Audience: Aimed at scientists, researchers and technicians all over the globe who rely upon computing to help them with their work.
BUSINESS: APPLIED SCIENCE & LABORATORIES

SCI-FI-LONDON
1791021U76A-203

Editorial Address: 145-157 St. John Street, LONDON, EC1V 4PY **Tel:** 020 3239 9277 **Fax:** 020 8983 9426
Email: chrisp@sci-fi-london.com
Web site: http://www.sci-fi-london.com
Publisher: Festival Biz
Date Launched: 2002
Frequency of update: Daily
Website Access: Free
Traffic Figures: 135,000 Unique Users (per month Publisher's Statement)
Editor: Chris Patmore
Summary of Content: Website featuring science fiction film, DVD, book and comic reviews as well as interviews with film directors, producers and actors.
Readership/Target Audience: Aimed at men aged 25 to 45 years old.
CONSUMER: MUSIC & PERFORMING ARTS: Cinema

SCOTSMAN.COM
634901U67C-37

Formerly: SCOTLAND on SUNDAY.COM
Editorial Address: 108 Holyrood Road, EDINBURGH, EH8
8AS **Tel:** 0131 620 8324 **Fax:** 0131 523 0227
Email: enquiries@scotsman.com
Web site: http://www.scotsman.com
Publisher: The Scotsman Publications Ltd
Date Launched: 2000
Frequency of update: 2444 times a year
Website Access: Free
Traffic Figures: 2,038,770 Unique Users (01/07/2008 To
31/12/2008 ABC/Electronic)
Editor: Alan Greenwood
Summary of Content: Website providing national and
international news and features with a focus on Scotland.
Readership/Target Audience: Aimed at those with an
interest in Scotland.
REGIONAL DAILY & SUNDAY NEWSPAPERS: Regional
Sunday Newspapers

SCOTTISH CONSTRUCTION NOW
1809328U4E-445

Editorial Address: For all contact details see main record,
Construction Now
Frequency of update: 250 times a year
BUSINESS: ARCHITECTURE & BUILDING: Building

SCOTTISH PROPERTY NETWORK
1622541U1E-358

Editorial Address: Empire House, 131 West Nile Street,
GLASGOW, G1 2RX **Tel:** 0141 561 7300 **Fax:** 0141 561 7319
Email: info@scottishproperty.co.uk
Web site: http://www.scottishproperty.co.uk
Publisher: CoStar UK Ltd
Date Launched: 1999
Frequency of update: Daily
Website Access: Free
Traffic Figures: 60,000 Unique Users (per month
WebTrends)
Editor: Fraser Collins
Summary of Content: Website containing information on
supply and market activity in Scottish industrial and
commercial property markets.
Readership/Target Audience: Aimed at the public and
private sectors of commercial property companies in
Scotland.
BUSINESS: FINANCE & ECONOMICS: Property

SCOTTISH RUGBY ONLINE
1663722U75C-465

Editorial Address: Murrayfield, EDINBURGH, EH12 5PJ
Tel: 0131 346 5000 **Fax:** 0131 346 5001
Email: graham.law@sru.org.uk
Web site: http://www.scottishrugby.org
Frequency of update: Daily
Website Access: Free
Editor: Graham Law
Summary of Content: Official site of Scottish Rugby Union
covering news, fixtures, results, player profiles and business.
Readership/Target Audience: Aimed at Scottish rugby
union fans around the world.
CONSUMER: SPORT: Rugby

SCOTTISHHOUSINGNEWS.COM
1776293U4D-410

Editorial Address: For all contact details see main edition,
housingnews.co.uk
Website Access: Free
BUSINESS: ARCHITECTURE & BUILDING: Planning &
Housing

SCOTWHEELS
1792875U77A-602

Editorial Address: Press Buildings, Campbell Street,
HAMILTON, ML3 6AX **Tel:** 01698 283200
Fax: 01698 891151
Email: icscotland@s-un.co.uk
Web site: http://www.scotwheels.co.uk
Publisher: Scottish and Universal Newspapers Hamilton
Date Launched: 2006
Frequency of update: Daily
Website Access: Free
Traffic Figures: 2,700 Unique Users (per week Publisher's
Statement)
Editor: Scott Sandlan
Summary of Content: Magazine covering new cars as well
as motoring news, car reviews, road tests, buying advice,
tips on finding the right car insurance and finance.

Readership/Target Audience: Aimed at Scottish
consumers looking to buy a car.
CONSUMER: MOTORING & CYCLING: Motoring

SCREENDAILY.COM
623121U76A-45_5

Editorial Address: Greater London House, 1 Hampstead
Road, LONDON, NW1 7EJ **Tel:** 020 7728 5000
Email: conor.dignam@emap.com
Web site: http://www.screendaily.com
Publisher: EMAP Inform
Date Launched: 2000
Frequency of update: Daily
Website Access: Paid
Editor: Conor Dignam
Summary of Content: Website covering business news for
the global movie and television industry. Also includes
interviews, reviews and box office.
Readership/Target Audience: Aimed at those with an
interest in the film and television industry.
CONSUMER: MUSIC & PERFORMING ARTS: Cinema

SCREENS.TV
1836874U53-704

Editorial Address: 6 Laurence Pountney Hill, LONDON,
EC4R 0BL **Tel:** 020 7933 8999
Email: info@screens.tv
Web site: http://www.screens.tv
Publisher: St. John Patrick Publishers Ltd
Frequency of update: Daily
Traffic Figures: 18,000 Unique Users (per year Publisher's
Statement)
Editor: Barnaby Page
Summary of Content: Website covering information and
news about digital signage.
Readership/Target Audience: Aimed at transport
operators, networkers, the leisure and hospitality industry
and anyone interested in digital signage.
BUSINESS: RETAILING & WHOLESALING

SCRIP WORLD PHARMACEUTICAL NEWS
38772U37-65

Editorial Address: Telephone House, 69-77 Paul Street,
LONDON, EC2A 4LQ **Tel:** 020 7017 5000
Fax: 020 7017 6965
Email: scrip.editorial@informa.com
Web site: http://www.scripnews.com
Publisher: Informa Healthcare
Date Launched: 1972
Frequency of update: Daily
Website Access: Paid
Editor: John Davis
Summary of Content: Publication providing news and
commentary about the pharmaceutical, biotech, generic and
healthcare sectors worldwide and the environments in which
they work. Including politics, pricing, regulatory affairs,
financial news, science and research and development.
Readership/Target Audience: Read by company
executives, investors, analysts, governmental agencies,
regulatory agencies and clinical researchers.
BUSINESS: PHARMACEUTICAL & CHEMISTS

SEA TROUT FISHING
1667897U92-107

Editorial Address: The Little Barn, Garmston,
SHREWSBURY, SY5 6RL **Tel:** 07870 666553
Email: hoppy@seatroutfishing.net
Web site: http://www.seatroutfishing.net
Date Launched: 1999
Frequency of update: Daily
Website Access: Free
Traffic Figures: 3,160 Unique Users (per month Publisher's
Statement)
Editor: Paul Hopwood
Summary of Content: Website containing a range of advice
on most aspects of Sea Trout Fishing including fishing by
day and night, fly fishing, bait fishing and where to fish.
The site also contains a web based forum, which is heavily
used, with users giving up to date information on river, catch
returns, fishing tactics and fly selection.
Readership/Target Audience: Aimed at anglers interested
in fishing for sea trout and salmon or those interested in
starting out.
CONSUMER: ANGLING & FISHING

SECURITY DOCUMENT WORLD
1741115U54C-326

Editorial Address: 6 Cardiff Road, St. Fagans, CARDIFF,
CF5 6EB **Tel:** 029 2056 0458 **Fax:** 029 2056 0458
Email: info@securitydocumentworld.com
Web site: http://www.securitydocumentworld.com
Publisher: Science Media Partners Ltd

Frequency of update: Daily
Website Access: Free
Editor: Mark Lockie
Summary of Content: Website focusing on the traditional
and electronic security document market, including
passports, ID cards, visas, driving licences and other
government issued identity documents.
Readership/Target Audience: Aimed at suppliers,
integrators, end users and government officials who are
being tasked to install security document solutions.
BUSINESS: SAFETY & SECURITY: Security

SECURITY INDUSTRY DIRECTORY
1912972U54C-342

Editorial Address: 18 Generator Hall, Electric Wharf,
COVENTRY, CV1 4JL **Tel:** 0870 199 4044
Fax: 0870 777 4360
Email: enquiries@simplymarcomms.co.uk
Web site: http://www.industrydirectory.co.uk
Publisher: Simply Marcomms
Frequency of update: Daily
Website Access: Free
Editor: Kirstie Colledge
Summary of Content: Directory containing the latest news
stories for the UK security industry. Includes news archives.
Readership/Target Audience: Aimed at Security
professionals, suppliers to the Security industry, Security
Industry PR & Marketing firms.
BUSINESS: SAFETY & SECURITY: Security

SECURITY INDUSTRY TODAY
1786629U54C-329

Editorial Address: PR by email only **Tel:** 0871 983 7368
Email: editor@security-industry-today.com
Web site: http://www.Security-Industry-Today.com
Publisher: EFE International
Frequency of update: Daily
Website Access: Free
Editor: R. Pas
Summary of Content: Website providing information on
global security risks and news and updates on advanced
technology and security industry developments, an events
calendar, and vendor directory. Sectors covered include
access control, biometrics, ITC, data fusion, detectors and
sensors, photonics, and other security related technologies,
plus their markets and developments.
Readership/Target Audience: Aimed at senior executives
and key decision-makers in the transportation, oil and gas,
utilities, construction and defence industries, and the ports
and airports, buildings, border control, and homeland
security sectors in the UK and internationally.
Other Features: Buyers Guide, Events Calendar,
Recruitment, Newsletter.
BUSINESS: SAFETY & SECURITY: Security

SECURITY INTERNATIONAL
1640531U54C-336

Editorial Address: 100 Chapel Street, TIVERTON, EX16
6BU **Tel:** 01884 244670 **Fax:** 01884 244671
Email: info@copybook.com
Web site: http://www.copybook.com/securitydirectory.asp
Publisher: Copybook Solutions Ltd
Date Launched: 1999
Frequency of update: Monthly
Website Access: Free
Editor: James Armstrong
Summary of Content: Online portal containing information
on security services and products, government policies on
protection, fire safety and health.
Readership/Target Audience: Aimed at governments,
buyers, specifiers and installers of products and services
related to the security industry.
BUSINESS: SAFETY & SECURITY: Security

SECURITY MANAGEMENT TODAY (SMT)
39918U54C-115_55

Formerly: SMT Security Management Today
Editorial Address: 7th Floor, Ludgate House, 245
Blackfriars Road, LONDON, SE1 9UY **Tel:** 020 7921 8286
Fax: 020 7921 8059
Email: brian.sims@ubm.com
Web site: http://www.info4security.com/smtonline
Publisher: UBM Information Ltd
Date Launched: 1961
Frequency of update: Daily
Website Access: Free
Traffic Figures: 7,514 Unique Users (Publisher's Statement)
Editor: Brian Sims; **Web Editor:** Anthony Hildebrand
Summary of Content: Website containing news, product
specifications, case studies of security system installations
and career development features. Majors on industry profiles
of leading players, employment legislation and regulation
and licensing of the private security sector.

Internet Media

Readership/Target Audience: Read by managers and directors in security industry, security chiefs in industry, security system end users, consultants and crime prevention officers and police officers.
BUSINESS: SAFETY & SECURITY: Security

SECURITY NEWS ONLINE
1808779U54C-333

Editorial Address: PO Box 623, Farlington, PORTSMOUTH, PO6 1XQ **Tel:** 023 9264 6159 **Fax:** 0870 133 7687
Email: paulrussell@securitynewsonline.net
Web site: http://www.securitynewsonline.net
Publisher: Paul Russell Media
Date Launched: 2004
Frequency of update: Daily
Website Access: Free
Traffic Figures: 15,000 Unique Users (Publisher's Statement)
Editor: Paul Russell
Summary of Content: Website providing information about security matters and products, details of exhibitions and events, job opportunities and suppliers' directory.
Readership/Target Audience: Aimed at providers of security services.
BUSINESS: SAFETY & SECURITY: Security

SECURITY PARK
626536U54C-306

Editorial Address: Britannia House, 11 Glenthorne Road, LONDON, W6 0LH **Tel:** 0870 745 3380
Email: editor@securitypark.co.uk
Web site: http://www.securitypark.co.uk
Publisher: Areza Ltd
Date Launched: 2000
Frequency of update: Daily
Website Access: Free
Traffic Figures: 395,000 Unique Users (per month Publisher's Statement)
Editor: Phillippe Marc
Summary of Content: Website covering news, features and product information about electronic security, IT and network security, CCTV, access control, biometrics, remote monitoring, surveillance, perimeter protection, intruder alarms, biometrics, physical security, manned security and security services.
Readership/Target Audience: Aimed at security professionals, manufacturers, installers, end-users and distributors.
Other Features: Directory, job forum, classifieds and email newsletter.
BUSINESS: SAFETY & SECURITY: Security

SECURIZINE
1795206U54C-331

Editorial Address: PR by email only **Tel:** 01795 435913
Email: news@prosecurizine.com
Web site: http://www.securizine.com
Publisher: Zenius (Croydon) Ltd
Date Launched: 2005
Frequency of update: Weekly
Website Access: Free
Traffic Figures: 4,800 Unique Users (Publisher's Statement)
Editor: Henry Lott
Summary of Content: Website and newsletter providing the latest police news, jobs and product information for the UK police service.
Readership/Target Audience: Aimed at police staff and uniformed officers.
BUSINESS: SAFETY & SECURITY: Security

SEMICONDUCTOR FABTECH
707581U18A-411_50

Formerly: semiconductor FABTECH Online
Editorial Address: Trans-World House, 100 City Road, LONDON, EC1Y 2BP **Tel:** 020 7871 0123
Fax: 020 7871 0101
Email: mosborne@fabtech.org
Web site: http://www.fabtech.org
Publisher: Semiconductor Media Ltd
Date Launched: 1994
Frequency of update: Daily
Website Access: Free
Traffic Figures: 13,741 Unique Users (per quarter Publisher's Statement)
Editor: Mark Osborne; **Editor-in-Chief:** Mark Osborne
Summary of Content: Website containing industry news, product reviews and technical articles divided into sections and online.
Readership/Target Audience: Aimed at leading-edge IC manufacturing engineers and management, world-wide.
BUSINESS: ELECTRONICS

SEMICONDUCTOR TECHNOLOGY
1616585U18A-9011

Editorial Address: Brunel House, 55-57 North Wharf Road, LONDON, W2 1LA **Tel:** 020 7915 9957 **Fax:** 020 7915 9720
Email: production@spgmedia.com
Web site: http://www.semiconductor-technology.com
Publisher: SPG Media Ltd
Date Launched: 2000
Frequency of update: Daily
Website Access: Free
Traffic Figures: 14,224 Unique Users (per month Publisher's Statement)
Editor: Duncan West
Summary of Content: Website covering semiconductor technology projects as well as general news, products and services and exhibitions and conferences.
Readership/Target Audience: Aimed at those working within the semiconductor industry.
BUSINESS: ELECTRONICS

SERVER MANAGEMENT
36023U5B-77

Formerly: Enterprise Server Magazine
Editorial Address: 15B St. Georges Mews, Primrose Hill, LONDON, NW1 8XE **Tel:** 020 7449 1500
Email: editorial@server-management.co.uk
Web site: http://www.server-management.co.uk
Publisher: Story Worldwide
Date Launched: 1996
Frequency of update: Daily
Website Access: Paid
Traffic Figures: 19,941 Unique Users (Publisher's Statement)
Editor: Sue Gee
Summary of Content: Website containing in-depth technical features, product news and product reviews relating to Windows Server and Microsoft's Enterprise Server applications.
Readership/Target Audience: Aimed at IT managers/directors working with, or responsible for Windows and Enterprise Server products.
BUSINESS: COMPUTERS & AUTOMATION: Data Processing

SERVERS
1836212U5E-9004

Editorial Address: City Tower, Piccadilly Plaza, MANCHESTER, M1 4BT **Tel:** 0844 576 3909
Fax: 0870 458 4545
Email: stephen.mcnamara@ukfast.co.uk
Web site: http://www.servers.co.uk
Publisher: UKFast.Net
Date Launched: 2007
Frequency of update: Daily
Website Access: Free
Editor: Stephen McNamara
Summary of Content: Website covering a series of online journals and press releases about the internet industry, specifically web hosting, managed hosting, dedicated hosting and technology and hardware.
Readership/Target Audience: Aimed at businesses, entrepreneurs and IT managers.
Other Features: FAQs, polls, request more information, internet news and hosting news with archive
BUSINESS: COMPUTERS & AUTOMATION: Data Transmission

SHADOWS ON THE WALL
1685686U76A-180

Editorial Address: 37 Holland Walk, LONDON, N19 3XT
Tel: 020 7686 2561
Email: shadows@wall.net
Web site: http://www.shadowsonthewall.co.uk
Date Launched: 1985
Frequency of update: Daily
Website Access: Free
Editor: Rich Cline
Summary of Content: Website covering film reviews, news and interviews.
Readership/Target Audience: Aimed at film lovers.
CONSUMER: MUSIC & PERFORMING ARTS: Cinema

SHARE MY POPCORN
1705976U76A-192

Editorial Address: 53 Newland Gardens, Hertford, HERTS, SG13 7WN
Email: melanie.dayasena@sharemypopcorn.co.uk
Web site: http://www.sharemypopcorn.co.uk
Date Launched: 2001
Frequency of update: Weekly
Website Access: Free
Editor: Melanie Dayasena
Summary of Content: Website covering movies showing at the cinema, coming soon section for films hitting the cinema

within the coming four to six weeks and film-related products out to buy (DVDs and soundtracks).
Readership/Target Audience: Aimed at a wide spectrum of mainstream movie goers.
CONSUMER: MUSIC & PERFORMING ARTS: Cinema

SHARECAST
639428U1F-404_50

Editorial Address: 4th Floor, Bankside House, 107 Leadenhall Street, LONDON, EC3A 4AF **Tel:** 020 7743 0050
Fax: 020 7504 3627
Email: info@sharecast.com
Web site: http://www.sharecast.com
Frequency of update: Daily. The site is updated hourly
Website Access: Free
Editor: Philip Whiterow
Summary of Content: Website containing news, views and information on the latest stock market happenings. Includes a broker recommendation, a real-time price alert and annual reports for business.
Readership/Target Audience: Aimed at investors.
BUSINESS: FINANCE & ECONOMICS: Investment

SHE
1902875U74A-1062

Editorial Address: 72 Broadwick Street, LONDON, W1F 9EP **Tel:** 020 7439 5000
Email: editor@shemagazine.co.uk
Web site: http://www.allaboutyou.com/she
Publisher: Hearst Digital
Frequency of update: 355 times a year
Website Access: Free
Editor: Bernadette Fallon
Summary of Content: Website covering fashion, features and lifestyle.
Readership/Target Audience: Aimed at women of all ages.
CONSUMER: WOMEN'S INTEREST CONSUMER MAGAZINES: Women's Interest

SHEERLUXE.COM
1800375U74A-1032

Editorial Address: Studio 2, 92 Lots Road, LONDON, SW10 0QD **Tel:** 020 7368 7852
Email: natalie.hughes@sheerluxe.com
Web site: http://www.sheerluxe.com
Date Launched: 2007
Frequency of update: Daily
Website Access: Free
Traffic Figures: 75,000 Unique Users (per month Publisher's Statement)
Editor: Natalie Hughes
Summary of Content: Website dedicated to online shopping and covering new fashion boutiques, beauty and lingerie brands, delis, and home and lifestyle stores.
Readership/Target Audience: Aimed at women aged 18 to 55 years old who appreciate the finer things in life.
CONSUMER: WOMEN'S INTEREST CONSUMER MAGAZINES: Women's Interest

SHEFFIELD MATTERS
1881671U72J-414

Email: comments@sheffield-matters.co.uk
Web site: http://www.sheffield-matters.co.uk
Frequency of update: Daily
Summary of Content: Website created to help people who care about local issues. Whether you need access to useful information, want to highlight a particular topic to other people, discuss ideas with like minded individuals or just show your support and keep up to date with current affairs in your area, Sheffield Matters is the place for you.
Readership/Target Audience: Aimed at residents in the local area of Sheffield.
LOCAL NEWSPAPERS: Community Newsletters

THE SHETLAND TIMES
629064U80E-250

Formerly: Shetlandtoday
Editorial Address: Gremista, LERWICK, ZE1 0PX
Tel: 01595 693622 **Fax:** 01595 694637
Email: editorial@shetland-times.co.uk
Web site: http://www.shetlandtimes.co.uk/
Date Launched: 1997
Frequency of update: Daily
Website Access: Free
Summary of Content: Website providing news and information on the Shetland Islands.
Readership/Target Audience: Aimed at Shetland residents, expatriates and visitors.
Other Features: Features include a chat forum, recruitment, an events calendar and archiving.
CONSUMER: RURAL & REGIONAL INTEREST: Regional Interest Scotland

SHIP TECHNOLOGY
1616310U45D-402

Editorial Address: Brunel House, 55-57 North Wharf Road, LONDON, W2 1LA **Tel:** 020 7915 9957 **Fax:** 020 7915 9720
Email: production@spgmedia.com
Web site: http://www.ship-technology.com
Publisher: SPG Media Ltd
Frequency of update: Daily
Traffic Figures: 102,005 Unique Users (Publisher's Statement)
Editor: Duncan West
Summary of Content: Website covering tankers, gas carriers, floating offshore facilities, cruise liners, dry cargo vessels, ferries and support vessels as well as marine equipment, products and services, and marine industry exhibitions, conferences and events.
Readership/Target Audience: Aimed at those working in the cruise and ship industries.
BUSINESS: MARINE & SHIPPING: Marine Engineering Equipment

SHOOTINGUK.CO.UK
1818701U75F-214

Editorial Address: 9th Floor, Blue Fin Buidling, 110 Southwark Street, LONDON, SE1 0SU **Tel:** 020 3148 5000
Email: barnaby_dracup@ipcmedia.com
Web site: http://www.shootinguk.co.uk
Publisher: IPC Inspire
Date Launched: 2007
Frequency of update: Daily
Website Access: Free
Editor: Barnaby Dracup
Summary of Content: Online shooting network with review of guns, news, features, forums, blogs and a market place to buy and sell equipment.
Readership/Target Audience: Aimed at the British shooting community.
Other Features: Forums, blogs, and newsletters
CONSUMER: SPORT: Shooting

SHOTS
1804957U84B-368

Editorial Address: 189 Snakes Lane East, WOODFORD GREEN, IG8 7JH **Tel:** 07951 996004
Email: shotseditor@yahoo.com
Web site: http://www.shotsmag.co.uk
Frequency of update: Daily
Website Access: Free
Traffic Figures: 17,000 Unique Users (per day Publisher's Statement)
Editor: Mike Stotter
Summary of Content: Website covering crime and thriller books with book reviews, features, interviews and competitions.
Readership/Target Audience: Aimed at fans of the genre and publishers.
CONSUMER: THE ARTS & LITERARY: Literary

SHOTS ONLINE
749202U2A-168_72

Editorial Address: Greater London House, Hampstead Road, LONDON, NW1 7EJ **Tel:** 020 7728 5000
Fax: 020 7728 4800
Email: news@shots.net
Web site: http://www.shots.net
Publisher: EMAP Communications
Frequency of update: Weekly
Website Access: Paid
Traffic Figures: 12,000 Unique Users (per week Publisher's Statement)
Editor: Danny Edwards
Summary of Content: Website concentrating on International advertising and creativity. Includes news, views, a directory of directors, agencies, production companies and post production companies.
Readership/Target Audience: Aimed at advertising and production professionals worldwide.
BUSINESS: COMMUNICATIONS, ADVERTISING & MARKETING

SHOUT99.COM
766720U14H-429

Editorial Address: 18 Goodwin Close, LONDON, SE16 3TR
Tel: 07703 486276
Email: susie@shout99.com
Web site: http://www.shout99.com
Date Launched: 2000
Frequency of update: Daily
Website Access: Free
Traffic Figures: 35,000 Unique Users (Publisher's Statement)
Editor: Susie Hughes
Summary of Content: Website covering news and views pertinent to consultants and contractors working in all business sectors including news, information, resources, letters to the editor and ask an expert.

Readership/Target Audience: Aimed at consultants, contractors and related parties including clients, accountants and others working in business both in the UK and abroad.
BUSINESS: COMMERCE, INDUSTRY & MANAGEMENT: Small Business

SHOWBIZWORKS.COM
1810329U64K-655

Formerly: showbizworks
Editorial Address: Communications House, 26 York Street, LONDON, W1U 6PZ **Tel:** 0845 638 1808 **Fax:** 01253 735899
Email: marina@showbizworks.com
Web site: http://www.showbizworks.com
Date Launched: 2006
Frequency of update: Daily
Website Access: Free
Editor: Marina Blore
Summary of Content: Entertainment agency website featuring show business breaking news, new talent, record signings, celebrity gossip, news of original live artistes and general live entertainment news.
Readership/Target Audience: Aimed at those interested in celebrity news and trends in live entertainment and celebrity bookers seeking to find performers or shows for international events.
BUSINESS: OTHER CLASSIFICATIONS: Cinema Entertainment

SHOW.ME.UK
1709126U84A-451

Editorial Address: PO Box 3470, BRIGHTON, BN1 1DA
Tel: 01273 623357
Email: newsdesk@24hourmuseum.org.uk
Web site: http://www.show.me.uk
Frequency of update: 104 times a year
Website Access: Free
Traffic Figures: 90,000 Unique Users (per month Publisher's Statement)
Editor: Anra Kennedy
Summary of Content: Website featuring interactive kids' content from UK museums and galleries, arty games and fun, drawing, news and places to go.
Readership/Target Audience: Aimed at children aged 4 to 11 years old.
CONSUMER: THE ARTS & LITERARY: Arts

SHOWSTUDIO
1902989U47A-594

Editorial Address: 1-9 Bruton Place, LONDON, W1J 6LT
Tel: 0207 3998225
Email: alex@showstudio.com
Web site: http://www.showstudio.com/
Frequency of update: Daily
Summary of Content: Website covering the award winning fashion website founded and directed by Nick Knight, pushing the boundaries of communicating fashion online.
Readership/Target Audience: Aimed at those interested in fashion, fashion shows and the fashion industry in general.
BUSINESS: CLOTHING & TEXTILES

SHROPSHIRE MATTERS
1881672U72J-415

Email: comments@shropshire-matters.co.uk
Web site: http://www.shropshire-matters.co.uk
Frequency of update: Daily
Summary of Content: Website created to help people who care about local issues. Whether you need access to useful information, want to highlight a particular topic to other people, discuss ideas with like minded individuals or just show your support and keep up to date with current affairs in your area, Shropshire Matters is the place for you.
Readership/Target Audience: Aimed at residents in the local area of Shropshire.
LOCAL NEWSPAPERS: Community Newsletters

SIGHT 'N SOUND
47602U85B-25

Formerly: AV Sight'n Sound
Editorial Address: 47 Dorset Street, LONDON, W1U 7ND
Tel: 020 7935 2580 **Fax:** 020 7486 1272
Email: simon@widescreen-centre.co.uk
Web site: http://www.widescreen-centre.co.uk
Publisher: The Widescreen Centre
Date Launched: 1995
Frequency of update: Weekly
Website Access: Free
Traffic Figures: 12,000 Unique Users (Publisher's Statement)
Editor: Simon Bennett
Summary of Content: Electronic newsletter reporting on astronomy, astro-photography, audio visual, exhibition and museum event installations, widescreen film systems in panoramic formats, 3-D, flight simulation and virtual reality and motion pictures.

Readership/Target Audience: Read by people interested in audio visual, astronomy, astro-photography, 3D and technological progress.
Other Features: Discussion forum for readers.
CONSUMER: PHOTOGRAPHY & FILM MAKING: Film Making

SIKH TIMES
1616497U90-923

Editorial Address: 160 Rolfe Street, SMETHWICK, B66 2AU
Tel: 0121 558 3020 **Fax:** 0121 275 6197
Email: gurjeet@emgonline.co.uk
Web site: http://www.emgonline.co.uk
Publisher: Eastern Media Group
Frequency of update: 260 times a year. Published Monday to Friday
Website Access: Free
Editor: Gurjeet Kaur Bains
Summary of Content: Online newspaper covering international news, events, history, culture and sport.
Readership/Target Audience: Aimed at Sikh and Asian communities within the UK.
CONSUMER: ETHNIC

SILICON.COM
42954U5R-679

Editorial Address: 5-11 Lavington Street, LONDON, SE1 0NZ **Tel:** 020 7021 1000
Email: editorial@silicon.com
Web site: http://www.silicon.com
Publisher: CBS Interactive
Date Launched: 1998
Frequency of update: Daily
Website Access: Free
Traffic Figures: 752,838 Unique Users (per month ABC/ Electronic)
Editor: Steve Ranger
Summary of Content: Website covering news in a combined text and video format, delivering editorial comment and analysis, interviews with industry figures and industry reports.
Readership/Target Audience: Aimed at CIOs, IT directors, managers and consultants, network managers, senior business professionals involved in IT and technology and telecoms analysts.
BUSINESS: COMPUTERS & AUTOMATION: Computers Related

SIMPLYDV.CO.UK
1685619U78R-497

Formerly: SimplyDV.com
Editorial Address: 29 Florin Close, Pennyland, MILTON KEYNES, MK15 8AG **Tel:** 01908 673294
Email: editor@simplydv.co.uk
Web site: http://www.simplydv.co.uk
Publisher: Simply DV Ltd
Date Launched: 2002
Frequency of update: Daily
Website Access: Free
Traffic Figures: 9,000 Unique Users (per day Publisher's Statement)
Editor: Colin Barrett
Summary of Content: Internet guide to choosing and using digital video technology including digital camcorders, video editing, DVD authoring, web authoring and other associated consumer video technologies.
Readership/Target Audience: Aimed at users and would be users of consumer video technology.
CONSUMER: CONSUMER ELECTRONICS: Consumer Electronics Related

SIXTYPLUSURFERS
1641985U74N-166

Editorial Address: 241 Chase Side, Southgate, LONDON, N14 5LD **Tel:** 020 8440 3340 **Fax:** 020 8866 3686
Email: murrayhj@live.co.uk
Web site: http://www.sixtyplusurfers.co.uk
Publisher: Sixtyplusurfers
Date Launched: 2004
Frequency of update: Monthly. Updated on the 1st of each month
Website Access: Free
Traffic Figures: 44,000 Unique Users (per month Publisher's Statement)
Editor: Murray Jacobs
Summary of Content: Website covering lifestyle, fitness, health, healthy eating, retirement, finance, travel, fashion, beauty, gifts, homes, gardens, mobility and competitions.
Readership/Target Audience: Aimed at the mature population over the age of 60 who want to live a fit, active and interesting life.
Other Features: Recruitment.
CONSUMER: WOMEN'S INTEREST CONSUMER MAGAZINES: Retirement

SKIDDLE.COM
1834261U89C-1108

Editorial Address: The Benchmark, Ribbleton Street, PRESTON, PR1 5BA **Tel:** 0870 896 6896
Email: editorial@skiddle.com
Web site: http://www.skiddle.com
Publisher: Skiddle Ltd
Date Launched: 2001
Frequency of update: Daily
Website Access: Free
Traffic Figures: 600,000 Unique Users (per month Publisher's Statement)
Editor: Ben Sebborn
Summary of Content: What's on guide covering live music, clubs and events, entertainment, restaurants and hotels.
Readership/Target Audience: Aimed at men and women of all ages in the UK.
Other Features: Music release reviews, public message board and large mailing list
CONSUMER: HOLIDAYS & TRAVEL: Entertainment Guides

THE SKINNY
1895212U89C-1134

Editorial Address: The Drill Hall, 30-38 Dalmeny Street, EDINBURGH, EH6 8RG **Tel:** 0131 467 4630
Email: rupert@theskinny.co.uk
Web site: http://www.theskinny.co.uk
Publisher: Radge Media Limited
Frequency of update: Daily
Website Access: Free
Traffic Figures: 44,500 Unique Users (Publisher's Statement)
Editor: Rupert Thomson
Summary of Content: Website featuring interviews and articles on music, art, film, comedy and other aspects of Scottish culture.
Readership/Target Audience: Anybody with an interest in cultural events in Scotland.
CONSUMER: HOLIDAYS & TRAVEL: Entertainment Guides

SKY STYLE
1833506U74A-1049

Editorial Address: 5th Floor, Fergusson House, 124-128 City Road, LONDON, ECIV 2NJ **Tel:** 020 7553 3353
Email: helen.oram@bskyb.com
Web site: http://www.sky.com/style
Publisher: BSkyB
Date Launched: 2007
Frequency of update: Daily
Website Access: Free
Editor: Helen Oram
Summary of Content: Website covering fashion, beauty and health.
Readership/Target Audience: Aimed at women aged 25 to 35 years old.
CONSUMER: WOMEN'S INTEREST CONSUMER MAGAZINES: Women's Interest

SKYMOVIES.COM
765749U76A-171

Editorial Address: SKY Movies, Grant Way, ISLEWORTH, TW7 5QD **Tel:** 020 7941 5038 **Fax:** 020 7805 8296
Email: richard.phippen@bskyb.com
Web site: http://www.skymovies.com
Publisher: BSkyB
Date Launched: 2002
Frequency of update: Daily
Website Access: Free
Editor: Richard Phippen
Summary of Content: Website featuring movie news, reviews, gossip, trailers and picture galleries. Includes TV and cinema listings and competitions.
Readership/Target Audience: Aimed at movie enthusiasts and BSkyB subscribers.
CONSUMER: MUSIC & PERFORMING ARTS: Cinema

SLINK
626545U74F-617

Formerly: BBC Teens
Editorial Address: Grafton House, 379-381 Euston Road, LONDON, NW1 3AU **Tel:** 020 7765 0604
Email: slink@bbc.co.uk
Web site: http://www.bbc.co.uk/teens
Date Launched: 2000
Frequency of update: Daily
Website Access: Free
Editor: Trevor Klein
Summary of Content: Website including features on fashion, relationships, celebrities, music, film reviews, mobile phones, paranormal stories, games and news.
Readership/Target Audience: Aimed at teenager girls in the 12 to 16 age group.
Other Features: Features include competitions.
CONSUMER: WOMEN'S INTEREST CONSUMER MAGAZINES: Teenage

SMALL SHIPS AND WORKBOATS
1775303U45A-516

Formerly: Small Ships Europe
Editorial Address: Hesketh House, 3 School Road, SALE, M33 7XY **Tel:** 0161 374 5615 **Fax:** 0161 374 6436
Email: it.marketing@itmagazine.uk.com
Web site: http://www.smallshipsandworkboats.co.uk
Publisher: New Wave Publishing
Website Access: Free
Editor: George Bennett
Summary of Content: Website covering all aspects of the small working marine vessel industry including building, supply, commissioning, operation, legislation, safety and equipment.
Readership/Target Audience: Aimed at builders, owners, operators and designers of working marine vessels up to 120 metres in length.
BUSINESS: MARINE & SHIPPING

SMALLBUSINESS.CO.UK
1639896U14H-412

Editorial Address: Octavia House, 50 Banner Street, LONDON, EC1Y 8ST **Tel:** 020 7250 7010
Fax: 020 7250 7011
Email: marc.barber@vitessemedia.co.uk
Web site: http://www.smallbusiness.co.uk
Publisher: Vitesse Media plc
Date Launched: 2002
Frequency of update: Daily
Website Access: Free
Traffic Figures: 150,000 Unique Users (per month Publisher's Statement)
Editor: Marc Barber
Summary of Content: Website focusing on small businesses. Includes information on start-ups, finance, IT, legal, sales and marketing, people and franchising.
Readership/Target Audience: Aimed at small business owners.
BUSINESS: COMMERCE, INDUSTRY & MANAGEMENT: Small Business

SMART CARD NEWS
707497U1G-107

Editorial Address: Anchor Springs House, Duke Street, LITTLEHAMPTON, BN16 6BP **Tel:** 01903 734677
Fax: 01903 734318
Email: info@smartcard.co.uk
Web site: http://www.smartcard.co.uk
Date Launched: 1992
Frequency of update: Daily
Website Access: Paid
Traffic Figures: 2,000 Unique Users (Publisher's Statement)
Editor: Lesley Dann
Summary of Content: Website featuring the latest news headlines, a directory of companies, smartcard exchange and market intelligence.
Readership/Target Audience: Aimed at anybody within the smart card and biometrics industry.
BUSINESS: FINANCE & ECONOMICS: Credit Trading

SMARTDEVICESDIRECT
1692635U78R-501

Formerly: Smart Devices
Editorial Address: The Reeds, Frensham, FARNHAM, GU10 3BP **Tel:** 0870 027 2127
Web site: http://www.smartdevicesdirect.com
Publisher: Smart Devices Ltd
Frequency of update: Daily
Website Access: Free
Editor: Nick France
Summary of Content: Website covering consumer electronics including PDAs, handhelds, smart phones and accessories, MP3 players, portable peripherals, satellite navigation solutions, VoIP and Wireless LAN products.
Readership/Target Audience: Aimed at the general consumer, consumer electronics resellers, IT resellers, IT managers and purchasing managers.
CONSUMER: CONSUMER ELECTRONICS: Consumer Electronics Related

SMART-QUOTES
1644408U74M-402

Formerly: SMART Quotes
Editorial Address: 1 Liverpool Street, LONDON, EC2M 7QD **Tel:** 0870 803 3758
Email: jackie.falls@smart-quotes.com
Web site: http://www.smart-quotes.com
Publisher: Smart-Quotes Ltd
Date Launched: 2002
Frequency of update: Monthly
Website Access: Free
Traffic Figures: 300,000 Unique Users (per quarter Publisher's Statement)
Editor: Jackie Falls

Summary of Content: Website covering loans, credit cards, bank accounts and insurance information.
Readership/Target Audience: Aimed at retail finance customers.
CONSUMER: WOMEN'S INTEREST CONSUMER MAGAZINES: Personal Finance

SMASH HITS
46259U76E-330

Editorial Address: Mappin House, 4 Winsley Street, LONDON, W1W 8HF **Tel:** 020 7182 8000
Fax: 020 3761 1313
Email: victoria.grosvenor@bauermedia.co.uk
Web site: http://www.smashhits.net
Publisher: Box TV Ltd
Date Launched: 1978
Frequency of update: 104 times a year
Website Access: Free
Traffic Figures: 70,000 Unique Users (Publisher's Statement)
Editor: Victoria Grosvenor
Summary of Content: Website covering all aspects of pop music, containing interviews and articles on fashion and cinema.
Readership/Target Audience: Aimed at teenagers.
CONSUMER: MUSIC & PERFORMING ARTS: Pop Music

SME WEB
1821866U14H-438

Editorial Address: 40 Bowling Green Lane, LONDON, EC1R 0NE **Tel:** 020 7074 7768 **Fax:** 020 7837 6135
Email: gary@atalink.co.uk
Web site: http://www.smeweb.com
Publisher: Atalink Ltd
Date Launched: 2007
Frequency of update: Daily
Website Access: Free
Editor: Gary Howes
Summary of Content: Website providing information to small and medium size enterprises and freelance professionals featuring news, personnel, finance, economy, technology, fleet management, health and safety, sales and marketing, travel, energy and lifestyle.
Readership/Target Audience: Aimed at small and medium-size enterprise professionals, senior SME decision makers and freelance professionals.
Other Features: News feeds, newsletter, message board and video.
BUSINESS: COMMERCE, INDUSTRY & MANAGEMENT: Small Business

SNL FINANCIAL
1865485U1A-348

Editorial Address: 8th Floor, 7 Birchin Lane, LONDON, EC3V 9BW **Tel:** 020 7398 0870 **Fax:** 020 7398 0871
Email: bmeggeson@snl.com
Web site: http://www.snl.com
Publisher: SNL Financial
Frequency of update: Daily
Website Access: Free
Editor: Ben Meggeson
Summary of Content: Emailed newsletter featuring news stories, industry events and advice on investments, mortgages, banks and investors.
Readership/Target Audience: Aimed at financial investors.
BUSINESS: FINANCE & ECONOMICS

SO ONLINE
1656468U1E-363

Formerly: Sold Out
Editorial Address: Telfords Yard, 6-8 The Highway, LONDON, E1W 2BS **Tel:** 0845 539 0309
Email: kyle.gray@3cliffsmedia.co.uk
Web site: http://www.soldout-online.co.uk
Publisher: 3 Cliffs Media
Date Launched: 2004
Frequency of update: Daily
Website Access: Paid
(Publisher's Statement)
Editor: Kyle Gray
Summary of Content: Website covering property news, estate agency news, technology, expert opinions, car reviews and luxury property reviews.
Readership/Target Audience: Aimed at Estate Agents.
BUSINESS: FINANCE & ECONOMICS: Property

SO SWITCHED ON
1800323U86C-739

Editorial Address: Ground Floor, 211 Old Street, LONDON, EC1V 9NR **Tel:** 020 7608 6324
Email: adamo@trojanpublishing.net
Web site: http://www.switchedonmagazine.co.uk
Publisher: Trojan Publishing
Date Launched: 2007
Frequency of update: Daily

Website Access: Free
Traffic Figures: 30,000 Unique Users (per month Publisher's Statement)
Editor: Adam Osborne; **Web Editor:** Adam Osborne
Summary of Content: Web based magazine covering gadgets, sport, travel, entertainment reviews, men's fashion and celebrity.
Readership/Target Audience: Aimed at men aged 19 to 40 years old.
CONSUMER: ADULT & GAY MAGAZINES: Men's Lifestyle Magazines

SOCCER INVESTOR DAILY   1623350U32H-458

Editorial Address: 16 Butlers & Colonial Wharf, LONDON, SE1 2PX **Tel:** 020 7403 4110
Email: admin@soccerinvestor.com
Web site: http://www.soccerinvestor.com
Publisher: Soccer Investor Ltd
Date Launched: 1998
Frequency of update: Daily
Website Access: Paid
Editor: Brian Sturgess
Summary of Content: Electronically delivered newsletter covering the financial and commercial side of football, including share movements and player transfers.
Readership/Target Audience: Aimed at football agents, football clubs, investors, banks, lawyers, sponsors and broadcasters.
BUSINESS: LOCAL GOVERNMENT, LEISURE & RECREATION: Leisure, Recreation & Entertainment

SOCCERNET   45778U75B-233

Editorial Address: Mail Code 615, 3 Queen Caroline Street, LONDON, W6 9PE **Tel:** 020 8222 1000 **Fax:** 020 8222 2805
Email: john.brewin@disney.com
Web site: http://www.soccernet.com
Publisher: ESPN
Date Launched: 1995
Frequency of update: Daily
Website Access: Free
Traffic Figures: 4,500,000 Unique Users (Publisher's Statement)
Editor: John Brewin
Summary of Content: Website covering the English and Scottish teams, in Europe and globally. Includes tables, match reports and other football commentaries. Also features an England team page, with 24-hour news.
Readership/Target Audience: Aimed at football fans.
CONSUMER: SPORT: Football

SOCIAL VISION & SOCIETY TODAY
1606352U32G-162

Editorial Address: 71 Quickswood, LONDON, NW3 3RT
Tel: 020 7722 0992 **Fax:** 020 7586 4102
Email: ethnicsociety@gmail.com
Web site: http://www.ethnicsociety.com
Frequency of update: Monthly
Website Access: Free
Traffic Figures: 30,000 Unique Users (per month Publisher's Statement)
Editor: Gautam Barua
Summary of Content: Website covering news, views and articles on community, community developments, social welfare, re-generation, social policy and development, social intelligence and information, ethnic community, race relations, corporate social responsibility, social exclusion, law, gender, immigration and social integration and equality issues.
Readership/Target Audience: Aimed at CEOs, social planners, social and economic researchers, central and local government senior officials and MPs and NGOs.
Other Features: Archiving, recruitment and message board.
BUSINESS: LOCAL GOVERNMENT, LEISURE & RECREATION: Community Care & Social Services

SOCIETY GUARDIAN.CO.UK   634108U74Q-927_50

Editorial Address: 90 York Way, LONDON, N1 9GU
Tel: 020 3353 2000
Email: editor@societyguardian.co.uk
Web site: http://www.societyguardian.co.uk
Publisher: Guardian News and Media
Date Launched: 2000
Frequency of update: Daily
Website Access: Free
Editor: Clare Horton
Summary of Content: Website containing news and information on a wide range of social issues including health, local government and charities.
Readership/Target Audience: Read by public and voluntary sector staff and those with an interest in social issues.

Other Features: Features include recruitment, an e-mail newsletter and archiving.
CONSUMER: WOMEN'S INTEREST CONSUMER MAGAZINES: Lifestyle

SOCIOLOGICAL RESEARCH ONLINE
40110U55-169_80

Editorial Address: Department of Sociology, University of Surrey, GUILDFORD, GU2 7XH **Tel:** 01483 686989
Fax: 01483 259551
Email: socres@surrey.ac.uk
Web site: http://www.socresonline.org.uk/socresonline
Publisher: Sociological Research Online Consortium
Date Launched: 1996
Frequency of update: 6 times a year
Website Access: Paid
Editor: Meirion Hood
Summary of Content: Website publishing fully peer-reviewed sociology looking at current issues. A purely online journal, we make use of new media and reach a wide and international readership. Also publishing special collections and rapid response articles, which address key issues in the public arena.
Readership/Target Audience: Aimed at professional sociologists, social researchers and students throughout the world.
BUSINESS: APPLIED SCIENCE & LABORATORIES

SOFTWARE EDITORIAL   1827967U78R-522

Editorial Address: 10B Crown Place, Lady Betty Road, NORWICH, NR1 2QU **Tel:** 0845 257 4354
Email: chriswatts@softwareeditorial.com
Web site: http://www.softwareeditorial.com
Frequency of update: Daily
Website Access: Free
Traffic Figures: 160,000 Unique Users (per year Publisher's Statement)
Editor: Chris Watts
Summary of Content: Website covering software and hardware for both Microsoft Window and Apple Mac applications with reviews, articles and news relating to the computer industry.
Readership/Target Audience: Aimed at professionals, home users and enthusiasts.
CONSUMER: CONSUMER ELECTRONICS: Consumer Electronics Related

SOGLOS.COM - THE ONLINE MAGAZINE FOR GLOUCESTERSHIRE   1809520U80C-5425

Formerly: SoGlos.com
Editorial Address: PR by email only **Tel:** 01242 210330
Email: info@soglos.com
Web site: http://www.SoGlos.com
Date Launched: 2007
Frequency of update: Daily
Website Access: Free
Traffic Figures: 62,000 Unique Users (Publisher's Statement)
Editor: Michelle Byrne
Summary of Content: Online lifestyle and entertainment magazine covering Gloucestershire restaurants, bars and pubs, nightclubs, music, film, theatre and comedy, sport and outdoor, health and beauty, art and culture, books, children, accommodation and competitions.
Readership/Target Audience: Aimed at residents and visitors to Gloucestershire.
CONSUMER: RURAL & REGIONAL INTEREST: Regional Interest English Counties

SOMERSET MATTERS   1881673U72J-416

Email: comments@somerset-matters.co.uk
Web site: http://www.somerset-matters.co.uk
Frequency of update: Daily
Summary of Content: Website created to help people who care about local issues. Whether you need access to useful information, want to highlight a particular topic to other people, discuss ideas with like minded individuals or just show your support and keep up to date with current affairs in your area, Somerset Matters is the place for you.
Readership/Target Audience: Aimed at residents in the local area of Somerset.
LOCAL NEWSPAPERS: Community Newsletters

SOMETHING DIFFERENT FOR WEDDINGS   1696194U74L-242

Editorial Address: 55 Dores Road, Upper Stratton, SWINDON, SN2 7QU **Tel:** 01793 700566
Email: info@somethingdifferentweddings.co.uk
Web site: http://www.somethingdifferentweddings.co.uk
Publisher: Something Different Magazine

Frequency of update: 6 times a year
Website Access: Free
Editor: Sonia Pawley
Summary of Content: Website covering all aspects of weddings including, bridal wear, men's wear, accessories, cakes and catering, hen and stag nights, venues, travel, wedding stationery, flowers, gifts, photography and jewellery.
Readership/Target Audience: Aimed at brides, grooms and wedding guests who are looking for something different.
CONSUMER: WOMEN'S INTEREST CONSUMER MAGAZINES: Brides

SOMETHING JEWISH   1826690U87-2049

Editorial Address: PO Box 585, EDGWARE, HA8 4DU
Tel: 020 7993 0092
Email: editorial@somethingjewish.co.uk
Web site: http://www.somethingjewish.co.uk
Publisher: JMT Ventures Ltd
Frequency of update: Daily
Website Access: Free
Editor: Leslie Bunder
Summary of Content: Website covering news and information relevant to the Jewish community we well as lifestyle articles.
Readership/Target Audience: Aimed at the Jewish Community.
CONSUMER: RELIGIOUS

SOURCINGFOCUS.COM   1828544U14A-591

Editorial Address: 44 Wardour Street, LONDON, W1D 6QZ
Email: editor@sourcingfocus.com
Web site: http://www.sourcingfocus.com
Publisher: OUT Group
Date Launched: 2008
Frequency of update: Daily
Website Access: Free
Editor: Joanna Quayle
Summary of Content: Community portal featuring news, editorial comment and analysis, interviews with industry figures, blogs and forums.
Readership/Target Audience: Aimed at both suppliers and end users in the outsourcing industry.
BUSINESS: COMMERCE, INDUSTRY & MANAGEMENT

SOUTH LANARKSHIRE MATTERS
1881674U72J-417

Email: comments@southlanarkshire-matters.co.uk
Web site: http://www.southlanarkshire-matters.co.uk
Frequency of update: Daily
Summary of Content: Website created to help people who care about local issues. Whether you need access to useful information, want to highlight a particular topic to other people, discuss ideas with like minded individuals or just show your support and keep up to date with current affairs in your area, South Lanarkshire Matters is the place for you.
Readership/Target Audience: Aimed at residents in the local area of South Lanarkshire.
LOCAL NEWSPAPERS: Community Newsletters

SOUTH YORKSHIRE MATTERS
1881675U72J-418

Email: comments@southyorkshire-matters.co.uk
Web site: http://www.southyorkshire-matters.co.uk
Frequency of update: Daily
Summary of Content: Website created to help people who care about local issues. Whether you need access to useful information, want to highlight a particular topic to other people, discuss ideas with like minded individuals or just show your support and keep up to date with current affairs in your area, South Yorkshire Matters is the place for you.
Readership/Target Audience: Aimed at residents in the local area of South Yorkshire.
LOCAL NEWSPAPERS: Community Newsletters

SOUTHEAST.HOUSINGNEWS.CO.UK
1776300U4D-417

Editorial Address: For all contact details see main edition, housingnews.co.uk
Website Access: Free
BUSINESS: ARCHITECTURE & BUILDING: Planning & Housing

SOUTHERN EUROPE UNQUOTE
1750389U1F-623

Editorial Address: 4th Floor, Haymarket House, 28-29 Haymarket, LONDON, SW1Y 4RX **Tel:** 020 7484 9700
Fax: 020 7004 7548
Email: francinia.protti-alvarez@incisivemedia.com
Web site: http://www.unquotenews.com
Publisher: Incisive Media Investments
Date Launched: 1998
Frequency of update: 10 times a year
Website Access: Paid
Editor: Francinia Protti-Alvarez
Summary of Content: Newsletter covering private equity transactions in the region of Southern Europe.
Readership/Target Audience: Aimed at people in the private equity industry.
BUSINESS: FINANCE & ECONOMICS: Investment

SOUTHWEST.HOUSINGNEWS.CO.UK
1776301U4D-418

Editorial Address: For all contact details see main edition, housingnews.co.uk
Website Access: Free
BUSINESS: ARCHITECTURE & BUILDING: Planning & Housing

SPACEFLIGHT NOW
1850010U6C-202

Editorial Address: PO Box 175, TONBRIDGE, TN10 4ZY
Tel: 01732 367542 **Fax:** 01732 300148
Email: editorial2009@astronomynow.com
Web site: http://spaceflightnow.com
Publisher: Pole Star Publications
Frequency of update: Daily
Website Access: Free
Traffic Figures: 400,000 Unique Users (per month Publisher's Statement)
Editor: Steven Young
Summary of Content: Website featuring coverage of space mission launches and other events, news, features and reviews.
Readership/Target Audience: Aimed at anybody interested in space flight in addition to aerospace professionals.
BUSINESS: AVIATION & AERONAUTICS: Space Research

SPALDING TODAY
629846U80C-2250

Editorial Address: Priory House, The Crescent, SPALDING, PE11 1AB **Tel:** 01775 725021 **Fax:** 01775 714744
Email: nick.woodhead@jpress.co.uk
Web site: http://www.spaldingtoday.co.uk
Publisher: Johnston Press plc
Date Launched: 1999
Frequency of update: Daily
Website Access: Free
Traffic Figures: 16,731 Unique Users (Publisher's Statement)
Editor: Nick Woodhead
Summary of Content: Website containing news, sport, information and features about Spalding and surrounding villages.
Readership/Target Audience: Read by residents and visitors to the local area.
Other Features: Features include recruitment, motors, property, reader holidays, business directory, seasonal features and archiving.
CONSUMER: RURAL & REGIONAL INTEREST: Regional Interest English Counties

SPIKED
712466U2A-170

Editorial Address: Signet House, 49-51 Farringdon Road, LONDON, EC1M 3JP **Tel:** 020 7404 0470
Email: general-enquiries@spiked-online.com
Web site: http://www.spiked-online.com
Date Launched: 2001
Frequency of update: Daily
Website Access: Free
Editor: Nathalie Rothschild
Summary of Content: Website providing a combination of comment, news and in-depth documentary on a range of topics. Subjects include Politics, IT, science, liberties and culture.
Readership/Target Audience: Aimed at those not satisfied by the mainstream press and those who enjoy enlightened thinking and freedom of expression in journalism.
BUSINESS: COMMUNICATIONS, ADVERTISING & MARKETING

SPINDRIFT
1693224U41A-331

Editorial Address: The Clock Tower, Southover, Spring Lane, Burwash, ETCHINGHAM, TN19 7JB
Tel: 01539 435012
Email: lb@digitaldots.org
Web site: http://www.digitaldots.org
Publisher: Digital Dots Ltd
Date Launched: 2003
Frequency of update: 10 times a year
Website Access: Paid
Traffic Figures: 3,000 Unique Users (Publisher's Statement)
Editor: Laurel Brunner
Summary of Content: Electronically delivered publication covering all aspects of print and publishing technologies.
Readership/Target Audience: Aimed at professionals in the graphic arts industry.
BUSINESS: PRINTING & STATIONERY: Printing

SPORT4MEDIA.COM
1828546U32H-476

Editorial Address: The Chandlery, 50 Westminster Bridge Road, LONDON, SE1 7QY **Tel:** 020 7953 7434
Fax: 020 7953 8773
Email: news.desk@sport4media.com
Web site: http://www.sport4media.com
Publisher: News4Media Ltd
Date Launched: 2007
Frequency of update: Daily
Website Access: Free
Traffic Figures: 5,000 Unique Users (Publisher's Statement)
Editor: Howard Salinger
Summary of Content: Online publication featuring sport, football, rugby, cricket, golf, tennis, athletics, Olympic sports, winter sports, water sports, motor racing, horse racing, sports personalities and sports products.
Readership/Target Audience: Aimed at sport brands, companies, clubs and organisations.
BUSINESS: LOCAL GOVERNMENT, LEISURE & RECREATION: Leisure, Recreation & Entertainment

SPORTBUSINESS.COM
628979U32H-270

Editorial Address: 33-41 Dallington Street, LONDON, EC1V 0BB **Tel:** 020 7954 3515
Email: newsdesk@sportbusiness.com
Web site: http://www.sportbusiness.com
Publisher: SPG Companys Ltd
Date Launched: 1996
Frequency of update: Daily
Website Access: Paid
Traffic Figures: 26,000 Unique Users (per day Publisher's Statement)
Editor: Miriam Sherlock
Summary of Content: Website focusing on the world of sport. Covers news, careers, broadcast, new media, finance, federations, brands, sponsorship and commercial opportunities within the sport industry.
Readership/Target Audience: Aimed at those involved within the sports industry.
BUSINESS: LOCAL GOVERNMENT, LEISURE & RECREATION: Leisure, Recreation & Entertainment

SPORT.CO.UK
1841982U75A-1034

Editorial Address: 77 Queen Victoria Street, LONDON, EC4V 4AY **Tel:** 020 7618 9000 **Fax:** 020 7618 9001
Email: feedback@sport.co.uk
Web site: http://www.sport.co.uk
Publisher: Media Corporation plc
Date Launched: 2008
Frequency of update: Daily
Website Access: Free
Editor: Nigel Brown
Summary of Content: Website covering all sports from football to ice-hockey with up to the minute news, daily blogs, features, punditry and opinion.
Readership/Target Audience: Aimed at sporting enthusiasts.
CONSUMER: SPORT

SPORTHULL.CO.UK
1813679U75A-1031

Editorial Address: Blundell's Corner, Beverley Road, HULL, HU3 1XS **Tel:** 01482 327111
Email: sport@mailnewsmedia.co.uk
Web site: http://www.sporthull.co.uk
Publisher: Mail News & Media Ltd
Date Launched: 2007
Frequency of update: Daily
Website Access: Free
Traffic Figures: 15,000 Unique Users (per month Publisher's Statement)
Editor: Paul Baxter
Summary of Content: Website covering East Yorkshire sport including the rugby league clubs Hull FC and Hull

Kingston Rovers, Hull City Football Club and the ice hockey team Hull Stingrays as well as other local sports.
Readership/Target Audience: Aimed at sports fans in Hull.
CONSUMER: SPORT

SPORTINDUSTRY.BIZ
1791913U32H-470

Editorial Address: 23-24 Henrietta Street, LONDON, WC2E 8ND **Tel:** 020 7240 7702 **Fax:** 020 7240 7703
Email: drew@sportindustry.biz
Web site: http://www.sportindustry.biz
Publisher: The Sport Industry Group
Frequency of update: Daily
Website Access: Free
Editor: Drew Barrand
Summary of Content: Website covering business issues within sport including sponsorship, TV rights, governance and commerce.
Readership/Target Audience: Aimed at the business community.
BUSINESS: LOCAL GOVERNMENT, LEISURE & RECREATION: Leisure, Recreation & Entertainment

SPORTINGLIFE
629002U75A-755

Editorial Address: Apsley House, 78 Wellington Street, LEEDS, LS1 2EQ **Tel:** 0113 399 2143 **Fax:** 0870 128 8333
Email: editorial@sportinglife.com
Web site: http://www.sportinglife.com
Date Launched: 1996
Frequency of update: Daily
Website Access: Free
Traffic Figures: 663,265 Unique Users (per month ABC/ Electronic)
Editor: Graham Shaw; **Web Editor:** Graham Shaw
Summary of Content: Website providing live worldwide sports news, results and betting information.
Readership/Target Audience: Aimed at sports and betting enthusiasts.
CONSUMER: SPORT

SPORT.SCOTSMAN.COM
1872674U75A-1035

Editorial Address: 108 Holyrood Road, EDINBURGH, EH8 8AS **Tel:** 0131 620 8620
Email: sport_ts@scotsman.com
Web site: http://sport.scotsman.com
Publisher: The Scotsman Publications Ltd
Frequency of update: Daily
Website Access: Free
Editor: Alan Greenwood; **Web Editor:** Alan Greenwood
Summary of Content: Website featuring national and international sporting news and stories with a focus on Scotland.
Readership/Target Audience: Aimed at sports enthusiasts..
CONSUMER: SPORT

SPORTSECHO.CO.UK
1813131U75A-1030

Editorial Address: Brayford Wharf East, LINCOLN, LN5 7AT
Tel: 01522 804390 **Fax:** 01522 804493
Email: sports@lincolnshireecho.co.uk
Web site: http://www.sportsecho.co.uk
Publisher: Lincolnshire Media Ltd
Date Launched: 2007
Frequency of update: Daily
Website Access: Free
Editor: John Pakey
Summary of Content: Website covering sport in Lincoln and surrounding areas including football, rugby union and rugby league, angling and cricket.
Readership/Target Audience: Aimed at sports fans of all ages.
CONSUMER: SPORT

SPORTSMEDIA.CO.UK
634715U75A-806

Formerly: sportonair.com
Editorial Address: Broadcast Centre, Suite 16, The Linen House, 253 Kilburn Lane, LONDON, W10 4BQ
Tel: 020 8964 5522 **Fax:** 020 8964 6565
Email: jonny.gould@sportsmedia.co.uk
Web site: http://sportsmedia.co.uk
Publisher: Sports Media Broadcasting
Date Launched: 1999
Frequency of update: Daily
Website Access: Free
Traffic Figures: 350,000 Unique Users (per month Publisher's Statement)
Editor: Jonny Gould
Summary of Content: Website containing the latest sporting news including features and interviews, mainly in the audio format. Also includes an online betting section.

Readership/Target Audience: Read by sports enthusiasts of all ages.
Other Features: Features include a message board and archiving.
CONSUMER: SPORT

SPORTSTELEGRAPH.CO.UK   45722U75A-850

Formerly: Sports Telegraph (Grimsby)
Editorial Address: 80 Cleethorpe Road, GRIMSBY, DN31 3EH **Tel:** 01472 360360 **Fax:** 01472 372257*
Email: sport@grimsbytelegraph.co.uk
Web site: http://www.sportstelegraph.co.uk
Publisher: Grimsby & Scunthorpe Media Group
Date Launched: 1890
Frequency of update: Daily
Website Access: Free
Traffic Figures: 16,619 Unique Users (01/01/2008 To 31/01/2008 visitors per month)
Editor: Simon Blow
Summary of Content: Website with daily coverage of sport in North East Lincolnshire.
Readership/Target Audience: Read by sports enthusiasts in the Grimsby and North Lincolnshire area.
Other Features: Message boards, petitions, slideshows, videos
CONSUMER: SPORT

SPORT.TELEGRAPH.CO.UK   633799U75A-851

Editorial Address: 111 Buckingham Palace Road, LONDON, SW1W 0DT **Tel:** 020 7931 2000
Email: chei.amlani@telegraph.co.uk
Web site: http://www.sport.telegraph.co.uk
Publisher: Telegraph Media Group Ltd
Date Launched: 1994
Frequency of update: Daily
Website Access: Free
Editor: Chei Amlani
Summary of Content: Website containing news and information on football, rugby, cricket, motor racing, golf, tennis, horse racing and other sports. Also includes fantasy football, cricket, rugby, tennis and golf games.
Readership/Target Audience: Aimed at sports enthusiasts.
Other Features: Features include an events calendar and archiving.
CONSUMER: SPORT

SQ FT PROPERTY INVESTOR MAGAZINE
1639839U74K-673

Formerly: Square Foot Magazine
Editorial Address: 3rd Floor, Castleton Mill, Armley Road, LEEDS, LS12 2DS **Tel:** 0113 227 0825
Email: michele@sqftmag.com
Web site: http://www.sqftmag.com
Publisher: Sq Ft Ltd
Date Launched: 2004
Frequency of update: Daily
Traffic Figures: 10,000 Unique Users (Publisher's Statement)
Editor: Michele Andrew
Summary of Content: On-line magazine with property reviews, investment news, design and architecture, hotels, economic profiles of cities, restaurants, contemporary furniture and commercial property news.
Readership/Target Audience: Aimed at property investors and home buyers across the UK.
CONSUMER: WOMEN'S INTEREST CONSUMER MAGAZINES: Home Purchase

SQM ONLINE   1775091U1E-394

Formerly: Sqm Magazine
Editorial Address: Unit 6, 5 Durham Yard, Teesdale Street, LONDON, E2 6QF **Tel:** 0870 850 3586 **Fax:** 020 7749 1280
Email: editorial@ddgm.co.uk
Web site: http://www.sqmonline.co.uk
Publisher: DDGM
Date Launched: 2005
Frequency of update: Daily
Website Access: Paid
(Publisher's Statement)
Editor: Mark Burgess
Summary of Content: Business and lifestyle website covering all aspects of estate agency work including sales and lettings.
Readership/Target Audience: Aimed at estate agents.
BUSINESS: FINANCE & ECONOMICS: Property

SQUASH NOW!   1664182U75H-913

Editorial Address: 56 Buckingham Avenue, LONDON, N20 9DE **Tel:** 020 8445 1497 **Fax:** 020 8343 9135

Email: colin@squashnow.com
Web site: http://www.squashnow.com
Frequency of update: Daily
Website Access: Free
Editor: Colin McQuillan
Summary of Content: Website covering squash worldwide with world news, action reports and reports on major tournaments.
Readership/Target Audience: Aimed at squash enthusiasts.
CONSUMER: SPORT: Racquet Sports

STAFFORD DISTRICT VOLUNTARY SERVICES HEADLINES   1847239U1P-287

Editorial Address: 131-141 North Walls, STAFFORD, ST16 3AD **Tel:** 01785 606670 **Fax:** 01785 606669
Email: ray@sdvs.org.uk
Web site: http://www.sdvs.org.uk/headlines
Frequency of update: Weekly
Website Access: Paid
Traffic Figures: 250 Unique Users (per week Publisher's Statement)
Editor: Ray Morris
Summary of Content: Website promoting any charitable activity for the benefit of the community in Staffordshire and the West Midlands with particular reference to the borough of Stafford. Including weekly headlines about social care, public safety, health and volunteering.
Readership/Target Audience: Aimed at third sector (voluntary, community, faith and social enterprise groups) in the Staffordshire District.
BUSINESS: FINANCE & ECONOMICS: Fundraising

STAFFORDSHIRE MATTERS   1881677U72J-420

Email: comments@staffordshire-matters.co.uk
Web site: http://www.staffordshire-matters.co.uk
Frequency of update: Daily
Summary of Content: Website created to help people who care about local issues. Whether you need access to useful information, want to highlight a particular topic to other people, discuss ideas with like minded individuals or just show your support and keep up to date with current affairs in your area, Staffordshire Matters is the place for you.
Readership/Target Audience: Aimed at residents in the local area of Staffordshire.
LOCAL NEWSPAPERS: Community Newsletters

THE STAGE   629074U64K-610

Editorial Address: 47 Bermondsey Street, LONDON, SE1 3XT **Tel:** 020 7403 1818 **Fax:** 020 7939 8478
Email: newsdesk@thestage.co.uk
Web site: http://www.thestage.co.uk
Date Launched: 1998
Frequency of update: 260 times a year
Website Access: Free
Traffic Figures: 424,511 Unique Users (01/03/2009 To 31/03/2009 ABC/Electronic)
Editor: Newsdesk
Summary of Content: Website focusing on theatre, dance, opera, light entertainment and their technical aspects. Contains news, reviews and feature articles.
Readership/Target Audience: Aimed at those who read the newspaper and actors, dancers, singers, comedians, speciality acts, musicians, playwrights, technicians, lighting designers, stage managers, agents, managers, municipal entertainment officers, drama students and teachers.
BUSINESS: OTHER CLASSIFICATIONS: Cinema Entertainment

STARTUPS.CO.UK   601198U14A-595

Editorial Address: Westminster House, Kew Road, RICHMOND, TW9 2ND **Tel:** 020 8334 1600
Fax: 020 8334 1601
Email: sarar@crimsonbusiness.com
Web site: http://www.startups.co.uk
Publisher: Crimson Business Ltd
Date Launched: 1999
Frequency of update: 730 times a year
Website Access: Free
Traffic Figures: 150,000 Unique Users (per month Publisher's Statement)
Editor: Sara Rizk
Summary of Content: Website providing information, advice, news, reviews and case studies on starting up in business. Features articles on finance, franchising, technology and office equipment.
Readership/Target Audience: Aimed at small business owners and entrepreneurs.
BUSINESS: COMMERCE, INDUSTRY & MANAGEMENT

STEEL BUSINESS BRIEFING   764937U27-201

Editorial Address: 2nd Floor, Peek House, 20 Eastcheap, LONDON, EC3M 1EB **Tel:** 020 7626 0600
Fax: 020 7929 4666
Email: info@steelbb.com
Web site: http://www.steelbb.com
Publisher: Steel Business Briefing
Date Launched: 2001
Frequency of update: 260 times a year
Website Access: Paid
Traffic Figures: 32,000 Unique Users (per day Publisher's Statement)
Editor: Paul Millbank
Summary of Content: Electronic newsletter containing up to date steel market, prices and company information.
Readership/Target Audience: Aimed at steel industry professionals, end users, and those serving the industry including analysts, lawyers, associations and government bodies, software companies, transportation companies and academics.
BUSINESS: METAL, IRON & STEEL

STORAGE.BIZ-NEWS.COM   1864880U5B-9023

Editorial Address: PR by email only **Tel:** 020 3051 4108
Email: dave@biz-news.com
Web site: http://storage.biz-news.com
Publisher: Biz-news.com
Frequency of update: Daily
Website Access: Free
Editor: David Montgomery
Summary of Content: Business to business website covering IT storage.
Readership/Target Audience: Aimed at professionals in the IT storage industry.
BUSINESS: COMPUTERS & AUTOMATION: Data Processing

STORM   1852993U1D-429

Editorial Address: 507 Clarkenwell Workshops, 27-31 Clarkenwell Close, LONDON, EC1R 0AT **Tel:** 020 7061 6332
Email: mp@storminvestor.com
Web site: http://www.storminvestor.com
Publisher: Cold Fountains Media
Date Launched: 2007
Frequency of update: Weekly
Website Access: Paid
Editor: Mark Pelham
Summary of Content: Publication covering all aspects of the alternative risk transfer markets from weather and insurance derivatives, catastrophe bonds and insurance linked securities to carbon and emissions trading.
Readership/Target Audience: Aimed at banks and brokers, insurance and reinsurance companies, senior executive officers at corporates and all potential product investors such as pension funds, hedge funds and asset managers.
BUSINESS: FINANCE & ECONOMICS: Insurance

STREETBRAND   1813663U87-2047

Editorial Address: Ground Floor GBN, BMS House, Oxlow Lane, DAGENHAM, RM10 8PS
Email: editor@streetbrand.com
Web site: http://www.streetbrand.com
Date Launched: 2004
Frequency of update: 5 times a year
Website Access: Free
Editor: Kofo Baptist
Summary of Content: Online Christian based, youth culture magazine covering music, films, books, celebrity interviews, fashion, style, relationships, health, fitness, money, careers and in your face columns.
Readership/Target Audience: Aimed at men and women aged 16 to 25 years old.
CONSUMER: RELIGIOUS

STRUCTURED RETAIL PRODUCTS
1844561U1F-651

Editorial Address: 12 Broadbent Close, 20-22 Highgate High Street, LONDON, N6 5JW **Tel:** 020 8347 3622
Fax: 020 8347 7872
Email: info@structuredretailproducts.com
Web site: http://www.srpmagazine.com
Publisher: Arete Consulting Ltd
Frequency of update: Monthly
Website Access: Paid
Editor: Kim Hunter
Summary of Content: Electronic magazine covering structured retail investment products. Features include a news service, analysis and research reports, portfolio and product scoring tools.

Internet Media

Readership/Target Audience: Aimed at structured products professionals and financial services companies.
BUSINESS: FINANCE & ECONOMICS: Investment

STUDENT 123.COM
1739970U83-295

Editorial Address: Unit 2.4, Paintworks, Bath Road, BRISTOL, BS4 3EH **Tel:** 0117 902 9977 **Fax:** 0117 902 9978
Email: lucy.reeves@wildfirecomms.co.uk
Web site: http://www.student123.com
Publisher: Wildfire Communications
Frequency of update: Daily
Website Access: Free
Traffic Figures: 30,000 Unique Users (per month Publisher's Statement)
Editor: Lucy Reeves
Summary of Content: Website covering all aspects of student life including reviews, entertainment, bands, student TV, live videos and competitions as well as a social networking site.
Readership/Target Audience: Aimed at students aged 16 to 25 years old.
Other Features: Newsletter and recruitment
CONSUMER: STUDENT PUBLICATIONS

STUDENT EXPRESS
629078U83-79_50

Editorial Address: 7 Bourne Road, BROMLEY, BR2 9PB
Tel: 020 8295 7000 **Fax:** 020 8295 7099
Email: editor@student-express.co.uk
Web site: http://www.student-express.co.uk
Publisher: Student Express Media
Date Launched: 1999
Frequency of update: Monthly
Website Access: Free
Traffic Figures: 4,000 Unique Users (Publisher's Statement)
Editor: Nigel Cribbs
Summary of Content: Magazine covering music, fashion and news.
Readership/Target Audience: Aimed at UK students and youth market.
CONSUMER: STUDENT PUBLICATIONS

STUDENTBONKERS.COM
1745414U83-275

Formerly: Student Bonkers
Editorial Address: Garden Flat, 45 Clifton Hill, LONDON, NW8 0QE **Tel:** 020 7328 3443
Email: info@studentbonkers.com
Web site: http://www.studentbonkers.com
Date Launched: 2006
Frequency of update: Weekly
Website Access: Paid
Editor: Jo Lynn
Summary of Content: Website with news on events, food, clothing, beauty, music and politics as well as other issues that impact on students including transport, finance, jobs, sexual health and student finances.
Readership/Target Audience: Aimed at students aged 18 to 25 years old.
CONSUMER: STUDENT PUBLICATIONS

STUDYZONE
47873U88A-74_50

Formerly: Studyzone Magazine
Editorial Address: 11-15 Emerald Street, LONDON, WC1N 3QL **Tel:** 020 7440 4025 **Fax:** 020 7440 4033
Email: bethan@hothousemedia.com
Web site: http://www.hothousemedia.com
Publisher: Hothouse Media
Date Launched: 1998
Frequency of update: Annual
Website Access: Free
Editor: Bethan Norris
Summary of Content: Website containing information and articles about studying overseas.
Readership/Target Audience: Aimed at students.
CONSUMER: EDUCATION

STUFF.TV
1808776U86C-738

Editorial Address: Teddington Studios, Broom Road, TEDDINGTON, TW11 9BE **Tel:** 020 8267 5885
Email: news@stuff.tv
Web site: http://www.stuff.tv
Publisher: Haymarket Network
Frequency of update: Daily
Website Access: Free
Traffic Figures: 320,000 Unique Users (per month Publisher's Statement)
Editor: Linsey Fryatt
Summary of Content: Men's lifestyle website with a focus on gadgets and innovation as well as multi-media content including videocasts and podcasts.

Readership/Target Audience: Aimed at men aged between 25 and 35 years old.
CONSUMER: ADULT & GAY MAGAZINES: Men's Lifestyle Magazines

STYLEFINDER.COM
1794218U74B-727

Editorial Address: 25 Maddox Street, LONDON, W1S 2QN
Tel: 020 7499 9080
Email: clare.alstin@condenast.co.uk
Web site: http://www.stylefinder.com
Publisher: Conde Nast Publications Ltd
Date Launched: 2007
Frequency of update: Daily
Website Access: Free
Traffic Figures: 200,000 Unique Users (Publisher's Statement)
Editor: Clare Alstin
Summary of Content: Online style and shopping guide covering designer and high street womenswear and accessories with a focus on who is wearing what on the street, what the celebrities are wearing and where to get it.
Readership/Target Audience: Aimed at women aged 15 to 45 years old.
CONSUMER: WOMEN'S INTEREST CONSUMER MAGAZINES: Women's Interest - Fashion

SUFFOLK MATTERS
1881678U72J-421

Email: comments@suffolk-matters.co.uk
Web site: http://www.suffolk-matters.co.uk
Frequency of update: Daily
Summary of Content: Website created to help people who care about local issues. Whether you need access to useful information, want to highlight a particular topic to other people, discuss ideas with like minded individuals or just show your support and keep up to date with current affairs in your area, Suffolk Matters is the place for you.
Readership/Target Audience: Aimed at residents in the local area of Suffolk.
LOCAL NEWSPAPERS: Community Newsletters

SUGARSCAPE.COM
1835392U74F-774

Editorial Address: 64 North Row, LONDON, W1K 7LL
Tel: 020 7150 7000
Email: mango@sugarscape.com
Web site: http://www.sugarscape.com
Publisher: Hachette Filipacchi (UK) Ltd
Date Launched: 2008
Frequency of update: Daily
Website Access: Free
Traffic Figures: 10,000 Unique Users (per month Publisher's Statement)
Editor: Mango Saul
Summary of Content: Social networking website that enables users to share their favourite sites with other users.
Readership/Target Audience: Aimed at 14 to 17 year4 olds.
CONSUMER: WOMEN'S INTEREST CONSUMER MAGAZINES: Teenage

THE SUN ONLINE
623632U65A-121

Editorial Address: 1 Virginia Street, LONDON, E98 1SN
Tel: 020 7782 4000 **Fax:** 020 7782 4597
Email: talkback@the-sun.co.uk
Web site: http://www.thesun.co.uk
Publisher: News Group Newspapers Ltd
Date Launched: 1998
Frequency of update: Daily. News updated continuously
Website Access: Paid
Traffic Figures: 25,094,107 Unique Users (01/07/2009 To 31/07/2009 ABC/Electronic)
Editor: Danny Rogers
Summary of Content: Website version of The Sun. Includes news, sport, show-biz news, film, music, trailers, lifestyle features, motoring, technology, gadgets and travel.
Twitter: http://twitter.com/thesun_news.
NATIONAL DAILY & SUNDAY NEWSPAPERS: National Daily Newspapers

SUNDERLAND MATTERS
1881679U72J-422

Email: comments@sunderland-matters.co.uk
Web site: http://www.sunderland-matters.co.uk
Frequency of update: Daily
Summary of Content: Website created to help people who care about local issues. Whether you need access to useful information, want to highlight a particular topic to other people, discuss ideas with like minded individuals or just show your support and keep up to date with current affairs in your area, Sunderland Matters is the place for you.

Readership/Target Audience: Aimed at residents in the local area of Sunderland.
LOCAL NEWSPAPERS: Community Newsletters

SUNDERLAND TODAY
629780U67B-1071

Editorial Address: Echo House, Pennywell, SUNDERLAND, SR4 9ER **Tel:** 0191 501 5800 **Fax:** 0191 534 5975
Email: echo.news@northeast-press.co.uk
Web site: http://www.sunderlandecho.com
Publisher: Northeast Press Ltd
Date Launched: 1998
Frequency of update: Daily
Website Access: Free
Traffic Figures: 137,760 Unique Users (per month Publisher's Statement)
Editor: Rob Lawson; **Web Editor:** Lee Hall
Summary of Content: Website containing news, sport, information and features about Sunderland.
Readership/Target Audience: Read by residents and visitors to the local area, expatriates in the US and other English-speaking countries.
Other Features: Features include recruitment and archiving.
REGIONAL DAILY & SUNDAY NEWSPAPERS: Regional Daily Newspapers

SUNSHINE.CO.UK
1864967U89E-260

Editorial Address: Centaur House, Ancells Business Park, Ancells Road, FLEET, GU51 2UJ **Tel:** 01252 762267
Fax: 01252 761105
Email: contact@sunshine.co.uk
Web site: http://www.sunshine.co.uk
Frequency of update: Daily
Website Access: Free
Traffic Figures: 2,700,000 Unique Users (2008 Publisher's Statement)
Editor: Chris Brown
Summary of Content: Website covering travel, holidays, reviews and news.
Readership/Target Audience: Aimed at people with an interest in cheap holidays.
CONSUMER: HOLIDAYS & TRAVEL: Holidays

SUPANET
629809U74Q-935_50

Editorial Address: Indigo House, Time Technology Park, Blackburn Road, Simonstone, BURNLEY, BB12 7NQ
Tel: 01282 681000 **Fax:** 01282 681001
Email: theeditor@supanet.net.uk
Web site: http://www.supanet.com
Publisher: Supanet Ltd
Date Launched: 1999
Frequency of update: Daily
Website Access: Free
Traffic Figures: 1,250,000 Unique Users (per month Publisher's Statement)
Editor: Dave Lancaster
Summary of Content: Website focusing on lifestyle issues including news, sport, entertainment, business, computing, health, motoring, travel, women's and men's websites, games and viral content.
Readership/Target Audience: Aimed at individuals looking for news and information on lifestyle issues.
Other Features: Features include an e-mail newsletter, exclusive competitions and archive facility. Accessible version of site also available.
CONSUMER: WOMEN'S INTEREST CONSUMER MAGAZINES: Lifestyle

SUPERYACHTSONLINE.COM
1776236U91A-292

Editorial Address: Bucklands, Loxwood Road, Rudgwick, HORSHAM, RH12 3DW **Tel:** 01403 823640
Fax: 01403 433332
Web site: http://www.superyachtsonline.com
Publisher: Big Blue Publishing Company Ltd
Date Launched: 2007
Frequency of update: Weekly
Website Access: Free
Editor: Giles Morgan; **Editor-in-Chief:** Giles Morgan
Summary of Content: Website covering everything regarding owning and upkeep of super-yachts, featuring craft no smaller than 20 metres as well as in-depth coverage of selected owners and their passions.
Readership/Target Audience: Aimed at billionaire and multi-millionaire owners of super-yachts worldwide.
Other Features: Search engines Superyachts for Sale and Superyachts for Charter
CONSUMER: RECREATION & LEISURE: Boating & Yachting

SUPPLIERBUSINESS.COM
1655075U31R-58

Editorial Address: 2 St. Pauls Street, STAMFORD, PE9 2BE
Tel: 01780 481712 **Fax:** 01780 482383

Email: edmund.chew@supplierbusiness.com
Web site: http://www.supplierbusiness.com
Publisher: SupplierBusiness.com
Date Launched: 2003
Frequency of update: Weekly
Website Access: Paid
Editor: Edmund Chew
Summary of Content: Electronically delivered newsletter focusing on analysis and research on the automotive supplier sector.
Readership/Target Audience: Aimed at senior executives.
BUSINESS: MOTOR TRADE: Motor Trade Related

SUPPLY CHAIN STANDARD   36537U10-77_50

Formerly: Logistics Europe
Editorial Address: St. Giles House, 50 Poland Street, LONDON, W1F 7AX **Tel:** 020 7970 4000 **Fax:** 020 7970 4493
Email: malory.davies@centaur.co.uk
Web site: http://www.supplychainstandard.com
Publisher: Centaur Communications Ltd
Frequency of update: 11 times a year. Published in the 1st week of the cover month
Website Access: Free
Traffic Figures: 13,988 Unique Users (Publisher's Statement)
Editor: Malory Davies
Summary of Content: Electronic magazine covering all aspects of logistics and supply chain management.
Readership/Target Audience: Read by logistics and supply chain professionals across Europe.
BUSINESS: MATERIALS HANDLING

SUPPORT INSIGHT   755512U14F-75_30

Editorial Address: 37 Evelyn Road, DUNSTABLE, LU5 4NG
Tel: 01582 696911 **Fax:** 01582 696913
Email: peter@comgen.co.uk
Web site: http://www.supportinsight.com
Date Launched: 2002
Frequency of update: Daily
Website Access: Free
Editor: Peter Friedman; **Web Editor:** Karen Appleby; **Online Journalist:** Karen Appleby
Summary of Content: Website featuring news stories and articles on critical and newly emerging issues and trends in the world of IT support, training, CRM, e-learning and call centres.
Readership/Target Audience: Aimed at executives and operatives involved in providing training, user support and call centres.
BUSINESS: COMMERCE, INDUSTRY & MANAGEMENT: Training & Recruitment

---

SURFCORE.CO.UK   1849712U75M-1004

Editorial Address: 1 West Smithfield, LONDON, EC1A 9JU
Tel: 020 7332 9700 **Fax:** 020 7332 9799
Email: paul.moore@factorymedia.com
Web site: http://www.surfcore.co.uk
Publisher: Factory Media
Frequency of update: Daily
Website Access: Free
Traffic Figures: 15,000 Unique Users (per month Publisher's Statement)
Editor: Paul Moore
Summary of Content: Website covering surf weather forecasting.
Readership/Target Audience: Aimed at surfers worldwide.
CONSUMER: SPORT: Water Sports

SURREY MATTERS   1881680U72J-423

Email: comments@surrey-matters.co.uk
Web site: http://www.surrey-matters.co.uk
Frequency of update: Daily
Summary of Content: Website created to help people who care about local issues. Whether you need access to useful information, want to highlight a particular topic to other people, discuss ideas with like minded individuals or just show your support and keep up to date with current affairs in your area, Surrey Matters is the place for you.
Readership/Target Audience: Aimed at residents in the local area of Surrey.
LOCAL NEWSPAPERS: Community Newsletters

SUSSEX MATTERS   1881681U72J-424

Email: comments@sussex-matters.co.uk
Web site: http://www.sussex-matters.co.uk
Frequency of update: Daily
Summary of Content: Website created to help people who care about local issues. Whether you need access to useful information, want to highlight a particular topic to other people, discuss ideas with like minded individuals or just

---

show your support and keep up to date with current affairs in your area, Sussex Matters is the place for you.
Readership/Target Audience: Aimed at residents in the local area of Sussex.
LOCAL NEWSPAPERS: Community Newsletters

SUSSEXFILM.CO.UK   1774819U76A-200

Editorial Address: 23 Meyrick Drive, Wash Common, NEWBURY, RG14 6SY **Tel:** 01635 600377
Email: info@sussexfilm.co.uk
Web site: http://www.sussexfilm.co.uk
Date Launched: 2001
Frequency of update: Daily
Website Access: Free
Traffic Figures: 950,000 Unique Users (per month Publisher's Statement)
Editor: Kirsty McKenzie; **Webmaster:** Kirsty McKenzie
Summary of Content: Website containing a complete guide to films and film making including technology reviews, films, history and guidance on how to make films and a preview into film-makers guidance to new technology.
Readership/Target Audience: Aimed at 18 to 70 year old men and women interested in films, film making, new releases, trialing new technology, digital camcorders, mobile devices, home entertainment equipment, protection and sound systems and comparing software and hardware from leading market providers.
Other Features: Site features include message boards and newsletter.
CONSUMER: MUSIC & PERFORMING ARTS: Cinema

SUSTAINABLE DEVELOPMENT INTERNATIONAL   766443U57-123

Editorial Address: Trans-World House, 100 City Road, LONDON, EC1Y 2BP **Tel:** 020 7871 0123
Fax: 020 7871 0101
Email: info@sustdev.org
Web site: http://www.sustdev.org
Publisher: Henley Media Group Ltd.
Frequency of update: Daily
Website Access: Paid
Traffic Figures: 30,000 Unique Users (Publisher's Statement)
Editor: Diva Rodriguez
Summary of Content: Electronic publication containing case studies and discussion on areas of renewable energy, agriculture and food security, reduction of poverty, clean water and sanitation.
Readership/Target Audience: Aimed at the government, IGOs, NGOs, decision makers and businesses.
BUSINESS: ENVIRONMENT & POLLUTION

SUTTON MATTERS   1881682U72J-425

Email: comments@sutton-matters.co.uk
Web site: http://www.sutton-matters.co.uk
Frequency of update: Daily
Summary of Content: Website created to help people who care about local issues. Whether you need access to useful information, want to highlight a particular topic to other people, discuss ideas with like-minded people or just show your support and keep up to date with current affairs in your area, Sutton Matters is the place for you.
Readership/Target Audience: Aimed at residents in the local area of Sutton.
LOCAL NEWSPAPERS: Community Newsletters

SWANSEA MATTERS   1881683U72J-426

Web site: http://www.swansea-matters.co.uk
Frequency of update: Daily
Summary of Content: Website created to help people who care about local issues. Whether you need access to useful information, want to highlight a particular topic to other people, discuss ideas with like minded individuals or just show your support and keep up to date with current affairs in your area, Swansea Matters is the place for you.
Readership/Target Audience: Aimed at residents in the local area of Swansea.
LOCAL NEWSPAPERS: Community Newsletters

T3   628917U78R-380

Formerly: T3 NETWORK
Editorial Address: 2 Balcombe Street, LONDON, NW1 6NW
Tel: 020 7042 4000
Email: t3@futurenet.com
Web site: http://www.t3.com
Publisher: Future Publishing Limited
Date Launched: 2000
Frequency of update: Daily
Website Access: Free

Traffic Figures: 500,000 Unique Users (per month Publisher's Statement)
Editor: Michael Brook
Summary of Content: Website focusing on consumer electronics from gadgets to computers and includes technical news.
Readership/Target Audience: Aimed at those interested in computers, cameras, electrical goods and gadgets.
CONSUMER: CONSUMER ELECTRONICS: Consumer Electronics Related

TAKELEGALADVICE.COM   1894695U44-3061

Editorial Address: Hereford House, 22-24 Smithfield Street, LONDON, EC1A 9LF **Tel:** 020 7332 2580
Fax: 020 7332 2599
Email: enquiries@takelegaladvice.com
Web site: http://www.takelegaladvice.com
Publisher: Polyview Media Ltd
Date Launched: 2006
Frequency of update: Daily
Website Access: Free
Editor: Mary Heaney
Summary of Content: Online search and comparison service giving individuals and businesses information on suitable lawyers to select for their needs.
Readership/Target Audience: Aimed at consumers and businesses looking to make informed choices on which law firm to choose.
BUSINESS: LEGAL

TALENTSCOTLAND   1852762U14F-266

Editorial Address: 150 Broomielaw, 5 Atlantic Quay, GLASGOW, G2 8LU **Tel:** 0141 248 2793 **Fax:** 0141 221 3217
Email: daniel.crowe@scotent.co.uk
Web site: http://www.talentscotland.com
Date Launched: 2001
Frequency of update: Daily
Website Access: Free
Traffic Figures: 40,000 Unique Users (Publisher's Statement)
Editor: Daniel Crowe
Summary of Content: Website designed to encourage individuals to work in Scotland in the energy, electronics, financial services and life science industries. Featuring company profiles, career interviews, recruitment, Scottish life sciences news, energy news, financial service news and electronics news.
Readership/Target Audience: Aimed at professional job seekers in the energy, life sciences, financial services and energy sectors looking to work in Scotland.
Other Features: Recruitment
BUSINESS: COMMERCE, INDUSTRY & MANAGEMENT: Training & Recruitment

---

TALKACNE   1791248U94F-1010

Editorial Address: PO Box 7383, Sherfield-on-Loddon, HOOK, RG27 7FX **Tel:** 0870 042 9500
Email: contact.acne@talkacne.com
Web site: http://www.talkacne.com
Publisher: TalkHealth Partnership Ltd
Date Launched: 2005
Frequency of update: Daily
Website Access: Free
Traffic Figures: 66,000 Unique Users (per year Publisher's Statement)
Editor: Deborah Mason
Summary of Content: Website covering acne care, news and new treatments, diet, alternative medicine, food allergies, features, real stories and competitions.
Readership/Target Audience: Aimed at carers and sufferers of acne.
CONSUMER: OTHER CLASSIFICATIONS: Disability

TALKALLERGY   1791250U94F-1012

Editorial Address: PO Box 7383, Sherfield-on-Loddon, HOOK, RG27 7FX **Tel:** 0870 042 9500
Email: contact.allergy@talkhealthpartnership.com
Publisher: TalkHealth Partnership Ltd
Date Launched: 2003
Frequency of update: Daily
Website Access: Free
Traffic Figures: 130,000 Unique Users (per year Publisher's Statement)
Editor: Samantha Cook
Summary of Content: Website covering allergies with news and new treatments, diet, alternative medicine, food allergies, features, real stories and competitions.
Readership/Target Audience: Aimed at carers and those suffering from allergies.
Other Features: Message board, registered members area, secure healthcare professional area.
CONSUMER: OTHER CLASSIFICATIONS: Disability

TALKASTHMA
1791247U94F-1009

Editorial Address: PO Box 7383, Sherfield-on-Loddon, HOOK, RG27 7FX **Tel:** 0870 042 9500
Email: contact.asthma@talkhealthpartnership.com
Web site: http://www.talkasthma.com
Publisher: TalkHealth Partnership Ltd
Frequency of update: Daily
Website Access: Free
Traffic Figures: 30,000 Unique Users (per year Publisher's Statement)
Editor: Deborah Mason
Summary of Content: Website covering asthmas care, news and new treatments, diet, alternative medicine, food allergies, features, real stories and competitions.
Readership/Target Audience: Aimed at carers and sufferers of asthma.
Other Features: Message board, registered members area, secure healthcare professionals area.
CONSUMER: OTHER CLASSIFICATIONS: Disability

TALKECZEMA
1667634U94F-998

Editorial Address: PO Box 7383, Sherfield-on-Loddon, HOOK, RG7 7FX **Tel:** 0870 042 9500
Email: contact.eczema@talkhealthpartnership.com
Web site: http://www.talkeczema.com
Publisher: TalkHealth Partnership Ltd
Date Launched: 2000
Frequency of update: Daily
Website Access: Free
Traffic Figures: 383,000 Unique Users (per year Publisher's Statement)
Editor: Lisa Anderson; **Web Editor:** Lisa Anderson
Summary of Content: Website covering eczema care, news and new treatments, diet, alternative medicine, food allergies, features, real stories and competitions.
Readership/Target Audience: Aimed at carers and sufferers of eczema.
Other Features: Message boards.
CONSUMER: OTHER CLASSIFICATIONS: Disability

TALKING PICTURES
46061U76A-70

Editorial Address: 1 Orchard Cottages, Orchard Lane, PLYMOUTH, PL7 4AJ **Tel:** 01752 347200
Email: nigelwatson1@gmail.com
Web site: http://www.talkingpix.co.uk
Publisher: Valis Books
Date Launched: 2001
Frequency of update: Weekly
Website Access: Free
Traffic Figures: 18,000 Unique Users (per month Publisher's Statement)
Editor: Nigel Watson
Summary of Content: Website providing a detailed look at popular and arthouse films. Also contains reviews of movie orientated computer software.
Readership/Target Audience: Read by people interested in all aspects of film, TV and video production.
CONSUMER: MUSIC & PERFORMING ARTS: Cinema

TALKINGRETAIL.COM
37942U22A-70

Formerly: Checkout
Editorial Address: 6th Floor, Davis House, 2 Robert Street, CROYDON, CR0 1QQ **Tel:** 020 8253 8704
Fax: 020 8253 8727
Email: david.shrimpton@metropolis.co.uk
Web site: http://www.talkingretail.com
Publisher: Metropolis International Group Ltd
Frequency of update: Daily
Website Access: Paid
(Publisher's Statement)
Editor: David Shrimpton
Summary of Content: Website providing information about grocery retail in the UK and overseas.
Readership/Target Audience: Aimed at multiple and independent wholesalers and retailers.
BUSINESS: FOOD

TALKPSORIASIS
1791249U94F-1011

Editorial Address: PO Box 7383, Sherfield-on-Loddon, HOOK, RG27 7FX **Tel:** 0870 042 9500
Email: contact.psoriasis@talkhealthpartnership.com
Web site: http://www.talkpsoriasis.com
Publisher: TalkHealth Partnership Ltd
Date Launched: 2005
Frequency of update: Daily
Website Access: Free
Traffic Figures: 60,000 Unique Users (per year Publisher's Statement)
Editor: Deborah Mason

Summary of Content: Website covering psoriasis care, news and new treatments, diet, alternative medicine, food allergies, features, real stories and competitions.
Readership/Target Audience: Aimed at carers and sufferers of psoriasis.
CONSUMER: OTHER CLASSIFICATIONS: Disability

TALKXBOX
1859795U78D-339

Editorial Address: 203 Whitton Avenue East, GREENFORD, UB6 0QG **Tel:** 020 8902 4639
Email: press@talkxbox.com
Web site: http://www.talkxbox.com
Date Launched: 2002
Frequency of update: Daily
Website Access: Free
Traffic Figures: 90,000 Unique Users (Publisher's Statement)
Editor: Press Office
Summary of Content: Talkxbox is a professional Xbox website with a blogging twist!.
Readership/Target Audience: Aimed at video game enthusiasts.
CONSUMER: CONSUMER ELECTRONICS: Games

TAX GUIDE
712611U1M-44

Formerly: Tax Guide 2001
Editorial Address: Octavia House, 50 Banner Street, LONDON, EC1Y 8ST **Tel:** 020 7250 7010
Fax: 020 7250 7011
Email: taxguide@growthcompany.co.uk
Web site: http://www.taxguide.co.uk
Publisher: Vitesse Media plc
Date Launched: 2001
Website Access: Free
Editor: Sara Williams
Summary of Content: Website focusing on tax news, tax-saving investments and 'how to' guides.
Readership/Target Audience: Aimed at financiers and the general public.
BUSINESS: FINANCE & ECONOMICS: Taxation

TAX PLANNING INTERNATIONAL ASIA PACIFIC FOCUS
35411U1M-48

Formerly: Tax Planning International Review
Editorial Address: Millbank Tower, 21-24 Millbank, LONDON, SW1P 4QP **Tel:** 020 7559 4800
Fax: 020 7559 4880
Email: lillianadams@bna.com
Web site: http://www.bnai.com
Publisher: BNA International
Date Launched: 1998
Frequency of update: 165 times a year
Website Access: Paid
Editor: Lillian Adams
Summary of Content: Online journal covering all aspects of international tax planning developments, tax treaties and significant national rules in the Asia-Pacific region.
Readership/Target Audience: Aimed at tax practitioners with a particular interest in the Asia-Pacific region.
BUSINESS: FINANCE & ECONOMICS: Taxation

TEACHING TIMES
1647248U62B-1405

Editorial Address: 215 The Green House, Gibb Street, Digbeth, BIRMINGHAM, B9 4AA **Tel:** 0121 224 7576
Fax: 0121 224 7565
Email: rchima@qiis.co.uk
Web site: http://www.teachingtimes.co.uk
Publisher: Imaginative Minds
Date Launched: 2000
Frequency of update: Daily
Website Access: Free
Editor: Raspal Chima
Summary of Content: Website covering the latest news from the education sector, from nursery education through to adult learning.
Readership/Target Audience: Aimed at those working within the education sector.
BUSINESS: CHURCH & SCHOOL EQUIPMENT & EDUCATION: Education Teachers

TEAMTALK
626402U75B-278

Editorial Address: Apsley House, 78 Wellington Street, LEEDS, LS1 2EQ **Tel:** 0113 399 2050 **Fax:** 0870 128 8333
Email: bl-365mediasubbing@bskyb.com
Web site: http://www.teamtalk.com
Publisher: 365 Media Group
Frequency of update: Daily
Website Access: Free

Traffic Figures: 2,000,000 Unique Users (per month Publisher's Statement)
Editor: Simon Wilkes
Summary of Content: Website containing news and information on the world of football.
Readership/Target Audience: Aimed at those interested in football.
Other Features: Features include a sports store, an online radio, archiving and recruitment.
CONSUMER: SPORT: Football

TECHEVENTGUIDE.COM
1826012U18A-9038

Editorial Address: Birdham Road, CHICHESTER, PO20 7DU **Tel:** 01243 531123 **Fax:** 01243 779070
Email: sales@techeventguide.com
Web site: http://www.techeventguide.com
Publisher: Napier Partnership Ltd
Date Launched: 2006
Frequency of update: Quarterly
Website Access: Free
Traffic Figures: 2,446 Unique Users (Publisher's Statement)
Editor: Leigh Swains
Summary of Content: Online guide to shows, seminars, training and conferences for the European electronics industry.
Readership/Target Audience: Aimed at those in the electronics industry including design engineers, purchasers, senior managers, production and testers.
Other Features: Newsletter
BUSINESS: ELECTRONICS

TECHNOLOGY4MEDIA.COM
1842851U5R-691

Editorial Address: Unit 11, The Chandlery, 50 Westminster Bridge Road, LONDON, SE1 7QY **Tel:** 020 7953 8770
Fax: 020 7953 8773
Email: news.desk@technology4media.com
Web site: http://www.technology4media.com
Publisher: News4Media Ltd
Date Launched: 2008
Frequency of update: Daily
Website Access: Free
Traffic Figures: 5,000 Unique Users (per month Publisher's Statement)
Editor: Henry Hemming
Summary of Content: Website covering all aspects of news from the technology industry.
Readership/Target Audience: Aimed at those working in the technology industry at all levels.
BUSINESS: COMPUTERS & AUTOMATION: Computers Related

TECHNOLOGY WEEKLY
1779750U2A-690

Editorial Address: St. Giles House, 50 Poland Street, LONDON, W1F 7AX **Tel:** 020 7970 4000 **Fax:** 020 7970 4925
Email: ellie.wallis@mad.co.uk
Web site: http://www.mad.co.uk/technologyweekly
Publisher: Centaur Communications Ltd
Date Launched: 2004
Frequency of update: Weekly
Website Access: Free
Traffic Figures: 50,000 Unique Users (per week Publisher's Statement)
Editor: Ellie Wallis
Summary of Content: Newsletter and website providing information for marketers on the technology involved in email, search engine, marketing, social networking and mobile marketing.
Readership/Target Audience: Aimed at marketers and those working in the digital sector.
BUSINESS: COMMUNICATIONS, ADVERTISING & MARKETING

TECHRADAR.COM
1752935U78R-510

Formerly: Tech.co.uk
Editorial Address: 30 Monmouth Street, BATH, BA1 2BW **Tel:** 01225 442244 **Fax:** 01225 732295
Email: news@techradar.com
Web site: http://www.tech.co.uk
Publisher: Future Publishing Ltd
Date Launched: 2006
Frequency of update: Daily
Website Access: Free
Editor: Patrick Goss
Summary of Content: Website covering daily product news and opinion on consumer technology.
Readership/Target Audience: Aimed at high spending technology enthusiasts.
Other Features: Newsletters, forums, RSS feeds, audio and video downloads, blogs, site search, comprehensive site filtering and content customisation.
CONSUMER: CONSUMER ELECTRONICS: Consumer Electronics Related

TECHTESTED.CO.UK
1752934U78R-509

Editorial Address: For all contact details see main record, TechRadar.com
Frequency of update: Daily
Website Access: Free
CONSUMER: CONSUMER ELECTRONICS: Consumer Electronics Related

TECHWORLD
1622482U5C-905

Editorial Address: 4th Floor, 101 Euston Road, LONDON, NW1 2RA **Tel:** 020 7756 2800
Email: editor@techworld.com
Web site: http://www.techworld.com
Publisher: IDG (International Data Group)
Date Launched: 2003
Frequency of update: Daily
Website Access: Free
Editor: Maxwell Cooter
Summary of Content: Website covering IT, computing, networking, software and hardware as well as the latest news and product reviews. Focuses on storage, security and operating systems.
Readership/Target Audience: Aimed at the IT and administration departments of large enterprise companies.
BUSINESS: COMPUTERS & AUTOMATION: Professional Personal Computers

TELECOMMUNICATIONS
37508U18B-1600

Formerly: Telecommunications International
Editorial Address: 16 Sussex Street, LONDON, SW1V 4RW
Fax: 020 7596 8739
Web site: http://www.telecomengine.com
Publisher: Horizon House Publications - Europe
Frequency of update: Daily
Website Access: Free
Traffic Figures: 64,262 Unique Users (01/01/2007 To 30/06/2007 BPA Worldwide)
Summary of Content: Online Journal covering news and information on the telecommunications industry.
Readership/Target Audience: Aimed at those involved in telecommunications.
BUSINESS: ELECTRONICS: Telecommunications

TELECOMREDUX
1692423U18B-1964

Editorial Address: PR by email only **Tel:** 01245 495213
Email: ichanning@telecomredux.com
Web site: http://www.telecomredux.com
Frequency of update: Daily
Website Access: Free
Editor: Ian Channing
Summary of Content: Website covering news and analysis on the IT, wireless, new media and telecommunications industry.
Readership/Target Audience: Aimed at senior executives in the telecommunications industry.
BUSINESS: ELECTRONICS: Telecommunications

TELECOMS INDUSTRY DIRECTORY
1912973U18B-2015

Editorial Address: 18 Generator Hall, Electric Wharf, COVENTRY, CV1 4JL **Tel:** 0870 199 4044
Fax: 0870 777 4360
Email: enquiries@industrydirectory.co.uk
Web site: http://www.industrydirectory.co.uk
Publisher: Simply Marcomms
Frequency of update: Daily
Website Access: Free
Editor: Kirstie Colledge
Summary of Content: Directory containing the latest news stories for the UK telecoms industry. Includes news archives.
Readership/Target Audience: Aimed at Telecoms professionals, suppliers to the Telecoms industry, Telecoms PR & Marketing firms.
BUSINESS: ELECTRONICS: Telecommunications

TELECOMTV
626431U18B-1935

Formerly: Telecomtv.com
Editorial Address: 3 London Wall Buildings, LONDON, EC2M 5PP **Tel:** 020 7448 1070 **Fax:** 020 7448 1099
Email: guy@telecomtv.com
Web site: http://www.telecomtv.com
Publisher: Decisive Media
Date Launched: 1998
Frequency of update: Daily
Website Access: Free
Traffic Figures: 30,000 Unique Users (per month Publisher's Statement)
Editor: Guy Daniels

Summary of Content: Website covering daily news and analysis for the global telecommunications industry.
Readership/Target Audience: Aimed at global telecommunications professionals.
BUSINESS: ELECTRONICS: Telecommunications

TELECOMVIEW
1646093U18B-1949

Editorial Address: 2 Hawkmoor Parke, Bovey Tracey, NEWTON ABBOT, TQ13 9NL **Tel:** 01626 834224
Email: iancox@telecomview.info
Web site: http://www.telecomview.info
Publisher: Hawkmoor Research
Date Launched: 2004
Frequency of update: 26 times a year
Website Access: Paid
Editor: Ian Cox
Summary of Content: Website focusing on the broadband industry. Includes articles on network convergence, broadband access, networks and broadband value added services.
Readership/Target Audience: Aimed at vendors, service providers, regulators and investors.
BUSINESS: ELECTRONICS: Telecommunications

TELECOMWORLDWIRE
37515U18B-1700

Editorial Address: PR via email only **Tel:** 020 7047 0200
Email: m2pw@m2.com
Web site: http://www.m2.com
Publisher: M2 Communications Ltd
Frequency of update: Daily
Website Access: Paid
Editor: Jamie Ayres
Summary of Content: Electronically mailed news service covering global telecommunications, computing and information technology markets.
Readership/Target Audience: Aimed at users, buyers, consultants, sector groups, researchers and educators.
BUSINESS: ELECTRONICS: Telecommunications

THE TELEGRAPH AND ARGUS
706772U67B-9001

Formerly: THIS IS BRADFORD & DISTRICT
Editorial Address: Hall Ings, BRADFORD, BD1 1JR **Tel:** 01274 729511
Email: newsdesk@telegraphandargus.co.uk
Web site: http://www.telegraphandargus.co.uk
Publisher: Newsquest Yorkshire and North East (Bradford)
Date Launched: 1998
Frequency of update: Daily
Website Access: Paid
Traffic Figures: 212,115 Unique Users (01/01/2009 To 30/06/2009 ABC/Electronic)
Editor: News Desk
Summary of Content: Website focusing on news, sport, entertainment and general stories in the Bradford area.
Readership/Target Audience: Aimed at those who live in Bradford and surrounding areas.
Other Features: Other features include buyer's guide, recruitment, chat forums, e-mail newsletter, events calendar, directory search and archiving.
REGIONAL DAILY & SUNDAY NEWSPAPERS: Regional Daily Newspapers

TELEGRAPH MONEY
707439U74M-287

Editorial Address: 111 Buckingham Palace Road, LONDON, SW1W 0DT **Tel:** 020 7931 2000
Fax: 020 7931 2760
Email: dtnews@telegraph.co.uk
Web site: http://money.telegraph.co.uk
Publisher: Telegraph Media Group Ltd
Date Launched: 2001
Frequency of update: Daily
Website Access: Free
Traffic Figures: 151 Unique Users (ABC/Electronic)
Editor: Paul Farow
Summary of Content: Website featuring news on money and investment and opinions on marketing.
Readership/Target Audience: Aimed at those aged 30 and upwards.
Other Features: Features include an e-mail newsletter and archiving.
CONSUMER: WOMEN'S INTEREST CONSUMER MAGAZINES: Personal Finance

TELEGRAPH.CO.UK
601708U65A-125

Editorial Address: 111 Buckingham Palace Road, LONDON, SW1W 0DT **Tel:** 020 7931 2000
Email: newsfeedback@telegraph.co.uk
Web site: http://www.telegraph.co.uk

Publisher: Telegraph Media Group Ltd
Date Launched: 1994
Frequency of update: Daily. News updated continuously
Traffic Figures: 26,479,638 Unique Users (01/07/2009 To 31/07/2009 ABC/Electronic)
Editor: Duncan Hooper
Summary of Content: Website version of The Daily Telegraph and The Sunday Telegraph. Covers UK and international news, city and financial news, reviews, features and sport.
Twitter: http://twitter.com/dailytelegraph.
Other Features: Also includes 'Booksonline', 'Connected2' (technology and science), 'Internet for Schools' (a support site for the education community) and 'Gallery' (features art exhibitions).
NATIONAL DAILY & SUNDAY NEWSPAPERS: National Daily Newspapers

TELEGRAPH.CO.UK/EARTH
1813760U94X-293

Editorial Address: 111 Buckingham Palace Road, LONDON, SW1W 0DT **Tel:** 020 7931 2000
Email: louise.gray@telegraph.co.uk
Web site: http://www.telegraph.co.uk/earth
Publisher: Telegraph Media Group Ltd
Date Launched: 2007
Frequency of update: Daily
Website Access: Free
Traffic Figures: 1,500,000 Unique Users (Publisher's Statement)
Editor: Louise Gray
Summary of Content: Website covering all aspects of the environment including climate change, the natural world and energy.
Readership/Target Audience: Aimed at anyone with an interest in the environment.
CONSUMER: OTHER CLASSIFICATIONS: Miscellaneous

TELEGRAPH.CO.UK/MOTORING
713769U77A-330

Formerly: motoring.telegraph.co.uk
Editorial Address: 111 Buckingham Palace Road, LONDON, SW1W 0DT **Tel:** 020 7931 2000
Fax: 020 7931 2879
Email: motoring.desk@telegraph.co.uk
Web site: http://www.telegraph.co.uk/motoring
Publisher: Telegraph Media Group Ltd
Date Launched: 2001
Frequency of update: Daily
Website Access: Free
Traffic Figures: 3,189,241 Unique Users (per month ABC/Electronic)
Editor: Nick Cowen
Summary of Content: Website covering motoring news and information on test drives, finance, insurance, breakdown services and company cars. Includes information on classic and used cars and a car valuation section.
Readership/Target Audience: Aimed at motoring and motor sport enthusiasts.
Other Features: Features include a buyer's guide, a chat forum, an e-mail newsletter and archiving.
CONSUMER: MOTORING & CYCLING: Motoring

TELEGRAPH.CO.UK/PROPERTY
713979U74K-360

Formerly: property.telegraph.co.uk
Editorial Address: 111 Buckingham Palace Road, LONDON, SW1W 0DT **Tel:** 020 7931 2000
Email: sharon.keene@telegraph.co.uk
Web site: http://www.telegraph.co.uk/property
Publisher: Telegraph Media Group Ltd
Date Launched: 2001
Frequency of update: Daily. For circulation figure see telegraph.co.uk
Website Access: Free
Editor: Sharon Keene
Summary of Content: Website providing expert advice, news and information about the property market. Also includes home improvement ideas, buying and selling new homes, moving house and a property finder section.
Readership/Target Audience: Aimed at those wanting to buy or sell property.
CONSUMER: WOMEN'S INTEREST CONSUMER MAGAZINES: Home Purchase

TELEGRAPH.CO.UK/TRAVEL
704828U89A-575

Formerly: travel.telegraph.co.uk
Editorial Address: 111 Buckingham Palace Road, LONDON, SW1W 0DT **Tel:** 020 7931 2000
Fax: 020 7538 6158
Email: francesca.hoyles@telegraph.co.uk
Web site: http://www.telegraph.co.uk/travel

Internet Media

Publisher: Telegraph Media Group Ltd
Date Launched: 2001
Frequency of update: Daily
Website Access: Free
Editor: Francesca Hoyles
Summary of Content: Website containing information on cruises, city breaks, UK holidays and family holidays. Includes travel news, a weather report from all over the world and a currency converter.
Readership/Target Audience: Aimed at those interested in travelling.
CONSUMER: HOLIDAYS & TRAVEL: Travel

TELEGRAPH.CO.UK/ULTRATRAVEL

1779479U89A-736

Editorial Address: 111 Buckingham Palace Road, LONDON, SW1W 0DT **Tel:** 020 7931 2000
Fax: 020 7931 2767
Email: traveldesk@telegraph.co.uk
Web site: http://www.telegraph.co.uk/ultratravel
Publisher: Telegraph Media Group Ltd
Frequency of update: Weekly
Website Access: Free
Editor: Francesca Hoyles
Summary of Content: Website covering luxury travel, the latest travel news and destination features as well as interactive, multimedia content such as video.
Readership/Target Audience: Aimed at armchair travellers and top-end luxury travellers.
Other Features: Weekly newsletter.
CONSUMER: HOLIDAYS & TRAVEL: Travel

TELEPRESENCE AND VIDEOCONFERENCING INSIGHT NEWSLETTER

1837335U2D-154

Formerly: Videoconferencing Insight Newsletter
Editorial Address: ATM House, 28 Roman Road, HOVE, BN3 4LF **Tel:** 01273 381300
Email: editor@vcinsight.com
Web site: http://www.tpandvc-insight.com
Publisher: IMP Publications
Date Launched: 1996
Frequency of update: Weekly
Website Access: Free
Editor: Richard Line
Summary of Content: Newsletter reporting on the telepresence and videoconferencing industry from a user perspective. Features user application case studies, interviews and industry news and includes a reference data bank of 500 user applications in 25 user vertical categories such as manufacturing, industry, financial services, hospitals, telemedicine and education.
Readership/Target Audience: Aimed at users and potential users of telepresence and videoconferencing.
BUSINESS: COMMUNICATIONS, ADVERTISING & MARKETING: Broadcasting

TES CONNECT

1924905U62B-1415

Editorial Address: 26 Red Lion Square, LONDON, WC1R 4HQ **Tel:** 020 3194 3000 **Fax:** 020 3194 3300
Email: newsdesk@tes.co.uk
Web site: http://www.tes.co.uk
Publisher: TSL Education Ltd
Frequency of update: Daily
Traffic Figures: 1,300,000 Unique Users (per month Publisher's Statement)
Summary of Content: TES Connect is a social network that allows teachers to network, share resources and search for jobs. Split into five user-friendly sections including jobs, community, resources and My TES, the site gives teachers access to tools that have the potential to transform lesson planning and the quality of lessons taught.
BUSINESS: CHURCH & SCHOOL EQUIPMENT & EDUCATION: Education Teachers

TEXTILE DYER

1846835U47A-591

Editorial Address: 80 Featherstone Lane, Featherstone, PONTEFRACT, WF7 6LR **Tel:** 01977 708488
Fax: 0700 609 0531
Email: editor@textiledyer.com
Web site: http://www.textiledyer.com
Publisher: Mowbray Communications Ltd
Date Launched: 2008
Frequency of update: Daily
Website Access: Paid
Traffic Figures: 2,200 Unique Users (per month Publisher's Statement)
Editor: Phil Patterson
Summary of Content: Online magazine covering new textiles dyes, chemicals and auxiliaries, commercial news, new machinery and processing techniques.

Readership/Target Audience: Aimed at the textile dying and finishing industries.
BUSINESS: CLOTHING & TEXTILES

THEBATHROOM.INFO

760719U74C-806

Formerly: Soak
Editorial Address: The Bathroom Works, National Avenue, HULL, HU5 4HS **Tel:** 0870 202 2202 **Fax:** 01484 686690
Email: editorial@thebathroom.info
Web site: http://www.thebathroom.info
Publisher: American Standard Plumbing
Date Launched: 2004
Frequency of update: Monthly
Website Access: Free
Editor: Zoe Alderson
Summary of Content: Website for BASIS (the Bathroom & Shower Information Service), covering bathroom design trends, new products, style and colour with advice from leading interior designers.
Readership/Target Audience: Aimed at those with a general interest in interior design, as well as those in the process of updating an existing bathroom or planning a new one.
CONSUMER: WOMEN'S INTEREST CONSUMER MAGAZINES: Home & Family

THEBUSINESSDESK.COM/NORTHWEST

1853137U63B-2590

Editorial Address: 6th Floor, Peter House, Oxford Street, MANCHESTER, M1 5AN **Tel:** 0161 209 3612
Fax: 0161 209 3618
Email: nwoffice@thebusinessdesk.com
Web site: http://www.thebusinessdesk.com/northwest/
Publisher: TheBusinessDesk Ltd
Date Launched: 2008
Frequency of update: 260 times a year
Website Access: Free
Traffic Figures: 6,650 Unique Users (per month Publisher's Statement)
Editor: David Parkin
Summary of Content: Regional news service covering up to date business news and features.
Readership/Target Audience: Aimed at professionals and senior managers across the North West.
BUSINESS: REGIONAL BUSINESS: Regional Business English Counties

THEBUSINESSDESK.COM/YORKSHIRE

1827966U63B-2586

Formerly: thebusinessdesk.com
Editorial Address: The Round Foundry Media Centre, Foundry Street, LEEDS, LS11 5QP **Tel:** 0113 394 4321
Fax: 0113 394 4322
Email: news@thebusinessdesk.com
Web site: http://www.thebusinessdesk.com/yorkshire/
Publisher: TheBusinessDesk Ltd
Date Launched: 2007
Frequency of update: 260 times a year
Website Access: Free
Traffic Figures: 44,000 Unique Users (per month Publisher's Statement)
Editor: David Parkin
Summary of Content: Regional news service covering up to date business news and features. Promoting events as well as company results, deals, people moves, commercial property, professional services and the public sector.
Readership/Target Audience: Aimed at professionals and senior managers across the Yorkshire region.
BUSINESS: REGIONAL BUSINESS: Regional Business English Counties

THEDIGITALLIFESTYLE.COM

1825785U78R-519

Editorial Address: 3 Osborne Drive, Clayton-le-Woods, CHORLEY, PR6 7SR **Tel:** 0161 886 4270
Email: ian@thedigitallifestyle.com
Web site: http://www.thedigitallifestyle.com
Date Launched: 2007
Frequency of update: Daily
Website Access: Free
Traffic Figures: 40,000 Unique Users (per month Publisher's Statement)
Editor: Ian Dixon
Summary of Content: Website covering a digital lifestyle, home entertainment, software and consumer electronics around the home related to personal computers.
Readership/Target Audience: Aimed at enthusiast of home theatre and digital computer electronics.
CONSUMER: CONSUMER ELECTRONICS: Consumer Electronics Related

THELONDONPAPER.COM

1829844U67B-9070

Editorial Address: 1 Pennington Street, LONDON, E98 1XY
Tel: 020 7782 4848
Email: online@thelondonpaper.com
Web site: http://www.thelondonpaper.com
Publisher: News International Ltd
Frequency of update: Daily
Website Access: Free
Traffic Figures: 1,000,000 Unique Users (per month Publisher's Statement)
Editor: Kat Brown
Summary of Content: Interactive website featuring news, show-biz, blogging, going out, drinking, dating, competitions, television, sport, property, travel and jobs with a focus on London.
REGIONAL DAILY & SUNDAY NEWSPAPERS: Regional Daily Newspapers

THELUXURYROOM.COM

1776237U74Q-1333

Editorial Address: Bucklands, Loxwood Road, Rudgwick, HORSHAM, RH12 3DW **Tel:** 01403 823640
Fax: 01403 433332
Email: editorial@theluxuryroom.com
Web site: http://www.theluxuryroom.com
Publisher: Big Blue Publishing Company Ltd
Date Launched: 2006
Frequency of update: Weekly
Website Access: Free
Editor: Giles Morgan; **Editor-in-Chief:** Giles Morgan
Summary of Content: Website covering everything luxury including a what's on guide, calendar, homes, fashion, celebrity, travel, business, luxury goods, shopping, food and drink, motoring, listings and beauty.
Readership/Target Audience: Aimed at millionaires and high-net-worth consumers.
Other Features: Newsletter
CONSUMER: WOMEN'S INTEREST CONSUMER MAGAZINES: Lifestyle

THEME MAGAZINE ONLINE

1924473U9A-272

Editorial Address: UBM Information, Ludgate House, 245 Blackfriars Road, LONDON, SE1 9UY **Tel:** 020 7955 3807
Email: allan.taylor@ubm.com
Web site: http://www.thememagazine.co.uk
Frequency of update: Daily
Traffic Figures: 40,000 Unique Users (per month Publisher's Statement)
Summary of Content: Website of a magazine providing information on UK bar and restaurant industry.
BUSINESS: DRINKS & LICENSED TRADE: Drinks, Licensed Trade, Wines & Spirits

THENORTHERNECHO.CO.UK

629110U80C-1375

Formerly: THIS IS THE NORTH EAST
Editorial Address: PO Box 14, Priestgate, DARLINGTON, DL1 1NF **Tel:** 01325 381313 **Fax:** 01325 380539
Email: newsdesk@nne.co.uk
Web site: http://www.thenorthecho.co.uk
Publisher: Newsquest Yorkshire and North East (Darlington)
Frequency of update: Daily
Website Access: Free
Traffic Figures: 100,000 Unique Users (per month Publisher's Statement)
Editor: Michael Atkinson
Summary of Content: Website containing news and information on the North East of England. Includes sport, business, leisure, weather, music, education and travel.
Readership/Target Audience: Aimed at those living in or interested in the North East.
Other Features: Features include archiving.
CONSUMER: RURAL & REGIONAL INTEREST: Regional Interest English Counties

THEONLINEMAIL.CO.UK

1902249U72C-520

Editorial Address: 14 Eastgate Street, CAERNARFON, LL55 1AG **Tel:** 01492 574334
Email: paul.scott@northwalesnews.co.uk
Web site: http://www.theonlinemail.co.uk
Frequency of update: Daily
Website Access: Free
Editor: Paul Scott; **Web Editor:** Paul Scott
Summary of Content: Website featuring local news and sport.
Readership/Target Audience: Aimed at residents living Gwynnedd and the Isle of Anglesey.
LOCAL NEWSPAPERS: Local Newspapers Wales

THESHEEPDIP.CO.UK

1779803U87-2044

Editorial Address: 10 Amity Street, READING, RG1 3LP
Tel: 07985 413641
Email: shepherd@thesheepdip.co.uk
Web site: http://www.thesheepdip.co.uk
Publisher: Phil Creighton
Frequency of update: Monthly
Website Access: Paid
Editor: Phil Creighton
Summary of Content: Website with downloadable testimonies, news, focuses on Christian charities, opinions, Bible studies, Church history and humour.
Readership/Target Audience: Aimed at editors of church/parish newsletters and magazines.
Other Features: Links to Christian businesses/printers
CONSUMER: RELIGIOUS

THESITE.ORG

629252U74Q-927

Formerly: The Site.org
Editorial Address: 1st Floor, 50 Featherstone Street, LONDON, EC1Y 8RT **Tel:** 020 7250 5700
Fax: 020 7250 3695
Email: hannah.jolliffe@youthnet.org
Web site: http://www.thesite.org
Publisher: YouthNet
Date Launched: 1995
Frequency of update: Daily
Website Access: Free
Traffic Figures: 500,000 Unique Users (per month Publisher's Statement)
Editor: Hannah Jolliffe
Summary of Content: Website focusing on advice based on lifestyle issues. Includes information on money, health, drugs, careers, students, housing, sex and relationships.
Readership/Target Audience: Aimed at 16 to 25 year olds.
Other Features: Features include discussion forums, real life articles, competitions, games, polls and surveys.
CONSUMER: WOMEN'S INTEREST CONSUMER MAGAZINES: Lifestyle

THESTUDENTPLANNER.ORG

1641849U83-294

Formerly: TheStudentPlanner.co.uk
Editorial Address: 201 Houldsworth Mill, Waterhouse Way, STOCKPORT, SK5 6DD **Tel:** 07841 500222
Email: martin@thestudentplanner.com
Web site: http://www.thestudentplanner.org
Publisher: Student Planner UK
Date Launched: 2004
Frequency of update: Weekly
Website Access: Free
Traffic Figures: 100,000 Unique Users (per month Publisher's Statement)
Editor: Martin Dallaghan
Summary of Content: Website covering news, entertainment, competitions and advice.
Readership/Target Audience: Aimed at 6th form and further education college students aged 16 to 19 years old.
CONSUMER: STUDENT PUBLICATIONS

THE-VOID.CO.UK

1811098U76A-209

Editorial Address: 17 Cromwell Road, CANTERBURY, CT1 3LB **Tel:** 07779 004643
Email: mrshaw@the-void.co.uk
Web site: http://www.the-void.co.uk
Date Launched: 2007
Frequency of update: Daily
Website Access: Free
Traffic Figures: 67,000 Unique Users (per month Publisher's Statement)
Editor: Mike Shaw; **Editor-in-Chief:** Mike Shaw
Summary of Content: Website covering all genres of movies as well as music, TV, video games, books, comics and gadgets.
Readership/Target Audience: Aimed at 18 to 35 year olds who enjoy all forms of entertainment.
CONSUMER: MUSIC & PERFORMING ARTS: Cinema

THEWEDDINGNETWORK.CO.UK

1799655U74L-261

Editorial Address: Springfield Lyons Business Centre, Springfield Lyons Approach, Springfield, CHELMSFORD, CM2 5TH **Tel:** 01245 235199
Email: editorial@theweddingnetwork.co.uk
Web site: http://www.theweddingnetwork.co.uk
Date Launched: 2004
Frequency of update: Weekly
Website Access: Free
Traffic Figures: 68,000 Unique Users (per week Publisher's Statement)
Editor: Jacinda Love

Summary of Content: Website covering all aspects of weddings including planning, bridal wear and grooms wear, beauty, health, venues, overseas weddings, honeymoons, hen nights and stag weekends.
Readership/Target Audience: Aimed at brides and grooms to be.
Other Features: Interactive planning tools including profile, photo and video posting, dress and suit finder, checklist, budget planner, guest list, table planner and speeches, local network with other brides, monthly newsletters, competitions and directory of local wedding suppliers. Resident online wedding experts including Annie, the wedding agony aunt.
CONSUMER: WOMEN'S INTEREST CONSUMER MAGAZINES: Brides

THINKBABY.CO.UK

1696010U74D-615

Editorial Address: 8th Floor, Caxton House, 2 Farringdon Road, LONDON, EC1M 3HN **Tel:** 020 7861 9869
Email: editor@thinkbaby.co.uk
Web site: http://www.thinkbaby.co.uk
Publisher: Magicalia Ltd
Frequency of update: Daily
Website Access: Free
Traffic Figures: 110,000 Unique Users (per month Omniture)
Editor: Laura Lee
Summary of Content: Website covering conception, pregnancy, birth, babies and parenting as well as product reviews.
Readership/Target Audience: Aimed at parents-to-be and those with children aged 0 to two years old.
CONSUMER: WOMEN'S INTEREST CONSUMER MAGAZINES: Child Care

THINKNATURAL

626172U74G-75

Editorial Address: Elizabethan Way, LUTTERWORTH, LE17 4ND **Tel:** 0845 601 1948 **Fax:** 01455 557971
Email: editorial@thinknatural.com
Web site: http://www.thinknatural.com
Date Launched: 1999
Frequency of update: Daily
Website Access: Free
Traffic Figures: 30,000 Unique Users (per month Publisher's Statement)
Editor: Mia Hyde
Summary of Content: Website covering all aspects of health. Includes articles on alternative therapies, herbs and plants and products, vitamins and nutritional vitamin supplements.
Readership/Target Audience: Aimed at those interested in health topics.
CONSUMER: WOMEN'S INTEREST CONSUMER MAGAZINES: Slimming & Health

THINKPACKAGING.COM

38692U35-350

Formerly: PackNews Today
Editorial Address: Glaisdale Drive East, Bilborough, NOTTINGHAM, NG8 4JJ **Tel:** 0115 942 8912
Fax: 0115 929 0490
Email: patricia@tdk.co.uk
Web site: http://www.thinkpackaging.com
Publisher: TDK Business Technologies Ltd
Date Launched: 1996
Frequency of update: Daily
Editor: Patricia Cullen
Summary of Content: Website covering all aspects of packaging including machinery, materials, developments and events, employment opportunities and prospective employees, case studies and an online auction.
Readership/Target Audience: Read by management and decision makers in the packaging industry and potential employees.
BUSINESS: PACKAGING & BOTTLING

THIS IS LONDON

623004U67B-9010

Editorial Address: Northcliffe House, 2 Derry Street, LONDON, W8 5TT **Tel:** 020 7938 7236
Email: editor@thisislondon.co.uk
Web site: http://www.thisislondon.co.uk
Publisher: Evening Press Ltd
Date Launched: 1997
Frequency of update: Daily. News updated continuously
Website Access: Free
Traffic Figures: 2,066,288 Unique Users (01/10/2007 To 31/10/2007 ABC/Electronic)
Editor: Neil Hunter
Summary of Content: Website version of the Evening Standard and London Lite. Covers general news, city news, sport, lifestyle features, entertainment, local listings and tourist information. Classified sections covering jobs, property and holiday.

Readership/Target Audience: Aimed at those who live in the London area.
Other Features: Features include recruitment and archiving.
REGIONAL DAILY & SUNDAY NEWSPAPERS: Regional Daily Newspapers

THIS IS MONEY

45561U74M-290

Editorial Address: Northcliffe House, 2 Derry Street, LONDON, W8 5TT **Tel:** 020 7938 6000 **Fax:** 020 7937 7614
Email: editor@thisismoney.co.uk
Web site: http://www.thisismoney.co.uk
Publisher: Associated Northcliffe Digital
Date Launched: 1999
Frequency of update: Daily. News updated continuously
Website Access: Free
Traffic Figures: 572,624 Unique Users (per month ABC/Electronic)
Editor: Andrew Oxlade
Summary of Content: Website covering all aspects of personal finance including share prices, savings and investments, mortgages, pensions, tax, insurance and City news.
Readership/Target Audience: Aimed at small investors and a wider audience interested in personal finance.
Other Features: Features include an eight-year archive, chat forum, reader comments, a weekly email newsletter, calculators and money-saving tools in Money Shop.
CONSUMER: WOMEN'S INTEREST CONSUMER MAGAZINES: Personal Finance

THIS IS NOTTINGHAM

628992U80C-2535

Editorial Address: Castle Wharf House, NOTTINGHAM, NG1 7EU **Tel:** 0115 948 2000 **Fax:** 0115 964 4032
Email: newsdesk@nottinghameveningpost.co.uk
Web site: http://www.thisisnottingham.co.uk
Publisher: Nottingham Post Media Group Ltd
Date Launched: 1999
Frequency of update: Daily
Website Access: Free
Traffic Figures: 347,578 Unique Users (01/01/2009 To 30/06/2009 ABC/Electronic)
Editor: Martin Done
Summary of Content: Website providing news, sports news, business news and general lifestyle information about the Nottingham area.
Readership/Target Audience: Aimed at anyone interested in the Nottingham area.
Other Features: Features include a what's on guide, a buyer's guide, recruitment, a chat forum and archiving.
CONSUMER: RURAL & REGIONAL INTEREST: Regional Interest English Counties

THIS IS THE WEST COUNTRY

704823U80C-5481

Tel: 01752 206600 **Fax:** 01752 206163
Email: newsdesk@countygazette.co.uk
Web site: http://www.thisisthewestcountry.co.uk
Date Launched: 2000
Frequency of update: Daily
Website Access: Free
Summary of Content: Website containing information on local towns in Devon, Somerset and Cornwall including news, business news, leisure, weather and sport.
Readership/Target Audience: Aimed at those who live or are interested in local events for the above towns.
Other Features: Features include archiving.
CONSUMER: RURAL & REGIONAL INTEREST: Regional Interest English Counties

THOMSONLOCALMONEY

1827402U74M-431

Editorial Address: Thomson House, 296 Farnborough Road, FARNBOROUGH, GU14 7NU **Tel:** 01252 390506
Email: mark.cox@thomsonlocal.com
Web site: http://www.thomonlocalmoney.com
Publisher: Thomson Local
Date Launched: 2007
Frequency of update: Daily
Website Access: Free
Editor: Mark Cox
Summary of Content: Website aimed at helping consumers find the best deals on a wide range of financial products and services including car insurance, debt management, home insurance, pensions and bank accounts.
Readership/Target Audience: Aimed at consumers looking for financial advice.
CONSUMER: WOMEN'S INTEREST CONSUMER MAGAZINES: Personal Finance

TIGHTSPLEASE

1685474U74B-713

Editorial Address: Albion Court, 18-20 Frederick Street, Hockley, BIRMINGHAM, B1 3HE **Tel:** 07977 820213

Email: annalie@annalieevanspr.co.uk
Web site: http://www.tightsplease.co.uk
Date Launched: 2004
Frequency of update: 6 times a year
Website Access: Free
Traffic Figures: 120,000 Unique Users (per month Publisher's Statement)
Editor: Annalie Maher
Summary of Content: Website covering fashion, health and beauty with tips for leg care, fashion advice, latest trends, interviews with fashion, health and beauty experts, prizes and giveaways.
Readership/Target Audience: Aimed at women aged 25 and over.
CONSUMER: WOMEN'S INTEREST CONSUMER MAGAZINES: Women's Interest - Fashion

TILLLATE.COM
1777544U89C-1088

Editorial Address: 14 Laburnum Street, LONDON, E2 8AY
Tel: 020 7739 9240
Email: info@tilllate.com
Web site: http://www.tilllate.com
Frequency of update: Daily
Website Access: Free
Traffic Figures: 1,300,000 Unique Users (per month Publisher's Statement)
Editor: Marco Rohr
Summary of Content: Website covering night-life across Europe including events, bars and clubs.
Readership/Target Audience: Aimed at 18 to 30 year old party goers.
CONSUMER: HOLIDAYS & TRAVEL: Entertainment Guides

TIMBERWEB
713768U46-43

Editorial Address: Fern Court, 39 Park Road, ALDEBURGH, IP15 5ET **Tel:** 01728 451010 **Fax:** 01728 451019
Email: keith@timberweb.com
Web site: http://www.timberweb.com
Date Launched: 1996
Frequency of update: 2704 times a year. Continuous updates throughout the day
Website Access: Paid
Traffic Figures: 40,000 Unique Users (per month Publisher's Statement)
Editor: Keith Richmond
Summary of Content: Website focusing on serving the global timber industry. Includes daily news, online trading, current rates and import-export statistics. Members have extra access to global contacts, new customers and trading information.
Readership/Target Audience: Aimed at buyers and sellers of timber and those interested in the global timber industry.
Other Features: Jobs, Technical Information, Global Events Guide.
BUSINESS: TIMBER, WOOD & FORESTRY

TIME OUT FILM
1659847U76A-175

Editorial Address: Universal House, 251 Tottenham Court Road, LONDON, W1T 7AB **Tel:** 020 7813 3000
Fax: 020 7813 6128
Email: film@timeout.com
Web site: http://www.timeout.com/film
Publisher: Time Out Group Ltd
Date Launched: 2004
Frequency of update: Daily
Website Access: Free
Editor: David Jenkins
Summary of Content: Website featuring news, reviews and film listings.
Readership/Target Audience: Aimed at cinema goers.
CONSUMER: MUSIC & PERFORMING ARTS: Cinema

TIMEOUT.COM
1829384U89C-1106

Editorial Address: Universal House, 251 Tottenham Court Road, LONDON, W1T 7AB **Tel:** 020 7813 3000
Email: alanrutter@timeout.com
Web site: http://www.timeout.com
Publisher: Time Out Group Ltd
Frequency of update: Weekly
Website Access: Free
Traffic Figures: 1,500,000 Unique Users (per month Publisher's Statement)
Editor: Alan Rutter
Summary of Content: Website covering London arts and entertainment.
Readership/Target Audience: Aimed at those aged 20 to 40 years old interested in experiencing the best London has to offer.
Other Features: Other features on site include newsletter and travel.
CONSUMER: HOLIDAYS & TRAVEL: Entertainment Guides

THE TIMES HIGHER EDUCATION
629268U62F-800

Formerly: THE TIMES HIGHER EDUCATION SUPPLEMENT
Editorial Address: 26 Red Lion Square, LONDON, WC1R 4HQ **Tel:** 020 3194 3000 **Fax:** 020 3194 3300
Email: editor@tsleducation.com
Web site: http://www.timeshighereducation.co.uk
Publisher: TSL Education Ltd
Frequency of update: Weekly
Website Access: Paid
Traffic Figures: 27,500 Unique Users (per month Publisher's Statement)
Editor: Phil Baty; **Web Editor:** Sarah Knowles
Summary of Content: Website focusing on higher education news and information.
Readership/Target Audience: Aimed at professionals working in higher education.
BUSINESS: CHURCH & SCHOOL EQUIPMENT & EDUCATION: Adult Education

THE TIMES LITERARY SUPPLEMENT ONLINE
629266U84B-190

Editorial Address: Times House, 1 Pennington Street, LONDON, E98 1BS **Tel:** 020 7782 5000 **Fax:** 020 7782 4966
Email: tls_internet_editor@newsint.co.uk
Web site: http://www.the-tls.co.uk
Publisher: Times Literary Supplement Ltd
Frequency of update: Weekly
Website Access: Paid
Traffic Figures: 56,535 Unique Users (per week Publisher's Statement)
Summary of Content: Website focusing on reviews and information on new releases in the literary world, theatre, opera and the film industry.
Readership/Target Audience: Aimed at professionals and enthusiasts of art and literature.
Other Features: Features include archiving of back issues and a weekly newsletter.
CONSUMER: THE ARTS & LITERARY: Literary

TIMESONLINE.CO.UK
629298U65A-131

Formerly: thetimes.co.uk
Editorial Address: 1 Pennington Street, LONDON, E98 1TT
Tel: 020 7782 5000 **Fax:** 020 7782 3768
Email: online.editor@thetimes.co.uk
Web site: http://www.timesonline.co.uk
Publisher: Times Newspapers Ltd
Date Launched: 1996
Frequency of update: 364 times a year
Website Access: Free
Traffic Figures: 18,873,975 Unique Users (01/07/2009 To 31/07/2009 ABC/Electronic)
Editor: Brigid Callaghan
Summary of Content: Website version of The Times providing news and online opinion and analysis. Contains news from The Times as well as original editorial with features, business news, sport, arts, book reviews and law content.
Twitter: http://twitter.com/TimesOnline.
Other Features: Features include e-mail news bulletins, news ticker and student e-mail service and archiving.
NATIONAL DAILY & SUNDAY NEWSPAPERS: National Daily Newspapers

TISCALI
629490U74Q-936

Editorial Address: 20 Broadwick Street, LONDON, W1F 8HT **Tel:** 020 7087 2000 **Fax:** 020 7087 2272
Web site: http://www.tiscali.co.uk
Date Launched: 1999
Frequency of update: Daily
Website Access: Free
Traffic Figures: 6,800,000 Unique Users (per month Publisher's Statement)
Editor: Bridie Pritchard
Summary of Content: Website covering motoring, money, business, music, sport, travel, finance, jobs, news, entertainment, film, TV, games, property, lifestyle, reference, green, homes and gardens, shopping and health issues.
Readership/Target Audience: Aimed at consumers and business executives.
Other Features: Features include channel and commercial newsletters and a members area. Video and audio content, e.g. news and weather broadcasts, test drives, music videos, film and tv clips. Forums and chat rooms.
CONSUMER: WOMEN'S INTEREST CONSUMER MAGAZINES: Lifestyle

TNT MAGAZINE
629059U89A-550

Formerly: TNT live!
Editorial Address: 14-15 Child's Place, Earls Court, LONDON, SW5 9RX **Tel:** 020 7373 3377 **Fax:** 020 7341 6600

Email: enquiries@tntmagazine.com
Web site: http://www.tntonline.co.uk
Publisher: TNT Publishing
Date Launched: 2001
Frequency of update: Daily
Website Access: Free
Traffic Figures: 268,000 Unique Users (per month Publisher's Statement)
Editor: Krysten Booth
Summary of Content: Website containing a guide for independent travellers. Provides up-to-date travel and lifestyle information including news, arts, entertainment and sport. Includes a message board featuring flats to rent.
Readership/Target Audience: Aimed at 18 to 35 year olds interested in travelling, working and living around the world.
Other Features: Features include recruitment, a chat forum, an e-mail newsletter, events listings, competitions and archiving.
CONSUMER: HOLIDAYS & TRAVEL: Travel

TOMORROW'S CLEANING
1903396U4F-111

Editorial Address: Bollinbrook House, Beech Lane, MACCLESFIELD, SK10 2XZ **Tel:** 01625 614 787
Email: charlotte@opusbusinessmedia.co.uk
Web site: http://www.tomorrowscleaning.com
Frequency of update: Daily
Editor: Charlotte Taylor
Summary of Content: Website covering online cleaning magazine.
Readership/Target Audience: Aimed at those interested in cleaning and cleaning publications.
BUSINESS: ARCHITECTURE & BUILDING: Cleaning & Maintenance

TOP GAYER
1789859U86B-178

Editorial Address: 4 South Bank, CHELTENHAM, GL51 8DN **Tel:** 01242 696314 **Fax:** 020 7117 3380
Email: rich@topgayer.eu
Web site: http://www.topgayer.net
Publisher: TANG Media
Date Launched: 2005
Frequency of update: Daily
Website Access: Free
Traffic Figures: 2,500,000 Unique Users (Publisher's Statement)
Editor: Rich Tuckwell
Summary of Content: Website covering motoring news, cars, entertainment, gossip and shopping.
Readership/Target Audience: Aimed at gay men and women aged 18 to 40 years old.
CONSUMER: ADULT & GAY MAGAZINES: Gay & Lesbian Magazines

TOP GRADUATE
47922U88C-130

Formerly: Top Graduate Career Guide
Editorial Address: 1 Tranley Mews, Fleet Road, LONDON, NW3 2DG **Tel:** 020 7284 7213 **Fax:** 020 7284 7201
Email: d.nelkin@qsnetwork.com
Web site: http://www.topgraduate.com
Publisher: QS Quacquarelli Symonds Ltd
Date Launched: 1992
Frequency of update: Monthly
Website Access: Free
Editor: David Nelkin
Summary of Content: A comprehensive career guide containing executive interviews, job vacancies, news and advice with an aim to help students throughout Europe make informed decisions regarding careers.
Readership/Target Audience: Aimed at undergraduates in their final year.
CONSUMER: EDUCATION: Careers

TOP GRADUATE: QS BUSINESS & TECHNOLOGY
47923U88C-135

Formerly: Top Technical Graduate/Top Engineer
Editorial Address: 1 Tranley Mews, Fleet Road, LONDON, NW3 2DG **Tel:** 020 7284 7200 **Fax:** 020 7284 7201
Email: d.nelkin@qsnetwork.com
Web site: http://www.topgraduate.com
Publisher: QS Quacquarelli Symonds Ltd
Frequency of update: Quarterly
Website Access: Free
Editor: David Nelkin
Summary of Content: Website providing a link between business, IT and engineering, with a focus on recruitment advice and careers for students.
Readership/Target Audience: Aimed at engineers, computer scientists and professionals in industry technology.
CONSUMER: EDUCATION: Careers

TOPBIKE
626450U77B-612

Formerly: TOP bike
Editorial Address: Press releases by email
Tel: 01302 842676
Email: nigel.clarke@gianthand.com
Web site: http://www.topbike.com
Publisher: Gianthand.com Ltd
Date Launched: 1999
Frequency of update: Weekly
Website Access: Free
Traffic Figures: 10,000 Unique Users (per month WebTrends)
Editor: Nigel Clarke; **Web Editor:** Nigel Clarke
Summary of Content: Website focusing on top-end and high performance motorbikes.
Readership/Target Audience: Aimed at enthusiasts and those working in the motorcycle industry.
CONSUMER: MOTORING & CYCLING: Motorcycling

TOP-CONSULTANT.COM
1640353U14A-516

Formerly: Management Consultancy Newsletter
Editorial Address: 18B Charles Street, LONDON, W1J 5DU
Tel: 020 7667 6880 **Fax:** 020 7667 6400
Email: sophia@top-consultant.com
Web site: http://www.top-consultant.com
Date Launched: 2000
Frequency of update: Daily
Website Access: Free
Traffic Figures: 150,000 Unique Users (per month Publisher's Statement)
Editor: Sophia Karadov
Summary of Content: Website including news, trends and interviews relevant to business, management and IT consulting industry.
Readership/Target Audience: Aimed at business, management and IT consultants.
Other Features: Recruitment, forum, newsletter, monthly e-magazine
BUSINESS: COMMERCE, INDUSTRY & MANAGEMENT

TOPGEAR.COM
46304U77A-55

Formerly: BBC Top Gear Online
Editorial Address: 2nd Floor, Energy Centre, 201 Wood Lane, LONDON, W12 7TQ **Tel:** 020 8433 1236
Fax: 020 8433 3754
Email: jamie.hibbard@bbc.com
Web site: http://www.topgear.com
Publisher: BBC Worldwide Publishing
Frequency of update: Daily
Website Access: Free
Traffic Figures: 962,000 Unique Users (per month Publisher's Statement)
Editor: Jamie Hibbard
Summary of Content: Website covering motoring news with features on new products and developments in the motor industry. Includes buying advice, road tests, advice and book reviews.
Readership/Target Audience: Aimed at those interested in cars/car culture, thinking of purchasing a new or used car and looking for advice on what to buy.
Other Features: Competitions, features, road tests, buying guides, user's cars and a newsletter.
CONSUMER: MOTORING & CYCLING: Motoring

TOPTABLE
1789573U74P-951

Editorial Address: 9 Hayne Street, LONDON, EC1A 9HH
Tel: 020 299 2949
Email: ros.choate@toptable.com
Web site: http://www.toptable.com
Frequency of update: Daily
Website Access: Free
Traffic Figures: 800,000 Unique Users (Publisher's Statement)
Editor: Ros Choate
Summary of Content: Website covering on-line restaurant bookings and reviews of restaurants, bars and clubs as well as news and gossip about the restaurant scene.
Readership/Target Audience: Aimed at the web savvy who dine in restaurants.
CONSUMER: WOMEN'S INTEREST CONSUMER MAGAZINES: Food & Cookery

TORPEDO
40730U57-56

Editorial Address: Glaucus House, 14 Corbyn Crescent, SHOREHAM-BY-SEA, BN43 6PQ **Tel:** 01273 465433
Email: glaucus@hotmail.com
Web site: http://www.glaucus.org.uk/Torpedo2.htm
Publisher: British Marine Life Study Society
Date Launched: 1996
Frequency of update: Monthly
Website Access: Paid

Traffic Figures: 8,000 Unique Users (per month Publisher's Statement)
Editor: Andy Horton; **Web Editor:** Andy Horton
Summary of Content: Website containing news and information on all aspects of marine life and ocean environment in the seas surrounding the British Isles.
Readership/Target Audience: Aimed at members of the BMLSS worldwide and anyone interested in this subject matter.
BUSINESS: ENVIRONMENT & POLLUTION

TOTAL TELECOM ONLINE
37517U18B-1750

Editorial Address: Wren House, 43 Hatton Garden, LONDON, EC1N 8EL **Tel:** 020 7092 1000
Email: mary.lennighan@totaltele.com
Web site: http://www.totaltele.com
Publisher: Terrapinn Holdings Ltd.
Date Launched: 1997
Frequency of update: 260 times a year
Website Access: Paid
Editor: Mary Lennighan
Summary of Content: Website focusing on news and analysis covering the international telecommunications industry.
Readership/Target Audience: Aimed at global network professionals.
BUSINESS: ELECTRONICS: Telecommunications

TOTALLY JEWISH
713134U87-214_30

Editorial Address: PO Box 34296, LONDON, NW5 1YW
Tel: 020 7692 6929 **Fax:** 020 7692 6689
Email: newsdesk@totallyplc.com
Web site: http://www.totallyjewish.com
Date Launched: 2000
Frequency of update: Daily
Website Access: Paid
Editor: Zeddy Lawrence
Summary of Content: Website providing news and information on culture, shopping, health, beauty, parenting, dating and food. Also covers travel, weddings, rugby, cricket and football.
Readership/Target Audience: Aimed at the Jewish community living in the UK.
Other Features: Features include recruitment, a chat forum, an e-mail newsletter and archiving.
CONSUMER: RELIGIOUS

TOTALLYMOTOR.CO.UK
1862084U77A-612

Editorial Address: South Quay Plaza, 183 Marsh Wall, LONDON, E14 9SH **Tel:** 020 7517 2268 **Fax:** 020 7517 2233
Email: matt.west@adfero.co.uk
Web site: http://www.totallymotor.co.uk
Publisher: Adfero
Date Launched: 2008
Frequency of update: Daily
Website Access: Paid
Editor: Matthew West
Summary of Content: Website dedicated to providing the latest motor news. Features information on the latest car developments and a reference archive.
Readership/Target Audience: Aimed at car enthusiasts.
CONSUMER: MOTORING & CYCLING: Motoring

TOUCH OIL AND GAS
1913435U33-95

Editorial Address: Saffron House, 6-10 Kirby Street, LONDON, EC1N 8TS **Tel:** 020 7452 5000
Fax: 020 7452 5050
Email: enquiries@touchoilandgas.com
Web site: http://www.touchoilandgas.com/
Publisher: Touch Briefings
Frequency of update: Daily
Webmaster: Webmaster
Summary of Content: Website covering oil and gas, the environment and technology.
Readership/Target Audience: Aimed at those interested in the Oil and Gas industry.
BUSINESS: OIL & PETROLEUM

TOWER HAMLETS MATTERS
1881684U72J-427

Email: comments@towerhamlets-matters.co.uk
Web site: http://www.towerhamlets-matters.co.uk
Frequency of update: Daily
Summary of Content: Website created to help people who care about local issues. Whether you need access to useful information, want to highlight a particular topic to other people, discuss ideas with like minded individuals or just show your support and keep up to date with current affairs in your area, Tower Hamlets Matters is the place for you.

Readership/Target Audience: Aimed at residents in the local area of Tower Hamlets.
LOCAL NEWSPAPERS: Community Newsletters

TOWN & COUNTRY CLUB
1776230U74Q-1334

Editorial Address: Bucklands, Loxwood Road, Rudgwick, HORSHAM, RH12 3DW **Tel:** 01403 823640
Fax: 01483 433332
Email: mail@townandcountryclub.net
Web site: http://www.townandcountryclub.net
Publisher: Big Blue Publishing Company Ltd
Frequency of update: Weekly
Website Access: Free
Traffic Figures: 6,000 Unique Users (Publisher's Statement)
Editor: Giles Morgan; **Editor-in-Chief:** Giles Morgan
Summary of Content: Portal covering VIP offers, promotions, incentives, and invitations as well as what's on guide, calendar, homes, fashion, celebrity, travel, business, luxury goods, shopping, food and drink, motoring, listings and beauty.
Readership/Target Audience: Aimed at wealthy families in each county.
Other Features: Monthly newsletter.
CONSUMER: WOMEN'S INTEREST CONSUMER MAGAZINES: Lifestyle

TOY UPDATE
1658995U79F-83

Editorial Address: 15 Ravens Close, Knaphill, WOKING, GU21 2LD **Tel:** 01483 888378
Email: editor@toyupdate.co.uk
Web site: http://www.toyupdate.co.uk
Date Launched: 2005
Frequency of update: Weekly
Website Access: Paid
Editor: Ian Murphy
Summary of Content: Website covering toys from infants to grown ups.
Readership/Target Audience: Aimed predominantly at parents.
CONSUMER: HOBBIES & DIY: Games & Puzzles

TOYTALK
1837394U79F-111

Editorial Address: 5 Lache Park Avenue, CHESTER, CH4 8HR **Tel:** 01244 679103
Email: davidsmith@toytalk.co.uk
Web site: http://www.toytalk.co.uk
Publisher: Huckelberry Media
Date Launched: 2006
Frequency of update: Daily
Website Access: Free
Traffic Figures: 14,000 Unique Users (per month Publisher's Statement)
Editor: David Smith
Summary of Content: Website covering new toy releases for the UK market, features, reviews and interviews with those involved in the toy industry.
Readership/Target Audience: Aimed mainly at consumers of all ages as well as toy industry personnel.
CONSUMER: HOBBIES & DIY: Games & Puzzles

TPM ONLINE
629315U94X-190_10

Editorial Address: Dunstan House, 14A St. Cross Street, LONDON, EC1N 8XA **Tel:** 020 7841 1959
Fax: 020 7242 1474
Email: editor@philosophers.co.uk
Web site: http://www.philosophers.co.uk
Publisher: The Philosophy Press Ltd
Date Launched: 1997
Frequency of update: 182 times a year
Website Access: Free
Traffic Figures: 50,000 Unique Users (per week Publisher's Statement)
Editor: Julian Baggini
Summary of Content: Website focusing on philosophy. Includes news and features.
Readership/Target Audience: Aimed at professionals, students and those interested in philosophy.
Other Features: Features include an e-mail newsletter and various interactive activities.
CONSUMER: OTHER CLASSIFICATIONS: Miscellaneous

TRAINING REFERENCE
1644265U14F-236

Editorial Address: PO Box 3621, FROME, BA11 1ZR
Tel: 01373 300693 **Fax:** 01373 300693
Email: news@trainingreference.co.uk
Web site: http://www.trainingreference.co.uk
Date Launched: 2003
Frequency of update: Daily
Website Access: Free

Section 5 Internet Media

Traffic Figures: 60,784 Unique Users (Publisher's Statement)
Editor: Steve Haines
Summary of Content: Website covering training and development topics including awards; blended learning; business & professional skills; case studies/project announcements; conferences & events; e-learning; evaluation and return of investment; Government initiatives/agencies; IT user skills; IT professional skills; learning/skills management systems; research studies and reports and trainer skills.
Readership/Target Audience: Aimed at training, HR, IT and business professionals and managers.
Other Features: Buyers guide and newsletter.
BUSINESS: COMMERCE, INDUSTRY & MANAGEMENT: Training & Recruitment

TRAININGZONE
626272U14F-195

Editorial Address: 100 Victoria Street, BRISTOL, BS1 6HZ
Tel: 01453 768855 **Fax:** 0117 915 9630
Email: features@trainingzone.co.uk
Web site: http://www.trainingzone.co.uk
Publisher: Sift Media Ltd
Date Launched: 1998
Frequency of update: Daily
Website Access: Free
Traffic Figures: 45,000 Unique Users (Publisher's Statement)
Editor: Claire Savage
Summary of Content: Website containing features, news, comment, resources and information on training, learning and development.
Readership/Target Audience: Aimed at training professionals.
BUSINESS: COMMERCE, INDUSTRY & MANAGEMENT: Training & Recruitment

TRANSPORT INDUSTRY DIRECTORY
1912974U49A-427

Editorial Address: 18 Generator Hall, Electric Wharf, COVENTRY, CV1 4JL **Tel:** 0870 199 4044
Fax: 0870 777 4360
Email: enquiries@industrydirectory.co.uk
Web site: http://www.industrydirectory.co.uk
Publisher: Simply Marcomms
Frequency of update: Daily
Website Access: Free
Editor: Kirstie Colledge
Summary of Content: Directory containing the latest news stories for the UK transport industry. Includes news archives.
Readership/Target Audience: Aimed at Transportation & Logistics professionals, suppliers to the Transportation & Logistics industry, Transportation & Logistics PR & Marketing firms.
BUSINESS: TRANSPORT

TRANSPORT NEWS BRIEF
767258U49D-357

Formerly: CV News Brief
Editorial Address: Forbes House, Halkin Street, LONDON, SW1X 7DS **Tel:** 020 7344 9222
Email: rdickeson@smmt.co.uk
Web site: http://www.smmt.co.uk
Publisher: SMMT Ltd
Date Launched: 2001
Frequency of update: Weekly
Website Access: Free
Traffic Figures: 55,500 Unique Users (Publisher's Statement)
Editor: Robin Dickeson
Summary of Content: Email newsletter covering brief details on vans, trucks, buses and coaches, the aftermarket and road freight logistics.
Readership/Target Audience: Aimed at commercial vehicle and road transport industry professionals, senior civil servants, academics and commercial vehicle, road transport and automotive aftermarket industry journalists.
BUSINESS: TRANSPORT: Commercial Vehicles

TRAVEL CONNECT
1775364U89A-734

Editorial Address: Madeira House, Madeira Walk, WINDSOR, SL4 1EU **Tel:** 01753 860700
Email: dedwards@utmedia.co.uk
Web site: http://www.travelconnect.co.uk
Publisher: UTMedia
Date Launched: 2006
Frequency of update: Daily
Website Access: Free
Traffic Figures: 900,000 Unique Users (Publisher's Statement)
Editor: Newsdesk

Summary of Content: Website with travel guides, features, travel news, competitions and user reviews in Spain, France, USA, Italy, Thailand, luxury travel, activities and more.
Readership/Target Audience: Aimed at people of all ages looking to go on holiday. Including travel deals and travel reviews.
CONSUMER: HOLIDAYS & TRAVEL: Travel

TRAVEL WEEKLY ONLINE
713844U50-162

Editorial Address: Quadrant House, The Quadrant, SUTTON, SM2 5AS **Tel:** 020 8652 8230 **Fax:** 020 8652 3956
Email: michelle.perrett@travelweekly.co.uk
Web site: http://www.travelweekly.co.uk
Publisher: Reed Business Information
Date Launched: 2000
Frequency of update: Weekly
Website Access: Free
Traffic Figures: 24,000 Unique Users (per month Publisher's Statement)
Editor: Michelle Perrett; **Web Editor:** Nathan Midgley
Summary of Content: Website containing the latest travel news and information. Also includes offer of the week.
Readership/Target Audience: Aimed at travel agents, the travel industry, students looking to travel and tourists.
BUSINESS: TRAVEL & TOURISM

TRAVELBITE.CO.UK
1666799U89E-240

Editorial Address: South Quay Plaza, 183 Marsh Wall, LONDON, E14 9SH **Tel:** 020 7517 2268 **Fax:** 020 7517 2229
Email: news@travelbite.co.uk
Web site: http://www.travelbite.co.uk
Publisher: Adfero
Date Launched: 2004
Frequency of update: Daily
Website Access: Free
Traffic Figures: 45,000 Unique Users (per month Publisher's Statement)
Editor: Natasha von Geldern
Summary of Content: Website covering holiday destination features and travel news. The site carries news about specific destinations, as well as details of travel advice, last minute bargains and general travel trends.
Readership/Target Audience: Aimed at those planning a holiday and looking for holiday ideas, as well as those on extended breaks thinking about where to go next.
CONSUMER: HOLIDAYS & TRAVEL: Holidays

TRAVELINNOVATOR.COM
1882154U50-245

Editorial Address: PR by email only **Tel:** 0871 989 8619
Email: editordir@travelinnovator.com
Web site: http://www.travelinnovator.com
Publisher: EFE International
Frequency of update: Daily
Website Access: Free
Editor: Editorial Department
Summary of Content: Website featuring destination guides and news, sustainable tourism and travel updates, eco tourism, tourism and travel activities including trekking, diving, cruises, wildlife and nature, cultural travel, spas and wellness. Also offers accommodation information, flights, an events calendar, book reviews and a jobs and career section.
Readership/Target Audience: Aimed at the travel trade, event organisers, business travellers, societies, clubs and media.
BUSINESS: TRAVEL & TOURISM

TRAVELINTELLIGENCE.COM
1813573U89A-744

Editorial Address: PO Box, 44 Newman Street, LONDON, W1T 1QD **Tel:** 020 7580 2663 **Fax:** 020 7691 7535
Email: jeroen@travelintelligence.com
Web site: http://www.travelintelligence.com
Frequency of update: Daily
Website Access: Free
Traffic Figures: 150,000 Unique Users (per month Publisher's Statement)
Editor: Nadia Latif
Summary of Content: Website covering all aspects of luxury travel and providing an online booking service for 3000 hotels worldwide with reviews, articles and travel information.
Readership/Target Audience: Aimed at high spending travellers aged 25 years old and over.
CONSUMER: HOLIDAYS & TRAVEL: Travel

TRAVELMAIL.CO.UK
1813801U89A-745

Editorial Address: 2nd Floor, Northcliffe House, 2 Derry Street, LONDON, W8 5TT **Tel:** 020 7938 6000
Email: joanna.tweedy@travelmail.co.uk
Web site: http://www.travelmail.co.uk

Publisher: Associated Northcliffe Digital
Frequency of update: Daily
Website Access: Free
Editor: Joanna Tweedy
Summary of Content: Website covering inspiration, destination guides, reader reviews and expert advice.
Readership/Target Audience: Aimed at readers of the Daily Mail.
CONSUMER: HOLIDAYS & TRAVEL: Travel

TRAVELMOLE.COM
623544U50-61

Editorial Address: Heathcote, HASLEMERE, GU27 3QL
Tel: 01428 642765
Email: editor@travelmole.com
Web site: http://www.travelmole.com
Publisher: TravelMole Ltd
Date Launched: 1998
Frequency of update: Daily
Website Access: Free
Traffic Figures: 341,606 Unique Users (Publisher's Statement)
Editor: Bev Fearis
Summary of Content: Website covering the latest developments in the travel and tourism industry. Includes a travel industry reference directory of travel agents, tour operators, trade suppliers, airlines, airports, training providers, consultants, venues for training and conferences.
Readership/Target Audience: Aimed at travel agents, tour operators and trade suppliers to the travel industry.
BUSINESS: TRAVEL & TOURISM

TRAVMEDIA.COM
1666158U32H-463

Editorial Address: The Chandlery, 50 Westminster Bridge Road, LONDON, SE1 7QY **Tel:** 020 7953 8768
Fax: 020 7953 8773
Email: howard.salinger@travmedia-uk.com
Web site: http://www.travmedia.com
Frequency of update: Daily
Website Access: Paid
Traffic Figures: 8,000 Unique Users (Publisher's Statement)
Editor: Howard Salinger
Summary of Content: Online news site focusing on the travel and tourism industry, including industry contact details and a calendar of industry travel events.
Readership/Target Audience: Aimed at journalists and PR managers.
BUSINESS: LOCAL GOVERNMENT, LEISURE & RECREATION: Leisure, Recreation & Entertainment

TREASURY MANAGEMENT INTERNATIONAL
629522U1R-320

Editorial Address: Temple House, 20 Holywell Row, LONDON, EC2A 4XH **Tel:** 0118 947 8057
Fax: 0118 947 8062
Email: tmi@treasury-management.com
Web site: http://www.treasury-management.com
Publisher: P4 Publishing Ltd
Frequency of update: Monthly
Website Access: Free
Editor: Robin Page
Summary of Content: Website containing treasury information and topics such as the globalisation of business, the rising importance of the European, NSBP, Asian and emerging markets, and news of international treasury associations.
Readership/Target Audience: Read by multinational treasurers and professionals working within the treasury management industry.
BUSINESS: FINANCE & ECONOMICS: Financial Related

TRENDSTOP
1693380U47A-580

Editorial Address: The Qudarant, Units 28-39, 135 Salusbury Road, LONDON, NW6 6RJ **Tel:** 0870 788 6888
Fax: 0870 788 6886
Email: info@trendstop.com
Web site: http://www.trendstop.com
Date Launched: 2002
Frequency of update: Daily
Website Access: Paid
Traffic Figures: 20,000 Unique Users (Publisher's Statement)
Editor: Roisin Moloney
Summary of Content: Website providing fashion trend forecasting and information.
Readership/Target Audience: Aimed at all members of the fashion industry including retailers, students and designers.
BUSINESS: CLOTHING & TEXTILES

TRUSTEDREVIEWS.COM
1665341U78R-496

Formerly: TrustedReviews
Editorial Address: The Brackens, London Road, ASCOT, SL5 8BJ **Tel:** 01344 898480 **Fax:** 01344 898489
Email: editor@trustedreviews.com
Web site: http://www.trustedreviews.com
Publisher: IPC Media Ltd
Date Launched: 2003
Frequency of update: Daily
Website Access: Free
Traffic Figures: 2,456,763 Unique Users (01/11/2008 To 30/11/2008 ABC/Electronic)
Editor: Riyad Emeran; **Editor-in-Chief:** Riyad Emeran
Summary of Content: Website covering IT news, reviews, editorial and features. Specialist website includes notebooks, PCs, mobile phones and devices, digital cameras and camcorders, TVs, monitors, software, gaming, multimedia, MP3s, graphics, CPUs, memory, storage, networking and peripherals.
Readership/Target Audience: Aimed at consumers, businesses, IT enthusiasts and technology professionals.
CONSUMER: CONSUMER ELECTRONICS: Consumer Electronics Related

TRUSTNET
35314U1F-490

Editorial Address: 6th Floor, Roxburghe House, 273-287 Regent Street, LONDON, W1B 2HA **Tel:** 020 7408 8000
Fax: 020 7408 8001
Email: jonathan.boyd@financialexpress.net
Web site: http://www.trustnet.com
Publisher: Financial Express Limited
Date Launched: 1995
Frequency of update: Daily
Website Access: Free
Traffic Figures: 1,950,000 Unique Users (per year Publisher's Statement)
Editor: Jonathan Boyd; **Editor-in-Chief:** Jonathan Boyd
Summary of Content: Website providing UK investment fund information and educational material, with daily updates, interactive price and performance data, plus fund fact sheets, performance charts, dividend histories, fund ratings, portfolio management and analysis. Also includes education guides, specialist fund news services, search facilities and investment forums.
Readership/Target Audience: Aimed at private investors, financial advisers and financial industry professionals.
BUSINESS: FINANCE & ECONOMICS: Investment

TTG BUSINESS.COM
1805219U50-233

Editorial Address: 1st Floor, Ludgate House, 245 Blackfriars Road, LONDON, SE1 9UY **Tel:** 020 7921 8029
Fax: 020 7921 8032
Email: lhuxley@ttglive.com
Web site: http://www.ttgbusiness.com
Publisher: UBM Information Ltd
Date Launched: 2004
Frequency of update: Daily
Website Access: Free
Editor: Lucy Huxley
Summary of Content: Website featuring articles about business travel, interviews with industry leaders, green issues, city guides, airline reviews, statistical information and previews of industry events.
Readership/Target Audience: Aimed at business travel agents.
BUSINESS: TRAVEL & TOURISM

TUCO
1739879U11A-213

Editorial Address: Unit 2.4, Paintworks, Bath Road, BRISTOL, BS4 3EH **Tel:** 0117 902 9977 **Fax:** 0117 902 9978
Email: webmaster@tuco.org
Web site: http://www.tuco.org
Publisher: Wildfire Communications
Frequency of update: Daily
Website Access: Paid
Editor: Matthew Robinson
Summary of Content: Website of the University Caterers Organisation. Covers news, information and promotions.
Readership/Target Audience: Aimed at catering managers, chefs, university staff and colleges in the UK.
BUSINESS: CATERING: Catering, Hotels & Restaurants

TWOHUNDREDBY200
1698076U84A-447

Editorial Address: 16 Linton Place, Rosyth, DUNFERMLINE, KY11 2YY **Tel:** 01383 417667
Email: info@twohundredby200.co.uk
Web site: http://www.twohundredby200.co.uk
Publisher: twohundredby200
Date Launched: 2003
Frequency of update: 6 times a year
Website Access: Free

Traffic Figures: 5,000,000 Unique Users (per month Publisher's Statement)
Editor: Sean Makin
Summary of Content: Website focusing on the creative arts including graphic design, cgi graphics, motion graphics, web design, print design, computer art, software, computer related products, alternative culture, photography, poetry, illustration, music and literature.
Readership/Target Audience: Aimed at creatives, designers, students and artists.
Other Features: Daily creative related news feed and competitions.
CONSUMER: THE ARTS & LITERARY: Arts

TYNE AND WEAR MATTERS
1881685U72J-428

Email: comments@tyneandwear-matters.co.uk
Web site: http://www.tyneandwear-matters.co.uk
Frequency of update: Daily
Summary of Content: Website created to help people who care about local issues. Whether you need access to useful information, want to highlight a particular topic to other people, discuss ideas with like-minded people or just show your support and keep up to date with current affairs in your area, Tyne and Wear Matters is the place for you.
Readership/Target Audience: Aimed at residents in the local area of Tyne and Wear.
LOCAL NEWSPAPERS: Community Newsletters

TYRES ONLINE
38327U31A-180

Editorial Address: PO Box 320, CREWE, CW2 6WY
Tel: 01270 668718 **Fax:** 01270 668801
Email: tyres-online@tyres-online.co.uk
Web site: http://www.tyres-online.co.uk
Publisher: Retreading Business Ltd
Date Launched: 1996
Frequency of update: Daily
Website Access: Free
Traffic Figures: 50,000 Unique Users (per month Publisher's Statement)
Editor: David Wilson
Summary of Content: Website covering information and news about the tyre trade, plus consumer interest features.
Readership/Target Audience: Aimed at both consumers and those who work in the tyre trade.
BUSINESS: MOTOR TRADE: Motor Trade Accessories

TYRETRADE NEWS ONLINE
749229U31A-202

Editorial Address: 6B Acorn Farm Business Centre, Cublington Road, WING, LU7 0LB **Tel:** 01296 681424
Fax: 01296 682628
Email: tyres@tyretradenews.co.uk
Web site: http://www.tyretradenews.co.uk
Publisher: Technique Publishing Co Ltd
Date Launched: 1993
Frequency of update: Daily
Website Access: Free
Editor: Mike Scanlon
Summary of Content: Website containing the latest news and retail reviews in the tyre industry.
Readership/Target Audience: Aimed at those working in the tyre industry.
BUSINESS: MOTOR TRADE: Motor Trade Accessories

UK FUNDRAISING
711751U1P-245

Editorial Address: 17 Errington Road, COLCHESTER, CO3 3EA **Tel:** 01206 579081 **Fax:** 07092 028510
Email: hlake@fundraising.co.uk
Web site: http://www.fundraising.co.uk
Publisher: Fundraising UK Ltd
Date Launched: 1994
Frequency of update: Daily
Website Access: Free
Traffic Figures: 21,000 Unique Users (Publisher's Statement)
Editor: Howard Lake
Summary of Content: Website focusing on helping charities to use the Internet as a fundraising tool. Provides information about events for fundraisers, fundraising bookshop, links to fundraising news and organisations providing information and services useful to UK charity fundraisers.
Readership/Target Audience: Aimed at UK and international charities involved in fundraising.
Other Features: 14 years of archived news. A discussion forum with 12 years of archives, suppliers directory and a fortnightly email newsletter. Latest jobs listings, blogs by leading fundraising thinkers/practitioners, Ireland section (Republic and Northern Ireland), suppliers directory, extensive RSS feeds available, and aggregated feeds from other fundraising-related sites.
BUSINESS: FINANCE & ECONOMICS: Fundraising

UK HOT MOVIES.COM
1696116U76A-184

Editorial Address: 52 Bloomsbury Street, LONDON, WC1B 3QT **Tel:** 0870 870 2222 **Fax:** 0870 870 2223
Email: support@UKHotMovies.com
Web site: http://www.ukhotmovies.com
Frequency of update: Daily
Website Access: Free
Traffic Figures: 220,000 Unique Users (Publisher's Statement)
Editor: Michael Laker
Summary of Content: Website covering film reviews, box office charts, competitions and games.
Readership/Target Audience: Aimed at 18 to 45 year olds interested in the latest film releases.
CONSUMER: MUSIC & PERFORMING ARTS: Cinema

THE UK INSOLVENCY HELPLINE
629602U74M-97

Editorial Address: 788-790 Finchley Road, LONDON, NW11 7TJ **Tel:** 0 845 612 2626
Email: ian@insolvencyhelpline.co.uk
Web site: http://www.insolvencyhelpline.co.uk
Frequency of update: Weekly
Website Access: Free
Traffic Figures: 30,000 Unique Users (per month Publisher's Statement)
Summary of Content: Website focusing on promoting the UK bankruptcy and insolvency profession with debt and credit advice. Includes official announcements and notices regarding insolvency.
Readership/Target Audience: Aimed at the general public.
CONSUMER: WOMEN'S INTEREST CONSUMER MAGAZINES: Personal Finance

UK THEATRE NETWORK
1748244U76B-352

Editorial Address: PO Box 3009, Old Kilpatrick, GLASGOW, G60 5ET **Tel:** 0870 760 6033 **Fax:** 0870 760 6033
Email: editor@uktheatre.net
Web site: http://www.uktheatre.net
Publisher: Interactors Management (Scotland) Ltd
Date Launched: 2001
Frequency of update: Daily
Website Access: Paid
Traffic Figures: 20,000 Unique Users (per month Publisher's Statement)
Editor: Douglas McFarlane
Summary of Content: Website covering theatre and Internet TV with interviews, reviews, previews and feature articles.
Readership/Target Audience: Aimed at audiences and those who work in the profession.
CONSUMER: MUSIC & PERFORMING ARTS: Theatre

UK THEATRE WEB
46080U76B-300

Editorial Address: 37 Severn Avenue, WESTON-SUPER-MARE, BS23 4DG **Tel:** 01934 626344
Email: info@uktw.co.uk
Web site: http://www.uktw.co.uk
Date Launched: 1995
Frequency of update: Daily
Website Access: Free
Traffic Figures: 5,000 Unique Users (per day Publisher's Statement)
Editor: Frances Iles
Summary of Content: Website providing information about theatres and performing art groups within the UK.
Readership/Target Audience: Aimed at those interested in plays, musicals, opera, dance and films.
Other Features: Features include a discussion forum and archiving.
CONSUMER: MUSIC & PERFORMING ARTS: Theatre

UKAUTHORITY.COM
766092U32A-252

Editorial Address: PO Box 2087, SHOREHAM-BY-SEA, BN43 5ZF **Tel:** 01273 273941
Email: helen@infopub.co.uk
Web site: http://www.ukauthority.com
Publisher: Informed Publications Ltd
Date Launched: 2001
Frequency of update: Daily
Website Access: Free
Editor: Helen Olsen
Summary of Content: Website reporting news on the development of local e-government and policy.
Readership/Target Audience: Aimed at local government officers involved in the implementation of local e-government.
BUSINESS: LOCAL GOVERNMENT, LEISURE & RECREATION: Local Government

Internet Media

UKGAYNEWS.ORG.UK
1844884U86B-185

Editorial Address: PR by email only
Email: editorial@ukgaynews.org.uk
Web site: http://www.ukgaynews.org.uk
Frequency of update: Daily
Website Access: Free
Traffic Figures: 500,000 Unique Users (per month Publisher's Statement)
Editor: Andy Harley
Summary of Content: Website covering lgbt news worldwide, human rights and events.
Readership/Target Audience: Aimed at lgbt communities.
CONSUMER: ADULT & GAY MAGAZINES: Gay & Lesbian Magazines

UK-GOLFGUIDE.COM
45831U75D-280

Formerly: UK-GOLF
Editorial Address: Tigh Osda, Charleston, North Kessock, INVERNESS, IV1 3YA **Tel:** 01463 731566
Email: ms@uk-golfguide.com
Web site: http://www.uk-golfguide.com
Publisher: Cosys Management Information Services
Date Launched: 1995
Frequency of update: Daily
Website Access: Free
Traffic Figures: 250,000 Unique Users (per month Publisher's Statement)
Editor: John Tuach
Summary of Content: Website providing details of UK golf courses, hotels, services and suppliers.
Readership/Target Audience: Aimed at travelling golfers.
Other Features: Features include a chat forum and an e-mail newsletter.
CONSUMER: SPORT: Golf

UKPETS
630341U81X-500

Editorial Address: Lynnwood Business Centre, Lynnwood Terrace, NEWCASTLE UPON TYNE, NE4 6UL
Tel: 0191 284 4131
Email: admin@ukpets.co.uk
Web site: http://www.ukpets.co.uk
Publisher: UKPets Partnership
Date Launched: 1999
Frequency of update: Daily
Website Access: Free
Traffic Figures: 20,000 Unique Users (per month Publisher's Statement)
Editor: Steve O'Malley
Summary of Content: Website containing news and information for the pet industry and pet owners in the UK. Includes up to date news regarding the pet industry and a directory listing all pets services in the UK, charities, clubs and journals.
Readership/Target Audience: Read by those with pets looking to locate pet products, pet shops, groomers and vets.
Other Features: Features include a discussion forum, recruitment, an e-mail newsletter and archiving.
CONSUMER: ANIMALS & PETS

UNIQUE
1667146U62G-424

Editorial Address: 43 Scotland Road, NELSON, BB9 7UT
Tel: 01282 604387 **Fax:** 01282 604326
Email: karen@looppublishing.co.uk
Web site: http://www.unique-magazine.co.uk
Publisher: Loop Publishing Ltd
Date Launched: 2005
Frequency of update: Daily
Website Access: Free
Editor: Karen Shaw
Summary of Content: Online magazine focusing on special educational needs that bridges the gap between mainstream and specialist education.
Readership/Target Audience: Aimed at colleges, resource centres and schools, teachers, head teachers, parents and educational professionals.
BUSINESS: CHURCH & SCHOOL EQUIPMENT & EDUCATION: Special Needs Education

UNQUOTENEWS.COM
1750390U1F-619

Editorial Address: 4th Floor, Haymarket House, 28-29 Haymarket, LONDON, SW1Y 4RX **Tel:** 020 7004 7526
Fax: 020 7004 7548
Email: kimberly.romaine@incisivemedia.com
Web site: http://www.unquote.com
Publisher: Incisive Media Investments
Date Launched: 2006
Frequency of update: Daily
Website Access: Free
Traffic Figures: 6,332 Unique Users (Publisher's Statement)

Editor: Kimberly Romaine; **Editor-in-Chief:** Kimberly Romaine
Summary of Content: Website providing daily breaking news stories on private equity, venture capital and fund raising.
Readership/Target Audience: Aimed at private equity companies and advisers.
BUSINESS: FINANCE & ECONOMICS: Investment

UNSTRUNG
763550U18B-1944

Editorial Address: 42 Hookfield, EPSOM, SURREY, KT19 8JG **Tel:** 020 8224 8268
Email: lemaistre@lightreading.com
Web site: http://www.unstrung.com
Publisher: Light Reading Inc
Date Launched: 2000
Frequency of update: Daily
Website Access: Free
Editor: Ray Le Maistre
Summary of Content: Website that's the 'Home of 4G' covering the wireless network, infrastructure markets, daily news coverage of the wireless industry as well as monthly reports, CEO interviews and webinars.
Readership/Target Audience: Aimed at telecommunications professionals.
BUSINESS: ELECTRONICS: Telecommunications

UPSTART
48443U91D-5

Formerly: 95 Per Cent
Editorial Address: Fairways House, Mount Pleasant Road, SOUTHAMPTON, SO14 0QB **Tel:** 023 8063 0960
Fax: 023 8063 2949
Email: virginia@artswork.org.uk
Web site: http://www.artswork.org.uk
Publisher: Artswork
Frequency of update: Daily
Website Access: Paid
Editor: Virginia Haworth
Summary of Content: Website dedicated to promoting youth arts work and raising the profile of young people's creativity.
Readership/Target Audience: Read by youth arts workers.
CONSUMER: RECREATION & LEISURE: Children & Youth

URBANPLANET.CO.UK
1800268U89C-1100

Editorial Address: Madeira House, Madeira Walk, WINDSOR, SL4 1EU **Tel:** 01753 860700
Email: dedwards@utmedia.co.uk
Web site: http://www.urbanplanet.co.uk
Publisher: UTMedia
Frequency of update: Daily
Website Access: Free
Traffic Figures: 900,000 Unique Users (Publisher's Statement)
Editor: Newsdesk
Summary of Content: Website covering music, unsigned bands, entertainment, indie, rock and roll, hip hop, interviews, celebrities, DVDs, competitions, events, festivals, what's on, clubbing, music reviews, new bands, band interviews, gig guides, Ibiza and competitions.
Readership/Target Audience: Aimed at those aged 18 to 35 years old interested in music, clubbing, gigging and going out.
CONSUMER: HOLIDAYS & TRAVEL: Entertainment Guides

UTALKMARKETING
1800066U2A-693

Editorial Address: Suite 2.1B, The Old Fire Station, 140 Tabernacle Street, LONDON, EC2A 4SD **Tel:** 020 7300 7333
Email: news@utalkmarketing.com
Web site: http://www.utalkmarketing.com
Publisher: McKinney Media
Date Launched: 2006
Frequency of update: Daily
Website Access: Free
Traffic Figures: 131,000 Unique Users (Publisher's Statement)
Editor: Clark Turner
Summary of Content: News and community website for the marketing and PR industry showcasing advertising creative and featuring best practice, white papers, help and advice.
Readership/Target Audience: Aimed at marketing and PR professionals.
BUSINESS: COMMUNICATIONS, ADVERTISING & MARKETING

UVONLINE
626493U49R-400_1

Editorial Address: 268 Bath Road, SLOUGH, SL1 4DX
Tel: 01753 727001 **Fax:** 01753 727002
Email: news@uvonline.com
Web site: http://www.uvonline.com

Publisher: The Shephard Group
Date Launched: 2000
Frequency of update: Daily
Website Access: Free
Traffic Figures: 43,000 Unique Users (per month Publisher's Statement)
Editor: Darren Lake
Summary of Content: Website covering news, contracts, trends and developments for the unmanned vehicle industry.
Readership/Target Audience: Aimed at military and civilian professionals in the unmanned vehicles industry.
BUSINESS: TRANSPORT: Transport Related

V3.CO.UK
36137U5B-231_50

Formerly: vnunet.com
Editorial Address: 32-34 Broadwick Street, LONDON, W1A 2HG **Tel:** 020 7316 9000 **Fax:** 020 7316 9440
Email: madeline.bennett@incisivemedia.com
Web site: http://www.v3.co.uk/
Publisher: Incisive Media
Frequency of update: Daily
Website Access: Free
Traffic Figures: 170,364 Unique Users (ABC/Electronic)
Editor: Madeline Bennett
Summary of Content: Website containing news, features, business and technical information on IT.
Readership/Target Audience: Read by Internet users interested in consumer and business technology news.
BUSINESS: COMPUTERS & AUTOMATION: Data Processing

VEHICLE ENGINEER
38330U31A-253

Editorial Address: Pike's Peak, Finchampstead, WOKINGHAM, RG40 4RD **Tel:** 0118 973 3435
Fax: 0118 932 8185
Email: ve@pikespeak.demon.co.uk
Web site: http://www.vehicle-engineer.com
Publisher: Motor Industry Publishing Ltd
Date Launched: 1988
Frequency of update: Updated when new information is received
Website Access: Free
Editor: Anne Hope
Summary of Content: Journal covering vehicle design, body structures, body equipment, powertrain and running gear, oil and all components in vehicle (car, trucks, hybrid and other vehicles) manufacture, engineering and design.
Readership/Target Audience: Aimed at vehicle engineering specialists and those interested in automotive design.
Other Features: News, Archive material, reviews, events and industry.
BUSINESS: MOTOR TRADE: Motor Trade Accessories

VERDICT ON CARS
1706842U77A-594

Editorial Address: 2 Shad Thames, LONDON, SE1 2YU
Tel: 020 7234 0221 **Fax:** 020 7403 8096
Email: jnagley@redspy.co.uk
Web site: http://www.verdictoncars.com
Date Launched: 2003
Frequency of update: Daily
Website Access: Free
Traffic Figures: 38,000 Unique Users (per month Publisher's Statement)
Editor: Jay Nagley
Summary of Content: Website covering daily news, vehicle road tests and specifications of new cars.
Readership/Target Audience: Aimed at those looking to buy a new car.
CONSUMER: MOTORING & CYCLING: Motoring

VETNURSE.CO.UK
1755674U64H-245

Editorial Address: Frog Pond Farm, Ansty Coombe Lane, Ansty, SALISBURY, SP3 5PY **Tel:** 020 7183 2511
Email: support@vetnurse.co.uk
Web site: http://www.vetnurse.co.uk
Publisher: Guthrie Communications Ltd
Date Launched: 2000
Frequency of update: Daily
Website Access: Free
Editor: Arlo Guthrie
Summary of Content: Online information resource providing news, clinical articles, diary events, training materials and job opportunities of interest to the veterinary profession.
Readership/Target Audience: Aimed at veterinary nurses, assistants, students and practice support staff.
BUSINESS: OTHER CLASSIFICATIONS: Veterinary

VETSURGEON.ORG
1823978U64H-247

Editorial Address: Frog Pond Farm, Ansty Coombe Lane, Ansty, SALISBURY, SP3 5PY **Tel:** 020 7183 2511
Email: editor@vetsurgeon.org
Web site: http://www.vetsurgeon.org
Publisher: Guthrie Communications Ltd
Date Launched: 2007
Frequency of update: Daily
Website Access: Free
Editor: Arlo Guthrie
Summary of Content: Website covering all aspects of veterinary medicine and practice featuring a newsfeed, veterinary forums, products and services, jobs and a CPD and events diary.
Readership/Target Audience: Aimed at veterinary surgeons and practice managers.
BUSINESS: OTHER CLASSIFICATIONS: Veterinary

VIEW.CO.UK
1848133U89C-1111

Editorial Address: D304, 116 Commercial Street, LONDON, E1 6NF **Tel:** 020 7247 1525
Email: lisa.ellwood@view.co.uk
Web site: http://www.view.co.uk
Publisher: 2View Group
Frequency of update: Daily
Website Access: Free
Traffic Figures: 1,400,000 Unique Users (per month Publisher's Statement)
Editor: Lisa Ellwood
Summary of Content: Website with entertainment guides for British cities including what's on, pubs, clubs and restaurants, cinema reviews, hotels, experiences and competitions.
Readership/Target Audience: Aimed at local residents in cities across the UK aged 18 to 45 years old.
CONSUMER: HOLIDAYS & TRAVEL: Entertainment Guides

VIEWLONDON.CO.UK
1615356U89C-952

Editorial Address: D304, 116 Commercial Street, LONDON, E1 6NF **Tel:** 020 7247 1525
Email: lisa.ellwood@view.co.uk
Web site: http://www.viewlondon.co.uk
Publisher: 2View Group
Date Launched: 2001
Frequency of update: Daily
Website Access: Free
Traffic Figures: 1,400,000 Unique Users (per month Publisher's Statement)
Editor: Lisa Ellwood
Summary of Content: Website providing a listings and entertainment guide for those who live or work in London. Also contains daily changing lifestyle features and reviews of venues in London. Restaurant, bar, club and cinema reviews.
Readership/Target Audience: Aimed at Londoners between 18 and 45 years old.
Other Features: Newsletters
CONSUMER: HOLIDAYS & TRAVEL: Entertainment Guides

VIP
1641628U14A-519

Editorial Address: 4-6 Station Approach, ASHFORD, TW15 2QN **Tel:** 0870 141 7474
Web site: http://www.vivavip.com
Publisher: Free Pint Limited
Date Launched: 2003
Frequency of update: Monthly
Website Access: Paid
Editor: Tim Buckley Owen
Summary of Content: PDF magazine focusing on business information products and information people, including product reviews and comparisons, monitoring of research and interviews, news comment and analysis.
Readership/Target Audience: Aimed at business information professionals.
Other Features: LiveWire editorial blog from Senior Editor and other contributors commenting on news in the industry.
BUSINESS: COMMERCE, INDUSTRY & MANAGEMENT

VIRTUAL BRIGHTON AND HOVE
48150U89C-503

Editorial Address: The Brighton Media Centre, 9-12 Middle Street, BRIGHTON, BN1 1AL **Tel:** 01273 381100
Fax: 01273 381120
Email: rowan.richardson@brighton.co.uk
Web site: http://www.brighton.co.uk
Publisher: NTD
Date Launched: 1995
Frequency of update: Daily
Website Access: Free
Traffic Figures: 1,000,000 Unique Users (per year Publisher's Statement)

Editor: Rowan Richardson
Summary of Content: Website providing information on local facilities and entertainment in the Brighton and Hove area.
Readership/Target Audience: Aimed at tourists, ex-pats, locals, students and conference delegates.
Other Features: Features include chat forums, recruitment, an email newsletter, message board and archiving.
CONSUMER: HOLIDAYS & TRAVEL: Entertainment Guides

VIRTUAL LONDON
1613621U80B-386

Editorial Address: Weston Bank, Weston-under-Lizard, SHIFNAL, TF11 8JU **Tel:** 01952 852200 **Fax:** 01952 850445
Email: rowbothams@vip-internet.com
Web site: http://www.virtual-london.com
Publisher: VIP Internet Ltd
Date Launched: 1995
Frequency of update: Daily
Website Access: Free
Traffic Figures: 340,000 Unique Users (Publisher's Statement)
Editor: Stuart Rowbotham
Summary of Content: A comprehensive guide to London's attractions, theatres and leisure venues.
Readership/Target Audience: Aimed at UK and overseas tourists visiting the capital.
CONSUMER: RURAL & REGIONAL INTEREST: Regional Interest Greater London

VIRUS BULLETIN
36309U5R-487

Editorial Address: The Pentagon, Abingdon Science Park, ABINGDON, OX14 3YP **Tel:** 01235 555139
Fax: 01865 543153
Email: editorial@virusbtn.com
Web site: http://www.virusbtn.com
Publisher: Virus Bulletin Ltd
Date Launched: 1989
Frequency of update: Monthly
Website Access: Paid
Traffic Figures: 1,000 Unique Users (Publisher's Statement)
Editor: Helen Martin
Summary of Content: Website featuring reports and analysis of malicious computer programs. Monitors new developments in virus and spam prevention and removal.
Readership/Target Audience: Aimed at those involved with anti-virus computer security.
BUSINESS: COMPUTERS & AUTOMATION: Computers Related

VISION ONLINE
765132U64E-76

Editorial Address: Elmtree Business Park, Elmswell, BURY ST EDMUNDS, IP30 9HR **Tel:** 01359 243400
Fax: 01359 242921
Email: editor@visionline.co.uk
Web site: http://www.visionline.co.uk
Publisher: AT Veterinary Systems Ltd
Frequency of update: Weekly
Website Access: Free
Traffic Figures: 10,000 Unique Users (Publisher's Statement)
Editor: Amanda Smith
Summary of Content: Website providing relevant news for all members of the veterinary profession.
Readership/Target Audience: Aimed at veterinary workers, practice managers, universities, animal welfare workers, animal charities, veterinary research institutes and all veterinary organisations.
Other Features: Features include mailing lists, newsletter and archiving.
BUSINESS: OTHER CLASSIFICATIONS: Pet Trade

VISIT LONDON
1642359U80B-416

Editorial Address: 2 More London Riverside, LONDON, SE1 2RR **Tel:** 020 7234 5800
Email: editorial@visitlondon.com
Web site: http://www.visitlondon.com
Frequency of update: Daily
Website Access: Free
Traffic Figures: 1,000,000 Unique Users (per month Publisher's Statement)
Editor: Julie Chappell
Summary of Content: Website covering travel, sport, theatre, what's on, restaurants, attractions, shopping and accommodation.
Readership/Target Audience: Aimed at overseas and resident visitors to London as well as those who live and work there.
CONSUMER: RURAL & REGIONAL INTEREST: Regional Interest Greater London

VISITBORNEO.COM
754518U50-185

Editorial Address: PR by email only **Tel:** 0871 983 7367
Fax: 0871 983 7368
Email: editor@visitborneo.com
Web site: http://www.visitborneo.com
Publisher: EFE International
Date Launched: 2000
Frequency of update: Daily
Website Access: Free
Traffic Figures: 350,000 Unique Users (Publisher's Statement)
Editor: R. Pas; **Web Editor:** R. Pas
Summary of Content: Website covering travel and destination features, tours, accommodation, hotels, overseas property, flights, diving, golf, wildlife, nature, trekking, adventure, eco tourism and eco projects, sustainable developments, activity and wildlife holidays, travel info, spas, culture and an events calendar.
Readership/Target Audience: Aimed at leisure and business travellers and travel trade.
BUSINESS: TRAVEL & TOURISM

VISITSCOTLAND.COM
1639215U80E-355

Editorial Address: 6 Fairways Business Park, Deer Park Avenue, LIVINGSTON, EH54 8AF **Tel:** 01506 832100
Fax: 01506 832111
Email: editorial@visitscotland.com
Web site: http://www.visitscotland.com
Publisher: visitscotland.com
Frequency of update: Daily
Website Access: Free
Traffic Figures: 100,000 Unique Users (per week Publisher's Statement)
Editor: James Carney
Summary of Content: Website covering tourist-related information including accommodation-booking, attractions, events and travel.
Readership/Target Audience: Aimed at those planning to visit Scotland and those who have already booked to do so.
Other Features: Other features include online late-offer accommodation booking, newsletter, mailing lisat and book purchase.
CONSUMER: RURAL & REGIONAL INTEREST: Regional Interest Scotland

VISORDOWN.COM
1809922U77B-721

Editorial Address: 15-18 White Lion Street, Islington, LONDON, N1 9PD **Tel:** 020 7843 8819
Email: news@visordown.com
Web site: http://www.visordown.com
Publisher: Magicalia Ltd
Frequency of update: Daily
Website Access: Free
Traffic Figures: 248,000 Unique Users (per month Publisher's Statement)
Editor: Ben Cope
Summary of Content: Online motorcycle community with daily motorcycle news, reviews, features and forums, product reviews and accessories.
Readership/Target Audience: Aimed at UK motorcyclists and anyone with an interest in motorcycles.
CONSUMER: MOTORING & CYCLING: Motorcycling

VOGUE ONLINE
45233U74B-650

Formerly: vogue.co.uk
Editorial Address: 25 Maddox Street, LONDON, W1S 2QN
Tel: 020 7152 3132 **Fax:** 020 7493 1469
Email: vogue.com.editor@condenast.co.uk
Web site: http://www.vogue.co.uk
Publisher: Conde Nast Publications Ltd
Date Launched: 1995
Frequency of update: Daily
Website Access: Free
Traffic Figures: 1,300,000 Unique Users (per month Publisher's Statement)
Editor: Dolly Jones
Summary of Content: Website covering daily news on fashion and beauty. Includes competitions.
Readership/Target Audience: Aimed at professional women aged 20 to 44 years of age.
Other Features: Features include recruitment and chat forums.
CONSUMER: WOMEN'S INTEREST CONSUMER MAGAZINES: Women's Interest - Fashion

VOLTIMUM
1623136U17-252

Formerly: Voltimum UK
Editorial Address: 54 Applesham Avenue, HOVE, BN3 8JJ
Tel: 01273 725322
Email: james.hunt11@btopenworld.com
Web site: http://www.voltimum.co.uk

Publisher: Voltimum UK & Ireland Ltd
Date Launched: 2002
Frequency of update: Daily
Website Access: Paid
Traffic Figures: 67,000 Unique Users (Publisher's Statement)
Editor: James Hunt
Summary of Content: Website providing a source of electrical installation news, product information and technical/ standards issues across the UK and Europe.
Readership/Target Audience: Aimed at electrical specifiers and contractors.
BUSINESS: ELECTRICAL

VOLUNTEERING
38501U32G-136_50

Editorial Address: Regent's Wharf, 8 All Saints Street, LONDON, N1 9RL **Tel:** 020 7520 8957 **Fax:** 020 7520 8910
Email: magazine@volunteeringengland.org
Web site: http://www.volunteering.org.uk
Publisher: The Volunteering England
Date Launched: 1995
Frequency of update: 10 times a year
Website Access: Free
Traffic Figures: 1,300 Unique Users (Publisher's Statement)
Editor: Penny Gee
Summary of Content: Website focusing on volunteering, covering policy and practical issues.
Readership/Target Audience: Read by managers and individuals working with volunteers.
BUSINESS: LOCAL GOVERNMENT, LEISURE & RECREATION: Community Care & Social Services

WAKEFIELD TODAY
629785U67B-1130

Editorial Address: Express House, Southgate, WAKEFIELD, WF1 1TE **Tel:** 01924 375111 **Fax:** 01924 433040
Email: editorial@wakefieldexpress.co.uk
Web site: http://www.wakefieldexpress.co.uk
Date Launched: 1999
Frequency of update: Daily
Website Access: Free
Editor: Lisa Rookes; **Web Editor:** John Baron
Summary of Content: Website containing news, sport, information and features about Wakefield.
Readership/Target Audience: Read by residents and visitors to the local area.
Other Features: Features include recruitment, discussion forums, a buyer's guide, an events calendar and archiving.
REGIONAL DAILY & SUNDAY NEWSPAPERS: Regional Daily Newspapers

WALTHAM FOREST MATTERS
1881686U72J-429

Web site: http://www.walthamforest-matters.co.uk
Frequency of update: Daily
Summary of Content: Website created to help people who care about local issues. Whether you need access to useful information, want to highlight a particular topic to other people, discuss ideas with like-minded people or just show your support and keep up to date with current affairs in your area, Waltham Forest Matters is the place for you.
Readership/Target Audience: Aimed at residents in the local area of Waltham Forest.
LOCAL NEWSPAPERS: Community Newsletters

WANDSWORTH MATTERS
1881687U72J-430

Email: comments@wandsworth-matters.co.uk
Web site: http://www.wandsworth-matters.co.uk
Frequency of update: Daily
Summary of Content: Website created to help people who care about local issues. Whether you need access to useful information, want to highlight a particular topic to other people, discuss ideas with like-minded people or just show your support and keep up to date with current affairs in your area, Wandsworth Matters is the place for you.
Readership/Target Audience: Aimed at residents in the local area of Wandsworth.
LOCAL NEWSPAPERS: Community Newsletters

WARC NEWS
623984U2F-80

Formerly: World Advertising & Marketing News
Editorial Address: 1 Farm Road, HENLEY-ON-THAMES, RG9 1EJ **Tel:** 01491 411000 **Fax:** 01491 418600
Email: news@warc.com
Web site: http://www.warc.com
Publisher: World Advertising Research Center
Date Launched: 2000
Frequency of update: Daily
Website Access: Free
Traffic Figures: 76,579 Unique Users (01/11/2008 To 30/11/2008 ABC/Electronic)

Editor: Peter Scott-Smith
Summary of Content: Electronically mailed newsletter covering the advertising and marketing industry.
Readership/Target Audience: Aimed at marketing and advertising professionals plus academics.
BUSINESS: COMMUNICATIONS, ADVERTISING & MARKETING: Selling

WARWICKSHIRE GOLF
707924U75D-290

Editorial Address: Westfield Lodge, Moreton Morrell, WARWICK, CV35 9DB **Tel:** 01926 650173
Email: editor@warksgolf.co.uk
Web site: http://www.warksgolf.co.uk
Publisher: FGA Ltd
Date Launched: 2001
Frequency of update: Daily
Website Access: Free
Traffic Figures: 68,000 Unique Users (Publisher's Statement)
Editor: David Morgan
Summary of Content: Website providing information about golf in Warwickshire. Includes clubs, competitions, league information, professional tournaments, interviews, course features, information about holiday destinations and cars.
Readership/Target Audience: Aimed at those interested in golf in Warwickshire and the Midlands and anyone who wants to visit Warwickshire.
Other Features: Features include a buyer's guide, recruitment, an events calendar and archiving.
CONSUMER: SPORT: Golf

WARWICKSHIRE MATTERS
1881688U72J-431

Email: comments@warwickshire-matters.co.uk
Web site: http://www.warwickshire-matters.co.uk
Frequency of update: Daily
Summary of Content: Website created to help people who care about local issues. Whether you need access to useful information, want to highlight a particular topic to other people, discuss ideas with like-minded people or just show your support and keep up to date with current affairs in your area, Warwickshire Matters is the place for you.
Readership/Target Audience: Aimed at residents in the local area of Warwickshire.
LOCAL NEWSPAPERS: Community Newsletters

THE WASTE PAPER
1743030U57-150

Formerly: The Waste Paper Magazine
Editorial Address: 57 Prince Street, BRISTOL, BS1 4QH **Tel:** 0117 903 0698 **Fax:** 0117 907 7214
Email: charles@resource.uk.com
Web site: http://www.crn.org.uk/wastepaper
Publisher: Resource Media Ltd
Date Launched: 1986
Frequency of update: Monthly
Website Access: Paid
Traffic Figures: 6,000 Unique Users (Publisher's Statement)
Editor: Charles Newman
Summary of Content: Electronic newsletter covering sustainable waste management, recycling, re-use, composting and waste minimisation.
Readership/Target Audience: Aimed at community waste organisations, local government recycling officers, central government waste officers and the private sector.
BUSINESS: ENVIRONMENT & POLLUTION

WATER BRIEFING
1776087U42C-762

Editorial Address: Castlemead, Lower Castle Street, BRISTOL, BS1 3AG **Tel:** 0117 917 5310 **Fax:** 0117 917 5005
Email: elaine.coles@imsplc.com
Web site: http://www.waterbriefing.org
Publisher: IMS
Date Launched: 2006
Frequency of update: Daily
Website Access: Free
Editor: Elaine Coles
Summary of Content: Web based and business intelligence portal covering water and wastewater supply and management, AMP4, environmental issues and legislation, market intelligence, forthcoming tender opportunities, situations vacant and user forum as well as in depth news, market analysis and intelligence and company and product information.
Readership/Target Audience: Aimed at buyers and specifiers in the European Water Industry.
Other Features: Online retrieval of news information from over 12000 sources, recruitment, buyers guide, FAQs, reader forum, white papers, application stories and industry intelligence reports.
BUSINESS: CONSTRUCTION: Water Engineering

WATER TECHNOLOGY
1616312U42C-752

Editorial Address: Brunel House, 55-57 North Wharf Road, LONDON, W2 1LA **Tel:** 020 7915 9957 **Fax:** 020 7915 9720
Email: production@spgmedia.com
Web site: http://www.water-technology.net
Publisher: SPG Media Ltd
Date Launched: 1999
Frequency of update: Daily
Website Access: Free
Traffic Figures: 42,276 Unique Users (per month Publisher's Statement)
Editor: Duncan West
Summary of Content: Website covering water technology projects both in production and under development as well as products and services, conferences, exhibitions and events.
Readership/Target Audience: Aimed at those working within the water industries.
BUSINESS: CONSTRUCTION: Water Engineering

WATERSTONES.COM
1849740U84B-372

Editorial Address: Capital Court, Capital Interchange Way, BRENTFORD, TW8 0EX **Tel:** 020 8742 3800
Email: greg.eden@waterstones.com
Web site: http://www.waterstones.com
Frequency of update: Daily
Website Access: Free
Traffic Figures: 1,000,000 Unique Users (per month Publisher's Statement)
Editor: Greg Eden
Summary of Content: Website covering book reviews, information on authors, book club, new books, best seller, forthcoming titles, bookshop events, children's books, book news and promotional offers.
Readership/Target Audience: Aimed at readers of all ages.
CONSUMER: THE ARTS & LITERARY: Literary

WAVE & TIDAL ENERGY NEWS
1856398U58-194

Editorial Address: Windmill Oast, Benenden Road, Rolvenden, CRANBROOK, TN17 4PF **Tel:** 01580 240055
Email: editor@wave-tidal-energy.com
Web site: http://www.wave-tidal-energy.com
Publisher: Bishop Rock Publishing
Date Launched: 2008
Frequency of update: Daily
Website Access: Free
Editor: Giles Clark
Summary of Content: Online publication covering the politics, technology and commerce of the wave and tidal energy sector.
Readership/Target Audience: Aimed at those involved in the wave and tidal energy sector including politicians, management and designers.
BUSINESS: ENERGY, FUEL & NUCLEAR

WEALTHBRIEFING
1805238U1F-637

Editorial Address: 27 Parsons Green Lane, LONDON, SW6 4HH **Tel:** 020 7736 8180 **Fax:** 020 8711 6025
Email: tom.burroughes@wealthbriefing.com
Web site: http://www.wealthbriefing.com
Publisher: ClearView Publishing
Date Launched: 2004
Frequency of update: Daily
Website Access: Paid
Traffic Figures: 12,000 Unique Users (Publisher's Statement)
Editor: Tom Burroughes
Summary of Content: Website covering strategic and structural changes across the private banking and wealth management sectors, mergers and acquisitions, people moves and profiles, fund management, tax, estate management and legal issues.
Readership/Target Audience: Aimed at wealth managers.
BUSINESS: FINANCE & ECONOMICS: Investment

WEALTH-BULLETIN.COM
1834715U1F-645

Editorial Address: 2nd Floor, Stapleton House, 29-33 Scrutton Street, LONDON, EC2A 4HU **Tel:** 020 7426 3333 **Fax:** 020 7426 3329
Email: dbain@efinancialnews.com
Web site: http://www.wealth-bulletin.com
Publisher: Efinancialnews.com
Date Launched: 2007
Frequency of update: 730 times a year
Website Access: Paid
Editor: David Bain
Summary of Content: Online news and analysis service featuring breaking news, analysis, features and columns.

Readership/Target Audience: Aimed at the global wealth management industry including wealth managers and their clients.
BUSINESS: FINANCE & ECONOMICS: Investment

WEB4WATER
1664224U42C-755

Editorial Address: Faversham House, 232A Addington Road, SOUTH CROYDON, CR2 8LE **Tel:** 020 8651 7161
Fax: 020 8651 7117
Email: newsdesk@edie.net
Web site: http://www.web4water.co.uk
Publisher: Faversham House Group Ltd
Date Launched: 2000
Frequency of update: Daily
Website Access: Free
Editor: Sam Bond
Summary of Content: Website covering current news from the water industry including waste water treatment, technology and infrastructure.
Readership/Target Audience: Aimed at professionals in the water industry.
BUSINESS: CONSTRUCTION: Water Engineering

WEBWEDDINGS
629241U74L-185

Editorial Address: 80-81 Tottenham Court Road, LONDON, W1T 4TE **Tel:** 020 7291 7600 **Fax:** 020 7291 7601
Email: carolr@confetti.co.uk
Web site: http://www.webweddings.co.uk
Publisher: Confetti Network
Date Launched: 1999
Frequency of update: Daily
Website Access: Free
Editor: Carol Richardson
Summary of Content: Website focusing on advice and ideas for the intermediate stages of wedding planning.
Readership/Target Audience: Aimed at those thinking about getting married.
Other Features: Features include a chat forum.
CONSUMER: WOMEN'S INTEREST CONSUMER MAGAZINES: Brides

WEDDINGGUIDEUK.COM
626335U74L-194

Formerly: Wedding GuideUK.com
Editorial Address: 80-81 Tottenham Court Road, LONDON, W1T 4TE **Tel:** 020 7291 7600 **Fax:** 020 7291 7601
Email: carolr@confetti.co.uk
Web site: http://www.weddingguideuk.com
Publisher: Confetti Network
Date Launched: 1996
Website Access: Free
Traffic Figures: 360,000 Unique Users (per month)
Editor: Carol Richardson
Summary of Content: Website covering all aspects of weddings, setting up home and parenting.
Readership/Target Audience: Aimed predominantly at women including brides-to-be and newly-weds..
Other Features: Features include archiving.
CONSUMER: WOMEN'S INTEREST CONSUMER MAGAZINES: Brides

WEDDINGMAGAZINE.CO.UK
1913586U74L-277

Editorial Address: Blue Fin Building, 110 Southwark Street, LONDON, SE1 OSU **Tel:** 020 3148 7800
Email: weddingweb@ipcmedia.com
Web site: http://www.weddingmagazine.co.uk
Publisher: IPC Southbank
Frequency of update: Daily
Website Access: Free
Editor: Beth Ivory
Summary of Content: Website providing inspirational ideas for modern brides.
Readership/Target Audience: Aimed at brides-to-be, bridegrooms and their families.
CONSUMER: WOMEN'S INTEREST CONSUMER MAGAZINES: Brides

WEDDINGPATH
1743096U74L-270

Editorial Address: 16 North Road, SURBITON, KT6 4DY
Tel: 020 8390 0162
Email: amanda@weddingpath.com
Web site: http://www.weddingpath.co.uk
Date Launched: 2004
Frequency of update: Daily
Website Access: Free
Traffic Figures: 80,000 Unique Users (per month Publisher's Statement)
Editor: Amanda Hinton
Summary of Content: Website covering all aspects of planning a wedding including bridal fashion and accessories,

health and beauty, venues, honeymoons, groom's fashion, wedding photography, flower, gifts, food and drink, real weddings and celebrity wedding gossip.
Readership/Target Audience: Aimed at brides, grooms and all those involved in planning a wedding.
Other Features: Shopping, supplier's directory, free personal wedding website, free downloadable wedding planning tools and forums.
CONSUMER: WOMEN'S INTEREST CONSUMER MAGAZINES: Brides

WEIGHTWATCHERS.CO.UK
1613611U74G-229

Editorial Address: Millennium House, Ludlow Road, MAIDENHEAD, SL6 2SL **Tel:** 01628 513011
Fax: 01628 513049
Email: cstokes@weightwatchers.co.uk
Web site: http://www.weightwatchers.co.uk
Publisher: WeightWatchers.co.uk Limited
Date Launched: 2002
Frequency of update: Daily
Website Access: Paid
Editor: Clair Stokes
Summary of Content: Website covering food and recipes, beauty, health and fitness, success stories and fashion.
Readership/Target Audience: Aimed at people interested in losing and maintaining weight, as well as health and fitness enthusiasts.
Other Features: Other features on site include an email newsletter and an online community.
CONSUMER: WOMEN'S INTEREST CONSUMER MAGAZINES: Slimming & Health

THE WELSH CONSUMER
45294U74C-557

Editorial Address: 5th Floor, Longcross Court, 47 Newport Road, CARDIFF, CF24 0WL **Tel:** 029 2025 5454
Fax: 029 2025 5464
Web site: http://www.wales-consumer.org.uk
Publisher: Welsh Consumer Council
Date Launched: 1999
Frequency of update: Weekly
Website Access: Paid
Traffic Figures: 1,300 Unique Users (Publisher's Statement)
Editor: Rhys Evans
Summary of Content: Bilingual, electronically delivered bulletin containing Welsh consumer news, research and campaigns.
Readership/Target Audience: Sent to local authorities, National Assembly members, Welsh MPs and MEPs, consumer organisations in Wales, UK and Europe, individuals, the top 100 companies in Wales, press and media in Wales, and individuals who subscribe.
CONSUMER: WOMEN'S INTEREST CONSUMER MAGAZINES: Home & Family

THE WELSH CONSUMER COUNCIL
629104U74C-553

Formerly: Wales Consumer Council
Editorial Address: 5th Floor, Longcross Court, 47 Newport Road, CARDIFF, CF24 0WL **Tel:** 029 2025 5454
Fax: 029 2025 5464
Email: info@wales-consumer.org.uk
Web site: http://www.wales-consumer.org.uk
Date Launched: 2001
Frequency of update: Daily
Website Access: Free
Editor: Angharad Griffiths
Summary of Content: Website focusing on consumer issues and information.
Readership/Target Audience: Aimed at politicians and policy makers in Wales.
CONSUMER: WOMEN'S INTEREST CONSUMER MAGAZINES: Home & Family

WEST MIDLANDS MATTERS
1881689U72J-432

Email: comments@westmidlands-matters.co.uk
Web site: http://www.westmidlands-matters.co.uk
Frequency of update: Daily
Summary of Content: Website created to help people who care about local issues. Whether you need access to useful information, want to highlight a particular topic to other people, discuss ideas with like-minded people or just show your support and keep up to date with current affairs in your area, West Midlands Matters is the place for you.
Readership/Target Audience: Aimed at residents in the local area of West Midlands.
LOCAL NEWSPAPERS: Community Newsletters

WEST SUSSEX COUNTY TIMES
629699U80C-3187

Editorial Address: 14-16 Market Square, HORSHAM, RH12 1HD **Tel:** 01403 751200 **Fax:** 01403 751248
Email: ct.news@sussexnewspapers.co.uk
Web site: http://www.wscountrytimes.co.uk
Frequency of update: Daily
Website Access: Free
Editor: Gary Shipton
Summary of Content: Website containing news, sport, information and features about Horsham.
Readership/Target Audience: Read by residents, expatriates and visitors to the local area.
Other Features: Features include recruitment, property, cars, pictures and archiving.
CONSUMER: RURAL & REGIONAL INTEREST: Regional Interest English Counties

WEST SUSSEX MATTERS
1881690U72J-433

Email: comments@westsussex-matters.co.uk
Web site: http://www.westsussex-matters.co.uk
Frequency of update: Daily
Summary of Content: Website created to help people who care about local issues. Whether you need access to useful information, want to highlight a particular topic to other people, discuss ideas with like-minded people or just show your support and keep up to date with current affairs in your area, West Sussex Matters is the place for you.
Readership/Target Audience: Aimed at residents in the local area of West Sussex.
LOCAL NEWSPAPERS: Community Newsletters

WEST YORKSHIRE MATTERS
1881691U72J-434

Email: comments@westyorkshire-matters.co.uk
Web site: http://www.westyorkshire-matters.co.uk
Frequency of update: Daily
Summary of Content: Website created to help people who care about local issues. Whether you need access to useful information, want to highlight a particular topic to other people, discuss ideas with like minded individuals or just show your support and keep up to date with current affairs in your area, West Yorkshire Matters is the place for you.
Readership/Target Audience: Aimed at residents in the local area of West Yorkshire.
LOCAL NEWSPAPERS: Community Newsletters

WESTERN GAZETTE
629086U72B-907

Editorial Address: Sherborne Road, YEOVIL, BA21 4YA
Tel: 01935 700500 **Fax:** 01935 426963
Email: newsdesk@westgaz.co.uk
Web site: http://www.westgaz.co.uk
Publisher: Northcliffe Media Ltd
Frequency of update: Weekly
Website Access: Free
Editor: Zena O'Rourke
Summary of Content: Website containing news, sport, horoscopes and information for the Somerset and Dorset region.
Readership/Target Audience: Aimed at citizens who live in the area.
Other Features: Features include recruitment and archiving.
LOCAL NEWSPAPERS: Local Newspapers English Counties

WESTMIDLANDS.HOUSINGNEWS.CO.UK
1776296U4D-413

Editorial Address: For all contact details see main edition, housingnews.co.uk
Website Access: Free
BUSINESS: ARCHITECTURE & BUILDING: Planning & Housing

WESTMINSTER MATTERS
1881692U72J-435

Email: comments@westminster-matters.co.uk
Web site: http://www.westminster-matters.co.uk
Frequency of update: Daily
Summary of Content: Website created to help people who care about local issues. Whether you need access to useful information, want to highlight a particular topic to other people, discuss ideas with like minded individuals or just show your support and keep up to date with current affairs in your area, Westminster Matters is the place for you.
Readership/Target Audience: Aimed at residents in the local area of Westminster.
LOCAL NEWSPAPERS: Community Newsletters

THE WESTMORLAND GAZETTE

629291U80C-960

Formerly: THIS IS THE LAKE DISTRICT
Editorial Address: 1 Wainwright's Yard, KENDAL, LA9 4DP
Tel: 01539 710161 **Fax:** 01539 720990
Email: kate.whiteside@kendal.newsquest.co.uk
Web site: http://www.thewestmorlandgazette.co.uk
Date Launched: 1999
Frequency of update: Daily
Website Access: Free
Editor: Mike Addison; **Web Editor:** Kate Whiteside
Summary of Content: Website covering news, sport, leisure and general entertainment topics for the Lake District.
Readership/Target Audience: Aimed at citizens in the region.
Other Features: Features include archiving.
CONSUMER: RURAL & REGIONAL INTEREST: Regional Interest English Counties

WGSN

42957U47A-562

Formerly: Worth Global Style Network
Editorial Address: Greater London House, Hampstead Road, LONDON, NW1 7EJ **Tel:** 020 7728 5000
Email: content@wgsn.com
Web site: http://www.wgsn.com
Date Launched: 1998
Frequency of update: Daily. News updated continuously
Website Access: Paid
Editor: Sandra Halliday
Summary of Content: Website covering B2B trends, research and news for the fashion industry. Contains store reports and photos, lifestyle and street reports, catwalk show reports, also technical and production news.
Readership/Target Audience: Aimed at professionals in the fashion, design and style-related industries.
BUSINESS: CLOTHING & TEXTILES

WHAT TO BUY FOR BUSINESS

38661U34-100

Editorial Address: 2nd Floor, 207-215 High Street, ORPINGTON, BR6 0PF **Tel:** 01689 899170
Fax: 01689 899171
Email: sara.white@purplems.com
Web site: http://www.whattobuyforbusiness.com
Publisher: Purple Media Solutions Ltd
Date Launched: 1980
Frequency of update: Monthly. Published on the 24th of the month prior to cover date
Website Access: Paid
Editor: Sara White
Summary of Content: Website containing advice on buying and running business equipment, technology and services.
Readership/Target Audience: Aimed at small to medium sized enterprises.
BUSINESS: OFFICE EQUIPMENT

WHATCAR? ONLINE

714080U77A-475_50

Editorial Address: Teddington Studios, Broom Road, TEDDINGTON, TW11 9BE **Tel:** 020 8267 5000
Fax: 020 8267 5750
Email: editorial@whatcar.com
Web site: http://www.whatcar.com
Publisher: Haymarket Media Group Ltd
Frequency of update: Daily
Website Access: Free
Editor: Leo Wilkinson; **Web Editor:** Iain Reid
Summary of Content: Website providing news and information about the car industry. Includes road tests and research, advice, used cars ads and valuations of used cars.
Readership/Target Audience: Aimed at UK car buyers.
Other Features: Features include a buyer's guide, an e-mail newsletter and archiving.
CONSUMER: MOTORING & CYCLING: Motoring

WHATGREENHOME.COM

1862035U74K-793

Editorial Address: PR by email only
Email: editor@whatgreenhome.com
Web site: http://www.whatgreenhome.com
Publisher: What Green Home Ltd
Date Launched: 2007
Frequency of update: Daily
Website Access: Free
Traffic Figures: 103,000 Unique Users (October 2008 Controlled Circulation)
Editor: Gordon Miller
Summary of Content: Internet portal featuring reviews of eco-friendly homes for sale worldwide.
Readership/Target Audience: Aimed at people interested in environmental issues relating to their home and the built environment.

Other Features: Bi-monthly newsletter
CONSUMER: WOMEN'S INTEREST CONSUMER MAGAZINES: Home Purchase

WHATHOUSE.CO.UK

45506U74K-530

Formerly: What House?
Editorial Address: 1st Floor, 1 East Poultry Avenue, LONDON, EC1A 9PT **Tel:** 020 7002 8300
Fax: 020 7002 8310
Web site: http://www.whathouse.co.uk
Publisher: Globespan Media Ltd
Frequency of update: Daily
Website Access: Free
Editor: Marc Da-Silva
Summary of Content: Website providing information on new and resale houses, mortgages, developing a property and interiors. Includes listings of 1000s of brand new homes for sale.
Readership/Target Audience: Aimed at everyone thinking of buying, selling or investing in property both in the UK and overseas.
CONSUMER: WOMEN'S INTEREST CONSUMER MAGAZINES: Home Purchase

WHAT'S NEW IN INDUSTRY

37672U19F-650

Editorial Address: Unit 2, Sugar Brook Court, Aston Road, BROMSGROVE, B60 3EX **Tel:** 01527 880827
Email: carolyn.ellison@centaur.co.uk
Web site: http://www.wnii.co.uk
Publisher: Centaur Media Plc
Date Launched: 1972
Frequency of update: 180 times a year
Website Access: Paid
(Publisher's Statement)
Editor: Carolyn Ellison
Summary of Content: Online magazine containing news and features on the latest products and industrial equipment.
Readership/Target Audience: Aimed at manufacturers, engineers and executives in the manufacturing industry.
BUSINESS: ENGINEERING & MACHINERY: Production & Mechanical Engineering

WHAT'S ON BRISTOL

753242U89C-510_25

Editorial Address: 62 North Street, Bedminster, BRISTOL, BS3 1HJ **Tel:** 0117 963 2263 **Fax:** 0117 963 2330
Email: nikki@whatsongroup.co.uk
Web site: http://www.whatsonbristol.co.uk
Publisher: What's on Group Limited
Date Launched: 2000
Frequency of update: Daily
Website Access: Free
Editor: Nikki Cook
Summary of Content: Entertainment, leisure and lifestyle Website covering restaurant reviews, outdoor and indoor leisure activities, cinema, clubs and places of interest in and around Bristol.
Readership/Target Audience: Read by residents and visitors to Bristol.
CONSUMER: HOLIDAYS & TRAVEL: Entertainment Guides

WHATS-ON-GUIDE

48166U89C-653

Formerly: Whats-on-guide.co.uk
Editorial Address: The Pavilion, Moulsham Hall Lane, Great Leighs, CHELMSFORD, CM3 1QP **Tel:** 01245 362412
Fax: 01245 361850
Email: jason@whats-on-guide.co.uk
Web site: http://www.whats-on-guide.co.uk
Publisher: What's On Guide UK Ltd
Frequency of update: Daily
Website Access: Free
Traffic Figures: 250,000 Unique Users (Publisher's Statement)
Editor: Jason Ferrando
Summary of Content: Website containing a comprehensive leisure and entertainment guide covering the theatre, arts, cinema, eating out, exhibitions, music, nightlife, sport, tourism, health, national news stories and reviews.
Readership/Target Audience: Aimed at those who want to know what's on, when and where in the UK.
Other Features: Features include an events calendar.
CONSUMER: HOLIDAYS & TRAVEL: Entertainment Guides

WHATSONSTAGE.COM

46081U76B-350

Editorial Address: 5th Floor, Palace Theatre, 109-113 Shaftsbury Avenue, LONDON, W1V 5AY **Tel:** 020 7317 9104
Email: editorial@whatsonstage.com
Web site: http://www.whatsonstage.com
Publisher: Bandwidth Communications Ltd.

Date Launched: 1996
Frequency of update: Daily
Website Access: Paid
Traffic Figures: 300,000 Unique Users (per month Publisher's Statement)
Editor: Terri Paddock; **Web Editor:** Terri Paddock
Summary of Content: Website containing daily news, reviews and features about theatre, with a listing guide to drama, ballet, opera and classical music events around the UK.
Readership/Target Audience: Aimed at theatregoers and those interested in the theatre and performing arts in the UK.
Other Features: Features include a message board, an e-mail newsletter and archiving.
CONSUMER: MUSIC & PERFORMING ARTS: Theatre

WHATSONTV.CO.UK

1804556U76C-833

Editorial Address: 6th Floor, Blue Fin Building, 110 Southwark Street, LONDON, SE1 0SU **Tel:** 020 3148 5000
Fax: 020 3148 8116
Email: patrick_mclennan@ipcmedia.com
Web site: http://www.whatsontv.co.uk
Publisher: IPC Media Ltd
Date Launched: 2007
Frequency of update: Daily
Website Access: Free
Traffic Figures: 516,247 Unique Users (01/12/2008 To 31/12/2008 ABC/Electronic)
Editor: Patrick McLennan
Summary of Content: Website with TV listings, soap story lines, news, star interviews, videos, photo galleries, online games and film reviews.
Readership/Target Audience: Aimed at fans of soaps, reality shows and prime time television shows, predominantly women aged 18 to 45 years old.
CONSUMER: MUSIC & PERFORMING ARTS: TV & Radio

WHATSONWHEN

749426U89C-510_50

Editorial Address: 91 Brick Lane, LONDON, E1 6QL
Tel: 020 7770 6050 **Fax:** 020 7770 6051
Email: editor@whatsonwhen.com
Web site: http://www.whatsonwhen.com
Date Launched: 1999
Frequency of update: Daily
Website Access: Free
Traffic Figures: 2,000,000 Unique Users (Publisher's Statement)
Editor: Derek Lock
Summary of Content: Website focusing on worldwide events and in depth travel guides. Includes news and information on adventure, classical music, clubs, film, food and drink, heritage, children and family, lifestyle, literature, music, performing arts, religion, sport, theatre, visual arts, travel and video.
Readership/Target Audience: Aimed at those who like to travel.
Other Features: Features include a buyer's guide, recruitment, an e-mail newsletter and an events calendar.
CONSUMER: HOLIDAYS & TRAVEL: Entertainment Guides

WHICHFRANCHISE.COM

1645687U14A-523

Editorial Address: 375 West George Street, GLASGOW, G2 4LW **Tel:** 0141 204 0050
Email: enquiry@whichfranchise.com
Web site: http://www.whichfranchise.com
Date Launched: 2001
Frequency of update: Daily
Website Access: Free
Editor: Suzanne Donald
Summary of Content: Website covering the pros and cons of investing in the franchise industry.
Readership/Target Audience: Aimed at those looking to start up their own business.
BUSINESS: COMMERCE, INDUSTRY & MANAGEMENT

WHISPER MAG

1843466U74A-1050

Formerly: whispermag.co.uk
Editorial Address: PR by email only **Tel:** 07736 933836
Email: press@whispermag.co.uk
Web site: http://www.whispermag.co.uk
Date Launched: 2008
Frequency of update: Daily
Website Access: Free
Editor: Liz Moores
Summary of Content: Online magazine covering fashion, beauty, music, movies, columns, advice, web-based content, opinion, news, gadgets and features.
Readership/Target Audience: Aimed at 18 to 30 year old women in the UK.

Other Features: Weekly newsletter, archive, RSS feed and social networking links.
CONSUMER: WOMEN'S INTEREST CONSUMER MAGAZINES: Women's Interest

WICKED COLORS
1645247U74F-758

Editorial Address: iBubble Ltd, Denny Lodge Business Park, Chittering, CAMBRIDGE, CB25 9PH
Tel: 01223 863843 **Fax:** 01223 864780
Email: editor@wickedcolors.com
Web site: http://www.wickedcolors.com
Frequency of update: Daily
Website Access: Free
Traffic Figures: 420,000 Unique Users (per month Publisher's Statement)
Editor: Peter Dabrowa
Summary of Content: Website covering show business, music, life, style, films and careers.
Readership/Target Audience: Aimed at the teen market, 10 to 16 years old.
CONSUMER: WOMEN'S INTEREST CONSUMER MAGAZINES: Teenage

WIKIJOB
1829342U88C-184

Editorial Address: 132 Nork Way, BANSTEAD, SM7 1HP
Tel: 07818 401787
Email: edward.mellett@wikijob.co.uk
Web site: http://www.wikijob.co.uk
Date Launched: 2007
Editor: Edward Mellett
Summary of Content: Website covering graduate recruitment in the UK.
Readership/Target Audience: Aimed at graduate jobseekers and recruitment professionals.
Other Features: Other features on site include message board, wiki profiles and a job posting area.
CONSUMER: EDUCATION: Careers

WILTSHIRE MATTERS
1881693U72J-436

Email: comments@wiltshire-matters.co.uk
Web site: http://www.wiltshire-matters.co.uk
Frequency of update: Daily
Summary of Content: Website created to help people who care about local issues. Whether you need access to useful information, want to highlight a particular topic to other people, discuss ideas with like-minded people or just show your support and keep up to date with current affairs in your area, Wiltshire Matters is the place for you.
Readership/Target Audience: Aimed at residents in the local area of Wiltshire.
LOCAL NEWSPAPERS: Community Newsletters

WINE & DINE
1647646U74P-917

Editorial Address: 27 Eddiscombe Road, LONDON, SW6 4TZ **Tel:** 07050 252738
Email: editor@winedine.co.uk
Web site: http://www.winedine.co.uk
Publisher: Winedine
Date Launched: 1995
Frequency of update: Monthly
Website Access: Free
Traffic Figures: 450,000 Unique Users (Publisher's Statement)
Editor: Antony le Ray-Cook
Summary of Content: Website covering wine, spirits, restaurants, travel, food and hotels.
Readership/Target Audience: Aimed at affluent people who have an interest in wine, food and travel.
CONSUMER: WOMEN'S INTEREST CONSUMER MAGAZINES: Food & Cookery

WINE.TELEGRAPH.CO.UK
713977U74P-905

Editorial Address: 111 Buckingham Palace Road, LONDON, SW1W 0DT **Tel:** 020 7931 2000
Fax: 020 7538 6158
Email: sharon.keene@telegraph.co.uk
Web site: http://www.wine.telegraph.co.uk
Publisher: Telegraph Media Group Ltd
Date Launched: 2001
Frequency of update: Weekly. Updated on a Saturday
Website Access: Free
Editor: Sharon Keene
Summary of Content: Website including information about wines, recipes, restaurants, healthy eating and expert information.
Readership/Target Audience: Aimed at wine lovers and dining enthusiasts.
CONSUMER: WOMEN'S INTEREST CONSUMER MAGAZINES: Food & Cookery

WIRELESS EUROPE
714464U18B-1902

Formerly: Wireless Europe online
Editorial Address: 4th Floor, BSG House, 226-236 City Road, LONDON, EC1V 2QY **Tel:** 020 7336 6100
Fax: 020 7549 9930
Email: james.watts@visiongainglobal.com
Web site: http://www.visiongainnews.com/
Publisher: Visiongain Ltd
Frequency of update: Daily
Traffic Figures: 20,000 Unique Users (per month Publisher's Statement)
Editor: James Watts
Summary of Content: Emailed newsletter covering over twenty five new stories for the wireless industry throughout Europe and the rest of the world.
Readership/Target Audience: Aimed at decision makers in the wireless industry across Europe.
BUSINESS: ELECTRONICS: Telecommunications

WOMANANDHOME.COM
1813027U74C-871

Editorial Address: Blue Fin Building, 110 Southwark Street, LONDON, SE1 0SU **Tel:** 020 3148 7834
Email: wandhmail@ipcmedia.com
Web site: http://www.womanandhome.com
Publisher: IPC Media Ltd
Frequency of update: Daily
Website Access: Free
Traffic Figures: 115,000 Unique Users (per month Publisher's Statement)
Web Editor: Louise O'Connell
Summary of Content: Website covering fashion, beauty, health, home decor, gardening, travel, fiction, relationships and people as well as an online community.
Readership/Target Audience: Aimed at women aged 35 years old and over.
CONSUMER: WOMEN'S INTEREST CONSUMER MAGAZINES: Home & Family

WOMENS EVERYTHING
1860152U74A-1057

Editorial Address: 4 Hockerley New Road, Whaley Bridge, HIGH PEAK, SK23 7GA **Tel:** 01663 719047
Email: info@womenseverything.com
Web site: http://www.womenseverything.com
Publisher: Womens Everything Ltd
Date Launched: 2008
Frequency of update: Daily
Website Access: Free
Editor: Maxine Muzzlewhite
Summary of Content: Online magazine providing factual information and advice about money, property, business, careers, travel, motoring, lifestyle, parenting and health as well as a website of the week.
Readership/Target Audience: Aimed predominantly at women aged between 25 and 45 years old.
CONSUMER: WOMEN'S INTEREST CONSUMER MAGAZINES: Women's Interest

WORCESTERSHIRE MATTERS
1881694U72J-437

Email: comments@worcestershire-matters.co.uk
Web site: http://www.worcestershire-matters.co.uk
Frequency of update: Daily
Summary of Content: Website created to help people who care about local issues. Whether you need access to useful information, want to highlight a particular topic to other people, discuss ideas with like-minded people or just show your support and keep up to date with current affairs in your area, Worcestershire Matters is the place for you.
Readership/Target Audience: Aimed at residents in the local area of Worcestershire.
LOCAL NEWSPAPERS: Community Newsletters

WORKINGMUMS.CO.UK
1872708U74D-677

Editorial Address: PO Box 53228, LONDON, N3 1YR
Tel: 020 8432 6094
Email: mandy@workingmums.co.uk
Web site: http://www.workingmums.co.uk
Frequency of update: Weekly
Website Access: Free
Traffic Figures: 20,000 Unique Users (per week Publisher's Statement)
Editor: Mandy Garner; **Web Editor:** Mandy Garner
Summary of Content: Website covering a jobsite for working parents, news and features, careers advice and blogs.
Readership/Target Audience: Aimed at working mothers.
CONSUMER: WOMEN'S INTEREST CONSUMER MAGAZINES: Child Care

WORKPLACE LAW NETWORK
1850196U44-3071

Editorial Address: 2nd Floor, Daedalus House, Station Road, CAMBRIDGE, CB1 2RE
Email: editorial@workplacelaw.net
Web site: http://workplacelaw.net
Frequency of update: Daily
Summary of Content: Website covering Workplace Law Network.
Readership/Target Audience: Aimed at people interested in employment law, health and safety and premises management.
BUSINESS: LEGAL

WORKSOPGUARDIAN.CO.UK
629834U67B-1165

Formerly: Worksop Today
Editorial Address: 21-27 Ryton Street, WORKSOP, S80 2AY **Tel:** 01909 500500 **Fax:** 01909 474849
Email: newsroom@worksop-guardian.co.uk
Web site: http://www.worksopguardian.co.uk
Frequency of update: Daily
Website Access: Free
Traffic Figures: 10,595 Unique Users (Publisher's Statement)
Editor: George Robinson
Summary of Content: Website containing news, sport, information and features on Worksop.
Readership/Target Audience: Read by residents and visitors to the local area.
Other Features: Features include recruitment, an e-mail newsletter and chat forums.
REGIONAL DAILY & SUNDAY NEWSPAPERS: Regional Daily Newspapers

WORKWITHUS.ORG
1694561U1P-281

Editorial Address: Mansfield Traquair Centre, 15 Mansfield Place, EDINBURGH, EH3 6BB **Tel:** 0131 556 3882
Fax: 0131 556 0279
Web site: http://www.workwithus.org/services
Frequency of update: Daily
Website Access: Paid
Editor: Administration
Summary of Content: Website providing internet services for charities and their supporters.
Readership/Target Audience: Aimed at voluntary sector workers in the U.K.
BUSINESS: FINANCE & ECONOMICS: Fundraising

WORLD ADVERTISING RESEARCH CENTER
629108U2A-380

Formerly: World Advertising Research
Editorial Address: 1 Farm Road, HENLEY-ON-THAMES, RG9 1EJ **Tel:** 01491 418639 **Fax:** 01491 418600
Email: editor@warc.com
Web site: http://www.warc.com
Publisher: World Advertising Research Center
Date Launched: 1998
Frequency of update: Daily
Website Access: Paid
Traffic Figures: 36,000 Unique Users (per month Publisher's Statement)
Editor: James Aitchison
Summary of Content: Online database of articles, case studies and research reports on all aspects of marketing communications, providing intelligence for the marketing, advertising, media and research communities world-wide.
Readership/Target Audience: Aimed at marketing, advertising, media, research and academic executives and organisations.
BUSINESS: COMMUNICATIONS, ADVERTISING & MARKETING

WORLD NUCLEAR ASSOCIATION
711857U58-155

Formerly: The Uranium Institute
Editorial Address: 22A St. James's Square, LONDON, SW1Y 4JH **Tel:** 020 7451 1520 **Fax:** 020 7839 1501
Email: wna@world-nuclear.org
Web site: http://www.world-nuclear.org/
Date Launched: 2001
Frequency of update: Daily
Website Access: Free
Editor: Jeremy Gordon
Summary of Content: Website covering news, reviews, reports and links about the nuclear power industry for electricity generation. Also includes an introduction to the nuclear fuel-cycle and other applications of nuclear energy in the civil field.
Readership/Target Audience: Aimed at those interested in recent developments relevant to the nuclear industry.
BUSINESS: ENERGY, FUEL & NUCLEAR

Internet Media

WORLD OF CARAVANS
1698561U91B-310

Editorial Address: 97 Link Road, Anstey, LEICESTER, LE7 7BZ **Tel:** 07711 583333 **Fax:** 0116 221 9942
Email: enquiries@ukwom.com
Web site: http://www.worldofcaravans.com
Publisher: World of Motorhomes Ltd
Date Launched: 2004
Frequency of update: Daily
Website Access: Free
Editor: Chris Apperley
Summary of Content: Website covering dealers, accessories, services, shows, magazines, clubs and information centre.
Readership/Target Audience: Aimed at caravanners and the leisure industry generally.
CONSUMER: RECREATION & LEISURE: Camping & Caravanning

WORLD OF MOTORHOMES
1698560U91B-309

Editorial Address: 97 Link Road, Anstey, LEICESTER, LE7 7BZ **Tel:** 07711 583333 **Fax:** 0870 429 9274
Email: enquiries@ukwom.com
Web site: http://www.worldofmotorhomes.com
Publisher: World of Motorhomes Ltd
Date Launched: 2004
Frequency of update: Daily
Website Access: Free
Editor: Chris Apperley
Summary of Content: Website covering dealers, accessories, services, shows, magazines, clubs and information centre.
Readership/Target Audience: Aimed at motor caravanners and the leisure industry generally.
CONSUMER: RECREATION & LEISURE: Camping & Caravanning

WORLD OF POWERBOATS
767413U75M-993

Formerly: Raceboat
Editorial Address: PO Box 4781, POOLE, BH15 1WH
Tel: 01202 625048
Email: info@blue-mediagroup.com
Web site: http://www.worldofpowerboats.com
Publisher: World Of PowerBoats
Date Launched: 1985
Frequency of update: 6 times a year
Website Access: Paid
Traffic Figures: 22,300 Unique Users (Publisher's Statement)
Editor: David Sewell
Summary of Content: Website covering high performance powerboats, including reviews, equipment, lifestyle and events.
Readership/Target Audience: Aimed at powerboat owners and enthusiasts.
CONSUMER: SPORT: Water Sports

WORLD OFF ROAD
629022U77A-500

Editorial Address: High View, Rock Place, Coedpoeth, WREXHAM, LL11 3RS **Tel:** 01978 753164
Email: tonyautonutz@aol.com
Web site: http://www.worldoffroad.com
Publisher: Worldoffroad.com Ltd
Date Launched: 1996
Frequency of update: Monthly
Website Access: Free
Traffic Figures: 80,000 Unique Users (per month Publisher's Statement)
Editor: Tony Pritchard
Summary of Content: Website focusing on 4x4 vehicles, with news and features.
Readership/Target Audience: Aimed at 4x4 owners and enthusiasts.
Other Features: Features include a buyer's guide, discussion forums and archiving.
CONSUMER: MOTORING & CYCLING: Motoring

WORLD PUMPS
719245U19D-622

Formerly: World Pumps Online
Editorial Address: The Boulevard, Langford Lane, KIDLINGTON, OX5 1GB **Tel:** 01865 843686
Fax: 01865 843973
Email: a.burrows@elsevier.co.uk
Web site: http://www.worldpumps.com
Publisher: Elsevier Ltd
Date Launched: 1949
Frequency of update: Monthly
Website Access: Free
Traffic Figures: 16,000 Unique Users (Publisher's Statement)
Editor: Alan Burrows

Summary of Content: Website providing information for pump users in the industrial sector. Includes industry news, new products, technical articles and features.
Readership/Target Audience: Aimed at users and manufacturers of pumps.
BUSINESS: ENGINEERING & MACHINERY: Hydraulic Power

WORLD SOCCER
707742U75B-261

Editorial Address: Blue Fin Building, 110 Southwark Street, LONDON, SE1 0SU **Tel:** 020 3148 5000 **Fax:** 020 3148 8130
Email: jamie_rainbow@ipcmedia.com
Web site: http://www.worldsoccer.com
Publisher: IPC Inspire
Date Launched: 2000
Frequency of update: Daily
Website Access: Free
Traffic Figures: 80,000 Unique Users (per month Publisher's Statement)
Editor: Jamie Rainbow
Summary of Content: Website containing world football news, results and fixtures on the world cup, champion league, UEFA Cup, African nations and Copa America.
Readership/Target Audience: Aimed at those interested in football.
CONSUMER: SPORT: Football

WORLD SOCCER NEWS.COM
634875U75B-263

Editorial Address: 326 Upper Richmond Road West, LONDON, SW14 7JN **Tel:** 020 8392 5050
Email: press@worldsoccernews.com
Web site: http://www.worldsoccernews.com
Date Launched: 1995
Frequency of update: Daily
Website Access: Free
Traffic Figures: 300,000 Unique Users (per month Publisher's Statement)
Editor: Anthony Appleby
Summary of Content: Website containing soccer news from around the world.
Readership/Target Audience: Read by soccer fans.
Other Features: Features include a chat forum, an e-mail newsletter, interviews, live coverage, an events calendar and archiving.
CONSUMER: SPORT: Football

WORLD STEEL EXPORTS - STAINLESS, HIGH SPEED AND OTHER ALLOY
37744U20-305

Editorial Address: 1 Carlton House Terrace, LONDON, SW1Y 5DB **Tel:** 020 7343 3916 **Fax:** 020 7343 3903
Email: publications@issb.co.uk
Web site: http://www.issb.co.uk
Publisher: ISSB Ltd (Iron and Steel Statistics Bureau)
Frequency of update: Quarterly
Website Access: Paid
Editor: Phil Hunt
Summary of Content: Electronically mailed spreadsheet detailing the export trade of 50 major steel producing countries in 40 selected alloy and stainless products to 100 export markets.
BUSINESS: IMPORT & EXPORT

WORLD TRANSPORT POLICY & PRACTICE
39595U49A-400

Editorial Address: 53 Derwent Road, LANCASTER, LA1 3ES **Tel:** 01524 63175
Email: j.whitelegg@btinternet.com
Web site: http://www.eco-logica.co.uk
Publisher: Eco-Logica Ltd
Date Launched: 1995
Frequency of update: Quarterly
Website Access: Free
Editor: John Whitelegg; **Editor-in-Chief:** John Whitelegg
Summary of Content: Website covering transport, public policy, the environment and infrastructure.
Readership/Target Audience: Aimed at scholars, researchers, transport operators, policy makers and those concerned with the marked lack of sustainability of current transport arrangements.
BUSINESS: TRANSPORT

WORLD TRAVEL GUIDE
626337U89A-650

Editorial Address: Media House, Azalea Drive, SWANLEY, BR8 8HU **Tel:** 01322 660070 **Fax:** 01322 616327
Email: worldtravelguide@nexusmedia.com
Web site: http://www.worldtravelguide.net
Date Launched: 1996
Frequency of update: Daily

Website Access: Free
Traffic Figures: 800,000 Unique Users (per month Publisher's Statement)
Editor: Susie Henderson
Summary of Content: Website focusing on world travel and tourism.
Readership/Target Audience: Aimed at those seeking tourist information on countries worldwide, business travellers and travel agents.
CONSUMER: HOLIDAYS & TRAVEL: Travel

WORLDCARGO NEWS ONLINE
1912903U49C-509

Editorial Address: Northbank House, 5 Bridge Street, LEATHERHEAD, KT22 8BL **Tel:** 01372 375511
Fax: 01372 370111
Email: vchampion@wcnpublishing.com
Web site: http://www.worldcargonews.com
Publisher: WCN Publishing
Frequency of update: Daily
Website Access: Free
Summary of Content: Website covering most kinds of cargo handling, containerisation, intermodalism and port development.
Readership/Target Audience: Aimed at cargo handling and transportation professionals worldwide.
BUSINESS: TRANSPORT: Freight

WORLDCONSTRUCTIONWEEK
1841578U4E-454

Editorial Address: Southfields, Southview Road, WADHURST, TN5 6TP **Tel:** 01892 784088
Fax: 01892 784086
Email: richard.high@khl.com
Web site: http://www.khl.com/enewsletter
Publisher: KHL Group
Date Launched: 2006
Frequency of update: Weekly. Published on Wednesday
Website Access: Paid
Traffic Figures: 25,000 Unique Users (Publisher's Statement)
Editor: Richard High
Summary of Content: Email newsletter covering construction, lifting, access, transportation, rental and demolition markets news.
Readership/Target Audience: Aimed at contractors, architects and buyers.
BUSINESS: ARCHITECTURE & BUILDING: Building

WORLDROVER
1665918U89A-719

Editorial Address: 26-28 Low Greens, BERWICK-UPON-TWEED, TD15 1LZ **Tel:** 01289 308654
Email: editor@worldrover.net
Web site: http://www.worldrover.net
Frequency of update: Quarterly
Website Access: Free
Traffic Figures: 68,000 Unique Users (per month Publisher's Statement)
Editor: Allan Rogers
Summary of Content: Website covering travel news and events, good travel experiences, destinations worldwide, food and drink.
Readership/Target Audience: Aimed at general travellers.
CONSUMER: HOLIDAYS & TRAVEL: Travel

WOTSIT
45935U75L-800

Editorial Address: Croft Farm, Spreyton, CREDITON, EX17 5EB **Tel:** 01647 231527
Email: editor@wotsit.co.uk
Web site: http://www.wotsit.co.uk
Publisher: Crofter Internet Ltd
Date Launched: 1996
Frequency of update: Weekly
Website Access: Free
Editor: Bruce Ross-Smith
Summary of Content: Website covering outdoor pursuits in the West Country.
Readership/Target Audience: Aimed at those with an interest in outdoor activities.
CONSUMER: SPORT: Outdoor

WRC.COM
1639028U77D-466

Formerly: WRC+
Editorial Address: 34 Fouberts Place, LONDON, W1F 7PX
Tel: 020 7478 7647
Email: feedback@wrc.com
Web site: http://www.wrc.com
Publisher: North One
Frequency of update: Daily

Website Access: Free
Editor: Nick Atkins
Summary of Content: Website covering the World Rally Championship with driver and team profiles, rally reports, previews and features.
Readership/Target Audience: Aimed at rally and motorsport enthusiasts.
Other Features: Other features include archiving and chat forums.
CONSUMER: MOTORING & CYCLING: Motor Sports

YACHTCREWONLINE.COM   1776234U91A-293
Editorial Address: Bucklands, Loxwood Road, Rudgwick, HORSHAM, RH12 3DW **Tel:** 01403 823640
Fax: 01403 433332
Email: editorial@yachtcrewonline.com
Web site: http://www.yachtcrewonline.com
Publisher: Big Blue Publishing Company Ltd
Date Launched: 2006
Frequency of update: Weekly
Website Access: Free
Editor: Giles Morgan; **Editor-in-Chief:** Giles Morgan
Summary of Content: Website covering everything relevant to yacht crew including provisioning, bars and restaurants.
Readership/Target Audience: Aimed at captains and crew of super-yachts.
Other Features: Recruitment and newsletter.
CONSUMER: RECREATION & LEISURE: Boating & Yachting

YACHTING & BOATING WORLD 48397U91A-230
Editorial Address: Blue Fin Building, 110 Southwark Street, LONDON, SE1 0SU **Tel:** 020 3148 5000 **Fax:** 020 3148 6439
Email: ybw.com@ipcmedia.com
Web site: http://www.ybw.com
Publisher: IPC Inspire
Date Launched: 1997
Frequency of update: Daily
Website Access: Free
Traffic Figures: 340,000 Unique Users (per month Publisher's Statement)
Editor: Dan Foley
Summary of Content: Website providing coverage of key high-spending, high-value communities including motorboats, sail yacht cruising, day sailing and performance racing.
Readership/Target Audience: Aimed at those interested in, who are passionate about, or earn their living from boating and marine recreation.
Other Features: Features include a buyer's guide, chat forums, a marine company directory, classified listings, weather and tide information and archiving.
CONSUMER: RECREATION & LEISURE: Boating & Yachting

YACHTING MONTHLY ONLINE 713149U91A-262
Editorial Address: Blue Fin Building, 110 Southwark Street, LONDON, SE1 0SU **Tel:** 020 3148 5000
Email: yachting_monthly@ipcmedia.com
Web site: http://www.yachtingmonthly.com
Publisher: IPC Inspire
Date Launched: 2000
Frequency of update: Daily
Website Access: Free
Editor: Dick Durham
Summary of Content: Website providing yachting news and information about boats and yachts.
Readership/Target Audience: Aimed at yachtsmen and people interested in yachting.
Other Features: Features include a buyer's guide and archiving.
CONSUMER: RECREATION & LEISURE: Boating & Yachting

YACHTS AND YACHTING ONLINE
628935U91A-281
Editorial Address: 196 Eastern Esplanade, SOUTHEND-ON-SEA, SS1 3AB **Tel:** 023 8045 8572 **Fax:** 01702 588434
Email: club@yachtsandyachting.com
Web site: http://www.yachtsandyachting.com
Publisher: Yachting Press Ltd
Date Launched: 1999
Frequency of update: Daily. News updated continuously
Website Access: Free
Traffic Figures: 58,961 Unique Users (per month Publisher's Statement)
Editor: Mark Jardine
Summary of Content: Website covering all aspects of sailing with news, information and events.
Readership/Target Audience: Aimed at sailors of all levels and abilities.
Other Features: Features include an events calendar, recruitment and archiving.
CONSUMER: RECREATION & LEISURE: Boating & Yachting

YAHOO MUSIC   40932U76E-776
Formerly: Launch
Editorial Address: 125 Shaftesbury Avenue, LONDON, WC2H 8AD **Tel:** 020 7131 1330
Email: benberry@yahoo-inc.com
Web site: http://uk.launch.yahoo.com
Publisher: Yahoo
Date Launched: 1996
Frequency of update: Daily
Website Access: Free
Traffic Figures: 1,254,679 Unique Users (per month ABC/Electronic)
Editor: Ben Berry
Summary of Content: Website covering the world of pop music with updates on the charts, news, reviews and features on pop music plus a major label music download service, free online music videos and radio services.
Readership/Target Audience: Aimed at those with an interest in current music between 16 and 34 years old.
CONSUMER: MUSIC & PERFORMING ARTS: Pop Music

YAHOO UK & IRELAND CARS 1696590U77A-572
Editorial Address: 125 Shaftesbury Avenue, LONDON, WC2H 8AD **Tel:** 020 7131 1000 **Fax:** 020 7171 1210
Email: tyrones@yahoo-inc.com
Web site: http://www.uk.cars.yahoo.com
Frequency of update: Daily
Website Access: Free
Traffic Figures: 800,000 Unique Users (per month Nielsen NetRatings)
Editor: Hazel Checkley
Summary of Content: Website covering news and reviews of new cars, used cars, and new cars, a database of new and used car classifieds for sale, car insurance, finance, breakdown cover, warranties, personal number plates and car maintenance as well as photo galleries.
Readership/Target Audience: Aimed at anyone researching, buying or selling a car and associated products.
Other Features: Forums and picture galleries.
CONSUMER: MOTORING & CYCLING: Motoring

YORKSHIRE MATTERS   1881695U72J-438
Email: comments@yorkshire-matters.co.uk
Web site: http://www.yorkshire-matters.co.uk
Frequency of update: Daily
Summary of Content: Website created to help people who care about local issues. Whether you need access to useful information, want to highlight a particular topic to other people, discuss ideas with like-minded people or just show your support and keep up to date with current affairs in your area, Yorkshire Matters is the place for you.
Readership/Target Audience: Aimed at residents in the local area of Yorkshire.
LOCAL NEWSPAPERS: Community Newsletters

YOUNGTALENT.ORG.UK   1732059U64K-652
Editorial Address: International House, Suite 501, 223 Regent Street, LONDON, W1H 2QD **Tel:** 020 7723 1209
Email: chanel@youngtalent.org.uk
Web site: http://www.youngtalent.org.uk
Publisher: Unique Talent Management Ltd
Date Launched: 2006
Frequency of update: 14 times a year
Website Access: Free
Traffic Figures: 8,752 Unique Users (per month Publisher's Statement)
Editor: Chanel Williams
Summary of Content: Website with features, advice and services covering health and beauty products and services, book reviews, celebrity biographies, music releases, events, theatre, film, concerts and up and coming auditions and competitions.
Readership/Target Audience: Aimed at aspiring and working dancers, actors, models and other performers.
BUSINESS: OTHER CLASSIFICATIONS: Cinema Entertainment

YOUR CANTERBURY   1827089U72B-4101_101
Editorial Address: Hythe Road, Smeeth, Ashford, KENT, TN25 6SR **Tel:** 01303 817100
Email: editorial@kosmedia.co.uk
Web site: http://www.yourcanterbury.co.uk
Frequency of update: Daily
Website Access: Free
(Publisher's Statement)
Summary of Content: Website covering political, cultural, sport news of Canterbury.
Readership/Target Audience: Aimed at people living in this area.
LOCAL NEWSPAPERS: Local Newspapers English Counties

YOUR FAMILY   1663299U74D-587
Editorial Address: 7 St. Martin's Place, LONDON, WC2N 4HA **Tel:** 020 7747 0862
Email: yourfamily.online@redwoodgroup.net
Web site: http://www.yourfamily.org.uk
Publisher: Redwood
Date Launched: 2005
Frequency of update: Daily
Website Access: Free
Traffic Figures: 394,307 Unique Users (Publisher's Statement)
Editor: Susannah Pearce
Summary of Content: Website helping parents get the most out of family life. With features on parenting babies to six year olds and older. Lifestyle content from shopping, fashion, and product reviews to recipe and day out ideas.
Readership/Target Audience: Aimed at parents.
CONSUMER: WOMEN'S INTEREST CONSUMER MAGAZINES: Child Care

YOUR FRIDGE DOOR   1786178U74Q-1340
Editorial Address: Compton House, School Lane, LIVERPOOL, L1 3BT **Tel:** 0151 707 0660
Email: sam@yourfridgedoor.com
Web site: http://www.yourfridgedoor.com
Publisher: Your Fridge Door Ltd
Date Launched: 2006
Frequency of update: Daily
Website Access: Free
Editor: Sam Gallagher
Summary of Content: Electronic daily web magazine and newsletter service covering music, fashion, style, lifestyle features, launches, openings, cultural events and product releases.
Readership/Target Audience: Aimed at creative people aged 23 to 35 year old.
Other Features: Soundtrack page featuring downloads from unsigned acts. Streetlife page featuring vox pops, photographs of interesting faces.
CONSUMER: WOMEN'S INTEREST CONSUMER MAGAZINES: Lifestyle

YOUR MEDWAY   1827092U72B-4101_104
Editorial Address: Hythe Road, Smeeth, Ashford, KENT, TN25 6SR **Tel:** 01303 817100
Email: editorial@kosmedia.co.uk
Web site: http://www.yourmedway.co.uk
Frequency of update: Daily
Website Access: Free
(Publisher's Statement)
Summary of Content: Website covering news and events in Medway.
Readership/Target Audience: Aimed at people living in this area.
LOCAL NEWSPAPERS: Local Newspapers English Counties

YOUR MONEY HAVEN   1852527U74M-435
Editorial Address: 0-2 River Court, 201 Busby Road, Clarkston, GLASGOW, G76 8DR **Tel:** 0141 644 1969
Email: marc@liquidkool.com
Web site: http://www.yourmoneyhaven.com
Date Launched: 2008
Frequency of update: Daily
Website Access: Free
Traffic Figures: 100 Unique Users (per day Publisher's Statement)
Editor: Marc Love
Summary of Content: Website covering credit cards, loans, insurance, banking, saving and mortgages as well as UK financial news.
Readership/Target Audience: Aimed at the general UK public.
CONSUMER: WOMEN'S INTEREST CONSUMER MAGAZINES: Personal Finance

---

YOUR SWALE   1827094U72B-4101_106
Editorial Address: KOS Media Ltd, Apple Barn, Hythe Road, Smeeth, ASHFORD, TN25 6SR **Tel:** 01303 817100
Email: editorial@kosmedia.co.uk
Web site: http://www.yourswale.co.uk
Frequency of update: Daily
Website Access: Free
(Publisher's Statement)
Summary of Content: Website covering news and events in Swale.
Readership/Target Audience: Aimed at people living in this area.
LOCAL NEWSPAPERS: Local Newspapers English Counties

Internet Media

YOURASHFORD 1827088U72B-4101_100

Editorial Address: Hythe Road, Smeeth, Ashford, KENT, TN25 6SR **Tel:** 01303 817070
Email: editorial@kosmedia.co.uk
Web site: http://www.yourashford.co.uk
Frequency of update: Daily
Website Access: Free
(Publisher's Statement)
Summary of Content: Website covering political, cultural, sports news of Ashford.
Readership/Target Audience: Aimed at people living in this area.
LOCAL NEWSPAPERS: Local Newspapers English Counties

YOURDOVER 1827090U72B-4101_102

Editorial Address: Hythe Road, Smeeth, Ashford, KENT, TN25 6SR
Email: editorial@kosmedia.co.uk
Web site: http://www.yourdover.co.uk
Frequency of update: Daily
Website Access: Free
(Publisher's Statement)
Summary of Content: Website covering political, cultural, sports news of Dover.
Readership/Target Audience: Aimed at people living in this area.
LOCAL NEWSPAPERS: Local Newspapers English Counties

YOUREABLE 711984U94F-990

Editorial Address: Unit 3, Sterling Park, Pedmore Road, BRIERLEY HILL, DY5 1TB **Tel:** 01384 473743
Email: jennifergodson@gmail.com
Web site: http://www.youreable.com
Date Launched: 2000
Frequency of update: Daily
Website Access: Free
Traffic Figures: 41,890 Unique Users
Editor: Jennifer Godson
Summary of Content: Website focusing on lifestyle issues concerning disabled people. Provides information, products and services enabling disabled people to live independent lives. Features equipment, community, penpals, travel, education, motoring, work, money, discounts, computing and health sections.
Readership/Target Audience: Aimed at disabled people, their carers, family and friends.

Other Features: Features include a buyer's guide, recruitment, a chat forum, an e-mail newsletter, a pen house directory and archiving.
CONSUMER: OTHER CLASSIFICATIONS: Disability

YOURMAIDSTONE 1827091U72B-4101_103

Editorial Address: Hythe Road, Smeeth, Ashford, KENT, TN25 6SR **Tel:** 01303 817100
Email: editorial@kosmedia.co.uk
Web site: http://www.yourmaidstone.co.uk
Frequency of update: Daily
Website Access: Free
(Publisher's Statement)
Summary of Content: Website covering news and events in Maidstone.
Readership/Target Audience: Aimed at people living in this area.
LOCAL NEWSPAPERS: Local Newspapers English Counties

YOURS.CO.UK 1923359U74N-189

Editorial Address: 4th Floor, Endeavour House, 189 Shaftesbury Avenue, LONDON, WC2H 8JG
Tel: 020 7182 8491
Email: gareth.hargreaves@bauermedia.co.uk
Web site: http://www.yours.co.uk
Publisher: Bauer Consumer Media Ltd (Media House)
Frequency of update: Daily
Website Access: Free
Editor: Gareth Hargreaves
Summary of Content: Website containing advice on a variety of topics including entertainment, health, cooking, personal finance, gardening, housing, social security benefits and celebrity features.
Readership/Target Audience: Aimed at men and women over 50 years old.
CONSUMER: WOMEN'S INTEREST CONSUMER MAGAZINES: Retirement

YOURSHEPWAY 1827093U72B-4101_105

Editorial Address: Hythe Road, Smeeth, Ashford, KENT, TN25 6SR **Tel:** 01303 817100
Email: editorial@kosmedia.co.uk
Web site: http://www.yourshepway.co.uk
Frequency of update: Daily
Website Access: Free

(Publisher's Statement)
Summary of Content: Website covering news and events in Shepway.
Readership/Target Audience: Aimed at people living in this area.
LOCAL NEWSPAPERS: Local Newspapers English Counties

YOURTECHTV.COM 1850504U10-225

Editorial Address: Latimer House, 189 High Street, POTTERS BAR, EN6 5DA **Tel:** 01707 664200
Fax: 01707 664800
Email: info@yourtechtv.com
Web site: http://www.yourtechtv.com
Publisher: Interactive Business Communications Ltd
Frequency of update: Daily
Website Access: Free
Traffic Figures: 38,000 Unique Users (per month Publisher's Statement)
Editor: Peter West
Summary of Content: Video upload and sharing web portal which allows companies to upload, share and view technology related videos.
Readership/Target Audience: Aimed at technology companies.
BUSINESS: MATERIALS HANDLING

ZDNET UK 36190U5C-800

Editorial Address: 5-11 Lavington Street, LONDON, SE1 0NZ **Tel:** 020 7021 1125
Email: karen.friar@zdnet.co.uk
Web site: http://www.zdnet.co.uk
Publisher: CBS Interactive
Date Launched: 1995
Frequency of update: 260 times a year
Website Access: Free
Traffic Figures: 2,118,578 Unique Users (01/11/2005 To 30/11/2005 ABC/Electronic)
Editor: Rupert Goodwins
Summary of Content: Website focusing on computer and business technology.
Readership/Target Audience: Aimed at Technology decision-makers in the business and the public sector in the U.K.
BUSINESS: COMPUTERS & AUTOMATION: Professional Personal Computers

Willings Volume 1
Section 6

Publishers
UK Publishers with the
titles they publish

All titles in Section 4 cross-refer with this section.
Information on publishers in Western Europe can be found in Volume 2
(Western European edition), Sections 16 and 17. Publishers in the rest of the
world (excluding Western Europe) can be located in Volume 3 (World Edition),
Sections 26 and 27.

UK Publishers & Their Titles

125 WORLD 1713414
5 Calvert Avenue, LONDON, E2 7JP **Tel:** 020 7613 2015
Titles:
125 MAGAZINE

THE 1990 TRUST 674810
Suite 12, Winchester House, 9 Cranmer Road, LONDON,
SW9 6EJ **Tel:** 020 7582 1990 **Fax:** 020 7793 8269
Email: bljnk1990@blink.org.uk
Titles:
BLACK INFORMATION LINK

2I MEDIA PLC 1654322
16-17 Little Portland Street, LONDON, W1W 8BP
Tel: 020 7299 7700
Titles:
INVESTOR SERVICES JOURNAL

2M MEDIA 1726900
2nd Floor, 11-13 Spear Street, MANCHESTER, M1 1JU
Tel: 0161 228 0044
Web site: http://www.2mmedia.com
Titles:
BODYCONFIDENTIAL.COM
LIVERPOOL CONFIDENTIAL

2M MEDIA LTD 1732871
11-13 Spear Street, MANCHESTER, M1 1JU
Tel: 0161 228 0044
Titles:
MANCHESTERCONFIDENTIAL.COM

2 N MEDIA LTD 1713664
Unit 2, Flag House, 47 Brunswick Court, LONDON, SE1 3LH
Tel: 020 7939 0790 **Fax:** 01404 871663
Titles:
MODERNSELLING.COM

2VIEW GROUP 1621730
D304, 116 Commercial Street, LONDON, E1 6NF
Tel: 020 7247 1525
Web site: http://www.viewlondon.co.uk
Titles:
VIEW.CO.UK
VIEWLONDON.CO.UK

328 MEDIA 1729057
5 St. Georges Place, BRIGHTON, BN1 4GA
Tel: 01273 808601 **Fax:** 0560 065 5815
Titles:
KITE WORLD

365 MEDIA GROUP 1640455
3rd Floor, 14 Waterloo Place, LONDON, SW1Y 4AR
Tel: 020 7004 2805
Titles:
TEAMTALK

3 CLIFFS MEDIA 1649742
Telfords Yard, 6-8 The Highway, LONDON, E1W 2BS
Tel: 0870 803 0146
Titles:
SO ONLINE

3-D MEDIA LTD 1626608
Seymour House, South Street, BROMLEY, BR1 1RH
Tel: 020 8460 6060 **Fax:** 020 8460 6050
Titles:
FQ MAGAZINE

4 SQUARE MEDIA 696741
The Old Coach House, 12 Main Street, HILLSBOROUGH,
BT26 6AE **Tel:** 028 9268 8888 **Fax:** 028 9268 8866
Email: info@4squaremedia.net
Web site: http://www.4squaremedia.net
Titles:
EXPORT & FREIGHT
PLANT & CIVIL ENGINEER
SUSTAINABLE IRELAND

50CONNECT LTD 1640089
Morley House, Badminton Court, Church Street,
AMERSHAM, HP7 0DD **Tel:** 01753 850606
Fax: 0800 634 2250
Email: admin@50connect.co.uk
Web site: http://www.50connect.co.uk
Titles:
50CONNECT.CO.UK

55 NORTH 1653326
Waterloo Chambers, 19 Waterloo Street, GLASGOW, G2
6AY **Tel:** 0141 222 2100 **Fax:** 0141 222 2177
Web site: http://www.55north.com
Titles:
CABLETALK
DATABASE MARKETING
ON TRADE SCOTLAND

5TH ELEMENT PUBLICATIONS LTD 625372
Ivy Lane Business Centre, 8A Victoria Road, DARTMOUTH,
TQ6 9SA **Tel:** 01803 839399 **Fax:** 01803 893398
Web site: http://www.thedesignermagazine.com
Titles:
THE DESIGNER

69 MAGAZINE LTD 621623
15 Leatherline House, 71 Narrow Lane, Aylestone,
LEICESTER, LE2 8NA **Tel:** 0871 426 9696
Email: manchester@69-247.com
Web site: http://www.69-247.com
Titles:
69 MAGAZINE MIDLANDS
69 MAGAZINE NORTH

A&A THORPE 14350
131A Furtherwick Road, CANVEY ISLAND, SS8 7AT
Tel: 01268 511300 **Fax:** 01268 510467
Titles:
PEM (PORT ENGINEERING MANAGEMENT)

A & D MEDIA LTD 622923
Jesses Farm, Snow Hill, Dinton, SALISBURY, SP3 5HN
Tel: 01722 717026 **Fax:** 01722 716926
Email: wiltshirelife@markallengroup.co.uk
Web site: http://www.markallengroup.com
Titles:
CARRIAGE DRIVING
FACILITIES-UK
HAMPSHIRE THE COUNTY MAGAZINE
PRO SHOP EUROPE
RECYCLING & WASTE WORLD MAGAZINE
RECYCLING WORLD HANDBOOK
WILTSHIRE LIFE

A.E. MORGAN PUBLICATIONS LTD 12723
8A High Street, EPSOM, KT19 8AD **Tel:** 01372 741411
Fax: 01372 744493
Email: info@aemorgan.co.uk
Titles:
CANALS & RIVERS
CARAVAN INDUSTRY AND PARK OPERATOR
CARAVAN INDUSTRY SUPPLIES & SERVICES
DIRECTORY
DANCE EXPRESSION
DENTAL PRACTICE
THE DENTAL TECHNICIAN
SIGN WORLD

A. ROMANES & SON LTD 15044
17 Bank Street, LOCHGELLY, KY5 9QQ **Tel:** 01592 780342
Fax: 01592 780342
Titles:
CENTRAL FIFE TIMES AND ADVERTISER

THE AA 1762147
Fanum House, Basing View, BASINGSTOKE, RG21 4EA
Tel: 01256 492926
Titles:
THE AA MEMBERS CLUB MAGAZINE

AAG PUBLISHING LTD 1615892
24 Bray Gardens, MAIDSTONE, ME15 9TR
Tel: 01622 744481
Titles:
MAVERICK

ABACABE PUBLISHING 16984
10 Messaline Avenue, LONDON, W3 6JX **Tel:** 020 8723 7376
Fax: 020 8723 7380
Titles:
BLUES IN BRITAIN

ABBEY PUBLISHING 1643389
Apex House, 28 Ruskin Avenue, WALTHAM ABBEY, EN9
3BP **Tel:** 0845 652 1012 **Fax:** 01992 767672
Email: ralph@abbeypublishing.co.uk
Web site: http://www.abbeypublishing.co.uk
Titles:
BUILDING AND FACILITIES MANAGEMENT
BULK SOLIDS TODAY
SUSTAINABLE FM

ABC MAGAZINE BERKSHIRE 1766879
PO Box 2780, BRIGHTON, BN1 5QR **Tel:** 01273 552842
Fax: 01273 542257
Email: berkshire@abcmag.co.uk
Web site: http://www.abcmag.co.uk
Titles:
ABC MAGAZINE BERKSHIRE

ABC MEDIA GROUP LTD 1731922
4 James Brindley House, Coventry Canal Basin, St. Nicholas
Street, COVENTRY, CV1 4LY **Tel:** 024 7671 7707
Email: info@smartmediacom.co.uk
Web site: http://www.smartmediacom.co.uk
Titles:
MIND YOUR BUSINESS

ABDO 14550
PO Box 233, CROWBOROUGH, TN6 9BD
Tel: 01892 667626 **Fax:** 01892 668547
Titles:
DISPENSING OPTICS

**ABERDEEN AND GRAMPIAN CHAMBER OF
COMMERCE** 671711
Greenhole Place, Bridge of Don Industrial Estate,
ABERDEEN, AB23 8EU **Tel:** 01224 343900
Fax: 01224 343943
Web site: http://www.agcc.co.uk
Titles:
ABERDEEN AND GRAMPIAN CHAMBER OF COMMERCE
BUSINESS BULLETIN

ABERDEEN JOURNALS LTD 14770
PO Box 43, Lang Stracht, Mastrick, ABERDEEN, AB15 6DF
Tel: 01224 343467
Titles:
ABERDEEN CITIZEN
ENERGY
EVENING EXPRESS (ABERDEEN)
THE PRESS & JOURNAL (ABERDEEN)

ABERDEEN PETROLEUM PUBLISHING LTD 14205
Unit 12, Wellheads Crescent Industrial Estate, Wellheads
Crescent, ABERDEEN, AB21 7GA **Tel:** 0870 438 0001
Fax: 0870 438 0002
Email: info@aproil.co.uk
Titles:
ABERDEEN PETROLEUM REPORT

ABERDEEN UNIVERSITY STUDENTS' ASSOCIATION 15755
University of Aberdeen, The Hub, ABERDEEN, AB24 3TU
Tel: 01224 272980 **Fax:** 01224 272977
Web site: http://www.ausa.org.uk
Titles:
GAUDIE

ABERDEEN-ANGUS CATTLE SOCIETY 17475
Pedigree House, 6 King's Place, PERTH, PH2 8AD
Tel: 01738 622477 **Fax:** 01738 636436
Titles:
ABERDEEN-ANGUS REVIEW

ABERGAVENNY CHRONICLE LTD 15013
Tindle House, 13 Nevill Street, ABERGAVENNY, NP7 5AA
Tel: 01873 852187 **Fax:** 01873 857677
Titles:
ABERGAVENNY CHRONICLE SERIES

ABM PUBLISHING LTD 17126
61 Great Whyte, Ramsey, HUNTINGDON, PE26 1HJ
Tel: 01487 814050 **Fax:** 01487 711361
Titles:
DOGS MONTHLY
FAMILY TREE MAGAZINE
PRACTICAL FAMILY HISTORY

ABR CO LTD 14329
The Barn, Ford Barn, Bradford Leigh, BRADFORD-ON-AVON, BA15 2RP **Tel:** 01225 868821 **Fax:** 01225 868831
Web site: http://www.tugandsalvage.com
Titles:
INTERNATIONAL TUG & SALVAGE

ABSOLUTE MEDIA LTD 1653936
42 Wilbury Villas, HOVE, BN3 6GD **Tel:** 0845 389 0662
Fax: 0845 389 0663
Titles:
ABSOLUTE BRIGHTON
ABSOLUTE LONDON

ABSOLUTE PUBLISHING LTD 17106
197-199 City Road, LONDON, EC1V 1JN **Tel:** 020 7253 9909
Fax: 020 7253 9907
Web site: http://www.absolutepublishing.com
Titles:
ABTA GOLF
ABTA MAGAZINE
SPA SECRETS MAGAZINE
WELCOME TO LONDON

ABUCON 12746
21A Vincent Square, LONDON, SW1P 2NA
Tel: 020 7834 1066 **Fax:** 020 7828 1828
Titles:
FREEHAND

YR ACADEMI GYMREIG 16340
3ydd Llawr, Ty Mount Stuart, Sgwar Mount Stuart, CARDIFF, CF10 5FQ **Tel:** 029 2047 2266 **Fax:** 029 2049 2930
Web site: http://www.academi.org
Titles:
A470 - WHAT'S ON IN LITERARY WALES
TALIESIN

ACADEMY OF EXPERTS 1713616
3 Gray's Inn Square, LONDON, WC1R 5AH
Tel: 020 7430 0333 **Fax:** 020 7430 0666
Email: admin@academy-experts.org
Web site: http://www.academy-experts.org
Titles:
THE EXPERT AND DISPUTE RESOLVER

ACCA 13302
29 Lincoln's Inn Fields, LONDON, WC2A 3EE
Tel: 020 7059 5700 **Fax:** 020 7059 7070
Titles:
FINANCIAL SERVICES REVIEW

ACCENT MAGAZINES LTD 13275
5-11 Causey Street, Gosforth, NEWCASTLE UPON TYNE, NE3 4DJ **Tel:** 0191 284 9994 **Fax:** 0191 284 9995
Web site: http://www.accentmagazines.co.uk
Titles:
ACCENT
NORTH EAST TIMES COUNTY MAGAZINE
NORTHEAST HOUSE HUNTER

ACCESS INTELLIGENCE LLC 13718
4-25 Scala Street, LONDON, W1T 2HP **Tel:** 020 7436 7676
Fax: 020 7436 3749
Web site: http://www.chemweek.com
Titles:
CHEMICAL WEEK

ACCOLADE PUBLISHING 1679929
Shetland House, 5-25 Scrutton Street, LONDON, EC2A 4HJ
Tel: 020 7613 7472
Email: puzzles@accoladepublishing.co.uk
Web site: http://www.totalpuzzles.co.uk
Titles:
COMPETITORS COMPANION
JUMBO CROSS
JUMBO CROSS COLLECTION
LOGICAL CHALLENGE
PUZZLE MONTHLY
PUZZLE MONTHLY COLLECTION
TEA BREAK QUICKIE CROSSWORDS
TOTAL SUDOKU

ACCOMMODATION SEARCH ENGINE 625243
Derlwyn, Hayscastle, HAVERFORDWEST, SA62 5PW
Tel: 01437 741543 **Fax:** 01437 741129
Web site: http://www.ase.net
Titles:
ASE.NETWORK

ACE PUBLISHING 1692148
4 Carriers Place, Blackham, TUNBRIDGE WELLS, TN3 9UQ
Tel: 01892 740869 **Fax:** 0870 762 8112
Titles:
CASINO LIFE

ACEVILLE PUBLICATIONS LTD 623741
21-23 Phoenix Court, Hawkins Road, COLCHESTER, CO2 8JY **Tel:** 01206 505900 **Fax:** 01206 505915
Web site: http://www.aceville.com
Titles:
COOK VEGETARIAN!
CRAFT BUSINESS
CRAFTS BEAUTIFUL
GARDEN WILDLIFE
GREAT BRITISH FOOD
GROW YOUR OWN
GUN MART
LET'S GROW VEG
LET'S KNIT
LET'S MAKE CARDS
NATURAL HEALTH
PERIOD IDEAS
SEW
SLIM AT HOME
SOUL & SPIRIT
SPECIALITY FOOD
WHAT GUN

ACG PUBLICATIONS 14717
The Publishing House, 119 Newland Street, WITHAM, CM8 1WF **Tel:** 01376 521900 **Fax:** 01376 521901
Titles:
ANGLIA BUSINESS

ACKRILL GROUP LTD 15005
1 Cardale Park, Beckwith Head Road, HARROGATE, HG3 1RZ **Tel:** 01423 564321 **Fax:** 01423 707440
Titles:
ACKRILL NEWSPAPER SERIES
ELEGANCE MAGAZINE
HARROGATEADVERTISER.NET

ACORN INTERNET LTD 1640330
18 Shepherds Close, Grove, WANTAGE, OX12 0NX
Tel: 01235 224633
Email: ewk@acorn-internet-ltd.co.uk
Web site: http://www.acorn-internet-ltd.co.uk
Titles:
EQUINE WORLD UK

ACP PUBLISHERS LTD 14005
Offices 2 & 3, Brixfield Farm, Sunrising Hill, Kineton, WARWICK, CV35 0ED **Tel:** 01926 691212
Fax: 01926 642060
Titles:
AMENITY MACHINERY & EQUIPMENT
FARM CONTRACTOR & LARGE SCALE FARMER
FARM MACHINERY DIRECTORY

ACP-NATMAG 1724004
33 Broadwick Street, LONDON, W1F 0DQ
Tel: 020 7439 5000
Titles:
REAL PEOPLE

ACT PUBLISHING 14084
Lion House, Church Street, MAIDSTONE, ME14 1EN
Tel: 01622 695656 **Fax:** 01622 663733
Email: info@actpub.co.uk
Web site: http://www.actpub.co.uk
Titles:
THE COMMERCIAL GREENHOUSE GROWER
THE FRUIT GROWER
THE VEGETABLE FARMER

ACTION AGAINST ALLERGY 14567
PO Box 278, TWICKENHAM, TW1 4QQ **Tel:** 020 8892 4949
Fax: 020 8892 4950
Email: aaa@actionagainstallergy.freeserve.co.uk
Web site: http://www.actionagainstallergy.co.uk
Titles:
ALLERGY NEWSLETTER

ACTION FOR SOUTH AFRICA (ACTSA) 17445
28 Penton Street, LONDON, N1 9SA **Tel:** 020 7833 3133
Fax: 020 7837 3001
Email: actsa@actsa.org
Web site: http://www.actsa.org
Titles:
ACTSA NEWS

ACTION MEDICAL RESEARCH 14589
Vincent House, HORSHAM, RH12 2DP **Tel:** 01403 210406
Fax: 01403 210541
Email: info@action.org.uk
Web site: http://www.action.org.uk
Titles:
TOUCHING LIVES

ACTIONAID 15684
Hamlyn House, Macdonald Road, LONDON, N19 5PG
Tel: 020 7561 7561 **Fax:** 020 7281 5146
Web site: http://www.actionaid.org.uk
Titles:
COMMON CAUSE

ACTIVE MAGAZINES LTD 1654028
PO Box 627, RICKMANSWORTH, WD3 0BQ
Tel: 0870 766 1653 **Fax:** 0870 766 8529
Email: info@activemagazines.co.uk
Web site: http://www.activemagazines.co.uk
Titles:
HOUSING ACTIVE
WINDOWS ACTIVE

ACUMEN PUBLICATIONS 1740132
6 The Mount, Higher Furzeham Road, BRIXHAM, TQ5 8QY
Tel: 01803 851098
Titles:
ACUMEN

AD SALES 700593
4 Beachfield Avenue, NEWQUAY, TR7 1DR
Tel: 01637 878298 **Fax:** 01637 878298
Titles:
THE NEWQUAY VOICE
ST. AUSTELL VOICE

ADDICTION RECOVERY FOUNDATION 14566
193 Victoria Street, LONDON, SW1E 5NE
Tel: 020 7233 5333 **Fax:** 020 7233 8123
Titles:
ADDICTION TODAY

ADDISON LEE PLC 1650170
35-37 William Road, LONDON, NW1 3ER
Tel: 020 7255 4224
Web site: http://www.addlee.com
Titles:
ADD LIB

ADFERO 1681292
South Quay Plaza, 183 Marsh Wall, LONDON, E14 9SH
Tel: 020 7517 2200 **Fax:** 020 7517 2233
Web site: http://www.adfero.co.uk
Titles:
ABOUTPROPERTY.CO.UK
INTHENEWS.CO.UK
MYFINANCES.CO.UK
POLITICS.CO.UK
TOTALLYMOTOR.CO.UK
TRAVELBITE.CO.UK

ADH PUBLISHING 674947
Doolittle Mill, Doolittle Lane, Totternhoe, DUNSTABLE, LU6 1QX **Tel:** 01525 222573 **Fax:** 01525 222574

UK Publishers & Their Titles

Web site: http://www.adhpublishing.com
Titles:
MILITARY ILLUSTRATED
MODEL AIRPLANE INTERNATIONAL
RADIO CONTROL CAR RACER
RADIO CONTROL MODEL FLYER
TAMIYA MODEL MAGAZINE INTERNATIONAL

ADMAN PUBLISHING LTD   1681945
5 University Street, BELFAST, BT7 1FY **Tel:** 028 6024 6624
Fax: 028 9024 6936
Email: info@admanpublishing.com
Web site: http://www.admanpublishing.com
Titles:
THE BELFAST BEAT
GAEL SPORTS
THE ULSTER TIPPLER

ADRENALINE MEDIA   1600645
8 Canfield Place, LONDON, NW6 3BT **Tel:** 0870 060 0663
Fax: 0870 060 0664
Email: ben@newsontheblock.com
Web site: http://www.newsontheblock.com
Titles:
NEWS ON THE BLOCK

ADVANCED TELEVISION LIMITED   1717418
Bondway Commercial Centre, 4th Floor, Unit 4.01, 71
Bondway, LONDON, SW8 1SQ **Tel:** 020 7793 8855
Fax: 020 7793 9955
Email: colin.mann@advanced-television.com
Web site: http://www.advanced-television.com
Titles:
ADVANCED-TELEVISION.COM

ADVANCED TELEVISION LTD   1621869
4th Floor, Unit 4.01, 71 Bondway, LONDON, SW8 1SQ
Tel: 020 7793 8855 **Fax:** 020 7793 9955
Web site: http://www.advanced-television.com
Titles:
EUROMEDIA
IPTV INTERNATIONAL

ADVANSTAR COMMUNICATIONS (U.K.) LTD   13550
Advanstar House, Park West, Sealand Road, CHESTER,
CH1 4RN **Tel:** 01244 378888 **Fax:** 01244 370011
Web site: http://www.advanstar.com
Titles:
APPLIED CLINICAL TRIALS
DENTAL PRODUCTS REPORT EUROPE
LCA•GC EUROPE
LICENSE! GLOBAL
OPHTHALMOLOGY TIMES EUROPE
PHARMACEUTICAL EXECUTIVE EUROPE
PHARMACEUTICAL TECHNOLOGY EUROPE

ADVANTAGE PUBLISHING LTD   1654029
3rd Floor, Alma House, Alma Road, REIGATE, RH2 0AX
Tel: 01737 735018 **Fax:** 01737 735195
Email: info@advantagepublishing.co.uk
Titles:
BREWERS' GUARDIAN

ADVANTAGE PUBLISHING (UK) LTD   1734536
1st Floor, Barry House, 20-22 Worple Road, LONDON,
SW19 4DH **Tel:** 020 8947 0100 **Fax:** 020 8947 0117
Titles:
BRITISH TENNIS

ADVERTISER & TIMES (HANTS)   14950
62 Old Milton Road, NEW MILTON, BH25 6EH
Tel: 01425 613009 **Fax:** 01425 638635
Web site: http://www.advertiserandtimes.co.uk
Titles:
ADVERTISER & TIMES SERIES

ADVERTISER NEWSPAPERS   16986
Bentham House, 147-149 Chorley New Road, Horwich,
BOLTON, BL6 5QE **Tel:** 01204 696916 **Fax:** 01204 691139
Email: advertiser@news4u.co.uk
Titles:
THE ADVERTISER (HORWICH, WESTHOUGHTON &
DISTRICT)

AEO   1692793
119 High Street, BERKHAMSTED, HP4 2DJ
Tel: 01442 873331 **Fax:** 01442 875551
Web site: http://www.aeo.org.uk
Titles:
EIA STANDARD

AESTHETICA MAGAZINE LTD   1746158
PO Box 371, YORK, YO23 1WL **Tel:** 01904 479168
Fax: 01904 479749
Email: info@aestheticamagazine.com
Web site: http://www.aestheticamagazine.com
Titles:
AESTHETICA

AFASIC   693802
20 Bowling Green Lane, LONDON, EC1R 0BD
Tel: 020 7490 9410 **Fax:** 020 7251 2834
Email: info@afasic.org.uk
Web site: http://www.afasic.org.uk
Titles:
AFASIC NEWS

AFION MEDIA LTD   1768099
6 Orchard Bank, Great Rissington, CHELTENHAM, GL54
2LT **Tel:** 01451 810377 **Fax:** 0870 199 1100
Titles:
ENERGY EFFICIENCY NEWS

AFRO MEDIA (UK) LTD   600534
Suite 2, 2nd Floor, AMC House, 12 Cumberland Avenue,
LONDON, NW10 7QL **Tel:** 020 8838 5900
Fax: 020 8838 3700
Titles:
AFRICA TODAY

AFT LTD   14169
7 Executive Suite, St. James Court, Wilderspool Causeway,
WARRINGTON, WA4 6PS **Tel:** 01925 444414
Email: ged59@hotmail.com
Web site: http://www.aft.org.uk
Titles:
CONTEXT NEWS MAGAZINE OF FAMILY THERAPY AND
SYSTEMIC PRACTICE IN THE UK

AFTERDARK MAGAZINE LTD   1729747
Studio 257, 20 Winchcombe Street, CHELTENHAM, GL52
2LY **Tel:** 07796 670273
Email: sales@afterdarkmagazine.co.uk
Web site: http://www.afterdarkmagazine.co.uk
Titles:
AFTERDARK MAGAZINE

AFV MODELLER LTD   1711981
176 New Bridge Street, NEWCASTLE UPON TYNE, NE1 2TE
Tel: 0191 209 1107 **Fax:** 0191 209 2002
Email: david@afvmodeller.com
Web site: http://www.airmodeller.com
Titles:
AFV MODELLER
AIR MODELLER

AGE CONCERN ENGLAND   18634
Astral House, 1268 London Road, LONDON, SW16 4ER
Tel: 020 8765 7200 **Fax:** 020 8765 7211
Email: ageagendabulletin@ace.org.uk
Web site: http://www.ageconcern.org.uk
Titles:
AGE AGENDA BULLETIN
AGE AGENDA BULLETIN

AGILE MEDIA   1757631
Gateway House, 42A East Park, CRAWLEY, RH10 6AS
Tel: 01293 590052
Titles:
DRINKS INTERNATIONAL
DRINKS INTERNATIONAL

THE AGILITY CLUB   15639
6 Fane Way, MAIDENHEAD, SL6 2TL **Tel:** 01628 680823
Titles:
AGILITY VOICE

AGORA LIFESTYLES LTD   17023
Sea Containers House, 7th Floor, 20 Upper Ground,
LONDON, SE1 9JD **Tel:** 020 7447 4073 **Fax:** 020 7447 4041
Web site: Http://www.shortcutpublications.co.uk
Titles:
NUTRITION & HEALING
SHORTCUT CONFIDENTIAL

AGRA INFORMA LTD   12440
80 Calverley Road, TUNBRIDGE WELLS, TN1 2UN
Tel: 020 7017 7500 **Fax:** 020 7017 7599
Web site: http://www.agra-net.com
Titles:
AGBIOTECH REPORTER
AGRA EUROPE
AGRAFOOD EAST EUROPE
AGRAFOOD EUROPE
CAP MONITOR
CHOCOLATE & CONFECTIONERY INTERNATIONAL
DAIRY MARKETS
ENVIRONMENTAL LAW MONTHLY
EU FOOD LAW WEEKLY
EUROCHEM MONITOR
EUROFOOD
EUROFOOD MONITOR
EUROPEAN ENVIRONMENTAL LAW FOR INDUSTRY
EUROPEAN POTATO MARKETS
FARM LAW
FISH FARMING INTERNATIONAL
F.O. LICHT'S INTERNATIONAL COFFEE REPORT
F.O. LICHT'S INTERNATIONAL SUGAR & SWEETENER
REPORT
F.O. LICHT'S WORLD ETHANOL & BIOFUELS REPORT
F.O. LICHT'S WORLD GRAIN MARKETS REPORT
F.O. LICHT'S WORLD MOLASSES & FEED INGREDIENTS
REPORT
F.O. LICHT'S WORLD TEA MARKETS MONTHLY
FOOD & DRINK LAW MONTHLY
FOODNEWS
FRUIT AND VEGETABLE MARKETS
INTERNATIONAL SUGAR JOURNAL
LIVESTOCK & MEAT
MILK PRODUCTS
POTATO MARKETS WEEKLY
PRESERVED MILK
THE PUBLIC LEDGER
RURAL EUROPE
SUGAR CANE INTERNATIONAL
WORLD DRINKS REPORT
WORLD FOOD LAW
WORLD POULTRYMEAT
WORLD SUGAR YEARBOOK
WORLDFISH REPORT

AGRI PUBLISHING INTERNATIONAL LTD   600463
Goblands Farm, Court Lane, Hadlow, TONBRIDGE, TN11
0EB **Tel:** 01732 852383 **Fax:** 01732 852488
Titles:
PROFI INTERNATIONAL

AGRICULTURAL COMMUNICATIONS LTD   1643385
11 Sunnyside Gardens, Drumoak, BANCHORY, AB31 5EZ
Tel: 01330 811616 **Fax:** 01330 811616
Email: eddie.gillanders@btopenworld.com
Titles:
FARM NORTH EAST

AGRICULTURAL LAW ASSOCIATION   672202
Kimblewick Cottage, Prince Albert Road, West Mersea,
COLCHESTER, CO5 8AZ **Tel:** 01206 383521
Email: geoff@geoffwhittaker.com
Web site: http://www.ala.org.uk
Titles:
ALA BULLETIN

AGUDAS YISROEL OF GREAT BRITAIN   15891
8 Grosvenor Way, LONDON, E5 9ND **Tel:** 020 8806 1978
Fax: 020 8806 5556
Titles:
JEWISH TRIBUNE

AIA   1643874
Staithes 3, The Watermark, Metro Riverside, NEWCASTLE
UPON TYNE, NE11 9SN **Tel:** 0191 493 0277
Fax: 0191 493 0278
Email: aia@aiaworldwide.com
Web site: http://www.aiaworldwide.com
Titles:
INTERNATIONAL ACCOUNTANT

THE AIB-ASSOCIATION FOR INTERNATIONAL BROADCASTING   696735
PO Box 141, CRANBROOK, TN17 9AJ **Tel:** 020 7993 2557
Fax: 020 7993 8043
Email: info@aib.org.uk
Web site: http://www.aib.org.uk
Titles:
    THE CHANNEL

AID LTD   18566
Fairview, 31 Cape Road, WARWICK, CV34 4JP
Tel: 01926 410040 **Fax:** 01926 776252
Email: info@eagleAID.com
Web site: http://www.eagleAID.com
Titles:
    AID AUTOMOTIVE INDUSTRY DATA NEWSLETTER

AIR CARGO MEDIA LTD   17075
Headline House, Chaucer Road, ASHFORD, TW15 2QT
Tel: 01784 255000 **Fax:** 01784 246189
Titles:
    AIR CARGO NEWS

THE AIR LETTER   12315
42 Markham Court, CAMBERLEY, GU15 3HJ
Tel: 01276 502571 **Fax:** 01276 501654
Titles:
    THE AIR LETTER

AIR TRANSPORT PUBLICATIONS LTD   623436
16 Hampden Gurney Street, LONDON, W1H 5AL
Tel: 020 7724 3456 **Fax:** 020 7724 2632
Email: info@airtransportpubs.com
Web site: http://www.airtransportpubs.com
Titles:
    AIR CARGO YEARBOOK
    AIRCRAFT MAINTENANCE & ENGINEERING DIRECTORY
    AIRLINE CARGO MANAGEMENT
    AIRPORT EQUIPMENT & SERVICES BUYERS' GUIDE
    MRO MANAGEMENT

AIR-BRITAIN (HISTORIANS) LTD   1649369
Whitmore, Rockshaw Road, MERSTHAM, RH1 3BZ
Tel: 01737 642527 **Fax:** 01737 644442
Titles:
    AVIATION WORLD

AIRCRAFT VALUE ANALYSIS CO   13617
23 Cherry Lane, Bearley, STRATFORD-UPON-AVON, CV37 0SX **Tel:** 01789 730283 **Fax:** 01789 730309
Titles:
    AIRCRAFT VALUE JOURNAL

AIRPORTS PUBLISHING NETWORK LTD   13627
The Stables, Willow Lane, Paddock Wood, TONBRIDGE, TN12 6PF **Tel:** 01892 839200 **Fax:** 01892 839210
Titles:
    GROUND HANDLING INTERNATIONAL

AIRSTREAM COMMUNICATIONS LTD   12470
59-61 The Broadway, HAYWARDS HEATH, RH16 3AS
Tel: 01444 440188 **Fax:** 01444 414813
Web site: http://www.airstream.co.uk
Titles:
    BRUSHWORK
    TOOL BUSINESS + HIRE

AITEC   13611
8 High Street, Croxton, ST. NEOTS, PE19 6SX
Tel: 01480 880774 **Fax:** 01480 880765
Titles:
    COMPUTING AND COMMUNICATIONS AFRICA

AKHBAR LIBYA CULTURAL LTD   1713364
PO Box 268, SOUTH CROYDON, CR2 0EB
Tel: 0845 370 1102
Titles:
    AKHBAR LIBYA

ALAD LTD   14291
Bat and Ball Studio, 168 St. Johns Hill, SEVENOAKS, TN13 3PF **Tel:** 01732 459683
Web site: http://www.aladltd.co.uk

Titles:
    HIGHWAYS
    STADIUM & ARENA MANAGEMENT

ALAIN CHARLES PUBLISHING LTD   13770
University House, 11-13 Lower Grosvenor Place, LONDON, SW1W 0EX **Tel:** 020 7834 7676 **Fax:** 020 7973 0076
Web site: http://www.alaincharles.com
Titles:
    AFRICA AND MIDDLE EAST TEXTILES
    AFRICAN FARMING AND FOOD PROCESSING
    AFRICAN REVIEW OF BUSINESS AND TECHNOLOGY
    COMMUNICATIONS AFRICA
    CTO WORLD
    FAR EASTERN AGRICULTURE
    OIL REVIEW MIDDLE EAST
    TECHNICAL REVIEW MIDDLE EAST

ALAIN CHARLES PUBLISHING (TRAVEL) LTD   676697
University House, 11-13 Lower Grosvenor Place, LONDON, SW1W 0EX **Tel:** 020 7834 6661 **Fax:** 020 7834 7519
Web site: http://www.travelbulletin.co.uk
Titles:
    TRAVEL BULLETIN

ALAN FAIRBAIRN PROMOTIONS   15456
Unit 15F, Follingsby Avenue, GATESHEAD, NE10 8HQ
Tel: 0191 418 3970 **Fax:** 0191 418 3973
Titles:
    POST OFFICE MOTORING MAGAZINE

AL-ARAB PUBLISHING HOUSE   1681938
Office W123, Westminster Business Square, 1-45 Durham Street, LONDON, SE11 5JH **Tel:** 020 7021 0966
Fax: 020 7021 0917
Web site: http://www.alarab.co.uk
Titles:
    AL-ARAB

ALBANY MEDIA   1763662
Albany Villas, 74 Eastworth Road, CHERTSEY, KT16 8DR
Titles:
    INTERSEC

ALBANY PUBLISHING   1640131
R&J Offices, New Cut East, IPSWICH, IP3 0EA
Tel: 01473 214444 **Fax:** 01473 214088
Titles:
    LIVING SPAIN

ALBATROSS PUBLICATIONS   12889
PO Box 523, HORSHAM, RH12 4WL **Tel:** 01293 871201
Titles:
    KENNEL AND CATTERY MANAGEMENT
    PRESTIGE HOTEL AND HIGH STREET INTERIORS
    PROFESSIONAL LANDSCAPER & GROUNDSMAN

ALCHEMY MEDIA   1627128
Gainsborough House, 2 Sheen Road, RICHMOND, TW9 1AE
Tel: 020 8973 2611
Web site: http://www.alchemymedia.co.uk
Titles:
    CLASS MAGAZINE
    CLUB HOUSE
    CLUB REPORT
    THE JOURNAL OF THE INSTITUTE OF
        TELECOMMUNICATIONS PROFESSIONALS
    PREVIEW

ALCOHOL CONCERN   623700
64 Leman Street, LONDON, E1 8EU **Tel:** 020 7264 0510
Fax: 020 7488 9213
Email: contact@alcoholconcern.org.uk
Web site: http://www.alcoholconcern.org.uk
Titles:
    STRAIGHT TALK

ALDERNEY JOURNAL LTD   15625
2A Olivier Court, Ollivier Street, Alderney, GUERNSEY, GY9 3TD **Tel:** 01481 823243 **Fax:** 01481 823824
Titles:
    ALDERNEY JOURNAL

ALDERSHOT NEWS LTD   14951
35-39 High Street, ALDERSHOT, GU11 1BH
Tel: 01252 339760 **Fax:** 01252 339770
Titles:
    ALDERSHOT MAIL AND NEWS SERIES

ALFA MEDIA GROUP   1644404
PO Box 72, CALDICOT, NP26 3ZG **Tel:** 01633 889419
Fax: 0870 787 7413
Email: admin@alfamedia.co.uk
Titles:
    CLASSIC CHARTER & CRUISE
    READYMEALSINFO

ALFOL LTD   674308
21 The Timber Yard, Drysdale Street, LONDON, N1 6ND
Tel: 020 7324 7540 **Fax:** 020 7739 7789
Titles:
    CREATIVE HEAD

ALIBI PUBLISHING LTD   1741166
1 The Square, King Street, WIMBORNE, BH21 1DY
Tel: 01202 841114 **Fax:** 01202 842314
Titles:
    OCC COUNTRY
    OCC OUTDOOR

ALISTAIR MCCONNACHIE   624603
268 Bath Street, GLASGOW, G2 4JR **Tel:** 0141 332 2214
Fax: 0141 353 6900
Titles:
    PROSPERITY
    SOVEREIGNTY

ALL ENGLAND NETBALL ASSOCIATION LTD   15330
Netball House, 9 Paynes Park, HITCHIN, SG5 1EH
Tel: 01462 442344 **Fax:** 01462 442343
Titles:
    NETBALL MAGAZINE

ALL THAT WOMEN WANT   624611
125 Elmore, Eldene, SWINDON, SN3 3TN
Email: editor@allthatwomenwant.com
Web site: http://www.allthatwomenwant.com
Titles:
    ALL THAT WOMEN WANT

ALL TOGETHER NOW! LTD   1653348
The Bradbury Centre, Youens Way, LIVERPOOL, L14 2EP
Tel: 0151 230 0307
Email: news@alltogethernow.org.uk
Web site: http://www.alltogethernow.org.uk
Titles:
    ALL TOGETHER NOW!

ALLENBRIDGE GROUP PLC   13373
17 Hill Street, Mayfair, LONDON, W1J 5NZ
Tel: 020 7409 1111 **Fax:** 020 7629 7026
Email: info@allenbridge.co.uk
Web site: http://www.allenbridge.co.uk
Titles:
    THE TAX SHELTER REPORT

ALLIANCE PUBLISHING TRUST   1731140
76 Sistova Road, LONDON, SW12 9QS **Tel:** 020 7608 1862
Fax: 020 7608 1862
Email: alliance@alliancemagazine.org
Web site: http://www.alliancemagazine.org
Titles:
    ALLIANCE MAGAZINE

ALLIANCE TRACE MEDIA LTD   1646143
2nd Floor, Farringdon House, 105-107 Farringdon Road, LONDON, EC1R 3BU **Tel:** 020 7014 9549
Fax: 020 7251 8051
Titles:
    TRACE

ALLPAY.NET LTD   1735128
Fortis et Fides, Whitestone Business Park, Whitestone, HEREFORD, HR1 3SE **Tel:** 0870 774 2315
Email: news@allpay.net

UK Publishers & Their Titles

Titles:
24HOUSING

ALLSCOT 14215
PO Box 6, HADDINGTON, EH41 3NQ **Tel:** 01620 822578
Fax: 01620 825079

Titles:
ALLSCOT NEWS LETTER

ALLSTAR SERVICES LTD 16346
25 Forward Drive, Christchurch Business Centre, HARROW, HA3 8NT **Tel:** 020 8861 6440 **Fax:** 020 8861 3134

Titles:
FORWARD THOUGHT

ALMANACH DE GOTHA LTD 17567
328 Linen Hall, 162-168 Regent Street, LONDON, W1B 5TD
Tel: 020 7249 9988 **Fax:** 020 8404 2629

Titles:
THE ALMANACH DE GOTHA REVIEW OF ROYAL BOOKS

ALMEIDA CAPITAL LIMITED 1692550
Burleigh House, 357 Strand, LONDON, WC2R 0HS
Tel: 020 7845 7575 **Fax:** 020 7845 7599
Email: info@almediacapital.com
Web site: http://www.almeidacapital.com

Titles:
ALTASSETS

ALPHA NEWSPAPER GROUP 15081
Unit 179, Moygashel Mills, DUNGANNON, BT71 7HB
Tel: 028 8772 2274

Titles:
ANTRIM GUARDIAN SERIES
ATHLONE VOICE
THE COUNTY DOWN OUTLOOK
TYRONE CONSTITUTION AND STRABANE WEEKLY
NEWS SERIES

ALPHABET PUBLISHING LTD 16826
PO Box 2780, BRIGHTON, BN1 5QR **Tel:** 01273 542257
Fax: 01273 542257

Titles:
ABC MAGAZINE SUSSEX

ALPHAPRINT COLCHESTER LTD 671957
Unit 2, Challenge Way, Hythe Hill, COLCHESTER, CO1 2LY
Tel: 01206 795546 **Fax:** 01206 793379

Titles:
WOODLAND HERITAGE JOURNAL

ALSTEAD CONSULTING 700149
14 Maritime Street, Leith, EDINBURGH, EH3 5LS
Tel: 0131 551 5500
Email: webmaster@hogmanay.net
Web site: http://www.hogmanay.net

Titles:
HOGMANAY.NET

ALTERNATIVE INVESTMENT MANAGEMENT ASSOCIATION 1735662
167 Fleet Street, LONDON, EC4A 2EA **Tel:** 020 7822 8380
Fax: 020 7822 8381
Web site: http://www.aima.org

Titles:
AIMA JOURNAL

ALTERNATIVE SPORTS MEDIA 1650954
27 The Brambles, CROWTHORNE, RG45 6EF
Tel: 0781 555 7325

Titles:
RACER READY

ALTERNATIVE ULSTER 1680975
56 Bradbury Place, BELFAST, BT7 1RU **Tel:** 028 9032 4455

Titles:
A U MAGAZINE

AMATEUR ROWING ASSOCIATION 15302
6 Lower Mall, Hammersmith, LONDON, W6 9DJ
Tel: 0870 060 7100 **Fax:** 0870 060 7101
Email: info@ara-rowing.org

Web site: http://www.ara-rowing.org
Titles:
ROWING & REGATTA

AMATEUR SWIMMING ASSOCIATION 17569
Harold Fern House, Derby Square, LOUGHBOROUGH, LE11 5AL **Tel:** 01509 618700 **Fax:** 01509 610720

Titles:
AMATEUR SWIMMING ASSOCIATION HANDBOOK

AMBASSADOR PRODUCTIONS LTD 1690364
Providence House, Ardenlee Street, BELFAST, BT6 8QJ
Tel: 028 9045 0010 **Fax:** 028 9073 9659
Web site: http://www.ambassador-productions.com

Titles:
LIFE TIMES

AMBIT 18627
17 Priory Gardens, LONDON, N6 5QY **Tel:** 020 8340 3566

Titles:
AMBIT

AMERICAN ASSOC. FOR THE ADVANCEMENT OF SCIENCE 14486
Science International, Bateman House, 82-88 Hills Road, CAMBRIDGE, CB2 1LQ **Tel:** 01223 326500
Fax: 01223 326501
Web site: http://www.aaas.org

Titles:
SCIENCE

THE AMERICAN CHEMICAL SOCIETY 17161
41 Galveston Road, LONDON, SW15 2RZ
Tel: 020 8870 6884 **Fax:** 020 8874 4633

Titles:
CHEMICAL AND ENGINEERING NEWS

AMERICAN IN BRITAIN 16116
PO Box 921, SUTTON, SM1 2WB **Tel:** 020 8661 0186
Fax: 020 8652 3564

Titles:
AMERICAN IN BRITAIN

AMERICAN STANDARD PLUMBING 697078
The Bathroom Works, National Avenue, HULL, HU5 4HS
Tel: 01482 499621

Titles:
THEBATHROOM.INFO

AMG LTD 1731737
Kingfisher House, 21-23 Elmfield Road, BROMLEY, BR1 1LT
Tel: 020 8135 6682 **Fax:** 020 8315 6555
Email: admin@aboutmygeneration.com

Titles:
ABOUTMYGENERATION

AMNESTY INTERNATIONAL UK 15676
17-25 New Inn Yard, LONDON, EC2A 3EY
Tel: 020 7033 1500 **Fax:** 020 7033 1503

Titles:
AMNESTY

AMOC LTD 15447
Drayton St. Leonard, WALLINGFORD, OX10 7BG
Tel: 01865 400400 **Fax:** 01865 400200
Email: hqstaff@amoc.org
Web site: http://www.amoc.org

Titles:
AM QUARTERLY

AMPLEFORTH ABBEY TRUSTEES 15857
Ampleforth College, YORK, YO62 4EY **Tel:** 01439 766867
Fax: 01439 788182

Titles:
THE AMPLEFORTH JOURNAL

AMSPAR 14488
Tavistock House North, Tavistock Square, LONDON, WC1H 9LN **Tel:** 020 7387 6005 **Fax:** 020 7388 2648
Email: info@amspar.com
Web site: http://www.amspar.co.uk

Titles:
AMSPAR MAGAZINE

AN: THE ARTISTS INFORMATION COMPANY 625633
1st Floor, 7-15 Pink Lane, NEWCASTLE UPON TYNE, NE1 5DW **Tel:** 0191 241 8000 **Fax:** 0191 241 8001

Titles:
AN MAGAZINE

ANCIENT EGYPT MAGAZINE LTD 700080
1 Newton Street, MANCHESTER, M1 1HW
Tel: 0161 872 3319 **Fax:** 0161 872 4721

Titles:
ANCIENT EGYPT

ANDREW BOND 16479
Vine House, Church Road, Harrietsham, MAIDSTONE, ME17 1HJ **Tel:** 01622 858251 **Fax:** 01622 858976

Titles:
INDUSTRIAL AUTOMATION INSIDER

ANGEL BUSINESS COMMUNICATIONS LTD 13314
Unit 6, Bow Court, Fletchworth Gate Industrial Estate, Burnsall Road, COVENTRY, CV5 6SP **Tel:** 024 7671 8970
Fax: 024 7671 8971
Web site: http://www.angelbc.com

Titles:
EUROASIA SEMICONDUCTOR
MNS MICRO NANO SYSTEMS
SNS EUROPE

ANGELS & URCHINS LTD 1638465
PO Box 32654, LONDON, W14 0EW **Tel:** 020 7603 1366
Fax: 020 7602 7208
Web site: http://www.angelsandurchins.co.uk

Titles:
ANGELS & URCHINS

ANGLIA NEWSPAPERS 1653304
Kings Road, BURY ST. EDMUNDS, IP33 3ET
Tel: 01284 768911

Titles:
BURYFREEPRESS (ON-LINE)

ANGLIA RUSKIN STUDENTS UNION 15731
Room 125, Helmore Building, East Road, CAMBRIDGE, CB1 1PT **Tel:** 01223 460008 **Fax:** 01223 417718

Titles:
THE APEX

ANGLIA RUSKIN UNIVERSITY 16339
Alumni Office, Anglia Ruskin University, Rivermead Gate, Bishop Hall Lane, CHELMSFORD, CM1 1SQ
Tel: 0845 196 4714
Email: alumni@anglia.ac.uk
Web site: http://www.anglia.ac.uk

Titles:
ASPECTS

ANGLING PUBLICATIONS LTD 16101
Regent House, 101 Broadfield Road, SHEFFIELD, S8 0XH
Tel: 0114 258 0812 **Fax:** 0114 258 2728
Email: info@anglingpublications.co.uk
Web site: http://www.anglingpublications.co.uk

Titles:
CARPWORLD
CRAFTY CARPER

ANGLO AMERICAN MEDIA LTD 18489
58 The Terrace, TORQUAY, TQ1 1DE **Tel:** 01803 400000
Fax: 01803 407390

Titles:
CAKE CRAFT AND DECORATION
CAKE CRAFT & DECORATION MAGAZINE MONTHLY

ANGLO-HELLENIC LEAGUE 624576
16-18 Paddington Street, LONDON, W1U 5AS
Tel: 020 7486 9410
Email: info@anglohellenicleague.org
Web site: http://www.anglohellenicleague.org

Titles:
THE ANGLO-HELLENIC REVIEW

ANGUS BIRD PUBLISHING 622836
31 Manor Way, CHESHAM, HP5 3BH
Email: fmbpereira@gmail.com
Titles:
KNIT & STITCH TODAY
THE THEORIST

ANGUS COUNTY PRESS LTD 14026
117-119 Castle Street, FORFAR, DD8 3AH
Tel: 01307 464899 **Fax:** 01307 466923
Email: dispatchnews@forfardispatch.com
Web site: http://www.forfardispatch.co.uk
Titles:
ARBROATH HERALD & GAZETTE SERIES
BRECHIN ADVERTISER
THE BUTEMAN
DEESIDE PIPER AND HERALD SERIES
THE ELLON TIMES AND EAST GORDON ADVERTISER
FORFAR DISPATCH SERIES
INVERURIE HERALD

ANIMAL AID 15636
The Old Chapel, Bradford Street, TONBRIDGE, TN9 1AW
Tel: 01732 364546 **Fax:** 01732 366533
Email: info@animalaid.co.uk
Web site: http://www.animalaid.co.uk
Titles:
OUTRAGE

ANIMAL DEFENDERS INTERNATIONAL 600681
Millbank Tower, Millbank, LONDON, SW1P 4QP
Tel: 020 7630 3340 **Fax:** 020 7828 2179
Email: pr@ad-international.org
Web site: http://www.navs.org.uk
Titles:
ANIMAL DEFENDER AND THE CAMPAIGNER

ANJA PUBLICATIONS LTD 16143
43A Jerningham Road, LONDON, SE14 5NQ
Tel: 020 7639 7314 **Fax:** 020 7639 7314
Titles:
PHILOSOPHY NOW

ANORAK UK LTD 1767074
Tel: 0 7980 578831
4 Water Gardens, STANMORE, HA7 3QA **Tel:** 07980 578831
Email: psorene@anorak.co.uk
Web site: http://www.anorak.co.uk
Titles:
ANORAK

ANTHEM PUBLISHING LTD 1621287
Suite 6, Piccadilly House, London Road, BATH, BA1 6PL
Tel: 01225 489984 **Fax:** 01225 489980
Titles:
CALCIO ITALIA
ITALIA!
MUSIC TECH MAGAZINE
TASTE ITALIA

THE ANTIQUARIAN HOROLOGICAL SOCIETY 13653
New House, High Street, Ticehurst, WADHURST, TN5 7AL
Tel: 01580 200155 **Fax:** 01580 201323
Titles:
ANTIQUARIAN HOROLOGY

ANTIQUE COLLECTORS' CLUB LTD 15504
Sandy Lane, Old Martlesham, WOODBRIDGE, IP12 4SD
Tel: 01394 389950 **Fax:** 01394 389999
Web site: http://www.antiquecollectorsclub.com
Titles:
ANTIQUE COLLECTING

ANTIQUES DIARY 13657
PO Box 6271, CHRISTCHURCH, BH23 9BF
Tel: 01425 280340
Titles:
ANTIQUES DIARY

ANTIQUES INFORMATION SERVICES LTD 18786
Wallsend House, PO Box 93, BROADSTAIRS, CT10 3YR
Tel: 01843 862069 **Fax:** 01843 862014
Web site: http://www.antiques-info.co.uk
Titles:
ANTIQUES INFO

ANTIQUES NEWS 625132
PO Box 3369, CHIPPENHAM, SN15 9DU **Tel:** 01225 742240
Titles:
ANTIQUESNEWS

ANTIQUITY PUBLICATIONS LTD 1640005
King's Manor, YORK, YO1 7EP **Tel:** 01904 433994
Fax: 01904 433994
Web site: http://www.antiquity.ac.uk
Titles:
ANTIQUITY

ANTONVILLE LTD 15753
Building D, Berkeley Works, Berkley Grove, LONDON, NW1 8XY **Tel:** 020 7449 0900 **Fax:** 020 7449 0901
Titles:
FRESH DIRECTION

AP PUBLICATIONS LTD 13581
58 Ryecroft Way, LUTON, LU2 7TU **Tel:** 01582 722219
Titles:
DATABASE AND NETWORK JOURNAL
SOFTWARE WORLD

APAP 18645
6 The Old Brewery, Charlton Estate, SHEPTON MALLET, BA4 5QE **Tel:** 0870 167 0999 **Fax:** 01749 342042
Titles:
AMBULANCE ASSESSMENT

APITS LTD 1759854
2nd Floor, Rear West Office, 16 Winchester Walk, LONDON, SE1 9AQ
Titles:
A PLACE IN THE SUN

APPLIED MARKET INFORMATION LTD 1761243
AMI House, 45-47 Stokes Croft, BRISTOL, BS1 3QP
Tel: 0117 924 9442 **Fax:** 0117 989 2128
Titles:
COMPOUNDING WORLD
FILM AND SHEET EXTRUSION
PIPE AND PROFILE EXTRUSION

THE APPOINTMENT LTD 16476
The Old Bank, 349 Archway Road, Highgate, LONDON, N6 5AA **Tel:** 020 8340 3366 **Fax:** 020 8340 8866
Web site: http://www.theappointment.co.uk
Titles:
THE APPOINTMENT

THE ARAB MAGAZINE 1744704
27 Old Gloucester Street, LONDON, WC1N 3AX
Tel: 020 7100 6017
Titles:
THE ARAB

ARAB-BRITISH CHAMBER OF COMMERCE 13771
43 Upper Grosvenor Street, LONDON, W1K 2NJ
Tel: 020 7235 4363 **Fax:** 020 7235 1748
Web site: http://www.abcc.org
Titles:
ARAB-BRITISH BUSINESS
ECONOMIC FOCUS

ARCHANT DIALOGUE 697243
Prospect House, Rouen Road, NORWICH, NR1 1RE
Tel: 01603 664242
Web site: http://www.archant.co.uk
Titles:
HOG TALES
SAAB MAGAZINE

ARCHANT EAST LONDON & ESSEX 697240
Media House, 539 High Road, ILFORD, IG1 1UD
Tel: 020 8478 4444 **Fax:** 020 8478 6606
Web site: http://www.archant.co.uk
Titles:
ILFORD RECORDER SERIES
NEWHAM RECORDER
ROMFORD AND HAVERING WEEKLY POST
ROMFORD RECORDER

ARCHANT HERTS & CAMBS 697234
Bank House, Primett Road, STEVENAGE, SG1 3EE
Tel: 01438 866000
Web site: http://www.archant.co.uk
Titles:
CAMBRIDGE AGENDA
CAMBS TIMES
THE COMET SERIES
DUNMOW BROADCAST AND RECORDER
ELY STANDARD SERIES
HERTS ADVERTISER
THE HUNTS POST
THE REPORTER (SAFFRON WALDEN, STANSTED & SAWSTON)
ROYSTON CROW
WELWYN & HATFIELD TIMES & HERALD SERIES
WISBECH STANDARD

ARCHANT LIFE 697244
Prospect House, Rouen Road, NORWICH, NR1 1RE
Tel: 01603 772101
Web site: http://www.archantlife.co.uk
Titles:
ANGEL & NORTH
CORNWALL LIFE
COTSWOLD LIFE
COTSWOLD WEDDINGS
DEVON LIFE
DORSET
THE ENGLISH GARDEN
THE ENGLISH HOME
FRANCE MAGAZINE
FRENCH PROPERTY NEWS
THE GREEN
THE GUIDE MAGAZINE
HEREFORDSHIRE LIFE
HERITAGE
THE HILL
KENT LIFE
LIVING FRANCE
LIVING SOUTH
NORTH MAGAZINE
NORTHWEST MAGAZINE
THE ORACLE CHELTENHAM
THE ORACLE GLOUCESTER
THE RESIDENT (LONDON)
SOUTHWEST
STAFFORDSHIRE COUNTY
SUSSEX LIFE
WARWICKSHIRE LIFE
WESTSIDE MAGAZINE

ARCHANT LIFE CAMBRIDGESHIRE, HERTFORDSHIRE AND ESSEX 1638645
28 Teville Road, Worthing, WEST SUSSEX, BN11 1UG
Tel: 020 8504 0455 **Fax:** 020 8504 0488
Web site: http://www.archantlife.co.uk
Titles:
BUCKINGHAMSHIRE LIFE
ESSEX LIFE
HERTFORDSHIRE LIFE

ARCHANT LIFE (MIDLANDS) LTD 1724447
Archant House, Oriel Road, CHELTENHAM, GL50 1BB
Tel: 01527 831733
Web site: http://www.archant.co.uk
Titles:
SHROPSHIRE LIFE
WORCESTERSHIRE LIFE

ARCHANT LIFE (NORTH) PLC 697451
61 Friar Gate, DERBY, DE1 1DJ **Tel:** 01772 722022
Fax: 01772 736496
Web site: http://www.archantlife.co.uk
Titles:
DERBYSHIRE LIFE & COUNTRYSIDE
LAKE DISTRICT LIFE
LANCASHIRE LIFE
THE LEICESTERSHIRE MAGAZINE
LIVINGEDGE
NORTH EAST LIFE
PEAK DISTRICT LIFE
PURE WEDDINGS

ARCHANT LONDON 1675354
Media House, 539 High Road, ILFORD, IG1 1UD
Tel: 020 8478 4444 **Fax:** 020 8478 6606
Titles:
BARKING AND DAGENHAM POST
THE DOCKLANDS AND PENINSULA SERIES
H & F NEWS
HACKNEY GAZETTE
HAM & HIGH SERIES
ISLINGTON GAZETTE & JOURNAL SERIES

NORTH WEST LONDON NEWSPAPER SERIES
PROPERTY MART
TIMES AND REPORTER SERIES (KENT)

ARCHANT NORFOLK　697231
Prospect House, Rouen Road, NORWICH, NR1 1RE
Tel: 01603 628311
Web site: http://www.archant.co.uk
Titles:
ANGLIA ADVERTISER SERIES
ANGLIA AFLOAT
CHESHIRE LIFE
DORSET ONLINE
EASTERN DAILY PRESS NORFOLK MAGAZINE
EASTERN DAILY PRESS (NORWICH)
GREAT YARMOUTH ADVERTISER SERIES
GREAT YARMOUTH MERCURY
LET'S TALK!
LOWESTOFT JOURNAL
NORFOLK COUNTY WEEKLIES SERIES
NORWICH EVENING NEWS
ON BUSINESS
THE PINK 'UN (NORWICH)
SURREY LIFE
YORKSHIRE LIFE
YORKSHIRE RELISH

ARCHANT REGIONAL　1640211
Prospect House, Rouen Road, NORWICH, NR1 1RE
Tel: 01603 772824 **Fax:** 01603 631226
Web site: http://www.archant.co.uk
Titles:
EAST LONDON ADVERTISER
HARLOW HERALD
STRATFORD & NEWHAM EXPRESS

ARCHANT SOUTH EAST　1744201
28 Teville Road, WORTHING, BN11 1UG **Tel:** 01903 703730
Titles:
HAMPSHIRE LIFE
WEST ESSEX LIFE

ARCHANT SOUTH WEST　697241
Fair Oak Close, Exeter Airport Business Park, Clyst Honiton, EXETER, EX5 2UL **Tel:** 01392 888400 **Fax:** 01392 888470
Web site: http://www.archant.co.uk
Titles:
ADMAG (WESTON-SUPER-MARE)
COUNTRY LANDOWNER
COUNTRY SMALLHOLDING
THE JOURNAL SERIES (EXMOUTH)
MIDWEEK HERALD
NORTH DEVON GAZETTE
SHOOTING & CONSERVATION
SIDMOUTH HERALD SERIES
VIEWS
WESTON & SOMERSET MERCURY SERIES

ARCHANT SPECIALIST LTD　697245
3 The Courtyard, Denmark Street, WOKINGHAM, RG40 2AZ
Tel: 0118 989 7212
Web site: http://www.archant.co.uk
Titles:
SPORTING SHOOTER

ARCHANT SPECIALIST LTD (SAFFRON WALDEN)　1737764
3 The Courtyard, 3 The Courtyard, WOKINGHAM, RG40 2AZ
Tel: 0118 989 7215
Titles:
BPI
CANAL BOAT
PHOTOGRAPHY MONTHLY
PILOT
PROFESSIONAL PHOTOGRAPHER
SPORTDIVER

ARCHANT SPECIALIST (WOKINGHAM)　15262
3 The Courtyard, Denmark Street, WOKINGHAM, RG40 2AZ
Tel: 020 7751 4800 **Fax:** 020 7751 4848
Titles:
AIR GUNNER
AIRGUN WORLD

ARCHANT SUFFOLK　697232
Press House, 30 Lower Brook Street, IPSWICH, IP4 1AN
Tel: 01473 230023 **Fax:** +44 01473 324626
Web site: http://www.archant.co.uk

Titles:
ADVERTISER SERIES (IPSWICH)
BUSINESS EAST
EA WEEK
EADT SUFFOLK BUSINESS
EAST ANGLIAN DAILY TIMES
EAST ANGLIAN DAILY TIMES SUFFOLK
EVENING STAR
GREEN 'UN (IPSWICH)
MERCURY SERIES

ARCHERS ADDICTS　675115
The Village Voice Company, The Mansley Centre, Timothys Bridge Road, STRATFORD-UPON-AVON, CV37 9NQ
Tel: 08708 744400 **Fax:** 01789 207481
Email: dum.di.dum@archers-addicts.com
Web site: http://www.archers-addicts.com
Titles:
THE AMBRIDGE VOICE

THE ARCHITECTS' REGISTRATION BOARD　18220
8 Weymouth Street, LONDON, W1W 5BU
Tel: 020 7580 5861 **Fax:** 020 7436 5269
Titles:
REGISTER OF ARCHITECTS

ARCHITECTURAL ASSOCIATION　17436
36 Bedford Square, LONDON, WC1B 3ES
Tel: 020 7887 4000 **Fax:** 020 7414 0782
Email: publications@aaschool.ac.uk
Web site: http://www.aaschool.info/publications/
Titles:
AA FILES

ARCHITECTURE TODAY PLC　13489
161 Rosebery Avenue, LONDON, EC1R 4QX
Tel: 020 7837 0143 **Fax:** 020 7837 0155
Web site: http://www.architecturetoday.co.uk
Titles:
ARCHITECTURE TODAY
AT HANDBOOK

ARCWIND LTD　15307
The Blue Barns, Tew Lane, Wootton, WOODSTOCK, OX20 1HA **Tel:** 01993 811181 **Fax:** 01993 811481
Titles:
KITESURF MAGAZINE
PITPILOT
POWERKITE
WINDSURF MAGAZINE

AREMI LTD　14037
2 The Hill, Almondsbury, BRISTOL, BS32 4AE
Tel: 01454 615118
Email: edit@potatoreview.com
Web site: http://www.potatoreview.com
Titles:
POTATO REVIEW

ARENA　1733110
70 Copthorne Avenue, BROMLEY, BR2 8NN
Tel: 020 3087 2378
Titles:
AROUND ARENA

ARETE CONSULTING LTD　1753229
12 Broadbent Close, 20-22 Highgate High Street, LONDON, N6 5JW **Tel:** 020 8347 0203 **Fax:** 020 8347 7872
Titles:
STRUCTURED RETAIL PRODUCTS

AREZA LTD　623042
Britannia House, 11 Glenthorne Road, LONDON, W6 0LH
Tel: 0870 745 3380
Titles:
CAR NEWS PORTAL
CONSTRUCTION NEWS PORTAL
ECO FRIEND NEWS
ELECTRICAL PORTAL
GIFT OR PRESENT
GOLD AND PRECIOUS METALS
NEWBORN TO TEEN
PLUMBING PARK
SECURITY PARK

ARGUS MEDIA LTD　699409
175 St. John Street, LONDON, EC1V 4LW
Tel: 020 7780 4200 **Fax:** 020 7780 4201
Email: sales@argusmediagroup.com
Web site: http://www.argusmediagroup.com
Titles:
ARGUS FSU ENERGY
ARGUS FUNDAMENTALS
PETROLEUM ARGUS GAS CONNECTIONS
PETROLEUM ARGUS LPG WORLD
WEEKLY PETROLEUM ARGUS

ARGYLL COMMUNICATIONS　625090
29 Charlemont Lane, Clontarf, DUBLIN 3 **Tel:** +353 1 83 30 560
Web site: http://www.argyllcommunications.ie
Titles:
COMMERCIAL PROPERTY & INTERIORS
MOVING IN MAGAZINE

ARK GROUP LTD　16192
266-276 Upper Richmond Road, LONDON, SW15 6TQ
Tel: 020 8785 2700 **Fax:** 020 8785 9373
Web site: http://www.ark-group.com
Titles:
ELDERLY CLIENT ADVISER
FD LEGAL
INSIDE KNOWLEDGE
MANAGING PARTNER

ARLIS/UK & IRELAND　17461
Word and Image Department, Victoria and Albert Mus, Cromwell Road, South Kensington, LONDON, SW7 2RL
Tel: 020 7942 2317
Email: arlis@vam.ac.uk
Web site: http://www.arlis.org.uk
Titles:
ARLIS/UK & IRELAND ANNUAL DIRECTORY
ART LIBRARIES JOURNAL

ARNFORD LTD　14004
PO Box 100, Benniworth, MARKET RASEN, LN8 6LE
Tel: 01507 313798 **Fax:** 01507 313997
Titles:
PIG WORLD

ARNOLD STRATEGY　1710857
31 Burroway Road, Langley, SLOUGH, SL3 8EH
Tel: 01753 542810
Titles:
OCTOPUSH NEWS

AROQ LTD　622411
Seneca House, Buntsford Hill Business Park, Buntsford Park Road, BROMSGROVE, B60 3DX **Tel:** 01527 573600
Fax: 01527 577423
Web site: http://www.aroq.com
Titles:
JUST-AUTO.COM
JUST-DRINKS.COM
JUST-FOOD.COM
JUST-STYLE.COM

AROUND KENT PUBLICATIONS　15963
Flat 1, Ashley House, Royal Crescent, MARGATE, CT9 5AJ
Tel: 01843 571500
Titles:
AROUND CANTERBURY

ART 21 LTD　16377
Suite K 101, Tower Bridge Business Complex, 100 Clements Road, LONDON, SE16 4DG **Tel:** 020 7740 1704
Fax: 020 7252 3510
Email: brian@art-21.co.uk
Web site: http://www.art-21.co.uk
Titles:
CONTEMPORARY

THE ART FUND　15808
Millais House, 7 Cromwell Place, LONDON, SW7 2JN
Tel: 020 7225 4800 **Fax:** 020 7225 4848
Web site: http://www.artfund.org
Titles:
ART QUARTERLY

ARTETECH PUBLISHING COMPANY 698853
PO Box 972, Thelwall, WARRINGTON, WA4 9DP
Tel: 07813 075509 **Fax:** 0870 706 1858
Titles:
THE INTERNATIONAL JOURNAL OF METEOROLOGY

ARTFEKS PUBLISHING 16824
Building D, Templar Business Park, off Torrington Avenue,
COVENTRY, CV4 9AP **Tel:** 024 7646 5000
Web site: http://www.bizworldonline.com
Titles:
BUSINESS WORLD
LONDON BUSINESS WORLD
WEST MIDLANDS HERALD

ARTHRITIS CARE 14568
18 Stephenson Way, LONDON, NW1 2HD
Tel: 020 7380 6500 **Fax:** 020 7380 6505
Email: info@arthritiscare.org.uk
Web site: http://www.arthritiscare.org.uk
Titles:
ARTHRITIS NEWS

ARTHRITIS TODAY 1726520
Copeman House, St. Marys Court, St. Marys Gate,
CHESTERFIELD, S41 7TD **Tel:** 01246 541107
Fax: 01246 558007
Web site: http://www.arc.org.uk
Titles:
ARTHRITIS TODAY

ARTIKOL 13725
39 Cromwell Road, BECKENHAM, BR3 4LL
Tel: 020 8658 2621 **Fax:** 020 8402 1544
Email: regadams@artikol.com
Web site: http://www.artikol.com
Titles:
TIO2 WORLDWIDE UPDATE

THE ARTISTS' PUBLISHING COMPANY LTD 15521
Caxton House, 63-65 High Street, TENTERDEN, TN30 6BD
Tel: 01580 763673 **Fax:** 01580 765411
Web site: http://www.painters-online.co.uk
Titles:
THE ARTIST (INC. ART & ARTISTS)
LEISURE PAINTER

ARTREVIEW LTD 15809
1 Sekforde Street, LONDON, EC1R 0BE **Tel:** 020 7107 2760
Fax: 020 7107 2761
Web site: http://www.art-review.co.uk
Titles:
ARTREVIEW

ARTROCKER MAGAZINE LTD 1729597
16 Cholmeley Place, READING, RG1 3NH
Titles:
ARTROCKER MAGAZINE

ARTS INTELLIGENCE LTD 674041
PO Box 1010, Histon, CAMBRIDGE, CB24 9WH
Tel: 01223 200200 **Fax:** 01223 200201
Titles:
ARTSPROFESSIONAL

ARTS RESEARCH LIMITED 623709
Corbridge Business Centre, Tinklers Yard, CORBRIDGE,
NE45 5SB **Tel:** 01434 636089
Email: enquiries@arts-research-digest.com
Web site: http://www.arts-research-digest.com
Titles:
ARTS RESEARCH DIGEST

ARTSWORK 1718360
Fairways House, Mount Pleasant Road, SOUTHAMPTON,
SO14 0QB **Tel:** 023 8063 0960
Titles:
UPSTART

AS&K SKYLIGHT 1622265
3rd Floor, Commonwealth House, 1 New Oxford Street,
LONDON, WC1A 1NU **Tel:** 020 7759 2999
Fax: 020 7759 2901

Email: info@ask-mediapartnership.com
Web site: http://www.ask-partnership.com
Titles:
QP

ASAP PUBLISHING LTD 622181
PO Box 4173, WIMBORNE, BH21 1YX **Tel:** 01202 842222
Fax: 01202 848494
Titles:
SOFT DRINKS INTERNATIONAL

ASEMPA LIMITED 1732870
Vine House, Fair Green, Reach, CAMBRIDGE, CB5 0JD
Tel: 01638 743633 **Fax:** 01638 743998
Titles:
AFRICA ASIA CONFIDENTIAL
AFRICA CONFIDENTIAL

ASHDOWN.CO.UK LTD 13008
Ancient Lights, 19 River Road, ARUNDEL, BN18 9EY
Tel: 01903 884988 **Fax:** 01903 885514
Email: ashdown@ashdown.co.uk
Web site: http://www.ashdown.co.uk
Titles:
BEAD
CAT WORLD
CAT WORLD ONLINE
DOLLS HOUSE WORLD
THE TEDDY BEAR CLUB INTERNATIONAL

ASHFORD BOROUGH COUNCIL 1676025
Civic Centre, Tannery Lane, ASHFORD, TN23 1PL
Tel: 01233 331111
Web site: http://www.ashford.gov.uk
Titles:
ASHFORD VOICE

ASHLEY AND DUMVILLE PUBLISHING LTD 1757258
Regent House, Bexton Lane, KNUTSFORD, WA16 9AB
Tel: 01565 653283 **Fax:** 01565 755607
Web site: http://www.ashleyanddumville.co.uk
Titles:
RENEWABLE ENERGY INSTALLER

ASHLEY MARK PUBLISHING CO. 15360
1-2 Vance Court, Trans Britannia Enterprise Park, BLAYDON
ON TYNE, NE21 5NH **Tel:** 0191 414 9000
Fax: 0191 414 9001
Email: info@ashleymark.co.uk
Web site: http://www.fretsonly.com
Titles:
CLASSICAL GUITAR

ASHRIDGE COMMUNICATIONS 1731736
Berkhamsted House, 121 High Street, BERKHAMSTED, HP4
2DJ **Tel:** 01442 877992 **Fax:** 01442 870148
Email: info@ashridgecommunications.com
Web site: http://www.ashridgecommunications.com
Titles:
HEALTH MANAGEMENT

ASHTON WEEKLY NEWSPAPERS LTD 14941
Park House, 5 Acres Lane, STALYBRIDGE, SK15 2JR
Tel: 0161 303 1910 **Fax:** 0161 303 1922
Titles:
ASHTON-UNDER-LYNE REPORTER SERIES

THE ASIAN ART LTD 624200
PO Box 22521, LONDON, W8 4GT **Tel:** 020 7229 6040
Fax: 020 7565 2913
Web site: http://www.asianartnewspaper.com
Titles:
ASIAN ART NEWSPAPER

ASIAN BUSINESS PUBLICATIONS LTD 14440
Unit 2, Karma Yoga House, 12 Hoxton Market, LONDON, N1
6HW **Tel:** 020 7749 4082 **Fax:** 020 7749 4081
Web site: http://www.abplgroup.com
Titles:
ASIAN VOICE
GUJARAT SAMACHAR

THE ASIAN EXPRESS NEWSPAPER 18458
211 Piccadilly, LONDON, W1J 9HF **Tel:** 020 7917 2744
Fax: 020 7537 2141
Web site: http://www.asianexpressnewspaper.com
Titles:
THE ASIAN EXPRESS NEWSPAPER

ASIAN INTERACTIVE MEDIA 694586
The Accessory House, Cox Lane, CHESSINGTON, KT9 1SD
Tel: 0870 755 5501 **Fax:** 020 8880 6837
Web site: http://www.asianwomanmag.com
Titles:
ASIAN BRIDE
ASIAN WOMAN

ASIAN TRADE PUBLICATIONS LTD 14039
Garavi Gujarat House, 1 Silex Street, LONDON, SE1 0DW
Tel: 020 7928 1234 **Fax:** 020 7261 0055
Email: tanuja@gujarat.co.uk
Web site: http://www.asiantrader.biz
Titles:
ASIAN TRADER
PHARMACY BUSINESS

ASIAN VOICE GROUP 1621191
PO Box 15, BATLEY, WF17 7YY **Tel:** 01924 510512
Fax: 01924 510513
Titles:
AWAAZ

ASLEF 13859
9 Arkwright Road, Hampstead, LONDON, NW3 6AB
Tel: 020 7317 8600 **Fax:** 020 7794 6406
Email: journal@aslef.org.uk
Web site: http://www.aslef.org
Titles:
ASLEF LOCOMOTIVE JOURNAL

**ASLIB - ASSOCIATION FOR INFORMATION
MANAGEMENT** 13451
The Holywell Centre, 1 Phipp Street, LONDON, EC2A 4PS
Tel: 020 7613 3031 **Fax:** 020 7613 5080
Web site: http://www.aslib.com
Titles:
MANAGING INFORMATION

ASOS 1764013
Greater London House, Hampstead Road, LONDON, NW1
7SB **Tel:** 020 7756 1000
Titles:
ASOS

ASPECT MEDIA 1715170
Bakehouse Unit J108, 100 Clements Road, LONDON, SE16
4DG **Tel:** 020 7064 8400 **Fax:** 020 7231 1231
Web site: http://www.aspectmediauk.com
Titles:
THE BRIDGE
CLOSE UP

ASPERMONT 14101
Albert House, 1 Singer Street, LONDON, EC2A 4BQ
Tel: 020 7216 6060 **Fax:** 020 7216 6050
Titles:
GEODRILLING INTERNATIONAL
MINING ENVIRONMENTAL MANAGEMENT
MINING JOURNAL
MINING JOURNAL
MINING MAGAZINE
WORLD TUNNELLING/TRENCHLESS WORLD

ASSERTIVE MEDIA GROUP LIMITED 1653829
28 Sandford Street, LICHFIELD, WS13 6QA
Tel: 0870 242 7021 **Fax:** 0870 242 7023
Titles:
ACQUISITION FINANCE

ASSET INTERNATIONAL 12163
150 Borough High Street, LONDON, SE1 1LB
Tel: 020 7148 4280 **Fax:** 020 7148 4292
Email: newsdesk@globalcustodian.com
Web site: http://www.globalcustodian.com
Titles:
GLOBAL CUSTODIAN

UK Publishers & Their Titles

ASSOCIA LTD 622016
Agriculture House, North Gate, Uppingham, OAKHAM, LE15
9NX **Tel:** 01572 824600 **Fax:** 01572 824651
Email: info@associa.co.uk

Titles:
BRITISH FARMER AND GROWER
COUNTRYSIDE MAGAZINE
FARMING WALES YR AMAETHWR
NFU BRITISH FARMER AND GROWER (EAST ANGLIA)
NFU BRITISH FARMER AND GROWER (EAST
 MIDLANDS)
NFU BRITISH FARMER AND GROWER (NORTH EAST)
NFU BRITISH FARMER AND GROWER (NORTH WEST)
NFU BRITISH FARMER AND GROWER (SOUTH EAST)
NFU BRITISH FARMER AND GROWER (SOUTH WEST)
NFU BRITISH FARMER & GROWER (WEST MIDLANDS)
NFU HORTICULTURE
TOWNSWOMAN

ASSOCIATED NEWSPAPERS LTD 14816
Northcliffe House, 2 Derry Street, LONDON, W8 5TT
Tel: 020 7938 6000 **Fax:** 020 7937 3745
Web site: http://www.dmgt.co.uk

Titles:
DAILY MAIL
DAILY MAIL (CITY OFFICE)
DAILY MAIL (MANCHESTER OFFICE)
DAILY MAIL ONLINE
DAILY MAIL WEEKEND
FMWF FINANCIAL MAIL WOMEN'S FORUM
HOMESANDPROPERTY.CO.UK
LIVE
LONDON LITE
THE MAIL ON SUNDAY
METRO (LONDON)
METRO (SCOTLAND)
METRO.CO.UK
SCOTTISH DAILY MAIL
SCOTTISH MAIL ON SUNDAY
YOU MAGAZINE THE MAIL ON SUNDAY

ASSOCIATED NORTHCLIFFE DIGITAL 1723456
Northcliffe House, 2 Derry Street, LONDON, W8 5TT
Tel: 020 7938 6000 **Fax:** 020 7937 7614

Titles:
THIS IS MONEY
TRAVELMAIL.CO.UK

**ASSOCIATION FOR CONSULTANCY AND
ENGINEERING** 17443
Alliance House, 12 Caxton Street, LONDON, SW1H 0QL
Tel: 020 7222 6557 **Fax:** 020 7222 0750

Titles:
ACE DIRECTORY

**ASSOCIATION FOR INTERACTIVE MEDIA &
ENTERTAINMENT** 691194
2-5 Manchester Street, BRIGHTON, BN2 1TF
Tel: 0844 582 8828
Email: toby@aimelink.org
Web site: http://www.aimelink.org

Titles:
AIME

THE ASSOCIATION FOR LANGUAGE LEARNING 17616
University of Leicester, University Road, LEICESTER, LE1
7RH **Tel:** 0116 229 7453 **Fax:** 0116 229 7456
Email: info@all-languages.org.uk
Web site: http://www.all-languages.org.uk

Titles:
FRANCOPHONIE

**THE ASSOCIATION FOR MANAGEMENT EDUCATION &
DEVELOPMENT** 13801
7-8 Roman Way, Small Business Park, London Road,
Godmanchester, HUNTINGDON, PE29 2LN
Tel: 01480 459575 **Fax:** 01480 450721
Web site: http://www.amed.org.uk

Titles:
AMED NEWS
ORGANISATIONS & PEOPLE

ASSOCIATION FOR ORGANICS RECYCLING 1681961
3 Burystead Place, WELLINGBOROUGH, NN8 1AH
Tel: 0870 160 3270 **Fax:** 0870 160 3280
Email: enquiries@organics-recycling.org.uk
Web site: http://www.organics-recycling.org.uk

Titles:
COMPOSTING NEWS

ASSOCIATION FOR PERIOPERATIVE PRACTICE 14522
Daisy Ayris House, 6 Grove Park Court, HARROGATE, HG1
4DP **Tel:** 01423 508079 **Fax:** 01423 531613
Web site: http://www.afpp.org.uk

Titles:
JOURNAL OF PERIOPERATIVE PRACTICE

ASSOCIATION FOR PHYSICAL EDUCATION 14188
Building 25, London Road, READING, RG1 5AQ
Tel: 0118 378 6240 **Fax:** 0118 378 6242
Web site: http://www.afpe.org.uk

Titles:
PHYSICAL EDUCATION MATTERS

THE ASSOCIATION FOR SCIENCE EDUCATION 14485
College Lane, HATFIELD, AL10 9AA **Tel:** 01707 283000
Fax: 01707 266532
Web site: http://www.ase.org.uk

Titles:
EDUCATION IN SCIENCE
PRIMARY SCIENCE REVIEW
SCHOOL SCIENCE REVIEW

**ASSOCIATION OF BRITISH HEALTH-CARE
INDUSTRIES** 14604
111 Westminster Bridge Road, LONDON, SE1 7HR
Tel: 020 7960 4360 **Fax:** 020 7960 4361

Titles:
FOCUS

ASSOCIATION OF BRITISH SCIENCE WRITERS - ABSW
600512
Wellcome Wolfson Building, 165 Queen's Gate, LONDON,
SW7 5HE **Tel:** 0870 770 3361 **Fax:** 0870 770 7102
Email: press@kenward.eu
Web site: http://www.absw.org.uk

Titles:
THE SCIENCE REPORTER

ASSOCIATION OF BUILDING ENGINEERS 13490
Lutyens House, Billing Brook Road, NORTHAMPTON, NN3
8NW **Tel:** 01604 404121 **Fax:** 01604 784220
Email: building.engineers@abe.org.uk
Web site: http://www.abe.org.uk

Titles:
BUILDING ENGINEER

**ASSOCIATION OF CHARITY INDEPENDENT
EXAMINERS** 697097
ACIE, Bentley Resource Centre, High Street, Bentley,
DONCASTER, DN5 0AA **Tel:** 01302 828338
Email: info@acie.org.uk
Web site: http://www.acie.org.uk

Titles:
INDEPENDENT EXAMINER

ASSOCIATION OF CHRISTIAN TEACHERS 16293
94A London Road, ST. ALBANS, AL1 1NX
Tel: 01727 840298 **Fax:** 01727 848966
Web site: http://www.christian-teachers.org.uk

Titles:
ACT NOW

THE ASSOCIATION OF CORPORATE TREASURERS
13301
51 Moorgate, LONDON, EC2R 6BH **Tel:** 020 7847 2540
Fax: 020 7374 8744
Web site: http://www.treasurers.org

Titles:
THE TREASURER

ASSOCIATION OF EDUCATIONAL PSYCHOLOGISTS
18630
26 The Avenue, DURHAM, DH1 4ED **Tel:** 0191 384 9512
Fax: 0191 386 5287

Titles:
AEP APPOINTMENTS BROADSHEET

ASSOCIATION OF ILLUSTRATORS 1713022
2nd Floor, Back Building, 150 Curtain Road, LONDON,
EC2A 3AT **Tel:** 020 7613 4328 **Fax:** 020 7613 4417
Email: info@theaoi.com
Web site: http://www.theaoi.com

Titles:
VAROOM

ASSOCIATION OF INDEPENDENT MUSEUMS 14811
Lindford Cottage, Church Lane, Cocking, MIDHURST, GU29
0HW **Tel:** 01730 812419 **Fax:** 01730 812419
Email: heavyhorse@mistral.co.uk
Web site: http://www.aim-museums.co.uk

Titles:
ASSOCIATION OF INDEPENDENT MUSEUMS (AIM)
 BULLETIN

ASSOCIATION OF INTERIOR SPECIALISTS 621525
Olton Bridge, 245 Warwick Road, SOLIHULL, B92 7AH
Tel: 0121 707 0077 **Fax:** 0121 706 1949
Email: interiorsfocus@ais-interiors.org.uk
Web site: http://www.ais-interiors.org.uk

Titles:
INTERIORS FOCUS

ASSOCIATION OF LIGHTHOUSE KEEPERS 625386
3 Exeter Road, DAWLISH, EX7 9JD **Tel:** 01986 894937

Titles:
LAMP

ASSOCIATION OF PHOTOGRAPHERS 14244
81 Leonard Street, LONDON, EC2A 4QS **Tel:** 020 7739 6669
Fax: 020 7739 8707
Web site: http://www.the-aop.org

Titles:
IMAGE

ASSOCIATION OF REVENUE AND CUSTOMS 12387
8 Leake Street, LONDON, SE1 7NN **Tel:** 020 7401 5555
Fax: 020 7401 5550
Email: arc@fda.org.uk

Titles:
ARC

ASSOCIATION OF SCHOOL AND COLLEGE LEADERS
1654067
130 Regent Road, LEICESTER, LE1 7PG **Tel:** 0116 299 1122
Fax: 0116 299 1123
Web site: http://www.ascl.org.uk

Titles:
LEADER

THE ASSOCIATION OF TEACHERS OF MATHEMATICS
15920
Unit 7 Prime Industrial Park, Shaftesbury Street, DERBY,
DE23 8YB **Tel:** 01332 346599 **Fax:** 01332 204357
Web site: http://www.atm.org.uk

Titles:
MT MATHEMATICS TEACHING INCORPORATING
 MICROMATH

ASSOCIATION OF WELDING DISTRIBUTORS 1731819
Securehold Business Centre, Studley Road, REDDITCH, B98
7LG **Tel:** 01952 290036 **Fax:** 01952 290037
Email: info@awd.org.uk
Web site: http://www.awd.org.uk

Titles:
AWD WELDING BUSINESS BULLETIN

ASTHMA ENTERPRISES LIMITED 623287
Summit House, 70 Wilson Street, LONDON, EC2A 2DB
Tel: 020 7786 4900 **Fax:** 020 7256 6075

Titles:
ASTHMA MAGAZINE

ASTON STUDENTS GUILD 15736
Aston Students Guild, Aston Triangle, BIRMINGHAM, B4
7ES **Tel:** 0121 359 6531 **Fax:** 0121 333 4218
Email: guild.editor@aston.ac.uk
Web site: http://www.astonguild.org.uk

Titles:
ASTON TIMES

AT REVIEW PUBLISHING 1730537
PO Box 6098, NEWBURY, RG14 9BN **Tel:** 01635 297000
Fax: 01635 297000

Titles:
WANTAGE AND GROVE REVIEW

AT VETERINARY SYSTEMS LTD 698838
Elmtree Business Park, Elmswell, BURY ST EDMUNDS, IP30
9HR **Tel:** 01359 243400 **Fax:** 01359 242921
Titles:
VISION ONLINE

THE AT WORK PARTNERSHIP LTD 1719951
19 Bishops Avenue, Elstree, BOREHAMWOOD, WD6 3LZ
Tel: 0845 017 6986 **Fax:** 020 8275 8469
Web site: http://www.atworkpartnership.co.uk
Titles:
OCCUPATIONAL HEALTH AT WORK

ATALINK LTD 1622318
40 Bowling Green Lane, LONDON, EC1R 0NE
Tel: 020 7074 7700 **Fax:** 020 7837 6135
Email: hq@atalink.com
Web site: http://www.atalink.co.uk
Titles:
DIRECTOR OF FINANCE ONLINE
SME WEB
WOMAN'S HEALTH
WOMAN'S WORLD

ATE / CLARION EVENTS 625370
Earls Court Exhibition Centre, Warwick Road, LONDON,
SW5 9TA **Tel:** 020 7370 8560
Titles:
COINSLOT INTERNATIONAL

ATHENE PUBLISHING 1686926
1st Floor, Axe and Bottle Court, 70 Newcomen Street,
LONDON, SE1 1YT **Tel:** 0844 477 4740 **Fax:** 020 7940 4843
Web site: http://www.credittoday.co.uk
Titles:
CREDIT TODAY

ATHOLE DESIGN AND PUBLISHING LTD 1724356
Tolastadh, 18 Corsie Drive, Kinnoull, PERTH, PH2 7BU
Tel: 01738 639747
Email: athole@atholedesign.com
Web site: http://www.atholedesign.com
Titles:
FARMING SCOTLAND MAGAZINE

ATL 15940
7 Northumberland Street, LONDON, WC2N 5RD
Tel: 020 7930 6441 **Fax:** 020 7925 0529
Web site: http://www.atl.org.uk
Titles:
REPORT

ATLANTIC COMMUNICATIONS 17088
The Arena, Stockley Park, UXBRIDGE, UB11 1AA
Tel: 020 8899 1765 **Fax:** 020 8534 5396
Web site: http://www.oilonline.com
Titles:
ASIAN OIL & GAS
OFFSHORE ENGINEER

ATLANTIC PUBLISHERS 13010
83 Parkanaur Avenue, SOUTHEND-ON-SEA, SS1 3JA
Tel: 01702 580409 **Fax:** 01702 588970
Email: tr@atlanticpublishers.com
Web site: http://www.atlanticpublishers.com
Titles:
GARDEN RAIL
NARROW GAUGE WORLD

ATLANTIC PUBLISHING COMPANY LTD 16319
Coates House, Upper Largo, LEVEN, KY8 6JF
Tel: 01333 360606 **Fax:** 01333 360607
Email: editorial@luxury-briefing.com
Web site: http://www.luxury-briefing.com
Titles:
LUXURY BRIEFING

ATLAS MAGAZINE 17734
16 Talfourd Road, LONDON, SE15 5NY **Tel:** 020 7701 7245
ATLAS MAGAZINE

ATOM PUBLISHING LTD 16478
45-47 Clerkenwell Green, LONDON, EC1R 0EB
Tel: 020 7490 5595 **Fax:** 020 7490 4957
Email: emma@atompublishing.co.uk
Web site: http://www.atompublishing.co.uk
Titles:
RIBA JOURNAL
RICS BUSINESS

ATTEND 18815
11-13 Cavendish Square, LONDON, W1G 0AN
Tel: 020 7307 2570 **Fax:** 020 7307 2571
Web site: http://www.attend.org.uk
Titles:
FRIENDS CONNECT

ATTIC MEDIA NETWORK 1649636
Unit 1.08 Clerkenwell Workshops, 31 Clerkenwell Close,
LONDON, EC1R 0AT **Tel:** 020 7014 3777
Fax: 020 7014 3776
Titles:
KICK
NATIONAL GEOGRAPHIC KIDS

AUDIENCE MEDIA LTD 1720996
26 Dorset Street, LONDON, W1U 8AP **Tel:** 020 7486 7007
Fax: 020 7486 2002
Web site: http://www.audience.uk.com
Titles:
AUDIENCE
LIVE UK

AUDIO PUBLISHING LTD 15472
Unit G4, Argo House, Kilburn Park Road, LONDON, NW6
5LF **Tel:** 020 7625 3134 **Fax:** 020 7328 1844
Titles:
HI-FI WORLD

AUGUST MEDIA 1710432
Zetland House, 5-25 Scrutton Street, LONDON, EC2A 4HJ
Tel: 020 7749 3300 **Fax:** 020 7749 3325
Email: info@augustmedia.com
Web site: http://www.augustmedia.com
Titles:
@HOME
IKEA FAMILY LIVE
WEEKENDER

AURORA PUBLICATIONS LTD 18017
14 Old Bond Street, LONDON, W1S 4PP **Tel:** 020 7495 2590
Fax: 020 7591 1595
Titles:
MINERVA. THE INTERNATIONAL REVIEW OF ANCIENT
ART AND ARCHAEOLOGY

AUTHENTIC MEDIA 673306
PO Box 300, Kingstown Industrial Estate, CARLISLE, CA3
0QS **Tel:** 01228 554332 **Fax:** 01228 393388
Titles:
SCIENCE & CHRISTIAN BELIEF

AUTHORIT PUBLISHING LTD 1690406
38 Digby Crescent, LONDON, N4 2HR **Tel:** 07971 161234
Titles:
NEWSWIRELESS.NET

AUTOBUS REVIEW PUBLICATIONS LTD 14398
42 Coniston Avenue, Queensbury, BRADFORD, BD13 2JD
Tel: 01274 881640
Titles:
BUS FAYRE

AUTOMETRIX PUBLICATIONS 15461
Campion House, 1 Greenfield Road, Westoning, BEDFORD,
MK45 5JD **Tel:** 01525 750500 **Fax:** 01525 750700
Email: mail@autometrix.co.uk
Web site: http://www.autometrix.co.uk
Titles:
AUDI DRIVER
VOLKSWAGEN DRIVER

AUTOMOTIVE RETAIL LTD 1644319
44 Station Road, Woodford Halse, DAVENTRY, NN11 3RB
Tel: 01327 264188 **Fax:** 01327 264189
Titles:
AUTO RETAIL BULLETIN

AVAKADO LTD 698831
Global House, 13 Market Square, HORSHAM, RH12 1EU
Tel: 01403 220760 **Fax:** 01403 220761
Email: mark@avakado.eu
Titles:
LIFE SCIENCE CLUSTERS
SP2

AVENUES PUBLISHING 1653882
Arden House, Arden Grove, HARPENDEN, AL5 4SJ
Tel: 01582 984940
Email: info@avenuesonline.co.uk
Web site: http://www.avenuespublishing.co.uk
Titles:
AVENUES SERIES

AVIA PRESS ASSOCIATES 13642
75 Elm Tree Road, Locking, WESTON-SUPER-MARE, BS24
8EL **Tel:** 01934 822524 **Fax:** 01934 822400
Email: editorial@aviapress.fsnet.co.uk
Web site: http://www.helidata.rotor.com
Titles:
HELICOPTER INTERNATIONAL
HELICOPTER INTERNATIONAL
HELIDATA NEWS & CLASSIFIED
HELIDATA SHOW DAILY

AVIATION ECONOMICS 18208
James House, 1st Floor, 22-24 Corsham Street, LONDON,
N1 6DR **Tel:** 020 7490 5215 **Fax:** 020 7490 5218
Email: info@aviationeconomics.com
Web site: http://www.aviationeconomics.com
Titles:
AVIATION STRATEGY

AVRIL NICOLL BUSINESS 621626
33 Kinnear Square, LAURENCEKIRK, AB30 1UL
Tel: 01561 377415 **Fax:** 01561 377415
Web site: http://www.speechmag.com
Titles:
SPEECH & LANGUAGE THERAPY IN PRACTICE

THE AWARD SCHEME LTD 16091
Gulliver House, Madeira Walk, WINDSOR, SL4 1EU
Tel: 01753 727400 **Fax:** 01753 810666
Titles:
AWARD JOURNAL

AWARENESS MAGAZINE LTD 1712722
Tel: 0845 338 0373 **Fax:** 0845 338 0373
PO Box 18727, ABERDEEN, AB25 2ZU **Tel:** 0845 338 0373
Fax: 0845 338 0373
Titles:
AWARENESS MAGAZINE

AXA PPP HEALTHCARE 1749668
Phillips House, Crescent Road, TUNBRIDGE WELLS, TN1
2PL **Tel:** 01892 512345
Titles:
BE

AXIS PUBLICATIONS LTD 1649458
Harlow Enterprise Hub, Kao Hockham Building, Edinburgh
Way, HARLOW, CM20 2NQ **Tel:** 01920 885162
Fax: 01920 885172
Email: info@axispublications.co.uk
Titles:
AXIS MAGAZINE

AXON PUBLISHING LTD 13836
11 Plough Yard, LONDON, EC2A 3LP **Tel:** 020 7684 7111
Fax: 020 7684 7122
Titles:
LIVE IT, THE CONRAN MAGAZINE
NOTEWORTHY

UK Publishers & Their Titles

AYRSHIRE CATTLE SOCIETY 14001
17 Barns Street, AYR, KA7 1XB **Tel:** 01292 267123
Fax: 01292 611973
Email: society@ayrshirescs.org
Web site: http://www.ayrshirescs.org
Titles:
THE AYRSHIRE JOURNAL

A-Z GROUP LTD 17312
Darby House, Bletchingley Road, Merstham, REDHILL, RH1
3TT **Tel:** 01737 645777 **Fax:** 01737 645888
Email: info@a-zgroup.net
Web site: http://www.azfreight.com
Titles:
ACW AIR CARGO WEEK
A-Z AIR FREIGHTERS GUIDE
A-Z WORLD AIRPORTS GUIDE
A-Z WORLDWIDE AIRFREIGHT DIRECTORY

AZILLA LTD 1654380
118 Green Lanes, Newington Green, LONDON, N16 9EH
Tel: 020 7275 7610 **Fax:** 020 7241 1908
Titles:
AVRUPA NEWSPAPER

AZTEC MEDIA SERVICES LTD 628831
1 Bankside, Churt Road, HINDHEAD, GU26 6NR
Tel: 01428 605605 **Fax:** 01428 714278
Email: info@aztecxpress.com
Web site: http://www.aztec-media.com
Titles:
TRANSPORT ENGINEER

B2BZINES.NET 1677037
The Oast Cottage, Stream Lane, Hawkhurst, CRANBROOK,
TN18 4RD **Tel:** 01580 754667 **Fax:** 01580 754669
Email: johnausten@mac.com
Web site: http://www.thecleanzine.com
Titles:
CLEANZINE

B5 MEDIA 1744256
502 Clerkenwell Workshops, 27-31 Clerkenwell Close,
LONDON, EC1R 0AU **Tel:** 020 7014 3438
Titles:
ART WORLD

B & S PUBLICATIONS 16294
3 Crescent Terrace, CHELTENHAM, GL50 3PE
Tel: 01242 510760 **Fax:** 01242 226626
Titles:
TECHNOLOGY IN EDUCATION

BABTAC LTD 697044
Ambrose House, Meteor Court, Barnett Way, Barnwood,
GLOUCESTER, GL4 3GG **Tel:** 0845 065 9000
Titles:
VITALITY

BABYWORLD.COM LTD 1634338
The Slate Barn, Mongewell Park Farm, Mongewell,
WALLINGFORD, OX10 8BY **Tel:** 01491 821870
Titles:
BABYWORLD.CO.UK

BACKCARE - THE CHARITY FOR HEALTHIER BACKS
16 Elmtree Road, TEDDINGTON, TW11 8ST 14600
Tel: 020 8977 5474 **Fax:** 020 8943 5318
Titles:
TALKBACK

BACKPASS LTD 1752559
Greystones, Beechgrove, KINGTON, HR5 3RH
Tel: 01544 230317
Titles:
BACKPASS

BADGER PUBLICATIONS 15593
PO Box 1, CASTLE CARY, BA7 7BG
Titles:
THE VISITOR

BAKERS, FOOD AND ALLIED WORKERS' UNION 13852
Stanborough House, Great North Road, WELWYN GARDEN
CITY, AL8 7TA **Tel:** 01707 260150 **Fax:** 01707 261570
Email: joe.marino@bfawu.org
Web site: http://www.bfawu.org
Titles:
FOOD WORKER

BALANCE LIFE LTD 1655432
Howletts, Chignal St. James, CHELMSFORD, CM1 4TP
Tel: 01245 441994 **Fax:** 01245 442012
Email: enquiries@balancelifemagazine.com
Titles:
BALANCELIFE

B.A.L.P.A. 13860
BALPA House, 5 Heathrow Boulevard, 278 Bath Road,
WEST DRAYTON, UB7 0DQ **Tel:** 020 8476 4000
Fax: 020 8476 4077
Email: communications@balpa.org
Web site: http://www.balpa.org
Titles:
THE LOG

BALTIC PUBLICATIONS LTD 1643803
Baltic Business Centre, Saltmeadows Road, GATESHEAD,
NE8 3DA **Tel:** 0191 442 4001 **Fax:** 0191 442 4002
Email: balticpub@blueyonder.co.uk
Titles:
F.C. BUSINESS
PATHFINDER

BANBRIDGE CHRONICLE PRESS LTD 15070
14 Bridge Street, BANBRIDGE, BT32 3JS
Tel: 028 4066 2322 **Fax:** 028 4062 4397
Titles:
BANBRIDGE CHRONICLE

BANDWIDTH COMMUNICATIONS LTD. 695790
5th Floor, Palace Theatre, 109-113 Shaftsbury Avenue,
LONDON, W1V 5AY **Tel:** 020 7317 9104
Titles:
WHAT'S ON STAGE
WHATSONSTAGE.COM

BANGLA POST MEDIA SERVICES LTD 1687242
Unit 4G, Room 5, BJ House, 10-14 Holly Bush Gardens,
LONDON, E2 9QP **Tel:** 020 7729 5295 **Fax:** 020 8983 4959
Titles:
BANGLA POST

BANK HOUSE COMMUNICATIONS LTD 17171
Bank House, Great Rissington, CHELTENHAM, GL54 2LP
Tel: 01451 821982 **Fax:** 01451 821972
Web site: http://www.andycouchman.com
Titles:
HEALTHCARE INSURANCE REPORT

BANKSIDE PRESS 1645348
27 Blackfriars Road, LONDON, SE1 8NY **Tel:** 020 7633 0766
Fax: 020 7401 2521
Email: office@banksidepress.com
Web site: http://www.banksidepress.com
Titles:
IN SE 1
LONDON SE1

BANNISTER PUBLICATIONS 1676172
118 Saltergate, CHESTERFIELD, S40 1NG
Tel: 01246 550488 **Fax:** 01246 555420
Titles:
REFLECTIONS

BAPH PUBLICATIONS 673753
24 Heol Beca, Monument Hill, CARMARTHEN, SA31 3LS
Tel: 01305 816482
Titles:
THE QUARTERLY

BAPTIST HISTORICAL SOCIETY 17722
Regents Park College, Pusey Street, OXFORD, OX1 2LB
Tel: 01865 288120 **Fax:** 01865 288121
Email: john.briggs@regents.ox.ac.uk

Web site: http://www.baptisthistory.org.uk
Titles:
BAPTIST QUARTERLY

BAPTIST MEN'S MOVEMENT 18363
35 Ock Street, ABINGDON, OX14 5AG
Titles:
MEN MATTERS

BAPTIST TIMES LTD. 15859
Baptist House, PO Box 54, 129 Broadway, DIDCOT, OX11
8XB **Tel:** 01235 517670 **Fax:** 01235 517678
Web site: http://www.baptisttimes.co.uk
Titles:
BAPTIST TIMES

BARB WIRE ENTERPRISES LTD 1643778
102 Mallinson Road, Battersea, LONDON, SW11 1BN
Tel: 0870 765 5503 **Fax:** 020 7207 6503
Email: all3mags@yahoo.co.uk
Web site: http://www.barbwire-enterprises.co.uk
Titles:
BLACK HERITAGE
LIVE LISTINGS
THE OFFICIAL GUIDE TO INTERNATIONAL WOMEN'S
MONTH

BARKER BROOKS MEDIA 675480
Barker Brooks House, 4 Greengate, Cardale Park,
HARROGATE, HG3 1GY **Tel:** 01423 851150
Fax: 01423 851151
Email: info@barkerbrooks.co.uk
Web site: http://www.barkerbrooks.co.uk
Titles:
ETC
THE LEEDS & YORKSHIRE LAWYER
LEGAL & MEDICAL
STEP JOURNAL

BARNARDO'S 17741
Tanners Lane, Barkingside, ILFORD, IG6 1QG
Tel: 020 8550 8822 **Fax:** 020 8550 0429
Email: info@barnados.org.uk
Web site: http://www.barnardos.org.uk
Titles:
BARNARDO'S TODAY

**BARNSLEY AND ROTHERHAM CHAMBER OF
COMMERCE** 1706554
2 Genesis Park, Sheffield Road, ROTHERHAM, S60 1DX
Tel: 01709 386200
Titles:
CHAMBER BULLETIN

BARNSLEY CHRONICLE LTD 15007
47 Church Street, BARNSLEY, S70 2AS **Tel:** 01226 734734
Titles:
BARNSLEY CHRONICLE & INDEPENDENT SERIES

BARRETT, BYRD ASSOCIATES 17035
Linden House, Linden Close, TUNBRIDGE WELLS, TN4 8HH
Tel: 01892 524455 **Fax:** 01892 524456
Email: two@barrett-byrd.com
Web site: http://www.barrett-byrd.com
Titles:
MODERN ASPHALTS
NEW STEEL CONSTRUCTION
TRANSPORTATION PROFESSIONAL

BARRINGTON PUBLICATIONS 13660
54 Uxbridge Road, LONDON, W12 8LP **Tel:** 020 8740 7020
Fax: 020 8740 7020
Web site: http://www.barringtonpublications.com
Titles:
GALLERIES

BARTS AND THE LONDON ALUMNI ASSOCIATION
625728
Queen Mary University of London, Alumni Relations Office,
Mile End Road, LONDON, E1 4NS **Tel:** 020 7882 3732
Fax: 020 7882 3706
Email: batlaa@qmul.ac.uk
Web site: http://www.batlaa.org
Titles:
BARTS AND THE LONDON CHRONICLE

BASBWE 16585
Y Fron, Llansadwrn, MENAI BRIDGE, LL59 5SL
Tel: 01248 811285
Web site: http://www.basbwe.org
Titles:
WINDS

BASS MEDIA LTD 1626606
Oyster House, Hunter's Lodge, KENTISBEARE, EX15 2DY
Tel: 01884 266100 **Fax:** 01884 266101
Titles:
BASS GUITAR MAGAZINE

BATH & WELLS DIOCESAN BOARD OF FINANCE 17731
The Old Deanery, WELLS, BA5 2UG **Tel:** 01749 670777
Fax: 01749 674240
Titles:
BATH & WELLS DIOCESAN DIRECTORY

BATH NEWS & MEDIA 18936
Westpoint, James Street West, BATH, BA1 2DA
Tel: 01225 322322 **Fax:** 01225 322292
Web site: http://www.thisisbath.co.uk
Titles:
THE BATH CHRONICLE
MID SOMERSET NEWS & MEDIA
SOMERSET STANDARD & GUARDIAN SERIES
THIS IS BATH

THE BATH PARENT 1753055
70 Warminster Road, BATH, BA2 6RU **Tel:** 01225 421984
Titles:
THE BATH PARENT

BATTLE OF BRITAIN INTERNATIONAL LTD 16148
The Mews, Hobbs Cross House, OLD HARLOW, CM17 0NN
Tel: 01279 418833 **Fax:** 01279 419386
Titles:
AFTER THE BATTLE

BATTLESPACE PUBLICATIONS 1622114
2nd Floor Flat, 8 Sinclair Gardens, LONDON, W14 0AT
Tel: 020 7610 5520 **Fax:** 020 7610 5520
Web site: http://www.battle-technology.com
Titles:
BATTLESPACE NEWS

BAUER CONSUMER MEDIA LTD (MAPPIN HOUSE) 1744482
Mappin House, 4 Winsley Street, LONDON, W1W 8HF
Tel: 020 7182 8000
Titles:
ARENA HOMME PLUS
EMPIRE
EMPIRE ONLINE
FHM
FHM (ONLINE)
KERRANG!
MOJO
MOJO4MUSIC
Q4MUSIC
Q MAGAZINE
ZOO

BAUER CONSUMER MEDIA LTD (MEDIA HOUSE) 1744481
Media House, Lynchwood, Peterborough Business Park,
PETERBOROUGH, PE2 6EA **Tel:** 01733 468000
Fax: 01733 468888
Titles:
BIKE
BIRD WATCHING
CAR
CLASSIC BIKE
CLASSIC CARS
COMPANY CAR DRIVER
COUNTRY WALKING
DIGITAL PHOTO
FLEET NEWS ONLINE
LAND ROVER OWNER INTERNATIONAL MAGAZINE
MATCH
MAX POWER
MAX POWER.CO.UK
MCN MOTOR CYCLE NEWS
MOTORCYCLENEWS.COM
PARKER'S CAR PRICE GUIDE
PARKER'S ONLINE
PERFORMANCE BIKES

PRACTICAL CLASSICS
PRACTICAL PHOTOGRAPHY
RIDE
TODAY'S GOLFER
TRAIL
WHAT BIKE?
YOURS
YOURS.CO.UK

BAUER MEDIA 1744483
Endeavour House, Shaftesbury Avenue, LONDON, WC2H
8JG **Tel:** 020 7437 9011
Web site: http://www.bauer.co.uk
Titles:
CLOSER
CLOSERDIETS.COM
CLOSERONLINE.CO.UK
GRAZIA
HEAT
HEATWORLD.COM
MORE
MORE ONLINE
MOTHER & BABY
PREGNANCY & BIRTH
TOP SANTE HEALTH & BEAUTY

BAUER MEDIA LTD (ORTON) 1744440
Bushfield House, Orton Centre, PETERBOROUGH, PE2
5UW **Tel:** 01733 237111 **Fax:** 01733 465779
Web site: http://www.bauer.co.uk
Titles:
AM
ANGLING TIMES
FLEET NEWS
FLEET VAN
GARDEN ANSWERS
GARDEN NEWS
GOLF WORLD
IMPROVE YOUR COARSE FISHING
MODEL RAIL
PPM PET PRODUCT MARKETING
PRACTICAL FISHKEEPING
RAIL
SEA ANGLER
STEAM RAILWAY
TROUT AND SALMON
TROUT FISHERMAN
UK CARP
YOUR HORSE

BAY PUBLISHING LTD 1603053
1st Floor, Suite One, St. Albans Chambers, 15-16 St. Alban
Street, WEYMOUTH, DT4 8PY **Tel:** 01305 785199
Fax: 01305 772722
Email: info@baysafety.com
Titles:
AWE INTERNATIONAL
HEALTH AND SAFETY INTERNATIONAL

BAYLIS & CO. 14903
48 Bell Street, MAIDENHEAD, SL6 1HX **Tel:** 01628 417834
Fax: 01628 678245
Titles:
BERKSHIRE LIVING
BUSINESS MONTHLY
MAIDENHEAD ADVERTISER SERIES
SLOUGH EXPRESS
WEDDINGS ETC

BAYVIEW PUBLISHING LTD 1734119
57A-59 Prospect Road, BANGOR, BT20 5DF
Tel: 028 9147 8703 **Fax:** 028 9147 2045
Titles:
IRISH BATHROOMS
IRISH KITCHENS
NI HOMES & LIFESTYLE

BBC 1654899
Room 2425, White City, 201 Wood Lane, LONDON, W12
7TS **Tel:** 020 8008 4224
Titles:
ARIEL
BBC LIFESTYLE
BBC LOCAL HUMBERSIDE
BBC LOCAL NORTHAMPTONSHIRE
BBC WATCHDOG

BBC CHILDREN'S MAGAZINES 18130
Media Centre, 201 Wood Lane, LONDON, W12 7TQ
Tel: 020 8433 2000 **Fax:** 020 8433 2941

Titles:
ALL ABOUT ANIMALS
CBEEBIES ANIMALS
TOYBOX
WAYBULOO

BBC MAGAZINES 12859
Media Centre, 201 Wood Lane, LONDON, W12 7TQ
Tel: 020 8433 2000 **Fax:** 020 8433 3867
Web site: http://www.bbcworldwide.com
Titles:
BBC GARDENERS' WORLD MAGAZINE
CBEEBIES ART
DOCTOR WHO ADVENTURES
IN THE NIGHT GARDEN
MATCH OF THE DAY MAGAZINE

BBC MAGAZINES BRISTOL 1715980
14th Floor, Tower House, Fairfax Street, BRISTOL, BS1 3BN
Tel: 0117 927 9009 **Fax:** 0117 934 9008
Web site: http://www.bbcmagazinesbristol.com
Titles:
ABOUT THE HOUSE
BBC FOCUS
BBC HISTORY MAGAZINE
BBC HOMES & ANTIQUES
BBC KNOWLEDGE MAGAZINE
BBC MUSIC MAGAZINE
BBC SKY AT NIGHT MAGAZINE
BBC WHO DO YOU THINK YOU ARE? MAGAZINE
BBC WILDLIFE MAGAZINE
BBCWHODOYOUTHINKYOUARE.COM
CINEWORLD UNLIMITED
COUNTRYFILE
GARDENS ILLUSTRATED
HMV CHOICE

BBC WORLD SERVICE 15690
Room 345, Centre Block, Bush House, The Strand,
LONDON, WC2B 4PH **Tel:** 020 7557 2956
Fax: 020 7240 4899
Web site: http://www.bbcworldservice.com
Titles:
BBC FOCUS ON AFRICA MAGAZINE
BBC WORLD AGENDA

BBC WORLDWIDE PUBLISHING 13216
Media Centre, 201 Wood Lane, LONDON, W12 7TQ
Tel: 020 8433 2000 **Fax:** 020 8433 3754
Web site: http://www.bbcmagazines.com
Titles:
BBC EASY COOK
BBC GOOD FOOD
BBC TOP GEAR MAGAZINE
BBCGOODFOOD.COM
GARDENERSWORLD.COM
GIRL TALK
GIRL TALK EXTRA
LONELY PLANET MAGAZINE
OLIVE
RADIO TIMES
RADIOTIMES.COM
TOP OF THE POPS
TOPGEAR.COM

BBR 17223
Elsecar Heritage Centre, Wath Road, Elsecar, BARNSLEY,
S74 8HJ **Tel:** 01226 745156 **Fax:** 01226 745156
Web site: http://www.onlinebbr.com
Titles:
BRITISH BOTTLE REVIEW INCORPORATING
COLLECTORS MART

BC INSIGHT 1732830
Southbank House, Black Prince Road, LONDON, SE1 7SJ
Tel: 020 7793 2567 **Fax:** 020 7793 2577
Web site: http://www.bcinsight.com
Titles:
FERTILIZER INDUSTRY DIRECTORY
FERTILIZER INTERNATIONAL
NITROGEN & SYNGAS
SULPHUR

BC PUBLICATIONS 13523
27 Norwich Road, HALESWORTH, IP19 8BX
Tel: 01986 834250 **Fax:** 01986 834255
Titles:
AI
ANGLIA FARMER
FORESTRY & TIMBER NEWS
MOTOR CARAVANNER

UK Publishers & Their Titles

BCR PUBLISHING LTD   16950
3 Cobden Court, Wimpole Close, BROMLEY, BR2 9JF
Tel: 020 8466 6987 **Fax:** 020 8466 0654

Titles:
THE WORLD FACTORING YEARBOOK

BCS   1621031
1st Floor, Block D, North Star House, North Star Avenue,
SWINDON, SN2 1FA **Tel:** 01793 417417
Web site: http://www.bcs.org

Titles:
ITNOW

BCTGA   18696
13 Wolrige Road, EDINBURGH, EH16 6HX
Tel: 0131 664 1100 **Fax:** 0131 664 2669
Email: rogermhay@btinternet.com
Web site: http://www.bctga.co.uk

Titles:
CHRISTMAS TREE NEWSLETTER

BD COMMUNICATIONS   1649943
153 Simpson, MILTON KEYNES, MK6 3AH
Tel: 01908 660856 **Fax:** 01908 660856

Titles:
RUN OFF AND RESTRUCTURING

BDP MEDIA   1751832
Unit 11-12; The Leather Market, Weston Street, LONDON,
SE1 3ER **Tel:** 020 7407 7060
Web site: http://www.bdpmedia.com

Titles:
DADS SPACE

BEARPARK PUBLISHING   13562
63 Gee Street, LONDON, EC1V 3RS **Tel:** 020 7336 0666
Fax: 020 7336 0866
Email: vsjmag@bearpark.co.uk
Web site: http://www.vsj.co.uk

Titles:
VISUAL SYSTEMS JOURNAL

BEAU BUSINESS MEDIA LTD   623680
Publishing House, Windrush, Ash Lane, Hopwood,
Alvechurch, BIRMINGHAM, B48 7TS **Tel:** 0121 445 6961
Fax: 0121 445 4436
Email: beau.media@btconnect.com

Titles:
COACH TOURING
GROUP TRAVEL TODAY

BEAUMONDE PUBLICATIONS LTD   15553
PO Box 5, HITCHIN, SG5 1GJ **Tel:** 01462 431237
Fax: 01462 422015

Titles:
BUCKINGHAMSHIRE COUNTRYSIDE
HERTFORDSHIRE COUNTRYSIDE

BEAUMONT PUBLISHING LTD   18954
PO Box 161, CONGLETON, CW12 3WJ **Tel:** 01260 278044
Fax: 01260 278044
Email: editor@armourer.co.uk
Web site: http://www.armourer.co.uk

Titles:
THE ARMOURER

BEAUTIFUL BRITAIN LTD   1731855
PO Box 52, CHELTENHAM, GL50 1YQ **Tel:** 01242 537900

Titles:
BEAUTIFUL BRITAIN

BEB MEDIA LTD   1751953
7B Lower Ballinderry Road, Upper Ballinderry, LISBURN,
BT28 2JB **Tel:** 028 9265 2773 **Fax:** 028 9265 2773
Email: beryl@bebmedia.com

Titles:
ABILITY NORTHERN IRELAND
FOOD TECHNOLOGY & PACKAGING

BECKHOUSE MEDIA LTD   14623
22 Warwick Street, Adlington, CHORLEY, PR7 4JQ
Tel: 01257 481878 **Fax:** 01257 474975

Titles:
ENVIRONMENT TIMES

BECTU   13870
373-377 Clapham Road, LONDON, SW9 9BT
Tel: 020 7346 0900 **Fax:** 020 7346 0901
Email: info@bectu.org.uk
Web site: http://www.bectu.org.uk

Titles:
STAGE SCREEN & RADIO

BEDFORDSHIRE COUNTY COUNCIL   14700
County Hall, Cauldwell Street, BEDFORD, MK42 9AP
Tel: 01234 363222 **Fax:** 01234 228937

Titles:
WE LOVE BEDFORDSHIRE

BEE3 LTD   1717984
Unit 28B Harris Business Park, Hanbury Road, Stoke Prior,
BROMSGROVE, B60 4DJ **Tel:** 01527 871747

Titles:
AGA LIVING
WARWICKSHIRE LIVING
WORCESTERSHIRE LIVING

BEE CRAFT LTD   15671
107 Church Street, Werrington, PETERBOROUGH, PE4 6QF
Tel: 01733 771221 **Fax:** 01733 771221
Email: secretary@bee-craft.com
Web site: http://www.bee-craft.com

Titles:
BEE CRAFT

BEES FOR DEVELOPMENT   15672
PO Box 105, MONMOUTH, NP25 9AA **Tel:** 01600 713648
Fax: 01600 716167
Email: info@beesfordevelopment.org
Web site: http://www.beesfordevelopment.org

Titles:
BEES FOR DEVELOPMENT JOURNAL

**BELFAST CITY CENTRE MANAGEMENT & BELFAST
CHAMBER OF TRADE & COMMERCE**   1685984
Sinclair House, 2nd Floor, 95-101 Royal Avenue, BELFAST,
BT1 1FE **Tel:** 028 9024 2111 **Fax:** 028 9023 0809

Titles:
CITY BUSINESS

BELFAST MEDIA GROUP   18628
Teach Basil, 2 Hannahstown Hill, BELFAST, BT17 0LT
Tel: 028 9061 9000 **Fax:** 028 9062 0602
Web site: http://www.belfastmediagroup.com

Titles:
ANDERSONSTOWN NEWS SERIES
NORTH BELFAST NEWS
SOUTH BELFAST NEWS

BELFAST TELEGRAPH NEWSPAPERS LTD   15071
124-144 Royal Avenue, BELFAST, BT1 1EB
Tel: 028 9026 4000

Titles:
COMMUNITY TELEGRAPH SERIES

BELGIAN-LUXEMBOURG CHAMBER OF COMMERCE
                    13978
105 Ferriby Road, HESSLE, HU13 0HX **Tel:** 0870 246 1610
Fax: 0870 429 2148
Email: info@blcc.co.uk
Web site: http://www.blcc.co.uk

Titles:
BELUX

BELL JOHNSTONE COMMUNICATIONS   1653862
34 Bernard Street, EDINBURGH, EH6 6PR
Tel: 0131 554 1129 **Fax:** 0131 555 1622

Titles:
FACTS
SCOTS AUTO SCENE
THE SCRUM

BELL PUBLISHING LTD   675006
The Maltings, 57 Bath Street, GRAVESEND, DA11 0DF
Tel: 01474 532202 **Fax:** 01474 532203

Web site: http://www.bellpublishing.com

Titles:
CANTECH INTERNATIONAL
CONFECTIONERY PRODUCTION
DAIRY INDUSTRIES INTERNATIONAL
FOOD & DRINK TECHNOLOGY

BELLCOURT LIMITED   623305
PO Box 8455, NEWARK, NG23 5WX **Tel:** 01636 525607
Web site: http://www.bellcourtltd.co.uk

Titles:
THE A & B NEWS
THE CATHOLIC NEWS
HALLAM NEWS
MENEVIA NEWS
NETWORKING - CATHOLIC EDUCATION TODAY
OUR DIOCESAN FAMILY
THE SHERWOOD VILLAGER
UNITY
THE VINE

THE BELLMONT AGENCY LTD   14202
1st Floor, Clifton House, 4A Goldington Road, BEDFORD,
MK40 3NF **Tel:** 0870 749 0220 **Fax:** 0870 749 0221
Web site: http://www.pirnet.co.uk

Titles:
CUSTODIAL REVIEW
PIR CARE HOME MANAGEMENT
PIR CONSTRUCTION
PIR EDUCATION
PIR HOSPITALITY BUSINESS

BENHAM PUBLISHING LIMITED   1688396
4th Floor, Orleans House, Edmund Street, LIVERPOOL, L3
9NG **Tel:** 0151 236 4141 **Fax:** 0151 236 0440
Email: blueprint@behampublishing.com
Web site: http://www.benhampublishing.com

Titles:
THE BILL OF MIDDLESEX
BLUEPRINT
THE SURREY LAWYER

BENNETT PUBLISHING LTD   16252
2-3 The Centre, WESTON-SUPER-MARE, BS23 1US
Tel: 01934 622000 **Fax:** 01934 622123
Email: enquiries@propnews.co.uk
Web site: http://www.propnews.co.uk

Titles:
PROPERTY NEWS MIDLANDS
PROPERTY NEWS SOUTH
PROPERTY NEWS SOUTH WEST & SOUTH WALES

BENT LTD   1643429
APN House, Temple Crescent, LEEDS, LS11 8BP
Tel: 0871 220 1518 **Fax:** 0870 122 2666
Web site: http://www.mag.bent.com

Titles:
BENT

BEONA PUBLISHING   1764631
PO Box 198, DARLINGTON, DL1 9FW

Titles:
WEST END DIRECTORY
WEST PARK DIRECTORY

BERG PUBLISHERS   16514
1st Floor, Angel Court, 81 St. Clements Street, OXFORD,
OX4 1AW **Tel:** 01865 245104 **Fax:** 01865 791165
Web site: http://www.bergpublishers.com

Titles:
FASHION THEORY
TEXTILE: THE JOURNAL OF CLOTH AND CULTURE

BERKOFF DESIGN & COMMUNICATIONS   1709899
17 Station Road, NEW BARNET, EN5 7NW
Web site: http://www.berkoffdesign.co.uk

Titles:
CITY SECURITY

BERKSHIRE MEDIA GROUP LTD   1739752
50 Portman Road, READING, RG30 1BA

Titles:
BRACKNELL NEWS SERIES
READING CHRONICLE SERIES
SLOUGH & WINDSOR OBSERVER SERIES
THE VILLAGER

BERLINGUER LTD 1686301
1st Floor, Rennie House, 57-60 Aldgate High Street, LONDON, EC3N 1AL **Tel:** 020 7680 5151
Fax: 020 7680 5155
Email: priority@berlinguer.com
Web site: http://www.berlinguer.com
Titles:
EMERGING MARKETS REPORT
FTSE GLOBAL MARKETS

BERRYDALES PUBLISHING 15169
5 Lawn Road, LONDON, NW3 2XS **Tel:** 020 7722 2866
Fax: 020 7722 7685
Titles:
FOODS MATTER

BERW CYF 15716
PO Box 44, ABERYSTWYTH, SY23 3ZZ **Tel:** 01970 611255
Fax: 01970 611197
Titles:
PLANET - THE WELSH INTERNATIONALIST

BEST ASIAN MEDIA 1627096
48 Milkstone Road, ROCHDALE, OL11 1EB
Tel: 01706 670119 **Fax:** 01706 649908
Web site: http://www.asianleader.co.uk
Titles:
ASIAN LEADER (NORTHWEST AND YORKSHIRE EDITION)

BESTADVICE.NET 1747448
Denvilles House, 33 Emsworth Road, HAVANT, PO9 2SN
Tel: 020 7639 5120
Titles:
CLEAN SLATE
NICHE COMMERCIAL FINANCE

BESTWAY & BATLEYS CASH & CARRY 1753100
The Studio, 5 Philpotts Yard, Beare Green, DORKING, RH5 4QU **Tel:** 0845 644 1870
Titles:
ESSENTIALLY CATERING

BETRESCUE LTD 1742968
Chelwood House, Chelwood Drive, LEEDS, LS8 2AT
Tel: 0845 833 0909 **Fax:** 0845 833 0910
Email: david@betrescue.com
Titles:
BETTING MONTHLY

BEZIER 1712154
HQ Bellway Court, WAKEFIELD, WF5 9TL
Tel: 01924 362921 **Fax:** 01924 291868
Email: enquiries@bezier.co.uk
Web site: http://www.bezier.co.uk
Titles:
RETAIL MARKETING NEWS

BFP BOOKS 17633
Focus House, 497 Green Lanes, LONDON, N13 4BP
Tel: 020 8882 3315 **Fax:** 020 8886 3933
Titles:
FREELANCE PHOTOGRAPHER'S MARKET HANDBOOK

THE BGROUP 1653575
6 Charlotte Square, NEWCASTLE UPON TYNE, NE1 4XF
Tel: 0191 261 1333 **Fax:** 0191 261 6012
Email: info@thebgroup.co.uk
Web site: http://www.thebgroup.co.uk
Titles:
THE BDAILY NEWS

BH PUBLICATIONS 1766047
Unit 8 Branksome Business Park, POOLE, BH12 1DW
Tel: 01202 765988
Titles:
BH EXCLUSIVE
NEW FOREST EXCLUSIVE

BHF PUBLISHING 12467
Entrance B, Level 1, Salamander Quay West, Park Lane, HAREFIELD, UB9 6NZ **Tel:** 0870 205 2924
Fax: 0870 205 2934

Web site: http://www.bhfgroup.co.uk
Titles:
HARDWARE TODAY

BHR COMMUNICATIONS 16174
The White Cottage, The Street, Long Stratton, NORWICH, NR15 2XJ **Tel:** 0845 402 6527 **Fax:** 0845 402 6528
Email: roger@bhrcommunications.co.uk
Titles:
PRO VETERINARIO AUDIO MAGAZINE

BIALL 14670
1 Silk Street, LONDON, EC2Y 8HQ **Tel:** 020 7456 2442
Fax: 020 7456 2222
Titles:
BIALL BRITISH & IRISH ASSOCIATION OF LAW LIBRARIANS NEWSLETTER

THE BIG AGENCY 1641609
22 Stephenson Way, LONDON, NW1 2HD
Tel: 020 7380 8599 **Fax:** 020 7383 0357
Web site: http://www.big-agency.com
Titles:
HOUNSLOW MATTERS

BIG BEAR MUSIC GROUP 15371
PO Box 944, BIRMINGHAM, B16 8UT **Tel:** 0121 454 7020
Fax: 0121 454 9996
Web site: http://www.bigbearmusic.com
Titles:
THE JAZZ RAG

BIG BLUE PUBLISHING COMPANY LTD 1719328
Bucklands, Loxwood Road, Rudgwick, HORSHAM, RH12 3DW **Tel:** 01403 823640 **Fax:** 01483 433332
Titles:
SUPERYACHTSONLINE.COM
THELUXURYROOM.COM
TOWN & COUNTRY CLUB
YACHTCREWONLINE.COM

BIG CHEESE PUBLISHING LTD 16383
Unit 7, Clarendon Buildings, 25 Horsell Road, LONDON, N5 1XL **Tel:** 020 7607 0303 **Fax:** 020 7607 0303
Web site: http://www.bigcheesemagazine.com
Titles:
BIG CHEESE

THE BIG ISSUE IN SCOTLAND LTD 15678
1-5 Wandsworth Road, LONDON, SW8 2LN
Tel: 020 7526 3200
Titles:
THE BIG ISSUE IN SCOTLAND

THE BIG ISSUE LTD 15677
1-5 Wandsworth Road, LONDON, SW8 2LN
Tel: 020 7526 3200 **Fax:** 020 7526 3201
Titles:
THE BIG ISSUE
THE BIG ISSUE CYMRU

THE BIG ISSUE (SOUTH WEST) LTD 16988
5 Brunswick Court, Brunswick Square, BRISTOL, BS2 8PE
Tel: 0117 916 6593 **Fax:** 0117 916 6599
Titles:
THE BIG ISSUE SOUTH WEST

THE BIG LIFE COMPANY 18633
10 Swan Street, MANCHESTER, M4 5JN **Tel:** 0161 831 5550
Titles:
THE BIG ISSUE IN THE NORTH

BIG PUBLISHING 1621070
22 Stephenson Way, LONDON, NW1 2HD
Tel: 020 7383 2335
Titles:
LIFESTYLE
LUXURY MEETINGS

BIG SMOKE PROJECTS LTD 699089
PO Box 38799, LONDON, E10 5UV **Tel:** 0777 8717 2847
Email: dirtyharry@bigsmokelive.com

Web site: http://www.bigsmokelive.com/
Titles:
BIG SMOKE MAGAZINE

THE BIG SPARK 1642390
Bridgebank Industrial Estate, Taylor Street, Horwich, BOLTON, BL6 7PD **Tel:** 0161 909 0909 **Fax:** 0161 909 0919
Web site: http://www.bigspark.co.uk
Titles:
CAPITAL
CITY LIFE
CONNECTED
ECO-YOU BUSINESS
FLIGHT
GATEWAY
THE GIRLS' GUIDE TO PROPERTY
MY HOME IN THE SUN
RELAX
SOMERSET COUNTY NEWS
UK LANDSCAPE TODAY
THE VOLUNTEER

BIGGA 14781
Bigga House, Aldwark, Alne, YORK, YO61 1UF
Tel: 01347 833800 **Fax:** 01347 833801
Web site: http://www.bigga.org.uk
Titles:
GREENKEEPER INTERNATIONAL

BIGGIN HILL NEWS LTD 14882
Winterton House, High Street, WESTERHAM, TN16 1AT
Tel: 01959 564766 **Fax:** 01959 562760
Titles:
BROMLEY AND BIGGIN HILL NEWS SERIES
CHRONICLE SERIES
COUNTY BORDER NEWS SERIES

BII 625473
Wessex House, 80 Park Street, CAMBERLEY, GU15 3PT
Tel: 01276 684449 **Fax:** 01276 23045
Email: marketing@bii.org
Web site: http://www.bii.org
Titles:
BIIBUSINESS

BIKE SPORT NEWS LTD 1711783
Paddock 2, Donington Park, Castle Donington, DERBY, DE74 2RP **Tel:** 01332 818800
Titles:
BIKE SPORT NEWS

THE BINGO ASSOCIATION 698828
Lexham House, 75 High Street, DUNSTABLE, LU6 1JF
Tel: 01582 860921 **Fax:** 01582 860901
Titles:
BINGO LINK

BINLEYS 1744298
Binleys Beechwood, Christy Close, ESSEX SS15 6EF
Tel: 01268 495600 **Fax:** 01268 495602
Titles:
HD HOSPITAL DEVELOPMENT

THE BINSTED GROUP PLC 14225
Attwood House, Mansfield Park, Four Marks, ALTON, GU34 5PZ **Tel:** 01420 568900 **Fax:** 01420 565994
Email: info@binstedgroup.com
Web site: http://www.binstedgroup.com
Titles:
BINSTED'S BOTTLING DIRECTORY
CHP PACKER INTERNATIONAL
FOOD PACKER AND PROCESSOR DIRECTORY
FOOD PACKER & PROCESSOR INTERNATIONAL
INTERNATIONAL BOTTLER & PACKER

BIO-CENTURY PUBLICATIONS INC 17095
225 Banbury Road, OXFORD, OX2 7HQ **Tel:** 01865 512184
Fax: 01865 311195
Titles:
BIOCENTURY INTERNATIONAL

THE BIOCHEMICAL SOCIETY 14474
3rd Floor, Eagle House, 16 Procter Street, LONDON, WC1V 6NX **Tel:** 020 7280 4100 **Fax:** 020 7323 1136
Web site: http://www.biochemistry.org

UK Publishers & Their Titles

Titles:
THE BIOCHEMIST

BIOGS LTD   1728108
10 Tonbridge Chambers, Pembury Road, TONBRIDGE, TN9
2HZ **Tel:** 01732 358861 **Fax:** 01732 367947
Email: info@legalmoves.co.uk
Titles:
LEGAL-MOVES

BIOINDUSTRY ASSOCIATION   14473
14-15 Belgrave Square, LONDON, SW1X 8PS
Tel: 020 7565 7190 **Fax:** 020 7565 7191
Email: admin@bioindustry.org
Web site: http://www.bioindustry.org
Titles:
BIA NEWSCAST

BIP SOLUTIONS LTD   17397
300 Glasgow Road, Rutherglen, GLASGOW, G73 1SQ
Tel: 0141 332 8247 **Fax:** 0141 331 2652
Web site: http://www.bipsolutions.com
Titles:
CONTRAX WEEKLY
GOVERNMENT OPPORTUNITIES

BIPP   14248
1 Prebendal Court, Oxford Road, AYLESBURY, HP19 8EY
Tel: 01296 718530
Web site: http://www.bipp.com
Titles:
THE PHOTOGRAPHER

THE BIRCHLEY HALL PRESS   1740700
29 Pinewood Park, FARNBOROUGH, GU14 9LB
Tel: 01252 691590
Web site: http://www.birchleyhallpress.com
Titles:
BJHCIM (THE BRITISH JOURNAL OF HEALTHCARE
  COMPUTING & INFORMATION MANAGEMENT)
MEDICAL TECHNOLOGY BUSINESS EUROPE

BIRDING WORLD   16395
Sea Lawn, Coast Road, Cley-next-the-Sea, HOLT, NR25
7RZ **Tel:** 01263 740913 **Fax:** 01263 741173
Web site: http://www.birdingworld.co.uk
Titles:
BIRDING WORLD

BIRDLIFE INTERNATIONAL   674212
Wellbrook Court, Girton Road, CAMBRIDGE, CB3 0NA
Tel: 01223 277318 **Fax:** 01223 277200
Email: birdlife@birdlife.org
Web site: http://www.birdlife.org
Titles:
WORLD BIRDWATCH

BIRMINGHAM101   697924
214 Brandwood Road, Kings Heath, BIRMINGHAM, B14
6LD **Tel:** 0121 444 4723
Titles:
BIRMINGHAM 101

BIRMINGHAM CITY COUNCIL   1653574
Council House, Victoria Square, BIRMINGHAM, B1 1BB
Tel: 0121 303 9944
Titles:
FORWARD

BIRMINGHAM CITY COUNCIL CHILDREN'S SERVICES
                    15916
Council House Extension, Margaret Street, BIRMINGHAM,
B3 3BU **Tel:** 0121 675 2243 **Fax:** 0121 464 2387
Email: cypfcomms@birmingham.gov.uk
Web site: http://www.birmingham.gov.uk/brighterfutures
Titles:
BRIGHT FUTURES

BIRMINGHAM CITY UNIVERSITY   15747
Union of Students, Franchise Street, Perry Barr,
BIRMINGHAM, B42 2SZ **Tel:** 0121 331 6801
Fax: 0121 331 6802
Email: union.comms@bcu.ac.uk
Web site: http://www.uceunion.com

Titles:
SJ (SPAGHETTI JUNCTION)

BIRMINGHAM JEWISH CULTURAL SOCIETY   15860
PO Box 13512, BIRMINGHAM, B32 9BX **Tel:** 0121 428 3347
Email: admin@recorder.org.uk
Titles:
THE BIRMINGHAM JEWISH RECORDER

BIRMINGHAM UNIVERSITY GUILD OF STUDENTS 15785
The Guild Of Students, Edgbaston Park Road, Edgbaston,
BIRMINGHAM, B15 2TU **Tel:** 0121 251 2300
Web site: http://www.bugs.bham.ac.uk
Titles:
REDBRICK

THE BIRSTALL POST SOCIETY   17453
Longslade College, Wanlip Lane, Birstall, LEICESTER, LE4
4GH **Tel:** 0116 267 4213 **Fax:** 0116 267 4213
Titles:
THE BIRSTALL POST

BISHOP ROCK PUBLISHING   1718301
Windmill Oast, Benenden Road, Rolvenden, CRANBROOK,
TN17 4PF **Tel:** 01580 240055
Email: info@bishop-rock.co.uk
Titles:
BIOFUEL REVIEW
WAVE & TIDAL ENERGY NEWS

BITEBACK MEDIA   1744821
7 Cowley Street, LONDON, SW1P 3NB **Tel:** 020 7654 5567
Web site: http://www.bitebackmedia.com
Titles:
TOTAL POLITICS

BIZ MEDIA   1762146
80-82 Chiswick High Road, LONDON, W4 1SY
Tel: 020 8995 9345
Titles:
INFORMATION WORLD REVIEW

BIZMEDIA LTD   623347
Royal Station Court, Station Road, Twyford, READING,
RG10 9NF **Tel:** 0118 960 2820 **Fax:** 0118 960 2821
Web site: http://www.bizmedia.co.uk
Titles:
E.LEARNING AGE

BIZ-NEWS.COM   1759299
Tel: 020 3051 4108
PR by email only **Tel:** 020 3051 4108
Titles:
STORAGE.BIZ-NEWS.COM

B.L. JOURNALS   1690370
PO Box 280, GRAVESEND, DA13 9WB **Tel:** 01634 256794
Fax: 01634 256798
Titles:
WELSH BOWLER

BLACK DOG   1638408
33 Wingrove Avenue, NEWCASTLE, NE4 9AN
Tel: 0191 245 6516
Titles:
THE JOURNAL OF ONE DAY SURGERY

BLACK LETTER PUBLISHING   1616840
55 Millbrook Drive, Shenstone, LICHFIELD, WS14 0JL
Tel: 07875 493586
Email: info@itreviewed.co.uk
Web site: http://www.itreviewed.co.uk
Titles:
BCW

THE BLACK SOLICITORS NETWORK   1752882
c/o Webster Dixon, 4th Floor, Thavies Inn House, 3-4
Holborn Circus, LONDON, EC1N 2HA **Tel:** 020 7366 6311
Web site: http://www.blacksolicitorsnetwork.co.uk
Titles:
DIVERSITY LEAGUE TABLE

BLACK UK PUBLICATIONS LTD   1728110
PO Box 574, BURY ST. EDMUNDS, IP33 9BW
Tel: 0845 193 4431 **Fax:** 0845 193 4438
Email: admin@keepthefaith.co.uk
Web site: http://www.blackukonline.com
Titles:
BLACK UK ONLINE
KEEP THE FAITH MAGAZINE

BLACKBALL MEDIA LTD   1745339
PO Box 227, GOSPORT, PO12 9DE **Tel:** 07747 600855
Titles:
CAR DEALER

BLACKFISH PUBLISHING LTD   1733071
20 Monmouth Place, BATH, BA1 2AY **Tel:** 01225 338828
Fax: 01225 338890
Email: mail@blackfishpublishing.com
Web site: http://www.blackfishpublishing.com
Titles:
DEATH RAY
FILMSTAR

BLACKFOX CREATIVE LTD   696681
Suite W, 27 Hastings Road, BROMLEY, BR2 8NA
Tel: 020 8462 7733
Titles:
THE GLADES MAGAZINE

BLACKMORE VALE MEDIA   16295
High Street, Stalbridge, STURMINSTER NEWTON, DT10
2LH **Tel:** 01963 365117 **Fax:** 01963 364029
Titles:
BLACKMORE VALE MAGAZINE
FOSSE WAY MAGAZINE
THE STOUR & AVON MAGAZINE

**BLACKWELL PUBLISHING AND THE REMOTE
SENSING AND PHOTOGRAMMETRY SOCIETY** 1738770
9600 Garsington Road, Cowley, OXFORD, OX4 2DQ
Tel: 01865 776868 **Fax:** 01865 714591
Web site: http://www.blackwellpublishing.com
Titles:
THE PHOTOGRAMMETRIC RECORD

BLADONMORE   1652947
10-11 Percy Street, LONDON, W1T 1DA **Tel:** 020 7631 1250
Email: info@bladonmore.com
Web site: http://www.bladonmore.com
Titles:
CORPORATE FINANCIER
THE POINT

BLAG UK LTD   1691989
Tel: 0870 138 9430
PR by email only **Tel:** 0870 138 9430 **Fax:** 0870 138 9430
Titles:
BLAG

BLAH BLAH MAGAZINE   18365
PO Box 2622, READING, RG1 9DJ **Tel:** 0118 975 3577
Titles:
BLAH BLAH

BLANK CANVAS (PUBLISHING) LTD   1684917
Suite C, 30A Church Road, TUNBRIDGE WELLS, TN1 1JP
Tel: 01892 532467 **Fax:** 01892 676282
Web site: http://www.blankcanvaspublishing.com
Titles:
PRO AUDIO ASIA
PRO AUDIO MIDDLE EAST

BLAZE PUBLISHING LIMITED   164987
Lawrence House, Morrell Street, LEAMINGTON SPA, CV32
5SZ **Tel:** 01926 339808
Email: info@blazepublishing.co.uk
Web site: http://www.blazepublishing.co.uk
Titles:
CLAY SHOOTING
GUN TRADE NEWS
HARLOT
SCARLET

BLIND MICE MEDIA LTD 1639938
Unit 1 Beehive Works, Milton Street, SHEFFIELD, S3 7WL
Tel: 0114 275 7709 **Fax:** 0114 275 7750
Web site: http://www.exposedmagazine.co.uk
Titles:
EXPOSED

BLOCKHEAD MEDIA LTD 1721336
Crown Lane, Tinwell, STAMFORD, PE9 3UF
Tel: 01780 758800
Titles:
PRACTICAL PERFORMANCE CAR

BLOW 1676007
29-35 Rathbone Street, LONDON, W1T 1NJ
Titles:
BLOW

BLUE AND GREEN LTD 697462
Tormore House, 150 High Street, DEAL, CT14 6BG
Tel: 01304 239988
Web site: http://www.avnews.co.uk
Titles:
AV NEWS

BLUE DOME 695778
6 Anselms Court, Werneth, OLDHAM, OL8 4EG
Tel: 0161 628 3885
Web site: http://www.bluedome.co.uk
Titles:
BLUE DOME

BLUE EDGE PUBLISHING 1717657
Old Byre House, East Knoyle, SALISBURY, SP3 6AW
Tel: 01747 830520
Titles:
THE AMERICAN

BLUE GREEN MEDIA LTD 1681186
14 Deanway, HOVE, BN3 6DG **Tel:** 01273 556377
Titles:
GOLF NEWS
GOLF NEWS NORTH

BLUE SAX PUBLISHING LTD 600363
86 Colston Street, BRISTOL, BS1 5BB **Tel:** 0117 914 3434
Fax: 0117 914 3444
Titles:
THE SPARK

BLUE SKY PUBLICATIONS LTD 1654441
Unit 7, Commodore House, Juniper Drive, LONDON, SW18
1TW **Tel:** 0845 456 4910 **Fax:** 0845 456 4912
Web site: http://www.blueskygroup.co.uk
Titles:
AUSTRALIAN TIMES
NEW ZEALAND TIMES
SOUTH AFRICAN

BLUES & SOUL LTD 15355
153 Praed Street, LONDON, W2 1RL **Tel:** 020 8656 5651
Web site: http://www.bluesandsoul.com
Titles:
BLUES & SOUL

BMF PUBLISHING 1725064
Davidson House, Glenavy Road Business Park, Moira,
CRAIGAVON, BT67 0LT **Tel:** 028 9261 9933
Fax: 028 9261 9951
Email: info@bmfbusinessservices.com
Web site: http://www.bmfbusinessservices.com
Titles:
AGENDANI

BMI PUBLICATIONS LTD 13631
Suffolk House, George Street, CROYDON, CR9 1SR
Tel: 020 8649 7233 **Fax:** 020 8649 7234
Email: enquiries@bmipublications.com
Web site: http://www.bmipublications.com
Titles:
THE BUSINESS TRAVEL MAGAZINE
ONBOARD HOSPITALITY

SELLING LONG HAUL
SHORT BREAKS & HOLIDAYS

BMJ PUBLISHING GROUP 12612
BMA House, Tavistock Square, LONDON, WC1H 9JR
Tel: 020 7387 4499 **Fax:** 020 7383 6418
Email: customerservices@bmjgroup.com
Web site: http://www.group.bmj.com
Titles:
BMJ.COM
BRITISH JOURNAL OF OPHTHALMOLOGY
DRUG & THERAPEUTICS BULLETIN
EMERGENCY MEDICINE JOURNAL
OCCUPATIONAL AND ENVIRONMENTAL MEDICINE
POSTGRADUATE MEDICAL JOURNAL
STUDENT BMJ

BNA INTERNATIONAL 13377
Millbank Tower, 21-24 Millbank, LONDON, SW1P 4QP
Tel: 020 7559 4800 **Fax:** 020 7559 4880
Web site: http://www.bnai.com
Titles:
TAX PLANNING INTERNATIONAL ASIA PACIFIC FOCUS
TAX PLANNING INTERNATIONAL EUROPEAN TAX
SERVICE
TAX PLANNING INTERNATIONAL INDIRECT TAXES
TAX PLANNING INTERNATIONAL TRANSFER PRICING

BO PUBLICATIONS LTD 1739870
18 Salisbury Road, LONDON, E10 5RG **Tel:** 020 8279 0831
Titles:
VIYA

BOADICEA PUBLICATIONS LTD 12203
176 Swievelands Road, Biggin Hill, WESTERHAM, TN16
3QS **Tel:** 01959 572444 **Fax:** 0870 706 3074
Titles:
SALESFORCE

BOARDROOM EDGE LLP 1742430
PR by email only
Titles:
BOARDROOM EDGE

BOAT SHOP 24 LTD 695697
44A North Street, CHICHESTER, PO19 1NF
Tel: 01243 533394
Email: sales@boatshop24.co.uk
Web site: http://www.boatshop24.co.uk
Titles:
BOAT TRADER
BOATS & YACHTS FOR SALE

THE BOOKPLATE SOCIETY 17679
11 Nella Road, LONDON, W6 9PB **Tel:** 020 7385 3099
Titles:
THE BOOKPLATE JOURNAL

BOOKS & LIFE LTD 1653394
17-21 Wyfold Road, LONDON, SW6 6SE **Tel:** 0845 257 2930
Fax: 020 7391 8444
Email: director@society-today.com
Titles:
SOCIETY TODAY

BOOKSELLER PUBLICATIONS 16197
5th Floor, Endeavour House, 189 Shaftesbury Avenue,
LONDON, WC2H 8TJ **Tel:** 020 7420 6000
Fax: 020 7420 6103
Titles:
BACK TO SCHOOL BOOKSELLER
THE BOOKSELLER.COM

**THE BOOKSELLERS ASSOCIATION OF THE UK &
IRELAND LTD** 14658
272 Vauxhall Bridge Road, LONDON, SW1V 1BA
Tel: 020 7802 0802 **Fax:** 020 7802 0803
Titles:
BOOKSELLING ESSENTIALS

BOOMBERG 1764807
Manor House, Manor Park, ALDERSHOT, GU12 4JU

Titles:
LET'S GO WITH THE CHILDREN IN BRISTOL, BATH,
GLOS, WILTS (COTSWOLDS, FOREST OF DEAN)

BORDER EVENTS.COM LTD 1692058
2 Heatherlie Park, SELKIRK, TD7 5AL **Tel:** 01750 725480
Email: info@borderevents.com
Web site: http://www.borderevents.com
Titles:
BORDEREVENTS

BORDER PUBLISHING LTD 1655207
Salop House, Salop Road, OSWESTRY, SY11 2NS
Tel: 01691 662709
Email: info@borderpublishing.com
Web site: http://www.borderpublishing.com
Titles:
COUNTRY & BORDER LIFE MAGAZINE

BORDER WEEKLIES LTD 15039
113 High Street, GALASHIELS, TD1 1SB **Tel:** 01896 758395
Fax: 01896 758395
Titles:
BORDER TELEGRAPH
PEEBLESSHIRE NEWS

BOSTON HANNAH INTERNATIONAL 16177
21-24 Bruges Place, Randolph Street, LONDON, NW1 0TF
Tel: 020 7870 9000 **Fax:** 020 7870 9095
Web site: http://www.bostonhannah.co.uk
Titles:
COLLECTIONS

BOTANICAL SOCIETY OF THE BRITISH ISLES 18322
c/o Botany Department, The Natural History Museum,
Cromwell Road, LONDON, SW7 5BD
Titles:
WATSONIA

BOUNDARY I MEDIA 675204
Priory Park, Beech Green Lane, Withyham, HARTFIELD, TN7
4DB **Tel:** 01892 771047 **Fax:** 01892 771048
Titles:
INSURANCE DIRECTORY
INTERNATIONAL LEATHER GUIDE

BOUNTY HUNTER PUBLICATIONS 1735943
44 Herbs End, Cove, FARNBOROUGH, GU14 9YD
Tel: 01252 373658 **Fax:** 01252 373658
Email: bigcarpmagazine@hotmail.com
Web site: http://www.bigcarpmagazine.co.uk
Titles:
BC BIG CARP MAGAZINE

THE BOW GROUP 18500
Can Mezzanine Building, 32-36 Loman Street, LONDON,
SE1 0EH **Tel:** 020 7922 7718 **Fax:** 020 7431 6668
Titles:
CROSSBOW

BOWLERS' WORLD 15323
2 Braunton Road, WALLASEY, CH45 5HL
Tel: 07984 348341
Titles:
BOWLERS WORLD

BOX TV LTD 1744503
Mappin House, 4 Winsley Street, LONDON, W1W 8HF
Tel: 020 7182 8000
Titles:
SMASH HITS

GEORGE BOYDEN & SON 15002
York House, 17 Rother Street, STRATFORD-UPON-AVON,
CV37 6NB **Tel:** 01789 266261 **Fax:** 01789 269519
Email: publishing@stratford-herald.com
Web site: http://www.stratford-herald.com
Titles:
STRATFORD-UPON-AVON HERALD SERIES

UK Publishers & Their Titles

BPC MAGAZINES 1676919
Media House, 5 Broadway Court, High Street, CHESHAM,
HP5 1EG **Tel:** 01494 771144 **Fax:** 01494 771277
Email: info@bpcmagazines.com
Web site: http://www.bpcmagazines.com

Titles:
ANTRIM BOROUGH COUNCIL GUIDE
THE ARDS VISITOR GUIDE
BURNHAM TOWN GUIDE
CHILTERN DISTRICT COUNCILLORS GUIDE
ENNISKILLEN AIRSHOW PROGRAMME
EXCLUSIVE (CHILTERNS)
EXCLUSIVE (LONDON)
LONDON'S OWN
ULSTER AIRSHOW PROGRAMME

BPG (STAMFORD) LTD 15267
Roebuck House, 33 Broad Street, STAMFORD, PE9 1RB
Tel: 01780 754900 **Fax:** 01780 766416
Email: info@bournepublishinggroup.co.uk
Web site: http://www.bournepublishinggroup.com

Titles:
FIELDSPORTS
HORSE + PONY
THE SCOTTISH SPORTING GAZETTE & INTERNATIONAL
  TRAVELLER
YOUR CAT
YOUR DOG

BPL BUSINESS MEDIA LTD 13574
3rd Floor, Armstrong House, 38 Market Square, UXBRIDGE,
UB8 1TG **Tel:** 01895 421111 **Fax:** 01895 431252
Web site: http://www.bpl-business.com

Titles:
8020 EUROPA
C2M
IBE INTERNATIONAL BROADCAST ENGINEER
IT EUROPA
RETAIL TECHNOLOGY

BPM MEDIA (MIDLANDS) 16240
Floor 6, Fort Dunlop, Fort Parkway, BIRMINGHAM, B24 9FF
Tel: 0121 234 5000 **Fax:** 0121 234 5625
Email: magazines@mrn.co.uk
Web site: http://www.livingseries.co.uk

Titles:
THE BIRMINGHAM POST
LIVING
SOLIHULL NEWS
SUNDAY MERCURY (BIRMINGHAM)

BRADGATE PUBLISHING 1740907
9-10 Havelock Street, ILKESTON, DE7 5RJ
Tel: 0115 944 2344

Titles:
IN BUSINESS

BRANCH & MOBILE LIBRARIES GROUP 621658
3 Spring Garden, Hensall, GOOLE, DN14 0QL
Tel: 01977 663143 **Fax:** 01226 773955
Email: ian_bmlg@hotmail.com

Titles:
SERVICE POINT

THE BRASS HERALD 1711733
2 The Coppice, Impington, CAMBRIDGE, CB24 9PP
Tel: 01223 234090

Titles:
THE BRASS HERALD

BRAVE ENTERPRISE AGENCY 16259
The Coach House Small Business Centre, 2 Upper York
Street, BRISTOL, BS2 8QN **Tel:** 0117 944 5330
Fax: 0117 944 5661

Titles:
BRAVE

BRAVE NEW WORLD INTERNATIONAL LTD 17880
Orchardton Hall, Auchencairn, CASTLE DOUGLAS, DG7
1QL **Tel:** 0845 130 6249
Email: edit@bnw.demon.co.uk

Titles:
ANIMALS WRITE
BOOKREVIEW ONLINE
CAR NEWS INTERNATIONAL
CENTRAL LONDON INDEPENDENT
DIESELMOTORING.COM
DIY DOG
HAPPY FAMILIES

HAPPY FAMILIES ONLINE
INTERNATIONAL CONNECTION
MOTOR NEWS
MOVIE CLUB NEWS
TOP REVIEW

**BRAZILIAN CHAMBER OF COMMERCE IN GREAT
BRITAIN** 13772
32 Green Street, LONDON, W1K 7AT **Tel:** 020 7221 7179
Fax: 020 7221 7179

Titles:
BRAZIL BUSINESS BRIEF

BREAKTHROUGH BREAST CANCER 1643805
Third Floor, Weston House, 246 High Holborn, LONDON,
WC1V 7EX **Tel:** 020 7025 2470

Titles:
PURPLE

BREAKTIME MAGAZINES LTD 1745972
Breaktime House, 2 Glencoe Road, POOLE, BH12 2DW
Tel: 01202 722458 **Fax:** 0871 218 0096
Email: breaktime@breaktimemagazine.co.uk
Web site: http://www.breaktimemagazine.co.uk

Titles:
BREAKTIME MAGAZINE

BRECON AND RADNOR EXPRESS LTD 13247
11 The Bulwark, BRECON, LD3 7AE **Tel:** 01874 610111

Titles:
BRECON AND RADNOR EXPRESS
VITA

BREEZI PUBLISHING LTD 1710754
PO Box 75, BRIGHOUSE, HD6 3WF **Tel:** 01484 401353

Titles:
FARMINGUK
POULTRY GAZETTE

BREWIN BOOKS LTD 1653071
56 Alcester Road, STUDLEY, B80 7LG **Tel:** 01527 854228
Fax: 01527 852746
Email: admin@brewinbooks.com
Web site: http://www.brewinbooks.com

Titles:
LOCAL HISTORY MAGAZINE

BRIDGE FOR DESIGN 1761812
Unit 16, Millbrook Trading Estate, Sybron Way,
CROWBOROUGH, TN6 3DZ **Tel:** 01732 461090

Titles:
BRIDGE FOR DESIGN

BRIGHT PUBLISHING LTD 1724966
Bright house, 82 High Street, Sawston, CAMBRIDGE, CB22
3HJ **Tel:** 01223 499450

Titles:
CAMBRIDGE MATTERS
DIGITAL SLR USER
PHOTO PRO MAGAZINE

BRIGHTDAY 1680241
38 High Street, BISHOPS CASTLE, SY9 5BQ
Email: news@learningsupport.co.uk

Titles:
LEARNING SUPPORT

BRIGHTON PEARL 1710684
10 Queen Victoria Avenue, HOVE, BN3 6WN
Tel: 01273 249751 **Fax:** 01273 264413

Titles:
FISH & CHIPS AND FAST FOOD

BRIGHTON SOURCE LTD 1749652
PO Box 3313, BRIGHTON, BN1 4BJ **Tel:** 01273 609955

Titles:
THE BRIGHTON SOURCE

BRILLIANT PRODUCTIONS 1642258
90 Furness Road, LONDON, NW10 5UE **Tel:** 020 8933 1659
Fax: 020 8933 1659

Titles:
HOWTOLOOKGOOD

BRISTOL NEWS AND MEDIA 1640065
1 Clarence Parade, CHELTENHAM, GL50 3NY
Tel: 0117 934 3000
Email: wdnews@bepp.co.uk
Web site: http://www.westerndailypress.co.uk

Titles:
PRIMARY TIMES IN AVON
RIDERS
WESTERN DAILY PRESS BRISTOL

BRISTOL NEWS & MEDIA LTD 14832
Temple Way, BRISTOL, BS99 7HD **Tel:** 0117 934 3000

Titles:
BRISTOL OBSERVER SERIES
EVENING POST (BRISTOL)
WEST COUNTRY LIFE

BRITAIN'S ASIAN ASSETS 1644586
Tel: 020 8907 3071
PR by email only, LONDON **Tel:** 07976 205185

Titles:
ASSETS WORLD
ASSETSWORLD

BRITANNIA ART PUBLICATIONS 15806
4th Floor, 28 Charing Cross Road, LONDON, WC2H 0DB
Tel: 020 7240 0389 **Fax:** 020 7497 0726

Titles:
ART MONTHLY

BRITISH AGENTS REGISTER 13884
5A Cheltenham Mount, HARROGATE, HG1 1DW
Tel: 01423 560608 **Fax:** 01423 561204
Email: info@agentsregister.com
Web site: http://www.agentsregister.com

Titles:
BRITISH COMMERCIAL AGENTS REVIEW

BRITISH AIRWAYS COMMUNICATIONS DEPARTMENT
13647
Waterside (HCB3), PO Box 365, Harmondsworth, WEST
DRAYTON, UB7 0GB

Titles:
BRITISH AIRWAYS NEWS
TOUCHDOWN BRITISH AIRWAYS

BRITISH AMATEUR GYMNASTICS ASSOCIATION 15284
Ford Hall, Lilleshall National Sports Centre, NEWPORT, TF10
9NB **Tel:** 0845 129 7129 **Fax:** 0845 124 9089
Web site: http://www.british-gymnastics.org

Titles:
THE GYMNAST

BRITISH AND IRISH ORTHOPTIC SOCIETY 17710
Tavistock House North, Tavistock Square, LONDON, WC1H
9HX **Tel:** 020 7387 7992 **Fax:** 020 7383 2584
Web site: http://www.orthoptics.org.uk

Titles:
BRITISH AND IRISH ORTHOPTIC JOURNAL

BRITISH ART JOURNAL 673861
46 Grove Lane, LONDON, SE5 8ST **Tel:** 020 7787 6944
Fax: 020 7701 3299
Web site: http://www.britishartjournal.co.uk

Titles:
THE BRITISH ART JOURNAL

**BRITISH ASSOCIATION FOR ADOPTION AND
FOSTERING** 14157
Saffron House, 6-10 Kirby Street, LONDON, EC1N 8TS
Tel: 020 7421 2600 **Fax:** 020 7421 2601
Email: mail@baaf.org.uk
Web site: http://www.baaf.org.uk

Titles:
ADOPTION & FOSTERING

BRITISH ASSOCIATION FOR COUNSELLING & PSYCHOTHERAPY 14170
BACP House, Unit 15, St. John's Business Park, LUTTERWORTH, LE17 4HB **Tel:** 01455 883300
Fax: 01455 550243
Email: bacp@bacp.co.uk
Web site: http://www.bacp.co.uk
Titles:
COUNSELLING AT WORK
THERAPY TODAY

BRITISH ASSOCIATION FOR THE ADVANCEMENT OF SCIENCE 15922
165 Queen's Gate, LONDON, SW7 5HD **Tel:** 020 7019 4930
Fax: 020 7019 4923
Email: wendy.barnaby@the-ba.net
Web site: http://www.the-ba.net/spa
Titles:
PEOPLE & SCIENCE

BRITISH ASSOCIATION OF COMMUNICATORS IN BUSINESS 13470
Woodlands Business Park, Breckland, Linford Wood West, MILTON KEYNES, MK14 6EY **Tel:** 01908 313755
Fax: 01908 313661
Email: enquiries@cib.uk.com
Web site: http://www.cib.uk.com
Titles:
COMMUNICATORS

BRITISH ASSOCIATION OF DENTAL NURSES 14542
PO Box 4, Room 200, Hillhouse International Business Centre, THORNTON-CLEVELEYS, FY5 4QD
Tel: 01253 338360
Email: editor@badn.org.uk
Web site: http://www.badn.org.uk
Titles:
THE BRITISH DENTAL NURSES' JOURNAL

THE BRITISH ASSOCIATION OF LANDSCAPE INDUSTRIES 14632
Landscape House, Stoneleigh Park, KENILWORTH, CV8 2LG **Tel:** 024 7669 0333 **Fax:** 024 7669 0077
Email: contact@bali.org.uk
Web site: http://www.bali.org.uk
Titles:
LANDSCAPE NEWS

BRITISH ASSOCIATION OF SOCIAL WORKERS 14179
16 Kent Street, BIRMINGHAM, B5 6RD **Tel:** 0121 622 3911
Fax: 0121 622 4860
Web site: http://www.basw.co.uk
Titles:
PROFESSIONAL SOCIAL WORK

BRITISH ASSOCIATION OF TEACHERS OF THE DEAF 1622116
41 The Orchard, Leven, BEVERLEY, HU17 5QA
Web site: http://www.batod.org.uk
Titles:
THE BATOD MAGAZINE

THE BRITISH ASTRONOMICAL ASSOCIATION 16137
Burlington House, Piccadilly, LONDON, W1J 0DU
Tel: 020 7734 4145
Web site: http://www.britastro.org
Titles:
JOURNAL OF THE BRITISH ASTRONOMICAL ASSOCIATION

BRITISH AUTOMOBILE RACING CLUB 15445
Thruxton Circuit, ANDOVER, SP11 8PN **Tel:** 01264 882200
Fax: 01264 882233
Email: info@barc.net
Web site: http://www.barc.net
Titles:
STARTLINE

BRITISH BALLOON & AIRSHIP CLUB 18182
1 Home Farm Cottages, Lenham Heath Road, Sandway, MAIDSTONE, ME17 2HX **Tel:** 01622 858956
Fax: 01622 853817
Titles:
AEROSTAT

BRITISH BANDSMAN LTD 671630
66-78 Denington Road, Denington Industrial Estate, WELLINGBOROUGH, NN8 2QH **Tel:** 01933 445442
Fax: 01933 445435
Titles:
THE BRITISH BANDSMAN

BRITISH BIRDS 15664
4 Harlequin Gardens, ST. LEONARDS-ON-SEA, TN37 7PF
Tel: 01424 755155 **Fax:** 01424 755155
Titles:
BRITISH BIRDS

BRITISH CACTUS & SUCCULENT SOCIETY 16105
Old Oak Farm, Moor Edge Low Side, Harden, BINGLEY, BD16 1LD **Tel:** 01535 273615
Email: dequail@tiscali.co.uk
Web site: http://www.bcss.org.uk
Titles:
CACTUSWORLD JOURNAL OF THE BRITISH CACTUS AND SUCCULENT SOCIETY

BRITISH CANOE UNION 16072
18 Market Place, Bingham, NOTTINGHAM, NG13 8AP
Tel: 0845 370 9500 **Fax:** 0845 370 9501
Email: info@bcu.org.uk
Web site: http://www.bcu.org.uk
Titles:
CANOE FOCUS

BRITISH CHESS MAGAZINE LIMITED 15490
44 Baker Street, LONDON, W1U 7RT **Tel:** 020 7486 8222
Fax: 020 7486 3355
Email: editor@bcmchess.co.uk
Web site: http://www.bcmchess.co.uk
Titles:
BRITISH CHESS MAGAZINE

BRITISH CHIROPRACTIC ASSOCIATION 14599
59 Castle Street, READING, RG1 7SN **Tel:** 0118 950 5950
Fax: 0118 958 8946
Web site: http://www.chiropractic-uk.co.uk
Titles:
CONTACT (BRITISH CHIROPRACTIC ASSOCIATION)

BRITISH COMPUTER SOCIETY 1734340
1st Floor, Block D, North Star House, North Star Avenue, SWINDON, SN2 1FA **Tel:** 01793 417417 **Fax:** 01793 417444
Web site: http://www.bcs.org
Titles:
IT TRAINING

BRITISH CYCLING 1642293
National Cycling Centre, Stuart Street, MANCHESTER, M11 4DQ **Tel:** 0161 274 2035
Titles:
RACING CALENDAR

BRITISH DEAF ASSOCIATION 1640088
10th Floor, Coventry Point, Market Way, COVENTRY, CV1 1EA **Tel:** 0870 770 3300 **Fax:** 020 7588 3527
Email: midlands@signcommunity.org.uk
Web site: http://www.bda.org.uk
Titles:
BRITISH DEAF NEWS

BRITISH DEER FARMERS ASSOCIATION 1653563
PO Box 7522, MATLOCK, DE4 9BR **Tel:** 08456 344758
Fax: 08456 344759
Email: info@bdfa.co.uk
Web site: http://www.bdfa.co.uk
Titles:
DEER FARMING

BRITISH DENTAL ASSOCIATION 14541
64 Wimpole Street, LONDON, W1G 8YS **Tel:** 020 7935 0875
Fax: 020 7487 5232
Web site: http://www.bda.org
Titles:
BDA NEWS

THE BRITISH DENTAL TRADE ASSOCIATION 1767688
The British Dental Trade Association, Mineral Lane, CHESHAM, HP5 1NL **Tel:** 01494 782873
Titles:
DENTAL TRADER

BRITISH DESIGN INNOVATION 18570
9 Pavilion Parade, BRIGHTON, BN2 1RA **Tel:** 01273 621378
Fax: 01273 622144
Email: info@britishdesign.co.uk
Web site: http://www.britishdesign.co.uk
Titles:
DESIGN & INNOVATION NEWS WIRE

THE BRITISH ECOLOGICAL SOCIETY 14611
26 Blades Court, Deodar Road, LONDON, SW15 2NU
Tel: 020 8871 9797 **Fax:** 020 8871 9779
Titles:
THE BULLETIN

BRITISH EDITORIAL SOCIETY OF BONE AND JOINT SURGERY 18442
22 Buckingham Street, LONDON, WC2N 6ET
Tel: 020 7782 0010 **Fax:** 020 7782 0995
Email: council@jbjs.org.uk
Web site: http://www.jbjs.org.uk
Titles:
JOURNAL OF BONE & JOINT SURGERY (BRITISH VOLUME)

THE BRITISH FEDERATION OF FESTIVALS 17700
Festival House, 198 Park Lane, MACCLESFIELD, SK11 6UD
Tel: 01625 428297 **Fax:** 01625 503229
Email: info@federationoffestivals.org.uk
Web site: http://www.federationoffestivals.org.uk
Titles:
THE BRITISH AND INTERNATIONAL FEDERATION OF FESTIVALS FOR MUSIC, DANCE & SPEECH

BRITISH FENCING ASSOCIATION 15335
Baron's Gate, 33 Rothschild Road, LONDON, W4 5HT
Tel: 020 8742 3032 **Fax:** 020 8674 2245
Email: british_fencing@compuserve.com
Web site: http://www.britishfencing.com
Titles:
THE SWORD

BRITISH FILM INSTITUTE 15341
21 Stephen Street, LONDON, W1T 1LN **Tel:** 020 7255 1444
Fax: 020 7436 2327
Titles:
SIGHT & SOUND

BRITISH FLUTE SOCIETY 15379
1 Doveridge Gardens, LONDON, N13 5BJ
Tel: 020 8882 2627 **Fax:** 020 8882 2728
Web site: http://www.bfs.org.uk
Titles:
PAN

BRITISH FREE RANGE EGG PRODUCERS ASSOCIATION 1733263
Po Box 75, BRIGHOUSE, HD6 3WF **Tel:** 01484 400 666
Fax: 01484 400 661
Titles:
RANGER

THE BRITISH FUCHSIA SOCIETY 17641
PO Box 178, EVESHAM, WR11 3WY **Tel:** 01386 45158
Web site: http://www.thebfs.org.uk
Titles:
FUCHSIA ANNUAL

BRITISH GEOLOGICAL SURVEY 14617
Kingsley Dunham Centre, Keyworth, NOTTINGHAM, NG12 5GG **Tel:** 0115 936 3100 **Fax:** 0115 936 3385
Email: enquiries@bgs.ac.uk
Web site: http://www.bgs.ac.uk
Titles:
EARTHWISE

UK Publishers & Their Titles

BRITISH GLIDING ASSOCIATION LTD 15309
Kimberley House, Vaughan Way, LEICESTER, LE1 4SE
Tel: 0116 253 1051
Titles:
SAILPLANE & GLIDING

BRITISH GOAT SOCIETY 17703
34-36 Fore Street, Bovey Tracey, NEWTON ABBOT, TQ13
9AD **Tel:** 01626 833168 **Fax:** 01626 834536
Titles:
BRITISH GOAT SOCIETY MONTHLY JOURNAL
BRITISH GOAT SOCIETY YEAR BOOK
HERD BOOK

**BRITISH HANG GLIDING AND PARAGLIDING
ASSOCIATION** 15310
The Old School Room, Loughborough Road, LEICESTER,
LE4 5PJ **Tel:** 0116 261 1322
Titles:
SKYWINGS

BRITISH HOLIDAY AND HOME PARKS ASSOCIATION
14426
6 Pullman Court, Great Western Road, GLOUCESTER, GL1
3ND **Tel:** 01452 526911 **Fax:** 01452 508508
Web site: http://www.ukparks.com
Titles:
JOURNAL - BRITISH HOLIDAY & HOME PARKS
ASSOCIATION

BRITISH HOMEOPATHIC ASSOCIATION 17136
Hahnemann House, 29 Park Street West, LUTON, LU1 3BE
Tel: 0870 444 3950 **Fax:** 0870 444 3960
Email: info@trusthomeopathy.org
Web site: http://www.trusthomeopathy.org
Titles:
HEALTH & HOMEOPATHY

THE BRITISH HOROLOGICAL INSTITUTE 14436
Upton Hall, Main Street, Upton, NEWARK, NG23 5TE
Tel: 01636 817601 **Fax:** 01636 812258
Web site: http://www.bhi.co.uk
Titles:
HOROLOGICAL JOURNAL

BRITISH HORSERACING BOARD 18156
Weatherbys Thoroughbred Ltd, Sanders Road,
WELLINGBOROUGH, NN8 4BX **Tel:** 01933 440077
Fax: 01933 440807
Titles:
THE PROGRAMME BOOKS

BRITISH HOSPITALITY ASSOCIATION 1690158
55-56 Lincoln's Inn Fields, LONDON, WC2A 3BH
Tel: 0845 880 7744 **Fax:** 020 7404 7799
Web site: http://www.bha.org.uk
Titles:
BRITISH HOSPITALITY: TRENDS AND DEVELOPMENTS

BRITISH INSTITUTE OF NON-DESTRUCTIVE TESTING
14480
1 Spencer Parade, NORTHAMPTON, NN1 5AA
Tel: 01604 630124 **Fax:** 01604 231489
Email: info@bindt.org
Web site: http://www.bindt.org
Titles:
CONDITION MONITOR
INSIGHT

BRITISH INSURANCE BROKERS ASSOCIATION 16909
8th Floor, John Stow House, 18 Bevis Marks, LONDON,
EC3A 7JB **Tel:** 0844 770 0266 **Fax:** 020 7626 9676
Email: enquiries@biba.org.uk
Web site: http://www.biba.org.uk
Titles:
THE BROKER

BRITISH INTERPLANETARY SOCIETY 13635
27-29 South Lambeth Road, LONDON, SW8 1SZ
Tel: 020 7735 3160 **Fax:** 020 7820 1504
Web site: http://www.bis-spaceflight.com
Titles:
SPACEFLIGHT

BRITISH IRIS SOCIETY 17885
Edgebolton, Shawbury, Shrewsbury, SHROPSHIRE, SY4
4EL **Tel:** 01939 251173 **Fax:** 01939 251311
Titles:
THE IRIS YEAR BOOK

THE BRITISH JUDO ASSOCIATION 625669
Suite B, Loughborough Technology Centre, Epinal Way,
LOUGHBOROUGH, LE11 3GE **Tel:** 01509 631692
Fax: 01509 631680
Web site: http://www.britishjudo.org.uk
Titles:
MATSIDE MAGAZINE

**BRITISH KINEMATOGRAPH, SOUND & TELEVISION
SOCIETY** 14802
17 Winterslow Road, Porton, SALISBURY, SP4 0LW
Tel: 01980 610544 **Fax:** 01980 590611
Titles:
CINEMA TECHNOLOGY

BRITISH LIBRARY 18179
96 Euston Road, LONDON, NW1 2DB **Tel:** 020 7412 7000
Titles:
THE ELECTRONIC BRITISH LIBRARY JOURNAL

BRITISH LUNG FOUNDATION 1748367
73-75 Goswell Road, LONDON, EC1V 7ER
Tel: 020 7688 5555 **Fax:** 020 7688 5556
Email: breathing.space@blf-uk.org
Web site: http://www.lunguk.org
Titles:
BREATHING SPACE

BRITISH MARINE FEDERATION 1709778
Marine House, Thorpe Lea Road, EGHAM, TW20 8BF
Tel: 01784 223678
Titles:
BRITISH MARINE NEWS

BRITISH MARINE LIFE STUDY SOCIETY 17792
Glaucus House, 14 Corbyn Crescent, SHOREHAM-BY-SEA,
BN43 6PQ **Tel:** 01273 465433
Web site: http://www.glaucus.org.uk
Titles:
TORPEDO

BRITISH MEDICAL ASSOCIATION 14491
BMA House, Tavistock Square, LONDON, WC1H 9JP
Tel: 020 7387 4499 **Fax:** 020 7383 6418
Web site: http://www.bma.org
Titles:
BMA NEWS
BMJ BRITISH MEDICAL JOURNAL
STUDENT BMA NEWS

BRITISH MENSA LTD 16141
St. Johns House, St. Johns Square, WOLVERHAMPTON,
WV2 4AH **Tel:** 01902 772771 **Fax:** 01902 422327
Email: enquiries@mensa.org.uk
Web site: http://www.mensa.org.uk
Titles:
MENSA MAGAZINE

BRITISH MICROLIGHT AIRCRAFT ASSOCIATION 13652
The Bull Ring, Deddington, BANBURY, OX15 0TT
Tel: 01869 338888 **Fax:** 01869 337116
Titles:
MF MICROLIGHT FLYING

BRITISH MODEL FLYING ASSOCIATION 17510
Chacksfield House, 31 St. Andrews Road, LEICESTER, LE2
8RE **Tel:** 0116 244 0028 **Fax:** 0116 244 0645
Web site: http://www.bmfa.org
Titles:
BMFA NEWS

BRITISH MOUNTAINEERING COUNCIL 16592
177-179 Burton Road, MANCHESTER, M20 2BB
Tel: 0161 445 4747 **Fax:** 0161 445 4500
Email: office@thebmc.co.uk
Web site: http://www.thebmc.co.uk

Titles:
SUMMIT

BRITISH MUSEUM FRIENDS 18521
British Museum, Great Russell Street, LONDON, WC1B 3DG
Tel: 020 7323 3000 **Fax:** 020 7323 8614
Titles:
BRITISH MUSEUM MAGAZINE

BRITISH NATURAL HYGIENE SOCIETY 17828
Shalimar, The Weavers, Farndon Road, NEWARK ON
TRENT, NG24 4RY **Tel:** 01636 682 941
Titles:
THE HYGIENIST

BRITISH NUTRITION FOUNDATION 16429
High Holborn House, 52-54 High Holborn, LONDON, WC1V
6RQ **Tel:** 020 7404 6504 **Fax:** 020 7404 6747
Web site: http://www.nutrition.org.uk
Titles:
BRITISH NUTRITION FOUNDATION NEWS

BRITISH PARKING ASSOCIATION 16351
Stuart House, 41-43 Perrymount Road, HAYWARDS HEATH,
RH16 3BN **Tel:** 01444 447300 **Fax:** 01444 447311
Titles:
CIVIL ENFORCEMENT NOW
PARKING NEWS

BRITISH PEST CONTROL ASSOCIATION 13992
Gleneagles House, Vernon Gate, South Street, DERBY, DE1
1UP **Tel:** 01332 294288 **Fax:** 01332 295904
Web site: http://www.bpca.org.uk
Titles:
PEST

BRITISH PLASTICS FEDERATION 1685911
Tel: 020 7457 5000 **Fax:** 020 7457 5045
6 Bath Place, Rivington Street, LONDON, EC2A 3JE
Tel: 020 7457 5000 **Fax:** 020 7457 5045
Web site: http://www.bpf.co.uk
Titles:
BPF WEEKLY NEWSLETTER

BRITISH POLIO FELLOWSHIP 14571
Unit A, Eagle Office Centre, The Runway, SOUTH RUISLIP,
HA4 6SE **Tel:** 0800 018 0586 **Fax:** 0845 450 0226
Titles:
THE BULLETIN OF THE BRITISH POLIO FELLOWSHIP

THE BRITISH PSYCHOLOGICAL SOCIETY 12617
St. Andrews House, 48 Princess Road East, LEICESTER,
LE1 7DR **Tel:** 0116 254 9568 **Fax:** 0116 227 1314
Email: mail@bps.org.uk
Web site: http://www.bps.org.uk
Titles:
BRITISH JOURNAL OF DEVELOPMENT PSYCHOLOGY
BRITISH JOURNAL OF EDUCATIONAL PSYCHOLOGY
BRITISH JOURNAL OF MATHEMATICAL & STATISTICAL
PSYCHOLOGY
BRITISH JOURNAL OF PSYCHOLOGY
THE PSYCHOLOGIST
PSYCHOLOGIST APPOINTMENTS

BRITISH SAFETY COUNCIL 14457
70 Chancellors Road, LONDON, W6 9RS
Tel: 020 8741 1231 **Fax:** 020 8741 0835
Titles:
HEALTH & SAFETY AT WORK ACT NEWSLETTER
SAFETY MANAGEMENT

THE BRITISH SCHOOL AT ROME 18119
The British Academy, 10 Carlton House Terrace, LONDON,
SW1Y 5AH **Tel:** 020 7969 5202 **Fax:** 020 7969 5401
Titles:
PAPERS OF THE BRITISH SCHOOL AT ROME

THE BRITISH SIMMENTAL CATTLE SOCIETY LTD
621959
National Agricultural Centre, Stoneleigh Park,
KENILWORTH, CV8 2LG **Tel:** 024 7669 6513
Fax: 024 7669 6724

Titles:
THE SIMMENTAL REVIEW

THE BRITISH SOCIETY OF DENTAL HYGIENE AND THERAPY 14545
19 Cwrt-y-Vil Road, PENARTH, CF64 3HN
Tel: 029 2071 0042 **Fax:** 029 2071 0042
Titles:
DENTAL HEALTH

BRITISH SOCIETY OF DOWSERS 18000
2 St. Anns Road, MALVERN, WR14 4RG **Tel:** 01684 576969
Fax: 01684 576969
Web site: http://www.britishdowsers.org
Titles:
DOWSING TODAY

BRITISH SUGAR PLC 14032
Sugar Way, PETERBOROUGH, PE2 9AY **Tel:** 01733 422278
Fax: 01733 422080
Titles:
BRITISH SUGAR BEET REVIEW
SUGAR EXTRACTS

BRITISH SULPHUR PUBLISHING 13715
31 Mount Pleasant, LONDON, WC1X 0AD
Tel: 020 7837 5600 **Fax:** 020 7837 0292
Web site: http://www.britishsulphur.com
Titles:
FERTILIZERWEEK

BRITISH TELECOMMUNICATIONS PLC 13926
Post Point A5E, 81 Newgate Street, LONDON, EC1A 7AJ
Tel: 020 7356 6543 **Fax:** 020 7356 6546
Titles:
BT TODAY

BRITISH TRUST FOR ORNITHOLOGY 15661
The Nunnery, THETFORD, IP24 2PU **Tel:** 01842 750050
Fax: 01842 750030
Web site: http://www.bto.org
Titles:
BTO NEWS

BRITISH VETERINARY ASSOCIATION 14794
7 Mansfield Street, LONDON, W1G 9NQ **Tel:** 020 7636 6541
Fax: 020 7908 6349
Email: bvahq@bva.co.uk
Web site: http://www.bva.co.uk
Titles:
IN PRACTICE
THE VETERINARY RECORD

BRITISH WATER SKI FEDERATION LIMITED 15298
The Tower, Thorpe Road, CHERTSEY, KT16 8PH
Tel: 01932 570885 **Fax:** 01932 566719
Email: info@bwsf.co.uk
Web site: http://www.britishwaterski.org.uk
Titles:
BRITISH WATER SKI & WAKEBOARD

BROADBAND TV NEWS 1649368
PO Box 499, CAMBRIDGE, CB1 0AH **Tel:** 01223 475381
Email: office@broadbandtvnews.com
Web site: http://www.broadbandtvnews.com
Titles:
BROADBAND TV NEWS
NEW TELEVISION INSIDER

BROADGATE PUBLICATIONS 1648998
37 The Towers, Lower Mortlake Road, RICHMOND, TW9
2JR **Tel:** 020 8948 8561 **Fax:** 020 8940 6009
Titles:
INSIDE SATELLITE TV
RAPID TV NEWS

BROCKWELL PUBLISHING 1649585
7 Eurolink Business Centre, Effra Road, LONDON, SW2 1BZ
Tel: 020 7733 0088 **Fax:** 020 7733 4988
Titles:
THE BABY DIRECTORY

THE BROOKLANDS SOCIETY LTD 15436
Copse House, Coxheath Road, Church Crookham, FLEET,
GU52 6QG **Tel:** 01252 408877 **Fax:** 01252 408878
Titles:
THE BROOKLANDS SOCIETY GAZETTE

BROWN, SON & FERGUSON LTD 14331
4-10 Darnley Street, GLASGOW, G41 2SD
Tel: 0141 429 1234 **Fax:** 0141 420 1694
Email: info@skipper.co.uk
Web site: http://www.skipper.co.uk
Titles:
THE NAUTICAL MAGAZINE

BRUNTON BUSINESS PUBLICATIONS LTD 14226
1 Salisbury Office Park, London Road, SALISBURY, SP1
3HP **Tel:** 01722 337038
Web site: http://www.brunton.co.uk
Titles:
BOARD CONVERTING NEWS INTERNATIONAL
FOLDING CARTON INDUSTRY
INTERNATIONAL PAPER BOARD INDUSTRY
RECOVERED FIBRE NEWS INCORPORATING
RECYCLING MARKETS

BRUSH EXPERT LTD 698763
44 Boleyn Close, Maidenbower, CRAWLEY, RH10 7QJ
Tel: 01293 884103 **Fax:** +33 5 49 29 03 08
Web site: http://www.brushexpert.com
Titles:
BRUSH EXPERT

THE BRYANSGROUND PRESS 1677457
Bryans Ground, Stapleton, PRESTEIGNE, LD8 2LP
Tel: 01544 260001 **Fax:** 01544 260015
Titles:
HORTUS: A GARDENING JOURNAL

BSAVA 1724965
Woodrow House, 1 Telford Way, GLOUCESTER, GL2 2AV
Tel: 01452 726100 **Fax:** 01452 726701
Web site: http://www.bsava.co.uk
Titles:
JOURNAL OF SMALL ANIMAL PRACTICE

BSKYB 700652
Online Business Unit, BSkyB, 9th Floor, Great West 1, Great
West Road, BRENTFORD, TW8 9DF **Tel:** +44 020 7705 3000
Fax: 020 7805 8296
Titles:
SKY STYLE
SKYMOVIES.COM

BSKYB PUBLICATIONS LTD 1762493
Grant Way, ISLEWORTH, TW7 5QD **Tel:** 020 7198 3000
Titles:
SKY MAG

BTO 18243
The Nunnery, THETFORD, IP24 2PU **Tel:** 01842 750050
Fax: 01842 750030
Titles:
RINGING & MIGRATION

BUCHAN ASSOCIATES 1686207
10 Rose Street, PETERHEAD, AB42 1DB **Tel:** 01779 480851
Fax: 01779 480851
Titles:
NORTH EAST WEEKLY

BUCKLEY PUBLICATIONS 623804
Upper Newtownards Road, BELFAST, BT4 3JF
Tel: 028 9047 4490 **Fax:** 028 9047 4495
Web site: http://www.businesseye.co.uk
Titles:
BUSINESS EYE

BUD UK 1752560
176 Shortwood Road, Pucklechurch, BRISTOL, BS16 9PH
Tel: 0117 937 3483
Email: nigel@bud.uk.com
Web site: http://www.bud.uk.com

Titles:
BRISTOL BRIEFING

BUDGERIGAR SOCIETY 15665
Spring Gardens, NORTHAMPTON, NN1 1DR
Tel: 01604 624549 **Fax:** 01604 627108
Titles:
THE BUDGERIGAR

BUFVC 15953
77 Wells Street, LONDON, W1T 3QJ **Tel:** 020 7393 1511
Fax: 020 7393 1555
Titles:
VIEWFINDER

BUILDER MAGAZINES 676114
PO Box 8, MARKFIELD, LE67 9ZT **Tel:** 01530 244069
Fax: 01530 249557
Email: info@buildermagazines.co.uk
Web site: http://www.buildermagazines.co.uk
Titles:
GROBY & FIELD HEAD SPOTLIGHT
THE HERALD
LEICESTERSHIRE BUILDER MAGAZINE

BUILDING AND FACILITIES NEWS 1733285
Suite 4.4B, 4th Floor, Maybrook House, Queensway,
HALESOWEN, B63 4AH **Tel:** 0121 504 3671
Fax: 0121 550 7482
Email: bafn@btconnect.com
Web site: http://www.buildingandfacilitiesnews.co.uk
Titles:
BUILDING AND FACILITIES NEWS

BULL NELSON LTD 1749699
PO Box 4136, Upper Basildon, READING, RG8 6BS
Tel: 01491 671998
Titles:
INDEPENDENT SCHOOLS MAGAZINE

BULLDOG PUBLISHING 18949
1 Church Lane, Whittlesford, CAMBRIDGE, CB22 4NX
Tel: 01223 499880 **Fax:** 01223 499889
Titles:
QUEST

BULLIVANT MEDIA LIMITED 18964
Webb House, 20A Church Green East, REDDITCH, B98 8BP
Tel: 01527 588688 **Fax:** 01527 584371
Web site: http://www.observerstandard.com
Titles:
COVENTRY OBSERVER
EVESHAM OBSERVER SERIES
LEAMINGTON & STRATFORD OBSERVER SERIES
REDDITCH AND BROMSGROVE STANDARD SERIES
THE RUGBY OBSERVER SERIES
SOLIHULL, SHIRLEY & ARDEN OBSERVER SERIES
THE WORCESTER STANDARD

BURDA MEDIA 18818
32-34 Great Marlborough Street, LONDON, W1V 1HA
Tel: 020 7439 2444 **Fax:** 020 7439 2555
Titles:
BURDA MODEMAGAZIN

BUREAU OF FREELANCE PHOTOGRAPHERS 13442
Focus House, 497 Green Lanes, LONDON, N13 4BP
Tel: 020 8882 3315 **Fax:** 020 8886 5174
Email: mail@thebfp.com
Web site: http://www.thebfp.com
Titles:
MARKET NEWSLETTER

THE BURLINGTON MAGAZINE PUBLICATIONS LTD
15813
14-16 Duke's Road, LONDON, WC1H 9AD
Tel: 020 7388 1228 **Fax:** 020 7388 1230
Titles:
THE BURLINGTON MAGAZINE

BURMA STAR ASSOCIATION 17739
4 Lower Belgrave Street, LONDON, SW1W 0LA
Tel: 020 7823 4273 **Fax:** 020 7730 7882

UK Publishers & Their Titles

Titles:
DEKHO!

BUSINESS ADVANTAGE GROUP   697360
Pel House, 35 Station Square, ORPINGTON, BR5 1LZ
Tel: 01689 873636 **Fax:** 01689 878070
Web site: http://www.business-advantage.com
Titles:
ICT SPAGHETTI

BUSINESS AND INDUSTRY TODAY LTD   1753017
Suite 4.4B, 4th Floor, Maybrook House, HALESOWEN, B63
4AH **Tel:** 0121 550 4823 **Fax:** 0121 550 7940
Titles:
BUSINESS & INDUSTRY TODAY
TRADEX NEWS

BUSINESS AND PROFESSIONAL WOMEN UK LTD   13729
74 Fairfield Rise, BILLERICAY, CM12 9NU
Tel: 01225 837251
Email: info@bpwuk.co.uk
Web site: http://www.hpwuk.co.uk
Titles:
BPW NEWS

BUSINESS & TECHNICAL COMMUNICATIONS   13576
35 Station Square, Petts Wood, ORPINGTON, BR5 1LZ
Tel: 01689 616000 **Fax:** 01689 826622
Web site: http://www.btc.co.uk
Titles:
COMPUTING SECURITY
CONSTRUCTION COMPUTING
DOCUMENT MANAGER
GREEN I.T.
NETWORK COMPUTING

BUSINESS BRIEF LTD   17511
9th Floor, Albany House, Hurst Street, BIRMINGHAM, B5
4BD **Tel:** 07803 053056
Titles:
BUSINESS BRIEF

BUSINESS CAR MANAGER LTD   1747698
95 Station Road, HAMPTON, TW12 2BD **Tel:** 020 8783 0999
Web site: http://www.businesscarmanager.co.uk
Titles:
BUSINESS CAR MANAGER
BUSINESS VAN MANAGER

BUSINESS CONNEXION$ 16964
6 Querrin Street, LONDON, SW6 2SJ **Tel:** 07050 600420
Titles:
BUSINESS CONNECTION$
WIN.MAC.LINUX

THE BUSINESS (DORSET) LTD   14715
9 Gainsborough Road, Ashley Heath, RINGWOOD, BH24
2HY **Tel:** 01425 471500 **Fax:** 01425 475600
Web site: http://www.bizmag.co.uk
Titles:
THE BUSINESS, THE INDEPENDENT MAGAZINE
(DORSET, WEST HANTS & SOUTH WILTSHIRE)

BUSINESS FIRST   1746013
Unit 84, Mackley Industrial Estate, Small Dole, HENFIELD,
BN5 9XE **Tel:** 01903 885191
Titles:
BUSINESS FIRST MAGAZINE

BUSINESS INDEPENDENT PUBLISHING   699583
Suite 1, 2nd Floor, 26-32 Hill Street, POOLE, BH15 1NR
Tel: 01202 666602 **Fax:** 01202 666609
Titles:
BUSINESS INDEPENDENT
NATIONAL FARMER

BUSINESS LINK   671749
Crossbow House, 40 Liverpool Road, SLOUGH, SL1 4QZ
Tel: 0845 600 9006
Web site: http://www.businesslink.gov.uk/southeast
Titles:
BUSINESS NEWS

BUSINESS MAGAZINE PUBLISHING   1644346
4th Floor, 63 Church Street, BIRMINGHAM, B3 2DP
Titles:
BUSINESS EAST MIDLANDS
PROPERTY EAST MIDLANDS

BUSINESS MONEY LTD   15410
Bowdens Business Centre, Hambridge, LANGPORT, TA10
0BP **Tel:** 01458 253536 **Fax:** 01458 253538
Email: info@business-money.com
Web site: http://www.business-money.com
Titles:
BUSINESS MONEY
BUSINESS MONEY (ONLINE)

BUSINESS MONITOR INTERNATIONAL LTD   13782
Mermaid House, 2 Puddle Dock, LONDON, EC4V 3DS
Tel: 020 7248 0468 **Fax:** 020 7248 0467
Web site: http://www.businessmonitor.com
Titles:
AFRICA MONITOR
ASIA MONITOR
CORPORATE FINANCING WEEK
EMERGING EUROPE MONITOR
THE EMERGING MARKETS MONITOR
MIDDLE EAST MONITOR
NORTH AFRICA MONITOR
SOUTHERN AFRICA MONITOR
TELECOMS INSIGHT
WEST & CENTRAL AFRICA MONITOR

BUSINESS PUBLICATION COMPANY (NI) LTD   1748666
3 Wellington Park, Malone Road, BELFAST, BT9 6DJ
Tel: 028 9092 3347 **Fax:** 028 9092 3348
Email: info@bpcmagazines.com
Web site: http://www.bpcmagazines.com
Titles:
CITY MATTERS

BUSINESS PUBLICATIONS UK LTD   12276
3rd Floor, Armstrong House, 38 Market Square, UXBRIDGE,
UB8 1TG **Tel:** 01895 421111 **Fax:** 01895 431252
Titles:
COMMS DEALER

BUSINESS REPORT LTD   1762616
The Creative Industries Centre, Glaisher Drive,
Wolverhampton Science Park, WOLVERHAMPTON, WV10
9TG **Tel:** 01902 710078 **Fax:** 01922 663400
Titles:
BUSINESS REPORT (BLACK COUNTRY)

BUSINESS REVIEW UK   1757185
2nd Floor, Churchill House, Hagley Street, HALESOWEN,
B63 4RH
Titles:
BUSINESS REVIEW UK

BUTLER PUBLISHING LTD   1707381
McDermott Chambers, 2 The Green, Kings Norton,
BIRMINGHAM, B38 8SD **Tel:** 0121 451 3037
Fax: 0121 459 2179
Email: lee.butler@buildingnews.co.uk
Web site: http://www.buildingnews.co.uk
Titles:
BUILDING NEWS

BUTTERICK COMPANY LTD   12865
New Lane, HAVANT, PO9 2ND **Tel:** 0870 777 9966
Fax: 023 9249 2769
Web site: http://www.sewdirect.com
Titles:
SEW TODAY
SEW TODAY'S SEW BRIDAL

BUY-SELL   17753
123 Main Street, FRODSHAM, WA6 7AF **Tel:** 01928 736220
Fax: 01928 736208
Web site: http://www.buysell.co.uk
Titles:
BUY SELL (FLINTSHIRE EDITION)
BUY SELL (MID CHESHIRE & CHESTER EDITION)
BUY-SELL (SOUTH CHESHIRE & NORTH SHROPSHIRE)

BUZZ MAGAZINE   621503
6 Glenview Terrace, CRUMLIN, BT29 4XX
Tel: 028 9445 9758
Titles:
THE BIG BUZZ

BVRLA   16222
River Lodge, Badminton Court, AMERSHAM, HP7 0DD
Tel: 01494 434747 **Fax:** 01494 434499
Email: info@bvrla.co.uk
Web site: http://www.bvrla.co.uk
Titles:
BVRLA NEWS

BYTESTART LTD   1747672
6 Sonic Court, 21 Woodbridge Road, GUILDFORD, GU1
1DZ **Tel:** 01483 577326
Email: editor@bytestart.co.uk
Web site: http://www.bytestart.co.uk
Titles:
BYTESTART.CO.UK

C & C BUSINESS UK LTD   1712077
Suite 7, Sherwood House, 89 Lillie Road, LONDON, SW6
1UD **Tel:** 020 7385 6486 **Fax:** 020 7117 1563
Email: info@candcbusiness.com
Titles:
C & C BUSINESS MAGAZINE

C21 MEDIA LTD   673971
2nd Floor, 148 Curtain Road, LONDON, EC2A 3AT
Tel: 020 7729 7460 **Fax:** 020 7729 7461
Titles:
CHANNEL 21 INTERNATIONAL
FUTUREMEDIA

C&M PUBLICATIONS LTD   13322
3A Market Place, UPPINGHAM, LE15 9QH
Tel: 01572 820088 **Fax:** 01572 820099
Email: publisher@cm-media.net
Web site: http://www.cardworldonline.com
Titles:
CARD WORLD
CARD WORLD AND FRAUD WATCH USER GUIDE
DIRECTORY
FRAUD WATCH
LOYALTY MAGAZINE

C SQUARED COMMUNICATIONS   1679768
115 Southwark Bridge Road, LONDON, SE1 0AX
Tel: 020 7367 6990
Web site: http://www.cmdglobal.com
Titles:
CREAM
MM MEDIA & MARKETING

CABBELL PUBLISHING LTD   13105
Woodman Works, 204 Durnsford Road, LONDON, SW19
8DR **Tel:** 020 8971 8450 **Fax:** 020 8971 8480
Web site: http://www.cabbell.co.uk
Titles:
NATIONAL THEATRE PROGRAMMES

CABI   12441
Nosworthy Way, WALLINGFORD, OX10 8DE
Tel: 01491 832111 **Fax:** 01491 833508
Email: cabi@cabi.org
Web site: http://www.cabi.org
Titles:
AGBIOTECH NEWS AND INFORMATION
CROP PHYSIOLOGY ABSTRACTS
DAIRY SCIENCE ABSTRACTS
GRASSLANDS & FORAGE ABSTRACTS
LEISURE, RECREATION & TOURISM ABSTRACTS
LEISURETOURISM.COM
MAIZE ABSTRACTS
PIG NEWS & INFORMATION
PLANT GROWTH REGULATOR ABSTRACTS
POSTHARVEST NEWS AND INFORMATION
POTATO ABSTRACTS
REVIEW OF AROMATIC AND MEDICINAL PLANTS
RURAL DEVELOPMENT ABSTRACTS
SEED ABSTRACTS
SOILS & FERTILIZERS
SUGAR INDUSTRY ABSTRACTS
WEED ABSTRACTS
WHEAT, BARLEY & TRITICALE ABSTRACTS
WORLD AGRICULTURAL ECONOMICS & RURAL
SOCIOLOGY ABSTRACTS

CADUCEUS JOURNAL LTD 15163
9 Nine Acres, MIDHURST, GU29 9EP **Tel:** 01730 816799
Web site: http://www.caduceus.info
Titles:
  CADUCEUS

CAER PUBLISHING GROUP 1712496
45 Dyer Street, CIRENCESTER, GL7 2PP **Tel:** 01285 650661
Fax: 01285 650620
Email: simon@cotswoldmedia.co.uk
Titles:
  COTSWOLD BUSINESS NEWS

CALL CENTRE HELPER 1751061
Trevethin, Dixton Road, MONMOUTH, NP25 3PR
Tel: 01600 714546
Email: newsdesk@callcentrehelper.com
Web site: http://www.callcentrehelper.com
Titles:
  CALL CENTRE HELPER

THE CALLIGRAPHY & LETTERING ARTS SOCIETY
  673774
54 Boileau Road, LONDON, SW13 9BL **Tel:** 020 8741 7886
Titles:
  THE EDGE

CAM PUBLISHING 1676874
30 York Road, WORTHING, BN11 3EN **Tel:** 0870 190 0220
Fax: 0870 190 0210
Email: info@camcentral.co.uk
Web site: http://www.camcentral.co.uk
Titles:
  TFT - THE FEMALE TOUCH

CAMBRIAN NEWS (ABERYSTWYTH) LTD 15017
Unit 7, Cefn Llan Science Park, ABERYSTWYTH, SY23 3AH
Tel: 01970 615000 **Fax:** 01970 624699
Email: edit@cambrian-news.co.uk
Web site: http://www.aberystwyth-today.co.uk
Titles:
  THE CAMBRIAN NEWS SERIES
  Y CYMRO
  Y DYDD

CAMBRIDGE NEWSPAPERS LTD 14834
Winship Road, Milton, CAMBRIDGE, CB24 6PP
Tel: 01223 434434 **Fax:** 01223 434415
Web site: http://www.cambridge-news.co.uk
Titles:
  CAMBRIDGE NEWS
  CAMBRIDGE WEEKLY NEWS & CRIER SERIES
  CAMBRIDGESHIRE JOURNAL
  OUR TIME
  PROPERTY NEWS
  STYLE
  STYLE WEDDINGS

CAMBRIDGE PUBLISHERS LTD 622187
275 Newmarket Road, CAMBRIDGE, CB5 8JE
Tel: 01223 477411 **Fax:** 01223 327356
Web site: http://www.campublishers.com
Titles:
  RECREATION

CAMBRIDGE UNIVERSITY PRESS 12180
The Edinburgh Building, Shaftesbury Road, CAMBRIDGE,
CB2 8RU **Tel:** 01223 326070 **Fax:** 01223 325150
Email: journals@cambridge.org
Web site: http://www.cambridge.org/uk
Titles:
  AGEING AND SOCIETY
  THE BULLETIN OF THE SCHOOL OF ORIENTAL AND
    AFRICAN STUDIES
  THE CAMBRIDGE LAW JOURNAL
  THE CHINA QUARTERLY
  THE CLASSICAL QUARTERLY
  THE CLASSICAL REVIEW
  EXPERIMENTAL AGRICULTURE
  GREECE & ROME
  INTERNATIONAL AND COMPARATIVE LAW QUARTERLY
  THE JOURNAL OF NAVIGATION
  LEGAL INFORMATION MANAGEMENT
  NEW THEATRE QUARTERLY
  ORYX - THE INTERNATIONAL JOURNAL OF
    CONSERVATION
  POPULAR MUSIC
  PRIMARY HEALTH CARE RESEARCH & DEVELOPMENT
  PROCEEDINGS OF THE EDINBURGH MATHEMATICAL
    SOCIETY
  RELIGIOUS STUDIES
  REVIEW OF INTERNATIONAL STUDIES
  ROBOTICA
  TEMPO
  THEATRE RESEARCH INTERNATIONAL
  UTILITAS

CAMERAPIX MAGAZINES LTD 16006
32 Friars Walk, LONDON, N14 5LP **Tel:** 020 8361 2942
Email: camerapixuk@btinternet.com
Web site: http://www.camerapix.com
Titles:
  SELAMTA
  SILHOUETTE

CAMPAIGN AGAINST EURO-FEDERALISM 17758
PO Box 46295, LONDON, W5 2UG **Tel:** 0845 345 8902
Email: caef@caef.org.uk
Web site: http://www.caef.org.uk
Titles:
  THE DEMOCRAT

CAMPAIGN FOR PRESS & BROADCASTING FREEDOM
  13437
Vi and Garner Smith House, 23 Orford Road, LONDON, E17
9NL **Tel:** 020 8521 5932 **Fax:** 020 7837 8868
Email: freepress@cpbf.org.uk
Web site: http://www.cpbf.org.uk
Titles:
  FREE PRESS

CAMPAIGN FOR REAL ALE LTD 13677
230 Hatfield Road, ST. ALBANS, AL1 4LW
Tel: 01727 867201 **Fax:** 01727 867670
Email: camra@camra.org.uk
Web site: http://www.camra.org.uk
Titles:
  THE FULL PINT MAGAZINE
  LONDON DRINKER
  WHAT'S BREWING

CAMPAIGN FOR STATE EDUCATION 18120
98 Erlanger Road, LONDON, SE14 5TH **Tel:** 020 8942 2826
Titles:
  CASENOTES

CAMPBELL MARSH COMMUNICATIONS 1768098
128 Warwick Street, LEAMINGTON SPA, CV32 4QY
Tel: 01926 420660 **Fax:** 01926 420990
Titles:
  SPECIALIST BUILDING FINISHES

CAMPDEN PUBLISHING LTD 673792
1 St. John's Square, LONDON, EC1M 4PN
Tel: 020 7214 0500 **Fax:** 020 7214 0501
Email: editorial@campden.com
Web site: http://www.campden.com
Titles:
  CAMPDEN FB
  HOSPITAL IMAGING & RADIOLOGY EUROPE
  HOSPITAL PHARMACY EUROPE
  MANAGEMENT IN PRACTICE
  NURSING IN PRACTICE
  OFFSHORE RED

THE CAMPING AND CARAVANNING CLUB 16082
Greenfields House, Westwood Way, COVENTRY, CV4 8JH
Tel: 024 7647 5300 **Fax:** 024 7647 5413
Web site: http://www.campingandcaravanningclub.co.uk
Titles:
  CAMPING & CARAVANNING

CAMPRO ENTERTAINMENT 698783
PO Box 18542, LONDON, E17 5UY **Tel:** 020 8527 2720
Fax: 020 8531 6050
Titles:
  G MAG

CANARY LTD 621695
PO Box 9, GUILDFORD, GU3 2WZ **Tel:** 01483 226279
Fax: 01483 295911
Titles:
  CR ADVISOR

CANON COMMUNICATIONS 1650913
Kent House, Romney Place, MAIDSTONE, ME15 6LH
Tel: 01622 662511 **Fax:** 01622 661687
Web site: http://www.cancom.com
Titles:
  EUROPEAN MEDICAL DEVICE MANUFACTURER
  MEDICAL DEVICE & DIAGNOSTICS INDUSTRY
  MEDICAL PRODUCTS MANUFACTURING NEWS

CANON COMMUNICATIONS LLC 1714933
Murlain Business Centre, Union Street, CHESTER, CH1 1QP
Tel: 01244 357201 **Fax:** 01244 357246
Web site: http://www.devicelink.com
Titles:
  MEDICAL DEVICE TECHNOLOGY

LA CANTINA 1691149
7 Alicia Gardens, HARROW, HA3 8JB
Titles:
  FICTION

CAPACITY MEDIA 673875
9B Millennium House, 21 Eden Street, KINGSTON UPON
THAMES, KT1 1BL **Tel:** 020 8549 2449 **Fax:** 020 8549 1249
Titles:
  CAPACITY

CAPITAL BUSINESS MEDIA 1720245
17 Ensign House, Canary Wharf, LONDON, E14 9XQ
Tel: 020 7148 3861 **Fax:** 0845 638 0341
Email: info@cbmeg.co.uk
Web site: http://www.cbmeg.co.uk
Titles:
  BUSINESS MATTERS
  FUND MANAGER TODAY

CAPITAL IDEAS FINANCIAL PUBLISHING LIMITED
  12726
Sophia House, 76-80 City Road, LONDON, EC1Y 2BJ
Tel: 020 3326 2000
Email: s.bolton@capitalideasplc.com
Titles:
  THE CORPORATE REGISTER

CAPITAL PUBLISHING 18515
6 Freskyn Place, East Mains Industrial Estate, BROXBURN,
EH52 5NF **Tel:** 01506 508001 **Fax:** 01506 508002
Email: enquiries@capitalgroupuk.com
Web site: http://www.capitalgroupuk.com
Titles:
  ENTERPRISING SCOTLAND
  HOME PLUS SCOTLAND
  LIFESTYLE DIRECTORY

CAR PR LTD 1639939
52 Sunnybank, WARLINGHAM, CR6 9SS **Tel:** 01883 372085
Fax: 01883 624964
Titles:
  TKC MAG

THE CARAVAN CLUB 16084
East Grinstead House, Wood Street, EAST GRINSTEAD,
RH19 1UA **Tel:** 01342 326944 **Fax:** 01342 410258
Email: enquiries@caravanclub.co.uk
Web site: http://www.caravanclub.co.uk
Titles:
  THE CARAVAN CLUB MAGAZINE

CARDIFF UNION SERVICES LTD 15754
Cardiff University, Students Union, Park Place, CARDIFF,
CF10 3QN **Tel:** 029 2078 1436 **Fax:** 029 2078 1407
Titles:
  GAIR RHYDD

CARDIFF UNIVERSITY 18745
Public Relations and Communications Division, Cardiff
University, Park Place, CARDIFF, CF10 3AT
Tel: 029 2087 4731 **Fax:** 029 2087 0401
Email: publicrelations@cardiff.ac.uk
Web site: http://www.cardiff.ac.uk/schoolsanddivisions/
divisions/prcom
Titles:
  CARDIFF UNIVERSITY NEWS

UK Publishers & Their Titles

CARE CHOICES LTD 1642294
Valley Court Offices, ROYSTON, SG8 0HF
Tel: 01223 207770 **Fax:** 01223 207135
Web site: http://www.carechoices.co.uk
Titles:
   CARE MANAGEMENT MATTERS

CAREER MEDIA LTD 1650183
70 West Regent Street, GLASGOW, G2 2QZ
Tel: 0141 333 6665 **Fax:** 0141 333 1116
Email: info@careermedia.co.uk
Web site: http://www.careermedia.co.uk
Titles:
   CARE APPOINTMENTS

CAREERMAKEOVER LTD 1733111
93 Blackamoor Lane, MAIDENHEAD, SL6 8RJ
Tel: 07092 276160 **Fax:** 07092 276160
Email: morrisey@btopenworld.com
Web site: http://www.careermakeover.co.uk
Titles:
   CAREERMAKEOVER

CARERS UK 623656
20 Great Dover Street, LONDON, SE1 4LX
Tel: 020 7490 8818 **Fax:** 020 7490 8824
Web site: http://www.carersuk.org
Titles:
   CARING

CARIBBEAN COUNCIL 622020
2 Belgrave Square, LONDON, SW1X 8PJ
Tel: 020 7235 9484 **Fax:** 020 7823 1370
Titles:
   CARIBBEAN INSIGHT

CARIC PRESS 1747285
Rickets Green, Lionheart Close, Bearwood,
BOURNEMOUTH, BH11 9UB **Tel:** 01202 574577
Fax: 01202 574578
Web site: http://www.caricpress.co.uk
Titles:
   THE COURIER (ABERYSTWYTH)

CARNYX GROUP LTD 12186
4th Floor, The Mercat Building, 26 Gallowgate, GLASGOW,
G1 5AB **Tel:** 0141 552 5858 **Fax:** 0141 559 6050
Web site: http://www.carnyx.com
Titles:
   THE DRUM
   THE DRUM YEARBOOK
   FIRM SCOTLAND
   PROSPECT

CAROLE BALDOCK 1653560
17 Greenhow Avenue, WIRRAL, CH48 5EL
Tel: 0151 625 1446
Email: carolebaldock@hotmail.com
Web site: http://www.poetrymagazines.org.uk
Titles:
   KUDOS
   ORBIS INTERNATIONAL LITERARY JOURNAL

CAROUSEL 15830
The Saturn Centre, 54-76 Bissell Street, BIRMINGHAM, B5
7HX **Tel:** 0121 622 7458 **Fax:** 0121 643 3152
Titles:
   CAROUSEL THE GUIDE TO CHILDREN'S BOOKS

CARP FISHING NEWS LTD 16100
Sandholme Grange, NEWPORT, HU15 2QG
Tel: 01430 440624 **Fax:** 01430 441319
Titles:
   CARP TALK

CARS FOR THE CONNOISSEUR 1676056
Prospect House, Shaftesbury Road, East Knoyle,
SALISBURY, SP3 6AR **Tel:** 01747 830977
Fax: 01747 830857
Web site: http://www.carsfortheconnoisseur.com
Titles:
   CARS FOR THE CONNOISSEUR

CARTER ROE LTD 625351
The Old Bakery, 31 Huntly Grove, PETERBOROUGH, PE1
4DJ **Tel:** 01733 890888 **Fax:** 01733 890711
Titles:
   HOSPITALITY INTERIORS

CASPIAN PUBLISHING 16345
198 Kings Road, LONDON, SW3 5XP **Tel:** 020 7368 7100
Fax: 020 7368 7201
Web site: http://www.caspianpublishing.co.uk
Titles:
   THE ACQUIRER
   BUSINESS STANDARDS
   BUSINESS VOICE
   FINANCIAL MANAGEMENT
   REAL BUSINESS
   REAL DEALS
   REAL FD

CATALOGUE DEVELOPMENT CENTRE LTD 14441
151 High Street, ILFRACOMBE, EX34 9EZ
Tel: 01271 866221 **Fax:** 01271 866281
Email: info@catalog-biz.com
Web site: http://www.catalog-biz.com
Titles:
   CATALOGUE E-BUSINESS

THE CATALOGUE E-TAIL LTD 1630338
Innovation Studios, 159 Shelbourne Road,
BOURNEMOUTH, BH8 8RD **Tel:** 0845 838 6077
Fax: 0700 345 1606
Titles:
   MULTICHANNEL MARKETING

CATALYST CREATIVE MEDIA 1655221
85-89 Duke Street, LIVERPOOL, L1 5AP **Tel:** 0151 709 9948
Email: mail@catalystmedia.org.uk
Web site: http://www.catalystmedia.org.uk
Titles:
   NERVE

CATHEDRAL COMMUNICATIONS 697376
Jubilee House, High Street, TISBURY, SP3 6HA
Tel: 01747 871717 **Fax:** 01747 871718
Email: context@cathcomm.demon.co.uk
Web site: http://www.buildingconservation.com
Titles:
   CONTEXT

CATHERINE SAINT PUBLICITY 676957
4 Kenwood Road, SHEFFIELD, S7 1NP **Tel:** 0114 255 9686
Email: catherine.saint@yahoo.co.uk
Titles:
   THE DECORATOR

CATHOLIC HERALD LTD 15862
Herald House, 15 Lamb's Passage, Bunhill Row, LONDON,
EC1Y 8TQ **Tel:** 020 7588 3101 **Fax:** 020 7256 9728
Email: editorial@catholicherald.co.uk
Web site: http://www.catholicherald.co.uk
Titles:
   THE CATHOLIC HERALD
   CATHOLIC HERALD (& STANDARD)
   SCOTTISH CATHOLIC OBSERVER

THE CATHOLIC RECORD SOCIETY 18211
c/o 12 Melbourne Place, WOLSINGHAM, DL13 3EH
Tel: 01388 527747
Titles:
   RECUSANT HISTORY

CATS PROTECTION 15649
National Cat Centre, Chelwood Gate, HAYWARDS HEATH,
RH17 7TT **Tel:** 0870 770 8649 **Fax:** 0870 770 8265
Web site: http://www.thecat.org.uk
Titles:
   THE CAT

CAVENDISH GROUP 1649578
15-19 Great Chapel Street, LONDON, W1F 8FN
Tel: 020 7758 3000 **Fax:** 020 7758 3001
Web site: http://www.cavendishgroup.co.uk
Titles:
   AUTOMOTIVE MANUFACTURER

   OIL & GAS TECHNOLOGY
   PHARMATECHNOLOGY

CAVYRESCUE 1714628
10 College Gardens, Westgate-On-Sea, CT8 8EY
Tel: 07932 750271
Web site: http://www.cavyrescue.co.uk
Titles:
   CAVYRESCUE.CO.UK

CBD RESEARCH LTD 17515
Chancery House, 15 Wickham Road, BECKENHAM, BR3
5JS **Tel:** 020 8650 7745 **Fax:** 020 8650 0768
Web site: http://www.cbdresearch.com
Titles:
   COUNCILS, COMMITTEES & BOARDS
   CURRENT BRITISH DIRECTORIES
   DIRECTORY OF BRITISH ASSOCIATIONS

CBI LONDON 14622
Centre Point, 103 New Oxford Street, LONDON, WC1A 1DU
Tel: 020 7379 7400 **Fax:** 020 7497 2597
Titles:
   CBI SUSTAINABILITY UPDATE

CBS INTERACTIVE 18359
5-11 Lavington Street, LONDON, SE1 0NZ
Tel: 020 7021 1000
Web site: http://www.cnetnetworks.co.uk
Titles:
   CNET.CO.UK
   GAMESPOT UK
   SILICON.COM
   ZDNET UK

CCBN 16129
30-32 Wycliffe Road, NORTHAMPTON, NN1 5JF
Tel: 01604 620361 **Fax:** 01604 230176
Titles:
   BRITISH NATURISM

CCH 1743849
145 London Road, KINGSTON UPON THAMES, KT2 6SR
Tel: 020 8547 3333
Titles:
   PAY MAGAZINE

CCP LTD 17333
Premier Media Group, 22 Chapter Street, LONDON, SW1P
4NP **Tel:** 020 7316 1450 **Fax:** 020 7233 6706
Web site: http://www.premier.org.uk
Titles:
   CHRISTIAN MARKETPLACE
   CHRISTIANITY
   YOUTHWORK

CCS PUBLISHING LTD 1758776
4 Elms Lane, Shareshill, WOLVERHAMPTON, WV10 7JS
Tel: 01922 415233 **Fax:** 01922 415208
Titles:
   RETAIL SECURITY FRAUD & LOSS PREVENTION

CCTV MEDIA LTD 1643715
16 Greenhill Mews, LICHFIELD, WS13 6LF
Tel: 01543 250456 **Fax:** 01543 415044
Email: peter.mawson@cctvmedia.co.uk
Web site: http://www.cctvimage.com
Titles:
   CCTV IMAGE

CECILE PARK PUBLISHING LTD 622365
17 The Timber Yard, Drysdale Street, LONDON, N1 6ND
Tel: 020 7012 1380 **Fax:** 020 7729 6093
Titles:
   E-COMMERCE LAW AND POLICY
   E-COMMERCE LAW REPORTS
   WORLD ONLINE GAMBLING LAW REPORT

CEDAR COMMUNICATIONS 12181
85 Strand, LONDON, WC2R 0DW **Tel:** 020 7550 8000
Fax: 020 7550 8250
Web site: http://www.cedarcom.co.uk
Titles:
   BUSINESS LIFE

FIRST LIFE
HIGH LIFE
HIGH LIFE SHOP!
HORIZONS
THE LONDON MAGAZINE
NIKON PRO
REAL HOLIDAYS
TESCO: THE MAGAZINE

CELLO PRESS LIMITED 1763574
Office G18 Spinners Court, 55 West End, Witney, OXON,
OX28 1NH **Tel:** 01993 701002
Email: cellomail@pt.cellopress.co.uk
Titles:
PRINTMAKING TODAY

CELTIC NEWSPAPERS LTD 15021
Thomson House, Havelock Street, CARDIFF, CF10 1XR
Tel: 029 2028 3611
Titles:
GLAMORGAN GAZETTE SERIES
MERTHYR EXPRESS SERIES

CENTAUR BUSINESS INTELLIGENCE 600600
St. Giles House, 50 Poland Street, LONDON, W1F 7AX
Tel: 020 7970 4000 **Fax:** 020 7943 8172
Web site: http://www.centaur.co.uk
Titles:
ABC AND D ARCHITECT BUILDER CONTRACTOR &
DEVELOPER

CENTAUR COMMUNICATIONS LTD 12258
St. Giles House, 50 Poland Street, LONDON, W1F 7AX
Tel: 020 7970 4000
Web site: http://www.centaur.co.uk
Titles:
CREATIVE REVIEW
DATA STRATEGY
DESIGN WEEK
DESIGN WEEK
THE LAWYER.COM
LENDING STRATEGY
LOGISTICS MANAGER - THE SUPPLY CHAIN BUSINESS
MONEY MARKETING
PERIOD LIVING
RECRUITER
SUPPLY CHAIN STANDARD
TECHNOLOGY WEEKLY

CENTAUR MEDIA PLC 16789
St. Giles House, 50 Poland Street, LONDON, W1F 7AX
Tel: 020 7970 4000 **Fax:** 020 7970 4189
Web site: http://www.centaur.co.uk
Titles:
CORPORATE ADVISER
EMPLOYEE BENEFITS
THE ENGINEER
THE ENGINEER ONLINE
FUND STRATEGY
THE LAWYER
LOAN DISTRIBUTOR
MAD.CO.UK
MARKETING WEEK
METALWORKING PRODUCTION
MORTGAGE STRATEGY
NEW MEDIA AGE
NMA.CO.UK
PROCESS ENGINEERING
PUBLICPRIVATEFINANCE.COM
TECHNOLOGY HORIZONS
WHAT'S NEW IN INDUSTRY

CENTAUR SPECIAL INTEREST MEDIA 13522
2 Sugar Brook Court, Aston Road, BROMSGROVE, B60 3EX
Tel: 01527 834400 **Fax:** 01527 574388
Web site: http://www.centaur.co.uk
Titles:
HOMEBUILDING & RENOVATING
PUBLIC SECTOR BUILDING
REAL HOMES MAGAZINE

CENTOR PUBLISHING LTD 674347
86-88 Nelson Road, Wimbledon, LONDON, SW19 1HX
Tel: 020 8287 3312
Email: subs@sportex.net
Web site: http://www.sportex.net
Titles:
SPORTEX HEALTH
SPORTEX MEDICINE

CENTRAL BANKING PUBLICATIONS 18485
Incisive Media, Haymarket House, 28-29 Haymarket,
LONDON, SW1Y 4RX **Tel:** 020 7930 9700
Fax: 020 7930 2238
Titles:
SPEED

CENTRAL COUNTIES NEWSPAPERS SOUTH LTD 12819
The Gatehouse, Gatehouse Way, AYLESBURY, HP19 8DB
Tel: 01296 619700 **Fax:** 01296 393451
Titles:
AYLESBURY TODAY
BANBURY GUARDIAN REVIEW SERIES
BH THE MAGAZINE
BUCKINGHAM ADVERTISER SERIES
BUCKS ADVERTISER & THAME GAZETTE SERIES
THE BUCKS HERALD SERIES
DAVENTRY EXPRESS AND REVIEW SERIES
DAVENTRY TODAY.CO.UK
GAZETTE & HERALD EXPRESS SERIES (HEMEL
HEMPSTEAD)
LEAMINGTON SPA COURIER SERIES

CENTRAL INDEPENDENT NEWS & MEDIA LTD 16981
Bitterscote, Ventura Park Road, TAMWORTH, B78 3LZ
Tel: 01827 848586 **Fax:** 01827 848640
Titles:
ADMAG NEWSPAPERS SERIES
THE JOURNAL MAGAZINE
LICHFIELD MERCURY SERIES
SUTTON COLDFIELD OBSERVER SERIES
WALSALL ADVERTISER

CENTRAL SCHOOL OF SPEECH & DRAMA 600730
Embassy Theatre, 64 Eton Avenue, LONDON, NW3 3HY
Tel: 020 7722 8183 **Fax:** 020 7722 4132
Titles:
THE ALUMNI NEWSLETTER

THE CENTRE FOR FOOD AND HEALTH STUDIES LTD 14048
Crown House, 72 Hammersmith Road, LONDON, W14 8TH
Tel: 020 7617 7032 **Fax:** 020 7900 1937
Titles:
NEW NUTRITION BUSINESS

CENTRE FOR NEW WRITING 1759316
University of Manchester, Oxford Road, MANCHESTER,
M13 9PL **Tel:** 0161 275 3167
Titles:
THE MANCHESTER REVIEW

CERAM RESEARCH LTD 17762
Queens Road, Penkhull, STOKE-ON-TRENT, ST4 7LQ
Tel: 01782 764444 **Fax:** 01782 412331
Web site: http://www.ceram.com
Titles:
CERAMICNEWS
ENVIRONMENT BULLETIN

CERAMIC REVIEW PUBLISHING LTD 13707
25 Fouberts Place, LONDON, W1F 7QF **Tel:** 020 7439 3377
Fax: 020 7287 9954
Titles:
CERAMIC REVIEW

CERDAC 15072
6 Market Place, CARRICKFERGUS, BT38 7AW
Tel: 028 9336 3651 **Fax:** 028 9336 3092
Titles:
EAST ANTRIM GAZETTE SERIES

CERTIFIED ACCOUNTANTS EDUCATIONAL TRUST 13303
29 Lincoln's Inn Fields, LONDON, WC2A 3EE
Tel: 020 7059 5970 **Fax:** 020 7059 5957
Titles:
STUDENT ACCOUNTANT

CERTIFIED ACCOUNTANTS PUBLICATIONS LIMITED 17117
29 Lincoln's Inn Fields, LONDON, WC2A 3EE
Tel: 020 7059 5000 **Fax:** 020 7059 5050
Web site: http://www.accaglobal.com

Titles:
ACCOUNTING & BUSINESS

CFA UK 625025
2nd Floor, 135 Cannon Street, LONDON, EC4N 5BP
Tel: 020 7796 3000 **Fax:** 020 7796 3333
Titles:
PROFESSIONAL INVESTOR

CFES PUBLISHING 1706592
63 Amberley Slope, Werrington, PETERBOROUGH, PE4
6QQ **Tel:** 01733 571858
Titles:
MOBILITYTODAY

THE CGA 1644416
Chalke House, Station Road, Codford, WARMINSTER, BA12
0JX **Tel:** 01985 850706 **Fax:** 01985 850378
Web site: http://www.thecga.co.uk
Titles:
COUNTRY THE MAGAZINE OF THE CGA

CGES 621814
17 Knightsbridge, LONDON, SW1X 7LY **Tel:** 020 7309 3610
Fax: 020 7235 4338
Email: marketing@cges.co.uk
Web site: http://www.cges.co.uk
Titles:
MONTHLY OIL REPORT

CH PUBLICATIONS LTD 15405
Nimax House, 20 Ullswater Crescent, Ullswater Business
Park, COULSDON, CR5 2HR **Tel:** 020 8655 6400
Fax: 020 8763 1001
Email: chp@chpltd.com
Web site: http://www.chpltd.com
Titles:
911 & PORSCHE WORLD
AMERICAN CAR WORLD
AUTO ITALIA
JAPANESE PERFORMANCE
ULTRA VW

CHADWICK HOUSE GROUP LTD 14140
Chadwick Court, 15 Hatfields, LONDON, SE1 8DJ
Tel: 020 7928 6006 **Fax:** 020 7827 5862
Web site: http://www.cieh.org
Titles:
ENVIRONMENTAL HEALTH NEWS - EHN
ENVIRONMENTAL HEALTH PRACTITIONER

CHALLENGER SOCIETY FOR MARINE SCIENCE 18064
National Oceanography Centre, Waterfront Campus,
SOUTHAMPTON, SO14 3ZH **Tel:** 023 8059 6097
Fax: 023 8059 6149
Web site: http://www.challenger-society.org.uk
Titles:
OCEAN CHALLENGE

**CHAMBER OF COMMERCE HEREFORDSHIRE AND
WORCESTERSHIRE** 1715945
Severn House, Prescott Drive, Warndon Business Park,
WORCESTER, WR4 9NE **Tel:** 0845 641 1641
Web site: http://www.hwchamber.co.uk
Titles:
NEW DIRECTION

CHAMBERLAIN DUNN ASSOCIATES 621807
Gothic House, 3 The Green, RICHMOND, TW9 1PL
Tel: 020 8334 4500 **Fax:** 020 8332 7201
Email: mail@chamberdunn.co.uk
Web site: http://www.chamberlaindunn.com
Titles:
EMPLOYING DOCTORS & DENTISTS
EMPLOYING NURSES & MIDWIVES

CHAMBERS & PARTNERS 17063
23 Long Lane, LONDON, EC1A 9HL **Tel:** 020 7606 1300
Fax: 020 7606 0906
Web site: http://www.chambersandpartners.com
Titles:
CHAMBERS CLIENT REPORT

UK Publishers & Their Titles

CHAMELEON BUSINESS MEDIA LTD 1747709
1 Cantelupe Mews, Cantelupe Road, EAST GRINSTEAD,
RH19 3BG
Titles:
SPECIALIST PRINTING

CHAMP MEDIA GROUP 18539
Woodland Place, Hurricane Way, Wickford Business Park,
WICKFORD, SS11 8YB **Tel:** 01268 766515
Fax: 01268 766516
Titles:
CASINO & GAMING INTERNATIONAL
RELIEF & DEVELOPMENT (ASIA PACIFIC, MIDDLE EAST
& AFRICA DIRECTORY)

CHAMPION MEDIA GROUP 14977
Clare House, 166 Lord Street, SOUTHPORT, PR9 0QA
Tel: 01704 392392 **Fax:** 01704 531327
Email: editorial@champnews.com
Web site: http://www.champnews.com
Titles:
LINEDANCER
SOUTHPORT, ORMSKIRK & FORMBY CHAMPION
SERIES

CHANCERY PALLADIUM LLP 1750635
4 The Willows, Mill Farm Courtyard, Beachampton, MILTON
KEYNES, MK19 6DS **Tel:** 01908 566800 **Fax:** 01908 566802
Web site: http://www.chancerypaladium.co.uk
Titles:
INVEST TODAY

CHANNELFLY PLC 629259
59-61 Worship Street, LONDON, EC2A 2DU
Tel: 020 7688 9000
Titles:
THE FLY

THE CHAP LTD 1752529
17 Ardmere Road, LONDON, SE13 6EL **Tel:** 020 8305 0244
Titles:
THE CHAP

CHAPELFIELD SHOPPING CENTRE 1747908
Plain Speaking PR Limited, 24 North Walsham Road,
NORWICH, NR6 7QB **Tel:** 01603 727729
Titles:
THE CHAPELFIELD MAGAZINE

CHAPMAN PUBLISHING 15832
4 Broughton Place, EDINBURGH, EH1 3RX
Tel: 0131 557 2207
Titles:
CHAPMAN

CHARACTER GRAPHICS 1744186
56 Station Road, TAUNTON, TA1 1NS **Tel:** 01823 279008
Fax: 01823 279011
Titles:
WHAT'S ON SOMERSET

**CHARTERED INSTITUTE OF ARCHITECTURAL
TECHNOLOGISTS** 12217
397 City Road, LONDON, EC1V 1NH **Tel:** 020 7278 2206
Fax: 020 7837 3194
Email: info@ciat.org.uk
Web site: http://www.ciat.org.uk
Titles:
ARCHITECTURAL TECHNOLOGY

**CHARTERED INSTITUTE OF BUILDING SERVICES
ENGINEERS** 1762492
PR by email only **Tel:** 01223 273520
Titles:
CIBSE JOURNAL

THE CHARTERED INSTITUTE OF JOURNALISTS 13439
2 Dock Offices, Surrey Quays Road, LONDON, SE16 2XU
Tel: 020 7252 1187 **Fax:** 020 7232 2302
Email: memberservices@cioj.co.uk

Titles:
INTERNATIONAL JOURNALIST
THE JOURNAL

**CHARTERED INSTITUTE OF LIBRARY &
INFORMATION PROFESSIONALS** 12669
7 Ridgmount Street, LONDON, WC1E 7AE
Tel: 020 7255 0500 **Fax:** 020 7255 0581
Email: information@cilip.org.uk
Web site: http://www.cilip.org.uk/publishing
Titles:
IMPACT (JOURNAL OF THE CAREER DEVELOPMENT
GROUP)
LIBRARY + INFORMATION GAZETTE
LIBRARY & INFORMATION UPDATE

THE CHARTERED INSTITUTE OF LINGUISTS 15948
Saxon House, 48 Southwark Street, LONDON, SE1 1UN
Tel: 020 7940 3100 **Fax:** 020 7940 3101
Email: info@iol.org.uk
Web site: http://www.iol.org.uk
Titles:
THE LINGUIST

**THE CHARTERED INSTITUTE OF LOGISTICS AND
TRANSPORT UK** 13685
Earlstrees Court, Earlstrees Court, CORBY, NN17 4AX
Tel: 01536 740100 **Fax:** 01536 740103
Email: enquiry@ciltuk.org.uk
Web site: http://www.ciltuk.org.uk
Titles:
LOGISTICS & TRANSPORT FOCUS

**CHARTERED INSTITUTE OF MANAGEMENT
ACCOUNTANTS** 13315
26 Chapter Street, LONDON, SW1P 4NP **Tel:** 020 7663 5441
Fax: 020 7663 5442
Web site: http://www.cimaglobal.com
Titles:
CIMA INSIGHT
CIMA SYNERGY
CIMA VELOCITY

THE CHARTERED INSTITUTE OF PUBLIC RELATIONS 13466
32 St. James's Square, LONDON, SW1Y 4JR
Tel: 020 7766 3333 **Fax:** 020 7490 0588
Email: info@cipr.co.uk
Web site: http://www.cipr.co.uk
Titles:
PROFILE

THE CHARTERED MANAGEMENT INSTITUTE 13758
3rd Floor, 2 Savoy Court, Strand, LONDON, WC2R 0EZ
Tel: 020 7421 2710 **Fax:** 020 7497 0463
Web site: http://www.managers.org.uk
Titles:
PROFESSIONAL MANAGER

CHARTERED QUALITY INSTITUTE 13843
12 Grosvenor Crescent, LONDON, SW1X 7EE
Tel: 020 7245 6676 **Fax:** 020 7245 6755
Web site: http://www.thecqi.org
Titles:
QUALITYWORLD

CHARTERED SOCIETY OF DESIGNERS 12386
1 Cedar Court, Royal Oak Yard, Bermondsey Street,
LONDON, SE1 3GA **Tel:** 020 7407 9878
Titles:
THE DESIGNER

THE CHARTERED SOCIETY OF PHYSIOTHERAPY 14608
14 Bedford Row, LONDON, WC1R 4ED **Tel:** 020 7306 6666
Fax: 020 7306 6611
Email: enquiries@csp.org.uk
Web site: http://www.csp.org.uk
Titles:
PHYSIOTHERAPY FRONTLINE

CHARTERHOUSE BUSINESS PUBLICATIONS 13418
PO Box 66, WOKINGHAM, RG41 5FS **Tel:** 0870 241 4466
Web site: http://www.sponsorshipnews.com

Titles:
SPONSORSHIP NEWS

CHARTIST EDITORIAL COLLECTIVE 15682
PO Box 52751, LONDON, EC2P 2XF **Tel:** 0845 456 4977
Titles:
CHARTIST MAGAZINE

CHEERING WORDS 17484
22 Victoria Road, STAMFORD, PE9 1HB **Tel:** 01780 763780
Titles:
CHEERING WORDS

THE CHELSEA MAGAZINE COMPANY 1733448
26-30 Old Church Street, Chelsea, LONDON, SW3 5BY
Tel: 020 7349 3150
Titles:
ARTISTS & ILLUSTRATORS MAGAZINE
BRITAIN
CRUISE INTERNATIONAL

CHELTENHAM NEWSPAPER COMPANY LTD 14937
1 Clarence Parade, CHELTENHAM, GL50 3NY
Tel: 01242 271900 **Fax:** 01242 271848
Titles:
GLOUCESTERSHIRE ECHO

CHEMICAL MATTERS LTD 13716
Chapel House, 7 Schoolbell Mews, Arbery Road, LONDON,
E3 5BZ **Tel:** 020 8981 3309
Email: hilfra@chemicalmetters.net
Titles:
CHEMICAL MATTERS

CHERRINGTON ADVERTISING LTD 1649551
45 Atkinson Gardens, Aycliffe, NEWTON AYCLIFFE, DL5
6LH **Tel:** 01325 304360 **Fax:** 01325 314283
Email: sue@cherrington.onyxnet.co.uk
Titles:
DARLINGTON TODAY
TEESSIDE HIGHLIGHTS
WEST PARK

CHERRY PUBLISHING 694265
22-26 Albert Embankment, LONDON, SE1 7TJ
Tel: 020 7735 4900 **Fax:** 020 7840 0443
Titles:
REAL WORLD

CHESS & BRIDGE LTD 15489
369 Euston Road, LONDON, NW1 3AR **Tel:** 020 7388 2404
Fax: 020 7388 2407
Titles:
BRIDGE
CHESS MONTHLY

CHESTER CITY COUNCIL 1713618
Chester City Council, The Forum, CHESTER, CH1 2HS
Titles:
WHAT'S ON IN CHESTER & CHESHIRE GUIDE

CHEW VALLEY GAZETTE LTD 14899
5 South Parade, Chew Magna, BRISTOL, BS40 8SH
Tel: 01275 332266 **Fax:** 01275 333067
Email: editorial@chewvalleygazette.co.uk
Web site: http://www.chewvalleygazette.co.uk
Titles:
CHEW VALLEY GAZETTE

**CHICHESTER DIOCESAN FUND AND BOARD OF
FINANCE INC.** 15866
Diocesan Church House, 211 New Church Road, HOVE,
BN3 4ED **Tel:** 01273 421021 **Fax:** 01273 421041
Titles:
THE CHICHESTER MAGAZINE

THE CHILDREN'S LEGAL CENTRE LTD 14164
University of Essex, Wivenhoe Park, COLCHESTER, CO4
3SQ **Tel:** 01206 872466 **Fax:** 01206 874026
Email: clc@essex.ac.uk
Web site: http://www.childrenslegalcentre.com

Titles:
CHILDRIGHT

CHILTERN & THAMES RIDER 1680977
Suite 108, Crystal House, New Bedford Road, LUTON, LU1
1HS **Tel:** 0870 224 1263
Web site: http://www.chilternrider.co.uk
Titles:
CHILTERN & THAMES RIDER

CHINA-BRITAIN BUSINESS COUNCIL 13779
1 Warwick Row, LONDON, SW1E 5ER **Tel:** 020 7802 2000
Fax: 020 7802 2029
Web site: http://www.cbbc.org
Titles:
CHINA BRITAIN BUSINESS REVIEW

CHOICE PUBLISHING LTD 1605937
1st Floor, 2 King Street, PETERBOROUGH, PE1 1LT
Tel: 01733 555123 **Fax:** 01733 427500
Titles:
CHOICE

CHRIS LEWIS 1752677
High View, Toothill Road, UTTOXETER, ST14 8JU
Tel: 01889 568183
Titles:
MOTOINFO

CHRISTCHURCH PUBLISHERS LTD 12909
2 Caversham Street, LONDON, SW3 4AH
Tel: 020 7351 4995 **Fax:** 020 7351 4995
Titles:
BOOK WORLD

CHRISTIAN AID 15867
PO Box 100, LONDON, SE1 7RT **Tel:** 020 7620 4444
Fax: 020 7620 0712
Web site: http://www.christian-aid.org
Titles:
CHRISTIAN AID NEWS
CTRL+ALT+SHIFT

CHRISTIAN EDUCATION PUBLICATIONS 15921
1020 Bristol Road, Selly Oak, BIRMINGHAM, B29 6LB
Tel: 0121 472 4242 **Fax:** 0121 472 7575
Email: lat@retoday.org.uk
Web site: http://www.retoday.org.uk
Titles:
RETODAY

CHRISTIAN PUBLISHING & OUTREACH LTD 17309
CPO, Garcia Estate, Canterbury Road, WORTHING, BN13
1BW **Tel:** 01903 264556 **Fax:** 01903 537321
Email: sales@cpo.org.uk
Web site: http://www.cpo.org.uk
Titles:
INSPIRE
WOMAN ALIVE

CHRISTIE'S INTERNATIONAL PLC 15814
8 King Street, St. James's, LONDON, SW1Y 6QT
Tel: 020 7839 9060 **Fax:** 020 7389 2429
Titles:
CHRISTIE'S MAGAZINE

CHRISTINE STALKER 1719952
PO Box 533, NORTHWICH, CW9 9DZ **Tel:** 01565 755033
Titles:
BED & BREAKFAST NEWS

CHRONICLE PUBLICATIONS LTD 14958
102 Boothferry Road, GOOLE, DN14 6AE **Tel:** 01405 720110
Fax: 01405 720003
Titles:
GOOLE TIMES
SELBY POST

CHURCH ARMY 18091
Marlowe House, 109 Station Road, SIDCUP, DA15 7AD
Tel: 020 8309 9991 **Fax:** 020 8309 3500
Email: info@churcharmy.org.uk

Web site: http://www.churcharmy.org.uk
Titles:
SHAREIT!

CHURCH HOUSE PUBLISHING 18456
Church House, Great Smith Street, LONDON, SW1P 3AZ
Tel: 020 7898 1451 **Fax:** 020 7898 1449
Email: publishing@c-of-e.org.uk
Web site: http://www.chpublishing.co.uk
Titles:
CHURCH OF ENGLAND YEAR BOOK

CHURCH LANE PUBLISHING LTD 622821
The Clock Tower, 6 Market Gate, Market Deeping,
PETERBOROUGH, PE6 8DL **Tel:** 01778 342814
Fax: 01778 342814
Email: info@bestofbritishmag.co.uk
Web site: http://www.bestofbritishmag.co.uk
Titles:
BEST OF BRITISH

THE CHURCH MONUMENTS SOCIETY 17596
Department of History of Art and Film, Leicester University,
University Road, LEICESTER, LE1 7RH **Tel:** 0116 252 2866
Fax: 0116 252 5128
Email: so4@leicester.ac.uk
Web site: http://www.churchmonumentssociety.org
Titles:
CHURCH MONUMENTS

THE CHURCH OF IRELAND PRESS 15870
3 Wallace Avenue, LISBURN, BT27 4AA **Tel:** 028 9267 5743
Fax: 028 9267 7580
Email: gazette@ireland.anglican.org
Web site: http://www.gazette.ireland.anglican.org
Titles:
CHURCH OF IRELAND GAZETTE

CHURCH OF SCOTLAND PUBLICATIONS 17603
121 George Street, EDINBURGH, EH2 4YN
Titles:
LIFE AND WORK

CHURCH SOCIETY 15872
Dean Wace House, 16 Rosslyn Road, WATFORD, WD18
0NY **Tel:** 01923 235111 **Fax:** 01923 800362
Titles:
CHURCHMAN
CROSS WAY

CIBSE 629257
222 Balham High Road, LONDON, SW12 9BS
Titles:
THE CIBSE ELECTRONIC NEWSLETTER

CILIP 17592
Department of Information Studies, Llanbadarn Fawr,
ABERYSTWYTH, SY23 3AS **Tel:** 01970 622174
Fax: 01970 622190
Web site: http://user.aber.ac.uk/hle
Titles:
Y DDOLEN

CIM LLP 1645385
Barham Court, Teston, MAIDSTONE, ME18 5BZ
Tel: 01622 618799 **Fax:** 01622 618793
Web site: http://www.cimltd.co.uk
Titles:
BAR MAGAZINE
CONSTRUCTOR AND ARCHITECT
IN DESIGN
THE SALON MAGAZINE
STAND OUT

CIMEX MEDIA 1640082
53-55 Scrutton Street, LONDON, EC2A 4XL
Tel: 020 7324 7780 **Fax:** 020 7324 7781
Web site: http://www.cimex.com
Titles:
NEED2KNOW

CIMTECH LTD 13597
University of Hertfordshire, Innovation Centre, College Lane,
HATFIELD, AL10 9AB **Tel:** 01707 281060 **Fax:** 01707 281061

Email: c.cimtech@herts.ac.uk
Web site: http://www.cimtech.co.uk
Titles:
INFORMATION MANAGEMENT & TECHNOLOGY
INFORMATION MANAGEMENT & TECHNOLOGY
(IM@T.ONLINE)

CINNAMON PRESS 1639877
Ty Meirion, Glan yr afon, Tanygrisiau, BLAENAU
FFESTINIOG, LL41 3SU **Tel:** 01766 832112
Titles:
ENVOI

CIO CONNECT 1622356
21 Whitefriars Street, LONDON, EC4Y 8JJ
Tel: 020 7842 7999 **Fax:** 020 7842 7998
Web site: http://www.cio-connect.com
Titles:
CIO CONNECT

CIPD 1755900
151 The Broadway, LONDON, SW19 1JQ
Tel: 020 8612 6200 **Fax:** 020 8612 6201
Web site: http://www.cipd.co.uk
Titles:
COACHING AT WORK

CIRCLE OF WINE WRITERS 17354
34 Frobisher Court, Sydenham Rise, LONDON, SE23 3XH
Tel: 020 8699 3173
Web site: http://www.winewriters.org
Titles:
CIRCLE UPDATE

CIRCLE PUBLISHING 676677
One Victoria Villas, RICHMOND, TW9 2GW
Tel: 020 8332 8400 **Fax:** 020 8332 9307
Titles:
ACTIVE
DIVE MAGAZINE
GEOGRAPHICAL
GEOGRAPHICAL ONLINE
SNOW

CIRCULATION FACTORS 13436
49 New Road, LITTLEHAMPTON, BN17 5AT
Tel: 020 8668 8525 **Fax:** 020 8763 1710
Titles:
CIRCULATION FACTORS

CIRCUS FRIENDS ASSOCIATION OF GREAT BRITAIN 16899
Fir Tree Cottage, Little Hormead, BUNTINGFORD, SG9 0LU
Tel: 01763 289543
Titles:
KING POLE CIRCUS MAGAZINE

CISION UK LTD 18636
Chess House, 34 Germain Street, CHESHAM, HP5 1SJ
Tel: 0870 736 0010 **Fax:** 0870 736 0011
Web site: http://uk.cision.com
Titles:
CISION MEDIA UPDATES - UK

CITIZEN NEWSPAPERS LTD 1640440
11A Ravenoak Road, CHEADLE HULME, SK8 5LL
Tel: 0161 491 5700 **Fax:** 0161 491 5200
Email: cheshirestylemag@aol.com
Web site: http://www.stylemag.co.uk
Titles:
CHESHIRE STYLE MAGAZINE
STOCKPORT CITIZEN

CITY AM 1686020
12-14 Dowgate Hill, LONDON, EC4R 2SU
Tel: 020 7015 1200 **Fax:** 020 7015 1299
Titles:
CITY A.M.

CITY GUIDES LTD 691235
PO Box 6160, BIRMINGHAM, B16 8XA **Tel:** 0121 245 0000
Fax: 0121 245 0009

UK Publishers & Their Titles

Titles:
WHATSONUK GUIDES

CITY KIDZ MEDIA   1758398
6-14 Underwood Street, LONDON, N1 7JQ
Email: grownups@londonkidz.co.uk
Titles:
LONDONKIDZ

CITY LIFE MEDIA LTD   1649739
Halifax House, Halifax Place, NOTTINGHAM, NG1 1QN
Tel: 0115 924 2433 **Fax:** 0115 924 3433
Email: enquiries@citylifemedia.com
Web site: http://www.citylifemedia.com
Titles:
CITY LIFE & COUNTY LIVING MAGAZINE (EAST MIDLANDS)

CITY OF LONDON & DOCKLAND TIMES   697746
10 College East, Gunthorpe Street, LONDON, E1 7RL
Tel: 020 7247 2524
Titles:
CITY OF LONDON & DOCKLAND TIMES

CITY PUBLICATIONS   700192
Enterprise House, 127 Bute Street, CARDIFF, CF10 5LE
Tel: 029 2045 0532 **Fax:** 029 2045 0533
Web site: http://www.citypublications.org
Titles:
AT HOME IN WALES
BUSINESS IN FOCUS
KIDZ LIFE

CITY UNIVERSITY STUDENTS' UNION   15770
City University, Northampton Square, LONDON, EC1V 0HB
Tel: 020 7505 5606 **Fax:** 020 7505 5601
Titles:
MASSIVE

CITYGATE DEWE ROGERSON   1654295
3 London Wall Buildings, LONDON, EC2M 5SY
Tel: 020 7638 9571
Titles:
PERSUADER

CITYWIRE   623617
1st Floor, 87 Vauxhall Walk, LONDON, SE11 5HJ
Tel: 020 7840 2250
Titles:
CITYWIRE
CITYWIRE FUNDS INSIDER
FUND SELECTOR
NEW MODEL ADVISER

CIVIL SERVICE PENSIONERS' ALLIANCE   15199
1st Floor, 102-104 Park Lane, CROYDON, CR0 1JB
Tel: 020 8688 8418 **Fax:** 020 8760 9806
Web site: http://www.cspa.co.uk
Titles:
THE CIVIL SERVICE PENSIONER

CJ MEDIA   1762408
Valley House, Trimpley, BEWDLEY, DY12 1PG
Tel: 07980 770701
Titles:
PLAYERS CLUB

CLARINET & SAXOPHONE SOCIETY (CASS)   15359
Y Fron, Llansadwrn, MENAI BRIDGE, LL59 5SL
Tel: 01248 352585 **Fax:** 01248 352585
Titles:
CLARINET & SAXOPHONE

CLARITY PUBLISHING LTD   1711937
7 Midshires Business Park, Smeaton Close, AYLESBURY,
HP19 8HL **Tel:** 0845 057 0514 **Fax:** 01296 468549
Email: info@claritypublishing.co.uk
Web site: http://www.policeprofessional.com
Titles:
POLICE PROFESSIONAL

CLARK WHITE PUBLICATIONS LTD   13934
70-74 City Road, LONDON, EC1Y 2BJ **Tel:** 020 7324 3500
Fax: 020 7324 3511
Titles:
MOBILE NEWS

CLARK WHITE PUBLISHING LTD   13939
3rd Floor, 102-108 Clerkenwell Road, LONDON, EC1M 5SA
Tel: 020 7324 3500
Titles:
WHAT MOBILE

CLARKE DESIGN & MEDIA LTD   14249
Wisteria House, Stump Cross Lane, Swineshead, BOSTON,
PE20 3JJ **Tel:** 0845 388 0281 **Fax:** 0845 388 0283
Email: enquiries@clarke-media.co.uk
Web site: http://www.clarke-media.co.uk
Titles:
QUBE MAGAZINE

CLASH MAGAZINE LTD.   1641474
143C Nethergate, DUNDEE, DD1 4DP **Tel:** 01382 808808
Fax: 01382 909909
Titles:
CLASH

CLASSIC BUS LTD   15516
15 Starfield Road, LONDON, W12 9SN
Titles:
CLASSIC BUS

CLASSIC TITLES   625279
PMA House, Free Church Passage, ST. IVES, PE27 5AY
Tel: 01480 463565 **Fax:** 01480 494146
Web site: http://www.classictitles.com
Titles:
CLASSIC ANGLING

CLEANTECH INVESTOR   1768103
PO Box 63865, LONDON, SE1 3SN **Tel:** 020 7394 7110
Fax: 020 7252 0910
Titles:
CLEANTECH

CLEARVIEW PUBLISHING   1731142
27 Parsons Green Lane, LONDON, SW6 4HH
Tel: 020 7736 8180 **Fax:** 020 7504 3610
Web site: http://www.clearviewpublishing.com
Titles:
THE BARNSLEY EYE
EXECUTIVE COMPENSATION BRIEFING
THE HUDDERSFIELD EYE
WEALTHBRIEFING

CLICK IT LTD   622842
Hampshire Gate, Langley, LISS, GU33 7JR
Tel: 01730 895614 **Fax:** 0870 033 3104
Web site: http://www.incisor.tv
Titles:
INCISOR

CLICKWORKS LTD   17198
24A Market Square, Potton, SANDY, SG19 2NP
Tel: 01767 261620
Email: info@theventurer.co.uk
Web site: http://www.ukbusinessexchange.com
Titles:
IOD HERTFORDSHIRE
THE VENTURER

CLIMATE AND ENVIRONMENT MEDIA LTD   1655303
The Studio, Denton, PETERBOROUGH, PE7 3SD
Tel: 01733 246850 **Fax:** 01733 243322
Web site: http://www.climateandenvironmentmedia.com
Titles:
ENVIRONMENT JOURNAL

THE CLUB CRICKET CONFERENCE   17234
128 High Street, Hampton Hill, HAMPTON, TW12 1NS
Titles:
CLUB CRICKET CONFERENCE YEARBOOK
EXTRA COVER

CLYDE & FORTH PRESS GROUP   15046
Pitreavie Business Park, DUNFERMLINE, KY11 8QS
Tel: 01383 728201 **Fax:** 01383 737040
Email: editorial@cfpress.co.uk
Titles:
ALLOA AND HILLFOOTS ADVERTISER
ARDROSSAN & SALTCOATS HERALD
AYR ADVERTISER SERIES
CLYDEBANK POST
CUMNOCK CHRONICLE
DUMBARTON AND VALE OF LEVEN REPORTER
GREENOCK TELEGRAPH
HELENSBURGH ADVERTISER
INVERCLYDE EXTRA
IRVINE TIMES
LARGS & MILLPORT WEEKLY NEWS
THE PAISLEY AND RENFREWSHIRE GAZETTE SERIES

CMM PUBLICATIONS   16477
PO Box 129, BOLTON, BL3 4YQ **Tel:** 01204 657212
Fax: 01204 652764
Titles:
CLASSIC MOTOR MONTHLY

CMYK DESIGN   1645323
91 East London Street, EDINBURGH, EH7 4BQ
Tel: 0131 556 2220
Email: info@cmyk-design.co.uk
Web site: http://www.cmyk-design.co.uk
Titles:
SCOTLAND IN TRUST

CN PUBLISHING   14374
9A Kings Road, Flitwick, BEDFORD, MK45 1ED
Tel: 01525 718890 **Fax:** 01525 718026
Titles:
IMAGES

COAST PUBLISHING LTD   1713762
St Josephs, St. Mawgan, NEWQUAY, TR8 4EN
Tel: 01637 860031
Email: info@coast-publishing.co.uk
Web site: http://www.coast-publishing.co.uk
Titles:
ADVENTURE CORNWALL

COATES & PARKER LTD   15004
36 Market Place, WARMINSTER, BA12 9AN
Tel: 01985 213030 **Fax:** 01985 217680
Email: sales@coatesandparker.co.uk
Web site: http://www.coatesandparker.co.uk
Titles:
WARMINSTER JOURNAL

COBWEB INFORMATION LTD   1640413
1st Floor, Northumbria House, 5 Delta Bank Road, Metro
Riverside Park, GATESHEAD, NE11 9DJ **Tel:** 0191 461 8000
Fax: 0191 461 8001
Email: enquiries@cobwebinfo.com
Web site: http://www.cobwebinfo.com
Titles:
BAD NEWS
BETTER BUSINESS

CODE BLUE PUBLISHING LIMITED   698366
17 Old Leeds Road, HUDDERSFIELD, HD1 1SG
Tel: 01484 441400 **Fax:** 01484 441421
Web site: http://www.codebluegroup.co.uk
Titles:
CONSTRUCTION INDUSTRY NEWS
CONSTRUCTION INDUSTRY NEWS IRELAND
FMCG
INDUSTRY UK

COELIAC UK   1638844
Suite A-D, Octagon Court, HIGH WYCOMBE, HP11 2HS
Tel: 01494 437278 **Fax:** 01494 474349
Email: contact@coeliac.org.uk
Web site: http://www.coeliac.org.uk
Titles:
CROSSED GRAIN

COGNITIVE PUBLISHING LTD   694499
Suite 102, International House, 82-86 Deansgate,
MANCHESTER, M3 2ER **Tel:** 0161 833 6320
Fax: 0161 832 0571
Web site: http://www.cognitivepublishing.com

Titles:
NATIONAL HEALTH EXECUTIVE
PUBLIC SECTOR EXECUTIVE
RAIL TECHNOLOGY MAGAZINE

COIL WINDING INTERNATIONAL LTD   13914
East by North, Tudor Road, Newton, Alderney, GUERNSEY,
GY9 3XP **Tel:** 01481 823292 **Fax:** 01202 736018
Email: office@coilwinding.e7even.com
Web site: http://www.coilwindingmgazine.com

Titles:
COIL WINDING INTERNATIONAL AND ELECTRICAL
INSULATION MAGAZINE

COLD CHAIN NEWS LIMITED   13479
7 Ship Street Gardens, BRIGHTON, BN1 1AJ
Tel: 07796 297350

Titles:
COLD CHAIN NEWS

COLD FOUNTAINS MEDIA   1719699
507 Clarkenwell Workshops, 27-31 Clarkenwell Close,
LONDON, EC1R 0AT **Tel:** 020 7438 1160
Fax: 020 7117 3664

Titles:
SCI STRUCTURED CREDIT INVESTOR
STORM

THE COLLECTOR LTD   17678
32 Swift Way, Thurlby, BOURNE, PE10 0QA
Tel: 01778 338095 **Fax:** 01778 338096
Email: info@thebookcollector.co.uk
Web site: http://www.thebookcollector.co.uk

Titles:
THE BOOK COLLECTOR

THE COLLEGE OF OCCUPATIONAL THERAPISTS LTD
14601
106-114 Borough High Street, LONDON, SE1 1LB
Tel: 020 7450 2339 **Fax:** 020 7450 2350
Email: editorial@cot.co.uk
Web site: http://www.cot.org.uk

Titles:
OCCUPATIONAL THERAPY NEWS

COLOURFAST GROUP LTD   17430
Colourfast Studio, 36 Cheltenham Place, BRIGHTON, BN1
4AB **Tel:** 01273 674321 **Fax:** 01273 609135

Titles:
CSN COPY SHOP NEWS

COMMERCIAL CRIME SERVICES LTD   14461
Cinnabar Wharf, 26 Wapping High Street, LONDON, E1W
1NG **Tel:** 020 7423 6960

Titles:
COMMERCIAL CRIME INTERNATIONAL

COMMITTEE OF GKT MEDICAL SCHOOLS   671736
2nd Floor, Doyles House, 19 Newcomen Street, LONDON,
SE1 1UL **Tel:** 020 7848 6983 **Fax:** 020 7848 6984
Email: office@gktgazette.com
Web site: http://www.gktgazette.com

Titles:
GKT GAZETTE

COMMONWEALTH BROADCASTING ASSOCIATION
17296
17 Fleet Street, LONDON, EC4Y 1AA **Tel:** 020 7583 5550
Fax: 020 7583 5549
Email: cba@ba.org.uk
Web site: http://www.cba.org.uk

Titles:
COMMONWEALTH BROADCASTER

COMMONWEALTH FORESTRY ASSOCIATION   14362
The Crib, Dinchope, CRAVEN ARMS, SY7 9JJ
Tel: 01588 672868

Titles:
INTERNATIONAL FORESTRY REVIEW

COMMONWEALTH PARLIAMENTARY   18121
Suite 700, Westminster House, Millbank, LONDON, SW1P
3JA **Tel:** 020 7799 1460 **Fax:** 020 7222 6073

Web site: http://www.cpahq.org
Titles:
THE PARLIAMENTARIAN

COMMUNICATION WORKERS UNION   13849
150 The Broadway, LONDON, SW19 1RX
Tel: 020 8971 7286 **Fax:** 020 8971 7437
Web site: http://www.cwu.org

Titles:
CWU VOICE

COMMUNICATIONS INTERNATIONAL GROUP   12517
207 Linen Hall, 162-168 Regent Street, LONDON, W1B 5TB
Tel: 020 7434 1530 **Fax:** 020 7437 0915

Titles:
BEAUTY MAGAZINE
COSMETICS INTERNATIONAL
COSMETICS PRODUCTS REPORT
THE INDEPENDENT COMMUNITY PHARMACIST
P3
PHARMACY MAGAZINE
TM TRAINING MATTERS

COMMUNICORP   1655126
Banklands, Ferry Lane, Wraysbury, STAINES, TW19 6HG
Tel: 01784 483281 **Fax:** 01784 483600

Titles:
CLERKS AND COUNCILS DIRECT
INVEST IN THE UK

COMMUNITY   13469
Swinton House, 324 Gray's Inn Road, LONDON, WC1 8DD
Tel: 020 7239 1200 **Fax:** 020 7278 8378
Email: info@community-tu.org
Web site: http://www.community-tu.org

Titles:
STRONGER TOGETHER

COMMUNITY & CO-OPERATIVE PUBLISHIND LIMITED
13887
Princes House, 5 Shadwick Place, EDINBURGH, EH2 4RG
Tel: 0131 229 7257 **Fax:** 0131 221 9798

Titles:
NEW SECTOR

COMMUNITY MATTERS   14165
12-20 Baron Street, LONDON, N1 9LL **Tel:** 020 7837 7887
Fax: 020 7278 9253
Email: communitymatters@communitymatters.org.uk
Web site: http://www.communitymatters.org.uk

Titles:
COMMUNITY

COMMUNITY NEWSPAPER SUPPORT ASSOCIATION
1650247
1st Floor Offices, Shildon Town Council, Civic Hall Square,
SHILDON, DL4 1AH **Tel:** 01388 775896 **Fax:** 01388 775896
Email: record@talk21.com

Titles:
COMMUNITY NEWSPAPER SERIES

COMMUNITY TIMES UK LTD   1767062
39 Jay Close, BICESTER, OX26 6XN **Tel:** 01869 660082

Titles:
BICESTER COMMUNITY TIMES

COMMUNITY TRANSPORT ASSOCIATION   14400
Highbank, Halton Street, HYDE, SK14 2NY
Tel: 0870 774 3586 **Fax:** 0870 774 3581
Email: info@ctauk.org
Web site: http://www.ctauk.org

Titles:
CTA JOURNAL

THE COMPANY OF BIOLOGISTS LTD   17810
Bidder Building, 140 Cowley Road, CAMBRIDGE, CB4 0DL
Tel: 01223 425525 **Fax:** 01223 423520

Titles:
JOURNAL OF EXPERIMENTAL BIOLOGY

COMPASSION IN WORLD FARMING   15629
2nd Floor, River Court, Mill Lane, GODALMING, GU7 1EZ
Tel: 01483 521950 **Fax:** 01483 861639

Email: supporters@ciwf.org
Web site: http://www.ciwf.org
Titles:
FARM ANIMAL VOICE

COMPASSSPORT   1716011
6 Glenmore Park, TUNBRIDGE WELLS, TN2 5NZ
Tel: 07720 952241
Web site: http://www.compasssport.co.uk

Titles:
COMPASS SPORT

COMPLETE CIRCULATION AND MARKETING LTD
699967
Unit 8, Netherhall Yard, Mill Lane, Newick, LEWES, BN8 4JL
Tel: 01825 724623 **Fax:** 01825 724623
Email: c.dann@completecircmktg.co.uk
Web site: http://www.completecircmktg.co.uk

Titles:
DIRECT DISTRIBUTION NEWSLETTER
INSULATION - THE ENERGY EFFICIENCY NEWSLETTER
PAINT & RESIN TIMES

COMPLETE MEDIA & MARKETING LTD   674300
6 Harforde Court, John Tate Road, Foxholes Business Park,
HERTFORD, SG13 7NW **Tel:** 01992 538001
Fax: 01992 538002
Email: info@cm-2.co.uk
Web site: http://www.nutrition2me.com

Titles:
CN FOCUS
COMPLETE NUTRITION

COMPLINET   1653555
3rd Floor, Vinter's Place, Upper Thames Street, LONDON,
EC4V 3BJ **Tel:** 0870 042 6400 **Fax:** 020 8661 5879
Email: clientsupport@complinet.com
Web site: http://www.complinet.com

Titles:
COMPLINET

COMPULSION MEDIA   1640223
BCM Compulsion, LONDON, WC1N 3XX **Tel:** 0870 011 8168
Fax: 0870 011 8168
Web site: http://www.compulsion-media.com

Titles:
HCD

CONCEPT FOR LIVING LTD   700382
The Old School, Higher Kinnerton, CHESTER, CH4 9AJ
Tel: 01244 663400
Email: info@conceptforliving.co.uk
Web site: http://www.conceptforliving.co.uk

Titles:
CONCEPT FOR LIVING

THE CONCRETE SOCIETY   14280
Riverside House, 4 Meadows Business Park, Station
Approach, Blackwater, CAMBERLEY, GU17 9AB
Tel: 01276 607140 **Fax:** 01276 607141
Email: enquirires@concrete.org.uk
Web site: http://www.concrete.org.uk

Titles:
CONCRETE
CONCRETE ENGINEERING INTERNATIONAL

CONDE NAST INTERACTIVE   1735478
Vogue House, 1 Hanover Square, LONDON, W1S 1JU
Tel: 0207 499 9080
Web site: http://www.condenast.co.uk

Titles:
BRIDESMAGAZINE.CO.UK

CONDE NAST PUBLICATIONS LTD   15097
Vogue House, 1 Hanover Square, LONDON, W1S 1JU
Tel: 020 7499 9080 **Fax:** 020 7493 1345
Web site: http://www.condenast.com

Titles:
CNTRAVELLER
CONDE NAST BRIDES
CONDE NAST TRAVELLER
EASY LIVING
EASYLIVINGMAGAZINE.COM
GLAMOUR
GLAMOUR.COM
GQ
GQ ONLINE

UK Publishers & Their Titles

GQ STYLE
HOUSE & GARDEN
MAYBOURNE STYLE MAGAZINE
MO
THE OFFICIAL FERRARI MAGAZINE
STYLEFINDER.COM
TATLER
VANITY FAIR
VOGUE
VOGUE ONLINE
WIRED
THE WORLD OF INTERIORS

CONFERENCE & TRAVEL PUBLICATIONS LTD 13443
Kings House, Cantelupe Road, EAST GRINSTEAD, RH19
3BE **Tel:** 01342 306700
Titles:
ASSOCIATION MEETINGS INTERNATIONAL
MEETINGS & INCENTIVE TRAVEL
WORLDWIDE CONVENTION CENTRES DIRECTORY

CONFERENCE COMMUNICATION 672231
Monks Hill, Tilford, FARNHAM, GU10 2AJ
Tel: 01252 783111
Email: info@maintenanceonline.co.uk
Web site: http://www.maintenanceonline.co.uk
Titles:
MAINTENANCE AND ENGINEERING

CONFETTI NETWORK 674981
80-81 Tottenham Court Road, LONDON, W1T 4TE
Tel: 020 7291 7600
Web site: http://www.confetti.co.uk
Titles:
CONFETTI.CO.UK
WEBWEDDINGS
WEDDINGGUIDEUK.COM

CONGLETON CHRONICLE LTD 14907
11 High Street, CONGLETON, CW12 1BW
Tel: 01260 280687 **Fax:** 01260 280687
Titles:
CONGLETON CHRONICLE SERIES
MOORLANDS TRADER

CONNECT 621767
30 St. Georges Road, Wimbledon, LONDON, SW19 4BD
Tel: 020 8971 6000 **Fax:** 020 8971 6002
Web site: http://www.connectuk.org
Titles:
CONNECTED

CONNECT COMMUNICATIONS 1640353
Studio 2001, Mile End, PAISLEY, PA1 1JS
Tel: 0141 561 0300 **Fax:** 0141 561 0400
Titles:
CA MAGAZINE

CONNOLLY PUBLICATIONS LTD 17887
244 Gray's Inn Road, LONDON, WC1X 8JR
Tel: 020 7833 3022
Titles:
IRISH DEMOCRAT

CONROY MEDIA 1642385
24 Stacey Road, CARDIFF, CF24 1DU **Tel:** 029 2019 0224
Fax: 029 2019 0226
Titles:
RED HANDED

CONSCIENCE - THE PEACE TAX CAMPAIGN 15685
Archway Resource Centre, 1B Waterlow Road, LONDON,
N19 5NJ **Tel:** 020 7561 1061 **Fax:** 020 7281 6508
Web site: http://www.peacepays.org
Titles:
CONSCIENCE UPDATE

CONSORTIUM PUBLISHING LTD 17076
PO Box 30, CROWBOROUGH, TN6 3ZY **Tel:** 01892 661166
Fax: 01892 661122
Web site: http://www.consortiumpublishing.co.uk
Titles:
YOUR CONSORTIUM

CONSTRUCTION BIBLE LTD 1723528
The Quadrus Centre, Woodstock Way, Boldon Business
Park, BOLDON COLLIERY, NE35 9PF **Tel:** 0191 519 7268
Fax: 0191 519 7201
Email: info@constructionbible.co.uk
Web site: http://www.constructionbible.eu
Titles:
CONSTRUCTION BIBLE

CONSTRUCTIVE MEDIA 1731702
Brecon House, Mamhilad Park Estate, PONTYPOOL, NP4
0HZ **Tel:** 01495 740050 **Fax:** 01495 740050
Email: sales@constructivemedia.co.uk
Web site: http://www.constructivemedia.co.uk
Titles:
UNIMER NEWS

CONSUMER MEDICAL REPORTS LTD 16608
Unit 10, Woodman Works, 204 Durnsford Road, LONDON,
SW19 8DR **Tel:** 020 8944 9555 **Fax:** 020 8944 9888
Titles:
PROOF!

CONSYL PUBLISHING & PUBLICITY LTD 16008
13 London Road, BEXHILL-ON-SEA, TN39 3JR
Tel: 01424 223111 **Fax:** 01424 224992
Email: consylpublishing@btconnect.com
Web site: http://www.consylpublishing.co.uk
Titles:
AUSTRALIAN OUTLOOK
NEW ZEALAND OUTLOOK
TRAVEL AUSTRALIA & NEW ZEALAND

CONTACT 94 SALES LTD 675167
PO Box 243, ST HELIER, JE4 5PL **Tel:** 01534 504800
Titles:
ENJOY JERSEY MAGAZINE

CONTACT CENTRE MEDIA LTD 1751995
16 Rosewood Way, West End, WOKING, GU24 9PF
Tel: 01296 857950
Titles:
CONTACTCENTREJOBS.CO.UK
CONTACTCENTRELINK.COM

CONTACTLESS INTELLIGENCE 1760514
PR by email only
Titles:
C-IQ

CONTAINER MANAGEMENT LTD 1677030
213 Drury House, Marsh Wall, LONDON, E14 9FJ
Tel: 020 7510 0015
Email: publisher@lngjournal.com
Web site: http://www.container-mag.com
Titles:
CONTAINER MANAGEMENT

CONTENT CONSULTANTS 1649370
The Genome Centre, Norwich Research Park, Colney,
NORWICH, NR4 7UH **Tel:** 01603 450987 **Fax:** 01603 450986
Web site: http://www.contentconsultants.co.uk
Titles:
BABYCENTRE

CONTINYOU 15915
31-33 Bondway, Vauxhall, LONDON, SW8 1SJ
Tel: 024 7658 8440 **Fax:** 024 7658 8441
Email: info@continyou.org.uk
Web site: http://www.continyou.org.uk
Titles:
THE LEARNING EXCHANGE

CONWAY MARITIME PRESS 15476
10 Southcombe Street, LONDON, W14 0RA
Tel: 020 7605 1400 **Fax:** 020 7605 1505
Email: conway@anovabooks.com
Web site: http://www.anovabooks.com
Titles:
MODEL SHIPWRIGHT

CO-OPERATIVE PRESS LTD 14653
Holyoake House, Hanover Street, MANCHESTER, M60 0AS
Tel: 0161 214 0870 **Fax:** 0161 214 0878
Email: editorial@thenews.coop
Web site: http://www.thenews.coop
Titles:
CO-OPERATIVE NEWS

COPYBOOK SOLUTIONS LTD 624211
100 Chapel Street, TIVERTON, EX16 6BU **Tel:** 01884 244670
Fax: 01884 244671
Titles:
AIRPORT INTERNATIONAL
ARMED FORCES INTERNATIONAL
SECURITY INTERNATIONAL

CORES PUBLICATIONS INC. 13913
PO Box 107, BICESTER, OX25 4WA **Tel:** 01869 347644
Titles:
CEMA CONSUMER ELECTRONICS

CORGI 1676023
1 Elmwood, Crockford Lane, Chineham Business Park,
Chineham, BASINGSTOKE, RG24 8WG **Tel:** 0870 401 2200
Fax: 0870 401 2600
Email: enquiries@corgi-gas.com
Web site: http://www.corgi-group.com
Titles:
THE GAS INSTALLER

CORNERSTONE VISION 1650278
28 Old Park Road, Peverell, PLYMOUTH, PL3 4PY
Tel: 01752 225623 **Fax:** 01752 673441
Email: info@cornerstonevision.com
Web site: http://www.cornerstonevision.com
Titles:
THE PLYMOUTH MAGAZINE
PORTSMOUTH PEOPLE
THE SARUM LINK
THE WEY

CORNISH & DEVON POST 16296
Tindle House, Westgate Street, LAUNCESTON, PL15 7AL
Tel: 01566 772424 **Fax:** 01566 776976
Titles:
CORNISH & DEVON POST SERIES

CORNISH TIMES GROUP 18944
The Tindle Suite, Webbs House, The Parade, LISKEARD,
PL14 6AH **Tel:** 01579 342174
Titles:
PRIME OF LIFE
WESTERN COUNTIES BUSINESS NEWS

CORNWALL & DEVON MEDIA LIMITED 14914
Harmsworth House, City Wharf, Malpas Road, TRURO, TR1
1QH **Tel:** 01872 271451 **Fax:** 01872 247435
Web site: http://www.thisiscornwall.co.uk
Titles:
CORNISH GUARDIAN SERIES
THE CORNISHMAN
CORNWALL TODAY
NORTH DEVON JOURNAL SERIES
WAVELENGTH
THE WEST BRITON SERIES

CORNWALL & DEVON MEDIA LTD 600669
Sherborne Road, YEOVIL, BA21 4YA **Tel:** 01935 700500
Fax: 01935 432266
Titles:
COUNTRY GARDENER

CORNWALL FAMILY HISTORY SOCIETY 16131
5 Victoria Square, TRURO, TR1 2RS **Tel:** 01872 264044
Titles:
CORNWALL FAMILY HISTORY SOCIETY JOURNAL

CORPORATE CITIZENSHIP 13463
5th Floor, Holborn Gate, 330 High Holborn, LONDON, WC1V
7QG **Tel:** 020 7861 1616 **Fax:** 020 7861 3908
Email: editor@corporate-citizenship.co.uk
Web site: http://www.corporate-citizenship.com
Titles:
CORPORATE CITIZENSHIP BRIEFING

CORPORATE PUBLICATIONS   17186
PO Box 49, HAYLING ISLAND, PO11 9YJ
Tel: 023 9246 5631

Titles:
  DECISION

CORPS OF ROYAL ENGINEERS   1652966
RHQ RE, Brompton Barracks, CHATHAM, ME4 4UG
Tel: 01634 822122 **Fax:** 01634 822397
Email: corps.secretary@rhqre.co.uk
Web site: http://www.royalengineers.org

Titles:
  THE SAPPER

CORUS   14094
PO Box 1, Brigg Road, SCUNTHORPE, DN16 1BP
Tel: 01724 405761 **Fax:** 01724 405383

Titles:
  CORUS NEWS

COSMIC PUBLICATIONS LTD   1735857
PO Box 9844, COLCHESTER, CO1 9EE **Tel:** 01322 340207

Titles:
  COMICS INTERNATIONAL

COSTAR LTD   1735086
10 Great Pulteney Street, LONDON, W1F 9NB
Tel: 020 3214 0100 **Fax:** 020 3214 0126
Web site: http://www.costar.co.uk

Titles:
  COSTAR GROUP

COSTAR UK LTD   1627001
Empire House, 131 West Nile Street, GLASGOW, G1 2RX
Tel: 0141 561 7300 **Fax:** 0141 561 7319
Email: info@scottishproperty.co.uk
Web site: http://www.scottishproperty.co.uk

Titles:
  SCOTTISH PROPERTY NETWORK

COSYS MANAGEMENT INFORMATION SERVICES 16752
Tigh Osda, Charleston, North Kessock, INVERNESS, IV1
1YA **Tel:** 01463 731566
Email: admin@uk-golfguide.com
Web site: http://www.uk-golfguide.com

Titles:
  UK-GOLFGUIDE.COM

COTLOOK LTD   13393
Outlook House, 458 New Chester Road, Rock Ferry,
BIRKENHEAD, CH42 2AE **Tel:** 0151 644 6400
Fax: 0151 644 8550

Titles:
  COTTON OUTLOOK

COTSWOLD WATER PARK MEDIA LTD   1744009
The Marketing House, Meadow Road, CIRENCESTER, GL7
1YA **Tel:** 01285 715776

Titles:
  COTSWOLD WATER PARK LIFE

THE COUNCIL OF CHRISTIANS AND JEWS   15873
1st Floor, Camelford House, 87-89 Albert Embankment,
LONDON, SE1 7TP **Tel:** 020 7820 0090 **Fax:** 020 7820 0504
Email: cjrelations@ccj.org.uk
Web site: http://www.ccj.org.uk

Titles:
  COMMON GROUND

COUNCIL OF MORTGAGE LENDERS   13390
North West Wing, Bush House, Aldwych, LONDON, WC2B
4PJ **Tel:** 020 7437 0075 **Fax:** 020 7434 3791
Email: bernard.clarke@cml.org.uk
Web site: http://www.cml.org.uk

Titles:
  CML NEWS & VIEWS

COUNTIES NEWSPAPERS LTD   1762318
4 Copthall House, Station Square, COVENTRY, CV1 2FY

Titles:
  COUNTIES TODAY

COUNTRY AND TOWN HOUSE LTD   1733113
The Studio, 1 Linver Road, LONDON, SW6 3RA
Tel: 020 7731 9470

Titles:
  COUNTRY AND TOWN HOUSE
  SCHOOL HOUSE MAGAZINE

COUNTRY DOCTOR   17398
17 Symonds Road, HITCHIN, SG5 2JJ **Tel:** 01462 434515
Web site: http://www.countrydoctor.co.uk

Titles:
  COUNTRYDOCTOR.CO.UK

COUNTRY PUBLICATIONS LTD   15562
The Water Mill, Broughton Hall, SKIPTON, BD23 3AG
Tel: 01756 701 033 **Fax:** 01756 701326

Titles:
  THE COUNTRYMAN
  CUMBRIA
  DALESMAN
  DOWN YOUR WAY

COUNTRY WAY   621502
Arthur Rank Centre, National Agricultural Centre,
STONELEIGH PARK, CV8 2LG **Tel:** 024 7669 6460
Fax: 024 7669 6460

Titles:
  COUNTRY WAY

COUNTRYSIDE ALLIANCE   695493
367 Kennington Road, LONDON, SE11 4PT
Tel: 020 7840 9200 **Fax:** 020 7793 9200
Web site: http://www.countryside-alliance.org

Titles:
  THE COUNTRYSIDE ALLIANCE

COUNTRYSIDE RECREATION NETWORK   15531
Unit 10, Sheffield Science Park, Howard Street, SHEFFIELD,
S1 2LX **Tel:** 0114 225 4494 **Fax:** 0114 225 2197
Web site: http://www.countrysiderecreation.org.uk

Titles:
  COUNTRYSIDE RECREATION

COUNTRYWIDE PUBLICATIONS   13477
27 Norwich Road, HALESWORTH, IP19 8BX
Tel: 01986 834216 **Fax:** 01986 834270
Email: countrywide@micropress.co.uk
Web site: http://www.micropress.co.uk

Titles:
  CONTACT
  THE PISTE
  VAN USER

COUNTY BUSINESS PUBLISHING LTD   13344
26 Wood Street, SWINDON, SN1 4AB **Tel:** 01793 615393
Fax: 01793 488517
Email: info@swindon-business.net
Web site: http://www.swindon-business.net

Titles:
  ESTATES WEST BULLETIN
  SWINDON BUSINESS NEWS

COUNTY ECHO NEWSPAPERS LTD   15020
Parc Y Shwt, FISHGUARD, SA65 9AP **Tel:** 01348 874445
Fax: 01348 873651

Titles:
  COUNTY ECHO AND ST. DAVIDS CITY CHRONICLE

COUNTY LIFE LTD   15587
County House, 9 Checkpoint Court, Sadler Road, LINCOLN,
LN6 3PW **Tel:** 01522 527127 **Fax:** 01522 560035

Titles:
  LINCOLNSHIRE LIFE

COUNTY MAGAZINE PUBLICATIONS LTD   692425
2 Bexley Cottages, The Street, Horton Kirby, DARTFORD,
DA4 9BU **Tel:** 01322 860100 **Fax:** 01322 860200
Email: info@countymag.co.uk
Web site: http://www.countymag.co.uk

Titles:
  THE COUNTY MAGAZINE
  NEW SHOOTS DIRECTORY

THE COUNTY PRESS   15666
The County Press Buildings, Station Road, BALA, LL23 7PG
Tel: 01678 520262 **Fax:** 01678 521262

Titles:
  BUDGERIGAR WORLD

COURIER MEDIA GROUP LTD   14962
Longfield Road, TUNBRIDGE WELLS, TN2 3HL
Tel: 01892 681000 **Fax:** 01892 510400
Email: editor@courier.co.uk
Web site: http://www.courier.co.uk

Titles:
  KENT & SUSSEX COURIER SERIES
  SEVENOAKS CHRONICLE SERIES
  TODAY KENT & SUSSEX

COX PUBLICATIONS   1764259
Northam Road, Drivers Wharf, SOUTHAMPTON, SO14 0PF
Tel: 0845 686 0645

Titles:
  WHATBOAT?

CPA   14281
27-28 Newbury Street, Barbican, LONDON, EC1A 7HU
Tel: 020 7796 3366 **Fax:** 020 7796 3399
Web site: http://www.cpa.uk.net

Titles:
  THE CONSTRUCTION PLANT-HIRE ASSOCIATION
  BULLETIN

CPC LTD   14071
Napier House, 11 Surrey Street, LOWESTOFT, NR32 1LJ
Tel: 01502 517115 **Fax:** 01502 517117
Web site: http://www.craftsmanpublishing.co.uk

Titles:
  BATHROOM JOURNAL
  FURNITURE JOURNAL
  KITCHEN JOURNAL

CPL LTD   1743847
275 Newmarket Road, CAMBRIDGE, CB5 8JL
Tel: 01223 477411 **Fax:** 01223 327356
Web site: http://www.cpl.biz/index.htm

Titles:
  EAST CAMBRIDGESHIRE MAGAZINE

CPL MEDIA LTD   625064
Unit 5, The Oast, 62 Bell Road, SITTINGBOURNE, ME10
4HC **Tel:** 01795 599191 **Fax:** 01795 599282

Titles:
  CYCLING WORLD
  HERITAGE HOMES
  TRADITIONAL HOMES & INTERIORS

CPRW   694143
Ty Gwyn, 31 High Street, WELSHPOOL, SY21 7YD
Tel: 01938 552525 **Fax:** 01938 552741
Web site: http://www.cprw.org.uk

Titles:
  RURAL WALES

CRACK LTD   622956
1 Pink Lane, NEWCASTLE UPON TYNE, NE1 5DW
Tel: 0191 230 3038 **Fax:** 0191 230 4484
Web site: http://www.thecrackmagazine.com

Titles:
  THE CRACK
  THE CRACK GUIDE TO THE NORTH EAST

CRAFTS COUNCIL   15932
44A Pentonville Road, Islington, LONDON, N1 9BY
Tel: 020 7278 7700 **Fax:** 020 7837 0858

Titles:
  CRAFTS

CRAIGMILLAR COMMUNITY NEWSPAPER LTD   15613
Unit 9A, Castlebrae Business Centre, Peffer Place,
EDINBURGH, EH16 4BB **Tel:** 0131 661 0791

Titles:
  THE CHRONICLE

UK Publishers & Their Titles

CRAIN COMMUNICATIONS LTD 16851
3rd Floor, 21 St. Thomas Street, LONDON, SE1 9RY
Tel: 020 7457 1400 **Fax:** 020 7457 1440
Web site: http://www.crain.com
Titles:
BUSINESS INSURANCE
CRAIN'S MANCHESTER BUSINESS
EUROPEAN PLASTICS NEWS
EUROPEAN RUBBER JOURNAL
PENSIONS & INVESTMENTS
PRW PLASTICS & RUBBER WEEKLY
URETHANES TECHNOLOGY INTERNATIONAL

CRANBROOK MEDIA LTD 1761866
The Coach House, Angley Road, CRANBROOK, TN17 2LE
Titles:
QUALITY MANUFACTURING TODAY

CRASH MEDIA GROUP LTD 1646181
No 1 Silverstone Innovation Centre, Silverstone Circuit,
SILVERSTONE, NN12 8GX **Tel:** 0870 350 5044
Fax: 0870 350 5088
Titles:
CRASH.NET

CRAVEN PUBLISHING LTD 17270
15-39 Durham Street, Kinning Park, GLASGOW, G41 1BS
Tel: 0141 419 0044 **Fax:** 0141 419 0077
Email: edit@cravenpublishing.co.uk
Web site: http://www.cravenpubishing.co.uk
Titles:
ABLE
CIVVY STREET
END OF TERM

CRAVENHILL PUBLISHING 1765431
26-32 Voltaire Road, LONDON, SW4 6DH
Tel: 020 7498 7008
Titles:
COMMUNICATE MAGAZINE

CRE8 1684981
The Old Brewery, Priory Lane, BURFORD, OX18 4SG
Tel: 01993 822811
Web site: http://www.cre8ing.com
Titles:
ARSENAL
CELTIC VIEW
RANGERS NEWS

CREATE PUBLISHING 697702
15-16 Lower Park Row, BRISTOL, BS1 5BN
Tel: 0117 945 1913 **Fax:** 0117 927 7825
Titles:
IDJ
REAL TRAVEL

CREATE UK 17392
4 Kemp House, Sewardstone Road, LONDON, E2 9JL
Tel: 020 8980 8635
Titles:
THE CULINARY GUIDE
IMPURE MAGAZINE
TASTE

CREATIVE COPY LTD 17376
2-4 The Fradgan, Newlyn, PENZANCE, TR18 5BE
Tel: 01736 334800 **Fax:** 01736 334808
Email: mail@insidecornwall.co.uk
Web site: http://www.insidecornwall.co.uk
Titles:
INSIDE CORNWALL

CREATIVE CRAFTS PUBLISHING LTD 12864
Well Oast, Brenley Lane, Boughton-under-Blean,
FAVERSHAM, ME13 9LY **Tel:** 01227 750215
Fax: 01227 750813
Titles:
MARY HICKMOTT'S NEW STITCHES

CREATIVE JUICES LTD 1744824
39 Bocking Street, LONDON, E8 3GL **Tel:** 020 8144 8588
Titles:
EAST EIGHT

CREATIVE MEDIA LTD 1676120
318C High Road, Off Meggison Way, BENFLEET, SS7 5HB
Tel: 0870 444 3531 **Fax:** 01268 754429
Email: info@caraudioretailer.co.uk
Web site: http://www.caraudioretailer.co.uk
Titles:
MOBILE ELECTRONICS NEWS

CREATIVEMATCH 1649496
Building 3, Chiswick Park, 566 Chiswick High Road,
LONDON, W4 5YA **Tel:** 0845 676 2250 **Fax:** 0845 676 2251
Web site: http://www.creativematch.co.uk
Titles:
CREATIVEMATCH

CREDITFLUX 1650325
2-6 Northburgh Street, LONDON, EC1V 0AY
Tel: 020 7253 9510
Email: mail@creditflux.com
Web site: http://www.creditflux.com
Titles:
CREDITFLUX

CREDITON COUNTRY COURIER 14921
102 High Street, CREDITON, EX17 3LF **Tel:** 01363 774263
Fax: 01363 773545
Email: editor@creditoncouriernewspaper.co.uk
Web site: http://www.creditoncouriernewspaper.co.uk
Titles:
CREDITON COUNTRY COURIER

CRESCENDO 15364
13 Buckfast House, Priory Close, Southgate, LONDON, N14
4AZ **Tel:** 020 8440 5526 **Fax:** 020 8440 5526
Titles:
CRESCENDO & JAZZ MUSIC

CRESCENT MOON PUBLISHING 671987
PO Box 393, MAIDSTONE, ME14 5XU **Tel:** 01622 729593
Titles:
PASSION

CREST PUBLICATIONS 18189
O'Dell House, Hunters Road, Weldon North Industrial Estate,
CORBY, NN17 5JE **Tel:** 01536 266576 **Fax:** 01536 264509
Web site: http://www.nsalg.org.uk
Titles:
ALLOTMENT & LEISURE GARDENER

CRICINFO 624541
3 Queen Caroline Street, Hammersmith, LONDON, W6 9PE
Tel: 020 8222 1665
Web site: http://www.cricinfo.com
Titles:
CRICINFO

CRICKET WORLD MEDIA LTD 671719
24-26 London Road, GRANTHAM, NG31 6EJ
Tel: 01476 565569 **Fax:** 01476 572901
Email: info@cricketworld.com
Web site: http://www.cricketworld.com
Titles:
CRICKET WORLD
CRICKET WORLD

CRICNET MAGAZINES LTD 1643283
c/o Trinorth Ltd, The Brit Oval, Kennington, LONDON, SE11
5SS **Tel:** 020 7953 7403 **Fax:** 020 7953 8329
Email: comments@alloutcricket.co.uk
Web site: http://www.alloutcricket.co.uk
Titles:
ALL OUT CRICKET

CRIER MEDIA GROUP 13663
1st Floor Offices, 1-3 Station Road East, OXTED, RH8 0BD
Tel: 01883 734582 **Fax:** 01883 713649
Web site: http://www.crier.co.uk
Titles:
ASIA-PACIFIC BAKER
BISCUIT WORLD
EUROPEAN BAKER
POTATO PROCESSING INTERNATIONAL
POTATO STORAGE INTERNATIONAL

CRIME TIME PUBLISHING LTD 18980
7A King Henry's Walk, Islington, LONDON, N1 4NX
Tel: 020 7249 5940
Web site: http://www.crimetime.co.uk
Titles:
CRIME TIME

CRIMSON BUSINESS LTD 18986
Westminster House, Kew Road, RICHMOND, TW9 2ND
Tel: 020 8334 1600 **Fax:** 020 8334 1601
Web site: http://www.crimsonbusiness.co.uk
Titles:
GROWING BUSINESS
GROWINGBUSINESS.CO.UK
MYBUSINESS.CO.UK
STARTUPS.CO.UK

CRIMSON COMMUNICATIONS 18955
Meridian House, Royal Hill, LONDON, SE10 8RD **Tel:** +44
020 8305 6905
Titles:
ADVANCE PRODUCTION NEWS

CRITERION PUBLISHING LTD 13541
2 Darsham Walk, Lums Yard, 32 High Street, CHESHAM,
HP5 1EP **Tel:** 01494 791222 **Fax:** 01494 792223
Titles:
EUROPEAN CLEANING JOURNAL

CRM PUBLISHING LTD 1640079
BT3 Business Centre, 10 Dargan Crescent, BELFAST, BT3
9JP **Tel:** 028 9077 5577
Web site: http://www.crmpublishing.com
Titles:
HOOKER RUGBY

CROFTER INTERNET LTD 16802
Croft Farm, Spreyton, CREDITON, EX17 5EB
Tel: 01647 231527
Titles:
WOTSIT

CRONER GROUP LTD 12306
145 London Road, KINGSTON UPON THAMES, KT2 6SR
Tel: 020 8547 3333 **Fax:** 020 8547 3637
Email: info@croner.co.uk
Web site: http://www.croner.co.uk
Titles:
CRONER'S HEALTH & SAFETY AT WORK
CRONER'S PAY & BENEFITS SOURCEBOOK
CRONER'S PERSONNEL ASSISTANT'S HANDBOOK
ENERGY MANAGEMENT BRIEFING
SCHOOL LEADERSHIP

CROQUET ASSOCIATION 12941
Cheltenham Croquet Club, Old Bath Road, CHELTENHAM,
GL53 7DF **Tel:** 01242 242318
Titles:
THE CROQUET GAZETTE

CROSS & COCKADE INTERNATIONAL 17551
Cragg Cottage, The Cragg, BRAMHAM WETHERBY, LS23
6QB **Tel:** 01937 845320
Titles:
CROSS & COCKADE INTERNATIONAL

CROSS BORDER LTD 13366
Churchill House, 142-146 Old Street, LONDON, EC1V 9BW
Tel: 020 7251 7500 **Fax:** 020 7490 4349
Email: mail@thecrossbordergroup.com
Web site: http://www.thecrossbordergroup.com
Titles:
IR MAGAZINE

CROSS RHYTHMS 625200
PO Box 1110, STOKE-ON-TRENT, ST1 1XR
Tel: 0870 011 8008 **Fax:** 0870 011 7002
Web site: http://www.crossrhythms.co.uk
Titles:
CROSS RHYTHMS ONLINE

CROSS-BORDER INFORMATION   13786
19 Wellington Square, HASTINGS, TN34 1PB
Tel: 01424 721667 **Fax:** 01424 721721
Titles:
   AFRICAN ENERGY
   GULF STATES NEWSLETTER

CROWN WOOD PUBLICATIONS LTD   14689
PO Box 249, ASCOT, SL5 0BZ **Tel:** 01344 459528
Fax: 01344 862569
Email: crownwood@btconnect.com
Web site: http://www.cwponline.co.uk
Titles:
   MAINTENANCE & EQUIPMENT NEWS FOR CHURCHES
      AND SCHOOLS
   SCHOOLS EQUIPMENT NEWS DIRECT

CRU INTERNATIONAL LTD   13721
31 Mount Pleasant, LONDON, WC1X 0AD
Tel: 020 7903 2023 **Fax:** 020 7837 3558
Web site: http://www.crugroup.com
Titles:
   CIA
   CRU STEEL NEWS

CRUISING ASSOCIATION   16074
CA House, 1 Northey Street, Limehouse Basin, LONDON,
E14 8BT **Tel:** 020 7537 2828 **Fax:** 020 7537 2266
Titles:
   CRUISING - JOURNAL OF THE CRUISING ASSOCIATION

CRYSTAL COMMUNICATIONS   14107
Crystal House, 14 London Road, RAINHAM, ME8 6YX
Tel: 01634 261262 **Fax:** 01634 360514
Email: sales@aftermarket.co.uk
Web site: http://www.aftermarketnetwork.com
Titles:
   AFTERMARKET

THE CRYSTAL PALACE FOUNDATION   17553
58 Laurier Road, CROYDON, CR0 6JQ **Tel:** 07956 587257
Fax: 0870 133 7920
Email: crystalpalacefoundation@gmail.com
Web site: http://www.crystalpalacefoundation.org.uk
Titles:
   CRYSTAL PALACE FOUNDATION NEWS
   CRYSTAL PALACE MATTERS

CSC METROCENTRE LTD   1717683
Centre Management Offices, MetroCentre, GATESHEAD,
NE11 9YG **Tel:** 0191 493 0200 **Fax:** 0191 493 2756
Titles:
   METROCENTRE MAGAZINE

CSF MEDICAL COMMUNICATIONS LTD   1622486
Suite 119, Eagle Tower, Montpellier Drive, CHELTENHAM,
GL50 1TA **Tel:** 01242 223890
Web site: http://www.csfmedical.com
Titles:
   DRUGS IN CONTEXT

CSL PUBLISHING LTD   13214
Alliance House, 49 Sidney Street, CAMBRIDGE, CB2 3HX
Tel: 01223 460490 **Fax:** 01223 315960
Titles:
   4X4 MART
   ALL AT SEA
   BOAT MART
   CLASSIC CAR MART
   JET SKIER & PERSONAL WATERCRAFT MAGAZINE
   SPORTSBOAT & RIB MAGAZINE

CSMA LTD   15455
Britannia House, 21 Station Street, BRIGHTON, BN1 4DE
Tel: 01273 744744
Email: magazine@csma.uk.com
Web site: http://www.csma.uk.com
Titles:
   CSMA CLUB MAGAZINE

CSC SPORTS AND LEISURE   700591
4-8 Buckingham Place, Bellfield Road, HIGH WYCOMBE,
HP13 5HW **Tel:** 01494 888430 **Fax:** 01494 888437
Titles:
   LEISURE SCENE

C-STREAM   622960
2nd Floor, Kenilworth House, 79-80 Margaret Street,
LONDON, W1W 8TA **Tel:** 020 7079 2801
Titles:
   GTNEWS.COM

C.T.N   14787
Transport House, 128 Theobalds Road, LONDON, WC1X
8TN
Titles:
   CAB TRADE NEWS

CUBA SOLIDARITY CAMPAIGN   15689
c/o Unite - Woodberry, 218 Green Lanes, LONDON, N4 2HB
Tel: 020 8800 0155 **Fax:** 020 8800 9844
Email: office@cuba-solidarity.org.uk
Web site: http://www.cuba-solidarity.org.uk
Titles:
   CUBASI

CULLUM PUBLISHING   16648
8 Sovereign Park, Cleveland Way, HEMEL HEMPSTEAD,
HP2 7DA **Tel:** 01442 233656 **Fax:** 01442 258853
Titles:
   HEADLINES
   PRODUCTION JOURNAL

CULT TV PUBLISHING   18084
PO Box 1701, PETERBOROUGH, PE7 1ER
Tel: 01733 205009
Email: editor@cult.tv
Web site: http://www.cult.tv
Titles:
   CULT TV - THE OFFICIAL MAGAZINE

CULTURE AND SPORT GLASGOW   1735332
20 Trongate, GLASGOW, G1 5ES **Tel:** 0141 257 4350
Fax: 0141 287 5199
Web site: http://www.csglasgow.org
Titles:
   PREVIEW GLASGOW MUSEUMS MAGAZINE

CULTURESHOCK MEDIA LTD   1630601
27B Tradescant Road, LONDON, SW8 1XD
Tel: 020 7735 9263 **Fax:** 020 7735 5052
Email: info@cultureshockmedia.co.uk
Web site: http://www.cultureshockmedia.co.uk
Titles:
   V&A MAGAZINE

CUMBERLAND & WESTMORLAND HERALD   674653
14 King Street, PENRITH, CA11 7AH **Tel:** 01768 862313
Fax: 01768 890363
Email: mail@cwherald.com
Web site: http://www.cwherald.com
Titles:
   CUMBERLAND & WESTMORLAND HERALD ONLINE
   CUMBERLAND & WESTMORLAND HERALD SERIES

CUMBRIAN NEWSPAPERS LTD   14835
PO Box 7, Newspaper House, Dalston Road, CARLISLE,
CA2 5UA **Tel:** 01228 612600 **Fax:** 01228 612640
Email: news@cngroup.co.uk
Web site: http://www.newsandstar.co.uk
Titles:
   THE ADVERTISER BARROW AND WEST CUMBERLAND
   CARLISLE LIVING
   THE CUMBERLAND NEWS & GAZETTE SERIES
   CUMBRIA LIFE
   NEWS & STAR (CARLISLE)
   TIMES AND STAR SERIES
   WHITEHAVEN NEWS

CUMBRIAN PRESS GROUP   14019
3 Chatsworth Square, CARLISLE, CA1 1HB
Tel: 01228 547144 **Fax:** 01228 514747
Titles:
   CUMBRIAN EXECUTIVE
   CUMBRIAN FARMING
   GUIDE TO CUMBRIA MAGAZINE
   GUIDE TO INDUSTRY & COMMERCE IN CUMBRIA

CURRENCY PUBLICATIONS LTD   1689828
2A High Street, SHEPPERTON, TW17 9AW
Tel: 01932 267232 **Fax:** 01932 269918

Email: info@currency-news.com
Web site: http://www.currency-news.com
Titles:
   CURRENCY NEWS

CURRENT ARCHAEOLOGY   17559
Barley Mow Centre, 10 Barley Mow Passage, LONDON, W4
4PH **Tel:** 0845 644 7707 **Fax:** 020 7916 2405
Email: publisher@archaeology.co.uk
Web site: http://www.archaeology.co.uk
Titles:
   CURRENT ARCHAEOLOGY

CURRENT MEDICINE GROUP LTD   1739630
11-12 Paul Street, LONDON, EC2A 4JU **Tel:** 020 7562 2957
Fax: 020 7562 2931
Email: lucy.piper@medwire-news.md
Web site: http://www.currentmedicinegroup.com
Titles:
   MEDWIRENEWS

CURRENT PUBLISHING   1632831
Lamb House, Church Street, LONDON, W4 2PD
Tel: 0845 644 7707 **Fax:** 0845 644 7708
Titles:
   CURRENT ARCHAEOLOGY
   CURRENT WORLD ARCHAEOLOGY

CURRY LIFE LTD   1728345
Suite 9, 5 Durham Yard, Teesdale Street, LONDON, E2 6QF
Tel: 020 7729 0999 **Fax:** 020 7729 0222
Titles:
   CURRY LIFE

C.V PUBLISHERS LTD   18472
8 The Crescent, SOUTHALL, UB1 1BE **Tel:** 020 8571 1127
Fax: 020 8571 2604
Email: mail@despardesweekly.co.uk
Titles:
   DES PARDES

CW PUBLISHING   17059
1A Circus Street, OXFORD, OX4 1JR **Tel:** 01865 205522
Fax: 01865 205533
Titles:
   DESPATCH MANAGER

CW PUBLISHING GROUP   1640141
134 Liverpool Road, LONDON, N1 1LA **Tel:** 020 7665 1111
Fax: 020 7665 2222
Email: cwadmin@cwcomms.com
Web site: http://www.cwcomms.com
Titles:
   THE ALFRED DUNHILL LINKS CHAMPIONSHIP
   MANAGING GROWTH
   MUM PLUS ONE
   MYHOME
   YOU & YOUR FAMILY

CYBER COMMUNICATIONS LTD   17139
St Albans House, 98 East Hill, DARTFORD, DA1 1SB
Tel: 01322 228239 **Fax:** 01322 228239
Web site: http://www.elevation.co.uk
Titles:
   ELEVATION MAGAZINE

CYCLISTS' TOURING CLUB   15430
Parklands, GUILDFORD, GU2 9JX **Tel:** 0870 873 0060
Fax: 0870 873 0064
Web site: http://www.ctc.org.uk
Titles:
   CTC CYCLE DIGEST
   CYCLE

CYHOEDDWYR CYMRICA CYFYNGEDIG   16915
PO Box 22, CARMARTHEN, SA32 7LX **Tel:** 01267 290188
Email: admin@cambriamagazine.com
Titles:
   CAMBRIA THE NATIONAL MAGAZINE OF WALES

CYMDEITHAS BOB OWEN   15512
Tan-Y-Castell, Llanuwchllyn, Y BALA, LL23 7TA
Tel: 01678 540652

UK Publishers & Their Titles

Titles:
Y CASGLWR (THE COLLECTOR)

CYTGORD   15394
Ffordd Llanllechid, Llanllechid, BANGOR, LL57 3EE
Tel: 01248 602267 **Fax:** 01248 602267
Titles:
SOTHACH (ROCK MAGAZINE)

CYWU/UNITE THE UNION   1744054
128 Theobald's Road, Holborn, LONDON, WC1X 8TN
Tel: 020 7611 2500 **Fax:** 020 7611 2555
Titles:
RAPPORT CYWU

D.E. ALEXANDER & SONS LTD.   15073
91 Main Street, BANGOR, BT20 4AF **Tel:** 028 9127 0270
Fax: 028 9127 1544
Titles:
COUNTY DOWN SPECTATOR AND ULSTER STANDARD
SERIES

D. RILEY CARRINGTON & CO. PUBLICATIONS   17988
Oxbrook Farm, Hoby Road, Thrussington, LEICESTER, LE7
4TH **Tel:** 01664 424752 **Fax:** 01664 424678
Titles:
PRINT AND PAPER BUYER

DAIRY UK   696100
93 Baker Street, LONDON, W1U 6RL **Tel:** 020 7486 7244
Fax: 020 7487 4234
Email: info@dairyuk.org
Web site: http://www.dairyuk.org
Titles:
MILK INDUSTRY

DAISYBAKERS   1605491
Whitehill Farmhouse, Crawick, SANQUHAR, DG4 6JW
Tel: 01659 50942 **Fax:** 0870 123 1659
Titles:
NITHSDALE NEWS

DALES LIFE   692421
Suite 2 Market Chambers, 14 Market Place, BEDALE, DL8
1EQ **Tel:** 01429 835888 **Fax:** 01429 835977
Titles:
DALES LIFE

DALLAS BRETT PUBLISHING   18768
East End Farm, East End, North Leigh, WITNEY, OX29 6PX
Tel: 01993 886885 **Fax:** 01993 882660
Titles:
POLO TIMES

DAMTE LTD   1735390
38 West Street, Great Gransden, SANDY, SG19 3AU
Tel: 01767 677620
Email: info@damte.com
Web site: http://www.damte.com
Titles:
EFFICIENTENERGY.NET
MACHINEBUILDING.NET

DANCE EUROPE   16712
PO Box 12661, LONDON, E5 9TZ **Tel:** 020 8985 7767
Fax: 020 8525 0462
Titles:
DANCE EUROPE

DANCE NEWS LTD.   15402
Hamble House, Meadrow, GODALMING, GU7 3HJ
Tel: 01483 428679 **Fax:** 01483 417650
Email: editor@dance-news.co.uk
Web site: http://www.dance-news.co.uk
Titles:
DANCE NEWS

THE DANCING TIMES LTD   15399
45-47 Clerkenwell Green, LONDON, EC1R 0EB
Tel: 020 7250 3006 **Fax:** 020 7253 6679
Web site: http://www.dancing-times.co.uk

Titles:
DANCE TODAY
DANCING TIMES

DARK ARTS LTD   1606081
Unit 36, 10-50 Willow Street, LONDON, EC2A 4BH
Tel: 020 7739 7666 **Fax:** 020 7739 0544
Titles:
TERRORIZER

DARK HORSE PR   1630178
Oliver House, 54 Edward Road, West Bridgford,
NOTTINGHAM, NG2 5GB **Tel:** 0115 981 4421
Email: enquiries@darkhorsepr.co.uk
Titles:
BMI DIAMOND CLUB MAGAZINE

DARK NEON LTD   1744411
PR by email only **Tel:** 01237 441527
Titles:
BITWISE MAGAZINE

DARK SUMMER LTD   1736250
143 Walkley Crescent Road, SHEFFIELD, S6 5BA
Titles:
DARK SUMMER

DARKSIDE PUBLISHING LTD   15513
PO Box 36, LISKEARD, PL14 4YT **Tel:** 01579 340400
Fax: 01579 340400
Titles:
THE DARK SIDE

DARWIN PUBLISHING   1622111
Greenways, Bridge Road, Lower Hardres, CANTERBURY,
CT4 7AG **Tel:** 01227 464739
Titles:
WILDSCAPE

DATA MEDIA AND RESEARCH LTD.   1642407
Tel: 07092 511049 **Fax:** 07092 516002
2-3 The Academy Suite, Sheffield United Academy, Firshill
Crescent, SHEFFIELD, S4 7DR **Tel:** 0114 281 5760
Fax: 0114 281 5767
Titles:
CARSOURCE

DATA TRANSCRIPTS   12455
PO Box 14, DORKING, RH5 4YN **Tel:** 01306 884473
Fax: 01306 884473
Email: info@datatranscripts.com
Web site: http://www.woodpanelsonline.com
Titles:
FILM EXTRUSION MATERIALS AND MARKETS
BULLETIN
FLEXPACK MATERIALS & MARKETS BULLETIN
PMP DIGEST
PRESSURE SENSITIVE INDUSTRY YEARBOOK
SELF-ADHESIVE MATERIALS AND MARKETS BULLETIN

DATACENTERDYNAMICS LTD   623232
70 Clifton Street, LONDON, EC2A 4HB **Tel:** 020 7377 1907
Fax: 020 7377 9583
Web site: http://www.datacenterdynamics.com
Titles:
DATACENTREDYNAMICS FOCUS

DATATEAM PUBLISHING LTD   12325
15A London Road, MAIDSTONE, ME16 8LY
Tel: 01622 687031 **Fax:** 01622 757646
Email: info@datateam.co.uk
Web site: http://www.datateam.co.uk
Titles:
BKU MAGAZINE
BUILDING SERVICES & ENVIRONMENTAL ENGINEER
CASINO INTERNATIONAL
CONNECTING INDUSTRY
CONNECTINGINDUSTRY.COM AUTOMATION
CONNECTINGINDUSTRY.COM DESIGN SOLUTIONS
CONNECTINGINDUSTRY.COM ELECTRONICS
CONNECTINGINDUSTRY.COM ENERGY MANAGEMENT
CONNECTINGINDUSTRY.COM INSTRUMENTATION
CONNECTINGINDUSTRY.COM IRISH MANUFACTURING
CONNECTINGINDUSTRY.COM PROCESS & CONTROL
EDUCATION TODAY
ELECTRICAL ENGINEERING

ELECTRICAL WHOLESALER
EUROSLOT MAGAZINE
FACTORY EQUIPMENT
FOOTWEAR TODAY
GARDEN CENTRE UPDATE
THE INDEPENDENT ELECTRICAL RETAILER
NURSERY INDUSTRY
PARK WORLD
PLASTICS & BOARD INDUSTRIES FEDERATION
MAGAZINE
PRINTWEAR & PROMOTION
SCREEN PROCESS AND DIGITAL IMAGING
SGB GOLF
SGB SPORTS & OUTDOOR
STATIONERY & OFFICE UPDATE
VENDING INTERNATIONAL

DATEL/THIN ICE MEDIA   600419
Datel, Stone Business Park, Stafford Road, STONE, ST15
0DG **Tel:** 01785 810800 **Fax:** 01785 810820
Web site: http://www.thinicemedia.co.uk
Titles:
CODEJUNKIES

DAVID HALL PUBLISHING LTD   16243
2 Stephenson Close, Drayton Fields Industrial Estate,
DAVENTRY, NN11 8RF **Tel:** 01327 311999
Fax: 01327 311190
Web site: http://www.dhponline.com
Titles:
ADVANCED CARP FISHING
ADVANCED POLE FISHING
IRISH ANGLER
MATCH FISHING MAGAZINE
TACKLE & GUNS
TACKLE TRADE WORLD
TOTAL CARP
TOTAL COARSE FISHING
TOTAL FLYFISHER
TOTAL SEA FISHING

DAVID PUBLISHING LTD   16751
1 Friary Chambers, Whitefriargate, HULL, HU1 2HA
Tel: 01482 585735 **Fax:** 01482 229593
Titles:
HOSPITAL BULLETIN
INSIDE HOSPITALS

DAWLISH NEWSPAPERS LTD   14922
Gazette Office, 6 Park Road, DAWLISH, EX7 9LQ
Tel: 01626 864161 **Fax:** 01626 888518
Web site: http://www.internet-today.co.uk
Titles:
DAWLISH GAZETTE
TEIGNMOUTH NEWS

DAY TRIPPER   625255
239 Stoke Newington, Church Street, LONDON, N16 9HP
Web site: http://www.day-tripper.net
Titles:
DAY TRIPPER

DAYS OUT PUBLISHING LTD   1639682
41 Parkland Avenue, UPMINSTER, RM14 2EX
Tel: 01708 222394 **Fax:** 01708 228339
Web site: http://www.daysout.co.uk
Titles:
DAYS OUT

THE DAZED MAGAZINE GROUP   67409
112-116 Old Street, LONDON, EC1V 9BG
Tel: 020 7336 0766 **Fax:** 020 7336 0966
Titles:
ANOTHER MAGAZINE
ANOTHER MAN

D.C. THOMSON & CO LTD   163968
Albert Square, DUNDEE, DD1 9QJ **Tel:** 01382 223131
Fax: 01382 228812
Email: courier@dcthomson.co.uk
Web site: http://www.dcthomson.co.uk
Titles:
ANIMALS AND YOU
THE BEANO
BEANOMAX
BRATZ
CHUGGINTON
CLASSIC STITCHES
THE COURIER AND ADVERTISER

THE DANDY XTREME
EVENING TELEGRAPH & POST (DUNDEE)
THE FIRESIDE BOOK OF DAVID HOPE
GOODIE BAG MAGAZINE
I'M PREGNANT!
MY WEEKLY
PEOPLE'S FRIEND
POST PLUS
THE SCOTS MAGAZINE
SHOUT MAGAZINE
THE SUNDAY POST (DUNDEE)
THE SUNDAY POST (GLASGOW OFFICE)
THE SUNDAY POST (LONDON OFFICE)
THE WEEKLY NEWS

DCE PUBLICATIONS   1650918
The Oaks, Wesleyan Road, Ashley, MARKET DRAYTON,
TF9 4JT **Tel:** 01630 673000 **Fax:** 01630 673247
Web site: http://www.dcep.co.uk
Titles:
 EXTERNAL ENVIRONMENT - PRODUCT REVIEW
 ROOFS, FLOORS & WALLS PRODUCT REVIEW

DDGM   1717930
Unit 6, 5 Durham Yard, Teesdale Street, LONDON, E2 6QF
Tel: 0870 850 3586 **Fax:** 020 7749 1280
Web site: http://www.ddgm.co.uk
Titles:
 THE ESTATE AGENCY TIMES
 LETS FOCUS
 SQM ONLINE

THE DEAL   623186
107-111 Fleet Street, LONDON, EC4A 2AB
Tel: 020 7936 9037
Web site: http://www.thedeal.com
Titles:
 THE DAILY DEAL
 THE DEAL

DEALER-WORLD.COM   623575
Kenwood House, 1 Upper Grosvenor Road, TUNBRIDGE
WELLS, TN1 2DU **Tel:** 01892 511516 **Fax:** 01892 511517
Titles:
 AMERICAN MOTORCYCLE DEALER
 INTERNATIONAL DEALER NEWS

DECISIVE MEDIA   698841
3 London Wall Buildings, LONDON, EC2M 5PP
Tel: 020 7448 1070 **Fax:** 020 7448 1099
Titles:
 TELECOMTV

DEEBAX INTERNATIONAL   1641682
8 Sam Road, Diggle, OLDHAM, OL3 5PU **Tel:** 01457 829845
Titles:
 CUE SPORT

DEFENCE ANALYSIS LTD   699778
PO Box 29478, LONDON, NW1 8GF **Tel:** 020 7284 0331
Titles:
 DEFENCE ANALYSIS
 MILITARY LOGISTICS INTERNATIONAL

DEFENDER NEWSPAPERS   1740737
PO BOX 7731, DERBY, DE1 0RW **Tel:** 0845 46 300 46
Titles:
 THE NATIONAL STUDENT
 THE NATIONAL STUDENT MAGAZINE

DEHAVILLAND   625187
Greater London House, Hampstead Road, LONDON, NW1
7EJ **Tel:** 020 7728 5000
Web site: http://www.dehavilland.co.uk
Titles:
 DEHAVILLAND

DELANE PRESS   17506
157 Vicarage Road, Leyton, LONDON, E10 5DU
Tel: 020 8539 3876 **Fax:** 020 8539 3876
Email: keys@fsmail.net
Titles:
 CENTREPOINT
 CONTRASTS
 THE KEYS OF PETER
 THE LAITY

NAPOLEON
WARFARE

DENBY PRINT LTD   1686769
Mexborough Business Centre, College Road,
MEXBOROUGH, S64 9JP **Tel:** 01709 581400
Fax: 01709 581339
Titles:
 ROTHERHAM GAZETTE SERIES

DENEHOLME PUBLISHING   12381
2 West Street, Blackhall, HARTLEPOOL, TS27 4LJ
Tel: 0191 518 4281
Email: editor@thebusinessinformer.co.uk
Titles:
 BUSINESS INFORMER

DENNIS PUBLISHING LTD   13557
Dennis Publishing Ltd, 30 Cleveland Street, LONDON, W1T
4JD **Tel:** 020 7907 6000
Web site: http://www.dennis.co.uk
Titles:
 AUTO EXPRESS
 AUTO EXPRESS ONLINE
 BIT-TECH.NET
 BIZARRE
 COMPUTER SHOPPER
 COMPUTER SHOPPER.CO.UK
 CUSTOM PC
 DIGITAL SLR PHOTOGRAPHY
 EVO
 THE FIRST POST
 FORTEAN TIMES
 FORTEANTIMES ONLINE
 IGIZMO
 IMOTOR
 INSIDEPOKER
 IT PRO
 MACUSER
 MEN'S FITNESS
 MICRO MART
 MONKEY
 OCTANE
 PC PRO
 PC PRO ONLINE
 POKER PLAYER
 VIZ
 THE WEEK

DENTAL LABORATORIES ASSOCIATION LTD   14546
44-46 Wollaton Road, Beeston, NOTTINGHAM, NG9 2NR
Tel: 0115 925 4888 **Fax:** 0115 925 4800
Email: info@dla.org.uk
Web site: http://www.dla.org.uk
Titles:
 DENTALLAB JOURNAL

THE DENTAL PRACTITIONERS' ASSOCIATION   14548
61 Harley Street, LONDON, W1G 8QU **Tel:** 020 7636 1072
Fax: 020 7636 1086
Email: info@uk-dentistry.org
Web site: http://www.uk-dentistry.org
Titles:
 THE GDP

DENTAL TRIBUNE INTERNATIONAL   1759284
4th Floor, Treasure House, 19-21 Hatton Garden, LONDON,
EC1N 8BA **Tel:** 020 7400 8964 **Fax:** 020 7400 8988
Titles:
 DENTAL TRIBUNE

DEPARTMENT FOR BUSINESS   12603
1 Victoria Street, LONDON, SW1H 0ET **Tel:** 020 7215 4117
Fax: 020 7215 3609
Email: dti.news@dti.gsi.gov.uk
Web site: http://www.dti.gov.uk
Titles:
 INTERFACE

DEPARTMENT FOR INTERNATIONAL DEVELOPMENT
     17254
1 Palace Street, LONDON, SW1E 5HE **Tel:** 020 7023 0000
Fax: 020 7023 0016
Email: enquiry@dfid.gov.uk
Web site: http://www.dfid.gov.uk
Titles:
 DEVELOPMENTS

DERBY DAILY TELEGRAPH LTD   12801
Northcliffe House, Meadow Road, DERBY, DE1 2BH
Tel: 01332 291111 **Fax:** 01332 253011
Web site: http://www.thisisderbyshire.co.uk
Titles:
 DERBY EXPRESS AND MESSENGER SERIES
 DERBY TELEGRAPH
 THE DERBYSHIRE MAGAZINE

DERBYSHIRE COUNTY COUNCIL   1763838
Derbyshire County Council, County Hall, MATLOCK, DE4
3AG
Titles:
 QUIDS IN

DERBYSHIRE TIMES NEWSPAPER GROUP   14917
37 Station Road, CHESTERFIELD, S41 7XD
Tel: 01246 504500 **Fax:** 01246 504584
Web site: http://www.derbyshiretimes.co.uk
Titles:
 BUXTON ADVERTISER AND TIMES SERIES
 CHESTERFIELD & DRONFIELD ADVERTISER SERIES
 CHESTERFIELD EXPRESS
 EASTWOOD & KIMBERLEY ADVERTISER
 RIPLEY & HEANOR NEWS

DERRY JOURNAL LTD   15074
22 Buncrana Road, LONDONDERRY, BT48 8AA
Tel: 028 7127 2200 **Fax:** 028 7127 2260
Web site: http://www.derrytoday.com
Titles:
 DERRY JOURNAL SERIES
 DONEGAL ON SUNDAY
 DONEGAL PEOPLE'S PRESS
 SUNDAY JOURNAL

DESCARTES PUBLISHING LTD   600518
81 Park Road, PETERBOROUGH, PE1 2TN
Tel: 01733 808550 **Fax:** 01733 898443
Titles:
 ATHLETICS WEEKLY

THE DESIGN AND TECHNOLOGY ASSOCIATION   13149
16 Wellesbourne House, Walton Road, Wellesbourne,
WARWICK, CV35 9JB **Tel:** 01789 470007
Fax: 01789 841955
Web site: http://www.data.org.uk
Titles:
 D & T NEWS
 D&T PRACTICE
 DESIGN AND TECHNOLOGY EDUCATION: AN
  INTERNATIONAL JOURNAL
 DESIGNING

THE DESIGN ROOM   1706884
Salamander Lodge, 80 Sandford Road, Ranalagh, DUBLIN 6
Tel: 01 49 79 022
Email: info@designroom.ie
Web site: http://www.designroom.ie
Titles:
 THE PROPERTY PROFESSIONAL

DESIGNS FOR YOU LTD   1763612
Oak Court, Sandridge Park, Porters Wood, ST ALBANS, AL3
6PH **Tel:** 01727 731812
Titles:
 CHROMATOGRAPHY TODAY

DESIRABLE FISH MARKETING   1724380
31B Gaskell Street, Stockton Heath, WARRINGTON, WA4
2UN **Tel:** 01925 262839
Email: info@desirablefish.com
Web site: http://www.desirablefish.com
Titles:
 PENDRO MAGAZINE

THE DESPATCH ASSOCIATION   17077
Lamb's End House, 36 Church Road, Magdalen, KING'S
LYNN, PE34 3DG **Tel:** 01553 813479 **Fax:** 01553 813479
Email: phil@despatch.co.uk
Web site: http://www.despatch.co.uk
Titles:
 DESPATCHES

UK Publishers & Their Titles

DESTINATION MAPS & MEDIA LTD 694134
Brook House, Brook Street, Hazel Grove, STOCKPORT, SK7
4QX **Tel:** 0161 292 3432 **Fax:** 0161 292 3299
Titles:
 CONSTRUCTION HOUSING
 CONSTRUCTION NATIONAL
 ECCLESIASTICAL AND HERITAGE WORLD
 YOUR WITNESS

DETAIL EXTRA LTD 17667
Media House, Hallidays Yard, Radcliffe Road, STAMFORD,
PE9 1ED **Tel:** 01780 765960 **Fax:** 01780 765904
Titles:
 GIFTWARE REVIEW

THE DEUX CHEVAUX CLUB OF GREAT BRITAIN 15446
PO Box 602, CRICK, NN6 7BR
Email: press@2cvgb.com
Web site: http://www.2cvgb.com
Titles:
 2CVGB NEWS

DEVELOPMENT CONTROL SEVICES LTD 1737069
Suite1, Fullers Court, Lower Quay Street, GLOUCESTER,
GL1 2LW **Tel:** 01452 835820 **Fax:** 01452 835822
Email: dcs@haymarket.com
Web site: http://www.planningresource.co.uk/dcs
Titles:
 MINERAL PLANNING
 WASTE PLANNING

DEVELOPMENT HELL LTD 1621025
90-92 Pentonville Road, LONDON, N1 9HS
Tel: 020 7520 8625 **Fax:** 020 7833 9900
Titles:
 MIXMAG
 THE WORD

DEVON & CORNWALL NEWSPAPERS LTD 14924
Old Manor House, 63 Wolborough Street, NEWTON ABBOT,
TQ12 1NE **Tel:** 01626 355577 **Fax:** 01626 334595
Titles:
 DEVON DIARY
 MID-DEVON ADVERTISER SERIES

DEVON BEEKEEPERS ASSOCIATION 621519
Landscore, Eastern Road, Ashburton, NEWTON ABBOT,
TQ13 7AR **Tel:** 01364 652640
Titles:
 BEEKEEPING

DEVON COUNTY COUNCIL AND TORBAY COUNCIL
 673711
Adult & Community Services Directorate, County Hall,
Topsham Road, EXETER, EX2 4QR **Tel:** 01392 382332
Fax: 01392 382363
Web site: http://www.devon.gov.uk
Titles:
 DEVON LINK

DEWBERRY REDPOINT LTD 13691
Progressive House, 2 Maidstone Road, Sidcup,
PULBOROUGH, DA14 5HZ **Tel:** 0845 000 2500
Web site: http://www.dewberryredpoint.co.uk
Titles:
 ASPIRE
 THE BULLETIN
 COST SECTOR CATERING
 EAT OUT
 FD
 FOODSERVICE UPDATE
 THE LONDON SOURCE
 STOCKPOT

DEWSBURY REPORTER GROUP 15012
1 Market Street, CLECKHEATON, BD19 3RT
Tel: 01274 874635 **Fax:** 01274 851304
Titles:
 SPENBOROUGH GUARDIAN

DFA MEDIA LTD 1653951
Cape House, 60A Priory Road, TONBRIDGE, TN9 2BL
Tel: 01732 370340 **Fax:** 01732 360034
Email: ian@dfamedia.co.uk
Web site: http://www.pwemag.co.uk

Titles:
 DRIVES & CONTROLS
 HYDRAULICS & PNEUMATICS
 PLANT & WORKS ENGINEERING

DH PUBLISHING LTD 622199
Imperial House, Imperial Park, 46-48 Towerfield Road,
Shoeburyness, SOUTHEND-ON-SEA, SS3 9QT
Tel: 0870 766 8530 **Fax:** 0870 766 9582
Titles:
 ONLINE RECRUITMENT

DIA INTERNATIONAL LTD 14127
Safety House, Beddington Farm Road, CROYDON, CR0 4XZ
Tel: 020 8665 5151 **Fax:** 020 8665 5565
Titles:
 DRIVING INSTRUCTOR
 DRIVING MAGAZINE

DIABETES UK 12649
10 Parkway, Camden, LONDON, NW1 7AA
Tel: 020 7424 1000 **Fax:** +44
Web site: http://www.diabetes.org.uk
Titles:
 BALANCE

DIAL-A-CAB 16852
Dial-a-Cab House, 39-47 East Road, LONDON, N1 6AH
Tel: 020 7251 0581 **Fax:** 020 7250 0581
Web site: http://www.dial-a-cab.co.uk
Titles:
 CALL SIGN

DIAMOND PUBLISHING LTD 15392
Diamond Publishing Ltd, Unit 101, 140 Wales Farm Road,
LONDON, W3 6UG **Tel:** 020 8752 8181 **Fax:** 020 8752 8185
Web site: http://www.metropolis.co.uk
Titles:
 THE COUNTRYMAN'S WEEKLY
 FAMILY HISTORY MONTHLY
 RECORD COLLECTOR

DIANA ZEUNA 16671
Lindford Cottage, Church Lane, Cocking, MIDHURST, GU29
0HW **Tel:** 01730 812419 **Fax:** 01730 812419
Email: heavyhorse@mistral.co.uk
Web site: http://www.heavyhorseworld.co.uk
Titles:
 HEAVY HORSE WORLD

THE DIARY 17993
30 Harcourt Street, LONDON, W1H 4AA **Tel:** 020 7724 7770
Fax: 020 7724 7357
Email: gail@diaryd.com
Titles:
 DIARY
 DIARY DIRECTORY

DIESEL & GAS TURBINE PUBLICATIONS 13945
120 Long Acre, Covent Garden, LONDON, WC2E 9ST
Tel: 020 7632 9580 **Fax:** 020 7632 9585
Web site: http://www.dieselpub.com
Titles:
 DIESEL & GAS TURBINE WORLDWIDE
 DIESEL PROGRESS INTERNATIONAL

DIGEST PUBLISHING 18736
PO Box 45358, LONDON, SE14 5ZP **Tel:** 020 8677 4701
Email: editor@theridersdigest.co.uk
Titles:
 THE RIDER'S DIGEST

DIGITAL DOTS LTD 1681288
The Clock Tower, Southover, Spring Lane, Burwash,
ETCHINGHAM, TN19 7JB **Tel:** 01435 883565
Web site: http://www.digitaldots.org
Titles:
 SPINDRIFT

DIGITAL LOOK LTD 1733298
4th Floor, Bankside House, 107 Leadenhall Street,
LONDON, EC3A 4AF **Tel:** 020 7743 0050
Fax: 020 7504 3627
Web site: http://www.digitallook.com

Titles:
 AIM BULLETIN

DIGITALSHIP LTD 625362
Drewry House, 213 Marsh Wall, LONDON, E14 9FJ
Tel: 020 7510 0015 **Fax:** 020 7510 2344
Titles:
 DIGITAL SHIP

DIOCESE OF BATH & WELLS 15884
The Old Deanery, WELLS, BA5 2UG
Titles:
 THE GRAPEVINE

DIOCESE OF CHELMSFORD 18076
Diocesan Office, 53 New Street, CHELMSFORD, CM1 1AT
Tel: 01245 294400 **Fax:** 01245 294477
Email: mail@chelmsford.anglican.org
Web site: http://www.chelmsford.anglican.org
Titles:
 THE MONTH (INCORPORATING EAST WINDOW)
 NB

THE DIOCESE OF DURHAM 1691143
Diocesan Office, Auckland Castle, Market Place, BISHOP
AUCKLAND, DL14 7QJ **Tel:** 01388 604515
Email: diocesan.secretary@durham.anglican.org
Web site: http://www.durham.anglican.org
Titles:
 DURHAM NEWSLINK

DIOCESES OF HEREFORD 1649908
The Palace, HEREFORD, HR4 9BL **Tel:** 01432 373300
Fax: 01432 352952
Email: thenewspaper@hereford.anglican.org
Web site: http://www.hereford.anglican.org
Titles:
 THE NEWSPAPER

DIRECT MARKETING INTERNATIONAL LTD 13416
New Broad Street House, New Broad Street, LONDON, EC2
M1NH **Tel:** 020 7043 9008 **Fax:** 020 7023 4954
Email: sally@dmi.news.com
Web site: http://www.dmionline.net
Titles:
 DIRECT MARKETING INTERNATIONAL

DIRECT PUBLISHING LTD 13415
Kentons House, 24 Blendon Road, BEXLEY, DA5 1BW
Tel: 0870 701 3536
Email: directpublishing@ntlworld.com
Web site: http://www.directpublishing.webeden.co.uk
Titles:
 BUILDING & CONSTRUCTION
 ELECTRONIC PRODUCTION
 ENGINEERING & TECHNOLOGY
 FOOD & BEVERAGE
 GARDEN & HORTICULTURE
 HOME & INTERIOR WORLD
 TEST MAGAZINE
 TOURISM, TRAVEL & HOTELS

DIRECTOR PUBLICATIONS LTD 13739
116 Pall Mall, LONDON, SW1Y 5ED **Tel:** 020 7839 1233
Fax: 020 7766 8840
Titles:
 AFTER HOURS
 DIRECTOR

DIRECTORS GUILD OF GREAT BRITAIN 13456
4 Windmill Street, LONDON, W1T 2HZ **Tel:** 020 7836 3602
Fax: 020 7836 3603
Titles:
 DIRECT

DISCOVERY BOOKS & PUBLICATIONS 164471
29 Hacketts Lane, WOKING, GU22 8PP **Tel:** 01932 400800
Fax: 01932 346201
Email: discoverybooks@ntlworld.com
Titles:
 SPA WELLBEING

DISTINCTIVE PUBLISHING   1653919
24 Lancaster Street, Summerhill, NEWCASTLE UPON TYNE,
NE4 6EU **Tel:** 0191 298 3571 **Fax:** 0191 298 3561
Titles:
    NORTH WORKS
    WAY TO GO

DIVERSIFIED BUSINESS COMMUNICATIONS   624627
Blenheim House, 119-120 Church Street, BRIGHTON, BN1
1UD **Tel:** 01273 645110 **Fax:** 01273 645169
Titles:
    NATURAL PRODUCTS

DIVINE MARKETING LTD   1744316
1st Floor, 43 Market Place, WETHERBY, LS22 6LN
Tel: 01937 589777 **Fax:** 01937 587788
Web site: http://www.divineagency.co.uk
Titles:
    CLOUD NINE

D.J. MURPHY (PUBLISHERS) LTD   15655
Headley House, Headley Road, Grayshott, HINDHEAD,
GU26 6TU **Tel:** 01428 601020 **Fax:** 01428 601030
Email: djm@djmurphy.co.uk
Titles:
    HORSE & RIDER
    PONY MAGAZINE

DJ MAGAZINE LTD   1729641
183 Kingston Road, LONDON, SW19 1LH
Tel: 020 8545 0955
Web site: http://www.djmag.com
Titles:
    DJ

DJ MEDIA   1757259
PO Box 716, WORCESTER, WR2 4WN **Tel:** 01905 429018
Web site: http://www.energy-now.co.uk
Titles:
    ENERGY NOW

DJA DESIGN   14786
PO Box 3472, BARNET, EN5 9HF **Tel:** 020 8440 3333
Titles:
    THE CAB DRIVER
    STEERING WHEEL

DMA LTD   17777
13 College Approach, Greenwich, LONDON, SE10 9HY
Tel: 020 8858 9771
Email: dmaltd@dma.eclipse.co.uk
Titles:
    CENTRAL

DMC PUBLISHING LTD   13236
PO Box 89, SLOUGH, SL1 8NA **Tel:** 01628 667124
Fax: 01628 605246
Titles:
    UPDATE

DMG BUSINESS MEDIA   1686208
Westgate House, 120-130 Station Road, REDHILL, RH1 1ET
Tel: 01737 855000 **Fax:** 01737 855474
Web site: http://www.dmgworldmedia.com
Titles:
    ALUMINIUM INTERNATIONAL TODAY
    EAS EUROPEAN ADHESIVES AND SEALANTS
    FURNACES INTERNATIONAL
    GLASS INTERNATIONAL
    OILS & FATS INTERNATIONAL
    SPECIALITY CHEMICALS MAGAZINE
    STEEL TIMES INTERNATIONAL INCORPORATING STEEL
      TIMES

DMG WORLD MEDIA   698710
Equitable House, Lyon Road, HARROW, HA1 2EW
Tel: 01737 855066
Web site: http://www.dmgworldmedia.com
Titles:
    APCJ ASIA PACIFIC COATINGS JOURNAL
    DAILY MAIL SKI & SNOWBOARD MAGAZINE
    PPCJ POLYMERS PAINT COLOUR JOURNAL

DNG MEDIA   15047
96 High Street, ANNAN, DG12 6EJ **Tel:** 01461 202417
Fax: 01461 205659
Web site: http://www.dumfriescourt.co.uk
Titles:
    ANNANDALE OBSERVER SERIES

DODS   1653690
Westminster Tower, 3rd Floor, 3 Albert Embankment,
LONDON, SE1 7SP **Tel:** 020 7091 7500 **Fax:** 020 7091 7525
Web site: http://www.dodsparlicom.com
Titles:
    CIVIL SERVICE WORLD
    EPOLITIX.COM
    THE HOUSE MAGAZINE
    PUBLIC AFFAIRS NEWS

DOG WORLD LTD   15642
Somerfield House, Wotton Road, ASHFORD, TN23 6LW
Tel: 01233 621877 **Fax:** 01233 645669
Web site: http://www.dogworld.co.uk
Titles:
    DOG WORLD

DOGS TRUST   18839
17 Wakley Street, LONDON, EC1V 7RQ **Tel:** 020 7837 0006
Web site: http://www.dogstrust.org.uk
Titles:
    WAG

THE DOLMETSCH FOUNDATION   17492
Jesses, Grayswood Road, HASLEMERE, GU27 2BS
Tel: 01458 851561
Titles:
    THE CONSORT, EARLY MUSIC JOURNAL

**DORSET BUSINESS - THE CHAMBER OF COMMERCE
AND INDUSTRY**   14716
Chamber House, Office Park, Ling Road, Tower Park,
POOLE, BH12 4NZ **Tel:** 01202 714800
Email: contact@dorsetbusiness.net
Titles:
    DORSET BUSINESS

THE DORSET MAGAZINE LTD   17002
7 The Leanne, Sandford Lane, WAREHAM, BH20 4DY
Tel: 01929 551264 **Fax:** 01929 552099
Titles:
    DORSET LIFE THE DORSET MAGAZINE

DOUGLAS MCLEAN PUBLISHING   671731
The New Building, Ellwood Road, Milkwall, COLEFORD,
GL16 7LE **Tel:** 01594 833366
Titles:
    DEAF WORLDS: THE INTERNATIONAL JOURNAL OF
      DEAF STUDIES

DOW JONES & CO INC.   14824
10 Fleet Place, Limeburner Lane, LONDON, EC4M 7QN
Tel: 020 7842 9200 **Fax:** 020 7842 9201
Titles:
    THE WALL STREET JOURNAL EUROPE

DOW JONES INTERNATIONAL, LTD.   1200813
90 Long Acre, LONDON, WC2E 9PR **Tel:** 020 7842 9608
Fax: 020 7842 9650
Web site: http://www.traderdaily.co.uk
Titles:
    TRADER MONTHLY MAGAZINE

DP MEDIA   17491
Unit 25, The Coach House, 2 Upper York Street, BRISTOL,
BS2 8QN **Tel:** 0117 904 1283 **Fax:** 0117 904 0085
Email: sales@dpmedia.co.uk
Web site: http://www.dpmedia.co.uk
Titles:
    ARC MAGAZINE
    ICON NEWS

DPA PUBLISHING   13896
PO Box 419, FOLKESTONE, CT20 3GU **Tel:** 01303 238002
Fax: 01303 237996

Titles:
    THE PROFESSIONAL PAINTER & DECORATOR

DPS PUBLISHING LIMITED   1675641
Green Hedges, Melfort Road, CROWBOROUGH, TN6 1QT
Tel: 01892 664555 **Fax:** 01560 1256390
Titles:
    TURF BUSINESS

DR HARNISCH VERLAGSGES MBH   1654962
2 Kilvinton Drive, ENFIELD, EN2 0BD **Tel:** 020 8363 3052
Titles:
    WOODWORKING INTERNATIONAL

**DRAGON MARKETING FOR THE HAIRDRESSING
COUNCIL**   13893
Dragon Studios, Blackhouse Road, Colgate, HORSHAM,
RH13 6HS **Tel:** 01293 851101 **Fax:** 01293 851112
Web site: http://www.dragon-marketing.co.uk
Titles:
    THE HAIRDRESSER

DRAGOON PUBLISHING LTD   1653875
Dane Mill Business Centre, Broadhurst Lane, CONGLETON,
CW12 1LA
Titles:
    SKIRMISH

DRAIN TRADER LTD   18370
Units 6-8, Home Farm, Quat Goose Lane, Swindon Village,
CHELTENHAM, GL51 9RP **Tel:** 01242 576777
Fax: 01242 577733
Web site: http://www.draintraderltd.com
Titles:
    DRAIN TRADER MAGAZINE

DRIFT MAGAZINE   1714848
22 Church Lane, Clifton, BRISTOL, BS8 4TR
Tel: 0117 929 1390
Titles:
    DRIFT

DRIVEMEDIA LTD   1649710
45 Queen Street, EDINBURGH, EH2 3NH **Tel:** 01578 750693
Fax: 0131 225 6317
Web site: http://www.cateringscotland.com
Titles:
    CATERING IN SCOTLAND

DRUGSCOPE   1653564
Prince Consort House, 109-111 Farringdon Road, LONDON,
EC1R 3BW
Titles:
    DRUGLINK

DSA PUBLISHING   17704
26A Queens Road, SWANAGE, BH19 2ER
Tel: 01929 421974 **Fax:** 01929 421974
Titles:
    GEAR WHEELS INCORPORATING WESSEX WHEELS

DSN PUBLISHING   14128
The Lansdowne Building, Crowhurst Road, Hollingbury,
BRIGHTON, BN1 8AF **Tel:** 01273 566058
Fax: 01273 566059
Titles:
    ADINEWS

DTZ   1741543
199 St. Vincent Street, GLASGOW, G2 5QD
Titles:
    HILLSTREET MAGAZINE

DUNDEE UNIVERSITY PUBLICATIONS BOARD   13096
University of Dundee, Students Association, Perth Road,
DUNDEE, DD1 4HN **Tel:** 01382 386060
Web site: http://www.dusa.co.uk
Titles:
    THE MAGDALEN

UK Publishers & Their Titles

THE DUNFERMLINE PRESS GROUP 15033
Pitreavie Business Park, Queensferry Road, DUNFERMLINE,
KY11 8QS **Tel:** 01383 728201 **Fax:** 01383 737040
Email: enquiries@dunfermlinepress.co.uk
Web site: http://www.dunfermlinepress.com

Titles:
    DUNFERMLINE PRESS AND WEST OF FIFE ADVERTISER
    EAST LOTHIAN COURIER
    FIFE AND KINROSS EXTRA
    THE SCOTTISH CURLER
    STIRLING NEWS INCORPORATING ALLOA AND
        HILLFOOT WEEKENDER

DUNSTANS PUBLISHING 18675
Stodmarsh Enterprise Centre, Stodmarsh, CANTERBURY,
CT3 4BE **Tel:** 01227 722227 **Fax:** 01227 787658

Titles:
    ETHICAL PERFORMANCE

DUNWOODY MARKETING COMMUNICATIONS 1621016
First Floor Suite, 65 The Broadway, HAYWARDS HEATH,
RH16 3AS **Tel:** 01635 35599 **Fax:** 01635 845811
Web site: http://www.dunwoody.co.uk

Titles:
    GLOUCESTER RUGBY FOOTBALL CLUB MATCHDAY
        MAGAZINE
    THOROUGHBRED OWNER & BREEDER
    UP FRONT THE OFFICIAL MAGAZINE OF GLOUCESTER
        RUGBY CLUB

DURIAN PUBLICATIONS LTD 15816
81 Rivington Street, LONDON, EC2A 3AY
Tel: 020 3372 6111 **Fax:** 020 3178 7042
Web site: http://www.frieze.com

Titles:
    FRIEZE

DUTCH PUBLISHING 1691147
16 Tedder Road, Halton Camp, AYLESBURY, HP22 5QE

Titles:
    CONTEMPORARY ZONE

DUVAN LTD 18651
98 Hillfield Avenue, Hornsey, LONDON, N8 7DN
Tel: 020 8292 0822
Email: tmbweekly@btinternet.com

Titles:
    TMB WEEKLY: THE MAGAZINE BUSINESS WEEKLY

DV8 PUBLICATIONS LTD 16495
28 Poole Hill, BOURNEMOUTH, BH2 5PS
Tel: 01202 388388 **Fax:** 01202 250869
Email: mail@dv8online.co.uk
Web site: http://www.dv8online.co.uk

Titles:
    DV8 MAGAZINE BOURNEMOUTH

DVD TIMES 1642257
49 Elgar Close, SWINDON, SN25 2HG **Tel:** 01793 703714

Titles:
    DVD TIMES

DVV MEDIA UK LTD 1735330
9 Sutton Court Road, SUTTON, SM1 4SZ
Tel: 020 8652 5200 **Fax:** 020 8652 5210
Email: sales@railwaygazette.com
Web site: http://www.railwaygazette.com

Titles:
    RAIL BUSINESS INTELLIGENCE
    RAILWAY GAZETTE INTERNATIONAL

DYNAMIS PLC 1716376
Dynamis House, 6-8 Sycamore Street, LONDON, EC1Y 0SW
Tel: 020 7324 1930 **Fax:** 020 7324 1931
Web site: http://www.dynamis.co.uk

Titles:
    BUSINESSESFORSALE.COM
    BUSINESSWINGS.CO.UK
    FRANCHISESALES.COM

E. & R. INGLIS 15049
219 Argyll Street, DUNOON, PA23 7QT **Tel:** 01369 706854
Fax: 01369 703458

Titles:
    DUNOON OBSERVER & ARGYLLSHIRE STANDARD

EAC PUBLISHING 15967
Suite 3, 2nd Floor, 1-7 Castle Street, CARDIFF, CF10 2BS
Tel: 029 2025 6881

Titles:
    BUZZ

EAP GROUP BUSINESS MEDIA 18383
Suite 207, Parkway House, Sheen Lane, LONDON, SW14
8LS **Tel:** 020 8392 1122 **Fax:** 020 8392 1422
Email: info@eapgroup.com
Web site: http://www.eapgroup.com

Titles:
    ARAB BANKER
    INTERNATIONAL BUSINESS OPPORTUNITIES
    THE MIDDLE EAST IN EUROPE

EAPGROUP INTERNATIONAL MEDIA 15815
PO Box 13666, LONDON, SW14 8WF **Tel:** 020 8392 1122
Fax: 020 8392 1422
Email: main@eapgroup.com
Web site: http://www.eapgroup.com

Titles:
    EASTERN ART REPORT
    EASTERN ART REPORT ON LINE

EARLYBIRD FARMING PUBLICATIONS LTD 14023
Parkside, London Road, IPSWICH, IP2 0SS
Tel: 01473 691888 **Fax:** 01473 691886
Web site: http://www.farmersguide.co.uk

Titles:
    FARMERS GUIDE

EAST AYRSHIRE COUNCIL 1654174
Council Headquarters, London Road, KILMARNOCK, KA3
7BU **Tel:** 01563 576000 **Fax:** 01563 576500
Email: the.council@east-ayrshire.gov.uk
Web site: http://www.east-ayrshire.gov.uk

Titles:
    HEADLINES

EAST LANCASHIRE NEWSPAPERS LTD 14734
Bull Street, BURNLEY, BB11 1DP **Tel:** 01282 426161
Fax: 01282 618626

Titles:
    BURNLEY EXPRESS AND REPORTER SERIES
    LEADER TIMES SERIES

EAST MIDLANDS NEWSPAPERS LTD 17178
New Telegraph House, 57 Priestgate, PETERBOROUGH,
PE1 1JW **Tel:** 01733 555111 **Fax:** 01733 555188

Titles:
    THE CITIZEN (LYNN & DISTRICT)
    ET BUSINESS
    THE LOCAL (BOURNE, THE DEEPINGS)
    LYNN NEWS SERIES
    PETERBOROUGHTODAY

EAST OF SCOTLAND GOLF ALLIANCE 1654117
21 Castle Street, DUNDEE, DD1 3AA

Titles:
    EAST OF SCOTLAND GOLF

EAST SURREY & SUSSEX NEWSPAPERS PLC 17528
Trinity House, 51 London Road, REIGATE, RH2 9PR
Tel: 01737 732000 **Fax:** 01737 732119

Titles:
    ADVERTISER SERIES (SURREY)

EASTCASTLE PUBLISHING 674564
Julia House, 40-44 Newman Street, LONDON, W1T 1QD
Tel: 020 7436 1088

Titles:
    E-TID.COM

EASTERN MEDIA GROUP 1639977
160 Rolfe Street, SMETHWICK, B66 2AU
Tel: 0121 523 0115 **Fax:** 0121 523 0107

Titles:
    EASTERN VOICE
    SIKH TIMES

EASTWICK PUBLISHING LTD 622310
15 Whitecliff Road, POOLE, BH14 8DU **Tel:** 01202 737678
Fax: 01202 710544

Titles:
    ENJOY DORSET & HAMPSHIRE MAGAZINE

EAT ME MEDIA 1680893
Mappin House, 4 Winsley Street, LONDON, W1W 8HF
Tel: 020 7247 6504 **Fax:** 020 7247 6556

Titles:
    DISORDER MAGAZINE

EATON PUBLICATIONS 15301
55 High Street, TEDDINGTON, TW11 8HA
Tel: 020 8943 4288 **Fax:** 020 8943 4312
Email: enquiries@divermag.com
Web site: http://www.divernet.com

Titles:
    DIVER
    DIVERNET

EBCON PUBLISHING 1714935
2 Shaw Close, Peneden Heath, MAIDSTONE, ME14 5DN
Tel: 01622 692885

Titles:
    AIRSOFT INTERNATIONAL
    RAIDER

EBEA 16763
The Forum, 277 London Road, BURGESS HILL, RH15 9QU
Tel: 01444 240150 **Fax:** 01444 240101 .
Email: office@ebea.org.uk
Web site: http://www.ebea.org.uk

Titles:
    TEACHING BUSINESS AND ECONOMICS

EBONY MEDIA LTD 16561
PO Box 25, LISKEARD, PL14 6XX **Tel:** 01579 340100
Fax: 01579 340400

Titles:
    WORKBOX

EBONYONLINE COMMUNICATIONS LTD 1717437
Coopers Yard (Amani Training), Westow Hill, LONDON, SE19
1TQ **Tel:** 020 8670 8200

Titles:
    BREEZE MAGAZINE
    EBONYONLINE

EBURY PRESS 1653657
13 Little London, CHICHESTER, PO19 1NZ

Titles:
    THE IDLER

EC MEDIA LTD. 16633
23 Uvedale Road, ENFIELD, EN2 6HA **Tel:** 020 8366 3331
Fax: 020 8366 3331

Titles:
    PANEL PRODUCTION

ECHO NEWSPAPERS 13049
Newspaper House, Chester Hall Lane, BASILDON, SS14
3BL **Tel:** 01268 522792 **Fax:** 01268 532060

Titles:
    SOUTHEND STANDARD SERIES

ECI PUBLISHING LIMITED 1737535
Finsbury Business Centre, 40 Bowling Green Lane,
LONDON, EC1R 0NE **Tel:** 020 7415 7099
Email: mail@ec1publishing.com

Titles:
    F2 FREELANCE PHOTOGRAPHER

ECO LTD 1742725
PO Box 900, BROMLEY, BR1 9FF **Tel:** 020 8315 7565
Fax: 0870 137 2360
Email: info@ecoharmony.com
Web site: http://www.ecoharmony.com

Titles:
    BOILING POINT

ECO-LOGICA LTD 16688
53 Derwent Road, LANCASTER, LA1 3ES **Tel:** 01524 63175
Titles:
WORLD TRANSPORT POLICY & PRACTICE

ECONOMATTERS LTD 14075
35 New Bridge Street, LONDON, EC4V 6BW
Tel: 020 7650 1460 **Fax:** 020 7650 1461
Titles:
GAS MATTERS
LNG FOCUS

ECONOMIST INTELLIGENCE UNIT 13396
26 Red Lion Square, LONDON, WC1R 4HQ
Tel: 020 7576 8000 **Fax:** 020 7576 8485
Email: london@eiu.com
Web site: http://www.eiu.com
Titles:
BUSINESS AFRICA
BUSINESS EUROPE
EUROPEAN POLICY ANALYST
WORLDWIDE COST OF LIVING SURVEY

THE ECONOMIST NEWSPAPER LTD 15087
25 St. James's Street, LONDON, SW1A 1HG
Tel: 020 7830 7000
Web site: http://www.economist.com
Titles:
THE ECONOMIST
INTELLIGENT LIFE
MOREINTELLIGENTLIFE.COM
THE WORLD IN

THE ECONOMY NEWS 1764346
29 Links Avenue, MORDEN, SM4 5AE **Tel:** 07874 085952
Titles:
THE ECONOMY NEWS

ECOSYSTEMS LTD 1640333
118 Commercial Street, LONDON, E1 6NF
Tel: 020 7422 8100 **Fax:** 020 7422 8101
Email: ecosystems@theecologist.org
Web site: http://www.theecologist.org
Titles:
THE ECOLOGIST
THE ECOLOGIST ONLINE

ECR PUBLISHING PARTNERSHIP 13324
The Granary, High Street, Blakeney, HOLT, NR25 7AL
Tel: 01263 741126 **Fax:** 01263 741183
Email: alex@europeancardreview.com
Web site: http://www.europeancardreview.com
Titles:
PAYMENTS CARDS & MOBILE

ECRA PUBLISHING LTD 12851
Unit 21, 41 Old Birley Street, MANCHESTER, M15 5RF
Tel: 0161 226 2929 **Fax:** 0161 226 6277
Web site: http://www.ethicalconsumer.org
Titles:
ETHICAL CONSUMER
THE ETHICAL CONSUMER

EDDIE MAYS 1605993
Sheridan, Rutland Gardens, Bursledon, SOUTHAMPTON,
SO31 8FZ **Tel:** 023 8040 2194
Web site: http://www.eddiemays.com
Titles:
GYBE

EDEN PUBLISHING COMPANY 14010
37 Valiant House, Vicarage Crescent, LONDON, SW11 3LU
Tel: 020 7228 3674
Titles:
DAIRY INDUSTRY NEWSLETTER

THE EDGE 697313
65 Guinness Buildings, Hammersmith, LONDON, W6 8BD
Tel: 0845 456 9337
Titles:
THE EDGE

EDGE MEDIA AND RESEARCH 1740924
Suite 207, Linen Hall, 162-168 Regent Street, LONDON, WIB
5TB
Titles:
HM HEALTH MATTERS

EDGEMOOR PUBLISHING LTD 1748873
Wykeham House, 3 Station Road, OKEHAMPTON, EX20
1DY **Tel:** 01837 659224
Titles:
DARTMOOR MAGAZINE

EDINBURGH GUIDE 625194
14 Maritime Street, EDINBURGH, EH6 6SB
Tel: 01875 822694 **Fax:** 01875 822314
Web site: http://www.edinburghguide.com
Titles:
EDINBURGH GUIDE.COM

EDINBURGH HOUSE PUBLISHING 1650326
8 Oxford Terrace, EDINBURGH, EH4 1PX
Tel: 0131 315 4443 **Fax:** 0131 315 4443
Titles:
YOUNG COMPANY FINANCE

EDINBURGH UNIVERSITY PRESS LTD 12713
22 George Square, EDINBURGH, EH8 9LF
Tel: 0131 650 4222 **Fax:** 0131 662 0053
Web site: http://www.eupjournals.com
Titles:
ARCHITECTURAL HERITAGE
DANCE RESEARCH
INTERNATIONAL JOURNAL OF HUMANITIES AND ARTS
COMPUTING
TRANSLATION & LITERATURE

**EDINBURGH UNIVERSITY STUDENT NEWSPAPER
SOCIETY** 15794
60 The Pleasance, EDINBURGH, EH8 9TJ
Tel: 0131 650 2363 **Fax:** 0131 650 2358
Web site: http://www.studentnewspaper.org
Titles:
EDINBURGH STUDENT

EDISEA LTD 16070
Hartfield House, 41-42 Hartfield Road, LONDON, SW19 3RQ
Tel: 020 8547 2662 **Fax:** 020 8547 1201
Titles:
BOAT INTERNATIONAL
SAILING TODAY

EDITION MAGAZINE LTD 1643221
PO Box 500, Happisburgh, NORWICH, NR12 0WX
Tel: 01692 650837 **Fax:** 01692 651158
Web site: http://www.edition-mag.co.uk
Titles:
EDITION MAGAZINE

EDITIONS PUBLISHING LTD 18187
The Loft, Bonnington Mill, 72 Newhaven Road,
EDINBURGH, EH6 5QG **Tel:** 0131 476 2502
Fax: 0131 476 2672
Titles:
CHARTERED BANKER

EDITORIAL DESIGN CONCEPTS 1634334
79 Essex Road, Islington, LONDON, N1 2SF
Tel: 020 7354 5577 **Fax:** 020 7354 8827
Web site: http://www.chandlergooding.co.uk
Titles:
DIAL

EDITORIAL SOLUTIONS LTD 1735845
The Annexe, 7 Birchin Lane, LONDON, EC3V 9BW
Tel: 020 7148 3688
Email: info@editorial-solutions.com
Web site: http://www.editorial-solutions.com
Titles:
GLOBAL BROKER & UNDERWRITER

EDITORIALE LARIANA 17154
21 South Square, LONDON, NW11 7AJ **Tel:** 020 8458 4860
Fax: 020 8458 0994

Titles:
ITALIAN WINES & SPIRITS

THE EDITORS OF THE OBSERVATORY 625718
16 Swan Close, Grove, WANTAGE, OX12 0QE
Tel: 01235 767509
Email: obs@astro1.bnsc.rl.ac.uk
Web site: http://www.ulo.ucl.ac.uk/obsmag
Titles:
THE OBSERVATORY MAGAZINE

EDPIC 1728374
1.1.2 The Leather Market, 11 Weston Street, LONDON, SE1
3ER **Tel:** 020 7407 9351
Titles:
MEGASTAR

EDUCATION AND MEDIA SERVICES LTD. 1768074
2nd floor Chiswick Gate, 598-608 Chiswick High Road,
Chiswick, LONDON, W4 5RT
Titles:
EMBODY FOR YOU

THE EDUCATION PUBLISHING CO LTD 16216
Devonia House, 4 Union Terrace, CREDITON, EX17 3DY
Tel: 01363 774455
Email: info@educationpublishing.com
Web site: http://www.educationpublishing.com
Titles:
EDUCATION & TRAINING PARLIAMENTARY MONITOR
EDUCATION JOURNAL
LITERACY TODAY

**EDUCATIONAL INSTITUTE OF SCOTLAND,
EDINBURGH** 13868
46 Moray Place, EDINBURGH, EH3 6BH **Tel:** 0131 225 6244
Fax: 0131 220 3151
Titles:
SCOTTISH EDUCATIONAL JOURNAL

EDUTECH MEDIA LTD 1763840
6th Floor, 223 Regent Street, LONDON, W1B 2QD
Tel: 0871 508 8918
Email: info1@edutechmedia.com
Web site: http://www.edutechmedia.com
Titles:
LLM DIRECTORY

EDWARD HODGETT LTD 15083
4 Margaret Street, NEWRY, BT34 1DF **Tel:** 028 3026 7633
Fax: 028 3026 3157
Titles:
NEWRY REPORTER

EFE INTERNATIONAL 677118
6th Floor, 223 Regent Street, LONDON, W1B 2QD
Tel: 0870 759 3697 **Fax:** 0871 508 0938
Titles:
ANGLOGERMANTRADE.COM
DISTINGUISHED SPAS
MBA SPECTRUM
MBAINUK.COM
SECURITY INDUSTRY TODAY
TRAVELINNOVATOR.COM
VISITBORNEO.COM

EFFECTIVE BUSINESS MEDIA 1767139
Ferneberga House, Alexandra Road, HAMPSHIRE, GU14
6DQ
Titles:
EFFECTIVE BUSINESS

EFFECTIVE TECHNOLOGY MARKETING LTD 17502
PO Box 171, GRIMSBY, DN35 0TP **Tel:** 01472 816660
Fax: 01472 816660
Web site: http://www.dataresources.co.uk
Titles:
BUSINESS INFORMATION SEARCHER

EFINANCIALNEWS.COM 624349
2nd Floor, Stapleton House, 29-33 Scrutton Street,
LONDON, EC2A 4HU **Tel:** 020 7426 3333
Fax: 020 7426 3329
Email: news@efinancialnews.com

Web site: http://www.efinancialnews.com

Titles:
BRUMMELL
EFINANCIAL NEWS
FINANCIAL NEWS
FINANCIAL NEWS
PRIVATE EQUITY NEWS
WEALTH-BULLETIN.COM

EFM PUBLISHING   1654181
Homelands, Exford, MINEHEAD, TA24 7NY
Tel: 01643 831635 **Fax:** 01643 831015
Email: info@efmpublishing.com

Titles:
EFM

E.G. ENTERPRISES LTD   17022
Apartment 41, Hampton Court Palace, EAST MOLESEY,
KT8 9AU **Tel:** 020 8943 1229 **Fax:** 020 8977 9882

Titles:
EMBROIDERY
STITCH WITH THE EMBROIDERERS' GUILD

EGMONT MAGAZINES UK   16675
239 Kensington High Street, LONDON, W8 6SA
Tel: 020 7761 3500 **Fax:** 020 7761 3510
Web site: http://www.egmont.co.uk

Titles:
BARBIE
DISNEY & ME
DISNEY'S PRINCESS
DORA THE EXPLORER
FIREMAN SAM
GO GIRL
POWER RANGERS
THOMAS & FRIENDS
THOMAS & FRIENDS PLAY & LEARN
TINKER BELL
TOXIC

E.GOLFBUSINESS.COM LTD   14780
5-7 High Street, Dorchester-on-Thames, WALLINGFORD,
OX10 7HH **Tel:** 01865 340759

Titles:
GOLF BUSINESS NEWS.COM

E-HEALTH MEDIA LTD   1682696
Southbank House, Black Prince Road, LONDON, SE1 7SJ
Tel: 020 7785 6900 **Fax:** 020 7785 6908
Email: info@e-health-media.com

Titles:
E-HEALTH INSIDER
E-HEALTH INSIDER PRIMARY CARE

ELCOT PUBLICATIONS LTD   14704
2 The Courtyard, The Old Dairy House, Dark Lane,
Maidenhatch, Pangbourne, READING, RG8 8HP
Tel: 0118 974 5330 **Fax:** 0118 974 4110
Email: solent@elcot.co.uk
Web site: http://www.elcot.co.uk

Titles:
THE BUSINESS MAGAZINE

ELECTRIC MARKETING   17766
22 John Street, LONDON, WC1N 2BY **Tel:** 020 7419 7999
Fax: 020 7419 7999
Web site: http://www.electricmarketing.co.uk

Titles:
BUSINESS TO BUSINESS MARKETING APPOINTMENTS

ELECTRIC WORD   674836
3rd Floor, 33-41 Dallington Street, LONDON, EC1V 0BB
Tel: 020 7954 3506 **Fax:** 020 7954 3515
Email: sportsdesk@tvsportsmarkets.com
Web site: http://www.tvsportsmarkets.com

Titles:
TV SPORTS MARKETS

ELECTRIC WORDS PLC   1710401
33-41 Dallington Street, LONDON, EC1V 0BB
Tel: 0845 450 6414 **Fax:** 0845 450 6405
Web site: http://www.mychild.co.uk

Titles:
MY CHILD

ELECTROPAGES LIMITED   600489
Unit 4, The Axium Centre, POOLE, BH16 6FE
Tel: 01202 632441
Email: info@electropages.com
Web site: http://www.electropages.com

Titles:
ELECTROPAGES.COM

ELFANDE LTD   17494
Surrey House, 31 Church Street, LEATHERHEAD, KT22 8EF
Tel: 01372 220330 **Fax:** 01372 220340

Titles:
CONTACT ILLUSTRATORS & CONTACT
PHOTOGRAPHERS (2 VOLUMES)

ELITE MEDIA MARKETING   15101
Trehwbwb, St. Lythan's, CARDIFF, CF5 6BQ
Tel: 029 2059 3310 **Fax:** 029 2059 3310

Titles:
ELITE MAGAZINE

ELIXIR MAGAZINE LTD   1723530
7 Munroe House, Lorne Close, LONDON, NW8 7JN
Tel: 020 7569 8676
Web site: http://www.elixirnews.com

Titles:
ELIXIR

ELIXIR PRESS LTD   1735391
Suite D211, Macmillan House, Paddington Station,
LONDON, W2 1FT

Titles:
ELIXIR NEWS

ELLOUGHTON-CUM-BROUGH PARISH COUNCIL 621774
PO Box 124, BROUGH, HU15 1YH **Tel:** 01482 665600
Fax: 01482 665600

Titles:
PETUARIA PRESS

ELMBRIDGE BOROUGH COUNCIL   18514
Civic Centre, High Street, ESHER, KT10 9SD
Tel: 01372 474474 **Fax:** 01372 474972
Email: contactus@elmbridge.gov.uk
Web site: http://www.elmbridge.gov.uk

Titles:
THE ELMBRIDGE REVIEW

ELSEVIER   698752
The Boulevard, Langford Lane, KIDLINGTON, OX5 1GB
Tel: 01865 843000 **Fax:** 01865 843933
Web site: http://www.elsevier.com

Titles:
CARBOHYDRATE POLYMERS
CLINICAL ONCOLOGY
ENVIRONMENTAL SCIENCE & POLICY
FOCUS ON CATALYSTS
FOCUS ON PIGMENTS
FOCUS ON SURFACTANTS
PHYSIOTHERAPY

ELSEVIER HEALTH SCIENCES   1622055
32 Jamestown Road, LONDON, NW1 7BY
Tel: 020 7424 4200
Web site: http://www.elsevier.com

Titles:
THE LANCET
THE LANCET ONCOLOGY
NURSE EDUCATION TODAY
THE PRACTISING MIDWIFE

ELSEVIER LONDON LTD   621733
32 Jamestown Road, LONDON, NW1 7BY
Tel: 020 7424 4200
Web site: http://www.elsevier.com

Titles:
DRUG DISCOVERY TODAY
JOURNAL OF FELINE MEDICINE & SURGERY
TRENDS IN BIOCHEMICAL SCIENCES
TRENDS IN BIOTECHNOLOGY
TRENDS IN CELL BIOLOGY
TRENDS IN COGNITIVE SCIENCES
TRENDS IN ECOLOGY & EVOLUTION
TRENDS IN IMMUNOLOGY
TRENDS IN MICROBIOLOGY
TRENDS IN MOLECULAR MEDICINE
TRENDS IN PARASITOLOGY

TRENDS IN PHARMACOLOGICAL SCIENCES
TRENDS IN PLANT SCIENCE

ELSEVIER LTD   12226
The Boulevard, Langford Lane, Kidlington, OXFORD, OX5
1GB **Tel:** 01865 843000 **Fax:** 01865 843933
Web site: http://www.elsevier.com

Titles:
ADDITIVES FOR POLYMERS
ADVANCES IN ENGINEERING SOFTWARE
BEST PRACTICE & RESEARCH CLINICAL
ENDOCRINOLOGY & METABOLISM
BIOMETRIC TECHNOLOGY TODAY
CARD TECHNOLOGY TODAY
COMPLEMENTARY THERAPIES IN CLINICAL PRACTICE
COMPLEMENTARY THERAPIES IN MEDICINE
COMPUTER FRAUD & SECURITY
THE COMPUTER LAW AND SECURITY REPORT
ENERGY POLICY
FILTRATION+SEPARATION
FILTRATION INDUSTRY ANALYST
FOOD CHEMISTRY
FOOD QUALITY AND PREFERENCE
FUTURES
HOMEOPATHY
INFORMATION SECURITY TECHNICAL REPORT
INFOSECURITY
INJURY
INTENSIVE AND CRITICAL CARE NURSING
INTERNATIONAL JOURNAL OF ADHESION &
ADHESIVES
INTERNATIONAL JOURNAL OF MACHINE TOOLS AND
MANUFACTURE
INTERNATIONAL JOURNAL OF PROJECT
MANAGEMENT
JOURNAL OF CONSTRUCTIONAL STEEL RESEARCH
JOURNAL OF THE EUROPEAN CERAMIC SOCIETY
JOURNAL OF FORENSIC AND LEGAL MEDICINE
MATERIALS & DESIGN
MATERIALS TODAY
MEMBRANE TECHNOLOGY NEWSLETTER
METAL POWDER REPORT
NDT & E INTERNATIONAL
NETWORK SECURITY
PLASTICS ADDITIVES & COMPOUNDING
PRACTICE NURSE
PUMP INDUSTRY ANALYST
REINFORCED PLASTICS
RENEWABLE ENERGY FOCUS
RESPIRATORY MEDICINE
SEALING TECHNOLOGY NEWSLETTER
TRENDS IN FOOD SCIENCE & TECHNOLOGY
TRENDS IN NEUROSCIENCES
WORLD PUMPS
WORLD PUMPS

EM & EN MEDIA   1747435
26 Sandown Road, Hazel Grove, STOCKPORT, SK7 4SH
Tel: 0161 483 1790

Titles:
ROCHDALE STYLE

EMAP COMMUNICATIONS   12754
Greater London House, Hampstead Road, LONDON, NW1
7EJ **Tel:** 020 7728 5000 **Fax:** 020 7728 4800
Web site: http://www.emap.com

Titles:
SHOTS
SHOTS ONLINE

EMAP COMMUNICATIONS LTD   1738800
Greater London House, Hampstead Road, LONDON, NW1
7EJ
Web site: http://www.emap.com

Titles:
BROADCAST
MEED
PROFESSIONAL BEAUTY

EMAP INFORM   1256
Greater London House, Hampstead Road, LONDON, NW1
7EJ **Tel:** 020 7391 5000 **Fax:** 020 7728 4000
Web site: http://www.emap.com

Titles:
CONSTRUCTION NEWS
DRAPERS
HEALTH SERVICE JOURNAL
JEWELLERY IN BRITAIN
LGC LOCAL GOVERNMENT CHRONICLE
LIGHTING
RAC PLUS
SCREEN INTERNATIONAL
SCREENDAILY.COM
THE SPECIFIER'S GUIDE

EMAP INSIGHT   13485

Greater London House, Hampstead Road, LONDON, NW1
7EJ **Tel:** 020 7728 5000 **Fax:** 020 7728 4000
Web site: http://www.emap.com

Titles:
AJ SPECIFICATION
THE ARCHITECTS' JOURNAL
ARCHITECTSJOURNAL.CO.UK
THE ARCHITECTURAL REVIEW
BROADCASTNOW
GROUND ENGINEERING
H&V NEWS
INFRASTRUCTURE JOURNAL
LGCNET
MRW
NCE
NEW CIVIL ENGINEER
NEW CIVIL ENGINEER INTERNATIONAL
RAC - REFRIGERATION AND AIR CONDITIONING

EMAP PUBLIC SECTOR   621740

Greater London House, Hampstead Road, LONDON, NW1
7EJ **Tel:** 020 7874 0200

Titles:
NURSING TIMES

EMAP RETAIL   622694

Greater London House, Hampstead Road, LONDON, NW1
7EJ **Tel:** 020 7728 5000
Web site: http://www.emap.com

Titles:
THE PROFESSIONAL BEAUTY DIRECTORY
RETAIL JEWELLER
RETAIL WEEK

EMEL MEDIA LTD   1689835

Barakat House, 116 Finchley Road, LONDON, NW3 5HT
Tel: 020 7431 5300 **Fax:** 020 7431 5324
Web site: http://www.emel.com

Titles:
EMEL

EMERALD GROUP PUBLISHING LTD   12144

Howard House, Wagon Lane, BINGLEY, BD16 1WA
Tel: 01274 777700 **Fax:** 01274 785201
Web site: http://www.emeraldinsight.com

Titles:
ACCOUNTING, AUDITING & ACCOUNTABILITY
    JOURNAL
AIRCRAFT ENGINEERING AND AEROSPACE
    TECHNOLOGY: AN INTERNATIONAL JOURNAL
ANTI-CORROSION METHODS & MATERIALS
ASSEMBLY AUTOMATION
BRITISH FOOD JOURNAL
CAREER DEVELOPMENT INTERNATIONAL
CIRCUIT WORLD
CLINICAL GOVERNANCE: AN INTERNATIONAL
    JOURNAL
COMPEL
CORPORATE COMMUNICATIONS: AN INTERNATIONAL
    JOURNAL
DEVELOPMENT AND LEARNING IN ORGANIZATIONS
DISASTER PREVENTION AND MANAGEMENT
EDUCATION & TRAINING
THE ELECTRONIC LIBRARY
ENGINEERING COMPUTATIONS
ENGINEERING, CONSTRUCTION AND ARCHITECTURAL
    MANAGEMENT
EUROPEAN BUSINESS REVIEW
FACILITIES
FORESIGHT
HEALTH EDUCATION
INDUSTRIAL & COMMERCIAL TRAINING
INDUSTRIAL LUBRICATION & TRIBOLOGY
INDUSTRIAL MANAGEMENT & DATA SYSTEMS
THE INDUSTRIAL ROBOT
INFO
INTERLENDING & DOCUMENT SUPPLY
INTERNATIONAL JOURNAL OF BANK MARKETING
INTERNATIONAL JOURNAL OF CONTEMPORARY
    HOSPITALITY MANAGEMENT
INTERNATIONAL JOURNAL OF HEALTH CARE QUALITY
    ASSURANCE
INTERNATIONAL JOURNAL OF MANPOWER
INTERNATIONAL JOURNAL OF NUMERICAL METHODS
    FOR HEAT & FLUID FLOW
INTERNATIONAL JOURNAL OF PRODUCTIVITY &
    PERFORMANCE MANAGEMENT
INTERNATIONAL JOURNAL OF RETAIL & DISTRIBUTION
    MANAGEMENT
THE JOURNAL OF BUSINESS STRATEGY
JOURNAL OF COMMUNICATION MANAGEMENT
THE JOURNAL OF CONSUMER MARKETING
JOURNAL OF CORPORATE REAL ESTATE
JOURNAL OF HEALTH, ORGANISATION AND
    MANAGEMENT

JOURNAL OF ORGANIZATIONAL CHANGE
    MANAGEMENT
THE JOURNAL OF RISK FINANCE INCORPORATING
    BALANCE SHEET
THE JOURNAL OF SERVICES MARKETING
JOURNAL OF WORKPLACE LEARNING
LIBRARY HI TECH NEWS
LIBRARY LINK
LIBRARY REVIEW
MICROELECTRONICS INTERNATIONAL
NEW LIBRARY WORLD
NUTRITION & FOOD SCIENCE
ONLINE INFORMATION REVIEW
PIGMENT & RESIN TECHNOLOGY
PROGRAM: ELECTRONIC LIBRARY AND INFORMATION
    SYSTEMS
QUALITY ASSURANCE IN EDUCATION
RAPID PROTOTYPING JOURNAL
RECORDS MANAGEMENT JOURNAL
SENSOR REVIEW
SOLDERING & SURFACE MOUNT TECHNOLOGY
STRATEGIC DIRECTION
STRATEGIC HR REVIEW
STRUCTURAL SURVEY
SUPPLY CHAIN MANAGEMENT: AN INTERNATIONAL
    JOURNAL
TRAINING & MANAGEMENT DEVELOPMENT METHODS
VINE: THE JOURNAL OF INFORMATION AND
    KNOWLEDGE MANAGEMENT SYSTEMS
YOUNG CONSUMERS

EML PUBLISHING   1677095

32 The Slopes, Portadown, Ballydougan, CRAIGAVON,
BT63 5NT **Tel:** 028 3834 4333

Titles:
EMERALD RUGBY

EMMA MEDIA   1649718

67-69 Whitfield Street, LONDON, W1T 4HS
Tel: 020 7636 1233

Titles:
EMMA MAGAZINE

EMMS INTERNATIONAL   17901

7 Washington Lane, EDINBURGH, EH11 2HA
Tel: 0131 313 3828 **Fax:** 0131 313 4662
Email: info@emms.org
Web site: http://www.emms.org

Titles:
THE HEALING HAND

EMP MEDIA   12857

EMP House, 2 Pembroke Road, LONDON, N10 2HR
Tel: 020 8444 3401 **Fax:** 020 8883 9504
Email: info@emp.plc.uk
Web site: http://www.empgroup.co.uk

Titles:
AT HOME
INVEST IN SUCCESS
OUTSOURCE

EMPHASIS MEDIA UK LTD   1759555

The Old Truman Brewery, Unit 23-24, 91 Brick Lane,
LONDON, E1 6QL **Tel:** 020 3355 8262

Titles:
CNN TRAVELLER

EMPLOYEE SHARE OWNERSHIP CENTRE   16410

2 Ridgmount Street, LONDON, WC1E 7AA
Tel: 020 7436 9936 **Fax:** 020 7580 0016
Web site: http://www.hurlstons.com/esop

Titles:
IT'S OUR BUSINESS

EMR-NAMNEWS LTD   16933

Venture House, 2 Arlington Square, Downshire Way,
BRACKNELL, RG12 1WA **Tel:** 01344 742816

Titles:
NAMNEWS

EMTRAD   18151

Unit 24, Eldon Business Park, Eldon Road, Attenborough,
NOTTINGHAM, NG9 6DZ **Tel:** 0115 925 5227
Fax: 0115 922 9645
Email: emtrad@freeuk.com

Titles:
HRM HOTEL & RESTAURANT MANAGER
THE NATIONAL BARTENDER

ENERGY INFORMATION CENTRE LTD   14645

Rosemary House, Lanwades Business Park, NEWMARKET,
CB8 7PW **Tel:** 01638 751400 **Fax:** 01638 751801
Email: info@eic.co.uk
Web site: http://www.eic.co.uk

Titles:
PULSE

ENERGY INSTITUTE   14217

61 New Cavendish Street, LONDON, W1G 7AR
Tel: 020 7467 7100 **Fax:** 020 7637 0086
Web site: http://www.energyinst.org.uk

Titles:
ENERGY WORLD
PETROLEUM REVIEW

ENERGY INTELLIGENCE GROUP   16845

8th Floor, Holborn Tower, 137-144 High Holborn, LONDON,
WC1V 6PW **Tel:** 020 7632 4700 **Fax:** 020 7404 1766
Web site: http://www.energyintel.com

Titles:
INTERNATIONAL OIL DAILY
NEFTE COMPASS

ENERGY STORAGE PUBLISHING LTD   1622353

70 Goring Road, GORING-BY-SEA, BN12 4AB
Tel: 0845 194 7338
Email: gerry@bestmag.co.uk
Web site: http://www.bestmag.co.uk

Titles:
BATTERIES AND ENERGY STORAGE TECHNOLOGY

ENGAGE GROUP LTD   1752856

24 Ainslie Place, EDINBURGH, EH3 6AJ **Tel:** 0131 225 9979
Web site: http://www.engagegroup.co.uk

Titles:
AMBITIONS

ENGAGE UK NETWORKS LIMITED   1717718

Waterfront Studios, 1 Dock Road, LONDON, E16 1AH
Tel: 020 8350 9443 **Fax:** 020 7476 6655
Email: craig@engagemagazine.co.uk
Web site: http://www.engagemagazine.co.uk

Titles:
ENGAGE

THE ENGINEERING INTEGRITY SOCIETY   16583

18 Oak Close, Bedworth, WARWICKSHIRE, CV12 9AJ
Tel: 0114 262 1155
Email: catherine@cpinder.com
Web site: http://www.e-i-s.org.uk

Titles:
ENGINEERING INTEGRITY

ENGINEERING MAGAZINE LTD   1732466

6A New Street, WARWICK, CV34 4RX **Tel:** 01926 408242
Fax: 01926 408206

Titles:
ENGINEERING

THE ENGLISH AND MEDIA CENTRE   1641752

18 Compton Terrace, LONDON, N1 2UN **Tel:** 020 7359 8080
Fax: 020 7354 0133
Email: info@englishmedia.co.uk
Web site: http://www.englishmedia.co.uk

Titles:
MEDIA MAGAZINE

THE ENGLISH ASSOCIATION   18304

University of Leicester, University Road, LEICESTER, LE1
7RH **Tel:** 0116 252 3982 **Fax:** 0116 252 2301
Email: engassoc@le.ac.uk
Web site: http://www.le.ac.uk/engassoc

Titles:
THE USE OF ENGLISH

ENGLISH BASKETBALL ASSOCIATION   17347

English Institute Of Sport, Coleridge Road, SHEFFIELD, S9
5DA **Tel:** 0114 223 5693 **Fax:** 0114 242 6419
Email: info@englandbasketball.co.uk
Web site: http://www.englandbasketball.co.uk

Titles:
ENGLAND BASKETBALL

UK Publishers & Their Titles

ENGLISH CHESS FEDERATION 17497
The Watch Oak, Chain Lane, BATTLE, TN33 0YD
Tel: 01424 775222 **Fax:** 01424 775904
Email: office@englishchess.org.uk
Web site: http://www.bcf.org.uk
Titles:
CHESSMOVES

ENGLISH CHURCHMAN TRUST 15877
64 Ripley Road, WORTHING, BN11 5NH **Tel:** 01903 505555
Email: englishchurchman.admin@ntlworld.com
Titles:
ENGLISH CHURCHMAN

ENGLISH FOLK DANCE AND SONG SOCIETY 17860
Cecil Sharp House, 2 Regent's Park Road, LONDON, NW1
7AY **Tel:** 020 7485 2206 **Fax:** 020 7284 0534
Email: info@efdss.org
Web site: http://www.efdss.org
Titles:
FOLK MUSIC JOURNAL

ENGLISH LACROSSE ASSOCIATION 15329
The Belle Vue Centre, Pink Bank Lane, Longsight,
MANCHESTER, M12 5GL **Tel:** 0161 227 3626
Fax: 0161 227 3625
Titles:
LACROSSE TALK

ENGLISH SPEAKING BOARD LTD 18274
26A Princes Street, SOUTHPORT, PR8 1EQ
Tel: 01704 501730 **Fax:** 01704 539637
Web site: http://www.esbuk.org
Titles:
SPEAKING ENGLISH

THE ENGLISH VOLLEYBALL ASSOCIATION 16266
Suite B, Loughborough Technology Centre, Epinal Way,
LOUGHBOROUGH, LE11 3GE **Tel:** 01509 631699
Fax: 01509 631689
Web site: http://www.volleyballengland.org.uk
Titles:
3TOUCH VOLLEYBALL

ENTERBRAIN INC. 1638638
16 Weare Gifford, Shoeburyness, SOUTHEND-ON-SEA, SS3
8AB **Tel:** 01702 589169
Titles:
FAMITSU PLAYSTATION+

ENTERTAINMENT TECHNOLOGY PRESS LTD 1616845
The Studio, High Green, Great Shelford, CAMBRIDGE, CB2
5EG **Tel:** 01223 550805 **Fax:** 01223 550806
Web site: http://www.etnow.com
Titles:
ENTERTAINMENT TECHNOLOGY
SIGHTLINE

ENTHUSIAST PUBLISHING LTD 15462
PO Box 153, CRANLEIGH, GU6 8ZL **Tel:** 01483 268818
Fax: 01483 268993
Titles:
THE AUTOMOBILE

**ENTOMOLOGIST'S RECORD & JOURNAL OF
VARIATION** 17862
14 West Road, BISHOP'S STORTFORD, CM23 3QP
Tel: 01279 507697 **Fax:** 01279 507697
Titles:
ENTOMOLOGIST'S RECORD & JOURNAL OF VARIATION

ENTS24 LTD 1723493
16-18 Whiteladies Road, BRISTOL, BS8 2LG
Tel: 0117 973 0548 **Fax:** 0117 973 0152
Email: info@ents24.com
Web site: http://www.ents24.com
Titles:
ENTS24.COM

ENVIROMEDIA LTD 1759204
254A Bury New Road, Whitefield, MANCHESTER, M45 8QN
Tel: 07791 227303
Email: alex@enviromedia.ltd.uk

Titles:
ENVIRONMENT INDUSTRY MAGAZINE

ENVIRONMENTAL INDUSTRIES COMMISSION 14615
45 Weymouth Street, LONDON, W1G 8ND
Tel: 020 7935 1675 **Fax:** 020 7486 3455
Web site: http://www.eic-uk.co.uk
Titles:
ENVIRO-TECH NEWS

ENVIRONMENTAL TECHNOLOGY PUBLICATIONS LTD 18655
Oak Court Business Centre, Sandridge Park, Porters Wood,
ST. ALBANS, AL3 6PH **Tel:** 01727 858840
Fax: 01727 840310
Email: info@iet-pub.com
Web site: http://www.iet-pub.com
Titles:
ASIAN ENVIRONMENTAL TECHNOLOGY
INTERNATIONAL ENVIRONMENTAL TECHNOLOGY
PETRO INDUSTRY NEWS
POLLUTION SOLUTIONS

ENVOY MEDIA LTD 1747200
11 Grosvenor Crescent, LONDON, SW1X 7EE
Tel: 020 7245 6794 **Fax:** 020 7823 2679
Email: info@diplomatmagazine.com
Web site: http://www.diplomatmagazine.com
Titles:
DIPLOMAT

EPILEPSY ACTION 17242
New Anstey House, Gate Way Drive, Yeadon, LEEDS, LS19
7XY **Tel:** 0113 210 8800 **Fax:** 0113 391 0300
Email: echampion@epilepsy.org.uk
Web site: http://www.epilepsy.org.uk
Titles:
EPILEPSY TODAY

THE EPOCH TIMES 1739629
Unit LG 1, 88-94 Wentworth Street, LONDON, E1 7SA
Tel: 020 7247 2719
Titles:
THE EPOCH TIMES

EPP PUBLICATIONS 12656
6 Eastbourne Road, LONDON, W4 3EB **Tel:** 020 8400 1601
Titles:
LAND CONTAMINATION & RECLAMATION

EQUESTRIAN MANAGEMENT CONSULTANTS LTD 17017
Stockeld Park, WETHERBY, LS22 4AW **Tel:** 01937 582111
Fax: 01937 582778
Titles:
BRITISH EQUESTRIAN DIRECTORY
EQUESTRIAN TRADE NEWS
TRADE SUPPLIERS DIRECTORY

EQUINE CANINE AND COUNTRY LIFE 1742721
Westside, Bow Farm, Badgworth, AXBRIDGE, BS26 2QA
Tel: 01934 751171
Titles:
EQUINE CANINE AND COUNTRY LIFE

EQUINE MARKETING LTD 1649374
Aberbanc, Penrhiwllan, LLANDYSUL, SA44 5NP
Tel: 01559 371994 **Fax:** 01559 371995
Email: info@equinemarketing.co.uk
Web site: http://www.equinemarketing.com
Titles:
WELSH COUNTRY

EQUINE VETERINARY JOURNAL LTD 14793
Mulberry House, 31 Market Street, Fordham,
CAMBRIDGESHIRE, CB7 5LQ **Tel:** 01638 720250
Fax: 01638 721868
Web site: http://www.evj.co.uk
Titles:
EQUINE VETERINARY EDUCATION
EQUINE VETERINARY JOURNAL

EQUIPMENT PUBLICATIONS 17339
31A Hibernia Street, HOLYWOOD, BT18 9JE
Tel: 028 9042 4924 **Fax:** 028 9042 7378
Titles:
EQUIP

EQUITY 13851
Guild House, Upper St Martin's Lane, LONDON, WC2H 9EG
Tel: 020 7379 6000 **Fax:** 020 7379 7001
Email: info@equity.org.uk
Web site: http://www.equity.org.uk
Titles:
EQUITY JOURNAL

EQUITYLINK LTD 13371
84 Addiscombe Road, CROYDON, CR0 5PP
Tel: 020 8656 4648 **Fax:** 020 8656 0111
Titles:
MOMENTUM
THE SMALL COMPANY SHAREWATCH

THE ERGONOMICS SOCIETY 14479
Elms Court, Elms Grove, LOUGHBOROUGH, LE11 1RG
Tel: 01509 234904
Web site: http://www.ergonomics.org.uk
Titles:
THE ERGONOMIST

THE EROTIC PRINT SOCIETY 1732277
Lower Ria, 31 Sinclair Road, LONDON, W14 0NS
Tel: 020 7371 1532 **Fax:** 020 7603 8378
Titles:
EROTIC REVIEW

ESEN GROUP 18193
Unit N4, Chorley Business & Technology Centre, Euxton
Lane, Euxton, CHORLEY, PR7 6TE **Tel:** 01257 231900
Fax: 01257 249389
Web site: http://www.esengroup.co.uk
Titles:
BUILDING SCOTLAND
CONSTRUCTION IRELAND
UK CONSTRUCTION MAGAZINE

ESKDALE & LIDDESDALE NEWSPAPERS 15053
Commercial House, High Street, LANGHOLM, DG13 0JH
Tel: 01387 380012 **Fax:** 01387 380979
Titles:
ESKDALE AND LIDDESDALE ADVERTISER

ESP MAGAZINE LTD 17116
PO Box 431, PETERBOROUGH, PE6 7FG
Tel: 01733 579707 **Fax:** 01733 579708
Email: office@espmag.co.uk
Titles:
ESP MAGAZINE

ESPC (UK) LIMITED 15176
90A George Street, EDINBURGH, EH2 3DF
Tel: 0131 624 8000 **Fax:** 0131 624 8570
Web site: http://www.espc.com
Titles:
ESPCHOMEPAGES

ESPICOM LTD 16850
Lincoln House, City Fields Business Park, City Fields Way,
Tangmere, CHICHESTER, PO20 2FS **Tel:** 01243 533322
Fax: 01243 533418
Web site: http://www.espicom.com
Titles:
ANTI-INFECTIVE DRUG NEWS
AUTOIMMUNE DRUG FOCUS
CANCER DRUG NEWS
CARDIOVASCULAR DRUG NEWS (CVDN)
CNS DRUG NEWS
THE DIABETES REPORT
DRUG DELIVERY INSIGHT
INTERNATIONAL PHARMACEUTICAL AGREEMENTS
MEDICAL DEVICE COMPANIES ANALYSIS
MEDICAL INDUSTRY WEEK
MEDISTAT
NEURO DRUG FOCUS (NDF)
PHARMA AGREEMENT NEWS (PAN)
PHARMA COMPANY INSIGHT

ESPN 674518
Mail Code 615, 3 Queen Caroline Street, LONDON, W6 9PE
Tel: 020 8222 1000 **Fax:** 020 8222 2805
Titles:
SOCCERNET

ESSENTIAL LOCAL MARKETING 1751426
149 Ramsden Road, LONDON, SW12 8RF
Tel: 020 8675 7697
Email: richard@essentiallocal.com
Web site: http://www.essentiallocal.com
Titles:
ESSENTIAL LOCAL
INSIDECLAPHAM.CO.UK

ESSEX CHRONICLE MEDIA GROUP LTD 700396
Westway, CHELMSFORD, CM1 3BE **Tel:** 01245 600700
Fax: 01245 603353
Web site: http://www.totalessex.co.uk
Titles:
BRENTWOOD GAZETTE SERIES
ESSEX CHRONICLE SERIES

ESSEX COUNTY NEWSPAPERS 12688
Oriel House, 43-44 North Hill, COLCHESTER, CO1 1TZ
Tel: 01206 506000 **Fax:** 01206 508274
Titles:
ESSEX COUNTY STANDARD
GAZETTE AND STANDARD SERIES (EAST ESSEX)
WEEKLY NEWS SERIES (COLCHESTER)

ESSEX JEWISH NEWS LTD 14932
Suite 314, Premier House, 112-114 Station Road,
EDGWARE, HA8 7AQ **Tel:** 020 8952 9526
Titles:
ESSEX JEWISH NEWS

THE ESSEX RIDER 700248
175 Waldegrave, BASILDON, SS16 5EL **Tel:** 01268 288088
Fax: 01268 288088
Titles:
THE ESSEX RIDER

THE ESTATES GAZETTE 17714
1 Proctor Street, LONDON, WC1V 6EU **Tel:** 020 7911 1825
Fax: 020 7911 1900
Titles:
THE ESTATES GAZETTE LAW REPORTS

ESTATES PRESS LTD 13341
Keenans Mill, Lord Street, LYTHAM ST. ANNES, FY8 2ER
Tel: 01253 783206 **Fax:** 01253 783217
Titles:
ESTATE AGENCY NEWS

ESTETICA UK 13892
118 Piccadilly, Mayfair, LONDON, W1J 7NW
Tel: 020 7569 6779 **Fax:** 020 7569 6778
Titles:
ESTETICA UK

ETA SERVICES LTD 1652861
68 High Street, WEYBRIDGE, KT13 8RS **Tel:** 0845 389 1010
Fax: 01932 829015
Email: eta@eta.co.uk
Web site: http://www.eta.co.uk
Titles:
THE APPLE

ETHICAL PUBLISHING 1742967
PO Box 282, STAMFORD, PE9 9BW **Tel:** 0845 643 2499
Titles:
ETHICAL LIVING

ETHNIC MEDIA GROUP 16413
Unit 2, Whitechapel Technology Centre, 65 Whitechapel
Road, LONDON, E1 1DU **Tel:** 020 7650 2000
Fax: 020 7650 2001
Titles:
EASTERN EYE
NEW NATION

THE ETHNIC MINORITY INFORMATION & ADVISORY
CENTRE 1726521
Suite C, Queensway House, 275-285 High Street, Stratford,
LONDON, E15 2TF **Tel:** 020 8534 2255 **Fax:** 020 8519 5564
Titles:
AFRICAN ECHO

E-TRADE MEDIA LTD 1621553
47 Bucknalls Lane, WATFORD, WD25 9NE
Tel: 01923 461527 **Fax:** 01923 337823
Titles:
THE GL@ZINE

ETTA THE ENGLISH TABLE TENNIS ASSOCIATION
LTD 16595
Queensbury House, 3rd Floor, Havelock Road, HASTINGS,
TN34 1HF **Tel:** 01424 722525 **Fax:** 01424 422103
Titles:
TABLE TENNIS NEWS

EUPHONY COMMUNICATIONS LTD 1680895
Belvedere, Basing View, BASINGSTOKE, RG21 4HG
Tel: 01256 857000
Web site: http://www.euphony.com
Titles:
EUMAGAZINE

EURO PUBLISHING CONSULTANCY 1758446
Unit 2, Chowley Oak Lane, Tattenhall, CHESTER, CH3 9GA
Tel: 01829 770037 **Fax:** 01829 770047
Email: sales@britishplastics.co.uk
Web site: http://www.britishplastics.co.uk
Titles:
BRITISH PLASTICS & RUBBER

EUROGAMER NETWORK LTD 1640313
Wenlock House, 41 North Street, BRIGHTON, BN1 1RH
Tel: 01273 382521 **Fax:** 01273 555989
Email: contact@eurogamer.net
Web site: http://www.eurogamer.biz
Titles:
GAMESINDUSTRY.BIZ

EUROMEDIA ASSOCIATES LTD 698742
Unit 8, Chorley West Business Park, Ackhurst Road,
CHORLEY, PR7 1NL **Tel:** 0870 444 8955
Fax: 0870 444 8956
Email: sales@euromedia-al.com
Web site: http://www.euromedia-al.com
Titles:
ARCHITEXT
CARE AND NURSING ESSENTIALS
DISABLED & SUPPORTIVE CARER INCORPORATING
   CHALLENGE
EDUCATION FOR EVERYBODY
ELECTROFACTS
GREEN TOURISM AND HERITAGE GUIDE
QA EDUCATION
WHAT'S ON AND WHERE TO GO - A NATIONWIDE
   GUIDE

EUROMONEY INSTITUTIONAL INVESTOR PLC 18865
Nestor House, Playhouse Yard, LONDON, EC4V 5EX
Tel: 020 7779 8888
Email: hotline@euromoneyplc.com
Web site: http://www.euromoneyplc.com
Titles:
AIRFINANCE ANNUAL
AIRFINANCE JOURNAL
COMPLIANCE REPORTER
DERIVATIVES WEEK
EUROMONEY
EUROMONEY.COM
EUROWEEK
FOW
FUTURES AND OPTIONS INTELLIGENCE
GLOBAL INVESTOR
GLOBAL MONEY MANAGEMENT
GLOBAL TELECOMS BUSINESS
INSTITUTIONAL INVESTOR
INTERNATIONAL FINANCIAL LAW REVIEW
INTERNATIONAL FINANCIAL LAW REVIEW 1000
INTERNATIONAL TAX REVIEW
ISF INTERNATIONAL SECURITIES FINANCE
LIQUID REAL ESTATE
MANAGING INTELLECTUAL PROPERTY
MBM - METAL BULLETIN MONTHLY
METAL BULLETIN
METALBULLETIN.COM
PROJECT FINANCE

REACTIONS
TOTAL SECURITIZATION
TRADE FINANCE
WORLD LEASING YEARBOOK

EUROPA SCIENCE LTD 1630517
The Spectrum Building, Michael Young Centre, Purbeck
Road, CAMBRIDGE, CB2 8PD **Tel:** 01223 211170
Fax: 01223 211107
Email: info@europascience.com
Web site: http://www.europascience.com
Titles:
ELECTRO OPTICS
IMAGING AND MACHINE VISION EUROPE
RESEARCH INFORMATION
SCIENTIFIC COMPUTING WORLD
SCIENTIFIC COMPUTING WORLD

EUROPEAN MAGAZINE SERVICES LIMITED 15105
Lombard House, 10-20 Lombard Street, BELFAST, BT1
1BW **Tel:** 028 9032 8777 **Fax:** 028 9032 8555
Email: administration@offshoreinvestment.com
Web site: http://www.offshoreinvestment.com
Titles:
OFFSHORE INVESTMENT

EUROPEAN RESELLER LTD 622879
Berkeley House, Barnet Road, London Colney, ST. ALBANS,
AL2 1BG **Tel:** 01727 742975 **Fax:** 01727 742976
Email: andy@europeanreseller.com
Web site: http://www.europeanreseller.com
Titles:
EUROPEAN RESELLER MAGAZINE

EUROPHARM MANAGEMENT EDUCATION LTD 14241
The Coach House, 173 Sheen Lane, East Sheen, LONDON,
SW14 8NA **Tel:** 020 8878 8566 **Fax:** 020 8876 8834
Titles:
PHARMA TIMES

EUROPUBLISHING CONSULTANCY LTD 16725
Unit 2, Chowley Court, Chowley Oak Lane, Tattenhall,
CHESTER, CH3 9GA **Tel:** 01829 770037 **Fax:** 01829 770047
Titles:
EUROPEAN PHARMACEUTICAL MANUFACTURER
EUROPEAN PLASTIC PRODUCT MANUFACTURER

EUSA 691263
The Potterrow, 5/2 Bristo Square, EDINBURGH, EH8 9AL
Tel: 0131 650 2656 **Fax:** 0131 650 4177
Web site: http://www.eusa.ed.ac.uk
Titles:
HYPE

THE EVANGELICAL ALLIANCE 18793
Whitefield House, 186 Kennington Park Road, LONDON,
SE11 4BT **Tel:** 020 7207 2100 **Fax:** 020 7207 2150
Email: info@eauk.org
Web site: http://www.eauk.org
Titles:
IDEA MAGAZINE

EVANGELICAL MOVEMENT OF WALES 15878
Bryntirion, BRIDGEND, CF31 4DX **Tel:** 01656 655886
Fax: 01656 665919
Titles:
THE EVANGELICAL MAGAZINE

EVANGELICAL TIMES 1649940
Faverdale North, DARLINGTON, DL3 0PH
Tel: 01325 380232 **Fax:** 01325 466153
Email: office@evangelicaltimes.org
Web site: http://www.evangelicaltimes.org
Titles:
EVANGELICAL TIMES

EVEGATE PUBLISHING LTD 14030
Tel: 01303 233880
PR br email only
Email: newsdesk@southeastfarmer.net
Titles:
SOUTH EAST BUSINESS
SOUTH EAST FARMER

EVENING PRESS LTD 1760499
c/o Northcliffe House, 2 Derry Street, LONDON, W8 5TT
Titles:
LONDON EVENING STANDARD
THIS IS LONDON

EVENING STANDARD CO LTD 14819
Northcliffe House, 2 Derry Street, Kensington, LONDON, W8 5EE **Tel:** 020 7938 6000 **Fax:** 020 7937 9302
Titles:
ES MAGAZINE

THE EVENT PARTNERSHIP 1724435
Watergate House, Watergate Street, CHESTER, CH1 2LF
Tel: 01244 346347 **Fax:** 01244 344833
Titles:
DESIGN ET AL

EVENTICA 1630181
12 Skylines Village, Limeharbour, LONDON, E14 9TS
Tel: 020 7510 2560 **Fax:** 020 7510 2561
Web site: http://www.eventica.co.uk
Titles:
RUSSIAN INVESTMENT REVIEW

EVERTON'S NEWS AGENCY 15334
Hayley Green Court, 130 Hagley Road, Hayley Green, HALESOWEN, B63 1DY **Tel:** 0121 585 9188
Fax: 0121 585 7117
Titles:
SNOOKER SCENE

EVERY INVESTOR LTD 1734500
1 Vincent Square, LONDON, SW1P 2PN **Tel:** 020 7932 4158
Web site: http://www.everyinvestor.co.uk
Titles:
EVERYINVESTOR.CO.UK

EVOLVE 1650171
Unit 8, Woodcock Hill Industrial Estate, Harefield Road, RICKMANSWORTH, WD3 1PQ **Tel:** 01923 774111
Fax: 01923 721818
Email: info@evolve-print.com
Web site: http://www.evolve-print.com
Titles:
AT EASE
OUTLOOK

EVOLVE DIGITAL PUBLISHING 1762145
Unit 3, The Old Estate Yard, North Stoke lane, Upton Cheyney, BRISTOL, BA2 3DZ **Tel:** 0117 932 3586
Titles:
AUSTRALIA & NEW ZEALAND
FRENCH MAGAZINE
TRAVELLER IN FRANCE

THE EXAMINER 1656195
Rathkeeland House, 1 Blaney Road, Crossmaglen, NEWRY, BT35 9JJ **Tel:** 028 3086 8500 **Fax:** 028 3086 8580
Titles:
THE EXAMINER

EXCEL PRINTING LTD 1706557
351 Lichfield Road, Aston, BIRMINGHAM, B6 7ST
Tel: 0121 326 3496 **Fax:** 0121 328 3806
Titles:
THE ECHO

EXCEL PUBLISHING COMPANY LTD 13525
Portland Buildings, 127-129 Portland Street, MANCHESTER, M1 4PZ **Tel:** 0161 236 2782 **Fax:** 0161 236 2783
Email: info@excelpublishing.co.uk
Web site: http://www.excelpublishing.co.uk
Titles:
BUILDER & ENGINEER
BUSINESS WEST
COMMERCE GM
CONNECT
CONSTRUCTION SCOTLAND
DECORATING MATTERS
EN THE MAGAZINE FOR ENTREPRENEURS (NORTH WEST)
FIRST MOVE CONSTRUCTION
FIRST MOVE HEALTHCARE
FIRST MOVE HOSPITALITY, LEISURE AND TOURISM

FIRST MOVE NORTH WEST
FLEET TIMES
FOCUS
FOOD SCIENCE AND TECHNOLOGY
GLASGOW BUSINESS
INSITE
LOCAL GOVERNMENT EXECUTIVE
NORTHERN HOUSING
PLUMB HEAT
PUBLIC SECTOR CONSTRUCTION
RETAIL PROPERTY AND DEVELOPMENT
SOUTH LONDON BUSINESS
TIMBER IN CONSTRUCTION

EXCELL PUBLISHING 13831
Portland Building, 127-129 Portland Street, MANCHESTER, M1 4PZ **Tel:** 0161 661 4150
Web site: http://www.excelpublishing.co.uk
Titles:
C & W IN BUSINESS
LONDON BUSINESS MATTERS
MSA NEWSLINK
PROSPER

EXCHANGE ENTERPRISES LTD 1687142
Robert Rogers House, New Orchard, POOLE, BH15 1LU
Tel: 01202 207750 **Fax:** 01202 207755
Web site: http://exchangeandmart.co.uk
Titles:
AUTO EXCHANGE
EXCHANGE & MART

EXCLUSIVE LONDON GROUP 1712789
Office 6231, 2nd Floor, 49 Greenwich High Road, LONDON, SE10 8JL **Tel:** 0870 350 9459 **Fax:** 0870 429 9459
Titles:
EXCLUSIVE LONDON

EXECUTARY INTERNATIONAL MAGAZINE LTD 18756
Groves Business Centre, Milton-under-Wychwood, CHIPPING NORTON, OX7 6JF **Tel:** 01993 832555
Fax: 01993 832999
Web site: http://www.executarynews.co.uk
Titles:
EXECUTARY NEWS

EXECUTIVE GRAPEVINE INTERNATIONAL LTD 600465
New Barnes Mill, Cottonmill Lane, ST. ALBANS, AL1 2HA
Tel: 01727 844335 **Fax:** 01727 844779
Web site: http://www.askgrapevine.com
Titles:
DIRECTORY OF EXECUTIVE RECRUITMENT - INTERNATIONAL EDITION
THE GRAPEVINE
UK DIRECTORY OF TALENT MANAGEMENT

EXECUTIVE HIRE NEWS LTD 13545
Hartham Park, CORSHAM, SN13 0RP **Tel:** 01249 700607
Fax: 01249 700235
Email: ehnteam@executivehirenews.co.uk
Web site: http://www.executivehirenews.co.uk
Titles:
EXECUTIVE HIRE NEWS

EXECUTIVE MAGAZINES LTD 14287
Bakers House, 25 Bakers Road, UXBRIDGE, UB8 1RG
Tel: 01895 819350 **Fax:** 01895 457457
Email: info@phe.co.uk
Web site: http://www.phe.co.uk
Titles:
PHE - PLANT HIRE EXECUTIVE

EXECUTIVE PUBLICATIONS 13191
Media House, Cronkbourne, DOUGLAS, IM4 4SB
Tel: 01624 696555 **Fax:** 01624 661655
Web site: http://www.manninmedia.co.im
Titles:
MANX TAILS
MONEY MEDIA

EXETER UNIVERSITY GUILD OF STUDENTS 15749
University of Exeter, Cornwall House, St. Germans Road, EXETER, EX4 6TG **Tel:** 01392 263513 **Fax:** 01392 263560
Titles:
EXEPOSÉ

EXIT LTD 674025
205 Regent Street, LONDON, W1B 4HB **Tel:** 020 7734 5299
Fax: 020 7734 5392
Titles:
EXIT

THE EXMOOR SOCIETY 1676026
The Parish Rooms, Rosemary Lane, DULVERTON, TA22 9DP **Tel:** 01398 323335 **Fax:** 01398 323335
Email: exmoorsociety@yahoo.co.uk
Web site: http://www.exmoorsociety.org.uk
Titles:
EXMOOR REVIEW

EXPANSIVE MEDIA LTD 1741927
The Basement, Woodlands, 79 High Street, GREENHITHE, DA9 9RD **Tel:** 01322 386444 **Fax:** 01322 386660
Titles:
ENTERTAIN

EXPAT NETWORK LTD 16119
Advertiser House, 19 Bartlett Street, SOUTH CROYDON, CR2 6TB **Tel:** 020 8256 0311 **Fax:** 020 8256 0312
Titles:
NEXUS

EXPATRIATE LIVING LTD 1745743
Suite 46, 24-28 St. Leonards Road, WINDSOR, SL4 3BB
Tel: 0845 056 9611 **Fax:** 01784 242051
Titles:
EXPATRIATE MAGAZINE

EXPERIENCE PRESS AND PR 1715851
PO Box 1469, HUDDERSFIELD, HD1 9EB
Tel: 01484 311089 **Fax:** 01484 311089
Email: editor@fff-uk.co.uk
Web site: http://www.fff-uk.co.uk
Titles:
FRYER & FAST FOOD

EXPO PUBLISHING 1638432
37 Tyndall Court, Commerce Road, Lynch Wood, PETERBOROUGH, PE2 6LR **Tel:** 01733 405730
Fax: 01733 405745
Titles:
CDC NEWS
COACH MONTHLY
ROUTE ONE

EXPORTA PUBLISHING & EVENTS LTD 1745794
3C Hillgate Place, LONDON, SW12 9ER **Tel:** 020 8673 9666
Fax: 020 8673 8662
Titles:
EMEA FINANCE MAGAZINE
GLOBAL TRADE REVIEW

EXPOSURE ORGANISATION LTD 600511
The Bigger Shoe Box, Muswell Hill Centre, Hillfield Park, LONDON, N10 3QJ **Tel:** 020 8883 0260 **Fax:** 020 8883 2906
Titles:
EXPOSURE

EXPRESS & STAR LTD 12820
51-53 Queen Street, WOLVERHAMPTON, WV1 1ES
Tel: 01902 313131 **Fax:** 01902 319467
Web site: http://www.expressandstar.com
Titles:
THE CANNOCK & LICHFIELD CHRONICLE SERIES
DUDLEY CHRONICLE SERIES
SANDWELL AND GREAT BARR CHRONICLE SERIES
THE STAFFORD & STONE CHRONICLE
WALSALL CHRONICLE
WOLVERHAMPTON CHRONICLE

EXPRESS NEWSPAPERS LTD 14815
The Northern & Shell Building, 10 Lower Thames Street, LONDON, EC3R 6EN **Tel:** 0871 434 1010
Fax: 0871 520 7766
Titles:
DAILY EXPRESS
DAILY EXPRESS SATURDAY
DAILY STAR
DAILY STAR (GLASGOW OFFICE)
DAILY STAR ONLINE
DAILY STAR SUNDAY

DAILY/SUNDAY EXPRESS ONLINE
HOTTV
NEW!
NEW-MAGAZINE.CO.UK
S THE SUNDAY EXPRESS
SCOTTISH DAILY EXPRESS (GLASGOW)
SCOTTISH SUNDAY EXPRESS
SUNDAY EXPRESS
SUNDAY EXPRESS REVIEW
TAKE 5

EXTREME PUBLISHING LTD   15429
PO Box 9845, LONDON, W13 9WP
Titles:
   SUPERMOTO MAGAZINE
   TRAILBIKE AND ENDURO MAGAZINE

EYE MAGAZINE LTD   1747673
Studio 6, The Lux Building, 2-4 Hoxton Square, LONDON,
N1 6NU **Tel:** 020 7684 6530 **Fax:** 020 7684 6525
Email: john.walters@eyemagazine.com
Web site: http://www.eyemagazine.com
Titles:
   EYE: THE INTERNATIONAL REVIEW OF GRAPHIC
      DESIGN

EYE SPY PUBLISHING LTD   674101
PO Box 10, SKIPTON, BD23 5US **Tel:** 01756 770199
Fax: 01756 770199
Email: editor@eyespymag.com
Web site: http://www.eyespymag.com
Titles:
   EYE SPY INTELLIGENCE MAGAZINE

FAB   12715
Taeselbury, High Street, Tisbury, SALISBURY, SP3 6LD
Tel: 0870 742 2278 **Fax:** 01747 871873
Email: information@fabcats.org
Web site: http://www.fabcats.org
Titles:
   CATCARE

FABIAN SOCIETY   17570
11 Dartmouth Street, LONDON, SW1H 9BN
Tel: 020 7227 4900
Titles:
   FABIAN REVIEW

FACILITIES MANAGEMENT ONLINE LIMITED   621995
Cefn Tew, Tynlon, Llanddeusant, HOLYHEAD, LL65 4AU
Tel: 01248 470477 **Fax:** 01248 470003
Email: info@fmonline.co.uk
Web site: http://www.fmonline.co.uk
Titles:
   FACILITIES MANAGEMENT ONLINE

FACTORY MEDIA   1677213
1 West Smithfield, LONDON, EC1A 9JU **Tel:** 020 7332 9700
Fax: 020 7332 9799
Web site: http://www.factorymedia.com
Titles:
   ADRENALINTRIP.NET
   THE BICYCLE BUYER
   COOLER
   DIG BMX MAGAZINE
   DIRT
   KINGPIN SKATEBOARDING EUROPA
   ONBOARD
   SIDEWALK SKATEBOARDING MAGAZINE
   SURF EUROPE
   SURFCORE.CO.UK
   THE SURFER'S PATH
   WHITE LINES SNOWBOARD MAGAZINE

FACTORY MEDIA LTD   15433
1 West Smithfield, LONDON, EC1A 9JU **Tel:** 01202 606118
Titles:
   MOTO MAGAZINE
   RIDE BMX MAGAZINE

FACTORY PUBLISHING LTD.   1653647
Flat 1, 30 Bramham Gardens, LONDON, SW5 0HF
Tel: 020 7370 2430 **Fax:** 020 7370 2430
Email: info@factory-publishing.com
Web site: http://www.factory-publishing.com
Titles:
   FACTORY: THE FILM INDUSTRY MAGAZINE

FAIRCHILD PUBLICATIONS   12480
20 Shorts Gardens, LONDON, WC2H 9AU
Tel: 020 7240 0420 **Fax:** 020 7240 0290
Web site: http://www.fairchildpub.com
Titles:
   W
   WOMEN'S WEAR DAILY
   WWD BEAUTY BIZ

FAIRGAME PUBLISHING   1653689
Baltic Business Centre, Saltmeadows Road, GATESHEAD,
NE8 3DA **Tel:** 0191 442 4001
Titles:
   FAIRGAME

FAIRMEAD COMMUNICATIONS LTD   16079
5 Britannia Place, Station Street, LYMINGTON, SO41 3BA
Tel: 01590 671899 **Fax:** 01590 671116
Titles:
   SEAHORSE INTERNATIONAL SAILING

FAIRTRADE MEDIA   1650952
3 Charnwood Street, DERBY, DE1 2GT **Tel:** 01954 211262
Titles:
   IRISH BEAUTY

THE FAIRWAY   18988
216 Christchurch Road, NEWPORT, NP19 8BJ
Tel: 01633 666700 **Fax:** 01633 277766
Email: enquiries@fairway.org.uk
Web site: http://www.fairway.org.uk
Titles:
   THE FAIRWAY GOLFING NEWS

FAIRWAY TO GREEN LTD   1621953
Floor 1, Room 113, Brook Drive, READING, RG2 6UB
Tel: 0800 043 3055 **Fax:** 0118 949 7001
Email: sales@fairwaytogreen.com
Titles:
   FAIRWAY TO GREEN

FALL LINE MEDIA LIMITED   15268
South Wing, Broadway Court, Broadway,
PETERBOROUGH, PE1 1RP **Tel:** 01733 293250
Fax: 01733 293269
Web site: http://www.fall-line.co.uk
Titles:
   DOCUMENT SNOWBOARD
   FALL LINE SKIING
   OUTDOOR ADVENTURE GUIDE

FAMEDRAM PUBLISHERS LTD.   15964
PO Box 3, ELLON, AB41 9EA **Tel:** 01651 842429
Fax: 01651 842180
Web site: http://www.artwork.co.uk
Titles:
   ARTWORK

FAMILIES MAGAZINES LTD   15136
PO Box 4302, LONDON, SW16 1ZS **Tel:** 020 8696 9680
Fax: 020 8696 9679
Email: publisher@familiesmagazine.co.uk
Web site: http://www.familiesmagazine.co.uk
Titles:
   FAMILIES BRISTOL
   FAMILIES CHILTERN
   FAMILIES EAST LONDON
   FAMILIES EDINBURGH
   FAMILIES EPSOM, SUTTON & CROYDON
   FAMILIES HERTS
   FAMILIES IN THE VALE OF YORK
   FAMILIES LEEDS
   FAMILIES LIVERPOOL
   FAMILIES LONDON
   FAMILIES MANCHESTER
   FAMILIES SOLENT EAST
   FAMILIES SOLENT WEST
   FAMILIES SOUTH EAST
   FAMILIES SURREY EAST
   FAMILIES SURREY WEST
   FAMILIES SUSSEX COAST
   FAMILIES SW LONDON
   FAMILIES THAMES VALLEY EAST
   FAMILIES THAMES VALLEY WEST
   FAMILIES UPON AVON
   FAMILIES UPON THAMES
   FAMILIES WEST

FAMILIES NORTH WEST MAGAZINE   1744157
PO Box 4302, LONDON, SW16 1ZS **Tel:** 020 8696 9680
Fax: 020 8696 9679
Email: publisher@familiesnw.co.uk
Titles:
   FAMILIES NORTH WEST

FAMILY INTEREST MAGAZINE   1744271
PO Box 395, SEVENOAKS, TN13 3YG **Tel:** 01732 227888
Fax: 01732 227881
Email: info@familyinterest.co.uk
Web site: http://www.familyinterest.co.uk
Titles:
   FAMILY INTEREST MAGAZINE

FAMILY MAGAZINE LTD   672113
5 Shaw Bridge Street, CLITHEROE, BB7 1LY
Tel: 01200 453004 **Fax:** 01200 453009
Email: editor@familymagazine.co.uk
Web site: http://www.familymagazine.co.uk
Titles:
   FAMILY MAGAZINE

FAMILY PLANNING ASSOCIATION   12647
50 Featherstone Street, LONDON, EC1Y 8QU
Tel: 020 7608 5240 **Fax:** 0845 123 2349
Email: susannaw@fpa.org.uk
Web site: http://www.fpa.org.uk
Titles:
   IN BRIEF

FAR AND WIDE PUBLISHERS LTD   15693
PO Box 3394, FARINGDON, SN7 7FN **Tel:** 0845 833 9626
Email: mail@tfa.net
Web site: http://www.tfa.net
Titles:
   FREEDOM TODAY

FARMERS CLUB JOURNAL   674105
3 Whitehall Court, LONDON, SW1A 2EL **Tel:** 020 7930 3751
Fax: 020 7839 7864
Web site: http://www.thefarmersclub.com
Titles:
   FARMERS CLUB JOURNAL

FARMERS' UNION OF WALES   14031
Llys Amaeth, Plas Gogerddan, ABERYSTWYTH, SY23 3BT
Tel: 01970 820820 **Fax:** 01970 820821
Email: head.office@fuw.org.uk
Web site: http://www.fuw.org.uk
Titles:
   WELSH FARMER (Y TIR)

FARMING MONTHLY LTD   18746
15-17 Dugdale Street, NUNEATON, CV11 5QJ
Tel: 024 7635 3537 **Fax:** 024 7635 3571
Titles:
   FARMING MONTHLY NATIONAL

FARNHAM CASTLE NEWSPAPERS LTD   14991
114-115 West Street, FARNHAM, GU9 7HL
Tel: 01252 725224 **Fax:** 01252 899267
Email: farnham-herald@internet-today.co.uk
Titles:
   FARNHAM HERALD SERIES

FARNHAM CASTLE PUBLICATIONS   627706
114-115 West Street, FARNHAM, GU9 7HL
Tel: 01252 899297
Titles:
   THE VILLAGE ECHO

FARSCAPE LTD   1650126
123-126 Trafalgar House, Grenville Place, LONDON, NW7
3SA **Tel:** 020 8906 7772 **Fax:** 020 8906 7773
Email: info@property-investor-news.com
Web site: http://www.property-investor-news.com
Titles:
   PROPERTY INVESTOR NEWS

FASHION WEB LTD   1735753
15 Cottenham Road, Histon, CAMBRIDGE, CB24 9ES
Tel: 0845 644 2284 **Fax:** +44 0845 126 0752

UK Publishers & Their Titles

Titles:
FASHIONWEB.CO.UK

FAST FERRY INFORMATION LTD   13641
14 Marston Gate, WINCHESTER, SO23 7DS
Tel: 01962 869842 **Fax:** 01962 843863
Titles:
FAST FERRY INTERNATIONAL

FAST FIX EURO LTD   1603064
PO Box 22894, LONDON, NW9 6ZE **Tel:** 020 8905 9511
Fax: 020 8905 9512
Titles:
F & F MAGAZINE

FASTENER FAIRS LIMITED   18760
18 Alban Park, Hatfield Road, ST. ALBANS, AL4 0JJ
Tel: 01727 739150 **Fax:** 01727 831033
Web site: http://www.fastenerfair.com
Titles:
FASTENER & FIXING MAGAZINE

FAVERSHAM HOUSE GROUP LTD   12535
Faversham House, 232A Addington Road, SOUTH
CROYDON, CR2 8LE **Tel:** 020 8651 7100
Fax: 020 8651 7117
Web site: http://www.fhgmedia.co.uk
Titles:
ACR NEWS
BMJ BUILDERS MERCHANTS JOURNAL
CONVERTER
DIY WEEK
EDIE
HARDWARE & GARDEN REVIEW
HOUSEWARES DIRECTORY
HOUSEWARES MAGAZINE
HVR
LOCAL AUTHORITY WASTE & RECYCLING
SUSTAINABLE BUSINESS
WATER & WASTEWATER TREATMENT
WEB4WATER
WET NEWS

THE FAWCETT SOCIETY   15725
1-3 Berry Street, LONDON, EC1V 0AA **Tel:** 020 7253 2598
Fax: 020 7253 2599
Titles:
STOPGAP

FC PUBLISHING   698799
7-9 Fashion Street, LONDON, E1 6PX **Tel:** 020 7375 7561
Fax: 020 7375 7511
Titles:
ETHICAL CORPORATION MAGAZINE

FDA   17036
8 Leake Street, LONDON, SE1 7NN **Tel:** 020 7401 5555
Fax: 020 7401 5550
Web site: http://www.fda.org.uk
Titles:
FOCUS
PUBLIC SERVICE MAGAZINE

FDI WORLD DENTAL PRESS LTD   14543
5 Battery Green Road, LOWESTOFT, NR32 1DE
Tel: 01502 511522 **Fax:** 01502 583152
Email: wdp@dbgp.co.uk
Web site: http://www.fdi.org.uk
Titles:
COMMUNITY DENTAL HEALTH
EUROPEAN JOURNAL OF PROSTHODONTICS AND
   RESTORATIVE DENTISTRY
INTERNATIONAL DENTAL JOURNAL

**FEDERATION OF BURIAL AND CREMATION
AUTHORITIES**   14809
41 Salisbury Road, CARSHALTON, SM5 3HA
Tel: 020 8669 4521
Titles:
RESURGAM

**THE FEDERATION OF COMMUNICATION SERVICES
LTD**   13596
Burnhill Business Centre, Provident House, Burrell Row,
BECKENHAM, BR3 1AT **Tel:** 020 8249 6363
Fax: 0870 120 5927
Web site: http://www.fcs.org.uk
Titles:
FCS BULLETIN

FEDERATION OF HOLISTIC THERAPISTS   17230
18 Shakespeare Business Centre, Hathaway Close,
EASTLEIGH, SO50 4SR **Tel:** 0844 875 2022
Fax: 023 8062 4398
Email: info@fht.org.uk
Web site: http://www.fht.org.uk
Titles:
INTERNATIONAL THERAPIST

FEDERATION OF PETROLEUM SUPPLIERS   14221
6 Royal Court, Tatton Street, KNUTSFORD, WA16 6EN
Tel: 01565 631313 **Fax:** 01565 631314
Email: vc@fpsonline.com
Web site: http://www.fpsonline.co.uk
Titles:
DOWNSTREAM

FEDERATION OF SMALL BUSINESSES   622084
PO Box 109, CHIPPING NORTON, OX7 6GL
Tel: 01993 832357 **Fax:** 01993 832366
Web site: http://www.fsb.org.uk/103
Titles:
THAMES VALLEY NEWS

FEELGOOD MEDIA   1684879
13 Coaledge, FIFE, KY4 8HB **Tel:** 0141 416 4055
Titles:
HI-TECH SCOTLAND

FELIXSTOWE TOWN CRIER LTD   1733857
Unit 1, Mannings Amusement Park, Mackle Gate Road,
FELIXSTOWE, IP11 2DN **Tel:** 01394 270811
Web site: http://www.felixstowetowncrierltd.com
Titles:
FELIXSTOWE TOWN CRIER

FELLOWS MEDIA   621977
The Gallery, Manor Farm, Southam, CHELTENHAM, GL52
3PB **Tel:** 01242 259240 **Fax:** 01242 259248
Web site: http://www.fellowsmedia.com
Titles:
BUTTERFLY

FELLOWSHIP OF ST ALBAN & ST SERGIUS   18249
1 Canterbury Road, OXFORD, OX2 6LU **Tel:** 01865 552991
Fax: 01865 316700
Titles:
SOBORNOST (INCORPORATING EASTERN CHURCHES
   REVIEW)

FENMAN LTD   17405
28 St. Thomas Place, Cambridgeshire Business Park, ELY,
CB7 4EX **Tel:** 01353 654877 **Fax:** 01353 663644
Titles:
TJ

FENS   17503
10 Wiseton Road, LONDON, SW17 7EE **Tel:** 020 8672 3191
Fax: 020 8672 2282
Titles:
THE CELEBRITY BULLETIN

THE FERRARI OWNERS CLUB LTD   15451
14 Lynn Road, Snettisham, KING'S LYNN, PE317PT
Tel: 01485 544500 **Fax:** 01485 544515
Email: ever.focuk@btinternet.com
Web site: http://www.ferrariownersclub.co.uk
Titles:
FERRARI MAGAZINE
FERRARI NEWS

FERRY PUBLICATIONS LTD   16158
PO Box 33, Ramsey, ISLE OF MAN, IM99 4LP
Tel: 01624 898445 **Fax:** 01624 898449

Titles:
EUROPEAN FERRY SCENE

FESPA   14268
Association House, 7B West Street, REIGATE, RH2 9BL
Tel: 01737 240788 **Fax:** 01737 240778
Titles:
THE FESPA WORLD

FESTIVAL BIZ   1726817
145-157 St. John Street, LONDON, EC1V 4PY
Tel: 020 3239 9277
Titles:
SCI-FI-LONDON

FFESTINIOG RAILWAY SOCIETY   15496
Harbour Station, PORTHMADOG, LL49 9NF
Tel: 01766 530670 **Fax:** 0870 706 3351
Email: secretary@ffestiniograilway.org.uk
Web site: http://www.ffestiniograilway.org.uk
Titles:
FFESTINIOG RAILWAY MAGAZINE

FGA LTD   698074
9 Byron Road, STRATFORD-UPON-AVON, CV37 7JP
Tel: 01926 650173
Titles:
GB.GOLF
PEGITUP
WARWICKSHIRE GOLF

FHG GUIDES   13165
Abbey Mill Business Centre, Seedhill, PAISLEY, PA1 1TJ
Tel: 0141 887 0428 **Fax:** 0141 889 7204
Email: admin@fhguides.co.uk
Web site: http://www.holidayguides.com
Titles:
BRITAIN'S BEST LEISURE AND RELAXATION GUIDE
FAMILY BREAKS IN BRITAIN
FHG COAST & COUNTRY HOLIDAYS
THE GOLF GUIDE: WHERE TO PLAY/ WHERE TO STAY
GUIDE TO CARAVAN & CAMPING HOLIDAYS
PETS WELCOME!
RECOMMENDED COUNTRY HOTELS OF BRITAIN
RECOMMENDED INNS & PUBS OF BRITAIN
RECOMMENDED SHORT BREAK HOLIDAYS IN BRITAIN

FIDGET LTD   1751819
The Drill Hall, 30-38 Dalmeny Street, EDINBURGH, EH6 8RG
Tel: 07929 381197
Email: josh@square-go.com
Web site: http://www.square-go.com
Titles:
SQUARE-GO

FIGURE 8 MEDIA   1759337
20 Portland Square, BRISTOL, BS2 8SJ **Tel:** 0117 230 8844
Titles:
ECOIDEAS

FILM MAKER PUBLICATIONS LTD   15843
40 Runnymeade, Swinton, MANCHESTER, M27 5WA
Tel: 0161 794 6743 **Fax:** 0161 794 6743
Titles:
FILM AND VIDEO MAKER

FINANCE PUBLICATIONS OFFSHORE LTD   17260
PO Box 726, St. Helier, JERSEY, JE4 0XJ **Tel:** 01534 625228
Fax: 01534 625227
Web site: http://www.financeoffshore.com
Titles:
GLOBAL ASSETS

FINANCIAL EXPRESS LIMITED   16654
7 Chertsey Road, WOKING, GU21 5AB **Tel:** 01483 783900
Fax: 01483 783901
Web site: http://www.financialexpress.net
Titles:
INVESTEGATE
TRUSTNET

FINANCIAL I LTD   1686182
40 Bowling Green Lane, LONDON, EC1R 0NE
Tel: 020 7415 7169 **Fax:** 020 7415 7172

Titles:
FINANCIAL I

FINANCIAL INDUSTRY GAZETTE   699894
Room SA301, St. Andrews House, St. Andrews Street,
NORWICH, NR2 4TP **Tel:** 01603 773722
Email: info@fignorfolk.com

Titles:
FINANCIAL INDUSTRY GAZETTE

THE FINANCIAL INFORMATION COMPANY LTD   13517
Fifth Floor, 57a Great Suffolk Street, LONDON, SE1 0BB
Tel: 020 7934 0166 **Fax:** 020 7934 0179
Email: socialhousing@socialhousing.co.uk
Web site: http://www.socialhousing.co.uk

Titles:
SOCIAL HOUSING

FINANCIAL TIMES   12361
1 Southwark Bridge, LONDON, SE1 9HL **Tel:** 020 7873 3000
Fax: 020 7873 3194
Web site: http://www.ft.com

Titles:
CHINA CONFIDENTIAL
FINANCIAL TIMES
FINANCIAL TIMES (BIRMINGHAM OFFICE)
FINANCIAL TIMES (EDINBURGH OFFICE)
FINANCIAL TIMES (MANCHESTER OFFICE)
FINANCIAL TIMES WEEKEND MAGAZINE
FT.COM
FTFM
HIGH NET WORTH MAGAZINE
HOW TO SPEND IT
PENSIONS MANAGEMENT

FINDLAY MEDIA LTD   12420
Hawley Mill, Hawley Road, DARTFORD, DA2 7TJ
Tel: 01322 221144 **Fax:** 01322 221188
Web site: http://www.findlay.co.uk

Titles:
AUTOMOTIVE DESIGN ASIA
EUREKA
EUROPEAN AUTOMOTIVE DESIGN
MACHINERY
MACHINERY BUYERS' GUIDE
MACHINERY CLASSIFIED
MACHINERY CLASSIFIED INTERNATIONAL
MANUFACTURING COMPUTER SOLUTIONS
NEW ELECTRONICS
THE PLANT ENGINEER
WORKS MANAGEMENT

FINE & COUNTRY LTD   1644581
121 Park Lane, LONDON, W1K 7AG **Tel:** 020 7079 1515
Fax: 020 7629 2329

Titles:
FINE & COUNTRY

THE FINE ART TRADE GUILD   14814
16-18 Empress Place, LONDON, SW6 1TT
Tel: 020 7381 6616 **Fax:** 020 7381 2596
Web site: http://www.fineart.co.uk

Titles:
ART BUSINESS TODAY

FINEXTRA RESEARCH   674931
101 St. Martin's Lane, LONDON, WC2N 4AZ
Tel: 020 3100 3670

Titles:
FINEXTRA

FINLAYSON MEDIA COMMUNICATIONS LTD   14547
1 Hertford House, Hugo Gryn Way, Farm Close, SHENLEY,
WD7 9AB **Tel:** 01923 851777 **Fax:** 01923 851778
Web site: http://www.fmc.co.uk

Titles:
DENTISTRY
DENTISTRY.CO.UK
ENDODONTIC PRACTICE
IRISH DENTIST
PREVENTIVE DENTISTRY
PRIVATE DENTISTRY

FINNYBANK LTD   18400
30 Finny Bank Road, SALE, M33 6LR **Tel:** 0161 969 9820
Fax: 0870 051 9527
Web site: http://www.finnybank.com

Titles:
QERCUS

FIPP   13441
Queens House, 55-56 Lincoln's Inn Fields, LONDON, WC2A
3LJ **Tel:** 020 7404 4169 **Fax:** 020 7404 4170
Email: info@fipp.com
Web site: http://www.fipp.com

Titles:
FIPP WORLD MAGAZINE TRENDS BOOK 2007/2008
MAGAZINE WORLD

FIRA INTERNATIONAL LTD   16278
Maxwell Road, STEVENAGE, SG1 2EW **Tel:** 01438 777700
Fax: 01438 777800

Titles:
ASKFIRA NEWS
FIRA INTERNATIONAL LIMITED

FIRE BRIGADES UNION   621737
Bradley House, 68 Coombe Road, KINGSTON UPON
THAMES, KT2 7AE **Tel:** 020 8541 1765 **Fax:** 020 8546 5187

Titles:
FIREFIGHTER

FIRE PROTECTION ASSOCIATION   14450
London Road, MORETON-IN-MARSH, GL56 0RH
Tel: 01608 812500 **Fax:** 01608 812501
Web site: http://www.thefpa.co.uk

Titles:
FIRE RISK MANAGEMENT

FIRE PUBLISHING   1736739
UKD House, Norstead Place, LONDON, SW15 3SA
Tel: 020 7228 6366 **Fax:** 020 7228 6330

Titles:
DVD WORLD
HUSTLER

FIREPLACE MARKETING COMPANY LIMITED   13268
Haseley Manor, Birmingham Road, WARWICK, CV35 7LS
Tel: 024 7624 7246 **Fax:** 024 7624 7266
Email: sales@firemarketing.co.uk
Web site: http://www.fireplace.co.uk

Titles:
FIRES & FIREPLACES

FIREWATER PUBLISHING   1748470
Office 14, Newport Market, Dock Street, NEWPORT, NP20
1DD **Tel:** 01633 251800

Titles:
BIGSCREEN

FIREWORKS   623458
PO Box 40, BEXHILL-ON-SEA, TN40 1GX
Tel: 01424 733050 **Fax:** 01424 733050
Email: editor@fireworks-mag.org
Web site: http://www.fireworks-mag.org

Titles:
FIREWORKS

FIRST CITY MEDIA   699587
28A Jubilee Trade Centre, Jubilee Road, LETCHWORTH
GARDEN CITY, SG6 1SP **Tel:** 01462 678300
Fax: 01462 481622
Email: editorial@firstcitymedia.co.uk
Web site: http://www.firstcitymedia.co.uk

Titles:
CONSULTING ENGINEER REVIEW
THE PRINT BUSINESS
PRINT MEDIA MANAGEMENT
SPECIFIER REVIEW

FIRST CONFERENCES   697566
7-9 Fashion Street, LONDON, E1 6PX **Tel:** 020 7375 7575

Titles:
TELEMATICS UPDATE MAGAZINE

FIRST MAGAZINE LIMITED   13744
56 Haymarket, LONDON, SW1Y 4RN **Tel:** 020 7389 9650
Fax: 020 7389 9644

Titles:
FIRST
WORLD PETROLEUM

FIRST TRUST BANK   1654819
4 Queen's Square, BELFAST, BT1 3DJ **Tel:** 028 9032 5599
Fax: 028 9023 5480

Titles:
ECONOMIC OUTLOOK AND BUSINESS REVIEW

FIRSTSTAR LTD   16772
2nd Floor, 23 Denmark Street, LONDON, WC2H 8NH
Tel: 020 7379 7887 **Fax:** 020 7379 7525

Titles:
QX MAGAZINE

FISH MEDIA GROUP LTD   1733073
6 Albany Chambers, 26 Bridge Road East, WELWYN
GARDEN CITY, AL7 1HL **Tel:** 0844 800 8439

Titles:
HARPENDEN LIFE

FISH MEDIA LTD   1733012
Chamber House, 25 Pier Road, St. Helier, JERSEY, JE1 4HF
Tel: 01534 619882

Titles:
THE GUERNSEY LIFE
THE JERSEY LIFE

THE FISHING LODGE STUDIO   623665
77 Bulbridge Road, Wilton, SALISBURY, SP2 0LE
Tel: 01722 743207 **Fax:** 01722 743207

Titles:
FLORA INTERNATIONAL

FISHING WAREHOUSE   625211
69 Browmere Drive, Croft, WARRINGTON, WA3 7HS

Titles:
FISHINGWAREHOUSE

FITNESS PROFESSIONALS LTD   14191
Kalbarri House, 107-113 London Road, LONDON, E13 0DA
Tel: 020 8586 0101 **Fax:** 020 8586 0685
Email: publish@fitpro.com
Web site: http://www.fitpro.com

Titles:
FITPRO
FITPRO BUSINESS
FITPRO NETWORK

FITWISE   622876
Drumcross Hall, BATHGATE, EH48 4JT **Tel:** 01506 811077
Fax: 01506 811477
Email: info@fitwise.co.uk
Web site: http://www.fitwise.co.uk

Titles:
THE MEDICAL DEVICE DECONTAMINATION

FLAG NEWSPAPERS   1630315
BCM The Flag, LONDON, WC1N 3XX **Tel:** 07071 226074
Fax: 07071 226074
Web site: http://www.the-flag.co.uk

Titles:
THE FLAG

FLAGSHIP MEDIA GROUP LTD   16190
48-50 York Street, BELFAST, BT15 1AS **Tel:** 028 9031 9008
Fax: 028 9072 7800
Web site: http://www.flagshipmedia.co.uk

Titles:
THE BIG LIST
KEYSTONE IRELAND
REGIONAL FILM & VIDEO

FLAVOUR MAGAZINE LTD   1731673
PO Box 55748, LONDON, E16 3XY **Tel:** 07949 310050
Email: info@flavourmag.co.uk

Titles:
FLAVOUR MAGAZINE
FLAVOUR MAGAZINE ONLINE

FLAXDALE PRINTERS   15193
5 Malvern Drive, WOODFORD GREEN, IG8 0JR
Tel: 020 8504 6862

Titles:
INVESTMENT TRUSTS

UK Publishers & Their Titles

FLEET STREET PUBLICATIONS LTD 12126
7th Floor, Sea Containers House, 20 Upper Ground,
LONDON, SE1 9JD **Tel:** 020 7447 4000 **Fax:** 020 7447 4041
Web site: http://www.fleetstreetpublications.co.uk
Titles:
  MONEY WEEK
  PROFIT WATCH
  PROFIT WATCH RECOMMENDS
  RED HOT PENNY SHARES

FLEMING INFORMATION SERVICES 16370
123 Adams Gardens, LONDON, SE16 4JH
Tel: 020 7237 9777
Titles:
  CONFERENCE CALENDAR

FLOREO 33 1735105
Brambletyne Close, Angmering, LITTLEHAMPTON, BN16
4DD **Tel:** 01903 774345
Email: euprosene@floreo.org
Web site: http://www.euphrosenelabon.com
Titles:
  FLOREO COMMUNITY

FLOURISH PUBLICATIONS (SCOTLAND) LTD 15881
196 Clyde Street, GLASGOW, G1 4JY **Tel:** 0141 226 5898
Fax: 0141 225 2600
Email: flourish@rcag.org.uk
Titles:
  FLOURISH

GERALDINE FLOWER PUBLICATIONS 12419
229 Acton Lane, LONDON, W4 5DD **Tel:** 020 8747 8028
Fax: 020 8747 8054
Web site: http://www.green-pages.co.uk
Titles:
  GREEN PAGES THE DIRECTORY OF AGRICULTURE
    FOR THE UK

FLUTEWISE ORGANISATION 16714
8-9 Beaconsfield Road, PORTSLADE, BN41 1XA
Tel: 01273 702367
Web site: http://www.flutewise.com
Titles:
  FLUTEWISE

FLUX PUBLICATIONS 600650
42 Edge Street, MANCHESTER, M4 1HN **Tel:** 0161 832 0300
Fax: 0161 819 1196
Titles:
  FLUX

FLYFISHERS CLUB 16104
69 Brook Street, LONDON, W1K 4ER **Tel:** 020 7629 5958
Titles:
  FLYFISHERS' JOURNAL

FLYING PIG PUBLISHING 1641545
3 Basset Place, FALMOUTH, TR11 2SS **Tel:** 01326 314242
Titles:
  BLACKBIRD PIE

FMB CONSULTANTS LTD 13720
FMB House, 6 Windmill Road, Hampton Hill, HAMPTON,
TW12 1RH **Tel:** 020 8979 7866 **Fax:** 020 8979 4573
Email: fmb@fmb-group.co.uk
Web site: http://www.fmb-group.co.uk
Titles:
  FERTILIZER FOCUS

FMS PUBLISHING 1600516
New Barn, Fanhams Grange, Fanhams Hall Road, WARE,
SG12 7QA **Tel:** 01920 467492 **Fax:** 01920 460149
Titles:
  BENTLEY MAGAZINE
  THE RITZ
  SUNSEEKER

FOCUS MEDIA PUBLICATIONS LTD 1716406
Cranes Point, Gardiners Lane South, BASILDON, SS14 3AP
Tel: 01268 286070
Titles:
  THE PARENTS GUIDE UK

FOCUS NEWSPAPERS LTD 696694
PO Box 238, ST. ALBANS, AL1 1WE **Tel:** 01582 414876
Fax: 01582 654327
Titles:
  FOCUS SERIES

FOCUS PUBLISHING LTD 1675502
100 Bridge Street, PETERBOROUGH, PE1 1DY
Tel: 01733 566933 **Fax:** 01733 566776
Email: sales@focuspublishing.co.uk
Web site: http://www.focuspublishing.co.uk
Titles:
  CV DEALER MONTHLY

FOCUS WORLDWIDE PUBLICATIONS LTD 621604
59 Carlton Hill, St. John's Wood, LONDON, NW8 0EN
Tel: 020 7624 3433 **Fax:** 020 7604 4433
Titles:
  FOCUS

THE FOOD COMMISSION 1712999
94 White Lion Street, LONDON, N1 9PF
Email: enquires@foodcomm.org.uk
Web site: http://www.foodcomm.org.uk
Titles:
  THE FOOD MAGAZINE

FOOD TRADE PRESS LTD 14055
Station House, Hortons Way, WESTERHAM, TN16 1BZ
Tel: 01959 563944 **Fax:** 01959 561285
Email: info@foodtradepress.com
Web site: http://www.foodtradepress.com
Titles:
  BINSTED'S DIRECTORY OF FOOD TRADE MARKS &
    BRAND NAMES
  FOOD TRADE REVIEW

THE FOOTBALL ASSOCIATION 1739874
Tel: 020 7745 4545
25 Soho Square, LONDON, W1D 4FA **Tel:** 020 7745 4545
Fax: 020 7745 5684
Titles:
  REFEREEING

THE FOOTBALL PAPER LTD 1720393
Lower Ground Floor, Tuition House, St. Georges Road,
LONDON, SW19 4EU **Tel:** 020 8971 4333
Fax: 020 8971 4366
Titles:
  THE NON-LEAGUE PAPER

FORBES INC 1685501
36-38 Piccadilly, LONDON, W1J 0DP **Tel:** 020 7286 6251
Titles:
  FORBES

THE FORCES PENSION SOCIETY 15202
68 South Lambeth Road, Vauxhall, LONDON, SW8 1RL
Tel: 020 7582 0469 **Fax:** 020 7820 9948
Titles:
  PENNANT

FORD MOTOR COMPANY LTD 691154
Eagle Way, BRENTWOOD, CM13 3BW **Tel:** 01277 252880
Fax: 01277 253097
Web site: http://www.ford.co.uk
Titles:
  FORD NEWS

THE FORENSIC SCIENCE SOCIETY 14155
18A Mount Parade, HARROGATE, HG1 1BX
Tel: 01423 566973 **Fax:** 01423 566391
Web site: http://www.forensic-science-society.org.uk
Titles:
  SCIENCE & JUSTICE

FOREST MACHINE JOURNAL 1744257
PO Box 7570, DUMFRIES, DG2 8YD **Tel:** 01387 880359
Fax: 01387 880722
Email: info@forestryjournal.co.uk
Web site: http://www.forsetryjournal.co.uk
Titles:
  FORESTRY JOURNAL

FOREST OF DEAN & WYE VALLEY REVIEW LTD 14938
The Tindle Suite, Kings Buildings, Hill Street, LYDNEY, GL15
5HE **Tel:** 01594 841113 **Fax:** 01594 842386
Titles:
  FOREST OF DEAN AND WYE VALLEY REVIEW

FORTH INDEPENDENT NEWSPAPERS 700661
10 Mar Street, ALLOA, FK10 1HR **Tel:** 01259 724724
Titles:
  ALLANWATER NEWS
  ALLOA AND HILLFOOTS WEE COUNTY NEWS
  EAST KILBRIDE MAIL

FORTH NATURALIST AND HISTORIAN 18412
Department of Biology, University of Stirling, STIRLING, FK9
4LA **Tel:** 01786 833409
Web site: http://www.fnh.stir.ac.uk
Titles:
  THE FORTH NATURALIST & HISTORIAN

FORUM FOR THE FUTURE 16290
Overseas House, 19-23 Ironmonger Row, LONDON, EC1V
3QN **Tel:** 020 7608 2332 **Fax:** 020 7608 2333
Email: post@greenfutures.org.uk
Web site: http://www.greenfutures.org.uk
Titles:
  GREEN FUTURES

FORUM MEDIA LTD 700270
Bradford Buildings, 27 Mawdsley Street, BOLTON, BL1 1LN
Tel: 01204 418866 **Fax:** 01204 418890
Web site: http://www.forummedia.org.uk
Titles:
  CONSTRUCTION FORUM

THE FORUM OF PRIVATE BUSINESS 13832
Ruskin Chambers, Drury Lane, KNUTSFORD, WA16 6HA
Tel: 01565 634467 **Fax:** 0870 241 9570
Email: info@fpb.org
Web site: http://www.fpb.org
Titles:
  ENEWSLETTER

THE FORWARD GROUP 12345
84-86 Regent Street, LONDON, W1B 5RR
Tel: 020 7734 2303 **Fax:** 020 7494 2570
Web site: http://www.theforwardgroup.com
Titles:
  LONDON LOOP
  LONDON LOOP WEEKEND
  PATEK PHILIPPE
  SMART INVESTOR
  TESCO BABY & TODDLER CLUB

THE FOSTERING NETWORK 14172
87 Blackfriars Road, LONDON, SE1 8HA **Tel:** 020 7620 6400
Fax: 020 7620 6401
Email: info@fostering.net
Web site: http://www.fostering.net
Titles:
  FOSTER CARE MAGAZINE

FOUR SHIRES PUBLISHING 18546
7 Borough House, Marlborough Road, BANBURY, OX16
5TH **Tel:** 01295 273138 **Fax:** 01295 273139
Web site: http://www.fourshires.co.uk
Titles:
  FOUR SHIRES MAGAZINE

FOURSIGHT PUBLICATIONS LTD 15498
20 Park Street, Kings Cliffe, PETERBOROUGH, PE8 6XN
Tel: 01780 470086 **Fax:** 01780 470060
Titles:
  RAIL EXPRESS

FOURWAYS SALES & MARKETING 16806
1A Melbourn Street, ROYSTON, SG8 7BP
Tel: 01763 243760 **Fax:** 01763 249396
Email: info@teachers-guide.co.uk
Web site: http://www.teachers-guide.co.uk
Titles:
  THE TEACHER'S GUIDE

FRANCHISE DEVELOPMENT SERVICES LTD 13746
Franchise House, 56 Surrey Street, NORWICH, NR1 3FD
Tel: 01603 620301 **Fax:** 01603 630174
Email: enquiries@fdsltd.com
Web site: http://www.fdsfranchise.com
Titles:
EUROPEAN FRANCHISING
FRANCHISE INTERNATIONAL
THE FRANCHISE MAGAZINE
THE IRISH FRANCHISE MAGAZINE
THE SCOTTISH FRANCHISE MAGAZINE

FRANCHISE WORLD 13747
Highlands House, 165 The Broadway, LONDON, SW19 1NE
Tel: 020 8605 2555 **Fax:** 020 8605 2556
Web site: http://www.franchiseworld.co.uk
Titles:
FRANCHISE WORLD

FRANCHISEEK LIMITED 1646236
129A High Street, LYMINGTON, SO41 9AQ
Tel: 01590 689755 **Fax:** 01590 688978
Email: sales@franchiseek.com
Web site: http://www.franchiseek.com
Titles:
FRANCHISE FOCUS

FRANK PUBLISHING LTD 700141
86 Sandyhurst Lane, ASHFORD, TN25 4NT
Tel: 01233 622001
Titles:
FIELD MARKETING AND BRAND X

FRASER PUBLICATIONS LTD 1737568
PO Box 503, WINCHESTER, SO23 3DG **Tel:** 01962 711756
Fax: 01962 713126
Titles:
AFRICA OIL AND GAS

**FREE CHURCH OF SCOTLAND COMMUNICATIONS
COMMITTEE** 18457
15 North Bank Street, EDINBURGH, EH1 2LS
Tel: 0131 226 5286 **Fax:** 0131 220 0597
Email: offices@freechurchofscotland.org.uk
Web site: http://www.freechurch.org
Titles:
THE MONTHLY RECORD OF FREE CHURCH OF
SCOTLAND

FREE PINT LIMITED 623099
4-6 Station Approach, ASHFORD, TW15 2QN
Tel: 0870 141 7474
Web site: http://www.freepint.com
Titles:
FREE PINT
VIP

FREELANCE.COM LTD 1747723
15 Loraine Gardens, ASHTEAD, KT21 1PD
Tel: 01372 274059 **Fax:** 01372 274059
Email: mail@davidmurphy.org
Titles:
MOBILE MARKETING MAGAZINE

FREEWAY MEDIA LTD 16897
20 Orange Street, LONDON, WC2H 7EF **Tel:** 020 7014 1368
Fax: 020 7490 3476
Email: info@freewaymedia.com
Web site: http://www.freewaymedia.com
Titles:
PRIDE OF BRITAIN MAGAZINE

FREIGHT TRANSPORT ASSOCIATION 1646274
Hermes House, St. Johns Road, TUNBRIDGE WELLS, TN4
9UZ **Tel:** 01892 526171 **Fax:** 01892 552352
Web site: http://www.fta.co.uk
Titles:
FREIGHT

**FRENCH CHAMBER OF COMMERCE IN GREAT
BRITAIN** 13789
21 Dartmouth Street, LONDON, SW1H 9BP
Tel: 020 7304 4040 **Fax:** 020 7304 7034
Email: mail@ccfgb.co.uk
Web site: http://www.ccfgb.co.uk

Titles:
INFO

FRESH MEDIA UK LTD 1654419
5th Floor, Scala House, Holloway Circus, BIRMINGHAM, B1
1EQ **Tel:** 0121 687 1041 **Fax:** 0121 687 1051
Titles:
BEST PRACTICE
BUSINESS UPDATE
LIFESTYLES TODAY
THE SOLIHULL JOURNAL
SOLUTIONS FOR INDUSTRY

THE FRESH NETWORK LIMITED 1713188
Unit 4, Aylsham Business Park, Shepheards Close,
NORWICH, NR11 6SZ **Tel:** 0845 833 7017
Fax: 08700 940077
Email: info@fresh-network.com
Web site: http://www.fresh-network.com
Titles:
GET FRESH

FRESHWOOD PUBLISHING 1745643
Ampney St. Peter, CIRENCESTER, GL7 5SH
Tel: 01285 580481
Titles:
BRITISH WOODWORKING MAGAZINE

FRIDAY HOLDINGS LTD 15652
London Road, Sayers Common, HASSOCKS, BN6 9HS
Tel: 0800 163 0163 **Fax:** 0870 162 9090
Email: info@friday-ad.co.uk
Web site: http://www.friday-ad.co.uk
Titles:
HOMES
NATIONAL HORSEMART
NATIONAL HORSEMART

THE FRIEND PUBLICATIONS LTD 15883
Friends House, 173 Euston Road, LONDON, NW1 2BJ
Tel: 020 7663 1010 **Fax:** 020 7663 1182
Email: editorial@thefriend.org
Web site: http://www.thefriend.org
Titles:
THE FRIEND

FRIENDS OF CLASSICS 1759442
51 Achilles Road, LONDON, NW6 1DZ **Tel:** 020 7431 5088
Titles:
AD FAMILIARES

FRIENDS OF THE EARTH 12658
26-28 Underwood Street, LONDON, N1 7JQ
Tel: 020 7490 1555 **Fax:** 020 7490 0881
Email: info@foe.co.uk
Web site: http://www.foe.co.uk
Titles:
EARTHMATTERS
ENEWS
FRIEND

FRONT PAGE PUBLISHING 699000
112-114 High Street, RICKMANSWORTH, WD3 1AQ
Tel: 0845 094 8022
Titles:
RECRUITMENT CONSULTANT

FRUKT MUSIC 1713715
c/o FRUKT, 56 Compton Street, LONDON, EC1V 0ET
Tel: 020 7017 8181 **Fax:** 020 7017 8199
Email: anthony@fructmusic.com
Web site: http://www.fructmusic.com
Titles:
FIVE EIGHT

FSB PUBLICATIONS 1676228
Sir Frank Whittle Way, Blackpool Business Park,
BLACKPOOL, FY4 2FE **Tel:** 01253 336000
Fax: 01253 348046
Email: nigel.duncan@fsb.org.uk
Titles:
BUSINESS NETWORK

FSG COMMUNICATIONS LTD 17062
Vine House, Fair Green, Reach, CAMBRIDGE, CB5 0JD
Tel: 01638 743633 **Fax:** 01638 743998
Titles:
AFRICA HEALTH

FSJ COMMUNICATIONS 14807
The Media Centre, Garcia Estate, Canterbury Road,
WORTHING, BN13 1EH **Tel:** 01903 602104
Fax: 01903 537321
Email: advertising@fsj.co.uk
Titles:
FUNERAL SERVICE JOURNAL

FSN PUBLISHING LTD 16651
Clarendon House, 125 Shenley Road, BOREHAMWOOD,
WD6 1AG **Tel:** 020 8445 2688 **Fax:** 020 8445 7172
Email: fsn@btconnect.com
Titles:
FSN

FSP FIRE SAFETY PROFESSIONAL 1621545
Fair View, Wissett Road, HALESWORTH, IP19 8BT
Tel: 01986 874526
Titles:
FSP FIRE SAFETY PROFESSIONAL

FSR 697723
PO Box 416, SURBITON, KT5 2ZF **Tel:** 020 8399 4831
Email: groveint@aol.com
Web site: http://www.fedrest.com
Titles:
MOOD FOOD

FST 1747445
58-60 Stamford Street, LONDON, SE1 9LX
Tel: 020 7921 9019 **Fax:** 020 7921 9145
Titles:
TONI & GUY MAGAZINE

FT FINANCE 16855
1 Southwark Bridge, LONDON, SE1 9HL **Tel:** 020 7873 4617
Fax: 020 7873 3937
Titles:
FTYOURMONEY

FT GROUP 17064
1 Southwark Bridge, LONDON, SE1 9HL **Tel:** 020 7873 3000
Titles:
THE BANKER
EPN EUROPEAN PENSIONS & INVESTMENT NEWS
FDI
FINANCIAL ADVISER
FINANCIAL TIMES MANDATE
FTADVISER.COM
INVESTMENT ADVISER
INVESTORS CHRONICLE
MONEY MANAGEMENT
PENSIONS WEEK
PENSIONSNEWS.COM
PROFESSIONAL WEALTH MANAGEMENT

FUEL OIL NEWS 1605924
Regent House, Bexton Lane, KNUTSFORD, WA16 9AB
Tel: 01565 653283 **Fax:** 01565 755607
Email: mail@fueloilnews.co.uk
Web site: http://www.fueloilnews.co.uk
Titles:
FUEL OIL NEWS

FULL ON PUBLICATIONS LTD 1600523
The Busworks, United House, North Road, LONDON, N7
9DP **Tel:** 020 7609 4254 **Fax:** 020 7609 4424
Titles:
FULL ON!
LOUD

FULTON PUBLISHING 622410
22-24 Corsham Street, LONDON, N1 6DR
Tel: 020 7251 9151 **Fax:** 020 7251 9161
Titles:
CARBON FINANCE
ENVIRONMENTAL FINANCE

UK Publishers & Their Titles

FUNDRAISING UK LTD 676116
17 Errington Road, COLCHESTER, CO3 3EA
Tel: 01206 579081 **Fax:** 07092 028510
Web site: http://www.fundraising.co.uk
Titles:
UK FUNDRAISING

FUNDS EUROPE LIMITED 1744504
4th Floor, Broadgate Court, 199 Bishopsgate, LONDON,
EC2M 3TY **Tel:** 020 3178 5872 **Fax:** 020 3178 4002
Titles:
FUNDS EUROPE

FURNESS NEWSPAPERS LTD 16500
Newspaper House, Abbey Road, BARROW-IN-FURNESS,
LA14 5QS **Tel:** 01229 821835 **Fax:** 01229 832141
Email: news@nwemail.co.uk
Titles:
NORTH WEST EVENING MAIL (BARROW)

THE FURNITURE HISTORY SOCIETY 17647
1 Mercedes Cottages, St. Johns Road, HAYWARDS HEATH,
RH16 4EH **Tel:** 01444 413845 **Fax:** 01444 413875
Email: furniturehistorysociety@hotmail.com
Web site: http://www.furniturehistorysociety.com
Titles:
FURNITURE HISTORY

FUSED 676669
315 The Greenhouse, Gibb Square, Gibb Street,
BIRMINGHAM, B9 4AA **Tel:** 0121 246 1946
Web site: http://www.fusedmagazine.com
Titles:
FUSED MAGAZINE

FUSS LIMITED 1712786
Q1 Capital Park, Capital Business Park, Parkway, CARDIFF,
CF3 2PU **Tel:** 029 2077 8918 **Fax:** 029 2079 3508
Email: mikes@smeuk.com
Titles:
CONTRACT FURNISHING CONCEPTS

FUTURE PUBLISHING LIMITED 1691088
2 Balcombe Street, LONDON, NW1 6NW
Tel: 020 7042 4000
Web site: http://www.futurenet.com
Titles:
CLASSIC ROCK
DVD & BLU-RAY REVIEW
HI-FI CHOICE
HOME CINEMA CHOICE
METAL HAMMER
ODEON MAGAZINE
OFFICIAL NINTENDO MAGAZINE
THE OFFICIAL TOUR DE FRANCE GUIDE
PC ZONE
PCZONE
PROCYCLING
SKY MOVIES
T3
T3 THE GADGET MAGAZINE
TOTAL FILM
WHAT LAPTOP
WHAT PLASMA AND LCD TV
WHAT SATELLITE & DIGITAL TV
WHAT VIDEO AND HIGH-DEFINITION TV
XBOX 360 THE OFFICIAL XBOX MAGAZINE

FUTURE PUBLISHING LTD 12281
30 Monmouth Street, BATH, BA1 2BW **Tel:** 01225 442244
Fax: 01225 446019
Web site: http://www.futurenet.co.uk
Titles:
.NET
.NET MAGAZINE
3D WORLD
BIKERADAR.COM
CLASSIC FORD
CLASSICS MONTHLY
COMPUTER ARTS
COMPUTER ARTS ONLINE
COMPUTER ARTS PROJECTS
COMPUTER MUSIC
COMPUTER MUSIC (ONLINE)
CROSS STITCH COLLECTION
CROSS STITCHER
CYCLING PLUS
DIGITAL CAMERA MAGAZINE
EDGE
EDGE ONLINE
FAST BIKES

FAST CAR MAGAZINE
FAST FORD
FASTCAR.CO.UK
FUTURE MUSIC
GAMES MASTER
GAMESRADAR
GUITAR TECHNIQUES
GUITARIST
HMV GAMES
IMAGINEFX
THE KNITTER
LINUX FORMAT
MACFORMAT
MICROSOFT WINDOWS XP: THE OFFICIAL MAGAZINE
MINI MAGAZINE
MOUNTAIN BIKING UK
MUSICIAN
NGAMER
NITRO
OFFICIAL PLAYSTATION MAGAZINE
PAPERCRAFT INSPIRATIONS
PC ANSWERS
PC ANSWERS ONLINE
PC FORMAT
PC GAMER
PC PLUS
PC PLUS ONLINE
PHOTO PLUS
PSM3
QUICK & EASY GUIDE
REDLINE
RHYTHM
SCRAPBOOK INSPIRATIONS
SFX
SIMPLY KNITTING
TECHRADAR.COM
TOTAL GUITAR
TOTAL VAUXHALL
TRIATHLON PLUS
TRUCKING
TRUCKSTOP NEWS
WHAT MOUNTAIN BIKE
WINDOWS VISTA: THE OFFICIAL MAGAZINE
XBOX WORLD 360
YOUR FAMILY TREE

FYNE ASSOCIATES LTD 1622160
Linde Buildings, 7 Nuffield Way, ABINGDON, OX14 1RJ
Tel: 01235 468428 **Fax:** 01235 468427
Titles:
FYNE TIMES

G2 MEDIA 1731677
50 The Craig Road, DOWNPATRICK, BT30 9BG
Tel: 028 4483 1862 **Fax:** 028 4483 2956
Titles:
UNITED NEWS

G.W. MCKANE & SON 16310
32-34 Station Street, KESWICK, CA12 5HF
Tel: 01768 772140 **Fax:** 01768 771203
Titles:
THE KESWICK REMINDER

G&T MEDIA LTD 1748597
2nd Floor, 145-157 St. John Street, LONDON, EC1V 4PY
Tel: 020 7608 5137 **Fax:** 0870 428 5885
Email: ka@ainalmusafer.com
Web site: http://www.ainalmusafer.com
Titles:
AIN ALMUSAFER MAGAZINE

GABRIEL COMMUNICATIONS LTD 13528
4th Floor, Landmark House, Station Road, Cheadle Hulme,
CHEADLE, SK8 7JH **Tel:** 0161 488 1700
Web site: http://www.totalcatholic.com
Titles:
CATHOLIC LIFE
CATHOLIC TIMES
CHURCH BUILDING
TOTAL CATHOLIC
WESTMINSTER RECORD

B GADD COMMUNICATIONS 622372
Blenheim Cottage, Millers Lane, Hornton, BANBURY, OX15
6BS **Tel:** 01295 670639 **Fax:** 01295 670043
Web site: http://www.centralhorsenews.co.uk
Titles:
CENTRAL HORSE NEWS

GALAXY PUBLICATIONS 15845
PO Box 312, WITHAM, CM8 3SZ **Tel:** 01376 534538
Fax: 01376 534546
Titles:
FIESTA
KNAVE
RAVERS DVD

THE GALPIN SOCIETY 18180
24 Gloucester Road, TEDDINGTON, TW11 0NU
Tel: 020 8977 2756
Titles:
GALPIN SOCIETY JOURNAL

GAME & WILDLIFE CONSERVATION TRUST 17649
Burgate Manor, FORDINGBRIDGE, SP6 1EF
Tel: 01425 652381 **Fax:** 01425 655848
Web site: http://www.gct.org.uk
Titles:
GAME & WILDLIFE CONSERVATION TRUST ANNUAL
REVIEW
GAME & WILDLIFE CONSERVATION TRUST MAGAZINE:
GAMEWISE

GAMES PRESS LTD 1638643
255 Staines Road, Laleham, STAINES, TW18 2RS
Tel: 020 7193 2246
Email: mail@gamespress.co.uk
Web site: http://www.gamespress.com
Titles:
GAMES PRESS

GAMES WORKSHOP LTD 15514
Willow Road, Lenton, NOTTINGHAM, NG7 2WS
Tel: 0115 916 8000 **Fax:** 0115 916 8008
Web site: http://www.games-workshop.co.uk
Titles:
WHITE DWARF

GAMING BUSINESS MEDIA 1719334
Bolton Technology Exchange, 33 Queensbrook, BOLTON,
BL1 4AY **Tel:** 01204 396397
Titles:
BETTING BUSINESS

GAMING FLOOR.COM LTD 1630307
72 New Bond Street, LONDON, W1S 1RR
Tel: 0870 011 3020 **Fax:** 0870 011 3021
Web site: http://www.gamingfloor.com
Titles:
GAMING FLOOR

GANDA PUBLISHING 16892
7 Phrosso Road, WORTHING, BN11 5SJ **Tel:** 01903 240517
Email: edit@essentiallyworthing.co.uk
Web site: http://www.essentiallyworthing.co.uk
Titles:
ESSENTIALLY WORTHING

GARAVI GUJARAT PUBLICATIONS LTD 16036
Garavi Gujarat House, 1 Silex Street, LONDON, SE1 0DW
Tel: 020 7928 1234 **Fax:** 020 7261 0055
Email: garavi@gujarat.co.uk
Web site: http://www.gg2.net
Titles:
GARAVI GUJARAT
GG2.NET

**THE GARDEN COMMUNICATION & MEDIA COMPANY
LTD** 694339
4th Floor, Churchgate, New Road, PETERBOROUGH, PE1
1TT **Tel:** 01733 775700 **Fax:** 01733 775900
Web site: http://www.growretail.co.uk
Titles:
GARDEN TRADE NEWS

GARDENFORUM LTD 163838
Stourton House, High Street, Stourton, WARMINSTER,
BA12 6QF **Tel:** 01747 841457 **Fax:** 01747 841394
Email: info@gardenforum.co.uk
Web site: http://www.gardenforum.co.uk
Titles:
GARDENFORUM.CO.UK

GARNETT DICKINSON GROUP LTD 15008
Brookfields Way, Manvers, Wath Upon Dearne,
ROTHERHAM, S63 5DL **Tel:** 01709 768000
Titles:
DEARNE VALLEY WEEKENDER
ROTHERHAM ADVERTISER AND RECORD SERIES
SOUTH YORKSHIRE BUSINESS

GAS TECHNOLOGY NEWS LTD 1759894
9 Ridgeway Drive, NEWPORT, NP20 5AR **Tel:** 01633 222661
Email: jon@gastechnologynews.net
Titles:
GAS TECHNOLOGY NEWS

GATEACRE PRESS 14452
260 Picton Road, Wavertree, LIVERPOOL, L15 4LP
Tel: 0151 734 3038 **Fax:** 0151 734 2860
Titles:
IN ATTENDANCE
ON THE BELL

THE GATESHEAD HOUSING COMPANY 1733856
Keelman House, Fifth Avenue Business Park, Team Valley
Trading Estate, GATESHEAD, NE11 0XA **Tel:** 0191 433 5382
Fax: 0191 433 5354
Titles:
MYPADGATESHEAD.CO.UK

GAY BRITAIN NETWORK 625202
PO Box 6991, LEICESTER, LE1 6YS **Tel:** 0870 345 5600
Fax: 0870 345 5584
Titles:
GAY BRITAIN NETWORK

GAZETTE MEDIA COMPANY LTD 621506
Barton Road, Riverside Park Road, MIDDLESBROUGH, TS2
1UT **Tel:** 01642 245401 **Fax:** 01642 232014
Web site: http://www.gazettelive.co.uk
Titles:
EVENING GAZETTE (MIDDLESBROUGH)
EVENING GAZETTE SPORTS (MIDDLESBROUGH)
GAZETTELIVE.CO.UK

EL GAZETTE NEW MEDIA LTD 18583
3 Constantine Court, Fairclough Street, LONDON, E1 1PW
Tel: 020 7481 6700 **Fax:** 020 7488 9240
Titles:
EL GAZETTE

GAZETTE PUBLICATIONS (LEICESTER) LIMITED
1650102
PO Box 8454, LEICESTER, LE9 2WU **Tel:** 0116 239 4284
Email: gazette@aol.com
Titles:
ANSTEY SCENE
GLENFIELD GAZETTE

BAKHANDA PUBLISHING 1654297
Chapeltown Enterprise Centre, 231 Chapeltown Road,
LEEDS, LS7 3DX **Tel:** 0113 262 6333
Titles:
THE NORTHERN JOURNAL

GDN MEDIA GROUP 1751583
Moorcrest Road, HUDDERSFIELD, HD4 5PT
Tel: 07913 148613
Titles:
GAMERSDAILYNEWS.COM

DR PUBLICATIONS LTD 1622205
Global House, 47A Tottenham Lane, LONDON, N8 9BD
Tel: 020 8347 6406 **Fax:** 020 8347 6427
mail: info@ets-news.com
Web site: http://www.cbreview.com
Titles:
CHEMICAL BIOLOGICAL WARFARE REVIEW
ETS NEWS
GLOBAL DEFENCE REVIEW

DS PUBLISHING 1709745
Queen Square House, 18-21 Queen Square, BRISTOL, BS1
NH **Tel:** 0117 921 4000 **Fax:** 0117 926 7444
Web site: http://www.gdsinternational.com

Titles:
BUSINESS MANAGEMENT
CXO (EUROPE)
FST FINANCIAL SERVICES TECHNOLOGY (EUROPE)

GEARING MEDIA GROUP 14070
4 Red Barn Mews, High Street, BATTLE, TN33 0AG
Tel: 01424 774982 **Fax:** 01424 775880
Email: info@gearingmediagroup.com
Web site: http://www.nigelgearing.com
Titles:
CARPET & FLOORING REVIEW
FURNITURE NEWS
FURNITURE PRODUCTION
TILE UK

GEE PUBLISHING LTD 13290
100 Avenue Road, Swiss Cottage, LONDON, NW3 3PF
Tel: 020 7393 7000 **Fax:** 020 7393 7010
Titles:
AIR QUALITY MANAGEMENT
COMPANY COMPLIANCE MONITOR

GEMINI NETWORK MEDIA 1735860
5th Floor, Telford Plaza 2, Ironmasters Way, TELFORD, TF3
4NT
Titles:
WOMEN & GOLF

GEMINI PUBLISHING & DESIGN 18830
62 Exe Vale Road, Countess Wear, EXETER, EX2 6LF
Tel: 01392 427576
Email: geminipublishing@blueyonder.co.uk
Web site: http://www.geminipublishing.net
Titles:
EXECITE!
GUIDE FOR THE BRIDE

GEMMOLOGICAL ASSOCIATION OF GREAT BRITAIN
17654
27 Greville Street, LONDON, EC1N 8TN **Tel:** 020 7404 3334
Fax: 020 7404 8843
Email: information@gem-a.com
Web site: http://www.gem-a.com
Titles:
GEMS & JEWELLERY
THE JOURNAL OF GEMMOLOGY

GENERAL COMMUNICATIONS INTERNATIONAL LTD
1751840
Waterfront Studios, 1 Dock Road, LONDON, E16 1AG
Tel: 020 7476 9400 **Fax:** 020 7476 9450
Titles:
ASIAN ENTERPRISE

THE GENERAL OSTEOPATHIC COUNCIL 17258
Osteopathy House, 176 Tower Bridge Road, LONDON, SE1
3LU **Tel:** 020 7357 6655 **Fax:** 020 7357 0011
Email: editor@osteopathy.org.uk
Web site: http://www.osteopathy.org.uk
Titles:
THE OSTEOPATH

GENESIS 1675653
Nithsdale House, 159 Cambridge Street, AYLESBURY,
HP20 1BQ **Tel:** 01296 434381
Email: studio@genesis-prepress.co.uk
Web site: http://www.genesis-prepress.co.uk
Titles:
PRINTERS WORKSHOP

GEO:CONNEXION LIMITED 600608
PO Box 594, CAMBRIDGE, CB1 0FY **Tel:** 01223 279151
Fax: 01223 279148
Email: maiward@geoconnexion.com
Web site: http://www.geoconnexion.com
Titles:
CONTINGENCYTODAY.COM
GEO:CONNEXION INTERNATIONAL
GEO:CONNEXION UK

THE GEOGRAPHICAL ASSOCIATION 15933
160 Solly Street, SHEFFIELD, S1 4BF **Tel:** 0114 296 0088
Fax: 0114 296 7176
Web site: http://www.geography.org.uk

Titles:
GEOGRAPHY

THE GEOLOGICAL SOCIETY PUBLISHING HOUSE 12537
Unit 7, Brassmill Enterprise Centre, Brassmill Lane, BATH,
BA1 3JN **Tel:** 01225 445046 **Fax:** 01225 442836
Web site: http://www.geolsoc.org.uk
Titles:
GEOSCIENTIST
SCOTTISH JOURNAL OF GEOLOGY

GEORGE WARMAN PUBLICATIONS (UK) LTD 14530
Unit 2, Riverview Business Park, Walnut Tree Close,
GUILDFORD, GU1 4UX **Tel:** 01483 304944
Fax: 01483 303191
Email: office@georgewarman.co.uk
Web site: http://www.the-dentist.co.uk
Titles:
DENTAL UPDATE
THE DENTIST
PRACTICE MANAGEMENT

GERARD DUGDILL 18131
41 Green Lane, LONDON, SE9 2AF **Tel:** 020 7407 4700
Fax: 020 7407 4704
Email: info@pinkribbon.co.uk
Web site: http://www.pinkribbon.co.uk
Titles:
PINK RIBBON

GFJ PUBLISHING LTD 1627153
80 Rosebery Road, EPSOM, KT18 6AA **Tel:** 01372 277377
Titles:
EUROPEAN RETAIL
INTERNAL COMMUNICATION

GFMS WORLD GOLD 1750703
153-155 Hedges House, Regent Street, LONDON, W1B 4JE
Tel: 020 7478 1777 **Fax:** 020 7478 1779
Titles:
WORLD GOLD

GHYLL HOUSE PUBLISHING 674527
5A The Maltings, Stowupland Road, STOWMARKET, IP14
5AG **Tel:** 01449 677500 **Fax:** 01449 770028
Email: info@ghyllhouse.co.uk
Web site: http://www.ghyllhouse.co.uk
Titles:
COUNTRYSIDE BUILDING

GIANTHAND.COM LTD 698016
Tel: 0870 046 7728 **Fax:** 0870 046 7729
Press releases by email **Tel:** 01302 842676
Web site: http://www.gianthand.com
Titles:
TOPBIKE

GILDENBURGH LTD 1744313
30 Stapledon Road, Orton Southgate, PETERBOROUGH,
PE2 6TD **Tel:** 01733 391181
Email: siterecorder@gildenburgh.co.uk
Titles:
SITE RECORDER

GIRAFFE MEDIA LTD 1638428
8 Hammet Street, TAUNTON, TA1 1RZ **Tel:** 01823 288344
Fax: 01823 288239
Email: info@giraffe-media.com
Web site: http://www.giraffe-media.co.uk
Titles:
WEDDING IDEAS

GIRL GUIDING UK 16094
17-19 Buckingham Palace Road, LONDON, SW1W 0PT
Tel: 020 7834 6242 **Fax:** 020 7828 8317
Web site: http://www.girlguiding.org.uk
Titles:
GUIDING MAGAZINE

THE GLADE 16750
Withnell Farm, Bury Lane, Withnell, CHORLEY, PR6 8SD
Tel: 020 8397 2603 **Fax:** 020 8397 5193
Web site: http://www.theglade.co.uk

UK Publishers & Their Titles

Titles:
THE GLADE

GLASGOW CITY COUNCIL 16444
City Chambers, George Square, GLASGOW, G2 1DU
Tel: 0141 287 3799 **Fax:** 0141 287 0925
Web site: http://www.glasgow.gov.uk
Titles:
INSIDER

GLASGOW UNIVERSITY S R C 15757
John McIntyre Building, University Avenue, GLASGOW, G12
8QQ **Tel:** 0141 337 3557
Titles:
GLASGOW UNIVERSITY GUARDIAN

GLASS'S INFORMATION 1642398
1 Princes Road, WEYBRIDGE, KT13 9TU **Tel:** 01932 823787
Fax: 01932 823798
Email: editor@autowired.co.uk
Web site: http://www.autowired.co.uk
Titles:
AUTOWIRED

GLENBUCK PUBLISHING LTD 1733902
7B High Street, BARNET, EN5 5UE **Tel:** 020 8275 5561
Titles:
INTERNATIONAL BULK JOURNAL

GLEN-HOLLAND LTD 14397
The Publishing Centre, 1 Woolram Wygate, SPALDING,
PE11 1NU **Tel:** 01775 711777 **Fax:** 01775 711737
Email: karen.wright@coachtoursuk.com
Web site: http://www.coachtoursuk.com
Titles:
BUS & COACH BUYER
COACH TOURS UK

GLENRAVEL PUBLICATIONS 1679855
Lepper Street, BELFAST, BT15 2DN **Tel:** 028 9074 2255
Fax: 028 9035 1326
Email: glenravel@ashtoncentre.com
Web site: http://www.glenravel.com
Titles:
BELFAST MAGAZINE

GLOBAL COLOR RESEARCH 1751575
1 Queen Anne Terrace, Sovereign Court, The Highway,
LONDON, E1W 3HH **Tel:** 020 7481 1507 **Fax:** 020 7481 1548
Titles:
MIX FUTURE INTERIORS

GLOBAL FINANCE 12133
123-127 Cannon Street, LONDON, EC4N 5AX
Tel: 020 7583 7588 **Fax:** 020 7583 7580
Titles:
GLOBAL FINANCE

GLOBAL MARKETS MEDIA LTD 1686402
Jeffries House, 1-5 Jeffries Passage, GUILDFORD, GU1 4AP
Tel: 020 7833 1441 **Fax:** 020 7520 7915
Titles:
THE TECHNICAL ANALYST

GLOBAL MEDIA LTD 1760999
Gibbs Yard, Auchincruive, AYR, KA6 5HN
Tel: 01292 525970
Email: info@gmexpos.com
Web site: http://www.scottishhealthcare.com
Titles:
SKILLS 4 NURSES

GLOBAL MEDIA PUBLISHING LTD 600538
Global House, 13 Market Square, HORSHAM, RH12 1EU
Tel: 01403 220750 **Fax:** 01403 220751
Web site: http://www.gmp.uk.com
Titles:
WORLDWIDE INDEPENDENT POWER

GLOBALCOM LTD 13603
26 Windridge Close, ST. ALBANS, AL3 4JP
Tel: 01727 851761 **Fax:** 01727 753454

Email: info@dvd-intelligence.com
Web site: http://www.dvd-intelligence.com
Titles:
DVD & BEYOND
DVD INTELLIGENCE

GLOBE BUSINESS PUBLISHING LTD 1640597
New Hibernia House, Winchester Walk, LONDON, SE1 9AG
Tel: 020 7234 0606
Titles:
INTERNATIONAL LAW OFFICE

GLOBE WHITE PAGE LTD 1640032
New Hibernia House, Winchester Walk, LONDON, SE1 9AG
Tel: 020 7234 0606 **Fax:** 020 7234 0808
Web site: http://www.globewhitepage.com
Titles:
IAM-MAGAZINE
INTELLECTUAL ASSET MANAGEMENT

GLOBESPAN MEDIA LTD 1738775
1st Floor, 1 East Poultry Avenue, LONDON, EC1A 9PT
Tel: 020 7002 8300 **Fax:** 020 7002 8310
Web site: http://www.globespanmedia.com
Titles:
HOMES OVERSEAS
SHOW HOUSE
WHATHOUSE.CO.UK

GLOUCESTERSHIRE MEDIA 14939
1 Clarence Parade, Cheltenham, GLOUCESTER, GL50 3NY
Tel: 01452 424442 **Fax:** 01452 420664
Web site: http://www.thisisgloucestershire.co.uk
Titles:
THE CITIZEN (GLOUCESTER)
THE FORESTER (FOREST OF DEAN)
GLOUCESTER AND CHELTENHAM NEWS SERIES
STROUD LIFE
WEST WEDDINGS

GMC PUBLICATIONS LTD 14368
86 High Street, LEWES, BN7 1XN **Tel:** 01273 477374
Fax: 01273 487692
Web site: http://www.thegmcgroup.com
Titles:
BLACK & WHITE PHOTOGRAPHY
THE DOLLS HOUSE MAGAZINE
FURNITURE AND CABINETMAKING
GUILD NEWS
KNITTING
MAKING JEWELLERY
OUTDOOR PHOTOGRAPHY
WOODCARVING
WOODTURNING
WOODWORKING PLANS & PROJECTS

GO PUBLISHING LTD 1713912
PO Box 874, Taunton, SOMERSET, TA1 9HB
Tel: 020 7637 5900
Titles:
SWIMMING POOL NEWS
UK LEISURE NEWS
WHAT POOL & HOT TUB

GOFAR ENTERPRISES 625225
Singletrack, Lockside Mill, Dale Street, TODMORDEN, OL14
5PX **Tel:** 01706 813344 **Fax:** 01706 813356
Web site: http://www.singletrackworld.com
Titles:
SINGLETRACK

GOING FOR GOLF 694202
134 Sandon Road, Pitsea, BASILDON, SS14 1TS
Tel: 01268 554100 **Fax:** 01268 552000
Email: admin@goingforgolf.com
Titles:
GOING FOR GOLF MAGAZINE

GOLD PRIZE MEDIA LTD 18621
46G Greatorex Street, LONDON, E1 5NP **Tel:** 020 7247 6280
Fax: 020 7247 9993
Email: news@notundin.com
Web site: http://www.notundin.com
Titles:
NOTUN DIN BENGALI NEWSWEEKLY

GOLDCREST BROADCASTING LTD 13461
21 West St. Helen Street, ABINGDON, OX14 5BL
Tel: 01536 418558 **Fax:** 01536 418539
Titles:
THE RADIO MAGAZINE

GOLDEN GATE PRODUCTION COMPANY LTD 18869
2 Brickfield Business Park, Woolpit, BURY ST. EDMUNDS,
IP30 9QS **Tel:** 01359 240066 **Fax:** 01359 244221
Email: hq@lrm.co.uk
Titles:
LRM LAND ROVER MONTHLY

GOLDSCHMIDT & HOWLAND 1715899
1 Heath Street, LONDON, NW3 6TP **Tel:** 020 7504 0350
Fax: 020 7345 0595
Web site: http://www.g-h.co.uk
Titles:
LONDON INSIGHTS

GOLF INTERNATIONAL SERVICES 16782
10 Buckingham Place, LONDON, SW1E 6HX
Tel: 020 7828 3003
Email: info@golfinternationalmag.com
Web site: http://www.golfinternationalmag.com
Titles:
GOLF INTERNATIONAL

GOLF RANGE NEWS LTD 1653955
Polmood, Sissinghurst, CRANBROOK, TN17 2AJ
Tel: 01580 715248 **Fax:** 01580 714516
Titles:
GOLF RANGE NEWS

GOLWG CYF 15696
PO Box 4, LAMPETER, SA48 7LX **Tel:** 01570 423529
Fax: 01570 423538
Web site: http://www.golwg.com
Titles:
GOLWG

GONE TO PRESS LTD 1653038
156 High Street, Wootton Bassett, SWINDON, SN4 7AB
Tel: 01793 849928 **Fax:** 01749 870471
Titles:
THE FAMILY GRAPEVINE

GONIEC LTD 1712156
Tel: 020 3067 1020 **Fax:** 020 3067 1010
48 Haven Green, LONDON, W5 2NX **Tel:** 020 3067 1020
Fax: 020 3067 1010
Web site: http://www.goniec.com
Titles:
GONIEC POLSKI

THE GOOD BOOK GUIDE 17798
29-30 Monument Business Park, CHALGROVE, OX44 7RW
Tel: 01865 893434
Web site: http://www.thegoodbookguide.com
Titles:
THE GOOD BOOK GUIDE

THE GOOD LIFE PRESS LTD 1745304
PO Box 536, PRESTON, PR2 9ZY **Tel:** 01772 652693
Titles:
HOME FARMER

GOOD NEWS FELLOWSHIP 676870
21 Holmewood Crescent, Holme, PETERBOROUGH, PE7
3PY **Tel:** 01487 831888
Titles:
GOOD NEWS

GOODLIFE MEDIA PR AND PROMOTIONS LTD 15217
Suite 58, 235 Earls Court Road, LONDON, SW5 9FE
Tel: 020 7373 7282 **Fax:** 020 7373 3215
Email: production.goodlifemedia@virgin.net
Titles:
GOODLIFE MAGAZINE
LONDON HOTEL MAGAZINE

GOODPOINT PRESS LLP 1762491
28 John Finnie Street, KILMARNOCK, KA1 1DD
Tel: 01563 539611 **Fax:** 01563 543956
Titles:
EMIGRANT

GOODWOOD ESTATE 600417
Goodwood House, CHICHESTER, PO18 0PX
Tel: 01243 755000 **Fax:** 01243 755005
Web site: http://www.goodwood.co.uk
Titles:
GOODWOOD MAGAZINE

GOVERNANCE PUBLISHING AND INFORMATION SERVICES LTD. 17163
Watchfield House, Watchfield, HIGHBRIDGE, TA9 4RD
Tel: 01278 793300 **Fax:** 01278 783750
Email: info@governance.co.uk
Web site: http://www.governance.co.uk
Titles:
GOVERNANCE

GOVERNORS' ASSOCIATION 18855
2nd Floor SBQ1, 29 Smallbrook Queensway, BIRMINGHAM, B5 4HE **Tel:** 0121 643 5787 **Fax:** 0121 633 7141
Email: governorhq@nga.org.uk
Web site: http://www.nasg.org.uk
Titles:
MATTERS ARISING

GOVNET COMMUNICATIONS 18431
9th Floor, St. James's Buildings, Oxford Street, MANCHESTER, M1 6PP **Tel:** 0161 211 3000
Fax: 0161 211 3008
Email: editorial@govnet.co.uk
Web site: http://www.govnet.co.uk
Titles:
CJM
DEFENCE DIRECTOR
GOVERNMENT IT
HEALTH DIRECTOR
MODERNGOV
SDUK

GP LONDON 17628
32 Fredericks Place, LONDON, N12 8QE **Tel:** 020 8446 3604
Titles:
THE ANTIQUE TRADE CALENDAR

GRADUATE PROSPECTS LTD. 13147
Prospects House, Booth Street East, MANCHESTER, M13 9EP **Tel:** 0161 277 5200
Titles:
PHOENIX

GRAFIK LTD 1680248
Third Floor, 104 Great Portland Street, LONDON, W1W 6PE
Tel: 020 7637 5900
Titles:
GRAFIK

THE GRAHAM CUMMING GROUP 1640505
Willow Walk Business Centre, 8-11 Willow Walk, Farmborough, ORPINGTON, BR6 7AA **Tel:** 01843 282500
Fax: 01843 282501
Titles:
LONDON P.A.

GRAND LODGE PUBLICATIONS LTD 1640044
Freemasons Hall, 60 Great Queen Street, LONDON, WC2B 5AZ **Tel:** 020 7831 9811 **Fax:** 020 7395 9307
Web site: http://www.grandlodge-england.org
Titles:
FREEMASONRY TODAY

THE GRAND ORANGE LODGE OF IRELAND 1677456
Schomberg House, 368 Cregagh Road, BELFAST, BT6 9EY
Tel: 028 9070 1122 **Fax:** 028 9040 3700
Email: info@grandorangelodge.co.uk
Web site: http://www.grandorange.co.uk
Titles:
ORANGE STANDARD

GRANDFLAME LTD 12707
Flame House, 12 Kings Park, Primrose Hill, KINGS LANGLEY, WD4 8ST **Tel:** 01923 272960 **Fax:** 01923 270760
Email: warehouse@flame1.com
Web site: http://www.grandflame.com
Titles:
FOOTBALL & SPORTS ARENA
THE GROCERY TRADER
WAREHOUSE & LOGISTICS NEWS

GRANGE NOW 18512
Palace Studio, Main Street, GRANGE-OVER-SANDS, LA11 6AB **Tel:** 01539 535453 **Fax:** 01539 534544
Web site: http://www.grange-now.co.uk
Titles:
GRANGE NOW

GRANTA PUBLICATIONS 15833
12 Addison Avenue, LONDON, W11 4QR
Tel: 020 7605 1360 **Fax:** 020 7605 1361
Titles:
GRANTA

GREAT EXPLORERS LTD 1724448
The Minories, STRATFORD-UPON-AVON, CV37 6NF
Tel: 0870 879 3743
Titles:
SMALL WORLD

GREAT ORMOND STREET HOSPITAL 1686096
GOSH marketing and communications, 40 Bernard Street, LONDON, WC1N 1LE **Tel:** 020 7239 3127
Web site: http://www.gosh.nhs.uk
Titles:
CHILDREN FIRST FOR HEALTH

GREATER LONDON PUBLISHING 13507
103 Camden Mews, LONDON, NW1 9BU
Tel: 020 7267 5224
Web site: http://www.greaterlondonpublishing.com
Titles:
CITY PLANNING
WESTMINSTER PLANNING

GREATROOM LTD 1630349
Unit 13, 10 High Craighall Road, GLASGOW, G4 9UD
Tel: 0141 581 2646 **Fax:** 0141 588 1410
Titles:
UPTOWN MAGAZINE

GREEN ARBOR PUBLISHING LTD 1736819
Unit 7, Woodman Works, 204 Durnsford Road, LONDON, SW19 8DR **Tel:** 020 8971 8452 **Fax:** 020 8971 8452
Titles:
BRITAIN AT WAR MAGAZINE

GREEN BUILDING PRESS 1630334
PO Box 32, LLANDYSUL, SA44 5ZA
Web site: http://www.greenbuildingpress.co.uk
Titles:
GREEN BUILDING

GREEN EVENTS 625461
48 Clifftown Gardens, HERNE BAY, CT6 8DE
Titles:
GREEN EVENTS

THE GREEN ORGANISATION 1645352
The Mill House, Mill Lane, Earls Barton, NORTHAMPTON, NN6 0NR **Tel:** 01604 810507 **Fax:** 01604 810507
Email: rogerwolens@btconnect.com
Web site: http://www.thegreenorganisation.info
Titles:
ECO-ECHO.COM

GREEN PARENT PUBLICATIONS 1740740
Tel: 01825 872858
PO Box 104, East Hoathly, LEWES, BN7 9AX
Tel: 01825 872858
Titles:
THE GREEN PARENT

GREEN PARTY 15697
1A Waterlow Road, LONDON, N19 5NJ **Tel:** 01252 330506
Fax: 01252 330506
Email: office@greenparty.org.uk
Web site: http://www.greenparty.org.uk
Titles:
GREEN WORLD

GREEN PEA PUBLISHING 1650375
Suite 51, The Business Centre, Ingate Place, LONDON, SW8 3NS **Tel:** 020 7501 0511 **Fax:** 020 7501 0510
Email: gregor.rankin@foodandtravel.com
Web site: http://www.foodandtravel.com
Titles:
FOOD AND TRAVEL

GREEN SHEET MEDIA 1749669
13 Caird's Wynd, BANCHORY, AB31 5XU
Tel: 024 7625 4957 **Fax:** 024 7638 2319
Titles:
IDMI

GREENHOUSE PUBLISHING 18663
12 Southgate Street, WINCHESTER, SO23 9EF
Tel: 0845 458 8420
Titles:
RETAIL FARMER

GREENLIGHT PUBLISHING 15488
119 Newland Street, WITHAM, CM8 1WF **Tel:** 01376 521900
Fax: 01376 521901
Titles:
TREASURE HUNTING

GREENPEACE LTD 14627
Canonbury Villas, LONDON, N1 2PS **Tel:** 020 7865 8100
Fax: 020 7865 8203
Titles:
GREENPEACE BUSINESS

GREENS COURT ADVERTISING LTD. 1653857
18 Brewer Street, LONDON, W1F 0SH **Tel:** 020 7025 6120
Fax: 020 7025 6109
Titles:
BOYZ

GREENSHIRES PUBLISHING LTD 16263
Telford Way, Telford Way Industrial Estate, KETTERING, NN16 8UN **Tel:** 01536 382500 **Fax:** 01536 382501
Web site: http://www.greenshirespublishing.com
Titles:
BRITISH DRESSAGE
CLIMB
OUTDOOR REVIEW

GREENSPACE 1653953
Caversham Court, Church Road, Caversham, READING, RG4 7AD **Tel:** 0118 946 9066 **Fax:** 0118 946 9061
Web site: http://www.green-space.org.uk
Titles:
SPACES&PLACES

GREER PUBLICATIONS LTD 13537
5B Edgewater Business Park, Belfast Harbour Estate, BELFAST, BT3 9JQ **Tel:** 028 9078 3200 **Fax:** 028 9078 3210
Web site: http://www.greerpublications.com
Titles:
CARSPORT
GARAGE TRADER
HOSPITALITY REVIEW NI
INDUSTRIAL & MANUFACTURING ENGINEER
NORTHERN WOMAN
SPECIFY
ULSTER BUSINESS
ULSTER GROCER

GREY MOON DESIGN 671848
39 Eslington Terrace, NEWCASTLE UPON TYNE, NE2 4RN
Tel: 0191 209 4228 **Fax:** 0191 281 0462
Web site: http://www.polsinelli.co.uk
Titles:
GATESHEAD COUNCIL NEWS
THE GATESHEAD HOUSING COMPANY NEWS

UK Publishers & Their Titles

GREYCOAT PUBLISHING LTD 14531
106 Earls Court Road, Kensington, LONDON, W8 6EG
Tel: 020 7937 6233 **Fax:** 020 7937 0933
Email: mail@greycoatpublishing.co.uk
Web site: http://www.greycoatpublishing.co.uk
Titles:
BRITISH JOURNAL OF INTENSIVE CARE
INTERNATIONAL JOURNAL OF INTENSIVE CARE

GRIMSBY & SCUNTHORPE MEDIA GROUP 14837
80 Cleethorpe Road, GRIMSBY, DN31 3EH
Tel: 01472 360360 **Fax:** 01472 372257
Titles:
GRIMSBY TELEGRAPH
LIFE
SCUNTHORPE TARGET
SCUNTHORPE TELEGRAPH
SPORTSTELEGRAPH.CO.UK

THE GROUP AUTO UNION UK & IRELAND LTD 14118
Roydsdale Way, Euroway Industrial Estate, BRADFORD,
BD4 6SE **Tel:** 01274 654600 **Fax:** 01274 654610
Web site: http://www.gau.co.uk
Titles:
MOTOR FACTOR

GROUP TRAVEL ORGANISER LTD 14422
47 Wellington Square, HASTINGS, TN34 1PN
Tel: 0845 166 8120 **Fax:** 01424 200478
Web site: http://www.grouptravelorganiser.com
Titles:
GROUP TRAVEL ORGANISER

GROUPS WELCOME 17452
The Old Police House, The Green, Tysoe, WARWICK, CV35
0SN **Tel:** 01295 688263 **Fax:** 01295 688263
Email: info@groupswelcome.co.uk
Web site: http://www.groupswelcome.co.uk
Titles:
GROUPS WELCOME

GROVE HOUSE PUBLISHING 1603380
Hendal Oast, Hendal Farm, Groombridge, KENT, TN3 9NU
Tel: 01892 861993
Titles:
FARM BUSINESS
FARM BUSINESS AGRONOMIST
OVER THE COUNTER
PIG MARKETING

GS1 UK 16885
Staple Court, 11 Staple Inn Building, LONDON, WC1V 7QH
Tel: 020 7655 9035 **Fax:** 020 7681 2296
Titles:
GSQ

GSCENE LTD 1730114
111 Western Road, HOVE, BN3 1DD **Tel:** 01273 722457
Email: info@gscene.com
Web site: http://www.gscene.com
Titles:
GSCENE

GTC 13943
Ewell House, Graveney Road, Goodstone, FAVERSHAM,
ME13 8UP **Tel:** 01795 535468 **Fax:** 01795 535469
Email: enquiries@deeson.co.uk
Web site: http://www.deeson.co.uk
Titles:
THE ARK
THE ASSESSOR
ENGINEERING DESIGNER
GREEN PLACES
GREEN PLACES INCORPORATING LANDSCAPE DESIGN
THE GROUNDSMAN
MANAGEMENT SERVICES
PULL!
SYNERGY - IMAGING AND THERAPY PRACTICE
ZERB

GTI SPECIALIST PUBLISHERS 18591
The Barns, Preston Crowmarsh, WALLINGFORD, OX10 6SL
Tel: 01491 826262 **Fax:** 01491 826401
Titles:
RECOVERY

GTS MEDIA 1714811
53 Harvey Gardens, LONDON, SE7 8AJ **Tel:** 020 8858 4223
Titles:
CREDIT COLLECTIONS AND RISK

GUARDIAN MEDIA GROUP PLC 13282
3-7 Herbal Hill, LONDON, EC1R 5EJ **Tel:** 0161 832 7200
Fax: 0161 832 0155
Web site: http://www.gmgplc.co.uk
Titles:
ASIAN NEWS
FAMILY
THE GUARDIAN
THE GUARDIAN (LEEDS OFFICE)
THE GUARDIAN (MANCHESTER OFFICE)
THE GUARDIAN WEEKEND
THE GUARDIAN WEEKLY
GUARDIAN.CO.UK
GUARDIAN.CO.UK/FILM
GUARDIAN.CO.UK/TRAVEL
THE GUIDE (GUARDIAN)
LEARNTHINGS
THE OBSERVER
THE OBSERVER FOOD MONTHLY
OBSERVER MUSIC MONTHLY
THE OBSERVER SPORT MONTHLY
OBSERVER WOMAN
THE OBSERVER.CO.UK
OM THE OBSERVER MAGAZINE
PUBLIC

GUARDIAN NEWS AND MEDIA 15698
90 York Way, LONDON, N1 9GU **Tel:** 020 3353 2000
Titles:
GUARDIAN.CO.UK/POLITICS
SOCIETY GUARDIAN.CO.UK

GUARDIAN SERIES 1640534
53 Corporation Street, COVENTRY, CV1 1GX
Tel: 024 7663 0550 **Fax:** 024 7622 0745
Email: guardianseries@tiscali.co.uk
Titles:
GUARDIAN SERIES (WILTSHIRE, HAMPSHIRE AND
SURREY)

GUERNSEY PRESS CO LTD 14855
PO Box 57, Braye Road, Vale, GUERNSEY, GY1 3BW
Tel: 01481 240240 **Fax:** 01481 240235
Email: newseditor@guernsey-press.com
Web site: http://www.guernsey-press.com
Titles:
GUERNSEY GLOBE
GUERNSEY NOW
GUERNSEY PRESS AND STAR
GUERNSEY WEEKLY PRESS AND STAR
THE VISITOR (GUERNSEY)

GUIDELINE PUBLICATIONS LTD 1676865
Unit 3, Enigma building, Bilton Road, Bletchley, MILTON
KEYNES, MK1 1HW **Tel:** 01908 270400 **Fax:** 01908 270614
Web site: http://www.guidelinepublications.co.uk
Titles:
MILITARY MODELCRAFT INTERNATIONAL

GUILD OF AIR TRAFFIC CONTROL OFFICERS 13634
4 St. Marys Road, Bingham, NOTTINGHAM, NG13 8DW
Tel: 01949 876405
Email: caf@gatco.org
Web site: http://www.gatco.org
Titles:
TRANSMIT

THE GUILD OF ARCHITECTURAL IRONMONGERS 13542
8 Stepney Green, LONDON, E1 3JU **Tel:** 020 7790 3431
Fax: 020 7790 8517
Titles:
ARCHITECTURAL IRONMONGERY JOURNAL

THE GUILD OF FINE FOOD LTD 14047
Guild House, Station Road, Wincanton, SOMERSET, BA9
9FE **Tel:** 01963 824464 **Fax:** 01963 824651
Email: info@finefoodworld.co.uk
Web site: http://www.finefoodworld.co.uk
Titles:
FINE FOOD DIGEST
GOOD CHEESE

GUILD PRESS LTD 16318
3 Charnwood Street, DERBY, DE1 2GT **Tel:** 01332 227680
Fax: 01332 227688
Email: info@beautyserve.net
Web site: http://www.beautyserve.com
Titles:
GUILD NEWS
TANNING WORLD

GUISE MARKETING 1646187
4 Froxfield Close, WINCHESTER, SO22 6JW
Tel: 01962 620320
Titles:
NEWBOOKS

GULF CENTRE FOR STRATEGIC STUDIES 1734339
Davina House, 137-149 Goswell Road, LONDON, EC1V 7ET
Tel: 020 7490 7101 **Fax:** 020 7490 7102
Email: gcss@btconnect.com
Titles:
GULF AFFAIRS JOURNAL

GUTHRIE COMMUNICATIONS LTD 1715129
Frog Pond Farm, Ansty Coombe Lane, Ansty, SALISBURY,
SP3 5PY **Tel:** 020 7183 2511
Titles:
VETNURSE.CO.UK
VETSURGEON.ORG

GUTHRUM HOUSE LTD 18639
Guthrum House, 145 Angel Street, Hadleigh, IPSWICH, IP7
5BY **Tel:** 01473 822061 **Fax:** 01473 822839
Titles:
SHIPPING & TRANSPORT INTERNATIONAL

GUY FOX HISTORY PROJECT LIMITED 1757733
Unit LF.B4, The Leathermarket, Weston Street, LONDON,
SE1 3HN **Tel:** 020 7407 4785 **Fax:** 020 7407 4785
Email: info@guyfox.org.uk
Web site: http://www.guyfox.org.uk
Titles:
THE GUY FOX FAMILY NEWSLETTER

GV MEDIA LTD 15107
Northern and Shell Tower, 6th Floor, 4 Selsdon Way,
LONDON, E14 9GL **Tel:** 020 7510 0340 **Fax:** 020 7510 0341
Web site: http://www.jamaica-gleaner.com
Titles:
THE VOICE
THE WEEKLY GLEANER
YOUNG VOICES

GVZ LTD 1761422
Starting Points, 16 Pickering Road, BARKING, IG11 8PG
Tel: 020 3288 2269
Titles:
GVZ

GWASG AERON PRINTERS 1746012
2 Market Street, ABERAERON, SA46 0AS
Tel: 01545 570573 **Fax:** 01545 570573
Email: aeron.printers@virgin.net
Web site: http://www.gwasgaeronprinters.com
Titles:
Y CARDI BACH

GWASG CARREG GWALCH 15609
12 Iard Yr Orsaf, Conwy, LLANRWST, LL26 0EH
Tel: 01492 642031 **Fax:** 01492 641502
Titles:
LLAFAR GWLAD (WELSH FOLKLORE)

GWASG PANTYCELYN 15840
Gwasg y Bwthyn, Lon Ddewi, CAERNARFON, LL55 1ER
Tel: 01286 672018 **Fax:** 01286 677823
Web site: http://www.ebcpcw.org.uk
Titles:
Y TRAETHODYDD (THE ESSAYIST)

GWASG Y SIR 15025
County Press Buildings, Station Road, BALA, LL23 7PG
Tel: 01678 520262

Titles:
NORTH WALES SERIES

H2B JOURNAL LTD   1739873
1 Cottage Road, LEEDS, LS6 4DD **Tel:** 0113 274 1308
Titles:
H2B JOURNAL

H3B MEDIA LTD   1760985
15 Onslow Gardens, WALLINGTON, SM6 9QL
Tel: 020 8254 9406 **Fax:** 020 8647 0045
Email: info@h3bmedia.com
Web site: http://www.thinkinghighways.com
Titles:
ETC, ETC
THINKING HIGHWAYS EUROPE/REST OF THE WORLD
EDITION
THINKING HIGHWAYS NORTH AMERICAN EDITION

H40 LTD   1758448
Stockwell House, Monksford Street, KIDWELLY, SA17 4TW
Tel: 07828 114358
Titles:
DEFENSEFILE

H. BAUER PUBLISHING   17072
Academic House, 24-28 Oval Road, LONDON, NW1 7DT
Tel: 020 7241 8000 **Fax:** 020 7241 8056
Web site: http://www.bauer.co.uk
Titles:
BELLA
CRISS CROSS
EAT IN
FATE & FORTUNE
SPIRIT & DESTINY
TAKE A BREAK
TAKE A BREAK SPECIALS
THAT'S LIFE
TOTAL TV GUIDE
TV QUICK
TVCHOICE

HABIA   1630390
Oxford House, Sixth Avenue, Sky Business Park, Robin
Hood Airport, DONCASTER, DN9 3GG **Tel:** 0845 230 6080
Fax: 01302 774949
Web site: http://www.habia.org.uk
Titles:
HABIA NEWS

HACHETTE FILIPACCHI MAGAZINES   15409
64 North Row, LONDON, W1K 7LL **Tel:** 020 7150 7000
Fax: 020 7150 7675
Titles:
PSYCHOLOGIES

HACHETTE FILIPACCHI (UK) LTD   15156
64 North Row, LONDON, W1K 7LL **Tel:** 020 7150 7000
Fax: 020 7150 7001
Web site: http://www.hf-uk.com
Titles:
ALL ABOUT SOAP
ELLE
ELLE DECORATION
ELLEUK.COM
INSIDE SOAP
PSYCHOLOGIES
RED
SUGAR
SUGARSCAPE.COM

HALI PUBLICATIONS LTD   13661
Studio 30, Liddell Road, LONDON, NW6 2EW
Tel: 020 7578 7228 **Fax:** 020 7578 7221
Email: info@hali.com
Web site: http://www.hali.com
Titles:
HALI
HALI
MODERN CARPETS + TEXTILES

HALIFAX COURIER LTD   14838
PO Box 19, King Cross Street, HALIFAX, HX1 2SF
Tel: 01422 260200 **Fax:** 01422 330021
Titles:
CALDERDALE NEWS
EVENING COURIER (HALIFAX)

HALLAM STUDENTS UNION   18492
The Hubs, Paternoster Row, SHEFFIELD, S1 2QQ
Tel: 0114 225 4571 **Fax:** 0114 225 4571
Titles:
SHU PRINT

HALLDALE MEDIA LTD   13619
Pembroke House, 8 St. Christophers Place,
FARNBOROUGH, GU14 0NH **Tel:** 01252 532000
Fax: 01252 512714
Email: cat@halldale.com
Web site: http://www.halldale.com
Titles:
CAT - CIVIL AVIATION TRAINING
MS & T

HALL-MCCARTNEY LIMITED   16112
PO Box 21, Heritage House, BALDOCK, SG7 5SH
Tel: 01462 896688 **Fax:** 01462 896677
Email: pgpublications@hall-mccartney.co.uk
Web site: http://www.hall-mccartney.co.uk
Titles:
HISTORIC HOUSE
THE PROFESSIONAL GARDENER

THE HAMBLIN VISION   18266
Bosham House, Main Road, Bosham, CHICHESTER, PO18
8PJ **Tel:** 01243 572109 **Fax:** 01243 572109
Email: office@thehamblinvision.org.uk
Web site: http://www.thehamblintrust.org.uk
Titles:
NEW VISION

HAMERVILLE MAGAZINES LTD   13006
Regal House, Regal Way, WATFORD, WD24 4YF
Tel: 01923 237799 **Fax:** 01923 246901
Email: office@hamerville.co.uk
Web site: http://www.hamerville.co.uk
Titles:
COMMERCIAL VEHICLE WORKSHOP
HOUSING ASSOCIATION BUILDING & MAINTENANCE
KITCHENS & BATHROOMS NEWS
LOCAL AUTHORITY BUILDING & MAINTENANCE
PROFESSIONAL BUILDER
PROFESSIONAL BUILDERS MERCHANT
PROFESSIONAL ELECTRICIAN AND INSTALLER
PROFESSIONAL HAIRDRESSER
PROFESSIONAL HEATING AND PLUMBING INSTALLER
PROFESSIONAL HOUSEBUILDER & PROPERTY
DEVELOPER
PROFESSIONAL MOTOR FACTOR
PROFESSIONAL MOTOR MECHANIC
WINDOW FABRICATOR AND INSTALLER

HAMMOND PUBLISHING   622373
PO Box 199, SCARBOROUGH, YO11 3GT
Tel: 01723 506326
Titles:
MODEL RAILWAY EXPRESS

HAMODIA   18806
113 Fairview Road, LONDON, N15 6TS **Tel:** 020 8442 7777
Fax: 020 8442 7778
Titles:
HAMODIA

HAMPSHIRE FAMILY PUBLICATIONS LTD   1737537
38 Lynford Avenue, WINCHESTER, SO22 6BN
Tel: 01962 620331 **Fax:** 01962 620331
Titles:
ABC MAGAZINE HAMPSHIRE

HAMPSHIRE MEDIA LTD   694790
20 Moorside Road, WINCHESTER, SO23 7RX
Tel: 01962 859559
Web site: http://www.hantsmedia.co.uk
Titles:
THE INDEPENDENT OBSERVER SERIES
THERE'S MORE TO LIFE

HAND TO MOUTH PUBLISHING LTD   1728849
Derw Mill North, Pentre-Cwrt, LLANDYSUL, SA44 5DB
Tel: 01599 363190 **Fax:** 01559 363186
Titles:
ROCK'N'REEL

HANDBAG PUBLISHING GROUP   1714809
5th Floor, 7 Swallow Place, LONDON, W1B 2AG
Tel: 020 7292 0020 **Fax:** 020 7292 0021
Titles:
ALLABOUTYOU

HANDBELL RINGERS OF GREAT BRITAIN   18235
87 The Woodfields, Sanderstead, SOUTH CROYDON, CR2
0HJ **Tel:** 01626 774131 **Fax:** 020 8651 2663
Titles:
REVERBERATIONS

THE HARDY GROUP   1735137
101 Back Church Lane, LONDON, E1 1LU
Tel: 020 7709 0303 **Fax:** 020 7709 1227
Email: info@hardyprinting.co.uk
Web site: http://www.thehardygroup.co.uk
Titles:
BRITISH HORSE

HARDY MEDIA   1758927
Churchill House, 142-146 Old Street, LONDON, EC1V 9BW
Tel: 020 7250 0607 **Fax:** 020 3014 8612
Titles:
CORPCOMMS

THE HARDY PLANT SOCIETY   16107
Little Orchard, Great Comberton, PERSHORE, WR10 3DP
Tel: 01386 710317 **Fax:** 01386 710117
Email: admin@hardy-plant.org.uk
Web site: http://www.hardy-plant.org.uk
Titles:
THE HARDY PLANT

**HARINGEY COUNCIL COMMUNICATIONS AND
CONSULTATIONS UNIT**   16662
8th Floor, Riverpark House, 225 High Road, LONDON, N22
8HQ **Tel:** 020 8862 2997 **Fax:** 020 8888 5484
Web site: http://www.haringey.gov.uk
Titles:
HARINGEY PEOPLE

HARLEY-DAVIDSON EUROPE   16488
Oxford Business Park, 6000 Garsington Road, Cowley,
OXFORD, OX4 2DQ **Tel:** 0870 850 1903 **Fax:** 0870 850 2003
Web site: http://www.harley-davidson.com
Titles:
HOG TALES

HARMSWORTH PRINTING LTD   1759829
Journal House, 18 Curzon Street, DERBY, DE1 1LL
Tel: 01332 384988 **Fax:** 01332 202671
Titles:
SOUTH BUCKS AND BERKSHIRE NEWS SERIES

HARMSWORTH PRINTING (STAVERTON) LTD   1744961
PO Box 8667, LEICESTER, LE1 8BE **Tel:** 01792 514309
Fax: 01792 514990
Titles:
THE MEON VALLEY NEWS

HARRIMAN CHEMSULT LTD   14254
24-25 Scala Street, LONDON, W1T 2HP **Tel:** 020 7462 1860
Fax: 020 7462 1861
Titles:
VINYL CHLORIDE REPORT

HARROW BOROUGH   18477
Communications Unit, M12, London Borough of Harrow,
Civic Centre, Station Road, HARROW, HA1 2XF
Tel: 020 8424 1290 **Fax:** 020 8424 1966
Titles:
HARROW PEOPLE

HART PUBLISHING LTD   600361
16C Worcester Place, OXFORD, OX1 2JW
Tel: 01865 517530 **Fax:** 01865 510710
Email: mail@hartpub.co.uk
Web site: http://www.hartjournals.co.uk
Titles:
EUROPEAN LAW REPORTS

UK Publishers & Their Titles

HARTSWOOD MEDIA 1744105
Tralee, Hillcrest Road, EDENBRIDGE, TN8 6JS
Tel: 01732 505724 **Fax:** 01732 860052
Email: pmdmagazine@btinternet.com
Web site: http://www.pmdmagazine.com
Titles:
    PAPER MAKING & DISTRIBUTION

HARVEY NICHOLS 1710872
67 Brompton Road, LONDON, SW3 1DB **Tel:** 020 7201 8717
Fax: 020 7201 8717
Web site: http://www.harveynichols.com
Titles:
    HARVEY NICHOLS EDIT

HAVERSHAM PUBLICATIONS LTD 625292
Freebournes House, Freebournes Road, WITHAM, CM8 3US
Tel: 01376 534500 **Fax:** 01376 534546
Titles:
    BLACKHAIR
    HAIRFLAIR & BEAUTY
    HAIRSTYLES ONLY

HAWKER CONSUMER PUBLICATIONS LTD 600753
2nd Floor, Culvert House, Culvert Road, Battersea,
LONDON, SW11 5DH **Tel:** 020 7720 2108
Fax: 020 7498 3023
Titles:
    BLACK BEAUTY & HAIR

HAWKER PUBLICATIONS 14160
2nd Floor, Culvert House, Culvert Road, Battersea,
LONDON, SW11 5DH **Tel:** 020 7720 2108
Fax: 020 7498 3023
Web site: http://www.careinfo.org
Titles:
    CARING TIMES
    COMMUNITY CONNECTING
    THE JOURNAL OF DEMENTIA CARE
    NURSERY MANAGEMENT TODAY

HAWKMOOR RESEARCH 1644747
2 Hawkmoor Parke, Bovey Tracey, NEWTON ABBOT, TQ13
9NL **Tel:** 01626 834224
Titles:
    TELECOMVIEW

HAWTHORNE PUBLISHING 1759998
Scott County, Sherwood Industrial Estate, Sherwood
Terrace, BONNYRIGG, EH19 3LB
Titles:
    THE PROPERTY GUIDE

HAXTON MARKETING LTD 1638843
96 Netherwood Park, LIVINGSTON, EH54 8RW
Tel: 01506 200890 **Fax:** 01506 203419
Titles:
    SCOTTISH WOMAN

AL HAYAT PUBLISHING 14868
Kensington Centre, 66 Hammersmith Road, LONDON, W14
8YT **Tel:** 020 7602 9988 **Fax:** 020 7371 4215
Titles:
    AL HAYAT

HAYCHART LTD 12699
Armstrong House, Armstrong Street, GRIMSBY, DN31 2QE
Tel: 01472 310305 **Fax:** 01472 310317
Email: fdi@blmgroup.co.uk
Web site: http://www.blmgroup.co.uk
Titles:
    BUSINESS LINK (YORKSHIRE & LINCOLNSHIRE)
    FOOD & DRINK INTERNATIONAL
    LINCOLNSHIRE TODAY
    YORKSHIRE TODAY

HAYES PRESS 1650978
The Barn, Flaxlands Manor Farm, Flaxlands, Wootton
Bassett, SWINDON, SN4 8DY **Tel:** 01666 510153
Email: info@hayespress.org
Web site: http://www.hayespress.org
Titles:
    PLUS & EAGLE WINGS

HAYMARKET AUTOSPORT AND CLASSIC PUBLICATIONS 693990
26-30 Old Church Street, LONDON, SW3 5BY
Tel: 020 8943 5000
Web site: http://www.haymarketgroup.com
Titles:
    MOTORSPORT NEWS

HAYMARKET BRAND MEDIA 1738611
174 Hammersmith Road, LONDON, W6 7JP
Tel: 020 8267 5000 **Fax:** 020 8267 4927
Titles:
    EVENT
    MANAGEMENT TODAY
    PPAJOBS.CO.UK
    PR WEEK
    PROMOTIONS & INCENTIVES
    REVOLUTION
    REVOLUTIONJOBS.CO.UK

HAYMARKET BUSINESS MEDIA LTD 13412
174 Hammersmith Road, LONDON, W6 7JP
Tel: 020 8267 5000 **Fax:** 020 8267 4987
Email: campaign@haymarket.com
Web site: http://www.haymarket.com
Titles:
    AUTOCAR
    AV INTERNATIONAL NEWSLETTER
    BRAND REPUBLIC
    CAMPAIGN
    ENDS EUROPE DAILY
    THE ENDS REPORT
    HORTICULTURE WEEK
    HUMAN RESOURCES
    MEDIA WEEK
    MEDIAWEEKJOBS.CO.UK
    MT MANGEMENTTODAY.COM
    NURSERY WORLD
    NURSERY WORLD
    PACKAGING NEWS
    PLANNING
    PRINTWEEK
    REGENERATION AND RENEWAL
    SC MAGAZINE
    THIRD SECTOR

HAYMARKET CONSUMER MEDIA 17783
Teddington Studios, Broom Road, TEDDINGTON, TW11
9BE **Tel:** 020 8267 5000 **Fax:** 020 8267 5777
Web site: http://www.haymarketgroup.co.uk
Titles:
    CLASSIC FM MAGAZINE
    FOUR FOUR TWO
    THE GRAMOPHONE
    GRAMOPHONE ONLINE
    PISTONHEADS.COM
    PRACTICAL CARAVAN
    PRACTICAL MOTORHOME
    STUFF
    WHAT HI-FI? SOUND AND VISION

HAYMARKET MEDIA GROUP LTD 14113
Teddington Studios, Broom Road, TEDDINGTON, TW11
9BE **Tel:** 020 8267 5000 **Fax:** 020 8267 5725
Web site: http://www.haymarketgroup.com
Titles:
    AUTOSPORT
    AUTOSPORT.COM
    CAT (CAR & ACCESSORY TRADER)
    CLASSIC & SPORTS CAR
    F1 RACING
    JAGUAR MAGAZINE
    WHAT CAR?
    WHATCAR? ONLINE

HAYMARKET MEDICAL PUBLICATIONS LTD 14500
174 Hammersmith Road, LONDON, W6 7JP
Tel: 020 8267 4850
Web site: http://www.haymarket.com
Titles:
    GP INCORPORATING MEDECONOMICS
    HEALTHCAREREPUBLIC.COM
    INDEPENDENT NURSE
    MIMS

HAYMARKET MOTORING 1622487
Teddington Studios, Broom Road, TEDDINGTON, TW11
9BE **Tel:** 020 8267 5000 **Fax:** 020 826 5725
Web site: http://www.haymarket.co.uk
Titles:
    EVECARS.COM

HAYMARKET NETWORK 622390
Teddington Studios, Broom Road, TEDDINGTON, TW11
9BE **Tel:** 020 8267 5000 **Fax:** 020 8267 5922
Web site: http://www.haymarketgroup.co.uk
Titles:
    CHAMPIONS
    GREENSIDE
    INSIDE UNITED
    SKY SPORTS MAGAZINE
    SONY MAGAZINE
    SPIKES
    STUFF.TV
    UNITED REVIEW

HAYMARKET PROFESSIONAL PUBLICATIONS LTD 1621864
174 Hammersmith Road, LONDON, W6 7JP
Tel: 020 8267 4706 **Fax:** 020 8267 4728
Web site: http://www.haymarketgroup.co.uk
Titles:
    CHILDREN & YOUNG PEOPLE NOW
    CHILDREN & YOUNG PEOPLE NOW

HAYMARKET SPECIALIST PUBLICATIONS 13424
174 Hammersmith Road, LONDON, W6 7JP
Tel: 020 8267 5000 **Fax:** 020 8267 4927
Web site: http://www.haymarket.com
Titles:
    AV INTERACTIVE
    AV MAGAZINE
    CONFERENCE & INCENTIVE TRAVEL
    MARKETING
    MARKETING DIRECT
    MARKETINGMAGAZINE.CO.UK
    PR WEEK BLACK BOOK

HAYWARD MEDICAL COMMUNICATIONS LTD 12616
8-10 Dryden Street, Covent Garden, LONDON, WC2E 9NA
Tel: 020 7240 4493 **Fax:** 020 7240 4479
Web site: http://www.hayward.co.uk
Titles:
    BRITISH JOURNAL OF RENAL MEDICINE
    DERMATOLOGY IN PRACTICE
    EUROPEAN JOURNAL OF PALLIATIVE CARE

HAZARDS PUBLICATIONS LTD 14455
PO Box 4042, Kent Road, SHEFFIELD, S8 9RL
Tel: 0114 201 4265
Titles:
    HAZARDS

HEADSTAR 700495
68 Middle Street, BRIGHTON, BN1 1AL **Tel:** 01273 267173
Fax: 01273 232119
Email: info@headstar.com
Web site: http://www.headstar.com
Titles:
    E-ACCESS BULLETIN
    E-GOVERNMENT BULLETIN

HEALTH CARE PUBLICATIONS 14536
The Old Vicarage, Beck Hill, BARTON-UPON-HUMBER,
DN18 5EY **Tel:** 01652 661510 **Fax:** 01652 661512
Web site: http://www.healthcarepublications.co.uk
Titles:
    HOSPITAL MANAGEMENT
    IN CONTROL
    NOW FOR HOSPITALS

HEALTH ISSUES LIMITED 1622264
The Elms, Radclive Road, Gawcott, BUCKINGHAM, MK18
4JB **Tel:** 01280 821211
Web site: http://www.iconmag.co.uk
Titles:
    ICON (INTEGRATED CANCER AND ONCOLOGY NEWS)

HEALTH SECTOR PUBLISHING 1732828
Unit 4, Clarks Courtyard, 145 Granville Street,
BIRMINGHAM, B1 1SB **Tel:** 0870 609 2834
Fax: 0870 609 2836
Web site: http://www.healthpublishing.co.uk
Titles:
    ON TARGET

HEALTH SQUARED COMMUNICATIONS 165296
69 Wigmore Street, LONDON, W1U 1PZ **Tel:** 020 7486 6660

Titles:
NUTRITION REVIEW

THE HEALTH STORE 18929
Unit 10, Blenheim Park Road, NOTTINGHAM, NG6 8YP
Tel: 0115 955 5255 **Fax:** 0115 955 5290
Titles:
THE HEALTH STORE MAGAZINE

HEALTHINVESTOR 1651167
2nd Floor, Griffin House, West Street, WOKING, GU21 6BS
Tel: 01483 749020 **Fax:** 01483 749021
Titles:
HEALTHINVESTOR

HEALTHY SOUL 1758449
PO Box 1073, COULSDON, CR5 3ZU
Web site: http://www.healthysoul.co.uk
Titles:
HEALTHYSOUL.CO.UK

HEARING CONCERN 14580
19 Hartfield Road, EASTBOURNE, BN21 2AR
Tel: 020 7440 9871
Titles:
HEARING CONCERN

HEARST DIGITAL 1763397
7 Swallow Place, LONDON, W1B 2AG
Titles:
COAST
COUNTRY LIVING
GOOD HOUSEKEEPING
HANDBAG.COM
HOUSE BEAUTIFUL
SHE

HEDGE FUND INTELLIGENCE 1719216
Nestor House, Playhouse Yard, LONDON, EC4V 5EX
Tel: 020 7779 7330 **Fax:** 020 7779 7331
Web site: http://www.hedgefundintelligence.com
Titles:
ABSOLUTE RETURN
AFRICAHEDGE
ASIAHEDGE
EUROHEDGE
INVESTHEDGE

HEDGE FUND PUBLISHING LTD 1650461
31 Davies Street, LONDON, W1K 4LW **Tel:** 020 7409 0888
Fax: 020 7629 7272
Titles:
THE HEDGE FUND JOURNAL

HELEN GILCHRIST 1653956
The Ground Floor, 1 South Harbour, Harbour Village,
PENRYN, TR10 8LR **Tel:** 01326 376500
Web site: http://www.stranger-mag.com
Titles:
STRANGER

HELLO! LTD 15218
Wellington House, 69-71 Upper Ground, LONDON, SE1 9PQ
Tel: 020 7667 8700 **Fax:** 020 7667 8716
Titles:
HELLO!

HEMMING GROUP LTD 12327
32 Vauxhall Bridge Road, LONDON, SW1V 2SS
Tel: 020 7973 6400 **Fax:** 020 7973 4647
Web site: http://www.hgluk.com
Titles:
THE BAPCO JOURNAL
BRIDGE DESIGN & ENGINEERING
COMPANY CLOTHING
FIRE & RESCUE
FIRETRADE ASIA AND MIDDLE EAST
HVP HEATING, VENTILATING & PLUMBING
INDUSTRIAL FIRE JOURNAL
LAPV LOCAL AUTHORITY PLANT & VEHICLES
LINGERIE BUYER
LOCAL GOVERNMENT NEWS
THE MJ
MUNICIPAL YEAR BOOK
RDA NEWS
THE RETAIL DIRECTORY - UK

SECURITY EUROPE
SURVEYOR
TEC TRAFFIC ENGINEERING & CONTROL

HEMMING INFORMATION SERVICES 12211
Hereford House, Bridle Path, CROYDON, CR9 4NL
Tel: 020 8680 4200 **Fax:** 020 8681 5049
Titles:
BUILDERS' MERCHANTS NEWS

HENLEY MEDIA GROUP LTD. 699278
Trans-World House, 100 City Road, LONDON, EC1Y 2BP
Tel: 020 7871 0123 **Fax:** 020 7871 0101
Web site: http://www.henleymediagroup.com
Titles:
INTERNATIONAL AID + TRADE REVIEW
PORT TECHNOLOGY INTERNATIONAL
SUSTAINABLE DEVELOPMENT INTERNATIONAL

**HENRY GEORGE FOUNDATION OF GREAT BRITAIN
LTD** 16229
212 Piccadilly, LONDON, W1J 9HG **Tel:** 020 7377 8885
Fax: 020 8881 4429
Email: office@landandliberty.net
Web site: http://www.landandliberty.net
Titles:
LAND AND LIBERTY

HENRY STEWART PUBLICATIONS 13421
Little Russell House, 28-30 Little Russell Street, LONDON,
WC1A 2HN **Tel:** 020 7404 3040 **Fax:** 020 7404 2081
Web site: http://www.henrystewart.com/publications.html
Titles:
JOURNAL OF TELECOMMUNICATIONS MANAGEMENT

HERALD PUBLISHING 697459
York House, 17 Rother Street, STRATFORD-UPON-AVON,
CV37 6NB **Tel:** 01789 266261
Titles:
FOCUS MAGAZINE SOUTH WARWICKSHIRE AND THE
COTSWOLDS
THE HERALD

THE HERB SOCIETY 13221
Sulgrave Manor, Sulgrave, BANBURY, OX17 2SD
Tel: 01295 768899
Web site: http://www.herbsociety.org.uk
Titles:
HERBS

HERON MEDIA LTD 1762110
Admirals Offices, The Historic Dockyard, CHATHAM, ME4
4TZ **Tel:** 01634 812530
Titles:
THE PENINSULA TIMES

THE HERTFORDSHIRE BUSINESS INDEPENDENT
700150
Simon James House, 17A Mill Lane, WELWYN, AL6 9EU
Tel: 01438 841310 **Fax:** 01438 841311
Email: sales@businessindependent.co.uk
Web site: http://www.businessindependent.co.uk
Titles:
THE HERTFORDSHIRE BUSINESS INDEPENDENT

HERTS & ESSEX NEWSPAPERS LTD 14934
The Media Centre, 40 Ware Road, HERTFORD, SG13 7HU
Tel: 01992 526600 **Fax:** 01992 526612
Email: mercury@hertsessexnews.co.uk
Web site: http://www.hertsessexnews.co.uk
Titles:
HARLOW STAR
HERTFORDSHIRE MERCURY SERIES
THE HERTS AND LEA VALLEY STAR
MERCURY SERIES (HODDESDON)

HERTS & ESSEX OBSERVER NEWSPAPERS 673681
The Media Centre, 40 Ware Road, HERTFORD, SG13 7HU
Tel: 01992 526625 **Fax:** 01279 306195
Titles:
HERTS & ESSEX OBSERVER SERIES

HEXUS LTD. 1685291
37 High Street, Purton, SWINDON, SN5 4BE
Tel: 07775 775115
Email: publisher@hexus.net
Web site: http://www.hexus.net
Titles:
HEXUS.NET

HG PUBLISHING 1622419
The Barn, Church Farm, Chalvington, HAILSHAM, BN27 3TD
Tel: 01323 811662 **Fax:** 01323 811486
Titles:
HUMAN GIVENS

H.H SAUDI RESEARCH & MARKETING UK LTD 16056
Arab Press House, 184 High Holborn, LONDON, WC1V 7AP
Tel: 020 7831 8181 **Fax:** 020 7831 2310
Web site: http://www.hhsaudi.com
Titles:
ASHARQ AL-AWSAT

HIFICRITIC LTD 1743871
PO Box 59214, LONDON, NW3 9EZ **Fax:** 020 7433 3220
Email: info@hificritic.com
Web site: http://www.hificritic.co.uk
Titles:
HIFICRITIC

HIGGS GROUP 16976
Caxton House, 1 Station Road, HENLEY-ON-THAMES, RG9
1AD **Tel:** 01491 419444 **Fax:** 01491 419401
Titles:
HENLEY STANDARD

HIGH POWER MEDIA 1734121
Whitfield House, Cheddar Road, WEDMORE, BS28 4EJ
Tel: 01934 713811 **Fax:** 020 8497 2102
Email: simon@highpowermedia.com
Web site: http://www.highpowermedia.com
Titles:
RACE ENGINE TECHNOLOGY

HIGHEND LTD 1749023
Rowmec Business Park, Plumpton Road, HODDESDON,
EN11 0EE **Tel:** 01992 445689 **Fax:** 01992 444966
Titles:
HIGHEND MAGAZINE

HIGHLEC PUBLISHING 1732100
Bowden House, 1 Church Street, HENFIELD, BN5 9NS
Tel: 01273 491462 **Fax:** 01273 495832
Email: hen@hilec.co.uk
Web site: http://www.highlec.co.uk
Titles:
HIGHWAY ELECTRICAL NEWS

HIGHPOINT MEDIA 1711332
Herberts House, High Laver, ONGAR, CM5 0DZ
Tel: 01732 750650
Titles:
OPEN CHAMPIONSHIP MAGAZINE

HIGHWOOD HOUSE PUBLISHING LTD 1648992
Highwood House, Winters Lane, Redhill, BRISTOL, BS40
5SH **Tel:** 0870 170 0666 **Fax:** 01934 861028
Email: admin@maturetimes.co.uk
Web site: http://www.maturetimes.co.uk
Titles:
MATURE TIMES

HIJ PUBLISHING LTD 17236
307 Bridge Road, Sutton Bridge, SPALDING, PE12 9SL
Tel: 0870 350 0280 **Fax:** 0870 350 0281
Email: mail@hijpublishing.com
Web site: http://www.hijpublishing.com
Titles:
INDUSTRIAL PRODUCT & SERVICE BULLETIN

HILL MEDIA LTD 12317
Marash House, 2-5 Brook Street, TRING, HP23 5ED
Tel: 01442 826826 **Fax:** 01442 823400
Email: hilmedia@aol.com

UK Publishers & Their Titles

Titles:
SURFACE WORLD
TROPHY & ENGRAVING NEWS INC. INDUSTRIAL &
INCENTIVE MARKING

HILLAINE PUBLISHING LTD   1605938
26 Blairs Road, Letham, FORFAR, DD8 2PE
Tel: 0845 130 7669 **Fax:** 0845 130 7669
Email: info@snequestrian.com
Web site: http://www.snequestrian.com
Titles:
THE NATIVE PONY
THE SCOTTISH AND NORTHERN EQUESTRIAN
THE SCOTTISH EQUESTRIAN DIRECTORY

HILLCLIMB & SPRINT ASSOCIATION   15444
42B Edwards Avenue, RUISLIP, HA4 6UT
Tel: 020 8845 9491 **Fax:** 020 8845 9491
Titles:
SPEEDSCENE

HILS PUBLICATIONS LTD   15103
1 Kings Road, CARDIFF, CF11 9BZ **Tel:** 029 2039 6600
Fax: 029 2039 6611
Titles:
LADIES FIRST
TIARA

HIRST KIDD & RENNIE LTD   14845
PO Box 47, 172 Union Street, OLDHAM, OL1 1EQ
Tel: 0161 633 2121 **Fax:** 0161 652 2111
Titles:
CHRONICLE WEEKEND OLDHAM
OLDHAM CHRONICLE ONLINE
OLDHAM EVENING CHRONICLE

THE HISTORIC GARDENS FOUNDATION   691186
34 River Court, Upper Ground, LONDON, SE1 9PE
Tel: 020 7633 9165 **Fax:** 020 7401 7072
Titles:
HISTORIC GARDENS REVIEW

HISTORIC MOTOR RACING NEWS LTD   628464
Unit 38, Chelsea Wharf, 15 Lots Road, LONDON, SW10 0QJ
Tel: 020 7349 8484
Email: contact@historicmotorracingnews.com
Titles:
HISTORIC MOTOR RACING NEWS

HISTORIC UK LTD   625236
Mill House, Mill Farm Close, Dunchurch, RUGBY, CV22 6QL
Tel: 01788 522341 **Fax:** 01788 522341
Email: info@historic-uk.com
Web site: http://www.historic-uk.com
Titles:
HISTORIC-UK.COM

HISTORY TODAY LTD   15699
20 Old Compton Street, LONDON, W1D 4TW
Tel: 020 7534 8000
Titles:
HISTORY TODAY

HMPR   672235
14A Eccleston Street, LONDON, SW1W 9LT
Tel: 020 7730 1100 **Fax:** 020 7730 2213
Titles:
ASPHALT NOW

HOAR OAK PUBLISHING   1752370
Martinhoe Cleave, Martinhoe, Parracombe, BARNSTAPLE,
EX31 4PZ **Tel:** 0845 224 1203
Email: hoaroak.publishing@googlemail.com
Titles:
EXMOOR - THE COUNTRY MAGAZINE

HOBBIES (DEREHAM) 1985 LTD   18003
Units 8-11, The Raveningham Centre, NORWICH, NR14 6NU
Tel: 01508 549330 **Fax:** 01508 549331
Titles:
HOBBIES HANDBOOK

HOG FEVER LTD   1720282
2 Alexandra Gate, Ffordd Pengam, CARDIFF, CF24 2SA
Tel: 029 2089 4888 **Fax:** 029 2089 4889
Email: actionadcopy@aol.com
Web site: http://www.actionmag.org
Titles:
ACTION NETWORK

HOLDERNESS NEWSPAPERS LTD   14956
1 Seaside Road, WITHERNSEA, HU19 2DL
Tel: 01964 612933 **Fax:** 01964 615303
Email: news@holderness-gazette.co.uk
Titles:
HOLDERNESS GAZETTE SERIES

HOLSTEIN UK   13997
Scotsbridge House, Scots Hill, RICKMANSWORTH, WD3
3BB **Tel:** 01923 695200 **Fax:** 01923 770003
Titles:
HOLSTEIN JOURNAL

HOLYROOD COMMUNICATIONS LTD   700397
14-16 Holyrood Road, EDINBURGH, EH8 8AF
Tel: 0131 272 2113 **Fax:** 0131 272 2116
Web site: http://www.holyrood.com
Titles:
HOLYROOD MAGAZINE
HOLYROOD TODAY

HOLYWOOD ADVERTISER   1675468
99 Princess Gardens, HOLYWOOD, BT18 0PW
Tel: 028 9042 7115
Titles:
HOLYWOOD ADVERTISER

HOMECARE PUBLISHING LIMITED   18308
The Stables, 16C High Street, RUSHTON, NN14 1RQ
Tel: 01536 710050 **Fax:** 01536 418280
Titles:
THIIS THE HOMECARE INDUSTRY INFORMATION
SERVICE

HONDA OWNERS CLUB (GB)   15423
Unit 1B & 5B, Kemps Quay Industrial Park, Quayside Road,
SOUTHAMPTON, SO18 1BZ
Web site: http://www.hoc.org.uk
Titles:
GOLDEN WING

HORIZON HOUSE PUBLICATIONS - EUROPE   18589
46 Gillingham Street, LONDON, SW1V 1HH
Tel: 020 7596 8730 **Fax:** 020 7596 8739
Titles:
TELECOMMUNICATIONS

HORIZON HOUSE PUBLICATIONS LTD   625102
46 Gillingham Street, LONDON, SW1V 1HH
Tel: 020 7596 8700 **Fax:** 020 7596 8739
Titles:
MICROWAVE JOURNAL

HORSESHOE MEDIA LTD   1733021
Marshall House, 124 Middleton Road, MORDEN, SM4 6RW
Titles:
BIOFUELS INTERNATIONAL
TANK STORAGE MAGAZINE

HOT PRESS PUBLICATIONS   12888
254 Cowbridge Road East, CARDIFF, CF5 1GZ
Tel: 029 2030 3900 **Fax:** 029 2040 2745
Email: cardiff.advertiser@virgin.net
Web site: http://www.thecardiffandsouthwalesadvertiser.co.
uk
Titles:
THE CARDIFF & SOUTH WALES ADVERTISER
NEW HOMES WALES AND THE SOUTH WEST

HOTCOURSES   1686799
150-152 King Street, LONDON, W6 0QU **Tel:** 020 8600 5307
Fax: 020 8741 7716
Titles:
FLOODLIGHT
HCSTUFF

HOTCOURSES
POST GRADUATE GUIDE

HOTDIGITS NEW MEDIA   1741147
34 Coniston Road, NESTON, CH64 0TD **Tel:** 0151 336 6199
Fax: 0151 336 6199
Titles:
GET READY TO ROCK!

HOTEL REVIEW WORLD   1676084
127 Broughton Road, EDINBURGH, EH7 4JH
Titles:
HOTEL REVIEW EDINBURGH
HOTEL REVIEW MADEIRA
HOTEL REVIEW SCOTLAND

HOTHOUSE MEDIA   17919
11-15 Emerald Street, LONDON, WC1N 3QL
Tel: 020 7440 4020 **Fax:** 020 7440 4035
Web site: http://www.hothousemedia.com
Titles:
EDUCATION TRAVEL MAGAZINE
LANGUAGE TRAVEL MAGAZINE
STUDYZONE

HOTHOUSE PUBLISHING LTD   1734365
171 Eagle Way, Hampton Vale, PETERBOROUGH, PE7 8EL
Tel: 01733 427502 **Fax:** 01733 427500
Titles:
MG ENTHUSIAST
MG ENTHUSIAST MAGAZINE

HOUSE OF WORDS LTD   13382
7 Greding Walk, Hutton, BRENTWOOD, CM13 2UF
Tel: 01277 225402 **Fax:** 0870 137 5688
Email: info@creditcontrol.co.uk
Web site: http://www.creditcontrol.co.uk
Titles:
CREDIT CONTROL
GETTING PAID
RED ALERT

HOUSEBUILDER MEDIA   13508
7-9 St. James's Street, LONDON, SW1A 1EE
Tel: 020 7960 1630 **Fax:** 020 7960 1631
Web site: http://www.house-builder.co.uk
Titles:
HOUSEBUILDER

HOUSING NEWS LTD   1739300
Avian House, 87 Brook Street, Broughty Ferry, DUNDEE,
DD5 1DJ **Tel:** 01382 427035 **Fax:** 01382 427006
Email: news@housingnews.co.uk
Web site: http://www.housingnews.co.uk
Titles:
HOUSINGNEWS.CO.UK

HOVERCRAFT CLUB OF GREAT BRITAIN LTD   16727
PR by email only
Web site: http://www.hovercraft.org.uk
Titles:
LIGHT HOVERCRAFT

THE HOVERCRAFT MUSEUM   13644
Argus Gate, Broom Way, Lee on Solent, GOSPORT, PO13
9NY **Tel:** 023 9255 2090 **Fax:** 023 9255 2090
Titles:
THE HOVERCRAFT NEWSLETTER

HOWARD PUBLICITY SERVICES LTD   1650972
PO Box 29407, Cupar, FIFE, KY14 7WW **Tel:** 0845 680 0049
Fax: 0845 458 0370
Titles:
GOLF LINKS

H.P. PUBLISHING   13656
Castle Ash, Birmingham Road, Blakedown,
KIDDERMINSTER, DY10 3JE **Tel:** 01562 701490
Fax: 01562 700001
Titles:
THE ANTIQUES FAIRS & CENTRES GUIDE

HP PUBLISHING LTD. 1640445
Samson House, 457 Manchester Road, MANCHESTER, M29 7BR **Tel:** 01942 879291 **Fax:** 01942 879291
Titles:
  G3 GLOBAL GAMES & GAMING MAGAZINE

HPC PUBLISHING 12313
Drury Lane, ST. LEONARDS-ON-SEA, TN38 9BJ
Tel: 01424 720477 **Fax:** 01424 443693
Email: admin@hpcpublisher.com
Web site: http://www.hpcpublishing.com
Titles:
  AVIATION NEWS
  WARSHIPS INTERNATIONAL FLEET REVIEW

HPCI MEDIA LTD 1758447
Poulton House, 8 Shepherdess Walk, LONDON, N1 7LB
Tel: 020 7549 8620
Titles:
  CLEANROOM TECHNOLOGY
  MANUFACTURING CHEMIST
  MANUFACTURING CHEMIST
  SPC (SOAP, PERFUMERY & COSMETICS)

THE HR DIRECTOR 1649569
Brook Farm, Heathend, Cromhall, GLOUCESTER, GL12 8AT
Tel: 01454 292060 **Fax:** 01454 294787
Email: info@thehrdirector.com
Web site: http://www.thehrdirector.com
Titles:
  THEHRDIRECTOR

HRC LEICESTER LTD 18072
PO Box 4, LEICESTER, LE1 3ZL **Tel:** 0116 253 7271
Fax: 0116 253 1875
Titles:
  THE OFFICIAL ELVIS PRESLEY FAN CLUB MAGAZINE

HSE BOOKS 1723429
PO Box 1999, SUDBURY, CO10 2WA **Tel:** 01787 881165
Fax: 01787 313995
Email: hsebooks@prolog.uk.com
Web site: http://www.hse.gov.uk
Titles:
  HEALTH AND SAFETY NEWSLETTER

HUBERT BURDA MEDIA UK 1691616
The Tower, Phoenix Square, Wyncolls Road, Severalls Industrial Park, COLCHESTER, CO4 9HU
Web site: http://www.hubert-burda-media.com
Titles:
  ESSENTIAL KITCHEN & BATHROOM BUSINESS
  THE ESSENTIAL KITCHEN, BATHROOM, BEDROOM MAGAZINE
  FULL HOUSE
  HEALTH & FITNESS MAGAZINE
  KITCHEN SPECIALIST MAGAZINE
  LOVE IT!
  PERIOD HOUSE
  YOUR HOME

HUCKELBERRY MEDIA 1746302
5 Lache Park Avenue, CHESTER, CH4 8HR
Tel: 01244 679103
Web site: http://www.huckleberrymedia.co.uk
Titles:
  TOYTALK

HULL & HUMBER CHAMBER OF COMMERCE INDUSTRY & SHIPPING 14732
34-38 Beverley Road, HULL, HU3 1YE **Tel:** 01482 324976
Fax: 01482 213962
Email: press@hull-humber-chamber.co.uk
Web site: http://www.hull-humber-chamber.co.uk
Titles:
  BUSINESS INTELLIGENCE

HULL CITY COUNCIL 15606
Guildhall, Alfred Gelder Street, HULL, HU1 2AA
Tel: 01482 613852 **Fax:** 01482 613845
Web site: http://www.hullcc.gov.uk
Titles:
  HULL IN PRINT

HURLINGHAM MEDIA 1677035
47-49 Chelsea Manor Street, LONDON, SW3 5RZ
Tel: 020 3239 9347
Email: hurlingham@hpa-polo.co.uk
Web site: http://www.hurlinghammedia.com
Titles:
  HURLINGHAM

HUSSAIN MEDIA 1720606
779 High Road, Leytonstone, LONDON, E11 4QS
Tel: 020 8558 9127 **Fax:** 020 8558 9127
Titles:
  ASIAN POST
  THE PAKISTAN POST

HYMNS ANCIENT & MODERN 15871
13-17 Long Lane, LONDON, EC1A 9PN **Tel:** 020 7776 1060
Titles:
  CARIS
  CHURCH TIMES
  CRUCIBLE
  HOME WORDS
  THE SIGN
  THIRD WAY

HYPER @ FALLON 1737281
67-69 Beak Street, LONDON, W1F 9SW
Titles:
  PETHEALTHCARE.CO.UK

I AND I MEDIA LTD 1644383
Tower Bridge Business Centre, 46-48 East Smithfield, LONDON, E1W 1AW **Tel:** 020 8983 6626
Fax: 020 8983 7453
Titles:
  ASIANA

IA PUBLICATIONS 1650060
22 Leydene Avenue, BOURNEMOUTH, BH8 9JG
Tel: 01202 300033 **Fax:** 01202 399998
Email: tony@internalaffairs.co.uk
Web site: http://www.ptreview.co.uk
Titles:
  PTR

IALS 625855
Charles Clore House, 17 Russell Square, LONDON, WC1B 5DR
Titles:
  AMICUS CURIAE

IAM GROUP SERVICES LTD 16854
510 Chiswick High Road, LONDON, W4 5RJ
Tel: 020 8996 9600 **Fax:** 020 8996 9601
Web site: http://www.iam.org.uk
Titles:
  ADVANCED DRIVING

IAN ALLAN PUBLISHING LTD 13616
Riverdene Business Park, Molesey Road, HERSHAM, KT12 4RG **Tel:** 01932 266600 **Fax:** 01932 266601
Email: info@ianallanpublishing.co.uk
Web site: http://www.ianallanpublishing.com
Titles:
  AIRCRAFT ILLUSTRATED
  BUSES
  COMBAT AIRCRAFT
  HORNBY MAGAZINE
  MODERN RAILWAYS
  RAILWAYS ILLUSTRATED
  THE SQUARE
  VINTAGE ROADSCENE

IBS PUBLISHING 13572
12-14 Barkat House, 116-118 Finchley Road, LONDON, NW3 5HT **Tel:** 020 7245 0404 **Fax:** 020 7245 9769
Email: info@ibspublishing.com
Web site: http://www.ibspublishing.com
Titles:
  THE INTERNATIONAL BANKING SYSTEMS JOURNAL
  NEWHORIZON

IC PUBLICATIONS LTD 13769
7 Coldbath Square, LONDON, EC1R 4LQ
Tel: 020 7841 3210 **Fax:** 020 7841 3211
Email: icpubs@africasia.com
Web site: http://www.africasia.com
Titles:
  AFRICAN BUSINESS
  THE MIDDLE EAST
  NEW AFRICAN

ICE CREAM ALLIANCE LTD 14060
3 Melbourne Court, Pride Park, DERBY, DE24 8LZ
Tel: 01332 203333 **Fax:** 01332 208420
Email: info@ice-cream.org
Web site: http://www.ice-cream.org
Titles:
  ICE CREAM MAGAZINE

ICHCA INTERNATIONAL 14402
Suite 2, 85 Western Road, ROMFORD, RM1 3LS
Tel: 01708 735295 **Fax:** 01708 735225
Titles:
  CARGO WORLD - THE NEWSLETTER

ICHILD 1740432
7th Floor, Artillery House, 11-19 Artillery Row, LONDON, SW1P 1RT **Tel:** 020 7227 3737 **Fax:** 020 7222 5949
Titles:
  ICHILD.CO.UK

ICIS HEREN 14074
1 Procter Street, LONDON, WC1V 6EU **Tel:** 020 7911 1920
Fax: 020 7911 1851
Email: info@icisheren.com
Web site: http://www.icis.com/heren
Titles:
  EUROPEAN DAILY ELECTRICITY MARKETS
  EUROPEAN GAS MARKETS
  EUROPEAN SPOT GAS MARKETS
  I & C ENERGY SNAPSHOT
  LNG MARKETS

ICON PUBLICATIONS LTD 12520
Maxwell Place, Maxwell Lane, KELSO, TD5 7BB
Tel: 01573 226032 **Fax:** 01573 226000
Email: iconmags@btconnect.com
Web site: http://www.iconpublications.com
Titles:
  MASTER PHOTO DIGITAL
  PHOTOWORLD

ICSA INFORMATION AND TRAINING 1741440
16 Park Crescent, LONDON, W1B 1AH **Tel:** 020 7580 4741
Fax: 020 7612 7034
Web site: http://www.icsa.co.uk
Titles:
  CHARTERED SECRETARY

IDG (INTERNATIONAL DATA GROUP) 12268
4th Floor, 101 Euston Road, LONDON, NW1 2RA
Tel: 020 7756 2800
Web site: http://www.idg.co.uk
Titles:
  CIO CHIEF INFORMATION OFFICER
  COMPUTERWORLD UK
  DIGITAL ARTS
  IPOD USER
  MACWORLD
  MACWORLD UK (ONLINE)
  PC ADVISOR
  PC ADVISOR
  TECHWORLD

IDOX 17916
Tontine House, 8 Gordon Street, GLASGOW, G1 3PL
Tel: 0141 248 8541 **Fax:** 0141 248 8277
Web site: http://www.planet.co.uk
Titles:
  SCOTTISH PLANNING AND ENVIRONMENTAL LAW

IGI GLOBAL 1766955
Room G5.80A, De Montfort University, The Gateway, LEICESTER, LE1 9BH **Tel:** 0116 207 8252
Fax: 0116 207 8159
Titles:
  INTERNATIONAL JOURNAL OF TECHNOLOGY AND HUMAN INTERACTION

UK Publishers & Their Titles

IGNITION PUBLICATIONS　　　　1732106
The Hawk Creative Business Park, Hawkhills, Easingwold,
YORK, YO61 3FE **Tel:** 01347 825270
Email: ignitionpublications@mac.com
Titles:
　LEEDS LEEDS LEEDS

IIC　　　　1685161
6 Buckingham Street, LONDON, WC2N 6BA
Tel: 020 7839 5975 **Fax:** 020 7976 1564
Email: iic@conservation.org
Web site: http://www.iiconservation.org
Titles:
　NEWS IN CONSERVATION
　REVIEWS IN CONSERVATION
　STUDIES IN CONSERVATION

ILEACH　　　　1711416
Main Street, BOWMORE, PA43 7JH **Tel:** 01496 810355
Fax: 01496 810647
Web site: http://www.ileach.co.uk
Titles:
　ILEACH

THE ILLUSTRATED LONDON NEWS LTD　　　　15089
Central Point, 45 Beech Street, LONDON, EC2Y 8AD
Tel: 020 7805 5555 **Fax:** 020 7805 5911
Email: iln@iln.co.uk
Web site: http://www.iln.co.uk
Titles:
　LIVEWIRE
　SPHERE
　SPHERE ASIA

ILLUSTRATION MAGAZINE　　　　1712241
39 Elmsleigh Road, TWICKENHAM, TW2 5EF
Tel: 07766 280221
Titles:
　ILLUSTRATION

IMAGINATIVE MINDS　　　　1741581
215 The Green House, Gibb Street, Digbeth, BIRMINGHAM,
B9 4AA **Tel:** 0121 224 7599 **Fax:** 0121 224 7598
Email: enquiries@imaginativeminds.co.uk
Titles:
　E-LEARNING TODAY
　PROFESSIONAL DEVELOPMENT TODAY
　SCHOOL LEADERSHIP TODAY
　TEACHING TIMES

IMAGINE 8 INTERNATIONAL LTD　　　　1654222
87 Loopland Drive, Castlereagh Road, BELFAST, BT6 9DW
Tel: 028 9073 8008 **Fax:** 028 9045 5684
Email: enquire@imagine8withus.com
Web site: http://www.imagine8withus.com
Titles:
　ISLAND CONNECTIONS
　RESIDENTIAL ESSENTIALS
　TIME FOR U
　WELCOME ABOARD

IMAGINE PUBLISHING　　　　1685022
Richmond House, 33 Richmond Hill, BOURNEMOUTH, BH2
6EZ **Tel:** 01202 586200
Web site: http://www.imagine-publishing.co.uk
Titles:
　3D ARTIST
　360
　ADVANCED PHOTOSHOP
　COREL PAINTER OFFICIAL MAGAZINE
　DIGITAL CAMERA ESSENTIALS
　DIGITAL PHOTOGRAPHER
　GAMES TM
　ICREATE
　LINUX USER & DEVELOPER
　NOWGAMER.COM
　NREVOLUTION
　PHOTOSHOP CREATIVE
　PLAY
　POKEMON WORLD
　POWERSTATION
　RETRO GAMER
　SCIFI NOW
　SMARTPHONE & PDA ESSENTIALS
　TOTAL 911
　TOTAL PC GAMING
　WEB DESIGNER
　X360

IMAREST　　　　14211
80 Coleman Street, LONDON, EC2R 5BJ **Tel:** 020 7382 2600
Fax: 020 7382 2669
Web site: http://www.imarest.org
Titles:
　THE MARINE SCIENTIST
　MARITIME IT & ELECTRONICS
　MER MARINE ENGINEERS REVIEW
　OFFSHORE TECHNOLOGY
　SHIPPING WORLD & SHIPBUILDER

IMAS PUBLISHING (UK) LTD　　　　622741
1st Floor, 1 Cabot House, Compass Point Business Park,
Stocks Bridge Way, ST. IVES, PE27 5JL **Tel:** 01480 461555
Fax: 01480 461550
Email: mail@audiomedia.com
Web site: http://www.audiomedia.com
Titles:
　AUDIO MEDIA
　TV TECHNOLOGY EUROPE

IMAX LTD　　　　17928
The Old Cart House, Applesham Farm, COOMBES, BN15
0RP **Tel:** 01273 464777 **Fax:** 01273 463999
Email: office@imaxweb.co.uk
Titles:
　PARROTS

IMIS　　　　16724
5 Kingfisher House, New Mill Road, ORPINGTON, BR5 3QG
Tel: 0700 002 3456 **Fax:** 0700 002 3023
Email: central@imis.org.uk
Web site: http://www.imis.org.uk
Titles:
　IMIS JOURNAL

IML GROUP PLC　　　　12406
Blair House, 184-186 High Street, TONBRIDGE, TN9 1BQ
Tel: 01732 359990 **Fax:** 01732 770049
Web site: http://www.imlgrouponthenet.net
Titles:
　CONTROL ENGINEERING EUROPE
　CONTROL ENGINEERING UK
　DPA
　ELECTRONIC PRODUCT DESIGN
　ELECTRONICS MANUFACTURE & TEST
　EPA
　FM REPORT
　FOOD PROCESSING
　HAZARDEX: THE JOURNAL
　HAZARDOUS AREA INTERNATIONAL
　INAVATE
　PANEL & SYSTEM BUILDING
　PFM (PREMISES & FACILITIES MANAGEMENT)

IMP PUBLICATIONS　　　　1746194
ATM House, 28 Roman Road, HOVE, BN3 4LF
Tel: 01273 381300
Titles:
　TELEPRESENCE AND VIDEOCONFERENCING INSIGHT
　NEWSLETTER

IMPACT!　　　　13955
Media House, 55 Old Road, LEIGHTON BUZZARD, LU7 2RB
Tel: 01525 370013 **Fax:** 01525 382487
Email: info@impact-now.co.uk
Web site: http://www.impact-now.co.uk
Titles:
　PROJECT

IMPERATIVE MEDIA LTD　　　　1745682
PO Box 39450, LONDON, N10 1WJ **Tel:** 07934 630287
Titles:
　MHA MAGAZINE

IMPERIAL COLLEGE UNION MEDIA GROUP　　　　15751
Beit Quad, Prince Consort Road, LONDON, SW7 2BB
Tel: 020 7594 8072 **Fax:** 020 7594 8065
Titles:
　FELIX

IMPROMPTU PUBLISHING LTD　　　　622269
2nd Floor, Century House, 11 St. Peters Square,
MANCHESTER, M2 3DN **Tel:** 0161 236 9526
Email: info@impromptupublishing.com
Web site: http://www.impromptupublishing.com

Titles:
　BRASS BAND WORLD
　GIG
　LINK
　MUSO

IMS　　　　1744671
Castlemead, Lower Castle Street, BRISTOL, BS1 3AG
Tel: 0117 929 3041 **Fax:** 0117 929 3041
Titles:
　WATER BRIEFING

IMS HEALTH　　　　14243
7 Harewood Avenue, LONDON, NW1 6JB
Tel: 020 7393 5000 **Fax:** 020 7393 5345
Titles:
　PHARMA PRICING & REIMBURSEMENT
　R&D FOCUS

IMS MARKETING COMMUNICATIONS GROUP PLC　　　　18398
Castlemead, Lower Castle Street, BRISTOL, BS1 3AG
Tel: 0117 917 5310 **Fax:** 0117 917 5005
Titles:
　ELEMENTS FOR ENVIRONMENTAL DECISIONS

IMTC　　　　1655031
Cranley Hill, Woodgrange Road, Hollymount,
DOWNPATRICK, BT30 8JE **Tel:** 028 4483 9167
Titles:
　IRISH COUNTRY SPORTS & COUNTRY LIFE

IN AND AROUND LTD　　　　1653448
19 Shorts Gardens, LONDON, WC2H 9AW
Tel: 020 7240 9731 **Fax:** 020 7836 3137
Titles:
　IN AND AROUND COVENT GARDEN

IN BUSINESS PUBLISHING　　　　1645420
14 Pierpoint Street, WORCESTER, WR1 1TA
Tel: 01905 20500 **Fax:** 01905 20360
Web site: http://www.inbusinesspublishing.com
Titles:
　IN BUSINESS EAST ENGLAND
　IN BUSINESS MIDLANDS
　IN BUSINESS NORTH WEST
　IN BUSINESS SOUTH WEST

IN POSITION MEDIA LTD　　　　12516
426 Drumoyne Road, GLASGOW, G51 4DA
Tel: 0141 810 9000 **Fax:** 0141 810 9009
Web site: http://www.inpositionmedia.co.uk
Titles:
　SCOTTISH DENTIST
　SCOTTISH PRIMARY CARE

IN PUBLICATIONS LTD　　　　1655266
2nd Floor, 9 The Broadway, WOODFORD GREEN, IG8 0HL
Tel: 0871 226 2690 **Fax:** 020 8505 8252
Titles:
　IN

INCAPITALHEALTH LTD　　　　1760449
c/o Carol Colinswood & Co, Dorchester House, 15
Dorchester Place, THAME, OX9 2DL **Tel:** 01844 338000
Email: bob@incapitalhealth.co.uk
Web site: http://www.incapitalhealth.com
Titles:
　INCAPITALHEALTH

INCISIVE MEDIA　　　　12278
32-34 Broadwick Street, LONDON, W1A 2HG
Tel: 020 7316 9000
Web site: http://www.incisivemedia.com
Titles:
　ACCOUNTANCY AGE
　ACCOUNTANCYAGE.COM
　ACCOUNTINGANDFINANCE365
　THE ACTUARY
　BJPONLINE
　BRITISH JOURNAL OF PHOTOGRAPHY
　BUSINESSGREEN.COM
　COMPUTER ACTIVE ONLINE
　COMPUTERACTIVE
　COMPUTING

COMPUTING BUSINESS
CRN
FINANCIAL DIRECTOR
GLOBALPENSIONS.COM
THE INQUIRER
INSURANCE AGE
LEGAL WEEK
POST MAGAZINE & INSURANCE WEEK
PROFESSIONAL BROKING
REINSURANCE
V3.CO.UK

INCISIVE MEDIA INVESTMENTS 13365
Haymarket House, 28-29 Haymarket, LONDON, SW1Y 4RX
Tel: 020 7484 9700
Web site: http://www.incisivemedia.com
Titles:
ASIA RISK
BENELUX UNQUOTE
BUY-SIDE TECHNOLOGY
CENTRAL BANKING
COVER
CREDIT
DEALING WITH TECHNOLOGY
DEUTSCHE UNQUOTE
ENERGY RISK
EXCHANGE TRADED FUNDS MAGAZINE
FX WEEK
GLOBAL PENSIONS
HEDGE FUNDS REVIEW
IFAONLINE
INSIDE REFERENCE DATA
INTERNATIONAL CUSTODY AND FUND
ADMINISTRATION
INVESTMENT WEEK
MORTGAGE SOLUTIONS
NORDIC UNQUOTE"
OPRISK & COMPLIANCE
PRIVATE EQUITY EUROPE
PROFESSIONAL ADVISER MAGAZINE
PROFESSIONAL PENSIONS
RETIREMENT PLANNER
RISK
SOUTHERN EUROPE UNQUOTE
STRUCTURED PRODUCTS
UNQUOTE
UNQUOTENEWS.COM
YOUR MONEY
YOUR MORTGAGE

INCOMES DATA SERVICES 13811
23 College Hill, LONDON, EC4R 2RP **Tel:** 020 7429 6800
Fax: 020 7393 8081
Email: ids@incomesdata.co.uk
Web site: http://www.incomesdata.co.uk
Titles:
IDS BRIEF
IDS EXECUTIVE COMPENSATION REVIEW
IDS HR STUDIES
IDS PENSIONS BULLETIN
IDS PENSIONS LAW REPORTS

INCORPORATED ASSOCIATION OF ORGANISTS 15378
17 Woodland Road, Northfield, BIRMINGHAM, B31 2HU
Tel: 0121 475 4408 **Fax:** 0121 475 4408
Web site: http://www.iao.org.uk
Titles:
ORGANISTS' REVIEW

INCORPORATED SOCIETY OF MUSICIANS (ISM) 17840
10 Stratford Place, LONDON, W1C 1AA **Tel:** 020 7629 4413
Fax: 020 7408 1538
Web site: http://www.ism.org
Titles:
MUSIC JOURNAL

INDEPENDENT & SPECIALIST TRAVEL 16436
5 Alscott Workshop, Alscot Park, Atherstone On Stour,
STRATFORD-UPON-AVON, CV37 8BL **Tel:** 01789 450000
Fax: 01789 459046
Titles:
ADVENTURE TRAVEL

INDEPENDENT CATHOLIC NEWS 1638661
147A Leighton Road, LONDON, NW5 2RB
Tel: 020 7267 3616
Titles:
INDEPENDENT CATHOLIC NEWS

INDEPENDENT EDUCATIONAL PUBLISHING LTD 622845
Independent House, 191 Marsh Wall, LONDON, E14 9RS
Tel: 020 7005 2000 **Fax:** 020 7005 2292
Titles:
CAREER GUIDANCE TODAY

INDEPENDENT HEALTHCARE MEDIA LTD 1687266
Marble Arch Tower, 55 Bryanston Street, LONDON, W1H
7AJ **Tel:** 020 7868 8522 **Fax:** 020 7868 8744
Titles:
INDEPENDENT HEALTHCARE

INDEPENDENT INVESTOR SERVICES LTD 1749709
42-44 Carter Lane, LONDON, EC4V 5EA
Titles:
INVESTING FOR GROWTH

INDEPENDENT NEWS & MEDIA GROUP 625220
Independent House, 191 Marsh Wall, LONDON, E14 9RS
Tel: 020 7005 5077
Titles:
INTERNATIONAL RUGBY NEWS
RYDER CUP MAGAZINE

INDEPENDENT NEWS AND MEDIA (UK) LTD 600541
Northcliffe House, 2 Derry Street, LONDON, W8 5TT
Tel: 020 7005 2000 **Fax:** 020 7005 2435
Web site: http://www.independent.co.uk
Titles:
BELFAST TELEGRAPH
EVERYTHING AEROSPACE
EXAM RESULTS
THE INDEPENDENT
THE INDEPENDENT MAGAZINE
THE INDEPENDENT ON SUNDAY
THE INFORMATION
LIFE
THE NEW REVIEW
RETAIL THERAPY
SUNDAY LIFE (BELFAST)
WHICH COURSE?

THE INDEPENDENT PORSCHE ENTHUSIASTS CLUB 1654047
10 Whitecroft Gardens, Woodford Halse, DAVENTRY, NN11
3PY **Tel:** 0121 288 6006
Email: tipec2003@yahoo.co.uk
Web site: http://www.tipec.org.uk
Titles:
ALL TORQUE

INDIALINK (UK) LTD 1689833
42 Farm Avenue, HARROW, HA2 7LR **Tel:** 020 8866 8421
Fax: 020 8868 7462
Email: indialink@hotmail.com
Titles:
INDIA LINK INTERNATIONAL

INDICATOR LIMITED 16965
Calgarth House, 39-41 Bank Street, ASHFORD, TN23 1DQ
Tel: 01233 653500 **Fax:** 01233 647200
Email: editorial@indicator.co.uk
Web site: http://www.indicator.co.uk
Titles:
TIPS & ADVICE COMPANY DIRECTOR
TIPS & ADVICE INTERNET
TIPS & ADVICE PERSONNEL
TIPS & ADVICE TAX

INDICES PUBLICATIONS LTD 1644371
1st Floor, Entrance B, Salamander Quay West, Park Lane,
HAREFIELD, UB9 6NZ **Tel:** 0870 205 2924
Fax: 0870 205 2934
Email: info@indices.co.uk
Web site: http://www.indices.co.uk
Titles:
BAGMA BULLETIN
HOME DECOR & FURNISHINGS

INDUSTRIAL MINERALS INFORMATION 13394
16 Lower Marsh, LONDON, SE1 7RJ **Tel:** 020 7827 9977
Fax: 020 7827 6441
Web site: http://www.indmin.com

Titles:
INDUSTRIAL MINERALS
MINERAL PRICEWATCH

INFAMOUS INK LTD 671690
PO Box 392, CAMBRIDGE, CB1 3WH **Tel:** 01223 210536
Fax: 01223 210546
Email: hhc@hiphop.com
Web site: http://www.hhcmagazine.com
Titles:
HIP-HOP CONNECTION

INFO VALLEY LTD 1734364
1 Wood Street, STRATFORD-UPON-AVON, CV37 6JE
Tel: 0845 468 5627
Titles:
CALL-CENTRES.COM

INFORMA CARGO INFORMATION 600549
Telephone House, 69-77 Paul Street, LONDON, EC2A 4LQ
Tel: 020 7017 5000
Web site: http://www.informa.com
Titles:
CARGO SYSTEMS
CONTAINERISATION INTERNATIONAL
HAZARDOUS CARGO BULLETIN
INTERNATIONAL FREIGHTING WEEKLY
LLOYD'S CASUALTY WEEK
LLOYD'S LIST
LLOYDS SHIP MANAGER
LLOYD'S SHIPPING ECONOMIST

INFORMA HEALTHCARE 1713670
Telephone House, 69-77 Paul Street, LONDON, EC2A 4LQ
Tel: 020 7017 5000
Web site: http://www.informaworld.com/journals
Titles:
BRAIN INJURY
CLINICA WORLD MEDICAL TECHNOLOGY NEWS
CURRENT MEDICAL RESEARCH AND OPINION
DISABILITY AND REHABILITATION
EXPERT OPINION ON DRUG DISCOVERY
GOOD CLINICAL PRACTICE JOURNAL
INTERNATIONAL JOURNAL OF LANGUAGE AND
COMMUNICATION DISORDERS
INTERNATIONAL REVIEW OF PSYCHIATRY
JOURNAL OF NUTRITIONAL & ENVIRONMENTAL
MEDICINE
JOURNAL OF OBSTETRICS & GYNAECOLOGY
SCRIP WORLD PHARMACEUTICAL NEWS

INFORMA PHARMA 13714
Telephone House, 69-77 Paul Street, LONDON, EC2A 4LQ
Tel: 020 7017 5000 **Fax:** 020 7017 6795
Email: pjb.enquiries@informa.com
Web site: http://www.pjbpubs.com
Titles:
ANIMAL PHARM - WORLD ANIMAL HEALTH AND
NUTRITION NEWS
EURALEX
THE REGULATORY AFFAIRS JOURNAL: DEVICES

INFORMA PLC 18622
Telephone House, 69-77 Paul Street, LONDON, EC2A 4LQ
Tel: 020 7017 4600 **Fax:** 020 7017 4111
Web site: http://www.informa.com
Titles:
ALTERNATIVE INSURANCE CAPITAL
BANKING TECHNOLOGY
BUILDING LAW MONTHLY
THE BUYER
CI ONLINE
COMMERCIAL LEASES
COMPETITION LAW INSIGHT
COMPLIANCE MONITOR
CONSTRUCTION INDUSTRY LAW LETTER
CONSUMER LAW TODAY
CORPORATE BRIEFING
EDUCATION LAW MONITOR
FARM TAX BRIEF
FINANCE & CREDIT LAW
FINANCIAL INSTRUMENTS TAX & ACCOUNTING
REVIEW
FINANCIAL REGULATION INTERNATIONAL
FRAUD INTELLIGENCE
HEALTH INSURANCE & PROTECTION
INSURANCE DAY
INSURANCE NEWS 24
INSURANCE REGULATION & ACCOUNTING
INTERNATIONAL CONSTRUCTION LAW REVIEW
INTERNATIONAL PAYMENTS
INTERNATIONAL TAX REPORT
INTERNATIONAL TRADE FINANCE

UK Publishers & Their Titles

LIABILITY, RISK & INSURANCE
THE LITIGATION LETTER
LLOYD'S LAW REPORTS
LLOYD'S MARITIME AND COMMERCIAL LAW
    QUARTERLY
MARITIME RISK INTERNATIONAL
MONEY LAUNDERING BULLETIN
MUSIC & COPYRIGHT
THE PENSION SCHEME TRUSTEE
PENSIONS TODAY
THE RE REPORT
THE REVIEW - WORLDWIDE REINSURANCE
TRUSTS & ESTATES
WORLD INSURANCE REPORT

INFORMA TELECOMS AND MEDIA GROUP   14805
Mortimer House, 37-41 Mortimer Street, LONDON, W1T 3JH
Tel: 020 7017 5000
Web site: http://www.informatm.com

Titles:
    ASIACOM
    CONVERGING MEDIA
    MOBILE FRONTIERS
    SCREEN FINANCE

INFORMA UK LIMITED   697739
Informa House, 30-32 Mortimer Street, LONDON, W1W 7RE
Tel: 020 7017 4600 **Fax:** 020 7436 8414

Titles:
    AGROW WORLD CROP PROTECTION NEWS
    CONTAINERISATION INTERNATIONAL YEARBOOK
    LLOYD'S LOADING LIST

INFORMATION EXPRESS   1654528
PO Box 2077, Verney Park, BUCKINGHAM, MK18 1WQ
Tel: 01280 820560 **Fax:** 01280 820554
Web site: http://www.riderresearch.com

Titles:
    THE ONLINE REPORTER
    THE ONLINE REPORTER

INFORMATION FACILITIES MANAGEMENT LTD.   674406
18 Princess Park Manor, Royal Drive, LONDON, N11 3FL
Tel: 020 8922 7491 **Fax:** 020 8368 3794

Titles:
    I-FM

INFORMED PUBLICATIONS LTD   14139
PO Box 2087, SHOREHAM-BY-SEA, BN43 5ZF
Tel: 01273 273941
Email: info@infopub.co.uk
Web site: http://www.infopub.co.uk

Titles:
    LOCAL GOVERNMENT IT IN USE
    TOWN HALL
    UKAUTHORITY.COM

INFORMER MAGAZINE LTD   1742979
PO Box 72, HEXHAM, NE47 9YY **Tel:** 0191 286 5020

Titles:
    THE INFORMER

INK PUBLISHING   623711
141-143 Shoreditch High Street, LONDON, E1 6JE
Tel: 020 7613 8777 **Fax:** 020 7613 8776
Web site: http://www.cnbceb.com

Titles:
    BRADMANS.COM
    B.SPIRIT!
    B.THERE!
    CNBC EUROPEAN BUSINESS
    CNN TRAVELLER ASIA PACIFIC
    EASYJET INFLIGHT
    GULF LIFE
    HOTLINE
    JETAWAY
    RYANAIR MAGAZINE
    THOMAS COOK TRAVEL MAGAZINE
    VELOCITY - VLM INFLIGHT MAGAZINE
    VOYAGER
    WIZZIT
    YEAHBABY

THE INKWELL PRESS LIMITED   622790
Kettle Chambers, 21 Stone Street, CRANBROOK, TN17 3HF
Tel: 01580 713993 **Fax:** 01580 715983
Email: info@inkwellpress.co.uk
Web site: http://www.inkpellet.co.uk

Titles:
    INK PELLET

INLAND WATERWAYS ASSOCIATION   16080
PO Box 114, RICKMANSWORTH, WD3 1ZY
Tel: 01923 711114 **Fax:** 01923 897000
Email: iwa@waterways.org.uk
Web site: http://www.waterways.org.uk

Titles:
    WATERWAYS

INNER DESIGN   1767065
Redfern House, 347 Margate Road, Northwood,
RAMSGATE, CT12 6SG **Tel:** 01843 592802
Fax: 01843 593145

Titles:
    ID INNER DESIGN

INNERPLACE   1766300
International House, 1-6 Yarmouth Place, Mayfair, LONDON,
W1J 7BU **Tel:** 020 3167 0077
Email: newsletter@innerplace.co.uk
Web site: http://www.innerplace.co.uk

Titles:
    INNERPLACE

INNOVATIVE WRITING LTD   623179
Unit 3A, 13 North Bank Street, EDINBURGH, EH1 2LP

Titles:
    ATLANTA UK MAGAZINE

INPUBLISHING LTD   1638377
Hawthorns, Station Road, Eynsford, DARTFORD, DA4 0EJ
Tel: 07808 638643

Titles:
    INPUBLISHING

INQUIRER PUBLISHING CO. LTD.   15887
Essex Hall, Essex Street, LONDON, WC2R 3HU
Tel: 020 8445 1654 **Fax:** 020 8446 9997

Titles:
    THE INQUIRER

INSIDE72   1720738
46 Collingwood Road, Long Eaton, NOTTINGHAM, NG10
1DR **Tel:** 0115 919 5231

Titles:
    INSIDE72

INSIDE BUSINESS   18423
151 Silbury Boulevard, MILTON KEYNES, MK9 1LH
Tel: 01908 545380 **Fax:** 01908 545389
Email: info@insidebusiness.co.uk
Web site: http://www.insidebusiness.co.uk

Titles:
    INSIDE BUSINESS MILTON KEYNES
    INSIDE BUSINESS READING
    INSIDE LIVING MILTON KEYNES

INSIDER PUBLISHING LTD   698531
2nd Floor, Asia House, 31-33 Lime Street, LONDON, EC3M
7HT **Tel:** 020 7398 0615 **Fax:** 020 7398 0614
Email: info@insiderquarterly.com

Titles:
    THE INSURANCE INSIDER
    IQ

INSIGHT EVENTS   1742736
Unit 4, Tetbury Industrial Estate, Cirencester Road,
TETBURY, GL8 8EZ **Tel:** 0870 011 7575 **Fax:** 0870 011 7676
Email: info@insightevents.co.uk
Web site: http://www.newstartsscotland.com

Titles:
    NEW START

INSIGHT MAGAZINE   1724756
SIG Roofing Supplies Group, Harding Way, ST. IVES, PE27
3YJ **Tel:** 01480 466777 **Fax:** 01480 300269
Email: editor@insightmag.co.uk
Web site: http://www.insightmag.co.uk

Titles:
    INSIGHT MAGAZINE

INSIGHT MEDIA LTD   17400
26-30 London Road, TWICKENHAM, TW1 3RW
Tel: 020 8831 7500 **Fax:** 020 8891 0123
Web site: http://www.insightgrp.co.uk

Titles:
    AIRPORT WORLD

THE INSPIRING FUTURES FOUNDATION   1743811
1st Floor, St. George's House, Knoll Road, CAMBERLEY,
GU15 3SY **Tel:** 01276 687500 **Fax:** 01276 28258

Titles:
    CAREERSCOPE

INSTANT PUBLICATIONS   1746303
Tel: 07968 198032
Whittingehame House, HADDINGTON, EH41 4QA
Tel: 07968 198032

Titles:
    INSTANT

INSTITUTE FOR COMPLEMENTARY MEDICINE   1764347
Can Mezzanine, 32-36 Loman Street, LONDON, SE1 0EH
Tel: 0845 456 2537 **Fax:** 0845 456 2538
Web site: http://www.icnm.org.uk

Titles:
    ICNM JOURNAL

INSTITUTE FOR INDEPENDENT BUSINESS   18792
Clarendon House, Bridle Path, WATFORD, WD17 1UB
Tel: 01903 239543 **Fax:** 01903 239643
Email: info@iib.ws
Web site: http://www.iib.org.uk

Titles:
    INDEPENDENT BUSINESS TODAY

INSTITUTE FOR SPORT, PARKS & LEISURE   14193
Abbey House, 1650 Arlington Business Park, Theale,
READING, RG7 4SA **Tel:** 0845 603 8734 **Fax:** 01491 874801
Email: info@ispal.org.uk
Web site: http://www.ispal.org.uk

Titles:
    ISPAL E-ZINE

INSTITUTE OF ACOUSTICS   14470
77A St. Peters Street, ST. ALBANS, AL1 3BN
Tel: 01727 848195 **Fax:** 01727 850553

Titles:
    ACOUSTICS BULLETIN

INSTITUTE OF BIOLOGY   14783
9 Red Lion Court, LONDON, EC4A 3EF **Tel:** 020 7936 5900
Fax: 020 7936 5901
Web site: http://www.iob.org

Titles:
    BIOLOGIST
    JOURNAL OF BIOLOGICAL EDUCATION

INSTITUTE OF BREWING & DISTILLING   13675
33 Clarges Street, LONDON, W1J 7EE **Tel:** 020 7499 8144
Fax: 020 7499 1156
Email: enquiries@ibd.org.uk
Web site: http://www.ibd.org.uk

Titles:
    THE BREWER & DISTILLER INTERNATIONAL
    IBD MEMBERS HANDBOOK

THE INSTITUTE OF CAST METALS ENGINEERS   621811
I C M E, National Metalforming Centre, 47 Birmingham
Road, WEST BROMWICH, B70 6PY **Tel:** 0121 601 6979
Fax: 0121 601 6981
Web site: http://www.icme.org.uk

Titles:
    CASTINGS BUYER
    FOUNDRY TRADE JOURNAL

INSTITUTE OF CHARTERED FORESTERS   1742950
59 George Street, EDINBURGH, EH2 2JG
Tel: 0131 240 1425 **Fax:** 0131 240 1424

Titles:
    CHARTERED FORESTER

THE INSTITUTE OF CHIROPODISTS AND PODIATRISTS　14563
27 Wright Street, SOUTHPORT, PR9 0TL **Tel:** 01704 546141
Fax: 01704 500477
Email: secretary@inst-chiropodist.org.uk
Web site: http://www.inst-chiropodist.org.uk
Titles:
　PODIATRY REVIEW

INSTITUTE OF COST AND EXECUTIVE ACCOUNTANTS EDUCATIONAL TRUST　16251
Akhtar House, 2 Shepherds Bush Road, LONDON, W6 7PJ
Tel: 020 8749 7126 **Fax:** 020 8749 7127
Titles:
　EXECUTIVE ACCOUNTANT

INSTITUTE OF CREDIT MANAGEMENT　13383
The Water Mill, Station Road, South Luffenham, OAKHAM, LE15 8NB **Tel:** 01780 722910 **Fax:** 01780 721271
Email: editorial@icm.org.uk
Web site: http://www.icm.org.uk
Titles:
　CREDIT MANAGEMENT

INSTITUTE OF CUSTOMER SERVICE　622528
2 Castle Court, St. Peter's Street, COLCHESTER, CO1 1EW
Tel: 01206 571716 **Fax:** 01206 546688
Email: customerfirst@icsmail.co.uk
Web site: http://www.instituteofcustomerservice.co.uk
Titles:
　CUSTOMERFIRST

INSTITUTE OF ECOLOGY AND ENVIRONMENTAL MANAGEMENT　14619
43 Southgate Street, WINCHESTER, SO23 9EH
Tel: 01962 868626 **Fax:** 01962 868625
Titles:
　ECOLOGY & ENVIRONMENTAL MANAGEMENT - IN PRACTICE

THE INSTITUTE OF EXPLOSIVES ENGINEERS　693712
Wellington Hall, Cranfield University, Shrivenham Campus, SWINDON, SN6 8LA **Tel:** 01729 840765 **Fax:** 01729 840765
Titles:
　EXPLOSIVES ENGINEERING

THE INSTITUTE OF FINANCIAL SERVICES　1710695
IFS House, 4-9 Burgate Lane, CANTERBURY, CT1 2XJ
Tel: 01227 762600 **Fax:** 01227 763788
Titles:
　FINANCIAL WORLD

INSTITUTE OF FISHERIES MANAGEMENT　18604
22 Rushworth Avenue, West Bridgford, NOTTINGHAM, NG2 7LF **Tel:** 0115 982 2317 **Fax:** 0115 982 6150
Titles:
　FISH

THE INSTITUTE OF HORTICULTURE　14087
9 Red Lion Court, LONDON, EC4A 3EF **Tel:** 020 7936 5957
Fax: 020 7936 5958
Web site: http://www.horticulture.org.uk
Titles:
　THE HORTICULTURIST

INSTITUTE OF HOSPITALITY　1739509
Trinity Court, 34 West Street, SUTTON, SM1 1SH
Tel: 020 8661 4900 **Fax:** 020 8661 4901
Email: sophie.allcock@instituteofhospitality.org
Web site: http://www.instituteofhospitality.org
Titles:
　HOSPITALITY

INSTITUTE OF INTERNAL AUDITORS (UK)　13311
13 Abbeville Mews, 88 Clapham Park Road, LONDON, SW4 7BX **Tel:** 020 7498 0101 **Fax:** 020 7978 2492
Titles:
　INTERNAL AUDITING

INSTITUTE OF LEADERSHIP & MANAGEMENT　13817
1 Giltspur Street, LONDON, EC1A 9DD **Tel:** 020 7294 2470
Fax: 020 7294 2402

Email: editorial@i-l-m.com
Web site: http://www.i-l-m.com
Titles:
　EDGE
　LOCAL GOVERNMENT MANAGER

THE INSTITUTE OF LEGAL CASHIERS AND ADMINISTRATORS　13312
2nd Floor, Marlowe House, 109 Station Road, SIDCUP, DA15 7ET **Tel:** 020 8294 2933 **Fax:** 020 8859 1682
Web site: http://www.ilca.org.uk
Titles:
　LEGAL ABACUS

INSTITUTE OF LEGAL EXECUTIVES　14321
Kempston Manor, Kempston, BEDFORD, MK42 7AB
Tel: 01234 845721 **Fax:** 01234 841999
Email: ipa@legal-executive-journal.co.uk
Web site: http://www.ilexjournal.com
Titles:
　THE LEGAL EXECUTIVE

THE INSTITUTE OF MATHEMATICS & ITS APPLICATIONS　13142
Catherine Richards House, 16 Nelson Street, SOUTHEND-ON-SEA, SS1 1EF **Tel:** 01702 354020 **Fax:** 01702 354111
Titles:
　MATHEMATICS TODAY

INSTITUTE OF MEASUREMENT & CONTROL　13555
87 Gower Street, LONDON, WC1E 6AF **Tel:** 020 7387 4949
Fax: 020 7388 8431
Titles:
　MEASUREMENT & CONTROL

THE INSTITUTE OF THE MOTOR INDUSTRY　14119
Fanshaws, Brickendon, HERTFORD, SG13 8PQ
Tel: 01992 511521 **Fax:** 01992 511548
Titles:
　MOTOR INDUSTRY MAGAZINE

INSTITUTE OF OPERATIONS MANAGEMENT　13885
CILT (UK) Earlstrees Court, Earlstrees Industrial Estate, CORBY, NN17 4AX **Tel:** 01536 740105 **Fax:** 01536 740103
Email: journal@iomnet.org.uk
Web site: http://www.iomnet.org.uk
Titles:
　OPERATIONS MANAGEMENT

INSTITUTE OF PAYROLL PROFESSIONALS　17111
Shelly House, Farmhouse Way, Monkspath, SOLIHULL, B90 4EH **Tel:** 0121 712 1000 **Fax:** 0121 712 1001
Titles:
　PAYROLL PROFESSIONAL

INSTITUTE OF RACE RELATIONS　18186
2-6 Leeke Street, LONDON, WC1X 9HS **Tel:** 020 7837 0041
Fax: 020 7278 0623
Titles:
　RACE & CLASS

THE INSTITUTE OF SALES & MARKETING MANAGEMENT　13468
Harrier Court, Woodside Road, Lower Woodside, LUTON, LU1 4DQ **Tel:** 01582 840001 **Fax:** 01582 849142
Titles:
　WINNING EDGE

INSTITUTE OF TRANSPORT ADMINISTRATION　14395
The Old Studio, 25 Greenfield Road, Westoning, BEDFORD, MK45 5JD **Tel:** 01525 634940 **Fax:** 01525 750016
Email: director@iota.org.uk
Web site: http://www.iota.org.uk
Titles:
　TRANSPORT MANAGEMENT

THE INSTITUTION OF AGRICULTURAL ENGINEERS　14006
Barton Road, Silsoe, BEDFORD, MK45 4FH
Tel: 01525 861096 **Fax:** 01525 861660
Web site: http://www.iagre.org

Titles:
　LANDWARDS

INSTITUTION OF CHEMICAL ENGINEERS　17193
Davis Building, 165-189 Railway Terrace, RUGBY, CV21 3HQ **Tel:** 01788 578214 **Fax:** 01788 560833
Web site: http://www.icheme.org
Titles:
　CHEMICAL ENGINEERING RESEARCH AND DESIGN
　LOSS PREVENTION BULLETIN
　TCE

INSTITUTION OF CIVIL ENGINEERING SURVEYORS　18118
Dominion House, Sibson Road, SALE, M33 7PP
Tel: 0161 972 3100 **Fax:** 0161 972 3118
Email: surco@ices.org.uk
Web site: http://www.ices.org.uk
Titles:
　CONSTRUCTION LAW REVIEW

INSTITUTION OF DIAGNOSTIC ENGINEERS　13551
7 Weir Road, Kibworth, LEICESTER, LE8 0LQ
Tel: 0116 279 6772 **Fax:** 0116 279 6884
Email: editor@diagnosticengineers.org
Web site: http://www.diagnosticengineers.org
Titles:
　DIAGNOSTIC ENGINEERING

THE INSTITUTION OF DIESEL & GAS TURBINE ENGINEERS　18148
Bedford Heights, Manton Lane, BEDFORD, MK4 7PH
Tel: 01234 214340 **Fax:** 01234 355493
Titles:
　THE POWER ENGINEER

THE INSTITUTION OF ENGINEERING AND TECHNOLOGY　12238
Michael Faraday House, Six Hills Way, STEVENAGE, SG1 2AY **Tel:** 01438 313311 **Fax:** 01438 765526
Email: enquiries@theiet.org
Web site: http://www.theiet.org/ee
Titles:
　ELECTRONICS EDUCATION
　ENGINEERING AND TECHNOLOGY
　FLIPSIDE
　THE IET STUDENT & YOUNG PROFESSIONAL MAGAZINE
　WIRING MATTERS

INSTITUTION OF GAS ENGINEERS AND MANAGERS　14076
IGEM House, High Street, KEGWORTH, DE74 2DA
Tel: 0844 375 4436
Titles:
　GAS INTERNATIONAL (ENGINEERING AND MANAGEMENT)

INSTITUTION OF STRUCTURAL ENGINEERS　14290
11 Upper Belgrave Street, LONDON, SW1X 8BH
Tel: 020 7235 4535 **Fax:** 020 7201 9109
Web site: http://www.thestructuralengineer.org.uk
Titles:
　THE STRUCTURAL ENGINEER

INSURANCE PUBLISHING & PRINTING CO　13333
7 Stourbridge Road, Lye, STOURBRIDGE, DY9 7DG
Tel: 01384 895228 **Fax:** 01384 893666
Titles:
　INSURANCE BROKERS' MONTHLY

INTELLECT LTD　12260
The Mill, Parnall Road, Fishponds, BRISTOL, BS16 3JG
Tel: 0117 958 9910 **Fax:** 0117 958 9911
Email: info@intellectbooks.com
Web site: http://www.intellectbooks.co.uk
Titles:
　ART DESIGN & COMMUNICATION IN HIGHER EDUCATION
　EUROPEAN JOURNAL OF AMERICAN CULTURE
　INTERNATIONAL JOURNAL OF EDUCATION THROUGH ART
　INTERNATIONAL JOURNAL OF FRANCOPHONE STUDIES
　INTERNATIONAL JOURNAL OF IBERIAN STUDIES

UK Publishers & Their Titles

INTERNATIONAL JOURNAL OF MEDIA AND CULTURAL
  POLITICS
INTERNATIONAL JOURNAL OF PERFORMANCE ARTS
  AND DIGITAL MEDIA
INTERNATIONAL JOURNAL OF TECHNOLOGY
  MANAGEMENT AND SUSTAINABLE DEVELOPMENT
JOURNAL OF MEDIA PRACTICE
JOURNAL OF VISUAL ARTS PRACTICE
NEW CINEMAS
ORGANISATIONAL TRANSFORMATION AND SOCIAL
  CHANGE
PORTUGUESE JOURNAL OF SOCIAL SCIENCE
THE RADIO JOURNAL
STUDIES IN EUROPEAN CINEMA
STUDIES IN FRENCH CINEMA
STUDIES IN HISPANIC CINEMA
STUDIES IN THEATRE AND PERFORMANCE

INTELLIGENCE RESEARCH LTD　　17026
61 Old Street, LONDON, EC1V 9HW **Tel:** 020 7251 0012
Fax: 020 7253 8193
Email: info@intelligenceresearch.com
Web site: http://www.intelligenceresearch.com
Titles:
  ASIAN INFRASTRUCTURE
  INFORME LATINOAMERICANO
  LATIN AMERICAN INFORMES ESPECIALES
  LATIN AMERICAN NEWSLETTERS
  LATIN AMERICAN REGIONAL REPORT - BRAZIL AND
    SOUTHERN CONE REPORT
  LATIN AMERICAN REGIONAL REPORT - CARIBBEAN &
    CENTRAL AMERICA REPORT
  LATIN AMERICAN REGIONAL REPORT - MEXICO &
    NAFTA REPORT
  LATIN AMERICAN REGIONAL REPORTS - ANDEAN
    GROUP REPORT
  LATIN AMERICAN WEEKLY REPORT

THE INTELLIGENT BUSINESS COMPANY　1743175
24 Cardinal Crescent, Coombeside, NEW MALDEN, KT3
3EF **Tel:** 01386 700195
Titles:
  HOUSING TECHNOLOGY

INTELLIGENT MEDIA SOLUTIONS　　1638715
Suite 223, Business Design Centre, 52 Upper Street,
LONDON, N1 0QH **Tel:** 020 7288 6833 **Fax:** 020 7288 6834
Email: info@intelligentmedia.co.uk
Web site: http://www.intelligentmedia.co.uk
Titles:
  DEALER SUPPORT
  EDUCATION EXECUTIVE
  KEEP IT REAL
  OLÉ
  PRACTICE BUSINESS
  USP MAGAZINE

INTENT MEDIA　　18190
Saxon House, 6A St Andrew Street, HERTFORD, SG14 1JA
Tel: 01992 535646 **Fax:** 01992 535648
Email: lisa.foster@intentmedia.co.uk
Titles:
  AUDIO PRO INTERNATIONAL
  BIKE BIZ
  CASUALGAMING.BIZ
  DEVELOP
  MCV - THE MARKET FOR HOME COMPUTING & VIDEO
    GAMES
  MI PRO INCORPORATING MUSIC TRADE NEWS
  MOBILE ENTERTAINMENT
  PC RETAIL INCORPORATING CTO
  TOYNEWS

INTERACTIVE BUSINESS COMMUNICATIONS LTD
　　16902
Latimer House, 189 High Street, POTTERS BAR, EN6 5DA
Tel: 01707 664200 **Fax:** 01707 664800
Titles:
  IT RESELLER
  LOGISTICS & HANDLING
  MANUFACTURING AND LOGISTICS IT
  RETAIL TECHNOLOGY REVIEW
  YOURTECHTV.COM

INTERACTIVE DATA (EUROPE) LIMITED　691131
Fitzroy House, 13-17 Epworth Street, LONDON, EC2A 4DL
Tel: 020 7825 8000 **Fax:** 020 7608 2032
Titles:
  THE BONDHOLDER
  CREDIT RATINGS INTERNATIONAL
  WEEKLY CAPITAL EVENT DIARY

INTERACTIVE INVESTOR TRADING LTD　18463
Standon House, 1st Floor, 21 Mansell Street, LONDON, E1
8AA **Tel:** 020 7680 3600
Titles:
  INTERACTIVE INVESTOR

INTERACTORS MANAGEMENT (SCOTLAND) LTD
　　1712994
PO Box 3009, Old Kilpatrick, GLASGOW, G60 5ET
Tel: 0870 760 6033 **Fax:** 0870 760 6033
Titles:
  UK THEATRE NETWORK

INTERCITY PRINT PLC　　623005
35 St. Augustine Mews, COLCHESTER, CO1 2PF
Tel: 01206 862136
Titles:
  ESSEX JOURNAL

INTERFLORA (BU) LTD　　14086
Interflora House, SLEAFORD, NG34 7TB **Tel:** 01529 304141
Fax: 01529 304462
Titles:
  MERCURY

INTERGAME LTD　　14778
Office Block 1, Southlink Business Park, Hamilton Street,
OLDHAM, OL4 1DE **Tel:** 0161 633 0100 **Fax:** 0161 627 0009
Titles:
  INTERGAME
  INTERGAMING
  INTERPARK

INTERIORS MEDIA　　1741746
124 Pembury Road, TONBRIDGE, TN9 2JJ
Tel: 01732 766333 **Fax:** 01732 352063
Email: akidd@interiorsmonthly.co.uk
Web site: http://www.interiorsmonthly.co.uk
Titles:
  INTERIORS MONTHLY

**INTERNATIONAL ASSOC. OF MARINE AIDS TO
NAVIGATION AND LIGHTHOUSE AUTHORITIES**　627597
No 3 The Green, Ketton, STAMFORD, PE9 3RA
Tel: 01780 721628 **Fax:** 01780 721980
Titles:
  IALA BULLETIN

**INTERNATIONAL ASSOCIATION OF INSTITUTES OF
NAVIGATION IAIN**　　14357
No 3 The Green, Ketton, STAMFORD, PE9 3RA
Tel: 01780 721628 **Fax:** 01780 721980
Titles:
  IAIN

INTERNATIONAL BAR ASSOCIATION　　14316
10th Floor, 1 Stephen Street, LONDON, W1T 1AT
Tel: 020 7691 6868 **Fax:** 020 7691 6544
Web site: http://www.ibanet.org
Titles:
  BUSINESS LAW INTERNATIONAL
  INTERNATIONAL BAR NEWS
  JOURNAL OF ENERGY & NATURAL RESOURCES LAW

INTERNATIONAL BEE RESEARCH ASSOCIATION　15670
16 North Road, CARDIFF, CF10 3DY **Tel:** 029 2037 2409
Fax: 05601 135640
Email: mail@ibra.org.uk
Web site: http://www.ibra.org.uk
Titles:
  JOURNAL OF APICULTURAL RESEARCH

INTERNATIONAL BUSINESS MEDIA GROUP LTD.
　　699393
68 Lombard Street, LONDON, EC3V 9LJ **Tel:** 020 3145 1240
Web site: http://www.newbusiness.co.uk
Titles:
  EXECUTIVE GOLF
  NEW BUSINESS

**THE INTERNATIONAL CENTRE FOR FAMILIES IN
BUSINESS**　　1735475
St. Augustines Yard, Orchard Lane, BRISTOL, BS1 5DE
Tel: 0117 314 5678 **Fax:** 0117 314 5679
Email: info@icfib.com
Web site: http://www.icfib.com
Titles:
  GENERATION

INTERNATIONAL FUND INVESTMENT　　16991
337 City Road, LONDON, EC1V 1LJ **Tel:** 020 7713 8748
Fax: 020 7837 7346
Email: fieldhouse@ifiglobal.com
Web site: http://www.ifilive.com
Titles:
  IAI INSTITUTIONAL ALTERNATIVE INVESTMENT
  INTERNATIONAL FUND INVESTMENT

INTERNATIONAL HARBOUR MASTERS' ASSOCIATION
　　1718405
PO Box 314, Wickham, FAREHAM, PO17 5XZ
Titles:
  THE HARBOURMASTER

INTERNATIONAL INSIDER PUBLISHING CO　13326
18 King William Street, LONDON, EC4N 7BP
Tel: 020 7236 0532 **Fax:** 020 7248 3859
Titles:
  INTERNATIONAL INSIDER

INTERNATIONAL JEWISH VEGETARIAN SOCIETY 15209
853-855 Finchley Road, LONDON, NW11 8LX
Tel: 020 8455 0692 **Fax:** 020 8455 1465
Titles:
  THE JEWISH VEGETARIAN

INTERNATIONAL LABMATE LTD　　14481
Oak Court Business Centre, Sandridge Park, Porters Wood,
ST. ALBANS, AL3 6PH **Tel:** 01727 855574
Fax: 01727 841694
Email: info@intlabmate.com
Web site: http://www.labmate-online.com
Titles:
  INTERNATIONAL LABMATE
  LAB ASIA
  LABMATE UK & IRELAND

**INTERNATIONAL MARINE PURCHASING
ASSOCIATION**　　18958
East Bridge House, East Street, COLCHESTER, CO1 2TX
Tel: 01206 798900 **Fax:** 01206 798909
Email: info@impa.net
Web site: http://www.impa.net
Titles:
  MARINE TRADER

THE INTERNATIONAL MASONRY SOCIETY　13532
c/o British Ceramic Research, Queens Road, Penkhull,
STOKE-ON-TRENT, ST4 7LQ **Tel:** 01782 279051
Fax: 01782 215354
Titles:
  MASONRY INTERNATIONAL

INTERNATIONAL NEWSLETTERS　　14091
9A Victoria Square, DROITWICH, WR9 8DE
Tel: 0870 165 7210 **Fax:** 0870 165 7212
Email: in@intnews.com
Web site: http://www.intnews.com
Titles:
  ADVANCED CERAMICS REPORT
  ADVANCED COMPOSITES BULLETIN
  ADVANCES IN TEXTILES TECHNOLOGY
  BIOMEDICAL MATERIALS
  HIGH PERFORMANCE PLASTICS
  MEDICAL TEXTILES
  NEW MATERIALS ASIA
  SMART TEXTILES AND NANOTECHNOLOGY
  TECHNICAL TEXTILES INTERNATIONAL

**INTERNATIONAL PLANNED PARENTHOOD
FEDERATION**　　17203
4 Newhams Row, LONDON, SE1 3UZ **Tel:** 020 7939 8280
Fax: 020 7939 8300
Titles:
  X-PRESS

INTERNATIONAL PUBLISHING GROUP 1653549
27 John Street, LONDON, WC1N 2BX **Tel:** 020 7269 8900
Fax: 020 7269 8909
Titles:
 EXPAT INVESTOR

INTERNATIONAL TOURISM PARTNERSHIP 623267
15-16 Cornwall Terrace, Regent's Park, LONDON, NW1 4QP
Tel: 020 7467 3620 **Fax:** 020 7467 3610
Email: tourismpartnership@iblf.org
Web site: http://www.tourismpartnership.org
Titles:
 GREENHOTELIER

INTERNATIONAL TRADE PUBLICATIONS 12333
3-4 Marshall's Court, Spring Garden, LINCOLNSHIRE, DN21
2AG **Tel:** 01724 850095 **Fax:** 01724 850012
Email: info@itp95.com
Web site: http://www.itp95.com
Titles:
 INTERNATIONAL SUPERMARKET NEWS

**INTERNATIONAL VISUAL COMMUNICATION
ASSOCIATION** 14303
19 Pepper Street, Glengall Bridge, LONDON, E14 9RP
Tel: 020 7512 0571 **Fax:** 020 7512 0591
Web site: http://www.ivca.org
Titles:
 IVCA UPDATE

INTERNATIONALSPORTGROUP 1681155
4 The Spinney, Chester Road, Poynton, STOCKPORT, SK12
1HB **Tel:** 07766 576834
Web site: http://www.isportgroup.com
Titles:
 BADMINTON
 INTERNATIONAL SQUASH MAGAZINE

INTERVAL INTERNATIONAL LTD 16537
Coombe Hill House, Beverley Way, LONDON, SW20 0AR
Tel: 020 8336 9573 **Fax:** 020 8336 9398
Titles:
 VACATION INDUSTRY REVIEW

INTRAFISH MEDIA AS 1745303
6th Floor, Eldon House, 2 Eldon Street, LONDON, EC2M
7LS
Titles:
 FISHING NEWS
 FISHING NEWS INTERNATIONAL
 SEAFOOD INTERNATIONAL
 SEAFOOD PROCESSOR

INTRAS LTD 12430
46 Holly Walk, LEAMINGTON SPA, CV32 4HY
Tel: 01926 334137 **Fax:** 01926 314755
Email: intras@intras.co.uk
Web site: http://www.intras.co.uk
Titles:
 EUROWIRE
 TUBE & PIPE TECHNOLOGY
 WIRE & CABLE ASIA

INTUITION COMMUNICATION 1737884
The Wilderness, 3 Churchgates, BERKHAMSTED, HP4 2UB
Tel: 0870 777 0401 **Fax:** 01442 817818
Web site: http://www.intuition-communication.co.uk
Titles:
 PRIVATE HEALTHCARE UK

INVERNESS CHAMBER OF COMMERCE 1718304
PO Box 5512, INVERNESS, IV2 3ZE **Tel:** 01463 718131
Fax: 01463 231523
Titles:
 INBUSINESS

INVESTORS IN PEOPLE 1649375
7-10 Chandos Street, LONDON, W1G 9DQ
Tel: 020 7467 1900 **Fax:** 020 7636 2386
Email: lucyh@iipuk.co.uk
Web site: http://www.investorsinpeople.co.uk
Titles:
 RAISING THE STANDARD

INVOLVEMENT & PARTICIPATION ASSOCIATION 12738
42 Colebrooke Row, LONDON, N1 8AF **Tel:** 020 7354 8040
Fax: 020 7354 8041
Titles:
 IPA BULLETIN

IOM COMMUNICATIONS LTD 1650100
1 Carlton House Terrace, LONDON, SW1Y 5DB
Tel: 020 7451 7300 **Fax:** 020 7451 1702
Web site: http://www.iom3.org
Titles:
 CLAY TECHNOLOGY
 MATERIALS WORLD
 THE PACKAGING PROFESSIONAL

IOP PUBLISHING 13579
Dirac House, Temple Back, BRISTOL, BS1 6BE
Tel: 0117 929 7481 **Fax:** 0117 925 1942
Email: custserv@iop.org
Web site: http://publishing.iop.org
Titles:
 CERN COURIER
 COMPOUND SEMICONDUCTOR
 FIBRESYSTEMS EUROPE
 MEASUREMENT SCIENCE & TECHNOLOGY
 NANOTECHNOLOGY
 OPTICS & LASER EUROPE
 PHYSICS WORLD

IOTAMEDIA 1736736
11 Chiltern Court, Asheridge Road Industrial Estate,
Asheridge Road, CHESHAM, HP5 2PX **Tel:** 0845 127 4600
Email: info@iotamedia.co.uk
Web site: http://www.iotamedia.com
Titles: .
 FIVE MINUTE LIFESTYLE

IOV FOCUS LTD 14302
PO Box 625, LOUGHTON, IG10 3GZ **Tel:** 020 8502 3817
Fax: 020 8508 9211
Email: info@iov.co.uk
Titles:
 IOV FOCUS

IP PUBLISHING LTD 17177
258 Belsize Road, LONDON, NW6 4BT **Tel:** 020 7316 1870
Titles:
 OUTLOOK ON AGRICULTURE

IPC CONNECT LTD 622370
Blue Fin Building, 110 Southwark Street, LONDON, SE1 0SU
Tel: 020 3148 5000
Web site: http://www.ipcmedia.com
Titles:
 CELEBRITY DIET NOW
 CHAT
 CHAT IT'S FATE
 GOODTOKNOW
 LOOK
 NOW
 NOWMAGAZINE.CO.UK
 PICK ME UP
 WOMAN

IPC IGNITE! 675393
Blue Fin Building, 110 Southwark Street, LONDON, SE1 0SU
Tel: 020 3148 5000 **Fax:** 020 7148 8170
Web site: http://www.ipc.co.uk
Titles:
 LOADED
 NME
 UNCUT

IPC INSPIRE 1734387
Blue Fin Building, 110 Southwark Street, LONDON, SE1 0SU
Tel: 020 3148 5000
Web site: http://www.ipcmedia.com
Titles:
 AEROPLANE MONTHLY
 AMATEUR GARDENING
 AMATEUR PHOTOGRAPHER
 ANGLER'S MAIL
 BRITISH COINS MARKET VALUES
 CAGE & AVIARY BIRDS
 CARAVAN BUYER
 CARAVAN MAGAZINE
 CLASSIC BOAT MAGAZINE
 COUNTRY LIFE
 COUNTRY LIFE INTERNATIONAL

 COUNTRY LIFE ONLINE
 CYCLE SPORT
 CYCLING WEEKLY
 DECANTER
 EUROPEAN BOATBUILDER
 EVENTING
 THE FIELD
 THE FIELD ONLINE
 GOLF MONTHLY
 GUITAR & BASS
 HEALTH & FITNESS FOR CYCLISTS
 HI-FI NEWS
 HORSE
 HORSE AND HOUND
 IBI
 IBI INTERNATIONAL BOAT INDUSTRY
 MBR
 MINIWORLD
 MODEL COLLECTOR
 MOTOR BOAT & YACHTING
 MOTOR BOAT & YACHTING ONLINE
 MOTOR BOATS MONTHLY
 MOTOR BOATS MONTHLY ONLINE
 MOTOR CARAVAN MAGAZINE
 NEWMINI.ORG
 PARK HOME & HOLIDAY CARAVAN
 PRACTICAL BOAT OWNER
 PREDICTION
 PREDICTION ANNUAL
 RACECAR ENGINEERING
 THE RAILWAY MAGAZINE
 RUGBY WORLD
 SAILPOWER.COM
 THE SHOOTING GAZETTE
 SHOOTING TIMES AND COUNTRY MAGAZINE
 SHOOTINGUK.CO.UK
 SPORTING GUN
 STAMP MAGAZINE
 SUPER YACHT WORLD
 SUPERBIKE
 SUPERSAIL WORLD
 SUPERYACHT BUSINESS
 TOP YACHTS
 VOLKSWORLD
 VOLKSWORLD CAMPER & BUS
 WHAT DIGITAL CAMERA
 WORLD SOCCER
 WORLD SOCCER
 YACHTING & BOATING WORLD
 YACHTING MONTHLY
 YACHTING MONTHLY ONLINE
 YACHTING WORLD

IPC MEDIA LTD 13071
Blue Fin Building, 110 Southwark Street, LONDON, SE1 0SU
Tel: 020 3148 5000 **Fax:** 020 3148 8119
Web site: http://www.ipcmedia.com
Titles:
 ESSENTIALS
 HAIR
 NUTS
 PICK ME UP
 SHIPS MONTHLY
 TRUSTEDREVIEWS.COM
 WALLPAPER*
 WEB USER
 WHATSONTV.CO.UK
 WOMAN&HOME
 WOMANANDHOME.COM
 WOMAN'S OWN
 WOMAN'S WEEKLY

IPC SOUTHBANK 1734533
Blue Fin Building, 110 Southwark Street, LONDON, SE1 0SU
Tel: 020 3148 5000 **Fax:** 020 3148 8168
Web site: http://www.ipcmedia.com
Titles:
 25 BEAUTIFUL HOMES
 BEAUTIFUL KITCHENS
 COUNTRY HOMES & INTERIORS
 HOMES & GARDENS
 HOUSETOHOME
 IDEAL HOME
 IN STYLE
 LIVING-ETC
 MARIE CLAIRE
 MARIECLAIRE.CO.UK
 WEDDING
 WEDDING FLOWERS MAGAZINE
 WEDDINGMAGAZINE.CO.UK

IPC TX 18911
Blue Fin Building, 110 Southwark Street, LONDON, SE1 0SU
Tel: 020 3148 5000
Web site: http://www.ipcmedia.com
Titles:
 SOAPLIFE
 TV & SATELLITE WEEK
 TV EASY

UK Publishers & Their Titles

TV TIMES
WHAT'S ON TV

IPE INTERNATIONAL PUBLISHERS LIMITED　16602
320 Great Guildford House, 30 Great Guildford Street,
LONDON, SE1 0HS **Tel:** 020 7261 0666 **Fax:** 020 7928 3332
Titles:
INVESTMENT & PENSIONS EUROPE
IPE REAL ESTATE

IPG　1735944
27 John Street, LONDON, WC1N 2BX
Web site: http://www.ipgaustralia.com
Titles:
NON LEAGUE TODAY
NON-LEAGUE-DAILY.COM

IPRA FRONTLINE LTD　674865
International Public Relations Association, 12 Dunley Hill
Court, Ranmore Common, DORKING, RH5 6SX
Tel: 01483 280130 **Fax:** 01483 280131
Email: info@ipra.org
Web site: http://www.ipra.org
Titles:
IPRA FRONTLINE

IPSWICH ARTS ASSOCIATION　15817
Town Hall, Kings Street, IPSWICH, IP1 1DH
Tel: 01473 836448
Titles:
IMAGES

IQPS LTD　18791
Suite 464, 24-28 St. Leonards Road, WINDSOR, SL4 3BB
Tel: 01628 625007 **Fax:** 01628 624990
Web site: http://www.iqps.org
Titles:
OFFICE PROFESSIONAL

IRELAND'S HOMES INTERIORS AND LIVING　676978
PO Box 42, BANGOR, BT19 7AD **Tel:** 028 9147 3979
Fax: 028 9145 7226
Email: enquiries@ihil.net
Web site: http://www.ihil.net
Titles:
THE ALL IRELAND KITCHEN GUIDE
IRELAND'S HOMES, INTERIORS & LIVING

IRISH NEWS LTD　14854
113-117 Donegall Street, BELFAST, BT1 2GE
Tel: 028 9032 2226 **Fax:** 028 9033 7505
Web site: http://www.irishnews.com
Titles:
FARMWEEK
THE IRISH NEWS

IRON & STEEL PUBLISHING (MMC)　1758399
Gresham House, 54 High Street, SHOREHAM-BY-SEA,
BN43 5DB **Tel:** 01273 453033 **Fax:** 01273 453085
Email: info@mmcpublications.co.uk
Web site: http://www.mmcpublications.co.uk
Titles:
IRON & STEEL TODAY

IRRV　16230
41 Doughty Street, LONDON, WC1N 2LF
Tel: 020 7691 8975 **Fax:** 020 7831 2048
Email: enquiries@irrv.org.uk
Web site: http://www.irrv.org.uk
Titles:
IRRV BENEFIT
IRRV INSIGHT
IRRV VALUER

IRS　13297
Quadrant House, The Quadrant, Brighton Road, SUTTON,
SM2 5AS **Tel:** 020 8652 3500
Web site: http://www.XpertHR.co.uk
Titles:
EUROPEAN EMPLOYMENT REVIEW
HEALTH CARE RISK REPORT

ISHERWOOD PRODUCTION　16837
39 Thurloe Place, LONDON, SW7 2HP **Tel:** 020 7584 0000
Fax: 020 7584 0022
Email: gish@commodities-now.com
Web site: http://www.commodities-now.com
Titles:
COMMODITIES NOW
COMMODITIES NOW ONLINE

ISKATE PUBLICATIONS LLP　1724379
Albion House, 11 The Chase, CROWTHORNE, RG45 6HT
Tel: 01344 774839 **Fax:** 01344 774340
Email: news@iskatemagazine.com
Web site: http://www.iskatemagazine.com
Titles:
ISKATE

ISLE OF MAN NEWSPAPERS LTD　13067
Publishing House, Peel Road, DOUGLAS, IM1 5PZ
Tel: 01624 695695 **Fax:** 01624 611149
Titles:
ISLE OF MAN TODAY

ISLE OF WIGHT COUNTY PRESS LTD　14959
Brannon House, 123 Pyle Street, NEWPORT, PO30 1ST
Tel: 01983 521333 **Fax:** 01983 527204
Web site: http://www.iwcp.co.uk
Titles:
ISLE OF WIGHT COUNTY PRESS
ISLE OF WIGHT COUNTY PRESS ONLINE

ISSB LTD (IRON AND STEEL STATISTICS BUREAU)　17878
1 Carlton House Terrace, LONDON, SW1Y 5DB
Tel: 020 7343 3916 **Fax:** 020 7343 3902
Email: phil.hunt@issb.co.uk
Web site: http://www.issb.co.uk
Titles:
INTERNATIONAL STEEL STATISTICS
UK IRON AND STEEL INDUSTRY: ANNUAL STATISTICS
WORLD STEEL EXPORTS - ALL QUALITIES
WORLD STEEL EXPORTS - STAINLESS, HIGH SPEED
　AND OTHER ALLOY
WORLD STEEL STATISTICS MONTHLY

ISTC　1653830
Airport House, Purley Way, CROYDON, CR0 0XZ
Tel: 020 8253 4506 **Fax:** 020 8253 4510
Email: istc@istc.org.uk
Web site: http://www.istc.org.uk
Titles:
COMMUNICATOR
INFOPLUS+

IT ANALYSIS COMMUNICATIONS LTD　624268
8 Priors Park, Emerson Valley, MILTON KEYNES, MK4 2BT
Tel: 01908 880760 **Fax:** 01908 880761
Email: admin@it-analysis.com
Web site: http://www.it-director.com
Titles:
IT-ANALYSIS.COM
IT-DIRECTOR.COM

ITALIA UK LTD　625131
3 Brooklands Place, Brooklands Road, SALE, M33 3SD
Tel: 0161 976 1212 **Fax:** 0161 976 1313
Email: gr@italiauk.net
Web site: http://www.italiauk.net
Titles:
ITALIAUK.NET

ITCHY GROUP　1641546
Unit 2, White Horse Yard, 78 Liverpool Rd, LONDON, N1
09Q **Tel:** 020 7288 9810
Web site: http://www.itchycity.co.uk
Titles:
ITCHY CITY

ITCM LIMITED　14425
Market House, 19-21 Market Place, WOKINGHAM, RG40
1AP **Tel:** 0118 979 3277 **Fax:** 0118 979 3499
Email: itcm@incentivetravel.co.uk
Web site: http://www.incentivetravel.co.uk
Titles:
INCENTIVE TRAVEL & CORPORATE MEETINGS

IT'S MANCHESTER LTD　1650373
12 Roche Gardens, Cheadle Hulme, CHEADLE, SK8 7QT
Tel: 0161 439 4694 **Fax:** 0161 439 4694
Titles:
EARLY TIMES LANCASHIRE
PRIMARY TIMES IN LANCASHIRE

ITSECURITY LTD　1747320
9 River Valley Road, Chudleigh Knighton, Chudleigh,
NEWTON ABBOT, TQ13 0HP **Tel:** 01626 854125
Titles:
QUANTASECURITY.COM

ITSMF　16955
150 Wharfedale Road, Winnersh Triangle, WOKINGHAM,
RG41 5RB **Tel:** 0118 926 0888 **Fax:** 0118 926 3073
Titles:
SERVICETALK THE JOURNAL

IVILLAGE LTD　674806
Propect House, 80-110 New Oxford Street, LONDON, WC1A
1HB **Tel:** 020 7079 6000 **Fax:** 020 7079 6497
Titles:
IVILLAGE UK

IVY HOUSE SPORT LAW PUBLICATIONS LTD　1649873
Ivy Dene, East End, Hook Norton, BANBURY, OX15 5LG
Tel: 01608 730595 **Fax:** 01608 730623
Email: info@ivyhousepublications.co.uk
Titles:
SPORTS LAW ADMINISTRATION AND PRACTICE

IW CHAMBER OF COMMERCE　14726
Mill Court, Furrlongs, NEWPORT, PO30 2AA
Tel: 01983 520777 **Fax:** 01983 554555
Email: chamber@iwchamber.co.uk
Web site: http://www.iwchamber.co.uk
Titles:
ISLAND BUSINESS

I.W. PUBLICATIONS LTD　16043
934 North Circular Road, LONDON, NW2 7JR
Tel: 020 8453 7800 **Fax:** 020 8208 1103
Titles:
THE IRISH WORLD

IWA PUBLISHING　14296
Alliance House, 12 Caxton Street, LONDON, SW1H 0QS
Tel: 020 7654 5500 **Fax:** 020 7654 5555
Web site: http://www.iwapublishing.com
Titles:
WATER21
WATER ASSET MANAGEMENT INTERNATIONAL

IWC MEDIA　622551
Kensington Village, Avonmore Road, LONDON, W14 8RF
Tel: 020 7013 4000 **Fax:** 020 7013 4001
Web site: http://www.iwcmedia.co.uk
Titles:
4CAR

IWM BUSINESS SERVICES LTD　14142
9 Saxon Court, St. Peter's Gardens, NORTHAMPTON, NN1
1SX **Tel:** 01604 620426 **Fax:** 01604 604467
Titles:
CIWM

IWO (INSTITUTION OF WATER OFFICERS)　14295
4 Carlton Court, Team Valley, GATESHEAD, NE11 0AZ
Tel: 0191 422 0088 **Fax:** 0191 422 0087
Email: info@iwo.org.uk
Web site: http://www.iwo.org.uk
Titles:
IWO JOURNAL

J & M GROUP LTD.　16373
Association House, 18C Moor Street, CHEPSTOW, NP16
5DB **Tel:** 01291 628103 **Fax:** 01291 630402
Titles:
CAFÉ CULTURE
EVENT ORGANISER
INTERNATIONAL SANDWICH & SNACK NEWS
PIZZA, PASTA & ITALIAN FOOD MAGAZINE

J & M PUBLISHING   15037
9 Gordon Street, HUNTLY, AB54 8AJ **Tel:** 01466 793622
Titles:
  BANFFSHIRE ADVERTISER
  BANFFSHIRE HERALD
  HUNTLY EXPRESS

J. CATHERALL & CO (PRINTERS) LTD   14980
Beaumont Street, HEXHAM, NE46 3NA **Tel:** 01434 602351
Fax: 01434 607872
Titles:
  HEXHAM COURANT

J LATKE PUBLISHING   14038
PO Box 125, STOWMARKET, IP14 1PB **Tel:** 01449 771200
Email: info@ameft.com
Web site: http://www.ameft.com
Titles:
  ASIA AND MIDDLE EAST FOOD TRADE

JACKDAW NEWSLETTERS LTD   1639976
93 Clissold Crescent, LONDON, N16 9AS
Tel: 020 7254 4027 **Fax:** 020 7254 4027
Web site: http://www.thejackdaw.co.uk
Titles:
  THE JACKDAW

JAGUAR DAIMLER HERITAGE TRUST   1728464
Browns Lane, Allesley, COVENTRY, CV5 9DR
Tel: 024 7640 1288
Web site: http://www.jdht.com
Titles:
  JAGUAR HERITAGE ARCHIVE

THE JAGUAR DRIVERS CLUB   15454
Jaguar House, 18 Stuart Street, LUTON, LU1 2SL
Tel: 01582 419332 **Fax:** 01582 455412
Titles:
  THE JAGUAR DRIVER

JAMES PEMBROKE PUBLISHING LTD   1719660
90 Walcot Street, BATH, BA1 5BG **Tel:** 01225 337777
Email: lucyc@jppublishing.co.uk
Web site: http://www.jppublishing.co.uk
Titles:
  THE CLERK
  GARDEN DESIGN JOURNAL
  REFLEXIONS

JANE'S INFORMATION GROUP   12741
Sentinel House, 163 Brighton Road, COULSDON, CR5 2YH
Tel: 020 8700 3700 **Fax:** 020 8763 1006
Email: info@janes.com
Web site: http://www.janes.com
Titles:
  JANE'S AERO-ENGINES
  JANE'S AIR LAUNCHED WEAPONS
  JANE'S AIR TRAFFIC CONTROL
  JANE'S AIRCRAFT COMPONENT MANUFACTURERS
  JANE'S AIRCRAFT UPGRADES
  JANE'S AIRPORT REVIEW
  JANE'S AIRPORTS AND HANDLING AGENTS
  JANE'S AIRPORTS, EQUIPMENT & SERVICES
  JANE'S ALL THE WORLD'S AIRCRAFT
  JANE'S AMMUNITION HANDBOOK
  JANE'S ARMOUR & ARTILLERY
  JANE'S ARMOUR & ARTILLERY UPGRADES
  JANE'S AVIONICS
  JANE'S C4I SYSTEMS
  JANE'S DEFENCE INDUSTRY
  JANE'S DEFENCE WEEKLY
  JANE'S EXPLOSIVE ORDNANCE DISPOSAL
  JANE'S FIGHTING SHIPS
  JANE'S FOREIGN REPORT
  JANE'S HELICOPTER MARKETS & SYSTEMS
  JANE'S INFANTRY WEAPONS
  JANE'S INTELLIGENCE REVIEW
  JANE'S INTELLIGENCE REVIEW
  JANE'S INTERNATIONAL ABC AEROSPACE DIRECTORY
  JANE'S INTERNATIONAL DEFENCE DIRECTORY
  JANE'S INTERNATIONAL DEFENCE REVIEW
  JANE'S INTERNATIONAL DEFENCE REVIEW
  JANE'S LAND-BASED AIR DEFENCE
  JANE'S MARINE PROPULSION
  JANE'S MERCHANT SHIPS
  JANE'S MILITARY COMMUNICATIONS
  JANE'S MILITARY VEHICLES & LOGISTICS
  JANE'S MINES & MINE CLEARANCE
  JANE'S MISSILES & ROCKETS
  JANE'S NAVAL CONSTRUCTION & RETROFIT MARKETS
  JANE'S NAVAL WEAPONS SYSTEMS

  JANE'S NAVY INTERNATIONAL
  JANE'S NAVY INTERNATIONAL ONLINE
  JANE'S NUCLEAR, BIOLOGICAL AND CHEMICAL
    DEFENCE
  JANE'S POLICE & HOMELAND SECURITY EQUIPMENT
  JANE'S POLICE REVIEW
  JANE'S RADAR AND ELECTRONIC WARFARE
  JANE'S SIMULATION & TRAINING SYSTEMS
  JANE'S SPACE SYSTEMS AND INDUSTRY
  JANE'S TERRORISM & SECURITY MONITOR
  JANE'S TRANSPORT FINANCE
  JANE'S UNDERWATER SECURITY SYSTEMS AND
    TECHNOLOGY
  JANE'S UNDERWATER WARFARE SYSTEMS
  JANE'S UNMANNED AERIAL VEHICLES & TARGETS
  JANE'S URBAN TRANSPORT SYSTEMS
  JANE'S WORLD AIR FORCES
  JANE'S WORLD AIRLINES
  JANE'S WORLD ARMIES
  JANE'S WORLD INSURGENCY & TERRORISM
  JANE'S WORLD RAILWAYS

JANG PUBLICATIONS LTD   14871
1 Sanctuary Street, LONDON, SE1 1ED **Tel:** 020 7403 5833
Fax: 020 7378 1653
Web site: http://www.jang.com.pk
Titles:
  THE DAILY JANG LONDON

JAPAN JOURNALS LTD   16045
7-8 Market Place, LONDON, W1W 8AG **Tel:** 020 7307 3210
Fax: 020 7307 3218
Email: info@japanjournals.com
Web site: http://www.japanjournals.com
Titles:
  WEEKLY JOURNEY

JAZZ JOURNAL LTD   15370
3 Forest Road, LOUGHTON, IG10 1DR **Tel:** 020 8532 0456
Fax: 020 8532 0440
Titles:
  JAZZ JOURNAL INTERNATIONAL

JAZZ MUSIC SOCIETY   676761
44 Rawlins Road, Bradwell, MILTON KEYNES, MK13 9DL
Tel: 01908 312392
Titles:
  JAZZ GUIDE

JAZZ NEWSPAPERS LTD   15372
26 The Balcony, Castle Arcade, CARDIFF, CF10 1BY
Tel: 029 2066 5161 **Fax:** 029 2066 5160
Email: jazzuk.cardiff@virgin.net
Web site: http://www.jazzservices.org.uk
Titles:
  JAZZ UK

JAZZ PUBLISHING   17191
The Old School, Higher Kinnerton, CHESTER, CH4 9AJ
Tel: 01244 663400 **Fax:** 01244 660611
Email: info@jazzpublishing.co.uk
Web site: http://www.jazzpublishing.co.uk
Titles:
  100% BIKER
  DVD MONTHLY
  SKIN DEEP
  VOLKSWAGEN CAMPER AND COMMERCIAL

JAZZWISE PUBLICATIONS LTD   600198
2B Gleneagle Mews, Ambleside Avenue, LONDON, SW16
6AE **Tel:** 020 8769 7725 **Fax:** 020 8677 7128
Email: magazine@jazzwise.com
Web site: http://www.jazzwise.com
Titles:
  JAZZWISE

JEALOUS NOSH MEDIA LTD   1649556
7 Corsham Street, LONDON, N1 6DP **Tel:** 020 7608 3770
Fax: 020 7608 3736
Titles:
  CHROMA

JENNIFER PROWSE MEDIA SERVICES LTD   1763185
21 The Maltings, Bures, SUFFOLK, CO8 5EJ
Titles:
  OUR BEST FRIENDS

JEREMY PRATT   1760862
c/o Airplan Flight Equipment Ltd, 1a Ringway Trading Estate,
Shadowmoss Ross, MANCHESTER, M22 5LH
Tel: 0161 499 0023
Email: afe@afeonline.com
Titles:
  FLIGHT SAFETY

JERSEY CATTLE SOCIETY OF THE UNITED KINGDOM
                                                          13998
Scotsbridge House, Scots Hill, RICKMANSWORTH, WD3
3BB **Tel:** 01923 695203 **Fax:** 01923 695303
Titles:
  THE JERSEY Q

JERSEY EVENING POST LTD   14777
PO Box 582, Five Oaks, St. Saviour, JERSEY, JE4 8XQ
Tel: 01534 611611 **Fax:** 01534 611622
Web site: http://www.jerseyeveningpost.com
Titles:
  JERSEY EVENING POST

JESUITS & FRIENDS   17956
11 Edge Hill, LONDON, SW19 4LR **Tel:** 020 8946 0466
Fax: 020 8946 2292
Web site: http://www.jesuitmissions.org.uk
Titles:
  JESUITS & FRIENDS

JEWISH CHRONICLE NEWSPAPER LTD   15889
25 Furnival Street, LONDON, EC4A 1JT **Tel:** 020 7415 1500
Fax: 020 7405 9040
Web site: http://www.thejc.com
Titles:
  JEWISH CHRONICLE

JEWISH LITERARY TRUST   15834
Haskell House, 152 West End Lane, LONDON, NW6 1SD
Tel: 020 7443 5155
Titles:
  THE JEWISH QUARTERLY

JEWISH NEWS AND MEDIA GROUP   17007
PO Box 34296, LONDON, NW5 1YW **Tel:** 020 7692 6929
Fax: 020 7692 6689
Titles:
  THE JEWISH NEWS

JEWISH TELEGRAPH LTD   15890
Telegraph House, 11 Park Hill, Bury Old Road, Prestwich,
MANCHESTER, M25 0HH **Tel:** 0161 740 9321
Fax: 0161 740 9325
Email: mail@jewishtelegraph.com
Web site: http://www.jewishtelegraph.com
Titles:
  JEWISH TELEGRAPH

J.F. MEDIA LTD   1728607
Unit 3, The Sussex Innovation Centre, Science Square,
BRIGHTON, BN1 9SD
Titles:
  FOOTBALL PUNK
  GOLF PUNK

JLD MEDIA   1759769
34 Porchester Road, LONDON, W2 6ES **Tel:** 020 7563 6665
Titles:
  PURE BEAUTY
  SHOPPING CENTRE

JLIFESTYLE LTD   1743623
PO Box 585, EDGWARE, HA8 4DU **Tel:** 020 7993 0092
Fax: 020 7657 4438
Email: editorial@jlifestyle.co.uk
Web site: http://www.jlifestyle.co.uk
Titles:
  JLIFESTYLE

JMT VENTURES LTD   1741747
PO Box 585, EDGWARE, HA8 4DU **Tel:** 020 7993 0092
Titles:
  JEWTASTIC
  SOMETHING JEWISH

UK Publishers & Their Titles

JNB PUBLISHING 1650977
The Treacle Factory, 2A Reginald Street, LUTON, LU2 7QZ
Tel: 01582 416171 **Fax:** 01582 416328
Web site: http://www.jnbpublishing.co.uk
Titles:
  DISCOVER BEDFORDSHIRE
  LUTON & DUNSTABLE AT LARGE

JOEM PR FAR EAST 1735331
The Courtyard, Sondes Road, DEAL, CT14 7BW
Tel: 01304 368688 **Fax:** 01304 375181
Titles:
  CONSTRUCTION EQUIPMENT ASIA

JOHN BROWN GROUP 15211
136-142 Bramley Road, LONDON, W10 6SR
Tel: 020 7565 3000 **Fax:** 020 7565 3050
Email: info@johnbrowngroup.co.uk
Web site: http://www.johnbrowngroup.co.uk
Titles:
  EDITION
  SKY KIDS MAGAZINE
  TEACHERS MAGAZINE
  WAITROSE FOOD ILLUSTRATED

JOHN CATT EDUCATIONAL LTD 17668
12 Deben Mill Business Centre, Melton, WOODBRIDGE,
IP12 1BL **Tel:** 01394 389850 **Fax:** 01394 386893
Web site: http://www.johncatt.com
Titles:
  BOARDING SCHOOL
  PREP SCHOOL

JOHN HORNBY SKEWES & CO. LTD 1630093
Salem House, Parkinson Approach, Garforth, LEEDS, LS25
2HR **Tel:** 0113 286 5381 **Fax:** 0113 286 8515
Titles:
  GEAR

JOHN LAMB MEDIA LTD 1691211
Pellingbrook House, Lewes Road, Scaynes Hill, HAYWARDS
HEATH, RH17 7NG **Tel:** 01444 831226
Email: jtlamb@onetel.com
Titles:
  ABILITY

JOHN WILEY & SONS LTD 12247
The Atrium, Southern Gate, CHICHESTER, PO19 8SQ
Tel: 01243 779777 **Fax:** 01243 770432
Web site: http://www.wiley.com
Titles:
  APPLIED COGNITIVE PSYCHOLOGY
  ARCHITECTURAL DESIGN
  THE BRITISH JOURNAL OF SURGERY
  CHILD ABUSE REVIEW
  CRIMINAL BEHAVIOUR & MENTAL HEALTH
  DYSLEXIA
  EUROPEAN JOURNAL OF PERSONALITY
  EUROPEAN JOURNAL OF SOCIAL PSYCHOLOGY
  FLAVOUR & FRAGRANCE JOURNAL
  HYDROLOGICAL PROCESSES
  INPHARM.COM
  INTERNATIONAL INSOLVENCY REVIEW
  INTERNATIONAL JOURNAL OF HEALTH PLANNING &
    MANAGEMENT
  JOURNAL OF CHEMICAL TECHNOLOGY AND
    BIOTECHNOLOGY
  JOURNAL OF CONSUMER BEHAVIOUR
  JOURNAL OF THE SCIENCE OF FOOD AND
    AGRICULTURE
  LUBRICATION SCIENCE
  LUMINESCENCE
  MICROSCOPY AND ANALYSIS
  PEST MANAGEMENT SCIENCE
  PHARMAFOCUS
  PHYTOCHEMICAL ANALYSIS
  PHYTOTHERAPY RESEARCH
  POLYMER INTERNATIONAL
  POLYMERS FOR ADVANCED TECHNOLOGIES
  PRACTICAL DIABETES INTERNATIONAL
  PRENATAL DIAGNOSIS
  PROGRESS IN NEUROLOGY & PSYCHIATRY
  PROGRESS IN PHOTOVOLTAICS
  RAPID COMMUNICATIONS IN MASS SPECTROMETRY
  REVIEWS IN MEDICAL VIROLOGY
  SPECTROSCOPY EUROPE
  TRENDS IN UROLOGY, GYNAECOLOGY & SEXUAL
    HEALTH
  WEATHER
  WIND ENERGY

JOHNSON MATTHEY PLC 18128
Orchard Road, ROYSTON, SG8 5HE **Tel:** 01763 256323
Fax: 01763 256259
Email: jmpmr@matthey.com
Titles:
  PLATINUM METALS REVIEW
  SELF STORAGE FOCUS

JOHNSTON (FALKIRK) LTD 18716
Redbrae Road, Camelon, FALKIRK, FK1 4ZA
Tel: 01324 624959 **Fax:** 01324 629079
Web site: http://www.johnstonpress.co.uk
Titles:
  CUMBERNAULD NEWS AND KILSYTH CHRONICLE
    SERIES
  THE FALKIRK HERALD
  LINLITHGOWSHIRE JOURNAL AND GAZETTE SERIES
  MILNGAVIE & BEARSDEN HERALD
  MOTHERWELL TIMES SERIES

JOHNSTON PRESS 13985
2 Esky Drive, Carn Industrial Estate, Portadown,
CRAIGAVON, BT63 5YY **Tel:** 028 3839 3939
Fax: 028 3839 5599
Titles:
  BELFAST NEWS
  FARMING LIFE
  NEWS LETTER
  THE TIMES SERIES

JOHNSTON PRESS (FALKIRK) 697237
Park House, Academy Park, Gower Street, Pollokshields,
GLASGOW, G51 1PT **Tel:** 0141 427 7878
Fax: 0141 427 9780
Titles:
  THE GLASGOW EXTRA SERIES

JOHNSTON PRESS OFF ROAD PORTFOLIO 13699
12 Victoria Street, MORECAMBE, LA4 4AG
Tel: 01524 833111 **Fax:** 01524 425469
Titles:
  TRIALS & MOTOCROSS NEWS

JOHNSTON PUBLISHING LTD 671635
Church Lane, HORNCASTLE, LN9 5HW **Tel:** 01507 526868
Fax: 01507 522025
Email: horncastle.news@jpress.co.uk
Web site: http://www.horncastletoday.co.uk
Titles:
  HORNCASTLE NEWS

**JOINT CENTRAL CTTEE POLICE FEDERATION (ENG./
WALES)** 14152
Federation House, Highbury Drive, SURREY, KT22 7UY
Tel: 01372 352000
Web site: http://www.polfed.org
Titles:
  POLICE

JORDAN PUBLISHING LTD 14309
21 St. Thomas Street, BRISTOL, BS1 6JS
Tel: 0117 923 0600 **Fax:** 0117 925 0486
Web site: http://www.jordanpublishing.co.uk
Titles:
  CHILD AND FAMILY LAW QUARTERLY
  EDUCATION LAW REPORTS
  FAMILY LAW

THE JOURNAL OF CHINESE MEDICINE 14507
22 Cromwell Road, HOVE, BN3 3EB **Tel:** 01273 777760
Fax: 01273 748588
Email: info@jcm.co.uk
Web site: http://www.jcm.co.uk
Titles:
  THE JOURNAL OF CHINESE MEDICINE

JOURNAL OF INDUSTRY AND TECHNOLOGY 676969
8 Matthew Wren Close, Little Downham, ELY, CB6 2UL
Tel: 01353 699094 **Fax:** 01353 699094
Email:
williamhammerton_thejournalofindustryandtechnology@
hotmail.co.uk
Web site: http://www.thejournalofindustryandtechnology.biz
Titles:
  EURO TECHNOLOGY

INDUSTRIAL ANALYTICAL INSTRUMENTATION
THE JOURNAL OF INDUSTRY AND TECHNOLOGY

JPC 1709537
8F Blackburnes Mews, LONDON, W1K 2LG
Tel: 020 7495 1697 **Fax:** 020 7487 4776
Web site: http://www.j-p-c.tv
Titles:
  CITYTECH
  CITYWEALTH
  SOUTHERN COUNTIES TELEGRAPH

JPC GROUP 14981
Journal House, 18 Curzon Street, DERBY, DE1 1LL
Tel: 01332 242044
Titles:
  JOURNAL & ADVERTISER SERIES

JPC LTD 14746
Journal House, 18 Curzon Street, DERBY, DE1 1LL
Tel: 01332 384988 **Fax:** 01332 202671
Titles:
  EAST STAFFORDSHIRE JOURNAL INCORPORATING
    STAFFS BUSINESS TIMES
  GREATER LONDON CHRONICLE
  MIDLANDS FOCUS
  SOUTHERN GAZETTE

JPS MEDIA LIMITED 1653540
21 Stone Street, CRANBROOK, TN17 3HF
Tel: 01580 714705 **Fax:** 01580 715983
Email: info@wealdentimes.co.uk
Web site: http://www.wealdentimes.co.uk
Titles:
  WEALDEN TIMES

JRS CORPORATE LTD 1677403
Charles House, 148-149 Great Charles Street Queensway,
BIRMINGHAM, B3 3HT **Tel:** 0121 236 0411
Fax: 0121 233 3874
Web site: http://www.corp-uk.com
Titles:
  CORPORATE UK

JS PUBLICATIONS 18297
PO Box 505, NEWMARKET, CB8 7TF **Tel:** 01638 561590
Fax: 01638 560924
Email: info@jspubs.com
Web site: http://www.jspubs.com
Titles:
  THE UK REGISTER OF EXPERT WITNESSES

JTC ASSOCIATES LTD 13733
4 Elms Lane, Shareshill, WOLVERHAMPTON, WV10 7JS
Tel: 01922 415233 **Fax:** 01922 415208
Titles:
  PROFESSIONAL SECURITY

JUKE BLUES MAGAZINE 18549
PO Box 4083, BATH, BA1 0FA **Tel:** 01225 758375
Fax: 01225 758375
Email: juke@jukeblues.com
Web site: http://www.jukeblues.com
Titles:
  JUKE BLUES MAGAZINE

JULIA BASKERVILLE PUBLICATIONS 18864
25 Southworth Way, THORNTON-CLEVELEYS, FY5 2WW
Tel: 01253 829431 **Fax:** 01253 829431
Titles:
  LIVERPOOL LAW SOCIETY BULLETIN
  THE MESSENGER

JUNCTION 19 MEDIA LIMITED 1767686
PO Box 7, KNUTSFORD, WA16 7PP **Tel:** 01565 872107
Fax: 01565 873943
Titles:
  INCHESHIRE

JUNGLE DRUMS LTD 1742765
PO Box 49713, LONDON, WC1X 8WW **Tel:** 020 7242 5140
Fax: 020 7242 5140
Titles:
  JUNGLEDRUMS MAGAZINE

JUNKK.COM 1650231
Kyrle House, Edde Cross Street, ROSS-ON-WYE, HR9 7BZ
Tel: 01989 762269
Email: info@junkk.com
Web site: http://www.junkk.com
Titles:
JUNKK.COM

JUSTICE 16735
SchNews c/o Community Base, 113 Queens Road,
BRIGHTON, BN1 3XG **Tel:** 01273 685913
Titles:
SCHNEWS

K9 MEDIA LTD 1641498
21 High Street, Warsop, MANSFIELD, NG20 0AA
Tel: 0870 011 4115
Titles:
K9 MAGAZINE
VIVO MAGAZINE

K J PARTNERSHIP LTD 1653039
PO Box 753, Flackwell Heath, HIGH WYCOMBE, HP10 9XG
Tel: 01628 530323 **Fax:** 01628 530212
Email: mail@drcreview.com
Web site: http://www.kjpartnership.co.uk
Titles:
DRAG, ROD & CLASSIC REVIEW

K W MEDIA LTD 1649548
Rye House, 15 North Street, ASHFORD, TN25 8LF
Tel: 01233 650888 **Fax:** 01233 650888
Email: editor.kwmedia@virgin.net
Titles:
KENTISH WAYS

KABLE 16562
20-24 Kirby Street, LONDON, EC1N 8TS **Tel:** 020 7061 3220
Fax: 020 7061 3289
Web site: http://www.kablenet.com
Titles:
GC MAGAZINE

KADIUM LTD 13599
Brassey House, New Zealand Avenue, WALTON-ON-
THAMES, KT12 1QD **Tel:** 01932 886537 **Fax:** 01932 886539
Web site: http://www.kadiumonline.net
Titles:
EASTERN EUROPEAN WIRELESS COMMUNICATIONS
NETWORKING +
NORTHERN AFRICAN WIRELESS COMMUNICATIONS
SOUTHERN AFRICAN WIRELESS COMMUNICATIONS

KAL MEDIA 1750358
Units 6-8 87 Trowbridge Road, BRADFORD ON AVON,
BA15 1EG **Tel:** 01225 309270
Titles:
YARN FORWARD

KANE 1766896
2-4 Noel Street, LONDON, W1F 8GB **Tel:** 020 3358 3305
Titles:
FRONT

KAREN MCAVOY PUBLISHING LTD 1707338
The Forge, 13B Lisburn Road, Moira, CRAIGAVON, BT67
0JR **Tel:** 028 9261 2990 **Fax:** 028 9261 2091
Email: info@kmpltd.co.uk
Web site: http://www.kmpltd.co.uk
Titles:
EXTRACTION INDUSTRY IRELAND
GUIDES TO INDUSTRIAL ESTATES IN NORTHERN
IRELAND
NORTHERN BUILDER
NORTHERN IRELANDS ELECTRICAL MAGAZINE
PLUMBING & HEATING IN NORTHERN IRELAND

KAV PUBLICITY LTD 14410
Wheatsheaf House, Montgomery Street, The Village, East
Kilbride, GLASGOW, G74 4JS **Tel:** 01355 279077
Fax: 01355 279088
Titles:
TRANSPORT NEWS
YACHTING LIFE

KAVA MEDIA 622929
PO Box 23, DURSLEY, GL11 5WA **Tel:** 01453 861390
Fax: 01453 860483
Titles:
3G SOLUTIONS FOR OPERATORS

KCM MEDIA 1710884
62 Castlepark Drive, Fairlie, LARGS, KA29 0DG
Tel: 01475 560177 **Fax:** 01475 568117
Email: info@kcmmedia.co.uk
Titles:
ABILITY NEEDS MAGAZINE

KEELE STUDENTS' UNION 621556
KUSU, Keele University, NEWCASTLE, ST5 5BJ
Tel: 01782 583702 **Fax:** 01782 712671
Titles:
CONCOURSE

**KEIGHLEY & WORTH VALLEY RAILWAY
PRESERVATION SOCIETY** 15497
Keighley & Worth Valley Railway, The Railway Station,
Haworth, KEIGHLEY, BD22 8NJ **Tel:** 01535 645214
Fax: 01535 647317
Titles:
PUSH AND PULL

KELSEY PUBLISHING LTD 15408
Cudham Tithe Barn, Berrys Hill, Berrys Green, Cudham,
WESTERHAM, TN16 3AG **Tel:** 01959 541444
Fax: 01959 541400
Email: fhec.info@kelsey.co.uk
Web site: http://www.kelsey.co.uk
Titles:
4X4
CAR MECHANICS
CLASSIC AND VINTAGE COMMERCIALS
CLASSIC CAR WEEKLY
CLASSIC MILITARY VEHICLE
CLASSIC PLANT & MACHINERY
CLASSIC VAN AND PICK-UP
COUNTRY KITCHEN
CUSTOM CAR
GOOD HOMES
GROW IT
JAGUAR ENTHUSIAST
JAGUAR WORLD MONTHLY
LAND ROVER WORLD
LOCALRIDER MAGAZINE
MODERN MINI
PERFORMANCE FRENCH CARS
PRACTICAL REPTILE KEEPING
RUNNING FITNESS
STATIONARY ENGINE
TOTAL BMW
TRACTOR & FARM TRADER
TRACTOR & MACHINERY
TRIUMPH WORLD
VOLKSWAGEN GOLF+

KEMPS PUBLISHING LTD 14758
11 Swan Courtyard, Charles Edward Road, BIRMINGHAM,
B26 1BU **Tel:** 0121 765 4144 **Fax:** 0121 706 3491
Titles:
BUSINESS ISSUES FOR LEICESTERSHIRE
CHAMBERLINK

KENNEDY'S PUBLICATIONS LTD 12321
First Floor Offices, Stafford House, 16 East Street,
TONBRIDGE, TN9 1HG **Tel:** 01732 371510
Fax: 01732 361385
Email: post@kennedys.co.uk
Web site: http://www.kennedysconfection.com
Titles:
THE CONFECTIONERY TRADE BUYER
HEALTHY FOODS AND SNACKS
KENNEDY'S CONFECTION

THE KENNEL CLUB 15646
1-5 Clarges Street, Piccadilly, LONDON, W1J 8AB
Tel: 020 7518 1038 **Fax:** 020 7518 1028
Titles:
KENNEL GAZETTE

KENSINGTON WEST PRODUCTIONS LTD 18933
5 Cattle Market, HEXHAM, NE46 1NJ **Tel:** 01434 609933
Fax: 01434 600066
Email: livingnorth@btconnect.com

Titles:
LIVING NORTH

KENT CHRISTIAN PRESS 600462
57 Neal Road, West Kingsdown, SEVENOAKS, TN15 6DG
Tel: 01474 852474
Email: kcpress@church-media.co.uk
Web site: http://www.church-media.co.uk
Titles:
THE BRIDGE
CANTERBURY OUTLOOK
ROCHESTER LINK

KENT MESSENGER GROUP 12791
Messenger House, New Hythe Lane, Larkfield, AYLESFORD,
ME20 6SG **Tel:** 01622 717880 **Fax:** 01622 715225
Web site: http://www.kentonline.co.uk
Titles:
CANTERBURY EXTRA SERIES
DARTFORD MESSENGER
EXPRESS EXTRA SERIES KENT
FOCUS
GRAVESEND MESSENGER SERIES
KENT BUSINESS
KENT MESSENGER GROUP NEWSPAPERS
KENT ONLINE
KENTISH GAZETTE SERIES
KM EXTRA SERIES (MAIDSTONE, TONBRIDGE AND
TUNBRIDGE WELLS)
MEDWAY MESSENGER AND EXTRA SERIES
MERCURY SERIES (KENT)
SHEERNESS TIMES GUARDIAN
WEDDING DAY
WHAT'S ON

KENT REGIONAL NEWS AND MEDIA 14961
Newspaper House, Simmonds Road, Wincheap,
CANTERBURY, CT1 3YR **Tel:** 01227 767321
Fax: 01227 788422
Titles:
ADSCENE (CANTERBURY)
ISLE OF THANET GAZETTE SERIES
MEDWAY NEWS SERIES
WHITSTABLE & HERNE BAY TIMES SERIES

KEW MAGAZINE 1724705
Royal Botanic Gardens, Kew, RICHMOND, TW9 3AB
Titles:
KEW MAGAZINE

KEY PUBLISHING LTD 13016
PO Box 100, STAMFORD, PE9 1XQ **Tel:** 01780 755131
Fax: 01780 757261
Web site: http://www.keypublishing.com
Titles:
AIR INTERNATIONAL
AIRFORCES MONTHLY
AIRLINER WORLD
AIRPORTS INTERNATIONAL
AIRPORTS OF THE WORLD
BOWLS INTERNATIONAL INCORPORATING WORLD
BOWLS
FLYPAST
PC PILOT
TODAY'S PILOT

KEYBOARD PLAYER 15373
48 Mereway Road, TWICKENHAM, TW2 6RG
Tel: 020 8241 3695
Titles:
KEYBOARD PLAYER

KEYNOTE 672726
Field House, 72 Oldfield Road, HAMPTON, TW12 2HQ
Tel: 01223 208512
Web site: http://www.keynote.co.uk
Titles:
BUSINESS RATIO

KEYPRINT 1606101
28 Saville Road, Westwood, PETERBOROUGH, PE3 7PR
Tel: 01733 331500 **Fax:** 01733 331511
Titles:
POWERPLAY

KEYWAYS PUBLISHING GROUP 14532
PO Box 100, CHICHESTER, PO18 8HD **Tel:** 01243 576444
Fax: 01243 576456

Email: admin@keywayspublishing.com
Web site: http://www.keywayspublishing.com
Titles:
THE JOURNAL OF FAMILY PLANNING AND
  REPRODUCTIVE HEALTH CARE
POLICING TODAY

KEYWAYS PUBLISHING LIMITED 1731676
PO Box 100, CHICHESTER, PO18 8HD **Tel:** 01243 576444
Fax: 01243 576456
Email: admin@keywayspublishing.com
Web site: http://www.keywayspublishing.com
Titles:
FIRE
FIRE
JOURNAL OF FAMILY HEALTH CARE
PUBLIC SECURITY
SCHOOL HEALTH

KHL GROUP 600289
Southfields, Southview Road, WADHURST, TN5 6TP
Tel: 01892 784088 **Fax:** 01892 784086
Email: mail@khl.com
Web site: http://www.khl.com
Titles:
ACCESS INTERNATIONAL
CONSTRUCTION EUROPE
DEMOLITION AND RECYCLING INTERNATIONAL
INTERNATIONAL CONSTRUCTION
INTERNATIONAL CRANES AND SPECIALIZED
  TRANSPORT
INTERNATIONAL RENTAL NEWS
WORLDCONSTRUCTIONWEEK

KICKIN' CUTS LTD 15362
PO Box 75, ATTLEBOROUGH, NR17 1WL
Tel: 01953 853068
Titles:
COUNTRY MUSIC PEOPLE

KICK-START PUBLISHING LTD 621508
The Oast, Great Danegate, Eridge, EAST SUSSEX, TN18
9HU **Tel:** 01892 752400 **Fax:** 01892 752405
Email: bobby.butler@kick-startpublishing.co.uk
Titles:
CFJ CONTRACT FLOORING JOURNAL
TILE & STONE JOURNAL

KIDAROUND LTD 1654821
1st Floor, Dolphin House, 126 Hythe Hill, COLCHESTER,
CO1 2NP **Tel:** 01206 863737 **Fax:** 01206 792823
Email: info@kidaround.biz
Web site: http://www.kidaround.biz
Titles:
KIDAROUND MAGAZINE LTD

KIDS LIFE LTD 1736820
PO Box 255, LETCHWORTH, SG6 9AZ **Tel:** 01462 679992
Titles:
ABC MAGAZINE HERTFORDSHIRE

KIMMERSTON DESIGN 18593
Tynemouth House, 33 Preston Road, NORTH SHIELDS,
NE29 0ND **Tel:** 0191 272 8283 **Fax:** 0191 272 8283
Email: nepa@kimmerston.co.uk
Web site: http://www.nepaonline.org.uk
Titles:
NEPA NEWS

KINDRED SPIRIT LTD 16138
Unit 2, Lynher House, 3 Bush Park, PLYMOUTH, PL6 7RG
Tel: 01752 762970 **Fax:** 01752 772107
Email: mail@kindredspirit.co.uk
Web site: http://www.kindredspirit.co.uk
Titles:
KINDRED SPIRIT

KINGPIN 622292
54 Hamilton Road, OXFORD, OX2 7PZ **Tel:** 01865 559509
Titles:
KINGPIN

KINGSLEY HOUSE (PUBLISHING) 699498
Home Close, Teffont, SALISBURY, SP3 5QY
Tel: 01722 716268 **Fax:** 01722 716781

Titles:
THE BEAT
SALISBURY SPORT
SOULSTAR CHATBUSTERS
VALLEY NEWS

KINGSMOOR PUBLICATIONS LTD 14562
PO Box 7861, BRAINTREE, CM7 4YZ **Tel:** 01371 812960
Fax: 01371 812969
Titles:
RAD MAGAZINE

KINGSWOOD MEDIA LTD 18430
4 New Cottages, Green Farm Lane, Shorne, GRAVESEND,
DA12 3HQ **Tel:** 01474 824711
Web site: http://www.binfo.co.uk
Titles:
BUSINESS INFO MAGAZINE
PEN 2 PAPER

KIT CARS INTERNATIONAL LTD 15468
11 Meadow Close, HOVE, BN3 6QQ **Tel:** 01273 55910
Titles:
KIT CAR

KL ENERGY PUBLISHING LTD 1761246
Tel: 020 7286 6055
PR by email only **Tel:** 020 7286 6055
Titles:
NORTH SEA REPORTER

KLINE DAVIS LTD 625302
Broseley House, Newlands Drive, WITHAM, CM8 2UL
Tel: 01376 514000 **Fax:** 01376 514555
Email: info@klinedavis.com
Web site: http://www.klinedavis.com
Titles:
AN ESSEX WEDDING
ATTIRE ACCESSORIES
ATTIRE BRIDAL
CRAFT FOCUS MAGAZINE
GIFT FOCUS
YOUR BERKS & BUCKS WEDDING
YOUR HAMPSHIRE WEDDING
YOUR HERTS & BEDS WEDDING
YOUR KENT WEDDING
YOUR SURREY WEDDING
YOUR SUSSEX WEDDING

KLUWER LAW INTERNATIONAL 14308
250 Waterloo Road, LONDON, SE1 8RD **Tel:** 020 8247 1694
Fax: 020 8247 1607
Web site: http://www.kluwerlaw.com
Titles:
BUSINESS LAW REVIEW

KMT PUBLISHING LTD 1653345
PO Box 10038, Sudbury, SUFFOLK, CO10 7WL
Tel: 01787 242100 **Fax:** 01787 242161
Titles:
TOTAL TATTOO

KNIGHT INTERNATIONAL LTD 16291
PO Box 697, Chelsea, LONDON, SW3 2BL
Tel: 020 7584 3939
Titles:
HOT GOSSIP UK

KNIGHTON ENTERPRISES LTD 14220
PO Box 27, CHELTENHAM, GL53 0YH **Tel:** 01242 574027
Fax: 01242 574102
Titles:
SUBSEA ENGINEERING NEWS

KNIGHTWRITER PUBLISHING 1680546
23 Padua Road, LONDON, SE20 8HF **Tel:** 020 8778 2215
Email: editor@londonsalsascene.co.uk
Web site: http://www.londonsalsascene.co.uk
Titles:
LONDON SALSA SCENE

KNOWLEDGE MEDIA LTD 1638632
18 (1F2) Gladstone Terrace, EDINBURGH, EH9 1LS
Tel: 0131 668 4864 **Fax:** 0131 668 4864

Titles:
HISTORY SCOTLAND

KNOWSHARE LTD 621535
PO Box 7003, WESTCLIFF-ON-SEA, SS0 0TH
Tel: 01702 343343 **Fax:** 01702 353588
Email: admin@publicnet.co.uk
Titles:
PUBLICNET

KNOWSLEY BOROUGH COUNCIL 1654148
PO Box 21, Archway Road, Huyton, LIVERPOOL, L36 9YU
Tel: 0151 443 3397 **Fax:** 0151 443 3507
Web site: http://www.knowsley.gov.uk
Titles:
KNOWSLEY NEWS

KOAN LTD 1739895
Big Red Office, 101 Princess Street, MANCHESTER, M1
6DD **Tel:** 0161 237 9994 **Fax:** 0845 299 1419
Titles:
ALL4HORSES.TV

KODAK LIMITED & EASTMAN KODAK COMPANY 16181
Kodak Business Centre, Hemel One, Boundary Way, HEMEL
HEMPSTEAD, HP2 7YU **Tel:** 01442 846945
Fax: 01422 846594
Email: laura.watson@kodak.com
Web site: http://www.kodak.com/go/motion
Titles:
INCAMERA

KOGAN PAGE LTD 17548
120 Pentonville Road, LONDON, N1 9JN **Tel:** 020 7278 0433
Fax: 020 7837 6348
Web site: http://www.kogan-page.co.uk
Titles:
TRANSPORT MANAGER'S & OPERATOR'S HANDBOOK

KOS MEDIA LTD 1603083
KoS Media Ltd, Apple Barn, Hythe Road, Smeeth,
ASHFORD, TN25 6SR **Tel:** 01303 817000
Titles:
KENT ON SATURDAY
KENT ON SUNDAY
YOURKENT SERIES

KSA PARTNERSHIP 14126
97 Front Street, Whickham, NEWCASTLE UPON TYNE,
NE16 4JL **Tel:** 0191 488 1947
Email: office@tradeindustry.net
Web site: http://www.tradeindustry.net
Titles:
BICYCLE TRADE AND INDUSTRY
SCOOTER TRADE AND INDUSTRY

KT PRESS 624575
38 Bellot Street, East Greenwich, LONDON, SE10 0AQ
Tel: 020 8858 3331 **Fax:** 020 8858 3331
Email: ktpress@ktpress.co.uk
Web site: http://www.ktpress.co.uk
Titles:
N.PARADOXA

KT PUBLICATIONS 1653480
25 Burges Close, DUNSTABLE, LU6 3EU **Tel:** 01582 477886
Email: info@keepingtrack.co.uk
Web site: http://www.keepingtrack.co.uk
Titles:
RAIL MANAGMENT

KUMUKA WORLDWIDE 1732279
40 Earls Court Road, LONDON, W8 6EJ **Tel:** 020 7937 8855
Fax: 020 7937 6664
Titles:
VENTURE

LABAN 15404
Laban, Creekside, LONDON, SE8 3DZ **Tel:** 020 8691 8600
Fax: 020 8691 8400
Web site: http://www.laban.co.uk
Titles:
DANCE THEATRE JOURNAL

THE LADY LTD 15104
39-40 Bedford Street, LONDON, WC2E 9ER
Tel: 020 7379 4717 **Fax:** 020 7497 2137
Titles:
 THE LADY

LAG EDUCATION & SERVICE TRUST LTD 14320
242 Pentonville Road, LONDON, N1 9UN
Tel: 020 7833 2931 **Fax:** 020 7837 6094
Titles:
 LEGAL ACTION

LAING & BUISSON 14166
29 Angel Gate, City Road, LONDON, EC1V 2PT
Tel: 020 7833 9123 **Fax:** 020 7833 9129
Web site: http://www.laingbuisson.co.uk
Titles:
 COMMUNITY CARE MARKET NEWS
 HEALTHCARE MARKET NEWS

LAKEBOURNE LTD 13983
6 Cley Road, HOLT, NR25 6JD **Tel:** 01263 711844
Fax: 01263 711845
Titles:
 FARM BRIEF

LAMBERT AND TUTTON COLOUR PRODUCTIONS 15557
Summerhill Cottages, Macclesfield Road, ALDERLEY EDGE,
SK9 7BG **Tel:** 01625 599909 **Fax:** 01625 599919
Titles:
 MACCLESFIELD & DISTRICT LIFESTYLE MAGAZINE

LAMDA PUBLICITY LTD 13960
Odeon House, 146 College Road, HARROW, HA1 1BH
Tel: 020 8863 2767 **Fax:** 020 8863 3917
Titles:
 INDUSTRIAL DIAMOND REVIEW

LAMONT PUBLICATIONS 15533
Hillrising House, 115 Potters Lane, Send, WOKING, GU23
7AW **Tel:** 01483 750692 **Fax:** 01483 750692
Titles:
 SURREY OCCASIONS

LANCASHIRE CONSTABULARY 14150
PO Box 77, Hutton, PRESTON, PR4 5SB **Tel:** 01772 618444
Fax: 01772 618356
Titles:
 CONTEXT

LANCASHIRE COUNTY CRICKET CLUB 1651308
Tel: 0161 282 4000 **Fax:** 0161 282 4030
County Ground, Brian Statham Way, Old Trafford,
MANCHESTER, M16 0PX **Tel:** 0161 282 4000
Fax: 0161 282 4064
Titles:
 LANCASHIRE SPIN

LANCASHIRE EVENING POST LTD 14022
Olivers Place, Eastway, Fulwood, PRESTON, PR2 9ZA
Tel: 01772 254841 **Fax:** 01772 880173
Email: lep.newsdesk@lep.co.uk
Web site: http://www.lep.co.uk
Titles:
 CHORLEY GUARDIAN SERIES
 THE GARSTANG & LONGRIDGE COURIER & NEWS
  SERIES
 LANCASHIRE EVENING POST
 LONGRIDGE & RIBBLE VALLEY NEWS AND
  ADVERTISER
 PRESTON REPORTER SERIES

LANCASHIRE PUBLICATIONS LTD 15502
PO Box 168, LEEDS, LS1 1RF **Tel:** 01942 228000
Titles:
 LEIGH REPORTER
 ST. HELENS REPORTER SERIES

LANCASHIRE PUBLICATIONS LTD (WIGAN) 1747874
Martland Mill, Martland Mill Lane, WIGAN, WN5 0LX
Titles:
 WIGAN EVENING POST

LANCASTER AND MORECAMBE NEWSPAPERS 1687069
12 Victoria Street, MORECAMBE, LA4 4AG
Tel: 01524 833111 **Fax:** 01524 834024
Titles:
 LAKELAND ECHO
 LANCASTER AND MORECAMBE REPORTER
 LANCASTER GUARDIAN SERIES
 VISITOR (MORECAMBE)

LANCASTER UNIVERSITY STUDENTS' UNION 15789
Slaidburn House, Bailrigg, LANCASTER, LA1 4YA
Tel: 01524 592613 **Fax:** 01524 846732
Web site: http://www.lusu.co.uk
Titles:
 SCAN

LANCE PUBLISHING LTD 1758899
1st Floor Tailby House, Bath Road, KETTERING, NN16 8NL
Tel: 01536 512624 **Fax:** 01536 515481
Web site: http://www.lancepublishing.co.uk
Titles:
 MENORAH

THE LANCET PUBLISHING GROUP 623198
32 Jamestown Road, LONDON, NW1 7BY
Tel: 020 7424 4910
Web site: http://www.thelancet.com
Titles:
 THE LANCET INFECTIOUS DISEASES

LAND RESEARCH UNIT LTD 13514
Studio Crown & Gallery Reach, 149A Grosvenor Road,
LONDON, SW1V 3JY **Tel:** 020 7834 9471
Fax: 020 7834 9470
Email: planninginlondon@mac.com
Titles:
 PLANNING IN LONDON

LANDOR PUBLISHING 13520
359 Kennington Lane, LONDON, SE11 5QY
Tel: 0845 270 7901 **Fax:** 0845 270 7960
Web site: http://www.parkingreview.co.uk
Titles:
 CINEMA BUSINESS
 LOCAL TRANSPORT TODAY
 NEW TRANSIT
 PARKING REVIEW

LANG SYNE PUBLISHERS LTD 15612
Strathclyde Business Centre, 120 Carstairs Street,
GLASGOW, G40 4JD **Tel:** 0141 554 9944
Fax: 0141 554 9955
Titles:
 SCOTTISH MEMORIES

LANGLEY & ALLEN LTD 1643301
PO Box 941A, SURBITON, KT1 9RQ **Tel:** 020 8661 5353
Fax: 020 3163 0287
Email: surrey@abcmag.co.uk
Web site: http://www.abcmag.co.uk
Titles:
 ABC MAGAZINE SURREY

LANGUTEC MEDIA LTD 1692020
Unit 1, 10-14 Hollybush Gardens, LONDON, E2 9QP
Tel: 020 7247 4614 **Fax:** 020 7613 5862
Titles:
 BANGLA MIRROR

LANSDOWNE PUBLISHING PARTNERSHIP LTD 13695
11-12 School House, Second Avenue, Trafford Park Village,
MANCHESTER, M17 1DZ **Tel:** 0161 872 6667
Fax: 0161 872 6668
Web site: http://www.lansdownepublishing.com
Titles:
 HOSPITAL CATERER

LARCHDRIFT PROJECTS LTD 13759
Unit 12, Moor Place Farm, Plough Lane, Bramshill, HOOK,
RG27 0RF **Tel:** 0118 932 6665 **Fax:** 0118 932 6663
Titles:
 PROJECT MANAGER TODAY

LARGE PUBLISHING LTD 1764808
60 Port Street, MANCHESTER, M1 2EQ **Tel:** 0161 235 7270
Fax: 0871 115 3137
Titles:
 LARGE MANCHESTER
 LARGE STUDENTS

LAST WORD MEDIA 1734098
4th Floor, 120 Moorgate, LONDON, EC2M 6SS
Titles:
 EXPERT INVESTOR EUROPE (EIE)
 INTERNATIONAL ADVISER
 PORTFOLIO ADVISER

LATEST HOMES LTD 18444
Unit 6, Level 5 North, New England House, New England
Street, BRIGHTON, BN1 4GH **Tel:** 01273 818150
Fax: 01273 818152
Email: accounts@thelatest.co.uk
Titles:
 LATEST 7
 LATEST HOMES
 WAVE

LAW BUSINESS RESEARCH LTD 629262
87 Lancaster Road, LONDON, W11 1QQ **Tel:** 020 7908 1184
Fax: 020 7229 6910
Titles:
 GLOBAL COMPETITION REVIEW
 LATIN LAWYER

THE LAW SOCIETY 14312
113 Chancery Lane, LONDON, WC2A 1PL
Tel: 020 7841 5400 **Fax:** 020 7841 5585
Web site: http://www.lawsociety.org.uk
Titles:
 LAW SOCIETY GAZETTE
 LITIGATION FUNDING

THE LAW SOCIETY OF NORTHERN IRELAND 18758
40 Linenhall Street, BELFAST, BT2 8BA **Tel:** 028 9023 1614
Fax: 028 9023 2606
Titles:
 THE WRIT

THE LAW SOCIETY OF SCOTLAND 14317
26 Drumsheugh Gardens, EDINBURGH, EH3 7YR
Tel: 0131 226 7411 **Fax:** 0131 225 2934
Web site: http://www.lawscot.org.uk
Titles:
 JOURNAL OF THE LAW SOCIETY OF SCOTLAND
 LAW SOCIETY OF SCOTLAND

LAWN GRAPHICS LTD 676318
70 Singer Way, Woburn Road Industrial Estate, KEMPSTON,
MK42 7PU **Tel:** 01234 843902 **Fax:** 01234 843901
Web site: http://www.lgdigital.co.uk
Titles:
 INVESTMENT NOW

LAWRAND LIMITED (MEDICAL PUBLISHING) 671858
PO Box 51, PONTYCLUN, CF72 9YY **Tel:** 020 7100 2867
Fax: 07092 097696
Email: admin@lawrand.com
Web site: http://www.lawrand.com
Titles:
 THE OPERATING THEATRE JOURNAL

LAWTEXT PUBLISHING LTD 623515
Office G18, Spinners Court, 55 West End, WITNEY, OX28
1NH **Tel:** 01993 706183 **Fax:** 01993 709410
Web site: http://www.lawtext.com
Titles:
 BIOSCIENCE LAW REVIEW
 CONTEMPORARY ISSUES IN LAW
 ENVIRONMENTAL LAW AND MANAGEMENT
 ENVIRONMENTAL LIABILITY
 INFORMATION TECHNOLOGY LAW REPORTS
 JOURNAL OF INTERNATIONAL MARITIME LAW
 THE JOURNAL OF WATER LAW
 UTILITIES LAW REVIEW

LAZY CATS MEDIA LTD 1711371
5 Alford Street, LONDON, W1K 2AF **Tel:** 020 7493 2030
Fax: 020 7493 2040

UK Publishers & Their Titles

Section 6 UK Publishers & Their Titles

Titles:
THE PLAYER

LCD PUBLISHING   16196
Suite 2.1, Level 2, Renslade House, Bonhay Road, EXETER, EX4 3AY **Tel:** 01392 664141 **Fax:** 01392 221794
Titles:
GIRL
LIVERPOOL MONTHLY
STAR GIRL MAGAZINE
TELLY-TIME FAVOURITES

LDI MEDIA (UK)   1763889
366 Bethnal Green Road, LONDON, E2 0AH
Tel: 020 7033 9410
Titles:
DESIGN EXCHANGE
DESIGN FOOTPRINT

LEAD MEDIA LTD   623215
6 Harford Court, John Tate Road, HERTFORD, SG13 7NW
Tel: 0871 622 6690 **Fax:** 0871 226 6691
Titles:
ACCEO MATTERS
VRL VEHICLE RECOVERY LINK
WEM (WATER AND ENVIRONMENT MAGAZINE)

LEAGUE AGAINST CRUEL SPORTS   15638
83-87 Union Street, LONDON, SE1 1SG **Tel:** 020 7403 6155
Fax: 020 7378 6940
Web site: http://www.league.org.uk
Titles:
CAMPAIGN UPDATE

LEAGUE PUBLICATIONS LTD   15250
Wellington House, Briggate, BRIGHOUSE, HD6 1DN
Tel: 01484 401895 **Fax:** 01484 401995
Web site: http://www.rugbytimes.com
Titles:
RUGBY LEAGUE WORLD
RUGBY LEAGUER & LEAGUE EXPRESS
RUGBY TIMES

LEAGUE WEEKLY   1654035
1 Oates Street, DEWSBURY, WF13 1BB **Tel:** 01924 666433
Email: editor@league-weekly.com
Web site: http://www.league-weekly.com
Titles:
LEAGUE WEEKLY

LEARNING THROUGH LANDSCAPES   1686540
3rd Floor, Southside Offices, The Law Courts, WINCHESTER, SO23 9DL **Tel:** 01962 846258
Email: schoolgrounds-uk@ltl.org.uk
Web site: http://www.ltl.org.uk
Titles:
OUTDOORS

LEEDS GUIDE LTD   17229
80 North Street, LEEDS, LS2 7PN **Tel:** 0113 244 1000
Fax: 0113 244 1002
Web site: http://www.leedsguide.co.uk
Titles:
THE LEEDS GUIDE
THE LEEDS GUIDE STUDENT GUIDE
PLUSH

LEEDS STUDENT UNION   15766
PO Box 157, LEEDS, LS1 1UH **Tel:** 0113 243 4727
Fax: 0113 246 7953
Titles:
LEEDS STUDENT

LEGAL TECHNOLOGY INSIDER   625439
Oak Lodge, Darrow Green Road, Denton, HARLESTON, IP20 0AY **Tel:** 01986 788666 **Fax:** 01986 788808
Titles:
LEGAL TECHNOLOGY INSIDER

LEGALEASE LTD   14311
Kensington Square House, 12-14 Ansdell Street, LONDON, W8 5BN **Tel:** 020 7396 9292 **Fax:** 020 7396 9302
Web site: http://www.legalease.co.uk

Titles:
FAMILY LAW JOURNAL
IN-HOUSE LAWYER
LEGAL BUSINESS
PRACTICAL LAWYER
PROPERTY LAW JOURNAL

LEICESTER CITY COUNCIL   15585
New Walk Centre, Welford Place, LEICESTER, LE1 6ZG
Tel: 0116 252 6394 **Fax:** 0116 254 5391
Web site: http://www.leicester.gov.uk/link
Titles:
LEICESTER LINK

LEICESTER CITY FOOTBALL CLUB   17427
Walkers Stadium, Filbert Way, LEICESTER, LE2 7FL
Tel: 0870 040 6000 **Fax:** 0116 291 1254
Web site: http://www.lcfc.com
Titles:
CITY MATCHDAY MAGAZINE

LEICESTER MERCURY MEDIA GROUP LTD   14842
St. George Street, LEICESTER, LE1 9FQ **Tel:** 0116 222 4627
Fax: 0116 262 4669
Web site: http://www.thisisleicestershire.co.uk
Titles:
LEICESTER MAIL SERIES
LEICESTER MERCURY
LEICESTERSHIRE & RUTLAND LIFE
THE MESSENGER SERIES (LEICESTERSHIRE & RUTLAND)
SPORTING BLUE

LEICESTERSHIRE CHAMBER OF COMMERCE   627364
Charnwood Court, 5B New Walk, LEICESTER, LE1 6TE
Tel: 0116 247 1800 **Fax:** 0116 247 0430
Email: leics@chamberofcommerce.co.uk
Web site: http://www.chamberofcommerce.co.uk
Titles:
CHAMBER NEWS

LEIGH TIMES LTD   15567
106 The Broadway, LEIGH-ON-SEA, SS9 1AB
Tel: 01702 477666 **Fax:** 01702 478910
Titles:
LEIGH TIMES SERIES

LEISURE CONNECTION   1655002
Low Lane, Horsforth, LEEDS, LS18 4ER **Tel:** 07971 264204
Email: harpers4life@leisureconnection.co.uk
Web site: http://www.lesiureconnection.co.uk
Titles:
HARPERS 4 LIFE

THE LEISURE MEDIA COMPANY LTD   14192
Portmill House, Portmill Lane, HITCHIN, SG5 1DJ
Tel: 01462 431385 **Fax:** 01462 433909
Email: newsdesk@leisuremedia.com
Web site: http://www.leisuremedia.com
Titles:
ATTRACTIONS MANAGEMENT
HEALTH CLUB MANAGEMENT
LEISURE MANAGEMENT
LEISURE OPPORTUNITIES
SPA BUSINESS
SPA OPPORTUNITIES
SPORTS MANAGEMENT

LEISURE PUBLISHING   13055
Unit 5, Bank Street, Stalham, NORWICH, NR12 9BA
Tel: 01692 582287
Titles:
TOWN AND COUNTRY NEWS NORTH NORFOLK & BROADLAND

LEMA PUBLISHING   14275
1 Churchgates, The Wilderness, BERKHAMSTED, HP4 2UB
Tel: 01442 289930 **Fax:** 01442 289950
Email: mark@lemapublishing.co.uk
Web site: http://www.lemapublishing.co.uk
Titles:
ART BUYER
GIFTS TODAY
GREETINGS TODAY
LICENSING TODAY WORLDWIDE
NURSERY TODAY
PARTY PARTY

THE PICTURE BUSINESS
TABLEWARE INTERNATIONAL
TOYS 'N' PLAYTHINGS

LEOPARD MAGAZINE LTD   15620
Auld Logie, Pitcaple, INVERURIE, AB51 5EE
Tel: 01467 625666
Email: ianhamilton@leopardmag.co.uk
Web site: http://www.leopardmagazine.co.uk
Titles:
LEOPARD MAGAZINE

THE LEOPOLD KOHR   600782
The Close, 26 High Street, Purton, SWINDON, SN5 4AE
Tel: 01793 772214
Titles:
FOURTH WORLD REVIEW

THE LEPROSY MISSION   18044
Goldhay Way, Orton Goldhay, PETERBOROUGH, PE2 5GZ
Tel: 01733 370505 **Fax:** 01733 404880
Email: post@tlmew.org.uk
Web site: http://www.leprosymission.org.uk
Titles:
NEW DAY

THE LESBIAN & GAY FOUNDATION   1684249
Princess House, 105-107 Princess Street, MANCHESTER, M1 6DD **Tel:** 0161 235 8035 **Fax:** 0161 235 8036
Email: info@lgf.org.uk
Web site: http://www.lgf.org.uk
Titles:
OUTNORTHWEST

LET THEM EAT CAKE LTD   1752734
Unit 206, Colourworks, 22-24 Abbot Street, LONDON, E8 3DP **Tel:** 07711 256182
Titles:
LET THEM EAT CAKE

LETSRECYCLE.COM   698840
154 Buckingham Palace Road, LONDON, SW1W 9TR
Tel: 020 7633 4500 **Fax:** 020 7633 4519
Titles:
LETSRECYCLE.COM
RESOURCE MANAGEMENT AND RECOVERY

LETTERPRINT LTD   13357
PO Box 1638, LONDON, W8 4QR **Tel:** 020 7937 7879
Fax: 020 7937 7364
Titles:
CHART BREAKOUT
THE QUANTUM LEAP STOCKMARKET LETTER

LEVELPRINT LTD   15154
124 Tabernacle Street, LONDON, EC2A 4SA
Tel: 020 7490 9710 **Fax:** 020 7490 9737
Titles:
I-D MAGAZINE

LEXINGTON PRESS LTD   16951
Tower House, Fishergate, YORK, YO10 4UA
Web site: http://www.thepolitician.org
Titles:
PARLIAMENTARY BRIEF

LEXISNEXIS   13398
Halsbury House, 35 Chancery Lane, LONDON, WC2A 1EL
Tel: 020 7400 2500
Web site: http://www.lexisnexis.co.uk
Titles:
COUNSEL
INSOLVENCY LAW & PRACTICE
JUSTICE OF THE PEACE
LOCAL GOVERNMENT REPORTS
NEW LAW JOURNAL
OCCUPATIONAL PENSIONS
PAY & BENEFITS MAGAZINE
THE SCOTTISH LAW DIRECTORY
SIMON'S WEEKLY TAX INTELLIGENCE
TAXATION
TOLLEY'S COMPANY SECRETARY'S REVIEW
TOLLEY'S PRACTICAL AUDIT & ACCOUNTING
TOLLEY'S PRACTICAL NIC SERVICE
TOLLEY'S PRACTICAL TAX NEWSLETTER

LEXISNEXIS BUTTERWORTHS 676990
Halsbury House, 35 Chancery Lane, LONDON, WC2A 1EL
Tel: 020 7400 2500
Web site: http://www.lexisnexis.co.uk
Titles:
THE TIMES LAW REPORTS
TOLLEY'S EMPLOYMENT LAW NEWSLETTER

LEXISNEXIS UK 629256
2 Addiscombe Road, CROYDON, CR9 5AF
Tel: 020 7400 2500 **Fax:** 020 7400 2842
Web site: http://www.lexisnexis.co.uk
Titles:
ENVIRONMENT IN BUSINESS
FACILITIES MANAGEMENT
HEALTH AND SAFETY AT WORK
PENSIONS WORLD
PENSIONS WORLD ONLINE
THE TAX JOURNAL

LIBERAL DEMOCRATS 15703
4 Cowley Street, LONDON, SW1P 3NB **Tel:** 020 7222 7999
Fax: 020 7222 7904
Titles:
LIBERAL DEMOCRAT NEWS

THE LIBERAL PUBLICATIONS LIMITED 1650917
208-210A High Road, LONDON, N2 9AY **Tel:** 020 8444 1944
Fax: 020 8444 5413
Email: info@theliberal.co.uk
Web site: http://www.theliberal.co.uk
Titles:
THE LIBERAL

THE LIBERTARIAN ALLIANCE 15692
Suite 35, 2 Lansdowne Row, LONDON, W1J 6HL
Tel: 0870 242 1712
Titles:
FREE LIFE

LIBRARIANS' CHRISTIAN FELLOWSHIP 17961
34 Thurlestone Avenue, Seven Kings, ILFORD, IG3 9DU
Tel: 020 8599 1310
Email: secretary@librarianscf.org.uk
Web site: http://www.librarianscf.org.uk
Titles:
CHRISTIAN LIBRARIAN

LICENSED TAXI DRIVERS' ASSOCIATION 14790
Taxi House, 11 Woodfield Road, LONDON, W9 2BA
Tel: 020 7286 1046 **Fax:** 020 7286 2494
Web site: http://www.ltda.co.uk
Titles:
TAXI NEWSPAPER

LIFE CHANGERS 1743592
203B Island Business Centre, 18-36 Wellington Street,
LONDON, SE18 6PS **Tel:** 0844 884 3384
Fax: 020 8854 1484
Email: info@life-changers.org.uk
Web site: http://www.life-changers.org.uk
Titles:
NOVELTY MAGAZINE

LIFECYCLE MARKETING LIMITED 15135
1 Globeside Business Park, Field House Lane, MARLOW,
SL7 1HY **Tel:** 01628 891644 **Fax:** 01628 816883
Titles:
EMMA'S DIARY PREGNANCY GUIDE

LIFESCAPE MAGAZINE LTD 1709957
PO Box 456, POTTERS BAR, EN6 9DS **Tel:** 01707 859805
Titles:
LIFESCAPE

LIGHTHOUSE PUBLISHING 1723729
1 Chartwell Lodge, 9 Brackley Road, BECKENHAM, BR3
1SW **Tel:** 020 8639 0538
Titles:
H&K
PARENTS' WORLD

LIMA PUBLISHING 1731791
9 Pump Place, Old Statford, MILTON KEYNES, MK19 6DL
Tel: 01908 562433
Titles:
ICT FOR EDUCATION

LINCOLNSHIRE LANCASTER ASSOCIATION 1649568
2 Village Street, Careby, STAMFORD, PE9 4EA
Tel: 01780 410016 **Fax:** 01780 410016
Web site: http://www.pa474.f9.co.uk
Titles:
MEMORIAL FLIGHT

LINCOLNSHIRE MEDIA LTD 14024
Brayford Wharf East, LINCOLN, LN5 7AT **Tel:** 01522 820000
Fax: 01522 804493
Web site: http://www.thisislincolnshire.co.uk
Titles:
FAMILY WEEKENDER
LINCOLN TARGET SERIES
LINCOLNSHIRE ECHO
RETFORD GAINSBOROUGH AND WORKSOP TIMES
SPORTSECHO.CO.UK
TARGET SERIES
THIS IS THE BUSINESS

LINCOLNSHIRE NEWSPAPERS LTD 14970
5-6 Church Lane, BOSTON, PE21 6ND **Tel:** 01205 311433
Fax: 01205 352913
Titles:
BOSTON STANDARD AND CITIZEN SERIES
MARKET RASEN MAIL

LINDBERG DELANEY PUBLICATIONS 1643804
3 Woodfield Grove, NEWTOWNABBEY, BT37 0ZP
Tel: 028 9086 2777 **Fax:** 028 9086 5000
Titles:
MODERN MUM

LINE UP PUBLICATIONS LTD 13459
PO Box 208, Havant, HAMPSHIRE, PO9 9BQ
Tel: 0300 400 8427 **Fax:** 0870 762 1557
Email: publisher@lineup.biz
Web site: http://www.lineup.biz
Titles:
LINE UP

LINK2.MEDIA BUSINESS PUBLISHING LTD 1638396
16 Parker Court, Dyson Way, Staffordshire Technology,
STAFFORD, ST18 0WP **Tel:** 01785 330634
Fax: 0845 862 8639
Email: info@link2media.co.uk
Web site: http://www.link2media.co.uk
Titles:
BUILDING INNOVATIONS
THE ESSENTIAL BUILDING PRODUCT REVIEW
GO PUBLIC

LINK PUBLISHING 700341
1st Floor Offices, 27-31 Church Road, Lawrence Hill,
BRISTOL, BS5 9JJ **Tel:** 0117 954 7370 **Fax:** 0117 954 1476
Web site: http://www.linkpublishing.co.uk
Titles:
PRINT MONTHLY
SIGN-LINK

LIPPINCOTT WILLIAMS & WILKINS 17990
250 Waterloo Road, LONDON, SE1 8RD **Tel:** 020 7981 0600
Fax: 020 7981 0601
Web site: http://www.lww.com
Titles:
AIDS
ANTI-CANCER DRUGS
BLOOD PRESSURE MONITORING
CURRENT OPINION IN NEUROLOGY
EUROPEAN JOURNAL OF CARDIOVASCULAR
PREVENTION AND REHABILITATION
EUROPEAN JOURNAL OF GASTROENTEROLOGY &
HEPATOLOGY

THE LIST LTD 16985
14 High Street, EDINBURGH, EH1 1TE **Tel:** 0131 550 3050
Fax: 0131 557 8500
Web site: http://www.list.co.uk
Titles:
THE LIST

LITERARY REVIEW 693767
44 Lexington Street, LONDON, W1F 0LW
Tel: 020 7437 9392 **Fax:** 020 7734 1844
Email: editorial@literaryreview.co.uk
Web site: http://www.literaryreview.co.uk
Titles:
LITERARY REVIEW

LITTLE RED MARKETING LTD 1643354
Office 1, 40 Stockhill Road, BRADFORD, BD10 9AX
Tel: 01274 610101 **Fax:** 01274 633653
Titles:
FARMERS MART MAGAZINE
FENCING AND LANDSCAPING NEWS

THE LITTLE SHIP CLUB (MEMBERS) LTD 16075
Bell Wharf Lane, Upper Thames Street, LONDON, EC4R 3TB
Tel: 020 8480 1683
Titles:
THE LITTLE SHIP

LIVERPOOL CHARITY AND VOLUNTARY SERVICES 13403
151 Dale Street, LIVERPOOL, L2 2AH **Tel:** 0151 227 5177
Fax: 0151 237 3998
Email: link@lcvs.org.uk
Web site: http://www.lcvs.org.uk
Titles:
LIVERPOOL LINK

LIVERPOOL CITY COUNCIL 1685573
Municipal Buildings, Dale Street, LIVERPOOL, L69 2DH
Tel: 0151 233 3000
Web site: http://www.liverpool.gov.uk
Titles:
CITY

LIVERPOOL DAILY POST & ECHO LTD 14738
PO Box 48, Old Hall Street, LIVERPOOL, L69 3EB
Tel: 0151 227 2000 **Fax:** 0151 472 2474
Web site: http://www.icliverpool
Titles:
CROSBY HERALD & BOOTLE TIMES SERIES
Y DAILY POST CYMRAEG
THE EVERTONIAN
FORMBY TIMES
THE KOP
LDP BUSINESS
LIVERPOOL DAILY POST
LIVERPOOL ECHO
ORMSKIRK ADVERTISER SERIES
SOUTHPORT VISITER SERIES

LIVERPOOL STUDENT MEDIA 600542
PO Box 187, Guild of Students, Liverpool University, 160
Mount Pleasant, LIVERPOOL, L69 7BR **Tel:** 0151 794 4121
Fax: 0151 794 4174
Titles:
LIVERPOOL STUDENT

LIVERPOOL UNIVERSITY PRESS 13158
4 Cambridge Street, LIVERPOOL, L69 7ZU
Tel: 0151 794 2237 **Fax:** 0151 794 2235
Web site: http://www.liverpool-unipress.co.uk
Titles:
IDPR INTERNATIONAL DEVELOPMENT PLANNING
REVIEW
TPR TOWN PLANNING REVIEW

THE LIVING TRADITION LTD 18586
PO Box 1026, KILMARNOCK, KA2 0LG **Tel:** 01563 571220
Email: admin@livingtradition.co.uk
Web site: http://www.folkmusic.net
Titles:
THE LIVING TRADITION

LLOYD'S REGISTER-FAIRPLAY LTD 14409
3rd Floor, Lombard House, 3 Princess Way, REDHILL, RH1
1UP **Tel:** 01737 379000 **Fax:** 01737 379001
Web site: http://www.lrfairplay.com
Titles:
DPC
FAIRPLAY INTERNATIONAL SHIPPING WEEKLY
FAIRPLAY SOLUTIONS
PORTS & HARBORS

UK Publishers & Their Titles

SAFETY AT SEA INTERNATIONAL
WORLD SHIPPING DIRECTORY

LNA ASSOCIATES LTD   1640468
33 Donkin House, Galleywall Road, LONDON, SE16 3PQ
Tel: 07984 021973
Email: publishers@lnaassociates.com
Web site: http://www.lnaassociates.com
Titles:
   EXECUTIVE TRAVELLER

THE LOCAL GOVERNMENT ASSOCIATION   16659
Local Government House, Smith Square, LONDON, SW1P
3HZ **Tel:** 020 7664 3000 **Fax:** 020 7664 3250
Email: info@lga.gov.uk
Web site: http://www.lga.gov.uk
Titles:
   LOCAL GOVERNMENT FIRST

LOCAL GOVERNMENT INFORMATION UNIT   14203
22 Upper Woburn Place, LONDON, WC1H 0TB
Tel: 020 7554 2800 **Fax:** 020 7554 2801
Web site: http://www.lgiu.gov.uk
Titles:
   COUNCILLOR

THE LOCAL HISTORY PRESS LTD   16139
3 Devonshire Promenade, Lenton, NOTTINGHAM, NG7 2DS
Tel: 0115 970 6473
Email: editors@local-history.co.uk
Web site: http://www.local-history.co.uk
Titles:
   LOCAL HISTORY ONLINE

LOCAL LIVING LTD   1649549
PO Box 208, STAMFORD, PE9 9FY **Tel:** 01780 765571
Fax: 01780 765571
Email: localliving@btopenworld.com
Web site: http://www.locallivingltd.co.uk
Titles:
   ESSENTIAL LIVING
   STAMFORD LIVING

LOCAL PUBLICATIONS (SAFFRON WALDEN) LTD   14935
10 Emson Close, SAFFRON WALDEN, CB10 1HL
Tel: 01799 516161 **Fax:** 01799 520561
Titles:
   WALDEN LOCAL

LOCKWOOD PRESS LTD   14085
430-438 Market Towers, 1 Nine Elms Lane, New Covent
Garden, LONDON, SW8 5NN **Tel:** 020 7501 0300
Fax: 020 7720 2047
Web site: http://www.freshinfo.com
Titles:
   FRESH PRODUCE JOURNAL

LODGEMARK PRESS   15467
15 Moorfield Road, ORPINGTON, BR6 0XD
Tel: 01689 897123 **Fax:** 01689 890998
Titles:
   KARTING

LOEWY GROUP   14219
11 Southwark Street, LONDON, SE1 1RQ
Tel: 020 7798 2000
Email: enquire@loewygroup.com
Web site: http://www.loewygroup.com
Titles:
   SPE REVIEW

LOGISTICS BUSINESS MAGAZINE LTD   600429
The Anderson Centre, Unit D(A), Spitfire Close, Ermine
Business Park, HUNTINGDON, PE29 6XY
Tel: 01480 455660 **Fax:** 01480 455661
Titles:
   LOGISTICS BUSINESS IT
   LOGISTICS BUSINESS MAGAZINE

LOGISTICS BUSINESS PUBLISHING LTD   1759997
The Anderson Centre, Unit D (A), Spitfire Close, Ermine
Business Park, HUNTINGDON, PE29 6XY
Tel: 01480 455660 **Fax:** 01480 455661

Titles:
   TRANSPORT DISTRIBUTION EUROPE

LOLFA TAL-Y-BONT (ABERYSTWYTH)   1649377
Lolfa, Taly-Y-Bont, ABERYSTWYTH
Titles:
   YR ANGOR (ABERYSTWYTH)

THE LONDON ARCHAEOLOGIST ASSOCIATION   16140
46 Eagle Wharf Road, LONDON, N1 7ED **Tel:** 020 7566 9331
Fax: 020 7490 3955
Titles:
   LONDON ARCHAEOLOGIST

LONDON AT LARGE LTD   18481
Zenith House, 155 Curtain Road, LONDON, EC2A 3QY
Tel: 020 7613 2299 **Fax:** 020 7613 4492
Web site: http://www.londonatlarge.com
Titles:
   ADVANCE LIST
   FILM AND TV MONTHLY

THE LONDON BOROUGH OF CAMDEN   1630167
Room 303, Town Hall, Judd Street, LONDON, WC1H 9JE
Tel: 020 7974 6021 **Fax:** 020 7974 5718
Web site: http://www.camden.gov.uk
Titles:
   YOUR CAMDEN

LONDON BOROUGH OF HACKNEY   1638410
Comminications, 2 Hillman Street, LONDON, E8 1FB
Tel: 020 7356 3275 **Fax:** 020 8356 3118
Web site: http://www.hackney.gov.uk
Titles:
   HACKNEY TODAY

LONDON BOROUGH OF HILLINGDON   15541
Corporate Communications, 3 East/07, Civic Centre, High
Street, UXBRIDGE, UB8 1UW **Tel:** 01895 250828
Fax: 01895 277233
Web site: http://www.hillingdon.gov.uk
Titles:
   HILLINGDON PEOPLE

LONDON BOROUGH OF MERTON   1630323
Merton Civic Centre, London Road, MORDEN, SM4 5DX
Tel: 020 8545 3327 **Fax:** 020 8545 4054
Titles:
   MY MERTON

LONDON BOROUGH OF NEWHAM   18859
Newham Town Hall, East Ham, LONDON, E6 2RP
Tel: 020 8430 4533 **Fax:** 020 8430 1549
Web site: http://www.newham.gov.uk
Titles:
   THE NEWHAM MAG

LONDON CITY MISSION   18271
175 Tower Bridge Road, LONDON, SE1 2AH
Tel: 020 7407 7585 **Fax:** 020 7403 6711
Email: enquiries@lcm.org.uk
Web site: http://www.lcm.org.uk
Titles:
   CHANGING LONDON - LONDON CITY MISSION
   MAGAZINE

LONDON CORN CIRCULAR   16330
The Palace Hall, Darthill Road, MARCH, PE15 8HP
Tel: 07916 671194 **Fax:** 01733 560702
Titles:
   LONDON CORN CIRCULAR

LONDON COUNCILS   692552
59½ Southwark Street, LONDON, SE1 0AL
Tel: 020 7934 9715 **Fax:** 020 7934 9991
Email: info@alg.gov.org
Web site: http://londoncouncils.gov.uk
Titles:
   LONDON BULLETIN

LONDON CYCLING CAMPAIGN LTD   15432
2 Newhams Row, LONDON, SE1 3UZ **Tel:** 020 7234 9310
Fax: 020 7234 9319
Email: office@lcc.org.uk
Web site: http://www.lcc.org.uk
Titles:
   LONDON CYCLIST

LONDON ESSENCE MAGAZINE LTD   1731820
6 Forsyth Gardens, Kennington, LONDON, SE17 3NE
Tel: 020 3216 0039
Titles:
   LONDON ESSENCE MAGAZINE

LONDON FIELDS PUBLISHING LTD   697195
Unit 4, 25A Vyner Street, LONDON, E2 9DG
Tel: 020 8982 1987
Email: tim@societymedia.co.uk
Web site: http://www.societymedia.co.uk
Titles:
   SOCIAL ENTERPRISE

LONDON MACADAM LTD   1643742
Suite 239, 2 Old Brompton Road, LONDON, SW7 3DQ
Tel: 020 7602 2773 **Fax:** 020 7602 2527
Email: pub@londonmacadam.com
Web site: http://www.londonmacadam.com
Titles:
   LONDON MACADAM

**THE LONDON MAGAZINE & ASSOCIATED
PUBLICATIONS LTD**   1644680
32 Addison Grove, LONDON, W4 1ER **Tel:** 020 8400 5882
Fax: 020 8994 1713
Web site: http://www.thelondonmagazine.net
Titles:
   THE LONDON MAGAZINE

**LONDON METROPOLITAN UNIVERSITY STUDENTS'
UNION**   15741
2 Goulston Street, LONDON, E1 7TP **Tel:** 020 7320 2223
Fax: 020 7230 2223
Titles:
   ISM

THE LONDON MIDDLE EAST INSTITUTE   1724760
SOAS, University of London, Thornhaugh Street, Russell
Square, LONDON, WC1H 0XG **Tel:** 020 7898 4442
Fax: 020 7898 4329
Web site: http://www.lmei.soas.ac.uk
Titles:
   THE MIDDLE EAST IN LONDON

LONDON NET LIMITED   1638387
Hopping Wood Farm, Robin Hood Way, LONDON, SW20
0AB **Tel:** 020 8949 5363 **Fax:** 020 8949 5364
Email: sales@londonnet.co.uk
Web site: http://www.londonnet.co.uk
Titles:
   LONDONNET

LONDON ROAD MEDIA LIMITED   1762809
1C The Courtyard, Market Square, WESTERHAM, TN16 1AZ
Tel: 0845 290 3774
Titles:
   PROFESSIONAL DRIVER

**LONDON SCHOOL OF ECONOMICS STUDENTS' UNION
(LSE SU)**   15735
East Building, Houghton Street, LONDON, WC2A 2AE
Web site: http://www.lsesu.com
Titles:
   THE BEAVER

THE LONDON SOCIETY   17917
Mortimer Wheeler House, 46 Eagle Wharf Road, LONDON,
N1 7ED **Tel:** 020 7253 9400
Email: info@londonsociety.org.uk
Web site: http://www.londonsociety.org.uk
Titles:
   JOURNAL OF LONDON SOCIETY

LONDON VOICE PUBLISHING 1621341
11 Heather Close, LONDON, SW8 3BS **Tel:** 020 7720 4150
Fax: 020 7720 4150
Titles:
LONDON VOICE SERIES

LONDRA GAZETE LTD 16046
177 Green Lanes, Palmers Green, LONDON, N13 4UR
Tel: 020 8889 5025 **Fax:** 020 8889 5101
Email: news@londragazete.com
Web site: http://www.londragazete.com
Titles:
LONDRA GAZETE

LONSDALE PRESS 676906
Archbishop's House, Ambrosden Avenue, LONDON, SW1P
1QJ **Tel:** 020 7798 9055 **Fax:** 020 7798 9077
Titles:
WESTMINSTER YEAR BOOK

LOOP PUBLISHING LTD 1654702
43 Scotland Road, NELSON, BB9 7UT **Tel:** 01282 604387
Fax: 01282 604326
Email: studio@looppublishing.co.uk
Web site: http://www.looppublishing.co.uk
Titles:
NORTHERN LIFE KIDS
NORTHERN LIFE MAGAZINE
UNIQUE

LOOP PUBLISHING (UK) LTD 1752854
9 The Mill Courtyard, Copley Hill Business Park, Babraham,
CAMBRIDGE, CB22 3GN **Tel:** 01280 846786
Titles:
LIGHT AVIATION

LOUD & CLEAR PUBLISHING LTD 1741959
3 Brownlow Road, REDHILL, RH1 6AW **Tel:** 01737 769175
Fax: 01737 773241
Email: carolfulford@marinaworld.com
Titles:
MARINA WORLD

LOUGHBOROUGH STUDENTS' UNION 15774
Ashby Road, LOUGHBOROUGH, LE11 3TT
Tel: 01509 635000 **Fax:** 01509 635003
Titles:
LABEL

LRB LTD 15836
28 Little Russell Street, LONDON, WC1A 2HN
Tel: 020 7209 1101 **Fax:** 020 7209 1102
Web site: http://www.lrb.co.uk
Titles:
LONDON REVIEW OF BOOKS

LRD PUBLICATIONS LTD 13764
78 Blackfriars Road, LONDON, SE1 8HF **Tel:** 020 7902 9812
Fax: 020 7928 0621
Email: info@lrd.org.uk
Web site: http://www.lrd.org.uk
Titles:
LABOUR RESEARCH
WORKPLACE REPORT

LRE MEDIA LTD 1642389
40 Stapeley Avenue, EDINBURGH, EH7 6QP
Titles:
LAND ROVER ENTHUSIAST

LRTA PUBLISHING 1733897
PO BOX 26, Sawtry, CAMBRIDGESHIRE, PE285WY
Tel: 01487 830001 **Fax:** 01487 832001
Web site: http://www.lrta.org
Titles:
TRAMWAYS & URBAN TRANSIT

LSC PUBLISHING 1765430
Unit 11 La Gare, 51 Surrey Row, LONDON, SE1 0BZ
Titles:
MARYLEBONE JOURNAL

LSN MEDIA 14901
22 Mill Street, BEDFORD, MK40 3HD **Tel:** 01234 300888
Fax: 01234 308612
Titles:
BEDFORDSHIRE ON SUNDAY
LUTON & DUNSTABLE EXPRESS & NEWS SERIES
MK NEWS
NORTHANTS HERALD AND POST SERIES

LTP PUBLICATIONS 1763611
PR By email only **Tel:** 07879 012344
Titles:
LONDON PROPERTY

LUCKY3 PUBLISHERS 1735737
PO Box 487, WOOTTON, NN4 6XY **Tel:** 0844 800 2885
Fax: 01604 708515
Titles:
GOREZONE

LUXE PUBLISHING LTD 1684986
1st Floor, 11 Poland Street, LONDON, W1F 8QA
Tel: 020 7494 3211 **Fax:** 020 7494 3255
Titles:
LUXOS

THE LUXURY DIRECTORY LTD 1741275
Hillgarth, 2A Pump Hill, LOUGHTON, IG10 1RT
Tel: 020 8502 0801
Email: info@the-luxury-directory.com
Web site: http://www.the-luxury-directory.com
Titles:
LA DOLCE VITA

LVC LTD 1690490
26 York Street, LONDON, W1U 6PZ **Tel:** 020 7788 7547
Titles:
TW MAGAZINE
W1 MAGAZINE

LYCEUM PUBLISHING 1640249
5th Floor, 124 Victoria Street, LONDON, 1E 5LA
Tel: 020 7828 2244 **Fax:** 020 7828 2299
Titles:
IGAMING BUSINESS
ONLINECASINONEWS.COM

LYONSDOWN LTD 1744693
Dephna House, 24-26 Arcadia Avenue, LONDON, N3 2JU
Tel: 020 8349 7192 **Fax:** 020 8349 7193
Web site: http://www.lyonsdown.co.uk
Titles:
YOUR BABY

LYRICAL COMMUNICATIONS 1750273
Unit 7, Oakridge Office Park, Southampton Road, Whaddon,
SALISBURY, SP5 3HT **Tel:** 01722 711332
Email: emcmanus@lyricalcomms.com
Titles:
INBLOOM

M2 COMMUNICATIONS LTD 12198
Tel: 020 7047 0200
PR by email only **Tel:** 020 7047 0200
Web site: http://www.m2.com
Titles:
AIRLINE INDUSTRY INFORMATION
CORPORATE IT UPDATE
EQUITY BITES
INTERNET BUSINESS NEWS
M2PRESSWIRE
NORDIC BUSINESS REPORT
TELECOMWORLDWIRE
WORLDWIDE COMPUTER PRODUCTS NEWS

M A HEALTHCARE 1622514
St. Judes Church, Dulwich Road, LONDON, SE24 0PB
Tel: 020 7738 5454 **Fax:** 020 7733 2325
Web site: http://www.markallengroup.com
Titles:
BRITISH JOURNAL OF COMMUNITY NURSING
BRITISH JOURNAL OF HEALTHCARE MANAGEMENT
THE BRITISH JOURNAL OF HOSPITAL MEDICINE
BRITISH JOURNAL OF MIDWIFERY
BRITISH JOURNAL OF NURSING

INTERNATIONAL JOURNAL OF THERAPY AND
REHABILITATION
NURSEPRESCRIBING
NURSING AND RESIDENTIAL CARE
PRACTICE NURSING

MA EDUCATION LTD 1626583
St. Jude's Church, Dulwich Road, LONDON, SE24 0PB
Tel: 020 7738 5454 **Fax:** 020 7733 8174
Web site: http://www.markallengroup.co.uk
Titles:
5 TO 7 EDUCATOR
EYE
SECED

MA HEALTH CARE LTD 1638869
St. Judes Church, Dulwich Road, LONDON, SE24 0PB
Tel: 020 7738 5454 **Fax:** 020 7733 2325
Titles:
THE BRITISH JOURNAL OF HEALTHCARE ASSISTANTS
BRITISH JOURNAL OF SCHOOL NURSING
INTERNATIONAL JOURNAL OF PALLIATIVE NURSING

MA HEALTHCARE 676863
St. Jude's Church, Dulwich Road, LONDON, SE24 0PB
Tel: 020 7738 5454 **Fax:** 020 7978 8316
Titles:
EQUIPMENT SERVICES
JOURNAL OF WOUND CARE

MAD PUBLICATIONS LTD 1739872
Suites 1 & 7, Albion Mills, BRADFORD, BD10 9TQ
Tel: 01274 420091 **Fax:** 01274 347291
Email: editor@madpublications.co.uk
Titles:
HERE & NOW
THE LOCAL FOCAL

MADE PUBLISHING LTD 1740701
Mill 7, Mabgate Mill, LEEDS, LS9 7DZ **Tel:** 0113 244 3619
Fax: 0113 234 1555
Titles:
MADE IN LEEDS

MADE UP MEDIA 1740761
9 Arundel Mews, 13-18 Arundel Place, BRIGHTON, BN2
1GD **Tel:** 01273 819826 **Fax:** 01273 547029
Titles:
#5
CATFLAP

MAGAZINE DESIGN & PUBLISHING CO LTD 17986
PO Box 735, LONDON, SE26 5NQ **Tel:** 020 8778 0514
Fax: 020 8776 8260
Titles:
MASTER DETECTIVE
TRUE CRIME

THE MAGAZINE PEOPLE 1748871
14B Chapel Place, High Street, TUNBRIDGE WELLS, TN1
1YQ **Tel:** 01892 616103 **Fax:** 01892 513547
Titles:
SO TUNBRIDGE WELLS

MAGENTA PRESS LTD 1757791
45 Centurion House, Centurion Way, Leyland Business Park,
Farington, LEYLAND, PR25 3GR **Tel:** 01772 459418
Web site: http://www.healthcaretoday.org.uk
Titles:
FLYING START PARENTING MAGAZINE
HEALTHCARE TODAY

MAGEZINE PUBLISHING LTD. 676133
The Turbine, Shireoaks Triangle Business Park, Coach
Close, Shireoaks, WORKSOP, S81 8AP **Tel:** 01909 512111
Fax: 01909 512147
Email: info@magezinepublishing.co.uk
Web site: http://www.magezinepublishing.co.uk
Titles:
EPHOTOZINE

THE MAGHREB REVIEW 600527
45 Burton Street, LONDON, WC1H 9AL **Tel:** 020 7388 1840
Fax: 020 7388 1840

UK Publishers & Their Titles

Titles:
THE MAGHREB REVIEW

THE MAGIC CIRCLE 17978
5 Folkington Corner, Woodside Park, LONDON, N12 7BH
Tel: 020 8445 7607 **Fax:** 020 8445 7607

Titles:
THE MAGIC CIRCULAR (MAGAZINE)

MAGICALIA LTD 1759087
15-18 White Lion Street, Islington, LONDON, N1 9PD
Tel: 020 7843 8800 **Fax:** 020 7843 8999
Web site: http://www.magicalia.com

Titles:
AVREVIEW.CO.UK
BIKEMAGIC
FISHINGMAGIC
GOLFMAGIC
JUNIOR
JUNIOR PREGNANCY & BABY
OUTDOORSMAGIC
PRACTICAL PARENTING
ROADCYCLINGUK
THINKBABY.CO.UK
TWO WHEELS ONLY
VISORDOWN.COM

THE MAGISTRATES' ASSOCIATION 14322
28 Fitzroy Square, LONDON, W1T 6DD

Titles:
THE MAGISTRATE

MAGNA PUBLISHING CO. (UK) LTD 15342
PO Box 5095, LONDON, W1A 7WG **Tel:** 020 7486 8409

Titles:
STARDUST INTERNATIONAL

MAGNESIUM MEDIA LTD 1686882
Unit 1, Adlington Court, London Road, Adlington Park,
MACCLESFIELD, SK10 4NL **Tel:** 01625 855036
Fax: 01625 855039
Email: info@magnesiummedia.com
Web site: http://www.magnesiummedia.com

Titles:
PC TOOLS
PC UTILITIES
TIP STATION

MAGNET PUBLICATIONS 15600
18 Silver Oaks Farm, Waldron, HEATHFIELD, TN21 0RS
Tel: 0845 872 2885 **Fax:** 01435 810472

Titles:
MAGNET

MAGPIE PUBLICATIONS 15506
70 Winifred Lane, Aughton, ORMSKIRK, L39 5DL
Tel: 01695 423470 **Fax:** 01695 420185

Titles:
CARD TIMES

MAI PUBLICATIONS 14256
Revenue Chambers, St. Peters Street, HUDDERSFIELD,
HD1 1DL **Tel:** 01484 435011 **Fax:** 01484 422177
Web site: http://www.impactmoviemagazine.co.uk

Titles:
COMBAT AND SURVIVAL MAGAZINE
THE EQUESTRIAN LIFESTYLE MAGAZINE
IMPACT
IRELAND'S EQUESTRIAN

MAIL NEWS & MEDIA LTD 14840
Blundell's Corner, Beverley Road, HULL, HU3 1XS
Tel: 01482 327111 **Fax:** 01482 315353
Web site: http://www.thisishull.co.uk

Titles:
THE BUSINESS
HORNSEA & DISTRICT POST
HULL ADVERTISER SERIES
HULL DAILY MAIL
THE JOURNAL (HULL)
THE JOURNAL (LINCOLN)
SPORTHULL.CO.UK

MAIL PUBLICATIONS LTD 18642
2 Forge House, Bearsted Green Business Park, Bearsted,
MAIDSTONE, ME14 4DT **Tel:** 01622 630330
Fax: 01622 631131

Titles:
DOWNS MAIL SERIES

THE MAILOUT TRUST 15820
87 New Square, CHESTERFIELD, S40 1AH
Tel: 01246 207070 **Fax:** 01246 238319
Email: admin@e-mailout.org
Web site: http://www.e-mailout.org

Titles:
MAILOUT

MANAGEMENT-ISSUES.COM LTD 1680465
New Broad Street House, 35 New Broad Street, LONDON,
EC2M 1NH **Tel:** 020 7183 6000
Email: editor@management-issues.com
Web site: http://www.management-issues.com

Titles:
MANAGEMENT-ISSUES.COM

MANCHESTER EVENING NEWS LTD 12691
1 Scott Place, Hardman Street, MANCHESTER, M3 3RN
Tel: 0161 832 7200 **Fax:** 0161 831 7418
Email: newsdesk@men-news.co.uk
Web site: http://www.manchestereveningnews.co.uk

Titles:
JOBS NORTH WEST
MANCHESTER CITY MAGAZINE
MANCHESTER EVENING NEWS

MANCHESTER MEDIA LIMITED 1650277
Crown House, Trafford Park Road, Trafford Park,
MANCHESTER, M17 1HG **Tel:** 0161 848 9222
Fax: 0161 848 9444
Email: connect@manchester-media.com
Web site: http://www.manchester-media.com

Titles:
0161 MAGAZINE

MANCHESTER TEACHERS ASSOCIATION 17980
NUT Office, Rackhouse Primary School, Yarmouth Drive,
MANCHESTER, M23 0BT **Tel:** 0161 945 5061

Titles:
THE MANCHESTER TEACHER

MANEY PUBLISHING 624199
Dept of Cardiovascular Sciences, University of Leicester,
LEICESTER **Tel:** 0113 243 2800 **Fax:** 0113 386 8178
Email: maney@maney.co.uk
Web site: http://www.maney.co.uk

Titles:
CORROSION ENGINEERING, SCIENCE & TECHNOLOGY
FAMILY & COMMUNITY HISTORY JOURNAL
THE IMAGING SCIENCE JOURNAL
IRONMAKING AND STEELMAKING INCORPORATING
  STEEL WORLD
JOURNAL OF ORTHODONTICS
MATERIALS SCIENCE & TECHNOLOGY
PACKAGING, TRANSPORT, STORAGE AND SECURITY
  OF RADIOACTIVE MATERIAL
POWDER METALLURGY
PROGRESS IN PALLIATIVE CARE
SURFACE ENGINEERING
TRANSACTIONS OF THE INSTITUTE OF METAL
  FINISHING
ULTRASOUND

MANNING PUBLISHING LTD 13787
The Irwin Centre, Scotland Road, Dry Drayton,
CAMBRIDGE, CB23 8AR **Tel:** 01954 212906
Fax: 01954 212105
Email: info@manpublishing.co.uk

Titles:
CABINET MAKER
SOUTH CAMBS MAGAZINE

MAP MAGAZINE LTD 1745465
13 Perth Road, DUNDEE, DD1 4HT **Tel:** 01382 381018

Titles:
MAP

MARBLE MEDIA PUBLISHING LTD 1717716
4 Steine Street, BRIGHTON, BN2 1TE **Tel:** 0870 620 1360
Fax: 01273 676201

Titles:
3SIXTY
ONE80NEWS

MARCH PUBLISHING LTD 1685163
South Fens Conference Centre, Fenton Way, Chatteris,
CAMBRIDGESHIRE, PE16 6TT **Tel:** 01354 695599
Fax: 01354 651770
Email: info@internationaltradefocus.co.uk
Web site: http://www.marchpublishing.co.uk

Titles:
INTERNATIONAL TRADE FOCUS

THE MARINE CONSERVATION SOCIETY 14633
Unit 3, Wolf Business Park, ROSS-ON-WYE, HR9 5NB
Tel: 01989 566017 **Fax:** 01989 567815
Web site: http://www.mcsuk.org

Titles:
MARINE CONSERVATION

THE MARINE SOCIETY & SEA CADETS 18052
202 Lambeth Road, LONDON, SE1 7JW **Tel:** 020 7654 7000
Fax: 020 7928 8914

Titles:
SEAFARER

MARITIME BOOKS 15525
Lodge Hill, LISKEARD, PL14 4EL **Tel:** 01579 343663
Fax: 01579 346747

Titles:
WARSHIP WORLD

MARITIME INTELLIGENCE LTD 18581
Maritime Centre, F5 Northney Marina, HAYLING ISLAND,
PO11 0NH **Tel:** 023 9246 0111 **Fax:** 023 9246 0123
Email: editor@maritimecontracts.com
Web site: http://www.maritimecontracts.com

Titles:
MARITIME CONTRACTS JOURNAL

MARITIME MEDIA LTD 18614
The Diary House, Rickett Street, LONDON, SW6 1RU
Tel: 020 7386 6100
Web site: http://www.mar-media.com

Titles:
THE BALTIC
WORLD BUNKERING

MARK 1 PROMOTIONS 15424
77 Urbal Road, Coagh, COOKSTOWN, BT80 0DR
Tel: 028 7973 7170 **Fax:** 028 7973 7170

Titles:
IRISH BIKE

MARKET HOUSE PUBLISHING 17839
Market House, Market Place, ALSTON, CA9 3HS
Tel: 01434 382264
Email: info@markethouse.info
Web site: http://www.markethouse.info

Titles:
IN-THE-STICKS

MARKET INTELLIGENCE LTD 14083
1 Nine Elms Lane, LONDON, SW8 5NQ **Tel:** 020 7501 3700
Fax: 020 7498 6472
Email: info@fruitnet.com
Web site: http://www.fruitnet.com

Titles:
AMERICAFRUIT MAGAZINE
ASIAFRUIT MAGAZINE
EUROFRUIT MAGAZINE

THE MARKET RESEARCH SOCIETY 12187
15 Northburgh Street, LONDON, EC1V 0JR
Tel: 020 7490 4911 **Fax:** 020 7490 0608

Titles:
RESEARCH

MARKET SCOPE EUROPE LTD 16498
6 Torcross Grove, Calcot, READING, RG31 7AT
Tel: 0118 941 7539 **Fax:** 0118 942 0014

Titles:
CROP PROTECTION MONTHLY

MARKETING COMMUNICATIONS MEDIA LTD 1639905
PO Box 881, WOKING, GU22 7ZN **Tel:** 01483 715539
Fax: 01483 755447
Titles:
   WORLD ENERGY REVIEW

THE MARKETING GUILD 13432
Regency House, Westminster Place, York Business Park,
YORK, YO26 6RW **Tel:** 01904 520820
Titles:
   STRATEGIC MARKETING

MARKETING SUPPORT SERVICES 17360
5 Paxford Close, REDDITCH, B98 8RH **Tel:** 01527 660940
Fax: 01527 660940
Email: mss@goldmine.cix.co.uk
Titles:
   MINING TIMES

MARKETLETTER (PUBLICATIONS) LTD 14239
Appleton House, 139 King Street, LONDON, W6 9JG
Tel: 020 8735 6625 **Fax:** 020 8735 6688
Titles:
   NUTRACEUTICALS INTERNATIONAL
   PHARMA MARKETLETTER

MARKETSKIL LTD 13697
54 Crockhamwell Road, Woodley, READING, RG5 3LB
Tel: 0118 969 5008
Email: jack@laundryandcleaningtoday.net
Titles:
   LAUNDRY & CLEANING TODAY

MARKETTIERS4DC PUBLISHING 13454
Northburgh House, 10A Northburgh Street, LONDON, EC1V
0AT **Tel:** 020 7253 8888 **Fax:** 020 7253 8885
Email: info@markettiers4dc.com
Web site: http://www.markettiers4dc.com
Titles:
   QSHEET

MARMALADYA LTD 1731703
65A Aylesford Street, LONDON, SW1V 3RJ
Tel: 020 7834 0330
Titles:
   MARMALADYA.COM

MARSHWOOD VALE LTD 1627188
Lower Atrim, BRIDPORT, DT6 5PX **Tel:** 01308 423031
Email: info@marshwoodvale.com
Web site: http://www.marshwoodvale.com
Titles:
   THE MARSHWOOD VALE MAGAZINE

MARSTON CONSULTING LTD TA DIRECTOR-E.COM
622979
South House 3A, Suite 4, Bond Estate, Bond Avenue,
Bletchley, MILTON KEYNES, MK1 1SW **Tel:** 0870 870 4578
Fax: 0870 870 4679
Email: hannah@director-e.com
Web site: http://www.director-e.com
Titles:
   CORPORATE CLOTHING DIRECTOR-E
   FABRICDIRECTOR-E

MARTEC INTERNATIONAL LTD 622125
Martec House, 40 High Street, TAUNTON, TA1 3PN
Tel: 01823 333469 **Fax:** 01823 332423
Email: info@martec-international.com
Web site: http://www.martec-international.com
Titles:
   RETAIL DIRECTIONS

MARTIAL ARTS LTD 15319
Revenue Chambers, St. Peter's Street, HUDDERSFIELD,
HD1 1DL **Tel:** 01484 435011 **Fax:** 01484 422177
Email: martialartsltd@btconnect.com
Web site: http://www.martialartsltd.co.uk
Titles:
   MARTIAL ARTS ILLUSTRATED

MARTIAL ARTS PUBLICATIONS LTD 15322
Unit 20, Maybrook Business Park, Maybrook Road, Sutton
Coldfield, BIRMINGHAM, B76 1BE **Tel:** 0121 344 3737
Fax: 0121 356 7300
Email: karate@martialartsinprint.com
Web site: http://www.karatemag.co.uk
Titles:
   COMBAT MARTIAL ARTS MAGAZINE
   FIGHTERS & KICK BOXING NEWS
   TAEKWONDO & KOREAN MARTIAL ARTS MAGAZINE
   TRADITIONAL KARATE

MARTIN AUSTEN PUBLISHING LTD 1686132
Woodlands Annexe, 79 High Street, GREENHITHE, DA9 9RD
Tel: 01322 387555 **Fax:** 01322 385444
Web site: http://www.martinaustenpublishing.co.uk
Titles:
   COMMERCIAL PROPERTY REGISTER

MARYVALE INSTITUTE 625388
Maryvale House, Old Oscott Hill, BIRMINGHAM, B44 9AG
Tel: 0121 360 8118 **Fax:** 0121 366 6786
Titles:
   THE SOWER

MASH MEDIA 624454
Faraday House, 39 Thornton Road, Wimbledon, LONDON,
SW19 4NQ **Tel:** 020 8971 8282 **Fax:** 020 8971 8283
Web site: http://www.mashmedia.net
Titles:
   C+MW
   CONFERENCE NEWS
   EXHIBITING
   EXHIBITION BULLETIN
   EXHIBITION NEWS

THE MASTER LOCKSMITHS ASSOCIATION 14463
5D Great Central Way, Woodford Halse, DAVENTRY, NN11
3PZ **Tel:** 01327 262255 **Fax:** 01327 262539
Titles:
   KEYWAYS

MATCHMAKER INTERNATIONAL LTD 17872
PO Box 430, PINNER, HA5 2TW **Tel:** 020 8868 1879
Web site: http://www.perfect-partner.com
Titles:
   M.I.L. MATCHMAKER

THE MATHEMATICAL ASSOCIATION 17864
259 London Road, LEICESTER, LE2 3BE **Tel:** 0116 221 0013
Fax: 0116 212 2835
Email: office@m-a.org.uk
Web site: http://www.m-a.org.uk
Titles:
   THE MATHEMATICAL GAZETTE
   MATHEMATICAL PIE
   MATHEMATICS IN SCHOOL
   PRIMARY MATHEMATICS

MATRIX PRINT 1746011
11 Desborough Road, Rothwell, KETTERING, NN14 6JG
Tel: 01536 713811 **Fax:** 01536 711463
Email: gary@matrixprint.com
Titles:
   THE LIGHTING JOURNAL

MATT PUBLISHING 17281
7 Unity Street, BRISTOL, BS1 5HH **Tel:** 0117 930 0255
Titles:
   DNJ ONLINE
   HARDCOPY

MAURITIUS PUBLISHERS CO LTD 16994
583 Wandsworth Road, LONDON, SW8 3JD
Tel: 020 7498 3066 **Fax:** 020 7498 3066
Titles:
   MAURITIUS NEWS

MAX PUBLISHING LTD 14438
United House, North Road, LONDON, N7 9DP
Tel: 020 7700 6740 **Fax:** 020 7607 6411
Titles:
   PROGRESSIVE GIFTS & HOME WORLDWIDE
   PROGRESSIVE GREETINGS WORLDWIDE
   PROGRESSIVE HOUSEWARES
   PROGRESSIVE PARTY

MAXIMVS 698958
1st Floor, 70 Newcomen Street, LONDON, SE1 1YT
Tel: 020 7940 4801 **Fax:** 020 7940 4843
Titles:
   PAYROLL WORLD

MAYDEN HEALTH 1761868
Manor Farm Stables, Biddestone, CHIPPENHAM, SN14 7DH
Tel: 01249 701100 **Fax:** 01249 715785
Titles:
   HC2D

MAYER HOUSE BUSINESS MEDIA LIMITED 1735126
Mayer House, 70 Collington Avenue, BEXHILL-ON-SEA,
TN39 3RA **Tel:** 01424 217888 **Fax:** 01424 211005
Web site: http://www.mayerhousebusinessmedia.co.uk
Titles:
   PRINTWEAR TODAY

THE MAYHEW ANIMAL HOME 17379
Trenmar Gardens, Kensal Green, LONDON, NW10 6BJ
Tel: 020 8969 7110 **Fax:** 020 8964 3221
Email: info@mayhewanimalhome.org
Web site: http://www.mayhewanimalhome.org
Titles:
   THE MAYHEW

MAYO MEDIA LTD 671976
Caddsdown Business Centre, Caddsdown Industrial Park,
Clovelly Road, BIDEFORD, EX39 3DX **Tel:** 01237 422660
Fax: 01237 422661
Email: admin@dealernews.co.uk
Titles:
   BRITISH DEALER NEWS

MAYVILLE PUBLISHING CO LTD 14073
219 West Ella Road, West Ella, HULL, HU10 7SD
Tel: 01482 659396 **Fax:** 01482 659397
Email: info@mayvillepublishing.co.uk
Titles:
   THE STOCKLISTS WITH FLOORING NEWS

MAZE MEDIA (2000) LTD 12585
21-23 Phoenix Court, Hawkins Road, COLCHESTER, CO2
8JY **Tel:** 01206 505915 **Fax:** 01206 505915
Titles:
   DISABILITY PRODUCT NEWS
   PROM
   SHOOTING SPORTS
   TEACH PRIMARY!

MB MEDIA LTD 676862
Alexander House, Forehill, ELY, CB7 4ZA **Tel:** 01353 665577
Fax: 01353 662489
Email: info@mbmediagroup.co.uk
Titles:
   DRUMMER
   GUITAR BUYER

MBO 700226
Langton Road, Langton Green, TUNBRIDGE WELLS, TN3
0EG **Tel:** 01892 860925 **Fax:** 01892 861363
Web site: http://www.mercedesclub.org.uk
Titles:
   MERCEDES OWNER

MC PUBLISHING LTD 1605939
25 Milsom Street, BATH, BA1 1DG **Tel:** 01225 424499
Fax: 01225 426677
Titles:
   THE BATH MAGAZINE
   THE BRISTOL MAGAZINE

MCCLELLAND PUBLISHING 13536
Deansgate Mews, 253 Deansgate, MANCHESTER, M3 4EN
Tel: 0161 950 4500 **Fax:** 0161 834 3344
Email: info@sustainmagazine.com
Web site: http://www.sustainmagazine.com
Titles:
   SUSTAIN

THE MCCLOSKEY GROUP LTD 600258
Unit 6, Rotherbrook Court, Bedford Road, PETERSFIELD,
GU32 3QG **Tel:** 01730 265095 **Fax:** 01730 260044
Email: marketing@mccloskeycoal.com
Web site: http://www.mccloskeycoal.com
Titles:
MCCLOSKEY'S COAL REPORT
MCCLOSKEY'S COAL UK
MCCLOSKEY'S STEAM COAL FORECASTER
MCCLOSKEY'S UK POWERFOCUS

MCDERMOTT PUBLISHING LTD 13493
McDermott Chambers, 2 The Green, Kings Norton,
BIRMINGHAM, B38 8SD **Tel:** 0121 451 3037
Fax: 0121 433 3082
Web site: http://www.mcdermottpublishing.com
Titles:
THE BUILDER
DABS

THE MCGRAW-HILL COMPANIES 17176
Shoppenhangers Road, MAIDENHEAD, SL6 2QL
Tel: 01628 502500 **Fax:** 01628 770224
Titles:
AVIATION WEEK & SPACE TECHNOLOGY
BUSINESSWEEK
EUROPEAN POWER DAILY
PLATTS OILGRAM NEWS

MCKENZIE PUBLISHING LTD 15279
Longhouse, 460 Bath Road, Longford, WEST DRAYTON,
UB7 0EB **Tel:** 01753 775511 **Fax:** 01753 775512
Titles:
THE SQUASH PLAYER
THE SQUASH PLAYER - ENGLAND SQUASH PLAYER
EDITION

MCKINNEY MEDIA 1739303
Suite 2.1B, The Old Fire Station, 140 Tabernacle Street,
LONDON, EC2A 4SD **Tel:** 020 7300 7333
Titles:
UTALKMARKETING

MDM PUBLISHING LTD 641655
The Abbey Manor Business Centre, The Abbey, Preston
Road, YEOVIL, BA20 2EN **Tel:** 01935 426428
Fax: 01935 426926
Web site: http://www.mdmpublishing.com
Titles:
APF ASIA PACIFIC FIRE
INTERNATIONAL FIRE FIGHTER
INTERNATIONAL FIRE PROTECTION

MDS STUDIO LTD 1732461
3 New Burlington Place, LONDON, W1S 2HR
Tel: 020 7851 0828
Titles:
THE BROADCASTER'S BULLETIN

ME MEDIA LTD 1621113
Eton House, 66 Eton Avenue, WEMBLEY, HA0 3AU
Tel: 0845 013 8401
Titles:
CLICKWALLA.COM
DIWALI UK
EID UK
VAISAKHI UK

ME PUBLISHING 700406
6 Kendal Court, Railway Road, NEWHAVEN, BN9 0AY
Tel: 01273 616040 **Fax:** 01273 516333
Titles:
MOTORCYCLE TRADER
QUAD

MEANS OF ESCAPE PUBLICATIONS LTD 1712155
Wins House, Bentalls, Pipps Hill Industrial Estate,
BASILDON, SS14 3BS **Tel:** 01268 242340
Fax: 01268 284046
Email: info@means-of-escape.com
Web site: http://www.means-of-escape.com
Titles:
MEANS OF ESCAPE

MEDALYER PUBLIC RELATIONS 1747720
Elizabeth House, 39 York Road, LONDON, SE1 7NQ
Titles:
NEW ENERGY FOCUS

MEDIA 10 1622039
National House, 121-123 High Street, EPPING, CM16 4BD
Tel: 01992 570030 **Fax:** 01992 570031
Web site: http://www.onofficemagazine.com
Titles:
GRAND DESIGNS
ICON
M MAGAZINE
ONOFFICE
SELFBUILDER

MEDIA 247 1744855
PR by email only **Tel:** 07852 334711
Titles:
BIZASIA.CO.UK

MEDIA ANALYTICS LTD 1654271
The Jam Factory, 27 Park End Street, OXFORD, OX1 1HU
Tel: 01865 204208 **Fax:** 01865 204209
Titles:
GLOBAL WATER INTELLIGENCE

MEDIA CLASH 1627035
Circus Mews House, Circus Mews, BATH, BA1 2PW
Tel: 01225 475800 **Fax:** 01225 475801
Email: info@mediaclash.co.uk
Web site: http://www.mediaclash.co.uk
Titles:
BATH LIFE
CARDIFF LIFE
CLIFTON LIFE
EXETER LIVING
SALISBURY LIFE

THE MEDIA COMPANY 694503
21 Royal Circus, EDINBURGH, EH3 6TL **Tel:** 0131 226 7766
Fax: 0131 225 4567
Titles:
LIVING ABROAD
SPAIN MAGAZINE

MEDIA CORPORATION PLC 1748368
77 Queen Victoria Street, LONDON, EC4V 4AY
Tel: 020 7618 9000 **Fax:** 020 7618 9001
Titles:
SPORT.CO.UK

MEDIA GENERATION EVENTS LTD 1603081
34 Ellerker Gardens, RICHMOND, TW10 6AA
Tel: 020 8241 1912 **Fax:** 020 8940 6211
Email: info@all-energy.co.uk
Web site: http://www.all-energy.co.uk
Titles:
NEWS@ALL-ENERGY

MEDIA MAD 1735473
Host Media Centre, Savile Mount, LEEDS, LS7 3HZ
Tel: 0845 052 2911 **Fax:** 0845 052 2912
Web site: http://www.media-mad.co.uk
Titles:
HOSPITALITY & EVENTS NORTH
J LIFE

MEDIA MAKER PUBLISHING LTD 1641749
The Studio, 64 Old Station Road, NEWMARKET, CB8 8AA
Tel: 01638 751300 **Fax:** 01638 601937
Email: info@definitionmagazine.com
Web site: http://www.definitionmagazine.com
Titles:
HIGH DEFINITION

MEDIA MANAGEMENT CORPORATION LTD 1733905
21A-23A Dudden Hill Lane, LONDON, NW10 2ET
Tel: 0870 766 2715
Titles:
THE BARRISTER

MEDIA ON SCREEN 1649579
Unit 2, The Old School, Church Street, BIGGLESWADE,
SG18 0JS **Tel:** 01767 601040
Titles:
EROTIC TRADE ONLY

MEDIA ONE COMMUNICATIONS LTD. 17267
4th Floor, Geneva House, Park Road, PETERBOROUGH,
PE1 2UX **Tel:** 01733 756555 **Fax:** 01733 760505
Web site: http://www.onecoms.co.uk
Titles:
ARCHITECTS CHOICE
BRITISH BUILDER & DEVELOPER
COMMERCIAL INTERIORS
DEPARTMENT STORE BUYER
FMCG NEWS
GARDEN AND HARDWARE NEWS
GIFTS AND HOUSEWARES MAGAZINE
INTERIOR DESIGN TODAY
PACKAGING GAZETTE

MEDIA PUBLISHING 12653
Media House, 48 High Street, SWANLEY, BR8 8BQ
Tel: 01322 660434 **Fax:** 01322 666539
Web site: http://www.mediapublishingcompany.com
Titles:
AMBULANCE UK
EMERGENCY & URGENT CARE TODAY
GASTROENTEROLOGY TODAY
TODAY'S ANAESTHETIST

MEDIA SOUTH 15597
1A Theaklen Drive, Ponswood Industrial Estate, ST.
LEONARDS-ON-SEA, TN38 9AZ **Tel:** 01424 201696
Fax: 01424 201696
Titles:
ASPECT COUNTY

MEDIA TODAY SOUTH LTD 1649586
Trinity House, Trinity Street, LEAMINGTON SPA, CV32 5YN
Tel: 0845 179 9001 **Fax:** 0845 179 9003
Titles:
BUSINESS TODAY

MEDIA WALES LTD 12825
6 Park Street, CARDIFF, CF10 1XR **Tel:** 029 2022 3333
Fax: 029 2058 3416
Web site: http://www.walesonline.co.uk
Titles:
BUSINESS IN WALES
CARDIFF POST SERIES
CAREER TRACK
CONFERENCE WALES
CYNON VALLEY LEADER
FORWARD WALES
ICWALES.CO.UK
NEATH GUARDIAN SERIES
RHONDDA LEADER
SOUTH WALES ECHO
WALES ON SUNDAY
WESTERN MAIL (CARDIFF)
WM
WM BRIDE
WM HOME

MEDIA WEST 2001 LTD 14697
10-12 Queens Road, Portishead, BRISTOL, BS20 8HT
Tel: 01275 845846 **Fax:** 01275 817585
Titles:
BRISTOL SECRETARY
THAMES VALLEY SECRETARY

MEDIA WORLD LTD 16728
Upper Floor, Finnieston House, 1 Stables Yard, 1103 Argyle
Street, GLASGOW, G3 8ND **Tel:** 0141 221 6965
Fax: 0141 221 6561
Titles:
DRAM - DRINKS RETAILING & MARKETING
REPERTOIRE

MEDIA WORLD SERVICES LTD 16030
25-27 Mossop Street, LONDON, SW3 2LY
Tel: 020 7052 9600 **Fax:** 020 7052 9609
Titles:
AL MUSHAHID ASSIYASI

MEDIADIRECT　1621478
2 The Laurels, BASINGSTOKE, RG21 4JP
Tel: 01256 817063
Titles:
　DYINGTOTELL.CO.UK

MEDIAHUSET　600526
86 Overdale, ASHTEAD, KT21 1PU **Tel:** 01372 271692
Fax: 01372 817737
Web site: http://www.mediahuset.se
Titles:
　DIRECTORY OF CARDIOLOGY
　DIRECTORY OF GASTROENTEROLOGY

MEDIAMARK LTD　13089
Studio 111, Finsbury Business Centre, 40 Bowling Green
Lane, LONDON, EC1R 0NE **Tel:** 020 7415 7100
Email: info@mediamark.co.uk
Web site: http://www.mediamark.co.uk
Titles:
　HIGHFLYERS
　OPTIMUM NUTRITION
　TRUST

MEDIASTORM PUBLISHING　1718695
Suite 3, Newspaper House, Brook Street, LEEK, ST13 5JE
Tel: 01538 384400 **Fax:** 01538 384777
Web site: http://www.m-storm.co.uk
Titles:
　EDUC8 MAGAZINE

MEDICAL COMMUNICATIONS LTD　18732
10 Dargan Crescent, Duncrue Industrial Estate, BELFAST,
BT3 9JP **Tel:** 028 9080 9090 **Fax:** 028 9080 9097
Titles:
　NORTHERN IRELAND MEDICAL REVIEW/LONDON
　　CHEMIST REVIEW
　SCOTTISH CHEMIST REVIEW
　ULSTER CHEMIST REVIEW

MEDICAL FUTURES　1622359
The Royal Institution of Great Britain, 21 Albemarle Street,
LONDON, W1S 4BS **Tel:** 0844 870 0056 **Fax:** 0844 870 0057
Email: mail@medicalfutures.co.uk
Web site: http://www.medicalfutures.co.uk
Titles:
　MEDICAL FUTURES

MEDICAL INDEMNITY REGISTER　16442
PO Box 44375, LONDON, SW19 8WA **Tel:** 020 8739 0066
Fax: 020 8739 0077
Titles:
　MIR NEWS

THE MEDICINE PUBLISHING COMPANY　17299
The Boulevard, Langford Lane, KIDLINGTON, OX5 1GB
Tel: 01235 542800 **Fax:** 01235 554692
Web site: http://www.medicinepublishing.co.uk
Titles:
　MEDICINE
　SURGERY

MEDILEXICON INTERNATIONAL　1760025
PO Box 193, BEXHILL-ON-SEA, TN40 9BA
Tel: 0161 408 2546 **Fax:** 0161 332 8215
Email: peter@medilexicon.com
Web site: http://www.medicalnewstoday.com
Titles:
　MEDICAL NEWS TODAY

MEDINEWS CARDIOLOGY LTD.　600801
9 Langton Street, LONDON, SW10 0JL **Tel:** 020 7823 3315
Fax: 020 8785 4603
Web site: http://www.bjcardio.co.uk
Titles:
　BRITISH JOURNAL OF CARDIOLOGY

MEDPRESS　16323
1 Canada Square, Canary Wharf, LONDON, E14 5AP
Tel: 020 7772 8466 **Fax:** 020 7772 8597
Email: peter.sayer@oceanmedia.co.uk
Web site: http://www.gerimed.co.uk
Titles:
　G M JOURNAL

MEDWAY COUNCIL　1640118
Gun Wharf, Dock Road, CHATHAM, ME4 4TR
Tel: 01634 332782 **Fax:** 01634 332743
Web site: http://www.medway.gov.uk
Titles:
　MEDWAY MATTERS

MEEJA　1650059
3rd Floor, 102 Dean Street, LONDON, W1D 3TQ
Tel: 020 7631 0644
Titles:
　DIGITAL-LIFESTYLES.INFO

THE MEETINGS FORUM　13426
29A Market Square, BIGGLESWADE, SG18 8AQ
Tel: 01767 316255 **Fax:** 01767 316430
Titles:
　CONFERENCE VENUE MARKETPLACE
　CORPORATE HOSPITALITY AND PARTY UPDATE
　EVENT ORGANISERS UPDATE
　MEETINGS FILE

MEKO LTD　677151
1 Blackdown Road, Deepcut, CAMBERLEY, GU16 6SH
Tel: 01252 835385 **Fax:** 01252 838621
Email: news@meko.co.uk
Web site: http://www.meko.co.uk
Titles:
　DISPLAY MONITOR

MELCRUM PUBLISHING LTD　17135
322B King Street, LONDON, W6 0AX **Tel:** 020 8600 4670
Fax: 020 8741 9975
Email: info@melcrum.com
Web site: http://www.melcrum.com
Titles:
　THE INTERNAL COMMS HUB
　KNOWLEDGE MANAGEMENT REVIEW
　STRATEGIC COMMUNICATION MANAGEMENT

MELLOR MEDIA LTD　1764809
West Hill House, West Hill, DARTFORD, DA1 2EU
Titles:
　BUSINESS NORTH WEST MAGAZINE

MEN MEDIA　624595
1 Scott Place, MANCHESTER, M3 3RN **Tel:** 0161 832 7200
Fax: 0161 342 2997
Titles:
　ACCRINGTON OBSERVER
　ADVERTISER SERIES (ASHTON)
　HEYWOOD ADVERTISER
　MACCLESFIELD EXPRESS AND TIMES SERIES
　MIDDLETON & NORTH MANCHESTER GUARDIAN &
　　ADVERTISER SERIES
　THE OLDHAM ADVERTISER
　ROCHDALE OBSERVER SERIES
　ROSSENDALE FREE PRESS
　SALFORD ADVERTISER SERIES
　SOUTH MANCHESTER REPORTER
　STOCKPORT EXPRESS AND TIMES SERIES
　TRAFFORD METRO NEWS
　URBAN LIFE
　WILMSLOW EXPRESS

MENCAP　12648
123 Golden Lane, LONDON, EC1Y 0RT **Tel:** 020 7696 5599
Fax: 020 7696 6930
Email: viewpoint@mencap.org.uk
Web site: http://www.mencap.org.uk
Titles:
　VIEWPOINT

MENDIP TIMES LTD　1739512
Coombe Lodge, Bourne Lane, Blagdon, BRISTOL, BS40
7RG **Tel:** 01761 463888 **Fax:** 01761 463890
Email: news@mendiptimes.co.uk
Web site: http://mendiptimes.co.uk
Titles:
　THE MENDIP TIMES

MEN'S HEALTH FORUM　1638768
32-36 Loman Street, LONDON, SE1 0EH **Tel:** 020 7922 7908
Web site: http://www.menshealthforum.org.uk
Titles:
　MALEHEALTH
　MEN'S HEALTH FORUM

MERCATOR MEDIA LTD　14330
The Old Mill, Lower Quay, FAREHAM, PO16 0RA
Tel: 01329 825335 **Fax:** 01329 825330
Web site: http://www.mercatormedia.com
Titles:
　BOATING BUSINESS
　ENGINEERING CAPACITY
　MARITIME JOURNAL
　THE MOTOR SHIP
　NAVIGATION NEWS
　PORT STRATEGY
　WORLD FISHING MAGAZINE

MERCEDES-BENZ(UK) LTD　17050
Mercedes-Benz Centre, Tongwell, MILTON KEYNES, MK15
8BA **Tel:** 01908 245000 **Fax:** 01908 245096
Titles:
　MERCEDESMAGAZINE

MERGE MAGAZINE LTD　1684825
3rd Floor, 27 Old Compton Street, LONDON, W1D 5JP
Tel: 020 7494 4550 **Fax:** 020 7494 2918
Titles:
　MERGE MAGAZINE

MERIDIAN LINE PUBLISHING LTD　16928
8 The Village, Charlton, LONDON, SE7 8UD
Tel: 020 8319 0555 **Fax:** 020 8319 4555
Titles:
　MERIDIAN MAGAZINE

MERIT PUBLICATIONS LTD　1748034
1 Paradise Square, SHEFFIELD, S1 2DE **Tel:** 0114 275 8840
Titles:
　PURE BUXTON

MERRICKS PUBLISHING LTD　622661
Wessex Buildings, Somerton Business Park, Bancombe
Road, SOMERTON, TA11 6SB **Tel:** 01458 274447
Fax: 01458 274059
Email: info@merricksmedia.com
Titles:
　HOLIDAY COTTAGES MAGAZINE
　HOLIDAY VILLAS MAGAZINE

MERSEA ISLAND COMMUNICATIONS　698305
46 High Street, West Mersea, COLCHESTER, CO5 8QA
Tel: 01206 382935
Email: infomic@btconnect.com
Titles:
　THE TRIBUNE & COURIER SERIES

MERSEY MIRROR　16927
36 Henry Street, LIVERPOOL, L1 5BS **Tel:** 0151 236 2426
Fax: 0151 236 2216
Titles:
　CATHOLIC PICTORIAL
　THE CHALLENGE

METAL BULLETIN PLC　13360
Nestor House, Playhouse Yard, LONDON, EC4V 5EX
Tel: 020 7827 9977 **Fax:** 020 7928 6539
Web site: http://www.metalbulletin.com
Titles:
　BASE METALS MONTHLY
　INDMIN.COM

METHOD PUBLISHING　14261
Sutherland Press House, Main Street, GOLSPIE, KW10 6RA
Tel: 01408 633871 **Fax:** 01408 633876
Web site: http://www.methodpublishing.co.uk
Titles:
　AFF JOURNAL
　ROYAL ARMY DENTAL CORPS BULLETIN
　THE THIN RED LINE

METHOD UK LTD　1753099
6 Graphite Square, Vauxhall Walk, LONDON, SE11 5EE
Tel: 020 7091 0922
Web site: http://www.thisismethod.co.uk
Titles:
　MANAGER - THE INSTITUTE OF ADMINISTRATIVE
　　MANAGEMENT

UK Publishers & Their Titles

METHODIST NEWSPAPER CO. LTD. 15893
122 Golden Lane, LONDON, EC1Y 0TL **Tel:** 020 7251 8414
Fax: 020 7608 3490
Titles:
METHODIST RECORDER

METROCREST LTD 16102
2 Harcourt Way, Meridian Business Park, Braunstone Town,
LEICESTER, LE19 1WP **Tel:** 0116 289 4567
Fax: 0116 289 4889
Titles:
COARSE FISHERMAN

METROPOLIS INTERNATIONAL GROUP LTD 1739511
6th Floor, Davis House, 2 Robert Street, CROYDON, CR0
1QQ **Tel:** 020 8253 8604 **Fax:** 020 2253 4603
Web site: http://www.metropolis.co.uk
Titles:
BUILDING PRODUCTS
DUTY FREE NEWS INTERNATIONAL
FRONTIER
INDEPENDENT RETAIL NEWS
LABORATORY NEWS
THE LANDSCAPER
MORTGAGE FINANCE GAZETTE
MOTOR TRADER
PERSONAL FINANCE & SAVINGS
TALKINGRETAIL.COM
TRAVEL RETAILER INTERNATIONAL INC.TAX FREE
TRADER
WHAT MORTGAGE

METROPOLIS INTERNATIONAL (UK) LIMITED 16201
140 Wales Farm Road, LONDON, W3 6UG
Tel: 020 8752 8181 **Fax:** 020 8752 8185
Email: metropolis@metropolis.co.uk
Web site: http://www.metropolis.co.uk
Titles:
FRONTIER BRANDS
THE TRADER

METROPRESS LTD. 13658
115 Shaftesbury Avenue, LONDON, WC2H 8AD
Tel: 020 7420 6600 **Fax:** 020 7420 6605
Titles:
ANTIQUES TRADE GAZETTE
ANTIQUES TRADE GAZETTE

MG CAR CLUB LTD 15458
Kimber House, PO Box 251, ABINGDON, OX14 1FF
Tel: 01235 555552 **Fax:** 01235 533755
Email: mgcc@mgcc.co.uk
Web site: http://www.mgcc.co.uk
Titles:
SAFETY FAST!

MG OWNERS CLUB 15437
Octagon House, Swavesey, CAMBRIDGE, CB24 4QZ
Tel: 01954 231125 **Fax:** 01954 232106
Email: mgmagazine@mgownersclub.co.uk
Web site: http://www.mgownersclub.co.uk
Titles:
ENJOYING MG

MH MEDIA INTERACTIVE LTD 1751605
Redfern House, 347 Margate Road, RAMSGATE, CT12 6SG
Tel: 01843 592802 **Fax:** 01843 593214
Web site: http://www.pecm.co.uk
Titles:
PECM PROCESS ENGINEERING, CONTROL &
MAINTENANCE

MH MEDIA SOLUTIONS LTD 1709747
Redfern House, 347 Margate Road, RAMSGATE, CT12 6SG
Tel: 01843 592802 **Fax:** 01843 593214
Titles:
DESIGN BUY BUILD
REFURB & RENOVATION NEWS

MICROPRESS 17669
27 Norwich Road, HALESWORTH, IP19 8BX
Tel: 01986 834200 **Fax:** 01986 834225
Titles:
COMMUNITY NEWS SERIES
HALESWORTH & SOUTHWOLD COMMUNITY NEWS
WOODBRIDGE AND MELTON COMMUNITY NEWS

MICROSOFT LTD. 1724074
Cardinal Place, 100 Victoria Street, LONDON, SW1E 5JL
Tel: 0870 601 0100
Web site: http://www.microsoft.com/uk
Titles:
MSN CARS
MSN TRAVEL

MID SUSSEX DISTRICT COUNCIL 600532
Oaklands, Oaklands Road, HAYWARDS HEATH, RH16 1SS
Tel: 01444 458166 **Fax:** 01444 450027
Titles:
MID SUSSEX MATTERS

THE MID YORKSHIRE CHAMBER OF COMMERCE 14763
The Stable Block, Brewery Drive, Lockwood Park,
HUDDERSFIELD, HD4 6EN **Tel:** 0844 9800 045
Web site: http://www.mycci.co.uk
Titles:
CLOSE-UP

MIDASCODE LTD 624477
5 Azure Suites, Churchill Court, 112 The Street, Rustington,
LITTLEHAMPTON, BN16 3DA **Tel:** 01903 779538
Titles:
DINE ONLINE

MIDDLESEX CRICKET CLUB 1741322
Lord's Cricket Ground, St. Johns Wood Road, LONDON,
NW8 8QN
Titles:
SCORECARD

MIDDLESEX UNIVERSITY STUDENTS' UNION 15782
Cat Hill, BARNET, EN4 8HT **Tel:** 020 8411 6473
Fax: 020 8411 6473
Titles:
MUD

MIDLAND NEWS ASSOCIATION 14848
51-53 Queen Street, WOLVERHAMPTON, WV1 1ES
Tel: 01902 313131 **Fax:** 01902 319721
Titles:
EXPRESS & STAR
EXPRESS & STAR (CITY/LONDON OFFICE)
NEWPORT & MARKET DRAYTON ADVERTISER SERIES
SHROPSHIRE STAR
SHROPSHIRE STAR (CITY/LONDON OFFICE)

MIDLAND NEWSPAPERS LTD 12437
Corporation Street, COVENTRY, CV1 1FP
Tel: 024 7663 3633 **Fax:** 024 7655 0869
Web site: http://www.coventrytelegraph.net
Titles:
COVENTRY TELEGRAPH
COVENTRY TIMES
FARM AD (INCORPORATING AGRI ADS)
THE MIDWEEK PINK

MIDLAND WEEKLY MEDIA 17573
103-106 High Green Court, Newhall Street, CANNOCK,
WS11 1AB **Tel:** 01543 501700 **Fax:** 01543 501793
Titles:
CHASE POST SERIES (LICHFIELD & RUGELEY)

MIDLANDS BUSINESS MEDIA LTD 1731675
65 Church Street, BIRMINGHAM, B3 2DP
Tel: 0121 262 3727
Email: enquiries_bfm@yahoo.co.uk
Titles:
BFM - BUSINESS AND FINANCE MIDLANDS

MIDO PUBLICATIONS LTD 13988
PO Box 1, WHITLAND, SA34 0HZ **Tel:** 01994 240978
Fax: 01994 240978
Email: editor@farmideas.co.uk
Titles:
PRACTICAL FARM IDEAS QUARTERLY

**MIDSOMER NORTON, RADSTOCK & DISTRICT
JOURNAL** 1639693
7 Frome Road, RADSTOCK, BA3 3PT **Tel:** 01761 432309
Fax: 01761 437810

Titles:
MIDSOMER NORTON, RADSTOCK & DISTRICT
JOURNAL

MIDWIVES INFORMATION AND RESOURCE SERVICE 14528
9 Elmdale Road, Clifton, BRISTOL, BS8 1SL
Tel: 0117 925 1791 **Fax:** 0117 925 1792
Titles:
MIDIRS MIDWIFERY DIGEST

MIGRAINE ACTION ASSOCIATION 18015
27 East Street, LEICESTER, LM1 6NB **Tel:** 0116 275 8317
Fax: 0116 254 2023
Email: info@migraine.org.uk
Web site: http://www.migraine.org.uk
Titles:
MIGRAINE ACTION NEWS

THE MIGRAINE TRUST 14582
2nd Floor, 55-56 Russell Square, LONDON, WC1B 4HP
Tel: 020 7436 1336 **Fax:** 020 7436 2880
Email: info@migrainetrust.org
Web site: http://www.migrainetrust.org
Titles:
MIGRAINE NEWS

MILES PUBLISHING LTD 700443
White House, Commercial Road, TUNBRIDGE WELLS, TN1
2RR **Tel:** 01892 538348 **Fax:** 01892 515724
Web site: http://www.cbmagazine.co.uk
Titles:
COMMS BUSINESS
MOBILE BUSINESS

MILES-BRAMWELL EXECUTIVE SERVICES LTD 17127
Clover Nook Road, Somercotes, ALFRETON, DE55 4RF
Tel: 01773 546071
Titles:
SLIMMING WORLD

MILL COTTAGE NEW MEDIA 1692057
Brant Lea, 2 Black Dyke Road, Arnside, CARNFORTH, LA5
0HH **Tel:** 01524 762653
Titles:
THE RECKLESS GARDENER

MILL DESIGN & PRINT 1747122
Harracles Mill, Dunwood Lane, Rudyard, LEEK, ST13 8RG
Tel: 01538 737308
Titles:
THE SNACKS MAGAZINE

MILLENNIUM PUBLISHING GROUP 16337
Room D701, London School of Economics and Political
Science, Houghton Street, LONDON, WC2A 2AE
Tel: 020 7955 6188 **Fax:** 020 7955 7438
Titles:
MILLENNIUM - JOURNAL OF INTERNATIONAL STUDIES

MILLENNIUM STEEL PUBLISHING 670261
11 Clacton Road, LONDON, E17 8AP **Tel:** 020 8509 3145
Fax: 020 8521 6999
Email: millenium.steel@virgin.net
Web site: http://www.millenium-steel.com
Titles:
MILLENNIUM STEEL

MILLIONNAIRE LIFESTYLE MEDIA LTD 1742380
Tel: 07918 937437
Press releases by email only **Tel:** 020 7183 7330
Titles:
MILLIONAIRE LIFESTYLE

MILLIVRES-PROWLER LTD 13123
Unit M, Spectrum House, 32-34 Gordon House Road,
LONDON, NW5 1LP **Tel:** 020 7424 7400 **Fax:** 020 7424 7401
Web site: http://www.millivres.co.uk
Titles:
AXM
DIVA
GT

PINK PAPER
PUFFTA.CO.UK

MIMI MEDIA   1717419
46A Carnaby Street, LONDON, W1F 9PS **Tel:** 020 7292 9779
Titles:
  BEAUTYANDTHEDIRT.CO.UK

MIND - THE MENTAL HEALTH CHARITY   17109
Granta House, 15-19 Broadway, LONDON, E15 4BQ
Tel: 020 8519 2122 **Fax:** 020 8522 1725
Titles:
  OPENMIND

MINERALOGICAL SOCIETY   17439
12 Baylis Mews, Amyand Park Road, TWICKENHAM, TW1
3HQ **Tel:** 020 8891 6600 **Fax:** 020 8891 6599
Email: info@minersoc.org
Web site: http://www.minersoc.org
Titles:
  CLAY MINERALS

MINERVA FUND MANAGERS   17197
Kelston View, Corston, BATH, BA2 9AH **Tel:** 01225 872300
Titles:
  THE NEW MINERVA REPORT

MINISTRY OF DEFENCE   1650215
HQ MOD, Main Building, Whitehall, LONDON, SW1A 2HB
Tel: 0870 607 4455
Titles:
  DESIDER
  SOLDIER

MINISTRY OF SOUND   18169
103 Gaunt Street, LONDON, SE1 6DP **Tel:** 020 7740 8600
Fax: 020 7403 5348
Web site: http://www.ministryofsound.com
Titles:
  MINISTRY OF SOUND

THE MISSION TO SEAFARERS   14335
St. Michael Paternoster Royal, College Hill, LONDON, EC4R
2RL **Tel:** 020 7248 5202 **Fax:** 020 7248 4761
Email: general@missiontoseafarers.org
Web site: http://www.missiontoseafarers.org
Titles:
  THE SEA

MIT PUBLISHING   17013
Featherstone House, 375 High Street, ROCHESTER, ME1
1DA **Tel:** 01634 830566 **Fax:** 01634 408488
Titles:
  AEROSPACE MANUFACTURING
  PRODUCTION ENGINEERING SOLUTIONS

MITRE HOUSE PUBLISHING LTD   13291
PO Box 29, SOUTH PETHERTON, TA13 5WE
Tel: 01460 241106 **Fax:** 01460 241091
Web site: http://www.mitrehousepublishing.co.uk
Titles:
  CHARITIES MANAGEMENT

MIX MEDIA LTD   697633
Wenden Court, Station Road, Wendens Ambo, SAFFRON
WALDEN, CB11 4LB **Tel:** 01799 541841 **Fax:** 0870 762 8551
Email: mixinteriors@aol.com
Titles:
  MIX INTERIORS

MIXED PHASE MEDIA LTD   15344
Suite 404 Albany House, 324-326 Regent Street, LONDON,
W1B 3HH **Tel:** 0870 233 2244
Titles:
  AMATEUR STAGE
  BEIGE MAGAZINE

MM PUBLISHING LTD   13948
Wadham House, 6 Blyth Road, BROMLEY, BR1 3RX
Tel: 020 8460 4224 **Fax:** 020 8290 1668
Titles:
  MACHINERY MARKET

MMG PUBLISHING LIMITED   1654654
MMG House, Connors Yard, Beeches Road,
CROWBOROUGH, TN6 2AH **Tel:** 01892 613400
Fax: 01892 613402
Titles:
  ELECTRONICS SOURCING

MMP FULFILMENT   13340
Challenge House, 616 Mitcham Road, CROYDON, CR9 3AU
Tel: 020 8683 6422 **Fax:** 020 8683 6426
Titles:
  COMMERCIAL PROPERTY MONTHLY

MODA MEDIA   1642388
5th Floor, White House, 111 New Street, BIRMINGHAM, B2
4EU **Tel:** 0121 631 6101 **Fax:** 0121 336 1936
Email: contact@modamedia.co.uk
Web site: http://www.modamedia.co.uk
Titles:
  MIDLANDS HOMES & INTERIORS
  PRIMARY TIMES IN DERBYSHIRE
  PRIMARY TIMES WEST MIDLANDS AND BLACK
    COUNTRY

MODEL ACTIVITY PRESS LTD   16381
Unit 5, Chiltern Business Centre, 63-65 Woodside Road,
AMERSHAM, HP6 6AA **Tel:** 01494 433453
Fax: 01494 433456
Titles:
  AVIATION MODELLER INTERNATIONAL
  FLYING SCALE MODELS
  MILITARY MACHINES INTERNATIONAL

MODERN HUMANITIES RESEARCH ASSOCIATION
    17613
Carlton House Terrace, LONDON, SW1Y 5DB
Tel: 01223 845512 **Fax:** 01223 845512
Email: mhra@mhra.org.uk
Web site: http://www.mhra.org.uk
Titles:
  ANNUAL BIBLIOGRAPHY OF ENGLISH LANGUAGE &
    LITERATURE
  PORTUGUESE STUDIES

MODERN MEDIA COMMUNICATIONS LTD   18419
Gresham House, 54 High Street, SHOREHAM-BY-SEA,
BN43 5DB **Tel:** 01273 453033 **Fax:** 01273 453085
Email: info@mmcpublications.co.uk
Web site: http://www.mmcpublications.co.uk
Titles:
  ALUMINIUM TIMES
  CAST METAL & DIECASTING TIMES
  EMERGENCY SERVICES TIMES
  FIRE TIMES

MODERN METALS PUBLICATIONS LTD   13709
PO Box 1187, GERRARDS CROSS, SL9 7ND
Tel: 01753 885968 **Fax:** 01753 882980
Titles:
  STAINLESS STEEL INDUSTRY
  WORLD CERAMICS & REFRACTORIES

MODERN MIDDLE EAST PUBLISHING LTD   1748494
Milk Studios, 34 Southern Row, LONDON, W10 5AN
Tel: 020 8962 2006 **Fax:** 020 8962 2006
Titles:
  ALEF

MODERN WELSH PUBLICATIONS LTD   697740
32 Garth Drive, LIVERPOOL, L18 6HW
Titles:
  YR ANGOR (LIVERPOOL)

MONDAQ   624581
16 West Barnes Lane, LONDON, SW20 0BU
Tel: 020 8544 8300 **Fax:** 020 8544 8340
Titles:
  MONDAQ

MONDIALE PUBLISHING LTD   16187
Waterloo Place, Watson Square, STOCKPORT, SK1 3AZ
Tel: 0161 476 8370 **Fax:** 0161 429 7214
Email: mondo@mondiale.co.uk
Web site: http://www.mondiale.co.uk

Titles:
MONDO*ARC
MONDO*DR
NIGHT MAGAZINE
TOTAL PRODUCTION INTERNATIONAL

MONDO VISIONE LTD   1692314
PO Box 36, Datchworth, KNEBWORTH, SG3 6WE
Tel: 01438 817018 **Fax:** 01438 817656
Titles:
  THE HANDBOOK OF WORLD STOCK DERIVATIVES &
    COMMODITY EXCHANGES
  TRADING PLACES

MONEYEXTRA.COM LTD   623743
Sigma House, Beverley Business Park, Oldbeck Road,
BEVERLEY, HU17 0JS **Tel:** 0207 029 4269
Titles:
  MONEYEXTRA

MONEYFACTS GROUP   16256
Moneyfacts House, 66-70 Thorpe Road, NORWICH, NR1
1BJ **Tel:** 0845 168 9690
Web site: http://www.moneyfacts.co.uk
Titles:
  BUSINESS MONEYFACTS
  INVESTMENT, LIFE & PENSIONS MONEYFACTS
  MONEYFACTS

MONEYSAVINGEXPERT.COM   699083
G12.1, Shepherds Studios, Charecroft Way, Shepherds
Bush, LONDON, W14 0DA **Tel:** 020 7384 9100
Fax: 0870 831 7286
Titles:
  MONEYSAVINGEXPERT.COM

MONEYWISE PUBLISHING   1653541
1st Floor, Standon House, 21 Mansell Street, LONDON, E1
8AA **Tel:** 020 7680 3600
Titles:
  MONEY OBSERVER
  MONEYWISE
  MONEYWISE.CO.UK

MONOMAX LTD   12753
Quadrant House, 250 Kennington Lane, LONDON, SE11
5RD **Tel:** 020 7582 0222 **Fax:** 020 7582 5444
Titles:
  IMBIBE
  SQUARE MEAL LIFESTYLE

MONTESSORI ST NICHOLAS   18603
18 Balderton Street, LONDON, W1K 6TG
Tel: 020 7493 8300 **Fax:** 020 7493 9936
Titles:
  MONTESSORI INTERNATIONAL

MOONSCAPE MEDIA LTD   1645305
33 Wood Lane, Sonning Common, READING, RG4 9SJ
Tel: 0845 880 1777 **Fax:** 0845 880 1770
Titles:
  PRIMARY TIMES IN BERKSHIRE

MORAY & NAIRN NEWSPAPER CO LTD   15038
74-76 South Street, ELGIN, IV30 1JG **Tel:** 01343 548777
Fax: 01343 545629
Titles:
  THE BANFFSHIRE JOURNAL
  FORRES GAZETTE
  NORTHERN SCOT AND MORAY & NAIRN EXPRESS
  STRATHSPEY & BADENOCH HERALD

MORE SPORT LTD   1639667
19 Great Ancoats Street, MANCHESTER, M60 4BT
Tel: 0161 236 4466
Titles:
  ADULT SPORT

MORIANA MEDIA GROUP   1747556
85 Waterhouse Business Centre, Cromar Way,
CHELMSFORD, CM1 2QE **Tel:** 07734 315506
Email: info@morianmediagroup.com
Web site: http://www.mcubedigital.com

Titles:
COMSEUROPA
CONVERGENCE WORLD
WIRELESS BUSINESS REVIEW

MORRIS INTERNATIONAL ASSOCIATES LTD   15727
The Studio, 143 Lavender Hill, LONDON, SW11 5QJ
Tel: 020 7228 1060 **Fax:** 020 7228 1191
Titles:
VOICE OF THE ARAB WORLD

MORTON NEWSPAPERS LTD   12833
2 Esky Drive, PORTADOWN, BT63 5YY **Tel:** 028 3839 3939
Fax: 028 3839 3940
Email: production@mortonnewspapers.com
Web site: http://www.mortonnewspapers.com
Titles:
BALLYMONEY AND MOYLE TIMES
COLERAINE TIMES
CRAIGAVON ECHO
LEADER (COUNTY DOWN SERIES)
LISBURN ECHO
LURGAN MAIL
MID ULSTER MAIL SERIES
PORTADOWN TIMES INC. CRAIGAVON NEWS
TYRONE TIMES AND DUNGANNON GAZETTE
ULSTER STAR

MORTONS HERITAGE MEDIA   18915
Media Centre, Morton Way, HORNCASTLE, LN9 6JR
Tel: 01507 523456 **Fax:** 01507 527840
Web site: http://www.mortons.co.uk
Titles:
BLUEBELL NEWS
HERITAGE COMMERCIALS
HERITAGE RAILWAY
WRIGHTS FARMING REGISTER

MORTONS MEDIA GROUP LTD   18725
Media Centre, Morton Way, HORNCASTLE, LN9 6JR
Tel: 01507 529529 **Fax:** 01507 529495
Email: info@mortonsmediagroup.co.uk
Web site: http://www.mortonsmediagroup.com
Titles:
CHERWELL
THE CLASSIC BIKE GUIDE
CLASSIC DIRTBIKE MAGAZINE
THE CLASSIC MOTORCYCLE
THE CLASSIC MOTORCYCLE
CLASSIC MOTORCYCLE MECHANICS
CLASSIC RACER
CLASSIC RACER ONLINE
CLASSIC SCOOTERIST SCENE MAGAZINE
ISLAND RACER
THE KITCHEN GARDEN
MOTOR CYCLE MONTHLY
MOTORCYCLE RACER
MOTORCYCLE SPORT AND LEISURE
OLD BIKE MART
OLD GLORY
ORGANIC GARDEN AND HOME
SCOOTERING
SOUTH EAST WALKER
TOWPATH TALK
TRACTOR
TWIST & GO MAGAZINE
USED BIKE GUIDE

THE MOTLEY FOOL UK   622535
18 Soho Square, LONDON, W1D 3QL **Tel:** 020 7025 8057
Fax: 020 7025 8112
Web site: http://www.fool.co.uk
Titles:
THE MOTLEY FOOL

MOTOPIA CREATIVE LTD   1741479
24 Beamont Way, Amesbury, SALISBURY, SP4 7UA
Tel: 07500 978201 **Fax:** 01980 590997
Email: melissa@motopia.co.uk
Titles:
MOTOPIA

MOTOPLAY LTD   1735844
Alexander House, 38 Forehill, ELY, CB7 4ZA
Tel: 01353 616104
Titles:
MOTOX

MOTOR INDUSTRY PUBLISHING LTD   14121
Pike's Peak, Finchampstead, WOKINGHAM, RG40 4RD
Tel: 0118 973 3435 **Fax:** 0118 932 8185
Email: ve@pikespeak.demon.co.uk
Web site: http://www.vehicle-engineer.com
Titles:
VEHICLE ENGINEER

MOTORBAR   694034
3 Cromers Road, SITTINGBOURNE, ME10 4HP
Tel: 01795 425520
Titles:
MOTORBAR

MOTORING AND HOME LIFE MAGAZINES LTD   12975
CIDO Business Complex, Charles Street, Lurgan,
CRAIGAVON, BT66 6HG **Tel:** 028 3832 4006
Fax: 028 3832 5213
Email: sales@homelifemagazines.co.uk
Titles:
HOME-LIFE MAGAZINE

MOUNTAIN LEISURE LTD   674011
Parman House, 30-36 Fife Road, KINGSTON UPON
THAMES, KT1 1SY **Tel:** 020 8547 9822
Email: info@goodholidayideas.com
Web site: http://www.goodskiguide.com
Titles:
GOOD HOLIDAY MAGAZINE
GOOD SKI GUIDE
GOOD SKI GUIDE A-Z
WORLD SKI GUIDE

MOUNTAIN MARKETING LTD   16228
PO Box 386, SEVENOAKS, TN13 1AQ **Tel:** 0845 310 8303
Titles:
THE SKIER AND SNOWBOARDER MAGAZINE

MOURNE OBSERVER LTD.   15082
Castlewellan Road, NEWCASTLE, BT33 0JX
Tel: 028 4372 2666 **Fax:** 028 4372 4566
Titles:
MOURNE OBSERVER SERIES

MOUSETRAP MEDIA LTD   1644744
68 Middle Street, BRIGHTON, BN1 1AL **Tel:** 01273 384293
Fax: 01273 232179
Email: info@mousetrapmedia.co.uk
Web site: http://www.mousetrapmedia.co.uk
Titles:
JOURNALISM.CO.UK

MOVE PUBLISHING   1649373
36 Henry Street, LIVERPOOL, L1 5BS **Tel:** 0151 709 3871
Fax: 0151 707 1678
Titles:
GO OUT
YOUR MOVE

MOVIE MAG INTERNATIONAL UK   1643219
20 Station Road, Hanwell, LONDON, W7 3JE
Tel: 020 8574 2222 **Fax:** 020 8813 9911
Titles:
MOVIE MAG INTERNATIONAL

MOWBRAY COMMUNICATIONS LTD   1750466
80 Featherstone Lane, Featherstone, PONTEFRACT, WF7
6LR **Tel:** 01977 708488 **Fax:** 0700 609 0531
Titles:
ECOTEXTILE NEWS
KNITTING TRADE JOURNAL
TEXTILE DYER

MPI GROUP LTD   14339
Peel House, Upper South View, FARNHAM, GU9 7JN
Tel: 01252 849707 **Fax:** 01252 849708
Web site: http://www.mpigroup.co.uk
Titles:
DRYDOCK

MPP LTD   13503
Sparta Works, 487 Blackfen Road, SIDCUP, DA15 9NP
Tel: 020 8298 6490 **Fax:** 020 8301 5304

Web site: http://www.floorpoint.com
Titles:
CHT CLEANING & HYGIENE TODAY
THE FLOORING MAGAZINE
FMJ THE FACILITIES MANAGEMENT JOURNAL
HEALTHCARE HYGIENE MANAGEMENT

MRWEB.COM   1729017
Langdale House, 11 Marshalsea Road, LONDON, SE1 1EN
Tel: 020 7515 6040
Web site: http://www.mrweb.com
Titles:
MRWEB.COM

MS PUBLICATIONS (2001) LTD   623182
2nd Floor, Ewer House, 44-46 Crouch Street,
COLCHESTER, CO3 3HH **Tel:** 01206 506250
Fax: 01206 500180
Web site: http://www.aceville.com
Titles:
CAR PARTS AND ACCESSORIES MART
CLASSIC CARS FOR SALE
HOTEL BUSINESS
RETAIL PACKAGING

MS SOCIETY   12642
372 Edgware Road, LONDON, NW2 6ND
Tel: 020 8438 0700 **Fax:** 020 8438 0701
Email: info@mssociety.org.uk
Web site: http://www.mssociety.org.uk
Titles:
MS MATTERS

MSL MEDIA   1744314
Cobalt House, Centre Court, Sir Thomas Longley Road,
ROCHESTER, ME2 4BQ **Tel:** 020 7993 3355
Fax: 01634 242611
Titles:
EMS ENGINEERING MAINTENANCE SOLUTIONS

MSLEXIA PUBLICATIONS LTD   1871
Holy Jesus Hospital, City Road, NEWCASTLE UPON TYNE,
NE1 2AS **Tel:** 0191 261 6656 **Fax:** 0191 261 6636
Email: postbag@mslexia.co.uk
Web site: http://www.mslexia.co.uk
Titles:
MSLEXIA

MSM INTERNATIONAL LTD   600388
Thames House, 18 Park Street, LONDON, SE1 9ER
Tel: 020 7378 7131 **Fax:** 020 7378 1605
Web site: http://www.moneyam.com
Titles:
SHARES

MSP PUBLISHING   1687
PO Box 582, JERSEY, JE4 8XQ **Tel:** 01534 611600
Fax: 01534 611610
Titles:
BUSINESS BRIEF CHANNEL ISLANDS
BUSINESS BRIEF/CONFIDENTIAL
JERSEY ALMANAC AND TRADES DIRECTORY
JERSEY NOW

MT PUBLICATIONS LTD   1357
Prudence Place, Proctor Way, LUTON, LU2 9PE
Tel: 01582 772460
Titles:
AUTOMOTIVE ELECTRONICS
MICRO TECHNOLOGY EUROPE

MTI LTD   167979
Appleby House, Headley Road, LEATHERHEAD, KT22 8PT
Tel: 01474 855505 **Fax:** 01372 373876
Titles:
MACHINERY TRADE INTERNATIONAL

MTV NETWORKS EUROPE   1875
17-29 Hawley Crescent, Camden Town, LONDON, NW1 8T
Tel: 020 7284 7430
Titles:
MTV ONLINE UK & IRELAND

MU ENTERPRISES LTD   1641013
The Mary Summer House, 24 Tufton Street, LONDON,
SW1P 3RB **Tel:** 020 7222 5533 **Fax:** 020 7222 1591
Titles:
  FAMILIES FIRST

MUD HUT PUBLISHING   1649552
Winchfield Lodge, Old Portbridge Road, Winchfield, HOOK,
RG27 8TB **Tel:** 01252 849051 **Fax:** 01420 88633
Email: terry@gcmagazine.co.uk
Web site: http://www.gcmagazine.co.uk
Titles:
  GET CONNECTED MAGAZINE

MULBERRY PUBLICATIONS LTD   1622131
Suite 209, 2nd Floor, Wellington House, Butt Road,
COLCHESTER, CO3 3DA **Tel:** 01206 767797
Fax: 01206 767532
Titles:
  FUNERAL SERVICE TIMES
  JEWELLERY FOCUS

MULTIHULL REVIEW LTD   1737070
Regus House, Southampton International Business Park,
George Curl Way, SOUTHAMPTON, SO18 2RZ
Titles:
  MULTIHULL REVIEW

MULTIMEDIA INFORMATION AND TECHNOLOGY 18901
45 Gwenllian Morgan Court, Heol Gouesnou, BRECON, LD3
7EE **Tel:** 01874 610412
Titles:
  MULTIMEDIA INFORMATION AND TECHNOLOGY

THE MULTIPLE SCLEROSIS RESOURCE CENTRE
                                          622958
7 Peartree Business Centre, Peartree Road, Stanway,
COLCHESTER, CO3 0JN **Tel:** 01206 505444
Fax: 01206 505449
Email: info@msrc.co.uk
Web site: http://www.msrc.co.uk
Titles:
  NEW PATHWAYS

MULTI-SCIENCE PUBLISHING CO LTD   12664
5 Wates Way, BRENTWOOD, CM15 9TB **Tel:** 01277 224632
Fax: 01277 223453
Email: mscience@globalnet.co.uk
Web site: http://www.multi-science.co.uk
Titles:
  NOISE & VIBRATION WORLDWIDE

MULTISERVICE ASSOCIATION LTD   1677192
PO Box 9378, NEWARK, NG24 9FE **Tel:** 01400 281298
Fax: 01400 282326
Email: info@msauk.biz
Web site: http://www.msauk.biz
Titles:
  SHOE SERVICE

MULTITRAX UK LTD   1731978
The Sail Loft, 3-11 Dod Street, LONDON, E14 7EQ
Tel: 0870 608 0001 **Fax:** 0870 042 0102
Web site: http://www.multitraxuk.com
Titles:
  TRAX

MUSCLE NEWS   15314
10 Alpha Court, Denton, MANCHESTER, M34 3RB
Tel: 0161 320 5123
Titles:
  THE BEEF

MUSCULAR DYSTROPHY CAMPAIGN   14590
61 Southwark Street, LONDON, SE1 0HL
Tel: 020 7803 4800 **Fax:** 020 7401 3495
Email: info@muscular-dystrophy.org
Web site: http://www.muscular-dystrophy.org
Titles:
  TARGET MD

MUSEUMS ASSOCIATION   14813
24 Calvin Street, LONDON, E1 6NW **Tel:** 020 7426 6969
Fax: 020 7426 6962
Email: info@museumsassociation.org
Web site: http://www.museumsassociation.org
Titles:
  MUSEUM PRACTICE
  MUSEUMS & GALLERIES YEARBOOK
  MUSEUMS JOURNAL

MUSHTAK PARKER ASSOCIATES   16756
30 Chelmsford Square, LONDON, NW10 3AR
Tel: 020 8459 4310
Titles:
  ISLAMIC BANKER

MUSIC HQ LTD   1651142
4th Floor, 2 Plough Yard, LONDON, EC2A 3LP
Tel: 0870 046 6622 **Fax:** 0870 046 6611
Titles:
  NOTION

MUSIC SCOTLAND LTD   18079
Trojan House, Phoenix Business Park, PAISLEY, PA1 2BH
Tel: 0141 840 5980 **Fax:** 0141 840 5995
Titles:
  TILLLATE

MUSIC TODAY LTD   1621129
PO Box 49554, LONDON, E17 9WB **Tel:** 020 8520 6646
Fax: 020 8520 2130
Titles:
  RECORD OF THE DAY

MUSICAL OPINION LTD   15375
1 Exford Road, LONDON, SE12 9HD **Tel:** 020 8857 1582
Web site: http://www.musicalopinion.com
Titles:
  MUSICAL OPINION
  THE ORGAN

MUSICAL STAGES   15345
PO Box 8365, LONDON, W14 0GL **Tel:** 020 7603 2227
Fax: 020 7603 2221
Titles:
  MUSICAL STAGES

MUSIC-ZINE LTD   1720706
PO Box 9080, BISHOPS STORTFORD, CM23 4XW
Tel: 01279 865070 **Fax:** 08704 860812
Web site: http://www.music-zine.com
Titles:
  MUSIC-ZINE

MUSTARD SEEDS PUBLISHING   1729807
The Cricketers, Station Road, Amberley, ARUNDEL, BN18
9LT **Tel:** 01798 839338
Titles:
  BATTERIES INTERNATIONAL

MVP EUROPE   15977
233 High Holborn, LONDON, WC1V 7DN **Tel:** 020 7242 5222
Fax: 020 7242 4184
Web site: http://www.morrisvisitorpublications.com
Titles:
  IN LONDON
  LONDON PLANNER
  WHERE LONDON

MY HOBBY STORE MEDIA   1710341
Berwick House, 8-10 Knoll Rise, ORPINGTON, BR6 0EL
Tel: 0844 412 2262
Email: feedback@myhobbystore.com
Web site: http://www.myhobbystore.com
Titles:
  GETWOODWORKING.COM
  GOOD WOODWORKING
  MILITARY MODELLING
  MODEL BOATS
  MODEL ENGINEER
  MODEL ENGINEERS' WORKSHOP
  POPULAR PATCHWORK
  PRACTICAL WOODWORKING
  RADIO CONTROL MODELS & ELECTRONICS
  THE WOODWORKER

MY MOVIES.NET LTD   18942
40 Oxford Drive, 7-25 Bermondsey Street, LONDON, SE1
2FB **Tel:** 01474 533655 **Fax:** 01474 535551
Titles:
  MY MOVIES.NET

MY TV ONLINE   1767077
The Old School Room, 358 Old Birmingham Road,
BIRMINGHAM, B45 8ES **Tel:** 0121 445 0668
Titles:
  EDUCATION NEWS

MY VILLAGE LOCAL   1634315
The Workplace, 105 Ladbroke Grove, LONDON, W11 1PG
Tel: 020 7792 0624
Titles:
  MYVILLAGE

MY WEBSITE LIMITED   1745168
Lilacs Thurston Road, Great Barton, BURY ST. EDMUNDS,
IP31 2PL **Tel:** 01359 233404
Email: editor@mywebsite.ltd.uk
Web site: http://mywebsite.ltd.uk
Titles:
  THE GARDENING WEBSITE

MYBRUM.TV   1648999
The Old School Room, 358 Old Birmingham Road, Lickey,
BIRMINGHAM, B45 8ES **Tel:** 0121 445 0668
Email: enquiries@birminghamindependent.co.uk
Web site: http://www.birminghamindependent.co.uk
Titles:
  BIRMINGHAM INDEPENDENT

MYKINDAPLACE LTD   624487
5th Floor, Fergusson House, 124-128 City Road, LONDON,
EC1V 2NJ **Tel:** 020 7553 3360 **Fax:** 020 7490 4837
Web site: http://www.mykindaplace.com
Titles:
  MONKEYSLUM
  MYKINDAPLACE.COM

MYPEC LTD   1649939
The Old Pottery, Fulneck, PUDSEY, LS28 8NT
Tel: 0113 255 6896 **Fax:** 0113 255 6887
Titles:
  ASSOCIATION MANAGEMENT QUARTERLY

N16 PUBLISHING LTD   1638624
PO Box 44624, LONDON, N16 5WN **Tel:** 020 7249 9943
Titles:
  N16: THE MAGAZINE AT THE HEART OF STOKE
  NEWINGTON

NADFAS ENTERPRISES LTD   15822
NADFAS House, 8 Guilford Street, LONDON, WC1N 1DA
Tel: 020 7430 0730 **Fax:** 020 7242 0686
Titles:
  NADFAS REVIEW

NAFAS ENTERPRISES LIMITED   15518
Osborne House, 12 Devonshire Square, LONDON, EC2M
4TE **Tel:** 020 7247 5567 **Fax:** 020 7247 7232
Titles:
  THE FLOWER ARRANGER

NAFEMS   13968
Prospect House, Stanley Boulevard, Hamilton Intnl
Technology Park, Blantyre, GLASGOW, G72 0BN
Tel: 01355 225688 **Fax:** 01698 823311
Titles:
  BENCHMARK

NAIRNSHIRE TELEGRAPH   18977
10 Leopold Street, NAIRN, IV12 4BG **Tel:** 01667 453258
Fax: 01667 455277
Titles:
  NAIRNSHIRE TELEGRAPH

UK Publishers & Their Titles

NAK (UK) LIMITED   674478
Technology Centre, Technology Drive, BATLEY, WF17 6ER
Tel: 01924 500366 **Fax:** 01924 500355
Web site: http://www.corpreports.co.uk
Titles:
CORPORATE REPORTS

NAM PUBLICATIONS   14487
Lincoln House, 1 Brixton Road, LONDON, SW9 6DE
Tel: 020 7840 0050 **Fax:** 020 7735 5351
Email: info@nam.org.uk
Web site: http://www.aidsmap.com
Titles:
HIV TREATMENT UPDATE

NAPIER PARTNERSHIP LTD   1741347
Donnington Park, Birdham Road, CHICHESTER, PO20 7DU
Tel: 01243 531123 **Fax:** 01243 779070
Titles:
TECHEVENTGUIDE.COM

NASEN   14553
Nasen House, 4-5 Amber Business Village, Amber Close,
Amington, TAMWORTH, B77 4RP **Tel:** 01827 311500
Fax: 01827 313005
Email: welcome@nasen.org.uk
Web site: http://www.nasen.org.uk
Titles:
SPECIAL

NASUWT   13850
Hillscourt Education Centre, Rose Hill, Rednal,
BIRMINGHAM, B45 8RS **Tel:** 0121 453 6150
Fax: 0121 457 6208
Email: nasuwt@mail.nasuwt.org.uk
Web site: http://www.teachersunion.org.uk
Titles:
TEACHING TODAY

NATIONAL AIR TRAFFIC SERVICES   625853
4000 Parkway, WHITELY, P015 7FL **Tel:** 01489 615804
Titles:
PULSE

THE NATIONAL ARCHIVES   694301
Ruskin Avenue, RICHMOND, TW9 4DU **Tel:** 020 8392 5370
Fax: 020 8392 5266
Web site: http://www.nationalarchives.gov.uk
Titles:
ANCESTORS

**NATIONAL ASSOCIATION FOR ENVIRONMENTAL
EDUCATION (UK)**   1762615
University of Wolverhampton, Walsall Campus, Gorway,
WALSALL, WS1 3BD **Tel:** 01922 631200
Email: info@naee.org.uk
Web site: http://www.naee.org.uk
Titles:
ENVIRONMENTAL EDUCATION

**NATIONAL ASSOCIATION OF AGRICULTURAL
CONTRACTORS**   14035
Samuelson House, 62 Forder Way, Hampton,
PETERBOROUGH, PE7 8JB **Tel:** 0845 6448 748
Fax: 01733 363921
Web site: http://www.naac.co.uk
Titles:
CONTRACTING BULLETIN

**NATIONAL ASSOCIATION OF CITIZENS ADVICE
BUREAUX**   621640
The Development Centre, Wolverhampton Science Park,
WOLVERHAMPTON, WV10 9RT **Tel:** 01902 310568
Fax: 01902 710068
Web site: http://www.advisermagazine.org.uk
Titles:
THE ADVISER

THE NATIONAL ASSOCIATION OF ESTATE AGENTS
    13342
PO Box 234, UCKFIELD, TN22 9AH **Tel:** 01825 733843
Fax: 01825 731845
Web site: http://www.naea.co.uk

Titles:
AGREEMENT
COMMERCIAL MOVES
THE ESTATE AGENT
GAVEL

**THE NATIONAL ASSOCIATION OF FUNERAL
DIRECTORS**   14806
618 Warwick Road, SOLIHULL, B91 1AA **Tel:** 0845 230 1343
Fax: 0121 711 1351
Email: info@nafd.org.uk
Web site: http://www.nafd.org.uk
Titles:
THE FUNERAL DIRECTOR MONTHLY

THE NATIONAL ASSOCIATION OF GOLDSMITHS 671738
78A Luke Street, LONDON, EC2A 4XG **Tel:** 020 7613 4445
Fax: 020 7613 4450
Web site: http://www.jewellers-online.org
Titles:
THE JEWELLER

NATIONAL ASSOCIATION OF HEAD TEACHERS   15935
1 Heath Square, Boltro Road, HAYWARDS HEATH, RH16
1BL **Tel:** 01444 472472 **Fax:** 01444 472473
Email: info@naht.org.uk
Web site: http://www.naht.org.uk
Titles:
LEADERSHIP FOCUS

NATIONAL ASSOCIATION OF LOCAL COUNCILS   18615
109 Great Russell Street, LONDON, WC1B 3LD
Tel: 020 7290 0308 **Fax:** 020 7436 7451
Email: lcr@nalc.gov.uk
Web site: http://www.nalc.gov.uk
Titles:
LOCAL COUNCIL REVIEW

NATIONAL ASSOCIATION OF ROUND TABLES   16145
Marchesi House, 4 Embassy Drive, Calthorpe Road,
Edgbaston, BIRMINGHAM, B15 1TP **Tel:** 0121 456 4402
Fax: 0121 456 4185
Email: hq@roundtable.org.uk
Web site: http://roundtable.org.uk
Titles:
TABLER

THE NATIONAL AUTISTIC SOCIETY   14573
393 City Road, LONDON, EC1V 1NG **Tel:** 020 7833 2299
Fax: 020 7833 9666
Email: nas@nas.org.uk
Web site: http://www.nas.org.uk
Titles:
COMMUNICATION

NATIONAL BACK EXCHANGE   18524
Linden Barns, Greens Norton Road, TOWCESTER, NN12
8AW **Tel:** 01327 358855 **Fax:** 01327 353778
Web site: http://www.nationalbackexchange.org.uk
Titles:
THE COLUMN

NATIONAL CHILDMINDING ASSOCIATION   14186
Royal Court, 81 Tweedy Road, BROMLEY, BR1 1TG
Tel: 0845 880 0044 **Fax:** 0845 880 0043
Email: info@ncma.org.uk
Web site: http://www.ncma.org.uk
Titles:
WHO MINDS?

THE NATIONAL COMPUTING CENTRE   13575
National Computing Centre, Oxford Road, MANCHESTER,
M1 7ED **Tel:** 0161 242 2121 **Fax:** 0161 242 2499
Web site: http://www.ncc.co.uk
Titles:
IT ADVISER

THE NATIONAL DEAF CHILDREN'S SOCIETY   17277
15 Dufferin Street, LONDON, EC1Y 8UR **Tel:** 020 7490 8656
Fax: 020 7251 5020
Web site: http://www.ndcs.org.uk
Titles:
NATIONAL DEAF CHILDREN'S SOCIETY MAGAZINE

NATIONAL DRAMA PUBLICATIONS   15945
University of Strathclyde, Southbrae Drive, GLASGOW, G13
1PP
Titles:
DRAMA

NATIONAL ECZEMA SOCIETY   12655
Hill House, Highgate Hill, LONDON, N19 5NA
Tel: 020 7281 3553 **Fax:** 020 7281 6395
Titles:
EXCHANGE

NATIONAL ENERGY SERVICES   1642228
The National Energy Centre, Davy Avenue, MILTON
KEYNES, MK5 8NA **Tel:** 01908 672787 **Fax:** 01908 662296
Titles:
ENERGY BYTES

**NATIONAL EXECUTIVE COMMITTEE OF THE POLICE
SUPERINTENDENTS' ASSOCIATION OF ENGLAND
AND WALES**   1654999
67A Reading Road, Pangbourne, READING, RG8 7JD
Tel: 0118 984 4005
Titles:
THE SUPERINTENDENT

NATIONAL FEDERATION OF 18 PLUS GROUPS   15233
210 Commerce House, High Street, SUTTON COLDFIELD,
B72 1AB **Tel:** 0870 879 4960
Titles:
PLUS NEWS

NATIONAL FEDERATION OF FISH FRIERS   13705
New Federation House, 4 Greenwood Mount, Meanwood,
LEEDS, LS6 4LQ **Tel:** 0113 230 7044 **Fax:** 0113 230 7010
Titles:
FISH FRIERS REVIEW

**THE NATIONAL FEDERATION OF MEAT AND FOOD
TRADERS**   14058
1 Belgrove, TUNBRIDGE WELLS, TN1 1YW
Tel: 01892 541412 **Fax:** 01892 535462
Web site: http://www.nfmft.co.uk
Titles:
FOOD TRADER FOR BUTCHERS

NATIONAL FEDERATION OF SUBPOSTMASTERS 13889
Evelyn House, 22 Windlesham Gardens, SHOREHAM-BY-
SEA, BN43 5AZ **Tel:** 01273 452324 **Fax:** 01273 465403
Web site: http://www.subpostmasters.org.uk
Titles:
THE SUBPOSTMASTER

NATIONAL FEDERATION OF WOMEN'S INSTITUTES
    15119
104 New King's Road, Fulham, LONDON, SW6 4LY
Tel: 020 7731 5777 **Fax:** 020 7736 4061
Titles:
WI LIFE

NATIONAL GEOGRAPHIC SOCIETY   18418
Lansbury Estate, Lower Guildford Road, WOKING, GU21
2EP **Tel:** 01483 522068 **Fax:** 01483 522069
Web site: http://www.nationalgeographic.com
Titles:
NATIONAL GEOGRAPHIC MAGAZINE

NATIONAL HAIRDRESSERS' FEDERATION   18666
1 Abbey Court, Fraser Road, Priory Business Park,
BEDFORD, MK44 3WH **Tel:** 0845 345 6500
Fax: 01234 838875
Email: enquiries@nhf.info
Web site: http://www.nhf.biz
Titles:
SALON FOCUS

**NATIONAL INSTITUTE OF ADULT CONTINUING
EDUCATION**   15925
21 De Montfort Street, LEICESTER, LE1 7GE
Tel: 0116 204 4200 **Fax:** 0116 285 4215
Email: enquiries@niace.org.uk
Web site: http://www.niace.org.uk

Titles:
ADULT LEARNING YEARBOOK
ADULTS LEARNING
CONCEPT
THE JOURNAL OF ADULT CONTINUING EDUCATION
STUDIES IN THE EDUCATION OF ADULTS

NATIONAL LANDLORDS ASSOCIATION   18135
22-26 Albert Embankment, LONDON, SE1 7TJ
Tel: 020 7840 8900
Email: info@landlords.org.uk
Web site: http://www.landlords.org.uk
Titles:
UK LANDLORD

NATIONAL MAGAZINE COMPANY LTD   15100
National Magazine House, 72 Broadwick Street, LONDON,
W1F 9EP **Tel:** 020 7439 5000
Web site: http://www.natmags.co.uk

Titles:
ALLABOUTYOU.COM/GOODHOUSEKEEPING
BABYEXPERT.COM
BEST
COAST
COMPANY MAGAZINE
COSMOPOLITAN
COSMOPOLITAN BRIDE
COSMOPOLITAN.CO.UK
COUNTRY LIVING
ESQUIRE
GOOD HOUSEKEEPING
HARPER'S BAZAAR
HARPERSBAZAAR.CO.UK
HOUSE BEAUTIFUL
PRIMA
PRIMA BABY & PREGNANCY
REVEAL
SHE
YOU & YOUR WEDDING
ZEST

NATIONAL OSTEOPOROSIS SOCIETY   1709746
NOS, Skinners Hill, Camerton, BATH, BA2 0PJ
Tel: 01761 471771 **Fax:** 01761 471104
Web site: http://www.nos.org.uk
Titles:
OSTEOPOROSIS NEWS

THE NATIONAL PAWNBROKERS ASSOCIATION   14446
Chiltern Court, St. Peters Avenue, Caversham, READING,
RG4 7DH **Tel:** 0845 612 0640
Email: des.milligan@thenpa.com
Web site: http://www.thenpa.com
Titles:
THE PAWNBROKER

NATIONAL PEST TECHNICIANS' ASSOCIATION   16785
NPTA House, Hall Lane, Kinoulton, NOTTINGHAM, NG12
3EF **Tel:** 01949 81133 **Fax:** 01949 823905
Email: officenpta@aol.com
Web site: http://www.npta.org.uk
Titles:
TODAY'S TECHNICIAN

NATIONAL PHYSICAL LABORATORY   621941
The National Physical Laboratory, Hampton Road,
TEDDINGTON, TW11 0LW **Tel:** 020 8977 3222
Fax: 020 8943 6458
Web site: http://www.npl.co.uk
Titles:
ENGINEERING PRECISELY

NATIONAL PIPING CENTRE   1651341
National Piping Centre, 30-34 McPhater Street,
Cowcaddens, GLASGOW, G4 0HW **Tel:** 0141 353 0220
Fax: 0141 353 1570
Web site: http://www.thepipingcentre.co.uk
Titles:
PIPING TODAY

NATIONAL PRESS PUBLISHERS LTD   15191
Tel: 0870 350 1893
PR only accepted via e-mail **Tel:** 0870 350 1892
Email: editorial@constabularymagazine.co.uk
Web site: http://www.constabulary.org.uk
Titles:
CONSTABULARY MAGAZINE

NATIONAL RIFLE ASSOCIATION   15266
Bisley Camp, Brookwood, WOKING, GU24 0PB
Tel: 01483 797777 **Fax:** 01483 797285
Web site: http://www.nra.org.uk
Titles:
NATIONAL RIFLE ASSOCIATION JOURNAL

NATIONAL SOCIETY FOR EPILEPSY   1690662
Chesham Lane, CHALFONT ST PETER, SL9 0RJ
Tel: 01494 601300 **Fax:** 01494 871927
Web site: http://www.epilepsynse.org.uk
Titles:
EPILEPSY REVIEW

THE NATIONAL TRUST   15532
Heelis, Kemble Drive, SWINDON, SN2 2NA
Tel: 01793 817575
Titles:
ACTIVE
THE NATIONAL TRUST MAGAZINE

NATIONAL UNION OF JOURNALISTS   13856
Headland House, 308 Gray's Inn Road, LONDON, WC1X
8DP **Tel:** 020 7278 7916 **Fax:** 020 7837 8143
Titles:
THE JOURNALIST

NATIONAL UNION OF TEACHERS   13873
Hamilton House, Mabledon Place, LONDON, WC1H 9BD
Tel: 020 7380 4708 **Fax:** 020 7387 8458
Titles:
THE TEACHER

NATIONAL WOMEN'S REGISTER   18039
23 Vulcan House, Vulcan Road North, NORWICH, NR6 6AQ
Tel: 01603 406767 **Fax:** 01603 407003
Email: office@nwr.org.uk
Web site: http://www.nwr.org.uk
Titles:
THE REGISTER - NWR NATIONAL MAGAZINE

THE NATIONAL YOUTH AGENCY   15730
Eastgate House, 19-23 Humberstone Road, LEICESTER,
LE5 3GJ **Fax:** 0116 242 7444
Email: nya@nya.org.uk
Web site: http://www.nya.org.uk
Titles:
RUCKUS
YOUTH & POLICY

NATIONWIDE CATERERS ASSOCIATION   1627036
Association House, 89 Mappleborough Road, Shirley,
SOLIHULL, B90 1AG **Tel:** 0121 603 2524
Fax: 0121 474 3938
Titles:
MOBILE & OUTSIDE CATERING

NATIONWIDE GROUP STAFF UNION   18204
Middleton Farmhouse, 37 Main Road, Middleton Cheney,
BANBURY, OX17 2QT **Tel:** 01295 710767
Fax: 01295 712580
Web site: http://www.ngsu.co.uk
Titles:
RAPPORT

NATM   14286
Unit 6A, Wharf Road, Ealand Industrial Estate, EALAND,
DN17 4JW **Tel:** 01724 712255 **Fax:** 01724 712266
Titles:
NATM

NATMAG RODALE LTD   15285
33 Broadwick Street, LONDON, W1F 0DQ
Tel: 020 7339 4400 **Fax:** 020 7339 4450
Web site: http://www.natmags.co.uk
Titles:
COMPANY.CO.UK
MEN'S HEALTH
MENSHEALTH.CO.UK
RUNNER'S WORLD
RUNNERSWORLD.CO.UK

NATURE PUBLISHING GROUP   621598
The Macmillan Building, 4 Crinan Street, LONDON, N1 9XW
Tel: 020 7833 4000 **Fax:** 020 7843 4640
Email: exec@nature.com
Web site: http://www.nature.com
Titles:
BDJ BRITISH DENTAL JOURNAL
BONE MARROW TRANSPLANTATION
THE EMBO JOURNAL
GENE THERAPY
NATURE
NATURE: INTERNATIONAL WEEKLY JOURNAL OF
    SCIENCE
NATURE MATERIALS
NATURE REPORTS CLIMATE CHANGE
NATURE REVIEWS DRUG DISCOVERY

NATURE'S SUNSHINE   621575
Unit 5, Hortonwood 32, TELFORD, TF1 7YL
Tel: 01952 671600 **Fax:** 01952 671601
Titles:
HORIZONS

THE NAUTICAL INSTITUTE   600296
202 Lambeth Road, LONDON, SE1 7LQ **Tel:** 020 7928 1351
Fax: 020 7401 2817
Web site: http://www.nautinst.org
Titles:
SEAWAYS

NAUTILUS UK   13874
Oceanair House, 750-760 High Road, Leytonstone,
LONDON, E11 3BB **Tel:** 020 8989 6677 **Fax:** 020 8530 1015
Web site: http://www.numast.org
Titles:
NAUTILUS UK TELEGRAPH

NAVY NEWS   14263
HMS Nelson, Queen Street, PORTSMOUTH, PO1 3HH
Tel: 023 9229 4228 **Fax:** 023 9283 8845
Email: edit@navynews.co.uk
Web site: http://www.navynews.co.uk
Titles:
NAVY NEWS
NAVY NEWS ONLINE

NBM LTD   696834
68 King James Way, ROYSTON, SG8 7EF
Tel: 01763 244366
Titles:
ECHOES

NCC (UK) LTD   12255
Cavendish House, Cavendish Court, 44-47 Hill Avenue,
AMERSHAM, HP6 5FA **Tel:** 0870 908 8767
Fax: 0870 134 0931
Email: info@ncc.co.uk
Web site: http://www.ncc.co.uk
Titles:
CONSPECTUS
MANAGEMENT CONSULTANTS NEWS

NCG MEDIA   17125
60 Churchill Square, Kings Hill, WEST MALLING, ME19 4YU
Tel: 01732 525800 **Fax:** 01732 525801
Web site: http://www.ncgmedia.co.uk
Titles:
THE EXPORT GUIDE
THE INTERNATIONAL FIRE BUYERS' GUIDE
THE INTERNATIONAL SECURITY BUYERS GUIDE
YOUR NEW HOME
YOUR OVERSEAS PROPERTY
YOUR SHOW HOME

NCJ MEDIA LTD   14856
Groat Market, NEWCASTLE UPON TYNE, NE1 1ED
Tel: 0191 232 7500 **Fax:** 0191 230 4144
Web site: http://www.icnewcastle.co.uk
Titles:
EVENING CHRONICLE (NEWCASTLE)
GOLF NORTH EAST
THE JOURNAL (NEWCASTLE)
NORTH EAST VISION
SUNDAY SUN

UK Publishers & Their Titles

THE NCT 1653885
Alexandra House, Oldham Terrace, LONDON, W3 6NH
Tel: 0844 243 6000 **Fax:** 0844 243 6001
Web site: http://www.nct.org.uk
Titles:
BUMPS & BABIES
NEWGEN

NCVO 13405
Regent's Wharf, 8 All Saints Street, LONDON, N1 9RL
Tel: 020 7713 6161 **Fax:** 020 7713 6300
Web site: http://www.ncvo-vol.org.uk
Titles:
ENGAGE MAGAZINE

NEA 14643
St. Andrew's House, 90-92 Pilgrim Street, NEWCASTLE
UPON TYNE, NE1 6SG **Tel:** 0191 261 5677
Fax: 0191 261 6496
Titles:
ENERGY ACTION

NEEDLE & HANDICRAFTS 623746
1 Castle Close, ROMFORD, RM3 7LN **Tel:** 01708 379897
Fax: 01708 379804
Email: sales@hobbycrafts.net
Web site: http://www.hobbycrafts.net
Titles:
NEEDLE & HANDICRAFTS

NEF (NEW ECONOMICS FOUNDATION) 15707
3 Jonathan Street, LONDON, SE11 5NH **Tel:** 020 7820 6300
Fax: 020 7820 6301
Email: info@neweconomics.org
Web site: http://www.neweconomics.org
Titles:
RADICAL ECONOMICS

NEIL STEWART ASSOCIATES 1649910
PO Box 39976, LONDON, EC1M 5YT **Tel:** 020 7324 4330
Fax: 020 7490 8830
Email: info@neilstewartassociates.co.uk
Web site: http://www.neilstewartassociates.com
Titles:
POLICY REVIEW MAGAZINE

NELSON MEDIA LTD 1726501
Diamond House, 36-38 Hatton Garden, LONDON, EC1N
8EB **Tel:** 020 7841 2950
Titles:
OFFICE PRODUCTS INTERNATIONAL

NELSON PUBLISHING LTD 14082
25A New Street, SALISBURY, SP1 2PH **Tel:** 01722 414245
Fax: 01722 414561
Web site: http://www.nelsoncommunications.co.uk
Titles:
SERVICE DEALER
TURF PROFESSIONAL

NELTON PUBLICATIONS 14229
The Old Sun, Crete Hall Road, GRAVESEND, DA11 9AA
Tel: 01474 536535 **Fax:** 01474 536552
Email: wwn@nelton.co.uk
Web site: http://www.nelton.co.uk
Titles:
FURNITURE PRODUCTS
IRISH WOODWORKING & FURNITURE NEWS
PAC PALLET AND CASE INDUSTRY
WOODWORKING NEWS
WOODWORKING PRODUCTS

NET COMMUNITIES LTD 1676052
4th Floor, 90-93 Cowcross Street, LONDON, EC1M 6BF
Tel: 020 7291 0770
Titles:
ITPROPORTAL.COM

THE NET IMPERATIVE LIMITED 622978
Mare Street Studios, Unit 303, 203-213 Mare Street,
LONDON, E8 3QE **Tel:** 020 8986 7797
Email: editorial@netimperative.com
Web site: http://www.netimperative.com
Titles:
NETIMPERATIVE

NET LOANS LTD 1741437
The Loading Bay, Albion Works, 12-18 Pollard Street,
MANCHESTER, M4 7AJ **Tel:** 0800 019 7180
Titles:
NETLOANS.CO.UK

NETCARS LTD 1741390
The Loading Bay, 12-18 Pollard Street, MANCHESTER, MA
7AJ **Tel:** 0800 019 7180
Titles:
MOTORCARLOANS.COM
NETCARS.CO.UK

NETMEDIAEUROPE 1761867
54 Poland Street, LONDON, W1F 7NJ
Titles:
EWEEKEUROPE UK

NETRO42 LTD 625171
39-51 Highgate Road, LONDON, NW5 1RT
Tel: 020 7267 7002 **Fax:** 020 7267 7544
Email: info@netro42.com
Web site: http://www.netro42.com
Titles:
NEW CAR NET

NETWORK PUBLISHING LTD 1744045
Network House, 28 Ballmoor, Celtic Court, Buckingham
Industrial Estate, BUCKINGHAM, MK18 1RQ
Tel: 01280 829300 **Fax:** 01280 829350
Web site: http://www.networkpublishingltd.com
Titles:
HISTORIC GRAND PRIX CARS ASSOCIATION
MAGAZINE

NETWORKS BUSINESS PUBLICATIONS 600533
Suite 3, Independent House, Imberhorne Lane, EAST
GRINSTEAD, RH19 1TU **Tel:** 01342 300070
Fax: 01342 300060
Titles:
CONTRACT FLOORS
RETAIL FLOORS MAGAZINE

NEW ASIAN MEDIA 625185
37 Hampshire Drive, BIRMINGHAM, B15 3NY
Tel: 07973 198066
Titles:
ASIAN SOCIETY

NEW ASIAN MEDIA LTD 1752541
EMF House, 12 Charlotte Street, MANCHESTER, M1 4FL
Tel: 0161 245 3257 **Fax:** 0161 245 3333
Titles:
ASIAN LITE

THE NEW BLACK PUBLISHERS 1711819
15 Gardens Court, 231-232 Ladywood, Middleway,
BIRMINGHAM, B16 8EU **Tel:** 0121 454 2238
Fax: 0121 454 2238
Email: sholaadenekan@thenewblackmagazine.com
Web site: http://www.thenewblackmagazine.com
Titles:
THE NEW BLACK MAGAZINE

THE NEW BRIDGE 16376
27A Medway Street, LONDON, SW1P 2BD
Tel: 020 7976 0779 **Fax:** 020 7976 0767
Titles:
INSIDE TIME

NEW CENTURY PUBLISHING GROUP 1622485
New Century House, Stadium Road, INVERNESS, IV1 1FG
Tel: 01463 732222 **Fax:** 01463 732220
Titles:
EXECUTIVE MAGAZINE
HIGHLAND LIFE MAGAZINE

NEW ENERGY FINANCE 1768100
2nd Floor, 283-288 High Holborn, LONDON, WC1V 7HP
Tel: 020 7092 8800 **Fax:** 020 7092 0801
Titles:
NEW ENERGY FINANCE
NEW ENERGY FINANCE BRIEFING

NEW ENERGY WORLD PRESS LTD 1768102
357 Strand, LONDON, WC2R 0HS
Titles:
NEWNET

NEW FREEDOM PUBLICATIONS LTD 16700
Burlington Court, Carlisle Street, GOOLE, DN14 5EG
Tel: 01405 760298 **Fax:** 01405 763815
Email: newfreedom@btinternet.com
Titles:
H & E NATURISM

THE NEW IMBIBER 1710860
16 Mount Street, LEWES, BN7 1HL **Tel:** 01273 486787
Titles:
THE NEW IMBIBER

NEW INTERNATIONALIST PUBLICATIONS LTD. 15710
55 Rectory Road, OXFORD, OX4 1BW **Tel:** 01865 811400
Fax: 01865 793152
Email: ni@newint.org
Web site: http://www.newint.org
Titles:
NEW INTERNATIONALIST

NEW JOURNAL ENTERPRISES LTD 14891
40 Camden Road, LONDON, NW1 9DR **Tel:** 020 7419 9000
Fax: 020 7482 7317
Titles:
JOURNAL SERIES

NEW LEAF PUBLISHING 17644
Studio 2 Willowfield Studios, 67A Willowfield Road,
EASTBOURNE, BN22 8AP **Tel:** 01323 431313
Fax: 01323 731136
Titles:
AQUILA MAGAZINE

NEW LEFT REVIEW LTD 622950
6 Meard Street, LONDON, W1F 0EG **Tel:** 020 7734 8830
Fax: 020 7439 3869
Email: mail@newleftreview.org
Web site: http://www.newleftreview.org
Titles:
NEW LEFT REVIEW

NEW LIFE PUBLISHING COMPANY 15892
PO Box 777, NOTTINGHAM, NG11 6ZZ **Tel:** 01158 240777
Fax: 0115 984 5251
Email: info@newlifepublishing.co.uk
Web site: http://www.newlifepublishing.co.uk
Titles:
DIRECTION
JOY MAGAZINE
NEW LIFE NEWSPAPER

NEW MEDIA REPUBLIC LTD 1751793
The Forge, Blisworth Hill Farm, Stoke Road, BLISWORTH,
NN7 3BD **Tel:** 01604 858524
Titles:
DRIVERS-REPUBLIC.COM

NEW MILLENNIUM PUBLISHING 18777
69 Grand Parade, BRIGHTON, BN2 9TS **Tel:** 05601 169695
Web site: http://www.nmp-eu.com
Titles:
ISLAMIC BANKING AND FINANCE

NEW POWER CONSULTING 1765839
Fair Snape, Gote Lane, RINGMER, BN8 5HT
Titles:
NEW POWER

NEW START PUBLISHING LTD 18738
The Workstation, Paternoster Row, SHEFFIELD, S1 2BX
Tel: 0114 281 6130
Email: info@newstartmag.co.uk
Web site: http://www.newstartmag.co.uk
Titles:
NEW START
NEW START

NEW STATESMAN LTD 15090
1st Floor, Boundary House, 91-93 Charterhouse Street, LONDON, EC1M 6HR **Tel:** 020 7730 3444
Fax: 020 7259 0181

Titles:
NEW STATESMAN

NEW VISION PRINT & PUBLISHING LTD 1735388
43A Esplanade, GREENOCK, PA16 7RY **Tel:** 01475 783000
Fax: 01475 728145
Email: cbjewell@btinternet.com
Web site: http://www.newvisionpublishing.co.uk

Titles:
BARRHEAD PRESS
INVERCLYDER
MEARNS PRESS

NEW WAVE MEDIA INC 1640386
12 Braehead, BO'NESS, EH51 0BZ **Tel:** 01506 822240

Titles:
MARINE TECHNOLOGY REPORTER
MARITIME REPORTER AND ENGINEERING NEWS

NEW WAVE PUBLISHING 13953
Hesketh House, 3 School Road, SALE, M33 7XY
Tel: 0161 374 5615 **Fax:** 0161 374 6436
Email: it.info@itmagazine.uk.com

Titles:
INDUSTRIAL TECHNOLOGY
INDUSTRIAL TECHNOLOGY
LIQUIDS AND GAS HANDLING
SMALL SHIPS AND WORKBOATS

NEW WELSH REVIEW LTD 18326
PO Box 170, ABERYSTWYTH, SY23 1WZ
Tel: 01970 626230 **Fax:** 01970 626230
Email: admin@newwelshreview.com
Web site: http://www.newwelshreview.com

Titles:
NEW WELSH REVIEW

NEW WORLD PRESS 600247
64B Grange Road, SUTTON, SM2 6SN **Tel:** 020 8643 3967
Fax: 020 8286 0468
Web site: http://www.new-world.ws

Titles:
NEW WORLD

NEW WORLD WEEKLY LTD 16048
234 Holloway Road, LONDON, N7 8DA **Tel:** 020 7700 2673
Fax: 020 7607 6706

Titles:
NEW WORLD

THE NEW WRITER 14679
PO Box 60, CRANBROOK, TN17 2ZR **Tel:** 01580 212626
Fax: 01580 212041

Titles:
THE NEW WRITER

NEW ZEALAND LTD 17291
Suite 5, Eden House, 59 Fulham High Street, LONDON, SW6
3JJ **Tel:** 020 7731 0202
Web site: http://www.nznewsuk.co.uk

Titles:
NEW ZEALAND INSPIRED

NEWARK ADVERTISER LTD 14975
Appleton Gate, NEWARK, NG24 1JX **Tel:** 01636 681234
Fax: 01636 681122
Email: post@newarkadvertiser.co.uk
Web site: http://www.newarkadvertiser.co.uk

Titles:
NEWARK ADVERTISER SERIES

NEWBURY WEEKLY NEWS (PRINTERS) LTD 16480
Newspaper House, Faraday Road, NEWBURY, RG14 2DW
Tel: 01635 564500 **Fax:** 01635 522922
Email: editor@newburynews.co.uk
Web site: http://www.newburytoday.co.uk

Titles:
NEWBURY BUSINESS TODAY
NEWBURY WEEKLY NEWS SERIES

NEWBYCOM LTD 1639899
Crendon House, Crendon Industrial Park, LONG CRENDON,
HP18 9BB **Tel:** 01844 202027 **Fax:** 01844 202267

Titles:
FAST FASTENING ADHESIVES ASSEMBLY & JOINING
TECHNOLOGY
FASTENING SOLUTIONS

NEWCASTLE CITY COUNCIL 622794
Civic Centre, Barras Bridge, NEWCASTLE UPON TYNE,
NE99 2BN **Tel:** 0191 211 5093 **Fax:** 0191 211 4888
Web site: http://www.newcastle.gov.uk

Titles:
CITYLIFE

NEWDESIGN MAGAZINE LTD 1644316
6A New Street, WARWICK, CV34 4RX **Tel:** 01926 408207
Fax: 01926 408206
Email: info@newdesignmagazine.co.uk
Web site: http://www.newdesignmagazine.co.uk

Titles:
NEW DESIGN

NEWHALL PUBLICATIONS LTD 15112
Newhall Lane, Hoylake, WIRRAL, CH47 4BQ
Tel: 0844 545 8102 **Fax:** 0844 545 8103
Web site: http://www.candis.co.uk

Titles:
CANDIS

NEWS4MEDIA LTD 1716854
Unit 11, The Chandlery, 50 Westminster Bridge Road,
LONDON, SE1 7QY **Tel:** 020 7953 8770 **Fax:** 020 7953 8773
Web site: http://www.news4media.com

Titles:
BEAUTY4MEDIA.COM
BUSINESS4MEDIA.COM
ENTERTAINMENT4MEDIA.COM
FASHION4MEDIA.COM
HEALTH4MEDIA.COM
HOMES4MEDIA
MONEY4MEDIA.COM
MOTORING4MEDIA.COM
PROPERTY4MEDIA.COM
SPORT4MEDIA.COM
TECHNOLOGY4MEDIA.COM

NEWS & MEDIA LTD 15700
Suite B, 233 Seven Sisters Road, LONDON, N4 2DA
Tel: 020 7263 1417 **Fax:** 020 7272 8934

Titles:
IMPACT INTERNATIONAL

NEWS GROUP NEWSPAPERS LTD 12956
1 Virginia Street, LONDON, E98 1NW **Tel:** 020 7782 4000
Web site: http://www.newsint.co.uk

Titles:
FABULOUS
NEWS OF THE WORLD
NEWS OF THE WORLD (GLASGOW OFFICE)
NEWS OF THE WORLD (MANCHESTER OFFICE)
NEWS OF THE WORLD ONLINE
THE SCOTTISH SUN (GLASGOW OFFICE)
THE SUN
THE SUN (BIRMINGHAM OFFICE)
THE SUN ONLINE
THE TV MAG

NEWS INTERNATIONAL LTD 1718407
1 Pennington Street, LONDON, E98 1XY **Tel:** 020 7782 6000

Titles:
THE SUNDAY TIMES TRAVEL MAGAZINE
THELONDONPAPER.COM

NEWS INTERNATIONAL (SCOTLAND) LTD 14823
6th Floor, Guildhall, 57 Queen Street, GLASGOW, G1 3EN
Tel: 0141 420 5100 **Fax:** 0141 420 5262

Titles:
ECOSSE
THE SUNDAY TIMES SCOTLAND

NEWSBRIDGE LTD 1711780
First News House, 95 The Street, West Horsley,
LEATHERHEAD, KT24 6DD **Tel:** 01483 281005

Titles:
FIRST NEWS

NEWSCAN LTD. 18505
21 Grosvenor Crescent, EDINBURGH, EH12 5EE
Tel: 0131 225 6357 **Fax:** 0131 346 7247

Titles:
INSPIRES

NEWSCO INSIDER LTD 14721
Boulton House, 17-21 Chorlton Street, MANCHESTER, M1
3HY **Tel:** 0161 907 9711 **Fax:** 0161 236 9862
Web site: http://www.newsco.com

Titles:
INSIDER (NORTH WEST BUSINESS INSIDER)
INSIDER (SOUTH WEST BUSINESS INSIDER)
INSIDERWEEKLY (EAST MIDLANDS)
INSIDERWEEKLY (WEST MIDLANDS)
MIDLANDS BUSINESS INSIDER
WALES BUSINESS INSIDER
YORKSHIRE BUSINESS INSIDER

NEWSLINK 696689
Flaxfield, Wittons Lane, Hoxne, EYE, IP21 5AE
Tel: 01379 669157 **Fax:** 01379 669157

Titles:
WEEKLY TRIBUNE

THE NEWSPAPER SOCIETY 13438
St. Andrew's House, St. Andrew Street, LONDON, EC4A
3AY **Tel:** 020 7636 7400 **Fax:** 020 7632 7401
Web site: http://www.newspapersoc.org.uk

Titles:
COMMERCIAL FOCUS
NS NEWS

NEWSPOST LTD 697414
Edward Latham House, 1 Oates Street, DEWSBURY, WF13
1BB **Tel:** 01924 439498 **Fax:** 01924 457994
Email: info@newspost.co.uk

Titles:
THE PRESS (DEWSBURY)

NEWSQUEST 1711089
Gazette House, Pelton Road, BASINGSTOKE, RG21 6YD
Tel: 01256 461131 **Fax:** 01256 840369

Titles:
BASINGSTOKE AND NORTH HANTS GAZETTE SERIES

NEWSQUEST (BLACKBURN) LTD 697172
Newspaper House, High Street, BLACKBURN, BB1 1HT
Tel: 01254 678 678

Titles:
ASIAN IMAGE

NEWSQUEST (ESSEX) LTD 17581
Wickham House, 1 Northgate Street, COLCHESTER, CO1
1HA **Tel:** 01206 506000 **Fax:** 01206 508195

Titles:
BRAINTREE & WITHAM TIMES & GAZETTE SERIES
CASTLE POINT ECHO INCLUDING RAYLEIGH &
ROCHFORD
DAILY GAZETTE
ECHO (BASILDON)
LIMITED EDITION THE MAGAZINE FOR ESSEX
MALDON & BURNHAM STANDARD SERIES
THURROCK GAZETTE
WEEKLY NEWS SERIES (CHELMSFORD)

NEWSQUEST HERALD & TIMES LTD 1627246
200 Renfield Street, GLASGOW, G2 3QB
Tel: 0141 302 7000 **Fax:** 0141 302 6699

Titles:
EVENING TIMES (GLASGOW)
EVENING TIMES WEE RED BOOK
THE HERALD BUSINESS MAGAZINE
THE HERALD (GLASGOW)
THE HERALD (GLASGOW) (CITY/LONDON OFFICE)
THE HERALD (GLASGOW) (EDINBURGH OFFICE)
THE HERALD MAGAZINE
THE SCOTTISH FARMER
SCOTTISH JOBS
SCOTTISH MOUNTAINEER
SUCCESS
TGO THE GREAT OUTDOORS

NEWSQUEST LANCASHIRE LIMITED 16321
Newspaper House, High Street, BLACKBURN, BB1 1HT
Tel: 01254 678678

UK Publishers & Their Titles

Titles:
BLACKBURN CITIZEN
CHORLEY CITIZEN

NEWSQUEST (LANCS)   670292
Newspaper House, Churchgate, BOLTON, BL1 1DE
Tel: 01204 522345 **Fax:** 01204 537427
Web site: http://www.theboltonnews.co.uk
Titles:
THE BOLTON NEWS
LIMITED EDITION (BOLTON)

NEWSQUEST (LET/CITIZEN) LTD   623502
Newspaper House, High Street, BLACKBURN, BB1 1HT
Tel: 01254 678678
Titles:
LANCASHIRE TELEGRAPH

NEWSQUEST MEDIA GROUP   14830
Unecol House, 819 London Road, SUTTON, SM3 9BN
Tel: 020 8329 9244
Web site: http://www.newsquest.co.uk
Titles:
BERROWS WORCESTER JOURNAL
BOATING CORNWALL
BOLTON JOURNAL
BRIDPORT & LYME REGIS NEWS SERIES
BROMSGROVE ADVERTISER SERIES
BUCKS FREE PRESS SERIES
THE BURNLEY AND PENDLE CITIZEN
BURY TIMES SERIES
CRAVEN HERALD & PIONEER
CROYDON GUARDIAN
DAILY ECHO (BOURNEMOUTH)
EVESHAM JOURNAL SERIES
GUARDIAN & NEWS SERIES (SUTTON)
HARROW TIMES
HEREFORD SOCIETY
HEREFORD TIMES
JOBS & CAREERS WEEKLY LONDON & ESSEX
LEIGH, TYLDESLEY AND ATHERTON JOURNAL
LUDLOW ADVERTISER SERIES
MALVERN GAZETTE & LEDBURY REPORTER SERIES
NEWPORT & CWMBRAN WEEKLY ARGUS
NEWS SHOPPER SERIES
THE PACKET SERIES
REDDITCH ADVERTISER AND CHRONICLE SERIES
RUNCORN & WIDNES WORLD
SALE & ALTRINCHAM MESSENGER SERIES
THE SHUTTLE INCORPORATING KIDDERMINSTER
   TIMES AND STOURPORT NEWS
SOUTHERN PROPERTY ADVERTISER
ST. HELENS STAR
STOURBRIDGE NEWS
SURREY COMET
TIMES SERIES (RICHMOND)
WALTHAM FOREST GUARDIAN & INDEPENDENT
   SERIES
WANSTEAD AND WOODFORD GUARDIAN
WORCESTER NEWS

NEWSQUEST (MEDIA GROUP) LTD   18658
Newspaper House, Test Lane, Redbridge, SOUTHAMPTON,
SO16 9JX **Tel:** 023 8042 4777 **Fax:** 023 8042 4545
Web site: http://www.newsquest.co.uk
Titles:
ADVERTISER SERIES (POOLE & SWANAGE)
ANDOVER ADVERTISER SERIES
BANBURY CAKE
BARRY & DISTRICT NEWS SERIES
CAERPHILLY CAMPAIGN SERIES
CHARD & ILMINSTER NEWS
DORSET ADVERTISER
DORSET ECHO
DORSET SOCIETY
THE FREE PRESS NEWSPAPER SERIES
GLOUCESTERSHIRE GAZETTE SERIES
HAMPSHIRE CHRONICLE SERIES
HAMPSHIRE SOCIETY MAGAZINE & WINCHESTER
   SOCIETY
INDEPENDENT SERIES (GLOUCESTERSHIRE)
LIFETIME
LIMITED EDITION
MERCURY AND WEEKLY NEWS SERIES
NEW FOREST POST INCORPORATING FOREST &
   WATERSIDE OBSERVER
THE NEWS EXTRA AND ADVERTISER SERIES
THE PINK SOUTHAMPTON
THE SAINTS MAGAZINE
SOMERSET COUNTY GAZETTE SERIES
SOUTH WALES GUARDIAN SERIES
SOUTH WEST FARMER
THE SOUTHERN DAILY ECHO (SOUTHAMPTON)
STAR AND EXPRESS SERIES
WESTERN TELEGRAPH SERIES
WILTS & GLOUCESTERSHIRE STANDARD SERIES

NEWSQUEST MIDLANDS (SOUTH) LTD   14027
Severn House, Prescott Drive, Warndon Business Park,
WORCESTER, WR4 9NE **Tel:** 01905 748200
Titles:
DUDLEY NEWS & COUNTY EXPRESS
HALESOWEN NEWS

NEWSQUEST MIDLANDS SOUTH LTD (STOURBRIDGE)
                                                            1733236
St. Johns House, St. Johns Road, STOURBRIDGE, DY8 1EH
Tel: 01384 358050 **Fax:** 01384 357115
Titles:
LIMITED EDITION NORTH

NEWSQUEST MIDLANDS SOUTH LTD (WORCESTER)
                                                            1733237
Berrows House, Hylton Road, WORCESTER, WR2 5JX
Tel: 01905 748200
Titles:
LIMITED EDITION SOUTH

NEWSQUEST (NORTH LONDON)   16569
Observer House, Caxton Court, Caxton Way, Watford
Business Park, WATFORD, WD18 8RJ **Tel:** 01923 216216
Fax: 01923 243738
Titles:
BOREHAMWOOD & ELSTREE TIMES
GUARDIAN AND INDEPENDENT SERIES
HENDON TIMES SERIES
LIMITED EDITION THE MAGAZINE FOR
   HERTFORDSHIRE
NEWSQUEST HERTFORDSHIRE, BUCKINGHAMSHIRE &
   MIDDLESEX
REVIEW SERIES
WATFORD OBSERVER SERIES

NEWSQUEST (NORTHWEST) LTD   17640
Crossford Court, Dane Road, SALE, M33 7BZ
Tel: 01925 434000 **Fax:** 01925 434115
Titles:
CREWE GUARDIAN SERIES
LIFESTYLE
LIFESTYLE
MID-CHESHIRE GUARDIAN SERIES
WARRINGTON GUARDIAN SERIES
WIRRAL GLOBE SERIES

NEWSQUEST (OXFORDSHIRE) LTD   17444
Newspaper House, Osney Mead, OXFORD, OX2 0EJ
Tel: 01865 425262 **Fax:** 01865 425554
Email: inquiries@nqo.com
Titles:
BICESTER ADVERTISER
HERALD AND TIMES SERIES OXON
IN BUSINESS THE OXFORD TIMES
JOBS AND CAREERS
OXFORD MAIL
OXFORD STAR
OXFORDMAIL.CO.UK
OXFORDSHIRE HOMES
OXFORDSHIRE LIMITED EDITION
WITNEY AND WEST OXFORDSHIRE GAZETTE

NEWSQUEST PLC   1711138
3 Falmouth Business Park, Bickland Water Road,
FALMOUTH, TR11 4SZ **Tel:** 01326 213333
Fax: 01326 212108
Titles:
SMALLHOLDER

NEWSQUEST (SOUTH LONDON)   14889
Newspaper House, 34-44 London Road, MORDEN, SM4
5BX **Tel:** 020 8646 6336 **Fax:** 020 8254 5367
Web site: http://www.newsquest.co.uk
Titles:
LIMITED EDITION

NEWSQUEST SPECIALIST MEDIA LTD   1630409
30 Cannon Street, LONDON, EC4M 6YJ **Tel:** 020 7618 3456
Fax: 020 7618 3459
Web site: http://www.newsquestspecialistmedia.com
Titles:
BOXING NEWS
ENGAGED INVESTOR
FIGHTING FIT
THE FUND BUSINESS
GLOBAL REINSURANCE
INSURANCE TIMES

INSURANCETIMES ONLINE
PENSIONS INSIGHT
STRATEGIC RISK

NEWSQUEST SUNDAY HERALD LTD   1627247
200 Renfield Street, GLASGOW, G2 3QB
Tel: 0141 302 7800
Email: news@sundayherald.com
Web site: http://www.sundayherald.com
Titles:
FRESH
SUNDAY HERALD
SUNDAY HERALD (EDINBURGH)
SUNDAY HERALD MAGAZINE

NEWSQUEST (SUSSEX) LTD   16574
Argus House, Crowhurst Road, Hollingbury, BRIGHTON,
BN1 8AR **Tel:** 01273 544544 **Fax:** 01273 566114
Titles:
THE ARGUS
BRIGHTON AND HOVE LEADER SERIES
THE GUIDE
REDHILL REIGATE HORLEY LIFE

NEWSQUEST WALES & GLOUCESTERSHIRE   1644475
Cardiff Road, NEWPORT, NP20 3QN **Tel:** 01633 810000
Titles:
MILFORD & WEST WALES MERCURY
MONMOUTHSHIRE COUNTY LIFE
SOUTH WALES GOLFER
STROUD NEWS AND JOURNAL
TIVY-SIDE ADVERTISER

NEWSQUEST (WILTSHIRE) LTD   16522
100 Victoria Road, SWINDON, SN1 3BE **Tel:** 01793 528144
Fax: 01793 501888
Email: digitalmedia@swindonadvertiser.co.uk
Web site: http://www.newsquestwiltshire.co.uk
Titles:
SWINDON ADVERTISER
SWINDON STAR
WILTSHIRE BUSINESS
WILTSHIRE GAZETTE AND HERALD SERIES
WILTSHIRE TIMES & NEWS SERIES

**NEWSQUEST YORKSHIRE AND NORTH EAST
(BRADFORD)**   17283
Hall Ings, BRADFORD, BD1 1JR **Tel:** 01274 729511
Fax: 01274 723634
Titles:
ASIAN EYE
BRADFORD TARGET SERIES
ILKLEY GAZETTE
KEIGHLEY NEWS SERIES
TELEGRAPH & ARGUS
THE TELEGRAPH AND ARGUS
WHARFEDALE & AIREDALE OBSERVER

**NEWSQUEST YORKSHIRE AND NORTH EAST
(DARLINGTON)**   17745
PO Box 14, Priestgate, DARLINGTON, DL1 1NF
Tel: 01325 381313 **Fax:** 01325 464637
Titles:
ADVERTISER SERIES (DURHAM)
DARLINGTON & STOCKTON TIMES SERIES
DURHAM TIMES
THE NORTHERN ECHO (DARLINGTON)
THENORTHERNECHO.CO.UK

NEWSQUEST YORKSHIRE AND NORTH EAST (YORK)
                                                            18960
PO Box 29, 76-86 Walmgate, YORK, YO1 9YN
Tel: 01904 653051 **Fax:** 01904 612853
Titles:
HOME & GARDEN
THE PRESS (YORK)
STAR SERIES (SELBY & YORK)
THE YORK FREE GUIDE
YORKSHIRE LIVING

NEWSTRAID BENEVOLENT FUND   16165
Barnetson Court, Braintree Road, DUNMOW, CM6 1HS
Tel: 01371 874198 **Fax:** 01371 873816
Titles:
NEWS FROM NEWSTRAID

NEWTON MANN LTD 13687
The Derwent Business Centre, Clarke Street, DERBY, DE1
2BU **Tel:** 01332 290460 **Fax:** 01332 345680
Email: admin@newtonmann.co.uk
Web site: http://www.newtonmann.co.uk
Titles:
CATERING MANAGER
FORGE

NEWTON MEDIA LTD 1726784
15-17 Newton Way, Woolsthorpe By Colsterworth,
GRANTHAM, NG33 5NR **Tel:** 01476 861737
Fax: 020 7681 1248
Email: info@newtonmedia.co.uk
Web site: http://www.bermudareinsurancemagazine.com
Titles:
BERMUDA REINSURANCE
CAYMAN FUNDS

NEWTON PRESS 14930
St. Cuthberts Way, Aycliffe Business Park, NEWTON
AYCLIFFE, DL5 6DX **Tel:** 01325 300212 **Fax:** 01325 312893
Web site: http://www.gonp.co.uk
Titles:
NEWTON NEWS

NEWTOWNARDS CHRONICLE LTD 15084
25 Frances Street, NEWTOWNARDS, BT23 7DT
Tel: 028 9181 3333 **Fax:** 028 9182 0087
Email: news@ardschronicle.co.uk
Titles:
NEWTOWNARDS CHRONICLE

NEWTRADE PUBLISHING LTD 14678
11 Angel Gate, City Road, LONDON, EC1V 2SD
Tel: 020 7689 0600 **Fax:** 020 7689 0700
Email: info@newtrade.co.uk
Web site: http://www.newtrade.co.uk
Titles:
RETAIL EXPRESS
RETAIL NEWSAGENT

NEWZEYE LTD 17172
The Chapel, Wellington Road, LONDON, NW10 5LJ
Tel: 020 8969 1008 **Fax:** 020 8969 1334
Email: customerservice@newzeye.com
Web site: http://www.newzeye.com
Titles:
BROWNFIELD BRIEFING
PROPERTY FORECAST
SUSTAINABLE BUILDING

NEXUS INTERNET LTD 16639
3 The Glen, Shepherdswell, DOVER, CT15 7PF
Tel: 01304 832470
Titles:
GOLF TODAY

NFSE (SALES LTD) 13827
275 Newmarket Road, CAMBRIDGE, CB5 8JE
Tel: 01223 477411 **Fax:** 01223 327356
Titles:
FIRST VOICE OF BUSINESS

NFU SCOTLAND 18067
Rural Centre-West Mains, Ingliston, NEWBRIDGE, EH28 8LT
Tel: 0131 472 4000 **Fax:** 0131 472 4010
Titles:
SCOTTISH FARMING LEADER

NH PUBLISHING LTD 1719333
Suite 1 Freshfield Hall, The Square, Lewes Road, FOREST
ROW, RH18 5ES
Web site: http://www.nhdmag.com
Titles:
NETWORK HEALTH DIETITIANS

N.I. MEDIA LTD 1707358
Lakeland Manor, HILLSBOROUGH, BT26 6RE
Tel: 028 9268 8577 **Fax:** 028 9268 8655
Titles:
NORTHERN IRELAND INTERIORS & LIVING

NICE ONE PUBLISHING LTD 1709548
43 Award Road, WIMBORNE, BH21 7NT **Tel:** 0845 193 3600
Fax: 0845 193 3602
Titles:
MONITORING MONTHLY

NICHOLAS HALL & COMPANY 13891
35 Alexandra Street, SOUTHEND-ON-SEA, SS1 1BW
Tel: 01702 220200 **Fax:** 01702 430787
Titles:
NICHOLAS HALL INSIGHT WESTERN EUROPE

NICK FLETCHER & ASSOCIATES 1649441
Bracken House, Queens Park Avenue, Dresden, STOKE-
ON-TRENT, ST3 4AU **Tel:** 01782 312119 **Fax:** 01782 314152
Email: mail@roadtests.co.uk
Web site: http://www.roadtests.co.uk
Titles:
ROADTESTS.CO.UK

NIELSEN BUSINESS MEDIA 697357
5th Floor, Endeavour House, 189 Shaftesbury Avenue,
LONDON, WC2H 8TJ **Tel:** 020 7420 6006
Fax: 020 7420 6014
Titles:
BILLBOARD
THE BOOKSELLER
THE HOLLYWOOD REPORTER

NIGEL J. CLARKE PUBLICATIONS 18461
Befferlands Farm Workshop, Charmouth, DORSET, DT6
6RD **Tel:** 01297 561577 **Fax:** 01297 561577
Web site: http://www.njcpublications.co.uk
Titles:
TIDE TIMES

NIMROD PUBLICATIONS 672242
Suite 2B, Bishops Wheel House, Albion Way, HORSHAM,
RH12 1AH **Tel:** 01403 230302 **Fax:** 01403 230525
Titles:
AIRCRAFT COMMERCE

NOBLE HOUSE MEDIA LTD 16534
14-16 Great Pulteney Street, LONDON, W1F 9ND
Tel: 020 7440 3823 **Fax:** 020 7437 4250
Titles:
MOBILE
MOBILE CHOICE
MOBILE CHOICE FOR BUSINESS

THE NOBLE PUBLISHING COMPANY 1654103
The Old Corn Store, Heartenoak Road, Hawkhurst,
CRANBROOK, TN18 4DZ **Tel:** 01580 752404
Fax: 01580 752604
Email: noblepublishing@aol.com
Titles:
NOBLESVENUES.COM

NOOZZ.COM LTD 1751940
40 Grosvenor Gardens, LONDON, SW1W 0EB
Tel: 020 7259 9000 **Fax:** 020 7259 9020
Email: info@noozz.com
Web site: http://www.noozz.com
Titles:
NOOZZ.COM

NORTH CORNWALL ADVERTISER LTD 15561
Tindle House, 2 Trevanson Street, WADEBRIDGE, PL27
7AW **Tel:** 01208 815096 **Fax:** 01208 815935
Web site: http://www.cornwalladvertisers.co.uk
Titles:
MID CORNWALL ADVERTISER
NORTH CORNWALL ADVERTISER

NORTH EDINBURGH NEWS 622091
222 Crewe Road North, EDINBURGH, EH5 2NS
Tel: 0131 467 3972 **Fax:** 0131 467 3973
Web site: http://www.northedinburghnews.co.uk
Titles:
NORTH EDINBURGH NEWS (NEN)

NORTH LONDON CHAMBER OF COMMERCE 14696
Enfield Business Centre, 201 Hertford Road, ENFIELD, EN3
5JH **Tel:** 020 8443 3833 **Fax:** 020 8443 3822
Titles:
BUSINESS LEADER

NORTH NOTTS NEWSPAPERS LTD 12816
121 Newgate Lane, MANSFIELD, NG18 2PA
Tel: 01623 456789 **Fax:** 01623 464749
Titles:
CHAD SERIES MANSFIELD

NORTH OF SCOTLAND NEWSPAPERS 15059
42 Union Street, WICK, KW1 5ED **Tel:** 01955 602424
Fax: 01955 604822
Titles:
JOHN O'GROAT JOURNAL SERIES

NORTH ONE 1713940
34 Fouberts Place, LONDON, W1F 7PX **Tel:** 020 7478 7647
Titles:
WRC.COM

NORTH POINT PUBLISHING 1676003
East Park Lodge, East Park Road, BLACKBURN, BB1 8DW
Tel: 01254 295580 **Fax:** 01254 295381
Titles:
LANCASHIRE BUSINESS VIEW

NORTH SOMERSET AND MEDIA LTD 14900
Elton House, Albert Road, CLEVEDON, BS21 7SW
Tel: 01275 335142 **Fax:** 01275 335147
Titles:
CLEVEDON NEWSPAPERS SERIES

NORTH SURREY AND LONDON NEWSPAPERS 12792
89 Eastworth Road, CHERTSEY, KT16 8DX
Tel: 01932 561111 **Fax:** 01932 563316
Titles:
HOUNSLOW CHRONICLE

NORTH WALES INDEPENDENT PUBLICATIONS 18971
Vale Road, Llandudno Junction, CONWAY, LL31 9SL
Tel: 01492 584321 **Fax:** 01492 593664
Titles:
THE CAERNARFON HERALD SERIES

NORTH WEST FEDERATION OF FOLK CLUBS 17632
36 The Oaks, Eaves Green, CHORLEY, PR7 3QU
Tel: 01257 263678
Titles:
FOLK NORTH WEST

NORTH WEST NEWS LTD 623720
52 Walton Road, Stockton Heath, WARRINGTON, WA4 6NL
Tel: 01925 600601 **Fax:** 01925 264102
Email: info@southwarringtonnews.co.uk
Titles:
SOUTH WARRINGTON NEWS

NORTHAMPTONSHIRE NEWSPAPERS LTD 14978
Upper Mounts, NORTHAMPTON, NN1 3HR
Tel: 01604 467000 **Fax:** 01604 467200
Email: editor@northantsnews.co.uk
Titles:
IMAGE
NORTHAMPTON CHRONICLE AND ECHO
NORTHAMPTON MERCURY
NORTHAMPTONCHRON.CO.UK
NORTHANTS MERCURY & CITIZEN SERIES

NORTHCLIFFE MEDIA LTD 14714
31-32 John Street, LONDON, WC1N 2QB
Tel: 020 7400 1401 **Fax:** 020 7400 1111
Web site: http://www.thisisnorthcliffe.co.uk
Titles:
ADSCENE, HERALD & EXPRESS SERIES (FOLKESTONE)
ADVERTISER SERIES (SOUTH CHESHIRE)
ADVERTISER SERIES (STOKE-ON-TRENT)
BRIDGWATER TIMES
CRAWLEY NEWS
CROYDON ADVERTISER & POST SERIES
EAST GRINSTEAD COURIER & OBSERVER

EAST KENT GAZETTE SERIES
THE GUIDE
HOLDTHEFRONTPAGE.CO.UK
POST & TIMES SERIES
SURREY MIRROR SERIES
TAMWORTH HERALD SERIES
WESTERN GAZETTE

NORTHEAST PRESS LTD 14839
Echo House, Pennywell, SUNDERLAND, SR4 9ER
Tel: 0191 501 5800 **Fax:** 0191 534 5975

Titles:
FOOTBALL ECHO (SUNDERLAND)
HARTLEPOOL MAIL
MORPETH HERALD INC PONTELAND OBSERVER
NORTH EAST HOMES
NORTHUMBERLAND GAZETTE
THE SHIELDS GAZETTE
STAR SERIES
SUNDERLAND ECHO
SUNDERLAND TODAY

NORTHERN ALPHA NEWSPAPER GROUP 15069
20 Railway Road, COLERAINE, BT52 1PD
Tel: 028 7034 3344 **Fax:** 028 7034 3606

Titles:
THE CHRONICLE AND LEADER SERIES (COLERAINE)
NORTHERN CONSTITUTION SERIES

NORTHERN & SHELL PLC 12904
10 Lower Thames Street, LONDON, EC3R 6EN
Tel: 0871 434 1010

Titles:
HOT STARS
OK!
STAR

NORTHERN BEE BOOKS 16335
Scout Bottom Farm, Mytholmroyd, HEBDEN BRIDGE, HX7
5JS **Tel:** 01422 882751 **Fax:** 01422 886157

Titles:
THE BEEKEEPERS QUARTERLY

NORTHERN CROSS TRUSTEES 15896
St. Joseph's Parish Centre, St. Paul's Road, HARTLEPOOL,
TS26 9EY **Tel:** 01429 274305 **Fax:** 01429 274328
Email: norcross@btconnect.com

Titles:
NORTHERN CROSS

NORTHERN EARTH 16641
10 Jubilee Street, Mytholmroyd, HEBDEN BRIDGE, HX7
5NP **Tel:** 01422 882441 **Fax:** 01422 882441
Web site: http://www.northernearth.co.uk

Titles:
NORTHERN EARTH

NORTHERN IRELAND TRAVEL AND LEISURE NEWS
15959
Unit 1, Windsor Business Park, 16-18 Lower Windsor
Avenue, BELFAST, BT9 7DW **Tel:** 028 9066 6151
Fax: 028 9068 3819
Web site: http://www.nitravelnews.com

Titles:
ESCAPE
NORTHERN IRELAND TRAVEL NEWS

NORTHSTAR PUBLISHING LTD 1645322
Spitfire Studios, 61 Collier Street, LONDON, N1 9BE
Tel: 020 7833 7410 **Fax:** 020 7833 7411

Titles:
THE AUDI MAGAZINE
MY BRENT CROSS

NORTHUMBRIA STUDENTS' UNION 1710755
2 Sandyford Road, NEWCASTLE UPON TYNE, NE1 8SB
Tel: 0191 227 3737

Titles:
NORTHUMBRIA STUDENT

NORTH-WEST OF IRELAND PTG. & PUB. CO. LTD 15075
14 John Street, OMAGH, BT78 1DT **Tel:** 028 8224 3444
Fax: 028 8224 2206

Titles:
DONEGAL NEWS (DERRY PEOPLE)

FERMANAGH HERALD
ULSTER HERALD SERIES

NOTICIAS LATIN AMERICA 18918
PO Box 34783, LONDON, N7 7WD **Tel:** 020 7686 1633
Fax: 020 7686 1662
Email: informacion@noticias.co.uk
Web site: http://www.noticias.co.uk

Titles:
NOTICIAS LATIN AMERICA

NOTTINGHAM POST MEDIA GROUP LTD 14844
Castle Wharf House, NOTTINGHAM, NG1 7EU
Tel: 0115 948 2000

Titles:
FOOTBALL POST (NOTTINGHAM)
NOTTINGHAM EVENING POST
NOTTINGHAMSHIRE COMMERCIAL PROPERTY
WEEKLY
NOTTINGHAMSHIRE TODAY
THIS IS NOTTINGHAM
WEST NOTTS & DERBYSHIRE RECORDER SERIES

NOTTINGHAM TRENT UNIVERSITY STUDENTS' UNION
697332
D H Lawrence House, Clifton Campus, NOTTINGHAM,
NG11 8NS **Tel:** 0115 848 1511 **Fax:** 0115 848 1401
Web site: http://www.su.ntu.ac.uk

Titles:
PLATFORM

NOTTINGHAM UNIVERSITY PRESS 1732803
Manor Farm, Church Lane, Thrumpton, NOTTINGHAM,
NG11 0AX **Tel:** 0115 983 1011 **Fax:** 0115 983 1003
Email: keeling@nupsales.co.uk
Web site: http://www.nup.com

Titles:
BIOTECHNOLOGY & GENETIC ENGINEERING REVIEWS

NOUSE NEWSPAPERS 15777
Grimston House, Vanbrugh College, University of York,
Heslington, YORK, YO10 5DD **Tel:** 01904 434425
Fax: 01904 434425

Titles:
NOUSE (UNIVERSITY OF YORK STUDENT NEWSPAPER)

NOVEMBER PUBLICATIONS LTD 15728
BCM Box 928, LONDON, WC1N 3XX **Tel:** 020 7254 8444
Email: office@cpgb.org.uk

Titles:
WEEKLY WORKER

NS3UK LTD 1676020
Swift House, Market Place, WOKINGHAM, RG40 1AP
Tel: 0118 979 8686 **Fax:** 0118 979 8786
Web site: http://www.ns3.co.uk

Titles:
THE NUTRITION PRACTITIONER

NTD 16770
The Brighton Media Centre, 9-12 Middle Street, BRIGHTON,
BN1 1AL **Tel:** 01273 381100 **Fax:** 01273 381120
Web site: http://www.brighton.co.uk

Titles:
VIRTUAL BRIGHTON AND HOVE

NURSERY ONLINE LTD 1747197
Tel: 07736 180017
PR by email only **Tel:** 07736 180017

Titles:
NURSERY ONLINE

NUS SERVICES LTD 15772
Snape Road, MACCLESFIELD, SK10 2NZ
Tel: 01625 413200 **Fax:** 01625 413400
Email: enquiries@nussl.co.uk
Web site: http://www.nussl.co.uk

Titles:
NUSSL TN MAGAZINE
NUSSL TRADING DIRECTORY

NUTWOOD UK LTD 13916
Eddystone Court, De Lank Lane, St. Breward, BODMIN,
PL30 4NQ **Tel:** 01208 851530 **Fax:** 01208 850871

Web site: http://www.theemcjournal.com
Titles:
THE EMC JOURNAL

NWN MEDIA LTD 14849
Mold Business Park, Wrexham Road, MOLD, CH7 1XY
Tel: 01352 707707 **Fax:** 01352 752180

Titles:
CHESTER STANDARD SERIES
DENBIGHSHIRE FREE PRESS SERIES
EVENING LEADER
FLINTSHIRE STANDARD
THE JOURNAL RHYL, PRESTATYN AND ABERGELE
NORTH WALES CHRONICLE
OSWESTRY AND BORDER COUNTIES ADVERTIZER
THE PIONEER (NORTH WALES)
POWYS COUNTY TIMES, EXPRESS & GAZETTE
WREXHAM LEADER

NWN (PRINTERS) LTD 15982
Newspaper House, Faraday Road, NEWBURY, RG14 2DW
Tel: 01635 564530 **Fax:** 01635 522922

Titles:
OUT & ABOUT

O PUBLISHING 1740768
The Old Brewery, Priory Lane, BURFORD, OX18 4SG
Tel: 01993 822811

Titles:
TOTAL YOUTH FOOTIE

OAKHILL MEDIA LTD 694207
Oakhill House, 22 Williams Grove, SURBITON, KT6 5RN
Tel: 020 8398 9048 **Fax:** 0870 762 0434
Email: pwh@oakhillmedia.com
Web site: http://www.oakhillmedia.com

Titles:
BULK DISTRIBUTOR

OAST PUBLISHING LTD 1690044
PO Box 2780, BRIGHTON, BN1 5QR **Tel:** 01273 552842
Fax: 01273 542257

Titles:
ABC MAGAZINE KENT

OBSERVER NEWSPAPERS NORTHERN IRELAND LTD
17169
Ann Street, DUNGANNON, BT70 1ET **Tel:** 028 8772 2557
Fax: 028 8772 7334

Titles:
DUNGANNON OBSERVER SERIES
ULSTER FARMER

**OBSERVER STANDARD NEWSPAPERS MAGAZINE
DIVISION** 1715090
The Old Library, Church Green West, REDDITCH, B97 4DU
Tel: 01527 453726 **Fax:** 01527 453724

Titles:
FLAVOUR
INSIDE OUT
YOUR WEDDING

OCCUCOM LTD 12914
Colchester Business Centre, 1 George Williams Way,
COLCHESTER, CO1 2JS **Tel:** 01206 369448
Fax: 01206 369437

Titles:
METROPOLITAN LIFE
OFF DUTY
POLICE LIFE

OCEAN MEDIA GROUP LTD 12414
1 Canada Square, 19th Floor, Canary Wharf, LONDON, E14
5AP **Tel:** 020 7772 8300 **Fax:** 020 7772 8584
Web site: http://www.oceanmedia.co.uk

Titles:
ACCESS ALL AREAS
BACK STREET HEROES
BRIDAL BUYER
BUILD IT
HOUSING MAGAZINE
INSIDE HOUSING
INSIDE HOUSING ONLINE
NEGOTIATOR
STREETFIGHTERS

OCTOBER BUILDING MEDIA LTD 1726786
Unit 6, Crown Yard, Bedgebury Estate, Bedgebury Road,
Goudhurst, CRANBROOK, TN17 2QZ **Tel:** 01580 213500
Fax: 01580 213600
Email: baseline@octoberbuildingmedia.co.uk
Titles:
BASELINE MAGAZINE
TOUCHBASE

ODS-PETRODATA UK LTD 14206
2nd Floor, The Exchange, Market Street, ABERDEEN, AB11
5PJ **Tel:** 01224 597800 **Fax:** 01224 580320
Web site: http://www.ods-petrodata.com
Titles:
THE AQUANAUT
INTERNATIONAL RIG REPORT
NORTH SEA RIG REPORT
OFFSHORE MARINE MONTHLY
PETRO DAILY: EUROPEAN MARINE
PETRO DAILY: NORTH AMERICAN CONSTRUCTION
PETRODAILY NEWS: EUROPEAN CONSTRUCTION
PETRODAILY NEWS: INTERNATIONAL CONSTRUCTION
PETRODAILY NEWS: INTERNATIONAL SUBSEA
PETRODAILY NEWS: NORTH AMERICAN
   CONSTRUCTION

OFAS 1621784
Manhattan House, 140 High Street, CROWTHORNE, RG45
7AY **Tel:** 01344 779438 **Fax:** 01344 779143
Email: ofas@ofas.org.uk
Web site: http://www.ofas.org.uk
Titles:
OFAS NEWSLETTER

OFFICE FUTURES 18920
14 Amy Road, OXTED, RH8 0PX **Tel:** 01883 713074
Fax: 0871 433 5581
Email: rgw@office-futures.com
Web site: http://www.office-futures.com
Titles:
OFFICE JOTTER

OFFICE SOLUTIONS MEDIA LIMITED 1640987
Progressive House, Maidstone Road, Foots Cray, SIDCUP,
DA14 5HZ **Tel:** 020 8269 7700 **Fax:** 020 8269 7877
Email: swight@progressivemediagroup.com
Titles:
CHANNEL INFO
OEN

OFFSHORE INTELLIGENCE 14213
PO Box 2779, LONDON, W2 6ZW **Tel:** 020 7386 5703
Titles:
EUROPE AFRICA NEWSLETTER
NORTH SEA WEEKLY NEWSLETTER
ONSHORE REPORT EUROPE/AFRICA

OFFSTAGE PUBLICATIONS LTD 697883
PO Box 46288, Ealing Green, LONDON, W5 5WZ
Tel: 0870 199 8493 **Fax:** 07092 342376
Titles:
OFFSTAGE

OGILVIE PUBLISHING LTD 628519
Quatro House, Lyon Way, FRIMLEY, GU16 7ER
Tel: 01276 804508 **Fax:** 01276 804513
Titles:
EUROPEAN OFFSHORE PETROLEUM NEWSLETTER
OGILVIE'S E & P DAILY

OIL & COLOUR CHEMISTS' ASSOCIATION 13898
Priory House, 967 Harrow Road, WEMBLEY, HA0 2SF
Tel: 020 8908 1086 **Fax:** 020 8908 1219
Email: publications@occa.org.uk
Web site: http://www.occa.org.uk
Titles:
SURFACE COATINGS INTERNATIONAL

OILC 698672
9 Carmelite Street, ABERDEEN, AB11 6NQ
Tel: 01224 210118 **Fax:** 01224 210095
Email: gensec@oilc.org
Web site: http://www.oilc.org
Titles:
BLOWOUT

OILDOM PUBLISHING CO 13966
PO Box 437, MAIDSTONE, ME14 4RB **Tel:** 01622 721222
Fax: 01622 721333
Titles:
PIPELINE & GAS JOURNAL

OINK NEWS CORPORATION LTD 1630391
7 Hampstead Gate, 1A Frognal, LONDON, NW3 6AL
Tel: 0870 755 0820 **Fax:** 020 7449 9851
Web site: http://www.oinknewspapers.com
Titles:
OINK!

OKSAR LTD 1728922
57 Connaught Works, 251 Old Ford Road, LONDON, E3 5PS
Titles:
ANORAK

OLAY NEWSPAPER LTD 1654381
100 Green Lanes, LONDON, N16 9EH **Tel:** 020 7923 9090
Fax: 020 7923 9080
Email: info@olaygazete.co.uk
Web site: http://www.olaygazete.co.uk
Titles:
OLAY NEWSPAPER

OLDIE PUBLICATIONS LTD 1649617
65 Newman Street, LONDON, W1T 3EG **Tel:** 020 7436 8801
Fax: 020 7436 8804
Web site: http://www.theoldie.co.uk
Titles:
THE OLDIE

OMNIA MEDIA 1686481
2 Mornington Place, BELFAST, BT7 3LD **Tel:** 028 9069 2334
Fax: 028 9069 2335
Titles:
FYI

ON THE BALL PUBLICATIONS 15331
11 Cliff Road, SHERINGHAM, NR26 8BJ **Tel:** 01263 837764
Fax: 01263 821463
Titles:
GO TENPIN

ON THE ROAD 17659
Riverside Lodge, Collier Close, Camerton, BATH, BA2 0QB
Tel: 01761 479645 **Fax:** 01761 479663
Email: info@chalkfarmpublishing.co.uk
Web site: http://www.ontheroad.co.uk
Titles:
ON THE ROAD

ONE 18577
19 Heddon Street, LONDON, W1B 4BG **Tel:** 020 7993 3833
Fax: 020 7437 4209
Email: info@oneismore.com
Web site: http://www.oneismore.com
Titles:
THE MAB BULLETIN
THE OFFICER
ROYAL MILITARY POLICE JOURNAL

ONEHUNDREDPERCENT PUBLISHING LTD 1654033
9 Albany Mews, Albany Road, LONDON, SE5 0DQ
Tel: 020 7701 7601 **Fax:** 020 7701 7601
Titles:
CENT

ONEUP MAGAZINE LTD 1712454
18 Lower Holt Street, Earls Colne, COLCHESTER, CO6 2PH
Tel: 01787 223557
Email: editor@oneupmagazine.co.uk
Web site: http://www.oneupmagazine.co.uk
Titles:
ONEUP

OPEN AIR MISSION 17987
4 Harrier Court, Woodside Road, Slip End, LUTON, LU1 4DQ
Tel: 01582 841141 **Fax:** 01582 841145
Titles:
MASTER & MULTITUDE

OPEN HOUSE PUBLISHING LTD 1649376
PO Box 7574, BILLERICAY, CM12 9XF **Tel:** 01277 650037
Fax: 0870 762 1039
Titles:
GD PRO
INTERNATIONAL SIGN MAGAZINE

OPEN MEDIA PUBLICATIONS LTD 1654529
Shine, Harehills Road, LEEDS, LS8 5HS **Tel:** 0870 360 8606
Fax: 0870 360 8605
Titles:
AD GUIDE
ASIAN CHOICE MAGAZINE
ASIAN EXPRESS NEWSPAPER
BRADFORD MELA

OPEN SPACES SOCIETY 18085
25A Bell Street, HENLEY-ON-THAMES, RG9 2BA
Tel: 01491 573535 **Fax:** 01491 573051
Titles:
OPEN SPACE

THE OPEN UNIVERSITY 15790
Walton Hall, MILTON KEYNES, MK7 6AA **Tel:** 01908 653761
Fax: 01908 652247
Titles:
SESAME

OPERA MAGAZINE LTD 15398
36 Black Lion Lane, LONDON, W6 9BE **Tel:** 020 8563 8893
Fax: 020 8563 8635
Email: editor@opera.co.uk
Web site: http://www.opera.co.uk
Titles:
OPERA

THE OPERATIONAL RESEARCH SOCIETY 13757
Seymour House, 12 Edward Street, BIRMINGHAM, B1 2RX
Tel: 0121 233 9300 **Fax:** 0121 233 0321
Web site: http://www.orsoc.org.uk
Titles:
INSIDE OR
OR INSIGHT

OPTICAL WORLD LTD 14551
258A Fairfax Drive, WESTCLIFF-ON-SEA, SS0 9EJ
Tel: 01702 345443 **Fax:** 01702 431806
Email: info@optical-world.co.uk
Web site: http://www.optical-world.co.uk
Titles:
OPTICAL WORLD

OPTIMA MAGAZINE LTD 622990
20 Sparrows Herne, BUSHEY, WD23 1FX
Tel: 020 8420 4488 **Fax:** 020 8386 4141
Web site: http://www.optimamagazine.co.uk
Titles:
OPTIMA MAGAZINE

OPTIMUS EDUCATION 627664
33-41 Dallington Street, LONDON, EC1V 0BB
Tel: 020 7954 3400 **Fax:** 020 7251 9045
Web site: http://www.optimuspub.co.uk
Titles:
EXTERNAL FUNDING BULLETIN
PE AND SPORT TODAY
SCHOOL FINANCIAL MANAGEMENT
SPECIAL CHILDREN
TEACHING AND LEARNING

OPUS BUSINESS MEDIA 1766899
Bollinbrook House, Beech Lane, MACCLESFIELD, SK10 2XZ
Tel: 01625 426054
Titles:
TOMORROW'S CLEANING

ORCA PUBLICATIONS 15299
Berry Road Studios, Berry Road, NEWQUAY, TR7 1AT
Tel: 01637 878074 **Fax:** 01637 850226
Titles:
CARVE SURFING MAGAZINE
SURF GIRL
THREESIXTY BODYBOARDING MAGAZINE

UK Publishers & Their Titles

THE ORCADIAN LTD 15062
50 Albert Street, KIRKWALL, KW15 1HQ **Tel:** 01856 878000
Fax: 01856 878001
Email: bookshop@orcadian.co.uk
Web site: http://www.orcadian.co.uk
Titles:
 THE ORCADIAN

ORCHESTRATE LTD 15644
PO Box 49, LETCHWORTH, SG6 2XB **Tel:** 01462 679439
Fax: 01462 485512
Titles:
 GREYHOUND STAR

ORIGIN PUBLISHING LTD 17225
9th Floor, Tower House, Fairfax Street, BRISTOL, BS1 3BN
Tel: 0117 927 9009 **Fax:** 0117 934 9008
Web site: http://www.originpublishing.co.uk
Titles:
 220 TRIATHLON
 BEAUTIFUL CARDS
 BLONDE HAIR
 CARDMAKING & PAPERCRAFT
 CRAFTBUBBLE.COM
 CROSS STITCH CRAZY
 CROSS STITCH GOLD
 HAIR IDEAS
 KNIT TODAY
 KOI
 LOVEYOURHAIR.COM
 PERFECT WEDDING
 QUICK CARDS MADE EASY
 THE WORLD OF CROSS STITCHING
 YOUR HAIR

ORKNEY TODAY LTD 1630619
Unit 1, Kiln Corner, Ayre Road, KIRKWALL, KW15 1QX
Tel: 01856 888810 **Fax:** 01856 888811
Email: editorial@orkneytoday.co.uk
Web site: http://www.orkneytoday.co.uk
Titles:
 ORKNEY TODAY

**ORPHEUS PORTFOLIO AT NEWSQUEST SPECIALIST
MEDIA LTD** 1627193
2nd Floor, 30 Cannon Street, LONDON, EC4M 6YJ
Tel: 020 7618 3456 **Fax:** 020 7618 3483
Titles:
 INTERNATIONAL PIANO
 THE STRAD

ORTON ASSOCIATES 13549
19 Lincoln Croft, Shenstone, LICHFIELD, WS14 0ND
Tel: 01543 480322 **Fax:** 01543 480864
Titles:
 PERIMETER SYSTEMS

OTC PUBLICATIONS LTD 14237
54 Creynolds Lane, Shirley, SOLIHULL, B90 4ER
Tel: 01564 777550 **Fax:** 01564 777524
Email: info@generics-bulletin.com
Web site: http://www.otc-bulletin.com
Titles:
 GENERICS BULLETIN
 OTC BULLETIN

THE OTHER SIDE MAGAZINE 1735846
20 Hollickwood Avenue, LONDON, N12 0LT
Tel: 07937 938805
Titles:
 THE OTHER SIDE

OUP 12122
Great Clarendon Street, OXFORD, OX2 6DP
Tel: 01865 353907 **Fax:** 01865 353485
Email: jnls.cust.serv@oupjournals.org
Web site: http://www.oxfordjournals.org
Titles:
 AFRICAN AFFAIRS
 AGE AND AGEING
 ALCOHOL & ALCOHOLISM
 APPLIED LINGUISTICS
 BEHAVIORAL ECOLOGY
 BIOINFORMATICS
 BIOMETRIKA
 BIOSTATISTICS
 BJA: BRITISH JOURNAL OF ANAESTHESIA
 BRAIN

 THE BRITISH JOURNAL FOR THE PHILOSOPHY OF
  SCIENCE
 THE BRITISH JOURNAL OF AESTHETICS
 THE BRITISH JOURNAL OF CRIMINOLOGY
 THE BRITISH JOURNAL OF SOCIAL WORK
 CAMBRIDGE JOURNAL OF ECONOMICS
 THE CAMBRIDGE QUARTERLY
 CARCINOGENESIS
 COMMUNITY DEVELOPMENT JOURNAL
 EARLY MUSIC
 ELT JOURNAL
 THE ENGLISH HISTORICAL REVIEW
 ENTERPRISE AND SOCIETY: THE INTERNATIONAL
  JOURNAL OF BUSINESS HISTORY
 ESSAYS IN CRITICISM
 EUROPEAN JOURNAL OF ECHOCARDIOGRAPHY
 EUROPEAN JOURNAL OF INTERNATIONAL LAW
 THE EUROPEAN JOURNAL OF ORTHODONTICS
 FAMILY PRACTICE
 FORESTRY
 FORUM FOR MODERN LANGUAGE STUDIES
 FRENCH HISTORY
 FRENCH STUDIES
 HEALTH EDUCATION RESEARCH
 HEALTH POLICY & PLANNING
 HISTORY WORKSHOP JOURNAL
 HOLOCAUST AND GENOCIDE STUDIES
 HUMAN MOLECULAR GENETICS
 HUMAN REPRODUCTION
 HUMAN REPRODUCTION UPDATE
 IEICE TRANSACTIONS ON ELECTRONICS
 IEICE TRANSACTIONS ON FUNDAMENTALS OF
  ELECTRONICS, COMMUNICATIONS & COMPUTER
  SCIENCE
 IEICE TRANSACTIONS ON INFORMATION AND
  SYSTEMS
 IMA JOURNAL OF APPLIED MATHEMATICS
 IMA JOURNAL OF MANAGEMENT MATHEMATICS
 IMA JOURNAL OF MATHEMATICAL CONTROL &
  INFORMATION
 IMA JOURNAL OF NUMERICAL ANALYSIS
 INDUSTRIAL & CORPORATE CHANGE
 INDUSTRIAL LAW JOURNAL
 INTERNATIONAL JOURNAL OF EPIDEMIOLOGY
 INTERNATIONAL JOURNAL OF LAW, POLICY & THE
  FAMILY
 INTERNATIONAL JOURNAL OF LEXICOGRAPHY
 JOURNAL OF AFRICAN ECONOMIES
 THE JOURNAL OF ANTIMICROBIAL CHEMOTHERAPY
 JOURNAL OF CONFLICT AND SECURITY LAW
 JOURNAL OF DESIGN HISTORY
 JOURNAL OF ECONOMIC GEOGRAPHY
 JOURNAL OF ELECTRON MICROSCOPY
 JOURNAL OF ENVIRONMENTAL LAW
 JOURNAL OF EXPERIMENTAL BOTANY
 JOURNAL OF THE HISTORY OF COLLECTIONS
 JOURNAL OF INTERNATIONAL ECONOMIC LAW
 JOURNAL OF ISLAMIC STUDIES
 THE JOURNAL OF LAW, ECONOMICS AND
  ORGANISATION
 JOURNAL OF LOGIC & COMPUTATION
 JOURNAL OF MOLLUSCAN STUDIES
 JOURNAL OF PLANKTON RESEARCH
 JOURNAL OF THE ROYAL MUSICAL ASSOCIATION
 JOURNAL OF SEMANTICS
 JOURNAL OF SEMITIC STUDIES
 JOURNAL OF THEOLOGICAL STUDIES
 JOURNAL OF TROPICAL PAEDIATRICS
 THE LIBRARY
 LITERARY AND LINGUISTIC COMPUTING
 LITERATURE & THEOLOGY
 LOGIC JOURNAL OF IGPL
 MATHEMATICAL MEDICINE AND BIOLOGY: A JOURNAL
  OF THE IMA
 MIND
 MOLECULAR HUMAN REPRODUCTION
 MUSIC & LETTERS
 THE MUSICAL QUARTERLY
 MUTAGENESIS
 NOTES & QUERIES
 NUCLEIC ACIDS RESEARCH
 OCCUPATIONAL MEDICINE
 THE OPERA QUARTERLY
 OXFORD ART JOURNAL
 OXFORD JOURNAL OF LEGAL STUDIES
 OXFORD REVIEW OF ECONOMIC POLICY
 PAST & PRESENT
 PROCEEDINGS OF THE LONDON MATHEMATICAL
  SOCIETY
 PROTEIN ENGINEERING, DESIGN AND SELECTION
 QJM: AN INTERNATIONAL JOURNAL OF MEDICINE
 THE QUARTERLY JOURNAL OF MATHEMATICS
 QUARTERLY JOURNAL OF MECHANICS AND APPLIED
  MATHEMATICS
 RADIATION PROTECTION DOSIMETRY
 REFUGEE SURVEY QUARTERLY
 RHEUMATOLOGY
 SCREEN
 STATUTE LAW REVIEW
 TEACHING MATHEMATICS AND ITS APPLICATIONS
 TRUSTS & TRUSTEES
 TWENTIETH CENTURY BRITISH HISTORY

OUR DOGS CENTENARY LTD 15648
1 Lund Street, MANCHESTER, M16 9EJ **Tel:** 0161 236 2660
Fax: 0161 236 2539
Web site: http://www.ourdogs.co.uk
Titles:
 OUR DOGS

OUR LADY'S NEWSLETTER 1712973
St. Benedicts, 1 Manor Road, Kemp Town, BRIGHTON, BN2
5EA **Tel:** 01273 680720
Titles:
 OUR LADY'S NEWSLETTER

OUREBI LTD 1739514
DMC House, Pullman Business Park, Pullman Way,
RINGWOOD, BH24 1HD **Tel:** 020 7503 0163
Titles:
 AXIOM

OUT GROUP 1742953
44 Wardour Street, LONDON, W1D 6QZ **Tel:** 020 7292 8680
Fax: 020 7287 2905
Titles:
 SOURCINGFOCUS.COM

OUT OF HAND LTD 1657607
Hebron House, Sion Road, BRISTOL, BS3 3BD
Tel: 0117 953 6363 **Fax:** 0117 953 6364
Email: info@outofhand.co.uk
Web site: http://www.outofhand.co.uk
Titles:
 247
 247 MAGAZINE - WEST AND WALES
 OUT OF HAND

OUTBOUND MEDIA AND EXHIBITIONS 16007
1 Commercial Road, EASTBOURNE, BN21 3XQ
Tel: 01323 726040 **Fax:** 01323 649249
Web site: http://www.emigrate2.co.uk
Titles:
 EMIGRATE
 EMIGRATE AMERICA
 EMIGRATE AUSTRALIA
 EMIGRATE CANADA
 EMIGRATE NEW ZEALAND
 WORLD OF PROPERTY MAGAZINE

OVUM 1675482
Shire Thorne House, 37-43 Prospect Street, HULL, HU2 8PX
Tel: 01482 586149 **Fax:** 01482 323577
Web site: http://www.butlergroup.com
Titles:
 AUTOMOTIVE BUSINESS REVIEW
 BUTLER GROUP REVIEW

OXERA 13375
Park Central, 40-41 Park End Street, OXFORD, OX1 1JD
Tel: 01865 253000 **Fax:** 01865 251172
Email: enquiries@oxera.com
Web site: http://www.oxera.com
Titles:
 AGENDA

OXFAM 13254
Oxfam House, John Smith Drive, Cowley, OXFORD, OX4
2JY **Tel:** 01865 312106 **Fax:** 01865 312393
Titles:
 GENDER & DEVELOPMENT

OXFORD DIOCESAN PUBLICATIONS LTD 17310
Diocesan Church House, North Hinksey Lane, Botley,
OXFORD, OX2 0NB **Tel:** 01865 208227 **Fax:** 01865 790470
Titles:
 THE DOOR

OXFORD UNIVERSITY STUDENT UNION 15778
Thomas Hull House, New Inn Hall Street, OXFORD, OX1
2DH **Tel:** 01865 288450 **Fax:** 01865 288450
Email: finance@ousu.org
Web site: http://www.ousu.org
Titles:
 THE OXFORD STUDENT

OXYGEN 10   1750274
21-24 Bruges Place, Baynes Street, LONDON, NW1 0TF
Tel: 020 7870 9000
Web site: http://www.oxygen10.com
Titles:
    THE CELEBRITY ANGELS SERIES

P1 MEDIA LTD   1724967
194A Upper Richmond Road West, LONDON, SW14 8AN
Tel: 020 8240 8901
Titles:
    TRACK & RACE CARS
    TRACK DRIVER

P4 PUBLISHING LTD   1739259
Temple House, 20 Holywell Row, LONDON, EC2A 4XH
Titles:
    TREASURY MANAGEMENT INTERNATIONAL
    TREASURY MANAGEMENT INTERNATIONAL

P & L SERVICES   623431
Suite 26, London Fruit Exchange, Brushfield Street,
LONDON, E1 6EU **Tel:** 020 7377 6383
Titles:
    ACI BRIEFING
    PROFIT AND LOSS

P M GROUP   622835
Vincent House, Vincent Lane, DORKING, RH4 3JD
Tel: 01306 740777 **Fax:** 01306 741069
Web site: http://www.pmlive.com
Titles:
    COMMUNIQUÉ
    PHARMACEUTICAL MARKETING
    PHARMACEUTICAL MARKETING EUROPE

PA BUSINESS   13374
292 Vauxhall Bridge Road, LONDON, SW1V 1AE
Tel: 020 7963 7680 **Fax:** 020 7963 7682
Email: info@telecomfinance.com
Web site: http://www.telecomfinance.com
Titles:
    LUXURYFINANCE
    MEDIA FINANCE
    TELECOM FINANCE

PACKET NEWSPAPERS   17801
Ponsharden, FALMOUTH, TR10 8AP **Tel:** 01326 213333
Fax: 01326 212108
Titles:
    THE ROYAL CORNWALL

PAGE & PULFORD   1649712
6 Whittle Road, Ferndown Industrial Estate, WIMBORNE,
BH21 7RU **Tel:** 01202 870270 **Fax:** 01202 870370
Email: mags@mags4dorset.co.uk
Titles:
    TOWN & VILLAGE COMMUNITY MAGAZINE
    THE VERWOOD & WIMBOURNE VIEWPOINT

PAGEANT MEDIA LTD   1649584
1st Floor, Dunstan House, 14A St. Cross Street, LONDON,
EC1N 8XA **Tel:** 020 7269 7575 **Fax:** 020 7269 7570
Web site: http://www.pageantmedia.com
Titles:
    CAPTIVE REVIEW
    EGAMING REVIEW
    HFM WEEK

PAGEPRINT PUBLISHING LIMITED   18572
PO Box 666, EDINBURGH, EH7 5YW **Tel:** 0131 539 0666
Fax: 0131 539 2999
Titles:
    SCOTSGAY

PAINT RESEARCH ASSOCIATION   1747558
14 Castle Mews, High Street, HAMPTON, TW12 2NP
Tel: 020 8487 0807 **Fax:** 020 8487 0801
Email: comet@pra-world.com
Web site: http://www.pra-world.com
Titles:
    COATINGS COMET

PALGRAVE MACMILLAN LTD   14504
Brunel Road, Houndmills, Basingstoke, HAMPSHIRE, RG21
6XS **Tel:** 0121 233 9300 **Fax:** 0121 233 0321
Web site: http://www.palgrave-journals.com
Titles:
    JORS-JOURNAL OF THE OPERATIONAL RESEARCH
      SOCIETY
    JOURNAL OF ASSET MANAGEMENT
    THE JOURNAL OF BRAND MANAGEMENT
    JOURNAL OF DATABASE MARKETING & CUSTOMER
      STRATEGY MANAGEMENT
    JOURNAL OF DERIVATIVES AND HEDGE FUNDS
    JOURNAL OF FINANCIAL SERVICES MARKETING
    JOURNAL OF TARGETING, MEASUREMENT AND
      ANALYSIS FOR MARKETING

PALLADIAN PUBLICATIONS LTD   14282
15 South Street, FARNHAM, GU9 7QU **Tel:** 01252 718999
Fax: 01252 718992
Email: mail@palladian-publications.com
Web site: http://www.palladian-publications.com
Titles:
    HYDROCARBON ENGINEERING
    WORLD CEMENT
    WORLD COAL
    WORLD PIPELINES

PANACEA MARKETING LTD   1757395
2 New Street, WARWICK, CV34 4RX **Tel:** 01926 493330
Fax: 01926 492203
Web site: http://www.panaceamarketing.co.uk
Titles:
    AUTOMOTIVATION

PANACEA PUBLISHING   1723928
Cardinal House, 39-40 Albemarle Street, LONDON, W1S
4TE **Tel:** 020 7647 6330 **Fax:** 020 7647 6331
Email: enquiries@panaceapublishing.co.uk
Web site: http://www.panaceapublishinginternational.com
Titles:
    AIR & BUSINESS TRAVEL NEWS
    AIR & BUSINESS TRAVEL NEWS
    BUYING BUSINESS TRAVEL

PANINI UK LTD   16596
Brockbourne House, 77 Mount Ephraim, TUNBRIDGE
WELLS, TN4 8BS **Tel:** 01892 500100 **Fax:** 01892 545666
Web site: http://www.paninicomics.co.uk
Titles:
    ART ATTACK
    THE AVENGERS UNITED
    BLISS
    DISNEY GIRL
    DR WHO MAGAZINE
    ESSENTIAL X-MEN
    HIGH SCHOOL MUSICAL
    LOONEY TUNES PRESENTS
    MIZZ
    SCOOBY DOO
    SHOWTIME
    SPECTACULAR SPIDERMAN
    SPIDERMAN & FRIENDS
    TOM AND JERRY
    TRACTOR TOM
    WOLVERINE AND DEADPOOL

PANSTADIA PUBLISHING LTD   674304
Head Office, Hall Farm House, 9 High Street, CASTLE
DONINGTON, DE74 2PP **Tel:** 01332 814555
Fax: 01332 853410
Email: subs@panstadia.com
Web site: http://www.panstadia.com
Titles:
    PANSTADIA

PAP PUBLICATIONS   1644476
Technology House, 8 Norroy Road, LONDON, SW15 1PF
Tel: 0871 237 4787
Email: marketingtechnologymagazine@googlemail.com
Titles:
    MARKETING TECHNOLOGY

PARAGRAPH PUBLISHING   18462
St. Faiths House, Mountergate, NORWICH, NR1 1PY
Tel: 01603 633808 **Fax:** 01603 632808
Titles:
    BEERS OF THE WORLD
    SCOTLAND MAGAZINE
    WHISKY MAGAZINE

PARAMOUNT PUBLICATIONS   1687349
Suite 15, Hardmans Business Centre, New Hall Hey Road,
ROSSENDALE, BB4 6HH **Tel:** 01706 212200
Fax: 01706 211782
Email: info@paramountpublications.co.uk
Web site: http://www.paramountpublications.co.uk
Titles:
    RETAIL & LEISURE INTERNATIONAL

PARENT PUBLISHING LTD   1715944
PO Box 9308, DUNMOW, CM6 2WP **Tel:** 01371 832116
Fax: 01371 832116
Titles:
    ABC MAGAZINE ESSEX

PARENT TALK   621521
Horton House, 8 Ditton Street, ILMINSTER, TA19 0BQ
Tel: 01460 259673 **Fax:** 01460 259678
Titles:
    PARENT TALK

PARENTS NEWS UK   15986
10 The Manor Drive, WORCESTER PARK, KT4 7LG
Tel: 020 8337 6337 **Fax:** 020 8337 8363
Email: info@parents-news.co.uk
Web site: http://www.parents-news.co.uk
Titles:
    PARENTS NEWS
    PARENTS NEWS (ONLINE)

PARENTS ONLINE   622655
28 Holly Hill Lane, Sarisbury Green, SOUTHAMPTON, SO31
7AD **Tel:** 01489 559111
Titles:
    PARENTS ONLINE

PARIKIAKI   17331
140 Falkland Road, LONDON, N8 0NP **Tel:** 020 8341 0751
Fax: 020 8341 9391
Titles:
    PARIKIAKI

PARISH COUNCIL (KIRBY MUXLOE)   1745482
Parish Council Office, Station Road, Kirby Muxloe,
LEICESTER, LE9 2EN **Tel:** 0116 238 6408
Fax: 0116 238 6408
Titles:
    KIRBY COMMENT

PARK LANE PUBLISHING   16828
2 Park Lane, Earls Colne, COLCHESTER, CO6 2RJ
Tel: 01787 222434 **Fax:** 01787 220465
Email: pedwards.parklane@virgin.net
Titles:
    BIFALINK

PARK LANE PUBLISHING LTD   14212
Cubic Business Centre, 533 Stanningley Road, LEEDS, LS13
4EN **Tel:** 0113 218 0117
Email: info@parklanepublishing.co.uk
Web site: http://www.parklanepublishing.co.uk
Titles:
    MOTOR EXCHANGE
    TAXI-TODAY

PARK VIEW PUBLISHING LTD   14755
Park View House, 19 The Avenue, EASTBOURNE, BN21
3YD **Tel:** 01323 411601 **Fax:** 01323 411654
Web site: http://www.parkview-publishing.co.uk
Titles:
    CAPTURE
    CAREWEEK
    OCEAN VIEW
    PET OWNER
    PIXEL
    SBT SUSSEX BUSINESS TIMES

PARKER ELLIS PUBLISHING LTD   697010
Cointronic House, Station Road, HEATHFIELD, TN21 8DF
Tel: 01435 863500 **Fax:** 01435 863897
Web site: http://www.parkerellis.eu
Titles:
    ARCHITECTS DATAFILE
    CPB CIVIC & PUBLIC BUILDING
    HOUSEBUILDER & DEVELOPER

UK Publishers & Their Titles

INTERIOR LINKS
SELFBUILDER & HOMEMAKER

PARKINSON'S DISEASE SOCIETY OF THE UK　14584
215 Vauxhall Bridge Road, LONDON, SW1V 1EJ
Tel: 020 7931 8080 **Fax:** 020 7233 9908
Web site: http://www.parkinsons.org.uk
Titles:
　THE PARKINSON MAGAZINE

PARLIAMENTARY & SCIENTIFIC COMMITTEE　1677093
3 Birdcage Walk, LONDON, SW1H 9JJ **Tel:** 020 7222 7085
Fax: 020 7222 7189
Email: lloyda@pandsctte.demon.co.uk
Web site: http://www.scienceinparliment.org.uk
Titles:
　SCIENCE IN PARLIAMENT

THE PARLIAMENTARY MARITIME GROUP　14332
No 3 The Green, Ketton, STAMFORD, PE9 3RA
Tel: 01780 721628 **Fax:** 01780 721980
Titles:
　THE PARLIAMENTARY MARITIME REVIEW

PARNELL PUBLICATIONS　1654231
58 Parnell Square, DUBLIN 1 **Tel:** +353 1 87 33 611
Fax: +353 1 87 33 074
Titles:
　AN PHOBLACHT

PARTNERS IN MEDIA PUBLISHING　1710885
Studio 52, Old Truman Brewery, 91 Brick Lane, LONDON,
E1 6QL **Tel:** 020 7655 0995
Email: info@pimpguides.com
Web site: http://www.pimpguides.com
Titles:
　PIMP

PARTNERSHIP PUBLISHING LIMITED　17264
2 Crown Street, Wellington, TELFORD, TF1 1LP
Tel: 01952 415334 **Fax:** 01952 245077
Web site: http://www.onlinerecovery.co.uk
Titles:
　GARAGE & MOT PROFESSIONAL
　PROFESSIONAL RECOVERY
　WELLINGTON NEWS

PARTRIDGE PUBLICATIONS　16504
49 Old Steine, BRIGHTON, BN1 1NH **Tel:** 01273 748675
Titles:
　MAKING MONEY
　SPORTS INSIGHT
　WHAT FRANCHISE

PARTRIDGE PUBLICATIONS (2000) LTD　1622134
21-23 Phoenix Court, Hawkins Road, COLCHESTER, CO2
8JY **Tel:** 01206 505900 **Fax:** 01206 505929
Titles:
　SMARTLIFE INTERNATIONAL
　SVI MAGAZINE

PASSFIELD BUSINESS PUBLICATIONS LTD　13964
Unit 40B, Passfield Business Centre, Lynchborough Road,
LIPHOOK, GU30 7SB **Tel:** 01428 751188 **Fax:** 01428 751199
Titles:
　PROCESS INDUSTRY INFORMER

PATHART LIMITED　1709930
31 High Street, Martin, LINCOLN, LN4 3QY
Tel: 01526 378703
Email: pathart.ltd@virgin.net
Web site: http://www.edimag.co.uk
Titles:
　ELECTRONICS DISTRIBUTOR ON-LINE

PAUL RAYMOND PUBLICATIONS LTD　15844
2 Archer Street, LONDON, W1D 7AW **Tel:** 020 7292 8000
Fax: 020 7734 5030
Web site: http://www.paulraymond.com
Titles:
　CLUB INTERNATIONAL
　ESCORT
　MAYFAIR

MEN ONLY
MENSWORLD

PAUL RUSSELL MEDIA　1734534
PO Box 623, Farlington, PORTSMOUTH, PO6 1XQ
Tel: 023 9264 6159 **Fax:** 0870 133 7687
Titles:
　SECURITY NEWS ONLINE

PAVILION JOURNALS (BRIGHTON) LTD　600413
Suite N4, The Old Market, Upper Market Street, HOVE, BN3
1AS **Tel:** 01273 623222 **Fax:** 01273 625526
Web site: http://www.pavpub.com
Titles:
　THE BRITISH JOURNAL OF FORENSIC PRACTICE
　DRUGS AND ALCOHOL TODAY
　HOUSING, CARE & SUPPORT
　THE JOURNAL OF ADULT PROTECTION
　JOURNAL OF INTEGRATED CARE
　THE JOURNAL OF PUBLIC MENTAL HEALTH
　LEARNING DISABILITY TODAY
　A LIFE IN THE DAY
　THE MENTAL HEALTH REVIEW JOURNAL
　MENTAL HEALTH TODAY
　QUALITY IN AGEING
　SAFER COMMUNITIES
　TIZARD LEARNING DISABILITY REVIEW
　WORKING WITH OLDER PEOPLE

PAWPRINT PUBLISHING LTD　1755903
Creative Media Centre, Robertson Street, HASTINGS, TN34
1HL **Tel:** 01424 205428 **Fax:** 01424 205436
Titles:
　PANEL, WOOD & SOLID SURFACES

PCBT PHOTOGRAPHY & PBT MEDIA RELATIONS LTD.
　1651046
4A Post Office Avenue, SOUTHPORT, PR9 0US
Tel: 01704 513569
Web site: http://www.pcbtphotography.co.uk
Titles:
　MERSEY AND SOUTHPORT REPORTER SERIES

PCD MEDIA (EAST ANGLIA) LTD　15651
Home Barn, Grove Hill, Belstead, IPSWICH, IP8 3LS
Tel: 01473 731220 **Fax:** 01473 731227
Email: pcdmedialtd@btconnect.com
Titles:
　ABSOLUTE HORSE

PCS　13863
160 Falcon Road, LONDON, SW11 2LN **Tel:** 020 7924 2727
Fax: 020 7924 1847
Titles:
　PCS VIEW

PDR ONLINE LTD.　1712644
An Garadh, Gallachoille, TAYVALLICH, PA31 8PG
Tel: 01546 870356
Email: pdrmail@aol.com
Web site: http://www.carkeys.co.uk
Titles:
　CARKEYS

PDSA　694515
Whitechapel Way, Priorslee, TELFORD, TF2 9PQ
Tel: 01952 290999 **Fax:** 01952 291035
Web site: http://www.pdsa.org.uk
Titles:
　COMPANIONS

PEACE NEWS LIMITED　15714
5 Caledonian Road, LONDON, N1 9DY **Tel:** 020 7278 3344
Fax: 020 7278 0444
Titles:
　PEACE NEWS

PEACOCK PRESS　15368
Scout Bottom Farm, Mytholmroyd, HEBDEN BRIDGE, HX7
5JS **Tel:** 01422 882751 **Fax:** 01422 886157
Titles:
　PRIMARY MUSIC TODAY
　THE RECORDER MAGAZINE

PEARSON EDUCATION LTD　17531
Edinburgh Gate, HARLOW, CM20 2JE **Tel:** 01279 623623
Fax: 01279 431059
Web site: http://www.pearsoned.co.uk
Titles:
　DIRECTORY OF VOCATIONAL AND FURTHER
　EDUCATION

PEARSON PRESS LIMITED　1713744
2nd Floor, 42 Whitechapel, LIVERPOOL, L1 6DZ
Tel: 0151 707 6688 **Fax:** 0151 707 6665
Titles:
　EQUALITY BRITAIN

PECKISH MEDIA LTD　1752738
67-69 Sutherland Road, LONDON, E17 6BH
Tel: 0845 260 1236 **Fax:** 0845 230 5256
Titles:
　RANDOM MAGAZINE

PECO PUBLICATIONS & PUBLICITY LTD.　15477
Underleys, Beer, SEATON, EX12 3NA **Tel:** 01297 20580
Fax: 01297 20229
Titles:
　CONTINENTAL MODELLER
　RAILWAY MODELLER

PEDESTRIANS ASSOCIATION　18317
31-33 Bondway, LONDON, SW8 1SJ
Web site: http://www.livingstreets.org.uk
Titles:
　LIVING STREETS

PEEBLES MEDIA GROUP LTD　621669
Bergius House, 20 Clifton Street, GLASGOW, G3 7LA
Tel: 0141 567 6000 **Fax:** 0141 331 1395
Web site: http://www.peeblesmedia.com
Titles:
　THE BEST SCOTTISH WEDDINGS
　ENVIROTEC
　HOMES & INTERIORS SCOTLAND
　HOMES & INTERIORS SCOTLAND ONLINE
　OS MAGAZINE
　PACKAGING SCOTLAND
　PROJECT PLANT
　PROJECT SCOTLAND
　SCOTTISH GROCER
　SCOTTISH LICENSED TRADE NEWS

THE PEERAGE GROUP LTD　16676
PO Box 5135, Strand-on-the-Green, Chiswick, LONDON,
W4 3WN **Tel:** 020 8560 0897 **Fax:** 020 8560 0897
Email: peerage@aol.com
Titles:
　FISHING IN BRITAIN & EUROPE
　GOLFING AROUND THE M25
　GOLFING IN BRITAIN & EUROPE
　PEERAGE MAGAZINE

PEGASUS　1627065
Regency House, 6-7 Elwick Road, ASHFORD, TN23 1PD
Tel: 01233 628496
Titles:
　PEGASUS

PEI MEDIA LTD　1738656
Sycamore House, Sycamore Street, LONDON, EC1Y 0SG
Titles:
　PRIVATE EQUITY INTERNATIONAL
　PRIVATE EQUITY ONLINE

PELICAN MAGAZINES LTD　18037
2 Cheltenham Mount, HARROGATE, HG1 1DL
Tel: 01423 569676 **Fax:** 01423 569677
Email: info@pelgrp.com
Titles:
　ACCOMMODATION MANAGEMENT
　EUROPEAN ORTHOPAEDIC PRODUCT NEWS

PEMBERLEY BOOKS　1739472
18 Bathurst Walk, IVER, SL0 9AZ **Tel:** 01735 631114
Fax: 01735 631115
Email: publishing@pemberleybooks.com
Web site: http://www.pemberleybooks.com

Titles:
ENTOMOLOGIST'S GAZETTE
ENTOMOLOGIST'S MONTHLY MAGAZINE

PEMBROKESHIRE & CANINE PRESS 15641
6 High Street, FISHGUARD, SA65 9AR **Tel:** 01348 875011
Fax: 01348 875013
Titles:
DOG TRAINING WEEKLY

PEN PEOPLE UK 1642381
113 High Street, NEWCASTLE-UNDER-LYME, ST5 1PS
Tel: 01782 611628
Email: penpeople2002@hotmail.com
Web site: http://www.penpeople.org.uk
Titles:
PEN PEOPLE UK

PENDRAGON PUBLISHING 1641676
PO Box 3, Easingwold, YORK, YO61 3YS **Tel:** 01347 824397
Fax: 01347 824397
Email: pendragonpublishing@btinternet.com
Web site: http://www.pendragonpublishing.co.uk
Titles:
BACKTRACK

PENN HOUSE PUBLISHING LTD 15654
PO Box 7, KNUTSFORD, WA16 7PP **Tel:** 01565 872107
Fax: 01565 873943
Titles:
HOOFPRINT

PENNINE PENS 16623
32 Windsor Road, HEBDEN BRIDGE, HX7 8LF
Tel: 01422 843724 **Fax:** 01422 843724
Titles:
HEBDEN BRIDGE WEB

PENNWELL CORPORATION 1742573
16 Arlington Villas, Clifton, BRISTOL, BS8 2EG
Tel: 0117 941 5378 **Fax:** 0117 941 5899
Titles:
LEDS MAGAZINE

PENNWELL PUBLICATIONS INTERNATIONAL LTD
1715171
Warlies Park House, Horseshoe Hill, Upshire, WALTHAM
ABBEY, EN9 3SR **Tel:** 01992 656600 **Fax:** 01992 656700
Web site: http://www.pennwell.com
Titles:
COSPP - COGENERATION AND ON-SITE POWER
  PRODUCTION
POWER ENGINEERING INTERNATIONAL
RENEWABLE ENERGY WORLD
WASTE MANAGEMENT WORLD

PENNWELL PUBLISHING LTD 14214
Warlies Park House, Horseshoe Hill, Upshire, WALTHAM
ABBEY, EN9 3SR **Tel:** 01992 656600
Web site: http://www.pennwell.com
Titles:
OFFSHORE
WATER & WASTEWATER INTERNATIONAL

PENSION PUBLICATIONS LTD 13386
East Wing, Fourth Floor, Hope House, 45 Great Peter Street,
LONDON, SW1P 3LT **Tel:** 020 7222 0288
Fax: 020 7799 2163
Titles:
BENEFITS & COMPENSATION INTERNATIONAL

PENSIONS MANAGEMENT INSTITUTE 13387
PMI House, 4-10 Artillery Lane, LONDON, E1 7LS
Tel: 020 7247 1452 **Fax:** 020 7375 0603
Titles:
PMI NEWS

PENTASTIC LTD 1717416
PO Box 4435, Cubbington, LEAMINGTON SPA, CV31 9EA
Tel: 01926 339661
Web site: http://www.pentastic.co.uk
Titles:
FUNDING FOR INDEPENDENT SCHOOLS

PENTLANDS PUBLISHING LTD 1643243
Station Road, Great Longstone, BAKEWELL, DE45 1TS
Tel: 01246 584002 **Fax:** 01246 584006
Titles:
FEED COMPOUNDER

PENTON MEDIA 12407
34A West Street, MARLOW, SL7 2NB **Tel:** 01628 477775
Fax: 01628 481111
Titles:
AIR TRANSPORT WORLD

PENTON PUBLICATIONS LTD 14447
Penton House, 38 Heron Road, Sydenham Business Park,
BELFAST, BT3 9LE **Tel:** 028 9045 7457 **Fax:** 028 9045 6611
Email: info@pentongroup.com
Web site: http://www.pentongroup.com
Titles:
GO BELFAST
IRELAND'S FORECOURT AND CONVENIENCE RETAILER
IRELAND'S WEDDING JOURNAL
LCN LICENSED & CATERING NEWS
NEIGHBOURHOOD RETAILER
NORTHERN IRELAND VETERINARY TODAY
NORTHERN IRELAND VISITORS JOURNAL

PENTREATH INDUSTRIES 623340
PO Box 71, PENZANCE, TR18 2ZR **Tel:** 01736 365896
Titles:
CORNISH WORLD

PEOPLES PRESS PRINTING SOCIETY 14820
William Rust House, 52 Beachey Road, LONDON, E3 2NS
Tel: 020 8510 0815 **Fax:** 020 8986 5694
Titles:
MORNING STAR

THE PEQUOT PUBLISHING GROUP 18909
8 Spencer Hill, Wimbledon, LONDON, SW19 4NY
Tel: 020 8946 5347
Titles:
GAS TURBINE WORLD

PERENDALE 1634372
7 St. Georges Terrace, St. James Square, CHELTENHAM,
GL50 3PT **Tel:** 01242 267700 **Fax:** 01242 267701
Email: info@perendale.co.uk
Web site: http://www.perendale.co.uk
Titles:
GRAIN & FEED MILLING TECHNOLOGY
INTERNATIONAL AQUAFEED
INTERNATIONAL MILLING DIRECTORY

PERFORMANCE PUBLISHING LTD 17224
County House, 3 Shelley Road, WORTHING, BN11 1TT
Tel: 01903 236268
Titles:
COMPLETE KIT CAR?

PERFORMING ARTS TRUST 15347
33A Lurline Gardens, LONDON, SW11 4DD
Tel: 020 7720 1950 **Fax:** 020 7720 1950
Titles:
PLAYS INTERNATIONAL

PERRY PUBLICATIONS LTD 16010
2nd Floor, Cardinal House, 39-40 Albemarle Street,
LONDON, W1S 4TE **Tel:** 020 7647 6330
Titles:
BUSINESS TRAVELLER

PERSIMMON PUBLISHING LTD 1640610
311 Shoreham Street, SHEFFIELD, S2 4FA
Email: info@persimmonpublishing.com
Titles:
FAST-AUTOS.COM

PERSONAL FINANCE SOCIETY 1739260
42-48 High Road, South Woodford, LONDON, E18 2JP
Tel: 020 8530 0852 **Fax:** 020 8530 3052
Titles:
FINANCIAL SOLUTIONS

PERSONALISED EDUCATION NOW 1742578
15 Campbell Close, WALSALL, WS4 2EJ **Tel:** 01922 624097
Titles:
PERSONALISED EDUCATION NOW

PERSONNELZONE 1627068
Heath House, Firfields, WEYBRIDGE, KT13 0UD
Tel: 01932 830111 **Fax:** 01932 821592
Email: contact@personnelzone.com
Web site: http://www.personnelzone.com
Titles:
HEALTHANDSAFETYZONE.COM
PERSONNELZONE

PERSPECTIVE INTERNATIONAL LTD 1746306
87 Station Road, ASHINGTON, NE63 8RS
Tel: 07775 607903 **Fax:** 020 8113 2345
Titles:
PERSPECTIVE MAGAZINE

PERSPECTIVE PUBLISHING LTD 13335
6th Floor, 3 London Wall Buildings, LONDON, EC2M 5PD
Tel: 020 7562 2401 **Fax:** 020 7374 2701
Web site: http://www.perspectivepublishing.com
Titles:
THE CHARITY BUYERS GUIDE
CHARITY TIMES
CONTINUITY, INSURANCE & RISK
CSI CABLE & SATELLITE INTERNATIONAL
EUROPEAN PENSIONS
FST FINANCIAL SECTOR TECHNOLOGY
PENSIONS AGE
RETAIL SYSTEMS
RISK MANAGEMENT PROFESSIONAL

PEST CONTROL NEWS LTD 13991
PO Box 2, OSSETT, WF5 9NA **Tel:** 01924 168400
Fax: 01924 264646
Email: editor@pestcontrolnews.com
Titles:
PEST CONTROL NEWS

PET SUBJECTS LTD 15643
Town Mill, Bagshot Road, Chobham, WOKING, GU24 8BZ
Tel: 01276 858880 **Fax:** 01276 858860
Titles:
DOGS TODAY

PETPLANET.CO.UK LTD 677103
10 Lindsay Square, Deans Industrial Estate, Deans,
LIVINGSTON, EH54 8RL **Tel:** 0845 601 2765
Fax: 0845 345 0723
Email: info@petplanet.co.uk
Web site: http://www.petplanet.co.uk
Titles:
PETPLANET.CO.UK

PETROLEUM ECONOMIST LTD 12310
69 Carter Lane, LONDON, EC4V 5EQ **Tel:** 020 7779 8800
Fax: 020 7779 8896
Titles:
PETROLEUM ECONOMIST

PETROSPOT LIMITED 1642395
Petrospot House, Somerville Court, Trinity Way, Adderbury,
BANBURY, OX17 3SN **Tel:** 01295 279393
Fax: 01295 273079
Titles:
CARGO SECURITY INTERNATIONAL

THE PEVEREL GROUP 670304
Queensway House, 11 Queensway, NEW MILTON, BH25
5NR **Tel:** 01425 638863 **Fax:** 01425 638838
Email: peverelnews@peverel.co.uk
Web site: http://www.peverel.co.uk
Titles:
PEVEREL LIFE AND STYLE

PFI MEDIA LTD 1690315
1 Red Lion Street, RICHMOND, TW9 1RE
Tel: 020 8332 4600 **Fax:** 020 8332 4639
Email: info@opp.org.uk
Titles:
OVERSEAS PROPERTY PROFESSIONAL
OVERSEAS PROPERTY PROFESSIONAL ONLINE

UK Publishers & Their Titles

PGRO 1752315
The Research Station, Great North Road, Thornhaugh,
PETERBOROUGH, PE8 6HJ **Tel:** 01780 782585
Titles:
PGRO PULSE MAGAZINE

PHARMACEUTICAL SERVICES NEGOTIATING COMM 14238
59 Buckingham Street, AYLESBURY, HP20 2PJ
Tel: 01296 432823 **Fax:** 01296 392181
Titles:
PSNC COMMUNITY PHARMACY NEWS

PHARMEDIA INTERNATIONAL 14049
6 Tobin Close, Livingstone Park, EPSOM, KT19 8AE
Tel: 01372 742347
Titles:
GROCER.ME
PAEDIATRICS.ME
PHARMACY.ME

PHARMIWEB SOLUTIONS 1733323
Clarenden House, Grenville Place, BRACKNELL, RG12 1BP
Tel: 01344 677433 **Fax:** 01344 677434
Titles:
PHARMIWEB.COM

PHARMWEB 625180
3 Kilmory Fold, GLOSSOP, SK13 7PH **Tel:** 07902 030763
Fax: 07902 030763
Titles:
PHARMWEB

PHAROS INTERNATIONAL 699806
1st Floor, Brecon House, 16-16A Albion Place, MAIDSTONE,
ME14 5DZ **Tel:** 01622 688292 **Fax:** 01622 686698
Titles:
PHAROS INTERNATIONAL

PHEONIX PUBLISHING 13011
PO Box 56556, LONDON, SW18 9EP **Tel:** 020 7183 0468
Titles:
KMAG

PHIL CREIGHTON 1721375
10 Amity Street, READING, RG1 3LP **Tel:** 07985 413641
Web site: http://www.thesheepdip.co.uk
Titles:
THESHEEPDIP.CO.UK

PHILATELIC EXPORTER 15479
7 Parkside, Christchurch Road, RINGWOOD, BH24 3SH
Tel: 01903 821082 **Fax:** 01903 537321
Titles:
THE PHILATELIC EXPORTER

PHILIP BARTLAM 13654
16 Dartmouth Court, Dartmouth Grove, LONDON, SE10 8AS
Tel: 020 8691 4820 **Fax:** 020 8691 2489
Email: philipbartlam@tiscali.co.uk
Titles:
ANTIQUE DEALER & COLLECTORS GUIDE

PHILIPPINE SERVICE CORPORATION 1645243
313 Brompton Road, LONDON, SW3 2DY
Tel: 020 7581 8100
Titles:
PLANET PHILIPPINES

PHILOSOPHY PRESS LTD 1718361
Dunstan House, 14A St. Cross Street, LONDON, EC1N 8XA
Tel: 020 7841 1959 **Fax:** 020 7242 1474
Titles:
THE PHILOSOPHERS' MAGAZINE
TPM ONLINE

PHOENIX 2 15994
Lantern House, Lodge Drove, Woodfalls, SALISBURY, SP5
2NH **Tel:** 01725 512200 **Fax:** 01725 511819
Titles:
WHAT'S ON IN DORSET & THE NEW FOREST

PHOENIX INTERNATIONAL PUBLISHING 697096
PO Box 615, HORSHAM, RH13 5WF **Tel:** 01403 276091
Fax: 01403 241614
Email: postmaster@phoenixip.com
Titles:
ESSENTIALLY AMERICA

PHOENIX MEDICAL SUPPLIES LTD 697377
Rivington Road, Whitehouse Industrial Estate, RUNCORN,
WA7 3DJ **Tel:** 01928 750500 **Fax:** 01928 750750
Web site: http://www.myp-i-n.co.uk
Titles:
PHOENIXFILE

PHOTO MARKETING ASSOCIATION INTL. (UK) LTD 14246
Wisteria House, 28 Fulling Mill Lane, WELWYN, AL6 9NS
Tel: 0870 240 4542 **Fax:** 01438 715022
Web site: http://www.pmai.org
Titles:
PMA MAGAZINE

**THE PHOTOGRAPHIC COLLECTORS CLUB
INTERNATIONAL LTD.** 15510
5 Buntingford Road, Puckeridge, WARE, SG11 1RT
Tel: 01920 821611
Titles:
PHOTOGRAPHICA WORLD

PHOTO-I 1743868
20 Green Lane, CHISLEHURST, BR7 6AG
Titles:
DVCAMERA.CO.UK

PICKWICK SWALES LTD 693204
6 The Rickyard, Clifton Reynes, OLNEY, MK46 5LQ
Tel: 01234 714644 **Fax:** 01234 714633
Email: info@pbwnews.com
Web site: http://www.pickwickswales.com
Titles:
PBW NEWS
THATCHED LIVING

PICTURE RESEARCH ASSOCIATION 1748665
c/o 1 Willow Court, off Willow Street, LONDON, E2A 4QB
Tel: 020 7739 8544 **Fax:** 020 7782 0011
Email: chair@picture-research.co.uk
Web site: http://www.picture-research.org.uk
Titles:
MONTAGE

PICTURE-BOX MEDIA LTD 1639728
Dulwich Lodge, 62 Pemberton Road, EAST MOLESEY, KT8
9LH **Tel:** 020 8941 0249 **Fax:** 020 8941 1088
Email: info@picture-box.com
Web site: http://www.picture-box.com
Titles:
AG

PINEDE PUBLISHING 16439
Suite 16-18, Hawkesyard Hall, Armitage Park, RUGELEY,
WS15 1PU **Tel:** 01889 577222 **Fax:** 01889 579177
Email: info@pinedepublishing.co.uk
Titles:
EIBI ENERGY IN BUILDINGS & INDUSTRY
PLUMBING, HEATING & AIR MOVEMENT NEWS

PINEGEN LTD 15419
9 Coppergate Mews, Brighton Road, SURBITON, KT6 5NE
Tel: 020 8335 1100
Titles:
SPEEDWAY STAR

PINK LOCAL DIRECTORY LTD 17713
St. Augustines House, St. Augustines Way, South Wootton,
KING'S LYNN, PE30 3TE **Tel:** 01553 675885
Fax: 01553 670007
Email: mail@pinklocaldirectory.co.uk
Web site: http://www.pinklocaldirectory.co.uk
Titles:
KING'S LYNN PINK LOCAL DIRECTORY
THETFORD & BRANDON PINK LOCAL DIRECTORY
WISBECH PINK LOCAL DIRECTORY

PINK UNLIMITED 1712787
Phoenix Yard, 65 King's Cross Road, LONDON, WC1X 9LW
Titles:
PINKNEWS.CO.UK

PINOY SERVICES LTD 1743934
Suite 19-20, Network Business Centre, 329-339 Putney
Bridge Road, LONDON, SW15 2PG **Tel:** 020 8780 3152
Titles:
ONE PHILIPPINES

PINPOINT SCOTLAND LTD 14498
9 Gayfield Square, EDINBURGH, EH1 3NT
Tel: 0131 557 4184 **Fax:** 0131 557 4701
Web site: http://www.pinpointmedical.com
Titles:
CARDIOLOGY NEWS
ENT NEWS
EYE NEWS
SCOTLAND'S NEW HOMEBUYER
UROLOGY NEWS

PIPE TEN LTD 1640326
15 Paternoster Row, SHEFFIELD, S1 2BX
Tel: 0114 279 6511 **Fax:** 0114 279 6522
Email: info@pipeten.com
Web site: http://www.pipeten.com
Titles:
COLDSWELL.COM

PIPERS PUBLISHING LTD. 1763419
26 Store Street, LONDON, WC1E 7BT **Tel:** 020 7636 4044
Titles:
THE LONDON PROPERTY REVIEW

PIRA INTERNATIONAL 12509
Cleeve Road, LEATHERHEAD, KT22 7RU **Tel:** 01372 802000
Fax: 01372 802079
Web site: http://www.intertechpira.com
Titles:
ACTIVE AND INTELLIGENT PACK NEWS
BRAND PROTECTION NEWS
BRAND - THE JOURNAL OF BRAND PROTECTION
DIGITAL DEMAND - THE JOURNAL OF PRINTING AND
    PUBLISHING TECHNOLOGY
FLEXIBLE - THE JOURNAL OF PLASTICS & PACKAGING
    TECHNOLOGY
NANOMATERIALS WORLD
PACKAGING MONTH
PAPERBASE ABSTRACTS
PLASTICS PACKAGING INNOVATIONS NEWS
+ PLASTIC ELECTRONICS
PRESS
PRINTED AND DISPOSABLE ELECTRONICS NEWS

PIREME PUBLISHING LTD 13009
Main Street, Strelley Hall, NOTTINGHAM, NG8 6PE
Tel: 0115 906 1218
Titles:
MINIATURE WARGAMES

PISCES MEDIA LTD 1630357
PO Box 234, UCKFIELD, TN22 9AH **Tel:** 01825 733843
Fax: 01825 731845
Web site: http://www.written-image.com
Titles:
THE SOROPTIMIST

PISON PUBLISHING 1685630
1 Warwick Road, BEACONSFIELD, HP9 2PE
Tel: 01494 677362 **Fax:** 01494 675385
Email: editorial@chichat.co.uk
Web site: http://www.chicchat.co.uk
Titles:
CHIC CHAT

PITA 14235
5 Frecheville Court, BURY, BL9 0UF **Tel:** 0161 764 5858
Fax: 0161 764 5353
Email: info@pita.co.uk
Web site: http://www.pita.co.uk
Titles:
PAPER TECHNOLOGY

PITCHCARE.COM LIMITED   1706552
The Technology Centre, Wolverhampton Science Park,
WOLVERHAMPTON, WV10 9RU **Tel:** 01902 440252
Fax: 01902 440253
Email: editor@pitchcare.com
Web site: http://www.pitchcare.com

Titles:
PITCHCARE

PJ DESIGN   15615
1 Beveridge Row, Belhaven, DUNBAR, EH42 1TP
Tel: 01368 863593 **Fax:** 01368 863593

Titles:
EAST LOTHIAN LIFE

THE PLAIN TRUTH LTD   14878
PO Box 4421, WORTHING, BN14 8WQ **Tel:** 01638 741549
Fax: 01638 744190
Web site: http://www.plain-truth.org.uk

Titles:
PLAIN TRUTH

PLANET 21   15715
60 Twisden Road, LONDON, NW5 1DN **Tel:** 020 7485 3136
Email: planet21@totalise.co.uk
Web site: http://www.peopleandplanet.net

Titles:
PEOPLEANDPLANET.NET

THE PLANET GROUP (UK) LTD   17162
7 Bay Hall, Willow Lane, Birkby, HUDDERSFIELD, HD1 5EN
Tel: 01484 321000 **Fax:** 01484 321001
Email: produce@planet-group.co.uk
Web site: http://www.planet-group.co.uk

Titles:
BRAND LABEL UK
CONSTRUCTION MAGAZINE
FOOD & DRINK NEWS
PRIVATE LABEL UK MAGAZINE
PRODUCE NEWS

PLANET INK LTD   1711815
Suite 3.4, 111 Union Street, GLASGOW, G1 3TA
Tel: 0141 248 5595
Web site: http://www.planetinkltd.co.uk

Titles:
ECOFORYOU

PLANET MEDIA PUBLISHING   1720704
G1 Unit 121, The Old Truman Brewery, 91 Brick Lane,
LONDON, E1 6QL **Tel:** 020 7375 2297 **Fax:** 020 7375 2296

Titles:
ATM MAGAZINE

PLASA   624213
Redoubt House, 1 Edward Road, EASTBOURNE, BN23 8AS
Tel: 01323 524120 **Fax:** 01323 524121
Email: info@plasa.org
Web site: http://www.plasa.org

Titles:
L&SI ONLINE (PLASA)

PLASTICS & RUBBER LTD   1640620
The Stables, Willow Lane, Paddock Wood, TONBRIDGE,
TN12 6PF **Tel:** 01892 839200 **Fax:** 01892 839210

Titles:
PLASTICS & RUBBER ASIA

PLASTIQUE MAGAZINE LTD   1732107
Suite 13, 93 Shepperton Road, LONDON, N1 3DF
Tel: 020 7288 1828 **Fax:** 020 7288 1828

Titles:
PLASTIQUE

PLATFORM 5 PUBLISHING LTD   15503
3 Wyvern House, Sark Road, SHEFFIELD, S2 4HG
Tel: 0114 255 2625 **Fax:** 0114 255 2471

Titles:
TODAY'S RAILWAYS UK

PLATFORM MEDIA LTD   16857
Woodburn Road, Blackburn Industrial Estate, Kinellar,
ABERDEEN, AB21 0RX **Tel:** 01224 791123
Fax: 01224 791147
Email: sales@platform-media.co.uk
Web site: http://www.platform-oilandgas.com

Titles:
PLATFORM

PLATFORM PUBLISHING & MEDIA LTD   1606029
16 The Square, Alvechurch, BIRMINGHAM, B48 7LA
Tel: 0121 445 6757 **Fax:** 0870 705 3041
Email: info@platformpublishing.co.uk
Web site: http://www.platformpublishing.co.uk

Titles:
THE VILLAGE

PLATTS   691219
20 Canada Square, Canary Wharf, LONDON, E14 5LH
Tel: 020 7176 7000 **Fax:** 020 7176 6260
Web site: http://www.platts.com

Titles:
ENERGY ECONOMIST
ENERGY IN EAST EUROPE
EU ENERGY
EUROPEAN NATURAL GAS
INTERNATIONAL COAL REPORT
INTERNATIONAL GAS REPORT
PLATTS METALS WEEK
POWER IN ASIA
POWER IN EUROPE
RENEWABLE ENERGY REPORT

PLAZA PUBLISHING LTD   13296
15 Prescott Place, LONDON, SW4 6BS **Tel:** 020 7819 1200
Fax: 020 7819 1219

Titles:
CHARITY FINANCE
CIVIL SOCIETY IT
GOVERNANCE
PROFESSIONAL FUNDRAISING

PLENHAM LTD   14112
The Firs, High Street, Whitchurch, AYLESBURY, HP22 4JU
Tel: 01296 642800 **Fax:** 01296 640044

Titles:
BODYSHOP BUYERS GUIDE
BODYSHOP MAGAZINE
THE TRUCK & CV DIRECTORY

PLUK   1653543
13 Masons Yard, LONDON, SW1Y 6BU **Tel:** 020 7839 9300
Fax: 020 7321 0496

Titles:
PLUK

PLUM PUBLISHING LIMITED   1649963
Suite 1, Cornerstone House, Stafford Park 13, TELFORD,
TF3 3AZ **Tel:** 01952 204920 **Fax:** 01952 204929
Web site: http://www.plumbpublishing.co.uk

Titles:
BUS AND COACH PROFESSIONAL
COACH TOURISM PROFESSIONAL
VEHICLE SALVAGE PROFESSIONAL

PMB MEDIA   1690042
Airedale Lodge, Stafford Road, Eccleshall, STAFFORD,
ST21 6JP **Tel:** 01785 851660 **Fax:** 01785 850173

Titles:
ART OF ENGLAND

POCKET LONDON LTD   600471
3 Stewart's Court, 218-220 Stewart's Road, LONDON, SW8
4UB **Tel:** 020 7720 1166 **Fax:** 020 7720 1177

Titles:
POCKET LONDON

THE POETRY SOCIETY   15837
22 Betterton Street, LONDON, WC2H 9BX
Tel: 020 7420 9880 **Fax:** 020 7240 4818

Titles:
POETRY REVIEW

POETRY WALES PRESS LTD   15838
c/o Seren Books, First Floor, 38-40 Norton Street,
BRIDGEND, CF31 3BN **Tel:** 01656 883018
Fax: 01656 649226

Titles:
POETRY WALES

POINTBLANK PUBLISHING   1730110
4B Kellaway Avenue, BRISTOL, BS6 7XR
Tel: 0117 924 5328
Web site: http://www.pointblankpublishing.com

Titles:
AREA MAGAZINE

POKE-IN-THE-EYE PUBLISHING LTD   1675961
PO Box 587, LONDON, WC1H 9WB **Tel:** 020 7833 0500
Email: info@nudemagazine.co.uk
Web site: http://www.nudemagazine.co.uk

Titles:
NUDE

POLE STAR PUBLICATIONS   16128
PO Box 175, TONBRIDGE, TN10 4ZY **Tel:** 01732 367542
Fax: 01732 356230

Titles:
ASTRONOMY NOW
SPACEFLIGHT NOW

POLICE AVIATION RESEARCH   1646267
7 Windmill Close, WALTHAM ABBEY, EN9 3BQ
Tel: 01992 714162
Email: info@policeaviationnews.com
Web site: http://www.policeaviationnews.com

Titles:
POLICE AVIATION NEWS

POLICY DIALOGUE INTERNATIONAL LIMITED   1745466
132 Walham Green Court, Moore Park Road, LONDON,
SW6 2PX

Titles:
EGOV MONITOR

THE POLICY PRESS   15717
4th Floor, Beacon House, Queens Road, BRISTOL, BS8
1QU **Tel:** 0117 331 4054 **Fax:** 0117 331 4093
Web site: http://www.policypress.org.uk

Titles:
BENEFITS
EVIDENCE AND POLICY
POLICY & POLITICS

THE POLISH DAILY (PUBLISHERS) LTD   16032
63 Jeddo Road, LONDON, W12 9ED **Tel:** 020 8740 1991
Fax: 020 8746 1661
Email: dziennik@dziennikpolski.co.uk

Titles:
DZIENNIK POLSKI

POLISH EXPRESS   1711936
603 Cumberland House, 80 Scrubs Lane, LONDON, NW10
6RF **Tel:** 020 8964 4488 **Fax:** 020 8964 4788
Email: info@polishexpress.co.uk
Web site: http://www.polishexpress.co.uk

Titles:
POLISH EXPRESS

POLYVIEW MEDIA LTD   1731550
Hereford House, 22-24 Smithfield Street, LONDON, EC1A
9LF **Tel:** 020 7332 2580 **Fax:** 020 7332 2599

Titles:
THE EUROPEAN LAWYER
INSIDEDIVORCE.COM
TAKELEGALADVICE.COM

PORSCHE CLUB GREAT BRITAIN   698212
Cornbury House, Cotswold Business Village, London Road,
MORETON-IN-MARSH, GL56 0JQ **Tel:** 01608 652911
Fax: 01608 652944
Email: cluboffice@porscheclubgb.com
Web site: http://www.porscheclubgb.com

Titles:
PORSCHE POST

PORTAL PUBLISHING LTD 1635467
PO Box 1393, HUDDERSFIELD, HD1 9TN
Tel: 01484 300750
Titles:
BUSINESS CONTINUITY JOURNAL
CONTINUITY CENTRAL

PORTER & PORTER LTD 17672
PO Box 2, TENBURY WELLS, WR15 8XX **Tel:** 01584 781588
Fax: 01584 781630
Titles:
XK GAZETTE

PORTFOLIO PUBLISHING, LONDON 1757281
Panstar House (1-2), 13-15 Swakeleys Road, UXBRIDGE, UB10 8DF **Tel:** 01895 678629
Email: kevin.odonnell@portfoliopublishing.co.uk
Web site: http://www.portfoliopublishing.co.uk
Titles:
FINANCIAL PLANNER

PORTFOLIO PUBLISHING LTD 1741731
Suite 114, 2 Old Brompton Road, LONDON, SW7 3DQ
Tel: 020 7731 0942
Titles:
EPICUREAN LIFE

PORTICO PUBLISHING LTD 1640438
1st Floor, Southgate House, St. George's Way, STEVENAGE, SG1 1HG **Tel:** 01438 759000
Fax: 01438 759007
Email: info@portico.uk.com
Web site: http://www.portico.uk.com
Titles:
MODERN BUILDING SERVICES

PORTLAND PRESS LTD 16304
Third Floor, Eagle House, 16 Procter Street, LONDON, WC1V 6NX **Tel:** 020 7280 4110 **Fax:** 020 7280 4169
Web site: http://www.portlandpress.com
Titles:
BIOTECHNOLOGY AND APPLIED BIOCHEMISTRY

PORTMAN PUBLISHING & COMMUNICATIONS LTD 16742
Deben House, Main Road, Martlesham, WOODBRIDGE, IP12 4SE **Tel:** 0870 241 4678 **Fax:** 01394 380594
Web site: http://www.portman.uk.com
Titles:
GOLF MANAGEMENT EUROPE

PORTSMOUTH & DISTRICT POST 1690005
120 London Road, North End, PORTSMOUTH, PO2 0NB
Tel: 02392 656903 **Fax:** 02392 656910
Titles:
PORTSMOUTH & DISTRICT POST

PORTSMOUTH & SOUTH EAST HAMPSHIRE CHAMBER OF COMMERCE 1627197
Regional Business Centre, Harts Farm Way, HAVANT, PO9 1HR **Tel:** 023 9244 9449 **Fax:** 023 9244 9444
Email: businessnews@chamber.org.uk
Web site: http://www.chamber.org.uk
Titles:
BUSINESS NEWS (SOUTH EAST HAMPSHIRE)

PORTSMOUTH PUBLISHING & PRINTING LTD 12886
The News Centre, Hilsea, PORTSMOUTH, PO2 9SX
Tel: 023 9266 4488 **Fax:** 023 9267 7777
Web site: http://www.thenews.co.uk
Titles:
HAYLING ISLANDER
JOURNAL SERIES PORTSMOUTH
LITTLEHAMPTON GAZETTE
THE NEWS (PORTSMOUTH)
PETERSFIELD POST SERIES
WORTHING ADVERTISER AND HERALD SERIES

POSITIVE ACTION PUBLICATIONS LTD 14002
PO Box 4, DRIFFIELD, YO25 9DJ **Tel:** 01377 241724
Fax: 01377 253640
Email: info@positiveaction.co.uk
Web site: http://www.positiveaction.co.uk

Titles:
INTERNATIONAL DAIRY TOPICS
INTERNATIONAL FOOD HYGIENE
INTERNATIONAL HATCHERY PRACTICE
INTERNATIONAL PIG TOPICS
INTERNATIONAL POULTRY PRODUCTION

POSITIVE NEWS PUBLISHING LTD 18559
Unit 5-6, Bicton Enterprise Centre, Bicton, Clun, CRAVEN ARMS, SY7 8NF **Tel:** 01588 640022 **Fax:** 01588 640033
Titles:
POSITIVE NEWS FROM AROUND THE WORLD

POSITIVE PUBLICATIONS LTD 13788
Alkmaar House, Alkmaar Way, NORWICH, NR6 6BF
Tel: 01603 414444 **Fax:** 01603 406543
Titles:
INDUSTRY EUROPE
PACKAGING EUROPE

POST NEWS 13384
STOKE-SUB-HAMDON, TA14 6BR **Tel:** 01935 881245
Titles:
POST NEWS

POST NEWS GROUP LTD 1710863
Central House, Summerland Place, MINEHEAD, TA24 5BT
Tel: 01643 888215 **Fax:** 01643 709677
Email: info@westsomersetpost.com
Web site: http://www.spostnews.blogspot.com
Titles:
WEST SOMERSET POST

POTTS PRINTERS LTD 629269
Stuart House, 1 High Flatworth, NORTH SHIELDS, NE29 7UZ **Tel:** 0191 257 0817
Titles:
DN

POUNDBURY PUBLISHING LTD 15258
Middle Farm, Middle Farm Way, Poundbury, DORCHESTER, DT1 3RS **Tel:** 01305 266360 **Fax:** 01305 262760
Web site: http://www.poundbury.co.uk
Titles:
ITALY
MINOR MONTHLY

POWDENE PUBLICITY LTD 14779
Unit 17, St. Peters Wharf, NEWCASTLE UPON TYNE, NE6 1TZ **Tel:** 0191 265 0040 **Fax:** 0191 265 0040
Email: info@powdene.com
Web site: http://www.powdene.com
Titles:
CLUB JOURNAL
THE NORTHUMBRIAN

POWER PUBLISHING 600700
PO Box 16, ST. LEONARDS-ON-SEA, TN37 6YE
Tel: 01424 465543
Titles:
THE ALTERNATIVE GUIDE

POYNTON POST 600769
PO Box 174, Poynton, STOCKPORT, SK12 1WF
Tel: 01625 874164 **Fax:** 01625 858847
Titles:
POYNTON POST

PPA 18106
Queen's House, 28 Kingsway, LONDON, WC2B 6JR
Tel: 020 7404 4166 **Fax:** 020 7404 4167
Titles:
MAGAZINE NEWS

PPASS LTD 18799
3 St. Johns Court, Moulsham Street, CHELMSFORD, CM2 0JD **Tel:** 01245 358877 **Fax:** 01245 357767
Titles:
INTERNATIONAL HOMES LUXURY COLLECTION

PPL RESEARCH LTD 627370
PO Box 2002, WATFORD, WD25 9ZT **Tel:** 01923 894777
Fax: 01923 894888
Email: enquiries@pplresearch.co.uk
Web site: http://www.pplresearch.co.uk
Titles:
BOARD MARKET DIGEST
PAPER MARKET DIGEST

PPMA LTD 14228
New Progress House, 34 Stafford Road, WALLINGTON, SM6 9AA **Tel:** 020 8773 8111 **Fax:** 020 8773 0022
Email: publishing@ppma.co.uk
Web site: http://www.ppma.co.uk
Titles:
MACHINERY UPDATE

PPS 12887
Banner House, Briar Close, EVESHAM, WR11 4XA
Tel: 01386 765832 **Fax:** 01386 40650
Email: info@ppsprint.co.uk
Web site: http://www.ppsprint.co.uk
Titles:
BRIDGEND & DISTRICT PROPERTY NEWS
HOMESFORSALEANDTOLET.COM
ROSSENDALE PROPERTY NEWS
SPAREROOM

PPS PUBLICATIONS LTD 16446
3A Gatwick Metro Centre, Balcombe Road, HORLEY, RH6 9GA **Tel:** 01293 783851 **Fax:** 01293 782959
Email: post@pps-publications.com
Web site: http://www.pps-publications.com
Titles:
THE AIRPORT OPERATOR
COMMUNIQUE AIRPORT BUSINESS

PQ PUBLISHING 1650061
4th Floor, Central House, 142 Central Street, LONDON, EC1V 8AR **Tel:** 020 7216 6444
Titles:
NQ MAGAZINE
PQ MAGAZINE

PRA 13897
14 Castle Mews, High Street, HAMPTON, TW12 2NP
Tel: 020 8487 0800 **Fax:** 020 8487 0801
Web site: http://www.pra-world.com
Titles:
RADNEWS
WATERBORNE & HIGH SOLIDS COATINGS

PRACTICAL ACTION PUBLISHING 13835
Bourton Hall, Bourton, RUGBY, CV23 9QZ
Tel: 01926 634501 **Fax:** 01926 634502
Web site: ukhttp://www.practicalaction.org.uk
Titles:
ENTERPRISE DEVELOPMENT AND MICROFINANCE
WATERLINES

PRACTICAL FACILITIES MANAGEMENT 1653551
30 The Copse, St. Georges, WESTON-SUPER-MARE, BS22 7SL **Tel:** 01934 521224 **Fax:** 01934 521224
Email: newsdesk@practicalfm.co.uk
Titles:
PRACTICAL FACILITIES MANAGEMENT

PRACTICAL LAW COMPANY LTD 14323
19 Hatfields, LONDON, SE1 8DJ **Tel:** 020 7202 1200
Fax: 020 7202 1211
Web site: http://www.practicallaw.com
Titles:
PLC CROSS-BORDER QUARTERLY
PLC MAGAZINE

PRACTICAL PUBLISHING INTERNATIONAL LTD 1685290
Unit 1 Adlington Court, Adlington Industrial Estate, Adlington, MACCLESFIELD, SK10 4NL **Tel:** 0844 561 1202
Web site: http://www.practicalpublishing.co.uk
Titles:
COMPLETE CARD MAKING
PAPERCRAFT ESSENTIALS
SCRAPBOOK MAGAZINE
SIMPLY CARDS & PAPERCRAFT

PRACTICE MANAGEMENT INTERNATIONAL LLP 13430
Warnford Court, 29 Throgmorton Street, LONDON, EC2N
2AT **Tel:** 020 7786 9786 **Fax:** 020 7786 9799
Web site: http://www.pmforum.co.uk

Titles:
PROFESSIONAL MARKETING

PRAYER BOOK SOCIETY 15880
The Studio, Copyhold Farm, Goring Heath, READING, RG8
7RT

Titles:
PRAYER BOOK SOCIETY JOURNAL

PRC ASSOCIATES LTD 14472
Dept. Clinical Biochemistry, City Hospital, Dudley Road,
BIRMINGHAM, B18 7QH **Tel:** 0121 507 5353
Fax: 0121 765 4224

Titles:
ACB NEWS

PRCA 18181
Willow House, Willow Place, LONDON, SW1P 1JH
Tel: 020 7233 6026
Email: pressoffice@prca.org.uk
Web site: http://www.prca.org.uk

Titles:
PUBLIC RELATIONS CONSULTANTS ASSOCIATION
YEAR BOOK

PRECIOUS ONLINE MAGAZINE AND NETWORK 1743869
7 Crayford House, Staple Street, LONDON, SE1 4BU
Tel: 07950 814371
Web site: http://www.preciousonline.co.uk

Titles:
PRECIOUS ONLINE MAGAZINE AND NETWORK

PREDATOR PUBLICATIONS LTD 16935
Sandholme Grange, Newport, BROUGH, HU15 2QG
Tel: 01430 440624 **Fax:** 01430 441319

Titles:
COARSE ANGLING TODAY
PIKE & PREDATORS

PREMIER COLOUR 13848
12 Campbell Court, Bramley, TADLEY, RG26 5EG
Tel: 01256 885837 **Fax:** 01256 882961

Titles:
THE ORBITAL

PREMIER NEWSPAPERS 16093
Napier House, 2 Auckland Park, Bond Avenue, Bletchley,
MILTON KEYNES, MK1 1BU **Tel:** 01908 651263
Fax: 01908 371115
Web site: http://www.miltonkeynes.co.uk

Titles:
CHILL OUT

PREMIER PUBLISHING LTD 1740925
2nd Floor, 73 Robertson Street, GLASGOW, G2 8QD
Tel: 0141 248 6331 **Fax:** 0141 248 6472

Titles:
SOUTHSIDE NEWS

PRESBYTERIAN CHURCH IN IRELAND 15899
Church House, Fisherwick Place, BELFAST, BT1 6DW
Tel: 028 9032 2284 **Fax:** 028 9041 7307
Web site: http://www.presbyterianireland.org

Titles:
PRESBYTERIAN HERALD

PRE-SCHOOL LEARNING ALLIANCE 15952
Fitzpatrick Building, 188 York Way, LONDON, N7 9AD
Tel: 020 7697 2500 **Fax:** 020 7697 8607
Email: info@pre-school.org.uk
Web site: http://www.pre-school.org.uk

Titles:
UNDER 5

PRESENT DAY PUBLISHING LIMITED 15900
Workspace House, 28-29 Maxwell Road, PETERBOROUGH,
PE2 7JE **Tel:** 01733 239090 **Fax:** 01733 239090
Email: editorial@swordpdp.com
Web site: http://www.swordpdp.com

Titles:
SWORD

PRESS ASSOCIATION 1649497
Bridgegate, Howden, GOOLE, DN14 7AE
Tel: 020 7963 7417 **Fax:** 020 7963 7419
Email: information@pa.press.net
Web site: http://www.pa-entertainment.co.uk

Titles:
MEDIA LAWYER
THE MORNING BRIEFING
SATELLITE FINANCE

PRESS ASSOCIATION SPORT SERVICES 18850
292 Vauxhall Bridge Road, LONDON, SW1V 1AE
Tel: 020 7963 7888 **Fax:** 020 7963 7894
Web site: http://www.pressassociation.com/sport

Titles:
FOOTBALL INSIDER
FOOTBALL INSIDER
SPORTSMEDIA

PRESSBUS PUBLISHING SERVICES 1739729
PO Box 636, PORTSMOUTH, PO2 9XR **Tel:** 023 9265 5224

Titles:
BUS & COACH PRESERVATION

PRESSDRAM LTD 15093
6 Carlisle Street, LONDON, W1D 3BN **Tel:** 020 7437 4017
Fax: 020 7437 0705
Email: strobes@private-eye.co.uk

Titles:
PRIVATE EYE

PRESSHOLDINGS 15096
22 Old Queen Street, LONDON, SW1H 9HP
Tel: 020 7916 0200

Titles:
APOLLO
THE SPECTATOR
SPECTATOR BUSINESS

PRESTIGE MEDIA LTD 600236
Suite 117, 70 Churchill Square, Kings Hill, WEST MALLING,
ME19 4YU **Tel:** 01732 844017 **Fax:** 01732 523509

Titles:
VANILLAPLUS MAGAZINE

PRG LTD 14078
The Point, College Road, EASTBOURNE, BN21 4JJ
Tel: 01323 646076 **Fax:** 01323 411050
Email: ppl@prgltd.co.uk

Titles:
LP GAS

PRIDE MAGAZINE LTD 16285
Hamilton House, 55 Battersea Bridge Road, LONDON,
SW11 3AX **Tel:** 020 7228 3110 **Fax:** 020 7228 3129

Titles:
PRIDE MAGAZINE

PRIDE PUBLICATIONS LTD 14705
14 Middletons Road, Yaxley, PETERBOROUGH, PE7 3LR
Tel: 01733 242312 **Fax:** 01733 244035
Web site: http://www.pridepublications.co.uk

Titles:
CAMBRIDGESHIRE PRIDE MAGAZINE
EASTERN DIRECTOR
HERTS DIRECTOR
KENT DIRECTOR
SURREY DIRECTOR

PRIMARY TIMES 15141
St. James House, 118 Greys Road, HENLEY-UPON-
THAMES, RG6 1QW **Tel:** 01491 845801
Web site: http://www.primarytimes.net

Titles:
PRIMARY TIMES GLASGOW & WEST OF SCOTLAND
PRIMARY TIMES IN BEDFORDSHIRE & LUTON
PRIMARY TIMES IN BELFAST, COUNTIES ANTRIM,
DOWN & ARMAGH
PRIMARY TIMES IN CAMBRIDGESHIRE
PRIMARY TIMES IN CARDIFF & SOUTH WALES
PRIMARY TIMES IN DUBLIN
PRIMARY TIMES IN EDINBURGH & THE LOTHIANS
PRIMARY TIMES IN ESSEX

PRIMARY TIMES IN FIFE, TAYSIDE & CENTRAL
SCOTLAND
PRIMARY TIMES IN HERTFORDSHIRE
PRIMARY TIMES IN LEICESTERSHIRE & RUTLAND
PRIMARY TIMES IN LEINSTER
PRIMARY TIMES IN NORTH LONDON
PRIMARY TIMES IN OXFORDSHIRE
PRIMARY TIMES IN SOUTH EAST LONDON
PRIMARY TIMES IN SOUTH LONDON
PRIMARY TIMES IN THE TEES VALLEY
PRIMARY TIMES IN WEST YORKSHIRE
PRIMARY TIMES SOUTH

PRIMARY TIMES LIVERPOOL 1734120
Ashill Court, Ashill, CULLOMPTON, EX15 3NQ
Tel: 01884 840994

Titles:
PRIMARY TIMES IN MERSEYSIDE

PRIMARY TIMES NEWPORT & MONMOUTHSHIRE 1650289
38 Pencisely Rise, CARDIFF, CF5 1DY **Tel:** 029 2065 2311
Fax: 029 2065 2311
Web site: http://www.primarytimes.net

Titles:
PRIMARY TIMES IN NEWPORT & MONMOUTHSHIRE

PRIMARY TIMES NORTH YORKSHIRE 1711935
10 Meadow Park, DAWLISH, EX7 9BS **Tel:** 01430 861474

Titles:
PRIMARY TIMES IN NORTH YORKSHIRE

PRIMARY TIMES NOTTINGHAM 1740941
81 Chestnut Crescent, Chudleigh, NEWTON ABBOT, TQ13
0PT **Tel:** 0116 286 6136 **Fax:** 0116 286 9083

Titles:
PRIMARY TIMES IN NOTTINGHAMSHIRE

PRINCIPAL MEDIA LTD 621898
19 Hurst Park, MIDHURST, GU29 0BP **Tel:** 01730 817600
Fax: 01730 817602

Titles:
INSIDE LEARNING TECHNOLOGIES

PRINT WORKSHOP PUBLICATIONS 18140
17 Ashcroft Court, Burnham, SLOUGH, SL1 8JT
Tel: 01628 666176 **Fax:** 01628 666176
Email: innovations@tinyworld.co.uk
Web site: http://www.innovfoodtech.com

Titles:
INNOVATIONS IN FOOD TECHNOLOGY
INNOVATIONS IN PROCESSING AND PACKAGING

PRINTING FOR PLEASURE LTD 16247
Elder House, The Street, Chattisham, IPSWICH, IP8 3QE
Tel: 01473 652789 **Fax:** 01473 652788

Titles:
FUR AND FEATHER INCORPORATING RABBITS

THE PRISON OFFICERS' ASSOCIATION 13854
Cronin House, 245 Church Street, LONDON, N9 9HW
Tel: 020 8803 0255 **Fax:** 020 8803 1761
Email: gatelodge@poauk.org.uk
Web site: http://www.poauk.org.uk

Titles:
GATELODGE

THE PRISON SERVICE 699137
Room 717, Cleland House, Page Street, LONDON, SW1P
4LN **Tel:** 020 7217 2118 **Fax:** 020 7217 2156
Web site: http://www.hmprisonservice.gov.uk

Titles:
PRISON SERVICE NEWS

PRIVACY LAWS AND BUSINESS 18146
2nd Floor, Monument House, 215 Marsh Road, PINNER,
HA5 5NE **Tel:** 020 8868 9200 **Fax:** 020 8868 5215

Titles:
PRIVACY LAWS & BUSINESS

PRIVATE HIRE & TAXI MONTHLY LTD 14789
PHTM House, 501 Oldham Road, Failsworth,
MANCHESTER, M35 9AB **Tel:** 0161 688 7777
Fax: 0161 688 7788

UK Publishers & Their Titles

Email: info@phtm.co.uk
Titles:
PRIVATE HIRE AND TAXI MONTHLY

PRIZE MAGAZINES 15494
PO Box 263, OXFORD, OX1 9GB **Tel:** 01865 760917
Fax: 01865 308490
Email: alastair@prizemags.co.uk
Titles:
COMPETITIONS GALORE
LUCKY BREAK
PRIZE QUEST
PRIZES & PUZZLES SPECIAL
PRIZES GALORE

PRO PUBLICATIONS INTERNATIONAL LTD 18617
1st Floor, Adelphi Court, 1 East Street, EPSOM, KT17 1BB
Tel: 01372 743837 **Fax:** 01372 743838
Web site: http://www.propubs.com
Titles:
GLOBAL CEMENT MAGAZINE
GLOBAL GYPSUM MAGAZINE

PRO PUBLISHING LTD 1735474
The Old School, Colchester Road, Wakes Colne,
COLCHESTER, CO6 2BY **Tel:** 01787 221396
Fax: 01787 221394
Email: info@propub.co.uk
Web site: http://www.propub.co.uk
Titles:
UTOPIA KITCHEN & BATHROOM

PRO-ACTIV PUBLICATIONS LTD 12594
PO Box 332, DARTFORD, DA1 9FF **Tel:** 020 8295 1414
Fax: 020 8295 1401
Email: info@proactivpubs.co.uk
Titles:
BENCHMARK
PSI (PROFESSIONAL SECURITY INSTALLER)
RISK UK

PROBUS TRADING 621908
2 Wychbold Farm Barns, Crown Lane, Wychbold,
DROITWICH, WR9 0BX **Tel:** 01527 861066
Fax: 01527 861066
Titles:
PROBUS MAGAZINE

PROCESS AND CONTROL TODAY LTD 623721
PO Box 223, TUNBRIDGE WELLS, TN2 9HU
Tel: 01892 619616 **Fax:** 01892 619616
Email: info@pandct.com
Web site: http://www.pandct.com
Titles:
FACTORYEQUIPMENT.COM
PROCESS AND CONTROL TODAY

PROFESSIONAL ENGINEERING PUBLISHING LTD 17335
1 Birdcage Walk, LONDON, SW1H 9JJ **Tel:** 020 7973 1299
Fax: 020 7973 0462
Email: pe@pepublishing.com
Web site: http://www.pepublishing.com
Titles:
AUTOMOTIVE ENGINEER
ENVIRONMENTAL ENGINEERING
PROFESSIONAL ENGINEERING

PROFESSIONAL LIGHTING & SOUND ASSOCIATION
  14686
Redoubt House, 1 Edward Road, EASTBOURNE, BN23 8AS
Tel: 01323 524120 **Fax:** 01323 524121
Email: news@plasa.org
Web site: http://www.plasa.org
Titles:
LIGHTING & SOUND INTERNATIONAL

THE PROFESSIONAL SERVICES MARKETING GROUP
  1644496
Phoebe Suite, 5-6 Carlos Place, Mayfair, LONDON, W1K
3AP **Tel:** 020 7907 9990
Email: editor@psmg.co.uk
Web site: http://www.psmg.co.uk
Titles:
PSMG MAGAZINE

PROFILE COMMUNICATION UK LTD 1600649
Blakemere Craft Centre, Unit 21, Chester Road, Sandiway,
NORTHWICH, CW8 2EB **Tel:** 01606 888111
Fax: 01606 882266
Email: info@profilecommunication.com
Web site: http://www.profilecommunication.com
Titles:
BUSINESS UPDATE MAGAZINE

THE PROFILE GROUP (UK) LTD 16947
The Johnson Building, 77 Hatton Garden, LONDON, EC1N
8JS **Tel:** 020 7190 7777 **Fax:** 020 7190 7797
Email: info@profilegroup.co.uk
Web site: http://www.profilegroup.co.uk
Titles:
ENTERTAINMENT NEWS

PROFILE LOCATIONS 1652942
Spray Hill, Hastings Road, Lamberhurst, TUNBRIDGE
WELLS, TN3 8JB **Tel:** 01892 891334 **Fax:** 01892 891336
Email: accounts@profilelocations.co.uk
Web site: http://www.profilelocations.co.uk
Titles:
RE:LOCATE

PROFILE MEDIA LTD 1627106
PO Box 246, REIGATE, RH2 9FL **Tel:** 01737 243433
Fax: 01737 888048
Titles:
MOULD TECHNOLOGY

PROFILE PUBLISHING & DESIGN 15196
101 Thunder Lane, NORWICH, NR7 0JG **Tel:** 01603 433972
Email: profilepublishing@hotmail.co.uk
Titles:
THE BEACON
STOWMARKET COMMUNITY NEWS
WAVENEY PROFILE
WHAT'S ON IN EAST ANGLIA

PROFILE PUBLISHING & DESIGN LTD 1630324
Unit 13 Ormeau Business Park, The Gasworks, Cromac
Avenue, BELFAST, BT6 2JA **Tel:** 028 9043 4112
Fax: 028 9043 4116
Email: info@profilepublishing.com
Titles:
PHARMACY IN FOCUS

PROFINDER MAGAZINES LTD 13710
6 Glencoe Apartment, 15 Harold Road, FRINTON-ON-SEA,
CO13 9BE **Tel:** 01255 673311 **Fax:** 01255 678364
Email: chris.sims@profinder.eu
Web site: http://www.profinder.eu
Titles:
THE FABRICATOR
THE INSTALLER

PROFYLE MAGAZINE LTD 1744423
Tel: 020 7987 9862 **Fax:** 020 7987 9862
Galleon House, Glengarnock Avenue, Tower Hamlets,
LONDON, E14 3DL **Tel:** 020 7987 9862 **Fax:** 020 7987 9862
Titles:
PROFYLE

PROGRAMME MASTER LTD 1724707
Stamford Bridge, Fulham Road, LONDON, SW6 1HS
Tel: 020 7958 2168 **Fax:** 020 7332 2001
Titles:
CHELSEA MAGAZINE

PROGRAMMEMASTER LTD 18905
1st Floor, Mermaid House, 2 Puddle Dock, LONDON, EC4V
3DS **Tel:** 020 7332 2000 **Fax:** 020 7332 2001
Web site: http://www.profile-pursuit.co.uk
Titles:
JUMP
ZEE MAGAZINE

PROGRESSIO 17194
Unit 3, Canonbury Yard, 190A New North Road, LONDON,
N1 7BJ **Tel:** 020 7288 8600 **Fax:** 020 7359 0017
Email: enquiries@progressio.org.uk
Web site: http://www.progressio.org.uk
Titles:
INTERACT

PROGRESSIVE MEDIA 13962
33-35 Cantelupe Road, EAST GRINSTEAD, RH19 3BE
Tel: 01342 316390 **Fax:** 01342 333701
Email: sales@progressive-media.co.uk
Titles:
CLEANING MATTERS
FMX
WATER, ENERGY & ENVIRONMENT JOURNAL

PROGRESSIVE MEDIA GROUP 1761424
7 Carmelite Street, LONDON, EC4Y 0DR **Tel:** 020 7915 9931
Titles:
ENERGY BUSINESS REVIEW
PRESS GAZETTE

PROGRESSIVE MEDIA PUBLICATIONS 1603082
Progressive House, 2 Maidstone Road, Foots Cray, SIDCUP,
DA14 5HZ **Tel:** 020 8269 7864
Titles:
BLUEPRINT
BUSINESSCAR
COMPUTER BUSINESS REVIEW
CONVERTING TODAY
CRANES TODAY
CRANES TODAY BUYERS GUIDE
EUROPEAN COSMETIC MARKETS
FX
HOIST
IDFX
INTERNATIONAL WATER POWER & DAM
   CONSTRUCTION
LAUNDRY & CLEANING NEWS
LEATHER INTERNATIONAL
MODERN POWER SYSTEMS
NUCLEAR ENGINEERING INTERNATIONAL
PACKAGING TODAY
RED
TIMBER BUILDING
TTJ
TTJ ADDRESS BOOK & BUYERS GUIDE
TUNNELS & TUNNELLING INTERNATIONAL
WHAT VAN?
WOOD BASED PANELS INTERNATIONAL
X2

PROJECT MANAGER TODAY PUBLICATIONS 674578
Unit 12, Moor Place Farm, Plough Lane, Bramshill, HOOK,
RG27 0RF **Tel:** 0118 932 6665 **Fax:** 0118 932 6663
Web site: http://www.pmtoday.co.uk
Titles:
PROJECT CONTROL PROFESSIONAL

PROLIFIC PUBLICATIONS LTD 600812
The Old Courthouse, New Road Avenue, CHATHAM, ME4
6BE **Tel:** 01444 831512 **Fax:** 01444 831512
Email: sunnycroftclose@btinternet.com
Web site: http://www.kentprofile.com
Titles:
KENT PROFILE

PROMOTE ENVIRONMENTAL COMMUNICATION
  1724759
Barbour Square, High Street, Tattenhall, CHESTER, CH3
9RF **Tel:** 01244 401811 **Fax:** 01244 401787
Web site: http://www.promotedesign.com
Titles:
GREEN-CAR-GUIDE.COM

PROPERTY PAPERS LTD 18907
Albion House, Broad Street, BRISTOL, BS1 2HL
Tel: 0117 929 2990 **Fax:** 0117 929 2655
Titles:
NEW HOMES

PROPHETIC WITNESS MOVEMENT INTERNATIONAL
  15913
PO Box 109, LEYLAND, PR25 1WB **Tel:** 01772 452846
Fax: 01772 452846
Titles:
PROPHETIC WITNESS

PROSPECT 69416
New Prospect House, 8 Leake Street, LONDON, SE1 7NN
Tel: 020 7902 6654 **Fax:** 020 7902 6665
Email: profile@prospect.org.uk
Web site: http://www.prospect.org.uk
Titles:
PROFILE

PROSPECT PUBLISHING LTD   15094
2 Bloomsbury Place, LONDON, WC1A 2QA
Tel: 020 7255 1281 **Fax:** 020 7255 1279
Email: publishing@prospect-magazine.co.uk
Web site: http://www.prospect-magazine.co.uk
Titles:
  PROSPECT

PROSPORT MEDIA LTD   15237
45 Woodside Gardens, SITTINGBOURNE, ME10 1SG
Tel: 01795 424631 **Fax:** 01795 424631
Titles:
  THE PGA PROFESSIONAL

PROSTATE RESEARCH CAMPAIGN UK   18772
10 Northfields Prospect, Putney Bridge Road, LONDON,
SW18 1PE **Tel:** 020 8877 5840 **Fax:** 020 8877 2609
Email: info@prostate-research.org.uk
Web site: http://www.prostate-research.org.uk/
Titles:
  UPDATE

PRO-TALK LTD   622874
St. Giles House, 50 Poland Street, LONDON, W1F 7AX
Tel: 020 7970 4941 **Fax:** 020 7970 4599
Email: admin@pro-talk.com
Web site: http://www.pro-talk.com
Titles:
  BUILDINGTALK
  ELECTRONICSTALK
  ENGINEERINGTALK
  LABORATORYTALK
  MANUFACTURINGTALK
  MARKETINGSERVICESTALK
  PRINTINGTALK
  PROCESSINGTALK

PROTESTANT TRUTH SOCIETY (INC.)   13132
184 Fleet Street, LONDON, EC4A 2HG **Tel:** 020 7405 4960
Fax: 020 7405 4960
Titles:
  PROTESTANT TRUTH

PROTEUS MEDIA   1724157
123 Sutherland Street, COVENTRY, CV5 7NH
Tel: 0560 132 6260 **Fax:** 0871 733 5046
Email: info@proteus-media.co.uk
Web site: http://www.proteus-media.co.uk
Titles:
  BUSINESS FOCUS
  BUSINESS-FOCUS.NET

PSA PEUGEOT CITROEN DRRH/DRHI   18116
Pinley House, 2 Sunbeam Way, COVENTRY, CV3 1ND
Tel: 024 7688 4000 **Fax:** 024 7688 4001
Titles:
  PSA PEUGEOT CITROEN TIMES

PSB DESIGN & PRINT CONSULTANTS LTD   16341
PO Box 5, DRIFFIELD, YO25 8JD **Tel:** 01377 255213
Email: info@craftanddesign.net
Web site: http://www.craftanddesign.net
Titles:
  CRAFTSMAN CRAFT&DESIGN MAGAZINE

PSCA INTERNATIONAL LTD   700111
Ebenezer House, Ryecroft, NEWCASTLE-UNDER-LYME,
ST5 2UB **Tel:** 01782 620088
Email: editorial@publicservice.co.uk
Web site: http://www.publicservice.co.uk
Titles:
  CENTRAL GOVERNMENT
  DEFENCE MANAGEMENT JOURNAL
  THE PPP JOURNAL
  PUBLIC SERVANT
  PUBLIC SERVICE REVIEW AND TRANSPORT

PSP PUBLISHING LTD   600672
50 High Craighall Road, GLASGOW, G4 9UD
Tel: 0141 353 2222 **Fax:** 0141 332 3811
Email: sales@psp.uk.net
Web site: http://www.prosportsltd.co.uk
Titles:
  BUNKERED
  ENGLISH CLUB GOLFER
  NATIONWIDE BOWLER
  NO.1

SCOTTISH CLUB GOLFER
WELSH CLUB GOLFER

PSP RARE PUBLISHING   15111
3rd Floor, 21 Great Sutton Street, LONDON, EC1V 0DY
Tel: 020 7099 2933 **Fax:** 020 7490 1723
Web site: http://www.psprarepublishing.co.uk
Titles:
  CONNECT
  THE SOMERFIELD MAGAZINE

PSPRARE PUBLISHING   1605992
3rd Floor, 21-22 Great Sutton Street, Farringdon Barbican,
LONDON, EC1V 0DY **Tel:** 020 7566 9910
Web site: http://www.psprarepublishing.com
Titles:
  EUREKA
  HEART HEALTH

PSYCHIATRIC REHABILITATION ASSOCIATION 18107
Bayford Mews, Bayford Street, LONDON, E8 3SF
Tel: 020 8985 3570 **Fax:** 020 8986 1334
Titles:
  THE PRA NEWSLETTER

PSYCHIC PRESS (1995) LTD   16125
The Coach House, Stansted Hall, Burton End, STANSTED,
CM24 8UD **Tel:** 01279 817050 **Fax:** 01279 817051
Email: pnadverts@btconnect.com
Web site: http://www.psychicnewsbookshop.org.uk
Titles:
  PSYCHIC NEWS

PTI DERBY LTD   674610
21 Cotton Brook Road, Sir Francis Ley Industrial Park,
DERBY, DE23 8YJ **Tel:** 01332 372851
Titles:
  PANJAB TIMES INTERNATIONAL
  PERDESAN MONTHLY

PTM PUBLISHERS LTD   14527
Westmead House, 123 Westmead Road, SUTTON, SM1 4JH
Tel: 020 8642 0162 **Fax:** 020 8661 5879
Titles:
  JOURNAL OF COMMUNITY NURSING

PUBLIC AND COMMERCIAL SERVICES UNION   13847
160 Falcon Road, LONDON, SW11 2LN **Tel:** 020 7801 2884
Fax: 020 7801 2888
Web site: http://www.pcs.org.uk
Titles:
  ORACLE

PUBLIC LIBRARIES GROUP OF CILIP   14674
Public Libraries Group of Cilip, 7 Ridgmount Street,
LONDON, WC1E 7AE
Web site: http://www.cilip.org.uk/plg
Titles:
  PUBLIC LIBRARY JOURNAL

PUBLIC SECTOR PUBLISHING LTD   17316
226 High Road, LOUGHTON, IG10 1ET **Tel:** 020 8532 0055
Fax: 020 8532 0066
Email: info@publicsectorpublishing.co.uk
Web site: http://www.publicsectorpublishing.co.uk
Titles:
  EDUCATION BUSINESS
  GOVERNMENT BUSINESS
  GOVERNMENT TECHNOLOGY
  GREENFLEET
  HB HEALTH BUSINESS
  TRANSPORT BUSINESS INTERNATIONAL

PUBLICATION 1969 LTD   16044
Unit 2, 20B Spelman Street, LONDON, E1 5LQ
Tel: 020 7377 6032 **Fax:** 020 7247 0141
Titles:
  JANOMOT BENGALI NEWSWEEKLY

PUBLICATIONS INTERNATIONAL LTD   1684984
PO Box 10, UPMINSTER, RM14 1LQ **Tel:** 01708 229354
Fax: 01708 220017
Email: barry@pubint.co.uk

Titles:
  SECURITY MIDDLE EAST

PUBLICIS BLUEPRINT LTD   18974
12 Dorset Street, LONDON, W1U 6QS **Tel:** 020 7462 7777
Fax: 020 7462 7467
Web site: http://www.publicis-blueprint.co.uk
Titles:
  VIA INMARSAT

PUBLISHING BUSINESS   15534
Blandel Bridge House, 56 Sloane Square, LONDON, SW1W
8AX **Tel:** 020 7259 1050 **Fax:** 020 7901 9042
Web site: http://www.pubbiz.com
Titles:
  BELGRAVIA
  MAYFAIR TIMES
  THE PORTMAN
  SLOANE SQUARE

THE PUBLISHING GROUP LTD   1748469
Davina House, 137-149 Goswell Road, LONDON, EC1V 7ET
Tel: 020 7490 0588 **Fax:** 020 7490 7069
Email: info@thepublishinggroup.co.uk
Web site: http://www.thepublishinggroup.co.uk
Titles:
  MORTGAGE INTRODUCER

THE PUBLISHING PARTNERSHIP   14741
16 York Road, NORTHAMPTON, NN1 5QG
Tel: 01604 259900 **Fax:** 01604 259901
Titles:
  BUSINESS TIMES

PUNTERS PUBLISHING LTD   14117
PO Box 6118, OAKHAM, LE15 6BR **Tel:** 01753 646591
Fax: 01753 643555
Email: subs@motester.co.uk
Web site: http://www.motester.co.uk
Titles:
  MOT TESTING

PURPLE MEDIA   1739020
Seton Business Centre, Scorrier, REDRUTH, TR16 5AW
Tel: 01209 315646
Titles:
  CORNISH BRIDES

PURPLE MEDIA SOLUTIONS LTD   1732087
2nd Floor, 207-215 High Street, ORPINGTON, BR6 0PF
Tel: 01689 899170 **Fax:** 01689 899171
Web site: http://www.purplems.com
Titles:
  ELECTRICAL TIMES
  HOTEL SPEC
  THE PROBE
  SHOP SPEC
  SMILE
  WHAT TO BUY FOR BUSINESS

PUSH HOCKEY LTD   1710691
17A South Street, LANCING, BN15 8AE **Tel:** 0870 803 4891
Email: info@pushhockey.co.uk
Titles:
  HKY WORLD
  HOCKEY SCOTLAND
  PUSH

PUTNAM NEWSPAPERS LTD   14913
Tindle Suite, Webbs House, The Parade, LISKEARD, PL14
6AH **Tel:** 01529 342174 **Fax:** 01529 341851
Titles:
  CORNISH TIMES & GAZETTE SERIES
  FOOD & CATERING SOUTH WEST

PUZZLER MEDIA LTD   15492
Stonecroft, 69 Station Road, REDHILL, RH1 1EY
Tel: 01737 378700 **Fax:** 01737 781800
Email: enquiries@puzzlermedia.com
Web site: http://www.puzzlermedia.com
Titles:
  100 CROSSWORDS
  FUNDOKU
  JUNIOR PUZZLES
  KRISS KROSS
  LOGIC PROBLEMS

UK Publishers & Their Titles

POCKET WORDSEARCH
PUZZLE COMPENDIUM
PUZZLE CORNER SPECIAL
QUIZKIDS
SUDOKU
WORD SEARCH

PV PUBLICATIONS   1650915
Suite L, 17 Park Place, STEVENAGE, SG1 1DU
Tel: 01438 352617 **Fax:** 01438 351989
Titles:
GIS PROFESSIONAL

PV PUBLICATIONS LTD.   13504
Suite L, 17 Park Place, STEVENAGE, SG1 1DU
Tel: 01438 352617 **Fax:** 01438 351989
Email: editor@pvpubs.demon.co.uk
Web site: http://www.pvpubs.com
Titles:
ENGINEERING SURVEYING SHOWCASE
GEOMATICS WORLD

PW MEDIA & PUBLISHING LTD   1603015
Richardson House, 21-24 New Street, WORCESTER, WR1
2DP **Tel:** 01905 723011 **Fax:** 01905 612039
Email: dawn@pw-media.co.uk
Titles:
AUTOMOTIVE INSIGHT
BIRMINGHAM LAW SOCIETY BULLETIN
EMBODY
PRIMARY TIMES IN SURREY

PW PUBLISHING LTD   15486
Arrowsmith Court, Station Approach, BROADSTONE, BH18
8PW **Tel:** 0845 803 1979 **Fax:** 01202 659950
Web site: http://www.pwpublishing.ltd.uk
Titles:
THE FALCONERS & RAPTOR CONSERVATION
   MAGAZINE
PRACTICAL WIRELESS
RADIO USER

PYBUS EVENTS AND PUBLICATIONS LIMITED   1645337
Suite 1, Bexley House, 77 Bexley High Street, BEXLEY, DA5
1JX **Tel:** 01322 526089 **Fax:** 01322 528172
Email: pybuspromotions@btconnect.com
Web site: http://www.cateringpromotions.co.uk
Titles:
FRY MONTHLY
FRY ONLINE
OOH (OUT OF,HOME) MAGAZINE

PYSCHIC WORLD PUBLISHING   18172
PO Box 14, GREENFORD, UB6 0UF **Tel:** 020 8903 1993
Fax: 020 8903 1987
Titles:
PSYCHIC WORLD

PZ PUBLISHING   699439
22 Station Road, Dunton Green, SEVENOAKS, TN13 2XA
Tel: 01732 462796 **Fax:** 01732 462820
Titles:
THE LINK

Q COMMUNICATIONS LTD   12700
The Old Horse Yard, Toft, CAMBRIDGE, CB23 2RY
Tel: 01223 264864 **Fax:** 01223 264665
Email: contact@businessweekly.co.uk
Web site: http://www.businessweekly.co.uk
Titles:
BUSINESS WEEKLY

QMJ PUBLISHING LTD   16280
7 Regent Street, NOTTINGHAM, NG1 5BS
Tel: 0115 941 1315 **Fax:** 0115 948 4035
Email: mail@qmj.co.uk
Web site: http://www.qmj.co.uk
Titles:
MQR (MINERALS, QUARRYING & RECYCLING)
NATURAL STONE SPECIALIST
QUARRY MANAGEMENT

QMSU   15745
Queen Mary College Students Union, 432 Bancroft Road,
LONDON, E1 4DH **Tel:** 020 7882 0841 **Fax:** 020 8981 0802

Titles:
CUB

QS QUACQUARELLI SYMONDS LTD   624283
1 Tranley Mews, Fleet Road, LONDON, NW3 2DG
Tel: 020 7284 7200 **Fax:** 020 7284 7201
Web site: http://www.qsnetwork.com
Titles:
TOP GRADUATE
TOP GRADUATE: QS BUSINESS & TECHNOLOGY
TOPMBA CAREER GUIDE

QUARTO MAGAZINES LTD   15170
226 City Road, LONDON, EC1V 2TT **Tel:** 020 7700 6700'
Fax: 020 7253 4370
Web site: http://www.quartomagazines.com
Titles:
THE WORLD OF FINE WINE

QUARTZ PUBLISHING   1653282
Armstrong House, 38 Market Square, UXBRIDGE, UB8 1LH
Tel: 01895 454600 **Fax:** 01895 454643
Email: robfisher@quartzltd.com
Web site: http://www.quartzltd.com
Titles:
CLEANING & MAINTENANCE
SOLIDS AND BULK HANDLING
STORAGE HANDLING DISTRIBUTION

QUE PASA COMMUNICATIONS LTD   1649331
Exmouth House, 3 Pine Street, LONDON, EC1R 0JH
Tel: 020 7278 9584 **Fax:** 020 7278 9659
Web site: http://www.quepasacomms.co.uk
Titles:
VIRGIN MOBILE BITES

**QUEEN ELIZABETH'S FOUNDATION FOR DISABLED
PEOPLE**   17636
Leatherhead Court, LEATHERHEAD, KT22 0BN
Tel: 01372 841100 **Fax:** 01372 844657
Web site: http://www.qef.org.uk
Titles:
HAPPENINGS

QUEST MEDIA LTD   17128
7th Floor, Ludgate House, 245 Blackfriars Road, LONDON,
SE1 9UY **Tel:** 020 7378 1188 **Fax:** 020 7378 1199
Web site: http://www.quest-media.com
Titles:
CUSTOMER STRATEGY

QUOIN PUBLISHING   1649426
17 North Street, MIDDLESBROUGH, TS2 1JP
Tel: 01642 252023
Titles:
NOW & THEN

QUORN HOUSE PUBLISHING LTD   15167
Quorn House, Meeting Street, Quorn, LOUGHBOROUGH,
LE12 8EX **Tel:** 01509 620444 **Fax:** 01509 620555
Email: qhp@freenetname.co.uk
Titles:
ROSEMARY CONLEY DIET & FITNESS MAGAZINE

R3 GROUP LTD   18778
Globe House, 24 Turret Lane, IPSWICH, IP4 1DL
Tel: 01473 384036 **Fax:** 01473 230561
Email: enquiries@r3group.com
Web site: http://www.r3group.com
Titles:
PROFESSIONAL FITNESS MAGAZINE

RA PUBLICATIONS   15824
Royal Academy of Arts, Burlington House, Piccadilly,
LONDON, W1J 0BD **Tel:** 020 7300 5820 **Fax:** 020 7300 5881
Titles:
RA MAGAZINE

RABBIT WELFARE ASSOCIATION   674218
PO Box 603, HORSHAM, RH13 5WL **Tel:** 0870 046 5249
Web site: http://www.rabbitwelfare.co.uk
Titles:
RABBITING ON

RACECAR GRAPHIC LTD   15442
841 High Road, Finchley, LONDON, N12 8PT
Tel: 020 8446 2100 **Fax:** 020 8446 2191
Email: info@racetechmag.com
Web site: http://www.racetechmag.com
Titles:
BERNOULLI
MOTO TECH
RACE TECH

RACEFORM LTD   15261
Raceform House, High Street, Compton, NEWBURY, RG20
6NL **Tel:** 01635 578080 **Fax:** 01635 578101
Titles:
RACEFORM UPDATE
RACING & FOOTBALL OUTLOOK

RACING AHEAD LTD   1742381
Office 113, Imperial Court, Exchange Street East,
LIVERPOOL, L3 2AB **Tel:** 0845 638 0704
Titles:
RACING AHEAD MAGAZINE

RACING AHEAD WEEKEND LTD   1742382
The Old Brewery, Priory Lane, BURFORD, OX18 4SG
Tel: 01993 822811
Titles:
RACING AHEAD WEEKEND

RADCLIFFE PUBLISHING LTD.   14602
18 Marcham Road, ABINGDON, OX14 1AA
Tel: 01235 528820 **Fax:** 01235 528830
Email: contactus@radcliffemed.com
Web site: http://www.radcliffe-oxford.com
Titles:
EDUCATION FOR PRIMARY CARE
THE INTERNATIONAL JOURNAL OF CLINICAL
   LEADERSHIP
QUALITY IN PRIMARY CARE

RADGE MEDIA LIMITED   1762319
The Drill Hall, 30-38 Dalmeny Street, EDINBURGH, EH6 8RG
Tel: 0131 467 4630
Titles:
THE SKINNY
THE SKINNY

RAE-LIN COMMUNICATIONS   627409
PO Box 6, HADDINGTON, EH41 3NQ **Tel:** 01620 822578
Fax: 01620 822578
Titles:
BUILDING POWER SCOTLAND
BUSINESS POWER SCOTLAND
LOTHIAN LEADER
OIL CITY NEWS
OIL NEWS AND GAS INTERNATIONAL

RAF   14265
Royal Air Force Headquarters, Strike Command, Naphill,
HIGH WYCOMBE, HP14 4UE **Tel:** 01494 495566
Fax: 01494 495569
Titles:
RAF NEWS

RAFATRAD LTD   14255
117 ½ Loughborough Road, LEICESTER, LE4 5ND
Tel: 0116 266 5224
Web site: http://www.rafatrad.co.uk
Titles:
AIR MAIL

RAIL MEDIA GROUP   1683819
Ashby House, Bath Street, ASHBY-DE-LA-ZOUCH, LE65
2FH **Tel:** 01530 560021 **Fax:** 01530 412166
Titles:
THE RAIL ENGINEER
RAILSTAFF

RAIL PROFESSIONAL LTD   1752505
275 Newmarket Road, CAMBRIDGE, CB5 8JE
Tel: 01223 477411 **Fax:** 01223 327356
Web site: http://www.railpro.co.uk
Titles:
RAIL PROFESSIONAL

RAILFUTURE 16433
12 Home Close, Bracebridge Heath, LINCOLN, LN4 2LP
Web site: http://www.railfuture.org.uk
Titles:
RAILWATCH

RAILNEWS LTD 16528
King's Cross Business Centre, Room 007, 180-186 King's
Cross Road, LONDON, WC1X 9DE **Tel:** 020 7278 6100
Fax: 020 7278 6145
Titles:
RAILNEWS

RAILWAY HERALD LTD 1760816
PO Box 252, SCUNTHORPE, DN17 2WY **Tel:** 01904 500175
Titles:
RAILWAY HERALD

RAILWAY PHILATELIC GROUP 18201
5 Garth Lane, Widdrington, MORPETH, NE61 5EN
Tel: 01670 760252
Titles:
RAILWAY PHILATELY

RAINBOW MEDIA 697049
Sybrig House, Ridge Way, Donibristle Industrial Park,
Hillend, DUNFERMLINE, KY11 9JN **Tel:** 0870 443 0270
Fax: 0870 443 0271
Titles:
COURIER DIRECT

THE RAMBLERS' ASSOCIATION 15295
2nd Floor, Camelford House, 87-90 Albert Embankment,
LONDON, SE1 7TW **Tel:** 020 7339 8500 **Fax:** 020 7339 8501
Email: ramblers@ramblers.org.uk
Web site: http://www.ramblers.org.uk
Titles:
THE RAMBLERS' ASSOCIATION
WALK

RAPID NEWS PUBLICATIONS 1640247
Unit 2, Chowley Court, Chowley Oak Lane, Tattenhall,
CHESTER, CH3 9GA **Tel:** 01829 770037 **Fax:** 01829 770047
Titles:
MICRO MANUFACTURING MAGAZINE
TCT MAGAZINE

RAPPORT LEARNING LTD 671880
Unit 1, Crumplin's Business Court, Odiham, HAMPSHIRE,
RG29 1DU **Tel:** 01256 704288 **Fax:** 01256 703447
Email: info@rapportlearning.com
Web site: http://www.rapportgroup.com
Titles:
HEADTEACHER UPDATE
SCHOOL VISITS

RAPRA TECHNOLOGY LTD 17508
Shawbury, SHREWSBURY, SY4 4NR **Tel:** 01939 250383
Fax: 01939 251118
Email: info@rapra.net
Web site: http://www.rapra.net
Titles:
INTERNATIONAL POLYMER SCIENCES & TECHNOLOGY
POLYMERS & POLYMER COMPOSITES
PROGRESS IN RUBBER, PLASTICS & RECYCLING
TECHNOLOGY

RAS PUBLISHING LTD 14369
The Old Town Hall, Lewisham Road, Slaithwaite,
HUDDERSFIELD, HD7 5AL **Tel:** 01484 846069
Fax: 01484 846232
Web site: http://www.ras-publishing.com
Titles:
CWB CHILDRENSWEAR BUYER
FE FOOTWEAR AND FASHION EXTRAS
MWB MENSWEAR BUYER
WWB WOMENSWEAR BUYER

RATING PUBLISHERS LIMITED 14144
80 Fleet Street, LONDON, EC4A 2HG **Tel:** 01483 233571
Fax: 01483 234804
Titles:
RATING & VALUATION REPORTER

RATIONALIST ASSOCIATION 15709
1 Gower Street, LONDON, WC1E 6HD **Tel:** 020 7436 1171
Fax: 020 7079 3588
Titles:
NEW HUMANIST

RAVENSWORLD LTD 15645
Rose Cottage, Hughley, SHREWSBURY, SY5 6NX
Tel: 01746 785637
Email: linda.sagar@yahoo.co.uk
Titles:
HOUNDS

RAW VISION LTD 16692
1 Watford Road, RADLETT, WD7 8LA **Tel:** 01923 856644
Fax: 01923 859897
Titles:
RAW VISION

RAZZ UK LTD 1738551
The Forge, Fore Street, Kenton, EXETER, EX6 8LF
Tel: 01626 891944 **Fax:** 01626 891936
Titles:
PRIMARY TIMES IN DEVON

RBC PUBLISHING LIMITED 625134
Suite 4, Roddis House, Old Christchurch Road,
BOURNEMOUTH, BH1 1LG **Tel:** 01202 552333
Fax: 01202 552666
Titles:
THE CARER
THE CATERER, LICENSEE & HOTELIER NEWS GROUP

RBP LTD 1640969
Schipol Way, Humberside International Airport, Kirmington,
ULCEBY, DN39 6GB **Tel:** 01652 680060 **Fax:** 01652 680070
Email: rbp@rbplimited.co.uk
Web site: http://www.rbp-ltd.co.uk
Titles:
GREENEYE
MOTORCYCLE RIDER

RCI EUROPE 600806
Kettering Parkway, KETTERING, NN15 6EY
Tel: 01536 310101 **Fax:** 01536 374682
Email: helen.foster@rci.com
Titles:
RCI VENTURES

RCN PUBLISHING CO LTD 14177
The Heights, 59-65 Lowlands Road, HARROW, HA1 3AW
Tel: 020 8423 1066 **Fax:** 020 8872 3193
Titles:
EMERGENCY NURSE
LEARNING DISABILITY PRACTICE
MENTAL HEALTH PRACTICE
NURSING MANAGEMENT
NURSING OLDER PEOPLE
NURSING STANDARD
PAEDIATRIC NURSING
PRIMARY HEALTH CARE

RCOG PRESS 1600339
Publications Department RCOG, 27 Sussex Place, Regents
Park, LONDON, NW1 4RG **Tel:** 020 7772 6200
Fax: 020 7772 6273
Web site: http://www.rcog.org.uk
Titles:
THE OBSTETRICIAN & GYNAECOLOGIST

RCSLT 14572
2 White Hart Yard, LONDON, SE1 1NX **Tel:** 020 7378 3012
Fax: 020 7613 3854
Email: postmaster@rcslt.org
Web site: http://www.rcslt.org
Titles:
BULLETIN OF THE ROYAL COLLEGE OF SPEECH AND
LANGUAGE THERAPISTS

RDB MEDIA 1650099
Unit 4, 4 Stanhope Road, LONDON, N6 5LR
Tel: 020 8341 0037
Titles:
GARDEN CENTRE MONTHLY

READER'S DIGEST ASSOCIATION LTD 14879
11 Westferry Circus, Canary Wharf, LONDON, E14 4HE
Tel: 020 7715 8000 **Fax:** 020 7715 8716
Web site: http://www.readersdigest.co.uk
Titles:
READER'S DIGEST

READYMADE MAGAZINE 1742549
Studio 4, 94 Dalston Lane, LONDON, E8 1NG
Titles:
MAURICE MAGAZINE

REAL WORLD PUBLISHING LTD 18333
108 Wick Street, LITTLEHAMPTON, BN17 7JS
Tel: 0845 450 6605 **Fax:** 0845 450 6606
Email: studio@realworldpublishing.com
Titles:
WHAT'S ON & WHERE IN KENT
WHAT'S ON & WHERE IN SUSSEX

REBELLION 691128
Riverside House, Osney Mead, OXFORD, OX2 0ES
Tel: 01865 792201 **Fax:** 01865 792254
Titles:
2000 AD
THE JUDGE DREDD MEGAZINE

RECONNAISSANCE INTERNATIONAL LTD 1712075
2A High Street, SHEPPERTON, TW17 9AW
Tel: 01932 269917 **Fax:** 01932 269918
Email: info@reconnaissance-intl.com
Web site: http://www.reconnaissance-intl.com
Titles:
AUTHENTICATION NEWS
HOLOGRAPHY NEWS

RECORDER NEWSPAPERS 12793
Prospect House, Rouen Road, NORWICH, NR1 1RE
Tel: 01603 628311 **Fax:** 01603 612930
Titles:
B & G (BRIDES & GROOMS)

RECOVERY OPERATOR LTD. 1622277
1 Bath Street, RUGBY, CV21 3JF **Tel:** 01788 572850
Fax: 01788 572850
Web site: http://www.avrouk.com
Titles:
RECOVERY OPERATOR

RECRUITMENT PUBLICATIONS LTD. 13818
2nd Floor, Lynton House, Station Approach, WOKING, GU22
7PT **Tel:** 01483 740874
Titles:
RECRUITMENT INTERNATIONAL

THE RECYCLER LTD 675648
12 Spinners Court, West End, WITNEY, OX28 1NH
Tel: 01993 899800 **Fax:** 01993 899801
Web site: http://www.therecycler.com
Titles:
RECYCLER TRADE MAGAZINE

RED BARN PUBLICATIONS LTD 1728643
18 Princess Street, SHREWSBURY, SY1 1LP
Tel: 01743 232181
Email: mail@redbarnpublications.com
Titles:
TASTE SHROPSHIRE & THE MARCHES

RED BULLETIN 1761230
14 Soho Square, LONDON, W1D 3QG **Tel:** 020 7434 8600
Titles:
THE RED BULLETIN

RED DOT PUBLICATIONS 1684909
T9 Dungannon Business Park, Coalisland Road,
DUNGANNON, BT71 6JT **Tel:** 028 8772 2788
Fax: 028 8772 2288
Titles:
GETTING MARRIED IN NORTHERN IRELAND

UK Publishers & Their Titles

RED LEAF MEDIA LTD 1713760
Flockton House, Audby Lane, WETHERBY, LS22 7FD
Tel: 01937 581400 **Fax:** 01937 581444
Email: news@excellemagazine.co.uk
Web site: http://www.excellemagazine.co.uk
Titles:
EXCELLE MAGAZINE

REDACTIVE MEDIA GROUP 13816
17 Britton Street, LONDON, EC1M 5TP **Tel:** 020 7880 6200
Fax: 020 7880 7553
Web site: http://www.redactive.co.uk
Titles:
CONNECTIONS
CPO AGENDA
FM WORLD
LEGION
THE MARKETER
MIDWIVES
PEOPLE MANAGEMENT
PEOPLE MANAGEMENT
PUBLIC FINANCE
RECRUITMENT MATTERS
SUPPLY MANAGEMENT

REDAN PUBLISHING 17226
Suite 2, Prospect House, Belle Vue Road, SHREWSBURY,
SY3 7NR **Tel:** 01743 364433 **Fax:** 01743 271528
Web site: http://www.redan.co.uk
Titles:
BAG-O-FUN
FUN TO LEARN PEPPA PIG
REDAN FUN TO LEARN BARNEY MAGAZINE
REDAN FUN TO LEARN DISCOVERY
REDAN FUN TO LEARN FAVOURITES
SPARKLE WORLD

REDGAUNTLET PUBLICATIONS LTD 15500
PO Box 2471, BOURNEMOUTH, BH7 7WF
Tel: 01202 752601 **Fax:** 01202 752601
Titles:
STEAM DAYS

REDPIN PUBLISHING LTD 1687272
Unit 2, Devizes Trade Centre, Hopton Park, DEVIZES, SN10
2EH **Tel:** 0845 644 2236 **Fax:** 0845 430 8678
Web site: http://www.redpin.co.uk
Titles:
ALL HORSE
EQUESTRIAN PLUS
RIDGEWAY RIDER
WELSH RIDER

REDWOOD 12343
7 St. Martin's Place, LONDON, WC2N 4HA
Tel: 020 7747 0700 **Fax:** 020 7747 0701
Web site: http://www.redwoodgroup.net
Titles:
BOOTS HEALTH & BEAUTY
ELECTRIC!
ENGAGE
HOMEBASE GARDEN LIVING
LAND ROVER ONELIFE
LIV
MAZDA MAGAZINE
UPLOAD
YOUR FAMILY
YOUR M&S MAGAZINE

REED BUSINESS INFORMATION 16494
Quadrant House, The Quadrant, SUTTON, SM2 5AS
Tel: 020 8652 3500 **Fax:** 020 8652 4005
Web site: http://www.reedbusiness.com
Titles:
AIR TRANSPORT INTELLIGENCE
AIRLINE BUSINESS
CATERER AND HOTELKEEPER
CATERER AND HOTELKEEPER DIRECTORY
CATERERSEARCH.COM
CHINA CHEMICALS
CLI CLINICAL LABORATORY INTERNATIONAL
COMMERCIAL MOTOR
COMMUNITY CARE
COMPUTER WEEKLY
COMPUTERWEEKLY.COM
CONTRACT JOURNAL
CROPS
EDN EUROPE
EGI
EGTV
ELECTRONICS WEEKLY
ELECTRONICSWEEKLY.COM

EMPLOYERS LAW
EMPLOYMENT LAW BULLETIN
ESTATES GAZETTE
EUROPROPERTY
EUROPROPERTY (ONLINE)
FARMERS WEEKLY
THE FARMERS WEEKLY AGRICULTURAL REGISTER
FARMERS WEEKLY INTERACTIVE
FARMLAND MARKET
FLIGHT INTERNATIONAL
HAIRDRESSERS JOURNAL INTERNATIONAL
HEALTH & BEAUTY SALON
ICIS CHEMICAL BUSINESS
ICIS NEWS
INSIGHT
IRS EMPLOYMENT REVIEW
IRS PAY INTELLIGENCE
MICROSCOPE
MOTOR TRANSPORT
NEW SCIENTIST
NEWSCIENTIST.COM
OCCUPATIONAL HEALTH JOURNAL
OPTICIAN
PAY AND BENEFITS BULLETIN
PERSONNEL TODAY
PMJ - PLANT MANAGERS JOURNAL
POULTRY WORLD
RECRUITMENT & RETENTION
ROADTRANSPORT.COM
TRAINING & COACHING TODAY
TRAVEL WEEKLY
TRAVEL WEEKLY ONLINE
TRAVOLUTION
TRUCK AND DRIVER
UTILITY WEEK
VARIETY

REED ELECTRONICS RESEARCH 628613
Harvard House, Grove Technology Park, WANTAGE, OX12
9FF **Tel:** 01235 227310 **Fax:** 01235 227322
Web site: http://www.rer.co.uk
Titles:
EUROPEAN ELECTRONICS MARKETS FORECAST

REFERENCE TECHNOLOGY 623864
1-3 The Pavilions, Amber Close, TAMWORTH, B77 4RP
Tel: 01827 61666 **Fax:** 01827 61661
Web site: http://www.reftech.co.uk
Titles:
MEETINGS INDUSTRY NEWS

REFLECTIONS OF A BYGONE AGE 15511
15 Debdale Lane, Keyworth, NOTTINGHAM, NG12 5HT
Tel: 0115 937 4079 **Fax:** 0115 937 6197
Titles:
PICTURE POSTCARD MONTHLY

THE REGATTA MAGAZINE LTD 1738655
56 Brook Street, WATLINGTON, OX49 5EH
Tel: 01491 614040
Titles:
BLADES

REGIONAL GOLF LTD 17215
The Old Chapel, The Mead, Farmborough, BATH, BA2 0AF
Tel: 01761 472468 **Fax:** 01761 472851
Email: info@regionalgolf.co.uk
Web site: http://www.regionalgolf.net
Titles:
GOLF NOW

REGIONAL MAGAZINE COMPANY 18842
RMC House, Broadfield Court, Broadfield Business Park,
SHEFFIELD, S8 0XF **Tel:** 0114 250 6300 **Fax:** 0114 255 5881
Web site: http://www.northernlifestyle.com
Titles:
FIRST FOR BUSINESS
IMAGE MAGAZINE
MOVING HOUSE MAGAZINE
SHEFFIELD SIXER
WESTSIDE MAGAZINE
YQ MAGAZINE

REGIONS PUBLISHING LTD 13793
26 Ives Street, LONDON, SW3 2ND **Tel:** 020 7581 6300
Fax: 020 7581 6400
Titles:
SHANG YE XIAN FENG (BUSINESS TO BUSINESS
MAGAZINE FOR CHINA)

RELIGIOUS INTELLIGENCE LTD 1721097
14 Great College Street, LONDON, SW1P 3RX
Tel: 020 7878 1001 **Fax:** 020 7878 1031
Web site: http://www.religiousintelligence.com
Titles:
THE CHURCH OF ENGLAND NEWSPAPER

REMPLOY LTD 14588
Stonecourt, Siskin Drive, COVENTRY, CV3 4FJ
Tel: 024 7651 5870 **Fax:** 024 7651 5860
Titles:
REMPLOY NEWS

REMUS 1640329
Easons Barn, Easons Green, Framfield, UCKFIELD, TN22
5RB **Tel:** 01825 873444 **Fax:** 01825 873555
Titles:
EQUESTRIAN

RENAISSANCE PUBLISHING LTD 675221
PO Box 28849, LONDON, SW13 0WA **Tel:** 020 8876 1891
Fax: 020 8392 1339
Titles:
JEWISH RENAISSANCE

RENAISSANCE UNIVERSAL 17044
3A Cazenove Road, LONDON, N16 6PA **Tel:** 020 8806 4250
Fax: 020 8806 4250
Web site: http://www.ru.org
Titles:
NEW RENAISSANCE

RENEWS LTD 698992
PO Box 27, CHELTENHAM, GL53 0YH **Tel:** 01962 829819
Fax: 01242 574102
Email: renewsltd@btconnect.com
Web site: http://www.renews.biz
Titles:
POWERHOUSE
RENEWS

REPHOTO PUBLISHING LTD 13704
Rephoto House, Plough Road, Smallfield, HORLEY, RH6
9EZ **Tel:** 01342 844444 **Fax:** 01342 844488
Email: info@rephotopublishing.co.uk
Web site: http://www.rephotopublishing.co.uk
Titles:
AUTO VENDING
AUTOVENDING
CAFÉ BUSINESS
CUSTOM INSTALLER

THE REPORTER LTD 12824
17 Wellington Road, DEWSBURY, WF13 1HQ
Tel: 01924 468282 **Fax:** 01924 457652
Email: thereporterlimited@ywng.co.uk
Titles:
BATLEY NEWS SERIES
DEWSBURY REPORTER AND ADVERTISER SERIES

REPTILE CARE UK LTD 1736249
126-128 Gloucester Road North, Filton, BRISTOL, BS34
7BQ **Tel:** 0117 969 3013
Titles:
REPTILE CARE

RESEARCH INFORMATION LTD 13915
Grenville Court, Britwell Road, Burnham, SLOUGH, SL1 8DF
Tel: 01628 600499 **Fax:** 01628 600488
Email: info@researchinformation.co.uk
Web site: http://www.researchinformation.co.uk
Titles:
APPROPRIATE TECHNOLOGY
FOOD PACKAGING BULLETIN
INTERNATIONAL JOURNAL OF MICROGRAPHICS &
OPTICAL TECHNOLOGY
INTERNATIONAL PEST CONTROL
INTERNATIONAL PESTICIDE DIRECTORY
OUTLOOKS ON PEST MANAGEMENT
WORLD FOOD REGULATION REVIEW

RESEARCH RESEARCH LTD 14484
Unit 111, 134-146 Curtain Road, LONDON, EC2A 3AR
Tel: 020 7216 6500 **Fax:** 020 7216 6501
Email: info@researchresearch.com

Titles:
RESEARCH EUROPE
RESEARCH FORTNIGHT

RESIDUA LTD   14652
Yellow Cottatge, Draughton, SKIPTON, BD23 6EA
Tel: 01756 711362 **Fax:** 01756 711360
Titles:
WARMER BULLETIN

RESOURCE MEDIA LTD   1710864
57 Prince Street, BRISTOL, BS1 4QH **Tel:** 0117 907 4107
Fax: 0117 907 7216
Web site: http://www.resourcepublishing.co.uk
Titles:
THE LOOP MAGAZINE
MATERIAL MATTERS MAGAZINE
RESOURCE
THE WASTE PAPER

RESULT CUSTOMER COMMUNICATIONS   1745314
1 Liverpool Street, LONDON, EC2M 7QD **Tel:** 020 7956 2792
Fax: 020 7956 2281
Email: info@resultmarketing.co.uk
Titles:
MORRISONS

RESURGENCE LTD   16674
Ford House, Hartland, BIDEFORD, EX39 6EE
Tel: 01237 441293 **Fax:** 01237 441203
Titles:
RESURGENCE

RETAIL BANKING RESEARCH LTD   13317
304 Sandycombe Road, Kew Gardens, RICHMOND, TW9
3NG **Tel:** 020 8940 1398 **Fax:** 020 8940 1527
Web site: http://www.rbrlondon.com
Titles:
BANKING AUTOMATION BULLETIN

RETAIL BULLETIN MEDIA LTD   1766302
Gatton Bottom, REIGATE, RH2 0TU
Titles:
THE RETAIL BULLETIN

RETAIL EVENTS   1758612
Imperial House, St. Nicholas Circle, LEICESTER, LE1 4LF
Tel: 0116 242 4054 **Fax:** 0116 242 4048
Titles:
RETAIL FRAUD

RETAIL MOTOR INDUSTRY FEDERATION LTD   14114
201 Great Portland Street, LONDON, W1W 5AB
Tel: 020 7580 9122 **Fax:** 020 7580 6376
Titles:
FORECOURT

RETHINK RESEARCH ASSOCIATES   1630597
4 Metro Central Heights, 119 Newington Causeway,
LONDON, SE1 6BA **Tel:** 020 7407 9848 **Fax:** 020 7900 2225
Email: info@rethinkresearch.biz
Web site: http://www.rethinkresearch.biz
Titles:
FAULTLINE
WIRELESS WATCH

RETRA   1627278
Retra House, St. John's Terrace, 1 Ampthill Street,
BEDFORD, MK42 9EY **Tel:** 01234 269110
Fax: 01234 269609
Email: alert@retra.co.uk
Web site: http://www.retra.co.uk
Titles:
ALERT MAGAZINE

RETREADING BUSINESS LTD   17082
PO Box 320, CREWE, CW2 6WY **Tel:** 01270 668718
Fax: 01270 668801
Titles:
TYRES ONLINE

RETRO SPEEDWAY   700122
103 Douglas Road, HORNCHURCH, RM11 1AW
Tel: 01708 734502
Titles:
CLASSIC SPEEDWAY

REVIEW MEDIA LTD.   15591
Media House, Building 9, Stanmore Industrial Estate,
BRIDGNORTH, WV15 5HR **Tel:** 01746 766848
Fax: 01746 764226
Titles:
THE SHROPSHIRE REVIEW

REVIEWER LTD   1749020
99 Falmouth Avenue, LONDON, E4 9QR **Tel:** 020 8527 8935
Titles:
DVD REVIEWER
MY REVIEWER

REVOLUTION PUBLISHING   1761231
145-147 St. John Street, LONDON, EC1V 4PY
Tel: 020 8407 0107
Web site: http://www.revolution-publishing.com
Titles:
ESCAPISM TRAVEL MAGAZINE

REWIND CREATIVE MEDIA   1724738
Unit 10-13, The Leather Market, Weston Street, LONDON,
SE1 3ER **Tel:** 020 7939 7600 **Fax:** 020 7367 6184
Titles:
RWD

REX PUBLICATIONS LTD   15231
64 Charlotte Street, LONDON, W1T 4QD **Tel:** 020 7436 4006
Fax: 020 7436 3458
Titles:
MAJESTY

R.G. ENTERPRISES LTD   625599
The Maltings, 50 Bath Street, GRAVESEND, DA11 0DF
Tel: 01474 335087
Titles:
CASINO WORLD

RGO EXHIBITIONS & PUBLICATIONS LTD   14115
Oakapple Cottage, Furnace Lane, Broad Oak Brede, RYE,
TN31 6ES **Tel:** 01424 882702 **Fax:** 01424 882702
Email: info@rgoltd.co.uk
Web site: http://www.rgoltd.co.uk
Titles:
ENGINE REPAIR & REMANUFACTURE
VEHICLE ELECTRICS & ELECTRONICS DIAGNOSTIC &
EMISSIONS (INCORPORATING FUEL INJECTION
NEWS)

RHINEGOLD PUBLISHING LTD   13862
239-241 Shaftesbury Avenue, LONDON, WC2H 8TF
Tel: 020 7333 1746 **Fax:** 020 7333 1769
Web site: http://www.rhinegold.co.uk
Titles:
CHOIR & ORGAN
CLASSICAL MUSIC
CLASSROOM MUSIC
EARLY MUSIC TODAY
MUSIC TEACHER
OPERA NOW
PIANO
THE SINGER
TEACHING DRAMA

RHS MEDIA   700180
4th Floor, Churchgate, New Road, PETERBOROUGH, PE1
1TT **Tel:** 0845 260 0909 **Fax:** 01733 341633
Titles:
THE GARDEN
THE ORCHID REVIEW
THE PLANTSMAN

RIAS   13491
15 Rutland Square, EDINBURGH, EH1 2BE
Tel: 0131 229 7545 **Fax:** 0131 228 2188
Email: smccord@rias.org.uk
Web site: http://www.rias.org.uk
Titles:
THE CHARTERED ARCHITECT

RIB INTERNATIONAL LTD   16076
Oyster House, Hunters Lodge, Kentisbeare, CULLOMPTON,
EX15 2DY **Tel:** 01884 266100 **Fax:** 01884 266101
Email: hms@ribmagazine.com
Web site: http://www.ribmagazine.com
Titles:
RIB INTERNATIONAL

RICH MEDIA LTD   1741783
17 Carlton Place, SOUTHAMPTON, SO15 2DY
Tel: 023 8063 8500
Titles:
OPEN GOAL

RICHARD BETTS   1640262
PO Box 33874, LONDON, N8 7XN **Tel:** 020 8340 4328
Titles:
EURO-INSIDER

RICHMOND AVIATION   1640594
The Studio, Kettys Close, Withiel, BODMIN, PL30 5NR
Tel: 01208 832975 **Fax:** 01208 832995
Titles:
GENERAL AVIATION

RICHMOND GREEN GROUP   1762303
1 Lion House, Red Lion Street, RICHMOND, TW9 1RE
Titles:
OPP RUSSIA

RICHMOND HOUSE PUBLISHING CO LTD   17717
70-76 Bell Street, LONDON, NW1 6SP **Tel:** 020 7224 9666
Fax: 020 7224 9688
Web site: http://www.rhpco.co.uk
Titles:
ARTISTS AND AGENTS

RIDINGS PUBLISHING CO.   15582
Seasiders Way, Bloomfield Road, BLACKPOOL, FY1 6JJ
Tel: 01253 405357
Titles:
LANCASHIRE MAGAZINE
YORKSHIRE RIDINGS MAGAZINE

RIGDEN THORNE   1763396
Queen anne House, LUCTON, HR6 9PN **Tel:** 0845 658 0068
Fax: 0845 658 0069
Titles:
BOOK PEOPLE

RILA PUBLICATIONS LTD   14494
73 Newman Street, LONDON, W1A 4PG **Tel:** 020 7631 1299
Fax: 020 7580 7166
Titles:
CLINICAL FOCUS

RIMS MEDIA   1654442
Unit 21, Highview, High Street, BORDON, GU35 0AX
Tel: 01420 473716 **Fax:** 01420 487799
Email: info@rimsmedia.co.uk
Titles:
EYES

THE RINGING WORLD LTD   16144
Eagleside House, 7-9 Chantry Street, ANDOVER, SP10 1DE
Tel: 01264 366620 **Fax:** 01264 360594
Titles:
THE RINGING WORLD

RIVER PUBLISHING LTD   13319
1 Neal Street, Covent Garden, LONDON, WC2H 9QL
Tel: 020 7306 0304 **Fax:** 020 7306 0314
Web site: http://www.riverltd.co.uk
Titles:
BM
CO-OP TRAVELLER
DARE
DREAM
THE HARRODS MAGAZINE
HEALTHY
HEALTHY FOR MEN
SWING
WEIGHT WATCHERS MAGAZINE

UK Publishers & Their Titles

THE RIVER THAMES GUIDE   1638429
100-102 George Lane, LONDON, E18 1AD
Tel: 020 8989 2041
Email: riverthames@btconnect.com
Web site: http://www.riverthames.co.uk
Titles:
  THE RIVER THAMES GUIDE

RIVIERA MARITIME MEDIA   676800
Mitre House, 66 Abbey Road, ENFIELD, EN1 2QN
Tel: 020 8363 1551 **Fax:** 020 8364 1331
Email: info@rivieramm.com
Web site: http://www.rivieramm.com
Titles:
  MARINE PROPULSION & AUXILIARY MACHINERY
  PASSENGER SHIP TECHNOLOGY
  TANKER SHIPPING & TRADE

RJ COMMUNICATIONS & MEDIA LTD   625360
39 Vineyard Path, Mortlake, LONDON, SW14 8ET
Tel: 020 8487 5656 **Fax:** 020 8487 5666
Email: robert@rjcoms.com
Titles:
  DRUG DISCOVERY WORLD

RLA PUBLISHING LTD   18385
1 Roebuck Lane, SALE, M33 7SY **Tel:** 0845 666 5000
Web site: http://www.rla.org.uk
Titles:
  RESIDENTIAL PROPERTY INVESTOR

RMT PUBLISHING   13866
39 Chalton Street, LONDON, NW1 1JD **Tel:** 020 7387 4771
Fax: 020 7387 4123
Titles:
  RMT NEWS

THE RNID   14569
19-23 Featherstone Street, LONDON, EC1Y 8SL
Tel: 020 7296 8000
Web site: http://www.rnid.org.uk
Titles:
  ONE IN SEVEN MAGAZINE

RNSA   16078
10 Haslar Marina, Haslar Road, GOSPORT, PO12 1NU
Tel: 023 9252 1100 **Fax:** 023 9252 1122
Titles:
  ROYAL NAVAL SAILING ASSOCIATION JOURNAL

ROAD HAULAGE ASSOCIATION LTD   17884
Roadway House, 35 Monument Hill, WEYBRIDGE, KT13
8RN **Tel:** 01932 841515 **Fax:** 01932 838916
Web site: http://www.rha.net
Titles:
  ROADWAY

ROADWAY PUBLISHING   1736182
Roadway House, 35 Monument Hill, WEYBRIDGE, KT13
8RN **Tel:** 01932 838922 **Fax:** 01932 852516
Email: roadway@rha.net
Web site: http://www.rha.net
Titles:
  FASTFORWARD

THE ROBERT BURNS WORLD FEDERATION LTD 13115
1 Cairnsmore Road, CASTLE DOUGLAS, DG7 1BN
Tel: 01556 504448 **Fax:** 01556 504448
Email: peter@cairnsmore1.freeserve.co.uk
Titles:
  THE BURNS CHRONICLE

ROBERT SCOTT PUBLISHING LIMITED   16709
The Old Barn, Ball Lane, Tackley, KIDLINGTON, OX5 3AG
Tel: 01869 331741 **Fax:** 01869 331641
Email: robert@rspl.eu
Web site: http://www.rspl.eu
Titles:
  EOS MAGAZINE

ROBIN ALTWOOD PUBLICATIONS   1723929
PO Box 793, Badley, IPSWICH, IP6 8WN **Tel:** 01449 722505

Titles:
  SHOWING WORLD

ROBIN RAMSAY   1650955
214 Westbourne Avenue, Princes Avenue, HULL, HU5 3JB
Tel: 01482 447558
Titles:
  LOBSTER MAGAZINE

ROCK SOUND LTD   18692
Unit 22, Jack's Place, 6 Corbet Place, LONDON, E1 6NN
Tel: 020 7877 8770 **Fax:** 020 7377 0455
Titles:
  ROCK SOUND
  ROCKSOUND.TV

ROCKCLIFFE LTD   1720998
20A Hillgate Place, 18-20 Balham Hill, LONDON, SW12 9ER
Tel: 020 8675 7770 **Fax:** 020 8675 0950
Email: dotter@pppbulletin.co.uk
Web site: http://www.pppbulletin.com
Titles:
  PPP BULLETIN
  PPP BULLETIN

ROGER BARBER PUBLISHING   1630325
Triumph House, Station Approach, Sanderstead Road,
SOUTH CROYDON, CR2 0PL **Tel:** 020 8916 0022
Fax: 020 8916 0033
Email: roger@rbpublishing.co.uk
Web site: http://www.rogerbarberpublishing.com
Titles:
  ENGINEERING SUBCONTRACTOR
  GRINDING AND SURFACE FINISHING

ROGER BOOTH STUDIOS LTD   1720328
48 Keymer Road, HASSOCKS, BN6 8AR **Tel:** 01273 842550
Fax: 01273 842246
Titles:
  SOUTH DOWNS LIVING

ROLLING RIVER PUBLICATIONS LTD   16103
The Locus Centre, The Square, ABERFELDY, PH15 2DD
Tel: 01887 829868 **Fax:** 01887 829856
Web site: http://www.flyfishing-and-flytying.co.uk
Titles:
  FLY-FISHING AND FLY-TYING

ROLLINS PROMOTIONS LTD   1682636
26 The Oaks, NEWTOWNARDS, BT23 8GZ
Tel: 028 9182 8211 **Fax:** 028 9182 7463
Titles:
  ROAD RACING IRELAND

ROLLS-ROYCE PLC   12311
65 Buckingham Gate, LONDON, SW1E 6AT
Tel: 020 7227 9139 **Fax:** 020 7227 9178
Web site: http://www.rolls-royce.com
Titles:
  THE ROLLS ROYCE MAGAZINE

ROMA PUBLICATIONS LTD   1644580
1 Livsey Street, ROCHDALE, OL16 1ST **Tel:** 01706 719972
Fax: 01706 719057
Titles:
  PREMIER CONSTRUCTION

ROMAN CATHOLIC DIOCESE LANCASTER   1681300
Balmoral Road, LANCASTER, LA1 3BT
Titles:
  THE CATHOLIC VOICE OF LANCASTER

ROOFING TODAY MAGAZINE LTD   1619199
85-89 Duke Street, LIVERPOOL, L1 5AP **Tel:** 0151 709 0904
Fax: 0151 709 0905
Titles:
  ROOFING TODAY

ROOM 501 PUBLISHING   1763078
Unit 10, Baird Close, Stephenson Industrial Estate,
Washington, TYNE AND WEAR, NE37 3HL
Tel: 0191 419 3321

Web site: http://www.room501.co.uk
Titles:
  BQ MAGAZINE

ROSEMAPLE MEDIA LTD   17774
PO Box 46249, LONDON, W5 2YN **Tel:** 020 8840 9765
Email: info@canadapost.co.uk
Web site: http://www.canadapost.co.uk
Titles:
  THE CANADA POST

ROSKILL INFORMATION SERVICES LTD   18405
27A Leopold Road, LONDON, SW19 7BB
Tel: 020 8944 0066 **Fax:** 020 8947 9568
Email: info@roskill.co.uk
Web site: http://www.roskill.co.uk
Titles:
  ROSKILL'S LETTER FROM JAPAN
  ROSKILL'S LITHIUM DIGEST

THE ROSS GAZETTE LTD   18934
54A Broad Street, ROSS-ON-WYE, HR9 7DY
Tel: 01989 562007 **Fax:** 01989 768023
Titles:
  THE ROSS GAZETTE

**ROTARY INTERNATIONAL IN GREAT BRITAIN AND
IRELAND**   14180
Kinwarton Road, ALCESTER, B49 6BP **Tel:** 01789 765411
Fax: 01789 765570
Email: secretary@ribi.org
Web site: http://www.rotary-ribi.org
Titles:
  ROTARY TODAY

ROUNCY MEDIA LTD   1691613
3 The Office Village, Cygnet Park, Forder Way, Hampton,
PETERBOROUGH, PE7 8GX **Tel:** 01733 293240
Fax: 0845 280 2927
Titles:
  COACH AND BUS WEEK

ROUND AND ABOUT PUBLICATIONS LTD.   15590
The Old Coach House, The Street, Crowmarsh Gifford,
WALLINGFORD, OX10 8EH **Tel:** 01491 837621
Fax: 01491 826809
Email: editor@roundandabout.co.uk
Web site: http://www.roundandabout.co.uk
Titles:
  ROUND & ABOUT OXFORDSHIRE

ROUND SUN LTD   1650290
1 Denehead Cottages, Hexham Road, Wabottle,
NEWCASTLE UPON TYNE, NE15 9RX **Tel:** 0191 264 5909
Titles:
  PRIMARY TIMES IN NEWCASTLE, NORTH TYNESIDE &
    NORTHUMBERLAND
  PRIMARY TIMES IN SUNDERLAND & DURHAM

ROUSTABOUT PUBLICATIONS LTD   14218
Suite 5, International Base, Greenwell Road, East Tullos,
ABERDEEN, AB12 3AX **Tel:** 01224 876582
Fax: 01224 879757
Email: editor@energyinternat.com
Web site: http://www.energyinternat.com
Titles:
  ROUSTABOUT ENERGY INTERNATIONAL

ROUTE ONE PUBLISHING LTD   14278
Horizon House, Azalea Drive, SWANLEY, BR8 8JR
Tel: 0161 603 0891
Titles:
  ITS INTERNATIONAL
  WORLD HIGHWAYS/ROUTES DU MONDE

ROUTLEDGE CAVENDISH PUBLISHING LTD   12546
Building 2, Floor 2, Social Sciences, 2 Park Square, Milton
Park, ABINGDON, OX14 4RN **Tel:** 020 7017 6000
Fax: 020 7278 8080
Titles:
  LANGUAGE LEARNING JOURNAL
  STUDENT LAW REVIEW

ROUTLEDGE, TAYLOR & FRANCIS 12340
4 Park Square, Milton Park, ABINGDON, OX14 4RN
Tel: 020 7017 6000
Web site: http://www.tandf.co.uk/journals
Titles:
THE ADELPHI PAPERS (IISS)
AIDS CARE
BRITISH JOURNAL OF GUIDANCE & COUNSELLING
BRITISH JOURNAL OF RELIGIOUS EDUCATION
BUSINESS HISTORY
CONTEMPORARY PHYSICS
EDUCATION AND THE LAW
ENVIRONMENTAL POLITICS
EUROPEAN PLANNING STUDIES
FOOD & AGRICULTURAL IMMUNOLOGY
HISTORY OF PHOTOGRAPHY
INDEX ON CENSORSHIP
INTERNATIONAL JOURNAL OF CONTROL
INTERNATIONAL JOURNAL OF THE ECONOMICS OF
   BUSINESS
INTERNATIONAL JOURNAL OF ELECTRONICS
INTERNATIONAL JOURNAL OF HERITAGE STUDIES
JOURNAL OF CHANGE MANAGEMENT
JOURNAL OF CONTEMPORARY AFRICAN STUDIES
JOURNAL OF EDUCATION AND WORK
JOURNAL OF ENGINEERING DESIGN
JOURNAL OF HERITAGE TOURISM
JOURNAL OF NATURAL HISTORY
THE JOURNAL OF SOCIAL WELFARE & FAMILY LAW
JOURNAL OF SOUTHERN AFRICAN STUDIES
THE JOURNAL OF THE TEXTILE INSTITUTE
JOURNAL OF VISUAL COMMUNICATION IN MEDICINE
LANGUAGE CULTURE & CURRICULUM
MEDICAL INFORMATICS AND THE INTERNET IN
   MEDICINE
MEDICAL TEACHER
MENTORING & TUTORING
MOLECULAR PHYSICS
PERFORMANCE RESEARCH JOURNAL
POLICY STUDIES
PRACTICE
REVIEW OF AFRICAN POLITICAL ECONOMY
SEXUAL & RELATIONSHIP THERAPY
SOCIAL IDENTITIES
STRATEGIC SURVEY
STUDIES IN THE HISTORY OF GARDENS & DESIGNED
   LANDSCAPES
SURVIVAL
THIRD TEXT
URBAN WATER JOURNAL
WASAFIRI

ROXBY MEDIA LTD 18607
The Diary House, Rickett Street, LONDON, SW6 1RU
Tel: 020 7386 6100 **Fax:** 020 7381 8890
Email: inbox@mar-media.com
Web site: http://www.roxby-media.com
Titles:
COMMUNITY HEALTH & SOCIAL CARE
NETWORK NEW YORK/LONDON

ROYAL ACADEMY OF DANCE 12973
36 Battersea Square, LONDON, SW11 3RA
Tel: 020 7326 8000
Titles:
DANCE GAZETTE

ROYAL AERONAUTICAL SOCIETY 13614
4 Hamilton Place, LONDON, W1J 7BQ **Tel:** 020 7670 4300
Fax: 020 7670 4359
Email: publications@raes.org.uk
Web site: http://www.aerosociety.com
Titles:
THE AERONAUTICAL JOURNAL
AEROSPACE INTERNATIONAL
THE AEROSPACE PROFESSIONAL

ROYAL AIR FORCE CHARITABLE TRUST ENTERPRISES 18217
Douglas Bader House, Horcott Hill, FAIRFORD, GL7 4DL
Tel: 01285 713300 **Fax:** 01285 713268
Web site: http://www.airtattoo.com
Titles:
THE ROYAL AIR FORCE YEARBOOK

ROYAL ANTHROPOLOGICAL INSTITUTE 16126
50 Fitzroy Street, LONDON, W1T 5BT **Tel:** 020 7387 0455
Fax: 020 7383 4235
Web site: http://www.therai.org.uk
Titles:
JOURNAL OF THE ROYAL ANTHROPOLOGICAL
   INSTITUTE (INC. MAN)

ROYAL ASSOCIATION FOR DISABILITY & REHABILITATION 14587
12 City Forum, 250 City Road, LONDON, EC1V 8AF
Tel: 020 7250 3222 **Fax:** 020 7250 0212
Email: radar@radar.org.uk
Web site: http://www.radar.org.uk
Titles:
RADAR NEW BULLETIN

ROYAL BRITISH LEGION SCOTLAND 16111
New Haig House, Logie Green Road, EDINBURGH, EH7
4HR **Tel:** 0131 557 2782 **Fax:** 0131 557 5819
Web site: http://www.rblscotland.org
Titles:
SCOTTISH LEGION NEWS

ROYAL COLLEGE OF GENERAL PRACTITIONERS 14518
14 Princes Gate, LONDON, SW7 1PU **Tel:** 020 7581 3232
Fax: 020 7584 6716
Web site: http://www.rcgp.org.uk
Titles:
BRITISH JOURNAL OF GENERAL PRACTICE

ROYAL COLLEGE OF PHYSICIANS 14509
11 St Andrews Place, LONDON, NW1 4LE
Tel: 020 7935 1174 **Fax:** 020 7486 5425
Web site: http://www.rcplondon.ac.uk
Titles:
CLINICAL MEDICINE

ROYAL COLLEGE OF PHYSICIANS OF EDINBURGH 18516
9 Queen Street, EDINBURGH, EH2 1JQ **Tel:** 0131 225 7324
Fax: 0131 220 3939
Email: enquiries@rcpe.ac.uk
Web site: http://www.rcpe.ac.uk
Titles:
JOURNAL OF THE ROYAL COLLEGE OF PHYSICIANS
   OF EDINBURGH

ROYAL COLLEGE OF PSYCHIATRISTS 14595
17 Belgrave Square, LONDON, SW1X 8PG
Tel: 020 7235 2351 **Fax:** 020 7259 6507
Titles:
THE BRITISH JOURNAL OF PSYCHIATRY
PSYCHIATRIC BULLETIN

ROYAL FORESTRY SOCIETY 14365
102 High Street, TRING, HP23 4AF **Tel:** 01442 822028
Fax: 01442 890395
Email: rfshq@rfs.org.uk
Web site: http://www.rfs.org.uk
Titles:
QUARTERLY JOURNAL OF FORESTRY

ROYAL HIGHLAND FUSILIERS 1654225
518 Sauchiehall Street, GLASGOW, G2 3LW
Tel: 0141 332 0961 **Fax:** 0141 353 1493
Titles:
JOURNAL OF THE ROYAL HIGHLAND FUSILIERS

THE ROYAL INSTITUTE OF INTERNATIONAL AFFAIRS 12368
Chatham House, 10 St. James's Square, LONDON, SW1Y
4LE **Tel:** 020 7957 5700 **Fax:** 020 7957 5710
Web site: http://www.riia.org
Titles:
THE WORLD TODAY

THE ROYAL INSTITUTE OF PUBLIC HEALTH 14555
28 Portland Place, LONDON, W1N 4DE **Tel:** 020 7580 2731
Fax: 020 7580 6157
Web site: http://www.riph.org.uk
Titles:
HEALTH & HYGIENE

ROYAL INSTITUTION OF CHARTERED SURVEYORS 622034
12 Great George Street, Parliament Square, LONDON,
SW1P 3AD **Tel:** 020 7222 7000
Web site: http://www.rics.org
Titles:
BUILDING CONSERVATION JOURNAL
BUILDING CONTROL JOURNAL

THE ROYAL INSTITUTION OF NAVAL ARCHITECTS 14337
10 Upper Belgrave Street, LONDON, SW1X 8BQ
Tel: 020 7235 4622 **Fax:** 020 7245 6959
Web site: http://www.rina.org.uk
Titles:
THE NAVAL ARCHITECT
SHIP & BOAT INTERNATIONAL
SHIPREPAIR AND CONVERSION TECHNOLOGY
WARSHIP TECHNOLOGY

THE ROYAL LIFE SAVING SOCIETY UK 14469
River House, High Street, Broom, ALCESTER, B50 4HN
Tel: 01789 773994 **Fax:** 01789 773995
Titles:
LIFESAVERS

ROYAL MAIL GROUP LTD 17712
Royal Mail, 35-50 RathbonePlace, LONDON, W1T 1HQ
Tel: 020 7441 4744
Email: john.r.holman@royalmail.co.uk
Web site: http://www.royalmail.com
Titles:
BRITISH PHILATELIC BULLETIN
BRITISH POSTMARK BULLETIN

ROYAL METEOROLOGICAL SOCIETY 14810
104 Oxford Road, READING, RG1 7LL **Tel:** 0118 956 8500
Fax: 0118 956 8571
Titles:
QUARTERLY JOURNAL OF THE ROYAL
   METEOROLOGICAL SOCIETY

ROYAL NATIONAL INSTITUTE OF BLIND PEOPLE 14583
PO Box 173, PETERBOROUGH, PE2 6WS
Tel: 0845 702 3153
Email: cservices@rnib.org.uk
Web site: http://www.rnib.org.uk
Titles:
APHRA
BIG PRINT
INSIGHT
NB
PROGRESS
SP

ROYAL NATIONAL INSTITUTE OF THE BLIND 1729016
105 Judd Street, LONDON, WC1H 9NE **Tel:** 020 7391 2018
Titles:
ACCESS JOURNAL
VISION

ROYAL NATIONAL LIFEBOAT INSTITUTION 14468
West Quay Road, POOLE, BH15 1HZ **Tel:** 0845 122 6999
Fax: 0845 126 1999
Email: info@rnli.org.uk
Web site: http://www.lifeboats.org.uk
Titles:
THE LIFEBOAT

THE ROYAL NATIONAL ROSE SOCIETY 16109
Chiswell Green, ST. ALBANS, AL2 3NR **Tel:** 01727 850461
Fax: 01727 850360
Titles:
THE ROSE

THE ROYAL OPERA HOUSE COVENT GARDEN LTD. 18230
Royal Opera House, Covent Garden, LONDON, WC2E 9DD
Tel: 020 7212 9362 **Fax:** 020 7212 9362
Titles:
ROYAL OPERA HOUSE NIGHTLY PROGRAMME BOOK

ROYAL OVER-SEAS LEAGUE 16142
Over-Seas House, Park Place, St. James's Street, LONDON,
SW1A 1LR **Tel:** 020 7408 0214 **Fax:** 020 7499 6738
Email: info@rosl.org.uk
Web site: http://www.rosl.org.uk
Titles:
OVERSEAS

THE ROYAL PHILATELIC SOCIETY 17975
41 Devonshire Place, LONDON, W1N 1PE
Tel: 020 7486 1044 **Fax:** 020 7486 0803

UK Publishers & Their Titles

Titles:
LONDON PHILATELIST

THE ROYAL PHOTOGRAPHIC SOCIETY 14245
Finsbury Business Centre, 40 Bowling Green Lane,
LONDON, EC1R 0NE **Tel:** 020 7415 7096
Web site: http://www.rps.org
Titles:
RPS JOURNAL

ROYAL PIGEON RACING ASSOCIATION 15324
The Reddings House, CHELTENHAM, GL51 6RN
Tel: 01452 713529
Titles:
BRITISH HOMING WORLD

THE ROYAL SCHOOL OF CHURCH MUSIC 15358
19 The Close, SALIBURY, SP1 2EB **Tel:** 01722 424848
Fax: 01722 424849
Email: enquiries@rscm.com
Web site: http://www.rscm.com
Titles:
CHURCH MUSIC QUARTERLY

ROYAL SCOTTISH FORESTRY SOCIETY 14366
Hagg-on-Esk, CANONBIE, DG14 0XE **Tel:** 01387 371518
Fax: 01387 371418
Email: rsfs@ednet.co.uk
Web site: http://www.rsfs.org
Titles:
SCOTTISH FORESTRY

THE ROYAL SOCIETY 18071
6-9 Carlton House Terrace, LONDON, SW1Y 5AG
Tel: 020 7839 5561 **Fax:** 020 7976 1837
Web site: http://www.pubs.royalsoc.ac.uk
Titles:
PHILOSOPHICAL TRANSACTIONS OF THE ROYAL
SOCIETY: BIOLOGICAL
PROCEEDINGS OF THE ROYAL SOCIETY SERIES:
MATHS, PHYS. & ENG.SC.

THE ROYAL SOCIETY FOR PUBLIC HEALTH 14605
38A St. George's Drive, LONDON, SW1V 4BH
Tel: 020 7630 0121 **Fax:** 020 7976 6847
Email: rsph@rsph.org
Web site: http://www.rsph.org
Titles:
PROSPECTIVE IN PUBLIC HEALTH

**ROYAL SOCIETY FOR THE PREVENTION OF
ACCIDENTS** 14454
Edgbaston Park, 353 Bristol Road, Edgbaston,
BIRMINGHAM, B5 7ST **Tel:** 0121 248 2000
Fax: 0121 248 2001
Web site: http://www.rospa.com
Titles:
CARE ON THE ROAD
THE ROSPA OCCUPATIONAL SAFETY & HEALTH
BULLETIN
THE ROSPA OCCUPATIONAL SAFETY & HEALTH
JOURNAL
SAFETY EDUCATION
SAFETY EXPRESS
STAYING ALIVE

**THE ROYAL SOCIETY FOR THE PROTECTION OF
BIRDS** 18331
The Lodge, SANDY, SG19 2DL **Tel:** 01767 680551
Fax: 01767 683262
Web site: http://www.rspb.org.uk
Titles:
BIRD LIFE
BIRDS - THE MAGAZINE OF THE RSPB
WINGBEAT

ROYAL SOCIETY OF CHEMISTRY 12336
Thomas Graham House, Science Park, Milton Road,
CAMBRIDGE, CB4 0WF **Tel:** 01223 420066
Fax: 01223 420247
Web site: http://www.rsc.org
Titles:
ANALYST
ANALYTICAL ABSTRACTS
CHEMICAL COMMUNICATIONS
CHEMICAL HAZARDS IN INDUSTRY
CHEMICAL SOCIETY REVIEWS

CHEMISTRY WORLD
EDUCATION IN CHEMISTRY
FARADAY DISCUSSIONS
GREEN CHEMISTRY
JOURNAL OF ANALYTICAL ATOMIC SPECTROMETRY
JOURNAL OF ENVIRONMENTAL MONITORING
LAB ON A CHIP
LABORATORY HAZARDS BULLETIN
METHODS IN ORGANIC SYNTHESIS
NATURAL PRODUCT REPORT
ORGANIC & BIOMOLECULAR CHEMISTRY
PHYSICAL CHEMISTRY CHEMICAL PHYSICS

THE ROYAL SOCIETY OF MEDICINE PRESS LTD 18597
1 Wimpole Street, LONDON, W1G 0AE **Tel:** 020 7290 2900
Fax: 020 7290 2929
Web site: http://www.rsmpress.co.uk
Titles:
THE JOURNAL OF THE ROYAL SOCIETY OF MEDICINE

**ROYAL UNITED SERVICES INSTITUTE FOR DEFENCE
& SECURITY STUDIES** 14264
Whitehall, LONDON, SW1A 2ET **Tel:** 020 7930 5854
Fax: 020 7321 0943
Titles:
RUSI DEFENCE SYSTEMS
RUSI JOURNAL

ROYAL YACHTING ASSOCIATION 16077
RYA House, Ensign Way, Hamble, SOUTHAMPTON, SO31
4YA **Tel:** 023 8060 4100 **Fax:** 023 8060 4293
Email: rya.magazine@rya.org.uk
Web site: http://www.rya.org.uk
Titles:
RYA MAGAZINE

RPA PUBLISHING LIMITED 15150
PO Box 1479, MAIDENHEAD, SL6 8YX **Tel:** 01628 783080
Fax: 01628 633250
Email: rpapublishinh@yahoo.co.uk
Titles:
MACHINE KNITTING MONTHLY

RPS PUBLISHING 14234
1 Lambeth High Street, LONDON, SE1 7JN
Tel: 020 7572 2271
Web site: http://www.rpspublishing.com
Titles:
CLINICAL PHARMACIST
THE PHARMACEUTICAL JOURNAL

THE RSE SCOTLAND FOUNDATION 18429
22-26 George Street, EDINBURGH, EH2 2PQ
Tel: 0131 240 5000 **Fax:** 0131 240 5024
Titles:
PROCEEDINGS OF ROYAL SOCIETY OF EDINBURGH
(SECTION A, MATHS)
RESOURCE

RSPCA 15630
Wilberforce Way, Southwater, HORSHAM, RH13 9RS
Tel: 0300 123 0100 **Fax:** 0300 123 0048
Web site: http://www.rspca.org.uk
Titles:
ANIMAL ACTION
ANIMAL LIFE
RSPCA

RTS 14301
Kildare House, 3 Dorsett Rise, LONDON, EC4Y 8EH
Tel: 020 7822 2810
Web site: http://www.rts.org.uk
Titles:
TELEVISION

RUBBISH 1710715
326 Kensal Road, LONDON, NW10 5BZ **Tel:** 020 8960 8263
Titles:
RUBBISH

RUBENSTEIN PUBLISHING 1741145
PO Box 61064, LONDON, SE1P 5BQ **Tel:** 020 7953 8796
Web site: http://www.rubensteinpublishing.com
Titles:
EQUAL OPPORTUNITIES REVIEW

RUGBY ADVERTISER 1713395
2 Albert Street, RUGBY, CV21 2RS **Tel:** 01788 539977
Fax: 01788 541274
Web site: http://www.rugbyadvertiser.co.uk
Titles:
RUGBY ADVERTISER.CO.UK

RUN WILD MEDIA - LONDON 1716342
16 Heron Quay, Canary Wharf, LONDON, E14 4JB
Tel: 020 7987 4320 **Fax:** 020 7005 0045
Email: info@runwildmedia.com
Web site: http://www.runwildmedia.com
Titles:
CANARY WHARF CITY LIFE MAGAZINE
THE CITY MAGAZINE

RUN WILD MEDIA LTD - MANCHESTER 1748998
623 Stretford Road, MANCHESTER, M16 0QA
Tel: 0161 877 6437 **Fax:** 0161 876 0771
Titles:
LIVE CHESHIRE
LIVE MANCHESTER

RUSH MEDIA LTD 1622243
4th Floor, Mercat Building, 26 Gallowgate, GLASGOW, G1
5AB **Tel:** 0141 552 5858 **Fax:** 0141 559 6050
Titles:
THE DRUM

RUSSELL PUBLISHING LTD 14415
Court Lodge, Hogtrough Hill, Brasted, WESTERHAM, TN16
1NU **Tel:** 01959 563311 **Fax:** 01959 563123
Email: info@russellpublishing.com
Web site: http://www.russellpublishing.com
Titles:
EUROPEAN PHARMACEUTICAL REVIEW
EUROPEAN RAILWAY REVIEW
EUROTRANSPORT
FX & MM
INTERNATIONAL AIRPORT REVIEW
NEW FOOD

RUSSIAN MEDIA HOUSE 1741784
12 Devereux Court, 215 Strand, LONDON, WC2R 1AP
Tel: 020 7353 5370
Web site: http://www.russianmedia.co.uk
Titles:
EXCLUSIVE LONDON
NEW STYLE
PULSE UK

THE RUSSO-BRITISH CHAMBER OF COMMERCE 13774
42 Southwark Street, LONDON, SE1 1UN
Tel: 020 7403 1706 **Fax:** 020 7403 1245
Titles:
RUSSO-BRITISH CHAMBER OF COMMERCE BULLETIN

RUSU 13103
Reading University Students Union, PO Box 230,
Whiteknights, READING, RG6 6AZ **Tel:** 0118 986 5140
Web site: http://www.rusu.co.uk
Titles:
SPARK*

RUXBURY PUBLICATIONS 17214
Scout Bottom Farm, Mytholmroyd, HEBDEN BRIDGE, HX7
5JS **Tel:** 01422 882751 **Fax:** 01422 886157
Titles:
EARLY MUSIC PERFORMER
HARPSICHORD & FORTEPIANO

RX COMMUNICATIONS 1760500
2 Long Barn, Pistyll Farm, Nercwys, MOLD, CH7 4EW
Tel: 01352 706190 **Fax:** 01352 756260
Titles:
HEALTH OUTCOMES COMMUNICATOR

RYANS HOLDINGS LTD 18307
Arlington Mews, Overton Road, LEICESTER, LE5 0JB
Tel: 0116 212 2555 **Fax:** 0116 246 0352
Titles:
COUNTRYSIDE LA VIE

THE RYEDALE GROUP 600720
Kirkdale Road, Kirkbymoorside, YORK, YO62 6YB
Tel: 01751 432505 **Fax:** 01751 432536
Titles:
  YORKSHIRE ADVERTISER (RYEDALE AND NORTH YORK
  MOORS)

S&G PUBLISHING (SCOTLAND) LTD 14429
71 Henderson Street, Bridge of Allan, STIRLING, FK9 4HG
Tel: 01786 834238 **Fax:** 01786 834295
Email: info@stannews.co.uk
Titles:
  STAN SCOTTISH TRAVEL AGENTS NEWS

S AND K PUBLISHING LIMITED 1655125
6 Yarde Hill Orchard, SIDMOUTH, EX10 9JZ
Tel: 01395 516122 **Fax:** 01395 516122
Email: sandk.publishing@which.net
Titles:
  NUCLEAR FUTURE

SAAB OWNERS CLUB OF GB 17930
PO Box 250, CARLISLE, CA2 7YB **Tel:** 07071 719000
Fax: 01228 380859
Titles:
  SAAB DRIVER

SACRED HOOP 1638451
BCM Sacred Hoop, LONDON, WC1N 3XX
Tel: 01239 682029 **Fax:** 0870 054 8946
Titles:
  SACRED HOOP

THE SAFE ENERGY JOURNAL 622925
24 Parkhead View, EDINBURGH, EH11 4RT
Tel: 0131 444 1445 **Fax:** 0131 444 1445
Web site: http://www.no2nuclearpower.org.uk
Titles:
  THE SAFE ENERGY JOURNAL

THE SAFETY & RELIABILITY SOCIETY 14460
Clayton House, 59 Piccadilly, MANCHESTER, M1 2AQ
Tel: 0161 228 7824 **Fax:** 0161 236 6977
Email: info@sars.org.uk
Web site: http://www.sars.org.uk
Titles:
  SAFETY & RELIABILITY

SAFETY SPECIALIST (SOS) LTD 1744328
18 High Street, Seal, SEVENOAKS, TN15 0AJ
Tel: 07918 765068
Email: safetyspecialist@btinternet.com
Web site: http://www.safetyspecialist.co.uk
Titles:
  SAFETY SPECIALIST

SAGA PUBLISHING LTD 15206
Saga Building, Enbrook Park, FOLKESTONE, CT20 3SE
Tel: 01303 771111 **Fax:** 01303 776699
Web site: http://www.saga.co.uk
Titles:
  SAGA MAGAZINE

SAGE PUBLICATIONS 16460
1 Oliver's Yard, 55 City Road, LONDON, EC1Y 1SP
Tel: 020 7324 8500 **Fax:** 020 7324 8600
Web site: http://www.sagepub.co.uk
Titles:
  AUTISM
  BODY & SOCIETY
  THE BRITISH JOURNAL OF DIABETES & VASCULAR
  DISEASE
  THE BRITISH JOURNAL OF VISUAL IMPAIRMENT
  BRITISH JOURNALISM REVIEW
  BUSINESS INFORMATION REVIEW
  CHILD LANGUAGE TEACHING AND THERAPY
  CHILDHOOD
  CLINICAL CHILD PSYCHOLOGY & PSYCHIATRY
  CLINICAL REHABILITATION
  CONVERGENCE
  CRITICAL SOCIAL POLICY
  CULTURAL GEOGRAPHIES
  CURRENT SOCIOLOGY
  DISCOURSE & SOCIETY
  ETHNOGRAPHY
  EUROPEAN JOURNAL OF ARCHAEOLOGY
  EUROPEAN JOURNAL OF COMMUNICATION

  EUROPEAN JOURNAL OF CULTURAL STUDIES
  EUROPEAN JOURNAL OF INDUSTRIAL RELATIONS
  EUROPEAN JOURNAL OF INTERNATIONAL RELATIONS
  EUROPEAN JOURNAL OF SOCIAL THEORY
  EUROPEAN PHYSICAL EDUCATION REVIEW
  EUROPEAN UNION POLITICS
  EUROPEAN URBAN AND REGIONAL STUDIES
  EVALUATION
  EXPOSITORY TIMES
  FEMINISM & PSYCHOLOGY
  FEMINIST THEORY
  GERMAN HISTORY
  GROUP ANALYSIS
  GROUP PROCESSES & INTERGROUP RELATIONS
  HEALTH
  THE HEALTH EDUCATION JOURNAL
  HISTORY OF THE HUMAN SCIENCES
  THE HOLOCENE
  HUMAN RELATIONS
  IMPROVING SCHOOLS
  INTERNATIONAL COMMUNICATION GAZETTE
  INTERNATIONAL JOURNAL OF CULTURAL STUDIES
  INTERNATIONAL POLITICAL SCIENCE REVIEW
  INTERNATIONAL REVIEW FOR THE SOCIOLOGY OF
  SPORT
  INTERNATIONAL SOCIAL WORK
  JOURNAL OF COMMONWEALTH LITERATURE
  JOURNAL OF CONTEMPORARY HISTORY
  JOURNAL OF EUROPEAN SOCIAL POLICY
  JOURNAL OF HEALTH PSYCHOLOGY
  JOURNAL OF INFECTION PREVENTION
  JOURNAL OF INTELLECTUAL DISABILITIES
  JOURNAL OF LIBRARIANSHIP & INFORMATION
  SCIENCE
  JOURNAL OF MATERIAL CULTURE
  JOURNAL OF PSYCHOPHARMACOLOGY
  JOURNAL OF THEORETICAL POLITICS
  JOURNALISM
  LANGUAGE AND LITERATURE
  LANGUAGE TEACHING RESEARCH
  LANGUAGE TESTING
  MANAGEMENT LEARNING
  MEDIA, CULTURE & SOCIETY
  MULTIPLE SCLEROSIS
  NATIONAL INSTITUTE ECONOMIC REVIEW
  NEW MEDIA & SOCIETY
  ORGANIZATION
  PALLIATIVE MEDICINE
  PARTY POLITICS
  PERFUSION
  PROBATION JOURNAL
  PROGRESS IN HUMAN GEOGRAPHY
  PROGRESS IN PHYSICAL GEOGRAPHY
  RATIONALITY & SOCIETY
  SCHOOL PSYCHOLOGY INTERNATIONAL
  SECOND LANGUAGE RESEARCH
  SECURITY DIALOGUE
  SEXUALITIES
  SOCIAL & LEGAL STUDIES
  SOCIAL COMPASS
  SOCIAL SCIENCE INFORMATION
  SOCIAL STUDIES OF SCIENCE
  STATISTICAL METHODS IN MEDICAL RESEARCH
  THEORY & PSYCHOLOGY
  THEORY, CULTURE & SOCIETY
  TIME & SOCIETY
  TOURIST STUDIES
  TRANSCULTURAL PSYCHIATRY
  TRAUMA
  URBAN STUDIES
  VASCULAR MEDICINE
  WAR IN HISTORY

SAHARA PUBLICATIONS 14512
Sahara House, 38 Greyhound Road, LONDON, W6 8NX
Tel: 020 7610 1387 **Fax:** 020 7610 0078
Titles:
  HEALTH CARE UPDATE FOR EASTERN & CENTRAL
  EUROPE
  LABORATORY EQUIPMENT FOR THE MIDDLE EAST &
  EASTERN EUROPE
  THE MEDICAL DIGEST MIDDLE EAST & N. AFRICA

SAILING MEDIA LTD. 1632065
10 Melina Road, LONDON, W12 9HZ **Tel:** 020 8740 6318
Titles:
  THE DAILY SAIL

SAILORS' SOCIETY 14328
350 Shirley Road, SOUTHAMPTON, SO15 3HY
Tel: 023 8051 5950 **Fax:** 023 8051 5951
Web site: http://www.sailors-society.org
Titles:
  CHART & COMPASS

THE SAINT 621559
Students' Association Building, St. Mary's Place, ST.
ANDREWS, KY16 9UZ **Tel:** 01334 422737
Fax: 01334 462716
Titles:
  THE SAINT

ST. ALBANS DIOCESE 18074
Holywell Lodge, 41 Holywell Hill, ST. ALBANS, AL1 1HE
Tel: 01727 854532 **Fax:** 01727 844469
Titles:
  ST. ALBANS DIOCESAN DIRECTORY

ST. IVES PRINTING AND PUBLISHING COMPANY 14915
High Street, ST. IVES, TR26 1RS **Tel:** 01736 795813
Fax: 01736 795020
Titles:
  ST. IVES TIMES & ECHO SERIES

ST. JOHN PATRICK PUBLISHERS LTD 12302
6 Laurence Pountney Hill, LONDON, EC4R 0BL
Tel: 020 7933 8999 **Fax:** 020 7933 8998
Web site: http://www.stjohnpatrick.com
Titles:
  DDR DIGITAL DISPLAY FOR RETAIL
  ELECTRICAL REVIEW
  ELECTRONICS WORLD
  EUROPEAN COMMUNICATIONS
  IMAGE REPORTS
  INTERNET RETAILING
  MOBILE EUROPE
  SCREEN MEDIA MAGAZINE
  SCREENS.TV

ST. MARTIN'S MAGAZINES PLC 15657
93-95 Wigmore Street, LONDON, W1U 1HH
Tel: 020 7935 0888 **Fax:** 020 7935 0898
Email: info@countryclubuk.com
Web site: http://www.countryclubuk.com
Titles:
  COUNTRY ILLUSTRATED
  COUNTRYCLUBUK

SALES PROMOTION PUBLISHING LTD 1739513
Arena House, 66-68 Pentonville Road, LONDON, N1 9HS
Tel: 020 7689 5572 **Fax:** 020 7837 5326
Email: sales@salespromo.co.uk
Web site: http://www.salespromo.co.uk
Titles:
  SALES PROMOTION

SALISBURY DISTRICT COUNCIL 18445
Bourne Hill, SALISBURY, SP1 3UZ **Tel:** 01722 434238
Fax: 01722 434440
Web site: http://www.visitsalisbury.com
Titles:
  THE SALISBURY AND STONEHENGE VISITORS GUIDE

SALISBURY NEWSPAPERS LTD 17406
Rollestone House, 8-12 Rollestone Street, SALISBURY, SP1
1DY **Tel:** 01722 426526 **Fax:** 01722 321854
Web site: http://www.thisissalisbury.co.uk
Titles:
  SALISBURY JOURNAL & AVON ADVERTISER SERIES
  WILTSHIRE SOCIETY

SALISBURY SARUM LTD 18100
PO Box 1523, LONDON, N2 9HZ **Tel:** 020 8442 0654
Fax: 020 8442 1640
Email: powderfax@btinternet.com
Web site: http://www.powdereporter.co.uk
Titles:
  PI DIRECTORY (POWDER INDUSTRY)
  POWDEREPORTER ONLINE

SALON GOLD PUBLISHING LTD 621751
223 Wickham Road, CROYDON, CR0 8TG
Tel: 020 3253 0140 **Fax:** 020 8656 8324
Email: info@salonbusiness.co.uk
Web site: http://www.salonbusiness.co.uk
Titles:
  SALON BUSINESS

SALT MEDIA LTD 1651032
1st Floor, 5 Cross Street, BARNSTAPLE, EX31 1BA
Tel: 01271 859299 **Fax:** 01271 859292
Email: info@saltmedia.co.uk
Web site: http://www.saltmedia.co.uk
Titles:
  FOOD

SALUTIONS LTD 1731735
St. James House, 676 Wilmslow Road, MANCHESTER, M20
2DM **Tel:** 0161 445 2883 **Fax:** 0161 445 2881
Web site: http://www.salutions.co.uk
Titles:
  DIDSBURY MAGAZINE
  HALE & BOWDON MAGAZINE

THE SALVATION ARMY 13139
101 Newington Causeway, LONDON, SE1 6BN
Tel: 020 7367 4910
Web site: http://www.salvationarmy.org.uk
Titles:
  KIDS ALIVE!
  THE WAR CRY

SALVATION ARMY (INTERNATIONAL) 1649743
101 Queen Victoria Street, LONDON, EC4V 4EH
Tel: 020 7332 0101 **Fax:** 020 7192 3413
Email: websa@salvationarmy.org
Web site: http://www.salvationarmy.org
Titles:
  SALVATION ARMY YEAR BOOK

SAM LTD 697324
Media House, 21 Kingsway, BEDFORD, MK42 9BJ
Tel: 0870 733 3733 **Fax:** 0870 733 3744
Titles:
  MODEL AIRCRAFT MONTHLY
  SCALE AVIATION MODELLER INTERNATIONAL
  SCALE MODELS COLLECTOR INTERNATIONAL

SAMAD PUBLICATIONS LTD 16900
218 Jubilee Street, LONDON, E1 3BS **Tel:** 020 7423 9270
Fax: 020 7423 9122
Titles:
  POTRIKA

SAMEDAN LTD 12350
16 Hampden Gurney Street, LONDON, W1H 5AL
Tel: 020 7724 3456 **Fax:** 020 7724 2632
Email: info@samedanltd.com
Web site: http://www.samedanltd.com
Titles:
  EUROPEAN PHARMACEUTICAL CONTRACTOR
  PMPS PHARMACEUTICAL MANUFACTURING &
    PACKING SOURCER

SAMEDAN PHARMACEUTICAL PUBLISHERS LTD
  1645340
16 Hampden Gurney Street, LONDON, W1H 5AL
Tel: 020 7724 3456 **Fax:** 020 7724 2632
Email: info@samedanltd.com
Web site: http://www.samedanltd.com
Titles:
  INNOVATIONS IN PHARMACEUTICAL TECHNOLOGY

SANDMAN MAGAZINE 1654104
PO Box 4250, SHEFFIELD, S8 2EL **Tel:** 0114 278 6727
Titles:
  SANDMAN

SANDRON PUBLISHING LTD 13890
87 Roundwood Way, BANSTEAD, SM7 1EJ
Tel: 01737 373099
Titles:
  ESPRIT

SARA-INT LTD 1713742
1A Salisbury Pavement, Dawes Road, LONDON, SW6 7HT
Tel: 020 7386 9499 **Fax:** 020 7386 3771
Web site: http://www.saraint.co.uk
Titles:
  COOLTURA

SATRA FOOTWEAR TECHNOLOGY CENTRE 14096
Technology Centre, Wyndham Way, Telford Way Industrial
Estate, KETTERING, NN16 8SD **Tel:** 01536 410000
Fax: 01536 410626
Email: info@satra.co.uk
Web site: http://www.satra.co.uk
Titles:
  SATRA BULLETIN

SAVA 1642229
PO Box 5603, MILTON KEYNES, MK5 8XR
Web site: http://www.sava.org.uk
Titles:
  THE HOME INSPECTOR

SAYERS PUBLISHING GROUP LTD 14089
Durand House, Manor Royal, CRAWLEY, RH10 9PY
Tel: 01293 435100 **Fax:** 01293 619988
Email: canmaker@sayers-publishing.com
Web site: http://www.sayers-publishing.com
Titles:
  THE CANMAKER
  PLASTICS IN PACKAGING

SAYONE MEDIA 1744072
Britannia House, 45-53 Prince of Wales Road, NORWICH,
NR1 1BL **Tel:** 01603 671300
Web site: http://www.sayonemedia.com
Titles:
  THE MANUFACTURER

SCALABRINI FATHERS 16122
20 Brixton Road, LONDON, SW9 6BU **Tel:** 020 7735 5164
Fax: 020 7793 0385
Titles:
  LA VOCE DEGLI ITALIANI

SCHOFIELD PUBLISHING LTD 600401
Unit 10, Cringleford Business Centre, Intwood Road,
Cringleford, NORWICH, NR4 6AU **Tel:** 01603 274130
Fax: 01603 274131
Web site: http://www.schofieldmediagroup.com
Titles:
  CONSTRUCTION TODAY
  EUROPEAN SUPPLY CHAIN MANAGEMENT
  FOODCHAIN
  MANUFACTURING TODAY EUROPE
  MODERN UTILITY MANAGEMENT
  RAILWAY STRATEGIES
  VENTURE

SCHOLASTIC UK LTD 15931
Villiers House, Clarendon Avenue, LEAMINGTON SPA, CV32
5PR **Tel:** 01926 887799 **Fax:** 01926 883331
Web site: http://www.scholastic.co.uk
Titles:
  CHILD EDUCATION PLUS
  JUNIOR EDUCATION PLUS
  LITERACY TIME PLUS
  NURSERY EDUCATION PLUS

SCHOOL BOOKSHOP ASSOCIATION LTD 15943
1 Effingham Road, LONDON, SE12 8NZ **Tel:** 020 8852 4953
Fax: 020 8318 7580
Email: enquiries@booksforkeeps.co.uk
Web site: http://www.booksforkeeps.co.uk
Titles:
  BOOKS FOR KEEPS

SCHOOL LIBRARY ASSOCIATION 14675
Unit 2, Lotmead Business Village, Lotmead Farm,
Wanborough, SWINDON, SN4 0UY **Tel:** 01793 791787
Fax: 01793 791786
Titles:
  THE SCHOOL LIBRARIAN

SCHOOLS PUBLISHING LIMITED 1762155
St. James House, 118 Greys Road, HENLEY-ON-THAMES,
RG9 1QW **Tel:** 01491 411848 **Fax:** 01491 411416
Titles:
  BUILDING FOR EDUCATION
  FURTHER EDUCATION TODAY
  INDEPENDENT EDUCATION TODAY

SCIENCE BUSINESS PUBLISHING LTD 1686482
11 Fulready Road, LONDON, E10 6DT **Tel:** 020 8539 1052
Fax: 0870 130 5680
Email: info@sciencebusiness.net
Web site: http://www.sciencebusiness.net
Titles:
  SCIENCE|BUSINESS

SCIENCE MEDIA PARTNERS LTD 1710342
6 Cardiff Road, St. Fagans, CARDIFF, CF5 6EB
Tel: 029 2056 0458 **Fax:** 029 2056 0458
Titles:
  SECURITY DOCUMENT WORLD

SCIENTIFIC PRESS LTD 12502
PO Box 21, BEACONSFIELD, HP9 1NS **Tel:** 01494 675139
Fax: 01494 670155
Titles:
  JOURNAL OF PETROLEUM GEOLOGY

SCIENTIFIC SURVEYS LTD 13956
PO Box 21, BEACONSFIELD, HP9 1NS **Tel:** 01494 675139
Fax: 01494 670155
Titles:
  GLOBAL PIPELINE MONTHLY

THE SCILLONIAN 1717952
The Paper Shop, Hugh Street, St. Mary's, ISLES OF SCILLY,
TR21 0LL **Tel:** 01720 422438
Titles:
  THE SCILLONIAN

SCISSORHANDS MEDIA 698720
211 Old Street, LONDON, EC1V 9NR **Tel:** 020 7608 6300
Titles:
  CELEBRITY HAIR NOW
  HAIR & BEAUTY INSPIRATIONS
  PERFECT HAIR

SCOPE 14577
6 Market Road, LONDON, N7 9PW **Tel:** 020 7619 7100
Web site: http://www.scope.org.uk
Titles:
  DISABILITY NOW

SCOTS INDEPENDENT (NEWSPAPERS) LTD 15621
51 Cowane Street, STIRLING, FK8 1JW **Tel:** 01259 730099
Fax: 0131 334 1739
Email: comment@scotsindependent.org
Web site: http://www.scotsindependent.org
Titles:
  SCOTS INDEPENDENT

THE SCOTSMAN PUBLICATIONS LTD 14851
108 Holyrood Road, EDINBURGH, EH8 8AS
Tel: 0131 620 8620 **Fax:** 0131 620 8491
Web site: http://www.scotsman.com
Titles:
  EVENING NEWS (EDINBURGH)
  THE GAZETTE SERIES (EDINBURGH)
  HERALD AND POST SERIES (EDINBURGH)
  THE PULSE EDINBURGH
  SCOTLAND ON SUNDAY
  SCOTLAND ON SUNDAY (CITY/LONDON OFFICE)
  THE SCOTSMAN
  THE SCOTSMAN (CITY/LONDON OFFICE)
  THE SCOTSMAN (GLASGOW OFFICE)
  THE SCOTSMAN MAGAZINE
  SCOTSMAN.COM
  SPECTRUM MAGAZINE SCOTLAND ON SUNDAY
  SPORT.SCOTSMAN.COM

SCOTT TAYLOR PUBLISHING LTD 18602
Beacon House, 2 Beacon Hill, LONDON, N7 9LY
Tel: 020 7609 5100 **Fax:** 020 7609 5100
Titles:
  BRITISH STYLE
  SAVILEROW-STYLE.COM

**SCOTTISH AND UNIVERSAL NEWSPAPERS
HAMILTON** 1643244
Press Buildings, Campbell Street, HAMILTON, ML3 6AX
Tel: 01698 283200
Web site: http://www.icscotland.co.uk

Titles:
ICSCOTLAND
THE IRVINE HERALD AND KILWINNING CHRONICLE
RUTHERGLEN REFORMER
SCOTWHEELS

SCOTTISH & UNIVERSAL NEWSPAPERS LTD   15032
Hamilton International Technology Park, Stanley Boulevard,
BLANTYRE, G72 04X **Tel:** 01698 710055 **Fax:** 01698 717509
Titles:
AIRDRIE & COATBRIDGE ADVERTISER
AYRSHIRE POST
AYRSHIRE WORLD SERIES
CLYDE WEEKLY NEWS
DUMFRIES AND GALLOWAY NEWS SERIES
DUMFRIES & GALLOWAY STANDARD
HAMILTON ADVERTISER
KILMARNOCK STANDARD
LANARK & CARLUKE ADVERTISER
LANARKSHIRE WORLD
LENNOX SERIES
PAISLEY DAILY EXPRESS
PERTHSHIRE ADVERTISER SERIES
RENFREWSHIRE WORLD
SCOTTISH RECRUITMENT
STIRLING OBSERVER SERIES
STIRLING SHOPPER SERIES
STRATHEARN HERALD
WISHAW PRESS

SCOTTISH BRAILLE PRESS   15236
Craigmillar Park, EDINBURGH, EH16 5NB
Tel: 0131 662 4445 **Fax:** 0131 662 1968
Web site: http://www.scottish-braille-press.org
Titles:
THE BRAILLE SPORTING RECORD

SCOTTISH CARAVANNER   671822
Suite 7, Buko Tower, Dalton Road, GLENROTHES, KY6 2SS
Tel: 01592 610421 **Fax:** 01592 755315
Web site: http://www.scottishcaravanner.com
Titles:
SCOTLAND AND NORTH OF ENGLAND PARKS GUIDE
SCOTTISH CARAVANNER

SCOTTISH CHILDMINDING ASSOCIATION   16198
7 Melville Terrace, STIRLING, FK8 2ND **Tel:** 01786 445377
Fax: 01786 449062
Email: information@childminding.org
Web site: http://www.childminding.org
Titles:
CHILDMINDING

SCOTTISH CND   15711
15 Barrland Street, GLASGOW, G41 1QH
Tel: 0141 423 1222 **Fax:** 0141 423 1231
Titles:
NUCLEAR FREE SCOTLAND

**THE SCOTTISH COUNCIL DEVELOPMENT AND
INDUSTRY**   18769
Campsie House, 17 Park Circus Place, GLASGOW, G3 6AH
Tel: 0141 332 9119 **Fax:** 0141 333 0039
Email: chris.watson@scdi.org.uk
Web site: http://www.scdi.org.uk
Titles:
POINTER

**SCOTTISH COUNCIL FOR VOLUNTARY
ORGANISATIONS**   14159
Mansfield Traquair Centre, 15 Mansfield Place,
EDINBURGH, EH3 6BB **Tel:** 0131 556 3882
Fax: 0131 556 0279
Email: info@scvo.org.uk
Web site: http://www.scvo.org.uk
Titles:
THIRD FORCE NEWS

SCOTTISH DAILY RECORD & SUNDAY MAIL LTD   15055
1 Central Quay, GLASGOW, G3 8DA **Tel:** 0141 309 3000
Titles:
BUSINESS 7
BUSINESS7
DAILY RECORD DIGITAL
THE GLASWEGIAN SERIES
INSIDER
SUNDAY MAIL

THE SCOTTISH LAW AGENTS SOCIETY   14326
166 Buchanan Street, GLASGOW, G1 2LW
Tel: 0141 352 4522 **Fax:** 0141 353 3819
Email: secretart@slas.co.uk
Web site: http://www.slas.co.uk
Titles:
SCOTTISH LAW GAZETTE

SCOTTISH PRE-SCHOOL PLAY ASSOCIATION   18885
21 Granville Street, GLASGOW, G3 7EE **Tel:** 0141 221 4148
Fax: 0141 221 6043
Web site: http://www.sppa.org.uk
Titles:
FIRST FIVE

SCOTTISH PROVINCIAL PRESS   15063
New Century House, Stadium Road, INVERNESS, IV1 1FG
Tel: 01463 246575
Titles:
GAZETA Z HIGHLAND
HIGHLAND NEWS SERIES
INVERNESS COURIER SERIES
NORTH STAR
ROSS-SHIRE JOURNAL AND HERALD SERIES

SCOTTISH REVIEW OF BOOKS   1654657
42 New Street, MUSSELBURGH, EH21 6JN
Tel: 0131 718 6443
Titles:
SCOTTISH REVIEW OF BOOKS

SCOTTISH SPCA   699713
603 Queensferry Road, EDINBURGH, EH4 6EA
Tel: 0131 339 0222 **Fax:** 0131 339 4777
Titles:
SCOTTISH SPCA NEWS

THE SCOTTISH SUB-AQUA CLUB   15304
The Cockburn Centre, 40 Bogmoor Place, GLASGOW, G51
4TQ **Tel:** 0141 425 1021 **Fax:** 0141 425 1021
Titles:
SCOTTISH DIVER

THE SCOTTISH WEDDING DIRECTORY   697412
Unit 26, 6 Harmony Row, GLASGOW, G51 3BA
Tel: 0141 445 5545 **Fax:** 0141 445 4468
Titles:
THE SCOTTISH WEDDING DIRECTORY

SCOTTISH WILDLIFE TRUST   1682645
Cramond House, Kirk Cramond, Cramond Glebe Road,
EDINBURGH, EH4 6NS **Tel:** 0131 312 7765
Fax: 0131 312 8705
Web site: http://www.swt.org.uk
Titles:
SCOTTISH WILDLIFE

SCOTTISH WOMEN'S RURAL INSTITUTES   15622
42 Heriot Row, EDINBURGH, EH3 6ES **Tel:** 0131 225 1724
Fax: 0131 225 8129
Email: swri@swri.demon.co.uk
Web site: http://www.swri.org.uk
Titles:
SCOTTISH HOME & COUNTRY

THE SCOUT ASSOCIATION   16097
Gilwell Park, Chingford, LONDON, E4 7QW
Tel: 020 8433 7100 **Fax:** 020 8433 7103
Web site: http://www.scouts.org.uk
Titles:
SCOUTING

SCREEN DIGEST LTD   14803
30-31 Lyme Street, LONDON, NW1 0EE **Tel:** 020 7424 2820
Fax: 020 7580 0060
Titles:
SCREEN DIGEST

SCREENTRADE MEDIA LTD   692572
PO Box 144, ORPINGTON, BR6 6LZ **Tel:** 01689 833117
Fax: 01689 833117
Email: philip@screentrademagazine.co.uk
Web site: http://www.screentrademagazine.co.uk

Titles:
SCREENTRADE MAGAZINE

SCRIPTURE UNION   17448
207-209 Queensway, Bletchley, MILTON KEYNES, MK2 2EB
Tel: 01908 856000 **Fax:** 01908 856111
Email: media@scriptureunion.org.uk
Web site: http://www.scriptureunion.org.uk
Titles:
DAILY BREAD
THE LIFE

SDI   1685628
21 High Street, Green Street Green, ORPINGTON, BR6 6BG
Tel: 01689 889100 **Fax:** 01689 889227
Email: marketing@hdi-europe.com
Web site: http://www.hdi-europe.com
Titles:
SUPPORTWORLD

SEA ANGLING NEWS LTD   1760515
27 Lower Bere Wood, WATERLOOVILLE, PO7 7NQ
Tel: 023 9226 5445 **Fax:** 023 9226 5445
Titles:
SEA ANGLING NEWS

SEA BREEZES PUBLICATIONS LTD   14336
Media House, Cronkbourne, Douglas, ISLE OF MAN, IM4
4SB **Tel:** 01624 696565 **Fax:** 01624 696565
Titles:
SEA BREEZES

SEAGER PUBLISHING LTD   15519
9 Riverside Court, Lower Bristol Road, BATH, BA2 3DZ
Tel: 01225 481440 **Fax:** 01225 481262
Titles:
FLYER
FLYER AIR-PORTAL

SEASCAPE MEDIA LTD   1675959
28 Ballmoor, Celtic Court, BUCKINGHAM, MK18 1RQ
Tel: 01329 834 545 **Fax:** 023 9238 8010
Web site: http://www.seascapemedia.co.uk
Titles:
DINGHY SAILING MAGAZINE

SEATRADE COMMUNICATIONS LTD   14346
Seatrade House, 42 North Station Road, COLCHESTER,
CO1 1RB **Tel:** 01206 545121 **Fax:** 01206 545190
Web site: http://www.seatrade-global.com
Titles:
SEATRADE
SEATRADE CRUISE REVIEW

SEED PUBLISHING LTD   1646294
1 The Courtyard, Market Square, WESTERHAM, TN16 1AZ
Tel: 01959 547000 **Fax:** 01959 565119
Web site: http://www.scratchmagazine.co.uk
Titles:
SCRATCH

SELECT PUBLICATIONS   698805
20A Swan Street, BRECHIN, DD9 6EF **Tel:** 01356 625080
Fax: 01356 622214
Titles:
RALLYACTION UK

SELECT PUBLISHER SERVICES   1724355
PO Box 6337, BOURNEMOUTH, BH1 9EH
Tel: 01202 586848
Web site: http://www.selectps.com
Titles:
SWEET MAGAZINE
WRITERS' FORUM

SELECT PUBLISHING   17736
PO Box 32, BIGGLESWADE, SG18 8TE **Tel:** 01462 819496
Fax: 01462 819496
Titles:
BEDFORDSHIRE COUNTY LIFE MAGAZINE
CAMBRIDGESHIRE COUNTY LIFE MAGAZINE

UK Publishers & Their Titles

SELFBUILD IRELAND LTD　1654813
119 Cahard, Saintfield, CO.DOWN, BT24 7LA
Tel: 028 9751 0570 **Fax:** 028 9751 0576
Email: info@selfbuild.ie
Web site: http://www.selfbuild.ie
Titles:
　SELF BUILD, EXTEND & RENOVATE

SELVEDGE　1638859
PO Box 40038, LONDON, N6 5UW **Tel:** 020 8341 9721
Fax: 020 8341 9721
Web site: http://www.selvedge.org
Titles:
　SELVEDGE

SELWOOD HOUSING SOCIETY　1726489
Bryer Ash Business Park, Bradford Road, TROWBRIDGE,
BA14 8RT **Tel:** 01225 715715 **Fax:** 01225 715950
Email: info@selwoodhousing.com
Web site: http://www.selwoodhousing.com
Titles:
　WORKING TOGETHER

SEMICONDUCTOR MEDIA LTD　1744958
Trans-World House, 100 City Road, LONDON, EC1Y 2BP
Tel: 020 7871 0123 **Fax:** 020 7871 0101
Web site: http://www.fabtech.org
Titles:
　SEMICONDUCTOR FABTECH
　SEMICONDUCTOR FABTECH

SEMINAR BOOKS　1685913
Swedenborg House, 20-21 Bloomsbury Way, LONDON,
WC1A 2TH
Titles:
　OUTLOOK

SEN MAGAZINE LTD　1749729
5 Shaw Bridge Street, CLITHEROE, BB7 1LY
Tel: 01200 453000 **Fax:** 0120 453009
Web site: http://www.senmagazine.co.uk
Titles:
　SEN SPECIAL EDUCATION NEEDS

SENA JULIA PUBLICATUS LTD　16645
PO Box 3278, 805 Finchley Road, LONDON, NW11 8DP
Tel: 020 8201 9978 **Fax:** 020 8201 9965
Titles:
　ROYALTY

**SENSE, NATIONAL DEAFBLIND & RUBELLA
ASSOCIATION**　14592
11-13 Clifton Terrace, Finsbury Park, LONDON, N4 3SR
Tel: 084 5127 0060 **Fax:** 084 5127 0061
Email: info@sense.org.uk
Web site: http://www.sense.org.uk
Titles:
　TALKING SENSE

THE SEQUAL TRUST　14558
3 Ploughmans Corner, Wharf Road, ELLESMERE, SY12 0EJ
Tel: 01691 624222 **Fax:** 01691 624222
Titles:
　SEQUAL NEWS

SER EDITORIAL BOARD　18075
School of Educational Studies, University of Dundee,
DUNDEE, DD1 4HN **Tel:** 01382 344387 **Fax:** 01382 221057
Titles:
　SCOTTISH EDUCATIONAL REVIEW

SETFORM LTD　13310
Europa House, 13-17 Ironmonger Row, LONDON, EC1V
3QG **Tel:** 020 7253 2545 **Fax:** 020 7608 1600
Titles:
　ASIA-PACIFIC ENGINEER
　EFOOD
　ENGINEERLIVE
　EUROPEAN CHEMICAL ENGINEER
　EUROPEAN DESIGN ENGINEER
　EUROPEAN ELECTRONICS ENGINEER
　EUROPEAN PROCESS ENGINEER
　INTERNATIONAL OIL & GAS ENGINEER

SEVEN PUBLISHING　1638376
Sea Containers House, 20 Upper Ground, LONDON, SE1
9PD **Tel:** 020 7775 7775 **Fax:** 020 7775 7705
Email: info@7publishing.co.uk
Titles:
　DELICIOUS
　FAMILY WORDSEARCH
　SAINSBURY'S MAGAZINE

SEVEN SQUARED　14668
Sea Containers House, 20 Upper Ground, LONDON, SE1
9PD **Tel:** 020 7775 5777 **Fax:** 020 7775 5711
Web site: http://www.sevensquared.co.uk
Titles:
　ACE TENNIS MAGAZINE
　GALA BUZZ
　GO TO...
　HERITAGE TODAY
　INSPIRE
　THE JOB
　LIGHTER LIFE
　SAINSBURY'S FRESH IDEAS
　SAINSBURY'S FRESH IDEAS FOR YOUNG FAMILIES
　WATERSTONE'S BOOKS QUARTERLY

SFEDI LTD　17138
PO Box 5753, MILTON KEYNES, MK10 1AE
Tel: 01525 211145 **Fax:** 01525 211145
Web site: http://www.sfedi.co.uk
Titles:
　THE SUCCESSFUL OWNER MANAGER

SFHA　1643857
Pegasus House, 375 West George Street, GLASGOW, G2
4LW **Tel:** 0141 332 8113 **Fax:** 0141 332 9684
Titles:
　HOUSING SCOTLAND

S.G. MEDIA PUBLICATIONS LTD　15973
39 Little Mount Sion, TUNBRIDGE WELLS, TN1 1YS
Tel: 01892 517320 **Fax:** 01892 547370
Titles:
　THE INDEX MAGAZINE

SGC MEDIA LTD　1649711
216 St. Vincent Street, GLASGOW, G2 5SG
Tel: 0870 011 5010 **Fax:** 0141 221 8434
Titles:
　PROPERTY EXECUTIVE MAGAZINE

THE SHAKESPEARE BIRTHPLACE TRUST　1606031
Shakespeare Centre, Henley Street, STRATFORD-UPON-
AVON, CV37 6QW **Tel:** 01789 204016 **Fax:** 01789 296083
Email: magazine@shakespeare.org.uk
Web site: http://www.shakespeare.org.uk
Titles:
　SHAKESPEARE AT THE CENTRE

THE SHAKESPEARE GLOBE TRUST　621719
21 New Globe Walk, Bankside, LONDON, SE1 9DT
Tel: 020 7902 1400 **Fax:** 020 7902 1401
Web site: http://www.shakespeares-globe.org
Titles:
　AROUND THE GLOBE

SHANKILL COMMUNITY MEDIA LTD　1656154
177-179 Shankill Road, BELFAST, BT13 1FP
Tel: 028 9031 2882 **Fax:** 028 9072 9002
Titles:
　SHANKILL MIRROR

SHARE INTERNATIONAL　627619
PO Box 3677, LONDON, NW5 1RU **Tel:** 020 7482 1113
Titles:
　SHARE INTERNATIONAL

SHAW & SONS LTD　18027
Shaway House, 21 Bourne Park, Bourne Road, CRAYFORD,
DA1 4BZ **Tel:** 01322 621100 **Fax:** 01322 550553
Web site: http://www.shaws.co.uk
Titles:
　NAPO PROBATION DIRECTORY
　PROBATION BULLETIN

　SHAW'S DIRECTORY OF COURTS IN THE UNITED
　　KINGDOM
　SHAW'S LOCAL GOVERNMENT DIRECTORY

SHEEN PUBLISHING LTD　13530
50 Queens Road, BUCKHURST HILL, IG9 5DD
Tel: 020 8504 1661 **Fax:** 020 8505 4336
Web site: http://www.sheenpublishing.co.uk
Titles:
　MACHINERY WORLD
　PLANT WORLD
　REFURB
　SECURE TIMES

SHEENGATE PUBLISHING LTD　17288
Unit A4, Kingsway Business Park, Oldfield Road,
HAMPTON, TW12 2HD **Tel:** 020 8939 5600
Fax: 020 8939 5610
Web site: http://www.sheengate.co.uk
Titles:
　THE ELMBRIDGE LIFESTYLE MAGAZINE
　THE GUILDFORD MAGAZINE
　KINGSTON MAGAZINE
　THE RICHMOND MAGAZINE
　THE WOKING LIFESTYLE MAGAZINE

SHEFFIELD MERCURY LTD　1649005
PO Box 3689, SHEFFIELD, S2 7WS **Tel:** 01142 763644
Fax: 01142 763644
Web site: http://www.mercurynewspaper.co.uk
Titles:
　THE MERCURY NEWSPAPER

SHEFFIELD NEWSPAPERS LTD　13060
York Street, SHEFFIELD, S1 1PU **Tel:** 0114 276 7676
Fax: 0114 275 3551
Titles:
　PROFILE (SHEFFIELD)
　SHEFFIELD JOURNAL SERIES
　SHEFFIELD TELEGRAPH
　SHEFFIELD WEEKLY GAZETTE
　THE STAR GREEN 'UN (SHEFFIELD)
　THE STAR SHEFFIELD

SHELTER　13516
88 Old Street, LONDON, EC1V 9HU **Tel:** 0844 515 2000
Fax: 0844 515 2167
Web site: http://www.shelter.org.uk
Titles:
　ROOF

THE SHEPHARD GROUP　13643
268 Bath Road, SLOUGH, SL1 4DX **Tel:** 01753 727001
Fax: 01753 727002
Email: publishing@shephard.co.uk
Web site: http://www.shephard.co.uk
Titles:
　DEFENCE HELICOPTER
　INFLIGHT ONLINE
　LOW-FARE & REGIONAL AIRLINES
　UNMANNED VEHICLES
　UNMANNED VEHICLES HANDBOOK
　UVONLINE

SHEPHERD PUBLISHING LTD　16327
The Sheep Centre, MALVERN, WR13 6PH
Tel: 01684 565533 **Fax:** 01684 565577
Email: info@shepherdpublishing.co.uk
Titles:
　BEEF FARMER
　SHEEP FARMER

SHERBORNE GIBBS　1644402
3 Duchess Place, BIRMINGHAM, B16 8NH
Tel: 0121 4544114 **Fax:** 0121 454 1190
Web site: http://www.sherbornegibbs.co.uk
Titles:
　THE BRITISH JOURNAL OF PRIMARY CARE NURSING
　THE BRITISH JOURNAL OF PRIMARY CARE NURSING -
　　RESPIRATORY DISEASES AND ALLERGY

SHERBORNE PUBLISHING　15721
PO Box 42184, LONDON, SW8 2WD **Tel:** 020 7819 1170
Titles:
　SOCIALIST REVIEW

SHERWIN PUBLICATIONS LTD 13480
PO Box 88, EDENBRIDGE, TN8 6ZW **Tel:** 01732 868288
Fax: 01732 865874

Titles:
 FROZEN & CHILLED FOODS
 TCS&D

THE SHETLAND PONY STUD-BOOK SOCIETY 18102
22 York Place, PERTH, PH2 8EH **Tel:** 01738 623471
Fax: 01738 442274
Email: enquiries@shetlandponystudbooksociety.co.uk
Web site: http://www.shetlandponystudbooksociety.co.uk

Titles:
 THE SHETLAND PONY STUD-BOOK SOCIETY
 MAGAZINE

THE SHETLAND TIMES LTD 15064
Gremista Industrial Estate, Gremista, Lerwick, SHETLAND,
ZE1 0PX **Tel:** 01595 693622 **Fax:** 01595 694637
Web site: http://www.shetlandtoday.co.uk/shetlandlife

Titles:
 SHETLAND LIFE
 THE SHETLAND TIMES

SHIATSU SOCIETY 15168
PO Box 4580, RUGBY, CV21 9EL **Tel:** 0845 130 4560
Fax: 01788 555052
Email: admin@shiatsusociety.org
Web site: http://www.shiatsusociety.org

Titles:
 SHIATSU SOCIETY NEWS

SHORTHORN CATTLE SOCIETY 18878
4th Street, NAC, Stoneleigh Park, KENILWORTH, CV8 2LG
Tel: 024 7669 6549 **Fax:** 024 7669 6729

Titles:
 SHORTHORN JOURNAL

SHORTLIST MEDIA LTD 1740410
6-8 Emerald Street, LONDON, WC1N 3QA
Tel: 020 7611 9700 **Fax:** 020 7611 9701

Titles:
 SHORTLIST

SHOUT! PUBLICATIONS 17363
PO Box YR46, LEEDS, LS9 6XG **Tel:** 0113 248 5700
Fax: 0113 295 6097
Web site: http://www.shoutweb.co.uk

Titles:
 SHOUT!

SHOW MEDIA LTD 1634295
Ground Floor, 1-2 Ravey Street, LONDON, EC2A 4QP
Tel: 020 3222 0101 **Fax:** 020 7739 1369
Email: info@showmedia.net
Web site: http://www.showmedia.net

Titles:
 EMPORIUM
 THE QUARTERLY
 ST FASHION
 ST MEN

SHROPSHIRE NEWSPAPERS LTD 12449
Waterloo Road, Ketley, TELFORD, TF1 5HU
Tel: 01952 242424 **Fax:** 01952 254605
Email: starmail@shropshirestar.co.uk

Titles:
 BRIDGNORTH JOURNAL
 CHRONICLE & JOURNAL SERIES
 THE FARMER
 THE SHROPSHIRE MAGAZINE
 TELFORD JOURNAL

SIEMEX INTERNATIONAL LTD 13682
Office 8, Unit 1-2 Wyvern Estate, Beverley Way, NEW
MALDEN, KT3 4PH **Tel:** 020 8949 0088 **Fax:** 020 8949 0160
Email: info@simex.biz
Web site: http://www.coffeeandcocoa.net

Titles:
 COFFEE AND COCOA INTERNATIONAL
 COFFEE INTERNATIONAL DIRECTORY

SIFT MEDIA LTD 622019
100 Victoria Street, BRISTOL, BS1 6HZ **Tel:** 0117 915 3344
Fax: 0117 915 9630

Email: info@siftmedia.co.uk
Web site: http://www.siftmedia.co.uk

Titles:
 ACCOUNTINGWEB.CO.UK
 BUSINESS MANAGEMENT ZONE
 BUSINESSZONE
 HR ZONE
 MYCUSTOMER.COM
 TRAININGZONE

SIGN UPDATE LTD 16921
Allens Orchard, Chipping Warden, BANBURY, OX17 1LX
Tel: 01295 660666 **Fax:** 0506 112 0149
Email: roger@sign-update-magazine.co.uk
Web site: http://www.sign-update-magazine.co.uk

Titles:
 SIGN UPDATE

SIGNATURE PUBLISHING LTD 1740693
Headley House, Headley Road, Grayshott, HINDHEAD,
GU26 6TU **Tel:** 01428 601020 **Fax:** 01428 601027
Email: info@signaturepl.co.uk
Web site: http://www.signaturepl.co.uk

Titles:
 DINOMITE
 EASY PEAZY
 FUNTASTIC
 THE HOME MAGAZINE

SILVER BULLET PUBLISHING 1644349
1st Floor, Colonial Buildings, 59-61 Hatton Garden,
LONDON, EC1N 8LS **Tel:** 020 7798 2136
Fax: 020 7798 2031
Email: info@b2bm.biz
Web site: http://www.b2bm.biz

Titles:
 B2B MARKETING

SILVER SEA PRESS 1715943
Bay Street Cottage, The Street, Dallington, HEATHFIELD,
TN21 9NH **Tel:** 07828 978328

Titles:
 SCOTTISH ISLANDS EXPLORER

SILVERDART PUBLISHING 1653302
211 Linton House, 164-180 Union Street, LONDON, SE1
OLH **Tel:** 020 7928 7770
Web site: http://www.silverdart.co.uk

Titles:
 INFORMED

SIMMONS-BOARDMAN PUBLISHING CORPORATION
 14416
46 Killigrew Street, FALMOUTH, TR11 3PP
Tel: 01326 313945 **Fax:** 01326 211576
Web site: http://www.railjournal.com

Titles:
 INTERNATIONAL RAILWAY JOURNAL

SIMON MOUNSEY LTD 1643242
Rye House, 47 Oakfield Avenue, Somersall,
CHESTERFIELD, S40 3LE **Tel:** 01246 569967
Fax: 01246 567932
Email: mail@simonmounsey.com
Web site: http://www.simonmounsey.com

Titles:
 FEED STATISTICS
 HANDBOOK OF FEED ADDITIVES

SIMPLE WORLD LTD 1751837
Brecon House, 16 Albion Place, MAIDSTONE, ME14 5DZ
Tel: 0845 094 1747

Titles:
 OVERSEAS PROPERTY TRADER

SIMPLY DV LTD 1676085
29 Florin Close, Pennyland, MILTON KEYNES, MK15 8AG
Tel: 01908 673294
Email: info@simplydv.co.uk
Web site: http://www.simplydv.co.uk

Titles:
 SIMPLYDV.CO.UK

SIMPLY MARCOMMS 1645392
18 Generator Hall, Electric Wharf, COVENTRY, CV1 4JL
Tel: 0870 199 4044 **Fax:** 0870 777 4360
Email: info@simplymarcomms.co.uk
Web site: http://www.simplymarcomms.co.uk

Titles:
 AEROSPACE INDUSTRY DIRECTORY
 AGRICULTURE INDUSTRY DIRECTORY
 ARCA NEWS
 ASBESTOS INDUSTRY DIRECTORY
 AUTOMOTIVE INDUSTRY DIRECTORY
 CHEMICALS INDUSTRY DIRECTORY
 CONSTRUCTION INDUSTRY DIRECTORY
 CONSTRUCTION PRODUCTS INDUSTRY DIRECTORY
 DEMOLITION INDUSTRY DIRECTORY
 ENERGY & ENVIRONMENT INDUSTRY DIRECTORY
 ENGINEERING INDUSTRY DIRECTORY
 FACILITIES MANAGEMENT & MAINTENANCE INDUSTRY
 DIRECTORY
 FINANCE INDUSTRY DIRECTORY
 HEALTH & SAFETY INDUSTRY DIRECTORY
 HVAC INDUSTRY DIRECTORY
 IT INDUSTRY DIRECTORY
 MANUFACTURING INDUSTRY DIRECTORY
 NUCLEAR INDUSTRY DIRECTORY
 PACKAGING INDUSTRY DIRECTORY
 PHARMACEUTICAL INDUSTRY DIRECTORY
 PLANT HIRE INDUSTRY DIRECTORY
 PR & MARKETING INDUSTRY DIRECTORY
 RECYCLING & WASTE INDUSTRY DIRECTORY
 ROOFING INDUSTRY DIRECTORY
 SECURITY INDUSTRY DIRECTORY
 TELECOMS INDUSTRY DIRECTORY
 TRANSPORT INDUSTRY DIRECTORY

SING TAO (UK) LTD 16061
1st Floor, Unit 3, Technology Park, Colindeep Lane,
LONDON, NW9 6BX **Tel:** 020 8732 7628 **Fax:** 020 8732 7630
Web site: http://www.singtaoeu.com

Titles:
 EAST WEEK
 SING TAO DAILY (EUROPEAN EDITION)

SITUATION PUBLISHING LTD. 17407
33 Glasshouse Street, LONDON, W1B 5DG
Tel: 020 3178 6500 **Fax:** 020 3178 6484

Titles:
 THE REGISTER

SIXTYPLUSURFERS 1645349
241 Chase Side, Southgate, LONDON, N14 5LD
Tel: 020 8440 3340 **Fax:** 020 8866 3686
Web site: http://www.sixtyplusurfers.co.uk

Titles:
 SIXTYPLUSURFERS

SKETCH NEWS 1691148
Davina House, Suite 205, 137-149 Goswell Road, LONDON,
EC1V 7ET **Tel:** 020 7328 7251

Titles:
 THE WESTMINSTER NEWS

SKI CLUB OF GB 15274
The White House, 57-63 Church Road, Wimbledon,
LONDON, SW19 5SB **Tel:** 020 8410 2000
Fax: 0845 458 0781
Email: skiers@skiclub.co.uk
Web site: http://www.skiclub.co.uk

Titles:
 SKI+BOARD

SKI SOLUTIONS LTD 1745942
84 Pembroke Road, LONDON, W8 6NX
Web site: http://www.skisolutions.com

Titles:
 IFYOUSKI.COM

SKIDDLE LTD 1744808
The Benchmark, Ribbleton Street, PRESTON, PR1 5BA
Tel: 0870 896 6896

Titles:
 SKIDDLE.COM

SLEEPER MEDIA LTD 1751802
Waterloo Place, Watson Square, STOCKPORT, SK1 3AZ
Tel: 020 476 8390 **Fax:** 020 476 7214

Titles:
 SLEEPER

UK Publishers & Their Titles

SLS LEGAL PUBLICATIONS (NI)   12541
50 Malone Road, BELFAST, BT9 5BS **Tel:** 028 9066 7711
Fax: 028 9066 6773
Titles:
  BULLETIN OF NORTHERN IRELAND LAW

SMALL WORLD PUBLISHING LTD   691218
26 Carnarvon Road, Redlands, BRISTOL, BS6 7DU
Tel: 0117 942 6977 **Fax:** 0117 907 0717
Web site: http://www.smallworldpublishing.co.uk
Titles:
  THE PRODUCER

SMART CARD NEWS LTD   13385
3 Anchor Springs, Duke Street, LITTLEHAMPTON, BN17
6BP **Tel:** 01903 734677 **Fax:** 01903 734318
Email: info@smartcard.co.uk
Web site: http://www.smartcard.co.uk
Titles:
  SMART CARD AND IDENTITY NEWS

SMART DEVICES LTD   1681109
The Reeds, Frensham, FARNHAM, GU10 3BP
Tel: 0870 027 2127
Web site: http://www.smartdevicesdirect.com
Titles:
  SMARTDEVICESDIRECT

SMART GROUP   15175
Western House, St. James Place, High Street, CRANLEIGH,
GU6 8RL **Tel:** 01483 276788 **Fax:** 01483 277646
Titles:
  PA ENEWS
  SMART BUSINESS TRAVEL
  SMART PA

SMART-QUOTES LTD   1643836
1 Liverpool Street, LONDON, EC2M 7QD **Tel:** 020 7932 4157
Web site: http://www.smart-quotes.com
Titles:
  SMART-QUOTES

G.H. SMITH & SON   15006
Advertiser Office, The Market Place, Easingwold, YORK,
YO61 3AB **Tel:** 01347 821329 **Fax:** 01347 822576
Email: info@ghsmith.com
Web site: http://www.ghsmith.com
Titles:
  EASINGWOLD ADVERTISER & WEEKLY NEWS

SMITHS NEWS   1690182
Wakefield House, Pipers Way, SWINDON, SN3 1RF
Tel: 01793 616161 **Fax:** 01793 542088
Email: info@smithsnews.co.uk
Web site: http://www.smithsnews.co.uk
Titles:
  CONNECT2U

SMMT LTD   17192
Forbes House, Halkin Street, LONDON, SW1X 7DS
Tel: 020 7235 7000 **Fax:** 020 7235 7112
Web site: http://www.smmt.co.uk
Titles:
  TRANSPORT NEWS BRIEF

SMS LTD   16270
Commerce House, 6 Grove Road, HITCHIN, SG5 1SE
Tel: 01462 620222 **Fax:** 01462 642464
Titles:
  STORAGE TODAY

SNG PUBLISHING LTD   1728606
Unit 22, Midsomer Enterprise Park, Radstock Road,
Midsomer Norton, RADSTOCK, BA3 2BB
Tel: 0870 774 3049 **Fax:** 0870 758 5906
Email: info@sng-publishing.co.uk
Web site: http://www.sng-publishing.co.uk
Titles:
  THE ESSENTIAL BOOK: HIP! HEATING ENGINEERS,
    INSTALLERS AND PLUMBERS
  THE ESSENTIAL BOOK: SPARKS
  THE HIP! MAGAZINE: HEATING ENGINEERS,
    INSTALLERS AND PLUMBERS
  SPARKS MAGAZINE

SNL FINANCIAL   1759491
8th Floor, 7 Birchin Lane, LONDON, EC3V 9BW
Tel: 020 7398 0870 **Fax:** 020 7398 0871
Titles:
  SNL FINANCIAL

SNS PUBLICATIONS   1638818
117 Whitechapel Road, LONDON, E1 1DT
Tel: 020 7377 1919 **Fax:** 020.7377 5004
Titles:
  THE MUSLIM WEEKLY

SO ESTEEM LTD   1743317
16 Stratford Place, LONDON, W1C 1BF **Tel:** 0870 765 6110
Fax: 0870 765 6120
Titles:
  SO ESTEEM

SOCCER INVESTOR LTD   1627198
16 Butlers & Colonial Wharf, LONDON, SE1 2PX
Tel: 020 7934 9179 **Fax:** 020 7934 9200
Titles:
  CENTRE CIRCLE
  SOCCER INVESTOR DAILY

SOCIAL AFFAIRS UNIT MAGAZINES LTD   1748047
11 Manchester Square, LONDON, W1U 3PW
Tel: 020 7563 9840 **Fax:** 020 7563 9841
Titles:
  STANDPOINT

**SOCIALIST ENVIRONMENT & RESOURCES
ASSOCIATION**   15708
1 London Bridge, 2nd Floor, Downstream Buildings,
LONDON, SE1 9BG **Tel:** 020 7022 1985
Web site: http://www.sera.org.uk
Titles:
  NEW GROUND

SOCIALIST NEWSPAPER PUBLICATIONS   15718
1B Waterlow Road, LONDON, N19 5NJ **Tel:** 020 7281 7024
Fax: 020 7263 9345
Titles:
  RED PEPPER
  REDPEPPER ONLINE

THE SOCIETY FOR COMPUTERS & LAW   14310
The Coach House, Black Dog Hill, Studley, CALNE, SN11
9LT **Tel:** 01249 822400 **Fax:** 01249 822522
Email: lseastham@aol.com
Web site: http://www.scl.org
Titles:
  COMPUTERS & LAW

THE SOCIETY FOR GENERAL MICROBIOLOGY   12709
Marlborough House, Basingstoke Road, Spencers Wood,
READING, RG7 1AG **Tel:** 0118 988 1800
Fax: 0118 988 5656
Web site: http://www.sgm.ac.uk
Titles:
  MICROBIOLOGY TODAY

SOCIETY FOR POPULAR ASTRONOMY   17350
c/o SPA Secretary, 36 Fairway, Keyworth, NOTTINGHAM,
NG12 5DU **Tel:** 0115 937 3610 **Fax:** 0115 937 3610
Web site: http://www.popastro.com
Titles:
  POPULAR ASTRONOMY

**SOCIETY FOR THE PROMOTION OF HELLENIC
STUDIES**   17945
Senate House, Malet Street, LONDON, WC1E 7HU
Tel: 020 7862 8730 **Fax:** 020 7862 8731
Titles:
  JOURNAL OF HELLENIC STUDIES

SOCIETY FOR UNDERWATER TECHNOLOGY   16814
80 Coleman Street, LONDON, EC2R 5BJ **Tel:** 020 7382 2601
Fax: 020 7382 2684
Email: info@sut.org
Web site: http://www.sut.org

Titles:
  UNDERWATER TECHNOLOGY

SOCIETY GOLF MAGAZINE LTD   15256
P.O. Box 1252, BRIGHTON, BN1 2YN **Tel:** 0870 600 5566
Fax: 01273 726153
Titles:
  SOCIETY GOLF

SOCIETY OF ANAESTHETISTS OF THE SW REGION
  14490
Department of Anaesthesia, Royal Devon and Exeter
Hospital, Barrack Road, EXETER **Tel:** 01392 411611
Titles:
  ANAESTHESIA POINTS WEST

THE SOCIETY OF ANTIQUARIES OF LONDON   18464
Burlington House, Piccadilly, LONDON, W1J 0BE
Tel: 020 7479 7089 **Fax:** 020 7287 6967
Email: admin@sal.org.uk
Web site: http://www.sal.org.uk
Titles:
  ANTIQUARIES JOURNAL

SOCIETY OF AUTHORS   15829
84 Drayton Gardens, LONDON, SW10 9SB
Tel: 020 7373 6642 **Fax:** 020 7373 5768
Email: info@societyofauthors.org
Web site: http://www.societyofauthors.org
Titles:
  AUTHOR

SOCIETY OF AUTOMOTIVE HISTORIANS IN BRITAIN
  1760876
55 Howletts Lane, RUISLIP, HA4 7SA
Titles:
  SAHB TIMES

SOCIETY OF BUSINESS ECONOMISTS   13284
11 Baytree Walk, WATFORD, WD17 4RX **Tel:** 01923 237287
Titles:
  THE BUSINESS ECONOMIST

**THE SOCIETY OF CABLE AND TELECOMMUNICATION
ENGINEERS**   1751606
Communications House, 41A Market Street, WATFORD,
WD18 0PN **Tel:** 01923 815500 **Fax:** 01923 803203
Titles:
  BROADBAND

THE SOCIETY OF CHIROPODISTS AND PODIATRISTS
  14564
1 Fellmongers Path, Tower Bridge Road, LONDON, SE1 3LY
Tel: 0845 450 3720 **Fax:** 0845 450 3721
Email: enquiries@scpod.org
Web site: http://www.feetforlife.org
Titles:
  PODIATRY NOW

SOCIETY OF DYERS & COLOURISTS   13722
PO Box 244, Perkin House, 82 Grattan Road, BRADFORD,
BD1 2JB **Tel:** 01274 725138 **Fax:** 01274 392888
Web site: http://www.sdc.org.uk
Titles:
  COLORATION TECHNOLOGY

THE SOCIETY OF FOOD, HYGIENE AND TECHNOLOGY
  14065
The Granary, Middleton House Farm, Tamworth Rd,
STAFFORDSHIRE, B78 2BD **Tel:** 01827 872500
Fax: 01827 875800
Email: admin@sofht.co.uk
Web site: http://www.sofht.co.uk
Titles:
  SOFHT FOCUS

SOCIETY OF GENEALOGISTS ENTERPRISES LTD   16130
14 Charterhouse Buildings, Goswell Road, LONDON, EC1M
7BA **Tel:** 020 7251 8799 **Fax:** 020 7250 1800
Titles:
  GENEALOGISTS' MAGAZINE

SOCIETY OF GLASS TECHNOLOGY 13712
Unit 9, Twelve O'Clock Court, 21 Attercliffe Road, SHEFFIELD, S4 7WW **Tel:** 0114 263 4455
Fax: 0114 263 4411
Web site: http://www.sgt.org
Titles:
GLASS TECHNOLOGY
PHYSICS & CHEMISTRY OF GLASSES

SOCIETY OF HOMEOPATHS 17204
11 Brookfield, Duncan Close, Moulton Park Industrial Estate, NORTHAMPTON, NN3 6WL **Tel:** 0845 450 6611
Fax: 0845 450 6622
Email: info@homeopathy-soh.org
Web site: http://www.homeopathy-soh.org
Titles:
THE HOMEOPATH

SOCIETY OF LEATHER TECHNOLOGISTS AND CHEMISTS 13723
49 North Park Street, DEWSBURY, WF13 4LZ
Tel: 01924 460864 **Fax:** 01924 460864
Web site: http://www.sltc.org
Titles:
JOURNAL OF THE SOCIETY OF LEATHER TECHNOLOGISTS AND CHEMISTS

THE SOCIETY OF LONDON THEATRE 17976
32 Rose Street, LONDON, WC2E 9ET **Tel:** 020 7557 6700
Fax: 020 7557 6799
Titles:
THE LONDON THEATRE GUIDE

SOCIOLOGICAL RESEARCH ONLINE CONSORTIUM 621643
Department of Sociology, University of Surrey, GUILDFORD, GU2 7XH **Tel:** 01483 876989
Web site: http://www.socresonline.org.uk
Titles:
SOCIOLOGICAL RESEARCH ONLINE

SOIL ASSOCIATION 13986
South Plaza, Marlborough Street, BRISTOL, BS1 3NX
Tel: 0117 314 5000 **Fax:** 0117 314 5001
Email: info@soilassociation.org
Web site: http://www.soilassociation.org
Titles:
LIVING EARTH
ORGANIC FARMING

SOLO PUBLISHING LTD 15663
B403A The Chocolate Factory, 5 Clarendon Road, LONDON, N22 6XJ **Tel:** 020 8881 0550 **Fax:** 020 8881 0990
Titles:
BIRDWATCH

SOLUTIONS PUBLISH LTD 1603373
15-17 Black Friars Lane, LONDON, EC4V 6ER
Tel: 020 7236 1118 **Fax:** 020 7489 5809
Titles:
EXECUTIVE PA
PTA

SOMA DIGITAL LTD 1711818
PO Box 55106, LONDON, N12 9WU **Tel:** 020 8445 8041
Titles:
MANSIZED

SOMETHING DIFFERENT MAGAZINE 1685627
55 Dores Road, Upper Stratton, SWINDON, SN2 7QU
Tel: 01793 700566
Titles:
SOMETHING DIFFERENT FOR WEDDINGS

THE SON NEWSPAPER 1655222
PO Box 3070, LITTLEHAMPTON, BN17 6WX
Tel: 01903 732190 **Fax:** 01903 733492
Titles:
THE SON NEWSPAPER
SORTED

SONGLINES PUBLICATIONS LTD 1728109
PO Box 54209, LONDON, W14 0WU **Tel:** 020 7317 2777
Fax: 020 7371 2220
Email: info@songlines.co.uk
Web site: http://www.songlines.co.uk
Titles:
SONGLINES

SONIC NETWORK 695831
3rd Floor, 74 Great Eastern Street, LONDON, EC2A 3JL
Tel: 020 7613 0555
Web site: http://www.sonicnetwork.net
Titles:
CLICKMUSIC

SOROPTIMIST INTERNATIONAL 17877
87 Glisson Road, CAMBRIDGE, CB1 2HG
Tel: 01223 311833 **Fax:** 01223 467951
Email: hq@soroptimistinternational.org
Web site: http://www.soroptimistinternational.org
Titles:
INTERNATIONAL SOROPTIMIST

SOS PUBLICATIONS LTD 16689
Media House, Trafalgar Way, Bar Hill, CAMBRIDGE, CB23 8SQ **Tel:** 01954 789888 **Fax:** 01954 789895
Email: sos.feedback@soundonsound.com
Titles:
PERFORMING MUSICIAN
SOUND ON SOUND

SOUND CULTURE LTD 1744822
80 New North Road, HUDDERSFIELD, HD1 5NE
Tel: 01484 451730 **Fax:** 01484 451729
Titles:
ALIVE.CO.UK

SOUND SENSE 17927
Riverside House, Rattlesden, BURY ST EDMUNDS, IP30 0SF
Titles:
SOUNDING BOARD

SOUNDAROUND ASSOCIATIONS 600343
74 Glentham Road, Barnes, LONDON, SW13 9JJ
Tel: 020 8741 3332
Web site: http://www.soundaround.org
Titles:
SOUNDAROUND

SOUTH AMERICAN MISSION SOCIETY 18090
Allen Gardiner Cottage, Pembury Road, TUNBRIDGE WELLS, TN2 3QU **Tel:** 01892 538647 **Fax:** 01892 525797
Web site: http://www.samsgb.org
Titles:
SHARE

SOUTH EAST BIKER 1768191
Wirral Acre, Eridge Road, CROWBOROUGH, TN6 2SP
Tel: 01892 610808
Titles:
SOUTH EAST BIKER

SOUTH NEWS PLC 622460
Spectrum House, Hillview Gardens, Hendon, LONDON, NW4 2JR **Tel:** 020 8203 5100
Titles:
INFORMER (RICHMOND & TWICKENHAM)

SOUTH WALES ARGUS LTD 14850
Cardiff Road, Maesglas, NEWPORT, NP20 3QN
Tel: 01633 810000 **Fax:** 01633 777202
Titles:
SOUTH WALES ARGUS

SOUTH WEST COAST PATH ASSOCIATION 18270
Bowker House, Lee Mill Bridge, Devon, IVYBRIDGE, PL21 9EF **Tel:** 01752 896237 **Fax:** 01752 893654
Email: info@swcp.org.uk
Web site: http://www.swcp.org.uk
Titles:
SOUTH WEST COAST PATH ANNUAL GUIDE

SOUTH WEST MEDIA GROUP LTD 16163
17 Brest Road, Derriford, PLYMOUTH, PL6 5AA
Tel: 01852 765500
Titles:
DEVON WEDDINGS
THE EXETER TIMES
EXPRESS & ECHO (EXETER)
THE EXTRA (PLYMOUTH)
THE GAZETTE SERIES (MID DEVON)
HERALD EXPRESS
THE HERALD (PLYMOUTH)
TORBAY WEEKENDER SERIES
WESTERN MORNING NEWS

SOUTH WEST WALES MEDIA LTD 17213
PO Box 14, Adelaide Street, SWANSEA, SA1 1QT
Tel: 01792 510000 **Fax:** 01792 514697
Email: postnews@swwmedia.co.uk
Web site: http://www.thisisswansea.co.uk
Titles:
THE COURIER SERIES (NEATH & PORT TALBOT)
JOURNAL SERIES (CARMARTHEN)
LLANELLI STAR SERIES
NEATH AND PORT TALBOT TRIBUNE
NEGESYDD
SOUTH WALES EVENING POST
SWANSEA HERALD OF WALES

SOUTH YORKSHIRE NEWSPAPERS LTD 14955
Sunny Bar, DONCASTER, DN1 1NB **Tel:** 01302 819111
Fax: 01302 814324
Email: editorial@doncastertoday.co.uk
Web site: http://www.doncasterfreepress.co.uk
Titles:
COMMUNITY NEWSLETTER SERIES
DONCASTER ADVERTISER
DONCASTER FREE PRESS
THE EPWORTH BELLS & CROWLE ADVERTISER
GAINSBOROUGH NEWS AND STANDARD SERIES
GOOLE, HOWDEN COURIER
GUARDIAN SERIES (WORKSOP)
RETFORD TRADER GUARDIAN
SELBY TIMES SERIES
SOUTH YORKSHIRE TIMES
THORNE AND DISTRICT GAZETTE
WORKSOP TRADER

SOUTHAMPTON CITY COUNCIL 15575
Corporate Communications, Southampton City Council, Civic Centre, SOUTHAMPTON, SO14 7LY
Tel: 023 8083 3660 **Fax:** 023 8023 4537
Web site: http://www.southampton.gov.uk
Titles:
SOUTHAMPTON CITY VIEW

SOUTHERN PUBLICATIONS LTD 622993
Homelife House, 26-32 Oxford Road, BOURNEMOUTH, BH8 8EZ **Tel:** 01202 310011 **Fax:** 01202 298577
Titles:
COMPASS MAGAZINE

SOUTHERN RAG LTD 15366
PO Box 337, LONDON, N4 1TW **Tel:** 020 8340 9651
Fax: 020 8348 5626
Titles:
FROOTS

SOUTHERN ROCK LTD 1719659
PO Box 2113, LEIGH-ON-SEA, SS9 5WW
Tel: 01702 512512
Titles:
UK ROCK

SOUTHWARD NEWSPAPER LTD. 14897
Unit A302, Tower Bridge Business Complex, Clements Road, LONDON, SE16 4DG **Tel:** 020 7237 1578
Titles:
SOUTHWARK NEWS SERIES

SOVEREIGN PUBLICATIONS LTD 18922
32 Woodstock Grove, LONDON, W12 8LE
Tel: 020 7616 0800 **Fax:** 020 7616 0810
Web site: http://www.sovereign-publications.com
Titles:
ALUMINIUM WORLD
AUTO
HOSPITAL DECISIONS

Section 6 UK Publishers & Their Titles

UK Publishers & Their Titles

SPA PUBLISHING   1762997
47 - 49 Borough High Street, LONDON, SE1 1NB
Titles:
 EUROPEAN SPA

SPA WORLD MAGAZINE LTD   1630294
5-7 The Shambles, WETHERBY, LS22 6NG
Tel: 01937 585800
Web site: http://www.spaworld.tv
Titles:
 SPA WORLD

SPAB   16114
37 Spital Square, LONDON, E1 6DY **Tel:** 020 7377 1644
Fax: 020 7247 5296
Email: info@spab.org.uk
Web site: http://www.spab.org.uk
Titles:
 CORNERSTONE

SPAFAX   1680580
13-16 Jacobs Well Mews, LONDON, W1U 3DY
Tel: 020 7906 2001 **Fax:** 020 7906 2022
Web site: http://www.spafax.com
Titles:
 ROYAL WINGS

SPAR UK LTD   14051
The Hygeia Building, 66-68 College Road, HARROW, HA1
1BE **Tel:** 020 8426 3700 **Fax:** 020 8426 3701
Titles:
 SPAR INTOUCH

SPCK   18851
36 Causton Street, LONDON, SW1P 4ST **Tel:** 020 7592 3900
Fax: 020 7592 3939
Email: theology@spck.co.uk
Web site: http://www.spck.org.uk
Titles:
 THEOLOGY

SPEAR MEDIA   1709538
5 Jubilee Place, LONDON, SW3 3TD **Tel:** 020 7985 0002
Fax: 020 7792 9244
Web site: http://www.spearswms.com
Titles:
 ASPINALL'S MAGAZINE

SPECIAL PUBLICATIONS   1622054
Craigcrook Castle, Craigcrook Road, EDINBURGH, EH4 3PE
Tel: 0131 312 4550 **Fax:** 0131 312 4551
Titles:
 FISH FARMER

SPECIAL T PUBLISHING   13974
41 High Street, Morcott, OAKHAM, LE15 9DN
Tel: 01572 747472 **Fax:** 01572 747576
Web site: http://www.mechaid.com
Titles:
 MECHAID

SPECIALIST BUSINESS MEDIA   1767443
8-10 Dryden Street, LONDON, WC2E 9NA
Titles:
 CIE

SPECIALIST (UK) LTD   14467
Fanum House, Basing View, BASINGSTOKE, RG21 4EA
Tel: 0117 925 1696 **Fax:** 0117 925 1808
Email: info@specialistuk.com
Web site: http://www.specialistuk.com
Titles:
 RAPPORT
 SMILEGUIDE

SPECIFIER PUBLISHING   14456
32 Portland Street, CHELTENHAM, GL52 2PE
Tel: 01242 236336 **Fax:** 01242 222331
Titles:
 HEALTH & SAFETY SPECIFIER
 SECURITY SPECIFIER

SPEEDIE CONSULTANTS LTD   1685571
10 College Gardens, Westgate-On-Sea, KENT, CT8 8EY
Tel: 01843 831088
Titles:
 PROTECTION INSURANCE

SPG COMPANYS LTD   16843
33-41 Dallington Street, LONDON, EC1V 0BB
Tel: 020 7934 9000 **Fax:** 020 7934 9201
Titles:
 SPORT BUSINESS INTERNATIONAL
 SPORTBUSINESS.COM

SPG MEDIA LTD   623873
Brunel House, 55-57 North Wharf Road, LONDON, W2 1LA
Tel: 020 7915 9600 **Fax:** 020 7915 9776
Email: info@spgmedia.com
Web site: http://www.spgmedia.com
Titles:
 AEROSPACE TECHNOLOGY
 AIRFORCE TECHNOLOGY
 AIRPORT TECHNOLOGY
 ARMY TECHNOLOGY
 CEO
 CHEMICALS TECHNOLOGY
 DESIGNBUILD-NETWORK.COM
 FINANCE DIRECTOR EUROPE
 FUTURE AIRPORT
 HOTEL MANAGEMENT INTERNATIONAL
 HYDROCARBONS TECHNOLOGY
 MEDICAL DEVICE DEVELOPMENTS
 MINING TECHNOLOGY
 MOBILECOMMS TECHNOLOGY
 NAVAL TECHNOLOGY
 OFFSHORE TECHNOLOGY
 PACKAGING-GATEWAY.COM
 PHARMACEUTICAL TECHNOLOGY
 POWER TECHNOLOGY
 PRACTICAL PATIENT CARE
 RAILWAY TECHNOLOGY
 ROAD TRAFFIC TECHNOLOGY
 SEMICONDUCTOR TECHNOLOGY
 SHIP TECHNOLOGY
 WATER TECHNOLOGY
 THE WEALTH COLLECTION
 WORLD CRUISE INDUSTRY REVIEW
 WORLD PHARMACEUTICAL FRONTIERS

SPICE BUSINESS MAGAZINE   623366
211 Firtree Road, Driftbridge, EPSOM DOWNS, KT17 3LB
Tel: 01737 210022 **Fax:** 01737 211903
Email: info@spicebusiness.co.uk
Web site: http://www.spicebusiness.co.uk
Titles:
 SPICE BUSINESS MAGAZINE

SPICE COURT PUBLICATIONS LTD   623326
17 Spice Court, Plantation Wharf, Battersea, LONDON,
SW11 3UE **Tel:** 020 7924 5885 **Fax:** 020 7924 1882
Email: info@spicepublishing.com
Web site: http://www.spicepublishing.com
Titles:
 FULFILMENT AND E.LOGISTICS
 M.LOGISTICS

SPLAT PUBLISHING LTD   671681
141B Lower Granton Road, EDINBURGH, EH5 1EX
Tel: 0131 331 3200
Titles:
 CLOCKS

THE SPORT INDUSTRY GROUP   1728107
23-24 Henrietta Street, LONDON, WC2E 8ND
Tel: 020 7240 7702 **Fax:** 020 7240 7703
Web site: http://www.sportindustry.biz
Titles:
 SPORTINDUSTRY.BIZ

SPORT NEWSPAPERS LTD   14818
19 Great Ancoats Street, MANCHESTER, M60 4BT
Tel: 0161 236 4466 **Fax:** 0161 236 4535
Titles:
 DAILY SPORT
 SUNDAY SPORT

SPORTECH PLC   1761001
101 Wigmore Street, LONDON, W1U 1QU
Tel: 020 7268 2400
Web site: http://www.sportechplc.com

Titles:
 4THEGAME.COM

SPORTS MEDIA BROADCASTING   1732249
Broadcast Centre, Suite 16, The Linen House, 253 Kilburn
Lane, LONDON, W10 4BQ **Tel:** 020 8964 5522
Fax: 020 8964 6565
Titles:
 FOOTBALLAUDIO.COM
 SPORTSMEDIA.CO.UK

SPORTS PUBLICATIONS LTD.   15254
1st Floor, 18-22 Market Street, CLECKHEATON, BD19 5AJ
Tel: 01274 851323 **Fax:** 01274 852687
Titles:
 LADY GOLFER
 NATIONAL CLUB GOLFER
 PIN HIGH!

SPORTSPRO MEDIA   1711978
Kemp House, 152 - 160 City Road, LONDON, EC1V 2NX
Tel: 020 7837 6240 **Fax:** 020 7837 6243
Titles:
 SPORTSPRO

SPRINGER   14516
Ashbourne House, The Guildway, Old Portsmouth Road,
Artington, GUILDFORD, GU3 1LP **Tel:** 01483 734433
Fax: 01483 734411
Email: journalslondon@springer.com
Web site: http://www.springerlink.com
Titles:
 CLINICAL RHEUMATOLOGY
 COMPARATIVE CLINICAL PATHOLOGY
 FORMAL ASPECTS OF COMPUTING
 INTERNATIONAL UROGYNAECOLOGY JOURNAL
 MCSS MATHEMATICS OF CONTROL, SIGNAL AND
  SYSTEMS
 NEURAL COMPUTING & APPLICATIONS
 OSTEOPOROSIS INTERNATIONAL
 PATTERN ANALYSIS & APPLICATIONS
 PERSONAL & UBIQUITOUS COMPUTING
 VIRTUAL REALITY

SPROUTS   1736201
St Aidens, 1 Yarmouth Road, Ditchingham, BUNGAY, NR35
2PF **Tel:** 01986 892335
Titles:
 SPROUTS

SPYDER REDSPY   1747726
2 Shad Thames, LONDON, SE1 2YU **Tel:** 020 7234 0221
Fax: 020 7403 8096
Web site: http://www.redspy.co.uk
Titles:
 FIFTHGEAR.FIVE.TV

SQ FT LTD   1639989
3rd Floor, Castleton Mill, Armley Road, LEEDS, LS12 2DS
Tel: 0113 227 0825
Titles:
 SQ FT PROPERTY INVESTOR MAGAZINE

SQUARE ONE ADVERTISING AND DESIGN   1600344
90 Totley Brook Road, SHEFFIELD, S17 3QT
Tel: 0114 255 7911 **Fax:** 0114 258 3076
Email: enquiries@squareone.co.uk
Web site: http://www.squareone.co.uk
Titles:
 CORROSION MANAGEMENT

SQUARE PEG MEDIA   700154
37 Ivor Place, LONDON, NW1 6EA **Tel:** 020 7258 1777
Fax: 020 7258 1787
Titles:
 G3 MAGAZINE
 OUT IN THE CITY

SQUARE UP MEDIA LTD   1686925
4 Tun Yard, Peardon Street, LONDON, SW8 3HT
Tel: 020 7819 9999 **Fax:** 020 7819 9840
Titles:
 HEDGE MAGAZINE
 SM SQUARE MILE MAGAZINE

SQUIRES KITCHEN MAGAZINE PUBLISHING   15152
Alfred House, Hones Business Park, FARNHAM, GU9 8BB
Tel: 0845 225 5671 **Fax:** 0845 225 5673
Email: editorial@squires-group.co.uk
Web site: http://www.squires-group.co.uk
Titles:
 CAKES & SUGARCRAFT
 WEDDING CAKES - A DESIGN SOURCE
 WEDDING DRESSES - A DESIGN SOURCE

SR MEDIA LTD   15924
101 Southwark Street, LONDON, SE1 0JF
Tel: 020 7401 7333 **Fax:** 020 7078 4930
Email: info@srmedia.net
Titles:
 STUDY OVERSEAS

SRPBA   15619
Studio 2001, Mile End, Abbey Mill Business Centre,
PAISLEY, PA1 1JS **Tel:** 0141 561 0300 **Fax:** 0141 561 0400
Web site: http://www.srpba.com
Titles:
 LAND BUSINESS

SSAFA FORCES HELP   16993
19 Queen Elizabeth Street, LONDON, SE1 2LP
Tel: 020 7403 8783 **Fax:** 020 7403 8815
Titles:
 NEWS & VIEWS

ST MARY'S COLLEGE   621560
St. Mary's College, Waldegrave Road, Strawberry Hill,
TWICKENHAM, TW1 4SX **Tel:** 020 8240 4039
Fax: 020 8240 4255
Titles:
 THE SIMMARIAN

STABLE PUBLISHING LTD   696715
SBC House, Restmor Way, WALLINGTON, SM6 7AH
Tel: 020 8288 1080 **Fax:** 020 8288 1099
Email: editor@stablepublishing.co.uk
Web site: http://www.stablepublishing.co.uk
Titles:
 BUILDING FOR LEISURE
 EDB

STAFFORDSHIRE MEDIA LTD   1650094
Park Hall Works, Sutherland Road, STOKE-ON-TRENT, ST3
1HB **Tel:** 01782 597500 **Fax:** 01782 318537
Titles:
 STAFFORDSHIRE LIVING

STAFFORDSHIRE NEWSPAPERS LTD   14833
65-68 High Street, BURTON-ON-TRENT, DE14 1LE
Tel: 01283 512345 **Fax:** 01283 515351
Email: editor@burtonmail.co.uk
Web site: http://www.burtonmail.co.uk
Titles:
 ASHBOURNE NEWS TELEGRAPH
 THE BURTON & SOUTH DERBYSHIRE ADVERTISER
 BURTON MAIL
 NUNEATON NEWS
 STAFFORDSHIRE LIFE
 STAFFORDSHIRE NEWSLETTER SERIES
 UTTOXETER ADVERTISER
 YOUR LEEK PAPER

STAFFORDSHIRE SENTINEL NEWS & MEDIA LTD 14847
Sentinel House, Etruria, STOKE-ON-TRENT, ST1 5SS
Tel: 01782 602525 **Fax:** 01782 280781
Web site: http://www.thisisthesentinel.co.uk
Titles:
 THE NORTH STAFFORDSHIRE MAGAZINE
 THE SENTINEL STOKE-ON-TRENT

STAFFORDSHIRE UNIVERSITY   15761
Graduate Relations, Staffordshire University, College Road,
STOKE-ON-TRENT, ST4 2DE **Tel:** 01782 294942
Fax: 01782 295703
Titles:
 HORIZON

STAG PUBLICATIONS LTD   17332
18 Alban Park, Hatfield Road, ST. ALBANS, AL4 0JJ
Tel: 01727 739160 **Fax:** 01727 739169

Titles:
 FLEET INDUSTRY CONFIDENTIAL (FIC)
 FLEET WORLD
 INTERNATIONAL FLEET WORLD
 VAN FLEET WORLD

THE STAGE NEWSPAPER LTD   15348
Stage House, 47 Bermondsey Street, LONDON, SE1 3XT
Tel: 020 7403 1818 **Fax:** 020 7357 9287
Titles:
 THE STAGE

STAINLESS STEEL FOCUS LIMITED   14092
Morgan House, Gilbert Drive, Wyberton Fen, BOSTON, PE21
7TR **Tel:** 01205 290844 **Fax:** 01205 290847
Web site: http://www.stainless-steel-focus.com
Titles:
 STAINLESS STEEL FOCUS

STANBOROUGH PRESS LTD   17630
Alma Park, GRANTHAM, NG31 9SL **Tel:** 01476 591700
Fax: 01476 577144
Titles:
 FOCUS MAGAZINE
 MESSENGER

STANDFIRST   17950
66 John Finnie Street, KILMARNOCK, KA1 1BS
Tel: 01563 530830 **Fax:** 01563 549503
Titles:
 SOURCES

STANDFIRST MEDIA LIMITED   1739915
Webster House, Dudley Road, TUNBRIDGE WELLS, TN1
1LE **Tel:** 01892 533456 **Fax:** 01892 535417
Web site: http://www.standfirst-media.com
Titles:
 PLAYMUSIC PICKUP
 RUNNINGFREE MAGAZINE

STANDISH MEDIA SERVICES LTD   1650129
Suite 116, The Standish Centre, Cross Street, Standish,
WIGAN, WN6 0HQ **Tel:** 01257 400026 **Fax:** 01257 400078
Titles:
 WIGAN COURIER

STANLEY GIBBONS LTD   15478
7 Parkside, Christchurch Road, RINGWOOD, BH24 3SH
Tel: 01425 472363 **Fax:** 01425 470247
Web site: http://www.stanleygibbons.com
Titles:
 GIBBONS STAMP MONTHLY

STANSTED NEWS LTD   13622
134 South Street, BISHOP'S STORTFORD, CM23 3BQ
Tel: 01279 714511 **Fax:** 01279 714519
Web site: http://www.stanstednews.com
Titles:
 AIRFRAMER
 EUROPEAN BUSINESS AIR NEWS
 EUROPEAN BUSINESS AIR NEWS
 INFANT
 INFANT

STANWORTH COMMUNICATIONS   12412
PO Box 220, WALTON-ON-THAMES, KT12 1YQ
Tel: 01932 254400 **Fax:** 01932 240294
Email: editor@call-centre-europe.com
Web site: http://www.call-centre-europe.com
Titles:
 CALL CENTRE EUROPE

STASH PUBLICATIONS   1685625
3rd Floor, Deansgate Court, Milton Hall, 244 Deansgate,
MANCHESTER, M3 4BQ **Tel:** 0161 832 7222
Fax: 0161 832 8414
Email: publisher@stashmag.com
Titles:
 HNW JOURNAL

STEAM WORLD PUBLISHING   600212
1st Floor, 2 King Street, PETERBOROUGH, PE1 1LT
Tel: 01733 555123 **Fax:** 01733 427500

Titles:
 STEAM WORLD

STEEL BUSINESS BRIEFING   698901
2nd Floor, Peek House, 20 Eastcheap, LONDON, EC3M 1EB
Tel: 020 7626 0600 **Fax:** 020 7929 4666
Web site: http://www.steelbb.com
Titles:
 STEEL BUSINESS BRIEFING

STEEL MEDIA LTD   1742379
17 Wilmar Close, UXBRIDGE, UB8 1AS **Tel:** 07811 135982
Web site: http://www.steelmedia.co.uk
Titles:
 POCKETGAMER.CO.UK
 POCKETPICKS.CO.UK

STEP AHEAD LTD   1729808
1st Floor, 299-301 London Road, BENFLEET, SS7 2BN
Tel: 01702 555990 **Fax:** 01702 555880
Titles:
 STEP AHEAD

STEP COMMUNICATIONS LTD   625293
Step House, North Farm Road, TUNBRIDGE WELLS, TN2
3DR **Tel:** 01892 518877 **Fax:** 01892 616177
Titles:
 ASIA PACIFIC PERSONAL CARE
 THE CLINICAL SERVICES JOURNAL
 HEALTH ESTATE JOURNAL

STEP FORWARD PUBLISHING LTD   16453
St. Jude's Church, Dulwich Road, LONDON, SE24 0PB
Tel: 01926 420046 **Fax:** 01926 420042
Titles:
 CHILD CARE
 PRACTICAL PRE-SCHOOL

STEP PUBLISHING LTD   14475
Step House, North Farm Road, TUNBRIDGE WELLS, TN2
3DR **Tel:** 01892 518877
Titles:
 THE BIOMEDICAL SCIENTIST
 BRITISH JOURNAL OF BIOMEDICAL SCIENCE

STEPHEN BARRY PUBLICITY   16962
11 Noblefield Heights, Great North Road, LONDON, N2 0NX
Tel: 020 8341 6660 **Fax:** 0870 135 7143
Email: stephenbarry@clara.co.uk
Titles:
 UNITY NEWS

STEPHEN WARD PHOTOGRAPHY (LEEDS) LTD 1711934
19 Marsh Street, Rothwell, LEEDS, LS26 0AG
Tel: 0113 282 6661 **Fax:** 0113 288 7429
Titles:
 ROTHWELL AND DISTRICT RECORD

STEPHENS & GEORGE MAGAZINES   14009
Goat Mill Road, Dowlais, MERTHYR TYDFIL, CF48 3TD
Tel: 01685 388888 **Fax:** 01685 721904
Web site: http://www.stephensandgeorge.co.uk
Titles:
 NFU POULTRY FORUM MAGAZINE

STEPPE INTERNATIONAL LTD   1726901
Manor Farm, High Street, Nettlebed, HENLEY-ON-THAMES,
RG9 5DA **Tel:** 01491 641914
Titles:
 STEPPE

STEVE WELCH MEDIA   13942
6A New Street, WARWICK, CV34 4RX **Tel:** 01926 408242
Fax: 01926 408206
Titles:
 ENERGY ENGINEERING

STEVENSON PUBLICATIONS LTD   14690
19 Wharfdale Road, LONDON, N1 9SB **Tel:** 020 7833 3772
Fax: 020 7833 3830
Web site: http://www.gsmagazine.co.uk

UK Publishers & Their Titles

Titles:
GS MAGAZINE

STILLS AUDIO MOTION LTD   1706591
Hoadsbrook, Mockbeggar Lane, East End, BENENDEN,
TN17 4BG **Tel:** 01580 243441
Titles:
CUE ENTERTAINMENT

STIRLING UNIVERSITY STUDENTS ASSOCIATION 15738
The Robbins Centre, The University of Stirling, STIRLING,
FK9 4LA **Tel:** 01786 467166 **Fax:** 01786 467176
Titles:
BRIG

STOCKTON BOROUGH COUNCIL   621565
PO Box 11, Church Road, STOCKTON-ON-TEES, TS18 1LD
Tel: 01642 393020 **Fax:** 01642 393026
Web site: http://www.stockton.gov.uk
Titles:
STOCKTON NEWS

STONE CROSS PUBLISHING LTD   698725
85 Elwyn Road, MARCH, PE15 9DB **Tel:** 01354 656555
Fax: 01354 660999
Web site: http://www.autotimes.co.uk
Titles:
AUTOTIMES

STONE LEISURE LTD   16086
Andrew House, Granville Road, SIDCUP, DA14 4BN
Tel: 020 8302 6150 **Fax:** 020 8300 2315
Web site: http://www.stoneleisure.com
Titles:
BEXLEY CHRONICLE SERIES
MOTORHOME MONTHLY

STONEWALL   18447
Tower Building, York Road, LONDON, SE1 7NX
Tel: 020 7881 9440 **Fax:** 020 7881 9444
Web site: http://www.stonewall.org.uk
Titles:
FRIENDS

STORY PUBLISHING LTD   1653389
Studio 209, Curtain House, 134-146 Curtain Road,
LONDON, EC2A 3AR **Tel:** 020 7729 3675
Titles:
HUCK
LITTLE WHITE LIES MAGAZINE

STORY WORLDWIDE   12250
15B St. Georges Mews, Primrose Hill, LONDON, NW1 8XE
Tel: 020 7449 1500 **Fax:** 020 7722 3598
Web site: http://www.storyworldwide.com
Titles:
BLUEWATER
HOLIDAY THE RCI MAGAZINE
INSIDE TRACK
LEXUS
SERVER MANAGEMENT

STRACHAN & LIVINGSTON LTD   15050
23 Kirk Wynd, KIRKCALDY, KY1 1EP **Tel:** 01592 261451
Fax: 01592 204180
Web site: http://www.fifetoday.co.uk
Titles:
EAST FIFE MAIL
FIFE HERALD INC. FIFE NEWS AND KINROSSHIRE
ADVERTISER
FIFE LEADER AND FREE PRESS SERIES
GLENROTHES GAZETTE LESLIE AND MARKINCH NEWS
HERALD AND POST FIFE
ST. ANDREWS CITIZEN

STRAIGHT LINE PUBLISHING LTD   14284
29 Main Street, Bothwell, GLASGOW, G71 8RD
Tel: 01698 853000 **Fax:** 01698 854208
Email: info@straightlinepublishing.com
Web site: http://www.straightlinepublishing.com
Titles:
ENTERPRISING NEWS
WIREIN

STRANRAER & WIGTOWNSHIRE FREE PRESS 15068
St. Andrew Street, STRANRAER, DG9 7EB
Tel: 01776 702551 **Fax:** 01776 706695
Email: info@stranraer-freepress.co.uk
Web site: http://www.stranraer-freepress.co.uk
Titles:
STRANRAER & WIGTOWNSHIRE FREE PRESS

THE STRATEGIC PLANNING SOCIETY   12356
Buxton House, 7 Highbury Hill, LONDON, N5 1SU
Tel: 0845 056 3663 **Fax:** 0870 751 8216
Titles:
STRATEGY

STRATFIELD LTD   1726533
26-30 Old Church Street, Chelsea, LONDON, SW3 5BY
Tel: 020 7349 3150 **Fax:** 020 7349 3160
Titles:
MOTOR SPORT

STRATHCLYDE POLICE HQ   16202
173 Pitt Street, GLASGOW, G2 4JS **Tel:** 0141 532 2659
Fax: 0141 532 2409
Titles:
UPBEAT

**STRATHCLYDE UNIVERSITY STUDENTS
ASSOCIATION**   15793
Strathclyde Student Association, 90 John Street,
GLASGOW, G1 1JH **Tel:** 0141 567 5000 **Fax:** 0141 552 5050
Web site: http://www.strathstudents.com
Titles:
STRATHCLYDE TELEGRAPH

STREAM PUBLISHING LTD   1759981
The Courtyard, Ladycross Farm, Hollow Lane, Dormansland,
LINGFIELD, RH7 6PB **Tel:** 01342 872020
Titles:
FLYBE UNCOVERED
THE RENAULT MAGAZINE
V - THE VAUXHALL MAGAZINE
THE WHEELS OF BUSINESS

STRI   16718
St. Ives Estate, BINGLEY, BD16 1AU **Tel:** 01274 565131
Fax: 01274 561891
Email: info@stri.co.uk
Web site: http://www.stri.co.uk
Titles:
INTERNATIONAL TURFGRASS BULLETIN

THE STROKE ASSOCIATION   14591
Stroke House, 240 City Road, LONDON, EC1V 2PR
Tel: 020 7566 0300 **Fax:** 020 7490 2686
Email: info@stroke.org.uk
Web site: http://www.stroke.org.uk
Titles:
STROKE NEWS

STUDENT DIRECT LTD   623393
University of Manchester, Student Union, Oxford Road,
MANCHESTER, M13 9PR **Tel:** 0161 351 5402
Fax: 0161 737 1633
Email: studendirect@salford.ac.uk
Web site: http://www.student-direct.co.uk
Titles:
STUDENT DIRECT

STUDENT EXPRESS MEDIA   625297
7 Bourne Road, BROMLEY, BR2 9PB **Tel:** 020 8295 7000
Fax: 020 8295 7099
Web site: http://www.student-express.co.uk
Titles:
STUDENT EXPRESS

STUDENT PLANNER UK   1741957
201 Houldsworth Mill, Waterhouse Way, STOCKPORT, SK5
6DD **Tel:** 07841 500222
Email: enquiries@thestudentplanner.com
Web site: http://thestudentplanner.org
Titles:
THESTUDENTPLANNER.ORG

STUDENTS UNION BANGOR   18844
University of Wales, Deiniol Road, BANGOR, LL57 2TH
Tel: 01248 388017
Titles:
Y DDRAENEN
SEREN

STUDENTS UNION UNIVERSITY OF GREENWICH 15788
Cooper Building, King William Walk, Greenwich, LONDON,
SE10 9JH **Tel:** 020 8331 9964 **Fax:** 020 8331 8591
Titles:
SARKY CUTT

SUBCONTINENT PUBLISHING   13703
Alexander House, 14-16 Peterborough Road, LONDON,
SW6 3BN **Tel:** 020 7348 7997 **Fax:** 020 7348 7996
Titles:
TANDOORI MAGAZINE

SUBCONTINENT PUBLISHING LTD   1728347
14-16 Peterborough Road, Fulham, LONDON, SW6 3BN
Tel: 020 7348 7997 **Fax:** 020 7348 7996
Titles:
INDUBAI

SUBLIME MAGAZINE LTD   1717389
167 Southwood Lane, Highgate, LONDON, N6 5TA
Tel: 020 8374 7695
Email: info@sublimemagazine.com
Titles:
SUBLIME

SUBU   1627126
Talbot Campus, Fern Barrow, POOLE, BH12 5BB
Tel: 01202 965653 **Fax:** 01202 535990
Web site: http://www.subu.org.uk
Titles:
NERVE MAGAZINE

THE SUFFOLK BOOK LEAGUE   624208
115 Anglesea Road, IPSWICH, IP1 3PJ **Tel:** 01473 250949
Titles:
BOOKTALK

SUGAR MEDIA LTD   1712721
Studio 4, Hiltongrove, 14 Southgate Road, LONDON, N1
3LY **Tel:** 020 7407 7747 **Fax:** 020 7407 6800
Web site: http://www.sugarmedia.co.uk
Titles:
STUDENT TIMES

SUIT YOURSELF LTD   1733026
17 Eastwood Road, BRISTOL, BS4 4RN **Tel:** 0117 370 2722
Titles:
SUIT YOURSELF MAGAZINE

SUMMERSAULT COMMUNICATIONS   1714806
122 Warwick Street, LEAMINGTON SPA, CV32 4QY
Tel: 01926 339949
Email: reception@summersault.co.uk
Web site: http://www.summersault.co.uk
Titles:
ESCAPE
PROMOTIONS BUYER

SUN GROUP LANARKSHIRE REGION   15051
2 Olympia Arcade, Town Centre, EAST KILBRIDE, G74 1LX
Tel: 01355 265000 **Fax:** 01355 264488
Titles:
EAST KILBRIDE NEWS

S.U.N LTD   15054
20-22 King Street, BATHGATE, EH48 1AX
Tel: 01506 633544 **Fax:** 01506 650578
Titles:
WEST LOTHIAN COURIER

SUNDAY NEWSPAPERS LTD   18620
3-5 Commercial Court, Off Hill Street, BELFAST, BT1 2NB
Tel: 028 9023 8118 **Fax:** 028 9023 8120

Titles:
SUNDAY WORLD NORTHERN IRELAND EDITION

SUNDAY PUBLISHING   1710135
Studio 7, 3rd Floor, Enterprise House, 1-2 Hatfields,
LONDON, SE1 9PG **Tel:** 020 7793 2460 **Fax:** 020 7953 7056
Email: ollie@sundaypublishing.com
Web site: http://www.sundaypublishing.com

Titles:
PET PEOPLE
TODAY TOMORROW

SUNDIAL MAGAZINES LTD   676917
Sundial House, 17 Wickham Road, BECKENHAM, BR3 5JS
Tel: 020 8639 4400 **Fax:** 020 8639 4411
Email: info@sundialmagazines.co.uk
Web site: http://www.sundialmagazines.co.uk

Titles:
CLASSIC TRACTOR
EARTHMOVERS
MERCEDES ENTHUSIAST

SUNSHINE PUBLISHING   1654052
PO Box 800, UXBRIDGE, UB8 2YY **Tel:** 01895 812594
Email: publishing@sunshinemagazine.co.uk

Titles:
SUNSHINE MAGAZINE HILLINGDON

SUPANET LTD   1654049
Indigo House, Time Technology Park, Blackburn Road,
Simonstone, BURNLEY, BB12 7NQ **Tel:** 01282 681000
Fax: 01282 681001
Web site: http://www.supanet.com

Titles:
SUPANET

SUPER SUPER MEDIA LTD   1692094
2nd Floor, 182 Commercial Road, LONDON, E1 2JY
Tel: 020 7240 1174

Titles:
THE SUPER SUPER

SUPPLIERBUSINESS.COM   1649353
2 St. Pauls Street, STAMFORD, PE9 2BE **Tel:** 01780 481712
Fax: 01780 482383

Titles:
SUPPLIERBUSINESS.COM

SURCO LTD   17367
Dominion House, Sibson Road, SALE, M33 7PP
Tel: 0161 972 3110 **Fax:** 0161 972 3119

Titles:
CIVIL ENGINEERING SURVEYOR

SURMA NEWS GROUP LTD   16065
Unit 10B Quaker Street, LONDON, E1 6SZ
Tel: 020 7377 9787 **Fax:** 020 8981 8829

Titles:
SURMA

SURREY & BERKSHIRE MEDIA GROUP   17404
Stoke Mill, Woking Road, GUILDFORD, GU1 1QA
Tel: 01483 508700 **Fax:** 01483 508701
Web site: http://www.surreyad.com

Titles:
BRACKNELL FOREST & WOKINGHAM STANDARD
  SERIES
READING POST SERIES
SURREY TIMES & ADVERTISER SERIES
WOKING NEWS & MAIL SERIES
WOKING REVIEW SERIES
WOKINGHAM AND BRACKNELL TIMES SERIES

SURREY WILDLIFE TRUST   625350
School Lane, Pirbright, WOKING, GU24 0JN
Tel: 01483 705466 **Fax:** 01483 486505
Web site: http://www.surreywildlifetrust.co.uk

Titles:
SURREY NATURE

SUSSEX NEWSPAPERS (HORSHAM) LTD   1649351
14-16 Market Square, HORSHAM, RH12 1HD
Tel: 01403 751200 **Fax:** 01403 751248

Titles:
EMS VALLEY GAZETTE
WEST SUSSEX COUNTY TIMES SERIES

SUSSEX NEWSPAPERS LTD   14997
12 The Boulevard, CRAWLEY, RH10 1XY **Tel:** 01293 562929
Fax: 01293 519052

Titles:
BOGNOR REGIS AND CHICHESTER GUARDIAN
CRAWLEY OBSERVER, TIMES AND HERALD SERIES
SHOREHAM & STEYNING HERALD SERIES

SUSSEX POLICE PRESS OFFICE   14151
Sussex Police HQ, Malling House, LEWES, BN7 2DZ
Tel: 01273 404177 **Fax:** 01273 404280

Titles:
PATROL

SUSSEX (SOUTHERN) NEWSPAPERS LTD   17004
7-9 South Road, HAYWARDS HEATH, RH16 4LE
Tel: 01444 452201 **Fax:** 01444 416611

Titles:
MID SUSSEX TIMES AND CITIZEN SERIES

SUSSEX UNIVERSITY STUDENTS' UNION   15783
Falmer House, Falmer, BRIGHTON, BN1 9QF
Tel: 01273 678555 **Fax:** 01273 678875
Email: communications@ussu.sussex.ac.uk
Web site: http://www.ussu.info

Titles:
THE PULSE SUSSEX

SUSSEX WILDLIFE TRUST   674297
Woods Mill, Shoreham Road, HENFIELD, BN5 9SD
Tel: 01273 492630 **Fax:** 01273 494500

Titles:
WILDLIFE (SUSSEX WILDLIFE TRUST)

SWEET & MAXWELL LTD   12542
100 Avenue Road, Swiss Cottage, LONDON, NW3 3PF
Tel: 020 7393 7000 **Fax:** 020 7393 7010
Web site: http://www.sweetandmaxwell.co.uk

Titles:
THE BAR DIRECTORY
BRITISH TAX REVIEW
COMPUTER & TELECOMMUNICATIONS LAW REVIEW
CRIMINAL LAW REVIEW
EIPR EUROPEAN INTELLECTUAL PROPERTY REVIEW
ENTERTAINMENT LAW REVIEW
EUROPEAN COMPETITION LAW REVIEW - ECLR
EUROPEAN PATENT OFFICE REPORTS
INTERNATIONAL ENERGY LAW REVIEW
JOURNAL OF BUSINESS LAW
JOURNAL OF INTERNATIONAL BANKING LAW AND
  REGULATION
LEGAL HUB

SWEET & MAXWELL YORKSHIRE   624190
The Hatchery, Hall Bank Lane, Mytholmroyd, HEBDEN
BRIDGE, HX7 5HQ **Tel:** 01422 888000 **Fax:** 01422 888001

Titles:
THE CONVEYANCER & PROPERTY LAWYER
INSOLVENCY INTELLIGENCE
JOURNAL OF PLANNING & ENVIRONMENT LAW
LAW QUARTERLY REVIEW

THE SWIMMING TEACHERS' ASSOCIATION   1616902
Anchor House, Birch Street, WALSALL, WS2 8HZ
Tel: 01922 645097 **Fax:** 01922 720628

Titles:
SWIM & SAVE

SWIMMING TIMES LTD   15305
41 Granby Street, LOUGHBOROUGH, LE11 3DU
Tel: 01509 632230 **Fax:** 01509 632233
Email: swimmingtimes@swimming.org
Web site: http://www.britishswimming.org

Titles:
SWIMMING TIMES MAGAZINE

SWINDON PUBLICATIONS LTD   15603
71 Basepoint, Rivermead Drive, Westlea, SWINDON, SN5
7EX **Tel:** 01793 608840
Email: publisher@swindonlink.com
Web site: http://www.swindonlink.com

Titles:
SWINDON LINK MAGAZINE

SWPP & BPPA   1735430
6 Bath Street, RHYL, LL18 3EB **Tel:** 01745 345935

Titles:
PROFESSIONAL IMAGEMAKER PHOTOGRAPHIC
  MAGAZINE
THE SHOW GUIDE

SWR MEDIA LTD   1651031
Suite 115, St Williams Court, 1 Gifford Street, LONDON, N1
0GN **Tel:** 01763 208876 **Fax:** 01763 208876
Email: info@swrmedia.co.uk
Web site: http://www.swrmedia.co.uk

Titles:
LUSSO

SYHA   16089
7 Glebe Crescent, STIRLING, FK8 2JA **Tel:** 01786 891400
Fax: 01786 891333

Titles:
SCOTTISH HOSTELLER

SYMPOSIUM LTD   13933
PO Box 700, GREAT MISSENDEN, HP16 9JA
Tel: 01494 862104 **Fax:** 01494 890788
Email: admin@landmobile.co.uk
Web site: http://www.landmobile.co.uk

Titles:
LAND MOBILE

SYNCHRO CITY UK LTD   1761950
22 Mary Seacole Road, PLYMOUTH, PL1 3JY

Titles:
THE PLYMOUTH DIARY

SYNONYM LTD   1655068
15 Ravens Close, Knaphill, WOKING, GU21 2LD
Tel: 01483 888378

Titles:
DATACENTRE TIMES

SYPHA   16788
Great Brownings, College Road, LONDON, SE21 7HP
Tel: 020 8761 1042

Titles:
HIDDENWIRES

SYSTEM THREE COMMUNICATIONS   1751617
254-258 Goswell Road, LONDON, EC1V 7EB
Tel: 020 7689 6841 **Fax:** 020 7689 6827

Titles:
THE IWSR DRINKS RECORD

T1PS.COM LIMITED   1712972
3rd Floor, Henry Thomas House, 5-11 Worship Street,
LONDON, EC2A 2BH **Tel:** 020 7562 3370
Fax: 020 7628 3815
Web site: http://www.t1ps.com

Titles:
THE AIM & PLUS DEAL MONITOR
THE AIM AND PLUS NEWSLETTER
SMALL CAP SHARES

T A PUBLISHING LTD   696968
PO Box 271, ROCHDALE, OL12 7YS **Tel:** 01706 861662
Fax: 01706 861673
Email: info@ta-publishing.co.uk
Web site: http://www.ta-publishing.co.uk

Titles:
OPENINGS

T&F INFORMA GROUP PLC   625184
Mortimer House, 37-41 Mortimer Street, LONDON, W1T 3JH
Tel: 020 7017 5537
Web site: http://www.informamedia.com

Titles:
3 G WIRELESS BROADBAND
DIGITAL TV EUROPE
MOBILE COMMUNICATIONS EUROPE
MOBILE COMMUNICATIONS INTERNATIONAL
MOBILE MEDIA
NEW MEDIA MARKETS

UK Publishers & Their Titles

OSS/BSS ANALYST
TBI TELEVISION BUSINESS INTERNATIONAL
TELECOM MARKETS
TV INTERNATIONAL
TV INTERNATIONAL DAILY

T MAGAZINE LTD 13820
Alex Wood Hall, Norfolk Street, CAMBRIDGE, CB1 2LD
Tel: 01223 358700 **Fax:** 01223 358766
Titles:
'T' MAG

T.R. BECKETT LTD 14996
Beckett House, 1 Commercial Road, EASTBOURNE, BN21 3XQ **Tel:** 01323 722091 **Fax:** 01323 431387
Titles:
ADNEWS SERIES (BEXHILL & HASTINGS)
EASTBOURNE HERALD & GAZETTE SERIES
HASTINGS OBSERVER SERIES

T SNAPE & CO LTD 1621214
Boltons Court, PRESTON, PR1 3TY **Tel:** 01772 254553
Fax: 01772 204697
Email: info@tsnapeprinters.co.uk
Titles:
CATHOLIC VOICE (MIDDLESBROUGH)

TABLET PUBLISHING CO. LTD. 15907
1 King Street Cloisters, Clifton Walk, LONDON, W6 0GY
Tel: 020 8748 8484 **Fax:** 020 8748 1550
Email: thetablet@thetablet.co.uk
Web site: http://www.thetablet.co.uk
Titles:
THE PASTORAL REVIEW
THE TABLET

TALKHEALTH PARTNERSHIP LTD 1726821
PO Box 7383, Sherfield-on-Loddon, HOOK, RG27 7FX
Tel: 0870 042 9500
Titles:
TALKACNE
TALKALLERGY
TALKASTHMA
TALKECZEMA
TALKPSORIASIS

TALYLLYN RAILWAY PRESERVATION SOCIETY 18290
Talyllyn Railway, Wharf Station, TYWYN, LL36 9EY
Tel: 01654 710472 **Fax:** 01654 711755
Email: enquiries@talyllyn.co.uk
Web site: http://www.talyllyn.co.uk
Titles:
TALYLLYN NEWS

TAMBA 15145
2 The Willows, Gardner Road, GUILDFORD, GU1 4PG
Tel: 0870 770 3305
Titles:
TWINS TRIPLETS AND MORE MAGAZINE

TANG MEDIA 1743377
4 South Bank, CHELTENHAM, GL51 8DN
Tel: 01242 696314
Titles:
TOP GAYER

TANK PUBLICATIONS LTD 674313
Princess House, 50-60 Eastcastle Street, LONDON, W1W 8EA **Tel:** 020 7323 3475 **Fax:** 020 7434 9232
Titles:
TANK

TANKER OPERATOR LTD 1600448
213 Marsh Wall, LONDON, E14 9FJ **Tel:** 020 7510 4933
Fax: 020 7510 2344
Web site: http://www.tankeroperator.com
Titles:
LNG JOURNAL
TANKER OPERATOR

TANNER STILES PUBLISHING LTD 17237
Grosvenor House, Central Park, TELFORD, TF2 9TW
Tel: 01952 234000 **Fax:** 01952 234003
Email: info@tspltd.co.uk

Web site: http://www.tspltd.co.uk
Titles:
HOTEL SPORT & LEISURE BUILDING & INTERIORS
LANDSCAPE & AMENITY PRODUCT UPDATE
SPECIFICATION MAGAZINE

TARGET PUBLISHING LTD 14061
The Old Dairy, Hudsons Farm, Fieldgate Lane, Ugley Green, BISHOP'S STORTFORD, CM22 6HJ **Tel:** 01279 816300
Fax: 01279 816496
Web site: http://www.targetpublishing.com
Titles:
CAM
HEALTH FOOD BUSINESS
NATURAL LIFESTYLE MAGAZINE
OE OUTDOOR ENTHUSIAST
OE RETAILER
ORGANIC AND NATURAL BUSINESS

TARGET RESPONSE 17490
PO Box 100, EDENBRIDGE, TN8 6ZN **Tel:** 01732 866122
Fax: 01732 866926
Titles:
CONFERENCE & SEMINAR SELECTOR PACK

TARSUS GROUP PLC 14227
9th Floor, Metro Building, 1 Butterwick, Hammersmith, LONDON, W6 8DW **Tel:** 020 8846 2700 **Fax:** 020 8846 2801
Titles:
LABELS & LABELLING INTERNATIONAL

TATE ENTERPRISES LTD 1641436
Tate Britian, Millbank, LONDON, SW1P 4RG
Tel: 020 7887 8888 **Fax:** 020 7887 8007
Web site: http://www.tate.org.uk
Titles:
TATE ETC

TAVISTOCK NEWSPAPERS LTD 14928
Tindle House, 14 Brook Street, TAVISTOCK, PL19 0HD
Tel: 01822 613666 **Fax:** 01822 613666
Email: tavistock@tavistock-today.co.uk
Web site: http://www.tavistock-today.co.uk
Titles:
SOUTH WEST BUILDING AND CONSTRUCTION
TAVISTOCK TIMES GAZETTE SERIES

TAYLIST MEDIA 1762157
Equitable House, Lyon Road, HARROW, HA1 2EW
Titles:
ERT
ERT IRELAND
KBBREVIEW
KITCHENS BEDROOMS & BATHROOMS MAGAZINE

TAYLOR MADE PUBLISHING 1723432
3 East Avenue, BOURNEMOUTH, BH3 7BW
Tel: 01202 317557
Titles:
DVD MAKER

TCPH LTD 1684983
Unit 2C, 2nd Floor, 289 Cricklewood Broadway, LONDON, NW2 6NX **Tel:** 020 8452 5244 **Fax:** 020 8452 5388
Titles:
ISLAMIC TOURISM MAGAZINE

TDK BUSINESS TECHNOLOGIES LTD 18206
Glaisdale Drive East, Bilborough, NOTTINGHAM, NG8 4JJ
Tel: 0115 929 3419 **Fax:** 0115 929 0490
Titles:
SAFETY.CO.UK
THINKPACKAGING.COM

THE TEAM 1764481
11 Southwark Street, LONDON, SE1 1RQ
Tel: 020 7089 5800
Web site: http://www.theteam.co.uk
Titles:
REGISTERED GAS ENGINEER

TEAM PUBLISHING 1687563
2 Claridge Court, Lower Kings Road, BERKHAMSTED, HP4 2AF **Tel:** 01442 870829 **Fax:** 01442 870617

Titles:
INTERNATIONAL MINING

TEAMPRINT LTD 16067
167c Stroud Green Road, LONDON, N4 3PZ
Tel: 020 7272 9702 **Fax:** 020 7272 9704
Titles:
TA NEA

TECH DATA GROUP 1653132
Computer 2000, Hampshire House, Wade Road, BASINGSTOKE, RG24 8NE **Tel:** 0870 060 3344
Fax: 0870 060 7998
Email: stickleback@meredith.cix.co.uk
Web site: http://www.living-it.co.uk
Titles:
LIVING IT

TECH INSIGHTS EUROPE, UNITED BUSINESS MEDIA 1747250
Ludgate House, 245 Blackfriars Road, LONDON, SE1 9UY
Tel: 020 7921 8271 **Fax:** 020 7921 8499
Web site: http://www.techinsights-europe.com
Titles:
EE TIMES EUROPE
MECHANICAL DESIGN (MCADONLINE)

TECHINSIGHTS 1752679
Ludgate House, 245 Blackfriars Road, LONDON, SE1 9UY
Tel: 020 7921 5000
Titles:
EMBEDDED SYSTEM EUROPE

TECHMEDIA INTERNATIONAL 624622
Kildonan, St. Marys Road, Wrotham, SEVENOAKS, TN15 7AP **Tel:** 01732 886495 **Fax:** 01732 886149
Titles:
POWER ELECTRONICS EUROPE

TECHNIQUE PUBLISHING CO LTD 14123
6B Acorn Farm Business Centre, Cublington Road, WING, LU7 0LB **Tel:** 01296 681424 **Fax:** 01296 682628
Email: tyres@tyretradenews.co.uk
Web site: http://www.tyretradenews.co.uk
Titles:
TYRE TRADE NEWS
TYRETRADE NEWS ONLINE

TECHNOLOGY NETWORKS LIMITED 1654116
Woodview, Bull Lane Industrial Estate, Bull Lane, Acton, SUDBURY, CO10 0BD **Tel:** 01787 319234
Fax: 01787 319235
Email: admin@technologyworks.net
Web site: http://www.technologyworks.net
Titles:
COMBICHEM.NET

TECHNOLOGY PUBLISHING COMPANY 17320
26 Chatsworth Road, SUTTON, SM3 8PN
Tel: 020 8644 9977 **Fax:** 020 8644 9937
Titles:
JOURNAL OF ARCHITECTURAL COATINGS

TEE PUBLISHING LTD 1606083
The Fosse, Fosse Way, LEAMINGTON SPA, CV31 1XN
Tel: 01926 614101 **Fax:** 01926 614293
Email: info@engineeringinminiature.co.uk
Web site: http://www.engineeringinminiature.co.uk
Titles:
ENGINEERING IN MINIATURE
STEAM HERITAGE MUSEUMS AND RALLY GUIDE

TEES VALLEY WILDLIFE TRUST 15635
Margrove Heritage Centre, Margrove Park, Boosbeck, SALTBURN-BY-THE-SEA, TS12 3BZ **Tel:** 01287 636382
Fax: 01287 636383
Titles:
GREENBITS

TEESDALE MERCURY LTD 14931
24 Market Place, BARNARD CASTLE, DL12 8NB
Tel: 01833 637140 **Fax:** 01833 638633
Email: editorial@teesdalemercury.co.uk
Web site: http://www.teesdalemercury.co.uk

Titles:
TEESDALE MERCURY
WEAR VALLEY MERCURY

TELEGEOGRAPHY 13607
3 Colleton Crescent, EXETER, EX2 4DG **Tel:** 01392 315567
Fax: 01392 315556
Email: info@telegeography.com
Web site: http://www.telegeography.com
Titles:
GLOBALCOMMS DATABASE & COMMS UPDATE NEWS
SERVICE

TELEGRAPH MEDIA GROUP LTD 14822
111 Buckingham Palace Road, LONDON, SW1W 0DT
Tel: 020 7931 2000
Web site: http://www.telegraph.co.uk
Titles:
ARTS.TELEGRAPH.CO.UK
THE DAILY TELEGRAPH
THE DAILY TELEGRAPH (CITY OFFICE)
THE DAILY TELEGRAPH (EDINBURGH OFFICE)
THE DAILY TELEGRAPH (MANCHESTER OFFICE)
THE DAILY TELEGRAPH (MIDLANDS OFFICE)
FASHION.TELEGRAPH.CO.UK
GARDENING.TELEGRAPH.CO.UK
HEALTH.TELEGRAPH.CO.UK
SEVEN
SPORT.TELEGRAPH.CO.UK
STELLA
THE SUNDAY TELEGRAPH
THE SUNDAY TELEGRAPH (CITY OFFICE)
THE TELEGRAPH
TELEGRAPH MAGAZINE
TELEGRAPH MONEY
TELEGRAPH.CO.UK
TELEGRAPH.CO.UK/EARTH
TELEGRAPH.CO.UK/MOTORING
TELEGRAPH.CO.UK/PROPERTY
TELEGRAPH.CO.UK/TRAVEL
TELEGRAPH.CO.UK/ULTRATRAVEL
ULTRATRAVEL
WINE.TELEGRAPH.CO.UK

TELEVISUAL MEDIA UK LTD 1726765
48 Charlotte Street, LONDON, W1T 2NS **Tel:** 020 3008 5750
Fax: 020 3008 5784
Web site: http://www.televisual.com
Titles:
TELEVISUAL

THE TELEWORK ASSOCIATION 17205
Swan House, Darvel, AYERSHIRE, KA17 0LP
Tel: 0800 616008
Titles:
21ST CENTURY WORKER

TELL-IT MEDIA PROMOTIONS 1640444
Suite 4, Goldlay House, Parkway, CHELMSFORD, CM2 7PR
Tel: 01245 292841 **Fax:** 01245 292858
Titles:
TOTAL HOSPITALITY
TOTAL LIGHTING
TOTAL RETAIL

TEMPLE DESIGN PUBLISHING SOLUTIONS 1621541
371 Bury Old Road, Prestwich, MANCHESTER, M25 1QA
Tel: 0161 798 7662 **Fax:** 0161 798 7662
Titles:
BODY & SOUL

TEN ALPS PUBLISHING 14719
Trelawney House, Chestergate, MACCLESFIELD, SK11
6DW **Tel:** 01625 613000 **Fax:** 01625 435038
Web site: http://www.tenalpspublishing.com
Titles:
AUTO SERVICE & REPAIR
BUSINESS VOICE THAMES VALLEY CHAMBER OF
COMMERCE
THE CHAMBER
CHEMISTRY & INDUSTRY
COMMUNITY PRACTITIONER
ENERGY AND ENVIRONMENTAL MANAGEMENT
MAGAZINE
FREIGHT INDUSTRY TIMES
INBUSINESS
IQ EDUCATION
MARINE & PORTS REVIEW
MENTAL HEALTH NURSING
MUSEUMS & HERITAGE
NORTH EAST BUSINESS

PRIMARY CARE TODAY
RIGHT START
SITELINES
SUSTAINABLE COMMUNITIES MAGAZINE
UK POWER AND PROCESS ENGINEERING
UK QUARRIES & MINES
WASTE MANAGEMENT YEARBOOK
WATER & SEWERAGE JOURNAL

TEN ALPS PUBLISHING PLC 1741273
9 Savoy Street, LONDON, WC2E 7HR **Tel:** 020 7878 2300
Titles:
INSURANCE PROFESSIONAL MAGAZINE
OT
YOUNG PERFORMER

TENBY OBSERVER LTD 15027
Tindle House, Warren Street, TENBY, SA70 7JY
Tel: 01834 843262 **Fax:** 01834 844774
Web site: http://www.tenby-today.co.uk
Titles:
TENBY, NARBERTH & WHITLAND OBSERVER SERIES

TENNIS TODAY LTD 15281
14 Sykes Lane, Balderton, NEWARK, NG24 3LT
Tel: 01636 689169 **Fax:** 01636 707952
Email: info@t4ennistodayltd.co.uk
Web site: http://www.tennis-today.net
Titles:
TENNIS TODAY

TERRAPINN HOLDINGS LTD. 629273
Wren House, 43 Hatton Garden, LONDON, EC1N 8EL
Tel: 020 7092 1000 **Fax:** 020 7242 1548
Web site: http://www.terrapinn.com
Titles:
TOTAL TELECOM MAGAZINE
TOTAL TELECOM ONLINE

TERRINGTON PUBLICATIONS LTD 1622011
Alexander House, Forehill, ELY, CB7 4ZA **Tel:** 01353 616100
Fax: 01353 665619
Titles:
ECN ELECTRICAL CONTRACTING NEWS
NCN NETWORK COMMUNICATIONS NEWS

THE TEXTILE INSTITUTE 14377
1st Floor, St. James's Building, Oxford Street,
MANCHESTER, M1 6FQ **Tel:** 0161 237 1188
Fax: 0161 236 1991
Web site: http://www.textileinstitute.org
Titles:
INTERNATIONAL TEXTILE CALENDAR
TEXTILE PROGRESS
TEXTILES

TEXTILE MEDIA SERVICES LTD 1622156
2A Bridge Street, Silsden, KEIGHLEY, BD20 9NB
Tel: 01535 656489 **Fax:** 0870 094 0868
Email: info@textilemedia.com
Web site: http://www.textilemedia.com
Titles:
CENTRAL AND EASTERN EUROPE TEXTILE BUSINESS
REVIEW
TEXTILES EASTERN EUROPE
TEXTILES SOUTH EAST ASIA

TEXTILES INTELLIGENCE LTD 621882
Suite 6, 1st Floor, Alderley House, Alderley Road,
WILMSLOW, SK9 1AT **Tel:** 01625 536136
Fax: 01625 536137
Email: info@textileintelligence.com
Web site: http://www.textilesintelligence.com
Titles:
PERFORMANCE APPAREL MARKETS
TECHNICAL TEXTILE MARKETS
TEXTILE OUTLOOK INTERNATIONAL

TFA GROUP 1729881
40 Bowling Green Lane, LONDON, EC1R 0NE
Tel: 020 7415 7070 **Fax:** 020 7415 7074
Titles:
BUDDYPOWER.NET
GRUB4LIFE.ORG.UK

THAMES GATEWAY LONDON PARTNERSHIP 1622240
8th Floor, Anchorage House, East India Dock, 2 Clove
Crescent, LONDON, E14 2BE **Tel:** 020 7017 2011
Fax: 020 7017 2099
Titles:
RENEW

THE MASTER CHEFS OF GREAT BRITAIN 698800
Woodmans, Brithem Bottom, CULLOMPTON, EX15 1NB
Tel: 01884 35104
Email: masterchefs@msn.com
Web site: http://www.masterchefs.co.uk
Titles:
MASTER CHEFS

THEATRE RECORD 622472
131 Sherringham Avenue, LONDON, N17 9RU
Tel: 020 8960 0740 **Fax:** 020 8962 0655
Web site: http://www.theatrerecord.com
Titles:
THEATRE RECORD

THEBUSINESSDESK LTD 1742547
The Round Foundry Media Centre, Foundry Street, LEEDS,
LS11 5QP **Tel:** 0113 394 4321 **Fax:** 0113 394 4322
Web site: http://www.thebusinessdesk.com/yorkshire/
Titles:
THEBUSINESSDESK.COM/NORTHWEST
THEBUSINESSDESK.COM/YORKSHIRE

THERAILWAYCENTRE.COM LTD 1710404
PO Box 45, DAWLISH, EX7 9XY **Tel:** 01626 862320
Email: editor@therailwaycentre.com
Web site: http://www.therailwaycentre.com
Titles:
THE RAILWAYCENTRE.COM

THETA PRESS 623706
26 Brickfields Close, Lychpit, BASINGSTOKE, RG24 8UX
Tel: 01256 352 221 **Fax:** 01256 352221
Titles:
CARE OF THE CRITICALLY ILL

THG PUBLISHING 16696
121 Dunkirk Lane, LEYLAND, PR26 7SQ **Tel:** 0870 609 8045
Fax: 0871 522 7035
Email: editorial@my-hospitality.com
Web site: http://www.thgpublishing.co.uk
Titles:
MY-HOSPITALITY.COM
NORTH WEST HOSPITALITY MAGAZINE

THINK PUBLISHING 1745644
20-23 Woodside Place, GLASGOW, G3 7QF
Titles:
TREE NEWS

THINK PUBLISHING LTD 1621731
The Pall Mall Deposit, 124-128 Barlby Road, LONDON, W10
6BL **Tel:** 020 8962 3020 **Fax:** 020 8962 8689
Web site: http://www.thinkpublishing.co.uk
Titles:
ACCOUNTING TECHNICIAN
COUNTRYSIDE VOICE
IP REVIEW
SUMMIT
WATERLIFE

THIRD AGE TRUST 17276
19 East Street, BROMLEY, BR1 1QE **Tel:** 020 8466 6139
Fax: 020 8466 5749
Titles:
U3A NEWS

THIS IS LONDON MAGAZINE LTD 15992
42 Conduit Street, LONDON, W1R 9FB **Tel:** 020 7434 1281
Fax: 020 7287 0592
Web site: http://www.til.com
Titles:
THIS IS LONDON

UK Publishers & Their Titles

THOMAS COOK TOUR OPERATIONS LTD   12351
PO Box 227, Coningsby Road, Thomas Cook Business Park,
PETERBOROUGH, PE3 8SB **Tel:** 01733 416477
Web site: http://www.thomascookpublishing.com
Titles:
THOMAS COOK EUROPEAN RAIL TIMETABLE

THOMAS CROSBIE HOLDINGS LTD   15076
45 Hill Street, NEWRY, BT34 1AF **Tel:** 028 3025 1250
Fax: 028 3025 1017
Titles:
NEWRY DEMOCRAT

THOMAS PUBLICATION   18771
St. Anne's House, France Street, BLACKBURN, BB2 1LX
Tel: 01254 59240 **Fax:** 01254 56884
Titles:
EDGES

THOMAS TELFORD LTD   17317
Thomas Telford House, 1 Heron Quay, LONDON, E14 4JD
Tel: 020 7665 2453 **Fax:** 020 7538 4101
Web site: http://www.thomastelford.com
Titles:
CIVIL ENGINEERING
PROCEEDINGS OF ICE, BRIDGE ENGINEERING
PROCEEDINGS OF ICE, ENGINEERING HISTORY AND
   HERITAGE
PROCEEDINGS OF ICE, GROUND IMPROVEMENT

THOMSON HEALTHCARE   18560
11A Sycamore Close, Audlem, CREWE, CW3 0EZ
Tel: 01270 812775
Titles:
BIOWORLD INTERNATIONAL

THOMSON LOCAL   1742277
Thomson Local, 296 Farnborough Road, FARNBOROUGH,
GU14 7NU **Tel:** 01252 516111
Titles:
THOMSONLOCALMONEY

THOMSON REUTERS   13356
Aldgate House, 33 Aldgate High Street, LONDON, EC3N
1DL **Tel:** 020 7369 7000
Web site: http://www.thomsonreuters.com
Titles:
ACQUISITIONS MONTHLY
EUROPEAN VENTURE CAPITAL AND PRIVATE EQUITY
   JOURNAL
IFR BUYOUTS EUROPE
IFR INTERNATIONAL FINANCING REVIEW
INTERNATIONAL SECURITISATION REPORT
PROJECT FINANCE INTERNATIONAL

THOMSON REUTERS LTD   12774
The Thomson Reuters Building, South Colonnade, LONDON,
E14 5EP **Tel:** 020 7250 1122
Web site: http://thomsonreuters.com
Titles:
REUTERS CLUB
REUTERS.CO.UK/FOOTBALL

THRIVE   17463
The Geoffrey Udall Centre, Beech Hill, READING, RG7 2AT
Tel: 0118 988 5688 **Fax:** 0118 988 5677
Email: info@thrive.org.uk
Web site: http://www.thrive.org.uk
Titles:
GROWTHPOINT

TIM WOODWARD PUBLISHING LTD   629289
BCM Box 2071, LONDON, WC1N 3XX **Tel:** 020 8487 9528
Email: mail@twpublishing.co.uk
Web site: http://www.skintwo.com
Titles:
SKIN TWO

TIME & LEISURE   622363
14 The Apprentice Shop, Merton Abbey Mills, 12 Watermill
Way, LONDON, SW19 2RD **Tel:** 020 8545 6777
Fax: 020 8545 6778
Web site: http://www.timeandleisure.co.uk
Titles:
TIME & LEISURE CLAPHAM, BATTERSEA AND FULHAM

TIME & LEISURE EPSOM AND SUTTON
TIME & LEISURE KINGSTON
TIME & LEISURE, WIMBLEDON, PUTNEY &
   WANDSWORTH

TIME INC.   12348
Blue Fin Building, 110 Southwark Street, LONDON, SE1 0SU
Tel: 020 3148 3000
Titles:
FORTUNE
PEOPLE WEEKLY MAGAZINE

TIME MAGAZINES EUROPE LIMITED   15098
8th Floor, Blue Fin Building, 110 Southwark Street,
LONDON, SE1 0SU **Tel:** 020 3148 3000 **Fax:** 020 3148 8514
Email: edit_office@timemagazine.com
Web site: http://www.time.com
Titles:
TIME MAGAZINE

TIME OUT GROUP LTD   16882
Universal House, 251 Tottenham Court Road, LONDON,
W1T 7AB **Tel:** 020 7813 3000 **Fax:** 020 7813 6001
Web site: http://www.timeout.com
Titles:
TIME OUT FILM
TIME OUT LONDON
TIME OUT LONDON SHOPS & SERVICES
TIMEOUT.COM

TIMES & ECHO NEWSPAPERS   12818
18 Tape Street, Cheadle, STOKE-ON-TRENT, ST10 1BD
Tel: 01538 752214 **Fax:** 01538 754465
Titles:
CHEADLE TIMES & ECHO SERIES

TIMES LITERARY SUPPLEMENT LTD   1688356
Times House, 1 Pennington Street, LONDON, E98 1BS
Tel: 020 7782 5000 **Fax:** 020 7782 4966
Email: letters@the-tls.co.uk
Titles:
THE TIMES LITERARY SUPPLEMENT
THE TIMES LITERARY SUPPLEMENT ONLINE

TIMES NEWSPAPERS LTD   14821
1 Pennington Street, LONDON, E98 1ST **Tel:** 020 7782 5000
Fax: 020 7782 5988
Titles:
CAREER
LUXX
PLAYLIST
THE SUNDAY TIMES
THE SUNDAY TIMES CULTURE
THE SUNDAY TIMES (IRELAND)
THE SUNDAY TIMES MAGAZINE
THE SUNDAY TIMES STYLE
THE TIMES
THE TIMES (EDINBURGH OFFICE)
THE TIMES (GLASGOW OFFICE)
THE TIMES MAGAZINE
THE TIMES (MANCHESTER OFFICE)
TIMESONLINE.CO.UK
WEEKEND

TIMES PUBLISHING LIMITED   1731958
18 Guildford Road, Urmston, MANCHESTER, M41 0SD
Tel: 0161 747 8390 **Fax:** 0161 747 3683
Titles:
GLASS TIMES

Y TINCER COMMITTEE   697401
Rhos Helyg, 23 Maes Yr Efail, Penrhyn-coch,
ABERYSTWYTH, SY23 3HE **Tel:** 01970 828017
Titles:
Y TINCER

TINDLE NEWSPAPERS LTD   14983
114-115 West Street, FARNHAM, GU9 7HL
Tel: 01252 723938 **Fax:** 01252 723950
Web site: http://www.tindlenews.co.uk
Titles:
ALTON POST GAZETTE, TIMES & MAIL SERIES
FARINGDON FOLLY
GAZETTE, ADVERTISER AND PRESS NEWSPAPER
   SERIES
THE GAZETTE - SERVING THE ISLE OF PURBECK & THE
   FROME VALLEY

GEM SERIES
THE MERCURY AND POST SERIES
THE MESSENGER
MONMOUTHSHIRE BEACON AND MERLIN SERIES
PULMANS WEEKLY NEWS AND ADVERTISER SERIES
SOUTH HAMS NEWSPAPERS GROUP
SOUTH LONDON PRESS SERIES
SUNDAY INDEPENDENT (PLYMOUTH)
TENBY TIMES
WELLINGTON WEEKLY NEWS
WEST SOMERSET FREE PRESS SERIES
YELLOW ADVERTISER GROUP SERIES (ESSEX)

TITAN MAGAZINES   13278
Titan House, 144 Southwark Street, LONDON, SE1 0UP
Tel: 020 7620 0200
Web site: http://www.titanmagazines.co.uk
Titles:
24 THE OFFICIAL MAGAZINE
BART SIMPSON
BATMAN LEGENDS
CSI: CRIME SCENE INVESTIGATION
DREAMWATCH
DREAMWORKS TALES
HEROES
INDIANA JONES THE OFFICIAL MAGAZINE
LAZY TOWN
NODDY
SIMPSONS COMIC
SPONGEBOB SQUAREPANTS
STAR TREK MAGAZINE
STAR WARS INSIDER
STARGATE
SUPERMAN LEGENDS
SUPERNATURAL MAGAZINE
TORCHWOOD

TNS MEDIA   600653
66 Wilson Street, LONDON, EC2A 2JX **Tel:** 020 7868 6100
Web site: http://www.tnsmi.co.uk
Titles:
PRESSWATCH COMPANY RANKINGS
PRESSWATCH FINANCIAL PRODUCTS
PRESSWATCH SECTOR SUMMARIES

TNT PUBLISHING   674192
Thatcham Business Village, Colthrop Way, THATCHAM,
RG19 4LW **Tel:** 01635 292800 **Fax:** 020 8879 1879
Web site: http://www.tradermedia.co.uk
Titles:
AUTO TRADER
AUTO TRADER
DEALER UPDATE
SA TIMES
TNT MAGAZINE
TNT MAGAZINE
TRUCK AND PLANT TRADER

TODAY MAGAZINES LTD   15125
The Publishing House, Station Road, Framlingham,
WOODBRIDGE, IP13 9EE **Tel:** 01728 622030
Fax: 01728 622031
Email: todaymagazines@btopenworld.com
Web site: http://www.todaymagazines.co.uk
Titles:
FANCY FOWL
SUFFOLK NORFOLK LIFE
WI NEWS (ESSEX)
WI NEWS MAGAZINE (SUFFOLK EAST)
WI NEWS MAGAZINE (SUFFOLK WEST)
WI NEWS MAGAZINE (WEST KENT)

TOFFEE PUBLICATIONS LTD   1643413
PO Box 28, HARLESTON, IP20 0WT **Tel:** 01986 788899
Fax: 01986 788655
Titles:
CARPOLOGY

TOKEN PUBLISHING LTD   15487
Orchard House, Duchy Road, Heathpark, HONITON, EX14
1YD **Tel:** 01404 46972 **Fax:** 01404 44788
Email: info@tokenpublishing.com
Web site: http://www.tokenpublishing.com
Titles:
COIN NEWS INC. BANKNOTE NEWS
COIN YEARBOOK
MEDAL NEWS

TOMORROW'S BUSINESS LTD   18744
Creative Media Centre, 45 Robertson Street, HASTINGS,
TN34 1NL **Tel:** 01424 439683 **Fax:** 01424 205401
Web site: http://www.officemanagement.uk.com

Titles:
UNLIMITED MAGAZINE

TONICK BUSINESS PUBLISHING LTD   1738537
The Old Farmhouse, Nancemellin, CAMBORNE, TR14 0DW
Tel: 01209 718688
Email: info@businesscornwall.co.uk
Web site: http://www.businesscornwall.co.uk
Titles:
BUSINESS CORNWALL

TOONTASTIC PUBLISHING   17269
Office Block 1, Southlink Business Park, Hamilton Street,
OLDHAM, OL4 1DE **Tel:** 0161 624 0414 **Fax:** 0161 628 4655
Titles:
LUCKY BAG COMIC
PRETTY PONY CLUB
RUGRATS

TOPAZ PUBLICATIONS   622248
1 Granville Walk, Chadderton, OLDHAM, OL9 6SR
Tel: 0161 284 6602 **Fax:** 0161 284 3790
Titles:
TODAY'S THERAPIST

TOPLUM POSTASI   1747842
117 Green Lanes, LONDON, N16 9DA **Tel:** 020 7354 4424
Fax: 020 7354 0313
Titles:
LONDON COMMUNITY POST
TOPLUM POSTASI

TOPPER NEWSPAPERS LTD   14982
Maychalk House, 8 Musters Road, West Bridgford,
NOTTINGHAM, NG2 7PL **Tel:** 0115 969 6000
Fax: 0115 982 1874
Email: enquires@toppernewspapers.co.uk
Web site: http://www.toppernewspapers.co.uk
Titles:
NOTTINGHAM AND LONG EATON TOPPER

TOPWAVE LTD   15318
40 Morpeth Road, LONDON, E9 7LD **Tel:** 020 8986 4141
Fax: 020 8986 4145
Titles:
BOXING MONTHLY

TORY REFORM GROUP   15719
83 Victoria Street, LONDON, SW1H 0HW
Tel: 020 3008 4991 **Fax:** 07092 879366
Email: trg@trg.org.uk
Web site: http://www.trg.org.uk
Titles:
REFORMER (CON)

TOTAL LICENSING LTD   1627051
4 Wadhurst Business Park, Faircrouch Lane, WADHURST,
TN5 6PT **Tel:** 01892 782220 **Fax:** 01892 782226
Email: subscriptions@totallicensing.com
Web site: http://www.totallicensing.com
Titles:
TOTAL LICENSING

TOTALLY MEDIA LTD   1726715
The Brewery House, 74 High Street, MARLOW, SL7 1AH
Tel: 01628 488388
Titles:
TOTALLY MEDIA LTD

TOTTEL PUBLISHING   1652859
Maxwelton House, 41-43 Boltro Road, HAYWARDS HEATH,
RH16 1BJ **Tel:** 01444 416119 **Fax:** 01444 440426
Web site: http://www.tottelpublishing.com
Titles:
COMMUNICATIONS LAW
HEALTH AND SAFETY AT WORK NEWSLETTER
JOURNAL OF IMMIGRATION ASYLUM AND
   NATIONALITY LAW
TRUST LAW INTERNATIONAL

TOTTENHAM HOTSPUR FOOTBALL CLUB   1748634
Bill Nicholson Way, 748 High Road, LONDON, N17 0AP
Tel: 0844 499 5000

Titles:
HOTSPUR

TOUCH BRIEFINGS   1766269
Saffron House, 6-10 Kirby Street, LONDON, 6-10 KIRBY
Tel: 020 7452 5600 **Fax:** 020 7452 5606
Email: hr@touchbriefings.com
Web site: http://www.touchbriefings.com/index.htm
Titles:
TOUCH OIL AND GAS

TOUCHLINE PUBLISHING   1649424
3-5 Spafield Street, LONDON, EC1R 4QB
Tel: 020 7841 0340
Web site: http://www.touchline.com
Titles:
MED LIFE

TOURISM SOCIETY   14430
Trinity Court, 34 West Street, SUTTON, SM1 1SH
Tel: 020 8661 4636 **Fax:** 020 8661 4637
Email: flo@tourismsociety.org
Web site: http://www.tourismsociety.org
Titles:
TOURISM

TOWER BUSINESS MEDIA   13343
37-42 Compton Street, LONDON, EC1V 0AP
Tel: 020 7014 0300 **Fax:** 020 7014 0302
Titles:
ESTATES REVIEW
EUROPEAN CEO
OVERSEAS LIVING

TOWER HAMLETS COUNCIL   14885
Mulberry Place, 5 Clove Crescent, LONDON, E14 2BG
Tel: 020 7364 5000 **Fax:** 020 7364 4917
Web site: http://www.towerhamlets.gov.uk
Titles:
EAST END LIFE

TOWER HAMLETS SUMMER UNIVERSITY   1719953
Ground Floor, 24-26 Fournier Street, LONDON, E1 6QE
Tel: 020 7183 3222
Email: nangmagazine@hotmail.com
Web site: http://www.summeruni.org
Titles:
NANG!

TOWN & COUNTRY PLANNING ASSOCIATION   13518
17 Carlton House Terrace, LONDON, SW1Y 5AS
Tel: 020 7930 8903 **Fax:** 020 7930 3280
Titles:
TOWN & COUNTRY PLANNING

TOWN TALK TEAM   625347
c/o The White Hill Centre, White Hill, CHESHAM, HP5 1AG
Tel: 01494 775190
Titles:
CHESHAM TOWN TALK

TRADELINK PUBLICATIONS LTD   14099
British Fields, Ollerton Road, Tuxford, NEWARK, NG22 0PQ
Tel: 01777 871007 **Fax:** 01777 872271
Email: accounts@mqworld.com
Web site: http://www.tradelinkpub.co.uk
Titles:
COAL INTERNATIONAL
INTERNATIONAL GUIDE TO THE COALFIELDS
MINING & QUARRY WORLD

TRADER MEDIA PUBLISHING   628822
Optimum House, Clippers Quay, Salford Quays, SALFORD,
M50 3XP **Tel:** 0161 877 9977
Titles:
CLASSIC AMERICAN

TRADESHIP PUBLICATIONS LTD   12528
Old Kings Head Court, 15 High Street, DORKING, RH4 1AR
Tel: 01306 740363 **Fax:** 01306 740660
Titles:
INTERNATIONAL CEMENT REVIEW

TRADING STANDARDS INSTITUTE   627674
1st Floor, 1 Sylvan Court, Sylvan Way, Southfields Business
Park, BASILDON, SS15 6TH **Tel:** 0870 872 9000
Web site: http://www.tsi.org.uk
Titles:
TS TODAY

TRAFALGAR PUBLICATIONS LTD   677017
7 Castle Street, BRIDGWATER, TA6 3DT **Tel:** 020 8123 6704
Email: news@globalsmt.net
Web site: http://www.globalsmt.net
Titles:
GLOBAL SMT AND PACKAGING
GLOBAL SOLAR TECHNOLOGY

TRAFFORD CENTRE   1761291
Management Suite, Trafford Centre, MANCHESTER, M17
8AA **Tel:** 0161 746 7777 **Fax:** 0161 749 1599
Titles:
THE TRAFFORD MAGAZINE

TRAMP MEDIA LTD   1735476
72 New Bond Street, LONDON, W1S 1RR
Tel: 020 7514 9990 **Fax:** 020 7514 5811
Titles:
TRAMP

TRANSITION EDITIONS   1713582
Unit 25A, Regent Studios, 8 Andrews Road, LONDON, E8
4QN **Tel:** 020 7254 4202
Titles:
GARAGELAND

TRANSPORT & GENERAL WORKERS' UNION   13871
128 Theobalds Road, LONDON, WC1X 8TN
Tel: 020 7611 2500 **Fax:** 020 7611 2555
Web site: http://www.tgwu.org.uk
Titles:
T & G RECORD
TOGETHER

TRANSPORT INTELLIGENCE LTD   1626596
Brinkworth House, Brinkworth, Wiltshire, CHIPPENHAM,
SN15 5DF **Tel:** 01666 511880 **Fax:** 0870 460 2165
Web site: http://www.transportintelligence.com
Titles:
LOGISTICS BRIEFING

TRANSPORT JOURNAL   14394
Unit 64, 14-20 George Street, BIRMINGHAM, B12 9RG
Tel: 0121 440 3003 **Fax:** 0121 440 4644
Titles:
TRANSPORT JOURNAL

TRANSPORT PRESS SERVICES   14396
38 Portobello Road, LONDON, W11 3DH **Tel:** 020 7727 0253
Fax: 020 7229 5909
Email: jds@transportpressservices.com
Titles:
TRANSPORT NEWS DIGEST

TRANSPORT SALARIED STAFFS' ASSOCIATION   13872
Walkden House, 10 Melton Street, LONDON, NW1 2EJ
Tel: 020 7387 2101 **Fax:** 020 7383 0656
Web site: http://www.tssa.org.uk
Titles:
TSSA JOURNAL

TRANSPORT TIMES LTD   1684882
Suite 21, Grosvenor Gardens House, 35-37 Grosvenor
Gardens, LONDON, SW1W 0BS **Tel:** 020 7828 3804
Titles:
TRANSPORT TIMES

TRAPLET PUBLICATIONS LTD   15151
Traplet House, Pendragon Close, MALVERN, WR14 1GA
Tel: 01684 588500 **Fax:** 01684 578558
Web site: http://www.traplet.com
Titles:
BEADS & BEYOND
CRAFT STAMPER
MARINE MODELLING INTERNATIONAL
MILITARY IN SCALE

UK Publishers & Their Titles

MODEL HELICOPTER WORLD
PATCHWORK & QUILTING
QEFI QUIET & ELECTRIC FLIGHT INTERNATIONAL
RADIO CONTROL JET INTERNATIONAL
RADIO CONTROL MODEL WORLD
RADIO RACE CAR INTERNATIONAL
SEWING WORLD
TRUCK MODEL WORLD

TRAVEL AFRICA LTD   18484
4 Rycote Lane Farm, Milton Common, OXFORD, OX9 2NZ
Tel: 01844 278883 **Fax:** 01844 278893
Titles:
  MSAFIRI
  TRAVEL AFRICA MAGAZINE

TRAVEL AGENTS NEWS   695849
14 Chapel Lane, WILMSLOW, SK9 5HX **Tel:** 01625 530580
Fax: 01625 535225
Email: editorial@travelagentsnews.co.uk
Titles:
  TRAVEL AGENTS NEWS

TRAVEL & LEISURE MAGAZINES LTD   13168
First Floor, 114 Cranbrook Road, ILFORD, IG1 4LZ
Tel: 020 8554 4456 **Fax:** 020 8554 4443
Email: choice@tlmags.com
Titles:
  CHOICE DAYS OUT & ATTRACTIONS
  CHOICE HOLIDAY PARKS & COTTAGES
  CHOICE VILLAS & APARTMENTS
  THE TRAVEL & LEISURE MAGAZINE

TRAVEL DAILY   1729089
PR by email only **Tel:** 0845 686 1220 **Fax:** 0845 686 1221
Web site: http://www.traveldaily.co.uk
Titles:
  TRAVEL DAILY

TRAVEL PUBLICATIONS   692795
19 Morley Crescent, EDGWARE, HA8 8XE
Tel: 020 8905 4851 **Fax:** 020 8933 4307
Web site: http://www.thetravelmagazine.co.uk
Titles:
  THE TRAVEL MAGAZINE

TRAVEL TALES   1654323
45 Salford Road, Aspley Guise, MILTON KEYNES, MK17 8HZ **Tel:** 01908 282363 **Fax:** 01908 282363
Titles:
  TRAVEL TALES (TALL AND TRUE)

TRAVELMOLE LTD   622832
Unit 6, City Business Centre, 6 Brighton Road, HORSHAM, RH13 5BP **Tel:** 01403 865800
Web site: http://www.travelmole.com
Titles:
  TRAVELMOLE.COM

TRAVELPLUS MEDIA LIMITED   1622434
Hunters Lodge, Cottesmore Road, Ashwell, OAKHAM, LE15 7LJ
Web site: http://www.travelplus.co.uk
Titles:
  TRAVELPLUS MAGAZINE

TRAVELSCOPE PUBLICATIONS   14432
3rd Floor, Foundation House, Perseverance Works, 38 Kingsland Road, LONDON, E2 8DD **Tel:** 020 7729 4337
Fax: 020 7729 1716
Email: travelgbi@talk21.com
Web site: http://www.travelgbi.com
Titles:
  TRAVEL GBI

TRAVISION LIMITED   700137
12 Heathgate, Wickham Bishops, WITHAM, CM8 3NZ
Tel: 01621 893557
Web site: http://www.travision.com
Titles:
  MARINER.CO.UK

TREACLE PRODUCTIONS LTD   1737042
Suite 9, 2 Commercial Street, EDINBURGH, EH6 6JA
Tel: 0131 555 4126 **Fax:** 0131 554 9303
Titles:
  I-ON EDINBURGH
  I-ON GLASGOW

TREND PUBLICATIONS LTD   1741958
The Bank, 292 Rosemount Place, ABERDEEN, AB25 2YA
Tel: 01224 631141 **Fax:** 01224 622288
Titles:
  TREND

TRENTHAM BOOKS LTD   12366
Westview House, 734 London Road, Oakhill, STOKE-ON-TRENT, ST4 5NP **Tel:** 01782 745567 **Fax:** 01782 74553
Web site: http://www.trentham-books.co.uk
Titles:
  RACE EQUALITY TEACHING

TRI MEDIA GROUP   14747
9-11 Cholswell Court, Cholswell Road, Shippon, ABINGDON, OX13 6HX **Tel:** 01235 547819
Fax: 01235 554465
Email: journal.news@youroxfordshire.co.uk
Titles:
  BREAKOUT (ABINGDON)
  OXFORD JOURNAL
  OXFORDSHIRE LIVING

TRIBUNE PUBLICATIONS LTD   15726
9 Arkwright Road, LONDON, NW3 6AN **Tel:** 020 7433 6410
Fax: 020 7433 6419
Email: mail@tribunemagazine.co.uk
Web site: http://www.tribunemagazine.co.uk
Titles:
  TRIBUNE

TRIDENT MEDIA   1630180
Unit 2A Stoney House, 26-30 Stoney Street, The Lacemarket, NOTTINGHAM, NG1 1LL **Tel:** 0115 924 2681
Fax: 0115 950 6075
Email: mail@fhpmagazine.co.uk
Web site: http://www.fhpmagazine.co.uk
Titles:
  FHP MAGAZINE

TRIDENT MIDLAND NEWSPAPERS   14972
Bridge Road, COALVILLE, LE67 3QP **Tel:** 01530 813101
Fax: 01530 811361
Titles:
  TRIDENT MIDLAND NEWSPAPERS SERIES

TRILOGY SERVICES LTD   1729138
Little Troys, Faulkbourne, WITHAM, CM8 1SL
Tel: 01376 513215
Titles:
  BRITISH VETERANS NEWS

TRI-MEDIA PUBLISHING   622298
Milestone House, 20 Marcham Road, ABINGDON, OX14 1AA **Tel:** 01235 547800 **Fax:** 01235 547801
Titles:
  BASINGSTOKE OBSERVER

TRINITY COLLEGE LONDON   12964
Trinity College London, 89 Albert Embankment, LONDON, SE1 7TP **Tel:** 020 7820 6100 **Fax:** 020 7820 6161
Titles:
  FLOURISH

TRINITY MIRROR   1638426
PO Box 48, Old Hall Street, LIVERPOOL, L69 3EB
Tel: 0151 227 2000 **Fax:** 0151 472 2474
Titles:
  BIRMINGHAM MAIL
  BIRMINGHAM MAIL EXTRA
  BIRMINGHAM POST (CITY/LONDON OFFICE)
  CELEBS ON SUNDAY
  CHRONICLE EXTRA SERIES (TYNE & WEAR)
  DAILY MIRROR
  DAILY MIRROR (BELFAST)
  DAILY MIRROR (BIRMINGHAM OFFICE)
  DAILY MIRROR (OLDHAM OFFICE)
  DAILY POST (WALES)

DAILY RECORD
DAILY RECORD (EDINBURGH OFFICE)
DISCOVER
EXAMINER WEEKLY
FEEL ALIVE
FLINTSHIRE CHRONICLE
GWENT GAZETTE
HERALD AND POST SERIES (TEESSIDE)
THE HINCKLEY TIMES & HERALD SERIES
HUDDERSFIELD DAILY EXAMINER
LIVERPOOL WEEKLY MERSEYMART & STAR SERIES
LIVERPOOL.COM
LIVERPOOL.COM
LOUGHBOROUGH ECHO SERIES
THE MAGAZINE
NORTH WALES WEEKLY NEWS SERIES
NUNEATON TRIBUNE
THE OFFICIAL LFC MAGAZINE
THE PEOPLE
PONTYPRIDD AND LLANTRISANT OBSERVER
RACING POST
RACING POST WEEKENDER
RACINGPOST.CO.UK
ROAD RECORD
THE RUGBY TIMES
SATURDAY PLUS
SCOTTISH BUSINESS INSIDER
SCOTTISH DAILY MIRROR (GLASGOW OFFICE)
SEVEN DAYS
SKYPORT HEATHROW
SUNDAY MIRROR
SUNDAY MIRROR (BELFAST)
SUNDAY MIRROR (GLASGOW OFFICE)
TAKE IT EASY
THIS IS ANFIELD
THE TICKET
TIMES SERIES (COVENTRY, LEAMINGTON, WARWICK & KENILWORTH)
UXBRIDGE GAZETTE SERIES
VISITOR SERIES
WE LOVE TELLY!
THE WHARF
WIRRAL NEWS SERIES
YOUR VALE

TRINITY MIRROR CHESHIRE   14906
Chronicle House, Commonhall Street, CHESTER, CH1 2AA
Tel: 01244 340151
Web site: http://www.iccheshireonline.co.uk
Titles:
  CHESTER CHRONICLE SERIES
  THE CHRONICLE
  CHRONICLE SERIES (CREWE)
  ELLESMERE PORT PIONEER
  RUNCORN & WIDNES NEWS & HERALD SERIES
  WHITCHURCH HERALD
  WREXHAM CHRONICLE

TRINITY MIRROR HUDDERSFIELD LTD   16590
Queen Street South, HUDDERSFIELD, HD1 3DU
Tel: 01484 430000 **Fax:** 01484 437789
Titles:
  EXPRESS & CHRONICLE
  KIRKLEES BUSINESS NEWS

TRINITY MIRROR MIDLANDS   16576
103-106 High Green Court, Newhall Street, CANNOCK, WS11 1AB **Tel:** 01543 501700 **Fax:** 01543 501748
Titles:
  CHASE POST SERIES BURNTWOOD & CANNOCK
  THE NEWS & OBSERVER SERIES
  STAFFORD POST SERIES
  SUTTON COLDFIELD NEWS

TRINITY MIRROR SOUTHERN   636782
326 Station Road, HARROW, HA1 2DR **Tel:** 01895 451000
Fax: 020 8427 5796
Titles:
  THE BUCKINGHAMSHIRE EXAMINER AND ADVERTISER SERIES
  THE GAZETTE AND LEADER SERIES
  HARROW OBSERVER & LEADER SERIES
  INFORMER SERIES (KINGSTON)
  LONDON NEWSPAPER GROUP SERIES
  STAINES INFORMER SERIES

TRMG LTD   17323
Winchester Court, 1 Forum Place, Fiddlebridge Lane, HATFIELD, AL10 0RN **Tel:** 01707 273999
Fax: 01707 276555
Web site: http://www.trmg.co.uk
Titles:
  BUSINESS EDGE
  ENGLAND RUGBY

INTERNATIONAL SHEET METAL REVIEW
MOTOR SPORTS NOW!

TROJAN PUBLISHING   1716418
211 Old Street, Ground Floor, LONDON, EC1V 9NR
Tel: 020 7608 6500 **Fax:** 020 7608 6320
Email: info@trojanpublishing.co.uk
Titles:
  ATTITUDE
  BEST OF FORUM
  DESIRE
  FLUSH
  FORUM
  SO SWITCHED ON
  WHAT DIESEL
  WOMEN'S FITNESS

TROPICANA HEALTH AND FITNESS   15311
Fort Dunlop, Fort Parkway, BIRMINGHAM, B24 9FE
Titles:
  MUSCLEMAG INTERNATIONAL

TRP MAGAZINES   14355
Lansdowne House, 3-7 Northcote Road, LONDON, SW11
1NG **Tel:** 020 7924 4004 **Fax:** 020 7924 1004
Web site: http://www.synfo.com
Titles:
  THE CREW REPORT
  THE YACHT REPORT GROUP

TRUCK AND BUS BUILDER PUBLISHING LTD   14411
PO Box 15, Williton, TAUNTON, TA4 4YP **Tel:** 01984 639300
Fax: 01984 618708
Email: info@truckandbusbuilder.com
Web site: http://www.truckandbusbuilder.com
Titles:
  TRUCK & BUS BUILDER
  THE WORLD BUS AND COACH MANUFACTURING
   INDUSTRY

TRU-EST GROUP   18757
22 Buckingham Gate, LONDON, SW1E 6LB
Tel: 020 7674 0413 **Fax:** 020 7674 0404
Web site: http://www.tru-est.com
Titles:
  WEALTH MANAGEMENT

THE TRUMPET   1645353
44A Selby Road, Leytonstone, LONDON, E11 3LT
Tel: 020 8522 6600 **Fax:** 020 8522 6699
Email: info@the-trumpet.com
Web site: http://www.the-trumpet.com
Titles:
  THE TRUMPET

TSL EDUCATION LTD   15923
26 Red Lion Square, LONDON, WC1R 4HQ
Tel: 020 3194 3000 **Fax:** 020 3194 3100
Email: help@tes.co.uk
Web site: http://www.tsleducation.co.uk
Titles:
  TES CONNECT
  TES CYMRU
  THE TES MAGAZINE
  TES THE TIMES EDUCATIONAL SUPPLEMENT
  TESS
  TIMES HIGHER EDUCATION
  THE TIMES HIGHER EDUCATION

TSO   1718320
The Stationery Office, 24 Seward Street, City Central Two
Estate, LONDON, EC1V 3PA **Tel:** 020 7772 4200
Web site: http://www.tso.co.uk
Titles:
  BELFAST GAZETTE
  EDINBURGH GAZETTE
  LONDON GAZETTE
  THE RETAILER MAGAZINE

TTA PRESS   600326
5 Martins Lane, Witcham, ELY, CB6 2LB **Tel:** 01353 777931
Fax: 01353 777931
Titles:
  THE BLACK STATIC
  CRIMEWAVE
  INTERZONE

THE TUDOR PRESS   697457
Unit 7, Avonside Industrial Park, Avonside Road, BRISTOL,
BS2 0UQ **Tel:** 0117 300 5766 **Fax:** 0117 300 5776
Titles:
  GOOD NEIGHBOURS NEWS

TUDOR ROSE HOLDINGS LTD   600411
Tudor House, 6 Friar Lane, LEICESTER, LE1 5RA
Tel: 0116 222 9900 **Fax:** 0116 222 9901
Titles:
  FINANCE ON WINDOWS
  GOLF COURSE ARCHITECTURE
  MICROSOFT CONNECTIONS IN COMMUNICATIONS
  RETAILSPEAK

TURRET GROUP LTD.   16609
173 High Street, RICKMANSWORTH, WD3 1AY
Tel: 01923 692660 **Fax:** 01923 692679
Web site: http://www.turretgroup.com
Titles:
  BLINDS & SHUTTERS
  CONSERVATORY INDUSTRIES
  DATA CENTRE MANAGEMENT
  FINISHING
  WINDOW INDUSTRIES

TUTOR2U LTD   1734890
Boston House, 214 High Street, Boston Spa, WETHERBY,
LS23 6AD **Tel:** 0844 800 0085 **Fax:** 01937 529236
Web site: http://www.tutor2u.net
Titles:
  LATTE

TWEEDDALE PRESS GROUP   14979
90 Marygate, BERWICK-UPON-TWEED, TD15 1BW
Tel: 01289 306677 **Fax:** 01289 307377
Web site: http://www.tweeddalepress.co.uk
Titles:
  BERWICK ADVERTISER AND GAZETTE SERIES
  BERWICKSHIRE NEWS AND EAST LOTHIAN HERALD
  BORDER LIFE
  HAWICK NEWS
  SELKIRK WEEKEND ADVERTISER
  SOUTHERN REPORTER

TWENTY 4 MEDIA LTD   694509
Suite 5A, 5th Floor, Medusa House, St. Johns Road,
STOURBRIDGE, DY8 1YS
Titles:
  MIDLAND EDITION

TWOHUNDREDBY200   1686800
16 Linton Place, Rosyth, DUNFERMLINE, KY11 2YY
Tel: 01383 417667
Email: info@twohundredby200.co.uk
Web site: http://www.twohundredby200.co.uk
Titles:
  TWOHUNDREDBY200

TYLER PUBLISHING   1630129
Premier House, 11 Marlborough Place, BRIGHTON, BN1
1UB **Tel:** 01273 670003 **Fax:** 01273 609040
Web site: http://www.motheratwork.co.uk
Titles:
  MOTHER@WORK

TYPESTYLE LTD   17426
Independent House, Radford Business Centre, Radford
Way, BILLERICAY, CM12 0AA **Tel:** 01277 627300
Fax: 01277 655925
Titles:
  ESSEX ENQUIRER SERIES
  VEGGIETIMES

TYRE INDUSTRY PUBLICATIONS LTD   14124
Unit 1, Magnolia Centre, Telford Road, CLACTON-ON-SEA,
CO15 4LP **Tel:** 01255 222233 **Fax:** 01255 222234
Email: info@tyrepress.com
Web site: http://www.tyrepress.com
Titles:
  TYRES & ACCESSORIES

TYRONE PRINTING CO LTD   15078
58 Scotch Street, DUNGANNON, BT70 1BD
Tel: 028 8772 2271 **Fax:** 028 8772 6171

Titles:
  DUNGANNON NEWS & TYRONE COURIER

TYRRELL BURGESS ASSOCIATES   15926
34 Sandilands, CROYDON, CR0 5DB **Tel:** 020 8656 1770
Titles:
  HIGHER EDUCATION REVIEW

UANDI DESIGN   1714629
PO Box 801, TAUNTON, TA1 9DS **Tel:** 0845 094 2034
Email: info@uandi-design.com
Web site: http://www.uandi-design.com
Titles:
  BIKERESS

UBM AVIATION   13640
Ludgate House, 245 Blackfriars Road, LONDON, SE1 9UY
Tel: 020 7579 4840 **Fax:** 020 7579 4848
Email: simonb@aviation-industry.com
Web site: http://www.aviationindustrygroup.com
Titles:
  AIRCRAFT TECHNOLOGY ENGINEERING &
   MAINTENANCE
  AIRLINE FLEET MANAGEMENT

UBM INFORMATION LTD   1758184
Ludgate House, 245 Blackfriars Road, LONDON, SE1 9UY
Tel: 020 7921 5000
Titles:
  BSD BUILDING SUSTAINABLE DESIGN
  BUILDING
  BUILDING DESIGN
  CARING BUSINESS
  CCF
  CONSTRUCTION MANAGER
  DALTONS WEEKLY
  ELECTRICAL & MECHANICAL CONTRACTOR
  FSE
  INFO4SECURITY
  INSTALLATION EUROPE
  INSTALLATION EUROPE
  INTERNATIONAL FOOD INGREDIENTS
  MUSIC WEEK
  ONE TO ONE
  PRO SOUND NEWS EUROPE
  PROPERTY DIRECT
  PROPERTY WEEK
  PROPERTY WEEK GLOBAL
  PROPERTYWEEK.COM
  PULSE
  RESIDENTIAL SYSTEMS EUROPE
  SAFETY AND HEALTH PRACTITIONER
  SECURITY INSTALLER
  SECURITY MANAGEMENT TODAY (SMT)
  THEME MAGAZINE
  TRAVEL TRADE GAZETTE
  TTG BUSINESS.COM
  TTG LUXURY
  TVB EUROPE
  WORLD ARCHITECTURE

UBM INFORMATION (PRESTON)   1600384
Unit 4, Fulwood Business Park, Caxton Road, Fulwood,
PRESTON, PR2 9NZ **Tel:** 020 7921 5000
Titles:
  FARMERS GUARDIAN

UBM INFORMATION (TONBRIDGE)   1600382
Riverbank House, Angel Lane, TONBRIDGE, TN9 1SE
Tel: 01732 364422
Web site: http://www.farmersguardian.com
Titles:
  CHEMIST + DRUGGIST
  CHEMIST+DRUGGIST
  DAIRY FARMER
  OVER THE COUNTER

UBM LIVE   1760998
245 Blackfriars Road, LONDON, SE1 9UY
Tel: 020 7921 5000
Web site: http://www.cmpi.biz
Titles:
  INTERIORS HUB
  THE PUBLICAN.COM
  SERVICE MANAGEMENT

UCAS   15927
Rosehill, New Barn Lane, CHELTENHAM, GL52 3LZ
Tel: 01242 544861 **Fax:** 01242 544806
Web site: http://www.ucas.ac.uk

UK Publishers & Their Titles

Titles:
YOU CAN!

UCATT 16308
UCATT House, 177 Abbeville Road, LONDON, SW4 9RL
Tel: 020 7223 6192 **Fax:** 020 7720 4081
Titles:
UCATT BUILDING WORKER

UCLAN STUDENTS UNION 18413
University of Central Lancashire Students Union, Fylde
Road, PRESTON, PR1 2TQ **Tel:** 01772 893000
Fax: 01772 893994
Titles:
PLUTO

UCU 1715168
27 Britannia Street, LONDON, WC1X 9JP
Tel: 020 7670 9700 **Fax:** 020 7670 9749
Web site: http://www.ucu.org.uk
Titles:
UC

UDSU 16394
Students Union, University of Derby, Kedleston Road,
DERBY, DE22 1GB **Tel:** 01332 591507 **Fax:** 01332 591501
Titles:
DUSTED

UFM WORLDWIDE 17965
145 Faringdon Road, SWINDON, SN1 5DL
Tel: 01793 610515 **Fax:** 01793 432255
Email: ufm@ufm.org.uk
Web site: http://www.ufm.org.uk
Titles:
4 CORNERS

UK COAL PLC 674655
Harworth Park, Blyth Road, Harworth, DONCASTER, DN11
8DB **Tel:** 01302 751751 **Fax:** 01302 751707
Titles:
UK COAL NEWSCENE

UK COBRA REPLICA CLUB LTD 16269
18 Neptune Road, FAREHAM, PO15 6SW
Tel: 01329 312011
Web site: http://www.cobraclub.com
Titles:
SNAKE TORQUE

UK DISTRIBUTION SERVICES LTD 1759938
UKD House, Norstead Place, LONDON, SW15 3SA
Tel: 020 8246 5900 **Fax:** 020 8246 5920
Email: info@ukltd.com
Web site: http://www.ukdistributionservices.com
Titles:
FIGHTSPORT

THE UK FLIGHT SAFETY COMMITTEE 13625
Graham Suite, Fairoaks Airport, Chobham, WOKING, GU24
8HX **Tel:** 01276 855193 **Fax:** 01276 855195
Titles:
FOCUS ON COMMERCIAL AVIATION SAFETY

UK HARBOUR MASTERS ASSOCIATION 18594
F5 Northney Marina, HAYLING ISLAND, PO11 0NH
Tel: 023 9246 0111 **Fax:** 023 9246 0123
Titles:
QUAY NOTES

UK LUBRICANTS ASSOCIATION LIMITED 17037
Berkhamsted House, 121 High Street, BERKHAMSTED, HP4
2DJ **Tel:** 01442 230589 **Fax:** 01442 259232
Email: lube@ukla.org.uk
Web site: http://www.ukla.org.uk
Titles:
LUBE

UK YOUTH 16098
Avon Tyrrell, Bransgore, CHRISTCHURCH, BH23 8EE
Tel: 01425 672347 **Fax:** 01425 675108
Web site: http://www.ukyouth.org

Titles:
THE SOURCE

UKEN LTD 16616
35 Hollywood Road, LONDON, SW10 9HT
Tel: 020 7351 3954 **Fax:** 020 7351 3954
Web site: http://www.ukendata.com
Titles:
UK ENVIRONMENT NEWS

UKFAST.NET 1745683
City Tower, Piccadilly Plaza, MANCHESTER, M1 4BT
Tel: 0870 421 1585 **Fax:** 0870 458 4545
Web site: http://www.ukfast.net
Titles:
SERVERS

UKIP MEDIA & EVENTS LTD 13954
Abinger House, Church Street, DORKING, RH4 1DF
Tel: 01306 743744 **Fax:** 01306 742525
Web site: http://www.ukipme.com
Titles:
AEROSPACE TESTING INTERNATIONAL
AIR TRAFFIC TECHNOLOGY INTERNATIONAL
AIRCRAFT INTERIORS INTERNATIONAL
AUDITORIA
AUTOMOTIVE TESTING TECHNOLOGY INTERNATIONAL
BUSINESS JET INTERIORS INTERNATIONAL
ELECTRIC & HYBRID VEHICLE TECHNOLOGY
ENGINE TECHNOLOGY INTERNATIONAL
EUROPEAN AUTOMOTIVE COMPONENTS NEWS
IVT INTERNATIONAL
PASSENGER TERMINAL WORLD
PASSENGERTERMINALTODAY.COM
POSTAL TECHNOLOGY INTERNATIONAL
PROFESSIONAL MOTORSPORT WORLD
RAILWAY INTERIORS INTERNATIONAL
STADIA
TIRE TECHNOLOGY INTERNATIONAL
TRAFFIC TECHNOLOGY INTERNATIONAL
VEHICLE DYNAMICS INTERNATIONAL

UKMPA 16807
Canterbury Gate House, Ash Road, SANDWICH, CT13 9HZ
Tel: 01304 613020 **Fax:** 01304 613020
Titles:
THE MARITIME PILOT

UKPETS PARTNERSHIP 1741876
Lynnwood Business Centre, Lynnwood Terrace,
NEWCASTLE UPON TYNE, NE4 6UL
Titles:
UKPETS

ULSTER GAZETTE (ARMAGH) LTD. 15086
56 Scotch Street, ARMAGH, BT61 7DQ **Tel:** 028 3752 2639
Fax: 028 3752 7029
Email: newsdesk@ulstergazette.co.uk
Web site: http://www.ulstergazette.co.uk
Titles:
ULSTER GAZETTE

ULSTER JOURNALS LTD 15993
39 Boucher Road, BELFAST, BT12 6UT **Tel:** 028 9066 3311
Fax: 028 9038 1915
Email: edit@ulstertatler.com
Web site: http://www.ulstertatler.com
Titles:
PERSPECTIVE
THE POLICE SERVICE GAZETTE INCORPORATING
   CONSTABULARY GAZETTE
SOUTH BELFAST LIFE
ULSTER BRIDE
ULSTER TATLER
ULSTER TATLER INTERIORS
ULSTER TATLER INTERIORS
WINE & DINE IN NORTHERN IRELAND

ULSTER SPEED PROMOTIONS 1706556
6 Parkland Avenue, LISBURN, BT28 3JW
Tel: 028 9266 4336 **Fax:** 028 9266 4336
Titles:
ULSTER ROAD RACING IN FOCUS

ULTIMA MEDIA LTD 16799
Lamb House, Church Street, LONDON, W4 2PD
Tel: 020 8987 0900 **Fax:** 020 8987 0901
Email: info@ultimamedia.com
Web site: http://www.ultimamedia.com

Titles:
AUTOMOTIVE LOGISTICS
AUTOMOTIVE MANUFACTURING SOLUTIONS
CAR DESIGN NEWS
FINISHED VEHICLE LOGISTICS
INTERIOR MOTIVES

ULTRA-FIT PUBLICATIONS LTD 15316
Champions House, 5 Princes Street, PENZANCE, TR18 2NL
Tel: 01736 350204 **Fax:** 01736 368587
Titles:
ULTRA-FIT MAGAZINE

UMBERTO ALLEMANDI & CO. PUBLISHING, TURIN 15807
70 South Lambeth Road, LONDON, SW8 1RL
Tel: 020 7735 3331 **Fax:** 020 7735 3332
Titles:
THE ART NEWSPAPER

UNCOOKED MEDIA LTD 1689801
B10 Arena Business Centre, Holyrood Close, POOLE, BH17
7BA **Tel:** 01202 606385 **Fax:** 01202 606386
Email: customerservice@uncookedmedia.com
Titles:
360 GAMER
FIGHTING SPIRIT
NEO

UNDERLINES LTD 16864
Room 102, Curtain House, 134-146 Curtain Road, LONDON,
EC2A 3AR **Tel:** 020 7729 3664 **Fax:** 020 7729 3701
Titles:
UNDERLINES

UNDERWATER WORLD PUBLICATIONS LTD 622767
55 High Street, TEDDINGTON, TW11 8HA
Tel: 020 8943 4288 **Fax:** 020 8943 4312
Email: ios@divermag.co.uk
Web site: http://www.intoceansys.co.uk
Titles:
INTERNATIONAL OCEAN SYSTEMS
UNDERWATER CONTRACTOR INTERNATIONAL

UNILEVER PLC 18302
PO Box 68, Unilever House, LONDON, EC4P 4BQ
Tel: 020 7822 5252 **Fax:** 020 7822 5128
Titles:
UNILEVER MAGAZINE

UNION OF BRUNEL STUDENTS 15765
Cleveland Road, UXBRIDGE, UB8 3PH **Tel:** 01895 269269
Web site: http://www.brunelstudents.com
Titles:
LE NURB

UNION OF STUDENTS 16877
University of Sheffield, Union of Students, Western Bank,
SHEFFIELD, S10 2TG **Tel:** 0114 222 8540
Fax: 0114 222 8542
Titles:
UNION

UNION OF UEA STUDENTS 15742
PO Box 410, NORWICH, NR4 7TB **Tel:** 01603 250558
Fax: 01603 506822
Titles:
CONCRETE

UNION PRESS LTD 18584
Unit 222-223, 30 Great Guildford Street, LONDON, SE1 0HS
Tel: 020 7803 2420 **Fax:** 020 7803 2421
Titles:
THE DRINKS BUSINESS
GOLF CLUB MANAGEMENT
THE SPIRITS BUSINESS

THE UNION SOCIETY 15744
University of Newcastle-Upon-Tyne, Kings Walk,
NEWCASTLE UPON TYNE, NE1 8QB **Tel:** 0191 232 4050
Fax: 0191 222 1876
Titles:
THE COURIER

UNIQUE TALENT MANAGEMENT LTD 1706558
International House, Suite 501, 223 Regent Street, LONDON,
W1H 2QD **Tel:** 020 7723 1209
Email: chanel@utm.org.uk
Web site: http://www.utm.org.uk

Titles:
ITGIRL WORLD
YOUNGTALENT.ORG.UK

UNITE 15208
Unit 6, Imperial Court, Laporte Way, LUTON, LU4 8FE
Tel: 01582 721652 **Fax:** 01582 450906
Web site: http://www.pensioneronline.com

Titles:
UNITE MAGAZINE

UNITE THE UNION 1746038
35 King Street, LONDON, WC2E 8JG **Tel:** 020 7420 8900
Fax: 020 7611 2555
Web site: http://www.tgwu.org.uk

Titles:
LANDWORKER
UNITED MAGAZINE

UNITED AWARENESS PUBLISHING LTD 1711140
Goss Chambers, Goss Street, CHESTER, CH1 2BG
Tel: 01244 624022 **Fax:** 01244 624023
Web site: http://www.uapl.co.uk

Titles:
THE BURNING ISSUE

UNITED BUSINESS MEDIA INTERNATIONAL LIMITED
623293
630 Chiswick High Road, LONDON, W4 5BG
Tel: 01732 364422
Web site: http://www.ubm.com

Titles:
CONTENT MANAGEMENT 365
THE PUBLICAN

UNITED KINGDOM HOME CARE ASSOCIATION LTD
14173
2nd Floor, Group House, 52 Sutton Court Road, SUTTON,
SM1 4SL **Tel:** 020 8288 5291 **Fax:** 020 8288 5290

Titles:
HOMECARER

THE UNITED REFORMED CHURCH (LONDON) 17947
86 Tavistock Place, LONDON, WC1H 9RT
Tel: 020 7916 2020 **Fax:** 020 7916 2121
Email: urc@urc.org.uk
Web site: http://www.urc.org.uk

Titles:
REFORM

UNITY MEDIA PLC 13535
Becket House, Vestry Road, SEVENOAKS, TN14 5EJ
Tel: 01732 748000 **Fax:** 01732 748001
Web site: http://www.unity-media.co.uk

Titles:
BANZAI MAGAZINE
BMW CAR
CONSERVATORY MAGAZINE
GLASS AND GLAZING PRODUCTS
GT PURELY PORSCHE
HEATING & PLUMBING MONTHLY
PERFORMANCE BMW
PERFORMANCE CAR
PERFORMANCE FORD
PERFORMANCE VW
PLUMBZINE
PSLG BUILDING
RCI DIRECTORY
RCI (ROOFING, CLADDING & INSULATION)
RETRO FORD

UNIVERSITIES FEDERATION FOR ANIMAL WELFARE
18295
The Old School, Brewhouse Hill, Wheathampstead, ST.
ALBANS, AL4 8AN **Tel:** 01582 831818 **Fax:** 01582 831414
Email: ufaw@ufaw.org.uk
Web site: http://www.ufaw.org.uk

Titles:
ANIMAL WELFARE

UNIVERSITY COLLEGE LONDON 15780
University College, London Union, 25 Gordon Street,
LONDON, WC1H 0AH **Tel:** 020 7679 7985
Fax: 020 7209 8533

Titles:
PI

**UNIVERSITY OF BATH & LONDON SCHOOL OF
ECONOMICS** 17946
University of Bath, The Avenue, Claverton Down, BATH, BA2
7AY **Tel:** 01225 386302 **Fax:** 01225 386767
Email: jtep@management.bath.ac.uk
Web site: http://www.jtep.com

Titles:
JOURNAL OF TRANSPORT ECONOMICS & POLICY

UNIVERSITY OF BATH STUDENTS' UNION 15798
University of Bath, Claverton Down, BATH, BA2 7AY
Tel: 01225 826883 **Fax:** 01225 826562
Web site: http://www.bathstudent.com

Titles:
STUDENT IMPACT

UNIVERSITY OF BIRMINGHAM 17114
University of Birmingham, Edgbaston, BIRMINGHAM, B15
2TT **Tel:** 0121 414 4986 **Fax:** 0121 414 4989
Email: ca.afowler@bham.ac.uk
Web site: http://www.inlogov.bham.ac.uk

Titles:
CRITICAL POLICY ANALYSIS

UNIVERSITY OF BRISTOL UNION 15748
Queens Road, Clifton, BRISTOL, BS8 1LN
Tel: 0117 954 5857 **Fax:** 0117 954 5817
Web site: http://www.ubu.org.uk

Titles:
EPIGRAM

UNIVERSITY OF CAMBRIDGE DEVELOPMENT OFFICE
16397
1 Quayside, Bridge Street, CAMBRIDGE, CB5 8AB
Tel: 01223 332288 **Fax:** 01223 764476

Titles:
CAM CAMBRIDGE ALUMNI MAGAZINE

UNIVERSITY OF ESSEX STUDENTS UNION 15750
Wivenhoe Park, COLCHESTER, CO4 3SQ
Tel: 01206 863211 **Fax:** 01206 870915
Web site: http://www.essexstudent.com

Titles:
THE RABBIT

UNIVERSITY OF KENT STUDENTS' UNION 15763
Mandela Building, University Of Kent, CANTERBURY, CT2
7NZ **Tel:** 01227 824200 **Fax:** 01227 464625

Titles:
INQUIRE
INQUIRELIVE.CO.UK

UNIVERSITY OF LEICESTER STUDENTS UNION 15787
Percy Gee Building, University of Leicester, University Road,
LEICESTER, LE1 7RH **Tel:** 0116 223 1216
Fax: 0116 223 1112

Titles:
RIPPLE

UNIVERSITY OF LONDON UNION 15768
Malet Street, LONDON, WC1E 7HY **Tel:** 020 7664 2056
Fax: 020 7664 2055

Titles:
LONDON STUDENT

UNIVERSITY OF NOTTINGHAM STUDENT UNION 621561
Portland Building, University Park, NOTTINGHAM, NG7 2RD
Tel: 0115 846 8716 **Fax:** 0115 935 1101

Titles:
IMPACT (NOTTINGHAM)

THE UNIVERSITY OF READING 16443
DARO, Blandford Lodge, PO Box 217, READING, RG6 6AH
Tel: 0118 378 8006 **Fax:** 0118 378 6587
Web site: http://www.reading.ac.uk

Titles:
UNIVERSITY OF READING MAGAZINE

UNIVERSITY OF SHEFFIELD STUDENT UNION 1709777
Western Bank, SHEFFIELD, S10 2TG **Tel:** 0114 222 8500

Titles:
FORGE PRESS

UNIVERSITY OF SUSSEX STUDENTS UNION 17818
Falmer House, Falmer, BRIGHTON, BN1 9QF
Tel: 01273 678555
Web site: http://www.ussu.net

Titles:
THE BADGER

**UNIVERSITY OF THE WEST OF SCOTLAND
ASSOCIATION** 15732
University of the West of Scotland, Storie Street, PAISLEY,
PA1 2HB **Tel:** 0141 849 4166 **Fax:** 0141 849 4158

Titles:
THE BANTER

UNIVERSITY OF WESTMINSTER STUDENT UNION 15792
32-38 Wells Street, LONDON, W1P 4DJ **Tel:** 020 7911 5850

Titles:
THE SMOKE

UNIVERSITY PRESS 1739897
School of Law, The Queen's University, 30 University
Square, BELFAST, BT7 1NN **Tel:** 028 9033 5224
Fax: 028 9032 6308

Titles:
NORTHERN IRELAND LEGAL QUARTERLY

UNLIMITED MEDIA 628837
3rd Floor, Unicorn House, 221-222 Shoreditch High Street,
LONDON, E14 9YT **Tel:** 0870 744 2643 **Fax:** 070 9231 4982
Email: info@unlimitedmedia.co.uk
Web site: http://www.unlimitedmedia.co.uk

Titles:
CMU DAILY
THREE WEEKS

URBAN MEDIA LTD 1641052
1162 Coventry Road, Yardley, BIRMINGHAM, B25 8DA
Tel: 0871 990 2305 **Fax:** 0871 990 2306
Email: info@urbanmedialtd.com
Web site: http://www.urbanmedialtd.com

Titles:
THE ASIAN TODAY

URDD GOBAITH CYMRU 13157
Swyddfa'r Urdd, Llanbadarn Road, ABERYSTWYTH, SY23
1EY **Tel:** 01970 613118 **Fax:** 01970 626120
Web site: http://www.urdd.org

Titles:
BORE DA
CIP
IAW!

URTU 13879
Almond House, Oak Green, Stanley Green Business Park,
CHEADLE HULME, SK8 6QL **Tel:** 0161 486 2103
Fax: 0161 485 3109

Titles:
WHEELS

USDAW 1719657
188 Wilmslow Road, MANCHESTER, M14 6LJ
Tel: 0161 224 2804 **Fax:** 0161 249 2490
Web site: http://www.usdaw.org.uk

Titles:
ARENA
USDAW NETWORK

UT2 PUBLISHING 1741878
7 Allens Orchard, Brampton, HUNTINGDON, PE28 4NW
Tel: 01480 370007
Email: john.howes@ntlworld.com
Web site: http://www.ut-2.com

Titles:
UT2

UK Publishers & Their Titles

UTEK EUROPE 1643428
Pera Innovation Park, Nottingham Road, MELTON MOWBRAY, LE13 0PB **Tel:** 01664 503700
Fax: 01664 503705
Titles:
  PHARMALICENSING

UTMEDIA 1717973
Madeira House, Madeira Walk, WINDSOR, SL4 1EU
Tel: 01753 860700
Web site: http://www.utmedia.co.uk
Titles:
  FINANCE DAILY
  JUSTCOMPETITIONS.CO.UK
  JUSTOVERSEAS.CO.UK
  KEEP THE DOCTOR AWAY
  TRAVEL CONNECT
  URBANPLANET.CO.UK

UWESU STUDENT PUBLICATIONS 15734
Univ. of West of England S.U., Coldharbour Lane, Frenchay Campus, BRISTOL, BS16 1QY **Tel:** 0117 965 6261
Fax: 0117 976 3909
Titles:
  WESTWORLD

V P PUBLISHING LIMITED 1745968
30 Diamond Ridge, CAMBERLEY, GU15 4LD
Tel: 01276 686654 **Fax:** 01276 686654
Email: teamwork@ukonline.co.uk
Web site: http://www.veterinary-practice.com
Titles:
  VETERINARY PRACTICE

V V MEDIA 1763394
48 Langham Street, LONDON, W1W 7AY
Titles:
  VV MAGAZINE

VALE PUBLISHING 1712198
7-8 St. Stephens Mews, LONDON, W2 5QZ
Tel: 020 7727 8000 **Fax:** 020 7221 6212
Web site: http://www.valepublishing.com
Titles:
  THE LONDON VISITOR MAGAZINE

VALIS BOOKS 15343
34 Darwin Crescent, Laira, PLYMOUTH, PL3 6DX
Tel: 01752 347200 **Fax:** 01752 347200
Titles:
  TALKING PICTURES

VAN UK LTD 1650957
The Old Police Station, Golden Hill, LEYLAND, PR25 4YE
Tel: 01772 433303 **Fax:** 01772 433772
Email: editor@vanandlighttruck.co.uk
Web site: http://www.vanandlighttruck.co.uk
Titles:
  PROFESSIONAL VAN & LIGHT TRUCK

VARIANT 1680195
1/2 189B Maryhill Road, GLASGOW, G20 7XJ
Tel: 0141 333 9522
Web site: http://www.variant.org.uk
Titles:
  VARIANT

VARIETY CLUB OF GREAT BRITAIN 15228
Variety Club House, 93 Bayham Street, LONDON, NW1 0AG
Tel: 020 7428 8100 **Fax:** 020 7428 8111
Titles:
  THE BARKER

VARSITY PUBLICATIONS LTD 15799
Old Examination Hall, Free School Lane, CAMBRIDGE, CB2 3RF **Tel:** 01223 337575 **Fax:** 01223 352913
Web site: http://www.varsity.co.uk
Titles:
  BLUESCI
  VARSITY

VATHEK PUBLISHING 18421
Bridge House, DALBY, IM5 3BP **Tel:** 01624 863256
Fax: 01624 863254
Email: mlw@vathek.com
Web site: http://www.vathek.com
Titles:
  COMMON LAW WORLD REVIEW

VAUXHALL MOTORS LTD 622464
Griffin House, Osborne Road, LUTON, LU1 3YT
Tel: 01582 721122 **Fax:** 01582 427400
Titles:
  HPM
  THE VOICE

THE VEGAN SOCIETY LTD 15210
21 Hylton Street, Hockley, BIRMINGHAM, B18 6HJ
Email: info@vegansociety.com
Web site: http://www.vegansociety.com
Titles:
  THE VEGAN

THE VEGETARIAN SOCIETY 12898
Parkdale, Dunham Road, ALTRINCHAM, WA14 4QG
Tel: 0161 925 2000 **Fax:** 0161 926 9182
Web site: http://www.vegsoc.org
Titles:
  THE VEGETARIAN

VEHICLE BUILDERS & REPAIRERS ASSOCIATION 14129
Belmont House, 102 Finkle Lane, Gildersome, LEEDS, LS27 7TW **Tel:** 0113 253 8333 **Fax:** 0113 238 1892
Email: body@vbra.co.uk
Web site: http://www.vbra.co.uk
Titles:
  BODY MAGAZINE

VELO AGENCY 1759891
82 Dean Street, LONDON, W1D 3HA
Titles:
  DEBENHAM'S DESIRE

VENTURE MARKETING GROUP 1762134
Carlton Plaza, 111 Upper Richmond Road, LONDON, SW15 2TJ
Titles:
  BUSINESS FRANCHISE

VENUE PUBLISHING 16774
2nd Floor, Bristol News & Media, Temple Way, BRISTOL, BS99 7HD **Tel:** 0117 942 8491 **Fax:** 0117 934 3566
Web site: http://www.venue.co.uk
Titles:
  EATING OUT WEST
  FOLIO
  VENUE

VERITAS FOUNDATION PUBLICATIONS CENTRE 1712719
63 Jeddo Road, LONDON, W12 9EE **Tel:** 020 8749 4957
Fax: 020 8749 4965
Titles:
  GAZETA NIEDZIELNA

VERITE CM LTD 1649965
8 St John's Parade, Alinora Crescent, Goring-by-Sea, WORTHING, BN12 4HJ **Tel:** 0845 166 8463
Fax: 0845 166 8459
Email: enquiries@veritecm.com
Web site: http://www.veritecm.com
Titles:
  CHALLENGE NEWSLINE INCORPORATING THE GOOD NEWSPAPER

THE VERTIKAL PRESS 621703
18 Cross Lane, Helmdon, BRACKLEY, NN13 5QL
Tel: 01295 768340 **Fax:** 01295 768223
Titles:
  CRANES & ACCESS

VETERAN CAR SERVICES LTD 15464
Jessamine Court, 15 High Street, Ashwell, BALDOCK, SG7 5NL **Tel:** 01462 742818 **Fax:** 01462 742997

Titles:
  VETERAN CAR

VETERINARY BUSINESS DEVELOPMENT LTD 14796
Olympus House, Werrington Centre, PETERBOROUGH, PE4 6NA **Tel:** 01733 325522 **Fax:** 01733 352212
Web site: http://www.vetsonline.com
Titles:
  THE VETERINARY BUSINESS JOURNAL
  VETERINARY TIMES
  THE VN TIMES

VETSTREAM LTD 621872
Three Hills Farm, Bartlow, CAMBRIDGE, CB21 4EN
Tel: 01223 895818 **Fax:** 01223 895820
Web site: http://www.vetstream.com
Titles:
  VETSTREAM

VIA MEDIA LTD 1676169
Oak House Mews, 43 The Parade, Claygate, ESHER, KT10 0PD **Tel:** 01392 202591 **Fax:** 01372 478961
Web site: http://www.via-medialtd.com
Titles:
  AUTO ID EUROPE
  NUTRACEUTICAL BUSINESS & TECHNOLOGY
  PHARMA
  SUPPLY CHAIN EUROPE

VICE UK LTD 1600524
Ground Floor, 77 Leonard Street, LONDON, EC2A 4QS
Tel: 020 7613 5981 **Fax:** 020 7729 6884
Titles:
  VICE MAGAZINE

VICTORIAN MILITARY SOCIETY 18262
PO Box 5837, NEWBURY, RG14 7FJ **Tel:** 01635 48628
Email: vmsdan@msn.com
Web site: http://www.victorianmilitarysociety.org.uk
Titles:
  SOLDIERS OF THE QUEEN
  SOLDIERS SMALL BOOK

THE VICTORIAN SOCIETY 16115
1 Priory Gardens, Bedford Park, LONDON, W4 1TT
Tel: 020 8994 1019 **Fax:** 020 8747 5899
Email: admin@victorian-society.org.uk
Web site: http://www.victoriansociety.org.uk
Titles:
  THE VICTORIAN

VIE EUROPE LTD 1715977
Studio 3C, 249-251 Kensal Road, LONDON, W10 5DB
Tel: 020 8969 3069 **Fax:** 020 8969 3069
Web site: http://www.matchboxmag.com
Titles:
  MATCHBOX

VIGILANTE PUBLICATIONS 15388
Alliance House, 37 Holybrook Road, READING, RG1 6DG
Tel: 0845 644 5513 **Fax:** 0870 705 8562
Titles:
  EP MAGAZINE

VINEYARD PUBLISHING 1766870
1 Chartwell Lodge, 9 Brackley Road, BECKENHAM, BR3 1SW **Tel:** 020 8650 3645
Titles:
  FLY

VINTAGE TRACTOR 1655129
30 Hallow Lane, Lower Broadheath, WORCESTER, WR2 6QL **Tel:** 01905 640306
Titles:
  MODEL TRACTOR
  VINTAGE TRACTOR

VINYL FACTORY PUBLISHING LTD 1630282
Basement Studio, 45 Foubert's Place, LONDON, W1F 7QH
Tel: 020 7025 1385 **Fax:** 020 7287 4912
Web site: http://www.vinylfactory.co.uk
Titles:
  FACT

VIP INTERNET LTD 1621030
Weston Bank, Weston-under-Lizard, SHIFNAL, TF11 8JU
Tel: 01952 852200

Titles:
VIRTUAL LONDON

VIP PUBLISHING 622837
Graphic House, 46 Alcester Street, BIRMINGHAM, B12 0PH
Tel: 0121 766 8830 **Fax:** 0121 766 8832

Titles:
PHARMACY PRODUCT GUIDE

VIRUS BULLETIN LTD 14466
The Pentagon, Abingdon Science Park, ABINGDON, OX14
3YP **Tel:** 01235 555139 **Fax:** 01235 531889
Web site: http://www.virusbtn.com

Titles:
VIRUS BULLETIN

VISAGE COMMUNICATIONS 1640246
Unit 1B Melrose Nurseries, Longland Lane, Farnsfield,
NEWARK, NG22 8HD **Tel:** 01623 882398

Titles:
SIGN DIRECTIONS

VISION ONLINE 1649329
Elmtree Business Park, Elmswell, BURY ST. EDMUNDS,
IP30 9HR **Tel:** 01359 243400 **Fax:** 01359 242921
Email: enquiries@visionline.co.uk

Titles:
PETFOCUS
VETERINARY MANAGEMENT FOR TODAY

VISIONGAIN LTD 621704
4th Floor, BSG House, 226-236 City Road, LONDON, EC1V
2QY **Tel:** 020 7336 6100
Web site: http://www.visiongain.com

Titles:
WIRELESS EUROPE

VISIT LONDON 16732
6th Floor, 2 More London Riverside, LONDON, SE1 2RR
Tel: 020 7234 5800 **Fax:** 020 7234 5750
Web site: http://www.visitlondon.com/business

Titles:
EVENT PLANNER'S GUIDE

VISIT YORK 16393
20 George Hudson Street, YORK, YO1 6WR
Tel: 01904 554455 **Fax:** 01904 554460
Web site: http://www.visityork.org

Titles:
YORK WHAT'S ON

VISITBRITAIN 14420
Thames Tower, Blacks Road, LONDON, W6 9EL
Tel: 020 8846 9000 **Fax:** 020 8563 3153
Web site: http://www.visitbritain.com

Titles:
ANGLOFILE
BRITAIN CALLING

VISITCREST LTD 16047
PO Box 380, HARROW, HA2 6LL **Tel:** 020 8863 8586
Fax: 020 8863 9370

Titles:
THE MUSLIM NEWS

VISITSCOTLAND 18053
Ocean Point One, 94 Ocean Drive, EDINBURGH, EH6 6JH
Tel: 0131 472 2222 **Fax:** 0131 472 2250
Web site: http://www.visitscotland.com

Titles:
SCOTLAND: CARAVAN & CAMPING, WHERE TO STAY
GUIDE
SCOTLAND: HOTELS & GUEST HOUSES, WHERE TO
STAY GUIDE
SCOTLAND: SELF CATERING, WHERE TO STAY GUIDE

VISITSCOTLAND.COM 1639719
6 Fairways Business Park, Deer Park Avenue, LIVINGSTON,
EH54 8AF **Tel:** 01506 832100 **Fax:** 01506 832111
Web site: http://www.visitscotland.com

Titles:
VISITSCOTLAND.COM

VISUAL IMAGINATION LTD 15337
9-10 Blades Court, Deodar Road, LONDON, SW15 2NU
Tel: 020 8875 1520 **Fax:** 020 8875 1588
Web site: http://www.visimag.com

Titles:
CULT TIMES
FILM REVIEW
SHIVERS
STARBURST
STARBURST SPECIAL
TV ZONE
ULTIMATE DVD
XPOSÉ

VISUAL TALENT LTD 1685150
133 Notting Hill Gate, LONDON, W11 3LB
Tel: 020 7243 9966 **Fax:** 020 7243 9967

Titles:
MAN ABOUT TOWN
WONDERLAND

VITAL PUBLISHING 1640074
4th Floor, Intergen House, 65-67 Western Road, HOVE, BN3
2JQ **Tel:** 01273 311289

Titles:
CLEAR PROFIT
FUTURE HEALTH BULLETIN

VITESSE MEDIA PLC 622967
Octavia House, 50 Banner Street, LONDON, EC1Y 8ST
Tel: 020 7250 7010 **Fax:** 020 7250 7011
Email: info@vitessemedia.co.uk
Web site: http://www.vitessemedia.com

Titles:
BUSINESS XL
GROWTH COMPANY INVESTOR
GROWTH COMPANY INVESTOR ONLINE
GROWTHBUSINESS
INFORMATION AGE
MANDADEALS.CO.UK
MERGERS & ACQUISITIONS MAGAZINE
SMALLBUSINESS.CO.UK
TAX GUIDE
WHAT INVESTMENT

VIVA PUBLISHING LTD 1709904
27 Old Gloucester Street, LONDON, WC1N 3XX
Tel: 0870 850 3085
Email: info@salontoday.co.uk
Web site: http://www.salontoday.co.uk

Titles:
SALON TODAY

VOICE OF THE LISTENER & VIEWER 696988
101 Kings Drive, GRAVESEND, DA12 5BQ
Tel: 01474 352835 **Fax:** 01474 351112
Email: info@vlv.org.uk
Web site: http://www.vlv.org.uk

Titles:
VLV BULLETIN

VOICE: THE UNION FOR EDUCATION PROFESSIONAL
12747
2 St. James' Court, Friar Gate, DERBY, DE1 1BT
Tel: 01332 372337 **Fax:** 01332 290310
Email: enquiries@voicetheunion.org.uk
Web site: http://www.voicetheunion.org.uk

Titles:
YOUR VOICE

VOLCANO PUBLISHING 1743870
5 Altmore, Cherry Garden Lane, MAIDENHEAD, SL6 3QG
Tel: 01628 825652 **Fax:** 01628 821148

Titles:
SHINDIG

VOLTIMUM UK & IRELAND LTD 1627140
3rd Floor, Bishop's Park House, 25-29 Fulham High Street,
LONDON, SW6 3JH **Tel:** 020 7751 3900
Email: enquiries@voltimum.co.uk
Web site: http://www.voltimum.co.uk

Titles:
VOLTIMUM

VOLUNTEER DEVELOPMENT SCOTLAND 18414
Stirling Enterprise Park, STIRLING, FK7 7RP
Tel: 01786 479593 **Fax:** 01786 449285
Email: spectrum@vds.org.uk
Web site: http://www.vds.org.uk

Titles:
SPECTRUM

THE VOLUNTEERING ENGLAND 16182
Regent's Wharf, 8 All Saints Street, LONDON, N1 9RL
Tel: 0845 305 6979 **Fax:** 020 7520 8910

Titles:
VOLUNTEERING

VOYAGEUR PUBLISHING 1616854
43 Colston Street, BRISTOL, BS1 5AX **Tel:** 0117 922 6600
Fax: 0117 925 2040
Email: info@voyageur.co.uk
Web site: http://www.voyageur.co.uk

Titles:
ITIJ INTERNATIONAL TRAVEL INSURANCE JOURNAL

VRA MEDIA 1640083
PO Box 324, FLEET, GU51 3ZH **Tel:** 01252 621513
Fax: 01252 761333

Titles:
GOLF & TRAVEL
GOLFANDTRAVELMAG.COM

VRL KNOWLEDGE BANK LTD 12145
The Colonnades, 34 Porchester Road, LONDON, W2 6ES
Tel: 020 7563 5631 **Fax:** 020 7563 5601
Web site: http://www.vrlknowledgebank.com

Titles:
THE ACCOUNTANT
CARDS INTERNATIONAL
ELECTRONIC PAYMENTS INTERNATIONAL (EPI)
INTERNATIONAL ACCOUNTING BULLETIN
LEASING LIFE
MOTOR FINANCE
PRIVATE BANKER INTERNATIONAL
RETAIL BANKER INTERNATIONAL

VSCC LTD 15463
The Old Post Office, West Street, CHIPPING NORTON, OX7
5EL **Tel:** 01608 644777 **Fax:** 01608 644888
Email: info@vscc.co.uk
Web site: http://www.vscc.co.uk

Titles:
BULLETIN OF THE VINTAGE SPORTS CAR CLUB

VSM MEDIA LTD. 1731700
Unit 14, 20 Palmers Road, LONDON, E2 0SY
Tel: 0845 077 2887
Web site: http://www.vsnmedia.co.uk

Titles:
MOC MAGAZINE

W. GREEN THOMSON REUTERS 17468
21 Alva Street, EDINBURGH, EH2 4PS **Tel:** 0131 225 4879
Fax: 0131 225 2104
Web site: http://www.wgreen.thomson.com

Titles:
GREENS WEEKLY DIGEST
THE SCOTS LAW TIMES

W. HOBBY LTD 18536
Knights Hill Square, LONDON, SE27 0HH
Tel: 020 8761 4244 **Fax:** 020 8761 8796

Titles:
HOBBY'S ANNUAL

W.M. WALTON & CO LTD 14731
Upper Spring Street, GRIMSBY, DN31 1QP
Tel: 01472 359036 **Fax:** 01472 599910
Email: post@waltonspublications.com
Web site: http://www.waltonspublications.com

Titles:
COMMERCE & INDUSTRY
FOOD AND DRINK NETWORK UK
'LINCOLNSHIRE IN FOCUS'

W. PETERS AND SON LTD 15031
16 High Street, TURRIFF, AB53 4DS **Tel:** 01888 563589
Fax: 01888 563936

UK Publishers & Their Titles

Titles:
ADVERTISER SERIES IN ABERDEENSHIRE

W.Y. CRICHTON & CO LTD 15077
2-4 Church Street, DOWNPATRICK, BT30 6EJ
Tel: 028 4452 3456 **Fax:** 028 4461 4624
Titles:
DOWN RECORDER

WADDELL LTD 15386
112-116 Old Street, LONDON, EC1V 9BG
Tel: 020 7336 0766 **Fax:** 020 7336 0966
Titles:
DAZED & CONFUSED
DAZED DIGITAL

WALES COUNCIL FOR VOLUNTARY ACTION 14176
Baltic House, Mount Stuart Square, CARDIFF, CF10 5FH
Tel: 029 2043 1700 **Fax:** 029 2043 1701
Titles:
NETWORK WALES

WALKER AGENCY 18506
Wootton Grange, Wootton Mount, BOURNEMOUTH, BH1
1PJ **Tel:** 01202 414200 **Fax:** 01202 414244
Email: ideas@thewalkeragency.co.uk
Web site: http://www.walkeragency.co.uk
Titles:
ENSIGN

WALKING WALES LTD 1710870
3 Glantwymyn Village Workshop, Cemmaes Road,
MACHYNLLETH, SY20 8LY **Tel:** 01650 511314
Email: walking_wales@perroto.co.uk
Titles:
WALKING WALES

WALLFLOWER PRESS 1737610
6 Market Place, LONDON, W1W 8AF **Tel:** 01582 727330
Email: info@wallflowerpress.co.uk
Web site: http://www.wallflowerpress.co.uk
Titles:
ELECTRIC SHEEP
FILM & FESTIVALS
THE INTERNATIONAL FILM GUIDE

WANDERLUST PUBLICATIONS 16024
PO Box 1832, WINDSOR, SL4 1YT **Tel:** 01753 620426
Fax: 01753 620474
Email: info@wanderlust.co.uk
Web site: http://www.wanderlust.co.uk
Titles:
WANDERLUST

WARBURG INSTITUTE 17948
The Warburg Institute, University of London, Woburn
Square, LONDON, WC1H 0AB **Tel:** 020 7862 8949
Fax: 020 7862 8955
Email: warburg@sas.ac.uk
Web site: http://www.warburg.sas.ac.uk/
Titles:
JOURNAL OF THE WARBURG AND COURTAULD
INSTITUTES

WARC LTD 624326
Farm Road, HENLEY-ON-THAMES, RG9 1EJ
Tel: 01491 411000 **Fax:** 01491 418600
Web site: http://www.warc.com
Titles:
ADMAP

WARDOUR 1742377
Walmour House, 296 Regent Street, LONDON, W1B 3AW
Tel: 020 7016 2555 **Fax:** 020 7970 4820
Web site: http://www.wardour.co.uk
Titles:
MASTERCLASS

WARDOUR PUBLISHING AND DESIGN 1638548
Walmar House, 296 Regent Street, LONDON, W1B 3AW
Tel: 020 7016 2555 **Fax:** 020 7907 4820
Web site: http://www.wardour.co.uk
Titles:
B2L

LANDSCAPE MAGAZINE
THE MARKET
RSA JOURNAL
SECURITIES & INVESTMENT REVIEW
VISTA

WARNERS GROUP PUBLICATIONS PLC 16560
The Maltings, West Street, BOURNE, PE10 9PH
Tel: 01778 391000 **Fax:** 01778 392079
Web site: http://www.warnersgroup.co.uk
Titles:
ACR TODAY
AIR CADET
BOAT FISHING MONTHLY
BOOK AND MAGAZINE COLLECTOR
BRITISH RAILWAY MODELLING
CAMPING MAGAZINE
CANOE AND KAYAK MAGAZINE UK
CARAVAN MOTORHOME & CAMPING MART
CLIMBER
COLLECT IT!
COLLECTORS GAZETTE
CONSULTING ENGINEER
THE DIECAST COLLECTOR
DOLLS HOUSE AND MINIATURE SCENE
GO CARAVAN
GOOD MOTORING
LAKELAND WALKER
THE LION
MASTER BUILDER
MMM MOTORCARAVAN MOTORHOME MONTHLY
MOBILISE
PARK & HOLIDAY HOMES
PHARMACEUTICAL FIELD
PIANIST
PLUMBING & HEATING ENGINEERING MAGAZINE
ROOFING
SKYDIVE MAG
STAMP & COIN MART
TAXI GLOBE
TRACTION
WHICH CARAVAN
WHICH MOTORCARAVAN
WRITERS' NEWS
WRITING MAGAZINE

WATER ACTIVE LTD. 1690609
Unit 2, 57 Bushey Grove Road, BUSHEY, WD23 2JW
Tel: 01923 233550 **Fax:** 01923 252220
Email: info@wateractive.co.uk
Web site: http://www.wateractive.co.uk
Titles:
WATER ACTIVE

WATERFRONT MAGAZINES LTD 1749022
4 Stable Court, Water Lane, Tarbock Green, PRESCOT, L35
1RD **Tel:** 0151 487 6900 **Fax:** 0151 487 5300
Titles:
WATERFRONT

WATERLAND PUBLISHING LIMITED 1711370
17 Sedgeway Business Park, Witchford, ELY, CB6 2HY
Tel: 01353 666663 **Fax:** 01353 666664
Email: info@waterlandpublishing.co.uk
Web site: http://www.waterlandpublishing.co.uk
Titles:
POOL AND SPA INDUSTRY

WATERLOW 1748043
6-14 Underwood Street, LONDON, N1 7JQ
Tel: 020 7324 2322 **Fax:** 020 7566 8238
Titles:
CARITAS MAGAZINE
CHARITY FUNDING REPORT
CODICIL

WATERLOW PROFESSIONAL PUBLISHING 621867
3rd Floor, 6-14 Underwood Street, LONDON, N1 7JQ
Tel: 020 7490 0049 **Fax:** 020 7324 2366
Web site: http://www.waterlow.com
Titles:
SOLICITORS' JOURNAL

WATERSHED MEDIA 1644271
Eagle Building, Wylam Wharf, Low Street, SUNDERLAND,
SR1 2AX **Tel:** 0191 514 3598 **Fax:** 0191 565 7672
Titles:
COLLECTIVE MAGAZINE

WATT PUBLISHING CO 14003
Lavant House, Lavant Street, PETERSFIELD, GU32 3EL
Web site: http://www.WATTpoultry.com
Titles:
FEED INTERNATIONAL
PIG INTERNATIONAL
POULTRY INTERNATIONAL

WAVERLEY COMMUNICATIONS LTD 12531
11 Galena Close, Amington Industrial Estate, TAMWORTH,
B77 4AS **Tel:** 01827 311800 **Fax:** 01827 301199
Email: press@wavcoms.co.uk
Web site: http://www.wavcoms.co.uk
Titles:
HA HOUSING ASSOCIATION
MMC
REFURB & REGENERATION JOURNAL
SCHOOL BUILDING

WAYMARK 600265
PO Box 78, SKIPTON, BD23 4UP **Tel:** 07000 782318
Web site: http://www.iprow.co.uk
Titles:
WAYMARK

WB PUBLISHING LTD 13993
8 Oakhill Drive, WELWYN, AL6 9NW **Tel:** 01438 716220
Fax: 01438 716230
Titles:
BRITISH DAIRYING

WCN PUBLISHING 14408
Northbank House, 5 Bridge Street, LEATHERHEAD, KT22
8BL **Tel:** 01372 375511 **Fax:** 01372 370111
Web site: http://www.wcnpublishing.com
Titles:
BULK MATERIALS INTERNATIONAL
COALTRANS INTERNATIONAL
WORLDCARGO NEWS
WORLDCARGO NEWS ONLINE

THE WEALDEN ADVERTISER 1737803
Cowden Close, Horns Road, Hawkhurst, CRANBROOK,
TN18 4QT **Tel:** 01580 753322 **Fax:** 01580 754104
Web site: http://www.wealdenad.co.uk
Titles:
FRESHWATER INFORMER
PROPERTY SOUTH EAST
TOWN & COUNTRY POST
THE WEALDEN ADVERTISER

WEARDALE GAZETTE & PUBLISHING CO LTD 1622271
6 Market Place, Stanhope, BISHOP AUCKLAND, DL13 2UJ
Tel: 01388 527706 **Fax:** 01388 527706
Titles:
WEARDALE GAZETTE

WEATHERBYS VENTURES LTD 17697
Sanders Road, Finedon Road Industrial Estate,
WELLINGBOROUGH, NN8 4BX **Tel:** 01933 440077
Fax: 01933 440807
Email: e-mail@weatherbys.co.uk
Web site: http://www.weatherbys.co.uk
Titles:
THE RETURN OF MARES
THE STALLION BOOK

WEB4LAW LTD 696774
2 Crown Lane, 4 Oaks, SUTTON COLDFIELD, B74 4SU
Tel: 01933 316488 **Fax:** 01933 316488
Web site: http://www.web4law.biz
Titles:
MANAGING RISK

WEBNET MEDIA 1627148
40 Longshut Lane West, STOCKPORT, SK2 6RX
Tel: 0845 310 1780 **Fax:** 0845 310 1781
Titles:
PPPFOCUS.COM

WEBTRAFIX LTD 670315
33 Pages Lane, Muswell Hill, LONDON, N10 1PU
Tel: 020 8444 7819
Email: cruisetradenews@aol.com

Titles:
CRUISE TRADE NEWS

WEDDING VENUES LTD 622733
215 London Road, HEMEL HEMPSTEAD, HP3 9SE
Tel: 01442 260178 **Fax:** 01442 266940
Email: info@weddingvenues.co.uk
Web site: http://www.weddingvenues.co.uk
Titles:
WEDDING VENUES & SERVICES MAGAZINE

WEED WORLD 1640213
PO Box 1332, COVENTRY, CV8 3YA **Tel:** 01974 821518
Fax: 01974 821518
Email: info@weedworld.co.uk
Web site: http://www.weedworld.co.uk
Titles:
WEED WORLD

WEEKEND CITY PRESS REVIEW LTD 600497
2 Clifton Villas, LONDON, W9 2PH **Tel:** 020 7289 9784
Fax: 020 7266 1991
Titles:
FINANCIAL REGULATORY BRIEFING

WEF PUBLISHING UK LTD 1732455
6 Brewery Square, LONDON, EC1V 4LE **Tel:** 020 7251 8778
Fax: 020 7336 0377
Web site: http://www.wef.org
Titles:
WORLD WATER & ENVIRONMENTAL ENGINEERING

WEIDER PUBLISHING LTD 15312
10 Windsor Court, Clarence Drive, HARROGATE, HG1 2PE
Tel: 01423 504516 **Fax:** 01423 561494
Email: ukpub@weideruk.com
Web site: http://www.muscle-fitness.co.uk
Titles:
FLEX
MUSCLE & FITNESS

WEIGHT MANAGEMENT UK LTD 697120
47 St Mary's Court, Huntly Street, ABERDEEN, AB10 1TH
Tel: 01224 211868 **Fax:** 01224 646943
Web site: http://www.scottishslimmers.com
Titles:
BOOST YOUR WEIGHT LOSS!

WEIGHTWATCHERS.CO.UK LIMITED 1621026
Millennium House, Ludlow Road, MAIDENHEAD, SL6 2SL
Tel: 01628 513000
Titles:
WEIGHTWATCHERS.CO.UK

THE WEIR GROUP PLC 18324
20 Waterloo Street, GLASGOW, G2 6DB **Tel:** 0141 637 7111
Fax: 0141 221 9789
Web site: http://www.weir.co.uk
Titles:
WEIR BULLETIN

WELLBEING MAGAZINE LTD 1762653
2 The Hall, Turners Green Road, WADHURST, TN5 6TR
Tel: 01892 782697
Titles:
WELLBEING MAGAZINE

WELSH CONSUMER COUNCIL 15132
5th Floor, Longcross Court, 47 Newport Road, CARDIFF,
CF24 0WL **Tel:** 029 2025 5454 **Fax:** 029 2025 5464
Web site: http://www.wales-consumer.org.uk
Titles:
THE WELSH CONSUMER

WENTWORTH PUBLISHING LTD 12894
17 Fleet Street, LONDON, EC4Y 1AA **Tel:** 020 7353 6606
Fax: 020 7353 6533
Email: wentworth@online.rednet.co.uk
Titles:
GOVERNMENT AUCTION NEWS
THE SCHMIDT REPORT

WESLEY HISTORICAL SOCIETY 18184
26 Roe Cross Green, Mottram, HYDE, SK14 6LP
Tel: 01457 763485
Titles:
PROCEEDINGS OF WESLEY HISTORICAL SOCIETY

WESLEYAN REFORM UNION 15868
Church House, 123 Queen Street, SHEFFIELD, S1 2DU
Tel: 0114 272 1938 **Fax:** 0114 272 1938
Titles:
CONTACT

WESSEX SCENE 600624
S.U. Southampton University, University Road, Highfield,
SOUTHAMPTON, SO17 1BJ **Tel:** 023 8059 5226
Fax: 023 8059 5252
Titles:
WESSEX SCENE

WEST END REVIEW 1690664
77 Oxford Street, LONDON, W1D 2ES **Tel:** 020 7659 2728
Fax: 01483 480462
Titles:
WEST END REVIEW

WEST HIGHLAND PUBLISHING CO. LTD 15067
Industrial Estate, Isle of Skye, BROADFORD, IV49 9AP
Tel: 01471 822464 **Fax:** 01471 822694
Titles:
WEST HIGHLAND FREE PRESS

WEST POINT MEDIA PUBLICATIONS 674184
113 Fazeley Street, BIRMINGHAM, B5 5RX
Tel: 0121 202 1586
Titles:
MASALA

THE WESTENDER 18823
25 Horsell Road, LONDON, N5 1XL **Tel:** 020 7607 6060
Fax: 020 7607 2299
Titles:
THE WESTENDER

WESTERN ALCOHOL & DRUGS EDUCATION SOCIETY 17795
Best View, Upton Lane, Dundry, BRISTOL, BS41 8NS
Tel: 0117 964 4088
Web site: http://www.wades-charity.org.uk
Titles:
THE ADVOCATE

WESTERN BUSINESS PUBLISHING 1742723
33-35 Cantelupe Road, EAST GRINSTEAD, RH19 3BE
Tel: 01342 314300 **Fax:** 01342 333700
Email: sales@western-bp.co.uk
Titles:
HANDLING & STORAGE SOLUTIONS
HEALTH & SAFETY MATTERS
IP&E INDUSTRIAL PLANT & EQUIPMENT
IP&E INDUSTRIAL PLANT & EQUIPMENT IRELAND

THE WESTERN GAZETTE CO. LTD 14984
Sherborne Road, YEOVIL, BA21 4YA **Tel:** 01935 700500
Fax: 01935 426963
Titles:
WESTERN GAZETTE AND YEOVIL TIMES SERIES

WESTERN MORNING NEWS & MEDIA LTD 14926
17 Brest Road, Derriford Business Park, PLYMOUTH, PL6
5AA **Tel:** 01752 765500 **Fax:** 01752 765670
Titles:
HOMESEEKER

WESTERN REGIONAL PUBLISHING 18269
1 Buckingham Court, Beaufort Business Park, Bradley,
Stoke North, BRISTOL, BS32 4NF **Tel:** 01454 616161
Fax: 01454 615159
Titles:
WESTERN & SOUTH WALES AUTO TRADER

WESTMINSTER TIMES LTD 1741289
112 Barnfield Avenue, KINGSTON ON THAMES, KL2 5RT
Tel: 020 7267 9093
Titles:
KENSINGTON AND CHELSEA TIMES

WESTMORLAND GAZETTE NEWSPAPERS 13039
1 Wainwright's Yard, KENDAL, LA9 4DP **Tel:** 01539 720100
Fax: 01539 720990
Web site: http://www.thewestmorlandgazette.co.uk
Titles:
WESTMORLAND GAZETTE NEWSPAPER SERIES

WESTPOINT PUBLISHING 1706589
113 Fazeley Street, Digbeth, BIRMINGHAM, B5 5RX
Tel: 0121 202 1595 **Fax:** 0121 202 1598
Titles:
THE GAZETTE SERIES

WESTSIDE COMMUNICATIONS LTD 1650898
10 Greycoat Place, LONDON, SW1P 1SB
Tel: 0871 989 8206 **Fax:** 0871 989 8207
Titles:
URBAN LIFE

WEXAS 16022
45-49 Brompton Road, Knightsbridge, LONDON, SW3 1DE
Tel: 020 7589 0500 **Fax:** 020 7581 1357
Web site: http://www.wexas.com
Titles:
TRAVELLER

WEYBRIDGE PRESS AND PROMOTIONS LTD 674404
3rd Floor, 2-4 St. Georges Road, Wimbledon, LONDON,
SW19 4DP **Tel:** 020 8181 5594 **Fax:** 020 8247 3820
Email: wppl@btconnect.com
Titles:
YOUR HEALTH

WFGA 18343
175 Gloucester Street, CIRENCESTER, GL7 2DP
Tel: 01285 658339
Titles:
WOMEN'S FARM & GARDEN ASSOCIATION

WHARFEDALE (PUBLISHING) LTD 628469
20 Wharfedale Road, IPSWICH, IP1 4JP **Tel:** 01473 400632
Fax: 01473 400633
Titles:
GREATER IPSWICH COMMUNITY NEWS SERIES

WHARNCLIFFE PUBLISHING LTD 12497
47 Church Street, BARNSLEY, S70 2AS **Tel:** 01226 734333
Titles:
ASSISTIVE TECHNOLOGIES
CARING UK
DESTINATION UK
HORSE HEALTH
MAIN EVENT
OUT ON A LIMB
WEDDING PROFESSIONAL
WORK OUT

WHAT DOCTORS DON'T TELL YOU PLC 16610
Satellite House, 2 Salisbury Road, LONDON, SW19 4EZ
Tel: 020 8944 9555 **Fax:** 020 8944 9888
Email: info@wddty.co.uk
Web site: http://www.wddty.com
Titles:
WHAT DOCTORS DON'T TELL YOU

WHAT GREEN HOME LTD 1758765
PR by email only
Email: info@whatgreenhome.com
Titles:
WHATGREENHOME.COM

WHAT'S ON GROUP LIMITED 1644469
62 North Street, Bedminster, BRISTOL, BS3 1HJ
Tel: 01275 891482
Titles:
WHAT'S ON BRISTOL

UK Publishers & Their Titles

WHAT'S ON GUIDE UK LTD 18764
The Pavilion, Moulsham Hall Lane, Great Leighs,
CHELMSFORD, CM3 1QP **Tel:** 01245 362412
Titles:
  WHATS-ON-GUIDE

WHAT'S ON MAGAZINE GROUP 15383
4-5 Dogpole, SHREWSBURY, SY1 1EN **Tel:** 01743 281777
Fax: 01743 281744
Titles:
  MIDLANDS WHAT'S ON
  MIDLANDS ZONE
  STAFFORDSHIRE WHAT'S ON
  THE STOCKPORT DIARY

WHAT'S ON PUBLICATIONS 15997
208-210 Great Junction Street, EDINBURGH, EH6 5LW
Tel: 0131 555 6667
Titles:
  WHAT'S ON EDINBURGH & LOTHIANS

WHEN SATURDAY COMES LTD 15248
17A Perseverance Works, 38 Kingsland Road, LONDON, E2
8DD **Tel:** 020 7729 1110 **Fax:** 020 7729 9417
Web site: http://www.wsc.co.uk
Titles:
  WHEN SATURDAY COMES

WHICH? LTD 15134
2 Marylebone Road, LONDON, NW1 4DF
Tel: 020 7770 7000 **Fax:** 020 7770 7655
Web site: http://www.which.co.uk
Titles:
  GARDENING WHICH?
  WHICH?
  WHICH? COMPUTING
  WHICH? HOLIDAY
  WHICH? MONEY

WHITE DIGITAL MEDIA LTD 1741274
Grosvenor House, Prince of Wales Road, NORWICH, NR1
1NS **Tel:** 01603 217530 **Fax:** 01603 617082
Web site: http://www.whitedm.com
Titles:
  EXEC UK
  FOOD AND DRINK DIGITAL

WHITE WEDDING PAGES LTD 1739932
90 Main Street, Saintfield, BALLYNAHINCH, BT24 7AB
Tel: 028 9751 2665 **Fax:** 028 9751 1030
Titles:
  WHITE WEDDING PAGES

WHITMAR PUBLICATIONS LTD 12508
30 London Road, Southborough, TUNBRIDGE WELLS, TN4
0RE **Tel:** 01892 514437 **Fax:** 01892 546693
Web site: http://www.paperandprint.com
Titles:
  DIGITAL PRINTER
  FLEXOTECH
  PRINT & PAPER MONTHLY

THE WHO CARES? TRUST 14185
Kemp House, 152-160 City Road, LONDON, EC1V 2NP
Tel: 020 7251 3117 **Fax:** 020 7251 3123
Web site: http://www.thewhocarestrust.org.uk
Titles:
  WHO CARES?

WHO'S JACK 1732111
93 Barker Drive, Camden, LONDON, NW1 0JG
Tel: 07789 393118
Titles:
  WHO'S JACK

WIDEMEDIA LTD 17206
PO Box 38185, LONDON, W10 4WF **Tel:** 020 8968 3149
Email: contact@widemedia.com
Titles:
  FUK.CO.UK

THE WIDESCREEN CENTRE 14797
47 Dorset Street, LONDON, W1U 7ND **Tel:** 020 7935 2580
Fax: 020 7486 1272
Email: call@widecreen-centre.co.uk
Web site: http://www.widescreen-centre.co.uk
Titles:
  SIGHT 'N SOUND

WIGMORE MEDICAL LIMITED 1737014
2D Wimpole Street, LONDON, W1G 0EB **Tel:** 01273 606799
Titles:
  BODY LANGUAGE

WIKI DESIGN 1741712
PO Box 586, FOLKESTONE, CT19 6WA
Email: wikidesign@mac.com
Web site: http://www.wikidesign.co.uk
Titles:
  GEEKANOIDS

WILD PLACES PUBLISHING 18035
PO Box 100, ABERGAVENNY, NP7 9WY **Tel:** 01873 737707
Web site: http://www.caving.uk.com
Titles:
  DESCENT - THE MAGAZINE OF UNDERGROUND
    EXPLORATION

WILD PUBLISHING LTD 1690371
22A Iliffe Yard, LONDON, SE17 3QA **Tel:** 020 7277 4517
Fax: 020 7703 8718
Email: info@wildpublishing.com
Web site: http://www.wildpublishing.com
Titles:
  REFRESH
  TRADITIONAL BOATS & TALL SHIPS

WILD SWAN PUBLICATIONS LTD 15475
1-3 Hagbourne Road, DIDCOT, OX11 8DP
Tel: 01235 816478
Titles:
  BRITISH RAILWAY JOURNAL

WILDFIRE COMMUNICATIONS 17188
Unit 2.4, Paintworks, Bath Road, BRISTOL, BS4 3EH
Tel: 0117 902 9977 **Fax:** 0117 902 9978
Web site: http://www.wildfirecomms.co.uk
Titles:
  IMAGINE
  IRISH DANCING AND CULTURE MAGAZINE
  STUDENT 123.COM
  TUCO
  UNIVERSITY CATERER

WILEY INTERFACE LTD 13590
The Atrium, Southern Gate, CHICHESTER, PO19 8SQ
Tel: 01243 770237 **Fax:** 01243 770144
Titles:
  FUTURE PRESCRIBER
  PRESCRIBER

WILEY-BLACKWELL 14612
The Atrium, Southern Gate, CHICHESTER, PO19 8SQ
Tel: 01243 779777
Web site: http://www.wiley.com
Titles:
  BUSINESS STRATEGY AND THE ENVIRONMENT
  THE ECONOMIC HISTORY REVIEW
  SUSTAINABLE DEVELOPMENT

WILEY-BLACKWELL PUBLISHING 1742575
9600 Garsington Road, Cowley, OXFORD, OX4 2DQ
Tel: 01865 776868 **Fax:** 01865 714951
Titles:
  ADDICTION
  AFRICAN JOURNAL OF ECOLOGY
  ANAESTHESIA
  ANNUAL BULLETIN OF HISTORICAL LITERATURE
  ANTHROPOLOGY TODAY
  AQUACULTURE NUTRITION
  AQUACULTURE RESEARCH
  THE ART BOOK
  ASTRONOMY & GEOPHYSICS
  BJU INTERNATIONAL
  BRITISH JOURNAL OF DERMATOLOGY
  BRITISH JOURNAL OF INDUSTRIAL RELATIONS
  BRITISH JOURNAL OF SPECIAL EDUCATION
  CEPHALALGIA

  CLINICAL & EXPERIMENTAL IMMUNOLOGY
  DIABETIC MEDICINE
  DISASTERS
  ECONOMIC AFFAIRS
  GRASS & FORAGE SCIENCE
  HEALTH INFORMATION AND LIBRARIES JOURNAL
  HIV MEDICINE
  IBIS
  INTERNATIONAL ENDODONTIC JOURNAL
  INTERNATIONAL JOURNAL OF CLINICAL PRACTICE
  THE INTERNATIONAL JOURNAL OF PSYCHOANALYSIS
  JOURNAL OF ADVANCED NURSING
  JOURNAL OF APPLIED RESEARCH IN INTELLECTUAL
    DISABILITY
  JOURNAL OF CLINICAL PHARMACY & THERAPEUTICS
  JOURNAL OF FISH BIOLOGY
  JOURNAL OF NURSING MANAGEMENT
  JOURNAL OF PSYCHIATRIC AND MENTAL HEALTH
    NURSING
  JOURNAL OF ZOOLOGY
  THE MODERN LAW REVIEW
  NURSING IN CRITICAL CARE
  NUTRITION BULLETIN
  OIL AND ENERGY TRENDS
  PEDIATRIC ANESTHESIA
  PUBLIC POLICY RESEARCH
  RENAISSANCE STUDIES
  SUPPORT FOR LEARNING
  TROPICAL MEDICINE & INTERNATIONAL HEALTH
  UK VET COMPANION ANIMAL
  UK VET LIVESTOCK
  VNJ VETERINARY NURSING JOURNAL
  WATER AND ENVIRONMENT JOURNAL

WILFRED EDMUNDS 1731946
121 Newgate Lane, MANSFIELD, NG18 2PA
Tel: 01623 456789 **Fax:** 01623 464749
Titles:
  ALFRETON CHAD
  HUCKNALL & BULWELL DISPATCH
  HUCKNALL AND BULWELL DISPATCH
  MANSFIELD AND ASHFIELD OBSERVER
  PORT TALBOT GUARDIAN
  PROFILE

WILFRED EDMUNDS LTD 14919
37 Station Road, CHESTERFIELD, S41 7XD
Tel: 01246 504500 **Fax:** 01246 504590
Titles:
  BELPER NEWS
  DERBYSHIRE TIMES SERIES
  MATLOCK MERCURY

WILL TO CHARITY LTD 12724
8 Hamble House, Meadrow, GODALMING, GU7 3HJ
Tel: 01483 429800 **Fax:** 01483 429500
Web site: http://www.willtocharity.co.uk
Titles:
  THE UK'S REGIONAL CHARITY FINDER

WILLIAM JOSEPH 1747722
21 Little Portland Street, LONDON, W1W 8BT
Tel: 020 7637 5077 **Fax:** 020 7580 7899
Web site: http://www.williamjoseph.co.uk
Titles:
  PAWS

WILLIAM REED BUSINESS MEDIA 13351
Broadfield Park, CRAWLEY, RH11 9RT **Tel:** 01293 613400
Web site: http://www.william-reed.co.uk
Titles:
  BRITISH BAKER
  CONVENIENCE STORE
  FOOD MANUFACTURE
  FORECOURT TRADER
  THE GROCER
  THE GROCER DIRECTORY OF MANUFACTURERS &
    SUPPLIERS
  HARPERS WINE & SPIRIT
  HARPERS WINE AND SPIRIT
  HOTEL REPORT
  M&C REPORT
  MEAT TRADES JOURNAL
  MEAT TRADES JOURNAL ONLINE
  MORNING ADVERTISER
  MTJ EXTRA
  OFF LICENCE NEWS
  OLN OFF LICENCE NEWS
  PRO WHOLESALER
  PRO WHOLESALER CASH & CARRY BIG BOOK
  PRO WHOLESALER DELIVERED BIG BOOK
  RESTAURANT
  SCOTTISH LOCAL RETAILER (SLR)
  SHOPPING CENTRE IRELAND

WILLIAM TRIMBLE LTD   15080
8-10 East Bridge Street, ENNISKILLEN, BT74 7BT
Tel: 028 6632 4422 **Fax:** 028 6632 5047
Titles:
IMPARTIAL REPORTER
LAKELAND EXTRA

WILLIS PLIMMER PUBLISHING LTD   1741184
White Cottage, 520 Bradgate Road, Newtown Linford,
LEICESTER, LE6 0HB **Tel:** 01530 242232
Fax: 01827 281143
Titles:
PRODUCT & IMAGE SECURITY INCORPORATING
PACKAGE PRINT & CONVERTING

WILLOWE MAGAZINES LIMITED   14363
29 High Street, RYE, TN31 7JG **Tel:** 01797 224816
Titles:
INDUSTRIAL WOODWORKER
KITCHEN MAKER
SHOP, BAR & OFFICE FITTER

WILMINGTON BUSINESS INFORMATION   622015
Paulton House, 8 Shepherdess Walk, LONDON, N1 7LB
Tel: 020 7490 0049
Titles:
SPC SOAP, PERFUMERY & COSMETICS ASIA

WILSON MARKETING LTD   1649747
Suite 26, 151 High Street, SOUTHAMPTON, SO14 2BT
Tel: 023 8046 4675 **Fax:** 023 8046 6677
Titles:
EUROPEAN COMPUTER SUPPORT

WILTSHIRE PUBLICATIONS LTD   16555
31 Market Place, MELKSHAM, SN12 6ES **Tel:** 01225 704761
Fax: 01225 708081
Titles:
THE MELKSHAM INDEPENDENT NEWS SERIES

WIMBORNE PUBLISHING LIMITED   15485
Sequoia House, 398A Ringwood Road, FERNDOWN, BH22
9AU **Tel:** 01202 873872 **Fax:** 01202 874562
Titles:
EVERYDAY PRACTICAL ELECTRONICS
HOROSCOPE
RADIO BYGONES

WINCKLEY PRESS   15668
5 Winckley Street, PRESTON, PR1 2AA **Tel:** 0870 417 8910
Fax: 0870 417 8910
Web site: http://www.winckley.co.uk
Titles:
FEATHERED WORLD

WINEDINE   1717660
27 Eddiscombe Road, LONDON, SW6 4TZ
Tel: 07050 252738
Email: tlc@winedine.co.uk
Web site: http://www.winedine.co.uk
Titles:
WINE & DINE

WINGALE PUBLISHING   1711091
64 Uplands Road, LONDON, N8 9NJ **Tel:** 020 8292 5509
Email: winskill@blueyonder.co.uk
Titles:
THE HORNSEY MAGAZINE

WINKONTENT   1725066
20 Boston Place, Marylebone, LONDON, NW1 6ER
Tel: 020 7725 4343 **Fax:** 020 7725 5711
Titles:
MONOCLE

WINLOVE PUBLICATIONS LTD   14052
PO Box 366, EAST GRINSTEAD, RH19 4ZE
Tel: 01342 303042 **Fax:** 01342 303052
Email: mail.winlove@btconnect.com
Titles:
CASH & CARRY MANAGEMENT INC. CASH & CARRY
WHOLESALER

THE WIRE MAGAZINE LTD   17983
23 Jack's Place, 6 Corbet Place, LONDON, E1 6NN
Tel: 020 7422 5010 **Fax:** 020 7422 5011
Titles:
THE WIRE

WISDEN CRICKETER PUBLISHING LTD   17217
2nd Floor, 123 Buckingham Palace Road, LONDON, SW1W
9SL **Tel:** 020 7705 4911
Titles:
THE WISDEN CRICKETER

WISEBUY PUBLICATIONS   622964
PR by email only
Titles:
INVESTMENTGUIDE.CO.UK

WOBURN MEDIA LTD   18575
Suite 433C, Midsummer House, Midsummer Boulevard,
MILTON KEYNES, MK9 3BN **Tel:** 01908 394501
Fax: 01908 394502
Email: news@businessmk.co.uk
Web site: http://www.businessmk.co.uk
Titles:
BUSINESS MK
BUSINESS TO BUSINESS

WODCON ASSOCIATION   14351
South Place, Derby Road, HASLEMERE, GU27 1BP
Tel: 01428 642208 **Fax:** 01428 642208
Titles:
WORLD DREDGING, MINING & CONSTRUCTION

WOKING BOROUGH COUNCIL   18478
Civic Offices, Gloucester Square, WOKING, GU21 6YL
Tel: 01483 743024 **Fax:** 01483 743055
Web site: http://www.woking.gov.uk
Titles:
THE WOKING MAGAZINE

WOLTERS KLUWER (UK) LTD   1654299
145 London Road, KINGSTON UPON THAMES, KT2 6SR
Tel: 020 8547 3333 **Fax:** 020 8547 3637
Email: info@croner.co.uk
Web site: http://www.croner.co.uk
Titles:
ACCOUNTANCY
ACCOUNTANCYMAGAZINE.COM
ACCOUNTING & BUSINESS RESEARCH
CHEMICAL SAFETY BRIEFING
CONSTRUCTION RISKS SPECIAL REPORT
CONSTRUCTION SAFETY BRIEFING
CRONER TRADE INTERNATIONAL DIGEST
CRONER'S EMPLOYMENT CASE LAW INDEX
CRONER'S ENVIRONMENT BRIEFING
CRONER'S ENVIRONMENT MAGAZINE
CRONER'S GUIDE TO CREDIT MANAGEMENT
CRONER'S IMPORTER'S BRIEFING
CRONER'S OFFICE HEALTH & SAFETY
CRONER'S PERSONNEL IN PRACTICE : RECORDS &
PROCEDURES
CRONER'S ROAD TRANSPORT OPERATION: RECORDS
& PROCEDURES
PASS
PERSONNEL MANAGEMENT NEWSLETTER
REFERENCE BOOK FOR EXPORTERS
TAX ADVISER

WOMEN'S ENGINEERING SOCIETY   13950
Michael Faraday House, Six Hills Way, Stevenage,
HERTFORDSHIRE, SG1 2AY **Tel:** 01483 765506
Email: info@wes.org.uk
Web site: http://www.wes.org.uk
Titles:
THE WOMAN ENGINEER

WOMENS EVERYTHING LTD   1758493
PO Box 78, Whaley Bridge, HIGH PEAK, SK23 7WD
Titles:
WOMENS EVERYTHING

WOMEN'S NEWS   1685220
Cathedral Quarter Managed Workspace, 109-113 Royal
Avenue, BELFAST, BT1 1FF **Tel:** 028 9032 2823
Fax: 028 9043 8788
Email: editorwomensnews@btconnect.com
Web site: http://www.womensnewsmagazine.org

Titles:
WOMEN'S NEWS

WOMEN'S ROYAL VOLUNTARY SERVICE   15234
Garden House, Milton Hill, Steventon, ABINGDON, OX13
6AD **Tel:** 01235 442900 **Fax:** 01235 861166
Web site: http://www.wrvs.org.uk
Titles:
WRVS ACTION

WOOD GREEN ANIMAL SHELTERS   15631
King's Bush Farm, London Road, Godmanchester,
HUNTINGDON, PE29 2NH **Tel:** 0870 190 4090
Fax: 01480 832379
Web site: http://www.woodgreen.org.uk
Titles:
ANIMALS MATTER

THE WORD WORKS PARTNERSHIP LIMITED   1650463
Suite 60, Enterprise House, Balloo Avenue, BANGOR, BT19
7QT **Tel:** 028 9147 0739 **Fax:** 028 9147 0738
Titles:
BUSINESS FIRST

THE WORDHOUSE PUBLISHING GROUP LTD   16721
68 First Avenue, Mortlake, LONDON, SW14 8SR
Tel: 020 8939 6470 **Fax:** 020 8878 9983
Email: info@thewordhouse.co.uk
Web site: http://www.fandwb.com
Titles:
THE FLORIST & WHOLESALE BUYER

WORDPLAY PUBLISHING LTD   1654593
41 Canning Street, LIVERPOOL, L8 7NN **Tel:** 0151 708 8864
Titles:
AMBULANCE TODAY

THE WORDS WORKSHOP LTD   1733284
26 Swanwick Lane, Broughton Leys, MILTON KEYNES,
MK10 9LD **Tel:** 01908 695500 **Fax:** 01908 690099
Email: rands@theworkshop.co.uk
Web site: http://www.thewordworkshop.co.uk
Titles:
REMOVALS & STORAGE

WORDWIDE COMMUNICATIONS   670263
4-8 Rodney Street, LONDON, N1 9JH **Tel:** 020 7841 8721
Web site: http://www.word-wide.co.uk
Titles:
LIFE
PELL-MELL AND WOODCOTE
SKIPTON LIFE

WORKING SHEEPDOG NEWS   17325
5 Vale Crescent, Bishop Wilton, YORK, YO42 1SU
Tel: 01759 368577 **Fax:** 01759 368577
Titles:
INTERNATIONAL SHEEPDOG NEWS

WORLD ADVERTISING RESEARCH CENTER   13409
1 Farm Road, HENLEY-ON-THAMES, RG9 1EJ
Tel: 01491 411000 **Fax:** 01491 418600
Email: enquiries@warc.com
Web site: http://www.warc.com
Titles:
MARKET LEADER THE JOURNAL OF THE MARKETING
SOCIETY
WARC NEWS
WORLD ADVERTISING RESEARCH CENTER

WORLD AVIATION COMMUNICATIONS LTD   600395
Cowleaze House, 39 Cowleaze Road, KINGSTON UPON
THAMES, KT2 6DZ **Tel:** 020 8255 4000 **Fax:** 020 8255 4300
Web site: http://www.avbuyer.com
Titles:
WORLD AIRCRAFT SALES MAGAZINE

WORLD GROUP   1640385
1A Northumberland Avenue, LONDON, WC2N 5BW
Tel: 020 7887 1916 **Fax:** 020 7843 6890
Titles:
BREAKING TRAVEL NEWS

UK Publishers & Their Titles

WORLD ILLUSTRATED LTD 697941
29-31 Saffron Hill, LONDON, EC1N 8SW **Tel:** 020 7421 6000
Fax: 020 7421 6006

Titles:
HOTSHOE INTERNATIONAL

WORLD MAGAZINES LTD 15326
28 Arrol Road, BECKENHAM, BR3 4PA **Tel:** 020 8650 6580
Fax: 020 8654 4343

Titles:
DARTS PLAYER
DARTS WORLD

WORLD NEWS MEDIA 1675656
37-42 Compton Street, LONDON, EC1V 0AP
Tel: 020 7014 0330

Titles:
BUSINESS DESTINATIONS
WORLD FINANCE

WORLD OF CRUISING LTD 1651307
Softec House, London Road, Albourne, HASSOCKS, BN6
9BN **Tel:** 0870 429 2686 **Fax:** 0870 429 2683

Titles:
WORLD OF CRUISING

WORLD OF INFORMATION 17462
11 Clarendon Street, CAMBRIDGE, CB1 1JU
Tel: 01223 351584 **Fax:** 01223 351584
Web site: http://www.worldinformation.com

Titles:
THE AFRICA REVIEW
THE AMERICAS REVIEW
THE ASIA & PACIFIC REVIEW
THE EUROPE REVIEW
THE MIDDLE EAST REVIEW

WORLD OF MOTORHOMES LTD 1687105
97 Link Road, Anstey, LEICESTER, LE7 7BZ
Tel: 0115 954 2206 **Fax:** 0116 221 9942
Email: enquiries@ukwom.com
Web site: http://www.worldofmotorhomes.com

Titles:
WORLD OF CARAVANS
WORLD OF MOTORHOMES

WORLD OF POWERBOATS 700006
PO Box 4781, POOLE, BH15 1WH **Tel:** 07946 230630

Titles:
WORLD OF POWERBOATS

THE WORLD SHIP TRUST 622917
No 3 The Green, Ketton, STAMFORD, PE9 3RA
Tel: 01780 721628 **Fax:** 01780 721980

Titles:
WORLD SHIP REVIEW

THE WORLD SIKH FOUNDATION 16060
33 Wargrave Road, HARROW, HA2 8LL **Tel:** 020 8864 9228

Titles:
WORLD SIKH FOUNDATION INCORPORATING THE SIKH
COURIER

WORLD SOCIETY FOR THE PROTECTION OF ANIMALS 16452
89 Albert Embankment, LONDON, SE1 7TP
Tel: 020 7587 5000 **Fax:** 020 7793 0208
Web site: http://www.wspa-international.org

Titles:
ANIMALS INTERNATIONAL

WORLD TELEMEDIA LTD 1744669
Virginia Cottage, Nash Lane, Scaynes Hill, HAYWARDS
HEATH, RH17 7NJ **Tel:** 0870 732 7327

Titles:
TELEMEDIA MAGAZINE

WORLD TEXTILE PUBLICATIONS LTD 13395
Perkin House, 1 Longlands Street, BRADFORD, BD1 2TP
Tel: 01274 378800 **Fax:** 01274 378811
Email: info@world-textile.net
Web site: http://www.inteletex.com

Titles:
DIGITAL TEXTILE
FUTURE MATERIALS
INTELETEX
INTERNATIONAL CARPET BULLETIN
INTERNATIONAL DYER
KNITTING INTERNATIONAL
NONWOVENS REPORT INTERNATIONAL
NONWOVENS REPORT INTERNATIONAL NEWSLETTER
TEXTILE HORIZONS
TEXTILE MONTH
TWIST - THE NEW WOOL RECORD
WOOL RECORD'S WEEKLY MARKET REPORT

WORLD TRADES PUBLISHING LTD 14378
36 Crosby Road North, LIVERPOOL, L22 0QN
Tel: 0151 928 9288 **Fax:** 0151 928 4190
Web site: http://www.worldleather.co.uk

Titles:
WORLD FOOTWEAR
WORLD LEATHER
WSA

WORLD TRAVEL MEDIA LTD 1605492
55 Kensington West, Blythe Road, LONDON, W14 0JQ
Tel: 020 7751 1689 **Fax:** 020 7371 2096

Titles:
CARIBBEAN WORLD

WORLDOFFROAD.COM LTD 1641630
The Granary, Hinton Lodge, Hinton, SAXMUNDHAM, IP17
3RG **Tel:** 01502 478000 **Fax:** 01502 478001
Web site: http://www.worldoffroad.com

Titles:
WORLD OFF ROAD

THE WORLD'S FAIR LTD 14079
3rd Floor, Hollinwood Business Centre, Albert Street,
OLDHAM, OL8 3QL **Tel:** 0161 683 8000 **Fax:** 0161 683 8001
Web site: http://www.worldsfair.co.uk

Titles:
FACILITIES MANAGEMENT UK
FOOTBALL AND STADIUM MANAGEMENT
IS OPPORTUNITIES
MARKET TRADER
WORLD'S FAIR

WORLDWIDE PURCHASING 1686920
3rd Floor, Roman House, 296 Golders Green Road,
LONDON, NW11 9PY **Tel:** 020 8764 9696

Titles:
AUTOMOTIVE INDUSTRIES

WORLDWIDE SPORTING PUBLICATIONS 14149
54 Alderley Road, WILMSLOW, SK9 1NY **Tel:** 01625 535081
Fax: 01625 537487
Web site: http://www.sportingpublications.com

Titles:
RACING INTERNATIONAL
WORLDWIDE GOLF

WPR MEDIA 1644745
PO BOX 222, DEWSBURY, WF13 3WN **Tel:** 01924 437820

Titles:
MATERIALS HANDLING WORLD MAGAZINE

THE WRITE PARTNERSHIP 600495
PO Box 25, Clawton, HOLSWORTHY, EX22 6WZ
Tel: 01409 271411 **Fax:** 01409 271414
Email: enquiries@twpltd.com
Web site: http://www.twpltd.com

Titles:
MILITARY TRAINING & SIMULATION NEWS

THE WRITE TECHNOLOGY LTD 1740461
Apsley Mills Cottage, London Road, Apsley, HEMEL
HEMPSTEAD, HP3 9RL **Tel:** 01442 242960
Email: enquiries@dpnow.com
Web site: http://www.dpnow.com

Titles:
DIGITAL PHOTOGRAPHY NOW

THE WRITERS BUREAU 1600376
Sevendale House, 7 Dale Street, MANCHESTER, M1 1JB
Tel: 0161 228 2362 **Fax:** 0161 228 3533
Web site: http://www.writersbureau.com

Titles:
FREELANCE MARKET NEWS

W.S. MANEY AND SON LTD 1646266
Suite 1C, Joseph's Well, Hanover Walk, LEEDS, LS3 1AB
Tel: 0113 243 2800 **Fax:** 0113 386 8178
Web site: http://www.maney.co.uk

Titles:
ITALIAN STUDIES

WW MAGAZINES 16081
151 Station Street, BURTON-ON-TRENT, DE14 1BG
Tel: 01283 742950 **Fax:** 01283 742957
Email: admin@wwonline.co.uk
Web site: http://www.wwmagazines.com

Titles:
DESTINATION FRANCE
PLANET 4X4
SELFBUILD AND DESIGN
SPIN
TOTAL OFF-ROAD
VINTAGE SPIRIT
WATERWAYS WORLD

WWF-UK 16147
Panda House, Weyside Park, GODALMING, GU7 1XR
Tel: 01483 426444 **Fax:** 01483 426409
Web site: http://www.wwf.org.uk

Titles:
WWF ACTION

WYTHENSHAWE WORLD LTD 14949
495 Altrincham Road, Baguley, MANCHESTER, M23 1AR
Tel: 0161 998 4786 **Fax:** 0161 998 2486

Titles:
WYTHENSHAWE WORLD

WYVEX MEDIA GROUP 12831
PO Box 1, Crannog Lane, OBAN, PA34 4HB
Tel: 01631 568000 **Fax:** 01631 568001
Web site: http://www.obantimes.co.uk

Titles:
ARGYLLSHIRE ADVERTISER
THE ARRAN BANNER
CAMPBELTOWN COURIER
OBAN TIMES & WEST HIGHLAND TIMES
SCOTTISH FIELD

X3D MEDIA 1750666
93A Rivington Street, LONDON, EC2A 3AY
Tel: 020 3355 7310 **Fax:** 020 3355 7319
Web site: http://www.x3dmedia.com

Titles:
AEC MAGAZINE
DEVELOP 3D
EXPERIENCE BUILDING
EXPERIENCE MANUFACTURING

XCESS MEDIA LTD 1730112
PO Box 158, BROMLEY, BR1 4YH **Tel:** 020 8352 7816
Fax: 020 8325 8352

Titles:
EVERY MAN
INTHEPINK
WISH

XENOGAMY LIMITED 1710150
The Old Bakery, 55A Belmont Road, WALLINGTON, SM6
8TE **Tel:** 020 8773 3404 **Fax:** 020 8773 3704
Email: racingnews@xenogamy-plc.co.uk
Web site: http://www.brscc.co.uk

Titles:
BRSCC RACING NEWS
BRSCC RACING NEWS

XTREME INFORMATION 1654023
45 Fouberts Place, LONDON, W1F 7QH **Tel:** 020 7575 1880
Fax: 020 7575 1888
Web site: http://www.xtremeinformation.com

Titles:
AMMO
AMMO WEEKLY BULLETIN
CONTAGIOUS
PROGRAMME NEWS BULLETIN

YACHTING PRESS LTD 16621
196 Eastern Esplanade, SOUTHEND-ON-SEA, SS1 3AB
Tel: 01702 582245 **Fax:** 01702 588434
Titles:
BOARDS
YACHTS AND YACHTING
YACHTS AND YACHTING ONLINE

YAHOO 1649936
125 Shaftesbury Avenue, LONDON, WC2H 8AD
Tel: 020 7131 1000
Titles:
YAHOO MUSIC

YAM PUBLICATIONS LTD 12840
Suite 9, 2nd Floor, 73 Robertson Street, GLASGOW, G2
8QD **Tel:** 0141 226 4898 **Fax:** 0141 226 4708
Email: yam@sol.co.uk
Titles:
LOCAL NEWS (GLASGOW) SERIES

YANDELL PUBLISHING LIMITED 14057
PO Box 5116, Tongwell, MILTON KEYNES, MK15 8ZQ
Tel: 01908 613323 **Fax:** 01908 210656
Email: info@yandellmedia.com
Web site: http://www.yandellmedia.com
Titles:
COACHING VENUES & EXCURSIONS GUIDE
CRUISE MAGAZINE FOR GROUPS
GROUP LEISURE

YBA PUBLICATIONS 15443
York House, 22 Frederick Street, BIRMINGHAM, B1 3HE
Tel: 0121 233 3468 **Fax:** 0121 236 4230
Titles:
SHORT CIRCUIT MAGAZINE

YELLOWHAWK LTD 1717965
40 Handside Lane, WELWYN GARDEN CITY, AL8 6SJ
Tel: 01707 891840
Email: contact@yellowhawk.co.uk
Web site: http://www.yellowhawk.co.uk
Titles:
GADGET SPEAK

YES CHEF! MAGAZINE LTD 1734945
28 Ballmoor, Celtic Court, BUCKINGHAM, MK18 1RQ
Tel: 01280 829300 **Fax:** 01280 829350
Email: info@yeschefmagazine.com
Web site: http://www.yeschefmagazine.com
Titles:
YES CHEF! MAGAZINE

YOGA MAGAZINE LTD 1653002
26 York Street, LONDON, W1U 6PZ
Email: info@yogamagazine.co.uk
Web site: http://www.yogamagazine.co.uk
Titles:
YOGA MAGAZINE (MIND BODY SPIRIT)

YOGA TODAY LTD 15527
101 Matilda House, St. Katherine's Way, LONDON, E1W 9LF
Tel: 020 7480 5456 **Fax:** 020 7480 5456
Titles:
YOGA AND HEALTH

YORK & COUNTY PRESS 12704
PO Box 29, 76-86 Walmgate, YORK, YO1 9YN
Tel: 01904 653051 **Fax:** 01904 612853
Titles:
GAZETTE & HERALD (RYEDALE & SCARBOROUGH)
LOOK IT UP
YORK TWENTY4SEVEN
YORKSHIRE LIVING BRIDES

YORK PUBLISHING SERVICES LTD 1621317
64 Hallfield Road, Layerthorpe, YORK, YO31 7ZQ
Tel: 01904 431213
Titles:
THE CONSERVATOR

YORK UNIVERSITY STUDENTS' UNION 673701
Grimston House, University of York, Heslington, YORK,
YO10 5DD **Tel:** 01904 433720 **Fax:** 01904 433720
Titles:
THE YORKER

YORKSHIRE FORWARD 18856
Victoria House, 2 Victoria Place, LEEDS, LS11 5AE
Tel: 0113 394 9600 **Fax:** 0113 243 9211
Titles:
INFORM

YORKSHIRE NATURALISTS' UNION 623682
Dept. of Geography & Environmental Science, University of
Bradford, BRADFORD, BD7 1DP **Tel:** 01274 234212
Fax: 01274 234231
Titles:
NATURALIST

YORKSHIRE POST NEWSPAPERS LTD 12448
PO Box 168, Wellington Street, LEEDS, LS1 1RF
Tel: 0113 243 2701 **Fax:** 0113 244 3430
Web site: http://www.yorkshireeveningpost.co.uk
Titles:
LEEDS BUSINESS UPDATE
LEEDS WEEKLY NEWS SERIES
LEEDSTODAY
MOORTOWN TODAY
YORKSHIRE EVENING POST
YORKSHIRE SPORT

YORKSHIRE REGIONAL NEWSPAPERS LTD 12811
17-23 Aberdeen Walk, SCARBOROUGH, YO11 1BB
Tel: 01723 363636 **Fax:** 01723 383825
Email: editorial@yrnltd.co.uk
Titles:
BRIDLINGTON FREE PRESS SERIES
DRIFFIELD TIMES SERIES
THE MERCURY SERIES (SCARBOROUGH)
POCKLINGTON POST
SCARBOROUGH EVENING NEWS
TRADER SCARBOROUGH, FILEY AND HUNMANBY
WHITBY GAZETTE SERIES

YORKSHIRE WEEKLY NEWSPAPER GROUP LTD 15010
Express House, Southgate, WAKEFIELD, WF1 1TE
Tel: 01924 375111 **Fax:** 01924 433033
Titles:
HEMSWORTH AND SOUTH ELMSALL EXPRESS
MORLEY OBSERVER & ADVERTISER
PONTEFRACT & CASTLEFORD EXPRESS & EXTRA
SERIES
WAKEFIELD EXPRESS SERIES

YORKSHIRE WOMEN'S LIFE MAGAZINE 699086
PO Box 113, LEEDS, LS8 2WX **Tel:** 0113 262 1409
Fax: 0113 240 7199
Email: ywlmagenquiries@btinternet.com
Web site: http://www.yorkshirewomenslife.co.uk
Titles:
YORKSHIRE WOMEN'S LIFE MAGAZINE

YOU FOOD LTD 1756524
16 Lower Road, Higher Denham, UXBRIDGE, UB9 5EA
Tel: 01865 832259
Titles:
YOU FOOD

YOU ME BABY LTD 1763890
The Coach House, Calehill Park, Little Chart, ASHFORD,
TN27 0QG **Tel:** 01233 713774
Titles:
YOU ME BABY

YOUNG COMMUNICATIONS MEDIA LTD 15869
20-26 Brunswick Place, LONDON, N1 6DZ
Tel: 020 7878 1034 **Fax:** 020 7878 1035
Titles:
AUTOMOTIVE QUARTERLY REVIEW

YOUNG MEDIA HOLDINGS LTD 1634304
PO Box 400, BRIDGWATER, TA6 9DT **Tel:** 0870 240 5845
Titles:
THE NEWSPAPER

YOUNG SCOT MAGAZINE 18968
Rosebery House, 9 Haymarket Terrace, EDINBURGH, EH12
5EZ **Tel:** 0131 313 2488 **Fax:** 0131 313 6800
Email: info@youngscot.org
Web site: http://www.youngscot.org
Titles:
YOUNG SCOT PORTAL

YOUNGMINDS 1736818
48-50 St. John Street, LONDON, EC1M 4DG
Tel: 020 7336 8445 **Fax:** 020 7336 8446
Titles:
YOUNGMINDSMAGAZINE

YOUR FRIDGE DOOR LTD 1723943
Compton House, School Lane, LIVERPOOL, L1 3BT
Titles:
YOUR FRIDGE DOOR

YOUR LEEK PAPER 1630105
19 Getliffes Yard, Derby Street, LEEK, ST13 6HU
Tel: 01538 371800
Titles:
TIMES GONE BY

YOUR LOCAL LINK LTD 1744846
Oaktree Farm, The Moor, Haxby, YORK, YO32 2LH
Tel: 01904 767881 **Fax:** 01904 764843
Titles:
THE YORK NEWS & TIMES

YOUTH COMMUNICATIONS NETWORK CIC 1744694
50-54 Mount Pleasant, LIVERPOOL, L3 5SD
Tel: 0151 702 6960
Titles:
YOUTH LIVE

YOUTH FOR CHRIST 15888
Coombswood Way, HALESOWEN, B62 8BH
Tel: 0121 502 9620 **Fax:** 0121 561 4035
Web site: http://www.yfc.co.uk
Titles:
INTERFACE NEWSLETTER
INTO VIEW

YOUTHNET 1744420
1st Floor, 50 Featherstone Street, LONDON, EC1Y 8RT
Tel: 020 7250 5700
Titles:
THESITE.ORG

ZAC PUBLISHING 694151
Unit 15, Archer Street Studios, 10-11 Archer Street,
LONDON, W1D 7AZ **Tel:** 020 7434 0042 **Fax:** 020 7434 0071
Titles:
10 MAGAZINE

ZENITH INTERNATIONAL 624624
7 Kingsmead Square, BATH, BA1 2AB **Tel:** 01225 327890
Fax: 01225 327891
Email: info@zippublishing.com
Web site: http://www.zippublishing.com
Titles:
BEVERAGE INNOVATION
COOLER INNOVATION
DAIRY INNOVATION
FUNCTIONALDRINKS
WATER INNOVATION

ZENITH INTERNATIONAL PUBLISHING 1741848
Lodge House, Lodge Lane, Langham, COLCHESTER, CO4
5NE **Tel:** 01206 233156 **Fax:** 01206 233157
Web site: http://www.zippublishing.com
Titles:
ALIMENTOS Y BEBIDAS, LATINOAMÉRICA
FOOD AND BEVERAGE INTERNATIONAL

ZENITH OPTIMEDIA GROUP 600697
24 Percy Street, LONDON, W1T 2BS **Tel:** 020 7961 1196
Fax: 020 7291 1199
Email: publications@zenithoptimedia.com
Web site: http://www.zenithoptimedia.com

Section 6 UK Publishers & Their Titles

UK Publishers & Their Titles

Titles:
ADVERTISING EXPENDITURE FORECASTS
MARKET & MEDIAFACT POCKET BOOKS

ZENIUS (CROYDON) LTD   1710882
PO Box 46, HOCKHURST, TN18 4RD **Tel:** 020 8656 9878
Titles:
THE K&BZINE
PROSECURIZINE
SECURIZINE

ZIETGEIST   1733461
PO Box 13499, EDINBURGH, EH6 8YL **Tel:** 07966 389732
Titles:
METAL4LIFE

THE ZIMBABWEAN LTD   1654027
PO Box 248, HYTHE, SO45 4WX **Tel:** 023 8084 5271
Web site: http://www.thezimbabwean.co.uk
Titles:
THE ZIMBABWEAN

ZINE MEDIA PUBLISHING LTD   1626590
Office F2-F3, Holme Suite, Oaks Business Park, Oaks Lane,
BARNSLEY, S71 1HT **Tel:** 01226 321450 **Fax:** 01226 240202
Web site: http://www.zmpl.co.uk
Titles:
CLEARVIEW
THE PROFESSIONAL INSTALLER

ZONE LTD   1680550
168A Camden Street, LONDON, NW1 9PT
Tel: 020 7267 4774

Email: info@zonecontent.com
Web site: http://www.zoneworldwide.com
Titles:
ICONS

ZONEAST PRODUCTION   622207
Unit 1, Dolphin House, Smugglers Way, LONDON, SW18
1DE **Tel:** 020 8870 7088
Titles:
ZONEAST

THE ZOOLOGICAL SOCIETY OF LONDON   17881
Regents Park, LONDON, NW1 4RY **Tel:** 020 7449 6281
Fax: 020 7449 6411
Email: yearbook@zsl.org
Web site: http://www.zsl.org
Titles:
INTERNATIONAL ZOO YEARBOOK

Willings Volume 1
Section 7

Advertising Representatives

These firms, mostly UK based, are generally known as UK Reps, and they handle advertising (but not subscriptions or editorial) for international newspapers and periodicals.

Advertising Representatives

ADLINK INTERNATIONAL
1200166

15 Kensington High Street, LONDON, W8 5NP
Tel: 0845 950 1312 **Fax:** 020 7938 4168
Email: info@adlinkinternational.co.uk
Web site: http://www.adlinkinternational.co.uk
Countries Represented: Bahamas, Bangladesh, Barbados, Belize, Bermuda, Bhutan, Botswana, Burundi, Cambodia, Cayman Islands, Croatia, Grenada, Guyana, India, Indonesia, Israel, Jamaica, Kazakhstan, Kenya, Kuwait, Laos, Malawi, Maldives, Malta, Mozambique, Namibia, Nepal, Netherlands Antilles, Nigeria, Pakistan, Romania, Seychelles, Sierra Leone, South Africa, Sri Lanka, St Lucia, Suriname, Swaziland, Tanzania, Thailand, Trinidad & Tobago, Turkey, Uganda, Yemen, Zambia, Zimbabwe

Titles:
ALASIRI, Tanzania
AMANDALA, Belize
ASSAM TRIBUNE, India
AUTO INDIA, India
BOTSWANA GUARDIAN, Botswana
BUSINESS RECORDER, Pakistan
CAYMANIAN COMPASS, Cayman Islands
CHRONICLE, Zimbabwe
CONCORD TIMES, Sierra Leone
DAILY DISPATCH (MAIN BODY), South Africa
DAILY NATION, Kenya
DAILY NATION (BARBADOS), Barbados
DAILY NEWS (TANZANIA), Tanzania
DAILY STAR, Jamaica
DAILY TIMES, Malawi
DAINIK ITTEFAQ, Bangladesh
DAINIK JAGRAN, India
DECCAN HERALD, India
DOMINGO, Mozambique
EAST AFRICAN, Uganda
FINANCIAL GAZETTE, Zimbabwe
FRIENDS MAGAZINE, Barbados
GRENADIAN VOICE, Grenada
GUARDIAN, Nigeria
GUARDIAN, Tanzania
GUYANA CHRONICLE, Guyana
HAVEERU DAILY, Maldives
HERALD, India
HERALD, Zimbabwe
HIMAL SOUTHASIAN, Nepal
HINDU, India
ISLAND, Sri Lanka
JAWA POS, Indonesia
KAZAKHSTANSKAYA PRAVDA, Kazakhstan
KRUNGTHEP TURAKIJ, Thailand
KUENSEL, Bhutan
KWAYEDZA, Zimbabwe
MALAWI NEWS, Malawi
MANICA POST, Zimbabwe
MID-OCEAN NEWS, Bermuda
MIDWEEK SUN, Botswana
MUMENT, Malta
NAMIBIAN, Namibia
NASSAU GUARDIAN, Bahamas
NATION, Thailand
NAZZJON, Malta
NEWSDAY, Trinidad & Tobago
NIGERIAN TRIBUNE, Nigeria
ORIZZONT, Malta
PHNOM PENH POST, Cambodia
PIONEER, India
PRENSA, Netherlands Antilles
PUNCH, Bahamas
RAI, Kuwait
RENOUVEAU DU BURUNDI, Burundi
ROMANIA LIBERA, Romania
SEYCHELLES NATION, Seychelles
SHAI, Israel
SPORTS MONTHLY, Kenya
STABROEK NEWS, Guyana
STANDARD, Kenya
SUNDAY GLEANER, Jamaica
SUNDAY MAIL (ZIMBABWE), Zimbabwe
SUNDAY NEWS (ZIMBABWE), Zimbabwe
SUNDAY OBSERVER, Sri Lanka
SWAZI OBSERVER, Swaziland
TICARET GAZETESI, Turkey
TIMES OF ZAMBIA, Zambia
TORCA, Malta
TRIBUNE, India
TRINIDAD GUARDIAN, Trinidad & Tobago
VEČERNJI LIST, Croatia
VIENTIANE TIMES, Laos
VOICE, St Lucia
WARE TIJD, Suriname
WEEKEND STAR, Jamaica
YEMEN TIMES, Yemen
ZAMBIA DAILY MAIL, Zambia

AFRICA MEDIA INTERNATIONAL
1200162

Whicham Hill, Whicham, MILLOM, LA18 5LX
Tel: 01229 776575
Email: carol.ibb@btinternet.com
Web site: http://www.btinternet.com/~carol.ibb
Countries Represented: South Africa, Zimbabwe

Titles:
INDWE, South Africa
SKYHOST, Zimbabwe

CARA-LYN REYNOLDS INTERNATIONAL MEDIA
600470

PO Box 3345, COVENTRY, CV6 6YD
Tel: 0247 636 1888
Email: info@cri-media.com
Countries Represented: Australia, Belgium, Denmark, Greece, Italy, Netherlands

Titles:
ADFORESULT, Netherlands
ARBO, Netherlands
AUSTRALIAN JOURNAL OF CIVIL ENGINEERING, Australia
AUSTRALIAN MINING, Australia
AUTOWEEK, Netherlands
B & T WEEKLY, Australia
COMPUTER GIA OLOUS, Greece
CONSTRUCTION CONTRACTOR, Australia
COSMOPOLITAN, Netherlands
DONALD DUCK EXTRA, Netherlands
ELECTRONICS NEWS, Australia
ENGINEERS AUSTRALIA (CIVIL), Australia
EUROMAN, Denmark
EUROWOMAN, Denmark
FACTO MAGAZINE, Netherlands
FANCY, Netherlands
FLAIR, Netherlands
FOOD MAGAZINE, Australia
GRASDUINEN, Netherlands
GROTER GROEIEN, Netherlands
GTO, Netherlands
KIJK, Netherlands
KNIPPIE BABY, Netherlands
LIV', Netherlands
MARIE CLAIRE, Netherlands
MIKRO GIDS, Netherlands
MORE THAN CLASSIC, Netherlands
NCRV-GIDS, Netherlands
NEGEN MAANDEN MAGAZINE, Netherlands
NOUVEAU, Netherlands
OUDERS VAN NU, Netherlands
PACKAGING, Australia
PANORAMA, Netherlands
PC-MASTER, Greece
PLAYBOY, Netherlands
PUB MAGAZINE, Belgium
PUBLISH, Netherlands
REVU, Netherlands
RI RASSEGNA DELL'IMBALLAGGIO, Italy
SALES MANAGEMENT, Netherlands
SECURITY MANAGEMENT, Netherlands
SESAMSTRAAT, Netherlands
SISTEMI DI TELECOMUNICAZIONI, Italy
SKI MAGAZINE, Netherlands
STORY, Netherlands
TELEVIZIER, Netherlands
TIJDSCHRIFT ADMINISTRATIE, Netherlands
TIJDSCHRIFT CONTROLLING, Netherlands
TIJDSCHRIFT VOOR MARKETING, Netherlands
TINA, Netherlands
VARAGIDS, Netherlands
VERPAKKEN, Netherlands
VERZEKERINGSBLAD, Netherlands
VIVA, Netherlands
VORSTEN ROYALE, Netherlands
VT WONEN, Netherlands
YES, Netherlands
ZOZITDAT, Netherlands

CHRIS SHAW MEDIA LTD
1200360

3 Brynlow Drive, MIDDLEWICH, CW10 0PD
Tel: 01606 833891 **Fax:** 01606 833891
Email: webmail@chrisshawmedia.co.uk
Web site: http://www.chrisshawmedia.co.uk
Countries Represented: Hong Kong

Titles:
CHINA TEXTILE & APPAREL JOURNAL, Hong Kong

CHRISTOPHER C STEVENS ASSOCIATES
692391

62 Rosebery Avenue, LONDON, EC1R 4RR
Tel: 020 7833 5533 **Fax:** 020 7689 3404
Email: chris@c-stevens.com
Countries Represented: Germany, Spain

Titles:
CAMBIO 16, Spain
HORIZONT, Germany
IDE - INFORMACIÓN DEL ENVASE Y EMBALAJE, Spain

CRANE MEDIA PARTNERS LTD
1201442

St Edmunds House, 13 Quarry Street, GUILDFORD, GU1 3UY **Tel:** 01483 461770 **Fax:** 020 8748 6580
Email: info-cmp@cranemedia.co.uk
Web site: http://www.cranemediapartners.com
Countries Represented: Brazil, Czech Republic, Denmark, Estonia, Finland, Germany, Hungary, Italy, Netherlands, Norway, Poland, Romania, Russian Federation, Slovakia, Sweden, Switzerland, Turkey, Ukraine

Titles:
AAMULEHTI, Finland
ADESSO, Germany
ANNA, Finland
AUTO FACHMANN, Germany
AUTOMOBIL INDUSTRIE, Germany
BAUEN MIT HOLZ, Germany
BAUGEWERBE, Germany
BERLINGSKE TIDENDE, Denmark
BLICK, Switzerland
BLIKK, Hungary
B.T., Denmark
BUSINESS SPOTLIGHT, Germany
CAPITAL, Romania
CARO, Germany
CHIP, Germany
CHIP, Hungary
CHIP, Italy
CHIP, Netherlands
CHIP, Poland
CHIP, Russian Federation
CHIP, Turkey
CHIP, Ukraine
CHIP COMPUTER & COMMUNICATIONS, Romania
COMPUTER EASY, Netherlands
DAGBLADET; NYHETSREDAKSJONEN, Norway
DAGENS NYHETER, Sweden
DDH DAS DACHDECKER-HANDWERK, Germany
ÉCOUTE, Germany
EDELWEISS, Switzerland
EE-MAIL -LEHTI, Finland
EKONOMI, Finland
ELEKTRONIK PRAXIS, Germany
ÉPOCA, Brazil
ETZ, Germany
EVA, Slovakia
FASSADENTECHNIK, Germany
FLIESEN & PLATTEN, Germany
FYENS STIFSTIDENDE, Denmark
GLOBO, Brazil
GÖTEBORGS-POSTEN, Sweden
HEBDO, Switzerland
HELSINGIN SANOMAT, Finland
HUFVUDSTADSBLADET, Finland
HYMY, Finland
ILLUSTRÉ, Switzerland
JORNAL DA TARDE, Brazil
KFZ-BETRIEB, Germany
KODUTOHTER, Estonia
KOMMERSANT, Russian Federation
KONSTRUKTIONS PRAXIS, Germany
KOTILIESI, Finland
LANCE!, Brazil
LEVEL, Turkey
LIBERTATEA, Romania
MAGYAR HÍRLAP, Hungary
MARIE CLAIRE (BRAZIL), Brazil
MARKT IN GRÜN, Germany
MARKT UND MITTELSTAND, Germany
MM MASCHINENMARKT DAS INDUSTRIE MAGAZIN, Germany
MOOTTORI, Finland
MOTORIST, Finland
NEMZETI SPORT, Hungary
NÉPSZABADSÁG, Hungary
NEWSWEEK POLSKA, Poland
PC GURU, Hungary
PHARMATEC, Germany
PIRKKA, Finland
PROCESS, Germany
REFLEX, Czech Republic
RZECZPOSPOLITA, Poland
SCHWEIZER ILLUSTRIERTE, Switzerland

SEURA, Finland
SONNTAGS BLICK, Switzerland
SPORT, Czech Republic
SPOT ON, Germany
SPOTLIGHT, Germany
SUOSIKKI, Finland
SYDSVENSKAN, Sweden
TALOUSSANOMAT, Finland
TEKNIIKAN MAAILMA, Finland
TELE, Switzerland
TROCKENBAU AKUSTIK, Germany
TURUN SANOMAT, Finland
UNICA, Romania
VAUHDIN MAAILMA, Finland
VDI NACHRICHTEN, Germany
VECKANS AFFÄRER, Sweden
VLAST, Russian Federation
WINDOWS NET MAGAZINE, Turkey
ZIMMERMANN, Germany
ZIVOT, Slovakia

DAVID TODD ASSOCIATES LTD 1201385
32-33 Skylines Village, Limeharbour, LONDON, E14 9TS
Tel: 020 7538 5811 **Fax:** 020 7538 4911
Email: graeme@dta.gb.com
Web site: http://www.dta.gb.com
Countries Represented: Austria, Canada, China,
Finland, Germany, Netherlands, Norway, South Africa,
Sweden, Switzerland, USA

Titles:
ADRESSEAVISEN, Norway
BEELD (MAIN BODY), South Africa
BERGENS TIDENDE, Norway
BILAN, Switzerland
BURGER, (W. CAPE MON-FRI), South Africa
CANADIAN BUSINESS, Canada
CHINA AVIATION NEWS, China
CHINA DAILY, China
CHINA SPACE NEWS, China
CHINA YOUTH DAILY, China
CIM CONFERENCE & INCENTIVE MANAGEMENT,
  Germany
CITY PRESS (MAIN BODY), South Africa
DAGENS INDUSTRI, Sweden
DRUM, South Africa
ECONOMIC DAILY, China
ESQUIRE, Netherlands
FAIR LADY, South Africa
FHM (FOR HIM MAGAZINE), Netherlands
HUISGENOOT, South Africa
INSIG, South Africa
LANDBOUWEEKBLAD, South Africa
MARKKINOINTI & MAINONTA, Finland
NATIONAL GEOGRAPHIC MAGAZINE, USA
NATIONAL GEOGRAPHIC TRAVELER, USA
PAARL POST, South Africa
PEOPLE'S DAILY, China
PRIVÉ, Netherlands
PROFIT, YOUR GUIDE TO BUSINESS SUCCESS,
  Canada
RAPPORT (MAIN BODY), South Africa
RESIDENCE, Netherlands
SARIE, South Africa
SOMERSET WEST: DISTRICT MAIL, South Africa
STAVANGER AFTENBLAD, Norway
SUNDAY SUN, South Africa
TALOUSELÄMÄ, Finland
TEKNIIKKA & TALOUS, Finland
TRUE LOVE, South Africa
TV PLUS!, South Africa
TYGERBURGER, South Africa
URATIE, Finland
VISTA, South Africa
VOETBAL MAGAZINE, Netherlands
VOLKSBLAD (MAIN BODY), South Africa
WIRTSCHAFTSBLATT, Austria
WITNESS, South Africa
WOMAN'S VALUE, South Africa
YOU, South Africa
ZEIT, Germany

THE FALSTEN PARTNERSHIP 1600226
23 Walsingham Road, HOVE, BN3 4FE
Tel: 01273 771020 **Fax:** 01273 770070
Email: sales@falsten.com
Web site: http://www.falsten.com
Countries Represented: Hong Kong

Titles:
CHINA PLASTIC & RUBBER JOURNAL, Hong Kong

GREG CORBETT ASSOCIATES 625425
5 Lower Belgrave Street, LONDON, SW1W 0NR
Tel: 020 7730 6033 **Fax:** 020 7730 6628
Email: gca@gca-international.co.uk
Web site: http://www.gca-international.co.uk
Countries Represented: Belgium, France, Germany,
Italy, Norway, Spain

Titles:
AFFARI & FINANZA (LA REPUBBLICA), Italy
AGEFI HEBDO, France
AGENZIA DI VIAGGI, Italy
ARGUS DE L'ASSURANCE JOURNAL
  INTERNATIONAL DES ASSURANCES, France
AUTOCAD MAGAZIN, Germany
CA M'INTERESSE, France
CAPITAL, France
CB NEWS, France
CHALLENGES, France
COM!, Germany
CUISINE ACTUELLE, France
DE MORGEN, Belgium
DIGITALBUSINESS, Germany
DINE PENGER, Norway
ECHO TOURISTIQUE, France
EDITUR, Spain
ESPRESSO, Italy
EUROPE 1 PARIS 104.7, France
FEMME ACTUELLE, France
GALA, France
GEO, France
GUIDE CUISINE, France
INTERVIU, Spain
INVESTIR, France
INVESTIR MAGAZINE, France
IT MANAGEMENT, Germany
IT SECURITY, Germany
JALOUSE, France
J'APPRENDS A LIRE (6-8 ANS), France
JULIE (FILLES 9-13 ANS), France
LAN NEWS / ELECTRONICS HIGH-TECH, Belgium
LSA ATTENTION : LIGNES DIRECTES EN COURS DE
  CHANGEMENT, France
MAN, Spain
MANAGEMENT, France
MAXIM MAGAZINE, Italy
MOCI LE MONITEUR DU COMMERCE
  INTERNATIONAL, France
MONDE, France
MONDE MAGAZINE, France
MUSICA, Italy
MUTEEN, France
NATIONAL GEOGRAPHIC, France
NEORESTAURATION MAGAZINE ATTENTION :
  LIGNES DIRECTES EN COURS DE CHANGEMENT,
  France
NOUVEL OBSERVATEUR, France
OFFICIEL, France
OPTIMUM, France
PC PLUS, Spain
PERIÓDICO DE CATALUNYA, Spain
PICOTI (9 MOIS-3 ANS), France
PLAYSTATION 2, Spain
PRIMA, France
PRIMA-CUISINE GOURMANDE, France
PRIMERA LÍNEA, Spain
REPUBBLICA, Italy
RFM PARIS 103.9, France
SCIENCES ET AVENIR, France
SCIENZE, Italy
SKYROCK PARIS 96.0, France
SUPER JUEGOS, Spain
TELE 2 SEMAINES, France
TELE LOISIRS, France
TIEMPO DE HOY, Spain
TOBOGGAN (5-7 ANS), France
TOUPIE (3-5 ANS), France
TRIBUNE, France
USINE NOUVELLE ATTENTION : LIGNES DIRECTES
  EN COURS DE CHANGEMENT, France
VOGUE ESPAÑA, Spain
VOICI, France
WAKOU (3-7 ANS), France
WAPITI (7-13 ANS), France
WOMAN, Spain

HOLMES & BRADFIELD LLP 1201206
The Media Centre, East Rudham, KING'S LYNN, PE31
8RD **Tel:** 01485 528020 **Fax:** 01485 528022
Email: mcentre@aol.com
Countries Represented: Germany

Titles:
AEROKURIER, Germany
FLUG REVUE, Germany

HUSON EUROPEAN MEDIA 698341
Cambridge House, Gogmore Lane, CHERTSEY, KT16
9AP **Tel:** 01932 564999 **Fax:** 01932 564998
Email: sales@husonmedia.com
Web site: http://www.husonusa.com
Countries Represented: Australia, Finland, Germany,
Hungary, India, Italy, Netherlands, Spain, Sweden, USA

Titles:
AUTOMAZIONE OGGI, Italy
COMPUTER & AUTOMATION, Germany
ELECTRICAL SOLUTIONS, Australia
ELECTRONIC PRODUCTS, USA
ELEKTRO-DATA, Netherlands
ELEKTRONET, Hungary
ELEKTRONICA, Netherlands
ELEKTRONIK, Germany
ELEKTRONIK AUTOMOTIVE, Germany
ELEKTRONIKTIDNINGEN, Sweden
ELETTRONICA OGGI, Italy
EO NEWS, Italy
FUNKSCHAU, Germany
FUNKSCHAU HANDEL, Germany
FUTURE MUSIC, Spain
IEEE NETWORK, USA
IEEE WIRELESS COMMUNICATIONS, USA
INTERNET MAGAZIN, Germany
PC GO, Germany
PC MAGAZIN, Germany
PC PRO, Spain
PCQUEST, India
PROSESSORI, Finland
SUSTAINABILITY MATTERS, Australia
VIDEO HOMEVISON, Germany
VOICE&DATA, Australia
WHAT'S NEW IN ELECTRONICS, Australia
WHAT'S NEW IN LAB TECHNOLOGY, Australia
WHAT'S NEW IN PROCESS TECHNOLOGY, Australia

IDG GLOBAL SOLUTIONS 1200049
29-31 Kingston Road, STAINES, TW18 4LH
Tel: 01784 210210 **Fax:** 01784 210200
Web site: http://www.idgglobalsolutions.com
Countries Represented: Australia, Austria, Belgium,
Bulgaria, Canada, China, Czech Republic, Denmark,
Ecuador, Finland, France, Germany, Hungary, Italy,
Lithuania, Myanmar (Burma), Netherlands, New
Zealand, Norway, Philippines, Poland, Romania,
Russian Federation, Serbia, South Africa, Spain,
Sweden, Switzerland, USA, Ukraine, United Arab
Emirates

Titles:
AUSTRALIAN PC WORLD, Australia
BIOTECHNOLOGY FOCUS, Canada
CAP & DESIGN, Sweden
CEO & CIO CHINA, China
CHANNELPARTNER, Germany
CHANNELWORLD, Netherlands
CHINA COMPUTER WORLD, China
CHINA NETWORK WORLD, China
CIO, Germany
CIO, USA
CIO BUSINESS WORLD, Czech Republic
CIO CANADA, Canada
CIO SWEDEN, Sweden
COMPUTER NEWS MIDDLE EAST, United Arab
  Emirates
COMPUTER SWEDEN, Sweden
COMPUTER WORLD, Bulgaria
COMPUTER WORLD/UKRAINA, Ukraine
COMPUTERS, Bulgaria
COMPUTERWELT, Austria
COMPUTERWOCHE, Germany
COMPUTERWOCHE.DE, Germany
COMPUTERWORLD, Czech Republic
COMPUTERWORLD, Ecuador
COMPUTERWORLD, Hungary
COMPUTERWORLD, Norway
COMPUTERWORLD, Romania
COMPUTERWORLD, Spain
COMPUTERWORLD, Switzerland
COMPUTERWORLD AUSTRALIA, Australia
COMPUTERWORLD CANADA, Canada
COMPUTERWORLD ITALIA, Italy
COMPUTERWORLD NEW ZEALAND, New Zealand
COMPUTERWORLD PHILIPPINES, Philippines
COMPUTERWORLD RUSSIA, Russian Federation
COMPUTING SA, South Africa
COMUNICACIONES WORLD, Spain
DEALER WORLD, Spain
DISTRIBUTIQUE.COM (SITE INTERNET), France
ELECTRONIC DESIGN AND APPLICATION WORLD,
  China
ELECTRONIC ENGINEER & PRODUCT WORLD,
  China
ENTERPRISE, Philippines

Advertising Representatives

GAMEPRO, Germany
GAMEPRO, USA
GAMESTAR, Germany
GAMESTAR, Hungary
IMPARJA NEWS NT PARLIAMENTARY PRESS
    GALLERY, Australia
INFORMATION AGE, Australia
INTERNETWORLD, Sweden
IT.BRANSCHEN, Sweden
KOMPIUTERIJA, Lithuania
LABORATORY FOCUS, Canada
LAN MAGAZINE, Netherlands
MACWELT, Germany
MACWORLD, Spain
MACWORLD, Sweden
MACWORLD, USA
MACWORLD ITALIA, Italy
MICRO HEBDO, France
MIKROPC, Finland
MIKRO/PC WORLD, Serbia
MIR PK, Russian Federation
NETTVERK & KOMMUNIKASJON, Norway
NETWORK WORLD, Romania
NETWORK WORLD, USA
NETWORK WORLD CANADA, Canada
NETWORK WORLD ITALIA (COMPUTERWORLD),
    Italy
NETWORK WORLD MIDDLE EAST, United Arab
    Emirates
ORDINATEUR INDIVIDUEL, France
PC FÖR ALLA, Sweden
PC WELT, Germany
PC WELT, Germany
PC WORLD, Belgium
PC WORLD, Hungary
PC WORLD, Romania
PC WORLD, Spain
PC WORLD CHINA, China
PC WORLD ECUADOR, Ecuador
PC WORLD EKSTRA, Norway
PC WORLD ITALIA, Italy
PC WORLD KOMPUTER, Poland
PC WORLD MYANMAR, Myanmar (Burma)
PC WORLD NORGE, Norway
PC WORLD PHILIPPINES, Philippines
PCTIPP, Switzerland
PCWORLD.DK, Denmark
RESELLER WORLD MIDDLE EAST, United Arab
    Emirates
TIETOVIIKKO, Finland
ZOOM.NL, Netherlands

INTERNATIONAL PUBLICITY SERVICES
1200063

27 Great Queen Street, LONDON, WC2B 5BB
Tel: 020 7404 6533 **Fax:** 020 7404 6544
Email: ips@adafrica-ips.co.uk
Countries Represented: Algeria, Botswana, Burkina
Faso, Cameroon, Cape Verde Islands, Egypt, Ghana,
Ivory Coast, Jordan, Lebanon, Madagascar, Malawi,
Mali, Mauritius, Morocco, Niger, Nigeria, Saudi Arabia,
Senegal, South Africa, Tunisia, Uganda

Titles:
AD-DUSTOUR, Jordan
AHRAM, Egypt
ALAM, Morocco
ASSAHRAE AL MAGHRIBIA, Morocco
CAMEROON TRIBUNE, Cameroon
DAILY CHAMPION, Nigeria
DAILY GRAPHIC, Ghana
ECONOMISTE, Morocco
ESSOR, Mali
EXPRESS DE MADAGASCAR, Madagascar
EXPRESS (MAURITIUS), Mauritius
FRATERNITÉ MATIN, Ivory Coast
GHANAIAN TIMES, Ghana
HAYAT - SAUDI EDITION, Saudi Arabia
ITTIHAD AL ICHTIRAKI, Morocco
JORDAN TIMES, Jordan
JOURNAL DE TANGER, Morocco
KHABAR, Algeria
LAHA, Lebanon
LIBERTÉ, Algeria
MAIL & GUARDIAN (MAIN BODY), South Africa
MAROC HEBDO INTERNATIONAL, Morocco
MATIN, Morocco
MESSAGER, Cameroon
MIDI MADAGASIKARA, Madagascar
MIRROR (GHANA), Ghana
MMEGI, Botswana
NATION, Malawi
NEW VISION, Uganda
NEWSWATCH, Nigeria
OBSERVATEUR PAALGA, Burkina Faso
OPINION, Morocco

PRESSE DE TUNISIE, Tunisia
RAI, Jordan
SAHEL, Niger
SEMANA, Cape Verde Islands
SIDWAYA QUOTIDIEN, Burkina Faso
SOLEIL, Senegal
STAR, Jordan
TEMPS, Tunisia
THIS DAY, Nigeria
VIE ECO, Morocco
WATAN, Algeria

JLA
1200432

Mitre House, 66 Abbey Road, ENFIELD, EN1 2QN
Tel: 020 8364 1441 **Fax:** 020 8364 1331
Email: sales@j-l-a.com
Web site: http://www.j-l-a.com
Countries Represented: Japan, Korea (South), USA

Titles:
COMPASS, Japan
MARINE LOG, USA
MARITIME KOREA, Korea (South)

AL KHALEEJIAH INTERNATIONAL
1200239

Arab Press House, High Holborn, LONDON, WC1V 7AP
Tel: 020 7404 6950 **Fax:** 020 7404 6963
Email: sales@alkhaleejiah.co.uk
Web site: http://www.alkhaleejiah.com.
Countries Represented: Saudi Arabia

Titles:
ARAB NEWS, Saudi Arabia
ARRIYADIAH, Saudi Arabia
EQTISADIAH, Saudi Arabia
URDU MAGAZINE, Saudi Arabia
URDU NEWS, Saudi Arabia

LGA LAGARDERE GLOBAL
ADVERTISING
1200570

64 North Row, LONDON, W1K 7LL **Tel:** 020 7150 7430
Fax: 020 7150 7439
Email: enquires@lgalondon.co.uk
Web site: http://www.i-g-a.com
Countries Represented: Argentina, Belgium, Canada,
China, Czech Republic, France, Germany, Hong Kong,
India, Italy, Japan, Korea (South), Mexico, Netherlands,
Norway, Poland, Portugal, Romania, Russian
Federation, Singapore, South Africa, Spain, Sweden,
Taiwan, Thailand, Turkey, USA

Titles:
AIR FRANCE MADAME, France
AIR FRANCE MAGAZINE, France
AMERICAN WAY, USA
AR LA REVISTA DE ANA ROSA, Spain
AUTO & FUORISTRADA, Italy
AUTOMOBILES CLASSIQUES, France
AUTO-MOTO, France
BABAR (3-6 ANS), France
BIBA, France
BUNTE, Germany
CAFÉ, Sweden
CAMPAGNE DECORATION, France
CAR & DRIVER, China
CAR AND DRIVER, Spain
CAR AND DRIVER, USA
CASA DIEZ, Spain
CONNAISSANCE DES ARTS, France
CRECER FELIZ, Mexico
CRECER FELIZ, Spain
D LIRE (9-13 ANS), France
DEVIAJES, Spain
DIEZ MINUTOS, Spain
ELLE, Argentina
ELLE, China
ELLE, Czech Republic
ELLE, France
ELLE, Germany
ELLE, India
ELLE, Italy
ELLE, Korea (South)
ELLE, Netherlands
ELLE, Norway
ELLE, Poland
ELLE, Portugal
ELLE, Romania
ELLE, Russian Federation
ELLE, Singapore
ELLE, South Africa
ELLE, Spain
ELLE, Sweden
ELLE, Thailand
ELLE, Turkey

ELLE A TABLE, France
ELLE CANADA, Canada
ELLE DECO, Spain
ELLE DECO (JAPAN EDITION), Japan
ELLE DECOR, Italy
ELLE DECOR, USA
ELLE DECORATION, Belgium
ELLE DECORATION, France
ELLE DECORATION, Germany
ELLE ETEN, Netherlands
ELLE HONG KONG, Hong Kong
ELLE INTERIÖR, Sweden
ELLE (JAPAN EDITION), Japan
ELLE MAT & VIN, Sweden
ELLE QUEBEC, Canada
ELLE TAIPEI, Taiwan
EMPRENDEDORES, Spain
ENFANT MAG, France
ENTREVUE, France
EQUIPE, France
EQUIPE MAGAZINE, France
EVA TREMILA, Italy
FILM, Poland
FOCUS, Germany
FOCUS MONEY, Germany
FOTOGRAMAS & DVD, Spain
FREUNDIN, Germany
FREUNDIN WELLFIT, Germany
GENTE, Italy
GENTE MOTORI, Italy
GENTE VIAGGI, Italy
GIOIA, Italy
HISTORIA, France
I LOVE ENGLISH JUNIOR (9-11 ANS), France
IMAGES DOC (8-12 ANS), France
J'AIME LIRE (7-11 ANS), France
JE BOUQUINE (10-15 ANS), France
JEUNE ET JOLIE, France
JEUNE ET JOLIE (15/25 ANS), Belgium
JOURNAL DE LA MAISON, France
JOURNAL DU DIMANCHE, France
MARIE CLAIRE, Italy
MARIE CLAIRE, Russian Federation
MAXIM, USA
METROPOLITAN HOME, USA
MICASA, Spain
MON JARDIN & MA MAISON, France
NUMERO, France
OKAPI (10-15 ANS), France
ONZE MONDIAL, France
PARENTS, France
PARENTS / KIND & CO, Belgium
PARIS MATCH, Belgium
PARIS MATCH, France
PARISIEN ET AUJOURD'HUI EN FRANCE PAGES
    HIPPIQUES, France
PELERIN, France
PHOSPHORE, France
PHOTO, France
PLUS LE MAGAZINE DES ABONNES DE CANAL+,
    France
POINT, France
POMME D'API (3-7 ANS), France
POPI (1-3 ANS), France
PREMIERE, Belgium
PREMIERE, France
QUÉ LEER, Spain
QUÉ ME DICES, Spain
QUO, Mexico
QUO, Spain
QUOTE, Netherlands
RAGAZZA, Spain
RAKAM, Italy
ROAD & TRACK, USA
SAMO ZDROWIE, Poland
SANTÉ, Netherlands
SAVEURS, France
SCIENCE & VIE, France
SUPERTELE, Spain
TECHNIKART, France
TELE 7 JOURS, France
TELECABLE SATELLITE HEBDO, France
TELEINDISCRETA, Spain
TELENOVELA, Spain
TENNIS MAGAZINE, France
TODAY IN ENGLISH, France
VERSION FEMINA, France
VERVE, Taiwan
VOTRE BEAUTE, France
WOMAN'S DAY, China
WOMAN'S DAY, USA
YOUPI (5-8 ANS), France

M W MEDIA
1200243

PO Box 125, STOWMARKET, IP14 1PB
Tel: 01449 771200

Email: info@mwmedia.uk.com
Countries Represented: Austria, Denmark, Germany, Israel, Italy, Netherlands, Norway, Portugal, South Africa, Spain, Sweden, Tunisia, USA

Titles:
AMERICA JOURNAL, Germany
CONGRESS TODAY & INCENTIVE TRAVEL, Italy
EVENTS, Germany
FIERE NEL MONDO, Italy
GSA TRAVEL MARKETING MAGAZINE, South Africa
GUIDA VIAGGI, Italy
HOSTELTUR, Spain
INCENTIVARE, Italy
ISRAEL TOURIST GUIDE MAGAZINE, Israel
JAX FAX TRAVEL MARKETING MAGAZINE, USA
KONFERENSVÄRLDEN, Sweden
MC MEETING E CONGRESSI, Italy
PUBLITURIS, Portugal
STAND BY, Denmark
SUITE, Italy
TAI TOURISMUSWIRTSCHAFT AUSTRIA & INTERNATIONAL, Austria
TOURISME INFO, Tunisia
TOURISTIK AKTUELL, Germany
TRAVEL NEWS, Norway
TRAVEL NEWS, Sweden
TRAVEL ONE, Germany
TURISMO D'AFFARI, Italy
TURISMO D'ITALIA, Italy
ZAKENREIS, Netherlands

MARSHALL CAVENDISH LTD   1200375
5th Floor, 32-38 Saffron Hill, LONDON, EC1N 8FH
Tel: 020 7421 8120 **Fax:** 020 7421 8121
Email: chris.jenner@marshallcavendish.com
Web site: http://www.marshallcavendish.co.uk
Countries Represented: Hong Kong

Titles:
CARGONEWS CHINA, Hong Kong

MEDIA NETWORK EUROPE   1500097
University House, 11-13 Lower Grosvenor Place, LONDON, SW1W 0EX **Tel:** 020 7834 7676
Fax: 020 7973 0076
Email: media@alaincharles.com
Web site: http://www.alaincharles.com
Countries Represented: Germany, Turkey, USA

Titles:
AUTOMOTIVE ENGINEERING INTERNATIONAL, USA
BTH HEIMTEX, Germany
HAUSTEX, Germany
HÜRRIYET, Turkey
LEBENSMITTEL TECHNIK, Germany
MECHANICAL ENGINEERING, USA
SECURITY MANAGEMENT, USA
WRP, Germany

MEDIAFORCE INTERNATIONAL   1200537
1 Gunpowder Square, Fleet Street, LONDON, EC4A 3EP **Tel:** 020 7583 0202 **Fax:** 020 7353 2111
Email: mediaforce-international@mediaforce.co.uk
Web site: http://www.mediaforceinternational.com
Countries Represented: Antigua & Barbuda, Argentina, Bermuda, Bolivia, Brazil, Chile, Colombia, Costa Rica, Dominica, Ecuador, Guatemala, Honduras, Jamaica, Mexico, Nicaragua, Paraguay, Peru, Puerto Rico, South Africa, Uruguay, Venezuela

Titles:
ABC COLOR, Paraguay
ANTIGUA SUN, Antigua & Barbuda
ATHLONE NEWS, South Africa
ATLANTIC SUN, South Africa
BOLANDER, South Africa
CAPE ARGUS (MAIN BODY), South Africa
CAPE TIMES (MAIN BODY), South Africa
CARETAS, Peru
CHRONICLE, Dominica
CLARÍN, Argentina
COMERCIO, Ecuador
COMERCIO (PERU), Peru
CONSTANTIABERG BULLETIN, South Africa
COSAS, Ecuador
DEBER, Bolivia
DIAMOND FIELDS ADVERTISER (MAIN BODY), South Africa
DIARIO, Bolivia
DIARIO EL MERCURIO, Chile
DIARIO ESTRATEGIA, Chile
DINERO, Colombia
ESPECTADOR, Colombia
EXCELSIOR, Mexico

FALSE BAY ECHO, South Africa
FOLHA DE SÃO PAULO, Brazil
GESTIÓN, Peru
GLEANER, Jamaica
MERCURY (MAIN BODY), South Africa
NACIÓN, Argentina
NACIÓN, Costa Rica
NACIONAL, Venezuela
NUEVA ECONOMÍA, Bolivia
OBSERVADOR, Uruguay
PAÍS, Uruguay
PLAINSMAN, South Africa
PRENSA, Honduras
PRENSA, Nicaragua
PRENSA LIBRE, Guatemala
PRETORIA NEWS (MAIN BODY), South Africa
PRETORIA NEWS WEEKEND, South Africa
ROYAL GAZETTE ONLINE, Bermuda
SAN JUAN STAR, Puerto Rico
SATURDAY STAR (MAIN BODY), South Africa
SEMANA, Colombia
SENTINEL NEWS, South Africa
SOUTHERN MAIL, South Africa
SOUTHERN SUBURBS TATLER, South Africa
STAR (MAIN BODY), South Africa
SUNDAY INDEPENDENT (MAIN BODY), South Africa
TABLETALK, South Africa
TIEMPO, Colombia
TRIBUNA, Honduras
TYGERTALK (BELLVILLE/DUBANVILLE), South Africa
TYGERTALK(PAROW/GOODWOOD), South Africa
UNIVERSAL, Venezuela
UNIVERSO, Ecuador
VUKANI, South Africa
WEEKEND CAPE ARGUS, South Africa

MERCURY PUBLICITY LTD   1200058
25 John Street, LONDON, WC1N 2DL
Tel: 020 7611 1900 **Fax:** 020 7404 4674
Email: sales@mercury-publicity.com
Web site: http://www.mercury-publicity.com
Countries Represented: Czech Republic, France, Hungary, Poland, Portugal, Russian Federation, Spain, Taiwan, USA

Titles:
ABC, Spain
CAPITAL, Spain
COSMOPOLITAN, Spain
DINERO, Spain
FIGARO, France
FIGARO MAGAZINE, France
FIGAROSCOPE SUPPLEMENT DU FIGARO, France
FIGYELO, Hungary
GACETA DE LOS NEGOCIOS, Spain
GAZETA WYBORCZA, Poland
GEO, Spain
HVG, Hungary
IZVESTIA, Russian Federation
MADAME FIGARO, France
MADAME FIGARO (TAIWAN EDITION), Taiwan
MARIE CLAIRE, Spain
MÁXIMA, Portugal
MÁXIMA INTERIORES, Portugal
MÍA, Spain
MLADÁ FRONTA DNES, Czech Republic
MOSCOW TIMES, Russian Federation
MUY INTERESANTE, Spain
PROPRIETES DE FRANCE, France
SER PADRES HOY, Spain
TV MAGAZINE, France
VEDOMOSTI, Russian Federation
WIRED, USA
WPROST, Poland

MWA INTERNATIONAL   1200562
No 2 Aura House, 53 Oldridge Road, LONDON, SW12 8PP **Tel:** 020 8772 1345 **Fax:** 020 8772 1035
Email: michael@mwa-media.com
Web site: http://www.mwa-media.com
Countries Represented: Argentina, Australia, Belgium, Brazil, Colombia, Czech Republic, France, Germany, Israel, Italy, Portugal, South Africa, Spain

Titles:
ALPIN, Germany
AM AUTOMESE, Italy
ÁMBITO FINANCIERO, Argentina
AMI DES JARDINS ET DE LA MAISON, France
AUTO, Italy
AUTO JOURNAL, France
AUTO PLUS, France
AUTOSPRINT, Italy
AVANTAGES, France
BATEAUX, France

CAMERA VIDEO & MULTIMEDIA, France
CARTA CAPITAL, Brazil
CHASSEUR FRANCAIS, France
COMPUTER, Czech Republic
CONNECT!, Czech Republic
CONSOLES +, France
CORRIERE DELLO SPORT-STADIO, Italy
COSMOPOLITAN, France
CRIATIVA, Brazil
CYCLE, France
DAG ALLEMAAL + EXPRES, Belgium
DATAWEEK: ELECTRONICS & COMMUN. TECHNOLOGY SA, South Africa
DIAPASON, France
DOCE REVISTA, Brazil
EMPIRE, Australia
ENTREPRENDRE, France
FAMILI, France
FHM, Australia
FHM (FOR HIM MAGAZINE), France
FHM FOR HIM MAGAZINE, Germany
FILM FRANCAIS, France
FRANCE FOOTBALL, France
GIORNO, Italy
GOED GEVOEL, Belgium
GOLF EUROPEEN, France
GOLF MAGAZINE, France
GRAND GIBIER, France
GUERIN SPORTIVO, Italy
HA'ARETZ, Israel
IN MOTO, Italy
JOEPIE (12/17 ANS), Belgium
KICKER SPORTMAGAZIN, Germany
LIBERATION, France
MARIE CLAIRE, France
MARIE CLAIRE BELGIQUE/ MARIE CLAIRE VLAAMSE EDITIE, Belgium
MARIE CLAIRE IDEES, France
MARIE CLAIRE MAISON, France
MARIE FRANCE, France
MARKETING DIRECT, France
MARKETING MAGAZINE, France
MICRO PRATIQUE, France
MICRO SIMULATEUR, France
MICROMANÍA, Spain
MODES ET TRAVAUX, France
MOTOSPRINT, Italy
NAZIONE, Italy
NOUS DEUX, France
NOUVEL ECONOMISTE, France
OFFICIEL DU CYCLE, DE LA MOTO ET DU QUAD, France
ONDA TV, Italy
PC TODAY, Spain
PECHE ET LES POISSONS, France
PECHE MOUCHE, France
PLAY2MANÍA, Spain
PLEINE VIE, France
PORTAFOLIO, Colombia
REPONSES PHOTO, France
RESTO DEL CARLINO, Italy
REVUE NATIONALE DE LA CHASSE, France
ROTAS & DESTINOS, Portugal
SPORT-AUTO, France
TELERAMA, France
TUTTOSPORT, Italy
TV-FAMILIE - BLIK, Belgium
ULYSSE/COURRIER INTERNATIONAL, France
UNTERWASSER, Germany
VALOR ECONÔMICO, Brazil
VELO MAGAZINE, France
WOEF, Belgium

OLIVER SMITH & PARTNER   1757483
Tel: 020 79 78 14 40
Web site: http://www.osp-uk.com
Countries Represented: Spain

Titles:
REDES & TELECOM, Spain

OLIVER SMITH & PARTNERS LTD   1200033
18 Abbeville Mews, 88 Clapham Park Road, LONDON, SW4 7BX **Tel:** 020 7978 1440 **Fax:** 020 7978 1550
Email: david@osp-uk.com
Web site: http://www.osp-uk.com
Countries Represented: Belgium, Canada, Denmark, Finland, France, Germany, Italy, Japan, Norway, Portugal, Russian Federation, Spain, Sweden, Thailand, USA

Titles:
ACTUALIDAD ECONÓMICA, Spain
ACTUALITE, Canada
AFFÄRSVÄRLDEN, Sweden
ALT OM DATA, Denmark

Advertising Representatives

BIZZ, Belgium
CIO INSIGHT, USA
COMPUTER ZEITUNG, Germany
DAILY YOMIURI, Japan
DATATID, Denmark
DATORMAGAZIN, Sweden
DIÁRIO ECONÓMICO, Portugal
EKSTRA BLADET; NYHEDER, Denmark
EWEEK, USA
EXPANSION, France
EXPANSIÓN, Spain
EXPRESS, France
EXPRESSEN, Sweden
FAST COMPANY, USA
GOLF DIGEST, Spain
GRANDE, Belgium
GT, Sweden
HLN - HET LAATSTE NIEUWS / DE NIEUWE GAZET,
  Belgium
INC., USA
ITVIIKKO, Finland
IX, Germany
KAPITAL, Norway
KNACK, Belgium
LANLINE, Germany
LIRE, France
MACLEAN'S, Canada
MAISON FRANCAISE, France
MAISON MAGAZINE, France
MARCA, Spain
MIEUX VIVRE VOTRE ARGENT, France
MIKROBITTI, Finland
MUNDO DEL SIGLO VEINTIUNO, Spain
NATIONAL POST, Canada
NY TEKNIK, Sweden
PC GAMER, Sweden
PC MAGAZINE, Belgium
PC MAGAZINE, Russian Federation
PC MAGAZINE THAILAND, Thailand
PC PROFESSIONALE, Italy
PC WEEK, Russian Federation
PLUS MAGAZINE, Belgium
POLITIKEN, Denmark
PVD, Spain
SMART BUSINESS STRATEGIES, Belgium
SPORT FOOT MAGAZINE, Belgium
SUPER PLAY, Sweden
TELEPRO MAGAZINE, Belgium
TELVA, Spain
TIETOKONE, Finland
TRENDS, Belgium
VG, Norway
VIF - L'EXPRESS, Belgium
WEEKEND ECONÓMICO, Portugal
WEEKEND KNACK, Belgium
YOMIURI SHIMBUN, Japan

THE PUBLICITAS
1600277

Gordon House, Greencoat Place, LONDON, SW1P 1PH
Tel: 020 7592 8300 **Fax:** 020 7592 8301
Email: london@publicitas.com
Web site: www.publicitas.com/uk
Countries Represented: Australia, Austria,
Bangladesh, Belgium, Canada, China, Denmark, Egypt,
France, Germany, Greece, Hong Kong, Italy, Japan,
Korea (South), Kuwait, Lebanon, Malaysia, Mauritius,
Mexico, New Zealand, Oman, Pakistan, Philippines,
Portugal, Saudi Arabia, Singapore, South Africa, Spain,
Switzerland, Taiwan, Thailand, USA, United Arab
Emirates

Titles:
4 X 4 AUSTRALIA, Australia
AERA, Japan
AFFAIRES, Canada
AGRI, Switzerland
AHRAM IKTISADI, Egypt
AKHBAR, Egypt
AKHBAR EL-YOM, Egypt
ALT FOR DAMERNE, Denmark
ANNABELLE, Switzerland
AN-NAHAR, Lebanon
ARAB TIMES, Kuwait
ASAHI CAMERA, Japan
ASAHI SHIMBUN, Japan
ASAHI WEEKLY, Japan
ASIAN HOTEL AND CATERING TIMES, Hong Kong
ATLANTA JOURNAL-CONSTITUTION, USA
AUSTRALIAN AUTO ACTION, Australia
AUSTRALIAN GOOD FOOD MAGAZINE, Australia
AUSTRALIAN HOUSE & GARDEN, Australia
AUSTRALIAN MOTORCYCLE NEWS, Australia
AUSTRALIAN PC USER, Australia
AUSTRALIAN WOMEN'S WEEKLY, Australia
BANGKOK POST, Thailand
BANGLADESH OBSERVER, Bangladesh
BAYAN, United Arab Emirates

BEIJING EVENING NEWS, China
BELLE, Australia
BØRSEN, DAGBLADET, Denmark
BÖRSEN-ZEITUNG, Germany
BOSTON GLOBE, USA
BUND, Switzerland
BURKE'S BACKYARD MAGAZINE, Australia
BUSINESS DAY, South Africa
CARAVAN WORLD, Australia
CHICAGO TRIBUNE, USA
CHINA POST, Taiwan
CLEO, Australia
CLEO MAGAZINE (NZ EDITION), New Zealand
CLICKX MAGAZINE, Belgium
COSMOPOLITAN, Australia
COUNTRY, Germany
DAILY EXPRESS, Malaysia
DALLAS MORNING NEWS, USA
DE GENTENAAR/NIEUWSBLAD, Belgium
DEALS ON WHEELS, Australia
DEPARTURES MAGAZINE, USA
DETROIT FREE PRESS, USA
DH LES SPORTS, Belgium
DIÁRIO DE NOTÍCIAS, Portugal
DOLLY, Australia
DS - DE STANDAARD, Belgium
EARTHMOVERS & EXCAVATORS, Australia
EGYPTIAN GAZETTE, Egypt
EVITA, Belgium
EXAME, Portugal
EXAME INFORMÁTICA, Portugal
EXECUTIVE DIGEST, Portugal
EXPRESSO, Portugal
FARMS & FARM MACHINERY, Australia
FASHION QUARTERLY, New Zealand
FEELING, Belgium
FEINSCHMECKER, Germany
FEMMES D'AUJOURD'HUI, Belgium
FINANCIAL MAIL, South Africa
FOXTEL MAGAZINE, Australia
FRANKFURTER RUNDSCHAU, Germany
FÜR SIE, Germany
FVW, Germany
GAEL, Belgium
GAEL MAISON / FEELING WONEN, Belgium
GAZET VAN ANTWERPEN, Belgium
GOING PLACES, Malaysia
GQ JAPAN, Japan
GUANGZHOU DAILY, China
GULF NEWS, United Arab Emirates
HANDELSZEITUNG & THE WALL STREET JOURNAL,
  Switzerland
HANKYUNG BUSINESS WEEKLY, Korea (South)
HARPER'S BAZAR, Mexico
HASNAA - LEVANT EDITION, Lebanon
HAWAA, Egypt
HENDES VERDEN, Denmark
HERALD, Pakistan
HET BELANG VAN LIMBURG, Belgium
HJEMMET, Denmark
HOME JOURNAL, Hong Kong
HONG KONG BUSINESS, Hong Kong
HOUSTON CHRONICLE, USA
HUMO, Belgium
INVESTOR'S BUSINESS DAILY, USA
ITTIHAD, United Arab Emirates
JYLLANDS-POSTEN, MORGENAVISEN, Denmark
KATHIMERINI, Greece
KHALEEJ, United Arab Emirates
KHALEEJ TIMES, United Arab Emirates
KLIK, Greece
KOREA HERALD, Korea (South)
KUWAIT TIMES, Kuwait
LAS VEGAS REVIEW-JOURNAL, USA
LIBELLE, Belgium
LIBRE ENTREPRISE (SUPP. LA LIBRE BELGIQUE),
  Belgium
LOS ANGELES TIMES, USA
MAKEDONIA, Greece
MALAYSIA TATLER, Malaysia
MANILA BULLETIN, Philippines
MARIE CLAIRE, Mexico
MAURITIUS TIMES, Mauritius
MEETING NEWS, USA
MEN MODE, Singapore
MENZO, Belgium
MERIAN, Germany
MIAMI HERALD, USA
MILITANT, Mauritius
MINERVA CHIRURGICA, Italy
MONEY MAGAZINE, Australia
NAFTEMPORIKI, Greece
NEUE LUZERNER ZEITUNG, Switzerland
NEW ZEALAND HERALD, New Zealand
NIKKEI WEEKLY, Japan
NORTH & SOUTH, New Zealand
NW, Australia

OFFICIAL SONY PLAYSTATION 2 MAGAZINE,
  Australia
OMAN DAILY OBSERVER, Oman
PAÍS, Spain
PEOPLE, Australia
PETRA, Germany
PHILADELPHIA DAILY NEWS, USA
PHILADELPHIA INQUIRER, USA
PLAIN DEALER, USA
PRESSE, Austria
PROFIL, Austria
PROFIL FEMME, Switzerland
PROGRÈS EGYPTIEN, Egypt
PÚBLICO, Portugal
RALPH, Australia
RHEINISCHE POST, Germany
RIYADH, Saudi Arabia
SAN FRANCISCO CHRONICLE, USA
SAWASDEE, Hong Kong
SCIENTIFIC AMERICAN, USA
SEATTLE TIMES, USA
SELBER MACHEN, Germany
SEYASSAH, Kuwait
SHUKAN ASAHI, Japan
SILKROAD, Hong Kong
SOIR - SIEGE SOCIAL, Belgium
SOUTH CHINA MORNING POST, Hong Kong
ST. GALLER TAGBLATT, Switzerland
STAR, Malaysia
STOCKS, Switzerland
STORY, Belgium
STUTTGARTER ZEITUNG, Germany
SUCCESSFUL MEETINGS, USA
SÜDDEUTSCHE ZEITUNG, Germany
TAGES ANZEIGER, Switzerland
TAKE 5, Australia
TELE POCKET, Belgium
TEVE BLAD, Belgium
TIMES OF OMAN, Oman
TOUR HEBDO, France
TRADE-A-BOAT, Australia
TRAVEL MAGAZINE, Belgium
TRAVEL TALK, Germany
TREND, Austria
TRIBUNE DE GENÈVE, Switzerland
TÚ, Mexico
UNIQUE CARS, Australia
VANGUARDIA, Spain
VIE CATHOLIQUE, Mauritius
VITAL, Germany
WASHINGTON POST, USA
WATAN, Kuwait
WATAN, Oman
WELTWOCHE, Switzerland
WEST AUSTRALIAN, Australia
WHEELS, Australia
WOMAN'S DAY, Australia
XINMIN EVENING NEWS, China
ZAHRAT AL KHALEEJ, United Arab Emirates
ZUHAUSE WOHNEN, Germany
ZUHAUSE WOHNEN EXTRA, Germany

PUBLIEUROPE LTD
697721

Ariel House, 74A Charlotte Street, LONDON W1T 4QJ
Tel: 020 7927 9800
Email: infolondon@publieurope.com
Web site: http://www.publieurope.com
Countries Represented: Belgium, Germany, Italy,
Spain

Titles:
AUTO OGGI, Italy
AUTOMOBILE CLUB, Italy
AVVENIRE, Italy
BANCAFINANZA, Italy
CAMBIO PANORAMAUTO, Italy
CASA FACILE, Italy
CASA IDEA (DONNA MODERNA), Italy
CASABELLA, Italy
CASAVIVA, Italy
CHI, Italy
COSMOPOLITAN, Italy
CUCINA MODERNA, Italy
DONNA MODERNA, Italy
ESPANSIONE, Italy
FAMIGLIA CRISTIANA, Italy
FOCUS, Italy
GIORNALE, Italy
GRAZIA, Italy
GRAZIA CASA, Italy
HP TRASPORTI CLUB, Italy
INTERNI, Italy
JACK, Italy
KABEL EINS, Germany
MEN'S HEALTH, Italy
MI CARTERA DE INVERSIÓN, Spain
PANORAMA, Italy

PANORAMA TRAVEL, Italy
PC MAGAZINE, Italy
PRO SIEBEN, Germany
RADIO DIMENSIONE SUONO, Italy
RADIO ITALIA SOLO MUSICA IT. - NOTIZIE, Italy
SALE & PEPE, Italy
SAT.1, Germany
STARBENE, Italy
TOP GIRL, Italy
TOPOLINO, Italy
TU STYLE, Italy
TV SORRISI & CANZONI, Italy
VILLEGIARDINI, Italy
VT4, Belgium

READER'S DIGEST
1200106

11 Westferry Circus, Canary Wharf, LONDON, E14 4HE
Tel: 020 7715 8000 **Fax:** 020 7715 8701
Email: scott_mineikis@readersdigest.co.uk
Web site: http://www.readersdigest.com/
globaladvertising
Countries Represented: Belgium, Brazil, Canada,
Finland, Germany, Hungary, India, Korea (South),
Netherlands, Russian Federation, South Africa,
Thailand, USA

Titles:
READER'S DIGEST, Canada
READER'S DIGEST, Hungary
READER'S DIGEST, India
READER'S DIGEST, South Africa
READER'S DIGEST, Thailand
READER'S DIGEST, USA
READER'S DIGEST DEUTSCHLAND, Germany
READER'S DIGEST, HET BESTE, Netherlands
READER'S DIGEST (KOREA), Korea (South)
READER'S DIGEST (RUSSIA), Russian Federation
READER'S DIGEST - SELECTION BELGIQUE/ HET
   BESTE VOOR BELGIE, Belgium
SELEÇÕES - READER'S DIGEST, Brazil
VALITUT PALAT, Finland

ROBERT G. HORSFIELD INTL. PUBLISHERS REPRESENTATIVES
1200618

Daisy Bank, Leaden Knowle, Chinley, HIGH PEAK,
SK23 6DA **Tel:** 01663 750242 **Fax:** 01663 750973
Email: ekania@btopenworld.com
Countries Represented: Canada, France, India, Italy,
Portugal, South Africa, USA

Titles:
CASTINGS SA, South Africa
CONSTRUCTION WORLD, South Africa
IMPIANTO ELETTRICO, Italy
INDIAN TEXTILE JOURNAL, India
INDUSTRIE TEXTILE, France
LUCE E DESIGN, Italy
MACHINES PRODUCTION, France
METALWORKING NEWS, South Africa
MINING WEEKLY, South Africa
MODERN MACHINE SHOP, USA
NOVA TÊXTIL, Portugal
ORGANI DI TRASMISSIONE, Italy
TEXTILE JOURNAL/LA REVUE DU TEXTILE, Canada
TEXTILE WORLD, USA
TEXTILES PANAMERICANOS, USA
TUT - LA REVUE DES UTILISATEURS DE TEXTILES A
   USAGES TECHNIQUES, France

SMYTH INTERNATIONAL
625111

PO Box 333, HERTFORD, SG13 9GU
Tel: 020 8446 6400 **Fax:** 020 8446 6402
Email: mail@smyth-international.com
Web site: http://www.smyth-international.com
Countries Represented: Australia, Denmark, Finland,
France, Germany, Italy, Malta, New Zealand, Norway,
Sweden, USA

Titles:
7 PÄIVÄÄ, Finland
AL VOLANTE, Italy
ALLAS VECKOTIDNING, Sweden
ALLERS, Sweden
ALLERS TRÄDGÅRD, Sweden
ANTIK & AUKTION, Sweden
ANTIK & AUKTION, Denmark
ÅRET RUNT, Sweden
BAZAR, Denmark
COMPUTER ARTS, France
COMPUTER ARTS, Italy
COMPUTER MAGAZINE, Italy
COURIER MAIL, Australia
DAGENS NÆRINGSLIV, Norway
DAILY TELEGRAPH, Australia

DESIGN&ELEKTRONIK, Germany
DHF INTRALOGISTIK, Germany
DIMA, Germany
DOMINION POST, New Zealand
ERHVERVSBLADET.DK, Denmark
FEMINA, Sweden
FOTO, Sweden
GIOCHI PER IL MIO COMPUTER, Italy
GIRLFRIEND, Australia
HÄNT EXTRA, Sweden
HEMMETS VECKOTIDNING, Sweden
HERALD SUN, Australia
HOB DIE HOLZBEARBEITUNG, Germany
IN SELLA, Italy
INGENIØREN, Denmark
INTERNET PRATIQUE, France
ITALIA OGGI, Italy
JEUX VIDEO MAGAZINE, France
KAUPPALEHTI, Finland
KAUPPALEHTI OPTIO, Finland
KOTI JA KEITTIÖ, Finland
LINUXMAGASINET, Norway
MÅ BRA, Sweden
MAD & BOLIG, Denmark
MARKT&TECHNIK, Germany
MATMAGASINET, Sweden
MERCURY, Australia
MIO COMPUTER, Italy
NET TV, Malta
NEW IDEA, Australia
NEW YORK POST, USA
NINTENDO LE MAGAZINE OFFICIEL, France
NZ INFOTECH, New Zealand
PC ACHAT, France
PC JEUX, France
PSM3, France
QUI TOURING, Italy
RHEINISCHER MERKUR, Germany
SE & HÖR, Sweden
SECOLO XIX, Italy
SPECCHIO+ (LA STAMPA), Italy
STAMPA, Italy
SUNDAY HERALD SUN, Australia
SUNDAY MAIL (QLD), Australia
SUNDAY MAIL (SA), Australia
SUNDAY TASMANIAN, Australia
SUNDAY TELEGRAPH, Australia
SUNDAY TERRITORIAN, Australia
SUNDAY TIMES, Australia
SVENSK DAMTIDNING, Sweden
SVENSKA DAGBLADET, Sweden
T3, Italy
TEMPO, Italy
THAT'S LIFE, Australia
TV HITS, Australia
TV WEEK, Australia
UNITA', Italy
VI UNGE, Denmark
WINDOWS NEWS, France
XBOX 360 LE MAGAZINE OFFICIEL, France

SOUTH AFRICAN SUGAR ASSOCIATION
1200080

Watermans Hall, 16 St. Mary At Hill, LONDON, EC3R
8EF **Tel:** 020 7626 1844 **Fax:** 020 7623 2715
Email: sasaldn@btinternet.com
Web site: http://www.sugar.org.za
Countries Represented: South Africa

Titles:
SUGAR JOURNAL, SA, South Africa

SPAFAX
1201134

The Pump House, 13-16 Jacobs Well Mews, LONDON,
W1U 3DY **Tel:** 020 7906 2001 **Fax:** 020 7906 2022
Email: info@spafax.com
Web site: http://www.spafax.com
Countries Represented: Austria, Germany, Japan,
Netherlands, Spain, USA, United Arab Emirates
Titles:
AGORA, Japan
AMERICAN AIRLINES NEXOS, USA
EMIRATES TV & RADIO, United Arab Emirates
FLYING DUTCHMAN, Netherlands
LUFTHANSA MAGAZIN, Germany
RONDA IBÉRIA, Spain
SKYLINES, Austria

SSM GLOBAL MEDIA LTD
1200338

1st Floor, SSM House, 1 Cobden Court, Wimpole Close,
BROMLEY, BR2 9JF **Tel:** 020 8464 5577
Fax: 020 8464 5588

Email: sales@ssm.co.uk
Web site: http://www.ssm.co.uk
Countries Represented: Australia, Belgium, Cyprus,
Denmark, Finland, Germany, Gibraltar, Lebanon, Malta,
Monaco, Netherlands, Poland, Romania, Singapore,
Spain, Sweden, USA, United Arab Emirates

Titles:
AANDRIJFTECHNIEK, Netherlands
AANNEMER, Netherlands
ABSOLUTE MARBELLA, Spain
ACHABAKA, Lebanon
ADHÄSION KLEBEN & DICHTEN, Germany
ANDALUCÍA GOLF, Spain
ARAB DEFENCE JOURNAL, Lebanon
AS, MAANDBLAD VOOR DE ACTIVITEITENSECTOR,
   Netherlands
ASIA IMAGE, Singapore
ASSAYAD, Lebanon
ATZ AUTOMOBILTECHNISCHE ZEITSCHRIFT,
   Germany
AUSTRALIAN TELECOM, Australia
AUTO & MOTORTECHNIEK, Netherlands
B&C BROADCASTING & CABLE, USA
BANKER MIDDLE EAST, United Arab Emirates
BARCELONA METROPOLITAN, Spain
BIKE EUROPE, Netherlands
BIT, Netherlands
BIZZ, Netherlands
BLOEM EN BLAD, Netherlands
BOOMKWEKERIJ, Netherlands
BOUWMARKT, Netherlands
BOUWWERELD, Netherlands
BOVAGKRANT, Netherlands
BUCHAREST BUSINESS WEEK, Romania
BUILDING DESIGN & CONSTRUCTION, USA
BULK, Netherlands
THE BULLETIN, Belgium
CALL CENTER PROFI, Germany
CHEM.INFO, USA
CHROMATOGRAPHIA, Germany
CONSTRUCTION EQUIPMENT, USA
CONSULTING - SPECIFYING ENGINEER, USA
CONTROLLERS MAGAZINE, Netherlands
COSTA BLANCA NEWS, Spain
CYPRUS MAIL, Cyprus
CYPRUS WEEKLY, Cyprus
DANSK GOLF, Denmark
DEDICA, Germany
EDP-AUDITOR, Netherlands
ELEMENT + BAU, Germany
ELSEVIER RETAIL, Netherlands
EURO WEEKLY NEWS, Spain
FAIRUZ INTERNATIONAL, Lebanon
FEESTELIJK ZAKENDOEN MAGAZINE, Netherlands
FNG FOOD, NONFOOD & GETRÄNKE, Germany
FOOD MANUFACTURING, USA
FOOD TECHNOLOGIE, Germany
GEBOUWBEHEER, Netherlands
GETRÄNKE!, Germany
GIBRALTAR CHRONICLE, Gibraltar
GOLF, Finland
GOLF JOURNAL, Germany
GULF TODAY, United Arab Emirates
ICT ZORG, Netherlands
INDUSTRIAL MAINTENANCE & PLANT OPERATION,
   USA
ISLAND CONNECTIONS, Spain
LAND + WATER, Netherlands
LATIN TRADE, USA
MALTA BUSINESS WEEKLY, Malta
MANAGEMENT KINDEROPVANG, Netherlands
MANUFACTURING BUSINESS TECHNOLOGY, USA
MARKT EN HANDEL, Netherlands
MEDICAL DESIGN TECHNOLOGY, USA
MEDISCH CONTACT, Netherlands
METAAL MAGAZINE, Netherlands
MTZ MOTORTECHNISCHE ZEITSCHRIFT, Germany
MUSICMAKER, Netherlands
NEDERLANDS TIJDSCHRIFT VOOR
   ANESTHESIOLOGIE, Netherlands
NEDERLANDS TIJDSCHRIFT VOOR
   DERMATOLOGIE & VENEREOLOGIE, Netherlands
NEDERLANDS TIJDSCHRIFT VOOR UROLOGIE,
   Netherlands
NIEUWSBLAD TRANSPORT, Netherlands
NURSING, Netherlands
ORACLE MAGAZINE, USA
PADDESTOELEN, Netherlands
PIPELINE MAGAZINE, United Arab Emirates
PLANT ENGINEERING, USA
PLUIMVEEHOUDERIJ, Netherlands
POWDER/BULK SOLIDS, USA
PRODUCT DESIGN AND DEVELOPMENT, USA
PRODUCTS4ENGINEERS, Netherlands
PROFESSIONAL BUILDER, USA
PROFIT: THE EXECUTIVE'S GUIDE TO ORACLE
   APPLICATIONS, USA

Advertising Representatives

PURCHASING MAGAZINE, USA
RADIO RIVIERA MONACO 106.3, Monaco
RECYCLING MAGAZINE BENELUX, Netherlands
REVALIDATIE MAGAZINE, Netherlands
SALES BUSINESS, Germany
SCHAAP, Netherlands
SCHILDERSVAKKRANT, Netherlands
SCIENTIFIC COMPUTING, USA
SLAGERSWERELD.NL, Netherlands
SNACKKOERIER, Netherlands
SPEELTUIN, Netherlands
SUN GOLF, Spain
SUR, Spain
SURGICAL PRODUCTS, USA
SVENSK GOLF, Sweden
TBS-THE BROADSHEET, Spain
TIMES, Malta
TRANSPORT + OPSLAG, Netherlands
TREKKER, Netherlands

TTM (TRUCK & TRANSPORT MANAGEMENT),
  Netherlands
TVV, TIJDSCHRIFT VOOR VERZORGENDEN,
  Netherlands
TVZ, TIJDSCHRIFT VOOR VERPLEEGKUNDIGEN,
  Netherlands
TWEEWIELER, Netherlands
VARKENSHOUDERIJ - VAKDEEL VAN BOERDERIJ,
  Netherlands
VEEHOUDERIJ TECHNIEK, Netherlands
VIS MAGAZINE, Netherlands
WARSAW BUSINESS JOURNAL, Poland
WIRELESS DESIGN & DEVELOPMENT, USA
WIRELESS WEEK, USA
WIRTSCHAFTSINFORMATIK, Germany
WORKING@OFFICE, Germany
ZAKENAUTO, Netherlands
ZONVAK MAGAZINE, Netherlands

ZORG + WELZIJN, Netherlands
ZORGVISIE, Netherlands

TRAVELLING MEDIA   1200078
28 Bruton Street, LONDON, W1J 6QW
Tel: 020 7659 5567 **Fax:** 020 7659 5568
Email: info@travellingmedia.com
Web site: http://www.travellingmedia.com
Countries Represented: South Africa, USA, United
Arab Emirates

Titles:
  CONTINENTAL, USA
  HEMISPHERES, USA
  OPEN SKIES, United Arab Emirates
  SAWUBONA, South Africa
  SKY, USA

Willings Volume 1
Section 8

International Media Consultants

UK-based consultants handling titles internationally:
media planning and buying, analysis and
media research. Listings give UK details and
countries represented where known.

International Media Consultants

AD MEDICA 600563
Haddington, EAST LOTHIAN, EH41 4PU **Tel:** 01620 823383
Fax: 01620 823325
Email: pnoble@admedica.co.uk
Personnel: Finance: David Scott; **Managing Director:** Pam Noble; **Partner:** David Noble
Date established: 1986.

AMS MEDIA GROUP LTD 600562
150-158 King's Cross Road, LONDON, WC1X 9DH
Tel: 020 7843 6900 **Fax:** 020 7843 6960
Email: mail@amsgroup.co.uk
Web site: http://www.amsgroup.co.uk
Personnel: Managing Director: Paul Phelps
Date established: 1975. **Memberships:** CRCA, ITVA, MPA, NS, PPA.

JOHN AYLING & ASSOCIATES LTD 600564
27 Soho Square, LONDON, W1D 3QR **Tel:** 020 7439 6070
Fax: 020 7437 8473
Email: jaa@jaa-media.co.uk
Web site: http://www.jaa-media.co.uk
Personnel: Managing Director: John Ayling; **Financial Director:** Angela Hickey; **Director:** Colin Mark; **Director:** Peter McGill; **Director:** Peter Merry

Date established: 1978. **Memberships:** AMCO, ITVA, NPA, NS, PPA.

BILLETT MEDIA CONSULTING 600565
2nd Floor, The Registry, Royal Mint Court, LONDON, EC2N 4QN **Tel:** 020 7650 9600 **Fax:** 020 7650 9650
Email: theteam@billetts.com
Web site: http://www.billetts.com
Date established: 1995. **Memberships:** AMCO, MS.

CARAT GLOBAL MANAGEMENT 600568
Parker Tower, 43-49 Parker Street, LONDON, WC2B 5PS
Tel: 020 7430 6000 **Fax:** 020 7430 6319
Email: nick.gracie@carat.com
Web site: http://www.carat-int.com
Personnel: Europe: Claire Corrigan; **Development Director:** Kate Rowlinson; **Chief Executive Officer:** Jerry Buhlman
Date established: 1978. **Memberships:** NPA, PPA.
Represented in: Austria, Belgium, Bulgaria, Croatia, Czech Republic, Denmark, Estonia, Finland, France, Germany, Greece, Hungary, Ireland, Italy, Latvia, Lithuania, Netherlands, Norway, Poland, Portugal, Russia, Slovakia, Slovenia, Spain, Sweden, Switzerland, Turkey, Ukraine, UK.

FARRAR MEDIA INTERNATIONAL LTD
600570
63 Catherine Place, LONDON, SW1E 6DY
Tel: 020 7630 6657 **Fax:** 020 7233 9312
Email: john.farrar@farrarmedia.com
Web site: http://www.farrarmedia.com
Personnel: Managing Director: John Farrar; **Director:** Peter Wright
Date established: 1988. Represented in 43 countries worldwide.

SIGMA COMMUNICATIONS LTD 600579
The Clock House, Bramshaw, LYNDHURST, SO43 7JG
Tel: 023 8081 3952 **Fax:** 023 8081 3951
Personnel: Director: Stephen Bennison; **Director:** Susan Bennison
Date established: 1988. **Memberships:** ITVA, PPA.

ZENITHOPTIMEDIA 600578
24 Percy Street, LONDON, W1T 2BS **Tel:** 020 7961 1000
Fax: 020 7961 1113
Email: info@zenithoptimedia.com
Web site: http://www.zenithoptimedia.com
Date established: 1992. **Memberships:** IPA, ITVA, NPA, NS, PPA.

Willings Volume 1
Section 9

Broadcasting
UK Broadcasting & Other Media

Television, radio and teletext. The section is preceded by an
alphabetical index to all stations and organisations, with
page number references.

Index to UK Broadcasting & Other Media

Section 9 UK Broadcasting

Index to UK Broadcasting & Other Media

Quick reference guide to regional radio and television by area, national stations are not included and may be found on pages 1322, 1324, 1329 and 1330

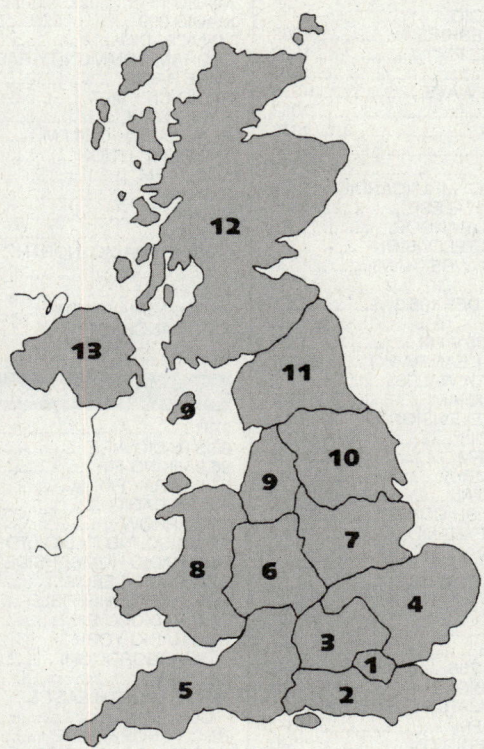

Regional Radio & Television

Section 9 UK Broadcasting

UK Broadcasting & Other Media

TELEVISION

NATIONAL TV STATIONS

THE BABY CHANNEL
1666062
Bentima House, 168-172 Old Street, LONDON, EC1V 9BP
Tel: 020 7608 8650
Email: info@babychanneltv.com
Web site: http://www.babychanneltv.com
News Editor: Deborah Daley

BABYTV
1800333
Unit 3.4, Shepherd's Studio East, Charecroft Way, LONDON, W14 0EE **Tel:** 020 7751 7599 **Fax:** 020 7751 7699
Email: info@babytvchannel.com
Web site: http://www.babytvchannel.com
News Editor: Debbie Hunt

BBC BREAKFAST NEWS PLANNING
41903
Room 1605, Television Centre, Wood Lane, LONDON, W12 7RJ **Tel:** 020 8624 9696 **Fax:** 020 8576 7101
Email: breakfastplanning@bbc.co.uk
Web site: http://www.bbc.co.uk/breakfast
Editor: Alison Ford; **News Editor:** Planning Desk
Twitter: http://twitter.com/bbcbreakfast.

BBC ECONOMICS AND BUSINESS UNIT (TELEVISION)
41904
Room 4220, Television Centre, Wood Lane, LONDON, W12 7RJ **Tel:** 020 8576 7486
Email: bizplan@bbc.co.uk
Web site: http://www.bbc.co.uk/news
Editor: Jeremy Hillman; **News Editor:** Planning Desk
Twitter: http://twitter.com/bbcbusiness.

BBC FACTUAL FEATURES AND FORMATS
1775356
Room 6060, TV Centre, Wood Lane, LONDON, W12 7RJ
Tel: 020 8743 8000
Email: commissioning.guide@bbc.co.uk
Web site: http://www.bbc.co.uk/commissioning/tv/network/genres/factual_features.shtml
Twitter: http://twitter.com/bbc.

BBC LEARNING
41905
MC4,A6, Media Centre, BBC White City, 201 Wood Lane, LONDON, W12 7TQ **Tel:** 020 8743 8000
Web site: http://www.bbc.co.uk
News Editor: Press and Publicity
Twitter: http://twitter.com/bbc.

BBC NATURAL HISTORY UNIT
1638753
Broadcasting House, Whiteladies Road, Clifton, BRISTOL, BS8 2LR **Tel:** 0117 974 2114 **Fax:** 0117 793 3583
Email: natural.history@bbc.co.uk
News Editor: Emma Lippiatt
Twitter: http://twitter.com/bbc.

BBC NEWS (PLANNING)
41906
The News Centre, Room 1624, Television Centre, Wood Lane, LONDON, W12 7RJ **Tel:** 020 8624 9141
Email: uknewsplan@bbc.co.uk
Editor: Dominic Ball; **News Editor:** News Planning
Twitter: http://twitter.com/bbcnews.

BBC NEWS PLANNING, NEWS GATHERING (TELEVISION)
41907
Room 1624, News Centre, Wood Lane, LONDON, W12 7RJ
Tel: 020 8624 9141
Email: uknewsplan@bbc.co.uk
News Editor: News Planning Desk
Twitter: http://twitter.com/bbcnews.

BBC PARLIAMENT
1697360
4 Millbank, LONDON, SW1P 3JA **Tel:** 020 7580 4468
Fax: 020 7233 2070
Email: parliament@bbc.co.uk
Web site: http://www.bbc.co.uk/parliament
News Editor: Peter Knowles

BBC POLITICAL PROGRAMMES (TELEVISION)
41909
1st Floor, 4 Millbank, LONDON, SW1P 3JQ
Tel: 020 7973 6000 **Fax:** 020 7973 6336
News Editor: Newsroom
Twitter: http://twitter.com/bbcpolitics.

BBC RELIGIOUS PROGRAMMES (TV)
601207
5th Floor, New Broadcasting House, Oxford Road, MANCHESTER, M60 1SJ **Tel:** 0161 200 2020
Fax: 0161 244 3183
Web site: http://www.bbc.co.uk/religion
News Editor: Press Office

BBC SCIENCE AND NATURE (TELEVISION)
41911
Room 4631, BBC White City, 201 Wood Lane, LONDON, W12 7TS **Tel:** 020 8752 5252 **Fax:** 020 8752 6989
Web site: http://www.bbc.co.uk/sn
Twitter: http://twitter.com/bbc.

BBC SPORT NEWS (TELEVISION)
41908
Room 2640, BBC Television Centre, Wood Lane, LONDON, W12 7RJ **Tel:** 020 8624 9690 **Fax:** 020 8624 9219
Email: kate.wademan@bbc.co.uk
Editor: Mark Wilkin; **News Editor:** Kate Wademan
Twitter: http://twitter.com/bbcsport.

BBC TRAFFIC NEWS (TELEVISION)
718524
91 Charterhouse Street, LONDON, EC1M 6HR
Tel: 020 7012 3555 **Fax:** 020 7012 3556
Email: london@trafficlink.co.uk
Web site: http://www.trafficlink.co.uk
News Editor: Peter Lees
Twitter: http://twitter.com/BBCTravelAlert.

BBC UK SPECIALISTS (TELEVISION)
41912
Room 1502, Stage 5, Television Centre, Wood Lane, LONDON, W12 7RJ **Tel:** 020 8624 9010 **Fax:** 020 8624 9101
Email: uknewsplan@bbc.co.uk
News Editor: Melanie Fanstone
Twitter: http://twitter.com/bbcnews.

BBC WORLD AFFAIRS UNIT (TELEVISION)
41914
Room 2505, Television Centre, Wood Lane, LONDON, W12 7RJ **Tel:** 020 8624 8550 **Fax:** 020 8743 7591
News Editor: News Desk
Twitter: http://twitter.com/bbcworld.

CBBC
758575
TV Centre, Room EM20, East Tower, Wood Lane, LONDON, W12 7RJ **Tel:** 020 8743 8000
Email: steven.alderton@bbc.co.uk
Web site: http://www.bbc.co.uk/cbbc
News Editor: Steven Alderton; **Executive Editor:** Anne Gilchrist

CBBC EXTRA
1742068
TV Centre, E1100 East Tower, Wood Lane, LONDON, W12 7RJ **Tel:** 020 8225 7312 **Fax:** 020 8576 9272
Email: cbbcextra@bbc.co.uk
Web site: http://www.bbc.co.uk/cbbc
News Editor: James Steel

CBEEBIES
758597
TV Centre, Room EM20, East Tower, Wood Lane, LONDON, W12 7RJ **Tel:** 020 8576 2416
Email: angela.young@bbc.co.uk
Web site: http://www.bbc.co.uk/cbeebies
News Editor: Angela Young

CHANNEL 4 NEWS
41918
200 Gray's Inn Road, LONDON, WC1X 8XZ
Tel: 020 7833 3000 **Fax:** 020 7430 4607
Email: c4home@itn.co.uk
Web site: http://www.channel4.com/news
News Editor: News Desk
Twitter: http://twitter.com/Channel4News.

CHANNEL 4 NEWS ECONOMICS AND BUSINESS UNIT
713866
200 Gray's Inn Road, LONDON, WC1X 8XZ
Tel: 020 7430 4601
Email: c4home@itn.co.uk
Web site: http://www.channel4.co.uk/news
News Editor: Neil Macdonald
Twitter: http://twitter.com/Channel4News.

CHANNEL 4 NEWS SCIENCE BUREAU
1657660
200 Gray's Inn Road, LONDON, WC1X 8XZ
Tel: 020 7430 4601
Email: c4home@itn.co.uk
Web site: http://www.channel4.com/news
News Editor: Tom Clarke
Twitter: http://twitter.com/Channel4News.

CHANNEL 4 TELEVISION
41915
124 Horseferry Road, LONDON, SW1P 2TX
Tel: 020 7396 4444
Email: newsdesk@itn.co.uk
Web site: http://www.channel4.com
News Editor: News Desk; **Managing Editor:** Janey Walker
Twitter: http://twitter.com/channel4.

CITV
1743277
20th Floor, The London Television Centre, Upper Ground, LONDON, SE1 9LT **Tel:** 020 7157 3040
Email: greg.taylor@itv.com
Web site: http://www.citv.co.uk
News Editor: Greg Taylor

THE COUNTRY CHANNEL
1749195
Unit 2, Gate Farm Offices, Park Road, Kiddington, WOODSTOCK, OX20 1DB **Tel:** 01608 678824
Email: enquiries@countrychannel.co.uk
Web site: http://www.countrychannel.tv
News Editor: Paul Aitken; **Managing Director:** Paul Aitken

FIVE
41916
22 Long Acre, LONDON, WC2E 9LY **Tel:** 020 7550 5555
Fax: 020 7550 5545
Web site: http://www.five.tv
Editor: Bethan Corney; **News Editor:** Press Office;
Managing Director: Mark White

FIVE NEWS
41917
BSKYB, Unit 1, Grant Way, ISLEWORTH, TW7 5QD
Tel: 020 7800 2705 **Fax:** 020 7800 2707
Email: news@five.tv
Web site: http://www.five.tv/news
News Editor: Forward Planning Desk; **Editor-in-Chief:** David Kermode

FIVE USA
1780892
22 Long Acre, LONDON, WC2E 9LY **Tel:** 020 7550 5558
Fax: 020 7550 5545
Email: rachel.moore@five.tv
Web site: http://www.five.tv
News Editor: Rachel Moore

FIVER
1780887
22 Long Acre, LONDON, WC2E 9LY **Tel:** 020 7550 5558
Fax: 020 7550 5545
Email: rachel.moore@five.tv
Web site: http://www.five.tv
News Editor: Rachel Moore

GMTV POLITICAL UNIT
629614
GMTV News, 4th Floor, London Television Centre, Upper Ground, LONDON, SE1 9TT **Tel:** 020 7827 7000
Fax: 020 7827 7249
Email: caroline.sigley@gm.tv
Web site: http://www.gm.tv
News Editor: Caroline Sigley
Twitter: http://twitter.com/GMTV.

GREEN TV
1744950
120 Long Acre, Covent Garden, LONDON, WC2E 9ST
Tel: 020 7240 0357 **Fax:** 020 7240 0909
Email: polly.jackson@green.tv
Web site: http://www.green.tv
News Editor: Polly Jackson

ITN BUSINESS UNIT
633992

200 Gray's Inn Road, LONDON, WC1X 8XZ
Tel: 020 7430 4878
Email: daisy.mcandrew@itn.co.uk
Web site: http://www.itv.com/news
News Editor: Peter Robinson
Twitter: http://twitter.com/ITN_NEWS.

ITN INDEPENDENT TELEVISION NEWS
41921

200 Gray's Inn Road, LONDON, WC1X 8XZ
Tel: 020 7833 3000 **Fax:** 020 7430 4598
Email: ben.faulks@itn.co.uk
Web site: http://www.itn.co.uk
Editor: Chris Choi; **News Editor:** Ian Rumsey
Twitter: http://twitter.com/ITN_NEWS.

ITN SCIENCE AND HEALTH UNIT
1657651

200 Grays Inn Road, LONDON, WC1X 8XZ
Tel: 020 7430 4349
Email: rob.white@itn.co.uk
Web site: http://www.itv.com/news
News Editor: Rob White
Twitter: http://twitter.com/ITN_NEWS.

ITV SPORT
1655748

London Television Centre, Upper Ground, LONDON, SE1
9LT **Tel:** 020 7849 7826 **Fax:** 020 7827 7610
Email: tony.pastor@itv.com
Web site: http://www.itv.com/sport
News Editor: Tony Pastor
Twitter: http://twitter.com/ITVFootball.

LA MUSCLE TV
1893476

3 Oliver Business Park, Oliver Road, LONDON, NW10 7JB
Tel: 020 8965 1177 **Fax:** 020 8965 1188
Email: jon@lamuscle.tv
Web site: http://www.lamuscle.tv
News Editor: Jon Lopera

METRO TV
1793921

Northcliffe House, 2 Derry Street, LONDON, W8 5TT
Tel: 020 7651 5200 **Fax:** 020 7651 5342
Email: ryan.battles@ukmetro.co.uk
Web site: http://www.metro.co.uk
News Editor: Ryan Battles

THE REEL SHOW
1861138

PR by email only. **Tel:** 01273 276665
Email: steve@reel-show.tv
Web site: http://www.reel-show.tv
Editor: Steve Parker; **News Editor:** Steve Parker

STUFF TV
1793967

Teddington Studios, Broom Road, TEDDINGTON, TW11
9BE **Tel:** 020 8267 5036 **Fax:** 020 8267 5019
Email: stuff@haymarket.com
Web site: http://stuff.tv
News Editor: Tom Wiggins

TELEGRAPH TV
1832505

111 Buckingham Palace Road, LONDON, SW1W 0DT
Tel: 020 7931 2000
Email: guy.ruddle@telegraph.co.uk
Web site: http://www.telegraph.co.uk/tv
Editor: Guy Ruddle; **News Editor:** Guy Ruddle

VEGGIE VISION
1792512

Independent House, Radford Business Centre, Radford
Way, BILLERICAY, CM12 0BZ **Tel:** 01277 627300
Email: info@veggievision.co.uk
Web site: http://www.veggievision.co.uk
News Editor: Karin Ridgers

YOURBUSINESSCHANNEL
1791207

Unit 11, 179 Whiteladies Road, BRISTOL, BS8 2AG
Tel: 020 8144 3184
Email: media@yourbusinesschannel.com
Web site: http://www.yourbusinesschannel.com
News Editor: David Chandler; **Features Editor:** Mark
Sinclair

REGIONAL TV STATIONS

ANGLIA TELEVISION
42613

Anglia House, NORWICH, NR1 3JG **Tel:** 01603 753057
Fax: 01603 622574
Email: anglianews@itv.com
Web site: http://www.itvlocal.com/anglia
News Editor: James Bush; **Managing Director:** Neil
Thompson

BBC 2W
754173

Broadcasting House, Llantrisant Road, Llandaff, CARDIFF,
CF5 2YQ **Tel:** 029 2032 2000
Email: newsgathering.wales@bbc.co.uk
Web site: http://www.bbc.co.uk/wales/commissioning
News Editor: Gail Morris-Jones

BBC EAST
42614

The Forum, Millennium Plain, NORWICH, NR2 1BH
Tel: 01603 619331 **Fax:** 01603 667865
Email: look.east@bbc.co.uk
Web site: http://www.bbc.co.uk/lookeast
News Editor: Jackie Leggett

BBC LONDON
42595

BBC London, 35C Marylebone High Street, LONDON, W1U
4QA **Tel:** 020 7208 9660
Email: ldn-planning@bbc.co.uk
Web site: http://www.bbc.co.uk/london
News Editor: Forward Planning; **Executive Editor:** Mike
Macfarlane

BBC MANCHESTER
42608

PO Box 27, New Broadcasting House, Oxford Road,
MANCHESTER, M60 1SJ **Tel:** 0161 244 3144
Fax: 0161 244 3172
Email: nwt@bbc.co.uk
Web site: http://www.bbc.co.uk/manchester
Editor: Caroline Le Beau; **News Editor:** News Planning
Desk

BBC NORTHERN IRELAND
42630

Broadcasting House, Ormeau Avenue, BELFAST, BT2 8HQ
Tel: 028 9033 8000 **Fax:** 028 9033 8806
Email: ni_news@bbc.co.uk
Web site: http://www.bbc.co.uk/northernireland
News Editor: Tom Coulter

BBC SOUTH
42619

Broadcasting House, Havelock Road, SOUTHAMPTON,
SO14 7PU **Tel:** 023 8022 6201 **Fax:** 023 8033 9931
Email: newsg.south@bbc.co.uk
Web site: http://www.bbc.co.uk/southtoday
News Editor: Greg Clark

BBC SOUTH EAST
712047

Great Hall Arcade, Mount Pleasant Road, TUNBRIDGE
WELLS, TN1 1QQ **Tel:** 01892 670000 **Fax:** 01892 549118
Email: southeasttoday@bbc.co.uk
Web site: http://www.bbc.co.uk/southeasttoday
News Editor: Forward Planning Desk

BBC SOUTH WEST
42617

Seymour Road, Mannamead, PLYMOUTH, PL3 5BD
Tel: 01752 229201 **Fax:** 01752 234595
Email: spotnews@bbc.co.uk
Web site: http://www.bbc.co.uk/spotlight
Editor: Simon Willis; **News Editor:** Simon Read

BBC TV EAST MIDLANDS
42615

London Road, NOTTINGHAM, NG2 4UU **Tel:** 0115 955 0500
Fax: 0115 902 1984
Email: emt@bbc.co.uk
Web site: http://www.bbc.co.uk/nottingham
News Editor: Emma Agnew

BBC TV MIDLANDS
42593

The Mailbox, BIRMINGHAM, B1 1RF **Tel:** 0121 567 6135
Fax: 0121 567 6005
Email: midlandstoday@bbc.co.uk
Web site: http://www.bbc.co.uk/midlandstoday
News Editor: Planning Desk

BBC TV NORTH EAST & CUMBRIA
42611

Barrack Road, NEWCASTLE UPON TYNE, NE99 2NE
Tel: 0191 232 1313 **Fax:** 0191 221 0112
Email: newcastlenews@bbc.co.uk
Web site: http://www.bbc.co.uk/looknorthnecumbria
News Editor: Forward Planning Desk

BBC TV SCOTLAND
42628

BBC Scotland, 40 Pacific Quay, GLASGOW, G51 1DA
Tel: 0141 422 7000 **Fax:** 0141 422 7900
Web site: http://www.bbc.co.uk/scotland
News Editor: Jim Gough

BBC TV SCOTLAND (EDINBURGH)
1745537

The Tun, Holyrood Road, EDINBURGH, EH8 8PJ
Tel: 0131 248 4215
Web site: http://www.bbc.co.uk/scotland
News Editor: Planning Desk

BBC TV WEST
42597

Broadcasting House, Whiteladies Road, Clifton, BRISTOL,
BS8 2LR **Tel:** 0117 973 2211 **Fax:** 0117 973 8815
Email: pointswest@bbc.co.uk
Web site: http://www.bbc.co.uk/bristol
Editor: Roger Farrant; **News Editor:** Dickon Hooper

BBC TV YORKSHIRE
42600

Broadcasting Centre, 2 St. Peters Square, LEEDS, LS9 8AH
Tel: 0113 244 1188 **Fax:** 0113 224 7316
Email: look.north@bbc.co.uk
Web site: http://www.bbc.co.uk/looknorthyorkslincs
Editor: Tim Smith; **News Editor:** Planning Desk

BBC TV YORKSHIRE & LINCOLNSHIRE
1752744

Queen's Court, Queen's Gardens, HULL, HU1 3RH
Tel: 01482 323232 **Fax:** 01482 226409
Email: looknorth@bbc.co.uk
Web site: http://www.bbc.co.uk/humberside
News Editor: Mark Hayman; **Managing Editor:** Simon
Pattern

BBC WALES TELEVISION
42622

Llantrisant Road, CARDIFF, CF5 2YQ **Tel:** 029 2032 2000
Fax: 029 2055 5960
Email: newsgathering.wales@bbc.co.uk
Web site: http://www.bbc.co.uk/walesnews
News Editor: News Gathering

CHANNEL 4 NEWS (MIDLANDS BUREAU)
1642158

Terry Lloyd House, 1 Regan Way, NOTTINGHAM, NG9 6RZ
Tel: 0844 881 6615
Email: c4midlands@itn.co.uk
Web site: http://www.channel4.com/news
News Editor: Mark Power

CHANNEL TELEVISION (GUERNSEY)
42632

Television House, Bulwer Avenue, St. Sampsons,
GUERNSEY, GY2 4LA **Tel:** 01481 241888
Fax: 01481 241889
Email: broadcast.gsy@channeltv.co.uk
Web site: http://www.channelonline.tv
News Editor: News Editor

CHANNEL TELEVISION (JERSEY)
42633

Television Centre, La Pouquelaye, St. Helier, JERSEY, JE1
3ZD **Tel:** 01534 816816 **Fax:** 01534 816817
Email: broadcast@channeltv.co.uk
Web site: http://www.channelonline.tv
News Editor: Allan Watts; **Managing Director:** Karen
Rankine

CITV
707554

ITV Granada, Quay Street, MANCHESTER, M60 9EA
Tel: 0161 835 6487
Email: tim.west@itv.com
Web site: http://www.granadamedia.com
News Editor: Tim West

UK Broadcasting & Other Media

Section 9 UK Broadcasting

GRANADA TELEVISION (LIVERPOOL) 42602
ITV Granada, 1st Floor, Liver Building, Pier Head,
LIVERPOOL, L3 1HU **Tel:** 0844 881 5350
Fax: 0844 881 5380
Email: granada.reports@itv.com
Web site: http://www.granadamedia.com
News Editor: Forward Planning Desk

ITV1 WESTCOUNTRY REGION 42618
Western Wood Way, Langage Science Park, PLYMOUTH,
PL7 5BQ **Tel:** 0844 881 4900
Email: news@westcountry.co.uk
Web site: http://www.itvlocal.com/west
News Editor: News Desk; **Managing Director:** Jane
McCloskey

ITV BORDER 42599
The Television Centre, CARLISLE, CA1 3NT
Tel: 0844 881 5850 **Fax:** 01228 594229
Email: btvnews@itv.com
Web site: http://www.itvlocal.com/border
News Editor: Newsdesk; **Managing Director:** Douglas
Merrall

ITV CENTRAL (BIRMINGHAM) 713909
Gas Street, BIRMINGHAM, B1 2JT **Tel:** 0844 881 4000
Email: centralnews@itv.com
Web site: http://www.itvlocal.com/central
News Editor: Marcus Bennett

ITV CENTRAL NEWS (BIRMINGHAM) 42594
ITV Central, Gas Street, BIRMINGHAM, B1 2JT
Tel: 0844 881 4000
Email: centralnews@itv.com
Web site: http://www.itvlocal.com/central
News Editor: Gary Newby

ITV CENTRAL NEWS (EAST) 42616
1 Regan Way, Chilwell, Beeston, NOTTINGHAM, NG9 6RZ
Tel: 0844 881 4000 **Fax:** 0844 881 4606
Email: centralnewseast@itv.com
Web site: http://www.itvlocal.com/central
News Editor: Chris Hesketh

ITV CENTRAL (NOTTINGHAM) 1825703
Terry Lloyd House, 1 Regan Way, NOTTINGHAM, NG9 6RZ
Tel: 0844 881 4000 **Fax:** 0844 881 4606
Email: centralnewseast@itv.com
Web site: http://www.itv.com/central
News Editor: Alan Rook

ITV GRANADA 42609
Quay Street, MANCHESTER, M60 9EA **Tel:** 0161 952 1000
Fax: 0161 953 0290
Email: granada.reports@itv.com
Web site: http://www.itvlocal.com/granada
News Editor: Forward Planning Desk

ITV LONDON 42606
ITV, 200 Gray's Inn Road, LONDON, WC1X 8XZ
Tel: 020 7430 4000
Email: planning@itvlondon.com
Web site: http://www.itvlocal.com/london
News Editor: Forward Planning Desk

ITV LONDON NEWS 42605
200 Gray's Inn Road, LONDON, WC1X 8XZ
Tel: 020 7430 4000 **Fax:** 020 7430 4138
Email: planning@itvlondon.com
Web site: http://www.itvlocal.com
News Editor: Forward Planning Desk

ITV MERIDIAN 42610
Forum 1, Solent Business Park, Whiteley, FAREHAM, PO16
7PA **Tel:** 0844 881 2000
Email: meridiantonight@itv.com
Web site: http://www.itvlocal.com/meridian
News Editor: Robin Britton

ITV TYNE TEES 42612
Television House, The Watermark, GATESHEAD, NE11 9SZ
Tel: 0844 881 5100 **Fax:** 0844 881 5010
Email: net@itv.com
Web site: http://www.itvlocal.com/tynetees
News Editor: Julie Jude

ITV TYNE TEES TELEVISION (BILLINGHAM) 26694
20 Manor Way, Belasis Park, BILLINGHAM, TS23 4HN
Tel: 0844 881 5336
Email: belasis.news@itv.com
Web site: http://www.itvlocal.com/tynetees
News Editor: Gregg Easteal

ITV WALES 42623
The TV Centre, Culverhouse Cross, CARDIFF, CF5 6XJ
Tel: 0844 881 0200
Email: news@itvwales.com
Web site: http://www.itvlocal.com/wales
News Editor: Sarah Drew

ITV WALES (CARMARTHEN) 42625
Top Floor, 19-20 Lammas Street, CARMARTHEN, SA31 3AL
Tel: 01267 236806 **Fax:** 01267 238228
Email: news@itvwales.com
Web site: http://www.itvlocal.com/wales
News Editor: Catharine Evans-Williams

ITV WEST 42598
Television Centre, Bath Road, BRISTOL, BS4 3HG
Tel: 0844 881 2345
Email: itvwestnews@itv.com
Web site: http://www.itvlocal.com/west
News Editor: John Alcock

ITV YORKSHIRE 42601
104 Kirkstall Road, LEEDS, LS3 1JS **Tel:** 0113 222 8700
Fax: 0113 243 3655
Email: calendar@yorkshiretv.com
Web site: http://www.yorkshiretv.com
News Editor: Gordon Stott

ITV YORKSHIRE TELEVISION (HULL) 1828596
23 The Prospect Centre, Prospect Street, HULL, HU2 8PN
Tel: 01482 324488 **Fax:** 01482 586028
Email: calendar@yorkshiretv.com
Web site: http://www.itv.com/yorkshire
News Editor: News Desk

ITV YORKSHIRE TELEVISION (SHEFFIELD) 26689
104 Kirkstall Road, LEEDS, LS1 3JS **Tel:** 0113 222 8785
Email: dick.taylor@itv.com
Web site: http://www.itvlocal.com/yorkshire
News Editor: Dick Taylor

ITV YORKSHIRE TELEVISION (YORK) 42621
St. John's College, YORK, YO31 7EX **Tel:** 01904 610066
Fax: 01904 610067
Email: calendar@yorkshiretv.com
Web site: http://www.itv.com/yorkshire
News Editor: News Desk

KENT TV 1831298
Maidstone Studios, Vinters Park, New Cut Road,
MAIDSTONE, ME14 5NZ **Tel:** 01622 684403
Email: info@kenttv.com
Web site: http://www.kenttv.com
News Editor: Evy Barry

MENDIP TV 1826305
Coombe Lodge, Bourne Lane, Blagdon, BRISTOL, BS40
7RG **Tel:** 01761 463888 **Fax:** 01761 463890
Email: enquiries@mendiptv.com
Web site: http://www.mendiptv.co.uk
News Editor: Steve Egginton

S4C 42624
Parc Ty Glas, Llanishen, CARDIFF, CF14 5DU
Tel: 029 2074 7444 **Fax:** 029 2075 4444
Email: s4c@s4c.co.uk
Web site: http://www.s4c.co.uk
News Editor: Hannah Thomas

STV (CENTRAL) 42629
Pacific Quay, GLASGOW, G51 1PQ **Tel:** 0141 300 3000
Fax: 0141 300 3200
Email: scotlandtoday@stv.tv
Web site: http://www.stv.tv
News Editor: Ken Bryson; **Managing Director:** Bobby Hain

STV (NORTH) 42627
Television Centre, Craigshaw Business Park, West Tullos,
ABERDEEN, AB12 3QH **Tel:** 01224 848848
Fax: 01224 848800
Email: northtonight@stv.tv
Web site: http://www.stv.tv
News Editor: Donald John-MacDonald

STV (NORTH) (DUNDEE) 26702
3rd Floor, Sea Braes, Greenmarket, DUNDEE, DD1 4QB
Tel: 01382 591000 **Fax:** 01382 591010
Email: craig.millar@stv.tv
Web site: http://www.stv.tv
News Editor: Craig Millar

UTV 42631
Havlock House, Ormeau Road, BELFAST, BT7 1EB
Tel: 028 9032 8122 **Fax:** 028 9026 2219
Email: newsroom@utvplc.com
Web site: http://www.u.tv
News Editor: Chris Hagan; **Features Editor:** Jeannie
Johnston; **Managing Director:** Michael Wilson

YORK AT 54 1639148
Tower House Studios, Askham Bryan, YORK, YO23 3NU
Tel: 01904 700464
Email: programming@york.tv
Web site: http://www.york.tv
News Editor: Phil Howden

CABLE & SATELLITE

SATELLITE TV

ALIBI 1644371
160 Great Portland Street, LONDON, W1W 5QA
Tel: 020 7299 5000 **Fax:** 020 7299 5412
Email: zoe.clapp@uktv.co.uk
Web site: http://uktv.co.uk/alibi
News Editor: Zoë Clapp

ALPHA ETC PUNJABI 1644131
Unit 7, Belvue Business Centre, Belvue Road, NORTHOLT,
UB5 5QQ **Tel:** 020 8839 4000 **Fax:** 020 8839 4061
Email: chiragh@zeetv.co.uk
Web site: http://www.zeetv.co.uk
News Editor: Chiragh Cherian

ANIMAL PLANET INTERNATIONAL 26336
Discovery House, Chiswick Park Building 2, 566 Chiswick
Road, LONDON, W4 5YB **Tel:** 020 8811 3000
Fax: 020 8811 3100
Email: lindsay_mcclelland@discovery-europe.com
Web site: http://www.animalplanet.co.uk
News Editor: Lindsay McClelland

ARSENAL TV 1832400
8 Waterloo Place, LONDON, SW1Y 4BE **Tel:** 020 7766 8484
Fax: 020 7766 8485
Email: julianne.mckeigue@setanta.com
Web site: http://tv.arsenal.com
News Editor: Julianne McKeigue

ARY DIGITAL 1644156
65 North Acton Road, Park Royal, LONDON, NW10 6PJ
Tel: 020 8838 6300 **Fax:** 020 8838 6122
Email: mails@arydigital.tv
Web site: http://www.arydigital.tv
News Editor: Mohammad Shahzad Alam

ATTHERACES 760706
18-21 Corsham Street, LONDON, N1 6DR
Tel: 020 7954 3000 **Fax:** 020 7954 3001
Email: julie.phelps@attheraces.com
Web site: http://www.attheraces.com
News Editor: Julie Phelps

THE AUDI CHANNEL 1665157
6 Hoxton Square, LONDON, N1 6NU **Tel:** 020 7012 1200
Fax: 020 7729 9540
Email: info@definition.tv
Web site: http://www.audi.co.uk
News Editor: John Beck; **Managing Director:** James
Jegede

BANGLA TV
1644159
67 Rothbury Road, LONDON, E9 5HA **Tel:** 0870 005 6778
Fax: 020 8985 7116
Email: info@banglatv.co.uk
Web site: http://www.banglatv.co.uk
News Editor: M Shamsul Alam Liton

BBC WORLD NEWS
26190
Room MC2B4, Media Centre, 201 Wood Lane, LONDON,
W12 7TQ **Tel:** 020 8433 2000 **Fax:** 020 8743 9256
Email: bbcworldplanning@bbc.co.uk
Web site: http://www.bbcworld.com
News Editor: Bbc News Gathering

BID TV
1644119
Sit-up Ltd, Sit-up House, 179-181 The Vale, LONDON, W3
7RW **Tel:** 020 8600 9700 **Fax:** 020 8746 2606
Email: steve.hart@sit-up.tv
Web site: http://www.sit-up.tv
News Editor: Steve Hart

THE BIOGRAPHY CHANNEL
626342
BSKYB, Grant Way, ISLEWORTH, TW7 5QD
Tel: 020 7941 5199 **Fax:** 020 7941 5187
Email: joanna.mitchell@bskyb.com
Web site: http://www.thebiographychannel.co.uk
News Editor: Joanna Mitchell

BITETV
1644705
11 Marlborough Place, BRIGHTON, BN1 1UB
Tel: 01273 728802
Email: info@bitetv.com
Web site: http://www.bitetv.co.uk
News Editor: Sean Mahoney; **Managing Director:** Sean
Mahoney

BLIGHTY
1644386
160 Great Portland Street, LONDON, W1W 5QA
Tel: 020 7299 5000 **Fax:** 020 7299 6914
Email: danielle.kemble@uktv.co.uk
Web site: http://www.loveblighty.co.uk
News Editor: Danielle Kemble

BLISS
1644133
37 Harwood Road, LONDON, SW6 4QP **Tel:** 020 7371 5999
Fax: 020 7384 9003
Email: info@chartshow.tv
Web site: http://www.cscmediagroup.com
News Editor: Stephanie Faleo

BLOOMBERG TELEVISION
41926
City Gate House, 39-45 Finsbury Square, LONDON, EC2A
1PQ **Tel:** 020 7330 7797
Email: newsalert@bloomberg.net
Web site: http://www.bloomberg.com/media/tv
News Editor: Andy Clarke

BOOMERANG
26527
Turner House, 16 Great Marlborough Street, LONDON, W1F
7HS **Tel:** 020 7693 1000 **Fax:** 020 7693 1020
Web site: http://www.cartoonnetwork.co.uk
News Editor: Catherine Hayes

THE BOX
42688
Mappin House, 4 Winsley Street, LONDON, W1W 8HF
Tel: 020 7182 8000 **Fax:** 020 7376 1313
Web site: http://www.thebox.co.uk
News Editor: Melissa Pine; **Managing Director:** Gidon Katz

BRAVO
41927
Flextech Television, 160 Great Portland Street, LONDON,
W1W 5QA **Tel:** 020 7299 5000 **Fax:** 020 7299 5516
Email: jakki_lewis@virginmedia.co.uk
Web site: http://www.bravo.co.uk
News Editor: Jakki Lewis

BRAVO 2
1787188
Flextech Television, 160 Great Portland Street, LONDON,
W1W 5QA **Tel:** 020 7299 5000 **Fax:** 020 7299 5516
Email: jakki.lewis@virginmedia.co.uk
Web site: http://www.bravo.co.uk
News Editor: Jakki Lewis

BRIGHT ENTERTAINMENT NETWORK (BEN)
1666255
2C Berol Court, 25 Ashley Road, LONDON, N17 9LJ
Tel: 020 8808 8800 **Fax:** 020 8808 8800
Email: marketinge@bentelevision.com
Web site: http://www.bentelevision.com
News Editor: Ebere Nzewuji; **Managing Director:** Ebere
Nzewuji

BRITISH EUROSPORT
41935
Broadcast Media Centre, Sussex House, 2 Plane Tree
Crescent, Felthambrook Industrial Estate, FELTHAM, TW13
7HF **Tel:** 020 8818 1400 **Fax:** 020 8818 1450
Web site: http://www.eurosport.yahoo.co.uk
News Editor: Matt Horler

BRITISH EUROSPORT 2
749714
Broadcast Media Centre, Sussex House, 2 Plane Tree
Crescent, Felthambrook Industrial Estate, FELTHAM, TW13
7HF **Tel:** 0845 672 1010 **Fax:** 020 8818 1450
Web site: http://www.eurosport.yahoo.co.uk
News Editor: Matt Horler

CARTOON NETWORK
41931
Turner Broadcasting System Europe Ltd, 16 Great
Marlborough Street, LONDON, W1F 7HS **Tel:** 020 7693 1000
Web site: http://www.cartoonnetwork.co.uk
News Editor: Catherine Hayes

CARTOONITO
1841063
Turner House, 16 Great Marlborough Street, LONDON, W1F
7HS **Tel:** 020 7693 1000 **Fax:** 020 7693 1224
Web site: http://www.cartoonito.co.uk
News Editor: Catherine Hayes

CARTOONNETWORK.CO.UK
1773016
Turner Broadcasting System Europe Ltd, 16 Great
Marlborough Street, LONDON, W1F 7HS **Tel:** 020 7693 1000
Fax: 020 7693 1065
Web site: http://www.cartoonnetwork.co.uk
News Editor: News Editor

CHALLENGE
41932
Flextech Television, 160 Great Portland Street, LONDON,
W1W 5QA **Tel:** 020 7299 5000 **Fax:** 020 7299 5440
Email: jakki.lewis@flextech.co.uk
Web site: http://www.challengetv.co.uk
News Editor: Jakki Lewis

CHANNEL U
1644162
Unit 4, 3 Lever Street, LONDON, EC1V 3QU
Tel: 020 7054 9010 **Fax:** 020 7054 9011
Email: cat@vitv.co.uk
Web site: http://www.channelu.tv
News Editor: Cat Park

CHART SHOW TV
49962
8 Chelsea Gate Studios, 115 Harwood Road, LONDON,
SW6 4QP **Tel:** 020 7371 5999 **Fax:** 020 7384 9003
Email: reception@chartshow.tv
Web site: http://www.chartshow.tv
News Editor: Sarah Gaughan

CNBC
41928
10 Fleet Place, LONDON, EC4M 7QS **Tel:** 020 7653 9427
Fax: 020 7653 9393
Email: anjuli.davies@cnbc.com
Web site: http://www.cnbc.com
News Editor: News Desk

CNN CABLE NEWS NETWORK
41929
Turner House, 16 Great Malborough Street, LONDON, W1F
7HS **Tel:** 020 7693 1000 **Fax:** 020 7693 1552
Email: cnnlondon@cnn.com
Web site: http://www.cnn.com
News Editor: Deborah Rayner; **Managing Editor:** Deborah
Rayner

COMEDY CENTRAL
1644245
Paramount Comedy, 180 Oxford Street, LONDON, W1D 1DS
Tel: 020 7478 5328 **Fax:** 020 7478 5442
Email: zoe.diver@comedycentral.co.uk
Web site: http://www.comedycentral.co.uk
News Editor: Zoe Diver; **Managing Director:** Jill Offman

CRIME & INVESTIGATION NETWORK
1766177
BSKYB, Grant Way, ISLEWORTH, TW7 5QD
Tel: 020 7941 5199 **Fax:** 020 7941 5187
Email: joanna.mitchell@bskyb.com
Web site: http://www.crimeandinvestigation.co.uk
News Editor: Joanna Mitchell

DAVE
1666014
160 Great Portland Street, LONDON, W1W 5QA
Tel: 020 7299 6200
Web site: http://www.uktv.co.uk
News Editor: Zoë Clapp

DEEPAM TV
1644733
161-163 Staines Road, HOUNSLOW, TW3 3JZ
Tel: 020 8814 6565 **Fax:** 020 8814 1144
Email: info@deepamtv.tv
Web site: http://www.deepamtv.tv
News Editor: Anton Mariyithasan

DISCOVERY CHANNEL
26198
Discovery House, Chiswick Park Building 2, 566 Chiswick
Road, LONDON, W4 5YB **Tel:** 020 8811 3000
Fax: 020 8811 3100
Email: rebecca_vase@discovery-europe.com
Web site: http://www.discoveryeurope.com
News Editor: Rebecca Vase

DISCOVERY KNOWLEDGE
707840
Discovery House, Chiswick Park Building 2, 566 Chiswick
Road, LONDON, W4 5YB **Tel:** 020 8811 3000
Fax: 020 8811 3100
Email: kate_buddle@discovery-europe.com
Web site: http://www.discoveryeurope.com
News Editor: Kate Buddle

DISCOVERY REAL TIME
26499
Discovery House, Chiswick Park Building 2, 566 Chiswick
Road, LONDON, W4 5YB **Tel:** 020 8811 3000
Fax: 020 8811 3191
Email: caroline_watt@discovery-europe.com
Web site: http://www.discoveryeurope.com
News Editor: Caroline Watt

DISCOVERY SCIENCE
707843
Discovery House, Chiswick Park Building 2, 566 Chiswick
Road, LONDON, W4 5YB **Tel:** 020 8811 3000
Fax: 020 8811 3100
Email: kate_buddle@discovery-europe.com
Web site: http://www.discoveryeurope.com
News Editor: Kate Buddle

DISCOVERY TRAVEL & LIVING
707841
1st Floor, Discovery House, Chiswick Park Building 2, 566
Chiswick High Road, LONDON, W4 5YB **Tel:** 020 8811 3000
Email: caroline_watt@discovery-europe.com
Web site: http://www.travelandliving.co.uk
News Editor: Caroline Watt

DISCOVERY TURBO
1804096
Discovery House, Chiswick Park, Building 2, Chiswick High
Road, LONDON, W4 5YB **Tel:** 020 8811 3000
Fax: 020 7462 3795
Email: kate_buddle@discovery-europe.com
Web site: http://www.discoveryeurope.com
News Editor: Kate Buddle

DISNEY CHANNEL INTERNATIONAL
49889
BVITV, 3 Queen Caroline Street, LONDON, W6 9PE
Tel: 020 8222 1000 **Fax:** 020 8222 1196
Email: charlotte.scott@disney.com
Web site: http://www.bvitv.com
News Editor: Charlotte Scott

DISNEY CHANNEL UK
1644120
Building 12, 566 Chiswick High Road, LONDON, W4 5AN
Tel: 020 8636 2000 **Fax:** 020 8636 2200
Email: charlotte.scott@disney.com
Web site: http://www.disneychannel.co.uk
News Editor: Charlotte Scott

UK Broadcasting & Other Media

DIVA TV
1842276
Sparrowhawk Entertainment, 234A Kings Road, LONDON, SW3 5UA **Tel:** 020 7368 9100 **Fax:** 020 7368 9101
Email: anna.morgan@nbcuni.com
Web site: http://www.divatv.co.uk
News Editor: Anna Morgan

EDEN
1644369
160 Great Portland Street, LONDON, W1W 5QA
Tel: 020 7299 5000 **Fax:** 020 7299 5412
Email: danielle.kemble@uktv.co.uk
Web site: http://www.uktvdocumentary.co.uk
News Editor: Danielle Kemble

EMMA
1644746
67-69 Whitfield Street, LONDON, W1T 4HF
Tel: 020 7636 1233 **Fax:** 020 7636 1255
Email: mail@emma.tv
Web site: http://www.emmainteractive.com
News Editor: Bobby Syed; **Managing Director:** Bobby Syed

ESPN AMERICA
1644235
Mail Code 611, 3 Queen Caroline Street, LONDON, W6 9PE
Tel: 020 8222 2174 **Fax:** 020 8222 2805
Email: virginie.bernon@disney.com
Web site: http://www.espnamerica.com
News Editor: Virginie Bernon

ESPN CLASSIC
1666178
3 Queen Caroline Street, LONDON, W6 9PE
Tel: 020 8222 2693
News Editor: Alex Lowe; **Managing Director:** Geoff Ellis

EXTREME SPORTS CHANNEL
41936
105-109 Salusbury Road, LONDON, NW6 6RG
Tel: 020 7328 8808
Email: ben.hobson@chellozone.com
Web site: http://www.extreme.com
News Editor: Ben Hobson

FILM 24
1753006
Film 24 Ltd, Room 661 to 668, Pinewood Studios, Pinewood Road, IVER, SL0 0NH **Tel:** 01753 630040
Fax: 01753 630830
Email: erica.banks@film24.co.uk
Web site: http://www.film24.co.uk
News Editor: Erica Banks

FILM4 CHANNEL
1644172
124 Horseferry Road, LONDON, SW1P 2TX
Tel: 020 7396 4444 **Fax:** 020 7306 8366
Email: spinder@channel4.co.uk
Web site: http://www.filmfour.com
News Editor: Steve Pinder

FLAUNT
1644173
115 Harwood Road, 8 Chelsea Gate Studios, LONDON, SW6 4QL **Tel:** 020 7371 5999 **Fax:** 020 7384 2026
Email: info@chartshow.tv
Web site: http://www.loveflaunt.com
News Editor: Keeley Gray

FLAVA
1835194
8 Chelsea Gate Studios, 115 Harwood Road, LONDON, SW6 4QP **Tel:** 020 7371 5999 **Fax:** 020 7384 2026
Email: info@chartshow.tv
Web site: http://www.essentialflava.com
News Editor: Sarah Gaughan

GEO TV
1791205
1 Sanctuary Street, LONDON, SE1 1ED **Tel:** 020 7403 5833
Fax: 020 7378 1653
Email: yaser.khan@geo.tv
Web site: http://www.geo.tv/uk
News Editor: Yaser Aziz-Khan

GOD TV
41934
Angel House, Borough Road, SUNDERLAND, SR1 1HW
Tel: 0191 568 0800 **Fax:** 0191 568 0808
Email: info@god.tv
Web site: http://www.god.tv
News Editor: Alistair Gibson

GOLD
41962
160 Great Portland Street, LONDON, W1W 5QA
Tel: 020 7299 6200 **Fax:** 020 7299 6194
Web site: http://www.uktv.co.uk
News Editor: Zoë Clapp

HALLMARK CHANNEL
1644180
234A Kings Road, LONDON, SW3 5UA **Tel:** 020 7368 9100
Fax: 020 7368 9101
Email: anna.morgan@nbcuni.com
Web site: http://www.hallmarkchannel.com
News Editor: Anna Morgan

HIGH STREET TV
1666157
1st Floor, Bentima House, 168-172 Old Street, LONDON, EC1V 9BP **Tel:** 020 7608 8650 **Fax:** 020 7608 8651
Email: catherine.daniel@simplymedia.tv
Web site: http://www.simplymedia.tv
News Editor: Catherine Daniel

HISTORY
26355
BSKYB, Grant Way, ISLEWORTH, TW7 5QD
Tel: 020 7941 5199 **Fax:** 020 7941 5187
Email: joanna.mitchell@bskyb.com
Web site: http://www.thehistorychannel.co.uk
News Editor: Joanna Mitchell

HORSE & COUNTRY TV
1749197
National Agricultural Centre, Stoney Park, KENILWORTH, CV18 2LG **Tel:** 024 7669 2269
Email: nickl@horseandcountry.tv
Web site: http://www.horseandcountry.tv
News Editor: Nick Ludlow

IDEAL WORLD 2
1666155
Ideal Home House, Newark Road, PETERBOROUGH, PE1 5WG **Tel:** 0870 0777 002
Email: customer.relations@idealshoppingdirect.co.uk
Web site: http://www.idealshoppingdirect.co.uk
News Editor: Charlotte Capper

INFORMATION TV
1644218
Information TV Ltd, 1 Stephen Street, LONDON, W1T 1AL
Tel: 020 7131 6693 **Fax:** 020 7131 6698
Email: info@information.tv
Web site: http://www.information.tv
News Editor: Fred Perkins

ISLAM CHANNEL
1806071
14 Bonhill Street, LONDON, EC2A 4BX **Tel:** 020 7374 4511
Fax: 020 7374 4602
Email: news@islamchannel.tv
Web site: http://www.islamchannel.tv
News Editor: Annabelle Drummond

ITV4
1700489
20th Floor, London Television Centre, Upper Ground, LONDON, SE1 9LT **Tel:** 020 7620 1620 **Fax:** 020 7157 3060
Email: janice.troup@itv.com
Web site: http://www.itv.com

AL JAZEERA ENGLISH
1789858
1 Knightsbridge, LONDON, SW1X 7XW **Tel:** 020 7201 2800
Email: press.int@aljazeera.net
Web site: http://english.aljazeera.net
News Editor: Newsdesk

THE JEWELLERY CHANNEL
1666156
1st Floor, Betima House, 168-172 Old Street, LONDON, EC1V 9BP **Tel:** 020 7608 8650 **Fax:** 020 7608 8651
Email: catherine.daniel@simplymedia.tv
Web site: http://www.simplymedia.tv
News Editor: Catherine Daniel

KISS TV
624654
Mappin House, 4 Winsley Street, LONDON, W1W 8HF
Tel: 020 7436 1515 **Fax:** 020 7376 1313
Web site: http://www.totalkiss.com
News Editor: David Young; **Managing Director:** Gidon Katz

KIX
1842557
8 Chelsea Gate Studios, 115 Harwood Road, LONDON, SW6 4QL **Tel:** 020 7371 5999 **Fax:** 020 7384 9003
Email: francesca@chartshow.tv
Web site: http://www.cscmediagroup.com
News Editor: Francesca Newington

KTV
1666093
3 Southbank, THAMES DITTON, KT7 0UD
Tel: 020 8335 6780 **Fax:** 020 8335 6790
Email: suntv@suntvuk.com
Web site: http://www.suntvuk.com
News Editor: S. Balamurali

LEGAL TV
1704686
Unit 3, Avenue Road, Aston, BIRMINGHAM, B6 4DY
Tel: 0121 380 1050 **Fax:** 0121 359 8839
Email: info@legaltv.co.uk
Web site: http://www.legaltv.co.uk
News Editor: D Bal

LIFE TELEVISION
1644721
Springfield House, MAIDSTONE, ME12 2LP
Tel: 0560 341 68 87 **Fax:** 01622 683979
Web site: http://www.lifetvmedia.com
News Editor: John Hammond

LIVING
41941
Virgin Media Television, 160 Great Portland Street, LONDON, W1W 5QA **Tel:** 020 7299 5000
Fax: 020 7299 6000
Web site: http://www.livingtv.co.uk
News Editor: Judy Wells

LIVING2
1666021
Virgin Media Television, 160 Great Portland Street, LONDON, W1W 5QA **Tel:** 020 7299 5000
Fax: 020 7299 6000
Email: jessica.littlewood@virginmediatv.co.uk
Web site: http://www.livingtv.co.uk
News Editor: Judy Wells

LOCAL GOVERNMENT CHANNEL
1703339
2nd Floor, Great Titchfield House, 14-18 Great Titchfield Street, LONDON, W1W 8BD **Tel:** 020 7612 1830
Fax: 020 7636 7446
Email: newsdesk@websedge.com
Web site: http://www.localgovernmentchannel.com
News Editor: Kelly Davis

MAGIC TV
767747
Mappin House, 4 Winsley Street, LONDON, W1W 8HP
Tel: 020 7436 1515 **Fax:** 020 7376 1313
Email: ppoole@channel4.co.uk
Web site: http://www.channel4.co.uk
News Editor: Phil Poole; **Managing Director:** Gidon Katz

MATV NATIONAL
1667375
Unit 213, Stanley House, Orchard Close, WEMBLEY, HA0 4JB **Tel:** 020 8795 0025 **Fax:** 020 8795 0026
Email: info@matv.co.uk
Web site: http://www.matv.co.uk
News Editor: Kuldeep Singh

MEN & MOTORS
623417
200 Grays Inn Road, LONDON, WC1X 8HF
Tel: 0844 881 8000
Web site: http://www.menandmotors.co.uk

MILITARY HISTORY
1849450
BSKYB, Grant Way, ISLEWORTH, TW7 5QD
Tel: 020 7941 5199 **Fax:** 020 7941 5187
Email: joanna.mitchell@bskyb.com
Web site: http://www.thehistorychannel.co.uk
News Editor: Joanna Mitchell

MORE4
1666805
124 Horseferry Road, LONDON, SW1P 2TX
Tel: 020 7306 8444 **Fax:** 020 7340 9735
Email: jbower@channel4.co.uk
Web site: http://www.channel4.com
Editor: Tabitha Jackson; **News Editor:** Justine Bower

MTV
1644823
Hawley Crescent, LONDON, NW1 8TT **Tel:** 020 7284 7777
Fax: 020 7284 7788
Web site: http://www.mtv.co.uk
News Editor: Mandy Hershon

MTV2
634725
17-29 Hawley Crescent, LONDON, NW1 8TT
Tel: 020 7284 7777 **Fax:** 020 7284 7511
Email: moore.joeleen@mtvne.com
Web site: http://www.mtv2.co.uk
News Editor: Joleen Moore

MTV BASE
41943
17-29 Hawley Crescent, LONDON, NW1 8TT
Tel: 020 7284 7777 **Fax:** 020 7284 7511
Email: stafford.zoe@mtvne.com
Web site: http://www.mtvbase.com
News Editor: Zoë Stafford

MTV R: RATED AND RECOMMENDED
1834445
17-29 Hawley Crescent, LONDON, NW1 8TT
Tel: 020 7284 7777 **Fax:** 020 7284 7511
Email: hershon.mandy@mtvne.com
Web site: http://www.mtv.co.uk/mtvr
News Editor: Mandy Hershon

MTV UK/IRELAND
41944
17-29 Hawley Crescent, LONDON, NW1 8TT
Tel: 020 7284 7777 **Fax:** 020 7284 6466
Web site: http://www.mtv.co.uk
News Editor: Lisa Stokoe

MUSIC CHOICE
1644128
Old Trumen Brewery, 91 Brick Lane, LONDON, E1 6QL
Tel: 020 3107 0300 **Fax:** 020 3107 0301
Email: contactus@musicchoice.co.uk
Web site: http://www.musicchoice.co.uk
News Editor: Ellen Lesemann-Andreadis

AL MUSTAKILLAH TELEVISION
1644612
49 Gorst Road, LONDON, NW10 6LS **Tel:** 020 8838 2884
Fax: 020 8838 2989
Email: atv@almustakillah.com
Web site: http://www.almustakillah.com
News Editor: News Desk; **Managing Director:** M. Hamdi

MUTV
1644129
274 Deansgate, MANCHESTER, M3 4JB **Tel:** 0161 834 1111
Fax: 0161 827 1190
Web site: http://www.manutd.com
News Editor: Kiera Barlow

NAT GEO WILD
1644130
Shepherds Building East, Richmond Way, LONDON, W14
0DQ **Tel:** 020 7751 7700 **Fax:** 020 7751 7699
Email: natgeoweb@bskyb.com
Web site: http://www.natgeochannel.co.uk
News Editor: Luigia Minichiello

NATIONAL GEOGRAPHIC CHANNEL
26500
National Geographic Channel, Shepherds Building East,
Richmond Way, LONDON, W14 0DQ **Tel:** 020 7751 7681
Fax: 020 7751 7699
Email: natgeoweb@bskyb.com
Web site: http://www.nationalgeographic.co.uk
News Editor: Luigia Minichiello

NICK JR.
601045
Nickelodeon UK, 15-18 Rathbone Place, LONDON, W1T
1HU **Tel:** 020 7462 1000 **Fax:** 020 7462 1040
Email: rachel.williams@nickelodeon.co.uk
Web site: http://www.nickjr.co.uk
News Editor: Rachel Williams

NICK JR. 2
1748206
Nickelodeon UK, 15-18 Rathbone Place, LONDON, W1T
1HU **Tel:** 020 7462 1000 **Fax:** 020 7462 1040
Email: rachel.williams@nickelodeon.co.uk
Web site: http://www.nickjr.co.uk
News Editor: Rachel Williams

NICKELODEON
41947
Nickelodeon UK, 15-18 Rathbone Place, LONDON, W1T
1HU **Tel:** 020 7462 1000 **Fax:** 020 7462 1040
Email: rachel.williams@nickelodeon.co.uk
Web site: http://www.nicktv.co.uk
News Editor: Rachel Williams

NICKTOONS TV
1606170
Nickelodeon UK, 15-18 Rathbone Place, LONDON, W1T
1HU **Tel:** 020 7462 1000 **Fax:** 020 7462 1040
Email: rachel.williams@nickelodeon.co.uk
Web site: http://www.nick.co.uk/nicktoonstv
News Editor: Rachel Williams

NME TV
1832464
8 Chelsea Gate Studios, 115 Harwood Road, LONDON,
SW6 4QL **Tel:** 020 7371 5999
Email: keeley@chartshow.tv
Web site: http://www.nme.com
News Editor: Keeley Gray

NUTS TV
1826936
Turner House, 16 Great Marlborough Street, LONDON, W1F
7HS **Tel:** 020 7693 1000 **Fax:** 020 7693 1065
Email: ann.rosen@turner.com
Web.site: http://www.nuts.tv
News Editor: Dan Alexis

OPEN ACCESS
1644240
6 Hoxton Square, LONDON, N1 6NU **Tel:** 020 7012 1200
Fax: 020 7729 9540
Email: info@openaccess.tv
Web site: http://www.openaccess.tv
News Editor: Matthew Andrew

OPEN ACCESS 2
1665021
6 Hoxton Square, LONDON, N1 6NU **Tel:** 020 7012 1200
Fax: 020 7729 9540
Email: info@openaccess.tv
Web site: http://www.openaccess.tv
News Editor: Matthew Andrew

PHOENIX CNE (PCNE)
1644717
7th Floor, Chiswick Centre, 414 Chiswick High Road,
LONDON, W4 5TF **Tel:** 020 8987 4320 **Fax:** 020 8987 4333
Email: info@phoenixcnetv.com
Web site: http://www.pcne.tv
News Editor: Pikwan Cheng

PLAY JAM
1644793
Ground Floor, 5 Old Street, LONDON, EC1V 9HL
Tel: 020 7250 1244 **Fax:** 020 7253 8396
Web site: http://www.playjam.com
News Editor: Annabel Allen

PLAYBOY TV
1666251
Aquis House, Station Road, HAYES, UB3 4DX
Tel: 020 8581 7000 **Fax:** 020 8581 7007
Email: oliver.spring@playboytv.com
Web site: http://www.playboytv.co.uk
News Editor: Oliver Spring

PLAYHOUSE DISNEY
1644510
Building 12, Chiswick High Road, LONDON, W4 5AN
Tel: 020 8636 2000
Email: charlotte.scott@disney.com
Web site: http://www.disney.co.uk/disneychannel/
playhouse
News Editor: Charlotte Scott

THE POKER CHANNEL
1666804
1 Down Place, LONDON, W6 9JH **Tel:** 020 8762 6150
Fax: 020 8762 6152
Email: info@pokerchanneleurope.com
Web site: http://www.pokerchanneleurope.com
News Editor: Angus Gairdner

POP
1644247
115 Harwood Road, LONDON, SW6 4QL **Tel:** 020 7371 5999
Fax: 020 7384 9003
Email: francesca@chartshow.tv
Web site: http://www.chartshow.tv
News Editor: Francesca Newington

POP GIRL
1832730
115 Harwood Road, LONDON, SW6 4QL **Tel:** 020 7371 5999
Fax: 020 7384 9003
Email: francesca@chartshow.tv
Web site: http://www.chartshow.tv
News Editor: Francesca Newington

PRICE-DROP TV
1644249
Sit-up Ltd, Sit-up House, 179-181 The Vale, LONDON, W3
7RW **Tel:** 020 8600 9700 **Fax:** 020 8746 2606
Email: steve.hart@sit-up.tv
Web site: http://www.sit-up.tv
News Editor: Steve Hart

PRIME TV
1644863
PAK (UK) TV Ltd, 8th Floor, Crown House, North Circular
Road, LONDON, NW16 7PN **Tel:** 020 8965 0333
Fax: 020 8965 5723
Email: ali.raza@primetv.tv
Web site: http://www.primetv.tv
News Editor: Ali Raza; **Managing Director:** Haroon Khan

PRIMEMAX
1644864
4-5 Hazlitt Mews, LONDON, W14 0JZ **Tel:** 020 7605 7900
Fax: 020 7610 4485
Email: info@eclipsesat.com
News Editor: Press Office

PRIMEMAX 2
1644868
4-5 Hazlitt Mews, LONDON, W14 0JZ **Tel:** 020 7605 7900
Fax: 020 7610 4485
Email: info@eclipsesat.com
News Editor: Press Office

Q TV
767748
Mappin House, 4 Winsley Street, LONDON, W1W 8HP
Tel: 020 7436 1515 **Fax:** 020 7376 1313
Email: ppoole@channel4.co.uk
Web site: http://www.emap.com
News Editor: Phil Poole; **Managing Director:** Gidon Katz

RACING UK
1666941
3rd Floor, Gillingham House, 38-44 Gillingham Street,
LONDON, SW1V WHU **Tel:** 0870 735 9150
Fax: 0870 735 9151
Email: info@racinguk.tv
Web site: http://www.racinguk.tv
News Editor: Zenia Wright

REALLY
1666058
160 Great Portland Street, LONDON, W1W 5QA
Tel: 020 7299 5000 **Fax:** 020 7299 5412
Email: rebecca.schutze@uktv.co.uk
Web site: http://www.uktv.co.uk
News Editor: Rebecca Schutze

REVELATION TV
1644264
61 Victoria Road, SURBITON, KT6 4JX **Tel:** 020 8972 1400
Email: info@revelationtv.com
Web site: http://www.revelationtv.com
News Editor: Howard Conder

ROCK ON TV
41950
St Brandon's House, 29 Great George Street, BRISTOL, BS1
5QT **Tel:** 020 3051 2160
Email: cleveland.salmon@eicom.co.uk
Web site: http://www.rock-ontv.co.uk
News Editor: Cleveland Salmon

ROUGE TV
1644907
4 -5 Hazlitt Mews, LONDON, W14 0JZ **Tel:** 020 7605 7900
Fax: 020 7610 4485
Email: info@eclipsesat.com
News Editor: Press Office

RUSSIAN HOUR
1644910
4th Floor, 193 Wardour Street, LONDON, W1F 8ZF
Tel: 020 7287 9962 **Fax:** 020 7287 9810
Email: i@russianhour.tv
Web site: http://www.russianhour.tv
News Editor: Press Office

UK Broadcasting & Other Media

S4C 2   1666019
Parc Ty Glas, Llanishen, CARDIFF, CF14 5DU
Tel: 029 2074 7444 **Fax:** 029 2075 4444
Email: hotline@s4c.co.uk
Web site: http://www.s4c.co.uk
News Editor: Hot Line

SCREENSHOP   1644268
Sit-up Ltd, Sit-up House, 179-181 The Vale, LONDON, W3 7RW **Tel:** 020 8600 9700 **Fax:** 020 8746 2606
Email: steve.hart@sit-up.tv
Web site: http://www.sit-up.tv
News Editor: Steve Hart

SCUZZ   1644224
115 Harwood Road, 8 Chelsea Gate Studios, LONDON, SW6 4QL **Tel:** 020 7371 5999 **Fax:** 020 7384 9003
Email: moshpit@scuzz.tv
Web site: http://www.scuzz.com
News Editor: Magda Gannon

SKY ARTS   1818816
New Horizon Court 4, Grant Way, ISLEWORTH, TW7 5QD
Tel: 020 7805 8226
Email: hannah.fayz@bskyb.com
Web site: http://www.skyarts.co.uk
News Editor: Hanna Fayaz

SKY BUSINESS NEWS   622691
BSKYB, Grant Way, ISLEWORTH, TW7 5QD
Tel: 020 7585 4535
Email: business.plan@bskyb.com
Web site: http://www.sky.com/news
News Editor: John Holliday

SKY MOVIE CHANNELS   41953
1st Floor, NHC 1, BSKYB, Grant Way, ISLEWORTH, TW7 5QD **Tel:** 020 7705 3000
Web site: http://www.skymovies.com
News Editor: Mark Aldridge

SKY NEWS (BRITISH SKY BROADCASTING)   41954
BSKYB, Grant Way, ISLEWORTH, TW7 5QD
Tel: 020 7705 3000 **Fax:** 020 7705 2966
Email: news.plan@bskyb.com
Web site: http://www.sky.com/news
Editor: Adam Boulton; **News Editor:** News Desk
Twitter: http://twitter.com/SKYnews.

SKY SPORTS 1   1644229
6 Centaurs Business Centre, Grant Way, ISLEWORTH, TW7 5QD **Tel:** 020 7705 3000 **Fax:** 020 7805 7570
Email: ssn-planning@bskyb.com
Web site: http://www.skysports.com

SKY SPORTS 2   1644232
6 Centaurs Business Centre, Grant Way, ISLEWORTH, TW7 5QD **Tel:** 020 7705 3000 **Fax:** 020 7805 7570
Email: ssn-planning@bskyb.com
Web site: http://www.skysports.com

SKY SPORTS 3   1644233
6 Centaurs Business Centre, Grant Way, ISLEWORTH, TW7 5QD **Tel:** 020 7705 3000 **Fax:** 020 7805 7570
Email: ssn-planning@bskyb.com
Web site: http://www.skysports.com

SKY SPORTS EXTRA   1644234
6 Centaurs Business Centre, Grant Way, ISLEWORTH, TW7 5QD **Tel:** 020 7705 3000 **Fax:** 020 7805 7570
Email: ssn-planning@bskyb.com
Web site: http://www.skysports.com

SKY SPORTS NEWS   41955
BSKYB, Grant Way, ISLEWORTH, TW7 5QD
Tel: 020 7705 3000 **Fax:** 020 7805 7570
Email: ssn-planning@bskyb.com
Web site: http://www.skysports.com
News Editor: Planning Desk

SONY ENTERTAINMENT TELEVISION ASIA   41956
24 Park Royal Metro Centre, Britannia Way, LONDON, NW10 7PA **Tel:** 0845 671 1001 **Fax:** 0845 671 1002
Web site: http://www.setasia.tv
News Editor: Shalin Patel

STAR GOLD   1793367
950 Great West Road, 2nd Floor, Profile West, BRENTFORD, TW8 9ES **Tel:** 020 3008 2000
Email: hema.patel@uk.startv.com
Web site: http://www.staruk.indya.com
News Editor: Hema Patel

STAR NEWS   760633
950 Great West Road, 2nd Floor, Profile West, BRENTFORD, TW8 9ES **Tel:** 020 3008 2000
Email: hema.patel@uk.startv.com
Web site: http://www.uk.startv.com
News Editor: Hema Patel

STAR ONE   1793368
950 Great West Road, 2nd Floor, Profile West, BRENTFORD, TW8 9ES **Tel:** 020 3008 2000
Email: hema.patel@uk.startv.com
Web site: http://uk.startv.com
News Editor: Hema Patel

STAR PLUS   634588
2nd Floor, Profile West, 950 Great West Road, BRENTFORD, TW8 9ES **Tel:** 020 3008 2000
Fax: 020 3255 3000
Email: hema.patel@uk.startv.com
Web site: http://www.uk.startv.com
News Editor: Hema Patel

STARZ TV   1644760
Studio 4, 3 Lever Street, LONDON, EC1V 3QU
Tel: 020 7054 9010 **Fax:** 020 7054 9011
Email: joe@mushroomtv.co.uk
Web site: http://www.starztv.co.uk
News Editor: Joe Broadfoot

STOP & SHOP   1645025
99 Farringdon Road, LONDON, EC1R 3BN
Tel: 020 7843 5800
Web site: http://www.thanedirect.co.uk
News Editor: Thomas Parrot; **Managing Director:** Thomas Parrot

SUN TV UK LTD   1645786
3 Southbank, THAMES DITTON, KT7 0UD
Tel: 020 8335 6780 **Fax:** 020 8335 6790
Email: suntv@suntvuk.com
Web site: http://www.suntvuk.com
News Editor: S. Balamurali

TCM 2   1746713
Turner House, 16 Great Marlborough Street, LONDON, W1F 7HS **Tel:** 020 7693 1000 **Fax:** 020 7693 1224
Email: ann.rosen@turner.com
Web site: http://www.tcm2.co.uk
News Editor: Ann Rosen

TEACHERS TV   1665351
16-18 Berners Street, LONDON, W1T 3LN
Tel: 020 7182 7430 **Fax:** 020 7580 3656
Email: info@teachers.tv
Web site: http://www.teachers.tv
News Editor: Communications

TELEVISION X THE FANTASY CHANNEL   41959
1st Floor, Orviss House, Queen Street, St. Helier, JERSEY, JE2 4WD **Tel:** 01534 703700 **Fax:** 01534 703760
Email: sales@rhf.je
Web site: http://www.televisionx.co.uk
News Editor: Chris Ratcliff

TINY POP   1644248
115 Harwood Road, LONDON, SW6 4QL **Tel:** 020 7371 5999
Fax: 020 7384 9003
Email: francesca@chartshow.tv
Web site: http://www.chartshow.tv
News Editor: Francesca Newington

TRAVEL CHANNEL INTERNATIONAL LTD   1644298
64 Newman Street, LONDON, W1T 3EF **Tel:** 020 7034 2511
Fax: 020 7636 6424
Email: petra@travelchannel.co.uk
Web site: http://www.travelchannel.co.uk
News Editor: Petra Shepherd

TRAVEL DEALS DIRECT   1644300
64 Newman Street, LONDON, W1T 3EF **Tel:** 020 7034 2511
Fax: 020 7636 6424
Email: petra@travelchannel.co.uk
Web site: http://www.traveldealsdirect.com
News Editor: Petra Shepherd

TROUBLE   41961
160 Great Portland Street, LONDON, W1W 5QA
Tel: 020 7299 5000 **Fax:** 020 7299 5440
Email: jakki.lewis@virginmediatv.co.uk
Web site: http://www.trouble.co.uk
News Editor: Jakki Lewis

TRUE MOVIES 1   1842559
8 Chelsea Gate Studios, 115 Harwood Road, LONDON, SW6 4QL **Tel:** 020 7371 5999
Email: danielle@chartshow.tv
Web site: http://www.cscmediagroup.com

TRUE MOVIES 2   1842563
8 Chelsea Gate Studios, 115 Harwood Road, LONDON, SW6 4QL **Tel:** 020 7371 5999
Email: danielle@chartshow.tv
Web site: http://www.cscmediagroup.com
News Editor: Danielle Benton

TURNER CLASSIC MOVIES   41957
Turner House, 16 Great Marlborough Street, LONDON, W1F 7HS **Tel:** 020 7693 1000 **Fax:** 020 7693 1224
Email: ann.rosen@turner.com
Web site: http://www.tcmonline.co.uk
News Editor: Ann Rosen

TV8   1645832
Viasat Broadcasting, Building 11, Floor 2 Chiswick Park, 566 Chiswick High Road, LONDON, W4 5XR **Tel:** 020 8742 5100
Fax: 020 8742 5179
Email: nils.gjerstad@viasat.co.uk
Web site: http://www.mtg.se
News Editor: Nils Gjerstad

TV WAREHOUSE ONE   1666154
JML House, Regis Road, LONDON, NW5 3EG
Tel: 020 7691 3800 **Fax:** 020 7691 3801
Email: jonathanoconnor@johnmillsltd.co.uk
Web site: http://www.jmldirect.com
News Editor: Jonathan O'Connor

TVBS EUROPE (THE CHINESE-CHANNEL LTD)   1644310
Teddington Studios, Broom Road, Teddington, MIDDLESEX, TW11 9NT **Tel:** 020 8614 8300 **Fax:** 020 8943 0982
Email: tvbseurope@chinese-channel.co.uk
Web site: http://www.chinese-channel.co.uk
News Editor: Stanley Mo

VAULT   1666036
8 Chelsea Gate Studios, 115 Harwood Road, LONDON, SW6 4QP **Tel:** 020 7371 5999 **Fax:** 020 7384 2026
Email: info@chartshow.tv
Web site: http://www.chartshow.tv
News Editor: Sarah Gaughan

VH1   41963
17-29 Hawley Crescent, LONDON, NW1 8TT
Tel: 020 7284 7777 **Fax:** 020 7284 6466
Email: joeleen.moore@mtvne.com
Web site: http://www.vh1.co.uk
News Editor: Joeleen Moore

VH1 CLASSIC   41964
17-29 Hawley Crescent, LONDON, NW1 8TT
Tel: 020 7284 7777 **Fax:** 020 7284 6466
Email: joeleen.moore@mtvne.com
Web site: http://www.vh1.co.uk
News Editor: Joeleen Moore

VIASAT SPORT 2
1666105
Building 11, Chiswick Park, 556 Chiswick High Road, LONDON, W4 5XR **Tel:** 020 8742 5100 **Fax:** 020 8742 5179
Email: nils.gjerstad@viasat.co.uk
Web site: http://www.mtg.se
News Editor: Nils Gjerstad

VIASAT SPORT 3
1666108
Building 11, Chiswick Park, 566 Chiswick High Road, LONDON, W4 5XR **Tel:** 020 8742 5100 **Fax:** 020 8742 5179
Email: nils.gjerstad@viasat.co.uk
Web site: http://www.mtg.se
News Editor: Nils Gjerstad

VIRGIN 1
1824866
Virgin Media Television, 160 Great Portland Street, LONDON, W1W 5QA **Tel:** 020 7299 5000
Fax: 020 7299 5516
Email: jakki.lewis@virginmediatv.co.uk
Web site: http://www.virgin1.co.uk
News Editor: Jakki Lewis

WATCH
1924744
160 Great Portland Street, LONDON, W1W 5QA
Tel: 020 7299 6200 **Fax:** 020 7299 6194
Web site: http://www.justwatch.co.uk
News Editor: Nicola Barrigan

WEDDING TV
1793873
44 Clipstone Street, LONDON, W1W 5DW
Tel: 020 7255 6240 **Fax:** 020 7255 6241
Email: info@weddingtv.com
Web site: http://www.weddingtv.com
News Editor: Anthony Jarvis

XPLICIT
1638699
The TV Group, Unit 415, Bondway Commercial Centre, 69-71 Bondway, LONDON, SW8 1SQ **Tel:** 0845 241 4791
Email: peter@thetvgroup.tv
News Editor: Peter Nellemann; **Managing Director:** Peter Nellemann

ZEE CINEMA
1644397
Units 7-9, Belvue Business Centre, Belvue Road, Northolt, MIDDLESEX, UB5 5QQ **Tel:** 020 8839 4000
Fax: 0870 197 3498
Email: shaney.burney@zeetv.co.uk
Web site: http://www.zeetv.co.uk
News Editor: Shaney Burney

ZEE MUSIC
1644401
Units 7-9, Belvue Business Centre, Belvue Road, Northolt, MIDDLESEX, UB5 5QQ **Tel:** 020 8839 4000
Fax: 0870 197 3498
Email: chiragh@zeetv.co.uk
Web site: http://www.zeetv.co.uk
News Editor: Chiragh Cherian

ZEE TV
41965
Unit 8, Belvue Business Centre, Belvue Road, NORTHOLT, UB5 5QQ **Tel:** 020 8839 4000 **Fax:** 020 8841 6123
Email: sangraam.marathe@zeetv.co.uk
Web site: http://www.zeetelevision.com
News Editor: Amey Bapat

ZONE EUROPA
1666266
Zone Media, 105-109 Salusbury Road, LONDON, NW6 6RG
Tel: 020 7644 7170 **Fax:** 020 7624 3652
Email: jon.moxey@chellozone.com
Web site: http://www.zonemedia.net
News Editor: Jon Moxey

ZONE HORROR
1851932
Chello Zone, 105-109 Salusbury Road, LONDON, NW6 6RG
Tel: 020 7328 8808 **Fax:** 020 7328 8858
Email: jon.moxey@chellozone.com
Web site: http://www.zonehorror.tv
News Editor: Jon Moxey

ZONE REALITY
1644817
Chello Zone, 105-109 Salusbury Road, LONDON, NW6 6RG
Tel: 020 7328 8808 **Fax:** 020 7328 8858
Email: jon.moxey@chellozone.com
Web site: http://www.zonereality.tv
News Editor: Jon Moxey

ZONE ROMANTICA
1644905
Zonemedia, 105-109 Salusbury Road, LONDON, NW6 6RG
Tel: 020 7644 7104 **Fax:** 020 7624 3652
Email: jon.moxey@chellozone.com
Web site: http://www.zoneromantica.net
News Editor: Jon Moxey

ZONE THRILLER
1851929
Chello Zone, 105-109 Salusbury Road, LONDON, NW6 6RG
Tel: 020 7328 8808 **Fax:** 020 7328 8858
Email: jon.moxey@chellozone.com
Web site: http://www.zonethriller.tv
News Editor: Jon Moxey

CABLE TV

CHANNEL M
622536
Urbis, Cathedral Gardens, MANCHESTER, M4 3BG
Tel: 0161 919 5250 **Fax:** 0161 919 5388
Email: newsdesk@channelm.co.uk
Web site: http://www.channelm.co.uk
News Editor: Zenna Barry

FILMFLEX
1743274
PR by email only **Tel:** 020 7323 6963
Email: sheena@pagetbaker.com
Web site: http://www.filmflexmovies.com
News Editor: Sheena Bhattessa

MATV CHANNEL 6
1667286
Unit 213, Stanley House, Orchard Close, WEMBLEY, HA0 4JB **Tel:** 020 8795 0025 **Fax:** 020 8795 0026
Email: info@matv.co.uk
Web site: http://www.matv.co.uk
News Editor: Kuldeep Singh

STOIC TV
42692
Imperial College Union, Prince Consort Road, LONDON, SW7 2BB **Tel:** 020 7594 8104
Email: info@stoictv.com
Web site: http://www.stoictv.com
News Editor: John Anderson

DIGITAL

NATIONAL DIGITAL TV

4MUSIC
1601422
Mappin House, 4 Winsley Street, LONDON, W1W 8HF
Tel: 020 7436 1515 **Fax:** 020 7376 1313
Email: ppoole@channel4.co.uk
Web site: http://4music.channel4.com/
News Editor: Phil Poole; **Managing Director:** Gidon Katz

AVENUE 11
1825347
Simply Media TV Ltd, 1st Floor, Bentima House, 168-172 Old Street, LONDON, EC1V 9BP **Tel:** 020 7608 8691
Email: aaron.hutchinson@simplymedia.tv
Web site: http://www.avenue11.com
News Editor: Aaron Hutchinson

B4U MOVIES
601035
Transputec House, 19 Heather Park Drive, WEMBLEY, HA0 1SS **Tel:** 020 8795 7171 **Fax:** 020 8795 7181
Email: info@b4network.com
Web site: http://www.b4utv.com
News Editor: Kevin Rego

B4U MUSIC
767590
Transputec House, 19 Heather Park Drive, WEMBLEY, HA0 1SS **Tel:** 020 8795 7171 **Fax:** 020 8795 7181
Email: info@b4network.com
Web site: http://www.b4utv.com
News Editor: Kevin Rego

BBC FOUR
41967
201 Wood Lane, LONDON, W12 7RJ **Tel:** 020 8743 8000
Email: david.okuefuna@bbc.co.uk
Web site: http://www.bbc.co.uk/bbcfour
News Editor: David Okuefuna

BBC THREE
41966
Room 6239, Television Centre, Wood Lane, LONDON, W12 7RJ **Tel:** 020 8743 8000 **Fax:** 020 8576 8955
Web site: http://www.bbc.co.uk/bbcthree

BEAUTYZONE
1825348
Simply Media TV, 1st Floor, Bentima House, 168-172 Old Street, LONDON, EC1V 9BP **Tel:** 020 7608 8654
Email: rachel.rosser@simplymedia.tv
Web site: http://www.beautyzone.tv
News Editor: Rachel Rosser

BOOK ZONE
1825351
Videobite Limited, Gainsborough House, 81 Oxford Street, LONDON, W1D 2EU **Tel:** 0845 224 3601
Email: editorial@bookzone.tv
Web site: http://www.bookzone.tv
News Editor: Editorial Team

DISCOVERY HOME AND HEALTH
625585
Discovery House, Chiswick Park Building 2, 566 Chiswick High Road, LONDON, W4 5YB **Tel:** 020 8811 3000
Fax: 020 8811 3193
Email: caroline_watt@discovery-europe.com
Web site: http://www.discoveryhealth.co.uk
News Editor: Caroline Watt

FILM4
41970
124 Horseferry Road, LONDON, SW1P 2TX
Tel: 020 7306 8274 **Fax:** 020 7340 9738
Email: spinder@channel4.co.uk
Web site: http://www.filmfour.com
News Editor: Steve Pinder

FOOD ZONE
1825352
Simply Media TV Ltd, 1st Floor, Bentima House, 168-172 Old Street, LONDON, EC1V 9BP **Tel:** 020 7608 8670
Email: aaron.hutchinson@simplymedia.tv
Web site: http://www.foodzone.tv
News Editor: Aaron Hutchinson

FTN
1601275
160 Great Portland Street, LONDON, W1W 5QA
Tel: 020 7299 5000 **Fax:** 020 7299 5482
Email: jakki.lewis@virginmediatv.co.uk
Web site: http://www.virgin1.co.uk
News Editor: Jakki Lewis

GARDENING TV
1825353
Simply Media TV Ltd, 1st Floor, Bentima House, 168-172 Old Street, LONDON, EC1V 9BP **Tel:** 020 7608 8672
Email: aaron.hutchinson@simplymedia.tv
Web site: http://www.gardening.tv
News Editor: Aaron Hutchinson

GOOD FOOD
714960
2nd Floor, 160 Great Portland Street, LONDON, W1W 5QA
Tel: 020 7299 5000
Email: tamsyn.zietsman@uktv.co.uk
Web site: http://www.goodfoodchannel.com
News Editor: Tamsyn Zietsman

HEALTH ZONE
1825350
Simply Media TV Ltd, 1st Floor, Bentima House, 168-172 Old Street, LONDON, EC1V 9BP **Tel:** 020 7608 8650
Email: david.harris@simplymedia.tv
Web site: http://www.healthzone.tv
News Editor: David Harris

HOME
41974
2nd Floor, 160 Great Portland Street, LONDON, W1W 5QA
Tel: 020 7299 5000
Email: tamsyn.zietsman@uktv.co.uk
Web site: http://www.ukstyle.tv
News Editor: Tamsyn Zietsman

ITV2
41971
20th Floor, London Television Centre, Upper Ground, LONDON, SE1 9LT **Tel:** 0844 881 3000 **Fax:** 020 7157 3060
Email: itv2@itv.com
Web site: http://www.itv.com/itv2
News Editor: Ben Webster

UK Broadcasting & Other Media

ITV3 1668038
20th Floor, London Television Centre, Upper Ground, LONDON, SE1 9LT **Tel:** 020 7156 6000
Email: janice.troup@itv.com
Web site: http://www.itv.com/itv3
News Editor: Janice Troup

KERRANG TV 711723
Mappin House, 4 Winsley Street, LONDON, W1W 8HF
Tel: 020 7436 1515 **Fax:** 020 7376 1313
Email: dyoung@channel4.co.uk
Web site: http://www.kerrang.com/tv
News Editor: David Young; **Managing Director:** Gidon Katz

MTV DANCE 707955
17-29 Hawley Crescent, LONDON, NW1 8TT
Tel: 020 7284 7777 **Fax:** 020 7284 6466
Email: stafford.zoe@mtvne.com
Web site: http://www.mtv.co.uk/dance
News Editor: Zoë Stafford

THE PUB CHANNEL 629909
BSKYB, Grant Way, ISLEWORTH, TW7 5QD
Tel: 020 7941 5084 **Fax:** 020 7941 5123
Email: alison.clarke@bskyb.com
Web site: http://www.pubchannel.com
News Editor: Alison Rattary-Clarke

SIMPLY ENTERTAINMENT 1825349
Simply Media TV Ltd, 1st Floor, Bentima House, 168-172 Old Street, LONDON, EC1V 9BP **Tel:** 020 7608 8668
Email: emma.holtham@simplymedia.tv
Web site: http://www.simplyentertainment.tv
News Editor: Emma Holtham

SKY REAL LIVES 1601458
BSKYB, Grant Way, ISLEWORTH, TW7 5QD
Tel: 020 7705 3000 **Fax:** 020 7805 8530
Email: bianca.simms@bskyb.com
Web site: http://www.sky.com/reallives
News Editor: Rebecca Cross

SMASH HITS CHANNEL 711721
Mappin House, 4 Winsley Street, LONDON, W1W 8HF
Tel: 020 7436 1515 **Fax:** 020 7376 1313
Email: ppoole@channel4.co.uk
Web site: http://www.smashhits.net
News Editor: Phil Poole; **Managing Director:** Gidon Katz

TMF THE MUSIC FACTORY 1601425
17-29 Hawley Crescent, LONDON, NW1 8TT
Tel: 020 7284 7777 **Fax:** 020 7284 6466
Email: hershon.mandy@mtvne.com
Web site: http://www.mtv.co.uk/tmf
News Editor: Mandy Hershon

YESTERDAY 1601272
2nd Floor, 160 Great Portland Street, LONDON, W1W 5QA
Tel: 020 7299 5000
Email: danielle.kemble@uktv.co.uk
Web site: http://www.uktv.co.uk/yesterday
News Editor: Danielle Kemble

TELETEXT

NATIONAL TELETEXT

CEEFAX 42916
Room 7540, BBC TV Centre, Wood Lane, LONDON, W12 7RJ **Tel:** 020 8225 7023 **Fax:** 020 8749 6734
Email: ceefax@bbc.co.uk
Editor: Patrick Heery

CEEFAX COMMUNITY MAGAZINE 42918
CSV Media, 237 Pentonville Road, LONDON, N1 9NJ
Tel: 020 7643 1425 **Fax:** 020 7833 5689
Email: ccooper@csv.org.uk

DEAFVIEW 42919
19-23 Featherstone Street, LONDON, EC1Y 8SL
Tel: 020 7296 8145 **Fax:** 020 7296 8021
Email: deafview@rnid.org.uk
Web site: http://www.rnid.org.uk
Editor: Tim Russell

TELETEXT 42922
Building 10, Chiswick Park, 566 Chiswick High Road, LONDON, W4 5TS **Tel:** 020 8323 5000 **Fax:** 020 8323 5001
Email: dutyeditor@teletext.co.uk
Web site: http://www.teletext.co.uk
Editor: Newsdesk

ZEETEXT 42923
EBS New Media Ltd, The Chequers, 28 Whitehorse Street, BALDOCK, SG7 6QQ **Tel:** 01462 895999 **Fax:** 01462 895777
Email: barry@ebsnewmedia.com
Web site: http://www.ebsnewmedia.com
Editor: Barry Swain

REGIONAL TELETEXT

CHANNEL TEXT 42924
Channel Television, Television Centre, La Pouquelaye, ST. HELIER, JE1 3ZD **Tel:** 01534 816760 **Fax:** 01534 816689
Email: broadcast@channeltv.co.uk
Web site: http://www.channelonline.tv
Editor: Russell Hookey; **News Editor:** Russell Hookey

TESTUN CYF 26627
Ty Norfolk, 57-59 Heol Siarl, CARDIFF, CF10 2GD
Tel: 029 2023 1722 **Fax:** 029 2023 1002
Email: post@testun.co.uk
Editor: Hywel Pennar; **Managing Director:** Hywel Pennar

RADIO

NATIONAL RADIO STATIONS

ABSOLUTE RADIO 41902
1 Golden Square, LONDON, W1F 9DJ **Tel:** 020 7434 1215
Fax: 020 7434 1197
Email: newsroom@absoluteradio.co.uk
Web site: http://www.absoluteradio.co.uk
News Editor: Andrew Bailey

AKASH RADIO 1647484
Unit 14, Arches Business Centre, Merrick Road, SOUTHALL, UB2 4AU **Tel:** 020 8843 0999
Email: info@akashradio.com
Web site: http://www.akashradio.com
News Editor: Sukhwinder Singh

AMAZING RADIO 1902482
19 Grey St, NEWCASTLE-UPON-TYNE, NE1 6EE
Tel: 0191 245 4444 **Fax:** 0191 245 3839
Email: info@amazingradio.co.uk
Web site: http://www.amazingradio.co.uk
News Editor: Paul Campbell

AMRIT BANI 1648404
Unit 1, 97 Western Road, SOUTHALL, UB2 5HN
Tel: 020 8606 9292 **Fax:** 020 8843 1210
Email: info@amritbani.com
Web site: http://www.amritbani.com
News Editor: Mani Bedi; **Managing Director:** Mani Bedi

ASIAN GOLD RADIO 766236
11A King Street, SOUTHALL, UB2 4DG **Tel:** 020 8571 7200
Fax: 020 8571 7300
Email: info@sukhsagarradio.co.uk
Web site: http://www.asiangoldradio.co.uk
News Editor: Zorawar Gakhal

BBC 1XTRA 759176
Yalding House, 152-156 Great Portland Street, LONDON, W1N 6AJ **Tel:** 020 7765 4649 **Fax:** 020 7765 3370
Email: karlene.pinnock@bbc.co.uk
Web site: http://www.bbc.co.uk/1xtra
News Editor: Jack Baine
Twitter: http://twitter.com/1Xtra.

BBC 6 MUSIC 759179
BBC 6 Music, c/o 99 Western House, LONDON, W1A 1AA
Tel: 020 8743 8000
Email: antony.bellekom@bbc.co.uk
Web site: http://www.bbc.co.uk/6music
Editor: Paul Rodgers; **News Editor:** Antony Bellekom;
Managing Editor: Antony Bellekom
Twitter: http://twitter.com/BBC6musicnews.

BBC ARTS UNIT (RADIO) 765744
Room 7028, Broadcasting House, Portland Place, LONDON, W1A 1AA **Tel:** 020 7765 4212
Email: theplanningunit@bbc.co.uk
Web site: http://www.bbc.co.uk/radio4/arts
News Editor: Planning Desk
Twitter: http://twitter.com/BBC.

BBC ASIAN NETWORK 42409
9 St. Nicholas Place, LEICESTER, LE1 5LB
Tel: 0116 201 6772
Email: asian.network@bbc.co.uk
Web site: http://www.bbc.co.uk/asiannetwork
Editor: Vijay Sharma; **News Editor:** Manjushri Mitra
Twitter: http://twitter.com/bbcasiannetwork.

BBC ECONOMICS AND BUSINESS UNIT (RADIO) 41885
Room 4220, Television Centre, Wood Lane, LONDON, W12 7RJ **Tel:** 020 8576 7486
Email: bizplan@bbc.co.uk
News Editor: Planning Desk
Twitter: http://twitter.com/bbcbusiness.

BBC EVENTS UNIT 41899
BC3 D3 Broadcast Centre, 201 Wood Lane, LONDON, W12 7TP
Email: pamela.paryag@bbc.co.uk
News Editor: Pamela Paryag
Twitter: http://twitter.com/bbc.

BBC GNS (RADIO) 41891
Room 1635, Television Centre, Wood Lane, LONDON, W12 7RJ **Tel:** 020 8624 9880 **Fax:** 020 8936 9220
News Editor: Peter Owen
Twitter: http://twitter.com/bbc.

BBC LONDON COMMUNITIES 41884
35 Marylebone High Street, LONDON, W1U 4QA
Tel: 020 7765 1325
Web site: http://www.bbc.co.uk
News Editor: Penny Wrout
Twitter: http://twitter.com/bbc.

BBC NEWS PLANNING, NEWS GATHERING (RADIO) 41886
Room 1624, News Centre, Wood Lane, LONDON, W12 7RJ
Tel: 020 8743 8000
Email: uknewsplan@bbc.co.uk
News Editor: News Planning Desk
Twitter: http://twitter.com/bbcnews.

BBC POLITICAL PROGRAMMES (RADIO) 41887
1st Floor, 4 Millbank, LONDON, SW1P 3JQ
Tel: 020 7973 6000 **Fax:** 020 7973 6336
News Editor: Newsroom
Twitter: http://twitter.com/bbcpolitics.

BBC RADIO 1 PRODUCTION DEPARTMENT (MUSIC) 41888
Yalding House, 152-156 Great Portland Street, LONDON, W1W 6AJ **Tel:** 020 7765 2413 **Fax:** 020 7765 1439
Web site: http://www.bbc.co.uk/radio1
News Editor: George Ergatoudis
Twitter: http://twitter.com/bbcradio1.

BBC RADIO 2 41889
Western House, 99 Great Portland Street, LONDON, W1A 1AA **Tel:** 020 7580 4468
Web site: http://www.bbc.co.uk/radio2
Editor: Robert Gallacher

BBC RADIO 3
41883
Broadcasting House, LONDON, W1A 1AA
Tel: 020 8743 8000
Web site: http://www.bbc.co.uk/radio3
Editor: Edwina Wolstencroft
Twitter: http://twitter.com/bbcradio3live.

BBC RADIO 4
26678
Broadcasting House, LONDON, W1A 1AA
Tel: 020 7580 4468
Web site: http://www.bbc.co.uk/radio4
Editor: Kate Rowland

BBC RADIO 5 LIVE
41890
Room 2605, Television Centre, Wood Lane, LONDON, W12
7RJ **Tel:** 020 8743 8000
Email: uknewsplan@bbc.co.uk
Web site: http://www.bbc.co.uk/fivelive
News Editor: Planning Desk
Twitter: http://twitter.com/BBC5Live.

BBC RADIO 7
759182
Room 4015, Broadcasting House, LONDON, W1A 1AA
Tel: 020 7756 0308 **Fax:** 020 7675 5077
Web site: http://www.bbc.co.uk/bbc7
News Editor: Sian Davis
Twitter: http://twitter.com/onbbc7now.

BBC RADIO AND MUSIC-FACTUAL
26663
Room 6026, BBC Broadcasting House, LONDON, W1A 1AA
Tel: 020 8743 8000 **Fax:** 020 7765 5454
Email: ruth.gardiner@bbc.co.uk
Editor: Edward Blakeman; **News Editor:** Ruth Gardiner
Twitter: http://twitter.com/bbc.

BBC RADIO ARTS (BRISTOL)
1614537
Room 16, BBC Broadcasting House, Whiteladies Road,
BRISTOL, BS8 2LR **Tel:** 0117 973 2211
Email: kate.chaney@bbc.co.uk
Editor: Clare McGinn; **News Editor:** Kate Chaney
Twitter: http://twitter.com/bbc.

BBC RADIO - AUDIO AND MUSIC FACTUAL (WEST)
26677
Broadcasting House, Whiteladies Road, BRISTOL, BS8 2LR
Tel: 0117 973 2211 **Fax:** 0117 946 7716
Email: kate.chaney@bbc.co.uk
Editor: Clare McGinn; **News Editor:** Kate Chaney
Twitter: http://twitter.com/bbc.

BBC RADIO ENTERTAINMENT NEWS UNIT
49702
Room 210, Yalding House, Clipstone Street, LONDON, W1N
4DJ **Tel:** 020 7765 4649 **Fax:** 020 7765 0002
Email: newsbeat@bbc.co.uk
News Editor: Frances Cronin
Twitter: http://twitter.com/BBCEntsTeam.

BBC RADIO SCIENCE
41892
Room 630, South East Wing, Bush House, The Strand,
LONDON, WC2B 4PH **Tel:** 020 7557 2471
Fax: 020 7557 3008
Email: radiosciencepress@bbc.co.uk
Web site: http://www.bbc.co.uk/radio4/science
News Editor: Planning Desk
Twitter: http://twitter.com/bbcscitech.

BBC RELIGIOUS PROGRAMMES (RADIO)
26660
5th Floor, New Broadcasting House, Oxford Road,
MANCHESTER, M60 1SJ **Tel:** 0161 200 2020
Fax: 0161 244 3183
Web site: http://www.bbc.co.uk/religion
News Editor: Press Office
Twitter: http://twitter.com/bbc.

BBC SPORTSNEWS
601641
Room 2640, Stage 6, BBC TV Centre, Wood Lane,
LONDON, W12 7RJ **Tel:** 020 8624 9690 **Fax:** 020 8624 9209
Email: kate.wademan@bbc.co.uk
Web site: http://www.bbc.co.uk/sport
News Editor: Kate Wademan
Twitter: http://twitter.com/bbcsport.

BBC TRAFFIC NEWS (RADIO)
718514
91 Charterhouse Street, LONDON, EC1M 6HR
Tel: 020 7012 3555 **Fax:** 020 7012 3501
Email: london@trafficlink.co.uk
Web site: http://www.trafficlink.co.uk
News Editor: Peter Lees
Twitter: http://twitter.com/BBCTravelAlert.

BBC UK SPECIALISTS (RADIO)
41893
Room 1502, Stage 5, Television Centre, Wood Lane,
LONDON, W12 7RJ **Tel:** 020 8624 9010 **Fax:** 020 8624 9101
Email: uknewsplan@bbc.co.uk
News Editor: Melanie Fanstone
Twitter: http://twitter.com/bbcnews.

BBC WORLD AFFAIRS UNIT (RADIO)
41894
Room 2505, Television Centre, Wood Lane, LONDON, W12
7RJ **Tel:** 020 8624 8550 **Fax:** 020 8743 7591
News Editor: News Desk
Twitter: http://twitter.com/bbcworld.

BBC WORLD SERVICE
41895
Room 500, North East, PO Box 76, Bush House, Strand,
LONDON, WC2B 4PH **Tel:** 020 7240 3456
Fax: 020 7836 0207
Email: peter.burdin@bbc.co.uk
Web site: http://www.bbc.co.uk/worldservice
News Editor: Peter Burdin

BFBS BRITISH FORCES BROADCASTING SERVICE
41896
SSVC, Chalfont Grove, Narcot Lane, CHALFONT ST.
PETER, SL9 8TN **Tel:** 01494 878723 **Fax:** 01494 870552
Email: admin.officer@bfbs.com
Web site: http://www.bfbs.com
News Editor: Josella Waldron; **Managing Director:** Alastair
Duncan

CALVARY CHAPEL RADIO
1647499
PO Box 647, BROMLEY, BR1 4WQ **Tel:** 020 8466 5365
Email: info@calvarychapelradio.co.uk
Web site: http://www.calvarychapelradio.co.uk
News Editor: Alison Johnston-White

CELTICA RADIO
766242
PO Box 48, BRIDGEND, CF32 9ZY **Tel:** 07005 963770
Email: info@celticaradio.com
Web site: http://www.celticaradio.com
News Editor: Bill Everatt; **Managing Director:** Bill Everatt

CHILL
1810525
PO Box 2000, BRISTOL, BS99 7SN **Tel:** 0117 900 5343
Fax: 0117 900 5308
Email: chill@helpmechill.com
Web site: http://www.helpmechill.com
News Editor: Bern Leckie
Twitter: http://twitter.com/ChillDAB.

CLASSIC FM
41898
30 Leicester Square, LONDON, WC2H 7LA
Tel: 020 7343 9000 **Fax:** 020 7344 2789
Email: anne-marie.minhall@classicfm.com
Web site: http://www.classicfm.co.uk
News Editor: Anne-Marie Minhall; **Managing Director:**
Darren Henley
Twitter: http://twitter.com/classicfm_1.

DEM RADIO
1852048
Media House, 10B Bury Road, LONDON, N22 6HS
Tel: 020 8889 6394 **Fax:** 020 8888 3550
Email: info@demradyo.com
Web site: http://www.demradyo.com
News Editor: Ipek Ozerim

GAYDAR RADIO
766120
PO Box 113, TWICKENHAM, TW1 4WI **Tel:** 020 8744 1287
Fax: 020 8744 1089
Email: contact@gaydarradio.com
Web site: http://www.gaydarradio.com
News Editor: Robin Crowley

GUARDIAN UNLIMITED PODCAST
1744743
King's Place, 90 York Way, LONDON, N1 9GU
Tel: 020 3353 3959
Email: podcasts@guardian.co.uk
Web site: http://www.guardian.co.uk/audio
News Editor: News Editor

HEAT RADIO
1647493
Castle Quay, Castlefield, MANCHESTER, M15 4PR
Tel: 0161 288 5000
Email: paul.mack@bauermedia.co.uk
Web site: www.heatworld.com/radio.aspx
News Editor: Paul Mack

IMMEDIA BROADCASTING
766809
7-9 The Broadway, NEWBURY, RG14 1AS
Tel: 01635 572800 **Fax:** 01635 572801
Email: steve.caldwell@immediaplc.com
Web site: http://www.immediaplc.com
News Editor: Steve Caldwell

INDEPENDENT RADIO NEWS (IRN)
48864
6th Floor, Grant Way, ISLEWORTH, TW7 5QD
Tel: 020 7585 4525 **Fax:** 020 7430 4092
Email: radio@bskyb.com
Web site: http://www.irn.co.uk
Editor: Jon Godel; **News Editor:** Forward Planning Desk;
Managing Director: John Perkins
Twitter: http://twitter.com/SKYnews.

IRN MONEY
633812
Grant Way, ISLEWORTH, TW7 5QD **Tel:** 020 7585 4525
Email: radio@bskyb.com

LIBERTY RADIO
1696668
199-201 Seven Sisters Road, LONDON, N4 3NG
Tel: 020 7686 6000
Email: info@libertyradio.co.uk
Web site: http://www.libertyradio.co.uk
News Editor: Richard Ashitey

THE MUSIC WELL
1752605
19 Manor Street, OTLEY, LS21 1AX **Tel:** 01943 462985
Email: info@themusicwell.co.uk
Web site: http://www.themusicwell.co.uk
News Editor: Phil Snell

NME RADIO
1841980
B2 Blue Fin Building, 110 Southwark Street, LONDON, SE1
0SU **Tel:** 020 7922 1991 **Fax:** 020 7922 1989
Email: katie.torrie@dx-media.co.uk
Web site: http://www.nmeradio.com
News Editor: Katie Torrie; **Managing Director:** Sammy
Jacob
Twitter: http://twitter.com/NMERadio.

PANJAB RADIO
766804
Panjab Radio House, Springfield Road, HAYES, UB4 0TY
Tel: 020 8848 8877 **Fax:** 020 8848 4422
Email: info@panjabradio.co.uk
Web site: http://www.panjabradio.co.uk
News Editor: Gurdeep Singh; **Managing Director:** Surjit
Singh Ghuman

PLANET ROCK
753146
54 Lisson Street, LONDON, NW1 5DF **Tel:** 020 7453 1639
Email: jon@planetrock.com
Web site: http://www.planetrock.com
News Editor: Jon Norman

Q RADIO
1647490
Mappin House, 4 Winsley Street, LONDON, W1W 8HF
Tel: 020 7182 8000
Email: ric.blaxill@bauermedia.co.uk
Web site: http://www.qthemusic.com
News Editor: Ric Blaxill
Twitter: http://twitter.com/Q_radio.

RADIO CAROLINE
1772528
426 Archway Road, Highgate, LONDON, N6 4JH
Tel: 020 8340 3831
Email: caroline_pirate@btconnect.com
Web site: http://www.radiocaroline.co.uk
News Editor: Peter Moore
Twitter: http://twitter.com/radiocaroline.

Section 9 UK Broadcasting

UK Broadcasting & Other Media

RADIO MAGNETIC   766088
Argyle House, 16 Argyle Court, 1103 Argyle Street,
GLASGOW, G3 8ND **Tel:** 0141 226 8808
Email: andy.m@radiomagnetic.com
Web site: http://www.radiomagnetic.com
News Editor: Andy McColgan

SKY NEWS RADIO   760634
BSKYB, Grant Way, ISLEWORTH, TW7 5QD
Tel: 020 7585 4525 **Fax:** 020 7585 4526
Email: radio@bskyb.com
Web site: http://www.sky.com/news
Editor: Andy Ivy; **News Editor:** Andy Ivy
Twitter: http://twitter.com/SKYnews.

SMASH HITS DIGITAL RADIO   758644
Castle Quay, Castlefield, MANCHESTER, M15 4PR
Tel: 0161 288 5000
Email: anthony.gay@thehitsradio.co.uk
Web site: http://www.smashhits.net
News Editor: Paul Mack

SOLAR RADIO   766847
PO Box 49300, LONDON, SE12 9XU **Tel:** 0870 949 0129
Email: tonymonson@solarradio.com
Web site: http://www.solarradio.com
News Editor: Clive Richardson

SUKH SAGAR   766238
11A King Street, SOUTHALL, UB2 4DG **Tel:** 020 8571 7200
Fax: 020 8571 7300
Email: info@sukhsagarradio.co.uk
Web site: http://www.sukhsagarradio.co.uk
News Editor: Zorawar Gakhal

TALKSPORT   41900
18 Hatfields, LONDON, SE1 8DJ **Tel:** 020 7959 7800
Email: press.releases@talksport.co.uk
Web site: http://www.talksport.net
News Editor: Matt Smith
Twitter: http://twitter.com/talkSPORT.

TOTAL ROCK   766245
1-6 Denmark Place, LONDON, WC2H 8NL
Tel: 020 7240 6665
Email: info@totalrock.com
Web site: http://www.totalrock.com
News Editor: Malcolm Dome

TRANS WORLD RADIO   766243
PO Box 606, ALTRINCHAM, WA14 2YS **Tel:** 0161 923 0270
Email: rfarnworth@twr.org.uk
Web site: http://www.twr.org.uk
News Editor: Russell Farnworth

UCB BIBLE   1660507
PO Box 255, STOKE-ON-TRENT, ST4 8YY
Tel: 01782 642000 **Fax:** 01782 641121
Email: bible@ucb.co.uk
Web site: http://www.ucb.co.uk/bible
News Editor: Peter Wooding

UCB INSPIRATIONAL   1660505
Broadcast Centre, Hanchurch Lane, STOKE-ON-TRENT,
ST4 8RY **Tel:** 01782 642000 **Fax:** 01782 641121
Email: inspirational@ucb.co.uk
Web site: http://www.ucb.co.uk/inspirational
News Editor: Peter Wooding

UCB TALK   1660501
PO Box 255, STOKE-ON-TRENT, ST4 8YY
Tel: 01782 642000 **Fax:** 01782 641121
Email: talk@ucb.co.uk
Web site: http://www.ucb.co.uk/talk
News Editor: Peter Wooding

UCB UK   41901
Broadcast Centre, Hanchurch Lane, STOKE-ON-TRENT,
ST4 8RY **Tel:** 01782 642000 **Fax:** 01782 641121
Email: news@ucb.co.uk
Web site: http://www.ucb.co.uk
News Editor: James Cantrill

WESTSIDE RADIO 89.6FM   766103
10 High Street, SOUTHALL, UB1 3DA **Tel:** 020 8571 9700
Fax: 0871 7142 896
Email: info@westsideradio.co.uk
Web site: http://www.westsideradio.co.uk
News Editor: Amar Chadha

REGIONAL RADIO STATIONS

102.4 WISH FM   42526
Orrell Lodge, Orrell Road, WIGAN, WN5 8HJ
Tel: 01942 761024 **Fax:** 01942 761024
Email: news@wish-fm.com
Web site: http://www.wishfm.net
News Editor: Lauren Moss

102.5 FM RADIO PEMBROKESHIRE 752745
14 Old School Estate, Station Road, NARBERTH, SA67 7DU
Tel: 01834 861071 **Fax:** 01834 861524
Email: news@radiopembrokeshire.com
Web site: http://www.radiopembrokeshire.com
News Editor: Sara Andrew

102.5 THE 'BRIDGE   1840063
PO Box 3968, STOURBRIDGE, DY8 5WR **Tel:** 01384 378537
Email: info@thebridgeradio.net
Web site: http://www.thebridgeradio.net
News Editor: Alex Totney

102.7 MERCURY FM   762763
Stanley Centre, Kelvin Way, CRAWLEY, RH10 9SE
Tel: 01293 636030
Email: news@mercuryfm.co.uk
Web site: http://www.mercuryfm.co.uk
News Editor: Cheryl Dennis

102 TOUCH RADIO (STRATFORD)   42510
Unit G3 Holly Farm Business Park, Honiley, KENILWORTH,
CV8 1NP **Tel:** 01926 485630
Email: stratford.newsroom@cnradio.co.uk
Web site: http://www.102touchradio.co.uk
News Editor: Nick Jewers; **Managing Director:** Chris
Arnold

103.6 FM TAMESIDE RADIO   1832728
Cavendish House, 85 Cavendish Street, ASHTON-UNDER-
LYNE, OL6 7QL **Tel:** 0161 343 8446
Email: news@tamesideradio.com
Web site: http://www.tamesideradio.com
News Editor: Gill Garston; **Managing Director:** Simon
Walker

104.9 IMAGINE FM   42504
1st Floor, Regent House, Heaton Lane, STOCKPORT, SK4
1BX **Tel:** 0161 609 1425
Email: news@imaginefm.net
Web site: http://www.imaginefm.net
News Editor: Helen Gray

106.1 ROCK RADIO   1840067
Laser House, Waterfront Quay, Salford Quays, SALFORD,
M50 3XW **Tel:** 0161 886 8800
Email: joe.radcliffe@rockradio.co.uk
Web site: http://www.rockradiomanchester.co.uk
News Editor: Malcolm Packer; **Managing Director:** Andy
Carter

106.3 BRIDGE FM   629433
Newby House, Neath Abbey Business Park, Neath Abbey,
NEATH, SA10 7DR **Tel:** 0845 890 4000 **Fax:** 0845 890 5000
Email: news@bridge.fm
Web site: http://www.bridge.fm
News Editor: News Desk

106 JACK FM   1813666
270 Woodstock Road, OXFORD, OX2 7NW
Tel: 01865 315987 **Fax:** 0870 220 7626
Email: news@jackfm.co.uk
Web site: http://www.jackfm.co.uk
News Editor: Greg Burke

107.1 RUGBY FM   718213
Unit G3, Holly Farm Business Park, Honiley, KENILWORTH,
CV8 1NP **Tel:** 01926 485630 **Fax:** 01926 485678
Email: rugby.newsroom@cnradio.co.uk
Web site: http://www.rugbyfm.co.uk
News Editor: Nick Jewers

107.2 THE WYRE   1666059
Foley House, Stourport Road, KIDDERMINSTER, DY11 7BW
Tel: 01562 641072 **Fax:** 01562 641073
Email: dj@thewyre.com
Web site: http://www.thewyre.com
News Editor: Dani Wozencroft

107.2 WIRE FM   42523
Warrington Business Park, Long Lane, WARRINGTON, WA2
8TX **Tel:** 01925 445545 **Fax:** 01925 431040
Email: news@wirefm.com
Web site: http://www.wirefm.com
News Editor: Louisa King

107.3 TOUCH RADIO   1836260
G3 Holly Farm Business Park, Honiley, KENILWORTH, CV8
1NP **Tel:** 01926 485630
Email: warwick.newsroom@cnradio.co.uk
Web site: http://www.1073touchradio.co.uk
News Editor: Nick Jewers

107.4 THE QUAY   42482
PO Box 1074, PORTSMOUTH, PO2 8YG **Tel:** 023 9236 4161
Fax: 023 9298 8633
Email: news@quayradio.com
Web site: http://www.quayradio.com
News Editor: News Desk

107.5 SOVEREIGN RADIO   42384
14 St. Mary's Walk, HAILSHAM, BN27 1AF
Tel: 01323 442700 **Fax:** 01323 442866
Email: news@1075sovereignradio.co.uk
Web site: http://www.sovereignradio.co.uk
News Editor: Saffron Swansborough

107.6 JUICE FM   42414
27 Fleet Street, LIVERPOOL, L1 4AR **Tel:** 0151 707 3107
Fax: 0151 707 3109
Email: news@juiceliverpool.com
Web site: http://www.juicefm.com
News Editor: Iain Fowler

107.6 KESTREL FM   42320
Suite Two, Paddington House, Festival Place,
BASINGSTOKE, RG21 7LJ **Tel:** 01256 694000
Fax: 01256 694133
Email: news@kestrelfm.com
Web site: http://www.kestrelfm.com
News Editor: Anna Baker

107.7 SPLASH FM   767516
Guildbourne Centre, WORTHING, BN11 1LZ
Tel: 01903 233005 **Fax:** 01903 233271
Email: news@splashfm.com
Web site: http://www.splashfm.com
News Editor: Lorraine White

107.7 THE WOLF   42527
2nd Floor, Mander House, WOLVERHAMPTON, WV1 3NB
Tel: 01902 571072 **Fax:** 01902 571079
Email: news@thewolf.co.uk
Web site: http://www.thewolf.co.uk
News Editor: News Desk

107.8 ARROW FM   42388
Priory Meadow Centre, HASTINGS, TN34 1PJ
Tel: 01424 461177 **Fax:** 01424 422662
Email: news@arrowfm.co.uk
Web site: http://www.arrowfm.co.uk
News Editor: Danielle Couchman

107.8 RADIO JACKIE   42402
110-112 Tolworth Broadway, SURBITON, KT6 7JD
Tel: 020 8288 1300 **Fax:** 020 8288 1312
Email: news@radiojackie.com
Web site: http://www.radiojackie.com
News Editor: Rod Bradbury

107 THE BEE
1697484
107 The Bee, 8 Dalton Road, DARWEN, BB3 0DG
Tel: 01254 778000 **Fax:** 01254 778001
Email: news@thebee.co.uk
Web site: http://www.thebee.co.uk
News Editor: Gina Millson

209RADIO
1839669
Citylife House, Sturton Street, CAMBRIDGE, CB1 2QF
Tel: 01223 488418 **Fax:** 01223 488419
Email: newsdesk@209radio.co.uk
Web site: http://www.209radio.co.uk
News Editor: Louise Hawes

2BR
622661
Unit 159, Lomeshaye Business Village, Turner Road,
NELSON, BB9 7DR **Tel:** 01282 677107 **Fax:** 01282 690001
Email: news@2br.co.uk
Web site: http://www.2br.co.uk
News Editor: Peter Mabb

3FM
1749433
45 Victoria Street, Douglas, ISLE OF MAN, IM1 3RS
Tel: 01624 616333 **Fax:** 01624 614333
Email: news@three.fm
Web site: http://www.three.fm
News Editor: Kelly Foran; **Managing Director:** Max Hailey

3TR FM
749624
Riverside Studios, WARMINSTER, BA12 9HQ
Tel: 01985 211111 **Fax:** 01985 211110
Email: news@3trfm.com
Web site: http://www.3trfm.com
News Editor: Jonathan Fido

7 WAVES COMMUNITY RADIO
1834593
Leasowe Community Centre, Twickenham Drive, Leasowe,
WIRRAL, CH46 1PF **Tel:** 0151 637 3790
Email: info@7waves.co.uk
Web site: http://www.7waves.co.uk
News Editor: Pauline Murphy

92.5 CHESHIRE FM
1808696
The Verdin Exchange, High Street, WINSFORD, CW7 2AN
Tel: 01606 555910
Email: garry.fuller@cheshirefm.com
Web site: http://www.cheshirefm.com
News Editor: Garry Fuller

95.8 CAPITAL FM
42420
30 Leicester Square, LONDON, WC2H 7LA
Tel: 020 7766 6000 **Fax:** 020 7766 6100
Email: jo.parkerson@lbc.co.uk
Web site: http://www.capitalradio.com
News Editor: News Desk
Twitter: http://twitter.com/958capitalfm.

96.3 RADIO AIRE
42404
51 Burley Road, LEEDS, LS3 1LR **Tel:** 0113 283 5500
Fax: 0113 283 5601
Email: news@radioaire.com
Web site: http://www.radioaire.co.uk
News Editor: Alice Bailey; **Managing Director:** Tracey
Eastwood

96.3 ROCK RADIO
42571
PO Box 101, Parkway Court, Glasgow Business Park,
GLASGOW, G69 6GA **Tel:** 0141 781 2206
Fax: 0141 781 1112
Email: news@rockradio.co.uk
Web site: http://www.rockradio.co.uk
News Editor: Heather Kane

96.4 EAGLE RADIO
42381
Dolphin House, North Street, GUILDFORD, GU1 4AA
Tel: 01483 468701 **Fax:** 01483 531612
Email: news@964eagle.co.uk
Web site: http://www.964eagle.co.uk
News Editor: Saffron Da Silva; **Managing Director:** Paul
Marcus

96.4 FM THE WAVE
42546
PO Box 964, Victoria Road, Gowerton, SWANSEA, SA4 3AB
Tel: 01792 511964 **Fax:** 01792 511964
Email: news@thewave.co.uk
Web site: http://www.thewave.co.uk
News Editor: Emma Grant

96.4FM-BRMB
42324
9 Brindley Place, 4 Oozells Square, BIRMINGHAM, B1 2DJ
Tel: 0121 566 5200 **Fax:** 0121 566 5429
Email: news@brmb.co.uk
Web site: http://www.brmb.co.uk
News Editor: Louise Easton

96.9 VIKING FM
42393
The Boat House, Commercial Road, HULL, HU1 2SG
Tel: 01482 320903 **Fax:** 01482 217703
Email: newsdesk@vikingfm.co.uk
Web site: http://www.vikingfm.co.uk
News Editor: News Desk

97.2 STRAY FM
42386
The Hamlet, Hornbeam Park, HARROGATE, HG2 8RE
Tel: 01423 522972 **Fax:** 01423 522922
Email: news@strayfm.com
Web site: http://www.strayfm.com
News Editor: Patrick Dunlop

97.4 ROCK FM
42483
PO Box 974, St. Paul's Square, PRESTON, PR1 1YE
Tel: 01772 477700 **Fax:** 01772 477701
Email: news@rockfm.co.uk
Web site: http://www.rockfm.co.uk
News Editor: Claire Hannah

99.9 RADIO NORWICH
1753137
Stanton House, 29 Yarmouth Road, NORWICH, NR7 0EE
Tel: 0845 365 8999 **Fax:** 0845 365 7999
Email: news@999radionorwich.com
Web site: http://www.999radionorwich.com
News Editor: Jen Dale; **Managing Director:** Gina Frost

ABSOLUTE CLASSIC ROCK
1667452
1 Golden Square, LONDON, W1F 9DJ **Tel:** 020 7434 1215
Fax: 020 7434 1197
Email: cat.macdonald@absoluteradio.co.uk
Web site: http://www.absoluteclassicrock.co.uk
News Editor: Cat MacDonald
Twitter: http://twitter.com/AbsoluteClassic.

ABSOLUTE XTREME
1697028
1 Golden Square, LONDON, W1F 9DJ **Tel:** 020 7434 1215
Email: david.lambert@absoluteradio.co.uk
Web site: http://www.absolutextreme.co.uk
News Editor: David Lambert
Twitter: http://twitter.com/AbsoluteXtreme.

AFAN FM
1826361
Aquadrome, Afan Lido, Princess Margaret Way, PORT
TALBOT, SA12 6QW **Tel:** 0845 467 1079
Email: studio@afanfm.co.uk
Web site: http://www.afanfm.co.uk
News Editor: Hannah Lewis

ALL FM
1646102
19 Albert Road, MANCHESTER, M19 2EQ
Tel: 0161 248 6888
Email: info@allfm.org
Web site: http://www.allfm.org
News Editor: Gavin White

ALPHA RADIO
42364
Radio House, 11 Woodland Road, DARLINGTON, DL3 7BJ
Tel: 01325 255550 **Fax:** 01325 255551
Email: news@alpharadio.co.uk
Web site: http://www.alpha1032.com
News Editor: Sarah Dobson

ANDOVER SOUND
1840531
The Andover Studios, 3 Eastgate House, East Street,
ANDOVER, SP10 1EP **Tel:** 01264 336000
Fax: 01264 366888
Email: news@andoversound.com
Web site: http://www.andoversound.com
News Editor: Ben McGrail; **Managing Director:** Ian Axton

ANGEL RADIO
1665266
56 Love Lane, COWES, PO31 7EU **Tel:** 01983 246810
Web site: http://angelradioisleofwight.moonfruit.com
News Editor: Chris Gutteridge

ARGYLL FM
601326
27-29 Longrow, CAMPBELTOWN, PA28 6ER
Tel: 01586 551800
Email: studio@argyllfm.co.uk
Web site: http://www.argyllfm.co.uk
News Editor: Iain Henderson

THE ARROW
1647015
1 The Square, 111 Broad Street, BIRMINGHAM, B15 1AS
Tel: 020 7314 7301
Web site: http://www.thearrow.co.uk
News Editor: Programme Director

ASIAN SOUND RADIO LTD
42448
42 Southall Street, MANCHESTER, M3 1LG
Tel: 0161 288 1000 **Fax:** 0161 288 9000
Email: news@asiansoundradio.co.uk
Web site: http://www.asiansoundradio.co.uk
News Editor: News Desk; **Managing Director:** Shujat Ali

ATLANTIC FM
1749922
10 Wheal Kitty Workshops, ST. AGNES, TR5 0RD
Tel: 01872 553400 **Fax:** 01872 554244
Email: news@atlantic.fm
Web site: http://www.atlantic.fm
News Editor: News Desk

AWAZ FM
763812
Craig House, 64 Darnley Street, GLASGOW, G41 2SE
Tel: 0141 420 6666
Email: javed@awazfm.co.uk
Web site: http://www.awazfm.co.uk
News Editor: Ali Malik; **Advertising Manager:** Ali Malik

BANBURY SOUND
1732403
9A Manor Park, Wildmere Industrial Estate, BANBURY,
OX16 3TB **Tel:** 01295 661070
Email: banbury.newsroom@cnradio.co.uk
Web site: http://www.www.banburysound.co.uk
News Editor: Rachel Brabbins

BANG RADIO
1837520
2nd Floor, 89-93 High Street, LONDON, NW10 4NX
Tel: 020 8963 9560 **Fax:** 020 8963 9561
Email: info@bangradio.fm
Web site: http://www.bangradio.fm
News Editor: Gabriella Incalza

BATH FM
601047
Station House, Ashley Avenue, Lower Weston, BATH, BA1
3DS **Tel:** 01225 471571
Email: news@bathfm.com
Web site: http://www.bathfm.com
News Editor: News Editor

THE BAY
42403
PO Box 969, St. Georges Quay, LANCASTER, LA1 3LD
Tel: 01524 848747
Email: baynews@cnradio.co.uk
Web site: http://www.thebay.co.uk
News Editor: Peter Storry

BAY RADIO
1833920
Newby House, Neath Abbey Business Park, Neath Abbey,
NEATH, SA10 7DR **Tel:** 0845 890 2000
Email: news@swanseabayradio.com
Web site: http://www.swanseabayradio.com
News Editor: Sara Andrew

BBC COVENTRY AND WARWICKSHIRE
42358
Priory Place, COVENTRY, CV1 5SQ **Tel:** 024 7655 1000
Fax: 024 7655 2000
Email: coventry.warwickshire@bbc.co.uk
Web site: http://www.bbc.co.uk/coventry
News Editor: Sue Curtis; **Managing Editor:** David Clargo

UK Broadcasting & Other Media

BBC ESSEX 42352
198 New London Road, CHELMSFORD, CM2 9XB
Tel: 01245 616066 **Fax:** 01245 492983
Email: essex@bbc.co.uk
Web site: http://www.bbc.co.uk/essex
Editor: Gerald Main; **News Editor:** Alison Hodgkins-Brown

BBC GUERNSEY 42588
Broadcasting House, Bulwer Avenue, St. Sampson,
GUERNSEY, GY2 4LA **Tel:** 01481 200600
Fax: 01481 200361
Email: bbcguernsey@bbc.co.uk
Web site: http://www.bbc.co.uk/guernsey
News Editor: News Desk; **Managing Editor:** Robert
Wallace

BBC HEREFORD & WORCESTER 42530
Hylton Road, WORCESTER, WR2 5WW **Tel:** 01905 748485
Fax: 01905 748006
Email: bbchw@bbc.co.uk
Web site: http://www.bbc.co.uk/herefordworcester
News Editor: Joe Baldwin; **Managing Editor:** James Coghill

BBC HEREFORD & WORCESTER (HEREFORD) 1639025
Hylton Road, WORCESTER, WR2 5WW **Tel:** 01905 337221
Fax: 01905 748006
Email: bbchw@bbc.co.uk
Web site: http://www.bbc.co.uk/worcester
News Editor: Joe Baldwin

BBC LONDON 94.9 42424
PO Box 94.9, 35 Marylebone High Street, LONDON, W1U
4QA **Tel:** 020 7224 2424 **Fax:** 020 7486 2442
Email: ldn-planning@bbc.co.uk
Web site: http://www.bbc.co.uk/london
News Editor: Forward Planning Desk

BBC NEWCASTLE 42460
Broadcasting Centre, Barrack Road, NEWCASTLE UPON
TYNE, NE99 1RN **Tel:** 0191 232 4141 **Fax:** 0191 221 0796
Email: radionewcastle.news@bbc.co.uk
Web site: http://www.bbc.co.uk/england/radionewcastle
News Editor: Rik Martin; **Managing Editor:** Andrew Robson

BBC RADIO BERKSHIRE 628856
Peppard Road, Caversham Park, READING, RG4 8FH
Tel: 0118 946 4200 **Fax:** 0118 946 4555
Email: radio.berkshire.news@bbc.co.uk
Web site: http://www.bbc.co.uk/radioberkshire
News Editor: News Desk

BBC RADIO BRISTOL 42339
PO Box 194, BRISTOL, BS99 7QT **Tel:** 0117 974 1111
Fax: 0117 923 8323
Email: radio.bristol@bbc.co.uk
Web site: http://www.bbc.co.uk/bristol
News Editor: Charlotte Callen; **Managing Editor:** Tim
Pemberton

BBC RADIO CAMBRIDGESHIRE 42344
104 Hills Road, CAMBRIDGE, CB2 1LQ **Tel:** 01223 259696
Fax: 01223 460832
Email: cambs@bbc.co.uk
Web site: http://www.bbc.co.uk/cambridgeshire
News Editor: Andy Burrows; **Managing Editor:** Jason
Horton

BBC RADIO CAMBRIDGESHIRE (PETERBOROUGH) 42476
Kings Chambers, Priestgate, PETERBOROUGH, PE1 1FG
Tel: 01733 312832 **Fax:** 01733 343768
Email: peterborough@bbc.co.uk
Web site: http://www.bbc.co.uk/cambridgeshire
News Editor: Steve Titman; **Managing Editor:** Jason
Horton

BBC RADIO CORNWALL 42522
Phoenix Wharf, TRURO, TR1 1UA **Tel:** 01872 275421
Fax: 01872 240679
Email: radio.cornwall@bbc.co.uk
Web site: http://www.bbc.co.uk/cornwall
News Editor: News Desk; **Managing Editor:** Pauline
Causey

BBC RADIO CUMBRIA 42348
Annetwell Street, CARLISLE, CA3 8BB **Tel:** 01228 592444
Fax: 01228 511195
Email: radio.cumbria@bbc.co.uk
Web site: http://www.bbc.co.uk/radiocumbria
Editor: Nigel Dyson; **News Editor:** Nigel Thompson

BBC RADIO CUMBRIA (FURNESS) 42319
Broadcasting House, Hartington Street, BARROW-IN-
FURNESS, LA14 5SL **Tel:** 01229 835252 **Fax:** 01229 870008
Email: radio.cumbria@bbc.co.uk
Web site: http://www.bbc.co.uk/cumbria
News Editor: John Bowness

BBC RADIO CYMRU (CARDIFF) 42539
Broadcasting House, Llantrisant Road, Llandaff, CARDIFF,
CF5 2YQ **Tel:** 029 2032 2787 **Fax:** 029 2055 5960
Email: newsgathering.wales@bbc.co.uk
Web site: http://www.bbc.co.uk/radiocymru
News Editor: News Desk

BBC RADIO DERBY 42365
PO Box 104.5, DERBY, DE1 3HL **Tel:** 01332 375044
Fax: 01332 290794
Email: radio.derby@bbc.co.uk
Web site: http://www.bbc.co.uk/derby
News Editor: Lisa Hay; **Managing Editor:** Simon Read

BBC RADIO DEVON (EXETER) 42371
Broadcasting House, PO Box 1034, EXETER, EX4 4DB
Tel: 01752 234511 **Fax:** 01392 424575
Email: radio.devon@bbc.co.uk
Web site: http://www.bbc.co.uk/devon
News Editor: Lidia Pearce; **Managing Editor:** Simon Read

BBC RADIO DEVON (PLYMOUTH) 42479
Broadcasting House, Seymour Road, Mannamead,
PLYMOUTH, PL3 5YQ **Tel:** 01752 234511
Fax: 01752 234595
Email: radio.devon@bbc.co.uk
Web site: http://www.bbc.co.uk/devon
News Editor: Lisa Hay; **Managing Editor:** Simon Read

BBC RADIO FOYLE 42584
8 Northland Road, LONDONDERRY, BT48 7GD
Tel: 028 7137 8678 **Fax:** 028 7137 8638
Email: foyle.newsroom@bbc.co.uk
Web site: http://www.bbc.co.uk/northernireland/radiofoyle

BBC RADIO GLOUCESTERSHIRE 42379
London Road, GLOUCESTER, GL1 1SW **Tel:** 01452 308585
Fax: 01452 309491
Email: radio.gloucestershire@bbc.co.uk
Web site: http://www.bbc.co.uk/gloucestershire
News Editor: Graham Day; **Managing Director:** Mark
Hurrell

BBC RADIO HUMBERSIDE 42394
Queen's Court, Queen's Gardens, HULL, HU1 3RH
Tel: 01482 323232 **Fax:** 01482 226409
Email: humberside.news@bbc.co.uk
Web site: http://www.bbc.co.uk/humberside
News Editor: Kate Slade; **Managing Editor:** Simon Pattern

BBC RADIO JERSEY 42589
18 and 21 Parade Road, St. Helier, JERSEY, JE2 3PL
Tel: 01534 870000 **Fax:** 01534 732569
Email: jersey@bbc.co.uk
Web site: http://www.bbc.co.uk/england/radiojersey
Editor: Denzil Dudley; **News Editor:** Matthew Price

BBC RADIO KENT 42350
The Great Hall, Mount Pleasant, TUNBRIDGE WELLS, TN1
1QQ **Tel:** 01892 670000
Email: radio.kent.news@bbc.co.uk
Web site: http://www.bbc.co.uk/kent
News Editor: Alex Bish; **Managing Editor:** Paul Leaper

BBC RADIO LANCASHIRE 42329
Darwen Street, BLACKBURN, BB2 2EA **Tel:** 01254 841001
Fax: 01254 680821
Email: lancsnews@bbc.co.uk
Web site: http://www.bbc.co.uk/lancashire
News Editor: Chris Rider; **Managing Editor:** John Clayton

BBC RADIO LEEDS 42405
Broadcasting Centre, 2 St. Peters Square, LEEDS, LS9 8AH
Tel: 0113 244 2131 **Fax:** 0113 224 7316
Email: radio.leeds@bbc.co.uk
Web site: http://www.bbc.co.uk/radioleeds
Editor: Rozina Breen; **News Editor:** Andy Evans; **Managing
Editor:** Mike Bettison

BBC RADIO LEICESTER 42410
9 St. Nicholas Place, LEICESTER, LE1 5LB
Tel: 0116 201 6660 **Fax:** 0116 251 1463
Email: radio.leicesternews@bbc.co.uk
Web site: http://www.bbc.co.uk/leicester
News Editor: Lucy Collins; **Managing Editor:** Kate Squire

BBC RADIO LINCOLNSHIRE 42412
Newport, LINCOLN, LN1 3XY **Tel:** 01522 511411
Fax: 01522 511058
Email: radio.lincolnshire@bbc.co.uk
Web site: http://www.bbc.co.uk/lincolnshire
News Editor: News Desk; **Managing Editor:** Charlie
Partridge

BBC RADIO MANCHESTER 42449
New Broadcasting House, PO Box 951, Oxford Road,
MANCHESTER, M60 1SD **Tel:** 0161 200 2000
Fax: 0161 236 5804
Email: radio.manchester@bbc.co.uk
Web site: http://www.bbc.co.uk/manchester/local_radio
News Editor: Mark Elliott; **Managing Editor:** John Ryan

BBC RADIO MERSEYSIDE 42415
PO Box 95.8, LIVERPOOL, L69 1ZJ **Tel:** 0151 708 6161
Fax: 0151 794 0909
Email: radio.merseyside.news@bbc.co.uk
Web site: http://www.bbc.co.uk/liverpool
News Editor: Liz Hughes; **Managing Editor:** Mick Ord

BBC RADIO NAN GAIDHEAL 26487
Rosebank, Church Street, STORNOWAY, HS1 2LS
Tel: 01851 705000 **Fax:** 01851 704633
Web site: http://www.bbc.co.uk/scotland/alba/radio
Editor: Marion MacKinnon; **News Editor:** News Desk

BBC RADIO NORFOLK 42466
The Forum, Millennium Plain, NORWICH, NR2 1BH
Tel: 01603 617411 **Fax:** 01603 284488
Email: radionorfolknews@bbc.co.uk
Web site: http://www.bbc.co.uk/norfolk
News Editor: Nicky Barnes; **Managing Editor:** David
Clayton

BBC RADIO NORTHAMPTON 42464
Broadcasting House, Abington Street, NORTHAMPTON,
NN1 2BH **Tel:** 01604 239100 **Fax:** 01604 230709
Email: mark.whall@bbc.co.uk
Web site: http://www.bbc.co.uk/radionorthampton
News Editor: Mark Whall

BBC RADIO NOTTINGHAM 42470
BBC Centre, London Road, NOTTINGHAM, NG2 4UU
Tel: 0115 955 0500 **Fax:** 0115 902 1983
Email: radio.nottingham@bbc.co.uk
Web site: http://www.bbc.co.uk/nottingham
News Editor: Aeneas Rotsos

BBC RADIO OXFORD 42474
269 Banbury Road, OXFORD, OX2 7DW **Tel:** 0845 931 1444
Fax: 0845 931 1555
Email: oxford@bbc.co.uk
Web site: http://www.bbc.co.uk/oxford
News Editor: Mike Day; **Executive Editor:** Steve Taschini

BBC RADIO SCOTLAND (ABERDEEN) 42551
Beechgrove Terrace, Beechgrove House, ABERDEEN, AB15
5ZT **Tel:** 01224 384888 **Fax:** 01224 384899
Email: news.aberdeen@bbc.co.uk
Web site: http://www.bbc.co.uk/scotland/radioscotland
News Editor: Sandy Bremner

BBC RADIO SCOTLAND (DUMFRIES) 42555
Elmbank, Lover's Walk, DUMFRIES, DG1 1NZ
Tel: 01387 268008
Email: dumfries@bbc.co.uk
Web site: http://www.bbc.co.uk/scotland/radioscotland
News Editor: Willie Johnston

BBC RADIO SCOTLAND (GLASGOW - HEAD OFFICE)
42562
40 Pacific Quay, GLASGOW, G51 1DA **Tel:** 0141 422 7000
Web site: http://www.bbc.co.uk/radioscotland
News Editor: Planning Desk
Twitter: http://twitter.com/bbcscotland.

BBC RADIO SCOTLAND (INVERNESS)
42565
Broadcasting House, 7 Culduthel Road, INVERNESS, IV2
4AD **Tel:** 01463 720720
Email: inverness.news@bbc.co.uk
Web site: http://www.bbc.co.uk/scotland/radioscotland
News Editor: Craig Swan

BBC RADIO SCOTLAND (ORKNEY)
42570
Castle Street, KIRKWALL, KW15 1DF **Tel:** 01856 873939
Fax: 01856 872908
Email: radio.orkney@bbc.co.uk
Web site: http://www.bbc.co.uk/scotland/radioscotland
News Editor: Dave Gray

BBC RADIO SCOTLAND (SELKIRK)
42574
Unit 001, Ettrick Riverside, Dunsdale Road, SELKIRK, TD7
5EB **Tel:** 01750 724567 **Fax:** 01750 724555
Email: selkirk.news@bbc.co.uk
Web site: http://www.bbc.co.uk/scotland/radioscotland
News Editor: Cameron Buttle

BBC RADIO SCOTLAND (SHETLAND)
42576
Pitt Lane, LERWICK, ZE1 0DW **Tel:** 01595 694747
Fax: 01595 694307
Email: radio.shetland@bbc.co.uk
Web site: http://www.bbc.co.uk/scotland/radioscotland
News Editor: John Johnston

BBC RADIO SHEFFIELD
42493
54 Shoreham Street, SHEFFIELD, S1 4RS
Tel: 0114 267 5440 **Fax:** 0114 267 5454
Email: radio.sheffield@bbc.co.uk
Web site: http://www.bbc.co.uk/southyorkshire
News Editor: News Desk; **Managing Editor:** Gary Keown

BBC RADIO SHROPSHIRE
42496
PO Box 96, SHREWSBURY, SY1 3WW **Tel:** 01743 237008
Fax: 01743 271702
Email: radio.shropshire@bbc.co.uk
Web site: http://www.bbc.co.uk/shropshire
News Editor: Sharon Simcock; **Managing Editor:** Tim
Beech

BBC RADIO STOKE
42507
Cheapside, Hanley, STOKE-ON-TRENT, ST1 1JJ
Tel: 01782 208080 **Fax:** 01782 289115
Email: radio.stoke@bbc.co.uk
Web site: http://www.bbc.co.uk/stoke/radiostoke
News Editor: Joel Moors; **Managing Editor:** Sue Owen

BBC RADIO SUFFOLK
42396
Broadcasting House, St. Matthews Street, IPSWICH, IP1
3EP **Tel:** 01473 250000 **Fax:** 01473 210887
Email: radiosuffolk@bbc.co.uk
Web site: http://www.bbc.co.uk/suffolk
News Editor: Lis Henderson; **Managing Editor:** Peter Cook

BBC RADIO SWINDON
1605077
Broadcasting House, Prospect Place, SWINDON, SN1 3RW
Tel: 01793 513626
Email: radio.swindon@bbc.co.uk
Web site: http://www.bbc.co.uk/england/radioswindon
News Editor: Jillian Moody

BBC RADIO ULSTER
42579
Broadcasting House, Ormeau Avenue, BELFAST, BT2 8HQ
Tel: 028 9033 8000 **Fax:** 028 9033 8806
Email: ni_news@bbc.co.uk
Web site: http://www.bbc.co.uk/northernireland/radioulster
News Editor: Kathleen Carragher
Twitter: http://twitter.com/bbcnireland.

BBC RADIO WALES
42540
Broadcasting House, Llantrisant Road, Llandaff, CARDIFF,
CF5 2YQ **Tel:** 029 2032 2000
Email: newsgathering.wales@bbc.co.uk
Web site: http://www.bbc.co.uk/wales/radiowales
Editor: Ruth Sully; **News Editor:** News Gathering
Twitter: http://twitter.com/bbcwales.

BBC RADIO WILTSHIRE
42514
Broadcasting House, Prospect Place, SWINDON, SN1 3RW
Tel: 01793 513626
Email: radio.wiltshire@bbc.co.uk
Web site: http://www.bbc.co.uk/wiltshire
News Editor: Kirsty Ward; **Managing Editor:** Rose Aston

BBC RADIO YORK
42534
20 Bootham Row, YORK, YO30 7BR **Tel:** 01904 622033
Fax: 01904 610937
Email: northyorkshire.news@bbc.co.uk
Web site: http://www.bbc.co.uk/york
News Editor: Nicola Lawrence; **Managing Editor:** Sarah
Drummond

BBC RADIO YORK (SCARBOROUGH)
1667500
Londesborough Lodge, The Crescent, SCARBOROUGH,
YO11 2PW **Tel:** 01723 352686 **Fax:** 01723 378614
Email: northyorkshirenews@bbc.co.uk
Web site: http://www.bbc.co.uk/northyorkshire
News Editor: Fay Yeomans

BBC SOLENT 96.1 FM (SOUTHAMPTON)
42499
Broadcasting House, 10 Havelock Road, SOUTHAMPTON,
SO14 7PU **Tel:** 023 8063 2811 **Fax:** 023 8033 9648
Email: radio.solent.news@bbc.co.uk
Web site: http://www.bbc.co.uk/radiosolent
News Editor: News Desk; **Managing Editor:** Chris Carnegy

BBC SOMERSET 95.5FM
42518
Broadcasting House, Park Street, TAUNTON, TA1 4DA
Tel: 01823 323956 **Fax:** 01823 332539
Email: somerset@bbc.co.uk
Web site: http://www.bbc.co.uk/somerset
Editor: Jess Rudkin; **News Editor:** News Editor

BBC SURREY
42382
Broadcasting Centre, GUILDFORD, GU2 7AP
Tel: 01483 734312 **Fax:** 01483 304952
Email: surrey@bbc.co.uk
Web site: http://www.bbc.co.uk/surrey
News Editor: Mark Carter

BBC SUSSEX
1898719
Broadcasting House, Queens Road, BRIGHTON, BN1 3XB
Tel: 01273 320400
Email: sussex@bbc.co.uk
Web site: http://www.bbc.co.uk/sussex
News Editor: Angus Moorat

BBC TEES
42457
PO Box 95FM, Broadcasting House, Newport Road,
MIDDLESBROUGH, TS1 5DG **Tel:** 01642 225211
Fax: 01642 211356
Email: tees.news@bbc.co.uk
Web site: http://www.bbc.co.uk/tees
Editor: Matthew Barraclough; **News Editor:** Angela
Johnston

BBC THREE COUNTIES RADIO
42445
Three Counties Radio, 1 Hastings Street, LUTON, LU1 5XL
Tel: 01582 637400 **Fax:** 01582 401467
Email: 3cr.news@bbc.co.uk
Web site: http://www.bbc.co.uk/england/threecounties
News Editor: News Desk; **Managing Editor:** Mark Norman

BBC WALES (BANGOR)
42537
Bryn Meirion, BANGOR, LL57 2BY **Tel:** 01248 370880
Fax: 01248 354976
Email: newsgathering.wales@bbc.co.uk
Web site: http://www.bbc.co.uk/wales/radiowales
News Editor: Bethan Williams

BBC WALES (WREXHAM)
42548
Library and Arts Centre, Rhosddu Road, WREXHAM, LL11
1AU **Tel:** 01978 221100 **Fax:** 01978 221102
Email: newsgathering.wales@bbc.co.uk
Web site: http://www.bbc.co.uk
News Editor: Cath Steward

BBC WM (BIRMINGHAM)
42325
The Mailbox, BIRMINGHAM, B1 1AY **Tel:** 0121 567 6000
Fax: 0121 567 6025
Email: bbcwm@bbc.co.uk
Web site: http://www.bbc.co.uk/birmingham/local_radio
News Editor: Jeremy Pollock; **Managing Editor:** Keith
Beech

BCB 106.6 FM
761394
11 Rawson Road, BRADFORD, BD1 3SH **Tel:** 01274 771677
Fax: 01274 771680
Email: news@bcbradio.co.uk
Web site: http://www.bcbradio.co.uk
Editor: Laura Rawlings; **News Editor:** Laura Rawlings

THE BEACH
42444
Radio House, 10 Oulton Road, LOWESTOFT, NR32 4QP
Tel: 0845 345 1035 **Fax:** 0845 345 1036
Email: news@thebeach.co.uk
Web site: http://www.thebeach.co.uk
News Editor: Ross Hutchinson; **Managing Director:** David
Blake

BEACON RADIO
42528
267 Tettenhall Road, WOLVERHAMPTON, WV6 0DE
Tel: 01902 461260 **Fax:** 01902 461266
Email: news@beaconradio.co.uk
Web site: http://www.beaconradio.co.uk
News Editor: Louise Easton

BELFAST CITY BEAT
42580
2nd Floor, Arena Building, Ormeau Road, BELFAST, BT7
1SH **Tel:** 028 9089 0140 **Fax:** 028 9089 0101
Email: newsdesk@citybeat.co.uk
Web site: http://www.citybeat.co.uk
News Editor: Barry Weir

BLACK DIAMOND 107.8 FM
1840758
67 Gardiner Place, NEWTONGRANGE, EH22 4RT
Tel: 0131 663 4811
Email: presenters@blackdiamondfm.com
Web site: http://www.blackdiamondfm.com
News Editor: John Ritchie

BLYTH VALLEY RADIO
1912252
The Bunker, Saint Felix School, Halesworth Road,
SOUTHWOLD, IP18 6SD **Tel:** 01502 723900
Email: studio@bvcr.co.uk
Web site: http://www.blythvalleycommunityradio.co.uk
News Editor: Amanda Humphry

BRANCH FM
1839629
17 Halifax Road, DEWSBURY, WF13 2JH **Tel:** 01924 465600
Email: studio@branchfm.co.uk
Web site: http://www.branchfm.co.uk
News Editor: Steve Hodgson

BRIGHT 106.4
707524
Unit 34, Market Place Shopping Centre, BURGESS HILL,
RH15 9NP **Tel:** 01444 248127 **Fax:** 01444 248553
Email: news@bright1064.com
Web site: http://www.bright1064.com
News Editor: Philip Keeler; **Managing Director:** Allan
Mould

BRISTOL COMMUNITY FM
1810696
The Beacon Centre, City Academy Bristol, Russell Town
Avenue, BRISTOL, BS5 9JH **Tel:** 05601 126659
Email: info@bcfm.org.uk
Web site: http://www.bcfm.org.uk
News Editor: Phil Gibbons

BRUNEL FM
1777096
Unit 4, Shrivenham Hundred Business Park, Majors Road,
Watchfield, SWINDON, SN6 8TZ **Tel:** 01793 784267
Email: news@brunelfm.com
Web site: http://www.brunelfm.com
News Editor: News Desk

UK Broadcasting & Other Media

Section 9 UK Broadcasting

CABLE RADIO MILTON KEYNES 42458
14 Vincent Avenue, Crownhill, MILTON KEYNES, MK8 0AB
Tel: 01908 265266
Web site: http://www.crmk.co.uk
News Editor: Mike Barry; **Managing Director:** Mike Barry

CALON FM 1839890
Mold Road, WREXHAM, LL11 2AW **Tel:** 01978 293393
Email: info@calonfm.com
Web site: http://www.calonfm.com
News Editor: Mike Wright

CENTRAL FM 42578
201-203 High Street, FALKIRK, FK1 1DU **Tel:** 01324 611164
Fax: 01324 611168
Email: news@centralfm.co.uk
Web site: http://www.centralfm.co.uk
News Editor: Tadek Kopszywa

CENTRAL RADIO 1858706
9-10 Eastway Business Village, Olivers Place, Fulwood,
PRESTON, PR2 9WT **Tel:** 01772 708001 **Fax:** 01772 708002
Email: news@centralradio.fm
Web site: http://www.centralradio.fm

CFM 42349
PO Box 964, CARLISLE, CA1 3NG **Tel:** 01228 810444
Fax: 01228 818444
Email: news@cfmradio.com
Web site: http://www.cfmradio.com
News Editor: Hayley Brewer; **Managing Director:** David
Bain

CHANNEL 103 FM 42590
6 Tunnell Street, St. Helier, JERSEY, JE2 4LU
Tel: 01534 888103 **Fax:** 01534 877177
Email: news@channel103.com
Web site: http://www.channel103.com
News Editor: Giulia Mausolle; **Managing Director:** Linda
Burnham

CHELMSFORD RADIO 42351
Icon Building, Western Esplanade, SOUTHEND-ON-SEA,
SS1 1EE **Tel:** 01702 455349
Email: news@chelmsfordradio.com
Web site: http://www.chelmsfordradio.com
News Editor: Nick Hull

CHESTER'S DEE 106.3 1614810
2 Chantry Court, CHESTER, CH1 4QN **Tel:** 01244 391030
Fax: 01244 391010
Email: news@dee1063.com
Web site: http://www.dee1063.com
News Editor: Jessica Forbes

CHOICE FM 42421
30 Leicester Square, LONDON, WC2H 7LA
Tel: 020 7766 6000 **Fax:** 020 7054 8009
Email: news@choicefm.com
Web site: http://www.choicefm.com
News Editor: Andre Morgan

CITYTALK 105.9 FM 1829345
St. John's Beacon, 1 Houghton Street, LIVERPOOL, L1 1RL
Tel: 0151 472 6800
Email: molly@radiocity.co.uk
Web site: http://www.citytalk.fm
News Editor: Steve Hothersall

CLUB ASIA 963/962 AM 765372
227-247 Gascoigne Road, BARKING, IG11 7LN
Tel: 020 8594 6662 **Fax:** 020 8594 3523
Email: info@clubasiaonline.com
Web site: http://www.clubasiaonline.com
News Editor: Ivor Etienne

CLYDE 1 42563
Clydebank Business Park, CLYDEBANK, G81 2RX
Tel: 0141 565 2345 **Fax:** 0141 565 2265
Email: clydenews@radioclyde.com
Web site: http://www.clyde1.com
News Editor: Lorraine Herbison

CLYDE TWO 601309
Clydebank Business Park, CLYDEBANK, G81 2RX
Tel: 0141 565 2345 **Fax:** 0141 565 2265
Email: clydenews@radioclyde.com
Web site: http://www.clyde2.com
News Editor: Lorraine Herbison

THE COAST 1779869
4th Floor, Roman Landing, Kingsway, SOUTHAMPTON,
SO14 1BN **Tel:** 023 8038 4100 **Fax:** 023 8082 9844
Email: news@thecoast106.com
Web site: http://www.thecoast106.com
Managing Director: Kevin Stewart

COMPASS FM 707997
26A Wellowgate, GRIMSBY, DN32 0RA **Tel:** 01472 346666
Fax: 01472 508811
Email: news@compassfm.co.uk
Web site: http://www.compassfm.co.uk
News Editor: Andy Marsh

CONNECT FM 42400
5 Church Street, PETERBOROUGH, PE1 1XB
Tel: 01733 898106 **Fax:** 01733 898107
Email: news@connectfm.com
Web site: http://www.connectfm.com
News Editor: Carlo Fiorentio

COOL FM 42581
Kiltonga Industrial Estate, NEWTOWNARDS, BT23 4ES
Tel: 028 9181 5211 **Fax:** 028 9181 7878
Email: news@downtown.co.uk
Web site: http://www.coolfm.co.uk
News Editor: Bob Huggins; **Managing Director:** Mark
Mahaffy

COUNTY SOUND RADIO 42383
Dolphin House, North Street, GUILDFORD, GU1 4AA
Tel: 01483 300964 **Fax:** 01483 531612
Email: news@964eagle.co.uk
Web site: http://www.964eagle.co.uk
News Editor: Saffron da Silva; **Managing Director:** Paul
Marcus

CROSS RHYTHMS CITY RADIO 761396
PO Box 1110, STOKE-ON-TRENT, ST1 1XR
Tel: 01782 251000 **Fax:** 01782 219718
Email: radio@crossrhythms.co.uk
Web site: http://www.crossrhythms.co.uk/radio
News Editor: News Desk

CROSS RHYTHMS PLYMOUTH 1839699
PO Box 12, PLYMOUTH, PL3 4WF **Tel:** 01752 225623
Email: info@crossrhythmsplymouth.co.uk
Web site: http://www.crossrhythms.co.uk/plymouth
News Editor: Chris Girdler; **Managing Director:** Ian
Pilkington

CUILLIN FM 765690
Stormyhill Road, PORTREE, IV51 9DY **Tel:** 01478 611797
Email: admin@cuillinfm.co.uk
Web site: http://www.cuillinfm.co.uk
News Editor: Ruth Taylor

DEARNE FM 1606920
Unit 7, Networkcentre, Zenith Park, Whaley Road,
BARNSLEY, S75 1HT **Tel:** 01226 321744 **Fax:** 01226 321755
Email: news@dearnefm.co.uk
Web site: http://www.dearnefm.co.uk
News Editor: May Norman

DELTA RADIO 42317
Tindle House, High Street, BORDON, GU35 0AY
Tel: 01420 473473 **Fax:** 01420 485186
Email: news@deltaradio.co.uk
Web site: http://www.deltaradio.co.uk
News Editor: Jenny Humphreys; **Managing Director:** Stuart
Clark

DESI RADIO 763862
30 Sussex Road, SOUTHALL, UB2 5EG **Tel:** 020 8574 9591
Fax: 020 8574 9850
Email: info@desiradio.org.uk
Web site: http://www.desiradio.org.uk
News Editor: Kulbinder Birring; **Advertising Manager:**
Jatinder Kundi

DIVERSITY FM 1826686
Lancaster and District YMCA, Heart of the City, Fleet
Square, LANCASTER, LA1 1HA **Tel:** 01524 383394
Fax: 01524 389184
Web site: http://www.diversityfm.co.uk
News Editor: Duncan Moore

DOWNTOWN RADIO (DTR) 42586
Kiltonga Industrial Estate, NEWTOWNARDS, BT23 4ES
Tel: 028 9181 5555 **Fax:** 028 9181 7878
Email: news@downtown.co.uk
Web site: http://www.downtown.co.uk
News Editor: Bob Huggins; **Managing Director:** Mark
Mahaffy

DREAM 100 FM 42356
Northgate House, St. Peter's Street, COLCHESTER, CO1
1HT **Tel:** 01206 715104 **Fax:** 01206 715102
Email: news@dream100.com
Web site: http://www.dream100.com
News Editor: Angharad Thomas

DRIVE 105.3 FM 1912767
71 Spencer Road, LONDONDERRY, BT47 6AE
Tel: 028 7131 3477
Email: admin@drive105.co.uk
Web site: http://www.drivefm.com
News Editor: Richard Moore

DUNE FM 42502
The Power Station, Victoria Way, SOUTHPORT, PR8 1RR
Tel: 01704 502502 **Fax:** 01704 502520
Email: news@dunefm.co.uk
Web site: http://www.dunefm.co.uk
News Editor: Sam Clack

DURHAM FM 1732515
3 Fram Well House, Framwelgate, DURHAM, DH1 5SU
Tel: 0191 383 5051 **Fax:** 0191 384 7735
Email: news@durhamfm.net
Web site: http://www.durhamfm.net
News Editor: Julie Howe

ENERGY FM 761515
100 Market Street, DOUGLAS, IM1 2PH **Tel:** 01624 611936
Fax: 01624 664699
Email: news@energyfm.net
Web site: http://www.energyfm.net
News Editor: Charles Turner; **Managing Director:** Charles
Turner

EXETER 107.3FM 1833394
6A Cranmere Court, Lustleigh Close, Matford Business Park,
Marsh Barton Trading Estate, EXETER, EX2 8PW
Tel: 01392 823557
Email: news@exeter.fm
Web site: http://www.exeter.fm
News Editor: Jo Rawlings

EXETER 107.3FM 1927078
6A Cranmere Court, Lustleigh Close, Matford Business Park,
Marsh Barton Trading Estate, EXETER, EX2 8PW
Tel: 01392 823557
Email: nes@exeter.fm
Web site: http://www.exeter.fm

EXPRESS FM 1824328
49 Arundel Street, PORTSMOUTH, PO1 1SA
Tel: 023 9284 5586
Email: news@expressfm.com
Web site: http://www.expressfm.com
News Editor: News Editor

FÉILE FM 103.2 1839994
Féile FM Studios, 1st Floor Conway Mill, 5-7 Conway Street,
BELFAST, BT12 2DE **Tel:** 028 9024 2002
Email: info@feilefm.com
Web site: http://www.feilefm.com
News Editor: Rosemary Whelan

FIRE RADIO
42334
The Picture House, 307 Holdenhurst Road,
BOURNEMOUTH, BH8 8BX **Tel:** 01202 443600
Fax: 01202 443601
Email: news@thenewfireradio.co.uk
Web site: http://www.fireradio.co.uk
News Editor: Simon Hancock

FIVE FM
1794335
Win Business Park, Canal Quay, NEWRY, BT35 6PH
Tel: 028 3025 4555 **Fax:** 028 3026 9005
Email: news@fivefm.co.uk
Web site: http://www.fivefm.co.uk
News Editor: Damien McGinley

FOREST FM
1732517
Unit 2, Enterprise Park, Black Moor Road, VERWOOD, BH31
6YS **Tel:** 01202 820003
Email: contact@forestfm.co.uk
Web site: http://www.forestfm.co.uk
News Editor: Steve Saville

FOREST OF DEAN RADIO
766953
Belle Vue House, Belle Vue Centre, Belle Vue Road,
CINDERFORD, GL14 2AB **Tel:** 01594 820722
Fax: 01594 820724
Email: contactus@fodradio.org
Web site: http://www.fodradio.org
News Editor: News Desk

FORTH 1
42560
Forth House, Forth Street, EDINBURGH, EH1 3LE
Tel: 0131 556 9255 **Fax:** 0131 558 3277
Email: forth-news@radioforth.com
Web site: http://www.forthone.com
News Editor: Paul Robertson

FORTH 2
42559
Forth House, Forth Street, EDINBURGH, EH1 3LE
Tel: 0131 556 9255 **Fax:** 0131 558 3277
Email: paul.robertson@radioforth.com
Web site: http://www.forth2.com
News Editor: Paul Robertson; **Managing Director:** Paul
Cooney

FRESH RADIO
42497
The Water Mill, Broughton Hall, SKIPTON, BD23 3AG
Tel: 0845 224 2052
Email: news@freshradio.co.uk
Web site: http://www.freshradio.co.uk
News Editor: James Wilson

FUN KIDS
758601
96A Curtain Road, LONDON, EC2A 3AA **Tel:** 020 7739 7879
Email: contact@funkidslive.com
Web site: http://www.funkidslive.com
News Editor: Matt Deegan; **Advertising Manager:** Jeff Link

FUTURE RADIO
1697074
The NR5 Project, The Neighbourhood Centre, Motum Road,
NORWICH, NR5 8EG **Tel:** 01603 250505 **Fax:** 01603 250505
Email: info@futureradio.co.uk
Web site: http://www.futureradio.co.uk
News Editor: Tom Buckham

GALAXY BIRMINGHAM
42326
1 The Square, 111 Broad Street, BIRMINGHAM, B15 1AS
Tel: 0113 308 5153
Email: news@galaxyfm.co.uk
Web site: http://www.galaxybirmingham.co.uk
News Editor: Kevin McGrath

GALAXY MANCHESTER
42451
Suite 1.1, 4 Exchange Quay, SALFORD, M5 3EE
Tel: 0161 662 4700 **Fax:** 0161 662 4759
Web site: http://www.galaxymanchester.co.uk
News Editor: News Desk

GALAXY NORTH EAST
42461
Kingfisher Way, Silverlink Business Park, WALLSEND, NE28
9NX **Tel:** 0191 444 2500 **Fax:** 0191 444 2509
Web site: http://www.galaxynortheast.co.uk
News Editor: Marie Christopher

GALAXY SCOTLAND
26460
1A, Four Winds Pavillion, Pacific Quay, GLASGOW, G51 1EB
Tel: 0141 566 6151 **Fax:** 0141 566 6189
Email: galaxynews@galaxyfm.co.uk
Web site: http://www.galaxyscotland.co.uk
News Editor: Louise Robertson

GALAXY SOUTH COAST
42376
Whittle Avenue, Segensworth West, FAREHAM, PO15 5SH
Tel: 01489 582556 **Fax:** 01489 589453
Email: news@oceanfm.co.uk
Web site: http://www.galaxy.co.uk
News Editor: Alison Law

GALAXY YORKSHIRE
42406
Joseph's Well, Hanover Walk, LEEDS, LS3 1AB
Tel: 0113 308 5153
Email: galaxynews@galaxyfm.co.uk
Web site: http://www.galaxyfm.co.uk
News Editor: Kevin McGrath

GOLD (1152)
766445
Earls Acre, Alma Road, PLYMOUTH, PL3 4HX
Tel: 01752 275600 **Fax:** 01752 275649
Email: news@plymouthsound.co.uk
Web site: http://www.mygoldmusic.co.uk
News Editor: Michaela Richards

GOLD (1260)
42340
One Passage Street, BRISTOL, BS2 0JF **Tel:** 0117 984 3200
Fax: 0117 984 3269
Email: news.bristol@heart.co.uk
Web site: http://www.classicgolddigital.com
News Editor: Cormac MacMahon; **Managing Director:**
Steve Jones

GOLD (1332)
42477
PO Box 225, Queensgate Centre, PETERBOROUGH, PE1
1XJ **Tel:** 01733 281400 **Fax:** 01733 281409
Email: peterborough.newsdesk@thisisglobal.com
News Editor: Katie Burnett

GOLD (1521)
42362
PO Box 1, CRAWLEY, RH10 9SE **Tel:** 01293 636030
Fax: 01293 636009
Email: crawley.newsdesk@thisisglobal.com
Web site: http://www.mygoldmusic.com
News Editor: Cheryl Dennis

GOLD (1548)
601338
30 Leicester Square, LONDON, WC2H 7LA
Tel: 020 7766 6000
Email: newsdesk@capitalradio.com
Web site: http://www.mygoldmusic.com
News Editor: News Desk

GOLD (1557)
601574
19-21 St. Edmunds Road, NORTHAMPTON, NN1 5DY
Tel: 01604 795691 **Fax:** 01604 795693
Email: northantsnews@heart.co.uk
Web site: http://www.mygoldmusic.com
News Editor: Richard Purvis

GOLD (774)
766593
Bridge Studios, Eastgate Street, GLOUCESTER, GL1 1SS
Tel: 01452 572430 **Fax:** 01452 572439
Email: news@severnsound.co.uk
News Editor: Duncan Cook

GOLD (990/1017)
42529
267 Tettenhall Road, WOLVERHAMPTON, WV6 0DE
Tel: 01902 461260 **Fax:** 01902 461266
Email: news@beaconradio.co.uk
Web site: http://www.beaconradio.co.uk
News Editor: Louise Easton

GOLD (BEDFORD)
26479
Chiltern Road, DUNSTABLE, LU6 1HQ **Tel:** 01582 676240
Fax: 01582 676249
Email: hbbnews@heart.co.uk
News Editor: Huw James; **Managing Director:** John Baish

GOLD (BIRMINGHAM)
42323
9 Brindley Place, 4 Oozells Square, BIRMINGHAM, B1 2DJ
Tel: 0121 566 5420 **Fax:** 0121 566 5429
Email: news@brmb.co.uk
Web site: http://www.brmb.co.uk
News Editor: Louise Easton

GOLD (BOURNEMOUTH)
42333
5-7 Southcote Road, BOURNEMOUTH, BH1 3LR
Tel: 01202 234930 **Fax:** 01202 234909
Email: news@2crfm.co.uk
Web site: http://www.2crfm.co.uk
News Editor: Luke Castiglione; **Managing Director:** John
Baish

GOLD (COVENTRY)
42359
Hertford Place, COVENTRY, CV1 3TT **Tel:** 024 7686 8233
Fax: 024 7686 8239
Email: tony.attwater@mercia.co.uk
Web site: http://www.mygoldmusic.com
News Editor: Tony Attwater

GOLD (DERBY)
1893798
Chapel Quarter, Maid Marian Way, NOTTINGHAM, NG1 6JR
Tel: 0115 873 1520 **Fax:** 0115 873 1529
Email: news@trentfm.co.uk
Web site: http://www.trentfm.co.uk
News Editor: Lewis Scrimshaw

GOLD (DEVON)
42373
Hawthorn House, Exeter Business Park, EXETER, EX1 3QS
Tel: 01392 354232 **Fax:** 01392 354239
Email: exeter.newsdesk@thisisglobal.com
Web site: http://www.musicradio.com
News Editor: Gareth Boulton

GOLD (ESSEX)
42500
Radio House, 31 Glebe Road, CHELMSFORD, CM1 1QG
Tel: 01245 524550 **Fax:** 01245 524559
Email: chelmsford.newsdesk@thisisglobal.com
Web site: http://www.essexfm.com
News Editor: Jessica Shiddell

GOLD (HAMPSHIRE)
42374
Whittle Avenue, Segensworth West, FAREHAM, PO15 5SX
Tel: 01489 582556 **Fax:** 01489 589453
Email: news@oceanfm.co.uk
Web site: http://www.mygoldmusic.co.uk
News Editor: Alison Law

GOLD (IPSWICH)
42397
Radio House, Alpha Business Park, Whitehouse Road,
IPSWICH, IP1 5LT **Tel:** 01473 467570 **Fax:** 01473 467579
Email: news.suffolk@heart.co.uk
News Editor: Sonia Clark

GOLD (KENT)
42524
Invicta FM News, PO Box 100, WHITSTABLE, CT5 3YR
Tel: 01227 774444 **Fax:** 01227 774489
Email: newsroom@invictafm.com
Web site: http://www.invictafm.com
News Editor: Charlotte O'Brien

GOLD (LUTON)
1893799
Chiltern Road, DUNSTABLE, LU6 1HQ **Tel:** 01582 676240
Fax: 01582 676249
Email: hbbnews@heart.co.uk
News Editor: Huw James; **Managing Director:** John Baish

GOLD (MANCHESTER)
766543
Suite 1.1, 4 Exchange Quay, SALFORD, M5 3EE
Tel: 0161 662 4790
Email: galaxynews@galaxyfm.co.uk
Web site: http://www.mygoldmusic.com
News Editor: Matthew Bowen

GOLD (NORWICH)
42468
47-49 St. Georges Plain, Colegate, NORWICH, NR3 1DB
Tel: 01603 671180 **Fax:** 01603 671189
Email: neil.perry@heart.co.uk
News Editor: Neil Perry; **Managing Director:** Sophie Hind

UK Broadcasting & Other Media

GOLD (NOTTINGHAM) 42472
Chapel Quarter, Maid Marian Way, NOTTINGHAM, NG1 6JR
Tel: 0115 873 1520 **Fax:** 0115 873 1529
Email: news@trentfm.co.uk
Web site: http://www.trentfm.co.uk
News Editor: Lewis Scrimshaw

GOLD (SOUTH WALES) 42542
Red Dragon Centre, Hemingway Road, CARDIFF, CF10 4DJ
Tel: 029 2094 2940
Email: news@reddragonfm.com
Web site: http://www.mygoldmusic.co.uk
News Editor: Vicky Etchells

GOLD (SUSSEX) 714927
Radio House, PO Box 2000, BRIGHTON, BN41 2SS
Tel: 01273 316940
Email: news@southernfm.com
Web site: http://www.mygoldmusic.co.uk
News Editor: Rob Gillett

GOLD (SWINDON) 42515
1st Floor, Chiseldon House, Stonehill Green, Westlea,
SWINDON, SN5 7HB **Tel:** 01793 663030 **Fax:** 01793 663009
Email: news.wiltshire@heart.co.uk
Web site: http://www.classicgold.com
News Editor: Charlotte Saker

GOLD (THAMES VALLEY) 42486
The Chase, Calcot, READING, RG31 7RB
Tel: 0118 928 8800 **Fax:** 0118 928 8809
Email: news@2tenfm.co.uk
Web site: http://www.heartberkshire.co.uk
News Editor: Anna Tyler

GOLD (WREXHAM) 42550
The Studios, Mold Road, Gwersyllt, WREXHAM, LL11 4AF
Tel: 01978 722230 **Fax:** 01978 722239
Email: news@marchersound.co.uk
News Editor: Alina Cavanagh

GTFM 107.9FM 763076
Pinewood Studios, Pinewood Avenue, Rhydyfelin,
PONTYPRIDD, CF37 5EA **Tel:** 01443 406111
Fax: 01443 492744
Email: news@gtfm.co.uk
Web site: http://www.gtfm.co.uk
News Editor: News Editor

HALLAM FM 42494
Radio House, 900 Herries Road, SHEFFIELD, S6 1RH
Tel: 0114 209 1010 **Fax:** 0114 285 5053
Email: news@hallamfm.co.uk
Web site: http://www.hallamfm.co.uk
News Editor: Lynn Dixon

HAYES FM 1824869
The Media Centre, 54A Station Road, HAYES, UB3 4DF
Tel: 020 8573 7992 **Fax:** 020 8573 8215
Email: office@hayesfm.org
Web site: http://www.hayesfm.org
News Editor: Sutish Sharma; **Managing Editor:** Sutish
Sharma

HEART 100-102 622626
Unit 1G, South Hams Business Park, Churchstow,
KINGSBRIDGE, TQ7 3QH **Tel:** 01548 854595
Fax: 01548 857345
Email: richard.spencer@heart.co.uk
Web site: http://www.heartsouthdevon.co.uk
News Editor: Steph Wright; **Managing Director:** Victoria
Ford

HEART 103 (CAMBRIDGE) 42346
PO Box 103, Vision Park, Histon, CAMBRIDGE, CB24 9WW
Tel: 01223 623800 **Fax:** 01223 623809
Email: cambridge.news@heart.co.uk
Web site: http://www.heartcambridge.co.uk
News Editor: Katie Burnett

HEART 106.2 (LONDON) 42425
30 Leicester Square, LONDON, WC2H 7LA
Tel: 020 7766 6000
Email: news@heart1062.co.uk
Web site: http://www.heart.co.uk
News Editor: Jonathan Richards
Twitter: http://twitter.com/heartlondon.

HEART 96.1 42357
Abbeygate Two, 9 Whitewell Road, COLCHESTER, CO2
7DE **Tel:** 01206 216130 **Fax:** 01206 216149
Email: sonia.clark@thisisglobal.com
Web site: http://www.heartcolchester.co.uk
News Editor: Sonia Clark

HEART 96.6 42465
19-22 St Edmunds Road, NORTHAMPTON, NN1 5DY
Tel: 01604 795600 **Fax:** 01604 795693
Email: richard.purvis@heart.co.uk
Web site: http://www.heartnorthants.co.uk
News Editor: Richard Purvis

HEART 97.2 AND 102.2 42516
1st Floor, Chiseldon House, Stonehill Green, Westlea,
SWINDON, SN5 7HB **Tel:** 01793 842600 **Fax:** 01793 663039
Email: news.wiltshire@heart.co.uk
Web site: http://www.heartwilts.co.uk
News Editor: Charlotte Saker

HEART (BATH) 1895425
1 Passage Street, BRISTOL, BS2 0JF **Tel:** 0117 984 3211
Email: news.bath@heart.co.uk
News Editor: Cormac MacMahon

HEART (BEDFORD) 42321
Chiltern Road, DUNSTABLE, LU6 1HQ **Tel:** 01582 676240
Fax: 01582 676239
Email: hbbnews@heart.co.uk
Web site: http://www.heart.co.uk
News Editor: Newsroom

HEART (BERKSHIRE) 42485
The Chase, READING, RG31 7RB **Tel:** 0118 928 8800
Fax: 0118 928 8809
Email: news1029@heart.co.uk
Web site: http://www.heart.co.uk
News Editor: Anna Tyler; **Managing Director:** Jo Lee

HEART BIRMINGHAM AND THE WEST MIDLANDS 42327
1 The Square, 111 Broad Street, BIRMINGHAM, B15 1AS
Tel: 0121 695 0000 **Fax:** 0121 633 3292
Email: news@heartfm.co.uk
Web site: http://www.heartfm.co.uk
News Editor: Emma Reid

HEART (BRISTOL) 42341
1 Passage Street, BRISTOL, BS2 0JF **Tel:** 0117 984 3200
Fax: 0117 984 3269
Email: news.bristol@heart.co.uk
Web site: http://www.heart.co.uk
News Editor: Cormac MacMahon; **Managing Director:**
Steve Jones

HEART (CYMRU) 42538
Y Stiwdios, Parc Menai, BANGOR, LL57 4BN
Tel: 01248 673433 **Fax:** 01248 673409
Email: newyddion@champion103.co.uk
Web site: http://www.heartcymru.co.uk
News Editor: Newsdesk

HEART DIGITAL 1614416
30 Leicester Square, LONDON, WC2H 7LA
Email: planning@lbc.co.uk
Web site: http://www.heart.co.uk
News Editor: Russ Evans

HEART (DORSET) 42332
5-7 Southcote Road, BOURNEMOUTH, BH1 3LR
Tel: 01202 234900 **Fax:** 01202 234909
Email: news@thisisglobal.com
Web site: http://www.heartdorset.co.uk
Managing Director: John Baish

HEART (DUNSTABLE) 42370
Chiltern Road, DUNSTABLE, LU6 1HQ **Tel:** 01582 676240
Fax: 01582 676249
Email: huw.james@thisisglobal.com
Web site: http://www.heartdunstable.co.uk
News Editor: Huw James

HEART (EAST MIDLANDS) 42471
City Link, NOTTINGHAM, NG2 4NG **Tel:** 0115 910 6100
Fax: 0115 910 6105
Email: news@heart106.com
Web site: http://www.hearteastmids.co.uk
News Editor: Newsroom

HEART (ESSEX) 42501
Radio House, 31 Glebe Road, CHELMSFORD, CM1 1QG
Tel: 01245 524550 **Fax:** 01245 524559
Email: chelmsford.newsdesk@thisisglobal.com
Web site: http://www.heartessex.co.uk
News Editor: Jessica Shiddell; **Managing Director:** Carlo
Triolo

HEART (EXETER AND TORBAY) 42372
Hawthorn House, Exeter Business Park, EXETER, EX1 3QS
Tel: 01392 354232 **Fax:** 01392 354239
Email: news.exeter@heart.co.uk
Web site: http://www.heartexeter.co.uk
News Editor: Gareth Boulton

HEART (GLOUCESTER) 42380
Bridge Studios, Eastgate Centre, GLOUCESTER, GL1 1SS
Tel: 01452 572430 **Fax:** 01452 572439
Email: news.gloucestershire@heart.co.uk
Web site: http://www.heartgloucestershire.co.uk
News Editor: Duncan Cook

HEART (HAMPSHIRE) 42375
Whittle Avenue, Segensworth West, FAREHAM, PO15 5SX
Tel: 01489 582556 **Fax:** 01489 589453
Email: news.hampshire@heart.co.uk
Web site: http://www.hearthampshire.co.uk
News Editor: Alison Law; **Managing Director:** Hugh Murray

HEART (IPSWICH) 42398
Radio House, Alpha Business Park, Whitehouse Road,
IPSWICH, IP1 5LT **Tel:** 01473 461000 **Fax:** 01473 467579
Email: sonia.clark@thisisglobal.com
Web site: http://www.heartipswich.co.uk
News Editor: Sonia Clark

HEART (KENT) 42525
Invicta FM Newscentre, PO Box 100, WHITSTABLE, CT5
3YR **Tel:** 01227 774444 **Fax:** 01227 774489
Email: newsroom@invictafm.com
Web site: http://www.heartkent.co.uk
News Editor: Charlotte O'Brien; **Managing Director:** Neil
Webster

HEART (MILTON KEYNES) 42459
14 Vincent Avenue, Crownhill, MILTON KEYNES, MK8 0AB
Tel: 01908 269111
Email: victoria.meakin@thisisglobal.com
Web site: http://www.heartmk.co.uk
News Editor: Victoria Meakin

HEART (MILTON KEYNES) 1925469
14 Vincent Avenue, Crownhill, MILTON KEYNES, MK8 0AB
Tel: 01908 269111
Email: victoria.meakin@thisisglboal.com
Web site: http://wwww.heartmk.co.uk
News Editor: Victoria Meakin

HEART (NORTH DEVON) 42322
Unit 2B, Lauder Lane, Roundswell Business Park,
BARNSTAPLE, EX31 3TA **Tel:** 01271 366381
Email: news.barnstaple@heart.co.uk
Web site: http://www.heart.co.uk
News Editor: Nicola Maxey

HEART (NORWICH) 42467
47-49 St. Georges Plain, Colegate, NORWICH, NR3 1DB
Tel: 01603 671180 **Fax:** 01603 671189
Email: neil.perry@heart.co.uk
Web site: http://www.heartnorwich.co.uk
News Editor: Neil Perry; **Managing Director:** Sophie Hind

HEART (OXFORD)
42475
Radio House, Pony Road, Cowley, OXFORD, OX4 2XR
Tel: 01865 871000 **Fax:** 01865 543359
Email: news.oxford@heart.co.uk
Web site: http://www.heart.co.uk
News Editor: John Stratford

HEART (PETERBOROUGH)
42478
PO Box 225, The Queensgate Centre, PETERBOROUGH,
PE1 1NS **Tel:** 01733 281400 **Fax:** 01733 281409
Email: peterborough.newsdesk@heart.co.uk
Web site: http://www.heartpeterborough.co.uk
News Editor: Katie Burnett

HEART (PLYMOUTH)
42481
Earls Acre, Alma Road, PLYMOUTH, PL3 4HX
Tel: 01752 275640 **Fax:** 01752 275649
Email: news.plymouth@heart.co.uk
Web site: http://www.heartplymouth.co.uk
News Editor: Michaela Richards

HEART (SOMERSET)
42519
Haygrove House, Shoreditch Road, TAUNTON, TA3 7BT
Tel: 01823 368330 **Fax:** 01823 368339
Email: news.taunton@heart.co.uk
Web site: http://www.heartsomerset.co.uk
News Editor: Nicola Maxey

HEART (SUSSEX)
42337
Radio House, Franklin Road, BRIGHTON, BN41 1AF
Tel: 01273 430111
Email: news.sussex@heart.co.uk
Web site: http://www.heartsussex.co.uk
News Editor: Rob Gillett

HEART (WELSH COAST)
42543
PO Box 963, BANGOR, LL57 4ZR **Tel:** 01248 673272
Fax: 01248 673409
Email: news@coast963.co.uk
Web site: http://www.heartwalescoast.co.uk/
News Editor: News Desk

HEART (WIRRAL)
623822
PO Box 971, BIRKENHEAD, CH41 6EY **Tel:** 0151 650 1700
Email: alina.cavanagh@thisisglobal.com
Web site: http://www.heartwirral.co.uk
News Editor: Alina Cavanagh

HEART (WREXHAM)
42549
The Studios, Mold Road, WREXHAM, LL11 4AF
Tel: 01978 722230
Email: news@marchersound.co.uk
Web site: http://www.heartwrexham.co.uk
News Editor: Alina Cavanagh; **Managing Director:** Clive
Douthwaite

HEARTLAND FM
42573
The Atholl Curling Rink, Lower Oakfield, PITLOCHRY, PH16
5HQ **Tel:** 01796 474040 **Fax:** 01796 474007
Email: mailbox@heartlandfm.co.uk
Web site: http://www.heartlandfm.co.uk
News Editor: Margaret Stevenson

HERTBEAT FM
623134
Knebworth Park, The Pump House, KNEBWORTH, SG3
6HQ **Tel:** 01438 810900 **Fax:** 01438 815100
Email: news@hertbeat.com
Web site: http://www.hertbeat.com
News Editor: Chris Hollis; **Managing Director:** Brett Harley

HERTFORDSHIRE'S MERCURY 96.6
42503
Unit 5, The Metro Centre, Dwight Road, WATFORD, WD18
9UP **Tel:** 01923 205470 **Fax:** 01923 205479
Email: simone.stewart@hertsmercury.co.uk
Web site: http://www.hertsmercury.co.uk
News Editor: Simone Stewart

HFM RADIO
1839501
Innovation House, Valley Way, MARKET HARBOROUGH,
LE16 7PS **Tel:** 01858 464666 **Fax:** 01858 464678
Email: news@harboroughfm.co.uk
Web site: http://www.harboroughfm.co.uk
News Editor: Nick Shaw

HIGH PEAK RADIO
1623287
PO BOX 106, HIGH PEAK, SK23 0DJ **Tel:** 01298 813144
Fax: 01298 813388
Email: info@highpeakradio.co.uk
Web site: http://www.highpeakradio.co.uk
News Editor: Ben Price

HOPE FM
1841111
Delta House, 56 Westover Road, BOURNEMOUTH, BH1
2BS **Tel:** 01202 569239 **Fax:** 01202 314219
Email: office@hopefm.com
Web site: http://www.hopefm.com
News Editor: Kevin Potter

INSIGHT RADIO
1647347
Centre for Sensory Impairment, 17 Gullane Street,
GLASGOW, G11 6AH **Tel:** 0141 357 3518
Email: info@insightradio.co.uk
Web site: http://www.insightradio.co.uk
News Editor: Ross MacFadyen

IPSWICH COMMUNITY RADIO
1826306
CSV Media Clubhouse, 120 Princes Street, IPSWICH, IP1
1RS **Tel:** 01473 418022
Email: nick@icrfm.co.uk
Web site: http://www.icrfm.co.uk
News Editor: Nick Greenland

ISLAND FM
42591
12 Westerbrook, St. Sampson, GUERNSEY, GY2 4QQ
Tel: 01481 242000 **Fax:** 01481 249676
Email: news@islandfm.com
Web site: http://www.islandfm.com
News Editor: Rob Moore; **Managing Director:** Linda
Burnham

ISLE OF WIGHT RADIO
42399
8 Dodnor Park, NEWPORT, PO30 5XE **Tel:** 01983 821777
Fax: 01983 821690
Email: news@iwradio.co.uk
Web site: http://www.iwradio.co.uk
News Editor: Michael Coombes

ISLES FM
42568
PO Box 333, STORNOWAY, HS1 2PU **Tel:** 01851 703333
Fax: 01851 703322
Email: studio@isles.fm
Web site: http://www.isles.fm
News Editor: Iain Maciver; **Managing Director:** David
Morrison

JUICE 107.2
42338
170 North Street, BRIGHTON, BN1 1EA **Tel:** 01273 386107
Fax: 01273 273107
Email: news@juicebrighton.com
Web site: http://www.juicebrighton.com
News Editor: Andrea Fox

KCFM 99.8
1818759
Planet House, Headen Road, HULL, HU9 1RJ
Tel: 01482 333999
Email: news@kcfm.co.uk
Web site: http://www.kcfm.co.uk
News Editor: Wesley Mallin

KERRANG! RADIO
1626000
Kerrang! House, 20 Lionel Street, BIRMINGHAM, B3 1AQ
Tel: 0845 053 1052
Email: news@kerrangradio.co.uk
Web site: http://www.kerrangradio.co.uk
News Editor: James Walshe

KEY 103 FM
42453
Castle Quay, Castlefield, MANCHESTER, M15 4PR
Tel: 0161 288 5000
Email: news@key103.co.uk
Web site: http://www.key103.com
News Editor: John Pickford; **Managing Director:** Michelle
Surrell

KICK FM
601577
The Studios, 42 Bone Lane, NEWBURY, RG14 5SD
Tel: 01635 841600 **Fax:** 01635 841010
Email: news@kickfm.co.uk
Web site: http://www.kickfm.co.uk
News Editor: Claire Gibbard

KINGDOM FM
42564
Haig House, Balgonie Road, Markinch, GLENROTHES, KY7
6AQ **Tel:** 01592 753753 **Fax:** 01592 612022
Email: news@kingdomfm.co.uk
Web site: http://www.kingdomfm.co.uk
News Editor: Laura Haldane; **Managing Director:** Kevin
Brady

KISMAT RADIO 1035 AM
1703140
Radio House, Bridge Road, SOUTHALL, UB2 4AT
Tel: 020 8574 6666 **Fax:** 020 8813 9700
Email: reception@kismatradio.com
Web site: http://www.kismatradio.com
News Editor: Ravi Sharma

KISS 100
42427
Mappin House, 4 Winsley Street, LONDON, W1W 8HF
Tel: 020 7182 8000
Web site: http://www.totalkiss.com
News Editor: Newsroom; **Managing Director:** Steve
Parkinson
Twitter: http://twitter.com/kiss100.

KISS 101
42342
Millenium House, 26 Baldwin Street, BRISTOL, BS1 1SE
Tel: 0117 901 0101 **Fax:** 0117 930 9149
Email: news101@totalkiss.com
Web site: http://www.totalkiss.com
News Editor: Newsroom

KISS 105-108
42343
Reflections House, The Anderson Centre, Olding Road,
BURY ST. EDMUNDS, IP33 3TA **Tel:** 01284 715300
Fax: 01284 715339
Email: news@totalkiss.com
Web site: http://www.totalkiss.com
News Editor: Glen White; **Advertising Manager:** Kelly
Snook

KL FM 96.7
42401
18 Blackfriars Street, KING'S LYNN, PE30 1NN
Tel: 01553 771778
Email: claire.gregory@klfm967.co.uk
Web site: http://www.klfm967.co.uk
News Editor: Claire Gregory; **Managing Director:** Pam
Lawton

KM FM
42347
Medway House, Ginsbury Close, Sir Thomas Longley Road,
Medway City Estate, ROCHESTER, ME2 4DU
Tel: 0845 080 0640
Email: radionews@kmfm.co.uk
Web site: http://www.kmfm.co.uk
News Editor: Susan Hilder

KMFM (ASHFORD)
1775676
Express House, 34-36 North Street, ASHFORD, TN24 8JR
Tel: 01233 895820
Email: radionews@kmfm.co.uk
Web site: http://www.kmfm.co.uk
News Editor: Susan Hilder

KMFM (FOLKESTONE AND DOVER)
42369
Messenger House, Ginsbury Close, Sir Thomas Longley,
Medway City Estate, STROOD, ME2 4DU
Tel: 0845 080 06 40 **Fax:** 01303 250287
Email: folkestonenewsdesk@kmfm.co.uk
Web site: http://www.kmfm.co.uk
News Editor: Jo Sword

KMFM FOR MEDWAY
42489
Medway City Estate, Strood, ROCHESTER, ME2 4DU
Tel: 01634 227821 **Fax:** 01634 719294
Email: rochesternewsdesk@kmfm.co.uk
Web site: http://www.kmfm.co.uk/medway
News Editor: Rhona Pinkerton

KMFM FOR WEST KENT
42363
1 East Street, TONBRIDGE, TN9 1AR **Tel:** 01732 369200
Fax: 01732 369201
Email: news@kmfm.co.uk
Web site: http://www.kmfm.co.uk
News Editor: Susan Hilder

UK Broadcasting & Other Media

Section 9 UK Broadcasting

KMFM (MAIDSTONE)   1646067
6-8 Mill Street, MAIDSTONE, ME15 6XH **Tel:** 01622 662500
Fax: 01622 662501
Email: maidstonenews@kmfm.co.uk
Web site: http://www.kmfm.co.uk
News Editor: Susan Hilder

KMFM (THANET)   42456
181-183 Northdown Road, Cliftonville, MARGATE, CT9 2PA
Tel: 01843 223999
Email: thanetnews@kmfm.co.uk
Web site: http://www.thanetextra.co.uk
News Editor: Martin Jefferies

LAKELAND RADIO   634917
Lakeland Food Park, Plumgarths, Crook Road, KENDAL,
LA8 8QJ **Tel:** 01539 737380 **Fax:** 01539 737390
Email: news@lakelandradio.co.uk
Web site: http://www.lakelandradio.co.uk
News Editor: News Desk

LBC 97.3 FM   42428
30 Leicester Square, LONDON, WC2H 7LA
Tel: 020 7766 6000
Email: planning@lbc.co.uk
Web site: http://www.lbc.co.uk
Editor: Jo Parkerson; **News Editor:** Jo Newsholme
Twitter: https://twitter.com/LBC973.

LBC NEWS 1152 AM   42436
LBC 97.3 FM, 30 Leicester Square, LONDON, WC2H 7LA
Tel: 020 7766 6000
Email: planning@lbc.co.uk
Web site: http://www.lbc.co.uk
News Editor: Forward Planning

LEICESTER SOUND   42408
6 Dominus Way, Meridian Business Park, LEICESTER, LE19
1RP **Tel:** 0116 256 1300
Email: news@leicestersound.co.uk
Web site: http://www.leicestersound.co.uk
News Editor: Yvonne Radley; **Managing Director:** Anita
Wright

LGR LONDON GREEK RADIO   42429
LGR House, 437 High Road, LONDON, N12 0AP
Tel: 020 8349 6950 **Fax:** 020 8349 6960
Email: al@lgr.co.uk
Web site: http://www.lgr.co.uk
News Editor: Tasos Zachariades

LINCS FM   42413
Witham Park, Waterside South, LINCOLN, LN5 7JN
Tel: 01522 549977 **Fax:** 01522 549911
Email: news@lincsfm.co.uk
Web site: http://www.lincsfm.co.uk
News Editor: News Desk

LITE FM   601181
Second Floor, 5 Church Street, PETERBOROUGH, PE1 1XB
Tel: 01733 898106 **Fax:** 01733 898107
Email: news@lite1068.com
Web site: http://www.lite1068.com
News Editor: Carlo Fiorentio

LOCHBROOM FM   26488
Radio House, Mill Street, ULLAPOOL, IV26 2UN
Tel: 01854 613131 **Fax:** 01854 613132
Email: radio@lochbroomfm.co.uk
Web site: http://www.lochbroomfm.co.uk
News Editor: Agnes Ferrier

LONDON TURKISH RADIO   26821
185B High Road, Wood Green, LONDON, N22 6BA
Tel: 020 8881 0606 **Fax:** 020 8881 5151
Email: info@londonturkishradio.org
Web site: http://www.londonturkishradio.org
News Editor: Deniz Demir; **Managing Director:** Erkan
Pastirmacioglu

MAGIC 105.4 FM   42433
Mappin House, 4 Winsley Street, LONDON, W1W 8HF
Tel: 020 7182 8233 **Fax:** 020 7975 8228
Email: studio@magic.fm
Web site: http://www.magic1054.co.uk
News Editor: Kit Li; **Managing Director:** Steve Parkinson
Twitter: http://twitter.com/MagicFM.

MAGIC 1152 (MANCHESTER)   42454
Castle Quay, Castlefield, MANCHESTER, M15 4PR
Tel: 0161 288 5070
Email: news@key103.co.uk
Web site: http://www.magicradio.com
News Editor: John Pickford; **Managing Director:** Michelle
Surrell

MAGIC 1152 (NEWCASTLE)   42462
55 Degrees North, Pilgrim Street, NEWCASTLE UPON
TYNE, NE1 6BF **Tel:** 0191 230 6100 **Fax:** 0191 421 0409
Email: news@metroandmagic.com
Web site: http://www.magic1152.co.uk
News Editor: News Desk; **Managing Director:** Sally
Aitchison

MAGIC 1161   42395
Commercial Road, HULL, HU1 2SG **Tel:** 01482 320903
Fax: 01482 217703
Email: newsdesk@vikingfm.co.uk
Web site: http://www.magic1161.co.uk
News Editor: Paul Dawson; **Managing Director:** Alexis
Thompson

MAGIC 1170   42505
Radio House, Yale Crescent, Thornaby, STOCKTON-ON-
TEES, TS17 6AA **Tel:** 01642 888222
Email: tfmnews@tfmradio.com
Web site: http://www.magic1170.co.uk
News Editor: Hayley Brewer; **Managing Director:** Sally
Aitchison

MAGIC 1548   42416
St. John's Beacon, 1 Houghton Street, LIVERPOOL, L1 1RL
Tel: 0151 472 6840 **Fax:** 0151 472 6841
Email: news@radiocity.co.uk
Web site: http://www.magic1548.co.uk
News Editor: Steve Hothersall

THE MAGIC 756   42545
The Studios, The Park, NEWTOWN, SY16 2NZ
Tel: 01686 623555 **Fax:** 01686 623666
Email: radio@magic756.net
Web site: http://www.magic756.net
News Editor: Emily Sandaman

MAGIC 828   42407
51 Burley Road, LEEDS, LS3 1LR **Tel:** 0113 283 5500
Fax: 0113 283 5601
Email: news@radioaire.com
Web site: http://www.magic828.co.uk
News Editor: Alice Bailey; **Managing Director:** Alexis
Thompson

MAGIC 999   42484
St. Paul's Square, PRESTON, PR1 1YE **Tel:** 01772 477700
Fax: 01772 477701
Email: news.users@rockfm.co.uk
Web site: http://www.magic999.co.uk
News Editor: Claire Hannah; **Managing Director:** Michelle
Surrell

MAGIC AM   42495
Radio House, 900 Herries Road, SHEFFIELD, S6 1RH
Tel: 0114 209 1010 **Fax:** 0114 285 5053
Email: news@hallamfm.co.uk
Web site: http://www.magicam.co.uk
News Editor: Lynn Dixon; **Managing Director:** Tracey
Eastwood

MANSFIELD 103.2   42455
Brunts Business Centre, Unit 4, Samuel Brunts Way,
MANSFIELD, NG18 2AH **Tel:** 01623 666020
Fax: 01623 666023
Email: news@mansfield103.co.uk
Web site: http://www.mansfield103.co.uk
News Editor: Ian Watkins; **Managing Director:** Tony
Delahunty; **Managing Editor:** Ian Watkins

MANX RADIO   42587
PO Box 1368, Broadcasting House, Douglas, ISLE OF MAN,
IM1 5BW **Tel:** 01624 682600 **Fax:** 01624 682604
Email: news@manxradio.com
Web site: http://www.manxradio.com
News Editor: Graham Bell

MEARNS FM   1902900
Stonehaven Town Hall, Allardyce, STONEHAVEN, AB39 2BU
Tel: 07871 052107
Email: info@mearnsfm.org.uk
Web site: http://www.mearnsfm.org.uk
News Editor: Charles Sands

MERCIA FM   42361
Hertford Place, COVENTRY, CV1 3TT **Tel:** 024 7686 8230
Fax: 024 7686 8239
Email: news@mercia.co.uk
Web site: http://www.mercia.co.uk
News Editor: Tony Attwater

METRO RADIO   42463
55 Degrees North, Pilgrim Street, NEWCASTLE UPON
TYNE, NE1 6BF **Tel:** 0191 230 6100 **Fax:** 0191 279 0409
Email: news@metroandmagic.com
Web site: http://www.metroradio.co.uk
News Editor: News Desk; **Managing Director:** Sally
Aitchison

**MIDWEST RADIO (BLANDFORD AND THE
VALE)**   42492
Longmead Studios, Shaftesbury, DORSET, SP7 8PL
Tel: 01747 855711 **Fax:** 01747 855974
Email: news@midwestradio.co.uk
Web site: http://www.midwestradio.co.uk
News Editor: News Desk

**MIDWEST RADIO (SOMERSET AND
DORSET)**   1637640
The Studios, Middle Street, YEOVIL, BA20 1DJ
Tel: 01935 848488 **Fax:** 01935 848489
Email: news@midwestradio.co.uk
Web site: http://www.midwestradio.co.uk
News Editor: Greg Bown

MINSTER FM   42535
PO Box 123, Dunnington, YORK, YO19 5ZX
Tel: 01904 486598 **Fax:** 01904 488811
Email: news@minsterfm.com
Web site: http://www.minsterfm.com
News Editor: Tracy Gee

MINSTER NORTHALLERTON   1813458
11 Woodland Road, DARLINGTON, DL3 7BJ
Tel: 01609 779599 **Fax:** 01609 775204
Email: news@minsternorthallerton.com
Web site: http://www.minsternorthallerton.com
News Editor: Sarah Dobson

MIX 96   42318
Friars Square Studios, 11 Bourbon Street, AYLESBURY,
HP20 2PZ **Tel:** 01296 399396 **Fax:** 01296 398988
Email: news@mix96.co.uk
Web site: http://www.mix96.co.uk
News Editor: Penny Harper

NATION RADIO   1812842
Newby House, Neath Abbey Business Park, NEATH, SA10
7DR **Tel:** 0845 025 1000 **Fax:** 0845 025 1001
Email: news@nationwales.com
Web site: http://www.nationwales.com
News Editor: Jason Briant

NE1 FM   1826986
NE1 Studios, The Old Methodist Church, 1 Clarence Street,
NEWCASTLE UPON TYNE, NE2 1YH **Tel:** 0191 240 1025
Email: studio@ne1fm.com
Web site: http://www.ne1fm.com
News Editor: Elaine Parker

NECR 630700
The Shed, School Road, Kintore, INVERURIE, AB51 0UX
Tel: 01467 632909 **Fax:** 01467 632969
Email: enquiries@necrfm.co.uk
Web site: http://www.necrfm.co.uk
Managing Director: Colin Strong

NEVIS RADIO 42567
Ben Nevis Industrial Estate, FORT WILLIAM, PH33 6PR
Tel: 01397 700007 **Fax:** 01397 701007
Email: david@nevisradio.co.uk
Web site: http://www.nevisradio.co.uk
News Editor: David Ogg

NEW STYLE RADIO 766958
339 Dudley Road, Winson Green, BIRMINGHAM, B18 4HB
Tel: 0121 456 3826 **Fax:** 0121 678 6030
Email: newstyle@acmccentre.co.uk
Web site: http://www.newstyleradio.co.uk
News Editor: Dennis Edwards

NORTH NORFOLK RADIO 1623352
The Studio, Breck Farm, STODY, NR24 2ER
Tel: 01263 860808 **Fax:** 01263 860809
Email: news@northnorfolkradio.com
Web site: http://www.northnorfolkradio.com
News Editor: Jen Dale; **Managing Director:** Gina Frost

NORTHSOUND ONE 42552
Abbotswell Road, West Tullos, ABERDEEN, AB12 3AJ
Tel: 01224 337002 **Fax:** 01224 633282
Email: news@northsound.co.uk
Web site: http://www.northsound1.com
News Editor: Joe Odber; **Managing Director:** Luke McCullogh

NORTHSOUND TWO 42553
Abbotswell Road, West Tullos, ABERDEEN, AB12 3AJ
Tel: 01224 337002 **Fax:** 01224 633282
Email: news@northsound.co.uk
Web site: http://www.northsound2.com
News Editor: Joe Odber; **Managing Director:** Luke McCullogh

NUSOUND RADIO 92 FM 1839870
PO Box 51092, LONDON, E7 8US **Tel:** 020 8472 9994
Email: info@nusoundradio.com
Web site: http://www.nusoundradio.com
News Editor: Sujata Sian

OAK FM 42443
3 Martins Court, Telford Way, COALVILLE, LE67 3HD
Tel: 01530 278200 **Fax:** 01530 278201
Email: news@oakfm.co.uk
Web site: http://www.oakfm.co.uk
News Editor: James Wall

OAK FM (LEICESTERSHIRE) 42390
3 Martins Court, Telford Way, Stephenson Industrial Estate, COALVILLE, LE67 3HD **Tel:** 01530 835108
Fax: 01530 278201
Email: news@oakfm.co.uk
Web site: http://www.oakfm.co.uk
News Editor: James Wall

OBAN FM 42569
132 George Street, OBAN, PA34 5NT **Tel:** 01631 570057
Fax: 01631 570530
Email: coll@obanfm.org.uk
Web site: http://www.obanfm.org.uk
News Editor: Coll MacDougall

OLDHAM COMMUNITY RADIO 1840069
PO Box 997, OLDHAM, OL1 9EB **Tel:** 0161 626 4004
Email: studio@oldhamcommunityradio.com
Web site: http://www.oldhamcommunityradio.com
News Editor: David McGealy; **Managing Director:** David McGealy

ORIGINAL 106.5 1809264
County Gates, Ashton Road, BRISTOL, BS3 2JH
Tel: 0117 966 1065
Email: news@originalbristol.com
Web site: http://www.originalbristol.com
News Editor: Journalists; **Managing Director:** Richard Johnson

ORIGINAL 106FM 1810739
Original House, Craigshaw Road, West Tullos Industrial Estate, ABERDEEN, AB12 3AR **Tel:** 01224 294860
Fax: 01224 896359
Email: info@originalfm.com
Web site: http://www.originalfm.com
News Editor: Neil Metcalf

OXFORD'S FM 107.9 42736
270 Woodstock Road, OXFORD, OX2 7NW
Tel: 01865 315987 **Fax:** 0870 220 7626
Email: news@jackfm.co.uk
Web site: http://www.fm1079.co.uk
News Editor: Greg Burke

PALM 105.5 1749513
Marble Court, Lymington Road, TORQUAY, TQ1 4AU
Tel: 01803 321050
Email: news@palm.fm
Web site: http://www.palm.fm
News Editor: Amy Capron

PASSION FOR THE PLANET 758604
Zeal House, Deer Park Road, LONDON, SW19 3GY
Tel: 020 8544 0091
Email: news@passionfortheplanet.com
Web site: http://www.passionfortheplanet.com
News Editor: Chantal Cooke

PEAK FM 42354
Radio House, Foxwood Road, CHESTERFIELD, S41 9RF
Tel: 01246 267132 **Fax:** 01246 267108
Email: news@peak107.com
Web site: http://www.peakfm.net
News Editor: Amy Meehan

PENNINE FM 42392
The Old Stable Block, Brewery Drive, Lockwood Park, HUDDERSFIELD, HD1 3UR **Tel:** 01484 319967
Fax: 01484 311107
Email: news@penninefm.com
Web site: http://www.penninefm.com
News Editor: Diane Bramell

PENWITH RADIO 1900175
Wharfside Shopping Centre, Market Jew Street, PENZANCE, TR18 2GB **Tel:** 01736 362884
Email: admin@penwithradio.org
Web site: http://www.penwithradio.org
News Editor: Julian Horner

PHOENIX FM 1826647
The Baytree Centre, Chapel High, BRENTWOOD, CM14 4BX
Tel: 01277 849929 **Fax:** 01277 849932
Email: steve@phoenixfm.com
Web site: http://www.phoenixfm.com
News Editor: Steve Mead

PHONIC FM 1851564
The Studios, The Exeter Phoenix, Bradninch Place, Gandy Street, EXETER, EX4 3LS **Tel:** 01392 427416
Email: info@phonic.fm
Web site: http://www.phonic.fm
News Editor: David Treharne

PIRATE FM 42488
Carn Brea Studios, Wilson Way, REDRUTH, TR15 3XX
Tel: 01209 314314 **Fax:** 01209 314345
Email: news@piratefm.co.uk
Web site: http://www.piratefm.co.uk
News Editor: Tristan Hunkin; **Managing Director:** Beverley Warne

PLAY RADIO 601013
St. Mary's Stadium, Britannia Road, SOUTHAMPTON, SO14 5FP **Tel:** 023 8033 0300 **Fax:** 023 8020 6400
Email: news@playradiouk.com
Web site: http://www.playradiouk.com
News Editor: News Desk

PREMIER CHRISTIAN RADIO 42437
22 Chapter Street, LONDON, SW1P 4NP **Tel:** 020 7316 1300
Fax: 020 7233 6706
Email: victoria.laurence@premier.org.uk
Web site: http://www.premier.org.uk
News Editor: Victoria Laurence

PULSE GOLD 26472
Pennine House, Forster Square, BRADFORD, BD1 5NE
Tel: 01274 203040
Email: news@pulse.co.uk
Web site: http://www.pulseclassicgold.co.uk
News Editor: Stephanie Otty

THE PULSE OF WEST YORKSHIRE 42335
Forster Square, BRADFORD, BD1 5NE **Tel:** 01274 203040
Email: news@pulse.co.uk
Web site: http://www.pulse.co.uk
News Editor: Mark Brow

PURE RADIO 1826651
PO Box 1078, STOCKPORT, SK3 0WH **Tel:** 0161 474 5964
Fax: 0161 491 6236
Email: pete@pureradio.org.uk
Web site: http://www.pureradio.org.uk
News Editor: Pete Liggins

Q101.2 WEST FM 713723
42A Market Street, OMAGH, BT78 1EH **Tel:** 028 8224 5777
Fax: 028 8225 9517
Email: news@q101west.fm
Web site: http://www.q101west.fm
News Editor: Damien McGinley; **Managing Director:** Robert Walshe

Q102.9 FM 42585
The Riverview Suite, 87 Rossdowney Road, Waterside, LONDONDERRY, BT47 5SU **Tel:** 028 7134 4449
Fax: 028 7131 2233
Email: news@sevenfm.co.uk
Web site: http://www.q102.fm
News Editor: Anna Quigley; **Managing Director:** Robert Walsh

Q97.2 FM CAUSEWAY COAST RADIO 628761
24 Cloyfin Road, COLERAINE, BT52 2NU
Tel: 028 7035 9100 **Fax:** 028 7032 6666
Email: news@sevenfm.co.uk
Web site: http://www.q972.fm
News Editor: Victoria Steveley; **Managing Director:** Robert Walshe

QUAY WEST 107.4 624217
Royal Clarence House, York Buildings, High Street, BRIDGWATER, TA6 3BH **Tel:** 01278 727701
Fax: 01278 727705
Email: studio@quaywest-radio.com
Web site: http://www.quaywest-radio.com
News Editor: Dave Englefield

QUAY WEST FM 26483
Harbour Studios, The Esplanade, WATCHET, TA23 0AJ
Email: news@quaywestradio.net
Web site: http://www.quaywest-radio.com
News Editor: Spencer Bishop

RADIO BORDERS 42575
Tweedside Park, Tweedbank, GALASHIELS, TD1 3TD
Tel: 01896 759444 **Fax:** 0845 345 7080
Email: news@radioborders.com
Web site: http://www.radioborders.com
News Editor: News Desk

RADIO CARMARTHENSHIRE AND SCARLET FM 1633125
PO Box 971, LLANELLI, SA15 1YH **Tel:** 0845 890 2000
Email: studio@scarletfm.com
Web site: http://www.radiocarmarthenshire.com
News Editor: Sara Andrew

RADIO CEREDIGION 42536
The Old Welsh School, Alexandra Road, ABERYSTWYTH, SY23 1LF **Tel:** 01970 627999 **Fax:** 01970 627206
Email: admin@ceredigionfm.co.uk
Web site: http://www.radioceredigion.net
News Editor: Ceryl Davies

UK Broadcasting & Other Media

RADIO CITY 96.7 42417
St. John's Beacon, 1 Houghton Street, LIVERPOOL, L1 1RL
Tel: 0151 472 6840 Fax: 0151 472 6841
Email: news@radiocity.co.uk
Web site: http://www.radiocity.co.uk
News Editor: Steve Hothersall

RADIO FAZA 762188
412-414 Radford Road, NOTTINGHAM, NG7 7NP
Tel: 0115 844 0047 Fax: 0115 844 0049
Email: mail@radiofaza.org.uk
Web site: http://www.radiofaza.org.uk
News Editor: Tasneem Ahmed; Advertising Manager:
Tasneem Ahmed

RADIO SCILLY 1697033
Unit 21 Porth Mellon, St. Mary's, ISLES OF SCILLY, TR21
0JY Tel: 01720 423417 Fax: 01720 423304
Email: studio@radioscilly.com
Web site: http://www.radioscilly.co.uk
News Editor: Keri Jones; Managing Director: Keri Jones

RADIO ST. AUSTELL BAY 1832406
Tregorrick Park, Tregorrick, ST. AUSTELL, PL26 7AG
Tel: 01726 65566
Email: g@rsab.org
Web site: http://www.rsab.org
News Editor: Graham Walker

RADIO TEESDALE 1851239
Enterprise House, Harmire Enterprise Park, BARNARD
CASTLE, DL12 8XT Tel: 01833 696750 Fax: 01833 631909
Email: studio@radioteesdale.co.uk
Web site: http://www.radioteesdale.co.uk
News Editor: Peter Dixon

RADIO TIRCOED 106.5 FM 1864277
Radio Tircoed Studio, Village Hall, Tircoed Forest Village,
Penllergaer, SWANSEA, SA4 9SF Tel: 01792 898628
Email: dj@radiotircoed.com
Web site: http://www.radiotircoed.com
News Editor: Phil England

RADIO VERULAM 1646069
PO Box 1092, ST ALBANS, AL1 9QB Tel: 01727 839926
Email: studio@radioverulam.com
Web site: http://www.radio-verulam.co.uk
News Editor: Phil Richards

RADIO WAVE 42330
965 Mowbray Drive, BLACKPOOL, FY3 7JR
Tel: 01253 650300 Fax: 01253 301965
Web site: http://www.wave965.com
News Editor: News Desk; Advertising Manager: Janice
Nandy

RADIO XL 42328
KMS House, Bradford Street, BIRMINGHAM, B12 0JD
Tel: 0121 753 5353 Fax: 0121 753 3111
Email: news@radioxl.net
Web site: http://www.radioxl.net
News Editor: News Desk; Managing Director: Arun Bajaj

RAIDIÓ FÁILTE 107.1 FM 1839828
An Chultúrlann, 216 Falls Road, BELFAST, BT12 6AH
Tel: 028 9031 0013
Email: oifig@raidiofailte.com
Web site: http://www.raidiofailte.com
News Editor: Máire Nic Fhionnahtaigh

RAM FM 42366
35-36 Iron Gate, DERBY, DE1 3GA Tel: 01332 324060
Fax: 01332 324009
Email: news@ramfm.co.uk
Web site: http://www.ramfm.co.uk
News Editor: Newsroom

READING 107 FM 768587
Radio House, Madejski Stadium, READING, RG2 0FN
Tel: 0118 945 0808 Fax: 0118 945 0809
Email: news@reading107fm.com
Web site: http://www.reading107fm.com
News Editor: Mel Bloor; Managing Director: Richard Codd

REAL RADIO 100-102 42378
Marquis Court, Team Valley Trading Estate, GATESHEAD,
NE11 0RU Tel: 0191 440 7555
Email: northeastnews@gmgradio.com
Web site: http://www.realradionortheast.co.uk
News Editor: Dan Entwisle; Managing Director: Debbie
Bowman

REAL RADIO 105.4 FM 42450
Laser House, Waterfront Quay, Salford Quays, SALFORD,
M50 3XW Tel: 0161 886 8860
Email: news@centuryradio.co.uk
Web site: http://www.realradionorthwest.co.uk
News Editor: News Desk; Managing Director: Andy Carter

REAL RADIO (CENTRAL SCOTLAND) 42561
1 Park Way Court, Glasgow Business Park, GLASGOW, G69
6GA Tel: 0141 781 2206 Fax: 0141 781 1112
Email: realnews@realradiofm.com
Web site: http://www.realradio-scotland.co.uk
Editor: David Treasurer; News Editor: Newsdesk;
Managing Director: Billy Anderson

REAL RADIO (WALES) 623857
PO Box 6105, Ty-Nant Court, CARDIFF, CF15 8YF
Tel: 029 2031 5110 Fax: 0845 051 0506
Email: news@realradio.co.uk
Web site: http://www.realradio.co.uk
News Editor: Sam Fleet

REAL RADIO (YORKSHIRE) 713782
1 Sterling Court, Tingley, WAKEFIELD, WF3 1EL
Tel: 0113 307 1444
Email: newscentre@realradio.co.uk
Web site: http://www.realradio.co.uk
News Editor: Justin Lockwood; Managing Director: Steve
South

RED DRAGON FM 42541
Red Dragon Centre, CARDIFF, CF10 4DJ
Tel: 029 2094 2940 Fax: 029 2066 2067
Email: news@reddragonfm.co.uk
Web site: http://www.reddragonfm.co.uk
News Editor: Vicky Etchells; Managing Director: Sally
Oldham

RESONANCE 104.4 FM 1646129
144 Borough High Street, LONDON, SE1 1LB
Tel: 020 7407 1210
Email: info@resonancefm.com
Web site: http://www.resonancefm.com
News Editor: Richard Thomas

THE REVOLUTION 622581
PO Box 962, OLDHAM, OL1 3JF Tel: 0161 621 6516
Fax: 0161 621 6521
Email: news@therevolution.uk.com
Web site: http://www.therevolution962.com
News Editor: Sara Cunningham

RIDINGS FM 600929
Unit 7, Network Centre, Zenith Park, Whaley Road,
BARNSLEY, S75 1HT Tel: 01924 598577 Fax: 01924 367133
Email: news@ridingsfm.co.uk
Web site: http://www.ridingsfm.co.uk
News Editor: Holly Hampshire

ROCK RADIO NORTH EAST 1836390
Marquis Court, Team Valley, GATESHEAD,
NE11 0RU Tel: 0191 440 7500 Fax: 0191 440 7501
Email: northeastnews@gmgradio.com
Web site: http://www.rockradionortheast.co.uk
News Editor: Myles Ashby

ROTHER FM 1780917
Aspen Court, Bessemer Way, ROTHERHAM, S60 1FB
Tel: 01709 369991 Fax: 01709 369993
Email: news@rotherfm.co.uk
Web site: http://www.rotherfm.co.uk
News Editor: Claire Whitfield

RUTLAND RADIO 42473
40 Melton Road, OAKHAM, LE15 6AY Tel: 01572 757868
Fax: 01572 757744
Email: news@rutlandradio.co.uk
Web site: http://www.rutlandradio.co.uk
News Editor: James Wall

SABRAS RADIO 42411
Radio House, 63 Melton Road, LEICESTER, LE4 6PN
Tel: 0116 261 0666 Fax: 0116 266 7776
Email: richard@sabrasradio.com
Web site: http://www.sabrasradio.com
News Editor: Richard Scarle; Managing Director: Don
Kotak

SEASIDE RADIO 1824650
27 Seaside Road, WITHERNSEA, HU19 2DL
Tel: 01964 611427 Fax: 01964 611427
Email: info@seasideradio.co.uk
Web site: http://www.seasideradio.co.uk
News Editor: Justin McCartney

SEVEN FM 1841117
1 Millenium Park, Woodside Road Industrial Estate,
Woodside Road, BALLYMENA, BT42 4QJ
Tel: 028 2564 8777 Fax: 028 2564 8778
Email: news@sevenfm.co.uk
Web site: http://www.sevenfm.co.uk
News Editor: Damien McGinley

SHROPSHIRE'S BEACON RADIO 1696578
267 Tettenhall Road, WOLVERHAMPTON, WV6 0DE
Tel: 01902 461260 Fax: 01902 461266
Email: news@beaconradio.co.uk
Web site: http://www.beaconradio.co.uk
News Editor: Louise Easton

SIBC 42577
Market Street, LERWICK, ZE1 0JN Tel: 01595 695299
Fax: 01595 695696
Email: news@sibc.co.uk
Web site: http://www.sibc.co.uk
News Editor: Ian Anderson; Managing Director: Inga
Walterson

SIGNAL 1 42508
Stoke Road, Shelton, STOKE-ON-TRENT, ST4 2SR
Tel: 01782 441300 Fax: 01782 441301
Email: news@signalradio.com
Web site: http://www.signal1.co.uk
News Editor: Paul Sheldon

SIGNAL 2 42509
Stoke Road, Shelton, STOKE-ON-TRENT, ST4 2SR
Tel: 01782 441300 Fax: 01782 441301
Email: news@signalradio.com
Web site: http://www.signal2.co.uk
News Editor: Paul Sheldon

SILK FM 42446
140 Moss Lane, MACCLESFIELD, SK11 7XE
Tel: 01625 268000 Fax: 01625 269010
Email: news@silkfm.com
Web site: http://www.silkfm.com
News Editor: Andy Bailey

SIREN FM 1824870
Brayford Pool, LINCOLN, LN6 7PS Tel: 01522 837337
Email: adavid@lincoln.ac.uk
Web site: http://www.sirenonline.co.uk
News Editor: Andrew David; Managing Editor: Andrew
David

SIX FM 763713
2C Park Avenue, COOKSTOWN, BT80 8AH
Tel: 028 8675 8696 Fax: 028 8676 1550
Email: news@sixfm.co.uk
Web site: http://www.sixfm.co.uk
News Editor: Debbie Burden

SKYLINE 1837524
The Old School House, St. Johns Road, Hedge End, SOUTHAMPTON, SO30 4AF **Tel:** 01489 799004
Fax: 01489 799008
Email: david.gates@skyline.fm
Web site: http://www.skyline.fm
News Editor: David Gates

SMOOTH RADIO (EAST MIDLANDS) 764742
Alder Court, Riverside Business Park, NOTTINGHAM, NG2 1RX **Tel:** 0115 986 1066 **Fax:** 0115 943 5075
Email: eastmidlandsnews@smoothradio.com
Web site: http://www.smoothradioeastmidlands.co.uk/
News Editor: Daryl Jackson; **Managing Director:** Samantha Fielding

SMOOTH RADIO (GLASGOW) 1654916
PO Box 101, Parkway Court, Glasgow Business Park, GLASGOW, G69 6GA **Tel:** 0141 781 2206
Fax: 0141 781 1112
Email: glasgownews@smoothradio.com
Web site: http://www.smoothradioglasgow.com
News Editor: Newsdesk; **Managing Director:** Billy Anderson

SMOOTH RADIO (LONDON) 42426
26-27 Castlereagh Street, LONDON, W1H 5DL
Tel: 020 7706 4100 **Fax:** 020 7298 7290
Email: news@smoothradio.co.uk
Web site: http://www.smoothradiolondon.com
News Editor: Bill Overton

SMOOTH RADIO (NORTH EAST) 1800277
Marquis Court, Team Valley Trading Estate, GATESHEAD, NE11 0RU **Tel:** 0191 440 7500 **Fax:** 0191 440 7501
Email: northeastnews@gmgradio.com
Web site: http://www.smoothradio.com
News Editor: Myles Ashby; **Managing Director:** Debbie Bowman

SMOOTH RADIO (NORTH WEST) 42452
Laser House, Waterfront Quay, Salford Quays, MANCHESTER, M50 3XW **Tel:** 0845 050 1004
Fax: 0845 054 1005
Email: newsroom@smoothradio.com
Web site: http://www.smoothradionorthwest.com
News Editor: News Desk

SMOOTH RADIO (WEST MIDLANDS) 712343
Crown House, 123 Hagley Road, BIRMINGHAM, B16 8LD
Tel: 0121 452 3262
Email: westmidlandsnews@smoothradio.com
Web site: http://www.smoothradiowest.com
News Editor: Colin Palmer; **Managing Director:** Andy Carter

SOUTH WEST SOUND FM 42556
Unit 40, Loreburne Centre, High Street, DUMFRIES, DG1 2BD **Tel:** 01387 250999 **Fax:** 01387 265629
Email: news.westsound@westsound.co.uk
Web site: http://www.southwestsound.co.uk
News Editor: Andrew Hynd; **Advertising Manager:** Fiona Blackwood

SOUTHEND RADIO 105.1 FM 1836207
The Icon Building, Western Esplanade, SOUTHEND-ON-SEA, SS1 1EE **Tel:** 01702 455080 **Fax:** 01702 455088
Email: info@southendradio.com
Web site: http://www.southendradio.com
News Editor: Nick Hull

SPECTRUM RADIO 42439
4 Ingate Place, Battersea, LONDON, SW8 3NS
Tel: 020 7627 4433 **Fax:** 020 7627 3409
Email: jogden@spectrumradio.net
Web site: http://www.spectrumradio.net
News Editor: Programming

SPICE FM 1852528
146 West Road, NEWCASTLE UPON TYNE, NE4 9QB
Tel: 0191 272 0883
Email: sand@spicefm.co.uk
Web site: http://www.spicefm.co.uk
News Editor: Sandeep Kapoor

SPIRE FM 42490
City Hall Studios, Malthouse Lane, SALISBURY, SP2 7QQ
Tel: 01722 416644 **Fax:** 01722 416688
Email: news@spirefm.co.uk
Web site: http://www.spirefm.co.uk
News Editor: Henrietta Creasey

SPIRIT FM 42355
9-10 Dukes Court, Bognor Road, CHICHESTER, PO19 8FX
Tel: 01243 773600 **Fax:** 01243 774814
Email: news@spiritfm.net
Web site: http://www.spiritfm.net
News Editor: Leon Jackson

STAR 107.5 FM 42353
First Floor West Suite, Cheltenham Film Studios, Arle Court, CHELTENHAM, GL51 6PN **Tel:** 01242 699555
Fax: 01242 699666
Email: news@star1075.co.uk
Web site: http://www.star1075.co.uk
News Editor: Damian Pickett

STAR RADIO BRISTOL 622573
County Gates, Ashton Road, BRISTOL, BS3 2JH
Tel: 0117 966 1065 **Fax:** 0117 953 1065
Email: news@starbristol.com
Web site: http://www.starbristol.com
News Editor: Roz Hutchins

STAR RADIO IN CAMBRIDGE 600902
Broadcast Centre, 20 Mercers Row, CAMBRIDGE, CB5 8HY
Tel: 01223 305107 **Fax:** 01223 309107
Email: news@star107.co.uk
Web site: http://www.star107.co.uk
News Editor: Emma Howgego

STAR RADIO (NORTH SOMERSET) 628824
Radio House, 11 Beaconsfield Road, WESTON-SUPER-MARE, BS23 1YE **Tel:** 01934 624455 **Fax:** 01934 629922
Email: darren.daley@star1077.co.uk
Web site: http://www.star1077.co.uk
News Editor: Darren Daley

STROUD FM 1799097
48C High Street, STROUD, GL5 1AN **Tel:** 01453 757492
Email: radio@stroudfm.co.uk
Web site: http://www.stroudfm.co.uk
News Editor: Claire Penketh

SUN FM 42512
PO Box 1034, SUNDERLAND, SR5 2YL **Tel:** 0191 548 1034
Fax: 0191 548 7171
Email: news@sun-fm.com
Web site: http://www.sun-fm.com
News Editor: Stephen McCabe

SUNRISE RADIO (LONDON) 42391
Radio House, Bridge Road, SOUTHALL, UB2 4AT
Tel: 020 8893 5900 **Fax:** 020 8893 5090
Email: news@sunriseradio.com
Web site: http://www.sunriseradio.com
News Editor: News Desk

SUNRISE RADIO (YORKSHIRE) 42336
55 Leeds Road, BRADFORD, BD1 5AF **Tel:** 01274 735043
Fax: 01274 728534
Email: news@sunriseradio.fm
Web site: http://www.sunriseradio.fm
News Editor: Gail Papworth

SUNSHINE 855 601325
Unit 11, Burway Trading Estate, LUDLOW, SY8 1EN
Tel: 01584 873795 **Fax:** 01584 875900
Email: studio1@sunshine-radio.info
Web site: http://www.sunshine-radio.info
News Editor: Kirsty Styles

SUNSHINE RADIO 42531
PO Box 262, WORCESTER, WR6 5LS **Tel:** 01905 740600
Fax: 01905 740608
Email: studio1@sunshine-radio.info
Web site: http://www.sunshinegold.co.uk
News Editor: Nigel Snow

SWANSEA SOUND 1170 MW 42547
Radio House, Victoria Road, Gowerton, SWANSEA, SA4 3AB **Tel:** 01792 511964 **Fax:** 01792 511171
Email: newsroom@swanseasound.co.uk
Web site: http://www.swanseasound.co.uk
News Editor: Emma Grant

SWINDON 105.5 1835393
Radio 105.5, County Ground, County Road, SWINDON, SN1 2ED **Tel:** 01793 611555 **Fax:** 01793 612517
Email: shirley@swindon1055.com
Web site: http://www.swindon1055.com
News Editor: Shirley Ludford

TAKEOVER RADIO 762028
PO Box 2000, LEICESTER, LE1 6YX **Tel:** 0116 299 9600
Fax: 0116 299 9654
Email: pq@takeoverradio.com
Web site: http://www.takeoverradio.co.uk
News Editor: Paul Quilter

TAY AM 42557
6 North Isla Street, DUNDEE, DD3 7JQ **Tel:** 01382 200800
Fax: 01382 423253
Email: newsroom@radiotay.co.uk
Web site: http://www.radiotay.co.uk
News Editor: Newsroom; **Managing Director:** Ally Ballingall

TAY FM 42558
6 North Isla Street, DUNDEE, DD3 7JQ **Tel:** 01382 200800
Fax: 01382 423253
Email: newsroom@radiotay.co.uk
Web site: http://www.radiotay.co.uk
News Editor: Newsroom; **Managing Director:** Ally Ballingall

TELFORD FM 42520
PO Box 1074, The Shropshire Star Building, TELFORD, TF1 5HU **Tel:** 01952 280011 **Fax:** 01952 280010
Email: news@telfordfm.co.uk
Web site: http://www.telfordfm.co.uk
News Editor: Dani Wozencroft; **Managing Director:** Peter Wagstaff

TEN 17 FM 42385
Latton Bush Centre, Southern Way, HARLOW, CM18 7BB
Tel: 01279 236680
Email: harlow.newsdesk@thisisglobal.com
Web site: http://www.ten17.co.uk

TFM RADIO 42506
Radio House, Yale Crescent, Thornaby, STOCKTON-ON-TEES, TS17 6AA **Tel:** 01642 888222 **Fax:** 01642 868290
Email: tfmnews@tfmradio.com
Web site: http://www.tfmradio.co.uk
News Editor: Hayley Brewer; **Managing Director:** Sally Aitchison

TIME 106.6 42498
Radio House, SOUTHALL, UB2 4AT **Tel:** 020 8893 5900
Email: news@time1066.com
Web site: http://www.time1066.com
News Editor: Matthew Lockwood

TIME FM 107.5 42419
Lambourne House, 7 Western Road, ROMFORD, RM1 3LD
Tel: 01708 728463 **Fax:** 01708 730383
Email: 1075news@timefm.com
Web site: http://1075.timefm.com
News Editor: Peter Stremes; **Managing Director:** Peter Stremes

TOUCH 96.2 (COVENTRY) 42360
Holly Farm Business Park, Honiley, KENILWORTH, CV8 1NP
Tel: 01926 485600 **Fax:** 01926 485678
Email: coventry.newsroom@cnradio.co.uk
Web site: http://www.962touchradio.co.uk
News Editor: Nick Jewers

TOUCH FM 42517
5-6 Aldergate, TAMWORTH, B79 7DJ **Tel:** 01827 318000
Fax: 01827 318002
Email: tamworth.newsroom@cnradio.co.uk
Web site: http://www.touchblt.co.uk
News Editor: Mathew Hulbert

UK Broadcasting & Other Media

TOWER FM
42331
The Mill, Brownlow Way, BOLTON, BL1 2RA
Tel: 01204 387444 **Fax:** 01204 534065
Email: news@towerfm.co.uk
Web site: http://www.towerfm.co.uk
News Editor: Sophie Hubberstey

TOWN 102
1791911
1st Floor, Radio House, Orion Court, Great Blakenham, IPSWICH, IP6 0LW **Tel:** 0845 365 1102 **Fax:** 0845 365 2102
Email: news@town102.com
Web site: http://www.town102.com
News Editor: Angharad Thomas

TRAX FM
42533
5 Sidings Court, White Rose Way, DONCASTER, DN4 5NU
Tel: 01302 738383 **Fax:** 01302 326104
Email: news@traxfm.co.uk
Web site: http://www.traxfm.co.uk
News Editor: Tina Masters

TRAX FM 107.9
1648459
5 Sidings Court, White Rose Way, DONCASTER, DN4 5NU
Tel: 01302 341166 **Fax:** 01302 326104
Email: news@traxfm.co.uk
Web site: http://www.traxfm.co.uk
News Editor: News Desk

TRENT FM
42469
Level 6, Chapel Quarter, Maid Marian Way, NOTTINGHAM, NG1 6JR **Tel:** 0115 873 1520 **Fax:** 0115 873 1529
Email: news@trentfm.co.uk
Web site: http://www.trentfm.co.uk
News Editor: Lewis Scrimshaw

TWO LOCHS RADIO
1616406
Harbour Centre, Pier Road, GAIRLOCH, IV21 2BQ
Tel: 0870 741 4657 **Fax:** 01445 712857
Email: press@2lr.co.uk
Web site: http://www.2lr.co.uk
News Editor: Alex Gray

U105
1698968
Havelock House, Ormeau Road, BELFAST, BT7 1EB
Tel: 028 9026 2261
Email: news@u105.com
Web site: http://www.u105.com
News Editor: Peter McVerry

UNITY 101
1839489
107 St. Mary's Road, SOUTHAMPTON, SO14 0AN
Tel: 023 8023 3239 **Fax:** 023 8023 3239
Email: kelly@unity101.org
Web site: http://www.unity101.org
News Editor: Ram Kalyan

VIBE RADIO
1835419
The Clinton Centre, East Bridge Street, ENNISKILLEN, BT74 6AA **Tel:** 028 6632 8160
Email: info@viberadio.fm
Web site: http://www.viberadio.fm
News Editor: Neil Wylie

WAVE 102
26445
8 South Tay Street, DUNDEE, DD1 1PA **Tel:** 01382 908020
Fax: 01382 908035
Email: bill.mcleod@wave102.co.uk
Web site: http://www.wave102.co.uk
News Editor: Alison McDonald; **Managing Director:** Adam Findley

WAVE 105.2 FM
42377
PO Box 105, FAREHAM, PO15 5YF **Tel:** 01489 481058
Fax: 01489 481060
Email: news@wave105.com
Web site: http://www.wave105.com
News Editor: Jason Beck; **Managing Director:** Martin Ball

WAVES RADIO
42572
7 Black Circle House, Black House Industrial Estate, PETERHEAD, AB42 1BN **Tel:** 01779 491012
Fax: 01779 490802
Email: glenn.moir@wavesfm.com
Web site: http://www.wavesfm.com
News Editor: Glenn Moir

WAYLAND RADIO
1925337
The Stables, Swaffham Road, Ashill, THETFORD, IP25 7BT
Tel: 01760 441161
Email: studio@waylandradio.com
Web site: http://www.wylandradio.com
News Editor: David Hatherly

WCR FM
766197
Newhampton Centre, Newhampton Road East, WOLVERHAMPTON, WV1 4AP **Tel:** 01902 572260
Fax: 01902 572261
Email: steve@wcrfm.com
Web site: http://www.wcrfm.com
News Editor: Steve Morris

WESSEX FM
42368
Radio House, Trinity Street, DORCHESTER, DT1 1DJ
Tel: 01305 250333 **Fax:** 01305 266885
Email: news@wessexfm.com
Web site: http://www.wessexfm.com
News Editor: Maria Greenwood

WEST FM
765917
Radio House, 54A Holmston Road, AYR, KA7 3BE
Tel: 01292 283662 **Fax:** 01292 262607
Email: west-news@westsound.co.uk
Web site: http://www.westsound.co.uk
News Editor: Ross Nixon

WEST MIDLAND'S BEACON RADIO
1696577
267 Tettenhall Road, WOLVERHAMPTON, WV6 0DE
Tel: 01902 461260 **Fax:** 01902 461266
Email: news@beaconradio.co.uk
Web site: http://www.beaconradio.co.uk
News Editor: Louise Easton

WEST SOUND AM
42554
Radio House, 54A Holmston Road, AYR, KA7 3BE
Tel: 01292 283662 **Fax:** 01292 283665
Email: west-news@westsound.co.uk
Web site: http://www.west-sound.co.uk
News Editor: Ross Nixon

WIGHTFM
1872995
Spithead Business Centre, Newport Road, SANDOWN, PO36 9PH **Tel:** 01983 409921
Email: news@wightfm.com
Web site: http://www.wightfm.com
News Editor: Justin Gladdis

WYTHENSHAWE FM
763814
First Floor, Alderman Gatley House, Hale Top, Civic Centre, Wythenshawe, MANCHESTER, M22 5RQ
Tel: 0161 499 7982
Email: info@wfmradio.org
Web site: http://www.wfmradio.org
News Editor: Jason Kenyon

WYVERN FM
42532
1st Floor, Kirkham House, John Comyn Drive, WORCESTER, WR3 7NS **Tel:** 01905 545500 **Fax:** 01905 545509
Email: news@wyvernfm.co.uk
Web site: http://www.wyvernfm.co.uk
News Editor: News Desk

X FM
42442
30 Leicester Square, LONDON, WC2H 7LA
Tel: 020 7054 8000 **Fax:** 020 7766 6601
Email: matt.dyson@xfm.co.uk
Web site: http://www.xfm.co.uk
News Editor: Matt Dyson

XFM MANCHESTER
1743069
Suite 1.1, 4 Exchange Quay, SALFORD, M5 3EE
Tel: 0161 662 4790 **Fax:** 0161 662 4799
Email: news@xfmmanchester.co.uk
Web site: http://www.xfmmanchester.co.uk
News Editor: James Brown

YORKSHIRE COAST RADIO
42491
PO Box 962, SCARBOROUGH, YO11 3ZP
Tel: 01723 581700 **Fax:** 01723 588990
Email: news@yorkshirecoastradio.com
Web site: http://www.yorkshirecoastradio.com
News Editor: Louisa Maher

YORKSHIRE COAST RADIO BRIDLINGTON
1665241
PO Box 962, SCARBOROUGH, YO11 3ZP
Tel: 01723 581700 **Fax:** 01723 588990
Email: news@yorkshirecoastradio.com
Web site: http://www.yorkshirecoastradio.com
News Editor: Rebecca O'Flynn

YORKSHIRE RADIO
1833504
Elland Road, LEEDS, LS11 0ES **Tel:** 0113 367 6177
Fax: 0113 367 6480
Email: onair@yorkshireradio.net
Web site: http://www.yorkshireradio.net
News Editor: Ben Fry

YOURRADIO
628879
Pioneer Park Studios, Unit 3, 80 Castlegreen Street, DUMBARTON, G82 1JB **Tel:** 01389 734422
Fax: 01389 734380
Email: news@yourradiofm.com
Web site: http://www.yourradiofm.com
News Editor: Gary Pews

NEWS INFORMATION SERVICES

24 DASH
1764850
Fortis et Fides, Whitestone Business Park, Whitestone, HEREFORD, HR1 3SE **Tel:** 01432 852522
Email: news@24dash.com
Web site: http://www.24dash.com
Editor: Jon Land

THE 451 GROUP
623986
37-41 Gower Street, LONDON, WC1E 6HH
Tel: 020 7299 7766
Email: william.fellows@the451group.com
Web site: http://www.the451group.com
Editor: William Fellows

ANANOVA
626427
Marshall Mill, Marshall Street, LEEDS, LS11 9YJ
Tel: 0113 367 4600
Email: newsdesk@ananova.com
Web site: http://www.ananova.com
Editor: Simon Glover; **News Editor:** Simon Glover

BESTADVICE.NET
758598
PR by email only **Tel:** 020 7639 5120
Email: newsdesk@bestadvice.net
Web site: http://www.bestadvice.net
Editor: News Desk

BONDWATCH
1790174
6th Floor, 18 King William Street, LONDON, EC4N 7BP
Tel: 020 7017 7003 **Fax:** 020 7017 7844
Email: andy.hicks@informa.com
Web site: http://www.informagm.com
Editor: Andy Hicks

DAILY MARKETING BULLETIN
1846833
Suite 2.1B, The Old Fire Station, 140 Tabernacle Street, LONDON, EC2A 4SD **Tel:** 020 7300 7333
Email: info@utalkmarketing.com
Web site: http://www.utalkmarketing.com
Editor: Clark Turner

THE LEISURE DATABASE COMPANY
42939
33 Bedford Street, Covent Garden, LONDON, WC2E 9EJ
Tel: 020 7379 3197 **Fax:** 020 7379 6174
Email: enquiries@theleisuredatabase.com
Web site: http://www.theleisuredatabase.com
Editor: David Minton

PERFECT INFORMATION
42940
35 Chiswell Street, LONDON, EC1Y 4SE **Tel:** 020 7892 4200
Fax: 020 7892 4201
Email: brendanm@perfectinfo.com
Web site: http://www.perfectinfo.com
Editor: Brendan Meehan

REUTERS ONLINE 1665479
Kildare House, 3 Dorset Rise, LONDON, EC4Y 8EN
Tel: 020 7542 6472 **Fax:** 020 7542 7921
Email: uk.online@reuters.com
Web site: http://uk.reuters.com
Editor: Astrid Zweynert

HOSPITAL RADIO

BAY TRUST RADIO 1641579
The Westmorland General Hospital, Burton Road, KENDAL,
LA9 7RG **Tel:** 0845 094 3096
Email: info@baytrustradio.co.uk
Web site: http://www.baytrustradio.co.uk
News Editor: John Williamson

BRIDGE FM 42664
The Tayside Hospital Broadcasting Group, Level 5,
Ninewells Hospital, DUNDEE, DD1 9SY **Tel:** 01382 496333
Email: manager@bridgefm.org.uk
Web site: http://www.bridgefm.org.uk
News Editor: Scott Young

**BRISTOL HOSPITAL BROADCASTING
SERVICE** 42634
Bristol Royal Infirmary, BRISTOL, BS2 8HW
Tel: 0117 929 3303
Email: iain.elliott@blueyonder.co.uk
Web site: http://mail.bris.ac.uk/~pmrie/bhbs.htm
News Editor: Iain Elliott

GRAMPIAN HOSPITAL RADIO 42637
Ashgrove House, Aberdeen Royal Infirmary, Foresterhill,
ABERDEEN, AB25 2ZA **Tel:** 01224 552964
Email: john.graham@arh.grampian.scot.nhs.uk
Web site: http://www.ghr.org.uk
News Editor: John Graham

HARROGATE HOSPITAL RADIO 623675
Harrogate District Hospital, Lancaster Park Road,
HARROGATE, HG2 7SX **Tel:** 01423 553342
News Editor: David Simister

HOSPITAL BROADCASTING SHEFFIELD 42641
Royal Hallamshire Hospital, Glossop Road, SHEFFIELD, S10
2JF **Tel:** 0114 271 2719 **Fax:** 0114 271 1969
Web site: http://www.hbsradio.co.uk
News Editor: Chris Fox

HOSPITAL RADIO BARNET 42642
Barnet Hospital, Wellhouse Lane, BARNET, EN5 3DJ
Tel: 020 8216 4796
Web site: http://www.hrb.org.uk
News Editor: Frank Heinley

HOSPITAL RADIO BEDSIDE 42643
The Studios, The Royal Bournemouth Hospital, Castle Lane
East, BOURNEMOUTH, BH7 7DW **Tel:** 01202 303887
Fax: 01202 704525
Email: webmaster@hospitalradiobedside.co.uk
Web site: http://www.hospitalradiobedside.co.uk
News Editor: Paul Sutton

HOSPITAL RADIO EXETER 42638
Royal Devon and Exeter Hospital (Wonford), Barrack Road,
EXETER, EX2 5DW **Tel:** 01392 402020 **Fax:** 01392 402020
Email: studio@hospitalradioexeter.co.uk
Web site: http://www.hospitalradioexeter.com
News Editor: Programme Controller

HOSPITAL RADIO MEDWAY 42639
Medway Maritime Hospital, Windmill Road, GILLINGHAM,
ME7 5NY **Tel:** 01634 406865
Email: studio@hospitalradiomedway.co.uk
Web site: http://www.hospitalradiomedway.co.uk
News Editor: Eunice Norman

HOSPITAL RADIO TUNBRIDGE WELLS 42645
Ashley Hale Suite, Kent and Sussex Hospital, Mount
Ephram, TUNBRIDGE WELLS, TN4 8AT **Tel:** 01892 528528
Fax: 01892 724804
Email: info@hrtw.org.uk
Web site: http://www.hrtw.org.uk
News Editor: Chris Manser

HOSPITAL RADIO WRIGHTINGTON 42646
Wrightington Hospital, Hall Lane, Appley Bridge, WIGAN,
WN6 9EP **Tel:** 01257 252435
Email: jrduffy@hotmail.co.uk
News Editor: John Duffy

MID-DOWNS HOSPITAL RADIO 762641
The Princess Royal Hospital, Lewes Road, HAYWARDS
HEATH, RH16 4EX **Tel:** 01444 441350
Email: studio@mdr.org.uk
Web site: http://www.mdr.org.uk
News Editor: Julia Mewes

MILLSIDE HOSPITAL RADIO 26490
King's Mill Hospital, Mansfield Road, SUTTON-IN-
ASHFIELD, NG17 4JL **Tel:** 01623 627596
Email: info@millsideradio.co.uk
Web site: http://www.millsideradio.co.uk
News Editor: Graham Collis

PADDINGTON'S HOSPITAL RADIO 42649
St. Mary's Hospital, Praed Street, LONDON, W2 1NY
Tel: 020 7402 8792 **Fax:** 020 7886 6200
Email: admin@phr.org.uk
Web site: http://www.phr.org.uk
News Editor: Peter Fielding

RADIO CHERWELL 42651
The Studio, Churchill Hospital, Headington, OXFORD, OX3
7LJ **Tel:** 01865 225522
Email: studio@radiocherwell.com
Web site: http://www.radiocherwell.com
News Editor: Natalie Higgs

RADIO LOLLIPOP (BRISTOL) 42660
Bristol Royal Hospital for Sick Children, Paul O'Gorman
Building, Upper Maudlin Street, BRISTOL, BS2 8BJ
Tel: 0117 342 8321
Web site: http://www.radiolollipop.org
News Editor: Paul Lindsay

RADIO LOLLIPOP (EDINBURGH) 42659
Royal Hospital for Sick Children, Sciennes Road,
EDINBURGH, EH9 1LF **Tel:** 0131 668 3097
Fax: 0131 536 0775
Email: edinburgh@radiolollipop.org
Web site: http://www.radiolollipop.org
News Editor: Louise Trow

RADIO MARSDEN 26493
Royal Marsden Hospital, Downs Road, SUTTON, SM2 5PT
Tel: 020 8661 3083
Email: secretary@radiomarsden.co.uk
Web site: http://www.radiomarsden.co.uk
News Editor: Steve Palmer

RADIO NIGHTINGALE 1641576
Rotherham General Hospital, Moorgate Road,
ROTHERHAM, S60 2UD **Tel:** 01709 304244
Email: admin@radionightingale.org.uk
Web site: http://www.radionightingale.org.uk
News Editor: Mel Jaques

RADIO NORTHWICK PARK 1641577
PO Box 615, HARROW, HA2 2BY **Tel:** 020 8869 3959
Email: press@radionorthwickpark.org
Web site: http://www.radionorthwickpark.org
News Editor: Stacie Souroukides

RADIO RAINBOW 42662
Ashgrove House, Aberdeen Royal Infirmary, Foresterhill,
ABERDEEN, AB25 2ZN **Tel:** 01224 550321
Web site: http://www.ghr.org.uk
News Editor: John Graham

RADIO ST. HELIER 42663
St. Helier Hospital, Wrythe Lane, CARSHALTON, SM5 1AA
Tel: 020 8296 2259 **Fax:** 020 8644 2603
Email: requests@radiosthelier.co.uk
Web site: http://www.radiosthelier.co.uk
News Editor: Kevin Horkan

RADIO TYNESIDE 42665
Radio Tyneside, Broadcast House, PO Box 1575,
NEWCASTLE UPON TYNE, NE99 2AW **Tel:** 0191 222 0789
Email: info@radiotyneside.co.uk
Web site: http://www.radiotyneside.co.uk
News Editor: Dave Nicholson

RADIO WEST MIDDLESEX 42667
West Middlesex University Hospital, Twickenham Road,
ISLEWORTH, TW7 6AF **Tel:** 020 8321 5166
Email: studio@radiowestmiddlesex.co.uk
Web site: http://www.radiowestmiddlesex.org.uk
News Editor: Alan Hardy

RADIO WEST SUFFOLK 1641595
The Friends Room, West Suffolk Hospital, Hardwick Lane,
BURY ST. EDMUNDS, IP33 2QZ **Tel:** 01284 713403
Web site: http://www.radiowestsuffolk.co.uk
News Editor: Julie MacLeod

RED DOT RADIO 42636
Royal Victoria Hospital, Craigleith Road, EDINBURGH, EH4
2DN **Tel:** 0131 537 5353
Email: chairman@ehbs.co.uk
Web site: http://www.reddotradio.co.uk
News Editor: Paul Coleman

RIDGEWAY RADIO 42668
Room 200, Dorset County Hospital, Williams Avenue,
DORCHESTER, DT1 2JY **Tel:** 01305 254227
Fax: 01305 255677
Email: enquires@ridgewayradio.org.uk
Web site: http://www.ridgewayradio.org.uk
News Editor: Peter Foster

RNA FM 42650
Rosemount Road, ARBROATH, DD11 2AT
Tel: 01241 879660
Email: info@radionorthangus.co.uk
Web site: http://www.radionorthangus.co.uk
News Editor: Malcolm Finlayson; **Managing Director:**
Malcolm Finlayson

**SOUTHAMPTON HOSPITAL
BROADCASTING ASSOCIATION** 42671
The Studio Centre, Tebourba Way, SOUTHAMPTON, SO16
4QE **Tel:** 023 8078 5151 **Fax:** 023 8078 5151
Email: hba@sohba.org
Web site: http://www.sohba.org
News Editor: Alan Lambourn

VICTORIA INFIRMARY RADIO 42673
South Glasgow Hospitals NHS Trust, Langside Road,
GLASGOW, G42 9TY **Tel:** 0141 201 5173
Web site: http://www.victoriainfirmaryradio.co.uk
News Editor: Craig McDougall

WYCOMBE RADIO 42676
Radio Room, Wycombe General Hospital, Queen Alexandra
Road, HIGH WYCOMBE, HP11 2TT **Tel:** 01494 425500
Email: whba@whba.org.uk
Web site: http://www.whba.org.uk
News Editor: Brian Sharman

STUDENT RADIO

1449 AM URB 26455
Students Union, University of Bath, Claverton Down, BATH,
BA2 7AY **Tel:** 01225 383629
Email: urb-manager@bath.ac.uk
Web site: http://www.1449urb.co.uk
News Editor: Tim Ayres

UK Broadcasting & Other Media

BAILRIGG FM 42707
Fylde College, Lancaster University, Bailrigg, LANCASTER, LA1 4YF **Tel:** 01524 593902
Email: news@bailriggfm.co.uk
Web site: http://www.bailriggfm.co.uk
News Editor: Head of News

BURN FM 42709
Guild of Students, University of Birmingham, Edgbaston Park Road, BIRMINGHAM, B15 2TU **Tel:** 0121 251 2300
Email: burnoff2@guild.bham.ac.uk
Web site: http://www.burnfm.com
News Editor: Station Manager

BURST FM 42710
Bristol University, Students' Union, Queens Road, Clifton, BRISTOL, BS8 1LN **Tel:** 0117 954 5777 **Fax:** 0117 954 5817
Email: studio@burstradio.org.uk
Web site: http://www.burstradio.org.uk
News Editor: Paras Shah

CRUSH 42715
Students' Union, University of Hertfordshire, College Lane, HATFIELD, AL10 9AB **Tel:** 01707 285005 **Fax:** 01707 286151
Email: uhsu.comms@herts.ac.uk
Web site: http://www.crushradio.co.uk
News Editor: Alec Sammon

CSR 42711
Mandela Building, University of kent, CANTERBURY, CT2 7NW **Tel:** 01227 824703
Email: press@csrfm.com
Web site: http://www.csrfm.com
News Editor: Will Jones

CUR 1350 (CAMBRIDGE UNIVERSITY RADIO) 42713
Churchill College, CAMBRIDGE, CB3 0DS
Tel: 01223 501004
Email: news@cur1350.co.uk
Web site: http://www.cur1350.co.uk
News Editor: Michael Brookes

DEMON FM 42716
De Montfort Students' Union, Campus Centre Building, Mill Lane, LEICESTER, LE2 7DR **Tel:** 0116 255 5576
Email: manager@demonfm.co.uk
Web site: http://www.demonfm.co.uk
News Editor: Andy Schooledge

EC1 FM 42705
City University, Department of Journalism, Northampton Square, LONDON, EC1V 0HB **Tel:** 020 7040 8228
Fax: 020 7040 8594
Email: b.schofield@city.ac.uk
Web site: http://www.ec1fm.org.uk
News Editor: Barbara Schofield

FLY FM 42720
Byron House, Shakespeare Street, NOTTINGHAM, NG1 4GH **Tel:** 0115 848 6200 **Fax:** 0115 848 6201
Email: flyfm@su.ntu.ac.uk
Web site: http://www.flyfm.co.uk
News Editor: David Walker

IC RADIO 42724
Beit Quad, Imperial College London, Prince Consort Road, South Kensington, LONDON, SW7 2BB **Tel:** 020 7594 8100
Fax: 020 7594 8101
Email: manager@icradio.com
Web site: http://www.icradio.com
News Editor: Station Manager

JAM RADIO 42727
University House, University of Hull, HULL, HU6 7RX
Tel: 01482 466999 **Fax:** 01482 466253
Email: stationmanager@ilovejamradio.co.uk
Web site: http://www.hull.au.uk/jam

JUNCTION11 42726
RUSU Whiteknights, University of Reading, READING, RG6 6AZ **Tel:** 0118 986 4152
Email: manager.junction11@reading.ac.uk
Web site: http://www.rusu.co.uk/junction11
News Editor: Carl Pendlebury

KUBE RADIO 42728
c/o Student Union Building, Keele University, STOKE-ON-TRENT, ST5 5BG **Tel:** 01782 583706
Email: tom@kuberadio.com
Web site: http://www.kuberadio.com
News Editor: Tom Darby

LCR 42729
Loughborough Students' Union, Union Building, Ashby Road, LOUGHBOROUGH, LE11 3TT **Tel:** 01509 635050
Fax: 01509 235593
Email: sm@lcrlive.co.uk
Web site: http://www.lufbra.net/lcr
News Editor: News Desk

LSRFM.COM 42730
Leeds University Union, PO Box 157, LEEDS, LS1 1UH
Tel: 0113 380 1280 **Fax:** 0113 380 1205
Email: info@lsrfm.com
Web site: http://www.lsrfm.com
News Editor: News Desk

LUSH FM 42732
University of Leicester, Percy Gee Building, University Road, LEICESTER, LE1 7RH **Tel:** 0116 223 1177
Fax: 0116 223 1112
Email: lush@le.ac.uk
News Editor: Gregory White

RADIO WELLSWAY 1741066
Wellsway School, Chandag Road, Keynsham, BRISTOL, BS31 1PH **Tel:** 0117 986 4751
Email: radio@wellsway.bathnes.sch.uk
News Editor: Roy Page

RADIOWAVE 42719
The Annex, FCA Tremough Campus, Penryn, FALMOUTH, TR10 9EZ **Tel:** 01326 370400 **Fax:** 01326 370445
Email: radiowave_ucf@hotmail.co.uk
News Editor: Station Manager

RAMAIR 1350 AM 42742
Communal Building, University of Bradford Union, Richmond Road, BRADFORD, BD7 1DP **Tel:** 01274 233267
Email: manager@ramair.co.uk
Web site: http://www.ramair.co.uk
News Editor: Andrew McSweeney

RARE FM 42743
UCL Union, 25 Gordon Street, LONDON, WC1H 0AY
Tel: 020 7679 2509
Email: manager.rarefm@ucl.ac.uk
Web site: http://www.rarefm.co.uk
News Editor: Station Manager

RAW RADIO WARWICK 42744
Students' Union, University of Warwick, COVENTRY, CV4 7AL **Tel:** 024 7657 3077 **Fax:** 024 7657 2759
Email: marketing@radio.warwick.ac.uk
Web site: http://www.radio.warwick.ac.uk
News Editor: Ted Gelety

RED 42752
Students Union, University of Essex, Wivenhoe Park, COLCHESTER, CO4 3SQ **Tel:** 01206 863211
Fax: 01206 870915
Web site: http://www.essexstudent.com/student_media/red
News Editor: Station Manager

SHOUT FM 1663238
Liverpool John Moores University, The Haigh Building, Maryland Street, LIVERPOOL, L1 9DE **Tel:** 0151 231 4946
Email: shoutradio@livjm.ac.uk
Web site: http://www.shoutradio.co.uk
News Editor: Station Manager

SIN RADIO 42745
Students Union, Southampton Solent University, East Park Terrace, SOUTHAMPTON, SO14 0YN **Tel:** 023 8031 9920
Email: station.manager@sinradio.co.uk
Web site: http://www.sinradio.co.uk
News Editor: Head of News

SURE RADIO 42746
The University of Sheffield, Union of Students, Western Bank, SHEFFIELD, S10 2TG **Tel:** 0114 222 8750
Email: stationmanager@sureradio.com
Web site: http://www.sureradio.com
News Editor: Station Manager

SURGE 42741
Southampton University Students' Union, University of Southampton, University Road, Highfield, SOUTHAMPTON, SO17 1BJ **Tel:** 0870 357 2252
Email: office@surgeradio.co.uk
Web site: http://www.surgeradio.co.uk
News Editor: Head of News

URF 42756
Norwich House, University of Sussex, BRIGHTON, BN1 9QS
Tel: 01273 678999
Email: stationmanager@urfonline.com
Web site: http://www.urfonline.com
News Editor: Station Manager

URN 42754
Students Union, Portland Building, University Park, NOTTINGHAM, NG7 2RD **Tel:** 0115 846 8722
Fax: 0115 935 1101
Email: news@urn1350.net
Web site: http://www.urn1350.net
News Editor: Ben Townsend

URY 42755
c/o Vanbrugh College, University of York, Heslington, YORK, YO10 5DD **Tel:** 01904 433840 **Fax:** 01904 433840
Email: station.manager@ury.york.ac.uk
Web site: http://www.ury.york.ac.uk
News Editor: Tim Wallace

XPRESS RADIO 42758
Cardiff University, Students Union, Park Place, CARDIFF, CF10 3QN **Tel:** 029 2078 1530 **Fax:** 029 2078 1522
Email: news@xpressradio.co.uk
Web site: http://www.xpressradio.co.uk
News Editor: Gareth Rees

XPRESSION FM 42753
Devonshire House, Stocker Road, EXETER, EX4 4PZ
Tel: 01392 263568
Email: stationmanager@xpressionfm.com
Web site: http://www.xpressionfm.com
News Editor: Ben Holt

XTREME RADIO 42759
Union House, Swansea University, Singleton Park, SWANSEA, SA2 8PP **Tel:** 01792 513008
Email: exec@xtremeradio.org
Web site: http://www.xtremeradio.org
News Editor: Juliet Beauvais

ZED FM 42714
Mid Kent College, Horsted Centre, Maidstone Road, CHATHAM, ME5 9UQ **Tel:** 01634 830633
Fax: 01634 830224
Email: sue.flipping@midkent.ac.uk
Web site: http://www.midkent.ac.uk
News Editor: Sue Flipping

Willings Volume 1
Section 10

Services
& Suppliers

Providers of services relating to the media and
publishing fields, listed alphabetically under subject
headings. The section is preceded by a classification
index, with page number references.

Headings

ISRAEL BROADCASTING AUTHORITY
21 Heleni HaMalka, PO Box 1082, JERUSALEM 91010, Israel
Tel: +972 2 5015555
National broadcasting authority of Israel focussing on TV and radio administration and freedom of speech.

ADVERTISEMENT MONITORING

PTM PUBLISHERS LTD
282 High Street, SUTTON, SM1 1PQ
Tel: 020 8642 0162 **Fax:** 020 8643 2275
Email: mail@ptmpublisher.com
Web site: http://www.jcn.co.uk
Contact: Stephen Mell, Director.

ADVERTISEMENT SPACE CONTRACTORS See also 'UK Newspaper Ad Sales Reps'

PRIMESIGHT LTD
Charlotte House, 14 Windmill Street, LONDON, W1T 2DY
Tel: 020 7908 4300 **Fax:** 020 7908 4399
Email: mail@primesight.co.uk
Web site: http://www.primesight.co.uk
Contact: Naren Patel, Managing Director. Nigel Clarkson, Sales Director.

PUBLICITAS
Gordon House, 10 Greencoat Place, LONDON, SW1P 1PH
Tel: 020 7592 8370 **Fax:** 020 7592 8371
Email: london@adnative.net
Web site: http://www.publicitas.com/uk
Alternative telephone number: +44 (0)20 7592 8300/8331. Alternative fax number: +44 (0)20 7592 8326/+44 (0)20 7630 9922.

TEN ALPS PUBLISHING
9 Savoy Street, LONDON, WC2E 7HR
Tel: 020 7878 2300 **Fax:** 020 7379 7118
Web site: http://www.tenalpspublishing.com

WYATT INTERNATIONAL LTD
Wyatt House, 72 Francis Road, Edgbaston, BIRMINGHAM, B16 8SP
Tel: 0121 454 8181 **Fax:** 0121 455 9785
Email: info@wyatt-inter.co.uk
Web site: http://www.wyattinternational.com

ZED MEDIA
22 Percy Street, LONDON, W1T 2BU
Tel: 020 7961 3501 **Fax:** 020 7961 3502
Email: info@zedmedia.co.uk
Web site: http://www.zedmedia.co.uk
Contact: Paul Constantine, Managing Director.

ZENITHOPTIMEDIA
24 Percy Street, LONDON, W1T 2BS
Tel: 020 7961 1000 **Fax:** 020 7961 1113
Email: info@zenithoptimedia.com
Web site: http://www.zenithoptimedia.com

ARTISTS, FREELANCE

ARTHUR WREN
32 Ganghill, GUILDFORD, GU1 1XF
Tel: 01483 533878
Email: arthurwren@btinternet.com
Contact: Arthur Wren MCSD, FRSA, Proprietor.

TERRY JAMES ASSOCIATES
8 London Road, AMERSHAM, HP7 0EZ
Tel: 01494 434394
Contact: Terry James, Proprietor.

ASSOCIATIONS / ORGANISATIONS

London

ACCOUNT PLANNING GROUP (APG)
16 Creighton Avenue, LONDON, N10 1NU
Tel: 020 8444 3692 **Fax:** 020 8883 9953
Email: mail@apg.org.uk
Web site: http://www.apg.org.uk
Contact: Steve Martin, General Manager.

THE ADVERTISING ASSOCIATION (AA)
7th Floor North, Artillery House, 11-19 Artillery Row, LONDON, SW1P 1RT
Tel: 020 7340 1100 **Fax:** 020 7222 1504
Email: aa@adassoc.org.uk
Web site: http://www.adassoc.org.uk
Contact: Mark Lund, Chairman. Jim Rothwell, Senior Public Affairs Manager. Sue Eustace, Director of Public Affairs.

THE ADVERTISING STANDARDS AUTHORITY LTD (ASA)
Mid City Place, 71 High Holborn, LONDON, WC1V 6QT
Tel: 020 7492 2222 **Fax:** 020 7242 3696
Email: enquiries@asa.org.uk
Web site: http://www.asa.org.uk
Contact: Matt Wilson, Press Officer.

ALLIANCE OF INTERNATIONAL MARKET RESEARCH INSTITUTES (AIMRI)
26 Granard Avenue, LONDON, SW15 6HJ
Tel: 020 8780 3343 **Fax:** 020 8246 6893
Email: rtchilton@aol.com
Web site: http://www.aimri.net
Contact: Richard Chilton, Company Secretary.

ASSOCIATION OF ILLUSTRATORS
2nd Floor, 150 Back Building, Curtain Road, LONDON, EC2A 3AT
Tel: 020 7613 4328 **Fax:** 020 7613 4417
Email: info@theaoi.com
Web site: http://www.theaoi.com
Contact: Paul Ryding, Membership Co-ordinator.

ASSOCIATION OF PHOTOGRAPHERS (AOP)
81 Leonard Street, LONDON, EC2A 4QS
Tel: 020 7739 6669 **Fax:** 020 7739 8707
Email: general@aophoto.co.uk
Web site: http://hub.the-aop.org

ASSOCIATION OF PUBLISHING AGENCIES (APA)
Queen's House, 55-56 Lincoln's Inn Fields, LONDON, WC2A 3LJ
Tel: 020 7404 4166 **Fax:** 020 7404 4167
Email: info@apa.co.uk
Web site: http://www.apa.co.uk
Contact: Julia Hutchison, Chief Operating Officer. Patrick Fuller, Chief Executive Officer.

ASSOCIATION OF REGIONAL FINANCIAL EDITORS (ARFE)
1 Fern Dene, LONDON, W13 8AN
Tel: 020 8997 6868
Email: john.heffernan@virgin.net
Contact: John Heffernan, Honorary Secretary.

BPA WORLD-WIDE
55 Russell Square, LONDON, WC1B 4HP
Tel: 020 7631 4809 **Fax:** 020 7631 4810
Email: swilkinson@bpaww.com
Web site: http://www.bpaww.com
Contact: Stuart Wilkinson, Director.

BPIF CARTONS
BPIF, Farringdon Point, 29-35 Farringdon Road, LONDON, EC1M 3JF
Tel: 020 7915 8300 **Fax:** 020 7405 7784
Web site: http://www.britishprint.com

BRITISH ASSOCIATION FOR PRINT & COMMUNICATION (BAPC)
Suite 2, Catalyst House, 720 Centennial Court, Centennial Park, Elstree, BOREHAMWOOD, WD6 3SY
Tel: 020 8736 5862 **Fax:** 020 8224 9090
Email: tony.honnor@bapc.co.uk
Web site: http://www.bapc.co.uk
Contact: Tony Honnor, Association Director.

BRITISH ASSOCIATION OF COMMUNICATORS IN BUSINESS (BACB)
Suite GA2, Oak House, Woodlands Business Park, Breckland, Linford Wood, MILTON KEYNES, MK14 6EY
Tel: 01908 313755 **Fax:** 01908 313661
Email: enquiries@cib.uk.com
Web site: http://www.cib.uk.com
Contact: Kathie Jones, Chief Executive. Tim Beynon, Membership Manager.

BRITISH KINEMATOGRAPH, SOUND & TELEVISION SOCIETY (BKSTS)
Pinewood Studios, Iverheath, IVER, SL0 0NH
Tel: 01753 656656
Email: info@bksts.com
Web site: http://www.bksts.com

BRITISH LIBRARY BUSINESS INFORMATION
Business and IP Centre, 96 Euston Road, LONDON, NW1 2DB
Tel: 020 7412 7454 **Fax:** 020 7412 7453
Email: bipc@bl.uk
Web site: http://www.bl.uk/bipc
Contact: Neil Infield, Manager of Business and Intellectual Property Information.

BRITISH PRINTING INDUSTRIES FEDERATION (BPIF)
Farringdon Point, 29-35 Farringdon Road, LONDON, EC1M 3JF
Tel: 020 7915 8300 **Fax:** 020 7405 7784
Email: info@bpif.org.uk
Web site: http://www.britishprint.com
Contact: Andrew Brown, Corporate Affairs Director.

CBI
Centre Point, 103 New Oxford Street, LONDON, WC1A 1DU
Tel: 020 7379 7400 **Fax:** 020 7497 2596
Email: press.office@cbi.org.uk
Web site: http://www.cbi.org.uk
Contact: Paul Latham, Head of News.

THE CHARTERED INSTITUTE OF JOURNALISTS (CIOJ)
2 Dock Offices, Surrey Quays Road, LONDON, SE16 2XU
Tel: 020 7252 1187 **Fax:** 020 7232 2302
Email: memberservices@cioj.co.uk
Web site: http://www.cioj.co.uk
Contact: Dominic Cooper, General Secretary and Production Editor; Andy Smith, Journal Editor.

CHARTERED INSTITUTE OF LIBRARY AND INFORMATION PROFESSIONALS
7 Ridgmount Street, LONDON, WC1E 7AE
Tel: 020 7255 0500 **Fax:** 020 7255 0501
Email: info@cilip.org.uk
Web site: http://www.cilip.org.uk

THE CHARTERED INSTITUTE OF PUBLIC RELATIONS (IPR)
52-53 Russell Square, LONDON, WC1B 4HP
Tel: 020 7631 6900 **Fax:** 020 7766 3344
Email: info@cipr.co.uk
Web site: http://www.cipr.co.uk
Contact: Ann Mealor, Assistant Director/Head of PR and Marketing.

CREATIVE CIRCLE
67-69 Whitfield Street, LONDON, W1T 4HF
Tel: 020 7636 1223
Email: janice@creativecircle.co.uk
Web site: http://www.creativecircle.co.uk
Contact: Janice Wilson, Administrator; Martin Denton, President.

D & AD
9 Graphite Square, Vauxhall Walk, LONDON, SE11 5EE
Tel: 020 7840 1111 **Fax:** 020 7840 0840
Email: info@dandad.co.uk
Web site: http://www.dandad.org
Contact: Maeve O'Sullivan, Media Relations Manager.

DATA PUBLISHERS ASSOCIATION (DPA)
Queens House, 28 Kingsway, LONDON, WC2B 6JR
Tel: 020 7405 0836 **Fax:** 020 7404 4167
Email: info@dpa.org.uk
Web site: http://www.dpa.org.uk

DIRECT SELLING ASSOCIATION
29 Floral Street, LONDON, WC2E 9DP
Tel: 020 7497 1234 **Fax:** 020 7497 3144
Email: info@dsa.org.uk
Web site: http://www.dsa.org.uk

Services & Suppliers

THE EDUCATIONAL PUBLISHERS COUNCIL
29B Montague Street, LONDON, WC1B 5BW
Tel: 020 7691 9191 **Fax:** 020 7691 9199
Email: mail@publishers.org.uk
Web site: http://www.publishers.org.uk
Contact: Nicola Swann, Executive Assistant. Graham Taylor, Director.

THE FOREIGN PRESS ASSOCIATION IN LONDON
11 Carlton House Terrace, LONDON, SW1Y 5AJ
Tel: 020 7930 0445 **Fax:** 020 7925 0469
Email: reception@foreign-press.org.uk
Web site: http://www.foreign-press.org.uk

HOME BUILDERS FEDERATION (HBF)
1st Floor, Byron House, 7-9 St. James's Street, LONDON, SW1A 1DW
Tel: 020 7960 1600 **Fax:** 020 7960 1601
Email: info@hbf.co.uk
Web site: http://www.hbf.co.uk
Contact: Steve Turner, Head of Communications.

HOUSE OF COMMONS
Information Office, House of Commons, Westminster, LONDON, SW1A 0AA
Tel: 020 7219 4272 **Fax:** 020 7219 5839
Email: hcinfo@parliament.uk
Web site: http://www.parliament.uk

INCORPORATED SOCIETY OF BRITISH ADVERTISERS LTD (ISBA)
1B Portland Place, LONDON, W1B 1PN
Tel: 020 7291 9020 **Fax:** 020 7291 9030
Email: info@isba.org.uk
Web site: http://www.isba.org.uk
Contact: Jackie Marlow, Director of Marketing Services.

INSTITUTE OF PRACTITIONERS IN ADVERTISING (IPA)
44 Belgrave Square, LONDON, SW1X 8QS
Tel: 020 7235 7020 **Fax:** 020 7245 9904
Email: info@ipa.co.uk
Web site: http://www.ipa.co.uk

INSTITUTE OF SALES PROMOTION (ISP) LTD
Arena House, 66-68 Pentonville Road, Islington, LONDON, N1 9HS
Tel: 020 7837 5340 **Fax:** 020 7837 5326
Email: enquiries@isp.org.uk
Web site: http://www.isp.org.uk
Contact: Clive Mishon, Chairman.

INTELLECT
Russell Square House, 10-12 Russell Square, LONDON, WC1B 5EE
Tel: 020 7331 2000 **Fax:** 020 7331 2040
Email: john.higgins@intellectuk.org
Web site: http://www.intellectuk.org
Contact: John Higgins, Director General.

INTERNATIONAL ADVERTISING ASSOCIATION (UK CHAPTER) LTD (IAA)
12 Rickett Street, LONDON, SW6 1RU
Tel: 020 7381 8777 **Fax:** 020 7610 0541
Email: office@iaauk.com
Web site: http://www.iaauk.com
Contact: Annika McCaskie, Office Manager.

INTERNATIONAL ADVERTISING FESTIVAL LTD
Greater London House, Hampstead Road, LONDON, NW1 7EJ
Tel: 020 7728 4040 **Fax:** 020 7728 4044
Email: info@canneslions.com
Web site: http://www.canneslions.com

INTERNATIONAL VISUAL COMMUNICATIONS ASSOCIATION LTD (IVCA)
19 Pepper Street, Glengall Bridge, LONDON, E14 9RP
Tel: 020 7512 0571 **Fax:** 020 7512 0591
Email: info@ivca.org
Web site: http://www.ivca.org
Contact: Marco Forgione, Chief Executive; Phillip Fey, Publications and Information Officer.

JOINT INDUSTRY COMMITTEE FOR REGIONAL PRESS RESEARCH (JICREG)
St. Andrews House, 18-20 St. Andrew Street, LONDON, EC4A 3AY
Tel: 020 7632 7400 **Fax:** 020 7632 7401
Email: steve@jicreg.co.uk
Web site: http://www.jicreg.co.uk
Contact: Steve Brown, Secretary.

THE LIST WARRANTY REGISTER (LWR)
DMA House, 70 Margaret Street, LONDON, W1W 8SS
Tel: 020 7291 3340 **Fax:** 020 7323 4124
Email: barbara@dma.org.uk
Web site: http://www.dma.org.uk
Contact: Barbara Holt, Accounts Manager.

LONDON CHAMBER OF COMMERCE & INDUSTRY (LCCI)
33 Queen Street, LONDON, EC4R 1AP
Tel: 020 7248 4444 **Fax:** 020 7203 1930
Email: lc@londonchamber.co.uk
Web site: http://www.londonchamber.co.uk

LONDON PRESS CLUB
St. Bride Institute, 14 Bride Lane, Fleet Street, LONDON, EC4Y 8EQ
Tel: 020 7353 7086 **Fax:** 020 7353 7087
Email: info@londonpressclub.co.uk
Web site: http://www.londonpressclub.co.uk
Contact: Steve Orham, Chairman. Peter Durrant, Secretary.

THE MAILING PREFERENCE SERVICE (MPS)
DMA House, 70 Margaret Street, LONDON, W1W 8SS
Tel: 020 7291 3315 **Fax:** 020 7323 4226
Email: mps@dma.org.uk
Web site: http://www.mpsonline.org.uk
Contact: Mike Lordan, Director of Consumer Services, Compliance and Accreditation.

THE MARKET RESEARCH SOCIETY (MRS)
15 Northburgh Street, LONDON, EC1V 0JR
Tel: 020 7490 4911 **Fax:** 020 7490 0608
Email: info@mrs.org.uk
Web site: http://www.mrs.org.uk

MARKETING COMMUNICATION CONSULTANTS ASSOCIATION (MCCA)
4 New Quebec Street, LONDON, W1H 7RF
Tel: 020 7535 3550 **Fax:** 020 7535 3551
Email: info@mcca.org.uk
Web site: http://www.mcca.org.uk
Contact: Samantha Gill, Information Manager.

THE MARKETING SOCIETY (MS)
1 Park Road, TEDDINGTON, TW11 0AR
Tel: 020 8973 1700 **Fax:** 020 8973 1701
Email: info@marketing-society.org.uk
Web site: http://www.marketing-society.org.uk
Contact: Helen Chowaniec, Events Assistant.

MEDIA RESEARCH GROUP (MRG)
Red Lion House, West Dean, SALISBURY, SP5 1JF
Tel: 01794 341337
Email: sally@mrg.org.uk
Web site: http://www.mrg.org.uk
Contact: Sally Hiddleston, Administrator.

NABS
47-50 Margaret Street, LONDON, W1W 8SB
Tel: 020 7462 3150 **Fax:** 020 7462 3151
Email: nabs@nabs.org.uk
Web site: http://www.nabs.org.uk
Contact: Lucy Owen, Chief Executive.

NATIONAL FEDERATION OF RETAIL NEWSAGENTS (NFRN)
Yeoman House, Sekforde Street, LONDON, EC1R 0HF
Tel: 020 7253 4225 **Fax:** 020 7017 8897
Email: info@nfrn.org.uk
Web site: http://www.nfrnonline.com

THE NATIONAL NEWSPAPERS' SAFE HOME ORDERING PROTECTION SCHEME (SHOPS)
18A King Street, MAIDENHEAD, SL6 1EF
Tel: 01628 641930 **Fax:** 01628 637112
Email: enquiries@shops-uk.org.uk
Web site: http://www.shops-uk.org.uk
Contact: Ron Davis, Chief Executive.

NATIONAL READERSHIP SURVEYS LTD (NRS)
40 Parker Street, LONDON, WC2B 5PQ
Tel: 020 7242 8111 **Fax:** 020 7242 8303
Email: roger@nrs.co.uk
Web site: http://www.nrs.co.uk

NATIONAL UNION OF JOURNALISTS (NUJ) PRESS & PR BRANCH
Headland House, 308-312 Gray's Inn Road, LONDON, WC1X 8DP
Tel: 020 7278 7916 **Fax:** 020 7837 8143
Email: info@nuj.org.uk
Web site: http://www.nuj.org.uk
Contact: Jeremy Dear, General Secretary.

NEWSPAPER MARKETING AGENCY
175 Piccadilly, LONDON, W1J 9EN
Tel: 020 7182 1700 **Fax:** 020 7182 1711
Email: enquiries@nmauk.co.uk
Web site: http://www.nmauk.co.uk

NEWSPAPER PUBLISHERS ASSOCIATION (NPA) LTD
8th Floor, St. Andrews House, 18-20 St. Andrew Street, LONDON, EC4A 3AY
Tel: 020 7632 4000 **Fax:** 020 7632 7401
Email: ns@newspapersoc.org.uk
Web site: http://www.newspapersoc.org.uk

THE NEWSPAPER SOCIETY (NS)
18-20 St. Andrew Street, LONDON, EC4A 3AY
Tel: 020 7632 7424
Email: ns@newspapersoc.org.uk
Web site: http://www.newspapersoc.org.uk
Contact: David Newell, Director.

OFCOM
Riverside House, 2A Southwark Bridge Road, LONDON, SE1 9HA
Tel: 020 7981 3000 **Fax:** 020 7981 3333
Email: contact@ofcom.org.uk
Web site: http://www.ofcom.org.uk
Contact: Julian Eccles, Communications Director.

OUTDOOR ADVERTISING ASSOCIATION OF GREAT BRITAIN LTD (OAA)
Summit House, 27 Sale Place, LONDON, W2 1YR
Tel: 020 7973 0315 **Fax:** 020 7973 0318
Email: ajames@oaa.org.uk
Web site: http://www.oaa.org.uk
Contact: Jali Mbali, Marketing Assistant. Alan James, Chief Executive.

PERIODICAL PUBLISHERS ASSOCIATION (PPA)
Queens House, 28 Kingsway, LONDON, WC2B 6JR
Tel: 020 7404 4166 **Fax:** 020 7404 4167
Email: info1@ppa.co.uk
Web site: http://www.ppa.co.uk

PRCA - PUBLIC RELATIONS CONSULTANTS ASSOCIATION LTD
Willow House, Willow Place, LONDON, SW1P 1JH
Tel: 020 7233 6026 **Fax:** 020 7828 4797
Email: communications@prca.org.uk
Web site: http://www.prca.org.uk
Contact: Richard Ellis, Communications Manager.

PRESS COMPLAINTS COMMISSION
Halton House, 22-23 Holborn, LONDON, EC1N 2JD
Tel: 020 7831 0022 **Fax:** 020 7831 0025
Email: complaints@pcc.org.uk
Web site: http://www.pcc.org.uk

THE PUBLISHERS ASSOCIATION (PA)
29B Montague Street, LONDON, WC1B 5BW
Tel: 020 7691 9191 **Fax:** 020 7691 9199
Email: mail@publishers.org.uk
Web site: http://www.publishers.org.uk
Contact: Anita Desilver, Secretary.

RADIO CENTRE
77 Shaftesbury Avenue, LONDON, W1D 5DU
Tel: 020 7306 2603 **Fax:** 020 7306 2505
Email: info@radiocentre.org
Web site: http://www.radiocentre.org

RADIO JOINT AUDIENCE RESEARCH LTD (RAJAR)
Paramount House, 162-170 Wardour Street, LONDON, W1F 8ZX
Tel: 020 7292 9040 **Fax:** 020 7292 9041
Email: info@rajar.co.uk
Web site: http://www.rajar.co.uk

ROYAL TELEVISION SOCIETY (RTS)
5th Floor, Kildare House, 3 Dorset Rise, LONDON, EC4Y 8EN
Tel: 020 7822 2810 **Fax:** 020 7822 2811
Email: info@rts.org.uk
Web site: http://www.rts.org.uk
Contact: Tasha Sutherland, Office Administrator.

SOCIETY OF AUTHORS
84 Drayton Gardens, LONDON, SW10 9SB
Tel: 020 7373 6642 **Fax:** 020 7373 5768
Email: info@societyofauthors.org
Web site: http://www.societyofauthors.org
Contact: Kate Pool, Deputy General Secretary.

THE TELEPHONE PREFERENCE SERVICE (TPS)
DMA House, 70 Margaret Street, LONDON, W1W 8SS
Tel: 020 7291 3320 **Fax:** 020 7323 4226
Email: tps@dma.org.uk
Web site: http://www.tpsonline.org.uk
Contact: Tessa Kelly, Director of Compliance
Operations.

UNITED KINGDOM WAREHOUSING
ASSOCIATION (UKWA)
Walter House, 418-422 Strand, LONDON, WC2R 0PT
Tel: 020 7836 5522 **Fax:** 020 7438 9379
Email: dg@ukwa.org.uk
Web site: http://www.ukwa.org.uk
Contact: Roger Williams, Chief Executive Officer.

WHICH?
2 Marylebone Road, LONDON, NW1 4DF
Tel: 020 7770 7000 **Fax:** 020 7770 7600
Email: press@which.co.uk
Web site: http://www.which.co.uk
Contact: Nikki Lehel, Head of Public Relations.

ASSOCIATIONS / ORGANISATIONS

Home Counties

ASSOCIATION OF EVENT ORGANISERS (AEO)
119 High Street, BERKHAMSTED, HP4 2DJ
Tel: 01442 285810 **Fax:** 01442 875551
Email: info@aeo.org.uk
Web site: http://www.aeo.org.uk

AUDIT BUREAU OF CIRCULATIONS LTD (ABC)
Saxon House, 211 High Street, BERKHAMSTED, HP4
1AD
Tel: 01442 870800 **Fax:** 01442 200702
Email: abcpost@abc.org.uk
Web site: http://www.abc.org.uk
Contact: Jan Pitt, Director of Magazines and
Exhibitions. Martyn Gates, Director of Newspapers.
Richard Gentle, Operations Manager. Lucy Palmer,
Marketing Manager. Jerry Wright, Chief Executive.

THE BOOK TRADE CHARITY (BTBS)
The Foyle Centre, The Retreat, KINGS LANGLEY, WD4
8LT
Tel: 01923 263128 **Fax:** 01923 270732
Email: david@btbs.org
Web site: http://www.btbs.org.uk
Contact: David Hicks, Chief Executive, Jackie Bright,
Housing Manager.

BRITISH INSTITUTE OF PROFESSIONAL
PHOTOGRAPHY (BIPP)
1 Prebendal Court, Oxford Road, AYLESBURY, HP19
8EY
Tel: 01296 718530 **Fax:** 01296 336367
Email: info@bipp.com
Web site: http://www.bipp.com
Contact: Chris Harper, Chief Executive.

BRITISH SOCIETY OF MAGAZINE EDITORS
Gill Branston & Associates, 137 Hale Lane, EDGWARE,
HA8 9QP
Tel: 020 8906 4664 **Fax:** 020 8959 2137
Email: admin@bsme.com
Web site: http://www.bsme.com
Contact: Gill Branston, Secretariat.

EVENTIA
5th Floor, Charles House, 148-149 Great Charles Street
Queensway, BIRMINGHAM, B3 3HT
Tel: 0121 212 1400 **Fax:** 0121 212 3131
Email: info@eventia.org.uk
Web site: http://www.eventia.org.uk

FOCAL INTERNATIONAL LTD
Pentax House, South Hill Avenue, SOUTH HARROW,
HA2 0DU
Tel: 020 8423 5853 **Fax:** 020 8933 4826
Email: info@focalint.org
Web site: http://www.focalint.org
Contact: Anne Johnson, Commercial Manager. Julie
Lewis, General Manager.

INDEPENDENT PUBLISHERS GUILD
PO Box 12, LLAIN, SA34 0WU
Tel: 01437 563335 **Fax:** 01437 563335
Email: info@ipg.com
Web site: http://www.ipg.uk.com
Contact: Bridget Shine, Executive Director.

THE INSTITUTE OF DIRECT MARKETING (IDM)
LTD
1 Park Road, TEDDINGTON, TW11 0AR
Tel: 020 8977 5705 **Fax:** 020 8943 2535
Email: enquiries@theidm.com
Web site: http://www.theidm.com
Contact: Derek Holder, Managing Director; Emma
Porch, Campaign Manager.

INSTITUTE OF SALES & MARKETING
MANAGEMENT (ISMM) LTD
Harrier Court, Lower Woodside, LUTON, LU1 4DQ
Tel: 01582 840001 **Fax:** 01582 849142
Email: sales@ismm.co.uk
Web site: http://www.ismm.co.uk
Contact: Stephen Wright, Commercial Director ; Denise
Edens, Education Director.

INSTITUTE OF TRANSLATION & INTERPRETING
(ITI)
Fortuna House, South Fifth Street, MILTON KEYNES,
MK9 2EU
Tel: 01908 325250 **Fax:** 01908 325259
Email: info@iti.org.uk
Web site: http://www.iti.org.uk
Contact: Georgina Dobbin, Commercial Development
Officer.

MARKETING GUILD (MG)
Regency House, Westminster Place, York Business
Park, YORK, YO26 6RW
Tel: 01904 520820 **Fax:** 01904 520899
Email: help@marketing-guild.com
Web site: http://www.marketing-guild.com
Contact: Jamie Austin, Divisional Director.

ASSOCIATIONS / ORGANISATIONS

South Eastern

THE CHARTERED INSTITUTE OF MARKETING
(CIM)
Moor Hall, Cookham, MAIDENHEAD, SL6 9QH
Tel: 01628 427500 **Fax:** 01628 427499
Email: rayjones@cim.co.uk
Web site: http://www.cim.co.uk
Contact: Ray Jones, Head of Communications.

DIGITAL AND SCREEN PRINTING ASSOCIATION
LTD (DSPA)
Association House, 7A West Street, REIGATE, RH2 9BL
Tel: 01737 240792 **Fax:** 01737 240770
Email: info@dspauk.co.uk
Web site: http://www.dspa.co.uk
Contact: Michael Turner, Managing Director.

NATIONAL TALKING NEWSPAPERS AND
MAGAZINES (TNAUK)
National Recording Centre, 10 Browning Road,
HEATHFIELD, TN21 8DB
Tel: 01435 866102 **Fax:** 01435 865422
Email: info@tnauk.org.uk
Web site: http://www.tnauk.org.uk

NEWSPAPER LICENSING AGENCY (NLA)
Wellington Gate, 7-9 Church Road, TUNBRIDGE
WELLS, TN1 1NL
Tel: 01892 525273 **Fax:** 01892 525275
Email: copy@nla.co.uk
Web site: http://www.nla.co.uk

ASSOCIATIONS / ORGANISATIONS

South Western

THE CONFEDERATION OF PAPER INDUSTRIES
1 Rivenhall Road, SWINDON, SN5 7BD
Tel: 01793 889600 **Fax:** 01793 878700
Email: cpi@paper.org.uk
Web site: http://www.paper.org.uk
Contact: Catherine Watson, Communications
Executive.

INSTITUTE OF COPYWRITING (IOC)
1-2 Overbrook Business Centre, WEDMORE, BS28 4PA
Tel: 01934 713563 **Fax:** 01934 713492
Email: copy@inst.org
Web site: http://www.inst.org/copy
Contact: Kit Sadgrove, Managing Director.

OUTDOOR ADVERTISING COUNCIL (OAC)
2 Bell Barn Road, Stoke Bishop, BRISTOL, BS9 2DA
Tel: 0117 904 7235 **Fax:** 0117 904 7236
Email: chris@oacuk.net
Web site: http://www.pa-entertainment.co.uk
Contact: Chris Thomas, Secretary.

ASSOCIATIONS / ORGANISATIONS

Eastern

ASSOCIATION FOR CONFERENCES & EVENTS
LTD (ACE)
Riverside House, High Street, HUNTINGDON, PE29
3SG
Tel: 01480 457595 **Fax:** 01480 412863
Email: ace@aceinternational.org

ASSOCIATION FOR QUALITATIVE RESEARCH
(AQR)
Suite 14, Davey House, 31 St. Neots Road, Eaton Ford,
ST NEOTS, PE19 7BA
Tel: 01480 407227 **Fax:** 01480 211267
Email: info@aqr.org.uk
Web site: http://www.aqr.org.uk
Contact: Rose Molloy, Secretary to Committee.

BRITISH SIGN & GRAPHICS ASSOCIATION LTD
(BSGA)
5 Orton Enterprise Centre, Bakewell Road, Orton
Southgate, PETERBOROUGH, PE2 6XU
Tel: 01733 230033 **Fax:** 01733 230993
Email: info@bsga.co.uk
Web site: http://www.bsga.co.uk

CONCORD VIDEO & FILM COUNCIL
Rosehill Centre, 22 Hines Road, IPSWICH, IP3 9BG
Tel: 01473 726012 **Fax:** 01473 274531
Email: sales@concordmedia.org.uk
Web site: http://www.concordmedia.org.uk
Contact: Lydia Vulliamy, Council Member.

THE INSTITUTE OF SCIENTIFIC & TECHNICAL
COMMUNICATORS LTD (ISTC)
Airport House, Purley Way, CROYDON, CR0 0XZ
Tel: 020 8253 4506 **Fax:** 020 8253 4510
Email: istc@istc.org.uk
Web site: http://www.istc.org.uk

OVERSEAS PRESS & MEDIA ASSOCIATION
(OPMA)
15 Magrath Avenue, CAMBRIDGE, CB4 3AH
Tel: 01223 512631 **Fax:** 01223 512631
Email: jackie.dunn@opma.co.uk
Web site: http://www.opma.co.uk
Contact: Jackie Dunn, Publisher, OPMA Guide.

SOCIETY OF EDITORS
Granta Place, Mill Lane, CAMBRIDGE, CB2 1RU
Tel: 01223 304080 **Fax:** 01223 304090
Email: info@societyofeditors.org
Web site: http://www.societyofeditors.org
Contact: Bob Satchwell, Executive Director.

ASSOCIATIONS / ORGANISATIONS

Midlands

CHARTERED INSTITUTE OF HOUSING (CIH)
Octavia House, Westwood Way, COVENTRY, CV4 8JP
Tel: 024 7685 1700 **Fax:** 024 7669 5110
Email: press@cih.org
Web site: http://www.cih.org
Contact: Gill Dwyer, Press Officer.

THE MEETINGS INDUSTRY ASSOCIATION (MIA)
PO Box 515, Kelmarsh, NORTHAMPTON, NN6 9XW
Tel: 0845 230 5508 **Fax:** 0845 230 7708
Email: info@mia-uk.org
Web site: http://www.mia-uk.org
Contact: Jane Evans, Chief Executive.

POINT OF PURCHASE ADVERTISING
INTERNATIONAL (POPAI) LTD
Highfields Farm, Huncote Road, Stoney Stanton,
LEICESTER, LE9 4DJ
Tel: 01455 271856 **Fax:** 01455 273918
Email: info@popai.co.uk
Web site: http://www.popai.co.uk
Contact: Phil Day, Business Manager.

Services & Suppliers

PROMOTA UK LTD
Concorde House, Trinity Park, Solihull, BIRMINGHAM, B37 7UQ
Tel: 0845 371 4335 **Fax:** 0845 371 4336
Email: info@promota.co.uk
Web site: http://www.promota.co.uk
Contact: Rod Duncan, Chairman.

ASSOCIATIONS / ORGANISATIONS

North Eastern

COMMUNITY MEDIA ASSOCIATION (CMA)
15 Paternoster Row, SHEFFIELD, S1 2BX
Tel: 0114 279 5219
Email: cma@commedia.org.uk
Web site: http://www.commedia.org.uk

MASTER PHOTOGRAPHERS ASSOCIATION (MPA)
Jubilee House, 1 Chancery Lane, DARLINGTON, DL1 5QP
Tel: 01325 356555 **Fax:** 01325 357813
Email: general@mpauk.com
Web site: http://www.thempa.com
Contact: Colin Buck, Chief Executive; Linda Buck, Company Secretary.

SOCIETY OF INDEXERS (SI)
Woodbourn Business Centre, 10 Jessell Street, SHEFFIELD, S9 3HY
Tel: 0114 244 9561 **Fax:** 0114 244 9563
Email: info@indexers.org.uk
Web site: http://www.indexers.org.uk
Contact: Wendy Burrow, Administrator.

ASSOCIATIONS / ORGANISATIONS

Scotland

THE SCOTTISH DAILY NEWSPAPER SOCIETY (SDNS)
21 Lansdowne Crescent, EDINBURGH, EH12 5EH
Tel: 0131 535 1064
Email: info@sdns.org.uk
Contact: James Raeburn, Director.

SCOTTISH NEWSPAPER PUBLISHERS ASSOCIATION (SNPA)
48 Palmerston Place, EDINBURGH, EH12 5DE
Tel: 0131 220 4353 **Fax:** 0131 220 4344
Email: info@snpa.org.uk
Web site: http://www.snpa.org.uk
Contact: Simon Fairclough, Director.

SCOTTISH PRINT EMPLOYERS FEDERATION (SPEF)
48 Palmerston Place, EDINBURGH, EH12 5DE
Tel: 0131 220 4353 **Fax:** 0131 220 4344
Email: info@spef.org.uk
Web site: http://www.spef.org.uk

BADGES

AAA BADGES OF QUALITY
Tumbleweed House, Hamsterley, BISHOP AUCKLAND, DL13 3RA
Tel: 01388 488733 **Fax:** 01388 488048
Email: enquiries@aaabadgesofquality.co.uk
Web site: http://www.aaabadgesofquality.co.uk
Contact: Brad Hallett, Chief Executive. Tracy Dunford, Sales Manager.

BOOKSELLERS

DAWSON BOOKS LTD
Foxhills House, Brindley Close, RUSHDEN, NN10 6DB
Tel: 01933 417500 **Fax:** 01933 417501
Email: bksales@dawsonbooks.co.uk
Web site: http://www.dawsonbooks.co.uk
Contact: George Hammond, Sales Manager.

CARTON MANUFACTURERS

BEAMGLOW LTD
Somersham Road, St Ives, HUNTINGDON, PE27 3LP
Tel: 01480 465012 **Fax:** 01480 494826
Email: cartons@beamglow.co.uk
Web site: http://www.beamglow.co.uk

CARTOON FEATURES

BILL BELCHER (CARTOONIST)
304 Kew Road, Kew, RICHMOND, TW9 3DU
Tel: 020 8940 5513
Contact: Bill Belcher, Proprietor.

GRAPHIC SYNDICATION
4 Reyntiens View, Odiham, HOOK, RG29 1AF
Tel: 01256 703004
Email: flantoons@btinternet.com
Contact: Mike Flanagan, Manager.

CELEBRITIES & PUBLIC SPEAKERS

NOEL GAY ARTISTS LTD
19 Denmark Street, LONDON, WC2H 8NA
Tel: 020 7836 3941
Email: info@noelgay.com
Web site: http://www.noelgay.com
Contact: David Corley, Financial Controller.

CONSULTANCY SERVICES

UK - GRANTS
Beach Field House, Lyme Green Business Park, Winterton Way, MACCLESFIELD, SK11 0LP
Tel: 0870 112 1871 **Fax:** 0870 112 1872
Email: hey@uk-grants.co.uk
Web site: http://www.uk-grants.co.uk
Contact: Patrick Heywood, Managing Director.

CORPORATE ENTERTAINMENT

ACE-TEC LEISURE
76 Graham Avenue, Portslade, BRIGHTON, BN41 2WL
Tel: 01273 430431
Email: ace-leisure@ntlworld.com
Web site: http://www.ace-leisure.com

ACTIVE CONSULTANCY LTD
Active House, 51 Wolsey Road, ESHER, KT10 8NT
Tel: 01372 461500 **Fax:** 01372 461501
Email: enquiries@getactive.co.uk
Web site: http://www.getactive.co.uk

CUSTOMER MAGAZINES (CONTRACT PUBLISHING)

AB
24-26 Great Suffolk Street, LONDON, SE1 0UE
Tel: 020 7922 5678 **Fax:** 020 7922 5679
Email: publishing@abcomm.co.uk
Web site: http://www.abcomm.co.uk

ANGEL BUSINESS COMMUNICATIONS LTD
Unit 6, Bow Court, Fletchworth Gate Industrial Estate, Burnstall Road, COVENTRY, CV5 6SP
Tel: 024 7671 8970
Email: info@angelbc.co.uk
Web site: http://www.angelbc.co.uk
Contact: Jessie Bhadan, Administration Assistant.

AXON PUBLISHING LTD
11 Plough Yard, LONDON, EC2A 3LP
Tel: 020 7684 7111 **Fax:** 020 7684 7122
Email: mail@axonpublish.com
Web site: http://www.axonpublish.com
Contact: Ellen Brush, Managing Director.

CAMBRIDGE PUBLISHERS LTD
275 Newmarket Road, CAMBRIDGE, CB5 8JE
Tel: 01223 477411 **Fax:** 01223 327356
Email: info@cpl.biz
Web site: http://www.cpl.biz

CASPIAN PUBLISHING

198 Kings Road, LONDON, SW3 5XP
Tel: 020 7368 7100 **Fax:** 020 7368 7201
Email: info@caspianpublishing.co.uk
Web site: http://www.caspianpublishing.co.uk

CEDAR COMMUNICATIONS

85 Strand, LONDON, WC2R 0DW
Tel: 020 7550 8000
Email: info@cedarcom.co.uk
Web site: http://www.cedarcom.co.uk
Contact: Clare Broadbent, Managing Director.

JOHN BROWN GROUP

The New Boathouse, 136-142 Bramley Road, LONDON, W10 6SR
Tel: 020 7565 3000 **Fax:** 020 7565 3050
Email: info@johnbrowngroup.co.uk
Web site: http://www.johnbrowngroup.co.uk
Contact: Dean Fitzpatrick, Managing Director. Andrew Hirsch, Chief Executive.

MEDIAMARK PUBLISHING LTD

Studio 111, Finsbury Business Centre, 40 Bowling Green Lane, LONDON, EC1R 0NE
Tel: 020 7415 7100 **Fax:** 020 7415 7002
Email: info@mediamark.co.uk
Web site: http://www.mediamark.co.uk
Contact: Andy Leach, Managing Director.

REDWOOD PUBLISHING LTD

7 St Martin's Place, LONDON, WC2N 4HA
Tel: 020 7747 0700 **Fax:** 020 7747 0701
Email: ian.sewell@redwoodgroup.net
Web site: http://www.redwoodgroup.net
Contact: Ian Sewell, Commercial Director.

STAIRWAY COMMUNICATION LTD

Baird House, 15-17 St Cross Street, Hatton Garden, LONDON, EC1 8UN
Tel: 020 7430 8221 **Fax:** 020 7430 8205
Email: design@domarn.co.uk
Web site: http://www.domarn.co.uk
Contact: Geoff Jenkins, Director.

STORY WORLDWIDE

15B St. Georges Mews, Primrose Hill, LONDON, NW1 8XE
Tel: 020 7449 1500
Email: lars.jorgensen@storyworldwide.com
Web site: http://www.storyworldwide.com
Contact: Lars Hemming Jorgensen, New Business Contact.

DIRECT MAIL SERVICES

ACCESS PLUS MARKETING LOGISTICS
Dorcan 300, Murdock Road, Dorcan, SWINDON, SN3 5HY
Tel: 0844 800 1050
Email: dorcan@accessplus.co.uk
Web site: http://www.accessplus.co.uk

ACXIOM LTD
Counting House, 53 Tooley Street, LONDON, SE1 2QN
Tel: 020 8213 5500
Web site: http://www.acxiom.co.uk
Contact: Pat Kelly, Marketing Director.

ADMAIL 4 INTERNATIONAL LTD
Vestry Road, SEVENOAKS, TN14 5EL
Tel: 01732 744000 **Fax:** 01732 453166
Email: sales@admail4.co.uk
Web site: http://www.admail4.co.uk

THE COMPACT DIRECT MAIL
Unit 2E, Deacon Trading Estate, Forstal Road, Aylesford, MAIDSTONE, ME20 7SP
Tel: 01622 719365 **Fax:** 01622 790659
Email: directmail@compactdirectmail.co.uk
Web site: http://www.compactgroup.co.uk
Contact: Tracey Gilbert, Client Services Director.

HAMILTON HOUSE MAILINGS LTD
Earlstrees Court, Earlstrees Road, CORBY, NN17 4HH
Tel: 01536 399000 **Fax:** 01536 399012
Email: sales@hamilton-house.com
Web site: http://www.hamilton-house.com
Contact: Stephen Mister, Managing Director. Tony Attwood, Chairman.

MAIL MARKETING (SCOTLAND) LTD
42 Methil Street, GLASGOW, G14 0SZ
Tel: 0141 950 2222 **Fax:** 0141 950 2726
Email: glasgow@mailmarkscot.com
Web site: http://www.mailmarkscot.com
Contact: Jan Morris, Managing Director.

MAILCOM PLC
1 Vincent Avenue, Crownhill, MILTON KEYNES, MK8 0AB
Tel: +44 0844 902 0844 **Fax:** +44 0844 902 0845
Email: contact@mailcom.co.uk
Web site: http://www.mailcom.co.uk
Contact: Eddie Shotton, Managing Director.

NOVA DIRECT MAIL
Edward Way, Victoria Business Park, BURGESS HILL, RH15 9UA
Tel: 01444 231400 **Fax:** 01444 232259
Email: sales@novadirectmail.co.uk
Web site: http://www.novadirectmail.co.uk
Contact: Andy Fry, Managing Director.

PARADE MARKETING LTD
Partnership House, 199 Tyburn Road, BIRMINGHAM, B24 8NB
Tel: 0870 066 4266 **Fax:** 0870 066 4267
Email: sales@paradedirect.co.uk
Web site: http://www.parademarketing.com

THE SCHOOLS REGISTER
64 Clarendon Road, WATFORD, WD17 1DA
Tel: 01923 281700 **Fax:** 01923 281723
Email: info@dlg.co.uk
Web site: http://www.dlg.co.uk/educationdata
Contact: Susmita Sarkar, Manager.

VIP MAIL SERVICES & CO LTD
60 Priory Road, REIGATE, RH2 8JB
Tel: 01737 242613
Email: enquiry@vipmail.co.uk
Web site: http://www.vipmail.co.uk
Contact: Louise Martin, Director.

DISTRIBUTION SERVICES

COMAG LTD
Tavistock Road, WEST DRAYTON, UB7 7QE
Tel: 01895 433600 **Fax:** 01895 433605
Email: hazel.isaacs@comag.co.uk
Web site: http://www.comag.co.uk
Contact: Hazel Isaacs, Business Development Director.

FRONTLINE LTD
Midgate, PETERBOROUGH, PE1 1TN
Tel: 01733 555161 **Fax:** 01733 562788
Email: information@flgroup.co.uk
Web site: http://www.frontline.ltd.uk

MAGAZINE MARKETING COMPANY LTD
Octagon House, White Hart Meadows, Ripley, WOKING, GU23 6HR
Tel: 01483 211222 **Fax:** 01483 224541
Email: newbusiness@mmcltd.co.uk
Web site: http://www.mmcltd.co.uk
Contact: Andy Scott, Managing Director.

MARKETFORCE (UK) LTD
Blue Fin Building, 110 Southwark Street, LONDON, SE1 0SU
Tel: 020 3148 3300 **Fax:** 020 3148 8105
Email: salesinnovation@marketforce.co.uk
Web site: http://www.marketforce.co.uk
Contact: Steve Brown, Business Manager.

MENZIES DISTRIBUTION LIMITED
2 Lochside Avenue, Edinburgh Park, EDINBURGH, EH12 9DJ
Tel: 0131 467 8070 **Fax:** 0131 469 4797
Web site: http://www.menziesdistribution.com
Contact: David Mcintosh Commercial & Marketing Director.

MMC LTD
Blacknest Industrial Estate, Blacknest Road, Blacknest, ALTON, GU34 4QE
Tel: 01420 525500 **Fax:** 01420 22642
Email: sales@mmcltd.com
Web site: http://www.mmcltd.com
Contact: Mark Smith, Head of Sales and Marketing.

NEWS INTERNATIONAL LTD
1 Virginia Street, LONDON, E98 1XY
Tel: 020 7782 6000 **Fax:** 020 7782 6097
Web site: http://www.newscorp.com
Contact: James McManus, Corporate Affairs Director.

ROYAL MAIL DOOR TO DOOR
Door to Door Sales & Service Centre, Kingsmead House, Oxpens Road, OXFORD, OX1 1RX
Tel: 0845 795 0950 **Fax:** 01865 796950
Email: doortodoor@royalmail.com
Web site: http://www.royalmail.com
Contact: Samantha Mason, Sales and Development Manager.

SEYMOUR DISTRIBUTION LTD
2 East Poultry Avenue, LONDON, EC1A 9PT
Tel: 020 7429 4000 **Fax:** 020 7429 4001
Email: info@seymour.co.uk
Web site: http://www.seymour.co.uk
Contact: Tracy O' Sullivan, Managing Director.

SMITHS NEWS
Wakefield House, Pipers Way, SWINDON, SN3 1RF
Tel: 0845 123 0000
Web site: http://www.smithsnews.co.uk
Contact: Jon Bunting, Commercial Director.

TIME OUT GUIDES
Universal House, 251 Tottenham Court Road, LONDON, W1T 7AB
Tel: 020 7813 3000 **Fax:** 020 7323 3438
Email: advertising@timeout.com
Web site: http://www.timeout.com

WARNERS (GROUP) PUBLICATIONS
The Maltings, West Street, BOURNE, PE10 9PH
Tel: 01778 391000 **Fax:** 01778 392079
Email: sales@warnersgroup.co.uk
Web site: http://www.warnersgroup.co.uk

EDITORIAL FEATURES

ADVANCE FEATURES
Stubbs Wood Cottage, Hammerwood, EAST GRINSTEAD, RH19 3QE
Tel: 01342 850480
Email: advancefeatures@aol.com
Web site: http://www.advancefeatures.uk.com
Contact: Peter Norman, News Editor.

ADVANCE LIST
Zenith House, 155 Curtain Road, LONDON, EC2A 3QY
Tel: 020 7613 2299 **Fax:** 020 7613 3822
Email: newsbreaks@londonatlarge.com
Web site: http://www.londonatlarge.com
Contact: Kerri Darn, Editor.

CELEBRITY & EVENT DIARY
Zenith House, 155 Curtain Road, LONDON, EC2A 3QY
Tel: 020 7613 2299 **Fax:** 020 7613 3822
Email: newsbreaks@londonatlarge.com
Web site: http://www.londonatlarge.com
Contact: Kerri Darn, Editor.

ENTERTAINMENT NEWS
The Profile Group UK Ltd, The Johnson Building, 77 Hatton Garden, LONDON, EC1N 8JS
Tel: 020 7190 7777 **Fax:** 020 7190 7860
Email: info@entnews.co.uk
Web site: http://www.entnews.co.uk
Contact: Jenny Priestley, Film Editor.

FORESIGHTNEWS
Dragon Court, 27-29 Macklin Street, LONDON, WC2B 5LX
Tel: 020 7190 7830 **Fax:** 020 7190 7858
Email: hotline@foresightnews.co.uk
Web site: http://www.foresightnews.co.uk
Contact: Chris Woods, Editor.

HISTORIC NEWSPAPERS

REMEMBER WHEN
2nd Floor, Suite 2, 1 Waterside, Station Road, HARPENDEN, AL5 4US
Tel: 0844 770 7689 **Fax:** 01582 469248
Email: mike@historic-newspapers.co.uk
Web site: http://www.remember-when.co.uk
Contact: Mike Herbert, Manager.

YESTERDAY'S NEWS
43 Dundonald Road, COLWYN BAY, LL29 7RE
Tel: 01492 531195
Email: elfedjones@hotmail.co.uk
Contact: Ed Jones, Proprietor.

INDEXERS

SOCIETY OF INDEXERS (SI)
Woodbourn Business Centre, 10 Jessell Street, SHEFFIELD, S9 3HY
Tel: 0114 244 9561 **Fax:** 0114 244 9563
Email: info@indexers.org.uk
Web site: http://www.indexers.org.uk
Contact: Wendy Burrow, Administrator.

LITERARY AGENTS

BLAKE FRIEDMANN, LITERARY, TV & FILM AGENCY LTD
122 Arlington Road, LONDON, NW1 7HP
Tel: 020 7284 0408 **Fax:** 020 7284 0442
Email: info@blakefriedmann.co.uk
Web site: http://www.blakefriedmann.co.uk
Contact: Michael Ambefhiki, Office Manager.

CHRISTOPHER LITTLE LITERARY AGENCY
10 Eel Brook Studios, 125 Moore Park Road, LONDON, SW6 4PS
Tel: 020 7736 4455 **Fax:** 020 7736 4490
Email: info@christopherlittle.net
Web site: http://www.christopherlittle.net
Contact: Christopher Little, Director.

FRANCES KELLY AUTHORS' AGENT
111 Clifton Road, KINGSTON UPON THAMES, KT2 6PL
Tel: 020 8549 7830 **Fax:** 020 8547 0051
Contact: Frances Kelly, Proprietor.

JONATHAN CLOWES LTD
10 Iron Bridge House, Bridge Approach, LONDON, NW1 8BD
Tel: 020 7722 7674 **Fax:** 020 7722 7677
Email: jonathanclowes@aol.com
Contact: Ann Evans, Director. Lisa Thompson, Agent.

SOLO SYNDICATION LTD
17-18 Hayward's Place, LONDON, EC1R 0EQ
Tel: 020 7566 0360 **Fax:** 020 7566 0388
Email: nyork@solosyndication.com
Web site: http://www.solopictures.com
Contact: William Gardiner, Managing Director.

MAILING (Bulk Despatch)

DHL GLOBAL MAIL
15 The Avenue, EGHAM, TW20 9AB
Tel: 01622 792111 **Fax:** 01622 718910
Email: sales@dhlglobalmail.co.uk
Web site: http://www.dhlglobalmail.co.uk
Contact: Billy McNamara, Sales Manager.

PACKPOST INTERNATIONAL LTD
Griffin House, Griffin Lane, AYLESBURY, HP19 8BE
Tel: 01296 487493 **Fax:** 01296 392369
Email: sales@packpost.co.uk
Web site: http://www.packpost.co.uk
Contact: Nicholas Rose, Managing Director.

MEDIA FOR THE BLIND

TALKING NEWSPAPER ASSOCIATION OF THE UNITED KINGDOM (TNAUK)
National Recording Centre, 10 Browning Road, HEATHFIELD, TN21 8DB
Tel: 01435 866102 **Fax:** 01435 865422
Email: info@tnauk.org.uk
Web site: http://www.tnauk.org.uk
Administration.

Services & Suppliers

MICROFILM SERVICES

EDOS COPYING & SCANNING
Unit V, Rose Industrial Estate, Marlow Bottom,
MARLOW, SL7 3ND
Tel: 01628 898800
Email: sales@edos.co.uk
Web site: http://www.edos.co.uk
Contact: Christopher J. Lovegrove, Manager.

IMAGING AND ARCHIVING GROUP LTD
424 Kingston Road, Raynes Park, LONDON, SW20 8LL
Tel: 020 8542 5151 **Fax:** 020 8544 0108
Email: enquiry@imagingandarchiving.co.uk
Web site: http://www.imagingandarchiving.co.uk
Contact: Yvonne Ellmers, Bureau Supervisor.

NEWS & PICTURE AGENCIES

London

AGENCE FRANCE PRESSE
Centre Point, 25th Floor, 101 - 103 New Oxford Street,
LONDON, WC1A 1DD
Tel: 020 7010 8750 **Fax:** 020 7010 8751
Email: london.economics@afp.com
Web site: http://www.afp.com

Material accepted: All international news and sports.
Serves: Worldwide.

AGENCIA EFE
299 Oxford Street, LONDON, W1C 2DZ
Tel: 020 7493 7313 **Fax:** 020 7493 7314
Email: efelondon@btclick.com
Web site: http://www.efe.com

Material accepted: International news and
photographs. Serves: Worldwide but mainly Spain and
Latin America.
Joaquin Rabago is the Bureau Chief to whom press
releases should be addressed.

ALPHA PRESS & PHOTOGRAPHIC AGENCY
3rd Floor, 36-37 Featherstone Street, LONDON, EC1Y
8QZ
Tel: 020 7253 7705 **Fax:** 020 7553 4040
Email: picture.desk@alphapress.com
Web site: http://www.alphapress.com

Material accepted: Worldwide - photos of celebrity,
film, television, British life, landscapes, sport, pop scene
and the Royal Family. Serves: Worldwide.
Mark Blumire is the Managing Director to whom press
releases should be addressed.

AMERICAN NEWS SERVICE
28 Pembridge Square, LONDON, W2 4DS
Tel: 020 7221 4964 **Fax:** 020 7221 4964

Material accepted: Political news of national and
international interest, also including business, cultural,
travel and special events. Serves: Worldwide.
Bruno F. R. Giorgi is the Editor in Chief to whom press
releases should be addressed.

ANATOLIA NEWS AGENCY
7 Bankside, Enfield, LONDON, EN2 8BN
Tel: 020 8362 1470 **Fax:** 020 8362 1480
Email: dkocabas@aol.com

Material accepted: National political, economic and
health. Serves: Turkey.
Dilek Kocabas is the Bureau Chief to whom press
releases should be addressed.

ANSA ITALIAN NEWS AGENCY
Minerva House, 26-27 Hatton Garden, LONDON, EC1N
8BR
Tel: 020 7841 5270 **Fax:** 020 7242 2499
Email: ansalondra@yahoo.com
Web site: http://www.ansa.it

Material accepted: UK news. Serves: Italy and other
ANSA subscribers worldwide.
Patrizio Nissirio is the Bureau Chief to whom press
releases should be addressed.

ASSOCIATED PRESS NEWS AGENCY
The Interchange, 32 Oval Road, Camden Lock,
LONDON, NW1 7DZ
Tel: 020 7427 4211 **Fax:** 020 7353 8118
Email: aplondon@ap.org
Web site: http://www.ap.org

Material accepted: All news and photographs. Serves:
Worldwide.

AUSTRALIAN ASSOCIATED PRESS
111 Buckingham Palace Road, LONDON, SW1W 0DT
Tel: 020 3262 0058 **Fax:** 020 7821 0851
Email: news.london@aap.com.au
Web site: http://www.aap.com.au

Material accepted: News of specific Australian
interest. Serves: All types of media in Australia.
Belinda Tasker is the London Bureau Chief to whom
press releases should be addressed.

BANG SHOWBIZ
28 Holmes Road, LONDON, NW5 3AB
Tel: 020 7428 7500
Email: ricksky@bangshowbiz.com
Web site: http://www.bangshowbiz.com

Material accepted: Entertainment news, entertainment
features, celebrity interview opportunities, music news,
film news, royal news and features. Serves: National
and regional newspapers, national and international
magazines, radio and websites.

BLOOMBERG NEWS
City Gate House, 39-45 Finsbury Square, LONDON,
EC2A 1PQ
Tel: 020 7330 7171 **Fax:** 020 7392 6666
Email: newsalert@bloomberg.net
Web site: http://www.bloomberg.com

Material accepted: Business, corporate, financial and
economic news worldwide. Serves: Worldwide.
Press releases should be addressed to the News Desk.

BRITISH SATELLITE NEWS
8 Fitzroy Square, LONDON, W1T 5HN
Tel: 020 7554 5888 **Fax:** 020 7380 0861
Email: rebecca.wood@world-television.com
Web site: http://www.bsn.org.uk

British TV news service funded by the Foreign and
Commonwealth Office. Material accepted:
Environment, culture, business, trade, politics, sport,
science, technology and any other topics of
international interest. Serves: Overseas broadcasters.

BUZZ PICTURES
14 Shanklin Road, LONDON, N8 8TJ
Tel: 020 8374 2596
Email: office@buzzpictures.co.uk
Web site: http://www.buzzpictures.co.uk

Material accepted: Photographic images of extreme
sports and travel. Serves: Worldwide.
Neale Haynes is the Managing Director to whom press
releases should be addressed.

CAMERA PRESS
21 Queen Elizabeth Street, LONDON, SE1 2PD
Tel: 020 7378 1300 **Fax:** 020 7278 5126
Email: editorial@camerapress.com
Web site: http://www.camerapress.com

**International picture agency specialising in
celebrities and members of the Royal Family. Also
covers art, science, technology, events and offbeat
issues. Serves:** Worldwide.

CAPITAL PICTURES
85 Randolph Avenue, LONDON, W9 1DL
Tel: 020 7286 2212
Email: sales@capitalpictures.com
Web site: http://www.capitalpictures.com

Material accepted: Photographs and information
regarding photo-calls and photo opportunities. Serves:
UK and worldwide.
Phil Loftus is the Managing Director to whom press
releases should be addressed.

CATCHLINE NEWS
28 Queensville Road, LONDON, SW12 0JJ
Tel: 020 8674 3494
Email: news@catchlinenews.co.uk
Web site: http://www.catchlinenews.co.uk

Material accepted: General news and features,
including, health, education, motoring and technology.
Serves: UK national and regional newspapers,
magazines and websites.

CENTRAL NEWS
Press Room, Central Criminal Court, Old Bailey,
LONDON, EC4M 7EH
Tel: 020 7236 0116
Email: news@centralnews.co.uk
Web site: http://www.courtnewsuk.co.uk

Material accepted: National criminal court and tribunal
proceedings. Serves: Worldwide.

COLORSPORT
The Old Saw Mill, Rusper Road, Capel, DORKING, RH5
5HF
Tel: 01306 712233 **Fax:** 01306 712260
Email: info@colorsport.co.uk
Web site: http://www.colorsport.co.uk

Material accepted: National and international sporting
photographs. Serves: Worldwide.

CZECH NEWS AGENCY
4 Glenhurst Avenue, LONDON, NW5 1PS
Tel: 020 7482 4995
Email: london@mail.ctk.cz
Web site: http://www.ctk.cz/english/index.html

Material accepted: All news relating to the Czech
Republic including topical political events, EU,
economics and sports. Serves: Media in the Czech and
Slovak Republics.
Sdanislav Mundil is the UK Correspondent to whom
press releases should be addressed.

DAVE SELBY EDITORIAL SERVICES
25 Downs Road, MALDON, CM9 5HG
Tel: 01621 854978

Material accepted: Classic motoring news, nautical
and maritime. Serves UK.
Dave Selby is the Proprietor to whom press releases
should be addressed.

DOW JONES ENERGY SERVICE
5th Floor, 10 Fleet Place, Limeburner Lane, LONDON,
EC4M 7QN
Tel: 020 7842 9340 **Fax:** 020 7842 9341
Email: leia.parker@dowjones.com
Web site: http://www.dowjones.com

Material accepted: Electricity, gas and oil news for the
UK and Continental Europe. Serves Worldwide.
Adam Smallman is the Editor to whom press releases
should be addressed.

DOW JONES NEWSWIRES
5th Floor, 10 Fleet Place, Limeburner Lane, LONDON,
EC4M 7QN
Tel: 020 7842 9300 **Fax:** 020 7842 9361
Email: djequitiesnews.london@dowjones.com
Web site: http://www.dowjones.com

Material accepted: International business and financial
news and information. Serves: Worldwide.
Ian Walker is the Assistant Managing Editor to whom
press releases should be addressed.

DOW JONES NEWSWIRES COMMODITIES
10 Fleet Place, Limeburner Lane, LONDON, EC4M 7QN
Tel: 020 7842 9300 **Fax:** 020 7842 9418
Web site: http://www.dowjones.com

Material accepted: Base and precious metals, grains,
feed-meal and softs markets. Serves: Worldwide.
Andrea Hotter is the Assistant News Editor to whom
press releases should be addressed.

DPA (GERMAN PRESS AGENCY)
30 Old Queen Street, St. James's Park, LONDON,
SW1H 9HP
Tel: 020 7233 2888 **Fax:** 020 7233 3534
Email: london@dpa.com
Web site: http://www.dpa.com

Material accepted: All news of interest to Europe, plus
items about German firms and organisations. Serves:
The German media.
Thomas Burmeister is the Bureau Chief to whom press
releases should be addressed.

EMIRATES NEWS AGENCY
The Studio, 143 Lavender Hill, LONDON, SW11 5QJ
Tel: 020 7228 1060 **Fax:** 020 7228 1191
Email: emirates@mia.gb.com

Material accepted: Political news concerning the
Middle East. Serves: All the national press in the UK.

EMPICS ENTERTAINMENT
2nd Floor, Press Association, 292 Vauxhall Bridge
Road, LONDON, SW1V 1AE
Tel: 020 7963 7000
Email: wai@empics.com
Web site: http://www.paphotos.com

Material accepted: Photos and news of celebrities,
photo-calls and major British events. Serves: National
and international newspapers and magazines.

HEADLINERS
Rich Mix, 35-47 Bethnal Green Road, LONDON, E1 6LA
Tel: 020 7749,9360
Email: enquiries@headliners.org
Web site: http://www.headliners.org
Children's charity which produces news and comment by children aged 8 to 18 years old for programmes of learning through journalism. **Serves:** Local and national media.
Fiona Wyton is the Director to whom press releases should be addressed.

INFOSTRADA HAYTERS
Image House, Station Road, LONDON, N17 9LR
Tel: 020 8808 3300 **Fax:** 020 8808 1122
Email: sport@infostradahayters.com
Material accepted: All sports news and events. **Serves:** UK and abroad.
Gerry Cox is the Chief Executive to whom press releases should be addressed.

INTERFAX EUROPE
3rd Floor, 2-3 Philpot Lane, LONDON, EC3M 8AQ
Tel: 020 7621 0595 **Fax:** 020 7929 4263
Email: europe@interfax.co.uk
Web site: http://www.interfax.com
Material accepted: UK cultural events. **Serves:** Russian national press, TV and radio.
Karen Whitney is the Office Manager to whom press releases should be addressed.

IPS PHOTO AGENCY
21 Delisle Road, LONDON, SE28 0JD
Tel: 020 8331 0207 **Fax:** 020 8855 1037
Email: info@ips-net.co.uk
Web site: http://www.ips-net.co.uk
Material accepted: Sports photography including football and big sporting occasions. **Serves:** National and International press in Japan, Italy and Holland.
Marcello Pozzetti is the Proprietor to whom press releases should be addressed.

IRNA ISLAMIC REPUBLIC NEWS AGENCY
3rd Floor, Imperial Life House, 390-400 High Road, WEMBLEY, HA9 6AS
Tel: 020 8903 1630 **Fax:** 020 8900 0705
Email: irna-london@yahoo.com
Web site: http://www.irna.ir
Material accepted: Economic, social, political and photographs. **Serves:** International.
Touraj Shiralilou is the Bureau Chief to whom press releases should be addressed.

ITAR - TASS NEWS AGENCY
Suite 12-20, 2nd Floor, Morley House, 314-322 Regent Street, LONDON, W1B 3BD
Tel: 020 7580 5543 **Fax:** 020 7580 5547
Email: tassinlondon@yahoo.co.uk
Web site: http://www.itar-tass.com
Material accepted: International political and economic news in English, French, German, Arabic and Russian. **Serves:** Russian and World media.
Vitaly Makarchev is the Bureau Chief to whom press releases should be addressed.

JIJI PRESS
4th Floor, International Press Centre, 76 Shoe Lane, LONDON, EC4A 3JB
Tel: 020 7936 2847 **Fax:** 020 7583 8353
Email: edit@jiji.co.uk
Web site: http://www.jiji.com
Japanese news wire service. **Material accepted:** News and events from around the globe. **Serves:** Worldwide.
Takashi Watanabe is the London Bureau Chief to whom press releases should be addressed.

KUWAIT NEWS AGENCY
5th Floor, New Premier House, 150 Southampton Row, LONDON, WC1B 5AL
Tel: 020 7278 5445 **Fax:** 020 7278 6232
Email: kuwait@btclick.com
Material accepted: General news and information from the UK. No photos. **Serves:** The Middle East.
Hosny Emam is the London Bureau Chief to whom press releases should be addressed.

KYODO NEWS
4th Floor, 20 Orange Street, LONDON, WC2H 7EF
Tel: 020 7766 4400 **Fax:** 020 7766 4411
Email: london@kyodonews.jp
Web site: http://home.kyodo.co.jp

Material accepted: General news concerning the UK, Ireland, Portugal and Scandinavia. **Serves:** English language newspapers in various parts of the world and all forms of media in Japan.
Juno Kondo is the London Bureau Chief to whom press releases should be addressed.

LONDON CORRESPONDENT'S BUREAU BILD GROUP
150-151 Fleet Street, LONDON, EC4A 2DQ
Tel: 020 7353 1414 **Fax:** 020 7353 1441
Email: cmaenz@bildlondon.com
Material accepted: UK news, sport, economic and entertainment news. **Serves:** Germany.
Christina Maenz is the Bureau Chief to whom press releases should be addressed.

MAGHREB ARABE PRESSE
35 Westminster Bridge Road, LONDON, SE1 7JB
Tel: 020 7401 8146 **Fax:** 020 7401 8148
Email: aouifia@aol.com
Web site: http://www.map.co.ma
Material accepted: UK news of interest to areas served. **Serves:** Middle East, Africa, the Mediterranean Basin and the Commonwealth.
Abdeljhani Awifia is the Bureau Chief to whom press releases should be addressed.

MALAYSIAN NATIONAL NEWS AGENCY
40 The Fairway, LONDON, W3 7PX
Tel: 020 8740 7758
Email: penawan@yahoo.co.uk
Material accepted: General European news. **Serves:** Malaysian media.

MARKET NEWS INTERNATIONAL
Market News International Inc, 50 Cannon Street, LONDON, EC4N 6JJ
Tel: 020 7634 1655 **Fax:** 020 7236 7126
Email: ukeditorial@marketnews.com
Web site: http://www.marketnews.com
News information service. Produces reports on monetary policy, currencies, bonds and derivatives. Distributed via major news agencies and across the Internet. **Serves:** Worldwide.
David Thomas is the Bureau Chief to whom press releases should be addressed.

MEDIA FEATURES
36 Holcroft Court, Carburton Street, LONDON, W1W 5DJ
Tel: 020 7436 3678
Email: leozanelli@aol.com
Material accepted: Literature, film, computing, gardening, food and drink as well as fraternal societies and Italian culture. **Serves:** Mainly UK.

NATIONAL NEWS
4/5 Academy Buildings, Fanshaw Street, LONDON, N1 6LQ
Tel: 020 7684 3000 **Fax:** 020 7684 3030
Email: news@nationalnews.co.uk
Material accepted: All press releases. **Serves:** UK.

NETHERLANDS PRESS ASSOCIATION
3 Moat Crescent, LONDON, N3 3DD
Tel: 020 8371 9909
Email: esthergotink@btinternet.com
Web site: http://www.gpd.nl
Material accepted: International news. **Serves:** Netherlands.
Esther Gotink is the UK Correspondent to whom press releases should be addressed.

NEWS LTD OF AUSTRALIA
1 Virginia Street, LONDON, E98 1NL
Tel: 020 7702 1355 **Fax:** 020 7702 1382
Web site: http://www.news.com.au
Material accepted: International news. **Serves:** News Corporation newspapers in Australia.
Charles Miranda is the Bureau Chief to whom press releases should be addressed.

NUNN SYNDICATION LTD
PO Box 56303, LONDON, SE1 2TD
Tel: 020 7357 9000 **Fax:** 020 7231 3912
Email: production@nunn-syndication.com
Web site: http://www.nunn-syndication.com
Material accepted: All press releases. **Serves:** Whole of the UK plus worldwide syndication outlet.
Robin Nunn is the Managing Director to whom press releases should be addressed.

ON LINE BROADCASTING
Box Tree House, Wroxton Lane, Horley, BANBURY, OX15 6BD
Tel: 020 7183 3833 **Fax:** 020 8960 7490
Email: simon@onlib.com
Web site: http://www.onlib.com
Material accepted: International sports stories. **Serves:** International television and radio broadcasters.

PA ENTERTAINMENT, ARTS AND EVENTS
PA Operations Centre, Bridgegate, Howden, GOOLE, DN14 7AE
Tel: 020 7963 7000 **Fax:** 020 7963 7805
Web site: http://www.pressassociation.com/
Provide listings information for newspapers.
Material accepted: TV, arts and entertainments. **Serves:** UK and Ireland.

PA VIDEO
Press Association, 292 Vauxhall Bridge Road, LONDON, SW1V 1AE
Tel: 020 7963 7000
Email: video@pressassociation.com
Web site: http://www.pressassociation.com/
Material accepted: News, sport and entertainment related events that can be filmed. **Serves:** Web-sites and broadcasters within the UK.
Press releases should be addressed to the News Desk.

PHOTOSHOT LTD
29-31 Saffron Hill, LONDON, EC1N 8SW
Tel: 020 7421 6000 **Fax:** 020 7421 6006
Email: info@photoshot.com
Web site: http://www.photoshot.com
Photographic news agency, interested in international news and personality stories. **Material accepted:** News, feature and photo-facility information. **Serves:** UK and international media. Full digital picture archive with transmission facilities by FTP or ISDN. Commercial photographic division with UK wide network of photographers available.

PLATT'S
20 Canada Square, Canary Wharf, LONDON, E14 5LH
Tel: 020 7176 7000 **Fax:** 020 7176 6108
Email: news@platts.com
Web site: http://www.platts.com
Material accepted: Oil and energy news items. **Serves:** Worldwide. Service includes live news service via satellite, daily newsletters, email, fax and telex market reports.

RACENEWS LIMITED
85 Blackstock Road, LONDON, N4 2JW
Tel: 020 7704 0326 **Fax:** 020 7704 6861
Email: racenews@racenewsonline.com
Web site: http://www.racenews.co.uk
Material accepted: Horse racing. **Serves:** Worldwide.

REX FEATURES LTD
18 Vine Hill, LONDON, EC1R 5DZ
Tel: 020 7278 7294 **Fax:** 020 7837 4812
Email: editorial@rexfeatures.com
Web site: http://www.rexfeatures.com
Photographic press agency. **Material accepted:** News, features, personality, human interest, travel, new products, technology and humour. **Serves:** UK and abroad.

RIA NOVOSTI
3 Rosary Gardens, LONDON, SW7 4NW
Tel: 020 7370 3002 **Fax:** 020 7244 7875
Email: ria@novosti.co.uk
Web site: http://www.rian.ru
Material accepted: General news, current affairs, politics, economics, science and finance relating to the Russian Federation from UK based organisations. **Serves:** UK and Russian media outlets and financial institutions.

SOUNDAROUND NEWS AGENCY
74 Glentham Road, BARNES, SW13 9JJ
Tel: 020 8741 3332
Email: nigel@soundaround.org
Web site: http://www.soundaround.org
Material accepted: News and features relevant to the blind and visually impaired. **Serves:** The blind and visually impaired in the English speaking world.
Nigel Verbeek is the Editor In Chief to whom press releases should be addressed.

Services & Suppliers

SPECIALIST NEWS SERVICES
27 Newton Street, LONDON, WC2B 5EL
Tel: 020 7831 3267 **Fax:** 020 7831 4351
Email: desk@snsnews.co.uk
Web site: http://www.specialistnews.co.uk

Material accepted: National and International material.
Serves: National daily newspapers.
Mark Solomons and Simon Worthington are the
Partners to whom press releases should be addressed.

**SPORT & GENERAL PHOTOGRAPHIC PRESS
AGENCY**
63 Gee Street, LONDON, EC1V 3RS
Tel: 020 7553 4044 **Fax:** 020 7553 4040
Email: alpha.library@alphapress.com
Web site: http://www.alphapress.com

Material accepted: All photographs and copy. Serves:
UK and abroad.
Kate Dollard is the Picture Editor to whom press
releases should be addressed.

SPORTSBEAT/NEWS ASSOCIATES
Tuition House, St. Georges Road, LONDON, SW19 4EU
Tel: 0870 445 0156 **Fax:** 0870 445 0157
Email: editorial@sportsbeat.co.uk
Web site: http://www.sportsbeat.co.uk

Material accepted: All sports news, pictures, results
and features. Serves: Worldwide for pictures and
television.

THOMSON REUTERS LTD
The Reuters Building, 30 South Colonnade, Canary
Wharf, LONDON, E14 5EP
Tel: 020 7250 1122 **Fax:** 020 7542 7921
Email: uk.online@reuters.com
Web site: http://www.thomsonreuters.com

Reuters World Service - material accepted: General
news of interest to a world audience, including sport.
Reuters Economic Services - material accepted:
Corporate, economic, financial and commodity news,
both domestic and international. Reuters Air Cargo
Service - material accepted: Air cargo and
transportation news, both domestic and international.
Serves: Worldwide.

TROIKA PHOTOS LTD
96 Farringdon Road, LONDON, EC1R 3EA
Tel: 020 7833 2330 **Fax:** 020 7278 9100
Email: pictures@troikaphotos.com

**Work on international and UK commissions. Archive
covers social, economic and political subjects in the
UK. Also includes material from Balkan countries,
Iraq and Iran.**

TV NEWS LONDON LTD
Brook House, 89 Station Road, New Barnet, BARNET,
EN5 1PX
Tel: 020 8275 8854 **Fax:** 020 8440 3368
Email: info@tvnewslondon.co.uk
Web site: http://www.tvnewslondon.co.uk

Material accepted: News about people and events in
London. Serves: UK.
Roz Morris is the Managing Director to whom press
releases should be addressed.

UK PRESS
3 The Drive, Great Warley, BRENTWOOD, CM13 3FR
Tel: 0870 114 2855
Email: info@ukpress.co.uk
Web site: http://www.ukpress.co.uk

Material accepted: National and International News.
Serves: Worldwide.
Julian Parker is the Picture Editor to whom press
releases should be addressed.

UNIQUE ENTERTAINMENT NEWS
50 Lisson Street, LONDON, NW1 5DF
Tel: 020 7453 1650 **Fax:** 020 7453 1688
Email: newsroom@unique.com
Web site: http://www.entertainmentnews.co.uk

Material accepted: Entertainment and celebrity news
and features.

WIREIMAGE
101 Bayham Street, LONDON, NW1 0AG
Tel: 020 7428 5120
Email: vickydearman@wireimage.com
Web site: http://www.wireimage.com

Material accepted: International news and photos
covering the entertainment industry including film,
music and fashion. Serves: National newspapers,
consumer magazines and online entertainment sites.
Vicky Dearman is the Assignment Head to whom press
releases should be addressed.

WORLD ENTERTAINMENT NEWS NETWORK
35 Kings Exchange, Tileyard Road, Kings Cross,
LONDON, N7 9AH
Tel: 020 7607 2757 **Fax:** 020 7700 4649
Email: info@wenn.com
Web site: http://www.wenn.com

Material accepted: Provides a 24 hour news and photo
service with a news-wire and bulletin feed covering
entertainment and showbiz news, current affairs, the
environment, science, health, and technology. Serves:
Newspapers, magazines, radio and TV networks and
online services worldwide.
Lloyd Beiny is the Chief Executive to whom press
releases should be addressed.

XINHUA NEWS AGENCY
8 Swiss Terrace, Belsize Road, Swiss Cottage,
LONDON, NW6 4RR
Tel: 020 7586 8271 **Fax:** 020 7722 8512
Email: xinhua.london@hotmail.com

Material accepted: National and International news
and stories related to China. Serves: Worldwide.
Mr Majian Guo Ma is the business writer to whom press
releases should be addressed.

NEWS & PICTURE AGENCIES

Home Counties

AUTO FEATURE SERVICES
12 Baas Lane, BROXBOURNE, EN10 7EH
Tel: 01992 307662 **Fax:** 01992 307662
Email: edward.wilkinson2@ntlworld.com

Materials accepted: Motoring information and tests.
Serves: UK.

CAR AND DRIVING
Heath House, Heath Business Centre, Salfords
Industrial Estate, 18 Bonehurst Road, Salfords,
REDHILL, RH1 5EN
Tel: 01293 774260 **Fax:** 01293 774261
Email: info@cardrive.demon.co.uk
Web site: http://www.caranddriving.com

Material accepted: All aspects of motoring. Serves:
Motoring publications and websites in the UK.

DRIVELINES MOTORING EDITORIAL AGENCY
120 North Road, HERTFORD, SG14 2BZ
Tel: 07710 259445 **Fax:** 01992 303234
Email: drivelines@ntlworld.com

Material accepted: Car road tests, motor industry and
motor sport. Serves: Regional newspapers and
magazines, motor trade and motor sport publications.
Adrian Foster is the Motoring Editor to whom press
releases should be addressed.

FERRARI PRESS AGENCY
7 Summerhill Road, DARTFORD, DA1 2LP
Tel: 01322 628444 **Fax:** 01322 628445
Email: news@ferraripress.com
Web site: http://www.ferraripress.com

Material accepted: National and local news, features
and pictures. Serves: National newspapers and
magazines.

SOUTH BEDS NEWS AGENCY
Bramingham Park Business Centre, Enterprise Way,
Bramingham Park, LUTON, LU3 4BU
Tel: 01582 572222 **Fax:** 01582 493486
Email: southbedsnews@btconnect.com

Material accepted: All news matters and pictures. PR
assignments undertaken. Serves: Bedfordshire,
Buckinghamshire, Hertfordshire and Northamptonshire.

NEWS & PICTURE AGENCIES

South Eastern

A2B NEWS
14 Waldegrave Road, BRIGHTON, BN1 6GE
Tel: 01273 279623
Email: andrew.baxter@a2bnews.com
Web site: http://www.a2bnews.com

Material accepted: All motoring and road transport
news. Serves: National daily and Sunday newspapers,
regional press and consumer magazines.
Andrew Baxter is the Proprietor to whom press
releases should be addressed.

**CASSIDY AND LEIGH (SOUTHERN NEWS
SERVICE)**
Exchange House, HINDHEAD, GU26 6AA
Tel: 01428 607330 **Fax:** 01428 606351
Email: news@cassidyandleigh.com

Material Accepted: Worldwide news, sports,
entertainment, show business and TV. Serves:
Worldwide.

CROWN HOUSE MEDIA
Crown House, Well Street, RUTHIN, LL15 1AE
Tel: 0870 850 8550 **Fax:** 0870 131 3597
Email: info@crownhousemedia.com
Web site: http://www.crownhousemedia.com

Material accepted: Football, cricket, motorsport,
mountain bike racing, sailing, horse racing, rugby and
golf. Serves: BBC and independent radio stations in the
UK and key radio stations worldwide.

**FEATS PRESS AND CELEBRITY NEWS SERVICE
(CNS)**
102 High Street, HURSTPIERPOINT, BN6 9PX
Tel: 01273 831138 **Fax:** 01273 836029
Email: info@featspress.com
Web site: http://www.featspress.com

Content: Celebrity interviews and features. Material
accepted: International entertainment and celebrity
news, photo-calls and events. Serves: Worldwide.
John Bedford is the Editorial Director to whom press
releases should be addressed.

FIRST ELEVEN SPORTS AGENCY
PO Box 11, READING, RG6 3DT
Tel: 0843 208 5390
Email: enquiries@firsteleven.co.uk
Web site: http://www.firsteleven.co.uk

Material accepted: Match results and statistics, news
and feature items on football, cricket, rugby union,
hockey, basketball, bowls, ice hockey, horse racing and
speedway in the Thames Valley. Serves: South England.
Bob Morrison is the Proprietor to whom press releases
should be addressed.

INS NEWS AGENCY LTD
145 Wharfedale Road, Winnersh Triangle, Winnersh,
READING, RG41 5RB
Tel: 0118 944 0600 **Fax:** 0118 922 9404
Email: newsdesk@insnews.co.uk
Web site: http://www.insnews.co.uk

Material accepted: National and regional news and
features.
Neil Hyde the Managing Director to whom press
releases should be addressed.

ISLE OF WIGHT NEWS AGENCY
123 Pyle Street, NEWPORT, PO30 1ST
Tel: 01983 522210 **Fax:** 01983 528920
Email: editor@iwcp2.demon.co.uk

Material accepted: General news and information
relating to the Isle of Wight. Serves: Mainly Isle of Wight
but the whole of the UK.

ITV MERIDIAN NEWS BUREAU (BOURNEMOUTH)
105D, Alum House, Discovery Court Business Park,
551-553 Wallisdown Road, POOLE, BH12 5AG
Tel: 01202 853131 **Fax:** 01202 853133
Email: martin.dowse@itv.com

Material accepted: News bureau serving Meridian
Broadcasting, covers regional news and current affairs.
Serves: Bournemouth and Dorset.
Martin Dowse is the Reporter to whom press releases
should be addressed.

JOHN CONNOR PRESS ASSOCIATES
57A High Street, LEWES, BN7 1XE
Tel: 01273 486851 **Fax:** 0870 706 0463
Email: news@jcpa.co.uk
Web site: http://www.jcpa.co.uk

Material accepted: Court cover at Lewes and Hove
Crown Courts and local Magistrates Courts. Serves:
Sussex.

M & Y NEWS AGENCY LTD
65 Osborne Road, SOUTHSEA, PO5 3LS
Tel: 023 9282 0311
Email: mail@mynewsagency.co.uk
Web site: http://www.mynewsagency.co.uk

Material accepted: National news, sport and features. Serves: National and regional newspapers, magazines and broadcasters.
Pat Symes and Alex Crook are the Director and Partner to whom press releases should be addressed.

MERIDIAN BROADCASTING LTD
The Forum, Solent Business Park, Whiteley, FAREHAM, PO15 7PA
Tel: 0844 881 2000
Email: thamesvalleynews@itv.com

Material accepted: News bureau serving Meridian Broadcasting, covers regional news and current affairs.
Kim Hewitt is the Producer to whom press releases should be addressed.

MONITOR PICTURE LIBRARY
The Forge, Roydon, HARLOW, CM19 5HH
Tel: 01279 792700 **Fax:** 01279 792600
Email: info@monitorpicturelibrary.com
Web site: http://www.monitorpicturelibrary.com

Material accepted: Political, business, government, law, art, sport, music, royal, showbiz and information on buildings and places. Serves: Worldwide.
Eleanore White is the Picture Editor to whom press releases should be addressed.

PRESS AGENCY (GATWICK)
1A Sunview Avenue, PEACEHAVEN, BN10 8PJ
Tel: 01273 583103
Email: petershirley2@hotmail.com

Material accepted: News stories from East and West Sussex. Serves: National newspapers.
Peter Shirley is the Editor to whom press releases should be addressed.

SOLENT NEWS AGENCY
23 Mitchell Point, Ensign Way, Hamble, SOUTHAMPTON, SO31 4RF
Tel: 023 8045 8800 **Fax:** 023 8045 8801
Email: news@solentnews.biz
Web site: http://www.solentnews.biz

Material accepted: News, PR and commercial photography. Serves: Hampshire, Wiltshire and the Isle of Wight.

SOUTHERN NEWS AND PICTURES
PR by email only
Tel: 07976 504832
Email: info@snapitnow.co.uk
Web site: http://www.snapitnow.co.uk

Material accepted: News and features from the South East. Serves: National and regional newspapers, magazines and broadcasters also PR agencies and local businesses.

TIM WOOD AGENCY
Victoria House, 148 Maldon Road, COLCHESTER, CO3 3AY
Tel: 020 7248 6858 **Fax:** 020 7236 8136
Email: obinsight@hotmail.com
Web site: http://www.old-bailey.com

Material accepted: Court cover at Old Bailey and the Crown courts at Southwark, Blackfriars and Middlesex Guildhall. Serves: UK.

WESSEX FEATURES AND PHOTOS LTD
Quill House, Charnham Lane, HUNGERFORD, RG17 0EY
Tel: 01488 686810 **Fax:** 01488 684463
Email: news@britishnews.co.uk
Web site: http://www.britishnews.co.uk

Material accepted: National general news, features and photographs. Serves: National and regional newspapers, radio, television and magazines.
Jim Hardy is the Editor to whom press releases should be addressed.

NEWS & PICTURE AGENCIES
South Western

BOURNEMOUTH NEWS & PICTURE SERVICE
Unit 1, 1st Floor Offices, 40-44 Holdenest Road, BOURNEMOUTH, BH8 8AD
Tel: 01202 558833 **Fax:** 01202 553875
Email: news@bnps.co.uk
Web site: http://www.bnps.co.uk

Material accepted: All general news, features and photographic material from central southern England. Serves: National and provincial press, radio and TV

throughout Dorset, Hampshire, Wiltshire and Devon. Apple-Picture transmission.

BRISTOL & WEST NEWS AGENCY LTD
80 Combe Avenue, Portishead, BRISTOL, BS20 6JT
Tel: 01275 842053
Material accepted: Sports coverage only. Serves: Bristol-UA, Gloucestershire and Somerset.
Richard Latham is the Managing Director to whom press releases should be addressed.

CALYX MULTIMEDIA
41 Churchward Avenue, Rodbourne Cheney, SWINDON, SN2 1NJ
Tel: 01793 520131
Email: calyxpix@ntlworld.com
Web site: http://www.calyxpix.com

Material accepted: Regional news, new pictures and specialist TV coverage - UK Royals Library footage. Serves: Wiltshire, North Hampshire, West Berkshire, North Dorset, M4 Corridor-West, South Midlands and Somerset.

COTSWOLD & SWINDON NEWS SERVICE
256 Marlborough Road, SWINDON, SN3 1NR
Tel: 01793 485461
Email: cotswin@stares.co.uk
Web site: http://www.stares.co.uk

Material accepted: News and features and journalism training courses. Serves: National and regional media.

DEVON NEWS LTD
Lower Barton, Higher Ashton, EXETER, EX6 7QR
Tel: 01647 252544
Email: devonnewslimited@aol.com

Material accepted: News and features relating to Devon. Serves: National newspapers.
Press releases should be addressed to the News Desk.

DRIVETIME (MOTORING PRESS AND PR)
46 Malvern Road, GLOUCESTER, GL1 3JT
Tel: 01452 522220
Email: drive_edit@yahoo.co.uk

Material accepted: Motoring, road safety, car maintenance. Serves: UK and Ireland.

FREEMANS
3 Youlston Close, Shirwell, BARNSTAPLE, EX31 4JW
Tel: 01271 850255
Email: freemans.pa@virgin.net
Web site: http://www.bipp.com/TonyFreeman

Material accepted: All subjects covering South West of England. Features: Women's interest, animals and unusual hobbies. Serves: Devon, Cornwall, Somerset and Wiltshire.

GLOUCESTERSHIRE NEWS SERVICE
26 Westgate Street, GLOUCESTER, GL1 2NG
Tel: 01452 522270
Email: stories@glosnews.com
Web site: http://www.glosnews.com

Provides coverage of court inquests, hard news events and information on Gloucester RFC. Serves: Gloucestershire.

ITV MERIDIAN NEWS (SOUTH)
ITV Meridian Broadcasting, Forum One, Parkway, Solent Business Park, WHITELEY, PO15 7PA
Tel: 0844 881 2000
Email: meridiantonight@itv.com

Material accepted: News bureau serving ITV Meridian, covers regional news and current affairs. Serves: Hampshire, Dorset, West Sussex and South Wiltshire.
Press releases should be addressed to the appropriate desk.

LAPPAS OF EXETER
7 Waylands Road, TIVERTON, EX16 6UT
Tel: 01884 254555
Email: lappas@freeuk.com
Web site: http://www.richardlappasimages.com

Material accepted: Photo-agency covering news, sport and lifestyle features. Serves: National daily newspapers.
Richard Lappas is the Managing Director to whom press releases should be addressed.

PA MOTORING
2nd Floor, BEPP Building, Temple Way, BRISTOL, BS99 7HD
Tel: 020 7963 7866
Email: motoring@pa.press.net
Web site: http://motoring.press.net

Material accepted: Motoring features press releases, travel where motoring related. Serves: UK and abroad.
Matt Joy is the Motoring Editor to whom press releases should be addressed.

PA NEWS (BRISTOL)
2nd Floor, Post & Press Building, Temple Way, BRISTOL, BS99 7HD
Tel: 0870 120 3200 **Fax:** 0870 830 6798
Email: pabristol@pa.press.net
Web site: http://www.pressassociation.press.net

Material accepted: General news and photographs. Serves: South West England.
All press releases should be addressed to the Reporters.

SOMERSET PHOTO NEWS
12 Jellalabad Court, The Mount, TAUNTON, TA1 3RZ
Tel: 01823 282053 **Fax:** 01823 282053
Email: somersetphotonews@boltblue.com

Material accepted: Local and national industrial and commercial photography. Serves: Worldwide.
Alain Lockyer is the Picture Editor to whom press releases should be addressed.

SOUTH COAST PRESS AGENCY
22 St. Peters Road, BOURNEMOUTH, BH1 2LE
Tel: 07980 978828

Material accepted: Photo calls and press events in Dorset and Hampshire. Serves: Dorset and Hampshire.

TORBAY NEWS AGENCY
43 Kilmorie, Ilsham Marine Drive, TORQUAY, TQ1 2HU
Tel: 01803 214555

Material accepted: Trade and technical news items. Serves: Torbay region.

WEST COAST NEWS LTD
Renaissance House, Parracombe, BARNSTAPLE, EX31 4QH
Tel: 01598 763296
Email: westcoast.news@dial.pipex.com

Material accepted: General news stories and features from the South West of England. Serves: National press.
Nick Constable is the News Editor and Karen Farrington is the Features Editor to whom press releases should be addressed.

NEWS & PICTURE AGENCIES
Eastern

ALBANPIX
Ivy House, Back Larre, Blakeney, HOLT, NR25 7NR
Tel: 01263 741600 **Fax:** 01263 741611
Email: mail@albanpix.com
Web site: http://www.albanpix.com

Material accepted: Photographs and features on news and sport covering East Anglia. Serves: Regional and national newspapers, magazines, television companies and PR companies.
Alban Donohoe is the Director to whom press releases should be addressed.

CNS CITY NEWS SERVICE & CNS ARTS WIRE
17 Kedleston Road, Heritage Park, PETERBOROUGH, PE2 8XL
Tel: 01733 345581
Email: citynewsuk@aol.com

Material accepted: Worldwide city and financial news. Theatre, arts and showbiz news and gossip. Club openings, gallery previews. Serves: Worldwide.

COI NEWS AND PR
Eastbrook, Shaftesbury Road, CAMBRIDGE, CB2 8DF
Tel: 01223 372780 **Fax:** 01223 372870
Email: cambridge@coi.gsi.gov.uk
Web site: http://nds.coi.gov.uk

Government news and press agency. Provides press and publicity services to Government departments, public sector organisations and the general public. Serves: Beds, Cambs, Essex, Herts, Norfolk and Suffolk.
Mick Lazarus is the Office Manager to whom press releases should be addressed.

Services & Suppliers

EAST ANGLIA NEWS SERVICE
32 Westerfield Road, IPSWICH, IP4 2UJ
Tel: 01473 221921 **Fax:** 01473 280333
Email: theyoungs@ntlworld.com
Web site: http://www.eanews.co.uk
Material accepted: General news from the East
Anglian region. Serves: National press.

JARROLDS PRESS AGENCY
45 Main Road, Kesgrave, IPSWICH, IP5 1AG
Tel: 01394 382810 **Fax:** 01394 382810
Email: darrenlennard@aol.com
Material accepted: General news and sports features
from the East Anglian region. Serves: Local TV and
radio, national media and trade press.
Darren Lennard is the Reporter to whom press releases
should be addressed.

KNS NEWS
Independent House, 18-20 Thorpe Road, NORWICH,
NR1 1RY
Tel: 01603 765188
Email: info@knsnews.co.uk
Web site: http://www.knsnews.co.uk
Material accepted: News concerning any organisations
in East Anglia.
Mark Houldey is the Managing Director to whom press
releases should be addressed.

MASONS NEWS LIMITED
Unit 10, Chesterton Mill, French's Road, CAMBRIDGE,
CB4 3NP
Tel: 01223 224400
Email: news@masons-news.co.uk
Material accepted: News concerning any organisations
and events linked with the East Anglian region in
addition to news regarding national events. Serves: East
Anglia and the East Midlands.

TONY SCASE NEWS SERVICE
Little Congham House, Congham, KING'S LYNN, PE32
1DR
Tel: 01485 600650 **Fax:** 01485 600672
Email: news@scase.co.uk
Web site: http://www.scase.co.uk
Material accepted: News, royal news and features for
the East Anglia area. Serves: National newspapers in
the United Kingdom and local television in East Anglia.
Hilary Scase is the Managing Director to whom press
releases should be addressed.

NEWS & PICTURE AGENCIES

Midlands

ASSOCIATED SPORTS PHOTOGRAPHY
21 Green Walk, LEICESTER, LE3 6SE
Tel: 0116 232 0310 **Fax:** 0116 231 1123
Email: asp@sports-photos.co.uk
Web site: http://www.sporting-heroes.net
Material accepted: National and international sport,
royal, political and travel. Serves: Worldwide.
George Herringshaw is the Managing Director to whom
press releases should be addressed.

CATERS NEWS AGENCY
Suite 40, Queens Gate, 121 Suffolk Street, Queensway,
BIRMINGHAM, B1 1LX
Tel: 0121 616 1100 **Fax:** 0121 616 2200
Email: news@catersnews.com
Web site: http://www.catersnews.com
Material accepted: News of events in the West
Midlands. Serves: National newspapers and magazines.

CHADWICKS PRESS AGENCY
Publicity House, 59 Long Street, Wigston, LEICESTER,
LE18 2AJ
Tel: 0116 288 1568 **Fax:** 0116 288 4672
Email: chris@chadwicksphoto.co.uk
Web site: http://www.chadwicksphoto.co.uk
Material accepted: All news material considered
covering the East Midlands. Serves: National and
regional newspapers.

CHAPMAN & PAGE
Denegate House, Amber Hill, BOSTON, PE20 3RL
Tel: 01205 290477 **Fax:** 01205 290477
Email: chapmanpage@internett.demon.co.uk
Material accepted: Crossword puzzles and feature
editorial for regional newspapers. Serves: UK.

COI COMMUNICATIONS EAST MIDLANDS
The Belgrave Centre, Stanley Place, Talbot Street,
NOTTINGHAM, NG1 5GG
Tel: 0115 971 2780 **Fax:** 0115 971 2791
Email: nottingham@coi.gsi.gov.uk
Web site: http://nds.coi.gov.uk
**Government press office. Provides press and
publicity services to Government and associated
departments. Communicates the policies of central
Government to the public through the regional
media. Provides 24 hour emergency service and
emergency planning. Serves:** the East Midlands.
Elizabeth Leonard is the Senior Press Officer to whom
press releases should be addressed.

COVENTRY NEWS SERVICE
2 Edison Building, Electric Wharf, Sandy Lane,
COVENTRY, CV1 4JA
Tel: 024 7663 3636 **Fax:** 024 7663 4906
Email: cns@leadstory.co.uk
Material accepted: News and sport from the West
Midlands. Serves: London newspapers, Press
Association, BBC, Central TV, ITN, provincial
newspapers and local radio.
Adam Dent is the Proprietor to whom press releases
should be addressed.

EASTERN NEWS SERVICE (LINCOLN)
Room SG10, Greetwell Place, 2 Lime Kiln Way,
LINCOLN, LN2 4US
Tel: 01522 533328 **Fax:** 01522 560589
Email: news@easternnews.plus.com
Material accepted: General news and features, sport
and legal features covering Lincolnshire. Serves: Local
and national press and national television.

ELLIOTT NEWS SERVICE
19-21 Main Street, Keyworth, NOTTINGHAM, NG12
5AA
Tel: 0115 937 6506
Email: elliottnews@btconnect.com
Material accepted: General regional news. Serves:
South Nottinghamshire, North Leicestershire and South
East Derbyshire.

EVERTON'S NEWS AGENCY
Hayley Green Court, 130 Hagley Road, Hayley Green,
HALESOWEN, B63 1DY
Tel: 0121 585 9188 **Fax:** 0121 585 7117
Email: clive.everton@talk21.com
Web site: http://www.snookerscene.co.uk
Material accepted: Snooker and cue sport related
material. Serves: Local and national media.
Clive Everton is the Proprietor to whom press releases
should be addressed.

FRONT PAGE NEWS AGENCY
The White House, 24 The Ridgeway, REDDITCH, B96
6LT
Tel: 0141 888 0909
Email: saralain@btopenworld.com
Web site: http://www.frontpageagency.co.uk
Material accepted: True life features and news
covering the UK. Serves: National media.
Sara Lain is the Features Editor to whom press releases
should be addressed.

M2 COMMUNICATIONS LTD
PO Box 4030, BATH, BA1 0EE
Tel: 020 7047 0200 **Fax:** 020 7057 0200
Email: info@m2.com
Web site: http://www.m2.com
Material accepted: General news worldwide, financial,
business, technology and science. Serves: International.

NEWS TEAM INTERNATIONAL LTD
35 Gas Street, BIRMINGHAM, B1 2JT
Tel: 0121 246 5511 **Fax:** 0121 246 5101
Email: info@newsteam.co.uk
Web site: http://www.newsteam.co.uk
Material accepted: All general news, features and
photographs. Commissioned work also undertaken for
the corporate and PR sector. Serves: International,
national provincial and trade media.

NOTTINGHAM NEWS SERVICE
56A Babington Lane, DERBY, DE1 1SX
Tel: 01332 340404 **Fax:** 0115 960 3522
Email: news@raymondspress.com
Web site: http://www.raymondspress.com
Material accepted: General news and pictures from
Nottinghamshire and Derbyshire. Serves: National
newspapers and magazines.

PA PHOTOS
Pavilion House, 16 Castle Boulevard, NOTTINGHAM,
NG7 1FL
Tel: 0115 844 7447 **Fax:** 0115 844 7448
Email: info@paphotos.com
Web site: http://www.paphotos.com
Material accepted: News and photos for International
and UK news, sport and entertainment. Serves:
Worldwide.

PAGE ONE PHOTOGRAPHY
11 West Avenue, West Bridgford, NOTTINGHAM, NG2
7NL
Tel: 0115 981 8880
Email: pictures@pageonephotography.com
Web site: http://www.pageonephotography.co.uk
Material accepted: National news and photographs.
Serves: Midlands.
Doug Marke is the Picture Editor to whom press
releases should be addressed.

RAYMONDS PRESS AGENCY (DERBY)
Abbots Hill Chambers, Gower Street, DERBY, DE1 1SD
Tel: 01332 340404 **Fax:** 01332 386036
Email: news@raymondspress.com
Web site: http://www.raymondspress.co.uk
Material accepted: National news, photos and sports
news. Serves: Derbyshire, Lincolnshire,
Nottinghamshire, Staffordshire, Leicestershire and
Rutland.

SMITH DAVIS PRESS
Queen's Chambers, 8 Westport Road, STOKE-ON-
TRENT, ST6 4AW
Tel: 01782 829850 **Fax:** 01782 812428
Email: agency@smith-davis.co.uk
Web site: http://www.smith-davis.co.uk
Material accepted: General news and features. Serves:
West Midlands and North West.
David Smith is the Managing Director to whom press
releases should be addressed.

WARWICKSHIRE NEWS & PICTURE AGENCY
42 Lucy's Mill, Mill Lane, STRATFORD-UPON-AVON,
CV37 6DE
Tel: 01789 295529
Email: barrietracey@gmail.com
Web site: http://www.napa.org.uk
Material accepted: National news stories, features and
pictures. Servers: Newspapers, magazines and
publications worldwide.
Barrie Tracey is the Editor to whom press releases
should be addressed.

NEWS & PICTURE AGENCIES

North Eastern

COMMUNITY NEWSWIRE
The Press Association, Bridgegate, Howden, GOOLE,
DN14 7AE
Tel: 0870 124 0866 **Fax:** 0870 124 0211
Email: communitynews@pa.press.net
Web site: http://www.communitynewswire.org
Material accepted: Charity or community group related
material that benefits or supports projects and events
within the voluntary sector. Serves: England.
Press releases can be sent via the website.

GOSNAY'S SPORTS AGENCY
Park House, 43 West End Drive, Horsrorth, LEEDS,
LS18 4JR
Tel: 0113 258 5864 **Fax:** 0113 258 7253
Email: gosnays@aol.com
Material accepted: Local sports news including
football, rugby and cricket. Serves: Leeds area.
John Wray is the Sports Editor to whom press releases
should be addressed.

HULL NEWS & PICTURES LTD
Room 115, The Microfirms Centre, 266-290
Wincolmlee, HULL, HU2 0PZ
Tel: 01482 210267 **Fax:** 01482 210267
Email: rich@hullnews.co.uk
Web site: http://www.hullnews.co.uk
Material accepted: Local and national news, features,
sport and photography.

NORTH NEWS AND PICTURES
The Newgate Centre, 69 Grainger Street, NEWCASTLE UPON TYNE, NE1 5JE
Tel: 0191 233 0223 **Fax:** 0191 230 0517
Email: copy@northnews.co.uk

Material accepted: Regional news and photographs including sport and stories of interest. Serves: National and regional newspapers and magazines.

THE ORIGINAL DOUBLE RED LTD
4 Gateway Court, Dankerwood Road, South Hykeham, LINCOLN, LN6 9UL
Tel: 01522 693278 **Fax:** 01469 531888
Email: j.wright@doublered.co.uk
Web site: http://www.doublered.co.uk
Material accepted: UK motor sports, especially motorcycle events. Also local news and events for Lincolnshire. Serves: UK.
James Wright is the Managing Director to whom press releases should be addressed.

PA NEWS (LEEDS)
Central Park, New Lane, LEEDS, LS11 5DZ
Tel: 0870 830 6822 **Fax:** 0870 124 0548
Email: paleeds@pressassociation.co.uk
Web site: http://www.thepagroup.com
Material accepted: News within Yorkshire, the Humber and North East Lincolnshire. Serves: National.
Alistair Keely is the Reporter to whom press releases should be addressed.

PA RACING PAGES
13 Bridgegate, Howden, EAST YORKSHIRE, DN14 7AE
Tel: 01430 455023 **Fax:** 0870 124 0811
Email: email@pa-sport.com
Web site: http://www.pressassociation.com
Material accepted: British and Irish horse racing information. Serves: Worldwide.
Jim Donnelly is the Head of Racing to whom press releases should be addressed.

PRESS ASSOCIATION SPORT
Bishops Manor, Market Place, HOWDEN, DN14 7BL
Tel: 01430 455000 **Fax:** 0870 124 0809
Email: pasport@pa.press.net
Web site: http://www.pressassociation.com/sport
Material accepted: Sport. Serves: United Kingdom.
David Balmforth is the Sports Editor to whom press releases should be addressed.

RIDINGS PRESS AND PUBLIC RELATIONS AGENCY
19 Hall Garth Lane, West Ayton, SCARBOROUGH, YO13 9JA
Tel: 01723 863395 **Fax:** 01723 865054
Email: cllr.david.jeffels@scarborough.gov.uk
Material accepted: General news. Serves: Eastern North Yorkshire.
David Jeffels is the Managing Director to whom press releases should be addressed.

ROSS PARRY AGENCY LTD
40 Back Town Street, FARSLEY, LS28 5LD
Tel: 0113 236 1842 **Fax:** 0113 236 1539
Email: newsdesk@rossparry.co.uk
Material accepted: General news, sport, features and photographs from Yorkshire and The Humber. Serves: National newspapers and magazines.

SOUTH YORKSHIRE SPORT
6 Sharman Walk, Apperknowle, SHEFFIELD, S18 4BJ
Tel: 01246 414767 **Fax:** 01246 414767
Email: nickjohnson@uwclub.net
Web site: http://www.nickjohnson.tv
Material accepted: Sports news covering in particular football and events relating to the North of England. Serves: North of England.

SPORTSPHOTO LTD
20 Clifton Street, SCARBOROUGH, YO12 7SR
Tel: 01723 367264 **Fax:** 01723 500117
Email: admin@sportsphoto.co.uk
Web site: http://www.sportsphoto.co.uk
Material accepted: Sport, politics and entertainment worldwide. Serves: Worldwide.

WEST RIDING NEWS & SPORTS SERVICE
Edward Latham House, 1 Oates Street, DEWSBURY, WF13 1BB
Tel: 01924 437555 **Fax:** 01924 457994
Email: martinwestriding@aol.com
Web site: http://www.westridingnews.co.uk

Material accepted: Local news, sport and pictures. Serves: West Yorkshire.

WHITE'S PRESS AGENCY
446 London Road, Heeley, SHEFFIELD, S2 4HP
Tel: 0114 255 3975
Email: news@whites-press-sheffield.co.uk
Material accepted: All local news except specialist trade. Serves: Sheffield, Barnsley, Rotherham & District.

NEWS & PICTURE AGENCIES

North Western

CAVENDISH PRESS
3rd Floor, Albert House, 17 Bloom Street, MANCHESTER, M1 3HZ
Tel: 0161 237 1066 **Fax:** 0161 237 5353
Email: newsdesk@cavendish-press.co.uk
Web site: http://www.cavendish-press.co.uk
Material accepted: General news, showbusiness, entertainment, celebrity, leisure, travel, food and wine, business, computing and legal issues for Manchester and the North West. Serves: North West.

COI COMMUNICATIONS NORTH WEST
25th Floor, City Tower, Piccadilly Plaza, MANCHESTER, M1 4BT
Tel: 0161 952 4513 **Fax:** 0161 228 0025
Email: manchester@coi.gsi.gov.uk
Web site: http://www.nds.coi.gov.uk
Government news and press agency. Provides press and publicity services to Government departments, public sector organisations and the general public.
Serves: North West.

INTERNATIONAL FASHION PRESS AGENCY
Penrose House, 56 Birtles Road, MACCLESFIELD, SK10 3JQ
Tel: 01625 615323 **Fax:** 01625 432284
Email: p.bentham@zen.co.uk
Material accepted: Fashion, beauty, health, medicine, science and technology, environmental and occupational health. Serves: National and regional daily and weekly newspapers, county magazines and international syndicates.
Peggy Bentham is the Director to whom press releases should be addressed.

MERCURY PRESS AGENCY LTD
Suite 218, Century Buildings, Tower Street, LIVERPOOL, L3 4BJ
Tel: 0151 709 6707 **Fax:** 0151 708 1908
Email: chrisjohnson@mercurypress.co.uk
Web site: http://www.mercurypress.co.uk
Material accepted: General text and newspress photos, both commercial and industrial from the North West of England and North Wales. Serves: National and local newspapers and magazines.
Chris Johnson is the Editor to whom press releases should be addressed.

NORTH WEST NEWS SERVICE
10 Broseley Avenue, MANCHESTER, M20 6JX
Tel: 07980 006606
Email: northwestnews@ntlworld.com
Web site: http://www.nw-news.co.uk
Material accepted: General news stories both UK wide and North-West based and including entertainment, health, sport news and hard news. Serves: National and regional newspapers, magazines, TV and radio.

PA NEWS (MANCHESTER)
230 Royal Exchange, Old Bank Street, MANCHESTER, M2 7EP
Tel: 0161 832 8302 **Fax:** 0161 839 2352
Email: pamanchester@pressassociation.co.uk
Web site: http://www.pa-mediapoint.press.net
Material accepted: National news stories from the North West, general news and information for the region and feature ideas. Serves: The North West.
Pat Hurst is the Reporter to whom press releases should be addressed.

SPACE PRESS NEWS AND PICTURES
Bridge House, Blackden Lane, GOOSTREY, CW4 8PZ
Tel: 01477 533403
Email: scoop2001@aol.com

Material accepted: General news and travel. Serves: North West of England.
John Williams is the Editor to whom press releases should be addressed.

NEWS & PICTURE AGENCIES

Scotland

7 DAY PRESS
132 West Nile Street, GLASGOW, G1 2RQ
Tel: 0141 572 0060 **Fax:** 0141 572 0265
Email: daypress@aol.com
Material accepted: Football news and information. Serves: Scotland.

ATMEDIA
Blairalan, Dargai Terrace, DUNBLANE, FK15 0AU
Tel: 01786 824671
Email: toby@atmedia.eclipse.co.uk
Material accepted: International news and features, including show business, politic, science and human interest. Serves: UK.

BG NEWS AGENCY
Margaretta Cottage, South Esplanade West, ABERDEEN, AB11 9AA
Tel: 01224 876873
Email: bgnewsagency@googlemail.com
Material accepted: Oil and gas industry news also business and finance news relevant to the area. Serves: Trade and regional press.
Bob Gibb is the Principal to whom press releases should be addressed.

CAPITAL PRESS AGENCY
14 Canongate Venture, New Street, EDINBURGH, EH8 8BH
Tel: 0131 652 3999 **Fax:** 0131 557 6086
Email: capitalnews@hemedia.co.uk
Web site: http://www.hemedia.co.uk
Material accepted: Scottish news and features. Serves: National newspapers and women's interest magazines.

CENTRAL SCOTLAND NEWS AGENCY LTD
10 Viewfield Place, STIRLING, FK8 1NQ
Tel: 01786 462423
Email: desk@thenewsagency.com
Material accepted: News and photos affecting Scotland including national news, Scottish news, human interest, celebrity, medical, animals, archaeology, research, science, politics, religion, crime, courts, fashion, music, technology and field sports. Serves: UK and Scottish national press and broadcasters: all of Scotland's daily, evening and Sunday newspapers and all of Scotland's broadcasters.
Tim Bugler is the News Editor to whom press releases should be addressed.

CENTRE PRESS AGENCY
Unit 15-16, M8 Business Complex, 259 Summerlee Street, Queenslie Industrial Estate, GLASGOW, G33 4DB
Tel: 0141 774 6969 **Fax:** 0141 774 4646
Email: centrenews@hemedia.co.uk
Web site: http://www.hemedia.co.uk
Material accepted: News and features covering Scotland. Serves: Scotland.

COPYLINE SCOTLAND
33 Academy Street, INVERNESS, IV1 1JN
Tel: 01463 710695 **Fax:** 01463 713695
Email: copylinescotland@aol.com
Material accepted: News and features relating to Scotland. Serves: Scottish and national press.

DEADLINE PRESS & PICTURE AGENCY
Bonnington Bond, 29 Breadalbane Street, EDINBURGH, EH6 5JW
Tel: 0131 561 2233 **Fax:** 0131-554 4340
Email: info@deadlinescotland.co.uk
Web site: http://www.deadlinescotland.co.uk
Material accepted: News, pictures and features covering Scotland and the UK. Serves: UK national and regional newspapers, broadcast media and magazines.

FOURTH ESTATE PRESS AGENCY
12 North Campbell Avenue, Milngavie, GLASGOW, G62 7AA
Tel: 0141 956 1540

Material accepted: Scottish parliamentary issues. Serves: Glasgow and EU.

FRANK RYAN NEWS SERVICE
Cargenriggs, Islesteps, DUMFRIES, DG2 8ES
Tel: 01387 253700 **Fax:** 01387 251121
Email: smeddum@btinternet.com

Material accepted: General news and features covering Scotland. Also features on travel worldwide. Serves: South West Scotland.

HEBRIDEAN PRESS SERVICE
37 Springfield Road, Stornoway, ISLE OF LEWIS, HS1 2PS
Tel: 01851 702737
Email: bill.hebpress@clara.co.uk

Material accepted: News, features and photographs covering the Outer Hebrides. Serves: Local and national media.
Bill Lucas is the Editor to whom press releases should be addressed.

HUGH FARMER PRESS AGENCY
68 Stamperland Drive, Clarkston, GLASGOW, G76 8HF
Tel: 0141 644 3253 **Fax:** 0141 571 8003
Email: farmernews@aol.com

Material accepted: National news, travel and religion. Serves: UK.
Hugh Farmer is the Managing Director to whom press releases should be addressed.

NEWSLINE SCOTLAND PRESS AGENCY
10 -12 Exchequer Row, ABERDEEN, AB11 5BW
Tel: 01224 594000 **Fax:** 01224 594001
Email: news@newsline-scotland.co.uk
Web site: http://www.newsline-scotland.co.uk

Material accepted: News, features, show-biz, sport and photography relevant to the North East of Scotland. Serves: National daily and regional press.

NIGEL DUNCAN MEDIA LTD
19 Lovedale Road, BALERNO, EH14 7DW
Tel: 0131 449 6682 **Fax:** 0131 449 7060
Email: nigeld@nigelduncanmedia.co.uk
Web site: http://www.nigelduncanmedia.co.uk

Material accepted: News, features, business and industrial including the drinks trade, arts, sports and sponsorship. Serves: National and regional press, leading magazines and broadcasting outlets.
Nigel Duncan is the Editor to whom press releases should be addressed.

NORTH SCOT PRESS AGENCY
18 Adelphi, ABERDEEN, AB11 5BL
Tel: 01224 212141 **Fax:** 01224 212163
Email: northscotnews@hemedia.co.uk
Web site: http://www.hemedia.co.uk

Material accepted: General news and features. Serves: National newspapers and magazines.

PRESS TEAM SCOTLAND LTD
22A St. John Street, COATBRIDGE, ML5 3EJ
Tel: 01236 440077 **Fax:** 01236 440066
Email: news@pressteam.co.uk
Web site: http://www.pressteam.co.uk

Material accepted: Hard news, local politics, court, and features. Serves: Lanarkshire, East Dunbartonshire and Glasgow.

READING SPORTS SERVICE
112 London Road, Ruscombe, READING, RG10 9HJ
Tel: 01189 345089
Email: readingsportsservice@yahoo.co.uk

Material accepted: National sports news but primarily football, golf, rugby union, ice hockey, speedway and boxing. Books, DVDs for review. Serves national media, Reading and surrounding area, plus Dubai sports publications.

SCOTTISH NEWS AGENCY
Avian House, 87 Brook Street, Broughty Ferry, DUNDEE, DD5 1DJ
Tel: 01382 427035 **Fax:** 01382 427006
Email: newsdesk@scottishnews.com
Web site: http://www.scottishnews.com

Material accepted: News and sport in Scotland. Regular features on construction, housing and tourism in Scotland. Serves: The Scottish press and several UK websites.
Graham Ogilvy is the Director to whom press releases should be addressed.

THE SCOTTISH PRESS ASSOCIATION
One Central Quay, GLASGOW, G3 8DA
Tel: 0870 830 6725 **Fax:** 0870 830 6726
Email: news@scottishpressassociation.co.uk
Web site: http://www.pa.press.net

Material accepted: General news, information and photographs for Scotland. Serves: National.
Iain Duff is the Editor to whom press releases should be addressed.

THE SCOTTISH PRESS ASSOCIATION (EDINBURGH)
Media Tower, Scottish Parliament, EDINBURGH, EH99 1SP
Tel: 0870 124 4188 **Fax:** 0870 124 4189
Email: scottishnews@pressassociation.com
Web site: http://www.pa.press.net/scotland

Material accepted: Scottish related political, parliamentary and general Edinburgh news. Serves: National press and broadcasters.
Joe Quinn is the Political Editor to whom press releases should be addressed.

SHETLAND NEWS AGENCY
The Knowes, Lunning, Vidlin, SHETLAND, ZE2 9QB
Tel: 01806 577332 **Fax:** 01806 577399
Email: news@shetland-news.co.uk
Web site: http://www.shetland-news.co.uk

Material accepted: General news and information on fishing, aqua culture and fish processing. Serves: Shetland Islands and Scotland.
Hans Marter is the Bureau Chief to whom press releases should be addressed.

SPINDRIFT PHOTO AGENCY
Claymore House, 149 Kilmarnock Road, GLASGOW, G41 3JA
Tel: 07836 507893
Email: spin@globalnet.co.uk

Material accepted: Press and magazine photographs and copy material and general news in Scotland. Serves: Worldwide.
Mike Gibbons is the Picture Editor to whom press releases should be addressed.

UNIVERSAL NEWS & SPORT (SCOTLAND)
PO Box 7448, GLASGOW, G42 8TY
Tel: 0141 416 2066 **Fax:** 0871 211 6065
Email: pictures@universalnewsandsport.com
Web site: http://www.universalnewsandsport.com
Material accepted: National news and sport. Serves: UK.

NEWS & PICTURE AGENCIES

Wales & The Marches

BELLIS NEWS AGENCY
Sea Breezes, 14B Kenelm Road, Rhos-on-Sea, COLWYN BAY, LL28 4ED
Tel: 01492 549503 **Fax:** 01492 543226
Email: bellisd@aol.com

Material accepted: News covering Caernarfon and Dolgellau Crown Courts and Magistrates Courts; general news and features. Serves: North and Mid Wales.

CHESTER NEWS SERVICE
Linen Hall House, Stanley Street, CHESTER, CH1 2LR
Tel: 01244 304500 **Fax:** 01244 351536
Email: news@chesterstandard.co.uk
Web site: http://www.chesterstandard.co.uk

Material accepted: Local news, sports, features and court news. Serves: Chester.

CHESTER PRESS BUREAUX
Riverside House, River Lane, Saltney, CHESTER, CH4 8RQ
Tel: 01244 678575 **Fax:** 01244 678749
Email: ron.quenby@btconnect.com

Material supplied: News and features. Serves: Cheshire, The Wirral and parts of North Wales.
Ron Quenby is the Chief Editorial contact to whom press releases should be addressed.

DRAGON NEWS & PICTURE AGENCY LTD
14 Brynmor Road, SWANSEA, SA1 4JQ
Tel: 01792 464800
Email: mail@dragon-pictures.com
Web site: http://www.dragon-pictures.com

Maintains a picture library covering all aspects of Wales and Welsh life. Serves: British daily and Sunday newspapers, national magazines, local authorities and government institutions, reporters and photographers.

GARETH MORGAN PHOTOGRAPHY
22 Tydfil Street, BARRY, CF63 3PY
Tel: 01446 411878 **Fax:** 01446 400556
Email: morganpix@ntlworld.com
Web site: http://www.morganpix.com

Material accepted: General news, sport and pictures. Serves: South, Mid and West Wales.
Gareth Morgan is the Managing Director to whom press releases should be addressed.

KIRAN RIDLEY
105 Ninian Road, CARDIFF, CF23 5ER
Tel: 029 2047 0490
Email: mail@kiranridley.com
Web site: http://www.kiranridley.co.uk

Material accepted: News, pictures and features across Wales and South West England. Provides a PR and corporate photographic service as well as a stock library of over 100,000 images including social documentary, travel and feature stories. International assignments undertaken. Serves: Photography for national and international newspapers and magazines as well as PR and advertising.
Kiran Ridley is the Picture Editor to whom press releases should be addressed.

PA NEWS (WALES)
8 Museum Place, CARDIFF, CF10 3BG
Tel: 029 2023 5852 **Fax:** 029 2023 1123
Email: pacardiff@pressassociation.co.uk

Material accepted: General news and sport relating to Wales. Serves: South & Mid Wales.
All press releases should be addressed to the News Reporters.

SHREWSBURY PRESS SERVICE
1A Victorian Arcade, Hill's Lane, SHREWSBURY, SY1 1PS
Tel: 01743 352710 **Fax:** 01743 247701
Email: shrewsburypress@btconnect.com

Material accepted: General news, agriculture, transport. Serves: Shropshire.

WALES NEWS & PICTURE SERVICE
5-7 Market Chambers, St Mary Street, CARDIFF, CF10 1AT
Tel: 029 2066 6366 **Fax:** 029 2066 4181
Email: news@walesnews.com
Web site: http://www.walesnews.com
Material accepted: News and features from Wales. Serves: National press.

NEWS & PICTURE AGENCIES

Northern Ireland

HARRISON PHOTOGRAPHY
37-39 Great Northern Street, BELFAST, BT9 7FJ
Tel: 028 9066 3100 **Fax:** 028 9066 4317
Email: mail@harrisonphotography.co.uk
Web site: http://www.harrisonphotography.co.uk

Material accepted: Northern Ireland news and feature photography with picture library. Serves: Worldwide.
John Harrison is the Managing Director to whom press releases should be addressed.

NORTH WEST NEWS AGENCY LTD
Lizzie's Cottage, 36 Terrydremont Road, LIMAVADY, BT49 0NL
Tel: 028 7776 8124 **Fax:** 028 7776 8124
Email: northwestnewsagency@yahoo.co.uk

Material accepted: All suitable press releases for inclusion in local press. Serves: Belfast based regional and national media including Londonderry Sentinel, Roe Valley Sentinel and North West Echo.
Frances Young is the Company Secretary to whom press releases should be addressed.

PA NEWS (BELFAST)
Scottish Provident Building, 7 Donegall Square West, BELFAST, BT1 6JH
Tel: 028 9024 5008 **Fax:** 028 9043 9246
Email: belfast@pressassociation.ie

Material accepted: General news, sport, information and photographs. Serves: Newspapers in UK, N Ireland and Irish Republic.
Deric Henderson is the Ireland Editor to whom press releases should be addressed.

PACEMAKER PRESS INTERNATIONAL LTD
Unait A19, 20 Heron Road, BELFAST, BT3 9LE
Tel: 028 9066 3191 **Fax:** 028 9068 2111
Email: david@pacemakerpressintl.com
Web site: http://www.pacemakerpressintl.com

Material accepted: National Court cover, general news, sport and photography. Serves: Northern Ireland and the Republic of Ireland.
David McCormick is the Editor to whom press releases should be addressed.

OVERSEAS CONSOLIDATION

BTB MAILFLIGHT LTD
Wolseley Road, Kempston, BEDFORD, MK42 7UA
Tel: 01234 840222 **Fax:** 01234 841041
Email: info@btbmf.co.uk
Web site: http://www.btbmf.co.uk

LEWIS DIRECT MAIL LTD
433 Caledonian Road, LONDON, N7 9BG
Tel: 020 7607 6505 **Fax:** 020 7607 0932
Email: info@ldm.co.uk
Web site: http://www.ldm.co.uk
Contact: James Phillips, Managing Director.

PHOTOGRAPHERS

Advertising

BRUCE FLEMING PHOTOGRAPHER
60 Wimpole Street, LONDON, W1G 8AG
Tel: 020 7486 4001
Email: mail@brucefleming.com
Web site: http://www.brucefleming.com
Contact: Bruce Fleming, Proprietor.

DAVID COCKROFT
10 Madrid Road, Barnes, LONDON, SW13 9PD
Tel: 020 8748 5117
Contact: David Cockroft, Proprietor.

GERRY CRANHAM'S COLOUR LIBRARY
28 Mindelheim Avenue, EAST GRINSTEAD, RH19 3UU
Tel: 01737 553688 **Fax:** 01342 300650
Email: mark@cranhamphoto.com
Contact: Mark Cranham, Partner.

FLASH PHOTOGRAPHICS LTD
750 Harrow Road, LONDON, NW10 5LE
Tel: 020 8964 6480 **Fax:** 020 8964 6499
Email: mail@flashphotodigital.co.uk
Web site: http://www.flashphotodigital.co.uk
Contact: Chris Bell, Director.

HANOVER SAFFRON LTD
29-31 Saffron Hill, LONDON, EC1N 8FH
Tel: 020 7404 4302 **Fax:** 020 7405 9002
Email: mailbox@hanoversaffron.co.uk
Web site: http://www.hanoversaffron.co.uk
Contact: Colin Shakespeare, Director.

VICTOR SHACK PHOTOGRAPHER
87 High Street, RICKMANSWORTH, WD3 1EF
Tel: 01923 772262 **Fax:** 01923 778940
Email: victorshack@aol.com
Web site: http://www.victorshackphotography.co.uk
Contact: Victor Shack, Director.

PHOTOGRAPHERS

Commercial & Industrial

ANTHONY MOSLEY PHOTOGRAPHER
16 Edgecombe Way, St Anns Chapel, GUNNISLAKE, PL18 9HJ
Tel: 01822 833204 **Fax:** 01822 833204
Email: info@anthonymosley-photographer.co.uk
Web site: http://www.anthonymosley-photographer.co.uk
Contact: Anthony Mosley, Proprietor. Sarah Mosley, Secretary.

BELLWOOD PHOTOGRAPHY LTD
6 & 8 Barlow Road, SHEFFIELD, S6 5HR
Tel: 0114 234 4746
Web site: http://www.bellwood.co.uk
Contact: Mike Bellwood, Director.

BMS IMAGING
Unit 17, Riverside Industrial Park, Wherstead Road, IPSWICH, IP2 8JX
Tel: 01473 601234 **Fax:** 01473 689065
Email: enquiries@bmsimaging.co.uk
Web site: http://www.bmsimaging.co.uk
Contact: Mr. R. Barcham, Proprietor.

MICHAEL BOOTH
16 Queen's Grove Road, North Chingford, LONDON, E4 7BT
Tel: 020 8529 3223
Email: michaelbooth@mac.com
Web site: http://www.michaelbooth.com

JOANNE O'BRIEN
2 Wesleyan Place, LONDON, NW5 1LG
Tel: 020 7485 7308 **Fax:** 020 7485 7308
Email: joanne@joanneobrien.co.uk
Web site: http://www.joanneobrien.co.uk
Contact: Joanne O'Brien, Photographer.

PHOTOCRAFT (HAMPSTEAD) LTD
4 Heath Street, LONDON, NW3 6TE
Tel: 020 7435 9932 **Fax:** 020 7435 3873
Email: info@photocraft-hampstead.com
Web site: http://www.photocraft-hampstead.com
Contact: Keith Wynn, Proprietor.

PHOTOSHOT LTD
29-31 Saffron Hill, LONDON, EC1N 8SW
Tel: 020 7421 6000 **Fax:** 020 7421 6006
Email: contacts@uppa.co.uk
Web site: http://www.photoshot.com
Contact: Commercial Department.

PREMIER PHOTOGRAPHY
Allestree, DERBY, DE22 2UG
Tel: 01332 550551
Email: justin@justinstrafford.co.uk
Web site: http://www.justinstrafford.co.uk
Contact: Justin Strafford, Photographer.

RAYMOND THATCHER STUDIOS
18 Queen Street, MAIDENHEAD, SL6 1HZ
Tel: 01628 625381 **Fax:** 01628 778921
Email: studio@raymondthatcher.co.uk
Web site: http://www.raymondthatcher.co.uk
Contact: Raymond Thatcher, Managing Director.

REALISTIC PHOTOGRAPHICS LTD
Stafford Studios, 129A Stafford Road, WALLINGTON, SM6 9BN
Tel: 020 8669 4900 **Fax:** 020 8773 0129
Email: info@realistic-digital.com
Web site: http://www.realistic-digital.com
Contact: Myles Grainger, Managing Director. Helen Delemos, Director.

VOLLANS PHOTOGRAPHY OF HARROGATE
26-28 Cheapside, KNARESBOROUGH, HG5 8AX
Tel: 01423 862626 **Fax:** 01423 869697
Email: vollansphotography@supanet.com
Web site: http://www.vollansphotography.co.uk
Contact: Bernard Vollans, Proprietor.

WINPENNY PHOTOGRAPHY
3 Wesley Street, OTLEY, LS21 1AZ
Tel: 01943 462597
Email: info@winpennyphoto.co.uk
Web site: http://www.winpennyphoto.co.uk
Contact: Christopher Winpenny, Partner.

PHOTOGRAPHERS

Press

DOBSONAGENCY.CO.UK
20 Seafield Avenue, Osgodby, SCARBOROUGH, YO11 3QG
Tel: 01723 860770 **Fax:** 0871 433 8973
Email: pix@dobsonagency.co.uk
Web site: http://www.dobsonagency.co.uk

Material accepted: National news and features. Press and Public Relations, corporate and commercial photography a speciality. Serves: UK.
Keith Meatheringham is the Proprietor to whom press releases should be addressed.

HARROGATE PRESS (PHOTO) AGENCY
26-28 Cheapside, Knaresborough, HARROGATE, HG5 8AX
Tel: 01423 862626 **Fax:** 01423 869697
Email: vollansphotography@supanet.com
Web site: http://www.vollansphotography.co.uk
Contact: Bernard Vollans, Proprietor.

PHOTOSHOT
29-31 Saffron Hill, LONDON, EC1N 8SW
Tel: 020 7421 6000 **Fax:** 020 7421 6006
Email: contacts@uppa.co.uk
Web site: http://www.photoshot.com
Contact: Peter Dare, News Editor.

REX FEATURES LTD
18 Vine Hill, LONDON, EC1R 5DZ
Tel: 020 7278 7294 **Fax:** 020 7837 4812
Email: enquiries@rexfeatures.com
Web site: http://www.rexfeatures.com
Contact: Dean Murray, Journalist.

TREVOR SMITH PHOTOGRAPHY
32 Somersall Park Road, Brampton, CHESTERFIELD, S40 3LD
Tel: 01246 567891 **Fax:** 01246 567891
Email: admin@trevorsmithphotography.co.uk
Web site: http://www.trevorsmithphotography.co.uk
Contact: Trevor Smith, Proprietor.

PICTURE LIBRARIES

ACQUIRE IMAGE MEDIA
16 Edgecombe Way, St. Anns Chapel, GUNNISLAKE, PL18 9HJ
Tel: 01822 833204 **Fax:** 01822 833204
Email: anthonymosley-photographer.co.uk
Web site: http://www.acquireimagemedia.com
Contact: Anthony Mosley, Proprietor. Sarah Mosley, Secretary.

ACTION PICTURES (UK) LTD
33 Aldgate High Street, LONDON, EC3N 1DL
Tel: 020 7003 5820 **Fax:** 020 8267 2035
Email: info@actionimages.com
Web site: http://www.actionimages.com

ALLSTAR PICTURE LIBRARY
20 Clifton Street, SCARBOROUGH, YO12 7SR
Tel: 01723 367264 **Fax:** 01723 500117
Email: library@allstarpl.com
Web site: http://www.allstarpl.com

ANDES PRESS AGENCY
26 Padbury Court, LONDON, E2 7EH
Tel: 020 7613 5417 **Fax:** 020 7739 3159
Email: news@andespressagency.com
Web site: http://www.andespressagency.com

Material accepted: Photos covering religious, political and economic issues, and travel. Serves: Worldwide.

ARDEA LTD WILDLIFE PETS ENVIRONMENT
35 Brodrick Road, LONDON, SW17 7DX
Tel: 020 8672 2067 **Fax:** 020 8672 8787
Email: ardea@ardea.com
Web site: http://www.ardea.com
Contact: Sophie Napier, Director.

ART DIRECTORS' AND TRIP PHOTO LIBRARY
57 Burdon Lane, Cheam, SUTTON, SM2 7BY
Tel: 020 8642 3593 **Fax:** 020 8395 7230
Email: images@artdirectors.co.uk
Web site: http://www.artdirectors.co.uk
Contact: Bob Turner, Partner. Helene Rogers, Joint Partner.

BEKEN OF COWES LTD
16 Birmingham Road, COWES, PO31 7BH
Tel: 01983 297311 **Fax:** 01983 291059
Email: beken@beken.co.uk
Web site: http://www.beken.co.uk
Contact: Kenneth Beken, Managing Director. Peter Mumford, Photography Manager.

Services & Suppliers

THE BRIDGEMAN ART LIBRARY
17-19 Garway Road, LONDON, W2 4PH
Tel: 020 7727 4065 **Fax:** 020 7792 8509
Email: info@bridgeman.co.uk
Web site: http://www.bridgeman.co.uk
Contact: Jenny Page, Picture Research Manager.
Additional Email: research@bridgeman.co.uk.

COLLECTIONS
13 Woodberry Crescent, LONDON, N10 1PJ
Tel: 020 8883 0083 **Fax:** 020 8883 9215
Email: collections@btinternet.com
Web site: http://www.collectionspicturelibrary.co.uk
Contact: Sal Shuel, Partner. Simon Shuel, Managing
Director.

CORBIS UK
111 Salusbury Road, LONDON, NW6 6RG
Tel: 020 7644 7400 **Fax:** 020 7644 7645
Email: sales.uk@corbis.com
Web site: http://www.corbis.com
Contact: Ivan Purdie, Sales Manager.

SYLVIA CORDAIY PHOTO LIBRARY LTD
45 Rotherstone, DEVIZES, SN10 2DD
Tel: 01380 728327 **Fax:** 01380 728328
Email: info@sylvia-cordaiy.com
Web site: http://www.sylvia-cordaiy.com
Contact: Sylvia Cordaiy, Proprietor.

DAVID HOFFMAN PHOTO LIBRARY
c/o BAPLA, 18 Vine Hill, LONDON, EC1R 5DZ
Tel: 020 8981 5041
Email: lib@hoffmanphotos.com
Web site: http://www.hoffmanphotos.com
Contact: David Hoffman, Manager.

DAVID HORWELL PHOTOGRAPHY
1-3 Brixton Road, LONDON, SW9 6DE
Tel: 020 7407 1478 **Fax:** 020 7407 0397
Email: info@selectlatinamerica.co.uk
Web site: http://www.selectlatinamerica.co.uk
Contact: David Horwell, Director.

JAMES DAVIS WORLDWIDE
65 Brighton Road, SHOREHAM-BY-SEA, BN43 6RE
Tel: 01273 440113 **Fax:** 01273 440116
Email: library@eyeubiquitous.com
Web site: http://www.eyeubiquitous.com
Contact: Paul Seheult, Proprietor.

MARY EVANS PICTURE LIBRARY
59 Tranquil Vale, Blackheath, LONDON, SE3 0BS
Tel: 020 8318 0034 **Fax:** 020 8852 7211
Email: pictures@maryevans.com
Web site: http://www.maryevans.com
Contact: Paul Brown, Managing Director.

FAMOUS PITCURES AND FEATURES AGENCY
13 Harwood Road, LONDON, SW6 4QP
Tel: 020 7731 9333 **Fax:** 020 7731 9330
Email: events@famous.uk.com
Web site: http://www.famous.uk.com
Contact: Rob Howard, Director.

THE GARDEN PICTURE LIBRARY
2nd Floor, Taxi House, Woodfield Road, LONDON, W9
2BA
Tel: 020 7228 4332 **Fax:** 020 7924 3267
Email: sales@gardenpicture.com
Web site: http://www.gardenpicture.com
Contact: James Cape, Sales Director.

LIVE PHOTOGRAPHY
1A Larchwood Close, BANSTEAD, SM7 1HE
Tel: 01737 373732
Email: live@livepix.biz
Contact: Steve Gillett, Photographer & Photo Library
Manager.

LONDON AERIAL PHOTO LIBRARY
Studio D1, Fairoaks Airport, Chobham, WOKING, GU24
8HU
Tel: +44 01483 233395 **Fax:** +44 01483 235258
Email: info@londonaerial.co.uk
Web site: http://www.londonaerial.co.uk
Contact: Amanda Campbell, General Manager.

LONDON FEATURES INTERNATIONAL LTD
Image House, Station Road, LONDON, N17 9LR
Tel: 020 7723 4204 **Fax:** 020 7723 9201
Email: sales@lfi.co.uk
Web site: http://www.lfi.co.uk
Press and photo agency covering all major show-
biz, celebrity and music events in London, Los

Angeles, New York, Sydney, Miami, Paris, Cannes,
Amsterdam, Madrid and Milan. Also contains a
photo library with subjects from '40s to date.
Serves: Worldwide.
Lynsey Carrott is the Picture Editor to whom press
releases should be addressed.

MARK GERSON PHOTOGRAPHY
3 Regal Lane, Regents Park Road, LONDON, NW1 7TH
Tel: 020 7485 6437 **Fax:** 020 7267 9246
Email: mark.gerson@virgin.net
Contact: Mark Gerson, Proprietor.

MIRRORPIX
20th Floor, 1 Canada Square, Canary Wharf, LONDON,
E14 5AP
Tel: 020 7293 3700 **Fax:** 020 7510 6141
Email: desk@mirrorpix.com
Web site: http://www.mirrorpix.com
Material accepted: photo, news, features and real life
stories of national and international interest. Serves:
newspapers, magazines and book publishing industries
based in the UK and overseas.

NATURAL SCIENCE PHOTOS
PO Box 397, Welwyn Garden City, HERTFORDSHIRE,
AL7 9BA
Tel: 01707 690561
Email: pics@naturalsciencephotos.com
Web site: http://www.naturalsciencephotos.com
Contact: Joe Carbonella, Partner.

NATURAL VISIONS
6 Vicarage Hill, FARNHAM, GU9 8HG
Tel: 01252 716700 **Fax:** 01252 727464
Email: info@naturalvisions.co.uk
Web site: http://www.naturalvisions.co.uk
Contact: Heather Angel, Proprietor.

PHIL HOLDEN PHOTOGRAPHY
Bali Hai, Michaels Field, Mumbles, SWANSEA, SA3 4JB
Tel: 01792 367571
Email: phil@philholdenphotography.com
Web site: http://www.philholdenphotography.com
Contact: Phil Holden, Director.

PHOTOLIBRARY GROUP
4th Floor, 83-84 Long Acre, LONDON, WC2E 9NG
Tel: 020 7836 5591 **Fax:** 020 7379 4650
Email: uksales@photolibrary.com
Web site: http://www.photolibrary.com
Contact: James Cape, Sales Director.

PPL (PHOTO AGENCY) LTD
Booker's Yard, The Street, Walberton, ARUNDEL, BN18
0PF
Tel: 01243 555561 **Fax:** 01243 555562
Email: ppl@mistral.co.uk
Web site: http://www.pplmedia.com
Contact: Barry Pickthall, Managing Director.

PR IMAGING INTERNATIONAL
Studio 12, 7 Wenlock road, LONDON, N1 7SL
Tel: 0845 094 6040
Email: simon@pr-imaging.org
Web site: http://www.pr-imaging.org
Contact: Simon Collyer, Director.

REALISTIC PHOTOGRAPHICS LTD
Stafford Studios, 129A Stafford Road, WALLINGTON,
SM6 9BN
Tel: 020 8669 4900 **Fax:** 020 8773 0129
Email: info@realistic-digital.com
Web site: http://www.realistic-digital.com
Contact: Myles Grainger, Managing Director. Helen
Delemos, Director.

REX FEATURES LTD
18 Vine Hill, LONDON, EC1R 5DZ
Tel: 020 7278 7294 **Fax:** 020 7837 4812
Email: library@rexfeatures.com
Web site: http://www.rexfeatures.com
Contact: Dean Murray, Journalist.

ROBERT HARDING PICTURE LIBRARY LTD
5th Floor, 58-59 Great Marlborough Street, LONDON,
W1F 7JY
Tel: 020 7478 4000 **Fax:** 020 7478 4161
Email: info@robertharding.com
Web site: http://www.robertharding.com
Contact: Robert Harding, Managing Director.

SCIENCE PHOTO LIBRARY LTD
327-329 Harrow Road, LONDON, W9 3RB
Tel: 020 7432 1100 **Fax:** 020 7286 8668
Email: info@sciencephoto.com
Web site: http://www.sciencephoto.com
Contact: Maria Storey, Sales and Marketing Director.

SKYSCAN PHOTOLIBRARY
Oak House, Toddington, CHELTENHAM, GL54 5BY
Tel: 01242 621357 **Fax:** 01242 621343
Email: info@skyscan.co.uk
Web site: http://www.skyscan.co.uk
Contact: Brenda Marks, Partner and Library Manager.

THE SUTCLIFFE GALLERY
1 Flowergate, WHITBY, YO21 3BA
Tel: 01947 602239
Email: photographs@sutcliffe-gallery.fsnet.co.uk
Web site: http://www.sutcliffe-gallery.co.uk
Contact: Mike Shaw, Partner.

TOPFOTO
PO Box 33, EDENBRIDGE, TN8 5PF
Tel: 01732 863939 **Fax:** 01732 860215
Email: requests@topfoto.co.uk
Web site: http://www.topfoto.co.uk
Contact: Alan Smith, Managing Director.

VINMAG ARCHIVE LTD
Vinmag House, 84-90 Digby Road, LONDON, E9 6HX
Tel: 020 8533 7588 **Fax:** 020 8533 7283
Email: piclib@vinmag.com
Web site: http://www.vinmagarchive.com
Contact: Angela McGuire, Director.

**WORLD PICTURES (FEATURE-PIX COLOUR
LIBRARY LTD)**
29-31 Saffron Hill, LONDON, EC1N 8SW
Tel: 020 7421 6004 **Fax:** 020 7421 6006
Email: mail@worldpictures.co.uk
Web site: http://www.worldpictures.co.uk
Contact: David Brenes, Manager.

THE ZOOLOGICAL SOCIETY OF LONDON
Regent's Park, LONDON, NW1 4RY
Tel: 020 7722 3333
Email: simon.rayner@zsl.org
Web site: http://www.zsl.org

PRESS AGENTS

ANGLO-DANISH PRESS AGENCY
Grosvenor Works, Mount Pleasant Hill, LONDON, E5
9NE
Tel: 020 8806 3232 **Fax:** 020 8806 3236
Email: mtbibelman@herzbi.com
Material accepted: National news, particularly
technical news about industry. Also accepts
photographs. Serves: Denmark.
Theo Bibelman is the Editorial Manager to whom press
releases should be addressed.

THE JOURDAN AGENCY
145-157 St. John Street, LONDON, EC1V 4PY
Tel: 020 7813 2520
Email: info@jourdanagency.com
Web site: http://www.jourdanagency.com
Contact: Ben Saer, Managing Director.

RICK MAYBURY LTD
73 Penrith Road, THORNTON HEATH, CR7 8PN
Tel: 020 8653 0316 **Fax:** 020 8653 0316
Email: rick@rickmaybury.com
Web site: http://www.rickmaybury.com
Contact: Richard Maybury, Proprietor.

ULTIMEDIA PUBLIC RELATIONS
Baystrait House, Station Road, BIGGLESWADE, SG18
8AL
Tel: 01767 601470 **Fax:** 01767 312323
Email: val@ultimediapr.co.uk
Contact: Valerie Jefferys, Senior Partner. Colin
Caldicott, Partner.

PRINT & PUBLISHING CONSULTANTS

KENT MESSENGER GROUP
Messenger House, New Hythe Lane, Larkfield,
AYLESFORD, ME20 6SG
Tel: 01622 717880 **Fax:** 01622 710926
Web site: http://www.kentonline.co.uk
Contact: Roy Bourner, Manager.

PRINTERS

Directories & Catalogues

BENHAM GOODHEAD PRINT
Chaucer Businees Park, Launton Road, BICESTER,
OX264Q7
Tel: 01869 363333 **Fax:** 01869 363365
Email: sales@bgprint.co.uk
Web site: http://www.bgprint.co.uk
Contact: Peter Simons, Sales Director. Bob Cayley,
Group Sales & Marketing Manager.

WOODFORD LITHO LTD
Freebournes Road, WITHAM, CM8 3UH
Tel: 01376 534500 **Fax:** 01376 534510
Email: rob.mcginlay@woodfordlitho.co.uk
Web site: http://www.woodfordlitho.co.uk
Contact: Rob McGinlay, Business Development
Manager.

PRINTERS

Magazines & Journals

HEADLEY BROTHERS LTD
The Invicta Press, Queens Road, ASHFORD, TN24 8HH
Tel: 01233 623131 **Fax:** 01233 612345
Email: stephen@headley.co.uk
Web site: http://www.headley.co.uk
Contact: Stephen Brind, Sales Manager.

THE MAGAZINE PRINTING COMPANY PLC
Mollison Avenue, Brimsdown, ENFIELD, EN3 7NT
Tel: 020 8805 5000 **Fax:** 020 8804 2432
Email: mpc@magprint.co.uk
Web site: http://www.magprint.co.uk
Contact: Finance Director.

THE NUFFIELD PRESS LTD
21 Nuffield Way, Ashville Trading Estate, ABINGDON,
OX14 1RL
Tel: 01235 554422 **Fax:** 01235 535445
Email: sales@nuffield.co.uk
Web site: http://www.nuffield.co.uk
Contact: Lucy Douglas, Marketing Manager.

STEPHENS & GEORGE MAGAZINES LTD
Goat Mill Road, Dowlais, MERTHYR TYDFIL, CF48 3TD
Tel: 01685 388888 **Fax:** 01685 385732
Email: sales@stephensandgeorge.co.uk
Web site: http://www.stephensandgeorge.co.uk
Contact: Andrew Jones, Managing Director.

PUZZLE FEATURES

BRAINWARP CROSSWORDS & PUZZLES
PO Box 51, Golborne, WARRINGTON, WA3 3NZ
Tel: 01942 271817
Email: trixie@brainwarp.com
Web site: http://www.brainwarp.com

CHAPMAN & PAGE
Denegate House, Amber Hill, BOSTON, PE20 3RL
Tel: 01205 290477 **Fax:** 01205 290477
Email: chapmanpage@internett.demon.co.uk
Contact: Graham Chapman, Editor.

THE PUZZLE HOUSE
Ivy Cottage, Battlesea Green, Stradbroke, EYE, IP21
5NE
Tel: 01379 384656 **Fax:** 01379 384656
Email: puzzlehouse@btinternet.com
Web site: http://www.thepuzzlehouse.co.uk
Contact: Roy Preston, Partner. Sue Preston, Partner.

SIRIUS MEDIA SERVICES
Suite 3, Stowmarket Business Centre, Meedham Road,
STOWMARKET, IP14 2AH
Tel: 01449 678878 **Fax:** 0870 130 2631
Email: mail@siriusmedia.co.uk
Web site: http://www.siriusmedia.co.uk
Contact: Tony Pickering, Director.

SUBSCRIPTION AGENTS

ANGLO-GULF BOOK SERVICES LTD
Unit 7, Longbridge Industrial Park, Floating Bridge
Road, SOUTHAMPTON, SO14 3FL
Tel: 023 8063 4963 **Fax:** 023 8022 4389
Contact: Martin Lawrence, Manager.

HAMMICKS LEGAL BOOKSHOP
191-192 Fleet Street, LONDON, EC4A 2NJ
Tel: 020 7405 5711 **Fax:** 020 7831 9849
Email: fleetstreet@hammicks.co.uk
Web site: http://www.hammickslegal.co.uk
Contact: Sue Gregory, Manager. .

HAMMICKS SUBSCRIPTION SERVICE
Allington House, 3 Station Approach, Ashford,
MIDDLESEX, TW15 2QN
Tel: 0870 224 4900 **Fax:** 01784 427959
Email: subs@hammicks.co.uk
Web site: http://www.hammickslegal.co.uk
Contact: Karen Baker, Supervisor.

SWETS
Swan House, Wyndyke Furlong, Abingdon Business
Park, ABINGDON, OX14 1UQ
Tel: 01235 857500 **Fax:** 01235 857501
Email: info@uk.swets.com
Web site: http://www.swets.com
Contact: Lucy McBride, Marketing Manager.

TELEPHONE MARKETING

MERCHANTS LTD
500 Avebury Boulevard, MILTON KEYNES, MK9 2BE
Tel: 01908 232323 **Fax:** 01908 242444
Email: info@merchants.co.uk
Web site: http://www.merchants.co.uk
Contact: Tessa Barfield, Sales and Marketing Director.

TRANSLATORS & CONFERENCE INTERPRETERS

UK

1ST TRANSLATION CO LTD
International Translation Centre, 24 Holborn Viaduct,
LONDON, EC1A 2BN
Tel: 020 7329 0032 **Fax:** 020 7329 0035
Email: welcome@1st-translation-co.com
Contact: Frances Glader, Managing Director.

LIONBRIDGE
Eaton House, Wigmore Place, Wigmore Lane, LUTON,
LU2 9EZ
Tel: 01582 702000 **Fax:** 01582 702222
Email: pr@lionbridge.com
Web site: http://www.lionbridge.com
Contact: John Harris, Business Development Manager.

THAMES TRANSLATIONS INTERNATIONAL LTD
Old Batford Mill, Lower Luton Road, HARPENDEN, AL5
5BZ
Tel: 0870 011 1130 **Fax:** 0870 011 1140
Email: info@thames.net
Web site: http://www.thames-translations.com
Contact: Simon George, Managing Director.

VSI
Aradco House, 132 Cleveland Street, LONDON, W1T
6AB
Tel: 020 7692 7700 **Fax:** 020 7692 7711
Email: info@vsi.tv
Web site: http://www.vsi.tv
Contact: Norman Darwood, Director.

**DORA WIRTH (LANGUAGES) LTD - MEDICAL
TRANSLATION AGENCY**
86-87 Campden Street, Kensington, LONDON, W8 7EN
Tel: 020 7229 2850 **Fax:** 020 7727 0744
Email: info@dwlanguages.com
Web site: http://www.dwlanguages.com
Contact: Sam Wirth, Managing Director.

TV/ SHOWBUSINESS FEATURES AGENCIES

STARPLUS
37 Cypress Close, Baswich, STAFFORD, ST17 0BB
Tel: 01785 245689
Email: starplusoffice@aol.com
Contact: Neil Bonner, News Editor.

UK NEWSPAPER AD SALES REPS
See also 'Advertisement Space Contractors'

AMRA LTD
62-65 Chandos Place, LONDON, WC2N 4LP
Tel: 020 7845 0100 **Fax:** 020 7845 0101
Web site: http://www.amra.co.uk
Contact: Gary McNish, Managing Director.

AMRA LTD (MANCHESTER)
Unit 12, Office Village, Exchange Quays,
MANCHESTER, M5 3EH
Tel: 0161 869 7800 **Fax:** 0161 848 8453
Email: manchester@amra.co.uk
Contact: Lee Bullmer, Provincial Sales Manager and
Associate Director. Jeff Lawrenson, Director.

CN GROUP LTD
Daleston Road, CARLISLE, CA2 5UA
Tel: 01228 612223 **Fax:** 01228 612601
Email: terry.hall@cumbrian-newspapers.co.uk
Web site: http://www.cngroup.co.uk
Contact: Terry Hall, Deputy Managing Director.

DAVID L. CLACKSON ORGANISATION
7 Baden Place, Crosby Row, LONDON, SE1 1YW
Tel: 020 7357 7979 **Fax:** 020 7357 0471
Email: marketing@clacksons.co.uk
Web site: http://www.clacksons.co.uk
Contact: Nick Wilson, Manager, Marketing and IT.

**DAVID L. CLACKSON ORGANISATION
(MANCHESTER)**
National Deposit House, 84 Talbot Road,
MANCHESTER, M16 0YY
Tel: 0161 877 7333 **Fax:** 0161 877 2590
Email: marketing@clacksons.co.uk
Web site: http://www.clacksons.co.uk
Contact: Adrian Worsley, Managing Director.

MEDIAFORCE LTD
1 Gunpowder Square, LONDON, EC4A 3EP
Tel: 020 7583 2100 **Fax:** 020 7353 2111
Contact: Malcolm Denmark, Managing Director.

NEWSQUEST DIGITAL MEDIA LTD
Berrows House, Hylton Road, WORCESTER, WR2 5JX
Tel: 01905 748200
Email: lindsay.ohara@midlands.newsquest.co.uk
Web site: http://www.newsquestmidlands.co.uk
Contact: Lindsay O'Hara, Operations and
Developement Manager.

NEWSQUEST MEDIA SALES (LONDON) LTD
3rd Floor, 30 Farringdon Street, LONDON, EC4A 4EA
Tel: 020 7489 4900 **Fax:** 020 7489 4991
Email: k.gallagher@newsquestmedia.co.uk
Web site: http://www.newsquestmedia.co.uk

**NEWSQUEST MEDIA SALES (MANCHESTER)
LTD**
94-96 Talbot Road, Old Trafford, MANCHESTER, M16
0PG
Tel: 0161 848 5200 **Fax:** 0161 848 5291
Email: k.leamy@newsquestmedia.co.uk
Web site: http://www.newsquestmedia.co.uk

Services & Suppliers

NEWSQUEST SOUTHERN
30 Farringdon Street, LONDON, EC4A 4EA
Tel: 020 7489 4900
Email: r.hughes@newsquestmedia.co.uk
Web site: http://www.newsquestmedia.co.uk
Contact: Rhys Hughes, Advertising Sales Manager.

NORTHCLIFFE MEDIA LTD
2 Derry Street, LONDON, W8 5TT
Tel: 020 7400 1400 **Fax:** 020 7400 1319
Web site: http://www.thisisnorthcliffe.co.uk
Contact: Daniel Jackman, Senior Sales Executive.

REGIONAL ADVERTISING COMPANY
Norman House, Heritage Gate, DERBY, DE1 1NU
Tel: 01332 293330 **Fax:** 01332 292125
Email: kevin@regionaladvertising.co.uk
Contact: Doug Price, Director. Kevin Curtis, Director.

THE SCOTSMAN PUBLICATIONS LTD
Barclay House, 108 Holyrood Road, EDINBURGH, EH8 8AS
Tel: 0131 620 8620 **Fax:** 0131 523 0373
Email: enquiries@scotsman.com
Web site: http://www.scotsman.com

WASTE PAPER MERCHANTS

INDEPENDENT WASTE PAPER PRODUCERS LTD
Heritage House, Vicar Lane, DAVENTRY, NN11 4GD
Tel: 01327 703223 **Fax:** 01327 300612
Email: admin@iwppa.co.uk
Web site: http://www.iwppa.co.uk

TGM ENVIRONMENTAL
55 New Lydenburg Street, LONDON, SE7 8ND
Tel: 020 8858 7799 **Fax:** 020 8858 1313
Email: sales@salterpaper.co.uk
Web site: http://www.tgmenvironmental.co.uk
Contact: Graham Coombes, Managing Director.

Willings Volume 1
Section 11

Master Index

Please note that in the Volume 1 Master Index which follows, the page numbers are in a variety of typestyles:

Numbers in **BOLD TYPEFACE** take you to the main listing for any newspaper or periodical in Section 4, or to Section 9 Broadcasting.

Numbers in MEDIUM TYPEFACE take you to Section 5: Internet Media; Section 6: Publishers; Section 7: Advertising Representatives; Section 8: International Media Consultants; or Section 10: Services & Suppliers.

Numbers in *ITALICS* take you to Section 2: UK Periodicals Index or Section 3: UK Newspaper Index.

The Appointment

BBC Where I Live Lincolnshire

British Journal of Industrial Relations

Section 11 Master Index

Centre Circle

Demolition and Recycling International

Emma's Diary Pregnancy Guide

The Gazette (Basingstoke and North Hants)

Health Information and Libraries Journal

Learning Disability Today

Mash Media

Nurseprescribing

Pinpoint Scotland Ltd

Purple Media Solutions Ltd

Russian London.com

Society of Business Economists

Surf Girl

Traveller in France

Welwyn & Hatfield Times & Herald Series

Section 11 Master Index

Your Wedding